MARCH'S
Thesaurus–Dictionary

FRANCIS ANDREW MARCH
LL.D., L.H.D., DC.L., Litt. D.

and
FRANCIS A. MARCH, Jr.
A.M., Ph. D.

Introduction by
CLARENCE L. BARNHART

Issued Under the Editorial Supervision of
NORMAN COUSINS

New Supplement by
R. A. GOODWIN

Hanover House
GARDEN CITY, NEW YORK

Originally published as *A Thesaurus Dictionary*
of the English Language

Library of Congress Catalog Card Number 57-9507

Printed in the United States of America

INTRODUCTION

Francis Andrew March: An Appreciation

By CLARENCE L. BARNHART

FRANCIS ANDREW MARCH was in the forefront of the development of the scientific study of language in the middle part of the nineteenth century.

Before the early part of that century there had been no clear understanding of the relationships among various languages that most of us now take almost for granted. Many diverse languages, utterly alien to each other, were grouped together and traced back to Hebrew as the parent language. The scientific study of language began with the observation of Sir William Jones, in 1786, that Sanskrit in relation to Greek and Latin "bears a stronger affinity, both in the roots of verbs and in the forms of grammar, than could possibly have been produced by accident; so strong, indeed, that no philologer [sic] could examine them all three without believing them to have sprung from some common source, which, perhaps, no longer exists; there is a similar reason, though not quite so forcible, for supposing that the Gothick [sic], and Celtick [sic], though blended with a very different idiom, had the same origin with the Sanskrit."

The great intellectual task of discovering a scientific basis for the comparative study of language began with the work of Rask on Old Norse, Bopp on the comparison of Greek, Latin, Persian, Germanic, and Sanskrit, and Grimm on the Germanic languages (1819, 1822) in discovering sound-laws that operated with consistency, methods of comparing inflections so that similarities between apparently diverse languages could be ascertained, in utilizing the identity of the common vocabulary of everyday terms to establish relationship, and in understanding the importance of common syntactical devices. These new methods of study resulted in the development of a new, and scientific, approach to language, sharply different in its attitude and emphasis from the older philological approach.

While various European scholars (notably Brugmann, Delbruck, and Paul) were building on the basic structure provided by the work of Rask, Bopp, Grimm, Schleicher, and others, Francis Andrew March pressed forward as the first American scholar in the field, and thus began the scientific study of language, especially of the English language, with which his name has now become identified.

According to Kemp Malone, one of the great modern linguistic scholars, writing in the Dictionary of American Biography, Professor March was "the first to apply exegesis in all its scientific rigor to the classroom study of English literary monuments." This interpretative and explanatory method of teaching, as distinguished from the lecture method, became widely popular in American teaching, being adopted and used at the Johns Hopkins University by March's great pupil, James W. Bright, and at Harvard by George L. Kittredge, the Shakespearean scholar (who did not, however, learn it directly from March).

March held the first professorship of the English language and comparative philology to be established in any college or university in the United States or Europe. Appointed to the professorship at Lafayette College, at Easton, Pa., in 1857, he held the chair for forty-nine years, until he retired at the age of eighty-two in 1907. His entire academic career was distinguished by its original reasearch and unflagging efforts to extend the field of linguistic knowledge, by the encouragement given to students, and by the popularization of the new science of linguistics.

In his *Lectures on the English Language* (1861) March makes the caustic comment that ". . . in our American system of education, the study of the English language has usually been almost wholly excluded from the collegial curriculum, and recently, indeed, from humbler seminaries, and, therefore, so great a novelty as its abrupt transfer from the nursery to the auditorium of a post-graduate course, may seem to demand both explanation and apology." When one considers the importance of the study of the English language and literature in American colleges and universities today it is difficult to imagine the time one hundred years ago when there were virtually no courses offered in this field. That English has been established as a serious discipline instead of an avocation is in no small part owing to March.

In 1869 March completed his most important scholarly work, *A Comparative Grammar of the Anglo-Saxon Language; in which its forms are illustrated by those of the Sanskrit, Greek, Latin, Gothic, Old Saxon, Old Friesic, Old Norse, and Old High German.* In his preface he outlines his purpose as follows: "Other Comparative Grammars have discussed several languages, each for the illustration of all, and of language in general; this book is an Anglo-Saxon Grammar, and uses forms of other tongues and general laws of language only so far as they illustrate the Anglo-Saxon. The hope has, however, been cherished that the methods of Comparative Grammar might be exemplified more fully than they have yet been for our students, in connection with the early forms of our mother tongue, and that in this way the Anglo-Saxon might be associated with the modern Science of Language, and share its honors."

How well founded this hope was is made clear by Kemp Malone's evaluation of the work upwards of sixty years later: "March's *Comparative Grammar* won instant and general recognition, in America and Europe alike, as a piece of research of the first order. He had laid the foundation on which all future historical grammarians in the field of English were destined to build, and his fame will ever rest secure as in a very real sense the founder of a science."

Greatly interested in the gathering of evidence with regard to the meanings and forms of English words, March supervised the American reading for quotations for the great historical dictionary of the English language, The Oxford English Dictionary. In the Historical Introduction to this work we find this statement: "Dr. Murray [James A. H. Murray, the original editor] then specially refers to the services rendered by Prof. Francis A. March of Lafayette College in directing the reading done in the United States at that time, and adds: There is another feature of American help to which I must allude, because it contrasts with that we have obtained in England—I refer to that offered to the Dictionary by men of Academic standing in the States. The number of Professors in American Universities and Colleges included among our readers is very large; and in several instances a professor has put himself down for a dozen works, which he has undertaken to read personally, and with the help of his students. We have had no such help from any college or university in Great Britain; only one or two Professors of English in this country have thought the matter of sufficient importance to talk to their students about it, and advise them to help us."

It is pleasing to know, as an American, that one of the greatest dictionaries of all time (perhaps no other reference work ever made, unless it be the Encyclopaedia Britannica, has been so widely consulted as this dictionary) was made with such significant aid from an American scholar. We may know of March's own great interest in the work from his own words—in the preface to his *Lectures on the English Language* he comments on the dictionary as follows: "These studies are, we may hope, soon to receive a new impulse and new aids from the publication of a complete dictionary of the English language —a work of prime necessity to all the common moral and literary interests of the British and American people, and which is now in course of execution by the London Philological Society, upon a plan, and with the command of facilities, that promise the most satisfactory results."

No doubt this experience in collecting quotations for a dictionary heightened March's interest in the English vocabulary, and gave him the general background necessary for the fresh approach to the study of synonyms, antonyms, and related words that was to make possible the great thesaurus he produced at the end of his career. Indeed, more than forty years before he published his Thesaurus, with his son's collaboration, March turned his attention to the study of English synonyms and worked out a theoretical basis for the book as it finally appeared. In his *Lectures* (1861) he says: "The Study of synonyms has always been regarded as one of the most valuable of intellectual disciplines, independently of its great importance as a guide to the right practical use of words. The habit of thorough investigation into the meaning of words, and of exact discrimination in the use of them, is indispensable to precision and accuracy of thought, and it is surprising how soon the process becomes spontaneous, and almost mechanical and unconscious, so that one often finds himself making nice and yet sound distinctions between particular words which he is not aware that he has ever made the subject of critical analysis,

The subtle intellect of the Greeks was alive to the importance of this study, and we not only observe just discrimination in the employment of language in their best writers, but we not infrequently meet with discussions as to the precise signification of words, which show that their exact import had become a subject of thoughtful consideration, before much attention had been bestowed upon grammatical forms."

From this it may surely be assumed that, although March was not to prepare a practical treatise giving exact discrimination of meanings of words for many years to come, he was already very conscious of the problem. Again, in the *Lectures,* we read: "Few languages are richer than English in approximate synonyms and conjugates; and it is much to be regretted that no competent scholar has yet devoted himself to the investigation of this branch of philology. The little manual, edited by Archbishop Whately, containing scarcely more than four hundred words, is, so far as it goes, the most satisfactory treatise we have on the subject. Crabb's Synonyms, much used in this country, is valuable chiefly for its exemplifications; but the author's great ignorance of etymology has led him into many errors; and it cannot pretend to compare with the many excellent works on the synonymy of the German, French, Danish, and other European languages. But in the increasing interest which the study of English is exciting, this, as well as other branches of lexicography, will doubtless receive a degree of attention, which will continue to give to the history of English a rank corresponding to the importance of that tongue, as one of the most powerful instruments of thought and action assigned by Providence to the service of man."

While there were many attempts to solve this problem, notably those of Roget in 1852 and of Soule in 1871, they were apparently unsatisfactory to March (the lists in Roget contained no definitions and so failed to make clear the distinctions between related and synonymous words, and in neither Soule nor Crabb was there a grouping of analogous and contrasting words so that the writer could find the exact word for the meaning he was striving to convey).

Working with his son, whom he had trained and who later succeeded him at Lafayette College, March published A Thesaurus Dictionary of the English Language in 1902. The work was a great success and went through some five editions. By combining the principles of the dictionary and the traditional thesaurus it was enabled to serve as a very practical reference tool for its users, whether as writer or reader. No doubt the experience of the younger March as assistant etymological editor on the staff of The Century Dictionary and Cyclopedia (1889–91) and as the head of the etymological department of the Standard Dictionary (1893–95) contributed much to the practical side of the collaboration, but the theoretical basis for the book had been worked out by the elder March many years before.

During the first third of the twentieth century March's Thesaurus-Dictionary was a standard reference book, but it gradually decreased in usefulness because of the great increase in scientific and technical vocabulary, a deficiency this edition seeks to correct. This need was perhaps anticipated by March himself when he commented on the rapid growth of scientific vocabulary in English: "In the meantime, and down to the present day, the rapid progress of physical science and industrial art has given birth to a great multitude of technical terms, a large part of which, in more or less appropriate applications, or in figurative senses, has entered into the speech of every-day life. Thus the means of articulate and written communication upon more familiar as well as more recondite subjects have been vastly extended, ever since the period when Shakespeare showed, by an experimental test, that English was already capable of exhibiting almost every conceivable phase of internal and external being in our common humanity."

The creation since then of many entirely new sciences, such as cybernetics, psychiatry, nuclear physics, electronics, etc., and the coming into importance of aviation, the automobile, guided missiles, and the great modifications of and additions to the nomenclature of chemistry, biology, geography, meteorology, and numerous other sciences and fields of study make this new edition of March's Thesaurus a practical necessity to many thousands of people.

The work of modernizing the book has been entrusted to Dr. R. A. Goodwin, a linguist, who has embodied in his supplement to the original thesaurus the same scholarly principles the first American linguist used in devising the original work. Dr. Goodwin has sometimes used a somewhat longer definition than did March, largely because of the need for fuller base definitions of many different terms in many new fields of knowledge. His supplement of synonymous and contrasting terms is the only single place that a modern reader or writer can turn for help with related terms in many new fields of study. As a result of his work, and because of the basic excellence of the original book, it seems to me that this newest edition of March's Thesaurus-Dictionary should prove fully as useful to modern users as the original was to previous generations of users.

FOREWORD

By NORMAN COUSINS

SELDOM have I met a March's Thesaurus-Dictionary owner who didn't express a devotion to the book verging on a literary mission to proclaim its virtues. When March's went out of print during World War II, its users constituted something of a proud and possessive band of the lexicographically privileged. For they regarded March's Thesaurus-Dictionary as one of the three or four handiest and most valuable reference books about words in the English language. Speaking personally, I can attest that there is no word book in my own library which has served me better or which I prize more highly than March's.

Clarence Barnhart's appreciation in the preceding pages concerns the man whose name is associated with this book. It is my purpose here to write about the book itself—how it came to be devised and compiled, why such an important book was allowed to go out of print, and how it happened that this special revised edition is now issued.

Francis Andrew March conceived of this book in response to the need for a single volume that would combine the main advantages of a thesaurus and a dictionary. In carrying out this purpose he put to work some carefully developed ideas for an all-purpose book about words that would enable any person who took pride in his use of the language to have a highly serviceable and creative aide within reach. March's ideas were aimed at providing both maximum speed of usage and a precise linguistic guide. The first great advance he made over the conventional thesaurus method was to eliminate the index system under which the user would be referred to several categories with the possible result that the word being sought might never be the key word of any particular grouping. March also wanted to keep cross-references down to a minimum. He used the direct alphabetical method, with each word given not only a compressed dictionary definition but a full range of associated words and phrases. Similarly, he believed it should not be necessary to consult two or more reference wordbooks in order to find related data—synonyms and antonyms and examples of usages. Hence, in the March system, a wide variety of purposes is served under each word listing.

Perhaps Francis March's greatest contribution to thesaurus making is in his system of juxtapositions. He believed that the full flavor of a word could best be brought out through contrast. Under the word "approval," for example, it will be seen that he follows the definition with a table called AP-PROVAL-DISAPPROVAL. In this table, divided into the categories of nouns, adjectives, verbs, and phrases, he brings into play all the color range, and depth of meaning, that help the user to rescue his language from the stale and flabby. And even where words do not lend themselves directly to the contrasting juxtapositions, March has associated the words that do.

This technique accounts in large part for the enthusiasm the March Thesaurus-Dictionary commands among its supporters. Whether the user is a professional writer or an educator or a businessman or scientist preparing a report for a general audience, his underlying purpose is usually the same: to find the word that *precisely* does the job intended for it but that does it with flavor and strength. As a result, people who enjoy and respect words have developed a profound affection for this book. Especially are they impressed with its enduring qualities. March never underestimated the striking power of new words, yet he knew that many expressions that spring into popular usage tend to drop out with equal suddenness. His yardsticks for determining which new words were likely to live have stood up over the years.

Professor March admired Peter Mark Roget, the English philologist whose great work was issued in 1852. But the Roget system made unreasonable demands on the user and tended to a certain cumbersomeness, a fault more recent editions of Roget have corrected by adopting the alphabetical rather than

index-plus-category method.   March, who was in the very front rank of American lexicographers and lin-
guists, believed that Roget's Thesaurus was a historic contribution to lexicography but that a new system was nonetheless necessary.

This new system served as the basis for the sustained efforts of Professor March and his son Francis
Andrew March, Jr., over a fifteen-year period.   After Professor March died in 1911, his son supervised
the issuance of new editions that were published in 1925 and 1930.   These and subsequent editions were
exhausted.   The book was allowed to go out of print in the early 1940's, following the death of Charles
W. Michener, president of the Historical Publishing Company, which issued the March Thesaurus.   Since
that time numberless orders from individuals and libraries have gone unfilled.

Negotiations for acquiring rights from the Michener estate were completed in early summer 1955,
and arrangements were made with Doubleday and Company to be the new publisher.   On the advice of
Clarence Barnhart the preparation of a new appendix was assigned to his associate, R. A. Goodwin.
The Appendix lists approximately 1800 new words from the sciences and professions and from contemporary usage.   Each word in the new section stands by itself, according to March's own system, but the section as a whole is integrated with the main body of the book through indicated connecting words or
terms.   A key to the new material immediately precedes the Appendix.

A final comment: the word "thesaurus" has come to have a single meaning, i.e., a book designed to
facilitate word use.   Actually "thesaurus" was the term used in early Greece to describe a treasure house.
It was natural perhaps that later use of the term linked it with a "storehouse of knowledge."   Francis
March's book should not be regarded solely as a linguistic aide; he intended it to fulfill the classical meaning of "thesaurus" as a treasure house as well.   For words are the working tiles of knowledge.   Their
creative and imaginative use makes possible not only rich new patterns of knowledge but new compre-
hensions of man's abilities and potentialities, the greatest source of his wealth.   It is in this sense that
the March Thesaurus-Dictionary seeks to make its principal contribution.

HOW TO USE THE THESAURUS

To the vast majority, the use of this Thesaurus-Dictionary of the English Language presents no more difficulties, for lack of understanding the plan adopted, than does any dictionary; but as its purpose is not limited to defining words, its wider sphere and usefulness being to suggest particular words or phrases as they may be required to definitely express a given idea, a brief explanation of how its fullest benefits may be obtained is appropriate.

All vocabulary words are printed in black face type; all definitions thereof appear in lower case Roman. The reference words are printed in small caps, under which heads the person consulting the dictionary must look to find any particular word desired. Thus, for example, take any word in the vocabulary, there will be found immediately following the definition, words printed in small caps, which are the reference words. These words must be looked up in their alphabetical position in the vocabulary, and under them will be found groups containing the word examined and words of related significance. Phrases and idioms are printed in black face type; foreign phrases appear in italics, and their phonetic pronunciation, in parentheses, are in lower case Roman. The foreign languages are indicated thus [F.], meaning French; [It.], Italian; [G.], German; [Sp.], Spanish; [L.], Latin; [Gr.], Greek. Those translations which appear in the vocabulary proper are printed in lower case Roman. Captions, to which the references direct, appear in capital letters, with positive and negative terms compounded, under which appear all associated words, printed in black face type, and the definitions in lower case Roman. The analysis of words, and their grammatical relationships, are printed under in small caps. Captions, denoting parts of speech and their relationship, are in italics. By observing these explanations no difficulty will ever be encountered in using the Thesaurus, or in obtaining the information which it is intended to supply.

THIS LINE IS CAPITAL LETTERS, USED IN CAPTIONS.
THIS LINE IS SMALL CAPS. (Used for reference words.)
This line is lower case Roman. (Used for definitions.)
This line is black face type. (Used for vocabulary words.)

A KEY TO PRONUNCIATION

The English words printed in this Thesaurus are easily pronounced by any one giving attention to the accent marks at the end of syllables. The single accent mark—thus, '—indicates the primary inflection, or the syllable upon which the greater stress must be laid. The double accent mark—thus, "—shows the secondary inflection, directing that some stress shall be laid, but less than that indicated by the primary accent.

Respellings for pronunciation have been given for all foreign words and phrases at their vocabulary places in this dictionary.

The Latin words have been pronounced according to the English method.

English words have been divided into syllables and the accented syllables marked.

In the respellings the ordinary Roman types have been use so far as possible.

The letters b, d, f, h, j, k, l, m, n, o, p, q, r, t, v, w, have been used with their ordinary normal values.

The following letters have been used with values as indicated:

a	as in far.	s	as in this.	ch	as in church.
a	as in cat.	ʊ	as in cup.	dh	as th in thou.
c	as in car.	u	as in rule.	iu	as u in mute.
e	as in met.	ü	as in G. über.	ng	as in sing.
ê	as in they.	x	as in box.	qu=cw	as in quit.
g	as in gun.	y	as in canyon.	sh	as in she.
i	as in din.	z	as in zebra.	th	as in thin.
î	as in machine.	ai	as in aisle.	zh	as g in mirage.
H	as ch in G. ach.	au	as ou in house.		
n˙	as n in F. bon.	au	as in author.		

A

Thesaurus Dictionary

OF THE

English Language.

A

A1. Excellent. Goodness-Badness.
A.B. Able-bodied seaman. Wayfarer-Seafarer.
a bene placito [It.] (a bê-ne pla-chî′-to). At pleasure. Volition-Obligation.
à bis ou à blanc [F.] (a bîs u a blan·). In one way or another; "by hook or by crook;" at all hazards. Craft-Artlessness, Determination-Vacillation.
à bon droit [F.] (a bon· drwa) With justice. Right-Wrong.
à bon marché [F.] (a bon· mar-shê′). At a good bargain, cheap. Costliness-Cheapness, Price-Discount.
a capite ad calcem [L.] (ê cap′-i-tî ad cal′-sem) From head to heel. Entirety-Deficiency.
à compte [F.] (a con't). On account. Credit-Debt.
à couvert [F.] (a cu-var′). Under cover. Enlightenment-Secrecy, Security-Insecurity.
à fond [F.] (a fon·). To the bottom Entirety-Deficiency.
à forfait [F.] (a for-fê′). By contract. Contract.
a fortiori [L.] (ê for-shi-o′-rai). With stronger reason. Supremacy-Subordinacy.
à l'américaine [F.] (a la-mê-ri-kên′). In the American style. Society-Ludicrousness.
à l'anglaise [F.] (a lan·-glêz′). In the English style. Society-Ludicrousness.
à outrance [F.] (a u-trans·′). To the utmost. Entirety-Deficiency.
à plomb [F.] (a plon·). Perpendicularly. Erectness-Flatness.
à propos [F.] (a pro-po′). To the point. Connection-Independence, Harmony-Discord, Opportuneness-Unsuitableness, Propriety-Impropriety.
à propos de bottes [F.] (a pro-po′ de bot). Not to the purpose. Connection-Independence.
a se [L.] (ê sî). From itself. Connection-Independence.
à temps, tout vient pour qui soit attendre [F.] (a tan·, tu vî-an′· pur kî swat at-tan·dr′). Everything comes in time to him who knows how to wait. Earliness-Lateness, Persistence-Whim.
ab actu ad posse valet consecutio [L.] (ab ac′-tiu ad pos′-sî vê′-let con-sî-kiu′-shi-o). From what has been to what may be. Ratiocination-Instinct.
ab alio exspectes, alteri quod feceris [L.] (ab ê′-li-o expec′-tîz, al′-ter-ai quod fes′-er-is). Expect to receive such treatment as you have given. Reprisal-Resistance.
ab extra [L.] (ab ex′-tra). From without. Outside-Inside.
ab inconvenienti [L.] (ab in-con-vî-ni-en′-tai). From the inconvenience involved. Difficulty-Facility.

ab initio [L.] (ab in-ish′-i-o). From the beginning. Beginning-End.
ab intra [L.] (ab in′-tra) From within. Outside-Inside.
ab origine [L.] ab o-rij′-i-nî). From the origin. Beginning-End.
ab ovo [L.] (ab o′-vo) From the egg. Beginning-End.
ab ovo usque ad mala [L.] (ab o′-vo us′-quî ad mê′-la). From egg to apples. Entirety-Deficiency.
ab uno disce omnes [L.] (ab yu′-no dis′-sî om′-nîz). From one learn all. Uniformity-Diversity.
ab′-a-cist. A calculator. Numbering.
a-back′. Backward. Anteriority-Posteriority; **take aback**, Expectation-Surprise.
ab′-a-cus. Calculating frame, the top member of a capital. Architecture, Numbering.
A-bad′-don. Apollyon. Angel-Satan, Heaven-Hell.
a-baft′. Toward the stern Anteriority-Posteriority.
ab-a′-li-en-ate. To transfer. Alienation.
ab-a″-li-en-a′-tion. A transfer. Alienation.
a-ban′-don. To give up. Arrival-Departure, Keeping-Relinquishment, Quest-Abandonment, Sociability-Privacy; **abandon hope**, Sanguineness-Hopelessness.
a-ban-don′. Ease of manner. Activity-Indolence, Craft-Artlessness.
a-ban′-doned. Depraved. Carefulness-Carelessness, Sociability-Privacy, Virtue-Vice.
a-ban′-don-ment. Desertion. Giving-Receiving, Quest-Relinquishment.
a-bas′. A Persian coin. Values.
a-base′. To degrade. Elevation-Depression, Self-Respect-Humbleness.
a-base′-ment. Humiliation. Elevation-Depression, Presumption-Obsequiousness, Reputation-Discredit.
a-bash′. To disconcert. Sanguineness-Timidity, Selfrespect-Humbleness.
a-bashed′. Disconcerted. Selfrespect-Humbleness.
a-bate′. To diminish. Costliness-Cheapness, Increase-Decrease.
a-bate′-ment. A reduction. Costliness-Cheapness, Increase-Decrease.
ab′-a-tis. An obstruction of felled trees. Attack-Defense.
a″-bat-toir′. A slaughter house. Life-Killing.
ab′-ba. Father. Parentage-Progeny.
ab′-ba-cy. Jurisdiction of an abbot. Church.

In parenthesis: fär, cat; met, thêy; din, machîne; cup, rule, G. über (*iu* nearly) ; canyon; aisle; au = house; author; iu = mute; c = k; church; dh = *thou*; go; н = G. ach; F. bon· = nearly song; quit; zh = mirage.

ab-ba′-tial. Like an abbey. CHURCH.
ab-bat′-ic-al. Like an abbey. CHURCH.
abbé [F.] (a-bê′). An abbot MINISTRY-LAITY.
ab′-bess. Lady superior of a nunnery. MINISTRY-LAITY.
ab′-bey. A monastery or nunnery. ARCHITECTURE, FANE.
ab′-bot. Superior of an abbey. MINISTRY-LAITY.
ab-bre′-vi-ate. To shorten. DIGEST, LENGTH-SHORTNESS.
ab-bre″-vi-a′-tion. An abridgment. DIGEST, LENGTH-SHORTNESS.
ab-bre′-vi-a-ture. A shortening. DIGEST, LENGTH-SHORTNESS.
A-B-C. The alphabet. BEGINNING-END, EDUCATION-MISTEACHING, LETTER.
ab′-dal. A Mohammedan devotee. MINISTRY-LAITY, ORTHODOXY-HETERODOXY.
ab′-di-cant. One who abdicates. COMMISSION-RETIREMENT.
ab′-di-cate. To withdraw from. COMMISSION-RETIREMENT, RULE-LICENSE.
ab″-di-ca′-tion. A giving up. COMMISSION-RETIREMENT, RULE-LICENSE.
ab′-di-to-ry. Place for concealing anything. DISCLOSURE-HIDINGPLACE.
ab-dom′-i-nal. Pertaining to the abdomen. ANATOMY.
ab-duce′. To lead away. ATTRACTION-REPULSION.
ab-du′-cent. Drawing away. ATTRACTION-REPULSION.
ab-duct′. To carry away wrongfully. ATTRACTION-REPULSION, TAKING-RESTITUTION, THEFT.
ab-duc′-tion. A carrying away. ATTRACTION-REPULSION, TAKING-RESTITUTION.
ab-duc′-tive. Carrying away. ATTRACTION-REPULSION.
a″-be-ce-da′-ri-an. Learner or teacher of the alphabet. INSTRUCTOR-PUPIL, LETTER.
a″-be-ce′-da-ry. An A-B-C book; pertaining to letters. SCHOOL, LETTER.
abends wird der Faule fleissig [G.] (a′-bents virt der Fau′-le flais′-sih). In the evening the lazy man becomes diligent. ACTIVITY-INDOLENCE.
ab-er′-rance. A departing from the correct way. AIM-ABERRATION.
ab-er′-rant. Wandering. AIM-ABERRATION, CONCENTRATION-RADIATION, CONVENTIONALITY-UNCONVENTIONALITY, TRUTH-ERROR.
ab″-er-ra′-tion. Deviation from a course. AIM-ABERRATION, CONCENTRATION-RADIATION, CONVENTIONALITY-UNCONVENTIONALITY, DEVIATION, SANENESS-LUNACY.
a-bet′. To encourage. OBSTRUCTION-HELP.
a-bet′-tor. One who abets. ANTAGONIST-ASSISTANT.
a-bey′-ance. Temporary inaction. DISCONTINUANCE-CONTINUANCE, EARLINESS-LATENESS, ENTITY-NONENTITY, EXPECTATION-SURPRISE; **in abeyance,** VIGOR-INERTIA.
a-bey′-ant. In a state of suspension. EXPECTATION-SURPRISE.
ab-hor′. To hate extremely. DESIRE-DISTASTE, LOVE-HATE.
ab-hor′-rence. Detestation. DESIRE-DISTASTE.
ab-hor′-rent. Hateful. LOVE-HATE, PLEASURABLENESS-PAINFULNESS.
a-bide′. To remain. DISCONTINUANCE-CONTINUANCE, EMOTION, EXCITABILITY-INEXCITABILITY, EXPECTATION-SURPRISE, LASTINGNESS-TRANSIENTNESS, MUTATION-PERMANENCE, PRESENCE-ABSENCE; **abide by,** ASSENT-DISSENT, OBSERVANCE-NONOBSERVANCE; **not abide,** DESIRE-DISLIKE.
a-bi′-ding. Enduring. LASTINGNESS-TRANSIENTNESS.
ab′-i-gail. A lady's maid. CHIEF-UNDERLING.
a-bil′-i-ty. Power. MIGHT-IMPOTENCE, MIND-IMBECILITY, SKILL-UNSKILFULNESS; **to the best of one's abilities,** TOIL-RELAXATION.

ab″-i-o-gen′-e-sis. Production of living from non-living matter. BIOLOGY, CREATION-DESTRUCTION.
ab′-ject. Despicable. PRESUMPTION-OBSEQUIOUSNESS, REPUTATION-DISCREDIT, UPRIGHTNESS-DISHONESTY; **abject fear,** BRAVERY-COWARDICE, SANGUINENESS-TIMIDITY.
ab-jec′-tion. Humiliation. UPRIGHTNESS-DISHONESTY.
ab′-ject″-ness. Meanness. REPUTATION-DISCREDIT.
ab-junc′-tion. Separation by means of a joint. UNION-DISUNION.
ab″-ju-ra′-tion. Renunciation. ASSERTION-DENIAL, BIGOTRY-APOSTASY, COMMISSION-RETIREMENT.
ab-jure′. To renounce under oath. COMMISSION-ABROGATION, PERSISTENCE-WHIM.
ab-jure′-ment. Renouncing. BIGOTRY-APOSTASY.
ab-la′-tion. Removal. ADDITION-SUBTRACTION, TAKING-RESTITUTION.
ab′-la-tive. The ablative case. GRAMMAR-SOLECISM, NOUN.
a-blaze′. On fire. HEAT-COLD, LIGHT-DARKNESS.
a′-ble. Having sufficient power. MIGHT-IMPOTENCE, SKILL-UNSKILFULNESS; **able seaman,** WAYFARER-SEAFARER.
a′-ble-bod″-ied. Robust. STRENGTH-WEAKNESS.
ab′-le-gate. A special papal envoy. DEPUTY, ESTABLISHMENT-REMOVAL.
a′-ble-ness. State of being able. MIGHT-IMPOTENCE.
ab′-lep-sy. Blindness. SIGHT-BLINDNESS.
ab-lude′. To differ. VARIATION.
ab-lu′-tion. A cleansing. CLEANNESS-FILTHINESS.
ab″-ne-ga′-tion. Denial. ASSERTION-DENIAL, MODERATION-SELFINDULGENCE, PROFFER-REFUSAL; **self-abnegation,** UNSELFISHNESS-SELFISHNESS.
ab-nor′-mal. Unnatural. CONVENTIONALITY-UNCONVENTIONALITY; **abnormal mind,** SANENESS-LUNACY.
abnormis sapiens [L.] (ab-nor′-mis sê′-pi-enz). An unusually wise man. SAGACITY-INCAPACITY.
ab-nor′-mi-ty. Monstrosity. CONVENTIONALITY-UNCONVENTIONALITY.
ab-nor′-mous. Unnatural. CONVENTIONALITY-UNCONVENTIONALITY.
a-board′. Upon. CONVEYANCE-VESSEL, PRESENCE-ABSENCE; **go aboard,** ARRIVAL-DEPARTURE.
a-bode′. A dwelling. DWELLER-HABITATION, EXTENSION-PLACE, PROPHECY; **take up one's abode,** DWELLER-HABITATION, ESTABLISHMENT-REMOVAL, MUTABILITY-STABILITY, PRESENCE-ABSENCE.
a-bode′-ment. An omen. PROPHECY.
a-bo′-ding. An omen. PROPHECY.
abois, aux [F.] (a-bwa′, oz). At bay. DIFFICULTY-FACILITY, LIFE-DEATH, SECURITY-INSECURITY.
a-bol′-ish. To do away with. PETITION-EXPOSTULATION.
a-bol′-ish-ment. Abolition. PETITION-EXPOSTULATION.
ab″-o-li′-tion. Extinction. CREATION-DESTRUCTION, PETITION-EXPOSTULATION.
a-bom′-i-na-ble. Very hateful. CLEANNESS-FILTHINESS, GOODNESS-BADNESS, LOVE-HATE.
a-bom′-i-nate. To detest. DESIRE-DISLIKE, LOVE-HATE.
a-bom″-i-na′-tion. Something disliked. CLEANNESS-FILTHINESS, DESIRE-DISTASTE, GOODNESS-BADNESS, LOVE-HATE.
a-bord′. To approach. POLITENESS-IMPOLITENESS.
ab″-o-rig′-i-nal. Native. BEGINNING-END, CAUSE-EFFECT.
ab″-o-rig′-i-nes. Original inhabitants. DWELLER-HABITATION.
a-bort′. To miscarry. SUCCESS-FAILURE.
a-bor′-tion. Act of bringing forth prematurely. PREPARATION-NONPREPARATION, SUCCESS-FAILURE.
a-bor′-tive. Brought forth prematurely. PREPARATION-NONPREPARATION, SUCCESS-FAILURE, USEFULNESS-USELESSNESS; **abortive attempt,** SUCCESS-FAILURE; **abortive efforts,** SUCCESS-FAILURE.

a-bound'. To be plentiful. ENOUGH.

a-bout'. Around; nearly; at the point. CONNECTION-INDEPENDENCE, ENVIRONMENT-INTERPOSITION, MAGNITUDE-SMALLNESS, REMOTENESS-NEARNESS; **be about,** OCCUPATION; **beat about,** MIDCOURSE-CIRCUIT; **come about,** BETTERMENT-DETERIORATION; **get about,** PUBLICITY, RENOVATION-RELAPSE; **going about,** TIDINGS-MYSTERY; **not know what one is about,** SKILL-UNSKILFULNESS; **put about,** ADVANCE-RETROGRESSION; **round about,** AIM-ABERRATION, CIRCUITION; **send about one's business,** COMMISSION-ABROGATION; **set about,** ENTERPRISE; **stir about,** ACTIVITY-INDOLENCE; **turn about,** REVERSAL; **what it is about,** CONCEPTION-THEME; **what one is about,** OCCUPATION; **about it and about it,** TERSENESS-PROLIXITY; **about to,** FUTURE-PAST; **about to be,** OCCURRENCE-DESTINY.

a-bove'. Overhead. EXPOSURE-HIDINGPLACE; **above all,** CONSEQUENCE-INSIGNIFICANCE, SUPREMACY-SUBORDINACY; **above board,** CRAFT-ARTLESSNESS, MANIFESTATION-LATENCY, UPRIGHTNESS-DISHONESTY; **above comprehension,** CLEARNESS-OBSCURITY; **above ground,** LIFE-DEATH; **above the mark,** SUPREMACY-SUBORDINACY; **above par,** GOODNESS-BADNESS, MAGNITUDE-SMALLNESS; **above praise,** VIRTUE-VICE; **above price,** COSTLINESS-CHEAPNESS; **above stairs,** HEIGHT-LOWNESS; **above suspicion,** INNOCENCE-GUILT; **above water,** SECURITY-INSECURITY.

a-bove'-men'-tioned. Referred to before. ANTECEDENCE-SEQUENCE, PRECEDENCE-SUCCESSION, RECURRENCE.

ab"-ra-ca-dab'-ra. Nonsensical words. DEVOTION-CHARM.

ab-rade'. To wear away. ADDITION-SUBTRACTION, FRIABILITY.

A'-bra-ham, sham. Feign sickness. TRUTHFULNESS-FALSEHOOD.

ab-rase'. To rub off. FRICTION-LUBRICATION.

ab-ra'-sion. Wearing away. ADDITION-SUBTRACTION, FRIABILITY, FRICTION-LUBRICATION.

a-breast'. Side by side. LATERALITY-CONTRAPOSITION.

abrégé [F.] (a-brê-zhê'). Abridged. ABRIDGMENT-DIGEST.

ab-rep'-tion. Snatching away. TAKING-RESTITUTION.

abri, tente d' [F.] (a-brî', tan·t d'). Shelter tent. COVER-LINING.

a-bridge'. To shorten. INCREASE-DECREASE, LENGTH-SHORTNESS; **abridge in writing,** DIGEST, TERSENESS-PROLIXITY.

a-bridged'. Shortened. DIGEST.

a-bridg'-ment. A condensed form. DIGEST, INCREASE-DECREASE, LENGTH-SHORTNESS, TERSENESS-PROLIXITY.

a-broach'. On tap. READINESS-RELUCTANCE.

a-broad'. At a great distance. CERTAINTY-UNCERTAINTY, CONSTITUENT-ALIEN, REMOTENESS-NEARNESS; **get abroad,** PUBLICITY.

ab'-ro-gate. To annul. COMMISSION-ABROGATION, COMMISSION-RETIREMENT.

ab'-ro-ga-ted. Annulled. COMMISSION-ABROGATION, COMMISSION-RETIREMENT.

ab"-ro-ga'-tion. Repeal. COMMISSION-ABROGATION, QUEST-RELINQUISHMENT.

ab-rupt'. Sudden. ELEGANCE-SUDDENNESS, ETERNITY-INSTANTANEITY, PARALLELISM-INCLINATION, TURBULENCE-CALMNESS.

ab-rup'-tion. A sudden breaking off. UNION-DISUNION.

ab-rupt'-ly. Suddenly. ETERNITY-INSTANTANEITY.

ab'-scess. An inflammatory tumor. HEALTH-SICKNESS.

ab-scind'. To cut off. ADDITION-SUBTRACTION, UNION-DISUNION.

ab-scis'-sa. An element of reference in the location of a point. MENSURATION.

ab-scis'-sion. Act of cutting off. ADDITION-SUBTRACTION, UNION-DISUNION.

ab-scond'. To depart secretly. ARRIVAL-DEPARTURE, QUEST-EVASION.

ab'-sence. Withdrawal from a place. ENTITY-NONENTITY, HOLDING-EXEMPTION, PLURALITY-ZERO, PRESENCE-ABSENCE; **absence of choice,** CHOICE-NEUTRALITY; **absence of elasticity,** ELASTICITY-INELASTICITY; **absence of intellect,** MIND-IMBECILITY; **absence of mind,** HEED-DISREGARD; **absence of motive,** MOTIVE-CAPRICE; **absence of preparation,** PREPARATION-NONPREPARATION; **absence of solidity,** SOLIDITY-RARITY; **absence of voice,** VOCALIZATION-MUTENESS.

absence d'esprit [F.] (ab-san·s' des-pri'). Absence of mind. HEED-DISREGARD, REFLECTION-VACANCY.

absens haeres non erit [L.] (ab-senz' hi'-rîz non î'-rit). The absent man will not be heir. REMEMBRANCE-FORGETFULNESS.

ab'-sent. Being away; absent-minded. HEED-DISREGARD, PRESENCE-ABSENCE, REFLECTION-VACANCY.

ab-sent' oneself. To withdraw. PRESENCE-ABSENCE.

ab-sen-tee'. One who is absent. PRESENCE-ABSENCE.

ab"-sen-tee'-ism. Practice of being absent. PRESENCE-ABSENCE.

ab"-sent—mind'-ed. Abstracted. HEED-DISREGARD.

ab'-sinth. A bitter, greenish liquor. REDNESS-GREENNESS.

ab'-so-lute. Independent; unqualified; despotic. ASSERTION-DENIAL, CERTAINTY-UNCERTAINTY, CHOICE-NEUTRALITY, DOMINANCE-IMPOTENCE, DUENESS-UNDUENESS, ENTIRETY-DEFICIENCY, ENTITY-NONENTITY, HARSHNESS-MILDNESS, HEED-DISREGARD, LIBERTY-SUBJECTION, MAGNITUDE-SMALLNESS, MIND-IMBECILITY, MOTIVE-CAPRICE, PRESENCE-ABSENCE; **absolute interest,** PROPERTY; **make absolute,** DECISION-MISJUDGMENT, EVIDENCE-COUNTEREVIDENCE.

ab'-so-lute ad-ver'-sa-tive. A conjunction expressing contrariety or opposition. PARTICLE.

ab'-so-lute-ly. Completely. MAGNITUDE-SMALLNESS.

ab'-so-lute-ness. State of being absolute. RULE-LICENSE, TYRANNY-ANARCHY.

ab"-so-lu'-tion. Remission of sin. DUTY-IMMUNITY, EXCULPATION-CONVICTION, PARDON-VINDICTIVENESS, RELEASE-RESTRAINT.

ab'-so-lu"-tism. Unlimited authority. HARSHNESS-MILDNESS, TYRANNY-ANARCHY.

ab-solv'-a-ble. Capable of being acquitted. ATONEMENT.

ab-solve'. To set free. ATONEMENT, DUTY-IMMUNITY, EXCULPATION-CONVICTION, PARDON-VINDICTIVENESS, JEALOUSY-ENVY, RELEASE-RESTRAINT.

ab'-so-nant. Unreasonable. MELODY-DISSONANCE, RATIOCINATION-CASUISTRY.

ab'-so-nous. Discordant. RATIOCINATION-CASUISTRY.

ab-sorb'. To take into. ADMISSION-EXPULSION, CHEMISTRY, COMPOSITION-RESOLUTION, EXCITATION, USE-DISUSE; **absorb the mind,** HEED-DISREGARD; **absorb the soul,** EXCITATION.

ab-sorbed'. Taken into; engrossed. HEED-DISREGARD.

ab-sorb'-ent. Tending to absorb. ADMISSION-EXPULSION.

ab-sorb'-ing. Tending to draw in. EMOTION, NEED.

ab-sorp'-tion. Act of absorbing. ADMISSION-EXPULSION, BIOLOGY, COMPOSITION-RESOLUTION, HEED-DISREGARD.

ab-sorp'-tive. Tending to absorb. ADMISSION-EXPULSION.

ab-squat'-u-late. To run away. QUEST-EVASION.

ab-stain'. To refrain. MODERATION-SELFINDULGENCE, QUEST-EVASION, USE-DISUSE; **abstain from action,**

Action-Passiveness; **abstain from voting,** Choice-Neutrality.

ab-stain'-er. One who abstains. Moderation-Self-indulgence, Teetotalism-Intemperance.

ab-ste'-mi-ous. Sparing. Moderation-Selfindulgence.

ab-ste'-mi-ous-ness. State of being sparing. Self-indulgence-Voluptuary.

ab-sten'-tion. A refraining. Quest-Evasion.

ab-sterge'. To make clean. Cleanness-Filthiness.

ab-ster'-sion. A cleansing. Cleanness-Filthiness.

ab-ster'-sive. Having cleansing qualities. Remedy-Bane.

ab'-sti-nence. Self-denial. Moderation-Selfindulgence, Quest-Evasion, Use-Disuse; **abstinence from action,** Action-Passiveness, Use-Disuse; **abstinence from voting,** Choice-Neutrality; **total abstinence,** Austerity, Moderation-Selfindulgence, Use-Disuse.

ab'-sti-nent. Continent. Moderation-Selfindulgence.

ab-stract'. To take away. Digest, Taking-Restitution, Terseness-Prolixity, Theft, Union-Disunion; **abstract idea,** Conception-Theme; **abstract oneself,** Heed-Disregard, **abstract noun,** Noun; **abstract thought,** Heed-Disregard, Reflection-Vacancy; **in the abstract,** Connection-Independence, Solitude-Company, Union-Disunion.

ab-stract'-ed. Separated. Heed-Disregard.

ab-stract'-ed-ly. Heedlessly. Union-Disunion.

ab-stract'-ed-ness. Heedlessness. Union-Disunion.

ab-strac'-tion. A separating; a taking. Addition-Subtraction, Heed-Disregard, Reflection-Vacancy, Taking-Restitution, Theft, Union-Disunion.

ab-struse'. Hidden. Clearness-Obscurity.

ab-surd'. Opposed to truth. Adage-Nonsense, Possibility-Impossibility.

ab-surd'-i-ty. A contradiction of sound reason. Adage-Nonsense, Society-Ludicrousness, Possibility-Impossibility.

ab-surd'-ness. State of being absurd. Adage-Nonsense.

A-bu'-na. The head of the Abyssinian Church. Chief-Underling, Ministry-Laity.

a-bun'-dance. Plenty. Enough.

a-bun'-dant. Plentiful. Enough, Entirety-Deficiency, Magnitude-Smallness.

abundanti cautela, ex [L.] (ab-un-dan'-tai cau-ti'-la, ex). From abundant caution. Security-Insecurity.

a-bun'-dant-ly. Plentifully. Magnitude-Smallness.

a-burst'. In a bursting condition. Excess-Lack.

a-buse'. To put to a bad use. Approval-Disapproval, Charitableness-Curse, Goodness-Badness, Purity-Impurity, Truthfulness-Falsehood, Use-Disuse; **abuse of language,** Word-Neology; **abuse of terms,** Interpretation-Misinterpretation, Word-Neology.

a-buse'-ful. Full of abuse. Usefulness-Uselessness.

a-bu'-sive. Hurtful; improper. Adulation-Disparagement, Approval-Disapproval, Charitableness-Menace, Politeness-Impoliteness.

a-but'. To touch end to end. Interspace-Contact, Suspension-Support.

a-but'-ment. A supporting structure. Attack-Defense, Interspace-Contact, Suspension-Support.

a-by'. To pay the penalty for. Emotion, Excitability-Inexcitability, Mutation-Permanence.

a-bysm'. A chasm. Interspace-Contact.

a-bys'-mal. Deep. Deepness-Shallowness.

a-byss'. A bottomless gulf. Extension-Inextension, Heaven-Hell, Interspace-Contact.

A. C. [L. *ante*]. Before Christ. Duration-Nearness.

ac''-a-dem'-ic. Classical. Education-Misteaching, School.

ac''-a-dem'-ic-al. Scholarly. Purity-Crudeness.

a-cad''-e-mi'-cian. A member of an academy. Scholar-Dunce; **Royal Academician,** Artist.

a-cad'-e-mist. An academician. Scholar-Dunce.

a-cad'-e-my. A place of instruction. School.

a-can'-thus. A plant. Architecture. Embellishment-Disfigurement.

acariâtre [F.] (a-ca-ri-atr'). Crabbed. Favorite-Quarrelsomeness.

a-cat''-a-lec'-tic. Not defective. Poetry.

a-cat''-a-lep-sy. The inconceivability of things. Certainty-Doubt.

accedas ad curiam [L.] (ac-si'das ad kiu'-ri-am). You may go to court. Litigation, Tribunal.

ac-cede'. To agree to. Assent-Dissent, Consent.

ac-cel'-er-ate. To quicken. Earliness-Lateness, Hurry-Leisure, Swiftness-Slowness, Turbulence-Calmness.

ac-cel''-er-a'-tion. A quickening. Hurry-Leisure, Swiftness-Slowness.

ac-cen'-sion. Act of setting fire to. Heating-Cooling.

ac'-cent. Stress of voice on a particular syllable. Rhetoric, Sound-Silence, Vocalization-Muteness; **broken accent,** Vocalization-Muteness.

ac-cen'-tu-ate. To pronounce with an accent. Consequence-Insignificance, Vocalization-Muteness.

ac-cen''-tu-a'-tion. Act of accentuating. Poetry-Prose, Vocalization-Muteness.

ac-cept'. To take when offered. Assent-Dissent, Consent, Giving-Receiving, Taking-Restitution.

accepta [L.] (ac-sep'ta). Receipts. Accounts, Security.

ac-cept'-a-ble. Pleasing. Pleasurableness-Painfulness, Propriety-Impropriety.

ac-cept'-ance. Act of accepting. Assent-Dissent, Consent, Giving-Receiving, Interpretation-Misinterpretation, Security.

ac''-cep-ta'-tion. Accepted meaning. Interpretation-Misinterpretation, Meaning-Jargon.

ac-cep'-tion. Favoritism. Interpretation-Misinterpretation.

ac'-cess. A coming near. Approach-Withdrawal; **easy of access,** Difficulty-Facility; **means of access,** Way.

ac-ces'-si-ble. Capable of being reached. Difficulty-Facility, Possibility-Impossibility.

ac-ces'-sion. Increase. Addition-Subtraction, Commission-Abrogation, Consent, Increase-Decrease, Rule-License.

ac-ces'-so-ry. Additional; aiding. Addition-Subtraction, Antagonist-Assistant, Increment-Remnant, Obstruction-Help, Solitude-Company.

acciaccatura [It.] (at-chac-ca-tu'-ra). A grace note in music. Melody-Dissonance.

ac'-ci-dence. Rudiments. Grammar-Solecism.

ac'-ci-dent. Event; chance; disaster. Good-Evil, Occurrence-Destiny, Rationale-Luck, Welfare-Misfortune; **fatal accident,** Life-Killing.

ac''-ci-den'-tal. Unexpected. Purpose-Luck, Rationale-Luck, Subjectiveness-Objectiveness.

ac''-ci-den'-tal-ly. Casually. Subjectiveness-Objectiveness.

ac'-ci-dents, trust to the chapter of. Purpose-Luck.

ac-cip'-i-ent. A receiver. Giving-Receiving.

ac-claim'. Applause. Approval-Disapproval.

ac''-cla-ma'-tion. Shout of assent. Approval-Disapproval, Assent-Dissent.

ac-cli''-ma-ti-za'-tion. An habituating. Habit-Desuetude

ac-cli'-ma-tize. To adapt to a new climate. DOMESTICATION-AGRICULTURE, HABIT-DESUETUDE.

ac-cliv'-i-ty. An upward slope. ASCENT-DESCENT, PARALLELISM-INCLINATION.

ac-cli'-vous. Sloping upward. PARALLELISM-INCLINATION.

ac-cloy'. To fill full. EXCESS-LACK.

ac"-co-lade'. Salutation of knighthood. POLITENESS-IMPOLITENESS.

ac-com'-mo-date. To oblige; furnish. EQUALITY-INEQUALITY, FIGHTING-CONCILIATION, GIVING-RECEIVING, HARMONY-DISCORD, LOAN-BORROWING, OBSTRUCTION-HELP; **accommodate oneself to,** CONVENTIONALITY-UNCONVENTIONALITY; **accommodate with,** GIVING-RECEIVING, LOAN-BORROWING.

ac-com'-mo-da"-ting. Obliging. CHARITABLENESS-MALEVOLENCE.

ac-com"-mo-da'-tion. Adjustment. FIGHTING-CONCILIATION, KEEPING-RELINQUISHMENT, OBSTRUCTION-HELP.

ac-com'-pa-ni-ment. Something added. ADDITION-SUBTRACTION, INCREMENT-REMNANT, MUSIC, SOLITUDE-COMPANY

ac-com'-pa-nist. One who accompanies. MUSICIAN.

ac-com'-pa-ny. To go with. ADDITION-SUBTRACTION, COEXISTENCE, MUSICIAN, SOLITUDE-COMPANY.

ac-com'-pa-ny-ing. Going with. SOLITUDE-COMPANY.

accompli, fait [F.] (ac-con'-pli', fêt). An accomplished deed. COMPLETION-NONCOMPLETION.

ac-com'-plice. An associate. ANTAGONIST-ASSISTANT.

ac-com'-plish. To carry out. COMPLETION-NONCOMPLETION, CREATION-DESTRUCTION, SUCCESS-FAILURE; **accomplish with difficulty,** DIFFICULTY-FACILITY.

ac-com'-plished. Carried out. SCHOLAR-DUNCE, SKILL-UNSKILFULNESS.

ac-com'-plish-ment. Completion. Anything that perfects. COMPLETION-NONCOMPLETION, KNOWLEDGE-IGNORANCE, SKILL-UNSKILFULNESS.

ac-compts'. Accounts. ACCOUNTS.

ac-cord'. To grant; harmony. ASSENT-DISSENT, GIVING-RECEIVING, HARMONY-DISCORD, LEAVE-PROHIBITION, MELODY-DISSONANCE, UNIFORMITY-DIVERSITY, VARIANCE-ACCORD; **in accord,** HARMONY-DISCORD; **of one's own accord,** READINESS-RELUCTANCE.

ac-cord'-ance. Agreement. ASSENT-DISSENT, GIVING-RECEIVING, HARMONY-DISCORD, LEAVE-PROHIBITION, UNIFORMITY-DIVERSITY; **accordance with reality,** NATURE-ART; **accordance with truth,** NATURE-ART; **in accordance,** CONVENTIONALITY-UNCONVENTIONALITY; **in accordance with,** HARMONY-DISCORD.

ac-cord'-ant. Harmonious. HARMONY-DISCORD; **be accordant,** HARMONY-DISCORD; **render accordant,** HARMONY-DISCORD.

ac-cord'-ing. Agreeing. **According as,** MODIFICATION; **according to,** EVIDENCE-COUNTEREVIDENCE; **according to circumstances,** CONDITION-SITUATION; **according to every reasonable expectation,** LIKELIHOOD-UNLIKELIHOOD; **according to law,** LAW-LAWLESSNESS; **according to regulation,** CONVENTIONALITY-UNCONVENTIONALITY; **according to rule,** CONVENTIONALITY-UNCONVENTIONALITY; **according to this occasion,** CONDITION-SITUATION.

ac-cord'-ing-ly. Suitably. CONDITION - SITUATION, RATIOCINATION-INSTINCT.

ac-cor'-di-on. A musical wind-instrument. MUSICAL INSTRUMENTS.

ac-cor'-di-on-ist. A player on the accordion. MUSICIAN

ac-cost'. To address. ADDRESS-RESPONSE.

ac-cou-cheur' (cu-shur). An assistant at childbirth. INSTRUMENTALITY, REMEDY-BANE.

ac-count'. A reckoning. ACCOUNT, ACCOUNTS, APPROVAL-DISAPPROVAL, CREDIT-DEBT, DECISION-MISJUDGMENT, ENLIGHTENMENT-SECRECY, NUMBERING, RECORD, REPUTATION-DISCREDIT; **call to account,** APPROVAL-DISAPPROVAL; **find one's account in,** SUCCESS-FAILURE, USEFULNESS-USELESSNESS; **make no account of,** OVERVALUATION-UNDERVALUATION; **not account for,** CLEARNESS-OBSCURITY; **on account of,** MOTIVE-CAPRICE, OBSTRUCTION-HELP, PURPOSE-LUCK, RATIONALE-LUCK; **on no account,** ASSERTION-DENIAL, LEAVE-PROHIBITION, PROFFER-REFUSAL; **send to one's account,** LIFE-KILLING; **take into account,** HEED-DISREGARD, MODIFICATION; **small account,** CONSEQUENCE-INSIGNIFICANCE; **to one's account,** PROPERTY; **turn to account,** BETTERMENT-DETERIORATION, GAIN-LOSS, SUCCESS-FAILURE, USE-DISUSE; **account as,** FAITH-MISGIVING; **account for,** INTERPRETATION-MISINTERPRETATION, RATIONALE-LUCK; **account with,** EXCHANGE, SETTLEMENT-DEFAULT

ACCOUNT.

Account. A written or spoken record.
Adventures. Hazardous events in a man's life.
Ana. A collection of sayings and anecdotes.
Anecdotes. Short stories.
Annals. Narrative of events divided into periods.
Apologue. Narrative of events to bring out some moral truth
Autobiography. A story of one's own life by himself.
Biography. The story of a person's life.
Chronography. History; record.
Circumstantial account. An account giving many details.
Confessions. Facts relative to the life of a person.
Delineation. Representing by drawing bold outlines.
Description. An account; a word portrayal.
Detailed account. A description giving minute details.
Essay. A composition on a subject less formal than a treatise.
Exposé [F.]. Statement; account; outline.
Fable. A fictitious story written to teach some moral.
Fairy tale. A recital of the deeds of a fairy; an invented story
Fortunes. Events which befall a person during his life.
Historiette. An historical treatise on a small scale.
Historiography. The writing of historic treatises; histories.
History. A written record of events.
Journal. An account of daily events.
Legend. A traditional story.
Memoir. A short biography; reminiscences; something memorable.
Memorial. A token or monument to perpetuate the memory of some one or something.
Minute account. A record in full.
Monograph. An essay upon a definite thing or special class.
Narration. The act of recounting the particulars of an event or series of events in the order of occurrence.
Narrative. A logical account of the successive events of something.
Necrology. A record of deaths.
Nursery tale. A story, or tale, for children.
Parable. A religious allegory, like the parables of Christ.
Particulars. A record in full.
Personal narration. A description about some particular person.
Recital. An account given in detail.
Record. Official proceedings entered in a book.
Rehearsal. A narration; a repeating of some performance to be rendered during some theatrical season.
Relation. A telling; a recital.
Report. A recountal of events.
Romance. A story of adventure or chivalry.
Sketch. A rough outline; a general delineation.
Specification. An account where every detail is specified.
Statement. A setting forth of certain opinions.
Statement of facts. Ground upon which evidence is to be considered.
Story. A tale; a history; a record.
Summary of facts. An epitome; a collection of the main points
Tale. A story; an account; statement.
Thesis. A subject prescribed to a student to write before granting him a degree.
Tradition. The handing down from one generation to another by word of mouth of the customs, deeds, attainments, etc., of a people
Treatise. A formal essay; a composition on a particular subject.
Work of fiction. A novel; a book of fiction.

ACCOUNT—*Associated Nouns.*

Biographer. One who writes biographies.
Clio. The muse of history.

Fabulist. A writer of fables; one who falsifies.
Guide book. A book of information for travelers and tourists.
Historian. A recorder and interpreter of events.
Historic muse. See CLIO.
Minerva Press. The press in London which printed a great many trashy novels in the eighteenth century.
Novelist. A writer of fiction.
Relator. One who recounts; narrator.

Account—*Verbs.*

Characterize. To set forth traits or well-known marks.
Descend to details, descend to particulars. To give descriptions in full.
Describe. To depict; delineate.
Draw a picture. To bring out the features of something with pencil and brush.
Enter into particulars. See DESCEND TO PARTICULARS.
Fight one's battles over again. Recall old adventures.
Give an account of. To describe; to tell about.
Make a report. To give a full account of; usually, written.
Narrate. To tell; to recount.
Particularize. Mention details.
Picture. To paint; to set forth in bold relief.
Portray. See DELINEATION.
Recapitulate. To repeat; to give a summary of.
Recite. Rehearse; repeat.
Recount. Relate; to tell.
Rehearse. To go over again; to relate.
Relate. To narrate; to report.
Render an account of. To give a true report.
Report. Give an account; to tell the facts.
Set forth. See ASSERTION
Sum up. To make a summary.
Unfold a tale. To relate a tale; to unravel a story.

Account—*Adjectives.*

Anecdotic. See *Nouns.*
Described. See *Verbs.*
Descriptive. Narrative; pictorial.
Epic. A recital of heroic exploits.
Graphic. Very clear and pronounced.
Historic. A part of history.
Legendary. Based on tradition.
Narrative. See ACCOUNT.
Storied. Connected with history.
Suggestive. Incidents which call forth others.
Traditional. Not authentic; based on legends.
Traditionary. Traditional.

Account—*Phrase.*

Furor scribendi [L.]. Rage for writing.

ac-count'-a-ble. Responsible. ACCOUNTS, DUTY-IMMUNITY.
ac-count'-a-ble-ness. Responsibility. DUTY-IMMUNITY.
ac-count'-ant. One skilled in accounts. ACCOUNTS, TREASURER.
ac-count'-ant gen'-er-al. Chief accountant. TREASURER.
ac-count'-ing. Reckoning. ACCOUNTS.
ac-counts'. Records. ACCOUNTS, MONEY.

ACCOUNTS.

Accompts. Accounts.
Account. Record of debits, credits, etc.
Account current. A running account.
Accounts. Record of business transactions.
Account settled. An account closed and verified.
Balance sheet. A sheet of paper on which the balance is put for inspection.
Bill. An orderly statement of small business transactions.
Budget. A financial statement put before a legislature.
Cash account. An account of ready money.
Compte rendu [F.]. A returned account.
Debtor and creditor account. An account in which debts and credits are exhibited.
Money matters. Financial statements or affairs.
Reckoning. An account stated; a score.
Running account. An open account.
Score. A bill.
Statistics. Classified facts. See NUMBERING.
Trial balance. In double-entry bookkeeping, a final statement of all balances in the ledger accounts.

Accounts—*Agency.*

Accountant. One who keeps or makes accounts.
Accounting party. One who is required to make an account.
Actuary. A calculating officer in an insurance company.
Auditor. One who examines accounts.
Bookkeeper. One who keeps account books.
Financier. One skilled in finance. See TREASURER.

Accounts—*Means.*

Account books. Books in which accounts are kept.
Books. A general name for all account books.
Cash books. Books in which cash transactions are recorded.
Day book. A journal of every item of daily business.
Journal. A register of daily transactions.
Ledger. Principal account book.
Pass book. A small book in which credits are kept.

Accounts—*Associated Nouns.*

Accepta [L.]. Receipts.
Acquit [F.]. Discharge from debt.
Audit. An examination of an account by proper persons.
Balance. An excess of credit over debtor side, or vice versa.
Bookkeeping. The method by which accounts are kept.
Commercial arithmetic. The science of mercantile transactions.
Double entry. A special method of keeping accounts.
Finance. The science of the proper management of monetary affairs.
Monetary arithmetic. Arithmetic of finance.

Accounts—*Verbs.*

Audit. To adjust an account.
Balance accounts. To make debit and credit sides of an account equal.
Book. Record in an account book.
Bring to book. Put a transaction in a book.
Carry over. To transfer an account from one book to another or from one page to another.
Cast up accounts. To compute accounts.
Cook an account. To tamper with an account.
Credit To enter upon credit side of accounts.
Debit. To enter upon debit side of accounts.
Doctor an account. To falsify an account.
Enter. To put on record; to enroll.
Falsify an account. To make an account false.
Garble an account. To mutilate an account.
Keep an account. To record accounts in a book.
Make accounts square. To make the accounts even.
Make up accounts. Compute accounts.
Post. To transfer accounts from journal to ledger.
Settle accounts. To balance or pay an account.
Square an account. To make an account balance.
Surcharge and falsify. To show an item in an account omitted or wrong.
Take stock. Take an account of merchandise.
Tax. To lay a burden upon; to assess.
Wind up accounts. To close accounts.

Accounts—*Adjectives.*

Accountable. Capable of being accounted.
Accounting. Computing; reckoning up.
Monetary. Of or pertaining to money or finance. See MONEY.

ac-coup'-le. To join. UNION-DISUNION.
ac-cou'-ter. To furnish. DRESS-UNDRESS, PREPARATION-NONPREPARATION.
ac-cou'-ter-ment. Trappings. DRESS, UNDRESS, INSTRUMENTS, PREPARATION-NONPREPARATION.
ac-coy'. To soothe. TURBULENCE-CALMNESS.
ac-cred'-it. To give authority to. ARTIST, CREDIT-DEBT, REPUTATION-DISCREDIT, TRUTHFULNESS-FALSEHOOD.
ac-cred'-it-ed. Believed. CREDIT-DEBT, FAITH-MISGIVING, HABIT-DESUETUDE; **accredited to,** COMMISSION-ABROGATION, REPRESENTATIVE.
ac-cre'-tion. Growth. BIOLOGY, COHESION-LOOSENESS, ENLARGEMENT-DIMINUTION, INCREASE-DECREASE.
ac-crim''-i-na'-tion. Accusation. JUSTIFICATION-CHARGE.
ac-croach'. To usurp. TAKING-RESTITUTION.

ac-cru′-al. Increase. INCREASE-DECREASE.

ac-crue′. To accumulate. ADDITION-SUBTRACTION, CAUSE-EFFECT, GAIN-LOSS, GIVING-RECEIVING, OUTLAY-INCOME.

ac-crust′. To become hard. HARDNESS-SOFTNESS.

ac″-cu-ba′-tion. Reclining. ERECTNESS-FLATNESS.

accueil [F.] (ac-cu-îy). Reception. POLITENESS-IMPOLITENESS.

ac-cum′-bent. Lying down. ERECTNESS-FLATNESS.

ac-cu′-mu-late. To collect. EXCESS-LACK, GATHERING-SCATTERING, STORE.

ac-cu″-mu-la′-tion. EXCESS-LACK, GATHERING-SCATTERING, STORE.

ac′-cu-ra-cy. Exactness. CAREFULNESS-CARELESSNESS, TRUTH-ERROR.

ac′-cu-rate. Exact. CAREFULNESS-CARELESSNESS, KNOWLEDGE-IGNORANCE, TRUTH-ERROR.

ac-curse′. Doom to evil. CHARITABLENESS-CURSE.

ac-cursed′. Miserable. GOODNESS-BADNESS, PLEASURE-PAIN, VIRTUE-VICE.

ac-cu′-sa-ble. Blameworthy. JUSTIFICATION-CHARGE.

accusare nemo se debet [L.] (ac-kiu-zê′-rî nî′-mo sî dî′-bet). No one is bound to accuse himself. LITIGATION.

ac″-cu-sa′-tion. A charge of crime. JUSTIFICATION-CHARGE, LITIGATION.

ac-cu′-sa-tive. The case of nouns which denotes the object of a transitive verb. NOUN.

ac-cu′-sa-to-ry. Accusing. JUSTIFICATION-CHARGE.

ac-cuse′. To charge with wrong-doing. APPROVAL-DISAPPROVAL, EXCULPATION-CONVICTION, JUSTIFICATION-CHARGE, LITIGATION.

ac-cused′. Charged. JUSTIFICATION-CHARGE.

ac-cus′-er. One who accuses. JUSTIFICATION-CHARGE.

ac-cus′-ing. Charging. JUSTIFICATION-CHARGE.

ac-cus′-tom. To make wonted. HABIT-DESUETUDE.

ac-cus′-tom-a-ry. Habitual. HABIT-DESUETUDE.

ac-cus′-tomed. Habituated. HABIT-DESUETUDE.

ace. A minute portion. MAGNITUDE-SMALLNESS, SOLITUDE-COMPANY; **within an ace,** REMOTENESS-NEARNESS.

A-cel′-da-ma. Place of bloody associations. LIFE-KILLING, LISTS.

a-cerb′. Harsh; sharp. SWEETNESS-ACIDITY.

ac′-er-bate. Embittered. ALLEVIATION-AGGRAVATION, BETTERMENT-DETERIORATION.

a-cerb′-ic. Severe. AUSTERITY.

a-cerb′-i-ty. Bitterness. CHARITABLENESS-MALEVOLENCE, FAVORITE-QUARRELSOMENESS, PALATABLENESS-UNPALATABLENESS, POLITENESS-IMPOLITENESS.

acerrima proximorum odia [L.] (a-ser′-rî-ma prox-i-mo′-rum o′-di-a). Fiercest the hatred of those nearest kin. LOVE-HATE.

a-cer′-vate. Massed together. GATHERING-SCATTERING.

acervatim [L.] (a-ser-vê-tim). In heaps. EXCESS-LACK. GATHERING-SCATTERING, MULTIPLICITY-PAUCITY.

ac″-er-va′-tion. Amassing. GATHERING-SCATTERING.

a-ces′-cent. Tart. SWEETNESS-ACIDITY.

a-cet′-ic. Sour. SWEETNESS-ACIDITY.

ac′-e-tone. An inflammable liquid. CHEMISTRY.

ac′-e-tous. Sour. CHEMISTRY, SWEETNESS-ACIDITY.

ac′-et-yl-ene″. An illuminating gas. CHEMISTRY.

acharné [F.] (a-shar-nê′). Ravenous. FAVORITE-ANGER.

acharnement [F.] (a-sharn-man′). Bloodthirstiness. FAVORITE-ANGER.

Achates, fidus [L.] (a-kê′-tîz, fai′-dus). Faithful Achates; trusty friend. FRIEND-FOE, UPRIGHTNESS-ROGUE.

ache. A pain. PLEASURE-PAIN, SENSUALITY-SUFFERING.

Ach′-e-ron, pit of. Hell. HEAVEN-HELL.

Acheronta, flectere si nequeo superos,—movebo [L.] (ak″-er-on′-ta, flec′-ter-î sai nî′-qui-o siu′-per-os,—

mo-vî′-bo). If I fail to move the powers above, I will move Acheron. SUCCESS-FAILURE.

Acherontis pabulum [L.] (ak-er-on′-tis pab′-yu-lum). Food for Acheron. GOOD MAN-BAD MAN.

a-chiev′-a-ble. Capable of being done. POSSIBILITY-IMPOSSIBILITY.

a-chieve′. To accomplish. ACTION-PASSIVENESS, BEGINNING-END, COMPLETION-NONCOMPLETION, CREATION-DESTRUCTION.

a-chieve′-ment. A successful action. ACTION-PASSIVENESS, BRAVERY-COWARDICE, COMPLETION-NONCOMPLETION, CREATION-DESTRUCTION, MARK-OBLITERATION.

Ach″-il-le′-an. Invulnerable; wrathful. FAVORITE-QUARRELSOMENESS, SECURITY-INSECURITY.

A-chil′-les, heel of (-kil′-). A vulnerable part. SECURITY-INSECURITY.

a′-ching. Suffering pain. PLEASURE-PAIN, SENSUALITY-SUFFERING; **aching heart,** PLEASURE-PAIN.

ach″-ro-mat′-ic. Colorless. COLOR-ACHROMATISM.

a-chro′-ma-tism. Quality of being colorless. COLOR-ACHROMATISM.

a-chro′-ma-tize. To make achromatic. COLOR-ACHROMATISM.

a-cic′-u-lar. Sharp-pointed. SHARPNESS-BLUNTNESS.

ac′-id. A sour substance. CHEMISTRY, SWEETNESS-ACIDITY.

a-cid′-i-fy. To make acid. SWEETNESS-ACIDITY.

a-cid′-i-ty. State of being acid. SWEETNESS-ACIDITY.

a-cid′-u-late. To embitter. SWEETNESS-ACIDITY.

a-cid′-u-la″-ted. Made acid. SWEETNESS-ACIDITY.

a-cid′-u-lous. Subacid. SWEETNESS-ACIDITY.

acierta errando [Sp.] (a-thî-er′-ta er-ran′-do). He blunders into the right. ADEPT-BUNGLER, PURPOSE-LUCK.

ac′-i-form. Needle-shaped. SHARPNESS-BLUNTNESS.

ac-knowl′-edge. To admit. ASSENT-DISSENT, ASSERTION-DENIAL, CONSENT, EVIDENCE-COUNTEREVIDENCE, EXPOSURE-HIDINGPLACE, INVESTIGATION-ANSWER, OBSERVANCE-NONOBSERVANCE, RECOMPENSE-PUNITION, REPENTANCE-OBDURACY, SAGACITY-INCAPACITY, SETTLEMENT-DEFAULT, THANKFULNESS-THANKLESSNESS.

ac-knowl′-edged. Admitted. HABIT-DESUETUDE.

ac-knowl′-edg-ment. Avowal; recognition; an official declaration. ASSENT-DISSENT, ASSERTION-DENIAL, CONSENT, EXPOSURE-HIDINGPLACE, INVESTIGATION-ANSWER, OBSERVANCE-NONOBSERVANCE, RECOMPENSE-PUNITION, REPENTANCE-OBDURACY, SETTLEMENT-DEFAULT, THANKFULNESS-THANKLESSNESS.

ac′-me. The highest point. TOP-BOTTOM; **acme of perfection,** FAULTLESSNESS-FAULTINESS.

a-col′-o-gy. Medical science. REMEDY-BANE.

a-col′-o-thyst. An attendant. MINISTRY-LAITY.

ac′-o-lyte. An attendant. MINISTRY-LAITY.

ac′-o-lyth. A Catholic priest. MINISTRY-LAITY.

a-co′-mi-a. Baldness. BEAUTY-UGLINESS.

ac′-o-nite. A medicinal plant. REMEDY-BANE.

a-cous′-tic. Pertaining to hearing. HEARING-DEAFNESS; acoustic organs. HEARING-DEAFNESS.

a-cous′-tics. Science of sound. SOUND-SILENCE.

ac-quaint′. To make familiar. **Acquaint oneself with,** EDUCATION-MISTEACHING, ENLIGHTENMENT-SECRECY; **acquaint with,** ENLIGHTENMENT-SECRECY.

ac-quaint′-ance. Knowledge of any person or thing. ENLIGHTENMENT-SECRECY, FRIEND-FOE, KNOWLEDGE-IGNORANCE; **make acquaintance with,** AMITY-HOSTILITY.

ac-quaint′-ed. Informed. SOCIABILITY-PRIVACY.

ac-quaint′-ed with. Known to. AMITY-HOSTILITY.

ac-quaint′-ing. Making familiar. ENLIGHTENING-SECRECY.

ac-quest′. Property acquired in any way except by inheritance. PROPERTY.

ac″-qui-esce′. To submit. ASSENT-DISSENT, CONSENT, EXCITABILITY-INEXCITABILITY.

ac″-qui-es′-cence. Submission. ASSENT-DISSENT, CONSENT.

ac″-qui-es′-cent. Yielding. ASSENT-DISSENT.

ac-quire′. To obtain. CREATION-DESTRUCTION, GAIN-LOSS, OUTLAY-INCOME; **acquire a habit**, HABIT-DESUETUDE; **acquire learning**, EDUCATION-LEARNING.

ac-quire′-ment. Attainment. EDUCATION-LEARNING, KNOWLEDGE-IGNORANCE, SKILL-UNSKILFULNESS.

ac″-qui-si′-tion. Anything gained. GAIN-LOSS, GIVING-RECEIVING, KNOWLEDGE-IGNORANCE.

ac-quis′-i-tive. Able to acquire. GAIN-LOSS.

ac-quit′. To free from. EXCULPATION-CONVICTION, INNOCENCE-GUILT, JUSTIFICATION-CHARGE, PARDON-VINDICTIVENESS, RELEASE-RESTRAINT; **acquit oneself**, CONDUCT, SETTLEMENT-DEFAULT; **acquit oneself of a debt**, SETTLEMENT-DEFAULT; **acquit oneself of a duty**, DUTY-DERELICTION; **acquit oneself of an obligation**, OBSERVANCE-NONOBSERVANCE.

acquit [F.] (ăc-kī′). Discharge. ACCOUNTS, CREDIT-DEBT.

ac-quit′-tal. Discharge. DUTY-IMMUNITY, EXCULPATION-CONVICTION, OBSERVANCE-NONOBSERVANCE, RELEASE-RESTRAINT.

ac-quit′-tance. Release. OBSERVANCE-NONOBSERVANCE, SECURITY, SETTLEMENT-DEFAULT.

ac-quit′-ted. Freed. EXCULPATION-CONVICTION.

a′-cre-age. Area in acres. EXTENSION-DISTRICT.

a′-cres. Measure of land. EXTENSION-DISTRICT, MEASURE, OCEAN-LAND, PROPERTY.

A′-cres, Bob. Character in *The Rivals;* a coward. BRAVERY-COWARDICE.

ac′-rid. Of a burning taste. PALATABLENESS-UNPALATABLENESS, PUNGENCY.

ac″-ri-mo′-ni-ous. Sarcastic; bitter. CHARITABLENESS-MALEVOLENCE, FAVORITE-ANGER, PALATABLENESS-UNPALATABLENESS, PRESUMPTION-OBSEQUIOUSNESS, PUNGENCY.

ac′-ri-mo-ny. Sharpness of speech or temper. CHARITABLENESS-CURSE, FAVORITE-ANGER, LOVE-HATE, ORDER, POLITENESS-IMPOLITENESS, VIGOR-INERTIA.

ac′-ri-tude. Bitterness. PUNGENCY, VIGOR-INERTIA.

ac″-ro-a-mat′-ic. Esoteric. KNOWLEDGE-IGNORANCE.

ac′-ro-a-mat″-ism. Quality of being oral. KNOWLEDGE-IGNORANCE.

ac′-ro-bat. A performer of gymnastic feats. ACTING, ADEPT-BUNGLER, STRENGTH-WEAKNESS, WAG.

Ac-rop′-o-lis. The citadel of an ancient Greek city. DWELLER-HABITATION.

a-cross′. Over. ANTAGONISM-CONCURRENCE, CROSSING.

ac″-ro-te′-ri-um. An ornament of whatever nature forming the apex of a building. ARCHITECTURE.

a-cros′-tic. A composition. LETTER, WITTINESS-DULNESS.

act. To perform. ACTING, ACTION-PASSIVENESS, AGENCY, DELINEATION-CARICATURE, IMITATION-ORIGINALITY, PRECEPT; **act a part**, ACTING, MANAGER, SOCIETY-AFFECTATION, TRUTHFULNESS-FALSEHOOD; **act as president**, PRESIDENT-MEMBER; **act one's part**, DUTY-DERELICTION, OCCUPATION; **act the tyrant**, TYRANNY-ANARCHY; **act upon**, ACTION-PASSIVENESS, AGENCY, MOTIVE-CAPRICE; **act up to**, OBSERVANCE-NONOBSERVANCE; **act well one's part**, VIRTUE-VICE; **act without authority**, RULE-LICENSE; **in the act**, ACTION-PASSIVENESS, INNOCENCE-GUILT.

act′-drop″. A curtain. ACTING.

ac′-ted upon. Passive. AGENCY.

act′-ing. Performing. ACTING, ACTION-PASSIVENESS, OCCUPATION, REPRESENTATIVE.

ACTING.

Acting. The performance of a dramatic part.
Dramaturgy. The art of composing and presenting a play.

Histrionic art. The art of dramatic representation.
Theatricals. Dramatic performances.
The drama. Theatrical composition.
The play. The performance of a dramatic composition.
The stage. The place of dramatic performance; hence, the drama.
The theater. The drama.

ACTING—*Forms of Dramatic Representation.*

After-piece, a farce after a play; *ballet* [F.], a spectacular dance; **burlesque,** a dramatic travesty; *burletta* [It.], a comic opera; **charade,** an enigma represented dramatically; *comédie drame* [F.], a dramatic comedy; *comédie larmoyante* [F.], a pathetic comedy; *comedietta* [It.], a short comedy; **comedy,** an amusing drama; *divertissement* [F.], an *entr'acte;* **drama,** a composition for the stage; *drame* [F.]; **duologue,** a dialogue; **exode,** the last part of a drama; *extravaganza* [It.], a drama wildly irregular; *fantoccini* [It.], dramatic representations with puppets as actors; **farce,** short extravagant comedy; **five-act play, long play;** **harlequinade,** **pantomime; interlude,** comedy performed between the acts of moralities; *lever de rideau* [F.], a curtain raiser; **light comedy, low comedy,** farcical comedy; **masque,** an allegorical play; **melodrama, melodrame,** a drama containing sensational incidents; **miracle play,** religious drama; **monodrame,** drama for single performer; **monologue,** a dramatic soliloquy; **morality,** allegorical play; **mystery,** rude religious drama; **opera,** musical drama; *opéra bouffe* [F.], farcical comic opera; **pantomime,** dumb show; **piece,** a play; **play,** dramatic composition; *proverbe* [F.], a short comedy with a proverb for its title; **Punch and Judy,** puppet show; **sensation drama,** sensational play; *spectacle* [F.], a play; **stage play,** play for stage; **acting; tragedy,** drama representing terrible emotions; **tragi-comedy,** a drama where comic and tragic scenes are mingled; **trilogy,** a group of three dramas; **vaudeville,** variety show.

ACTING—*Nouns of Agent.*

Acrobat. One who practises gymnastic feats.
Acting manager. The officiating manager of a dramatic company.
Actor. One who takes a dramatic part.
Amoroso [It.]. A lover in a drama.
Artiste [F.]. A high-class actor.
Ballet-dancer.
Ballet-girl. } One who dances in the ballet.
Buffo [It.], } A clown; a jester.
Buffoon.
Call-boy. A boy who calls actors to the stage.
Chorus singer. One who sings in a chorus.
Clown. A jester in a theater or circus.
Columbine. The mistress of Harlequin in pantomimes.
Comedian. An actor or writer of comedy.
Company. A number of players united for dramatic performances.
Contortionist. One who twists and contorts his body for a show.
Coryphee. A female premier dancer, leader of a ballet.
Costumier [F.]. One who prepares costumes for the theaters.
Danseuse. A female ballet-dancer.
Débutant, m.; *débutante*, f. [F.]. A person who makes his or her first public appearance.
Dramatic author. The writer of a dramatic composition.
Dramatic writer. One who writes concerning the drama.
Dramatist. One who writes dramas.
Entrepreneur [F.]. The proprietor of a dramatic entertainment.
Farceur [F.]. A comic actor.
Figurante [F.]. A ballet dancer.
First tragedian. The leading tragic actor.
General utility. An actor used for any part.
Genteel comedian. An actor of refined comedy.
Grimacier [F.]. One who makes grimaces or wry faces.
Guisard.
Guiser. } One who plays in a masquerade.
Gysart. A mummer.
Harlequin. A fancifully dressed character in pantomime.
Heavy father. An actor playing the part of a dignified father.
Impresario [It.]. One who manages an opera company.
Ingénue [F.]. An actress who fills the rôle of an artless character.
Jack Pudding. A buffoon.
Jeune premier [F.]. The leading young gentleman.
Jeune veuve [F.]. Young widow.
Light comedian. An actor of light comedy.
Low comedian. An actor of low comedy.
Machinist. One who attends to the machinery of the stage.
Manager. One who conducts a dramatic company or theater.
Masque. One who wears a masque; an actor.
Mime or **Mimer.** An actor in a mimic play.
Mimeographer. A writer of mimic plays.
Mountebank. A charlatan.

Mummer. A masked buffoon.

Mute. One whose part in a play consists only of dumb show

Pantaloon. A ridiculous character in Italian comedy.

Pantomimist. An actor in a dumb show.

Performer. One who shows skill in dramatic art.

Player. A dramatic actor.

Playwright, play-writer. One who writes plays.

Posture-master. A teacher or maker of artificial postures of the body.

Prima donna [It.]. The leading female singer in an opera.

Prompter. One who prompts the actors from behind the scenes in a theater.

Property-man. One in charge of the portable articles used in plays.

Protagonist. Leading actor in Greek dramas.

Pulcinella, Pulcinello [It.], PUNCH, PUNCHINELLO. The hero in a puppet show.

Stage-carpenter. The man who does the carpentry work for putting plays on the stage.

Stage-manager. One who superintends the production and performance of a play.

Stage-player. An actor on a stage.

Stager. An actor; a stage-horse.

Star. A brilliant and distinguished actor.

Strolling-player. An itinerant actor.

Super, Supernumerary. A person employed in addition to the regular number of actors, but who has no speaking part.

Thespian. An actor.

Tragedian. A tragic actor.

Tragédienne [F.]. A tragic actress.

Tumbler. One who plays the tricks of an acrobat or contortionist.

Walking gentleman. An actor filling parts requiring a gentlemanly appearance.

ACTING—*Associated Nouns.*

Act. A part of a drama.

Act-drop. The curtain drop at the end of an act.

Buffoonery. The practises and art of a buffoon; low drollery.

Character. A part assumed in a play.

Curtain. The movable screen in a theater concealing the stage.

Dramatis personæ [L.]. The characters of a drama.

Drop-scene. A painted picture dropped in front of the stage.

Epilogue. A speech or poem recited to the audience by an actor after a play.

Flat. The half of a scene.

Flies. The galleries running along the side of a stage where the scene ropes are worked.

Floats. A mechanical contrivance for elevating performers above the stage.

Foot-lights. A row of lights in front of and level with the stage to light it up.

Gag. An interpolation in his part introduced by an actor himself.

Gesture. See SIGN.

Impersonation. See DELINEATION.

Induction. The preface of a play.

Introduction. The part of a play which precedes the main part.

Jeu de théâtre [F.]. A stage trick.

Libretto [It.]. The words of an opera.

Marionettes [F.]. Puppets moved by strings.

Mezzanine floor. A stage.

Mise en scène [F.]. The putting on the stage.

Orchestra. The band which furnishes music for a theater.

Part. Character assigned to an actor in a play.

Performance. The exhibition of character on the stage.

Prologue. The speech or poem spoken before the beginning of a dramatic performance.

Proscenium. The part in a theater from the drop-curtain to the orchestra.

Répertoire [F.]. A list of performances which a dramatic company can render.

Representation. A dramatic performance.

Rôle [F.] A character taken by an actor.

Scene. A stage; the imaginary place wherein the action of a play occurs.

Screen. A partition concealing the stage from the audience.

Side-scene. A minor scene at the side of the stage.

Stage. The raised platform on which a theatrical performance takes place.

Stage-business. The calling of the stage, engaged in for a profession.

Staging. Preparing a piece for stage presentation.

Tableau. A picture scene in which the players remain silent.

Theatrical costume. Form of dress used in a theatrical performance.

Theatrical properties. The requisite goods for the presentation of a drama.

Transformation scene. A gorgeous scene at the conclusion of the burlesque of a pantomime, in which the principal characters are supposedly transformed into the leading actors in the following harlequinade.

Trap. A door in the floor of a stage.

Wing. One of the sides of the stage, or a piece of scenery for the side.

ACTING—*Nouns of Place*

Amphitheater. A theater built around an open space, with rising tiers of seats.

Auditorium. A building arranged for audiences

Auditory. A place for hearing.

Balcony. The seating part of a theater first below the gallery.

Boxes. Enclosed places in a theater furnished with seats.

Circus. A place of amusement where feats of horsemanship and acrobatic tricks form the chief display.

Coulisses [F.]. Spaces included between the side scenes on a stage

Dress circle. Seating part of a theater back of the parquet

Front of the house. The forepart of the theater

Gallery. The topmost seats in a theater.

Green-room. A room near the stage to which the actors retire between their parts.

Hippodrome. An ancient racecourse; also applied to a modern circus.

Music-hall. A building devoted to musical entertainments.

Opera-house. A theater where operas or musical dramas are rendered.

Parquet or Pit. Seating part of a theater on the floor next to the orchestra.

Playhouse. House devoted to the playing of dramas.

Stalls or Fauteuils. Theater seats separated from the others.

Theater. A building adapted to dramatic representations.

ACTING—*Figurative Expressions*

Buskin. A high shoe worn by tragic actors; hence, used figuratively to express the tragic drama.

Cothurnus [L.]. Buskin; hence, tragedy.

Melpomene and Thalia. The Grecian muses of tragedy and comedy, figuratively used for tragic and comic drama.

Roscius. Roman comedian; hence, an actor.

Sock. A shoe worn by ancient comedians; hence, used figuratively for comedy as distinguished from the buskin or tragedy.

The boards. Figurative expression for the stage of a theater.

Thespis. A leader of the early Greek drama.

ACTING—*Verbs.*

Act. To carry out a dramatic part.

Act a part, come out. To make a stage début.

Enact. To represent as in a play.

Gag. To introduce a gag. See *Associated Nouns.*

Go through a part, mimic. See IMITATE.

Perform. To act out, as on a stage.

Perform a part, personate. See DELINEATION.

Play a part, put on the stage.

Rant. To declaim boisterously.

Rehearse. To practise a play.

Spout. To utter or act for effect.

Star it. To take the part of a star. See *Associated Nouns.*

"Strut and fret one's hour upon a stage." From *As You Like It* wherein Shakespeare likens life to a part played on a stage.

Tread the boards, tread the stage. The profession of an actor.

ACTING—*Adjectives.*

Buskined. Wearing buskins, pertaining to tragedy.

Comic. Provoking mirth.

Dramatic. Pertaining to representation on the stage.

Farcical. Belonging to a farce or burlesque.

Histrionic. Pertaining to the stage.

Melodramatic. Pertaining to a melodrama, a romantic play full of startling incidents.

Operatic. Pertaining to the musical form of the drama.

Scenic. Dramatic; theatrical.

Stagey. Pertaining to the stage; theatrical.

Theatric, theatrical. Of the nature of dramatic representation; befitting the stage.

Tragic. Pertaining to tragedy.

Tragi-comic. Partly tragic and partly comic.

ACTING—*Adverbial Phrases.*

Before the floats; before an audience; behind the scenes; on the boards; on the stage.

act'-ing cor'-po-ral. A military officer. Chief-Underling.

ac-tin'-ic. Pertaining to radiation of light or heat. Light-Darkness.

ac'-tin-ism. Chemical effect of light. Light-Darkness.

ac''-ti-nom'-e-ter. Instrument for measuring radiation. Optical Instruments.

ac'-tion. Exertion of power. Action-Passiveness, Agency, Litigation, Strife-Peace; line of action, Conduct; put in action, Use-Disuse; suit the action to the word, Sign; thick of the action, Activity-Indolence.

ACTION—PASSIVENESS.

Achievement. A successful action.
Act. That which is done or doing.
Action. Exertion of power or force in doing something
Actor. One who acts, or takes part in any affair. See Agent.
Agency. The faculty of exerting power. See Agency.
Blow. A sudden or forcible act or effort.
Bout. As much of an action as is performed at one time.
Business. That which one has to do or should do. See Occupation.
Coup d'état [F.]. A violent measure of state in public affairs.
Coup de main [F.]. A sudden effort.
Dealings. Methods of business.
Deed. That which is done or effected by a responsible agent.
Doing. An action, good or bad. See *Verbs.*
Doings. Behavior; conduct.
Evolution. The prescribed movement of a body of troops, or a vessel or fleet.
Execution. A carrying into effect or to completion.
Exercise. Activity for the benefit or training of body or mind.
Exercitation. Practise; use.
Exploit. A deed of renown.
Feat. An act displaying skill, endurance, or daring.
Gest. A deed, or an action.
Handicraft. The application of skill and expertness in working with the hands.
Handiwork. Work done by the hands.
Job. A piece of work done, or to be done, as a whole.
Labor. Physical or mental action for some useful or desired end. See Toil.
Maneuver. A movement or change of position.
Measure. A specific act or course.
Move. An act in the carrying out of a plan.
Movement. A series of actions tending toward some end.
Operation. A mode of action.
Overt act. An open or manifest act.
Passage. The act of going from point to point.
Performance. Anything done or completed.
Perpetration. A doing; commonly used of doing something wrong.
Praxis [Gr.]. Exercise or discipline for a specific purpose.
Procedure. An act performed; the manner of moving forward. See Way.
Proceeding. An act, or course of action.
Step. A single action or proceeding regarded as leading to something.
Stitch. Space passed over at any one time.
Stroke. A powerful or sudden effort by which something is done.
Stroke of policy. A masterly effort; a successful attempt. See Design.
Touch. Any slight or delicate effort.
Tour de force [F.]. A feat of strength or skill. See Pomp.
Transaction. The doing or performing of any business.
Work. Exertion of strength or faculties.
Workmanship. The execution or manner of making anything.

Action—*Verbs.*

Achieve. To bring something difficult to a successful conclusion.
Act. To produce movement or effect.
Act a part in. To carry out or fulfil with others.
Act upon. To take action.
Be an actor. To be one who takes part in any work. See Agent.
Be a participant in, be a party to. To have a part or share of.
Bear a hand. To give aid.
Be at work. To be using one's powers mentally or physically.
Be in action. To put forth power.
Carry into execution. To finish. See Completion.
Commit. To perform.
Do. To bring to accomplishment.
Employ oneself. To have one's powers engaged.
Enact. To carry out in action.
Execute. To perform or accomplish something.
Exercise. To employ actively in order to train or develop.
Have a finger in the pie, have a hand in. To take part in some work.

Abstinence from action. Voluntary forbearance from labor.
Conservative policy. A settled method opposed to change.
Dolce far niente [It.]. Sweet idleness.
Fabian policy. A course of action avoiding a decisive contest.
Idle hours. Time not turned to appropriate use.
Inaction. Idleness; rest.
Inactivity. Want of energy. See Activity-Indolence.
Inoccupation. Want of any work to engage the time and attention.
Neglect. Failure to do or use anything. See Neglect, Carefulness-Carelessness.
Non-interference. Not taking part in the business of another.
Passiveness. Tendency to remain in a given state of motion or rest.
Quiescence. State of repose. See Movement-Rest.
Rest. Freedom from motion or labor. See Toil-Relaxation.
Sinecure. Any office or position which involves little or no active service.
Time hanging on one's hands. Time unemployed.
Want of occupation. Without work or employment.

Passiveness—*Verbal Expressions.*

Abstain from doing; beguile the time; be inactive; bide one's time; cool one's heels; desist; destroy; do away with; do nothing; fill up the time; fold one's arms; fold one's hands; have nothing to do; keep oneself from doing; keep quiet; kick one's heels; *laisser aller* [F.], let alone; *laisser faire* [F.], suffer to have its own way; leave alone; let alone; let be; let it have its way; let pass; let things take their course; let well alone; lie by; lie fallow; lie idle; lie in ordinary; lie in wait; lie on the shelf; lie to; lie upon one's oars; live and let live; not act; not attempt; not do; not lift a finger; not lift a foot; not lift a peg; not move; not stir; pass the time; pause; *quieta non movere* [L.], to be at rest; refrain; relax; remit one's efforts; rest and be thankful; rest upon one's oars; slug; spare; stand aloof; *stare super antiquas vias* [L.], to remain unchanged; stop; take down; take time; take to pieces; talk against time; tide it over; undo; wait; waste time; while away the tedious hours; while away the time; whistle for want of thought.

Passiveness—*Adjectives.*

Désoeuvré [F.]. Unemployed; idle.
Fallow. Untilled; neglected.
Not doing, not done. See *Verbs.*
Out of employ. Without work.
Out of work. Idle.
Passive. Not active, but acted upon.
Undone. Not worked or done; neglected.
Unemployed. Not engaged to work.
Unoccupied. Not working.

Passiveness—*Adverbs.*

At a stand. Unable to move.
Les bras croisés [F.]. With folded hands.
Pour passer le temps [F.]. To pass away the time.
Re infecta [L.]. The business being unfinished.
With folded arms, with the hands behind one's back, with the hands in the pockets. Figurative expressions for idleness.

Passiveness—*Interjections.*

Hands off! so let it be! stop!

Passiveness—*Phrase.*

Cunctando restituit rem [L.]. He restored the state by delaying.

Action—*Verbs—Continued.*

Have in hand. To have in one's power or control. See Business.
Have to do with. To make use of.
Inflict. To cause or produce by striking.
Labor. To strive to accomplish some purpose or work. See Toil.
Lend a hand, lift a finger. To help, or give assistance.

ACTION—VERBS—*Continued.*

Mix oneself up with. To take a part in when not wanted. See MED-
DLE.
Officiate. To act as an officer.
Operate. To put in action and supervise the working of.
Participate in. To have a part in.
Perform. To bring to completion.
Perform a part in. To do a part of a work.
Perpetrate. To do or carry through.
Play. Action without special aim or for amusement.
Play a part in. To be one of many engaged in a work.
Ply one's task. To work with steadiness.
Practise. To perform repeatedly and systematically by way of
training.
Prosecute. To follow up with a view to attain or accomplish.

Pull an oar. To give aid.
Pursue a course. To endeavor persistently to attain or gain.
Put in practise. To perform.
Put oneself in motion. To begin to work.
Run in a race. To take part in a work.
Shape one's course. To mark out one's actions. See CONDUCT.
Stretch forth one's hand. To give aid or help to.
Strike a blow. To be active in any occasion of employing force.
Take action. To begin to do something.
Take a part in. To be engaged with others in any work.
Take in hand. To attempt or undertake. See UNDERTAKING.
Take steps. To busy oneself with.
Transact. To carry through work.
Work. To put forth effort for the attainment of an object.

ACTION—*Adjectives.*

Acting. Doing.
Doing. Carrying out in action. See *Verbs.*
In action. At work.

In harness. In active duty.
In operation. In effect. See AGENCY.

ACTION—*Adverbs.*

Flagrante delicto [L.]. (Taken) in the flagrant fault.

**In the act, in the midst of, in the thick of, red-handed, while one's
hand is in.**

ACTION—*Phrases.*

Faire sans dire [F.]. To act without talking.
Fare, fac [L.]. Speak do.

Fronte capillata, post est occasio calva [L.]. Opportunity, though
she has hair in front, is bald behind.

ac'-tion-a-ble. Affording cause for lawsuit LAW-
LAWLESSNESS.
actions, les belles..cachées sont les plus estimables [F.]
(lê bel ac-si-on·', ca-shê' son· lê plüz es-ti-mabl').
Beautiful acts hidden are the most worthy of praise.
APPROVAL-DISAPPROVAL.

act'-ive. Agile. ACTIVITY-INDOLENCE, SWIFTNESS-
SLOWNESS, VIGOR-INERTIA; **active service,** FIGHT-
ING-CONCILIATION; **active thought,** HEED-DISRE-
GARD; **active voice,** VERB.
act'-ive-ly. Briskly. ACTIVITY-INDOLENCE.
ac-tiv'-i-ty. Exertion of energy. ACTIVITY-INDO-
LENCE, VIGOR-INERTIA.

ACTIVITY—INDOLENCE.

Abandon. Careless and easy activity.
Activity. The state of being active, nimble or brisk.
Ado. Unnecessary activity.
Agility. Activity in the movement of the limbs.
Alacrity. A cheerful, joyful activity, or promptitude.
Animation. Liveliness of the mind.
Ardor. Eagerness of passion, great activity.
Assiduity. Faithful careful activity.
Assiduousness. Unremitted effort. See *Adjectives.*
Bother. Having annoying activity; annoyance.
Briskness. Quick, sprightly activity.
Bustle. A stimulated activity.
Dabbling. Activity in a slight and careless way.
Dash. Spirited movement.
Despatch. Hasty, prompt execution; expedition.
Devotion. Zealous activity especially in religion. See DETERMINA-
TION.
Diligence. Assiduous activity. See PERSEVERING.
Dispatch. See DESPATCH.
Drudgery. Wearisome work; disgusting activity. See TOIL.
Eagerness. Anxious to do; excited by desire.
Earnestness. A permanent desire in the pursuit of good.
Empressement [F.]. Eagerness, forwardness.
Energy. Readiness for action.
Exertion. Act of putting in motion, or mental activity. See TOIL.
Expedition. Quickness in action.
Fidget. Nervous movements.
Fidgetiness. Quality of being fidgety.
Flurry. Sudden activity, a flutter. See HURRY.
Fuss. Unnecessary activity about small things.
Haste. Quickness of movement. See HURRY.
Industry. Earnest activity.
Insomnium [L.]. Sleeplessness; vigilance.
Intentness. The quality of having the mind firmly fixed on one pur-
pose.
Interference. Activity in taking part in the concerns of others.
Intermeddling. Interfering improperly in the affairs of others.
Interposition. A friendly mediation in the affairs of others.
Intrigue. A seeking of an end by sinister ways.
Life. Animation, spirit, vim.
Liveliness. Continuous feeling of life and vigor. See *Adjectives.*
Nimbleness. The quality of being very active.
Officiousness. Impertinently meddling in the affairs of others.

Dawdling. Aimless, trifling action. See *Verbs.*
Drowsiness. Disposition to sleep or inactivity. See *Adjectives.*
Dulness. Slowness of understanding; stupidity. See *Adjectives.*
Heaviness. The quality of being heavy or depressed.
Idleness. The state of being inactive.
Inaction. Cessation from action. See ACTION-PASSIVENESS.
Inactivity. Want of action.
Indiligence. Want of diligence.
Indolence. An indisposition to labor.
Inertness. Absence of activity. See VIGOR-INERTIA.
Languor. Condition in which there is no disposition to exertion.
Lentor. Slowness, delay.
Lethargy. A state of inaction or dulness.
Lull. Cessation from activity. See CONTINUANCE-DISCONTINUANCE.
Nodding. Lacking in care or diligence. See *Verbs.*
Obstinacy. Perseverance in one's own way. See BIGOTRY.
Oscitancy. Act of gaping, sluggishness.
Oscitation. See OSCITANCY.
Pandiculation. A stiffening of trunk and extremities, as in sleep
or fatigue.
Pottering. Walking sluggishly; trifling.
Procrastination. Habit of delaying. See EARLINESS-LATENESS.
Quiescence. A state of repose, or inactivity. See MOVEMENT-REST.
Relaxation. Remission from active duty. See COHESION-LOOSE-
NESS.
Remissness. Act of being careless in matters. See *Adjectives.*
Rust. Any addition or change coming from degeneration.
Rustiness. State of being rusty.
Segnitude. }
Segnity.   } Slowness, dulness.
Sloth. Strong indisposition to inactivity.
Sluggishness. State of being inactive. See SWIFTNESS-SLOWNESS.
Somnolence. Inclination to sleepiness.
Stupor. Great inactivity of the senses. See SENSITIVENESS-
APATHY.
Torpescence. State of becoming torpid.
Torpidity. State of being torpid.
Torpor. State in which power of exertion is lost.

INDOLENCE—*Nouns of Agent.*

Afternoon farmer; dawdle; do-little; dormouse; droil; drone; dummy;
farnéant [F.]; *fruges consumere natus* [L.] born to consume fruits;
idler; laggard; *lazzarone* [It.]; **loafer; lotus eater; lounger; lub-**

ACTIVITY—INDOLENCE—*Continued*.

Painstaking. Diligent and faithful in the performance of duty.
Perfervidum ingenium [L.]. Very eager nature.
Perseverance. Persistence in purpose. See PERSISTENCE.
Pervigilium [L.]. A watching all night.
Pottering. Being active to little purpose.
Promptitude. Acting upon the moment.
Punctuality. Done at a precise time. See EARLINESS.
Quickness. Quality of being quick. See *Adjectives*.
Racketing. An indulgence in boisterous pleasures.
Restlessness. The quality of being eager for change.
Sedulity. The quality of being persevering in effort.
Sleeplessness. Insomnia; vigilance.
Smartness. Quickness in action or thought.
Spirit. Energy; vivacity.
Stir. Activity in anything; public excitement.
Tampering with. Meddling with.
Velocity. Rapid motion, celerity. See SWIFTNESS.
Vigilance. Watchfulness. See CAREFULNESS.
Vigour. Vital strength; natural force. See VIGOR.
Wakefulness. Constant activity.
Zeal. Fervor in the pursuit of any object.

ACTIVITY—*Nouns of Agent*.

Blade; busy bee; busybody; devotee; enthusiast; housewife; inter-meddler; intriguer; meddler; new broom; pickthank; sharp fellow; zealot.

ACTIVITY—*Phrases*.

Battle of life; busy hum of men; great doings; habits of business; many irons in the fire; no sinecure; plenty to do; press of business; thick of the action.

ACTIVITY—*Verbs*.

Agitate. Stir up greatly.
Bestir. Arouse into action.
Bustle. Be very active and noisy.
Fuss Be active in small matters.
Hasten. Move swiftly.
Interfere. Meddle in the concerns of others.
Intermeddle. Be active in the affairs of others.
Interpose. Place oneself between persons at variance.
Intrigue. Effect a purpose by stratagem.
Meddle. Interfere.
Moil. Labor hard.
Obtrude. Thrust in without permission.
Outdo. Excel.
Overact. Act too well.
Overdo. Do too well.
Overlay. Cover completely.
Persist. Continue with determination in any course. See DETERMINATION.
Plod. Keep at a thing.
Push. Press onward.
Rise. Get up.
Speed. Cause to move with haste.
Stir. Move.
Toil. Labor. See TOIL.

ACTIVITY—*Verbal Phrases*.

Arouse oneself; be about; be active; be busy; bestir oneself; busy oneself in; dash off; do one's best; do wonders; elbow one's way; fight one's way; get up early; go ahead; go all lengths; have a finger in the pie; have a hand in; have all one's eyes about one; have much on one's hands; have one's fling; have one's hands full; have other fish to fry; have other things to do; improve the shining hour; keep moving; keep the pot boiling; keep up the ball; kick up a dust; kill two birds with one stone; lay about one; look sharp; lose no time; make a fuss; make a push; make a stir; make haste; make progress (see ADVANCE); make short work of; make the most; make the most of one's time; mix oneself up with; not have a moment that one can call his own; not have a moment to spare; not lose a moment; not suffer the grass to grow under one's feet; overshoot the mark; peg away; poke one's nose in; push forward; put in one's oar; raise a dust; rouse oneself; run riot; run the round of; seize the opportunity (see OPPORTUNE-NESS); steal a march; stick at nothing; stir about; stir one's stumps; take an active part; take pains; tamper with; thrust one's nose in; trouble one's head about; work wonders.

ACTIVITY—*Adjectives*.

Active. Having activity, quick in movement.
Afoot. On foot.
Agile. Having power of quick movement of body.
Agoing. In movement.
Alert. Active in watchfulness.
Alive. In a state of operation or activity.

bard; lubber; marmot; mopus; opium eater; sleeping partner; slow coach; slug; sluggard; slumberer; truant (see EVASION); waiter on Providence.

INDOLENCE—*Cause*

Lullaby. A song that causes sleep or rest.
Sedative. A medicine that allays pain and gives rest. See TURBULENCE-CALMNESS.
Torpedo. A numbfish.

INDOLENCE—*Accompaniment*.

Balmy sleep; coma; doze; dream; dull work; *ecstasis* [L.], trance; forty winks; heavy eyelids; heavy sleep; hibernation, wintering in a secluded place and torpid state; nap; siesta; sleep; slumber; snooze; snore; sound sleep; trance; wink of sleep.

INDOLENCE—*Associated Nouns*

Hypnology. Science of sleep.
Hypnotism. Art of producing sleep by artificial means, of producing a suspension of activity.
Indolence, Castle of. Figurative expression for a place to take one's ease; a poem by Thomson.
Morpheus. The god of dreams.

INDOLENCE—*Verbs*.

Dabble. Play in water; trifle.
Dawdle. Trifle away time.
Dilly-dally. Take matters easily.
Doze. Sleep lightly.
Drawl. Speak with a slow, lazy utterance.
Dream. Let the mind wander.
Droil. Work slowly.
Drowse. Be inclined to sleep.
Faddle. Trifle.
Fiddle-faddle. Talk foolishly.
Flag. Stop by a flag.
Fribble. Walk with tottering step; fritter.
Hibernate. Go into a comatose state during winter.
Lag. Move slowly.
Languish. Be dull and inactive.
Loaf. Spend time idly.
Loiter. Delay, or linger behind.
Loll. Lie at ease; act lazily.
Lounge. Lie about carelessly.
Mitigate. Make less severe; alleviate.
Nap. Take a short sleep.
Nod. Incline the head.
Oversleep. Sleep too long.
Peddle. Carry goods for sale from house to house; do an insignificant business.
Piddle. Occupy oneself with trifles.
Potter. Work without spirit.
Putter. Trifle.
Relax. Render languid.
Slouch. Move awkwardly.
Sluggardize. Make a sluggard.
Slumber. Sleep.
Snooze. Sleep for short time.
Snore. Make a rough noise during sleep.
Vegetate. Live an idle life.
Yawn. Open the mouth; gape.

INDOLENCE—*Verbal Phrases*.

Be asleep; be inactive; burn daylight; close the eyes; consume time; do nothing (see ACTION-PASSIVENESS); drop asleep; drop off; eat the bread of idleness; expend itself; fall asleep; fritter away time; get sleepy; go off to sleep; go to bed; go to sleep; hang back; hang fire; idle away time; kill time; lead an easy life; let the grass grow under one's feet; loll in the lap of indolence; loll in the lap of luxury; lose time; move slowly (see SWIFTNESS-SLOWNESS); render idle (see *Adjectives*); seal up the eyelids; seal up the eyes; settle off to sleep; sleep at one's post; sleep heavily; sleep like a dormouse; sleep like a log; sleep like a top; sleep soundly; spend time; spend time in; swim in the stream; take a nap (see *Nouns*); take it easy; take one's time; take things as they come; take time in; trifle away time; turn in; waste time; waste the precious hours; weigh down the eyelids.

INDOLENCE—*Adjectives*.

Asleep. In sleep.
Balmy. Soft, soothing.
Comatose. In the state of coma.
Dead asleep. In a deep sleep.
Dilatory. Delaying, lingering.
Dormant. Inactive.

ACTIVITY—INDOLENCE—*Continued.*

ACTIVITY—Adjectives—*Continued.*

Alive and frisking. Alive and active.
Animated. Full of vital activity.
Assiduous. Unremitting in activity or effort
Astir. On the move.
At call. Liable to be required at any time.
At work, awake. Come out of sleep, vigilant.
Brisk. Having life, vivacity, or spirit.
Brisk as a bee. Active.
Brisk as a lark. Very brisk.
Broad awake. Fully awake.
Business-like. Requiring attention and assiduity.
Bustling. Excitedly stirring about.
Busy. Active at anything.
Busy as a hen with one chicken.
Busy as a bee. } Continuous in application and effort.
Diligent.
Eager. Keenly desirous to obtain or perform something.
Enterprising. Having boldness and ability in business.
Eventful. Full of important events, hence full of life and activity.
Expeditious. Accomplished with speed.
Fast. Moving rapidly, quick. See SWIFTNESS.
Forward. Eager to presumptuousness.
Frisky. Inclined to playful activity.
Full of business, hard-working, hard at it, hard at work. Vigorously working. See TOIL.
Fussy. Taking active interest in trivial things.
Indefatigable. Incapable of being exhausted. See DETERMINATION.
Industrious. Working with diligence.
In earnest, in harness. At work.
In full swing. In active operation.
Intent. Having the mind directed to an object. See HEED.
Intrigant [F.]. Meddling.
Light-footed. Quick on the feet.
Lively. Full of vivacity and animation.
Meddlesome. Given to meddling.
Meddling. Participating without permission in the concerns of others. See *Verbs.*
Never tired. Never experiencing fatigue.
Nimble. Active in body.
Nimble as a squirrel, nimble-footed. Quick-footed.
Notable. Worthy of observation.
Occupied. Employed in an exclusive manner.
Officious. Unduly participating in others' concerns.
On duty, on foot, on one's legs. Ready.
On the alert. See CAREFULNESS.
Overofficious. Too officious.
Painstaking. Diligent and careful in labor.
Plodding. Laboriously toiling.
Pottering. Working unspiritedly.
Pushing. To advance with energy.
Quick.
Quick as a lamplighter. } Characterized by life or speed.
Resolute. Hainvg a steadfast purpose. See DETERMINATION.
Restless.
Restless as a hyena. } Never resting, eager for variety
Sedulous. Constant and persevering in effort.
Sharp. Keen and eager; active.
Smart. Quick in thought or action.
Spirited. Having spirit or vim.
Spry. Inclined to quick movement; nimble
Stirring. Moving vigorously.
Strenuous. Zealous in anything; ardently eager.
Tripping. Moving lightly and nimbly.
Unsleeping. Not sleeping.
Unwearied. Not wearied or fatigued.
Up and doing, up and stirring. Active and brisk.
Up to one's ears in. Deeply engrossed in.
Vivacious. Full of life and activity.
Wide awake. Perfectly awake. See SAGACITY.
Work a day. A week day.
Working. Toiling.
Zealous. Earnest in a cause.

ACTIVITY—Adverbs.

Actively. In an active manner. See *Adjectives.*
Featly. Nimbly and dexterously.
Fidgety. Nervously active.
Full tilt. With full force.
In mediis rebus [L.]. In the midst of affairs.
With haste. With speed. See HURRY.

INDOLENCE—Adjectives—*Continued.*

Dozy. Inclined to doze.
Dreamy. In a state of reverie.
Dronish. Like a drone; doing nothing.
Drony. Like a drone.
Drowsy. Disposed to sleep.
Dull. Not sharp, not animated.
Exanimate. Not animated.
Fast asleep. In a state of slumber.
Fiddle faddle. Bustling about trifles.
Flagging. Bringing to a stop by waving a flag.
Heavy. Dull, inactive.
Heavy with sleep. Overcome by sleep.
Hypnotic. Pertaining to hypnotism.
Idle. Not active.
Inactive. Wanting activity.
In a sound sleep. Completely asleep.
Indolent. Lazy by habit.
Inert. Devoid of the power of moving.
In the arms of Morpheus.
In the lap of Morpheus. } Asleep.
Lackadaisical. Languid and half-hearted.
Laggard. Falling behind.
Lagging. Inclined to move slowly. See *Verbs.*
Languid. Becoming spiritless.
Lazy. Indisposed to work.
Lazy as Ludlam's dog.
Leaden. Like lead, heavy, dull.
Lethargic.
Lethargical. } Being in a lethargy or a drowse.
Listless. Without active interest.
Lumpish. Like a lump, inert.
Lusk. Lazy.
Maudlin. Weak and foolish; weeping drunk. [St. Magdalen.]
Motionless. Without motion. See MOVEMENT-REST.
Napping. Inclined to take short sleeps.
Pottering. Moving without spirit. See *Verbs.*
Remiss. Careless in performance of duty.
Rusty. Affected with rust, impaired by inactivity.
Sedative. Soothing in effects. See TURBULENCE-CALMNESS.
Shilly shally. In an irresolute manner. See DETERMINATION-VACILLATION.
Slack. Relaxed and careless in activity.
Sleepful. Full of sleep.
Sleeping. See *Verbs.*
Sleepy. Inclined to sleep.
Slothful. Inclined to indolence.
Slow. Having little speed. See SWIFTNESS-SLOWNESS.
Sluggish. Inclined not to move, lazy.
Somniferous. Bringing sleep.
Somnific. Causing sleep.
Somnolent. Inclined to sleep.
Soporiferous. Tending to cause sleep.
Soporific. Producing sleep.
Soporous. Causing sleep.
Sound as a top. Asleep.
Sound asleep. Completely overcome by sleep.
Soulless. Without a soul, spiritless.
Supine. Lying on the back, careless, indolent.
Torpescent. Becoming torpid.
Torpid. In a comatose state.
Unawakened. Not roused from sleep, not active.
Unbusied. Not occupied at anything.
Unoccupied. Not possessing time of. See ACTION-PASSIVENESS.
Unwaked. Not stirred from sleep.

INDOLENCE—Adverbs.

At leisure. See HURRY-LEISURE.
Inactively See *Adjectives.*

INDOLENCE—Phrase.

The eyes begin to draw straws.

ACTIVITY—*Continued.*

ACTIVITY—Adverbs.

With life and spirit, with might and main. See TOIL.
With wings.

ACTIVITY—Interjections.

Age quod agis! [L.]. Beware what you do!
Be alive! be sharp! go ahead! keep moving! look alive! look sharp! move on! push on! stir your stumps!

Abends wird der Faule fleissig [G.]. In the evening the lazy man becomes diligent.

Carpe diem [L.]. Seize your opportunity　See OPPORTUNENESS

Catch a weasel asleep.

Dictum ac factum [L.]. No sooner said than done. [Terence, *Andrea*. 2, 3, 7.]

Nec mora nec requies [L.]. Neither delay nor rest. [Virgil, *Georgics*, iii, 110.]

No sooner said than done. See EARLINESS.

Nulla dies sine linea [L.]. Not a day without a line. [Pliny, *Nat. Hist*. 35.]

The plot thickens. Matters become interesting.

"*Veni, vidi, vici* [L.]. I came, saw, conquered. [Suetonius, *Cæsar*, 37.]

---

act'-or. One who performs or plays a part. ACTING, ACTION-PASSIVENESS, AGENT, GULL-DECEIVER, SOCIETY-AFFECTATION.

acts. Records; deeds. MARK-OBLITERATION, REVELATION-PSEUDOREVELATION.

ac'-tu-al. Real. ENTITY-NONENTITY, SAMENESS-CONTRAST, TIME.

ac'-tu-al-ism. The doctrine that all existence is active. ENTITY-NONENTITY.

ac''-tu-al'-ity. Realism ENTITY-NONENTITY.

ac'-tu-al-ly. In reality ENTITY-NONENTITY, TRUTH-ERROR.

ac'-tu-a-ry. A clerk. ACCOUNTS.

ac'-tu-ate. To move to action. MOTIVE-CAPRICE.

actum est [L.] (ac'-tum est). It is done. COMPLETION-NONCOMPLETION.

actum ne agas [L.] (ac'-tum nî ê'-gas). Do not do what is done. USEFULNESS-USELESSNESS.

actus me invito factus, non est meus actus [L.] (ac'-tus mî in-vai-to fac'-tus, non est mî'-us ac'-tus). An act I do against my will is not my act. VOLITION-OBLIGATION

a-cu'-i-ty. Sharpness. SHARPNESS-BLUNTNESS.

a-cu'-le-ate. Prickly. SHARPNESS-BLUNTNESS.

a-cu'-le-a''-ted. Made sharp. SHARPNESS-BLUNTNESS.

a-cu'-men. Mental quickness. SAGACITY-INCAPACITY

a-cu'-m na''-ted. Pointed. SHARPNESS-BLUNTNESS.

a-cu''-mi-na'-tion. Act of sharpening. SHARPNESS-BLUNTNESS.

a-cu'-mi-nous. Possessing keenness of intellect. SAGACITY-INCAPACITY.

ac''-u-punc'-ture. Pricking with a needle. APERTURE-CLOSURE.

a-cute'. Keen. CRAFT-ARTLESSNESS, EMOTION, FEELING - INSENSIBILITY, PLEASURABLENESS - PAINFULNESS, SAGACITY-INCAPACITY, SHARPNESS-BLUNTNESS, TURBULENCE-CALMNESS, VIGOR-INERTIA; **acute angle,** ANGULARITY; **acute ear,** HEARING-DEAFNESS; **acute note,** CACOPHANY.

a-cute'-ly. In an acute degree. MAGNITUDE-SMALLNESS.

a-cute'-ness. Discernment. SAGACITY-INCAPACITY.

acu tetigisti rem [L.] (ê'-kiu tet-i-jis'-tai rem). You have touched it with a needle. DIFFERENTIATION-INDISCRIMINATION, TRUTH-ERROR.

A. D. Abbreviation for Anno Domini. DURATION-NEVERNESS.

a-da'-ga. An Asiatic parrying weapon. WEAPON.

ad'-age. Well-known saying. ADAGE-NONSENSE.

ad astra per aspera [L.] (ad as'-tra per as'-per-ra). To the stars through difficulties. DIFFICULTY-FACILITY.

ad captandum [L.] (ad cap-tan'-dum). Big sounding. SOCIETY-AFFECTATION.

ad hominem [L.] (ad hom'-i-nem)　To the man. UNIVERSALITY-PARTICULARITY.

ad infinitum [L.] (ad in-fi-nai'-tum)　Indefinite INFINITY.

ad instar [L.] (ad in'-star). After the fashion. CONVENTIONALITY-UNCONVENTIONALITY.

ad interim [L.] (ad in'-ter-im). Meanwhile. DURATION-NEVERNESS.

ad rem [L.] (ad rem). To the point. HARMONY-DISCORD.

ADAGE—NONSENSE.

Adage. A brief saying that has obtained credit or force by long usage.

Aphorism. A brief statement of speculative or scientific truth.

Apophthegm. } A terse, instructive saying regarding practical matters.
Apothegm. }

Axiom. Any proposition that men universally accept as true.

By-word. A phrase or sentence that has become an object of derision or mockery.

Conclusion. See DECISION.

Dictum. A statement of some person or school, on whom it depends for authority.

Formula. A fixed form of words used as a guide for thought or action.

Maxim. A brief statement of some practical principle or proposition.

Moral. The lesson taught by a fable or the like.

Mot [F]. A witty saying.

Motto. An expressive word or pithy saying expressing some guiding principle

Phylactery. A strip of parchment inscribed with passages of Scripture setting forth guides to right living.

Principia [L.]. Principles.

Principle. A rule for action.

Protasis [Gr.]. A short introduction or an exposition of the subject.

Proverb. A brief saying condensing in witty or striking form the wisdom of experience.

Reflection. See CONCEPTION

Saw. A saying that is old, but worn and tiresome.

Saying. A statement current among common people, deriving its authority from its manifest truth and good sense.

Scholium. A remark or observation joined to a demonstration or reasoning.

Sentence. A short saying usually containing moral instruction.

Theorem. A proposition that is demonstrably true.

Truism. A self-evident or unquestionable statement.

Word. Any brief remark or phrase of no particular significance.

Absurdity. } Anything which is contrary to the first principles of
Absurdness. } reasoning. See *Adjectives*

Alogy. Unreasonableness of behavior

Amphigouri [F.]. Idle or foolish talk.

Anticlimax. Any speech which produces a ridiculous effect.

Bathos. Descent in speaking which is ridiculous.

Blunder. Mistake or error resulting from carelessness.

Boutade [F.]. Any action or saying destitute of ordinary good sense.

Bull. A verbal blunder, containing a laughable incongruity of ideas.

Escapade. Any act which breaks the rules of propriety.

Exaggeration. See GULL-HYPERBOLE.

Extravagance. Vain use of words.

Farce. Empty show of words.

Farrago. See REGULARITY-IRREGULARITY.

Fustian. Bombast or use of high-sounding words.

Galimathias [F.]. Speech that is so rapid, confused, or disguised as to be unintelligible.

Hibernicism. An Irish idiom or peculiarity of speech.

Imbecility. Foolishness growing out of mental feebleness. See SAGACITY-INCAPACITY.

Inconsistency. Self-contradiction.

Irishism. See HIBERNICISM.

Jargon. Confused or unintelligible speech.

Macaronic. Jumbled speech.

Monkey trick. A mischievous prank.

Moonshine. Speech without reality.

Muddle. Confusion of speech.

Mummery. Buffoonery.

Nonsense. An act worthy only to be laughed at.

Paradox. Anything which appears contradictory, yet may be true.

Pun. A play on words.

Rhapsody. A disconnected series of sentences.

Romance. Imaginative habit of mind.

Sciomachy. An imaginary combat with words.

ADAGE—*Associate Phrases*

Admitted maxim; common saying; commonplace saying; golden rule (see PRECEPT); hackneyed saying; profession of faith (see FAITH); received maxim; sage maxim; trite saying; true saying: wise maxim.

ADAGE—*Adjectives*

Aphoristic. Containing short, pithy statements
Axiomatic. Self-evident.
Phylacteric. Pertaining to phylacteries
Proverbial. Well known.

ADAGE—*Phrases*

As the saying is; as they say.

NONSENSE—*Adjectives—Continued from Column 2*

Senseless. Meaningless
Sophistical. False.
Unmeaning. Unintelligible

NONSENSE—*Interjections.*

Fiddle-de-dee! Pho! Pish!

NONSENSE—*Phrases.*

Credat Judæus Apella [L.]. Let Apella, the superstitious Jew, believe it. [Horace, *Satires*, I, v, 100.]
In the name of the Prophet—figs! [Horace Smith, *Johnson's Ghost.*]
Tell it to the marines.
Without rhyme or reason.

---

a-da-gio. Slow. MUSIC, SWIFTNESS-SLOWNESS.
Ad'-am. The first man. VIRTUE-VICE.
ad'-a-mant. A hard mineral. HARDNESS-SOFTNESS, STRENGTH-WEAKNESS.
ad''-a-man-te'-an. Very hard. HARDNESS-SOFTNESS.
ad''-a-man'-tine. Impenetrably hard. HARDNESS-SOFTNESS, STRENGTH-WEAKNESS.
ad''-a-man-tine'-ness. State of being hard. HARDNESS-SOFTNESS.
a-dapt'. To adjust. EQUALITY-INEQUALITY, HARMONY-DISCORD; adapt oneself to, CONVENTIONALITY-UNCONVENTIONALITY.
a-dapt'-a-ble. Capable of being adapted. USEFULNESS-USELESSNESS.
ad''-ap-ta'-tion. Act of being adapted. HARMONY-DISCORD.
a-dapt'-ed. Suited. HARMONY-DISCORD.

NONSENSE—*Continued.*

Sell. A deceitful speech.
Slip-slop. A weak discourse.
Sophism. See RATIOCINATION-INSTINCT.
Stuff. Trashy language.
Stultiloquence. ⎫ Talk that is contrary to practical good sense.
Stultiloquy. ⎬
Tomfoolery. Trifling talk.
Twaddle. Silly talk.
Vagary. A wandering of thoughts or speech.
Verbal quibble. A dispute about trifles.

NONSENSE—*Verbs.*

Anemolia bazein [Gr.]. To talk words of wind.
Battre la campagne [F.]. To beat about the bush; to speak wildly
Be absurd. To be unreasonable.
Parler à tort et à travers [F.]. To speak disconnectedly
Play the fool. To act contrary to good common sense
Talk nonsense. To utter words without any sense or meaning.

NONSENSE—*Adjectives.*

Absurd. Contrary to good reasoning.
Egregious. Greatly exceeding, usually in a bad sense.
Extravagant. Immoderate.
Foolish. Wanting in judgment.
Inconsistent. Self-contradictory.
Macaronic. Jumbled.
Nonsensical. Of no importance.
Preposterous. Impracticable.
Punning. Using a word in two senses.
Quibbling. Evading the point and speaking trifles.
Ridiculous. Laughable and comical.

(*Continued on Column* 1.)

---

add. To join together. ADDITION-SUBTRACTION, INCREASE-DECREASE, NUMBER.
add'-ed. Joined to. ADDITION-SUBTRACTION.
ad-den'-dum. An addition. ADDITION-SUBTRACTION, INCREMENT-REMNANT.
adde parvum parvo, magnus acervus erit [L.] (ad'-dĭ par'-vum pur'-vo, mag'-nus a-ser'-vus ĭ'-rit). Add a little to little, a great pile will be. ADDITION.
ad'-der. A viper. BENEFACTOR-EVILDOER.
ad-dict'. To give oneself up to. HABIT-DESUETUDE.
ad-dict'-ed. Devoted to. HABIT-DESUETUDE.
ad-dic'-tion. Bent. HABIT-DESUETUDE.
ad-dit'-a-ment. A thing added. ADDITION-SUBTRACTION, INCREMENT-REMNANT.
ad-di'-tion. Act of uniting. ADDITION-SUBTRACTION, INCREMENT-REMNANT.

ADDITION—SUBTRACTION

Accession. An addition; augmentation.
Accompaniment. Anything that attends or goes with
Addendum. Something to be added.
Additament. A thing added.
Addition. Act of giving an increase to something.
Adjection. The addition.
Annexation. The act of connecting; union
Increase. An addition.
Increment. That which is added.
Insertion. Act of putting in or together.
Interposition. Act of interceding or coming together. See ENVIRONMENT-INTERPOSITION.
Junction. Union of two or more things.
Reinforcement. An increase of strength.
Superaddition. An addition to an addition.
Superfetation. An unusual additional growth.
Superjunction. Act of joining or adding to.
Superposition. The laying of one thing on another.
Supplement. An addition that remedies a defect, or makes complete.

ADDITION—*Verbs*

Accrue. To accumulate naturally
Add. To give an increase to.
Advene. To come in addition; to be added.
Affix. To fasten or join to.

Ablation. A taking away.
Abrasion. A wearing away.
Abscission. A cutting away.
Abstraction. A withdrawal; removal; absent-mindedness.
Amputation. The cutting off of a part.
Curtailment. Lessening; reduction. See LENGTH-SHORTNESS.
Decrease. A becoming less, diminution. See INCREASE-DECREASE.
Deduction. A drawing away from.
Detruncation. A cutting off; a lopping.
Garbling. Act of mutilating.
Minuend. The number from which another is to be taken.
Mutilation. Deprivation of an essential part.
Recision. The cutting off.
Removal. Moving away; displacement.
Retrenchment. A cutting down; curtailment.
Suduction. Taking part from whole; a subtraction.
Sublation. A removal.
Subtraction. Act of deducting; deduction.
Subtrahend. That which is subtracted.

SUBTRACTION—*Verbs.*

Abrade. To rub away; wear off.
Abscind. To sever.
Amputate. To cut off a part; maim.
Bate. To lessen.

ADDITION—SUBTRACTION—*Continued.*

Annex. To join to; bind; unite.
Append. To hang to; add as supplemental.
Augment. To increase in size; enlarge; add.
Become added. To come into a state of addition.
Clap on. To quickly put in addition.
Ingraft. To insert as a part of; incorporate.
Insert. To put in as supplementary or remedial.
Introduce. To bring or put in. See Environment-Interposition.
Reinforce. To give an addition of force and strength.
Saddle on. To fix a load upon; encumber with an addition.
Saddle with. See Saddle on.
Sprinkle. To add to by scattering over.
Subjoin. To add at the end.
Superadd. Add to an addition.
Superpose. To put over another.
Supervene. To come as additional.
Swell the ranks of. To add to by recruits
Tack to. To add by affixing slightly.
Tag. To join closely.

Addition—*Adjectives.*

Accessory. Additional.
Added. Brought together to make a whole. See *Verbs.*
Additional. Supplemental; in the way of an addition.
Additive. Allowing to be added.
Adjectitious. Added to.
Adscititious. } Supplemental.
Ascititious. }
Extra. Beyond what is due.
Subjunctive. Joined at the end.
Supplement. Supplying a deficiency.
Supplemental. Added to supply a defect.
Supplementary. Serving as a supplement.
Suppletory. Supplying deficiencies.

Addition—*Particles.*

Along with; also; and; and also; and else; and so forth; and so on; as well as; besides; conjointly; coupled; else; extra; further; furthermore; in addition; in conjunction with; including; inclusive; into the bargain; item; jointly; likewise; more; moreover; over and above; plus; to boot; together with; too; with; withal.

Addition—*Phrases.*

Adde parvum parvo, magnus acervus erit [L.]. Add a little to little, a great pile will be.

ad-di'-tion-al. Supplementary. Addition-Subtraction, Increment-Remnant.
ad'-di-tive. That which may be added. Addition-Subtraction.
ad'-dle. Spoiled. Completion - Noncompletion, Fertility-Sterility, Success-Failure; **addle the wits,** Saneness-Lunacy.

Castrate. To cut out; remove anything.
Curtail. To cut off from; lessen.
Decimate. To destroy the tenth one; kill many.
Deduce. To draw off as a conclusion; infer.
Deduct. To take away; subtract.
Detract. To lessen in value; derogate.
Detruncate. To lop off a part.
Diminish. To lessen; abridge. See Increase-Decrease.
Eliminate. To take away entirely.
Excise. To cut out; remove.
File. To wear away with a file.
Garble. To select certain parts; mutilate.
Geld. To castrate.
Mutilate. To remove a part; maim.
Pare. To lessen by peeling.
Prune. To diminish by cutting away a little.
Remove. To take away; go away.
Retrench. To limit.
Scrape. To remove with a rough instrument.
Subduct. To remove.
Subtract. To take from.
Thin. To diminish gradually and become thin.
Withdraw. To draw apart; separate.

Subtraction—*Verbal Phrases.*

Cut away; cut off; cut out; deprive of; take away; take from

Subtraction—*Adjectives.*

Subtracted. Taken away from. See *Verbs.*
Subtractive. Having power to subtract.

Subtraction—*Particles.*

Except; excepting; exclusive of; in deduction; less; minus; save; save and except; short of; with a reservation; without; with the exception.

ADDITION—Phrases—*Continued.*

Au reste [F.]. As for the rest; besides.
Cum multis aliis [L.]. With many other things.
Et cetera [L.]. And other things.

ad'-dle-head''. A stupid person. Sage-Fool.
ad'-dle-head''-ed. Dull-witted. Sagacity-Incapacity.
ad'-dle-pate''. A dunce. Sagacity-Incapacity.
ad-dress'. To direct spoken words to. Address-Response, Petition-Expostulation, Sign, Skill-Unskilfulness; **address card,** Sign.

ADDRESS—RESPONSE.

Address. A speaking to.
Allocution. A formal address.
Alloquy. A speaking to another.
Apostrophe. A sudden breaking out in address.
Appeal. An address to the feelings.
Audience. An interview generally public. See Conversation
Dialogism. A feigned conversation.
Interpellation. A questioning.
Invocation. An address to a superior being.
Salutation. An address of welcome.
Speech. A formal talk. See Speech.
Word in the ear. A word in private.

Address—*Nouns of Place.*

Auditory. An auditorium.
Platform. A place where addresses are made.

Address—*Verbs.*

Accost. To address first.
Address. To speak to.

Response. See Investigation-Answer.

ADDRESS—Verbs—*Continued.*

Apostrophize. To appeal suddenly.
Halloo. To shout loudly.
Hail. To address; call after.
Invoke. To call on a superior being.
Lecture. To address in a formal manner. See Speech
Salute. To make an address of welcome.

Address—*Verbal Phrases.*

Appeal to; call to; make up to; speak to; take aside; take by the button; talk to in private.

Address—*Interjections.*

Halloo! hey! hist! soho!

ad-dress'-es. Devoted attention. BLANDISHMENT.

ad-duce'. To bring forward. ATTRACTION-REPULSION, EVIDENCE-COUNTEREVIDENCE.

ad-du'-cent. Drawing together. ATTRACTION-REPULSION.

ad-duc'-tion. The act of adducing. ATTRACTION-REPULSION.

ad-duct'-ive. Adducing. ATTRACTION-REPULSION.

a-deem'. To take away. TAKING-RESTITUTION.

a-demp'-tion. Satisfaction of a legacy. TAKING-RESTITUTION.

ad''-en-og'-ra-phy. A treatise on the glands. TEXTURE.

ad''-en-ol'-o-gy. A branch of anatomy. TEXTURE.

a-dept'. One fully skilled in any art. ADEPT-BUNGLER.

ADEPT—BUNGLER.

Acrobat. One skilled in gymnastics.
Adept. One especially skilled in anything.
Admirable Crichton. A Scotchman remarkable for his precociousness.
Chef de cuisine [F.]. A head cook.
Clean hand. One who does work skilfully and neatly.
Conjurer. A sleight of hand performer. See GULL-DECEIVER.
Connoisseur [F.]. A critical judge. See SCHOLAR.
Crack shot. An especially skilful shooter; hence, one skilled in anything.
Cracksman. One especially proficient in anything; burglar.
Cunning blade. An expert swordsman; hence, an expert in anything.
Cunning fellow. ⎫
Cunning man. ⎭ One especially skilful.
Dab. A skilful person.
Dead shot. A shooter whose shot always causes death; hence, an accurate person.
Experienced eye. A trained eye; a trained person.
Experienced hand. One who has attained skill in anything by long practise.
Expert. One having skill and dexterity either from education or experience.
First fiddle. The most skilful worker or leader of a body of men.
Funambulist. A rope-walker.
Genius. One capable of original work.
Good hand. A skilful worker.
Good shot. A sure shooter.
Jack of all trades. One who is fitted for different kinds of work.
Jobber. A middle man; an intriguer.
Man of business. One who goes about his work without trifling.
Man of the world. One versed in the tricks and practises of men.
Marksman. An expert shot.
Master. A person thoroughly competent in his work.
Master hand. An expert workman.
Master head. ⎫
Master mind. ⎬ The leader of men.
Master spirit. ⎭
Medallist. One who has been rewarded for special skill in his work.
Nice hand. One who does his work neatly and accurately.
Old campaigner. An experienced worker.
Old file. A shrewd, deep, or artful person.
Old hand. ⎫
Old soldier. ⎬ A worker of large experience.
Old stager. ⎭
Pantologist. An expert whose knowledge comprehends summarily all departments of human knowledge.
Picked man. One chosen for his special skill.
Politician. A crafty or artful person.
Practised eye. ⎫
Practised hand. ⎭ An experienced worker.
Prima donna [It.]. The leading lady.
Prize man. One who is rewarded for his work.
Prodigy of learning. A person whose knowledge is unusually wide.
Proficient. One who has attained great skill in any art.
Protagonist. The leading actor in the Greek drama.
Rope dancer. An expert rope-walker.
Sharp blade. ⎫
Sharp fellow. ⎭ A shrewd artful person.

Awkward squad. Untrained soldiers.
Bad hand. Weak, unskilful tool.
Bad shot. An awkward person.
Blanc-bec [F.]. A greenhorn.
Blunderer. One who blunders or acts clumsily.
Blunderhead. A stupid fellow.
Botcher. One who makes a botch.
Bungler. An awkward fellow.
Butter-fingers. One who awkwardly drops what he ought to hold.
Clod. A dull fellow.
Duffer. An awkward, worthless person.
Flat. A dunce; a dull fellow.
Fumbler. One who handles anything clumsily.
Greenhorn. An inexperienced person.
Gull. See GULL-DECEIVER.
Land lubber. A raw, awkward person on board a vessel.
Looby. An unskilful person.
Lubber. A heavy, awkward, clumsy person.
Marplot. One who frustrates a plan by his interference.
Muff. A bungler.
No conjurer. A clumsy person.
Novice. An untried person.
Poor hand. ⎫
Poor shot. ⎭ A bungler.
Quack. See GULL-DECEIVER.
Slattern. A woman careless in dress.
Sloven. A man who is careless in dress.
Slow coach. A stupid fellow.
Stick. One who is stupid.
Swab. A lubber or clumsy fellow.
Trapes. A slattern; a tramp.
Yokel. A countryman.

BUNGLER—*Figurative Expressions.*

Ass in lion's skin; fair weather sailor; fish out of water; fresh water sailor; horse-marine; jackdaw in peacock's feathers; lord of misrule.

BUNGLER—*Phrases.*

Acierta errando [Sp.]. He blunders into the right.
Aliquis in omnibus, nullus in singulis [L.]. Dabbler in all things, good for nothing in each particular thing.
Bis peccare in bello non licet [L.]. To blunder twice in war is not permitted.
He will never set the Thames on fire.
Il n'a pas inventé la poudre [F.]. He did not invent gunpowder.

ADEPT—*Continued.*

Strategist. ⎫
Tactician. ⎭ One who displays skill and forethought in carrying out his plans.
Top sawyer. One who stands above the timber in a sawpit; a superior.
Veteran. An experienced person.
Wizard. One who seems to use magic in his work.

---

ad'-e-qua-cy. State of being adequate. ENOUGH, USEFULNESS-USELESSNESS.

ad'-e-quate. Fully sufficient. ENOUGH, MIGHT-IMPOTENCE, USEFULNESS-USELESSNESS; **adequate adversative**, PARTICLE.

a''-des-pot'-ic. Not despotic. RULE-LICENSE.

ad-here'. To stick to. COHESION-LOOSENESS, INTERSPACE-CONTACT; **adhere like Dejani'ra's shirt,** COHESION-LOOSENESS; **adhere to,** HABIT-DESUE-TUDE, PERSISTENCE-WHIM; **adhere to an obligation,** OBSERVANCE-NONOBSERVANCE; **adhere to a duty,** DUTY-DERELICTION.

ad-her'-ence. Adhesion. COHESION-LOOSENESS.

ad-her'-ent. One devoted to a party, person or principle. ANTAGONIST-ASSISTANT.

ad-her'-er. One who stands by a principle. PATRIOTISM-TREASON.

ad-her'-ing. Sticking. COHESION-LOOSENESS.

ad-he′-sive. Sticky. COHESION-LOOSENESS, VISCIDITY-FOAM.

ad-he′-sive-ness. State of being adhesive. COHESION-LOOSENESS, VISCIDITY-FOAM.

ad-hib′-it. To apply. USE-DISUSE.

ad″-hi-bi′-tion. An admitting. USE-DISUSE.

ad″-hor-ta′-tion. Attempt to arouse or incite. ADVICE.

ad″-i-aph′-a-nous. Opaque. DIAPHANEITY-OPAQUENESS.

a-dieu′. Farewell. ARRIVAL-DEPARTURE, GAIN-LOSS.

ad′-i-po-cere. A light-colored fatty substance. PULPINESS-OIL.

ad′-i-pose″. Fatty. PULPINESS-OILINESS.

ad′-it. A passage. APERTURE-CLOSURE, WATERCOURSE-AIRPIPE, WAY.

ad-ja′-cent. Adjoining. REMOTENESS-NEARNESS.

ad-jec′-tion. Addition. ADDITION-SUBTRACTION.

ad″-jec-ti′-ti-ous. Added. ADDITION-SUBTRACTION.

ad′-jec-tive. A part of speech used to describe or define a noun. ADJECTIVE, INCREMENT-REMNANT; **adjective pronoun**, PRONOUN; **adjective verb**, VERB; **cardinal adjective**, ADJECTIVE; **common adjective**, ADJECTIVE; **compound adjective**, ADJECTIVE; **definitive adjective**, ADJECTIVE; **descriptive adjective**, ADJECTIVE; **indefinite numeral adjective**, ADJECTIVE; **indefinite quantitative adjective**, ADJECTIVE; **multiplicative adjective**, ADJECTIVE; **numeral adjective**, ADJECTIVE; **ordinal adjective**, ADJECTIVE; **participial adjective**, ADJECTIVE; **partitive adjective**, ADJECTIVE; **pronominal adjective**, ADJECTIVE; **proper adjective**, ADJECTIVE.

ADJECTIVE.

Adjective. Word used to describe or define a noun.

ADJECTIVE—*Kinds.*

Article. Adjective serving to reduce a noun, from a general to a particular signification.
Definite article. One pointing out some definite object.
Indefinite article. One pointing out one object but not which one. The definite article is *the*, the indefinite *a* or *an*. *A* is used before a consonant sound, *an* before a vowel sound.
Common adjective. One not derived from a proper name.
Compound adjective. One made up of two or more words.
Definitive adjective. One that defines or limits the meaning of a noun.
Descriptive adjective. One expressing some quality or condition of a noun.
Numeral adjective. One expressing number.
Cardinal. One answering the question "How many?" as *one*, *two*, etc.
Indefinite numeral. One expressing number indefinitely; as, *many, few*, etc.
Indefinite quantitative. One expressing quantity indefinitely; as, *great, little*, etc.
Multiplicative. One answering the question "How many fold?" as, *single, double*, etc.
Ordinal. One which answers the question "Which one?" as, *first, second*, etc.
Partitive. One denoting a part, as, *half, third*, etc.
Participial adjective. One that has the form of a participle.
Pronominal adjective. One that may be used either as a pronoun or an adjective. See PRONOUN.
Proper adjective. One derived from a proper name.

ADJECTIVE—*Associated Words.*

Comparative. The form expressing the greater or less degree of a quality.
Comparison. Change of adjectives to denote variation of quality.
Positive. The simple form of an adjective.
Superlative. The form expressing the greatest or least degree of a quality.

ad-join′. To border upon. INTERSPACE-CONTACT, REMOTENESS-NEARNESS.

ad-journ′. To put off to another day. EARLINESS-LATENESS, PRESIDENT-MEMBER.

ad-journ′-ment. Postponement. EARLINESS-LATENESS.

ad-judge′. To award. DECISION-MISJUDGMENT, JUDGE, LITIGATION.

ad-ju′-di-cate. To try and decide. DECISION-MISJUDGMENT.

ad-ju″-di-ca′-tion. Decision. DECISION-MISJUDGMENT.

ad-junct′. Something joined to. ANTAGONIST-ASSISTANT, INCREMENT-REMNANT, OBSTRUCTION-HELP, SOLITUDE-COMPANY.

ad″-ju-ra′-tion. A charging under oath. ASSERTION-DENIAL.

ad-jure′. To invoke earnestly. ASSERTION-DENIAL, ENGAGEMENT-RELEASE, PETITION-EXPOSTULATION.

ad-just′. To cause to fit; settle. FIGHTING-CONCILIATION, HARMONY-DISCORD, PREPARATION-NONPREPARATION; **adjust differences**, COMPOSITION.

ad-just′-ment. Arrangement. FIGHTING-CONCILIATION, HARMONY-DISCORD, PREPARATION-NONPREPARATION.

ad′-ju-tage. A spout or tube. APERTURE-CLOSURE, WATERCOURSE-AIRPIPE.

ad′-ju-tant. A military staff-officer. ANTAGONIST-ASSISTANT, CHIEF-UNDERLING.

ad-meas′-ure-ment. Act of measuring. MENSURATION.

ad-min′-is-ter. To have the charge of. MANAGEMENT, RULE-LICENSE; **administer correction**, RECOMPENSE-PUNITION; **administer oath**, ENGAGEMENT-RELEASE; **administer sacrament**, CEREMONIAL; **administer to**, GIVING-RECEIVING, OBSTRUCTION-HELP.

ad-min″-is-tra′-tion. Management. MANAGEMENT; **administration of justice**, JUDICATURE.

ad-min′-is-tra″-tive. Executive. JUDICATURE, RULE-LICENSE.

ad′-mi-ra-ble. Worthy of admiration. GOODNESS-BADNESS, VIRTUE-VICE.

ad′-mi-ra-ble Crichton. A clever Scotchman. ADEPT.

ad′-mi-ral. A naval officer of highest rank. CHIEF-UNDERLING.

ad′-mi-ral-ty. Naval department; court of admiralty. TRIBUNAL.

admirari, nil [L.] (ad-mi-rê′-rai, nil). To wonder at nothing. ASTONISHMENT-EXPECTANCE.

ad-mi-ra′-tion. An emotion of wonder and pleasure. APPROVAL-DISAPPROVAL, ASTONISHMENT-EXPECTANCE, LOVE-HATE, REGARD-DISRESPECT.

ad-mire′. To be pleased. APPROVAL-DISAPPROVAL, ASTONISHMENT-EXPECTANCE.

ad-mired′ dis-or′-der. Wondered at. REGULARITY-IRREGULARITY.

ad-mir′-er. A lover. LOVE-HATE.

ad-mis′-si-ble. Worthy of admittance. ADMISSION-EXPULSION, FAULTLESSNESS-FAULTINESS, HARMONY-DISCORD; **admissible in society**, SOCIETY-LUDICROUSNESS.

ad-mis″-si-bil′-i-ty. The quality of being admissible. HARMONY-DISCORD.

ad-mis′-sion. (1) Act of admitting. ADMISSION-EXCLUSION, ADMISSION-EXPULSION, ASSENT-DISSENT, EVIDENCE-COUNTEREVIDENCE, GIVING-RECEIVING, INCLUSION-OMISSION, LEAVE-PROHIBITION.

ad-mis′-sion. (2) A conceding. ADMISSION-EXCLUSION, ADMISSION-EXPULSION, ASSENT-DISSENT, EVIDENCE-COUNTEREVIDENCE, GIVING-RECEIVING, INCLUSION-OMISSION, LEAVE-PROHIBITION.

ADMISSION—EXCLUSION

Admission. The act of admitting, or the state of being admitted. **Composition.** See INCLUSION

Exclusion, etc. The act of excluding or the state of being excluded; debarment. See INCLUSION-OMISSION.

ADMISSION—*Continued.*

Comprehension. The act of including or taking in ideas, facts, etc.
Inclusion. The act of enclosing or comprising; the state of being enclosed.

Reception. The act of admitting or welcoming; the state of being received.

ADMISSION—*Verbs.*

Admit. To suffer to enter; allow to be included.
Arrange under. To include in proper order under.
Arrange with. To include in proper order with.
Be included in, etc. To be enclosed or comprised in
Belong to. To appertain to; be included in.
Come under. To be included under.
Comprehend. To include ideas, facts, etc.
Comprise. To include and consist of
Contain. To include and hold.
Embrace. To include in the arms.
Enclose, etc. See CONFINEMENT.
Enumerate among. To count or include among.
Fall under. To come under or within.

Include. To enclose; comprise.
Merge in. To be sunk or lost in.
Number among. To reckon as one of.
Pertain to. To belong to; to be included in.
Place under. To include under.
Place with. To include with.
Range under. To include in rows under.
Range with. To include in rows with.
Receive. To accept; contain; hold.
Reckon among. To include among.
Refer to. To assign to; include under.
Take into account. To take into consideration.

ADMISSION—*Adjectives.*

Congeneric. Included under the same genus or kind.
Congenerous. Belonging to the same genus or kind.
Included, etc. Comprised; enclosed. See *Verbs.*

Including, etc. Comprising; enclosing. See *Verbs.*
Inclusive. Comprising; embracing.
Of the same class, etc. See DIVISION.

ADMISSION—*Phrases.*

A maximis ad minima [L.]. From the greatest to the least.
Et cetera [L.]. And so on.

Et hoc genus omne [L.]. And everything of this kind.

ADMISSION—EXPULSION.

Absorption. Drawing in slowly, as through pores.
Admission. The act of admitting; permission to enter.
Admittance. See ADMISSION.
Drinking. Act of taking liquid into the stomach.
Eating. Act of taking food into the body.
Entrée [F.]. The act or right of entering.
Imbibition. The act of absorbing or drinking in.
Immission. The act of injecting.
Importation. The act of bringing from one country into another.
Ingestion. Taking in, as into the stomach.
Ingurgitation. The act of swallowing greedily or immoderately.
Inhalation. Taking in the breath; inspiration.
Insertion. The act of putting or placing in or among.
Interjection. A sudden throwing in.
Introduction. The act of bringing into notice or making acquainted.
Intromission. The act of permitting to enter.
Reception. The act of admitting or welcoming.
Sucking. Drawing in.
Suction. The act of causing to be drawn in by the force of a vacuum.

ADMISSION—*Verbs.*

Absorb. To draw in slowly as through pores.
Admit. To permit to enter; receive.
Bring in. To introduce.
Drink. To take in a liquid, usually through the mouth; more rapid action than imbibing. See NUTRIMENT.
Eat. To take in nourishment or food.
Engorge. To swallow greedily.
Engulf. To swallow up as in a gulf.
Give admittance to. To give the right of entering.
Give entrance to. To permit to enter.
Give the entrée. See *Nouns.*
Gulp. To swallow greedily and in large quantities.
Imbibe. To take in a liquid; drink.
Import. To bring from one country into another.
Ingurgitate. To swallow greedily.
Inhale. To draw in the breath.
Introduce. To bring into the presence of and make known to; bring in.
Intromit. To admit; allow to enter.
Let in. To permit to enter; insert.
Open the door to. To receive kindly; welcome.
Readmit. To admit again.
Reabsorb. To absorb again what has formerly been given out.
Receive. To welcome on their first arrival; said mostly of persons
Resorb. To reabsorb.
Snuff up. To draw in through the nose.
Suck in. To draw in by suction.
Swallow. To receive into the stomach through the gullet.

ADMISSION—*Adjectives.*

Absorbent. Tending to drink in or suck up.
Absorptive. That which takes in and incorporates.
Admissible. Worthy or capable of being entertained; allowable.
Admitted. Allowed to enter; received.
Admitting. Granting or ready to grant the privilege of entering.
Entrant. Admitting.

Clearage. The act of removing anything
Clearance. The act of clearing.
Deportation. The act of exiling.
Discharge. The act or process of relieving of a charge or load.
Dislodgment. The act of driving from a place of rest.
Drainage. The act of drawing off slowly, as a liquid.
Effusion. The act or process of pouring forth unrestrainedly.
Egestion. The act of casting forth or voiding.
Ejection. The act of casting forth hurriedly, usually with violence.
Emesis. Vomiting.
Emission. The act of sending forth or giving out, as sound or light.
Eructation. The act of throwing off wind from the stomach or of gaseous or solid matter from a volcano.
Evacuation. The act of making empty.
Eviction. The act of dispossessing by means of some legal title or proceedings.
Expulsion. The act of driving away by force or authority.
Extrusion. The act of forcing or thrusting out, as of fused matter through fissures.
Rejection. The act of rejecting.
Relegation. The act of sending off into some obscure position or into exile. See ERUCTATION.
Ructation. See ERUCTATION.
Tapping. The act of drawing off a liquid by removing the tap.
Trajection. The act of casting forth or over, usually with force.
Vomition. The act of ejecting from the stomach.

EXPULSION—*Denotations.*

Banishment. A driving out of the country. See RECOMPENSE-PUNITION.
Blood-letting. The act of drawing blood from, especially in surgery.
Paracentesis. In medicine the operation of drawing off fluid.
Phlebotomy. The operation of letting blood by opening a vein.
Venesection. The operation of opening a vein for drawing off blood.

EXPULSION—*Associated Words.*

Extradition. The delivering up by one government to another of any person who is a fugitive from justice.
Rogue's march. Music played in derision of a person when he is expelled or driven away in disgrace.

EXPULSION—*Verbs.*

Averruncate. To ward off; avert.
Bail out. To release a person from custody by giving security for his appearance.
Bale out. To empty of water, as a boat.
Banish. To compel to leave a country by authority of political decree or judicial sentence; exile. See EXCULPATION-PUNITION.
Belch. To send forth violently.
Belch out. To vent with vehemence.
Be let out. To permit to depart.
Blow. To drive a current of air out, as through a tube, or to impel by means of a current of air. See RIVER-WIND.
Bow out. To accompany separation with a a slight bow.
Break bulk. To begin to unload.
Breathe. To inhale and exhale air from the lungs; respire.

EXPULSION—Verbs—*Continued*.

Bring up.   To cause to advance, as an army

Broach.   To introduce for discussion.

Brush away.⎫
Brush off.⎭ To remove.

Bundle out.   To dismiss; to send away.

Cast adrift.   To throw overboard.

Cast up.   To throw up or raise.

Chasser [F.].   To pursue; drive out; banish

Clean out.   To remove dirt or impurities.

Clear away.   To remove out of the way.

Clear decks.   To prepare a man-of-war for action.

Clear off.   See CLEAR AWAY.

Clear out.   To remove; betake oneself away.

Clear the throat.   To remove any impediment to the speech.

Cut.   To sever; remove by incision.

Depopulate.   To drive out the inhabitants, as in war.

Deport.   To send away forcibly, as to a penal colony; banish.

Despatch.   To act with promptness; send in haste, as a messenger.

Detrude.   To thrust down forcibly.

Disbowel.   To take out the bowels of.

Discard.   To throw aside as worthless.

Discharge.   To send forth by propulsive force.

Disembowel.   To remove the bowels; eviscerate.

Disgorge.   To throw out from; eject.

Dislodge.   To force out from a place of rest or defense

Dispatch.   See DESPATCH.

Dispeople.   See DEPOPULATE.

Do away with.   To dispose of.

Drain.   To draw off slowly, as a liquid.

Drain to the dregs.   To draw off to the last drop

Draw off.   To withdraw; drain some fluid.

Drivel.   To have spittle flow from the mouth.

Effuse.   To pour forth unrestrainedly.

Eject.   To thrust out with violence or indignity.

Eliminate.   To get rid of as superfluous or unnecessary.

Embowel.   To eviscerate; rend.

Emit.   To send out or give forth as sound or light.

Empty.   To remove all the contents; make void.

Eructate.   To eject with noise.

Evacuate.   To eject by any of the excretory passages.

Evict.   To dispossess by some legal title or proceedings.

Eviscerate.   To remove the entrails.

Excern.   To excrete.

Excrete.   To separate and discharge waste matter from any animal body.

Exhale.   To send out the breath from the lungs.

Expectorate.   To discharge matter from the throat and lungs by coughing and spitting.

Expel.   To drive out summarily, usually with violence and disgrace.

Expend.   To pay out or use, as time or money.

Extravasate.   To permit or cause to flow out of the proper vessels, as blood out of arteries.

Extrude.   To force or thrust out, as fused matter through fissures

Get out.   To draw forth or disengage; betake oneself away.

Get rid of.   To dispose of; extricate oneself from.

Give exit to.   To permit to leave; grant a way of departure.

Give out.   To send out; publish or report.

Give the sack to.   To discharge, as a servant; to jilt, as a lover.

Give vent to.   To give expression or utterance to; to pour forth as anger or tears.

Gut.   To eviscerate; destroy the contents of.

Hawk.   To discharge phlegm from the throat by a forced cough.

Heck.   To heave, as in the act of vomiting.

Lade out.   To dip out with a ladle or dipper.

Let blood.   To draw blood by opening a vein.

Let out.   To extend, as a cord; release or permit to escape, as a prisoner.

Make a clean sweep of.   To clear away everything.

Ooze.   To flow gently, as through pores or small openings.

Open the flood-gates.   To turn on a great flow or flood of water

Open the sluices.   See OPEN THE FLOOD-GATES.

Oust.   To turn out by force or legal process.

Pack off.   To go off or be sent off peremptorily or in haste.

Perspire.   To excrete fluids and waste matter through the pores of the skin.

Pour forth.   See POUR OUT.

Pour out.   To cause to flow freely, as a liquid.

Puke.   To eject from the stomach.

Purge.   To cleanse from impurities.

Push aside.⎫
Push away.⎪
Push off.⎬ Reject.
Push out.⎭

Reject.   To cast away as worthless.

Relegate.   To send off, to consign.

Retch.   To strain as in vomiting.

Root out.   To tear up by the roots.

Root up.   See ROOT OUT.

Secern.   To secrete or separate in the animal body.

Secrete.   To separate from the blood or sap and form new substances, as saliva or gum.

Send about one's business.

Send adrift.   To give to the mercy of wind and wave.

Send away.   To dismiss.

Send away with a flea in the ear.   To send one away after having told him some secret or given him some warning or rebuke.

Send off.   To dismiss or despatch.

Send packing.   To discharge a person without ceremony.

Send to Coventry.   To send to some imaginary place of social banishment; exclude from social intercourse on account of some ungentlemanly conduct.

Send to Jericho.   To send to some remote and out-of-the-way place.

Send to the right-about.   To send in the opposite direction; reject.

Shake off.   To throw to one side.

Shed.   To lose or cast off something.

Shovel away.   To remove with a shovel.

Shovel out.   See SHOVEL AWAY.

Show the door to.   To point one to the door.

Slabber.   To drop liquid food from the mouth in eating.

Slaver.   To permit saliva to flow from the mouth in eating, as a horse.

Slop.   To cause to overflow.

Spend.   To use or waste that which is valuable, as time or money.

Spew.   To cast forth.

Spill.   To allow or cause to overflow.

Spit.   To discharge mucus or phlegm from the mouth.

Splutter.   To speak or act hastily and confusedly.

Sputter.   To scatter saliva in speaking.

Spurt.   To cause a liquid to flow out in a jet.

Squirt.   To cause to issue in a sudden jet.

Strike off the roll.   To erase the name from the list of members.   See COMMISSION-ABROGATION.

Suck.   To draw in by forming a vacuum, as by the action of mouth and tongue.

Suck off.   Remove by suction.

Sweep away.⎫
Sweep off.⎬ To remove.
Sweep out.⎭

Tap.   To draw off liquid by opening or removing the tap.

Throw aside.   To dispense with as useless.

Throw away.   To cast from.

Throw off.   To unload or get rid of.

Throw out.   To reject, as part of an account.

Throw overboard.   To cast from a ship into the water.

Turn adrift.   To unmoor and let float.

Turn away.   To reject, as an offer.

Turn off.   To send away or dismiss, as a servant.

Turn on the tap.   To cause or permit liquid to flow by opening the tap.

Turn out.   To put out.

Turn out head and shoulders.   To go into a thing with force and violence.

Turn out neck and crop.   To go into a thing all at once, in a summary manner.

Turn out neck and heels.   See TURN OUT NECK AND CROP.

Turn out of house and home.   To drive out of one's place of abode.

Unearth.   To dig up from the earth.

Unhouse.   To drive from one's house or habitation.

Unkennel.   To drive out from a kennel or retreat.

Unlade.   To unload.

Unload.   To remove a load.

Unpack.   To remove the contents of.

Unpeople.   To depopulate.

Unship.   To unload from a ship.

Void.   To quit; leave.

Vomit.   To eject the contents of the stomach.

Weed out.   To remove the weeds, as from a garden.

Whisk away.   To brush away with a light, rapid motion.

Whisk off.   To brush off, as dust from a table.

EXPULSION—*Adjectives*.

Emitting, etc.   See *Verbs*.   **Emitted, etc.**   See *Verbs*.

EXPULSION—*Continued.*

EXPULSION—*Interjections.*

Aroynt! Avaunt! Away! Away with! Be gone! Be off! Get along! Get along with you! Get away! Get you gone! Go! Go about your business! Go along! Go along with you! Go away! Go your way! Off with you!

ad-mit'. To allow to go in. ADMISSION-EXCLUSION, ADMISSION-EXPULSION, ASSENT-DISSENT, CONSENT, EXPOSURE-HIDINGPLACE, GIVING-RECEIVING, INCLUSION-OMISSION, LEAVE-PROHIBITION; admit exceptions, MODIFICATION; admit of, POSSIBILITY-IMPOSSIBILITY

ad-mit'-tance. Entrance. ENTRANCE-EXIT.

ad-mit'-ted. Accepted. HABIT-DESUETUDE; admitted maxim, etc., ADAGE-NONSENSE.

ad-mit'-ting. Allowing to enter. ADMISSION-EXPULSION, MODIFICATION.

ad-mix'-ture. A mixture. MIXTURE-HOMOGENEITY.

ad-mon'-ish. To warn. ADVICE, APPROVAL-DISAPPROVAL, WARNING.

ad''-mo-ni'-tion. Reprimand. ADVICE, WARNING.

ad-mon'-i-tive. Admonitory. ADVICE, WARNING.

ad-mon'-i-to-ry. Serving to warn. WARNING.

a-do'. Bustle. ACTIVITY-INDOLENCE, DIFFICULTY-FACILITY, TOIL-RELAXATION; make much ado about, CONSEQUENCE-INSIGNIFICANCE; much ado about nothing, CONSEQUENCE-INSIGNIFICANCE, OVERVALUATION-UNDERVALUATION, SKILL-UNSKILFULNESS.

ad''-o-les'-cence. Period from childhood to manhood. MANHOOD.

ad''-o-les'-cent. Pertaining to youth. MANHOOD.

A-do'-nis. A mythological youth. BEAUTY-UGLINESS.

ad'-o-nize. To dandify. EMBELLISHMENT-DISFIGUREMENT.

a-dopt'. To take as one's own. CHOICE-NEUTRALITY, ESTABLISHMENT-REMOVAL; adopt a cause, OBSTRUCTION-HELP; adopt a course, CONDUCT; adopt an opinion, FAITH-MISGIVING.

a-dopt'-ed. Accepted. GODLINESS-UNGODLINESS.

a-dopt''-i-bil'-i-ty. Capability of being assumed. FAITH-MISGIVING.

a-dop'-tion. Act of adopting. CHOICE-NEUTRALITY, GODLINESS-UNGODLINESS.

a-dor'-a-ble. Lovable. LOVE-HATE.

ad''-o-ra'-tion. Reverential love. DEVOTION-IDOLATRY, LOVE-HATE.

a-dore'. To worship. DEVOTION-IDOLATRY, LOVE-HATE.

a-dor'-er. A lover. LOVE-HATE.

adorer le veau d'or [F.] (a-do-ré' lc vo dor). To worship the golden calf. DEVOTION-IDOLATRY.

a-dorn'. To decorate. EMBELLISHMENT-DISFIGUREMENT.

a-dorn'-ment. An ornament. EMBELLISHMENT-DISFIGUREMENT.

a-down'. Downward. HEIGHT-LOWNESS.

a-drift'. Drifting. CERTAINTY-DOUBT, CONNECTION-INDEPENDENCE, GATHERING-SCATTERING, SKILL-UNSKILFULNESS, UNION-DISUNION; go adrift, AIM-ABERRATION; turn adrift, COMMISSION-ABROGATION, GATHERING-SCATTERING, RELEASE-RESTRAINT.

a-droit'. Expert. SKILL-UNSKILFULNESS.

a-droit'-ness. Expertness. SKILL-UNSKILFULNESS.

ad''-sci-ti'-tious. Supplemental. ADDITION-SUBTRACTION, COMMISSION-ABROGATION, SUBJECTIVENESS-OBJECTIVENESS.

adscriptus glebæ [L.] (ad-scrip'-tus glî'-bî). Bound to the soil. CHIEF-UNDERLING.

ad'-sum [L.]. I am present. Answer to a roll-call.

ad''-u-la'-tion. Flattery. ADULATION-DISPARAGEMENT.

ADULATION—DISPARAGEMENT.

Adulation. Servile flattery.

Blandiloquence. Language of compliment.

Blandishment. Caressing speech or actions to win the heart.

Blarney. Smooth, wheedling flattery.

Buncombe.
Bunkum. } Bombastic speech for political effect.

Butter. Flattery.

Cajolery. Act of duping by deceitful flattery.

Captation. Obtaining favor or applause by flattery or address.

Coquetry. Vain trifling in love.

Euphemism. An expression less offensive than one more directly expressive of the thought.

Fawning. Cringing flattery in hope of favor.

Flattery. Undue or insincere compliment.

Flummery. Empty compliment.

Flunkyism. A worshiper of rank or wealth.

Gloze. Flattery.

Honeyed words. Sweet flattery.

Incense. Complimentary language.

Lip homage.
Mouth honor. } Empty or insincere honor.

Placebo. A prescription by a physician, given to please rather than to cure.

Rosewater. Smooth talk.

Snobbishness. Aping of gentility by a vulgar person.

Soft sawder.
Soft soap. } Blarney; flattery.

Sycophancy. Base, servile flattery.

Taffy. Flattery; soft praises.

Toad eating. Sycophancy.

Tuft hunting. Flattery upon persons of position in hope of gain.

Unctuousness. Quality of being extremely bland or suave.

Voice of the charmer. Flattering voice.

Wheedling. Persuasion by flattering words.

Aspersion. Circulation of false and injurious charges.

Backbiting. Speaking secretly to one's injury.

Calumny. Invention and propagation of evil reports.

Chronique scandaleuse [F.]. Chronicle of scandals.

Criticism. Harsh or unfavorable judgment. See APPROVAL-DISAPPROVAL.

Cynicism. Contempt for others' doings and opinions.

Defamation. Injury to reputation by aspersions, etc.

Depreciation. Lessening the estimation of.

Detraction. Lessening of reputation by insinuation of base motives.

Detractor. One who finds fault with or defames another.

Disparagement. Injury done by speaking sightingly of.

Envenomed tongue. Bitter, hostile speech.

Evil-speaking. Harmful talk.

Invective. Harsh and reproachful accusations.

Lampoon. Personal, written satire.

Libel. Written defamation.

Obloquy. Censorious, abusive, and reproachful language.

Obtrectation. Act of calumniating.

Pasquinade. A short satirical publication.

Personality. Disparaging remark about a person.

Sarcasm. Sharp, scornful language.

Scandal. Defamatory talk, heedlessly or maliciously uttered.

Scandalum magnatum [L.]. Scandal concerning those of rank or dignity.

Scurrility. Foul or obscene language.

Skit. A brief satire.

Slander. Spoken defamation.

Spretæ injuria formæ [L.]. Wrong done to slighted beauty.

Traducement. Odious misrepresentation of one's conduct or character.

Vilification. Words intended to make a person or thing seem vile in another's eyes.

ADULATION—DISPARAGEMENT—*Continued.*

ADULATION—*Verbs.*

Beplaster. Thoroughly plaster.
Beslaver. Thoroughly slaver.
Beslubber. Thoroughly slubber.
Bespatter. Thoroughly spatter.
Butter. To flatter.
Cajole. To dupe by deceitful flattery.
Coax. To seek to persuade by fondling or flattery.
Cog. To cheat, as with loaded dice.
Collogue. To use flattery and deceit.
Coquet. To trifle vainly in love.
Court. To seek to obtain by assiduous attentions.
Creep into the good graces of. To get into favor by flattery or cajolery.
Curry favor with. To seek favor with by adulation or attentions.
Earwig. To gain favor by telling tales about others.
Exaggerate. To enlarge upon the truth.
Fawn.
Fawn upon. } To flatter cringingly in hope of favor.
Flatter. To give undue or insincere compliment.
Fool to the top of one's bent. To fool shamelessly
Gild the pill. To gloze.
Glaver. To wheedle.
Gloze. To gloss over with specious representation.
Hang on the sleeve of. To be a sycophant.
Humor. To gratify by yielding to some one's inclinations.
Lay it on thick. To flatter extravagantly.
Lay the flattering unction to one's soul. To use flattery.
Lick the dust. To cringe.
Make things pleasant. To gloss over.
Overestimate. To value too highly.
Overpraise. To praise beyond just due.
Pandar to.
Pander to. } To cater to the wishes of.
Pay court to. To court. See COURT.
Pet. To fondle and indulge.
Praise to the skies. To praise lavishly.
Puff. To praise unduly.
Slaver. To flatter.
Soothe. To calm with soft words.
Truckle to. To curry favor with servility.
Wheedle. To persuade with flattering words.

ADULATION—*Adjectives*

Adulatory. Servilely flattering.
Blandiloquent. In the language of compliment.
Courtierlike.
Courtierly. } Very courteous.
Fair-spoken. Bland in speech.
Fine. Nice, artful, subtle.
Flattering. Praising unduly or insincerely
Fulsome. Offensive from excess of praise.
Honeyed. Sweetly flattering.
Honey-mouthed. Having a flattering mouth.
Mealy-mouthed. Euphemistic.
Oily. Deceitfully affable in speech or manners.
Plausible. Apparently right.
Servile. Meanly obsequious.
Smooth. Suave, often deceitfully.
Smooth-tongued. Deceitfully pleasing in speech.
Soapy. Using flattery.
Specious. Appearing well at first sight, but really unsound.
Sycophantic. Like a sycophant, servile in flattery.
Unctuous. Extremely bland or suave.

ADULATION—*Adverbial Phrase.*

Ad captandum [L.]. To attract or please.

DISPARAGEMENT—*Noun of Agent.*

Detractor. A defamer; slanderer.

DISPARAGEMENT—*Verbs.*

Anathematize. To pronounce a curse against.
Asperse. To bespatter with injurious charges.
Avile. To vilify.
Backbite. To speak evil behind one's back.
Bear false witness against. To tell lies, especially before a magistrate.
Besmirch. To dim the reputation of.
Bespatter. To cover with slander or reproaches.
Blacken. To defame; vilify.
Blow upon. To taint; discredit.
Brand. To stamp with infamy.
Calumniate. To invent and spread evil reports.
Cast aspersions. To censure harshly and falsely.
Criticize. To judge harshly or unfavorably.
Cry down. To depreciate; decry.
Decry. To disparage loudly.
Defame. To injure reputation by evil or false reports concerning.
Depreciate. To lessen the estimation of.
Derogate. To lessen by taking away a part; to disparage.
Detract. To lessen reputation by insinuation of base motives.
Dip the pen into gall. To write bitterly.
Disparage. To injure by speaking slightingly of.
Fling dirt. To use abusive language.
Give a dog a bad name. Calumniate.
Lampoon. To indulge in written, personal satire.
Libel. To defame in writing.
Malign. To speak great evil of, especially falsely
Pick a hole in one's coat. To find fault with.
Pull to pieces. To criticize unsparingly.
Run down. To attempt to depreciate one in the estimation of others.
Slander. To utter malicious reports about.
Sneer at. To speak of in scornful contempt.
Speak ill of behind one's back. Slander.
Traduce. To odiously misrepresent one's conduct or character.
View in a bad light. To think unfavorably of.
Vilify. To attempt to make one seem vile in others' eyes.
Vilipend. To speak of disparagingly.

DISPARAGEMENT—*Adjectives.*

Abusive. Coarse and rude in reproach.
Calumniatory.
Calumnious. } Containing a false, malicious report or accusation.
Cynical. Contemptuous of others' doings and opinions.
Defamatory. Tending to bring disrepute upon.
Derogatory. Taking away a part, as from dignity.
Detracting, etc. See *Verbs.*
Detractory. Tending to lessen estimation of.
Disparaging. Tending to injure by unfavorable comparison.
Foul-mouthed.
Foul-spoken. } Using obscene and abusive language.
Foul-tongued.
Libelous. Containing anything damaging to character.
Sarcastic. Exhibiting contemptuous language.
Sardonic. Having a forced, sneering laugh or smile.
Satirical. Containing irony.
Scurrile.
Scurrilous. } Gross or vile in speech.
Slanderous. Containing false tales or reports.

DISPARAGEMENT—*Phrases.*

Assent with civil leer; damn with faint praise; without sneering, others teach to sneer.

---

ad'-u-la''-tor. A flatterer. FLATTERER-DEFAMER.
ad'-u-la-to-ry. Flattering. ADULATION-DISPARAGEMENT.
A-dul'-lam. A Biblical cave. **Cave of Adullam,** CONTENTEDNESS–DISCONTENTMENT, QUEST–EVASION, REGRET.
a-dult'. A fully developed person. MANHOOD.
a-dul'-ter-ate. To make impure. BETTERMENT-DETERIORATION, MIXTURE-HOMOGENEITY.

a-dul'-ter-a''-ted. Corrupted. TRUTHFULNESS-FRAUD.
a-dul''-ter-a'-tion. Condition of being adulterated. BETTERMENT-DETERIORATION, MIXTURE-HOMOGENEITY.
a-dul'-ter-er. A man guilty of adultery. PURITY-RAKE.
a-dul'-ter-ess. A female adulterer. PURITY-RAKE.
a-dul'-ter-ous. Illicit. PURITY-IMPURITY.
a-dul'-ter-y. Unchastity. PURITY-IMPURITY.

a-dult'-ness. State of being an adult. MANHOOD.

ad-um'-brate. To overshadow. DELINEATION-CARICATURE, LIGHT-DARKNESS, TROPE.

ad-um-bra'-tion. A shadow. COPY-MODEL, LIGHT-DARKNESS, MANIFESTATION-LATENCY, TROPE.

ad-un'-ci-ty. Condition of being hook-shaped. ANGULARITY.

ad-un'-cous. Hook-shaped. ANGULARITY.

a-dus'-tion. Process of drying or burning. HEATING-COOLING.

ad-vance'. To move forward. ASSERTION-DENIAL, BETTERMENT-DETERIORATION, INCREASE-DECREASE, LOAN-BORROWING, OBSTRUCTION-HELP, PERIOD-PROGRESS, SUCCESS-FAILURE; **advance against,** ATTACK-DEFENSE; **advance of learning,** KNOWLEDGE-IGNORANCE; **in advance,** ANTERIORITY-POSTERIORITY, LEADING-FOLLOWING, LOAN-BORROWING, PRECEDENCE-SUCCESSION; **in advance of,** SUPREMACY-SUBORDINACY; **in advance of one's age,** SAGACITY-INCAPACITY.

ADVANCE—RETROGRESSION.

Advance. The act of moving forward or proposing; progress.

Advancement. Forwarding; promotion.

Advancing. Progression. See *Verbs.*

Flood-tide. The rising tide.

Headway. Forward motion, particularly of a vessel; progress.

Improvement. Advancement in desirable qualities. See BETTERMENT.

March. Onward progress. See TRAVELING.

Ongoing. The act of going forward; progress.

Progress. A moving or going forward; an advance.

Progression. Motion forward or onward; a proceeding in a course.

Progressiveness. The quality of being progressive.

Rise. Ascent; advance as in rank, prosperity, or importance.

ADVANCE—*Verbs.*

Advance. To move forward; further; proceed.

Distance. To leave behind in a race; greatly to excel.

Proceed. To go forward; continue in progress.

Progress. To continue onward in course of action or development.

ADVANCE—*Verbal Expressions.*

Carve one's way; come ahead; come forward; come forwards; come on; edge one's way; elbow one's way; force one's way; gain ground; get ahead; get along; get forward; get forwards; get on; get over the ground; go ahead; go forward; go forwards; go on; go with the stream; hold on one's course; jog on; keep one's course; make advances; make head; make headway; make one's way; make progress; make rapid strides (see SWIFTNESS); make strides; make up leeway, make up for time lost; make way; move ahead; move forwards; move on; pass ahead; pass forward; pass forwards; pass on; press ahead; press forward; press forwards; press on; press onwards; push ahead; push forward; push forwards; push on; push one's way; rub on, go on with difficulty; shoot ahead; step forward; wag on; work one's way.

ADVANCE—*Adjectives.*

Advanced. Moved forward; promoted; furthered.

Advancing, etc. Progressing; improving. See *Verbs*

Ebbless. Not flowing back.

Profluent. Flowing forward.

Progressive. Advancing.

ADVANCE—*Adverbs.*

Ahead. In advance.

En route **for.** On the way to.

Forth. Forward in place, time, or order.

Forward. Onward; ahead.

In mid progress. Half achieved.

In progress. Advancing.

In transitu [L.]. On the passage. See TRANSFER.

On. With unbroken advance; forward.

On one's way to.
On the high road to.
On the road to.
On the way to. } In the act of going.

Onward. In the direction of progress; forward.

Under way. In motion, as a ship.

ADVANCE—*Phrases.*

Boutez en avant [F.]. Push forward.

Vestigia nulla retrorsum [L.]. No footsteps backward (At the mouth of the lion's den). [Horace.]

Backsliding. Falling back into sin or error; abandonment of faith or duty.

Backwater. Water set, thrown or held back.

Countermarch. A return march; any reversal of conduct or method.

Counter-motion. Motion in a contrary direction.

Counter-movement. Movement in opposition to another.

Crab-like motion. Motion backward.

Deterioration. The process of growing worse, or the state of having grown worse. See BETTERMENT-DETERIORATION.

Ebb. The reflux of tide-water to the ocean.

Fall. The act, process or result of dropping from a higher to a lower place or position.

Recess. A place or space left depressed in the thickness of a wall; a time of cessation from employment.

Recession. Withdrawal. See WITHDRAWAL.

Recidivation. A falling back; a backsliding.

Reculade [F.]. Falling back.

Reflection. The act of turning back, or the state of being turned back; the turning in of the mind upon itself. See IMPETUS-REACTION.

Refluence. A flowing back.

Reflux. A flowing back; ebb.

Regress. Passage back; return.

Regression. The act of moving back or returning; retrogression.

Regurgitation. The act of rushing back or of swallowing again.

Remigration. Migration back to the place from which one came.

Resilience. The act, power or result of springing back to a former position.

Retirement. The act of retiring or withdrawing; the state of being retired.

Retreat. The act of retreating, as an army before an enemy; retirement.

Retroaction. A reverse action.

Retrocession. Going or moving backward.

Retrogradation. The act or result of going, moving, or tending backward.

Retrogression. A going or moving backward; degeneration.

Return. The act, process or result of turning backward.

Tergiversation. Evasion of a point, as by subterfuge; inconstancy.

Turning point. See CONVERSION-REVERSION.

Veering. Direction to a different course.

Withdrawal. The act of withdrawing; retraction.

RETROGRESSION—*Verbs.*

Back. To reverse the action of; move rearward.

Countermarch. To march back.

Double. To turn and go back on the same or a parallel track.

Ebb. To flow back towards the ocean, as the tide; decline.

Jib. To move restively sidewise or backwards.

Rebound. To bound back. See IMPETUS-REACTION.

Recede. To move back; withdraw.

Regrade. To retire; go back.

Regurgitate. To throw or pour back; surge or be poured back.

Retire. To separate or withdraw; remove.

Retreat. To withdraw from a position; go into retirement.

Retrocede. To give back; restore ownership, possession, or control of.

Retrograde. To move, or cause to move, backward.

Return. To put, carry, or send back; turn or direct backward.

Revert. To reverse; come back.

Shrink. To draw back; recoil.

Shy. To start suddenly aside.

Turn. To change, alter or vary in nature, form or aspect; rotate or cause to rotate.

Veer. To turn to another course; change direction, as the wind.

Wheel. To perform or cause to perform a circular movement; take a new direction.

Withdraw. To draw or take away; take back.

RETROGRESSION—*Continued.*

RETROGRESSION—*Verbal Expressions.*

Back out, retreat or withdraw; **back water,** reverse the action of the oars, paddle, or propeller, so as to force the ship backward; **beat a retreat; come back; dance the back step; draw back; drop astern,** be left behind; **fall astern,** move or be driven backward; **fall back; get back; go back; go home; hark back,** go back for a fresh start; **lose ground; put about,** change the course of, as a ship; **put back; retrace one's steps; run back; sound a retreat; turn; turn back; turn one's back upon,** leave; **turn round; turn tail,** run away; **turn upon one's heel; veer; veer round,** direct to a different course, as a vessel.

RETROGRESSION—*Adjectives.*

Crab-like. Moving backward.
Reactionary. Tending toward a former or opposite state, etc. See IMPETUS-REACTION.
Receding. Withdrawing, as from a claim; moving back. See *Verbs.*
Recidivous. Liable to backslide.
Reflex. Turned or thrown backward; bent back.

Refluent. Flowing or rushing back.
Regressive. Passing back; retroactive.
Resilient. Having the quality of resilience.
Retrograde. Going, moving, or tending backward; declining toward a worse state of character.
Retrogressive. Going or moving backward; declining.

RETROGRESSION—*Adverbs.*

Back. To or toward the rear; behind.
Backwards. To the rear; into time past.

Reflexively. Bending or turned backwards.
To the right about. Toward the opposite point or quarter.

RETROGRESSION—*Phrases.*

As you were. In original condition.

Revenons à nos moutons [F.]. Let us return to our sheep; let us return to our subject.

ad-vanced'. Before. ADVANCE-RETROGRESSION; **advanced guard,** ANTERIORITY-POSTERIORITY; **advanced in life,** INFANCY-AGE; **advanced work,** ATTACK-DEFENSE.
ad-vance'-ment. Promotion. ADVANCE-RETROGRESSION, BETTERMENT-DETERIORATION.
ad-van'-ces. Anything supplied. **Make advances,** PROFFER-REFUSAL, TREASURY.
ad-vanc'-ing. Approaching. ADVANCE-RETROGRESSION, YELLOWNESS-PURPLE.
ad-van'-tage. Anything favorable to success. GOOD-EVIL, SUPREMACY-SUBORDINACY; **advantage over,** SUCCESS-FAILURE; **dressed to advantage,** EMBELLISHMENT-DISFIGUREMENT; **find one's advantage in,** USEFULNESS-USELESSNESS; **gain an advantage,** GAIN-LOSS, SUCCESS-FAILURE; **mechanical advantage,** INSTRUMENT; **set off to advantage,** BETTERMENT-DETERIORATION; **take advantage of,** SKILL-UNSKILFULNESS, USE-DISUSE.
ad"-van-ta'-geous. Favorable. GAIN-LOSS, GOODNESS-BADNESS, USEFULNESS-USELESSNESS.
ad-vene'. To come to. ADDITION-SUBTRACTION.
ad'-vent. Arrival. APPROACH-WITHDRAWAL, ARRIVAL-DEPARTURE, FUTURE-PAST, OCCURRENCE-DESTINY.
Ad'-vent. The coming of Christ. CEREMONIAL.
ad"-ven-ti'-tious. Incidental. CONDITION-SITUATION, RATIONALE-LUCK, SUBJECTIVENESS-OBJECTIVENESS.
ad-ven'-ture. A remarkable experience. OCCURRENCE-DESTINY, QUEST-EVASION, RATIONALE-LUCK, SECURITY-INSECURITY, VENTURE.
ad-ven'-tur-er. One who engages in dangerous undertakings. GENTILITY-DEMOCRACY, PURPOSE-LUCK, RECKLESSNESS-CAUTION, TRIAL, WAYFARER-SEAFARER.
ad-ven'-tures. Experiences. ACCOUNT.
ad-ven'-tur-ous. Venturesome. BRAVERY-COWARDICE, RECKLESSNESS-CAUTION.
ad'-verb. A part of speech which defines or limits a verb. PARTICLE; **adverbial pronoun,** PRONOUN.
ad"-ver-sa'-ri-a. A commonplace-book. MARK.
ad'-ver-sa-ry. An opposing party. ANTAGONIST-ASSISTANT.
ad-ver'-sa-tive. Conjunction expressing opposition. PARTICLE.
ad'-verse. In opposition. ANTAGONISM-CONCURRENCE, DESIRE-DISTASTE, WELFARE-MISFORTUNE, READINESS-RELUCTANCE; **adverse party,** ANTAGONIST-ASSISTANT; **adverse fate,** VOLITION-OBLIGATION.

ad-ver'-si-ty. Misfortune. GOOD-EVIL, WELFARE-MISFORTUNE.
ad-vert'. To turn to. HEED-DISREGARD.
ad-vert'-ence. Notice. HEED-DISREGARD.
ad-vert'-en-cy. Attentiveness. HEED-DISREGARD.
ad'-ver-tise". To make known publicly. PUBLICITY.
ad"-ver-tise'-ment. A public notice. PUBLICITY, SIGN.
ad-vice'. Counsel. ADVICE, ENLIGHTENMENT-SECRECY, MOTIVE-DEHORTATION, TIDINGS-MYSTERY.

ADVICE.

Adhortation. Advice.
Admonition. Friendly counseling or warning. See WARNING.
Advice. A speaking to in reference to some act or course.
Advocacy. The act of pleading for, defending of.
Charge. An instruction; advice to.
Conference. The act of advising together.
Consultation. The act of consulting, of deliberating.
Council. Act of deliberating.
Exhortation. Earnest advice to well doing. See MOTIVE.
Expostulation. Counseling against a certain course.
Guidance. The act of guiding or directing. See MANAGEMENT.
Hortatory. Giving or containing advice.
Injunction. Authoritative advice.
Instruction. The act of teaching, of directing.
Obtestation. The act of supplicating not to do a certain thing.
Pourparler [F.]. A parleying.
Recommendation. The act of counseling on a certain course.
Reference. The act of directing for a testimonial.
Referment. The act of referring.
Submonition. Suggestion.
Suggestion. Act of bringing up for consideration.

ADVICE—*Nouns of Instrument.*

Chart. A guiding map; a tabulated sheet. See ENLIGHTENMENT.
Guide. Something that serves to direct.
Manual. A small book often containing instructions.

ADVICE—*Nouns of Agent.*

Adviser. One who gives advice.
Arbiter. A judge between contestants. See JUDGE.
Archiater. The chief physician. [Used in Europe.]
Council. A body of men which gives advice.
Councilor. A member of council.
Counselor. One who gives advice.
Leech. A doctor.
Mentor. A wise and elderly guide.
Monitor. A warner, a cautioner.
Physician. One who advises on bodily ailments.
Prompter. One who incites; one who suggests what follows.
Senator. A member of the more stable of the legislative assemblies of states.
Teacher. One who instructs or educates. See INSTRUCTOR.

ADVICE—*Continued*.

ADVICE—*Figurative*.

Magnus Apollo [L.]. Great Apollo; the god of prophecy and advice.
Nestor. A faithful and wise counselor in the *Iliad*.

ADVICE—*Phrase*.

A word to the wise.

ADVICE—*Verbs*.

Admonish. To advise in a friendly way. See WARNING.
Advise. To commend or condemn a given course.
Advise with. To ask advice of.
Advocate. To defend publicly.
Be advised by. Accept advice.
Be closeted with. To be granted a private interview.
Call. To assemble for a purpose.
Call in. To invite together.
Call upon. Invite to speak.
Charge. To lay upon; instruct.
Compare notes. Compare information.
Confer. To enter into a consultation with.
Consult. To receive advice from.
Consult together. To interchange advice.
Counsel. To give advice to.
Deliberate. To weigh in the mind.
Dictate. To enjoin positively.
Enforce. To put into effect; urge forcibly.
Enjoin. To charge; advise strongly.
Exhort. To warn against a certain course. See MOTIVE.
Expostulate. To earnestly warn against. See MOTIVE-DEHORTATION.
Follow advice. To act upon advice.
Give advice.
Give a piece of advice. } To advise.
Give counsel.
Have at one's elbow. To have within easy reach.
Hold a council. Confer.
Instruct. To impart knowledge and directions.
Lay heads together. To consider in union.
Prescribe. To lay out beforehand; direct.
Prompt. To incite to activity; point to the next.
Recommend. To give a favorable opinion of; advise.
Refer to. Mention.
Submonish. To suggest.
Suggest. To bring to the notice of.
Take advice. Accept counsel.
Take one's cue from. To get a hint from.

ADVICE—*Adjectives*.

Admonitory. Serving to warn or reprove. See WARNING.
Dehortatory. Fitted to dissuade. See MOTIVE-DEHORTATION.
Hortatory. Fitted to encourage in a given course. See MOTIVE.
Recommendatory. Having a recommendation.

ADVICE—*Interjection*.

Go to!

ADVICE—*Phrases*.

Verbum sat sapienti [L.]. A word to the wise is sufficient.
Vive memor leti [L.]. Live mindful of death.

ad-vi'-sa-ble. Expedient. PROPRIETY-IMPROPRIETY.
ad-vise'. To give counsel to. ADVICE, ENLIGHTENMENT-SECRECY, PROPHECY; **advise with one's pillow**, REFLECTION-VACANCY.
ad-vised'. Prudent. PREDETERMINATION-IMPULSE, PURPOSE-LUCK; **better advised**, BETTERMENT-DETERIORATION.
ad-vi'-sed-ly. Not hastily. PREDETERMINATION-IMPULSE, PURPOSE-LUCK.
ad-vi'-ser. One who advises. ADVICE, MANAGER.
ad'-vo-ca-cy. Pleading. APPROVAL-DISAPPROVAL, MOTIVE-DEHORTATION, OBSTRUCTION-HELP.
ad'-vo-cate. One who pleads the cause of another. ADVICE, ADVOCATE, ANTAGONIST-ASSISTANT, FRIEND-FOE, JUSTIFICATION-CHARGE, MOTIVE-CAPRICE, OBSTRUCTION-HELP; **the Advocate**, DIVINITY.

ADVOCATE.

Advocate. One who pleads for another before a judicial tribunal or court.
Attorney. One who is legally appointed by another to transact business for him.
Bar. The entire body of lawyers.
Barrister.
Barrister-at-law } One who practises in the courts.
Bencher. A member of the bar holding a place in one of the governing bodies.
Civilian. One learned in Roman or civil law.
Conveyancer. One whose business is to transfer titles to property.
Counsel. One who gives advice in legal matters.
Counselor. One who manages a cause for a client or gives legal advice.
Cursitor. A clerk in the Court of Chancery.
Equity draftsman. A lawyer who drafts equity pleadings.
Inner bar. The body of senior barristers.
Judge. The officer who presides over a court. See JUDGE.
Junior bar. The body of barristers who occupy a place beyond the crown's counsel.
Jurisconsult. A man learned in the law, who gives legal advice.
Jurist. One learned in the law; a judge.
K. C. Abbreviation for King's Counsel.
King's Counsel. A barrister appointed by the crown to plead its causes.
Lawmonger. One who practises law as if it were a trade.
Lawyer. A general term for persons versed in the law and employed to plead the cause of clients.
Leader. The principal attorney in a case.
Legal adviser. One who gives advice on law matters
Legal profession. The body of lawyers.
Legist. A writer on law.
Notary. } A public officer who has a seal and is empowered to
Notary public. } note protests, certify deeds, etc.
Outer bar. The body of junior barristers.
Pettifogger. A lawyer who uses short or dishonest methods.
Pleader. One who advocates the cause of another.
Proctor. An officer employed in admiralty and ecclesiastical causes.
Publicist. A writer on law.
Pundit. One versed in the laws of the Hindus.
Q. C. Abbreviation for Queen's Counsel.
Queen's Counsel. A barrister appointed by the crown to plead its causes, and not permitted afterwards to plead against it.
Scrivener. One who draws up deeds, contracts, etc.
Sergeant-at-law. The highest rank at the common law bar.
Special pleader. An expert in the drawing of pleadings.
Tubman. One of the two most experienced barristers in the Court of Exchequer.
Writer to the signet. A judicial officer who prepares writs, warrants, etc.

ADVOCATE—*Figurative Nouns*.

Gentlemen of the long robe. The legal profession.
Limb of the law. A lawyer.
Silk gown. The legal profession.

ADVOCATE—*Verbs*.

Be called to the bar.
Be called within the bar. } To be admitted to the rank of barrister.
Call to the bar.
Call within the bar. } To admit as a member of the legal profession.
Plead. To argue in defense of one.
Practise at the bar.
Practise within the bar. } To exercise law as a profession.
Take silk. To become king's or queen's counsel.

ADVOCATE—*Adjectives*.

At the bar. Before court.
Forensic. Belonging to courts, legal proceedings, etc.
Learned in the law. Versed in law.

ADVOCATE—*Phrases*

Banco regis [L.]. On the king's bench.

ad''-vo-ca'-tion. A pleading. PRETEXT.
ad-vou'-tress. An adulteress. PURITY-RAKE.
ad-vou'-try. Adultery. PURITY-IMPURITY.
ad-vow'-son. Patronage. CHURCH.
ad''-y-nam'-ic. Lacking physical strength. STRENGTH-WEAKNESS.

a-dyn'-a-my. Lack of strength. STRENGTH-WEAKNESS.

adytum [L.] (ad'-i-tum). A secret shrine. CONTENTS-RECEIVER, EXPOSURE-HIDINGPLACE, PROPHECY.

adze. A hand-cutting tool. SHARPNESS-BLUNTNESS.

ad'-zooks. Exclamation of wonder. ASTONISHMENT-EXPECTANCE.

ae'-dile. A Roman magistrate. JUDICATURE.

ae'-gis. A shield. ATTACK-DEFENSE.

aegrescit medendo [L.] (î-gres'-sit mî-den'-do). He grows worse by the remedy. BETTERMENT-DETERIORATION.

ae'-on. An age of the universe. DIVINITY.

aequam servare mentem [L.] (î'-quam ser-vê'-rî men'-tem). To keep a well-balanced mind. EXCITABILITY-INEXCITABILITY.

aequitas sequitur legem [L.] (eq'-ui-tas seq'-ui-ter lî'-gem). Equity follows law. LAW-LAWLESSNESS.

aequo animo [L.] (î'-quo an'-i-mo). With unmoved feelings. EXCITABILITY-INEXCITABILITY, SENSITIVENESS-APATHY.

aere perennius [L.] (î'-rî per-en'-ni-us). More lasting than bronze. REPUTATION-DISCREDIT.

a-e'-ri-al. Atmospheric. HEIGHT-LOWNESS, LIQUID-GAS, WATER-AIR; **aerial navigator,** WAYFARER-SEAFARER.

a'-er-ie. Nest of a bird of prey. DWELLER-HABITATION, HEIGHT-LOWNESS.

a'-er-i-form. Airy. LIQUID-GAS, WATER-AIR.

a''-er-o-dy-nam'-ics. Science of gaseous bodies. LIQUID-GAS, RIVER-WIND.

a''-er-og'-ra-phy. A treatise on air. WATER-AIR.

a'-er-o-lite. A mass from celestial space. ASTRONOMY, UNIVERSE.

a''-er-ol'-o-gy. Science of the atmosphere. WATER-AIR.

a''-er-o-man''-cy. Forecasting changes in weather; divination by appearances in the air. PROPHECY.

a''-er-om'-e-ter. Instrument for measuring density of gases. WATER-AIR.

a'-er-o-naut. One who navigates the air. WATER-AIR, WAYFARER-SEAFARER.

a''-er-o-naut'-ics. Treatment of air navigation. TRAVELING-NAVIGATION, WATER-AIR.

a'-er-o-scope. An air microscopic instrument. WATER-AIR.

a'-er-o-stat. A balloon. CONVEYANCE-VESSEL.

a''-er-o-stat'ic. Pertaining to aerostatics. TRAVELING-NAVIGATION.

a''-er-o-stat'-ics. Science of mechanical properties of air. LIQUID-GAS, TRAVELING-NAVIGATION.

a''-er-o-sta'-tion. Ballooning. TRAVELING-NAVIGATION, WATER-AIR.

aes alienum debitorem leve, gravius inimicum facit [L.] (îz ê-li-î'-num deb-i-to'rem lî'-vî, grê'-vi-us in-i-mai'-cum fê'-sit). A light sum owed makes a debtor, one too heavy an enemy. CREDIT-DEBT.

Æs''-cu-la'-pi-us. The god of medicine. REMEDY-BANE.

Æ-sop'. Author of fables. BEAUTY-UGLINESS.

æs-thet'-ic. Artistic. BEAUTY-UGLINESS, FEELING-INSENSIBILITY, TASTE-VULGARITY.

aetas, dum loquimur fugerit invidia [L.], (î'-tas, dum loq'-ui-mur fiu'-ji-rit in-vid'-i-a). While we talk envious time has been flying. LASTINGNESS-TRANSIENTNESS.

aeternum servans sub pectore vulnus [L.] (î-ter'-num ser'-vans sub pec'-to-rî vul'-nus). Keeping an everlasting wound in the heart. PARDON-VINDICTIVENESS.

ae''-ti-ol'-o-gy. The science of efficient causes. KNOWLEDGE-IGNORANCE, RATIONALE-LUCK.

a-far'. At a distance. REMOTENESS-NEARNESS.

af''-fa-bil'-i-ty. Courtesy of manner. POLITENESS-IMPOLITENESS, SELFRESPECT-HUMBLENESS.

af'-fa-ble. Courteous. POLITENESS-IMPOLITENESS, SELFRESPECT-HUMBLENESS.

af-fair'. Anything done. CONCEPTION-THEME, OCCUPATION, OCCURRENCE-DESTINY, STRIFE-PEACE; **affair of honor,** STRIFE-PEACE.

affaires, chargé'd [F.] (af-fêr', shar-zhêd'). A diplomatic agent. CONSIGNEE.

affaires, les—font les hommes [F.] (af-fêr', lez—fon' lez om). Experience of affairs makes men. KNOWLEDGE-IGNORANCE, SAGACITY-INCAPACITY.

af-fairs'. Business. OCCUPATION.

af-fect'. To put on. CONNECTION-INDEPENDENCE, DESIRE-DISTASTE, EXCITATION, INCLINATION, LOVE-HATE, TRUTHFULNESS-FRAUD.

af''-fec-ta'-tion. Display. SOCIETY-AFFECTATION.

af-fect'-ed. (1) Acted upon. **Affected with,** EMOTION, HEALTH-SICKNESS.

af-fect'-ed. (2) Pretended; loved. AFFECTIONS, PURITY-CRUDENESS, TRUTHFULNESS-FALSEHOOD.

af-fect''-i-bil'-i-ty. Quality of being affected. SENSITIVENESS-APATHY.

af-fect'-ing. Acting upon the feelings. PLEASURABLENESS-PAINFULNESS.

af-fec'-tion. Love. AMITY-HOSTILITY, EMOTION, LOVE-HATE.

af-fec'-tion-ate. Loving. LOVE-HATE.

af-fec'-tions. Natural tendency of feeling. AFFECTIONS

AFFECTIONS.

Affections. Mental feelings toward some object.

Bent. A decided and fixed tendency of the mind towards a particular mode of action.

Bias. A leaning of the mind.

Cast of mind. A characteristic inclination.

Character. The sum of qualities by which a person is distinguished from others; strength of mind.

Diathesis [Gr.] Particular disposition or habit of body, good or bad.

Disposition. Tendency to any action or state, resulting from natural constitution.

Frame of mind. Particular state of the mind.

Frame of soul. Manifestation of the moral nature.

Furore [It.] An overmastering passion or mania for anything

Grain. Natural temper.

Habit of mind. The state of mind, either natural or acquired, regarded as firmly retained.

Humor. State of mind, whether habitual or temporary.

Idiosyncrasy. A peculiarity of mental constitution or temperament.

Master passion. Any emotion or sentiment in a state of controlling activity.

Mettle. Spirit, especially as regards honor, courage, fortitude, etc.

Mood. Temporary state of the mind as regards passion or feeling.

Natural turn of mind. Inherent mental disposition.

Nature. Inherent or essential qualities or attributes.

Passion. The state of the mind when it is powerfully acted upon and influenced by something external to itself.

Pervading spirit. Controlling temper or mental condition.

Predilection. A previous liking, a prepossession of the mind for something.

Predisposition. Previous inclination, or tendency.

Proclivity. Facility; inclination.

Proneness. Inclination of mind or temper.

Propendency.
Propensedness.
Propension. } A leaning or bent of mind
Propensity.

Qualities. Acquired traits.

Ruling passion. See MASTER PASSION.

Spirit. The state of temper or mind as governing the actions.

Sympathy. The quality of being affected by the state or condition of another. See LOVE.

Temper. The constitution of the mind, particularly with regard to the passions and affections.

Temperament. The peculiar physical and mental character of an individual.

Tone. Characteristic tendency.

AFFECTIONS—*Continued.*

Turn.
Turn of mind. } A particular disposition or cast of genius.
Vein.

AFFECTIONS—*Figurative Expressions.*

Back-bone; bosom; breast; cockles of one's heart; heart; heart of hearts; heart's blood; heart's core; heart's strings; inmost heart; inmost soul; inner man; *penetralis mentis* [L.], secret recesses of the mind; secret and inmost recesses of the heart; soul.

AFFECTIONS—*Verbs.*

Be affected. To have the mind influenced. See *Adjectives*.
Be of a character. To have particular or peculiar qualities. See *Nouns*.
Breathe. To show or express one's affections or feelings.
Have affections. } See *Nouns*.
Possess affections. }

AFFECTIONS—*Adjectives.*

Affected. Regarded with affection; beloved.
Attempered. Regulated.
Cast. Formed.
Characterized. Distinguished by peculiar marks or traits.
Deep-rooted. Firmly implanted.
Disposed. Inclined.
Eaten up with. Of deep affection.
Formed. Modeled by discipline.
Framed. Regulated.
Having a bias. See *Nouns*.
Imbued with. Impressed.
Inborn. Implanted by nature.
Inbred. Bred within.
Inclined. Having a tendency or leaning toward.
Ineffaceable. Incapable of being blotted out.
Ingrained. Worked into the mental or moral constitution of.
Inveterate. Fixed and settled by long continuance.
Molded. Given a certain training.
Pathoscopic. Indicative of the passions.

AFFECTIONS—*Adverbs.*

At heart. Deeply felt.
Heart and soul. With all one s might. See EMOTION.
In one's heart. In one's thought or feelings. See *Nouns*.

af-fec'-tor. One who pretends. PRESUMPTION-OBSEQUIOUSNESS.

---

affettuoso [It.] (af-fet-tu-o'-zo). Soft in music. MUSIC.
af-fi'-ance. Pledge of faith. ENGAGEMENT-RELEASE, MATRIMONY-CELIBACY, SANGUINENESS-HOPELESSNESS.
af-fi'-anced. Engaged to be married. ENGAGEMENT-RELEASE, LOVE-HATE, MATRIMONY-CELIBACY.
af-fiche'. A poster. PUBLICITY.
af-ficher'. One who posts. PUBLICITY.
af"-fi-da'-tion. Act of promising. CONTRACT.
af"-fi-da'-vit. A sworn declaration. ASSERTION-DENIAL, LITIGATION, MARK-OBLITERATION.
af-fil'-i-a"-ted. Associated. CONNECTION-INDEPENDENCE, RELATIONSHIP.
af-fil"-i-a'-tion. Relationship. CONNECTION-INDEPENDENCE, RATIONALE-LUCK, RELATIONSHIP.
af-fin'-i-ty. Connection. CONNECTION-INDEPENDENCE, LIKENESS-UNLIKENESS.
af-firm'. To declare positively. ASSENT-DISSENT, ASSERTION-DENIAL.
af-firm'-ance. Affirmation. ASSENT-DISSENT, ASSERTION-DENIAL.
af"-fir-ma'-tion. A declaration. ASSENT-DISSENT, ASSERTION-DENIAL.
af-firm'-a-tive. Positive. ASSENT-DISSENT, ASSERTION-DENIAL.
af-firm'-a-tive-ly. In an affirmative side. ASSENT-DISSENT.
af-fix'. To join. ADDITION-SUBTRACTION, INCREMENT-REMNANT, LETTER, UNION-DISUNION.
af-fla'-tion. A breathing on. RIVER-WIND.
af-fla'-tus. Spiritual inspiration. REVELATION-PSEUDOREVELATION, RIVER-WIND.
af-flict'. To oppress with suffering. PLEASURABLENESS-PAINFULNESS; **afflict with illness,** HEALTH-SICKNESS.
af-flic'-tion. Distress. LIGHTHEARTEDNESS-DEJECTION, PLEASURE-PAIN, PLEASURABLENESS-PAINFULNESS, WELFARE-MISFORTUNE.
af'-flu-ence. Wealth. AFFLUENCE-PENURY, ENOUGH, WELFARE-MISFORTUNE.

AFFLUENCE—PENURY.

Affluence. An abundant supply of worldly goods.
Competence, etc. Sufficiency; enough property for a comfortable livelihood. See ENOUGH.
Easy circumstances. Moderate condition in regard to worldly estate.
Fortune. Estate; possessions; great wealth.
Good circumstances. Very good condition in regard to property, etc.
Handsome fortune. Ample or large possessions.
Independence. Sufficient means or wealth to support oneself.
Opulence. State of being rich or wealthy.
Riches. Abundance of whatever is precious.
Solvency. The condition of being able to pay all just debts.
Wealth. An extraordinary abundance of this world's goods; large possessions.

AFFLUENCE—*Associated Nouns.*

Alimony, sum allowed to a woman who is separated from her husband; capital; command of money; dowry, property which a woman brings to her husband on marriage; earnings, that which is earned; income, etc. (see OUTLAY-INCOME); livelihood; lucre; maintenance; means; money; pelf, wealth, generally in an ill-sense; property, etc. (see PROPERTY); provision; resources; round sum, etc. (see TREASURE-SUBSTANCE).

AFFLUENCE—*Figurative Nouns.*

Crœsus; Danae; Dives; *El Dorado* [Sp.], any country of great wealth in precious metals; *embarras de richesses* [F.], over-supply; filthy lucre; full purse; Golconda; heavy purse; loaves and fishes, items of personal gain or advantage; long purse; mammon, riches, generally in an ill sense. Midas; mine of wealth; mint of money; nabob, any European who has amassed wealth in the East; Pactolus; Plutus; Potosi, town famous for silver mines; purse of Fortunatus; Timon of Athens; well-lined purse.

AFFLUENCE—*Nouns of Agent.*

Capitalist. One possessing large means to engage in extensive business undertakings.

Bad circumstances.
Embarrassed circumstances.
Needy circumstances. } Expressions denoting poor financial standing.
Poor circumstances.
Reduced circumstances.
Straitened circumstances.
Destitution. Lack of the comforts, and in part even of the necessaries of life.
Difficulties. Embarrassment chiefly in money affairs.
Distress. Painful lack of what is useful or desirable.
Impecuniosity. State of being habitually without money.
Indigence. Lack of ordinary means of subsistence.
Lack. Deficiency; inadequate supply.
Narrow means. }
Slender means. } Expressions denoting a low state of resources.
Necessity. Condition of being in want.
Need. Pressing occasion for something; absence of means of action.
Neediness. State of being needy.
Pauperism. State of being thrown upon public charity for support.
Penury. Continuous cramping poverty.
Poverty. Lack of property or adequate means of support.
Privation. Deprived or destitute of something.
Straits. Narrow or restricted condition.
Want. Being without that which is a comfort, or an object of our desire.

PENURY—*Associated Nouns.*

Beggary; insolvency, etc. (see SETTLEMENT-DEFAULT); loss of fortune; mendicancy; mendicity.

PENURY—*Figurative Nouns.*

Beggarly account of empty boxes; broken fortune; empty pocket; empty purse; hand to mouth existence; light purse; low water; *res augustæ domi* [L.], narrow cirumstances at home; poverty; wolf at the door; poor as a church mouse.

AFFLUENCE—PENURY—*Continued.*

Man of substance. One who has great material possessions.
Millionaire. One who has a million of money; a very rich man.
Moneyed man. One who is rich in money.
Rich man. One who has large possessions.
Warm man. One who is well off as to property.

AFFLUENCE—*Nouns of Result.*

Plutocracy. A government in which the wealthy classes rule.
Timocracy. A government in which honors are distributed according to a rating of property.

AFFLUENCE—*Verbs*

Afford. To be able to bear expenses; have sufficient means for.
Become rich, etc. To come to a state of wealth or means. See *Adjectives*
Be rich, etc. To be wealthy; have ample means. See *Adjectives*.
Command a sum. To have at one's disposal a sum of money.
Command money. To have control of money.
Enrich. To make rich; increase the wealth of.
Feather one's nest. To amass money, especially from holding an office or place.
Fill one's pocket, etc. To collect and store as much wealth as possible. See TREASURY.
Hold one's head above water. To survive a financial crisis.
Imburse. To supply with money.
Make a fortune. To become rich; amass wealth.
Make both ends meet. To make the income pay the expenses.
Make money, etc. To earn or gain money. See GAIN.
Roll in wealth. To be exceedingly rich.
Wallow in riches. } To be exceedingly wealthy and avaricious.
Wallow in wealth. }
Well afford. To be in good financial condition.
Worship Mammon. } To devote one's time and energies to the
Worship the Golden Calf. } accumulation of riches.

AFFLUENCE—*Adjectives.*

Affluent. Rich in worldly goods; abounding in wealth.
All straight. Having money affairs in good condition.
Flush. Abundantly furnished with money.
Flush of cash. }
Flush of money. } Possessing plenty of ready money.
Flush of tin. }
In cash. }
In full feather. } Having a supply of money on hand.
In funds. }
Made of money. Plenteously supplied with money.
Moneyed. } Rich in money.
Monied. }
Opulent. Having large means; rich.
Out of debt. Freed from all encumbrances.
Pecunious. Having abundance of money; wealthy.
Provided for. Taken care of, financially, beforehand.
Rich. Possessing abundant means to supply wants.
Rich as a Jew. } Expressions signifying enormous wealth.
Rich as Crœsus. }
Rolling in riches. } Exceedingly wealthy.
Rolling in wealth. }
Solvent. Able to liquidate all just debts.
Warm. Easy and safe in money matters.
Wealthy. Having greater means than the generality of men.
Well off. Thriving; prosperous.
Well provided for. Generously taken care of beforehand.
Well to do. Easy in circumstances.
Worth much. Well supplied with worldly goods.

AFFLUENCE—*Phrases.*

Magna servitus est magna fortuna [L.]. Great fortune is great slavery.
Más vale saber que haber [Sp.]. Wisdom is better than wealth.
One's ship coming in. When one becomes wealthy.
Vera prosperità è non aver necessità [It.]. True wealth is to have no want.
Wie gewonnen, so zerronnen [G.]. As won, so flown; light come, light go.

PENURY—ADJECTIVES—*Continued from Column 2.*

Under hatches. In a state of depression or poverty.
Unmoneyed. Not having money.
Unportioned. Not endowed with portion or fortune.
Without a rap. Moneyless; extremely poor.

PENURY—*Phrases.*

À pobreza no hay vergüenza [Sp.]. Poverty has no shame.
In forma pauperis [L.]. As a poor man.
Zonam perdidit [L.]. He is in desperate circumstances.

PENURY—*Nouns of Agent.*

Beggar. One who is poor and asks charity.
Mendicant. A begging friar of a Roman Catholic religious order.
Mumper. A begging impostor.
Pauper. One supported or assisted by charity.
Pauvre diable [F.]. Poor devil; fellow; wretch.
Poor man. One lacking material riches or goods.
Starveling. An animal or plant weakened from want of nutriment.

PENURY—*Verbs.*

Beg one's bread. To ask or supplicate in charity.
Be poor, etc. To be destitute of property. See *Adjectives*.
Bring to the parish. To be dependent upon charity for livelihood.
Come upon the parish. To be supported by the parish.
Fleece. To fraudently deprive of money or property.
Go down in the world. To become poorer and poorer.
Go to the dogs. To leave the path of rectitude; to fail financially.
Go to wrack and ruin. To fall into decay; be brought to poverty.
Have seen better days. To have once been in a state of prosperity
Impoverish. To reduce to poverty; make poor.
Lack. To be deficient in; be destitute of.
Live from hand to mouth. To continue in an unsettled financial state
Not have a penny. } To be poor; be without money
Not have a shot in one's locker. } See MONEY.
Pauperize. To reduce to a condition of being supported by charity
Reduce. To bring to an inferior condition.
Reduce to poverty. To make poor; be without means of support.
Render poor, etc To cause to be or become poor. See *Adjectives*.
Ruin. To bring to poverty.
Run into debt, etc. To come or get into a state of debt. See CREDIT-DEBT.
Starve. To suffer extreme want.
Tirer le diable par la queue [F.]. To be hard put to it for a livelihood.
Want. To be without comforts or objects of desire.

PENURY—*Adjectives.*

Badly off. Unfortunately situated; not well off.
Bare footed. Having the feet bare; poor.
Beggarly. Miserably poor; mean.
Bereaved. Made destitute, as by the death of a relative.
Bereft. Deprived of something, as of hope and strength.
Destitute. Lacking comforts or necessaries of life.
Distressed. Painfully lacking what is useful or desirable.
Dowerless. Without a dowry.
Embarrassed. Involved in pecuniary difficulties.
Fleeced. Robbed or plundered.
Fortuneless. Without a fortune; luckless.
Hard up. In want of money; needy
Ill off. See BADLY OFF.
Impecunious. Without money; poor.
Indigent. Without the means of subsistence.
Insolvent, etc. Unable to pay debts. See NOT PAYING.
Involved, etc. Entangled financially. See IN DEBT.
In want. Very destitute in means of subsistence; needy.
Moneyless. Without money.
Necessitous. Pressed with poverty; very needy.
Needy. Very poor; lacking the means of living.
Not worth a rap, etc. Of little account or value. See MONEY.
Out at elbows. }
Out at heels. } In a poverty-stricken condition.
Out at pocket. }
Out of money. Destitute of money; lacking funds.
Penniless. Without money.
Pinched. In a starved or distressed condition.
Poor. Having small means.
Poor as a church mouse. }
Poor as a rat. } Destitute of material riches or goods.
Poor as Job. }
Poorly off. See BADLY OFF.
Poverty stricken. Suffering from poverty.
Put to one's last shifts. } On the last resources.
Put to one's shifts. }
Qui n'a pas le sou [F.]. One who has not a cent.
Reduced. See *Verbs.*
Seedy. Poor; shabbily dressed.
Short of cash. }
Short of money. } Without, or nearly without money.
Straitened. Pressed with poverty or other necessity.
Stripped. Made destitute; divested of possessions.
Unable to keep the wolf from the door. Incapable of supplying wants.
Unable to make both ends meet. Not able to make income cover expenses.

(Continued on Column 1.)

af'-flu-ent. A tributary. AFFLUENCE-PENURY, AP-PROACH-WITHDRAWAL, ENOUGH, RIVER-WIND.

af'-flux". Act of flowing to a point. APPROACH-WITHDRAWAL.

af-ford'. To have means for. AFFLUENCE-PENURY, GIVING-RECEIVING, OUTLAY-INCOME, PRICE-DISCOUNT; **afford aid,** etc., OBSTRUCTION-HELP.

af-fran'-chise. To liberate. LIBERTY-SUBJECTION, RELEASE-RESTRAINT.

af-fran'-chise-ment. Liberation. LIBERTY-SUBJEC-TION, RELEASE-RESTRAINT.

af-fray'. A public fight. STRIFE-PEACE.

af-fray'-ment. Public fighting. STRIFE-PEACE.

af-freet'. A devil. JOVE-FIEND.

af-fric'-tion. Friction. FRICTION-LUBRICATION.

af-fright'. Great fear. SANGUINENESS-TIMIDITY.

af-fright'-ment. Great fear. SANGUINENESS-TIMIDITY.

af-front'. To insult openly. CHARITABLENESS-MA-LEVOLENCE, FAVORITE-ANGER, PLEASURABLENESS-PAINFULNESS, REGARD-DISRESPECT; **affront danger,** BRAVERY-COWARDICE.

af-fuse'. To pour. WATER-AIR.

af-fy'. To promise in marriage. MATRIMONY-CELI-BACY.

a-field'. On the field. PRESENCE-ABSENCE.

a-float'. Floating. CONVEYANCE-VESSEL, ENTITY-NONENTITY, MUTABILITY-STABILITY, OCCURRENCE-DESTINY, OCEAN-LAND, PREPARATION-NONPREPA-RATION, TIDINGS-MYSTERY, TRAVELING-NAVIGATION; **keep oneself afloat,** WELFARE-MISFORTUNE.

a-foot'. In progress. ACTIVITY-INDOLENCE, OCCUPA-TION, PREPARATION-NONPREPARATION.

a-fore'. Before. ANTECEDENCE-SEQUENCE.

a-fore'-named". Named before. ANTECEDENCE-SE-QUENCE.

a-fore'-said". Said before. ANTECEDENCE-SEQUENCE, PRECEDENCE-SUCCESSION, RECURRENCE.

a-fore'-thought". Premeditation. PREDETERMINA-TION-IMPULSE.

a-fraid'. Filled with fear. SANGUINENESS-TIMIDITY; **afraid to say,** CERTAINTY-DOUBT; **be afraid,** DETER-MINATION-VACILLATION.

a-fresh'. Anew. NOVELTY-ANTIQUITY, RECURRENCE.

Af'-ric heat. Great heat. HEAT-COLD.

af'-rite. An evil genie. JOVE-FIEND.

aft. Toward the stern. ANTERIORITY-POSTERIORITY.

aft'-er. Behind. ANTECEDENCE-SEQUENCE, ANTE-RIORITY-POSTERIORITY, LEADING-FOLLOWING, OP-PORTUNENESS-UNSUITABLENESS, PRECEDENCE-SUC-CESSION, QUEST-EVASION; **after all,** COMPENSATION, MODIFICATION, RATIOCINATION-INSTINCT; **after time,** EARLINESS-LATENESS, FUTURE-PAST; **be after,** PURPOSE-LUCK, QUEST-EVASION; **go after,** LEADING-FOLLOWING.

aft'-er-ac"-cep-ta'-tion. After meaning. MEANING-JARGON.

aft'-er-age. Future time. NOVELTY-ANTIQUITY.

aft'-er-clap". An unexpected stroke. EXPECTATION-SURPRISE.

aft'-er-course". A later course. PREDECESSOR-CON-TINUATION.

aft'-er-din"-ner. Made or occurring after dinner. ANTECEDENCE-SEQUENCE.

aft'-er-glow". A glow in the western sky after sunset. INCREMENT-REMNANT.

aft'-er-life". The future life. OCCURRENCE-DESTINY.

aft"-er-noon'. Day between noon and sunset. MORN-ING-EVENING.

aft"-er-noon' far'-mer. A lazy person. ACTIVITY-INDOLENCE.

aft'-er-noon" par'-ty. A party. SOCIABILITY-PRIVACY.

aft'-er-part". That which follows. ANTERIORITY-POSTERIORITY, PREDECESSOR-CONTINUATION.

aft'-er-piece". A sequel. ACTING.

aft'-er-taste". Lingering taste in the mouth. SAVOR-TASTELESSNESS.

aft'-er-thought". A more deliberate thought. BIG-OTRY-APOSTASY, MIND-IMBECILITY, REMEMBRANCE-FORGETFULNESS.

aft'-er-time". Future. EARLINESS-LATENESS, FUTURE-PAST.

aft'-er-wards. At a later time. ANTECEDENCE-SEQUENCE.

a'-ga. Lower Turkish noble. CHIEF-UNDERLING.

agacerie [F.] (a-gas-rī'). Enticement. MOTIVE-CA-PRICE.

a-gain'. At another time. DOUBLING-HALVING, RE-CURRENCE; **again and again,** FREQUENCY-RARITY, RECURRENCE; **come again,** PERIODICITY-REGULAR-ITY; **fall off again,** RENOVATION-RELAPSE; **live again,** RENOVATION-RELAPSE.

a-gainst'. In opposition to. ANTAGONISM-CONCUR-RENCE, LATERALITY-CONTRAPOSITION, PREPARATION-NONPREPARATION; **against one's expectation,** EX-PECTATION-SURPRISE; **against one's will,** COERCION; **against one's wishes,** READINESS-RELUCTANCE; **against the grain,** ANTAGONISM-CONCURRENCE, DE-SIRE-DISTASTE, DIFFICULTY-FACILITY, PLEASURABLE-NESS-PAINFULNESS; **against the stream,** ANTAGO-NISM-CONCURRENCE, DIFFICULTY-FACILITY; **against the time when,** PREVISION; **chances against,** LIKELI-HOOD-UNLIKELIHOOD; **declaim against,** APPROVAL-DISAPPROVAL; **false witness against,** ADULATION-DIS-PARAGEMENT; **go against,** ANTAGONISM-CONCUR-RENCE; **raise one's voice against,** ASSENT-DISSENT; **set against,** LOVE-HATE; **set one's face against,** AN-TAGONISM-CONCURRENCE, APPROVAL-DISAPPROVAL, PROFFER-REFUSAL; **stand up against,** REPRISAL-RESISTANCE.

ag'-a-mist. One who opposes marriage. MATRIMONY-CELIBACY.

a-gape'. Gaping. ASTONISHMENT-EXPECTANCE, EX-PECTATION-SURPRISE, INQUISITIVENESS-INDIFFER-ENCE.

ag'-a-pe. The love-feast of the primitive Christians. CEREMONIAL.

Ag"-a-pem'-o-ne. A religious community. LOVE-HATE, PLEASURE-PAIN.

ag'-ate. A variety of quartz. EMBELLISHMENT-DIS-FIGUREMENT.

age. A period of time. DURATION-NEVERNESS, IN-FANCY-AGE, LASTINGNESS-TRANSIENTNESS, NOV-ELTY-ANTIQUITY, PERIOD-PROGRESS, TIME; **from age to age,** ETERNITY-INSTANTANEITY; **of age,** MAN-HOOD.

a'-ged. Old. INFANCY-AGE.

a'-gen-cy. Active power. ACTION-PASSIVENESS, AGENCY, COMMISSION-ABROGATION, INSTRUMENTAL-ITY, MANAGEMENT, USE-DISUSE.

AGENCY.

Action. Effect of power exerted on one body by another. See ACTION.

Agency. The means or mode of action.

Causation. The act or power by which an effect is produced. See CAUSE.

Exercise. Employment in the proper mode of activity.

Force. Capacity of exercising an influence or producing an effect.

Function. Any specific power of acting or operating that belongs to an agent.

Home stroke. A well aimed blow.

Influence. Controlling power quietly exerted. See DOMINANCE.

Instrumentality. Anything used as a means or an agency. See INSTRUMENTALITY.

Inter-action. Mutual or reciprocal action or influence.

Inter-working. Act of working in together.

Maintaining power. The power or force which supports or keeps up

Maintenance. That which supports or defends.

Modus operandi [L.]. Manner of operation.

Office. A special duty, trust, or charge

AGENCY—*Continued.*

Operation. Method of working.
Play. Liberty of action.
Quickening power. The act or agent which imparts energy or movement to.
Strain. Extreme tension; a violent effort.
Swing. Swaying motion; free course.
Work. Exertion of strength or faculties.
Working. Act of laboring.

AGENCY—*Verbs.*

Act. To exert power.
Act upon. To produce an effect upon.
Be in action, etc. To be exerting one's strength. See *Adjectives.*
Bring into operation. ⎫
Bring into play. ⎬ To bring into action; to work.
Bring to bear upon. ⎪
Come into operation. ⎭
Have free play. ⎫ To have freedom of action.
Have play. ⎬
Maintain. To support or keep up.
Operate. To exert power or strength, physical or mechanical.
Perform. To bring to completion.
Play. To put in action or motion.
Quicken. To make lively or active.
Strain. Overexert.
Strike. To deliver a quick blow or thrust.
Support. To bear by being under.
Sustain. To keep from falling.
Take effect. To accomplish an aim.
Work. To exert oneself for a purpose.

AGENCY—*Adjectives.*

Acted upon. Having some power exerted upon
Acting. Operating in any way. See ACTION.
At work. Laboring.
Effectual. Capable of bringing about a result.
Efficacious. Powerful to produce the effect intended.
Efficient. Marked by energetic and useful activity.
In action. Engaged in work.
In exercise. Using physical or mechanical powers.
In force. Driving; compelling.
In operation. Exerting power.
In play. Into use.
On foot. Doing.
Operative. Having the power of acting.
Practical. Capable of being turned to use or account.
Wrought upon. Having power acting upon.

AGENCY—*Adverbs.*

By means of. See MEANS.
By the agency of. See *Nouns*
Through. See INSTRUMENTALITY.

agenda [L.] (a-gen'-da). A program of business, OCCUPATION; **list of agenda,** DESIGN.
agendum [L.] (a-gen'-dum). A thing to be done. OCCUPATION.
a'-gent. One who has power to act. AGENT, CAUSE-EFFECT, CONSIGNEE; **anesthetic agent,** FEELING-INSENSIBILITY.

AGENT.

Actor. One who does anything in any way; a stage player.
Agent. One who has the power to act; one who acts.
Architect. One who constructs fine buildings.
Artificer. One who fashions.
Artisan. A skilled mechanical worker.
Artist. One who is skilled in fine arts.
Baker. One who bakes.
Blacksmith A smith who works in iron.
Bricklayer. One who puts bricks in place.
Builder. One who puts together.
Cabinet-maker. One who makes furniture.
Carpenter. One skilled in handling and constructing.
Chargeship. Office of a charge d'affaires.
Charwoman. A woman who works by the day.
Cordwainer. A worker in cordwain.
Coworker. One who works with another.
Craftsman. One who has manual skill, or belongs to a trade.
Day laborer. Laborer by day.

Demiurgus. Creator of the universe.
Doer. One who acts.
Dramatis Personæ. The persons of the play.
Drudge. One who works hard at servile tasks.
Engineer. One who runs an engine.
Executor. One who carries through, especially the provisions of a will.
Executrix. A female executor.
Factotum. An agent who does all sorts of work.
Fag. One who does menial service.
Farrier. A shoer of horses.
Forger. One who shapes metal.
Glazier. Fitter of window-panes.
Hack. A drudge.
Hand. A laborer.
Handicraft man. An artisan.
Hewers of wood and drawers of water. Humble workers.
Journeyman. One who has mastered his trade.
Laborer. ⎫ One who toils or labors.
Laboring man. ⎬
Machinist. One versed in construction of machines.
Maker. One who makes.
Man. Used of men who are employed.
Manufacturer. One engaged in the production of material objects.
Mason. One whose business is in stone.
Mechanic. One skilled in mechanic arts.
Mechanician. One who understands machines.
Milkman. One who sells milk from door to door.
Miller. One who tends a mill, particularly a grist-mill.
Minister. An agent, especially in religion. See INSTRUMENTALITY.
Navvy. One engaged in constructing canals, etc.
Needle-woman. One who uses a needle.
Operative. A person who works in a mill or factory.
Operator. One who looks after the working of any industry.
Particeps criminis [L.]. A partner in crime.
Participator in. One who has a word or part in.
Party to. One interested in.
Performer. One who carries through anything to completion
Perpetrator. One who carries through, in a bad sense.
Practitioner. One who practises.
Printer. One who sets type, or prints.
Puppet-man. A puppet-player.
Purveyor. One who provides victuals.
Quarryman. One who owns, operates, or works in a quarry.
Rag-man. One who buys rags.
Representative. One who represents another. See CONSIGNEE. See DEPUTY.
Sail-maker. One who makes sails.
Seamstress. A woman skilled in sewing.
Servant. A domestic laborer. See UNDERLING.
Servant of all work. One who does odd jobs.
Smith. One who shapes metal.
Stager. Actor.
Tailor. One who makes and fits clothes.
Tanner. One whose occupation is to tan hides.
Wheelwright. One who makes and repairs wheeled vehicles.
Worker. One who does something.
Workingman. A workman.
Workman. A man who works.
Workwoman. A woman who works.
Wright. One engaged in mechanical operations.

AGENT—*Figurative Nouns.*

Ant. An insect, the symbol of industry.
Bee. An insect that produces honey; a symbol of industry.
Laboring oar. A helper.
Mere tool. A low worker.
Vulcan. God of the forge.

AGENT—*Phrases.*

Faber est quisque fortunæ suæ [L.]. Every man is the artificer of his own fortune.
Quorum pars magna fui [L.]. Of which I have been a great part.

a'-gent–ship''. Office of an agent. COMMISSION-ABROGATION.
age quod agis [L.] (ê'-jî quod ê'-jis). Do what you do. ACTIVITY-INDOLENCE.
a'-ges. Long period of time. **Ages ago,** FUTURE-PAST; **for ages,** LASTINGNESS-TRANSIENTNESS.
ag-glom'-er-ate. Gathered into a mass. COHESION-LOOSENESS, GATHERING-SCATTERING.

ag-glom″-er-a′-tion. A mass. COHESION-LOOSENESS, GATHERING-SCATTERING.

ag-glu′-ti-nate. To stick together. COHESION-LOOSENESS.

ag-glu″-ti-na′-tion. Adhesion. COHESION-LOOSENESS.

ag′-gran-dize. To make greater. ENLARGEMENT-DIMINUTION, INCREASE-DECREASE, REPUTATION-DISCREDIT.

ag′-gran-dize″-ment. Exaltation. ENLARGEMENT-DIMINUTION, INCREASE-DECREASE, REPUTATION-DISCREDIT.

ag′-gra-va-ble. Tending to aggravate. ALLEVIATION-AGGRAVATION.

ag′-gra-vate. To add weight to; to anger. ALLEVIATION-AGGRAVATION, BETTERMENT-DETERIORATION, FAVORITE-ANGER, GULL-HYPERBOLE, INCREASE-DECREASE, TURBULENCE-CALMNESS.

ag′-gra-va″-ted. Increased. ALLEVIATION-AGGRAVATION.

ag′-gra-va″-ting. Irritating. ALLEVIATION-AGGRAVATION, PLEASURABLENESS-PAINFULNESS.

ag″-gra-va′-tion. Act of aggravating, ALLEVIATION-AGGRAVATION, GULL-HYPERBOLE, INCREASE-DECREASE.

ag′-gre-gate. To bring together. GATHERING-SCATTERING, WHOLE-PART.

ag″-gre-ga′-tion. Assemblage. COHESION-LOOSENESS.

ag-gres′-sion. An unprovoked attack. ATTACK-DEFENSE.

ag-grieve′. To cause sorrow to. GOODNESS-BADNESS, PLEASURABLENESS-PAINFULNESS.

ag-group′. To form a group. GATHERING-SCATTERING.

a-ghast′. Struck with terror. ASTONISHMENT-EXPECTANCE, EXPECTATION-SURPRISE, SANGUINENESS-TIMIDITY.

ag′-ile. Active. ACTIVITY-INDOLENCE, SWIFTNESS-SLOWNESS.

a-gil′-i-ty. Nimbleness. ACTIVITY-INDOLENCE.

ag′-i-o. Exchange premium. PRICE-DISCOUNT.

ag′-i-o-tage. Brokerage. EXCHANGE.

ag′-i-tate. To excite. ACTIVITY-INDOLENCE, AGITATION, EXCITATION, INVESTIGATION-ANSWER; **agitate a question,** RATIOCINATION-INSTINCT.

ag′-i-ta″-ted. Excited. AGITATION, MUTABILITY-STABILITY.

ag″-i-ta′-tion. Act of exciting. ACTIVITY-INDOLENCE, AGITATION, EMOTION, EXCITABILITY-INEXCITABILITY, EXCITATION, INVESTIGATION-ANSWER, MUTABILITY-STABILITY, VIGOR-INERTIA; **in agitation,** PREPARATION-NONPREPARATION.

AGITATION.

Agitation. Disturbance of mind which shows itself by physical excitement; state of being moved with violence or irregular action.

Bustle. Noisy stir.

Cahotage [F.]. A jolting; as the jolting of a car.

Commotion. A very violent agitation.

Convulsion. Any violent irregular motion; an abnormal muscular contraction of the body.

Dance. A series of rhythmic concerted movements and steps, usually to time marked by music.

Disquiet. An unsettled or disturbed condition.

Disturbance. A public tumult.

Ebullition. A violent bursting forth; the bubbling of a boiling liquid.

Effervescence. Irrepressible excitement or emotion; a bubbling caused otherwise than by boiling.

Epilepsy. A nervous disease characterized by fits and convulsive movements of the muscles.

Ferment. Internal motion or emotion.

Fermentation. A state of agitation or excitement, as of the intellect or the feelings.

Fits. A stroke of disease which causes convulsions; an impulsive and irregular action.

Flutter. A quick and irregular motion.

Fuss. Unnecessary or annoying activity about trifling matters.

Ground swell. A broad, deep rolling of the sea, due to a distant storm.

Heavy sea. A sea in which the waves run high.

Hubbub. A noisy disorder.

Hurly-burly. Tumult and uproar.

Jactitance. } A tossing about.
Jactitation. }

Jar. A trembling or shaking, as from a sudden shock.

Jerk. A short, sharp pull or twitch.

Jog. A slow, jolting motion.

Jolt. A sudden movement or shock.

Megrims. A sudden attack of sickness in a horse, which causes unconsciousness.

Palpitation. A rapid beating or throbbing.

Perturbation. A disturbance or irregular motion, produced by some force additional to that which causes regular motion.

Quaver. A rapid and tremulous vibration.

Quiver. A slight trembling motion.

Racket. Confused, clattering noise.

Restlessness. Unquietness; uneasiness. See MUTABILITY.

Ripple. A slight curling motion.

Rout. A disorderly flight.

Shake. A short and rapid motion.

Shock. A sudden and violent motion caused by dashing against something.

Shuffling. An awkward, clumsy movement. See *Verbs*.

Spasm. Any sudden or convulsive action.

Staggers. A disease causing unsteady, reeling movements.

Stir. General or public excitement.

Storm. A great whirling motion of the air.

Subsultus. Convulsive muscular twitching.

Succussion. A shaking.

Tempest. A violent commotion or agitation.

Throb. A rapid and strong beating.

Throe. A struggling caused by pain.

Tremor. A shivering or shaking.

Trepidation. An involuntary trembling caused by terror or fear.

Tumult. Commotion or agitation of a multitude.

Tumultuation. Irregular or disorderly motion.

Turbulence. A violent agitation or commotion.

Turmoil. Confused motion.

Twitter. A light tremulous motion.

Vortex. A rotating or whirling motion.

Whirlpool. A place in a body of water where the water moves round in a circle causing a depression into which objects are drawn; a disturbance caused by the meeting of two currents.

Whirlwind. A funnel-shaped column of air with a circular, spiral motion; a great disturbance. See RIVER-WIND.

AGITATION—*Verbs*.

Agitate. To disturb or shake irregularly.

Bandy. To pass along or knock back and forth.

Be agitated. Be disturbed or excited.

Beat. To dash or strike against.

Be the sport of the winds and waves. To be tossed to and fro without a purpose.

Bicker. To strike repeatedly; wrangle.

Bob. Move up and down.

Boil. To bubble up.

Boil over. To be so violently agitated as to run over.

Brandish. Raise and move in various directions.

Bubble. To form globules of air or gas.

Bubble up. To begin to boil.

Buffet. To strike with a hand.

Bustle. To stir about actively or excitedly.

Churn. To stir or mix up.

Convulse. To cause to have contraction of muscles.

Curvet. To prance.

Dance. To cause to move lightly up or down.

Disturb. To rouse from repose, rest.

Drive from post to pillar and from pillar to post. To drive backward and forward.

Effervesce. To give up bubbles of gas.

Ferment. To be excited into sensible internal motion.

Flap. To move rapidly to and fro.

Flicker. To be unsteady or wavering.

Flitter. To scatter; flutter.

Flop. To move loosely.

Flounce. To move about with an impatient movement.

Flounder. To stumble or struggle.

Flourish. To swing, fling, or toss about while holding in the hand.

Foam. To froth.

AGITATION—Verbs—*Continued.*

Go pit-a-pat. Move with light, quick steps or pulsations.
Hitch. To move with a jerking motion.
Hustle. To shake or shuffle together in confusion.
Jerk. To move with short, sharp pulls.
Jog. To move with a slow, trotting motion.
Joggle. To shake slightly with irregular motion.
Jolt. To move up and down with a jarring movement.
Jostle. To shake slightly
Jounce. Jolt.
Jump about. To move by springs or bounds.
Jump like a parched pea. To move quickly and unexpectedly.
Keep between hawk and buzzard. To move from one dangerous place to another.
Move from post to pillar and from pillar to post. To move to and fro.
Palpitate. To beat violently.
Prance. To spring or bound, as a horse.
Quake. To be agitated with quick, short, repeated motions
Quaver. To have a tremulous motion.
Quiver. To be agitated with a fluttering motion.
Reel. To stagger or sway in walking.
Reel to and fro like a drunken man. To sway from side to side.
Shake. To move rapidly and shortly to and fro or up and down.
Shake like an aspen leaf. To tremble.
Shake to its center. To shake violently or through and through.
Shake to its foundations. To shake thoroughly.
Shake up. To stir with a violent motion.
Shamble. To walk with a shuffling or unsteady gait.
Shiver. To tremble, as with cold or fear.
Shuffle. To move along with difficulty, listlessly, or awkwardly.
Simmer. To boil gently.
Stagger. To move unsteadily to one side and the other.
Stir. To cause to move.
Stumble. To move unsteadily or in a blundering manner.
Sway. To incline, bend, or swing.
Throb. To vibrate in any way.
Toss. To throw up with the hand.
Toss about. To throw oneself from side to side.
Totter. To waver, as if about to fall.
Tremble. To have a slight irregular vibratory motion.
Tremble like an aspen leaf. To tremble violently.
Tumble. To move in a careless or headlong manner.
Twine. To wind in curves.
Twitter. To be excited or agitated.
Vellicate. To cause to twitch or contract convulsively.
Wag. To move lightly and quickly one way and the other.
Waggle. To cause to move in short, quick movements.
Wallop. To flog; waddle.
Whip. To excite; to strike with a rod.
Whisk. A light sweeping movement.
Wield. To use with full effect.
Wriggle. To move with short turns and twists.
Wriggle like an eel. To squirm.
Writhe. To twist with violence.

AGITATION—*Adjectives.*

Agitated. Disturbed.
All of a twitter. Highly excited.
Convulsive. Spasmodic.
Desultory. Changeable.
Giddy-paced. Moving irregularly.
Restless. Unquiet.
Saltatory. Moving abruptly or by leaps.
Shaking. Vibrating. See *Verbs.*
Shambling. Unsteady.
Subsultory. Bounding.
Tremulous. Trembling.
Unquiet. Without rest.

AGITATION—*Adverbs*

By fits and starts. Irregularly.
Hop, skip and jump. Carelessly.
In convulsions. By starts.
In fits. Unstably.
Per saltum [L.]. By leaps.
Subsultorily. Bounding.

AGITATION—*Phrases.*

Tempête dans un verre d'eau [F.]. Tempest in a glass of water

ag'-let. An ornamental pendant. DELINEATION-CARICATURE.

ag'-nate. Related on the father's side. RELATIONSHIP.
ag-na'-tion. Relationship on father's side. RELATIONSHIP.
ag-ni'-tion. Recognition. CONSENT.
ag-nize'. To acknowledge. CONSENT.
ag-no'-men. An additional name. NAME-MISNOMER.
agnus Dei [L.] (ag'-nus Dï'-ai). The Lamb of God. CEREMONIAL, DEVOTION-CHARM.
a-go'. Gone past. FUTURE-PAST.
a-gog'. Excited with curiosity. ASTONISHMENT-EXPECTANCE, DESIRE-DISTASTE, EXPECTATION-SURPRISE.
a-go'-ing. In motion. ACTIVITY-INDOLENCE; **set agoing,** OBSTRUCTION-HELP.
ag'-o-nism. Contention for a prize. STRIFE-PEACE.
ag'-o-nize. To cause pain. PLEASURABLENESS-PAINFULNESS, SENSUALITY-SUFFERING.
ag'-o-ni''-zing. Suffering agony. EXCITABILITY-INEXCITABILITY, PLEASURABLENESS-PAINFULNESS.
ag'-o-ny. Intense suffering. PLEASURE-PAIN, SENSUALITY-SUFFERING; **agony of death,** LIFE-DEATH; **agony of excitement,** EXCITABILITY-INEXCITABILITY.
a-gram'-ma-tist. An ignorant man. SCHOLAR-DUNCE.
a-gra'-ri-an. Pertaining to land. DOMESTICATION-AGRICULTURE.
a-gree'. To be of one mind. ASSENT-DISSENT, COMPOSITION, CONSENT, CONTRACT, COOPERATION-OPPOSITION, HARMONY-DISCORD, VARIANCE-ACCORD; **agree in opinion,** ASSENT-DISSENT; **agree with,** HEALTHINESS-UNHEALTHINESS.
a-gree'-a-ble. Pleasurable. PLEASURABLENESS-PAINFULNESS, SENSUALITY-SUFFERING, WELFARE-MISFORTUNE.
a-gree'-a-ble-ness. Pleasurableness. PLEASURABLENESS-PAINFULNESS.
a-gree'-a-bly. Pleasingly. **Agreeably to,** CONVENTIONALITY-UNCONVENTIONALITY.
a-gree'-ing. Being of one mind. HARMONY-DISCORD, VARIANCE-ACCORD.
a-gree'-ment. Mutual assent. ASSENT-DISSENT, COMPOSITION, CONSENT, CONTRACT, COOPERATION-OPPOSITION, HARMONY-DISCORD, LIKENESS-UNLIKENESS, VARIANCE-ACCORD, UNIFORMITY-DIVERSITY.
a-gres'-tic. Rural. DOMESTICATION-AGRICULTURE.
ag'-ri-cul''-tor. A farmer. DOMESTICATION-AGRICULTURE.
ag''-ri-cul''-tur-al. Rustic. DOMESTICATION-AGRICULTURE.
ag'-ri-cul''-ture. Cultivation of soil. DOMESTICATION-AGRICULTURE.
ag''-ri-cul''-tur-ist. A farmer. DOMESTICATION-AGRICULTURE.
ag-ron'-o-my. Scientific husbandry. DOMESTICATION-AGRICULTURE.
a-ground'. Stranded. DIFFICULTY-FACILITY, MUTABILITY-STABILITY, SUCCESS-FAILURE.
a'-gue—fit''. A fever. SANGUINENESS-HOPELESSNESS.
aguets, aux [F.] (a-gê', oz). On the watch. EXPECTATION-SURPRISE, EXPOSURE-HIDINGPLACE.
a'-gu-ish. Chilly. HEAT-COLD.
a-ha'. Exclamation of joy. JUBILATION-LAMENTATION.
a-head'. In front. ADVANCE-RETROGRESSION, ANTERIORITY-POSTERIORITY, LEADING-FOLLOWING; **go ahead,** ADVANCE-RETROGRESSION; **rock ahead,** REFUGE-PITFALL, SECURITY-INSECURITY; **shoot ahead,** ACTIVITY-INDOLENCE, TRANSCURSION-SHORTCOMING.
ah me. Exclamation of grief. JUBILATION-LAMENTATION.
Ah'-ri-man. Evil deity. JOVE-FIEND.
Ah'-ri-man''-es [Gr.]. Ahriman. ANGEL-SATAN.
aid. Help. CHARITABLENESS-MALEVOLENCE, INSTRUMENTALITY, MEANS, OBSTRUCTION-HELP, SUSPEN-

SION-SUPPORT; **by the aid of,** INSTRUMENTALITY, MEANS, OBSTRUCTION-HELP.

aide'–de–camp''. A staff officer. ANTAGONIST-ASSISTANT, CHIEF-UNDERLING.

aide-toi, le ciel t'aidera [F.] (êd-twa', le si-el' têd-e-ra'). Help yourself and Heaven will help you. TOIL-RELAXATION.

aid'-ing. Helping. OBSTRUCTION-HELP.

aid'-less. Helpless. STRENGTH-WEAKNESS.

ai-grette'. Tuft of feathers. EMBELLISHMENT-DISFIGUREMENT.

ai-guille'. A rocky mountain-summit. SHARPNESS-BLUNTNESS.

aiguille, chercher une—dans une botte de foin [F.] (êgwîy', shêr-shê' ŭn—dan·z ŭn bot de fwan·). "To look for a needle in a haystack." DIFFICULTY-FACILITY, POSSIBILITY-IMPOSSIBILITY, USEFULNESS-USELESSNESS.

ai'-gu-let. An ornamental pendant. EMBELLISHMENT-DISFIGUREMENT.

ail. To be ill. HEALTH-SICKNESS, PLEASURE-PAIN.

ail'-ing. Being somewhat ill. HEALTH-SICKNESS.

ail'-ment. Slight sickness. HEALTH-SICKNESS.

aim. To direct. AIM-ABERRATION, PURPOSE-LUCK; **aim a blow at,** ATTACK-DEFENSE; **aim at,** PURPOSE-LUCK, QUEST-EVASION.

AIM—ABERRATION.

Alignment. Arrangement in a straight line.

Aim. Line of direction; design.

Bearing. The direction of a point as determined by the compass on a ship.

Bending. Deflection.

Collimation. The act of rendering parallel to a given straight line.

Course. Line of motion.

Dip. Inclination; change of angle.

Direction. The trend of a line as determined by its extremities.

Drift. The course along which anything moves.

Incidence. The course of a body in relation to a surface on which it falls.

Line. A route; course.

Set. Direction of, as of wind and current.

Steerage. The course in which the ship is kept.

Tack. Fastening down the corners of certain sails in passing from one point to another; hence, the course of sailing.

Tendency. See INCLINATION.

Tenor. A settled manner of progress; direction.

Trend. Inclination; tendency.

AIM—*Associated Nouns.*

Azimuth the arc of the horizon which a vertical plane passing through a heavenly body makes with the meridian of the place of observation; **cardinal points; line of collimation; path; point of the compass; quarter,** any special place or direction; **range,** space through which anything moves; **road; rhumb,** one of the thirty-two points on a compass.

AIM—*Points of Direction.*

East; east by north; east by south; east-northeast; east-southeast; north; north by east; north by west; northeast; northeast by east; northeast by north; north-northeast; north-northwest; northwest; northwest by north; northwest by south; south; south by east; south by west; southeast; southeast by east; southeast by south; southwest; southwest by south; southwest by west; south-south-east; south-southwest; west; west by north; west by south; west-northwest; west-southwest.

AIM—*Verbs.*

Aim at. To point in the direction of.

Align one's march. To lay out a plan or course to follow.

Ascertain one's aim.

Ascertain one's course. } To find out where one is going.

Ascertain one's direction.

Be bound for. Have one's course determined.

Bend. To turn from its first direction.

Bend one's course. To turn.

Bend one's steps towards. To go in a direction.

Bend towards. To cause to go in a direction.

Box the compass. To recite in consecutive order the thirty-two points of the compass.

Conduct to. To lead to.

Determine. To make up one's mind about some course.

Dip. Incline.

Direct one's course. To turn to; to regulate; to plan.

Easter. Shift to the east.

Go straight to the point. To take the shortest way.

Go to. To reach; to go in the direction of.

Hold a course. } Keep the same line, path, road, route.

Keep a course. }

Keep hold. To continue holding.

Level at. To take aim; to place in a perfectly horizontal position.

Make for. To set out for; to go toward.

March on. Travel in some direction.

Aberrance. A wandering from the right way.

Aberration. Wandering from the truth.

Declination. Deviation; departure.

Deflection. The act of turning aside.

Deflexure. The state of bending away from.

Detour. See MIDCOURSE-CIRCUIT.

Deviation. Going out of the way.

Digression. Turning aside from the right path.

Divergence. See CONCENTRATION-RADIATION.

Diversion. Pastime; amusement. A rest from work.

Evagation. Wandering about; excursion.

Flection. A turning, as of the eye.

Obliquation. Turning to one side, as the eyes.

Refraction. Bending the rays of light in passing from a denser to a rarer medium, or vice versa.

Sweep. A long movement.

Vagrancy. State of wandering about.

Wandering. Going out of the way.

Warp. A twisting from the right course.

ABERRATION—*Denotations.*

Bypaths and crooked ways; knight's move at chess; zigzag.

ABERRATION—*Verbs.*

Alter one's course. To change one's direction.

Bear off. To steer away.

Bend. To twist away from its former course.

Crook. To turn; to curve.

Deflect. To turn aside from a horizontal or right position.

Depart from. To leave; to go in a different direction.

Deviate. Turn aside.

Digress. To go out of the way; to touch upon some side topics.

Diverge. See CONCENTRATION-RADIATION.

Divert from its course. To turn aside from its fixed course, business or occupation.

Dodge. To escape by evading the point at issue.

Draw aside. To pull away; to withdraw.

Drift. To float; to go any direction.

Ease off. To slacken the rope to let the ship slowly change her direction.

Face about. To turn the face completely around.

Face to the right about. To turn the face completely to the right.

Fly off at a tangent. To fly off at right angles to the radius of a circle; to drop the main subject.

Go adrift. To float helplessly along in any direction.

Go astray. To wander away from known paths.

Glance off. To bound to a side; to fail to do injury.

Go out of one's way. See CIRCUIT.

Heel. To tip or lean to one side.

Intervert. To turn to another course or way.

Lose one's way. Fail to know which direction to go.

Make way for. To go out of the way; to open up a passage.

Meander. To wind; to twist; to turn at random.

Put on a new scent. Direct in a different way.

Ramble. To roam carelessly, without any definite point in view.

Rove. To wander about in a heedless manner.

Shift. To move from place to place.

Shunt. To switch off, like a train of cars.

Shy. To jump to a side suddenly.

Sidle. To move sideways, putting one side ahead.

Steer clear of. To go out of the way; to avoid.

Step aside. To make room for passage by getting out of the way.

Straggle. To roam in bypaths; to wander out of the way.

Stray. To lose one's course.

AIM—ABERRATION—*Continued.*

AIM—Verbs—*Continued.*

March on a point. To go to some definite place.
Point at. Aim at.
Point to. Direct attention to.
See which way the wind blows. Determine the direction of the wind.
Shape one's course. Outline a way for oneself.
S'orienter [F.]. To find one's bearings.
Steer one's course. To be one's own pilot.
Take aim. To direct the eye or weapon.
Tend towards. To go in a direction.
Trend. Incline.
Verge. Come near.

AIM—*Adjectives.*

Aligned with. Put in the rank, line.
Bound for. Going in some particular direction.
Direct. In a straight line.
Directed. See *Verbs.*
Directed towards. See *Verbs.*
Easterly. Tending toward the east.
North, etc.
Northerly, etc. } See Points of Direction.
Northern, etc.
Point towards. To direct one's attention to something.
Straight. Not crooked; keeping in the same path.
Straightforward. Upright; not deviating.
Undeviating. Not going out of the way.
Unswerving. Unflinching; carrying out one's plans without fear or trembling.

AIM—*Adverbs.*

As the crow flies. In a direct line.
Before the wind. In the direction of the wind.
By the way. Branching off, but connected with the main point.
Directly. Straightway.
Eastabout. }
Eastward. } Towards the east.
En avant [F.]. Forward.
From the four winds. From north, east, south, west.
Full tilt at. Straight ahead.
Hither. This way; this direction.
In the wind's eye. Directly towards the point from which the wind blows.
Near the wind. Close to the wind.
Point blank. Straight off; flatly.
Quaquaversum. Facing all directions; all sides.
Straight. Direct.
Thither. To that place or result.
Through. From end to end.

ABERRATION—Verbs—*Continued.*

Swerve. To turn aside from a fixed rule law or custom; to deviate from a straight line.
Tralineate. To stray; to wander.
Trend. To tend in a different direction; deviate.
Turn. Change front; revolve.
Turn a corner. To go around a corner; to take a different course.
Turn aside. To go out of the way; to leave the right path.
Turn away from. To leave; desert; to take another direction.
Twist. To turn from its former course.
Veer. To change direction of a ship as the wind changes.
Wabble. See Vibration.
Wander. To rove; to roam; to go about aimlessly.
Warp. To twist from its proper course.
Wheel. To turn about; to change direction.
Wheel about. To take a new direction.
Yaw. To steer wildly or out of the right course.

ABERRATION—*Adjectives.*

Aberrant. Wandering from the right course.
Circuitous. Roundabout; indirect.
Crablike. Moving sideways.
Desultory. Jumping from one thing to another, like a circus rider.
Deviating. Varying.
Devious. Straying; wandering; leaving the path of rectitude.
Discursive. Passing from one thing to another; rambling.
Errant. Wandering; wayward.
Erratic. Wandering; rambling in thought.
Excursive. Roving.
Indirect. Not straight to the point; round about.
Rambling. Roving; discursive.
Stray. Straying; irregular.
Undirected. Not guided; not knowing the way.
Vagrant. Wandering; erring.
Zigzag. Going from side to side, at angles.

ABERRATION—*Adverbs.*

All manner of ways; astray from; circuitously (see Circuitous); **like the move of a knight on a chessboard; obliquely; sideling; to the right about; wide of the mark.**

AIM—Adverbs—*Continued.*

Towards. In the direction of.
Versus. Against.
Via. By way of.

AIM—*Phrases.*

In a direct line—for,—to,—with; in a line with; in a straight line— for,—to,—with; in all directions; in all manner of ways; on the road to; on the high road to.

---

aimable, faire l' [F.] (ê-mà′bl, fêr l′). To do the amiable. Love-Hate.
aimer éperdument [F.] (ê-mê′ ê-pêr-dŭ-màn·′). To love to distraction. Love-Hate.
aim′-less. Without purpose. Motive-Caprice, Purpose-Luck.
air. The atmosphere. Appearance-Disappearance, Beginning-End, Chemistry, Heaviness-Lightness, Liquid-Gas, Music, River-Wind, Society-Ludicrousness, Substance-Nullity, Water-Air, Weariness-Refreshment; **beat the air,** Usefulness-Uselessness; **fill the air,** Loudness-Faintness; **fine air,** Healthiness-Unhealthiness; **fish in the air,** Usefulness-Uselessness; **fowls of the air,** Fauna-Flora; **rend the air,** Loudness-Faintness; **take air,** Publicity.
air′-bal-loon″. A balloon for aerial navigation. Conveyance-Vessel.
air′-built″. Fanciful. Fancy.
air′-drawn″. Imaginary. Fancy.
air′-gun″. A gun fired by compressed air. Weapon.
air′-ing. Exposure to the air. Traveling-Navigation.
air′-pipe″. Pipe for carrying air. Aperture-Closure, Entrance-Exit, Watercourse-Airpipe.
air′-pump″. A pump for exhausting air. River-Wind.
airs. Affectation. Conceit-Diffidence, Presump-

tion-Obsequiousness, Selfrespect-Humbleness, Society-Affectation.
air′-tight″. Excluding the air. Aperture-Closure.
air′-tube″. An air pipe. Watercourse-Airpipe.
air′-ward. Upward. Height-Lowness.
air′-y. Visionary. Appearance-Disappearance, Beginning - End, Consequence - Insignificance, Heaviness-Lightness, Lightheartedness-Dejection, Liquid-Gas, Music, River-Wind, Society-Ludicrousness, Substance-Nullity, Water-Air, Weariness-Refreshment; **airy hopes,** Sanguineness-Hopelessness; **give to airy nothing a local habitation and a name,** Fancy.
aisle. A passageway. Aperture-Closure, Fane, Way.
ait. A little island. Swamp-Island.
a-jar′. Slightly opened. Aperture-Closure, Variance-Accord.
a-jee′. Distorted. Parallelism-Inclination.
aj′-u-tage. A tube or nozzle. Aperture-Closure, Watercourse-Airpipe.
a-kim′-bo. Bent. Angularity; **stand akimbo,** Defiance.
a-kin′. Related by blood. Consanguinity, Likeness-Unlikeness.
al′-a-bas″-ter. A white gypsum. Whiteness-Blackness.

a-lack'. Exclamation of sorrow. Jubilation-Lamentation.

a-lac'-ri-ty. Willingness. Activity-Indolence, Lightheartedness-Dejection, Readiness-Reluctance; **want of alacrity,** Readiness-Reluctance.

A-lad'-din's lamp. A magic lamp. Devotion-Charm

a-larm'. Emotion of fear. Alarm, Sanguineness-Timidity, Security-Insecurity; Sign, Warning; **cause for alarm,** Security-Insecurity; **give an alarm,** Alarm, Sign.

ALARM—*Nouns.*

Alarm. Any sound or information to give notice of approaching danger; a call to arms.

Alarum. An alarming sound.

Alarm bell. A bell that gives notice of danger.

Alerte [F.]. Notice of danger.

Beat of drum. A succession of strokes, varied in different ways, to give notice of danger.

Blue lights. A night signal of danger at sea.

Bugaboo. Anything imaginary that causes needless fright.

Bugbear. Something used to excite needless fear.

Cry of wolf. A needless alarm.

Danger signal. A mark or sign that points out some impending evil

False alarm. Unjustified warning.

Fire-cross. An ancient signal in Scotland for the nation to take arms, consisting of two firebrands in the fashion of a cross and fixed upon a spear.

Fog horn. A horn that gives warning of danger in thick weather.

Fog signal. A contrivance that sounds an alarm, where the visible signals would be hidden in thick weather.

Head light. A light in front of a locomotive to aid the engineer.

Hue and cry. A written proclamation issued on the escape of a felon from prison, requiring all persons to aid in retaking him.

Larum. Alarum.

Note of alarm. A sound of danger.

Red flag. A flag of a red color displayed as a signal of danger.

Red light. A warning signal of danger.

Signal of distress. A sign made by persons in danger for relief.

Sound of trumpet. A danger signal sounded by a trumpet.

Tocsin. A ringing of a bell for the purpose of alarm.

War cry. A cry or signal used in war.

War whoop. A war cry, especially that of the American Indian.

Yellow flag. A quarantine flag; a flag carried on a vessel to denote that an infectious disease is on board.

ALARM—*Verbs.*

Alarm. To give notice of approaching danger.

Battre la générale [F.]. The tattoo; a signal at 9 p. m. to repair to quarters or tents.

Beat an alarm, etc. See *Nouns.*

Cry wolf. To excite needless alarm.

Give an alarm. See *Nouns.*

Raise an alarm. See *Nouns.*

Ring the tocsin. See *Nouns.*

Sound an alarm. See *Nouns.*

Warn, etc. To give notice of approaching or probable danger. See Warning.

ALARM—*Adjectives.*

Alarming, etc. See *Verbs.*

ALARM—*Interjection.*

Sauve qui peut [F.]! Save himself who can!

a-larm'-ing. Feeling fear. Alarm, Security-Insecurity.

a-larm'-ist. One who needlessly excites alarm. Bravery-Cowardice, Sanguineness-Timidity.

a-lar'-um. An alarming sound. Alarm, Sign, Warning.

a-las'. Exclamation of pain or sorrow. Jubilation-Lamentation.

alb. A priest's garment. Vestments.

al'-ba. A priest's garment. Vestments.

al-be'-do. The brightness of a reflecting surface. Astronomy.

al''-be'-it. Even though. Compensation.

al''-bi-fi-ca'-tion. Act of whitening. Whiteness-Blackness.

Al''-bi-gen'-sis. An old sect of religious reformers. Austerity, Orthodoxy-Heterodoxy.

al-bi'-no. An abnormally white person. Sight-Dimsightedness.

al'-bum. A photograph book. Digest, Missive-Publication.

al-bu'-men. The white of an egg. Organization-Inorganization, Viscidity-Foam.

al-bu'-min-ous. Pertaining to albumen. Viscidity-Foam.

al-ca'-ic. A Grecian meter. Poetry-Prose.

al-caid'. A jailer. Chief-Underling.

al-cal'-de. A Spanish magistrate. Chief-Underling.

al'-che-my. The chemistry of the middle ages. Conversion-Reversion.

al'-co-hol. The intoxicating principle of wines and liquors. Teetotalism-Intemperance.

al'-co-hol'-ic. Pertaining to alcohol. Teetotalism-Intemperance.

al'-co-hol-ism. A disease produced by alcohol. Teetotalism-Intemperance.

Al''-co-ran'. The Koran. Revelation-Pseudo-revelation.

al'-cove. A covered recess. Contents-Receiver, Convexity-Concavity.

Al-deb'-a-ran. The principal star in the constellation Taurus. Luminary-Shade.

al'-der-man. A municipal legislator. Chief-Underling, President-Member.

ale. A beverage. Nutriment-Excretion.

alea, jacta est [L.] (ê'-lĭ-a, jac''-ta est). The die has been cast. Volition-Obligation.

A-lec'-to. A mythological goddess, avenger of iniquity. Turbulence-Calmness.

a-lec'-tro-man''-cy. Divination by a cock picking up grains. Prophecy.

ale'-house. A place where ale is sold. Dweller-Habitation; **go to the alehouse,** Teetotalism-Intemperance.

a-lem'-bic. A distilling apparatus. Contents-Receiver, Conversion-Reversion, Oven-Refrigerator, Workshop.

alentours [F.] (ɑl-an·tur'). The grounds around. Remoteness-Nearness.

a-lert'. Watchful. Activity-Indolence, Carefulness-Carelessness.

alerte [F.] (ɑ-lert). Take care. Alarm.

a-lert'-ness. Watchfulness. Carefulness-Carelessness.

a-leu'-ro-man-cy. Divination by means of meal or flour. Prophecy.

Al''-ex-an'-drine. Pertaining to Alexandria. Poetry-Prose, Simplicity-Floridness.

a-lex''-i-phar'-mic. Antidotal. Remedy-Bane.

a-lex''-i-ter'-ic. A preventive against contagion. Remedy-Bane.

al'-ge-bra. A branch of mathematics. Numbering.

al'-ge-bra'-ic. Pertaining to algebra. Numbering.

al'-gid. Chilly. Heat-Cold.

al-gol'-o-gy. A branch of botany. Zoology-Botany.

Al-gon'-kin. One of the Algonkian families of North-American Indians. Geology.

al'-go-rithm. The decimal system of numeration. Numbering.

al'-gua-zil'. A Spanish constable. Judicature.

alguazil, cada uno tiene su [Sp.] (ɑl-gwɑ-thil' cɑ'-dɑ u'-no tĩ-en'-ê su). Everybody has his governor. Chief-Underling, Rule-License.

Al''-ham-bra'-ic. Like the Alhambra in style. Architecture.

a'-li-as. Otherwise called. Name-Misnomer.

al'-i-bi. Elsewhere. Presence-Absence

a'-lien. Foreign. ALIENATION, CONNECTION-INDE-PENDENCE, CONSTITUENT-ALIEN, GODLINESS-DIS-BELIEF.

a'-lien-a-ble. Capable of being alienated. ALIENATION.

a'-lien-ate. To cause to turn away. ALIENATION, AMITY-HOSTILITY, LOVE-HATE.

a'-lien-a''-ted. Estranged. AMITY-HOSTILITY.

a''-lien-a'-tion. Deprivation of mental power. ALIEN-ATION, AMITY-HOSTILITY, LOVE-HATE; **mental alien-ation,** SANENESS-LUNACY.

ALIENATION.

Abalienation. The transfer of the property title from one to the other.
Alienation. The act of transference.
Assignment. A transfer of property by writing.
Bargain and sale. A species of land conveyance.
Barter, etc. An exchange of goods. See EXCHANGE.
Conveyance. The act by which the title to property is transferred.
Conveyancing. The act of drawing writings for the transference of property.
Devise. The transference of the crown or an estate.
Enfeoffment. The act of giving a fief, or right in land.
Exchange. The act of giving or taking one thing in return for another. See COMMUTATION-PERMUTATION.
Lease and release. A mode of conveyance of freehold estates former-ly common in England and New York.
Limitation. A settling of an estate by specific rules.
Substitution. The act of putting one person or thing in place of another. See COMMUTATION.
Transfer. The act of transferring or state of being transferred.

ALIENATION—*Associated Nouns.*

Reversion; shifting trust; shifting use; succession.

ALIENATION—*Verbs.*

Abalienate. ⎫
Alien. ⎬ To transfer to another.
Alienate. ⎭
Assign. To transfer in behalf of another.
Change from one to another.
Change hands. To change owners.
Come into possession, etc. See GAIN.
Consign. To transfer; commit.
Convey. To transfer to another.
Devolve. To transfer; transmit.
Disinherit. To alienate an inheritance.
Dispossess. To transfer possession.
Exchange. To give in return for something.
Grant, etc. To transfer by deed, etc. See GIVING.
Hand. ⎫
Hand down. ⎬ To transmit as with the hand.
Hand over. ⎭
Make over. To transfer the title of.
Negotiate. To transfer for a valuable consideration.
Pass. To transfer from one person to another.
Substitute. To transfer in the place of another person or thing.
Succeed. To follow, or come immediately after.
Transfer. To make over to another; to remove from one person or place to another.
Transmit. To hand down; to transfer.

ALIENATION—*Adjectives.*

Alienable. Capable of being alienated or transferred.
Negotiable. That may be negotiated. See *Verbs.*

ALIENATION—*Phrase.*

Estate coming into possession. A present right or interest in lands not in possession but which may by possibility vest in possession in some future time.

aliéné [F.] (a-li-ê-nê'). Mad. SANENESS-LUNACY.
alieni appetens [L.] (ê-li-î'-nai ap'-pi-tenz). Greedy of other people's possessions DESIRE-DISTASTE, PAR-DON-ENVY, UNSELFISHNESS-SELFISHNESS.

a-light'. To get down; on fire. ARRIVAL-DEPARTURE, ASCENT-DESCENT, HEAT-COLD, MOVEMENT-REST.
a-lign'. To form in line. AIM-ABERRATION.
a-lign'-ment. Formation in line. AIM-ABERRATION.

a-like'. Having resemblance. LIKENESS-UNLIKE-NESS, SYNONYM-ANTONYM; **share and share alike,** PARTICIPATION.
al'-i-ment. Food. NUTRIMENT-EXCRETION.
al''-i-men'-ta-ry. Nutritious. NUTRIMENT-EXCRE-TION, REMEDY-BANE.
al''-i-men-ta'-tion. Maintenance. OBSTRUCTION-HELP.
al'-i-mo-ny. Means of living. AFFLUENCE-PENURY, OUTLAY-INCOME, PROPERTY.
al'-i-quot. Dividing without a remainder. NUMBER, WHOLE-PART.
aliter visum diis [L.] (al'-i-ter vai'-sum dai'-is). The gods have judged otherwise. VOLITION-OBLIGA-TION.
a-live'. Having life. ACTIVITY-INDOLENCE, LIFE-DEATH, SAGACITY-INCAPACITY; **alive to,** ENLIGHTEN-MENT-SECRECY, HEED-DISREGARD, KNOWLEDGE-IG-NORANCE, SENSITIVENESS-APATHY, SKILL-UNSKIL-FULNESS; **keep alive,** DISCONTINUANCE-CONTINU-ANCE, LIFE-DEATH; **keep the memory alive,** REMEM-BRANCE-FORGETFULNESS, SAGACITY-INCAPACITY.
al'-ka-hest. An imaginary chemical liquid. ELAS-TICITY-INELASTICITY.
al'-ka-li. A caustic substance which neutralizes acids. CHEMISTRY.
all. The entire number; altogether. ENTIRETY-DE-FICIENCY, UNIVERSALITY-PARTICULARITY, WHOLE-PART; **all absorbing,** CONSEQUENCE-INSIGNIFICANCE; **all agog,** ASTONISHMENT-EXPECTATION, DESIRE-DISTASTE, EXPECTATION-SURPRISE; **all along,** DURA-TION-NEVERNESS; **all along of,** CAUSE-EFFECT; **all at once,** ETERNITY-INSTANTANEITY, HURRY-LEISURE; **all but,** MAGNITUDE-SMALLNESS; **all colors,** VARIE-GATION; **all considered,** DECISION-MISJUDGMENT, MIND-IMBECILITY; **all day long,** LASTINGNESS-TRAN-SIENTNESS; **all fours,** DIFFICULTY-FACILITY, ENTER-TAINMENT-WEARINESS; **all hail,** ARRIVAL-DEPAR-TURE, POLITENESS-IMPOLITENESS, REGARD-DISRE-SPECT, REPUTATION-DISCREDIT, SOLEMNIZATION; **all hands,** UNIVERSALITY-PARTICULARITY; **all in all,** WHOLE-PART; **all in good time,** OCCURRENCE-DESTINY, OPPORTUNENESS-UNSUITABLENESS; **all in one's power,** TOIL-RELAXATION; **all manner of,** UNI-FORMITY - DIVERSITY, UNIFORMITY - MULTIFORMITY, VARIATION; **all of a heap,** GATHERING-SCATTERING; **all one,** EQUALITY-INEQUALITY, UNCONCERN; **all over,** BEGINNING-END, CREATION-DESTRUCTION, EXTEN-SION-INEXTENSION, UNIVERSALITY-PARTICULARITY; **all powerful,** DIVINITY, STRENGTH-WEAKNESS; **all right,** RIGHT-WRONG; **all searching,** INVESTIGATION-ANSWER; **all sorts,** MIXTURE-HOMOGENEITY, UNI-FORMITY - DIVERSITY, UNIFORMITY - MULTIFORMITY; **all talk,** SUBSTANCE-NULLITY; **all the time,** DURA-TION-NEVERNESS; **all the world and his wife,** UNIVER-SALITY-PARTICULARITY; **all things to all men,** POLITE-NESS-IMPOLITENESS; **all together,** WHOLE-PART; **all ways,** AIM-ABERRATION, PROPORTION-DEFORMITY; **at all events,** COMPENSATION, DETERMINATION-VACILLATION, MODIFICATION, TRUTH-ERROR; **at all points,** ENTIRETY-DEFICIENCY; **at all times,** FRE-QUENCY-RARITY; **in all ages,** ETERNITY-INSTAN-TANEITY; **in all directions,** AIM-ABERRATION; **in all quarters,** EXTENSION-INEXTENSION; **in all respects,** ENTIRETY-DEFICIENCY, TRUTH-ERROR; **of all work,** CHIEF-UNDERLING, USEFULNESS-USELESSNESS; **on all hands,** ASSENT-DISSENT; **on all sides,** ENVIRONMENT-INTERPOSITION; **with all one's might,** TOIL-RELAXA-TION; **with all respect,** REGARD-DISRESPECT
Al'-lah. God. JOVE-FIEND.
al-lay'. To relieve. ALLEVIATION-AGGRAVATION, FIGHTING-CONCILIATION, TURBULENCE-CALMNESS; **allay excitability,** EXCITABILITY-INEXCITABILITY.
al''-lec-ta'-tion. An enticing. MOTIVE-CAPRICE.

al-lect'-ive. Enticing. MOTIVE-CAPRICE.

al''-le-ga'-tion. The act of alleging. ASSERTION-DENIAL, PRETEXT.

al-lege'. To assert to be true. ASSERTION-DENIAL, EVIDENCE-COUNTEREVIDENCE, PRETEXT.

al-le'-giance. Obligation of fidelity. DUTY-DERELICTION, INSUBORDINATION-OBEDIENCE.

al''-le-gor'-ic-al. Figurative. RHETORIC, TROPE.

al'-le-go-rize. To use an allegory. TROPE.

al'-le-go-ry. A figurative description. COMPARISON, RHETORIC, TROPE.

allegresse [F.] (al-e-gres'). Light-heartedness. LIGHT-HEARTEDNESS-DEJECTION.

allegretto [It.] (al-lê-gret'-to). Slower than allegro. MUSIC.

allegro [It.] (al-lê'-gro). Lively; brisk time. LIGHT-HEARTEDNESS-DEJECTION, MUSIC.

al''-le-lu'-jah. Shout of praise. DEVOTION-IDOLATRY.

allemande [F.] (al-man-d'). A German dance. ENTERTAINMENT-WEARINESS.

aller à tâtons [F.] (a-lê' ata-ton'). To go a groping. TRIAL.

al-le'-vi-ate. To relieve. ALLEVIATION-AGGRAVATION, TURBULENCE-CALMNESS.

al-le''-vi-a'-tion. Partial relief. ALLEVIATION-AGGRAVATION, TURBULENCE-CALMNESS.

ALLEVIATION—AGGRAVATION.

Alleviation, etc. That which lessens pain or burdens. See *Verbs.*
Comfort. Relief from sorrow or distress.
Consolation. The lessening of unhappiness. See *Verbs.*
Deliverance. Release.
Encouragement, etc. Inspiration of heart, etc. See *Verbs.*
Mitigation. The act or process of mitigating. See *Verbs.*
Refreshment. Restoration of vigor.
Relief. The partial removal of any physical or mental want or distress.
Softening. See *Verbs.*
Solace. Comfort given in time of trouble or anxiety.
Soothing. See *Verbs.*

ALLEVIATION—*Nouns of Cause.*

Cushion. A bag of soft elastic material used to sit or lie on.
Easement. That which gives ease or relief.
Lenitive. Anything that allays passion or relieves pain.
Lullaby. A song sung to lull babes to rest.
Palliative. That which eases without curing.
Restorative. Anything which restores the health and vigor.

ALLEVIATION—*Figurative Expression.*

Crumbs of comfort.

ALLEVIATION—*Verbs.*

Allay. To relieve the intensity of, as a fever.
Alleviate. Literally, to lighten the burden of; to make easier, as pain or suffering.
Assuage. To calm that which is violent, as the feelings.
Bear up. To keep up the strength and spirits of.
Be relieved, etc. See RELIEVE.
Breathe more freely. To be less excited or in less distress.
Cheer. To comfort or encourage.
Cheer the heart. See CHEER.
Comfort. To give cheer and encouragement in time of trouble or distress.
Console. To give sympathy in time of great sorrow or grief.
Cure. To restore to health and soundness.
Disburden. To remove the burden; to alleviate.
Draw a long breath. To take a sigh of relief.
Dry the eyes. } To comfort until the tears cease to flow.
Dry the tears. }
Ease. To render relief.
Encourage. To give hope and encourage; to cheer.
Foment. To relieve by treating with hot water or poultices.
Give comfort. See *Nouns.*
Gladden the heart. To cheer and encourage.
Lay the flattering unction to one's soul. To cheer the mind by word of comfort and encouragement.
Mitigate. To alleviate.
Palliate. To try to extenuate or partially excuse by artful means.
Pat on the back. To encourage.
Poultice. To relieve by treating with poultices.
Pour balm into. To relieve by soothing medicine or comforting words.
Pour oil on. To allay excitement or pain.
Refresh. To give new vigor or strength.
Relieve. To free wholly or in part from any trouble or distress.
Remedy. To remove any disorder.
Salve. To ease; to give temporary relief.
Set at ease. Make comfortable.
Smooth the ruffled brow of care. To quiet the mind disturbed by anxiety and trouble.
Soften. } To mitigate.
Soften down. }

Aggravation. The act of making worse.
Exacerbation. Increased severity or violence of a disease.
Exaggeration. The act of carrying beyond reasonable bounds.
Exasperation. State of provocation with unrestrained anger.
Heightening. Intensifying.
Overestimation. Act of valuing too highly.

AGGRAVATION—*Verbs.*

Acerbate. To embitter; to irritate.
Add fuel to the fire. } To give additional cause, as of provocation
Add fuel to the flame. } in anger.
Aggravate. To make worse; used only of that which is already bad, as a fever or anger.
Embitter. To intensify or make worse what is already bad, as a feud.
Envenom. To poison with venom; to render hostile or bitter.
Exacerbate. To intensify what has already been rendered sour or bitter.
Exasperate. To make exceedingly angry.
Fan the flame. To increase the intensity of by giving additional cause.
Go from bad to worse. Intensify what is bad.
Heighten. To intensify or increase; used both of good and bad things.
Render worse. To make worse.
Sour. To make morose and disagreeable.

AGGRAVATION—*Adjectives.*

Aggravable. Inclined to aggravate.
Aggravated, etc. See *Verbs.*
Aggravating, etc. Annoying; causing irritation, etc. See *Verbs.*
Unrelieved. Without relief; no better.
Worse. More evil.

AGGRAVATION—*Adverbs.*

From bad to worse. From evil to a more evil state.
Out of the frying-pan into the fire. Usually said of one who, in trying to better his condition, gets into a worse one.
Worse and worse. Continuing to go from bad to worse.

AGGRAVATION—*Interjections.*

So much the worse!

--- --- ---

ALLEVIATION—VERBS—*Continued.*

Stupe. To foment.
Take comfort. To be comforted.
Take off a load of care. To relieve the mind of something that troubles.
Temper the wind to the shorn lamb. To prevent troubles from becoming too great.
Wipe the eyes. } To console or comfort.
Wipe the tears. }

ALLEVIATION—*Adjectives.*

Anodyne. Having the power of allaying pain.
Assuaging. See *Verbs.*
Assuasive. Tending to soothe.
Balmy. Refreshing or healing like balm.
Balsamic. Soothing like balsam.
Consolatory. Inclined to give comfort.
Curative. Possessing the power to cure.
Lenitive. Tending to allay or relieve.
Palliative. Giving temporary relief.
Soothing. Tending to quiet and calm.

al'-ley. A passageway. APERTURE-CLOSURE, CITY-COUNTRY, DWELLER-HABITATION, WAY.

al-li'-ance. Combination or union. ANTAGONISM-CONCURRENCE, ASSOCIATION, CONNECTION-INDEPENDENCE, COOPERATION-OPPOSITION, RELATIONSHIP, VARIANCE-ACCORD.

al-lied'. United. **Allied to,** CONNECTION-INDEPENDENCE, LIKENESS-UNLIKENESS, RELATIONSHIP, VARIANCE-ACCORD.

al''-li-ga'-tion. Act of tying together. UNION-DISUNION.

al-lign'. To form in line. AIM-ABERRATION.

al-lign'-ment. Formation in a line. AIM-ABERRATION.

al-lit''-er-a'-tion. Successive recurrence of the same initial sound or letter. LIKENESS-UNLIKENESS, SIMPLICITY-FLORIDNESS.

al-lit'-er-a-tive. Marked by alliteration. SIMPLICITY-FLORIDNESS.

all'-ness. Completeness. ENTIRETY-DEFICIENCY.

al''-lo-ca'-tion. Apportionment. ORGANIZATION-DISORGANIZATION.

al''-lo-cu'-tion. A formal address. ADDRESS-RESPONSE, SPEECH-INARTICULATENESS.

al-lo'-di-al. Absolutely owned. LIBERTY-SUBJECTION, PROPERTY.

al-lo'-di-um. Estate in lands held in fee simple. LIBERTY-SUBJECTION, PROPERTY.

al-lop-a-thy. A system of medical treatment REMEDY-BANE.

al'-lo-quy. Act of speaking to another. ADDRESS-RESPONSE.

al-lot'. To distribute by authority. ASSIGNMENT, ORGANIZATION-DISORGANIZATION, DUENESS-UNDUENESS.

al-lot'-ment. Distribution. ASSIGNMENT, ORGANIZATION-DISORGANIZATION.

al-low'. To permit. ASSENT-DISSENT, CONSENT, EXPOSURE-HIDINGPLACE, GIVING-RECEIVING, LEAVE-PROHIBITION, MODIFICATION, PRICE-DISCOUNT; **allow to have one's own way,** HARSHNESS-MILDNESS, PARDON-VINDICTIVENESS.

al-low'-a-ble. Permissible. DUENESS-UNDUENESS, GIVING-RECEIVING, LEAVE-PROHIBITION.

al-low'-ance. A portion or amount granted. ASSIGNMENT, GIVING-RECEIVING, MODIFICATION, PRICE-DISCOUNT, RECOMPENSE-PUNITION; **make allowance for,** EVIDENCE-COUNTEREVIDENCE, JUSTIFICATION-CHARGE, PARDON-VINDICTIVENESS; **with grains of allowance,** FAITH-MISGIVING, MODIFICATION.

al-lowed'. Permitted. DUENESS-UNDUENESS, GIVING-RECEIVING.

al-loy'. Compound of metals; reduce the purity of. BETTERMENT-DETERIORATION, CHEMISTRY, MIXTURE-HOMOGENEITY.

al-loy'-age. The act of alloying. MIXTURE-HOMOGENEITY.

all''-si''-ded. Developed in every direction. ENTIRETY-DEFICIENCY.

al-lude'. To refer to indirectly. ENLIGHTENMENT-SECRECY, HYPOTHESIS, MANIFESTATION-LATENCY, MEANING-JARGON, TROPE.

al-lure'. To attract. DESIRE-DISTASTE, MOTIVE-CAPRICE, PLEASURABLENESS-PAINFULNESS.

al-lure'-ment. Enticement. DESIRE-DISTASTE.

al-lur'-ing. Tempting. PLEASURABLENESS-PAINFULNESS.

al-lu'-sion. A suggestion. AMBIGUITY, MEANING-JARGON, MANIFESTATION-SECRECY.

al-lu'-sive. Suggestive. AMBIGUITY, CONNECTION-INDEPENDENCE, MEANING-JARGON, MANIFESTATION-SECRECY, TROPE.

al-lu'-vi-al. Of earthy material deposited by floods. ERECTNESS-FLATNESS, GULF-PLAIN, OCEAN-LAND.

al-lu'-vi-on. Flood deposits. OCEAN-LAND.

al-lu'-vi-um. Deposits of earthy matter in rivers. CLEANNESS – FILTHINESS, INCREMENT – REMNANT, OCEAN-LAND.

al-ly'. A friendly associate. ANTAGONIST-ASSISTANT, FRIEND-FOE, OBSTRUCTION-HELP.

al'-ma ma'-ter. Institution where one has been educated. SCHOOL.

al'-ma-nac. Calendar of days, weeks, months, etc. CHRONOLOGY-ANACHRONISM, MARK-OBLITERATION.

al'-ma-nack. Calendar. MARK-OBLITERATION.

al-might'-i-ness. All powerful. MIGHT-IMPOTENCE.

al-might'-y. Boundless in power. MIGHT-IMPOTENCE.

Al-might'-y. God. The Almighty. DIVINITY.

al'-mon-er. Official dispenser of alms. MINISTRY-LAITY, TREASURER.

al'-most. Very nearly. FAULTLESSNESS-FAULTINESS, MAGNITUDE-SMALLNESS; **almost all,** WHOLE-PART; **almost immediately,** EARLINESS-LATENESS.

alms. Charitable offerings. CHARITABLENESS-MALEVOLENCE, DEVOTION-IDOLATRY, GIVING-RECEIVING.

alms'-giv''-ing. Charity. GIVING-RECEIVING.

alms'-man. One supported by charity. GIVING-RECEIVING.

al''-mu-can'-tar. A parallel of altitude. ASTRONOMY.

Al-nas'-char. A character in the *Arabian Nights*. **Alnaschar's dream,** FANCY, SANGUINENESS-HOPELESSNESS.

al'-oes. A medicine of bitter taste. PALATABLENESS-UNPALATABLENESS.

a-loft'. Above. HEIGHT-LOWNESS.

al'-o-gy. Senselessness. ADAGE-NONSENSE.

a-lone'. Apart from others. OBSTRUCTION-HELP, SOLITUDE-COMPANY; **let alone,** ADDITION-SUBTRACTION, COMPLETION-NONCOMPLETION, CONVENTIONALITY - UNCONVENTIONALITY, LIBERTY - SUBJECTION, QUEST-EVASION, USE-DISUSE.

a-long'. Onward; in company. **Along of,** CAUSE-EFFECT; **along with,** ADDITION-SUBTRACTION, INSTRUMENTALITY, SOLITUDE-COMPANY; **get along,** ADVANCE-RETROGRESSION, MOVEMENT-REST; **go along,** ADMISSION-EXPULSION, ARRIVAL-DEPARTURE; **go along with,** ANTAGONISM-CONCURRENCE, ASSENT-DISSENT, COOPERATION-OPPOSITION.

a-long'-side. Close to the side. LATERALITY-CONTRAPOSITION, PARALLELISM-INCLINATION, REMOTENESS-NEARNESS.

a-loof'. At a distance. HEIGHT-LOWNESS, REMOTENESS-NEARNESS, SOCIABILITY-PRIVACY; **stand aloof,** ACTIVITY-INDOLENCE, PROFFER-REFUSAL, RECKLESSNESS-CAUTION.

a-loud'. Noisy. LOUDNESS-FAINTNESS; **think aloud,** CONVERSATION-MONOLOGUE, CRAFT-ARTLESSNESS.

al'-pen-stock''. A long, pointed staff for mountain climbing. SUSPENSION-SUPPORT.

al'-pha. The first letter in the Greek alphabet. BEGINNING-END; **alpha and omega,** WHOLE-PART.

al'-pha-bet. A series of symbols indicating sounds. BEGINNING-END, LETTER.

al''-pha-bet-a'-ri-an. One learning the alphabet. INSTRUCTOR-PUPIL.

al''-pha-bet'-ic-al. Relating to the alphabet. LETTER.

al-phit'-o-man''-cy. Divination with barley-meal. PROPHECY.

Al'-pine. Pertaining to the Alps. HEIGHT-LOWNESS.

Al'-pine Club. Organization of mountain-climbers. ASCENT-DESCENT, WAYFARER-SEAFARER.

Alps. Lofty mountains of Europe. HEIGHT-LOWNESS.

al-read'-y. Beforehand. ANTECEDENCE-SEQUENCE, FUTURE-PAST, TIME.

Al-sa'-tian. Pertaining to Alsatia; an adventurer. THEFT, VIRTUE-VICE.

Al-sa'-ti-an den. Debtor's den. VIRTUE-VICE.

al'-so. In addition. ADDITION-SUBTRACTION.

al'-tar. A place devoted to prayer. FANE, MATRIMONY-CELIBACY.

al'-ter. To change. MUTATION-PERMANENCE; **alter one's course,** AIM-ABERRATION; **alter the case,** EVIDENCE-COUNTEREVIDENCE.

al'-ter-a-ble. Capable of being changed. MUTABILITY-STABILITY.

alteram partem, audire [L.] (al'-ter-am par'-tem, au-dai'-rî). To hear the other side. EVIDENCE-COUNTEREVIDENCE, RIGHT-WRONG.

al'-ter-ant. Any medicine that changes. REMEDY-BANE.

al'-ter-a-tive. Tending to change. COMMUTATION-PERMUTATION, REMEDY-BANE.

al''-ter-ca'-tion. A quarrel. VARIANCE-ACCORD.

al'-tered. Changed. BETTERMENT-DETERIORATION, WEARINESS-REFRESHMENT; **altered for the worse,** BETTERMENT-DETERIORATION.

alter ego [L.] (al'-ter î'-go). A second self. ANTAGONIST-ASSISTANT, FRIEND-FOE, LIKENESS-UNLIKENESS, REPRESENTATIVE, SAMENESS-CONTRAST.

al'-ter-nate. To do by turns; one acting in place of another. CONTINUITY-INTERRUPTION, DETERMINATION-VACILLATION, INTERDEPENDENCE, MUTABILITY-STABILITY, PERIODICITY-IRREGULARITY, PRECEDENCE-SUCCESSION, VIBRATION.

al-ter'-nate-ly. In alternation. PERIODICITY-IRREGULARITY.

al'-ter-nate''-ness. State of being alternate. PERIODICITY-IRREGULARITY.

al'-ter-na''-ting. Changing. DETERMINATION-VACILLATION, MUTABILITY-STABILITY.

al''-ter-na'-tion. Occurrence in turn; permutation. CONTINUITY-INTERRUPTION, CONVERSION-REVERSION, DEVIATION, MUTABILITY-STABILITY, PERIODICITY-IRREGULARITY, VIBRATION.

al-ter'-na-tive. Something that may be chosen or done instead of something else. CHOICE-NEUTRALITY, COMMUTATION-PERMUTATION, DESIGN, MUTATION-PERMANENCE.

al-ter'-na-tive''-ness. State of being alternative. PERIODICITY-IRREGULARITY.

al-ter'-ni-ty. Counterchange of vowels. PERIODICITY-IRREGULARITY.

al-though'. Granting that. COMPENSATION, COOPERATION-OPPOSITION, MODIFICATION.

al-til'-o-quence. Bombast. SIMPLICITY-FLORIDNESS.

al-til'-o-quent. Bombastic. SIMPLICITY-FLORIDNESS.

al-tim'-e-try. Measurement of elevation. ANGULARITY, HEIGHT-LOWNESS, MENSURATION.

al'-ti-tude. Elevation above. HEIGHT-LOWNESS; **altitude and azimuth,** MENSURATION.

al'-to. The lowest female voice. CACOPHANY.

al''-to-geth'-er. Entirely. ENTIRETY-DEFICIENCY, WHOLE-PART.

alto–rilievo [It.] (al''-to-rî-lyê'-vo). Carved work in which the carving stands out very prominently. CONVEXITY-CONCAVITY, SCULPTURE.

al'-tru-ism. Devotion to the interest of others. CHARITABLENESS-MALEVOLENCE.

al'-um. A chemical compound. SWEETNESS-ACIDITY.

a-lum'-nus. A graduate. INSTRUCTOR-PUPIL.

al'-ve-o-lar. Full of cells. CONVEXITY-CONCAVITY.

al-ve'-o-lus. A small cavity or socket. CONVEXITY-CONCAVITY.

al'-ways. Through all time. DURATION-NEVERNESS, ETERNITY-INSTANTANEITY, HABIT-DESUETUDE, UNIFORMITY-DIVERSITY, UNIVERSALITY-PARTICULARITY.

A. M. Ante Meridiem; before noon. MORNING-EVENING.

am''-a-bil'-i-ty. Amiability; lovableness. PLEASURABLENESS-PAINFULNESS, POLITENESS-IMPOLITENESS.

a-main'. With full strength; quickly. HURRY-LEISURE, TURBULENCE-CALMNESS.

a-mal'-gam. An alloy of mercury with a metal. COMPOSITION-RESOLUTION, MIXTURE-HOMOGENEITY.

a-mal'-ga-mate. To unite a metal in an alloy with mercury. COMPOSITION-RESOLUTION, MIXTURE-HOMOGENEITY.

a-mal''-ga-ma'-tion. A union. COMPOSITION-RESOLUTION.

Am''-al-thæ'-a. The nurse of Zeus. **Amalthæa's horn,** ENOUGH.

amantes, amentes [L.] (a-man'-tîz, a-men'-tîz). Lovers, lunatics. LOVE-HATE.

amantium iræ [L.] (a-man'-shi-um ai'-rî). Lovers' quarrels. PARDON-VINDICTIVENESS.

a-man''-u-en'-sis. A secretary. RECORDER, WRITING-PRINTING.

am''-a-ran'-thine. Unfading, like the amaranth flower. ETERNITY-INSTANTANEITY.

amari aliquid [L.] (a-mê'-rai al'-i-quid). To love the other thing. FAULTLESSNESS-FAULTINESS, GOODNESS-BADNESS, PLEASURABLENESS-PAINFULNESS.

a-mar'-i-tude. Bitterness. SWEETNESS-ACIDITY.

a-mass'. To collect a great quantity of. GATHERING-SCATTERING, STORE, WHOLE-PART.

am''-a-teur'. One who does for the love of doing. DESIRE-DISTASTE, TASTE-VULGARITY.

am'-a-tive-ness. Sexuality. MODERATION-SELFINDULGENCE.

am'-a-to-ry. Designed to excite love. LOVE-HATE.

am''-au-ro'-sis. Loss of sight. SIGHT-BLINDNESS.

a-maze'. To bewilder with surprise. ASTONISHMENT-EXPECTANCE.

a-ma'-zed-ness. Astonishment. ASTONISHMENT-EXPECTANCE.

a-maze'-ment. Wonder. ASTONISHMENT-EXPECTANCE.

a-ma'-zing-ly. Wonderfully. MAGNITUDE-SMALLNESS.

Am'-a-zon. A race of female warriors. BELLIGERENT, BRAVERY-COWARDICE.

am-ba'-ges. A winding path; ambiguity. CIRCLE-WINDING, MIDCOURSE-CIRCUIT, TERSENESS-PROLIXITY.

am-ba'-gious. Characterized by roundabout methods. TERSENESS-PROLIXITY.

am-bas'-sa-dor. A person of the highest diplomatic rank. CONSIGNEE, MESSENGER.

am'-ber. A fossilized vegetable resin. PULPINESS-ROSIN; **amber-color,** YELLOWNESS-PURPLE.

am'-ber-gris. A gray, waxy matter. PULPINESS-OIL.

am''-bi-dex'-ter. One who uses both hands equally well; a double-dealer. BIGOTRY-APOSTASY, RIGHT-LEFT, SKILL-UNSKILFULNESS.

am''-bi-dex-ter'-ity. Duplicity. SKILL-UNSKILFULNESS.

am''-bi-dex'-tral. Ambidextrous. RIGHT-LEFT.

am''-bi-dex'-trous. Double-dealing. BIGOTRY-APOSTASY.

am''-bi-dex'-trous-ness. Duplicity. SKILL-UNSKILFULNESS.

am'-bi-ent. Anything that encompasses. ENVIRONMENT-INTERPOSITION.

ambigu [F.] (an'-bi-gü'). A feast. MIXTURE-HOMOGENEITY.

ambiguas spargere voces [L.] (am-big'-yu-as spar'-ge-rî vo'-sîz). To spread doubtful rumors. CERTAINTY-DOUBT, CONVERSATION-MONOLOGUE, CRAFT-ARTLESSNESS, TRUTHFULNESS-FALSEHOOD.

am''-bi-gu'-i-ty. The quality of being obscure or uncertain. AMBIGUITY, CERTAINTY-DOUBT, CLEARNESS-OBSCURITY, PERSPICUITY-OBSCURITY.

AMBIGUITY.

Ambiguity. Obscurity of meaning.
Ambiloquy. Doubtful language.
Amphibology.⎱ Double meaning arising from a doubtful construc-
Amphiboly. ⎰ tion in the sentence.

Double entendre [F.]. Double meaning.
Double meaning. Doubtfulness of expression.
Equivocalness. } Uncertainty of meaning arising from a doubtful
Equivocation. } meaning of an expression.
Equivoque [F.]. Equivocation.
Homonymy. The state of having sameness of sound and difference of meaning.

AMBIGUITY—*Denotations.*

Anagram. An expression formed from the letters of another expression.
Calembour [F.]. Pun.
Conundrum. A riddle in which some fancied likeness between things is to be found. See MYSTERY.
Homonym. A word having the same sound as another, but a different meaning.
Paragram. A pun.
Pun. Use of word of two meanings.
Quibble. Tricky avoidance of the real meaning of a word.
Sphinx. A person who uses ambiguous language. [Greek myth.]

AMBIGUITY—*Associated Words.*

Delphic oracle, a famous Greek oracle brought into disrepute by the ambiguity of its declarations on several important occasions; **mental reservation,** a reservation unexpressed; **sphinx,** a mythological monster, a mysterious person; **white lie,** an unimportant lie; **word-play,** the application of various meanings to words.

AMBIGUITY—*Verbs.*

Be equivocal. See *Adjectives.*
Equivocate, etc. To use expressions from which two meanings may be taken, etc. See TRUTHFULNESS-FALSEHOOD.
Have two meanings. See MEANING.

AMBIGUITY—*Adjectives.*

Ambiguous. Obscure in meaning.
Amphibolous. Pertaining to amphiboly.
Double-tongued. Lying.
Equivocal. Having two meanings, each of which may be taken.
Homonymous. Similar in sound, but different in meaning.

am-big′-u-ous. Obscure in meaning. AMBIGUITY CERTAINTY-DOUBT, CLEARNESS-OBSCURITY, PERSPICUITY-OBSCURITY.
am-bil′-o-quy. Use of ambiguous language. AMBIGUITY.
am′-bit. A boundary. OUTLINE.
am-bi′-tion. Inordinate desire for anything. DESIRE-DISTASTE, PURPOSE-LUCK.
am-bi′-tious. Eager. DESIRE-DISTASTE.
am′-ble. To walk with a careless pace. SWIFTNESS-SLOWNESS, TRAVELING-NAVIGATION.
am′-bo. The pulpit of the early church. FANE, SCHOOL.
ambo [L.] (am′-bo). Both. *Arcades ambo* [L.] (Ar-kê′-dîz am′-bo). Both Arcadians. FRIEND-FOE, GOOD MAN-BAD MAN, LIKENESS-UNLIKENESS.
am-bro′-sia. The food of the gods. NUTRIMENT-EXCRETION, PALATABLENESS-UNPALATABLENESS.
am-bro′-sial. Divinely sweet. PALATABLENESS-UNPALATABLENESS, PERFUME-STENCH.
am′-bu-lance. A wagon for conveying the sick. CONVEYANCE-VESSEL, REMEDY-BANE.
am′′-bu-la′-tion. Act of walking about. TRAVELING-NAVIGATION.
am′-bu-la-to-ry. Pertaining to walking. TRAVELING-NAVIGATION.
am′′-bus-cade′. A hiding-place. DISCLOSURE-HIDING-PLACE.
am′-bush. A concealed place; to waylay. DISCLOSURE-HIDINGPLACE, REFUGE-PITFALL, TRUTHFULNESS-FRAUD; **lie in ambush,** ENLIGHTENMENT-SECRECY.
am-bus′-tion. A burn or scald. HEATING-COOLING.
âme [F.] (am). Soul. *âme damnée* [F.] (am da-nê′),

a hireling; ANTAGONIST-ASSISTANT, CHIEF-UNDERLING, GOOD MAN-BAD MAN, PRESUMPTION-OBSEQUIOUSNESS. *âme de boue* [F.] (am de bu), a base soul; GOOD MAN-BAD MAN. *âme qui vive* [F.] (am kî vîv), a living soul; PLURALITY-ZERO, PRESENCE-ABSENCE.
a-meer′. The ruler of Afghanistan. GENTILITY-DEMOCRACY.
a-me′-lio-rate. To make more endurable. BETTERMENT-DETERIORATION.
a-me′′-lio-ra′-tion. Betterment. BETTERMENT-DETERIORATION.
a′′-men′. So be it. ASSENT-DISSENT, CONTENTEDNESS-DICONTENTMENT, YIELDING.
a-me′-na-ble. Liable to be called to account. DUTY-DERELICTION.
a-mend′. To change for the better. BETTERMENT-DETERIORATION.
amende honorable [F.] (a-man·d′ o-no-rabl′). Public penance. ATONEMENT.
a-mend′-ment. Change for the better. BETTERMENT-DETERIORATION, PRESIDENT-MEMBER.
a-mends′. Satisfaction. ATONEMENT, COMPENSATION, RECOMPENSE-PUNITION.
a-men′-i-ty. Agreeableness. PLEASURABLENESS-PAINFULNESS, POLITENESS-IMPOLITENESS.
a-men′-ti-a. Idiocy. SANENESS-LUNACY.
a-merce′. To punish by a fine. RECOMPENSE-PENALTY.
A-mer′-i-ca. A national hymn of the United States. PATRIOTISM-TREASON.
A-mer′-i-can-Ea′-gle. The national emblem of the United States. PATRIOTISM-TREASON.
A-mer′-i-can-ism. Peculiar to the United States. WORD-NEOLOGY.
am′-e-thyst. A variety of quartz of purple color. EMBELLISHMENT – DISFIGUREMENT, YELLOWNESS-PURPLE.
a′′-mi-a-bil′-i-ty. Lovableness. CHARITABLENESS-MALEVOLENCE, POLITENESS-IMPOLITENESS.
a′-mi-a-ble. Lovable. CHARITABLENESS-MALEVOLENCE, LOVE-HATE, POLITENESS-IMPOLITENESS.
am′-i-ca-ble. Peaceable. AMITY-HOSTILITY, OBSTRUCTION-HELP.
am′-i-ca-bly. Friendly. AMITY-HOSTILITY.
am′-i-cal. Friendly. AMITY-HOSTILITY.
am′-ice. A monk's hood and cape. VESTMENTS.
amici probantur rebus adversis [L.] (a-mai′-sai pro-ban′-tur rî′-bus ad-ver′-sis). Friends are tested by adversity. FRIEND-FOE, WELFARE-MISFORTUNE.
amicus [L.] (a-mai′-cus), a friend. *Amicus curiæ* [L.] (a-mai′-cus kiu′-ri-î), an adviser without personal interest in the case, ENLIGHTENMENT-SECRECY; *amicus humani generis* [L.] (a-mai′-cus hiu-mê′-nai jen′-e-ris), a friend of the human race, HUMANITARIANISM-MISANTHROPY; *amicus usque ad aras* [L.] (a-mai′-cus us′-quî ad ê′-ras), a friend even to the altars, FRIEND-FOE.
a-mid′. In the midst of. MIXTURE-HOMOGENEITY.
a-midst′. In the center of. ENVIRONMENT-INTERPOSITION, MIXTURE-HOMOGENEITY.
a-miss′. Out of order; faulty. GOOD-EVIL; **come amiss,** HARMONY-DISCORD, OPPORTUNENESS-UNSUITABLENESS, PROPRIETY-IMPROPRIETY; **do amiss,** VIRTUE-VICE; **go amiss,** SUCCESS-FAILURE; **nothing comes amiss,** CONTENTEDNESS-DISCONTENTMENT, SENSITIVENESS-APATHY; **take amiss,** DESIRE-DISTASTE, FAVORITE-ANGER.
am′-i-ty. Friendly or peaceful relations. AMITY-HOSTILITY, STRIFE-PEACE, VARIANCE-ACCORD.

AMITY—HOSTILITY.

Acquaintance. Knowledge of a person resulting from personal contact.
Affection, etc. Strong and tender attachment See LOVE.

Alienation. The act of estranging.
Animosity, etc. Active and vehement ill-will. See FAVORITE-ANGER.

AMITY—HOSTILITY—*Continued.*

Amity. Mutual good-will.
Ardent friendship. Strong and warm brotherly feeling.
Bosom friendship. Deep-seated and intimate friendship.
Brotherhood. Close and indestructible friendship, as that of brothers.
Confraternity. Brotherhood in a religious sense.
Cordial friendship. Hearty friendship.
Cordiality. Warmth of feeling.
Devoted friendship. Zealous and ardent friendship
Entente cordial [F.]. A cordial understanding.
Familiar friendship. Intimate friendship.
Familiarity. The state of knowing well from long acquaintance.
Fast friendship. Strong and lasting friendship.
Favoritism. Unjustifiable preference for one person over another.
Fellow-feeling. The quality of sharing another's emotions.
Fellowship. Friendly intercourse.
Firm friendship. Steadfast and enduring friendship.
Fraternity. The proper affection of brothers for each other.
Fraternization. The act of bringing into brotherly relations.
Friendliness. The state of regarding others with favor.
Friendship. Attachment resulting from mutual respect.
Good understanding. Friendly relations.
Good-will, etc. Kindly feeling. See CHARITABLENESS.
Harmony, etc. Agreement in sentiment and feeling. See ACCORD.
Intercourse. Connection by friendly dealings.
Intimacy. Close or confidential friendship.
Intimate friendship. Close or confidential friendship.
Introduction. The act of causing to become acquainted.
Knowledge of. Acquaintance with.
Lasting friendship. Enduring friendship.
Peace, etc. A state of unity of feeling or interest. See STRIFE-PEACE.
Rapprochement [F.]. The act of restoring to friendship
Response. A sympathetic action.
Sincere friendship. True friendship.
Sodality. A fellowship for devotional or charitable purposes.
Stanch friendship. Faithful friendship.
Sympathy. Feeling corresponding to what another feels.
Tried friendship. Friendship which has been put to the test and stood it.
Warm friendship. Earnest and fervent friendship.
Welcomeness. The state of being gladly received.

AMITY—*Verbs*

Be acquainted with, etc. See *Adjectives.*
Bear good-will, etc. See CHARITABLENESS
Become friendly, etc. See *Adjectives.*
Befriend. To aid in a friendly way   See OBSTRUCTION-HELP
Be friendly, etc. See *Adjectives.*
Be friends, etc. See FRIEND.
Be introduced to. To become acquainted with.
Break the ice. To open the way to acquaintanceship.
Embrace. To hug.
Extend the right hand of fellowship.} Profess friendship.
Extend the right hand of friendship.}
Fraternize. To bring into brotherly relations.
Gain the friendship of. Become a friend.
Get into favor. Become a favorite.
Have a leaning to. To favor somewhat
Have dealings with. Be associated with.
Have the ear of. To have the favorable attention of.
Hold communication with. Have intercourse with.
Hold out the right hand of fellowship.
Hold out the right hand of friendship.
Introduce to. To make acquainted with.
Keep company with, etc. See SOCIABILITY
Know. To be acquainted with.
Love. To regard with strong and tender affection. See LOVE.
Make acquaintance with. Become acquainted.
Make friends with, etc. See FRIEND.
Make much of. To regard highly.
Meet half-way. To concede something in becoming conciliated.
Pick acquaintance with. To seek to become friendly.
Receive with open arms. To receive with affection.
Scrape acquaintance with. To intrude oneself into a person's acquaintance.
Set one's horses together. To fraternize.
Shake hands with. Give hands as a salute.
Sympathize with. To share the feelings of another.
Take in good part. To receive in a friendly manner.
Throw oneself into the arms of. Become very intimate readily.

Discord, etc. Variance **or** strife, etc. See VARIANCE.
Dislike, etc. A slight degree of hatred. See DESIRE-DISTASTE
Enmity. The state of cherishing resentment towards another.
Estrangement. The act of turning from friendliness to hostility.
Hate, etc. Intense dislike combined with ill-will. See LOVE-HATE.
Heartburning. Secret hate.
Hostility. The state of being actively inimical.
Malevolence, etc. The state of having an evil disposition towards others, etc. See CHARITABLENESS-MALEVOLENCE.
Unfriendliness, etc. See *Adjectives.*—

HOSTILITY—*Verbs*

Alienate. To withdraw love or affection from.
Bear malice, etc. To have a disposition to injure. See CHARITABLENESS-MALEVOLENCE.
Be inimical, etc. See *Adjectives.*
Estrange. To be or become less intimate in friendship.
Fall out. To become hostile from a disagreement.
Harden the heart. To become indifferent in friendship to another
Hold at arm's length.} Not to be very friendly with.
Keep at arm's length.}
Take umbrage, etc. To feel injured because of envy   See FAVORITE-ANGER.

HOSTILITY—*Adjectives.*

Alienated. Having love or affection withdrawn from
At daggers drawn. At enmity with each other.
At enmity. Cherishing resentment.
At open war with. Hostile to.
At variance. Disagreeing in opinion.
Cold-hearted. Lacking sympathy.
Cool. Lacking cordiality.
Disaffected. Filled with discontent.
Estranged. On less intimate terms than formerly.
Hostile. Actively inimical.
In bad odor with. Out of favor with.
Inimical. Hating others.
Irreconcilable. Not to be recalled from a state of hostility.
Not on speaking terms. Not friendly.
On bad terms. Unfriendly.
Unfriendly. Not kind or favorable.
Up in arms against. Actively hostile to.

AMITY—*Continued*

AMITY—*Adjectives.*

Acquainted. Familiar or conversant with.
Amicable. Showing good-will.
Amical. Of or pertaining to friends.
At home with. Intimate.
Brotherly. Showing friendship like brothers.
Cordial. Having warmth of heart or feeling.
Familiar. Well acquainted.
Fraternal. Friendly; in a manner befitting a brother.
Free and easy. Friendly without formality.
Friends with. Very friendly.
Hail fellow well met. On very familiar or cordial terms.
Hand and glove. Very intimate.
Hand in hand with. Closely associated.
Hearty. Proceeding from the heart.
In one's good books.} Favored by someone.
In one's good graces.}
Intimate. Closely connected by friendship.
Neighborly. Disposed to be sociable.
On amicable-footing,—terms. On a mutual footing of good-will.
On familiar-footing,—terms. On terms of familiarity. See FAMILIAR.
On friendly-footing,—terms. On terms befitting friendship.
On good-footing,—terms. On a favorable footing.
On intimate-footing,—terms. On terms of close companionship.
On speaking terms. Friendly enough to speak.
On visiting terms. Friendly enough to interchange visits.
Sympathetic. Having a fellow-feeling for another.
Thick. Closely associated.
Unhostile. Not unfriendly.
Warm-hearted. Sympathetic and cordial.
Welcome. Received in a friendly manner.
Well-affected. Influenced in a good manner.
Well at home. Thoroughly familiar.
Well with. On good terms.

AMITY—*Adverbs*

Amicably, etc. See *Adjectives.*
Arm in arm. In an intimate manner.
Sans cérémonie [F.]. Without ceremony; in a sociable manner.
With open arms. Cordially.

am-mo'-ni-um. A volatile alkali. CHEMISTRY.

amor [L.] (ê'-mor). Love. LOVE-HATE. *amor nummi* [L.] (ê'-mor num'mai), love of the dollar, EXTRAVAGANCE-AVARICE; *amor patriæ* [L.] (ê'-mor pê'-tri-î), love of country, HUMANITARIANISM-MISANTHROPY, PATRIOTISM-TREASON; *ducit amor patriæ* [L.] (du'-sit ê'-mor pê'-tri-î), love of country leads me, HUMANITARIANISM-MISANTHROPY; *omnia vincit amor* [L.] (om'-ni-a vin'-sit ê'-mor), love conquers all things, LOVE-HATE, SUCCESS-FAILURE; *vincet amor patriæ* [L.] (vin'-set ê'-mor pê'-tri-î), love of country will conquer, HUMANITARIANISM-MISANTHROPY.

amore [It.] (a-mo'-rê). Love. *Con amore* [It.] (con a-mo'-rê), with love, EMOTION, LOVE-HATE.

am''-mu-ni'-tion. Anything used in the discharge of firearms. MATERIALS, WEAPON.

am'-nes-ty. An act of pardon. FIGHTING-CONCILIATION, PARDON-VINDICTIVENESS.

amnis [L.] (am'-nis). River. *Rusticus expectat dum amnis defluat* [L.] (rus'-ti-cus ex-pec'-tat dum am'-nis def'-lu-at). The rustic waits for the river to flow by. SANGUINENESS-HOPELESSNESS.

a-mong'. In the midst of. ENVIRONMENT-INTERPOSITION, MIXTURE-HOMOGENEITY.

a-mongst'. In the midst of. ENVIRONMENT-INTERPOSITION, MIXTURE-HOMOGENEITY.

amoroso [It.] (a-mo-ro'-so). Tender. ACTING, LOVE-HATE.

am'-o-rous. Ardent in affection. LOVE-HATE.

a-mor'-phism. Quality of being without shape. FORM-FORMLESSNESS.

a-mor'-phous. Unshapen. CONVENTIONALITY-UNCONVENTIONALITY, FORM-FORMLESSNESS, MINERALOGY.

a-mor''-ti-za'-tion. Giving of lands to a corporation. GIVING-RECEIVING.

a-mo'-tion. A removal. TRANSFER.

a-mount'. The sum total. MONEY, PRICE-DISCOUNT, QUANTITY-MEASURE; **amount to,** EQUALITY-INEQUALITY, NUMBERING; **gross amount,** WHOLE-PART, EQUALITY-INEQUALITY.

amour [F.] (a-mu'r). A love affair. LOVE-HATE, PURITY-IMPURITY; *amour propre* [F.] (a-mur' pro'-pr). Self-love, CONCEIT-DIFFIDENCE.

am''-ou-rette'. A pretty love affair. LOVE-HATE, PURITY-IMPURITY.

am-pere'. The unit of electric-current strength. ELECTRICITY.

am-phib'-i-ous. Living both on land and in water. CONVENTIONALITY-UNCONVENTIONALITY.

am'-phi-bol'-o-gy. A sentence ambiguous in construction. AMBIGUITY.

am-phib'-o-lous. Ambiguous. AMBIGUITY.

am-phib'-o-ly. Ambiguity. AMBIGUITY.

am-phic''-ty-on'-ic. Pertaining to the Grecian councils. **Amphictyonic council,** COUNCIL.

amphigouri [F.] (an'-fi-gu-rî'). Nonsense. ADAGE-NONSENSE.

am''-phi-pro'-style. An edifice with columns in front and behind, but not on the sides. ARCHITECTURE.

am''-phi-the'-a-ter. An arena, or place of public contest; range of vision. ACTING, ARCHITECTURE, LISTS, SCHOOL, SIGHT-BLINDNESS.

am-phit'-ry-on. A host. FRIEND-FOE.

am'-pho-ra. An earthenware jar. CONTENTS-RECEIVER.

am'-ple. Of large capacity; sufficient. BREADTH-NARROWNESS, EXTENSION-INEXTENSION, GREATNESS-LITTLENESS, MAGNITUDE-SMALLNESS.

am''-pli-fi-ca'-tion. Elaboration. RHETORIC, TERSENESS-PROLIXITY.

am'-pli-fy. To enlarge. ENLARGEMENT-DIMINUTION, GULL-HYPERBOLE, TERSENESS-PROLIXITY.

am'-pli-tude. Greatness of extent. BREADTH-NARROWNESS, ENOUGH, GREATNESS-LITTLENESS, QUANTITY-MEASURE.

am''-pli-tu'-din-ous. Great in extent. GREATNESS-LITTLENESS.

am'-ply. Largely. ENOUGH.

am'-pu-tate. To cut off. ADDITION-SUBTRACTION.

am''-pu-ta'-tion. A cutting off. ADDITION-SUBTRACTION.

am'-u-let. A charm. DEVOTION-CHARM.

amusare [It.] (a-mu-za'-rê). To please. *Per amusare la bocca* (pêr a-mu-za'-rê la boc-ca). To please the mouth. PALATABLENESS-UNPALATABLENESS.

a-muse'. To please. ENTERTAINMENT-WEARINESS, PLEASURABLENESS-PAINFULNESS.

a-mused'. Pleased. ENTERTAINMENT-WEARINESS.

a-muse'-ment. Enjoyment. ENTERTAINMENT-WEARINESS, PLEASURE-PAIN; **place of amusement,** PLEASURABLENESS-PAINFULNESS.

a-mus'-ing. Entertaining. ENTERTAINMENT-WEARINESS.

amussis [L.] (a-mus'-sis). A rule or level. *ad amussim* [L.] (ad a-mus'-sim). According to rule. TRUTH-ERROR.

am''-y-la'-ceous. Starchy. VISCIDITY-FOAM.

an. One; and if. HYPOTHESIS.

an'-a. Scraps of literature. ACCOUNT.

An''-a-bap'-tism. A religious rite. ORTHODOXY-HETERODOXY.

An''-a-bap'-tist. A religious sect in Germany. ORTHODOXY-HETERODOXY.

an-ach'-ro-nism. An error in assigning the date of an event. CHRONOLOGY-ANACHRONISM, OPPORTUNENESS-UNSUITABLENESS.

an''-a-co-lu'-thon. Lack of grammatical symmetry in a sentence. CONTINUITY-INTERRUPTION, RHETORIC.

an''-a-con'-da. A huge tropical serpent. BENEFACTOR-EVILDOER.

an-ac''-re-on'-tic. Amatory verse. POETRY-PROSE.

an''-a-cru'-sis. An unemphatic introductory syllable in lyric verse. POETRY-PROSE.

an'-a-glyph. An ornament in relief. DELINEATION-CARICATURE, SCULPTURE.

an''-a-glyp'-tic. Ornamental. SCULPTURE.

an''-a-go'-ge. Spiritual significance. MANIFESTATION-LATENCY, TROPE.

an''-a-gog'-ic-al. Mystical. TROPE.

an'-a-gram. The letters of a word transposed so as to make a different word. AMBIGUITY, LETTER, TIDINGS-MYSTERY, WITTINESS-DULNESS.

an''-a-gram-mat'-i-cism. A letter or word transposed to make a different word. LETTER.

an''-a-lec'-ta. A selection from a literary work. DIGEST.

an''-a-lec'-tic. Composed of selections. DIGEST.

an''-a-lep'-tic. Restorative to strength. REMEDY-BANE.

an''-a-log'-ic-al. Figurative. LIKENESS-UNLIKENESS.

an''-a-log-ic'-al-ness. Similarity. LIKENESS-UNLIKENESS.

a-nal'-o-gous. Related. LIKENESS-UNLIKENESS.

an'-a-logue. Anything analogous. LIKENESS-UNLIKENESS.

a-nal'-o-gy. Similarity of properties or relations. CONNECTION-INDEPENDENCE, LIKENESS-UNLIKENESS, RHETORIC.

an-al'-y-sis. Resolution into parts. COMPOSITION-RESOLUTION, DIGEST, INVESTIGATION-ANSWER, NUMBERING, ORGANIZATION-DISORGANIZATION, RATIOCINATION-INSTINCT, TRIAL.

an'-a-lyst. One who analyzes. INVESTIGATION-ANSWER, TRIAL.

an''-a-lyt'-ic. Proceeding by analysis. INVESTIGATION-ANSWER, MIXTURE-HOMOGENEITY.

an'-a-lyze. To make an analysis. INVESTIGATION-ANSWER, MIXTURE-HOMOGENEITY.

an'-a-ly"-zer. One who analyzes. TRIAL.

an"-a-mor'-pho-sis. A distorted representation of an object, so made that when viewed through an instrument a correct image is obtained. DELINEATION-CARICATURE, PROPORTION-DEFORMITY, SIGHT-DIM-SIGHTEDNESS.

ananké [Gr.] (an-an'-ké). Necessity. VOLITION-OBLIGATION.

an'-a-pest. A metrical foot. POETRY-PROSE, RHETORIC.

an"-a-pes'-tic. Composed of anapests. RHETORIC.

an-ar'-chic. Opposed to government. TYRANNY-ANARCHY.

an-ar'-chic-al. Lawless. REGULARITY-IRREGULARITY, RULE-LICENSE, TYRANNY-ANARCHY.

an'-arch-ism. Disbelief in government. REGULARITY-IRREGULARITY, TYRANNY-ANARCHY.

an'-arch-ist. An advocate of anarchy. BENEFACTOR-EVILDOER, INSUBORDINATION-OBEDIENCE, TYRANNY-ANARCHY.

an"-arch-is'-tic. Hatred for law. TYRANNY-ANARCHY.

an'-arch-y. Disregard of government. REGULARITY-IRREGULARITY, RULE-LICENSE, TYRANNY-ANARCHY.

an"-a-stat'-ic. In relief. **Anastatic printing.** ENGRAVING.

a-nas"-to-mo'-sis. A union or running together. CROSSING, UNION-DISUNION.

a-nas'-tro-phe, a-nas'-tro-phy. Inversion of the natural order of words. REVERSAL.

a-nath'-e-ma. A formal ban or curse. CHARITABLENESS-CURSE.

a-nath'-e-ma-tize. To pronounce a curse against. ADULATION - DISPARAGEMENT, APPROVAL - DISAPPROVAL, CHARITABLENESS-CURSE.

an"-a-tom'-ic. Structural. TEXTURE.

an"-a-tom'-ic-al. Structural. TEXTURE.

a-nat'-o-mize. To dissect a body for examination. INVESTIGATION-ANSWER, UNION-DISUNION.

a-nat'-o-my. Science of the structure of organisms. ANATOMY, BIOLOGY, BREADTH-NARROWNESS, ORGANIZATION-INORGANIZATION, TEXTURE, UNION-DISUNION, ZOOLOGY-BOTANY; **comparative anatomy,** ZOOLOGY-BOTANY

ANATOMY

ANATOMY—*Associated Nouns*

Abdomen. Cavity of the belly

Alimentary canal. Channel extending from the mouth to the anus.

Ankle. The joint connecting the foot and the leg.

Antihelix. The curved elevation of the cartilage of the ear, within or in front of the helix.

Antitragus. A prominence on the lower posterior portion of the concha of the external ear, opposite the tragus.

Aorta. Great artery that carries blood from heart to the body.

Arm. The upper limb of the human body, from shoulder to hand.

Artery. A tube that carries blood from the heart

Biceps. A muscle with two heads or origins.

Bladder. A membranous sac for holding the urine.

Blood. The red nourishing fluid that circulates in animals.

Blood-vessel. A tubular canal in which blood circulates, either an artery, a vein, or a capillary.

Bone. A hard, dense, porous structure forming the skeleton of vertebrate animals.

Cæcum. The blind gut, open at one end, connected with the large intestine, beyond the entrance of the small intestine.

Canthus. The corner where the upper and under eyelids meet on each side of the eye.

Capillary. A hair-like vein or nerve.

Carotid. An artery by which blood is carried from the aorta to the head.

Carpus. The wrist.

Cerebellum. Organ of the central nervous system; posterior part of the brain.

Cerebrum. Seat of thought or will; anterior part of the brain.

Chin. The central and anterior part of the lower jaw.

Choroid coat. The highly pigmented membrane which lines the sclerotic coat of the eye.

Clavicle. The collar-bone.

Coccyx. Caudal, or tail end of the spine.

Cochlea. One of the passages of the internal ear.

Colon. The large intestine.

Concha. Deepest hollow of the external ear, one of the thin shell-like structures in the cavity of the nose.

Cornea. The anterior transparent part of the outer coat of the eye.

Duodenum. Small intestine connected with the stomach.

Ear. The organ of hearing.

Elbow. The joint at the bend of the arm.

Esophagus. The membranous tube through which food passes from the pharynx to the stomach.

Eustachian tube. A canal connecting the pharynx with the middle ear.

Eye. The organ of sight.

Face. The anterior portion of the head.

Femur. The long bone that forms the skeleton of the thigh.

Fetus. The young in the womb or in the egg.

Fibula. The outer of the two bones of the lower leg.

Finger. One of the terminal members of the hand.

Flesh. Portion of an animal body that consists of the softer tissues.

Foot. The part below the ankle in man or other animals.

Forehead. Upper part of the face, between the eyes and the hair

Ganglion. An aggregation of nerve cells; a nerve center.

Gland. An organ by means of which constituents are removed from the blood, either as a specific secretion or as an excretion.

Hair. One of the filamentous structures that grow from the skin or outer covering of a mammal; any mass of such filaments.

Hand. The part of the fore limb that is attached to the lower extremity of the forearm.

Heart. The central organ of the vascular system of animals, a hollow structure of muscles that propels the blood by alternate contractions and dilatations.

Helix. The recurved border of the external ear.

Hip. The lateral part of the body between the brim of the pelvis and the free part of the thigh.

Humerus. The bone of the upper arm.

Ileum. The lower three-fifths of the small intestine.

Iris. The curtain across the aqueous chamber of the eye.

Jaw. One of the two structures forming the framework of the mouth.

Jugular. One of the large veins of the neck.

Kidney. One of the glandular organs that secrete urine.

Knee. The joint between the thigh and the leg.

Leg. The part of the lower limb between knee and ankle.

Liver. A large glandular organ in the upper part of the body.

Lobe. A protuberance or projecting part, as of the ear.

Lung. Either of the two organs for the aeration of the blood, situated in the thorax on each side of the heart.

Lymphatic. An absorbent vessel carrying lymph to the veins.

Maxilla. One of the jaw bones.

Medulla. The marrow of long bones.

Meibomian glands. The slender sebaceous glands of the eyelids, which discharge, through minute orifices in the edges of the lids, a fatty secretion serving to lubricate the adjacent parts.

Metacarpus. Part of the hand between wrist and fingers.

Muscle. An organ composed of contractile fibers by the action of which bodily movement is effected.

Nail. A thin horny plate or scale on the end of a finger or toe.

Neck. Part of an animal which connects the head with the trunk.

Nerve. A cord-like structure composed of delicate filaments by which sensations or stimulative impulses are transmitted to and from the brain and other organs.

Nervous system. The specialized coordinating apparatus which endows animals with sensation and volition.

Nose. That part of the face of an animal containing the nostrils and the organ of smell.

Occiput. Lower back part of the head.

Optic nerve. The special nerve of vision.

Ovary. Gland of the female essential to generation.

Pancreas. A gland connecting with the alimentary canal

Patella. Kneecap.

Pelvis. The part of the skeleton that forms a bony girdle by which the lower or hinder limbs are joined to the body.

Peritoneum. The serous membrane lining cavity of the abdomen.

Phalanges. The bones of the hand or foot, beyond the metacarpus.

Pharynx. The alimentary canal between the mouth and esophagus

Prostate. A gland in front of the bladder and joins the urethra.

Pubis. The ventral and anterior of the three principal bones composing either half of the pelvis.

Pupil. The round opening in the iris of the eye.

Radius. That one of the two long bones of the forearm that is on the same side as the thumb.

Retina. The inner coat of the eye, containing the nervous apparatus essential to vision.

Rib. One of the bones attached to the spine encircling the body-cavity.

Sacrum. A composite bone formed by the union of the vertebræ between the lumbar and caudal regions, constituting the dorsal part of the pelvis

Scaphoid fossa. The groove between the helix and the antihelix.

Scapula. The shoulder-blade

Sclerotic coat. The dense white membrane which with the cornea in front forms the outer coating of the eye around the iris.

Scrotum. The pouch that contains the testes.

Spine. The vertebral column of the back.

Spleen. A ductless, gland-like organ lying below the stomach, the melt.

Sternum. The breast-bone.

Stomach. Vessel in which the food is digested.

Tarsus. The ankle.

Temple. The region on each side of the head in front of the ear and above the cheek-bone.

Testes. The testicles; male organs of generation.

Thorax. The part of the body between the neck and the abdomen.

Thumb. The short thick digit on the radial side of the hand.

Tibia. The inner one of the two bones that constitute the skeleton of the leg below the knee.

Toe. One of the digits of a foot of a quadruped or a biped.

Tongue. Organ of taste and speech.

Tooth. A small bone attached to the jaw for chewing.

Tragus. Prominence in front of the opening of the ear.

Trunk. The body as distinguished from its appendages—limbs, neck, head, etc.

Tympanum. The middle ear; the ear drum.

Ulna. In vertebrates above fishes, that one of the two long bones of the forearm, or corresponding portion of the fore limb, that is on the same side as the little finger.

Ureter. Duct that conveys urine from the kidneys.

Urethra. Canal discharging the urine

Vein. One of the muscular tubular vessels that convey blood to the heart.

Vermiform appendix. A blind process of the cæcum.

Vertebra. One of the segments of the spine.

Windpipe. The tube for carrying air to and from the lungs.

Wrist. The part of the arm immediately joining the hand.

Zonule of Zinn. The suspensory ligament of the crystalline lens of the eye.

ANATOMY—*Verbs.*

Breathe. To inhale and exhale air.

Circulate. To move by a circuit back to the starting point.

Diffuse. To expand; to cause to flow.

Digest. To prepare in the stomach for conversion into the blood.

Exhale. To force air out of the lungs.

Inhale. To take into the lungs, as air.

Perspire. To sweat.

Respire. To take breath again; to breathe in and out.

Transfuse. To transfer, as blood, from the veins or arteries of one animal to those of another.

ANATOMY—*Adjectives.*

Abdominal. Of, or pertaining to the abdomen.

Axillary. Pertaining to the arm-pit.

Brachial. Belonging to the arm.

Celiac. Pertaining to the belly.

Cervical. Belonging to the neck.

Cubital. Pertaining to the ulna.

Ectad. Toward the outside or surface.

Ectal. Situated near the surface.

Epigastric. Pertaining to the upper and anterior part of the abdomen.

Femoral. Belonging to the thigh.

Frontal. Belonging to the forehead.

Hypochondriac. Pertaining to the hypochondria.

Hypogastric. Relating to the lower part of the abdomen.

Iliac. Pertaining to the third division of the lesser intestine.

Intercostal. Lying between the ribs

Lumbar. Pertaining to, or near the loins.

Mesial. Middle.

Muscular. Pertaining to the muscles.

Pancreatic. Pertaining to the pancreas.

Parietal. Pertaining to the bones of the upper part of the skull.

Pedal. Relating to the foot.

Pulmonary. Pertaining to the lungs.

Radial. Pertaining to the radius

Sciatic. Pertaining to the hip.

Temporal. Pertaining to the temples.

Tibial. Pertaining to the tibia.

Umbilical. Of, or relating to the navel.

Venal. Pertaining to the veins.

Vertebral. Pertaining to a vertebra; spinal.

an″-a-trip′-tic. Using friction as a remedy for disease. FRICTION-LUBRICATION.

an-ces′-tral. Inherited from an ancestor. FUTURE-PAST, INFANCY-AGE, NOVELTY-ANTIQUITY.

an′-ces-try. One's ancestors collectively. FUTURE-PAST, PARENTAGE-PROGENY.

an′-chor. An implement that retains a ship in a particular station; to become fixed. CONNECTIVE, ESTABLISHMENT-REMOVAL, MOVEMENT-REST, REFUGE-PITFALL, SANGUINENESS-HOPELESSNESS; **at anchor,** ESTABLISHMENT-REMOVAL, MOVEMENT-REST, MUTABILITY-STABILITY, SECURITY-INSECURITY; **cast anchor,** ARRIVAL-DEPARTURE, ESTABLISHMENT-REMOVAL; **sheet anchor,** MEANS, REFUGE-PITFALL, SANGUINENESS-HOPELESSNESS.

an′-chor-age. A place suitable for anchoring a vessel. ARRIVAL-DEPARTURE, DWELLER-HABITATION, ESTABLISHMENT-REMOVAL, REFUGE-PITFALL.

an′-chored. Firmly fixed. MUTABILITY-STABILITY.

an′-cho-ret, an′-cho-rite. A recluse. AUSTERITY, SOCIABILITY-PRIVACY.

an″-chy-lo′-sis. Growing together of two bones. MUTABILITY-STABILITY.

an′-cient. Of great age; an ensign or flag. NOVELTY-ANTIQUITY, SIGN; **ancient times,** FUTURE-PAST.

an′-cil-la-ry. Serving as an aid. OBSTRUCTION-HELP.

andante [It.] (an-dan′-tê). Moving moderately. MUSIC.

and′-i″-ron. Metallic support for wood in an open fireplace. OVEN-REFRIGERATOR.

An′-drew, Mer′-ry. A buffoon. WAG.

an-drog′-y-nal. Hermaphrodite. CONVENTIONALITY-UNCONVENTIONALITY.

an-drog′-y-nous. Uniting the characteristics of both sexes. CONVENTIONALITY-UNCONVENTIONALITY.

an′-ec-dote. A short story. ACCOUNT.

an″-ec-dot′-ic. Relating to a story. ACCOUNT.

an-ele′. To anoint. GODLINESS-UNGODLINESS.

an″-e-mog′-ra-phy. The art of recording the velocity and direction of winds. RIVER-WIND.

an″-e-mom′-e-ter. A wind-measuring instrument. RIVER-WIND.

anemolia bazein [Gr.] (a-ne-mo′-li-a bad′-zain). To talk words of wind. ADAGE-NONSENSE.

a-nent′. Opposite. CONNECTION-INDEPENDENCE.

anerithmon gelasma [Gr.] (a-nê′-rith-mon gel′-as-ma). The many-twinkling smile of ocean. RIVER-WIND.

an′-e-roid. Not containing or using a fluid. WATER-AIR.

an″-es-the′-si-a. Loss of sensation. FEELING-INSENSIBILITY.

an″-es-thet′-ic. Insensible. FEELING-INSENSIBILITY, SENSITIVENESS-APATHY.

a-new′. Again; in a new manner. NOVELTY-ANTIQUITY, RECURRENCE.

an-frac″-tu-os′-i-ty. Winding. CIRCLE-WINDING.

an′-gel. A spiritual being; a person of angelic qualities. ANGEL-SATAN, GOOD MAN-BAD MAN, LOVE-HATE; **fallen angel,** ANGEL-SATAN, GOOD MAN-BAD MAN; **guardian angel,** ANTAGONIST-ASSISTANT, BENEFACTOR-EVILDOER, SECURITY-INSECURITY.

ANGEL—SATAN

Angel. A heavenly being superior to man in power and knowledge.

Archangel. A chief angel.

Cherub. One of the second order of angels; representation of a beautiful child with wings.

Abaddon. The destroying angel of hell.

Ahrimanes. The evil principle in Persian theology.

Apollyon. The destroyer.

Beelzebub. The prince of fallen angels; a god of the Philistines

ANGEL—SATAN—*Continued.*

Cherubim.   Plural of cherub.
Heavenly host.   The multitude of beings who inhabit heaven.
Host of heaven.   Angels and archangels.
Madonna.   The Virgin Mary.
Ministering spirit.   Beings having the power to aid; an angel
Morning Star.   Figurative for angel.
Saint.   One of the sanctified beings in heaven.
Seraph.   One of the order of angels ranking next above the cherubim.
Seraphim.   Plural of seraph.
Sons of God.   Angels; more often simply human beings enjoying special Divine favor.

ANGEL—*Adjectives.*

Angelic.   Of or pertaining to angels.
Seraphic.   Having the nature or character of a seraph.

SATAN—NOUNS OF CHARACTER—*Continued from Column 2.*

Devilship.   State or office of the devil.
Manicheism.   The doctrine of two supreme beings.
Satanism.   Disposition of Satan.
The cloven foot.   A devilish character.

SATAN—*Adjectives*

Devilish.   Having the qualities of the devil.
Diabolic.   Pertaining to the devil; satanic.
Hell-born.   Born of hell.
Infernal.   Pertaining to the lower regions or hell.
Satanic.   Having the qualities of Satan; devilish.

---

an-gel′-ic.   Having the nature of an angel.   ANGEL-SATAN, VIRTUE-VICE.
an′-gels.   Heavenly guardians.   **Angels and ministers of grace defend us,** SANGUINENESS-TIMIDITY.
an′-ger.   Violent passion.   EXCITABILITY-INEXCITABILITY, FAVORITE-ANGER.
an″-gi-og′-ra-phy.   A treatise upon the vascular system.   TEXTURE.
an″-gi-ol′-o-gy.   Treatise upon lymphatics.   TEXTURE.
an′-gle.   An opening between two intersecting lines; to try shyly or artfully to get.   ANGULARITY, TRIAL; **at an angle,** PARALLELISM-INCLINATION.
An′-gli-can-ism.   The practise of the Church of England.   ORTHODOXY-HETERODOXY.
an′-gling.   Fishing with a rod.   QUEST-EVASION.
an′-gri-ly.   In an angry manner.   FAVORITE-ANGER, FAVORITE-QUARRELSOMENESS.
an′-gry.   Inflamed.   FAVORITE-ANGER, FAVORITE-QUARRELSOMENESS; **angry mood,** FAVORITE-ANGER.
anguille [F.] (ɑn′-gwîy′).   An eel.   *rompre l'anguille au genou* (ron′·pr lɑn′-gwîy′ o zhe-nu′).   To break an eel across the knee.   MIGHT-IMPOTENCE, POSSIBILITY-IMPOSSIBILITY.
an-guil′-li-form.   Having the appearance of an eel.   CIRCLE-WINDING, LAMINA-FIBER.
anguis [L.] (an′-gwis).   A snake.   *anguis in herba* (an′-gwis in her′-bɑ).   A snake in the grass, REFUGE-PITFALL.
an′-guish.   Mental distress.   PLEASURE-PAIN, SENSUALITY-SUFFERING.
an′-gu-lar.   Having an angle.   ANGULARITY; **angular velocity,** MOVEMENT-REST.
an″-gu-lar′-i-ty.   Irregular.   ANGULARITY.

ANGULARITY.

Aduncity.   Inward curvature, hookedness.
Angle.   The figure made by two lines which meet at a point called the vertex.
Angularity.   The quality or state of being angular or sharp-cornered.
Angularness.   The quality of being angular.
Bend.   Deflection from a straight line, a crook or curve.
Bifurcation.   A forking, or separation into two branches.
Corner.   Point formed by intersecting surfaces.
Crotch.   Point of division
Cusp.   One of the horns of the crescent moon.   That point of a curved line where the generating point stops and moves backward.

Belial.   Any reckless person; the devil.
Demon.   An evil spirit.   See FIEND.
Devil.   Ruler of hell.
Fallen angels.   Angels hurled from heaven with Satan.
Inhabitants of Pandemonium.   The satanic hosts.
Lucifer.   The morning star; Satan.
Sammael.   A demon in rabbinical mythology.
Satan.   The chief of bad spirits.
Tempter.   One who entices to wrong.
The author of evil. }
The common enemy. } The devil.
The devil incarnate.   The devil in the flesh; the devil having a human body.
The arch fiend.   Satan.
The evil spirit.   The devil.
The foul fiend.   An evil spirit.
The wicked one.   The devil.
Zammiel.   See SAMMAEL.

SATAN—*Figurative Nouns.*

Old Gooseberry; old Harry; old Horny; old Nick; old Scratch; the deuce; the dickens; the old serpent; the prince of darkness; the prince of the devils; the prince of the powers of the air; the prince of the world; the powers of darkness; the rulers of darkness.

SATAN—*Nouns of Character*

Devilism. }
Diabolism. } Characteristic quality of Satan.

(Continued on Column 1)

Fold, etc.   See PLICATURE.
Fork.   The place where a division or divergence occurs; a crotch.
Obliquity, etc.   Deviation from a perpendicular or from a right line by any angle except a right angle, etc.   See PARALLELISM-INCLINATION.

ANGULARITY—*Denotations.*

Ankle; crane, a hoisting-machine, a siphon: **crutch; elbow; fluke,** the part of an anchor which catches hold on the bottom **groin; knee; knuckle; niche,** a recess, as in a wall; **nook oriel,** a window projecting outward from a wall and resting on a bracket, **recess; scythe; sickle; zigzag.**

ANGULARITY—*Scientific Terms.*

Acute angle.   An angle less than a right angle.
Altimetry.   The art of measuring vertical angular elevations.
Angle of 45°.   Half a right angle.
Angular distance.   The angle made at a given point by lines drawn to it from two objects.
Angular elevation.   In gunnery, the angle which the axis of the gun makes with the horizon.
Angular measurement.   Measurement in angles.
Angular velocity.   The rate at which an angle increases.
Clinometer.   An instrument for measuring angular inclination.
Cotangent.   A trigonometric function.
Cube.   A solid body bounded by six equal square sides.
Decagon.   A plane figure with ten angles and ten sides.
Diamond.   A figure bounded by four equal straight sides and having two of its interior angles acute and two obtuse.
Dichotomy.   Separation into two parts or branches; forking.
Dodecahedron.   A solid having twelve plane faces.
Goniometer.   An instrument for measuring angles.
Goniometry.   The art of measuring angles.
Graphometer.   Instrument used by surveyors in measuring angles.
Heptagon.   A plane figure having seven angles and seven sides.
Hexagon.   A plane figure having six angles and six sides.
Hexahedron.   A solid bounded by six plane faces.
Icosahedron.   A solid bounded by twenty plane faces.
Lozenge.   A parallelogram having its four sides equal and with two of its interior angles acute and two obtuse.
Miter.   The junction of two bodies upon a line bisecting the angle of junction, as at the corner of a picture frame.
Obtuse angle.   An angle greater than a right angle.
Octagon.   A plane figure having eight angles and eight sides.
Octahedron.   A solid bounded by eight plane faces.
Octant.   Eighth of a circle.
Parallelogram.   A quadrilateral whose opposite sides are parallel.
Parallelopiped.   A prism bounded by six faces, all parallelograms.
Pentagon.   A plane figure having five angles and five sides.
Pentahedron.   A solid bounded by five plane faces.

Platonic bodies. Five geometrical solids; the regular tetrahedron, the cube, the octahedron, the dodecahedron and the icosahedron.

Polygon. A plane figure having many angles and sides.

Prism. A solid whose bases are any similar, equal and parallel plane figures, and whose lateral faces are parallelograms.

Pyramid. A solid whose base is a polygon and whose lateral faces are triangles meeting at a point called the vertex.

Quadrangle. A plane figure having four angles and four sides.

Quadrant. An arc of ninety degrees.

Quadrature. The relative position of two heavenly bodies distant from each other ninety degrees as viewed from the center of a third body.

Quadrilateral. A plane figure bounded by four straight lines and having four angles.

Rectangle. A parallelogram having four right angles.

Reentering angle. An angle in a fortification, the vertex of which is turned towards the protected place.

Rhomb. A parallelogram having equal sides and oblique angles.

Rhomboid. A parallelogram having its opposite sides equal, but containing no right angle.

Right angle, etc. An angle whose sides are perpendicular to each other, etc. See ERECTNESS.

Salient angle. An angle in a fortification, the point of which is turned away from the protected place.

Sextant. An arc of sixty degrees. An instrument for measuring angular distances.

Spherical angle. An angle made by the intersection of two great circles, which mutually cut each other on the surface of a globe.

Square. A figure with four equal sides and four right angles.

Tetrahedron. A solid bounded by four triangles.

Theodolite. An instrument used for measuring horizontal and vertical angles.

Triangle. Plane figure having three sides and three angles.

Trigon. A triangle; the triangle of reference employed in trilinear coordinates.

Trigonometry. The branch of mathematics that treats of the relations of the sides and angles of triangles.

Wedge. A right triangular prism with one very acute angle.

ANGULARITY—*Verbs.*

Bend. Deflect from a straight line.

Bifurcate. Separate into two branches.

Crinkle. Form wrinkles, bends or folds.

Fork. Separate into diverging parts.

ANGULARITY—*Adjectives.*

Aduncous. Bent like a hook; hooked.

Akimbo. Having the hands on the hips and the elbows bent sharply outward.

Angular. Having an angle or angles; measured by an angle.

Aquiline. Hooked; curving.

Bent. Turned from a straight line.

Bifurcate. Forked.

Crinkled. Formed with folds, ridges or wrinkles.

Crooked. Having angles; not straight.

Cubical. Having the shape or properties of a cube.

Cuneiform. Wedge-shaped.

Dovetailed. Interlocked by wedge-shaped tenons and spaces.

Falcated. Sickle-shaped; scythe-shaped.

Falciform. Falcate; having the shape of a scythe or sickle.

Forked. Divided into diverging parts like a fork.

Furcated. Forked.

Fusiform. Spindle-shaped; tapering at each end.

Geniculated. Having knee-like joints.

Jagged. Having ragged edges or notches.

Kimbo. Crooked; bent.

Knock-kneed. Having the knees bent inward.

Multilateral. Having many sides and consequently many angles.

Oblique, etc. Neither parallel to, nor at right angles from the base.

Polygonal, etc. Having many angles, etc. See *Nouns.*

Pyramidal. Of or like a pyramid.

Quadrangular. Having four angles.

Quadrilateral. Formed by four sides and having four angles.

Rectangular. Having one or more right angles.

Rhomboidal. Having the shape of a rhomboid.

Scalene. Having no two sides equal, said of triangles.

Serrated. Notched along the edge like a saw.

Square. Having four right angles and four equal sides.

Triangular. Having three angles and three sides; bounded by a triangle.

Trigonal. Having three angles; three-cornered.

Trilateral. Having three sides.

Uncinated. Hooked.

Wedge-shaped. Having the shape of a wedge.

Zigzag. Having short turns or angles alternating in a series from side to side.

---

an'-gu-lar-ness. State of being angular. ANGULARITY.

angusta res domi [L.] (an-gus'-ta rîz do'-mai). In difficult circumstances. AFFLUENCE-PENURY.

an''-gus-ta'-tion. Contraction. BREADTH-NARROW-NESS.

an''-he-la'-tion. Shortness of breath. WEARINESS-REFRESHMENT.

an-hy'-drous. Waterless. DAMPNESS-DRYNESS.

an'-ile. Like an old woman. INFANCY-AGE, SAGACITY-INCAPACITY.

an'-i-line. A colorless oily compound. **Aniline dyes,** YELLOWNESS-PURPLE.

a-nil'-i-ty. Old-womanishness. INFANCY-AGE, SAGACITY-INCAPACITY.

an''-i-mad-ver'-sion. Criticism. APPROVAL-DISAPPROVAL.

an''-i-mad-vert'. To observe; to censure. APPROVAL-DISAPPROVAL, HEED-DISREGARD, REFLECTION-VACANCY.

an'-i-mal. A sentient living being; pertaining to an animal. FAUNA-FLORA; **animal cries,** CRY-ULULATION; **animal economy,** LIFE-DEATH; **animal gratification,** SENSUALITY-SUFFERING; **animal life,** ANIMALITY-VEGETABILITY; **animal physiology,** ZOOLOGY-BOTANY; **animal spirits,** LIGHTHEARTEDNESS-DEJECTION.

an''-i-mal'-cule. An animal of microscopic smallness. FAUNA-FLORA, GREATNESS-LITTLENESS, MAGNITUDE-SMALLNESS.

an'-i-mal-ism. State of mere animals. MODERATION-SELFINDULGENCE.

an''-i-mal'-i-ty. Nature of an animal. ANIMALITY-VEGETABILITY.

ANIMALITY—VEGETABILITY.

Animality. The nature or state of an animal.

Animalization. The act of endowing with the properties of an animal

Animal life. The potential force, or principle by which the organs of animals are started and continued in the performance of their functions.

Animation. The act of giving life or spirit.

Breath. Air inhaled or exhaled during respiration.

Flesh. The softer tissues of an animal body.

Flesh and blood. Animal nature.

Physique [F.] The physical structure of persons or animals.

Strength. Physical vigor. See STRENGTH.

an''-i-mal-i-za'-tion. Act of making animals. ANIMALITY-VEGETABILITY.

an'-i-mate. To impart life to. EXCITATION, LIGHTHEARTEDNESS-DEJECTION, MOTIVE-CAPRICE.

Vegetable life. The principle by which plant organs are started and continued in their functions.

Vegetability. The quality or state of being vegetable.

Vegetation. The act of growing as a plant does.

VEGETABILITY—*Adjectives.*

Lush. Full of juice.

Rank. Luxuriant in growth.

ANIMALITY—*Continued.*

ANIMALITY—*Adjective.*

Fleshly. Pertaining to the animal nature; corporeal; carnal.

an'-i-ma''-ted. Enlivened. ACTIVITY-INDOLENCE, LIFE-DEATH, LIGHTHEARTEDNESS-DEJECTION.

an''-i-ma'-tion. State of possessing life; liveliness. ACTIVITY-INDOLENCE, ANIMALITY-VEGETABILITY, Ex-

CITATION, LIFE-DEATH, LIGHTHEARTEDNESS-DEJECTION; **suspended animation,** SENSITIVENESS-APATHY.

animo, ex [L.] (an'-i-mo, ex). Readily. READINESS-RELUCTANCE.

animo, quo [L.] (an'-i-mo, quo). With what intention. PURPOSE-LUCK.

an''-i-mos'-i-ty. Hatred. AMITY-HOSTILITY, DESIRE-DISTASTE, FAVORITE-ANGER, LOVE-HATE.

an'-i-mus. The animating thought. DESIRE-DISTASTE, PURPOSE-LUCK, READINESS-RELUCTANCE.

an'-i-on. The electro-negative constituent of a decomposed substance, appearing at the anode. ELECTRICITY.

an'-kle. Joint connecting the foot and leg. ANATOMY, ANGULARITY; **ankle-deep,** DEEPNESS-SHALLOWNESS.

an'-klet. An ornamental ring for the ankle. EMBELLISHMENT-DISFIGUREMENT.

an'-nal-ist. A historian. CHRONOLOGY-ANACHRONISM, RECORDER.

an'-nals. Record of events. ACCOUNT, CHRONOLOGY-ANACHRONISM, MARK-OBLITERATION.

an-neal'. To reduce the brittleness of. PREPARATION-NONPREPARATION.

an-nex'. To join. ADDITION-SUBTRACTION, UNION-DISUNION.

an''-nex-a'-tion. An adding to. ADDITION-SUBTRACTION, UNION-DISUNION.

annexe [F.] (an-nex'). That which is added. INCREMENT-REMNANT.

an-nex'-ion. Construct relation. UNION-DISUNION.

an-ni'-hi-late. To put out of existence. CREATION-DESTRUCTION, SUBSTANCE-NULLITY.

an-ni''-hi-la'-ted. Destroyed. SUBSTANCE-NULLITY.

an-ni''-hi-la'-tion. Destruction. CREATION-DESTRUCTION, SUBSTANCE-NULLITY.

an''-ni-ver'-sa-ry. Annual celebration of some event. PERIODICITY-IRREGULARITY.

anno [L.] (an'-no). In the year. DURATION-NEVERNESS.

an'-no-tate. To supply with comments. INTERPRETATION-MISINTERPRETATION.

an''-no-ta'-tion. Act of making notes; comments. INTERPRETATION-MISINTERPRETATION, SIGN.

an'-no-ta'-tor. A commentator. INTERPRETER.

an-not'-to. A yellowish-red dye. REDNESS-GREENNESS.

an-nounce'. To proclaim publicly. ASSERTION-DENIAL, ENLIGHTENMENT-SECRECY, PROPHECY, PUBLICITY.

an-nounce'-ment. Publication. ENLIGHTENMENT-SECRECY, PREVISION, PUBLICITY.

an-noy'. To be troublesome to. CHARITABLENESS-MALEVOLENCE, GOODNESS-BADNESS, PLEASURABLENESS-PAINFULNESS.

an-noy'-ance. That which causes trouble. GOODNESS-BADNESS, LOVE-HATE, PLEASURABLENESS-PAINFULNESS, PLEASURE-PAIN; **source of annoyance,** PLEASURABLENESS-PAINFULNESS.

an'-nu-al. Yearly; a book issued yearly. FAUNA-FLORA, MISSIVE-PUBLICATION, PERIODICITY-IRREGULARITY.

an-nu'-i-ty. An annual income. OUTLAY-INCOME.

an-nul'. To render void. COMMISSION-ABROGATION, CREATION-DESTRUCTION.

an-nul'-ment. A making void. COMMISSION-ABROGATION.

an'-nu-lar. Ring-shaped. CIRCLE-WINDING.

an'-nu-let. A small ring. ARCHITECTURE, CIRCLE-WINDING.

an'-nu-lus. A ring. CIRCLE-WINDING.

an-nun'-ci-ate. To make known publicly. ENLIGHTENMENT-SECRECY.

an-nun'-ci-a'-tion. A proclamation. ENLIGHTENMENT-SECRECY.

annus magnus [L.] (an'-nus mag'-nus). The time in which the constellations return to the same place. PERIOD-PROGRESS.

an'-ode. The positive voltaic pole of a galvanic battery. ELECTRICITY.

an'-o-dyne. Anything that relieves pain, or calms the feelings. ALLEVIATION-AGGRAVATION, REMEDY-BANE, TURBULENCE-CALMNESS.

an-oint'. To pour oil upon in sign of consecration. COVER-LINING, FRICTION-LUBRICATION, PULPINESS-OILINESS.

an-oint'-ed. A consecrated person. CHIEF-UNDERLING, DIVINITY.

an-oint'-ment. Consecration. FRICTION-LUBRICATION, PULPINESS-OILINESS.

a-nom''-a-lis'-tic. Irregular. ASTRONOMY, CONVENTIONALITY-UNCONVENTIONALITY.

a-nom'-a-lous. Exceptional. CONVENTIONALITY-UNCONVENTIONALITY, REGULARITY-IRREGULARITY.

a-nom'-a-lous-ness. State of being anomalous. CONVENTIONALITY-UNCONVENTIONALITY.

a-nom'-a-ly. Irregularity. ASTRONOMY, CONVENTIONALITY-UNCONVENTIONALITY, REGULARITY-IRREGULARITY.

a-non'. Soon. EARLINESS-LATENESS.

a-non'-y-mous. Not disclosing a name. NAME-MISNOMER.

an'-o-rex-y. Loss of appetite. DESIRE-DISTASTE.

an-oth'-er. Not the same. RECURRENCE, VARIATION; **another time,** TIME; **go upon another tack,** BIGOTRY-APOSTASY; **tell another story,** EVIDENCE-COUNTEREVIDENCE.

an'-swer. To make reply to. GAIN-LOSS, INTERPRETATION-MISINTERPRETATION, INVESTIGATION-ANSWER, LITIGATION, PROOF-DISPROOF, SUCCESS-FAILURE; **answer for,** CREDIT-DEBT, ENGAGEMENT-RELEASE, REPRESENTATIVE; **answer one's turn,** USEFULNESS-USELESSNESS; **answer the helm,** INSUBORDINATION-OBEDIENCE; **answer the purpose,** SUCCESS-FAILURE; **answer to,** CONNECTION-INDEPENDENCE; **I'll answer for it,** ASSERTION-DENIAL; **require an answer,** INVESTIGATION-ANSWER.

an'-swer-a-ble. Liable to be called to account. APPROVAL-DISAPPROVAL, CREDIT-DEBT, DUTY-DERELICTION.

an'-swer-ing. Replying. INVESTIGATION-ANSWER.

ant. An insect. AGENT.

an'-tæ. Pilasters opposite one another. ARCHITECTURE.

An-tæ'-us. A mythological giant. GREATNESS-LITTLENESS, STRENGTH-WEAKNESS.

an-tag'-o-nism. Mutual opposition. ANTAGONISM-CONCURRENCE, COOPERATION-OPPOSITION, SAMENESS-CONTRAST.

ANTAGONISM—CONCURRENCE.

Absence of aid. Lack of help. See OBSTRUCTION-HELP.

Antagonism. Opposition of action.

Clashing. Opposition of views, interests, or purposes.

Collision. A state of opposition.

Competition. Common strife for the same object.

Conflict. A strife for the mastery.

Contravention. A meeting in the way of opposition.

Counteraction. Action in opposition. See COOPERATION-OPPOSITION.

Alliance. A union or connection of interests.

A long pull, a strong pull and a pull all together.

Association. State of being united for a common purpose.

Clanship. State of being united together as a clan.

Coadjutancy. } Joint help.
Coadjuvancy. }

Coagency. State of working together.

Coalition. A voluntary union for the support of some common policy or action.

ANTAGONISM—CONCURRENCE—*Continued.*

Counterplot. A plot or artifice opposed to another.
Crossfire. Lines of fire from two or more points; hence, a dangerous obstruction.
Emulation. Zealous rivalry.
Head wind. A contrary or opposing wind; hence, an obstruction or hindrance.
Hindrance. Anything that prevents movement or action.
Impugnation. Act of attacking by words or arguments.
Opposition. An attempt to check, restrain or defeat.
Oppugnancy. Act of being in conflict with.
Oppugnation. Opposition.
Race. A trial of speed, strength, etc.
Resistance. Act of opposing or striving against.
Restraint. See RELEASE-RESTRAINT.
Rivalry. The state of being in competition with.
Two of a trade. Rivals.
Undercurrent. A hidden obstruction, or secret antagonism.

ANTAGONISM—*Verbs.*

Antagonize. To contend or struggle with.
Belie. To contradict.
Breast. To encounter or oppose.
Confront. To stand up against.
Contradict. To deny or oppose in speech.
Contravene. To obstruct or prevent action.
Control, etc. To hold in power or check. See RELEASE-RESTRAINT.
Counteract. To work in opposition.
Countermine. To obstruct the work of another secretly.
Counterwork. To work against.
Disfavor. To disapprove.
Emulate. To strive to excel. See STRIFE.
Encounter. To come against face to face.
Face. To meet for the purpose of stopping.
Hinder. To prevent movement or action.
Oppose. To act against.
Oppugn. To fight against.
Overthwart. To cross; to oppose.
Rival. To strive with another to excel.
Stem. To resist or make progress against.
Thwart. To run counter to.
Withstand. To stand against. See REPRISAL-RESISTANCE.

ANTAGONISM—*Verbal Expressions.*

Beat against; be at cross purposes; beat up against; breast the current; breast the flood; breast the tide; buffet the waves; come in conflict with; contend against; contend with; cope with; do battle against; do battle with; fall foul of; fly in the face of; go against; go dead against; grapple with; kick against; kick against the pricks; make a dead set; make a stand against; make head against; militate against; pit against; pitch against; play at cross purposes; raise one's voice against; run against; run counter to; set against; set at naught; set oneself against; set one's face against; slam the door in one's face; slap in the face; spoil one's trade; stem the current; stem the flood; stem the tide; turn one's back upon; vote against.

ANTAGONISM—*Adjectives.*

Adverse. Opposed or opposing.
Antagonistic. Working against each other.
At daggers drawn. In hostile state.
At issue. In dispute.
At variance. Not in agreement.
At war with. Contending against.
Competitive. Characterized by rivalry.
Contrary. In opposition to. See SAMENESS-CONTRAST.
Cross. Adverse to.
Emulous. Eager to excel another.
Front to front. Directly opposing.
Hostile. Showing the disposition of an enemy.
In hostile array. Ready for combat.
Inimical. At enmity with.
Opposed. } Working against. See *Verbs.*
Opposing. }
Resistant. In an opposing manner. See REPRISAL-RESISTANCE.
Unfavorable. Contrary; discouraging.
Unfriendly. Not adapted to promote or support any object.
Unpropitious. Not favorable.
Up in arms. In active opposition.
With crossed bayonets. In conflict.

ANTAGONISM—*Particles, Phrases*

Across. Over against.
Against. In opposition to

Coefficiency. The cooperation of two or more parties or forces for the attainment of some end.
Colleagueship. Partnership in office.
Collusion. Secret cooperation for some fraudulent purpose.
Combination. A union. See COMPOSITION.
Complicity. State of being an accomplice.
Concert. Combination of forces or powers.
Concord, etc. Union of feeling. See VARIANCE-ACCORD.
Concurrence. Agreement or consent, implying aid or contribution.
Confederation, etc. A combination for mutual advantage or benefit. See ASSOCIATION. A league among states.
Cooperation. Act of working together to accomplish some end.
Copartnership. State of having a joint interest in anything.
Esprit de corps [F.]. The common spirit pervading the members of an association.
Freemasonry. The practises of Freemasons.
Joint stock. Held in company.
Log rolling. A joining together of politicians to promote each other's schemes.
Participation. Act of sharing in common with others.
Partizanship. Feelings or conduct appropriate to a partizan.
Party spirit. The spirit or temper which binds men together in support of a common cause.
Unanimity. Quality of being of one mind. See ASSENT.
Union, etc. A cooperation. See UNION.

CONCURRENCE—*Verbs.*

Collude. To work together secretly.
Combine. To unite for the attainment of a common object.
Concert. To act together or agree.
Concur. To agree.
Conduce. To help to bring about. See COOPERATION.
Confederate. To associate or unite; to league together.
Conspire. To work together secretly, usually for some evil purpose.
Cooperate. To work together for some common purpose.
Fraternize. To unite in fellowship; to act as brothers.
Participate. To take part in.
Second, etc. To attend for the purpose of assisting. See OBSTRUCTION-HELP.

CONCURRENCE—*Verbal Expressions.*

Act in concert; band together; be a party to; bear part in; be banded together; be in league with; be in the same boat; cast in one's lot with; cling to one another; club together; come into the views of; come to; draw together; enter into partnership; espouse a cause; espouse a quarrel; follow the lead of; go along; go hand in hand; hang together; have a finger in the pie; have a hand in the pie; hold together; hunt in couples; join forces; join hands; join partnership with; keep together; lay one's heads together; league together; lend oneself to; make common cause with; mix oneself up with; pass over to; play into the hands of; play the game of; pull together; put shoulder to shoulder; rally round; row in the same boat; sail in the same boat; sail on the same tack; side with; stand shoulder to shoulder; strike in with; take part in; take part with; take sides with; take the part of; understand one another; unite one's efforts; unite with.

CONCURRENCE—*Adjectives.*

Coadjutant. } Working together.
Coadjuvant. }
Cooperating, etc. See *Verbs.*
Favorable to, etc. See OBSTRUCTION-HELP.
In cooperation, etc. See *Nouns.*
In league, etc. See ASSOCIATION.
Unopposed, etc. See ANTAGONISM.

CONCURRENCE—*Adverbs.*

As one man, etc. Unanimously. See ASSENT.
Shoulder to shoulder. In union of power.

ANTAGONISM—PARTICLES. PHRASES—*Continued.*

Against the current.
Against the grain.
Against the stream. } See *Verbs.*
Against the tide.
Against the wind.
At cross purposes. See *Verbs.*
Athwart. Lying across one's path.
Counter to. In opposition to.
Even. Yet.

ANTAGONISM—Particles, Phrases—*Continued*.

In conflict with.
In defiance. } Notwithstanding.
In despite. }
In spite.
In spite of one's teeth.   Against the strongest opposition.
In the face of.
In the teeth of.
In the way of.
Overthwart.   Over against.

Per contra [L.].   Contrary to.
Quand même [F.].   Notwithstanding.
Though.   Notwithstanding that.
Versus [L.].   Against.
Where the shoe pinches.
With a head wind.
With a wind ahead.
With the wind in one's teeth.

ANTAGONISM—*Phrase*.

Nitor in adversum [L.].   I struggle against adverse circumstances.

an-tag'-o-nist.   One who contends against another.   ANTAGONIST-ASSISTANT.

ANTAGONIST—ASSISTANT.

Adversary.   One who is turned against another with the design to oppose or resist.
Adverse party.   A person acting against or in a contrary direction to another.
Antagonist.   One who contends with another in combat.
Assailant.   One who attacks or assaults.
Brangler.   A quarrelsome person.
Brawler.   One who quarrels noisily and outrageously.
Competitor.   One who strives with another in order to excel.
Demagogue.   One who opposes prevailing rule to win popular favor.
Disputant.   One who argues in opposition to.
Enemy.   One who hates, and desires or attempts the injury of another. See FRIEND.
Fenian.   A member of a secret Irish organization having for its aim the overthrow of English rule in Ireland; hence, a plotter against existing rule.
Jacobin.   One of a society of violent agitators in France, during the revolution of 1789; hence, a plotter against existing government.
Malcontent.   A discontented subject of a government.
Obstructive.   One who opposes or delays.
Opponent.   One who opposes in an argument or combat.
Opposition.   A party opposed to a party in power.
Oppositionist.   One who belongs to an opposition party.
Reactionist.   One who opposes and seeks to undo political progress.
Rival.   One striving to reach or attain something which another is attempting to obtain.
Wrangler.   One who disputes noisily and angrily: an honor-man at a university.

ASSISTANT—*Continued from Column* 2.

Upholder.   One who sustains or defends a person or cause.
Votary.   One who is devoted or consecrated to a special service.

ASSISTANT—*Associated Nouns*.

Alter ego [L.].   Another self; hence, a very dear friend.
Ame damnée [F.].   An instrument or tool of another person.
Candle-holder.   One who holds a candle; hence, an assistant of little importance.
Catspaw.   One who is used by another as an instrument to accomplish his purpose.
Deus ex machina [L.].   A god let down by a machine; an interference.
Fidus Achates [L.].   Faithful Achates; hence, a devoted friend.
Guardian angel.   The deity that watches over a person; hence, a protector.
Jackal.   An animal supposed to kill game for other animals; hence, one who does work for another's advantage.
Jack at a pinch.   A person who takes the place of another in an emergency.
Particeps criminis [L.].   A companion in crime.
Puppet.   A figure moved by a wire in a play; hence, one controlled in his actions by the will of another.
Right hand.   A necessary assistant.
Satellite.   A secondary planet which revolves about another; hence, an attendant attached to a person of power.
Tool.   An instrument; hence, a person used as an instrument by another person.
Tutelary genius.   A protective spirit; hence, a person who protects or defends another.

an-tag''-o-nis'-tic.   Opposed.   ANTAGONISM-CONCURRENCE, COOPERATION-OPPOSITION, SAMENESS-CONTRAST.

Abettor.   One who incites or encourages to an act without taking part in its accomplishment.
Accessory.   One who accompanies as a subordinate, or aids in a secondary way.
Accessory after the fact.   A person who knowing a crime to have been committed receives or assists the criminal.
Accomplice.   One who cooperates or helps, especially in wrongdoing.
Adherent.   One who is attached to or follows a person or party.
Adjunct.   A person associated with another person in an auxiliary or subordinate relation.
Adjutant.   An officer who assists a commander.
Adjuvant.   A helper.
Advocate.   One who pleads the cause of another.
Aide-de-camp.   An officer who serves a general.
Ally.   A person connected with another in some relation of helpfulness.
Assistant.   One regularly associated with another as a helper.
Associate.   One who is joined with another in business, etc.
Auxiliary.   One who aids or helps.
Backer.   One who upholds by aid of money or influence.
Bottle-holder.   One who attends a pugilist in a prize fight.
Champion.   One who defends or upholds any person or cause.
Clerk.   A hired assistant in an office.
Coadjutor.   An associate in action.
Coadjutrix.   A female assistant.
Collaborator.   One who is associated with another, especially in literary or scientific pursuits.
Colleague.   An associate in a board, commission, or professional employment.
Complice.   See ACCOMPLICE.
Confederate.   One who is united with others in a league or agreement.
Confidant.   One to whom secrets are entrusted.
Confrère [F.].   A fellow-member of an organization.
Cooperator.   One who aids or works with another.
Friend, etc.   See FRIEND.
Friend at court.   A friend who has influence.
Friend in need.
Handmaid.   A female servant.
Help.
Helper.   } One who gives help or aid; one hired to do the work
Helping hand.   } of another.
Helpmate.
Marshal.   An officer who assists a commander.
Mate.   A companion or associate.
Mediator.   Any agent that stands or goes between.
Midwife.   A woman who assists at childbirth.
Pal.   An associate in crime.
Partizan.   A person blindly or passionately attached to a person or party.
Partner.   An associate in business.
Patron.   One who protects or supports a person.
Recruit.   One who has recently enlisted in a cause.
Seconder.   An attendant who supports or aids another.
Secretary.   One who attends to correspondence or does writing for another.
Sectarian. } An adherent or supporter of a particular sect or school.
Sectary. }
Servant, etc.   See CHIEF-UNDERLING.

(Continued on Column 1.)

an-tag'-o-nize.   To oppose.   ANTAGONISM-CONCURRENCE, COOPERATION-OPPOSITION, SAMENESS-CONTRAST.

ant-arc′-tic. Opposed to arctic LATERALITY-CONTRA-POSITION.

Antecedence. The state of going before in time
Anteriority. The state of being prior in time.
Precedence. The state of being before.
Precession, etc. The act of going before, etc. See LEADING
Preexistence. Existence prior to something.
Priority. The condition of being antecedent.
The past, etc. See FUTURE-PAST.

ANTECEDENCE—*Associated Words*

Precursor. One who goes before.
Premises. The first two propositions of a syllogism.

ANTECEDENCE—*Verbs.*

Anticipate. To take beforehand; to foresee.
Be beforehand, etc. See EARLINESS.
Come before.
Dawn. To begin to grow light.
Forerun. To go in advance of.
Forestall. To anticipate.
Gain the start.
Go before, etc. }See LEADING.
Have the start.
Precede. To go before.
Preexist. To exist previous to something else.
Presage, etc. To foreknow, etc. See PROPHECY.
Steal a march upon. To get ahead of.

ANTECEDENCE—*Adjectives.*

Above-mentioned. Spoken of before.
Aforesaid. Said before.
Antecedent. Going before in time.
Anterior. Prior in time.
Before-mentioned. Named before.
Foregoing. Coming before.
Former. Going before in time.
Introductory, etc. Serving to introduce, etc. See PREDECESSOR.
Precedent. Going before.
Preceding. See *Verbs.*
Preexistent. Existing before something else.
Preexisting. See *Verbs.*
Previous. Taking place before something else.
Prior. Preceding in time.
Said. Previously mentioned.

ANTECEDENCE—*Adverbs.*

Afore. Before.
Already. Previously.
Before. In advance.
Beforehand. By way of preparation.
Before now.
Before then.
Earlier. More timely; before.
Ere. Earlier or sooner than.
Ere now. Before now.
Ere then. Before then.
Erewhile. Some time ago.

an″-te-ce′-den-cy. Precedence. PRECEDENCE-SUCCESSION.
an″-te-ce′-dent. Occurring or going before. ANTECEDENCE-SEQUENCE, PRECEDENCE-SUCCESSION, PREDECESSOR-CONTINUATION.
an′-te-cham″-ber. A waiting room. CONTENTS-RECEIVER.
ante Christum [L.] (an′-tî kris′-tum). Before Christ. DURATION-NEVERNESS.
an′-te-date. An earlier date. CHRONOLOGY-ANACHRONISM.
an″-te-di-lu′-vi-an. Before the flood. NOVELTY-ANTIQUITY.

an″-te-ce′-dence. Act of going before. ANTECEDENCE-SEQUENCE, PRECEDENCE-SUCCESSION.

ANTECEDENCE—SEQUENCE.

Following, etc Act of coming after. See LEADING-FOLLOWING
Futurity, etc. Time to come, etc. See FUTURE.
Posteriority. State of being later.
Remainder. That which is left over.
Reversion. A return to or toward some former state or condition.
Sequel, etc. A following part, continuation, etc. See PREDECESSOR-CONTINUATION.
Sequence. The state of following; that which follows as a result
Subsequence. The state of following.
Succession. The act of succeeding or following in order.
Successor. One who or that which succeeds or follows a predecessor.
Supervention. The act or state of following close upon something

SEQUENCE—*Verbs.*

Come after.
Follow, etc. To succeed in order or in time. See LEADING-FOLLOWING.
Follow after.
Go after.
Step into the shoes of. To take the place of.
Succeed. To follow in proper order.
Supervene. To follow closely upon.

SEQUENCE—*Adjectives.*

After. Later in time.
After-dinner. Post-prandial.
Following. See *Verbs.*
Future, etc. Pertaining to time to come, etc. See FUTURE
Later. Longer delayed.
Postdiluvial. }Happening since Noah's flood.
Postdiluvian.
Posterior. Later in time or place.
Posthumous. Born after the father's death; published after the death of the author.
Postliminious. Done subsequently.
Postnate. Subsequent.
Subsequent. Coming after in time or in order of place.
Succeeding. See *Verbs.*

SEQUENCE—*Adverbs.*

After; after a time; after a while; afterwards; at a later period; at a subsequent period; close upon; eftsoons; from that moment; from that time; in the process of time; in the sequel; later; next; since; subsequently; thereafter; thereupon; upon which.

ANTECEDENCE—ADVERBS—*Continued.*

On the eve of. Just before.
Previously. See *Adjectives.*
Prior to. Before.
Theretofore. Up to that time
Yet. Until now.

ANTECEDENCE—*Phrase.*

Prior tempore, prior jure [L.]. First in time, first in right, 'first come, first served."

an′-te-lope. An animal allied to the deer and goat. SWIFTNESS-SLOWNESS.
an″-te-mun′-dane. Occurring before the existence of the world. NOVELTY-ANTIQUITY.
an-ten′-na. An appendage of the head of an insect. TOUCH.
an″-te-po-si′-tion. The placing of a word before another. PRECEDENCE-SUCCESSION.
an-te′-ri-or. Earlier; before. ANTECEDENCE-SEQUENCE, ANTERIORITY-POSTERIORITY, PRECEDENCE-SUCCESSION; anterior to reason, RATIOCINATION-INSTINCT.
an-te″-ri-or′-i-ty. Precedence in time, order, or place. ANTECEDENCE-SEQUENCE, ANTERIORITY-POSTERIORITY, PRECEDENCE-SUCCESSION.

ANTERIORITY—POSTERIORITY.

Anteriority. The state or condition of preceding in time or in situation.
Face. Side of an object presented to view.
Fore. That which is in front

After-part. That which forms the back of anything.
Back. Part of an object turned away from its front.
Background. The part of a scene which is behind the principal object of a picture.

ANTERIORITY—POSTERIORITY—*Continued.*

Forepart. The part most advanced, or first in time or place.
Front. The surface which seems to look out or be directed forward.
Frontage. Extent of front.

ANTERIORITY—*Denotations.*

Advanced guard. A body of troops which precedes the march of the main body.
Beak. Anything projecting or ending in a point, as the bill of a bird.
Bow. The forward part of a ship.
Brow. The forehead.
Countenance. The face
Disc. }
Disk. } A projecting, circular part of anything.
Face. The front of a building.
Fascia. A band about a column or pillar.
Foreground. The part of a scene represented which is nearest to the spectator.
Forehead. The front part of the head.
Forerank. The first rank.
Frontispiece. An ornamental picture fronting the first page of a book.
Frontrank. The first rank.
Mug. A slang expression for face.
Obverse. One side of a medal.
Outpost. A guard in front of an army.
Phiz. The face
Physiognomy. The outline of features.
Prore. }
Prow. } The fore part of a ship.
Rostrum. The beak or head of a ship.
Stem. A piece of timber to which the two sides of a ship are united at the fore.
Van. The advance of a moving body.
Vanguard. An advanced body of troops.
Visage. The face.

ANTERIORITY—*Associated Word.*

Metoposcopy. The study of the features of a person to discover character.

ANTERIORITY—*Verbs.*

Confront. To stand face to face.
Face. To meet front to front.
Front. To have the front towards.

ANTERIORITY—*Verbal Expressions.*

Be in front; bend forwards; come to the fore; come to the front; go to the front; stand in front; stand in the face of.

ANTERIORITY—*Adjectives.*

Anterior. Preceding in time or place.
Fore. At the front.
Frontal. Pertaining to the front; usually of the head.

ANTERIORITY—*Adverbs.*

Ahead; before; before one's eyes; before one's face; face to face; foremost; headmost; in advance; in the front; in the foreground; in the lee of; in the van; right ahead.

ANTERIORITY—*Phrases.*

Front à front [F.] Front to front.
Vis-à-vis [F.] Face to face.

Backside. The hinder part.
Posteriority. State of being in the rear or behind.
Rear. The last part of an object.
Reverse. The back or rear as distinguished from the front.

POSTERIORITY—*Denotations.*

Breech. Part of a gun or cannon behind the closed end of the bore.
Buttock. The posterior and lower part of the body.
Chine. The back, or back-bone of an animal.
Croup. Portion of a horse's back behind the saddle.
Crupper. The croup.
Dorsal region. The back.
Dorsum. The back.
Heel. The posterior part of the foot.
Heel-piece. Part of a stocking which encloses the heel.
Loins. Part of the body between the lower rib and the hip-bone
Lumbar region. The region of the loins.
Nape. The back of the neck.
Occiput. The lower back part of the head.
Other side of the shield.
Poop. The stern of a vessel.
Posteriors. The hinder parts of men and animals.
Rear guard. }
Rear rank. } The last part of a marching body.
Rump. The hinder parts of an animal.
Scut. A short tail.
Stern. The back part of a ship
Tail. The hindermost part of an animal.
Train. That which is drawn along behind.
Wake. Course over which anything has passed.

POSTERIORITY—*Verbal Phrases.*

Be behind; be in the rear; bend backwards; bring up the rear; fall astern.

POSTERIORITY—*Adjectives*

After. Coming behind.
Back. Behind.
Caudal. Pertaining to the tail of an animal.
Dorsal. Of, or pertaining to the back.
Hind. }
Hinder. } Pertaining to the rear part.
Hindermost. }
Hindmost. } Farthest back.
Lumbar. Pertaining to the loins.
Posterior. Back or behind.
Postern. Rear
Rear. Behind.

POSTERIORITY—*Adverbs.*

Aback. Backwards.
Abaft. At the stern of a ship.
Aft. In the direction of the stern.
After. Coming behind.
Astern. Behind the stern.
Behind. To the rear of.
Rearward. Toward the back.
Sternmost. Farthest behind.

POSTERIORITY—*Adverbial Expressions.*

At the back of; at the heels of; at the tail of; back to back; behind one's back; in the background; in the rear.

POSTERIORITY—*Phrase.*

Ogni medaglia ha il suo rovescio [It.] Every medal has its reverse.

---

an'-te-room. A waiting-room. CONTENTS-RECEIVER.
an''-te-vert'. To tip forward. OBSTRUCTION-HELP.
an'-them. A musical composition. DEVOTION-IDOLATRY.
an-the'-mi-on. The honeysuckle pattern in decorative designs. EMBELLISHMENT-DISFIGUREMENT.
an-thol'-o-gy. A collection of extracts from various authors. DIGEST, POETRY-PROSE.
an'-thra-cite. Hard mineral coal. COMBUSTIBLE.
an-throp'-ic. Human. MALE-FEMALE.
an''-thro-pog'-e-ny. The science of man. HUMANITY.
an''-thro-pog'-ra-phy. Descriptive anthropology. ETHNOLOGY, HUMANITY

an'-thro-poid. Manlike. HUMANITY.
an''-thro-po-log'-ic-al. Pertaining to man in any aspect. ETHNOLOGY.
an''-thro-pol'-o-gist. A student of anthropology. ETHNOLOGY.
an'-thro-pol-o-gy. The science of man. ETHNOLOGY, HUMANITY, ZOOLOGY-BOTANY.
an'-thro-po-man''-cy. Divination by inspection of human entrails. PROPHECY.
an''-thro-poph'-a-gi. Eater of human flesh. BENEFACTOR-EVILDOER.
an''-thro-poph'-a-gist. A cannibal. BENEFACTOR-EVILDOER.

an″-thro-po-pho′-bi-a. Unreasonable aversion to society. SOCIABILITY-PRIVACY.

an″-thro-pos′-co-py. Art of determining a man's character from physical features. PROPHECY.

an″-thro-pos′-o-phy. Wisdom about man. ETHNOLOGY, HUMANITY.

an′-tic. A funny action. ENTERTAINMENT-WEARINESS.

antichambre [F.] (an′-ti-shan·br′). An antechamber. *faire antichambre* (fêr an′-ti-shan·br′). To dance attendance. EARLINESS-LATENESS.

An′-ti-christ. A false Christ. ORTHODOXY-HETERODOXY.

an″-ti-chris′-tian. Opposed to Christ or Christianity. GODLINESS-DISBELIEF, ORTHODOXY-HETERODOXY.

an″-ti-chris″-ti-an′-i-ty. Anything antichristian. GODLINESS-DISBELIEF.

an-tich′-ro-nism. Deviation from the true order of time. CHRONOLOGY-ANACHRONISM.

an-tic′-i-pate. To foresee; to look forward to; to act sooner than. ANTECEDENCE-SEQUENCE, CHRONOLOGY-ANACHRONISM, EARLINESS-LATENESS, EXPECTATION-SURPRISE, FUTURE-PAST, PREPARATION-NONPREPARATION, SANGUINENESS-HOPELESSNESS.

an-tic″-i-pa′-tion. Act of anticipating. CHRONOLOGY-ANACHRONISM, EARLINESS-LATENESS, EXPECTATION-SURPRISE, PREPARATION-NONPREPARATION, SANGUINENESS-HOPELESSNESS.

an-tic′-i-pa-to-ry. Anticipating. EARLINESS-LATENESS.

an″-ti-cli′-max. A sudden descent; decrease in the importance of what is said. ADAGE-NONSENSE, INCREASE-DECREASE, SOCIETY-LUDICROUSNESS.

an-ti-cli′-nal. Forming a bend with the convex side upward. PARALLELISM-INCLINATION.

an″-ti-cline′. Strata dipping in opposite directions. GEOLOGY.

an′-ti-dote. Anything that will counteract the effects of poison. REMEDY-BANE.

an″-ti-grop′-e-los. Water-proof leggings. DRESS-UNDRESS.

an″-ti-he″-lix. The round ridge of the inner ear. ANATOMY.

an″-ti-log′-a-rithm. The number corresponding to a given logarithm. NUMBER.

an-til′-o-gy. Self-contradiction. RATIOCINATION-CASUISTRY.

an′-ti-mo-ny. A silver-white metallic element, largely used in medicine. REMEDY-BANE.

an″-ti-no′-mi-an. Pertaining to the doctrine that faith frees the man from the claims of the moral law. ORTHODOXY-HETERODOXY.

an-tin′-o-my. Self-contradiction in law. LAW-LAWLESSNESS.

An-tin′-o-us. A part of the constellation Aquila, named after a handsome page of the Emperor Hadrian. BEAUTY-UGLINESS.

an″-ti-par′-al-lel. Parallel but running in opposite directions. PARALLELISM-INCLINATION.

an-tip′-a-thy. Aversion or dislike. DESIRE-DISTASTE, LOVE-HATE.

an′-ti-phon. An alternation of responses, generally musical. DEVOTION-IDOLATRY, INVESTIGATION-ANSWER, MUSIC.

an-tiph′-o-ny. An alternating anthem. INVESTIGATION-ANSWER.

an-tiph′-ra-sis. Irony. WORD-NEOLOGY.

an-tip′-o-dal. Opposed. LATERALITY-CONTRAPOSITION.

an-tip″-o-de′-an. Antipodal. SAMENESS-CONTRAST.

an-tip′-o-des. A place on the opposite side of the earth; exactly opposite. LATERALITY-CONTRAPOSITION, REMOTENESS-NEARNESS, SAMENESS-CONTRAST.

an″-ti-qua′-ri-an. A student of antiquities. FUTURE-PAST, SCHOLAR-DUNCE.

an″-ti-qua′-ri-an-ism. The tastes or pursuits of the antiquary. FUTURE-PAST.

an′-ti-qua-ry. A student of antiquity from a particular point of view. FUTURE-PAST, RECORDER, SCHOLAR-DUNCE.

antiquas vias, super stare [L.] (an-tai′-quas vai′-as, siu′-per stê′-ri). To stand in the old ways. CONSERVATION, HABIT-DESUETUDE.

an′-ti-qua′-ted. Out of date. INFANCY-AGE.

an-tique′. Old. NOVELTY-ANTIQUITY.

an-tique′-ness. Oldness. FUTURE-PAST.

an-tiq′-ui-ty. Ancient times. FUTURE-PAST, NOVELTY-ANTIQUITY.

an-ti-scrip′-tur-al. Opposed to the principles or doctrines of Scripture. ORTHODOXY-HETERODOXY.

an″-ti-sep′-tic. Anything that destroys the growth of putrefactive organs. REMEDY-BANE.

an-ti-so′-cial. Averse to society. HUMANITARIANISM-MISANTHROPY.

an′-ti-spast. A metrical foot consisting of an iambus and a trochee. POETRY-PROSE.

an-tis′-tro-phe. The lines of an ode sung by a chorus in returning from left to right. POETRY-PROSE, RHETORIC.

an-tith′-e-sis. A figure of speech in which contrasted words are balanced against each other. PURITY-CRUDENESS, RHETORIC, SAMENESS-CONTRAST. SIMPLICITY-FLORIDNESS, SYNONYM-ANTONYM, VIGOR-WEAKNESS.

an″-ti-thet′-ic-al. Strongly contrasted. SAMENESS-CONTRAST, SIMPLICITY-FLORIDNESS, VIGOR-WEAKNESS.

an-tit′-ra-gus. A prominence on the external ear. ANATOMY.

an′-ti-type. The original of the type. COPY-MODEL.

ant′-ler. A sharp branched outgrowth on the head of a deer. SHARPNESS-BLUNTNESS.

ant″-on-o-ma′-si-a. The substitution of a title for a proper name. NAME-MISNOMER, TROPE.

an′-to-nym. A counter-term. SYNONYM-ANTONYM.

an′-vil. An iron block, on which metals are hammered. SUSPENSION-SUPPORT; **on the anvil,** OCCUPATION, PREPARATION-NONPREPARATION, PURPOSE-LUCK.

anx-i′-e-ty. Distress of mind. DESIRE-DISTASTE, PLEASURE-PAIN, SANGUINENESS-TIMIDITY.

anx′-ious. Distressed. DESIRE-DISTASTE; **anxious expectation,** EXPECTATION-SURPRISE.

an′-y. One; portion of; some of whatever kind. CHOICE-NEUTRALITY, QUANTITY-MEASURE, WHOLE-PART; **at any price,** DETERMINATION-VACILLATION, PERSISTENCE-WHIM; **at any rate,** CERTAINTY-DOUBT, COMPENSATION, DETERMINATION-VACILLATION, TRUTH-ERROR; **at any time,** TIME.

an′-y-bod″-y. Any person whatever. UNIVERSALITY-PARTICULARITY.

an′-y-how″. In any way whatever; indifferently. CAREFULNESS-CARELESSNESS, WAY.

an′-y-thing. A matter of any sort. **For anything one knows,** KNOWLEDGE-IGNORANCE.

a′-o-rist. Without any limitation of time. PERIOD-PROGRESS, TIME; **aorist tense,** VERB.

a″-o-ris′-tic. Relating to the aorist. PERIOD-PROGRESS, TIME.

a-or′-ta. The great artery of the body. WATERCOURSE-AIRPIPE.

a-pace′. Fast; soon. EARLINESS-LATENESS, HURRY-LEISURE, SWIFTNESS-SLOWNESS.

a-part′. Aside by itself. REMOTENESS-NEARNESS, SOLITUDE-COMPANY, UNION-DISUNION; **set apart,** STORE; **wide apart,** REMOTENESS-NEARNESS.

a-part′-ment. A room or portion of an interior. CONTENTS-RECEIVER; **apartments to let,** SAGACITY-INCAPACITY, SENSITIVENESS-APATHY.

ap″-a-thet′-ic. Impassive.

ap'-a-thy. Insensibility to emotion SENSITIVENESS-APATHY, UNCONCERN.
ape. To imitate absurdly. IMITATION-ORIGINALITY
A-pell'-es. A famous Greek painter. ARTIST
aperçu [F.] (a-per-sü') An estimate at sight DIGEST

a-pe'-ri-ent. A laxative. APERTURE-CLOSURE.
a-per'-tion. An aperture. APERTURE-CLOSURE.
a-pert'-ness. That which opens. GROOVE.
ap'-er-ture. An opening. APERTURE-CLOSURE.

APERTURE—CLOSURE

Adit. An opening into a mine.
Adjutage. An opening of a tube through which water is discharged
Airpipe. A pipe for the passage of air
Aisle. A passage into which the pews of a church open
Ajutage. See ADJUTAGE.
Alley. An opening or passage in a garden, park or city
Aperture. An opening.
Arcade. An arched or covered passageway.
Blind orifice. An opening closed at one end.
Bore. An opening made by boring; the cylindrical cavity of a gun
Caliber. The diameter of a round or cylindrical opening
Canal. An artificial channel for navigation.
Casement. A window.
Channel. An opening where a stream of water runs
Chasm. A breach or opening in the earth.
Chimney. A flue of brick or stone through which smoke passes.
Colander. A kitchen utensil with the bottom perforated with little holes for straining liquids.
Cribble. A coarse sieve or screen.
Cullender. A strainer.
Door. } An entrance way into a house or a room
Doorway. }
Embouchure [F.]. The mouth of a cannon
Embrasure. An opening in a wall through which cannon are pointed
Eye. A hole through anything to receive a rope, shaft, etc.
Eyelet. A small hole to receive a cord or fastener, in a garment.
Eye of a needle. The hole through the head of a needle to receive the thread.
Fan light. A fan window.
Fistula. An abnormal opening in the body caused by a diseased condition.
Flue. An enclosed passageway for directing a current of air.
Foramen. A small opening or orifice for performing organic functions
Funnel. A passage for a fluid or flowing substance
Gallery. A long and narrow passage for walking.
Gangway. A passage or way into any enclosed place.
Gate. An opening or passage in a wall or fence; a frame closing it.
Gateway. See GATE.
Glade. An open passage through a wood.
Gullet. The tube or opening by which food is carried to the stomach.
Gully. A channel or hollow worn in the earth by a current of water
Gut. A narrow passage through which water flows.
Hatch. } An opening in the deck of a ship
Hatchway. }
Hole. An opening through a solid body.
Honeycomb. The wax of bees perforated with small cells.
Inlet. An opening by which an enclosed place may be entered
Keyhole. A hole in a door or lock for receiving a key.
Lattice. A screen or other open work made by crossing laths
Light. A window.
Loophole. A small opening in the walls of a fortification
Lych-gate. A covered gate at a church through which the corpse is carried.
Main. A duct or pipe.
Mine. A subterranean cavity or passage.
Mouse hole. An opening through which mice pass
Mouth. The opening in the face.
Muzzle. The mouth of a thing.
Nozzle. The outlet of a hose or pipe
Opening. A hole or aperture.
Orifice. The mouth of a tube or pipe.
Ostiary. The mouth of a river.
Outlet. The opening by which anything is let out.
Passage. Channel or course through which one passes
Path. A way or course in which anything moves.
Peephole. A hole or crevice through which one may peep without being discovered.
Perforation. A hole made by boring or piercing.
Pigeon-hole. A small compartment in a desk.
Pinhole. A hole made by a pin.
Pipe. A tube for leading water.
Pit. A subterranean cavity.
Porch. A covered and enclosed entrance.
Pore. An opening or gland in the skin.
Portal. A way of entrance or exit.

Blind alley. A passage closed at one end.
Blind corner. Turn from which there is no opening.
Blockade. A shutting up.
Cæcum. A cavity open only at one end; the blind gut.
Closure. That which closes or shuts.
Constipation. A shutting up of the bowels.
Contraction. Act of shrinking or closing.
Cul de sac [F.]. A blind alley.
Imperforation. The act of closing as not to permit anything to pass through.
Impermeability. The quality of not permitting passage through.
Imperviousness, etc. See *Adjectives.*
Infarction. Act of stuffing or filling up.
Obstipation. Act of stuffing.
Obstruction. Anything which hinders a passage through.
Occlusion. Act of shutting up.
Shutting up. A closing. See *Verbs.*
Stopper. That which closes or stops. See STOPPER.

CLOSURE—*Verbs.*

Bar. To close an opening or entrance.
Blockade. To shut off.
Bolt. To shut by means of a bar.
Choke. To obstruct the passage of.
Clinch. To close as with a nail.
Close. To shut.
Cram. To push into by force.
Dam. To stop the flow of water.
Obstruct, etc. To hinder. See OBSTRUCTION
Occlude. To close up a passage.
Plug. To insert a plug in an opening.
Plumb. To close with lead.
Seal. To close tightly.
Stop. To prevent from passing.
Throttle. To prevent the passage of breath.
Trap. To shut as in a trap.

CLOSURE—*Verbal Expressions.*

Block up; bung up; button up; cork up; dam up; fill up; shut up; stop up; stuff up; put to the door; ram down; shut the door.

CLOSURE—*Adjectives.*

Airtight. Closed so that air cannot enter
Cæcal. Pertaining to the cæcum.
Closed, etc. Shut. See *Verbs.*
Hermetically sealed. Closed as to make airtight
Impassable. Not to be passed through.
Impenetrable. Not to be passed through.
Imperforate. Without holes.
Impermeable. } Not permitting a passage.
Impervious. }
Imporous. Without pores or holes.
Invious. Without a way or passage.
Operculated. Having a lid or cover.
Pathless. Unopened.
Shut. Closed.
Snug. Closely covered
Tight. Closed.
Unopened. Closed.
Unpassable. Not permitting a passage.
Unpierced. Without holes through.
Untrodden. Without a way.
Unventilated. Closed that air cannot pass through
Watertight. Impervious to water.
Wayless. Pathless.

APERTURE—*Continued.*

Porthole. An opening in a ship's side.
Postern. A gate in a fortification.
Puncture. An opening made by a sharp tool.
Riddle. A coarse sieve.
Screen. A long, coarse sieve.
Shaft. An opening or passage into a mine.

APERTURE—*Continued.*

Sieve. A utensil with a perforated bottom.
Skylight. An opening in a roof.
Sucker. A pipe through which anything is drawn.
Tap. A hole or pipe through which liquor is drawn.
Thoroughfare. A passage through.
Throat. The passage from the mouth to the gullet.
Trapdoor. An opening in a roof or floor.
Tube. An opening through which anything flows.
Tubule. A small tube.
Tunnel. A subterranean passage.

Vent. A passage for air or any fluid.
Vessel. Any tube or canal.
Vista. A passage between intervening objects.
Vomitory. A principal door of a large ancient building.
Waterpipe. A passage for water.
Way. Any walk or passage.
Weasand. The windpipe.
Wicket. A small gate.
Window. An opening in the wall of a building.
Wizen. The windpipe.

APERTURE—*Nouns of Action and Quality.*

Acupuncture. Act of pricking with a needle.
Apertion. Act of opening.
Apertness. State of being open.
Dehiscence. The act of gaping.
Empalement. Act of thrusting a sharpened stake into.
Hiation. Act of gaping.
Oscitancy. Act of yawning.
Pandiculation. Act of spreading out.
Patefaction. The act of opening.

Penetration. Act of making an opening in.
Perforation. Act of boring or piercing through.
Pertusion. Act of piercing with a pointed instrument.
Piercing. Act of making a hole in. See *Verbs.*
Porosity. }
Porousness. } The quality of being porous, or full of holes.
Puncture. The act of piercing.
Terebration. The act of boring.
Yawning. Act of opening wide or of gaping.

APERTURE—*Nouns of Instrument.*

Key. An instrument by which a lock is opened.
Master-key. A key adapted to open several different locks.

Opener. Any instrument which unlocks or opens.
Passe-partout [F.]. A master-key.

APERTURE—*Verbs.*

Bilge. To stave in the bottom of.
Bore. To make a hole by boring.
Cut a passage through.
Cut open.
Drill. To pierce or bore through.
Empierce. To pierce.
Enfilade. To pierce with shot.
Fly open.
Gape. To open the mouth wide.
Gore. To pierce with a sharp instrument.
Impale. To thrust a sharp stake through.
Lance. To pierce with a lance.
Lay open.
Make room for. }
Make way for. } To open a passage.
Mine. To dig a passage or cavity. See CONVEXITY-CONCAVITY.
Ope. }
Open. } To make passage possible.
Perforate. To make holes through.
Pierce. To make an opening in.
Pink. To stab with a pointed weapon.

Prick. To pierce with a fine sharp point.
Punch. To perforate with an instrument by pressure or by a blow.
Puncture. To make a hole with a sharp-pointed instrument.
Riddle. To make full of holes.
Rip open. To tear.
Spear. To pierce with a spear.
Spike. To pierce with a spike.
Spit. To pierce as on a spit.
Stab. To pierce with a sharp instrument.
Stave in. To fracture by a blow from the outside.
Stick. To thrust through.
Tap. To make a hole in a cask.
Throw open.
Transfix. To pierce with a pointed weapon.
Transpierce. To penetrate.
Tunnel. To make an underground passage.
Unclose. To open.
Uncover. To lay open.
Unrip. To tear apart.
Yawn. To open the mouth wide.

APERTURE—*Adjectives.*

Ajar. Open.
Aperient. Tending to open the bowels.
Cannular. Tube shaped.
Cribiform. Pierced with small holes.
Fistulous. Hollow.
Follicular. In the form of small tubes.
Foraminous. In the shape of a foramina.
Gaping. Displaying an opening.
Honey-combed. Full of cells or openings.
Infundibular. Funnel shaped.
Open. Not closed; permitting something to pass through.
Opening, etc. See *Verbs.*
Oscitant. Yawning or gaping.
Patent. Open.
Perforate. Full of holes.

Perforated. Pierced with holes. See *Verbs.*
Permeable. Capable of allowing liquids to pass through.
Pervious. Capable of being passed through.
Porous. Full of holes.
Riddled. Pierced with holes.
Tubular. }
Tubulous. } Having a tube-like form.
Tubulated. Provided with tubes
Unclosed. Open.
Unstopped. Not closed.
Vascular. Having vessels.
Vesicular. Like a cell.
Wide open.
Yawning. Standing wide open.

APERTURE—*Interjection.*

Open sesame! A charm used to open a door in the *Arabian Nights'* tale, "Ali Baba and the Forty Thieves."

a'-pex. The pointed or highest point. ASTRONOMY, TOP-BOTTOM.

aph-e'-li-on. The point in a planet's orbit farthest from the sun. ASTRONOMY, REMOTENESS-NEARNESS.

aph-er'-e-sis. The dropping of an unaccented syllable or a letter from the beginning of a word. RHETORIC.

a-pho'-ni-a. Loss of voice. VOCALIZATION-MUTENESS.

aph'-o-nous. Not representing a sound. VOCALIZATION-MUTENESS.

aph'-o-ny. Loss of voice. VOCALIZATION-MUTENESS.

aph'-o-rism. A brief statement of scientific matters. ADAGE-NONSENSE.

aph"-o-ris'-tic. Pertaining to an aphorism. ADAGE-NONSENSE.

a'-pi-a-ry. Place where bees are kept. DOMESTICATION-AGRICULTURE.

A-pi′cius. A Roman epicure. FASTING-GLUTTONY.

a-piece′. For each one. UNIVERSALITY-PARTICULARITY.

a′-pish. Like an ape. SAGACITY-INCAPACITY.

ap″-la-nat′-ic. Free from spherical chromatic aberration. COLOR-ACHROMATISM.

a-plomb′. Self-possession; erectness. ASSENT-DISSENT, DETERMINATION-VACILLATION, MUTABILITY-STABILITY.

A-poc′-a-lypse. The revelation to the Apostle John. REVELATION-PSEUDOREVELATION.

a-poc″-a-lyp′-tic. Relating to Revelations. REVELATION-PSEUDOREVELATION.

a-poc′-o-pe. A cutting off of the last letter or syllable of a word. RHETORIC.

A-poc′-ry-pha. Fourteen books in the Vulgate and Septuagint versions of the Bible. REVELATION-PSEUDOREVELATION.

A-poc′-ry-phal. Not canonical. CERTAINTY-DOUBT, ORTHODOXY-HETERODOXY, TRUTH-ERROR.

ap″-o-dic′-tic. Indisputable. PROOF-DISPROOF.

ap″-o-dic′-tic-al. Indisputable. PROOF-DISPROOF.

ap″-o-dix′-is. Absolute demonstration PROOF-DISPROOF.

ap′-o-gee. That point of the moon's orbit which is most distant from the earth. ASTRONOMY.

ap′-o-graph. A transcript or facsimile. COPY-MODEL.

A-pol′-lo. The god of the sun and of music; a statue of the god Apollo, the most perfect representation of the human form. BEAUTY-UGLINESS, LUMINARY-SHADE, MUSICIAN, UNIVERSE.

Apollo magnus [L.] (a-pol′-lo mag′-nus). Great Apollo. ADVICE, SAGE-FOOL.

A-pol′-lyon. The destroyer, Abaddon. ANGEL-SATAN.

a-pol″-o-get′-ic. Like an apology. JUSTIFICATION-CHARGE.

a-pol′-o-gist. A defender. JUSTIFICATION-CHARGE.

a-pol′-o-gize. To offer an excuse. ATONEMENT, JUSTIFICATION-CHARGE.

ap′-o-logue. A fable or moral tale. ACCOUNT, EDUCATION-MISTEACHING, TROPE.

a-pol′-o-gy. A disclaimer of intentional offense. ATONEMENT, JUSTIFICATION-CHARGE, PRETEXT, REPENTANCE-OBDURACY.

ap′-o-phthegm. [Approved spelling in England.] A terse pointed saying; An apothegm. ADAGE-NONSENSE.

a-poph′-y-sis. An outgrowth or protuberance. CONVEXITY-CONCAVITY.

ap′-o-plex-y. A stroke of paralysis or loss of power of motion. MIGHT-IMPOTENCE.

ap″-o-si-o-pe′-sis. A figure in which the speaker leaves a sentence incomplete. RHETORIC.

a-pos′-ta-sy. Departure from one's faith or religion. BIGOTRY-APOSTASY, ORTHODOXY-HETERODOXY, UPRIGHTNESS-DISHONESTY.

a-pos′-tate. A renegade. PATRIOTISM-TREASON.

a-pos′-ta-tize. To forsake a faith. BIGOTRY-APOSTASY.

a-pos′-tle. A follower of Christ; a messenger. INSTRUCTOR-PUPIL, REVELATION-PSEUDOREVELATION; **Apostles' Creed,** ORTHODOXY-HETERODOXY.

a-pos′-tle-ship. Office of Apostle. CHURCH.

ap′os-tol′-ic. Pertaining to an apostle. CHURCH, REVELATION-PSEUDOREVELATION; **apostolic church,** ORTHODOXY-HETERODOXY; **apostolic see,** CHURCH.

ap″-os-tol′-ic-al. Of the apostles. REVELATION-PSEUDOREVELATION.

a-pos′-tro-phe. A figure of speech. ADDRESS-RESPONSE, CONVERSATION-MONOLOGUE, PETITION-EXPOSTULATION, RHETORIC.

a-pos′-tro-phize. To speak in apostrophes. CONVERSATION-MONOLOGUE.

a-poth′-e-ca-ry. A druggist. REMEDY-BANE; **apothecary's weight,** HEAVINESS-LIGHTNESS.

ap′-o-thegm. A truth strikingly expressed in a few words. ADAGE-NONSENSE.

ap″-o-the′-o-sis. Deification. DEVOTION-IDOLATRY, HEAVEN-HELL, RENEWAL.

ap′-o-zem. A medicated infusion. HEATING-COOLING, LIQUEFACTION-VOLATILIZATION.

ap-pal′. To terrify. PLEASURABLENESS-PAINFULNESS, SANGUINENESS-TIMIDITY.

ap-pal′-ling. Horrifying. PLEASURABLENESS-PAINFULNESS.

ap′-pa-nage. A dependent territory. GIVING-RECEIVING, PROPERTY.

ap″-pa-ra′-tus. A machine for a special purpose. INSTRUMENT.

apparatus belli [L.] (ap″-pa-rê′-tus bel′-lai). Material of war. WEAPON.

ap-par′-el. Garments. DRESS-UNDRESS.

ap-par′-ent. Clearly perceived. APPEARANCE-DISAPPEARANCE, LIKELIHOOD-UNLIKELIHOOD, MANIFESTATION-LATENCY, VISIBILITY-INVISIBILITY; **heir apparent,** POSSESSOR.

ap″-pa-ri′-tion. A ghost. JOVE-FIEND, SIGHT-DIMSIGHTEDNESS.

ap-par′-i-tor. An official who served the orders of a magistrate. MESSENGER.

ap-peach′. To accuse. JUSTIFICATION-CHARGE.

ap-peach′-ment. Accusation. JUSTIFICATION-CHARGE.

ap-peal′. An earnest request; resort to higher power or final means; carrying a case from a lower to a higher court. ADDRESS-RESPONSE, PETITION-EXPOSTULATION; **appeal from Philip drunk to Philip sober,** BETTERMENT-DETERIORATION; **appeal motion,** LITIGATION; **appeal to,** ADDRESS-RESPONSE, EVIDENCE-COUNTEREVIDENCE, PETITION – EXPOSTULATION; **appeal to arms,** FIGHTING-CONCILIATION, STRIFE-PEACE; **appeal to for,** DUENESS-UNDUENESS; **court of appeals,** COUNCIL, TRIBUNAL.

ap-pear′. To come into view. APPEARANCE-DISAPPEARANCE, MANIFESTATION-LATENCY, VISIBILITY-INVISIBILITY; **appear for,** REPRESENTATIVE; **appear in print,** WRITING-PRINTING.

ap-pear′-ance. Act of coming into view. APPEARANCE-DISAPPEARANCE; VISIBILITY-INVISIBILITY; **make one's appearance,** ARRIVAL-DEPARTURE; **to all appearance,** APPEARANCE-DISAPPEARANCE, LIKELIHOOD-UNLIKELIHOOD.

APPEARANCE—DISAPPEARANCE.

Air. Appearance.

Appearance. A coming in sight; the look of a person; show.

Aspect. Appearance to eye or mind; look.

Contour. The outline of anything.

Coup d'œil [F.]. A glance of the eye.

Display. Opening of anything to the view.

Exposure. A placing out in view.

Expression. Act of representing; external aspect.

Face of the thing. The outside appearance.

Feature. Appearance of any part of the place; the aspect.

Guise. External appearance.

Insignia. Some distinguishing marks; a badge, as of office or honor. See SIGN.

Lineament. Marks on the face.

Departure. Act of going away, withdrawal.

Disappearance. Going out of sight, hidden from the senses.

Dissolving views. Magic lantern views that are made to gradually sink away.

Eclipse. Hiding from view by something coming between.

Evanescence. A slow disappearance from view.

Exit. A going out.

Fading. Losing its color.

Occultation. A covering from view.

Vanishing point. The point of disappearance.

DISAPPEARANCE—Verbs.

Avaunt. Depart.

Be gone. See *Adjectives.*

APPEARANCE—DISAPPEARANCE—*Continued.*

Lines. Limits of figures, outlines.
Look. The act of looking; general air of face.
Lookout. An act of looking for or watching.
Outline. The contour; the boundary.
Outlook. The aspect.
Outside. The external part; the exterior. See OUTSIDE.
Pageant. An imposing show.
Pageantry. Spectacles; pompous shows. See POMP.
Perspective. A distant view.
Phase. An appearance of things to anyone.
Phasis. Same as phase.
Phenomenon. An appearance.
Premonstration. A showing beforehand.
Presence. State of being present.
Profile. The outline of face.
Prospect. A looking forward; view.
Scene. An assemblage of objects brought to view.
Seeming. An appearance.
Shape. Anything having form; an appearance. See FORM.
Show. An exhibition; a setting forth.
Sight. The act of seeing; a spectacle.
Species. Visible appearance.
Spectacle. Something that is put up for show.
Tournure [F.]. Shape; figure.
Trait. A singular feature, as of character.
View. The act of looking closely and carefully.
Vista. A view through intervening objects.

APPEARANCE—*Associated Nouns.*

Bird's-eye view; carriage; cast; cast of countenance; color; complexion; cosmorama; countenance; *coup de théâtre* [F.]; demeanor; diorama; dissolving views; face; gallanty-show; georama; image; *jeu de théâtre* [F.]; landscape; light; magic lantern; mien; *mise en scène* [F.]; *ombres chinoises* [F.]; panorama; peepshow; phantasm; phantasmagoria; phantom (see DIMSIGHTEDNESS); phiz; physiognomy; picture; point of view; port; raree show; scenery; tableau; visage.

APPEARANCE—*Figurative Nouns.*

Cut of one's jib.
First blush.
Rising of the curtain.

APPEARANCE—*Scientific Noun.*

Metoposcopy. Science of physiognomy.

APPEARANCE—*Verbs.*

Appear. To come to view, to be evident itself to the senses.
Assume the appearance. To take upon oneself appearance, to affect the appearance.
Bear the appearance. To maintain the appearance.
Become visible. To be apparent.
Be visible. To be evident to the senses. See VISIBILITY.
Carry the appearance.
Cut a figure. To make an exhibition.
Exhibit the appearance.
Figure. To be noted and conspicuous.
Have the appearance.
Look. To discern that to which the eyes are directed.
Look like. To resemble.
Present the appearance of.
Present to the view.
Seem. To be manifest on reflection.

DISAPPEARANCE—*Verbs—Continued.*

Disappear. To withdraw from view.
Dissolve. To separate into its parts, to waste away, to disappear.
Efface. To make disappear. See MARK-OBLITERATION.
Fade. To slowly experience an effacement of.
Go.
Go off the stage. To disappear from active life.
Leave no track. To disappear entirely.
"Leave not a rack behind." To disappear completely. [*Tempest,* IV, 1.]
Lose sight of. To vanish.
Melt away. To disappear slowly.
Pass away. To go away.
Retire from sight. To disappear.
Suffer an eclipse. }
Undergo an eclipse. } To be put out of sight.
Vanish. To fade away.

DISAPPEARANCE—*Adjectives*

Disappearing. See *Verbs.*
Evanescent. Passing away by degrees.
Gone. Moved away.
Lost. Not to be found, wasted.
Lost to sight. }
Lost to view. } Disappeared, vanished.
Missing. Lost to sight.

DISAPPEARANCE—*Interjections.*

Avaunt. See INJECTION-EJECTION.
Disappear!
Vanish!

APPEARANCE—*Verbs—Continued.*

Show. Put forth into view. See MANIFESTATION.
Take on the appearance of.
Take the appearance.
Wear the appearance.

APPEARANCE—*Adjectives*

Apparent. Manifest to the senses.
On view. Visible.
Ostensible. Presented as real or true, avowed.
Seeming. Apparent to the mind on reflection.

APPEARANCE—*Adverbs.*

Apparently. In a seeming manner.
As it seems. Apparently.
At first sight. On the first view.
At the first blush. At the first appearance.
In the eyes of. In the mental view of.
On the face of. On external appearance.
Ostensibly. Affectedly, professedly.
Prima facie [L.]. On the first view.
Seemingly. In a seeming way.
To all appearance. }
To all seeming. } As far as we can see.
To the eye. To the view.

APPEARANCE—*Phrase.*

Editio princeps [L.]. First edition.

---

ap-pear'-ances. Aspect of the circumstances. **Keep up appearances,** SOCIETY-LUDICROUSNESS.
ap-pease'. To soothe. EXCITABILITY-INEXCITABILITY, TURBULENCE-CALMNESS.
ap-pel'-lant. One who appeals. DUENESS-UNDUENESS.
ap-pel'-late. Having jurisdiction of appeals. TRIBUNAL.
ap''-pel-la'-tion. The name or title by which a person or thing is called. NAME-MISNOMER.
ap-pend'. To add or attach. ADDITION-SUBTRACTION, PRECEDENCE-SUCCESSION, SUSPENSION-SUPPORT.
ap-pend'-age. Anything added. INCREMENT-REMNANT, PREDECESSOR-CONTINUATION.
ap-pen''-di-ci'-tis. Inflammation of the vermiform appendix of the cæcum. REMEDY-BANE.

ap-pen'-dix. Supplementary matter placed at the end of a book. PREDECESSOR-CONTINUATION.
ap''-per-cep'-tion. Self-consciousness. CONCEPTION-THEME.
ap''-per-tain'. To pertain or belong to. CONNECTION-INDEPENDENCE, CONSTITUENT-ALIEN, HOLDING-EXEMPTION, PROPERTY.
ap'-pe-tence. Strong craving. DESIRE-DISTASTE.
ap'-pe-ten-cy. Strong desire. DESIRE-DISTASTE.
ap'-pe-ti-ble. Exciting the appetite. DESIRE-DISTASTE.
ap'-pe-tite. Physical craving or desire. DESIRE-DISTASTE; **tickle the appetite,** PALATABLENESS-UNPALATABLENESS.

appetitus rationi obediant [L.] (ap″-pî-tai′-tus rĕ-shi-o′-nai o-bi′-di-ant). Let the appetites obey the reason. MODERATION-SELFINDULGENCE.

ap′-pe-tize. To give relish. DESIRE-DISTASTE.

ap′-pe-ti″-zing. Giving relish. DESIRE-DISTASTE, EXCITATION, PALATABLENESS-UNPALATABLENESS, PLEASURABLENESS-PAINFULNESS.

ap-plaud′. To express approval of APPROVAL-DISAPPROVAL.

ap-plaud′-ing. Expressing approval APPROVAL-DISAPPROVAL.

ap′-ple. Apple of discord. VARIANCE-ACCORD; **apple off another tree,** VARIATION; **apple of one's eye,** FAVORITE-ANGER, GOODNESS-BADNESS, LOVE-HATE; **apple-pie order,** REGULARITY-IRREGULARITY; **golden apple,** MOTIVE-CAPRICE; **how we apples swim,** CONCEIT-DIFFIDENCE.

ap′-ple–green″. The color of apples. REDNESS-GREENNESS.

ap-pli′-ance. Act of putting to use, anything by which something is done. USE-DISUSE; **appliances,** INSTRUMENT-MEANS.

ap″-pli-ca-bil′-i-ty. Fitness. HARMONY-DISCORD, PROPRIETY-IMPROPRIETY, USEFULNESS-USELESSNESS.

ap′-pli-ca-ble. Fitting. HARMONY-DISCORD, PROPRIETY-IMPROPRIETY, USEFULNESS-USELESSNESS.

ap′-pli-cant. A candidate. PETITIONER.

ap″-pli-ca′-tion. The fixing of the attention closely, employment of principles; a demand. HEED-DISREGARD, PETITION-EXPOSTULATION, REFLECTION-VACANCY, TROPE, USE-DISUSE.

ap-plied′ chem′-is-try. Chemistry of practise. CHEMISTRY

ap-ply′. To bring into contact with something. TROPE, USE-DISUSE; **apply a match,** HEATING-COOLING; **apply a remedy,** REMEDY-BANE; **apply the match to a train,** BEGINNING-END; **apply the mind,** HEED-DISREGARD.

appoggiato [It.] (ap″-po-ja′-to) Prolonged. MELODY-DISSONANCE.

appoggiatura [It.] (ap-poj″-a-tu′-ra). An extra note or musical ornament. MELODY-DISSONANCE.

ap-point′. To designate. ASSIGNMENT, ORDER.

ap-point′-ing. Assigning. ASSIGNMENT.

ap-point′-ment. A being chosen to fill an office, a meeting or time of meeting. ASSIGNMENT, COMMISSION-ABROGATION, ORDER, SOCIABILITY-PRIVACY

ap-point′-ments. Furnishings. INSTRUMENT

ap-por′-tion. To divide equitably. ASSIGNMENT, GATHERING-SCATTERING, ORGANIZATION-DISORGANIZATION, UNION-DISUNION

ap-por′-tion-ing. Dividing. ASSIGNMENT.

ap-por′-tion-ment. A just division. ASSIGNMENT, GATHERING-SCATTERING, ORGANIZATION-DISORGANIZATION

ap′-po-site. Suitable; fit; well-adapted.

ap″-po-si′-tion. Relation between two or more nouns; act of placing side by side or in contact. HARMONY-DISCORD, INTERSPACE-CONTACT, INTERPRETATION-MISINTERPRETATION.

ap-praise′. To estimate the value of MENSURATION, PRICE-DISCOUNT.

ap-praise′-ment. Estimation MENSURATION, PRICE-DISCOUNT.

ap-pre′-ci-ate. To be fully aware of the importance of; to increase in value. APPROVAL-DISAPPROVAL, DECISION-MISJUDGMENT, KNOWLEDGE-IGNORANCE, MENSURATION, MIND-IMBECILITY, REFLECTION-VACANCY, TASTE-VULGARITY.

ap-pre″-ci-a′-tion. True estimation. APPROVAL-DISAPPROVAL, DECISION-MISJUDGMENT, KNOWLEDGE-IGNORANCE.

ap″-pre-hend′. To grasp with the understanding; to arrest. FAITH-MISGIVING, KNOWLEDGE-IGNORANCE, LITIGATION, SANGUINENESS-TIMIDITY.

ap″-pre-hen′-sion. The result of grasping mentally; seizure of a person. CONCEPTION-THEME, KNOWLEDGE-IGNORANCE, LITIGATION, SAGACITY-INCAPACITY, SANGUINENESS-TIMIDITY, TAKING-RESTITUTION.

ap-pren′-tice. One serving to learn a trade; to bind oneself as an apprentice. INSTRUCTOR-PUPIL; **apprentice oneself,** ENTERPRISE.

ap-pren′-tice-ship. Method of learning of an apprentice. EDUCATION-MISTEACHING.

appris, ils n'ont rien . . . , ni rien oublié [F.] (il non' rî-an″ a-prî′, nî rî-an″ u-bli-ê′). They have learned nothing and forgotten nothing. BIGOTRY-APOSTASY.

ap-prize′. To warn. ENLIGHTENMENT-SECRECY; **apprized of,** KNOWLEDGE-IGNORANCE.

ap-proach′. To come near in time, place, degree or quality. APPROACH-WITHDRAWAL, FUTURE-PAST, OCCURRENCE-DESTINY, REMOTENESS-NEARNESS, WAY; **approaching time,** FUTURE-PAST

APPROACH—WITHDRAWAL

Access. A coming to, admission.
Advent. A coming of something important See FUTURE
Afflux. A flowing to.
Affluxion. Act of flowing to.
Approach. A coming nearer.
Appropinquation. The act of bringing near.
Approximation. Act of causing to approach without exactly coming together.
Appulse. A driving toward.
Pursuit. A following up close. See QUEST

APPROACH—*Verbs*

Approach. To come to or near.
Approximate. To make come near but not to coincide.
Bear up. To tend toward.
Come near.
Come to close quarters. To engage at short range, to come together
Draw near.
Drift. To float slowly toward.
Gain upon. To be approaching nearer
Get near.
Go near.
Hug the land. ⎫
Hug the shore. ⎬ To keep close to.
Make the land. To come to destined place
Make up to. To approach.
Move towards.

Departure. A going away. See ARRIVAL-DEPARTURE.
Flight. The act of flying or moving swiftly See QUEST-EVASION
Recession. An act of moving away.
Recoil. A shrinking back, a quick rebound.
Retirement. Withdrawal from one's associations
Retreat. A going away from, a withdrawal
Retrocession. A moving backward. See ADVANCE-RETROGRESSION
Withdrawal. A drawing or taking back.

WITHDRAWAL—*Verbs*

Come away. Withdraw.
Depart. See ARRIVAL-DEPARTURE
Drift away. To move away slowly
Fall back. Retreat.
Get away. Escape.
Go. Move from one place to the other
Go away. ⎫
Move from. ⎬ Withdraw
Move off. ⎭
Recede. To move away, to withdraw.
Remove. To change from one station to another
Retreat. To move back and away from a given place See ADVANCE-RETROGRESSION.
Retire. To separate oneself from.
Run away. To run off. See QUEST-EVASION
Sheer off. To move aside.
Shrink. To draw back as if in terror

APPROACH—WITHDRAWAL —*Continued.*

APPROACH—Verbs—*Continued.*

Near. To make come near or close; to move toward.
Pursue. To follow close after. See Quest.
Set in towards. To start after.
Tread on the heels of. To follow very closely.

APPROACH—*Adjectives.*

Affluent. Flowing to.
Approaching. Coming toward; nearing. See *Verbs.*
Approximative. Coming to without coinciding.
Imminent. Jutting towards. See Occurrence.
Impending. Hanging over.

APPROACH—*Adverb.*

On the road.

ap-proach'-ing. Coming nearer. APPROACH-WITH-DRAWAL.
ap-pro-ba'-tion. Commendation. APPROVAL-DISAPPROVAL, REGARD-DISRESPECT, REPUTATION-DISCREDIT.
ap''-pro-pin-qua'-tion. Act of coming near. APPROACH-WITHDRAWAL.
ap-pro'-pri-ate. Suitable for the purpose; to take for

WITHDRAWAL—Verbs—*Continued.*

Shunt. To shun.
Stand aside. Move apart.
Withdraw. To draw away; retire.

WITHDRAWAL—*Adjectives.*

Removing, etc. See *Verbs.*

APPROACH—*Continued.*

APPROACH—*Interjections.*

Approach; come; come here; come hither; here.

one's own use. ASSIGNMENT, HARMONY-DISCORD, PROPRIETY - IMPROPRIETY, TAKING - RESTITUTION, THEFT, UNIVERSALITY-PARTICULARITY.
ap-pro''-pri-a'-tion. Anything set apart for special use. ASSIGNMENT, TAKING-RESTITUTION, THEFT.
ap-prov'-al. Sanction. APPROVAL-DISAPPROVAL, ASSENT-DISSENT, CONSENT.

APPROVAL—DISAPPROVAL

Acclaim. A shout of applause or approval.
Acclamation. A shout, usually by a multitude, of applause or approval.
Account. Importance; estimation.
Admiration. Wonder and approbation.
Advocacy. Approbation and support or vindication.
Applause. Any expression of approval.
Appreciation. Approbation and just valuation or estimation.
Approbation. The act of commending or regarding as worthy, proper or right.
Approval. The act of approving; sanction.
Approvement. Approbation.
Benediction. Solemn invocation of the divine approval or blessing.
Benison. Blessing; benediction.
Blessing. Divine favor; benediction.
Cheer. A shout of approbation or applause.
Commendation. Approbation; praise.
Credit. Reliance on the truth of a statement or on the sincerity of a person.
Éloge [F.]. Eulogy; praise.
Encomium. Formal expression of great approval or praise.
Esteem. High regard and approval.
Estimation. Favorable opinion; regard.
Eulogium. Spoken or written praise of a person's life or character.
Eulogy. See Eulogium.
Homage. Reverential regard; deference.
Kydos [Gr.]. Renown; glory.
Laud. High praise or commendation.
Laudation. The act of lauding or praising; high commendation.
Love. Strong attachment induced by that which excites delight or admiration, etc. See Love.
Panegyric. A formal and elaborate encomium; laudation.
Plaudit. An expression of applause.
Popularity. The state of being esteemed or approved by the people.
Praise. Approbation expressed.
Regard. Respect; esteem; reverence.
Repute, etc. Estimation; honor, etc. See Reputation.
Sanction. Authoritative approbation; ratification.

APPROVAL—*Associated Nouns.*

Chorus of applause; clap; clapping; clapping of hands; golden opinions; good opinion; good word; hero worship; hosannah; meed of praise; nod of approbation; pæan, an ancient Greek hymn in honor of Apollo, any joyful song; peal of applause; Prytaneum, a public hall at Athens where hospitality was officially extended to distinguished citizens and strangers; shout of applause; thunders of applause; tribute of praise.

APPROVAL—*Verbs.*

Acclamate. Shout in order to show approval.
Admire. Wonder and approve.
Applaud. Express approval by some sign that may be heard or seen.
Appreciate. Esteem highly and adequately.

Abuse. Expression of disapproval prompted by anger, and in harsh and unseemly words.
Admonition. A gentle or friendly counseling against fault or error.
Animadversion. Remarks by way of criticism and censure from one having authority over.
Blacklist. A number of persons to be regarded with suspicion.
Blame. Censure.
Castigation. Severe criticism.
Censoriousness. Implication or expression of censure.
Censure. The act of finding fault with and condemning as wrong.
Chiding. A personal rebuke from one having little authority over
Condemnation. The act of pronouncing to be wrong or guilty.
Contumely. Expression of disapproval by showing rudeness, haughtiness and contempt toward.
Correction. The act of reproving or punishing habitual faults.
Criticism. A critical judgment passed or expressed.
Denunciation. A public accusation of fault or wrong.
Depreciation. An attempt to represent as of little value or claim to esteem.
Detraction. Act of taking away from the good name or reputation of another.
Disapprobation. An unfavorable opinion, whether held in the mind or expressed.
Disapproval. Unfavorable judgment.
Discommendation. Censure or ill favor.
Disesteem. Low estimation, inclining to dislike.
Dislike. A feeling of positive and permanent aversion See Desire-Distaste.
Disparagement. Lowering in rank or estimation.
Displacency. Envious displeasure.
Dispraise. Dishonor; blame.
Disvaluation. A lowering of reputation.
Exception. Objection or cause of offense.
Execration. A curse dictated by violent feelings of hatred.
Expostulation. Reasoning with a person against some impropriety of conduct.
Exprobation. An offensive accusation.
Fie. A word which expresses dislike.
Hypercriticism. Unjust severity or rigor of criticism. See Desire-Particularness.
Improbation. Expression of disapproval.
Increpation. A chiding; rebuke.
Innuendo. A remote allusion, usually derogatory to a person not named.
Insinuation. A hint or suggestion of disapproval or fault
Jobation. A long, tedious reproof.
Objection. Anything expressed or presented in opposition.
Objurgation. A reproof.
Obloquy. Language that casts contempt on men or their actions.
Odium. Quality that provokes hatred.
Ostracism. Exclusion from society.
Rebuke. A strong and authoritative expression of disapproval for some wrong committed.
Reflection. Reproach cast upon a person.

APPROVAL—DISAPPROVAL—*Continued.*

APPROVAL—Verbs—*Continued.*

Approve. Commend; regard as right or proper.
Bepraise. Praise greatly.
Bless. Praise; invoke God's approval and favor upon
Cheer. Applaud with cheers.
Clap. Applaud by clapping the hands.
Commend. Approve or express approval; praise.
Compliment. Express admiration, commendation or approval.
Countenance. Look upon with approval.
Encore. Call for the repetition of, as of an approved performance.
Endorse. } Give sanction or approval to; put your name on the back
Indorse. }
Esteem. Regard as worthy or excellent.
Eulogize. Praise in speech or writing.
Exalt. Highly honor; magnify.
Extol. Commend in the highest terms.
Flatter, etc. Praise or approve unduly or obsequiously. See ADU-
LATION.
Glorify. Make glorious; exalt to a state of glory.
Hail. Greet approvingly.
Honor. Regard with high esteem or respect.
Laud. Praise in word, or in word and song.
Like, etc. Incline approvingly toward, etc. See LOVE.
Magnify. Glorify; extol.
Panegyrize. Pronounce an elaborate eulogy upon.
Praise. Express approval of.
Prize. Esteem highly.
Puff. Praise unduly; flatter.
Recommend. Commend to the favorable treatment of another
Sanction. Approve authoritatively.
Swell. Puff up.
Uphold. Give approval to; regard with approval.
Value. Prize; esteem highly.
Laudari a laudato viro [L.]. To be praised by a man who is praised
Prôner [F.]. Cry up; extol.

APPROVAL—*Verbal Expressions.*

Applaud to the echo; applaud to the very echo; be in favor of; be in
favor with; be in high favor with; be praised, etc.; chant the
praises of; cheer to the echo; cheer to the very echo; clap on the
back; clap the hands; cry up; deserve praise, etc. (see sub *Noun*);
do credit to; do justice to; extol to the skies; find favor with; gain
credit; give a blessing to; give credit; hail with satisfaction; have
a good word for; hold in esteem; hold up; keep in countenance;
look up to; make much of; mark with a white mark; mark with
a white stone; pass muster, pass through an inspection without
censure; pat on the back; pay a tribute; receive honorable mention; recommend itself; redound the praises of; redound to the
credit of; redound to the honor of; redound to the praise of; ring
with the praises of; say a good word for; set great store by; set
great store on; sing praises to; sing the praises of; sound the
praises of; speak highly of; speak in high terms of; speak well of;
stand up for; stand well in the opinion of; stick up for; think good;
think highly of; think much of; think well of; win golden opinions;
wish Godspeed.

APPROVAL—*Adjectives.*

Approved. Commended; sanctioned.
Approving, etc. Commending, etc. See *Verbs.*
Benedictory. Expressing good wishes.
Beyond all praise. Above all praise.
Commendable. Creditable; worthy of approval.
Commendatory. Expressing approbation.
Complimentary. Expressing admiration, approbation, or the like
Creditable. Deserving or reflecting credit or approbation.
Deserving praise, etc. See *Nouns.*
Encomiastic. Bestowing praise or high approval.
Estimable. Deserving good opinion or approval.
Eulogistic. Bestowing high praise.
Good, etc. Having physical or moral qualities that may be ap-
proved, etc. See GOODNESS.
In favor. Favored; approved.
In favor of. On the side of; approving
In good odor. In favor; approved.
In high esteem, etc. Respected; highly approved, etc. See RE-
GARD.
In high power. Dominant, as a political party, and hence approved
by the majority.
Laudatory. Praising; eulogizing.
Lavish of praise. Bestowing praise extravagantly

Remonstrance. Earnest presentation of reasons in opposition to
something.
Reprehension. A calm, just, but severe disapproval of an act.
Reprimand. Official censure by a superior to an inferior.
Reproach. An open and violent censure, with deep feeling of grief or
anger.
Reprobation. Strong personal disapproval.
Reproof. An expression of blame or censure expressed to the face.
Sarcasm. A keen, reproachful expression uttered with some degree
of scorn or contempt.
Scolding. A harsh, rude and boisterous rebuke.
Stricture. A touch of adverse criticism.
Upbraiding. Charge of something wrong or disgraceful.
Vituperation. A severe and abusive censure.

DISAPPROVAL—*Associated Nouns.*

Bad compliment; bad language (see CHARITABLENESS - CURSE);
bitter words; black look; blow up; carping; catcall; cavil,
clamor; *coup de bec* [F.], blow of the beak; curtain lecture;
cutting words; diatribe, a strain of railing or abusive language;
dressing; evil-speaking; frown; hard words; hiss; hissing; hit;
home thrust; hue and cry; jeremiad, a tale of disappointment or
complaint; jeremiade (see JEREMIAD); lecture; left-handed compliment; outcry; personality; philippic; poor compliment; rap on
the knuckles; rating; sardonic grin; sardonic laugh; satire;
scowl; set down; sibilation; slap; slap on the face; sneer, etc.
(see REGARD-SCORN); taunt, etc. (see REGARD - DISRESPECT);
thunderation; tirade; trimming; wigging.

DISAPPROVAL—*Verbs.*

Abuse. To treat with rude and reproachful language.
Accuse. To charge with a crime or offense. See JUSTIFICATION-
CHARGE.
Admonish. To reprove of a fault, gently or kindly.
Anathematize. To condemn publicly as something accursed
Avile. To lower in esteem or reputation
Backbite. To speak evil of one absent.
Bespatter. To spread foul reports or false and injurious charges.
Blame. To find fault with.
Brand. To mark as criminal or infamous
Castigate. To punish with blows.
Cavil. To find fault without good reason.
Censure. To find fault with and condemn as wrong.
Chastise. To inflict pain upon for the purpose of punishment or
reformation.
Chide. To scold.
Clamor. To complain and make troublesome demands.
Clapperclaw. To abuse with the tongue
Condemn. To declare the guilt of.
Correct. To reprove or punish for faults or moral weaknesses
Criticize. To judge severely.
Decry. To declare faulty, mean or worthless.
Defame. To harm or destroy the good fame or reputation of. See
ADULATION-DISPARAGEMENT.
Denounce. To point out as deserving of censure or punishment
Deprecate. To disapprove of strongly.
Depreciate. To represent as of little claim to honor or esteem
Disapprove. To pass unfavorable judgment upon.
Discommend. To put out of the favor of any one.
Dislike. To regard with some hatred and displeasure. See DESIRE-
DISTASTE.
Disparage. To lower in rank or estimation by actions or words
Dispraise. To withdraw praise or honor from.
Disvalue. To rob of real worth or merit.
Execrate. To protest against as unholy or detestable. See CHARI-
TABLENESS-CURSE.
Expose. To lay open to public inspection, as something criminal or
shameful.
Expostulate. To reason earnestly with a person on some impro-
priety of conduct.
Exprobate. To charge as shameful or disgraceful.
Fronder [F.]. To cast disfavor upon.
Impeach. To call in question and bring discredit upon.
Improbate. To disapprove of.
Impugn. To attack by words or arguments.
Insinuate. To hint at something derogatory to one's reputation.
Jaw. To scold or clamor.
Lament. To express or feel sorrow for. See LAMENTATION.
Lampoon. To subject to abusive ridicule expressed in writing.
Lash. To censure with severity.
Lecture. To reprove formally and with authority.
Mob. To crowd about and attack or annoy.

APPROVAL—DISAPPROVAL—*Continued.*

APPROVAL—ADJECTIVES—*Continued.*

Lost in admiration. Occupied with admiring so as to be insensible to external things.
Meritorious. Praiseworthy; deserving high approval.
Of estimation. Commendable; estimable.
Panegyrical. Praising elaborately.
Plausible. Calculated to win approval or confidence.
Popular. Approved by the people.
Praised, etc. Commended and approved, etc. See *Verbs.*
Praiseworthy. Worthy of commendation and approval.
Uncensured Exempt from blame.
Uncritical. Approving without judgment.
Unimpeachable. Blameless; free from stain or fault; approved.
Unimpeached. Not called in question; not discredited.
Worthy of praise, etc. Worthy of commendation and approval, etc. See *Nouns.*

APPROVAL—*Adverbs.*

To admiration. Admirably.
Well, etc. In a commendable manner, etc. See GOOD.
With credit. Creditably; with approval.
With three times three. With three cheers thrice repeated.

APPROVAL—*Interjections.*

Bis! [L.], twice! *bravissimo!* [It.], very well done; *bravo!* [It.], well done! *encore!* [F.], once more! *esto perpetua* [L.], let it last forever; *euge!* [L.], bravo; *evviva!* [It.], hurrah; **Godspeed!** hear, hear! long life to! may you never be less! may your shadow never be less! one cheer more! *optime!* [L.], very well; **quite right; so far so good; that's right;** *valete ac plaudite* [L.], farewell and applaud; *viva!* [L.], live; **well done.**

APPROVAL—*Phrases.*

En mauvaise odeur [F.]. In bad odor.
Les belles actions cachées sont les plus estimables [F.]. Beautiful acts hidden are the most worthy of praise.
Tacent, satis laudant [L.]. They are silent, they give enough praise.
Vivat respublica! [L.]. Long live the republic.
Vivat rex! [L.]. Long live the king.

DISAPPROVAL—ADJECTIVES—*Continued from Column 2.*

Clamorous. Complaining in noisy language.
Condemnatory. Containing censure.
Critical. Inclined to criticize or find fault.
Cutting. Severe; sarcastic.
Cynical. Given to sneering at rectitude and the conduct of life by moral principles.
Damnatory. Expressing the highest condemnation.
Defamatory. Injurious to reputation. See sub DETRACTION.
Denunciatory. Accusing; threatening.
Disapproved. Regarded with disfavor.
Disapproving, etc. See *Verbs.*
Disparaging. Undervaluing.
Dry. Severe, grave or hard; withering.
Exceptionable. Objectionable.
Exploded. Rejected with open contempt.
Fastidious. Difficult to please. See DESIRE-PARTICULARNESS.
Grudging praise. Praising with envy.
Hard upon. Severe.
Hypercritical. Unreasonably or unjustly critical.
In bad odor. Out of all favor.
Not to be thought of.
Objurgatory. Expressing reproof.
Reprehensible. Worthy of blame.
Reproachful. Abusive.
Sarcastic. Scornfully severe.
Sardonic. Derisive; mocking.
Scandalized. Disgraced.
Severe. Very strict in judgment.
Sharp. Cutting in language.
Sparing of praise. Not giving full credit.
To blame. Guilty.
Trenchant. Keen; biting.
Unapproved. Unfavorable.
Unbewailed. Not mourned for.
Unblest. Accursed.
Uncommendable. Not worthy of praise.
Unlamented. Unwept for.

DISAPPROVAL—VERBS—*Continued.*

Objurgate. To rebuke severely.
Ostracize. To cast out from social, political, or private favor.
Overhaul. To examine thoroughly with a view to correction.
Rate. To scold or censure violently.
Rebuke. To restrain by expression of disapproval.
Recriminate. To return one charge or accusation with another.
Remonstrate. To present and urge reasons in opposition to an act, measure, or any course of proceeding.
Reprehend. To make charge of fault against.
Reprimand. To reprove publicly and officially.
Reproach. To bring disgrace or shame upon.
Reprobate. To disapprove with marks of extreme dislike.
Reprove. To chide to the face as blameworthy.
Revile. To address or abuse with mean and disgraceful language.
Revolt. To be disgusted, shocked or grossly offended with.
Satirize. To censure with keenness.
Scandalize. To bring shame or disgrace upon.
Scold. To chide with rudeness or clamor.
Shock. To strike with horror or disgust.
Snub. To treat with contempt or neglect.
Stigmatize. To set a mark of disgrace upon.
Taunt. To jeer at with insulting words. See REGARD-DISRESPECT.
Trim. To rebuke.
Trounce. To punish or beat severely.
Twit. To vex by reminding of a fault.
Upbraid. To charge with something wrong or disgraceful.
Vilify. To degrade or debase by false report.
Vilipend. To slight, to value lightly.
Vituperate. To overwhelm with wordy abuse.

DISAPPROVAL—*Verbal Expressions.*

Abuse like a pickpocket; animadvert upon; bark at; be censorious, etc. (see sub *Adjective*); bend the brows; be outspoken; be scandalized at; be under a cloud; blow up; bring a hornet's nest about one's ears; bring over the coals; bring to account; bring to book; bring to order; call by hard names; call by ugly names; call names; call over the coals; call to account; call to order; carp at; cast a slur upon; cast blame upon; cast reflection upon; cast reproach upon; come under the ferule; cry down; cry out against; cry shame upon; cut up; damn with faint praise; declare against; draw up a round robin, to draw up a written remonstrance, the signatures to which are made in a circle so as not to indicate who signed first; excite disapprobation; exclaim against; fall foul of; find fault with; forfeit one's good opinion; frown down; frown upon; fulminate against; get a bad name; give a rap on the knuckles; give it one; give it one finely; give one a lick with the rough side of the tongue; give one a wipe; glance at; have a fling at; have a snap at; have to answer for; have words with; hint a fault and hesitate dislike; hold up to execration; hold up to reprobation; incur blame; inveigh against; knit the brows; *laver la tête* [F.], to rate a person; lay blame upon; load with reproaches; look askance; look black upon; look grave; look with an evil eye; make a fuss about; make a wry face at; make a wry mouth at; nibble at; *nil admirari* [L.], to wonder at nothing; not speak well of; not to be able to say much for; object to; pass censure on; peck at; pick a hole; pick a hole in one's coat; pick holes; pick to pieces; pluck a crow with; point at; protest against; pull to pieces; pull up; rail at; rail in good set terms; raise a hue and cry against; raise one's voice against; read a lecture to; read a lesson to; reflect upon; run down; scoff at; set down; set one's face against; shake the head at; show up; shrug the shoulders; sign a round robin (see DRAW UP A ROUND ROBIN); snap one up; sneer at (see REGARD-SCORN); speak daggers; speak ill of; stand corrected; take blame; take down; take exception; take exception to; take to task; take up; think ill of; throw a stone at; throw a stone in one's garden; turn up the nose (see REGARD-SCORN); view with dark eyes; view with disfavor; view with jaundiced eyes.

DISAPPROVAL—*Adjectives.*

Abusive. Prone to ill treat by coarse, insulting words.
Answerable. Obliged to account for.
At a discount. Poorly esteemed.
Bad. Unfavorable or offensive. See sub BADNESS.
Biting. Cutting or sarcastic.
Blameworthy. Deserving blame.
Blown upon. Brought into discredit.
Captious. Apt to catch at faults.
Carping. Fault-finding.
Censorious. Severe in making remarks on others.
Chid. Scolded. See *Verbs.*

(*Continued on Column 1.*)

DISAPPROVAL—Adjectives—Continued.

Unpitied. Merciless.
Vicious. Spiteful.
Vituperative. Characterized by abuse

Weighed in the balance and found wanting. Unapproved.
Withering. Blighted.
Worthy of blame.

DISAPPROVAL—Adverbs

Reproachfully, etc   See *Adjectives*

With a wry face.

DISAPPROVAL—Interjections.

Away with! come! fie! fie for shame! fie upon it! forbid it Heaven! God forbid! Heaven forbid! it is too bad! it will never do! it won't do! marry come up! oh! *O tempora! O mores!* [L.], O the times!

O the manners! out on you! out upon it! 'sdeath! God's death: shame! tell it not in Gath! tut!

ap-prove'. To commend. APPROVAL-DISAPPROVAL

ap-proved'. Sanctioned. APPROVAL-DISAPPROVAL.

ap-prove'-ment. Commendation. APPROVAL-DISAPPROVAL.

ap-prov'-ing. Commending. APPROVAL-DISAPPROVAL.

ap-prox'-i-mate. Near in position, time, or character; to come close to. APPROACH-WITHDRAWAL, CONNECTION - INDEPENDENCE, LIKENESS - UNLIKENESS, NUMBERING, REMOTENESS-NEARNESS.

ap-prox''-i-ma'-tion. A bringing near. APPROACH-WITHDRAWAL, CONNECTION-INDEPENDENCE, LIKENESS-UNLIKENESS, NUMBERING.

ap-prox'-i-ma-tive. Approximate. APPROACH-WITHDRAWAL, CONNECTION-INDEPENDENCE.

ap'-pulse. Approach of one body towards another. APPROACH-WITHDRAWAL, CONCENTRATION-RADIATION, IMPETUS-REACTION, INTERSPACE-CONTACT.

ap-pur'-te-nance. A minor thing joined to a principal one. CONSTITUENT-ALIEN, PROPERTY, WHOLE-PART.

ap-pur'-te-nant. Belonging to something more important. CONNECTION-INDEPENDENCE.

après nous le déluge [F.] (a-prê' nu le dê-lüzh'). After us the deluge. UNSELFISHNESS-SELFISHNESS.

a'-pri-cot. A peach-like fruit of a yellow color **Apricot color,** BLUENESS-ORANGE.

A'-pril. Fourth month of the year. **April fool,** GULLDECEIVER, SOCIETY-LAUGHINGSTOCK; **April showers,** MUTABILITY-STABILITY; **make an April fool of,** TRUTHFULNESS-FRAUD, REGARD-DISRESPECT.

a'-pron. An article of clothing. ATTACK-DEFENSE, DRESS-UNDRESS, VESTMENTS.

a''-pro-pos'. Suited to the occasion; by the way CONNECTION - INDEPENDENCE, HARMONY - DISCORD, OPPORTUNENESS-UNSUITABLENESS.

a'-pro-type. Close type. WRITING-PRINTING.

apse. The bishop's seat in ancient churches. FANE.

ap'-si-des. A point of an electric orbit which is nearest to or farthest from the center of attraction. ASTRONOMY.

apt. Liable; naturally gifted. EDUCATION-MISTEACHING, HARMONY-DISCORD, INCLINATION, SKILL-UNSKILFULNESS.

apt'-i-tude. Quickness of understanding. HARMONY-DISCORD, INCLINATION, READINESS-RELUCTANCE, SKILL-UNSKILFULNESS.

apt-ness. Quickness. EDUCATION-MISTEACHING, HARMONY-DISCORD, INCLINATION, SKILL-UNSKILFULNESS.

a''-qua-ma-rine'. A bluish-green color MINERALOGY, REDNESS-GREENNESS.

a-qua'-ri-um. A place for keeping aquatic animals. DOMESTICATION-AGRICULTURE.

A-qua'-ri-us. The eleventh sign of the zodiac. **Waterbearer,** ASTRONOMY, RIVER-WIND.

a-quat'-ic. Pertaining to water. WATER-AIR.

a-quat'-ics. Aquatic sports. ENTERTAINMENT-WEARINESS, TRAVELING-NAVIGATION.

a''-qua-tin'-ta. A kind of engraving. ENGRAVING.

aq'-ue-duct. A water-conduit. WATERCOURSE-AIRPIPE.

a'-que-ous. Watery WATER-AIR.

aquila non capit muscas [L.] (aq'-ui-la non kê'-pit mus'-kas). An eagle does not catch flies. LIKELIHOOD-UNLIKELIHOOD.

aq'-ui-line. Hooked like a beak. ANGULARITY.

A. R. Anno Regni. In the year of the reign. DURATION-NEVERNESS.

Ar'-ab. An Arabian; a wanderer; an Arabian horse. CONVEYER, WAYFARER-SEAFARER.

a-ra'-ba. An ox-cart. CONVEYANCE-VESSEL.

ar''-a-besque'. Fanciful ornamentation. EMBELLISHMENT-DISFIGUREMENT.

A-ra'-bi-an. Pertaining to Arabia. **Arabian Nights,** FANCY; **Arabian perfumes,** PERFUME-STENCH.

ar'-a-ble. Fit for cultivation. DOMESTICATION-AGRICULTURE.

ar'-bi-ter. A judge. ADVICE, DECISION-MISJUDGMENT, JUDGE, MANAGER.

arbiter bibendi [L.] (ar'-bi-ter bi-ben'-dai). Toastmaster. ENTERTAINMENT-WEARINESS.

arbiter elegantiarum [L.] (ar'-bi-ter el-î-gan''-shi-ê'-rum). A polished judge. ENTERTAINMENT-WEARINESS, SOCIETY-LUDICROUSNESS, TASTE-VULGARITY.

ar-bit'-ra-ment. Decision of an arbitrator. DECISION-MISJUDGMENT; **arbitrament of the sword,** FIGHTING-CONCILIATION.

ar'-bi-tra-ri-ness. State of not being fixed by law LAW-LAWLESSNESS, TYRANNY-ANARCHY.

ar'-bi-tra-ry. Done at pleasure; tyrannical. BIGOTRY-APOSTASY, CONNECTION-INDEPENDENCE, CONVENTIONALITY-UNCONVENTIONALITY, HARSHNESS-MILDNESS, LAW-LAWLESSNESS, PERSISTENCE-WHIM, PRESUMPTION-OBSEQUIOUSNESS, RULE-LICENSE; **arbitrary power,** HARSHNESS-MILDNESS

ar'-bi-trate. To settle by arbitration. DECISION-MISJUDGMENT, MEDIATION.

ar''-bi-tra'-tion. A hearing and decision by arbitrators. DECISION-MISJUDGMENT, JUDGE, MEDIATION; **court of arbitration,** TRIBUNAL; **submit to arbitration,** COMPOSITION.

ar'-bi-tra''-tor. An arbiter DECISION-MISJUDGMENT.

arbitrium, ad [L.] (ar-bit'-ri-um, ad). According to the will or judgment. VOLITION-OBLIGATION.

arbitrium, liberum [L.] (ar-bit'-ri-um, lib'-er-um) Free will. VOLITION-OBLIGATION.

ar'-bor. A bower or summer house; principal shaft of a machine. CITY-COUNTRY, CONTENTS-RECEIVER, DWELLER - HABITATION, ENTERTAINMENT -WEARINESS, REVOLUTION-EVOLUTION, SUSPENSION-SUPPORT.

ar'-bor-a-ry. Pertaining to trees. FAUNA-FLORA.

ar-bo'-re-al. Relating to trees. FAUNA-FLORA.

ar''-bo-res'-cence. The state of being tree-like. PROPORTION-DEFORMITY.

ar''-bo-res'-cent. Tree-like. FAUNA-FLORA, PROPORTION-DEFORMITY, SMOOTHNESS-ROUGHNESS.

ar'-bor-i-cul''-ture. Cultivation of trees. DOMESTICATION-AGRICULTURE.

ar'-bor-i-form. Tree-like. PROPORTION-DEFORMITY.

arc. A bow. CURVATURE-RECTILINEARITY.

ar-cade'. Vaulted passageway or street. APERTURE-

Closure, Architecture, Curvature-Rectilinearity, Dweller-Habitation.

Arcades ambo [L.] (ar-kê'-dez am'-bo). Arcadians both. Friend-Foe, Good Man-Bad Man, Uniformity-Diversity.

Ar-ca'-di-a. A place where rustic simplicity and content prevails. City-Country, Heaven-Hell, Pleasure-Pain.

Ar-ca'-di-an. Rustic or pastoral. City-Country, Craft-Artlessness, Innocence-Guilt.

ar-ca'-num. A secret or mystery. Tidings-Mystery.

arch. A bow-like curve, structure, or object; sly; most important. Architecture, Convexity-Concavity, Craft-Artlessness, Curvation-Rectilinearity, Magnitude-Smallness, Sagacity-Incapacity, Suspension-Support; triumphal arch, Solemnization, Trophy; arch over, Curvation-Rectilinearity.

Ar-chæ'-an. Pertaining to the oldest period in geological history. Geology.

ar''-chæ-o-log'-ic-al. Versed in antiquity. Future-Past.

ar''-chæ-ol'-o-gist. One who investigates ancient relics and remains. Future-Past, Scholar-Dunce.

ar''-chæ-ol'-o-gy. Study of man through ancient records and remains. Future-Past.

ar-cha'-ic. Belonging to a former period. Novelty-Antiquity, Word-Neology.

ar'-cha-ism. Anything archaic. Future-Past, Word-Neology.

arch''-an'-gel. An angel of high rank. Angel-Satan.

arch''-bish'-op. The chief bishop of a province. Ministry-Laity.

arch''-bish'-op-ric. Office of an archbishop. Church.

arch''-dea'-con. A high church officer. Ministry-Laity.

arch''-duke'. Son of an emperor. Chief-Underling.

ar''-che-bi-o'-sis. Abiogenesis. Creation-Destruction.

arched. Bowed in a curve. Convexity-Concavity.

arch''-e-gen'-e-sis. First creation. Creation-Destruction.

arch'-er. One who uses bow and arrow. Belligerent, Push-Pull.

arch'-er-y. Art of shooting with a bow. Entertainment-Weariness, Push-Pull; archery ground, Entertainment-Weariness.

Arch'-es, Court of. An English ecclesiastical court of appeal. Church-Tribunal.

ar'-che-type. A model. Copy-Model.

ar-che'-us. The soul of the world. Life-Death.

arch'-fiend''. The devil. Angel-Satan.

ar''-chi-a'-ter. A chief physician. Advice.

ar''-chi-e-pis'-co-pa-cy. Rule of an archbishop. Church.

ar''-chi-e-pis'-co-pal. Pertaining to an archbishop. Church.

ar'-chi-pel'-a-go. A collection of islands. Swamp-Island.

ar'-chi-tect. One who plans something. Agent, Maker-Destroyer.

ar'-chi-tec''-ture. Science of designing and constructing buildings. Creation-Destruction, Embellishment-Disfigurement, Nature-Art, Organization-Disorganization, Texture.

ARCHITECTURE

Architecture. The science and art of designing and constructing buildings or other structures, a style or system of building.

Architecture—*Associated Nouns.*

Abacus. A tablet, panel or compartment in ornamented or mosaic work.

Abbey. The buildings of a monastery or nunnery, a place of worship

Acanthus. A conventionalized representation of the acanthus leaf.

Acroterium. A small pedestal.

Alhambra. The palace of the Moorish kings at Granada.

Amphiprostyle. A temple having columns at each end but not at the sides.

Amphitheater. An edifice of elliptical shape, constructed about a central open space, with tiers of seats sloping upward and backward.

Annulet. A small projecting molding.

Anta. A pier produced by thickening a wall at its termination

Antefix. An ornament at the eaves, or fixed upon a frieze.

Arcade. A vaulted passageway.

Arch. Any structure supported at the sides or ends only, and formed of distinct pieces no one of which spans the opening.

Arris. An external angle; the sharp ridge between two channels of a Doric column.

Astragal. A molding surrounding the top of a column in the form of a ring.

Atlantes. Male human figures, used in place of columns or pilasters.

Balcony. A balustraded platform projecting from a wall; a tier of seats in a theater.

Baldachin. A canopy of rich stuff, or of stone or metal.

Baluster. A small pillar, one of a series supporting a hand-rail.

Balustrade. A railing formed of a range of balusters supporting a hand-rail.

Bartizan. A turret, with loopholes, jutting out from a wall.

Base. The lowest or supporting part.

Bastion. A projecting work having two faces and two flanks.

Battlement. A parapet having in its upper line a range of indentations.

Bay window. A window-structure of angular plan, projecting outward from a wall and reaching to the ground.

Bema. That part of an early Christian church which was reserved for the higher clergy.

Billet. An ornament in Norman work.

Bossage. Rustic work, consisting of stones which seem to advance beyond the level of the building.

Bracket. A piece projecting from a vertical surface, so as to support shelf, mirror, coping, etc.

Bucrania. Sculptured ornaments.

Buttress. Any support or prop.

Canopy. A covering suspended over a throne, shrine, bed, etc.

Cantilever. A heavy bracket supporting a cornice or balcony

Capital. The upper member of a column, pillar, pier, or pilaster.

Caryatid. A draped female figure supporting an entablature.

Catherine-wheel window. A rose window or wheel window.

Chaptrel. An impost.

Chevrons. Rafters, in a gable roof, that meet at the ridge.

Cinquefoil. A five-cusped ornament or window

Clustered column. A column which is composed, or appears to be composed, of several columns collected together.

Column. A vertical shaft, usually cylindrical and having both a base and a capital, designed to support an entablature, balcony, etc.

Composite capital. A capital belonging to an order composed of Ionic grafted upon the Corinthian.

Composite order. An order which is composed of the Ionic order grafted upon the Corinthian.

Console. A corbel.

Corbel. One of a series of brackets, often ornamental, projecting from the face of a wall, the basket-shaped cushion of the Corinthian capital.

Corinthian order. The most ornamental of the three orders of architecture used by the Greeks.

Cornice. Ornamental molding, as one running around the walls of a room close to the ceiling.

Crenelated molding. A kind of indented molding used in Norman buildings.

Crocket. A projecting ornament usually terminating in a floral curve or roll.

Cupola. A dome.

Curb-roof. A roof having two sets of rafters, the upper ones having much less inclination than the lower.

Cyma recta. A cyma, hollow in its upper part and swelling below.

Cyma reversa. A cyma swelling out on the upper part and hollow below.

Dome. A roof in the form of a half globe.

Doric capital. A capital of the simplest order known to the Greeks.

Doric order. The oldest and simplest of the three orders of architecture used by the Greeks.

Dormer window. A window pierced in a roof, and so set as to be vertical while the roof slopes away from it.

Eaves. The projecting edge of a roof, serving to shed rain-water.

Eavings. Eaves.

Echeum. Bell-shaped vase used as a sounding-board in Greek theaters.

Echinus. The cushion of the capital of a Doric column.

Engaged column. A column engaged in a wall, so that only a part of its circumference projects from it.

Festoon. Ornamental carving hanging in a curve between two points.

Finial. An ornament at the apex of a spire, pinnacle or the like.

Flying buttress. A contrivance for taking up the thrust of a roof or vault which cannot be supported by ordinary buttresses.

Foils. Leaf-like divisions in architectural ornamentation.

Foliations. Decorations with foliated tracery.

Fret. Ornamental work in relief, done by carving or embossing.

Frieze. Flat part under the cornice of a column.

Gable. The triangular end of a wall, above the level of the eaves; the entire end wall of a building.

Gargoyle. A spout projecting from the roof gutter of a building, often carved grotesquely.

Groined arch. An arch built with groins.

Groins. Angular curve formed by the intersection of two arches.

Guilloche. An ornament in the form of two or more bands or strings twisted over each other in a continued series, leaving circular openings, which are filled with round ornaments.

Guttæ. Drop-like ornaments.

Hammer-beam roof. A roof so formed as not to have a tiebeam at the top of the wall.

Hance. That part of an elliptical or many-centered arch which has the shorter radius and immediately adjoins the impost.

Haunch. The shoulder of an arch.

Helices. Figures like the tendrils of a vine.

Hip-knob. An ornament at the intersection of the hip rafters and the ridge.

Hip-roof. A roof rising directly from the wall-plate on all sides and so having no gable.

Impost. The plane from which an arch springs.

Interlacing arches. Arches, usually circular, so constructed that their archivolts intersect and seem to be interlaced.

Inverted arches. Arches placed with crown downward.

Ionic order. An order of architecture invented by the Greeks, the distinguishing feature of which is a capital with spiral volutes.

Keystone. The central or topmost stone of an arch, which completes it and locks its members together.

King-post. A single vertical strut supporting the apex of a triangular truss and itself supported by a cross-beam.

Lancet-window. An acutely pointed window.

Lattice-window. Openwork formed by crossing or interlacing strips or bars, which cover a window.

Lattice-work. Any work of wood or metal, made by crossing laths, or thin strips, and forming a network.

Lean-to. A building having a single-pitched roof, with its apex against an adjoining wall or building.

Leaves. Hinged or sliding parts, as of a door, table, etc.

Linen-scroll. An ornament for filling panels.

Lintel. The horizontal top piece of a doorway.

Loggia. A covered gallery or portico, having a colonnade on one or more sides, open to the air; a large ornamental window.

Lotus. An ornament much used in Egyptian architecture.

Louver-window. A lantern-like cupola or turret on the roof of a medieval dwelling.

Lozenge-window. A window made of lozenge-shaped panes set diagonally.

Lunette. Opening in a concave ceiling to admit light.

Machicolation. An opening between a wall and a parapet to permit missiles or boiling liquids to be dropped upon an enemy.

Metope. A square slab, sculptured or plain, between triglyphs in a Doric frieze.

Minaret. A slender tower characteristic of mosques, built of several stories, each surrounded by a balcony.

Modillion. An ornamental bracket.

Moorish capital. The capital in the style of architecture developed by the Moors in the later Middle Ages.

Moresque. The Moresque style of architecture or decoration, consisting of interlacings, relief, etc., highly colored and gilded.

Mullion. A division-piece between the lights of windows, or the bays or panels in wainscoting.

Multifoil. An ornamental foliation consisting of more than five divisions or foils.

Mutule. One of a series of rectangular impending blocks under a Doric corona, with dependent drop-like ornaments called guttæ.

Nave. The main body of a church, between the aisles.

Niche. A recess in a wall, as for a statue.

Oriel. A window resting on a bracket or corbel.

Ovolo. A convex molding.

Patera. A circular ornament, resembling a dish, often worked in relief on friezes, and the like.

Pavilion. A movable or open structure for temporary shelter, entertainment, or dwelling.

Pedestal. A base or support, as for a column or statue.

Pediment. A triangular member having a small altitude compared with its base, framed in by a cornice, and surmounting a portico.

Pendant. A hanging ornament on roofs ceilings, etc.

Pentastyle. A portico having five columns.

Pent roof. A roof having only one slope or pitch.

Peristyle. A system of columns surrounding a building or an internal court.

Pilaster. A right-angled columnar projection from a pier or wall.

Pinnacle. A small turret or tall ornament, usually tapering, as on a parapet.

Quoin. A large square ashlar or stone at the angle of a wall; a wedge-shaped stone of an arch.

Roman Doric. Roman modification of the Doric order of architecture.

Scroll. Any spiral line used as an ornament.

Soffit. The under side of a staircase, entablature lintel, archway, or cornice.

Spandrel. The triangular space between the shoulder of an arch and the rectangular figure formed by the moldings, etc., over it.

Spire. The tapering or pyramidal roof of a tower the tapering part of a steeple.

Stall. A partially enclosed seat, as in the orchestra of a theater; a compartment in which a horse or bovine animal is confined and fed.

Steeple. A lofty structure rising above the roof of a church: usually a tower surmounted with a spire.

Straight arch. A form of arch in which the intrados is straight.

Tower. A structure larger than a pinnacle and less tapering than a steeple.

Tracery. Ornamental stonework formed of ramifying lines.

Trefoil. An architectural ornament resembling the three-leaved clover.

Triforium. Open gallery in the wall above the arches of the nave.

Triglyph. A grooved tablet in the frieze of the Doric order.

Tubular bridge. A bridge in the form of a hollow trunk, made of iron plates riveted together.

Turnstile. A frame in the form of a horizontal X pivoted on an upright post, to turn as people pass through it.

Turret. A small tower.

Tuscan capital. A capital of the Tuscan order of architecture.

Tuscan order. One of the five orders of architecture. It admits of no ornaments.

Veranda. An open portico or gallery extending along one or more sides of a building.

Volute. A spiral ornament characteristic of Ionic and Corinthian capitals; a scroll.

ARCHITECTURE—*Adjective.*

Inclave. Shaped like a series of dovetails.

ar'-chi-trave. A chief beam. Top-Bottom.

ar'-chive. A depository for documents; a document. Mark-Obliteration.

arch'-lute. A large double-necked lute. Musical Instruments.

arch'-ness. Roguishness. Craft-Artlessness.

ar'-chon. A chief magistrate. Chief-Underling, Judge, President-Member, Representative.

arch'-trai"-tor. The chief criminal. Uprightness-Rogue.

arc–lights. Large electric lights. Electricity.

arc'-tic. Cold; near the north pole. Heat-Cold, Laterality-Contraposition.

ar'-cu-ate. Arc-like. Curvation-Rectilinearity.

ar"-cu-a'-tion. Curvature. Curvation-Rectilinearity.

ar'-dent. Passionate; flashing. Desire-Distaste, Emotion, Heat-Cold, Love-Hate; ardent expectation, Expectation-Surprise; ardent imagination, Fancy.

ardet proximus [L.] (ar'-det prox'-i-mus). The next house burns. Refuge-Pitfall, Security-Insecurity.

ar'-dor. Intensity of passion; eagerness. Activity-Indolence, Desire-Distaste, Emotion.

ar'-du-ous. Involving great labor. Difficulty-Facility.

are. A land measure of the metric system. Measure.

a´-re-a. Extent of surface. EXTENSION-INEXTENSION.

ar´´-e-fac´-tion. A drying up. DAMPNESS-DRYNESS.

a-re´na. Place in which exhibitions are held; sphere of action. EXTENSION-DISTRICT, EXTENSION-INEXTENSION, LISTS, SIGHT-BLINDNESS.

ar´´-e-na´-ceous. Sandy. FRIABILITY.

ar´´-e-na´-ri-ous. Sandy. FRIABILITY.

ar´-e-nose. Full of sand. FRIABILITY.

a-re´-o-la. Small spaces marked out by veins on leaves. CIRCLE-WINDING.

a-re´-o-lar. Containing a network of small interspaces. CROSSING.

ar´´-e-om´-e-ter. Instrument for measuring specific gravity. SOLIDITY-RARITY.

Ar-e-op´-a-gus. The high court of ancient Greece. TRIBUNAL.

a-rete´. An abrupt mountain spur. SHARPNESS-BLUNTNESS.

ar´´-e-tol´-o-gy. Science of virtue. DUTY-DERELICTION.

Ar´-gand. Inventor of a lighting system. **Argand lamp,** LUMINARY-SHADE.

ar´-gent. Silvery. WHITENESS-BLACKNESS.

argent comptant [F.] (ar-zhan´ con´-tan´). Ready money. MONEY.

ar´-gen-tine. Silver-coated. VALUES, WHITENESS-BLACKNESS.

ar´´-gil-la´-ceous. Clayey. HARDNESS-SOFTNESS.

ar´-go-sy. A richly laden ship of commerce. CONVEYANCE-VESSEL.

ar´-got. Slang. WORD-NEOLOGY.

ar´-gue. To urge reasons for or against. EVIDENCE-COUNTEREVIDENCE, RATIOCINATION-INSTINCT, SIGN.

ar´-gu-er. One who discusses. RATIOCINATION-CASUISTRY.

ar´-gu-ment. A reason offered for or against. CONCEPTION-THEME, MEANING-JARGON, RATIOCINATION-INSTINCT; **have the best of an argument,** PROOF-DISPROOF.

ar´´-gu-men-ta´-tion. Debate. RATIOCINATION-CASUISTRY.

ar´-gu-men´-ta-tive. Consisting of argument. RATIOCINATION-CASUISTRY.

argumentum ad crumenam [L.] (ar-giu-men´-tum ad kriu-mî´-nam). Argument to the purse. MONEY.

argumentum ad hominem [L.] (ar-giu-men´-tum ad hom´-i-nem). Argument from an opponent's own position. JUSTIFICATION-CHARGE.

argumentum ad verecundiam [L.] (ar-giu-men´-tum ad ver-î-cun´-di-am). Argument from authority. REPUTATION-DISCREDIT, UPRIGHTNESS-DISHONESTY.

argumentum baculinum [L.] (ar-giu-men´-tum bak-yu-lai´-num). Appeal to physical force. COERCION, LAW-LAWLESSNESS, RECOMPENSE-PUNITION.

ar´-gus. A hundred-eyed giant. SIGHT-BLINDNESS; **argus-eyed,** CAREFULNESS-CARELESSNESS, SIGHT-BLINDNESS.

ar-gute´. Quick or sharp. SAGACITY-INCAPACITY.

a´-ri-a. An air or melody. MUSIC.

A´-ri-an-ism. A doctrine that denies the consubstantial nature of the Trinity. ORTHODOXY-HETERODOXY.

ar´-id. Parched with heat; without interest. DAMPNESS-DRYNESS, ENTERTAINMENT-WEARINESS, FERTILITY-STERILITY.

A´-ri-el. One of the chief angels; the inner satellite of Uranus. ASTRONOMY, JOVE-FIEND, MESSENGER, SWIFTNESS-SLOWNESS, WAYFARER-SEAFARER.

A´-ri-es. A constellation in the zodiac. ASTRONOMY.

a´´-ri-e-ta´-tion. Act of butting like a ram. IMPETUS-REACTION.

a´´-ri-et´-ta. A short melody. MUSIC.

a-right´. Correctly. GOOD-EVIL.

Ar´-i-man. The evil deity. ANGEL-SATAN, JOVE-FIEND.

a´´-ri-o-la´-tion. Act of foretelling. PROPHECY.

aris et focis, pro [L.] (ê´-ris et fo´-sis, pro). For our altars and firesides. ATTACK-DEFENSE, HUMANITARIANISM-MISANTHROPY.

a-rise´. To come into existence; to get up from lying down; to move to a higher place. ASCENT-DESCENT, BEGINNING-END, ENTITY-NONENTITY, OCCURRENCE-DESTINY, VISIBILITY-INVISIBILITY; **arise from,** CAUSE-EFFECT.

Ar´-is-tarch´´-us. A learned critic of Alexandria. TASTE-VULGARITY.

ar´-is-tar´´-chy. Rule by the best. RULE-LICENSE.

Ar´´-is-ti´-des. An Athenian statesman called "the Just." GOOD MAN-BAD MAN.

ar´´-is-toc´-ra-cy. Hereditary nobility. GENTILITY-DEMOCRACY, RULE-LICENSE.

ar´´-is-to-crat´-ic. Pertaining to an aristocracy. GENTILITY-DEMOCRACY, RULE-LICENSE.

ariston metron [Gr.] (a´-ris-ton met´-ron). The golden mean. MIDCOURSE-CIRCUIT, TURBULENCE-CALMNESS.

Ar´´-is-to-te´-li-an. A disciple of Aristotle. RATIOCINATION-INSTINCT.

ar´-ith-man´´-cy. Divination by numbers. PROPHECY.

a-rith´-me-tic. Science of numbers. NATURE-ART, NUMBERING.

ar´´-ith-met´-ic-al. Pertaining to arithmetic. NUMBERING.

a-rith´´-me-ti´-cian. One skilled in arithmetic. NUMBERING.

ark. A large floating vessel. DWELLER-HABITATION, REFUGE-PITFALL.

arm. Part of the body; to furnish with means; strength. ANATOMY, FIGHTING-CONCILIATION, INSTRUMENT, MIGHT-IMPOTENCE, PREPARATION-NONPREPARATION, PROVISION-WASTE, WEAPON, WHOLE-PART; **armchair,** SUSPENSION-SUPPORT; **arm in arm,** AMITY-HOSTILITY, SOCIABILITY-PRIVACY, SOLITUDE-COMPANY; **arm of the law,** LAW-LAWLESSNESS; **arm of the sea,** GULF-PLAIN; **in the arms of Morpheus,** ACTIVITY-INDOLENCE; **make a long arm,** LENGTH-SHORTNESS, TAKING-RESTITUTION.

ar-ma´-da. A fleet of warships. BELLIGERENT.

Ar-ma-ged´-don. Plain of Esdraelon, famous as a battlefield. STRIFE-PEACE.

ar´-ma-ment. War equipment. PREPARATION-NONPREPARATION, WEAPON.

ar´-ma-ture. Means of defense; a piece of soft iron joining the poles of a magnet. ELECTRICITY, WEAPON.

armed. Prepared for war. ATTACK-DEFENSE; **armed at all points,** ATTACK-DEFENSE, PREPARATION-NONPREPARATION; **armed force,** BELLIGERENT; **armed with patience,** EXCITABILITY-INEXCITABILITY.

ar´-mi-ger. A knight's armor-bearer. GENTILITY-DEMOCRACY.

ar-mig´-er-ent. An armor-bearer. BELLIGERENT.

ar-mig´-er-ous. Entitled to heraldic arms. FIGHTING-CONCILIATION.

ar´-mil-la-ry. Consisting of rings. **Armillary sphere,** ASTRONOMY, MENSURATION.

ar´-mis-tice. Temporary cessation of hostilities. FIGHTING-CONCILIATION.

arm´-less. Without arms. MIGHT-IMPOTENCE.

arm´-let. A band worn on the arm; an arm of the sea. CIRCLE-WINDING, GULF-PLAIN.

ar´-mor. Defensive covering. ATTACK-DEFENSE, WEAPON.

ar-mo´-ri-al. Relating to heraldry. SIGN.

ar´-mor-y. Place for storing arms. STORE, WEAPON.

arms. Weapons; deeds done in battle; mark of distinction. FIGHTING-CONCILIATION, INSTRUMENT, SIGN, TITLE, WEAPON; **clash of arms,** STRIFE-PEACE; **deeds of arms,** STRIFE-PEACE; **in arms,** INFANT-

Veteran; **throw oneself into the arms of,** Amity-Hostility, Refuge-Pitfall; **under arms,** Fighting-Conciliation; **up in arms,** Activity-Indolence, Amity-Hostility, Favorite-Anger, Reprisal-Resistance, Variance-Accord; **with arms akimbo,** Defiance; **with folded arms,** Activity-Indolence.

arm's length. At a distance. **At arm's length,** Remoteness-Nearness; **keep at arm's length,** Amity-Hostility, Attack-Defense, Attraction-Repulsion, Politeness-Impoliteness, Sociability-Privacy.

Arm'-strong. Inventor of a gun. **Armstrong gun,** Weapon.

ar'-my. A large organized body of men. Belligerent, Gathering-Scattering, Multiplicity-Paucity.

a-ro'-ma. Fragrance. Perfume-Stench.

ar''-o-mat'-ic. Having an aroma. Perfume-Stench.

ar''-o-mat'-ic se'-ri-es. A series of compounds derived from benzene. Chemistry.

a-round'. On all sides of. Environment-Interposition; **lie around,** Environment-Interposition, Outside-Inside.

a-rouse'. To stir up. Excitation, Motive-Caprice; **arouse oneself,** Activity-Indolence.

a-roynt'. To begone out of the way. Admission-Expulsion, Charitableness-Curse.

ar'-que-bus. A fifteenth century musket. Weapon.

ar''-que-bus-ade'. A discharge from an arquebus. Remedy-Bane.

ar-raign'. To call into court. Justification-Charge, Litigation.

ar-raign'-ment. Accusation. Justification-Charge, Litigation.

ar-range'. To put in order; to agree on terms. Composition, Design, Organization-Disorganization; **arrange in a series,** Continuity-Interruption; **arrange itself,** Regularity-Irregularity; **arrange** matters, Fighting-Conciliation; **arrange music,** Musician; **arrange under,** Admission-Exclusion; **arrange with creditors,** Settlement-Default.

ar-ranged'. Put in order. Organization-Disorganization, Regularity-Irregularity.

ar-range'-ment. Order. Composition, Design, Fighting-Conciliation, Organization-Disorganization, Preparation-Nonpreparation, Regularity-Irregularity, Settlement-Default; **temporary arrangement,** Lastingness-Transientness.

ar'-rant. Notoriously bad. Goodness-Badness, Magnitude-Smallness, Manifestation-Latency, Publicity, Reputation-Discredit, Uprightness-Dishonesty.

ar'-ras. A fabric woven with figures. Embellishment-Disfigurement.

ar-ray'. Regular order; display; clothing; collective body. Continuity-Interruption, Dress-Undress, Embellishment-Disfigurement, Gathering-Scattering, Multiplicity-Paucity, Pomp, Preparation-Nonpreparation, Regularity-Irregularity; **battle array,** Fighting-Conciliation.

ar-rear'. Back; a debt. **In arrear,** Credit-Debt, Entirety-Deficiency, Settlement-Default.

ar-rears'. Debts. Credit-Debt.

arrectis auribus [L.] (ar-rek'-tis au'-ri-bus). With ears pricked up. Expectation-Surprise, Hearing-Deafness.

ar-rest'. To stop; to take into custody; to fix the attention. Discontinuance-Continuance, Litigation, Release-Restraint; **arrest the attention,** Heed-Disregard.

ar''-res-ta'-tion. An arrest. Release-Restraint.

arrière pensée [F.] (ar-ri-ar' pan'-sê'). Mental reservation. Enlightenment-Secrecy, Motive-Caprice, Predecessor-Continuation, Purpose-Luck.

ar'-ris. An external angle. Architecture.

ar-ri'-val. Coming to anything. Arrival-Departure.

ARRIVAL—DEPARTURE.

Advent. An important arrival; a coming.
Arrival. Act of reaching a place from a distance.
Caller. One who makes a visit.
Completion. End of a journey. See Completion.
Debarkation. Act of coming ashore from a vessel.
Destination. Place set for the end of a journey.
Disembarkation. The act of coming from on board a vessel.
Encounter. A hostile meeting.
Landing. A bringing on shore.
Meeting. A coming together.
Reception. The act of being received or met.
Recursion. The act of coming back.
Remigration. Going back to the place from which one came.
Rencounter. Sudden hostile collision.
Return. Coming back to the same place.
Vin d'honneur [F.]. Wine offered to a newly arrived guest.
Visitant. One who pays a visit.
Welcome. A greeting upon arrival.

Arrival—*Nouns of Place.*

Anchorage; goal; halting ground; halting place; harbor; haven; home; landing place; landing stage; port; resting place; terminus.

Arrival—*Verbs.*

Alight. To descend, as from horseback.
Arrive. To reach a point started for.
Attain. To come to a place by effort.
Be in at the death. To have arrived at the end.
Bounce upon. ⎫
Burst upon. ⎭ To arrive unexpectedly.
Cast anchor. To drop an anchor to keep a ship at rest.
Come. To complete a movement toward a place.
Come across. To meet.
Come at. To arrive.
Come back. To return.
Come home. To return to one's house or family.
Come in. To enter. See Entrance.

Decampment. Departure from a camp.
Decession. A going away.
Departure. Removal from a place.
Embarkation. Going on board a vessel to depart.
Exit. A departure, as from the stage after performing a part.
Exodus. A large migration from a place.
Flight. A hasty departure to escape danger or expected evil.
Hegira. The flight of Mohammed from Mecca, September 13, 622 A.D.; any flight or exodus.
Outset. Beginning of a journey.
Removal. Going from one place to another.
Start. Commencement of a journey.

Departure—*Denotations*

Adieu; conge; farewell; good-bye; leave taking; stirrup-cup, a parting cup taken after mounting; valediction.

Departure—*Nouns of Place.*

Place of departure; place of embarkation; point of departure; point of embarkation; port of embarkation; starting-point; starting-post.

Departure—*Verbs.*

Abandon. To cast or drive out.
Abscond. To depart secretly and hide. See Quest-Evasion.
Be gone. To be away.
Be off. To start away.
Bid good-bye. See *Nouns.*
Cut one's stick. To run away.
Debouch. To march from a wood into open ground.
Decamp. To move away from a camping ground, usually by night or secretly.
Depart. To go away.
Disappear. To get out of sight. See Appearance-Disappearance.
Embark. To go on shipboard to depart.
Evacuate. To withdraw from.
Flit. To move rapidly from place to place.
Fly. To run away from.

ARRIVAL—DEPARTURE—*Continued.*

ARRIVAL—Verbs—*Continued.*

Come in contact. To meet.
Come to. To reach.
Come to hand. To arrive.
Come upon. To befall.
Come up to. To meet.
Come up with. To catch up with.
Complete. To end a journey. See sub COMPLETION.
Debark. } To come from on board a ship.
Disembark. }
Dismount. To come down from on horseback.
Drop in. To visit casually.
Encounter. To meet; come upon unexpectedly.
Fetch. To go and bring.
Get back. } To return.
Get home. }
Get to. To arrive.
Get to one's journey's end.
Go ashore. To come from on shipboard.
Hit. To meet unexpectedly.
Join. To meet with.
Land. To end a journey by water.
Light. To dismount.
Light upon. To meet.
Make. To complete.
Make one's appearance. To arrive.
Make the land. To come to shore.
Meet. To come into the presence of.
Overtake. To catch up with.
Pitch one's tent. To stop or rest.
Pitch upon. }
Plump upon. } To meet suddenly.
Pop upon. }
Put in. } To land.
Put into. }
Reach. To come to a point journeyed to.
Rejoin. To meet again.
Rencounter. To meet in a hostile manner.
Return. To come back from whence one started.
Sit down. To stop; to rest. See ESTABLISHMENT.
Visit. To go or come to see.

ARRIVAL—*Adjectives.*

Arriving, etc. See *Verbs.*
Homeward-bound. Returning to one's home or family.

ARRIVAL—*Adverbs.*

Here. At this place.
Hither. To this place.

ARRIVAL—*Interjections.*

All hail! good day! good morrow! hail! welcome!

DEPARTURE—*Continued from Column 2.*

DEPARTURE—*Interjections.*

Adieu! au revoir! begone! farewell! fare you well! God bless you! God speed you! good-bye! good day!

DEPARTURE—*Phrases.*

Au plaisir de vous revoir [F.]. Till I have the pleasure of seeing you again; adieu; auf wiedersehen.
Bon voyage [F.]. Prosperous voyage to you.
Glückliche Reise [G.]. Prosperous journey to you.
Vive, valeque [L.]. Life and health to you! farewell!

DEPARTURE—Verbs—*Continued*

Fly away. To move or go suddenly.
Get off. To start.
Get under way. To start a journey.
Go. To depart.
Go aboard. To get on ship to depart.
Go along. Be off.
Go away. To depart.
Go forth. To go away.
Go from home.
Go off. To depart.
Go off the stage. To retire from sight or notice.
Go on board. To be ready to depart.
Go one's way. To proceed on one's journey.
Go to sea. To make a journey by sea.
Hoist blue peter. To raise the blue flag to recall boats.
Issue. To go forth.
Leave a place. To depart.
Make one's exit. To take one's departure.
March off. To leave a place.
March out. To depart.
Move off. To go from land.
Pack off. To go with one's belongings.
Put off. To depart from.
Put to sea. To begin a voyage.
Quit. Leave.
Remove. To go from one place to another.
Retire. To go backwards.
Sail. To go on a voyage.
Sally. To rush or burst forth.
Sally forth. Rush out suddenly.
Say good-bye. To give greeting upon departure.
Set forward. To go on.
Set off. To begin to go.
Set out. To leave.
Set sail. To begin a voyage.
Spring. To hasten away.
Start. } To begin to go away.
Start off. }
Strike tents. To take down tents; to begin a march.
Take flight. To run away from impending danger.
Take leave. To depart from.
Take one's departure. } To leave.
Take oneself off. }
Take wing. To hasten away.
Vacate. To depart from a place.
Walk one's chalks. To be sent away.
Weigh anchor. To start on a voyage.
Whip away. } To depart hurriedly.
Whip off. }
Wing one's flight. To leave hurriedly and unknown.
Withdraw. To leave; retire.

DEPARTURE—*Adjectives.*

Departing, etc. See *Verbs.*
Outward bound. Going away from.
Valedictory. Suitable for an occasion of leave taking.

DEPARTURE—*Adverbs.*

Hence. From here.
On the move. Departing.
On the wing. Fleeing.
Thence. From that place.
Whence. From what place.
With a foot in the stirrup. Ready to depart.

(Continued on Column 1.)

---

ar-rive'. To reach the end; to occur. ARRIVAL-DEPARTURE, COMPLETION-NONCOMPLETION, DISCONTINUANCE-CONTINUANCE, OCCURRENCE-DESTINY; **arrive at a conclusion,** DECISION-MISJUDGMENT; **arrive at the truth,** DISCOVERY.

ar-ri'-ving. Reaching a place. ARRIVAL-DEPARTURE.

ar'-ro-gance. Haughtiness. HARSHNESS-MILDNESS, SELFRESPECT-HUMBLENESS.

ar'-ro-gant. Excessively proud; haughty. CONCEIT-DIFFIDENCE, HARSHNESS-MILDNESS, PRESUMPTION-OBSEQUIOUSNESS, SELFRESPECT-HUMBLENESS.

ar'-ro-gate. To demand or claim without reason. COMPLETION - NONCOMPLETION, DUENESS - UNDUE-NESS, PRESUMPTION-OBSEQUIOUSNESS; **arrogate to oneself,** DUENESS-UNDUENESS.

arrondissement [F.] (a-ron'-dis-man'). Subdivision of a French department. EXTENSION-DISTRICT.

ar-ro'-sion. A gnawing. FRICTION-LUBRICATION.

ar'-row. A missile shot from a bow. PUSH-PULL, SWIFTNESS-SLOWNESS, WEAPON.

ar'-row-head''. Sharp-pointed head of an arrow; shaped like an arrow. SHARPNESS-BLUNTNESS, WRITING-PRINTING.

ar'-row-head''-ed. Shaped like an arrow. SHARPNESS-BLUNTNESS.

ars artium omnium conservatrix [L.] (arz ar'-shi-um

om'-ni-um con-ser-vê'-trix). The art preservative of all arts TRUTHFULNESS-FALSEHOOD, WRITING-PRINTING.

ars celare artem [L.] (arz sel-ê'-rî ar'-tem). Art consists in hiding art. SKILL-UNSKILFULNESS.

ar'-se-nal. A place of deposit for arms. STORE

ar'-se-nic. A non-metallic poisonous element. REMEDY-BANE.

ar'-son. Malicious burning of property. HEATING-COOLING.

art. Practical application of knowledge; embodiment of beautiful thought in visible forms; mastery in works of taste. CRAFT-ARTLESSNESS, DELINEATION-CARICATURE, NATURE-ART, OCCUPATION, SKILL-UNSKILFULNESS; **fine art,** TASTE-VULGARITY; **work of art,** BEAUTY-UGLINESS, EMBELLISHMENT-DISFIGUREMENT.

ar'-ter-y. A channel; a blood-vessel. WATERCOURSE-AIRPIPE, WAY.

artes, hae tibi erunt [L.] (ar'-tîz, hî tib'-i î'-runt). These shall be your methods. WAY.

artes honorabit [L.] (ar'-tîz hon-or-ê'-bit). He will honor the arts. SKILL-UNSKILFULNESS.

ar-te'-sian well. A well in which the water pressure forces the water up. GULF-PLAIN.

art'-ful. Cunning; deceitful. CRAFT-ARTLESSNESS, TRUTHFULNESS-FALSEHOOD; **artful dodge,** CRAFT-ARTLESSNESS, TRUTHFULNESS-FALSEHOOD.

art'-ful-ness. State of being artful. TRUTHFULNESS-FALSEHOOD.

ar'-ti-choke. A thistle-like plant, part of which is edible. NUTRIMENT-EXCRETION.

ar'-ti-cle. A particular object; a brief composition; a point of doctrine; an adjective that limits a noun. ADJECTIVE, ESSAY, MATERIALITY-SPIRITUALITY, MERCHANDISE, MISSIVE-PUBLICATION, SUBSTANCE-NULLITY, WHOLE-PART; **definite article,** ADJECTIVE; **indefinite article,** ADJECTIVE.

ar'-ti-cled clerk. A servant bound by agreement. INSTRUCTOR-PUPIL.

ar'-ti-cles. Complete terms of religious belief. TERMS; **articles of agreement,** TERMS; **articles of faith,** THEOLOGY; **Thirty-nine Articles,** ORTHODOXY-HETERODOXY.

ar-tic'-u-late. Clear. VOCALIZATION-MUTENESS.

ar-tic''-u-la'-tion. Distinct utterance; act of joining. UNION-DISUNION, VOCALIZATION-MUTENESS.

articulo, in [L.] (ar-tic'-yu-lo, in). In a moment. LIFE-DEATH, LASTINGNESS-TRANSIENTNESS.

ar'-ti-fice. Cunning. CRAFT-ARTLESSNESS, DESIGN.

ar-tif'-i-cer. A mechanic. AGENT, LABOR-CAPITAL.

ar''-ti-fi'-cial. Manufactured; crafty. CRAFT-ARTLESSNESS, NATURE-ART, PURITY-CRUDENESS, SIMPLICITY-FLORIDNESS, SOCIETY-AFFECTATION, TRUTHFULNESS-FRAUD; **artificial language,** PURITY-CRUDENESS.

ar''-ti-fi''-ci-al'-i-ty. No genuineness or naturalness. CRAFT-ARTLESSNESS.

ar-til'-ler-y. Heavy cannon. BELLIGERENT, LOUDNESS-FAINTNESS, WEAPON.

ar-til'-ler-y-man. One who works artillery. BELLIGERENT.

ar'-ti-san. A trained workman. AGENT, LABOR-CAPITAL.

artisan, chacun est l' . . . *de sa fortune* [F.] (sha-cun'' ê lar-ti-zan'' de sa for-tün'). Every man is the architect of his own fortune. SUCCESS-FAILURE, WELFARE-MISFORTUNE.

art'-ist. An adept in a fine art. AGENT, ARTIST, DESIGN.

ARTIST.

Artist. Any one who is skilful in the fine arts, especially painting and sculpture.
Carver. One skilled in chiseling wood into figures.
Chaser. An engraver.
Coach painter. One adept in painting wagons.
Copyist. One who reproduces that which has been created, by imitating it.
Designer. One who creates artistic designs.
Draftsman. One who makes a draft or sketch.
Drawer. One who delineates with a pencil.
Enameler. One who is skilled in putting on enamel.
Enamelist. Same as enameler.
Engraver. An artist who cuts into the surface of materials.
Figuriste [F.]. A representer.
Flower painter. A painter who paints flowers only.
Historical painter. A painter who depicts historical scenes.
Landscape painter. A painter who represents natural scenery.
Limner. One who draws or paints.
Marine painter. A painter of sea-pictures.
Miniature painter. A painter of small pictures.
Modeler. One who makes a pattern.
Painter. An artist who decorates or represents with colors.
Portrait painter. One who makes a specialty of depicting the portraits of men.
Scene painter. A landscape painter.
Sculptor. An artist in wood, marble, etc.
Sign painter. A painter of boards, etc., for indicating places of business.
Sketcher. One who makes a hasty and incomplete outline or drawing.
Statuary. A maker of statues.

ARTIST—*Denotations.*

Apelles; Phidias; Praxiteles; Royal Academician.

ar-tiste' [F.] (ar-tîst'). A professional dancer or singer. ACTING, MUSICIAN.

ar-tis-tic. Correctly and tastefully executed. BEAUTY-UGLINESS, NATURE-ART, PURITY-CRUDENESS, SKILL-UNSKILFULNESS, TASTE-VULGARITY; **artistic language,** PURITY-CRUDENESS.

ar-tis'-tic-al. Conformable to art. BEAUTY-UGLINESS.

ar-tis'-tic-al-ly. In an artistic manner. SKILL-UNSKILFULNESS.

artium baccalaureus [L.] (ar'-shi-um bac-ca-lau'-ri-us). Bachelor of arts. SCHOLAR-DUNCE.

artium magister [L.] (ar'-shi-um ma-jis'-ter). Master of arts. SCHOLAR-DUNCE.

art'-less. Without deceit; simple. CRAFT-ARTLESSNESS, NATURE-ART.

art'-less-ness. Without craft or deceit. CRAFT-ARTLESSNESS.

arundo lethalis lateri haeret [L.] (a-run'-do leth-ê'-lis lat'-er-ai hî-ret). The fatal arrow clings fast in her side. PLEASURE-PAIN.

a-rus'-pex, a-rus'-pice. A soothsayer. SOOTHSAYER.

a-rus'-pi-cy. Divination. PROPHECY.

Ar'-yan. One of the primitive peoples of Central Asia. ETHNOLOGY.

as. Like; thus; because; while; a Roman coin. MOTIVE-CAPRICE, VALUES; **as broad as long,** EQUALITY-INEQUALITY; **as can be,** ENTIRETY-DEFICIENCY; **as good as,** EQUALITY-INEQUALITY; **as if,** HYPOTHESIS, LIKENESS-UNLIKENESS; **as it may be,** CONDITION-SITUATION, OCCURRENCE-DESTINY, RATIONALE-LUCK; **as it were,** LIKENESS-UNLIKENESS, TROPE; **as little as may be,** MAGNITUDE-SMALLNESS; **as much again,** DOUBLING-HALVING; **as soon as,** COEXISTENCE; **as the world wags,** OCCURRENCE-DESTINY; **as they say,** ADAGE-NONSENSE, TIDINGS-MYSTERY; **as things are,** CONDITION-SITUATION; **as things go,** HABIT-DESUETUDE, OCCURRENCE-DESTINY; **as to,** CONNECTION-INDEPENDENCE; **as usual,** CONVENTIONALITY-UNCONVENTIONALITY, HABIT-DESUETUDE; **as well as,** ADDITION-SUBTRACTION; **as you were,** ADVANCE-RETROGRESSION, RENOVATION-RELAPSE.

as-a-fet'-i-da. The juice of a plant of the family Ferula, which is used in medicine. PALATABLENESS-UNPALATABLENESS, REMEDY-BANE.

as-cend'. To go upward. ASCENT-DESCENT, BETTER-MENT-DETERIORATION, INCREASE-DECREASE.

as-cend'-an-cy. Superiority in power or rank. DOMINANCE-IMPOTENCE, MIGHT-IMPOTENCE, SUCCESS-FAILURE.

as-cend'-ant. Dominant. CONSEQUENCE-INSIGNIFICANCE, DOMINANCE-IMPOTENCE, REPUTATION-DISCREDIT, RULE-LICENSE, SUCCESS-FAILURE; **lord of the ascendant,** CHIEF-UNDERLING; **one's star in the ascendant,** WELFARE-MISFORTUNE.

as-cend'-ing. Moving upwards. PARALLELISM-INCLINATION.

as-cen'-sion. Act of rising; a vapor. ASCENT-DESCENT, BETTERMENT-DETERIORATION, HEATING-COOLING, INCREASE-DECREASE.

as-cent'. Act of ascending in space; an upward slope. ASCENT-DESCENT, BETTERMENT-DETERIORATION, INCREASE-DECREASE, PARALLELISM-INCLINATION, REPUTATION-DISCREDIT.

ASCENT—DESCENT.

Ascension. The act of moving upward.
Ascent. The act of rising.
Leap. The act of springing clear of the ground, with the feet. See SPRING.
Rise. Distance through which anything goes upward.
Rising. Act of moving upward. See *Verbs*.
Upgrowth. The process or result of growing up.

ASCENT—*Denotations*.

Acclivity; Alpine Club; flight of steps; flight of stairs; hill; ladder; lark; ratlines; rocket; sky-rocket; skylark.

ASCENT—*Verbs*.

Arise. To come up from a lower to a higher position.
Ascend. To go up; to climb.
Aspire. To seek to attain something high.
Clamber. To go upward with difficulty, or with hands and feet.
Climb. To ascend with much labor.
Escalade. To mount by means of ladders.
Float. To move on the surface of a fluid.
Get up. } To rise.
Go up. }
Hover. To be suspended in the air above something.
Leap. To spring clear of the ground, with the feet. See SPRING
Mount. To get up on anything, as a platform, or horse.
Plane. To cut off parts that are higher than others.
Ramp. To creep up.
Rise. To go from a lower position to a higher.
Scale. To climb by a ladder.
Scale the heights. To fight one's way upward.
Scramble. To climb with hands and knees.
Shoot up. To rise suddenly.
Soar. To mount upward, as on wings.
Spire. To shoot up in a spire.
Spring up. To rise hurriedly.
Start up. To rise unexpectedly.
Surge. To rise high and roll.
Surmount. To rise higher than something else.
Swim. To float on the top of the water.
Tower. To overtop.
Uprise. To appear from below the horizon; to rise to one's feet.
Work one's way up. To struggle upward with great effort.

ASCENT—*Adjectives*.

Buoyant. Tending to rise or float.
Rising, etc. See *Verbs*.
Scandent. Climbing.
Superfluitant. Floating above or on the surface.
Supernatant. Swimming.

ASCENT—*Adverbs*.

Uphill. Ascending.

DESCENT—*Continued from Column 2.*

DESCENT—*Adjectives*.

Deciduous. Falling off at a certain season.
Decurrent. Extending downward.
Decursive. Running down.
Descendent. Falling.
Descending, etc. See *Verbs*.
Labent. Sliding; gliding.
Nodding to its fall. Having the top bent forward.

DESCENT—*Adverbs*.

Downhill. Sloping.
Downward. From a higher place to a lower.

Cadence. Act or state of declining or sinking.
Cropper. A fall on one's head when riding at full speed.
Culbute [F.]. A somerset.
Declension. A downward sloping.
Declination. Act or state of bending downward.
Descension. The act of going downward.
Descent. Change of place from higher to lower.
Downfall. A sudden descent.
Fall. A descent by the force of gravity.
Falling. A sinking or dropping.
Fate of Icarus. A fall while soaring too high.
Lapse. A passing downward smoothly and gradually.
Lurch. A sudden falling.
Stumble. A fall in walking or running.
Subsidence. A sinking.
Tilt. A leaning to one side.
Titubation. The act of stumbling, rocking or rolling.
Trip. A loss of footing or balance causing a fall.

DESCENT—*Denotations*.

Avalanche; *débâcle*, a breaking or bursting forth of water; declivity; dip; landslip; hill.

DESCENT—*Verbs*.

Alight. To spring down, as from on horseback.
Come down. To descend.
Come down a cropper. To fall on the head while going at full speed.
Come down a peg. To descend a short distance.
Decline. To bend downward.
Descend. To pass from a higher to a lower part of.
Dismount. To bring down from an elevation.
Droop. To hang bending downward.
Drop. To cause to fall in one portion.
Drop down. To fall.
Fall. To descend gradually or suddenly.
Fall prostrate. To fall at full length.
Get down.
Go down.
Gravitate. To tend in any direction or toward any object.
Let fall.
Light. To fall upon.
Lurch. To roll or sway suddenly.
Pitch. To decline or slope.
Plump down. To drop or fall suddenly or heavily, like lead.
Precipitate oneself. To throw oneself downward.
Set. To sink out of sight.
Settle. To sink gradually.
Sink. To descend lower and lower.
Slide. To move down gradually.
Slip. To move downward smoothly and quickly.
Sprawl. To move, when lying down.
Stoop. To bend the upward part of the body downward and forward.
Stumble. To fall while walking or running.
Swag. To sink down by its weight.
Swoon. To fall on at once and seize.
Tilt. To lower one end and raise the other.
Titubate. To stumble.
Topple. To pitch or tumble down.
Topple down. } See TOPPLE.
Topple over. }
Trip. To cause to stumble.
Tumble. To fall suddenly and violently.
Tumble down. } See TUMBLE.
Tumble over. }

(Continued on Column 1.)

as"-cer-tain'. To learn with certainty. DECISION-MISJUDGMENT, MUTABILITY-STABILITY.

as"-cer-tained'. Made certain. CERTAINTY-DOUBT, KNOWLEDGE-IGNORANCE.

as-cet′-ic. Practising asceticism. AUSTERITY.

as-cet′-i-cism. Practise of the life of a recluse. AUSTERITY.

as″-ci-ti′-tious. Added from without. ADDITION-SUBTRACTION, ENTITY-NONENTITY, SUBJECTIVENESS-OBJECTIVENESS.

as-cribe′. To refer, as to a cause or source. RATIONALE-LUCK.

as-crip′-tion. Act of ascribing. RATIONALE-LUCK.

ash. Remains of an organic substance that has been burned. HEATING-COOLING; **ash-colored,** GRAY-BROWN.

a-shame′. To cause shame. SELFRESPECT-HUMBLENESS.

a-shamed′. Feeling shame. SELFRESPECT-HUMBLENESS.

ash′-en. Resembling ashes in color. GRAY-BROWN.

ash′-es. Dust; mortal remains of the dead; deathly pallor. CLEANNESS-FILTHINESS, LIFE-CORPSE; **lay in ashes,** CREATION-DESTRUCTION; **pale as ashes,** COLOR-ACHROMATISM, SANGUINENESS-TIMIDITY; **rise from one's ashes,** RENOVATION-RELAPSE.

a-shore′. On the shore. OCEAN-LAND; **go ashore,** ARRIVAL-DEPARTURE, OCEAN-LAND.

Ash Wednesday. The first day of Lent. PERIODICITY-IRREGULARITY.

ash′-y. Like ashes. COLOR-ACHROMATISM.

A′-sian mys′-ter-y. Mystery of an Asian character. TIDINGS-MYSTERY.

a-side′. To one side; away from thought; apart. CONVERSATION-MONOLOGUE, ENLIGHTENMENT-SECRECY, LATERALITY-CONTRAPOSITION, LOUDNESS-FAINTNESS; **say aside,** CONVERSATION-MONOLOGUE; **set aside,** ASSERTION-DENIAL, CAREFULNESS-CARELESSNESS, CHOICE-REJECTION, COMMISSION-ABROGATION, ESTABLISHMENT-REMOVAL, KEEPING-RELINQUISHMENT, USE-DISUSE; **step aside,** AIM-ABERRATION.

as′-i-nine. Ass-like; stupid. CONVEYER, SAGACITY-INCAPACITY.

asininus ad lyram [L.] (as″-i-nai′-nus ad lai′-ram). Ass at the lyre. HARMONY-DISCORD.

ask. To make a request or petition for. EXCHANGE, INVESTIGATION-ANSWER, PETITION-EXPOSTULATION, PRICE-DISCOUNT; **ask leave,** LEAVE-PROHIBITION.

a-skance′. With a side or indirect glance or meaning. PARALLELISM-INCLINATION; **eye askance,** SANGUINENESS-TIMIDITY; **look askance,** APPROVAL-DISAPPROVAL, ASSENT-DISSENT, DESIRE-DISTASTE, SIGHT-BLINDNESS, SIGHT-DIMSIGHTEDNESS.

asked in church. Engaged to be married. MATRIMONY-CELIBACY.

ask′-ing. Making a petition. PETITION-EXPOSTULATION.

a-skew′. In a twisted position or manner. PARALLELISM-INCLINATION, PROPORTION-DEFORMITY.

a-slant′. Across in a slanting direction. PARALLELISM-INCLINATION.

a-sleep′. In a state of sleep. ACTIVITY-INDOLENCE.

As″-mo-de′-us. A destructive demon. JOVE-FIEND.

a-so′-ma-tous. Without body. MATERIALITY-SPIRITUALITY.

asp. A venomous serpent. BENEFACTOR-EVILDOER, FAUNA-FLORA.

As-pa′-si-a. The mistress of Pericles of Athens. PURITY-RAKE.

as′-pect. Peculiar feature; appearance. APPEARANCE-DISAPPEARANCE, CONDITION-SITUATION, POSITION, SUBJECTIVENESS-OBJECTIVENESS.

as′-pects. Appearances. SUBJECTIVENESS-OBJECTIVENESS.

asp′-en leaf. Leaf of the poplar tree. **Shake like an aspen leaf,** AGITATION, SANGUINENESS-TIMIDITY.

as-per′-i-ty. Harshness; roughness. FAVORITE-ANGER, FAVORITE-QUARRELSOMENESS, POLITENESS-IMPOLITENESS, SMOOTHNESS-ROUGHNESS.

as′-per-ous. Harsh. SMOOTHNESS-ROUGHNESS.

as-perse′. To slander. ADULATION-DISPARAGEMENT.

as-per′-sion. Baptism by sprinkling. ADULATION-DISPARAGEMENT, CEREMONIAL.

as′-phalt. Mineral pitch. PULPINESS-ROSIN, SMOOTHNESS-ROUGHNESS.

as-phyx′-i-a. Suffocation. LIFE-DEATH.

as-phyx′-i-ate. To suffocate. LIFE-DEATH.

as′-pir-ant. One who seeks earnestly. DESIRE-DISTASTE, PETITIONER.

as′-pi-rate. To utter with a breathing. VOCALIZATION-MUTENESS.

as″-pi-ra′-tion. Exalted desire. DESIRE-DISTASTE, DEVOTION-IDOLATRY, SANGUINENESS-TIMIDITY.

as-pire′. To have an earnest desire for. ASCENT-DESCENT, DESIRE-DISTASTE, DEVOTION-IDOLATRY, PURPOSE-LUCK, SANGUINENESS-HOPELESSNESS.

ass. An equine quadruped. CONVEYER, SAGE-FOOL; **ass between two bundles of hay,** DETERMINATION-VACILLATION; **ass in lion's skin,** ADEPT-BUNGLER, GULL-DECEIVER; **ass's bridge,** CLEARNESS-OBSCURITY; **make an ass of,** TRUTHFULNESS-FRAUD.

as″-sa-foet′-i-da. A drug of an offensive odor; asafetida. PERFUME-STENCH.

as′-sa-gai. A spear. WEAPON.

as-sail′. To attack violently. ATTACK-DEFENSE, PLEASURABLENESS-PAINFULNESS.

as-sail′-ant. One who attacks. ANTAGONIST-ASSISTANT, ATTACK-DEFENSE, BELLIGERENT.

as-sas′-sin. One who kills secretly. LIFE-KILLING, TYRANNY-ANARCHY.

as-sas′-sin-ate. To kill treacherously. LIFE-KILLING, TYRANNY-ANARCHY.

as-sas″-sin-a′-tion. Killing. LIFE-KILLING, TYRANNY-ANARCHY.

as-sault′. A violent attack. ATTACK-DEFENSE; **assault and battery,** ATTACK-DEFENSE; **take by assault,** TAKING-RESTITUTION.

as-say′. To try. TRIAL.

as-say′-ing. Analyzing an ore to find its ingredients. CHEMISTRY.

as′-se-guai. A light spear. WEAPON.

as-sem′-blage. Association. CONCENTRATION-RADIATION, GATHERING-SCATTERING.

as-sem′-bled. Convened. GATHERING-SCATTERING.

as-sem′-bly. A gathering together. COUNCIL, GATHERING-SCATTERING, MINISTRY-LAITY, SOCIABILITY-PRIVACY, UNION-DISUNION.

as-sem′-bly-man. A member of a legislative assembly. PRESIDENT-MEMBER.

as-sem′-bly room. A gathering place. DWELLER-HABITATION.

as-sent′. Agreement. ASSENT-DISSENT, CONSENT, CONTENTEDNESS-DISCONTENTMENT, FAITH-MISGIVING, READINESS-RELUCTANCE, VARIANCE-ACCORD.

ASSENT—DISSENT.

Acceptance. An agreeing to terms or proposals by which a party is bound.

Acclamation. A shout of favor or assent.

Accord. Agreement of opinion, will, or action.

Accordance. Agreement or conformity.

Acknowledgment. A declaration or avowal of one's own act.

Acquiescence. A silent or passive agreement or submission.

Cavilling. Picking flaws; frivolous dissenting.

Contradiction, etc. Denial of the truth of a statement; gainsaying. See ASSERTION-DENIAL.

Difference of opinion. Disagreement in belief or judgment; dissent.

Disaffection. Discontent; alienation; disloyalty.

Discontent, etc. Dissatisfaction; uneasiness. See CONTENTEDNESS-DISCONTENTMENT

Admission. The granting of an argument or position not fully proved.

Affirmance. }
Affirmation. } A solemn declaration in place of a judicial oath.

Agreement. Harmony of opinion, statement, or action. See HARMONY.

Approval. A favorable opinion.

Assent. Act of the mind in admitting or agreeing to anything.

Assentment. Act of agreeing with.

Avowal. An open declaration.

Chorus. The simultaneous joining of a company in any noisy demonstration.

Common consent. Public approval.

Concord. }
Concordance. } A state of agreement or harmony.

Concurrence. Agreement of opinion. See COOPERATION.

Confession. Acknowledgment of a matter pertaining to oneself.

Confession of faith. A formula containing the articles of belief.

Confirmation. That which gives new strength to a statement or belief

Consent. Voluntary agreement with what is done or proposed by another. See CONSENT.

Cooperation. Concurrent effort or labor. See COOPERATION.

Corroboration. To confirm or declare the truth of.

Current belief. General acceptance of a fact or assertion as true.

Current opinion. The judgment of a community in regard to any point of knowledge or action.

Endorsement. Sanction or approval. See MARK.

Nod. A motion of the head giving assent.

Popular belief. Common assent to anything without immediate personal knowledge.

Popular opinion. Public or common judgment.

Public opinion. Notion or conviction of the people, founded upon probable evidence.

Ratification. Approval or sanction of an act.

Recognition. Knowledge confessed or avowed

Unanimity. The state of being of one mind.

Visa [L.]. An endorsement on a passport.

Vox populi [L.]. The voice of the people.

ASSENT—*Verbs.*

Accede. To agree or assent to a proposal or a view.

Accept. To receive with a consenting mind.

Accord. To bring to an agreement.

Acknowledge. To own or recognize in a particular character.

Acquiesce. To consent by silence, or by omitting to object.

Admit. To concede as true.

Affirm. To confirm; to declare positively.

Agree. To come to one mind concerning. See HARMONY

Allow. To approve of.

Approve. To think well of.

Assent. To express one's agreement.

Avow. To acknowledge and justify.

Coincide. To correspond exactly.

Concede. To yield or suffer to pass.

Concur. To unite or agree in action or opinion.

Confess. To acknowledge oneself to be guilty of.

Confirm. To strengthen by approval.

Consent. To agree in opinion or sentiment.

Corroborate. To make more certain. See sub EVIDENCE

Countersign. To sign in order to attest the authenticity of a writing

Echo. To repeat with assent.

Endorse. }
Indorse. } To give one's name or support to

Own. To admit to be true.

Permit. To allow or suffer to be done. See LEAVE.

Ratify. To give sanction to something done by an agent.

Receive. To take into mind by assent to.

Reciprocate. To give and receive mutually.

Recognize. To allow that one knows.

ASSENT—*Verbal Expressions.*

Abide by; agree in opinion; be at one with; be in every mouth; be in the fashion; chime in with; close with; come round to; come to an agreement; come to an understanding; come to terms; conform to; defer to; enter into one's views; give assent; give one's voice for; go along with; go with; go with the stream; join in the chorus; lend oneself to; nod assent; say amen to; say aye to; say ditto to; say yes to; strike in with; swim with the stream; vote for; yield assent.

ASSENT—*Adjectives.*

Acquiescent. Disposed to submit quietly.

Affirmative. See ASSERTION.

Discordance, etc. State of disagreeing; lack of harmony, etc. See HARMONY-DISCORD.

Dissension, etc. Angry or violent disagreement in opinion, etc. See VARIANCE.

Dissent. Disagreement in opinion; separation from an established church.

Diversity of opinion. Unlikeness or variety of opinion.

Non-compliance, etc. Failure to conform or acquiesce, etc. See PROFFER-REFUSAL.

Non-conformity, etc. Failure to conform or agree; refusal to adhere to the established church. See ORTHODOXY-HETERODOXY.

Protest. Solemn or formal dissent or objection.

Protestantism. The principles and system of doctrines of the Protestant churches, dissenting from the authority of the pope.

Recantation, etc. The act of withdrawing, as a former statement, or disavowing an opinion previously held, etc. See BIGOTRY-APOSTASY.

Recusancy. Persistent non-conformity to authoritative commands; refusal to conform to the Church of England.

Schism. Division of a church into factions because of dissenting opinions.

Secession, etc. Withdrawal from union or fellowship, etc. See QUEST-ABANDONMENT.

DISSENT—*Nouns of Agent.*

Dissenter. One who disagrees; one who refuses conformity to an established church.

Dissentient. A dissenter; one who disagrees.

Non-content. One who votes negatively.

Non-juror. A Scotch or English clergyman who refused to swear allegiance.

Protestant. Any Christian who stands opposed to Roman Catholicism.

Recusant. One who obstinately refuses to conform to authoritative commands; a non-conformist.

Schismatic. One who causes or takes part in a schism; one who dissents from an established church because of difference of opinion.

DISSENT—*Verbs.*

Call in question, etc. Doubt; disagree with; challenge, etc. See FAITH-MISGIVING.

Cavil. Object frivolously; pick flaws.

Contradict, etc. Deny; be inconsistent with. See ASSERTION-DENIAL.

Demur. Bring forward objections or difficulties; take exception.

Differ in opinion. Disagree; dissent.

Differ *toto cœlo.* Differ by the whole heaven; be entirely different.

Disagree. Differ; hold discordant views.

Dissent. Disagree in opinion; refuse adherence to an established church.

Have no notion of. Refuse.

Look askance. }
Look askant. } Regard with disdain or distrust.

Protest. Dissent formally or solemnly.

Raise one's voice against. Object to or protest against by speech.

Recant, etc. Retract, as a former statement; renounce an opinion previously held. See BIGOTRY-APOSTASY.

Refuse assent. Withhold approval; dissent.

Refuse to admit. Decline to acknowledge the truth of; disagree.

Repudiate. Disavow; renounce; refuse to acknowledge and pay.

Revolt at. Dissent with disgust or offense.

Revolt from the idea. Be disgusted, shocked, or offended with the idea.

Say no, etc. See ASSERTION-DENIAL.

Secede. Withdraw from fellowship, communion, or confederation.

Shake the head. Dissent by moving the head on its axis from side to side.

Shrug the shoulders. Raise up the shoulders in order to express dislike, doubt, etc.

DISSENT—*Adjectives.*

Denominational. Sectarian; characterized by different opinions.

Discontented, etc. Dissatisfied, etc. See CONTENTEDNESS-DISCONTENTMENT.

Dissentient. Dissenting; withholding approval.

Dissenting, etc. Disagreeing; refusing adherence, etc. See *Verbs.*

Dissident. Differing; dissenting.

Extorted. Obtained violently from an unwilling person.

Negative, etc. Characterized by contradiction or dissent, etc. See ASSERTION-DENIAL.

Non-content. Dissatisfied.

Non-juring. Refusing to swear allegiance.

Out of the question. Not worthy of thought or consideration.

Protestant. Protesting; formally dissenting.

ASSENT—DISSENT—*Continued*.

ASSENT—Adjectives—*Continued*.

Agreed. Of the same mind.
Agreed *nem. con.* No one speaking in opposition.
Agreed on all hands. Unanimous.
Assenting. Admitting or agreeing to anything.
At one with. Agreed.
Carried by acclamation. Passed by a shout of approval.
Carried *nem. con.* Carried without opposition.
Content. Agreeing without examination.
Of one accord.
Of one mind. }Unanimous.
Of the same mind.
Unanimous. Agreeing in opinion or determination.
Unchallenged. Left to pass without examination.
Uncontradicted. Without assertion to the contrary.
Uncontroverted. Undisputed.
Unquestioned. Not doubted.
Willing, etc. Received of choice, or without reluctance. See READINESS.

ASSENT—Adverbs.

Affirmatively. Positively.
Amen. So be it.
As one man. All together.
Assuredly. Certainly.
Ay. }
Aye. } Yes.
Be it so.
By common consent. See *Nouns.*
Certainly. Without doubt or question.
Certes. In truth.
Doubtless. Fixed in judgment.
Even so. Just so.
Exactly. Strictly according to rule.
Ex concesso [L.]. From what has been conceded.
Good. Expression of approval.
Granted. Admitted as true.
In chorus. Acting together.
Indeed. Truly; denoting concession.
In the affirmative. Positively, as opposed to negatively.
Just so.
Nem. con. [L.]. Abbreviation for *nemine contradicente.*
Nemine contradicente [L.]. No one speaking in opposition.
Nemine dissentiente [L.]. Without a dissenting voice.
No doubt. }
Of course. } Surely.
On all hands. }
One and all. } All together.
Precisely.
So be it. }
So let it be. } Exactly.
That's just it. }
Thou hast said it. } Conceded.
To a man. All together.

DISSENT—Adjectives—*Continued*.

Recusant. Obstinately refusing conformity.
Schismatic. Of or pertaining to schism or dissent.
Sectarian. Devotedly attached to the tenets of a denomination; dissenting from all but one sect.
Unacknowledged. Not confessed or avowed.
Unavowed. Not openly acknowledged.
Unconsenting, etc. Not agreeing, etc. See PROFFER-REFUSAL.
Unconverted. Not agreeing with the Christian religion; not changed in opinion.
Unconvinced. Not persuaded by argument; unsatisfied by evidence.
Unwilling, etc. See READINESS-RELUCTANCE.

DISSENT—Adverbs.

At issue with. Dissenting from; disputed.
At variance with. In disagreement with; in a condition of dissension.
No, etc. See ASSERTION-DENIAL.
Under protest. With formal and solemn dissent.

DISSENT—Interjections.

God forbid! I'll be hanged if; never tell me; not for the world; pardon me; your humble servant.

DISSENT—Phrases.

Il s'en faut bien [F.]. It is far from it.
Many men many minds. Diversity of opinion.
Quot homines tot sententiæ [L.]. Many men many minds.
Tant s'en faut [F.]. So far from it.

ASSENT—Adverbs—*Continued*.

To be sure. Certainly.
True. }
Truly. } Expressions of assent.
Unanimously. Of one mind.
Una voce [L.]. With one voice.
Unquestionably. Undisputed.
Very true. }
Very well. } Certainly.
Well. }
Well and good. } Just so.
Willingly, etc. Of one's own accord. See READINESS.
With one accord. }
With one consent. } See *Nouns.*
With one voice. }
Without a dissentient voice. Unanimously.
Yea. }
Yes. } Affirmative adverbs.

ASSENT—Phrases.

Avec plaisir [F.]. With pleasure.
Chi tace accousente [It.]. Silence gives consent.
Es korakas [Gr.]. To the crows.

---

assenti, gli hanno torto [It.] (as-sen'-tî, yî an'-no tor-to). The absent are in the wrong. JUSTIFICATION-CHARGE.

as-sert'. To state positively or plainly. ASSERTION-DENIAL, DUENESS-UNDUENESS.

as-ser'-tion. Positive or definite statement. ASSERTION-DENIAL.

ASSERTION—DENIAL.

Acknowledgment. Avowal of an obligation; confession. See ASSENT.
Adjuration. An impressive appeal or charge.
Affidavit. A written declaration under oath.
Affirmance. The act of openly declaring.
Affirmation. The act of declaring true; an assertion.
Allegation. Act of strongly declaring.
Assertion. The making of a statement as a conviction of the mind.
Asseveration. Emphatic affirmation.
Assurance. Declaration intended to dispel doubt.
Averment. Strong statement of the truth.
Avouchment. A declaration that the maker will stand by.
Dogmatism. Unyielding; positive assertion. See CERTAINTY.
Declaration. An open, formal expression of facts, etc.
Deposition. Written testimony sworn to. See MARK.
Dictum. An authoritative statement.
Emphasis. The act of bringing out forcibly.
Ipse dixit [L.]. He himself has said it. Incontestable statement.
Oath. A solemn appeal to God in support of the truth of a declaration.

Abjuration. Renouncing upon oath.
Abnegation. A denial, a renouncing.
Confutation. The act of refuting, of successfully denying. See PROOF-DISPROOF.
Contradiction. Denial of another's assertion.
Contravention. Opposition to the operation, as of a law.
Denial. The act of refusing to grant or admit, non-compliance.
Disavowal. Refusing to own, repudiation.
Disclaimer. A denying of any responsibility, etc.
Emphatic contradiction. Positive denial.
Emphatic denial. Absolute refusal to accept or to admit.
Flat contradiction. }
Flat denial. } Open and absolute denial or contradiction.
Prohibition. The act of forbidding or disallowing. See LEAVE-PROHIBITION.
Protest. A public objecting to.
Negation. Opposed to affirmation, a denial.
Qualification. A partial negation. See MODIFICATION.
Recusation. Persistent refusal to conform to established order.
Recusancy. Obstinacy in refusal. See ASSENT-DISSENT.

ASSERTION—DENIAL—*Continued.*

Observation.   A casual remark.
Position.   The act of laying down, as a principle, fact, etc.
Predication.   A statement of a principle belonging to something.
Profession.   A declaration of any kind as of faith, etc.
Protest.   A solemn declaration or objection.
Protestation.   Act of proclaiming or objecting to a thing.
Remark.   A brief statement without much thought.
Saying.   A common remark often repeated.
Sentence.   A group of words making sense.
Statement.   A declaration of things.
Swearing.   Solemn affirmation upon oath.
Voice.   An expression of judgment or preference.
Vote.   A formal expression of preference.
Voter.   One who casts a vote on a question.
Word.   A brief remark.

ASSERTION—*Noun of Agency.*

Dogmatist.   One who clings tenaciously to an opinion or declaration.

ASSERTION—*Verbs.*

Acknowledge.   To avow, confess.   See ASSENT.
Adjure.   To put to one's oath.   See ENGAGEMENT.
Advance.   To put forward as one's opinion.
Affirm.   To make a statement firm; to declare positively.
Allege.   To declare, to aver.
Announce.   To give public notice of; to declare.   See ENLIGHTENMENT.
Assert.   To affirm boldly.
Assert positively.
Assert roundly.
Asseverate.   To aver strongly.
Assure.   To make safe against doubts.
Attest.   To declare true.   See EVIDENCE.
Aver.   To assert that something is true.
Avouch.   To declare in favor of.
Avow.   To acknowledge openly.
Be sworn.
Broach.   To introduce a subject for the first time.
Call Heaven to witness.   To affirm solemnly.
Certify.   To make certain; to make declaration of the truth of.
Contend.   To hold to a statement.
Declare.   To make an open statement.
Depone.   To testify.
Depose.   To bear witness to under oath.
Dogmatize.   To make positive, arrogant statements.
Emphasize.   To utter with force.
Have one's say.   To give one's opinion and carry his point.
Have the last word.
Hold out.   Stick to.
Insist upon.   To assert emphatically; to demand forcibly.
Kiss the book.   To take the oath.
Lay down.   To assert vigorously.
Lay down the law.
Lay stress upon.   To subjoin great importance to.
Maintain.   To affirm as a doctrine, etc.
Make an affidavit.
Make an assertion.   See *Nouns.*
Make (take) one's oath.
Predicate.   To affirm one thing of another.
Pretend.   To claim, profess.
Profess.   To announce publicly.
Pronounce.   To declare.
Propose.   To place before.
Propound.   To formally propose.
Protest.   To assert emphatically.
Put forth.
Put forward.
Put in an affidavit.
Raise one's voice.   To attest, proclaim.
Rap out.   To speak out suddenly.
Reaffirm.   To affirm again.
Reassert.   To assert again.
Repeat.   To say over again.
Say.
Set forth.   To declare.
State.   To set out clearly.
Swear.   To affirm on oath.
Swear by.
Swear by bell, book and candle.
Swear till one is all blue.
Swear till one is black in the face.

Refusal.   A declining to comply or accept.   See PROFFER-REFUSAL.
Repudiation.   Refusal to have anything to do with.   See CHOICE-REJECTION.
Retraction.   The act or state of being retracted.   See BIGOTRY-APOSTASY.

DENIAL—*Verbs.*

Belie.   To make out false, to contradict.
Bring in question.   To throw doubt upon.   See FAITH-MISGIVING.
Call in question.
Contradict.   To deny the truth of.
Contravene.   To oppose the operation of.
Controvert.   To deny and to sustain the denial by arguments.
Deny.   To affirm that such and such are untrue, to disown.
Deny emphatically.
Deny entirely.
Deny flatly.
Deny peremptorily.
Deny wholly.
Disaffirm.   Not to affirm or declare.
Disavow.   To refuse to own or acknowledge.
Disclaim.   Not to claim.
Disown.   To decline to own; to disavow.
Dispute.   To contend in argument; to question the truth of.
Gainsay.   To say against; to deny.
Give the lie to.   To call a liar; to brand as a liar.
Ignore.   To decline to have any relations with.   See CAREFULNESS-CARELESSNESS.
Impugn.   To assail with arguments; to contradict.
Join issue upon.   To enter into a debate.
Negative.   To prove or declare untrue.
Qualify.   To negative partially.   See MODIFICATION.
Rebut.   To contradict with argument.   See PROOF-DISPROOF.
Recant.   To take back a former statement.
Refuse.   To decline, to deny.   See PROFFER-REFUSAL.
Repudiate.   To refuse to have anything to do with, to discard.   See CHOICE-REJECTION.
Revoke.   To declare void, to reverse.   See COMMISSION-ABROGATION.
Set aside.
Shake the head.   To call in question.
Traverse.   To make a formal denial.

DENIAL—*Adjectives.*

At issue upon.   In controversy.
Contradictory.   Affirming the opposite.
Denied.   Declared untrue.   See *Verbs.*
Denying.   Declaring untrue.   See *Verbs.*
Negative.   Opposed to positive.
Negatory.   Belonging to negation.
Recusant.   Obstinately declining to conform.   See ASSENT-DISSENT.

DENIAL—*Adverbial Expressions.*

By no manner of; by no means; far from it; in no respect; nay; negatively; no; no such thing; not; not a bit; not a jot; not at all; not a whit; nothing of the kind; nothing of the sort; not in the least; not so; nowise; on no account; quite the contrary; *tant s'en faut* [F.], so far from it; *tout au contraire* [F.], on the contrary.

DENIAL—*Phrases.*

I know better.
Non hæc in fœdera [L.].   Not in these compacts.
There never was a greater mistake.

ASSERTION—VERBS—*Continued.*

Take one's Bible oath.   To take a very solemn oath.
Take one's stand upon.   To emphatically affirm.
Vitam impendere vero [L.].   To risk one's life for the truth.
Vouch.   To certify to the truth of.
Vow.   To make a solemn promise.
Warrant.   To declare confidently.

ASSERTION—*Adjectives.*

Absolute.   Authoritative, peremptory.
Affirmatory.   Having affirmation.
Asserting.   Stating positively.   See *Verbs.*
Broad.   Plain, open, clear.
Categorical.   Without condition, absolute.
Certain.   Plain, evident, open.   See CERTAINTY.
Confident.   Being bold, self-reliant.
Decided.   Having decision, resolute.

ASSERTION—Adjectives—*Continued.*

Declaratory. Making an affirmation.
Definitive. Final, conclusive.
Distinct. Open, clear.
Dogmatic. Having positive beliefs.
Emphatic. Having force or emphasis.
Explicit. Plainly expressed. See MANIFESTATION.
Express. Declared with distinctness.
Flat. Unqualified, positive.
Formal. Done according to form.
Marked. Distinguished by a mark.
Peremptory. Positive in opinion, absolute.

Pointed. Having sharpness or point.
Positive. That which may be asserted.
Predicable. Capable of predication.
Predicatory. Able to be affirmed as a quality.
Pronunciative. Dogmatical.
Round. Unqualified, full.
Soi-disant [F.]. Pretended.
Solemn. Having gravity, done formally.
Trenchant. Keen, biting.
Unretracted. Not taken back; still affirmed.

ASSERTION—*Adverbial Expressions.*

Affirmatively, in an affirmative manner (see *Adjectives*); **be assured** (see FAITH); **by George; by jingo; by Jove; by my troth; egad,** by God; *ex cathedra* [L.], with authority; **forsooth; give me leave to say; I assure you; I'd have you to know; i' faith; I'll answer for it; I'll be bound; I'll engage for it; I'll take my oath; I'll venture to say; I'll warrant; I'll warrant you; I must say; in all con**science; in sober earnest; in sober sadness; in sober truth; in the affirmative; joking apart; let me tell you; marry; not to mince the matter; of a truth; perdie; sadly; seriously; so help me God; take my honor; take my oath; troth; truly; upon my word; upon oath; why; with emphasis; without fear of contradiction; yes** (see ASSENT); **you may be sure.**

ASSERTION—*Phrases.*

Dixi [L.]. I have said it.

Quoth he. Said he.

as-sess'. To fix the amount of tax. DECISION-MISJUDGMENT, MENSURATION, PRICE-DISCOUNT.
as-sess'-ment. Apportionment of taxes. DECISION-MISJUDGMENT, MENSURATION, PRICE-DISCOUNT.
as-sess'-or. An officer who levies taxes; an associate judge. JUDGE.
as'-sets. Property of an insolvent debtor. MONEY, PROPERTY.
as-sev'-er-ate. To declare positively. ASSERTION-DENIAL.
as-sev''-er-a'-tion. Emphatic declaration. ASSERTION-DENIAL.
as''-si-du'-i-ty. Close application. ACTIVITY-INDOLENCE.
as-sid'-u-ous. Devoted or constant. ACTIVITY-INDOLENCE.
as-sid'-u-ous-ness. Habits of close application. ACTIVITY-INDOLENCE.
as'-si-fy. To make an ass of. SENSITIVENESS-APATHY.
as'-sign'. To set apart for a particular use. ALIENATION, ASSIGNMENT, COMMISSION-ABROGATION, GIVING-RECEIVING; **assign as a duty,** DUTY-DERELICTION; **assign as cause,** RATIONALE-LUCK; **assign places,** ORGANIZATION-DISORGANIZATION.
as'-sig-nat. Promissory note of the French revolutionary government in 1789. MONEY.
as''-sig-na'-tion. Appointment; a meeting place. SOCIABILITY-PRIVACY; **place of assignation,** GATHERINGPLACE.
as''-sign-ee'. A trustee. GIVING-RECEIVING.
as-sign'-ment. Appointment; transfer of property. ASSIGNMENT, COMMISSION-ABROGATION, GIVING-RECEIVING.

ASSIGNMENT

Allotment. Anything set apart for a special use or to a distinct person.
Allowance. A share or portion of anything granted.
Appointment. Designation of a person to hold an office or discharge trust.
Apportionment. A dividing into just shares or parts.
Appropriation. Application for a special use or purpose.
Assignment. A grant for a particular purpose.
Consignment. Goods sent to an agent at one time.
Contingent. That which falls to one in a division.
Deal. A part or portion.
Dispensation. That which is dealt out or appointed.
Distribution. Arrangement into parts.
Dividend. A sum of money to be divided or distributed.
Division. The portion separated or set apart from another.
Dole. That which is dealt out.
Dose. The quantity of medicine given at one time.
Lot. A part which falls to one by chance.

Measure. The quantity determined by measuring.
Meed. That which is bestowed upon one in consideration of merit.
Mess. A quantity of food set on a table at one time.
Modicum [L.]. A small quantity.
Partition. A part divided off.
Pittance. A meager portion, quantity, or allowance.
Portion. A part considered by itself.
Proportion. The part one receives when the whole is distributed by rule.
Quantum [L.]. A definite portion.
Quota. A proportional part or share.
Ratio. A fixed relation of quantity, or degree.
Ration. A fixed daily allowance of provisions.
Repartition. An additional separation into parts.
Share. The part belonging to one of anything owned by a number.

ASSIGNMENT—*Verbs.*

Allot. To parcel into parts.
Apportion. To divide and assign in just proportion.
Billet. To quarter or place in lodgings.
Carve. To cut into parts for sharing.
Cast. To fix or distribute.
Deal. To give in portions.
Detail. To appoint for a particular service.
Dispense. To give out in portions.
Distribute. To divide among several or many.
Divide. To part.
Dole out. To give out in small portions.
Mete. To allot by quantity or capacity.
Parcel out. To divide and distribute by parts.
Portion out. To endow with a portion or inheritance.
Share. To receive a portion.

ASSIGNMENT—*Adjectives.*

Apportioning, etc. See *Verbs.*
Respective. Relating to particular persons or things, each to each.

ASSIGNMENT—*Adverbs.*

Each to each. Considered separately from everything else.
Respectively. Referred to each in order.

as-sim'-i-late'. To make like, or transform into the same substance. CONVERSION-REVERSION, HARMONY-DISCORD, IMITATION-ORIGINALITY, LIKENESS-UNLIKENESS, UNIFORMITY-DIVERSITY.
as-sim''-i-la'-tion. A transformation into the same substance. BIOLOGY, CONVERSION-REVERSION, HARMONY-DISCORD, IMITATION-ORIGINALITY.
as-sist'. To help. OBSTRUCTION-HELP.
as-sis'-tance. Help. OBSTRUCTION-HELP.
as-sist'-ant. One who helps another. ANTAGONIST ASSISTANT.
as-sist'-er. One who is present. PRESENCE-ABSENCE.
as-size'. Session of a court; to fix the weight of. MENSURATION, TRIBUNAL; **justice of assize,** JUDGE.

as-so'-ci-ate. To bring together; one very much in the company of a person. ANTAGONIST-ASSISTANT, ASSOCIATION, CONNECTION-INDEPENDENCE, FRIEND-FOE, GATHERING-SCATTERING, MIXTURE-HOMOGENEITY, SOLITUDE-COMPANY, UNION-DISUNION; **associate with,** MIXTURE-HOMOGENEITY, SOCIABILITY-PRIVACY, SOLITUDE-COMPANY.

as-so'-ci-a-ted. Joined to. CONNECTION-INDEPENDENCE.

as-so''-ci-a'-tion. Connection or relation. ANTAGONISM-CONCURRENCE, ANTAGONIST-ASSISTANT, ASSOCIATION, CONNECTION-INDEPENDENCE, FRIEND-FOE, GATHERING-SCATTERING, MIXTURE-HOMOGENEITY, SOLITUDE-COMPANY, UNION-DISUNION; **association of ideas,** HYPOTHESIS, MIND-IMBECILITY, RATIOCINATION-INSTINCT, REFLECTION-VACANCY.

ASSOCIATION.

Association. A body of persons united for a common purpose.

Band. A body of men associated for the execution of a specific object.

Body. A group of persons considered as a whole.

Brigue. A cabal; a faction.

Brotherhood. A number of men united by some fraternal bond or vow.

Cabal. A factious, intriguing body of men.

Camarilla [It.]. An irresponsible company of advisers.

Camorra [It.]. A secret society of Italy and Naples, organized in the nineteenth century, to watch the course of political events.

Circle. A company bound together by a common tie.

Clan. A body of persons of the same descent having a tribal society. See PARENTAGE.

Clique. An exclusive circle of persons, generally associated for a bad purpose.

Club. An association of persons for social purposes.

Combination. A joining together of a number for effecting a purpose.

Community. A number of persons having a common interest; society in general; a corporate body.

Confederation. The act of joining together; a league of states.

Confederacy. A number of states in league.

Confraternity. A body of men joined together for a common end.

Coterie. A circle of persons meeting together for a certain purpose.

Crew. A body of men associated for a specific work; the seamen of one vessel; any gang.

Denomination. A group of persons having a common name.

Dramatis personæ [L.]. The characters of a play.

Faction. A combination of politicians within a party acting for their own interest, in opposition to the government or general good.

Familistery. A community in which many persons unite as one family.

Family. A group of persons united by consanguinity or ties of blood.

Federation. A league of persons or of states.

Fellowship. A body of associated persons as companions.

Fraternity. A body of men associated together in a friendly manner for some purpose.

Freemasonry. Institutions of Freemasons, a secret organization for promotion of social intercourse and mutual assistance.

Free-soiler. An advocate for the non-extension of slavery.

Gang. A number in company acting together.

Horde. An irregular company, said generally of barbarous nomads.

Incorporation. Act of incorporating.

Institute. A society generally of literary or philosophical men.

Institution. A corporate body for a public purpose.

Junto. A secret council of men for political purposes.

Knot. A cluster, a group of men.

League. A union of persons, or states for effecting an end.

Locofoco. A name formerly given to a part of the Democratic party.

Luddite. A member of a riotous gang which for six years (1811-17) tried to keep labor-saving machines out of England.

Party. A body of persons opposed in opinion or policy to another body; a number of persons associated.

Phalanx. Any closely knit body of men.

Posse. A number of men selected by the sheriff to assist in the maintenance of order.

Ring. A combination of persons generally for corrupt political purposes or mercenary ends.

Set. A number of persons of same rank, profession, tastes, or thought.

Side. A party, a clique.

Sisterhood. A company of women associated together in common bonds of friendship.

Society. Any body of persons united by any tie.

Sodality. A brotherhood.

Staff. A body of persons attached to a commander-in-chief of an army.

Trade union. A combination of workmen for bettering their social and economic condition.

Union. A combination or association of any kind.

ASSOCIATION—*Denotations.*

Alliance, an agreement between parties; *bund* [G.], a league, especially said of the German Confederation; **coalition; defensive alliance; Knight Templar; Kuklux; offensive alliance; party spirit; solidarity,** a solid union of interests or feeling; **Tammany; Tory;** *verein* [G.], a voluntary union of persons for a definite end; **Whig;** *zollverein* [G.], a union in respect to trade and customs.

ASSOCIATION—*Place.*

Casino. A place for assemblage, etc.

ASSOCIATION—*Verbs.*

Associate. To join together in a common enterprise. See GATHERING.

Cement a party. To join its parts firmly together, to make it cooperate together.

Club together. To join together in a common end. See CONCURRENCE.

Enleague. To unite in a league.

Form a party. To join together into a party. See *Nouns.*

Join. To bring together, to associate.

Unite. To join, to bring together into a whole.

ASSOCIATION—*Adjectives.*

Banded together. United together as in a band.

Bonded together. Held together as with bonds.

Confederated. Leagued together in a common end.

Embattled. Marshaled in battle array.

Federative. Leagued together.

In alliance (see *Nouns*); **in league; in partnership.**

Joint. United, working together.

Linked together. Associated together as if with links.

ASSOCIATION—*Adverbs.*

En masse [F.], in mass; hand in hand; shoulder to shoulder; side by side.

as-soil'. To set free. EXCULPATION-CONVICTION.

as'-so-nance. Correspondence in sound. MELODY-DISSONANCE, POETRY-PROSE.

as'-so-nant. Corresponding in sound. MELODY-DISSONANCE.

as-sort'. To distribute into classes. ORGANIZATION-DISORGANIZATION.

as-sort'-ment. Classification. DIVISION, GATHERING-SCATTERING.

as-suage'. To allay or soothe. ALLEVIATION-AGGRAVATION, TURBULENCE-CALMNESS.

as-suage'-ment. Abatement. TURBULENCE-CALMNESS.

as-sua'-ging. Soothing. ALLEVIATION-AGGRAVATION.

as-sua'-sive. Soothing. ALLEVIATION-AGGRAVATION.

as''-su-e-fac'-tion. Habituation. HABIT-DESUETUDE.

as'-su-e-tude. State of being accustomed to. HABIT-DESUETUDE.

as-sume'. To undertake; to take for granted; to put on deceitfully. DUENESS-UNDUENESS, FAITH-MISGIVING, HYPOTHESIS, PRESUMPTION-OBSEQUIOUSNESS, TAKING-RESTITUTION, TRUTHFULNESS-FALSEHOOD; **assume a character,** DELINEATION-CARICATURE; **assume a form,** CONVERSION-REVERSION; **assume authority,** RULE-LICENSE; **assume command,** ORDER, RULE-LICENSE; **assume the offensive,** ATTACK-DEFENSE.

as-sumed'. Taken for granted. HYPOTHESIS; **assumed name,** NAME-MISNOMER.

as-su'-ming. Being presumptuous. PRESUMPTION-OBSEQUIOUSNESS.

as-sump'-tion. Taken for granted; arrogance. Conversion-Reversion, Dueness-Undueness, Faith-Misgiving, Harshness-Mildness, Hypothesis, Presumption - Obsequiousness, Sanguineness-Hopelessness, Taking-Restitution, Truthfulness-Falsehood.

as-sur'-ance. Confidence, boldness; evidence of the transfer of property. Assertion - Denial, Certainty-Doubt, Conceit-Diffidence, Engagement-Release, Faith-Misgiving, Hypothesis, Presumption - Obsequiousness, Rationale - Luck, Sanguineness-Hopelessness, Security; **make assurance doubly sure,** Certainty - Doubt, Recklessness-Caution, Security-Insecurity.

as-sure'. To give confidence to. Assertion-Denial, Engagement-Release, Faith-Misgiving, Sanguineness-Hopelessness, Security.

as-sur'-ed-ly. Without doubt. Assent-Dissent.

a-stat'-ic. In neutral equilibrium. Heaviness-Lightness.

as'-ter-isk. A star used to indicate in writing or printing. Sign.

a-stern'. Behind the ship. Anteriority-Posteriority; **fall astern,** Advance-Retrogression.

as'-ter-oid. A small planet. Astronomy, Universe.

As'-ter-oth. Female counterpart of Baal. Jove-Fiend.

as"-the-ni'-a. General debility. Strength-Weakness.

as-then'-ic. One generally weak. Strength-Weakness.

as"-tig-mat'-ic. Relating to astigmatism. Sight-Dim-sightedness.

a-stig'-ma-tism. An optical defect. Sight-Dim-sightedness.

a-stir'. In full activity. Activity-Indolence, Excitation; **set astir,** Excitation.

a-ston'-ish. To affect with wonder or surprise. Astonishment-Expectance, Expectation-Surprise.

a-ston'-ished at no'-thing. Cool-headed. Astonishment-Expectance.

a-ston'-ish-ing. Surprising. Magnitude-Smallness.

a-ston'-ish-ing-ly. Surprisingly. Magnitude-Smallness.

a-ston'-ish-ment. Amazement. Astonishment-Expectance.

ASTONISHMENT—EXPECTANCE.

Admiration. Wonder mingled with pleasing emotions; it includes delight and regard.
Amazedness, etc. The state of being amazed. See *Adjectives.*
Amazement. Pleasing or painful wonderment, especially affecting the intellect.
Astonishment. Momentary overwhelming of the mind by that which is beyond expectation, affecting the emotions especially.
Awe. Yielding of the mind to something grand in character or formidable in power.
Bewilderment. State of being led into perplexity or confusion.
Fascination. An unseen, but powerful influence over the affections or passions.
Flabbergastation. The state of being astonished.
Marvel. Something so out of the ordinary as to seem nearly or quite incredible.
Sensation. Mental impression resulting from internal or external stimulus, especially a powerful one.
Stound. Confusion of mind from sudden fear or other passion; consternation.
Stupefaction. State of insensibility; stolid state; dulness.
Stupor. Condition of the body in which the senses and faculties are suspended or greatly dulled.
Surprise, etc. The act of coming upon unawares, or of taking suddenly. See Expectation-Surprise.
Wonder. Surprise caused by something new, strange, or unexpected, which at the time appears inexplicable.
Wonderment. Surprise; astonishment.

Astonishment—*Denotation.*

Note of admiration.

Astonishment—*Scientific Noun.*

Thaumaturgy. The art of performing something wonderful.

Astonishment—*Verbs.*

Admire. To look upon with regard and delight.
Amaze. To confound with terror or wonder.
Astonish. To confound with surprise; affect the emotions strongly.
Astound. To strike dumb with amazement.
Baffle description. To foil or frustrate all attempts at description.
Beggar description. To outdo or exhaust description.
Be surprised, etc. To be taken unaware; to be struck with wonder. See *Adjectives.*
Bewilder. To confuse or perplex; daze.
Be wonderful. To be able to excite awe or high admiration. See *Adjectives.*
Confound. To throw into consternation; perplex with terror or surprise.
Dazzle. To excite admiration by any showy quality.
Dumfound. } To strike dumb; confound; confuse.
Dumfounder. }
Electrify. To excite suddenly; surprise with some brilliant effect.
Fascinate. To influence the passions or affections in an uncontrollable manner.

Expectance. Act or state of expecting. See Expectation.

Expectance—*Phrase.*

Nine days' wonder. Something that excites public wonder for a few days.

Expectance—*Verbs.*

Expect. To look for; wait for. See Expectation.
Make nothing of. To pay no attention to.
Nil admirari [L.]. To be surprised at nothing.
Not be surprised. To take things calmly.
Not wonder. Not to be affected with surprise or admiration. See Astonishment.

Expectance—*Adjectives.*

Astonished at nothing. Immovable.
Blasé [F.]. Sated with pleasure; used up. See Entertainment-Weariness.
Common. Often met with; customary.
Expected, etc. Looked for; anticipated. See *Verbs.*
Expecting, etc. Looking forward to; waiting for. See *Verbs.*
Foreseen. Seen or known beforehand.
Ordinary. Customary; usual. See Habit.
Unamazed. Not confounded or bewildered.

Expectance—*Interjections.*

No wonder! of course!

ASTONISHMENT—Verbs—*Continued.*

Flabbergast. To astonish; strike with wonder.
Gape. To open the mouth, as indicative of wonder, surprise, or the like.
Gloar. To squint; stare.
Hold one's breath. To be overcome with awe.
Look blank, etc. To have a stupid bewildered appearance, arising from an unpleasant announcement. See Expectation-Disappointment.
Look aghast. To appear stupefied with sudden fright.
Make one's hair stand on end. To strike with horror; frighten.
Make one stare. To compel one to gaze in wonderment.
Make one's tongue cleave to the roof of one's mouth. To make speechless by frightening.
Marvel. To wonder at or about.
Not be able to account for, etc. To be perplexed. See Clearness-Obscurity.
Not believe one's ears. } Not credit certain strange, wonderful
Not believe one's eyes. } phenomena.
Not believe one's senses. }
Not know whether one stands on one's head or on one's heels. To be bewildered; be confounded.
Open one's eyes. To look in amazement.
Open one's mouth. To gape out of wonder or surprise.
Petrify. To fix in dumb amazement.

ASTONISHMENT—Verbs—*Continued*.

Rub one's eyes. To be perplexed or confounded.
Stagger. To shock; overcome, as with surprise.
Stagger belief. To cause to doubt or hesitate.
Stand aghast. To be struck with horror.
Stand agog. To be excited with expectation.
Stare. To gaze in wonder, surprise, horror, etc.
Start. To make a sudden motion of the body, caused by any sudden feeling or emotion.
Startle. To excite by sudden alarm or surprise.
Strike. To impress strongly.
Strike dumb. To greatly astonish; confound.
Strike with awe. To impress with great fear, dread, or reverence for.
Strike with wonder. To be affected with surprise or slight astonishment.

Stun. To render helpless from astonishment.
Stupefy. To dull the senses or faculties; deaden.
Surprise. To confuse by presenting something suddenly to the view of the mind.
Take away one's breath. To startle; surprise suddenly.
Take by surprise. To come upon unexpectedly. See Expectation-Surprise.
Throw on one's beam ends. To greatly surprise; confound.
Tomber des nues [F.]. To fall from the clouds; surprise.
Turn the head. To look for something to which attention is suddenly called.
Turn up one's eyes. To be greatly astonished.
Wonder. To be affected by surprise.

ASTONISHMENT—*Adjectives*.

Agape. Having the mouth wide open, as in wonder or expectation.
Aghast. Stupefied with sudden fright or horror.
All agog. All eager.
Awe-struck. Impressed or struck with solemn dread.
Breathless. Out of breath; intense or eager.
Inconceivable. That cannot be imagined; incomprehensible.
Incredible. Impossible to be believed.
Indescribable. That cannot be described.
Ineffable. Incapable of being expressed in words.
Inexpressible. Unspeakable; unutterable.
Inimaginable. Incapable of being imagined.
Like a duck in thunder. Struck with consternation.
Lost in amazement. }
Lost in astonishment. } Extremely amazed.
Lost in wonder. }
Marvelous. Exciting wonder or some degree of surprise.
Miraculous. Manifesting power beyond the forces of nature; supernatural.
Monstrous. Out of the common course of nature.
Moon-struck. Amazed or confounded.
Mysterious, etc. Not revealed or explained. See Clearness-Obscurity.
Open-mouthed. Gaping, as in wonder or surprise.

Overwhelming. Irresistible; over-powering.
Passing strange. Exceedingly strange.
Planet-struck. Confounded.
Prodigious. Out of or above the ordinary; excessive.
Spell-bound. Arrested by a spell or charm.
Stupendous. Overcoming by its vastness; amazing.
Strange, etc. Causing surprise; exciting curiosity. See Conventionality-Unconventionality.
Striking, etc. Impressive; surprising. See *Verbs*.
Surprised, etc. Confounded; confused. See *Verbs*.
Surprising, etc. Of a nature to excite wonder or astonishment. See *Verbs*.
Thunder-struck. Shocked by surprise.
Unable to believe one's senses. Perplexed; dumfounded.
Unexpected, etc. Coming without warning; taken by surprise. See Expectation-Surprise.
Unheard of. Unparalleled; unprecedented.
Unimaginable. See Inimaginable.
Unspeakable. Beyond the power of speech.
Unutterable. Too great for verbal expression; inexpressible.
Wonderful. Having qualities that excite wonder or admiration.
Wonder-working. Accomplishing wonders.
Wondrous. Such as may excite surprise and astonishment.

ASTONISHMENT—*Adverbs*.

Fearfully. In a manner to impress fear or awe.
For a wonder.
In the name of wonder.
Mirabile dictu [L.]. Wonderful to tell.
Mirabile visu [L.]. Wonderful to be seen.

Strange to say. Wonderful to relate.
To one's great surprise. Very unexpectedly.
With gaping mouth; with open eyes; with upturned eyes; with wonder, etc. See *Nouns*. In a surprised or astonished manner.

ASTONISHMENT—*Interjections*.

Adzooks! bless my heart! bless us! can such things be! dear me! gad so! God bless me! good gracious! good heavens! good lack! goodness gracious! gracious goodness! halloo! Heaven bless the mark! Heaven save the mark! Heavens and earth! hem! hey day! hoity-toity! how now? humph! indeed! lack-a-daisy! lo, and behold! mercy on us! my goodness! my stars! Oh! odzookens! *O gemini* [L.]! only think! really! 'sdeath! strong! surely! well a day! what? what do you say to that? what in the world? what on earth? where am I? who would have thought it? etc. (see Expectation-Surprise); you don't say so? zounds!

ASTONISHMENT—*Phrases*.

Nous verrons [F.]. We shall see.
One's hair standing on end. Fright, fear, horror.

Vox faucibus hæsit [L.]. The voice stuck in the throat; speechless.

a-stound'. To stun with wonder. Astonishment-Expectance, Excitation, Sanguineness-Timidity.
astra, sic itur ad [L] (as'-tra, sic ai'-tur ad). Thus the journey to the stars. Life-Death, Reputation-Discredit.
a-strad'-dle. Astride. Suspension-Support.
As-træ'-a. Goddess of justice. Right-Wrong.
as'-tra-gal. A molding in the form of a string of beads. Architecture, Embellishment-Disfigurement.
as'-tral. Starry. Universe; **astral influence,** Volition-Obligation.
a-stray'. Away from the right path. Certainty-Doubt, Truth-Error; **go astray,** Aim-Aberration, Virtue-Vice.
as-tric'-tion. Act of binding close together. Union-Disunion.
a-stride'. With one leg on each side. Suspension-Support.
as-trin'-gen-cy. Binding together. Enlargement-Diminution.

as-trin'-gent. Having power to contract or draw together, as an acid. Enlargement-Diminution.
as'-tro-labe. An instrument for obtaining the altitudes of stars. Mensuration.
as-trol'-o-gy. Star-divination. Prophecy.
as-tron'-o-mer. An observer of the stars. Universe.
as-tron'-o-my. Science of the heavenly bodies. Astronomy, Nature-Art, Universe.

ASTRONOMY.

Astronomy. The science that treats of the heavenly bodies, their motions, magnitudes, distances, and physical constitutions.

ASTRONOMY—*Associated Nouns*.

Aerolite. A mass falling on the earth from celestial space.
Albedo. The ratio which the light reflected from an unpolished surface bears to the total light falling upon that surface.
Almucantar. A small circle of the celestial sphere drawn parallel to the horizon.

Anomaly. The angular distance of a planet from its perihelion, as seen from the sun; the angle measuring apparent irregularities in the motion of a planet.

Apex. That point of the heavens towards which the earth is moving in its orbit.

Aphelion. The point in an orbit, as of a planet, farthest from the sun.

Apogee. That point in the moon's orbit farthest from the earth.

Apsides. Points of eccentric orbits nearest to or farthest away from the center of attraction.

Aquarius. The eleventh sign of the zodiac; the Water-bearer.

Ariel. A satellite of Uranus.

Aries. The first of the twelve signs of the zodiac, which the sun enters at the vernal equinox. A constellation west of Taurus.

Armillary sphere. An ancient astronomical machine designed to represent the positions of the important circles of the celestial sphere.

Asteroids. A group of small planets between Mars and Jupiter of which about 340 have been discovered.

Azimuth. The arc of the horizon that a vertical plane passing through a heavenly body makes with the meridian of the place of observation.

Binary star. A double star whose members have a revolution round their common center of gravity.

Bode's law. An empirical formula supposed to express approximately the distances of the planets from the sun in terms of the distance from the sun of the innermost two.

Calendar. A system of fixing the order, length and subdivisions of years and months so as to define the dates of events; an almanac.

Cancer. The fourth sign of the zodiac which the sun enters at the summer solstice.

Capricornus. The tenth sign of the zodiac which the sun enters at the winter solstice.

Celestial latitude. Angular distance of a heavenly body from the ecliptic.

Celestial longitude. The distance in degrees, reckoned from the vernal equinox, on the ecliptic, to a circle at right angles to the ecliptic passing through the heavenly body whose longitude is designated.

Chromosphere. A layer of incandescent red gas surrounding the sun and resting on its luminous envelope.

Collimation. The act of adjusting the line of sight, as of a telescope.

Comet. A heavenly body, consisting of a coma surrounding a star-like nucleus, with a nebulous train.

Constellation. An arbitrary assemblage or group of stars, or the portion of the heavens occupied by such a group.

Corona. A luminous circle around one of the heavenly bodies.

Declination. Angular distance from the celestial equator.

Deimos. A satellite of Mars.

Earth. The globe on which we dwell, considered as a whole.

Eclipse. The obscuration of a heavenly body by its entering the shadow of another body, as when the moon enters the shadow of the earth, or by the intervention of another heavenly body.

Ecliptic. The apparent path of the sun around the celestial sphere.

Elongation. The angular distance of a planet from the sun.

Epicycle. In ancient astronomy, a circle whose center was conceived to move around the earth in a larger circle called the deferent, while a planet moved around its circumference.

Faculæ. Groups of small shining spots on the surface of the sun.

Galaxy. The milky way.

Gemination. Doubling of a star.

Gibbous phase. Phase of the moon between half-moon and full-moon.

Helium. A chemical element first believed to exist in the sun because of certain lines in the solar spectrum, now found existing on the earth.

Hour-angle. The angle at the pole between the hour-circle of a given body and the celestial meridian.

Hour-circle. A great circle of the celestial sphere which passes through the poles.

Hyperion. A satellite of Saturn.

Iapetus. The remotest satellite of Saturn.

Julian calendar. The calendar adjusted by Julius Cæsar, in which the year was made to consist of 365 days, each fourth year having 366 days.

Jupiter. Largest planet of the solar system

Leo. A northern constellation east of Cancer; the Lion, the fifth sign of the zodiac.

Libra. The Balance; the seventh sign of the zodiac which the sun enters at the autumnal equinox in September.

Libration. A real or apparent libratory motion, like that of a balance before coming to rest.

Limb. The border or edge of the disk of a heavenly body, especially of the sun and moon.

Mars. A planet conspicuous for its red light.

Mercury. A planet that is nearest the sun

Meteorite. A mass of stone or iron that has fallen upon the earth from space.

Micrometer. An instrument for measuring very small angles or dimensions.

Milky way. A luminous band encircling the heavens composed of distant stars and nebulæ.

Moon. A celestial body that revolves around the earth once in a little less than 27 days 8 hours, and accompanies it in its annual revolutions around the sun; a satellite of any planet.

Mural circle. A graduated circle, in the plane of the meridian, attached permanently to a perpendicular wall; used for measuring arcs of the meridian.

Nebula. Any luminous cloud-like object in the sky, as a distant star-cluster.

Neptune. The most remote planet of the solar system, distant from the sun about 2,760,000,000 miles.

Occultation. The hiding of a heavenly body from sight by the intervention of some other of the heavenly bodies.

Opposition. Aspect of heavenly bodies when 180° apart.

Orbit. The path in space along which a heavenly body moves about its center of attraction.

Orrery. A philosophical apparatus for exhibiting the relative motions and positions of the members of the solar system.

Parallax. Such difference of position, as of a star, as would appear if the object were viewed from two points, as from the earth's center and from a point of observation on its surface.

Perigee. Point in the orbit of the moon nearest the earth.

Perihelion. Point in the orbit of a planet nearest the sun.

Perturbation. A disturbance in the regular elliptic or other motion of a heavenly body, produced by some force additional to that which causes its regular motion.

Phases. The appearances or forms presented periodically by the moon and planets.

Pisces. The twelfth sign of the zodiac; a constellation.

Planets. Celestial bodies that revolve around the sun.

Precession of the equinoxes. The slow backward motion of the equinoctial points along the ecliptic, at the rate of 50.1″ annually.

Prime vertical. The vertical circle of the celestial sphere, which is perpendicular to the celestial meridian.

Principal constellations. Orion, Cassiopea, Great Bear, Pleides Leo, Southern Cross.

Pyrheliometer. An instrument for measuring the direct heating effect of the sun's rays.

Right ascension. Angle made at the celestial pole between the hour circle of a given star and the hour circle of the vernal equinox.

Sagittarius. The ninth of the twelve signs of the zodiac; a zodiacal constellation.

Satellite. A secondary planet which revolves about another planet.

Saturn. One of the planets of the solar system, next in magnitude to Jupiter, nearly 880,000,000 miles from the sun.

Scorpion. A sign and constellation.

Shooting stars. Star-like, luminous meteors that, appearing suddenly, dart quickly across some portion of the sky and then as suddenly disappear.

Solar prominences. Certain rose-colored masses on the limb of the sun which are seen to extend beyond the edge of the moon at the time of a solar eclipse.

Solar system. Group of celestial bodies, including the planets, that revolve round the sun.

Solstice. The point in the ecliptic at which the sun is farthest from the equator, north or south, namely, the first point of the sign Cancer and the first point of the sign Capricorn, the former being the summer solstice, the latter the winter solstice in northern latitudes;—so called because the sun apparently stands still in its northward or southward motion.

Spectroscope. An optical instrument for forming and analyzing the spectra of the rays emitted by bodies or substances.

Spring equinox. Time when the sun crosses the equator moving northward. The southward crossing is the autumnal equinox.

Star. A celestial body so distant as to appear like a luminous point: in common usage including the planets, but in astronomy limited to the fixed stars.

Sun. The luminous orb the light of which constitutes day, and its absence night.

Syzygy. The point of an orbit, as of the moon, at which it is in conjunction or opposition.

Taurus. The Bull; the second in order of the twelve signs of the zodiac. A zodiacal constellation, containing the clusters called the Pleiades and the Hyades.

Telescope. An optical instrument used in viewing distant objects.

Uranus. One of the primary planets, 36,000 miles in diameter.

Venus. A planet nearly the size of the earth, also called morning and evening star.

Terminator. The dividing line between the illuminated and the un-illuminated part of the moon.

Tide. The alternate rising and falling of the waters of the ocean, and of rivers, bays, etc., connected therewith.

Transit. The passage of a heavenly body over the meridian of a place or through the field of a telescope; the passage of a smaller body across the disk of the larger.

Uranolite. A meteorite or aerolite.

Ursa Major. A conspicuous constellation near the north pole. It contains the stars which form the Dipper or Charles's Wain.

Variable stars. Fixed stars which vary in their brightness, usually in more or less uniform periods.

Venus. One of the planets, the second in order from the sun, its orbit lying between that of Mercury and that of the earth.

Vernal equinox. The point where the sun crosses the equator going northward.

Vulcan. A planet, supposed by Leverrier to exist between Mercury and the sun, to account for certain unexplained perturbations of Mercury.

Winter. The season of the year in which the sun shines most obliquely upon any region.

Zenith. The point in the celestial sphere directly overhead.

Zodiac. An imaginary belt in the heavens, 16° to 18° broad, in the middle of which is the ecliptic, or sun's path.

ASTRONOMY—*Adjectives*

Anomalistic. Pertaining to the anomaly or angular distance of a planet from its perihelion.

Circumpolar. About the pole.

Geocentric. Relating to the earth as a center.

Orbital. Belonging or pertaining to an orbit.

Planetary. Pertaining to the planets.

Sidereal. Measured by the apparent motion of the stars.

Solar. Pertaining to the sun.

Telescopic. Pertaining to a telescope; small.

Tidal. Pertaining to tides.

Zodiacal. Pertaining to the zodiac.

as-tute′. Shrewd. CRAFT-ARTLESSNESS, SAGACITY-INCAPACITY.

a-sun′-der. Apart. REMOTENESS-NEARNESS, UNION-DISUNION; **asunder as poles,** LATERALITY-CONTRAPOSITION.

a-sy′-lum. A place of refuge. ATTACK-DEFENSE, REFUGE-PITFALL.

as′-ym-ptote. A line tangent to a curve at infinity. CONCENTRATION-RADIATION.

as″-ym-ptot′-ic-al. Pertaining to an asymptote. CONCENTRATION-RADIATION.

at. In the place; near; in pursuit of. **At one,** ATONEMENT, DIVINITY, RECOMPENSE - PUNITION; **be at,** PURPOSE-LUCK; **up and at them,** ATTACK-DEFENSE.

at′-a-ghan. A weapon of war. WEAPON.

a″-te-lier′. A workshop; a studio. PAINTING, WORKSHOP.

ath″-a-na′-si-a. Immortality. ETERNITY-INSTANTANEITY.

Ath″-a-na′-sian Creed. A creed of the Early Church. ORTHODOXY-HETERODOXY.

ath′-a-nor. An alchemist's furnace. OVEN-REFRIGERATOR.

a′-the-ism. Denial of the existence of God. GODLINESS-DISBELIEF, ORTHODOXY-HETERODOXY.

a′-the-ist. A holder of atheism. GODLINESS-DISBELIEF.

a″-the-is′-tic-al. Relating to atheism. GODLINESS-DISBELIEF.

ath′-el-ing. A young noble. GENTILITY-DEMOCRACY.

A-the′-ni-an. Marked by culture. PURITY-CRUDENESS.

a-thirst′. Thirsty. DESIRE-DISTASTE.

ath′-lete. One trained in physical exercise. BELLIGERENT, STRENGTH-WEAKNESS.

ath-let′-ic. Strong; pertaining to sports. STRENGTH-WEAKNESS; **athletic sports,** ENTERTAINMENT-WEARINESS, STRIFE-PEACE,

ath-let′-i-cism. State of being athletic. STRENGTH-WEAKNESS.

ath-let′-ics. Athletic exercises collectively. STRENGTH-WEAKNESS.

a-thwart′. Across the course of; against. ANTAGONISM-CONCURRENCE, CROSSING, PARALLELISM-INCLINATION.

At″-lan-te′-an. Pertaining to Atlas. STRENGTH-WEAKNESS.

at-lan′-tes. Male human figures used as columns. ARCHITECTURE.

At-lan′-tis. A mythical island. FANCY.

At′-las. A mythological giant; a volume of maps. DELINEATION-CARICATURE, STRENGTH-WEAKNESS, SUSPENSION-SUPPORT.

at′-mos-phere. The air. CHEMISTRY, ENVIRONMENT-INTERPOSITION, WATER-AIR.

at″-mos-pher′-ic. Pertaining to the air or like the air. BLUENESS-ORANGE; **atmospheric blue,** BLUENESS-ORANGE.

a-toll′. A ring-shaped coral island. SWAMP-ISLAND.

at′-om. A small particle. CHEMISTRY, EXTENSION-INEXTENSION, GREATNESS-LITTLENESS, MAGNITUDE-SMALLNESS.

a-tom′-ic. Relating to atoms. GREATNESS-LITTLENESS.

at′-oms. Small particles. **Crush to atoms,** CREATION-DESTRUCTION.

at-one′-ment. Satisfaction for wrong. ATONEMENT, DIVINITY, RECOMPENSE-PUNITION, TAKING-RESTITUTION.

ATONEMENT.

Amends. A satisfaction for crimes, a compensation.

Amende honorable [F.]. A full apology.

Apology. An excuse for an act, a justification.

Atonement. Something done by way of reparation for sin or an injury.

Burnt offering. An offering burnt on an altar as an expiation for sin.

Compensation. Payment for something. See COMPENSATION.

Composition. A settlement of a debt, etc.

Compromise. An arrangement by which a debt, etc., is settled.

Conciliation. Act of gaining over, of winning.

Expiation. Act of making satisfaction by suffering.

Fasting. Abstinence from meat on religious grounds.

Flagellation. Whipping of oneself in expiation of sins or injuries wrought.

Lustration. The act of purifying.

Maceration. A making lean by fasting.

Peace offering. Same as burnt offering.

Penance. Voluntary pain as an act of atonement.

Propitiation. Act of conciliating or appeasing.

Purgation. Act of cleansing, of vindicating.

Quittance. Release from a debt or obligation.

Quits. Discharge from an obligation.

Reclamation. Restoration to former state or better condition.

Redemption. Act of delivering.

Reparation. The making amends; reimbursement.

Sackcloth and ashes. A Jewish custom of expressing sorrow for sin; a self-abasement.

Sacrifice. The act of offering to the Deity as an atonement.

Shrift. Confession and absolution.

Satisfaction. The act of making amends or atonement.

Sin offering. An offering as atonement for sin.

White sheet. See *Verbs.*

ATONEMENT—*Associated Nouns.*

Purgatory. A place where sinful souls are absolved from their sins by suffering.

Scapegoat. A person who bears the blame for others.

ATONEMENT—*Verbs.*

Absolve. To free from the penalty of sin.

Apologize. To ask pardon for; to make verbal amends.

Atone.
Atone for. } To make amends, or make reparation.

Beg pardon. To request earnestly a pardon.

Come down on one's knees. To bend in respect.

Do penance. To undergo suffering on account of sin.

Expiate. To atone for by suffering.
Fall down on one's knees.
Fall down on one's marrow bones.
Faire l'amende honorable [F.]. To make full satisfaction.
Give satisfaction.
Make amends. Make satisfaction.
Make good. To indemnify.
Make matters up. To be reconciled.
Pay the forfeit. }
Pay the penalty. } To pay a fine or penalty for an offense.
Propitiate. To conciliate, to win over.
Purge. To cleanse.
Ransom. To redeem by payment of money.
Reclaim. To make better or put back in former state.
Redeem. To recover, to deliver as from sin.
Repair. To make amends, to restore.
Repent in sackcloth and ashes. To repent earnestly.
Set one's house in order. Make preparation for the future.
Shrive. To receive absolution from a priest.
Stand in a white sheet. To indicate repentance.

ATONEMENT—*Adjectives.*

Absolvable. Capable of being freed from the penalty of guilt.
Expiatory. Having character of an expiation.
Piacular. Atoning.
Piaculous. See PIACULAR.
Propitiatory. Pertaining to propitiation.
Sacrificial. Of a sacrifice, pertaining to a sacrifice.
Sacrificiatory. Offering sacrifice.

ATONEMENT—*Phrase.*

Crux, fidei coticula [L.]. The cross is the touchstone of faith.

at'-o-ny. Want of tone; want of power. STRENGTH-WEAKNESS.
at''-ra-bil'-ious. Melancholy. LIGHTHEARTEDNESS-DEJECTION.
at''-ra-men'-tous. Of the nature of ink. WHITENESS-BLACKNESS.
a'-tri-um. A court or hall. DWELLER-HABITATION.
a-tro'-cious. Extremely heinous. VIRTUE-VICE.
a-troc'-i-ty. Cruelty; wickedness. CHARITABLENESS-MALEVOLENCE, INNOCENCE-GUILT, VIRTUE-VICE.
at'-ro-phy. To cause to waste away. BETTERMENT-DETERIORATION, BIOLOGY, ENLARGEMENT-DIMINUTION, HEALTH-SICKNESS.
at-tach'. To connect; to hold for court. LITIGATION, LOVE-HATE, UNION-DISUNION; **attach importance to,** CONSEQUENCE-INSIGNIFICANCE.
at''-ta-che'. One attached to the suite of another; a diplomatic officer. CHIEF-UNDERLING, CONSIGNEE.
at-tached'. Added. LOVE-HATE.
at-tach'-ment. Adherence. UNION-DISUNION.
at-tack'. To make an onset against; to affect. ATTACK-DEFENSE, HEALTH-SICKNESS.

ATTACK—DEFENSE.

Aggression. The first act of injury, or first act leading to a war.
Aggressor. One who begins a quarrel or hostility.
Assailant. One who injures or makes an attack upon another.
Assault. A violent attempt with force or violence to do hurt to another.
Assault and battery. The crime of violently attacking and beating a man.
Attack. The act of falling upon with force or violence.
Balistica. An ancient weapon.
Base of operations. A point for which supplies are drawn for an attacking army.
Battue [F.]. Killing of game driven to the sportsman; wanton slaughter.
Billy. A policeman's club.
Boarding. The act of entering a ship by force in combat.
Bombardment. An attack upon a fortified place with shot or shells.
Broadside. A discharge of all the guns on one side of a ship at the same time.
Camisade [F.]. A night attack.
Cannonade. An attack with large guns, lasting some time.
Carte and tierce. Positions in fencing.
Charge. The act of rushing suddenly upon an enemy.
Coup de bec [F.]. A quick, sharp blow, as with a beak.
Coup de main [F.]. A sudden and unexpected movement or attack.
Cross fire. Lines of fire from two or more points crossing each other.
Cut. A wound made with a weapon like a sword.
Dead set at. A determined and continuing attack.
Devastation. A laying waste.
Dragonnade [F.]. A rapid and devastating incursion.
Eboulement [F.]. Crumbling of a fortress wall.
Echelon. Arrangement of troops in a step-like formation.
Escalade. An attack upon a fortified place, in which ladders are used to pass a ditch or mount a rampart.
Estrapade [F.]. The action of a horse, when, to get rid of his rider, he rears, plunges, and kicks furiously.
Feu d'enfer [F.]. A hellish fire.
File fire. The firing of each file independently of others.
Fire. Discharge of firearms.
Foray. A sudden or irregular incursion in border warfare.
Fusillade [F.]. A simultaneous discharge of firearms.
Home thrust. A well directed or effective thrust.
Incursion. A hostile entrance into a territory.
Inroad. The entrance of an enemy into a country with a hostile purpose.
Invader. One who enters with a view to conquest or plunder.
Invasion. A warlike entrance into the domains of another.
Investment. The act of surrounding or blocking up a town by an armed force.
Irruption. A sudden violent rushing into a place.
Jacquerie [F.]. A revolt of peasants; so called from the revolt of French peasants against the nobles in 1358.
Kick. A blow with the foot.

Coverture. Concealment.
Defense. Protection from violence or danger.
Guard. Security against injury or attack.
Guardianship. The office of guardian; protection; care.
Preservation. The act of keeping from destruction or injury. See CONSERVATION.
Propugnation. The act of contending or fighting for.
Protection. The act of shielding from loss, injury, or annoyance.
Rain proof. Protected from rain.
Resistance. Exertion of force against force. See sub RESISTANCE.
Self-defense. The act of protecting one's own person, property, or reputation.
Self-preservation. Defense of oneself from destruction or injury.
Shielding. To cover from danger. See *Verbs.*
Ward. State of being under guardianship.

DEFENSE—*Means of Defense.*

Abatis. } A means of defense formed by felled trees, the ends of
Abattis. } whose branches are sharpened and directed toward the
Abbatis. } enemy.
Abutment. A part of a wall or fortification which projects beyond any other part.
Advanced work. A fortification built beyond the usual military lines.
Ægis. The shield of Minerva; a shield or protective armor.
Apron. An article of dress to keep the clothes clean, to defend them from injury.
Armor. A covering worn to protect one's person in battle.
Asylum. A place of refuge and protection.
Bank. A ridge or mound-like formation used as a fortification.
Banquette [F.]. A raised way running along the inside of a parapet, on which soldiers stand when firing.
Barbacan. }
Barbican. } A tower or advanced work defending a castle or a city.
Barracoon. An enclosure where slaves or prisoners are quartered.
Barricade. A hasty fortification made of anything that will obstruct the enemy.
Barrier. A wooden work or stockade, made in a narrow way.
Bastion. A work projecting from the main enclosure of a fortification.
Battlement. The solid upright part of a parapet in ancient fortifications.
Bearskin. A cap made of bearskin, especially worn by soldiers.
Boom. A chain cable, or line of spars, extended across a river to obstruct navigation.
Breastplate. A plate of metal covering the breast, as defensive armor.
Breastwork. A defensive work of moderate height, hastily thrown up.
Buckler. A shield worn on one arm.
Buffer. A pad or cushion at the end of a fender which receives the blow.
Bulwark. Any means of defense or protection.
Buttress. A structure built against a wall to strengthen it.

ATTACK—DEFENSE—*Continued.*

Lunge. A sudden thrust or pass, as with a sword.

Obsession. The act of besieging.

Offense. An assault or attack.

Onset. A rushing or setting upon.

Onslaught. A furious or murderous attack.

Outbreak. A rising in arms.

Pass. A movement in fencing.

Passado [Sp.]. A thrust, as with a sword.

Platoon fire. Discharge of the arms of half a company of soldiers, at the same time.

Point of attack. The place against which the strength of an attacking force is directed.

Punch. A blow with the fist.

Raid. A sudden or rapid invasion by a cavalry force.

Raking fire. Scouring with shot or shell in the direction of the length.

Razzia [F.]. A plundering and destructive incursion.

Ruade [F.]. A kick.

Run against. } An attack.
Run at. }

Sally. A rush of troops from a besieged place to attack the besiegers.

Sharp shooting. A shooting with great precision and effect.

Siege. The sitting of an army around a fortified place to compel the garrison to surrender.

Sortie [F.]. The sudden issuing of troops from a besieged place to attack the besiegers.

Storm. } An attempt to take a fortified place by scaling the walls,
Storming. } forcing the gates, etc.

Thrust. A stab, or sword wound.

Volley. The simultaneous discharge of a number of small arms

Volley of grape. Discharge of cannon shot.

ATTACK—*Verbs.*

Assail. To attack with violence or in a hostile manner.

Assault. To make an attack upon by a sudden rush of armed men.

Attack. To fall upon with force.

Bait. To provoke or worry.

Bayonet. To stab.

Beleaguer. To surround with an army so as to cut off escape.

Beset. To attack on all sides.

Besiege. To surround with armed forces.

Board. To enter a ship by force in battle.

Bombard. To attack with heavy artillery.

Butt. To strike against with the head.

Charge. To rush upon.

Harry. To strip or lay waste.

Impugn. To attack by words or arguments.

Invade. To enter with a view to conquest or plunder.

Invest. To hem in with troops.

Kick. To strike a blow with the foot.

Lapidate. To stone.

Mine. To dig a passage under anything to overthrow it by explosives.

Pelt. To throw missiles.

Pepper. To shower shot or blows upon.

Sap. To advance by secretly undermining.

Shell. To bombard.

Stone. To beat or kill with stones.

Storm. To attack by scaling walls, ramparts, etc.

Strike. To hit with some force. See IMPETUS.

Whip. To defeat in battle; see sub PUNISH.

ATTACK—*Verbal Expressions.*

Advance against; aim a blow at; assume the offensive; attack tooth and nail; bear down upon; become the aggressor; be down upon; be hard upon; be the aggressor; break a lance with; bring to bay; close with; come on; come to close quarters; cut and thrust; dash at; deal a blow at; draw the sword; drive one hard; enter the lists; fall foul of; fall upon; fetch one a blow; fetch one a kick; fire a red-hot shot; fire a shot at; fire at; fire upon; fire a volley; fly at; give one a blow; give one a kick; have a cut at; have a fling at; have a shot at; have a shy at; have at; hurl against; hurl at; hurl at the head of; launch out against; lay about one; lay siege to; let fly at; let off a gun at; let out at; level at; lift a hand against; make a dash at; make a pass at; make a rush at; make a set at; make a thrust at; march against; march upon; open fire; open the trenches; pitch into; plant a battery; poke at; pop at; pounce upon; pour a broadside into; press one hard; ride full tilt against; run amuck; run at; run a tilt at; run down; scale the walls; set upon; shoot at; show fight; slap in the face;

DEFENSE—MEANS OF DEFENSE—*Continued.*

Capitol. A government house.

Carapace. The thick shell which covers the back of the turtle, etc.

Casemate. A bomb-proof enclosure.

Casque. A piece of armor for the head and neck.

Castle. A fortified residence.

Cavin. A natural hollow forming a means of defense.

Chevaux de frise [F.]. A piece of timber covered with iron-pointed spikes or spears, used to impede the advance of cavalry.

Circumvallation. A line of field works around a besieged place or the besieging army, to protect the besiegers from an attack without, or complete the blockade.

Citadel. A fortress commanding a city and its fortifications.

Coat of mail. A defensive garment of chain mail.

Contravallation. Field works built by besiegers to secure themselves and check sallies of the enemy.

Corner stone. A stone which lies at the corner of two walls and unites them.

Counterscarp. The exterior wall or slope of a ditch.

Csako [Hung.]. A military cap.

Cuirass. A piece of defensive armor covering the body from the neck to the girdle.

Curtain. That part of a fortification which is between two bastions or two gates.

Dead wall. A wall unbroken by windows or other openings.

Dike. An embankment for protection against overflowing water.

Ditch. A trench to prevent approach to a town or fortress.

Donjon. The chief tower of ancient fortifications.

Dyke. See DIKE.

Earthwork. Any construction of earth for attack or defense.

Embankment. A structure of earth to prevent water from overflowing.

Escarp. The side of a ditch next the parapet.

Fastness. A secure retreat.

Fence. An enclosing structure intended to prevent intrusion.

Fender. Any shield or screen which protects, as from fire, shock, etc.

Field work. A temporary fortification thrown up by an army in the field.

Fort. A strong or fortified place.

Fortalice. } A small fortification or outwork.
Fortelage. }

Fortification. A work built to defend a place against attack.

Fortress. A large and permanent fortification.

Fosse. A ditch or moat.

Gauntlet. A glove to defend the hand from wounds.

Glacis. That slope of way which inclines from the covered way to the open country.

Habergeon. A short coat of mail.

Haha. A fence, wall, or ditch not visible until one is close upon it.

Hauberk. A long coat of mail.

Helmet. A defensive covering for the head.

Hold. A fortified place.

Horn work. An outwork composed of two half bastions joined by a curtain and wings.

Intrenchment. Any defensive work consisting of at least a trench or ditch and a parapet.

Keep. The strongest part of a castle or fortification.

Lines. Dispositions made to cover extended positions, and presenting a front in but one direction to an enemy.

Loophole. An opening in walls or ship sides through which small arms may be discharged.

Lorication. A covering of scales or plates.

Machicolation. An opening in the floor for shooting or dropping missiles upon an enemy.

Mail. A flexible fabric made of metal rings, used for defensive armor.

Mantelet. A shield.

Mantlet. A musket-proof shield of rope, wood, or metal.

Martello tower. A stone building usually erected on the seacoast, with a gun on the summit, to be fired in any direction.

Mask. A screen for a battery.

Moat. A deep trench around a fortified place, sometimes filled with water.

Mole. A wall to protect a harbor from the violence of the waves.

Mound. An artificial hill or elevation of earth used as a fortification.

Muniment. A place or means of defense.

Munition. Whatever materials are used in war for offense or defense.

Out work. A minor defense constructed beyond the main body of a work.

Pah. A kind of stockaded intrenchment.

Paling. A fence formed with pales or pickets. See ENCLOSURE.

Palisade. A fence made of sharp stakes.

Panoply. A full set of armor.

ATTACK—DEFENSE—*Continuea.*

ATTACK—VERBAL EXPRESSIONS—*Continued.*

spring a mine; strike at; strike at the root of; strike home; strike the first blow; take the offensive; take up the cudgels; throw a stone; throw stones at; throw the first stone; thrust at; tilt at.

ATTACK—*Adjectives.*

Aggressive. Disposed to attack unjustly.
Attacking, etc. See *Verbs.*
Obsidional. Pertaining to a siege.
Offensive. Making the first attack.
Up in arms. In a state of hostility.

ATTACK—*Adverbial Phrase.*

On the offensive. Tending to make the first attack.

ATTACK—*Interjection.*

"Up and at them!"

ATTACK—*Phrase.*

Garde royale [F.]. Royal guard.

DEFENSE—VERBS—*Continued from Column 2.*

Propugn. To contend in another's behalf.
Repel. To resist or oppose effectually.
Screen. To protect by hiding.
Shield. To cover from danger.
Shroud. To protect completely.

DEFENSE—*Verbal Expressions.*

Act on the defensive; bear harmless; bear the brunt; beat off; fall back upon; fence around (see CIRCUMSCRIPTION)**; give a warm reception to; guard against; hold at bay; hold one's own; keep at arm's length; keep at bay; keep off; maintain one's ground; put to flight; show fight; stand by; stand in the gap; stand one's ground; stand on the defensive; stand the brunt; take care of** (see CAREFULNESS)**; ward off.**

DEFENSE—*Adjectives.*

Armed. Furnished with weapons.
Armed at all points. Completely armed.
Armed cap-a-pie. Armed from head to foot.
Ball-proof. Invulnerable by balls.
Casemated. Furnished with a bomb-proof covering.
Castellated. Built in the style of a castle.
Defended, etc. See *Verbs.*
Defending, etc. See *Verbs.*
Defensive. Serving to protect or defend.
Iron-clad. Protected or covered with iron.
Iron-plated. Covered with iron.
Loopholed. Provided with loopholes.
Machicolated. Having holes through the floor for discharging weapons.
Mural. Resembling a wall.
Panoplied. Dressed in complete armor.
Proof against. Able to resist.
To the teeth. In open opposition.

DEFENSE—*Adverbs.*

At bay. Obliged to face an enemy, when escape has become impossible.
Defensively. Resisting attack.
In defense. In behalf of.
On the defense.
On the defensive. } Resisting, in opposition to attacking.
Pro aris et focis [L.]. For our altars and firesides.

DEFENSE—*Interjection.*

No surrender!

DEFENSE—*Phrases.*

Defense, not defiance.
Dieu defend le droit [F.]. God defend the right.
Fidei defensor [L.]. Defender of the faith.

DEFENSE—MEANS OF DEFENSE—*Continued.*

Parapet. A wall or elevation of earth for covering soldiers from an enemy's fire.
Peel house. A small tower, fort, or castle.
Pickel-haube [Ger.]. A headpiece or helmet.
Rampart. A broad embankment of earth, upon which a parapet is raised.
Rath. A hill or mound.
Ravelin. A detached fortification with two embankments which make a salient angle.
Redan. A work having two parapets whose faces unite so as to form a salient angle toward the enemy.
Redoubt. A small, roughly constructed fort, used in fortifying tops of hills and passes.
Safeguard. A convoy or guard to protect a traveler or property. See sub SAFETY.
Sally port. An underground passage connecting the inner and outer works of a fortification.
Scarp. The slope of a ditch nearest the parapet
Sconce. A fortification or work of defense.
Screen. Anything that protects from danger or injury.
Shako. A military cap.
Shield. A broad piece of defensive armor carried on the arm.
Shore. A prop placed as a brace or support against the side of a building or other structure. See sub SUPPORT.
Stoccado [It.]. A stockade.
Stockade. A line of stout timbers with loopholes, to form a defensive fortification.
Stronghold. A place of security.
Sunk fence. A ditch or fence sunk in the ground to impede the advance of troops.
Thimble. A cover for the end of the finger for protection in sewing.
Tower. A projection from a line of wall, and higher than the rest of the wall.
Tower of strength. A stronghold or fortification.
Truncheon. A military staff of command. See WEAPON.
Vallum [L.]. A wall.
Vambrace. Armor for the forearm.
Vanfoss. A ditch around part of a fort.
Vinea. A shed used by the Romans to defend them in besieging
Wall. A work for defense.
Wooden walls. The old ships of war

DEFENSE—*Nouns of Agent.*

Body guard. A guard to protect or defend the person.
Champion. One who contended in single combat in behalf of another's rights and honor.
Defender. One who shields or protects from danger or injury.
Garrison. A body of troops stationed in a fort or fortified town.
Guardian. One to whom any person or thing is committed for protection or preservation. See SECURITY.
Knight-errant. A knight who traveled in search of adventures, and defended the weak and helpless.
Paladin. A distinguished knight.
Picket. A detached body of troops serving to guard an army against surprise.
Piquet. See PICKET.
Propugner. A defender.
Protector. One who defends or shields from injury or oppression.

DEFENSE—*Verbs.*

Defend. To repel danger or harm from.
Engarrison. To protect by a garrison.
Fence. To guard oneself against attack.
Fend. To act on the defensive, or in opposition.
Forfend. To prevent the approach of.
Guard. To secure against surprise, attack, or injury. See SECURITY.
Hinder. To oppose obstacles or impediments. See OBSTRUCTION.
Hold. To retain possession of, or authority over.
Intrench. To surround with fortifications.
Parry. To turn a blow aside.

(Continued on Column 1.)

---

at-tack'-ing. Assailing. ATTACK-DEFENSE.
at'-ta-ghan. A Turkish sword. WEAPON.
at-tain'. Arrive at; to gain. ARRIVAL-DEPARTURE, SUCCESS-FAILURE; **attain majority,** MANHOOD.
at-tain'-a-ble. Practicable. POSSIBILITY-IMPOSSIBILITY.
at-tain'-der. The extinction of all civil rights for a capital offense. FAULTLESSNESS-FAULTINESS.

at-tain'-ment. Accomplishment. EDUCATION-LEARNING, KNOWLEDGE-IGNORANCE, SKILL-UNSKILFULNESS.
at'-tar. Oil of roses. PERFUME-STENCH.
at-tem'-per. To soothe; to moderate by mixture. MIXTURE-HOMOGENEITY, TURBULENCE-CALMNESS.
at-tem'-pered. Made less harsh AFFECTIONS.
at-tempt'. A trial or effort. VENTURE; **attempt im-**

possibilities, POSSIBILITY-IMPOSSIBILITY; **vain attempt,** SUCCESS-FAILURE.

at-tend'. To be with; to take care of; to give heed; to serve. CHIEF-UNDERLING, HEED-DISREGARD, LEADING-FOLLOWING, OBSTRUCTION-HELP, PRESENCE-ABSENCE.

at-tend'-ance. A retinue, act of attending. PRESENCE-ABSENCE.

at-tend'-ance. A waiting upon. **Dance attendance on,** LEADING - FOLLOWING, POLITENESS - IMPOLITENESS, PRESUMPTION-OBSEQUIOUSNESS.

at-tend'-ant. A follower. CHIEF-UNDERLING, LEADING-FOLLOWING, SOLITUDE-COMPANY.

at-ten'-tion. Direction of mental powers to any specific object. CAREFULNESS-CARELESSNESS, HEED-DISREGARD, REGARD-DISRESPECT; **attract attention,** POMP; **call attention to,** SIGN; **call to attention,** HEED-DISREGARD; **pay attentions to,** POLITENESS-IMPOLITENESS; **pay one's attentions to,** BLANDISHMENT.

at-ten'-tive. Observant. HEED-DISREGARD.

at-ten'-u-ate. Made thin or slender. ENLARGEMENT-DIMINUTION, FRIABILITY, INCREASE-DECREASE.

at-ten'-u-a''-ted. Made narrow. BREADTH-NARROWNESS.

at-ten''-u-a'-tion. A weakening. ENLARGEMENT-DIMINUTION, FRIABILITY.

at-test'. To certify as accurate. ASSERTION-DENIAL, ENGAGEMENT - RELEASE, EVIDENCE - COUNTEREVIDENCE, SIGN.

at''-tes-ta'-tion. Act of attesting. EVIDENCE-COUNTEREVIDENCE, SIGN.

at-test'-ed. Witnessed. **Attested copy,** SECURITY.

at'-tic. Room next the roof; classic; witty. CONTENTS-RECEIVER, PURITY-CRUDENESS, TASTE-VULGARITY, TOP-BOTTOM, WITTINESS-DULNESS.

At'-ti-cism. Elegant expression. WITTINESS-DULNESS.

At'-til-a. A king of the Huns, called the "Scourge of God." BENEFACTOR-EVILDOER.

at-tire'. Garments. DRESS-UNDRESS.

at'-ti-tude. Physical position; settled purpose or opinion. CONDITION-SITUATION, FORM-FORMLESSNESS, POSITION.

at''-ti-tu''-di-na'-ri-an. One who studies and practises attitudes. POMP.

at''-ti-tu'-di-nize. To pose for effect. SOCIETY-AFFECTATION.

at-tol'-lent. Lifting. ELEVATION-DEPRESSION.

at-tor'-ney. A person acting for another; a lawyer. ADVOCATE, CONSIGNEE; **power of attorney,** COMMISSION-ABROGATION.

at-tract'. To draw to; to affect favorably. ATTRACTION-REPULSION, DESIRE-DISTASTE, LOVE-HATE, MOTIVE-CAPRICE, PLEASURABLENESS-PAINFULNESS; **attract the attention,** HEED-DISREGARD, VISIBILITY-INVISIBILITY.

at-tract''-a-bil'-i-ty. Attraction. MOTIVE-CAPRICE, PLEASURABLENESS-PAINFULNESS.

at-tract'-ing. Drawing to itself. ATTRACTION-REPULSION.

at-trac'-tion. Act of attracting; attractive power. ATTRACTION-REPULSION, DESIRE-DISTASTE, LOVE-HATE, MIGHT-IMPOTENCE, MOTIVE-CAPRICE, PLEASURABLENESS-PAINFULNESS.

ATTRACTION—REPULSION.

Adduction. The action by which the parts of a body are drawn towards its axis.

Attraction. An invisible power in a body by which it draws anything to itself.

Attraction of gravitation. The tendency of every particle of matter in the universe towards every other particle.

Attractiveness. Having the power or quality of drawing towards itself.

Drawing to. The act of pulling towards or attracting.

Gravity. The tendency of a mass of matter towards the center of attraction

Magnetism. That quality or agency by virtue of which certain bodies are productive of magnetic force or susceptible to its action.

Pulling towards.

ATTRACTION—Nouns of Agent.

Loadstar. A guiding star; the polestar.

Loadstone. A magnetic iron ore.

Magnet. A bar or mass of steel to which the properties of a magnet have been imparted.

Siderite. Formerly magnetic iron ore, or loadstone.

ATTRACTION—Verbs.

Adduce. To bring forward.

Attract. To cause to be drawn to.

Drag towards.

Draw towards.

Pull towards.

ATTRACTION—Adjectives.

Adducent. } Drawing or binding together.
Adductive. }

Attracting, etc. See Verbs.

Attractive. Having the quality of attracting.

Attrahent. Drawing to or towards something.

Abduction. The act of drawing apart.

Driving forth, etc. See Verbs.

Repulse. A driving back.

Repulsion. The act of being driven back.

REPULSION—Verbs.

Abduce. To draw to a different part.

Abduct. To take away by force.

Chase. To drive by following.

Dispel. To drive away by scattering.

Drive from. See IMPETUS.

Push from. To drive away by steady pressure.

Repel. To act with force in opposition to force.

Retrude. To thrust back.

Send away. } To cause to go in any manner.
Send off. }

REPULSION—Adjectives.

Abducent. Drawing away from a common center.

Abductive. Carrying away.

Repellent. Driving back by force.

Repelling, etc. See Verbs.

Repulsive. Resisting.

REPULSION—Phrases.

Give the cold shoulder.

Keep at arm's length.

Send away with a flea in one's ear.

Turn one's back upon. Turn the cold shoulder.

at-tract'-ive. Having the power to attract; pleasing. ATTRACTION-REPULSION, BEAUTY-UGLINESS, DESIRE - DISTASTE, LOVE - HATE, MOTIVE - CAPRICE, PLEASURABLENESS - PAINFULNESS.

at-tract'-ive-ness. Condition of being attractive. ATTRACTION-REPULSION, LOVE-HATE, MOTIVE-CAPRICE, PLEASURABLENESS-PAINFULNESS.

at'-tra-hent. Drawing towards. ATTRACTION-REPULSION.

at-trib'-u-ta-ble. Capable of being attributed. RATIONALE-LUCK.

at'-tri-bute. A quality; that which is inherent in a person or thing. MIGHT-IMPOTENCE; **attributes of the Deity,** DIVINITY.

at-trib'-u-ted. Ascribed. RATIONALE-LUCK.

at-trib'-ute to. Ascribe to, RATIONALE-LUCK.

at''-tri-bu'-tion. Act of ascribing as a property or quality. RATIONALE-LUCK.

at-trite′. Worn down. FRIABILITY.

at-tri′-tion. Act of rubbing away. FRICTION-LUBRICATION.

attroupement [F.] (at-trup-man′). A riotous assembly. GATHERING-SCATTERING.

at-tune. To adjust as a musical instrument. MUSIC, PREPARATION-NONPREPARATION.

at-tuned′. Accustomed. **Attuned to,** HABIT-DESUETUDE.

au′-burn. Reddish-brown. GRAY-BROWN.

A. U. C. *Ab Urbe Conditâ* [L.] From the city's (Rome) construction. DURATION-NEVERNESS.

auc′-tion. A public sale. BUYING-SALE.

auc″-tion-eer′. One who conducts a sale. BUYING-SALE, CONSIGNEE.

auctor pretiosa facit [L.] auc′-tor pri shi-o′-sa fê′-sit). The giver adds value to the gift. GIVING-RECEIVING.

au-da′-cious. Bold. PRESUMPTION-OBSEQUIOUSNESS.

au-dac′-i-ty. Boldness; impudence. BRAVERY-COWARDICE, PRESUMPTION-OBSEQUIOUSNESS, RECKLESSNESS-CAUTION.

audacter et sincere [L.] (au-dac′-ter et sin-si′-ri). Boldly and sincerely. BRAVERY-COWARDICE.

au désespoir [F.] (o dê-zes-pwar′). In despair. LIGHTHEARTEDNESS-DEJECTION, SANGUINENESS-TIMIDITY.

au″-di-bil′-i-ty. State of being audible. HEARING-DEAFNESS, SOUND-SILENCE.

au′-di-ble. Capable of being heard. SOUND-SILENCE; **become audible,** HEARING-DEAFNESS; **scarcely audible,** LOUDNESS-FAINTNESS.

au′-di-ence. An assembly of hearers; a hearing. CONVERSATION-MONOLOGUE, HEARING-DEAFNESS; **before an audience,** ACTING.

audire alteram partem [L.] (au-dai′-ri al′-ter-am par′-tem). To hear the other side. EVIDENCE-COUNTEREVIDENCE, RIGHT-WRONG, UPRIGHTNESS-DISHONESTY.

au′-dit. To examine, as accounts. ACCOUNTS, INVESTIGATION-ANSWER, NUMBERING.

au′-di-tor. One who examines accounts; a listener. ACCOUNTS, HEARING-DEAFNESS.

au″-di-to′-ri-um. A place for speaking. ACTING, ADDRESS-RESPONSE.

au′-di-to-ry. Pertaining to hearing; an audience room. ACTING, HEARING-DEAFNESS; **auditory apparatus,** HEARING-DEAFNESS.

au fait [F.] (o fê). Up to the mark; well taught. SKILL-UNSKILFULNESS.

aufgeschoben ist nicht aufgehoben [G.] (auf″-ge-sho′-ben ist niht auf″-ge-ho′-ben). Later on is not foregone. QUEST-ABANDONMENT.

au fond [F.] (o fon′). At the bottom; fundamentally. SUBJECTIVENESS-OBJECTIVENESS.

Au-ge′-an. Like the stables of Augeas; very filthy. **Augean stable,** CLEANNESS-FILTHINESS; **Augean task,** DIFFICULTY-FACILITY.

au′-ger. An instrument for boring. PERFORATER-STOPPER.

aught. Any part, even the smallest. WHOLE-PART; **for aught one cares,** CONSEQUENCE-INSIGNIFICANCE, UNCONCERN; **for aught one knows,** HYPOTHESIS, KNOWLEDGE-IGNORANCE, RATIONALE-LUCK.

aug-ment′. To enlarge or increase. ENLARGEMENT-DIMINUTION, INCREASE-DECREASE, INCREMENT-REMNANT.

aug″-men-ta′-tion. An enlargement. ENLARGEMENT-DIMINUTION, INCREASE-DECREASE, INCREMENT-REMNANT.

au′-gur. A soothsayer; to betoken. PROPHECY, SOOTHSAYER; **augur well,** SANGUINENESS-HOPELESSNESS.

au′-gu-rate. Foretell. PROPHECY.

au″-gu-ra′-tion. Augury PROPHECY

au-gu′-ri-al Pertaining to auguries. PROPHECY.

au′-gu-rous. Relating to auguries. PROPHECY.

au′-gu-ry. Foretelling by signs or omens. PARENT.

au-gust′. Venerable; dignified. REPUTATION-DISCREDIT.

Au′-gus-tin. An Augustinian monk. MINISTRY-LAITY.

aunt. Sister of one's father or mother. RELATIONSHIP

au′-ra. A light breeze; sensation as of a light vapor passing over the body. RIVER-WIND, TINGLING-NUMBNESS.

aurea mediocritas [L.] (au′-ri-a mi-di-oc′-ri-tas). The golden mean. MIDCOURSE-CIRCUIT.

au′-re-ate. Golden. YELLOWNESS-PURPLE.

au-re′-o-la. Circlet of light about the head of a divine being. LIGHT-DARKNESS.

au′-re-ole. Radiance around a body; to surround with an aureola. REPUTATION-DISCREDIT.

au-re′-o-lin. Cobalt yellow. YELLOWNESS-PURPLE.

au′-ri-cle. External ear. HEARING-DEAFNESS.

au-ric′-u-lar. Pertaining to the ear; confidential. ENLIGHTENMENT-SECRECY, HEARING-DEAFNESS; **auricular confession,** CEREMONIAL.

auri sacra fames [L.] (au′-rai sê′-cra fê′-miz). Accursed greed of gold. EXTRAVAGANCE-AVARICE.

au-rist′. One who treats affections of the ear. REMEDY-BANE.

au-ro′-ra. A phenomenon of the upper atmosphere; dawn. DIMNESS, LIGHT-DARKNESS, LUMINARY-SHADE, MORNING-EVENING; **aurora borealis,** northern lights, LUMINARY-SHADE.

aus″-cul-ta′-tion. A listening. HEARING-DEAFNESS.

aus′-pi-cal. Auguring. PROPHECY.

aus′-pice. An omen or sign. PORTENT.

aus′-pi-ces. Protection or favoring. DOMINANCE-IMPOTENCE, PROPHECY, SECURITY-INSECURITY; **under the auspices of,** RULE-LICENSE.

aus-pi′-cious. Conducive to good fortune. OPPORTUNENESS-UNSUITABLENESS, PROPHECY, SANGUINENESS-HOPELESSNESS, WELFARE-MISFORTUNE.

auspicium melioris ævi [L.] (au-spish′-i-um mi-li-o′-ris i′-vai). Augury of a happier time. PORTENT.

aussitôt dit, aussitôt fait [F.] (o-si-to′ di, o-si-to′ fê). "No sooner said than done." COMPLETION-NONCOMPLETION.

aus-tere′. Severe. AUSTERITY, HARSHNESS-MILDNESS, POLITENESS-IMPOLITENESS.

aus-ter′-i-ty. Rigor in conduct; severe simplicity; sour. AUSTERITY, GODLINESS-UNGODLINESS, HARSHNESS-MILDNESS, PALATABLENESS-UNPALATABLENESS, POLITENESS-IMPOLITENESS.

AUSTERITY.

Asceticism. Belief in excessive austerity, the state of excessive self-denial.

Austerity. Severity and sternness in conduct.

Cynicism. The state of being cynical, of sneering at moral uprightness.

Fasting. Total or partial abstinence from food on religious grounds. See FASTING.

Flagellation. Whipping oneself as a part of religious duty.

Maceration. Making lean and thin by fasting.

Martyrdom. The condition of a martyr, or of one who suffers for his beliefs.

Mortification. The act or state of mortifying, or the death of a part of the body.

Nephalism. Total abstinence from intoxicants.

Penance. Suffering or punishment as an atonement of sin. See ATONEMENT.

Puritanism. The state of being a Puritan, or excessively severe in conduct

Sabbatarianism. Asceticism in the observance of the Sabbath.

Total abstinence. Refusal to have anything to do with, as liquor, etc.

AUSTERITY—*Nouns of Agency.*

Anchoret. One who retires from the world to practise religion.

Anchorite. See ANCHORET.

Ascetic. One who practises asceticism.

AUSTERITY—Nouns of Agency—*Continued.*

Cynic. One who holds in contempt all virtues.

Essene. One of a sect of ascetic Jews.

Heauton timoroumenos [Gr.]. The Self-tormentor, name of a play by Menander.

Hermit. One who leaves the world and lives for religious contemplation. See Sociability.

Martyr. One who suffers for his beliefs.

Puritan. One who is very strict in conduct.

Sabbatarian. One who strictly observes the Jewish Sabbath.

Austerity—*Figurative Nouns.*

Sackcloth and ashes. Penance for sin, self-abasement.

Austerity—*Adjectives.*

Acerbic. Rigidly exact and stern.

Ascetic. Given to severe self-denial.

Austere. Severe; grave; stern.

Cynical. Inclined to moral skepticism.

Over-religious. Excessively religious.

Puritanical. Rigid.

Austerlitz, voila le soleil d'— [F.] (au-ster-litz', vwa-la' le so-lêy' d). Behold the sun of Austerlitz. Reputation-Discredit, Sanguineness-Hopelessness.

aus'-tral. Southern. Laterality-Contraposition.

aus'-tro-man''-cy. Divination by observation of the wind. Prophecy.

au-then'-tic. Credible. Certainty-Doubt, Truth-Error.

au-then'-ti-cate. To certify. Evidence-Counterevidence.

au-then''-ti-ca'-tion. Confirmation. Evidence-Counterevidence, Security.

au''-then-tic'-i-ty. State of being authoritative. Truth-Error.

au'-thor. A creator; a writer. Cause-Effect, Maker-Destroyer, Missive-Publication; **author of our being,** Divinity; **author of evil,** Angel-Satan; **dramatic author,** Acting.

au-thor'-i-ta-tive. Duly sanctioned. Certainty-Doubt, Order.

au-thor'-i-ta-tive-ness. Possession of power. Rule-License.

au-thor'-i-ties. Rulers. Chief-Underling.

au-thor'-i-ty. Right to command and enforce obedience; that appealed to in support of an opinion. Dominance-Impotence, Dueness-Undueness, Enlightenment-Secrecy, Evidence-Counterevidence, Leave-Prohibition, Might-Impotence, Rule-License, Sage-Fool; **do upon one's own authority,** Volition-Obligation; **ensign of authority,** Manager, Scepter; **person in authority,** Chief-Undreling, Rule-License.

au''-thor-i-za'-tion. Legal sanction. Prohibition.

au'-thor-ize. To empower. Commission-Abrogation, Dueness-Undueness, Leave-Prohibition, Rule-License.

au'-thor-ized. Endowed with authority. Commission-Retirement, Dueness-Undueness.

au'-thor-ship. Quality or function of an author. Creation-Destruction, Style, Writing-Printing.

au''-to-bi-og'-ra-phy. Story of one's own life. Account.

au-toch'-tho-nes. Aborigines. Dweller-Habitation.

au-toch'-thon-ous. Native. Dweller-Habitation.

au-toc'-ra-cy. Rule of an autocrat. Harshness-Mildness, Rule-License, Tyranny-Anarchy.

au'-to-crat. A supreme unrestricted ruler. Chief-Underling, Tyranny-Anarchy.

au''-to-crat'-ic. Having absolute power. Rule-License, Volition-Obligation.

auto da fé [Pg.] (au'-to da fê). An act of faith; bonfire. Heating-Cooling, Recompense-Punition.

au'-to-graph. One's own signature. Sign, Writing-Printing.

au-tog'-ra-phy. Autographs collectively considered. Sign.

Au-tol'-y-cus. A famous thief of mythology. Dealer, Robber.

au''-to-ma'-ni-ac. One who has worked himself into insanity Saneness-Maniac.

au''-to-mat'-ic. Acting from itself. Volition-Obligation.

au-tom'-a-ton. An automatic machine. Volition-Obligation.

au''-to-mo'-bile. A self-acting or self-regulating road wagon.

au-ton'-o-my. Self-government. Liberty-Subjection, Rule-License.

au'-top-sy. Examination of a body after death. Life-Funeral, Sight-Blindness.

au-top'-tic-al. Seen with one's own eyes. Manifestation-Latency, Visibility-Invisibility.

au'-to-type. Photograph process of printing. Engraving.

au'-tumn. Third season of the year. Morning-Evening.

au-tum'-nal. Relating to autumn. Morning-Evening.

aux-il'-i-a-ry. One who or that which helps. Antagonist-Assistant, Benefactor-Evildoer, Obstruction-Help; **auxiliary forces,** Belligerent.

a-vail'. To serve; to use for a purpose. Success-Failure, Use-Disuse, Usefulness-Uselessness; **avail oneself of,** Use-Disuse; **of no avail,** Usefulness-Uselessness.

a-vail'-a-ble. Usable. Usefulness-Uselessness.

av'-a-lanche''. A fall of snow down a mountain side; anything sudden and overwhelming. Ascent-Descent, Excess-Lack.

avaler les couleuvres [F.] (a-va-lê' lê cu-luvr'). To swallow the snakes. To bear an affront. Presumption-Obsequiousness, Yielding.

avant-coureur [F.] (a-van' cu-rur'). Forerunner. Predecessor-Continuation, Preparation-Nonpreparation.

avant-propos [F.] (a-van' pro-po'). Preface. Predecessor-Continuation.

av'-a-rice. Passion for riches. Extravagance-Avarice.

av-a-ri'-cious. Greedy of gain. Extravagance-Avarice.

a-vast'. Stop. Discontinuance-Continuance, Leave-Prohibition, Movement-Rest, Quest-Abandonment.

av''-a-tar'. Descent of the deity into incarnate existence. Devotion-Idolatry, Divinity, Mutation-Permanence.

a-vaunt'. Dismissal. Admission-Expulsion, Appearance-Disappearance.

a'-ve. Hail. Politeness-Impoliteness, Reputation-Discredit.

a-venge'. To take satisfaction for. Pardon-Vindictiveness.

a-venge'-ance. Vengeance. Pardon-Vindictiveness.

a-venge'-ment. Retaliation. Pardon-Vindictiveness.

a-ven'-ger. One who avenges. Pardon-Vindictiveness.

a-veng'-ing. Taking revenge. Pardon-Vindictiveness.

av'-e-nue. A street; approach to a residence. City-Country, Domestication-Agriculture, Way.

a-ver'. To assert as a fact. Assertion-Denial.

av'-er-age. Arithmetical mean; moderate character. Faultlessness-Faultiness, Medium; **average circumstances,** Mediocrity; **take an average,** Mensuration.

a-ver'-ment. Affirmation. Assertion-Denial.

Averni, facilis descensus [L.] (a-ver'-nai, fas'-i-lis de-sen'-sus). Easy is the descent to the lower world. Parallelism-Inclination, Security-Insecurity.

A-ver'-nus. The infernal regions. HEAVEN-HELL.

av''-er-run'-cate. To ward off. ADMISSION-EXPULSION, INJECTION-EJECTION.

av''-er-sa'-tion. Aversion. ASSERTION-DENIAL.

a-verse'. Moved by dislike or repugnance. READINESS-RELUCTANCE.

a-verse'-ness. Dislike. READINESS-RELUCTANCE.

a-ver'-sion. Opposition or dislike. DESIRE-DISTASTE, LOVE-HATE.

a-vert'. To turn aside. OBSTRUCTION-HELP; **avert the eyes,** SIGHT-BLINDNESS.

a'-vi-a-ry. A place where birds are kept. DOMESTICATION-AGRICULTURE.

avibus, bonis [L.] (av'-i-bus, bo'-nis). Under good auspices. SECURITY-INSECURITY.

av'-id. Eager. DESIRE-DISTASTE.

a-vid'-i-ty. Strong desire. DESIRE-DISTASTE, EXTRAVAGANCE-AVARICE.

a-vile'. To make vile. ADULATION-DISPARAGEMENT, APPROVAL-DISAPPROVAL.

avi numerantur avorum [L.] (ê'-vai niu-mer-an'-tur a-vor'-um). Ancestors of ancestors are counted unto me. PARENTAGE-PROGENY.

avise la fin [F.] (à-vîz' la fan·). Weigh well the end. PREVISION.

a-vi'-so. A despatch boat. TIDINGS-MYSTERY.

av''-o-ca'-tion. That which takes one from his regular calling. OCCUPATION.

a-void'. To shun. DESIRE-DISTASTE, READINESS-RELUCTANCE.

a-void'-ance. Act of shunning. QUEST-EVASION.

a-void'-less. Inevitable. CERTAINTY-DOUBT, VOLITION-OBLIGATION.

av''-oir-du-pois'. A system of weights. HEAVINESS-LIGHTNESS.

av''-o-la'-tion. Act of flying away. ESCAPE, QUEST-EVASION.

a-vouch'. To declare openly. ASSERTION-DENIAL.

a-vouch'-al. A declaring. ASSERTION-DENIAL.

a-vouch'-ment. Declaration. ASSERTION-DENIAL.

a-vow'. To acknowledge or declare frankly. ASSENT-DISSENT, ASSERTION-DENIAL, EXPOSURE-HIDINGPLACE.

a-vul'-sion. A forcible separation. INJECTION-EJECTION, UNION-DISUNION.

a-wait'. To wait for. EARLINESS-LATENESS, EXPECTATION-SURPRISE, FUTURE-PAST, OCCURRENCE-DESTINY.

a-wake'. To cease from sleep; to call into action; to be awake. ACTIVITY-INDOLENCE, CAREFULNESS-CARELESSNESS, HEED-DISREGARD, SAGACITY-INCAPACITY.

a-wa'-ken. To arouse from sleep; to stir up; to stir up interest. ENLIGHTENMENT-SECRECY, EXCITATION; **awaken the attention,** HEED-DISREGARD; **awaken the memory,** REMEMBRANCE-FORGETFULNESS.

a-ward'. To decide to be rightly due. DECISION-MISJUDGMENT, GIVING-RECEIVING.

a-ware'. Having knowledge of. KNOWLEDGE-IGNORANCE.

a-way'. Absent; at a distance; apart. ADMISSION-EXPULSION, PRESENCE-ABSENCE, REMOTENESS-NEARNESS; **away from,** CONNECTION-INDEPENDENCE; **away with,** ADMISSION-EXPULSION, APPROVAL-DISAPPROVAL, COMMISSION-ABROGATION, KEEPING-RELINQUISHMENT, REGARD-SCORN; **break away,** QUEST-

EVASION; **do away with,** ACTION-PASSIVENESS, COMMISSION-ABROGATION; **fly away,** ARRIVAL-DEPARTURE; **get away,** ESCAPE; **move away,** APPROACH-WITHDRAWAL, ESCAPE; **take away from,** TAKING-RESTITUTION; **throw away,** ADMISSION-EXPULSION, CHOICE-REJECTION, KEEPING-RELINQUISHMENT, PROVISION-WASTE.

awe. Dread mingled with reverence. ASTONISHMENT-EXPECTANCE, REGARD-DISRESPECT, SANGUINENESS-TIMIDITY.

awe'-in-spir''-ing. Stupefying. SANGUINENESS-TIMIDITY.

awe'-less. Fearless. BRAVERY-COWARDICE, PRESUMPTION-OBSEQUIOUSNESS, REGARD-DISRESPECT.

aw'-ful. Terrible; very great. MAGNITUDE-SMALLNESS, SANGUINENESS-TIMIDITY; **awful silence,** SOUND-SILENCE.

a-while'. For a short time. LASTINGNESS-TRANSIENTNESS.

awk'-ward. Ungraceful; clumsy. BEAUTY-UGLINESS, DIFFICULTY-FACILITY, PLEASURABLENESS-PAINFULNESS, PROPRIETY-IMPROPRIETY, SKILL-UNSKILFULNESS, SOCIETY-LUDICROUSNESS, TASTE-VULGARITY; **awkward squad,** ADEPT-BUNGLER.

awk'-ward-ness. Clumsiness. DIFFICULTY-FACILITY, TASTE-VULGARITY.

awl. A shoemaker's tool for boring. PERFORATER-STOPPER.

awn'-ing. A covering or shelter from the sun. COVER-LINING, LUMINARY-SHADE.

a-wry'. Out of proper form; evil. GOOD-EVIL, PARALLELISM-INCLINATION, PROPORTION-DEFORMITY.

axe. An edge-tool for cutting. IMPETUS-REACTION, RECOMPENSE-SCOURGE, SHARPNESS-BLUNTNESS, WEAPON.

ax'-i-al. Pertaining to an axis. CENTER.

ax'-il-la-ry. Pertaining to the axilla. ANATOMY.

ax'-i-no-man''-cy. Divination by means of an axe. PROPHECY.

ax'-i-om. A self-evident truth. ADAGE-NONSENSE.

ax'-i-o-mat'-ic. Self-evident. ADAGE-NONSENSE, CERTAINTY-DOUBT.

ax'-is. A line or support on which something rotates. CENTER, REVOLUTION-EVOLUTION, SUSPENSION-SUPPORT.

ax'-le. A cross-bar on which anything turns. REVOLUTION-EVOLUTION, SUSPENSION-SUPPORT; **wheel and axle,** INSTRUMENT.

ax'-le-tree''. An axle of wood. SUSPENSION-SUPPORT.

ay. Yes. ASSENT-DISSENT.

a'-yah. A nurse; a lady's-maid. CHIEF-UNDERLING, GUARD-PRISON.

aye. Always; yes. ASSENT-DISSENT, ETERNITY-INSTANTANEITY.

az'-i-muth. An astronomical arc. AIM-ABERRATION, ASTRONOMY, ERECTNESS-FLATNESS, MENSURATION; **azimuth circle,** ERECTNESS-FLATNESS.

a-zo'-ic. Without organic life. ORGANIZATION-INORGANIZATION.

az-ote'. An old name for nitrogen, which does not support life. REMEDY-BANE.

a-zot'-ic. Unable to support life. HEALTHINESS-UNHEALTHINESS.

az'-ure. A clear blue. BLUENESS-ORANGE.

az'-y-gous. Occurring singly. CENTER, SOLITUDE-COMPANY.

B

Ba'-al. A Semitic sun-god. DEVOTION-IDOLATRY, JOVE-FIEND, REVELATION-PSEUDOREVELATION.

bab'-ble. Senseless sound. CONVERSATION-MONOLOGUE, LOUDNESS-FAINTNESS, MEANING-JARGON, RIVER-WIND, TALKATIVENESS-TACITURNITY.

bab'-ble-ment. Idle talk. TALKATIVENESS-TACITURNITY.

bab'-bler. An idle talker. SAGE-FOOL, TALKATIVENESS-TACITURNITY.

bab'-bling. Senseless talk. SAGACITY-INCAPACITY.

babe. An infant. INFANT-VETERAN; **innocent as the babe unborn,** INNOCENCE-GUILT.

ba'-bel. Confusion of sounds. LANGUAGE, MELODY-DISSONANCE, REGULARITY-IRREGULARITY, TALKATIVENESS-TACITURNITY, WORD-NEOLOGY.

Ba'-bism. The principles and practises of the Babi. REVELATION-PSEUDOREVELATION.

Ba'-bist. One who believes in the principles of the Babi. REVELATION-PSEUDOREVELATION.

bab-oon'. A large ape. BEAUTY-UGLINESS.

ba'-by. A very young child. INFANT-VETERAN, SAGE-FOOL; **baby linen,** DRESS-UNDRESS.

ba'-by-farm''. A place where babies are nursed and brought up. DWELLER-HABITATION.

ba'-by-hood. Infancy. INFANCY-AGE, SAGACITY-INCAPACITY.

ba'-by-ish. Like an infant. INFANT-VETERAN, SAGACITY-INCAPACITY.

bac''-ca-lau''-re-ate. The degree of bachelor. SCHOOL.

bac''-ca-rat. A gambling card game. ENTERTAINMENT-WEARINESS.

bac'-chal. A drunken reveler. TEETOTALISM-INTEMPERANCE.

bac'-cha-nal. A drunken reveler. TEETOTALISM-INTEMPERANCE.

bac''-cha-na'-li-a. Drunken orgies. TEETOTALISM-INTEMPERANCE.

bac''-cha-na'-lian. A drunken reveler. TEETOTALISM-INTEMPERANCE.

bac'-cha-nals. Drunken revelry. TEETOTALISM-INTEMPERANCE.

bac'-chante. A priestess of Bacchus. TEETOTALISM-INTEMPERANCE.

Bac'-chus. The god of wine. TEETOTALISM-INTEMPERANCE; **devotee to Bacchus,** TEETOTALISM-INTEMPERANCE.

bach'-e-lor. An unmarried man. MATRIMONY-CELIBACY.

bach'-e-lor-hood. The bachelor's degree. MATRIMONY-CELIBACY.

bach'-e-lor-ship. The condition of being a bachelor. MATRIMONY-CELIBACY.

back. A portion of the body; the part opposite the front. ADVANCE-RETROGRESSION, ANTERIORITY-POSTERIORITY, CONVEXITY-CONCAVITY, OBSTRUCTION-HELP; **back out,** ADVANCE-RETROGRESSION; **back to back,** ANTERIORITY-POSTERIORITY; **back up,** OBSTRUCTION-HELP, SUSPENSION-SUPPORT; **behind one's back,** ANTERIORITY-POSTERIORITY, ENLIGHTENMENT-SECRECY, MANIFESTATION-LATENCY; **carry one's thoughts back,** REMEMBRANCE-FORGETFULNESS; **come back,** ARRIVAL-DEPARTURE; **fall back,** RENOVATION-RELAPSE; **give back,** TAKING-RESTITUTION; **go back,** ADVANCE-RETROGRESSION; **go back from,** OBSERVANCE-NONOBSERVANCE; **have at one's back,** SUSPENSION-SUPPORT; **hold back,** QUEST-EVASION; **keep back,** STORE; **look back,** REMEMBRANCE-FORGETFULNESS; **on one's back,** ERECTNESS-FLATNESS, MIGHT-IMPOTENCE, SUCCESS-FAILURE; **pat on the back,** ALLEVIATION-AGGRAVATION, APPROVAL-DISAPPROVAL, BRAVERY-COWARDICE, MOTIVE-CAPRICE; **pay back,** REPRISAL-RESISTANCE; **put back,** BETTERMENT-DETERIORATION, RENOVATION-RELAPSE; **put one's back up,** FAVORITE-ANGER; **send back,** PROFFER-REFUSAL; **set one's back up,** SELF-RESPECT-HUMBLENESS; **set one's back against the wall,** DETERMINATION-VACILLATION; **some time back,** FUTURE-PAST; **spring back,** ELASTICITY-INELASTICITY, IMPETUS-REACTION; **take back again,** TAKING-RESTITUTION; **trace back,** REMEMBRANCE-FORGETFULNESS; **turn back,** ADVANCE-RETROGRESSION; **turn one's back,** ADVANCE-RETROGRESSION, QUEST-EVASION; **turn one's back upon,** ADVANCE-RETROGRESSION, ANTAGONISM-CONCURRENCE, ATTRACTION-REPULSION, HEED-DISREGARD, POLITENESS-IMPOLITENESS, QUEST-EVASION, REGARD-DISREGARD, REGARD-SCORN, SOCIABILITY-PRIVACY.

back'-bite''. Calumniate secretly. ADULATION-DISPARAGEMENT, APPROVAL-DISAPPROVAL; **Sir Benjamin Backbite,** FLATTERER-DEFAMER.

back'-bi''-ter. A base traducer. FLATTERER-DEFAMER.

back'-bone''. The spine; firmness. AFFECTIONS, BRAVERY-COWARDICE, CENTER, PERSISTENCE-WHIM, SUBJECTIVENESS-OBJECTIVENESS, SUSPENSION-SUPPORT; **game to the backbone,** DETERMINATION-VACILLATION.

back'-cast''. Thrown back. WELFARE-MISFORTUNE.

back'-door''. Rear entrance or exit. METHOD.

back'-down''. Retraction. YIELDING.

back'-er. A supporter. ANTAGONIST-ASSISTANT.

back'-friend''. A secret foe. FRIEND-FOE.

back''-gam'-mon. A game. ENTERTAINMENT-WEARINESS.

back'-ground''. Ground in the rear. ANTERIORITY-POSTERIORITY, REMOTENESS-NEARNESS; **in the background,** ANTERIORITY-POSTERIORITY, ENLIGHTENMENT-SECRECY, MANIFESTATION-LATENCY, REPUTATION-DISCREDIT; **keep in the background,** CONCEIT-DIFFIDENCE, ENLIGHTENMENT-SECRECY, SOCIABILITY-PRIVACY; **put one in the background,** REPUTATION-DISCREDIT; **throw into the background,** CAREFULNESS-CARELESSNESS.

back'-log''. A large log placed at the back of the fire in an open fireplace. OVEN-REFRIGERATOR.

back'-plate''. A piece of armor which covers the back. WEAPON.

back'-set''. To replow land. RENOVATION-RELAPSE.

back'-set''-tler. One who inhabits the back-settlements of a country. DWELLER-HABITATION.

back'-shish. A gratuity. GIVING-RECEIVING.

back'-side''. The back part. ANTERIORITY-POSTERIORITY.

back-sli'-der. An apostate. BIGOTRY-APOSTASY, PATRIOTISM-TREASON.

back-sli'-ding. Apostatizing. ADVANCE-RETROGRESSION, BIGOTRY-APOSTASY, ORTHODOXY-HETERODOXY, RENOVATION-RELAPSE, VIRTUE-VICE.

back'-stairs''. Private stairs. EXPOSURE-HIDINGPLACE, METHOD; **backstairs influence,** CRAFT-ARTLESSNESS.

back'-ward. Directed to the rear; late; reluctant. ADVANCE - RETROGRESSION, EARLINESS - LATENESS, READINESS-RELUCTANCE.

back"-war-da'-tion. The premium paid for delaying the delivery of stock. PRICE-DISCOUNT.

back'-ward-ness. Reluctancy DESIRE-DISTASTE, READINESS-RELUCTANCE.

back'-wards. Towards the rear. ADVANCE-RETRO-GRESSION; **bend backwards,** ELASTICITY-INELAS-TICITY; **bend backwards and forwards,** COMMUTATION-PERMUTATION, VIBRATION.

back'-wa"-ter. Water held or forced back. ADVANCE-RETROGRESSION.

back'-woods". Sparsely settled districts. CITY-COUN-TRY.

back'-woods"-man. A frontiersman. DOMESTICATION-AGRICULTURE, DWELLER-HABITATION.

ba'-con. Cured hog's flesh. **Buttered upon bacon,** EXCESS-LACK; **save one's bacon,** CONSERVATION, SECURITY-INSECURITY.

Ba-co'-ni-an meth'-od. Induction. INVESTIGATION-ANSWER.

bac-te'-ri-a. Microbes. BIOLOGY, GREATNESS-LITTLE-NESS.

baculinum argumentum [L.] (bac-yu-lai'-num ar-giu-men'-tum). Club law. COERCION, LAW-LAWLESS-NESS, RECOMPENSE-PUNITION.

bad. Wicked; worthless. APPROVAL-DISAPPROVAL, CLEANNESS-FILTHINESS, GOOD-EVIL, GOODNESS-BAD-NESS, PERFUME-STENCH, RIGHT-WRONG; **bad blood,** CHARITABLENESS-MALEVOLENCE, LOVE-HATE; **bad business,** SANGUINENESS-HOPELESSNESS; **bad case,** RATIOCINATION-INSTINCT; **bad chance,** LIKELIHOOD-UNLIKELIHOOD; **bad debt,** CREDIT-DEBT; **bad fairy,** JOVE-FIEND; **bad faith,** OBSERVANCE-NONOBSERV-ANCE, UPRIGHTNESS-DISHONESTY; **bad grace,** POLITE-NESS-IMPOLITENESS; **bad habit,** HABIT-DESUETUDE; **bad hand,** ADEPT-BUNGLER, WRITING-PRINTING; **bad humor,** CONTENTEDNESS - DISCONTENTMENT, FAVOR-ITE - ANGER, FAVORITE - QUARRELSOMENESS, LIGHT-HEARTEDNESS-DEJECTION; **bad intent,** CHARITABLE-NESS-MALEVOLENCE; **bad job,** GOOD-EVIL, SANGUINE-NESS-HOPELESSNESS, SKILFULNESS-UNSKILFULNESS; **bad joke,** TASTE-VULGARITY; **bad language,** AP-PROVAL-DISAPPROVAL, CHARITABLENESS-CURSE; **bad luck,** WELFARE-MISFORTUNE; **bad man,** GOOD MAN-BAD MAN, UPRIGHTNESS-ROGUE; **bad name,** ADULA-TION-DISPARAGEMENT, APPROVAL-DISAPPROVAL, REP-UTATION-DISCREDIT; **bad odor,** PERFUME-STENCH; **bad repute,** REPUTATION-DISCREDIT; **bad smell,** PER-FUME-STENCH; **bad spirit,** JOVE-FIEND; **bad spirits,** LIGHTHEARTEDNESS-DEJECTION; **bad taste,** TASTE-VULGARITY; **bad temper,** FAVORITE-ANGER, FAVOR-ITE - QUARRELSOMENESS, FAVORITE - MOROSENESS, **bad time of it,** PLEASURE-PAIN, **bad turn,** CHARI-TABLENESS-MALEVOLENCE, GOOD-EVIL; **bad woman,** GOOD MAN-BAD MAN; **from bad to worse,** ALLEVIA-TION-AGGRAVATION; **go bad,** BETTERMENT-DETERIO-RATION, CLEANNESS-FILTHINESS; **in bad odor,** AMITY-HOSTILITY; **in a bad way,** BETTERMENT-DETERIORA-TION, HEALTH - SICKNESS, SECURITY - INSECURITY, WELFARE-MISFORTUNE; **not a bad idea,** SAGACITY-INCAPACITY; **on bad terms,** AMITY-HOSTILITY, VARI-ANCE-ACCORD, **put a bad construction on,** INTERPRE-TATION-MISINTERPRETATION; **take in bad part,** CON-TENTEDNESS - DISCONTENTMENT, FAVORITE - ANGER; **view in a bad light,** ADULATION-DISPARAGEMENT

badaud [F.] (ba-do') An idler SAGE-FOOL.

badge. A mark of distinction. SIGN; **badge of author-ity,** SCEPTER; **badge of infamy,** REPUTATION-DIS-CREDIT; **badge of slavery,** CHIEF-UNDERLING; **Badge of the Grand Army of the Republic,** PATRIOTISM-TREASON: **Badge of the Order of St. Andrew,** PATRIOT-ISM-TREASON, **Badge of the Order of St. Patrick,**

PATRIOTISM-TREASON; **Badge of the Order of the Golden Fleece,** PATRIOTISM-TREASON; **Badge of the Order of the Thistle,** PATRIOTISM-TREASON.

badg'-er. A burrowing mammal; to worry. PLEASUR-ABLENESS-PAINFULNESS; **badger dog,** FAUNA-FLORA.

ba"-di-nage'. Banter. SOCIETY-DERISION, WITTINESS-DULNESS.

bad lands. Waste area. GEOLOGY.

bad'-ly. Wickedly. GOODNESS-BADNESS; **badly off,** AFFLUENCE-PENURY, WELFARE-MISFORTUNE.

bad'-ness. The state of being bad. GOOD-EVIL, GOOD-NESS-BADNESS.

baf'-fle. To frustrate. OBSTRUCTION-HELP, SUCCESS-FAILURE; **baffle description,** ASTONISHMENT-EXPEC-TANCE, CONVENTIONALITY-UNCONVENTIONALITY

baf'-fle-ment. Frustration. OBSTRUCTION-HELP.

baf'-fler. One who or that which baffles. OBSTRUC-TION-HELP.

bag. A sack; to secure. ESTABLISHMENT-REMOVAL, GAIN-LOSS, RECEIVER, TAKING-RESTITUTION, THEFT; **bag and baggage,** PROPERTY.

bag"-a-telle'. A trifle; a kind of game. CONSEQUENCE-INSIGNIFICANCE; ENTERTAINMENT-WEARINESS.

bag'-gage. Luggage; a strumpet. MATERIALS, PROP-ERTY, PURITY-RAKE.

bag'-ga-la. A two-masted Arabian trading-vessel. CONVEYANCE-VESSEL, CONVEYER.

bag'-gy. Ill-fitting; loose. COHESION-LOOSENESS.

bag'-man. A traveling salesman. CONSIGNEE.

bagn'-io. A brothel. PURITY-IMPURITY.

bag'-pipe. A musical wind-instrument. MUSICAL IN-STRUMENTS.

bah. A contemptuous exclamation. REGARD-SCORN.

bail. Surety. SECURITY; **go bail,** CREDIT-DEBT; **leg-bail,** QUEST-EVASION.

bail'-a-ble. Admitting of bail. CREDIT-DEBT, SECURITY.

bai'-liff. An officer CHIEF-UNDERLING, CONSIGNEE, JUDICATURE, MANAGER.

bail'-i-wick. The limits of a bailiff's authority. JUDI-CATURE.

bai-ram'. A Turkish festival CEREMONIAL, ENTER-TAINMENT-WEARINESS.

bairn. A child. INFANT-VETERAN.

bait. A lure. ATTACK-DEFENSE, GIVING-RECEIV-ING, MOTIVE - CAPRICE, NUTRIMENT - EXCRETION, PLEASURABLENESS - PAINFULNESS, TRUTHFULNESS-FRAUD, WEARINESS-REFRESHMENT, **swallow the bait,** GULL-DECEIVER, READINESS-RELUCTANCE.

bake. To dry and harden. HEATING-COOLING.

bake'-house. A house for baking. OVEN-REFRIGERATOR.

ba'-ker. One who bakes, especially one who bakes bread. AGENT, CHIEF-UNDERLING, HEATING-COOLING.

ba'-ker's-dozen. Thirteen. FIVE-QUINQUESECTION

ba'-ker-y. A place where different foods are baked OVEN-REFRIGERATOR.

hak'-ing-heat. The heat required in baking. HEAT-COLD.

bal [F.] (bal). An assembly for dancing. ENTERTAIN-MENT-WEARINESS.

balais [F.] (ba-lè). The rosy-red ruby yarn. EMBEL-LISHMENT-DISFIGUREMENT.

bal'-ance. Equipoise. ACCOUNTS, COMPARISON, COM-PENSATION, DETERMINATION-VACILLATION, EQUAL-ITY-INEQUALITY, HEAVINESS-LIGHTNESS, INCRE-MENT-REMNANT, MEDIUM, MONEY, NUMBERING; **bal-ance accounts with,** SETTLEMENT-DEFAULT; **in the balance,** CERTAINTY-DOUBT; **off one's balance,** DE-TERMINATION-VACILLATION, SUCCESS-FAILURE; **the mind losing its balance,** SANENESS-LUNACY.

bal'-anced. Equipoised. MUTABILITY-STABILITY, PRO-PORTION-DEFORMITY; **balanced sentence,** RHETORIC.

bal-bu'-ci-nate. To stammer. SPEECH-INARTICULATE-NESS.

bal'-co-ny. A raised porch ARCHITECTURE, CON-VEXITY-CONCAVITY.

bald. Unadorned. BEAUTY-UGLINESS, DRESS-UNDRESS, EMBELLISHMENT-SIMPLICITY, ENTERTAINMENT-WEARINESS, FORCE-WEAKNESS.

bal'-da-chin. } An altar canopy. AR-
baldachino [It.] (bal-da-kǐ'-no). } CHITECTURE, FANE.

bal'-der-dash. Nonsense. MEANING-JARGON.

bald'-head''. One whose head is bald. BEAUTY-UGLINESS, ENTIRETY-DEFICIENCY, SMOOTHNESS-ROUGHNESS.

bald'-ness. The state of being bald. BEAUTY-UGLINESS.

bal'-dric. A girdle. CIRCLE-WINDING, OUTLINE.

bale. Sorrow; package. ADMISSION-EXPULSION, CONTENTS-RECEIVER, GATHERING-SCATTERING, GOOD-EVIL, MEASURE.

bale'-ful. Sorrowful. GOODNESS-BADNESS.

bal'-is-ter. A cross-bow. WEAPON.

bal''-is-tra'-ri-a. A loophole through which crossbowmen fire. ATTACK-DEFENSE.

ba-lize'. A sea-mark. SIGN.

balk. Thwart. EXPECTATION-DISAPPOINTMENT, OBSTRUCTION-HELP, TRUTHFULNESS-FALSEHOOD.

ball. A sphere; a game; dance. ENTERTAINMENT-WEARINESS, PUSH-PULL, ROUNDNESS, SOCIABILITY-PRIVACY, WEAPON; **ball at one's feet,** RULE-LICENSE, SUCCESS-FAILURE; **ball dress,** POMP; **keep up the ball,** ACTIVITY-INDOLENCE, DISCONTINUANCE-CONTINUANCE.

bal'-lad. A song. MUSIC, POETRY-PROSE.

bal'-lad-mon'-ger. A poetaster. MUSIC, POETRY-PROSE.

bal'-lad-ry. Ballad poetry. MUSIC, POETRY-PROSE.

bal'-la-rag. To threaten. CHARITABLENESS-MENACE.

bal'-last. Heavy material placed in the hold of a vessel to steady it. COMPENSATION, HEAVINESS-LIGHTNESS, SAGACITY-INCAPACITY; **without ballast,** RECKLESSNESS-CAUTION, VIRTUE-VICE.

bal'-let. A dance. ACTING, ENTERTAINMENT-WEARINESS; **ballet-girl,** ACTING.

bal'-let-dan'-cer. A dancer. ACTING.

bal-lis'-tics. The science of projectiles. FIGHTING-CONCILIATION, PUSH-PULL, WEAPON.

bal-loon'. A bag to fill with gas and rise in the air CONVEYANCE-VESSEL, TRAVELING-NAVIGATION.

bal-loon'-ist. An aeronaut. WAYFARER-SEAFARER.

bal-loon'-ry. The science of ballooning. TRAVELING-NAVIGATION.

bal'lot. Vote. CHOICE-NEUTRALITY.

ball'-proof. Capable of resisting balls from firearms. ATTACK-DEFENSE.

ball'-room. A dance hall. ENTERTAINMENT-WEARINESS.

balm. A remedy. ALLEVIATION-AGGRAVATION, PERFUME-STENCH, REMEDY-BANE, TURBULENCE-CALMNESS.

bal-mor'-al. A boot. DRESS-UNDRESS.

balm'-y. Soothing. ACTIVITY-INDOLENCE, PERFUME-STENCH.

bal'-ne-al. Pertaining to a bath. WATER-AIR.

bal-ne-a'-tion. Bathing. WATER-AIR.

balourdise [F.] (ba-lur-dîz'). Blunder. ADEPT-BUNGLER.

bal-sam. A tree. REMEDY-BANE.

bal''-sam-a'-tion. The process of embalming. REMEDY-BANE.

bal-sam'-ic. Like balsam ALLEVIATION-AGGRAVATION, REMEDY-BANE.

bal'-us-trade. A row of balusters. ARCHITECTURE, ENCLOSURE, SUSPENSION-SUPPORT.

bam. To cheat. TRUTHFULNESS-FALSEHOOD.

bam-bi'-no. A child. INFANT-VETERAN.

bam-boo'-zle. To deceive. ENLIGHTENMENT-SECRECY, TRUTHFULNESS-FRAUD.

ban. A decree. CHARITABLENESS-CURSE; **ban with bell, book, and candle,** CEREMONIAL; **under the ban,** CHARITABLENESS-MENACE, LEAVE-PROHIBITION.

banco regis [L.] (ban'-co rĭ'-jis). On the king's bench. ADVOCATE.

band. A stripe; party; ring. ASSOCIATION, CIRCLE-WINDING, CONNECTIVE, GATHERING-SCATTERING, LAMINA-FIBER, MUSIC, MUSICAL INSTRUMENTS, MUSICIAN, OUTLINE, RELEASE-PRISON; **band of hope,** TEETOTALISM-INTEMPERANCE; **band together,** ANTAGONISM-CONCURRENCE; **band with,** STRIFE-PEACE.

band'-age. A strip of cloth. CONNECTIVE, COVER-LINING, RELEASE-PRISON, REMEDY-BANE, SUSPENSION-SUPPORT, UNION-DISUNION; **the eyes bandaged,** SIGHT-BLINDNESS.

ban-dan'-na. A large, bright-colored handkerchief. CLEANNESS-FILTHINESS, MATERIAL.

band'-box''. A hat box. CONTENTS-RECEIVER.

band'-ed to-geth'-er. United. ASSOCIATION, COOPERATION-OPPOSITION, VARIANCE-ACCORD.

ban'-dit. An outlaw. ROBBER.

band'-mas''-ter. The leader of a musical band. CHIEF-UNDERLING, MUSICIAN.

ban'-dog''. A fierce dog. SECURITY-INSECURITY, WARNING.

band'-rol. A pennant. SIGN.

bands. Linen strips worn with certain clerical garments. VESTMENTS.

bandurria [Sp.] (ban-dur'-ri-a). A Spanish musical instrument. MUSICAL INSTRUMENTS.

ban'-dy. To exchange; contend. AGITATION, COMMUTATION-PERMUTATION, CURVATURE-RECTILINEARITY; **bandy about,** PUBLICITY; **bandy legged,** PROPORTION-DEFORMITY; **bandy words,** CONVERSATION-MONOLOGUE, RATIOCINATION-INSTINCT.

bane. Ruin. GOOD-EVIL, GOODNESS-BADNESS, REMEDY-BANE.

bane'-ful. Ruinous. GOODNESS-BADNESS, REMEDY-BANE.

bang. A heavy blow. CRASH-DRUMMING, IMPETUS-REACTION, REWARD-PUNITION.

ban'-ish. Expel. ADMISSION-EXPULSION, INCLUSION-OMISSION, REWARD-PUNITION, SOCIABILITY-PRIVACY.

ban'-ished. Exiled. SOCIABILITY-PRIVACY.

ban'-ish-ment. Exile. ADMISSION-EXPULSION, REWARD-PUNITION, SOCIABILITY-PRIVACY.

ban'-is-ter. Baluster. SUSPENSION-SUPPORT.

ban'-jo. A string-instrument. MUSICAL INSTRUMENTS.

bank. The margin of a river; a money depository. ATTACK-DEFENSE, CITY-COUNTRY, LABOR-CAPITAL, OCEAN-LAND, PARALLELISM-INCLINATION, REFUGE-PITFALL, STORE, TREASURY; **bank holiday,** ENTERTAINMENT-WEARINESS; **Bank of England,** LABOR-CAPITAL; **bank up,** CONSERVATION; **sea bank,** OCEAN-LAND.

bank'-er. One who conducts a bank. DEALER, TREASURER.

bank'-note. Paper money issued by a bank. MONEY.

bank'-rupt. Insolvent. SETTLEMENT-DEFAULT.

bank'-rupt-cy. Insolvency. SETTLEMENT-DEFAULT, SUCCESS-FAILURE.

banlieue [F.] (ban'-li-u''). Outskirts. ENVIRONMENT-INTERPOSITION, REMOTENESS-NEARNESS.

ban'-ner. A standard. SIGN; **enlist under the banners of,** OBSTRUCTION-HELP; **raise one's banner,** FIGHTING-CONCILIATION.

ban'-ner-et. A little banner. GENTILITY-DEMOCRACY, SIGN.

ban'-ne-rol. A little flag. SIGN.

banns. Formal announcement of intended marriage. **Forbid the banns,** LEAVE-PROHIBITION; **publish the banns,** MATRIMONY-CELIBACY, PETITION-EXPOSTULATION.

ban'-quet. A feast. ENTERTAINMENT-WEARINESS, NUTRIMENT-EXCRETION.

ban''-quette'. A foot-path in a fort. ATTACK-DEFENSE.

ban'-shee. A goblin. JOVE-FIEND.

ban'-tam. A braggart. BRAWLER.

ban'-ter. Ridicule. SOCIETY-DERISION, WITTINESS-DULNESS.

ban'-ter-er. One who banters. BRAWLER.

bant'-ling. A child. INTERDEPENDENCE, PARENTAGE-PROGENY.

ban'-yan. The Indian fig-tree. EXCESS-LACK; **banyan day,** FASTING-GLUTTONY.

bap'-tism. A religious ceremony. CEREMONIAL, NAME-MISNOMER.

bap-tis'-mal. Pertaining to baptism. CEREMONIAL.

Bap'-tist. One who accepts no baptism but immersion. ORTHODOXY-HETERODOXY.

bap'-tis-ter-y. A place for baptizing. FANE.

bap'-tize. To christen. CEREMONIAL, NAME-MISNOMER.

bar. A bolt; court of justice; liquor-counter. ADVOCATE, APERTURE-CLOSURE, ENCLOSURE, INCLUSION-OMISSION, LEAVE-PROHIBITION, LENGTH-SHORTNESS, MELODY-DISSONANCE, OBSTRUCTION-HELP, RELEASE-PRISON, SUSPENSION-SUPPORT, TRIBUNAL; **bar sinister,** FAULTLESSNESS-FAULTINESS, LAW-LAWLESSNESS, REPUTATION-DISCREDIT.

baragouin [F.] (bar''-a-gwan·'). Gibberish. MEANING-JARGON.

barb. A backward-projecting point. CONVEYER, SHARPNESS-BLUNTNESS; **barb the dart,** PLEASURABLENESS-PAINFULNESS.

bar'-ba-can. A gun-hole in a fort. ATTACK-DEFENSE.

Bar''-ba-resque'. Pertaining to Barbary. GENTILITY-DEMOCRACY.

bar-ba'-ri-an. Uncivilized. BENEFACTOR-EVILDOER, GENTILITY-DEMOCRACY.

bar-bar'-ic. Cruel. GENTILITY-DEMOCRACY, TASTE-VULGARITY.

bar'-ba-rism. The middle state of civilization. GENTILITY-DEMOCRACY, POLITENESS-IMPOLITENESS, PURITY-CRUDENESS, TASTE-VULGARITY, WORD-NEOLGY.

bar-bar'-i-ty. Inhumanity. GENTILITY-DEMOCRACY, PURITY-CRUDENESS.

bar'-ba-rize. To make barbarous. GENTILITY-DEMOCRACY.

bar'-ba-rous. Rude. CHARITABLENESS-MALEVOLENCE, FORM-FORMLESSNESS, GENTILITY-DEMOCRACY, PURITY-CRUDENESS.

bar'-ba-rous-ness. Rudeness. GENTILITY-DEMOCRACY.

barbed. Having barbs. SHARPNESS-BLUNTNESS.

bar'-bi-can. An outwork. ATTACK-DEFENSE.

barbouillage [F.] (bar-buî-yazh'). Scribble. WRITING-PRINTING.

bar'-con. A boat or barge. CONVEYANCE-VESSEL.

bard. A poet. MUSICIAN, POETRY-PROSE.

bare. Uncovered; empty. DRESS-UNDRESS, EXCESS-LACK, EXPOSURE-HIDINGPLACE, MAGNITUDE-SMALLNESS, MANIFESTATION-LATENCY; **bare bone,** BREADTH-NARROWNESS; **bare faced,** PRESUMPTION-OBSEQUIOUSNESS; **bare foot,** AFFLUENCE-PENURY, DRESS-UNDRESS; **bare headed,** REGARD-DISRESPECT; **bare possibility,** LIKELIHOOD-UNLIKELIHOOD; **bare supposition,** HYPOTHESIS; **scud under bare poles,** DIFFICULTY-FACILITY.

bare'-ness. Nakedness. DRESS-UNDRESS.

bar'-gain. Contract. CONTRACT, COSTLINESS-CHEAPNESS, EXCHANGE; **bargain for,** EXPECTATION-SURPRISE; **bargain and sale,** ALIENATION, EXCHANGE; **into the bargain,** ADDITION-SUBTRACTION.

barge. A boat. CONVEYANCE-VESSEL.

bar-gee'. A boatman. WAYFARER-SEAFARER.

barge'-mas''-ter. The owner or manager of a barge. CHIEF-UNDERLING.

bar'-ghest''. A goblin. JOVE-FIEND.

bar'-i-tone. Deep-toned. RESONANCE-NONRESONANCE.

bark. A short cry made by a dog or fox; a boat; cover of a tree. CONVEYANCE-VESSEL, COVER-LINING, CRY-ULULATION, MIXTURE-HOMOGENEITY; **bark at,** CHARITABLENESS-MENACE, UPRIGHTNESS-DISHONESTY; **bark worse than bite,** PRESUMPTION-OBSEQUIOUSNESS; **more bark than bite,** CHARITABLENESS-CURSE.

bar'-kan-tine. A sea-vessel. CONVEYANCE-VESSEL.

bark'-bound''. Having a hard bark which stops the growth of the tree. RELEASE-RESTRAINT.

bar'-keep''-er. One who serves liquor over a bar. CHIEF-UNDERLING.

bar'-ley-corn. A grain of barley. GREATNESS-LITTLENESS.

Bar'-ley-corn, Sir John. A personification of liquors. NUTRIMENT-EXCRETION.

barm. Yeast. HEAVINESS-LIGHTNESS, VISCIDITY-FOAM.

bar'-mas''-ter. A local judge among miners. JUDGE.

Bar'-me-cide. Unreal; one who gives an imaginary feast. FASTING-GLUTTONY.

bar'-mote. An English court having jurisdiction over controversies concerning groves, and the affairs of miners. TRIBUNAL.

barn. A stable; a grain-house. DWELLER-HABITATION.

bar'-na-cles. Spectacles. OPTICAL-INSTRUMENTS.

barn'-door''-fowl''. Any domestic fowl. FAUNA-FLORA.

ba-rom'-e-ter. A weather-gage. MENSURATION, WATER-AIR; **consult the barometer,** TRIAL.

bar'-on. Title of nobility. GENTILITY-DEMOCRACY, MATRIMONY-CELIBACY; **baron of the exchange,** JUDGE; **court baron,** TRIBUNAL.

bar'-on-et. Next lower in rank to a baron. GENTILITY-DEMOCRACY.

bar'-on-et-cy. The rank of a baronet. GENTILITY-DEMOCRACY.

ba-ro'-ni-al. Relating to a barony. SELFRESPECT-HUMBLENESS.

bar'-on-ry. The estate of a baron. PROPERTY.

baroque [F.] (ba-roc'). Outlandish. SOCIETY-LUDICROUSNESS.

bar'-o-scope. A kind of barometer. WATER-AIR.

ba-rouche'. A carriage. CONVEYANCE-VESSEL.

barque. A boat. CONVEYANCE-VESSEL.

bar'-rack. A soldier lodge. DWELLER-HABITATION.

bar-ra-coon'. A slave pen. ATTACK-DEFENSE.

bar'-ra-try. Fraud committed by mariners. UPRIGHTNESS-DISHONESTY.

barred. Closed. CROSSING, VARIEGATION.

bar'-rel. A cask. CONTENTS-RECEIVER, ROUNDNESS; **barrel organ,** MUSICAL INSTRUMENTS.

bar'-ren. Unfruitful. FERTILITY-STERILITY.

bar'-ren-ness. Unfruitfulness. FERTILITY-STERILITY.

bar-ri-cade'. A fortification. ATTACK-DEFENSE, ENCLOSURE, OBSTRUCTION-HELP, RELEASE-PRISON.

bar'-ri-er. A defense. ATTACK-DEFENSE, ENCLOSURE, OBSTRUCTION-HELP, RELEASE-PRISON.

bar'-ring. Except; keeping out. ADDITION-SUBTRACTION, CONVENTIONALITY-UNCONVENTIONALITY, INCLUSION-OMISSION, OBSTRUCTION-HELP; **barring out,** INSUBORDINATION-OBEDIENCE, REPRISAL-RESISTANCE.

bar'-ris-ter. A lawyer. ADVOCATE; **revising barrister,** JUDGE.

bar'-row. A mound; hand-carriage. CONVEYANCE-VESSEL, FUNERAL, HEIGHT-LOWNESS.

bar'-tend''-er. A barkeeper. CHIEF-UNDERLING.

bar'-ter. To exchange. ALIENATION, COMMUTATION-PERMUTATION, EXCHANGE, INTERDEPENDENCE.

bar'-ti-zan. A turret. ARCHITECTURE.

bar'-way''. A way closed by bars. ENTRANCE-EXIT.

bar'-y-tone. A male voice. RESONANCE-NONRESONANCE.

bas–bleu [F.] (ba''-blu'). A literary woman. SCHOLAR-DUNCE, SOCIETY-AFFECTATION.

base. Mean; the bottom. ARCHITECTURE, BRAVERY-COWARDICE, GENTILITY-DEMOCRACY, GOODNESS-BADNESS, PRESUMPTION-OBSEQUIOUSNESS, REPUTATION-DISCREDIT, SUSPENSION-SUPPORT, TOP-BOT-

TOM, UPRIGHTNESS-DISHONESTY, VIRTUE-VICE; **base born**, GENTILITY-DEMOCRACY; **base coin**, MONEY; **baseminded**, UPRIGHTNESS-DISHONESTY; **base note**, RESONANCE-NONRESONANCE; **base of operation**, ATTACK-DEFENSE, DESIGN, MUSICAL INSTRUMENTS.

base'-ball''. A game. ENTERTAINMENT-WEARINESS.

bas'-e-lard. A dagger. WEAPON.

base'-ness. Turpitude. BRAVERY-COWARDICE, REPUTATION-DISCREDIT, UPRIGHTNESS-DISHONESTY.

based. Supported. Based on. EVIDENCE-COUNTEREVIDENCE.

base'-less. Without foundation. ENTITY-NONENTITY, SUBSTANCE-NULLITY.

base'-ment. Cellar. CONTENTS-RECEIVER, HEIGHT-LOWNESS, TOP-BOTTOM.

ba-shaw'. A Turkish ruler. CHIEF-UNDERLING, HARSHNESS-MILDNESS.

bash'-ful. Shy. CONCEIT-DIFFIDENCE.

bashi–bazouk [Turk.] (bash''-i-ba-zuk'). A skirmisher. BELLIGERENT.

ba-sil'-i-ca. A church. FANE.

bas'-i-lisk. A fabulous serpent. GOOD MAN-BAD MAN, RULE-LICENSE, SIGHT-BLINDNESS, WEAPON.

ba'-sin. A small vessel to hold water. CONTENTS-RECEIVER, CONVEXITY-CONCAVITY, DWELLER-HABITATION, GEOLOGY, GULF-LAKE.

ba'-sis. Foundation. PREPARATION-NONPREPARATION, SUSPENSION-SUPPORT, TOP-BOTTOM.

bask. To lie in warmth. HEAT-COLD, PLEASURE-PAIN, SENSUALITY-SUFFERING, WELFARE-MISFORTUNE.

bas'-ket. A receptacle made of twigs. CONTENTS-RECEIVER; **basket of**, CONTENTS-RECEIVER.

bas'-re-lief''. Sculpture, whose figures extend only a little above the base. CONVEXITY-CONCAVITY, SCULPTURE.

bass. Low; deep musical note. MUSIC, MUSICAL INSTRUMENTS, RESONANCE-NONRESONANCE.

bass'-drum''. A musical instrument. MUSICAL INSTRUMENTS.

bas'-set-horn. A kind of clarionet. MUSICAL INSTRUMENTS.

bas'-si-net. A basket resembling and used for a cradle. CONTENTS-RECEIVER.

bas-soon'. A musical wind-instrument. MUSICAL INSTRUMENTS.

basso–profundo [It.] (bas'-so-pro-fun'-do). The lowest bass. RESONANCE-NONRESONANCE.

basso–rilievo [It.] (bas'-so-rî-lyê'-vo). Bas-relief. CONVEXITY-CONCAVITY, SCULPTURE.

bass'-vi''-ol. A stringed instrument resembling a violin, used for playing a bass part. MUSICAL INSTRUMENTS.

bas'-tard. A spurious child; base. DUENESS-UNDUENESS, TRUTHFULNESS-FRAUD.

baste. To beat; sew. IMPETUS-REACTION, RECOMPENSE-PUNITION.

Bas-tile'. An ancient prison in Paris. RELEASE-PRISON.

bas-ti-na'-do. A beating with a stick. RECOMPENSE-PUNITION.

bast'-ion. A mound of earth extending out from a rampart. ATTACK-DEFENSE.

bas-ton'. Molding. ARCHITECTURE.

bat. A club. IMPETUS-REACTION, WEAPON.

batch. Quantity of anything made at one time. GATHERING-SCATTERING, QUANTITY-MEASURE.

bate. Lessen. ADDITION-SUBTRACTION, INCREASE-DECREASE, PRICE-DISCOUNT.

ba-teau'. A long light river-boat. CONVEYANCE-VESSEL.

bated–breath. Low. ENLIGHTENMENT-SECRECY, EXPECTATION-SURPRISE, HUMBLENESS, LOUDNESS-FAINTNESS, SELF-RESPECT, VOCALIZATION-MUTENESS.

bath. Act of bathing. INJECTION-EJECTION, WATER-AIR; **bath-room**, CONTENTS-RECEIVER; **warm-bath**, OVEN-REFRIGERATOR.

bath'-chair. A hand-chair for invalids. CONVEYANCE-VESSEL.

bathe. To wash in a bath. INJECTION-EJECTION, SPRING-DIVE, WATER-AIR.

ba-thom'-e-ter. An instrument for taking deep-sea soundings. MENSURATION.

ba'-thos. Anticlimax. ADAGE-NONSENSE, SOCIETY-LUDICROUSNESS.

bat'-man. A man in charge of a horse carrying heavy military baggage. PROVISION-WASTE.

ba-ton'. A staff. IMPETUS-REACTION, SCEPTER.

bat'-ta. Extra pay to troops. RECOMPENSE-PUNITION.

bat-tal'-ia. Order of battle. BELLIGERENT.

bat-tal'-ion. A division of an army. BELLIGERENT.

bat'-ten. To feast. NUTRIMENT-EXCRETION.

bat'-ter. Dough; to beat down. CREATION-DESTRUCTION, IMPETUS-REACTION.

bat'-ter-ed. Beaten. BETTERMENT-DETERIORATION, WEARINESS-REFRESHMENT.

batterie de cuisine [F.] (bat-rî' de cwî-zîn'). Kitchen utensils. FASTING-GLUTTONY.

bat'-ter-ing-ram. An engine for battering down walls. IMPETUS-REACTION, WEAPON.

bat'-ter-ing-train. A train of siege-guns. WEAPON.

bat'-ter-y. A raised work for cannon. BELLIGERENT, ELECTRICITY, WEAPON; **floating battery**, BELLIGERENT; **plant a battery**, ATTACK-DEFENSE.

bat'-tle. A fight. FIGHTING-CONCILIATION, STRIFE-PEACE; **battle array**, FIGHTING-CONCILIATION, ORGANIZATION-DISORGANIZATION, PREPARATION-NONPREPARATION; **battle-ax**, WEAPON; **battle-cry**, SIGN; **battle-field**, LISTS; **battle-ground**, LISTS, VARIANCE-ACCORD; **battle-ship**, BELLIGERENT: **battle with**, ANTAGONISM-CONCURRENCE, FIGHTING-CONCILIATION; **half the battle**, CONSEQUENCE-INSIGNIFICANCE, SUCCESS-FAILURE; **win the battle**, SUCCESS-FAILURE.

bat'-tle-dore''-and-shut'-tle-cock''. A flat bat; a game. COMMUTATION-PERMUTATION, ENTERTAINMENT-WEARINESS.

bat'-tle-ment. An indented parapet. ARCHITECTURE, ATTACK-DEFENSE, INDENTATION.

bat-tol'-o-gize. To repeat. RECURRENCE.

bat-tol'-o-gy. Repetition. RECURRENCE, TERSENESS-PROLIXITY.

battre la campagne [F.] (batr la can -pany'). To beat the bush. ADAGE-NONSENSE, EXCITABILITY-INEXCITABILITY, TERSENESS-PROLIXITY.

battre la générale [F.] (batr la zhê-nê-ral'). To beat the general. ALARM.

battre l'eau avec un baton [F.] (batr lo a-vec' un ba-ton'). To beat the water with a stick. USEFULNESS-USELESSNESS.

battre le fer sur l'enclume [F.] (batr le far sur lan'-clüm'). To beat the iron on the anvil. OPPORTUNENESS-UNSUITABLENESS.

battre, ne que d'une aile [F.] (batr, ne ke dün êl). The affair is in a bad way. ACTIVITY-INDOLENCE.

battre, se contre des moulins [F.] (batr, se con'tr de mu-lan'). To fight against bugbears. USEFULNESS-USELESSNESS.

battue [F.] (ba-tü'). The driving of game from cover. ATTACK-DEFENSE, QUEST-EVASION.

bau'-ble. A trinket. CONSEQUENCE-INSIGNIFICANCE, ENTERTAINMENT-WEARINESS.

ba-var''-dage'. Idle chatter. MEANING-JARGON, TALKATIVENESS-TACITURNITY.

bawd. A procuress. PURITY-RAKE.

bawd'-y–house''. A house of ill-repute. PURITY-IMPURITY.

bawl. Wail. CRY-ULULATION.

bawn. An enclosure. DWELLER-HABITATION.

bay. An inlet; to bark. CONVEXITY-CONCAVITY, CRY-ULULATION, GRAY-BROWN, GULF-LAKE; **at bay**, ATTACK-DEFENSE; DIFFICULTY-FACILITY, REPRISAL-

RESISTANCE, SECURITY-INSECURITY; **bay the moon,** CRY-ULULATION, USEFULNESS-USELESSNESS; **bring to bay,** ATTACK-DEFENSE.

ba''-ya-dere'. A dancing girl of Hindustan. ENTERTAINMENT-WEARINESS.

bay'-ard. A hand-barrow; a horse. CONVEYER.

bayer aux corneilles [F.] (bê-yê' o cor-nêîy'). To gape at the crowd. REFLECTION-VACANCY.

bay'-o-net. A dagger-like weapon attached to a gun. ATTACK-DEFENSE, LIFE-KILLING, WEAPON; **at the point of the bayonet,** COERCION, FIGHTING-CONCILIATION, HARSHNESS-MILDNESS, TURBULENCE-CALMNESS; **crossed bayonets,** ANTAGONISM-CONCURRENCE.

bays. A cloth. TROPHY-TITLE.

bay win'-dow. Projecting window. ARCHITECTURE.

ba-zaar'. A fancy fair. MARKET.

B. C. Before Christ. DURATION-NEVERNESS.

be. Exist. ENTITY-NONENTITY; **be all and end all,** CONSEQUENCE - INSIGNIFICANCE, PURPOSE - LUCK, WHOLE-PART; **be it so,** ASSENT-DISSENT, CONSENT; **be off,** ADMISSION-EXPULSION, ARRIVAL-DEPARTURE, OBSERVANCE-NONOBSERVANCE, QUEST-EVASION; **be that as it may,** COMPENSATION.

beach. A sandy shore. OCEAN-LAND.

bea'-con. A signal fire. SIGN, WARNING.

bead. A perforated ball. ROUNDNESS.

bead'-house''. A pay-hospital or almshouse. DWELLER-HABITATION.

bea'-dle. A court officer; petty town official. CLERGY-LAITY, JUDICATURE, PERFORATOR-STOPPER.

bea'-dle-dom. Petty officialism. RULE-LICENSE.

·bead'-roll''. A rosary. DEVOTION-IDOLATRY, MINISTRY-LAITY, RECORD.

beads. A rosary. **Tell one's beads,** CEREMONIAL, WORSHIP-IDOLATRY.

beads'-man. A resident of an almshouse. CHIEF-UNDERLING, MINISTRY-LAITY.

beads'-wom''-an. An almswoman. CHIEF-UNDERLING.

bea'-gle. A hound. FAUNA-FLORA.

beak. The bill of a bird; prow of a ship. ANTERIORITY-POSTERIORITY, CONVEXITY-CONCAVITY, JUDGE.

beak'-er. A wide-mouthed goblet; a chemical vessel. CHEMISTRY, CONTENTS-RECEIVER.

beam. Ray of light; a bar; to shine. BEAUTY-UGLINESS, HEAVINESS-LIGHTNESS, LIGHT-DARKNESS, SUSPENSION-SUPPORT; **on beam ends,** ASTONISHMENT-EXPECTANCE, ERECTNESS-FLATNESS, LATERALITY-CONTRAPOSITION, MIGHT-IMPOTENCE, SUCCESS-FAILURE.

beam'-ing. Shining. BEAUTY-UGLINESS, LIGHT-DARKNESS.

beam'-y. Radiant. BEAUTY-UGLINESS.

bear. Sustain; produce; suffer; press. EMOTION, EXCITABILITY - INEXCITABILITY, POSSIBILITY - IMPOSSIBILITY, SUSPENSION-SUPPORT, TRANSFER; **bear a hand,** ACTION-PASSIVENESS; **bear a sense,** MEANING-JARGON; **bear away,** TAKING-RESTITUTION; **bear away the bell,** GOODNESS-BADNESS, SUCCESS-FAILURE; **bear company,** DUALITY; **bear down,** TURBULENCE-CALMNESS; **bear down upon,** ATTACK-DEFENSE; **bear false witness,** ADULATION-DISPARAGEMENT, TRUTHFULNESS-FALSEHOOD; **bear fruit,** CREATION-DESTRUCTION, SUCCESS-FAILURE, USEFULNESS-USELESSNESS, WELFARE-MISFORTUNE; **bear hard upon,** GOODNESS-BADNESS; **bear harmless,** ATTACK-DEFENSE; **bear ill,** EXCITABILITY-INEXCITABILITY; **bear off,** AIM-ABERRATION, TAKING-RESTITUTION; **bear on,** SUSPENSION-SUPPORT; **bear out,** EVIDENCE-COUNTEREVIDENCE, JUSTIFICATION-CHARGE; **bear pain,** PLEASURE-PAIN; **bear the brunt,** ATTACK-DEFENSE, DIFFICULTY-FACILITY, EXCITABILITY-INEXCITABILITY; **bear the burden,** OCCUPATION; **bear the palm,** SUPREMACY-SUBORDINACY; **bear through,** OBSTRUCTION-HELP; **bear up,** ALLEVIATION-AGGRAVATION, APPROACH-WITHDRAWAL, BRAVERY-COWARD-

ICE, LIGHTHEARTEDNESS-DEJECTION, PERSISTENCE-WHIM; **bear up against,** BRAVERY-COWARDICE, REPRISAL-RESISTANCE; **bear upon,** CONNECTION-INDEPENDENCE, DOMINANCE-IMPOTENCE, HARMONY-DISCORD; **bear with,** EXCITABILITY-INEXCITABILITY, HARSHNESS-MILDNESS, LEAVE-PROHIBITION, PARDON-VINDICTIVENESS; **bring to bear,** USE-DISUSE; **more than flesh and blood can bear,** EXCITATION; **unable to bear,** DESIRE-DISTASTE, EXCITABILITY-INEXCITABILITY.

bear. A wild beast; depressor of stocks. CHARITABLENESS-MALEVOLENCE, LABOR-CAPITAL, POLITENESS-IMPOLITENESS; **bear-garden,** LISTS, REGULARITY-IRREGULARITY, VARIANCE-ACCORD; **bear-leader,** INSTRUCTOR-PUPIL; **bear-pit,** DOMESTICATION-AGRICULTURE; **bearskin,** DRESS-UNDRESS; **had it been a bear it would have bitten you,** HEED-DISREGARD.

bear'-a-ble. Tolerable. FAULTLESSNESS-FAULTINESS.

beard. The hair on a man's face; to meet face to face. BRAVERY-COWARDICE, DEFIANCE, LAMINA-FIBER, PRESUMPTION-OBSEQUIOUSNESS, SHARPNESS-BLUNTNESS, SMOOTHNESS-ROUGHNESS; **pluck by the beard,** REGARD-DISRESPECT.

beard'-less. Without a beard. INFANCY-AGE.

bear'-er. Carrier. CONVEYER.

bear'-ing. Endurance; deportment; connection; application. AIM-ABERRATION, CONDUCT, CONNECTION-INDEPENDENCE, MEANING-JARGON, SUSPENSION-SUPPORT; **bearing-rein,** RELEASE-PRISON.

bear'-ings. General tendency; mien; producing. CONDITION-SITUATION, POSITION, SIGN.

bear'-ish. Surly. FAVORITE-MOROSENESS.

bear'-ish-ness. Roughness. FAVORITE-MOROSENESS.

beast. An animal; a brutal person. CLEANNESS-FILTHINESS, FAUNA-FLORA, POLITENESS-IMPOLITENESS; **beast of burden,** AGENT, CONVEYER.

beast-ly. Brutish. CLEANNESS-FILTHINESS.

beat. Strike; excel; surpass; throb. AGITATION, CRASH-DRUMMING, EXTENSION-DISTRICT, FRIABILITY, IMPETUS-REACTION, OCCUPATION, PERIODICITY-IRREGULARITY, RECOMPENSE-PUNITION, SUCCESS-FAILURE, SUPREMACY-SUBORDINACY, TRANSCURSION-SHORTCOMING, WAY, VIBRATION; **beat about,** MIDCOURSE-CIRCUIT, TRIAL; **beat about the bush,** MIDCOURSE-CIRCUIT, RATIOCINATION-INSTINCT, TERSENESS-PROLIXITY, TRIAL, TRUTHFULNESS-FALSEHOOD; **beat against,** ANTAGONISM-CONCURRENCE, COOPERATION-OPPOSITION; **beat a retreat,** ADVANCE-RETROGRESSION, QUEST - EVASION, YIELDING; **beat down,** CREATION-DESTRUCTION, EXCHANGE, EXTRAVAGANCE-AVARICE, PRESUMPTION-OBSEQUIOUSNESS; **beat into,** EDUCATION-MISTEACHING; **beat of drum,** ALARM, FIGHTING-CONCILIATION, MUSICIAN, ORDER, POMP, PUBLICITY; **beat off,** ATTACK-DEFENSE; **beat one's breast,** JUBILATION-LAMENTATION; **beat the air,** USEFULNESS-USELESSNESS; **beat time,** CHRONOLOGY-ANACHRONISM, MUSICIAN; **beat up,** VISCIDITY-FOAM; **beat up against,** ANTAGONISM-CONCURRENCE; **beat up for,** PROVISION-WASTE; **beat up for recruits,** OBSTRUCTION-HELP, PREPARATION-NONPREPARATION; **beat up one's quarters,** INVESTIGATION-ANSWER, SOCIABILITY-PRIVACY; **without beat of drum,** CONCEIT-DIFFIDENCE, ENLIGHTENMENT-SECRECY.

beat'-en-track''. Usual course. HABIT-DESUETUDE, WAY; **leave the beaten track,** CONVENTIONALITY-UNCONVENTIONALITY; **tread the beaten track,** CONVENTIONALITY-UNCONVENTIONALITY.

beati [L.] (bî-ê'-tai). The happy. *medium tenuere beati* [L.] mî'-di-um ten-yu-î'-rî bî-ê'-tai). The happy hold the middle course. MEDIUM, MIDCOURSE-CIRCUIT.

be-at'-ic. Ecstatic. PLEASURE-PAIN.

be''-a-tif'-ic. Blissful. HEAVEN-HELL, PLEASURABLENESS-PAINFULNESS,

be-at″-i-fi-ca′-tion. The act of blessing. GODLINESS-UNGODLINESS.

be-at′-i-fied. Made happy. EMOTION.

beat-′ing high, the heart. Excited. EXCITATION.

be-at′-i-tude. Supreme felicity. PLEASURE-PAIN.

beau [F.] (bo). A lover; a fop. LOVE-HATE, MALE-FEMALE, SOCIETY-DANDY.

beau′-catch″-er. A small flat curl worn by women on the temple. CIRCLE-WINDING, EMBELLISHMENT-DISFIGUREMENT.

beau″-i-de′-al. Highest type of beauty or excellence. BEAUTY-UGLINESS, FAULTLESSNESS-FAULTINESS.

beau monde [F.] (bo mon'd). The fashionable world. SOCIETY-LUDICROUSNESS.

beau′-te-ous. Lovely. BEAUTY-UGLINESS.

beau′-ti-fied. Adorned. EMBELLISHMENT-DISFIGUREMENT, SIMPLICITY-FLORIDNESS.

beau′-ti-ful. Lovely. BEAUTY-UGLINESS, PROPORTION-DEFORMITY.

beau′-ti-fy. To adorn. BEAUTY-UGLINESS, EMBELLISHMENT-DISFIGUREMENT.

beau′-ti-fy″-ing. Adorning. BEAUTY-UGLINESS.

beau′-ti-less. Without beauty. BEAUTY-UGLINESS.

beau′-ty. Loveliness. BEAUTY-UGLINESS.

BEAUTY—UGLINESS.

Beauty. That quality of objects that appeals to and gratifies the esthetic faculty.

Beauty unadorned. Native beauty without decorations.

Belle tournure [F.]. Beautiful form.

Bloom. A state of development into beauty.

Brilliancy. Glitter.

Callesthetics. The science of the perception of beauty.

Charm. The power to please or allure.

Comeliness. Quality of being pleasing in person or manner.

Concinnity. Internal fitness of parts.

Decoration, etc. External embellishment. See EMBELLISHMENT

Delicacy. State of being delicate.

Elegance. State of being elegant.

Fairness. The quality of being fair.

Form. Outward appearance.

Gloss. Brightness of surface.

Good effect. } Quality of being pleasing in appearance.
Good looks. }

Gorgeousness. State of being gorgeous.

Grace. Beauty or harmony of attitude; ease or elegance of speech.

Je ne sais quoi [F.]. I know not what; indefinable charm.

Le beau ideal [F.]. The ideal of beauty.

Magnificence. State of being magnificent or grand in appearance.

Pleasurableness. State or quality of giving pleasure. See PLEASURABLENESS.

Polish. Refinement of manners.

Pulchritude. Physical beauty or charm.

Radiance. Quality of being radiant or brilliant.

Refinement. Delicacy of manners; freedom from coarseness.

Splendor. Pomp; magnificence.

Style. Mode of action approved as elegant.

Sublimification. Act of making sublime or beautiful.

Sublimity. State of being sublime

Symmetry, etc. Mutual adaptation or correspondence of parts, etc. See PROPORTION.

BEAUTY—Denotations.

Adonis. A youth beloved of Venus for his beauty.

Antinous. Favorite of the Emperor Hadrian.

Apollo. One of the great gods of the Greeks, whose figure is regarded as the most perfect representation of youthful manhood.

Bijou [F.]. A jewel.

Butterfly. An insect having beautifully colored wings.

Cupid. The god of love, represented as a beautiful winged boy.

Flower. A plant bearing beautifully colored blossoms.

Flow'ret gay. A colored flower.

Flower of. The best or choicest of.

Garden. A place where flowers are cultivated.

Hebe. The goddess of youth.

Houri. One of the beautiful damsels who, according to the Moslem faith, dwell in paradise.

Hyperion. The sun-god, the incarnation of light and beauty.

Jewel. Anything beautiful or precious.

Lily. A beautiful snow-white flower.

Narcissus. A youth fabled to have fallen in love with his own reflection and changed into the flower of the same name.

Peacock. A fowl noted for its brilliant plumage.

Peri. A fairy or elf.

Pink of. The most beautiful part of.

Rose. A variety of beautifully colored flowers.

The beautiful. The ideal of beauty.

The Graces. Three goddesses embodying grace, beauty, and joy.

Venus. Goddess of love and beauty.

Work of art. A masterpiece of beauty.

BEAUTY—Nouns of Cause.

Beautifying. The act of making beautiful.

Calisthenics. The science of bodily exercise for the promotion of beauty and strength.

Acomia. Absence of hair.

Deformity. Having an unnatural form.

Disfigurement, etc. See EMBELLISHMENT-DISFIGUREMENT.

Distortion. State of being twisted out of the right shape. See PROPORTION-DEFORMITY.

Forbidding aspect. Repulsive appearance.

Forbidding countenance. Unpleasant or repulsive appearance.

Hanging look. A look which should bespeak the halter for its possessor.

Inconcinnity. Lack of internal fitness.

Inelegance. Lack of grace or refinement.

Squalor, etc. The state of being filthy, etc. See CLEANNESS-FILTHINESS.

Ugliness. The quality of being ugly or unsightly.

Vinegar aspect. A sour look.

Want of symmetry.

Wry face. A distorted expression.

UGLINESS—Denotations.

Æsop. The writer of Æsop's fables, said to have been ugly and misshapen

Baboon. An ugly species of monkey.

Caliban. An uncouth monster in Shakespeare's *Tempest*.

Eyesore. Anything ugly or repulsive in appearance.

Figure. The appearance that a person or his conduct makes.

Fright. Anything very repulsive in appearance.

Hag. An ugly old woman.

Harridan. An ill-tempered old woman.

Monster. Anything hideous.

Object. Anything that attracts attention on account of its unusual appearance.

Satyr. An ugly woodland deity of the Greeks.

Scarecrow. An object set up to frighten birds from growing crops.

Sight. Something strange or remarkable.

Specter. A phantom of the dead.

Toad. An ugly amphibious animal.

Witch. An ugly, malignant old woman.

UGLINESS—Verbs.

Be ugly, etc. See *Adjectives.*

Blemish. To mar. See BETTERMENT-DETERIORATION.

Deface. To mar the external appearance.

Defigure. } To change for the worse the figure.
Disfigure. }

Distort. To twist out of shape.

Grin horrible a ghastly smile. [Milton, *Paradise Lost*, ii. 846.]

Look ill. To be displeasing to the sight; to look sick.

Make faces. Grimace.

Render ugly. Disfigure.

Soil. To make dirty.

UGLINESS—Adjectives.

Awkward. Lacking grace in bearing.

Bald. Devoid of hair.

Beautiless. Lacking beauty.

Cadaverous. Looking like a human corpse.

Clumsy. Devoid of grace or dexterity.

Crooked, etc. Not straight, etc. See PROPORTION-DEFORMITY

Curtailed of its fair proportions

Death-like. Looking like death.

Dingy, etc. Dusky in color, etc. See COLOR-ACHROMATISM.

Discolored. Changed in color.

Disfigured, etc. Marred as to figure, etc. See *Verbs.*

Dumpy, etc. Short and thick, etc. See LENGTH-SHORTNESS.

Evil-favored. Not having a good appearance.

Forbidding. Repulsive in appearance.

Foul, etc. Loathsome to the senses, etc. See CLEANNESS-FILTHINESS.

Frightful. Causing alarm.

BEAUTY—UGLINESS—*Continued.*

BEAUTY—Nouns of Cause—*Continued.*

Landscape gardening. The art of laying out grounds so as to produce an artistic effect.

BEAUTY—*Verbs.*

Beam. To give forth rays of light.
Beautify. . To make beautiful.
Be beautiful. See *Adjectives.*
Become one. To look well on a person. See HARMONY.
Bloom. To display health and vigor.
Burnish. To make smooth and bright.
Gild To heighten the beauty of. See SIMPLICITY-FLORIDNESS
Grace. To honor by an act of favor.
Polish. To rub off the coarseness.
Render beautiful.
Set off. To adorn.
Set out. To embellish.
Shine. To appear bright.
Snatch a grace beyond the reach of art. [Pope, *Essay on Criticism,* i, 152.]

BEAUTY—*Adjectives.*

Æsthetic. Relating to beauty See ESTHETIC.
Artistic. } In accord with the rules of art.
Artistical. }
Attractive, etc. Having power to attract, etc. See MOTIVE.
Beaming. Giving forth light.
Beamy. Radiant.
Beauteous. Full of beauty.
Beautiful. Possessing great beauty.
Becoming, etc. Fitting; suitable to, etc. See HARMONY
Blooming. Having beauty and vigor.
Bonny. Possessing homelike beauty.
Bright-eyed. Having brilliant eyes; hence beautiful.
Brilliant. Resplendent with luster.
Cherry-cheeked. Having red cheeks.
Comely. Handsome.
Curious. Skilfully wrought.
Dainty. Of delicate structure.
Dapper. Trim in appearance.
Dazzling. Exciting admiration by display.
Delicate. Of refined and gentle nature.
Elegant. Having acquired grace and beauty.
Enchanting. Having power to fascinate. See PLEASURABLENESS.
Esthetic. Relating to beauty; artistic.
Fair. Agreeable to the sight.
Fait à peindre [F.]. Picturesque.
Fine. Finished; hence beautiful.
Fit to be seen. Pleasing or fitted to the sight.
Gimp. Smart.
Glossy. Smooth and bright.
Glowing. Shining with intense heat.
Good looking. Handsome.
Goodly. Of agreeable appearance.
Gorgeous. Making a great show.
Graceful. Exhibiting beauty of action.
Grand. Imposing on account of vastness.
Handsome. Admirable; pleasing in appearance.
Harmonious. Symmetrical. See COLOR.
In full bloom. At the height of beauty.
Janty. } Of an affected manner.
Jaunty. }
Jimp. Handsome.
Lovely. Inspiring love.
Magnificent. Of imposing appearance.
Natty. Neat.
Neat. Free from disorder.
Not amiss. Pretty fair.
Ornamental. Serving to ornament.
Passable. Fairly good looking.
Personable. Having a handsome person.
Pictorial. Like a picture.
Picturesque. Having the kind of beauty that is pleasing in a picture.
Pretty. Possessing delicate or diminutive beauty.
Proper. Of a correct or becoming appearance.
Quaint. Curiously fashioned.
Refined. Having a delicate polish.
Resplendent. Refulgent with bright luster.
Rich. Highly endowed with beauty.
Rosy. Like a rose in color.
Rosy-cheeked. Ruddy.
Ruddy. Reddish in color, indicating health.
Seemly. Becoming in appearance.
Shapely. Having a good form.

UGLINESS—Adjectives—*Continued.*

Gaudy, etc. Showy, etc. See COLOR.
Gaunt, etc. Emaciated in looks. etc. See BREADTH-NARROWNESS.
Gawky. Ungainly in appearance.
Ghastly. Having a ghost-like appearance.
Ghost-like. Resembling a ghost.
Graceless. Lacking grace.
Grim. Having a forbidding aspect.
Grim-faced. } Ugly and dreadful.
Grim-visaged. }
Grisly. Frightful; fear-inspiring.
Gross. Not refined.
Gruesome. Horrid.
Haggard. Having wasted features.
Hard-favored. Not good looking.
Hard-featured. Possessing unattractive features.
Hard-visaged. Having a harsh expression.
Hideous. Frightful to look upon.
Homely, etc. Not handsome. See EMBELLISHMENT-SIMPLICITY.
Horrible. Exciting fear or dread.
Horrid. Fitted to awaken horror.
Hulking. }
Hulky. } Clumsy.
Ill-favored. Lacking beauty.
Ill-looking. Ugly.
Ill-made. Not well formed.
Ill-proportioned. In bad proportion.
Ill-shaped. Poorly shaped.
Inartistic. Not according to the standards of art.
Inelegant. Not elegant.
Lumbering. Clumsy.
Lumping. Possessing great bulk.
Lumpish. Lacking in motive power.
Misproportioned. Out of proportion.
Misshapen. Badly formed.
Monstrous. Of extraordinary ugliness.
Not fit to be seen.
Odious. Exciting disgust.
Ordinary. Undistinguished for beauty.
Plain. Devoid of adornment.
Repellent. Tending to repel.
Repulsive. Exciting dislike, disgust, horror, etc.
Rickety. Shaky; tottering.
Rough. Void of refinement; rude.
Rude. Lacking polish, refinement or delicacy.
Rugged. Unkempt; disordered.
Seemless. Not becoming.
Shapeless, etc. Void of regular form, etc. See FORM-FORMLESSNESS.
Shocking, etc. Very repulsive, etc. See PLEASURABLENESS-PAINFULNESS.
Sightless. Repulsive to the eye.
Slouching. Having an ungainly manner.
Squalid. Loathsome to the sight on account of filth.
Stiff. Starched, constrained.
Ugly. Not beautiful.
Ugly as a dead monkey. }
Ugly as a scarecrow. } Extremely ugly.
Ugly as a toad. }
Ugly as sin. }
Unbeauteous. Not beauteous.
Unbeautiful. Lacking beauty.
Uncanny. Devoid of pleasing qualities.
Uncomely. Not comely.
Uncouth. Characterized by awkwardness.
Ungainly. Lacking dexterity or skill.
Ungraceful. Not graceful.
Unlovely. Exciting dislike
Unornamental. Not ornamental.
Unprepossessing. Not inviting favor or confidence.
Unseemly. Not becoming.
Unshapely. Having a bad form.
Unsightly. Not pleasing to the sight.
Unwieldy. Not easily managed on account of bulk.

UGLINESS—*Phrases.*

Monstrum horrendum, informe, ingens, cui lumen ademptum [L.]. A horrid monster, ill-formed, gigantic, blind. [Virgil, *Æneid,* iii. 658.]
Spretæ injuria formæ [L.]. The insult of slighted beauty.

BEAUTY—Adjectives—*Continued*.

Shining. Conspicuous for pleasing qualities.
Showy. Of an appearance that attracts attention.
Sightly. Pleasing to look upon.
Sleek. Smooth; glossy.
Smart. Sprucely dressed; showy.
Sparkling. Very bright.
Specious. Pleasing to the view.
Splendid. Of an imposing appearance.
Spotless, etc. Without blemish, etc. See Faultlessness.
Spruce. Neat and trim in appearance.
Sublime. Awe-inspiring and elevating.
Superb. Possessing impressive beauty.
Symmetrical, etc. Having symmetry, etc. See Proportion.

Tidy. Distinguished by neatness.
Tight. Neat.
Tricksy. Crafty; artful.
Trim. Nicely adjusted.
Undefaced. Not marred.
Undeformed. Of a good form.
Unspotted. Without spot or blemish.
Well-composed. Of good carriage.
Well-favored. Endowed with beauty.
Well-formed. Having a good form.
Well-grouped. Nicely arranged.
Well-proportioned. Having a symmetrical form.
Well-varied. Presenting a pleasing diversity.

BEAUTY—*Phrase*.

Vedi Napoli, e poi muori [It.]. See Naples, and die.

bea'-ver. A small rat-like animal; a hat made of its fur. Dress-Undress.
be-calm'. To make still. Movement-Rest.
be-calmed'. Stilled. Movement-Rest.
be-cause'. For; since. Cause-Effect, Investigation-Answer, Motive-Caprice, Ratiocination-Instinct, Rationale-Luck.
be-chance'. Happen. Occurrence-Destiny.
beck. A brook; nod. Order, River-Wind, Sign; at one's beck, Insubordination-Obedience, Obstruction-Help.
beck'-on. To notify by nod. Motive-Caprice, Order, Sign.
be-cloud'. Darken. Enlightenment-Secrecy, Light-Darkness.
be-come'. Be worthy of; grace; grow to be. Conversion, Duty-Dereliction, Harmony-Discord; become of, Occurrence-Destiny.
be-com'-ing. Beginning to be; appropriate. Beauty-Ugliness, Dueness-Undueness, Embellishment-Disfigurement, Harmony-Discord, Propriety-Impropriety.
be-crip'-ple. Make lame. Might-Impotence.
bed. A couch to sleep on; the bottom of a stream; a layer; a foundation. Contents-Receiver, Domestication-Agriculture, Lamina-Fiber, Matrimony-Celibacy, Suspension-Support; **bedchamber,** Contents-Receiver; **bedfellow,** Friend-Foe; **bedgown,** Dress-Undress; **bedmaker,** Chief-Underling; **bedmate,** Friend-Foe; **bed of down,** Toil-Relaxation; **bed of roses,** Sensuality-Suffering, Welfare-Misfortune; **bedquilt,** Cover-Lining; **bedridden,** Health-Sickness; **bedroom,** Contents-Receiver; **bed-sore,** Remedy-Bane; **bedstead,** Suspension-Support; **bedtime,** Morning-Evening; **brought to bed,** Creation-Destruction; **death-bed,** Life-Death; **go to bed,** Activity-Indolence, Movement-Rest; **keep one's bed,** Health-Sickness; **put to bed with a shovel,** Life-Funeral; **smooth the bed of death,** Obstruction-Help.
be-dark'-en. Make dark. Light-Darkness.
be-daub'. Soil. Cleanness-Filthiness, Cover-Lining.
be-daz'-zle. Confuse. Light-Darkness.
bed'-ding. The furnishings for a bed. Suspension-Support.
be-deck'. Adorn. Embellishment-Disfigurement.
be'-del. A beadle. Judicature.
bedes'-man. A resident of an almshouse. Chief-Underling, Ministry-Laity.
be-dev'-il. Bewilder; bewitch. Devotion-Magic, Organization-Disorganization.
be-dev'-il-ment. Witchcraft. Devotion-Magic.
be-dew'. To moisten. Dampness-Dryness.
be-dight. Adorn. Embellishment-Disfigurement.
be-dim'. Darken. Dimness, Light-Darkness.
be-diz'-en. Adorn with tawdry splendor. Color-Achromatism, Embellishment-Disfigurement, Taste-Vulgarity.

be-diz'-ened. Dressed out. Taste-Vulgarity.
bed'-lam. A frenzied crowd; madhouse. **Bedlam broke loose,** Regularity-Irregularity; **candidate for Bedlam,** Saneness-Maniac.
bed'-lam-ite. A lunatic. Saneness-Maniac.
Bed'-ou-in. A nomadic Arab; vagabond. Robber.
be'-dwarf. Make smaller. Enlargement-Diminution.
bee. A four-winged insect. Agent; **bee in a bottle,** Crash-Drumming; **bee in one's bonnet,** Saneness-Lunacy; **beeswax,** Viscidity-Foam; **swarm like bees,** Multiplicity-Paucity.
beef. The flesh of any adult bovine animal. Nutriment-Excretion.
beef'-eat''-er. A yeoman of the British sovereign's guard. Belligerent.
beef'-head''-ed. Thick-headed. Sagacity-Incapacity.
beef'-steak''. A slice of beef broiled or ready for broiling. Nutriment-Excretion.
beef'-wit''-ted. Heavy-witted. Sagacity-Incapacity.
beef'-y. Fat; heavy. Heaviness-Lightness.
Be-el'-ze-bub. The devil. Angel-Satan.
beer. An intoxicant. Nutriment-Excretion.
beer'-y. Like beer. Teetotalism-Intemperance.
beet. The root of a biennial herb. Nutriment-Excretion.
bee'-tle. Any coleopterous insect; to jut out. Convexity-Concavity, Height-Lowness; **beetle head,** Sage-Fool; **blind as a beetle,** Sight-Blindness; **Colorado beetle,** Benefactor-Evildoer.
bee'-tling. Jutting. Height-Lowness.
be-fall'. Happen. Occurrence-Destiny.
be-fit'. Become; be suitable for. Dueness-Undueness, Duty-Dereliction, Harmony-Discord, Propriety-Impropriety.
be-fit'-ting. Suitable. Dueness-Undueness, Propriety-Impropriety.
be-fog'. To obscure; bewilder. Enlightenment-Secrecy.
be-fool'. Gull; outwit. Saneness-Lunacy, Truthfulness-Fraud.
be-fooled'. Victimized. Success-Failure.
be-fore'. In front of; prior to; in preference to. Antecedence-Sequence, Anteriority-Posteriority, Choice-Neutrality, Leading-Following, Precedence-Succession, Presence-Absence; **before Christ,** Duration-Neverness; **before long,** Earliness-Lateness; **before mentioned,** Antecedence-Sequence, Precedence-Succession; **before now,** Future-Past; **before one's eyes,** Manifestation-Latency, Visibility-Invisibility; **before one's time,** Earliness-Lateness; **set before one,** Manifestation-Latency.
be-fore'-hand''. In advance; in easy circumstances. Antecedence-Sequence, Earliness-Lateness, Prevision; **resolve beforehand,** Predetermination-Impulse.
be-foul'. Render impure. Cleanness-Filthiness.

be-friend'. To help; to treat as a friend. AMITY-HOSTILITY, OBSTRUCTION-HELP.

be'-fud"-dle. To become confused, as from liquor. TEETOTALISM-INTEMPERANCE.

beg. A Turkish governor of a town; to entreat; to ask alms. CHIEF-UNDERLING, PETITION-EXPOSTULATION; **beg leave,** LEAVE-PROHIBITION, PETITION-EXPOSTULATION; **beg one's bread,** PETITION-EXPOSTULATION; **beg one's life,** COMPASSION-RUTHLESSNESS; **beg pardon,** ATONEMENT, PARDON-VINDICTIVENESS, REPENTANCE-OBDURACY; **beg the question,** to assume an answer without proof in debate, RATIOCINATION-INSTINCT.

be-get'. Generate. CREATION-DESTRUCTION.

beg'-gar. One who asks alms. AFFLUENCE-PENURY, GENTILITY-DEMOCRACY, PETITIONER, REPUTATION-DISCREDIT; **beggar description,** to be indescribable, ASTONISHMENT-EXPECTANCE, CONVENTIONALITY-UNCONVENTIONALITY; **beggar my neighbor,** ENTERTAINMENT-WEARINESS; **sturdy beggar,** ROBBER.

beg'-gared. Bankrupt. AFFLUENCE-PENURY, SETTLEMENT-DEFAULT.

beg'-gar-ly. Mean; poor. AFFLUENCE-PENURY, CONSEQUENCE-INSIGNIFICANCE, GENTILITY-DEMOCRACY, PRESUMPTION-OBSEQUIOUSNESS, REPUTATION-DISCREDIT; **beggarly account of empty boxes,** AFFLUENCE-PENURY, EXCESS-LACK.

beg'-gar-y. Penury. AFFLUENCE-PENURY.

beg'-ging. Asking earnestly. PETITION-EXPOSTULATION; **begging letter,** PETITION-EXPOSTULATION; **go a begging,** EXCESS-LACK, LIBERTY-SUBJECTION, PETITION-EXPOSTULATION, PROFFER-REFUSAL, USEFULNESS-USELESSNESS.

be-gilt'. Made yellow like gold. EMBELLISHMENT-DISFIGUREMENT.

be-gin'. Commence. BEGINNING-END, ENTERPRISE; **begin again,** RECURRENCE.

be-gin'-ner. A founder; a novice. BEGINNING-END, INSTRUCTOR-PUPIL.

be-gin'-ning. Origin; the first part; source. BEGINNING-END.

BEGINNING—END.

Beginning. Something begun; a start.
Border. The outer edge. See BORDER.
Commencement. The first existence.
Début [F.]. The first attempt.
Elements. The first principles in any study.
Entrance. The act of entering upon or beginning.
Entry. The act of beginning.
First blush. First thought.
First glance. First look.
First impression. First effect on the senses.
First move. First attempt.
First sight. First glance.
First stage. Beginning.
Fresh start. New attempt.
Genesis. The act of originating.
Germ. The first source of anything. See CAUSE.
Head. Set division n a discourse; title.
Heading. A caption, title or the like.
Inauguration. The act of formally setting in operation.
Inception. The act of commencing.
Inchoation. The act or state of beginning.
Incipience. Inception.
Initiative. The first move.
Introduction. The act of introducing.
New departure. Unusual course.
Onset. A commencement.
Opening. The beginning.
Origin. The commencement of anything.
Outbreak. A sudden bursting forth.
Outset. A starting.
Rise. The act of originating.
Rudiment. The first principle of anything.
Rudiments. First principles.
Skirt. The border or edge.
Source. That from which something emanates.
Start. The act of going forth; the beginning.

BEGINNING—Denotations.

A B C. The first three letters of the alphabet.
Alpha. The first letter of the Greek alphabet.
Alphabet. The simplest rudiments.
Birth. The beginning of life.
Brunt. The utmost violence, marking the beginning of destruction.
Bud. A small growth containing the rudiments of future leaves.
Chops. The land on each side of the mouth of a river.
Grammar. The elementary principles of a science.
Infancy. The earliest period of life.
Initial. The first letter of a word.
Inlet. The beginning or opening of a passage.
Lips. The fleshy folds which surround the orifice of the mouth.
Mouth. The beginning of the alimentary canal.
Nativity. Birth.
Orifice. An opening into a passage.
Outlines. The lines which mark the outer limits.
Porch. A covered entrance to a building.
Portal. An opening or gate.
Portico. An entrance to a building.
Postern. A small door or gate.

Break up. The ending or separation, as of an assembly.
Close. The ending.
Commencement de la fin [F.]. The beginning of the end.
Conclusion. The final part.
Consummation. The state of being finished.
Desinence. The closing.
Destination. The end aimed at.
Determination. Bringing to a close.
End. The termination or close.
End of all things.
Expiration. The act or state of expiring.
Expiry. A coming to a close.
Extreme. The ultimate part.
Extremity. The most remote point or part.
Finale. The end or termination.
Finality. The state of being at an end.
Finis [L.]. The end or close.
Finish, etc. The concluding part, etc. See COMPLETION.
Last. The close.
Last stage. The concluding part.
Limit. That which sets a bound.
Termination. The act of closing.
Terminus [L.]. The close or termination.
Turning point. The critical or decisive point at which a change is effected.

END—Denotations.

Bonne bouche [F.]. A final good taste; a tidbit.
Butt end. The large end, or last part.
Coup de grâce [F.]. The finishing stroke.
Crack of doom. Judgment day.
Day of Judgment. The end of the world.
Dénouement [F.]. The outcome.
Death. See LIFE-DEATH.
Doom. Final judgment.
Fag-end. The end of the poorer quality.
Fall of the curtain. The end of an act; end of life.
Fate. The final lot.
Gable end. The end wall of a building.
Goal. End or aim of work or effort.
Nib. Sharp end of a pen.
Omega. Last letter of the Greek alphabet.
Period. The point marking the end of a sentence.
Peroration. Final part of an oration.
Point. The sharp end.
Tag. The close of an actor's speech.
Tail. See ANTERIORITY-POSTERIORITY.
Tail-end. The last part.
Tip. The end piece or part.

END—Noun of Agent.

Death blow. A blow that brings life to an end.

END—Verbs.

Achieve. To bring to a successful close. See COMPLETION.
Be all over. To be finished.
Bring to an end. See Nouns.
Close. To bring to a completion.
Come to a close. See Nouns.

BEGINNING—END—*Continued.*

BEGINNING—Denotations—*Continued.*

Propylon. An entrance to a building.
Starting-point. See ARRIVAL-DEPARTURE.
Title-page. The first page of a book.
Threshold. The place or point of entering or beginning.
Van, etc. See ANTERIORITY.
Vestibule. A place of opening.
Wicket. A small gate.

BEGINNING—*Phrases.*

Narrow end of the wedge.
Thin end of the wedge.

BEGINNING—*Figurative Nouns.*

Cradle. The earliest period of life.
Dawn. See MORNING.
Egg. That which contains the germ.
Embarkation. Act of beginning a voyage.
Le premier pas [F.]. The first step.
Rising of the curtain. The beginning of an act or scene.

BEGINNING—*Verbs.*

Air. To expose for the sake of notice.
Apply the match to a train. To start work or put in motion.
Arise. To begin to exist; to spring up.
Begin. To start; to commence.
Begin ab ovo. To begin from the egg or the beginning.
Begin again. Begin anew.
Begin at the beginning. Begin at the starting-point.
Begin de novo. Begin anew.
Break cover. To come out of concealment.
Burst forth. To emerge suddenly.
Break ground. To begin a foundation for a building.
Break out. To force out by breaking.
Break the ice. To master the difficulties of the first intercourse between strangers.
Broach. To bring to notice for the first time.
Come into existence. } Begin existence.
Come into the world. }
Commence. To make a start.
Conceive. To think out.
Crop up. To show itself above the surface.
Cross the Rubicon. To take the decisive step.
Cut the first turf. Start.
Dawn. To start to expand.
Embark in. To adventure upon.
Enter. To pass in.
Enter upon. To engage in.
Found. To establish or lay the foundation of. See CAUSE.
Head. To take the lead.
Handsel. To do for the first time with a view to a fortunate outcome.
Inaugurate. To make a formal beginning.
Initiate. To make a start.
Launch. To start anything going, as a ship.
Lay the first stone. Begin building, etc.
Lay the foundations. See PREPARATION.
Lead off. To make the beginning.
Lead the way. To act as a guide by going first.
Make a beginning. }
Make a fresh start. } Begin.
Make a start. }
Make one's début. To take the first step or enter upon something for the first time.
Open. To commence.
Open fire. } Open.
Open the ball. }
Open the door to. } Give opportunity.
Open up. }
Originate. To cause to exist.
Pass the Rubicon. To take the decisive step.
Recommence. To begin again.
Resume. To take up again.
Rise. To make a beginning.
Set about. To begin.
Set abroach. To tap.
Set agoing. To start.
Set in. To commence.
Set on foot. To start going.
Set out. To begin something, as a journey or career. See ARRIVAL-DEPARTURE.
Set the ball in motion. To make the start.
Set to work. To begin work.
Set up. To begin or found.

END—Verbs—*Continued.*

Conclude. To bring to a finish.
Determine. To make an end.
Die. To cease to live.
Draw to a close. See *Nouns.*
End. To close or finish.
Expire. To end life.
Finish. To come to an end.
Get through. To complete.
Have run its course. To come to a close.
Make an end of. Finish.
Pass away. To expire.
Put an end to. Close.
Run out. To come to an end.
Shut up shop. To quit business.
Terminate. To end.

END—*Adjectives.*

At an end. Finished.
Caudal. Pertaining to the tail.
Conclusive. Marking the close.
Conterminable. Ending at the same time or place.
Conterminate. Having the same limits.
Conterminous. Having common bounds.
Crowning, etc. Marking the end. See COMPLETION.
Decided. Not admitting of question.
Definite. Having fixed limits.
Ended. See *Verbs.*
Ending. See *Verbs.*
Final. Marking the end or close.
Fresh. Recently produced; marked by newness.
Hindermost. Furthest back.
Last. Coming after all the rest.
Last but one. Penultimate.
Last but two, etc. Antepenultimate, etc.
Over. Finished or ended.
Penultimate. The last but one.
Played out. Completely used up.
Rear, etc. Being in the hind part. See ANTERIORITY-POSTERIORITY.
Set at rest. Quieted; satisfied.
Settled. Determined upon; fixed.
Terminal. Marking the end or terminus.
Ultimate. Last.
Unbegun. Not begun.
Uncommenced. Not started.

END—*Adverbs.*

At the last. Finally.
Finally, etc. See *Adjectives.*
In fine. To sum up.
Once for all. To settle definitely.

END—*Phrases.*

Dimidium facti, qui cœpit, habet [L.]. What's well begun is half done.
En toute chose il faut considérer le fin [F.]. In everything one must consider the end.
Finem respice [L.]. Regard the end.
Ultimus Romanorum [L.]. Last of the Romans.

——————

BEGINNING—Verbs—*Continued.*

Shuffle the cards. To start in.
Spring up. To begin to make an appearance.
Stand at the head. } Lead.
Stand first. }
Stand for. To stand in place of.
Start afresh. Begin anew.
Take birth. To have its origin.
Take its rise. To have its beginning.
Take the first step. Begin.
Take the initiative. To make a beginning.
Take the lead. To make the start.
Undertake, etc. To set about anything, etc. See ENTERPRISE.
Usher in. To introduce.
Ventilate. To give publicity to; to air.

BEGINNING—*Adjectives.*

Aboriginal. Indigenous to the soil.
Beginning. See *Verbs.*
Begun. See *Verbs.*
Embryonic. In the embryo.
First. Having the foremost place.
Foremost. Of the first rank.

BEGINNING—Adjectives—Continued.

Inaugural. Pertaining to an inauguration.
Inceptive. Marking the beginning.
Inchoate. Just commenced.
Inchoative. Just begun.
Incipient. Coming into existence.
Initial. Marking the beginning.
Initiative. Relating to initiation.
Initiatory. Suited to introduce.
Introductory. Acting as an introduction.

Just begun. Begun now.
Leading. Having the foremost place.
Maiden. Initiative.
Nascent. Beginning to exist.
Natal. Dating from one's birth.
Primeval, etc. Dating from the first ages, etc. See NOVELTY-ANTIQUITY.
Primogenial. First born.
Rudimental. Relating to the rudiments.

BEGINNING—*Adverbs.*

Ab incunabilis [L.]. From the cradle.
Ab initio [L.]. From the beginning.
Ab origine [L.]. From the origin.
Ab ovo [L.]. From the egg.
At the beginning. At the starting-point.
First. Having priority in time or place.
First and foremost. At the head.
From its birth. From its beginning.

From the beginning. From the first.
Imprimis [L.]. First.
In embryo. In the incipient state.
In its infancy. In the start.
In limine [L.]. At the threshold.
In the beginning. In the first place.
In the bud. In the inceptive state.
In the first place. Leading off.

be-gird'. Surround. CONFINEMENT, ENVIRONMENT-INTERPOSITION.

beg'-ler-beg. The governor-general of a Turkish province. CHIEF-UNDERLING.

be-gone'. Depart. ADMISSION-EXPULSION, ARRIVAL-DEPARTURE, COMMISSION-ABROGATION; **begone dull care,** LIGHTHEARTEDNESS-DEJECTION.

be-grease'. To soil with grease. CLEANNESS-FILTHINESS, EMBELLISHMENT-DISFIGUREMENT.

be-grime'. Make foul. CLEANNESS-FILTHINESS.

be-grudge'. To envy one the possession of. EXTRAVAGANCE-AVARICE, PROFFER-REFUSAL, READINESS-RELUCTANCE.

be-guile'. Delude. CONTENTEDNESS-DISCONTENTMENT, TRUTH-ERROR, TRUTHFULNESS-FRAUD; **beguile the time,** ACTION-PASSIVENESS, ENTERTAINMENT-WEARINESS.

be'-gum. An East India princess. GENTILITY-DEMOCRACY.

be-gun'. Commenced. BEGINNING-END.

be-half'. Advantage; interest; matter. GOOD-EVIL, OBSTRUCTION-HELP; **in behalf of,** OBSTRUCTION-HELP, REPRESENTATION.

be-have'. Be good. CONDUCT, POLITENESS-IMPOLITENESS, SOCIETY-LUDICROUSNESS.

be-ha'-vior. Deportment. CONDUCT; **on one's good behavior,** VIRTUE-VICE.

be-head'. Decapitate. LIFE-KILLING, RECOMPENSE-PUNITION.

be-he'-moth. In the Bible, a monstrous beast. GREATNESS-LITTLENESS.

be-hest'. A command. ORDER.

be-hind'. At the back of; inferior to; at the rear. ANTERIORITY-POSTERIORITY, LEADING-FOLLOWING, PRECEDENCE-SUCCESSION; **behind one's back,** PRESENCE-ABSENCE; **behind the age,** KNOWLEDGE-IGNORANCE, NOVELTY-ANTIQUITY; **behind the scenes,** ACTING, CAUSE-EFFECT, ENLIGHTENMENT-SECRECY, KNOWLEDGE-IGNORANCE, MANIFESTATION-LATENCY, VISIBILITY-INVISIBILITY; **behind time,** EARLINESS-LATENESS; **speak ill of behind one's back,** ADULATION-DISPARAGEMENT.

be-hind'-hand". Late. EARLINESS-LATENESS, SETTLEMENT-DEFAULT, TRANSCURSION-SHORTCOMING, WELFARE-MISFORTUNE.

be-hold'. To look at. HEED-DISREGARD, ONLOOKER, SIGHT-BLINDNESS.

be-hold'-en. Indebted. DUTY-DERELICTION, THANKFULNESS-THANKLESSNESS.

be-hold'-er. A spectator. ONLOOKER.

be-hoof'. That which benefits one. GOOD-EVIL.

be-hoove'. To be right for. DUTY-DERELICTION.

be-'ing. Existing; entity. ENTITY-NONENTITY, SUBSTANCE-NULLITY; **created being,** FAUNA-FLORA; **human being,** HUMANITY; **time being,** DURATION-NEVERNESS.

Bel. One of the chief gods of the Babylonians. JOVE-FIEND.

be-la'-bor. Thrash. IMPETUS-REACTION, RECOMPENSE-PUNITION.

be-la'-ted. Benighted; made tardy. EARLINESS-LATENESS, KNOWLEDGE-IGNORANCE.

be-lay'. To surround. OBSTRUCTION-HELP, UNION-DISUNION.

belch. To emit wind from the stomach. ADMISSION-EXPULSION.

bel'-dam. A hag. BENEFACTOR-EVILDOER.

bel'-dame. A hag. TURBULENCE-CALMNESS.

be-lea'-guer. Besiege. ATTACK-DEFENSE.

bel"-es-prit'. A clever talker or writer. WAG.

bel'-fry. A bell-tower. FANE.

Be'-lial. The devil; the old Hebrew personification of lawlessness. ANGEL-SATAN, JOVE-FIEND; **sons of Belial,** GODLINESS-UNGODLINESS.

be-lie'. Contradict. ANTAGONISM-CONCURRENCE, ASSERTION-DENIAL, TRUTHFULNESS-FALSEHOOD.

be-lief'. Probable knowledge. FAITH-MISGIVING, GODLINESS-UNGODLINESS; **easy of belief,** LIKELIHOOD-UNLIKELIHOOD; **hug a belief,** BIGOTRY-APOSTASY.

be-lieve'. To credit. GODLINESS-UNGODLINESS, HYPOTHESIS; **believe who may,** FAITH-MISGIVING; **not believe one's senses,** ASTONISHMENT-EXPECTANCE; **reason to believe,** LIKELIHOOD-UNLIKELIHOOD.

be-lieved'. Credited. FAITH-MISGIVING.

be-liev'-er. One who believes; an adherent to some particular church sect. GODLINESS-UNGODLINESS; **true believer,** ORTHODOXY-HETERODOXY.

be-liev'-ing. Pious; crediting. FAITH-MISGIVING, GODLINESS-UNGODLINESS.

be-like'. Probably. LIKELIHOOD-UNLIKELIHOOD.

Belisario, date obolum [L.] (Bel-i-sê'-ri-o, dê'-tî ob'-o-lum). Give a penny to Belisarius. CHARITABLENESS-MALEVOLENCE.

bell. A hollow metallic instrument which rings when struck. MUSICAL INSTRUMENTS, SIGN; **alarm bell,** ALARM; **bear away the bell,** GOODNESS-BADNESS; REPUTATION-DISCREDIT, SUCCESS-FAILURE; **bell, book, and candle,** ASSERTION-DENIAL, CEREMONIAL, CHARITABLENESS-CURSE, DEVOTION-CHARM; **bell shape,** CONVEXITY-CONCAVITY, ROUNDNESS; **bell the cat,** BRAVERY-COWARDICE; **cracked bell,** RESONANCE-NONRESONANCE; **passing bell,** LIFE-FUNERAL.

bel"-la-don'-na. A poisonous herb used in medicine. REMEDY-BANE.

belle [F.] (bel). A reigning beauty. MALE-FEMALE.

belle étoile, à la [F.] (bel ê-twal', a la). In the open air. OUTSIDE-INSIDE, WATER-AIR.

belles-lettres [F.] (bel-letr'). Polite literature. LANGUAGE.

belli casus [L.] (bel'-lai kê'-sus). A cause of war. EXCITATION.

bel'-li-cose". Inclined to war. FIGHTING, STRIFE-PEACE.

bel'-lied. Having a belly. CONVEXITY-CONCAVITY.
bel-lig'-er-ent. One engaged in war. BELLIGERENT, FIGHTING-CONCILIATION, STRIFE-PEACE.

BELLIGERENT.

Amazon. A female warrior.
Archer. One skilled in the use of the bow and arrow.
Armigerent. One next in degree to a knight.
Artilleryman. A man who manages or assists in managing a large gun in firing.
Assailant. One who first attacks another.
Athlete. Any one trained to contend in exercises requiring great physical agility and strength.
Bashi-bazouk [Turk.]. An irregular Turkish volunteer.
Beefeater. One of the yeomen of the guard in England.
Belligerent. A nation or person recognized as rightfully engaged in war.
Bludgeon-man. One who uses the bludgeon.
Bombardier. An artilleryman.
Bowman. One skilled in the use of the bow.
Boxer. A pugilist; a Chinese rebel.
Bruiser. A boxer; a pugilist.
Bully. A blustering, tyrannical fellow.
Cadet. A young man in training for military or naval service.
Campaigner. An old soldier.
Cannoneer. A man who manages or fires cannon.
Carbineer. A soldier armed with a carbine.
Champion. The foremost in espousing a cause.
Charger. A steed.
Chasseur [F.]. Light infantry soldier.
Combatant. One who engages in a contest of violence.
Competitor. One of a number contending for a prize or something desirable.
Conscript. One taken by lot or compulsorily enrolled to serve as a soldier.
Controversialist. One who draws out an argument and disputes it point by point.
Coolie. A laborer transported from the East Indies, China, or Japan, for service in some other country.
Corrival. A fellow rival.
Cossack. A member of the race inhabiting the lower Don and Dnieper, Eastern Russia, etc.; military horsemen.
Croat. An irregular soldier, generally from Croatia.
Cuirassier [F.]. A soldier armed with a cuirass.
Destrier [F.]. A war-horse.
Disputant. One who argues in opposition to another.
Dragoon. A cavalryman.
Duelist. One who fights in single combat.
Engineer. An engine driver.
Ensign. A commissioned officer of the lowest grade in the navy.
Fencible. A soldier enlisted for home service only.
Fighter. One who fights; a combatant.
Fighting-cock. A cock trained to fight.
Fighting-man. Combatant.
Fire-eater. A quarrelsome person who seeks affrays.
Food for powder. Soldier.
Foot-soldier. A soldier who serves on foot.
Franc-tireur [F.]. French rifleman.
Fusileer. A soldier armed with a fusil.
Game-cock. The male game fowl.
Gendarme [F.]. Man at arms; policeman.
Gladiator. One who fought with weapons in public; one who engages in any fierce combat or controversy.
Grenadier. A member of a special regiment or corps; a member of a regiment composed of men of great stature.
Guardsman. A member of any military body called Guards.
Guerilla condottiere [It.]. An irregular soldiery.
Gunner. One who works a gun, whether on land or sea.
Hackster. A bully; a ruffian.
Halberdier. One who is armed with a halberd.
Heavy dragoon. A heavily armed cavalryman.
Heavyweight. The heaviest of the classes into which contestants are divided.
Horse soldier. A cavalryman.
Hussar. One of the light cavalry of European armies.
Infantryman. A foot soldier.
Irregular. A soldier not in regular service.
Janizary. A member of an unruly military force which for several centuries furnished the body-guard of the sultans of Turkey.
Lancer. A cavalry soldier carrying a lance as a weapon.
Legionary. }
Légionnaire [F.]. } A member of a legion.
Light dragoon. A light armed cavalryman

Litigant. One who is engaged in a lawsuit.
Mamaluke. } One of a celebrated cavalry corps of Egypt. (Thirteenth
Mameluke. } century to 1811.)
Man-at-arms. A soldier fully armed.
Man-of-war's man, etc. One who fights on an armed vessel belonging to a navy or military marine. See WAYFARER-SEAFARER.
Marine. Soldier serving on a war-vessel.
Matross. A gunner or gunner's mate.
Mercenary. A hired soldier in foreign service.
Military man. Soldier.
Mosstrooper. One of a class of bandits that formerly infested the border country between England and Scotland.
Musketeer. A soldier armed with a musket.
Myrmidon. One of a warlike people of ancient Thessaly; a petty officer of the law.
Officer. One appointed to some office in the army or navy. See CHIEF.
Paladin. Any one of the twelve peers of Charlemagne; a paragon of knighthood.
Pandour. A Hungarian foot-soldier; any inhuman soldier.
Peon. A foot-soldier.
Picket. A guard on the outskirts of a camp to warn against the enemy's approach.
Pikeman. A soldier armed with a pike.
Piquet. A picket.
Polemic. One who writes in support of any doctrine, opinion, etc.
Private. A common soldier.
Private soldier. A private.
Prize-fighter. One who fights publicly for a reward.
Pugilist. A professional prize-fighter.
Rajpoot [Hind.]. A Hindu of the military caste.
Recruit. A newly enrolled soldier or sailor.
Redcoat. A British soldier.
Rifleman. A soldier armed with a rifle.
Rival. A competitor.
Rough. A coarse bully.
Sabreur [F.]. Slasher.
Sapper. A soldier employed in making trenches.
Sapper and miner.
Sepoy. A native East-Indian soldier equipped and disciplined in European style.
Sharpshooter. One skilled with the rifle.
Skirmisher. A soldier assigned to skirmish duty.
Soldier. A person engaged in military service.
Spahee. }
Spahi. } One of a native Algerine corps in the French service.
Spearman. One who is armed with a spear.
Standard-bearer. One who carries the flag, ensign, or banner of an army.
Subaltern. A military officer ranking below a captain.
Swashbuckler. A swaggering, boastful fellow.
Swordsman. One who is skilful with or armed with a sword.
Tommy Atkins. Nickname of the English soldier.
Trooper. A cavalryman.
Uhlan. One of a certain description of militia among the Tartars.
Veteran. An old soldier.
Voltigeur [F.]. One of a picked company of irregular riflemen in each regiment.
War-horse. The horse of a cavalry soldier; a charger.
Warrior. A soldier; a champion.
Wrestler. One skilled in wrestling.
Yager. In the German army, one belonging to a body of light infantry armed with rifles.
Zouave. One of an active and hardy body of soldiers in the French service, originally Arabs, but now composed of Frenchmen who wear the Arab dress.

BELLIGERENT—*Collective Nouns*

Armada. A fleet of war-ships.
Armed force. }
Army. } A body of fighting men.
Artillery. The men of the artillery branch of an army.
Battalia. A body of soldiers on the march.
Battalion. A body of troops in battle array.
Battery. A company or division of artillery.
Brigade. A body of troops consisting of two or more regiments.
Cavalry. The military force which serves on horseback.
Cloud of skirmishers. A body of men sent ahead to cover the movements of an army.
Cohort. The tenth part of a legion.
Column. The division of an army.
Company. Subdivision of a regiment of troops.
Corps. An organized division of an army.
Corps d'armée [F.]. A corps organized as an army in itself.
Detachment. A body of troops or part of a fleet.

Division. Two or more brigades of soldiers.
Draft. Force of soldiers drawn by conscription.
File. A row of soldiers arranged one behind the other.
Fleet. A number of war-vessels.
Flotilla. A fleet of small vessels.
Flying column. A light-armed column of troops.
Forces. Bodies of troops.
Garrison. A body of soldiers in a fortified place.
Guard. A small detachment of troops.
Guards. Soldiers.
Horse. Cavalry.
Horse and foot. Mixed troops.
Horse artillery. Artillery drawn by horses.
Hosts. Armies.
Household troops. Troops appointed to attend a sovereign.
Infantry. Foot-soldiers.
Landsturm [G.]. Final reserves.
Landwehr [G.]. Militia.
Legion. A body of foot-soldiers numbering from four to six thousand.
Levy. A body of troops.
Life guards. A body of select troops attending a prince.
Light horse. Light-armed cavalry.
Light infantry. Light-armed foot-soldiers.
Line of battle. Regular infantry of an army.
Military. Whole body of soldiers.
Militia. The whole military force of a nation.
Mounted rifles. Mounted troops armed with rifles.
National guard. A body of militia, or local military organization.
Naval forces. Ships of war.
Navy. A fleet of ships.
Phalanx. A body of troops in close array.
Platoon. Half a company of soldiers.
Posse comitatus [L.]. The force which a sheriff may call to his assistance.
Rank. A row of soldiers.
Rank and file. Whole body of common soldiers.
Raw levies. New soldiers.
Regiment. Ten companies of soldiers.
Regulars. The standing army.
Reserve forces. A body of troops kept for an exigency.
Reserves. See RESERVE FORCES.
Rifles. Light-armed infantry.
Sabaoth. The hosts.
Section. A part of an army.
Soldiery. A body of soldiers.
Squad. A body of troops assembled for drill.
Squadron. A body of cavalry comprising two companies of troops.
Standing army. A permanent military force.
Subdivision. A part of a division of troops.
The army. The entire fighting force.
The fancy. Sporting characters taken collectively.
The line. Troops in battle array.
Trainband. The London militia.
Troops. Soldiers.
Troops of the line. The fighting soldiery.
Volunteers. Soldiers who enter the military service voluntarily.
Wing. Part of an army.
Wooden walls. Wooden war-ships.
Yeoman of the guard. }
Yeomanry. } Volunteer cavalry liable to service.

BELLIGERENT—*Naval Terms.*

Battle-ship. The heaviest armored and armed man-of-war.
Bomb-vessel. A small ketch or vessel, very strongly built, on which mortars are mounted to be used in naval bombardments.
Catamaran. A kind of raft or float, consisting of two or more logs or pieces of wood lashed together, and moved by paddles or sails.
Corvette. Same as sloop of war.
Cruiser. A swift, light-armored, heavily-armed ship for cruising.
First-rate. A war vessel of the highest grade.
Flag-ship. The vessel which carries the commanding officer of a fleet or squadron and flies his distinctive flag or pennant.
Floating battery. A battery erected on rafts or the hulls of ships, chiefly for the defense of a coast or the bombardment of a place.
Frigate. A steam war-vessel of high speed and great fighting capacity.
Guard-ship. The ship on guard-duty for the day; a ship of war stationed in a harbor for its protection.
Gunboat. A war-ship of light draft, carrying heavy guns.
Ironclad. A war-vessel sheathed with armor.
Line-of-battle ship. See SHIP OF THE LINE.
Man-of-war. An armed vessel belonging to a navy or military marine.
Monitor. An ironclad sitting very low in the water and having a flat deck, sharp stern, and one or more rotating deck-turrets carrying heavy guns.
Privateer. A vessel owned and officered by private persons, but carrying on maritime war under a commission from a belligerent state.
Ram. A war-vessel constructed for ramming.
Ship of the line. A ship of war large enough to have a place in the line of battle.
Sloop of war. Any war-vessel larger than a gunboat and carrying guns on one deck only.
Store-ship. A vessel used to carry naval stores for a fleet, garrison or the like.
Submarine boat. A vessel capable of traveling under water.
Tender. A vessel employed to attend other vessels, to supply them with provisions and other stores, to convey intelligence, or the like.
Torpedo-boat. A small, swift vessel designed to attack by launching torpedoes.
Transport. A vessel in government employ for transporting troops, military supplies, etc.
Troop-ship. A vessel built or fitted for the conveyance of troops.
Turret-ship. An ironclad vessel with low sides, on which heavy guns are mounted within one or more iron turrets, which may be rotated.

BELLIGERENT—*Phrases.*

Garde nationale [F.]. National guard.
Garde royale [F.]. Royal guard.
Hôtel des Invalides [F.]. Hospital for invalids, *i. e.,* invalid soldiers.

bell'-ing. The cry of rutting deer; baying of fox hounds. CRY-ULULATION.
bell'-man. A town crier. MESSENGER.
bell''-met''-al. Alloy used for making bells. MATERIALS.
bello flagrante [L.] (bel'-lo flê-gran'-tî). During hostilities. FIGHTING-CONCILIATION.
Bel-lo'-na. The goddess of war. FIGHTING-CONCILIATION.
bel'-low. A loud, hollow noise. CRY-ULULATION, JUBILATION-LAMENTATION, LOUDNESS-FAINTNESS.
bel'-lows. An instrument for sending air through a tube. RIVER-WIND, VOCALIZATION-MUTENESS.
bells. Metallic vessels which ring when struck. **Peal of bells,** CRASH-DRUMMING.
bell'-shape'. Like a bell in form. ROUNDNESS.
bell'-shaped'. Having the shape of a bell. CONVEXITY-CONCAVITY, CURVATION-RECTILINEARITY, ROUNDNESS.
bell'-weth''-er. The wether that leads a flock of sheep. MANAGER, PREDECESSOR-CONTINUATION.
bel'-ly. The abdomen. CONVEXITY-CONCAVITY, OUTSIDE-INSIDE; **bellyful,** ENTIRETY-DEFICIENCY; **belly god,** FASTING-GLUTTONY; **belly timber,** NUTRIMENT-EXCRETION.
bel'-o-man''-cy. Divination by arrows. PROPHECY.
be-long'. To be the property of; to adhere to. AD-MISSION-EXCLUSION, CONNECTION-INDEPENDENCE, CONSTITUENT-ALIEN, DUTY-DERELICTION, HOLDING-EXEMPTION, MIGHT-IMPOTENCE, PROPERTY.
be-long'-ings. What one has about him. PROPERTY.
be-lov'-ed. Dear to. LOVE-HATE.
be-low'. Under in time or place; inferior. **Below its full strength,** FAULTLESSNESS-FAULTINESS; **below par,** FAULTLESSNESS-FAULTINESS, GENTILITY-DE-MOCRACY, GOODNESS-BADNESS, HEIGHT-LOWNESS, MAGNITUDE-SMALLNESS, PRICE-DISCOUNT, SUPREM-ACY-SUBORDINACY; **below stairs,** HEIGHT-LOWNESS; **below the mark,** MAGNITUDE-SMALLNESS, SUPREM-ACY-SUBORDINACY; **here below,** UNIVERSE.
belt. A band; girdle. CIRCLE-WINDING, GULF-LAKE, OUTLINE; **swimming belt,** REFUGE-PITFALL.
belt'-ed. Having a mark like a belt. CIRCLE-WINDING.
Be'-lus. One of the chief gods of the Babylonians. JOVE-FIEND.
bel''-ve-dere'. A pavilion on the top of a house. SIGHT-BLINDNESS.
be'-ma. Sanctuary. ARCHITECTURE.
be-mask'. Cover with a mask. ENLIGHTENMENT-SECRECY.

be-min'-gle. To blend thoroughly. MIXTURE-HOMO-GENEITY.

be-mire'. To sink in the mire. CLEANNESS-FILTHI-NESS.

be-moan'. To express pity for. JUBILATION-LAMEN-TATION.

be-mused'. Stupefied. HEED-DISREGARD.

bench. A seat; a judge's seat; a body of judges. COUNCIL, SUSPENSION-SUPPORT, TRIBUNAL; **king's bench,** RELEASE-PRISON.

bench'-er. A senior member of the English bar. ADVOCATE.

bend. To deflect; submit; apply closely. AIM-ABER-RATION, ANGULARITY, CIRCUITION, CURVATION-RECTILINEARITY, ELEVATION-DEPRESSION, HARD-NESS-SOFTNESS, PARALLELISM-INCLINATION, YIELD-ING; **bend backwards,** ANTERIORITY-POSTERIORITY; **bend one's course,** AIM-ABERRATION; **bend one's look upon,** SIGHT-BLINDNESS; **bend one's steps,** QUEST-EVASION; **bend over,** CONVEXITY-CONCAVITY; **bend sinister,** REPUTATION-DISCREDIT; **bend the bow,** TOIL-RELAXATION; **bend the brows,** APPROVAL-DIS-APPROVAL; **bend the knee,** DEVOTION-IDOLATRY, ELEVATION-DEPRESSION, POLITENESS-IMPOLITENESS, PRESUMPTION - OBSEQUIOUSNESS, REGARD - DISRE-SPECT, SELFRESPECT-HUMBLENESS, YIELDING; **bend the mind,** HEED-DISREGARD, REFLECTION-VACANCY; **bend to,** INCLINATION; **bend to one's will,** RULE-LICENSE; **bend to rules,** CONVENTIONALITY-UNCON-VENTIONALITY; **bend towards,** AIM-ABERRATION.

be-neath'. Under; below. HEIGHT-LOWNESS; **beneath notice,** CONSEQUENCE-INSIGNIFICANCE; **beneath one,** UPRIGHTNESS-DISHONESTY.

ben'-e-dict [Shakespeare]. A newly married man. MATRIMONY-CELIBACY.

Ben'-e-dict Ar'-nold. American traitor. PATRIOTISM-TREASON.

ben''-e-dic'-tine. Pertaining to St. Benedict or his order. MINISTRY-LAITY.

ben''-e-dic'-tion. Blessing. APPROVAL-DISAPPROVAL, DEVOTION-IDOLATRY, THANKFULNESS-THANKLESS-NESS; **nuptial benediction,** MATRIMONY-CELIBACY.

ben''-e-dic'-to-ry. Blessing. APPROVAL-DISAPPROVAL.

ben''-e-fac'-tion. Charitable gift. GIVING-RECEIVING.

ben''-e-fac'-tor. One who confers a benefit. BENE-FACTOR-EVILDOER, GOOD MAN-BAD MAN.

BENEFACTOR—EVILDOER.

Auxiliary, etc. One who gives help, etc. See ANTAGONIST-ASSISTANT.

Benefactor. One who gives friendly help.

Benefactress. A female benefactor.

Good genius. A good spirit supposed to be attached to a person to influence their actions and fortunes for the good.

Good Samaritan [Bible]. One given to doing acts of charity.

Guardian angel. The particular spirit believed to have charge over a person from birth.

Pater patriæ [L.]. The father of his country.

Salt of the earth, etc. [Bible]. Those who shall purify the earth. See GOOD MAN.

Savior. One who saves from destruction.

Tutelary saint. A canonized person invested with the guardianship of a person or thing.

EVILDOER—DENOTATIONS—*Continued from Column 2.*

Cockatrice. A fabled serpent, whose look and breath were fatal.

Colorado beetle. A beetle which destroys potato plants.

Eumenides. The Furies.

Frankenstein's monster. A fabled monster, constructed by Frank-enstein, which destroyed its author.

Furies. Greek goddesses, the avengers of iniquities.

Gerfalcon. A large species of Arctic falcon.

Ghoul. An imaginary being supposed to feed on human beings.

Gorilla. A very large species of ape.

Gyrfalcon. See GERFALCON.

Harpy. A fabulous monster with the face of a woman and the body of a vulture.

Hell-hound. Fabulous guardians of hell.

Hornet. A large strong wasp.

Hyena. A large carnivorous animal.

Jezebel. A cruel queen of Israel.

Locust. A large insect, which preys upon growing crops.

Mohawk. } A member of a band of ruffians who infested the streets of
Mohock. } London in the time of Addison.

Monster. Any large and fierce animal.

Ogre. A hideous giant fabled to feed on human beings.

Rattlesnake. A snake whose bite is poisonous.

Savage. A wild or uncivilized person.

Scorpion. A stinging species of lizards.

Serpent. A snake.

Siren. One of the three sea-nymphs, said to allure passers by to destruction by sweet singing.

Tiger. A fierce animal.

Torpedo. An explosive cap.

Vampire. A ghost that sucks blood.

Viper. A venomous snake.

Vulture. A carnivorous bird.

Wild beast. A dangerous wild animal.

Wireworm. A species of beetles.

EVILDOER—*Phrase.*

Fœnum habet in cornu [L]. He has hay on his horn; hence, is dangerous.

Anarchist. One who seeks to overthrow all civil authority.

Anthropophagist. }
Anthropophagus. } One who eats human flesh; a cannibal.

Barbarian. One devoid of pity.

Beldam. An ugly old woman.

Blood sucker. A hard master.

Bludgeon-man. Man with a bludgeon or short stick.

Brute. An animal devoid of human reason.

Bully. A quarrelsome overbearing fellow.

Butcher. One causing needless loss of life.

Caitiff. A wicked wretch.

Cannibal. One who eats human flesh.

Communist. An advocate of equalizing social conditions.

Cut throat, etc. A murderer. See LIFE-KILLING.

Dangerous classes. Ruffian.

Demon in human shape. Unscrupulous scoundrel.

Desperado. A man without regard for law or life.

Destroyer. One who destroys.

Devil incarnate. One given to all manner of wickedness.

Evildoer. Criminal.

Evilworker. Worker of wickedness.

Fiend. A very wicked person.

Firebrand. A person causing mischief.

Hag. An ugly old woman.

Hangman. One whose business it is to hang people.

Hellhag. A hag fit for hell.

Iconoclast. One who assails cherished beliefs.

Incendiary. One who maliciously destroys property by fire.

Marplot. One who by meddling frustrates a plan.

Mischief maker. Causer of trouble.

Oppressor. One who oppresses.

Rough. }
Ruffian. } A brutal fellow.

Scourge of the human race. (Attila.)

Semibarbarian. One half civilized.

Snake in the grass. An evildoer who seeks to conceal his real character; a copperhead.

Terrorist. A partizan to the Reign of Terror in France.

Thief, etc. One who steals, etc. See ROBBER.

Tyrant. One exercising unlawful authority, especially cruelly.

Ugly customer. A disagreeable person, especially to fight.

Vandal. One who wilfully mutilates that which is beautiful or artistic.

Wrongdoer, etc. See BAD MAN.

EVILDOER—*Denotations.*

Adder. A serpent.

Anaconda. A large South American snake.

Asp. A poisonous serpent.

Attila. A king of the Huns, called "the Scourge of God."

Bane. That which destroys life. See REMEDY-BANE.

Blood-hound. A large dog used for tracking criminals.

Canker-worm. A moth which destroys fruit trees.

Cobra. A large poisonous snake.

(Continued on Column 1.)

ben''-e-fac'-tress. A female benefactor. BENEFACTOR-EVILDOER.

ben'-e-fice. A church living. CHURCH.

be-nef'-i-cence. Active goodness. CHARITABLENESS-MALEVOLENCE, GOODNESS-BADNESS.

be-nef'-i-cent. Delighting in good works. CHARITABLENESS-MALEVOLENCE, GOODNESS-BADNESS.

ben''-e-fi'-cial. Helpful. GOOD-EVIL, GOODNESS-BADNESS; beneficial interest, PROPERTY.

ben''-e-fi'-cial-ly. Advantageously. GOODNESS-BADNESS.

ben''-e-fi'-cia-ry. One who holds a benefice; one benefited by another. GIVING-RECEIVING, HOLDER, MINISTRY-LAITY.

ben'-e-fit. Advantage; favor bestowed. CHARITABLENESS-MALEVOLENCE, GAIN-LOSS, GOOD-EVIL, GOODNESS-BADNESS, OBSTRUCTION-HELP, PROPERTY, USEFULNESS-USELESSNESS; reap the benefit of, BETTERMENT-DETERIORATION, SUCCESS-FAILURE, USEFULNESS-USELESSNESS.

ben'-e-fits. Favors. Benefits forgot, THANKFULNESS-THANKLESSNESS.

bene, quamdiu se gesserit [L.] (bĭ'-nĭ, quam'-dai-yiu sĭ jes'-ser-it). During good behavior. DUTY-DERELICTION.

beneplacito, a vostro [It.] (bê-ne-pla-chĭ'-to, a vos'-tro). At your pleasure; as you will. VOLITION-OBLIGATION.

be-nev'-o-lence. Disposition to do good. CHARITABLENESS-MALEVOLENCE, GOOD MAN-BAD MAN, LOVE-HATE, PRICE-DISCOUNT; universal benevolence, HUMANITARIANISM-MISANTHROPY.

be-nev'-o-lent. Charitable. CHARITABLENESS-MALEVOLENCE.

Ben''-gal'. A division of India. Bengal heat, HEAT-COLD.

be-night'-ed. Ignorant. KNOWLEDGE-IGNORANCE, LIGHT-DARKNESS.

be-nign'. Kind. HEALTHINESS-UNHEALTHINESS.

be-nig'-nant. Gracious. CHARITABLENESS-MALEVOLENCE.

be-nig'-ni-ty. Kindliness. CHARITABLENESS-MALEVOLENCE.

ben'-i-son. A blessing. APPROVAL-DISAPPROVAL.

Ben'-ja-min. A corruption used only in compounds. Benjamin's mess, SUPREMACY-SUBORDINACY, WHOLE-PART.

ben'-shie. A fairy visitant. JOVE-FIEND.

bent. Curve; tendency. AFFECTIONS, ANGULARITY, DESIRE-DISTASTE, INCLINATION, READINESS-RELUCTANCE; bent on, DESIRE-DISTASTE, DETERMINATION-VACILLATION, PURPOSE-LUCK, READINESS-RELUCTANCE; fool to the top of one's bent, SOCIETY-DERISION.

Ben'-tham-ite. Philanthropist. HUMANITARIANISM-MISANTHROPY.

ben trovato [It.] (ben tro-va'-to). Well found. FANCY, LIKELIHOOD-UNLIKELIHOOD, TRUTHFULNESS-FABRICATION, WITTINESS-DULNESS.

be-numb'. Deaden. HEATING-COOLING, SENSITIVENESS-APATHY, SENSUALITY-SUFFERING.

be-plas'-ter. Cover with plaster. ADULATION-DISPARAGEMENT.

be-praise'. Commend. APPROVAL-DISAPPROVAL.

be-queath'. Give by will. GIVING-RECEIVING.

be-quest'. A legacy left by will. GIVING-RECEIVING.

be-reave'. Despoil. TAKING-RESTITUTION.

be-reave'-ment. A grievous loss. GAIN-LOSS, LIFE-DEATH, TAKING-RESTITUTION.

be-reft'. Deprived of. AFFLUENCE-PENURY, GAIN-LOSS, PROPERTY; bereft of reason, SANENESS-LUNACY.

berg. An iceberg. HEAT-COLD.

ber'-ga-mot. A kind of pear; snuff. PERFUME-STENCH.

ber'-lin. A four-wheeled carriage. CONVEYANCE-VESSEL.

ber-ret'-ta. A cardinal's red cap. DRESS-UNDRESS.

berth. A bed in a vessel; an office. DWELLER-HABITATION, OCCUPATION, SUSPENSION-SUPPORT.

ber'-yl. A greenish mineral or gem. EMBELLISHMENT-DISFIGUREMENT, REDNESS-GREENNESS.

be-seech'. To entreat. DEVOTION-IDOLATRY, PETITION-EXPOSTULATION.

be-seem'. Befit. DUTY-DERELICTION.

be-set'. To shut in on all sides. ATTACK-DEFENSE, ENVIRONMENT-INTERPOSITION, LEADING-FOLLOWING, PETITION-EXPOSTULATION, PLEASURABLENESS-PAINFULNESS; beset with difficulties, DIFFICULTY-FACILITY.

be-set'-ting. Constantly troubling. HABIT-DESUETUDE, UNIVERSALITY-PARTICULARITY; besetting sin, VIRTUE-VICE.

be-shrew'. To wish ill to. CHARITABLENESS-CURSE.

be-side'. At the side; except. CONVENTIONALITY-UNCONVENTIONALITY, LATERALITY-CONTRAPOSITION, REMOTENESS-NEARNESS; beside oneself, EXCITATION, SANENESS-LUNACY; beside the mark, CONNECTION-INDEPENDENCE, TRUTH-ERROR.

be-sides'. Over and above. ADDITION-SUBTRACTION.

be-siege'. To lay siege to. ATTACK-DEFENSE, PETITION-EXPOSTULATION.

besique [F.] (bê-zĭc'). A game of cards. ENTERTAINMENT-WEARINESS.

be-slav'-er. Bespatter; sully. ADULATION-DISPARAGEMENT.

be-slime'. Cover with slime. CLEANNESS-FILTHINESS.

be-slub'-ber. Bedaub. ADULATION-DISPARAGEMENT.

be-smear'. To soil. CLEANNESS-FILTHINESS, COVER-LINING.

be-smirch'. To defile. ADULATION-DISPARAGEMENT.

be'-som. A drab; broom. CLEANNESS-FILTHINESS.

be-sot'-ted. Stupefied in mind or morals. DECISION-MISJUDGMENT.

be-span'-gle. To adorn with spangles. EMBELLISHMENT-DISFIGUREMENT.

be-spat'-ter. To soil by spattering. ADULATION-DISPARAGEMENT, APPROVAL-DISAPPROVAL, CLEANNESS-FILTHINESS.

be-speak'. To ask for in advance. COMMISSION-ABROGATION, EARLINESS-LATENESS, EVIDENCE-COUNTEREVIDENCE, MEANING-JARGON, PETITION-EXPOSTULATION, RECKLESSNESS-CAUTION.

be-speck'-le. To cover with specks. VARIEGATION.

be-spot'. To cover with spots. VARIEGATION.

be-sprin'-kle. To scatter over. MIXTURE-HOMOGENEITY, VARIEGATION.

Bes'-se-mer. A kind of steel. CHEMISTRY.

best. First rate; most desirable. FAULTLESSNESS-FAULTINESS, GOODNESS-BADNESS; all for the best, CONTENTEDNESS-DISCONTENTMENT, GOOD-EVIL, SANGUINENESS-HOPELESSNESS, WELFARE-MISFORTUNE; best bib and tucker, EMBELLISHMENT-DISFIGUREMENT, POMP, PREPARATION-NONPREPARATION; best intentions, CHARITABLENESS-MALEVOLENCE; best is the best, GOODNESS-BADNESS; best part, MAGNITUDE-SMALLNESS, WHOLE-PART; do one's best, ACTIVITY-INDOLENCE, CAREFULNESS-CARELESSNESS, TOIL-RELAXATION, VENTURE; have the best of it, SUCCESS-FAILURE; make the best of it, COMPOSITION, EXCITABILITY-INEXCITABILITY, OVERVALUATION-UNDERVALUATION, SANGUINENESS-HOPELESSNESS, USE-DISUSE, YIELDING; make the best of one's time, HURRY-LEISURE; to the best of one's belief, FAITH-MISGIVING.

Beste ist gut genug, das [G.] (bes'-te ist gut ge-nuh', das). The best is good enough. ENOUGH, FAULTLESSNESS-FAULTINESS.

be-stead'. Help. USEFULNESS-USELESSNESS.

bes'-tial. Pertaining to beasts; brutish. PURITY-IMPURITY.

be-stir'. To move quickly. **Bestir oneself,** ACTIVITY-INDOLENCE, HURRY-LEISURE, TOIL-RELAXATION.

be-stow'. To confer. GIVING-RECEIVING; **bestow one's hand,** MATRIMONY-CELIBACY; **bestow thought,** REFLECTION-VACANCY.

be-stow'-al. Gift. GIVING-RECEIVING.

be-strad'-dle. To stand over. SUSPENSION-SUPPORT.

be-stride'. To get or sit upon astride. HEIGHT-LOWNESS, SUSPENSION-SUPPORT.

bet. A wager. PURPOSE-LUCK.

be-take'. To have recourse to. **Betake oneself to.** ENTERPRISE, OCCUPATION, TRAVELING-NAVIGATION, USE-DISUSE.

bête, pas si [F.] (bêt, pa sî). Not such a fool. SAGACITY-INCAPACITY.

bête noire [F.] (bêt nwar). A black beast; a bugbear. LOVE-HATE, SANGUINENESS-TIMIDITY.

beth'-el. A seaman's chapel. FANE.

be-think'. Consider. MIND-IMBECILITY, REMEMBRANCE-FORGETFULNESS.

be-thrall'. To enthrall. LIBERTY-SUBJECTION, RELEASE-RESTRAINT.

be-tide'. To befall. OCCURRENCE-DESTINY.

be-times'. Seasonably. EARLINESS-LATENESS.

be-to'-ken. To signify. EVIDENCE-COUNTEREVIDENCE, PROPHECY, SIGN.

be-tray'. To deliver up to an enemy; mislead. EXPOSURE-HIDINGPLACE, PATRIOTISM-TREASON, TRUTHFULNESS-FRAUD, UPRIGHTNESS-DISHONESTY; **betray itself,** VISIBILITY-INVISIBILITY.

be-tray'-al. Act of betraying. PATRIOTISM-TREASON, UPRIGHTNESS-DISHONESTY.

be-tray'-er. One who betrays. PATRIOTISM-TREASON, UPRIGHTNESS-ROGUE.

be-trim'. Array. PREPARATION-NONPREPARATION.

be-troth'. To engage to marry. ENGAGEMENT-RELEASE, MATRIMONY-CELIBACY.

be-troth'-al. Engagement to marry. ENGAGEMENT-RELEASE.

be-trothed'. Engaged to marry. LOVE-HATE.

be-troth'-ment. Mutual marriage contract. ENGAGEMENT-RELEASE.

bet'-ter. Preferable; superior. ENGRAVING, GULL-DECEIVER; **better half,** MATRIMONY-CELIBACY; **better sort,** GENTILITY-DEMOCRACY; **for better for worse,** CHOICE-NEUTRALITY, MATRIMONY-CELIBACY; **get better,** BETTERMENT-DETERIORATION, HEALTH-SICKNESS, RENOVATION-RELAPSE, WEARINESS-REFRESHMENT; **get the better of,** BETTERMENT-DETERIORATION, RENOVATION-RELAPSE, SUCCESS-FAILURE; **only better than nothing,** FAULTLESSNESS-FAULTINESS; **seen better days,** AFFLUENCE-PENURY, BETTERMENT-DETERIORATION, WELFARE-MISFORTUNE; **think better of,** BETTERMENT-DETERIORATION, REPENTANCE-OBDURACY.

bet'-ter-ment. Improvement. BETTERMENT-DETERIORATION.

BETTERMENT—DETERIORATION.

Advance. Progress; improvement. See ADVANCE.

Advancement. The act of advancing and improving.

Amelioration. The act of improving or of growing better; the state of being improved.

Amendment. The act of changing for the better by removing errors or defects.

Ascent, etc. See ASCENT.

Betterment. The act of moving or causing to move from one degree of excellence to a higher.

Civilization. National improvement or culture.

Correction. The removal of errors or evils; the act of setting right.

Cultivation. The act of tilling the soil with a view to improving it; improvement in mental, moral, or physical condition.

Culture. The result of cultivating; refinement in manners or speech; improvement in mental or moral condition.

Elaboration. The act of working out anything into detailed completeness by successive operations.

Elevation. An uplifting. See ELEVATION.

Emendation. The improvement of a document by the removal of errors or corruptions.

Improvement. The act of advancing toward what is better.

Increase. A growing larger or greater. See INCREASE.

Melioration. The act of improving or of making more tolerable; the state of being improved.

Mend. The condition or course of repairing, reforming, or helping.

Mending, etc. Repairing, reforming or helping, etc. See *Verbs.*

Preferment. The state of being advanced.

Promotion. The act of advancing or promoting.

Purification. The act of purifying. See CLEANNESS.

Radical reform. Fundamental or thoroughgoing reform.

Recovery, etc. Restoration, as from sickness. See RENOVATION.

Refinement. Personal cultivation; fineness or delicacy of thought, taste, etc.

Reform. Amendment of what is evil or defective.

Reformation. The act of changing from worse to better, or the state of being improved.

Repair, etc. Restoration after decay, injury, wasting away, etc. See RENOVATION.

Revise. A revision.

Revision. The act of revising or reexamining for correction.

BETTERMENT—*Denotations.*

March of intellect. Intellectual improvement.

New edition. A publication issued after its former publication.

Second thought. More mature and deliberate thought.

Adulteration. The act of making impure by mixing with other baser ingredients; the state of being adulterated.

Alloy. Combination of metals, resulting in their depreciation.

Atrophy. Wasting away or emaciation of the body or any part of the body.

Blight. Decay; mildew.

Caducity. Weakness of old age.

Collapse. Extreme dejection of the vital powers.

Contamination. The act of making impure or defiling by contact with something baser.

Corrosion. The act of gradually wearing away.

Corruption. The act of putrefying or causing to become putrid; pollution; deterioration.

Damage. Injury to person, property, or fame.

Debasement. The act of degrading or the state of being degraded; deterioration.

Decadence.⎫ A process of declining; deterioration.
Decadency.⎭

Decay. Gradual decline toward dissolution, corruption· deterioration.

Declension. Decline; deterioration.

Declination. The act or state of declining or deteriorating.

Decline. Deterioration; tendency to a worse condition.

Decrease. A becoming less; decay. See INCREASE-DECREASE.

Decrepitude. The state of being enfeebled by old age.

Defedation. The act of polluting.

Degeneracy. The state of having become inferior to the normal condition.

Degenerateness. Degeneracy.

Degeneration. The act or state of deteriorating.

Degradation. The act of debasing; the state of being debased.

Délabrement [F.] Ruin; decay. See CREATION-DESTRUCTION.

Delaceration. The act of tearing to pieces.

Demoralization. The act of debasing the morals of; the state of being debased in morals.

Depravation. The act of corrupting, especially in morals; the state of being corrupted or deteriorated.

Depravement. Depravity.

Depravity. The state of being depraved, or generally bad in character. See VIRTUE-VICE.

Deterioration. The act or process of growing worse, or the state of having grown worse.

Detriment. Something that causes loss or injury; injury.

Dilapidation. The process of falling into ruin or decay.

Discoloration. The act of altering the natural color of; the state of being discolored.

BETTERMENT—DETERIORATION—*Continued.*

BETTERMENT—*Nouns of Cause, etc.*

Limæ labor [L.]. The labor of the file; the polishing of a literary composition.

Radical. One who advocates extreme measures of change in social institutions with a view to improvement.

Reformer. One who counsels or works for reform.

BETTERMENT—*Verbs.*

Advance. Progress; improve. See ADVANCE.

Ameliorate. Improve or make better.

Amend. Change or correct in order to improve.

Appeal from Philip drunk to Philip sober. [Valerius Maximus, vi, 2.]

Ascend. Move upward. See ASCENT.

Be better, etc. Be improved, etc. See *Adjectives.*

Become better. Improve.

Be improved by. Be made better by.

Better. To improve the condition of.

Bolster up. To improve the condition of by propping up or encouraging.

Bring forward. Promote; advance.

Bring on. Cause to begin.

Brighten up. Improve by polishing.

Brush up. Improve; cleanse.

Come about. Change; improve.

Cook. To improve food by the agency of fire or heat.

Correct. To better by removing faults or errors; to set straight.

Cultivate. Better the soil by tillage; improve physical, mental, or moral condition.

Doctor, etc. Improve by applying remedies or by repairing, etc. See REMEDY.

Elaborate. Improve by working out into details.

Enhance. Better by increasing value or attractiveness.

Enrich. Improve by adorning or fertilizing.

Fatten. Make cattle ready for slaughter by feeding; better the soil by enriching.

Forward. Promote; further.

Foster, etc. Aid; encourage. See OBSTRUCTION-HELP

Fructify. Make fruitful.

Furbish up. Improve by brightening.

Get better. Improve.

Improve. Advance toward the better.

Improve upon. Better by amendments to or changes in.

Increase, etc. Grow larger or greater, etc. See INCREASE.

Infuse new blood into. Figurative for give life and strength to.

Invigorate. Improve by strengthening.

Lessen, etc., **an evil.** See INCREASE-DECREASE.

Make capital out of. Augment one's power or influence by taking advantage of anything.

Make corrections. Correct.

Make good use of. Use to the best advantage.

Make improvements, etc. Improve, etc. See Nouns.

Make the most of. Value highly; use completely.

Mature. Develop to completion.

Meliorate. Improve; better.

Mellow. To make mellow, as fruit; make perfect.

Mend. Repair; set right; improve.

Mitigate. Make less harsh; soften.

New model. Give a new and improved form to.

Palliate. Cloak; extenuate.

Pick up. Gradually improve.

Place to good account. Make good use of.

Polish. Make smooth; make polite; better by removing roughness and rudeness.

Profit by. Gain or improve by.

Promote. Advance; forward.

Prune. Improve by cutting off, as branches.

Purify, etc. Make clear; free from sin; etc. See CLEANNESS.

Put in order, etc. See ORGANIZATION.

Raise one's head. Figurative for improve.

Rally. Reunite; restore; revive.

Reap the benefit of. Receive the reward of.

Recover. Regain a former state or condition; restore See RENOVATION

Recruit. Furnish with fresh supplies.

Rectify. Set right; amend.

Refine upon. Improve in whatever constitutes excellence.

Reform. Change from worse to better; improve.

Refresh. Reinvigorate.

Relieve. Alleviate; lighten.

Remodel. Change the form so as to improve.

Render better. Improve.

Reorganize. Organize anew with a view to improvement.

Disorganization. The act of throwing into disorder.

Erosion. The act of wearing away, or the state of being worn away.

Falling off, etc. Decadence, etc. See *Verbs.*

Havoc. General destruction.

Impairment. The state of growing worse or being deteriorated.

Injury. Any wrong or hurt done to a person or thing.

Inquination. Pollution.

Loss. Damage; detriment; injury.

Marasmus. Wasting away of flesh when there is apparently no disease.

Moldiness. The state of being covered with any fungous growth.

Oxidation. The act of combining a compound with oxygen.

Outrage. Excessive injury; wanton mischief done to any person or thing.

Perversion. Deterioration from truth or right

Poisoning. Destroying with poison; corrupting.

Pollution. Deterioration from cleanness or purity.

Prostitution. The state of being devoted to lewdness; deterioration from chastity.

Recession. Retrocession; retrogression. See APPROACH - WITHDRAWAL.

Retrogradation, etc. Deterioration, etc. See ADVANCE-RETROGRESSION.

Retrogression. A going back; deterioration; degeneration.

Rottenness. The quality of being decayed.

Scath. Injury; harm; damage.

Venenation. Poisoning.

Vitiation. Depravation; corruption.

DETERIORATION—*Figurative Nouns.*

Dry-rot. The decay of timber; corruption of character.

Ebb. The falling of the tide; hence, a decreasing.

Honeycomb. The wax which encloses the honey.

Magni nominis umbra [L.]. [Lucan, *Pharsalia, i,* 135.] The shadow of a great name.

Mere wreck. Utter worthlessness.

Moth and rust. Anything which causes destruction. [Bible.]

Ravages of time. Wear and use caused by age.

Wane. The lessening of the moon; hence, a lessening.

Wear and tear. Destruction by use.

Wreck. A destruction.

DETERIORATION—*Nouns of Cause.*

Blight. That which blasts one's plans or hopes.

Canker. An ulcer producing corrosion; a disease peculiar to trees, which corrupts the bark and causes it to fall off

Inroad. A hostile attack producing disorganization.

Leaven. Any substance which produces fermentation.

Ravage. A violent action causing ruin or destruction.

DETERIORATION—*Verbs.*

Acerbate. To make worse by souring.

Adulterate. To deteriorate by mixing with baser ingredients.

Aggravate. Make worse or less tolerable.

Alloy. Form into an alloy; debase; deteriorate.

Become deteriorated, etc. Become worse in quality, etc See *Adjectives.*

Become worse. Deteriorate.

Be deteriorated, etc. Be worse in quality, etc. See *Adjectives.*

Be the worse for. Become less good for.

Be worse. Be less good.

Blemish. To make worse by deforming or defaming.

Blight. Blast; mar; ruin.

Break. Divide into parts by violence; destroy the utility of.

Break down. Fail; fail in health.

Break up. Separate into parts; scatter

Brutalize. Make or become beastly or inhuman.

Canker. Corrode; corrupt; deteriorate; eat as a canker.

Contaminate. Pollute by contact.

Corrode. Wear away gradually; impair

Corrupt. Deprave; make false; make worthless.

Crack. Deteriorate the value by splitting.

Cripple. Disable; render less useful.

Crumble. Deteriorate by falling into small pieces.

Damage. Harm; injure.

Damnify, etc. Injure; hurt; damage. See GOODNESS-BADNESS.

Deal a blow to. Injure; harm.

Debase. Degrade; depreciate.

Debauch. To make or become deteriorated in morals

Decay. Become rotten; deteriorate.

Decimate. Destroy a large part of; a tenth of.

Decline. Diminish; decay ; deteriorate.

Deface. Mar the face of; disfigure.

BETTERMENT—DETERIORATION—*Continued.*

BETTERMENT—Verbs—*Continued.*

Repair, etc.   Restore after decay, injury, etc.   See Renovation.
Review.   Examine to find the defects or excellences of.
Revise.   Improve by changes and corrections.
Ripen.   Mature; perfect.
Rub up.   Refresh one's memory.
Set off to advantage.   Adorn; embellish.
Sow one's wild oats.   To live a wild, reckless life.
Take a favorable turn.   Improve.
Think better of.   Improve one's opinion of.
Touch up.   Improve by touches.
Turn over a new leaf.   Change radically one's way of living.
Turn the corner.   Begin to improve.
Turn to best account. ⎫
Turn to good.   ⎬ Make profitable.
Turn to right.   ⎭
Vamp up.   Patch; repair.
View in a new light.   Consider from a new standpoint.
Warm up.   Improve in ardor; become animated.

Betterment—*Adjectives.*

All the better for.   Much improved for.
Better.   Preferable; improved in health.
Better advised.   Better informed.
Better for.   Improved for.
Better off.   In a better condition.
Corrigible.   That may be set right or amended.
Emendatory.   Relating to improvement.
Improvable.   That may be improved.
Improved, etc.   Bettered, etc.   See *Verbs.*
Improving, etc.   Growing better; turning to best account.
Progressive.   Improving.
Reformatory.   Tending to produce a change from worse to better.
Remedial, etc.   Corrective; affording a remedy.   See Remedy.
Reparatory, etc   Amending defects, etc.   See Renovation.

Betterment—*Adverbs.*

Ad melius inquirendum [L.].   After more thorough investigation.
On better advice.   After receiving further information.
On consideration.   After considering.
On reconsideration.   After reconsidering.
On second thoughts.   After thinking the matter over.

Betterment—*Phrase.*

Urbem lateritiam invenit, marmoream reliquit [L.].   He found the city brick, he (Augustus Cæsar) left it marble.

DETERIORATION—Verbs—*Continued from Column 2*

Prejudice.   Impair; injure.
Prostitute.   Apply to low or unworthy purposes.
Put back.   Delay; retard.
Rankle.   Fester or produce festering; inflame.
Ravage.   Lay waste; devastate; despoil.
Render vicious, etc.   See Virtue-Vice.
Retrograde.   Go backward; become worse.   See Advance-Retrogression.
Rot.   Corrupt; decay; decompose.
Run to seed.   Use up vitality in producing seed; figurative of to lose vital force.
Run to waste.   Become spoiled, useless or exhausted.
Rust.   To contract or become affected with rust; become useless from neglect or inaction.
Sap.   Undermine; weaken; destroy the foundation of.
Sap the foundations of.   Subvert by destroying the foundation of.
Scathe.   Harm severely; blast.
Scotch.   Cut slightly; chip.
Shake.   Weaken; render infirm.
Shend.   Injure; spoil; degrade.
Shrivel.   Wither.   See Enlargement-Diminution.
Sophisticate.   Make impure; adulterate.
Spoil.   Destroy the usefulness or value of; decay.
Spring a leak.   Begin to leak.
Stab.   Pierce with a pointed instrument, as a dagger; wound.
Stain, etc.   See Uncleanness.
Start.   Draw away the contents of; become dislocated.
Surbate.   To bruise; to fatigue.
Swale.   To waste away by melting; singe.
Sweal.   Scorch; swale; singe.
Taint.   Corrupt; infect; sully.
Tamper with.   Meddle with so as to injure.
Totter.   Waver.
Totter to its fall.   Stagger, threatening to fall.

DETERIORATION—Verbs—*Continued.*

Defile.   Make impure; pollute.
Deflower.   Take away the purity of.
Degenerate.   Become worse; deteriorate.
Degrade.   Debase; degenerate.
Demoralize.   Deteriorate in morals.
Denaturalize.   Make unnatural; deprive of citizenship.
Deprave.   Make bad or worse, especially in morals.
Despoil.   Deprive of by force; pillage.
Destroy.   Ruin; lay waste.   See Creation-Destruction.
Deteriorate.   Make or become worse; degenerate.
Die.   Lose life; expire.   See Life-Death.
Dilapidate.   Deteriorate like a stone wall; decay; fall into ruin.
Discolor.   Change the natural color of; put a false color on.
Disfigure.   Injure the form of; make worse in appearance.
Dismantle.   Divest of furniture and equipments.
Dismast.   Take away the mast or masts of.
Disorganize.   Throw into disorder; disarrange.
Do one's worst.   Put forth one's worst efforts.
Droop.   Let hang down; sink from lack of vigor or spirit; decline.
Ebb.   Fail; decline; recede, as the tide.
Embase.   Degrade; deteriorate.
Embitter.   Make bitter, sad, morose.
Empoison.   Make bitter; injure; deteriorate.
Envenom.   Poison; embitter.
Erode.   Eat away; corrode.
Exulcerate.   Corrode.
Fade.   Become indistinct; lose color, spirit, vigor.
Fall into decay.   Become corrupt; deteriorate.
"Fall into the sear and yellow leaf."   Wither.   [*Macbeth, V, i.*]
Fall off.   Deteriorate; depreciate.
Gnaw.   Waste away little by little; corrode.
Gnaw at the root of.   Eat away the root by slow degrees.
Go bad.   Go astray.
Go down, etc.   See Ascent-Descent.
Go down hill.   Get worse and worse.
Go farther and fare worse.   Go from bad to worse.
Go off.   Deteriorate; decline.
Go on from bad to worse.   Deteriorate.
Go to decay.   Become corrupt; deteriorate.
Hamstring.   Disable by cutting the tendons of the knee; hence incapacitate.
Harm.   Wrong; injure; damage.
Have seen better days.   Be in a deteriorated condition.
Hit between wind and water.   Injure at the load line, the danger-line of a ship.
Hough.   Disable; hamstring.
Hurt.   Harm; injure.
Impair.   Lessen in value or quantity.
Infect.   Corrupt; communicate infectious matter to.
Injure.   Harm; damage.
Inquinate.   Pollute; befoul.
Jump out of the frying pan into the fire.   Go from bad to worse.
Knock down.   Overthrow by a blow.
Labefy.   Impair; weaken.
Lame.   Make lame.
Lapse.   Deteriorate in moral conduct; slip from the right.
Leaven.   Ferment by the action of leaven; vitiate.
Maim.   Disable; impair.
Mangle.   Mutilate; make a blundering job of.
Mar.   Impair; injure.
Mine.   To ruin gradually and secretly.
Molder.   To crumble or waste away.
Mutilate.   Disfigure; maim.
Overrun.   Ravage; infest.
Perish.   Die; decay.   See Creation-Destruction.
Pervert.   Corrupt; turn from its proper use.
Pierce.   Penetrate; make an opening into.
Pillage.   Plunder; strip.   See Theft.
Play havoc among.   Spread destruction among.
Play havoc with.   Lay waste; destroy.
Play sad havoc among.
Play sad havoc with.
Play the deuce among.   Euphemistic for play the devil among.
Play the deuce with.   Euphemistic for play the devil with.
Play the mischief among. ⎫
Play the mischief with.   ⎬ Do much harm; throw into disorder.
Play the very devil among. ⎫
Play the very devil with. ⎬ Injure extremely.
Poison.   Administer poison to; corrupt; prejudice.
Pollute.   Corrupt; defile.

(*Continued on Column 1.*)

DETERIORATION—Verbs—*Continued*.

Undermine. To ruin secretly or stealthily.
Vitiate. Impair; contaminate.
Wane, etc. Decline gradually. See INCREASE-DECREASE.
Warp. Turn from its true path; deviate.
Waste. Use unnecessarily; squander; make desolate.

Weaken. Enfeeble; lessen in strength. See STRENGTH-WEAKNESS.
Wear away. Impair or destroy gradually; consume.
Wear out. Make useless; consume the strength of.
Wither. Deteriorate for want of moisture; blight; languish.
Wound. Hurt with violence; cause grief to.

DETERIORATION—*Adjectives*.

All the worse for. Injured on account of.
Altered. Changed.
Altered for the worse. Changed so as to be worse than before.
At a low ebb. In a low condition.
Battered. Beaten so as to be bruised or deteriorated.
Blighted. Blasted; marred.
Broken down. Enfeebled; dilapidated.
Cankered. Affected with canker; ill-natured.
Crumbling. Falling into decay or ruin; deteriorating.
Decayed, etc. Deteriorated as to physical or social condition; rotten, etc. See *Verbs*.
Deciduous. Falling off; subject to be shed periodically.
Decrepid. } Worn out; enfeebled.
Decrepit. }
Degenerate. Deteriorated in worth or goodness.
Deleterious, etc. Hurtful; pernicious. See GOODNESS-BADNESS.
Depraved, etc. Morally corrupt. See VIRTUE-VICE.
Deteriorated, etc. Having become worse, etc. See *Verbs*.
Dilapidated. Decayed; partially ruined.
Discolored. Altered in color; stained.
Done for. Tired out; destroyed.
Done up. Exhausted.
Effete. Not able to produce any longer; exhausted; sterile.
Faded. Deteriorated in color, freshness or brightness.
Far gone. Very much deteriorated.
Fatigued. Worn out; tired. See ENTERTAINMENT-WEARINESS.
Fit for the dust hole. Valueless; useless.
Fit for the waste-paper basket. Valueless; useless.
Imperfect. Defective. See FAULTLESSNESS-FAULTINESS.
In a bad way. Badly situated.
Injured, etc. Damaged; hurt; harmed. See *Verbs*.
Mildewed. Tainted with mildew.
Moldering. Crumbling into small pieces.
Moldy. Covered over with or containing mold.
Moss-grown. Grown over with moss.
Moth-eaten. Eaten by moths.
Nodding to its fall. See CREATION-DESTRUCTION.
On one's last legs. On the brink of ruin.
On the decline. Declining; deteriorating.
On the wane. Decreasing.
Out of repair. In bad condition.
Out of tune. Discordant; inharmonious.

Passé [F.]. Faded.
Past cure, etc. See SANGUINENESS-HOPELESSNESS.
Past work, etc. See USEFULNESS-USELESSNESS.
Reduced. Diminished in size, value, etc.
Reduced to a skeleton. Fleshless; emaciated.
Retrograde. Declining toward a worse state. See ADVANCE-RETROGRESSION.
Rotten. Decomposed naturally; putrid.
Rusty. Covered with rust; deteriorated from disuse.
Second-hand. Not new; of inferior grade.
Seedy. Like a plant run to seed; shabby.
Shabby. Ragged; paltry; despicable.
Shaken. Injured, as by a shock.
Spoiling, etc. Corrupting, etc. See *Verbs*.
Spotted. Stained with spots.
Sprung. Strained, cracked, so as to be useless.
Stale. Deteriorated from standing.
Tabid. Deteriorated gradually by the complaint called tabes.
Tainted. Deteriorated by being imbued with something odious, harmful or poisonous.
Time-worn. Worn out or deteriorated by time.
Tottering, etc. See SECURITY-INSECURITY.
The worse for. Impaired by.
The worse for wear. Impaired or deteriorated by wear.
Threadbare. Worn out to the threads.
Undermined. Secretly deteriorated.
Unimproved, etc. See BETTERMENT.
Used up. Consumed; exhausted.
Wasted. Needlessly deteriorated.
Weather-beaten. Deteriorated by exposure to the weather.
Weathered. Worn away by exposure to the atmosphere.
Wilted. Deteriorated by exposure to heat.
Withering. Tending to fade or wilt.
Worm-eaten. Deteriorated by being eaten by worms.
Worn. Deteriorated; impaired.
Worn out. Wholly deteriorated.
Worn to a shadow. }
Worn to a thread. }
Worn to rags. } Expressions denoting degrees of deterioration.
Worn to the stump. }
Worse. Less good. }

DETERIORATION—*Phrases*.

Aegrescit medendo [L.]. The remedy is worse than the disease.

Out of the frying pan into the fire. From bad to worse.

bet'-ting. Laying as a wager. PURPOSE-LUCK.
bet'-ting–house". Place for gambling. PURPOSE-LUCK.
bet'-ting–ring". Place for staking money. PURPOSE-LUCK.
be-tween'. In the middle. ENVIRONMENT-INTERPOSITION; **between ourselves,** ENLIGHTENMENT-SECRECY; **between two fires,** SECURITY-INSECURITY; **far between,** "like angels' visits," [Campbell], ENVIRONMENT-INTERPOSITION; **vibrate between two extremes,** MUTABILITY-STABILITY.
be-twixt'. Between. ENVIRONMENT-INTERPOSITION.
bev'-el. Slanting. PARALLELISM-INCLINATION.
be'-ver. A lunch between meals. NUTRIMENT-EXCRETION.
bev'-er-age. Drink. NUTRIMENT-EXCRETION.
be-vue'. Error. SUCCESS-FAILURE.
bev'-y. A flock of birds. GATHERING-SCATTERING, MULTIPLICITY-PAUCITY.
be-wail'. To lament. CONTENTEDNESS-REGRET, JUBILATION-LAMENTATION.
be-ware'. To be cautious. WARNING.
be-wil'-der. Puzzle. ASTONISHMENT-EXPECTANCE, CERTAINTY-DOUBT, HEED-DISREGARD.
be-wil'-der-ment. Entanglement. ASTONISHMENT-EXPECTANCE, KNOWLEDGE-IGNORANCE, CERTAINTY-DOUBT.

be-witch'. Charm. DEVOTION-MAGIC, LOVE-HATE, MOTIVE-CAPRICE, PLEASURABLENESS-PAINFULNESS.
be-witch'-ery. Fascination. DEVOTION-MAGIC.
be-witch'-ing. Charming. PLEASURABLENESS-PAINFULNESS.
bey. A Turkish governor. CHIEF-UNDERLING.
be-yond'. On the further side; surpassing. REMOTENESS-NEARNESS, SUPREMACY-SUBORDINACY; **beyond compare,** MAGNITUDE-SMALLNESS, SUPREMACY-SUBORDINACY; **beyond control,** POSSIBILITY-IMPOSSIBILITY; **beyond expression,** MAGNITUDE-SMALLNESS; **beyond hope,** SUCCESS-FAILURE, WELFARE-MISFORTUNE; **beyond measure,** EXCESS-LACK; **beyond one's depth,** CLEARNESS-OBSCURITY, DEEPNESS-SHALLOWNESS, VIGOR-INERTIA; **beyond one's grasp,** POSSIBILITY-IMPOSSIBILITY; **beyond possibility,** POSSIBILITY-IMPOSSIBILITY; **beyond praise,** APPROVAL-DISAPPROVAL, FAULTLESSNESS-FAULTINESS, VIRTUE-VICE; **beyond price,** COSTLINESS-CHEAPNESS; **beyond question,** CERTAINTY-DOUBT; **beyond reason,** POSSIBILITY-IMPOSSIBILITY; **beyond remedy,** SANGUINENESS-HOPELESSNESS; **beyond seas,** CONSTITUENT-ALIEN; **beyond the mark,** EXCESS-LACK, TRANSCURSION-SHORTCOMING; **go beyond,** TRANSCURSION-SHORTCOMING.

bi'-as. Weight on one side; partiality. AFFECTION, DECISION-MISJUDGMENT, INCLINATION, PARALLELISM-INCLINATION, SAGACITY-INCAPACITY.

bib. A cloth worn under the chin; tipple. DRESS-UNDRESS, TEETOTALISM-INTEMPERANCE.

bi-ba'-cious. Given to drinking. TEETOTALISM-INTEMPERANCE.

bib'-ber. An habitual drinker. JUBILATION-LAMENTATION, TEETOTALISM-INTEMPERANCE.

bib'-ble-bab''-ble. Prating. TALKATIVENESS-TACITURNITY.

bibendum est nunc [L.] (bi-ben'-dum est nunc). Now is the time for drinking. TEETOTALISM-INTEMPERANCE.

Bi'-ble. The sacred Scriptures. ASSERTION-DENIAL, REVELATION-PSEUDOREVELATION.

bib'-lic-al. Pertaining to the Bible. REVELATION-PSEUDO-REVELATION.

bib''-li-og''-ra-phy. A history of books. MISSIVE-PUBLICATION.

bib''-li-ol'-a-try. Book worship. DEVOTION-IDOLATRY, KNOWLEDGE-IGNORANCE, ORTHODOXY-HETERODOXY.

bib''-li-ol'-o-gy. Biblical literature; a treatise on books. MISSIVE-PUBLICATION.

bib'-li-o-man''-cy. Divination by Bible verses. PROPHECY.

bib''-lio-ma'-ni-a. Book madness. KNOWLEDGE-IGNORANCE.

bib''-lio-ma'-ni-ac. One who has a rage for possessing old books. SCHOLAR-DUNCE.

bib''-li-o-pole. A bookseller. MISSIVE-PUBLICATION.

bib''-li-op'-o-list. A bookseller. MISSIVE-PUBLICATION.

bib''-li-o-the'-ca. A library. MISSIVE-PUBLICATION.

bib'-u-lous. Apt to drink. NUTRIMENT-EXCRETION.

bice. A blue or green pigment. BLUENESS-ORANGE.

bi'-cen-ten''-ni-al. A fiftieth anniversary. PERIODICITY-IRREGULARITY.

bi'-ceps. A muscle of the arm. ANATOMY.

bick'-er. A petty dispute. AGITATION, VARIANCE-ACCORD.

bi-col'-or. Two colors. VARIEGATION.

bi-con'-ju-gate. Half conjugate. DOUBLING-HALVING.

bi-cus'-pid. Double-pointed. DOUBLING-HALVING.

bi'-cy-cle. A two-wheeled vehicle. CONVEYANCE-VESSEL.

bid. To offer; to command. ORDER, PROFFER-REFUSAL; **bid a long farewell,** QUEST-ABANDONMENT; **bid defiance,** DEFIANCE; **bid fair,** INCLINATION, LIKELIHOOD-UNLIKELIHOOD, PROPHECY, SANGUINENESS-HOPELESSNESS; **bid for,** EXCHANGE, PETITION-EXPOSTULATION, PROFFER-REFUSAL, PURPOSE-LUCK, **bid the banns,** MATRIMONY-CELIBACY.

bid'-der. One who bids. PETITIONER.

bide. To dwell. EARLINESS-LATENESS, EXCITABILITY-INEXCITABILITY, MUTATION-PERMANENCE; **bide one's time,** EXPECTATION-DISAPPOINTMENT, ACTION-PASSIVENESS, EARLINESS-LATENESS, EXPECTATION-SURPRISE.

bi-det'. A small horse. CONVEYER.

bien perdu, bien connu [F.] (bî-an·' per-dü', bî-an·' con-nü·'). Blessing flown is blessing known. OPPORTUNENESS-UNSUITABLENESS.

bien sans peine, nul [F.] (bî-an·' san· pên, nül). No good without pain. PLEASURABLENESS-PAINFULNESS.

bi-en'-ni-al. Occurring every two years. FAUNA-FLORA, PERIODICITY-IRREGULARITY.

bien''-se-ance'. Decorum. POLITENESS-IMPOLITENESS, SOCIETY-LUDICROUSNESS.

bier. A coffin. LIFE-FUNERAL.

bi-fa'-cial. Double-faced. DOUBLING-HALVING.

bi-fa'-ri-ous. Living on two substances. DOUBLING-HALVING.

bi'-fid. Two cleft. DOUBLING-HALVING.

bi'-fold. Two-fold. DOUBLING-HALVING.

bi'-form. Two-form. DOUBLING-HALVING.

bi-form'-i-ty. Doubleness of form. DUALITY.

bi-fur'-cate. Two-forked. ANGULARITY, DOUBLING-HALVING.

bi-fur'-ca-ted. Having two forks. DOUBLING-HALVING.

bi-fur-ca'-tion. Division into two branches. COVER-LINING, DOUBLING-HALVING.

bi-fur'-cous. Forked. DOUBLING-HALVING.

big. Large; fruitful. ENLARGEMENT-DIMINUTION, GREATNESS-LITTLENESS, MAGNITUDE-SMALLNESS; **big sounding,** LOUDNESS-FAINTNESS, SIMPLICITY-FLORIDNESS, SOCIETY-AFFECTATION; **big swoln,** ENLARGEMENT-DIMINUTION; **big with,** CREATION-DESTRUCTION; **big with the fate of,** PROPHECY; **look big,** DEFIANCE, PRESUMPTION-OBSEQUIOUSNESS, SELF-RESPECT-HUMBLENESS; **talk big,** AMITY-HOSTILITY, CHARITABLENESS-MENACE, PRESUMPTION-OBSEQUIOUSNESS.

big'-a-mist. One guilty of bigamy. MATRIMONY-CELIBACY.

big'-a-my. The crime of having two wives or husbands at once. MATRIMONY-CELIBACY.

big'-gin. A little pitcher. CONTENTS-RECEIVER.

bight. A small bay; the coil of a rope. GULF-LAKE.

big'-ness. Largeness. GREATNESS-LITTLENESS.

big'-ot. One unreasonably devoted to a party or creed. BIGOTRY-APOSTASY, CERTAINTY-DOUBT, DECISION-MISJUDGMENT, GODLINESS-UNGODLINESS, ORTHODOXY-HETERODOXY, PATRIOTISM-TREASON.

big'-ot-ed. Stubbornly attached to a cause or creed. BIGOTRY-APOSTASY, GODLINESS-UNGODLINESS, ORGANIZATION-DISORGANIZATION, ORTHODOXY-HETERODOXY.

big'-ot-ry. Obstinate attachment to a cause or creed. BIGOTRY-APOSTASY, CREDULOUSNESS-SKEPTICISM, GODLINESS-UNGODLINESS, ORGANIZATION-DISORGANIZATION, ORTHODOXY-HETERODOXY.

BIGOTRY—APOSTASY.

Bigotry. Obstinate and unreasonable attachment to a cause or creed.

Contumacy. Proud, insolent defiance of authority.

Dogmatism. Uncompromising or arrogant assertion.

Fanaticism. Extravagant or irrational zeal.

Immovability. Unchangeableness.

Indocility. Unteachableness.

Infatuation. Extravagant or irrational passion.

Inflexibility. Unyielding stiffness; obstinacy. See HARDNESS.

Intolerance. Illiberality; bigotry.

Monomania. Unreasonable pursuit of one idea.

Obduracy. Stubbornness.

Obduration. Obstinacy.

Obstinacy. Unreasonable adherence to an opinion

Obstinateness. Persistent and unreasonable resolution. See *Adjectives.*

Abjuration. Solemn rejection or repudiation.

Abjurement. Renunciation.

Afterthought. Reflection after an act.

Apostasy. Desertion of one's faith, principles, or party.

Backsliding. Falling back into sin or error.

Change of intention. Alteration of intention.

Change of mind. Alteration of mind.

Change of purpose. Alteration of purpose.

Coquetry. Trifling in love.

Defection. Abandoning of a person or cause to which one is bound by duty or allegiance. See ABANDONMENT.

Disavowal. Denial of anything. See DENIAL.

Going over, etc. See *Verbs.*

Palinode. An ode retracting a former one; retraction.

Palinody. See PALINODE.

Recantation. Disavowal of an opinion previously held.

BIGOTRY—APOSTASY—*Continued.*

Opiniativeness.
Opiniatry. } Determination to express one's opinions regardless of others.
Perseverance. Persistence in purpose and effort.
Pervicacity.
Pervicacy. } Obstinacy.
Resolution. Steadiness and firmness.
Self-will. Stubbornness; obstinacy.
Tenacity. Stubbornness; adhesiveness.
Zealotry. Immoderate partizanship.

BIGOTRY—*Associated Nouns.*

Blind side A nature which is unable to heed or endure the opinions of others, or the approach of danger.
Dogged resolution. Sullen or obstinate determination.
Fixed idea. Determination regarding.
Mule. An animal noted for its stubbornness; hence, a stubborn person.
Old school. A member of a class of persons opposed to change in ideas.
Ruling passion. An influence or power which controls or regulates one's thoughts or deeds. "Strong in death" [Pope].

BIGOTRY—*Nouns of Agent.*

Bigot. Unreasonable devotee of a party or creed.
Dogmatist. One who asserts positively without proof.
Enthusiast. One who imagines himself filled with some particular revelation; a zealot.
Fanatic. One filled with unreasonable zeal.
Opinator.
Opinionator. } One who is dogged in his own opinion.
Opinionationist.
Opinionist. } One who is conceited in his own opinions.
Stickler. An obstinate contender.
Zealot. An immoderate partizan.

BIGOTRY—*Verbs.*

Be obstinate, etc. See *Adjectives.*
Be wedded to an opinion. To be obstinate in an opinion.
Die hard. Not to give up easily.
Fight against destiny. To fight against what cannot be overcome.
Fly in the face of facts. To be unreasonably opinionated.
Have one's own way. To be stubborn, See VOLITION.
Have the last word. To insist on anything with great zeal.
Hug a belief. To insist irrationally upon a belief or doctrine.
Insist on having the last word. Argue to the end.
Not to yield an inch. Not to give way.
Opiniate. To persist.
Persist. To adhere firmly to an opinion. See PERSISTENCE.
Stand out. To continue in opposition.
Stickle. To contend about matters of slight importance.
Take no denial. Persist.

BIGOTRY—*Adjectives.*

Arbitrary. Despotic; fixed; obstinate.
Bigoted. Obstinate and unreasonable.
Case-hardened. Made callous to outside influences.
Contumacious. Rebellious; stubborn.
Cross-grained. Perverse; hard to persuade.
Deaf to advice. Stubborn.
Dogged. Obdurate; persistent like a dog.
Dogmatic. Arrogant; positively sure.
Entêté [F.]. Obstinate; headstrong.
Hard-mouthed. Having a hard mouth like a horse; therefore not easily controlled.
Headstrong. Insisting upon one's own way; stubborn.
Heady. Headstrong.
Hidebound. Narrow minded; fixed in one's opinions.
Immovable. Not to be moved.
Impersuasible. Not to be persuaded.
Impervious. Impenetrable.
Impervious to reason. Unreasonable; stubborn.
Impracticable. Difficult to get along with, unreasonable, headstrong.
Incorrigible. Not to be corrected.
Inert. Without the power to move; slow. See VIGOR-INERTIA.
Infatuated. Unreasonably filled with a desire for something.
Inflexible. Not to be turned from an opinion. See HARDNESS.
Intractable. Unruly, not easily controlled.
Mulish. Like a mule in stubbornness.
Not to be moved. Intractable.
Obdurate. Inexorable, unyielding.
Obstinate. Irrationally persistent in one's opinions.
Obstinate as a mule. Stubborn as a mule.
Perverse. Unreasonable; wilfully intractable.
Pervicacious. Very obstinate or stubborn.

Redintegratio amoris [L.]. Renewal of love.
Renunciation. Formal rejection or declination.
Repentance. Sorrow for something one has done or omitted to do. See REPENTANCE.
Retractation. } The act of recalling something which has been done
Retraction. } or said.
Reversal. The act of turning back.
Revocation.
Revokement. } The act of calling back a thing granted.
Tergiversation. Fickleness; the act of turning back.
Vacillation. Irresolution; unsteadiness of opinion. See DETERMINATION-VACILLATION.
Withdrawal. The act of taking back an assertion.

APOSTASY—*Nouns of Agent.*

Ambidexter. A double-dealer.
Apostate. One who has fallen away from his faith or belief.
Backslider. One who has returned to his former evil practises.
Convert. One who has been turned from his old belief.
Deserter. One who forsakes a duty, party, cause, or friend, or any one to whom he owes service.
Janus. A Latin deity represented with two faces looking in opposite directions; hence, a deceiver.
Pervert. One who has turned to error, especially in religion.
Proselyte. A convert to some religion or religious sect.
Rat. One who deserts his party or associates.
Renegade. One faithless to principle or party.
Time-pleaser. } One who complies with prevailing opinions whatever
Time-server. } they may be.
Timist. A time-server.
Trimmer. A time-server.
Turncoat.
Turntippet. } A renegade; deserter.
Vicar of Bray. Rev. Simon Alleyn, or one like him. He was Vicar through four reigns (Henry VIII — Elizabeth), papist twice, Protestant twice.
Weathercock. Fickle, inconstant person. See MUTABILITY-STABILITY.

APOSTASY—*Verbs.*

Abjure. Renounce upon oath.
Apostatize. Forsake one's faith.
Back out of. Retreat from an opinion or position.
Blow hot and cold. To appear to be in favor of both sides of a question, be inconsistent.
Box the compass. To go over the points of the compass in order and backwards.
Change from one side to another.
Change one's—intention,—mind,—note,—purpose.
Change sides. Change one's party.
Come back to one's first love. To return to one's first opinions.
Come,—over,—round—to an opinion.
Coquet. To trifle with.
Draw in one's horns. To restrain one's ardor.
Eat one's words. Retract.
Eat the leek. [Welsh.] To retract.
Flinch. To retreat in time of danger.
Forswear. To renounce, repudiate.
Go over from one side to another.
Go to the right about. To change one's opinion.
Go upon another tack. To follow another belief.
Hold with the hare, but run with the hounds. To wish to serve both sides; be inconsistent; be undecided.
Nager entre deux eaux [F.]. Swim between two waters; be undecided.
Pass from one side to another.
Play fast and loose. To try to serve both sides of a question.
Rat. To desert one's party, as rats a falling house.
Recall. To revoke.
Recant. To withdraw from a former opinion.
Renounce. To forswear; refuse to acknowledge.
Rescind. To cancel; repeal. See COMMISSION-ABROGATION.
Retrace one's steps. To go back; retract.
Retract. To withdraw from an opinion.
Return to one's first love. Return to one's first opinion.
Revoke. To make void by repealing.
Shift one's ground. To vacillate.
Shuffle. To change one's position; shift one's ground.
Skip from one side to another. To change one's position or ideas upon a subject.

BIGOTRY—APOSTASY—*Continued.*

BIGOTRY—Adjectives—*Continued.*

Pig-headed. Stupidly obstinate.
Positive. Certain of one's opinions.
Prejudiced. Biased.
Prepossessed. Biased; prejudiced.
Refractory. Not easy to control.
Restiff. } Recalcitrant; stubborn.
Restive. }
Resty. Restive.
Self-willed. Headstrong; stubborn.
Stiff-backed, -hearted, -necked. Not easily bent, stubborn.
Stubborn. Inflexible; opinionated.
Sulky. Morose; sullen.
Sullen. Untractable; obstinate.
Tenacious. Holding fast to.
Unaffected. Not to be moved in the feelings.
Unchangeable. Not to be turned away from one's opinions.
Uninfluenced. Not influenced.
Unmoved. Not moved.
Unpersuadible. Not to be persuaded.
Unruly. Not to be governed.
Untractable. Not easily ruled.
Unyielding. Not giving way.
Wayward. Disobedient.
Wilful. Determined to have one's own way.

BIGOTRY—Adverbs.

Obstinately, etc. Stubbornly; in an obstinate manner, etc. See *Adjectives.*

BIGOTRY—Phrases.

Ils n'ont rien appris ni rien oublié [F.]. They have learned nothing and forgotten nothing.
Non possumus [L.]. We cannot.
No surrender. Not to give up.

APOSTASY—Verbs—*Continued.*

Swallow the leek. Retract.
Swerve. To turn from any course or principle.
Think better of it. To hold in greater esteem.
Trim. To regulate one's conduct by the popular will.
Turn a *pirouette.* To turn a somersault; change sides completely.
Turn around. Change about.
Turn over a new leaf, etc. To repent, etc. See REPENTANCE-OBDURACY.
Unsay. To retract what one has said.
Veer around. Wheel about.
Wait to see how the—cat jumps,—wind blows. To bide one's time in making a decision.
Wheel around. To change entirely in one's opinions.
Withdraw from. To retract.

APOSTASY—Adjectives.

Ambidextrous. Two-sided, double-faced, with two right hands.
Changeful. Given to alteration. See MUTABILITY.
Coquetting, etc. Trifling, etc. See *Verbs.*
Ductile. Easily led.
Irresolute. Indecisive; hesitating. See DETERMINATION-VACILLATION.
Reactionary. Pertaining to the tendency to return to a former state.
Revocatory. Rescinding.
Slippery as an eel. Ready to use evasions.
Time-serving. Servile; complying with ruling powers.
Trimming. Fluctuating

APOSTASY—Phrase.

"A change came o'er the spirit of my dream." [Byron.]

big'-wig". A person of importance. GENTILITY-COMMONALTY, SAGE-FOOL, SCHOLAR-DUNCE.
bi"-jou'. A jewel. BEAUTY-UGLINESS, EMBELLISHMENT-DISFIGUREMENT, GOODNESS-BADNESS.
bil'-an-der. A small two-masted vessel. CONVEYANCE-VESSEL.
bi-lat'-er-al. Two-sided. DOUBLING-HALVING, LATERALITY-CONTRAPOSITION.
bil'-bo. A sword; a fetter. WEAPON.
bil'-boes. Fetters. RELEASE-PRISON; **put into bilboes,** RELEASE-RESTRAINT.
bile. A liquor secreted by the liver. FAVORITE-ANGER.
bilge. To cause to bulge; the flat part of a ship's bottom. APERTURE-CLOSURE, CONVEXITY-CONCAVITY, TOP-BOTTOM; **bilge-water,** CLEANNESS-FILTHINESS.
bil'-ious. Suffering from disordered condition of the liver. LIGHTHEARTEDNESS-DEJECTION.
bilk. Cheat. EXPECTATION-DISAPPOINTMENT, THEFT, TRUTHFULNESS-FRAUD.
bill. Beak of a bird; an account of debt. ACCOUNTS, DESIGN, LITIGATION, MISSIVE-PUBLICATION, MONEY, PRICE-DISCOUNT, PUBLICITY, RECORD, SECURITY, SHARPNESS-BLUNTNESS, SIGN, WEAPON; **bill and coo,** BLANDISHMENT; **bill of exchange,** MONEY, SECURITY; **bill of fare,** DESIGN, NUTRIMENT-EXCRETION, RECORD; **bill of indictment,** JUSTIFICATION-CHARGE; **bill of sale,** SECURITY; **bills of mortality,** LIFE-DEATH; **true bill,** LITIGATION.
bil'-let. Ornament. ARCHITECTURE.
bil'-let. To quarter soldiers. ASSIGNMENT, ESTABLISHMENT-REMOVAL, SIGN.
billet [F.] (bil-ê). A letter. MISSIVE-PUBLICATION.
billet-doux [F.] (bil"-ê-du'). A brief love-letter. BLANDISHMENT, MISSIVE-PUBLICATION.
bill'-head". A heading on paper used for making out bills. SIGN.
bill'-hook". A hook for bills. SHARPNESS-BLUNTNESS.
bil'-liard. A game. **Billiard-ball,** ROUNDNESS; **billiard-room,** CONTENTS-RECEIVER; **billiard-table,** ERECTNESS-FLATNESS.

bil'-liards. A game. ENTERTAINMENT-WEARINESS.
bil'-lings-gate". [A gate of London by the fish-market.] Vulgar language. CHARITABLENESS-CURSE, WORD-NEOLOGY.
bil'-lion. According to the English, a million millions; to the French, a thousand millions. FIVE-QUINQUESECTION.
bil'-low. A great wave. RIVER-WIND, OCEAN-LAND.
bil'-ly. A short club. ATTACK-DEFENSE, WEAPON.
bil'-ly-cock. A felt hat. DRESS-UNDRESS.
bil'-ly-goat. A he-goat. MALE-FEMALE.
bin. A box for holding. CONTENTS-RECEIVER.
bi'-na-ry. Double. DUALITY; **binary stars,** ASTRONOMY.
bind. To tie; to confine. COERCION, COVER-LINING, DUTY-DERELICTION, TERMS, UNION-DISUNION; **bind hand and foot,** RELEASE-RESTRAINT; **bind oneself,** ENGAGEMENT-RELEASE; **bind over,** COERCION; **bind up wounds,** RENOVATION-RELAPSE.
bine. A climbing stem of a plant. FAUNA-FLORA.
bin-oc'-u-lar. Having two eyes. OPTICAL INSTRUMENTS.
bi-no'-mi-al. Having two names. DUALITY.
bi"-o-gen'-e-sis. The doctrine that life is generated from living beings only. BIOLOGY, CREATION-DESTRUCTION.
bi-og"-ra-pher. Writer of lives. ACCOUNT, RECORDER.
bi-og'-ra-phy. A history of one's life and character. ACCOUNT.
bi-ol'-o-gy. The science of life. BIOLOGY, LIFE-DEATH, ORGANIZATION-DISORGANIZATION.

BIOLOGY.

BIOLOGY—*Associated Words*

Abiogenesis. Spontaneous generation.
Absorption. The taking up of food into the circulation.
Accretion. The growing together of parts normally separate.
Anatomy. Science of the structure of organisms.
Antherozoid. Male fecundating body in lowest plant life.
Assimilation. The changing of digested nutriment into the tissues and fluids of the body.
Atrophy. Stoppage of the growth of an organ.
Bacteria. Microscopic organisms, some of which cause diseases.

Biogenesis. Generation of life from living beings.

Cell. Smallest element of an organized body manifesting independent activity.

Conjugation. Union of cells or individuals for reproduction.

Digestion. The process of changing food so that it can be assimilated by the body.

Embryo. The undeveloped germ of an organism.

Excretion. The process of getting rid of waste matter in the body.

Fermentation. Decomposition of an organic compound caused by living organisms.

Fertilization. Process of the male element combining with the female.

Function. The action of an organ of the body.

Gemination. Duplication.

Germination. The sprouting of a seed, etc.

Hermaphrodite. An individual having the generative organs of both sexes.

Heterogamy. Alternating of sexual and parthenogenetic generation.

Histology. Microscopic anatomy.

Ingestion. Act of taking into the stomach.

Larva. The state of an animal in which a metamorphosis takes place before assuming the mature form.

Metabolism. Process of building and destruction of cells.

Metamorphosis. Change in form.

Metogenesis. The production of sexes by nonsexual means.

Molecule. Smallest part of a substance that can exist separately.

Monad. A primary element, changeless and indivisible.

Monogenesis. The opposite of metogenesis.

Morphology. Science of organic forms.

Nutrition. Process of promoting growth and replenishing the waste matter in living organisms.

Ontogeny. History of the development of the individual.

Oogenesis. Origin and development of the ovum.

Ovary. Organ of the female producing parts essential for generation.

Ovum. The cell in an ovary from which a new individual is produced.

Oxidation. The process of uniting something with oxygen.

Parthenogenesis. Production without the intervention of the male element.

Phylogeny. History of the development of a species.

Physiology. Science of the functions of the organs of the body.

Polymorphism. The condition of several forms of structure existing in the same species.

Protoplasm. Semi-liquid forming the principal portion of a cell.

Protozoa. A primary division, consisting of organisms of a single cell.

Putrefaction. Decaying of animal or vegetable matter.

Reproduction. The process of an animal or plant producing another of its kind.

Secretion. The process of taking from the blood or sap materials which are changed into new substances.

Spermary. Generative gland of the male.

Spermatozoon. Essential fertilizing element of the male.

Sterilization. Process of destroying bacteria; rendering barren.

Teratology. Science of abnormal growths.

bip'-a-rous. Twin-like. DUALITY.

bi-par'-tite. Two parted. DOUBLING-HALVING.

bi''-par-ti'-tion. Result of division into two parts. DOUBLING-HALVING.

bi''-plic'-i-ty. Doubleness. DUALITY.

bi-quad'-rate. A fourth power. QUADRUPLICATION-QUADRISECTION.

birch. A tree. EXCULPATION-PUNITION; **birch rod,** RECOMPENSE-SCOURGE.

bird. A feathered flying animal. **A little bird told me,** ENLIGHTENMENT-SECRECY; **bird in hand,** HOLDING-EXEMPTION, KEEPING-RELINQUISHMENT; **bird of ill omen,** PORTENT, SANGUINENESS-HOPELESSNESS, WARNING; **bird of passage,** WAYFARER-SEAFARER; **bird's-eye view,** APPEARANCE-DISAPPEARANCE, SIGHT-BLINDNESS; **birds of a feather,** LIKENESS-UNLIKENESS; **kill two birds with one stone,** ACTIVITY-INDOLENCE; **the bird has flown,** ESCAPE, PRESENCE-ABSENCE.

bird'-cage. DOMESTICATION-AGRICULTURE.

bird'-lime''. A bird bait. CONNECTIVE, TRUTHFULNESS-FRAUD.

bi-ret'-ta. Red cap worn by a cardinal. VESTMENTS.

bir'-law. Local custom. LAW-LAWLESSNESS.

birr. To make a whirring noise. SOUND-SILENCE.

bir'-rus. A hooded storm-cloak. DRESS-UNDRESS.

birth. The act of being born. BEGINNING-END, CREATION - DESTRUCTION, GENTILITY-COMMONALTY, PARENTAGE - PROGENY ; **birthday-suit,** DRESS - UNDRESS; **birthplace,** CAUSE-EFFECT; **birthright,** DUENESS-UNDUENESS.

birth'-day''. The anniversary of one's birth. PERIODICITY-IRREGULARITY.

birth'-mark''. A spot or stain on the body from birth. EMBELLISHMENT-DISFIGUREMENT.

bis. Twice. APPROVAL-DISAPPROVAL, RECURRENCE.

biscuits, s'embarquer sans [F.] (bis-cwî', san'-bar-kê' san'). To go to sea without biscuit. PREPARATION-NONPREPARATION.

bise. A cold northerly wind. RIVER-WIND.

bi-sect'. Divide into two parts. DOUBLING-HALVING.

bi-sec'-ted. Two-fold division. DOUBLING-HALVING.

bi-sec'-tion. The act of bisecting. DOUBLING-HALVING, MIDDLE.

bish'-op. The head of a diocese. MINISTRY-LAITY, NUTRIMENT-EXCRETION; **bishop's palace,** FANE; **bishop's purple,** YELLOWNESS-PURPLE.

bish'-op-dom. Episcopate. CHURCH.

bish'-op-ric. A diocese; the office of a bishop. CHURCH.

bis'-muth. Kind of metal. CHEMISTRY.

bisque. Biscuit. NUTRIMENT-EXCRETION.

bis-sex'-tile year. Leap-year. ASTRONOMY.

bis'-tou-ry. A knife used in surgery. SHARPNESS-BLUNTNESS.

bis'-tre. A brown pigment. GRAY-BROWN.

bi-sul'-cate. Two-grooved. GROOVE.

bi-sul'-cous. Two-furrowed. GROOVE.

bit. A tool for boring; a check; a small quantity. MAGNITUDE-SMALLNESS, RELEASE-PRISON, WHOLE-PART; **bit between the teeth,** REPRISAL-RESISTANCE; **bit by bit,** QUANTITY-MEASURE, SWIFTNESS-SLOWNESS, UNIVERSALITY-PARTICULARITY, WHOLE-PART.

bitch. A she-dog. MALE-FEMALE, PURITY-RAKE, SKILL-UNSKILFULNESS, SUCCESS-FAILURE.

bite. To seize with the teeth; a morsel of food; to cheat. ENGRAVING, GULL-DECEIVER, HEATING-COOLING, NUTRIMENT-EXCRETION, PLEASURABLENESS-PAINFULNESS, SENSUALITY-SUFFERING, TRUTHFULNESS-FRAUD; **bite in,** ENGRAVING, GROOVE; **bite the dust,** SUCCESS-FAILURE, YIELDING; **bite the thumb,** FAVORITE-ANGER, REGARD-DISRESPECT.

bi'-ter. One who bites. **Biter bit,** REPRISAL-RESISTANCE.

bi'-ting. Keen; nipping. APPROVAL-DISAPPROVAL, HEAT-COLD, PLEASURABLENESS-PAINFULNESS, POLITENESS-IMPOLITENESS, PUNGENCY.

bit'-ten. Wounded with the teeth. LOVE-HATE.

bit'-ter. Poignant; sharp. CHARITABLENESS-MALEVOLENCE, FAVORITE-ANGER, HEAT-COLD, LOVE-HATE, PALATABLENESS-UNPALATABLENESS, PLEASURABLENESS-PAINFULNESS, POLITENESS-IMPOLITENESS, PUNGENCY; **bitter pill,** LOVE-HATE, PLEASURABLENESS-PAINFULNESS, WELFARE-MISFORTUNE; **bitter words,** APPROVAL-DISAPPROVAL.

bit'-ter-ly. In a bitter manner. HEAT-COLD, MAGNITUDE-SMALLNESS.

bit'-ter-ness. Sharpness; deep resentment. CONTENTEDNESS-REGRET, FAVORITE-ANGER, LOVE-HATE, PLEASURE-PAIN.

bit'-ter-sweet''. A plant whose root has at first a bitter taste and afterwards a sweet one. PLEASURABLENESS-PAINFULNESS.

bi-tu'-men. Mineral pitch. PULPINESS-ROSIN.

bi-tu'-mi-nous. Containing bitumen. PULPINESS-ROSIN.

biv'-ouac. The night-watch of an army. DWELLER-HABITATION, ESTABLISHMENT-REMOVAL, MOVEMENT-REST, WARNING.

bi-week'-ly. Once in two weeks. PERIODICITY-IRREGULARITY.

bi-zarre'. Fantastic. CONVENTIONALITY-UNCONVEN-TIONALITY, SOCIETY-LUDICROUSNESS.

blab. To tell a secret. EXPOSURE-HIDINGPLACE.

blab'-ber. To prattle. TALKATIVENESS-TACITURNITY.

black. Destitute of color; a negro. LIGHT-DARK-NESS, WHITENESS-BLACKNESS, VIRTUE-VICE; black and blue, EXCULPATION-PUNITION; black and white, COLOR-ACHROMATISM, LIGHT-DARKNESS, MARK-OBLITERATION, WRITING-PRINTING; black art, DEVO-TION-MAGIC; black book, JUSTIFICATION-CHARGE; black eagle, PATRIOTISM-TREASON; black eye, EXCUL-PATION-PUNITION; black flag, FIGHTING-CONCILI-ATION; black hole, GATHERING-SCATTERING, RE-LEASE-PRISON; black in the face, ASSERTION-DENIAL, EMOTION, EXCITATION; black lead, PRINTING; black letter, NOVELTY-ANTIQUITY, WORD-NEOLOGY, WRIT-ING-PRINTING; black looks, APPROVAL-DISAPPROVAL, FAVORITE-MOROSENESS, POLITENESS-IMPOLITENESS; black mail, PLUNDER,RECOMPENSE-PUNITION,THEFT; black sheep, GOOD MAN-BAD MAN; black spots in the horizon, SANGUINENESS-HOPELESSNESS; black swan, CONVENTIONALITY-UNCONVENTIONALITY; look black, CONTENTEDNESS-DISCONTENTMENT, EMOTION, FA-VORITE-ANGER; prove the black is white, RATIOCINA-TION-INSTINCT

black'-a-moor. A negro. WHITENESS-BLACKNESS; wash a blackamoor white, POSSIBILITY-IMPOSSIBIL-ITY, USEFULNESS-USELESSNESS.

black'-ball". To reject by voting. INCLUSION-OMIS-SION, SOCIABILITY-PRIVACY.

black'-ber"-ry. The fruit of certain species of Rubus. NUTRIMENT-EXCRETION.

black'-board". A large slate used for writing upon with chalk. SCHOOL, SMOOTHNESS-ROUGHNESS, WRITING-PRINTING.

black'-browed". Gloomy; threatening. CHARITABLE-NESS-MENACE, FAVORITE-MOROSENESS.

black'-coat". A clergyman. MINISTRY-LAITY.

black'-death". An Oriental plague. HEALTH-SICK-NESS.

black'-en. To make black; to defame. ADULATION-DISPARAGEMENT, WHITENESS-BLACKNESS.

black'-guard. A low fellow. GOOD MAN-BAD MAN, POLITENESS-IMPOLITENESS, TASTE-VULGARITY, UP-RIGHTNESS-DISHONESTY, UPRIGHTNESS-ROGUE.

black'-guard-ism. The conduct of a blackguard. POLITENESS-IMPOLITENESS.

black'-leg. A sharper. ROBBER.

black'-list". A list of defaulters. APPROVAL-DIS-APPROVAL, LABOR-CAPITAL.

black'-mouthed". Using foul language. FLATTERER-DEFAMER.

black'-ness. Darkness; without color. LIGHT-DARK-NESS, WHITENESS-BLACKNESS.

black'-smith". A smith who works in iron. AGENT.

blad'-der. A vessel in the body containing some liquid. CONTENTS-RECEIVER.

blade. The cutting part of an instrument; a dull fellow. ACTIVITY-INDOLENCE, ADEPT-BUNGLER, INSTRU-MENT, MALE-FEMALE, SHARPNESS-BLUNTNESS, SO-CIETY-DANDY, WEAPON.

blague. To tell lies in jest. BRAGGING, TRUTHFUL-NESS-FALSEHOOD.

blain. A sore. CONVEXITY-CONCAVITY, EMBELLISH-MENT-DISFIGUREMENT.

blame. To censure; to find fault with. APPROVAL-DISAPPROVAL; lay blame on, APPROVAL-DISAPPRO-VAL, JUSTIFICATION-CHARGE; take blame, APPROVAL-DISAPPROVAL.

blame-less. Innocent. INNOCENCE-GUILT.

blame'-wor"-thy. Culpable. APPROVAL-DISAPPROVAL, INNOCENCE-GUILT, VIRTUE-VICE.

blanc-bec [F.] (blan -bec'). A greenhorn. ADEPT-BUNGLER.

blanch. To whiten; evade. COLOR-ACHROMATISM, WHITENESS-BLACKNESS.

blanched. Made white. WHITENESS-BLACKNESS.

blanc"-mange'. A jelly-like substance used in cooking. NUTRIMENT-EXCRETION.

bland. Gentle. POLITENESS-IMPOLITENESS, TURBU-LENCE-CALMNESS.

blan-dil'-o-quence. Language of courtesy. ADULA-TION-DISPARAGEMENT.

blan-dil'-o-quent. Flattering. ADULATION-DISPARAGE-MENT.

blan'-di-ment. Enticement. BLANDISHMENT.

blan'-dish-ment. Soothing; flattering. ADULATION-DISPARAGEMENT, BLANDISHMENT, MOTIVE-CAPRICE.

BLANDISHMENT.

Addresses. Loving attention.
Blandiment. Blandishment.
Blandishment. The use of flattery and caresses to win the heart.
Buss. Kiss.
Caress. Expression of tender feelings by words and actions.
Caterwauling. Making of cries, the blandishment of cats.
Coquetry. Art and practise of making oneself noticed and admired.
Courtship. Attendance on a lady for her love
Dalliance. Fondling.
Deosculation. A kissing.
Embrace. A holding in the arms.
Endearment. Acts expressive of affection.
Épanchement [F.]. An overflowing of feeling.
Flirtation.}
Flirting.} Pretended love-making. See Verbs.
Fondling. Tender feeling expressed by action.
Gallantry. Courteous attention on the ladies.
Honeymoon. Short period after marriage.
Kiss. A pressing of the lips on something, with a slight sound.
Osculation. A kissing.
Salute. An indication of respect on meeting.
Serenading. Music or noise made at night, especially at the place of a marriage.
Smack. A loud kiss.
Suit. Courtship.
Valentine. A sweetheart chosen on St. Valentine's day.
Wooing. Love-making, especially with promises and vows.

BLANDISHMENT—Associated Words.

Billet-doux [F.]. A love-letter.
Love-letter. A letter written by a lover.
Love-tale. A love-story.
Love-token. An article given by a lover as a mark of esteem.
Plighted-love. Love as a pledge for marriage.
Strephon and Chloe. Lovers in Sidney's Arcadia.
True-lovers' knot. An ornament given to be worn in token of love.

BLANDISHMENT—Verbs.

Buss. To kiss loudly.
Caress. To express love for by words and actions.
Cherish. To care for
Clasp. To hold tightly.
Coax. To persuade in a childish or trivial way.
Cocker. To indulge.
Cockle. To treat like a baby.
Coddle. To pamper.
Coquet. To try to attract notice and admirers.
Cosset. To pet.
Court. Make love to.
Cuddle. To hold in close embrace.
Dally. To play at caresses.
Dandle. To toss up and down in the arms.
Embrace. To hold in the arms.
Flirt. To love insincerely.
Fondle. To play with.
Foster. To nurture or encourage.
Galavant.}
Gallivant.} To run about with women.
Hug. To embrace tightly.
Kiss. To press the lips upon and make a slight noise.
Nestle. To lie up close to.
Nuzzle. To snuggle as a babe on its mother's bosom.
Ogle. To look at in a coquettish manner.
Pat. To hit lightly in a friendly manner.
Pet. To stroke with a show of affection.
Philander. To trifle at courtship.

BLANDISHMENT—Verbs—*Continued.*

Propose. To make an offer of marriage.
Salute. To give a friendly greeting.
Serenade. To make music or big noise at a marriage.
Smack. To kiss loudly.
Spoon. To make a show of loving.
Toy. To trifle.
Wheedle. To coax by artful and dishonest means.
Woo. To make love by promises and vows.

BLANDISHMENT—*Verbal Expressions.*

Be sweet upon; **bill and coo**; **blow a kiss**, to kiss the fingers and blow toward the person; **cast sheep's eyes on**, to ogle; **chuck under the chin**; **die for**; *faire les yeux doux* [F.], to ogle; **fall in love with**; **have an offer**; **look sweet upon**; **make an offer**; **make love**; **make much of**; **make of**; **pat on the cheek**; **pat on the head**; **pay one's addresses to**; **pay one's attentions to**; **pay one's court to**, to make love to; **plight one's faith**; **plight one's troth**, to promise oneself in marriage; **pop the question**, make an offer of marriage; **set one's cap at**, to seek to make love to; **smile upon**; **win the affections** (see LOVE).

BLANDISHMENT—*Adjectives.*

Caressed. Treated in a caressing manner
Caressing. Showing affection by words and actions.
Spoony. Addicted to spooning.
Love-sick, "sighing like furnace" [Shakespeare]. In love.

blank. Empty; a void space. ENTITY-NONENTITY, SUBSTANCE-NULLITY; **blank cartridge**, MIGHT-IMPOTENCE; **look blank**, ASTONISHMENT-EXPECTANCE, CONTENTEDNESS-DISCONTENTMENT, EXPECTATION-DISAPPOINTMENT; **point blank**, SIMPLICITY-FLORIDNESS.

blan'-ket. A woolen covering for a bed. COVER-LINING, HEATING-COOLING; **toss in a blanket**, REGARD-DISRESPECT; **wet blanket**, TURBULENCE-CALMNESS.

blare. A roar. CRY-ULULATION.

blar'-ney. To flatter. ADULATION-DISPARAGEMENT.

bla''-se'. Sated with pleasure. ASTONISHMENT-EXPECTANCE, DESIRE-REPLETION, ENTERTAINMENT-WEARINESS.

blas-pheme'. To speak irreverently of God. GODLINESS-UNGODLINESS.

blas-phe'-mer. Profane speaker. GODLINESS-UNGODLINESS.

blas'-phe-mous. Impious; irreverent. GODLINESS-UNGODLINESS.

blas'-phe-my. Profane speaking of God. GODLINESS-UNGODLINESS.

blast. A gust of wind; explosion of powder. CHARITABLENESS-CURSE, CREATION-DESTRUCTION, LOUDNESS-FAINTNESS, RIVER-WIND, TURBULENCE-CALMNESS, WELFARE-MISFORTUNE.

blast'-fur''-nace. Smelter. CHEMISTRY.

bla'-tant. Loud. CRY-ULULATION, SAGACITY-INCAPACITY.

blath'-er-skite. A blustering fellow. TALKATIVENESS-TACITURNITY.

blat'-ter. Clatter. CRY-ULULATION.

blaze. To flame; to publish. EXCITATION, HEAT-COLD, LIGHT-DARKNESS; **blaze abroad**, PUBLICITY.

bla'-zing. Glowing. LUMINARY-SHADE.

bla'-zon. Proclaim; a coat of arms. POMP, PUBLICITY, REPUTATION-DISCREDIT.

blé, manger son, en herbe [F.] (blé, man'-zhé' son', an' arb). To anticipate one's revenues. EXTRAVAGANCE-AVARICE.

bleach. Whiten. COLOR-ACHROMATISM, WHITENESS-BLACKNESS.

bleak. Exposed; cold. HEAT-COLD.

blear. To dim. SIGHT-DIMSIGHTEDNESS, TRUTHFULNESS-FRAUD.

blear'-eyed. Weak-sighted. SIGHT-DIMSIGHTEDNESS.

bleat. The cry of a sheep. CRY-ULULATION.

bleb. A blister. CONVEXITY-CONCAVITY.

bleed. To let blood. COSTLINESS-CHEAPNESS, OUTLAY-INCOME, PLEASURE-PAIN, REMEDY-BANE, SENSUALITY-SUFFERING; **bleed freely**, GENEROSITY-FRUGALITY; **make the heart bleed**, PLEASURABLENESS-PAINFULNESS.

bleed'-ing. Losing blood. NUTRIMENT-EXCRETION REMEDY-BANE; **bleeding heart**, PLEASURE-PAIN.

blem'-ish. To mar. BEAUTY-UGLINESS, BETTERMENT-DETERIORATION, EMBELLISHMENT-DISFIGUREMENT, FAULTLESSNESS-FAULTINESS.

blench. Flinch. QUEST-EVASION, SANGUINENESS-TIMIDITY.

blend. Mingle. COMPOSITION-RESOLUTION, MIXTURE-HOMOGENEITY.

blend'-ing. Combining. COMPOSITION-RESOLUTION.

bless. To make happy; to invoke a blessing upon. APPROVAL-DISAPPROVAL, DEVOTION-IDOLATRY, DIVINITY, PLEASURABLENESS-PAINFULNESS; **bless my heart**, ASTONISHMENT-EXPECTANCE; **bless one's stars**, JUBILATION-LAMENTATION, THANKFULNESS-THANKLESSNESS.

bless'-ed. Beatified. PLEASURE-PAIN; **abode of the blessed**, HEAVEN-HELL.

bless'-ed-ness. Happiness. **Single blessedness**, unmarried state, APPROVAL-DISAPPROVAL, GOOD-EVIL.

bless'-ings. Divine favors. WELFARE-MISFORTUNE.

blest. Beatified. PLEASURE-PAIN; **blest with**, HOLDING-EXEMPTION.

blet'-on-ism. The power to discover underground springs by sensation. PROPHECY.

blight. To blast; to ruin. BETTERMENT-DETERIORATION, WELFARE-MISFORTUNE; **blight hope**, EXPECTATION-DISAPPOINTMENT.

blight'-ed. Blasted. BETTERMENT-DETERIORATION.

blind. Destitute of sight; a shade. ENLIGHTENMENT-SECRECY, EXPOSURE-HIDINGPLACE, HEED-DISREGARD, KNOWLEDGE-IGNORANCE, LUMINARY-SHADE, PRETEXT, SENSITIVENESS-APATHY, SIGHT-BLINDNESS, TRUTHFULNESS-FRAUD, VOLITION-OBLIGATION; **blind alley**, APERTURE-CLOSURE; **blind bargain**, CERTAINTY-DOUBT, PURPOSE-LUCK, RECKLESSNESS-CAUTION; **blind hookey**, ENTERTAINMENT-WEARINESS; **blind lead the blind**, TEACHING-MISTEACHING; **blind man's buff**, ENTERTAINMENT-WEARINESS; **blind man's holiday**, LIGHT-DARKNESS; **blind of one eye**, SIGHT-DIMSIGHTEDNESS; **blind side**, BIGOTRY-APOSTASY, CREDULOUSNESS-SKEPTICISM, DECISION-MISJUDGMENT; **blind the eyes**, ENLIGHTENMENT-SECRECY, GULL-HYPERBOLE; **blind to one's own merits**, CONCEIT-DIFFIDENCE.

blind'-ed. Shut off from view. COLOR-ACHROMATISM, KNOWLEDGE-IGNORANCE, SIGHT-BLINDNESS.

blind'-fold''. Having the eyes bandaged. COLOR-ACHROMATISM, KNOWLEDGE-IGNORANCE, SIGHT-BLINDNESS, TRUTHFULNESS-FRAUD.

blind'-ness. Ignorance; want of sight. SIGHT-BLINDNESS.

blink. To wink. CAREFULNESS-CARELESSNESS, DETERMINATION-VACILLATION, QUEST-EVASION, SIGHT-DIMSIGHTEDNESS; **blink at**, SIGHT-BLINDNESS.

blink'-ard. One who blinks. SIGHT-DIMSIGHTEDNESS.

blink'-er. A blind for horses. EXPOSURE-HIDINGPLACE, SIGHT-DIMSIGHTEDNESS.

bliss. Blessedness. HEAVEN-HELL, PLEASURE-PAIN.

bliss'-ful. Supremely happy. PLEASURE-PAIN.

blis'-ter. A thin bladder on the skin. CONVEXITY-CONCAVITY.

blithe. Gay. LIGHTHEARTEDNESS-DEJECTION.

blithe'-some. Cheerful. LIGHTHEARTEDNESS-DEJECTION.

bloat'-ed. Puffed; swelled. CONVEXITY-CONCAVITY, ENLARGEMENT-DIMINUTION, PROPORTION-DEFORMITY; **bloated with pride**, SELFRESPECT-HUMBLENESS.

bloat'-ed bond'-hold''-er. Capitalist. CAPITAL-LABOR.

bloat'-er. A cured herring. Nutriment-Excretion.

block. A mass of wood, etc.; to hinder. Greatness-Littleness, Hardness-Softness, Obstruction-Help, Sage-Fool, Solidity-Rarity, Suspension-Support, Recompense-Scourge; **block of buildings,** Dweller-Habitation; **block out,** Form-Formlessness, Recompense-Penalty; **block printing,** Writing-Printing; **block up,** Aperture-Closure, Obstruction-Help, Preparation-Nonpreparation; **bring to the block,** Exculpation-Punition; **cut blocks with a razor,** Provision-Waste; **wood block,** Engraving.

block-ade'. Closure of a city to take it. Aperture-Closure, Obstruction-Help, Release-Restraint.

block'-head. A stupid fellow. Sage-Fool.

block'-ish. Stupid. Sagacity-Incapacity.

blonde. A fair person. Color-Achromatism, Whiteness-Blackness.

blood. Kindred; a red fluid which circulates in animals. Anatomy, Gentility-Democracy, Life-Killing, Liquid-Gas, Relationship, Society-Dandy; **blood boil,** Excitability-Inexcitability, Excitation; **blood for blood,** Pardon-Vindictiveness; **blood-heat,** Heat-Cold; **blood-horse,** Conveyer; **blood-hound,** Benefactor-Evildoer, Fauna-Flora; **blood-letting,** Admission-Expulsion, Remedy-Bane; **blood-money,** Price-Discount; **blood-red,** Redness-Greenness; **blood run cold,** Pleasurableness-Painfulness, Sanguineness-Timidity; **blood-stained,** Life-Killing; **blood-sucker,** Benefactor-Evildoer; **bloodthirsty,** Charitableness-Malevolence, Life-Killing; **blood up,** Excitation, Favorite-Anger; **dye with blood,** Harshness-Mildness; **hands in blood,** Charitableness-Malevolence; **in the blood,** Subjectiveness-Objectiveness; **life-blood,** Life-Death; **new blood,** Betterment-Deterioration, Excitation; **spill blood,** Fighting-Conciliation.

blood'-less. Without blood or color. Innocence-Guilt, Strife-Peace.

blood'-shed''. The shedding of blood. Fighting-Conciliation, Life-Killing.

blood'-shot''. Suffused with blood. Embellishment-Disfigurement.

blood'-stroke''. The loss of sensation resulting from hemorrhage. Health-Sickness.

blood'-ves''-sel. Tubes carrying blood. Anatomy.

blood'-y. Stained with blood. Charitableness-Malevolence, Cleanness-Filthiness, Life-Killing.

blood'-y-flux''. Dysentery. Health-Sickness.

blood'-y–mind'-ed. Cruel. Charitableness-Malevolence.

bloom. Blossom; the flush on the cheek. Beauty-Ugliness, Blueness-Orange, Health-Sickness, Infancy-Age, Welfare-Misfortune.

bloom'-ing. Blossoming. Beauty-Ugliness.

blos'-som. A flower. Fauna-Flora, Welfare-Misfortune.

blot. To spot; disgrace; obscure. Cleanness-Filthiness, Embellishment-Disfigurement, Innocence-Guilt, Mark-Obliteration, Reputation-Discredit, Truth-Error, Whiteness-Blackness; **blot out,** Creation-Destruction, Mark-Obliteration.

blotch. A spot or blot. Embellishment-Disfigurement.

blot'-ter. A sheet of blotting-paper. Cleanness-Filthiness.

blouse. A loose outer garment. Dress-Undress.

blow. A stroke; to make a current of air. Action-Passiveness, Admission-Expulsion, Exculpation-Punition, Expectation-Disappointment, Expectation-Surprise, Good-Evil, Impetus-Reaction, Pleasurableness-Painfulness, Pleasure-Pain, River-Wind, Stream, Success-Failure, Weariness-Refreshment, Welfare-Misfortune; **blow a kiss,** Blandishment; **blow down,** Creation-Destruction; **blow for blow,** Reprisal-Resistance; **blow-hole,** Watercourse-Airpipe; **blow hot and cold,** Bigotry-Apostasy, Determination-Vacillation, Persistence-Whim, Ratiocination-Instinct, Truthfulness-Falsehood; **blow off,** Gathering-Scattering; **blow one's brains out,** Life-Killing; **blow out,** Creation-Destruction, Fasting-Gluttony, Light-Darkness, Nutriment-Excretion; **blow over,** Future-Past; **blow-pipe,** River-Wind, Watercourse-Airpipe; **blow the coals,** Excitation; **blow the fire,** Heating-Cooling; **blow the horn,** Musician; **blow the trumpet,** Reputation-Discredit; **blow up,** Adulation-Disparagement, Approval-Disapproval, Creation-Destruction, Enlargement-Diminution, Excitation, River-Wind, Turbulence-Calmness; **come to blows,** Fighting-Conciliation, Strife-Peace; **deal a blow at,** Attack-Defense; **deal a blow to,** Betterment-Deterioration, Exculpation-Punition; **death-blow,** Life-Death, Life-Killing.

blown. Swollen; exhausted; stale. Selfrespect-Humbleness, Weariness; **blown upon,** Adulation-Disparagement, Approval-Disapproval, Reputation-Discredit; **storm blown over,** Security-Insecurity, Strife-Peace.

blow'-pipe''. Tube for blowing air through. Chemistry.

blowzed. Fat and high colored. Redness-Greenness.

blowz'-y. Red-faced. Enlargement-Diminution, Redness-Greenness.

blub'-ber. Mar; weep. Jubilation-Lamentation, Pulpiness-Rosin.

blu'-cher. A half boot. **Blucher boot,** Dress-Undress.

bludg'-eon. A club used as a weapon. Weapon; **bludgeon-man,** Belligerent, Benefactor-Evildoer.

blue. One of the primary colors. Blueness-Orange, Knowledge-Ignorance, Water-Air; **blue and red,** Yellowness-Purple; **blue and yellow,** Redness-Greenness; **blue-book,** Mark-Obliteration, Record; **blue devils,** Lightheartedness-Dejection; **blue-jacket,** Wayfarer-Seafarer; **blue-light,** Alarm, Sign; **blue-peter,** Arrival-Departure, Sign; **blue ribbon,** Title; **blue-ruin,** Teetotalism-Intemperance; **blue-stocking,** Scholar-Dunce, Society-Affectation; **bit of blue,** Sanguineness-Hopelessness; **look blue,** Contentedness-Discontentment, Emotion, Expectation-Disappointment, Reputation-Discredit; **swear till all's blue,** Assertion-Denial; **true-blue,** Truthfulness-Falsehood, Uprightness-Dishonesty.

Blue'-beard''. A cruel husband. Matrimony-Celibacy, Purity-Rake.

blue-ness. The state of being blue. Blueness-Orange.

BLUENESS—ORANGE.

Bice. A pale blue pigment.
Bloom. Freshness in hue.
Blue. One of the seven prismatic colors; color resembling that of the clear sky.
Blueness. The state of being blue.
Bluishness. The quality of being somewhat blue

Cadmium. An intense yellow or orange color.
Flame color, etc. See *Adjectives.*
Gold. A color like that of gold.
Mars orange. An artificial iron ocher.
Ocher. An earthy iron ore of an orange color used as a pigment.
Or. Orange or gold color.

BLUENESS—ORANGE—*Continued.*

Indigo. One of the seven prismatic colors; a deep blue.
Prussian blue. A dark blue pigment with a coppery luster.
Smalt. A deep blue pigment.
Syenite blue. A blue like Syenite.
Ultramarine. A blue pigment.
Watchet. A pale or light blue.
Zaffer. A blue pigment.

BLUENESS—*Associated Nouns.*

Cobalt. } Blue minerals used in making blue compounds.
Cyanogen. }
Garter-blue. The color of the badge of the Knights of the Garter.
Lapis lazuli [L.]. An aluminous mineral of rich blue color.
Opal. A silica stone of a milky appearance.
Sapphire. A blue mineral.
Turquoise. A blue mineral.

BLUENESS—*Adjectives.*

Atmospheric. Resembling the atmosphere in color.
Azure. Having a sky-blue color.
Blue. Having a color resembling that of the clear sky.
Bluish. Rather blue.
Cerulean. Sky-colored.
Cold. Having a bluish effect.
Opalescent. A pearly light, reflecting a play of opaline colors.

blu'-ish. Somewhat blue. BLUENESS-ORANGE.
blu'-ish-ness. Small degree of blue color. BLUENESS-ORANGE.
blue'-lights. Signal lights. ALARM.
bluff. Steep; bold; blunt. HEIGHT-LOWNESS, POLITENESS-IMPOLITENESS, PRESUMPTION-OBSEQUIOUSNESS, TURBULENCE-CALMNESS.
blun'-der. To mistake. ADAGE-NONSENSE, ADEPT-BUNGLER, SKILL-UNSKILFULNESS, SUCCESS-FAILURE, TRUTH-ERROR.
blun'-der-buss. A shotgun. WEAPON.
blun'-der-head''. A stupid person. ADEPT-BUNGLER.
blun'-der-head''-ed. Stupid. SAGACITY-INCAPACITY.
blunt. Dull; rude in manner; to weaken. CRAFT-ARTLESSNESS, FEELING-INSENSIBILITY, MONEY, MOTIVE-DEHORTATION, POLITENESS-IMPOLITENESS, SAGACITY-INCAPACITY, SENSITIVENESS-APATHY, SHARPNESS-BLUNTNESS, STRENGTH-WEAKNESS, TURBULENCE-CALMNESS, VIGOR-INERTIA; **blunt tool,** USEFULNESS-USELESSNESS; **blunt-witted,** SAGACITY-INCAPACITY.
blunt'-ness. Dulness. SMOOTHNESS-ROUGHNESS.
blur. A blot; to partly obscure. CLEANNESS-FILTHINESS, EMBELLISHMENT-DISFIGUREMENT, REPUTATION-DISCREDIT.
blurred. Blotted. VISIBILITY-INVISIBILITY.
blurt. To utter abruptly. **Blurt out,** EXPOSURE-HIDINGPLACE, SPEECH-INARTICULATENESS.
blush. To redden in the face. CONCEIT-DIFFIDENCE, EMOTION, REDNESS-GREENNESS, SELFRESPECT-HUMBLENESS; **at first blush,** APPEARANCE-DISAPPEARANCE, MANIFESTATION-LATENCY, SIGHT-BLINDNESS; **put to the blush,** POLITENESS-IMPOLITENESS, PRESUMPTION-OBSEQUIOUSNESS, REPUTATION-CREDIT, SELFRESPECT-HUMBLENESS.
blush'-ing. Coloring in the face. REDNESS-GREENNESS; **blushing honors** [Shakesp.]; CONCEIT-DIFFIDENCE, REPUTATION-DISCREDIT.
blus'-ter. To talk noisily; to blow. CHARITABLENESS-MENACE, DEFIANCE, PRESUMPTION-OBSEQUIOUSNESS, TURBULENCE-CALMNESS.
blus'-ter-er. One who talks noisily. BRAWLER, BRAGGING.
blus'-ter-ing. Talking noisily; blowing. PRESUMPTION-OBSEQUIOUSNESS, RIVER-WIND, TURBULENCE-CALMNESS.
Blut und Eisen [G.] (blut unt ai'-zen). Blood and iron. LIQUID-GAS, STRENGTH-WEAKNESS.

ORANGE.

Orange. One of the seven prismatic colors; the color resembling that of an orange.
Red and yellow. The two colors which make orange when mixed.

ORANGE—*Verbs.*

Gild. To cover with an orange or gold color.
Warm. To give an orange or reddish color to.

ORANGE—*Adjectives.*

Apricot-colored. Having the color of an apricot or an orange color.
Brass-colored. Of the color of brass.
Copper-colored. Like copper in color.
Flame-colored. Having the color of a flame of fire.
Glowing. Exhibiting a strong bright color.
Hot. Having a warm or yellowish red color.
Ocherous. Resembling ocher in color.
Orange. Of the color of an orange or reddish yellow.
Orange-colored. Possessing the color of an orange.
Warm. Yellowish red.

BLUENESS—ADJECTIVES—*Continued.*

Sky-blue. Of the color of the sky.
Sky-colored. Having the color of the sky.
Sky-dyed. Sky-colored.

bo. An exclamation. **Not say "bo" to a goose,** BRAVERY-COWARDICE.
bo'-a. A serpent; a woman's fur tippet. DRESS-UNDRESS.
boar. The wild hog. FAUNA-FLORA, MALE-FEMALE.
board. A piece of timber; food; a council. ATTACK-DEFENSE, COUNCIL, HARDNESS-SOFTNESS, LAMINA-FIBER, MANAGER, NUTRIMENT-EXCRETION, SUSPENSION-SUPPORT, TRIBUNAL; **board school,** SCHOOL; **festive board,** SOCIABILITY-PRIVACY; **go by the board,** CREATION-DESTRUCTION, MIGHT-IMPOTENCE; **go on board,** ARRIVAL-DEPARTURE; **on board,** CONVEYANCE-VESSEL, PRESENCE-ABSENCE; **preside at the board,** MANAGEMENT.
board'-ing. Going on board a ship. ATTACK-DEFENSE.
board'-ing-school''. Where scholars are instructed and lodged. SCHOOL.
boards. A stage. ACTING, LISTS.
boast. Brag. BRAGGING, CONCEIT-DIFFIDENCE, PRIDE-HUMBLENESS, SOCIETY-AFFECTATION; **not so much to boast of,** FAULTLESSNESS-FAULTINESS.
boast'-er. One who boasts. BRAGGING, BRAWLER.
boast'-ing. Bragging. BRAGGING, SOCIETY-AFFECTATION.
boast'-ful. Proud. BRAGGING.
boa'-ston. A game. ENTERTAINMENT-WEARINESS.
boat. A small open vessel. CONVEYANCE-VESSEL; **row in the same boat,** ANTAGONISM-CONCURRENCE, SOLITUDE-COMPANY.
boat'-ing. Traveling in a boat. TRAVELING-NAVIGATION.
boat'-man. One who manages a boat. WAYFARER-SEAFARER.
boat'-swain. An officer in charge of a ship's boats, rigging, etc. WAYFARER-SEAFARER.
bob. A plummet; a grapple; a cork on a line. AGITATION, ELEVATION-DEPRESSION, SPRING-DIVE, VIBRATION; **bob a curtsy,** POLITENESS-IMPOLITENESS; **bob for,** TRIAL.
bob'-a-dil. A blustering braggart. **Captain Bobadil,** BRAWLER.
bob-bin. A kind of spool. REVOLUTION-EVOLUTION.
bob'-bing. A fuel. COMBUSTIBLE.
bob'-bish. Hearty. HEALTH-SICKNESS; **bobbish pretty,** HEALTH-SICKNESS.
bob'-tailed''. Having the tail cut short. EMBELLISHMENT-DISFIGUREMENT.
bocage [F.] (bo-cazh') A grove. FAUNA-FLORA.

bocca, per amusare la [It.] (boc'-ca, pêr a-mu-za'-rê la). To delight the lips. PALATABLENESS-UNPALATABLE-NESS.

bod'-ice. A corset. DRESS-UNDRESS.

bode. To predict. PROPHECY.

bode'-ment. An omen. PROPHECY.

Bode's law. A law of the planets. ASTRONOMY.

bod'-i-ly. In person; wholly. MATERIALITY-SPIRITU-ALITY, SUBSTANCE-NULLITY, WHOLE-PART; **bodily enjoyment,** SENSUALITY-SUFFERING; **bodily fear,** SANGUINENESS-TIMIDITY; **bodily pain,** SENSUALITY-SUFFERING.

bod'-kin. A large needle; a long hairpin. ENVIRONMENT-INTERPOSITION, PERFORATOR-STOPPER.

bod'-y. A person; mass; corporation; system. ASSOCIATION, GATHERING-SCATTERING, HUMANITY, MATERIALITY-SPIRITUALITY, SUBSTANCE-NULLITY, WHOLE-PART; **body and blood of Christ,** GODLINESS-UNGODLINESS; **body clothes,** DRESS-UNDRESS; **body color,** PAINTING; **body forth,** DELINEATION-CARICATURE; **body-guard,** ATTACK-DEFENSE, GUARD-PRISONER; **body of doctrine,** KNOWLEDGE-IGNORANCE; **body of water,** RIVER-WIND; **body politic,** HUMANITY, RULE-LICENSE; **in a body,** SOLITUDE-COMPANY; **keep body and soul together,** HEALTH-SICKNESS, LIFE-DEATH.

Bœ-o'-tian. Pertaining to Bœotia; sluggish. GENTILITY-DEMOCRACY, SAGACITY-INCAPACITY, SAGE-FOOL, TASTE-VULGARITY.

bog. A fen or morass. CLEANNESS-FILTHINESS, SWAMP-ISLAND; **bog trotter,** GENTILITY-DEMOCRACY.

bog'-gart. A goblin. JOVE-FIEND.

bog'-gle. Doubt; hesitate; shy. DETERMINATION-VACILLATION, DIFFICULTY-FACILITY, SKILL-UNSKILFULNESS

bog'-gy. Full of bogs. SWAMP-ISLAND.

bo'-gie. A goblin. JOVE-FIEND.

bo'-gle. A goblin. JOVE-FIEND.

bo'-gus. Sham. TRUTHFULNESS-FRAUD.

bo'-gy. A goblin. JOVE-FIEND.

Bo-he'-mi-an. A vagabond. WAYFARER-SEAFARER.

boil. To bubble from heat. AGITATION, EXCITABILITY-INEXCITABILITY, EXCITATION, FAVORITE-ANGER, HEALTH-SICKNESS, HEAT-COLD, HEATING-COOLING, TURBULENCE-CALMNESS, VISCIDITY-FOAM.

boil'-ing. State of ebullition. HEATING-COOLING.

boil'-er. A cylindrical vessel used in cooking. OVEN-REFRIGERATOR.

bois'-ter-ous. Noisy. EXCITABILITY-INEXCITABILITY, HURRY-LEISURE, RIVER-WIND, TURBULENCE-CALMNESS.

bold. Brave. BRAVERY-COWARDICE, CONVEXITY-CONCAVITY, FORCE-WEAKNESS; **bold faced,** PRESUMPTION-OBSEQUIOUSNESS; **bold push,** VENTURE; **bold relief,** VISIBILITY-INVISIBILITY; **bold stroke,** BRAVERY-COWARDICE, DESIGN, SUCCESS-FAILURE; **make bold with,** POLITENESS-IMPOLITENESS; **show a bold front,** BRAVERY-COWARDICE, DEFIANCE.

bold'-ness. Courage. BRAVERY-COWARDICE, FORCE-WEAKNESS.

bole. The stem of a tree. WHOLE-PART.

bo-le'-ro. A Spanish dance. ENTERTAINMENT-WEARINESS.

Bol'-i-var. Bolivian coin. VALUES.

bol'-ster. A long underpillow. BETTERMENT-DETERIORATION, CONVEXITY-CONCAVITY, OBSTRUCTION-HELP; **bolster up,** JUSTIFICATION-CHARGE.

bolt. To fasten; to dart; a bar for a door; lightning. APERTURE-CLOSURE, CONNECTIVE, ESCAPE, FASTING-GLUTTONY, MIXTURE-HOMOGENEITY, NUTRIMENT-EXCRETION, OBSTRUCTION-HELP, PUSH-PULL, QUEST-EVASION, RELEASE-PRISON, SWIFTNESS-SLOWNESS, UNION-DISUNION; **bolt food,** FASTING-GLUTTONY, NUTRIMENT-EXCRETION; **bolt in,** RELEASE-RESTRAINT; **bolt the door,** LEAVE-PROHIBITION; **bolt**

upright, ERECTNESS-FLATNESS; **thunderbolt,** PHENOMENON, WEAPON.

bolt'-head". A chemist's vessel. CONTENTS-RECEIVER.

bo'-lus. A large pill. NUTRIMENT-EXCRETION, REMEDY-BANE.

bomb. An explosive shell. WEAPON; **bomb-vessel,** BELLIGERENT.

bom-bard'. To attack with bombs. ATTACK-DEFENSE.

bom"-bar-dier'. One who has charge of mortars. BELLIGERENT.

bom-bard'-ment. Assault with shot or shell. ATTACK-DEFENSE.

bom-bar'-don. A wind instrument. MUSICAL INSTRUMENTS.

bom'-bast. Cotton padding; extravagant language. BRAGGING, RHETORIC, MEANING-JARGON, SIMPLICITY-FLORIDNESS, SOCIETY-LUDICROUSNESS.

Bom-bas'-tes Fu-ri-o'-so. A burlesque opera by William Barnes Rhodes, produced in 1790. BRAWLER.

bom-bas'-tic. Inflated. GULL-HYPERBOLE, SIMPLICITY-FLORIDNESS, SOCIETY-LUDICROUSNESS.

bom"-bi-la'-tion. A humming. LOUDNESS-FAINTNESS.

bon augure, de [F.] (bon· o-gür', de). Of good omen. SANGUINENESS-TIMIDITY.

bon diable [F.] (bon· di-abl'). A good-natured fellow. WAG.

bon enfant [F.] (bon· an·-fan·'). A good fellow. SOCIABILITY-PRIVACY.

bon gré mal gré [F.] (bon· grê mal grê). Willing or unwilling. VOLITION-OBLIGATION.

bon mot [F.] (bon· mo). A witty expression. WITTINESS-DULNESS.

bon naturel [F.] (bon· na-tū-rel'). A good-natured fellow. LIGHTHEARTEDNESS-DEJECTION.

bon ton [F.] (bon· ton·). Good manners. SOCIETY-LUDICROUSNESS.

bon vivant [F.] (bon· vi-van·'). A boon companion. FASTING-GLUTTONY.

bona fide [L.] (bo'-na fai'-dî). In good faith. TRUTHFULNESS-FALSEHOOD, UPRIGHTNESS-DISHONESTY.

bona roba [It.] (bo'-na ro'-ba). A mistress. PURITY-RAKE.

bo-nan'-za. A lucky operation. EXCESS-LACK, GIVING-RECEIVING.

bon'-bon". A candy. SWEETNESS-ACIDITY.

bond. A band; a written obligation to pay money. CONNECTIVE, CONTRACT, DUENESS-UNDUENESS, GIVING-RECEIVING, MONEY, RELEASE-PRISON, SECURITY; **bond of union,** CONNECTION-INDEPENDENCE, CONNECTIVE.

bond'-age. Servitude. LIBERTY-SUBJECTION.

bond'-ed. Secured by bonds. **Bonded together,** ASSOCIATION.

bond'-hold"-er. One owning bonds. LABOR-CAPITAL; **bloated bondholder,** LABOR-CAPITAL.

bond'-maid". A female servant. CHIEF-UNDERLING.

bonds. Fetters. RELEASE-PRISON; **bonds of harmony,** VARIANCE-ACCORD; **in bonds,** CHIEF-UNDERLING; **tear asunder one's bonds,** RELEASE-RESTRAINT.

bonds'-man. A slave. CHIEF-UNDERLING.

bone. The solid framework of the body; a pair of clappers. ANATOMY, HARDNESS-SOFTNESS, LIFE-CORPSE, MUSICAL INSTRUMENTS, SOLIDITY-RARITY; **bone of contention,** STRIFE-PEACE, VARIANCE-ACCORD; **bone to pick,** DIFFICULTY-FACILITY, INVESTIGATION-ANSWER, VARIANCE-ACCORD; **break no bones,** GOODNESS-BADNESS; **bred in the bone,** SUBJECTIVENESS-OBJECTIVENESS; **make no bones,** DIFFICULTY-FACILITY, READINESS-RELUCTANCE; **one bone and one flesh,** MATRIMONY-CELIBACY.

bone'-black". Animal black. CHEMISTRY.

bone'-house". A dead house. LIFE-FUNERAL.

bone'-set". A bitter tonic. REMEDY-BANE.

bon'-fire". A triumphal fire. ENTERTAINMENT-WEARINESS, HEAT-COLD, SOLEMNIZATION; **make a bonfire of,** HEATING-COOLING.

bon"-ho-mie'. Good fellowship. CHARITABLENESS-MALEVOLENCE.

Bon-homme [F.] (bon'-om'). A religious order. MINISTRY-LAITY.

bon'-i-face. An innkeeper. FRIEND-FOE.

bonne [F.] (bon). A nursemaid. CHIEF-UNDERLING, GUARD-PRISONER.

bonne, à la . . . heure [F.] (a la bon ur). In good time. CONTENTEDNESS-DISCONTENTMENT, READINESS-RELUCTANCE.

bonne bouche [F.] (bon bush'). A good mouth, a tidbit; the best for last. BEGINNING-END.

bonne, de . . . volonté [F.] (de bon vo-lon'-tê'). With good will. READINESS-RELUCTANCE.

bon'-net. A covering for the head. DRESS-UNDRESS.

bon-ny. Merry; handsome. BEAUTY-UGLINESS, LIGHTHEARTEDNESS-DEJECTION.

bono, cui [L.] (bo'-no, cwai). Of what good is it? PURPOSE-LUCK, USEFULNESS-USELESSNESS.

bono, pro . . . publico [L.] (pro bo'-no pub'-li-co). For the public good. HUMANITARIANISM-MISANTHROPY, USEFULNESS-USELESSNESS.

bonum magnum [L.] (bo'-num mag'-num). A great good. GOOD-EVIL.

bo-nus. An extra payment. EXCESS-LACK, GIVING-RECEIVING, OUTLAY-INCOME.

bo'-ny. Hard. HARDNESS-SOFTNESS.

bonze. A Buddhist monk. MINISTRY-LAITY.

boo'-by. A dunce. SAGE-FOOL.

Boo'-dhism. Buddhism. ORTHODOXY-HETERODOXY.

Boo'-dhist. Buddhist. ORTHODOXY-HETERODOXY.

book. A volume; printed matter. ACCOUNTS, MARK-OBLITERATION, MISSIVE-PUBLICATION, RECORD; **at one's books,** TEACHING-LEARNING; **book learning,** KNOWLEDGE-IGNORANCE; **book of fate,** VOLITION-OBLIGATION; **bring to book,** ACCOUNTS, APPROVAL-DISAPPROVAL, EVIDENCE; **mind one's books,** TEACHING-LEARNING; **school book,** SCHOOL; **without book,** REMEMBRANCE-FORGETFULNESS.

book'-case". A case for books. CONTENTS-RECEIVER.

booked. About to die. LIFE-DEATH.

book'-ing. Registering in a book. MARK-OBLITERATION.

book'-ish. Studious. KNOWLEDGE-IGNORANCE.

book'-keep"-er. Accountant. RECORDER.

book'-keep"-ing. The art of keeping accounts. ACCOUNTS.

book'-learn"-ing. Knowledge from books. MISSIVE-PUBLICATION.

book'-less. Unscholarly. SCHOLAR-DUNCE.

book'-let. Little book. MISSIVE-PUBLICATION.

book'-mak"-ing. The art of compiling books. RATIONALE-LUCK.

book'-sell"-er. One who sells books. MISSIVE-PUBLICATION.

book'-worm". A close student. SCHOLAR-DUNCE.

boom. A hollow roar; to promote. ATTACK-DEFENSE, IMPETUS-REACTION, LOUDNESS-FAINTNESS', OBSTRUCTION-HELP, SWIFTNESS-SLOWNESS, SUSPENSION-SUPPORT, TRAVELING-NAVIGATION.

boom'-er-ang. A missile weapon of Australia. IMPETUS-REACTION, WEAPON.

boom'-ing. Roaring like distant guns. IMPETUS-REACTION.

boon. A gift. GIVING-RECEIVING, GOOD-EVIL; **boon companion,** FRIEND-FOE; **beg a boon,** PETITION.

boor. An ill-bred fellow. GENTILITY-DEMOCRACY.

boor'-ish. Clownish. POLITENESS-IMPOLITENESS, TASTE-VULGARITY.

boost. To raise from beneath. PUSH-PULL.

boot. A covering for the foot and leg. CONTENTS-RECEIVER, DRESS-UNDRESS, RECOMPENSE-SCOURGE.

boot. To benefit; an addition. CONSEQUENCE-INSIGNIFICANCE, GOOD-EVIL; **to boot,** ADDITION-SUBTRACTION; **what boots it?** CONSEQUENCE-INSIGNIFICANCE.

boot'-ed. Having boots on; ready. **Booted and spu:red,** PREPARATION-NONPREPARATION.

booth. A stall in a fair, market, etc. DWELLER-HABITATION, MARKET.

boot'-less. Useless. SUCCESS-FAILURE, USEFULNESS-USELESSNESS.

boots. An inn servant; coverings for foot and leg. GENTILITY-DEMOCRACY.

boo'-ty. Plunder. PLUNDER.

booze. To drink to excess. TEETOTALISM-INTEMPERANCE.

booz'-y. Tipsy. TEETOTALISM-INTEMPERANCE.

bo"-peep'. The game of peek'-a-boo. ENLIGHTENMENT-SECRECY, SIGHT-BLINDNESS.

bor'-del. A bawdy-house. PURITY-IMPURITY.

bor'-der. Adjoin; an edge; to adorn with a border. BEGINNING-END, BORDER, DOMESTICATION-AGRICULTURE, EMBELLISHMENT-DISFIGUREMENT, ENVIRONMENT-INTERPOSITION; **border upon,** INTERSPACE-CONTACT, REMOTENESS-NEARNESS.

BORDER.

Border.	Strip or stripe just inside or surrounding the edge.
Brim.	The top of the side of a containing vessel.
Brink.	Edge of a precipice or deep place.
Brow.	The upper part of a hill.
Edge.	Line marking the termination of a surface.
Marge.	Margin.
Margin.	Border of a book or of a piece of water.
Rim.	Edge of a vessel.
Skirt.	The outer part, as of a city.
Verge.	Extreme border of a place.

BORDER—*Denotations.*

Chaps. Chops.	The fleshy parts about the jaws; the jaws.
Coast.	The land bordering upon the ocean.
Door.	An opening in the wall of a house or of an apartment.
Edging.	That which forms an edge or border.
Flange.	A surrounding rim for strength, or for a guide.
Flounce.	An ornamental appendage about the skirt of a woman's dress.
Frame.	The skeleton of a structure; an open structure for enclosing or supporting things.
Frill.	A border secured at one edge, and left free at the other.
Fringe.	An ornamental appendage to the border of a piece of stuff.
Furbelow.	A flounce on a woman's garment.
Hem.	The edge or border of a garment.
Jaws.	The framework of the mouth.
List.	A strip forming the woven border of cloth
Mouth.	The aperture between the jaws.
Porch.	An entrance to a building.
Portal.	A doorway.
Selvedge.	The woven edge of cloth.
Skirting.	The border of a woman's skirt.
Threshold.	The border or entrance.
Trimming.	An ornamental bordering.
Valance.	Hanging drapery of a couch or window.
Welt.	A hem, border or fringe.

BORDER—*Adjectives.*

Border.	Lying on the edge.
Labial.	Having edges or lips.
Labiated.	Provided with edges or lips.
Marginal.	Pertaining to the margin.
Marginated.	Provided with margins.
Skirting.	Lying close to, running along the edge of.

bor'-der-er. One dwelling on the border. REMOTENESS-NEARNESS.

bor'-der-land". Land on the border. INTERSPACE-CONTACT, REMOTENESS-NEARNESS.

bore. To perforate; a tiresome affair. APERTURE-CLOSURE, BREADTH-NARROWNESS, DESIRE-REPLETION, ENTERTAINMENT-WEARINESS, PLEASURABLENESS-PAINFULNESS, PLEASURE-PAIN, RIVER-WIND.

bo'-re-al. Northern; pertaining to Boreas. HEAT-COLD, LATERALITY-CONTRAPOSITION.

Bo'-re-as. The north wind. RIVER-WIND.

bor'-er. One who or that which bores. PERFORATOR-STOPPER.

borgnes, au royaume des aveugles les . . . sont rois [F.] (o rwa-yom' dez a-vugl' le borny son· rwa). In the country of the blind the one-eyed are kings. CHIEF-UNDERLING, CONSEQUENCE-INSIGNIFICANCE.

Borgen macht Sorgen [G.] (bor'-hen maht sor'-hen). Borrowing makes sorrowing. LOAN-BORROWING.

born. Brought into being. **Born so,** SUBJECTIVENESS-OBJECTIVENESS; **born under a lucky star,** WELFARE-MISFORTUNE; **born under an evil star,** WELFARE-MISFORTUNE.

borne. Supported; carried. EXCITABILITY-INEXCITABILITY; **borne down,** LIGHTHEARTEDNESS - DEJECTION, SUCCESS-FAILURE.

borne' [F.] (bor-nê'). Narrow-minded. SAGACITY-INCAPACITY.

bor-nouse'. A garment of Arab origin. DRESS-UNDRESS.

bor'-ough. An incorporated town that is not a city. CITY-COUNTRY, DWELLER-HABITATION.

bor'-row. To take from another as a loan.. CREDIT-DEBT, LOAN - BORROWING ; **borrow of Peter to pay Paul,** COMMUTATION-PERMUTATION, LOAN-BORROWING, THEFT.

bor'-rowed. Loaned. **Borrowed plumes,** TRUTHFULNESS-FRAUD, LOAN-BORROWING.

bor'-row-er. One who borrows. CREDIT-DEBT.

bor'-row-ing. The act of obtaining loans. LOAN-BORROWING.

bosh. Folly. CONSEQUENCE-INSIGNIFICANCE, MEANING-JARGON, TRUTHFULNESS-FABRICATION.

bos'-om. The breast. AFFECTIONS, OUTSIDE-INSIDE, SAGACITY-INCAPACITY; **bosom-friend,** FRIEND-FOE; **bosom of one's family,** OUTSIDE-INSIDE; **in the bosom of,** CONFINEMENT.

boss. A knob. CONVEXITY-CONCAVITY.

boss'-age. Stone projecting from a wall. ARCHITECTURE.

bossed. Worked in relief. CONVEXITY-CONCAVITY.

boss'-ism. Political party management by bosses. PRESUMPTION-OBSEQUIOUSNESS, TYRANNY-ANARCHY.

boss'-y. Decorated with bosses. CONVEXITY-CONCAVITY.

bos'-ton. A game of cards. ENTERTAINMENT-WEARINESS.

bo-tan'-ic. Pertaining to botany. **Botanic garden,** ZOOLOGY-BOTANY.

bo-tan'-ic-al. Pertaining to botany. ZOOLOGY-BOTANY.

bot'-a-nist. One versed in botany. ZOOLOGY-BOTANY

bot'-a-nize. Study plants. ZOOLOGY-BOTANY.

bot'-a-no-man''-cy. Divination by plants. PROPHECY.

bot'-a-ny. Science of plants. FAUNA-FLORA, ORGANIZATION-INORGANIZATION, ZOOLOGY-BOTANY.

botch. Ill - finished work. RENOVATION - RELAPSE, SKILL-UNSKILFULNESS, SUCCESS-FAILURE.

botch'-er. A bungler. ADEPT-BUNGLER.

botch'-er-y. Bungling work. SKILL-UNSKILFULNESS, TRUTH-ERROR.

both. The two. **Burn the candle at both ends,** EXCESS-LACK; **butter one's bread on both sides,** EXCESS-LACK; **listen with both ears,** HEARING-DEAFNESS.

both'-er. To annoy. ACTIVITY-INDOLENCE, CERTAINTY - DOUBT, DIFFICULTY-FACILITY, PLEASURABLENESS-PAINFULNESS, PLEASURE-PAIN.

both''-er-a'-tion. Annoyance. PLEASURE-PAIN.

both'-er-ing. Annoying. PLEASURABLENESS-PAINFULNESS.

both'-y. A hut for. laborers; a cottage. DWELLER-HABITATION.

bot'-tle. A narrow mouthed vessel for liquids. CONSERVATION, CONTENTS-RECEIVER; **bee in a bottle,** CRASH-DRUMMING; **bottle-green,** REDNESS - GREENNESS; **bottle-holder,** ANTAGONIST-ASSISTANT, MEDIATION, TURBULENCE-CALMNESS; **bottle up,** ENLIGHTENMENT-SECRECY, RELEASE-RESTRAINT, REMEMBRANCE - FORGETFULNESS; **crack a bottle,** NUTRIMENT-EXCRETION; **pass the bottle,** TEETOTALISM-INTEMPERANCE; **smelling-bottle,** PERFUME-STENCH.

bot'-tom. The base; the keel of a ship; endurance. BRAVERY-COWARDICE, CONVEXITY-CONCAVITY, CONVEYANCE-VESSEL, PERSISTENCE-WHIM, SUSPENSION-SUPPORT, TOP-BOTTOM; **at bottom,** SUBJECTIVENESS-OBJECTIVENESS; **at the bottom of,** CAUSE-EFFECT; **bottom upwards,** REVERSAL; **from the bottom of one's heart,** EMOTION, TRUTHFULNESS-FALSEHOOD; **go to the bottom,** SPRING-DIVE; **probe to the bottom,** INVESTIGATION-ANSWER.

bot'-tom-less. Having no bottom. DEEPNESS-SHALLOWNESS; **angel of the bottomless pit,** ANGEL-SATAN; **bottomless pit,** DEEPNESS-SHALLOWNESS, HEAVEN-HELL.

bouche, bonne [F.] (bush, bon·). The best taste. BEGINNING-END, PALATABLENESS-UNPALATABLENESS, PLEASURABLENESS-PAINFULNESS, SENSUALITY-SUFFERING, STORE.

bouche à feu [F.] (bush a fu). Cannon. WEAPON.

bou'-der-ie. Pouting. FAVORITE-MOROSENESS.

bou'-doir''. A lady's private reception-room. CONTENTS-RECEIVER.

bouffe, opéra [F.] (buf, op-ê-ra'). A farcical comic operetta. ACTING.

bouge. The bulge of a cask. CONVEXITY-CONCAVITY.

bough. A large branch of a tree. CURVATION-RECTILINEARITY, FAUNA-FLORA, WHOLE-PART.

bought. Bending. CURVATION-RECTILINEARITY.

bou'-gie. A surgical instrument. LUMINARY-SHADE.

boul'-der. A large stone. ROUNDNESS.

bou'-le-vards. Broad city avenues. CITY, ENVIRONMENT-INTERPOSITION.

boule-verse'. Overthrow. EXCITATION.

boule-verse'-ment. A revolution. CREATION-DESTRUCTION, EXCITATION, REVOLUTION.

boule-ver'-ser. Revolutionist. EXCITATION.

bounce. A sudden leap; a lie; a boast. BRAGGING, PRESUMPTION - OBSEQUIOUSNESS, SPRING - DIVE, TRUTHFULNESS-FABRICATION, TURBULENCE-CALMNESS; **bounce upon,** ARRIVAL-DEPARTURE, EXPECTATION-DISAPPOINTMENT.

boun'-cing. Large. GREATNESS-LITTLENESS.

bound. Jump; confined; limit. CONFINEMENT, ENGAGEMENT-RELEASE, SPRING-DIVE, SWIFTNESS-SLOWNESS; **bound back,** IMPETUS-REACTION; **bound by,** DUTY-IMMUNITY; **bound for,** AIM-ABERRATION, PURPOSE-LUCK; **bound to,** DUTY-IMMUNITY, ENGAGEMENT-RELEASE; **I'll be bound,** ASSERTION-DENIAL.

bound'-a-ry. A limiting or dividing line. BOUNDARY.

BOUNDARY.

Boundary. That which indicates or fixes a limit, or extent, or marks a bound.

Boundary line. See BOUNDARY.

Confine. A common boundary.

Enclave. A territory within another, but independent of it.

Flood-gate. A gate which limits the flow of water.

Frontier. The boundary of a country or of civilization.

Hedgerow. A fence or boundary made of hedge.

Kerb-stone. The boundary of a pavement.

Landmark. A mark which indicates the extent of territory.
Limit. That which limits or bounds.
Line of circumvallation. A surrounding boundary.
Line of demarcation. A boundary or limit of extent of territory.
Marches. Territorial borders or frontiers
Ne plus ultra [L.]. No more beyond; hence, the limit.
Pale. An enclosure.
Pillars of Hercules. Two hills, between which are the Straits of Gibraltar, thrown up by Hercules to mark the limit of his labors, and of the world.
Precinct. A place marked by fixed lines
Rubicon. A small river separating Gaul from Italy, the crossing of which by Cæsar began his conquest of Italy.
Sluice. A channel for water.
Stint. A definite amount, as of work.
Termination. The end or limit.
Terminus. The end.
Verge. A border or limit.

BOUNDARY—*Adjectives.*

Definite. With fixed limits.
Conterminable. } With the same limits.
Conterminate. }
Frontier. Pertaining to the limits of a country.
Terminal. Pertaining to a boundary.

BOUNDARY—*Adverbs.*

Thus far. To this extent
Thus far and no further. To this extent only.

bound'-en. Binding. **Bounden duty,** DUTY-IMMUNITY.
bound'-less. Unlimited. EXTENSION-DISTRICT, INFINITY.
bounds. Limits; springs. **Bounds of possibility,** POSSIBILITY-IMPOSSIBILITY; **keep within bounds,** LEAVE-PROHIBITION, RELEASE-RESTRAINT, TRANSCURSION-SHORTCOMING, TURBULENCE-CALMNESS.
boun'-te-ous. Plentiful. GENEROSITY-FRUGALITY.
boun'-te-ous-ness. Munificence. GENEROSITY-FRUGALITY.
boun'-ti-ful. Free in giving. CHARITABLENESS-MALEVOLENCE, GENEROSITY-FRUGALITY.
boun'-ti-ful-ness. Liberality in the bestowment of gifts. GENEROSITY-FRUGALITY.
boun'-ty. Plenty. GENEROSITY-FRUGALITY, GIVING-RECEIVING, OBSTRUCTION-HELP.
bou'-quet. A bunch of flowers. EMBELLISHMENT-DISFIGUREMENT, PERFUME-STENCH.
bour-geois'. A kind of type; a Frenchman of middle rank. GENTILITY-DEMOCRACY, WRITING-PRINTING.
bour'-geon. Sprout, as a branch. ENLARGEMENT-DIMINUTION.
bourn. A limit. BOUNDARY.
bourse. A money-market. CITY-COUNTRY, MONEY.
bouse. To drink to excess. TEETOTALISM-INTEMPERANCE.
bout. A contest. ACTION-PASSIVENESS, ENTERTAINMENT-WEARINESS, PERIODICITY-IRREGULARITY, STRIFE-PEACE; **drinking bout,** MODERATION, SELF-INDULGENCE.
bou-tade'. An outbreak of speech. ADAGE-NONSENSE, PERSISTENCE-WHIM.
bout de son latin, au [F.] (bu de son· la-tan·', o). At the end of his Latin. DIFFICULTY-FACILITY, KNOWLEDGE-IGNORANCE, RATIOCINATION-INSTINCT.
bout du compte, au [F.] (bu dü con·t, o). Finally. RATIOCINATION-INSTINC .
boutez en avant [F.] (bu-têz' an· a-van·'). Push forward. ACTIVITY-INDOLENCE, ADVANCE-RETROGRESSION, ORDER.
bove majori discit arare minor, a [L.] (bo'-vî ma-jo'-rai dis'-sit a-rê'-rî mai'-nor, ê). From the older ox the younger learns to plow. EDUCATION-LEARNING, PREPARATION-NONPREPARATION.
bo'-vine. Ox-like. FAUNA-FLORA, SAGACITY-INCAPACITY.

bow. To incline; the prow of a ship; a weapon; a fiddlestick. ANTERIORITY-POSTERIORITY, CONVEXITY-CONCAVITY, CURVATION-RECTILINEARITY, ELEVATION-DEPRESSION, EMBELLISHMENT-DISFIGUREMENT, MUSICAL INSTRUMENTS, POLITENESS-IMPOLITENESS, PRESUMPTION-OBSEQUIOUSNESS, REGARD-DISRESPECT, WEAPON; **bend the bow,** ELEVATION-DEPRESSION, TOIL-RELAXATION; **bow down,** DEVOTION-IDOLATRY; **bow out,** ADMISSION-EXPULSION; **bow submission,** YIELDING.
Bow'-bells''. The bells of St. Mary-le-Bow, in the central part of London, in Cockneydom. **Born within sound of Bow-bells,** GENTILITY-DEMOCRACY.
bowed. Bent. **Bowed down,** CONVEXITY-CONCAVITY, CURVATURE-RECTILINEARITY, LIGHTHEARTEDNESS-DEJECTION, SELFRESPECT-HUMBLENESS.
bow'-el-less. Merciless. COMPASSION-RUTHLESSNESS.
bow'-els. The intestines. OUTSIDE-INSIDE; **bowels of compassion,** COMPASSION-RUTHLESSNESS; **bowels of the earth,** DEEPNESS-SHALLOWNESS.
bow'-er. A cottage; an arbor. CONTENTS-RECEIVER, COUNTRY, DWELLER-HABITATION; **bowers of bliss,** HEAVEN-HELL.
bow'-ie-knife''. A hunting knife, 15 inches by 1¼, worn as a weapon by Colonel J. Bowie, of Texas. WEAPON.
bowl. A concave vessel; a ball for rolling on level surfaces. CONTENTS-RECEIVER, REVOLUTION; **bowl along,** SWIFTNESS-SLOWNESS, TRAVELING-NAVIGATION; **flowing bowl,** TEETOTALISM-INTEMPERANCE.
bowl'-der. A large stone. ROUNDNESS.
bow'-legged''. Crooked-legged. CURVATURE-RECTILINEARITY, PROPORTION-DEFORMITY.
bowl'-ing-green''. A lawn for playing at bowls. ERECTNESS-FLATNESS, FORM-FORMLESSNESS.
bowls. A game. ENTERTAINMENT-WEARINESS, SMOOTHNESS-ROUGHNESS.
bow'-man''. An archer. BELLIGERENT, PUSH-PULL.
bow'-shot''. The distance an arrow can be shot from a bow. REMOTENESS-NEARNESS.
bow'-string''. A string for a bow; a Turkish punishment. EXCULPATION-PUNITION, LIFE-KILLING, RECOMPENSE-SCOURGE.
bow'-wow''. The bark of a dog. CRY-ULULATION.
box. A case; blow on the ear. ACTING, CONTENTS-RECEIVER, DWELLER-HABITATION, STRIFE-PEACE; **box the compass,** AIM-ABERRATION, BIGOTRY-APOSTASY, REVOLUTION-EVOLUTION; **box the ear,** FAVORITE-ANGER, RECOMPENSE-PUNITION; **box up,** RELEASE-RESTRAINT; **horse box,** CONVEYANCE-VESSEL; **musical box,** MUSICAL INSTRUMENTS; **wrong box,** DIFFICULTY-FACILITY, RIGHT-WRONG, SKILL-UNSKILFULNESS, TRUTH-ERROR.
box'-er. A pugilist. BELLIGERENT.
box'-ing. Pugilism. STRIFE-PEACE.
boy. A male child. INFANT-VETERAN, MALE-FEMALE.
boy'-cott. Refraining from intercourse, as with Capt. Boycott, A. D. 1880, an Irish landlord. LABOR-CAPITAL.
boy'-ar. An aristocrat. GENTILITY-DEMOCRACY
boy'-hood. State of a boy. INFANCY-AGE.
boy'-ish. Like a boy. INFANT-VETERAN.
brab'-ble. To squabble. STRIFE-PEACE, VARIANCE-ACCORD.
brab'-bler. A squabbler. FAVORITE-QUARRELSOMENESS.
brace. That which holds; a pair; a strut. CONNECTIVE, DUALITY, MELODY-DISSONANCE, STRENGTH-WEAKNESS, UNION-DISUNION, WEARINESS-REFRESHMENT.
brace'-let. A wrist ornament. CIRCLE-WINDING, EMBELLISHMENT-DISFIGUREMENT.
brach'-i-al. Belonging to the arm. ANATOMY, INSTRUMENT.

bra-chyg'-ra-phy. Stenography. WRITING-PRINTING.

bra'-cing. Invigorating. HEALTHINESS-UNHEALTHINESS, WEARINESS-REFRESHMENT.

brack'-en. Fern. FAUNA-FLORA.

brack'-et. A support. ARCHITECTURE, CONNECTIVE, DUALITY, SUSPENSION-SUPPORT, UNION-DISUNION.

brack'-ish. Saltish. PUNGENCY.

brad. A thin nail. CONNECTIVE.

brad'-awl". An awl to make holes for inserting brads. PERFORATOR-STOPPER.

Brad'-shaw. A guide-book to English railways. TRAVELING-NAVIGATION.

brae. A hillside. HEIGHT-LOWNESS.

brag. Boast; a game of cards. BRAGGING, ENTERTAINMENT-WEARINESS.

brag"-ga-do'-cio. A braggart. BRAGGING.

brag'-gard-ism. Boastfulness. BRAGGING.

brag'-gart. A boaster. BRAGGING, BRAWLER.

brag'-ging. Boasting. BRAGGING.

BRAGGING

Blague. Pretentious falsehood.
Boast. The act of boasting; bragging.
Boasting. Ostentatious speaking or display.
Bombast. High-sounding language.
Bounce. Audacious boasting.
Brag. Showy pretense.
Braggardism. The act of boasting or bragging.
Bravado. Boastful conduct.
Buncombe. } Anything said to gain public applause. It comes from
Bunkum. } a remark made by a Congressman from North Carolina that he was talking "Only for Buncombe," a county in his congressional district.
Chauvinism. Very showy and exaggerated patriotism. From N. Chauvin, a soldier of Napoleon.
Crake. Boasting; a boast.
Exaggeration, etc. The act of overstating the truth. See GULL-HYPERBOLE.
Exultation. The act of excessive rejoicing.
Fanfaronnade. A blustering speech or style; vain boasting.
Fine talking. Boastful speech.
Flourish. An ostentatious display of words and figures.
Flourish of trumpets. Great rejoicing.
Gasconade. Boasting; bragging like Gascons.
Gloriation. Boasting.
Glorification. The act of making glorious.
Jactancy. A bragging.
Jactitation. A false assertion repeated to the prejudice of another's rights.
Magniloquence. Bombastic discourse.
Much cry and little wool. Much noise but little product, as when one shears the swine.
Pretense. False show.
Pretension. An assumed right.
Puff. An empty expression of praise.
Puffery. The bestowment of interested public commendation.
Rodomontade. Like Rodomonte in *Orlando Furioso*. Vainglorious boasting.
Tall talk. Bragging.
Teratology. Affected sublimity.
Triumph, etc. Exultation for success, etc. See SOLEMNIZATION.
Vanity, etc. Idle show, etc. See CONCEIT.
Vaporing. Idle boasting.
Vaunt. Ostentatious display.
Venditation. Showy display.
Vox et præterea nihil [L.]. Voice and nothing else.

BRAGGING—*Nouns of Agent.*

Blusterer A noisy swaggerer. See BRAWLER.
Boaster. One who boasts; a braggart.
Braggadocio. A braggart; a boaster.
Braggart. A boaster.
Brutum fulmen [L.]. A harmless thunderbolt.
Charlatan. An impostor.
Fanfaron [F.]. A bully.
Foxy Quiller. Bragging comic detective.
Heroics. Poems which celebrate the deeds of heroes.
Jackpudding. A buffoon.
Pretender. One who lays claim or asserts a title to something.

Puppy, etc. A conceited and impertinent person. See SOCIETY-DANDY.
Soi-disant [F.]. A pretender.
Trumpeter. One who proclaims, publishes, or denounces

BRAGGING—*Verbs*

Ballarag. To boast.
Boast. To speak vaingloriously, especially of oneself or one's belongings.
Brag. To speak boastfully.
Chuckle. To laugh in an exulting or derisive manner.
Crack. } To talk boastfully; to crack up, as a whip.
Crake. }
Crow over. To exult triumphantly over, like a game-cock.
Exult. To rejoice triumphantly; to leap up.
Faire claquer son fouet [F.]. To crack a whip; hence, to make a noise in the world.
Halloo before one is out of the wood. To shout before one is out of danger.
Make a boast of. } Exult over.
Make a merit of. }
Neigh. To utter a cry like a horse; to scoff or jeer
Puff. To flatter or to praise excessively; to blow up, as a bladder.
Se faire valoir [F.]. To maintain one's dignity.
Show off. To make a display of oneself.
Sing *Io triumphe.* To sing as Roman soldiers at a triumph.
Strut. To walk about with affected dignity.
Swagger. To bluster or boast noisily.
Take merit to oneself. Assume credit.
Talk big. To brag; to speak great [Bacon, *Essay on Friendship*].
Throw up one's cap. To exult exceedingly, as over a victory.
Triumph. To gain a victory; to celebrate a victory.
Trumpet. To proclaim abroad.
Vapor. To indulge in idle talk; to boast; to blow off steam.
Vaunt. To make an ostentatious display of; to display with vanity.

BRAGGING—*Adjectives.*

Boastful. Disposed to boast.
Boasting. See *Verbs.*
Braggart. Boastful.
Cock-a-hoop. Exulting.
Elate. Puffed up by success.
Elated. Filled with exultation.
Exultant. Given to rejoicing.
Flaming. Very ardent.
Flushed. Glowing with excitement.
Flushed with victory.
Gasconading. Inclined to brag or boast like a Gascon.
In high feather. Exulting in spirit.
Jubilant. Shouting songs of triumph.
Magniloquent. Speaking in a pompous style.
On stilts. Elevated as if on stilts, hence pompous.
Pretentious. Inclined to claim more than is one's due.
Soi-disant. [F.] Self-styled.
Stilted. Bombastic.
Thrasonic. Pertaining to Thraso, a braggart soldier in Terence's *Eunuch*, hence boastful.
Triumphant. Exultant over victory.
Vainglorious. Possessed of empty pride. See CONCEIT.
Vaunted. See *Verbs.*

BRAGGING—*Adverbs.*

Vauntingly, etc. See *Adjectives.*

BRAGGING—*Phrases.*

Curæ leves loquuntur, ingentes stupent [L.]. Trivial anxieties talk, great ones stand mute.
Facta non verba [L.]. Deeds, not words.
"Let the galled jade wince." [Shakespeare, *Hamlet, III, ii.*]

Brah'-ma. The Hindu Supreme Creator. JOVE-FIEND.

Brah'-man. A member of the first caste of India. ORTHODOXY-HETERODOXY.

Brah'-min. A member of the first caste of India. MINISTRY-LAITY, ORTHODOXY-HETERODOXY.

Brah-min'-ic-al. Pertaining to the doctrines of the Brahmins. ORTHODOXY-HETERODOXY.

braid. To plait; sort of lace. CONNECTIVE, CROSSING, UNION-DISUNION, VARIEGATION.

brain. The understanding; to kill. LIFE-KILLING; MIND-IMBECILITY, SAGACITY-INCAPACITY; **blow one's**

brains out, LIFE-KILLING; **coinage of the brain,** FANCY; **suck one's brains,** INVESTIGATION-ANSWER; **rack one's brains,** FANCY, MIND-IMBECILITY.

brain'-less. Witless. SAGACITY-INCAPACITY.

brain'-pan''. The skull. MIND-IMBECILITY.

brain'-sick'': Mentally disordered. HEED-DISREGARD.

brain'-work''. Mental labor. REFLECTION-VACANCY.

brake. A fern; a harrow. FAUNA-FLORA, RELEASE-PRISON.

bram'-ble. A prickly shrub. REMEDY-BANE, SHARPNESS-BLUNTNESS.

bran. Husk. FRIABILITY.

bran'-card. A horse-litter. CONVEYANCE-VESSEL.

branch. A bough; a department. FAUNA-FLORA, PARENTAGE-PROGENY, WHOLE-PART; **branch off,** CONCENTRATION - RADIATION, DOUBLING - HALVING; **branch out,** DOUBLING-HALVING, TERSENESS-PROLIXITY.

branch'-ing. The act of sending forth branches. PROPORTION-DEFORMITY.

brand. A mark; a sword; a disgrace; a kind. ADULATION - DISPARAGEMENT, APPROVAL - DISAPPROVAL, COMBUSTIBLE, HEATING-COOLING, LUMINARY-SHADE, REPUTATION-DISCREDIT, SIGN, WEAPON; **brand of discord,** VARIANCE-ACCORD; **brand new,** NOVELTY-ANTIQUITY; **brand with reproach,** JUSTIFICATION-CHARGE.

bran'-dish. Flourish. AGITATION, POMP, VIBRATION.

bran'-gle. Brawl. VARIANCE-ACCORD.

bran'-gler. A wrangler. ANTAGONIST-ASSISTANT.

brank. To restrain. RECOMPENSE-SCOURGE.

bran'-ny. Like bran. FRIABILITY.

bras croisés, les [F.] (brɑ crwɑ-zě', le). With hands folded. ACTION-PASSIVENESS.

bras ouverts, à [F.] (brɑz u-var', ɑ). With open arms. POLITENESS-IMPOLITENESS.

brash. A transient attack of sickness. HEALTH-SICKNESS.

bra'-sier. A brass-worker. OVEN-REFRIGERATOR.

brass. An alloy of copper and zinc; boldness. BRAGGING; **brass band,** MUSICAL INSTRUMENTS; **brass-colored,** BLUENESS-ORANGE; **brass farthing,** CONSEQUENCE-INSIGNIFICANCE; **bold as brass,** BRAVERY-COWARDICE.

brat. A contemptuous name for a child. INFANT-VETERAN.

brat'-ling. An infant. INFANT-VETERAN.

bra-va'-do. A brag. BRAGGING.

brave. Fearless; bold; to dare. BRAVERY-COWARDICE, DEFIANCE, EMOTION, EXCITABILITY-INEXCITABILITY, HEALTH-SICKNESS; **brave a thousand years** [Campbell, *Ye Mariners of England*], LASTINGNESS-TRANSIENTNESS.

bra'-ver-y. Courage. BRAVERY-COWARDICE.

BRAVERY—COWARDICE.

Audacity. Excessive tendency to venture.

Backbone. Firmness.

Boldness, etc. Readiness to meet danger, etc. See *Adjectives.*

Bottom. Power of endurance. See PERSISTENCE.

Bravery. Sustained energy of soul in the presence of living or active opponents.

Bulldog courage. Determination; persistence.

Chivalry. Conduct becoming a knight.

Confidence. Trust in oneself or another.

Contempt of danger. Recklessness.

Courage. Calm and persistent bravery in the presence of moral as well as physical dangers; a stout heart.

Daring. Eagerness to encounter dangers.

Dash. Animation.

Defiance of danger. Utter recklessness.

Face. Effrontery.

Firmness. Persistence in an opinion or position. See DEFIANCE.

Fortitude. Firmness of mind in resisting dangers and sufferings.

Gallantry. Spirited and adventurous courage with gaiety.

Game. Gallantry; the spirit of a game-cock.

Hardihood. Boldness, united with firmness and constancy of mind.

Heart. Spirit.

Heart of grace. Courageousness.

Heart of oak. Courage, valor.

Heroism. The courage of a hero or demigod.

Intrepidity. The quality of sustaining the most extreme and appalling dangers unmoved.

Manhood. ⎫
Manliness. ⎬ Courage. virtue, etc

Mettle. Ardor. The metal of which a warrior is made.

Nerve. Fearlessness.

Pluck. Spirit; indomitable resolution.

Prowess. Bravery combined with skill.

Rashness, etc. Undue haste in action, etc. See RECKLESSNESS.

Resoluteness. Firmness in purpose.

Resolution. ⎫
Self-reliance. ⎬ Confidence in oneself.

Spirit. Vivacity; nerve, heart, pluck, stomach for a fight.

Spunk. Spirit, or pluck; touchwood; tinder.

Valor. Quality shown by refusing to yield and fly.

Virtue. Moral excellence; in early Rome, pluck.

BRAVERY—*Agents.*

Amazon. One of a fabulous race of female warriors in Scythia.

Bulldog. A fierce dog noted for its persistence; hence, a determined person.

Bully. A fellow, more insolent than courageous.

Demigod. A fabulous hero, the offspring of a deity and a mortal.

Fighting-cock. A male fowl kept for fighting; hence, a quarrelsome person.

Baseness. Dishonorableness.

Cowardice. ⎫
Cowardliness. ⎬ State or quality of being fearful. See *Adjectives.*

Dastardness. ⎫
Dastardly. ⎬ Base cowardice.

Effeminacy. Womanish delicacy or softness.

Fear. Feeling aroused by the expectation of danger. See SANGUINENESS-TIMIDITY.

Funk. Cowardly fright.

Poltroonery. Mean-spirited cowardliness.

Pusillanimity. Lack of firmness of heart.

Timidity. Disposition of being afraid of offending others, or experiencing ill from them.

COWARDICE—*Denotations.*

Alarmist. A person who is always on the lookout for danger.

Coistrel. A coward.

Coward. A person who lacks courage.

Dastard. A person who does mean, cowardly acts.

Midget. A person who does small, low deeds.

Milksop. An effeminate person.

Pessimist. A person who sees danger and evil in all change.

Poltroon. A base, cowardly person.

Recreant. One who has failed or proved false to a trust.

Runagate. See QUEST-EVASION.

Sneak. A person who does stealthy, mean deeds.

Terrorist. A person who finds cause of alarm in small deeds.

COWARDICE—*Figurative Terms.*

Bob Acres. Boasting coward. [Sheridan's *Rivals.*]

Dunghill-cock. Cock of ordinary breed.

Jerry Sneak. The type of a foolish, but good-hearted, hen-pecked husband. [Foote's *Mayor of Garratt.*]

One that cannot say "Bo" to a goose. A very timid person.

Shycock. An easily frightened person.

White-liver. A coward.

COWARDICE —*Verbs.*

Be a coward, etc. See *Nouns.*

Be cowardly, etc. See *Adjectives.*

Cower. To bend in fear or shame.

Flinch. To shrink from danger.

Funk. Flinch.

Quail, etc. To tremble from fear in the presence of danger, etc. See SANGUINENESS-TIMIDITY.

Run away, etc. See QUEST-EVASION.

Show the white feather. Act like a coward.

Shy. To act timidly.

Skulk. To hide or move about so as not to be seen.

BRAVERY—COWARDICE—*Continued.*

BRAVERY—Agents—*Continued.*

Fire-eater. See RECKLESSNESS.
Game-cock. See FIGHTING-COCK.
Hector. The Trojan hero of the Trojan war.
Lion. The king of beasts; hence, a brave man.
Man. A strong, courageous person.
Man of mettle. A brave, determined person.
Panther. A fierce wild animal; hence, a persistent fighter.
Tiger. A wild animal; hence, a fierce person.

BRAVERY—*Associated Words.*

Achievement. A deed accomplished by great bravery.
Bold stroke. A deed requiring courage.
Exploit. A remarkable achievement.
Feat. A notable deed.
Heroic act. }
Heroic deed. } An act worthy of a hero.

BRAVERY—*Verbs.*

Beard. To oppose openly.
Be courageous. To be brave. See *Adjectives.*
Brave. To resist with bravery.
Cheer. To urge on.
Dare. To call directly or indirectly to combat.
Defy. To hold of little worth that which opposes. See DEFIANCE.
Embolden. To make bold.
Encourage. To give courage; to hearten.
Face. To resist boldly.
Fire. To arouse spirit.
Inspirit. To infuse spirit in.
Make bold. To put on a show of bravery.
Meet. To combat with.
Nerve. To summon all one's self-control and courage together.
Rally. To restore animation in.
Reassure. To restore courage to.
Stand. To resist without yielding.
Venture. To dare in a hazardous manner.

BRAVERY—*Verbal Expressions.*

Affront danger, confront danger; **beard the lion in his den,** to venture or provoke an open combat against great odds; **bear up,** to stand; **bear up against; be courageous** (see *Adjectives*); **bell the cat,** to discuss a venture which none are brave enough to undertake; **brave danger; come to the scratch,** to show the required or expected amount of bravery; **come up to the scratch;** confront danger; **defy danger;** despise danger; **face danger; front danger; give courage;** go through fire and water, to brave any danger; **hold out,** etc. (see PERSISTENCE); **hold up one's head,** to be fearless; **infuse courage; inspire courage; keep in countenance,** to appear undisturbed; **look boldly in the face; look danger in the face; look full in the face; look in the face; make a man of,** to develop manly qualities in; **make bold,** to venture; **march up to the cannon's mouth,** to walk into danger unflinchingly; **meet in front; mock danger; muster courage; nerve oneself; pat on the back,** to encourage, or to praise; **pluck up courage; pluck up heart of grace,** to revive one's spirits; **present a bold front,** put a bold face upon, to act in a bold and fearless manner; **put upon one's mettle,** to call forth one's utmost endurance; **raise a rallying cry; run the gauntlet,** pass through dangerous experiences; **screw up one's courage to the sticking place; show a bold front; show fight; stand against; stand fire,** sustain an attack; **stand to one's guns,** be firm; **summon up courage; take courage; take heart, take heart of grace,** to revive one's courage; **take the bull by the horns,** to meet a danger boldly.

BRAVERY—*Adjectives.*

Adventurous. Inclined to hazard life in adventures.
Audacious. Impudently bold or daring.
Aweless. Not affected by awe.
Bold. Ready to meet danger.
Brave. Not losing heart in the face of living or active opponents.
Chivalrous. Acting like a knight.
Confident. Trusting in oneself or others.
Courageous. Calmly and persistently brave in moral and physical dangers.
Daring. Anxious for adventures.
Dashing. Spirited.
Dauntless. Not easily daunted.
Determined, etc. Not wavering etc. See DETERMINATION.
Dogged. Stubbornly persistent.

COWARDICE—Verbs—*Continued.*

Slink. To steal away quietly.
Sneak. To hide or steal away in a cowardly manner.
Turn tail. Flee.

COWARDICE—*Adjectives.*

Base. Dishonorable in dealing with others.
Coward. }
Cowardly. } Lacking in courage to meet danger.
Craven. Meanly seeking to escape danger by begging off.
Dastard. }
Dastardly. } Fearfully shrinking from danger.
Dunghill. Of low birth, or of little worth.
Effeminate. Weak-hearted.
Fearful. Constantly looking for ill to befall one.
Frightened. Paralyzed with sudden fear. See SANGUINENESS-TIMIDITY.
Milksop. Effeminate.
Recreant. Unfaithful to a pledge.
Shy. Distrustful.
Skittish. Easily frightened.
Sneaking. Keeping out of view because of cowardice.
Soft. Not determined; yielding easily.
Spiritless. Lacking spirit.
Timid. Fearing to offend or receive offense from others.
Timorous. Lacking in moral firmness.
Unmanned. Deprived of one's nerve or courage.
Unsoldier-like. Cowardly.

COWARDICE—*Adjective Expressions.*

Chicken-hearted, faint-hearted, cowardly; in face a lion but in heart a deer, apparently bold, but really cowardly; **infirm of purpose** (see DETERMINATION-VACILLATION); **lily-livered; milk-livered; pigeon-hearted; smock-faced; unable to say "Bo" to a goose; weak-hearted; weak-minded; white-livered.**

COWARDICE—*Interjections.*

Devil take the hindmost!
Sauve qui peut [F.]. Save himself who can.

COWARDICE—*Phrases.*

Ante tubam trepidat [L.]. He trembles even before the trumpet sounds.
Audendo magnus tegitur timor [L.]. Great fear is covered by a show of daring.
Canes timidi vehementius latrant quam mordent [L.]. Cowardly dogs bark more fiercely than they bite.
One's courage oozing out. Losing one's courage slowly. [Sheridan's *Rivals.*]

BRAVERY—Adjectives—*Continued.*

Doughty. Brave.
Dreadless. Not affected with dread.
Enterprising. Acting with a calculated boldness.
Fearless. Not affected with fear.
Fierce. Showing a cruel disposition.
Firm. Fixed. See MUTABILITY-STABILITY.
Gallant. Displaying gallantry.
Hardy. Able to endure.
Heroic. Of a hero.
Indomitable. Unconquerable. See PERSISTENCE.
Intrepid. Calm in the face of the greatest dangers.
Lion-hearted. Very brave.
Lion-like. Bold as a lion.
Manful. Displaying valor and prowess.
Manly. Becoming a man.
Mettlesome. Courageous.
Penthesilean. Brave, like Penthesilea.
Plucky. Possessing spirit.
Pugnacious, etc. Inclined to fight, etc. See sub STRIFE.
Reassured. Encouraged.
Resolute. Uninfluenced by the consequences of his own action.
Savage. Rejoicing in the pain of others.
Self-reliant. Trusting in one's own abilities.
Soldierly. Acting like a soldier. See FIGHTING.
Spirited. Possessing ardor.
Spiritful. Spirited.
Stout. Firm, resolute.

BRAVERY—ADJECTIVES—*Continued.*

Unabashed. Not confused.
Unalarmed. Not alarmed.
Unappalled. Not appalled.
Unapprehensive. Not expecting something fearful or evil.
Unawed. Not affected with awe.
Unblenched. Not having shown fear by paleness of the face.
Unblenching. Not betraying fear by whiteness of the face.
Undaunted. Fearless.

Undismayed. Not frightened.
Undreaded. Fearless.
Unfeared. Not frightened.
Unshrinking. Not shrinking.
Valiant. } Unyielding in the face of danger.
Valorous. }
Venturesome. } Risky.
Venturous. }

BRAVERY—*Adjective Expressions.*

Bold as a lion; bold as brass; bold-spirited; heart of oak, brave; **high-mettled**; high-spirited; iron-hearted, unmoved by fear; **one's blood being up**; stout-hearted; strong-minded; upon one's mettle, having all one's spirits aroused; **up to,** required of some one to show ability. power, etc.; **up to the scratch,** ready to enter a contest.

BRAVERY—*Phrases.*

Audacter et sincere [L.]. Bravely and sincerely.
Courage sans peur [F.]. Courage without fear.
Fortes fortuna adjuvat [L.]. Fortune favors the brave.
Il a le courage de ses convictions [F.]. He has the courage of his convictions.

Omne solum forti patria [L.]. Every soil is fatherland to the brave man.
One's blood being up. Roused.
Virtus ariete fortior [L.]. Valor is stronger than the battering-ram.
Virtus millia scuta [L.]. Valor is a thousand shields.
Virtus vincit invidiam [L.]. Virtue prevails over envy.

bravissimo [It.] (bra-vis'-si-mo). Superlative of bravo, brave. APPROVAL-DISAPPROVAL.
bravo [It.] (bra'-vo). A bandit; well done! APPROVAL-DISAPPROVAL, LIFE-KILLING, RECKLESSNESS-CAUTION.
bra-vu'-ra. A passage that requires dash. MUSIC.
brawl. A noisy quarrel; revel. CRY-ULULATION, ENTERTAINMENT-WEARINESS, VARIANCE-ACCORD.
brawl'-er. A noisy fellow. ANTAGONIST-ASSISTANT, BRAWLER, INSUBORDINATION-OBEDIENCE.

Captain Bobadil. A character in Ben Jonson's *Every Man in His Humor.*
Chrononhotonthologos. The hero of a tragedy of the same name produced by Henry Carey, burlesque of Fielding's *Tom Thumb.*
Hector. The bravest of the Trojan warriors in Homer's *Iliad.*
Parolles. A boastful coward in Shakespeare's *All's Well that Ends Well.*
Sir Lucius O'Trigger. A fortune-hunting Irishman in Sheridan's comedy *The Rivals.*
Sir Oracle. A title used by Gratiano in Shakespeare's *Merchant of Venice* to ridicule those who affect wisdom.
Thraso. A braggart soldier in Terence's *Eunuch.*

BRAWLER.

Blusterer. One who blusters or is characterized by noisy violence.
Braggart. One who indulges in boasting. See BRAGGING.
Brawler. One who becomes involved in noisy quarrels.
Bully. A threatening, quarrelsome fellow.
Dare-devil. A very reckless person.
Desperado. A man of a reckless, desperate character.
Doctrinaire. A propounder of dogmatic theories.
Dogmatist. A bold propounder of principles.
Drawcansir. A braggart. [Buckingham's *Rehearsal.*]
Fanfaron [F.]. A blusterer; a bully.
Fire-eater. A daring fellow always ready for a fight.
Fury. A violent woman. See TURBULENCE.
Hackster. A bravo.
Jackanapes. A conceited fellow.
Jack-in-office. An insulting fellow in office.
Malapert. A bold, saucy person; pert.
Minx. A bold or lewd girl.
Mohawk. One of a group of ruffians who formerly infested the streets of London like Indians. [*The Spectator,* 1712.]
Prig. A conceited fellow.
Puppy, etc. A contemptible, impertinent fellow, etc. See SOCIETY-DANDY.
Rodomonte. A braggart. [*Orlando Furioso,* by Ariosto]
Roisterer. A turbulent fellow.
Rough. A coarse fellow; a bully.
Rowdy. A ruffian.
Saucebox. An insolent person.
Swaggerer. One who brags noisily; a blusterer.
Swashbuckler. A blusterer or boastful fellow.
Terrorist. An advocate of terrorism; an agent of the revolutionary tribunal during the French Revolution.
Vaporer. A braggart.

BRAWLER—*Denotations.*

Bantam-cock. A small fighting cock; hence, a fighting person.
Bombastes Furioso. The hero of W. B. Rhodes' farce *Bombastes Furioso;* a burlesque of *Orlando Furioso.*

BRAWLER—*Phrase.*

Canes timidi vehementius latrant quam mordent [L.]. Cowardly dogs bark more fiercely than they bite. [Q. Curtius Rufus.]

brawn'-y. Strong, muscular. GREATNESS-LITTLENESS, STRENGTH-WEAKNESS.
bray. Grind; cry. CRY-ULULATION, FRIABILITY.
Bray. A parish in Berkshire, England. **Vicar of Bray,** BIGOTRY-APOSTASY, PRESUMPTION-OBSEQUIOUSNESS.
bra'-zen. Bold. PRESUMPTION-OBSEQUIOUSNESS.
breach. A break; quarrel. DUENESS-UNDUENESS, INTERSPACE-CONTACT, UNION-DISUNION, VARIANCE-ACCORD; **breach of faith,** UPRIGHTNESS-DISHONESTY; **breach of law,** CONVENTIONALITY-UNCONVENTIONALITY, LAW-LAWLESSNESS; **breach of the peace,** VARIANCE-ACCORD; **custom honored in the breach** [Shakespeare, *Hamlet,* I, iv], HABIT-DESUETUDE.
breach'-load-er. A gun. WEAPON.
bread. Food made of flour or meal. NUTRIMENT-EXCRETION; **beg bread,** PETITION-EXPOSTULATION, UNSELFISHNESS-SELFISHNESS; **bread of idleness,** ACTIVITY-INDOLENCE; **bread of life,** DIVINITY, GODLINESS-UNGODLINESS; **bread upon the waters,** PROVISION-WASTE; **quarrel with bread and butter,** SKILL-UNSKILFULNESS.
bread'-bas''-ket. A tray for carrying bread. CONTENTS-RECEIVER.
bread'-fruit''. The fruit of an African tree. NUTRIMENT-EXCRETION.
bread'-stuff''. Material for bread. NUTRIMENT-EXCRETION.
bread'-win''-ner. Producer. LABOR-CAPITAL.
breadth. Broadness. BREADTH-NARROWNESS, LIGHT-DARKNESS.

BREADTH—NARROWNESS.

Amplitude. Greatness of extent or surface.
Bore. The size of a hole or the interior diameter of a gun-barrel or rifle-barrel.
Breadth. The distance from one side of a thing to the other; width.

Angustation. The act of narrowing.
Closeness. The state of being close or narrow.
Coarctation. Restriction to a narrow space.
Constriction. The act of contracting.

BREADTH—NARROWNESS—*Continued.*

Caliber. Diameter of a cylindrical body, as of a gun-barrel.
Corpulence. Excessive fleshiness. See GREATNESS.
Crassitude. Thickness.
Diameter. The length of a straight line through the center of a plane figure or solid, terminated at the boundary thereof.
Dilation. The state of being expanded or enlarged. See ENLARGEMENT.
Latitude. Distance from side to side; specifically, distance north or south from the equator.
Radius. A semidiameter.
Superficial extent. The measure of surface.
Thickness. The quality of being thick.
Width. Distance from side to side; the state of being wide.

BREADTH—*Verbs.*

Be broad, etc. See *Adjectives.*
Became broad, etc. See *Adjectives.*
Expand. To widen out; to enlarge. See ENLARGEMENT.
Render broad, etc. See *Adjectives.*
Thicken. To render thick.
Widen. To make wide; to increase in breadth.

BREADTH—*Adjectives.*

Ample. Large; making a full supply for every want.
Broad. Extended from side to side; wide.
Discous. Like a disk or flat circular plate.
Dumpy. Short and thick.
Extended. Stretched out in length and breadth.
Fanlike. Shaped like a fan.
Outspread. Expanded.
Outstretched. Spread out; extended outside of or beyond.
Squab. Fat; bulky.
Squat. Short and thick, like an animal sitting on its hams or heels.
Thick. Having a great extent or depth from one surface to its opposite.
Thick as a rope. Not very thick; comparatively thin.
Thickset. Having a short, stout body.
Wide. Having great extent between the sides; greatly extended every way.
Wide as a church door. [*Romeo and Juliet, III, i.*]

NARROWNESS—ADJECTIVES—*Continued from Column 2.*

Lean as a rake. [Chaucer, Prolog. *Canterbury Tales.*]
Macilent. Lean; emaciated.
Marcid. Lean; thin.
Meager. Deficient in flesh; thin.
Narrow. Of little distance from side to side.
Rawboned. With but little flesh on the bones.
Scant. Meager; less than is needed for the purpose
Scanty. Lacking in extent; narrow; small.
Shriveled. Drawn into wrinkles; shrunken.
Skinny. Wanting in flesh.
Slender. Narrow in proportion to the length or height.
Slender as a thread. Very slender.
Slight-made. Slim or slender.
Slim. Thin in proportion to the length or height.
Spare. Lean; lacking flesh.
Starved. Reduced in flesh by hunger.
Starveling. Lean; emaciated with want.
Tabid. Affected by a progressive wasting away of the body.
Taper. Gradually narrowed toward the end.
Thin. Of little thickness or distance from one surface to its opposite.
Thin as a lath.
Thin as a wafer.　}Extremely thin.
Thin as a whipping-post.
Threadlike, etc. Thin like a thread, etc. See LAMINA-FIBER.
Unexpanded. Not spread out or diffused.
Weedy. Like a weed, especially of a rank but weakly growth.
Worn to a shadow. Thin.

Contraction. The state of being drawn together or lessened. See ENLARGEMENT-DIMINUTION.
Emaciation. The state of being greatly reduced in flesh.
Exiguity. Thinness. See GREATNESS-LITTLENESS.
Exility. Smallness; slenderness.
Macilency. Leanness.
Marcor. A withering or wasting away of flesh; emaciation.
Mere skin and bones. State of being extremely thin or wasted away.
Narrowing. The act of making or becoming less wide or extended.
Narrowness, etc. See *Adjectives.*
Stricture. Contraction of a duct or channel.
Tapering. The state of becoming gradually small toward one end.
Tenuity. The state or quality of being thin.
Thinness, etc. See *Adjectives.*

NARROWNESS—*De　ions.*

Anatomy. A skeleton.
Finger's breadth. The width of a finger.
Ghant [Hind.]. A mountain pass.
Hair's breadth. The thickness of a hair.
Hour-glass. An instrument for measuring the interval of an hour.
Isthmus. A narrow neck of land connecting two larger divisions of land.
Lantern-jaws. Long thin jaws; hence, a thin visage.
Line. That which has length, but not breadth or thickness.
Middle. The waist.
Neck. A narrow portion of land.
Pass. A narrow valley.
Ravine. A narrow pass. See INTERSPACE.
Ridge. A raised line or strip of ground.
Shadow. A reflected image.
Shaving. A thin slice or strip shaved off with a plane.
Skeleton. The framework of the body.
Slip. A slender piece. See LAMINA-FIBER.
Spindleshanks. A person with slim legs.
Streak. A line or long mark.
Strip. A narrow, long piece.
Thread-paper. Thin paper used in wrapping up thread.
Vein. A narrow mass of rock or mineral.
Waist. A girdle or belt for the waist.
Wasp. An insect having a long, slender body.

NARROWNESS—*Verbs.*

Be narrow, etc. See *Adjectives.*
Contract, etc. To draw together or lessen in extent. See ENLARGEMENT-DIMINUTION.
Narrow. To make less wide or to restrict.
Render narrow, etc. See *Adjectives.*
Taper. To become smaller toward one end.

NARROWNESS—*Adjectives.*

Attenuated. Made thin or rare.
Barebone. So thin or lean that the bones show their forms.
Close. Narrow; closely confined.
Contracted, etc. Drawn together or lessened, etc. See ENLARGEMENT-DIMINUTION.
Delicate. Slight or slender.
Emaciated. Wasted away in flesh.
Extenuated. Drawn out or made thin.
Fine. Not coarse; thin.
Finespun. Drawn out to a fine thread.
Gaunt. Lean; wasting.
Hatchet-faced. Having a sharp visage.
Herring-gutted. Thin in the waist.
Incapacious. Narrow; small.
Lank. Slender; poorly filled out.
Lanky. Somewhat lank or thin.
Lantern-jawed. Thin-jawed or thin-visaged.
Lean. Lacking flesh; thin.

(Continued on Column 1.)

---

break. To rend; drawn; become bankrupt; to fall out. COMMISSION-ABROGATION, CONTINUITY-INTERRUPTION, CONVEYANCE-VESSEL, DUTY-DERELICTION, EDUCATION-MISTEACHING, ENTIRETY-DEFICIENCY, EXPOSURE-HIDINGPLACE, INTERSPACE-CONTACT, MUTATION-PERMANENCE, OBSERVANCE-NONOBSERVANCE, SETTLEMENT-DEFAULT, TOUGHNESS-BRITTLENESS, UNION-DISUNION, WHOLE-PART; **apply the break,** SWIFTNESS-SLOWNESS; **break a habit,** HABIT-

DESUETUDE; **break a lance,** ATTACK-DEFENSE, FIGHTING-CONCILIATION; **break a law,** CONVENTIONALITY-UNCONVENTIONALITY; **break away,** QUEST-EVASION; **break bread,** NUTRIMENT-EXCRETION; **break bulk,** ADMISSION-EXPULSION; **break down,** BETTERMENT-DETERIORATION, CREATION-DESTRUCTION, SUCCESS-FAILURE, TRANSCURSION-SHORTCOMING; **break forth,** ENTRANCE-EXIT; **break ground,** BEGINNING-END; **break in,** DOMESTICATION-AGRICULTURE, EDUCATION-

MISTEACHING, ENTRANCE-EXIT, LIBERTY-SUBJECTION; **break in upon**, CONTINUITY-INTERRUPTION, ENTRANCE-EXIT, OBSTRUCTION-HELP, OPPORTUNENESS-UNSUITABLENESS, ORGANIZATION-DISORGANIZATION; **break loose**, ESCAPE, RELEASE-RESTRAINT; **break no bones**, GOODNESS-BADNESS; **break of**, RENOVATION-RELAPSE; **break of day**, DIMNESS, MORNING-EVENING; **break off**, COMMISSION-ABROGATION, DISCONTINUANCE-PERMANENCE, QUEST-ABANDONMENT; **break the circuit**, ELECTRICITY; **break one's neck**, LIFE-DEATH, MIGHT-IMPOTENCE; **break on the wheel**, PLEASURABLENESS-PAINFULNESS, PUNITION-PENALTY, RECOMPENSE, SENSUALITY-SUFFERING; **break out**, BEGINNING-END, EXCITABILITY-INEXCITABILITY, HEALTH-SICKNESS, TURBULENCE-CALMNESS; **break Priscian's head**, GRAMMAR-SOLECISM; **break prison**, RELEASE-RESTRAINT; **break short**, TOUGHNESS-BRITTLENESS; **break silence**, SPEECH-INARTICULATENESS; **break the heart**, LIGHTHEARTEDNESS-DEJECTION, PLEASURABLENESS-PAINFULNESS, PLEASURE-PAIN, **break the ice**, AMITY-HOSTILITY; **break the neck of**, ENTERPRISE, SUCCESS-FAILURE; **break the peace**, STRIFE-PEACE, TURBULENCE-CALMNESS; **break the ranks**, ORGANIZATION-DISORGANIZATION; **break the teeth**, PURITY-CRUDENESS; **break the thread**, CONTINUITY-INTERRUPTION; **break through the clouds**, EXPOSURE-HIDINGPLACE, VISIBILITY-INVISIBILITY; **break through a custom**, HABIT-DESUETUDE; **break up**, BEGINNING-END, BETTERMENT-DETERIORATION, COMPOSITION-RESOLUTION, CREATION-DESTRUCTION, REVOLUTION, UNION-DISUNION; **break up of the system**, HEALTH-SICKNESS, LIFE-DEATH, SECURITY-INSECURITY; **break with**, VARIANCE-ACCORD; **break with the past**, REVOLUTION; **break word**, TRUTHFULNESS-FRAUD, UPRIGHTNESS-DISHONESTY.

break'-er. A trainer; wave. RIVER-WIND, SWAMP-ISLAND, WAYFARER-SEAFARER.

break'-ers. Huge waves. REFUGE-PITFALL, RIVER-WIND; **breakers ahead**, SECURITY-INSECURITY; **surrounded by breakers**, DIFFICULTY-FACILITY.

break'-fast. The morning meal. NUTRIMENT-EXCRETION.

break'-neck". A steep place; rash. PARALLELISM-INCLINATION, RECKLESSNESS-CAUTION.

break'-wa"-ter. A wall to break the force of waves. OBSTRUCTION-HELP, REFUGE-PITFALL.

breast. The chest; to meet. AFFECTIONS, ANTAGONISM-CONCURRENCE, CONVEXITY-CONCAVITY, MIND-IMBECILITY, OUTSIDE-INSIDE; **at the breast**, INFANT-VETERAN; **breast high**, HEIGHT-LOWNESS; **breast the current**, REPRISAL-RESISTANCE; **in the breast of**, PURPOSE-LUCK.

breast'-plate". Armor for the breast. ATTACK-DEFENSE.

breast'-work". A low parapet for defense. ·ATTACK-DEFENSE.

breath. Air inhaled or exhaled; life; breeze. ANIMALITY-VEGETABILITY, ETERNITY-INSTANTANEITY, LIFE-DEATH, LOUDNESS-FAINTNESS, RIVER-WIND; **breath of new-mown hay**, CITY-COUNTRY; **hold breath**, ASTONISHMENT-EXPECTANCE, EXPECTATION-SURPRISE, MOVEMENT-REST; **in the same breath**, COEXISTENCE, ETERNITY-INSTANTANEITY; **not a breath of air**, HEAT-COLD, MOVEMENT-REST; **out of breath**, WEARINESS-REFRESHMENT; **shortness of breath**, WEARINESS-REFRESHMENT; **take away one's breath**, ASTONISHMENT-EXPECTANCE, EXPECTATION-SURPRISE, SANGUINENESS-TIMIDITY; **take breath**, MOVEMENT-REST, WEARINESS-REFRESHMENT; **with bated breath**, VOCALIZATION-MUTENESS.

breathe. To respire; to utter softly. ADMISSION-EXPULSION, ANATOMY, ENLIGHTENMENT-SECRECY, ENTITY-NONENTITY, EVIDENCE-COUNTEREVIDENCE,

EXPOSURE-HIDINGPLACE, MEANING-JARGON, LIFE-DEATH, LOUDNESS-FAINTNESS, RIVER-WIND, SPEECH-INARTICULATENESS, VOCALIZATION-MUTENESS, WEARINESS-REFRESHMENT; **breathe freely**, ALLEVIATION-AGGRAVATION, PLEASURE-PAIN; **breathe one's last**, LIFE-DEATH; **not breathe a word**, ENLIGHTENMENT-SECRECY.

breath'-ing. Respiring. LIFE-DEATH; **breathing time**, FIGHTING-CONCILIATION, TOIL-RELAXATION.

breath'-less. Out of breath; exhausted. ASTONISHMENT-EXPECTANCE, DESIRE-DISTASTE, EMOTION, HEED-DISREGARD, HURRY-LEISURE, SANGUINENESS-TIMIDITY, VOCALIZATION-MUTENESS, WEARINESS-REFRESHMENT; **breathless attention**, INQUISITIVENESS-INDIFFERENCE; **breathless expectation**, EXPECTATION-SURPRISE; **breathless impatience**, DESIRE-DISTASTE; **breathless speed**, HURRY-LEISURE.

breech. The hinder part of anything. ANTERIORITY-POSTERIORITY.

breech'-es. A man's garment. **Breeches maker**, DRESS-UNDRESS; **breeches pocket**, CONTENTS-RECEIVER, MONEY; **wear the breeches**, RULE-LICENSE.

breed. To hatch; instruct. CREATION-DESTRUCTION, DIVISION, DOMESTICATION-AGRICULTURE, EDUCATION-MISTEACHING, PARENTAGE-PROGENY.

breed'-ing. Training. DOMESTICATION-AGRICULTURE, POLITENESS-IMPOLITENESS, SOCIETY-LUDICROUSNESS.

breeze. A slight wind. RIVER-WIND, VARIANCE-ACCORD.

breez'-y. Airy. RIVER-WIND.

breth'-ren. Formal plural of brother. MINISTRY-LAITY

breve. A note in music. MELODY-DISSONANCE.

bre-vet'. A commission giving an officer rank above his pay. COMMISSION-ABROGATION, LEAVE-PROHIBITION, ORDER; **brevet rank**, REPUTATION-DISCREDIT.

brevet d'invention [F.] (bre-ve' dan'-van'-si-on'). A patent. LEAVE-PROHIBITION.

bre'-vi-a-ry. The prayer-book of the Roman Catholic Church. CEREMONIAL.

bre-vier'. A small printing letter. WRITING-PRINTING.

brev'-i-ty. Shortness. LENGTH-SHORTNESS, TERSENESS-PROLIXITY.

brew. Mingle; to make beer. MIXTURE-HOMOGENEITY, PREPARATION-NONPREPARATION.

brew'-ing. A preparing of liquor; impending. OCCURRENCE-DESTINY, PREPARATION-NONPREPARATION; **storm brewing**, SECURITY-INSECURITY.

bri'-ar. A prickly plant. REMEDY-BANE, SHARPNESS-BLUNTNESS.

Bri-a'-re-an. Many-handed. MULTIPLICITY-PAUCITY.

bri'-ar-y. Full of briars. SHARPNESS-BLUNTNESS.

bribe. To corrupt by gifts. GIVING-RECEIVING, MOTIVE-CAPRICE, OUTLAY-INCOME, PROFFER-REFUSAL, RECOMPENSE-PUNITION, UNIFORMITY-MULTIFORMITY.

bri'-ber-y. The act of giving bribes. BUYING-SALE.

brick. A block of burned clay. GOOD MAN-BAD MAN, HARDNESS-SOFTNESS, HEATING-COOLING, MATERIALS, UPRIGHTNESS-DISHONESTY; **brick color**, REDNESS-GREENNESS; **make bricks without straw**, POSSIBILITY-IMPOSSIBILITY.

brick'-bat". A fragment of a brick. PUSH-PULL, WEAPON.

brick'-lay"-er. One who lays bricks. AGENT.

bri'-dal. Nuptial. MATRIMONY-CELIBACY.

bride. A newly married woman. MATRIMONY-CELIBACY.

bride'-groom". A newly married man. MATRIMONY-CELIBACY.

brides'-maid". A young unmarried woman who attends a bride at her wedding. MATRIMONY-CELIBACY.

brides'-man''. A male friend who attends upon a bridegroom and bride at their wedding. MATRIMONY-CELIBACY.

Bride'-well. A lockup. RELEASE-PRISON.

bridge. A structure carrying a road over some impassable place. CONNECTIVE, WAY; **bridge over,** COMPOSITION-RESOLUTION, DIFFICULTY-FACILITY, FIGHTING-CONCILIATION, UNION-DISUNION.

bri'-dle. A part of a horse's harness. PRIDE-HUMBLENESS, RELEASE-RESTRAINT, SENSUALITY-SUFFERING; **bridle one's tongue,** RECKLESSNESS-CAUTION, TALKATIVENESS-TACITURNITY; **bridle-road,** WAY; **bridle up,** FAVORITE-ANGER.

brief. Short. ACCOUNT, DIGEST, LASTINGNESS-TRANSIENTNESS, LENGTH-SHORTNESS, TERSENESS-PROLIXITY.

brief'-ly. Shortly; **in a few words.** EARLINESS-LATENESS, LASTINGNESS-TRANSIENTNESS, TERSENESS-PROLIXITY.

brig. A vessel of two masts. CONVEYANCE-VESSEL.

bri-gade'. A division of troops. BELLIGERENT.

bri-gade'-ma''-jor. An officer appointed by the brigadier-general to assist him in his duties. CHIEF-UNDERLING.

brig''-a-dier'. The commanding officer of a brigade. CHIEF-UNDERLING.

brig'-and. A lawless fellow. ROBBER.

brig'-and-age. Robbery. THEFT.

brig'-an-tine. A two-masted vessel. CONVEYANCE-VESSEL.

bright. Clear; witty; intelligent; promising. COLOR-ACHROMATISM, LIGHT-DARKNESS, LIGHTHEARTEDNESS-DEJECTION, REPUTATION-DISCREDIT, SAGACITY-INCAPACITY, SANGUINENESS-HOPELESSNESS; **bright days,** WELFARE-MISFORTUNE; **bright-eyed,** BEAUTY-UGLINESS; **bright prospect,** SANGUINENESS-HOPELESSNESS, TIMIDITY; **bright side,** PLEASURABLENESS-PAINFULNESS; **bright thought,** DESIGN, SAGACITY-INCAPACITY, WITTINESS-DULNESS; **look at the bright side,** LIGHTHEARTEDNESS-DEJECTION, SANGUINENESS-HOPELESSNESS.

bright'-en. To make bright. **Brighten up,** BETTERMENT-DETERIORATION, LIGHT-DARKNESS, LIGHTHEARTEDNESS-DEJECTION.

bright'-ness. Clearness; brilliancy. LIGHT-DARKNESS.

brigue. To contend. ASSOCIATION, STRIFE-PEACE.

briller par son absence [F.] (bri-yē' par son˙ ab-san˙s'). To be conspicuous by one's absence. PRESENCE-ABSENCE.

bril'-lian-cy. Great brightness. BEAUTY-UGLINESS, LIGHT-DARKNESS.

bril'-liant. Shining; a gem; good. BEAUTY-UGLINESS, EMBELLISHMENT-DISFIGUREMENT, GOODNESS-BADNESS, REPUTATION-DISCREDIT; **brilliant idea,** WITTINESS-DULNESS.

brim. Rim; to be full of. BORDER; **brim over,** EXCESS-LACK.

brim'-ful''. Full to the top. ENTIRETY-DEFICIENCY.

brim'-mer. A brimming glass, as of wine. ENTIRETY-DEFICIENCY.

brim'-ming. Full to the brim. ENTIRETY-DEFICIENCY.

brim'-stone. Sulphur. COMBUSTIBLE.

brin'-ded. Brindle. VARIEGATION.

brin'-dled. Spotted. VARIEGATION.

brine. The ocean; salt-water. OCEAN-LAND, PUNGENCY.

bring. To convey to; persuade; to produce an increase. **Bring about,** CAUSE-EFFECT, COMPLETION-NONCOMPLETION; **bring back,** TAKING-RESTITUTION; **bring back to the memory,** REMEMBRANCE-FORGETFULNESS; **bring forth,** CREATION-DESTRUCTION, MANIFESTATION-LATENCY; **bring forward,** BETTERMENT-DETERIORATION, EDUCATION-MISTEACHING, EVIDENCE-COUNTEREVIDENCE, MANIFESTATION-LA-

TENCY; **bring gray hair to the grave,** PLEASURABLENESS-PAINFULNESS, WELFARE-MISFORTUNE; **bring grist to the mill,** GAIN-LOSS, USEFULNESS-USELESSNESS; **bring home,** GAIN-LOSS; **bring home to,** EVIDENCE-COUNTEREVIDENCE, FAITH-MISGIVING, JUSTIFICATION-CHARGE, RATIONALE-LUCK; **bring in,** ADMISSION-EXPULSION, OUTLAY-INCOME, PRICE-DISCOUNT; **bring in a verdict,** DECISION-MISJUDGMENT; **bring in its train,** SOLITUDE-COMPANY; **bring in question,** FAITH-MISGIVING, INVESTIGATION-ANSWER; **bring into being,** CREATION-DESTRUCTION; **bring into play,** USE-DISUSE; **bring low,** REPUTATION-DISCREDIT; **bring off,** RESCUE; **bring out,** DISCOVERY, MANIFESTATION-LATENCY, WRITING-PRINTING; **bring over,** FAITH-MISGIVING; **bring round,** FAITH-MISGIVING, MOTIVE-CAPRICE, RENOVATION-RELAPSE; **bring to,** BUYING-SALE, CONVERSION-REVERSION, MOVEMENT-REST; **bring to a crisis,** PERSISTENCE-WHIM; **bring to bear upon,** AGENCY, CONNECTION-INDEPENDENCE, USE-DISUSE; **bring to life,** LIFE-DEATH; **bring to light,** DISCOVERY, EXPOSURE-HIDINGPLACE, MANIFESTATION-LATENCY; **bring to maturity,** COMPLETION-NONCOMPLETION, PREPARATION-NONPREPARATION; **bring to mind,** REMEMBRANCE-FORGETFULNESS; **bring to perfection,** ENTERPRISE; **bring to a point,** GATHERINGPLACE; **bring to terms,** FIGHTING-CONCILIATION; **bring to trial,** LITIGATION; **bring together,** GATHERING-SCATTERING; **bring under one's notice,** HEED-DISREGARD; **bring up,** ADMISSION-EXPULSION, CREATION-DESTRUCTION, EDUCATION-MISTEACHING; **bring up the rear,** ANTERIORITY-POSTERIORITY; **bring word,** ENLIGHTENMENT-SECRECY.

brink. Edge. **Brink of the grave,** LIFE-DEATH; **on the brink,** FUTURE-PAST, MAGNITUDE-SMALLNESS, REMOTENESS-NEARNESS.

bri'-ny. Full of salt. PUNGENCY.

brisk. Active; gay. ACTIVITY-INDOLENCE, LASTINGNESS-TRANSIENTNESS, LIGHTHEARTEDNESS-DEJECTION, VIGOR-INERTIA.

bris'-tle. A short, stiff hair. **Bristle up,** CONVEXITY-CONCAVITY, FAVORITE-ANGER, SHARPNESS-BLUNTNESS; **bristle with,** ENOUGH, EXCESS-LACK; **bristle with arms,** FIGHTING-CONCILIATION.

bris'-tling. Becoming like bristles. SHARPNESS-BLUNTNESS.

Brit'-ish. Pertaining to Great Britain and its people. DWELLER-HABITATION; **British lion,** DETERMINATION-VACILLATION, PATRIOTISM-TREASON.

Brit'-on. British. **True Briton,** UPRIGHTNESS-DISHONESTY.

brit'-tle. Fragile. TOUGHNESS-BRITTLENESS.

brit'-tle-ness. Friability. TOUGHNESS-BRITTLENESS.

britz'-ska. A long carriage. CONVEYANCE-VESSEL.

broach. To utter; pierce; a tapering tool. ADMISSION-EXPULSION, ASSERTION-DENIAL, BEGINNING-END, CAUSE-EFFECT, PUBLICITY.

broad. Wide; ample; gross. ASSERTION-DENIAL, BREADTH-NARROWNESS, GULF-PLAIN, PURITY-IMPURITY, UNIVERSALITY-PARTICULARITY; **broad accent,** VOCALIZATION-MUTENESS; **broad awake,** ACTIVITY-INDOLENCE, CAREFULNESS-CARELESSNESS; **broad daylight,** LIGHT-DARKNESS, MANIFESTATION-LATENCY; **broad farce,** WITTINESS-DULNESS; **broad grin,** JUBILATION-LAMENTATION; **broad highway,** WAY; **broad hint,** ENLIGHTENMENT-SECRECY; **broad meaning,** MEANING-JARGON.

broad'-cast. Widely spread. GATHERING-SCATTERING; **sow broadcast,** EXTRAVAGANCE-AVARICE.

Broad Church. The liberal wing of any Church. ORTHODOXY-HETERODOXY.

broad'-heart''-ed. Generous. CHARITABLENESS-MALEVOLENCE.

broad'-sheet''. A newspaper. MISSIVE-PUBLICATION.

broad'–shoul''–dered. Wide across the shoulders. STRENGTH-WEAKNESS.

broad'-side. A discharge of all the guns on one side of a ship; a paper printed on only one side. ATTACK-DEFENSE, LATERALITY-CONTRAPOSITION, PUBLICITY.

broad'-sword''. A sword with a broad blade and a cutting edge. WEAPON.

Brob''-ding-nag'-i-an. [Swift, *Gulliver's Travels.*] Gigantic. GREATNESS-LITTLENESS.

bro-cade'. A fabric woven with raised figures. EMBELLISHMENT-DISFIGUREMENT.

brocatelle [F.] (broc-a-tel'). A yellow variegated marble. EMBELLISHMENT-DISFIGUREMENT.

bro-chure'. A short pamphlet. MISSIVE-PUBLICATION.

Brock'-en. A mountain in Germany. **Specter of the Brocken,** SIGHT-DIMSIGHTEDNESS.

broder [F.] (bro-dê'). To embellish. GULL-HYPERBOLE.

brogue. A boot; a dialect. DRESS-UNDRESS, WORD-NEOLOGY, SPEECH-INARTICULATENESS.

broi'-der-y. Embroidery. EMBELLISHMENT-DISFIGUREMENT.

broil. A noisy quarrel; to cook over the coals. HEAT-COLD, HEATING-COOLING, STRIFE-PEACE, VARIANCE-ACCORD.

bro'-ken. Torn apart; humbled; ruined; rough. CONTINUITY-INTERRUPTION, STRENGTH-WEAKNESS; **broken down,** BETTERMENT-DETERIORATION, LIGHTHEARTEDNESS-DEJECTION, SUCCESS-FAILURE; **broken English,** WORD-NEOLOGY; **broken fortune,** AFFLUENCE-PENURY, WELFARE-MISFORTUNE; **broken heart,** LIGHTHEARTEDNESS-DEJECTION, PLEASURE-PAIN, SANGUINENESS-HOPELESSNESS; **broken meat,** USEFULNESS-USELESSNESS; **broken reed,** SECURITY-INSECURITY; **broken voice,** SPEECH-INARTICULATENESS, VOCALIZATION-MUTENESS; **broken winded,** HEALTH-SICKNESS, WEARINESS.

bro'-ker. An agent. CONSIGNEE, DEALER.

bro'-ker-age. The business of a broker; his fee. PRICE-DISCOUNT.

bro'-ker-y. The business of a broker. EXCHANGE.

bron'-chi-a. The air-passages of the lungs. WATERCOURSE-AIRPIPE.

bron'-chus. One of the divisions of the trachea. WATERCOURSE-AIRPIPE.

bronze. A compound of copper and tin. GRAY-BROWN, SCULPTURE.

brooch. A breastpin. EMBELLISHMENT-DISFIGUREMENT.

brood. Offspring; sitting on eggs. MULTIPLICITY-PAUCITY, PARENTAGE-PROGENY; **brood over,** LIGHTHEARTEDNESS-DEJECTION, REFLECTION-VACANCY.

brood'-ing. Hatching eggs. PREPARATION-NONPREPARATION.

brook. A small stream; bear. EXCITABILITY-INEXCITABILITY, RIVER-WIND.

brook'-let. A small brook. RIVER-WIND.

broom. A brush for sweeping. CLEANNESS-FILTHINESS.

broth. Thin soup. NUTRIMENT-EXCRETION.

broth'-el. A bawdy house. PURITY-IMPURITY.

broth'-er. A son of the same parents; a companion. EQUALITY-INEQUALITY, LIKENESS-UNLIKENESS, RELATIONSHIP.

broth'-er-hood. Union. AMITY-HOSTILITY, ASSOCIATION, GATHERING-SCATTERING, LIKENESS-UNLIKENESS, RELATIONSHIP.

Broth'-er Jon'-a-than. [Biblical.] Washington's name for Jonathan Trumbull, Gov. of Connecticut; a Yankee; the American people. PATRIOTISM-TREASON.

broth'-er-ly. Affectionate; kind. AMITY-HOSTILITY, CHARITABLENESS-MALEVOLENCE, LOVE-HATE.

brough'-am. A light carriage. CONVEYANCE-VESSEL.

brought. Past tense of bring. **Brought to bed,** CREATION-DESTRUCTION.

brouillerie [F.] (bruî-ye-rî'). Disagreement. VARIANCE-ACCORD.

brouillon [F.] (bruî-yon'). Blundering. DESIGN.

brow. The forehead; an edge. ANTERIORITY-POSTERIORITY, BORDER, TOP-BOTTOM.

brow'-beat''. To bully. PRESUMPTION-OBSEQUIOUSNESS, REGARD-DISRESPECT, SANGUINENESS-TIMIDITY; **brow-beaten,** SELFRESPECT-HUMBLENESS.

brown. A dark olo . GRAY-BROWN; **brown Bess,** WEAPON; **brown study,** HEED-DISREGARD, REFLECTION-VACANCY.

Brown. A family name. **Brown, Jones and Robinson,** GENTILITY-DEMOCRACY.

Brown'-i-an. Pertaining to the Scotch botanist, Dr. Robert Brown. ORTHODOXY-HETERODOXY.

brown'-ie. A household spirit. JOVE-FIEND.

browse. To graze. NUTRIMENT-EXCRETION.

bru'-in. A bear. POLITENESS-IMPOLITENESS.

bruise. To crush; to injure with blows. FRIABILITY, GOODNESS-BADNESS, PURPOSE-LUCK.

bruis'-er. A pugilist. BELLIGERENT.

bruit. A loud noise; to noise abroad. PUBLICITY, TIDINGS-MYSTERY.

bru'-mal. Wintry. HEAT-COLD.

brum'-ma-gem. A sham. TRUTHFULNESS-FRAUD.

bru-nette'. A woman of dark complexion. GRAY-BROWN.

brunt. Shock; an assault. CONTINUITY-INTERRUPTION, IMPETUS-REACTION; **bear the brunt,** ATTACK-DEFENSE, DIFFICULTY-FACILITY, EMOTION, EXCITABILITY-INEXCITABILITY.

brush. An instrument to brush with; thicket; a fight. CLEANNESS-FILTHINESS, PAINTING, SMOOTHNESS-ROUGHNESS, STRIFE-PEACE, SWIFTNESS-SLOWNESS; **brush away,** ADMISSION-EXPULSION, COMMISSION-ABROGATION; **brush up,** BETTERMENT-DETERIORATION, PREPARATION-NONPREPARATION; **paint-brush,** PAINTING.

brush'-wood. A thicket of small trees. FAUNA-FLORA.

brusque. Rough; blunt in manners. HURRY-LEISURE, POLITENESS-IMPOLITENESS, TURBULENCE-CALMNESS.

brusquerie [F.] (brüs-ke-rî'). Abruptness. HURRY-LEISURE, POLITENESS-IMPOLITENESS.

brus'-tle. To rustle. CRASH-DRUMMING.

bru'-tal. Inhuman; vulgar. CHARITABLENESS-MALEVOLENCE, POLITENESS-IMPOLITENESS, TASTE-VULGARITY.

bru-tal'-i-ty. Savageness. CHARITABLENESS-MALEVOLENCE, MIND-IMBECILITY, POLITENESS-IMPOLITENESS, TASTE-VULGARITY, VIRTUE-VICE.

bru'-tal-ize. To make brutal; · corrupt. BETTERMENT-DETERIORATION, SENSITIVENESS-APATHY, VIRTUE-VICE.

brute. A beast; cruel; coarse. BENEFACTOR-EVILDOER, FAUNA-FLORA, POLITENESS-IMPOLITENESS; **brute force,** COERCION, HARSHNESS-MILDNESS, LAW-LAWLESSNESS, MIND-IMBECILITY, STRENGTH-WEAKNESS, TURBULENCE-CALMNESS; **brute matter,** MATERIALITY-SPIRITUALITY, ORGANIZATION-INORGANIZATION.

Brute, et tu [L.] (Bru'-tî, et tiu). Thou too, Brutus. THANKFULNESS-THANKLESSNESS.

bru'-ti-fy. Brutalize. POLITENESS-IMPOLITENESS.

bru'-tish. Stupid; cruel. CHARITABLENESS-MALEVOLENCE, GENTILITY-DEMOCRACY, MODERATION-SELFINDULGENCE, TASTE-VULGARITY.

brutum fulmen [L.] (bru'-tum ful'-men). A harmless thunderbolt. BRAGGING, MIGHT-IMPOTENCE, RULE-LICENSE, SUCCESS-FAILURE.

Bry'-an-ite. "A Bible Christian." [Founded by Wm. O'Bryan, a Cornishman, 1815.] ORTHODOXY-HETERODOXY.

bub-ble. A small bladder of water; a cheat; to rise in bubbles. AGITATION, CONSEQUENCE-INSIGNIFICANCE, GREATNESS-LITTLENESS, HEAVINESS-LIGHTNESS, LASTINGNESS-TRANSIENTNESS, RIVER-WIND, SUBSTANCE-NULLITY, TRUTH-ERROR, TRUTHFULNESS-FRAUD, VISCIDITY-FOAM; **bubble burst,** EXPECTATION-DISAPPOINTMENT, SUCCESS-FAILURE, TRANSCURSION-SHORTCOMING; **bubble reputation,** REPUTATION-DISCREDIT; **bubble up,** AGITATION.

bub'-bling. Forming bubbles. VISCIDITY-FOAM.

buc''-ca-neer'. A pirate. ROBBER, THEFT.

buc''-ca-neer'-ing. Pirating. ROBBER.

buc''-ca-nier'. A pirare. ROBBER.

Bu-ceph'-a-lus. Alexander's favorite horse. CONVEYER.

buck. The male of deer, goats, etc.; a fop. CLEANNESS-FILTHINESS, FAUNA-FLORA, MALE-FEMALE, SOCIETY-DANDY, SPRING-DIVE; **buck basket,** CONTENTS-RECEIVER; **buck jump,** SPRING-PLUNGE.

buck'-et. A vessel for carrying water. **Drop bucket in empty well,** USEFULNESS-USELESSNESS; **kick the bucket,** LIFE-DEATH; **like buckets in a well,** VIBRATION.

buck'-le. An instrument for fastening straps; a curl. CIRCLE-WINDING, CONNECTIVE, UNION-DISUNION; **buckle on one's armor,** PREPARATION-NONPREPARATION; **buckle to,** PERSISTENCE-WHIM, TOIL-RELAXATION; **buckle with,** STRIFE-PEACE.

buck'-led. Fastened with buckles. CIRCLE-WINDING.

buck'-ler. A shield. ATTACK-DEFENSE.

buck'-ram. Haughty; stiffness of manners. SELFRESPECT-HUMBLENESS, SOCIETY-AFFECTATION; **men in buckram,** GULL-HYPERBOLE.

bu-col'-ic. Pertaining to shepherds; a pastoral poem. CITY-COUNTRY, DOMESTICATION-AGRICULTURE, POETRY.

bu-cra'-ni-a. Ornaments. ARCHITECTURE.

bud. An undeveloped flower; to graft; expand. BEGINNING-END, CAUSE-EFFECT, ENLARGEMENT-DIMINUTION, INJECTION-EJECTION; **bud from,** CAUSE-EFFECT.

Bud'-dha. A religious teacher. JOVE-FIEND, REVELATION-PSEUDOREVELATION.

Bud'-dhism. The Hindu religion, widely prevalent in Asia. ORTHODOXY-HETERODOXY.

Bud'-dhist. One who accepts the teachings of Buddhism. ORTHODOXY-HETERODOXY.

bud'-ding. The beginning. INFANCY-AGE.

budge. To move. MOVEMENT-REST.

budg'-et. A bag; a financial statement; a store. ACCOUNTS, CONTENTS-RECEIVER, GATHERING-SCATTERING, STORE; **budget of news,** TIDINGS-MYSTERY.

buff. A light yellowish color. REDNESS-GREENNESS; **native buff,** DRESS-UNDRESS.

buff'-er. A non-concussion apparatus. ATTACK-DEFENSE, OBSTRUCTION-HELP.

buf'-fet. Thump; to struggle against. AGITATION, FAVORITE-ANGER, GOOD-EVIL, GOODNESS-BADNESS, IMPETUS-REACTION, RECOMPENSE-PUNITION; **buffet the waves,** ANTAGONISM-CONCURRENCE, DIFFICULTY-FACILITY.

buf-fet'. A cupboard. CONTENTS-RECEIVER.

buffo [It.] (buf'-fo). A comic actor. ACTING.

buf-foon'. A clown. ACTING, SOCIETY-LAUGHINGSTOCK, WAG.

buf-foon'-er-y. Jests. ACTING, ENTERTAINMENT-WEARINESS, SOCIETY-DERISION, SOCIETY-LUDICROUSNESS, WITTINESS-DULNESS.

bug. An insect of many species. CLEANNESS-FILTHINESS.

bug'-a-boo''. A specter. ALARM, SANGUINENESS-TIMIDITY.

bug'-bear. A frightful object. ALARM, FANCY, SANGUINENESS-TIMIDITY.

bug'-gy. A light carriage. CONVEYANCE-VESSEL.

bu'-gle. A horn. FIGHTING-CONCILIATION, MUSICAL INSTRUMENTS; **bugle call,** ORDER, SIGN.

build. Construct. CREATION-DESTRUCTION, FORM-FORMLESSNESS, **build up,** INCLUSION-OMISSION; **build upon,** FAITH-MISGIVING; **build upon a rock,** MUTABILITY-STABILITY.

build'-er. An architect. AGENT.

build'-ings. Edifices for any use. DWELLER-HABITATION.

built. Erected. **Built on,** TOP-BOTTOM.

bulb. A round root; to swell. CONVEXITY-CONCAVITY, ENLARGEMENT-DIMINUTION, ROUNDNESS.

bulb'-ous. Having or growing from bulbs. CONVEXITY-CONCAVITY, ENLARGEMENT-DIMINUTION, ROUNDNESS.

bulge. A swelling. CONVEXITY-CONCAVITY.

bulk. Size; mass. GREATNESS-LITTLENESS, WHOLE-PART.

bulk'-head''. A partition in a ship. OBSTRUCTION-HELP.

bulk'-y. Large; unwieldy. GREATNESS-LITTLENESS.

bull. The male of cattle; the pope's edict; stockdealer. ADAGE-NONSENSE, GRAMMAR-SOLECISM, INCREASE-DECREASE, LABOR-CAPITAL, MALE-FEMALE, ORDER, TRUTH-ERROR; **bull in a china shop,** REGULARITY-IRREGULARITY; **take the bull by the horns,** BRAVERY-COWARDICE, DETERMINATION-VACILLATION.

Bull. A family name. **John Bull,** a typical Englishman. [Arbuthnot, *Satire*, 1712.] DWELLER-HABITATION.

bull'-calf. A dull, stupid fellow. SAGE-FOOL.

bull'-dog. A ferocious dog. BRAVERY-COWARDICE, DETERMINATION-VACILLATION, FAUNA-FLORA, PERSISTENCE-WHIM.

bul'-let. A ball for a gun. ROUNDNESS, WEAPON.

bul'-le-tin. An official report. MISSIVE-PUBLICATION, TIDINGS-MYSTERY.

bull'-fight. A fight in an arena between men and bulls. STRIFE-PEACE.

bull'-head. Stubborn. SAGE-FOOL.

bul'-lion. Uncoined gold or silver. MONEY.

bull's'-eye. The center of a target; a policeman's lantern. CENTER, LUMINARY-SHADE, PURPOSE-LUCK.

bul'-ly. A noisy fellow; to terrorize. BELLIGERENT, BENEFACTOR-EVILDOER, BRAVERY-COWARDICE, BRAWLER, CHARITABLENESS-MENACE, CITY-COUNTRY, GOOD MAN-BAD MAN, HARSHNESS-MILDNESS, PRESUMPTION-OBSEQUIOUSNESS, RECKLESSNESS-CAUTION, SANGUINENESS-TIMIDITY.

bul'-rush''. A large rush growing in damp places. CONSEQUENCE-INSIGNIFICANCE.

bul'-wark. A fortification. ATTACK-DEFENSE.

bum-bail'-iff. A sheriff's deputy. JUDICATURE.

bum'-ble-dom. Extravagant authority shown by petty officials. JUDICATURE, RULE-LICENSE.

bum'-boat''. A clumsy boat. CONVEYANCE-VESSEL.

bump. To strike; an extension. CONVEXITY-CONCAVITY, IMPETUS-REACTION.

bump'-er. A cup or glass filled to the brim. ENTIRETY-DEFICIENCY.

bump'-kin. A clown; a rustic. GENTILITY-DEMOCRACY.

bump'-tious. Self-conceited; aggressive. PRESUMPTION-OBSEQUIOUSNESS, REGARD-SCORN, SELFRESPECT-HUMBLENESS.

bunch. A hunch; a cluster. CONVEXITY-CONCAVITY, GATHERING-SCATTERING.

bunch'-backed''. Hunchbacked. PROPORTION-DEFORMITY.

bun'-combe. A district in N. C.; speech made for it by its Congressman; political claptrap; bombastic utterance. ADULATION-DISPARAGEMENT, BRAGGING, TRUTHFULNESS-FALSEHOOD.

bund [G.] (bunt). A league, especially of German states. ASSOCIATION.

bun'-dle. A number of things bound together; a parcel; to dismiss. GATHERING-SCATTERING, MEASURE, TRAVELING-NAVIGATION; **bundle on,** HURRY-LEISURE, SWIFTNESS-SLOWNESS; **bundle out,** ADMISSION-EXPULSION.

bung. A stopper for a barrel. PERFORATOR-STOPPER; **bung up,** APERTURE-CLOSURE.

bun'-ga-low. A one-storied house. DWELLER-HABITATION.

bun'-gle. Work clumsily. SKILL-UNSKILFULNESS.

bun'-gler. A clumsy person. ADEPT-BUNGLER, SKILL-UNSKILFULNESS.

bun'-gling. Awkward. SKILL-UNSKILFULNESS.

bun'-ker. A chest. CONTENTS-RECEIVER.

bun'-kum. Buncombe.

bun'-ting. A thin stuff used for flags. SIGN.

buoy. Support; a guide to ships. ELEVATION-DEPRESSION, HEAVINESS-LIGHTNESS, SANGUINENESS-TIMIDITY.

buoy'-an-cy. Power to float on or in a liquid or gas. ELASTICITY-INELASTICITY, HEAVINESS-LIGHTNESS, SANGUINENESS-HOPELESSNESS.

buoy'-ant. Floating; cheerful; light. ASCENT-DESCENT, ELASTICITY-INELASTICITY, HEAVINESS-LIGHTNESS, LIGHTHEARTEDNESS-DEJECTION, SANGUINENESS-HOPELESSNESS.

bur. A prickly head of a plant; a ridge. ENGRAVING, SMOOTHNESS-ROUGHNESS.

bur'-den. A load; care; refrain. CONTENTS-RECEIVER, EXCESS-LACK, HEAVINESS-LIGHTNESS, MELODY-DISSONANCE, OBSTRUCTION-HELP, PLEASURABLENESS-PAINFULNESS; PLEASURE-PAIN, **burden of a song,** RECURRENCE; **burden the memory.** REMEMBRANCE-FORGETFULNESS.

bur'-den-some. Grievous. GOODNESS-BADNESS, HEAVINESS-LIGHTNESS, OBSTRUCTION-HELP.

bu'-reau. A desk; office; a department of business. CONTENTS-RECEIVER, MARKET, PURITY-IMPURITY, TRIBUNAL, WORKSHOP.

bu-reau'-cra-cy. Government by bureaus. RULE-LICENSE.

bu'-reau-crat. A member of a bureaucracy. MANAGER.

burg. Borough. CITY-COUNTRY.

bur'-gee. A pennant. SIGN.

bur'-geon. To sprout. ENLARGEMENT-DIMINUTION.

bur'-gess. A citizen. DWELLER-HABITATION, PRESIDENT-MEMBER.

burgh. An incorporated village. DWELLER-HABITATION.

burgh'-er. A citizen of a burgh. DWELLER-HABITATION.

burgh'-mote. The court of a burgh. TRIBUNAL.

bur'-glar. A thief. ROBBER.

bur'-gla-ry. Housebreaking by night. THEFT.

bur'-go-mas''-ter. A chief magistrate. CHIEF-UNDERLING, PRESIDENT-MEMBER.

bur'-grave. The magistrate of a fortified town. CHIEF-UNDERLING.

bur'-i-al. A funeral. CEREMONIAL, LIFE-FUNERAL.

bur'-ied. Interred. CONFINEMENT, DEEPNESS-SHALLOWNESS, ENLIGHTENMENT-SECRECY, LIFE-FUNERAL; **buried in a napkin** [Bible], CAREFULNESS-CARELESSNESS; **buried in oblivion,** REMEMBRANCE-FORGETFULNESS.

bu'-rin. An engraver's tool. ENGRAVING.

burke. To murder by suffocation. [An Irish murderer, 1829.] LIFE-KILLING.

bur-lesque'. Laughable imitation; a dramatic travesty. ACTING, COPY-MODEL, IMITATION-ORIGINALITY, REGARD-DISRESPECT, SOCIETY-DERISION, SOCIETY-LUDICROUSNESS.

burletta [It.] (bur-let'-ta). A comic opera. ACTING.

bur'-ly. Stout. GREATNESS-LITTLENESS.

burn. To destroy by heat; to be very active; to be full of passion. DISCOVERY, EXCITABILITY-INEXCITABILITY, HEAT-COLD, HEATING-COOLING, LOVE-HATE, RECOMPENSE-PUNITION, REMOTENESS-NEARNESS, RIVER-WIND; **burn daylight,** ACTIVITY-INDOLENCE; **burn in,** HEATING-COOLING; **burn one's fingers,** SKILL-UNSKILFULNESS; **burn out,** HEATING-COOLING; **burn the candle at both ends,** EXTRAVAGANCE-AVARICE, PROVISION-WASTE, TOIL-RELAXATION; **burn to,** DESIRE-DISTASTE.

burn'-er. A part of a lamp. LUMINARY-SHADE.

burn'-ing. Hot; passionate. DESIRE-DISTASTE, EMOTION, FAVORITE-ANGER, HEATING-COOLING; **burning pain,** SENSUALITY-SUFFERING; **burning shame,** REPUTATION-DISCREDIT; **burning with curiosity,** INQUISITIVENESS-INDIFFERENCE

bur'-nish. To polish. BEAUTY-UGLINESS, LIGHT-DARKNESS, SMOOTHNESS-ROUGHNESS.

bur'-nished. Polished. LIGHT-DARKNESS.

bur'-nish-er. One who burnishes; a tool for burnishing. SMOOTHNESS-ROUGHNESS.

bur'-noose. An Arabian garment. DRESS-UNDRESS.

bur'-nous. An Arabian garment. DRESS-UNDRESS.

burnt. Consumed by fire; scorched. HEATING-COOLING, REDNESS-GREENNESS; **burnt offering,** ATONEMENT, DEVOTION-IDOLATRY.

burr. A rough guttural sound. CACOPHONY.

bur'-rock. A small weir or dam in a river to direct the current to fish-traps at one side. OBSTRUCTION-HELP.

bur'-row. Excavate; a hole made by animals. CONVEXITY-CONCAVITY, ESTABLISHMENT-REMOVAL.

bur'-sar. A treasurer. TREASURER.

bur'-sa-ry. A treasury. TREASURER, TREASURY.

burst. To break; an explosion; to commence. CRASH-DRUMMING, ETERNITY-INSTANTANEITY, EXCITABILITY-INEXCITABILITY, FAVORITE-ANGER, TOUGHNESS-BRITTLENESS, TURBULENCE-CALMNESS, UNION-DISUNION; **bubble burst,** COMPLETION-NONCOMPLETION, EXPOSURE-HIDINGPLACE; **burst away,** QUEST-EVASION; **burst forth,** BEGINNING-END, ENLARGEMENT-DIMINUTION, VISIBILITY-INVISIBILITY; **burst in,** ENTRANCE-EXIT; **burst into a flame,** EXCITABILITY-INEXCITABILITY; **burst into tears,** JUBILATION-LAMENTATION; **burst of anger,** FAVORITE-ANGER; **burst of eloquence,** SPEECH-INARTICULATENESS; **burst of envy,** PARDON-ENVY; **burst of laughter,** JUBILATION-LAMENTATION; **burst out,** ENTRANCE-EXIT, EXCITABILITY-INEXCITABILITY, TURBULENCE-CALMNESS; **burst upon,** ARRIVAL-DEPARTURE, EXPECTATION-SURPRISE; **burst with grief,** JUBILATION-LAMENTATION; **ready to burst,** EXCESS-LACK, EXCITATION.

bur'-then. A load. CONTENTS-RECEIVER, EXCESS-LACK, HEAVINESS-LIGHTNESS, OBSTRUCTION-HELP.

bur'-y. To inter. CONFINEMENT, ENLIGHTENMENT-SECRECY, LIFE-FUNERAL; **bury one's talent,** LIFE-FUNERAL; **bury the hatchet,** FIGHTING-CONCILIATION.

bus'-by. A tall bushy fur cap. DRESS-UNDRESS.

bush. A low shrub; a thicket. FAUNA-FLORA, GULF-PLAIN, WHOLE-PART; **beat about the bush,** MIDCOURSE-CIRCUIT, TERSENESS-PROLIXITY.

bush'-el. A dry measure of four pecks. CONTENTS-RECEIVER, GREATNESS-LITTLENESS, MAGNITUDE-SMALLNESS, MULTIPLICITY-PAUCITY; **hid under a bushel,** CAREFULNESS-CARELESSNESS; **not hide light under a bushel,** SELFRESPECT-HUMBLENESS.

bush'—fight''-ing. Fighting under the cover of bushes. STRIFE-PEACE.

bush'-ran''-ger. An outlaw. ROBBER.

bush'-y. Overgrown. SMOOTHNESS-ROUGHNESS.

bus'-i-ness. Occupation; traffic. CONCEPTION-THEME, CONDUCT, EXCHANGE, OCCUPATION, OCCURRENCE-DESTINY, QUEST-EVASION; **full of business,** AC-

TIVITY-INDOLENCE; **man of business**, ADEPT-BUNGLER, CONSIGNEE; **mind one's business**, CAREFULNESS-CARELESSNESS, HEED-DISREGARD, INQUISITIVENESS-INDIFFERENCE; **send about one's business**, ADMISSION-EXPULSION; **stage business**, ACTING.

bus'-i-ness-like. Systematic; practical. ACTIVITY-INDOLENCE, CONDUCT, OCCUPATION, REGULARITY-IRREGULARITY, SKILL-UNSKILFULNESS.

bus'-kin. A half boot. ACTING, DRESS-UNDRESS.

bus'-kined. Having the feet laced in buskins; tragic. ACTING.

buss. A small two-masted vessel; a kiss. BLANDISHMENT, CONVEYANCE-VESSEL, POLITENESS-IMPOLITENESS.

bust. A statue of the head and shoulders. DELINEATION-CARICATURE.

bus'-tle. To stir quickly. ACTIVITY-INDOLENCE, AGITATION, DRESS-UNDRESS, HURRY-LEISURE, VIGOR-INERTIA.

bus'-tling. Hurrying. MUTABILITY-STABILITY.

bus'-y. Occupied. ACTIVITY-INDOLENCE, OCCUPATION.

bus'-y-bod''-y. A meddler with others' affairs. ACTIVITY-INDOLENCE.

but. Except; yet; save, etc. BOUNDARY, COMPENSATION, CONVENTIONALITY-UNCONVENTIONALITY, MODIFICATION; **but now**, TIME.

butch'-er. One who slaughters. BENEFACTOR-EVILDOER, LIFE-KILLING.

butch'-er-y. Wholesale slaughter; a slaughter house. LIFE-KILLING.

but'-ler. A servant in care of the liquors. CHIEF-UNDERLING.

butt. A limit; aim; one at whom fun is thrust. ATTACK-DEFENSE, CONTENTS-RECEIVER, IMPETUS-REACTION, PURPOSE-LUCK, SOCIETY-LAUGHINGSTOCK; **butt end**, BEGINNING-END.

butte. A conspicuous hill or low mountain range. HEIGHT-LOWNESS, GEOLOGY.

but'-ter. A substance obtained from cream. ADULATION-DISPARAGEMENT, HARDNESS-SOFTNESS; **butter bread on both sides**, EXCESS-LACK; **butter not melt in mouth**, POLITENESS-IMPOLITENESS.

but'-tered side. Side covered with butter. **Know on which side one's bread is buttered**, SKILL-UNSKILFULNESS, UNSELFISHNESS-SELFISHNESS; **not know on which side one's bread is buttered**, UNSELFISHNESS-SELFISHNESS.

but'-ter-fly''. A winged insect. BEAUTY-UGLINESS, DETERMINATION-VACILLATION, POMP, VARIEGATION; **break butterfly on wheel**, CHARITABLENESS-MALEVOLENCE, PROVISION-WASTE.

but'-ter-y. Containing butter. STORE.

but'-tock. The rump. ANTERIORITY-POSTERIORITY.

but'-ton. A knob for fastening. CONNECTIVE, CONSEQUENCE-INSIGNIFICANCE, CONVEXITY-CONCAVITY, GREATNESS-LITTLENESS, SUSPENSION-SUPPORT, UNION-DISUNION; **button up**, LEVELNESS, RELEASE-RESTRAINT; **button up one's pockets**, SETTLEMENT-DEFAULT; **take by the button**, ADDRESS-RESPONSE.

but'-toned up. Reserved. ENLIGHTENMENT-SECRECY.

but'-ton-hold''-er. A bore. ENTERTAINMENT-WEARINESS.

but'-ton-top. Top of a button; useless thing. USEFULNESS-USELESSNESS.

but'-tress. A support to a wall. ARCHITECTURE, ATTACK-DEFENSE, SUSPENSION-SUPPORT.

but''-y-ra'-ceous. Buttery. PULPINESS-OILINESS.

bux'-om. Plump; comely. LIGHTHEARTEDNESS-DEJECTION.

buy. Purchase. BUYING-SALE. **Buy a pig in a poke**, PURPOSE-LUCK; **buy and sell**, EXCHANGE.

buy'-ing. Purchasing. BUYING-SALE.

BUYING—SALE.

Bribery. The crime or offense of giving, offering, or accepting any gift, advantage, or emolument used corruptly to influence a public officer in his official action, or a private person in the discharge of a public duty.

Buying. Acquisition by payment of a price or value; purchasing.

Coemption. Buying the whole quantity of any commodity.

Emption. The act of buying.

Preemption. The act or right of purchasing before others.

Purchase. The act of seeking and acquiring property; buying for money or its equivalent.

Purchasing. Obtaining by the payment of money or its equivalent.

Refusal. The right of taking in preference to others.

Shopping. Visiting shops for the purchase of goods.

Slave-trade. The buying and selling of slaves.

BUYING—Nouns of Agent.

Buyer. One who buys.

Client. One who pays for advice from a legal adviser.

Customer. One who regularly makes purchases of a trader.

Employer. One who keeps men at work and pays them.

Emptor [L.]. Buyer.

Patron. One who protects, supports, or countenances.

Purchaser. One who purchases.

Vendee. The person to whom a thing is vended or sold.

BUYING—Verbs.

Bribe. Give a bribe to; corrupt with money or other reward.

Buy. Obtain for a price; purchase.

Buy in. Purchase stock in any fund or partnership.

Buy over the counter.

Complete a purchase. Make a purchase.

Go a shopping. Visit shops in order to purchase goods.

Invest in. Make an investment.

Keep in one's pay. Employ.

Make a purchase. Buy something.

Market. Buy in a market.

Pay. Make due return to, as for service rendered See SETTLEMENT.

Auction. A public sale of property to the highest bidder.

Custom. A tariff or duty assessed by law. See EXCHANGE.

Disposal. The act of disposing of something by gift, sale, or the like.

Dutch auction. The public offer of property at a price beyond its value, then gradually lowering the price, till some one accepts it as a purchaser.

Roup. A sale of goods by auction.

Sale. Exchange of property for money or its equivalent.

Vendibility. The quality or state of being vendible or salable.

Vendibleness. The quality or state of being vendible.

Vendue. A public sale at auction.

Vent. Sale; opportunity to sell; market.

SALE—Nouns of Agent.

Auctioneer. One who conducts a sale by auction.

Haberdasher. One who sells small articles of dress, thread, pins, etc.

Merchant. A person who buys and sells commodities as a business and for profit. See DEALER.

Seller. One who sells.

Vender. One who vends or sells; especially, a pedler.

Vendor. Same as VENDER, the common legal spelling.

SALE—Verbs.

Bring to market. Offer for sale.

Bring to the hammer. } Put up at auction.
Bring under the hammer.

Deal in, etc. Buy and sell; furnish, as a retailer. See EXCHANGE.

Dispense. Deal out in portions.

Dispose of. Part with; get rid of, as for money.

Effect a sale. Accomplish the sale of anything.

Hawk. Offer for sale by outcry in the street; peddle.

Let. Allow to be used or occupied for a compensation; rent

Mortgage, etc. Convey or make over by mortgage, etc. See SECURITY.

Offer. Tender or present for acceptance or rejection.

Offer for sale. Offer to give up for a price.

Put up for sale. Offer publicly for sale.

Put up to auction. Offer for sale at auction.

BUYING—SALE—*Continued.*

BUYING—Verbs—*Continued.*

Procure. Come into possession of by some means.
Purchase. Obtain as one's own by paying, or promising to pay, a price.
Rent. Secure the possession and use of for a consideration See LOAN-BORROWING.
Repurchase. Buy back or again.
Shop. Visit shops for the purpose of buying.
Spend. Pay out, as money, as in making purchases. See OUTLAY
Suborn. Induce or procure to commit perjury.

BUYING—*Adjectives*

Purchased, etc. Bought, etc. See *Verbs.*

BUYING—*Phrase.*

Caveat emptor [L Let the buyer beware.

SALE—Adjectives—*Continued from Column 2.*

Unsalable. Not salable; unmerchantable.
Vendible. Capable of being vended or sold; salable.

SALE—*Phrase*

Chose qui plaît est à demi vendue [F.]. A thing that pleases is half sold.

SALE—Verbs—*Continued.*

Realize. Obtain as a profit or return.
Resell. Sell over again.
Retail. Sell in small quantities to consumers.
Sell. Give up for a price; dispose of by sale.
Sell by auction, etc. See *Nouns.*
Sell off. Sell.
Sell out. Dispose of wholly or entirely.
Sell over the counter.
Turn into money. Sell for money.
Undersell. Sell cheaper than.
Vend. Transfer to another person for a pecuniary equivalent; sell.

SALE—*Adjectives.*

For sale. To be bought or sold.
In the market. On hand; for sale.
Marketable. Fit to be offered for sale in a market; salable.
On one's hands. In one's possession, care or management.
Salable. That may be sold; marketable
Unbought. Not bought; not sold.
Under the hammer. At auction.
Unpurchased. Unbought; not sold.

(*Continued on Column* 1.)

---

buzz. A low humming sound. CACOPHONY, CRY-ULULATION, PUBLICITY RESONANCE-SIBILATION, TIDINGS-MYSTERY.
buz'-zard. A bird of prey. SAGE-FOOL; **between hawk and buzzard,** AGITATION, PLEASURE-PAIN; **blind as a buzzard,** SIGHT-BLINDNESS.
by. Near; through means of, tc. INSTRUMENTALITY, LATERALITY-CONTRAPOSITION; **by and by,** EARLINESS-LATENESS, OPPORTUNENESS UNSUITABLENESS; **by itself,** SOLITUDE-COMPANY; **by means of,** AGENCY, MEANS; **by my tro.h,** etc., ASSERTION-DENIAL; **by no means,** MAGNITUDE-SMALLNESS; **by the card,** CONVENTIONALITY - UNCONVENTIONALITY; **by the hour,** etc., LOAN-BORROWING; **by the way,** CONNECTION-INDEPENDENCE, OPPORTUNENESS-UNSUITABLENESS, PURPOSE-LUCK; **go by,** TRANSCURSION-SHORTCOMING; **have by one,** HOLDING-EXEMPTION, PROVISION-WASTE.

bye. Secondary; **good bye.** God be with you. ARRIVAL-DEPARTURE, SOCIABILITY-PRIVACY.
by'-gone. Past. FUTURE-PAST, REMEMBRANCE-FORGETFULNESS; **let bygones be bygones,** PARDON-VINDICTIVENESS.
by'-law". A subordinate law or regulation. LAW-LAWLESSNESS.
by'-name". A nickname. NAME-MISNOMER.
by'-path". An obscure way. AIM-ABERRATION.
by'-play". A side-show. ENLIGHTENMENT-SECRECY, SIGN.
byre. A cow-stable. DWELLER-HABITATION.
bys'-sus. A kind of flax. SMOOTHNESS-ROUGHNESS.
by'-stand"-er. A looker-on. ONLOOKER, PRESENCE-ABSENCE, REMOTENESS-NEARNESS.
by'-way. A secluded way. WAY.
by'-word". A proverb; a nickname. ADAGE-NONSENSE, NAME-MISNOMER, REGARD-SCORN, WORD-NEOLOGY.

C

cab. A carriage. CONVEYANCE-VESSEL.

ca-bal'. Conspiracy of leaders. ASSOCIATION-DE-SIGN.

cab'-a-la. A mystic philosophy. DEVOTION-CHARM, ENLIGHTENMENT-SECRECY.

cab'-a-ret. A wine-shop. DWELLER-HABITATION.

cab'-bage. To pilfer. THEFT.

cab'-in. A small house. CONTENTS-RECEIVER, DWELLER-HABITATION.

cab'-ined, cribbed, con-fined'. Narrowly restrained. RELEASE-RESTRAINT.

cab'-i-net. A council; a chest of drawers; a private room. CONTENTS-RECEIVER, COUNCIL, RULE-LI-CENSE, WORKSHOP; **cabinet picture,** PAINTING.

ca'-ble. A heavy rope. CONNECTIVE; **slip cable,** MESSENGER, QUEST-EVASION.

cab'-man. A cab driver. MANAGER, MEASURE, WAY-FARER-SEAFARER.

ca-boose'. A nautical cooking place. OVEN-REFRIG-ERATOR.

cab"-ri-o-let'. A one-horse cab. CONVEYANCE-VESSEL.

cache. A place for storing. STORE.

cachet, lettre de [F.] (ca-shê', letr de). A sealed letter, RELEASE-RESTRAINT.

ca-chex'-i-a. } General bad health. HEALTH-SICKNESS,
ca-chex'y. } STRENGTH-WEAKNESS.

cach"-in-na'-tion. Loud laughter. JUBILATION-LA-MENTATION.

cack'-le. A shrill cry of a hen; idle talk; a chuckle. CONVERSATION-MONOLOGUE, CRY-ULULATION, JUBI-LATION-LAMENTATION, TALKATIVENESS-TACITURNITY.

cac"-o-de'-mon. An evil spirit. JOVE-FIEND.

cacoethes [L.] (ca-co-î'-thîz). A bad habit. DESIRE-DISTASTE, HABIT-DESUETUDE.

cacoethes loquendi [L.] (ca-co-î'-thîz lo-quen'-dai). The habit of talking. TALKATIVENESS-TACITURNITY.

cacoethes scribendi [L.] (ca-co-î'-thîz scri-ben'-dai). The habit of writing. WRITING-PRINTING.

cac-og'-ra-phy. Bad writing. WRITING-PRINTING.

cac-oph'-o-nous. Sounding harsh. CACOPHONY, MEL-ODY-DISSONANCE.

cac-oph'-o-ny. Disagreeable sound. CACOPHONY, MEL-ODY-DISSONANCE, PURITY-CRUDENESS.

CACOPHONY.

Acute note. A shrill and piercing note.

Alto. The lowest female voice or highest male.

Cacophony. A disagreeable sound.

Creak, etc. A prolonged, sharp sound made by friction. See *Verbs*.

Creaking, etc. A succession of creaks. See *Verbs*.

Discord, etc. A combination of sounds not in harmony. See MELODY-DISSONANCE.

Falsetto. The high artificial tones of the voice.

High note. A note high in the musical scale.

Roughness. The quality of being loud and grating upon the ears.

Sharpness, etc. The quality of being high in pitch and having a piercing sound, etc. See *Adjectives*.

Soprano. The highest female voice.

Stridor. A harsh grating sound.

Tenor. The highest male voice.

Treble. The highest of the four parts of music.

Voce di testa [It.]. The head-voice.

CACOPHONY—*Noun of Agent.*

Penny trumpet. Any instrument that makes a harsh disagreeable sound.

CACOPHONY—*Verbs.*

Burr. To pronounce with a rough whirring sound.

Buzz, etc. To produce a shrill murmuring sound like that of bees, etc. See RESONANCE-SIBILATION.

Clank. To produce a harsh metallic sound.

Clink. To produce a shrill metallic sound.

Creak. To produce a prolonged sharp sound by friction.

Grate. To produce a harsh sound by rubbing.

Jangle. To produce discordant sounds.

Jar. To produce a harsh rattling sound.

Pipe. To produce a shrill sound.

Scream, etc. To cry in a shrill voice, etc. See CRY.

Twang. To produce a quick, sharp noise; a nasal twang.

Yelp, etc. To bark in a sharp, shrill tone. See CRY-ULULATION.

CACOPHONY—*Verbal Expressions.*

Écorcher les oreilles [F.], to grate upon the ears; grate upon the ear; jar upon the ear; offend the ear; pierce the ears, pierce the head, to sound shrill and penetrating; set the teeth on edge, to sound so as to produce a disagreeable sensation in the teeth; split the ears, split the head, to have a piercing sound.

CACOPHONY—*Adjectives.*

Acute. Shrill and piercing.

Cacophonous. Having a disagreeable sound.

Coarse. Loud and harsh.

Cracked. Harsh and imperfect.

Creaking, etc. See *Verbs.*

Discordant, etc. Sounding together out of harmony, etc. See MELODY-DISSONANCE.

Ear-piercing. Sharp and penetrating in the highest degree.

Gruff. Rough and repulsive.

Grum. Harsh and guttural.

Harsh. Producing an unpleasant effect upon the ear.

High. Relatively acute.

Hoarse. Having a rough grating sound.

Horrisonous. Producing a terrible sound.

Piercing. Sharp and penetrating.

Rough. Loud and hoarse.

Sepulchral. Grave and low.

Sharp. Piercing and high in pitch.

Shrill. Intensely sharp.

Stridulous. Harsh and grating.

Trumpet-toned. Very loud and harsh.

Ca'-cus, den of. A robber's den. THEFT.

cad. A vulgar, low fellow. CHIEF-UNDERLING, GEN-TILITY-DEMOCRACY, TASTE-VULGARITY.

ca-das'-ter. A survey of lands. MENSURATION, REC-ORD.

ca-das'-tral. Pertaining to real estate. RECORD.

ca-dav'-er-ous. Resembling a corpse. BEAUTY-UG-LINESS, COLOR-ACHROMATISM, LIFE-CORPSE.

cad'-dy. A box. CONTENTS-RECEIVER.

cadeau [F.] (ca-do'). A present. GIVING-RECEIVING.

ca'-dence. Modulation of voice. ASCENT-DESCENT, MOVEMENT-REST, MUSIC, SOUND-SILENCE.

cadenza [It.] (ca-den'-za). A musical flourish. MUSIC.

cader va chi troppo alto sale, a [It.] (ca'-dêr va kî trop'-po al'-to sa'-lê, a). He goes to fall who climbs too high. RECKLESSNESS-CAUTION.

ca-det'. A pupil in a military academy. BELLIGER-ENT, CHIEF-UNDERLING, INFANT-VETERAN.

cadge. Act of begging. PETITION-EXPOSTULATION.

cadg'-er. A huckster, a beggar. DEALER, PETI-TIONER.

ca'-di. A judge. JUDGE.

cadit quæstio [L.] (kê'-dit ques'-ti-o). The question falls. PROOF-DISPROOF.

cad'-mi-um. A bluish-white element. YELLOWNESS-PURPLE, BLUENESS-ORANGE.

ca-du'-ce-us. The wand of Mercury. DEVOTION-CHARM.

ca-du'-ci-ty. Tendency to fall off. BETTERMENT-DETERIORATION, INFANCY-AGE, LASTINGNESS-TRANSIENTNESS.

cæ'-cal. Having an end closed. APERTURE-CLOSURE.

cæ'-cum. Cavity open only at one end. APERTURE-CLOSURE.

cælitus mihi vires [L.] (sî'-lit-us mai'-hai vai'-rîz). My strength is from heaven. STRENGTH-WEAKNESS.

Cæ'-sar. A Roman emperor. CHIEF-UNDERLING.

Cæsar, aut nullus, aut [L.] (Sî'-zar, aut nul'-lus, aut). Either Cæsar or nobody. DESIRE-DISTASTE, REPUTATION-DISCREDIT.

Cæ'-sar-ism. Unrestricted rule. TYRANNY-ANARCHY.

cæ-su'-ra. A break in a poetical foot or verse. CONTINUITY-INTERRUPTION, INTERSPACE-CONTACT, UNION-DISUNION.

cætera desunt [L.] (set'-er-a dî'-sunt). The remainder is wanting. ENTIRETY-DEFICIENCY.

ca''-fe'. A coffee-house. DWELLER-HABITATION.

caf'-tan. A Turkish undercoat. DRESS-UNDRESS.

cag. Keg. CONTENTS-RECEIVER.

cage. A place of confinement. CONTENTS-RECEIVER, DOMESTICATION-AGRICULTURE, RELEASE-PRISON, RELEASE-RESTRAINT.

Ca-gli-os'-tro. An Italian impostor. DEVOTION-MAGICIAN, GULL-DECEIVER.

cahotage [F.] (ca-o-tazh'). Jolting. HEAVINESS-LIGHTNESS.

Cain. First son of Adam. LIFE-KILLING.

ca-ique'. A narrow boat. CONVEYANCE-VESSEL.

cairn. A heap of stones. LIFE-FUNERAL, SIGN.

cais'-son. A military box; a water-tight box. CONTENTS-RECEIVER.

cai'-tiff. A vile, wicked wretch. BENEFACTOR-EVILDOER, GENTILITY-DEMOCRACY, GOOD MAN-BAD MAN.

ca-jole'. To dupe. MOTIVE-CAPRICE.

ca-jo'-ler-y. Deceitful speech. ADULATION-DISPARAGEMENT, MOTIVE-CAPRICE, TRUTHFULNESS-FALSEHOOD.

ca-jo'-ling. Duping. ADULATION-DISPARAGEMENT.

cake. A baked mass. COHESION-LOOSENESS, SOLIDITY-RARITY.

cal'-a-bash. A fruit; a vessel made of the fruit. CONTENTS-RECEIVER.

ca-lam'-i-tous. Disastrous. PLEASURABLENESS-PAINFULNESS, WELFARE-MISFORTUNE.

ca-lam'-i-ty. A misfortune. GOOD-EVIL, WELFARE-MISFORTUNE.

calamo currente [L.] (cal'-a-mo cur-ren'-tî). A running pen, a ready pen. WRITING-PRINTING.

ca-lash'. A carriage; a cap. CONVEYANCE-VESSEL, DRESS-UNDRESS.

cal-ced'-o-ny. Chalcedony. EMBELLISHMENT-DISFIGUREMENT.

cal''-ci-na'-tion. Roasting. HEATING-COOLING.

cal'-cine. To reduce to calx by heating. HEATING-COOLING.

cal'-ci-trate. To kick. IMPETUS-REACTION.

cal'-ci-tra'-tion. Act of kicking. IMPETUS-REACTION.

cal'-cu-late. To compute, to reckon. INVESTIGATION-ANSWER, NUMBERING, PURPOSE-LUCK; **calculated upon,** FAITH-MISGIVING.

cal'-cu-la''-ted. Computed. INCLINATION, PREDETERMINATION-IMPULSE.

cal'-cu-la''-ting. Computing; forecasting. EXPECTATION-SURPRISE, INVESTIGATION-ANSWER, RECKLESSNESS-CAUTION; **calculating machine,** NUMBERING.

cal'-cu-la''-tion. Computation; a forecast. EXPECTATION-SURPRISE, INVESTIGATION-ANSWER, NUMBERING, PURPOSE-LUCK, RECKLESSNESS-CAUTION.

cal'-cu-la''-tor. One, or a machine, that calculates. NUMBERING.

cal'-cu-lus. Calculation by algebraic symbols. NUMBERING; **calculus of differences,** NUMBERING.

cal'-dron. A boiling pot. CONTENTS-RECEIVER, CONVERSION-REVERSION, OVEN-REFRIGERATOR, WORKSHOP.

calèche [F.] (ca-lêsh'). Barouche. CONVEYANCE-VESSEL.

cal''-e-fac'-tion. A heating. HEATING-COOLING.

calembour [F.] (ca-lan-bur'). A pun. AMBIGUITY.

cal'-en-dar. A table of lengths of time. ASTRONOMY, CHRONOLOGY-ANACHRONISM, MARK-OBLITERATION, RECORD.

calendas Græcas [L.] (cal-en'-das grî'-cas). At the Greek calends. DURATION-NEVERNESS.

cal'-en-der. A smoothing machine. SMOOTHNESS-ROUGHNESS.

cal'-en-ture. A tropical fever. FANCY, HEALTH-SICKNESS, SANENESS-LUNACY.

calf. The young of cattle. FAUNA-FLORA, INFANT-VETERAN, SAGE-FOOL; **golden calf,** DEVOTION-IDOLATRY, REVELATION-PSEUDOREVELATION.

Cal'-i-ban. A monster. [*The Tempest.*] BEAUTY-UGLINESS.

cal'-i-ber. Internal diameter of; degree of mental power. APERTURE-CLOSURE, BREADTH-NARROWNESS, QUANTITY-MEASURE, REMOTENESS-NEARNESS, SAGACITY-INCAPACITY.

cal'-i-co. Cotton dress goods. DRESS-UNDRESS, MATERIALS.

ca-lid'-i-ty. Heat. HEAT-COLD.

ca'-lif. Caliph. CHIEF-UNDERLING.

cal'-if-ate. The office of calif. RULE-LICENSE.

cal-i-ga'-tion. Darkness. LIGHT-DARKNESS.

ca-lig'-i-nous. Dark. LIGHT-DARKNESS.

cal'-i-pers. An instrument like the compass for measuring diameters. INSTRUMENT, MENSURATION.

ca'-liph. A title of the successors of Mohammed. CHIEF-UNDERLING.

cal''-is-then'-ics. Art of exercise. BEAUTY-UGLINESS, EDUCATION-MISTEACHING.

cal'-i-ver. A 16th century hand gun. WEAPON.

calk. To make tight with oakum. RENOVATION-RELAPSE.

call. To summon; to be called divinely; a visit. CHURCH, DIVINITY, DUTY-DERELICTION, INNOCENCE-GUILT, MANAGEMENT, MOTIVE-CAPRICE, NAME-MISNOMER, ORDER, SIGN, SOCIABILITY-PRIVACY; **at one's call,** ACTIVITY-INACTIVITY, INSUBORDINATION-OBEDIENCE; **call attention to,** HEED-DISREGARD, SIGN; **call for,** NEED, ORDER, PETITION-EXPOSTULATION; **call forth,** EXCITATION, USE-DISUSE; **call in,** ADVICE; **call in question,** ASSERTION-DENIAL, FAITH-MISGIVING; **call into being,** CREATION-DESTRUCTION; **call into notice,** MANIFESTATION-LATENCY; **call into play,** USE-MISUSE; **call names,** ADULATION-DISPARAGEMENT, REGARD-DISRESPECT; **call of duty,** DUTY-DERELICTION; **call off the attention,** HEED-DISREGARD; **call out,** CRY-ULULATION, DEFIANCE; **call over,** NUMBERING; **call to,** ADDRESS-RESPONSE; **call to account,** APPROVAL-DISAPPROVAL, DUTY-DERELICTION; **call to mind,** REMEMBRANCE-FORGETFULNESS; **call to order,** ORDER, PRESIDENT-MEMBER; **call to the bar,** ADVOCATE; **call to the ministry,** MINISTER-LAITY; **call to witness,** EVIDENCE-COUNTEREVIDENCE; **call up,** EXCITATION, MOTIVE-CAPRICE, REMEMBRANCE-FORGETFULNESS; **call up from the vasty deep,** DEVOTION-MAGIC; **call upon,** ADVICE, DUENESS-UNDUENESS, DUTY-DERELICTION, MOTIVE-CAPRICE, ORDER, PETITION-EXPOSTULATION, SOCIABILITY-PRIVACY;

call up spirits, DEVOTION-MAGIC; **within call,** RE-MOTENESS-NEARNESS.

cal'-lant. A lad. INFANT-VETERAN.

call'-boy". A boy giving a summons. ACTING.

called, so. Called as stated. NAME-MISNOMER, TRUTH-FULNESS-FRAUD.

call'-er. One who pays a short visit to a person. AR-RIVAL-DEPARTURE.

cal"-les-thet'-ics. Science of the beautiful. BEAUTY-UGLINESS.

cal-lid'-i-ty. Shrewdness. SKILL-UNSKILFULNESS.

cal-lig'-ra-phy. Beautiful writing. WRITING-PRINTING.

call'-ing. Occupation. DUTY-DERELICTION, OCCUPA-TION.

Cal-li'-o-pe. A muse. POETRY-PROSE.

cal"-lis-then'-ics. Light gymnastics to promote grace. BEAUTY-UGLINESS.

cal'-li-thump". A noisy parade or serenade. TURBU-LENCE-CALMNESS.

cal-los'-i-ty. Hardened skin. HARDNESS-SOFTNESS.

cal'-lous. Unfeeling; hardened. FEELING-INSENSI-BILITY, SENSITIVENESS-APATHY.

cal'-lous-ness. State of being callous. SENSITIVE-NESS-APATHY.

cal'-low. Bare; youthful. DRESS-UNDRESS, INFANCY-AGE, INFANT-VETERAN.

calm. Absence of emotion; of hurry; of turmoil. ERECTNESS-FLATNESS, EXCITABILITY-INEXCITABIL-ITY, HURRY-LEISURE, MOTIVE-DEHORTATION, MOVE-MENT-REST, STRIFE-PEACE, TURBULENCE-CALMNESS; **calm before a storm,** CONVERSION-REVERSION; **calm belief,** FAITH-MISGIVING.

calm'-ness. State of being calm. SENSITIVENESS-APATHY.

cal'-o-mel. Chlorid of mercury. CHEMISTRY.

cal"-o-res'-cence. The production of bright heat-rays from obscure ones. HEATING-COOLING, REDNESS-GREENNESS.

ca-lor'-ic. Pertaining to heat. HEAT-COLD.

cal"-o-rif'-ic. Pertaining to heat. HEAT-COLD.

cal"-o-rim'-e-ter. A measurer of heat. THERMOMETER.

calotte [F.] (ca-lot'). A skullcap worn by Catholic clergy. VESTMENTS.

cal'-o-type. A method of taking photographic pic-tures. PAINTING.

cal'-o-yer. A monk. MINISTRY-LAITY.

cal'-u-met. An Indian tobacco-pipe. SIGN; **calumet of peace,** FIGHTING-CONCILIATION, STRIFE-PEACE; **calumet of war,** FIGHTING-CONCILIATION.

ca-lum'-ni-ate. Defame. ADULATION-DISPARAGEMENT.

ca-lum"-ni-a'-tor. One who slanders. FLATTERER-DEFAMER.

ca-lum'-ni-a-to-ry. Slanderous. ADULATION-DISPAR-AGEMENT.

ca-lum'-ni-ous. Slanderous. ADULATION-DISPARAGE-MENT.

cal'-um-ny. False report. ADULATION-DISPARAGE-MENT.

Cal'-va-ry. Place of Christ's crucifixion. FANE.

Cal'-vin-ism. System taught by Calvin. ORTHODOXY-HETERODOXY.

Cal'-vin-ist. Follower of Calvin. ORTHODOXY-HET-ERODOXY.

ca'-lyx. The outmost series of leaves of a flower. CON-TENTS-RECEIVER.

cam. A rotating piece. INSTRUMENT.

camarade [F.] (ca-ma-rad'). Comrade. FRIEND-FOE.

camarilla [Sp.] (ca-mar-il'-lya). A body of secret ad-visers. ASSOCIATION.

camarista [Sp.] (ca-mar-is'-ta). A maid of honor. CHIEF-UNDERLING.

cambio non è furto [It.] (cam'-bi-o non ê fur'-to). Ex-change is no robbery. EXCHANGE.

cam'-bist. One who deals in exchange bills. DEALER-TREASURER.

cam-boose'. Same as caboose. OVEN-REFRIGERATOR.

Cam'-bri-an pe'-ri-od. Portion of geological history. GEOLOGY.

cam'-bric. A white cotton or linen fabric. DRESS-UNDRESS, MATERIALS.

cam'-el. A ruminant of Asia and Africa. CONVEYER; **swallow a camel,** BIGOTRY-APOSTASY, SKILL-UN-SKILFULNESS.

cam'-e-o. A small convex stone carved in relief. CON-VEXITY-CONCAVITY, SCULPTURE.

camera lucida [L.] (cam'-er-a lu'-si-da). An optical in-strument. OPTICAL INSTRUMENTS.

camera obscura [L.] (cam'-er-a ob-sciu'-ra). An opti-cal instrument. OPTICAL INSTRUMENTS.

cam'-e-ra-ted. Arched over. CONTENTS-RECEIVER.

Camilla [L.] (ca-mil'-la). A swift-footed servant of Diana. SWIFTNESS-SLOWNESS.

camisade [F.] (ca-mi-zad'). A night attack; also a shirt worn by soldiers to distinguish comrades in the night-time. ATTACK-DEFENSE.

camisole [F.] (ca-mi-zol'). A short nightshirt. DRESS-UNDRESS.

camorra [Sp.] (ca-mor'-ra). A quarrel. ASSOCIATION.

camp. Quarters of a soldiery; a seat of action. DWEL-LER-HABITATION, ESTABLISHMENT-REMOVAL, LISTS.

campagna [It.] (cam-pa'-nya). Place; country. EX-TENSION-INEXTENSION, GULF-PLAIN.

cam-paign'. Organized action; a series of military operations. CONDUCT, FIGHTING-CONCILIATION, GULF-PLAIN.

cam-paign'-er. One who serves in a campaign. BEL-LIGERENT.

cam-paign'-ing. Conducting a campaign. FIGHTING-CONCILIATION, TRAVELING-NAVIGATION.

cam-pan'-i-form. Bell-shaped. CONVEXITY-CONCAV-ITY, ROUNDNESS.

cam"-pa-ni'-le. A bell-tower. HEIGHT-LOWNESS.

cam"-pa-nil'-i-form. Shaped like a campanile. ROUND-NESS.

cam-pan'-u-la"-ted. Bell-shaped. ROUNDNESS.

cam-pes'-tri-an. Pertaining to open fields. GULF-PLAIN.

cam'-phor. The solidified sap of an East Indian tree. PULPINESS-ROSIN.

cam'-pus. The grounds of a college. ERECTNESS-FLATNESS, GULF-PLAIN.

Campus Martius [L.] (cam'-pus mar'-shi-us). Place of assembly of Romans. LISTS.

can. To put up for conservation; a vessel; to be able. CONSERVATION, CONTENTS-RECEIVER, MIGHT-IMPO-TENCE; **best one can,** TOIL-RELAXATION.

ca"-naille'. Rabble. GENTILITY-COMMONALTY.

ca-nal'. An artificial waterway. APERTURE-CLOSURE, WATERCOURSE-AIRPIPE, WAY.

can"-a-lic'-u-la-ted. Grooved. GROOVE.

ca-nard'. A newspaper hoax. GULL-DECEIVER, TID-INGS-MYSTERY.

ca-na'-ry. A singing bird. FAUNA-FLORA.

can'-can. An indecorous dance. CONVERSATION-MONOLOGUE, ENTERTAINMENT-WEARINESS.

can'-cel. To mark out. COMMISSION-ABROGATION, MARK-OBLITERATION, OBSERVANCE-NONOBSERV-ANCE.

can'-cel-la"-ted. Latticed-like. CROSSING.

can-cel'-li. A lattice-work. CONTENTS-RECEIVER.

can'-cer. A malignant growth; a constellation. ASTRON-OMY, HEALTH-SICKNESS, PLEASURABLENESS-PAIN-FULNESS, REMEDY-BANE.

can"-de-la'-brum. A candlestick. LUMINARY-SHADE.

can'-dent. Heated to whiteness. HEATING-COOLING.

can'-did. Sincere in speech or spirit; white. CRAFT-

Artlessness, Truthfulness-Falsehood, Upright-ness-Dishonesty, Whiteness-Blackness.

can'-di-date. One who desires or is nominated to an office. Desire-Distaste, Petitioner.

can'-di-da-ture. The state of being a candidate. Proffer-Refusal.

can'-died. Hardened. Sweetness-Acidity.

can'-dle. A light-giving cylinder of fat. Combustible, Luminary-Shade; **bargain by inch of candle,** Contract; **burn candle at both ends,** Extravagance-Avarice, Toil-Relaxation; **candle-ends,** Generosity-Frugality, Increment-Remnant; **candle-holder,** Antagonist-Assistant; **candle-light,** Dimness; **candlestick,** Luminary-Shade; **hold candle to the sun,** Usefulness-Uselessness; **not fit to hold a candle to,** Supremacy-Subordinacy.

can'-dor. Openness; impartiality. Craft-Artlessness, Truthfulness-Falsehood, Uprightness-Dishonesty.

can'-dy. Thickened sugar. Solidity-Rarity.

cane. A walking-stick. Recompense-Punishment, Recompense-Scourge, Weapon.

ca-nes'-cent. Becoming white. Whiteness-Blackness.

canes timidi vehementius latrant quam mordent [L.] (kê-niz tim'-i-dai vî-hî-men'-shi-us lê'-trant quam mor'-dent). Cowardly dogs bark more fiercely than they bite. Bravery-Cowardice, Brawler.

can'-hook''. An instrument used for slinging barrels. Instrument.

Ca-nic'-u-la. The star Sirius. Luminary-Shade.

ca-nic'-u-lar. Relating to Sirius. Heat-Cold.

ca-nine'. Related to dogs. Fauna-Flora; **canine appetite,** Desire-Distaste.

canis in præsepi [L.] (kê'-nis in prî-sî'-pai). Dog in the manger. Unselfishness-Selfishness.

can'-is-ter. A metal box. Contents-Receiver.

can'-ker. Any ulcerous sore. Betterment-Deterioration, Contentedness-Discontentment, Health-Sickness, Remedy-Bane.

can'-kered. Infected with canker. Betterment-Deterioration, Favorite-Moroseness, Health-Sickness.

can'-ker-worm. A destructive worm. Benefactor-Evildoer, Maker-Destroyer, Pleasurableness-Painfulness, Remedy-Bane.

can'-ni-bal. One who eats human flesh. Benefactor-Evildoer.

can'-ni-bal-ism. State of being a cannibal. Virtue-Vice.

can'-non. A weapon of war. Impetus-Reaction, Lists, Loudness-Faintness; **cannon's mouth,** Bravery-Cowardice, Fighting-Conciliation.

can''-non-ade'. Continued firing of the cannon. Attack-Defense.

can'-non-ball.'' A ball shot from a cannon. Swiftness-Slowness.

can''-non-eer'. A gunner. Belligerent.

can'-nu-lar. Tubular. Aperture-Closure.

can'-ny. Shrewd. Craft-Artlessness, Sagacity-Incapacity.

ca-noe'. A small boat. Conveyance-Vessel; **paddle your own canoe,** Liberty-Subjection.

can'-on. (1) Rules of a religious order; gorge; a member of a cathedral. Ceremonial, Faith-Misgiving, Interspace-Contact, Law-Lawlessness, Minister-Laity, Music, Precept.

can'-on. (2) The inspired books of the Bible. Orthodoxy-Heterodoxy.

ca-non'-ic-al. Pertaining to the canon. Church, Conventionality-Unconventionality, Revelation-Pseudorevelation.

ca-non'-ic-als. Robes prescribed by canon. Dress-Undress, Vestments.

ca-non'-i-cate. Office of a canon. Church.

can'-on-ist. One skilled in canon law. Orthodoxy-Heterodoxy, Theology.

can''-on-i-za'-tion. A recognizing as part of the canons; a regarding as a saint. Ceremonial.

can'-on-ize. To regard as a saint. Ceremonial, Devotion-Idolatry, Reputation-Discredit.

can'-on law. Devotion-Idolatry, Law-Lawlessness.

can'-on-ry. The office of a canon. Church.

can'-o-py. A suspended covering. Architecture, Cover-Lining; **the canopy of heaven,** Universe.

canoræ nugæ [L.] (can-o'-rî niu'-jî). Melodious trifles. Wittiness-Dulness.

ca-no'-rous. Melodious. Melody-Dissonance.

cant. Pietistic talk; an inclination; any technical phraseology. Godliness-Ungodliness, Impetus-Reaction, Name-Misnomer, Parallelism-Inclination, Truthfulness-Falsehood, Word-Neology.

can-tan'-ker-ous. Given to wrangling. Favorite-Moroseness, Favorite-Quarrelsomeness.

can-ta'-ta. A choral composition. Music; **missa cantata,** Ceremonial.

can''-ta-tri'-ce. A female singer. Musician.

can-teen'. A soldier's flask; a sutler's shop. Contents-Receiver, Dweller-Habitation.

can'-ter. To cause to move in a canter. Swiftness-Slowness, Traveling-Navigation; **win at a canter,** Difficulty-Facility.

can'-ter-bur-y. A music stand. Contents-Receiver.

Can'-ter-bur-y tale. One of the tales of Chaucer. Truthfulness-Fabrication.

can-thar'-i-des. The Spanish fly. Vigor-Inertia.

can'-thus. Corner of the eye. Anatomy.

can'-ti-cle. A non-metrical hymn. Music.

cant'-ing. Speaking affectedly. Godliness-Ungodliness, Truthfulness-Falsehood.

can'-tle. A piece broken off. Whole-Part.

cant'-let. A small piece. Magnitude-Smallness, Whole-Part.

can'-to. A part of a large poem. Poetry-Prose.

can'-ton. A district. Extension-District.

can'-ton-ment. A camp for troops. Dweller-Habitation, Establishment-Removal.

can'-trap. A charm. Devotion-Charm.

can'-ty. Cheerful. Lightheartedness-Dejection.

can'-vas. A cloth for paintings; heavy cloth used for sails. Painting, Traveling-Navigation; **under press of canvas,** Swiftness-Slowness.

can'-vass. Act of soliciting; examination. Essay, Investigation-Answer, Petition-Expostulation, Ratiocination-Instinct.

can'-vass-er. One who canvasses. Petitioner.

can''-zo-net'. A short song. Music, Poetry-Prose.

caout'-chouc. India-rubber. Elasticity-Inelasticity.

cap. To complete; a covering; a hat; to tip; to salute; to excel. Completion-Noncompletion, Cover-Lining, Dress-Undress, Height-Lowness, Politeness-Impoliteness, Reprisal-Resistance, Supremacy-Subordinacy; **cap and bells,** Wag; **cap fits,** Harmony-Discord; **cap in hand,** Petition-Expostulation, Presumption-Obsequiousness, Regard-Disrespect; **cap of maintenance,** Scepter; **fling up one's cap,** Jubilation-Lamentation; **Fortunatus's cap,** Devotion-Charm; **set one's cap,** Blandishment, Love-Hate, Predecessor-Continuation.

ca''-pa-bil'-i-ty. Power of performing. Difficulty-Facility, Dominance-Impotence, Might-Impotence, Skill-Unskilfulness, Subjectiveness-Objectiveness.

ca'-pa-ble. Having ability. Might-Impotence, Skill-Unskilfulness.

ca-pa'-cious. Able to receive. Extension-Inextension, Greatness-Littleness; **capacious memory,** Remembrance-Forgetfulness.

ca-pac'-i-ty. Power to receive. Greatness-Littleness, Might-Impotence, Mind-Imbecility, Occupation, Sagacity-Incapacity, Skill-Unskilfulness, Subjectiveness-Objectiveness.

cap and bells, wear'-er of. Fool. Wag.

cap-a–pie. From head to foot. Entirety-Deficiency; **armed cap-a-pie,** Attack-Defense, Fighting-Conciliation, Preparation-Nonpreparation.

ca-par'-i-son. Decorative trappings. Dress-Undress.

cape. A sleeveless garment or cloak; a headland. Convexity-Concavity, Dress-Undress, Height-Lowness.

capella, alla [It.] (ca-pel'-la, al'-la) Church music. Music.

ca'-per. Frolicsomeness. Jubilation-Lamentation, Spring-Dive.

cap'-ful. Hatful. Magnitude-Smallness, Quantity-Measure; **capful of wind,** River-Wind.

ca-pil'-la-ment. A hairy covering. Lamina-Fiber.

cap'-il-la-ry. Hairlike. Lamina-Fiber.

ca-pil'-li-form. Formed like a hair. Lamina-Fiber.

cap'-i-tal. Resources; a city; a large letter; upper part of a column. Affluence-Penury, Architecture, City-Country, Dweller-Habitation, Consequence-Insignificance, Goodness-Badness, Labor-Capital, Letter, Money, Top-Bottom; **capital punishment,** Exculpation-Conviction; **make capital out of,** Betterment-Deterioration, Gain-Loss, Pretext; **print in capitals,** Consequence-Insignificance.

cap'-i-tal-ist. An owner of capital. Affluence-Penury, Labor-Capital.

cap'-i-tals. Large letters. Letter, Writing-Printing.

cap'-i-ta'-tion. Individual assessment. Numbering.

cap'-i-tol. Any state house. Attack-Defense.

ca-pit'-u-lar. Relating to an ecclesiastical chapter. Church, Ministry-Laity.

ca-pit'-u-late. To make terms. Yielding.

ca-pit''-u-la'-tion. Surrender. Yielding.

cap'-no-man''-cy. Divination by smoke. Prophecy.

ca-poch'. A monk's hood. Vestments.

ca'-pon. A gelded cock. Male-Female.

ca''-pote'. A hooded cloak. Dress-Undress.

cap'-ping. Saluting. Politeness-Impoliteness.

capriccio [It.] (ca-prit'-cho). A fantastic piece of music. Music, Persistence-Whim.

ca-price'. Any sudden change of mood. Persistence-Whim; **out of caprice,** Motive-Caprice.

ca-pri'-cious. Whimsical. Determination-Vacillation, Mutability-Stability, Periodicity-Irregularity, Persistence-Whim.

ca-pri'-cious-ness. State of being capricious. Persistence-Whim.

Cap'-ri-corn. Constellation. Astronomy.

cap'-ri-ole. An upward leap by a trained horse. Spring-Dive.

cap-size'. To upset. Reversal, Success-Failure.

cap-sized'. Upset. Success-Failure.

cap'-stan. A ship apparatus. Elevation-Depression, Instrument.

cap'-su-lar. Pertaining to a capsule. Contents-Receiver, Convexity-Concavity.

cap'-sule. A shallow dish; a seed vessel. Contents-Receiver, Covering-Lining.

cap'-tain. A chief or head. Chief-Underling, Manager, Supremacy-Subordinacy.

captandum, ad [L.] (cap-tan'-dum, ad). To attract. Adulation-Disparagement, Affectation, Ratiocination-Instinct.

captandum vulgus, ad [L.] (cap-tan'-dum vul'-gus, ad). For attracting the rabble. Pomp.

cap-ta'-tion. An attraction. Adulation-Disparagement.

cap'-tion. The taking of a person. Taking-Restitution.

cap'-tious. Apt to find fault. Approval-Disapproval, Favorite-Quarrelsomeness, Persistence-Whim.

cap'-tious-ness. Troublesomeness. Politeness-Impoliteness.

cap'-ti-vate. To engage the affections. Keeping-Relinquishment, Love-Hate, Motive-Dehortation, Pleasurableness-Painfulness, Release-Restraint.

cap'-ti-va''-ted. Charmed. Pleasure-Pain.

cap'-ti-va''-ting. Fascinating. Love-Hate, Pleasurableness-Painfulness.

cap'-tive. Taken prisoner; enthralled by passion. Guard-Prisoner, Love-Hate; **lead captive,** Liberty-Subjection; **make captive,** Release-Restraint.

cap-tiv'-i-ty. State of being captive. Release-Restraint.

cap'-tor. One who captures. Taking-Restitution.

cap'-ture. The act of capturing. Taking-Restitution.

Cap''-u-chin'. A Franciscan friar. Minister-Laity.

caput [L.] (kê'-put). Head. Council.

caput mortuum [L.] (kê'-put mor'-tiu-um). A dead body. Cleanness-Filthiness, Usefulness-Uselessness.

caquet [F.] (ca-ke') Idle talk. Talkativeness-Taciturnity.

car. A railroad vehicle. Conveyance-Vessel.

car''-a-bi-neer'. Carbineer. Belligerent.

car'-ack. A Portuguese merchantman. Conveyance-Vessel.

car'-a-cole. A sudden half-turn. Spring-Dive.

car'-a-co''-ler. One who makes caracoles. Traveling-Navigation.

caraffe [F.] (ca-raf'). A glass water-bottle. Contents-Receiver.

carambole [F.] (ca-ran'-bol') Impact of a cue-ball. Impetus-Reaction.

car'-a-mel. A kind of sweet candy Sweetness-Acidity.

car'-a-pace. Hard case of animals. Attack-Defense.

car'-at. A twenty-fourth part. Heaviness-Lightness.

car'-a-van. A camel train; a company Conveyance-Vessel, Traveling-Navigation.

car''-a-van'-sa-ry. An inn for caravans Dweller-Habitation.

car'-a-vel. A fast galley. Conveyance-Vessel

car'-bine. A short rifle. Weapon.

car''-bo–hy''-drate. A class of chemicals. Chemistry

car'-bon. A non-metallic element. Chemistry, Combustible, Heating-Cooling.

car-bo-na'-ceous. Pertaining to carbon. Combustible.

Car''-bo-na'-ro. A member of a secret society of Naples. Insubordination-Obedience.

car'-bon-ate. Salt of carbonic acid. Chemistry.

car''-bon-if'-er-ous pe'-ri-od. Period in geological history. Geology.

car'-bon-i-za''-tion. The act of carbonizing. Heating-Cooling.

car'-boy. A large glass bottle. Contents-Receiver

car'-bun''-cle. A brilliant, red gem; a boil. Convexity-Concavity, Embellishment-Disfigurement, Health-Sickness, Redness-Greenness.

car'-ca-net. An ornamental collar. Embellishment-Disfigurement.

car'-cass. A dead body; a bomb. LIFE-CORPSE, TEXTURE, WEAPON.

car'-cel-age. Prison-fees. RECOMPENSE-PENALTY

car''-ci-no'-ma. A cancer. HEALTH-SICKNESS.

card. A piece of pasteboard. DESIGN, ORGANIZATION-DISORGANIZATION, SIGN; **address cards,** SIGN; **by the cards,** CONVENTIONALITY-UNCONVENTIONALITY; **cards to play,** MEANS; **great cards,** REPUTATION-DISCREDIT; **house of cards,** TOUGHNESS-BRITTLENESS; **leave a card,** SOCIABILITY-PRIVACY; **on the cards,** OCCURRENCE-DESTINY, POSSIBILITY-IMPOSSIBILITY, VIGOR-INERTIA; **play one's best card,** TOIL-RELAXATION; **play one's cards,** CONDUCT; **play one's cards well,** SKILL-UNSKILFULNESS; **shuffle the cards,** BEGINNING-END, MUTATION-PERMANENCE, PREPARATION-NONPREPARATION, PURPOSE-LUCK; **speak by the card,** CAREFULNESS-CARELESSNESS, PHRASE, TRUTHFULNESS-FALSEHOOD; **throw up the cards,** COMMISSION-RETIREMENT; **ticklish cards,** DIFFICULTY-FACILITY; **trump card,** CONSEQUENCE-INSIGNIFICANCE, DESIGN, SUCCESS-FAILURE.

card'-case''. A case for holding cards. CONTENTS-RECEIVER.

car'-di-ac. Relating to the heart. LIGHTHEARTEDNESS-DEJECTION.

car-di'-ac-al. Pertaining to the heart. LIGHTHEARTEDNESS-DEJECTION.

car'-di-nal. A church dignitary; a short, hooded cloak. CHURCH, CONSEQUENCE-INSIGNIFICANCE, DRESS-UNDRESS, GOODNESS-BADNESS, MINISTRY-LAITY; **cardinal point,** CONSEQUENCE-INSIGNIFICANCE; **cardinal points,** AIM-ABERRATION; **cardinal virtues,** VIRTUE-VICE.

car'-di-nal-ate. Office of a cardinal. REVELATION-PSEUDOREVELATION.

car'-di-nal-ship. Office of a cardinal. REVELATION-PSEUDOREVELATION.

car'-di-o-graph. An instrument for tracing the force of the action of the heart. INSTRUMENT.

car'-di-oid. A heart-shaped curve. CURVATION-RECTILINEARITY.

cards. A game. ENTERTAINMENT-WEARINESS.

card'-sharp''-er. A cheat. THEFT.

card'-sharp''-ing. Cheating. TRUTHFULNESS-FRAUD.

care. Caution; watchfulness; anxiety; ground of care; solicitude. CAREFULNESS-CARELESSNESS, GENEROSITY - FRUGALITY, OCCUPATION, PLEASURABLENESS-PAINFULNESS, PLEASURE-PAIN, RELEASE-RESTRAINT, SANGUINENESS-TIMIDITY, WELFARE-MISFORTUNE; **begone dull care,** LIGHTHEARTEDNESS-DEJECTION; **care for,** CONSEQUENCE-INSIGNIFICANCE, CONSERVATION, DESIRE-DISTASTE, LOVE-HATE; **drive care away,** ENTERTAINMENT-WEARINESS; **for aught one cares,** CONSEQUENCE-INSIGNIFICANCE, DESIRE-DISTASTE; **have the care of,** MANAGEMENT; **take care,** CAREFULNESS-CARELESSNESS, RECKLESSNESS-CAUTION; **take care of,** CAREFULNESS-CARELESSNESS.

ca-reen'. To incline; to lean over to repair. PARALLELISM-INCLINATION, RENOVATION-RELAPSE.

ca-reer'. Procedure; course. CONDUCT, OCCUPATION.

care'-ful. Attentive. CAREFULNESS-CARELESSNESS, GENEROSITY-FRUGALITY.

care'-ful-ly. With care. CAREFULNESS-CARELESSNESS.

care'-ful-ness. An exercise of care. CAREFULNESS-CARELESSNESS.

CAREFULNESS—CARELESSNESS.

Accuracy, etc. See TRUTH.

Alertness, etc. See ACTIVITY

Attention, etc. See ATTENTION.

Attention to detail. Carefulness in small matters.

Care. Solicitous watchfulness.

Circumspection, etc. See RECKLESSNESS-CAUTION.

Eyes of Argus. (Fig.) Keenness of sight. [He had a hundred eyes, (Greek) transferred by Juno to the peacock's tail. Spenser, *Fairy Queen*, I, iv, 17.]

Forethought. See PREVISION.

Heed. Serious regard.

Heedfulness, etc. See *Adjectives*.

L'oeil du maître [F.]. The eye of the master.

Lookout. An attentive watchfulness for some object or event.

Minuteness. Great exactness.

Precaution, etc. See PREPARATION.

Prudence, etc. See RECKLESSNESS-CAUTION.

Scruple, etc. See UPRIGHTNESS.

Solicitude. Anxiety of the mind.

Surveillance. Watchful inspection.

Tidiness. See CLEANNESS, REGULARITY.

Vigil. Watchful care.

Vigilance. Guarding against danger.

Watch. Close and constant attention.

Watch and ward. Continuous vigil for the purpose of guarding.

Watchfulness, etc. See *Adjectives*.

CAREFULNESS—*Verbs.*

Protect, etc. See SECURITY.

Reck. To consider thoughtfully.

Watch. To guard with care and attention.

CAREFULNESS—*Verbal Expressions.*

Be careful, etc. (see *Adjectives*); **be heedful** (see *Adjectives*); **do one's best;** **have all one's eyes about one,** to be extremely watchful; **have all one's wits about one;** **have the eyes open,** to be on the lookout; **keep a good lookout;** **keep an eye upon;** **keep a sharp eye upon;** **keep a sharp lookout;** **keep in mind;** **keep in one's business;** **keep in sight;** **keep in view;** **keep one's eyes open;** **keep watch,** to be on guard; **keep watch and ward,** to keep continuous vigil;

Carelessness, etc. See *Adjectives*.

Default. A failure to perform a duty.

Heedlessness, etc. See *Adjectives*.

Improvidence, etc. See PREPARATION-NONPREPARATION.

Imprudence. Lack of ordinary caution.

Inattention, etc. See HEED-DISREGARD.

Inexactness, etc. See TRUTH-ERROR.

Insouciant. Careless unconcern.

Laches. Neglect to do at the proper time.

Neglect. Leaving a duty undone.

Negligence. Habitual non-performance of duty.

Nonchalance [F.]. Heedlessness. See SENSITIVENESS-APATHY.

Non-completion, etc. See COMPLETION-NONCOMPLETION.

Omission. Something left undone.

Paraleipsis. A pretended omission in speaking.

Recklessness, etc. See RECKLESSNESS.

Slovenliness. See FILTHINESS, IRREGULARITY

Supineness, etc. See ACTIVITY-INDOLENCE.

Trifling. Frivolity.

CARELESSNESS—*Nouns of Agent.*

Trifler. One careless of his responsibilities.

Waiter on Providence. One who shirks his responsibilities, trusting in luck or fate to meet them for him.

CARELESSNESS—*Verbs.*

Blink. To dodge one's duty.

Cut. To ignore intentionally.

Disregard. To pass unnoticed.

Effleurer [F.]. To graze; touch slightly.

Forget, etc. See REMEMBRANCE-FORGETFULNESS.

Fribble. To treat in a trifling manner.

Ignore. To consider unworthy of attention

Jump. To pass over.

Miss. To pass by.

Omit. To fail to treat or observe.

Overlook. To fail to notice.

Pretermit. To fail to give heed to.

Scamp. To do in a half-hearted, stinted manner

Shelve. To put away undone.

Sink. To keep out of sight.

Skim. To regard superficially

CAREFULNESS—CARELESSNESS—*Continued.*

CAREFULNESS—VERBAL EXPRESSIONS—*Continued.***

look about one; look after, to take solicitous interest in; look sharp; look to; look well with one's eyes, to see for one's ownself; mind one's business; mind one's P's and Q's, to be exact and careful; mount guard, to enter upon guard-duty; pay attention to, etc. (see HEED); pick one's steps, to act with caution; see after; see to, to give close attention to; set watch, to station a guard; sleep with one eye open, to sleep in anticipation of danger; speak by the card, to speak from sure knowledge; take care, etc. (see RECKLESSNESS-CAUTION); take care of, to give oversight and protection to; take precaution, etc. (see PREPARATION); watch for, etc. (see EXPECTATION).

CAREFULNESS—*Adjectives.*

Accurate, etc. See TRUTH.
Alert, etc. See ACTIVITY.
Argus-eyed. Sharp-sighted. See *above*
Awake. Not asleep.
Broad awake. Fully roused from slumber.
Careful. Cautious and prudent.
Cavendo tutus [L.]. Safe by taking heed. See SECURITY.
Considerate. Thoughtful and forbearing.
Guarded. Cautious.
Heedful. Regardful of advice and appearances.
Painstaking. Giving careful and scrupulous attention.
Particular. Careful of details.
Provident, etc. See PREPARATION.
Prudent, etc. See RECKLESSNESS-CAUTION.
Regardful. Closely attentive.
Scrupulous. Cautious from conscientious motives.
Sure-footed. Not liable to stumble.
Thoughtful, etc. See REFLECTION.
Tidy, etc. See CLEANNESS, REGULARITY.
Vigilant. Thoughtfully watchful.
Wakeful. Active.
Watchful. Full of caution.
Wide-awake, etc. See SAGACITY
Wistful. Contemplative.

CAREFULNESS—*Adjective Expressions.*

On one's guard, prepared for emergencies; **on the alert,** active; **on the lookout,** watchful; **on the** *qui vive,* expectant; **on the watch,** on guard; **on the watch for; taking care, taking heed,** etc (see *Verbs*).

CAREFULNESS—*Adverbs.*

Carefully, etc. See *Adjectives.*
Gingerly. Cautiously; trippingly.
Thoughtfully, etc. See *Adjectives.*
With care.

CAREFULNESS—*Phrases*

Ni bebas agua que no veas [Sp.]. Look at the water before you drink.
Quis custodiet ipsos custodes? [L.]. Who will guard the guards themselves?

CARELESSNESS—ADJECTIVES—*Continued from Column 2.*

Unwary. Careless.
Unwatchful. Not on the watch.
Unweighed. Not considered carefully

CARELESSNESS—*Adjective Expressions.*

Buried in a napkin, laid aside; unused [Bible, Luke xix, 20]; **hid under a bushel,** screened [Bible, Matthew v, 15]; **off one's guard,** unprepared; **unattended to; uncared for; unthought of.**

CARELESSNESS—*Adverbs.*

Anyhow. In a haphazard manner.
Negligently, etc. See *Adjectives*

CARELESSNESS—*Adverbial Expressions.*

Hand over head; in an unguarded moment, etc. (see EXPECTATION-SURPRISE); *per incuriam* [L.], through carelessness.

CARELESSNESS—*Interjections.*

Let it pass. Give it not attention
Never mind. Don't give it a thought.
No matter. It is of little consequence

CARELESSNESS—VERBS—*Continued.***

Skip. To pass over unnoticed.
Slight. To neglect or pass by.
Slur. To pass over triflingly.
Trifle. To treat as unimportant.

CARELESSNESS—*Verbal Expressions.*

Be caught napping; be negligent, etc. (see *Adjectives*); **cast aside,** to reject; **connive at,** to voluntarily fail to discover a wrong; **do by halves,** to do only half well; **give the go-by to,** to shun; **gloss over,** to hide the defects of; **jump over; keep out of sight; lay aside,** to abandon; **leave a loose thread,** to leave in a slack condition; **leave out of one's calculation,** not to take into consideration; **leave out of sight,** to leave undisclosed; **let go,** to desert; **let pass,** to pass unheeded; **let slip,** to lose by negligence; **let the grass grow under one's feet,** to remain idle; **lose sight of,** to miss; **miss,** to fail in an attempt; **neglect,** to fail to treat properly, or to leave undone; **not attend to,** etc. (see HEED); **not mind,** to give no thought to; **not trouble oneself about; not trouble oneself with; not trouble one's head about; not trouble one's head with; pass by,** to leave untreated; **pass over,** to leave unnoticed; **pay no regard to; play with,** to treat in a light, frivolous manner; **push aside,** to reject; **put aside; put off one's guard,** to deceive one by apparent neglect in competition, etc.; **refuse to hear; render neglectful,** etc. (see *Adjectives*); **set aside,** to leave unconsidered; **shut one's eyes to,** to ignore; **skim the surface; skip over; slight** (see REGARD-SCORN); **slip over; slur over; take a cursory view of** (see HEED); **take no account of,** to attach no importance to; **take no care of,** to neglect totally; **take no note of; take no notice of; take no thought of; throw into the background,** to abandon as unworthy of notice; **throw off one's guard,** to deceive; **trifle with; turn a deaf ear to,** to disregard; **wink at,** to avoid noticing.

CARELESSNESS—*Adjectives*

Abandoned. Forsaken.
Careless. Unconcerned with responsibility.
Heedless. Inconsiderate; rash.
Improvident, etc. See PREPARATION-NONPREPARATION.
Imprudent. Lacking in proper regard for consequences.
Inattentive, etc. See HEED-DISREGARD.
Incircumspect. See UNCIRCUMSPECT.
Inconsiderate. Disregardful.
Inexact, etc. See TRUTH-ERROR.
Insouciant [F.]. Heedless, etc. See SENSITIVENESS-APATHY
Neglected, etc. See *Verbs.*
Neglectful. Shiftless in the performance of duty.
Neglecting, etc. See *Verbs.*
Negligent. Given to omitting duty.
Offhand. Impromptu.
Perfunctory. Done merely for the sake of performing a duty.
Reckless, etc. See RECKLESSNESS.
Remiss. Slack in duty.
Shelved. See *Verbs.*
Shunted. Turned aside.
Slovenly, etc. See CLEANNESS-FILTHINESS, REGULARITY-IRREGULARITY.
Supine, etc. See ACTIVITY-INDOLENCE.
Thoughtless. Characterized by want of discretion.
Uncircumspect. Not cautious.
Unexamined. Not investigated.
Unexplored. Not searched through.
Unguarded. Left without a guard.
Unheeded. Disregarded.
Unmarked. Without a mark.
Unmindful. Not retaining in mind.
Unmissed. Not wanted.
Unnoted. Not recorded.
Unnoticed. Not observed.
Unobserved. Not perceived.
Unperceived. Not discerned.
Unregarded. Not cared for.
Unremarked. Not observed
Unscanned. Not scrutinized.
Unsearched. Not explored.
Unseen. Not seen.
Unsifted. Not analyzed.
Unstudied. Natural.

(*Continued on Column* 1.)

care'-less. Without care; unconcerned; easy; without anxiety. CAREFULNESS-CARELESSNESS, DESIRE-UNCONCERN, FORCE-WEAKNESS, HEED-DISREGARD, QUEST-EVASION, UNCONCERN.

care'-less-ness. State of being careless. CAREFULNESS-CARELESSNESS.

ca-ress'. To fondle. BLANDISHMENT.

ca-ressed'. Fondled. BLANDISHMENT.

ca-res'-sing. Fondling. BLANDISHMENT.

car'-et. A sign indicating omitted words, etc. ENTIRETY-DEFICIENCY, EXCESS-LACK.

care'-worn''. Burdened with care or pain. LIGHTHEARTEDNESS-DEJECTION, PLEASURE-PAIN.

Ca'-rey's chick'-en, Moth'-er. A stormy petrel. WARNING.

car'-go. Merchandise taken on a vessel. CONTENTS-RECEIVER, MAGNITUDE-SMALLNESS, MERCHANDISE, PROPERTY.

car''-i-ca-tur'-a. Caricature DELINEATION-CARICATURE, GULL-HYPERBOLE.

car'-i-ca-ture. An exaggerated imitation to produce an absurd effect. COPY-MODEL, DELINEATION-CARICATURE, DERISION, GULL-HYPERBOLE, IMITATION-ORIGINALITY.

car'-i-ca-tur-ist. Maker of caricatures. WAG.

ca'-ri-es. Decay of a bone. HEALTH-SICKNESS

car'-i-ole. A carriage. CONVEYANCE-VESSEL.

ca'-ri-ous. Decayed. CLEANNESS-FILTHINESS.

cark. To worry. PLEASURE-PAIN.

cark'-ing. Causing worry. PLEASURABLENESS-PAINFULNESS, PLEASURE-PAIN.

cark'-ing care. Wearing care. PLEASURABLENESS-PAINFULNESS.

carle. A rustic. GENTILITY-DEMOCRACY

car'-man. A truckman. MANAGER.

Car'-mel-ite. A friar of Mount Carmel. MINISTRY-LAITY.

car-min'-a-tive. A warming. REMEDY-BANE.

car'-mine. A reddish pigment. REDNESS-GREENNESS.

car'-nage. Bloody massacre. LIFE-KILLING.

car'-nal. Not spiritual; relating to bodily appetites. GODLINESS-DISBELIEF, MODERATION-SELFINDULGENCE, PURITY-IMPURITY

car-nal'-i-ty. Sensuality MODERATION-SELFINDULGENCE, PURITY-IMPURITY

car-na'-tion. A pink flower. REDNESS-GREENNESS.

car'-ni-val. A gay festival ENTERTAINMENT-WEARINESS.

Car-niv'-o-ra. A family of mammals. FAUNA-FLORA.

car-niv'-o-rous. Eating flesh. NUTRIMENT-EXCRETION.

car'-ol. A song of joy; a song. JUBILATION-LAMENTATION, LIGHTHEARTEDNESS-DEJECTION, MUSIC, MUSICIAN.

caro sposo [It.] (ca'-ro spo'-zo) Dear spouse. LOVE-HATE.

ca-rou'-sal. Revelry. ENTERTAINMENT-WEARINESS, MODERATION-SELFINDULGENCE, NUTRIMENT-EXCRETION.

ca-rouse'. A deep draft; a feast, to drink deeply. ADMISSION-EXPULSION, ENTERTAINMENT-WEARINESS, MODERATION-SELFINDULGENCE, TEETOTALISM-INTEMPERANCE.

ca-rous'-er. Reveler. TEETOTALISM-INTEMPERANCE.

carp at. To find fault with. APPROVAL-DISAPPROVAL

carpe diem [L.] (car'-pî dai'-em). Seize the opportunity. ACTIVITY-INDOLENCE, OPPORTUNENESS-UNSUITABLENESS.

car'-pen-ter. A builder with wood. AGENT.

carp'-er One who carps. FLATTERER-DEFAMER.

car'-pet. A covering for floors. TOP-BOTTOM; **carpet knight,** MODERATION-VOLUPTUARY, PRESUMPTION-OBSEQUIOUSNESS, SOCIETY-DANDY; **on the carpet,** CONCEPTION-THEME, DESIGN.

car'-pus. The wrist. ANATOMY.

carrefour [F.] (car-fur'). Across street. WAY.

car'-riage. Appearance; conduct; a vehicle. APPEARANCE-DISAPPEARANCE, CONDUCT, CONTENTS-RECEIVER, CONVEYANCE-VESSEL, CONVEYER, MOVEMENT-REST, TRANSFER; **keep one's carriage,** SOCIETY-LUDICROUSNESS.

car'-ried. Propelled. **Carried away by passion,** EXCITATION; **carried by acclamation,** ASSENT-DISSENT.

car'-ri-er. One who carries. CONVEYER; **carrier pigeon,** CONVEYER, MESSENGER.

car'-ri-on. Dead flesh. CLEANNESS-FILTHINESS, LIFE-CORPSE.

car''-ro-nade'. A short ordnance piece. WEAPON.

car'-rot-y. Reddish-yellow; edible vegetable. REDNESS-GREENNESS.

car'-ry. To influence; conduct; bear; transport. INCLINATION, MOTIVE-CAPRICE, SUSPENSION-SUPPORT, TRANSFER; **carry all before one,** SUCCESS-FAILURE; **carry a point,** SUCCESS-FAILURE; **carry by storm,** SUCCESS-FAILURE; **carry coals,** SELFRESPECT-HUMBLENESS; **carry conviction,** FAITH-MISGIVING; **carry in the mind,** REMEMBRANCE-FORGETFULNESS; **carry into execution,** COMPLETION-NONCOMPLETION, OBSERVANCE-NONOBSERVANCE; **carry matters with a high hand,** TYRANNY-ANARCHY; **carry off,** TAKING-RESTITUTION, THEFT; **carry oneself,** CONDUCT; **carry out,** COMPLETION-NONCOMPLETION, CONDUCT; **carry over,** ACCOUNTS, TRANSFER; **carry through,** COMPLETION-NONCOMPLETION, CONDUCT; **carry weight,** CONSEQUENCE-INSIGNIFICANCE, DOMINANCE-IMPOTENCE, EVIDENCE-COUNTEREVIDENCE; **carry with a high hand,** PRESUMPTION-OBSEQUIOUSNESS, RULE-LICENSE, SELFRESPECT-HUMBLENESS; **reap and carry,** GAIN-LOSS.

car'-ry-ing. Conveying. SWIFTNESS-SLOWNESS.

car'-ry on. To conduct; to keep going; to act badly. ACTION-PASSIVENESS, CONDUCT, DISCONTINUANCE-CONTINUANCE, QUEST-EVASION; **carry on an argument,** RATIOCINATION-INSTINCT; **carry on an inquiry,** INVESTIGATION-ANSWER; **carry on a trade,** EXCHANGE; **carry on business,** OCCUPATION; **carry on war,** FIGHTING-CONCILIATION.

cart. A heavy, two-wheeled vehicle. CONVEYANCE-VESSEL; **cart away,** ESTABLISHMENT-REMOVAL; **cart before the horse,** REGULARITY-IRREGULARITY, REVERSAL, SKILL-UNSKILFULNESS; **cart-horse,** CONVEYER; **cart-load,** CONTENTS-RECEIVER, MAGNITUDE-SMALLNESS; **work like a cart-horsr,** TOIL-RELAXATION.

cart'-age. The act of carting. TRANSFER.

carte [F.] (cart). A card or paper. RECORD; *carte blanche* [F.] (cart blan'sh), blank paper; free leave,, GENEROSITY-FRUGALITY, LEAVE-PROHIBITION; *carte de visite* [F.] (cart de vi-sît'), visiting card, SIGN; *carte du pays* [F.] (cart dü pê-î') map of the country, DESIGN.

carte and tierce. Positions in fencing. ATTACK-DEFENSE.

car'-tel. Written agreement between two governments; a challenge. CONTRACT, DEFIANCE, FIGHTING-CONCILIATION.

cart'-er. A teamster. WAYFARER-SEAFARER

cartes sur table [F.] (cart sür tabl). Acting openly. MANIFESTATION-LATENCY, TRUTHFULNESS-FALSEHOOD.

Carthago, delenda est [L.] (car-thê'-go, dî-len'-da est) Carthage must be destroyed. CHARITABLENESS-CURSE.

Car-thu'-sian. A monk. MINISTRY-LAITY.

car'-ti-lage. A gristle. HARDNESS-SOFTNESS, SOLIDITY-RARITY, TOUGHNESS-BRITTLENESS.

car''-ti-lag'-i-nous. Like cartilage. HARDNESS-SOFTNESS, TOUGHNESS-BRITTLENESS.

cart'-ing. Hauling. TRANSFER.

car-tog'-ra-phy. The art of drawing charts. DELINEATION-CARICATURE.

car-toon'. A design or drawing. PAINTING.

car-touche'. An ornamental tablet; a cartridge box. EMBELLISHMENT-DISFIGUREMENT, WEAPON.

car'-tridge. A charge for a firearm. WEAPON.

car'-tu-la-ry. A collection of records. CONSTITUENT-ALIEN, MARK-OBLITERATION.

carve. To cut designs upon; to cut to pieces. ASSIGNMENT, CREATION-DESTRUCTION, DELINEATION-CARICATURE, FORM-FORMLESSNESS, SCULPTURE, UNION-DISUNION; **carve one's way,** ADVANCE-RETROGRESSION.

car'-vel. A caravel. CONVEYANCE-VESSEL.

carv'-er. One who carves. ARTIST.

carv'-ing. Carved work. SCULPTURE.

car''-y-at'-id. } A column in the form of a female.
car''-y-at'-id-es. } SUSPENSION-SUPPORT.

casaque, tourner [F.] (ca-sak', tur-nê'). To turn one's coat; change one's party BIGOTRY-APOSTASY, MUTATION-PERMANENCE.

cas-cade'. A small waterfall. RIVER-WIND.

case (1) The state of things; a box; an action; a binding; physical condition. CONCEPTION-THEME, CONDITION-SITUATION, CONTENTS-RECEIVER, COUNCIL, COVER-LINING, ENCLOSURE, HEALTH-SICKNESS, MANIFESTATION-LATENCY, RATIOCINATION-INSTINCT; **be the case,** ENTITY-NONENTITY, TRUTH-ERROR; **case in point,** CONVENTIONALITY-UNCONVENTIONALITY, HARMONY-DISCORD; **in case,** CONDITION-SITUATION, HYPOTHESIS, OCCURRENCE-DESTINY; **in good case,** HEALTH-SICKNESS, WELFARE-MISFORTUNE; **make out a case,** DUENESS-UNDUENESS, EVIDENCE-COUNTEREVIDENCE.

case (2) A grammatical distinction. NOUN.

case'-hard''-en. To render insensible to outside influences. HABIT-DESUETUDE, STRENGTH-WEAKNESS.

case'-hard''-ened. Hardened against good influences. FEELING-INSENSIBILITY, PERSISTENCE-WHIM, SENSITIVENESS-APATHY.

case'-mate. A vaulted chamber ATTACK-DEFENSE, DWELLER-HABITATION.

case'-ma''-ted. Furnished with casemates. ATTACK-DEFENSE.

case'-ment. The sash of a window APERTURE-CLOSURE.

ca-sern'. A barrack for soldiers DWELLER-HABITATION.

cash. Current money; payment; Chinese coin. MONEY, SETTLEMENT-DEFAULT, VALUES; **cash account,** ACCOUNTS; **in cash,** AFFLUENCE-PENURY.

cash'-book''. Book containing the cash account. TREASURER.

cash-ier'. To dismiss; a custodian of money. COMMISSION-ABROGATION. TREASURER.

cash'-keep''-er. Cashier. TREASURER.

cash'-mere. A fine woolen dress-fabric. DRESS-UNDRESS.

ca'-sing. The framework of a window COVER-LINING.

ca-si'-no. A public resorting place. ASSOCIATION.

cask. A barrel-shaped wooden vessel. CONTENTS-RECEIVER, MEASURE.

cas'-ket. A small box or chest. CONTENTS-RECEIVER.

casque. A helmet. ATTACK-DEFENSE, DRESS, UNDRESS.

Cas-san'-dra. A Trojan prophetess. SOOTHSAYER, WARNING.

cas-si'-no. Casino. ENTERTAINMENT-WEARINESS.

cas'-sock. A long clerical coat DRESS-UNDRESS, VESTMENTS

cast. To throw; to form; to calculate; appearance; mien. AFFECTIONS, APPEARANCE-DISAPPEARANCE, ASSIGNMENT, CHOICE-REJECTION, COLOR-ACHROMATISM, COPY-MODEL, DESIGN, ELEVATION-DEPRESSION, EXCULPATION-CONVICTION, FORM-FORMLESSNESS, GATHERING-SCATTERING, GIVING-RECEIVING, INCLINATION, MAGNITUDE-SMALLNESS, PUSH-PULL, SCULPTURE; **cast about for,** TRIAL; **cast accounts,** ACCOUNTS; **cast adrift,** ADMISSION-EXPULSION, COMMISSION-ABROGATION, GATHERING-SCATTERING, RELEASE-RESTRAINT; **cast a gloom,** LIGHTHEARTEDNESS-DEJECTION; **cast a nativity,** DEVOTION-MAGIC, PROPHECY; **cast anchor,** ARRIVAL-DEPARTURE, MOVEMENT-REST; **cast a shade,** LIGHT-DARKNESS; **cast aside,** CAREFULNESS-CARELESSNESS, KEEPING-RELINQUISHMENT; **cast a slur,** JUSTIFICATION-CHARGE, REPUTATION-DISCREDIT; **cast a spell,** DEVOTION-MAGIC, VOLITION-OBLIGATION; **cast aspersions,** ADULATION-DISPARAGEMENT; **cast away,** CHOICE-REJECTION, KEEPING-RELINQUISHMENT, PROVISION-WASTE, SUCCESS-FAILURE; **cast away care,** LIGHTHEARTEDNESS-DEJECTION; **cast behind one,** KEEPING-RELINQUISHMENT, PROFFER-REFUSAL, REMEMBRANCE-FORGETFULNESS; **cast dishonor upon,** REPUTATION-DISCREDIT; **cast down,** ELEVATION-DEPRESSION, LIGHTHEARTEDNESS-DEJECTION; **cast eyes on,** SIGHT-BLINDNESS; **cast in a different mold,** REPRISAL-RESISTANCE; **cast in one's lot with,** CHOICE-NEUTRALITY; **cast in the same mold,** LIKENESS-UNLIKENESS; **cast iron,** HARDNESS-SOFTNESS; **cast lots,** PURPOSE-LUCK; **cast luster upon,** LIGHT-DARKNESS; **cast of countenance,** APPEARANCE-DISAPPEARANCE; **cast off,** COMMISSION-ABROGATION, DRESS-UNDRESS, KEEPING-RELINQUISHMENT; **cast off a habit,** HABIT-DESUETUDE; **cast off clothes,** USEFULNESS-USELESSNESS; **cast of the dice,** RATIONALE-LUCK; **cast of the mind,** AFFECTIONS; **cast one's net,** TRIAL; **cast overboard,** USE-MISUSE; **cast reflection upon,** ADULATION-DISPARAGEMENT; **cast the eyes back,** FUTURE-PAST; **cast the eyes over,** HEED-DISREGARD; **cast the parts,** ORGANIZATION-DISORGANIZATION; **cast the skin,** DRESS-UNDRESS; **cast to the dogs,** CREATION-DESTRUCTION, USE-DISUSE; **cast up,** ADMISSION-EXPULSION, NUMBERING, OCCURRENCE-DESTINY; **set on a cast,** PURPOSE-LUCK.

cas'-ta-net. An instrument rattled. MUSICAL INSTRUMENTS.

cast'-a-way. A reprobate; one wrecked. GOOD MAN-BAD MAN, SOCIABILITY-PRIVACY.

caste. An hereditary or artificial division. DIVISION, REPUTATION-DISCREDIT; **lose caste,** UPRIGHTNESS-DISHONESTY.

cas'-tel-lan. Keeper of a castle. CHIEF-UNDERLING, GUARD-PRISONER.

cast'-er. A cruet for condiments; a roller. CONTENTS-RECEIVER, REVOLUTION-EVOLUTION.

cas'-ti-gate. To punish sharply. APPROVAL-DISAPPROVAL, RECOMPENSE-PUNITION.

cas''-ti-ga'-tion. Whipping. APPROVAL-DISAPPROVAL, RECOMPENSE-PUNITION.

cas'-ti-ga''-tor. A punisher. FLATTERER-DEFAMER.

cast'-ing vote. Deciding vote. DECISION-MISJUDGMENT; **casting weight,** COMPENSATION, EQUALITY-INEQUALITY.

cas'-tle. A strong fortress; a chess block; a habitation. ATTACK-DEFENSE, COMMUTATION-PERMUTATION, DWELLER-HABITATION; **castle in the air,** FANCY, POSSIBILITY-IMPOSSIBILITY, SANGUINENESS-HOPELESSNESS.

Cas'-tle of In'-do-lence. A castle in the land of Drowsiness. [Thompson.] ACTIVITY-INDOLENCE.

cast'-ling. Abortion. COMMUTATION-PERMUTATION.

cas'-tor. A beaver hat. DRESS-UNDRESS.

Cas'-tor and Pol'-lux. Twin sons of Jupiter. DUALITY, FRIEND-FOE.

cas''-tra-me-ta'-tion. The laying out of a camp. DWELLER-HABITATION, FIGHTING-CONCILIATION.

cas'-trate. To remove the sexual organs. ADDITION-SUBTRACTION, CLEANNESS-FILTHINESS, MIGHT-IMPOTENCE.

cas'-u-al. Accidental. CERTAINTY-DOUBT, RATIONALE-LUCK.

cas'-u-al-ly. Unexpectedly. PURPOSE-LUCK, RATIONALE-LUCK.

cas'-u-al-ty. A chance; a fatal accident. GOOD-EVIL, LIFE-KILLING, OCCURRENCE-DESTINY, POSITION, RATIONALE-LUCK, WELFARE-MISFORTUNE.

cas'-u-ist. An expert in casuistry. RATIOCINATION-INSTINCT.

cas''-u-is'-tic-al. Pertaining to casuistry. DUTY-DERELICTION.

cas'-u-ist-ry. Sophistical reasoning. DUTY-DERELICTION, RATIOCINATION-CASUISTRY.

casus belli [L.] (kê'-sus bel'-lai). Cause of war. EXCITATION, FAVORITE-ANGER, VARIANCE-ACCORD.

casus fœderis [L.] (kê'-sus fed'-er-is). Cause of treaty. CONTRACT.

cat. A domestic animal. FAUNA-FLORA, RECOMPENSE-SCOURGE, SIGHT-BLINDNESS; **as the cat jumps,** OCCURRENCE-DESTINY; **cat and dog life,** VARIANCE-ACCORD; **catcall,** APPROVAL-DISAPPROVAL, MUSICAL INSTRUMENTS; **cat in pattens,** CONDUCT; **cat-o'-nine-tails,** RECOMPENSE-SCOURGE; **cat's concert,** MELODY-DISSONANCE; **cat's cradle,** CROSSING; **cat's paw,** ANTAGONIST-ASSISTANT, GULL-DECEIVER, INSTRUMENTALITY, USE-DISUSE; **gib-cat,** MALE-FEMALE; **let cat out of bag,** EXPOSURE-HIDINGPLACE; **rain cats and dogs,** RIVER-WIND; **see how the cat jumps,** BIGOTRY-APOSTASY, PREVISION, RECKLESSNESS-CAUTION; **tom-cat,** MALE-FEMALE.

cat''-a-chre'-sis. Misuse of a word; bad use of metaphors. INTERPRETATION-MISINTERPRETATION, TROPE.

cat''-a-chres'-tic-al. Far-fetched. TROPE.

cat'-a-clysm. A flood. CREATION-DESTRUCTION, REVOLUTION, RIVER-WIND.

cat'-a-comb. An underground burial gallery. LIFE-FUNERAL.

catadupe [F.] (ca-ta-düp'). A waterfall. RIVER-WIND.

cat'-a-falque. A draped funeral car. LIFE-FUNERAL.

cat'-a-lec'-tic. Lacking a syllable to complete a verse. MOVEMENT-REST, POETRY-PROSE.

cat'-a-lep-sy. A sudden suspension of action. MOVEMENT-REST.

cat'-a-logue. A list of names with method. ORGANIZATION-DISORGANIZATION, RECORD.

catalogue raisonné [F.] (ca-ta-log' re-zo-nê'). List of books. ACCOUNT, RECORD.

cat-al'-y-sis. Contact-action. COMPOSITION-RESOLUTION.

cat''-a-ma-ran'. A vessel of logs adapted to fighting. BELLIGERENT, CONVEYANCE-VESSEL.

cat'-a-plasm. A poultice. REMEDY-BANE.

cat'-a-pult. A military engine. PUSH-PULL, WEAPON.

cat'-a-ract. A flood of water; an affection of the eye. RIVER-WIND, SIGHT-BLINDNESS, SIGHT-DIMSIGHTEDNESS.

ca-tarrh'. An affection of the nose and throat. NUTRIMENT-EXCRETION.

cat-as'-tro-phe. Calamity. COMPLETION-NONCOMPLETION, GOOD-EVIL, WELFARE-MISFORTUNE.

cat'-call''. A shrill call or whistle; an instrument for producing this sound. CRY-ULULATION, MUSICAL INSTRUMENTS, VARIANCE-ACCORD.

catch. To perceive clearly; to overtake; that which seizes; a snatch; gain; a scrap of song. CLEARNESS-OBSCURITY, CONNECTIVE, DISCOVERY, GIVING-RECEIVING, IMITATION-ORIGINALITY, MUSIC, TAKING-

RESTITUTION, TRUTHFULNESS-FRAUD; **by catches,** CONTINUITY-INTERRUPTION; **catch a disease,** HEALTH-SICKNESS; **catch a glimpse,** SIGHT-BLINDNESS; **catch a likeness,** DELINEATION-CARICATURE; **catch an idea,** SAGACITY-INCAPACITY; **catch a sound,** HEARING-DEAFNESS; **catch at,** DESIRE-DISTASTE, READINESS-RELUCTANCE, TAKING-RESTITUTION; **catch a Tartar,** GULL-DECEIVER, INTERSPACE-CONTACT, REPRISAL-RESISTANCE; **catch at a straw,** CREDULOUSNESS-SKEPTICISM, OVERVALUATION - UNDERVALUATION, RECKLESSNESS-CAUTION, SANGUINENESS-HOPELESSNESS, SKILL-UNSKILFULNESS; **catch by surprise,** EXPECTATION-SURPRISE; **catch fire,** HEATING-COOLING; **catch in a trap,** TRUTHFULNESS-FRAUD; **catch one's death,** LIFE-DEATH; **catch the attention,** HEED-DISREGARD; **catch the breath,** RIVER-WIND; **catch the ear,** HEARING-DEAFNESS; **catch the eye,** VISIBILITY-INVISIBILITY; **catch the infection,** EMOTION, EXCITATION; **catch tripping,** DISCOVERY; **catch up,** TAKING-RESTITUTION; **no great catch,** FAULTLESSNESS-FAULTINESS.

catch'-ba'-sin. A basin for catching coarse matter not easily floated off in the sewer. CONTENTS-RECEIVER.

catch'-drain''. A drain made on a slope to catch the surface-water. CONTENTS-RECEIVER, WATERCOURSE-AIRPIPE.

catch'-ing. Infectious. HEALTHINESS-UNHEALTHINESS.

catch'-pen''-ny. Made to sell. CONSEQUENCE-INSIGNIFICANCE, COSTLINESS-CHEAPNESS, TRUTHFULNESS-FRAUD.

catch'-poll''. A bailif. JUDICATURE.

catch'-word''. A popular word. SIGN.

cat''-e-chet'-i-cal. Pertaining to questions and answers. INVESTIGATION-ANSWER.

cat'-e-chism. A collection of answers showing religious truth or creed. FAITH-MISGIVING, INVESTIGATION-ANSWER; **church catechism,** ORTHODOXY-HETERODOXY.

cat'-e-chist. One who catechizes. INVESTIGATION-ANSWER.

cat'-e-chize. To instruct in the elements of religion. INVESTIGATION-ANSWER.

cat''-e-chu'-men. A religious beginner. INSTRUCTOR-PUPIL, MINISTRY-LAITY.

cat''-e-go-re'-ma. Predicate. DIVISION.

cat'-e-gor'-ic-al. Absolute. ASSERTION-DENIAL, CERTAINTY-DOUBT, PROOF-DISPROOF.

cat''-e-gor'-ic-al-ly true. Unconditionally true. TRUTH-ERROR.

cat'-e-go''-ry. Highest class to which objects of knowledge can be reduced. CONDITION-SITUATION, DIVISION; **in the same category,** CONNECTION-INDEPENDENCE.

cat'-e-na-ry. A curve. CURVATION-RECTILINEARITY.

cat''-e-na'-tion. A chain-like series. CONTINUITY-INTERRUPTION.

ca'-ter. To provide food for entertainments. PROVISION-WASTE.

ca'-ter-er. A purveyor. PROVISION-WASTE.

ca'-ter-ess. A female caterer. PROVISION-WASTE.

cat'-er-waul. A cat-like cry. BLANDISHMENT, CRY-ULULATION, MELODY-DISSONANCE.

cat'-er-waul''-ing. Cat-cry. MELODY-DISSONANCE.

cates. Food; provisions. NUTRIMENT-EXCRETION.

cat'-gut-scra''-per. A violinist. MUSICIAN.

ca-thar'-tic. Purgative. CLEANNESS-FILTHINESS.

cathedra, ex [L.] (ca-thī'-dra, ex). From the chair. ASSERTION-DENIAL, PRESUMPTION-OBSEQUIOUSNESS, RULE-LICENSE, SCHOOL.

ca-the'-dral. A chief church of a diocese. FANE.

cath'-o-lic. Not heretical; universal in reach. GODLINESS-UNGODLINESS, UNIVERSALITY-PARTICULARITY;

Catholic Church, ORTHODOXY-HETERODOXY; **Roman Catholic Church,** ORTHODOXY-HETERODOXY.

ca-thol'-ic-al. Catholic. UNIVERSALITY-PARTICULARITY.

Ca-thol'-i-cism. Orthodox faith; liberality of sentiment. ORTHODOXY-HETERODOXY, UNIVERSALITY-PARTICULARITY.

cath''-o-lic'-i-ty. Breadth; acceptance by the whole Church. ORTHODOXY-HETERODOXY, UNIVERSALITY-PARTICULARITY.

ca-thol'-i-con. A panacea. REMEDY-BANE.

Cat'-i-line. A Roman conspirator. UPRIGHTNESS-ROGUE.

cat'-nip''. An aromatic herb used as a stimulant. ODOR-INODOROUSNESS, REMEDY-BANE.

cat-op'-sis. Clear sight. SIGHT-BLINDNESS.

cat-op'-trics. The science that investigates the reflection of light. LIGHT-DARKNESS.

ca-top'-tro-man''-cy. Divination by a mirror. PROPHECY.

cat'-tle. Bovine animals. CONVEYER, FAUNA-FLORA; **cattle truck,** CONVEYANCE-VESSEL.

Cau-ca'-sian. One of the Indo-European race. ETHNOLOGY.

Cau-ca'-sian mys'-ter-y. Mystery of the Caucasian peoples. THEOLOGY

cau'-cus. A private meeting. COUNCIL.

cau'-dal. Pertaining to the tail. ANTERIORITY-POSTERIORITY, BEGINNING-END.

cau'-date. Having a tail. SUSPENSION-SUPPORT.

cau'-dex. A stem. SUSPENSION-SUPPORT, TOP-BOTTOM.

cauf. A chest for fish. DOMESTICATION-AGRICULTURE.

caulk. To make tight. RENOVATION-RELAPSE.

causa causans [L.] (cau'-za cau'-zans). Underlying principle. CAUSE-EFFECT.

caus'-al con-junc'-tion. Conjunction indicating causal relations. PARTICLE.

causas, felix qui potuit rerum cognoscere [L.] (cau'-zas, fi'-lix quai pot'-iu-it ri'-rum cog-nos'-ser-i). Happy he who is able to ascertain the causes of things. CAUSE-EFFECT.

cau-sa'-tion. Act of causing. AGENCY, CAUSE-EFFECT

causa vera [L.] (cau'-za vi'-ra). The real cause. CAUSE-EFFECT.

cause. An efficient agent; a legal action. CAUSE-EFFECT, CREATION-DESTRUCTION, LITIGATION, **caused by,** CAUSE-EFFECT; **final cause,** PURPOSE-LUCK; **take up the cause of,** OBSTRUCTION-HELP, **tell the cause of,** INTERPRETATION-MISINTERPRETATION.

CAUSE—EFFECT.

Agent. An active power, or efficient cause of anything.
Causa causans [L.]. The causing cause.
Causality. The active power of a cause.
Causation. The act of producing.
Cause. That which brings about a result.
Derivation. Act of drawing from or causing to be.
Final cause. See PURPOSE.
Fons et origo [L.]. The source and origin.
Genesis. The act of bringing anything into existence.
Mainspring. The making cause of action.
Occasion. The reason to be.
Origin. That from which anything first proceeds.
Origination. Primary production.
Primum mobile [L.]. First cause of motion.
Production. Coming into existence.
Proximate cause. An immediately preceding cause.
Reason. The producing cause.
Reason why. Cause of being, or acting.
Remote cause. A cause far removed from its result.
Source. That from which anything takes its being.
Spring. An active, producing power.
Spring-head. Source.
Vera causa [L.]. The true cause.
Why and wherefore. The efficient reason.

CAUSE—*Associated Nouns.*

Author. One who begins, forms, or originates.
Birthplace. Environment or location at the time of being born.
Bud. An undeveloped stem or branch; hence, the earliest part of anything.
Cradle. An infant's bed; hence, place of origin
Descent. See PARENTAGE.
Egg. That which contains a germ, or origin.
Element. The first principle of a thing.
Embryo. The germ of anything.
Etymon. The root of a word.
Font. A source or fountain.
Foundation, etc. See SUSPENSION-SUPPORT.
Fountain. The source of a stream.
Fountain-head. Source of a stream; hence, an originating cause.
Germ. The rudimentary vital element.
Ground. The support or foundation.
Groundwork. That on which anything is built.
Hinge. The pivotal point on which anything depends for its effect or cause.
Hotbed. A place or condition favoring rapid growth.
Key. That which opens or prepares a way; as in a lock.
Leaven. Anything that works a general change; as in dough.
Lever. That which exerts, or through which one may exert, great power.

Consequence. A more remote effect.
Dénouement [F.]. The unraveling of the plot.
Derivation. Act of receiving from a source.
Derivative. Anything derived from another.
Development. The growth from a cause.
Effect. The immediate outcome of a cause.
End. The result or effect of work. See BEGINNING-END.
Issue. Outcome.
Outgrowth. A result or consequence.
Result. The most remote and comprehensive outcome of any cause or causes.
Resultance. } A result.
Resultant. }
Upshot. Final outcome.

EFFECT—*Denotations.*

Bud. The earliest growth of a stem or branch.
Creation. The act of God in bringing the world into existence.
Creature. That which has been created.
Crop. Things produced or grown.
Fabric. Something that has been constructed or put together.
First-fruit. The first outcome, result, or reward of anything.
Firstling. The first born of a flock.
Fruit. The growth from the seed of plants.
Handiwork. The result of one's work.
Harvest. The crop.
Offshoot. Something that branches off from a parent stock.
Offspring. A descendant.
Performance. The result of work.
Premises. First-fruits.
Work. Result achieved by labor.

EFFECT—*Verbal Expressions.*

Accrue from, to accumulate; **arise from; be due to,** be caused by; **be owing to; be the effect of,** etc. (see *Nouns*); **bud from; come from,** to have origin in; **come of,** to be derived from; **come out of; come to,** to aggregate to; **depend upon,** to rely upon for support or existence; **derive its origin from; emanate from,** to go out from; **flow from; follow from; germinate from; grow from; hang upon; hinge upon,** to be subject to a governing principle; **issue from; originate from; originate in; proceed from; result from; rise from; spring from,** to have birth or origin in; **sprout from,** to develop from, as a plant; **sow the wind and reap the whirlwind,** to suffer the consequences of error; **take its rise from,** to have its beginning; **take the consequences,** to assume responsibility for the outcome; **turn upon.**

EFFECT—*Adjectives.*

Derivative. Not original.
Hereditary. Passing naturally from parent to child.

CAUSE—EFFECT—*Continued.*

CAUSE—ASSOCIATED NOUNS—*Continued.*

Nest. The habitation of a bird, prepared for rearing its young.
Nidus [L.]. A nest.
Nucleus. The germ or seed.
Nursery. A place where the growth of anything is promoted.
Occasioner. One who or that which causes anything.
Pivot. That on which anything depends for its cause or effect.
Prime mover. The leader or cause of anything.
Principle. The source or cause from which a thing proceeds.
Radical. Essential nature.
Radix [L.]. A root.
Rationale. The logical basis of a statement.
Root. That from which anything derives origin.
Rudiment. The germ.
Seed. That from which a plant grows.
Stirps. A source of property-descent.
Stock. The main stem of a tree.
Tap-root. The principal root of a plant.
Trunk. The main body of a tree.
Turning-point. The place or time from which a force or conduct takes a different course.
Undercurrents. Silent or unseen sources.
Well. A source of water.
Womb. The organ in which young are developed.

CAUSE—*Verbs.*

Broach. To open primarily.
Cause. To produce; to be the reason for a result.
Contribute. To participate in the bringing about of a result.
Create, etc. See CREATION.
Decide. To fix the result of.
Determine. To shape the character of.
Elicit. To bring forth.
Entail. To fix as an inevitable result on a person or thing.
Evoke. To bring into play; to call forth.
Found. To set up; to establish.
Induce. To bring about.
Institute. To begin.
Kindle. To arouse.
Occasion. To move; to incite.
Operate. To work an effect upon.
Originate. To bring into being.
Procure. To bring on; to manage.
Produce. To bring forth; to cause to follow as a natural consequence.
Provoke. To instigate.
Set afloat. To put in action.
Set afoot. To start in motion.
Set up. To begin, as something new.
Superinduce. To bring on additionally.
Suscitate. To rouse into action or being

CAUSE—*Verbal Expressions.*

Be the cause of, be the reason of, etc. (see *Nouns*); **bring about,** to effect; **bring on,** to bring into existence; **bring to pass,** to accomplish; **conduce to,** etc. (see INCLINATION); **derive its origin** (see CAUSE-EFFECT); **draw down;** **give occasion to;** **give origin to;** **give rise to,** to occasion; **have a common origin;** **have a finger in the pie,** to be implicated in; **have a hand in the pie;** **lay the foundation of;** **lie at the root of;** **open the door to;** **sow the seeds of,** to start; **turn the scale,** to decide the result of.

caused. Effected. CAUSE-EFFECT.
cause'-less. Groundless; uncaused. PURPOSE-LUCK, RATIONALE-LUCK.
causerie [F.] (coz-rî') Talk CONVERSATION-MONOLOGUE.
cause'-way''. A raised road. WAY.
cau-sid'-ic-al. Pertaining to a lawsuit. JUDICATURE.
caus'-tic. Sarcastic; stinging; corroding. CHARITABLENESS-UNCHARITABLENESS, CURVATION-RECTILINEARITY, EMOTION, HEATING-COOLING, PLEASURABLENESS-PAINFULNESS, VIGOR-INERTIA.
caus-tic'-i-ty. State of being caustic. VIGOR-INERTIA
cau'-tel. Caution. RECKLESSNESS-CAUTION.
cautela, ex abundanti [L.] (cau-tî'-la, ex ab-un-dan'-

EFFECT—*Adjective Expressions.*

Caused by, etc. (see CAUSE); **dependent upon; derivable from; derived from; due to; evolved from; owing to; resulting from,** etc. (see *Verbs*).

EFFECT—*Adverbs.*

Consequently. As a natural result
Eventually. Ultimately; at last.
Naturally. Following the rule or law.
Necessarily. Inevitably.
Through. To a termination.

EFFECT—*Adverbial Expressions.*

All along of, because of; **as a consequence; in consequence;** for this reason; **it follows that;** of course, as a matter of common sequence or necessity.

EFFECT—*Phrases.*

Cela va sans dire [F.], that goes without saying; **thereby hangs a tale.**

CAUSE—*Continued.*

CAUSE—*Adjectives.*

Aboriginal. Of or pertaining to the first.
Causal. Productive of a result.
Caused, etc. See *Verbs*.
Connate. Of common birth.
Embryonic. Rudimentary.
Embryotic. In the earliest stage of development.
Germinal. Of the nature of a germ.
Original. First of its kind.
Originated, etc. See *Verbs*
Primary. Earliest.
Primitive. Pertaining to the beginning, or first state.
Primordial. Of the first order.
Radical. Pertaining to the root, or foundation.
Seminal. Pertaining to the seed, or first development.

CAUSE—*Adjective Expressions.*

At the bottom of, the chief cause of; **having a common origin; in embryo,** in an inceptive state; *in ovo* [L.], in embryo.

CAUSE—*Adverbial Expressions.*

Because, etc. See RATIONALE.
Behind the scenes. Familiar with the hidden cause.

CAUSE—*Phrases.*

Felix qui potuit rerum cognoscere causas [L.]. Happy he who is able to ascertain the causes of things.
Last straw that breaks the camel's back. The ultimate cause of defeat or downfall.
Les dessous des cartes [F.]. The secrets of an affair.

tai). Out of abundant caution. SECURITY-INSECURITY.
cau''-ter-i-za'-tion. Process of making callous. HEATING-COOLING.
cau'-ter-ize. To sear by burning. HEATING-COOLING.
cau'-ter-y. A searing by caustic. HEATING-COOLING.
cau'-tion. Care to avoid misfortune; a warning. SECURITY, WARNING; want of caution, RECKLESSNESS-CAUTION.
cau'-tion-a-ry. Admonitory. WARNING.
cau'-tious-ness. Carefulness. WARNING.
cav''-al-cade'. A company of riders. CONTINUITY-INTERRUPTION, TRAVELING-NAVIGATION.

cav″-a-lier′. A gallant; haughty; offhand; a lover; a horseman. POLITENESS-IMPOLITENESS, PRESUMPTION-OBSEQUIOUSNESS, RECKLESSNESS-CAUTION, REGARD-SCORN, WAYFARER-SEAFARER.

cavalière servente [It.] (cɑ-vɑ-lî-ê′-rê ser-ven′-tê). A cavalier servant; a lover LOVE-HATE, PRESUMPTION-OBSEQUIOUSNESS.

cav′-al-ry. Troops trained for fighting on horseback. BELLIGERENT.

ca″-va-ti′-na. A simple air. MUSIC.

cave. A natural cavity in the earth. CONTENTS-RECEIVER, CONVEXITY-CONCAVITY, DWELLER-HABITATION, OUTSIDE-INSIDE; **cave in,** CONVEXITY-CONCAVITY, TRANSCURSION-SHORTCOMING, YIELDING; **cave of Adullam,** CONTENTEDNESS-DISCONTENTMENT, QUEST-ABANDONMENT; **cave of despair,** LIGHTHEARTEDNESS-DEJECTION, SANGUINENESS-HOPELESSNESS; **cave of Eolus,** RIVER-WIND.

ca′-ve-at. A legal caution. ORDER, WARNING.

caveat actor [L.] (kê′-ve-at ac′-tor) Let the doer beware. WARNING.

caveat emptor [L.] (kê′-ve-at emp′-tor). Let the buyer beware. BUYING-SALE, CONTRACT.

cav′-en-dish. A brand of American tobacco. PUNGENCY, SWEETNESS-ACIDITY.

cavendo tutus [L.] (cɑ-ven′-do tiu′-tus). Safe through caution. CAREFULNESS-CARELESSNESS, RECKLESSNESS-CAUTION, SECURITY-INSECURITY.

cave quid dicis, quando, et cui [L.] (kê′-vî quid dai′-sis, quan′-do, et kai). Beware what you say, when, and to whom. TALKATIVENESS-TACITURNITY, WARNING.

cav′-ern. A cave. CONTENTS-RECEIVER, CONVEXITY-CONCAVITY, DWELLER-HABITATION.

cav′-ern-ous. Like a cavern. CONVEXITY-CONCAVITY, FUTURE-PAST.

cav″-i-are′. A condiment. CONDIMENT, PUNGENCY; **caviare to the general,** TASTE-VULGARITY.

cav′-il. To raise objections, to be captious. APPROVAL-DISAPPROVAL, ASSENT-DISSENT, RATIOCINATION-CASUISTRY.

cav′-il-er. One who cavils. FLATTERER-DEFAMER.

cav′-i-ty. A hole. CONVEXITY-CONCAVITY.

caw. The cry of a crow. CRY-ULULATION.

Cay-enne′. Red pepper. CONDIMENT, PUNGENCY.

ca-zique′. A prince or chief. CHIEF-UNDERLING.

cease. To leave off action. DISCONTINUANCE-CONTINUANCE; **cease to breathe,** LIFE-DEATH; **cease to exist,** ENTITY-NONENTITY.

cease′-less. Without stop ETERNITY-INSTANTANEITY.

ce′-ci-ty. Blindness. SIGHT-BLINDNESS.

ce′-dar. An evergreen tree. MARK-OBLITERATION, REDNESS-GREENNESS, STRENGTH-WEAKNESS.

cede. To give up; to abandon; to admit. GIVING-RECEIVING, KEEPING-RELINQUISHMENT, YIELDING.

ce-dil′-la. A mark under the letter " c " to give it the sound of " s." MARK-OBLITERATION, SIGN.

ceil′-ing. The overhead covering of a room. COVER-LINING, HEIGHT-LOWNESS, TOP-BOTTOM.

celare artem [L.] (sî lê′-rî ɑr′-tem). To conceal art. *Ars celare artem* [L.] (ɑrz sî-lê′-rî ɑr′-tem), the art to conceal art, SKILL-UNSKILFULNESS.

celare fraudem, fraus est [L.] (sî-lê′-rî frau′-dem, fraus est). It is a fraud to conceal a fraud. DECEPTION-FRAUD, VISIBILITY-INVISIBILITY.

cela va sans dire [F.] (se-la′ vɑ sɑn· dîr). That is, a matter of course. CAUSE-EFFECT, CONVENTIONALITY-UNCONVENTIONALITY, MELODY-DISSONANCE, MANIFESTATION-LATENCY.

cel′-e-brant. One who celebrates. DEVOTION-IDOLATRY.

cel′-e-brate. To observe. SOLEMNIZATION

cel′-e-bra″-ted. Observed; famous. REPUTATION-DISCREDIT, SOLEMNIZATION.

cel′-e-bra″-ting. Observing. SOLEMNIZATION.

cel′-e-bra′-tion. The act of celebrating. CEREMONIAL, REPUTATION-DISCREDIT, SOLEMNIZATION.

ce-leb′-ri-ty. One who is celebrated. GENTILITY-DEMOCRACY, REPUTATION-DISCREDIT.

ce-ler′-i-ty. Speed. SWIFTNESS-SLOWNESS.

ce-les′-tial. Heavenly. DIVINITY, HEAVEN-HELL, UNIVERSE; **celestial latitude,** ASTRONOMY; **celestial longitude,** ASTRONOMY.

ce′-li-ac. Abdominal. ANATOMY

cel′-i-ba-cy. The unmarried state MATRIMONY-CELIBACY.

cell. A small room, as for a prisoner; part of a battery. CONTENTS-RECEIVER, CONVEXITY-CONCAVITY, DWELLER-HABITATION, ELECTRICITY, RELEASE-PRISON, SOCIABILITY-PRIVACY.

cel′-lar. An underground room. CONTENTS-RECEIVER.

cel′-lar-et. A small cabinet for bottles. CONTENTS-RECEIVER.

cel′-lu-lar. Pertaining to a cell. CONTENTS-RECEIVER, CONVEXITY-CONCAVITY.

cel′-lule. Small cell. CONTENTS-RECEIVER.

cel′-lu-loid. A composition made in imitation of ivory, coral, etc. IMITATION-ORIGINALITY, MATERIALS.

cel′-lu-lose. Full of small cells. CONTENTS-RECEIVER.

Celt′-ic. Pertaining to one of the races of men. ETHNOLOGY.

ce-ment′. An adhesive substance; any bond of union. COHESION-LOOSENESS, CONNECTIVE, HARDNESS-SOFTNESS, MATERIALS.

ce-ment′-ed. United. VARIANCE-ACCORD.

cem′-e-ter-y. A burial ground. LIFE-FUNERAL.

cen′-o-bite. A monk. MINISTRY-LAITY, SOCIABILITY-PRIVACY.

cen′-o-taph. An empty tomb. LIFE-FUNERAL.

cen′-ser. A vessel for burning incense. CEREMONIAL.

cen′-sor. A critic; an official examiner. DECISION-MISJUDGMENT, FLATTERER-DEFAMER, JUDGE.

cen-so′-ri-ous. Faultfinding. APPROVAL-DISAPPROVAL.

cen-so′-ri-ous-ness. Faultfinding. APPROVAL-DISAPPROVAL.

cen′-sur-a-ble. Deserving censure. INNOCENCE-GUILT.

cen′-sure. To disapprove. APPROVAL-DISAPPROVAL.

cen′-sur-er. One who censures. FLATTERER-DEFAMER.

cen′-sus. A numbering of the people. NUMBERING, RECORD.

cen-tare′. Square meter. MEASURE.

cen′-taur. A monster CONVENTIONALITY-UNCONVENTIONALITY.

cen-ta′-vo. Mexican coin. VALUES.

cen″-te-na′-ri-an. One a hundred years old. INFANT-VETERAN.

cen′-te-na-ry. Pertaining to a century. FIVE-QUINQUESECTION, PERIODICITY-IRREGULARITY.

cen-ten′-ni-al. Hundredth anniversary. CONVENTIONALITY-UNCONVENTIONALITY, PERIODICITY-IRREGULARITY.

cen′-ter. The middle; a focal point. CENTER, GATHERINGPLACE, MIDDLE; **center round,** CONCENTRATION-RADIATION, GATHERING-SCATTERING; **shake to its center,** AGITATION

CENTER.

Axis. The line on which something rotates, or about which something is symmetrically arranged.

Center. A point equidistant from the extremities of a line, figure, or body.

Centricalness. Location in the center.

Focus. A center. See GATHERINGPLACE.

Middle, etc. See MIDDLE.

CENTER—*Denotations.*

Backbone. The spine or vertebral column of a person.
Bull's-eye. The central division of a target.
Core. The central or innermost part of a thing.
Heart. The chief, or central part.
Hotbed. The place from which any activity or growth arises.
Kernel. The central part round which other matter is gathered.
Marrow. The interior substance of anything.
Nave. The central part of a church; a hub.
Navel. A central part or point; the umbilicus.
Nucleolus. A center of growth.
Nucleus. A center of growth.
Pith. The spongy substance in the interior of stems or branches.
Pole. Either of the two points equidistant from every point of a circle of a sphere.
Umbilicus. The depression at the middle of the abdomen.

CENTER—*Associated Nouns.*

Centrality. Tendency toward the center.
Centralization. Act or process of reducing to a center.
Concentration. Act of directing toward a common center. See CONCENTRATION.
Symmetry. Due proportion of the parts of a body to each other.

CENTER—*Scientific Terms.*

Buoyancy. Property of floating on the surface.
Center of gravity. The balancing point in a body.
Center of oscillation. The point in a body at which if all the mass were concentrated the time of vacillation would continue the same as before.
Center of percussion. That point in a body revolving about a fixed axis at which it may strike an obstacle without communicating the shock to the axis.
Center of pressure. That point in a body at which the whole pressure may be applied with the same effect it would produce if distributed.
Metacenter. The point of intersection of a vertical line through the center of gravity of the fluid displaced by a floating body.

CENTER—*Verbs.*

Centralize. To make central.
Concentrate. To bring to a common central point.
Converge, etc. See CONCENTRATION.

CENTER—*Verbal Expressions.*

Be central; be concentric, etc. (see *Adjectives*); **bring to a focus; render central.**

CENTER—*Adjectives.*

Axial. Around an axis or center.
Azygous. Without a fellow; single.
Central. Relating to the middle; placed in the middle.
Centrical. Centrally located.
Concentric. Having a common center.
Focal. Pertaining or belonging to the central point or focus.
Homocentric. Having the same center.
Middle, etc. See MIDDLE.
Middlemost. Nearest the middle.
Umbilical. Pertaining to the navel; hence, in the center.

CENTER—*Adverbs.*

Centrally, etc. See *Adjectives.*
Middle. In the central part.
Midst. In the center.

cen-tes'-i-mal. One hundredth. FIVE-QUINQUESECTION.
cen'-ti-gram. Small weight. MEASURE.
cen'-ti-li''-ter. One hundredth of a liter. MEASURE.
cen'-ti-me''-ter. One hundredth of a meter. MEASURE.
cen'-ti-ped. Kind of worm. MULTIPLICITY-PAUCITY.
cen'-to. A musical medley. POETRY-PROSE.
cen-tral. Pertaining to the center. CENTER.
cen-tral'-i-ty. The state of being central. CENTER, PROPORTION-DEFORMITY.

cen''-tral-i-za'-tion. Act of centralizing. CENTER.
cen'-tral-ize. To bring to a center. COMPOSITION-RESOLUTION, CENTER.
cen'-tral-ly. In the center. CENTER.
cen'-tric-al. Pertaining to the center. CENTER.
cen'-tric-al-ness. State of being in the center. CENTER.
cen-trif'-u-gal. Directed from the center. CONCENTRATION-RADIATION.
cen-trip'-e-tal. Directed toward the center. CONCENTRATION-RADIATION.
cen'-tu-ple. Increased a hundredfold. FIVE-QUINQUESECTION.
cen-tu'-pli-cate. To increase a hundredfold. FIVE-QUINQUESECTION.
cen-tu'-ri-al. Pertaining to a century. FIVE-QUINQUESECTION.
cen-tu'-ri-ate. Pertaining to a century. FIVE-QUINQUESECTION.
cen-tu'-ri-on. A captain of a hundred men. CHIEF-UNDERLING.
cen'-tu-ry. A hundred years. FIVE-QUINQUESECTION, LASTINGNESS-TRANSIENTNESS, MEASURE, PERIOD-PROGRESS.
cer'-am'-ic. Pertaining to pottery. HEATING-COOLING; **ceramic ware,** SCULPTURE.
ce'-rate. A compound used for blisters. REMEDY-BANE.
Cer'-be-rus. A three-headed dog. PERFORATOR-STOPPER, SECURITY-INSECURITY; **sop for Cerberus,** MOTIVE-CAPRICE.
ce'-re-al. A grain. NUTRIMENT-EXCRETION.
ce''-re-a'-li-a. The cereals. NUTRIMENT-EXCRETION.
cer'-e-bral. Mental. MIND-IMBECILITY.
cer''-e-bra'-tion. Brain action. REFLECTION-VACANCY.
cer'-e-brum. The upper part of the brain. MIND-IMBECILITY.
cere'-cloth''. A cloth saturated with wax. LIFE-FUNERAL.
cere'-ment. A waxed cloth used as a winding sheet. COVER-LINING, LIFE-FUNERAL, PULPINESS-OIL.
cer''-e-mo'-ni-al. A ritual. CEREMONIAL, POLITENESS-IMPOLITENESS, POMP, VESTMENTS.

CEREMONIAL.

Ceremonial. A system of rules and forms, enjoined by law, or established by custom in religious worship.
Ceremonialism. Adherence to or fondness for ceremony.
Ceremony. A formal rite or observance.
Duty. Any service, business, or office.
Form. Stated method; prescribed practise; ceremony.
Formulary. Prescribed form or model.
Litany. The form of supplication in public worship.
Observance. Performance, as of rules, rites, and ceremonies.
Ordinance. Observance commanded; an established rite or ceremony.
Rite. A formal act or ceremonial of religion or other solemn duty.
Ritualism. Adherence to a prescribed form of divine service.
Sacrament. A sacred token or ceremony used to impress an obligation.
Service. Public religious worship or ceremony.
Solemnity. A rite or ceremony performed with religious reverence.

CEREMONIAL—*Denotations.*

Agape. The early Christian love-feast.
Aspersion. A sprinkling, as of water in a religious ceremony.
Auricular confession. Confidential or private confession to a priest.
Baptism. A sacrament or rite, in which water is made use of to acknowledge consecration to Christ
Baptismal regeneration. The doctrine that baptism is a means of being born into a new life, as brothers of Christ.
Burial. See LIFE-FUNERAL.
Canonization. The enrolling of a person in the calendar of saints.
Celebration. The ceremonial of the Lord's Supper.
Christening. See BAPTISM.
Circumcision. The custom of cutting off the foreskin of human males, as a pledge of spiritual purification.

Communion. The sacrament of the Lord's Supper.

Confirmation. The form of full induction into the church.

Consecration. Act of setting apart to a sacred use.

Consubstantiation. The actual, substantial presence of the body and blood of Christ with the bread and wine of the sacrament.

Discourse. A formal ceremonious talk.

Dry mass. A form of mass, without consecration.

Eaglewood. A wood burned for incense.

Eileton. The cloth on which the eucharistic elements are laid.

Encenia. A church wake.

Eucharist. The Lord's Supper.

Excommunication. An ecclesiastical censure whereby the person against whom it is pronounced is cast out of the communion of the church.

Extreme unction. The anointing of a dying person.

Farse. An addition to the Latin service.

Flagellation. A scourging.

High celebration. The ceremonial of the eucharist.

High mass. A mass celebrated with full ceremonial.

Homily. A serious discourse.

Impanation. Embodiment of the body of Christ in the bread of the eucharist.

Imposition of hands. Act of blessing.

Incantation, etc. A form of words sung in connection with ceremonies. See DEVOTION-CHARM.

Introit. A psalm read or sung at mass.

Invocation of saints. A form of prayer in which the blessing of the saints is invoked.

Laying on of hands. Act of blessing.

Lecture. An expository sermon.

Lord's Supper. The sacrament of the communion.

Low mass. Ordinary form of mass said by the priest without music.

Maceration. Act of expressing mortification by fasting.

Mass. A service that includes the holy communion and the liturgy.

Matrimony. See MATRIMONY.

Ministration. Service or ministry.

Missa cantata [L.]. A mass sung.

Offertory. An anthem chanted or played during the offering and first part of the mass.

Ordination. See CHURCH.

Pastoral. A letter from a bishop to his diocese.

Penance. See ATONEMENT.

Preaching. A discourse on religious subjects.

Predication. Act of delivering sermons.

Psalmody. Practise of singing psalms or sacred songs. See DEVOTION.

Real presence. The doctrine that the body of Christ is partaken of in the communion.

Sabbatarianism. The doctrine which teaches the strictest observance of the Sabbath, often including the day of the week specified in Exodus.

Sabbatism. The keeping of the Sabbath.

Sermon. A public discourse by a clergyman.

Seven sacraments. Baptism, confirmation, the eucharist, penance, holy orders, matrimony, and extreme unction.

Telling of beads. To recite prayers, checking them off by the beads of a rosary.

The holy sacrament. The Lord's Supper.

Thurification. Act of burning incense.

Transfiguration. A festival commemorating Christ's transfiguration.

Transubstantiation. The doctrine which teaches that the bread and wine of the eucharist is converted into the body and blood of Christ.

Viaticum [L.]. The communion given to dying persons.

Visitation of the sick. Act of visiting.

CEREMONIAL—*Nouns of Agent.*

Ritualist. One skilled in or attached to a ritual.

Sabbatarian. One who keeps the Sabbath holy.

CEREMONIAL—*Associated Words.*

Agnus Dei [L.]. The Lamb of God.

Bead-roll. A roll of prayers.

Beads. A rosary, hence, prayers.

Book of Common Prayer. Book of the ritual of the Episcopal Church.

Breviary. In the Roman Catholic Church, a book containing the daily offices which all who are in orders are bound to read.

Canon. A law or rule of doctrine.

Censer. A vase or pan in which incense is burned.

Chrism. A consecrated ointment of oil and balm for baptism, etc.

Cross. The ensign of the Christian religion.

Crucifix. A cross, or representation of a cross with the figure of Christ crucified upon it.

Elements. The bread and wine used in the eucharist.

Euchology. A formulary of prayers.

Font. The vessel used in churches as the repository of the baptismal water.

Holy water. In the Roman Catholic Church, salted water consecrated by the priest and used in certain rites and ceremonies.

Host. In the Roman Catholic Church, the consecrated wafer representing the body of Christ.

Hymnal. A collection of hymns, generally for use in public worship.

Hymn-book. A book containing a collection of hymns.

Hymnology. A collection of hymns.

Incense. The odors of spices and gums burned in religious rites.

Lectionary. A book, or list of lections, for reading in divine service.

Liturgy. An established formula for public worship.

Mass-book. } The book containing the service of the mass for the entire year.
Missal. }

Ordinal. A book containing the rubrics of the mass.

Patera. A saucerlike vessel of earthenware or metal used by the Greeks and Romans in libations and sacrifices.

Pax. The embrace in the sanctuary at high mass in Roman Catholic churches.

Pietas. A representation of the dead Christ attended by the Virgin Mary, or by holy women and angels.

Pix. A box or case containing the host.

Prayer-book. A book containing devotional prayers.

Psalm-book. A book containing versifications of the Scriptural psalms composed for use in churches.

Psalter. A psalm-book; a rosary consisting of 150 beads in accordance with the number of the psalms.

Pyx. Same as pix.

Relics. The body of a deceased saint or martyr.

Reliquary. A depository in which relics are kept.

Ritual. A prescribed form of performing divine service in a particular church or communion.

Rosary. A series of prayers arranged to be recited in order, on beads; also a string of beads on which the prayers are counted.

Rubric. The directions and rules for the conduct of service, formerly written or printed in red.

Sackcloth and ashes. A mode of apparel formerly signifying mourning or penitence.

CEREMONIAL—*Nouns of Time.*

Advent. The first season of the ecclesiastical year, including the four Sundays immediately preceding Christmas.

Bairam. The name of two Mohammedan festivals.

Christmas. The birthday of Christ.

Easter. The day of the resurrection of Christ.

Epiphany. A festival of the Christian Church celebrated in commemoration of the manifestation of Christ to the Gentiles, held the twelfth day after Christmas.

Fast. A period observed for religious fasting.

Feast. A day or season in commemoration of some great event.

Holiday. A day of exemption from labor.

Holy week. The week before Easter.

Lammas. A festival held August 1, in commemoration of the imprisonment of the Apostle Peter.

Lent. A fast of forty days before Easter.

Martinmas. Feast of St. Martin, the 11th of November.

Michaelmas. The feast of St. Michael, occurring September 29th.

Passion week. The week immediately preceding Easter.

Passover. A Jewish feast in commemoration of the passing over of the children of Israel when God smote the eldest born of the Egyptians.

Pentecost. A Jewish festival occurring fifty days after the Passover.

Ramadan. The great annual feast of the Mohammedans.

Ramazan. See RAMADAN.

Sabbath. The first day of the week.

Whitsuntide. The time of Pentecost.

Yule. Christmas.

CEREMONIAL—*Verbs.*

Anele. To anoint; to give extreme unction to.

Baptize. To administer the sacrament of baptism to.

Circumcise. To cut off the foreskin.

Communicate. To partake of the Lord's Supper; to commune.

Confirm. To administer the rites of confirmation to.

Dip. To immerse for baptism.

Excommunicate. To put out of communion.

Lecture. To deliver a familiar discourse.

Minister. To perform service in any office, sacred or secular.

Officiate. To conduct a public service.

Preach. To proclaim by public discourse.

CEREMONIAL—Verbs—*Continued.*

Predicate. To preach.
Sermonize. To deliver a formal sermon.
Sprinkle. To baptize by the application of a few drops of water.

CEREMONIAL—*Verbal Phrases.*

Administer extreme unction; administer the sacrament; attend the communion; attend the sacrament; ban with bell, book, and candle, a solemn mode of excommunication in the Roman Catholic Church, in which the clergyman pronounces the sentence of excommunication, the bell is tolled as for the dead, the book from which the formula was read is closed, and a lighted candle is cast upon the ground; **do duty; give the communion; give the sacrament; lay hands on; partake of communion; partake of the sacrament; perform service; receive the communion; receive the sacrament; take the communion; take the sacrament.**

CEREMONIAL—*Adjectives.*

Baptismal. Of or pertaining to baptism.
Ceremonial. Of, pertaining to, or characterized by outward form and ceremony.
Eucharistical. Pertaining to or of the nature of the eucharist.
Paschal. Of or pertaining to the Jewish Passover or the Christian Easter.
Ritual. Of, pertaining to, or consisting of a rite or **rites.**
Ritualistic Adhering or tending to or favoring ritualism.

CEREMONIAL—*Phrase.*

Eau bénite de cour [F.]. Holy water of the court.

cer″-e-mo′-ni-al-ism. Fondness of ceremony. VESTMENTS.
cer″-e-mo′-ni-ous. Formal. REGARD - DISRESPECT, VESTMENTS.
cer′-e-mo-ny. A formal act; observance of etiquette. CEREMONIAL, POMP.
ce′-ro-graph. Wax-engraving. ENGRAVING.
ce-rog′-ra-phy. Engraving with wax. ENGRAVING, WRITING-PRINTING.
ce′-ro-man″-cy. Divination by melted wax. PROPHECY.
ce″-ro-plas′-tic. Wax-modeling. SCULPTURE.
cer′-tain. Assured; indefinite; fixed; inevitable. ASSERTION-DENIAL, CERTAINTY-DOUBT, FAITH-MISGIVING, PLURALITY-FRACTION, TRUTH-ERROR, UNIVERSALITY-PARTICULARITY; **make certain of,** DISCOVERY; **of a certain age,** INFANCY-AGE; **to a certain degree,** MAGNITUDE-SMALLNESS.
cer′-tain-ly. Without doubt. CERTAINTY-DOUBT, ASSENT-DISSENT.
cer′-tain-ty. The quality of being certain. CERTAINTY-DOUBT.

CERTAINTY—DOUBT.

Assurance. The act of making certain; a pledge of confidence.
Certainty. Freedom from doubt or failure.
Certitude. Exemption from doubt.
Dead certainty. An emphatic reality.
Dogmatism. Positiveness in stating opinion.
Fact. Reality.
Fait accompli [F.]. An accomplished fact.
Infallibility. The quality of being incapable of error.
Infallibleness. See *Adjectives.*
Matter of fact. An absolute reality.
Moral certainty. A probability so strong that the possibility of the opposite may be wholly disregarded.
Necessity. Inevitableness. See VOLITION-OBLIGATION.
Positive fact. An occurrence or existence undeniable.
Positiveness. Certainty. See *Adjectives.*
Reliability. Trustworthiness.
Surety. The state of being certain.

CERTAINTY—*Associated Nouns.*

Bigot. An illiberal adherent to a creed, or party.
Church. The whole body of Christian believers.
Court of final appeal. A court to which a case may be taken from a lower court.
Doctrinaire. A person who applies abstract principles to practical concerns.
Dogmatist. One given to positive opinions and beliefs.
Dogmatizer. See DOGMATIST.
Gospel. That which is regarded as infallibly true.
Ipse dixit [L.]. He said it; a dogmatic assertion.
Opinionist. One given to having strong and unshaken opinions.
Pope. The head of the Roman Catholic Church.
Res judicata [L.] A case that has been determined.
Scripture. Infallible truth.
Sir Oracle. A title used by Gratiano in the *Merchant of Venice,* ridiculing those affecting wisdom.
Ultimatum. The final or only condition.

CERTAINTY—*Verbs.*

Assure. To make sure.
Clinch. To make fixed or conclusive.
Decide. To bring to a definite termination.
Determine. To fix upon; to certify.
Dogmatize. To affirm positively.
Ensure. Same as INSURE.
Insure. To render secure or certain.
Know. See FAITH.

Acatalepsy. The incomprehensibleness of things.
Ambiguity. See AMBIGUITY.
Bewilderment. Confused state of mind.
Contingency. Complexity.
Diaporesis. Doubt concerning the order of treating several subjects.
Dilemma. A case in which a choice between two equally undesirable courses is necessary.
Doubt. Absence of certain knowledge.
Doubtfulness. See *Adjectives.*
Dubiety. Doubtfulness.
Dubiousness. The state of being in doubt.
Dubitancy. Uncertainty.
Dubitation. The act of doubting.
Embarrassment. Uneasiness of mind caused by a perplexity.
Fallibility. Tendency to err.
Hesitation. Suspense of opinion or action because of uncertainty.
Incertitude. The state of being doubtful.
Indetermination. State of being wavering in mind.
Obscurity, etc. See LIGHT-DARKNESS.
Onus probandi [L.]. The burden of proving.
Open question. A question admitting of doubt.
Perplexity. State of not being able to determine an opinion or course of conduct.
Possibility upon possibility. A question admitting of many surmises.
Precariousness. The condition of being subject to risk of loss.
Something or other. A doubtful thing.
Suspense. State of indetermination.
Timidity, etc. See SANGUINENESS-TIMIDITY.
Uncertainty. Lack of resolution.
Vacillation, etc. Changeableness in opinions or conduct, etc. See DETERMINATION-VACILLATION.
Vagueness, etc. Indefiniteness, etc. See *Adjectives.*

DOUBT—*Figurative Nouns.*

Blind bargain. An exchange without seeing the article received.
Fog. Condensed vapor which obscures the view; hence, perplexity.
Haze. Anything that dims; hence, uncertainty.
Leap in the dark. Performance of an act without foresight.
Pig in a poke. A blind bargain.

DOUBT—*Verbs.*

Be uncertain, etc. See *Adjectives.*
Be undefined, etc. See *Adjectives.*
Bewilder. To make unsettled in mind.
Bother. To annoy by worrying.
Confound. To overwhelm the mental faculties.
Confuse. To make indistinct or unintelligible.

CERTAINTY—*Verbal Expressions.*

Be certain; be sure, etc. (see *Adjectives*) ; **lay down the law,** to make acquainted with existing rules or regulations; **"make assurance doubly sure"; make sure; render certain; set at rest,** to settle definitely; **stand to reason,** to be consistent with truth.

CERTAINTY—*Adjectives.*

Absolute. Self-determined.
Ascertained. Known or established with certainty.
Assured, etc. See *Verbs.*
Authentic. Genuinely accurate.
Authoritative. Positively established.
Avoidless. Not to be escaped.
Axiomatic. Self-evident.
Categorical. Admitting no exceptions or doubts.
Certain. Admitting neither doubt nor denial.
Clear. Free from doubt or misgiving.
Conclusive. Not able to be refuted or proved false.
Decided. Settled as to doubt.
Decisive. Having the power or quality of deciding.
Definite. Certain.
Determinate. Having the power of settling or limiting definitely.
Doubtless. Without doubt.
Evident. Easily manifest to both eye and mind.
Incontestable. Not to be denied or contradicted.
Incontrovertible. Too certain to be disputed.
Indisputable. Too obvious to admit of contradiction.
Indubious. Not doubtful.
Indubitable. Plainly certain.
Inevitable. Not to be evaded or resisted.
Infallible. Incapable of erring.
Insured, etc. See *Verbs.*
Irrefutable. See PROOF.
Known, etc. See *Verbs.*
Official. Derived from, or done by the proper authority.
Positive. Fully convinced or confident.
Questionless. Beyond question.
Reliable. Worthy of belief or dependence.
Self-evident. Producing certainty or conviction from mere consideration.
Solid. Worthy of credence or trust.
Sure. Worthy of dependence; certain to meet expectations.
Trustworthy. Meriting trust and confidence.
Unavoidable. Not to be escaped.
Unchangeable. Fixed in form or substance.
Uncontested. Not denied.
Undeniable. Not to be refuted.
Undisputed. Not contradicted.
Undoubted. Accepted without hesitation or doubt.
Unequivocal. Admitting of but a single, certain interpretation.
Unerring. Accurate.
Unimpeachable. Not to be reproached.
Unmistakable. Not doubted.
Unqualified. Unconditional; absolute.
Unquestionable. Not to be doubted or questioned.
Unquestioned. Not doubted.
Well founded. Clearly established.

CERTAINTY—*Adjective Expressions.*

Beyond a doubt; beyond all dispute; beyond all question; beyond question; clear as day; clear as the sun at noonday; past dispute; sure as a gun; sure as death and taxes, sure as fate, inevitable; **to be depended on; without a doubt; without a shade or shadow of doubt; without power of appeal,** settled decisively; **without question.**

CERTAINTY—*Adverbs.*

Certainly, etc. See *Adjectives.*
Certes. Verily.
Doubtless. Unquestionably.
Sure. Surely.
Surely, etc. See *Adjectives.*

CERTAINTY—*Adverbial Expressions.*

A coup sûr [F.], with certainty; **and no mistake; as a matter of course; at all events,** surely; **at any rate,** inevitably; **come what may; come what will;** *coûte-que-coûte* [F.], at any price; *coûte qu'il coûte*

DOUBT—VERBS—*Continued.*

Depend. To be or remain uncertain.
Doubt. To be undecided.
Embarrass. To disconcert.
Float in a sea of doubt. To be in a doubtful state.
Flounder. To stumble or waver in reasoning.
Hang in the balance. To be undecided.
Hesitate. To pause awaiting decision or action.
Keep in suspense. To keep in doubt.
Lose oneself. To be in a state of suspense as to memory and reason.
Lose one's head. To become utterly confused.
Lose the clew. ⎫ To lose the thread leading from an intricacy, as that
Lose the clue. ⎬ of Daedalus from the labyrinth of Crete.
Lose the scent. To lose track of.
Miss one's way. Lose one's path.
Moider. To distract; to confuse.
Muddle one's brains. To becloud the brain, as with drink.
Not know whether one stands on one's head or heels.
Not know which way to turn.
Not to know what to make of, etc. See CLEARNESS-OBSCURITY.
Perplex. To make obscure, or to confuse.
Pose. To embarrass by puzzling questions.
Put out. To disconcert.
Puzzle. To mystify.
Render uncertain, etc. See *Adjectives.*
Throw off the scent. To put in a state of uncertainty, as a hunting dog.
Tremble in the balance. To be in doubt or great danger; on wavering scales.
Wonder whether. To be doubtful about.

DOUBT—*Adjectives.*

Abroad. Uncertain, as in calculation.
Adrift. Aimless; without occupation.
Afraid to say. Not certain enough to say.
Ambiguous. Double in meaning.
Apocryphal. Of uncertain authenticity.
Astray. Wandering, as in reasoning.
At a loss. Unable to decide.
At a nonplus. Puzzled.
At fault. Embarrassed.
At one's wit's end. Entirely at a loss.
At sea. Ignorant of how to proceed.
Casual. Occurring without premeditation.
Changeable. See MUTABILITY.
Confused. See VISIBILITY-INVISIBILITY.
Contingent. Dependent on unknown circumstances.
Contingent on. Dependent on.
Controvertible. Deniable.
Debatable. Disputable.
Dependent on. Determined by.
Dependent on circumstances.
Désorienté [F.]. Having lost one's bearings.
Distracted. Unsettled in reason.
Distraught. Confused.
Doubtful. Having the character of ambiguity.
Dubious. Calling forth doubt.
Enigmatic. Not easily solved.
Equivocal. Capable of equally appropriate interpretations.
Experimental, etc. See TRIAL.
Fallible. Liable to err, or deceive.
Hypothetical. Taken as an unproved premise from which to deduct proof.
Ignorant, etc. See KNOWLEDGE-IGNORANCE.
In a cloud. Not knowing how to proceed.
In a maze. In a state of confusion.
In a state of uncertainty. Doubtful.
Indecisive. Not bringing to a definite end.
Indefinite. Not established or determined.
Indeterminate. Not precise.
In question, etc. See INVESTIGATION.
In suspense. In a state of uncertainty.
Lost. Bewildered.
Mystic. Secret.
Occasional. Pertaining to or occurring at irregular times or periods.
Open to discussion. Debatable.
Oracular. Doubtful, like lying oracles.
Out of one's reckoning. Wrong in calculation.

CERTAINTY—DOUBT—*Continued.*

CERTAINTY—ADVERBIAL EXPRESSIONS—*Continued.*

[F.], at any price; *flagrante delicto* [L.], in the commission of the crime; **for certain**; **happen what may**; **happen what will**; **if the worst comes to the worst**; in truth, etc. (see TRUTH); **no doubt**; **of course**; **sink or swim**; **sure enough**; **to a certainty**; **to be sure**; **whatever may happen**; **without fail.**

CERTAINTY—*Phrases.*

Cela va sans dire [F.], that goes without saying; *dictum de dicto* [L.], hearsay report; *más vale pájaro en mano que buitre volando* [Sp.], a sparrow on the hand is better than a vulture on the wing; *para todo hay remedio sinó para la muerte* [Sp.], there is a remedy for all things except death; **the die is cast,** the course has been decided upon; **there is no question**; **there is not a shadow of doubt**

DOUBT—*Continued from Column 2.*

Untrustworthy. Not worthy of trust or confidence.
Vague. Dim; unfixed.

DOUBT—*Phrases.*

Ambiguas in vulgum spargere voces [L.]. To stir up doubt in the minds of the people.
Heaven knows.
Pendente lite [L.] Pending the suit.
Who can tell!
Who shall decide when doctors disagree?

DOUBT—ADJECTIVES—*Continued.*

Paradoxical. Seemingly absurd, but possibly true.
Perplexing, etc. See *Verbs.*
Precarious. Not to be relied upon for certainty; unsteady.
Problematical. Involving doubt.
Puzzled, etc. See *Verbs.*
Questionable. Liable to be doubted or suspected.
Random, etc. See PURPOSE-LUCK.
Slippery. Elusive; tricky.
Subject to. Liable to.
Ticklish. Not fixed; easily affected.
Unascertained. Not definitely known.
Unauthentic. Not genuine; not reliable.
Unauthenticated. Not supported by sufficient authority.
Unauthoritative. Not derived from creditable sources.
Uncertain. Not sure or definite.
Unconfirmed. Not assured or verified.
Uncounted. Of uncertain number.
Undecided. Not settled upon.
Undefinable. Not to be described.
Undefined. Not clear.
Undemonstrated. Not made certain.
Undetermined. Not fixed upon.
Unreliable. Not to be depended upon.
Unsettled. Not steady or fixed.
Untold. Secret.

(Continued on Column 1.)

---

cer′-tes. Truly. ASSENT-DISSENT, CERTAINTY-DOUBT.

cer-tif′-i-cate. A writing used as legal evidence; a declaration in regard to qualifications EVIDENCE-COUNTEREVIDENCE, MARK-OBLITERATION, SECURITY.

cer′-ti-fy. To attest; to assure. ASSERTION-DENIAL, EVIDENCE-COUNTEREVIDENCE.

cer″-ti-o-ra′-ri. A writ from a superior to an inferior court. LITIGATION.

cer′-ti-tude. Confidence. CERTAINTY-DOUBT.

ce-ru′-le-an. Sky-blue. BLUENESS-ORANGE.

cer′-vi-cal. Pertaining to the neck. ANATOMY.

cess. A hole of filth; a public assessment. CLEANNESS-FILTHINESS, PRICE-DISCOUNT.

ces-sa′-tion. Discontinuance. DISCONTINUANCE-CONTINUANCE.

ces′-sion. A surrender. GIVING-RECEIVING, KEEPING-RELINQUISHMENT, YIELDING.

cess′-pool″. A pit of foulness. CLEANNESS-FILTHINESS.

cestui que trust [Law F.] (ses-twi′ ke trust). One to whom a trust is made. HOLDER.

ces′-tus. A girdle or belt. CIRCLE-WINDING, CONNECTIVE.

chafe. To fret; to make sore; to make warm by rubbing. CONTENTEDNESS-DISCONTENTMENT, EXCITABILITY-INEXCITABILITY, FAVORITE-ANGER, HEATING-COOLING, PLEASURABLENESS-PAINFULNESS, PLEASURE-PAIN, SENSUALITY-SUFFERING.

chaff. Trifles; banter; the envelopes of grain. CONSEQUENCE-INSIGNIFICANCE, GENTILITY-DEMOCRACY, SOCIETY-DERISION; **not to be caught with chaff,** CRAFT-ARTLESSNESS, SKILL-UNSKILFULNESS; **winnow chaff from the wheat,** CHOICE-NEUTRALITY.

chaf′-fer. To haggle. EXCHANGE.

cha′-fing. Annoying. EXCITABILITY-INEXCITABILITY.

cha′-fing-dish″. A vessel for heating. OVEN-REFRIGERATOR.

cha-grin′. Mortification. PLEASURE-PAIN.

cha-grined′. Mortified. EXCITABILITY-INEXCITABILITY.

chain. To join with a chain; bonds; an ornament; unit of length. CONNECTIVE, CONTINUITY-INTERRUPTION, CROSSING, EMBELLISHMENT-DISFIGUREMENT, LENGTH-SHORTNESS, MEASURE, RELEASE-PRISON, UNION-DISUNION; **drag a chain,** LIBERTY-SUBJECTION, OBSTRUCTION-HELP; **drag a lengthened**

chain, TOIL-RELAXATION; **in chains,** GUARD-PRISONER.

chain–shot. Cannon-balls chained together. WEAPON.

chair. A single seat; a seat of office; a presiding officer; a conveyance. CONVEYANCE-VESSEL, MANAGEMENT, MANAGER, PRESIDENT-MEMBER, SCEPTER, SCHOOL, SOLEMNIZATION, SUSPENSION-SUPPORT; **in the chair,** MANAGEMENT.

chair′-man. One who presides. MANAGER, PRESIDENT-MEMBER.

chaise. A vehicle. CONVEYANCE-VESSEL.

chal-ced′-o-ny. A waxy transparent quartz. EMBELLISHMENT-DISFIGUREMENT.

chal-cog′-ra-phy. Engraving on plates for printing. ENGRAVING.

cha″-let′. Peasant's cottage. DWELLER-HABITATION.

chal′-ice. A drinking cup. CONTENTS-RECEIVER.

chalk. A white calcareous earth. PAINTING, SIGN, WHITENESS-BLACKNESS; **chalk-engraving,** ENGRAVING; **chalk out,** DESIGN, PAINTING; **not know chalk from cheese,** KNOWLEDGE-IGNORANCE.

chalk′-y. Resembling chalk. WHITENESS-BLACKNESS.

chal′-lenge. To claim as one's due; to defy; to dispute. DEFIANCE, DUENESS-UNDUENESS, FAITH-MISGIVING, INVESTIGATION-ANSWER, JUSTIFICATION-CHARGE; **challenge comparison,** GOODNESS-BADNESS.

cham. A khan. CHIEF-UNDERLING.

cham′-ber. A room; an assembly hall. CONTENTS-RECEIVER, COUNCIL, DWELLER-HABITATION, MARKET; **sick-chamber,** HEALTH-SICKNESS.

cham′-ber-lain. An etiquette official. CHIEF-UNDERLING.

cham′-ber-maid″. A woman who takes care of bed-chambers. CHIEF-UNDERLING.

cha-me′-le-on. A lizard capable of changing colors. VARIEGATION.

cham′-fer. To cut a channel in. GROOVE.

cham′-ois. An antelope famed for agility. SPRING-DIVE.

champ. To bite; to gnash. NUTRIMENT-EXCRETION; **champ the bit,** EXCITABILITY-INEXCITABILITY, FAVORITE-ANGER, INSUBORDINATION-OBEDIENCE.

cham-pagne′. A sparkling wine. LIQUID-GAS, NUTRIMENT-EXCRETION.

cham-paign'. A flat piece of land. GULF-PLAIN.

cham-pain'. A mark of dishonor. REPUTATION-DISCREDIT.

Champ de Mars [F.] (shan· de marz). Field of Mars. LISTS.

champêtre, fête [F.] (shan·-pêtr', fêt) A rustic festival. ENTERTAINMENT-WEARINESS.

cham'-pi-on. One who fights in behalf of another; a victor. ANTAGONIST-ASSISTANT, ATTACK-DEFENSE, BELLIGERENT, PATRIOTISM-TREASON.

cham'-pi-on-ship. Position of a champion. OBSTRUCTION-HELP.

Champs Elysées [F.] (shan·z ê-li-zê'). Elysian fields. HEAVEN-HELL.

chance. Fortune; an opportunity. MOTIVE-CAPRICE, PURPOSE-LUCK, RATIONALE-LUCK; **as chance would have it,** OCCURRENCE-DESTINY; **one's chance,** OCCURRENCE-DESTINY; **chances against one,** SECURITY-INSECURITY; **game of chance,** ENTERTAINMENT-WEARINESS, PURPOSE-LUCK; **small chance,** LIKELIHOOD-UNLIKELIHOOD; **stand a chance,** CONTINGENCY, POSSIBILITY - IMPOSSIBILITY, PURPOSE - LUCK, **take one's chance,** PURPOSE-LUCK, VENTURE.

chan'-cel. A part of a church. FANE.

chan'-cel-lor. A keeper of the great seal; a judicial officer. ADVOCATE, CHIEF-UNDERLING, REPRESENTATIVE; **chancellor of the exchequer,** TREASURER.

chan'-cer-y. A court of equity. **Chancery suit,** EARLINESS-LATENESS; **court of chancery,** TRIBUNAL.

chan''-de-lier'. A branching frame for lights. LUMINARY-SHADE.

chandelle, le jeu ne vaut pas la [F.] (shan·-del', le zhu ne vo pa la). The game is not worth the candle. CONSEQUENCE-INSIGNIFICANCE, PROVISION-WASTE.

chand'-ler. A trader. DEALER.

change. An exchange; small coins; to alter. DETERMINATION-VACILLAT.ON, MARKET, MONEY, MUTATION-PERMANENCE; **change about,** MUTABILITY-STABILITY; **change color,** EMOTION; **change for,** COMMUTATION-PERMUTATION; **change hands,** ALIENATION, COMMUTATION-PERMUTATION; **change of mind,** BIGOTRY-APOSTASY; **change of opinion,** FAITH-MISGIVING; **interchange,** COMMUTATION-PERMUTATION; **radical change,** REVOLUTION; **sudden change,** REVOLUTION.

change'-a-ble. Unsteady. CERTAINTY-DOUBT, MUTABILITY-STABILITY, MUTATION-PERMANENCE.

change'-a-ble-ness. Inconstancy; capability of being changed. DETERMINATION-VACILLATION, LASTINGNESS-TRANSIENTNESS, MUTABILITY-STABILITY, MUTATION-PERMANENCE.

changed. Altered. MUTATION-PERMANENCE.

change'-ful. Full of change. BIGOTRY-APOSTASY, MUTABILITY-STABILITY.

change'-ling. Inconstant. COMMUTATION-PERMUTATION, SAGE-FOOL.

chang'-er. One who changes. DEALER.

chan'-nel. A conduit; a groove; deep part of a stream. APERTURE-CLOSURE, GROOVE, WATERCOURSE-AIR PIPE, WAY.

chant. A song; a psalm chanted. DEVOTION-IDOLATRY, MUSIC, MUSICIAN.

chant du cygne [F.] (shan· dü cîny). The song of the swan; the last strains of an author. LIFE-DEATH.

chant'-er. A singer. MUSICIAN.

chan'-ti-cleer. A cock. FAUNA-FLORA.

chant'-ry. A chapel. FANE.

cha'-o-man''-cy. Fortune-telling. PROPHECY.

cha'-os. A state of disorder. WHOLE-PART.

chap. Jaw; crack; a fellow. INTERSPACE-CONTACT, MALE-FEMALE.

cha-peau'. A plumed hat. DRESS-UNDRESS.

chap'-el. A small church. FANE.

chap'-er-on. An attendant. SECURITY-INSECURITY.

chap'-fal''-len. Dejected. SELFRESPECT-HUMBLENESS.

chap'-lain. A clergyman. CHURCH, MINISTRY-LAITY.

chap'-let. A wreath. CIRCLE-WINDING, EMBELLISHMENT-DISFIGUREMENT, TROPHY.

chap'-man. A pedler. DEALER.

chaps. Mouth and cheeks. BORDER.

chap'-ter. Division of a book; the clergy; a society. CHURCH, CONCEPTION-THEME, COUNCIL, MISSIVE-PUBLICATION, WHOLE-PART; **chapter of accidents,** RATIONALE-LUCK; **chapter and verse,** EVIDENCE-COUNTEREVIDENCE, TRUTH-ERROR.

chap'-trel. Impost. ARCHITECTURE.

char. To scorch. HEATING-COOLING.

char-à-bancs [F.] (shar-a-ban·). A long carriage. CONVEYANCE-VESSEL.

char'-ac-ter. A person in a play; reputation; sign; individuality. ACTING, AFFECTION, CONDITION-SITUATION, CONVENTIONALITY-UNCONVENTIONALITY, DIVISION, LETTER, NATURE-ART, SUBJECTIVENESS-OBJECTIVENESS.

char''-ac-ter-is'-tic. Marking. NATURE-ART, SIGN, SUBJECTIVENESS - OBJECTIVENESS, UNIVERSALITY - PARTICULARITY, VARIATION.

char'-ac-ter-ize. To describe; distinguish. ACCOUNT, NAME-MISNOMER.

char'-ac-ter-ized. Marked by. AFFECTIONS.

cha-rade'. An enigma represented. ACTING, TIDINGS-MYSTERY.

char'-coal''. A black substance used for fuel and in painting. COMBUSTIBLE, HEATING-COOLING, PAINTING, WHITENESS-BLACKNESS.

charge. An admonition; an attack; a position of care; a load of a firearm or a battery; a care; instruction; an accusation. ADVICE, ATTACK-DEFENSE, COMMISSION-ABROGATION, CONTENTS-RECEIVER, ELECTRICITY, ENTIRETY-DEFICIENCY, EXCHANGE, IMPETUS-REACTION, JUSTIFICATION-CHARGE, MANAGEMENT, OCCUPATION, ORDER, PRECEPT, PRICE-DISCOUNT, RELEASE-RESTRAINT; **charge on,** RATIONALE-LUCK; **charge with,** HOLDING-EXEMPTION; **in charge,** GUARD-PRISONER; **justifiable charge,** JUSTIFICATION-CHARGE; **take charge of,** SECURITY-INSECURITY.

charge'-a-ble. Capable of being charged. CREDIT-DEBIT; **chargeable on,** DUTY-IMMUNITY.

chargé d'affaires [F.] (shar-zhê' daf-far'). A diplomatic agent. CONSIGNEE.

char'-ger. A war-horse. BELLIGERENT, CONVEYANCE-VESSEL.

char-ge'-ship. The office of a *chargé d'affaires*. AGENT, CHIEF-UNDERLING, OCCUPATION.

Char'-ing Cross, pro-claim' at. Announce publicly. PUBLICITY.

char'-i-ot. A two-wheeled vehicle. CONVEYANCE-VESSEL; **drag at one's chariot wheels,** LIBERTY-SUBJECTION.

char''-i-ot-eer'. A chariot driver. MANAGER, WAYFARER-SEAFARER.

char'-i-ta-ble. Generous. CHARITABLENESS-MALEVOLENCE, GENEROSITY-FRUGALITY, GIVING-RECEIVING.

char'-i-ta-ble-ness. State of being charitable. CHARITABLENESS-MALEVOLENCE.

CHARITABLENESS—MALEVOLENCE.

Almsgiving. Gratuitous relieving of the poor by gifts.
Altruism. Charitableness towards others.
Amiability. Pleasantness of disposition.
Beneficence. Charity in action.
Benevolence. Desire for the happiness of others.
Benignity. Kindliness of disposition.
Bonhomie [F.]. Good nature.
Bounty. Liberality in giving.
Brotherly love. Fraternal affection.
Charitableness, etc. See *Adjectives.*
Charity. Generosity to the poor.
Christian charity. Charity of a believer in Christ.
Consideration. Kindly regard.
Fellow feeling. Sympathy.
Friendship, etc. State of sustaining friendly relations, etc. See AMITY.
Generosity. Nobleness of mind.
God's grace. } Divine charity.
God's love. }
Good feeling. Friendliness.
Good nature. Mildness of temper.
Goodness of heart. Good disposition.
Good-will. Benevolence.
Good wishes. Desire for the happiness of others.
Humanity. Disposition to relieve those in distress.
Kindheartedness. State of being kind-hearted.
Kindliness, etc. See *Adjectives.*
Knidness, etc. See *Adjectives.*
Love, etc. Kind feeling, etc. See LOVE.
Loving kindness. Affectionate feeling.
Mercy, etc. Inclination to relieve suffering, etc. See COMPASSION.
Milk of human kindness. [Fig.] Benevolence.
Philanthropy, etc. Readiness to do good to all mankind, etc. See HUMANITARIANISM.
Sympathy. Kind feeling toward the suffering growing out of similar previous experience.
Tenderness. State of being susceptible of compassion.
The luxury of doing good. Pleasure in benevolence.
Toleration. State of putting up with opinions or beliefs contrary to our own.
Unselfishness, etc. State of not being selfish, etc. See SELFISHNESS-UNSELFISHNESS.
Warmth of heart. Benevolence.

CHARITABLENESS—*Denotations.*

Acts of kindness. Expression of charity.
A good turn. A helpful deed.
Good offices. A service performed for another.
Good treatment. Kindness.
Good works. Kind and helpful deeds.
Kind offices. See GOOD OFFICES.
Kind treatment. See GOOD TREATMENT.

CHARITABLENESS—*Nouns of Agent.*

Bon enfant [F.]. A good fellow.
Good Samaritan. One given to deeds of kindness. [Bible.]
Sympathizer. One who sympathizes.

CHARITABLENESS—*Verbs.*

Aid, etc. To render assistance, etc. See OBSTRUCTION-HELP.
Benefit. To be of use to.
Fraternize. To treat as a companion.

CHARITABLENESS—*Verbal Expressions.*

Bear good-will; be benevolent, etc. (see *Adjectives*); be interested in; be of use; do a good turn; do as you would be done by; do good; enter into the feelings of others; feel an interest in; feel for; feel interested in; give comfort; have one's heart in the right place, to be generous; meet half way, to concede half of the difference in order to make a compromise; regard with an eye of favor; render a service; smooth the bed of death, to make one's last hours pleasant; sympathize with, to have a common feeling with; take an interest in; take in good part; treat well; view with an eye of favor; wish Godspeed; wish well.

CHARITABLENESS—*Adjectives.*

Accommodating. Given to doing kindnesses or granting favors.
Amiable. Having a pleasing disposition.
Beneficent. Doing good.

Acerbity. Harshness.
Atrocity. Extreme wickedness.
Bad blood. Ill feeling.
Bad intent. Evil purpose.
Bad intention. Ill design.
Barbarity. State of being brutal or uncivilized.
Brutality. The state or quality of being like a brute.
Churlishness, etc. Rudeness of temper, etc. See POLITENESS-IMPOLITENESS.
Cruelness, etc. See *Adjectives.*
Cruelty. A disposition to inflict unnecessary suffering on others.
Despite. Malicious hate.
Diskindness. State of being unkind.
Enmity, etc. The quality of being an enemy, etc. See AMITY-HOSTILITY.
Ferity. State of being wild or fierce in disposition.
Ferocity. Fierceness; cruelty.
Gall. Bitterness of feeling.
Hardness of heart. State of being void of sympathy.
Hate, etc. Intense dislike or aversion coupled with a desire to do injury, etc. See LOVE-HATE.
Heart of stone. Hard-heartedness.
Ill blood. Hatred.
Ill nature. Bad temper; peevishness.
Ill usage. Bad treatment of a person or thing.
Ill will. Enmity.
Immanity. The state of being atrocious or fierce.
Incompassionateness, etc. State of being void of pity, etc. See COMPASSION-RUTHLESSNESS.
Inhumanity. State of being inhumane or cruel.
Intolerance. Refusal to allow others to enjoy their rights.
Malevolence. A disposition to injure others.
Malice. Active malevolence.
Malice prepense. Deliberate purpose of doing evil.
Maliciousness, etc. See *Adjectives.*
Malignity. Cruel malevolence; love of harm for the sake of doing it.
Mordacity. The quality of being biting or sarcastic
Obduracy. State of being stubbornly wicked.
Persecution. The act of besetting with cruelty.
Rancor. Bitter hatred; spitefulness.
Rankling. State of inflamed passion.
Resentment, etc. Anger excited by a sense of personal injury, etc. See FAVORITE-ANGER.
Ruffianism. Conduct of a ruffian.
Savagery. The state of being savage.
Spite. Mean hatred; petty malice.
Tender mercies. Ironical expression for cruelty.
Torture. Infliction of extreme bodily pain.
Truculence. Fierceness of manners.
Uncharitableness, etc. See *Adjectives*
"Unkindest cut of all." [Shakespeare.] Injury hardest to bear.
Unkindness. See *Adjectives.*
Venom. Malice; spite.
Virulence. Bitter enmity.

MALEVOLENCE—*Associated Words.*

Affront. See REGARD-DISRESPECT.
Bad turn. An evil or harmful deed.
Cloven foot. A sign of a devilish character.
Evil eye. An eye supposed to inflict injury by some magical influence. The eye of envy.
Ill turn. A harmful act toward another.
Outrage. An act of violence or cruelty.
Vivisection. The cutting of an animal alive for the purpose of physiological investigation.

MALEVOLENCE—*Verbs.*

Annoy, etc. To disturb or vex, etc. See PLEASURABLENESS-PAINFULNESS.
Bait. To harass or worry.
Disoblige. To offend by an unkind act.
Dragoon. To enforce submission by violent means.
Grind. To oppress by harsh exactions; to bring to the grindstone.
Harass. To tire one with importunity or care.
Harm. To do injury to.
Harry. To tease or worry.
Haunt. To visit with a view to injury.

CHARITABLENESS—MALEVOLENCE—*Continued.*

CHARITABLENESS—Adjectives—*Continued.*

Benevolent.   Possessing a disposition to do good.
Benignant.   Kind; helpful in influence.
Bounteous.   Characterized by liberality.
Bountiful.   Liberal in giving.
Broad-hearted.   Generous; liberal.
Brotherly.   Having the nature of a brother; hence, kind, affectionate.
Charitable.   Good to the poor and helpless.
Complacent.   Self-approved; contented.
Complaisant, etc.   Anxious to please, etc.   See POLITENESS.
Fatherly.   Having the nature or disposition of a father.
Fraternal.   Brotherly.
Friendly, etc.   Disposed to help or assist others, etc.   See AMITY.
Good-humored.   Having a pleasant temper.
Good-natured.   Having a disposition to please and be pleased.
Gracious.   Showing mercy or grace.
Humane.   Disposed to treat man and lower animals with kindness.
Indulgent.   Inclined to yield to the desires of those under our care.
Kind.   Desirous of the happiness of others.
Kind-hearted.   Of a sympathetic nature.
Kindly.   Sympathetic.
Large-hearted.   Generous.
Maternal.   Motherly.
Merciful, etc.   Characterized by pity, etc.   See COMPASSION.
Motherly.   Having the disposition of a mother; hence, tender, compassionate.
Obliging.   Given to doing favors.
Paternal.   Fatherly.
Sisterly.   Having the disposition of a sister.
Spleenless.   Gentle; kind.
Sympathetic.   Given to sympathy.
Sympathizing, etc.   See *Verbs.*
Tender-hearted.   Very sensitive to impressions; affectionate.
Warm-hearted.   Possessed of strong affection.
Well-intentioned.   Having good purposes.
Well-meaning.   Of a good intention.
Well-meant.   Having had a good intention.
Well-natured.   Good-natured.

CHARITABLENESS —*Adverbial Expressions.*

With a good intention; with the best intentions.

CHARITABLENESS—*Interjections.*

Godspeed.   Success.
Much good may it do.

CHARITABLENESS—*Phrases.*

Date obolum Belisario [L.], give a penny to Belisarius; *de mortuis nil nisi bonum* [L.], of the dead say nothing but good.

MALEVOLENCE—Adjectives—*Continued from Column 2.*

Maleficent.   Causing harm or evil to others.
Malevolent.   Disposed to harm or injure others.
Malicious.   Delighting in harming others for its own sake.
Malign.   Evilly disposed toward others.
Malignant.   Virulently bent upon doing harm or evil.
Marble-hearted.   Unsympathetic; stony-hearted.
Mordacious.   Biting; severe.
Rancorous.   Characterized by rancor; intensely malignant.
Relentless, etc.   Void of pity or tenderness, etc.   See PARDON-VINDICTIVENESS.
Ruthless, etc.   Having no pity, etc.   See COMPASSION-RUTHLESSNESS.
Satanic.   Possessed of the qualities of Satan.
Spiteful.   Full of spite.
Stony-hearted.   Unsympathetic.
Sullen, etc.   Habitually sulky or morose, etc.   See FAVORITE-MOROSENESS.
Surly.   Crabbed; rough.
Tameless.   Not capable of being tamed.
Truculent.   Ferocious; cruel.
Unamiable.   Not friendly; ill-natured.
Unbenevolent.   Lacking benevolence
Unbenign.   Malignant.
Uncandid.   Not candid.

MALEVOLENCE—Verbs—*Continued.*

Hound.   To chase as with hounds.
Hurt, etc.   To inflict physical injury, etc.   See PLEASURE-PAIN.
Ill-treat.   To use badly.
Ill-use.   To mistreat.
Injure.   To harm or wrong.
Malign.   To defame; to treat with enmity.
Maltreat.   To treat badly.
Molest.   To annoy or interfere with.
Oppress.   To treat with excessive severity.
Outrage.   To treat with violence or abuse.
Persecute.   To continually annoy, especially on account of religion.
Tease.   To annoy by impertinent importunities.
Worry.   To vex with care and anxiety.
Wrong.   To treat unjustly.

MALEVOLENCE—*Verbal Expressions.*

Bear a grudge, etc.; **bear malice,** etc.; **bear spleen,** etc. (see *Nouns*); **be malevolent,** etc. (see *Adjectives*); **betray the cloven foot, to** betray an evil purpose; **break a butterfly on the wheel; dip one's hands in blood, to** commit murder; **do an ill office to; do harm; do one's worst; harbor a grudge, harbor malice, harbor spleen,** etc. (see *Nouns*); **have no mercy,** etc. (see COMPASSION-RUTHLESS-NESS); **hunt down, to** chase; **imbrue one's hands in blood, to** commit murder; **plant a thorn in the breast; play the devil with,** to greatly injure; **show the cloven foot, to** betray an evil purpose; **throw stones at,** to vex with slurs; **wreak one's malice on, to** injure maliciously.

MALEVOLENCE—*Adjectives*

Acrimonious.   Exhibiting bitterness of temper.
Atrocious.   Extremely wicked.
Barbarous.   Marked by coarseness and brutality, especially of speech.
Bitter.   Severe; harsh; cruel.
Bloodthirsty, etc.   Anxious to shed blood, etc.   See LIFE-KILLING.
Bloody-minded.   Bloodthirsty, cruel.
Brutal.   Having the characteristics of a brute.
Brutish.   Resembling a brute; coarse; sensual.
Caustic.   Burning; sarcastic.
Churlish, etc.   Like a churl; hence, rude, surly, etc.   See POLITENESS-IMPOLITENESS.
Cold-blooded.   Unsympathetic.
Cold-hearted.   Wanting in feeling.
Cruel.   Disposed to inflict pain, mental or physical; bloody.
Demoniacal.   Characteristic of a demon; devilish.
Despiteful.   Full of hatred or malice.
Devilish.   Possessed of the qualities of the devil.
Diabolic. } Like the devil; *i. e.,* the prosecutor of man in the court
Diabolical. } of God; nefarious.
Disobliging.   Not disposed to oblige or do a favor.
Envenomed.   Poisoned with hatred or malice.
Evil-disposed.   Inclined toward evil.
Evil-minded.   Wicked; atrocious.
Fell.   Cruel; savage.
Ferine.   Untamed; malignant.
Ferocious.   Savage or ravenous in disposition.
Fiendish. } Acting like a fiend; *i. e.,* one hating mankind.
Fiendlike. }
Flint-hearted.   Hard-hearted; unsympathetic.
Galling.   Irritating; vexing.
Grinding.   Very oppressing; pressing to the grindstone.
Hard-hearted. } Lacking in feeling; unsympathetic.
Hard of heart. }
Harsh.   Abusive; disagreeable
Hellish.   Like hell; diabolical.
Ill-conditioned.   In bad or unfavorable circumstances.
Ill-contrived.   Poorly planned or designed.
Ill-disposed.   Badly inclined.
Ill-intentioned.   Having an evil purpose.
Ill-natured.   Having a bad temper; surly.
Incendiary.   Kindling hate or factions.
Infernal.   Suitable for hell or its inhabitants.
Inhuman.   Void of human qualities; hence, brutal, cruel.
Inhumane.   Void of the feelings of humanity.
Inofficious.   Indifferent to obligation.
Invidious.   Provoking envy.

(*Continued on Column* 1.)

MALEVOLENCE—ADJECTIVES—Continued.

Uncharitable. Wanting in charity.
Unfriendly. Void of kindness or benevolence.
Ungracious. Not gracious.
Unkind. Lacking in sympathy or gratitude.

Unnatural. Contrary to nature.
Untamed. Not tamed.
Venomous. Poisonous; mischievous.
Virulent. Very active to do injury.

MALEVOLENCE—Adjective Expressions.

Savage as a bear; savage as a tiger.

MALEVOLENCE—Adverbs.

Malevolently, etc. See *Adjectives.* **With bad intent,** etc. See *Nouns.*

CHARITABLENESS—CURSE.

CURSE.

Abuse. Malignant condemnation.
Anathema. A formal ecclesiastical ban or curse.
Ban. An edict of official prohibition.
Commination. A denunciation or threatening.
Curse. Calamity invoked or threatened.
Cursing. Act of invoking evil upon another. See *Verbs.*
Denunciation. Proclamation, as of impending evil.
Excommunication. An expulsion from church membership and communion.
Execration. The act of calling down evil upon a person.
Fulmination. Censures or threats thundered against one.
Imprecation. A prayer that a curse or calamity may fall on any one.
Invective, etc. Something uttered or written, intended to cast disgrace, censure, or reproach on another, etc. See APPROVAL-DISAPPROVAL.
Malediction. An utterance, denoting bitter reproach, or wishes and predictions of evil.
Malison. A prayer invoking evil or injury upon any one.
Maranatha [Aramaic]. The Lord hath come; used to intensify ANATHEMA.
Oath. A careless and blasphemous use of the name of the divine Being.
Proscription. A dooming to death or exile; especially the dooming of a political enemy.
Threat. An attempt to alarm, with the promise of something evil or disagreeable.

CURSE—Denotations.

Bad language. Foul or blasphemous speech.
Billingsgate. Vulgar, abusive language, as of the fish-market near Billingsgate.
Evil speaking. Slanderous language.
Foul language. Abusive, profane, or obscene talk.
Profane swearing. Vulgar use of holy names in oaths and curses.
Sauce. Pert speech, which gives a sauce to one's good wit. [Shakespeare.]
Strong language. Speech characterized by violence.
Unparliamentary language. Language violating the rules of order.

CURSE—Verbs.

Accurse. To doom to misery or evil.
Anathematize. To condemn publicly as something accursed.

Beshrew. A very mild form of cursing a person.
Curse. To desire evil, upon oath or in the most solemn manner.
Damn. To doom to punishment in the future world.
Denounce. To point out as deserving of reprehension or punishment.
Excommunicate. To cut off from church membership and communion.
Execrate. To protest against as unholy or detestable.
Fulminate. To thunder censures or denunciations; especially menaces or censures uttered by an ecclesiastical authority.
Imprecate. To call down by prayer something hurtful or calamitous.
Proscribe. To outlaw.
Scold. To rebuke with severity.
Swear.
Swear at. } To speak emphatically; to utter profanity.
Threaten. To inspire with fear.

CURSE—Verbal Expressions.

Call down curses on the head of, to appeal to God for evil upon any one; **curse and swear,** to call upon God profanely for the fulfilment of an evil; **curse with bell, book, and candle,** to excommunicate from the Roman Catholic Church by tolling a bell, as for the dead, closing the book of worship and extinguishing a candle; **devote to destruction,** to doom to destruction by vow; **fall a cursing,** to use profanity; **hold up to execration,** to expose to strongest curses; **swear like a trooper,** to swear violently; "swore terribly in Flanders" [to my Uncle Toby, in *Tristram Shandy*, iii, 11, L. Sterne]; **thunder at,** to talk in a harsh loud tone.

CURSE—Interjections.

Aroynt! Begone! Beshrew! Blast! Confound! Confusion seize! Curse! Damn! Devil take! Hang! *Honi soit!* [F.], evil to you. **Ill betide! Out upon! Out with!** *Parbleu!* [F.], by God! **Plague upon!** *Ruat cœlum!* [L.], let the heavens fall! **Wo betide! Wo to!**

CURSE—Phrases.

Delenda est Carthago [L.]. Carthage must be destroyed. [Cato, the elder, in every speech.]
More bark than bite. Empty threats.
Thunders of the Vatican. The decrees and sentences of the Pope.

CHARITABLENESS—MENACE.

MENACE.

Abuse. Coarse, insulting language.
Commination, etc. A divine threatening or denunciation, etc. See CHARITABLENESS-CURSE.
Defiance. The act of provoking an encounter; a challenge, etc. See DEFIANCE.
Fulmination. The act of fulminating or thundering forth threats.
Intimidation. The act of making fearful or afraid by threats.
Menace. The show of an intention to do harm or evil.
Minacity. Disposition or inclination to threaten.
Threat. The expressed determination to inflict evil or injury on another.

MENACE—Figurative Expressions.

Gathering clouds, etc. A presaging or foreboding of a passionate outbreak, etc. See WARNING.

MENACE—Verbs.

Bark. To make a loud, explosive noise with the vocal organs, such as a dog makes; hence, to clamor.
Bluster. To utter boastful threats.
Bully. To intimidate by threats and an overbearing manner.
Defy, etc. To challenge or treat with contempt, etc. See DEFIANCE.
Fulminate. To utter or thunder forth threats.
Gnarl. To growl.
Growl. To utter an angry sound; to grumble.
Intimidate, etc. To make fearful, as by threats, etc. See SANGUINE-NESS-TIMIDITY.
Menace. To make a show of inflicting injury or evil upon.
Mutter. To utter in a low voice; to growl.
Snarl. To utter in a surly voice; to growl harshly.
Threat. To threaten
Threaten. To present the appearance of approaching evil or harm.
Thunder. To publish forth, as a threat or a menace

CHARITABLENESS—MENACE—*Continued.*

MENACE—*Verbal Expressions.*

Clinch the fist at, double the fist at, to defy; hold out *in terrorem* [L.], to give as a warning; hold up *in terrorem* [L.]; keep *in terrorem* [L.], to hold in suspense; look daggers, to look fiercely; shake the fist at; talk big, to speak in a menacing tone; use big words, to make boastful threats.

MENACE—*Adjectives.*

Abusive. Containing abuse or insulting words.
Black-browed. Threatening.
Comminatory. Threatening punishment.
Defiant, etc. Bold; insolent. etc. See DEFIANCE.
In terrorem [L.]. By way of warning.
Menacing, etc. See *Verbs.*

Minacious. Threatening.
Minatory. Threatening or menacing.
Ominous, etc. Presaging or foreboding evil; inauspicious, etc. See PROPHECY.
Threatening, etc. See *Verbs.*

MENACE—*Adjective Expression.*

Under the ban. Forbidden; excommunicated.

MENACE—*Interjections.*

At your peril!
Do your worst!

Væ victis! [L.] Wo to the vanquished.

char'-i-ty. Benevolence; almsgiving; liberality in giving. CHARITABLENESS-MALEVOLENCE, COMPASSION-RUTHLESSNESS, GENEROSITY-FRUGALITY, GIVING-RECEIVING; charity that begins at home, UNSELFISHNESS-SELFISHNESS; Christian charity, CHARITABLENESS-MALEVOLENCE; cold as charity, SENSITIVENESS-APATHY.

char''-i-var'-i. A serenade. CRASH-DRUMMING, LOUDNESS-FAINTNESS.

char'-la-tan. A quack; a mountebank. BRAGGING, GULL-DECEIVER, SCHOLAR-DUNCE, SOCIETY-AFFECTATION, WAG.

char'-la-tan-ism. The practise of charlatanry. AFFECTATION, TRUTHFULNESS-FALSEHOOD.

char'-la-tan-ry. Quackery. TRUTHFULNESS-FALSEHOOD.

Charles's Wain [Charlemagne]. The Great Bear. UNIVERSE.

Char'-ley [man of Charles I.]. A night-watchman. GUARD-PRISONER.

charm. Fascination; spell; amulet. BEAUTY-UGLINESS, DEVOTION-CHARM, DEVOTION-MAGIC, LOVE-HATE, MOTIVE-CAPRICE, PLEASURABLENESS-PAINFULNESS; bear a charmed life, SECURITY-INSECURITY, WELFARE-MISFORTUNE.

charmed. Fascinated. LOVE-HATE.

charm'-er. One who charms. DEVOTION-MAGICIAN; not listen to the voice of the charmer, PERSISTENCE-WHIM; voice of the charmer, ADULATION-DISPARAGEMENT.

charm'-ing. Fascinating. LOVE-HATE, PLEASURABLENESS-PAINFULNESS.

char'-nel-house''. A depository for dead bones. LIFE-FUNERAL.

chart. A map; a sheet showing facts. ADVICE, DELINEATION-CARICATURE, ENLIGHTENMENT-SECRECY.

char'-ter. The leasing of a vessel; an act of incorporation; the writing of incorporation. COMMISSION-ABROGATION, CONTRACT, DUENESS-UNDUENESS, LAW-LAWLESSNESS, LEAVE-PROHIBITION, SECURITY; charter poll, SECURITY.

char'-tered. Legally established. DUENESS-UNDUENESS, LAW-LAWLESSNESS; chartered libertine, PURITY-RAKE.

char'-wom''-an. A chore-woman. AGENT, CHIEF-UNDERLING.

char'-y. Frugal; cautious. EXTRAVAGANCE-AVARICE, GENEROSITY-FRUGALITY, RECKLESSNESS-CAUTION.

Cha-ryb'-dis. Fabled rock dangerous to mariners. REVOLUTION-EVOLUTION.

chase. Pursuit; part of a cannon; ornamentation; a game preserve. ATTRACTION-REPULSION, CONVEXITY-CONCAVITY, EMBELLISHMENT-DISFIGUREMENT, FAUNA-FLORA, LIFE-KILLING, QUEST-EVASION, SKILL-UNSKILFULNESS; wild goose chase, CHOICE-WHIM, USEFULNESS-USELESSNESS.

cha'-ser. One who chases or embosses. ARTIST.

chasm. A yawning hollow. APERTURE-CLOSURE, INTERSPACE-CONTACT.

chassemarée [F.] (shas-ma-rê'). A fish-boat. CONVEYANCE-VESSEL.

chasse'-pot. A gun. WEAPON.

chasser [F.] (sha-sê'). To pursue. ADMISSION-EXPULSION.

chasser balancer [F.] (sha-sê' ba-lan·-sê'). DETERMINATION-VACILLATION.

chas''-seur'. A light-armed soldier. BELLIGERENT.

chaste. Pure; undefiled. CIRCLE-WINDING, EMBELLISHMENT-SIMPLICITY, PURITY-CRUDENESS, PURITY-IMPURITY, SIMPLICITY-FLORIDNESS, TASTE-VULGARITY.

cha'-sten. To punish; to calm. RECOMPENSE-PUNITION, TURBULENCE-CALMNESS.

cha'-stened. Subdued. EXCITABILITY-INEXCITABILITY.

cha'-sten-ing. Chastisement. RECOMPENSE-PUNITION.

chas-tise'. To correct; to punish. APPROVAL-DISAPPROVAL, RECOMPENSE-PUNITION; chastise with scorpions, HARSHNESS-MILDNESS.

chas'-tise-ment. Punishment. RECOMPENSE-PUNITION.

chas'-ti-ty. Purity. EMBELLISHMENT-SIMPLICITY, PURITY-IMPURITY.

chas'-u-ble. A sleeveless mantle. VESTMENTS.

chat. Gossipy talk. CONVERSATION-MONOLOGUE.

château [F.] (sha-tó). A country mansion. DWELLER-HABITATION, FANCY.

château en Espagne [F.] (sha-tó an· es-pan'y'). A castle in Spain. FANCY, SANGUINENESS-HOPELESSNESS.

chat'-e-laine. A chain. EMBELLISHMENT-DISFIGUREMENT.

chatoyant [F.] (sha-twa-i-an·'). Shot-colored. VARIEGATION.

chat qui dort [F.] (sha kî dor). The cat which sleeps. REFUGE-PITFALL, WARNING.

chat'-tels. Any movable property. INSTRUMENT, PROPERTY.

chat'-ter. Idle prattle. TALKATIVENESS-TACITURNITY.

chat'-ter-box''. An idle prattler. TALKATIVENESS-TACITURNITY.

chat'-ter-er. Prattler. CONVERSATION-MONOLOGUE, TALKATIVENESS-TACITURNITY.

chat'-ter-ing. Prattling. TALKATIVENESS-TACITURNITY.

chat'-ter-ing of the teeth. Trembling. HEAT-COLD.

chat'-ty. Loquacious; gossipy. CONVERSATION-MONOLOGUE, SOCIABILITY-PRIVACY, TALKATIVENESS-TACITURNITY.

chauf-feur'. One who directs an automobile. MAN-AGER.

chaunt. Same as chant. DEVOTION-IDOLATRY, MUSIC, MUSICIAN.

chausse [F.] (shos). A stocking. DRESS-UNDRESS.

chau'-vin-ism. Extravagant patriotism. BRAGGING, PATRIOTISM-TREASON.

chau''-vin-is'-tic. Demonstrative in patriotism. PATRIOTISM-TREASON.

chaw'-ba''-con. A country bumpkin. GENTILITY-DEMOCRACY.

cheap. Worthless; of low price. CONSEQUENCE-INSIGNIFICANCE, COSTLINESS-CHEAPNESS; **hold cheap,** REGARD-SCORN.

cheap'-en. To make cheap. EXCHANGE, EXTRAVAGANCE-AVARICE.

cheap'-ness. State of being cheap. COSTLINESS-CHEAPNESS.

cheat. A fraud; a cheater. GULL-DECEIVER, TRUTHFULNESS-FRAUD.

check. Restraint; a mark for verification; to mark off; an order for money; a rebuke; curb; a printed design in squares. COOPERATION-OPPOSITION, EVIDENCE-COUNTEREVIDENCE, MENSURATION, MONEY, MOTIVE-DEHORTATION, NUMBERING, OBSTRUCTION-HELP, REFUGE-PITFALL, RELEASE-RESTRAINT, SIGN, SWIFTNESS-SLOWNESS, TRIAL, TURBULENCE-CALMNESS, VARIEGATION; **check oneself,** EXCITABILITY-INEXCITABILITY; **check the growth,** LENGTH-SHORTNESS.

check'-ered. Divided into squares of different colors. VARIEGATION.

check'-ers. A game. VARIEGATION.

check'-mate''. To defeat. SUCCESS-FAILURE.

check'-rein''. A bearing-rein. RELEASE-RESTRAINT.

check'-roll''. A record of checks. RECORD.

check'-string''. A check. **Pull the checkstring,** DISCONTINUANCE-CONTINUANCE.

cheek. Side of face. LATERALITY-CONTRAPOSITION; **cheek by jowl,** LATERALITY-CONTRAPOSITION, REMOTENESS-NEARNESS, SOLITUDE-COMPANY; **cheeks,** DUALITY.

cheep. A weak chirp. CRY-ULULATION.

cheer. Entertainment; state of mirth; applause; to encourage. ALLEVIATION-AGGRAVATION, APPROVAL-DISAPPROVAL, BRAVERY-COWARDICE, CRY-ULULATION, ENTERTAINMENT-WEARINESS, JUBILATION-LAMENTATION, LIGHTHEARTEDNESS-DEJECTION, NUTRIMENT-EXCRETION, OBSTRUCTION-HELP, PLEASURE-PAIN, POLITENESS-IMPOLITENESS, SOCIABILITY-PRIVACY; **good cheer,** FASTING-GLUTTONY, SANGUINENESS-HOPELESSNESS.

cheer'-ful. Joyous. CONTENTEDNESS-DISCONTENT, LIGHTHEARTEDNESS-DEJECTION.

cheer'-ful-ly. In a cheerful manner. LIGHTHEARTEDNESS-DEJECTION.

cheer'-ful-ness. State of being cheerful. LIGHTHEARTEDNESS-DEJECTION.

cheer'-ing. Encouraging. REGARD-DISRESPECT, SANGUINENESS-HOPELESSNESS.

cheer'-less. Without hope. LIGHTHEARTEDNESS-DEJECTION, PLEASURABLENESS-PAINFULNESS, REGARD-DISRESPECT.

cheer'-ly. Cheering. LIGHTHEARTEDNESS-DEJECTION.

cheer'-y. Joyous. LIGHTHEARTEDNESS-DEJECTION.

cheese'-par''-ings. Miserly; the remains. CLEANNESS-FILTHINESS, GENEROSITY-FRUGALITY, INCREMENT-REMNANT.

chef de cuisine [F.] (shef de cwî-zîn'). Head cook. ADEPT-BUNGLER, CHIEF-UNDERLING.

chef-d'œuvre [F.] (she-duvr'). Masterpiece. GOODNESS-BADNESS, SKILL-UNSKILFULNESS.

chem'-ic-al. Pertaining to chemistry. CHEMISTRY; **chemical crystallography,** MINERALOGY.

chemin de fleurs ne conduit à la gloire, aucun [F.] (she-man· de flur ne con'-dwît' a la glwar, o-cun·'). There is no pathway of flowers that leads to glory. DIFFICULTY-FACILITY, REPUTATION-DISCREDIT.

chemin faisant [F.] (she-man·' fe-zan·'). In passing. TRANSFER.

che-mise'. A woman's undergarment. DRESS-UNDRESS.

chem'-ist. One skilled in chemistry. CHEMISTRY.

chem'-is-try. Science of composition of substances. CHEMISTRY, CONVERSION-REVERSION; **organic chemistry,** ORGANIZATION-INORGANIZATION.

CHEMISTRY.

Chemistry. The science of the composition of bodies and the specific properties of matter.

CHEMISTRY—*Associated Words.*

Acetone. Inflammable liquid used in making chloroform.

Acetylene. A colorless, offensive gas that produces an intense light.

Acid. A compound of hydrogen with a base.

Air. Atmosphere, composed of oxygen and hydrogen, surrounding the earth.

Alkali. Compound of hydrogen and oxygen with metals like sodium; also a caustic base, such as soda, potash, ammonia.

Alloy. Mixture of metals by fusion.

Ammonium. Hypothetical alkali acting like sodium.

Applied chemistry. The study of the application and economic relation of chemistry to the arts.

Aromatic series. Substances derived from benzene.

Assaying. The process of making a chemical analysis of metals.

Atmosphere. The gases surrounding the earth.

Atom. The smallest portion into which matter can be divided.

Beaker. Cylindrical, glass vessel with a flaring top.

Bessemer steel. Steel made by the Bessemer process. [Henry Bessemer, English, 1856–58.]

Bismuth. One of the metallic elements.

Blast-furnace. Furnace in which heat is intensified by forcing in air.

Blowpipe. Tube through which air is blown to intensify a flame.

Bone-black. Fine carbon made by calcining bones.

Calomel. Mercurous chlorid used as a purgative.

Carbohydrate. Compound of carbon with hydrogen and oxygen.

Carbon. Non-metallic element.

Carbonate. Compound formed with carbonic acid.

Chemist. One versed in chemistry.

Chemitype. Method of making maps in relief by using chemicals.

Chemolysis. Chemical analysis.

Chlorid. Compound formed with chlorin.

Chlorine. An elementary substance, forming the compound of common salt. When isolated it appears as a greenish-yellow gas, exceedingly offensive and poisonous.

Chloroform. A volatile liquid formed by treating alcohol with chlorine and an alkali.

Coagulation filter. A system of filtering water.

Cobalt. A metallic element forming a blue pigment.

Concentration forces. Chemical forces or actions which reduce to one bulk or mass.

Condenser. Appliance for cooling steam.

Copper. Reddish metallic element.

Crucible. Fusing pot.

Crystal. Solid mathematical form assumed by homogeneous substances.

Cyanogen. A colorless, inflammable, poisonous gas, with peach-blossom odor.

Dalton's theory. The atomic theory of chemistry originated by John Dalton (1766–1844).

Davy's lamp. Safety-lamp invented by Sir Humphrey Davy in 1815.

Dialysis. Method of separating mixed substances.

Dioxide. An oxide containing two atoms of oxygen.

Distillation. Separation from a substance of parts easily volatilized by heating the substance and condensing the steam.

Distilled water.

Electrochemistry. The study of chemical changes affected by electricity.

Evaporation. Process of changing into vapor.

Fertilizer. Substance used to enrich the soil.

Filter-paper. Soft paper used for filtering.

Flask. Bottle.

Flint glass. Glass containing lead.

Flux. Substance that promotes the fusing of metals or minerals.

Fractional distillation. The process of redistilling the product of previous distillation.

Gas. The aeriform state of matter.

Glass tubing. Pipes made of glass.

Gold. Heavy, yellow, metallic element.

Graduate. A graduated vessel.

Graham's law. The law that "the velocity of the diffusion of gases varies inversely as the square root of their specific gravities," discovered by Thomas Graham (1805–1869).

Graphic symbols. Symbols for representing chemical substances.

Graphite. Dark, metallic variety of carbon.

Hard water. Water containing minerals in solution.

Hot blast. Hot air blown into a smelting-furnace.

Hydrochloric acid. Colorless, corrosive gas easily soluble in water.

Hydrogen. A gaseous element, found in great abundance in the air.

Hydroxid. Compound containing the hydroxyl group.

Hydrosulphite. A compound of hydrosulfurous acid and a base.

Hydroxyl. A compound of one atom of hydrogen and one of oxygen.

Inorganic chemistry. The chemistry of metals and non-metals excepting carbon.

Intermittent sand filtration. Method of filtering water.

Iodin. Crystalline element giving off violet fumes when heated.

Iron. Common metallic element.

Isocyanid. A hydrocarbon compound with cyanogen.

Lavoisier (Antoine Laurent). French chemist (1743–1794), founder of modern chemistry.

Lead. Metallic element.

Lithium. Metallic element, silver-white, and the lightest of metals.

Mercury. Bright, liquid, metallic element.

Metal. A substance that is opaque and possesses a peculiar luster.

Molecule. Smallest physical division of matter.

Mortar. Mixture of sand and slaked lime.

Naphtha. Light, colorless, inflammable oil from bituminous shale.

Nickel. Bright, hard, metallic element

Nitric acid. Colorless corrosive liquid.

Nitrogen. A gaseous, colorless, non-metallic element, comprising four-fifths of the atmosphere.

Organic chemistry. The chemistry of the compounds of carbon.

Oxid. Compound of oxygen.

Oxygen. A gaseous element forming twenty-three per cent (weight) of the atmosphere.

Ozone. Gaseous element.

Periodic law. Law suggested by Newlands that the properties of an element are a periodic function of its atomic weight.

Physiological chemistry. Chemistry applied to physiology.

Platinum. Steel-gray metallic element.

Potable water. Drinkable water.

Practical chemistry. Same as APPLIED CHEMISTRY.

Priestley's apparatus. Apparatus used in making oxygen. [English-American, 1733–94.]

Replacement. The operation of one substance taking the place of another in a compound.

Retort. Vessel used in distillation.

Roasting. Process of heating ores.

Safety-lamp. Lamp used without danger of explosion from gases

Salt. Compound of a base with an acid.

Silica. Silicon dioxid found as quartz and sand.

Silver. White metallic element.

Slag. Refuse from a blast-furnace.

Sodium. Silver-white alkaline metallic element.

Specific gravity. The comparative weight of unit volumes.

Spectroscope. An instrument for forming and analyzing the spectra of rays given off by substances.

Steel. Compound chiefly of iron and carbon.

Substitution. Same as REPLACEMENT.

Sugar. Sweet crystalline compound made chiefly from sugar-beets and sugar-cane.

Sulfate. Compound of a base with sulfuric acid.

Sulfur. Yellowish, crystalline, non-metallic element.

Sufuric acid. Oily, colorless, corrosive liquid compounded of hydrogen, sulfur, and oxygen.

Test-tube. Slender tube of glass, used in making experiments.

Tin. White metallic malleable element.

Tripod. Stand having three legs.

Tungsten. Grayish, heavy, metallic element.

Water. Colorless liquid compounded of hydrogen and oxygen.

Welsbach lamp. Gas-lamp in which the light is made by the gas heating a gauze made of several elements.

Zinc. Grayish white metallic element.

Zincite. Zinc ore.

Zincolysis. Decomposition of zinc compounds by electrolysis in which the action is referred to the zinc element.

CHEMISTRY—*Verbs.*

Absorb. To take up by chemical action.

Coagulate. To change into a curdlike state by chemical reaction.

Concentrate. To increase the strength of.

Crystallize. To assume a solid and symmetrical form.

Decompose. To undergo dissolution.

Diffuse. To cause to flow out and mingle chemically.

Displace. To remove one chemical element by another.

Distil. To extract by vaporization and condensation.

Effloresce. The act of becoming powdery.

Electrolyze. To resolve into chemical elements by electricity.

Electrotype. To make facsimile plates by an electrolytic process.

Explode. To transform suddenly into gas or vapor.

Filter. To remove impurities by passing through a porous substance.

Ignite. To set on fire.

Invert. To undergo rearrangement of the molecular structure.

Liberate. To free from chemical union.

Oxidize. To combine with oxygen.

Replace. To substitute one element for another in a chemical union.

Rust. To become affected with a reddish or yellowish oxid.

CHEMISTRY—*Adjectives.*

Acetic. Pertaining to vinegar.

Ferric. Pertaining to iron.

Inflammable. That can be set on fire.

Insoluble. That cannot be dissolved in a fluid.

Sulfuric. Pertaining to sulfur.

chem'-i-type. Relief plate for a map produced by chemical processes. CHEMISTRY.

che-mol'-y-sis. Chemical analysis. CHEMISTRY.

cheque. Check. MONEY.

cheq'-uer. Checker. VARIEGATION, RECORD.

cheq'-uered. Diversified. MUTABILITY-STABILITY.

chère amie [F.] (shêr a-mî'). Dear mistress. PURITY-RAKE.

cher'-ish. To indulge; to support. BLANDISHMENT, LOVE-HATE, OBSTRUCTION-HELP, PATRIOTISM-TREASON; cherish a belief, FAITH-MISGIVING; cherish an idea, REFLECTION-VACANCY, EMOTION.

cher'-ry. A fruit. Two bites of a cherry, MIDCOURSE-CIRCUIT, OVERVALUATION-UNDERVALUATION, SKILL-UNSKILFULNESS.

cher'-ry–cheeked. Red-cheeked. BEAUTY-UGLINESS.

cher'-ry–col''-ored. Reddish. REDNESS-GREENNESS.

cher'-ub (pl. cherubim, cherubs). An angelic being. ANGEL-SATAN.

Chesh'-ire cat, grin like a. To grin broadly. JUBILATION-LAMENTATION.

chess. A game. ENTERTAINMENT-WEARINESS.

chess'-board''. The board for playing chess. VARIEGATION.

chest. A large box. CONTENTS-RECEIVER, TREASURY.

chest'-nut–col''-or. A dark brown. GRAY-BROWN.

cheval-de-bataille [F.] (she-val' de ba-tay'). A war-horse. CONCEIT-DIFFIDENCE, DESIGN, PRETEXT.

chev-al'–glass. A large, swinging mirror. OPTICAL INSTRUMENTS.

chevalier d'industrie [F.] (she-va-li-ê' dan'-düs-trî'). A swindler. ROBBER.

chevaux de frise [F.] (she-vo' de frîz). Obstructing spikes. ATTACK-DEFENSE, SHARPNESS-BLUNTNESS.

chev'-ron. A sign of non-commissioned officers. SIGN.

chew. To grind with the teeth. ADMISSION-EXPULSION, PUNGENCY; chew the cud, REFLECTION-VACANCY; chew tobacco, PUNGENCY.

chiar''-os-cu'-ro. The lights and shades of a picture. GRAY-BROWN, LIGHT-DARKNESS, PAINTING, WHITENESS-BLACKNESS.

chic. Stylish. POMP.

chi-cane'. Specious trickery. CRAFT-ARTLESSNESS, RATIOCINATION-CASUISTRY, TRUTHFULNESS-FRAUD.

chi-ca'-ner-y. Scheming. RATIOCINATION-INSTINCT, TRUTHFULNESS-FRAUD.

chick'-en. A young fowl. FAUNA-FLORA, INFANT-VETERAN; reckon chickens before hatched, RECKLESSNESS-CAUTION, SANGUINENESS-HOPELESSNESS; tender as a chicken, COMPASSION-RUTHLESSNESS, HARDNESS-SOFTNESS, SENSITIVENESS-APATHY.

chick'-en–heart"-ed. Cowardly. BRAVERY-COWARDICE.
chid. Rebuked. APPROVAL-DISAPPROVAL.
chide. To scold. APPROVAL-DISAPPROVAL.
chid'-ing. Rebuking. APPROVAL-DISAPPROVAL.

chief. A leader. CHIEF-UNDERLING, CONSEQUENCE-INSIGNIFICANCE, PRESIDENT-MEMBER; **chief part,** MAGNITUDE-SMALLNESS; **evidence in chief,** EVIDENCE-COUNTEREVIDENCE.

CHIEF—UNDERLING.

Abuna. Head of Abyssinian Church.
Acting corporal. One performing the duties of a corporal.
Adjutant. A staff officer, who assists the colonel or commanding officer of a regiment or garrison.
Admiral. A naval officer of the highest rank. From Arabic *amir, emir.*
Admiralty. A department of government having supreme charge of naval affairs.
Aga. A Turkish noble.
Aide-de-camp [F.]. An officer who receives and transmits the orders of a general.
Alcaid. The chief officer of a Spanish castle or fortress; a jailer.
Alcalde [Sp.]. An officer or magistrate in a Spanish or Spanish-American town.
Alderman. A member of a city legislative body, having also certain judicial functions.
Anointed king. Legally crowned king.
Archduke. A son of the Austrian emperor.
Archon. A chief magistrate in ancient Athens.
Authorities. The persons or body exercising power or command.
Autocrat. A supreme ruler whose power is unrestricted and irresponsible.
Bandmaster. The leader of a band.
Bargemaster. A master of a barge.
Bashaw. An honorary title given to persons of high rank in Turkey.
Beg. } The governor of a Turkish town or province; a colonel in the
Bey. } Turkish army.
Beglerbeg. The ruler of a province in the Ottoman empire.
Brigade-major. An officer appointed by a brigadier to assist in the command of a brigade.
Brigadier. An officer who commands a brigade of soldiers.
Burgomaster. The chief officer of a municipal town in Holland.
Burgrave. One appointed to the command of a fortress or castle.
Cadet. A pupil in a military or naval school.
Cæsar. A Roman emperor; any emperor, or powerful ruler.
Caliph. The ruler of Turkey.
Captain. A leader; the chief officer of a company of soldiers; an officer entitled to command a war-ship.
Cazique. A prince or chief among the Indian tribes of Mexico and South America.
Centurion. The captain of a hundred soldiers in the Roman army.
Cham. A Tartar or Mogul ruler.
Chancellor. A judicial officer of high rank.
Chief. A person highest in rank or authority; especially among the Indian tribes of North America.
Chieftain. The civil or military head of a clan, tribe, army, or other body of men among the Scotch Highlanders.
Colonel. The highest officer of a regiment of soldiers.
Color-sergeant. A non-commissioned officer who carries the flag of a regiment.
Commandant. An officer in charge of a garrison or military post.
Commander. A military leader; a naval officer next below a captain in rank.
Commander-in-chief. One holding supreme command.
Commodore. The commander of a squadron or division of a fleet, ranking between captain and rear admiral.
Constable. A civil officer appointed to maintain the peace.
Cornet. The lowest commissioned cavalry officer.
Corporal. The lowest non-commissioned officer in a company of soldiers.
Corporal major. An officer who assists a corporal.
Corregidor [Sp.]. The chief magistrate of a Spanish town.
Czar. The emperor of Russia; an absolute monarch. [Cæsar.]
Czarina. The empress of Russia.
Despot. An absolute monarch; a hard master.
Dey. The ruler of Algiers, Tunis, or Tripoli.
Dictator. A person invested with absolute power, especially in an emergency.
Doge. The elective chief magistrate in Venice and Genoa.
Drum-major. The chief drummer of a regiment.
Duchess. The wife or widow of a duke, or a woman who is the sovereign of a duchy.
Duke. An English temporal peer of the highest rank. See GENTILITY.
Elector. One of the great princes who had the right of electing the emperor of Germany.

Abigail. A lady's waiting-maid. In *The Sorrowful Lady,* Beaumont and Fletcher.
Adscriptus glebæ [L.]. Belonging or attached to the soil; hence a servant who was sold or exchanged with the land.
Agent, etc. One who acts or serves for another, etc. See CONSIGNEE.
Âme damnée [F.]. A hireling.
Assistant secretary. One who serves or helps a secretary.
Attaché [F.]. One attached to the company or suite of another; as in a diplomatic embassy.
Attendant. One who waits upon or serves another.
Ayah [Sp.]. A native nurse for children; a lady's-maid.
Bailiff. A deputy of a sheriff.
Baker. One who bakes bread.
Barkeeper. } One who sells liquor over a bar.
Bartender. }
Beadsman. } A poor man, supported in an almshouse, and required
Bedesman. } to pray for the soul of its founder.
Beadswoman. An almswoman.
Bed-maker One who arranges a bed for sleeping.
Bondmaid. A female slave.
Bondslave. One whose person and liberty are subject to a master.
Bondsman. One who is bound as security for another; a male slave.
Bondswoman. A female slave.
Bonne [F.]. A female servant charged with the care of a young child.
Butler. A servant whose principal business is to take charge of the liquors, plate, etc.
Cad. A person who stands at the door of an omnibus to open and shut it, and to receive fares; a vulgar fellow.
Camarista [Sp.]. Maid of honor.
Castellan. A keeper of a castle.
Chamberlain. A palace official who regulates the etiquette of a court.
Chambermaid. A servant who has care of bedchambers.
Chargéship. Office of a *chargé d'affaires.*
Charwoman, etc. A woman hired for odd work or for single days, etc. See AGENT.
Chef de cuisine [F.]. Head cook.
Cinderella. A figurative expression for a kitchen servant. [A beautiful girl treated as a kitchen-girl by her elder sisters, but disclosed to the prince in the fairy tale current in many nations.]
Clerk. A hired assistant, who keeps records and accounts.
Client. One bound to another, and expected to give service.
Confidente [F.]. One to whom one's secrets are entrusted.
Cook. A servant whose occupation is to prepare food for the table.
Cordon bleu [F.]. A joking expression for a first-rate cook.
Cortège [F.]. A train of attendants.
Court. A body of persons composing the retinue of a sovereign or person in authority.
Creature. A person who owes his rise and fortune to another; a servile dependent.
Cupbearer. A servant whose duty is to fill and hand the cups at an entertainment.
Dependant. } One who relies on another for support or favor.
Dependent. }
Domestic. A hired household assistant.
Donzel. A servant of a knight; a page.
Employé [F.]. A workman in the service of another.
Equerry. A servant charged with the care of horses.
Femme de chambre [F.]. A chambermaid.
Fille de chambre [F.]. A waiting-maid; a lady's-maid.
Flunkey. A name for a liveried servant or footman, used in contempt.
Follower. An attendant; a dependent associate.
Footboy. A page; an attendant in livery.
Footman. A male servant whose duties are to attend the door, the carriage, the table, etc.
Gillie. A male servant in the Scottish Highlands.
Groom. A man or boy who has charge of horses or the stable.
Groom of the chambers. A servant in the English royal household.
Gyp. A college servant at Cambridge University.
Handmaid. A female servant that waits at hand.
Hanger on. One that sticks to a person or society longer than he is wanted.
Helot. A bondman or serf of the Spartans.

CHIEF—UNDERLING—*Continued.*

Emir. An independent prince or commander in the Mohammedan East.

Emperor. The ruler of an empire.

Empress. A woman who rules an empire; the wife or widow of an emperor.

Ensign. The lowest commissioned officer in the navy.

Etat major [F.]. The staff of an army.

Exarch. A governor of a province under the Byzantine Empire.

Field-marshal. An officer of the highest rank in the armies of several European nations.

Fonctionnaire [F.]. Public officer.

General. An officer who commands a body of troops not less than a brigade.

Generalissimo. A supreme military commander.

Government. The organization of power for the control of a state.

Governor. One who exercises executive control. Pilot of the ship of state.

Grand Turk. The sultan of Turkey.

Great mogul. The sovereign of Hindustan; a lord.

Hetman [Pol.]. The title of the general of the Cossacks.

High-priest. Principal priest among the Jews.

Hospodar. A title of the emperor of Russia.

Imaum. A Mohammedan prince.

Imperator [L.]. Commander or ruler; emperor.

Inca. An ancient native Peruvian emperor or chief.

Infanta. A princess of the blood royal in Spain or Portugal.

Jemidar [Per. and Hind.]. An officer in the native Indian army.

Judge. A public officer who is invested with authority to hear and determine cases.

Kaiser. The emperor of Germany. [Cæsar.]

Khan. An Eastern title of varying significance, from a Tartar sovereign to any gentleman.

Khedive. The title of the ruler of Egypt appointed by the sultan of Turkey.

King. The sovereign male ruler of a kingdom.

Knight-marshal. High officer of the sovereign's household.

Laird, etc. The owner of a landed estate, etc. [Scotch for *lord.*] See HOLDER.

Lama. A Buddhist priest.

Lance-corporal. An assistant to a corporal.

Landamman. The chief magistrate of Swiss cantons.

Landgrave. A German count.

Leader, etc. One who leads or conducts, etc. See MANAGER.

Liege. A lord; sovereign.

Liege lord. The lord to whom one owes service.

Lieutenant. An officer next below a captain in the army; a naval officer, in rank next below a lieutenant-commander.

Lieutenant-colonel. An army officer ranking next to a colonel.

Lieutenant-general. An army officer ranking between a major-general and general.

Lord. A title of nobility in Great Britain. [Loaf-ward, master of a family.]

Lord-mayor. An honorary title bestowed upon the chief magistrates of some English cities.

Lord paramount. Feudal king.

Magistrate. One having public civil authority.

Maharajah. A sovereign prince in India.

Majesty. A reigning monarch.

Major. A military officer next in rank above a captain.

Major-general. A military officer, in rank between a brigadier and a lieutenant-general.

Mandarin. A Chinese civil or military official.

Maréchal [F.]. A military officer of high rank.

Margrave. The governor of a German march or border.

Margravine. The wife of a margrave.

Marshal. A military officer of high rank.

Master. A male person who has authority over others; the commander of a merchant vessel.

Mate. A petty naval officer.

Mayor. The chief magistrate of a city.

Mayoralty. The office or term of a mayor.

Mikado. The ruler of Japan.

Mogul. A ruler among the Mongolian tribes.

Monarch. An hereditary constitutional sovereign. [Sole ruler.]

Nabob. A governor in India under the old Mogul empire.

Naik. A chief; a Sepoy corporal.

Navarck. The commander of a fleet.

Nawaub. A Moslem ruler or viceroy in India.

Nizam. The native sovereigns of Hyderabad, in India.

Non-commissioned officer. A subordinate officer not appointed by the chief executive or supreme authority of a state.

Help. A domestic servant, man or woman.

Henchman. A servant or follower. Now chiefly used as a political term, denoting a subordinate or servile agent.

Herdman. A servant who tends cattle.

Hireling. A person serving for hire; a mercenary.

Hostler. A servant who has the care of horses at an inn.

Housemaid. A girl or woman employed in doing housework.

Jockey. One employed to ride horses, especially at races.

Journeyman. Formerly, a man hired by the day; now, one who has mastered a handicraft or trade.

Kitchen-maid. A servant employed in the kitchen.

Lackey. A male servant who waits on a master.

Lady help. The servant of a lady.

Lady's-maid. A female attendant upon a lady.

Laundress. A washerwoman.

Led captain. A favorite that follows as if led by a string.

Liegeman. A vassal or bound person.

Livery servant. A servant wearing a peculiar dress by which the house of his master is distinguished.

Maid. A female servant.

Maid of all work. A female servant who does all manner of work.

Maid-servant. A female servant.

Majordomo [L.]. The steward of a royal household.

Man.
Man-servant. } An adult male servant.

Menial. One doing servile work: used generally in contempt.

Mercenary. A person working or serving only or chiefly for pay.

Messenger. A servant who bears messages.

Milkmaid. A dairymaid.

Negro. A person of the black race; a slave.

Nurse. A female who takes care of young children; or a person who cares for the sick, wounded, or enfeebled.

Nurse-maid. A maid-servant employed in nursing children.

Nursery-maid. A female servant who has charge of a place set apart for children.

Odalisque [Turk.]. A female slave in an Eastern harem.

Official. A subordinate executive officer or attendant.

Orderly. A servant who carries orders for his superior.

Ostler. A form for the word hostler. See sub HOSTLER.

Page. A male attendant, usually a lad.

Parasite, etc. One who lives at the expense of another, etc. See PRESUMPTION-OBSEQUIOUSNESS.

Parlor-maid. A female servant who receives visitors.

Pensionary.
Pensioner. } One who lives on the gifts or bounty of another.

Protégé [F.]. One especially cared for by another older or more powerful.

Puppet. A person slavishly subject to the will of another.

Retainer. One kept in the service of a person of rank or position.

Retinue. A body of servants attending a person of rank.

Ryot. In India, a tenant or tiller of the soil.

Satellite. One who attends upon a person in power.

Scout. A college servant at Oxford University.

Scullery-maid. A servant whose work is to clean kitchen utensils.

Scullion. A servant who cleans pots and kettles.

Secretary. One who attends to correspondence, keeps records, or does other writing for another.

Seneschal. A servant who had charge of feasts or ceremonies in the household of a noble.

Serf. A servant whose service is attached to the estate and is transferred with it.

Servant. A person employed to labor for the interest of another.

Servant of all work. A servant who does all kinds of work, usually household work.

Servitor. One who waits upon or serves another.

Sizer. An undergraduate in college allowed some gratuities for some service he performed.

Slave. One whose person is held as property. [The Slavic race furnished servants to the Germans.]

Soubrette [F.]. A meddlesome female servant.

Squire. A shield-bearer or armor-bearer who attended a knight.

Staff. A body of assistants serving to carry into effect the plans of a superintendent or manager.

Subaltern. A person of inferior rank or position.

Subject. One under the power or authority of another.

Subsidiary. One who contributes aid to another.

Suite. A company of attendants or followers.

Swineherd. A tender of swine.

Tapster. A servant who draws and serves liquors.

Tiger. A liveried groom.

Train-bearer. An attendant who holds the long train of a dress or robe.

CHIEF—UNDERLING—*Continued.*

Officer. One appointed to office in an army; one holding a civil position or authority. See sub JURISDICTION.
Official. One holding a public office.
Oligarch. One of a few persons in whose hands is the power of government.
Padishah. A title of the sultan of Turkey, and of the shah of Persia.
Padrone [It.]. A protector; a patron.
Palatine. One invested with royal rights and privileges within his domains.
Pasha. } An Ottoman or Egyptian high civil, military or naval
Pashaw. } officer.
Person in authority. One having power or control over others.
Port-admiral. The admiral commanding at a naval port.
Portreeve. The chief magistrate of a port or maritime town.
Potentate. One possessed of great power or sway.
Prefect. An ecclesiastical or civil officer.
President. The chief magistrate of a republic.
Prince. A male descendant of a royal house.
Princess. Wife of a prince; female member of a royal family.
Protector. A guard; one appointed as ruler of a kingdom during the minority or incapacity of the sovereign.
Provost. A person having charge or authority over others.
Queen. A female sovereign of a kingdom; wife of a king.
Queenhood. The state of a queen.
Rajah. A Hindu prince or chief of a tribal state in India.
Rear admiral. A naval officer, in rank between a commodore and vice-admiral.
Regent. One who rules in the name and place of a sovereign.
Ruler. One who has power or authority.
Sachem. One of the hereditary chiefs in a tribe of North American Indians.
Sagamore. Indian chief of secondary rank.
Satrap. A governor of a province in ancient Persia.
Scherif. A member of an Arab princely family descended from Mohammed.
Seignior. A lord in the countries of southern Europe.
Seneschal. A magistrate or military commander of the Middle Ages; an official who had charge of feasts and ceremonies.
Senior. One more advanced in rank than others.
Seraskier [Turk.]. A general or commander of land forces in the Turkish Empire.
Sergeant. A non-commissioned officer in a military company.
Sergeant-major. The highest non-commissioned officer in a regiment.
Seyyid. Title of the members of the Koreish tribe.
Shah. The ruler of Persia.
Sheik. The head of a family, village, tribe, or religious organization in Mohammedan countries.
Sirdar. A native chief in Hindustan.
Skipper. The master of a small trading or fishing vessel.
Soldan. Sultan.
Sophi. Title of the king of Persia.
Sovereign. One who possesses supreme authority or exercises absolute control.
Stadtholder. A governor of a province or town in the Netherlands.
Staff. A body of officers attached to a commander-in-chief of an army.
Staff-officer. An officer attached to a commander-in-chief.
Subaltern. A military officer ranking below a captain.
Subhadar. Governor of a province in India.
Sublieutenant. An inferior or second lieutenant.
Sultan. A Mohammedan ruler; especially the ruler of Turkey.
Sultana. A sultan's wife, daughter, or mother.
Suzerain. One having superior authority.
Syndic. An officer of the government having different powers in different countries.
Tête d'armée [F.]. Head of the army.
Tetrarch. The governor of one part of a country divided into four governments.
Three-tailed Bashaw. The title of the highest official in a Turkish province, so named from three horse-tails waving from a lance.

Underling. A subordinate; a servile person.
Undersecretary. An assistant to the secretary.
Understrapper. An inferior agent; a petty fellow.
Usher. A servant who has the care of the door of a court, hall, chamber, etc.
Valet. A servant who attends on a gentleman's person
Valet de chambre [F.]. An attendant; a footman.
Vassal. One who held land of a superior lord by a feudal tenure; a servant of any kind.
Villain. } A feudal tenant of the lowest class; a bondman.
Villein. }
Waiter. A servant in attendance, especially at a table.
Waiting-maid. A servant who waits upon a lady as a personal attendant.
Waitress. A female who serves at the table.
Ward. A person under the guardianship of another.
Yardman. Workman in a railroad's yards.

UNDERLING—*Associated Words.*

Badge of slavery. A mark or token of inferiority.
Bonds. Chains of a slave. See RELEASE-PRISON.

UNDERLING—*Verbs.*

Serve. To wait on.
Squire. To attend as an armor-bearer.
Tend. To be at one's command.

UNDERLING—*Verbal Expressions.*

Attend upon. Wait upon as a servant.
Dance attendance upon. To be in waiting at the beck and call of another, with a view to please or gain favor.
Hang on the sleeve of. To be dependent upon.
Pin oneself upon. To follow, in order to win favor.
Wait upon. To attend as a servant.

UNDERLING—*Adjective Expressions.*

At one's call, liable to be called to service at any time; **in bonds,** captive, in the state of slavery; **in one's employ,** at one's service; **in one's pay,** serving for pay; **in the train of,** among one's attendants.

CHIEF—*Continued.*

Tsar. The title of the ruler of Russia. [Cæsar]
Tycoon. An old title of the ruler of Japan.
Tyrant. One who exercises absolute or arbitrary power without legal warrant, whether ruling well or ill.
Vaivode. The title of governors of provinces and towns in Slavonic countries.
Vakeel. An Oriental commissioner residing at the East-Indian court.
Vexillary. A standard-bearer.
Vice-admiral. A naval officer next in rank to an admiral.
Viceroy. A ruler acting with royal authority in the place of a sovereign.
Waiwode. See VAIVODE.
Warden. A chief officer, as in a prison; a gate-keeper.
Waywode. See VAIVODE.

CHIEF—*Figurative Expressions.*

Cock of the roost; cock of the walk; crowned head; head; gray mare; lord of the ascendant; man in office; mistress; the powers that be.

CHIEF—*Phrases.*

Au royaume des aveugles les borgnes sont rois [F.] In the kingdom of the blind the one-eyed are kings.
Cada uno tiene su alguazil [Sp.]. Everybody has his governor.
Da locum melioribus [L.]. Give place to your betters.
Der Fürst ist der erste Diener seines Staats [G.]. The prince is the first servant of his state.
Homme de cour [F.]. Courtier.

---

chief'-dom. State of being chief. RULE-LICENSE.
chief-jus'-tice. The presiding judge. JUDGE, PRESIDENT-MEMBER.
chief'-ly. Especially. MAGNITUDE-SMALLNESS.
chief'-tain. The head of a tribe or clan. CHIEF-UNDERLING, REPUTATION-DISCREDIT.
chien et loup, entre [F.] (shi-an' ê lu, an·tr). Between dog and wolf. MORNING-EVENING.

chif''-fo-nier'. A rag-picker. GENTILITY-DEMOCRACY.
chiffonnière [F.] (shif-on-ni-ar'). A cabinet. CONTENTS-RECEIVER.
chi'-gnon. A mass of hair. DRESS-UNDRESS.
child. An offspring of man and woman. INFANT-VETERAN, PARENTAGE-PROGENY, SAGE-FOOL; **child of God,** GODLINESS-UNGODLINESS; **child's play,** CONSEQUENCE-INSIGNIFICANCE, DIFFICULTY-FACILITY.

child'-birth". Travail. CREATION-DESTRUCTION.

child'-hood. The time of being a child. INFANCY-AGE.

child'-ish. Like a child. CREDULOUSNESS-SKEPTICISM, FORCE-WEAKNESS, INFANT-VETERAN, SAGACITY-INCAPACITY; **childish treble,** VOCALIZATION-MUTENESS.

child'-like". Like a child. CRY-ULULATION.

chil'-i-ad. A thousand. FIVE-QUINQUESECTION.

chill. Coldness; a check to ardor, etc. HEAT-COLD, HEATING-COOLING, MOTIVE-DEHORTATION.

chill'-i-ness. Coolness. HEAT-COLD.

chill'-y. Cool. HEATING-COOLING.

Chil-tern Hun'-dreds, Accept the stew'-ard-ship of the. To retire from the English Parliament. COMMISSION-RETIREMENT.

chime. Harmonious sound; a set of bells. CRASH-DRUMMING, MELODY-DISSONANCE, RECURRENCE, RESONANCE-NONRESONANCE; **in chime with,** ASSENT-DISSENT, CONVENTIONALITY-UNCONVENTIONALITY, HARMONY-DISCORD, VARIANCE-ACCORD.

chi-me'-ra. An absurd fancy. CONVENTIONALITY-UNCONVENTIONALITY, FANCY.

chi-mer'-ic-al. Visionary. FANCY.

chi'-ming. Rhythmical. RECURRENCE.

chim'-ney. A passage for smoke. APERTURE-CLOSURE, WATERCOURSE-AIRPIPE.

chin. Part of the face. ANATOMY.

chi'-na. Porcelain. HEATING-COOLING, SCULPTURE.

Chi'-na to Pe-ru', from. Everywhere. [Dr. Johnson.] EXTENSION-INEXTENSION.

chine. A piece of backbone. ANTERIORITY-POSTERIORITY.

chink. A crack; a metallic sound; money. INTERSPACE-CONTACT, MONEY, RESONANCE-NONRESONANCE.

chi non s'arrischia non guadagna [It.] (kî non sar-risk'-î-a non gua-da'-nya). Nothing venture, nothing have. DETERMINATION-VACILLATION, VENTURE.

chip. A fragment. ENLARGEMENT-DIMINUTION, JUBILATION-LAMENTATION, LIGHTHEARTEDNESS-DEJECTION, MAGNITUDE-SMALLNESS, UNION-DISUNION, WHOLE-PART; **chip of the old block,** COPY-MODEL, LIKENESS-UNLIKENESS, PARENTAGE-PROGENY.

chip'-ping. Chip. MAGNITUDE-SMALLNESS.

chi'-rog'-ra-phy. Style of writing. WRITING-PRINTING.

chi-rol'-o-gy. The art of speaking by signs. SIGN.

chi'-ro-man"-cy. Palmistry. PROPHECY.

chirp. A short, cheery sound. CRY-ULULATION, JUBILATION-LAMENTATION, LIGHTHEARTEDNESS-DEJECTION, MUSICIAN.

chir'-rup. A chirp. CRY-ULULATION, JUBILATION-LAMENTATION, LIGHTHEARTEDNESS-DEJECTION, MUSICIAN.

chi-rur'-ge-ry. Surgery. REMEDY-BANE.

chi-rur'-gic-al. Surgical. REMEDY-BANE.

chis'-el. To cut or engrave. CREATION-PRODUCTION, FORM-FORMLESSNESS, SCULPTURE.

chit. A young woman. GREATNESS-SMALLNESS, INFANT-VETERAN.

chi tace accousenie [It.] (kî tach'-ê ac-cu-sen'-tê). Silence gives consent. ASSENT-DISSENT, CONSENT.

chit'-chat". Small talk. CONVERSATION-MONOLOGUE.

chi t'ha offeso, non ti perdona mai [It.] (kî ta of-fê'-zo, non tî pêr-don'-a ma'-î). Who has wronged you never forgives you. FAVORITE-RESENTMENT.

chit'-ter-lings. Small intestines of a pig. OUTSIDE-INSIDE.

chiv'-al-ric. Pertaining to chivalry. HUMANITARIANISM-MISANTHROPY, PATRIOTISM-TREASON.

chiv'-al-rous. Gallant. FIGHTING-CONCILIATION, UNSELFISHNESS-SELFISHNESS, UPRIGHTNESS-DISHONESTY.

chiv'-al-ry. Bravery; a body of warriors; courtesy; honor. BRAVERY-COWARDICE, FIGHTING-CONCILIATION, HOLDING-EXEMPTION, HUMANITARIANISM-MISANTHROPY, PATRIOTISM-TREASON, UNSELFISHNESS-SELFISHNESS, UPRIGHTNESS-DISHONESTY.

chla'-mys. An ancient robe. DRESS-UNDRESS.

chlo'-ral. An hypnotic. FEELING-INSENSIBILITY.

chlo'-rid. Compound of chlorin. CHEMISTRY.

chlo'-ro-form. An anesthetic compound. FEELING-INSENSIBILITY, SENSITIVENESS-APATHY.

chlo'-ro-formed. Subjected to chloroform. SENSITIVENESS-APATHY.

chlo-rot'-ic. Pertaining to chlorosis. HEALTH-SICKNESS.

chock'-full". Quite full. AGENCY, ENTIRETY-DEFICIENCY.

choc'-o-late. A brown beverage. GRAY-BROWN, NUTRIMENT-EXCRETION.

choice. Select; precious. CHOICE-NEUTRALITY, GOODNESS-BADNESS; **absence of choice,** CHOICE-NEUTRALITY; **by choice,** CHOICE-NEUTRALITY, VOLITION-OBLIGATION; **choice of words,** STYLE; **choice spirits,** REPUTATION-DISCREDIT.

CHOICE—NEUTRALITY.

Adoption. Act of taking by choice.

Alternative. An offer of two things, one of which may be chosen.

Choice. Act of selecting or separating, from two or more things, that which is preferred.

Cooptation. The act of choosing.

Decision. A choosing between two sides of a controversy. See DECISION.

Dilemma. A difficult choice.

Discretion. Freedom to choose one's own judgment. See VOLITION.

Eclecticism. Practise of choosing what is true or excellent in doctrines or opinions from various sources or systems.

Election. The act of choosing.

Embarras de choix [F.]. Difficulty of choosing.

Excerption. Act of gleaning or selecting.

Gleaning. Act of picking out or choosing.

Novation. A choosing of the new.

Option. The right of choice or election.

Predilection. Predisposition to choose or like. See DESIRE.

Preference. An expressed choice.

Prelation. Choosing or setting one above another.

Preoption. Right of first choice.

Selection. Choice by preference.

Voting. Choice by suffrage.

CHOICE—*Nouns of Means.*

Ballot. A paper that expresses a voter's choice.

Cumulative vote. A system of voting which allows a person as many votes as there are persons to be voted for, and permits him to cast all these votes for one person.

Indecision, etc. See DETERMINATION-VACILLATION.

Indifference. Unconcern; freedom from prejudice.

Neutrality. The state of taking no part on either side

NEUTRALITY—*Denotations.*

Any. An indefinite part or portion.

First come, first served. A dealing out without selection.

Hobson's choice. An unavoidable choice. [Tobias Hobson, livery-man of Cambridge, England, permitted his customers to take only the horse nearest the door.]

Necessity, etc. See VOLITION-OBLIGATION.

No choice. An unavoidable selection.

Not a pin to choose from. See EQUALITY.

The first that comes. A dealing out without choice.

NEUTRALITY—*Verb.*

Waive. To relinquish a right to.

NEUTRALITY—*Verbal Expressions.*

Abstain from voting; be neutral, etc. (see *Adjectives*); have no choice; leave undecided; make a virtue of necessity, to seem to do or accept from principle or from choice that which is a necessity; not vote; refrain from voting.

NEUTRALITY—*Adjectives.*

Either, etc. See CHOICE.

Indifferent. Free from prejudice; unconcerned.

Neuter. Of neither side.

Neutral. Taking no part with either side.

Undecided, etc. See DETERMINATION-VACILLATION.

CHOICE—NOUNS OF MEANS—*Continued*.

Electioneering. A canvassing for votes.
Plébiscite [F.]. A vote by universal male suffrage.
Plebiscitum [L.]. The expression of the choice of the plebeians of Rome.
Plumper. A vote given to one candidate only, when two or more are to be voted for.

Poll. The voting or registration of votes at an election.
Scissors and paste. Articles used for preparing votes or ballots.
Suffrage. Approval, as by a vote.
Voice. Expression of one's opinion.
Vote. An expression of one's choice.
Vox populi [L.]. The voice of the people.

CHOICE—*Nouns of Result*.

Cuttings. Something obtained by cutting.
Excerpta [L.]. Things chosen; passages extracted.

Gleanings. That which is collected with great labor.
Pick. That which has been chosen for excellence.

CHOICE—*Verbs*.

Adopt. To make one's own.
Choose. To select one thing rather than another.
Cull. To pick out.
Decide, etc. See DECISION.
Divide. To separate; to apportion.
Elect. To choose.
Embrace. To avail oneself of. [To take in the arms.]
Espouse. To declare oneself in favor of.
Fancy, etc. To prefer because of external appearance, etc. See DESIRE.

Glean. To collect gradually.
List, etc. See VOLITION.
Mark, etc. To distinguish by a sign, etc. See SIGN.
Poll. To cast a vote.
Prefer. To place above in estimation.
Select. To choose with the greatest care.
Settle. To decide.
Vote. To choose by suffrage.
Winnow. To separate, as chaff from grain, by a current of air.

CHOICE—*Verbal Expressions*.

Be persuaded. See MOTIVE.
Cast in one's lot with. To share the fate or fortune of.
Commit oneself to a course. Pledge.
Cross the Rubicon. To take a decisive step binding oneself to a dangerous course, as Cæsar crossed the stream.
Exercise one's discretion. To choose for oneself.
Exercise one's option. To use one's right to choose.
Fix upon. To determine.
Have as lief. To have as willingly
Have rather. To prefer.
Hold out the alternative. Offer for choice.
Hold up one's hand. To signify one's choice by raising the hand.
Indulge one's fancy. Take what one likes.
Make choice of. To select from.
Make one's choice. Decide.
Make up one's mind. See DETERMINATION.
Mark out for. To select for.
Offer for one's choice. } Present for choice.
Offer the alternative. }
Pass the Rubicon. To take the decisive step which commits one to a hazardous enterprise, as Cæsar crossed into Italy.
Pick. To choose from several or more.

Pick and choose. Cull.
Pick one's way. Go slowly and carefully.
Pick out. Select.
Pick up. Select here and there.
Pitch upon. To settle upon.
Present the alternative. Offer for choice.
Put to the vote. To ask a decision.
Separate the chaff from the wheat. To separate the bad from the good; to thrash out.
Set apart. To separate.
Set before. To offer to.
Sift the chaff from the wheat. Throw aside what is worthless.
Single out. To choose; select.
Take a decided step. Decide.
Take a decisive step. Settle.
Take for better or for worse. To accept with all accompanying responsibilities.
Take one's choice. Choose.
Take up. To favor.
Use one's discretion. Use one's judgment in choosing.
Use one's option. Choose.
Winnow the chaff from the wheat. Separate the good from the bad.

CHOICE—*Adjectives*.

Choice, etc. See GOODNESS.
Choosing, etc. See *Verbs*.
Chosen, etc. See *Verbs*.
Discretional, etc. See VOLITION.

Eclectic. Selecting at will from the productions of others.
Optional. Depending on choice.
Preferential. Having, showing, or constituting preference.

CHOICE—*Adverbs, Conjunctions*.

Before. Sooner than.
Either. In one of two (or sometimes more) cases.
Optionally. With free choice.

Or. Otherwise.
Rather. More to one's liking.

CHOICE—*Adverbial Expressions*.

At pleasure, etc. (see VOLITION); **at the option of,** at the free choice of; **by choice; by preference; either the one or the other; for one's money; in preference; once for all,** the last time; **whether or not.**

CHOICE—REJECTION.

REJECTION.

Exclusion. The act of thrusting out, or shutting out.
Refusal, etc. See PROFFER-REFUSAL.
Rejection. The act of casting from one.
Repudiation. The act of disavowing or renouncing.

Pluck. To reject at examinations in English universities.
Reject. To throw away; to refuse to grant or receive.
Repudiate. To disavow; to renounce.
Scout. To reject disdainfully.
Spin. To reject after examination.

REJECTION—*Verbs*.

Cast. To throw off; to throw.
Decline, etc. See PROFFER-REFUSAL.
Discard, etc. See ADMISSION-EXPULSION.
Disclaim, etc. See ASSERTION-DENIAL.
Except. To omit; to leave out.
Exclude. To shut or thrust out.

REJECTION—*Verbal Expressions*.

Cast away; cast overboard; cast to the dogs, throw away; cast to the winds; fling away; fling overboard; fling to the dogs; fling to the winds; give up, to surrender; **lay aside; send to the right about,** to dismiss; **set aside,** to leave out; **set at naught,** to despise; **throw away; throw overboard; throw to the dogs; throw to the winds; toss away; toss overboard; toss to the dogs; toss to the winds.**

CHOICE—REJECTION—*Continued.*

REJECTION—*Adjectives.*

Rejectaneous. Not chosen or received.
Rejected, etc. See *Verbs.*

Rejectitious. Implying or necessitating rejection.

REJECTION—*Adjective Expressions.*

Not chosen, etc (see CHOICE); **not to be thought of; out of the question.**

REJECTION—*Adverbs.*

Neither. Not either.

No, etc. See ASSERTION-DENIAL.

REJECTION—*Adverbial Expression.*

Neither the one nor the other.

REJECTION—*Phrase.*

Non hæc in fœdera [L.]. Not into such alliances as these.

choir. A company of singers in a church. FANE, MINISTRY-LAITY, MUSICIAN.
choke. To obstruct; to strangle; quite. APERTURE-CLOSURE, EXCESS-LACK, LIFE-DEATH, OBSTRUCTION-HELP; **choke-full,** ENOUGH, ENTIRETY-DEFICIENCY.
chol'-er. Wrath. FAVORITE-ANGER.
chol'-er-ic. Fiery. FAVORITE-QUARRELSOMENESS.
choose. To make a selection. CHOICE-NEUTRALITY; **do what one chooses,** LIBERTY-SUBJECTION, VOLITION-OBLIGATION.
choos'-ing. Selecting. CHOICE-WHIM.
chop. To cut into pieces. MUTATION-PERMANENCE, UNION-DISUNION; **chop logic,** RATIOCINATION-CASUISTRY; **chop up,** LENGTH-SHORTNESS.
chop'-fal''-len. Chapfallen. LIGHTHEARTEDNESS-DEJECTION.
chop'-ping. Cutting in pieces. GREATNESS-SMALLNESS; **chopping sea,** RIVER-WIND.
chops. A headland; jaw. BEGINNING-END, BORDER, NUTRIMENT-EXCRETION.
cho'-ral. Pertaining to a chorus. MUSIC.
chord. Harmonious combination of sounds. MELODY-DISSONANCE.
cho''-ri-am'-bus. A quadrisyllabic foot, composed of a choree and an iambus. POETRY-PROSE.
chor'-is-ter. Member of a choir. MINISTRY-LAITY, MUSICIAN.
cho-rog'-ra-phy. The mapping of regions. POSITION.
cho'-roid coat. Part of the eye. ANATOMY.
cho'-rus. A body of singers in opera; concord; a song. ASSENT-DISSENT, CRY-ULULATION, MUSIC, MUSICIAN, VARIANCE-ACCORD.
chose. Personal property. **Chose in action,** PROPERTY; **chose in possession,** HOLDING-EXEMPTION.
cho' sen. Selected. CHOICE-WHIM.
chose qui plait est à demi vendue [F.] (shoz ki plê ê-ta de-mî' van'-dü'). A thing that pleases is half sold. BUYING-SALE, PLEASURABLENESS-PAINFULNESS.
chouse. To cheat. TRUTHFULNESS-FRAUD.
choux gras, faire ses [F.] (shu grä, fêr sê). To delight in a thing. SENSUALITY-SUFFERING.
chow'-der. A dish of clams or fish stewed with vegetables, etc. NUTRIMENT-EXCRETION.
chres-tom'-a-thy. A collection of choice extracts. LANGUAGE.
chrism. A consecrated ointment. CEREMONIAL.
Christ. The Messiah. DIVINITY; **Church of Christ,** ORTHODOXY-HETERODOXY; **receive Christ,** GODLINESS-UNGODLINESS.

Christ'-cross''-row'. The alphabet. LETTER.
chris'-ten. To name in baptism. CEREMONIAL, NAME-MISNOMER.
Chris'-ten-dom. Christians. GODLINESS-UNGODLINESS, ORTHODOXY-HETERODOXY.
chris'-ten-ing. Baptism. CEREMONIAL.
Chris'-tian. Pertaining to Christians. GODLINESS-UNGODLINESS, ORTHODOXY-HETERODOXY; **Christian charity,** CHARITABLENESS-MALEVOLENCE.
Chris''-ti-an'-i-ty. Christian religion. ORTHODOXY-HETERODOXY.
Christ'-mas. A church festival. CEREMONIAL, PERIODICITY-IRREGULARITY.
Christ'-mas-box''. A Christmas gift. GIVING-RECEIVING.
chro-mat'-ic. Pertaining to color. COLOR-ACHROMATISM; **chromatic scale,** MELODY-DISSONANCE.
chro''-ma-to-pseu''-do-blep'-sis. Color blindness. SIGHT-DIMSIGHTEDNESS.
chro'-ma-trope. An optical instrument. OPTICAL INSTRUMENTS.
chro''-mo-lith'-o-graph. A print in colors. ENGRAVING.
chro''-mo-li-thog'-ra-phy. Printing in colors. ENGRAVING.
chro'-mo-sphere. A layer of the sun. ASTRONOMY, UNIVERSE.
chron'-ic. Inveterate. LASTINGNESS-TRANSIENTNESS.
chron'-i-cle. A register of events. CHRONOLOGY-ANACHRONISM, MARK-OBLITERATION.
chron'-i-cler. One who chronicles. RECORDER.
chron'-o-gram. Date written in numeral letters. CHRONOLOGY-ANACHRONISM.
chron''-o-gram-mat'-ic-al. Pertaining to a chronogram. CHRONOLOGY-ANACHRONISM.
chron'-o-graph. Instrument for measuring time. CHRONOLOGY-ANACHRONISM, ELECTRICITY.
chro-nog'-ra-pher. Chronicler. CHRONOLOGY-ANACHRONISM.
chro-nog'-ra-phy. The investigation of times. ACCOUNT, CHRONOLOGY-ANACHRONISM.
chro-nol'-o-ger. Chronologist. CHRONOLOGY-ANACHRONISM.
chron''-o-log'-ic-al. Pertaining to chronology. CHRONOLOGY-ANACHRONISM.
chro-nol'-o-gist. Annalist. CHRONOLOGY-ANACHRONISM.
chro-nol'-o-gy. The science of time. CHRONOLOGY-ANACHRONISM.

CHRONOLOGY—ANACHRONISM.

Chronology. The science which treats of the measurement of time by regular periods or divisions, and which assigns events to their proper dates.
Chronometry. The art of computing time.
Horology. The science of time measurement, or the principles and construction of time-measuring machines.

Anachronism. An error in the computation of time.
Antichronism. A departure from the true order of time.
Anticipation. Act of considering or taking up before the **proper** time.
Disregard of time. Heedlessness of time.
Intempestivity. See OPPORTUNENESS-UNSUITABLENESS.

CHRONOLOGY—ANACHRONISM—*Continued.*

Horometry. The art or science of measuring time by hours and lesser divisions.

Style. A mode of measuring time with regard to the Julian and Gregorian calendars.

CHRONOLOGY—*Associated Words.*

Almanac. A series of tables giving the days of the week corresponding to the days of the month throughout the year, and certain astronomical information.

Annals. A record of events in their chronological order.

Calendar. An almanac.

Chronicle. A register of facts and events in the order of time.

Chronogram. The record of a chronograph.

Chronograph. An instrument for recording intervals of time.

Date. The time assigned for some event.

Diary. A record of daily events.

Ephemeris. A table showing the calculated positions of heavenly bodies.

Epoch. A division of time.

Era. A space of time.

Journal. A daily record of events.

Register. A record of events.

Registry. See REGISTER.

CHRONOLOGY—*Nouns of Agency.*

Annalist. A writer of annals.

Chronographer. One who writes a history.

Chronologer. } One who investigates dates of past events and trans-
Chronologist. } actions.

CHRONOLOGY—*Nouns of Instrument.*

Chronograph. An instrument for recording intervals of time.

Chronometer. An instrument that measures time.

Chronoscope. An instrument to measure the duration of light impressions upon the retina.

Clepsydra. A water clock.

Clock. An instrument or machine for measuring time.

Dial. A graduated circular plate upon which time is indicated by means of hands or by the shadow of a gnomon.

Gnomon. The pin, whose shadow shows the hour on a dial.

Horologe. An instrument which indicates the time of day.

Hour-glass. An instrument which measures time by hours.

Pendulum. A weighted rod that swings to and fro to regulate the movements of clocks.

Repeater. A watch which strikes the hour, quarter, and sometimes the odd minutes at the touch of a spring.

Sun-dial. An instrument which shows the time of day by means of the shadow of a pin on a plate.

Timekeeper. Any instrument which measures time.

Timepiece. A clock watch, or other time-measuring instrument.

Watch. A small timepiece conveniently carried about the person.

chro-nom'-e-ter. Timepiece. CHRONOLOGY-ANACHRONISM.

chron''-o-met'-ric. Pertaining to a chronometer. CHRONOLOGY-ANACHRONISM.

chro-nom'-e-try. The measurement of time. CHRONOLOGY-ANACHRONISM.

chrononhotonthologos. A bombastic person, from the hero of Carey's burlesque. BRAWLER.

chron'-o-scope. Chronograph. CHRONOLOGY-ANACHRONISM.

chrys'-a-lis. The pupa of an insect. INFANT-VETERAN.

chrys'-o-lite. A vitreous, olive-green gem. EMBELLISHMENT-DISFIGUREMENT, FAULTLESSNESS-FAULTINESS.

chrys-ol'-o-gy. Science of wealth. MONEY.

chub'-by. Plump. GREATNESS-LITTLENESS.

chub'-by-faced''. Plump-faced. GREATNESS-LITTLENESS.

chub'-faced''. Plump-faced. GREATNESS-LITTLENESS.

chuck. To pitch; a fowl's call. CRY-ULULATION, PUSH-PULL; **chuck under the chin,** BLANDISHMENT.

chuck'-far''-thing. A game of chance. PURPOSE-LUCK.

chuck'-le. To cackle; to laugh. BRAGGING, CRY-ULULATION, ENTERTAINMENT-WEARINESS.

chuff. A boor. GENTILITY-DEMOCRACY.

chum. A dear companion. FRIEND-FOE.

church. A place of worship; an association of worshipers. CERTAINTY-DOUBT, CHURCH, FANE, OR-

Metachronism. An error in computing time by dating an event **after** its true date.

Misdate. A wrong date.

Neglect of time. Carelessness about time.

Oblivion of time. Forgetfulness of time.

Parachronism. A chronological error, made by dating an event later.

Prochronism. The antedating of an event.

Prolepsis. The antedating of an event.

ANACHRONISM—*Verbs.*

Antedate. To date before the actual time; to precede in order of time.

Anticipate. To do or consider something before the proper time; to take before in fact or in thought.

Misdate. To date wrongly.

Overdate. To mark with a date later than the true one.

Postdate. To mark the date of a writing later than the actual one

Take no note of time. [T. Young, *Night Thoughts,* 55.]

ANACHRONISM—*Adjectives.*

Misdated, etc. See *Verbs.*

Out of date. Not in fashion.

Overdue. Not appearing or occurring at the assigned time.

Undated. Bearing no date.

CHRONOLOGY—*Continued.*

CHRONOLOGY—*Verbs.*

Chronicle. To record in history.

Date. To note or fix the time of.

Register. To record for future use.

CHRONOLOGY—*Verbal Expressions.*

Bear date, to have the date named on the face of; **beat time,** to measure time by moving hand, etc.; **fix the time; mark the time, mark time,** to move the feet as if in marching, without advancing; **measure time.**

CHRONOLOGY—*Adjectives.*

Chronogrammatical. Concerning, or containing a chronogram.

Chronological. Containing a record of events in the order of time; according to the order of time.

Chronometrical. Pertaining to, or measured by a chronometer

CHRONOLOGY—*Adverb.*

O'clock. Of the clock.

THODOXY-HETERODOXY; **Church of Christ,** ORTHODOXY-HETERODOXY; **dignitaries of the Church,** MINISTRY-LAITY; **go to church,** DEVOTION-IDOLATRY-Broad Church, ORTHODOXY-HETERODOXY; **Free Church,** ORTHODOXY-HETERODOXY; **High Church,** ORTHODOXY-HETERODOXY; **Low Church,** ORTHODOXY-HETERODOXY.

CHURCH.

Christendom. The part of the world in which Christianity prevails; the whole body of Christians.

Church. The collective body of Christians; any body of worshipers.

Churchdom. The dominion or authority of the Church.

Ebenezer. Memorial of divine help. [Bible, I Sam. vii, 12.]

Monachism. The system of monastic life.

Monachy. Monasticism.

Monasticism. The monastic life, system or condition.

Monkhood. The character or condition of a monk.

Pale of the Church. The boundary or limit of the Church.

Popedom. The jurisdiction of the pope.

Religious sects, etc. Bodies of believers holding to particular creeds or practises, etc. See ORTHODOXY-HETERODOXY.

The apostolic see. The Church of Rome.

The Vatican. The papal government. [A hill at Rome; the pope's palace upon it.]

CHURCH—*Church Offices and Dignities.*

Abbacy. The dignity or jurisdiction of an abbot

Advowson. (Eng. Law.) The right of presenting to a vacant benefice or living in the Church.

CHURCH—Church Offices and Dignities—*Continued.*

Apostleship. The office of an apostle.
Archbishopric. The office and jurisdiction of an archbishop.
Archiepiscopacy. The official rank and rule of an archbishop.
Benefice. An ecclesiastical living.
Bishopdom. The jurisdiction of a bishop.
Bishopric. A diocese; the office of a bishop.
Canonicate. The office of a canon.
Canonry. The office or benefice of a canon.
Cardinalate. The office or dignity of a cardinal.
Cardinalship. The condition or office of a cardinal.
Chaplain, etc. An ecclesiastic who has a chapel, etc. See MINISTRY-LAITY.
Chaplaincy. The office or station of a chaplain.
Chaplainship. The office or business of a chaplain.
Deaconry. }
Deaconship. } The office or ministry of a deacon or deaconess.
Deanery. The office of a dean.
Diocese. The extent of a bishop's jurisdiction.
Episcopacy. Church government by bishops.
Episcopate. The office of a bishop.
Glebe. The land attached to an ecclesiastical benefice.
Incumbency. The state of holding a benefice.
Living. A benefice.
Pontificate. The office of the pope.
Prebend. A stipend received from the revenues of a cathedral or conventual church.
Prebendaryship. The office of a prebendary.
Prelacy. The office of a prelate or church government by prelates.
Presbytery. The system of church government by presbyters.
Priesthood. The office of a priest.
Primacy. The office or character of a primate or an archbishop.
Rectorship. The office or rank of a rector.
See. The jurisdiction of a bishop.
Stall. A seat in the choir of a church for one of the officiating clergy.
Vicariate. The office or oversight of a vicar.
Vicarship. The office of a vicar.

CHURCH—*Associated Words.*

Church government. The policy or laws by which the Church is ruled.
Clericalism. The policy of clerical control over education, marriage law, and the like.
Consecration. Setting aside for a sacred use.
Ecclesiography. Church history.
Ecclesiologist. One versed in the history of the development of the Church.
Ecclesiology. The department of religious science that treats of the organization and development of the Church.
Episcopalianism. The beliefs or religious practises of an Episcopalian.
Hierarchy. A body of ecclesiastical rulers.
Holy orders. State of being ordained to the ministry.
Induction. Installation of a person into a church living.
Institution. Investment of a clergyman into his office.
Ministry. The body of ministers of the gospel.
Odium theologicum [L.]. The hatred of theologians.
Ordination. Act of setting apart to the Christian ministry.
Preferment. A superior ecclesiastical rank.
Prelacy. System of church government by prelates or bishops.
Presentation. Nomination of a person to a church living.
Priestcraft. The policy of the priesthood, especially when dictated by selfish motives.
Reading in. Legal entrance upon the duties of office in the English Church.
Sacerdotalism. The character or methods of the priesthood.
Theocracy. Government by the immediate direction of God.
Translation. Act of removing from one office to another.
Ultramontanism. The principles of the Roman Catholic Church, maintaining extreme views on the supremacy of the pope. [Held beyond the Alps.]

CHURCH—*Church Assemblies.*

Chapter. An assembly of the clergy connected with a cathedral; a bishop's council.
Classis. A church council or court.
Conclave. The body of cardinals shut up in the conclave for the election of a pope.
Congé d'élire [F.]. Permission to elect.
Consistory. (R. C. Ch.) An assembly of the college of cardinals at Rome; (Eng. Ch.) the spiritual court of a diocesan bishop.
Consistorial court. Ecclesiastical court.
Convocation. (Eng. Ch.) An assembly of the clergy, by their representatives, to consult on church affairs.

Council, etc. An assembly of divines convened from the whole body of the Church to regulate matters of doctrine or discipline, etc. See sub COUNCIL.
Court of Arches. (Eng. Ch.) The court of appeal of the Archbishop of Canterbury.
Ecclesiastical courts. Church courts.
Sanhedrin. The supreme council of the Jewish nation.
Synod. An ecclesiastical council to consult on church matters.
Vestry. (Eng. Ch.) A parochial assembly; (Prot. Epis. Ch.) a body which regulates the temporal affairs of a parish.

CHURCH—*Verbs.*

Call. To designate for a religious office; to invite.
Consecrate. To set apart or dedicate to the service or worship of God.
Induct. To bring in or introduce to a benefice or office.
Ordain. To invest with ministerial or sacerdotal functions.
Prefer. To honor before another.
Present. To bestow upon.
Take orders. To enter some grade of the ministry.
Take the veil. To become a nun.
Take vows. To take an oath or solemn promise in entering some sacred office.
Translate. To remove, as a bishop, from one see to another.

CHURCH—*Adjectives.*

Abbatial. }
Abbatical. } Belonging to an abbey.
Apostolic. Of or pertaining to an apostle, according to the practises and principles of the apostles.
Archiepiscopal. Pertaining to the archbishop.
Canonical. Belonging to, according to, or derived from, the canons or the books of the Bible that are held to be inspired.
Capitular. Pertaining to an ecclesiastical chapter.
Clerical. Pertaining to the clergy.
Ecclesiastical. Relating to the government or polity of the Church.
Ecclesiological. Belonging to the science or theory of church building and decoration.
Episcopal. Governed by bishops; pertaining to the Anglican Church.
Episcopalian. Relating to the Episcopal Church, its polity, etc.
Hierarchical. Pertaining to a hierarchy.
Ministerial. Relating to or characteristic of a minister or the ministry.
Monachal. Of or pertaining to monks.
Monastic. Pertaining to monasteries; like monks, recluse.
Monkish. Like monks, withdrawn from the world.
Papal. Pertaining to the pope or the Roman Catholic system.
Pastoral. Relating to a pastor of a church or his duties.
Pontifical. Pertaining to a pontiff or high priest; hence, to the pope.
Prelatical. Relating to prelates or prelacy.
Presbyterian. Governed by elders.
Priestly. Relating to, befitting, a priest.
Priest-ridden. Completely under the domination of priests.
Sacerdotal. Of or pertaining to the priesthood or priests.
Theocratic. Pertaining to a theocracy, administered directly by God.
Ultramontane. Favoring or holding extreme views in regard to the supremacy of the pope.

church'-dom. Collective body of Christians. CHURCH.
church'-go''-er. One who goes regularly to church. GOODNESS-BADNESS.
church'-man. A member of a church. MINISTRY-LAITY.
church'-war''-den. An officer in a church. MINISTRY-LAITY.
church'-yard''. An enclosure of a church. FANE, LIFE-FUNERAL; churchyard cough, HEALTH-SICKNESS.
churl. Boor. EXTRAVAGANCE-AVARICE, GENTILITY-DEMOCRACY.
churl'-ish. Like a churl. CHARITABLENESS-MALEVOLENCE, EXTRAVAGANCE-AVARICE, MOROSENESS, POLITENESS-IMPOLITENESS.
churl'-ish-ness. Rudeness. CHARITABLENESS-MALEVOLENCE, FAVORITE-MOROSENESS, POLITENESS-IMPOLITENESS.
churn. To shake or agitate. AGITATION, VISCIDITY-FOAM.
chut. Exclamation of impatience. SOUND-SILENCE, TALKATIVENESS-TACITURNITY.

chyle. The milky fluid contained in the intestines during digestion. LIQUID-GAS, NUTRIMENT-EXCRETION.

ci-ba′-ri-ous. Pertaining to food. NUTRIMENT-EXCRETION.

cic′-a-trix. A scar. MARK-OBLITERATION.

cicatrix manet [L.] (sic′-a-trix mê-net). The scar remains. PARDON-VINDICTIVENESS.

cic″-a-tri-za′-tion. Formation of connective tissue. RENOVATION-RELAPSE.

cic′-a-trize. To form a cicatrix. RENOVATION-RELAPSE.

Cic′-e-ro. The Roman orator. SPEECH-INARTICULATENESS.

Cic″-e-ro′-ni-an. Pertaining to Cicero. PURITY-CRUDENESS.

cicerone [It.] (chî-chê-ro′-nê). A guide. ENLIGHTENMENT-SECRECY, INTERPRETER.

cicisbeo [It.] (chī″-chîs-bê′-o). A gallant. LOVE-HATE.

cic″-u-ra′-tion. A taming. DOMESTICATION-AGRICULTURE.

ci′-der. The expressed juice of apples. LIQUID-GAS, NUTRIMENT-EXCRETION.

ci″-de-vant′. Of the past. FUTURE-PAST.

ci-gar′. A roll of tobacco for smoking. PUNGENCY.

cig″-a-rette′. Little cigar. PUNGENCY.

cigît [F.] (sî-jî). Here lies. LIFE-FUNERAL.

cil′-i-a. Hair. SMOOTHNESS-ROUGHNESS.

cil′-i-a″-ted. Having cilia. SMOOTHNESS-ROUGHNESS.

cil′-i-um. Hair. LAMINA-FIBER.

cim′-e-ter. A sword. WEAPON.

Cim-me′-ri-an. Densely dark. LIGHT-DARKNESS.

cinc′-ture. A girdle. CIRCLE-WINDING.

cin′-der. Waste; charred matter. CLEANNESS-FILTHINESS, HEATING-COOLING.

Cin″-der-el′-la. A heroine of a fairy tale. CHIEF-UNDERLING, GENTILITY-DEMOCRACY, SCEPTER.

cin′-der-wench″. Laboring-woman. GENTILITY-DEMOCRACY.

cin′-e-ra-ry. Relating to ashes. LIFE-FUNERAL.

cin″-e-ra′-tion. Reduction to ashes. HEATING-COOLING.

ci-ne′-re-ous. Ash-colored. GRAY-BROWN.

cin′-gle. A belt. OUTLINE.

cin′-na-bar. A red ore. REDNESS-GREENNESS.

cin′-na-mon. Brown aromatic bark. GRAY-BROWN.

cinque [F.] (san·k). The number 5. FIVE-QUINQUESECTION.

cinque′-foil. Ornament. ARCHITECTURE.

ci′-pher. The character o; a worthless person. LETTER, NUMBER, NUMBERING, PLURALITY-ZERO, SIGN, SUBSTANCE-NULLITY, USEFULNESS-USELESSNESS; writing in cipher, WRITING-PRINTING.

Cir′-ce. An enchantress. DEVOTION-MAGICIAN, MOTIVE-CAPRICE; circean cup, MODERATION-SELFINDULGENCE, SENSUALITY-SUFFERING.

cir″-ci-na′-tion. State of being circinate. REVOLUTION-EVOLUTION.

cir′-cle. A surface bounded by a curve; company. ASSOCIATION, CIRCLE-WINDING, EXTENSION-DISTRICT; circle of acquaintances, SOCIABILITY-PRIVACY; circle of sciences, KNOWLEDGE-IGNORANCE; describe a circle, CIRCUITION, ROUNDNESS; great circle sailing, MIDCOURSE-CIRCUIT.

CIRCLE—WINDING.

Circle. A plane figure bounded by a curved line every point of which is equally distant from the center.

Circularity. State of forming a circle.

Rotundity, etc. Roundness of solid bodies, etc. See ROUNDNESS.

Roundness. State of having curved lines or surfaces.

CIRCLE—*Denotations.*

Amulet. A charm to ward off diseases, witchcraft, etc.

Annulus [L.]. A ring.

Areola. A halo surrounding the image of a brilliant body.

Armlet. An ornamental band worn on the upper arm.

Baldric. An ornamental belt worn over the shoulder and across the breast.

Band. A flexible strip used as an article of dress.

Belt. A band worn about the waist.

Bracelet. A band worn about the wrist.

Cestus. A belt or girdle.

Chaplet. A band of flowers worn about the head.

Cincture. Something bound about the waist.

Circlet. A small ornamental ring.

Collar. A band worn about the neck.

Cordon. An ornamental lace, or ribbon.

Corona. A halo surrounding a bright body.

Coronet. A small crown.

Crown. A decorative circlet or covering for the head.

Cycle. A wheel.

Eye. A circular hole in anything.

Fascia [L.]. A belt.

Fillet. An ornamental band worn about the head.

Garland. A circular band of flowers.

Girdle. A belt.

Hoop. A circular band of wood or metal.

Lasso. A line with a running noose for capturing cattle.

Loop. A fold or doubling of a string in the form of a ring.

Necklace. An ornament worn about the neck.

Noose. A loop.

Orb. A circle.

Orbit. A circular path.

Ovule. The rudimentary seed.

Ring. An ornament worn about the finger.

Ringlet. A small ring.

Roundlet. A little circle.

Rundle. A round or rung, as of a ladder.

Ambages [L.]. A winding or turning.

Anfractuosity. The state of having windings.

Circuit. The act of moving around.

Circumvolution. The act of rolling round.

Convolution. The act of rolling or twisting together.

Inosculation. To wind about to cause to become one.

Involution. Act of turning or winding about.

Meandering. A winding course.

Reticulation, etc. State of being netted, etc. See CROSSING.

Sinuation. A winding in and out.

Sinuosity. The quality of bending in and out.

Torsion. The act of turning or twisting.

Tortuosity. State of being twisted.

Twist. A bending.

Undulation. State of having a wave-like appearance.

Winding. A turn or turning.

WINDING—*Denotations.*

Beau-catcher. A curl worn on the temple.

Buckle. A bend; a curl of hair.

Circumbendibus. A roundabout course or method.

Coil. A ring or succession of rings formed by winding.

Corkscrew. A spirally twisted wire, to pierce and draw a cork.

Curl. Anything coiled, or spiral.

Eel. A fish which twists and winds its body.

Escallop. Semicircular curves along an edge for ornament.

Helix. A wire in the form of a screw-thread.

Labyrinth. A place of windings.

Roll. Anything of a cylindrical form.

Rundle. A round or rung of a ladder.

Scallop. } See ESCALLOP.
Scollop. }

Serpent. A creeping animal which twists its body into the shape of rings.

Spiral. A curve winding like a screw-thread.

Tendril. A young branch that grows in the shape of a ring.

Twirl. A curved flourish, as with a pen.

Volute. A spiral scroll-like ornament.

Wave. A rising curve on a surface, especially on the surface of the water.

Windings and turnings. Roundabout paths.

Worm. An animal which is able to twist its body into rings.

CIRCLE—WINDING—*Continued.*

CIRCLE—Denotations—*Continued.*

Sash. An ornamental band about the waist.
Snood. A fillet worn about the head.
Wheel. A circular rim and hub connected by spokes.
Wreath. A circular band of flowers.
Zone. A portion of the earth's surface.

CIRCLE—*Mathematical Terms.*

Circle. Plane figure bounded by a curved line, every point of which is equidistant from a point within called the center; the circumference of such a figure.
Cycloid. The curve described by a point in a circle that rolls along a straight line.
Ellipse. Plane curve such that the sum of the distances from any point on the curve to two fixed points is constant.
Ellipsoid. A solid, every plane section of which is an ellipse (or a circle).
Epicycle. Circle rolling upon the external or internal circumference of another circle.
Epicycloid. Curve traced by a point on the circumference of a circle which rolls upon the convex circumference of another circle.
Oval. Closed convex plane curve, larger in the middle than at the ends.
Semicircle. Half a circle.

CIRCLE—*Nouns of Instrument.*

Quadrant. Instrument provided with a graduated arc for measuring altitudes.
Sector. Instrument for measuring angles in the heavens.
Sextant. Instrument for measuring distance by angles.

CIRCLE—*Verbs.*

Describe a circle, etc. See CIRCUITION.
Encircle, etc. See ENVIRONMENT.
Go round. See CIRCUITION.
Make circular, etc. } See *Adjectives.*
Make round, etc. }
Round. To make circular.

CIRCLE—*Adjectives.*

Annular. Pertaining to, or formed like, a ring.
Belted. Having a belt.
Circular. Of, or pertaining to, a circle.
Coroniform. Having the shape of a crown.
Cycloidal, etc. Pertaining to a cycloid, etc. See *Nouns.*
Egg-shaped. Shaped like an egg.
Elliptic. } Pertaining or related to an ellipse.
Elliptical. }
Guttiform. Shaped like a drop.
Orbicular. Similar to an orb.
Oval. Shaped like an egg.
Ovate. Egg-shaped.
Pear-shaped. See CURVATION.
Round. Having a curved form.
Rounded. Made circular.
Spherical, etc. See ROUNDNESS.

WINDING—Adjectives—*Continued from Column 2.*

Vermicular. Shaped like, or having the motion of, a worm.
Vermiform. Having the shape of a worm.
Wavy. Full of waves.
Winding. Twisting from a straight line or even surface.
Wreathy. Twisted; spiral.

WINDING—*Adverbs.*

In and out.
Round and round.

cir´-clet. A small ring. OUTLINE.
cir´-cling. Surrounding. CIRCLE-WINDING.
cir´-cuit. A circular space, a district. CIRCLE-WINDING, CIRCUITION, ELECTRICITY, EXTENSION-DISTRICT, MIDCOURSE-CIRCUIT, OUTLINE.
cir´´-cu-i´-tion. A going around. CIRCUITION.

CIRCUITION.

Circuit, etc. See CIRCUIT.
Circuition. A going round.
Circulation. Motion through or around something back to the starting point.

WINDING—*Verbs.*

Be convoluted, etc. See *Adjectives.*
Coil. To wind in rings.
Contort. To twist together; to writhe.
Crape. To shape into ringlets.
Crimp. To form into plaits.
Crisp. To form little curls or ringlets.
Curl. To twist or wind into ringlets or rings.
Entwine. To twist together.
Frizz. To form into small curls, as the hair.
Frizzle. To curl the hair.
Indent. To cut, leaving a toothed edge.
Inosculate. To run together; to unite, as in kissing.
Intort. To twist; to writhe.
Intwine. To twist into, or together.
Meander. To wind or turn round, as the river Meander.
Roll. To move by turning on a surface.
Scallop. }
Scollop. } To mark or cut the edge of into segments of circles
Swirl. To form eddies.
Twill. To weave so as to produce diagonal markings.
Twine. To wind about.
Twirl. To whirl or turn around rapidly.
Twist. To wind; to turn.
Turn and twist. Wind about.
Undulate. To move with a wave-like motion.
Wave. To move like a wave.
Wind. To turn about something fixed; to encircle.
Wreathe, etc. See CROSSING.
Wring. To twist and strain with violence.
Wrinkle. To make uneven.

WINDING—*Adjectives.*

Anguilliform. In the form of an eel.
Buckled. Bent; curled.
Circling. Moving around.
Coiled. Wound around in the form of rings.
Complicated. Folded or twisted together.
Convoluted. Curved or rolled together.
Crêpé [F.]. Curled, as the hair.
Daedalian. Artistically worked, as by mythic Daedalus of Crete.
Flexous. Winding; bending.
Frizzly. Curled or crisped.
Helical. Of, or relating to, a helix.
Intricate. Having numerous windings and confused involutions.
Involved. Wound round; rolled up.
Labyrinthian. Winding; perplexed.
Labyrinthic. Like a labyrinth, as that of Crete.
Labyrinthine. Like a labyrinth.
Mazy. Confusing with turns and windings.
Peristaltic. Contracting in successive circles.
Perplexed. Confused.
Raveled, etc. See PERIODICITY-IRREGULARITY.
Serpentiform. Shaped like a serpent.
Serpentine. Having the shape of a serpent.
Sigmoidal. Curved in two directions.
Sinuous. Winding in and out.
Snake-like. Like a snake.
Snaky. Winding like a snake.
Spiral. Winding like a screw.
Tortile. Twisted; coiled.
Tortive. Wreathed; twisted.
Tortuous. Winding; bent in different directions.
Turbinated. Whirling; winding.
Twisted, etc. See *Verbs.*
Undate. Rising and falling in waves towards the margin, as a leaf.
Undulatory. Resembling, or pertaining to, the motion of waves.

(Continued on Column 1.)

Circumambulation. The act of walking round or about.
Circumnavigation. The act of sailing entirely around.
Circumvention. The act of surrounding, or getting around.
Evolution. Act of unrolling or unfolding.
Turn. The act of moving around or about, as on a hinge, pivot, or center.
Turning, etc. See *Verbs.*
Wrench. A sudden and forcible turn.

CIRCUITION—*Denotations.*

Coil. A ring or succession of rings formed by winding.
Corkscrew. A spiral-shaped wire.

CIRCUITION—DENOTATIONS—*Continued.*

Curvet. A movement made by a horse, by which the four feet are in the air at the same time.
Excursion. A pleasure journey.
Northwest passage. The passage around North America through Bering Straits.

CIRCUITION—*Verbs.*

Bend. To move out of a straight line; to curve.
Circulate. To move round and return to the same starting point.
Circumambulate. To walk round about.
Circumnavigate. To sail round about.
Circumvent. To surround entirely; to get around.
Describe a circle.
Describe a complete circle. } To trace out a circle.
Double a point. To go round a point.
Go about. To turn the head of a ship.
Go round. Encircle.
Go the round. Make the circuit.
Go through 180°. Go through a half circle.
Go through 360°. Go round a circle.
Go to the right-about. To turn in the opposite direction.
Heel. To spin round on the heel.
Make a circle.
Make a complete circle. } Encircle.
Make a detour, etc. See CIRCUIT.
Make the round of. To go the circuit of.
Meander. To run, turn, or wind round, as where "Meander's amber waves in lingering labyrinths creep." [T. Gray, *Progress of Poesy*, ii, 3.]
Pass through 180°. Pass through a half circle.
Pass through 360°. Pass round a circle.
Put about. To change direction.
Put a girdle round about the earth. To travel round the world. [Shakespeare, *Midsummer Night's Dream*, II, i.]
Round a corner. To turn a corner.
Turn. To cause to revolve; to give another direction to.
Turn a corner. Go round a corner.
Turn on one's heel. Wheel about.
Turn round. Revolve.
Turn to the right-about. To turn from the left in an opposite direction; right-about face.
Twirl. To revolve or be revolved rapidly.
Twist, etc. See CIRCLE-WINDING.
Wheel. To go round in a circuit.
Whisk. To move, or cause to move quickly, lightly, and suddenly.
Wind. To turn round something fixed; to encircle.

CIRCUITION—*Adjectives.*

Circuitous. Winding.
Circumfluent. Flowing round.
Circumforaneous. Going from place to place; strolling about.
Turning, etc.
Winding, etc. } See *Verbs.*

CIRCUITION—*Adverb.*

Round about.

cir-cu'-i-tous. Going around in a circle. AIM-ABERRATION, CIRCUITION; **circuitous method,** MIDCOURSE-CIRCUIT.
cir-cu'-i-tous-ly. Indirectly. ROUNDNESS.
cir'-cu-lar. Round. CIRCLE-WINDING, MISSIVE-PUBLICATION, PUBLICITY; **circular note,** CREDIT-DEBIT.
cir''-cu-lar'-i-ty. The state of being circular. HARMONY-DISCORD.
cir'-cu-late. To move around. ANATOMY, CIRCUITION, PUBLICITY, REVOLUTION-EVOLUTION.
cir'-cu-lat''-ing med'-i-um. Currency. MONEY.
cir''-cu-la'-tion. A passing round. CIRCUITION, OUTLAY-INCOME, PUBLICITY, REVOLUTION-EVOLUTION; **circulation in,** PUBLICITY, TIDINGS-MYSTERY.
cir''-cum-am'-bi-ence. A surrounding. ENVIRONMENT-INTERPOSITION.
cir''-cum-am'-bi-ent. Encompassing. ENVIRONMENT-INTERPOSITION.
cir''-cum-am'-bu-late. To walk around. CIRCUITION, TRAVELING-NAVIGATION.
cir''-cum-am''-bu-la'-tion. A going around. CIRCUITION.
cir''-cum-ben'-di-bus. A roundabout course. CIRCLE-WINDING.

cir'-cum-cise. To cut the foreskin. CEREMONIAL, UNION-DISUNION.
cir''-cum-ci'-sion. A Jewish rite of cutting off the prepuce. CEREMONIAL.
cir''-cum-duc'-tion. A leading around. MARK-OBLITERATION.
cir-cum'-fer-ence. The boundary-line of a circle. OUTLINE.
cir''-cum-fe-ren'-tial. Lying in the circumference. ENVIRONMENT-INTERPOSITION.
cir-cum'-flu-ent. Surrounding. CIRCUITION, ENVIRONMENT-INTERPOSITION.
cir''-cum-fo-ra'-ne-an. Vagrant. TRAVELING-NAVIGATION.
cir''-cum-fo-ra'-ne-ous. Strolling about. CIRCUITION, TRAVELING-NAVIGATION.
cir''-cum-fuse'. To pour around. GATHERING-SCATTERING.
cir''-cum-fu'-sion. A pouring around. GATHERING-SCATTERING.
cir''-cum-gy-ra'-tion. Rotation on axis. REVOLUTION-EVOLUTION.
cir''-cum-ja'-cence. Lying about. ENVIRONMENT-INTERPOSITION, OUTSIDE-INSIDE.
cir''-cum-ja'-cent. Surrounding. ENVIRONMENT-INTERPOSITION.
cir''-cum-lo-cu'-tion. Indirect expression. TERSENESS-PROLIXITY.
cir''-cum-loc'-u-to-ry. Roundabout. ROUNDNESS.
cir''-cum-nav'-i-gate. To sail around. CIRCUITION, TRAVELING-NAVIGATION.
cir''-cum-nav''-i-ga'-tion. A sailing around. CIRCUITION, TRAVELING-NAVIGATION.
cir''-cum-po'-lar. Near a pole. ASTRONOMY.
cir''-cum-ro-ta'-tion. A whirling. REVOLUTION-EVOLUTION.
cir''-cum-ro'-ta-to-ry. Rotatory. REVOLUTION-EVOLUTION.
cir''-cum-scribe'. To define. CONFINEMENT, ENLARGEMENT-DIMINUTION, LEAVE-PROHIBITION.
cir''-cum-scribed'. Defined. CONFINED.
cir''-cum-scrip'-tion. Restriction. CONFINEMENT.
cir''-cum-spec'-tion. Watchfulness. CAREFULNESS-CARELESSNESS, HEED-DISREGARD.
cir'-cum-stance. A condition of things. CONDITION-SITUATION, OCCURRENCE-DESTINY.
cir'-cum-stan-ces. Worldly estate. PROPERTY; **bad circumstances,** AFFLUENCE-PENURY; **depend on circumstances,** CERTAINTY-DOUBT; **good circumstances,** AFFLUENCE-PENURY; **under the circumstances,** CONDITION-SITUATION.
cir''-cum-stan'-tial. Particular; presumptive. CONDITION-SITUATION; **circumstantial account,** ACCOUNT; **circumstantial evidence,** EVIDENCE-COUNTEREVIDENCE, LIKELIHOOD-UNLIKELIHOOD.
cir''-cum-val-la'-tion. A throwing up of ramparts. ATTACK-DEFENSE, CONFINEMENT, ENCLOSURE; **line of circumvallation,** COVER-LINING.
cir''-cum-vent'. To prevent. CIRCUITION, CRAFT-ARTLESSNESS, ENVIRONMENT-INTERPOSITION, OBSTRUCTION-HELP, SUCCESS-FAILURE, TRUTHFULNESS-FRAUD.
cir''-cum-ven'-tion. Stratagem. CIRCUITION, SUCCESS-FAILURE, TRUTHFULNESS-FRAUD.
cir''-cum-vo-lu'-tion. Convolution. CIRCLE-WINDING, REVOLUTION-EVOLUTION.
cir''-cum-volve'. To cause to revolve. REVOLUTION-EVOLUTION.
cir'-cus. A place for acrobatic feats. ACTING, DWELLER-HABITATION, LISTS.
cir'-ro-cu'-mu-lus. A form of clouds. VISCIDITY-FOAM.
cir'-ro-stra'-tus. A cloud formation. VISCIDITY-FOAM.

cir'-rus. A form of cloud. VISCIDITY-FOAM.
Cis-ter'-cian. A monk. MINISTRY-LAITY.
cis'-tern. A reservoir. CONTENTS-RECEIVER, STORE.
cit. A citizen. DWELLER-HABITATION.
cit'-a-del. A fortress. ATTACK-DEFENSE.
ci-ta'-tion. Quotation; summons. EVIDENCE-COUN-TEREVIDENCE, JUSTIFICATION-CHARGE, LITIGATION, ORDER.
cite. To quote; to summon. CONVENTIONALITY-UN-

CONVENTIONALITY, EVIDENCE-COUNTEREVIDENCE, JUSTIFICATION-CHARGE, LITIGATION, ORDER.
cith'-ern. A lute. MUSICAL INSTRUMENTS.
cit'-i-zen. A city dweller. DWELLER-HABITATION; **citizen of the world,** HUMANITARIANISM-MISANTHROPY.
cit'-rine. Yellow-colored. YELLOWNESS-PURPLE.
city. An incorporated town. CITY-COUNTRY, DWELLER-HABITATION.

CITY—COUNTRY.

Borough. An incorporated town or village.
Burgh. A borough or incorporated town.
Capital. The city used as the seat of government of a nation.
City. A corporate town.
Metropolis. The chief city of a kingdom, state, or country.
Municipality. A municipal district.
Town. Any considerable collection of dwelling-houses.

CITY—*Associated Words.*

Alley. Narrow street.
Avenue. Broad street usually bordered with trees.
Bank. Institution which lends and cares for money.
Boulevard. Pleasure-street.
Bourse. Money-market; exchange.
Bully. Quarrelsome but generally cowardly fellow.
Cockney. A Londoner; his mother's darling.
Crossing. Place where streets pass each other.
Curbstone. Row of stones placed at the edge of a sidewalk or street.
Dark retreat. Slum.
Dives. Disreputable resorts.
Esplanade. Lawn.
Exchange. Place where business transactions are centered.
Fire-district. Section of a city protected by certain fire-stations.
Gamin. Street Arab.
Ghetto. The Jews' quarters.
Gutter. Channel at side of street for running off water.
Hoodlum. Street rowdy.
Low neighborhood. Disreputable portion of a city.
Man about town. Man of means and leisure.
Pavement. Hard surface-covering for walks and streets.
Plaza. Open square or market-place.
Police district. Section assigned to certain police officers.
Precinct. District made with reference to elections, policing, etc.
Promenade. Place for walking for pleasure.
Public park. Pleasure-ground for the public.
Rowdy. A rough.
Saloon. Place where spirituous liquors are sold. A large hall
Slums. Low filthy portions of a city.
Stock exchange. Place where stocks are bought and sold.
Street. Thoroughfare. A paved Roman road.
Street Arab. Child living on the streets.
Swell. Very fashionable person.
Tenderloin. Low district in New York City, between West Twenty-third street and West Thirty-fourth street.
Tough. Person given to vice and crime.
Urbanity. Refinement and agreeableness; city manners.
Ward. Division of a city made for convenience of government.

CITY—*Adjectives.*

Citylike. Having the manners of a city dweller.
Genteel. Stylish; well bred.
Oppidan. Relating to a town.
Polished. Refined and polite.
Urbane. Polite; suave.

COUNTRY—ADJECTIVES—*Continued from Column 2.*

Rural. Rustic.
Rustic. Rude; country.

cit'-y-like". Similar to a city. CITY-COUNTRY
civ'-et. A perfume. PERFUME-STENCH.
civ'-ic. Relating to a citizen. HUMANITY.
civ'-ic crown. Garland of honor among the Romans. TROPHY.
civ'-il. Relating to a citizen; courteous. MINISTRY-LAITY, POLITENESS-IMPOLITENESS, SOCIETY-LUDICROUSNESS; **civil law,** LAW-LAWLESSNESS; **civil war,** FIGHTING-CONCILIATION.

Arcadia. Any place where ideal rustic simplicity and content prevail.
Backwoods. Wild, sparsely settled districts.
Country. With the definite article, a rural region; outside the city.
Countryside. A section of country, or its inhabitants.

COUNTRY—*Associated Words.*

Arbor. Summer-house, consisting of lattice framework covered with vines.
Bower. Shady nook.
Breath of new-mown hay.
Bucolics. Pastoral poems, as those of Virgil.
Country churchyard.
Countryman. One living in the country.
Country-seat. Dwelling in the country.
Countrywoman. A woman living in the country.
Cottage. House in the country.
Curfew. Bell rung at nightfall, a Norman signal to cover fire. "The curfew tolls the knell of parting day." [Gray's *Elegy in a Country Churchyard*.]
Fold. Place where sheep are sheltered.
Forest. Tract of land covered with trees.
Green fields and pastures new. "To-morrow to fresh woods and pastures new." [Milton, *Lycidas*, 193.]
Hamlet. Village. [A little Saxon home.]
Landscape. A rural view.
Lawn. Plot of ground, usually around a house, covered with grass.
Lea. Meadow.
Little red schoolhouse.
May-day. First day of May, the coronation day of the May queen.
May-pole. Pole, decorated, and around which dancing took place on May-day.
Meadow-land. Meadow.
Milkmaid. Woman who milks cows.
Old homestead. Old family abode.
Old Oaken Bucket. Popular pastoral song written by Samuel Woodworth.
Orchard. Plot of land on which fruit is raised.
Park. Tract of land of natural or historic interest set apart by the government for the enjoyment of the public.
Pasture. Ground on which cattle can graze.
Rustic. Peasant.
Shepherd. Keeper of sheep.
Shepherdess. Female keeper of sheep.
Swain. Rustic gallant.
Thorp. } Small settlement.
Village. }
Village green. Grass-land in or near a village.
Vineyard. Collection of grape-vines.
Woodland. Land grown up with trees.
Yew tree. An evergreen, often found in British churchyards. "The yew tree's shade." [Gray's *Elegy.*]

COUNTRY—*Adjectives.*

Arcadian. Ideally rural or simple.
Bucolic. Pastoral.
Country. Of, or pertaining to, the region outside a city.
Pastoral. Pertaining to the life of shepherds and rustics.

(Continued on Column 1.)

ci-vil'-ian. One who understands civil law; a citizen. ADVOCATE, MINISTRY-LAITY.
ci-vil'-i-ty. Politeness. POLITENESS-IMPOLITENESS.
civ"-i-li-za'-tion. Refinement; culture. BETTERMENT-DETERIORATION, POLITENESS-IMPOLITENESS, SOCIETY-LUDICROUSNESS.
civ'-i-lize. Make civilized. POLITENESS-IMPOLITENESS.

icv'-i-lized. Educated from the savage to the cultured state. Politeness-Impoliteness.

civ'-i-lized life. Not savage. Society-Ludicrousness.

civitas magna, magna solitudo [L.] (siv'-i-tas mag'-na, mag'-na sol-i-tiu'-do). A great city, a great solitude. Sociability-Privacy.

civ'-ism. Devotion to public weal. Humanitarianism-Misanthropy.

clack. A sharp noise; continuous talk. Crash-Drumming, Cry-Ululation, Talkativeness-Taciturnity.

clad. Clothed. Dress-Undress.

claim. A right; a title; the thing claimed. Dueness-Undueness, Litigation, Order, Property; **claim the attention,** Heed-Disregard.

claim'-ant. One who makes a claim. Dueness-Undueness, Petitioner.

claim'-ing. Demanding. Dueness-Undueness.

clair-obscur [F.] (clar-ob-scür'). Light and shade. Light-Darkness.

clair-voy'-ance. Fortune-telling. Devotion-Magic.

clair-voy'-ant. One who practises clairvoyance. Devotion-Magician.

clam. A bivalve mollusk. Nutriment-Excretion.

clam'-ant. Calling for help. Cry-Ululation, Dueness-Undueness.

clam'-ber. To mount. Ascent-Descent.

clam'-my. Damp and cold. Viscidity-Foam.

clam'-or. To make loud cries. Approval-Disapproval, Cry-Ululation, Jubilation-Lamentation; **clamor for,** Petition-Expostulation.

clam'-or-ous. Made with clamor. Approval-Disapproval, Excitability-Inexcitability, Loudness-Faintness.

clamp. To join; a fastener. Connective, Obstruction-Help, Union-Disunion.

clan. A small tribe. Association, Division, Gathering-Scattering, Parentage-Progeny.

clan-des'-tine. Kept secret. Enlightenment-Secrecy.

clang. Loud sound. Loudness-Faintness.

clan'-gor. Repeated clanging. Cacophony.

clan'-gor-ous. Noisy. Loudness-Faintness.

clan'-nish-ness. State of being clannish. Decision-Misjudgment.

clan'-ship. Union under a chief. Antagonism-Concurrence.

clap. To applaud; to strike together. Approval-Disapproval, Crash-Drumming; **clap on the shoulder,** Motive-Caprice; **clap the hand,** Approval-Disapproval, Jubilation-Lamentation; **clap together,** Union-Disunion; **clap up,** Release-Restraint; **thunder clap,** Phenomenon.

clap'-per-claw". To slap. Approval-Disapproval, Strife-Peace.

clap'-ping. Striking together. Approval-Disapproval.

clap'-trap". Cheap artifice. Pomp, Ratiocination-Instinct, Truthfulness-Fabrication.

claqueur [F.] (cla-cur'). A paid applauder. Flatterer-Defamer.

claqueur, faire son fouet [F.] (cla-cur', fêr son· fu-ê'). To make a bustle in the world. Bragging.

clar'-ence. A carriage. Conveyance-Vessel.

clar'-et. A red table-wine. Nutriment-Excretion.

clar'-et–col"-or. Reddish. Redness-Greenness.

clar'-i-chord. Musical instrument. Musical Instruments.

clar'-i-fy. To make clear. Cleanness-Filthiness.

clar'-i-net. A wooden musical instrument. Musical Instruments.

clar'-i-on. Trumpet. Fighting-Conciliation, Musical Instruments.

clash. Opposition; to strike together; inharmonious sound. Antagonism-Concurrence, Cooperation-Opposition, Crash-Drumming, Harmony-Discord, Impetus-Reaction, Variance-Accord; **clash of arms,** Strife-Peace.

clash'-ing. Interfering. Antagonism-Concurrence, Cooperation-Opposition.

clasp. To embrace; hold firmly; a bond; a holding close. Blandishment, Cohesion-Looseness, Connective, Outline, Remoteness-Nearness, Taking-Restitution, Union-Disunion.

class. To divide; to arrange; a group of students. Division, Organization-Disorganization, School, Teacher-Pupil.

clas'-sic. Pertaining to Greek and Latin authors; pure. Novelty-Antiquity, Proportion-Deformity.

clas'-sic-al. Classic; pure; refined. Purity-Crudeness, Taste-Vulgarity; **classical education,** Education-Learning.

clas"-si-fi-ca'-tion. A grouping. Organization-Disorganization.

clas'-sis. An ecclesiastical body. Church, Ministry-Laity.

class'-man. One of a class in college; in English universities, a candidate for a degree who has won an honor on account of his standing at examinations. Friend-Foe, Reputation-Discredit, Solitude-Company.

class'-mate. A member of the same class. Friend-Foe, Solitude-Company.

clat'-ter. A rattling noise. Crash-Drumming, Loudness-Faintness.

clau'-di-cate. To limp. Swiftness-Slowness.

clau"-di-ca'-tion. A limping. Success-Failure, Swiftness-Slowness.

clause. A portion of a sentence or document. Missive-Publication, Terms, Whole-Part.

clausis januis [L.] (clau'-zis jan'-yu-is). With closed doors. Enlightenment-Secrecy.

claus'-tral. Pertaining to a cloister. Fane.

cla'-vate. Club-shaped. Convexity-Concavity.

cla'-va"-ted. Club-shaped. Convexity-Concavity.

clav'-i-chord. An early piano. Musical Instruments.

cla'-vi-er. A keyboard instrument. Musical Instruments.

claw. To tear. Giving-Receiving, Keeping-Relinquishment; **claw back,** Flatterer-Defamer.

clay. Soft earth; the human body; earth. Hardness-Softness, Life-Corpse, Materials, Ocean-Land.

clay'-cold". Clammy. Heat-Cold.

clay'-more". A broadsword. Weapons.

clean. Pure; well-proportioned. Cleanness-Filthiness, Entirety-Deficiency, Faultlessness-Faultiness; **clean bill of health,** Health-Sickness; **clean breast,** Exposure-Hidingplace; **clean forgotten,** Remembrance-Forgetfulness; **clean hand,** Adept-Bungler; **clean out,** Admission-Expulsion; **clean sweep,** Revolution; **with clean hands,** Innocence-Guilt, Uprightness-Dishonesty.

cleaned. Renovated. Cleanness-Filthiness.

clean'-ing. Renovating. Cleanness-Filthiness.

clean'-ly. Free from dirt. Cleanness-Filthiness.

clean'-ness. State of being clean. Cleanness-Filthiness

CLEANNESS—FILTHINESS.

Ablution. Cleaning by washing.

Abstersion. Cleansing by wiping away.

Cleaning, etc. The act of removing dirt from. See *Verbs.*

Cleanness. The state of being free from dirt.

Abomination. Extremely loathsome filthiness.

Contamination, etc. The state of being made filthy by contact, etc. See *Verbs.*

Defedation. The act of making filthy

CLEANNESS—FILTHINESS—*Continued.*

Colature. The process of cleaning by straining.
Defecation, etc. The act of freeing from impurities. See *Verbs.*
Detersion. Act of freeing from offensive or impure matter.
Disinfection. The process of freeing from contagious matter.
Drainage. The process of cleaning by a continuous flow of water.
Epurgation. A making pure.
Lavation. The process of cleansing by washing.
Lustration. The ceremony of cleansing by water.
Mundation. The act of cleansing.
Purgation. The act of cleansing from impurities.
Purification. The process of freeing from defilement.
Purity. The state of being free from defilement.
Sewerage. Drainage or cleaning by means of sewers.

CLEANNESS—*Nouns of Agent.*

Bandanna. A bright red handkerchief.
Besom. A broom made out of twigs.
Blotter. A sheet of absorbent paper.
Broom. A brush attached to a long handle for sweeping.
Cloth. A piece of clothing for mopping or drying.
Doily. ⎫ A small mat-like napkin.
Doyley. ⎭
Drugget. A coarse fabric used for table-covers.
Duster. Anything by which dust is removed.
Dustman. One whose business is the removal of ashes, etc.
Filter. An apparatus, or porous substance for straining impurities.
Handkerchief. A piece of cloth for wiping the face or nose.
Laundry. An establishment for washing.
Laundress. A woman employed in a laundry.
Lavatory. An apartment for washing.
Malkin. A cloth for cleaning an oven.
Mop. A cloth used for cleaning.
Rake. An implement for gathering loose material, or making a surface smooth or level.
Riddle. A coarse sieve.
Scavenger. A street cleaner.
Screen. A sieve.
Shovel. A flattened scoop with a handle, used to lift and throw loose substances.
Sieve. An apparatus for sifting.
Sponge. A substance used as an absorbent.
Sudary. A handkerchief for drying sweat.
Swab. A mop for drying and cleaning.
Sweep. One who, or that which, sweeps.
Towel. A cloth for drying anything by wiping.
Washerwoman. A woman whose business it is to wash clothes.
Wash-house. A place where washing is done.

CLEANNESS—*Medical Terms.*

Cathartic. A purgative medicine.
Detergent. A medicine that cleanses morbid parts.
Disinfectant. A substance used to destroy the germs of infectious diseases.
Lotion. A wash for a wound.
Purifier, etc. See *Verbs.*
Wash. A liquid preparation for washing injured parts.

CLEANNESS—*Verbs.*

Absterge. To clean by wiping.
Brush. To clean away with a brush.
Buck. To cleanse in running water by beating.
Castrate. To purify from objectionable passages, as a book.
Clarify. To free from impurities by chemical means.
Clean. To remove dirt from
Cleanse. To remove all filth.
Clear. To make perceptibly clean.
Comb. To clean with a comb.
Defecate. To cleanse by discharging impurities.
Deodorize. To clean so as not to have an odor.
Depurate. To free from physical impurities.
Despumate. To clean away impurities in scum.
Deterge. To free from offending matter, as an ulcer.
Disinfect. To free from contagious matter.
Edulcorate. To free from soluble acids or salts.
Elutriate. To cleanse by washing out.
Emasculate. To purify from coarseness, as a book.
Expurgate. To purify from what is unclean.
Filter. ⎫ To purify by passing through a porous substance.
Filtrate. ⎭
Flush. To purify by washing out with a continuous flow of water.
Full. To purify by scouring, as cloth in a fulling-mill.
Fumigate. To disinfect with smoke.
Launder. To clean by washing and ironing.

Defilement. The state of being made filthy.
Fetor, etc. A filthy smell, etc. See PERFUME-STENCH.
Immundicity. ⎫ Uncleanness.
Immundity. ⎭
Impurity. The state of being defiled.
Impurity of mind, etc. See PURITY-IMPURITY.
Slovenliness, etc. ⎫ The state of being careless in one's personal
Slovenry, etc. ⎭ habits, etc. See *Adjectives.*
Soiliness. Filth.
Soilure. The state of having been made unclean by filth.
Squalor. Filth resulting from improvident poverty.
Taint. ⎫ A trace of filth.
Tainture. ⎭

FILTHINESS—*Denotations.*

Alluvium. Deposits of sand and mud by the currents of rivers.
Ashes. The remains of a substance that has been burned.
Bilge-water. Foul water that collects in the bilge of a ship.
Bug. An insect, usually living in filthy places.
Caput mortuum [L.]. Dead head; worthless residuum from distillation.
Carrion. Putrefying flesh.
Cheese-parings. Parings or cuttings of cheese, sometimes becoming strong smelling.
Cinders. Remains of burning.
Clinker. A large cinder.
Cobweb. A spider's-web, a mark of filth or disuse.
Compost. Stable manure used as a fertilizer.
Coprolite. The petrified dung of extinct vertebrates.
Dandruff. A scurf that forms on the head and comes off in small scales.
Dirt. Any foul or filthy substance; "matter in the wrong place."
Dish-water. Water in which dishes have been washed.
Ditch-water. Foul and ill-smelling water.
Draff. Refuse.
Dregs. The sediment of beverages.
Dross. Impurity in melted metal.
Drossiness. Quality of being dross.
Dung. The excrement of animals.
Dust. Sweepings and refuse of housekeeping; earth pulverized.
Excrement. Refuse matter discharged from an animal body.
Excreta [L.]. Excrement. See NUTRIMENT-EXCRETION.
Exuviæ [L.]. Cast skins or shells of animals.
Fæces [L.]. Animal excrement.
Fecula. The washings of a farinaceous pulp.
Filth. Anything that soils or makes foul.
Flea. An insect, parasitic upon a mammal or bird.
Flue. The downy matter that is scraped from cloth or wool.
Froth. Any foamy excretion.
Fur. The crust deposited by a liquid, as wine.
Furfur. Dandruff.
Garbage. Waste of any kind.
Grime. That which soils, as smut or soot.
Grounds. Particles that settle at the bottom of a liquid preparation.
Guano. The excrement of sea-birds.
Heeltap. Liquor left in a glass after drinking.
Hogwash. Kitchen refuse, fed to hogs.
Lees. Dregs of a liquor.
Lienteria [L.]. A diarrhea in which partially digested food is passed.
Louse. A small insect parasitic on and sucking the blood of mammals.
Manure. Substance applied to soil to render it more fertile, as dung, decaying animal and vegetable matter, etc.
Mire. Deep mud.
Morphew. A scurfy eruption.
Mother. A film on the surface of alcoholic liquids.
Muck. Moist manure.
Mud. Moistened earth.
Offal. Rubbish or refuse of any kind.
Offscourings. Rejected matter.
Offscum. Refuse or scum.
Ordure. Offensive excrement.
Outscourings. That which is scoured or washed out.
Peccant humor. Corrupt and offensive matter; a sinning fluid among the five fluids of the body. [Bacon, *Ad. of Learning*, I, 52.]
Precipitate. A substance separated from a solution.
Pus. Secretion from inflamed tissues.
Quagmire. Soft, marshy ground.
Raff. Worthless stuff.
Recrement. Superfluous stuff.
Residuum. That which remains after any process of subtraction.
Riffraff. Miscellaneous rubbish.
Rinsings. Lees removed by rinsing.

CLEANNESS—FILTHINESS—*Continued.*

CLEANNESS—VERBS—*Continued.*

Lave. To clean by washing with a flow of water.
Lixiviate. To separate soluble from insoluble substances by washing.
Mop. To clean by wiping with a bundle of rags attached to a handle.
Mundify. To cleanse.
Pick. To clean by carefully gathering out.
Purge. To cleanse by removing foreign and impure matter.
Purify. To free from an undesirable admixture.
Rack. To separate liquor from its sediment.
Rake. To clean out searchingly.
Refine. To purify by freeing from extraneous matter.
Rinse. To cleanse for a last time with water.
Scour. To clean by a thorough washing and rubbing.
Scrub. To clean by hard washing and rubbing.
Shampoo. To lather, rub and wash the head. [Hindus.]
Sift. To clean out the fine parts by means of a sieve.
Sponge. To clean with a damp sponge.
Strain. To purify a liquid of its coarse particles by passing through some porous substance.
Swab. To clean with a soft cloth or rag.
Sweep. To clean with a broom.
Ventilate. To render pure by admitting fresh air.
Wash. To cleanse with a liquid.
Weed. To clean the weeds out of.
White-wash. To try to purify by covering dirt over with a coat of white; so of soiled characters.
Winnow. To clean the chaff from the grain.
Wipe. To clean by rubbing softly.
Wring. To separate the water from by squeezing or twisting tight.

CLEANNESS—*Verbal Expressions.*

Be clean, etc. (see *Adjectives*); **brush up; clear out; make a clean sweep of,** to clean out thoroughly; **render clean,** etc. (see *Adjectives*); **rout out,** to clean out by means of a thorough search; **sweep out.**

CLEANNESS—*Adjectives.*

Clean. Free from dirt.
Cleaned, etc. Freed from dirt, etc. See *Verbs.*
Cleanly. Disposed to be clean.
Gimp. Dressed in a careful and cleanly manner.
Immaculate. Perfect in purity; without spot.
Kempt. Arranged in good order.
Neat. Marked by strict cleanliness.
Pure. Free from defilement.
Spotless. Free from impurity.
Spruce. Neat in dress.
Stainless. Absolutely pure.
Tidy. Marked by order and cleanliness.
Trim. Perfect in order and neatness.
Uninfected. Free from contagion.
Unsoiled. Free from defilement.
Unspotted. Free from blemishes.
Unstained. Absolutely pure.
Untainted. Not made impure by an admixture of foul matter.

CLEANNESS—*Adjective Expressions.*

Clean as a new penny; like a cat in pattens, awkwardly and affectedly neat; **sweet as a nut.**

CLEANNESS—*Adverbs.*

Neatly, etc. See *Adjectives.*

CLEANNESS—*Adverbial Expression.*

Clean as a whistle. Neatly; smoothly; slick as a whistle.

FILTHINESS—FILTHY PERSONS—*Continued from Column 2.*

Dustman. One whose employment is to remove dirt and refuse.
Malkin. An untidy kitchen-maid.
Mudlark. A person who cleans sewers.
Scrub. One who lives meanly.
Slammerkin. An untidy woman.
Slattern. A woman of uncleanly habits.
Sloven. One negligent of neatness and order.
Slut. A disgustingly filthy woman.
Sweep. One whose business is to clean chimneys.

FILTHINESS—*Verbs.*

Befoul. To make offensive with filth.
Begrease. To cover with grease.

FILTHINESS—DENOTATIONS—*Continued.*

Scoria. Refuse of fused metals.
Scum. Impure matter that rises on the surface of liquids, as in boiling.
Scurf. Worthless or impure coating or covering.
Scurfiness. Condition of being scurfy.
Sediment. Matter that settles to the bottom of a liquid.
Settlement. Sediment.
Sewage. Waste matter carried off in sewers.
Sewerage. Draining by sewers.
Silt. Fine earthy sediment deposited by water.
Slag. Refuse fused substance separated in the reduction of ores.
Slime. A dirty and adhesive substance.
Slop. Waste and dirty water.
Slosh. Soft, sloppy material.
Slough. Dead tissue thrown off from a diseased part.
Sludge. Muddy refuse.
Slush. Soft, sloppy matter.
Smoke. A product of burning.
Smudge. Paint-pot scrapings and cleanings.
Smut. Blackening made by soot.
Soil. Foul matter.
Soot. A black substance from the smoke of wood or coal.
Sordes. A discharge from an ulcer.
Spawn. The ova or offspring of any animal.
Sprue. Dross.
Suppuration. Act of generating pus.
Tartar. An incrustation on the teeth.
Vermin. Parasitic insects.

FILTHINESS—*Nouns of Cause.*

Corruption. Act of corrupting or making putrid.
Decay. Tendency toward corruption and rottenness.
Dry-rot. A decay of timber.
Leaven. Anything which makes a general assimilating, especially a corruption.
Mildew. A growth on diseased or decaying substances.
Mold. A growth on damp or decaying organic matter.
Mucor. Mold.
Must. Anything foul, or sour and fetid.
Putrefaction. Act of putrefying or becoming rotten.
Putrescence. State of being putrid or rotten.
Rubigo [L.]. Rust.

FILTHINESS—*Nouns of Place.*

Augean stable. A type of a very filthy and never cleaned stable; cleansed by Hercules turning a river through it; government offices to be cleansed and occupied.
Bog. A quagmire filled with decayed vegetable matter.
Cess. Any receptacle of filth.
Cesspool. A drain to collect refuse.
Cloaca [L.]. A sewer.
Cloacina. The purifier. A Roman goddess.
Colluvies [L.]. A collection of filth.
Common sewer. A common place for the collection of refuse.
Den. A squalid place of resort.
Drain. A pipe for carrying off refuse matter.
Dunghill. A heap of dung.
Dusthole. An opening through which dust enters.
Jakes. A privy.
Lair. A burial place.
Latrine. A privy.
Laystall. A place where rubbish, dung, etc., are deposited.
Midden. }
Mixen.   } A dunghill.
Pigsty. A place where pigs are kept.
Privy. A backhouse.
Rookery. A breeding place of birds.
Sewer. A drain for carrying off filth.
Sink. A place where refuse is collected.
Sink of corruption. Any place filled with foul and decaying matter.
Slum. A foul back street of a city.
Sough. A drain.
Swamp. A place filled with decaying vegetable matter.

FILTHINESS—*Filthy Persons.*

Beast. A filthy person.
Dowdy. A slovenly woman.
Drab. A prostitute.
Draggletail. An untidy person.

(*Continued on Column* 1.)

FILTHINESS—Verbs—*Continued.*

Begrime. To soil thickly with dirt.
Bemire. To soil by passing through very wet mud.
Beslime. To daub with soft and viscid filth.
Besmear. To defile the surface of with any viscid substance.
Blot. To make a dirty spot, or spots upon.
Blur. To make indistinct by soiling.
Contaminate. To make unclean by contact.
Corrupt, etc. To destroy the purity of, etc. See BETTERMENT-DETERIORATION.
Dabble. To dirty a little by splashing.
Daub. To paint or smear in a heedless manner.
Debase. To lessen the purity of.
Defile. To render impure.
Dirt. To soil with filth.
Dirty. To make filthy.
Distain. To destroy the natural color of with filth.
Drabble. } To dirty by dragging in filth.
Draggle. }
Fester. To become foul with matter, as a sore.
Leaven. To spoil the character of by inward working.
Maculate. To impair the purity of; to spot.
Mold. To go bad because of a fungous growth.
Molder. To waste away gradually.
Pollute. To render entirely foul.

Putrefy. To become foul from decay with a vile odor.
Rankle. To become inflamed and offensive with gathered matter.
Reek. To give out foul-smelling fumes.
Roil. To render turbid by stirring up the sediment.
Rot. To become foul by decomposition.
Slabber. To soil with some liquid.
Slaver. To let saliva run from the mouth.
Slobber. To soil with some liquid.
Slubber. To act in a slovenly manner.
Smear. To dirty by spreading something sticky over.
Smirch. To dirty by rubbing with grime.
Smoke. To give a dirty appearance to, by means of smoke.
Smudge. To soil with dry dirt.
Smutch. To make a foul stain upon.
Soil. To dirty the surface of by contact.
Spatter. To soil by splashing.
Splash. To soil by dashing water upon.
Spot. To mark with dirt in one place or several.
Stain. To discolor with foreign matter.
Stink, etc. To have a filthy smell, etc. See PERFUME-STENCH.
Sully. To darken with impurity.
Taint. To impregnate with foulness.
Tarnish. To destroy the purity of.

FILTHINESS—*Verbal Expressions.*

Become unclean, etc. (see *Adjectives*); be unclean, etc.; cover with; cover with dust, etc. (see *Nouns*); drabble in the mud; go bad, etc., to become foul and inedible, etc. (see *Adjectives*); **wallow in the mire,** to roll about in filth.

FILTHINESS—*Adjectives.*

Abominable. Very loathsome and filthy
Bad. Foul and inedible.
Beastly. Having foul habits.
Bloody. Smeared with blood.
Carious. Having ulcered and decayed bones.
Coarse. Vile in manners.
Corrupt. Spoiled by decay.
Crapulous, etc. Diseased from overindulgence in drink, etc. See MODERATION-SELFINDULGENCE.
Dirty. Made foul with dirt.
Dowdy. Vulgar looking.
Draggletailed. Dirty in personal appearance.
Dreggy. Full of grounds.
Dusty. Covered with fine, dry dirt.
Effete. Worn out by decay.
Excrementitious. Disgustingly filthy, like excrement.
Fecal. Pertaining to animal excrement.
Feculent. Foul from animal excrement.
Fetid, etc. Giving out an evil odor, etc. See PERFUME-STENCH.
Filthy. Repulsively foul.
Flyblown. Tainted with the eggs of flies.
Foul. Offensive to the senses.
Fusty. Rank from moldiness.
Gory. Smeared with thick and clotted blood.
Grimy. Filthy with dry dirt.
Gross, etc. Marked by coarseness and impurity, etc. See PURITY-IMPURITY.
High. Slightly tainted, as meat.
Impetiginous. Having a skin made unclean by the running tetter.
Impure. Having lost purity.
Maggoty. Infested with the larvæ of flies.
Mildewed. Decayed by the action of a kind of fungus.
Moldy. Covered with a growth of minute fungi.
Moth-eaten. Eaten into by moths.
Mucid. Dirty from a slimy mold.
Musty. Having a rank smell due to decomposition.
Nasty. Nauseous and filthy.
Offensive. Exciting a feeling of displeasure.
Peccant. Corrupt and repulsive from disease.

Purulent. Filthy from the formation of pus.
Putrefied. Having a filthy smell as a result of decay.
Putrescent. Beginning to putrefy.
Putrid. In a state of decay with a fetid odor.
Rancid. Foul in smell and taste from decay.
Reasty. Rancid, as salt meat.
Reechy. Reeking, as with sweat ["reechy neck," Shakespeare, *Cor.*, ii, 1; "reechy kisses," *Hamlet*, iii, 4].
Reeky. Foul from smoke.
Rotten. Offensive from decomposition.
Rotting, etc. See *Verbs.*
Rusty. Dirty with rust.
Scurfy. Dirty from a scale-like affection of the skin.
Slimy. Dirty with wet filth.
Slovenly. Careless in one's personal habits.
Sluttish. Disgustingly filthy, like a slut.
Smoky. Dirty from smoke.
Smutty. Stained with soot or smoke.
Snuffy. Soiled with snuff.
Soiled. Having the surface dirtied by contact.
Sooty. Blackened with soot.
Squalid. Filthy from extreme poverty.
Stercoraceous. Dirty, like dung.
Tainted. Impregnated with foulness.
Thick. Dirty and muddy, as water.
Touched. Slightly affected with decay.
Turbid. Dirty from having the sediment stirred up.
Unclean.
Uncleanly.
Uncombed.
Unkempt.
Unpurified.
Unscoured. } See CLEANNESS.
Unstrained.
Unswept.
Untidy.
Unwashed.
Unwiped.

FILTHINESS—*Adjective Expressions.*

Gone bad, grown foul; **not to be handled with kid gloves,** dirty; **rotten as cheese,** rotten with a powerful stench; **rotten as a pear.**

cleanse. To clean. CLEANNESS-FILTHINESS.
clear. Pure; plain; unmixed; free from fault; indisputable. CERTAINTY-DOUBT, CLEANNESS-FILTHINESS, CLEARNESS-OBSCURITY, DIAPHANEITY-OPAQUENESS, DIFFICULTY-FACILITY, EXCULPATION-CONVICTION, GAIN-LOSS, INNOCENCE-GUILT, JUSTIFICATION-CHARGE, LIGHT-DARKNESS, MANIFESTATION-LA-TENCY, MELODY-DISSONANCE, MIXTURE-HOMOGENEITY, RELEASE-RESTRAINT, SETTLEMENT-DEFAULT, VISIBILITY-INVISIBILITY; **clear articulation,** VOCALIZATION-MUTENESS; **clear conscience,** INNOCENCE-GUILT; **clear for action,** PREPARATION-NONPREPARATION; **clear of,** REMOTENESS-NEARNESS; **clear off,** ADMISSION-EXPULSION, SETTLEMENT-DEFAULT; **clear**

out, Admission-Expulsion, Cleanness-Filthiness; **clear-sighted,** Sagacity-Incapacity, Sight-Blindness; **clear sky,** Sanguineness-Hopelessness; **clear stage,** Difficulty-Facility, Opportuneness-Unsuitableness, Right-Wrong; **clear the course,** Transmission; **clear the ground,** Difficulty-Facility; **clear the throat,** Admission-Expulsion; **clear up,** Clearness-Obscurity, Interpretation-Misinterpretation, Light-Darkness; **coast clear,** Security-Insecurity; **get clear off,** Escape; **keep**

clear of, Quest-Evasion, Remoteness-Nearness.
clear'-age. The act of removing. Admission-Expulsion.
clear'-ance. Clearage. Admission-Expulsion, Exculpation-Conviction, Preparation-Nonpreparation, Settlement-Default.
clear'-head"-ed. Sagacious. Sagacity-Incapacity.
clear'-ness. State of being clear. Clearness-Obscurity, Vocalization-Muteness.

CLEARNESS—OBSCURITY.

Clearness. The quality or state of being clear, intelligible, or distinct.
Explicitness, etc. Clearness; directness, etc. See *Adjectives*.
Intelligibility. The quality or state of being intelligible; perspicuity; definiteness.
Legibility. The quality of being legible; legibleness.
Lucidity. The quality or state of being clear or lucid.
Perspicuity. Clearness of expression or thought.
Phonanta synetoisi [Gr.]. A word to the wise.
Plain speaking, etc. See Manifestation.
Precision, etc. Exactness; accuracy; definiteness, etc. See Truth.

Clearness—*Verbs.*

Catch. Apprehend or perceive clearly.
Collect. Gain by information or observation; gather from premises.
Comprehend. Take into the mind; understand clearly and fully.
Elucidate, etc. Throw light upon; clear up, etc. See Interpretation.
Follow. Keep up with; keep the thread of, as in thought.
Grasp. Seize intellectually; comprehend.
Master. Comprehend in all its details.
Popularize. Make clear and acceptable to the common people.
Simplify. Make clear by plainer statement.
Take. To receive in thought.
Understand. To have the right idea of.

Clearness—*Verbal Expressions.*

Be intelligible, etc. (see *Adjectives*); clear up; come to an understanding; enter into the ideas of, understand; lie on the surface, to be clearly evident; make out, to find out; render intelligible, etc. (see *Adjectives*); see daylight, understand clearly; see one's way; see with half an eye, understand without any difficulty; speak for itself, require no explanation; speak volumes, express much and clearly in few words; take in, comprehend; tell its own tale, speak for itself.

Clearness—*Adjectives.*

Clear. Distinct; intelligible.
Definite, etc. Clear and known with exactness, etc. See Truth.
Distinct. Easily understood; clear to the mind.
Explicit. Plainly expressed.
Expressive, etc. Full of meaning, etc. See Meaning.
Graphic. Describing with pictorial effect.
Illustrative, etc. Designed to make clear by means of figures, comparisons, etc. See Interpretation.
Intelligible. Capable of being understood; clear.
Legible. That may be read.
Lucid. Intellectually clear.
Luminous. Light-bearing, radiant, clear.
Obvious, etc. Immediately evident, etc. See Manifestation.
Perspicuous. Translucent; clear; lucid.
Plain. That may be readily seen or understood.
Popularized. Made clear and acceptable to the common people.
Positive. Openly and plainly expressed; explicit.
Recognizable. Capable of being recognized.
Transparent. Easy to see through or understand.
Transpicuous. Transparent.
Unambiguous. Not ambiguous; clear; perspicuous.
Unconfused. Not confused; distinct.
Unequivocal. Unambiguous; certain.
Unmistakable, etc. Clear; plain; obvious; etc. See Manifestation.

Clearness—*Adjective Expressions.*

Clear as day; clear as noonday; easily understood; easy to understand; for the million; intelligible to the meanest capacity, clear to one of the poorest intellectual powers.

Clearness—*Adverbial Expressions.*

In plain English.
In plain terms. } Clearly.
In plain words.

Ambiguity, etc. Lack of grammatical sense, etc. See Ambiguity.
Doubtful meaning. Capable of more than one interpretation.
Imperspicuity. Lack of clearness of expression of thought.
Incomprehensibility. The quality of being impossible to be fully understood.
Inconceivableness. Quality of being unimaginable.
Latency, etc. State of being undeveloped, etc. See Manifestation-Latency.
Mystification, etc. Act of making obscure, etc. See Enlightenment-Secrecy.
Obscuram per obscurius [L.]. Explaining of an obscure thing by something more obscure.
Obscurity. Quality of being not easily understood: used in reference to subject-matter.
Perplexity, etc. Inability to fix an opinion, etc. See Regularity-Irregularity.
Spinosity. State of being full of difficulties or thorns.
Transcendentalism. Obscure speculation; climbing higher than the evidence of the senses.
Uncertainty, etc. The quality of not being certain, etc. See Certainty-Doubt.
Unintelligibility. Quality of not being easily understood.
Vagueness, etc. Lack of definiteness, etc. See *Adjectives*.

Obscurity—*Denotations.*

Dignus vindice nodus [L.]. A knot worthy to be loosened.
Freemasonry. The institutions and practises of a secret association.
Jargon, etc. See Meaning-Jargon.
Paradox. That which seems absurd but may be true in fact.
Riddle, etc. See Tidings-Mystery.
Sealed book. Anything which is unknown or kept secret.
Steganography. Art of writing in characters which are not intelligible except to persons who have the key; cryptography; cipher-writing.

Obscurity—*Figurative Nouns.*

Asses' bridge. The fifth proposition of the first book of Euclid.
Greek.
Hebrew. } Something unintelligible to the ignorant.
High Dutch.
Pons asinorum [L.]. The asses' bridge.

Obscurity—*Verbs.*

Bemuddle. To confuse.
Conceal, etc. To hide, etc. See Enlightenment-Secrecy.
Confuse, etc. To perplex the mind, etc. See Organization-Disorganization.
Darken, etc. To render unintelligible. See Light-Darkness.
Lose. Fail to keep.
Miss. Fail to perceive or learn.
Perplex, etc. To make difficult to form an opinion, etc. See Certainty-Doubt.
Wonder, etc. Feel doubt and curiosity, etc. See Astonishment.

Obscurity—*Verbal Expressions.*

Be able to make nothing of; be at sea, etc., be confused, etc. (see Doubt); be unintelligible, etc. (see *Adjectives*); give it up, cease from effort to understand it; have a doubtful meaning, be uncertain, be obscure; lose the clue, be confused, be unable to follow; not be able to account for; not be able to make either head or tail of, be unable to find anything distinct or definite about; not know what to make of; not understand, etc. (see Clearness); not understand one another; pass comprehension, be incomprehensible; play at cross purposes, etc., misunderstand or act counter to one another without intending it, etc. (see Interpretation-Misinterpretation); render unintelligible, etc. (see *Adjectives*); require explanation, etc. (see Interpretation); see through a glass darkly [Bible], etc. (see Knowledge-Ignorance).

CLEARNESS—OBSCURITY—*Continued.*

CLEARNESS—*Phrases.*

A word to the wise.
He that runs may read, etc.　It is so simple as to be intelligible to any-body, etc.　See MANIFESTATION.
Id est [L.].　That is it.

OBSCURITY—ADJECTIVES—*Continued from Column 2.*

Paradoxical.　Seemingly contradictory.
Perplexed, etc.　Confused; of a complicated character, etc.　See REGULARITY-IRREGULARITY.
Puzzling.　Bewildering; perplexing.
Recondite.　Secret; hidden from the mental view.
Searchless.　Inscrutable; impenetrable.
Transcendental.　Vaguely and ambitiously extravagant in specula-tion, imagery, or diction.
Unaccountable.　Inexplicable; strange.
Unconceived.　Not understood.
Undeciphered.　Undiscovered.
Undefinable.　Not capable of being made clear or of being defined by a definition.
Undetermined.　Not defined; indeterminate.
Undiscernible, etc.　Not to be seen through; obscure, etc.　See VISI-BILITY-INVISIBILITY.
Undiscoverable.　That cannot be discovered or found out.
Unexplained.　Not explained.
Unfathomable.　Incapable of being fathomed or sounded.
Unintelligible.　Not intelligible; not capable of being understood.
Unknowable.　Incapable of being known.
Vague.　Hazy; uncertain; doubtful.

OBSCURITY—*Adjective Expressions.*

Above comprehension; as Greek to one, unintelligible; **beyond com-prehension; beyond one's depth,** too profound for one; **clear as mud,** not clear; **past comprehension; seen through a mist,** obscure; **shrouded in mystery.**

---

clear′-ob-scure″.　Chiaroscuro.　LIGHT-DARKNESS.
cleav′-age.　A split.　GEOLOGY, TEXTURE, UNION-DISUNION.
cleave.　To split; to remain fast.　COHESION-LOOSE-NESS, DOUBLING-HALVING, UNION-DISUNION.
cleav′-er.　A sharp chopper.　SHARPNESS-BLUNTNESS.
clef.　A musical character.　MELODY-DISSONANCE.
cleft.　Divided; crevice.　DOUBLING-HALVING, INTER-SPACE-CONTACT; **in a cleft stick,** DIFFICULTY-FA-CILITY.
clem.　To starve.　FASTING-GLUTTONY.
clem′-en-cy.　Mercy.　COMPASSION - RUTHLESSNESS, HARSHNESS-MILDNESS.
clem′-ent.　Mild; lenient.　COMPASSION-RUTHLESSNESS, EXCITABILITY - INEXCITABILITY, HARSHNESS - MILD-NESS.
clench.　To grasp firmly.　CONTRACT, KEEPING-RE-LINQUISHMENT, TAKING-RESTITUTION.
clepe.　To name.　NAME-MISNOMER.
clep′-sy-dra.　A water clock.　CHRONOLOGY-ANACH-RONISM.
clere′-sto″-ry.　An elevated story of a church.　CON-TENTS-RECEIVER.
cler′-gy.　The ministry.　MINISTRY-LAITY.
cler′-ic-al.　Pertaining to the clergy.　CHURCH; **clerical error,** TRUTH-ERROR.
cler′-ic-al-ism.　Control of education, charities, etc., by the clergy.　CHURCH.
cler′-ic-als.　The clergy.　MINISTRY-LAITY.
clerk.　A secretary; a salesman; a clergyman; a learned person.　ANTAGONIST-ASSISTANT, CHIEF-UNDERLING, CONSIGNEE, MINISTRY-LAITY, RECORDER, SCHOLAR-DUNCE, WRITING-PRINTING; **articled clerk,** INSTRUC-TOR-PUPIL; **clerk of work,** MANAGER.
clerk′-ship.　The position of a clerk.　COMMISSION-ABROGATION.
cle′-ro-man″-cy.　Divination with dice or beans.　PROPHECY.

OBSCURITY—*Adjectives.*

Abstruse.　Hard to be understood.
Ambiguous.　Having a double meaning.
Crabbed.　Obscure; perplexing.
Dark.　Obscure; mysterious; hidden.
Dim.　Indistinct; obscure.
Enigmatic.
Enigmatical. } Obscure; puzzling.
Hidden, etc.　Concealed; secret, etc.　See ENLIGHTENMENT-SECRECY.
Illegible.　Incapable of being read.
Impenetrable.　Abstruse.
Inapprehensible.　Unintelligible; inconceivable.
Incognizable.　Incapable of being recognized, known, or distin-guished.
Incommunicable.　Incapable of being communicated.
Incomprehensible.　Not capable of being understood.
Inconceivable.　Incapable of being conceived by the mind.
Inconceptible.　Inconceivable.
Indefinite, etc.　Not explicit; uncertain, etc.　See VISIBILITY-IN-VISIBILITY.
Inexplicable.　Not explainable.
Inexpressible.　Not capable of expression in language; indescribable.
Inscrutable.　Unsearchable; obscure.
Insoluble.　Not to be solved or explained; inexplicable.
Insolvable.　Insoluble.
Latent, etc.　Hidden; invisible, etc.　See MANIFESTATION-LATENCY.
Loose.　Vague; rambling.
Misty, etc.　Lacking clearness; obscure, etc.　See DIAPHANEITY-OPAQUENESS.
Muddy.　Confused; cloudy in mind; vague.
Mysterious.　Involved in mystery; obscure.
Mystic.
Mystical. } Secret; dark; betokening a hidden meaning.
Nebulous.　Cloudy; misty; obscure.
Obscure.　Abstruse; indistinct.
Occult.　Hidden; mysterious.

(Continued on Column 1.)

---

clev′-er.　Gifted; adroit.　SAGACITY-INCAPACITY, SKILL-UNSKILFULNESS; **too clever by half,** CRAFT-ARTLESS-NESS.
clev′-er-ness.　Skilfulness.　SKILL-UNSKILFULNESS.
clew.　Something that leads to a solution; to coil into a ball.　INTERPRETATION-MISINTERPRETATION, ROUNDNESS, SIGN; **seek a clew,** INVESTIGATION-ANSWER.
click.　A short, sharp sound.　CRASH-DRUMMING.
cli′-ent.　Dependent; a buyer.　BUYING-SALE, CHIEF-UNDERLING.
cli′-ent-ship.　The position of a client.　LIBERTY-SUBJECTION.
cliff.　A steep slope.　ERECTNESS-FLATNESS, HEIGHT-LOWNESS, PARALLELISM-INCLINATION.
cli-mac′-ter-ic.　Relating to critical periods.　INFANCY-AGE.
cli′-mate.　Atmosphere; region.　EXTENSION-DISTRICT, WATER-AIR; **fine climate,** HEALTHINESS-UNHEALTHI-NESS.
cli″-ma-tol′-o-gy.　Science of climate.　WATER-AIR.
cli′-max.　Culmination.　RHETORIC, SUPREMACY-SUB-ORDINACY, TOP-BOTTOM.
climb.　To ascend.　ASCENT-DESCENT.
clime.　Region.　EXTENSION-DISTRICT.
cli′-nal.　Inclining.　PARALLELISM-INCLINATION.
clinch.　To secure firmly; to seize; a decisive argument.　APERTURE-CLOSURE, CERTAINTY-DOUBT, COMPLE-TION-NONCOMPLETION, KEEPING-RELINQUISHMENT, TAKING-RESTITUTION, UNION-DISUNION, WORD-NEOLOGY; **clinch an argument,** COHESION-LOOSE-NESS; **clinch the fist at,** CHARITABLENESS-MENACE.
cling.　To hold on to anything firmly; to hold to an opinion.　COHESION-LOOSENESS, PERSISTENCE-WHIM.
clink.　A short, ringing sound.　CACOPHONY, RESO-NANCE-NONRESONANCE.
clink′-er.　A clencher; a burnt mass.　CLEANNESS-FILTHINESS, HEATING-COOLING.

cli-nom'-e-ter. A measuring instrument. ANGU-LARITY, PARALLELISM-INCLINATION.

clin'-quant. Tinseled. EMBELLISHMENT-DISFIGURE-MENT, TASTE-VULGARITY.

Cli'-o. A muse. ACCOUNT.

clip. To cut off. LENGTH-SHORTNESS; **clip one's words,** SPEECH-INARTICULATENESS; **clip the wing,** LEAVE-PROHIBITION, MIGHT-IMPOTENCE, OBSTRUCTION-HELP, SWIFTNESS-SLOWNESS, USEFULNESS-USELESSNESS.

clip'-per. A swift vessel. CONVEYANCE-VESSEL.

clip'-ping. That clipped off. WHOLE-PART.

clique. A clannish set. ASSOCIATION, COUNCIL.

clo-a'-ca. A sewer. CLEANNESS-FILTHINESS, WATER-COURSE-AIRPIPE.

cloacina [L.] (clo-a-sai'-na). The purifier. CLEANNESS-FILTHINESS.

cloak. An outer garment; a pretext. DRESS-UNDRESS, ENLIGHTENMENT-SECRECY, EXPOSURE-HIDINGPLACE.

clock. A timepiece. CHRONOLOGY-ANACHRONISM; **clock-work,** INSTRUMENT.

clod. A mass of earth; a dull fellow. ADEPT-BUNGLER, GREATNESS-LITTLENESS, OBSTRUCTION-HELP, OCEAN-LAND, SAGE-FOOL.

clod'-hop''-per. A rustic. GENTILITY-DEMOCRACY

clod'-pate''. Blockhead. SAGE-FOOL.

clod'-pa''-ted. Being stupid. SAGACITY-INCAPACITY

clod'-poll. Blockhead. SAGE-FOOL.

clog. A shoe; an impediment. DRESS-UNDRESS, OBSTRUCTION-HELP.

clois'-ter. A monastery. FANE, RELEASE-RESTRAINT.

clois'-tered. Living in a cloister. FANE.

close. The end; near together; to terminate; land enclosed; not open or free; stingy; stifling; nearly alike; near; compact; with lips closed; terse. APERTURE-CLOSURE, BEGINNING-END, BREADTH-NARROWNESS, COMPLETION-NONCOMPLETION, DWELLER-HABITATION, ENLIGHTENMENT-SECRECY, EXTENSION-DISTRICT, EXTRAVAGANCE-AVARICE, HEAT-COLD, LIKENESS-UNLIKENESS, REMOTENESS-NEARNESS, SOLIDITY-RARITY, TALKATIVENESS-TACITURNITY, TERSENESS-PROLIXITY, UNION-DISUNION; **close at hand,** FUTURE-PAST, OCCURRENCE-DESTINY, REMOTENESS-NEARNESS; **close inquiry,** INVESTIGATION-ANSWER; **close in upon,** CONCENTRATION-RADIATION; **close one's eyes to,** HEED-DISREGARD, OBSERVANCE-NONOBSERVANCE; **close one's ranks,** PREPARATION-NONPREPARATION; **close prisoner,** GUARD-PRISONER; **close quarters,** APPROACH-WITHDRAWAL, ATTACK-DEFENSE, OBSERVANCE-NONOBSERVANCE, REMOTENESS-NEARNESS; **close study,** HEED-DISREGARD, REFLECTION-VACANCY; **close the eyes,** ACTIVITY-INDOLENCE, LIFE-DEATH, SIGHT-BLINDNESS; **close with,** ASSENT-DISSENT, ATTACK-DEFENSE, COHESION-LOOSENESS, CONCENTRATION-RADIATION, CONSENT, INTERSPACE-CONTACT, STRIFE-PEACE; **closely packed,** GATHERING-SCATTERING; **examined closely by,** HEED-DISREGARD; **keep close with,** ENLIGHTENMENT-SECRECY, KEEPING-RELINQUISHMENT; **tread close upon,** LEADING-FOLLOWING.

closed. Shut. APERTURE-CLOSURE.

close'-ness. Tightness; secrecy. BREADTH-NARROWNESS, ENLIGHTENMENT-SECRECY.

clos'-et. A small side-room. CONTENTS-RECEIVER, EXPOSURE-HIDINGPLACE.

clos'-et-ed with. In session with. ADVICE, CONVERSATION-MONOLOGUE.

close'-tongued''. Secretive. TALKATIVENESS-TACITURNITY.

clo'-sure. A shutting up. APERTURE-CLOSURE.

clot. A thick, viscid mass. OCEAN-LAND, SOLIDITY-RARITY.

cloth. A woven fabric; the clergy. CLEANNESS-FILTHINESS, MINISTRY-LAITY, OCCUPATION.

clothe. To dress. DRESS-UNDRESS.

clothes. Articles of wear. DRESS-UNDRESS; **grave-clothes,** LIFE-FUNERAL.

clothes'-horse''. A frame to hang clothes on. SUSPENSION-SUPPORT.

clothes'-press''. A wardrobe. CONTENTS-RECEIVER.

cloth'-ier. One who sells clothes. DRESS-UNDRESS.

cloth'-ing. Garments. COVER-LINING, DRESS-UNDRESS, HEATING-COOLING.

clot'-pate. Blockhead. SAGE-FOOL.

clot'-poll. A blockhead. SAGE-FOOL.

clot'-ted. Full of clots. VISCIDITY-FOAM.

cloud. Vapor; whatever confuses; a mass. DIAPHANEITY-OPAQUENESS, DIMNESS, EXPOSURE-HIDINGPLACE, GATHERING-SCATTERING, LIQUID-GAS, LUMINARY-SHADE, MULTIPLICITY-PAUCITY, VISCIDITY-FOAM, WATER-AIR, WELFARE-MISFORTUNE; **break through the cloud,** VISIBILITY-INVISIBILITY; **cloud-capped,** HEIGHT-LOWNESS; **cloud of dust,** FRIABILITY; **cloud of skirmishers,** BELLIGERENT; **cloud of smoke,** VISCIDITY-FOAM; **cloud of words,** TERSENESS-PROLIXITY; **clouds gathering,** LIGHT-DARKNESS, SECURITY-INSECURITY, WARNING; **clouded,** ENLIGHTENMENT-SECRECY, LIGHTHEARTEDNESS-DEJECTION, SANGUINENESS-HOPELESSNESS, VARIEGATION, WELFARE-MISFORTUNE; **clouded perception,** SAGACITY-INCAPACITY; **drop from the clouds,** EXPECTATION-SURPRISE; **in a cloud,** CERTAINTY-DOUBT, ENLIGHTENMENT-SECRECY; **in the clouds,** FANCY, HEED-DISREGARD, HEIGHT-LOWNESS; **under a cloud,** APPROVAL-DISAPPROVAL, JUSTIFICATION-CHARGE, REPUTATION-DISCREDIT, SOCIABILITY-PRIVACY, WELFARE-MISFORTUNE.

cloud'-i-ness. Obscurity. VISCIDITY-FOAM.

cloud'-land''. Fancy-land. FANCY.

cloud'-less. Clear; without trouble. LIGHT-DARKNESS, PLEASURE-PAIN, VISCIDITY-FOAM.

cloud'-topped''. Lofty. HEIGHT-LOWNESS.

cloud'-touch''-ing. Lofty. HEIGHT-LOWNESS.

cloud-y. Obscure; vague. DIAPHANEITY-OPAQUENESS, DIMNESS.

clough. A sluice. HEIGHT-LOWNESS.

clo'-ven. Parted. DOUBLING-HALVING.

clo'-ven foot. Satan. ANGEL-SATAN, CHARITABLENESS-MALEVOLENCE, VIRTUE-VICE; **see the cloven foot,** DISCOVERY; **show the cloven foot,** CHARITABLENESS-MALEVOLENCE.

clo'-ver. A plant. SENSUALITY-SUFFERING.

clown. A buffoon. ACTING, GENTILITY-DEMOCRACY, TASTE-VULGARITY, WAG.

clown'-ish. Coarse. GENTILITY-DEMOCRACY, TASTE-VULGARITY.

cloy. To satiate. EXCESS-LACK, REPLETION.

club. A weapon; a social organization. ASSOCIATION, DWELLER-HABITATION, GATHERINGPLACE, PRESIDENT-MEMBER; SOCIABILITY-PRIVACY, WEAPON; **club law,** COERCION, LAW-LAWLESSNESS, **club together,** ANTAGONISM-CONCURRENCE, ASSOCIATION, SOCIABILITY-PRIVACY.

club'-ba-ble. Sociable. SOCIABILITY-PRIVACY.

club'-bism. Association in clubs. SOCIABILITY-PRIVACY.

club'-foot''-ed. Having a distorted foot. PROPORTION-DEFORMITY.

club'-house''. A house occupied by a club. DWELLER-HABITATION.

cluck. The call of a hen. CRY-ULULATION.

clue. Spelling of the figurative senses of CLEW. INVESTIGATION-ANSWER, SIGN; **seek a clue,** INVESTIGATION-ANSWER.

clump. A compact group. CONVEXITY-CONCAVITY, GATHERING-SCATTERING; **clump of trees,** FAUNA-FLORA.

clum'-sy. Lacking ease. BEAUTY-UGLINESS, PROPRIETY-IMPROPRIETY, SKILL-UNSKILFULNESS.

Clu'-ri-chaune. A fairy fabled to help housewives. JOVE-FIEND.

clus'-ter. A group or bunch. GATHERING-SCATTERING.

clus'-tered col'-umn. Union of columns. ARCHITECTURE.

clutch. To seize eagerly. KEEPING-RELINQUISHMENT, TAKING-RESTITUTION.

clutch'-es. Tight grip. KEEPING-RELINQUISHMENT, RULE-LICENSE; in the clutches of, LIBERTY-SUBJECTION.

clut'-ter. To clatter. CRASH-DRUMMING.

co''-a-cer-va'-tion. A gathering. GATHERING-SCATTERING.

coach. A vehicle; an instructor. CONVEYANCE-VESSEL, EDUCATION-MISTEACHING, INSTRUCTOR-PUPIL; coach painter, ARTIST; coach road, WAY; coach up, EDUCATION-LEARNING; drive a coach and six through, LAW-LAWLESSNESS.

coach'-house''. Place for a coach. CONTENTS-RECEIVER.

coach'-man''. A driver. MANAGER, WAYFARER-SEAFARER.

co''-ac'-tion. Joint action. COERCION.

co''-ac'-tive. Acting together. COERCION.

co-ad'-ju-tan-cy. Cooperation. ANTAGONISM-CONCURRENCE, OBSTRUCTION-HELP.

co-ad'-ju-tant. Cooperating. ANTAGONISM-CONCURRENCE.

co''-ad-ju'-tor. An assistant. ANTAGONIST-ASSISTANT.

co''-ad-ju'-trix. Female assistant. ANTAGONIST-ASSISTANT.

co-ad'-ju-van-cy. Cooperation. ANTAGONISM-CONCURRENCE.

co-a'-gen-cy. Coworking. ANTAGONISM-CONCURRENCE, COOPERATION-OPPOSITION.

co-ag'-u-late. To curdle. CHEMISTRY, SOLIDITY-RARITY.

co-ag''-u-la'-tion. A curdling. SOLIDITY-RARITY; coagulation filters, CHEMISTRY.

co-ag'-u-lum. A clot. SOLIDITY-RARITY.

coal. A combustible material. COMBUSTIBLE, WHITENESS-BLACKNESS; call over the coals, APPROVAL-DISAPPROVAL; carry coals, SELFRESPECT-HUMBLENESS; carry coals to Newcastle, EXCESS-LACK, USEFULNESS-USELESSNESS; coal black, WHITENESS-BLACKNESS.

co''-a-lesce'. To fuse. COMPOSITION-RESOLUTION, SAMENESS-CONTRAST.

co''-a-les'-cence. Union. SAMENESS-CONTRAST.

co''-a-les'-cent. United. SAMENESS-CONTRAST.

co''-a-les'-cing. Uniting. SAMENESS-CONTRAST.

coal'-heav''-er. One who loads coal. Work like a coal-heaver, TOIL-RELAXATION.

co''-a-li'-tion. A combination. ANTAGONISM-CONCURRENCE, ASSOCIATION.

co''-ap-ta'-tion. Adjustment. HARMONY-DISCORD.

co-arc'-tate. To crowd. ENLARGEMENT-DIMINUTION.

co''-arc-ta'-tion. Stricture. BREADTH-NARROWNESS, ENLARGEMENT-DIMINUTION, INCREASE-DECREASE, OBSTRUCTION-HELP, RELEASE-RESTRAINT.

coarse. Indelicate; crude; vulgar; harsh in sound. CACOPHONY, CLEANNESS-FILTHINESS, PREPARATION-NONPREPARATION, PURITY-IMPURITY, TASTE-VULGARITY.

coarse'-grained''. Made of coarse particles. TEXTURE.

coarse'-ness. The state of being coarse. TASTE-VULGARITY.

coast. The seashore; to sail along. BORDER, OCEAN-LAND, TRAVELING-NAVIGATION.

coast'-guard''. Customs agents. GUARD-PRISONER.

coast'-ing. Sailing. TRAVELING-SAILING.

coat. A garment; an outside layer. COVER-LINING, DRESS-UNDRESS, LAMINA-FIBER; coat of arms, SIGN; coat of mail, ATTACK-DEFENSE; cut coat according to cloth, GENEROSITY-FRUGALITY, RECKLESSNESS-CAUTION, SKILL-UNSKILFULNESS.

coat'-ing. Covering. COVER-LINING, inner coating, COVER-LINING.

coax. To beg; to soothe. ADULATION-DISPARAGEMENT, BLANDISHMENT, MOTIVE-CAPRICE.

cob. A short-legged horse; to beat on the buttocks. CONVEYER, RECOMPENSE-PUNITION.

co'-balt. A steel-gray element. BLUENESS-ORANGE, CHEMISTRY.

cob'-ble. To repair. RENOVATION-RELAPSE.

cob'-bler. One who cobbles. DRESS-UNDRESS, RENOVATION-RELAPSE.

cob'-le. A fishing-boat. CONVEYANCE-VESSEL.

co'-bra. A venomous snake. BENEFACTOR-EVILDOER.

cob'-web''. A network of fine threads; a snare; anything flimsy. CLEANNESS-FILTHINESS, CONSEQUENCE-INSIGNIFICANCE, HEAVINESS-LIGHTNESS, TRUTHFULNESS-FRAUD; cobweb of antiquity, NOVELTY-ANTIQUITY; cobwebs of sophistry, RATIOCINATION-CASUISTRY.

coch'-i-neal. A dyestuff. REDNESS-GREENNESS.

cock. A male domestic fowl. FAUNA-FLORA, MALE-FEMALE; cock and bull story, TRUTHFULNESS-FABRICATION; cock boat, CONVEYANCE-VESSEL; cock of the roost, CHIEF-UNDERLING, GOODNESS-BADNESS; cock the eye, SIGHT-BLINDNESS; cock up, CONVEXITY-CONCAVITY, ERECTNESS-FLATNESS; game cock, BRAVERY-COWARDICE.

cock-ade'. A knot of ribbon. SIGN, TITLE.

cock'-a-hoop''. Elated; on a high horse. BRAGGING, LIGHTHEARTEDNESS-DEJECTION.

cock'-a-trice. A serpent. BENEFACTOR-EVILDOER, CONVENTIONALITY-UNCONVENTIONALITY, GOOD MAN-BAD MAN, GULL-DECEIVER, SIGHT-BLINDNESS.

cock'-crow''. Early morn. MORNING-EVENING.

cock'-er. To coddle; to fold up. BLANDISHMENT, PLICATURE.

Cock'-er. English teacher. SCHOOL; according to Cocker, CONVENTIONALITY-UNCONVENTIONALITY.

cock'-le. To wrinkle; wheedle. BLANDISHMENT, PLICATURE; cockles of one's heart, AFFECTIONS.

cock'-le-shell''. A small boat. CONVEYANCE-VESSEL.

cock'-loft''. A high loft. CONTENTS-RECEIVER.

cock'-ney. A foolish person; a low-bred person. CITY, GENTILITY-DEMOCRACY.

cock'-pit. A ring; a place for wounded. CONTENTS-RECEIVER, COUNCIL, LISTS.

cock'-shut. Twilight. DIMNESS.

cock'-spar''-row. Male sparrow. GREATNESS-LITTLENESS.

cock'-sure. Quite certain. FAITH-MISGIVING.

cock'-swain. Same as coxswain. WAYFARER-SEAFARER.

cock'-tail''. An iced drink made of spirits. NUTRIMENT-EXCRETION.

co'-coa. A beverage or food. NUTRIMENT-EXCRETION.

co-coon'. A case spun by the silk-worm before leaving its larva state. INFANT-VETERAN.

cocotte [F.] (co-cot'). A lewd woman. PURITY-RAKE.

coc'-tion. A boiling. HEATING-COOLING.

Co-cy'-tus. A river of Hades. HEAVEN-HELL.

cod. A pod. COVER-LINING.

cod'-dle. To pamper. BLANDISHMENT; coddle oneself, UNSELFISHNESS-SELFISHNESS.

code. A system of rules of conduct. LAW-LAWLESSNESS, PRECEPT.

co'-dex. A manuscript. MISSIVE-PUBLICATION.

codg'-er. A miserly man. EXTRAVAGANCE-AVARICE.

cod'-i-cil. A supplement. PREDECESSOR-CONTINUATION, SECURITY.

cod″-i-fi-ca′-tion. Collection. Law-Lawlessness.

cod′-i-fy. To systematize. Law-Lawlessness.

cod′-ling. A young cod. Infant-Veteran.

cœ′-cum. Same as cæcum. Aperture-Closure.

co″-ef-fi′-cien-cy. Cooperation. Antagonism-Concurrence, Solitude-Company.

co″-ef-fi′-cient. Acting together; a mathematical term. Antagonism-Concurrence, Number, Solitude-Company.

Cœ′-lebs. A bachelor desirous of marrying [Hannah More's *Cælebs in Search of a Wife*]. Matrimony-Celibacy.

co-emp′-tion. A buying. Buying-Sale.

co″-e′-qual. Of same rank. Equality-Inequality.

co-erce′. To compel. Coercion, Harshness-Mildness, Release-Restraint.

co-er′-cion. Constraint. Coercion, Harshness-Mildness, Release-Restraint.

COERCION.

Argumentum baculinum [L.]. Appeal to force; club law.

Brute force. Physical force.

Club law. Lynch law; anarchy.

Coaction. An impelling force.

Coercion. Act of compelling by authority and power.

Compulsion. The act of restraining the will or action of another.

Conscription. A compulsory enrolment of men for military or naval service.

Constraint. Any power, moral or physical, that compels to do or prevents the doing of some act.

Duress. Pressure; restraint of liberty.

Enforcement. Compulsion to yield obedience.

Force. Power; constraint.

Force majeure [F.]. Superior force.

Hobson's choice. A choice without an alternative.

Le droit du plus fort [F.]. The right of superior strength.

Main force. Violent effort.

Martial law. A law instituted for the carrying on of war.

Necessity, etc. See Volition-Obligation.

Physical force. Sheer bodily strength.

Press. Force; compulsion.

Restraint, etc. See Release-Restraint.

The sword. The force of weapons.

Ultima ratio [L.]. The last argument.

Coercion—*Verbs.*

Bind. To restrain.

Coerce. To dominate by advantage and authority.

Compel. To force to yield.

Constrain. Influence to do or not to do.

Drag into. To induce unwillingly.

Dragoon. To compel submission by violent measures.

Drive. To compel to move on.

Enforce. To constrain.

Extort. To wring from by force.

Force. To compel to do.

Insist upon. To demand authoritatively.

Make. To force to comply.

Necessitate. To make unavoidable, indispensable.

Oblige. To be duty bound.

Press. Coerce; compel.

Require. Demand.

Restrain, etc. See Release-Restraint.

Tax. To burden.

Coercion—*Verbal Expressions.*

Bind over, to put under bonds to do something; **cram down the throat**; **drag into**; **force down the throat**; **force upon,** to cause to accept; **insist upon**; **make a point of,** to attach special importance to; **pin down,** to hold in subjection; **put down,** force to give in; **put in force**; **put on the screw**; **say it must be done**; **take no denial,** to allow no refusal; **thrust down the throat**; **tie down,** to enslave; **turn on the screw,** to force obedience; **wring from,** to extort.

Coercion—*Adjectives.*

Coactive. Restrictive; constraining.

Coercive. Intended to coerce.

Compelled, etc. See *Verbs.*

Compelling, etc. See *Verbs.*

Compulsory. By force or constraint.

Compulsatory. Operating with force.

Forcible. Powerful; effective.

Inexorable, etc. See Harshness.

Irresistible, etc. See Volition-Obligation.

Obligatory. Binding in law or duty.

Peremptory. Decisive; compulsory.

Pulsive. Coercive.

Stringent. Binding strongly.

Coercion—*Adjective Expressions.*

Fain to, reluctantly willing; **not to be trifled with.**

Coercion—*Adverbial Expressions.*

Against one's will; **at the point of the bayonet**; **at the point of the sword**; **by a strong arm**; **by force** (see *Nouns*); **by force of arms**; **by stress of circumstances**; **by stress of weather**; **forcibly, powerfully**; **in spite of one's teeth**; *nolens volens* [L.], willingly or unwillingly (see Volition-Obligation); **on compulsion**; **perforce, by force**; **under press of**; **under protest**; **under the lash**; *vi et armis* [L.], by force and arms.

co-er′-cive. Compelling. Coercion, Harshness-Mildness.

co″-e-ta′-ne-an. A person of the same age as another. Coexistence.

co″-e-ta′-ne-ous. Of equal age. Coexistence.

co″-e-ter′-nal. Equally eternal. Coexistence, Eternity-Instantaneity.

cœur, à contre [F.] (cur, a con′tr). Against the grain. Readiness-Reluctance.

co-e′-val. Of same age. Coexistence.

co-e′-vous. Coeval. Coexistence.

co″-ex-ist′. To exist together. Coexistence, Interspace-Contact, Solitude-Contact.

co″-ex-ist′-ence. Concurrent existence. Coexistence, Entity-Nonentity, Interspace-Contact.

COEXISTENCE.

Coetanean. A person of the same age as another.

Coexistence. Existence at the same time.

Coincidence. The quality of happening at the same time.

Concomitance. Having the quality of accompanying or attending.

Concurrence. Agreement in opinion.

Contemporary. A person living at the same time.

Interim. A time between acts or periods.

Isochronism. The property of occurring at equal intervals of time.

Simultaneousness, etc. See *Adjectives.*

Synchronism. The simultaneity of two events in history.

Unity of time. The law of Aristotle that the supposed time of the action of a play should not exceed the actual time of performance.

Coexistence—*Verbs.*

Accompany. To go with, as associated, incidental, or concomitant.

Coexist. To exist at the same time.

Concur. To agree in opinion.

Synchronize. To make agree in time.

Coexistence—*Verbal Expressions.*

Go hand in hand, to coincide; **keep pace with,** to make equal progress with.

Coexistence—*Adjectives.*

Coetaneous. Of the same age.

Coeternal. Equally eternal.

Coeval. }
Coevous. } Existing from the same time.

Coexisting. To exist at the same time.

Coincident. Happening at the same time.

Concomitant. Accompanying or attending.

Concurrent. Agreeing in opinion.

Contemporaneous. }
Contemporary. } Living at the same time.

Isochronous. Occurring at equal intervals of time.

Simultaneous. Occurring at exactly the same time, as two sounds.

Synchronal. }
Synchronical. }
Synchronistical. } Pertaining to events of the same date.
Synchronous. }

COEXISTENCE—*Adverbs.*

Meanwhile. In the intervening time.
Simultaneously. See *Adjectives.*
Together. At the same time.

COEXISTENCE—*Adverbial Expressions.*

As soon as; at the same time; at the very moment; during the same time; in the interim; in the same breath; just as; *pari passu* [L.], **together, with equal pace.**

co″-ex-ist′-ing. Of the same period of time. COEXIST-ENCE.

co″-ex-ten′-sion. A being coextensive. EQUALITY-INEQUALITY, PARALLELISM-INCLINATION, PROPORTION-DEFORMITY,

co″-ex-ten′-sive. Having the same limits. PARALLELISM-INCLINATION.

cof′-fee. A black bean. NUTRIMENT-EXCRETION.

cof′-fee-house″. A house for coffee. DWELLER-HABITATION.

cof′-fer. A strong box for money. CONTENTS-RECEIVER, STORE, TREASURY,

cof′-fer-dam″. A water-tight enclosure sunk in a stream to expose the bottom. INCLUSION-OMISSION.

cof′-fin. Case for a corpse. LIFE-FUNERAL; **add a nail to one's coffin,** PLEASURABLENESS-PAINFULNESS.

cog. A rowboat; a trick; a projecting tooth; to cheat. ADULATION-DISPARAGEMENT, CONVEYANCE-VESSEL, SHARPNESS-BLUNTNESS, TRUTHFULNESS-FRAUD.

co′-gen-cy. Moral or logical force. MIGHT-IMPOTENCE.

co′-gent. Convincing. MIGHT-IMPOTENCE; **cogent reasoning,** RATIOCINATION-CASUISTRY.

cog′-ger-y. Flattery. TRUTHFULNESS-FRAUD.

cog′-i-tate. To meditate. REFLECTION-VACANCY.

cog″-i-ta′-tion. Reflection. REFLECTION-VACANCY.

cog′-i-ta-tive fac′-ul-ties. The mind. RATIOCINATION-CASUISTRY.

cogito, ergo sum [L.] (coj′-i-to, er-go sum). I think, therefore I am. ENTITY-NONENTITY.

cog′-nate. Allied. CONNECTION-INDEPENDENCE, RELATIONSHIP.

cog-na′-tion. Relationship. CONNECTION-INDEPENDENCE, HARMONY-DISCORD.

cog-ni′-tion. The act of knowing. KNOWLEDGE-IGNORANCE.

cog′-ni-tive. Knowing. KNOWLEDGE-IGNORANCE.

cog′-ni-za-ble. Capable of being examined. KNOWLEDGE-IGNORANCE.

cog′-ni-zance. Apprehension. KNOWLEDGE-IGNORANCE; **take cognizance of,** HEED-DISREGARD, MIND-IMBECILITY.

cog-no′-men. A surname. NAME-MISNOMER.

cog-nom′-i-nal. Pertaining to a cognomen. NAME-MISNOMER.

cog-nom″-i-na′-tion. Surname. NAME-MISNOMER.

cognosca occasionem [L.] (cog-nos′-ca oc-kê″-zi-o′-nem). Know the opportunity. OPPORTUNENESS-UNSUITABLENESS.

cog-nos′-cence. Knowledge. KNOWLEDGE-IGNORANCE.

cog-nos′-ci-ble. Knowable. KNOWLEDGE-IGNORANCE.

co-hab″-i-ta′-tion. Dwelling together. ESTABLISHMENT-REMOVAL, MATRIMONY-CELIBACY.

co′-heir. Joint heir. PARTICIPATION.

co-her′-ence. Conjunction. COHESION-LOOSENESS, UNION-DISUNION.

co-her′-ent. Sticking together. SOLIDITY-RARITY.

co-he′-sion. A holding together. COHESION-LOOSENESS.

COHESION—LOOSENESS.

Accretion. Increase by external additions.
Adherence. Attachment in a moral sense.
Adhesion. Attachment in a physical sense, usually of unlike substances.
Adhesiveness. The condition of being adhesive.
Agglomeration. Act of forming a mass by clinging together.
Agglutination. The state of being united by glue or other tenacious substance; a similar union of the elements of words.
Aggregation. Act of collecting together.
Cementation. The act of uniting or causing to adhere by the introduction of a third substance.
Coherence. Unification of the parts of the same body.
Cohesion. The force uniting like molecules.
Cohesiveness. The state of clinging together.
Concretion. Act of forming a mass from particles.
Conglomerate. A union of heterogeneous parts.
Conglomeration. Act of accumulating.
Conglutination. A union by means of some sticky substance.
Consolidation. Act of uniting.
Inseparability. The condition of being incapable of division.
Inseparableness. Same as INSEPARABILITY.
Set. Act of becoming fixed together.
Soldering. The process of uniting by means of a fusible alloy.
Sticking, Gluing, etc. See *Verbs.*
Stickiness, etc. See VISCIDITY.
Tenacity. Persistency in sticking together.
Toughness. The quality of greatly resisting division or fracture.

COHESION—*Denotations.*

Bur. A prickly seed vessel which clings to clothing, fur, or wool.
Concrete. A hardened mixture.
Remora. A fish which clings to other fish or floating bodies.

COHESION—*Verbs.*

Adhere. To cling together. See ADHESION.
Agglomerate. To gather into a mass.
Agglutinate. To cause to stick together.
Cake. To shape into a hardened mass.
Cement. To unite firmly.
Clasp. To fasten together as with a hook or buckle.
Cleave. To hold together.
Cling. To hold on firmly.

Disjunction, etc. See UNION-DISUNION.
Freedom. The state of being unbound.
Immiscibility. Incapability of being mixed or fused.
Incoherence. } Absence of connection.
Incohesion. }
Laxity. The state or quality of being loose or disconnected.
Looseness, etc. See *Adjectives.*
Loosening, etc; See *Verbs.*
Non-adhesion. See *Adjectives.*
Relaxation. The state of being loose.
Slackening, etc. See *Verbs.*
Slackness, etc. See *Verbs.*

LOOSENESS—*Figurative Noun.*

Rope of sand. Worthless attachment.

LOOSENESS—*Verbs.*

Detach. See UNION-DISUNION.
Loosen. To make less tight, firm, or compact.
Relax. To make loose.
Slacken. To reduce tension or to deprive of cohesion.
Unglue, etc. See COHESION.

LOOSENESS—*Verbal Expressions.*

Make loose, etc.; make slack, etc. (see *Adjectives*).

LOOSENESS—*Adjectives.*

Detached. Unconnected.
Disheveled. Loosely disordered.
Flapping. Waving loosely.
Immiscible. Not capable of being mixed.
Incoherent. Not attached.
Lax. Not in a close or firm state.
Loose. Unbound.
Non-adhesive. Not sticking.
Relaxed. In a loosened condition.
Segregated. Separated.
Slack. Loose.
Streaming. Hanging loosely.
Uncombined, etc. See COMPOSITION.
Unconsolidated, etc. See SOLIDITY.

LOOSENESS—*Adjective Expression.*

Like grains of sand.

COHESION—Verbs—*Continued.*

Cohere. To stick together. See COHESION.
Conglutinate. To unite by the intervention of some sticky substance.
Consolidate, etc. See SOLIDITY.
Glue. To fasten by means of a sticky substance.
Gum. To smear with a pasty substance.
Hold. To retain closely.

Hug. To embrace closely.
Lute. To seal up crevices with a soft adhesive mixture.
Paste. To stick with an adhesive compound.
Solder. To unite by means of a fusible alloy.
Stick. To cause to cleave by means of paste.
Weld. To unite by pressure.

COHESION—*Verbal Expressions.*

Adhere like a remora; adhere like Dejanira's shirt; cling like a bur; cling like ivy; close with, to join in action; grow together; hang together; hold fast; stick close; stick like a leech; stick like wax; take hold of; twine round, etc. (see UNION).

COHESION—*Adjectives.*

Adhering. Sticking to.
Adhesive. Tending to cling.
Clinging, etc. See *Verbs.*
Cohering, etc. See *Verbs.*
Cohesive. Tending to cohere in homogeneous bodies.
Compact. Closely joined.
Inextricable. Incapable of being disunited.
Infrangible. Incapable of being broken.

Inseparable. Not capable of being disjoined.
Sessile. Closely attached.
Sticky, etc. See VISCIDITY.
Tenacious. Holding fast.
Tough. Not easily parted or broken.
United. Made into one.
Unseparated. Not parted.

co-he′-sive. Belonging to cohesion. COHESION-LOOSENESS, SOLIDITY-RARITY.
co-he′-sive-ness. Stickiness. COHESION-LOOSENESS.
co-hib′-it. Restrain. LEAVE-PROHIBITION, RELEASE-RESTRAINT.
co-hi-bi′-tion. Restraint. MOTIVE-DEHORTATION.
co-hib′-i-tive. Restraining. RELEASE-RESTRAINT.
co″-ho-ba′-tion. Returning to a still. ESTABLISHMENT-REMOVAL, MATRIMONY-CELIBACY.
co′-hort. A company of soldiers. BELLIGERENT.
cohue [F.] (co-ü′). A crowd. GATHERING-SCATTERING.
coif. A hood. DRESS-UNDRESS.
coif′-fure. A head-dress. DRESS-UNDRESS.
coil. A succession of rings. CIRCLE-WINDING, CIRCUITION, DIFFICULTY-FACILITY, REGULARITY-IRREGULARITY; shuffle off this mortal coil, LIFE-DEATH.
coiled. Wound around. CIRCLE-WINDING.
coin. To fabricate; to invent; money. CREATION-DESTRUCTION, FANCY, MONEY; **coin money,** GAIN-LOSS; **coin words,** WORD-NEOLOGY.
coin′-age. Making of coins. CREATION-DESTRUCTION.
co″-in-cide′. To agree with; be the same as. ASSENT-DISSENT, CONTENTS-RECEIVER, SAMENESS-CONTRAST.
co-in′-ci-dence. Agreement. ASSENT-DISSENT, COEXTENSIVE, INTERSPACE-CONTACT, SAMENESS-CONTRAST.
co-in′-ci-dent. Agreeing. SAMENESS-CONTRAST.
co″-in-ci′-ding. Agreeing. SAMENESS-CONTRAST.
coin′-er. A counterfeiter. ROBBER.
cois′-tril. A knight's groom. BRAVERY-COWARDICE.
co-ju′-ror. A compurgator. LITIGATION, TRUTHFULNESS-FALSEHOOD.
coke. Heated coal. COMBUSTIBLE, HEATING-COOLING.
col′-an-der. A perforated vessel. APERTURE-CLOSURE.
col′-a-ture. Substance strained. CLEANNESS-FILTHINESS.
cold. Without heat; chilled; indifferent; weak to the senses. AMITY-HOSTILITY, BLUENESS-ORANGE COLOR-ACHROMATISM, FORCE-WEAKNESS, HEAT-COLD, UNCONCERN; **cold comfort,** CONTENTEDNESS-DISCONTENTMENT; **cold-hearted,** AMITY-HOSTILITY, CHARITABLENESS-MALEVOLENCE, SENSITIVENESS-APATHY; **cold shoulder,** POLITENESS-IMPOLITENESS, REGARD-SCORN; **cold steel,** WEAPON; **cold sweat,** SANGUINENESS-TIMIDITY; **cold water cure,** REMEDY-BANE; **in cold blood,** PREDETERMINATION-IMPULSE, PURPOSE-LUCK, SENSITIVENESS-APATHY, UNCONCERN; **throw cold water upon,** MOTIVE-CAPRICE, OBSTRUCTION-HELP, WITTINESS-DULNESS.
cold′-heart″-ed. Unsympathetic. CHARITABLENESS-MALEVOLENCE, FAVORITE-ANGER, SENSITIVENESS-APATHY.
cold′-ly. In a cold manner. HEAT-COLD.

cold′-ness. State of being cold. HEAT-COLD, UNCONCERN.
Col″-i-se′-um. Amphitheater of Rome. [" While stands the Coliseum, Rome shall stand." Byron, *Childe Harold,* iv, 145.] LISTS.
col-lab′-o-ra″-tor. One who is associated. ANTAGONIST-ASSISTANT.
col-lapse′. Extreme prostration; failure. BETTERMENT-DETERIORATION, COMPLETION-NONCOMPLETION, ENLARGEMENT-DIMINUTION, MIGHT-IMPOTENCE, SUCCESS-FAILURE, TRANSCURSION-SHORTCOMING, WEARINESS-REFRESHMENT.
col′-lar. Any article of dress worn about neck; to seize. CIRCLE-WINDING, DRESS-UNDRESS, RELEASE-PRISON, TAKING-RESTITUTION; **slip the ˘ collar,** ESCAPE, RELEASE-RESTRAINT.
col-late′. To compare critically. COMPARISON.
col-lat′-er-al. Secondary; parallel. LATERALITY-CONTRAPOSITION, RELATIONSHIP; **collateral evidence,** EVIDENCE-COUNTEREVIDENCE.
col-la′-tion. Comparison. COMPARISON, NUTRIMENT-EXCRETION.
col′-league. An associate. ANTAGONISM-CONCURRENCE, ANTAGONIST-ASSISTANT, SOLITUDE-COMPANY.
col′-league-ship. Association. ANTAGONISM-CONCURRENCE.
col-lect′. To gather; to infer; to get control of; a short prayer. CLEARNESS-OBSCURITY, DECISION-MISJUDGMENT, DEVOTION-IDOLATRY, GAIN-LOSS, GATHERING-SCATTERING, STORE; **collect evidence,** EVIDENCE-COUNTEREVIDENCE; **collect knowledge,** EDUCATION-LEARNING; **collect one's thoughts,** REFLECTION-VACANCY.
col″-lec-ta′-ne-a. A miscellany DIGEST, GATHERING-SCATTERING.
col-lect′-ed. Composed. EXCITABILITY-INEXCITABILITY.
col-lec′-tion. A gathering. GATHERING-SCATTERING.
col-lect′-ive. Taken together. UNIVERSALITY-PARTICULARITY.
col-lect′-ive-ly. Relating to an assembly; aggregately. SOLITUDE-COMPANY, WHOLE-PART.
col-lect′-ive-ness. State of being collected. WHOLE-PART.
col-lect′-ive noun. A noun which denotes plurality without a plural form. NOUN.
col′-lege. An educational institution. SCHOOL; **go to college,** EDUCATION-LEARNING.
col-le′-gi-ate. Pertaining to a college. SCHOOL; **collegiate school,** SCHOOL.
col-lide′. To come together violently. IMPETUS-REACTION.

col'-lie. A shepherd dog. FAUNA-FLORA.

col'-lier. A vessel. CONVEYANCE-VESSEL.

col'-li-gate. To group together. GATHERING-SCATTERING.

col''-li-ga'-tion. A grouping. GATHERING-SCATTERING.

col''-li-ma'-tion. Making parallel. AIM-ABERRATION, ASTRONOMY.

col'-li-quate. To melt. LIQUEFACTION-VOLATILIZATION.

col''-li-qua'-tion. Act of melting. LIQUEFACTION-VOLATILIZATION.

col-liq'-ua-tive. Exhaustive. LIQUEFACTION-VOLATILIZATION.

col-liq''-ue-fac'-tion. Fusion. LIQUEFACTION-VOLATILIZATION.

col-li'-sion. Clash; opposition; encounter. ANTAGONISM - CONCURRENCE, COOPERATION - OPPOSITION, IMPETUS-REACTION, STRIFE-PEACE.

col'-lo-cate. To put together. GATHERING-SCATTERING, ORGANIZATION-DISORGANIZATION.

col''-lo-ca'-tion. A grouping together. ESTABLISHMENT-REMOVAL, GATHERING-SCATTERING, ORGANIZATION-DISORGANIZATION.

col''-lo-cu'-tion. Conference. CONVERSATION-MONOLOGUE.

col-logue'. To cajole. ADULATION-DISPARAGEMENT.

col'-lop. A morsel. WHOLE-PART.

col-lo'-qui-al. Conversational. CONVERSATION-MONOLOGUE, TROPE, WORD-NEOLOGY.

col-lo'-qui-al-ism. Colloquial expression. TROPE, WORD-NEOLOGY.

col'-lo-quy. Dialogue. CONVERSATION-MONOLOGUE.

col-lude'. To connive. ANTAGONISM-CONCURRENCE.

col-lu'-sion. A secret agreement. ANTAGONISM-CONCURRENCE, TRUTHFULNESS-FRAUD.

col-lu'-sive. Acting by collusion. TRUTHFULNESS-FALSEHOOD.

col-lu'-so-ry. Marked by fraud. TRUTHFULNESS-FALSEHOOD.

col''-lu-ta'-tion. A strife. STRIFE-PEACE.

col-lu'-vi-es. Filth. CLEANNESS-FILTHINESS.

col-lyr'-i-um. An eye-wash. REMEDY-BANE.

co'-lon. A punctuation-mark. DISCONTINUANCE-CONTINUANCE.

colo'-nel. An officer. CHIEF-UNDERLING.

col'-o-nist. A settler. DWELLER-HABITATION.

col''-o-ni-za'-tion. Settling. ESTABLISHMENT-REMOVAL.

col'-o-nize. To settle. ESTABLISHMENT-REMOVAL.

col''-on-nade'. A row of columns. CONTINUITY-INTERRUPTION, DWELLER-HABITATION.

col'-o-ny. A body of emigrants. DWELLER-HABITATION, ESTABLISHMENT-REMOVAL.

col'-o-phon. An ancient index. PREDECESSOR-CONTINUATION.

col'-or. Any hue; paint; pretense. COLOR-ACHROMATISM, GULL-HYPERBOLE, LIKELIHOOD-UNLIKELIHOOD, PAINTING, PRETEXT, SEEMING, TRUTHFULNESS-FALSEHOOD, WHITENESS-BLACKNESS; **all colors,** PERFUME-STENCH; **change colors,** SELFRESPECT-HUMBLENESS; **color blindness,** SIGHT-DIMSIGHTEDNESS; **color-sergeant,** CHIEF-UNDERLING; **color too highly,** GULL-HYPERBOLE; **color up,** REDNESS-GREENNESS, SELFRESPECT-HUMBLENESS; **give a color to,** LIKELIHOOD-UNLIKELIHOOD, MODIFICATION, MUTATION-PERMANENCE, TRUTHFULNESS-FALSEHOOD; **lend a color to,** JUSTIFICATION-CHARGE, LIKELIHOOD-UNLIKELIHOOD, PRETEXT; **man of color,** WHITENESS-BLACKNESS; **show in true color,** TRUTHFULNESS-FALSEHOOD.

COLOR—ACHROMATISM.

Broken color. A color made by a mixture of two or more pigments.

Cast. Tinge.

Color. A property depending on the relations of light to the eye, by which differences in the hues and tints are apprehended.

Coloration. Characteristic arrangement of colors.

Coloring. Combined effect of colors

Complementary color. One of two colors which when combined produce white light.

Complexion. General appearance or aspect.

Dye Hue, tinge.

Flush.}
Glow.} A heightened color; a redness.

Hue. Compound of one or more colors.

Keeping. Harmony.

Key. The prevailing effect, whether bright, dull, etc.

Livery. Characteristic color or outward appearance.

Local color. Natural color.

Positive color. A color distinct in itself.

Primary colors. The principal colors into which white light is separated by a prism.

Pure color. A strong, distinct color.

Secondary color. A color formed by mixing two primary pigments.

Shade. Relative luminosity of a color.

Tertiary color. A color produced by a primary and secondary pigment.

Three primaries. The colors red green, blue, by mixture of which any others can be made.

Tincture. Tint.

Tinge. A faint trace of one color mixed with another.

Tint. A faint color.

Tone. Degree of a color.

COLOR—Nouns of Cause.

Coloring matter. Anything used for coloring or dyeing.

Distemper. A pigment mixed with something soluble in water.

Dye. A fluid used for coloring.

Logwood. A tree from which a red dye is made.

Medium. A liquid vehicle, as oil.

Mordant. Substance used in fixing a dye.

Oil-paint Paint made by mixing a pigment with oil.

Paint. A pigment or coloring substance.

Absence of color. State of being colorless.

Achromatism.}
Decoloration.} State of being colorless.

Discoloration. State of having an unnatural color.

Etiolation. Process of blanching plants.

Paleness. Lack of intensity of color.

Pallidity.}
Pallor.} State of being abnormally pale.

ACHROMATISM—Denotations.

Black and white. Uncertainty of tint.

Monochrome. Painting in a single color.

Neutral tint. Blue or gray

ACHROMATISM—Verbs.

Achromatize. To free from color.

Become colorless. Lose color.

Blanch. To whiten permanently or temporarily.

Bleach. To whiten permanently.

Decolorize. To deprive of color.

Deprive of color. Bleach.

Etiolate. To blanch plants.

Fade. To grow pale or dull in color.

Fly. To fade or disappear.

Go. To leave; to become faint.

Lose color, etc. See COLOR.

Pale. To turn pale or wan.

Tarnish. To lessen or destroy the luster

Tone down. To lower, soften, or subdue the tone of.

Turn pale. To become wan or pallid

Wash out. Remove by the application of a liquid.

ACHROMATISM—Adjectives.

Achromatic. Free from color

Aplanatic. Freed from spherical aberration by two lenses

Ashy. Ash-colored.

Blond. Having a fair skin, light eyes, and fair hair.

Cadaverous. Deathly pale.

Cold. Bluish in tone or effect.

Colorless. Without color.

Dead. Lusterless; dull.

Dingy. Of a dusky color

COLOR—ACHROMATISM—*Continued.*

COLOR—Nouns of Cause—*Continued.*

Pigment. Coloring material.
Stain. A dye.
Wash. Preparation used in coating.

COLOR—*Scientific Terms.*

Chromatic dispersion. The separation of a ray of light into its colors by a prism.
Chromatics. The science of colors.
Prism. Transparent triangular solid used in refracting light.
Spectroscope. Instrument for analyzing the spectra of rays emitted by bodies.
Spectrum. Image of radiant energy in which parts are arranged according to their wave-length.
Spectrum analysis. Chemical analysis by means of the spectra of a substance.

COLOR—*Verbs.*

Bedizen. To adorn in tawdry splendor.
Color. To infuse color into.
Dye. To fix a color in a substance by soaking.
Emblazon. To adorn with armorial ensigns.
Grain. To paint or stain in imitation of grain.
Illuminate. To decorate with ornamental colored figures.
Imbue. To tinge or dye deeply.
Ingrain. To dye with any lasting color.
Paint, etc. To adorn with colors, etc. See PAINTING.
Tinct. To tinge slightly.
Tinge. To imbue with a faint trace of color.
Tint. To give a delicate hue to.
Stain. To color by the use of a dye or stain.
Wash. To spread flat color lightly and evenly upon a surface.

COLOR—*Adjectives.*

Bright. Of brilliant color.
Chromatic. Pertaining to color.
Colored. Infused with color; having color.
Colorific. Of or pertaining to the production or sensation of color.
Crude. Having inharmonious colors.
Deep. Of intense or dark hue.
Deep colored. Dark.
Discordant. Out of harmony.
Double-dyed. Dyed twice over.
Flaring. Shining out in glaring colors.
Flashy. }
Flaunting. } Gaudy.
Florid. Of a lively, reddish hue.
Fresh. Retaining vividness or distinctness.
Full-colored.
Gairish. Garish.
Garish. Displaying a gaudy effect.

ACHROMATISM—Adjectives—*Continued.*

Discolored. Changed in color.
Dull. Without luster.
Dun. Of a dull dark-brown color.
Faint. Indistinct in color.
Fair. Having light or clear color.
Ghastly. Having a death-like appearance.
Glassy. Transparent.
Hueless. Without shade of color.
Lack-luster. Wanting luster; dim.
Leaden. Having the color of lead.
Light-colored. Of a faint or pale shade of color.
Muddy. Clouded.
Pale. Lacking in color and freshness.
Pale as a corpse. }
Pale as a ghost. }
Pale as ashes. } Unnaturally pale.
Pale as a witch. }
Pale as death. }
Pale-faced. Having a pale face.
Pallid. Of a pale or wan appearance.
Sallow. Of an unhealthy yellowish color.
Tallow-faced. Having a tallowy complexion.
Uncolored, etc. See COLOR.
Wan. Pale, as from sickness or anxiety.
White, etc. Of the color of snow, etc. See WHITENESS.

COLOR—Adjectives—*Continued.*

Gaudy. Brilliant in color.
Gay. Brilliant in color or appearance.
Glaring. Emitting an excessively bright light.
Gorgeous. Conspicuous by splendor of colors.
Harmonious. Symmetrical.
High-colored. Having a strong, deep, or glaring color
Inharmonious. Unsymmetrical.
Intense. Having strength or marked contrast.
Mellow. Agreeable to the senses.
Pearly. Resembling pearls in color and luster.
Polychromatic. Exhibiting many colors.
Prismatic. Exhibiting rainbow tints.
Raw. Untempered or without tone.
Rich. Pleasing in color.
Showy. Gaudy.
Sweet. Agreeable to the eye.
Tinctorial. Of or pertaining to color or hue.
Tingent. Capable of tingeing.
Unfaded. Not dulled in tint or color.
Vivid. Having intense luminosity or high chroma.

---

col'-or-able. Plausible. LIKELIHOOD-UNLIKELIHOOD, TRUTHFULNESS-FRAUD.

Col''-o-ra'-do bee'-tle. Potato bug. BENEFACTOR-EVILDOER.

col''-or-a'-tion. The use of colors. COLOR-ACHROMATISM.

col'-or-ing. The general colors; appearance. COLOR-ACHROMATISM, GULL-HYPERBOLE, MEANING-JARGON, MODIFICATION, TRUTHFULNESS-FALSEHOOD; **coloring matter,** COLOR-ACHROMATISM; **false coloring,** INTERPRETATION-MISINTERPRETATION.

col'-or-less. Without color. COLOR-ACHROMATISM.

col'-ors. An ensign or flag. SIGN, TITLE; **false colors,** TRUTHFULNESS-FALSEHOOD, TRUTHFULNESS-FRAUD; **flying colors,** POMP, SOLEMNIZATION; **lower one's colors,** WELFARE-MISFORTUNE; **nail one's colors to the mast,** PERSISTENCE-WHIM; **show one's colors,** EXPOSURE-HIDINGPLACE, MANIFESTATION-LATENCY, SIGN; **true to one's colors,** UPRIGHTNESS-DISHONESTY.

co-los'-sal. Large. GREATNESS-LITTLENESS.

Col''-os-se'-um. A large theater. [Coliseum.] LISTS.

co-los'-sus. A large statue. GREATNESS-LITTLENESS, HEIGHT-LOWNESS.

col'-por''-teur. An agent. DEALER.

col'-staff. A cowlstaff. SUSPENSION-SUPPORT.

col'-um-bine. Dove-like. ACTING.

col''-u-mel'-la. A plant support. SUSPENSION-SUPPORT.

col'-umn. A shaft; a prop; a vertical space or row. ARCHITECTURE, BELLIGERENT, CONTINUITY-INTERRUPTION, HEIGHT-LOWNESS, MARK-OBLITERATION, ROUNDNESS, SUSPENSION-SUPPORT, TRAVELING-NAVIGATION, WRITING-PRINTING.

col'-um-nar. Like a column. ROUNDNESS.

co-lures'. Great circles of the celestial sphere. UNIVERSE.

co'-ma. A stupor. ACTIVITY-INDOLENCE, SENSITIVENESS-APATHY.

co'-ma-tose. Abnormally sleepy. ACTIVITY-INDOLENCE.

comb. An instrument for the hair. CLEANNESS-FILTHINESS, RECOMPENSE-PUNITION, SHARPNESS-BLUNTNESS.

com'-bat. A battle. FIGHTING-CONCILIATION, STRIFE-PEACE.

combat, hors de [F.] (con'-ba', or dc). Out of fighting condition. HEALTH-SICKNESS, USEFULNESS-USELESSNESS, WEARINESS-REFRESHMENT.

com'-bat-ant. A fighter. BELLIGERENT.

com'-bat-ive. Pugnacious. STRIFE-PEACE.

com'-bat-ive-ness. Tendency to fight. FIGHTING-CONCILIATION, STRIFE-PEACE.

combe. A valley. CONVEXITY-CONCAVITY.

com''-bi-na'-tion. A joining; a union. ANTAGONISM-CONCURRENCE, ASSOCIATION, COMPOSITION-RESOLUTION, INCLUSION-OMISSION, MIXTURE-HOMOGENEITY, NUMBER, UNION-DISUNION.

com-bine'. To compound; organization. ANTAGONISM-CONCURRENCE, COMPOSITION-RESOLUTION, LABOR-CAPITAL.

com-bined'. United. COMPOSITION-RESOLUTION.

com-bus'-ti-ble. Burnable. COMBUSTIBLE, HEATING-COOLING.

COMBUSTIBLE.

Anthracite. A hard mineral coal.
Bobbing. A fagot of brushwood.
Brand. A burning piece of wood.
Brimstone. Sulfur.
Carbon. A combustible element forming the greater part of coal, charcoal, etc.
Charcoal. Impure carbon prepared from vegetable and animal substances.
Coal. A black, solid combustible substance consisting mainly of carbon.
Coke. Mineral coal deprived of bitumen, sulfur, and volatile matter.
Combustible. A substance which is liable to take fire and burn.
Congreve. A rocket, carrying a case shot filled with combustible material.
Culm. Anthracite coal in small masses.
Fagot. A bundle of sticks used for fuel.
Fire-ball. A ball filled with powder or other combustible.
Fire-barrel. A cylinder for carrying combustibles on a fire-ship.
Fire-brand. A piece of burning wood.
Firewood. Wood used for fuel.
Firing. Fuel.
Fuse. } A combustible cord used for firing shells or for blasting.
Fusee. }
Incense. Material burned in religious rites.
Locofoco. A friction match.
Log. Wood used for fuel.
Lucifer. A friction match.
Match. A splint of wood dipped at one end in a substance easily ignited.
Oil. A variety of combustible liquid substances.
Peat. Decomposed vegetable matter used for fuel.
Port-fire. A case of strong paper filled with niter and sulfur.
Spill. A roll of paper, or split of wood used as a lamplighter.
Sulfur. A non-metallic combustible element.
Tinder. Something very inflammable used for kindling fire.
Torch. A fire-brand.
Touchwood. Wood so decayed as to serve for tinder.
Turf. Peat prepared for fuel.
Vesta. A wax friction match.
Vesuvian. A cigar lighter.
Wallsend. A kind of coal.
Wick. A braided cord used to draw up the oil in a lamp.

COMBUSTIBLE—*Associated Nouns.*

Cinder. Product of combustion.
Ingle. A flame.
Light. A product of combustion.
Linstock. A pointed fork to hold a match in firing a cannon.

COMBUSTIBLE—*Adjectives.*

Carbonaceous. Containing carbon; hence, combustible.
Combustible. Capable of being set on fire.
Inflammable. Highly combustible.

com-bus''-ti-bil'-i-ty. Inflammability. HEATING-COOLING.

com-bus'-tion. Disturbance. HEATING-COOLING.

come. To happen; to approach; to move toward. APPROACH-WITHDRAWAL, APPROVAL-DISAPPROVAL, ARRIVAL-DEPARTURE, LIGHTHEARTEDNESS-DEJECTION, OCCURRENCE-DESTINY; **come about,** BETTERMENT-DETERIORATION, OCCURRENCE-DESTINY; **come across,** ARRIVAL-DEPARTURE, DISCOVERY; **come after,** ANTECEDENCE-SEQUENCE, PRECEDENCE-SUCCESSION; **come amiss,** HARMONY-DISCORD, OPPORTUNENESS-UNSUIT-

ABLENESS, VARIANCE-ACCORD; **come and go,** VIBRATION; **come at one's call,** INSUBORDINATION-OBEDIENCE; **come back,** ADVANCE-RETROGRESSION; **come before,** ANTECEDENCE-SEQUENCE, PRECEDENCE-SUCCESSION; **come by,** GAIN-LOSS; **come down with,** SETTLEMENT-DEFAULT; **come first,** MAGNITUDE-SMALLNESS, PRECEDENCE-SUCCESSION; **come forth,** ENTRANCE-EXIT, OCCURRENCE-DESTINY, VISIBILITY-INVISIBILITY; **come forward,** ADVANCE-RETROGRESSION, POMP, PROFFER-REFUSAL; **come from,** CAUSE-EFFECT; **come in,** ARRIVAL-DEPARTURE, ENTRANCE-EXIT, GIVING-RECEIVING; **come in for,** GAIN-LOSS, HOLDING-EXEMPTION, PARTICIPATION, PROPERTY; **come into existence,** BEGINNING-END, ENTITY-NONENTITY, OCCURRENCE-DESTINY; **come into operation,** AGENCY; **come into the view,** ANTAGONISM-CONCURRENCE; **come into the world,** BEGINNING-END, LIFE-DEATH; **come into use,** HABIT-DESUETUDE; **come into view,** VISIBILITY-INVISIBILITY; **come near,** APPROACH-WITHDRAWAL; **come of,** CAUSE-EFFECT; **come of age,** MANHOOD; **come off,** ESCAPE, PRETEXT, OCCURRENCE-DESTINY, UNION-DISUNION; **come off well,** SUCCESS-FAILURE; **come on,** ADVANCE-RETROGRESSION, ATTACK-DEFENSE, DEFIANCE, FUTURE-PAST, OCCURRENCE-DESTINY, PRECEDENCE-SUCCESSION; **come out,** ACTING, EXPOSURE-HIDINGPLACE, PUBLICITY, VISIBILITY-INVISIBILITY; **come out of,** CAUSE-EFFECT, ENTRANCE-EXIT; **come out with,** EXPOSURE-HIDINGPLACE, PUBLICITY, SPEECH-INARTICULATENESS; **come over,** CONSENT, MOTIVE-CAPRICE, TRUTHFULNESS-FRAUD; **come round,** ASSENT-DISSENT, BIGOTRY-APOSTASY, CONSENT, CONVERSION-REVERSION, FIGHTING-CONCILIATION, MOTIVE-CAPRICE, PERIODICITY-IRREGULARITY, RENOVATION-RELAPSE; **come short of,** SUPREMACY-SUBORDINACY, TRANSCURSION-SHORTCOMING; **come to,** ARRIVAL-DEPARTURE, CAUSE-EFFECT, CONVERSION-REVERSION, EQUALITY-INEQUALITY, HOLDING-EXEMPTION, LIFE-DEATH, MONEY, NUMBERING, PRICE-DISCOUNT, RENOVATION-RELAPSE, WHOLE-PART; **come to a determination,** DETERMINATION-VACILLATION; **come to a head,** COMPLETION-NONCOMPLETION, ENTIRETY-DEFICIENCY, SUPREMACY-SUBORDINACY; **come to a stand,** DISCONTINUANCE-CONTINUANCE; **come together,** CONCENTRATION-RADIATION, GATHERING-SCATTERING; **come to hand,** GIVING-RECEIVING; **come to nothing,** FERTILITY-STERILITY, SUCCESS-FAILURE; **come to oneself,** RENOVATION-RELAPSE; **come to one's knowledge,** ENLIGHTENMENT-SECRECY, KNOWLEDGE-IGNORANCE; **come to one's senses,** SANENESS-LUNACY; **come to pass,** CONDITION-SITUATION, OCCURRENCE-DESTINY; **come to pieces,** UNION-DISUNION; **come to terms,** ASSENT-DISSENT, COMPOSITION, CONSENT, CONTRACT, FIGHTING-CONCILIATION, TERMS, YIELDING; **come to the front,** CONSEQUENCE-INSIGNIFICANCE, TRANSCURSION-SHORTCOMING; **come to the point,** HEED-DISREGARD, TERSENESS-PROLIXITY, UNIVERSALITY-PARTICULARITY; **come to the rescue,** RESCUE; **come to the same thing,** EQUALITY-INEQUALITY; **come under,** ADMISSION-EXCLUSION; **come upon,** ARRIVAL-DEPARTURE, DUENESS-UNDUENESS, EXPECTATION-SURPRISE, GAIN-LOSS; **come what may,** CERTAINTY-DOUBT; **cut and come again,** ENOUGH, RECURRENCE; **to come,** FUTURE-PAST, OCCURRENCE-DESTINY.

co-me'-di-an. A player of comedy. ACTING, SOCIETY-LAUGHINGSTOCK.

co-me''-di-et'-ta. A short comedy. ACTING.

com'-e-dy. An entertaining drama. ACTING, SOCIETY-LUDICROUSNESS.

come'-li-ness. Gracefulness. BEAUTY-UGLINESS.

come'-ly. Graceful. BEAUTY-UGLINESS.

com-es'-ti-ble. Edible. NUTRIMENT-EXCRETION.

com-es'-ti-bles. Edibles. NUTRIMENT-EXCRETION.

com'-et. A heavenly body. ASTRONOMY, UNIVERSE, WAYFARER-SEAFARER.

com'-fit. Confection. SWEETNESS-ACIDITY.

com'-fort. Freedom from pain or anxiety. ALLEVIATION-AGGRAVATION, CONTENTEDNESS-DISCONTENTMENT, PLEASURE-PAIN, SENSUALITY-SUFFERING; **give comfort,** ALLEVIATION-AGGRAVATION, CHARITABLENESS-MALEVOLENCE.

com'-fort-a-ble. Having comfort. PLEASURABLENESS-PAINFULNESS, PLEASURE - PAIN, SENSUALITY - SUFFERING.

Com'-fort-er. Holy Spirit. DIVINITY.

com'-fort-er. Quilt. DRESS-UNDRESS.

com'-fort-ing. Giving comfort. SENSUALITY-SUFFERING.

com'-fort-less. Without comfort. LIGHTHEARTEDNESS-DEJECTION, PLEASURABLENESS-PAINFULNESS.

com'-ic. Ludicrous. ACTING, SOCIETY-LUDICROUSNESS-WITNESS, WITTINESS-DULNESS.

com'-ic-al. Droll. SOCIETY-LUDICROUSNESS.

com''-i-cal-i'-ty. Mirth. SOCIETY-LUDICROUSNESS, TINESS-DULNESS.

com'-ing. Approaching. APPROACH-WITHDRAWAL, ARRIVAL-DEPARTURE, FUTURE-PAST, OCCURRENCE-DESTINY; **coming events,** PROPHECY; **coming time,** FUTURE-PAST.

comitia [L.] (co-mish'-i-α). An assembly. COUNCIL.

com'-i-ty. Good-will. POLITENESS-IMPOLITENESS.

com'-ma. A punctuation-mark. DISCONTINUANCE-CONTINUANCE.

com-mand'. Ruling power; range of outlook. HEIGHT-LOWNESS, HOLDING-EXEMPTION, ORDER, RULE-LICENSE; **at one's command,** HOLDING-EXEMPTION, INSUBORDINATION-OBEDIENCE, RULE-LICENSE; **command a view of,** SIGHT-BLINDNESS; **command belief,** FAITH-MISGIVING; **command of language,** FORCE-WEAKNESS, SPEECH-INARTICULATENESS, STYLE; **command of money,** AFFLUENCE-PENURY; **command one's passions,** VIRTUE-VICE; **command respect,** REGARD-DISRESPECT.

com''-man-dant'. One in command. CHIEF-UNDERLING.

com-mand'-er. A leader. CHIEF-UNDERLING, CONSEQUENCE-INSIGNIFICANCE, HEIGHT-LOWNESS, HOLDING-EXEMPTION, ORDER, RULE-LICENSE.

com-mand'-er-in-chief'. The head of the army. CHIEF-UNDERLING.

com-mand'-ing. Ordering. ORDER.

com-mas'-see. Arabian coin. VALUES.

comme deux gouttes d'eau [F.] (com dʋ gut do). Like two drops of water. LIKENESS-UNLIKENESS.

comme il faut [F.] (com il fo). As it should be. GENTILITY-DEMOCRACY, SOCIETY, TASTE-VULGARITY.

com-mem'-o-rate. To fix in memory. DELINEATION-CARICATURE, REMEMBRANCE-FORGETFULNESS, SOLEMNIZATION.

com-mem''-o-ra'-tion. Remembrance; observance. MARK-OBLITERATION, REMEMBRANCE-FORGETFULNESS, SOLEMNIZATION.

com-mem'-o-ra-tive. Serving to remember. SOLEMNIZATION.

com-mence'. To begin. BEGINNING-END.

com-mence'-ment. Beginning. BEGINNING-END.

commencement de la fin [F.] (co-man's-man'' de la fan·). Beginning of the end. BEGINNING-END, CREATION-DESTRUCTION.

com-mend'. To approve. APPROVAL-DISAPPROVAL; **commend the poisoned chalice,** TRUTHFULNESS-FALSEHOOD.

com-mend'-a-ble. Laudable. GOOD-EVIL, VIRTUE-VICE.

com''-men-da'-tion. Approbation. APPROVAL-DISAPPROVAL.

com-men''-su-ra-bil'-i-ty. Quality of being commensurable. HARMONY-DISCORD.

com-men'-su-ra-ble. Measurable. NUMBERING.

com-men'-su-rate. Commensurable. ENOUGH, HARMONY-DISCORD, NUMBERING.

com'-ment. A note. DECISION-MISJUDGMENT, INTERPRETATION - MISINTERPRETATION, RATIOCINATION - CASUISTRY.

com'-men-ta-ry. An exposition. ESSAY, INTERPRETATION-MISINTERPRETATION.

com'-men-ta'-tor. An annotator. DECISION-MISJUDGMENT, INTERPRETER, ESSAY.

com'-merce. Intercourse; a card-game. CONVERSATION-MONOLOGUE, ENTERTAINMENT-WEARINESS, EXCHANGE.

com-mer'-cial a-rith'-me-tic. Mercantile arithmetic. ACCOUNTS.

com''-mi-na'-tion. A denunciation. CHARITABLENESS-CURSE, CHARITABLENESS-MENACE.

com-min'-a-to-ry. Threatening. CHARITABLENESS-MENACE.

com-min'-gle. To blend. MIXTURE-HOMOGENEITY.

com'-mi-nute. To couch. FRIABILITY, UNION-DISUNION.

com-mis'-er-ate. To pity. COMPASSION-RUTHLESSNESS.

com-mis''-er-a'-tion. Compassion. BENEFACTOR-EVILDOER.

com''-mis-sa'-ri-at. Food department. NUTRIMENT-EXCRETION, PROVISION-WASTE.

com'-mis-sa-ry. A commissioner. CONSIGNEE.

com-mis'-sion. COMMISSION-ABROGATION, OCCUPATION, RULE-LICENSE; **commission of the peace,** JUDICATURE.

COMMISSION—ABROGATION.

Accession. A coming to by right of inheritance.

Agency. } The office or power of one authorized to act for another.
Agentship.

Appointment. A selection to fill some position of responsibility.

Assignment. An allotting to a particular person for a particular time.

Brevet. A commission from the government, granting some privilege.

Charge. A responsibility; an obligation.

Clerkship. Office of a clerk.

Commission. A trust; a charge.

Consignment. A sending of goods to another person at a different place for sale.

Coronation. The ceremony of investing a prince with the insignia of royalty.

Delegation. The appointment of persons to represent others.

Deputation. The appointment of a deputy or representative.

Enthronement. The act of enthroning.

Errand. A commission to carry another's message.

Abolishment. The act of doing away with, as of slavery

Abolition. An annulling.

Abrogation. Act of annulling by authority.

Annulment. The act of making void.

Cancel. The striking out of worthless printed matter.

Canceling, etc. See *Verbs.*

Congé [F.]. The act of taking leave.

Countermand. Revocation of a former order.

Counter-order. A contradictory order.

Deconsecration. A deprivation of sacredness.

Defeasance. The act of rendering null.

Demission. Resignation of an office.

Deposal. Removal from office or throne.

Deposition. Removal from office.

Dethronement. Removal from regal power.

Disendowment. A depriving of endowments.

Disestablishment. Act of overthrowing or unsettling.

Dismissal. A sending away.

Dissolution. The breaking up of a body into parts.

COMMISSION—ABROGATION—*Continued.*

Inauguration. The ceremony of inducting into public office.
Installation. The act or ceremony of inducting into office.
Investiture. The ceremony of presenting the symbols of some office.
Mission. The office of a messenger or agent.
Nomination. A naming for an office.
Ordination. The rite of admitting to the Christian ministry.
Procuration. The management of another's business.
Regency. } The office of regent; vicarious government.
Regentship. }
Return. A passing back into possession.
Vicegerency. The office of a delegated authority.

COMMISSION—*Nouns of Instrument.*

Charter. A written evidence of things done, or power granted.
Diploma. A writing conferring some privilege, honor, or power.
Exequatur. A written recognition by a government to a consul authorizing him to exercise his power in the place to which he is assigned.
Permit. A written license or permission.
Power of attorney. A written authority from one person empowering him to transact business for another.

COMMISSION—*Nouns of Agent.*

Consignee. A person to whom goods are consigned.
Deputy. One who acts for another.
Embassy. A person or persons sent as envoys.
Legation. A diplomatic minister and his suite.
Viceroy. A governor who rules in the name of a sovereign. See Chief.

COMMISSION—*Verbs.*

Accredit. To invest with authority
Appoint. To commission; to delegate.
Assign. To give a certain work to perform.
Authorize, etc. See Leave.
Be accredited. See Accredit.
Be commissioned. See Commission.
Bespeak. To arrange for beforehand.
Charge. To entrust; to commission.
Commission. To grant authority to act.
Commit. To put in charge of.
Commit to the hands of. Hand over to the care of.
Consign. To give to the care of.
Crown. To invest with regal powers.
Delegate. To empower; to authorize.
Depute. To appoint as assistant.
Employ. To have in service.
Empower. To give power to act.
Engage. To place under obligation.
Enlist. To secure the services of.
Enroll. To record as a member.
Entrust. To commit with confidence.
Hire. To give employment.
Inaugurate. To invest with an office.
Induct. To put formally into possession.
Install. The ceremony of taking office.
Intrust. To deliver in trust; to confide.
Invest. To clothe with authority.
Name. To appoint; to choose to supervise.
Nominate. To entitle.
Ordain. To set apart for an office.
Place over. } Given authority to.
Put in command. }
Represent. To act as proxy for another.
Return. To regain possession of.
Send out. To delegate.
Set over. To appoint.
Stand for. }
Stand in the place of. }
Stand in the shoes of. } Act as deputy for.
Stand in the stead of. }

COMMISSION—*Adjectives.*

Commissioned, etc. See *Verbs*

ABROGATION—Adjectives—*Continued from Column 2.*

Functus officio [L.]. Having performed his office or duty; hence, out of office.

ABROGATION—*Interjections.*

Away with! begone! get along with you! go about your business!

Nullification. Act of declaring null and void.
Recantation, etc. See Bigotry-Apostasy.
Repeal. An annulment.
Repudiation. The act of refusing to pay a legally contracted debt.
Rescission. The act of abrogating, rescinding.
Retractation. Act of withdrawing something advanced.
Revocation. A recalling.
Revokement. Act of recalling or repealing.

ABROGATION—*Verbs.*

Abolish. To do away with.
Abrogate. To repeal with authority.
Annul. To make void.
Be abrogated. See Abrogate.
Break. To sever relations.
Break off. To become separated by violence.
Brush away. To remove as by a brush.
Cancel. To mark out by cross lines, latticework.
Cast adrift. To let float at random.
Cast aside. To reject.
Cast away. To throw away.
Cast behind. To let perish.
Cast off. To free oneself from.
Cast out. To expel.
Cast out of doors. Expel from the house.
Countermand. To cancel; to recall.
Counter-order. To order in.
Declare null and void. Annul.
Deconsecrate. To secularize.
Depose. To deprive of powers.
Dethrone. To take away the throne.
Disannul. To render of no effect.
Disbar. To expel from the legal profession.
Disbench. To drive from the bench.
Discard. To turn down.
Discharge. To send away.
Disclaim, etc. See Assertion-Denial.
Disendow. To deprive of one's natural powers.
Disenthrone. To depose from sovereign authority.
Disestablish. To deprive of fixed state or condition.
Dismiss. To send away.
Dissolve. To separate a body into minute particles.
Divest oneself. To strip; to dispossess.
Do away with. Abrogate.
Get rid of, etc. See Admission-Expulsion.
Ignore. Refuse to recognize.
Nullify. To revoke; to render invalid.
Oust. To eject; to turn out.
Override. To suppress; to destroy.
Overrule. To control by superior power.
Quash. To set aside; annul.
Recall. To revoke.
Recant, etc. See Bigotry-Apostasy.
Receive its quietus. To be brought to silence.
Repeal. To revoke.
Repudiate. To renounce; to have nothing to do with.
Rescind. To abrogate.
Retract. To withdraw from; to take back
Reverse. To make void; to revoke.
Scatter to the winds. Dissolve.
Send about one's business. }
Send away. } Dismiss.
Send off. }
Set aside. To ignore.
Strike off the roll. Dismiss; disbar.
Sweep away. To put out of the way.
Throw overboard. } Get rid of.
Throw to the dogs. }
Turn adrift. Send off.
Turn aside. Move away.
Turn away. }
Turn off. }
Turn out. } Discharge
Turn out of doors. }
Uncrown. To take away the crown.
Unfrock. To deprive of priestly character.
Unsaddle. To take away the saddle; to disarm.
Unseat. To deprive of office.
Unthrone. Dethrone.

ABROGATION—*Adjectives.*

Abrogated, etc. See *Verbs.*

(*Continued on Column 1.*)

COMMISSION—RETIREMENT.

RETIREMENT.

Abdication. The act of giving up (as sovereign power) voluntarily.
Abjuration. The act of disavowing what one has had connection with.
Renunciation. The act of refusing to acknowledge longer.
Resignation. The act of formally giving back a trust.
Retirement. Withdrawal from active service.

RETIREMENT—*Verbs*.

Abjure. To disavow what one has had connection with.
Abrogate, etc See COMMISSION-ABROGATION.
Accept the stewardship of the Chiltern Hundreds. To effect a virtual resignation from the House of Commons.
Deny, etc. To refuse to give, etc. See ASSERTION-DENIAL.
Desert, etc. To forsake in violation of duty, etc. See QUEST-ABANDONMENT.
Disclaim. To deny ownership, **merit,** or pretension.
Forego. To refrain from doing or enjoying.
Get rid of, etc. See QUEST-ABANDONMENT.
Give up. To desist from; to abandon or surrender.

Lay down. To resign.
Renounce. To refuse to acknowledge any longer.
Resign. To give back a trust formally.
Retire. To withdraw from active service.
Retract. To declare to be false, as one's own teaching, accusation, etc.
Tender one's resignation. Offer a resignation.
Throw up. To relinquish, as a situation.
Throw up the cards. To quit; resign.
Vacate. To cease from filling or occupying.
Vacate one's seat. Retire from one's seat.
Wash one's hands of. To have nothing more to do with.

RETIREMENT—*Adjective*.

Abdicant. Pertaining to one who abdicates.

RETIREMENT—*Phrase*.

"Othello's occupation's gone." [Shakespeare, *Othello*, III, iii.]

---

com-mis″-sion-aire′. A messenger. CONSIGNEE, MESSENGER, REPRESENTATIVE.
com-mis′-sioned. Appointed. COMMISSION-ABROGATION.
com-mis′-sion-er. A governmental head. CONSIGNEE.
com′-mis-sure. A junction. UNION-DISUNION.
commis-voyageur [F.] (co-mī″-vwɑ-yɑ-zhur′). A commercial traveler. CONSIGNEE.
com-mit′. To pledge; **to** consign to another; to be guilty of. ACTION-PASSIVENESS, ENTERTAINMENT-WEARINESS, LITIGATION, RELEASE-RESTRAINT; **commit an absurdity,** SOCIETY-LUDICROUSNESS; **commit oneself,** ENGAGEMENT-RELEASE, SKILL-UNSKILFULNESS; **commit oneself to a course,** CHOICE-NEUTRALITY; **commit sin,** VIRTUE-VICE; **commit to memory,** REMEMBRANCE-FORGETFULNESS; **commit to prison,** RELEASE-RESTRAINT; **commit to the flames,** HEATING-COOLING; **commit to writing,** MARK-OBLITERATION.
com-mit′-tal. Warrant for imprisonment. LITIGATION.
com-mit′-tee. A person or persons appointed for a purpose. CONSIGNEE, PRESIDENT-MEMBER, SKILL-UNSKILFULNESS; **committee of the whole,** PRESIDENT-MEMBER.
com-mix′. To intermix. MIXTURE-HOMOGENEITY.
com-mix′-tion. Mixture. MIXTURE-HOMOGENEITY.
com-mix′-ture. Mixture. MIXTURE-HOMOGENEITY.
com-mode′. A washstand; a night-stool. CONTENTS-RECEIVER.
com-mo′-di-ous. Suitable. USEFULNESS-USELESSNESS.
com-mod′-i-ty. Articles. MERCHANDISE.
com′-mo-dore. A naval officer. CHIEF-UNDERLING.
com′-mon. Commonplace; land; universal; frequent or usual. ASTONISHMENT-EXPECTANCE, CONSEQUENCE-INSIGNIFICANCE, CONVENTIONALITY-UNCONVENTIONALITY, GENTILITY-DEMOCRACY, GULF-PLAIN, HABIT-DESUETUDE; **common consent,** ASSENT-DISSENT; **common course,** HABIT-DESUETUDE; **common herd,** GENTILITY-DEMOCRACY; **common law,** LAW-LAWLESSNESS, NOVELTY-ANTIQUITY; **common measure,** NUMBER; **common origin,** CAUSE-EFFECT; **common parlance,** SIMPLICITY-FLORIDNESS; **commonplace book,** DIGEST, MARK-OBLITERATION; **common saying,** ADAGE-NONSENSE; **common sense,** SAGACITY-INCAPACITY; **common sewer,** CLEANNESS-FILTHINESS; **common stock,** PARTICIPATION; **common weal,** GOOD-EVIL, HUMANITARIANISM-MISANTHROPY, HUMANITY, USEFULNESS-USELESSNESS; **in common,** CONNECTION-INDEPENDENCE, PARTICIPATION; **make common cause,** ANTAGONISM-CONCURRENCE; **right of common,** PROPERTY; **tenant in common,** PARTICIPATION.

com′-mon-al-ty. The lower classes. GENTILITY-DEMOCRACY, SUPREMACY-SUBORDINACY.
com′-mon-er. Any of the commonalty. GENTILITY-DEMOCRACY, PRESIDENT-MEMBER.
com′-mon-ly. Generally. FREQUENCY-RARITY.
com′-mon me′-ter. Kind of stanza. RHETORIC.
com′-mon noun. Name of each of a kind. NOUN.
com′-mon-place″. Trite. CONSEQUENCE-INSIGNIFICANCE, HABIT-DESUETUDE, KNOWLEDGE-IGNORANCE, MEDIUM, WITTINESS-DULNESS.
Com′-mon Pleas. Ordinary courts of justice. **Court of Common Pleas,** TRIBUNAL.
com′-mons. Rations. NUTRIMENT-EXCRETION.
com′-mon-wealth″. A state. HUMANITY.
com′-mon year. Year of 365 days. MEASURE.
com′-mor-ant. A dwelling. DWELLER-HABITATION.
com-mo′-tion. Excitement. AGITATION, VARIANCE-ACCORD.
Com′-mune of Pa′-ris. Communists of Paris, 1871; revolutionary committee of Paris, 1789–94. TYRANNY-ANARCHY.
com-mune′ with. To converse with. CONVERSATION-MONOLOGUE; **commune with oneself,** REFLECTION-VACANCY.
communibus annis [L.] (com-miu′-ni-bus an′-nis). Common years. MEDIUM.
com-mu′-ni-ca-ble. Capable of being imparted. GIVING-RECEIVING.
com-mu′-ni-cant. A partaker of the Lord's Supper. DEVOTION-IDOLATRY.
com-mu′-ni-cate. To make known; to be connected; to give or receive communion. CEREMONIAL, ENLIGHTENMENT-SECRECY, GIVING-RECEIVING.
com-mu″-ni-ca′-tion. A letter. ENLIGHTENMENT-SECRECY, GIVING-RECEIVING, TIDINGS-MYSTERY, UNION-DISUNION; **oral communication,** CONVERSATION-MONOLOGUE, SPEECH-INARTICULATENESS.
com-mu′-ni-ca-tive-ness. Tendency to talk. ENLIGHTENMENT-SECRECY.
com-mu′-ni-ca-to-ry. Talkative. ENLIGHTENMENT-SECRECY.
com-mu′-nion. Fellowship. ASSOCIATION, CEREMONIAL, FRIABILITY, PARTICIPATION; **communion table,** FANE; **hold communion table,** AMITY-HOSTILITY.
communiquer [F.] (co-mŭ-ni-kê′). To communicate. ENLIGHTENMENT-SECRECY.
com′-mu-nism. A sharing in common. HUMANITARIANISM-MISANTHROPY, MERCHANDISE, TYRANNY-ANARCHY.
com′-mu-nist. One advocating communism. BENEFACTOR-EVILDOER, HUMANITARIANISM-MISANTHROPY,

Insubordination-Obedience, Participation, Tyranny-Anarchy.

com″-mu-nis′-tic. Shared in common. Participation, Tyranny-Anarchy.

com-mu′-ni-ty. A body politic. Association, Humanity, Participation; **community at large,** Humanity; **community of good,** Participation.

com″-mu-ta′-tion. A substitution, a reduction. Commutation-Permutation, Composition, Exchange, Uniformity-Multiformity.

COMMUTATION—PERMUTATION.

Commutation. Change of one kind of payment, service, or penalty for another
Substitution. Replacement of one thing by another.
Supersession. Act of displacing.
Supplanting, etc. See *Verbs.*

COMMUTATION—*Denotations.*

Alternative. Something which may be done or taken instead of something else.
Changeling. An ill-favored child substituted by the fairies for a better favored one stolen.
Consideration. Something given in return for services.
Double. A person closely resembling another.
Dummy. An object resembling something else superficially.
Equivalent. An equal in value.
Jury-mast. A mast rigged in an emergency.
Locum tenens [L.]. Proxy.
Makeshift. Something used in an emergency.
Metonymy. A figure of speech in which an object is named by one of its attributes.
Palimpsest. A parchment which has been written upon twice.
Pis aller [F.]. Last or worst shift.
Price. That, usually money, given in exchange for an article.
Purchase-money. The price.
Quid pro quo [L.]. One thing for another.
Representative. A person who transacts business for another.
Scapegoat. A person made to bear the fault of another. [Bible.]
Shift. An expedient.
Stop-gap. A temporary fixture.
Substitute. A person or thing taking the place of another.
Succedaneum [L.]. A substitute.
Warming-pan. A person holding office until the intended occupant is ready to take it.

COMMUTATION—*Verbs.*

Borrow of Peter to pay Paul. To take from one needy person to give to another.
Change for. Exchange.
Commute. To change one kind or thing, as service, or payment, for another, usually less severe.
Compound for. To settle or discharge for less than the sum required.
Cut out. To supplant, as a rival.
Give place to. Yield to.
Make a shift with. Get along with.
Make way for. Stand aside.
Put in the place of. Replace.
Put up with. To endure submissively.
Redeem. To regain by paying a price.
Replace. To put in the place of one removed.
Serve as a substitute. Act for.
Stand in the shoes of. To be in someone's place.
Step into the shoes of. To go into someone's place.
Substitute. To put into the place of someone or something else, often temporarily.
Supersede. To succeed by appointment.
Supplant. To take the place of artfully or treacherously.
Supply the place of. Take the place of.
Take the place of. Supplant.

COMMUTATION—*Adjectives.*

Subdititious. Secretly put in the place of something else.
Substituted, etc. See *Verbs.*
Vicarious. Made or performed by substitution.

COMMUTATION—*Adverbs.*

Faute de mieux [F.]. For want of something better.
In lieu of.
In place of.
In stead of. } As a substitute for.
In the room of.
In the stead.

com-mute′. To give or accept something in place of something else. Composition.
com-mu′-tu-al. Reciprocal. Interdependence.

Barter, etc. See Exchange.
Castling. Exchange of relative position by a king and a castle as in chess.
Commutation. See Commutation.
Exchange. Act of giving one thing in return for another regarded as its equivalent.
Interchange. Act of putting each in the place of the other; mutual and reciprocal exchange.
Interchangeability. } Quality or state of being interchangeable.
Interchangeableness.
Intermutation. Mutual interchange of elements.
Permutation. Act of making a mutual transference.
Quid pro quo [L.]. One thing for another.
Reciprocation. Mutual giving and receiving.
Shuffling. Act of disordering, as at cards.
Tit for tat, etc. Like for like, etc. See Reprisal.
Transposition. Act of reversing the order of, or changing the place of.

PERMUTATION—*Denotations.*

Battledore and shuttlecock. A game played with a bat and a cork stuck with feathers.
Cross-fire. Lines of fire crossing each other.
Hocus-pocus. A juggler's trick. [Part of a juggler's formula, in sham Latin; imitative of the priests of Rome saying *hoc est corpus* (this is the body) over the bread of the eucharist. Early 17th century.]

PERMUTATION—*Verbs.*

Bandy. To exchange, as hot words or blows.
Change hands. Change clasps.
Commute. See Commutation.
Counter-change. To cause to change places, or take an opposite place.
Exchange. To make an exchange. See *Nouns.*
Give and take. Interchange.
Interchange. To make an interchange. See *Nouns.*
Permute. To mutually transfer.
Play at battledore and shuttlecock. } To make many interchanges.
Play at puss in the corner.
Reciprocate. To give and receive mutually, as feelings, favors, etc.
Retaliate, etc. See Reprisal.
Return the compliment. Do to another what he has done to you.
Shuffle. To disorder, as in cards.
Swap. To trade.
Transpose. To reverse the order of, or to change the place of.

PERMUTATION—*Adjectives.*

Communicate. Ready to impart or talk.
Interchangeable. Capable of interchange.
Interchanged, etc. See *Verbs.*
Intercurrent. Coming among or between.
Mutual. Pertaining to what naturally exists between two persons as regard or love.
Reciprocal. Given in return, under obligation, or as a result of.

PERMUTATION—*Adverbs.*

Backwards and forwards.
By turns. Alternately.
Each in his turn.
Every one in his turn.
In exchange.
Mutatis mutandis [L.]. Things necessary having been changed.
Turn and turn about. Alternately.
Vice versa [L.]. The terms being reversed.

com′-pact. A covenant; condensed; solid; made up. Cohesion-Looseness, Contract, Enlargement-Diminution, Enterprise, Length-Shortness,

Solidity-Rarity, Solitude-Company, Terseness-Prolixity, Union-Disunion.

com-pact'-ness. State of being compact. Enlargement-Diminution.

compages [L.] (com-pê'-jîz). A union of parts. Regularity-Irregularity, Texture.

com-pag''-i-na'-tion. A joining together. Union-Disunion.

com-pan'-ion. Comrade. Friend-Foe, Solitude-Company.

com-pan'-ion-a-ble. Sociable. Sociability-Privacy.

com-pan'-ion-ship. State of being a company. Duality, Sociability-Privacy, Solitude-Company.

com'-pa-ny. An acting class; fellowship; guests; a fighting body of men. Acting, Association, Belligerent, Gathering-Scattering, Sociability-Privacy, Solitude-Company; **bear company,** Solitude-Company; **in company with,** Solitude-Company.

com'-pa-ra-ble. Similar. Comparison, Connection-Independence.

com-par'-a-tive. Relative; expressing a greater or lesser degree of an adjective. Adjective, Comparison, Quantity Measure; **comparative anatomy,** Zoology-Botany; **comparative physiology,** Zoology-Botany.

com-pare'. To liken. Comparison; **compare notes,** Advice, Comparison.

com-par'-i-son. A comparing. Adjective, Comparison, Connection-Independence.

COMPARISON.

Allegory. An extended simile with the words of comparison left out.
Collation. A critical comparison.
Comparison. The act of examining so as to perceive similarity or dissimilarity.
Contrast. The opposition between things similar in some respects.
Identification. The act of declaring and recognizing sameness
Simile. A comparison introduced by such words of comparison, as *like*, *as*, etc.
Similitude. Likeness; simile.

COMPARISON—*Verbs.*

Balance. To weigh in the mind by comparison.
Collate. To compare critically.

Compare notes. To make comparisons.
Compare to. Consider a person or thing in connection with another which we think it resembles.
Compare with. Consider a person or thing in connection with another to note agreement or difference.
Confront. To compare.
Contrast. To place or represent in comparison.
Draw a parallel to. To produce something similar
Identify. To declare or recognize to be the same.
Institute a comparison. To begin to compare.
Parallel. To place in comparison with.
Parva componere magnis [L.]. To compare small things with great.
Pit against one another. To match in a contest.
Place side by side, etc. To parallel, etc. See Remoteness-Nearness.
Set against one another. To put in contrast.

COMPARISON—*Adjectives.*

Comparable. That may be compared.
Comparative. Pertaining to, resulting from, or making use of comparisons.
Compared with. Put into contrast with.
Metaphorical, etc. Figurative, etc. See Trope.

COMPARISON—*Adverbs.*

As compared with. Comparatively.
Relatively, etc. In a relative manner, etc. See Connection.

com''-par-ti'-tion. A division. Union-Disunion.

com-part'-ment. A separate section. Contents-Receiver, Extension-District, Extension-Place, Whole-Part.

com'-pass. Reach; circuit; an instrument; due limits. Completion-Noncompletion, Environment-Interposition, Extension-District, Management, Mensuration, Purpose-Luck; **box the compass,** Aim-Aberration, Revolution-Evolution; **compass about,** Confinement; **compass of thought,** Sagacity-Incapacity; **in a small compass,** Greatness-Littleness; **keep within compass,** Generosity-Frugality, Transcursion-Shortcoming, Turbulence-Calmness; **points of compass,** Laterality-Contraposition.

com-pas'-sion. Commiseration. Compassion-Ruthlessness, Harshness-Mildness; **objects of compassion,** Pleasure-Pain.

COMPASSION—RUTHLESSNESS.

Bowels. Tenderness; compassion.
Bowels of compassion. Compassion.
Charity. Universal benevolence; Christian love.
Clemency. Mildness of temper or disposition.
Commiseration. A feeling of pity or compassion for.
Compassion. A sense of sorrow for the unfortunate and distressed.
Fellow-feeling. Sympathy.
Forbearance. Abstaining from retaliation or revenge; indulgence towards offenders.
Grace. The unmerited love and favor of God.
Humanity. The state or quality of being humane.
Leniency, etc. The state of being lenient, etc. See Harshness-Mildness.
Long-suffering. Patience under offense.
Mercy. Kind or compassionate treatment of the unfortunate and helpless.
Pity. A feeling of sorrow or compassion awakened by the sufferings or distresses of others.
Quarter. Clemency shown to an enemy.
Ruth. Sorrow for the distress of others.
Sympathy. A fellow-feeling for others in their joys or sorrows.
Tenderness. The quality of being tender or kind.
Yearning. Affection; tenderness.

COMPASSION—*Noun of Agent.*

Sympathizer. One who sympathizes.

COMPASSION—*Noun of Place.*

Locus penitentiæ [L.]. The place of repentance.

Inclemency. Lack of mildness of temper, unmercifulness.
Malevolence, etc. Disposition to injure others, etc. See Charitableness-Malevolence.
Pitilessness. The state of being without pity.
Severity, etc. The state of being severe or strict; inclemency, etc. See Harshness.

RUTHLESSNESS—*Verbs.*

Give no quarter. See *Nouns.*
Have no mercy. See *Nouns.*
Shut the gates of mercy, etc. See Compassion.

RUTHLESSNESS—*Adjectives.*

Bowelless. Having no pity.
Cruel, etc. Disposed to inflict pain or suffering; merciless, etc. See Charitableness-Malevolence.
Harsh, etc. Crabbed; abusive, etc. See Harshness.
Inclement. Wanting in a kind and gentle temper.
Incompassionate. Destitute of pity or tenderness.
Inexorable. That cannot be moved by entreaty or prayer; unyielding.
Merciless. Without mercy; cruel.
Pitiless. Destitute of pity.
Ruthless. Void of ruth; pitiless.
Uncompassionate. Not compassionate.
Unmerciful. Not merciful.
Unpitying. Not pitying.
Unrelenting, etc. See Pardon-Vindictiveness.

COMPASSION—*Continued.*

COMPASSION—*Nouns of Cause.*

Argumentum ad misericordiam [L.]   An argument appealing to the sympathies.

Melting mood.   A compassionate frame of mind.

COMPASSION—*Verbs.*

Ask for mercy. See *Nouns.*
Beg one's life. Pray for quarter.
Be sorry for. Regret; **have pity.**
Commiserate. To sympathize with in distress or misery.
Compassionate. To have compassion for.
Condole, etc. To grieve with another in distress or sorrow, etc. See CONDOLENCE.
Cry for quarter, etc. See *Nouns.*
Deprecate. To desire or pray for the removal of a present evil.
Disarm. To render harmless.
Enter into the feelings of. Sympathize with.
Excite pity, etc. See *Nouns.*
Feel for. Sympathize with.
Forbear. To treat with indulgence.
Give a *coup de grâce.* To give a finishing stroke; to end the misery of.
Give quarter. See *Nouns.*
Have pity. See *Nouns.*
Kneel. To bend the knee, especially in the act of worship.
Melt. To become tender or gentle.

Melt the heart. Soften the heart.
Parcere subjectis [L.]. To spare the conquered.
Pity. To have compassion for, or sympathy with, one in misery or distress. [*Pity* is from *piety.*]
Propitiate. To appease or conciliate.
Put out of one's misery. To end the life of one who is suffering.
Raise pity. See *Nouns.*
Relax. To become less rigorous.
Relent. To feel compassion.
Show pity. See *Nouns.*
Soften. To mitigate; to assuage.
Supplicate, etc. To ask earnestly for, etc. See PETITION.
Sympathize. To have common feelings with others.
Take pity. See *Nouns.*
Thaw. Fig.: To grow gentle.
Touch. To affect with tender feeling.
Weep. To lament or bewail.
Wipe the tears. Console.
Yearn for. To have a great uneasiness of feeling for.

COMPASSION—*Adjectives.*

Clement. Gentle in temper and disposition.
Compassionate. Full of compassion.
Exorable. That may be moved by pity.
Forbearing. See *Verbs.*
Humane. Kind; compassionate.
Humanitarian, etc. Benevolent, etc. See HUMANITARIANISM.
Lenient, etc. Clement; merciful, etc. See HARSHNESS-MILDNESS.
Melting. See *Verbs.*
Merciful. Having mercy.
Pitiful. Having pity; tender-hearted.
Pitying, etc. See *Verbs.*

Ruthful. Tender; pitiful.
Soft. Tender; sympathetic.
Soft-hearted. Having tenderness of heart.
Sympathetic. Inclined to, or produced by, sympathy.
Tender. Mild; gentle.
Tender as a chicken. } Easily moved.
Tender-hearted. }
Touched. See *Verbs.*
Unhardened. Not hardened or morally depraved.
Weak. Clement.

COMPASSION—*Interjections.*

Cry you mercy!   **For pity's sake!**   **God help you!**   **Have mercy!**   **Mercy!**   **Poor dear!**   **Poor fellow!**   **Poor thing**

COMPASSION—*Phrases.*

Haud ignara mali, miseris succurrere disco [L.]. Not ignorant of misfortune, I learn to succor the unfortunate. [*Æneid*, I, 630.]
One's heart bleeding for.

Quis talia fando temperet a lacrimis! [L.]. Who, in relating such things, can refrain from tears! [Virgil, *Æneid*, II, 6.]
Woe betide!

com-pas'-sion-ate. Merciful. COMPASSION-RUTHLESS-NESS.
com-pat''-i-bil'-i-ty. Congruity. HARMONY-DISCORD, POSSIBILITY-IMPOSSIBILITY.
com-pat'-i-ble. Congruous. HARMONY-DISCORD, POSSIBILITY-IMPOSSIBILITY.
com-pa'-tri-ot. A fellow citizen. DWELLER-HABITATION, FRIEND-FOE.
com-peer'. An equal. EQUALITY-INEQUALITY, FRIEND-FOE.
com-pel'. To coerce. COERCION, MIGHT-IMPOTENCE, VOLITION-OBLIGATION.
com''-pel-la'-tion. Appellation. NAME-MISNOMER.
com-pelled'. Forced. COERCION.
com-pel'-ling. Forcing. COERCION.
com'-pend. Abridgment. DIGEST.
com-pen'-di-ous. Succinct. DIGEST, LENGTH-SHORTNESS, TERSENESS-PROLIXITY.
com-pen'-di-um. An abstract. DIGEST, ENLARGEMENT-DIMINUTION.
com'-pen-sate. To make amends for. COMPENSATION, RECOMPENSE-PUNITION.
com''-pen-sa'-tion. Payment. ATONEMENT, COMPENSATION, COMPOSITION, RECOMPENSE-PUNITION, REPRISAL-RESISTANCE.

COMPENSATION.

Amends, etc. Satisfaction given for wrong done, etc. See ATONEMENT.
Casting-weight. Make-weight.

Commutation. The reduction or change of a penalty.
Compensation. A return for service done.
Compromise, etc. Settling by mutual concessions, etc. See COMPOSITION.
Counteraction, etc. Action in an opposite direction, etc. See ANTAGONISM.
Counterpoise. Counterbalance.
Equalization, etc. The act of making equal, etc. See EQUALITY.
Equation. A proposition expressing the equality of two quantities.
Equivalent. That which is the same in value, etc.
Indemnification. The act of compensating for damages.
Indemnity. The amount paid in compensation for damages.
Make-weight. Something thrown into the scale to make good weight.
Measure for measure. Like for like; expedient for expedient.
Neutralization. The process of making inactive.
Nullification. The act of making of no effect.
Offset. Something given in exchange.
Quid pro quo [L.]. Something for something.
Reaction. Tendency toward a former state.
Retaliation, etc. The act of returning an injury, etc. See REPRISAL.
Robbing Peter to pay Paul. Taking from one whose necessity is as great as the person who receives.
Set-off. Offset.

COMPENSATION—*Denotations.*

Ballast. That which gives uprightness or security.
Bribe. A price given with the object of perverting the judgment of a person.
Hushmoney. Money paid for keeping a thing secret.

COMPENSATION—*Verbs.*

Balance. To pay the difference between the debit and credit sides of an account.
Compensate. To make return for services.

Compense. To compensate.
Counteract. To hinder.
Counterbalance. Offset.
Counterpoise. }
Countervail. } To set an equal force against.
Cover. To restore to the treasury.
Equalize, etc. To make equal, etc. See EQUALITY.
Hedge. To bet on both sides so as to escape loss.
Indemnify. To make compensation for damages.
Neutralize. To make neutral.
Nullify. To make null.
Outbalance. }
Overbalance. } To weigh down.
Redeem, etc. To pay off, etc. See ATONEMENT.
Square. Settle.

COMPENSATION—*Verbal Expressions.*

Fill up; give and take; make compensation; make good, make compensation for; **make up for; make up leeway,** to make up for lost time; **set off,** to reckon against.

COMPENSATION—*Adjectives.*

Compensating. }
Compensatory. } Serving to make compensation.
Countervailing, etc. Opposing with a force equal to the opponent's, etc. See *Verbs.*
Equivalent, etc. Of the same value, etc. See EQUALITY.
In the opposite scale. In the balance.

COMPENSATION—*Adverbs.*

Albeit. Even though.
Although. Notwithstanding.
Howbeit. Be it as it may.
However. By whatever means.
Maugre [F.]. In spite of.
Nathless. Nevertheless.
Nevertheless. None the less.
Notwithstanding. In spite of the fact.
Still. Notwithstanding.
Though. Notwithstanding the fact that.
Yet. In addition.

COMPENSATION—*Adverbial Expressions.*

After all, after all is said and done, nevertheless; **at all events, at any rate,** yet; be that as it may; even so; **for all that,** notwithstanding all that; however that may be; **in consideration; in return; on the other hand;** *quand même* [F.], even though; *quoad minus* [L.], none the less; **taking one thing with another,** etc. (see MEDIUM).

com-pen'-sa-to-ry. Requiting. RECOMPENSE-PUNI-TION.
com-pense'. To compensate. COMPENSATION.

com'-pe-tence. Ability; means of livelihood. AFFLU-ENCE-PENURY, ENOUGH, MIGHT-IMPOTENCE, SKILL-UNSKILFULNESS.
com'-pe-tent. Qualified. ENOUGH, SKILL-UNSKILFUL-NESS.
com''-pe-ti'-tion. Rivalry. ANTAGONISM-CONCUR-RENCE, STRIFE-PEACE.
com-pet'-i-tive. Pertaining to a competition. ANTAG-ONISM-CONCURRENCE, STRIFE-PEACE.
com-pet'-i-tor. One who competes. ANTAGONIST-ASSISTANT, BELLIGERENT, PETITIONER.
com''-pi-la'-tion. A collection. DIGEST, GATHERING-SCATTERING, MISSIVE-PUBLICATION.
com-pile'. Compose. DIGEST.
com-pla'-cen-cy. Satisfaction. POLITENESS-IMPOLITE-NESS.
com-pla'-cent. Serene. CHARITABLENESS-MALEVO-LENCE, CONTENTEDNESS-DISCONTENTMENT, POLITE-NESS-IMPOLITENESS.
com-plain'. To find fault. JUBILATION-LAMENTATION.
com-plaint'. A statement of wrong; a cause of wrong. HEALTH-SICKNESS, JUBILATION-LAMENTATION; **lodge a complaint,** JUSTIFICATION-CHARGE.
com'-plai-sance''. Courtesy. POLITENESS-IMPOLITE-NESS.
com'-plai-sant''. Affable. CHARITABLENESS-MALEVO-LENCE, POLITENESS-IMPOLITENESS.
com'-ple-ment. An addition. ENTIRETY-DEFICIENCY, INCREMENT-REMNANT, NUMBER.
com''-ple-men'-ta-ry co'-lor. An accessory color. COLOR-ACHROMATISM, NUMBER.
com-plete'. To finish up. ARRIVAL-DEPARTURE, COM-PLETION-NONCOMPLETION, CONTRACT, ENTIRETY-DE-FICIENCY, FAULTLESSNESS-FAULTINESS, WHOLE-PART; **complete an answer,** PROOF-DISPROOF; **complete a circle,** CIRCUITION; **in a complete circle,** MAG-NITUDE-SMALLNESS.
com-ple'-ted. Finished. COMPLETION-NONCOMPLE-TION.
com-plete'-ly. In a complete manner. COMPLETION-NONCOMPLETION, ENTIRETY-DEFICIENCY.
com-plete'-ness. State of being complete. ARRIVAL-DEPARTURE, COMPLETION-NONCOMPLETION, EN-TIRETY-DEFICIENCY, MUTABILITY-STABILITY.
com-ple'-ting. Finishing. COMPLETION-NONCOMPLE-TION, ENTIRETY-DEFICIENCY.
com-ple'-tion. Accomplishment. COMPLETION-NON-COMPLETION, ENTIRETY-DEFICIENCY.

COMPLETION—NONCOMPLETION.

Accomplishment. Act of finishing or bringing to completion.
Achievement. Act of doing or finishing.
Close. Ending or termination. See BEGINNING-END.
Completion. The getting through to the end.
Conclusion. Coming to the close or last part.
Consummation. Act of bringing to completion.
Culmination. Raising to the highest point or degree.
Dénouement [F.]. Event; issue; end.
Despatch. }
Dispatch. } The finishing up of a business.
Elaboration. The act of working out or raising to a higher degree.
Execution. A carrying into effect or completion, as of a sentence.
Finale [It.]. End.
Finality. State of being finished or completed
Finish. The result of completed labor.
Fulfilment. Accomplishment; completion.
Issue. Final outcome or result.
Performance. Carrying into execution.
Terminus. The end. See ARRIVAL-DEPARTURE.
Upshot. The result.
Winding up. The completion or close of a work.

COMPLETION—*Nouns of Means.*

Catastrophe. A final event, usually of a disastrous nature.
Coping-stone. The highest course of masonry in a wall.
Coup de grâce [F.]. The death-blow,

Incompleteness, etc. See ENTIRETY-DEFICIENCY.
Inexecution. Failure to carry out.
Neglect, etc. See CAREFULNESS-CARELESSNESS.
Non-completion. Incompletion.
Non-fulfilment. Neglect to fulfil.
Non-performance. Failure.
Shortcoming. Failing to attain.

NONCOMPLETION—*Denotations.*

Drawn-battle. } A contest in which neither party secures an advan-
Drawn-game. } tage.
Work of Penelope. An endless task, like that of Penelope, the wife of Ulysses.

NONCOMPLETION—*Verbs.*

Be slow to. To hesitate; to lag.
Collapse, etc. See TRANSCURSION-SHORTCOMING.
Do things by halves. To do partially.
Fall short of, etc. See TRANSCURSION-SHORTCOMING.
Hang fire. To hold in suspense.
Leave undone. Leave unfinished.
Leave unfinished, etc. See *Adjectives.*
Let alone. Leave.
Let slip. To neglect; to cease to care for.
Lose sight of. To allow to drift.

COMPLETION—NONCOMPLETION—*Continued.*

COMPLETION—Nouns of Means—*Continued.*

Crowning of the edifice. The completion of a building.
Crowning stroke. }
Crowning touch. } The last work.
Fait accompli [F.]. Work accomplished
Final stroke. }
Final touch. }
Finishing stroke. } The finishing work.
Finishing touch. }
Keystone. The highest stone in an arch.
Last finish. }
Last stroke. } The last work done upon anything.
Last touch. }
Ne plus ultra [L.]. No more beyond (the Pillars of Hercules); the highest or best.
Superstructure. Structure used in building.
Work done. The finished task.

COMPLETION—*Verbs.*

Accomplish. To completely fulfil a plan.
Achieve. To work to a conclusion.
Attain the goal. To bring to completion, or reach what one has striven for in a race.
Be as good as one's word. To fulfil a promise.
Be at the death, etc. See PERSISTENCE.
Bring about. To bring to pass; to effect.
Bring through. To bring to a successful issue.
Bring to a close, etc. See BEGINNING-END.
Bring to a head. To bring to a climax.
Bring to bear. To cause to have influence.
Bring to maturity. To bring to completion.
Bring to pass. Cause to happen.
Bring to perfection. Make perfect.
Cap. To crown; to mark the climax.
Carry into effect. }
Carry into execution. } Accomplish.
Carry out. }
Carry through. }
Clinch. To make conclusive.
Complete. To finish; to perform fully.
Come to a crisis. To arrive at the critical stage.
Come to a head. To come to a climax.
Come to its end. Close.
Consummate. To bring to completion; to finish.
Crown. To form the topmost part of.
Crown all. To put on the finishing touches.
Culminate. Attain a final effect.
Die a natural death. End of itself.
Die of old age. Expire on account of the weakness of great age.
Discharge. To liberate; set free.
Dispatch. To complete in a hurry.
Dispose of. To get rid of.
Do. Perform; transact.
Effect. Bring about; to accomplish.
Effectuate. To achieve; to fulfil.
Elaborate. To carry out with labor and study.
Enact. To pass, as a law.
Execute. To complete; to finish.
Exhaust. To wear out the force of.
Finish. Complete; terminate.
Finish off. To round out; to smooth.
Fulfil. To perform; to complete.
Get in the harvest. To finish the harvest.
Get through. To come to the end.
Give the final touch to. Perform the finishing work.
Go the whole hog. Do all the work or none.
Go through. Complete.
Hammer out. To shape by hard intellectual labor.
Knock off. To finish.
Make. To produce; to bring into being.
Make short work of. Finish up promptly
Not do by halves. Do completely.
Perfect. To consummate.
Perform. To accomplish; to achieve.

NONCOMPLETION—Verbs—*Continued.*

Neglect, etc. See CAREFULNESS-CARELESSNESS.
Not complete, etc. See COMPLETION.
Scotch the snake, not to kill it. To wound slightly.

NONCOMPLETION—*Adjectives.*

Going on. In an unfinished state.
Incomplete. Lacking fulness.
In hand. }
In progress. } Under way.
In one's hands. Not finished.
Not completed, etc. See *Verbs.*
Proceeding. Advancing.
Sketchyaddle. Confused; wanting the power to progress.
Unaccomplished. Not accomplished.
Uncompleted. Not completed.
Unexecuted. Left in an unfinished state.
Unfinished. Not done.
Unperformed. Not performed.

NONCOMPLETION—*Adverb.*

Re infecta [L.]. The business being unfinished.

COMPLETION—Verbs—*Continued.*

Play out. Exhaust; to consume the force of.
Polish off. To put on the finishing touches.
Put in force. }
Put in practise. } Carry out.
Put the finishing hand to. }
Put the last hand to. } Finish off.
Reach. See ARRIVAL.
Reach the goal. Reach the end.
Realize. To effectuate.
Ripen. To come to a head.
Run its course. }
Run one's race. } Come to the end.
Seal. To designate the conclusion.
Set at rest. To satisfy.
Stamp. To attach the sign of completion; to label.
Wind up. To bring to a close.
Work out. To solve; to exhaust the vital force of.

COMPLETION—*Adjectives.*

Completed, etc. See *Verbs.*
Completing. Being in the state of completion.
Concluding. Drawing to an end.
Conclusive. Decisive; final.
Crowning, etc. See *Verbs.*
Done. Completed; finished.
Done for. Used up; destroyed.
Exhaustive. Treating thoroughly.
Final. Conclusive; allowing no appeal.
Highly wrought, etc. See PREPARATION.
Ripe, etc. See PREPARATION.
Thorough, etc. See ENTIRETY.

COMPLETION—*Adverbs.*

Completely. See ENTIRETY.
Out of hand. Promptly.
To crown all. To cap.

COMPLETION—*Phrases.*

Actum est [L.]. It is done.
Aussitôt dit, aussitôt fait [F.]. No sooner said than done.
Aut non tentaris aut perfice [L.]. Either do not attempt or else achieve. [Ovid, *Ars Am.*, I, 389.]
C'en est fait [F.]. It is finished.
Consummatum est [L.]. It is consummated.
Cosa ben fatta è fatta due volte [It.] A thing well done is twice done.
Finis coronat opus [L.]. The end crowns the work.
It is all over; the bubble has burst; the game is played out; the race is run.
Una golondrina no hace verano [Sp.]. One swallow does not make a summer.

---

com'-plex''. Composite. FERTILITY-STERILITY, REGULARITY-IRREGULARITY.
com'-plexed''. Intricate. REGULARITY-IRREGULARITY.
com-plex'-ion. The color of skin; character; aspect.

APPEARANCE - DISAPPEARANCE, COLOR - ACHROMATISM, CONDITION-SITUATION.

com-plex'-i-ty. State of being complex. REGULARITY-IRREGULARITY.

com-plex'-ness. Complexity. REGULARITY-IRREGU-LARITY.

com-pli'-ance. Complaisance. CONSENT, CONVENTIONALITY-UNCONVENTIONALITY, INSUBORDINATION-OBEDIENCE, OBSERVANCE-NONOBSERVANCE, READINESS-RELUCTANCE.

com-pli'-ant. Obedient. INSUBORDINATION-OBEDIENCE.

com'-pli-cate. Complex. ORGANIZATION-DISORGANIZATION.

com'-pli-ca''-ted. Complex; interwoven. CIRCLE-WINDING, DIFFICULTY-FACILITY, REGULARITY-IRREGULARITY.

com''-pli-ca'-tion. Complexity. REGULARITY-IRREGULARITY.

com'-plice. An associate. ANTAGONIST-ASSISTANT.

com-plic'-i-ty. Participation. OBSTRUCTION-HELP.

com'-pli-ment. An expression of admiration; a greeting. APPROVAL-DISAPPROVAL, INCREMENT-REMNANT, POLITENESS-IMPOLITENESS; **compliments of the season,** FELICITATION; **poor compliments,** APPROVAL-DISAPPROVAL.

com''-pli-men'-ta-ry. Expressing a compliment. APPROVAL-DISAPPROVAL.

com-plot'. To conspire. DESIGN.

com-ply'. To consent; obey. CONSENT, CONVENTIONALITY-UNCONVENTIONALITY, INSUBORDINATION-OBEDIENCE, OBSERVANCE-NONOBSERVANCE, REPRISAL-RESISTANCE.

com-ply'-ing. Obeying. INSUBORDINATION-OBEDIENCE.

com'-po. Composition of plaster. COVER-LINING, MATERIALS.

com-po'-nent. Constituent. CONSTITUENT-ALIEN.

componere lites magnas [L.]. (com-pon'-er-î lai'-tîz mag'-nas). To settle great disputes. MEDIATION.

componere lites, tantas [L.] (com-pon'-er-î lai'-tîz, tan'-tas). To settle so great disputes. FIGHTING-CONCILIATION.

com-port'. To conduct or behave. **Comport oneself,** CONDUCT; **comport with,** HARMONY-DISCORD.

com-port'-ment. Behavior. CONDUCT.

compos [L.] (com'-pos). Sound; sane. SANENESS-LUNACY.

com-pose'. To make up; to calm; to adjust; to set type; to make a musical work. CONSTITUENT-ALIEN, CREATION-DESTRUCTION, EXCITABILITY-INEXCITA-BILITY, FIGHTING-CONCILIATION, HEED-DISREGARD, INCLUSION-OMISSION, MUSIC, MUSICIAN, TURBULENCE-CALMNESS, WRITING-PRINTING.

com-posed'. Free from agitation. AFFECTIONS.

com-po'-ser. One who composes. MELODY-DISSONANCE, MUSIC, MUSICIAN.

com-po'-sing. Reconciling. FIGHTING-CONCILIATION.

com-pos'-ite. Compounded. MIXTURE-HOMOGENEITY; **composite capital,** ARCHITECTURE; **composite order,** ARCHITECTURE.

com''-po-si'-tion. A compromise; that which is composed; the act of composing. ATONEMENT, COMPOSITION, COMPOSITION-RESOLUTION, DELINEATION-CARICATURE, EXCHANGE, INCLUSION-OMISSION, MATERIALS, MUSIC, RHETORIC, STYLE, WRITING-PRINTING.

COMPOSITION.

Commutation. The substitution of one penalty or punishment for another of less severe kind.

Compensation, etc. The act of paying or making amends, etc. See COMPENSATION.

Composition. A union of two materials or opinions of different kinds.

Compromise. The settlement of differences by mutual concessions.

Mezzo termine [It.]. The middle term.

Middle term. The term between two extremes.

COMPOSITION—*Verbs.*

Abide by arbitration. To submit to peaceful settlement.

Adjust. To arrange suitably.

Adjust differences. To arrange controversies.

Agree. To come into a state of harmony.

Arrange. To adjust; put into proper order.

Bridge over. To get over a difficulty in some way.

Come to terms, etc. To make suitable arrangements, etc. See CONTRACT.

Commute. To put one thing in place of another.

Compound. To mingle different substances.

Compromise. To settle by mutual concessions.

Give and take. To make a mean of gain and loss.

Make the best of.⎫ To comply with a thing because it is
Make a virtue of necessity.⎭ necessary.

Meet half way. To compromise; settle by both parties making concessions.

Patch up. To repair.

Split the difference. To make a compromise.

Submit to arbitration. To abide by a peaceful settlement.

Take the mean. To take the average.

Take the will for the deed. Be satisfied with the intention.

COMPOSITION—RESOLUTION.

Absorption. The process of being taken up into the mass of something.

Amalgamation. The process of uniting with mercury; union of races, societies.

Blending. A gradual merging of things into each other.

Centralization. Union of individual societies under one control.

Coalescence. Temporary combination of persons to accomplish some purpose.

Combination. Connection.

Composition. The association of parts with design and in proportion.

Embodiment. Process of collecting into a whole.

Fusion. Coalescence; melting.

Impregnation. Saturation.

Incorporation. Mixture of elements, especially of drugs with a liquid or semi-liquid to give a certain consistency.

Junction. A coming together.

Mixture. A union of forces not joined by chemism. See MIXTURE.

Unification. The process of bringing together into one.

Union. A junction leaving no mark of identity of parts.

COMPOSITION—*Associated Nouns.*

Amalgam. An alloy of a metal with mercury.

Compound. A number of substances held together by chemism.

Resultant. A force equal to a combination of given forces.

Tertium quid [L.]. A third something; a supposed intermediate substance between mind and matter.

Analysis. Resolution of a thing into its elements by a person.

Catalysis. Change wrought in a chemical by an agent which remains stable.

Corruption. Dissolution.

Decomposition. Process of resolving a compound into its elements.

Disjunction, etc. Separation, etc. See UNION-DISUNION.

Dispersion, etc. Separation of rays of light of different colors by a prism, etc. See GATHERING-SCATTERING.

Dissection. A cutting to pieces for examination.

Dissolution. Process of breaking up into parts.

Resolution. Separation into component parts.

RESOLUTION—*Verbs.*

Analyze. To resolve into elements.

Break up. To separate into parts.

Crumble into dust. Fall into bits.

Decentralize. To withdraw from the center.

Decompose. To undergo dissolution.

Decompound. To mix compounds to form other compounds.

Disembody. To separate from the body.

Disperse, etc. To scatter; to separate, etc. See GATHERING-SCATTERING.

Dissect. To cut in pieces for examination.

Dissolve. To separate into component parts.

Electrolyze. To separate by the action of electricity.

Resolve into its elements. To reduce to elementary principles.

COMPOSITION—RESOLUTION—*Continued.*

COMPOSITION—*Scientific Terms:*

Crasis. A contraction of two vowels into one long vowel.
Synthesis. The uniting of elements to form a compound; composition.

COMPOSITION—*Verbs.*

Absorb. To suck up; to engross completely.
Amalgamate. To mix or blend together.
Blend. To unite so as to form a homogeneous mass.
Cement a union. To hold together firmly.
Centralize. To bring into control of a central organization.
Coalesce. To come together into one.
Combine. To bring into close union.
Consolidate. To unite in a coherent mass.
Embody. To make into a compact form.
Fuse. To unite or blend by melting.
Impregnate. To infuse with another substance.
Incorporate. To join with something else so as to form a harmonious mass.
Lump together. To heap indiscriminately.
Marry. To unite in matrimony.
Melt into one. To blend into one.

RESOLUTION—VERBS—*Continued.*

Separate into its elements. To take to pieces.
Unravel. To separate or unmix the threads of.

RESOLUTION—*Adjectives.*

Analytical. Resolving into first principles or elements.
Catalytic. Relating to a resolution into parts.
Decomposed. Resolved from existing combinations.

COMPOSITION—VERBS—*Continued.*

Merge. To cause the identity to be absorbed into something else.
Put together. To unite in one.
Reembody. To place in a compact mass.
Unite. To join together to form a whole.

COMPOSITION—*Adjectives.*

Combined. Bound together.
Impregnated with. Filled with.
Ingrained. Fixed deeply.
Synthetic. Constructive.

---

com-pos'-i-tor. A typesetter. WRITING-PRINTING.
com'-post. A fertilizing mixture. CLEANNESS-FILTHINESS.
com-po'-sure. Tranquillity. PLEASURABLENESS-PAINFULNESS.
com''-po-ta'-tion. A carouse. MODERATION-SELF-INDULGENCE.
com-pound'. To mix into a compound; to agree. COMPOSITION, COMPOSITION-RESOLUTION, MIXTURE-HOMOGENEITY; **compound àrithmetic,** MENSURATION; **compound for,** COMMUTATION-PERMUTATION, EXCHANGE; **compound noun,** NOUN.
com''-pra-dor'. A caterer. PROVISION-WASTE.
com''-pre-hend'. To understand fully; to include. ADMISSION-EXCLUSION, CLEARNESS-OBSCURITY, INCLUSION-OMISSION, KNOWLEDGE-IGNORANCE.
com''-pre-hen'-sion. Full understanding. ADMISSION-EXCLUSION, CLEARNESS-OBSCURITY, INCLUSION-OMISSION, KNOWLEDGE-IGNORANCE, SAGACITY-INCAPACITY.
com''-pre-hen'-sive. Inclusive. GREATNESS-LITTLENESS, UNIVERSALITY-PARTICULARITY; **comprehensive argument,** RATIOCINATION-CASUISTRY.
comprendre, c'est tout pardonner, tout [F.] (con·-prandr', sê tu par-do-nê', tu). To understand all is to pardon all. KNOWLEDGE-IGNORANCE, PARDON-VINDICTIVENESS.
com-press'. To condense. ENLARGEMENT-DIMINUTION, LENGTH-SHORTNESS, REMEDY-BANE, SOLIDITY-RARITY.
com-press''-i-bil'-i-ty. Power to be compressed. ENLARGEMENT-DIMINUTION, SOLIDITY-RARITY.
com-press'-i-ble. Capable of being compressed. ENLARGEMENT-DIMINUTION, SOLIDITY-RARITY.
com-pres'-sion. State of being compressed. DIGEST, ENLARGEMENT - DIMINUTION, TERSENESS - PROLIXITY.
com-prise'. To include. ADMISSION-EXCLUSION.
com''-pro-ba'-tion. Confirmation. EVIDENCE-COUNTEREVIDENCE, PROOF-DISPROOF.
com'-pro-mise. To compound; to expose to risks; to bind mutually. ATONEMENT, COMPENSATION, COMPOSITION, CONTRACT, DETERMINATION-VACILLATION, FIGHTING-CONCILIATION, MEDIATION, MEDIUM, MID-COURSE-CIRCUIT, SECURITY-INSECURITY.
com'-pro-mised. Adjusted. DUTY-DERELICTION, ENGAGEMENT-RELEASE.
compter [F.] (con·-tê'). To charge. MARKET.
compte rendu [F.] (con·t ran-dü'). An account. ACCOUNTS, MARK-OBLITERATION.

comptes nouvelles disputes, à vieux [F.] (con·t nu-vel' dis-püt', a vi-u'). Old accounts breed new disputes. FAVORITE-QUARRELSOMENESS.
comp-trol'-ler. A controller. MANAGER.
com-pul'-sa-to-ry. Tending to compel. COERCION.
com-pul'-sion. Coercion. COERCION, VOLITION-OBLIGATION.
com-pul'-so-ry. Coercive. COERCION, RULE-LICENSE, VOLITION-OBLIGATION.
com-punc'-tion. Uneasiness of mind. REPENTANCE-OBDURACY.
com''-pur-ga'-tion. A cleansing. EVIDENCE-COUNTEREVIDENCE, EXCULPATION-CONVICTION.
com-pu'-ta-ble. Capable of being reckoned. NUMBERING.
com''-pu-ta'-tion. Act of reckoning. NUMBERING.
com-pute'. To reckon. NUMBERING.
com'-rade. A companion. FRIEND-FOE.
com'-rade-ship. Good-fellowship. SOCIABILITY-PRIVACY.
con. To think over; to learn. EDUCATION-LEARNING, REFLECTION-VACANCY, REMEMBRANCE-FORGETFULNESS.
co-na'-tion. Faculty of volition. VOLITION-OBLIGATION.
conatu magnas nugas, magno [L.] (con-ê'-tiu mag'-nas niu'-gas, mag'-no). Great jokes from great attempts. CONSEQUENCE-INSIGNIFICANCE, PROVISION-WASTE.
con-cam'-er-ate. To arch over. CURVATION-RECTILINEARITY.
con-cat''-e-na'-tion. A chain-like series. CONTINUITY-INTERRUPTION, UNION-DISUNION.
con'-cave''. Hollow and rounded; having a cavity. CONCAVITY-CONVEXITY, CONTENTS-RECEIVER.
con-cav'-i-ty. A hollow. CONVEXITY-CONCAVITY.
con-ceal'. To hide. CLEARNESS-OBSCURITY, COVER-LINING, CRAFT-ARTLESSNESS, ENLIGHTENMENT-SECRECY, VISIBILITY-INVISIBILITY.
con-cealed'. Hidden. ENLIGHTENMENT-SECRECY, KNOWLEDGE-IGNORANCE, MANIFESTATION-LATENCY.
con-ceal'-ment. A hiding. ENLIGHTENMENT-SECRECY, VISIBILITY-INVISIBILITY.
con-cede'. To yield; to grant; to yield assent. ASSENT-DISSENT, CONSENT, CRAFT-ARTLESSNESS, EXPOSURE-HIDINGPLACE, GIVING-RECEIVING, LEAVE-PROHIBITION, MOTIVE-CAPRICE.
con-ceit'. Too much self-esteem; a fantastic notion; power of conceiving; clever thought. CONCEIT-DIFFIDENCE, CONCEPTION-THEME, FANCY, HYPOTHESIS, SAGACITY-INCAPACITY, SOCIETY-AFFECTATION, WITTINESS-DULNESS; **idle conceit,** WITTINESS-DULNESS.

CONCEIT—DIFFIDENCE.

Airs. Affectation.
Amour-propre [L.]. Self-love.
Assurance, etc. Excess of boldness, etc. See PRESUMPTION.
Conceit. Too much self-esteem.
Conceitedness. Overestimation of oneself.
Coxcombry. Foppishness
Egotism. Tendency or act of magnifying oneself.
Elation. Exaltation of mind resulting from success.
Gaudery. Showy ornament.
Mannerism. Excessive adherence to some peculiarity or manner.
Ostentation, etc. Display prompted by vanity, etc. See POMP.
Pretention. A claim falsely assumed.
Pride, etc. Self-approval based upon something one is or has done. See SELFRESPECT.
Priggishness. ⎫ The characteristics of a narrow-minded, conceited
Priggism. ⎬ person.
Self-admiration. Gratified contemplation of self.
Self-applause. ⎫ Approval of self.
Self-approbation. ⎬
Self-complacency. Quality of being pleased with oneself.
Self-conceit. Unduly high opinion of self.
Self-confidence. Confidence in one's own powers.
Self-esteem.. Good opinion of oneself.
Self-glorification. Boastfulness of oneself.
Self-gratulation. Satisfaction with self.
Selfishness. Disposition to seek for one's own advantage.
Self-love. Tendency to promote one's own well-being.
Self-praise. Praise of oneself.
Self-sufficiency. Tendency to disregard the opinions of others because of a high estimation of our own.
Vainglory. Excessive vanity.
Vanity. Great desire for applause or admiration.
Vox et præterea nihil [L.]. Voice and nothing else

CONCEIT—*Nouns of Agent.*

Cheval de bataille [F.]. A war-horse; a main reliance.
Coxcomb, etc. A vain, showy fellow, etc. See SOCIETY-DANDY.
Sir Oracle, etc. A person who affects wisdom, etc. ["I am Sir Oracle; and when I ope my lips let no dog bark." Shakespeare, *Merchant of Venice*, I, i.] See BRAWLER.

CONCEIT—*Verbs.*

Be vain, etc. ⎫ See *Adjectives.*
Be vain of. ⎬
Blind oneself as to one's own merit. To be deceived as to one's real worth.
Boast, etc. To speak of oneself with vanity, etc. See BRAGGING.
Fish for compliments. Indirectly to seek to draw forth flattery.
Give oneself airs. To show pride.
Have too high opinion of oneself. To show pride in one's abilities.
Have too high opinion of one's talents. To overestimate one's mental endowments.
Have an overweening opinion of oneself. To be unduly self-confident.
Have an overweening opinion of one's talents. To be overconfident of one's ability.
Inflate. To puff up, as with pride.
Inspire with vanity, etc. To arouse a feeling of shallow pride, etc. See *Nouns.*
Lay the flattering unction to one's soul. Pride oneself. [Shakespeare, *Hamlet*, III, iv.]
Not think *vin ordinaire* **of oneself.** ⎫ Not to think little of oneself.
Not to think small beer of oneself. ⎬
Pique oneself. To pride oneself.
Puff up. To inflate with pride or vanity.
Put oneself forward. Assume importance.
Render vain, etc. To make foolishly proud of one's personal charms or powers, etc. See *Adjectives.*
Turn one's head. To make one conceited.
Turn up. To bend or incline.
Be vain. To be elated with self-admiration.
Be vain of. To be proud of trifling or petty things.

CONCEIT—*Adjectives.*

Arrogant, etc. Giving oneself undue importance, etc. See PRESUMPTION
Conceited. Holding a flattering opinion of oneself.
Egotistic. Egotistical.
Egotistical. Addicted to or manifesting an excesive love of self.
Entêté [F.], etc. Obstinate, etc. See DECISION-MISJUDGMENT.
Flushed. Elated; being animated with joy.
Forward. Not reserved and modest.
Free and easy. Showing little regard for conventionality.
High-flown. Swelled.

Bashfulness, etc. Excessive modesty, etc. See *Adjectives.*
Constraint. Unnaturalness in manner resulting from timidity.
Demureness, etc. The show of modesty, etc. See *Adjectives.*
Diffidence. Distrust of oneself; modesty; bashfulness.
Humility, etc. A modest estimate of oneself, etc. See SELFRESPECT-HUMBLENESS.
Mauvaise honte [F.]. Shamefacedness.
Modesty. Freedom from boldness or forwardness.
Reserve. Repression of one's thoughts and feelings.
Timidity. Want of courage to face publicity.
Verecundity. Modesty; shyness.

DIFFIDENCE—*Associated Nouns.*

Blush. Color in the cheeks caused by modesty, etc.
Blushing. The appearance of reddish color upon the cheeks.
Blushing honors. Modest honors. [Shakespeare, *King Henry VIII*, III, ii.]
Self-knowledge. Knowledge of one's limitations.

DIFFIDENCE—*Verbs.*

Be modest, etc. See *Adjectives.*
Cast a sheep's eye. Cast a bashful glance. [He "cast a sheep's eye out of a calf's head at you." Swift, *Polite Conversation.*]
"Do good by stealth and blush to find it fame." To be modest. [Pope, *Satires*, i, 136.]
Draw in one's horns, etc. To check oneself or retract, etc. See SELFRESPECT-HUMBLENESS. ["They ganne to draw in thar horrnes, as a snayl among the thornes." A. D. 1300.]
Give way to. To yield with modesty.
Hide one's face. To keep out of sight.
Hide one's light under a bushel. Not to make a display of one's ability. [Bible, Matt. v, 15.]
Keep in the background. ⎫
Keep one's distance. ⎬ To refrain from putting oneself forward.
Keep private. ⎭
Pursue the noiseless tenor of one's way. To live modestly. [Gray, *Elegy in a Country Churchyard*, 19.]
Reserve oneself. To hold oneself aloof.
Retire. To seclude oneself.

DIFFIDENCE—*Adjectives.*

Bashful. Modest to excess.
Blushing. Showing reddish color upon the cheeks.
Constrained. Held in check by timidity.
Coy. Reserved through shyness.
Demure. Feigning modesty. ["Demurest of the tabby kind." Gray, *Favorite Cat*, 4.]
Diffident. Not self-reliant; modest.
Humble, etc. Not assuming, etc. See SELFRESPECT-HUMBLENESS.
Modest. Unpretentious.
Nervous. Easily disturbed.
Out of countenance, etc. Abashed, etc. See SELFRESPECT-HUMBLENESS.
Overmodest. Very bashful.
Poor in spirit. Humble. [Bible, Matt v, 3.]
Reserved. Keeping one's thoughts to oneself.
Shamefaced. Easily confused; from *shamefast*, firm in modesty. ["Shamefast she was in mayden's shamefastnesse." Chaucer, *Doctor's Tale*, i, 55.]
Sheepish. Awkwardly diffident.
Shy. Bashful.
Skittish. Timid; shy.
Timid. Shrinking from publicity.
Timorous. Shy.
Unaspiring. Unambitious.
Unassuming. Modest.
Unboastful. Not inclined to brag.
Unobtrusive. Not tending to obtrude.
Unostentatious. Not showy.
Unpretending. Without pretense; modest.
Unpretentious. Not characterized by pretension.
Verecund. Modest; shy.

DIFFIDENCE—*Adverbs.*

Humbly, etc. With modest submissiveness, etc. See *Adjectives.*
Privately. In a secret manner.
Quietly. Informally.
Sans façon [F.]. Informally.
Without beat of drum. Unostentatiously.
Without ceremony. Abruptly.

CONCEIT—ADJECTIVES—*Continued.*

Inflated. Bombastic.
Ostentatious, etc. Fond of making a display from vanity, etc. See POMP.
Overweening. Unduly self-confident.
Overwise. Affectedly wise.
Pert. Free in speech or behavior.
Pragmatical. Self-important.
Pretentious. Marked by conceit, pretense, or show.
Priggish. Conceited or affectedly precise in dress and manners.
Puffed up. Inflated with pride or vanity.
Self-admiring. Being pleased with self.
Self-applauding. Approving oneself.
Self-confident. Confident in one's own ability.
Self-flattering. Making complimentary speeches of self.

Self-glorious. Vainglorious.
Self-opinionated. Holding opinions of one's own in a conceited way stubbornly.
Self-satisfied. Self-complacent.
Self-sufficient. Having overweening confidence in one's powers.
Soi-disant [F.], etc. Self-styled; self-dubbed, etc. See BRAGGING.
Unabashed. Not disconcerted.
Unblushing. Not embarrassed.
Unceremonious. Informal.
Unconstrained. Not repressed.
Vain. Elated with self-admiration.
Vain as a peacock. Proud of one's person or dress.
Vainglorious. Overproud of one's achievements.
Wise in one's own conceit.

CONCEIT—*Adverb.*

Vainly. In a vain manner.

CONCEIT—*Phrase.*

How we apples swim! [Swift, *Brother Protestants.*]

con-ceit′-ed. Vain. CONCEIT-DIFFIDENCE, DECISION-MISJUDGMENT, SOCIETY-AFFECTATION.
con-ceit′-ed-ness. Vanity. CONCEIT-DIFFIDENCE.
con-ceiv′-a-ble. Imaginable. POSSIBILITY-IMPOSSIBILITY.
con-ceive′. To originate; to take possession of the mind; to imagine; to produce; to think. BEGINNING-END, FAITH-MISGIVING, FANCY, FERTILITY-STERIL-

ITY, KNOWLEDGE-IGNORANCE.
con-cent′. Harmony. MELODY-DISSONANCE.
con′-cen-trate. To concenter. CENTER, CHEMISTRY, CONCENTRATION-RADIATION, GATHERING-SCATTERING.
con″-cen-tra′-tion. Condensation. CENTER, CONCENTRATION-RADIATION, GATHERING-SCATTERING; **concentration forces,** CHEMISTRY.

CONCENTRATION—RADIATION.

Assemblage, etc. A group or collection of persons or things, etc. See GATHERING.
Concentration. A drawing together or accumulation around one point.
Concourse. A running together of men or things.
Concurrence. Agreement of persons on a question.
Confluence. }
Conflux. } A flowing together of streams, or meeting of people.
Congress. A deliberative body representative of a nation or nations.
Convergence. A turning toward one point.
Corradiation. The convergence of rays of light to a focus.
Meeting. Gathering of people to be addressed or to deliberate.
Resort, etc. Assembly, etc. See GATHERINGPLACE.

CONCENTRATION—*Denotations.*

Applause. Praise expressed, generally by clapping the hands, etc.
Asymptote. A line which continually approaches a curve but never reaches it.

CONCENTRATION—*Verbs.*

Concentrate. To gather around one point.
Concur. To agree.
Converge. To turn toward one point.
Meet. To come together.
Unite. To become one, to act together.

CONCENTRATION—*Verbal Expressions.*

Bring into a focus; center around; center in; close in upon; close with, to agree with, **to grapple with; come together, to meet, to fight; enter in; fall in with, to meet; gather together; pour in.**

CONCENTRATION—*Adjectives.*

Asymptotical. Approaching but never meeting.
Centripetal. Directed toward the center.
Concurrent. Agreeing.
Confluent. Flowing together.
Convergent. }
Converging, etc. } Turning toward one point, etc. See *Verbs.*

con-cen′-tric. Having a common center. CENTER.
con-cen′-tu-al. Harmonious. MELODY-DISSONANCE.
con-cep′-tion. The act of conceiving; a plan; an inven-

Aberration. Departure from a course of sober conduct.
Deviation. A turning, indifferent or blameworthy, from a course in words or actions. See AIM-ABERRATION.
Dispersion. State of being scattered. See GATHERING-SCATTERING.
Divarication. A forking.
Divergence. } Conscious or unconscious stepping from one path to
Divergency. } another.
Radiation. Emission in all directions from a center.
Ramification. A branching in all directions.
Separation. A parting, or state of being parted. See UNION-DISUNION.

RADIATION—*Verbs.*

Deviate, etc. To leave a set line or rule of action, etc. See AIM-ABERRATION.
Disperse, etc. To break up and scatter a compact body with force, etc. See GATHERING-SCATTERING.
Divaricate. }
Diverge. } To extend in different directions from a point.
Part, etc. To separate, etc. See UNION-DISUNION.
Radiate. To extend in all directions from a center.
Ramify. To form branches.
Scatter. To strew about in disorder.
Spread. To strew with design.

RADIATION—*Adjectives.*

Aberrant. Wandering.
Centrifugal. Tending from the center.
Divergent. Separating at a point.
Diverging, etc. See *Verbs.*
Radiant. Tending in different directions from a center.

tion. BEGINNING-END, CONCEPTION-THEME, FAITH-MISGIVING, FANCY, FERTILITY-STERILITY, KNOWLEDGE-IGNORANCE, MIND-IMBECILITY.

CONCEPTION—THEME.

Abstract idea. An idea separate from other accompanying ideas.
Apperception. Self-consciousness.
Apprehension. An estimate.
Conceit. Flattering opinion of oneself.
Conception. A general notion.
Consideration. The act of reflecting or of forming conceptions.

Affair. That which happens or is to be done.
Argument. That which is offered as a reason for or against anything.
Business. That which interests or occupies the attention of a person.
Case. Something to be or being discussed; an hypothesis.
Chapter. One of the divisions of a book.
Field of inquiry. Subjects for investigation.

CONCEPTION—THEME—*Continued.*

Eidolon [Gr.]. An image; a phantom.
Fancy. A visionary notion.
Field of view. The space within which objects may be seen.
Idea. A conception or image formed by the mind.
Image. Representation of anything according to one's conception of it.
Impression. An effect made on the mind or feelings.
Notion. An idea; an opinion.
Observation. A statement of one's opinion.
Perception. An idea formed as the result of an impression produced on the mind by a single object; direct knowledge of matter.
Phantasy, etc. An odd or whimsical notion, etc. See FANCY.
Point of view, etc. The position from which one considers any subject, etc. See APPEARANCE.
Reflection. The act of forming ideas.
Sentiment. An opinion concerning any practical or moral question.
Theory, etc. A plan formulated by the mind, etc. See HYPOTHESIS.
Thought. Any mental process; an intellectual state.
View, etc. Opinion; belief, etc. See FAITH.

THEME—*Continued from Column 2*

THEME—*Adverbs.*

In question. In debate.
In the mind. Under discussion.
On foot. Being executed or performed.
On the carpet. Being subject of deliberation.
Relative to, etc. Referring to; respecting, etc. See CONNECTION.
On the tapis. On the table-cover; under consideration.
Under consideration. Being subject of discussion.

Food for the mind. Subjects for consideration.
Head. Division of a speech or discourse.
Material for thought. Subjects for consideration.
Matter. A subject for discussion.
Matter in hand. The subject one is considering.
Mental *pabulum.* Mental food; subject for thought.
Moot point. A question for debate.
Motion. A formal proposition made in a deliberative body.
Noêmata [Gr.] A thought; purpose; design.
Point. Precise question for consideration.
Problem, etc. In mathematics, something to be done; a question for solution; a puzzling question, etc. See INVESTIGATION.
Proposition. A statement offered for acceptance or discussion.
Resolution. A proposition formally offered for adoption.
Subject. A topic for discussion.
Subject for thought. That which requires consideration.
Subject matter. Material for examination or discussion.
Text. Scriptural verse or verses selected as a subject for a sermon.
Theme. Subject for oral or written composition.
Theorem. A geometrical or algebraic proposition requiring proof.
Thesis. A proposition to be upheld by argumentation.
What it is about. Subject.

THEME—*Verbs.*

Float in the mind. To be vaguely under consideration.
Pass in the mind, etc. To go through the mind, etc. See REFLECTION.

THEME—*Adjectives.*

In petto [It.]. In secret; in reserve.
Thought of. Considered.
Uppermost in the mind. Holding the most important position in one's thoughts.

(Continued on Column 1.)

con-cern'. An affair; a business; interest; to engage; to relate to. CONNECTION-INDEPENDENCE, CONSEQUENCE-INSIGNIFICANCE, DEALER, OCCUPATION, OCCURRENCE-DESTINY, PLEASURE-PAIN; **concern oneself with,** OCCUPATION.
con-cerned'. Anxious. PLEASURE-PAIN.
con-cern'-ing. About. CONNECTION-INDEPENDENCE.
con-cert'. To arrange for; to contrive. **con'-cert.** A musical entertainment, an agreement. ANTAGONISM-CONCURRENCE, DESIGN, COOPERATION-OPPOSITION, HARMONY-DISCORD, MUSIC; **act in concert,** ANTAGONISM-CONCURRENCE; **in concert,** MELODY-DISSONANCE, VARIANCE-ACCORD.
con''-cer-ti'-na. Wind musical instrument. MUSICAL INSTRUMENTS.
con-cer'-to. Harmony. MUSIC.
con'-cert-room''. A room for concerts. ENTERTAINMENT-WEARINESS.
con-ces'-sion. The act of conceding. CONSENT, GIVING-RECEIVING, LEAVE-PROHIBITION.
concesso, ex [L.] (con-ses'-so, ex). From what has been conceded. ASSENT-DISSENT, RATIOCINATION-CASUISTRY.
con-cet'-to. Conceit. WITTINESS-DULNESS.
con'-cha. External ear. ANATOMY.
con'-choid. A curve. CURVATION-RECTILINEARITY.
con-choi'-dal. Shell-shaped. CURVATION-RECTILINEARITY.
con-chol'-o-gy. A branch of zoology. COVER-LINING.
con-cierge'. A janitor. GUARD-PRISONER.
con-cil'-i-ate. To pacify; gain. ATONEMENT, CONTENTEDNESS-DISCONTENTMENT, FIGHTING-CONCILIATION, MOTIVE-CAPRICE, PARDON-VINDICTIVENESS, POLITENESS-IMPOLITENESS.
con-cil''-i-a'-tion. Act of conciliating. ATONEMENT, FIGHTING-CONCILIATION, PARDON-VINDICTIVENESS, VARIANCE-ACCORD.
con-cil'-i-a-to-ry. Tending to reconcile. CONTENTEDNESS-DISCONTENTMENT, FIGHTING-CONCILIATION, PARDON-VINDICTIVENESS, POLITENESS-IMPOLITENESS, VARIANCE-ACCORD.
conciliatrix [L.] (con-sil-i-ê'-trix). A procuress. PURITY-RAKE.

con-cin'-ni-ty. Harmony; fitness. BEAUTY-UGLINESS, PURITY-CRUDENESS.
con-cise'. Exact. LENGTH-SHORTNESS, TERSENESS-PROLIXITY.
con-cise'-ly. Exactly. TERSENESS-PROLIXITY.
con-cise'-ness. State of being concise. LENGTH-SHORTNESS, TERSENESS-PROLIXITY.
con-ci'-sion. A schism. LENGTH-SHORTNESS.
con'-clave. A secret council. CHURCH, COUNCIL, GATHERING-SCATTERING.
con-clude'. To end; to complete; to decide; to stop. BEGINNING-END, COMPLETION-NONCOMPLETION, CONTRACT, DECISION-MISJUDGMENT, PERSISTENCE-WHIM.
con-clu'-ding. Ending. COMPLETION-NONCOMPLETION.
con-clu'-sion. End; a conviction; final decision; closing part. ASSENT-DISSENT, BEGINNING-END, COMPLETION-NONCOMPLETION, CONTRACT, DECISION-MISJUDGMENT, PERSISTENCE-WHIM; **foregone conclusion,** PREDETERMINATION-IMPULSE; **hasty conclusion,** DECISION-MISJUDGMENT; **try conclusions,** RATIOCINATION-CASUISTRY.
con-clu'-sive. Final; decisive. BEGINNING-END, COMPLETION-NONCOMPLETION, CERTAINTY-DOUBT, DECISION-MISJUDGMENT, INVESTIGATION-ANSWER, PROOF-DISPROOF; **conclusive reasoning,** RATIOCINATION-CASUISTRY.
con-clu'-sive-ness. Decisiveness. RATIOCINATION-INSTINCT.
con-coct'. To prepare by mixing; to contrive. DESIGN, TRUTHFULNESS-FALSEHOOD.
con-coc'-tion. Mixture. PREPARATION-NONPREPARATION.
con-com'-i-tance. Accompaniment. COEXISTENCE, SOLITUDE-COMPANY.
con-com'-i-tant. Attendant. COEXISTENCE, SOLITUDE-COMPANY.
con'-cord. Agreement; harmony. ASSENT-DISSENT, HARMONY-DISCORD, MELODY-DISSONANCE, VARIANCE-ACCORD.
con-cord'-ance. An index; concord. ASSENT-DISSENT, HARMONY-DISCORD, WORD-NEOLOGY.

con-cord'-ant. Consonance. HARMONY-DISCORD, VARIANCE-ACCORD.

con-cor'-dat. A compact. CONTRACT.

concordia discors [L.] (con-cor'-di-ɑ dis'-cors). Discordant harmony. HARMONY-DISCORD, REGULARITY-IRREGULARITY.

concours [F.] (con'-cur'). Competition. STRIFE-PEACE.

con'-course. An assembly. CONCENTRATION-RADIATION, GATHERING-SCATTERING.

con''-cre-ma'-tion. Cremation. HEATING-COOLING.

con'-crete. Joined together; a hard mass. COHESION-LOOSENESS, HARDNESS-SOFTNESS, MATERIALS, SOLIDITY-RARITY; **concrete noun,** NOUN.

con-cre'-tion. Solidification. COHESION-LOOSENESS, SOLIDITY-RARITY.

con-cu'-bi-nage. State of being or having concubines. PURITY-IMPURITY.

con'-cu-bine. A kept mistress. PURITY-RAKE.

con-cu'-pis-cence. Illicit desire. DESIRE-DISTASTE, PURITY-IMPURITY.

con-cu'-pis-cent. Carnal. PURITY-IMPURITY.

con-cur'. To agree; to cooperate; unite. ANTAGONISM-CONCURRENCE, ASSENT-DISSENT, COEXISTENCE, CONCENTRATION-RADIATION, COOPERATION-OPPOSITION.

con-cur'-rence. Cooperation. ASSENT-DISSENT, COEXISTENCE, CONCENTRATION-RADIATION, COOPERATION-OPPOSITION, HARMONY-DISCORD.

con-cur'-rent. Acting or occurring together. COEXISTENCE, CONCENTRATION-RADIATION, COOPERATION-OPPOSITION.

con-cur'-ring. Agreeing. COOPERATION-OPPOSITION.

con-cus'-sion. A violent shock. IMPETUS-REACTION.

con-demn'. Censure. APPROVAL-DISAPPROVAL, EXCULPATION-CONVICTION.

con''-dem-na'-tion. State of being or act of condemning. APPROVAL-DISAPPROVAL, EXCULPATION-CONVICTION, JUSTIFICATION-CHARGE.

con-dem'-na-to-ry. Condemning. APPROVAL-DISAPPROVAL, EXCULPATION-CONVICTION.

con-demned'. Convicted. EXCULPATION-CONVICTION.

con''-den-sa'-tion. Act of compressing. ENLARGEMENT-DIMINUTION, SOLIDITY-RARITY.

con-dense'. To compress. DIGEST, ENLARGEMENT-DIMINUTION, SOLIDITY-RARITY, TERSENESS-PROLIXITY.

con-dens'-er. Solidifying apparatus. CHEMISTRY.

con''-de-scend'. To be gracious. SELFRESPECT-HUMBLENESS.

con''-de-scend'-ing. Deigning. SELFRESPECT-HUMBLENESS.

con''-de-scen'-sion. Graciousness. SELFRESPECT-HUMBLENESS, POLITENESS-IMPOLITENESS.

con-dign'. Well deserved. DUENESS-UNDUENESS.

con'-di-ment. A sauce. CONDIMENT, NUTRIMENT-EXCRETION.

CONDIMENT.

Condiment. A sauce, relish, or spice.
Relish. A savory dish served to stimulate appetite.
Seasoning. Something added to food to give a higher relish.

CONDIMENT—*Denotations.*

Caviare. The roes of certain fish, prepared and salted.
Cayenne. A pungent pepper.
Curry. An East-Indian sauce of pepper and spice.
Garlic. A plant with a very pungent taste.
Mustard. A powder from mustard seed, used as a condiment.
Onion. A plant with a strong-flavored bulb, used as food.
Pepper. A pungently aromatic condiment.
Pickle. Any article of food preserved in vinegar.
Pot-herbs. Any plant, as spinach, the leaves of which are used for food.
Salt. Chloride of sodium, used for seasoning.
Sauce. A composition of appetizing ingredients.
Sauce piquante [F.]. A sharp sauce.
Spice. A vegetable production, fragrant or aromatic.

CONDIMENT—*Verbs.*

Season, etc. To increase the relish or savor of, etc. See PUNGENCY.

con''-dis-ci'-ple. A fellow student. INSTRUCTOR-PUPIL.

con-di'-tion. A state of being; a rank; hypothesis; qualification; a prerequisite. CONDITION-SITUATION, GENTILITY-DEMOCRACY, HYPOTHESIS, MODIFICATION, TERMS; **in condition,** GREATNESS-LITTLENESS; **in good condition,** GOODNESS-BADNESS, GREATNESS-LITTLENESS; **in perfect condition,** FAULTLESSNESS-FAULTINESS; **on condition,** TERMS; **physical condition,** MATERIALITY-SPIRITUALITY.

CONDITION—SITUATION.

Aspect, etc. A characteristic part of an appearance, etc. See APPEARANCE.
Case. The condition of things in a given instance.
Category. Condition; any comprehensive class of things.
Character. General outline or condition.
Complexion. General appearance.
Condition. Temporary state of something.
Constitution. The frame and vitality of any living or organized thing.
Diathesis. Predisposition to certain diseases.
Estate. State.
Fabric, etc. Make-up, etc. See TEXTURE.
Fashion. Appearance.
Fit. An adjustment to conditions.
Form, etc. Figure, etc. See FORM.
Frame. The entire make-up of things.
Guise. Fashion.
Habitude. Custom or habit.
Light. Aspect.
Lot. Condition or fortune.
Modality. Quality of being marked only by form and not by substance.
Mode. Regular way or manner.
Mold. Character.
Mood. State of the mind.
Pickle. An embarrassing condition.
Plight. A distressing condition.
Schesis. Condition.

Attitude. Physical position, as of the body.
Bearings. Situation of a distant object with regard to a ship's position.
Circumstance. Condition of things surrounding an event.
Conjunction. State of being joined together.
Contingency, etc. The union of a number of causes in producing a practical result, etc. See OCCURRENCE.
Crisis. The turning point in any affair.
Emergence. The process of emerging.
Emergency. An occurrence unforeseen and demanding immediate action.
Exigency. Emergency of minor moment.
Footing. Permanent situation.
How the land lies. Situation of an object with regard to its surroundings.
Juncture. Important occasion.
Occasion. State of affairs in general.
Pass. State of affairs.
Phase. Any one of the various appearances of the same object.
Pinch. Predicament; a tight place.
Place. A particular position.
Point. Step in the movement or gradation of something.
Position. The relative situation of a body.
Posture. Pose.
Predicament. A condition to escape from which is equally dangerous or undesirable in any direction.
Push. Extremity.
Régime. Manner of government; prevalent mode in society.

CONDITION—SITUATION—*Continued.*

Set.   Fixed form or position.
Stamp.   General character.
State.   Manner or mode of existing.
Style.   Mode.
Temper.   Constitution or disposition; mixture of humors.
Tenor.
Tone. } Stamp.
Trim.   General appearance.
Turn.   Form, cast, or shape.

CONDITION—*Verbs.*

Be in a state, etc. See *Nouns.*
Be on a footing.   Be in a condition.
Come to pass.   Happen.
Do.   To bring into a form or state.
Enjoy a state.   Be in a condition gladly.
Fare.   To be in any state or condition.
Labor under a state.   Be in a condition regretfully.
Possess a state.   Have a condition.

CONDITION—*Adjectives.*

Conditional.   Containing or depending upon conditions.
Formal.   Referring to form in contrast to substance.
Modal.   Having the form without the reality.
Organic.   Pertaining to an organ or organs.
Structural.   Pertaining to structure.

CONDITION—*Adverbs.*

As the matter stands.
As, things are. } Under the existing conditions.
Conditionally, etc.   Under certain conditions, etc. See *Adjectives.*
Such being the case, etc.   Under these circumstances, etc. See CONDITION-SITUATION.

con-di'-tion-al.   Not absolute. ANTAGONISM-CONCURRENCE, CONDITION-SITUATION, EVIDENCE-COUNTER-EVIDENCE.
con-di'-tion-al-ly.   Not absolutely. CONDITION-SITUATION, MODIFICATION, POSSIBILITY-IMPOSSIBILITY.
con-di'-tions.   Terms. TERMS.
con-dole'.   Sympathize. COMPASSION-RUTHLESSNESS.
con-do'-lence.   Sympathy. COMPASSION-RUTHLESSNESS, CONDOLENCE, FELICITATION, JUBILATION-LAMENTATION, POLITENESS-IMPOLITENESS.

CONDOLENCE.

Condolence.   Expression of sympathy with a person in trouble or misfortune.
Consolation.   The act of comforting or soothing the mind.
Lamentation, etc.   See JUBILATION-LAMENTATION.
Sympathy.   Feeling corresponding to that which affects another.

CONDOLENCE—*Verbs.*

Afford consolation.   Console.
Condole with.   To express sorrow at the misfortune of another.
Console.   To cheer the mind in distress or grief.
Express pity.   Pity.
Lament with, etc.   See JUBILATION-LAMENTATION.
Supply consolation.   Console.
Sympathize.   To share the feelings and mental states of another.
Testify pity.   Show pity.

con''-do-na'-tion.   Act of condoning. PARDON-VINDICTIVENESS.
con-done'.   To forgive. PARDON-VINDICTIVENESS.
con'-dor.   Chilian coin. VALUES.
con''-dot-tie'-re.   A mercenary chief. BELLIGERENT, WAYFARER-SEAFARER.
con-duce'.   To help effect; to contribute. CAUSE-EFFECT, COOPERATION-OPPOSITION, INCLINATION, USEFULNESS-USELESSNESS.
con-duce'-ment.   Tendency. INCLINATION.
con-du'-cive.   Helping. INCLINATION, USEFULNESS-USELESSNESS.
con-duct'.   To carry on; to convey. MANAGEMENT, TRANSFER; **conduct an inquiry,** INVESTIGATION-ANSWER; **conduct to,** AIM-ABERRATION.

Situation.   Place in connection with all its surroundings.
Standing.   Relative position.
Status [L.].   Condition.
Terms.   Conditions.
Turning-point.   Point of some decisive change.

SITUATION—*Adjectives.*

Adventitious, etc.   Forming only an incidental part, etc. See OBJECTIVENESS.
Circumstantial.   Dependent upon indirectly related incidents.
Conditional.   Depending on certain modifying terms.
Contingent.   Depending on something else.
Critical.   Pertaining to the turning-point in some event.
Given.   Granted.
Incidental.   Occurring along with something else.
Modal.   Denoting a manner.

SITUATION—*Adverbs.*

Accordingly, in a manner conformable to the circumstances; **according to the circumstances; according to the occasion; as it may be; as it may happen; as it may turn out; as the case may be; as the wind blows,** under the existing circumstances; **as things go; as times go; conditionally,** under certain modifying terms; **if, provided that; if it be so; if it so happen; if it so turn out; if so; if so be; in case,** under the condition that; **in such a case; in such a contingency; in such an event; in such wise,** in such a manner; **in the circumstances; in the event of,** provided that it happens; *pro re nata* [L.], according to the circumstances; **provided,** on condition; **provisionally,** for the present exigency; **seeing that,** taking that condition into account; **since, sith,** seeing that; **such being the case; that being so; that being the case; thus,** in this or that manner; **under the circumstances,** etc. (see *Nouns*); **under the conditions,** etc. (see CONDITION); **unless,** without the case that; **without,** excepting the circumstance that.

con'-duct.   Behavior; control. CONDUCT, MANAGEMENT; **safe conduct,** INSTRUMENTALITY, SECURITY-INSECURITY.

CONDUCT.

Bearing.   Manner in which one conducts oneself.
Behavior.   Manner of behaving, or mode of conducting oneself.
Business.   What one has to do or should do.
Campaign.   Course of operation.
Career.   General course of life.
Carriage.   Manner of carrying oneself; personal conduct.
Comportment.   Manner of acting.
Conduct.   Manner of guiding or carrying oneself.
Course.   Manner of procedure; line of conduct.
Course of action.   Line of action.
Course of conduct.   Line of conduct.
Course of procedure.   Line of procedure.
Dealing.   Method of business or intercourse.
Demeanor.   Behavior; mien.
Deportment.   Manner of acting with respect to the courtesies and duties of life.
Economics.   Science of conducting household affairs.
Economy.   Conduct of domestic affairs.
Execution.   Act or mode of performing.
Game.   One's method of operation.
Generalship.   Management.
Government.   Mode of governing or managing. See MANAGEMENT.
Guise.   Customary way of speaking or acting.
Housekeeping.   Management of domestic affairs.
Housewifery.   Female management of domestic concerns.
Husbandry.   Domestic management.
Life.   Certain way or manner of living.
Line of action.   Manner of acting.
Line of conduct.   Manner of carrying oneself.
Line of procedure.   Way of proceeding.
Maintien [F.].   Deportment or carriage.
Management.   Mode or way of handling.
Manipulation.   Artful management.
Manner.   Characteristic mode of acting or conducting oneself.
Ménage [F.].   Housekeeping.
Method.   Regular manner of doing anything.
Modus operandi [L.].   Regular method of operation.
Observance.   Customary action or service.
Path.   Regular course of conduct. See WAY.
Plan.   Method of action or procedure described or expressed in language. See DESIGN.
Policy.   Method by which any institution is administered.

Political economy. That branch of political science that treats of methods of production of wealth.
Polity. Recognized principles.
Practise. Customary or constant use.
Procedure. Act or manner of proceeding.
Process. Regular method of operation.
Race. Characteristic quality or disposition.
Régime [F.]. Mode or system of rule or management.
Rôle [F.]. A part or character which one performs.
Seamanship. Management of vessels.
Statesmanship. Method of conducting political affairs.
Stewardship. Management.
Strategics. } Military management.
Strategy. }
Tactics. System or method of procedure.
Transaction. Method of conducting business.
Treatment. Act or manner of treating.
Walk. Course of action.
Ways. Resolved mode of action or conduct.

CONDUCT—*Verbs.*

Acquit oneself. To bear or conduct oneself.
Adopt a course. To select for pursuit.
Behave oneself. To conduct; to carry.
Carry into effect. Execute.
Carry on. Behave.
Carry oneself. Conduct oneself.
Carry out. } Perform.
Carry through. }
Comport oneself. Behave.
Conduct, etc. See *Nouns.*
Conduct oneself. Behave.
Deal with. To treat in any manner.
Demean oneself. To comport; to conduct.
Despatch. } To send off hastily.
Dispatch. }
Discharge. To set free.
Enact. To establish by law.
Execute. Carry into effect.
Get through. Finish.
Go through. Transact.
Handle a case. Conduct the proceedings.
Have to do with. To be implicated in some way.
Lead a life. Conduct one's life.
Manage, etc. See MANAGEMENT.
Officiate, etc. See OCCUPATION.
Paddle one's own canoe. To go through life by one's own efforts.
Play a game. Act artfully.
Play one's cards. To put forth an effort at the right time.
Play one's part. To do one's duty.
Practise. To repeat many times to gain dexterity.
Proceed with. To continue.
Put into. To insert; to add.
Put into practise. Perform.
Run a race. Finish a course.
Shape one's course. To lay out one's own pathway.
Shift for oneself. Rely on one's own efforts for success.
Steer one's course. To be one's own pilot.
Take a course. }
Take measures. } To take means to attain one's end.
Take steps. }
Transact. To do; to perform.
Treat. To bear oneself toward.

CONDUCT—*Adjectives.*

Business-like. Well or precisely done.
Conducting, etc. See *Verbs.*
Executive. Possessing the power to control.
Practical. Applying knowledge to some useful end.
Strategical. Pertaining to or displaying foresight.

con-duct'-ing. Behaving. CONDUCT.
con-duc'-tion. Transmission. TRANSFER.
con-duc'-tive-ness. Power of conducting. INCLINATION.
con-duct'-or. A carrier; a manager. CONVEYER, ELECTRICITY, MANAGER; **lightning conductor,** REFUGE-PITFALL.
con'-duit. A passage or channel. ENTRANCE-EXIT, TRANSMISSION, WATERCOURSE-AIRPIPE.
con-du'-pli-cate. To fold together. DUALITY.
con'-dyle. A bony eminence. CONVEXITY-CONCAVITY.

cone. A round figure tapering to a point. ROUNDNESS, SHARPNESS-BLUNTNESS.
con-fab'-u-late. Gossip. CONVERSATION-MONOLOGUE.
con-fab''-u-la'-tion. Chat. CONVERSATION - MONO-LOGUE.
con-fec'-tion. A sweetmeat. SWEETNESS-ACIDITY.
con-fec'-tion-a-ry. Sweetmeat. SWEETNESS-ACIDITY.
con-fed'-er-a-cy. A number in a league. ASSOCIATION, ANTAGONISM-CONCURRENCE.
con-fed'-er-ate. An accomplice. ANTAGONISM-CONCURRENCE, ANTAGONIST-ASSISTANT.
con-fed'-er-a''-ted. Joined. ASSOCIATION.
con-fed''-er-a'-tion. Union. ANTAGONISM-CONCURRENCE, ANTERIORITY-POSTERIORITY, ASSOCIATION.
con-fer'. To hold a conference; to bestow. ADVICE, GIVING-RECEIVING; **confer benefit,** GOODNESS-BADNESS; **confer power,** MIGHT-IMPOTENCE; **confer privilege,** LEAVE-PROHIBITION; **confer right,** DUENESS-UNDUENESS; **confer with,** CONVERSATION-MONOLOGUE.
con'-fer-ence. An official consultation. ADVICE, CONVERSATION-MONOLOGUE, COUNCIL.
con-fer'-va. Fresh-water algæ. FAUNA-FLORA.
con-fess'. To own; to expose; to make confessions. ASSENT-DISSENT, EXPOSURE-HIDINGPLACE, REPENTANCE-OBDURACY; **confess and avoid,** JUSTIFICATION-CHARGE.
con-fes'-sion. Admission; advowal. ASSENT-DISSENT, EXPOSURE-HIDINGPLACE, REPENTANCE-OBDURACY; **auricular confession,** CEREMONIAL; **confession of faith,** ORTHODOXY-HETERODOXY.
con-fes'-sion-al. Pertaining to confessions and their place of being made. EXPOSURE-HIDINGPLACE, FANE.
con-fes'-sions. A disclosure. ACCOUNT.
con-fess'-or. One who confesses or hears confessions. MINISTRY-LAITY.
con'-fi-dant. One trusted. ANTAGONIST-ASSISTANT.
con''-fi-dante'. A female confidant. FRIEND-FOE.
con-fide'. Trust. SANGUINENESS-HOPELESSNESS.
con'-fi-dence. Self-assurance; belief in a person or thing. BRAVERY-COWARDICE, FAITH-MISGIVING, SANGUINENESS-HOPELESSNESS, SECURITY-INSECURITY; **in confidence,** ENLIGHTENMENT-SECRECY.
con'-fi-dent. Having confidence; self-reliant. ASSERTION-DENIAL, BRAVERY-COWARDICE, FAITH-MISGIVING, SANGUINENESS-HOPELESSNESS.
con''-fi-den'-tial. Trusted. ENLIGHTENMENT-SECRECY.
con''-fi-den'-tial-ly. Intimately. ENLIGHTENMENT-SECRECY.
con-fi'-ding. Trusting. FAITH-MISGIVING.
con-fig''-u-ra'-tion. Conformation. FORM-FORMLESSNESS.
con-fine'. To imprison; to restrict. CONFINEMENT, ENCLOSURE, RELEASE-RESTRAINT.
con-fined'. Restricted; brought to childbirth. DECISION-MISJUDGMENT, HEALTH-SICKNESS.
con-fine'-ment. A woman's lying-in. CONFINEMENT, CREATION-DESTRUCTION, RELEASE-RESTRAINT.

CONFINEMENT.

Circumscription. The process of limiting.
Circumvallation. The process of throwing a wall about.
Confinement. Lack of freedom.
Enclosure. State of being shut in.
Limitation. The act of keeping within certain bounds.

CONFINEMENT—*Denotations.*

Envelope, etc. That which envelops, or wraps up, especially the cover of a letter. See ENCLOSURE.
Wrapper. That which encases or surrounds. See ENCLOSURE.

CONFINEMENT—*Verbs.*

Bound. To limit the extension.
Bury. To hide or cover up.

Circumscribe. To limit in action, range, etc.
Compass about. To surround.
Confine. To shut up within an enclosure.
Enclose. To surround.
Enfold. To wrap up in.
Enshrine. To place in a shrine.
Fence round. To enclose with a fence.
Hedge in. To enclose with or as with a hedge.
Hedge round. To surround.
Imprison. To put in prison.
Incase. To enclose in a case.
Inclasp. To clasp within.
Limit. To set bounds to.
Pack up. To stow in any receptacle.
Picket. To fence with pickets.
Rail in. To shut in with rails.
Surround, etc. To shut in on all sides, etc. See ENVIRONMENT.
Wall in. To surround with walls.
Wrap up, etc. To enclose something, etc. See DRESS-UNDRESS.

CONFINEMENT—*Adjectives.*

Begirt. Surrounded as with a band.
Buried in. Absorbed in.
Circumscribed, etc. Confined within bounds, etc. See *Verbs.*
Embedded. Deposited in a partly enclosing mass.
Embosomed. Received into one's bosom.
Encysted. Enclosed in a membranous sac.
Immersed in. Dipped in.
Imprisoned, etc. Deprived of liberty, etc. See RELEASE-RESTRAINT.
In a ring fence. Surrounded by a ring fence.
In the bloom of. Covered with; in a flourishing condition.
Land-locked. Enclosed by land.
Lapt. Wrapped around. ["All thy friends are lapt in lead." Shakespeare, *P. Pilgrim*, 396.]
Mewed up. Shut up.

con'-fines. Limit. REMOTENESS-NEARNESS; **on the confines of**, REMOTENESS-NEARNESS.
con-firm'. To verify; to establish in church membership; to sanction; to strengthen. ASSENT-DISSENT, CEREMONIAL, CONTRACT, DECISION-MISJUDGMENT, EVIDENCE-COUNTEREVIDENCE.
con''-fir-ma'-tion. Act of confirming; proof. ASSENT-DISSENT, CEREMONIAL, CONSENT, EVIDENCE-COUNTEREVIDENCE.
con-firm'-a-to-ry. Helping to prove. EVIDENCE-COUNTEREVIDENCE.
con-firmed'. Fully established. MUTABILITY-STABILITY; **confirmed habit**, HABIT-DESUETUDE.
con'-fis-cate. To take for public funds. EXCULPATION-CONVICTION, RECOMPENSE-PENALTY, TAKING-RESTITUTION.
con''-fis-ca'-tion. Act of confiscating. RECOMPENSE-PENALTY, TAKING-RESTITUTION.
con'-fi-ture. A confection. SWEETNESS-ACIDITY.
con'-fla-gra'-tion. A burning. HEATING-COOLING.
con-flex'-ure. Curvation. CURVATION-RECTILINEARITY.
con'-flict. A strife; an antagonism. ANTAGONISM-CONCURRENCE, HARMONY-DISCORD, STRIFE-PEACE, VARIANCE-ACCORD.
con-flic'-ting. Contending. COOPERATION-OPPOSITION, SAMENESS-CONTRAST; **conflicting evidence,** EVIDENCE-COUNTEREVIDENCE.
con'-flu-ence. A junction; a concourse. CONCENTRATION-RADIATION, RIVER-WIND, UNION-DISUNION.
con'-flux. A confluence. CONCENTRATION-RADIATION, GATHERING-SCATTERING.
con-form'. To comply. ASSENT-DISSENT, PROPRIETY-IMPROPRIETY, UNIFORMITY-DIVERSITY.
con-form'-a-ble. Correspondent. HABIT-DESUETUDE, HARMONY-DISCORD.
con-form'-a-bly. Consistently. CONVENTIONALITY-UNCONVENTIONALITY.
con-form'-ance. Conformity. HARMONY-DISCORD, CONVENTIONALITY-UNCONVENTIONALITY.
con''-for-ma'-tion. Arrangement of parts. FORM-FORMLESSNESS.

con-form'-i-ty. Agreement. CONVENTIONALITY-UNCONVENTIONALITY, HABIT-DESUETUDE, HARMONY-DISCORD, UNIFORMITY-DIVERSITY, UNIFORMITY-MULTIFORMITY; **conformity with nature,** NATURE-ART.
con-found'. To bewilder; to perplex; to abash; to mix. ASTONISHMENT-EXPECTANCE, CERTAINTY-DOUBT, CHARITABLENESS-CURSE, CREATION-DESTRUCTION, DIFFERENTIATION-INDISCRIMINATION, ORGANIZATION-DISORGANIZATION, SUCCESS-FAILURE.
con-found'-ed. Abashed. GOODNESS-BADNESS.
con-found'-ed-ly. Greatly. MAGNITUDE-SMALLNESS.
con''-fra-ter'-ni-ty. Brotherhood. AMITY-HOSTILITY, ASSOCIATION.
confrère [F.]. (con'-frar'). A fellow member. ANTAGONIST-ASSISTANT, FRIEND-FOE.
con''-fri-ca'-tion. A rubbing together. FRICTION-LUBRICATION.
con-front'. To face defiantly; to put face to face. ANTAGONISM-CONCURRENCE, ANTERIORITY-POSTERIORITY, COMPARISON, REPRISAL-RESISTANCE; **confront danger,** BRAVERY-COWARDICE; **confront witnesses,** EVIDENCE-COUNTEREVIDENCE.
Con-fu'-ci-us. Chinese sage. REVELATION-PSEUDO-REVELATION.
con-fuse'. To perplex the mind; to confound; to derange. CERTAINTY-DOUBT, CLEARNESS-OBSCURITY, DIFFERENTIATION-INDISCRIMINATION, HEED-DISREGARD, ORGANIZATION-DISORGANIZATION, SELFRESPECT-HUMBLENESS.
con-fused'. Distracted; disordered. CERTAINTY-DOUBT, CLEARNESS-OBSCURITY, REGULARITY-IRREGULARITY, VISIBILITY-INVISIBILITY.
con-fu'-sed-ness. Disorder. REGULARITY-IRREGULARITY.
con-fu'-sion. Distraction; abashment. ORGANIZATION-DISORGANIZATION, REGULARITY-IRREGULARITY, SELFRESPECT-HUMBLENESS; **confusion of tongues,** LANGUAGE, WORD-NEOLOGY; **confusion of vision,** SIGHT-DIMSIGHTEDNESS; **confusion seize,** CHARITABLENESS-CURSE; **confusion worse confounded,** REGULARITY-IRREGULARITY.
con-fu'-ta-ble. Refutable. PROOF-DISPROOF.
con''-fu-ta'-tion. Disproof. ASSERTION-DENIAL, PROOF-DISPROOF.
con-fute'. Refute. PROOF-DISPROOF.
con-fu'-ted. Refuted. PROOF-DISPROOF.
con-fu'-ting. Refuting. PROOF-DISPROOF.
congé [F.] (con'-zhê'). Leave-taking. ARRIVAL-DEPARTURE, COMMISSION-ABROGATION, LEAVE-PROHIBITION.
congé d'élire [F.] (con'-zhê' dê-lîr'). Permission to elect. CHURCH.
con-geal'. To freeze hard or solid. HEATING-COOLING, SOLIDITY-RARITY.
con''-ge-la'-tion. Clot. HEATING-COOLING.
con'-ge-ner. One of the same kind. ADMISSION-EXCLUSION, LIKENESS-UNLIKENESS.
con-gen'-er-ous. Concurring in action. ADMISSION-EXCLUSION.
con-ge'-nial. Sympathetic; agreeable. HARMONY-DISCORD, LOVE-HATE, VARIANCE-ACCORD.
con-ge''-ni-al'-i-ty. Agreeableness. HARMONY-DISCORD.
con-gen'-i-tal. Born with one. SUBJECTIVENESS-OBJECTIVENESS.
con-gen'-ite. Born with one. SUBJECTIVENESS-OBJECTIVENESS.
con-ge'-ri-es. Mass. GATHERING-SCATTERING.
con-ges'-tion. Excess of blood. EXCESS-LACK, GATHERING-SCATTERING.
con-gla''-ci-a'-tion. A freezing solid. HEATING-COOLING.
con''-glo-ba'-tion. Gathering into a ball. GATHERING-SCATTERING.

con-glom'-er-ate. To gather into a mass. COHESION-LOOSENESS, GATHERING-SCATTERING, SOLIDITY-RARITY.

con-glom''-er-a'-tion. Concretion. COHESION-LOOSENESS.

con-glu'-ti-nate. To glue together. COHESION-LOOSENESS.

con-glu''-ti-na'-tion. Adherence. COHESION-LOOSENESS.

con-grat'-u-late. To felicitate. FELICITATION; **congratulate oneself,** FELICITATION, JUBILATION-LAMENTATION.

con-grat''-u-la'-tion. Act of congratulating. FELICITATION, JUBILATION-LAMENTATION.

con-grat'-u-la-to-ry. Expressing congratulation. FELICITATION.

con''-gre-ga'-tion. An assemblage for religious worship; a gathering. DEVOTION-IDOLATRY, GATHERING-SCATTERING, MINISTRY-LAITY.

Con''-gre-ga'-tion-al-ist. A member of the Congregational Church. ORTHODOXY-HETERODOXY.

con'-gress. An assembly; a coming together. CONCENTRATION-RADIATION, CONVERSATION-MONOLOGUE, COUNCIL, GATHERING-SCATTERING.

Con'-gress-man. Member of Congress. PRESIDENT-MEMBER.

con'-greve. A friction match. COMBUSTIBLE, WEAPON; **congreve rocket,** WEAPON.

con'-gru-ence. Appropriateness. HARMONY-DISCORD.

con-gru'-i-ty. Appropriateness. HARMONY-DISCORD.

con'-gru-ous. Appropriate. HARMONY-DISCORD.

con'-ic-al. Conic. ROUNDNESS, SHARPNESS-BLUNTNESS.

con-jec'-tur-al. Depending on conjecture. HYPOTHESIS.

con-jec''-tu-ral'-i-ty. Quality of being conjectural. HYPOTHESIS.

con-jec'-ture. To surmise. HYPOTHESIS.

con-join'. To unite. UNION-DISUNION

con-joint'. Associated. UNION-DISUNION.

con-joint'-ly. In association. ADDITION-SUBTRACTION.

con'-ju-gal. Matrimonial. MATRIMONY-CELIBACY.

con'-ju-gate. To give in order. DUALITY, WORD-NEOLOGY; **conjugate in all its tenses,** RECURRENCE.

con''-ju-ga'-tion. Conjunction. BIOLOGY, CONVERSION, DUALITY, GRAMMAR-SOLECISM, UNION-DISUNION, VERB.

con-junct'. Joined together. UNION-DISUNION.

con-junc'-tion A union. PARTICLE, UNION-DISUNION; **in conjunction with,** ADDITION-SUBTRACTION, UNION-DISUNION.

con''-ju-ra'-tion. Invocation. DEVOTION-MAGIC, TRUTHFULNESS-FRAUD.

con-jure'. To call on God; bewitch. DEVOTION-MAGIC, PETITION-EXPOSTULATION, TRUTHFULNESS-FRAUD; **conjure up a vision,** FANCY.

con'-jur-er. A juggler. DEVOTION-MAGICIAN, GULL-DECEIVER.

con-jur'-ing. Appealing to solemnly. TRUTHFULNESS-FRAUD.

connaître les dessous des cartes [F.] (co-nêtr' lê de-su' de cart). To know the under card. KNOWLEDGE-IGNORANCE.

con-nate'. Innate. CAUSE-EFFECT, SUBJECTIVENESS-OBJECTIVENESS.

con-nat'-u-ral. Congenital. LIKENESS-UNLIKENESS, UNIFORMITY-DIVERSITY.

con-nat''-u-ral'-i-ty. Natural similarity. UNIFORMITY-DIVERSITY.

con-nat'-u-ral-ize. To connect by nature. UNIFORMITY-DIVERSITY.

con-nat'-u-ral-ness. Natural connection. UNIFORMITY-DIVERSITY.

con-nect'. To join; to associate. CONNECTION-INDEPENDENCE, CONNECTIVE, UNION-DISUNION.

con-nect'-ed. United. CONNECTION-INDEPENDENCE.

con-nec'-tion. Union. CONNECTION-INDEPENDENCE, CONNECTIVE.

CONNECTION—INDEPENDENCE.

Affinity. A close relationship, whether artificial or natural.

Alliance. A union of any kind for giving mutual aid.

Analogy. A resemblance of relations.

Approximation, etc. The act or result of coming near to without actually reaching, etc. See REMOTENESS-NEARNESS.

Association. The relation of being frequently together, either actually or in thought.

Bearing. Relation to something.

Bond of union. That which serves to unite.

Cognation. Relationship by blood.

Comparison, etc. Relative resemblance, etc. See COMPARISON.

Concern. Interest felt in anything.

Connection. Relationship.

Correlation, etc. Reciprocal relation, etc. See INTERDEPENDENCE.

Filiation, etc. The relation of a child to a parent, etc. See RELATIONSHIP.

Homogeneity. Identity or similarity of nature or composition.

Homology. The condition of being similar in form or structure.

Interest. Importance; feeling of sympathy for or curiosity about something.

Link. That which binds together separate things

Proportion. Degree of relationship; ratio.

Ratio. Relative amount.

Reference. A slight relation; usually in a single point.

Relation. The condition of being in some way connected, associated, or similar.

Relevancy. The condition of being in some way suited or related to the matter in hand.

Similarity. Resemblance.

Tie. The feeling of relationship or connection.

CONNECTION—*Verbs.*

Affect. To influence or change in any way.

Answer to. To correspond to.

Appertain to. To have a proper relation to.

Associate. To connect in thought

Disassociation. Want of association.

Disconnection. The condition of lacking relation or connection.

Heterogeneity. Dissimilarity of quality or kind.

Impertinence. Irrelevancy.

Incommensurability. The quality or condition of two quantities having no common measure.

Inconnection. See DISCONNECTION.

Inconsequence. The condition of lacking logical connection.

Independence. State of not being bound to anything else.

Intrusion, etc. See HARMONY-DISCORD.

Irreconcilableness. The condition of not allowing to be reconciled or made to agree.

Irrelation. Lack of relation.

Irrelevancy. Quality of not pertaining to: as a statement to an argument.

Misrelation. Erroneous relation.

Multifariousness. Lack of common nature.

Nihil ad rem [L.]. Nothing to the purpose.

Unconformity. Lack of conformity, harmony, or agreement.

INDEPENDENCE—*Verbs.*

Bring in head and shoulders. To bring in by force or violence.

Drag in head and shoulders. Bring in unnecessarily.

Have no bearing upon.
Have no business there.
Have no business with. } **Have no connection with.**
Have no concern with.
Have no relation to.
Have nothing to do with.

Intrude. To force upon, or thrust in that which has no real connection, as in an argument.

Lug in head and shoulders. See BRING IN HEAD AND SHOULDERS.

INDEPENDENCE—*Adjectives.*

Adrift. Unmoored; floating; hence, without relation or connection.

Alien. Of different nature; foreign.

CONNECTION—INDEPENDENCE—*Continued.*

CONNECTION—Verbs—*Continued.*

Bear upon. To be so related as to affect or influence in some degree.
Belong to. To be related to.
Be related, etc. See *Adjectives.*
Bring into relation with. To bring into such a position as to affect.
Bring to bear upon. To cause to influence or affect.
Concern. To interest or draw the attention.
Connect. To unite or combine in any manner.
Draw a parallel. To make a comparison and point out the similarity.
Have a relation, etc. See *Nouns.*
Have to do with. To have concern or relations with.
Interest. To engage the attention or curiosity of.
Link, etc. To bind together separate things, etc. See UNION.
Pertain to. See APPERTAIN TO.
Refer to. To have relation to.
Regard. Same as REFER TO.
Relate to. To pertain to or be connected with.
Touch. To concern or affect.

CONNECTION—*Adjectives.*

Affiliated. Closely related.
Allied to. Bound to, as by treaty; also related by similarity of structure, etc.
Allusive. Pertaining to indirectly.
Approximating. Coming near to in any respect.
Approximative. Tending to, or obtained by, approximation.
Appurtenant to. Relating to something more important.
Associated. Connected in thought, etc.
Belonging to, etc. See *Verbs.*
Cognate. Related by blood.
Comparable. Allowing of comparison.
Connected. See *Verbs.*
Correlative. Having a reciprocal relation.
En rapport [F.]. In harmony or agreement.
Implicated. Connected with, or involved in; often in a bad sense.
In common with. Having the same part or interest as others.
In relation with. Related.
In the same category. Of the same kind or class.
Like. Similar.
Proportionable.
Proportional. } Varying as something else varies.
Proportionate.
Referable to. Capable of being considered in relation to.
Related. }
Relating. } See *Verbs.*
Relative. Having relation; pertaining.
Relative to. Pertaining to.
Relevant. See RELEVANCY.

CONNECTION—*Adverbs, etc.*

About; anent, concerning; in regard to; as far as; as for; as relates to; as respects; as to; by the bye; by the way; concerning; for as much as; in as much as; in connection with; in point of; in respect of; on the score of; pertinently, etc. (see HARMONY); *pro re nata* [L.], according to the circumstances; *quoad hoc* [L.], to this extent, as far as this; relating to; thereof; under the head; whereas; while speaking *à propos,* while speaking to the point; while speaking to; with reference to; with relation to; with respect to.

CONNECTION—*Phrase.*

Thereby hangs a tale. [Shakespeare, *As You Like It,* II, vii; *Taming of the Shrew,* IV, i.]

INDEPENDENCE—Adverbs—*Continued from Column 2.*

Parenthetically, etc. See *Adjectives.*
Without reference to. }
Without regard to. } Independently of.

---

con-nect′-ive. That which connects. CONNECTIVE, PARTICLE.

CONNECTIVE.

Connecting medium. Means of uniting.
Connective. That which connects.
Intermedium. Connective.

CONNECTIVE—*Denotations.*

Anchor. An iron instrument which by laying hold of the bottom retains a ship in a particular station.

INDEPENDENCE—Adjectives—*Continued.*

À propos de bottes [F.]. With reference to the boots; **without** relevancy.
Arbitrary. Without logical connection.
Away from the point.
Away from the purpose.
Away from the question.
Away from the transaction.
Beside the mark. } Not connected with the point, etc.
Beside the point.
Beside the purpose.
Beside the question.
Beside the transaction.
Detached. Disconnected.
Disconnected. Separated; disunited.
Discordant, etc. Contradictory; disagreeing, etc. See HARMONY-DISCORD.
Episodic. Out of the regular course of events; as an episode of an epic poem; not directly connected.
Exotic. Foreign; of another kind or nature.
Extraneous. Having no essential relation; irrelevant.
Far fetched. Studiously sought; not natural or obvious.
Forced. Not arising from natural causes or relations.
Foreign. Not native; having no relation.
Foreign to the point.
Foreign to the purpose. } Not pertinent.
Foreign to the question.
Foreign to the transaction.
Heterogeneous. Dissimilar in structure or kind.
Impertinent. Having no bearing on the subject; irrelevant.
Inapplicable. Not suited to the matter in hand.
Inapposite. Not pertinent.
Incidental. Happening by chance; without regularity or design.
Incommensurable. See *Nouns.*
Independent. Separate or disconnected; having no connections.
Insular. Standing alone; isolated.
Irrelative. Without mutual connection; unconnected.
Irrelevant. Foreign to the subject; impertinent.
Irrespective. Lacking relation.
Isolated. Detached or insular.
Misplaced. Placed out of natural relations.
Multifarious. Having great diversity or variety.
Neither here nor there. Foreign to the subject under discussion.
Not comparable. Not allowing of comparison.
Not pertinent. Not to the point.
Not to the purpose. Irrelevant.
Obiter dictum [L.]. Something spoken by the way or in passing.
Outlandish. Not according to usage; uncouth.
Out of the way. Foreign.
Parenthetical. Not essentially a part.
Quite another thing. An entirely different matter.
Remote. Having slight relation or connection.
Segregate. Separate; select.
Strange. Not related; belonging elsewhere.
Unallied. Not bound to; also, not similar in form or structure.
Unconformable. See CONVENTIONALITY-UNCONVENTIONALITY.
Unconnected. Not logically or naturally related.

INDEPENDENCE—*Adverbs.*

A se [L.]. By itself.
By the bye. By the way.
By the way. Incidentally.
En passant [F.]. In passing; by the way.
Incidentally. In a closely related way.
Irrespectively, etc. See *Adjectives.*
In the abstract. In its general meaning.

(*Continued on Column 1.*)

Bandage. A strip of cloth to retain dressings on wounds.
Birdlime. Sticky substance smeared on twigs to catch birds.
Bolt. A strong pin of iron used to hold something in place.
Bond. That which binds, ties, or fastens.
Bond of union. Anything that serves to join together.
Brace. That which holds or supports anything firmly; an arm.
Bracket. Anything used to support a weight; a mark of punctuation.
Brad. A small nail.
Braid. Woven tape.
Bridge. A roadway over a stream.
Buckle. A device for fastening things together.

Button. A catch of various materials to fasten the parts of dress.

Cable. A strong rope or chain used to retain a vessel at anchor.

Catch. That by which anything is fastened.

Cement. A calcined limestone mortar.

Cestus. A strap worn around the arm by ancient boxers.

Chain. A series of metal links used as a rope.

Clamp. Something rigid that holds fast or binds things together.

Clasp. An adjustable catch for holding two objects together.

Connection. Anything serving to unite two objects.

Copula. A word which unites the subject and the predicate.

Cord. A small rope or string.

Cordage. Ropes or cords collectively.

Corking-pin. A pin formerly used in attaching a woman's head-dress to a cork model.

Cramp. A mechanical device for binding pieces together.

Fastening. Anything used for uniting or joining.

Fiber. One of the threadlike portions of which the tissues of plants and animals are made up.

Fillet. A ribbon for encircling the head.

Garter. A band for fastening a stocking.

Girder. A beam bearing vertically upon its supports.

Girdle. A belt for holding articles of dress.

Girth. A band with which a saddle is fastened on a horse.

Glue. A substance for sticking.

Grappling-iron. A device having claws for fastening or holding.

Grout. A mortar.

Gum. A substance of sticky properties.

Halser. A cable.

Hank. Rope; one or more skeins of yarn.

Harness. A horse's equipment for drawing a wagon.

Hasp. A metal hook for fastening a door.

Hawser. A large rope.

Hinge. A device for holding a door fast to a building.

Holdfast. Anything used to secure or hold in place.

Hook. A piece of metal bent at an angle for catching anything.

Hook and eye. A wire hook and loop for holding the edges of a garment together.

Inkle. A tape or braid.

Isthmus. A narrow neck of land joining two larger portions.

Junction. That which serves as a connection. See UNION.

Knot. A fastening together of the parts or ends of one or more threads.

Lasso. A rope with a running noose.

Latch. That which fastens or holds.

Latchet. The string that fastens a shoe.

Ligament. A cord that unites bones and muscles in the body.

Ligature. Anything which serves to bind.

Line. A linen thread or string.

Lock. A fastening for a door.

Lute. A cement.

Moorings. That which serves to confine a ship to a place.

Mortar. A plaster made by mixing lime, cement, etc.

Nail. An iron pin for holding timbers together.

Noose. A running knot or loop.

Padlock. A lock which fastens by means of a bow fitting through a staple.

Painter. A rope used to fasten a boat.

Paste. Any substance used for sticking.

Pin. A piece of metal used for holding separate articles together.

Plaster. A substance or mixture used for holding stones together.

Post. A piece of timber used as a stay or support for something.

Prop. A piece of timber which is used for supporting anything.

Putty. A thick paste made of whiting and linseed oil.

Rein. The strap of a bridle by which the driver governs the horse.

Ribband. A ribbon.

Rigging. Ropes, as of a ship.

Rivet. A metallic pin, the end of which can be beaten to cover a large space.

Roller. A bandage rolled up.

Running knot. Knot made to slip along a noose.

Running rigging. Ropes controlling the sails.

Screw. A piece of metal with a thread winding around it spirally.

Shackle. A fetter for the legs.

Size. Sticky substance used in gilding.

Skewer. A wooden pin used to hold meat.

Solder. A metallic alloy easily melted, used for uniting edges of metallic articles.

Stake. A post for tying things to.

Standing rigging. Permanent ropes of sails.

Staple. A U-shaped piece of metal for holding the fastening of a padlock.

Stepping-stone. A connection.

Strap. A band of leather.

String. A small cord.

Stucco. Plaster used for external purposes.

Surcingle. A girth of a beast of burden, holding on the saddle or blanket.

Tack. A short nail.

Tackle. A mechanism of ropes, pulley blocks, etc., for raising and lowering weights.

Tag. A direction card or label.

Tendon. A cord to which muscles are attached.

Tendril. That part of a plant which winds itself about objects and supports the plant.

Thong. A long narrow strip of leather used for fastening.

Tie. A bond.

Tie beam. A timber that serves as a tie, as between walls.

Tooth. Projecting stones or bricks to which material is attached.

Traces. The straps of a harness attached to the vehicle.

Trennel. A slender piece of wood used in fastening timbers together.

Vinculum. A bond of union.

Wafer. A disk used in sealing letters.

Wire. A metal cord.

With. }
Withe. } A band made of twisted shoots of trees or shrubs.

Withy. A rope made of withes.

Yoke. A frame or cross-bar for coupling animals

CONNECTIVE—*Verbs.*

Bridge over. To make a passage over.

Connect, etc. To join together as by links or fastenings, etc. See UNION.

Hang, etc. To fasten or attach to some object above, etc. See SUSPENSION.

Span. To attach.

conned, well. Well learnt. KNOWLEDGE-IGNORANCE.

con-nex'-ion. Same as connection. CONNECTION-INDEPENDENCE, RELATIONSHIP, UNION-DISUNION; **in connexion with,** CONNECTION-INDEPENDENCE.

con-nex-ions. Connections. ENTERTAINMENT-WEARINESS.

con-ni'-vance. Act of conniving. LEAVE-PROHIBITION.

con-nive'. To look over. CAREFULNESS-CARELESSNESS, LEAVE-PROHIBITION.

con''-nois-seur'. A judge of art. ADEPT-BUNGLER, DECISION-MISJUDGMENT, SCHOLAR-DUNCE, TASTE-VULGARITY.

con'-no-tate. To indicate as by a word. SIGN.

con-no'-ta-tive. Implying a correlative. SIGN.

con-note'. To connotate. SIGN.

con-nu'-bi-al. Matrimonial. MATRIMONY-CELIBACY.

conoscente [It.] (co-no-shen'-tê). A knowing one. VULGARITY.

con'-quer. To overcome. SUCCESS-FAILURE.

con'-quered. Overcome. SUCCESS-FAILURE.

con'-quer-ing he'-ro comes. SOLEMNIZATION.

con'-quer-or. One who conquers. SUCCESS-FAILURE.

con'-quest. Something conquered. SUCCESS-FAILURE.

con''-san-guin'-e-ous. Akin. RELATIONSHIP.

con''-san-guin'-i-ty. Blood-relationship. RELATIONSHIP, PARENTAGE-PROGENY.

conscia recti, mens [L.] (con'-shi-a rec'-tai, menz). A mind conscious of rectitude. INNOCENCE-GUILT, SELFRESPECT-HUMBLENESS, UPRIGHTNESS-DISHONESTY.

con'-science. The moral sense. DUTY-DERELICTION, FEELING-INSENSIBILITY, KNOWLEDGE-IGNORANCE; **awakened conscience,** REPENTANCE-OBDURACY; **clear conscience,** INNOCENCE-GUILT; **in all conscience,** ASSERTION-DENIAL, MAGNITUDE-SMALLNESS; **qualms of conscience,** REPENTANCE-OBDURACY; **stricken conscience,** REPENTANCE-OBDURACY; **tender conscience,** DUTY-DERELICTION.

conscientia sana, murus æreus [L.] (con-si-en'-shi-a sê'-na, miu'-rus î'-rî-us). A sound conscience is a wall of brass. INNOCENCE-GUILT.

con''-sci-en'-tious. Governed by conscience. DUTY-DERELICTION, UPRIGHTNESS-DISHONESTY.

con''-sci-en'-tious-ness. Scrupulousness. DUTY-DERELICTION, KNOWLEDGE-IGNORANCE.

con'-scious. Aware of one's existence. KNOWLEDGE-IGNORANCE, MIND-IMBECILITY; **conscious of disgrace,** REPUTATION-DISCREDIT, SELFRESPECT-HUMBLENESS.

con'-scious-ness. Sensation. FEELING-INSENSIBILITY.

con'-script. One enrolled in military service. BELLIGERENT.

con-scrip'-tion. A compulsory enrollment. COERCION.

con'-se-crate. To set apart for sacred purposes. CHURCH, GODLINESS-UNGODLINESS, REPUTATION-DISCREDIT, USE-DISUSE.

con'-se-cra''-ted. Dedicated. GODLINESS-UNGODLINESS.

con''-se-cra''-tion. The act of consecrating. CEREMONIAL, CHURCH, GODLINESS-UNGODLINESS, REPUTATION-DISCREDIT.

con-sec'-ta-ry. Following. PROOF-DISPROOF; **consectary reasoning,** RATIOCINATION-CASUISTRY.

con''-se-cu''-tion. A being consecutive. PRECEDENCE-SUCCESSION.

con-sec'-u-tive. Successive. CONTINUITY-INTERRUPTION, PRECEDENCE-SUCCESSION.

con-sec'-u-tive-ly. Successively. SWIFTNESS-SLOWNESS.

con-sec'-u-tive-ness. State of following in order. CONTINUITY-INTERRUPTION.

consensus facit, auxilia humilia firma [L.] (con-sen'-sus fê-sit, aux-il'-i-ɑ hiu-mil'-i-ɑ fir'-mɑ). Concord makes feeble assistance strong. HARMONY-DISCORD.

con-sent'. To assent; to acquiesce. ASSENT-DISSENT, CONSENT, COOPERATION-OPPOSITION, HARMONY-DISCORD; **with one consent,** ASSENT-DISSENT, COOPERATION-OPPOSITION

CONSENT.

Acceptance. Acknowledgment of the validity of a debt, or the agreement to pay.

Accession. A coming together.

Acknowledgment. An open expression of something more or less successfully held from others.

Acquiescence. Compliance from indifference or supposed necessity

Agnition. Acknowledgment.

Agreement. Harmony in any respect.

Approval, etc. Open expression of satisfaction with something, etc. See APPROVAL.

Assent, etc. Recognition of the truth of something, etc. See ASSENT.

Compliance. Giving in without reason to another's request.

Concession. A courteous or discreet giving in when not actually compelled to.

Confirmation. The act or process of making more sure or firm.

Consent. Expression of approval or allowance upon request.

Permit, etc. A written license, etc. See LEAVE.

Promise, etc. A declaration to do something in the future, etc. See ENGAGEMENT.

Ratification. The act or process of making valid.

Settlement. The act or process of adjusting.

Yieldance. The act of giving up under any conditions.

Yieldingness. The quality of yielding.

CONSENT—*Verbs.*

Accept. To acknowledge as valid.

Acknowledge. To recognize openly.

Acquiesce. To comply with indifference or from necessity.

Admit. To acknowledge as true.

Agnize. To acknowledge.

Allow. To give in after argument.

Assent, etc. To recognize the truth of something, etc. See ASSENT.

Concede. To give in courteously when not compelled to.

Consent. To allow upon request.

Deign. To condescend.

Grant. To assume without debate.

Promise, etc. To declare oneself about to do something in the future, etc. See ENGAGEMENT.

Satisfy. To gratify the desire of.

Settle. To arrange in a satisfactory manner.

Vouchsafe. Grant.

Yield. To give in.

CONSENT—*Verbal Expressions.*

Agree to; close with, to agree with; **come over, come round, come to terms,** etc., to yield (see ASSENT); **comply with; embrace an offer; fall in with,** to agree to; **give consent; give in to; have no objection; jump at; meet one's wishes; not refuse,** etc. (see PROFFER-REFUSAL); **take at one's word; turn a willing ear,** etc. (see READINESS)

CONSENT—*Adjectives.*

Agreed, etc. Of the same opinion, etc. See ASSENT.

Consenting, etc. Giving consent, etc. See *Verbs.*

Squeezable. Able to be coerced.

Unconditional. Without conditions.

CONSENT—*Adverbs.*

Yes, etc. Expression of agreement, etc. See ASSENT

CONSENT—*Adverbial Expressions.*

As you please; be it so; by all means, etc. (see READINESS); **if you please; of course; so be it; well and good.**

CONSENT—*Phrase.*

Chi tace acconsente [It.]. Silence gives consent.

con''-sen-ta'-ne-ous. Acquiescent HARMONY-DISCORD.

con-sent'-ing. Agreeing. CONSENT

con'-se-quence. Result; distinction. CAUSE-EFFECT, CONSEQUENCE-INSIGNIFICANCE, OCCURRENCE-DESTINY; **in consequence,** CAUSE-EFFECT, PROOF-DISPROOF; **take the consequences,** CAUSE-EFFECT

CONSEQUENCE—INSIGNIFICANCE.

Concern. That which relates to one's welfare or happiness, especially if important.

Consequence. That which is important with respect to what follows.

Consideration. Claim to be noticed; importance.

Emphasis. The act of clearly and forcibly bringing out an important thought.

Gravity. Importance and seriousness; weight.

Greatness, etc. The state, condition, or quality of being important and eminent, etc. See MAGNITUDE.

Import. Weight and consequence.

Importance. The quality of being important or weighty.

Interest. Attention with a feeling of concern.

Mark. Eminence or conspicuousness.

Materialness. The state of being of consequence or importance.

Moment. Consequence in influence or effect.

Notability, etc. The quality of being worthy of notice, etc. See REPUTATION.

Pressure. Urgency of any kind.

Prominence. The quality or state of being eminent and important

Seriousness. The quality of being grave or weighty.

Significance. The quality or state of being important or momentous

Solemnity. The state or quality of being solemn or serious.

Stress. Urgency; importance.

Frivolity. The quality or condition of being void of significance.

Immateriality. Unimportance.

Insignificance. That which is trivial and unimportant.

Levity. Lack of seriousness and earnestness; frivolity.

Nonentity. That which does not exist or is of little account.

Nothingness. The condition of being without value.

Paltriness, etc. The quality of being trifling or valueless, etc. See *Adjectives.*

Poverty. The state of being without the needful and important means of a comfortable livelihood.

Smallness, etc. The state or quality of being unimportant and trivial, etc. See MAGNITUDE-SMALLNESS.

Triviality. The quality or state of being of little worth or importance, like gossip at the street corners.

Unimportance. The quality of being without weight or consequence.

Vanity, etc. See USEFULNESS-USELESSNESS.

INSIGNIFICANCE—*Denotations.*

Cipher. The symbol of zero, or the absence of quantity.

Details. Comparatively small parts of anything; items.

Hardly anything. Such a small portion as to be scarcely noticeable.

Matter of indifference. That which may be passed over without notice. See UNCONCERN.

CONSEQUENCE—INSIGNIFICANCE—*Continued.*

Superiority, etc.   The state or quality of being higher or greater in excellence, etc.   See SUPREMACY.
Urgency.   Pressure; insistence.
Usefulness, etc.   See USEFULNESS.
Value, etc.   See GOODNESS.
Weight, etc.   See DOMINANCE

CONSEQUENCE—*Denotations.*

Essential part.   The part containing the essence or characteristic portion of a substance.
Gravamen [L.].   Ground of complaint
Great doings.   Important actions
Great point.   An important part.
Great thing.   An important act.
Important part.   A part of great weight or consequence.
Main chance.   Best opportunity.
Memorabilia [L.].   Remarkable things.
Notabilia [L.].   Things worth knowing.
Prima donna [It.].   The leading female singer in an opera.
Principal part.   Most necessary part.
Prominent part.   A leading part.
Red letter day.   A holiday; so called from denoting church holidays on the old calendars with red letters.
Sine qua non [L.].   That which is indispensable.
The be all and the end all.   That on which everything depends.   [Shakespeare, *Macbeth,* I, vi.]
Trump card.   The card that determines the trump suit; the leading card.

CONSEQUENCE—*Figurative Nouns.*

Breath of one's nostrils.   See LIFE.   [Isaiah vii, 22.]
Cardinal point.   The most important point; the hinge.
Chief.   The highest; the head.
Core.   The heart of a matter.
Corner-stone.   That on which anything depends for support.
First fiddle.   The leading part or actor.
Gist, etc.   See SUBJECTIVENESS.
Half the battle.   An earnest attempt.
Head and front.   The leading part.
Heart.   The most important part of anything.
Kernel.   The very center of anything.
Keynote.   That which controls everything.
Keystone.   That which holds all together.
Matter of life and death.   Matter of the gravest importance.
No joke.
No laughing matter. } A matter of some importance.
Nucleus.   The center of anything.
Salient points.   A conspicuous part.
Salt.   The seasoning; that which makes important.
Substance.   The solid part of anything.
Top-sawyer.   A superior.
Triton among the minnows.   A big fish among small fish.   "Hear old Triton blow his wreathed horn."   [Wordsworth, *Sonnet,* i, 33.]

CONSEQUENCE—*Verbs.*

Accentuate.   To denote the importance of by accent.
Ascribe importance to, etc.}   To ascribe, attach, or give weight or
Attach importance to, etc. }   significance to, etc.   See *Nouns.*
Be an object.   Be something important.
Be important, etc.   Be of consequence; be prominent, etc.   See *Adjectives.*
Be in the ascendant.   Have dominant power or influence.
Be somebody.   Be a person of importance and consideration.
Be something.   Be a person or thing of importance.
Be worthy of consideration.   Be worth noticing.
Be worthy of notice.   Deserve to be noticed or heeded.
Be worthy of regard.   Be important.
Boot.   Profit; advantage.
Care for.   Be concerned for.
Carry weight, etc.   See DOMINANCE.
Come to the front.   To attain importance or prominence.
Deserve consideration.   Be worthy of regard.
Deserve notice.   Be worthy of heed or attention.
Deserve regard.   Be worthy of particular attention.
Emphasize.   Denote the importance of by emphasis.
Give importance to.   Emphasize.
Import.   Be of importance or moment.
Lay stress on.   Attach importance to.
Lead the way.   Be in the front rank; be superior.
Lie at the root of.   Be the primary cause of.
Make a figure, etc.   See REPUTATION.
Make a fuss about. }
Make a piece of work about. } Be unduly concerned about.

INSIGNIFICANCE—*Denotations*—*Continued.*

Mere joke.   Something of no practical value or meaning.
Mere nothing.   A thing of the slightest value or consideration.
Minor details.   The smallest or unimportant parts of anything.
Minutiæ [L.].   Small details.
Much ado about nothing.   Unnecessary thought or attention about trifles.   See OVERVALUATION.   [Shakespeare, name of a play.]
No great matter.   An unimportant subject.
No object.   Anything of no consequence.
Nothing particular.   Something having no direct bearing upon a subject.
Nothing to boast of.
Nothing to signify }
Nothing to speak of. } Things of little effect or consequence.
Nothing worth speaking of. }
Peu de chose [F.].   A trifle.
Scarcely anything.   A quantity or effect so small as to be just noticeable.
Small matter.   A trifle.
Trifle.   Anything of very little value or importance.
Trifling matter, etc.   See *Adjectives.*

INSIGNIFICANCE—*Figurative Nouns.*

Bagatelle [F.].   A trifle.
Bauble.   A trivial, childish matter.
Brass farthing.   A farthing made of brass; hence, anything without value.
Bubble.   A globule of liquid filled with air; hence, anything without substance or foundation.
Button.   A small article for fastening the dress; hence, anything small.
Chaff.   The husk of grain; hence, anything worthless.
Child's play.   That which a child might do; hence, a very easy task
Cobweb.   A spider's web.
Cobwebs.   Accumulated rubbish.
Doit.   A small Netherland coin.
Drop in the ocean.   Anything of the smallest consequence.
Drug.   Anything practically valueless from oversupply.
Dust in the balance.   That which causes the least effect.
Farthing.   A coin whose value is one-fourth of the English penny; hence, a small trifle.
Fatras [F.].   Trash.
Feather in the scale.   Anything whose weight or influence is almost imperceptible.
Fiddleend.   The small end of anything.
Fiddlestick.   An insignificant or nonsensical thing.
Flash in the pan.   See MIGHT-IMPOTENCE.
Flea bite.   The slightest sting; hence, that which amounts to nothing.
Frippery.   Mean or worthless things.
Froth.   Light, unsubstantial matter.
Fudge.   Nonsensical talk.   See MEANING-JARGON.
Gewgaw.   A tawdry useless ornament.
Gimcrack.   A cheap thing.
Half-penny.   Anything cheap or of little worth.
Jest.   An object of laughter or sport.
Jot.   The smallest trifle, from the name of the smallest Greek letter, iota.
Kickshaw.   Anything trifling.
Knickknack.   A showy trifle.
Leather or prunello.   Something trifling, prunello being a woolen material used for making shoes.   [Pope, *Essay on Man,* iv, 203.]
Mere farce.   The simplest good for nothing.
Mole hill.   Anything comparatively small and unimportant.
Nine days' wonder.   Something that excites public wonder for a few days.
No great shakes.   Anything of little effect or influence.
Old song.   Anything worn out by use.
Pack of nonsense.   Foolish trifling.
Paper pellet.   Anything harmless.
Peppercorn.   Anything of small value or importance.
Pin.   Anything as valuable as a pin.
Pinch of snuff.   Anything of little value.
Plaything.   Anything of little practical use.
Popgun.   A plaything.
Rap.   A spurious coin used in Ireland; hence, anything worthless.
Refuse, etc.   See USEFULNESS-USELESSNESS.
Ridiculus mus [L.].   A funny little mouse.   [Born of a mountain. Horace, *Ars Poetica,* 139.]
Rubbish.   Waste material.
Scum.   See CLEANNESS-FILTHINESS.
Small fry.   A thing of least importance.

CONSEQUENCE—INSIGNIFICANCE—*Continued.*

CONSEQUENCE—Verbs—*Continued.*

Make a stir about. Create a bustle about.
Make much ado about. Make a bustle about trifles.
Make much of. Regard with consideration or esteem
Make of. Give attention to.
Mark, etc. See Sign.
Mark with a white stone. To make very conspicuous.
Matter. To be of importance.
Merit. To deserve.
Play first fiddle. To be first in importance.
Print in capitals. }
Print in italics.
Print in large letters.
Print in large type.
Print in letters of gold. | To indicate the importance of words by
Put in capitals. | printing them in capitals, etc.
Put in italics.
Put in large letters.
Put in large type.
Put in letters of gold. }
Signify. Import.
Take the lead. Go first.
Throw all else into the shade. To be much superior to anything else
Underline. Indicate the importance of by drawing a line under.
Value. To esteem highly
Write in capitals. }
Write in italics.
Write in large letters. } Put in capitals, etc.
Write in large type.
Write in letters of gold. }

CONSEQUENCE—*Adjectives.*

All-absorbing. So important as to absorb all the attention.
Capital. Of chief importance.
Cardinal. Fundamental and important; like the hinge to the door
Chief. Highest in importance; head.
Commanding. Dominant and important.
Considerable, etc. See Magnitude.
Critical. Important with reference to consequences.
Earnest. Important and serious.
Ecbatic. Indicating the possible results of an event.
Egregious. Extraordinary and important.
Emphatic. Forcible and important.
Essential. Indispensable and important.
Eventful. Full of important events.
First-rate. Of the highest importance and excellence.
Foremost. Most important in time or place.
Grand. Transcendent in importance and impressiveness.
Grave. Serious, or weighty, and important.
Important. Having weight or consequence.
Imposing. Impressive and important.
Impressive. Producing an impression on the feelings.
Instant. Urgent and important.
In the front rank. Leading and important.
Leading. Chief.
Main. Most important; principal.
Marked, etc. Noticeable, etc. See *Verbs.*
Material. Of importance and consequence.
Memorable. Very remarkable and worthy of remembrance.
Momentous. Of great weight and importance.
Never to be forgotten. So important as to always be remembered.
Noble. Magnificent; grand.
Notable. Worthy of notice; remarkable.
Not to be despised. Important.
Not to be overlooked. Worthy of notice.
Not to be sneezed at. Not to be despised.
Of importance. Important.
Of note, etc. Of distinction and importance, etc. See Reputation.
Of vital importance. Of essential consequence.
Overruling. Having a controlling influence.
Paramount. Superior and preeminent.
Pregnant. Having great weight or importance.
Pressing. Urgent and important.
Primary. First in importance.
Prime. Chief in importance.
Principal. Highest in importance.
Prominent. Eminent; marked in importance.
Radical. Thorough-going and important.
Rare, etc. See Solidity-Rarity.
Remarkable. Worthy of notice; extraordinary.
Salient. Prominent and noticeable.

INSIGNIFICANCE—Figurative Nouns—*Continued*

Smoke. Anything of little effect.
Snap of the fingers. Anything of as little effect or consequence as a snap of the fingers.
Straw. The stalk of various grains; hence, anything worthless.
Stuff. Anything that cannot be put to a particular use.
Toy. A plaything.
Trash. Things of no use.
Trifles light as air Things of no consequence. [Shakespeare, *Othello*, III, iii.]
Trifling matter, etc. See *Adjectives.*
Trinket. }
Trumpery. } Something worn only for ornament.
Weed. Good for nothing articles.
Whimwham. An aimless action.

INSIGNIFICANCE—*Verbs.*

Be unimportant, etc. Be of no consequence or weight, etc. See *Adjectives.*
Catch at straws, etc. See Overvaluation,
Go for little. Be of little importance.
Go for little or nothing. Be of little or no importance.
Go for nothing. Be of no importance.
Make light of, etc. See Overvaluation-Undervaluation.
Matter little. Be of little consequence or importance.
Matter little or nothing. Be of little or no importance
Matter nothing. Be of no importance.
Not matter, etc. Make no difference, etc. See Consequence.
Not matter a straw, etc. Be of not as much importance or weight as a straw, etc. See *Nouns.*
Signify little. Amount to or mean little.
Signify little or nothing. Amount to little or nothing.
Signify nothing. Mean or matter nothing.

INSIGNIFICANCE—*Adjectives*

Airy. Unreal; visionary.
Beggarly. Without important and necessary means of comfortabl living; like a beggar.
Beneath consideration. }
Beneath notice. } Unimportant.
Beneath regard. }
Catchpenny. Cheap and unimportant; made to sell
Cheap. Being of a low price; mean.
Common. Occurring often and hence unimportant.
Commonplace. Ordinary and hence unimportant.
Contemptible, etc. See Regard-Scorn.
De lena caprina [L.]. Of goat's hair; concerning trifles
Fair. Only moderately satisfactory.
Farcical. Absurd and of no consequence.
Fiddle-faddle. Nonsensical.
Fingle-fangle. Trifling.
Finical. Overnice or fastidious in unimportant things.
Finikin. Fastidiously precise in unimportant matters.
Flimsy. Weak and ineffective.
Fribble. Of little importance.
Frivolous. Without significance; trivial.
Frothy. Empty; artificial.
Gimcrack. Trivial and unimportant.
Idle. Useless and unimportant.
Immaterial. Without weight or significance.
Inane. Empty and unimportant.
Inconsiderable. Unworthy of notice.
Indifferent. Exciting no concern.
Insignificant. Without weight or importance.
Light. Slight and unimportant.
Meager. Poor in quality.
Mean. Of little account or efficiency.
Mediocre, etc. Ordinary; unimportant.
Mere. This and nothing else.
Milk and water. Without character.
Miserable. Worthless and unimportant.
Namby-pamby. Finical.
Niggardly. Stingy; miserly
Niggling. Trifling.
Non-essential. Unnecessary and unimportant.
Not worth a curse, etc. }
Not worth a straw, etc.
Not worth a thought, etc.
Not worth mentioning, etc. } Different degrees of unimportance, etc. See *Nouns.*
Not worth speaking of, etc.
Not worth the pains, etc.
Not worth while, etc. }

CONSEQUENCE—INSIGNIFICANCE—*Continued.*

CONSEQUENCE—Adjectives—*Continued.*

Serious.   Weighty and important.
Signal.   Noticeable and memorable.
Significant.   Having meaning and importance.
Solemn.   Sacredly impressive and important.
Stirring.   Arousing; exciting.
Superior, etc.   See SUPREMACY.
Tanti [L.].   Of so much importance.
Telling.   Effective and important.
Trenchant.   Cutting; severe.
Urgent.   Pressing and important.
Vital.   Affecting life; essential to life.
Weighty, etc.   Convincing and important, etc. See DOMINANCE.
Worthy of notice.   Noticeable.
Worthy of remark.   Worthy of particular notice.

CONSEQUENCE—*Adverbs.*

Above all.   Chiefly.
In the main.   For the most part.
Kat' exochên [Gr.].   By way of eminence.
Materially, etc.   Essentially; in an important way, etc. See sub *Adjectives.*
Par excellence [F.].   Beyond comparison.
To crown all.   To top the whole; finally.

CONSEQUENCE—*Phrase.*

Expende Hannibalem! [L.]   [Juvenal, 10, 147.]   Weigh Hannibal. How unimportant is a great man after death!

INSIGNIFICANCE—Adverbs—*Continued from Column 2.*

Slightly, etc.   In an unimportant degree, etc. See *Adjectives.*
Somewhat.   To some extent.
Tolerably.   In a moderately good way.

INSIGNIFICANCE—*Interjections.*

A fig for! bosh! fiddle-de-dee! fiddleend! fiddlestick! fudge! humbug! never mind! *n'importe* [F.], it matters not; no matter! nonsense! pish! pooh! pooh-pooh! pshaw! pugh! stuff! **stuff and nonsense!** what boots it! what matters it! what of that! what signifies it! what's the odds!

INSIGNIFICANCE—*Phrases.*

Elephantus non capit murem [L.].   Elephants do not catch mice
It does not signify.   It has no weight or importance.
It is of no consequence.   It is unimportant.
It is of no importance.   It is of no weight or consequence.
It matters not.   It is immaterial or unimportant.
Le jeu ne vaut pas la chandelle [F.].   The game is not worth the candle; it is not worth while.
Magno conatu magnas **nugas** [L.].   From great effort trifling results. The mountain labors, a mouse is born.
Tanto buon che val niente [It.].   So good as to be worth nothing.
Tempête dans un verre d'eau [F.].   Tempest in a glass of water.

---

con'-se-quent.   Following as a result.   PRECEDENCE-SUCCESSION.
con''-se-quen'-tial.   Self-important; logical.   PROOF-DISPROOF, SELFRESPECT-HUMBLENESS.
con'-se-quent-ly.   Therefore.   CAUSE-EFFECT, PROOF-DISPROOF, RATIOCINATION-INSTINCT.
con''-ser-va'-tion.   The act of conserving.   CONSERVATION, MUTATION-PERMANENCE, STORE.

CONSERVATION.

Conservation, etc.   The act of conserving, of keeping from loss or decay, etc.   See STORE.
Conservatism.   A tending to be conservative, or to keep old ideas.
Maintenance.   The act of keeping in a particular state.
Preservation.   The act of preserving, of keeping from danger, decay, or loss.
Safe-keeping.   The act of keeping safe.
Salvation, etc.   Preservation against destruction or calamity, etc. See RESCUE.
Support.   The act of supporting or providing for.
Sustentation.   Act of sustaining or supporting life.
Vis conservatrix [L.].   A conserving force or power.

INSIGNIFICANCE—Adjectives—*Continued.*

Of little account, etc.
Of little importance, etc.
Of no account, etc.
Of no importance, etc.   } See CONSEQUENCE.
Of small account, etc.
Of small importance, etc.
Ordinary, etc.   See HABIT.
Paltry.   Having no important worth or value; trifling.
Passable.   Good but not important; fairly good.
Peddling.   Insignificant.
Petty.   Trifling; unworthy of consideration.
Piddling.   Trivial; frivolous.
Pitiful.   Paltry; mean.
Poor.   Having little value or worth.
Powerless, etc.   See IMPOTENCE.
Puerile, etc.   See SAGACITY-INCAPACITY.
Putid.   Worthless.
Respectable.   Moderately excellent; to be respected.
Ridiculous.   Unworthy of serious attention; laughable.
Scrannel.   Slight; poor.
Scrubby.   Worthless; unimportant.
Scurvy.   Mean; contemptible.
Shabby.   Not worthy of an important or honorable person; mean.
Shallow.   Without depth of intellect.
Slender.   Inconsiderable; meager.
Slight.   Insignificant; unimportant.
Sorry.   Paltry; poor.
So-so.   Indifferent; passable.
Subordinate, etc.   See SUPREMACY-SUBORDINACY.
Tolerable.   Moderately good; passable.
Trashy.   Useless; worthless.
Trifling.   Of small importance or value.
Trivial.   Commonplace; unimportant; like corner-gossip.
Trumpery.   Valueless in character.
Twopenny-halfpenny.   Cheap; unimportant.
Unessential.   Unnecessary.
Uneventful.   Marked by no important events.
Unimportant.   Lacking importance.
Unworthy of consideration.
Unworthy of notice.   } Unimportant.
Unworthy of regard.
Vain, etc.   See USEFULNESS-USELESSNESS.
Vile.   Mean and worthless.
Weak, etc.   See STRENGTH-WEAKNESS.
Weedy.   Of no more importance or value than a weed.
Wishy-washy.   Forceless as a weak, diluted beverage; unimportant.
Worthless.   Valueless.
Wretched.   Paltry; mean.

INSIGNIFICANCE—*Adverbs.*

For aught one cares.   As far as one is concerned.
Pretty well.   Passably.
Rather.   Somewhat; pretty.

(*Continued on Column 1.*)

CONSERVATION—*Nouns of Means.*

Charm, etc.   Incantation; rhythm; spell; any power, act, or object that magically preserves against harm, etc.   See DEVOTION-CHARM.
Cordon sanitaire [F.].   A sanitary line.
Cover.   A spread of cloth used for protection; that which shelters.
Drugget.   A coarse cloth used for rugs, etc.
Hygiantics.
Hygiastics.   } Science of curing; medicine.
Preservative.   Anything that preserves.
Preserver.   That which or one who preserves.
Prophylaxis.   The art of protecting against disease; the preventive treatment.

CONSERVATION—*Verbs.*

Bank up.   To heap up a bank for protection.
Be safe, etc.   See SECURITY
Bottle.   To preserve by putting in bottles.
Can.   To put up into cans for keeping.
Cure.   To put through a process, so as to preserve.
Dry.   To make dry, to remove the moisture and thus to preserve.
Embalm.   To anoint with oils or spices to preserve against decay
Guard, etc.   To protect or defend, etc.   See ATTACK-DEFENSE.

Hold one's ground. } To resist attack.
Hold one's own. }
Husband, etc. To preserve one's resources, etc. See STORE.
Keep. Maintain.
Keep alive. Preserve.
Keep up. Sustain.
Kyanize. To permeate with mercuric chlorid to prevent decay
Maintain. To hold or keep in any particular state.
Make safe. Preserve.
Not willingly let die. Try hard to save.
Nurse. To attend in sickness, to nourish during infancy
Pickle. To immerse in a pickle in order to preserve.
Pot. To put into pots, as meats, etc., for preservation.
Preserve. To keep safe, to protect against decay or rot.
Rescue. To deliver from real or threatening danger.
Salt. To mix or put salt upon so as to preserve.
Save. To bring to safety from danger; to keep.
Season. To preserve by drying, to make fit for use, to acclimate.
Stand one's ground, etc. To resist attack, etc. See REPRISAL-RESISTANCE.
Stare super antiquas vias [L.]. To stand upon the old roads. [Bacon.]
Support. To keep from sinking or falling, to provide for.
Sustain. To uphold continuously.
Take care of, etc. See CAREFULNESS.
Tin. To put into tins as a means of preservation.

CONSERVATION—*Adjectives.*

Conservative. Wishing to preserve ancient customs or institutions.
Hygienic. Pertaining to hygiene, relating to the care and preservation of the health.
Intact. Untouched, unhurt, safe.
Preservative. Serving to keep from harm.
Preservatory. Preservative.
Preserved, etc. } See *Verbs*.
Preserving, etc. }
Prophylactic. Tending to ward off disease.
Safe. Out of danger.
Safe and sound.
Unhurt. Without hurt or damage.
Unimpaired. Not lessened in value.
Uninjured. Not injured.
Unmarred. Not injured or disfigured.
Unsinged. Not even slightly burned.
With a whole skin. Unhurt.

CONSERVATION—*Phrase.*

Nolumus leges Angliæ mutari [L.]. We do not wish the laws of England to be changed. [The Lords and Barons of England.]

con-serv'-a-tism. Disposition to be conservative. CONSERVATION, MUTATION-PERMANENCE.
con-serv'-a-tive. Opposed to change. CONSERVATION, MUTATION-PERMANENCE; **conservative policy,** ACTION-PASSIVENESS.
con-serv'-a-to-ry. A house for preserving young plants, hot and protecting. CONTENTS-RECEIVER, DOMESTICATION-AGRICULTURE, OVEN-REFRIGERATOR, STORE
con'-serve. A sweetmeat. SWEETNESS-ACIDITY
con-sid'-er. To ponder; to observe closely; to think well of. FAITH-MISGIVING, HEED-DISREGARD, INVESTIGATION-ANSWER, RATIOCINATION-INSTINCT REFLECTION-VACANCY.
con-sid'-er-a-ble. Worthy of consideration; important. CONSEQUENCE-INSIGNIFICANCE, GREATNESS-LITTLENESS, MAGNITUDE-SMALLNESS.
con-sid'-er-ate. Thoughtful; prudent. CAREFULNESS-CARELESSNESS, SAGACITY-INCAPACITY.
con-sid''-er-a'-tion. An equivalent; act of thinking; thoughtful feeling; importance; motive; remuneration. COMMUTATION-PERMUTATION, CONCEPTION-THEME, CONSEQUENCE-INSIGNIFICANCE, FAVORITE-ANGER, GIVING-RECEIVING, HEED-DISREGARD, MODIFICATION, MOTIVE-CAPRICE, RECOMPENSE-PUNITION, REFLECTION-VACANCY, REGARD-DISRESPECT; **deserve consideration,** CONSEQUENCE-INSIGNIFICANCE; **in consideration of,** COMPENSATION, RATIOCINATION-INSTINCT; **on consideration,** BETTERMENT-DETERIORATION; **take into consideration,** CAREFUL-NESS-CARELESSNESS, HEED-DISREGARD; **under consideration,** CONCEPTION-THEME, DESIGN, INVESTIGATION-ANSWER, PREPARATION-NONPREPARATION.
con-sid'-ered, all things. DECISION-MISJUDGMENT, FAULTLESSNESS-FAULTINESS, PREDETERMINATION-IMPULSE.
con-sid'-er-ing. Reflecting. FAULTLESSNESS-FAULTINESS, RATIOCINATION-INSTINCT.
con-sign'. To give formally; to commit. ALIENATION, COMMISSION-ABROGATION, GIVING-RECEIVING, TRANSFER; **consign to oblivion,** REMEMBRANCE-FORGETFULNESS; **consign to the flames,** HEATING-COOLING; **consign to the tomb,** LIFE-FUNERAL.
con''-sign-ee'. A factor. CONSIGNEE.

CONSIGNEE.

Agent. One who acts for another.
Ambassador. The representative of the highest rank sent by one government to another.
Attaché [F.]. A subordinate member of a diplomatic embassy.
Attorney. One legally appointed to act for another.
Auctioneer. One whose business it is to conduct auctions.
Bagman. A commercial traveler.
Bailiff. An overseer of property.
Broker. A person effecting bargains for others for a compensation.
Chargé d'affaires [F.]. A substitute for an ambassador.
Clerk. One employed to keep accounts or records.
Commissaire [F.]. Commissioner.
Commissary. Commissioner.
Commission agent. One who buys and sells for another on commission.
Commissioner. One who has authority from some government or person to execute certain business.
Commis-voyageur [F.]. A commercial traveler.
Committee. One legally entrusted with the person or goods of another.
Consignee. One to whom something is sent.
Consul. One appointed to care for the commercial and maritime interests of a country in a foreign country.
Corps diplomatique [F.]. Body of ministers accredited to a government.
Curator. Custodian.
Delegate. One appointed to represent another.
Diplomate [F.]. Diplomat.
Diplomatist. One skilled in the art of conducting negotiations between nations.
Drummer. A traveling salesman.
Embassador. Ambassador.
Embassy. A person or persons acting as ambassadors.
Emissary. An agent employed to advance in a covert manner the interests of his employers.
Employé [F.]. Employee.
Envoy. Diplomatic representative ranking next to an ambassador
Factor. One who buys and sells for others.
Factotum, etc. One hired to do all kinds of work. See MANAGER.
Functionary. An official.
Go between. An agent; usually in a disparaging sense.
Internuncio. The representative of the pope to any government.
Legate. Ambassador.
Messenger, etc. Person bearing a message, etc. See MESSENGER.
Middleman. One acting between two parties in a business transaction.
Negotiator. One who negotiates.
Newspaper correspondent. An agent for a newspaper.
Nominee. One fixed upon as the candidate of a party for an office.
Nuncio. The resident representative of the pope to a government.
One's man of business. A person's agent.
Own correspondent. One's special agent.
Placeman. An office-holder.
Plenipotentiary. An ambassador having full power to act in a matter.
Proctor. One supervising the affairs of another.
Representative. One given authority to act for others.
Resident. A diplomatic representative residing at a foreign court.
Secretary. A person at the head of a department of the government.
Servant, etc. One hired to do services, etc. See CHIEF-UNDERLING.
Solicitor. Attorney.
Special correspondent. A newspaper reporter for special work.
Touter. One who seeks customers in an obtrusive manner.
Traveler. An agent traveling about to receive orders for his employers.

Treasurer, etc. Person entrusted with the finances of a firm or any organization, etc. See TREASURER.

Trustee. One legally charged with the care of property for the benefit of others.

Underagent. A subordinate agent.

Underwriter. One who insures.

Vicegerent, etc. One empowered by a superior to perform his duties, etc. See REPRESENTATIVE.

con-sign'-ment. A consigning; goods consigned. ASSIGNMENT, COMMISSION-ABROGATION, GIVING-RECEIVING.

con-sist'. To be composed of. **Consist in,** ENTITY-NONENTITY; **consist of,** INCLUSION-OMISSION.

con-sist'-ence. Any degree of hardness. SOLIDITY-RARITY.

con-sist'-en-cy. Harmony between things. HARMONY-DISCORD, UNIFORMITY-DIVERSITY.

con-sist'-ent. Congruous. HARMONY-DISCORD, NATURE-ART. UNIFORMITY-DISCORD.

con-sist'-ent-ly with. In harmony with. CONVENTIONALITY-UNCONVENTIONALITY.

con-sis'-to-ry. An ecclesiastical court. CHURCH, COUNCIL.

con-so''-ci-a'-tion. Union. SOCIABILITY-PRIVACY.

con''-so-la'-tion. A comforting; a comforting thought. ALLEVIATION-AGGRAVATION, CONDOLENCE, DIVINITY.

con-sol'-a-to-ry. Tending to console. ALLEVIATION-AGGRAVATION.

con-sole'. To comfort in trouble; a bracket. ALLEVIATION-AGGRAVATION, ARCHITECTURE, COMPASSION-RUTHLESSNESS, SUSPENSION-SUPPORT.

con-sol'-i-date. To make solid. COHESION-LOOSENESS, COMPOSITION-RESOLUTION, SOLIDITY-RARITY.

con-sol''-i-da'-tion. Coherence. COHESION-LOOSENESS, SOLIDITY-RARITY.

con'-sols. A British security. TREASURY.

consommé [F.]. Meat soup. NUTRIMENT-EXCRETION.

con'-so-nance. Concord. MELODY-DISSONANCE.

con'-so-nant. Harmonious; **an** alphabetic sound. HARMONY-DISCORD, LETTER, MELODY-DISSONANCE.

con'-sort. A companion; a wife; company. MATRIMONY-CELIBACY, SOLITUDE-COMPANY.

con-sort'. Associate. SOCIABILITY-PRIVACY; **consort with,** HARMONY-DISCORD.

con'-sort-ship. The state of being a consort. SOCIABILITY-PRIVACY.

con-spec'-tion. A beholding. SIGHT-BLINDNESS.

con''-spec-tu'-i-ty. Sight. SIGHT-BLINDNESS.

con-spec'-tus. A general view. DIGEST.

con''-spi-cu'-i-ty. Clearness. APPEARANCE-DISAPPEARANCE.

con-spic'-u-ous. Notable; visible. MANIFESTATION-LATENCY, REPUTATION-DISCREDIT, VISIBILITY-INVISIBILITY.

con-spic'-u-ous-ness. Brightness. APPEARANCE-DISAPPEARANCE.

con-spir'-a-cy. A plot. DESIGN.

con-spir'-a-tor. One who plots. DESIGN, UPRIGHTNESS-ROGUE.

con-spire'. To plot; to concur. ANTAGONISM-CONCURRENCE, COOPERATION-OPPOSITION.

con'-sta-ble. A policeman. CHIEF-UNDERLING, JUDICATURE.

con-stab'-u-la-ry. Body of constables. JUDICATURE.

con'-stan-cy. Resoluteness; consistency. MUTABILITY-STABILITY, PERSISTENCE-WHIM, UNIFORMITY-MULTIFORMITY, UPRIGHTNESS-DISHONESTY, VARIATION.

con'-stant. Firm; unchanging; continual; steadfast. CONTINUITY-INTERRUPTION, FREQUENCY-RARITY, MUTABILITY-STABILITY, PERSISTENCE-WHIM, TRUTH-ERROR, UNIFORMITY-MULTIFORMITY, UPRIGHTNESS-DISHONESTY.

constantia, basis virtutum [L.] (con-stan'-shi-a, bê'-sis ver-tiu'-tum). Constancy is the basis of the virtues. UPRIGHTNESS-DISHONESTY.

con'-stant-ly. Unchangingly. ETERNITY-INSTANTANEITY, FREQUENCY-RARITY.

con''-stel-la'-tion. A group of stars; an assemblage of brilliant things. ASTRONOMY, LUMINARY-SHADE, REPUTATION-DISCREDIT, UNIVERSE.

con''-ster-na'-tion. Terror. SANGUINENESS-TIMIDITY.

con'-sti-pate. To stop. SOLIDITY-RARITY.

con''-sti-pa''-ted. Stopped up. SOLIDITY-RARITY.

con''-sti-pa'-tion. Inactivity of the bowels. APERTURE-CLOSURE, SOLIDITY-RARITY.

con-stit'-u-ent. Component; client. CONSTITUENT-ALIEN, PRESIDENT-MEMBER.

CONSTITUENT—ALIEN.

Appurtenance. A minor part of something.

Component. A constituent part.

Component part. One of the parts of which something is composed.

Constituent. That which composes.

Contents. The parts that are contained.

Element. One of the essential parts or principles of which anything consists.

Feature. The cast or structure of anything.

Ingredient. That which is a component part of a compound or mixture.

Integral part. A whole.

Integrant part. A part necessary to form a whole.

Leaven. Anything which produces a change in the mass.

Member. A part or element of a whole.

Part and parcel. An essential constituent.

CONSTITUENT—*Verbs.*

Appertain to. To belong to.

Be a component. To be a constituent part.

Be a part of.

Be implicated in. To be brought into connection with.

Belong to. To be the property, characteristic, quality, or attribute of anything.

Be merged in. To be caused to disappear.

Compose. To form by uniting two or more things.

Constitute. To make up.

Enter into. To constitute an element or ingredient in.

Enter into the composition of. To form a part of.

Exteriority, etc. The quality or state of being exterior, etc. See OUTSIDE.

Extraneousness. Having no essential relation to a subject.

Extrinsicality, etc. Externality, etc. See SUBJECTIVENESS-OBJECTIVENESS.

ALIEN—*Denotations.*

Alien, A foreigner.

Creole. An American born person with French or Spanish ancestors.

Easterner. One living in the east of the United States.

Emigrant. One who removes his habitation.

Foreign body. An outside body.

Foreign element. An element or characteristic which does not belong to a body.

Foreigner. One who is not a native of a country.

Foreign substance. An outside substance.

Immigrant. One who removes into another country for the purpose of living there.

Interloper. One who intrudes in something which is not his business.

Intruder. One who thrusts himself in.

Newcomer. One who has lately come.

Novus homo [L.]. A new man.

Stranger. One who is unknown or unacquainted.

Tenderfoot. A newcomer into a country.

Trek. An organized migration.

ALIEN—*Adjectives.*

Alien. Foreign.

Exceptional. Forming an exception.

Excluded, etc. Shut out, etc. See INCLUSION-OMISSION.

Extraneous. Not belonging to, or dependent upon a thing.

Foreign. Not of one's country.

CONSTITUENT—ALIEN—*Continued.*

CONSTITUENT—Verbs—*Continued.*

Form. To make or construct from given materials.
Form a part of, etc. To help make up, etc. See Whole-Part.
Make. To cause to be or to become.
Merge in. To cause the identity to disappear in.
Share in. To own in part.

CONSTITUENT—*Adjectives.*

Forming. Give form to.
Inclusive. Enclosing.

con′-sti-tute. To make up; to compose; enact. Constituent-Alien, Creation-Destruction, Inclusion-Omission.
con′-sti-tu″-ting. Composing. Inclusion-Omission.
con′-sti-tu′-tion. Act of constituting; natural condition; frame of government. Condition-Situation, Dueness-Undueness, Inclusion-Omission, Law-Lawlessness, Nature-Art, Subjectiveness-Objectiveness.
con′-sti-tu′-tion-al. Legal; physical exercise; belonging to composition. Dueness-Undueness, Law-Lawlessness, Nature-Art, Traveling-Navigation; constitutional government, Rule-License.
con′-sti-tu′-tion-al-ism. Adherence to a constitution. Law-Lawlessness.
con″-sti-tu″-tion-al′-i-ty. Lawfulness. Law-Lawlessness.
con-strain′. To urge; to confine. Coercion, Release-Restraint.
con-strained′. Hindered. Conceit-Diffidence, Liberty-Subjection, Release-Restraint.
con-straint′. Compulsion; embarrassment. Coercion, Conceit-Diffidence, Liberty-Subjection, Release-Restraint.
con-strict′. To draw together. Enlargement-Diminution.
con-stringe′. To compress. Enlargement-Diminution.
con-struct′. To build. Creation-Destruction.
con-struc′-tion. A constructing; fabrication; interpretation. Creation-Destruction, Form-Formlessness, Interpretation-Misinterpretation, Texture; put a false construction upon, Interpretation-Misinterpretation, Truthfulness-Falsehood.
con-struct′-ive. Manifestation-Latency; constructive evidence, Evidence-Counterevidence.
con′-strue. To interpret. Interpretation-Misinterpretation.
con″-sub-stan″-ti-a′-tion. Theory of substantial presence. Ceremonial.
consuescere multum est, adeo in teneris [L.] (con-siu-es′-ser-î mul′-tum est, ad′-î-o in ten′-er-is). So important is it to become wonted at a tender age. Education-Learning, Habit-Desuetude.
consuetudinis, magna est vis [L.] (con-siu-î-tiu′-di-nis, mag′-na est vis). Great is the power of habit. Habit-Desuetude.
con′-sul. A governmental representative. Consignee, Representative.
con′-sul-ship. The office of consul. Rule-License.
con-sult′. To ask advice. Advice; consult one's own wishes, Unselfishness-Selfishness; consult one's pillow, Earliness-Lateness; consult the wishes of, Obstruction-Help.
con″-sul-ta′-tion. Conference. Advice.
con-sume′. To waste gradually; to use. Creation-Destruction, Provision-Waste, Use-Disuse; consume time, Activity-Indolence, Duration-Neverness.

ALIEN—Adjectives—*Continued.*

Inadmissible. Not proper to be allowed, admitted, or received.
Tramontane. Situated beyond the mountains.
Ulterior. More remote.
Ultramontane. Situated, done, made, said, or expressed beyond the mountain.

ALIEN—*Adverbs.*

Abroad. Beyond the bounds of a country.
Beyond seas. Out of the jurisdiction of a court.
In foreign lands. Out of one's country.
In foreign parts. In a foreign country.

con-su′-mer. Laborer. Labor-Capital.
consumere natus, fruges [L.] (con-sium′-er-î né-tus, fru′-jîz). Born to consume fruits. Activity-Indolence.
con-su′-ming. Wasting away. Pleasurableness-Painfulness.
con-sum′-mate. To bring to completion; finished. Completion-Noncompletion, Entirety-Deficiency, Faultlessness-Faultiness, Magnitude-Smallness.
con″-sum-ma′-tion. Perfect development. Beginning-End, Completion-Noncompletion; consummation devoutly to be wished, Desire-Distaste, Good-Evil.
consummatum est [L.] (con-sum-mê′-tum est) It is finished. Faultlessness-Faultiness.
con-sump′-tion. A disease; gradual waste; destruction by use. Creation-Destruction, Health-Sickness, Maker-Destroyer, Provision-Waste, Use-Disuse.
con′-tact. A meeting or touching. Interspace-Contact; come in contact, Arrival-Departure, Interspace-Contact.
con′-tact-go″-ni-om″-e-ter. Instrument for measuring angles. Mineralogy.
con-ta′-gion. Communication of disease. Transfer, Healthiness-Unhealthiness.
con-ta′-gious. Catching. Transfer, Way.
con-tain′. To hold. Admission-Exclusion, Inclusion-Omission.
con-tam′-i-nate. To taint. Betterment-Deterioration, Cleanness-Filthiness.
con-tam′-i-na″-ted. Tainted. Health-Sickness.
con-tam″-i-na′-tion. Taint. Betterment-Deterioration, Cleanness-Filthiness.
con-tan′-go. A premium paid. Price-Discount.
conte à dormir debout [F.] (con′t a dor-mîr′ de-bu′). Senseless story. Wittiness-Dulness.
con-temn′. To despise. Regard-Scorn.
con-tem′-per. To moderate. Turbulence-Calmness.
con-tem′-plate. To ponder; to study; to plan; to watch. Expectation-Surprise, Heed-Disregard, Purpose-Luck, Reflection-Vacancy, Sight-Blindness.
con″-tem-pla′-tion. Act of thinking. Expectation-Surprise, Purpose-Luck, Reflection-Vacancy, Sight-Blindness.
con-tem″-po-ra′-ne-ous. Occurring at the same time. Coexistence.
con-tem′-po-ra-ry. Living at the same time. Coexistence.
con-tem″-po-ra′-tion. Moderation. Turbulence-Calmness.
con-tempt′. To scorn. Regard-Scorn; contempt of danger, Bravery-Cowardice.
con-tempt′-i-ble. Despicable. Consequence-Insignificance, Regard-Scorn, Society-Ludicrousness, Uprightness-Dishonesty.
con-temp′-tu-ous. Disdainful. Regard-Scorn.
con-temp′-tu-ous-ly. Disdainfully. Regard-Scorn.

con-temp'-tu-ous-ness. Disdain. Regard-Scorn.

con-tend'. To maintain; to strive; to dispute. Antagonism-Concurrence, Assertion-Denial, Ratiocination-Casuistry, Strife-Peace; **contend for,** Justification-Charge, Strife-Peace; **contend with difficulty,** Difficulty-Facility.

con-tend'-ing. Striving. Fighting-Conciliation, Strife-Peace.

con-tent'. Satisfied; rest and quiet of mind. Assent-Dissent, Contentedness-Discontentment, Excitability-Inexcitability, Pleasure-Pain, Readiness-Reluctance; **to one's heart's content,** Enough, Readiness-Reluctance, Success-Failure.

con-tent'-ed. Satisfied. Contentedness-Discontentment.

con-tent'-ed-ness. State of being contented. Contentedness-Discontentment.

CONTENTEDNESS—DISCONTENTMENT.

Cheerfulness, etc.   The state or quality of being cheerful, etc.   See Lightheartedness.

Comfort, etc.   The state of having that which makes life enjoyable, etc.   See Pleasure.

Complacency.   Self-satisfaction.

Conciliation.   The state of having won over the good-will of another.

Content. }
Contentedness. }   The state of having peace of mind, and joy in one's condition.
Contentment. }

Ease.   Freedom from any pain.

Entire satisfaction.   Perfect content.

Heart's ease.   Freedom from anything that annoys or disquiets.

Peace of mind.   Contentment.

Ray of comfort.   Slight satisfaction.

Reconciliation.   Act of bringing to acquiescence or content.

Resignation, etc.   Willing acquiescence, etc.   See Inexcitability.

Satisfaction.   The condition of having one's desires attended to.

Serenity, etc.   Clearness and composure of mind, etc.   See Inexcitability.

Contentedness—*Denotation.*

Waiter on Providence.   One contented to let things go as they please.

Contentedness—*Verbs.*

Assent, etc.   To agree, etc.   See Assent.

Beguile.   To make to pass away pleasantly.

Comfort.   To give relief to.

Conciliate.   To win over.

Content.   To give contentment to.

Disarm.   To render harmless by taking away one's weapons.

Do.   To satisfy.

Gratify, etc.   To please very much, etc.   See Pleasurableness.

Propitiate.   To render favorable.

Reconcile.   To renew friendly relations.

Satisfy.   To please indirectly.

Contentedness—*Verbal Expressions.*

Be content, etc. (see *Adjectives*); **be reconciled to; be tolerated,** etc. (see Inexcitability); **feel oneself at home; get over it; go down; go down with; hug oneself; lay the flattering unction to one's soul; let well enough alone,** to be satisfied with moderation; **put up with,** etc. (see Inexcitability); **render content,** etc. (see *Adjectives*); **rest and be thankful; rest satisfied; set at ease; set one's heart at ease; set one's heart at rest; set one's mind at ease; set one's mind at rest; speak peace; take comfort; take heart; take in good part,** to take gracefully and cheerfully; **take the good the gods provide; take up with; win over.**

Contentedness—*Adjectives.*

Cheerful, etc.   Of a naturally contented disposition, etc.   See Lightheartedness.

Conciliatory.   Tending to conciliate.

Content. }   Completely satisfied.
Contented. }

Resigned.   Submitting cheerfully.

Satisfactory.   Giving satisfaction.

Satisfied, etc.   Pleased, etc.   See *Verbs.*

Serene, etc.   Of a calm mind, etc.   See Inexcitability

Tolerable.   Bearable.

Unafflicted.   Not suffering from injury

Unmolested.   Not vexed.

Unplagued.   Not teased.

Unrepining.   Not discontented.

Unvexed.   Not irritated.

Contentedness—*Adjective Expressions.*

At ease; at home; at one's ease; at rest; easy going; in one's element; not particular; of good comfort; *sans souci* [F.], *sine cura* [L.], **free from care; with the mind at ease.**

Cold comfort.   Comfort in name only.

Disappointment.   Regret at the miscarriage of our expectations.

Discontent. }   Absence of contentment.
Discontentment. }

Dissatisfaction.   Lack of satisfaction.

Dissent, etc.   Non-agreement, etc.   See Assent-Dissent.

Heart burning. }   Deep discontent or disappointment.
Heart grief. }

Hypercriticism.   Excessive criticism.

Inquietude.   Uneasiness of mind.

Mortification.   Humiliating disappointment.

Querulousness, etc.   Very complaining disposition, etc.   See Jubilation-Lamentation.

Regret, etc.   Feeling of wishing something to have gone differently from what it did, etc.   See Contentedness-Regret.

Repining.   Inward discontent.

Soreness.   State of being sore.

Taking on.   Wild expression of grief.

Vexation of spirit.   Disquiet; affliction.

Discontentment—*Associated Nouns.*

Cave of Adullam.   The cave at which four hundred discontented men gathered under the leadership of David.   [Bible, I Sam. xxii, 1.]

Croaker.   One who complains unreasonably.

Growler.   One who complains without cause.

Grumbler.   One who is constantly complaining.

Indignation meeting.   A public meeting for making a complaint.

Laudator temporis acti [L.].   One who praises the past.

Malcontent.   One who is discontented.

Winter of our discontent.   Season of discontent. [Shakespeare, *Henry VI*, Part III, ii, 1.]

Discontentment—*Verbs.*

Chafe.   To put into ill humor; fret.

Croak.   To complain.

Disappoint.   To cause expectations to fail.

Disconcert.   To confuse.

Dishearten.   To cause to lose hope.

Fret.   To vex very much.

Grumble.   To find fault in a surly manner.

Lament, etc.   To have grief for any misfortune, etc.   See Jubilation-Lamentation.

Mortify.   To cause an humiliating disappointment.

Regret, etc.   To feel pain at something which we would wish different, etc.   See Contentedness-Regret.

Repine.   To be discontented and complaining.

Discontentment—*Verbal Expressions.*

Be discontented, etc. (see *Adjectives*); **cause discontent,** etc. (see *Nouns*); **cut up,** to discourage; **knit one's brows, look black, look black as thunder,** to show dissatisfaction or anger; **look blank, look blue, look glum,** to look as if discomfited; **make a piece of work,** to cause much trouble; **make a wry face; pull a long face; put out,** to provoke; **quarrel with one's bread and butter,** to injure one's own good interests; **shrug the shoulders; take ill; take in bad part; take on,** make much ado; **take to heart; wish one at the bottom of the Red Sea,** to be incensed at one.

Discontentment—*Adjectives.*

Disappointing, etc.   See *Verbs.*

Discontented.   Not contented.

Dissatisfied, etc.   See *Verbs.*

Dissentient, etc.   Not agreeing, etc.   See Assent-Dissent.

Exacting.   Too severe in making demands.

Exigent.   Requiring immediate help.

Glum.   Sullen.

Hypercritical.   Excessively critical.

Malcontent.   Dissatisfied.

Regretful, etc.   Full of regret, etc.   See Contentedness-Regret.

Repining, etc.   Complaining to oneself, etc.   See *Verbs.*

CONTENTEDNESS—DISCONTENTMENT—*Continued.*

CONTENTEDNESS—*Adverbial Expressions.*

À la bonne heure [F.], at a good time; all for the best; to one's heart's content.

CONTENTEDNESS—*Interjections.*

Amen, etc. (see ASSENT); it cannot be helped; it will do; so much the better; that will do; very well; well and good.

CONTENTEDNESS—*Phrases.*

Ich habe genossen das irdische Glück, ich habe gelebt und geliebet [G.]. I have tasted the good of earth, I have lived and loved. [Schiller, *Piccolomini (Wallenstein,* Part I), 3, 7, Coleridge, *Translation,* I, ii, 6.
Nothing comes amiss.

DISCONTENTMENT—ADJECTIVES—*Continued.*

Sore. Distressed.
Sour. Having an unfriendly disposition.
Soured. Made sour.
Sulky. Obstinate.
Ungratified. Not gratified.
Unsatisfactory. Not satisfactory.
Unsatisfied. Not satisfied.

DISCONTENTMENT—*Phrases.*

It will never do.
Ne Jupiter quidem omnibus placet [L.].   Not even Jupiter pleases all.
So much the worse.
That will never do.

CONTENTEDNESS—REGRET.

REGRET.

Bitterness. Hatred.
Heartburning. Discontent.
Homesickness. Intense longing for home.
Lamentation, etc. Grief over any misfortune, etc. See JUBILATION-LAMENTATION.
Maladie du pays [F.].
Mal du pays [F.].   } Homesickness.
Nostalgia. Homesickness.
Penitence, etc. Sorrow for guilt, etc. See REPENTANCE.
Regret. Feeling of pain because of something turning out unsatisfactorily.
Repining. Inward discontent.

REGRET—*Agent.*

Laudator temporis acti [L.].   One who praises the past.

REGRET—*Verbs.*

Bewail, etc. To make a loud and unrestrained show of sorrow, etc. See JUBILATION-LAMENTATION.
Deplore. To be greatly dissatisfied.
Regret. To look back upon with pain.

Repent, etc. To have sorrow for the past, and resolving to do better in the future, etc. See REPENTANCE.
Repine. To feel secret discontent.
Rue. To be sorry for.

REGRET—*Verbal Expressions.*

Cast a longing, lingering look behind; have a weight on the mind, to be troubled by something; *infandum renovare dolorem* [L.], to recall unspeakable grief; leave an aching void, to leave an unsatisfied longing; prey on the mind, to give much anxiety to; rue the day; weigh on the mind, to cause anxiety.

REGRET—*Adjectives.*

Homesick. Having a longing for home.
Lamentable, etc. Sorrowful, etc. See GOODNESS-BADNESS.
Much to be regretted. Regrettable.
Regretful. Full of regret.
Regrettable. Able to be regretted.
Regretted, etc. See *Verbs.*
Regretting, etc. Feeling regret, etc. See *Verbs.*

REGRET—*Interjections.*

Hang it! what a pity!

REGRET—*Phrases.*

'Tis pity.
'Tis too true.

---

con-ten'-tion. Dispute. RATIOCINATION-INSTINCT, STRIFE-PEACE.
con-ten'-tious. Quarrelsome. FAVORITE-QUARRELSOMENESS.
con-ten'-tious-ness. Quarrelsomeness. FIGHTING-CONCILIATION, VARIANCE-ACCORD.
con-tent'-ment. Content. CONTENTEDNESS-DISCONTENTMENT.
con'-tents. All that a thing contains. CONSTITUENT-ALIEN, CONTENTS-RECEIVER, DIGEST, RECORD.

CONTENTS—RECEIVER.

Bale. Quantity of goods bound in cloth or by cords for shipment.
Basket of. As much of anything as a basket will contain. See CONTENTS-RECEIVER.
Burden. The carrying capacity of a vessel.
Cargo. The load of goods carried by a ship.
Cartload. Contents of a cart.
Contents. That which is contained in anything.
Cup of. As much as a cup will hold. See CONTENTS-RECEIVER.
Freight. Goods transported in cars on a railroad.
Inside, etc. A passenger carried inside a coach, etc. See OUTSIDE-INSIDE.
Lading. Freight whose weight and quantity have been formally recorded.
Load. That which is transported.
Shipload. Capacity of a ship.
Shipment. That which is shipp d.
Stuffing. Anything used to fill up vacant space.
Ullage. The space left vacant in a partially filled ship, cask, etc.

CONTENTS—*Verbs.*

Charge. To put into.
Fill. To leave no space vacant.
Lade.
Load. } To put a load upon or in.
Ship. To put aboard a ship for transportation
Stuff. To fill to distention.

Enclosure, etc. That which encloses, etc. See ENCLOSURE
Receiver. One who or that which receives.
Receptacle. That in which anything is received or held.
Recipient. Receiver.
Reservatory. A place in which things are preserved.

RECEIVER—*Denotations.*

Adytum. The innermost shrine in an ancient place of worship.
Alcove. Any embowered or secluded spot.
Alembic. A glass or metal vessel used for distilling.
Amphora. A tall two-handled earthenware jar.
Antechamber. The entry to a room.
Anteroom. A waiting-room.
Apartment. A room or set of rooms.
Arbor. A shaded walk; a summer-house.
Attic. A room next to the roof.
Bag. A sack or pouch, of cloth, leather, paper, etc.
Bandbox. A light paper or wooden box.
Barrel. A wooden vessel made of staves held together by hoops.
Basement. The lowest room of a house.
Basin. A shallow dish or vessel for holding liquids.
Basket. A vessel of woven woodwork.
Bassinet. A basket with a wicker hood, used as a cradle.
Bathroom. A room for bathing.
Beaker. A large wide-mouthed drinking-cup or goblet; a glass vessel with a flaring top, used for making solutions, etc.

RECEIVER—Denotations—*Continued*.

Bed. An article of furniture to sleep on. See Suspension-Support.

Bedchamber. } A sleeping-room.
Bedroom. }

Billiard-room. A room which contains a billiard table or tables.

Bin. A box for holding grain, etc.

Bladder. The sac in the pelvic cavity for the retention of the urine.

Bolthead. A glass vessel with a long slender neck, used in chemical operations.

Bookcase. A case with shelves for keeping books.

Boot. A covering for the foot and lower leg.

Bottle. A glass vessel with a slender neck, for holding liquids.

Boudoir. A lady's private room.

Bower. A covered retreat.

Bowl. A concave vessel used for holding liquids.

Box. A six-sided case of various materials.

Bread-basket. A basket for carrying bread. The stomach.

Breeches pocket. A pouch attached to the sides or back of a breeches.

Buckbasket. A basket for soiled clothes.

Bucket. A cylindrical wooden vessel.

Budget. A small sack.

Buffet. A cupboard for china, glass, etc.

Bunker. A large, fixed box for coal, etc.

Bureau. A case with drawers for keeping clothes, etc.

Bushel. A vessel holding a bushel.

Butt. A large cask for wine.

Cabin. A small room on a ship.

Cabinet. A room in which a council or cabinet meets.

Caddy. A box for keeping tea.

Cag. A keg.

Cage. A box-like structure for confining birds or beasts.

Caisson. An ammunition chest.

Calabash. A vessel made of the dry shell of the calabash.

Caldron. A large kettle.

Calyx. A cup-shaped part of a flower.

Can. A vessel made of tin.

Cancelli. The bars in the railing of a court.

Canister. A metal box for tea, coffee, etc.

Canteen. A soldier's drinking-flask.

Canterbury. A stand containing divisions for portfolios, music, etc.

Capsule. A small gelatinous case containing a dose of nauseous drug.

Caraffe. A glass water-bottle.

Carboy. A large glass bottle enclosed in a box or in wickerwork.

Cardcase. A pocket-case for calling-cards.

Carriage. See Conveyance.

Case. Anything that encloses or contains something.

Cask. A barrel-shaped wooden vessel.

Casket. A small box for keeping jewels.

Caster. A bottle or vessel for dispersing powders, liquids, etc.

Catch-basin. A pit or reservoir at the end of a pipe or sewer.

Cave. An underground cavity. See Convexity-Concavity.

Cellar. A room under a building.

Cellaret. A small case for bottles, etc.

Cellule. A small cell in a plant or animal organism.

Chalice. A consecrated cup used in the Lord's Supper.

Chamber. A room.

Chest. A large strong box.

Chest of drawers. A case containing drawers.

Chiffonière. A high narrow bureau.

Cistern. A hole in the ground for storing water. See Store.

Clerestory. The highest story of the nave and choir of a church.

Closet. A small room for storing articles.

Clothes-press. A closet for clothes.

Cockloft. A room under the peak of a roof.

Cockpit. A ring for cock-fighting.

Coffer. A chest or box for keeping money.

Commode. An article of furniture to contain things for convenience.

Compartment. One of the parts into which an enclosed space is subdivided.

Conservatory. An apartment where plants are grown.

Corbeille [F.]. A basket.

Corner. A retired spot.

Corridor. A passageway.

Court. A space enclosed on three sides.

Cove. A nook in the shore of any body of water.

Cradle. An infant's bed.

Cran. A measure of fresh herrings, equal to a barrel

Crate. A box made of a framework of slats.

Craw. The stomach of an animal.

Creel. A willow basket for carrying fish.

Crock. An earthen pot or jar.

Crop. The first stomach of a bird.

Crucible. A pot or vessel for melting metals.

Cruet. A small glass bottle for holding vinegar.

Cruise. A small jug.

Crypt. Any secret recess or vault.

Cup. A small drinking vessel.

Cupboard. A closet for keeping dishes.

Cyst. Any membranous sac in the body.

Dairy. A building or room where milk is kept.

Davenport. A writing-desk.

Decanter. An ornamental glass bottle for wine.

Demijohn. A glass bottle usually enclosed in wickerwork.

Den. An underground retreat.

Desk. A stand usually containing drawers.

Dish. A concave or hollow vessel.

Dormitory. Any large room in which a number of persons sleep.

Dorser. A basket for bread.

Dosser. } A sliding receptacle in a bureau for holding clothes, etc.
Drawer. }

Drawing-room. A reception-room.

Entresol [F.]. A half story of a house.

Epergne. An ornamental centerpiece for a dining-table to hold flowers, etc.

Ewer. A water pitcher.

Faience. A highly decorated ewer.

Firkin. A wooden hooped vessel to hold butter.

Flagon. A vessel used to serve liquors.

Flask. A small bottle.

Flasket. A shallow basket.

Flat. A portion of a floor divided into rooms.

Fob. A watch-pocket.

Follicle. A minute cavity, sac, or tube.

Galipot. A small glazed earthenware jar used by pharmacists.

Gallery. An elevated floor in a building.

Garret. The highest room of a house.

Gizzard. The second stomach of birds.

Glass. Any article made of glass; a drinking vessel.

Goblet. A drinking vessel with stem and standard.

Greenhouse. A house for raising plants.

Ground-floor. The lowest room in a house.

Grotto. A small cavern.

Hall. The apartment first entered in a building.

Hamper. A large wickerwork basket.

Haversack. A soldier's ration bag.

Hermitage. The cell of a hermit.

Hod. A box for carrying plaster.

Hold. Part of a ship below deck.

Hole. An opening in anything.

Hopper. A funnel-shaped spout or tank.

Horn. A drinking vessel made of horn.

Imperial. A baggage case on top of a carriage.

Jar. A deep vessel of earthenware or glass.

Jardinière. A jar or box for flowers.

Jorum. A drinking-bowl.

Jug. A drinking vessel for holding or serving liquids.

Keg. A strong barrel.

Kettle. A metallic cooking utensil.

Kilderkin. An old English measure.

Kit. A wooden tub or vessel.

Kitchen. The cooking-room of a house.

Knapsack. A bag or case of leather used by soldiers.

Knit. A small bundle.

Ladle. A large spoon.

Laundry. A room for washing purposes.

Lean-to. A building having a roof pitched toward another building.

Library. A room where books are kept.

Lobby. An entrance or passageway.

Locker. A small closet.

Lodging. A place where one dwells. See Dweller-Habitation.

Loft. The room next to the roof.

Lumber-room. A garret or chamber for lumber or waste articles.

Manger. A feeding-box for cattle.

Matrass. A long-necked round-bodied glass vessel.

Maund. A basket.

Maw. The stomach of a bird.

Mezzanine. A half story of a house.

Mouth. The orifice by which food is taken into the body.

Mug. A drinking-cup.

Net. A woven fabric for catching fish.

Niche. A recessed space or hollow.

Nipperkin. A small cup.

Noggin. A wooden mug.

RECEIVER—Denotations—*Continued*.

Nook. A retired place.
Nursery. A room set apart for children.
Office. A business room.
Offices. Business apartments.
Oriel. A window built out from a wall and resting on a bracket.
Outhouse. A small building standing apart from a house.
Outroom. Outlying apartment or office.
Pail. A conical vessel for carrying liquids.
Pan. A wide shallow tin vessel.
Pannier. A basket used for carrying burdens on the backs of animals.
Pantry. A room where cooking utensils are·kept.
Parlor. A reception-room.
Passage. A corridor, hall, or gallery.
Patella. A cup-like part of anything.
Patera. A vessel used by the Romans in pouring libations.
Paunch. The abdomen.
Penthouse. A structure in the form of a shed with a single slope.
Pew. A seat in a church.
Phial. A small bottle.
Pig. An earthen vessel.
Pigeon-hole. A small compartment in a desk for holding papers, etc.
Piggin. A small wooden tub having one stave projecting for a handle.
Pipkin. A small earthenware jar.
Pitcher. A vessel used for holding and pouring liquids.
Plate. A shallow vessel for holding food.
Platter. A large plate.
Pocket. A pouch attached to the clothes for carrying small articles.
Pocket-pistol. A small liquor flask.
Pod. A seed vessel of a plant.
Poke. A pocket or small bag.
Porch. A covered entrance.
Porringer. A porridge-dish.
Portfolio. A portable case for carrying writing materials, etc.
Portico. A porch.
Portmanteau. A case for carrying clothing.
Posnet. A small saucepan.
Pot. An earthenware vessel.
Potage. A vessel for holding soup.
Pottle. A drinking vessel.
Pouch. A small bag or sack.
Presence-chamber. The room in which an official receives assemblies.
Press. A closet for clothes.
Punch-bowl. A large bowl in which punch is mixed.
Puncheon. A liquor cask.
Pyx. A receptacle for coins.
Quiver. A case for carrying arrows. See Store.
Rack. An open framework on which clothing is hung.
Receiver. A vessel considered as a receptacle for gas or fluid.
Reception-room. A room in which guests are received.
Recess. A secret place.
Refectory. A hall set apart for meals.
Reliquary. A casket or coffer in which relics are kept.
Reticule. A small bag for carrying needlework, etc.
Retort. A vessel with a bulb and long stem, for distilling liquids.
Rez-de-chaussée [F.]. The ground-floor.
Room. A space in a building.
Rummer. A drinking-cup.
Rundlet. A small wine barrel.
Sac. A membranous pouch
Saccule. A little sac.
Sachel. A leather traveling-bag.
Sack. A bag, usually large, made of strong material.
Sɾddle-bag. A pouch attached to a saddle.
Safe. A strong metal chest for storing valuables.
Salle à manger [F.]. A dining-room.
Salon [F.]. An apartment in which company is received.
Saloon. A large room for receptions; a grog-shop.
Salver. A heavy tray.
Sanctum. A private room.
Satchel. A leather traveling-bag.
Saucepan. A small tin pan for cooking.

Saucer. A shallow dish for holding a cup.
Scabbard. A case for a sword.
School-room. A room where pupils meet for instruction.
Scrip. A wallet or small bag.
Scrutoir. A writing-desk.
Scullery. A room where cooking utensils are kept.
Scuttle. A metal vessel for holding coal.
Secrétaire [F.]. A writing-desk.
Sheath. A case into which a blade is thrust when not in use.
Shovel. A scoop for throwing coal, etc.
Sideboard. A cupboard for holding dishes.
Sitting-room. A room where guests are entertained.
Skillet. A small kettle or stew-pan.
Skippet. A box for carrying a seal.
Smoking-room. A room for smoking.
Socket. A cavity specially adapted to receive something.
Spatula. A long spoon-shaped instrument.
Spoon. A utensil used in eating food.
Stall. A place where cattle are kept.
Stateroom. A private sleeping apartment on a train or ship; a room of state.
Stomach. The organ of the body which receives the food.
Storeroom. A place where goods are stored. See Store.
Story. A floor of a house.
Stoup. A drinking-cup.
Studio. An artist's working-room.
Study. A room for study.
Suite of rooms. A number of connected apartments.
Summer-house. A small open structure.
Tablespoon. A utensil used for ladling food.
Tableware. Articles used on the table.
Tablinum. A room in a Roman house where family records were kept.
Tankard. A large drinking-cup.
Tazza. A flat ornamental cup supported by a high foot. [It.]
Teaspoon. A spoon used in a tea-cup.
Terrine. A soup-dish.
Thimble. A small metal case worn on the end of the finger when sewing.
Till. A money-drawer.
Toby. A beer-jug in the form of an old man wearing a three-cornered hat.
Tray. A large flat vessel.
Trencher. A wooden plate.
Trowel. A small scoop.
Trunk. A covered box used for carrying articles on a journey.
Tub. A broad open-topped vessel of wood, formed by staves held together by hoops.
Tumbler. A glass with a stand.
Tun. A large liquor cask.
Tureen. A soup-dish.
Tyg. A three-handled drinking-cup.
Udder. The milk-bag of cows.
Urceus. A one-handled jug or pitcher.
Urn. A vase.
Utensil. A vessel of any kind.
Utricle. A cell of an animal or plant.
Vacherie [F.]. A cow-house.
Valise. A small leather traveling-bag.
Vasculum. A botanist's collecting case.
Vase. A vessel for holding flowers, etc.
Vat. A large tub or cistern.
Vault. A strong room for storing valuables.
Venter. The belly.
Ventricle. A cavity of a hollow organ.
Veranda. A covered porch.
Vesicle. A small bladder-like cavity.
Vessel. Any hollow receptacle for holding a liquid.
Vestibule. An entrance to a building.
Wallet. A pouch for carrying money.
Watch-glass. A half-hour glass for dividing watches into periods.
Whisket. A straw basket for cattle provender.
Wisket. A basket.
Zarf. A metal cup-holder.

RECEIVER—*Adjectives*.

Camerated. Provided with chambers.
Capsular. Like a capsule.
Cellular. Containing cells.
Concave. Curved in.
Cystic. Containing cysts.

Locular. Having cells.
Marsupial. Having a pouch for retaining the young.
Multilocular. Having many cells.
Polygastric. Provided with many stomachs.
Recipient. Ready to receive.

RECEIVER—ADJECTIVES—*Continued.*

Saccular. In the form of a sac.
Sacculated. Provided with sacs.
Siliquose. }
Siliquous. } Like a pod.

Vascular. Having vessels.
Ventricular. Like a ventricle.
Vesicular. Containing air-bladders.

con-ter'-min-a-ble. Limitable. BEGINNING - END, COVER-LINING.
con-ter'-mi-nate. To end. BEGINNING-END, BOUNDARY.
con-ter'-mi-nous. Coextensive. BEGINNING-END, INTERSPACE-CONTACT.
con-tes''-sa-ra'-tion. An assembly. GATHERING-SCATTERING.
con'-test. A struggle. STRIFE-PEACE.
con''-tes-ta'-tion. Strife. STRIFE-PEACE.
con'-text. A portion of a discourse. SOLITUDE-COMPANY, WRITING-PRINTING.
con-tex'-ture. Constitution. TEXTURE.
con''-ti-gu'-i-ty. Nearness. INTERSPACE-CONTACT, REMOTENESS-NEARNESS.
con-tig'-u-ous. Adjacent. INTERSPACE-CONTACT.
con'-ti-nence. Self-restraint. PURITY-IMPURITY.
con'-ti-nent. Greatest body of land; chaste. OCEAN-LAND, PURITY-IMPURITY.
con''-ti-nen'-tal. Pertaining to a continent. OCEAN-LAND.
con-tin'-gen-cy. Possibility of happening. CONDITION-SITUATION, CONTINGENCY, POSSIBILITY-IMPOSSIBILITY, RATIONALE-LUCK.

CONTINGENCY.

Contingency. The possibility of coming to pass.
Liableness. Likelihood.
Liability. The state of being likely to happen; tendency to happen.
Possibility. Power of happening, being or existing.
Susceptibility. The capability of easily receiving impressions.
Susceptivity. The capacity of admitting.

CONTINGENCY—*Verbs.*

Be liable, etc. Be likely or open to, etc. See *Adjectives.*
Expose oneself to. To render oneself accessible to anything that may affect.
Incur. To expose oneself to.
Lay oneself open to. To expose oneself to.
Lie under. To be subject to or oppressed by.
Open a door to. To expose, lay open to access.
Run the chance. To incur the liability that a thing may happen.
Stand the chance. To take the chance.

CONTINGENCY—*Adjectives.*

Apt to. Likely to.
At the mercy of. To be completely in the power of.
Contingent. Liable but not certain to occur.
Dependent on. Subject to, inferior to.
Exposed to. Rendered accessible to anything.
Incidental. Happening as an accidental event.

CONTINGENCY—ADJECTIVES—*Continued.*

Incident to. Apt to occur.
In danger, etc. In a state of exposure to peril, pain, or any other evil, etc. See SECURITY-INSECURITY.
Liable. Likely, possible.
Obnoxious to. Exposed, liable.
On the cards. Probable.
Open to. Accessible to.
Possible. Likely or liable to come to pass or happen.
Subject. Exposed to; liable.
Unexempt from. Not free from.
Within range of. Within reach.

con-tin'-gent. A proportionate share; fortuitous; a quota of troops; liable to occur. ASSIGNMENT, CERTAINTY-DOUBT, CONDITION-SITUATION, CONTINGENCY, MODIFICATION, OBSTRUCTION-HELP, OUTLAY-INCOME, POSSIBILITY - IMPOSSIBILITY, RATIONALE-LUCK; **contingent interest,** PROPERTY; **contingents,** MATERIALS.
con-tin'-gent du'-ra-tion. Duration dependent upon some contingency. CONTINGENT DURATION.

CONTINGENT DURATION.

CONTINGENT DURATION—*Adverbs.*

During good behavior. As long as one behaves well.
During pleasure. As long as one is pleased.
Quamdiu se bene gesserit [L.]. As long as he carries himself well.
[For words denoting *definite* duration, see PERIOD-PROGRESS.]

con-tin'-u-al. Oft repeated; kept up without intermission. ETERNITY-INSTANTANEITY, FREQUENCY-RARITY.
con-tin'-u-ance. Duration. DISCONTINUANCE-CONTINUANCE, LASTINGNESS-TRANSIENTNESS, PERSISTENCE-WHIM.
con-tin''-u-a'-tion. The act of continuing or that which is added by continuing. INCREMENT-REMNANT, PRECEDENCE-SUCCESSION, PREDECESSOR-CONTINUATION, RENEWAL.
con-tin'-u-a'-tive. Kind of conjunction. PARTICLE.
con-tin'-ue. To endure; to persist. DISCONTINUANCE-CONTINUANCE, DURATION-NEVERNESS, LASTINGNESS-TRANSIENTNESS, PERSISTENCE-WHIM.
con-tin'-ued. Having extension of time, space, etc. CONTINUITY-INTERRUPTION; **continued success,** SUCCESS-FAILURE.
con''-ti-nu'-i-ty. The state or quality of being continuous. CONTINUITY-INTERRUPTION.

CONTINUITY—INTERRUPTION.

Array. Disposition in regular lines.
Catenation. The union or interlinking of parts, as in a chain.
Chain. Used figuratively for catenation.
Concatenation. Catenation.
Consecution. Consecutiveness.
Consecutiveness, etc. The quality of following in uninterrupted succession, etc. See *Adjectives.*
Continuity. Uninterrupted action, flow, etc.
Course. The advance or progress of anything.
Gradation. Arrangement in the regular order of degree.
Progression. Regular advance.
Round. Rotation.
Scale. Gradation.
Series. A connected succession.
Succession. The state of succeeding in order.
Suite. A number of things connected in a series.
Train. Succession considered as a whole.

Alternation. The changing from one thing or condition to another.
Break. The absence of a connective.
Crack. A partial break.
Cut. An open excavation through a mountain, etc.
Discontinuity. The quality of not being continuous.
Disjunction, etc. The state of being disunited, etc. See UNION-DISUNION.
Fault. Displacement of part of a stratum.
Flaw. A break and dislocation in a stratum.
Fracture. A partial breaking as in a bone.
Gap, etc. An opening; a ravine, etc. See INTERSPACE.
Intermission. Temporary cessation.
Interruption. Hindrance; breaking in upon.
Solution of continuity. Breaking up of continuity.

INTERRUPTION—*Denotations.*

Anacoluthon. Violation of the law of sequence in grammar.
Broken thread. A break in the thought in a story.

CONTINUITY—INTERRUPTION—*Continued.*

CONTINUITY—*Denotations.*

Array. A body of persons or things arranged in ranks.
Cavalcade. A company of riders on the march.
Colonnade. A range of columns.
Column. A body of troops with narrow front but extended rearward.
Cortège [F.]. A file.
File. An orderly succession of men or things.
Genealogy. A list of ancestors in the order of succession.
Hedge row. An orderly rank of shrubs or small trees.
Line. A series of objects in a straight row.
Lineage. Ancestral line of relationship.
Line of battle. Troops drawn up in regular ranks.
Pedigree. One's line of ancestors.
Procession. A body in marching order.
Race. A genealogical or family stock.
Range. A class of objects considered as making a rank or series.
Rank. A series of objects arranged in a row.
Rank and file. Rows regarded as running from side to side and from front to back.
Retinue. A body of persons attending a person of rank.
Row. A line of persons or things.
String. A connected series or succession of things.
Suit. A succession of things forming a series.
Team. Several persons who act together in a particular work.
Thread. A steady succession of thoughts or things.
Tier. A rank or row in a series.

CONTINUITY—*Verbs.*

File. To march one after the other.
Graduate. To arrange according to the degree of some quality.
Tabulate. To make a systematic record of.
Thread. To arrange on a thread.

CONTINUITY—*Verbal Expressions.*

Arrange in a series, etc. (see *Nouns*); **fall in,** get into line, **follow in a series; form in a series,** etc. (see *Nouns*); **string together.**

CONTINUITY—*Adjectives.*

Consecutive. Following in regular order.
Constant. Unchangeable.
Continued. Having but slight pauses or intervals.
Continuous. Absolutely without intervals or breaks.
Entire. Having all its parts.
Evergreen. Green the whole year.
Gradual. Proceeding by regular steps.
Immediate. Coming after with the loss of little time.
In a line. } See *Nouns.*
In a row. }
Linear. Continuous like a line.
Perennial. Continuing for many years.
Progressive. Advancing regularly.
Serial. Arranged in a series.
Successive. Following in order.
Unbroken. Not broken.
Unintermitting. Not ceasing.
Uninterrupted. Not hindered.
Unremitting. Not relaxing.

CONTINUITY—*Adverbs.*

Continuously. In a continuous manner.
Gradatim [L.]. } By degrees.
Gradually. }

INTERRUPTION—*Denotations—Continued.*

Cæsura. A pause in a metrical foot.
Dropping fire. Continued, irregular discharge of firearms.
Episode. An incident or story in a literary work, separable from it.
Parenthesis. An explanatory clause inserted in a sentence.
Patchwork. Work made up of misfitting materials.
Rhapsody. A series of utterances or sentences without natural connection.

INTERRUPTION—*Verbs.*

Alternate. To change from one to another.
Disconnect, etc. To sever the connection, etc. See UNION-DISUNION.
Discontinue. To leave off.
Intermit. To cease for a time.
Interpose, etc. To come between, etc. See ENVIRONMENT-INTERPOSITION.
Interrupt. To hinder by breaking in upon the course of.
Intervene. To come between.
Pause. A short stop.

INTERRUPTION—*Adjectives.*

Alternate. Following one after the other.
Broken. Lacking a connective.
Desultory. Skipping from one to another.
Disconnected. Not united.
Discontinuous. Not continuous.
"Few and far between." Scarce, "Like angel visits." [Campbell: *Pleasures of Hope,* ii, 378.]
Fitful, etc. Marked by great irregularity, etc. See REGULARITY-IRREGULARITY.
Intermittent. }
Intermitting, etc. } Ceasing at times, etc. See *Verbs.*
Interrupted. Broken in upon.
Recurrent, etc. Occurring again at stated times, etc. See PERIODICITY.
Spasmodic. Acting by starts.
Unconnected. Not connected.
Unsuccessive. Not successive.

INTERRUPTION—*Adverb.*

Skippingly. With omissions.

INTERRUPTION—*Adverbial Expressions.*

At intervals; by catches, by short intervals of action; **by fits and starts; by jerks; by skips; by snatches;** *longo intervallo* [L.], by a long interval; *per saltum* [L.], by a leap.

CONTINUITY—*Adverbs—Continued.*

Running. Continuously.
Seriatim [L.]. One after another.

CONTINUITY—*Adverbial Expressions.*

At a stretch, without interruption; **in a line** (see *Nouns*); **in column, in file, in Indian file, in single file,** marching one after the other; **in succession; in turn; step by step,** slowly.

-----

con-tort'. To twist. CIRCLE-WINDING, PROPORTION-DEFORMITY.
con-tor'-tion. Unnatural writhing or wryness. PROPORTION-DEFORMITY.
con-tor'-tion-ist. One who is trained to distort his limbs. ACTING.
con-tour'. Outline. APPEARANCE-DISAPPEARANCE, FORM-FORMLESSNESS, OUTLINE.
contra [L.] (con'-tra). Against; opposite; contrary. SAMENESS-CONTRAST.
contra bonos mores [L.] (con'-tra bo'-nos mo'-rîz). Against good manners. DUENESS - UNDUENESS, TASTE-VULGARITY, VIRTUE-VICE.
contra, per [L.] (con'-tra, per). On the contrary. ANTAGONISM-CONCURRENCE.

con'-tra-band. Forbidden. LAW-LAWLESSNESS, LEAVE-PROHIBITION, TRUTHFULNESS-FRAUD.
con'-tra-bas''-so. The double-bass viol. MUSICAL INSTRUMENTS.
con-tract'. To shrink; to make a contract. BREADTH-NARROWNESS, ENGAGEMENT, ENLARGEMENT-DIMINUTION; **contract a debt,** CREDIT-DEBT; **contract a habit,** HABIT-DESUETUDE; **contract an obligation,** ENGAGEMENT.
con'-tract. A formal agreement between two or more parties. CONTRACT, ENGAGEMENT, ENTERPRISE.

CONTRACT.

Affidation. Promise.
Agreement. An engagement that something shall be done or omitted.

Bargain. An agreement. between two parties as to the buying and selling of a piece of property.

Bond. A writing under seal by which a person binds himself to pay a sum of money.

Cartel. A written agreement between belligerents for the exchange of prisoners.

Charter. A written document given by the proper authority to a company of men, giving them certain privileges, rights, and franchises.

Compact. An agreement; a mutual contract.

Completion. The end of an agreement.

Compromise. A mutual agreement brought about by both sides making concessions.

Concordat. A covenant; a compact.

Contract. An agreement between two, stipulating what each one will do and what he will not do.

Convention. An agreement preliminary to a treaty.

Covenant. An agreement between God and man.

Indenture. A written agreement between two parties, of which each one keeps a duplicate.

Pact. An agreement.

Paction. See PACT.

Protocol. A preliminary treaty.

Settlement. An agreement giving possession under legal sanction.

Stipulation. A contract or bargain.

Treaty. An agreement or contract between nations.

CONTRACT—*Denotations.*

Magna Charta. A charter of English liberties secured from King John on the demand of the barons, June 15, 1215.

Pragmatic Sanction. An edict of Charles VI, of the House of Hapsburg, regulating the succession to the Austrian throne.

Sonderbund [G.]. A league of the Swiss states.

Zollverein [G.]. A tax-union of the German states.

CONTRACT—*Associated Nouns.*

Diplomacy. The art of transacting business between sovereign states.

Negotiator. One who transacts business. See CONSIGNEE.

Seal. The impression made by a stamp, attesting the genuineness of an instrument.

Sigil. A seal or signature.

Signature. The name of the author or party to an instrument.

Signet. A seal.

CONTRACT—*Verbs.*

Agree for. See HARMONY.

Bargain, etc. See EXCHANGE.

Bargain by inch of candle. To bargain closely.

Clench. To bind.

Close. To come to an agreement.

Close with. To end the bargain.

Come to an understanding. } Agree

Come to terms.

Complete. To fulfil.

Compromise, etc. See COMPOSITION.

Conclude. To end; to finish.

Confirm. To ratify; to sign.

Contract. To enter into an agreement.

Covenant. To contract for a single thing.

Endorse. To set one's signature to a check or note.

Engage, etc. See ENGAGEMENT.

Indent. To seal.

Indorse. To sign.

Make a bargain. } Agree.

Make terms.

Negotiate. To treat with.

Put the seal to. Seal.

Ratify. To make valid by approval.

Seal, etc To place a seal upon, etc. See EVIDENCE

Set at rest. Settle.

Settle. To come to an agreement.

Sign. To attach one's signature to.

Stipulate. To require in an agreement.

Strike a bargain. Come to an agreement.

Subscribe. To set one's name to a paper for the promise of paying a certain sum.

Take one at one's word. End a bargain.

Treat. To deal with.

Underwrite. To affix one's signature.

CONTRACT—*Adjectives.*

Agreed, etc. See *Verbs.*

Conventional. Pertaining to convention.

Under hand and seal. Ratified.

CONTRACT—*Phrases.*

À forfait [F.]. By contract.

Caveat emptor [L.]. Let the buyer beware.

con-tract'-ed. Drawn together. BREADTH-NARROWNESS.

con-tract'-ile. Producing contraction. ENLARGEMENT-DIMINUTION.

con"-trac-til'-i-ty. The inherent force by which bodies shrink. ENLARGEMENT-DIMINUTION.

con-tract'-ing. Drawing together. ENLARGEMENT-DIMINUTION.

con-trac'-tion. The act of contracting. APERTURE-CLOSURE, DIGEST, ENLARGEMENT-DIMINUTION, WRITING-PRINTING.

con"-tra-dict'. To deny; to oppose. ANTAGONISM-CONCURRENCE, ASSENT-DISSENT, ASSERTION-DENIAL, SAMENESS-CONTRAST.

con"-tra-dic'-tion. A gainsaying. SAMENESS-CONTRAST.

con"-tra-dict'-o-ry. Diametrically opposed. ASSERTION-DENIAL, EVIDENCE-COUNTEREVIDENCE, SAMENESS-CONTRAST.

con"-tra-dis-tinc'-tion. Distinction by contrast. VARIATION.

con"-tra-in'-di-cate. To indicate the opposite of. MOTIVE-DEHORTATION.

con"-tra-in"-di-ca'-tion. Unfavorable indication. MOTIVE-DEHORTATION.

contraire [F.] (con'-trar'). Contrary.

contraire, tout au [F.] (con'-trar', tut-o). Quite the contrary. ASSERTION-DENIAL.

con-tral'-to. The part between soprano and tenor. RESONANCE-NONRESONANCE.

con"-tra-po-si'-tion. A placing opposite. LATERALITY-CONTRAPOSITION, REVERSAL.

con"-tra-pun'-tist. One skilled in counterpoint. MELODY-DISSONANCE.

con-tra'-ri-ant. Opposing. SAMENESS-CONTRAST.

con-tra-ri'-e-ty. The quality or state of being contrary. COOPERATION-OPPOSITION, SAMENESS-CONTRAST.

con'-tra-ri-ly. Perversely. SAMENESS-CONTRAST.

con-tra'-ri-ous. Showing opposition. SAMENESS-CONTRAST.

con'-tra-ri-wise. Conversely. SAMENESS-CONTRAST.

con'-tra-ry. Antagonistic; captious; opposite in direction. ANTAGONISM-CONCURRENCE, COOPERATION-OPPOSITION, PERSISTENCE-WHIM, SAMENESS-CONTRAST; **contrary to expectation,** EXPECTATION-SURPRISE, LIKELIHOOD-UNLIKELIHOOD; **contrary to reason,** POSSIBILITY-IMPOSSIBILITY; **quite the contrary,** ASSERTION-DENIAL, SAMENESS-CONTRAST.

con'-trast. The opposition between things similar in some respects which are yet strikingly different. COMPARISON, SAMENESS-CONTRAST, VARIATION.

con-trast'-ed. Set in opposition. SAMENESS-CONTRAST.

con'-tra-val-la'-tion. A trench guarded by a parapet. ATTACK-DEFENSE.

con"-tra-vene'. To prevent. ANTAGONISM-CONCURRENCE, ASSERTION-DENIAL, EVIDENCE-COUNTEREVIDENCE, OBSTRUCTION-HELP, SAMENESS-CONTRAST.

contre cœur, à [F.] (con'tr cur, a). Against the grain. READINESS-RELUCTANCE.

contre-coup [F.] (con'tr-cu'). A rebound. IMPETUS-REACTION.

contre-temps [F.] (con'tr-tan'). A disappointment; a mischance. OBSTRUCTION-HELP, OPPORTUNENESS-UNSUITABLENESS, WELFARE-MISFORTUNE.

con-tri'-bute. To give aid to some object; to share in effecting a result. CAUSE-EFFECT, COOPERATION-OPPOSITION, GIVING-RECEIVING, INCLINATION, OBSTRUCTION-HELP.

con''-tri-bu'-tion. The act of contribution or that which is contributed. GIVING-RECEIVING; **lay under contribution,** DUENESS-UNDUENESS, TAKING-RESTITUTION.

con'-trite. Penitent. REPENTANCE-OBDURACY.

con-tri'-tion. Deep penitence; friction. FRICTION-LUBRICATION, REPENTANCE-OBDURACY.

con-tri'-vance. Device. DESIGN.

con-trive'. Invent; plot. CRAFT-ARTLESSNESS, CREATION-DESTRUCTION, DESIGN; **contrive to,** SUCCESS-FAILURE.

con-triv'-ing. Scheming. CRAFT-ARTLESSNESS.

con-trol'. Regulation. ANTAGONISM-CONCURRENCE, MANAGEMENT, MIGHT-IMPOTENCE, PRESIDENT-MEMBER, RELEASE-RESTRAINT, RULE-LICENSE; **board of control,** COUNCIL, MANAGEMENT; **under control,** INSUBORDINATION-OBEDIENCE, LIBERTY-SUBJECTION, RULE-LICENSE.

con''-tro-ver'-sial. Polemical; contentious. RATIOCINATION-CASUISTRY, VARIANCE-ACCORD.

con''-tro-ver'-sial-ist. A disputant. BELLIGERENT, RATIOCINATION-CASUISTRY.

con'-tro-ver''-sy. A disputation. RATIOCINATION-INSTINCT, STRIFE-PEACE.

con''-tro-vert'. To deny and endeavor to disprove. ASSERTION-DENIAL, RATIOCINATION-INSTINCT, VARIANCE-ACCORD.

con''-tro-vert'-i-ble. Disputable. CERTAINTY-DOUBT, RATIOCINATION-INSTINCT, TRUTH-ERROR.

con''-tro-ver'-tist. Debater. RATIOCINATION-INSTINCT.

con''-tu-ma'-cious. Rebellious. BIGOTRY-APOSTASY, INSUBORDINATION-OBEDIENCE.

con'-tu-ma-cy. Insolent and stubborn perseverance. BIGOTRY-APOSTASY, INSUBORDINATION-OBEDIENCE.

con''-tu-me'-li-ous. Rude. POLITENESS-IMPOLITENESS, PRESUMPTION - OBSEQUIOUSNESS, REGARD - DISRESPECT.

con'-tu-me-ly. Scornful insolence. APPROVAL-DISAPPROVAL, POLITENESS-IMPOLITENESS, REGARD-DISRESPECT, REGARD-SCORN.

con-tund'. To bruise by beating. FRIABILITY.

con-tuse'. To beat. FRIABILITY.

con-tu'-sion. A pulverizing. FRIABILITY.

co-nun'-drum. A riddle. AMBIGUITY, TIDINGS-MYSTERY, WITTINESS-DULNESS.

con''-va-les'-cence. Progressive restoration to health and strength after disease. RENOVATION-RELAPSE.

con''-va-les'-cent. Getting well. RENOVATION-RELAPSE.

con-vec'-tion. The act of conveying. TRANSFER.

con-vene'. To assemble. GATHERING-SCATTERING.

con-ve'-nienc-es. Those things which are convenient. MEANS.

con-ve'-nient. Conducive to comfort or ease. PROPRIETY-IMPROPRIETY.

con-ve'-nient-ly. Suitably. PROPRIETY-IMPROPRIETY.

con'-vent. The house occupied by a body of monks or nuns. FANE, SOCIABILITY-PRIVACY.

con-ven'-ti-cle. A religious meeting. COUNCIL, GATHERING-SCATTERING, FANE.

con-ven'-tion. A formal gathering of persons for some specific object; a compact. CONTRACT, COUNCIL, FIGHTING-CONCILIATION, GATHERING - SCATTERING; **conventions of society,** SOCIETY-LUDICROUSNESS.

con-ven'-tion-al. Established by custom. CONVENTIONALITY-UNCONVENTIONALITY, FERTILITY-STERILITY, HABIT-DESUETUDE, SOCIETY-LUDICROUSNESS.

con-ven'-tion-al-ism. Formality. HABIT-DESUETUDE.

con-ven''-tion-al'-i-ty. A formality. CONVENTIONALITY-UNCONVENTIONALITY, HABIT-DESUETUDE.

CONVENTIONALITY—UNCONVENTIONALITY.

Agreement, etc. Exact sameness, etc. See HARMONY.

Conformance. } Correspondence in form, character, etc.
Conformity.

Conventionality, etc. Adherence to certain forms and usages, etc. See HABIT.

Exemplification. A showing by example.

Naturalization. The act of making natural or conformable to habit or custom. Making a foreigner a citizen.

Observance. Adherence to rule.

CONVENTIONALITY—*Associated Nouns.*

Case in point. An instance supporting an argument.

Example. Anything used as a copy or model.

Illustration. A print, drawing, or picture of any kind.

Instance. A case offered as an exemplification.

Pattern. That after which something should be modeled. See MODEL.

Quotation. A passage from a book used as an illustration, and cited verbatim.

Sample. A part taken as the representative of the whole.

Specimen. A sample.

CONVENTIONALITY—*Verbs.*

Cite. To refer to by giving exact location.

Exemplify. To prove by an example.

Illustrate. To make clear by comparisons.

Quote. To give the substance of another's words.

CONVENTIONALITY—*Verbal Expressions.*

Accommodate oneself to; adapt oneself to; be guided by; bend to precedents, to do as has been done; **bend to rules; be regular,** etc. (see *Adjectives*), be regulated by; **chime in with,** to agree to; **comply with; conform to rule; do as others do; do at Rome as the Romans do,** to conform to one's surroundings; **fall into a custom; fall into a usage; fall in with,** to conform to; **follow precedents; follow rules; follow the fashion; follow the multitude; go by precedents; go by rules; go with the current; go with the stream; go with the tide;** *hurler avec les loups* [F.], to howl with the wolves; to do as others

Aberration. A wandering from a prescribed course.

Abnormality. The state of not being according to the usual natural condition or rule.

Anomalousness, etc. The state of being anomalous, etc. See *Adjectives*.

Anomaly. A rare exception to a rule.

Bizarrerie [F.]. Whim.

Breach of custom. Departure from the ordinary way of acting.

Breach of law. The doing of something contrary to law.

Breach of usage. Performance of anything not approved by usage.

Disconformity. Lack of conformity.

Eccentricity. The state of being odd, out of center.

Exception. A variation from a rule.

Exemption. Freedom from a common burden or obligation.

Idiosyncrasy. Mental peculiarity of a person.

Individuality. The state of having a combination of qualities peculiar only to one.

Informality. Absence of formality.

Infraction of custom. See BREACH OF CUSTOM.

Infraction of law. See BREACH OF LAW.

Infraction of usage. See BREACH OF USAGE.

Infringement of custom. See BREACH OF CUSTOM.

Infringement of law. See BREACH OF LAW.

Infringement of usage. See BREACH OF USAGE.

Irregularity. The state of not being regular.

Je ne sais quoi [F.]. I know not what.

Mannerism. Adherence to a certain manner or style.

Monstrosity. Great abnormality.

Non-conformity, etc. Neglect or refusal to conform, etc. See CONVENTIONALITY.

Oddity. Something the like of which cannot easily be found.

Originality. The power or state of being original.

Peculiarity. Quality belonging only to one.

Rarity. The state of being rare.

Salvo, etc. A proviso, etc. See MODIFICATION.

Singularity. The quality of being singular or rare.

Unconventionality. The state of not being conventional.

CONVENTIONALITY—UNCONVENTIONALITY—*Continued.*

CONVENTIONALITY—Verbal Expressions—*Continued.*

do; keep one in countenance, to stay in the favor of others; move in a groove, to become settled in habits, thought, etc.; obey precedents; obey rules; observe precedents; observe rules; pass muster, to pass a successful examination; produce an instance, etc. (see *Nouns*); put a case, give an example; rub off corners, to trim or train so as to make more suitable; swim with the current, swim with the stream, swim with the tide, tally with, to do as others do; tread the beaten track, etc., to be ruled by precedents, etc. (see HABIT).

CONVENTIONALITY—*Adjectives.*

Canonical. Pertaining to the canon of scripture.
Common. To be noticed everywhere or often.
Conventional, etc. Conformity to a fixed standard, etc. See HABIT.
Exemplary. Worthy to be taken as an example.
Formal. Inclined to the observance of forms.
Habitual. Settled by frequent practise.
Illustrative. Serving to illustrate.
Naturalized. Accepted as a citizen of a foreign country; accommodated to new surroundings.
Normal. Conforming to the general rule of nature.
Orderly. Nicely arranged.
Ordinary. Not above the average.
Orthodox. In accordance with the established belief.
Positive. Laid down arbitrarily.
Procrustean. Violently forcing into conformity, as did Procrustes, an Athenian highwayman, who made every one fit his bed by stretching him or cutting off his legs.
Regular, etc. Following some rule, etc. See UNIFORMITY.
Rigid. Not varying.
Sound. Well grounded.
Strict. Rigorous.
Technical. Pertaining to the principles of some profession.
Typical. Marked by the principal characteristics of a group.
Uncompromising. Not conceding anything.
Usual. Customary.

CONVENTIONALITY—*Adjective Expressions.*

According to Cocker, according to the best authority; according to regulation; according to rule; conformable to rule; *en règle* [F.], according to rule; in point; in the natural order of things; in the order of the day, on the program of the day's work; of daily occurrence; of every day occurrence; *secundum artem* [L.], according to rule; *selon les règles* [F.], according to rules; ship-shape, in good order; well regulated.

CONVENTIONALITY—*Adverbs.*

Conformably, etc. In conformity with, etc. See *Adjectives.*
Invariably, etc. Without variation, etc. See UNIFORMITY.

CONVENTIONALITY—*Adverbial Expressions.*

According to; *ad instar* [L.], after the manner of; agreeably to; as a matter of course; as usual; by rule; by the card, correctly; consistently with; *e. g.* [L.], for *exempli gratia* [L.], for the sake of an example; for example; for form's sake; for instance; for the sake of conformity; in accordance with; in conformity with; in keeping with; *instar omnium* [L.], the manner of all; *inter alia* [L.], among other things; *more majorum* [L.], in the manner of our forefathers; of course; *pro forma* [L.], for the sake of form; *solito majorum* [L.], according to the custom of our ancestors.

CONVENTIONALITY—*Phrases.*

Cela va sans dire [F.]. That goes without saying.
Ex pede Herculem [L.]. We recognize a Hercules by his foot.
Noscitur a sociis [L.]. One is known by the company he keeps.

UNCONVENTIONALITY—*Continued from Column 2.*

UNCONVENTIONALITY—*Scientific Noun.*

Teratology. That branch of biology which treats of abnormal growths.

UNCONVENTIONALITY—*Verbal Expressions.*

Baffle all description, beggar all description, to be unable to be described properly; be unconformable, etc. (see *Adjectives*); break a custom; break a habit; break a law; break a usage; drive a coach and six through; have no business there, to be out of place; infringe a custom; infringe a habit; infringe a law; infringe a usage; leave the beaten path, to err in any way; leave the beaten track; stretch a point, to make an exception to the dictates of one's conscience; violate a custom; violate a habit; violate a law; violate a usage.

Variety. Absence of sameness in things.
Violation of custom. See BREACH OF CUSTOM.
Violation of law. See BREACH OF LAW.
Violation of usage. See BREACH OF USAGE.

UNCONVENTIONALITY—*Denotations.*

Black swan. An Australian species of swan.
Centaur. A fabled monster, a horse having the body and head of man.
Character. Combination of qualities distinguishing any person or thing.
Chimera. A fire-breathing monster, a combination of lion, goat, and serpent.
Cockatrice. A winged and legged serpent.
Cross-breed. The offspring of different breeds.
Curiosity. An object that attracts attention by some peculiar characteristic.
Cyclops. A fabled race of one-eyed giants.
Dragon. A large winged lizard or serpent.
Fish out of water. Anything in an unusual condition.
Flying fish. A winged fish.
Freak of nature. Anything unnatural.
Griffin. }
Griffon. } A creature half lion and half eagle.
Half-blood. }
Half-breed. } One whose parents are of different races.
Half-caste. One whose parents are of European and East-Indian blood.
Hermaphrodite. An animal having the sexual characteristics of both sexes.
Hippocentaur. A centaur.
Hippogriff. A fabled beast having the head and claws of a griffin and the hoofs and tail of a horse.
Hybrid. An animal or plant produced from a mixture of different breeds.
Hydra. A nine-headed water-serpent.
Kraken. A fabulous sea-monster, said to be a mile and a half in circumference.
Lusus naturæ [L.]. A freak of nature.
Men whose heads do grow beneath their shoulders. Freaks. [Shakespeare, *Othello*, I, 3.]
Mermaid. A marine creature having the head and body of a woman and ending in the tail of a fish.
Métis [F.]. Any one of mixed blood.
Miracle. Any event beyond the power of ordinary natural agencies.
Mongrel. The offspring of different breeds.
Monster. A fabulous animal half human, half brute.
Mulatto. The offspring of a white person and a black person.
Mule. A hybrid between the ass and horse.
Neither fish, nor flesh, nor good red herring. Neither one thing nor another. [*Heywood's Proverbs*, A. D. 1546.]
Neither one thing nor another. Anything difficult to distinguish the species of.
Non-conformist. One who does not conform to established usage or law, especially in church matters.
Nondescript. A person or thing difficult to describe.
Nonsuch. Anything the like of which is not known.
Oasis. A fertile spot in a desert.
One in a thousand. A rare article.
One in a way. An odd thing.
Original. A person or thing which differs from any ordinary type.
Outcast. One cast out from home or country.
Outlaw. A person deprived of the benefit of the law.
Phœnix. A sacred bird which sacrificed itself by burning every 500 years, and rose out of the ashes young and beautiful.
Prodigy. Something so out of the ordinary as to excite wonder
Queer fish. A Caliban. [Shakespeare, *Tempest*, II, i.] An odd and droll person, A. D. 1750. "He was an odd fish." [Franklin's *Autobiography*.] "The queerest, coolest fish in Rugby." [Hughes, *Tom Brown*.]
Rara avis [L.]. A rare bird.
Roc. A fabulous bird of prey. [*The Arabian Nights.*]
Sagittary. A centaur.
Scab. A laborer who does not act with a labor-union.
Sea-serpent. A monster.
Sphinx. A winged monster with a woman's head and lion's body
Tertium quid [L.]. A third something.
Unicorn. A monster having the body of a horse and a single long horn projecting from the head.
Wonder. Any object that causes wonder.
Wyvern. A winged dragon, figured in heraldry. ["Blaze like a wyvern flying round the sun." Browning, *Paracelsus.*]
Xiphopagus. A double monster, such as the Siamese twins.

(Continued on Column 1.)

UNCONVENTIONALITY—*Continued.*

UNCONVENTIONALITY—*Adjectives.*

Aberrant. Deviating from a prescribed course.
Abnormal. }
Abnormous. } Not normal.
Amorphous. Irregular in shape.
Amphibious. Possessing two natures.
Androgynal. }
Androgynous. } Partaking of the nature of a male and a female.
Anomalistic. }
Anomalous. } Not conforming to a rule.
Arbitrary. Depending on no rule.
Bizarre [F.]. Fantastic.
Curious. Somewhat odd or strange.
Denaturalized. Made unnatural; deprived of citizenship.
Eccentric. Not conforming to any rule.
Egregious. Extraordinary.
Epicene. Common to both sexes.
Exceptional. Not ordinary.
Exclusive. Not including some things.
Exotic. Foreign.
Extraordinary. Out of the ordinary course.
Fantastic. Extremely fanciful.
Grotesque. Whimsical and uncouth.
Heteroclite. Anomalous. A noun declined from more than one stem.
Heterogeneous. Possessing characteristics of a number of different things
Hybrid. Produced from the mixture of two species.
Informal. Not formal.
Irregular. Not regular.
Lawless. Not restrained by law.
Misplaced. Bestowed in the wrong place.
Mongrel. Of mixed breed.

Monstrous. Very abnormal, so as to be an admonition from the gods.
Nondescript. Not able to be described.
Non-union. Opposed to trades-unions.
Noteworthy. Worthy of observation.
Odd. Not having anything to mate it.
Original. Not imitated or imitating.
Outlandish. Uncouth.
Outré [F.]. Extravagant.
Peculiar. Belonging to one.
Preternatural. Not governed by any known powers of nature.
Quaint. Not conforming to the present manner, style, etc.
Qualified, etc. Limited, etc. See MODIFICATION.
Queer. Slightly comical.
Rare. Occurring not very often; dear.
Remarkable. Extraordinary and noticeable.
Singular. Entirely different from others.
Strange. Not easily explained.
Stray. Not often met with.
Unaccountable. Not to be accounted for.
Unaccustomed. Not accustomed.
Uncommon. Not common.
Unconformable. Not conformable.
Unconventional. Not customary.
Uncustomary. Not usual.
Undescribed. Unheard of.
Unexampled. Unprecedented.
Unusual. Not usual.
Unwonted. Not customary.
Wandering. Not guided by anything definite.
Wanton. Free from restraint.
Wonderful, etc. Strange, etc. See ASTONISHMENT.

UNCONVENTIONALITY—*Adjective Expressions.*

New-fangled, out of keeping, not in harmony with; **out of one's element,** not in circumstances to which one is accustomed; **out of order; out of place; out of the beaten track,** not following precedents; **out of the common; out of the common run; out of the pale** of; **out of the way; out of tune;** *sui generis* [L.], of its own kind; *tombé des nues* [F.], fallen from the clouds, occurring when least expected; unheard of.

UNCONVENTIONALITY—*Adverbs, etc.*

Unconformably, etc. Not in conformity, etc. See *Adjectives.*

Barring; beside; but; except; however; let alone; save; save and except; unless; without; yet.

UNCONVENTIONALITY—*Interjections.*

What in the world! what on earth! Expressions to denote surprise.

UNCONVENTIONALITY—*Phrases.*

Never was heard the like; never was known the like; never was seen the like.

con-ven′-tu-al. Belonging to a convent. FANE, MINISTRY-LAITY.
con-verge′. To run together. CENTER, CONCENTRATION-RADIATION, REMOTENESS-NEARNESS.
con-ver′-gence. The act or state of coming toward one point. CONCENTRATION-RADIATION, GATHERING-SCATTERING, REMOTENESS-NEARNESS.
con-ver′-gent. Tending towards one point. CONCENTRATION-RADIATION.

con-ver′-ging. Convergent. CONCENTRATION-RADIATION.
con-vers′-a-ble. Affable. CONVERSATION-MONOLOGUE, SOCIABILITY-PRIVACY.
con-ver′-sant. Knowing fully. KNOWLEDGE-IGNORANCE, SKILL-UNSKILFULNESS.
con″-ver-sa′-tion. The speaking of two or more persons alternately with each other. CONVERSATION-MONOLOGUE.

CONVERSATION—MONOLOGUE.

Audience. A formal hearing.
Babble. Prattle; gossip.
Babblement. Babble.
Cackle. Idle or silly talk.
Cancan [F.]. Gossip; tittle-tattle.
Causerie [F.]. Talk; chat.
Chat. Easy and familiar speech.
Chit-chat. Careless familiar talk.
Collocution. Mutual discourse.
Colloquy. Conversation; dialogue.
Commerce. Intercourse.
Confabulation. Familiar conversation.
Conference. A formal consultation.
Congress. An assembly or conference. See COUNCIL.
Conversation. The speaking of two or more persons alternately. with each other. Association. *Bible.*

Apostrophe. A digressive address aside from the main purpose of a speaker or writer, as to an absent person.
Monologue. That which is spoken by one person alone; a dramatic soliloquy.
Soliloquy. A talking to oneself, regardless of the presence or absence of others; monologue.

MONOLOGUE—*Verbs.*

Apostrophize. Deliver an apostrophe; address by apostrophe.
Say aside. Say so as not to be heard by others.
Say to oneself. Talk alone.
Soliloquize. Utter a soliloquy; talk to oneself.
Talk to oneself. Talk alone.
Think aloud. Talk to oneself.

CONVERSATION—MONOLOGUE—*Continued.*

Conversazione [It.]. A conversation.
Converse. Conversation.
Debate. Discussing of any question; argumentation.
Dialogue. Formal conversation between two or more persons.
Discourse. Connected communication of thought; conversation.
Duologue. A literary composition for two speakers.
"Feast of reason and the flow of soul." [Pope, *Satires*, 1, ii, 127.]
Gossip. Familiar or idle talk; tattle.
Idle talk. Useless or vain talk.
Interlocution. Interchange of speech; conference.
Interview. An official consultation; a formal conversation.
Logomachy. A strife about mere words.
On dit [F.]. They say; hence, a flying rumor.
Oral communication. Communication by means of speech.
Palaver. Empty talk; especially, flattering talk.
Parley. An oral conference, as with an enemy on a battlefield.
Pourparler [F.]. A parley.
Prittle-prattle. Empty talk; prattle;—used in contempt or ridicule.
Small talk. Light or trifling conversation.
Table talk. Conversation at table or meals.
Talk. The act of talking or that which is said.
Talk of the town.
Talk of the village.
Tattle. Blabbing talk or gossip; idle talk.
Tea-table talk. Conversation at the tea-table.
Tête-à-tête [F.]. A private conversation.
Tittle-tattle. Useless, trivial talk; gossip.
Town talk. The common talk of a place.
Trialogue. A discourse or colloquy by three persons.
Tripotage [F.]. Medley; miscellany.
Verbal intercourse. Conversation.
Village talk. Common talk of the village.
War of words. Strife carried on with words.

CONVERSATION—*Associated Words.*

Durbar [Anglo-Ind.]. An official reception given by a native ruler or officer of rank in British India.
Hall of audience. A place for formal consultation.
Mollia tempora fandi [L.]. Times or opportunities favorable for speaking.
Reception. A formal meeting for consultation or conference.

CONVERSATION—*Nouns of Agent.*

Chatterer, etc. One who chatters, etc. See TALKATIVENESS.
Conversationist. One who converses much or excels in conversation.
Dialogist. A speaker in a dialogue; a maker of dialogues.
Gossip. One who gossips or tells idle or mischievous tales.
Interlocutor, etc. One who takes part in a conversation or oral discussion, etc. See SPEECH.
Paul Pry. The principal character, an impudent and meddlesome fellow, in a comedy of the same name by John Poole.
Tabby. A gossiping old maid; a tabby cat.
Tattler. One who tattles or tells in idle talk.

CONVERSATION—*Verbs.*

Bandy words. Give and receive words; reciprocate words.
Be closeted with. Be taken into a closet for a secret interview.

con″-ver-sa′-tion-al. Pertaining to conversation. CONVERSATION-MONOLOGUE, SOCIABILITY-PRIVACY.
con″-ver-sa′-tion-ist. Talker. CONVERSATION-MONOLOGUE.
conversazione [It.] (con-ver-sat-si-o′-nê). A meeting for conversation. CONVERSATION-MONOLOGUE, GATHERING-SCATTERING, SOCIABILITY-PRIVACY.

MONOLOGUE—*Adjectives.*

Soliloquizing, etc. Talking to oneself; speaking a soliloquy, etc. See *Verbs.*

MONOLOGUE—*Adverb.*

Aside. So as not to be overheard.

CONVERSATION—VERBS—*Continued.*

Carry on a conversation. Converse.
Chat. Converse in an easy or gossipy manner.
Commerce with. Hold intercourse with.
Commune with. Converse together with sympathy and confidence.
Confabulate. Talk familiarly together; chat.
Confer with. Have discourse with; consult.
Converse. Speak together informally and alternately.
Discourse with. Confer with; give an address.
Engage in a conversation. Converse.
Gossip. Tell idle or mischievous tales.
Hold a conversation.
Hold conference.
Hold converse. } Expressions for converse, confer.
Hold intercourse.
Join in a conversation. Converse.
Palaver. Use flattering speech to; talk idly and overmuch.
Parley. Hold a conference; prolong talk; take up the parable.
Prate, etc. Talk about vainly or foolishly, etc. See TALKATIVENESS.
Put in a word. Speak, with difficulty, while others are discoursing.
Shine in conversation. Exhibit brilliant intellectual powers in conversation.
Talk it over. Talk about it; confer respecting it.
Talk together. Converse; confer.
Talk with one in private. Converse privately.
Talk with one *tête-à-tête.* Talk with one head to head or confidentially.
Tattle. Tell in idle talk; tell tales.

CONVERSATION—*Adjectives.*

Chatty, etc. Loquacious; gossipy, etc. See SOCIABILITY.
Colloquial. Conversational.
Conversable. Qualified for conversation; free in discourse.
Conversational. Pertaining to conversation.
Conversing, etc. Holding conversation; interchanging thoughts and opinions in a free informal manner, etc. See *Verbs.*
Discursive. Inclined to converse; containing dialogue or conversation.
Discursive. Passing from one subject to another; wandering away from the point.
Interlocutory. Consisting of or pertaining to dialogue; conversational.

con-verse′. To speak together alternately. CONVERSATION-MONOLOGUE, SAMENESS-CONTRAST.
con-vers′-ing. Talking. CONVERSATION-MONOLOGUE.
con-ver′-sion. The act of converting. CONVERSION-REVERSION, MUTATION-PERMANENCE; **trover and conversion,** LAW-LAWLESSNESS.

CONVERSION—REVERSION.

Assimilation. The act of taking up and transforming into the same nature.
Assumption. The act of taking to oneself.
Conversion. A relative change from one use, condition, etc., to another.
Naturalization. The act of becoming a citizen of a nation.
Reduction. The process of taking out impurities.
Resolution. Analysis.
Transmutation. Change in the substance of a thing.

CONVERSION—*Nouns of Agent and Means.*

Alchemy. The immature chemistry of the middle ages.
Alembic. An apparatus used in distilling.

Alternation, etc. Change proceeding by turns, etc. See PERIODICITY.
Inversion, etc. The placing or occurrence in the opposite order, etc. See CROSSING.
Recoil, etc. Whirl backward, etc. See IMPETUS-REACTION.
Regression, etc. The act of passing back, etc. See ADVANCE-RETROGRESSION.
Relapse, etc. To return from a better to a worse condition, etc. See RENOVATION-RELAPSE.
Restoration, etc. The act of placing in or renewing the former condition, etc. See RENOVATION.
Return. A coming back.
Reversion. A conscious returning to a former state.
Revulsion. A violent separation; a change of feeling.

CONVERSION—REVERSION—*Continued.*

CONVERSION—NOUNS OF AGENT AND MEANS—*Continued.*

Apostate. One who forsakes a faith and principles that he formerly professed, especially the Christian faith.
Caldron. A large kettle or boiler.
Chemistry. That branch of science that treats of matter as composed of atoms and the relation of one kind of matter to another.
Conjugation. Union or fusion of two or more cells for reproduction.
Convert. A person turned over to a new faith.
Crucible. A metal vessel in which metals are melted.
Flux. The process of melting.
Growth. Gradual increase of a living thing by natural process.
Lapse. A gradual passing away.
Passage. Transition from one state or condition to another.
Pervert. One who forsakes a true doctrine for a false.
Phase. A stage of development.
Progress. Advancement in growth or development.
Renegade. One who denies or deserts his faith.
Shifting. Change from one form or development to another. See *Verbs.*
Transit. Act of passing through or over.
Transition. Change from one form to another.
Transmigration. The theory that souls pass from one body to another.

CONVERSION—*Verbs.*

Become. Change into.
Form, etc. To produce or make from different materials, etc. See FORM.
Get. To become.
Grow. To increase in a certain respect gradually.
Illapse. To pass.
Lapse. To pass or change slowly.
Make. To cause to be, to form.
Mature. To become ripe.
Mellow. To make soft.
Melt. To change from a solid to a liquid state.
Mold. To give shape to.
Reform. To change for the better.
Refound. To cast over.
Remodel. To change the structure of.
Render. To make clear by melting.
Reorganize. To make a new organization.
Shift. To move from one to another.
Wax. To grow.

CONVERSION—*Verbal Expressions.*

Assimilate to; assume a new phase; assume the character of; assume the form of; assume the nature of; assume the shape of; assume the state of; be converted into; bring to; come around to; come into; come to; convert into; fall into; glide into; grow into; merge into; new model; open into; pass into; reduce to; resolve into; resolve itself into; ripen into; run into; settle into; slide into; turn into; turn out; turn to; undergo a change.

con-vert'. To transform; to turn from a sinful course to a life of piety. BIGOTRY-APOSTASY, CONVERSION-REVERSION, FAITH-MISGIVING, GODLINESS-UNGODLINESS; **convert to use,** INTERPRETATION-MISINTERPRETATION.
con-vert''-i-bil'-i-ty. Ability to be changed. CONVERSION-REVERSION, SAMENESS-CONTRAST.

REVERSION—*Denotations.*

Calm before a storm. Quiet preparation for a violent change.
Status quo ante bellum [L.]. The condition before the war.
Turn of the tide. A changing.
Turning point. Point of time or place where a change takes place.

REVERSION—*Verbs.*

Recoil, etc. To whirl forcibly backward, etc. See IMPETUS-REACTION.
Relapse, etc. To fall back from a better to a worse condition, etc. See RENOVATION-RELAPSE.
Restore, etc. To put into a former condition, etc. See RENOVATION.
Retreat, etc. To make a reversion, etc. See ADVANCE-RETROGRESSION.
Revert. To return consciously to a former state.
Undo. }
Unmake. } To destroy the effect of.

REVERSION—*Verbal Expressions.*

Turn the scale; turn the tide, to decide.

REVERSION—*Adjectives.*

Reactionary. Tending to act in an opposite direction.
Retrorse. Turned backwards.
Reverting, etc. Turning back, etc. See *Verbs.*
Revulsive. Tending to cause a sudden change.

REVERSION—*Phrase.*

À rebours [F.]. Quite contrary.

CONVERSION—*Continued.*

CONVERSION—*Adjectives.*

Converted into, etc. See *Verbs.*
Convertible. Easily converted.
Naturalized. Admitted to citizenship in a nation.
Resolvable into. Able to be analyzed into.
Transitional. Involving transition.

CONVERSION—*Adverbs.*

Gradually, etc. Slowly, etc. See SWIFTNESS-SLOWNESS.
In transitu [L.], etc. In the change, in passing, etc. See TRANSFER.

con-vert'-i-ble. Capable of conversion; interchangeable. CONVERSION-REVERSION, EQUALITY-INEQUALITY, SAMENESS-CONTRAST; **convertible terms,** INTERPRETATION-MISINTERPRETATION, NAME-MISNOMER.
con'-vex''. Bulging out. CONVEXITY-CONCAVITY.
con-vex'-i-ty. Sphericity. CONVEXITY-CONCAVITY.

CONVEXITY—CONCAVITY.

Bulge. The swelled or most convex part.
Convexity. Roundness.
Embreastment. Swelling in the surface of the ground.
Gibbosity. Irregular roundness.
Projection. That which sticks out.
Prominence. That which stands out from the surrounding surface.
Protuberance. That which rises by a gradual ascent from the surrounding surface.
Protrusion. The act of thrusting beyond the usual limits.
Swelling. Enlargement.

CONVEXITY—*Denotations.*

Alto-rilievo [It.]. Sculptured or carved work in which the figures stand out very strongly from the background.
Apophysis. An outgrowth on the body.
Arch. A bow-like structure or object.
Back. That part of the body from the neck to the buttocks.

Cavity. Hole.
Concavity. Slight superficial cavity.
Dent. Depression caused by a blow.
Depression. Place lower than the surrounding surface.
Dint. Dent.
Dip. Inclination.
Excavation. Hollow formed in a solid by living or mechanical agency.
Hollow. Interior of a hollow body.
Hollowness. The state or quality of being hollow.
Indentation. A notch.
Pit. Cavity.
Sinus. A cavity formed by folding.
Trough, etc. A long, narrow depression, etc. See GROOVE.

CONCAVITY—*Denotations.*

Alcove. A covered recess connecting with a larger room.
Alveolus. A small cavity like an air-cell, or honeycomb cell,

CONVEXITY—CONCAVITY—*Continued.*

CONVEXITY—Denotations—*Continued.*

Balcony. A railed platform projecting from a wall.
Bas-relief. Carving in which the figures project but slightly.
Basso-rilievo [It.]. Bas-relief.
Beak. The projecting mouth-parts of various animals.
Belly. That part of the trunk not enclosed by the ribs.
Bilge. The bottom of a ship.
Blain. A tumor or blister.
Blister. A swelling on the cuticle containing a watery matter.
Boil. A highly inflammatory tumor. See HEALTH-SICKNESS.
Boss. Any circular prominence.
Bow. Anything bent or curved.
Breast. The front of the chest in man.
Bulb. A leaf-bud developed underground; any enlargement resembling a plant-bulb.
Bump. A swelling caused by a blow.
Bunch. A group or cluster of objects either growing or fastened together.
Button. A knob of metal, bone, or other material for holding parts of garments together.
Cameo. Carving or engraving in relief.
Cape. A point of land projecting into the water.
Carbuncle. An inflammatory tumor.
Clump. A compact group or cluster.
Condyle. The enlarged end of a bone.
Corn. A horny swelling on the cuticle.
Corporation. The human body, especially when large or unwieldy.
Cupola. A dome.
Dome. A hemispherical roof.
Dorsum [L.]. The back.
Dug. A teat of a suckling animal.
Eaves. Projecting edge of a roof.
Elbow. The region at the junction of the upper arm and forearm.
Embossment. The process of producing designs in relief.
Excrescence. A disfiguring outgrowth.
Exostosis. A bony outgrowth or tumor.
Flange. A projecting edge or rim.
Foreland. A projecting point of land.
Fungosity. State of being a sponge-like growth.
Fungus. A soft spongy growth or abnormal excrescence.
Furuncle. A boil.
Growth. Anything growing or produced.
Headland. A point of land extending into the water
High-relief. Carving or sculpture standing prominently from the background.
Hill. An elevation of land.
Hummock. A slight elevation of land; a pile of ice.
Hump. A protuberance, especially of a curved spine.
Hunch. A hump.
Intumescence. A swelling on the body.
Jetty. A structure extending into the water.
Jutty. See JETTY.
Knob. A rounded mountain.
Ledge. A rocky projection into the water.
Lip. One of the two muscular organs that bound the mouth.
Low relief. Carving in which the figures project but slightly from the background.
Mamelon. A low rounded hill. See HEIGHT.
Mammilla. A nipple or teat.
Mezzo-rilievo [It.]. Work in half relief.
Mole. A slight dark swelling on the skin.
Mull. A cape.
Neb. The beak of a bird.
Nipple. A cone-shaped growth on the breast.
Node. A knot-like protuberance.
Nodosity. A knot.
Nodule. A little knot.
Nose. That part of an animal containing the nostrils and organ of smell.
Nozzle. A projecting spout or pipe.
Pap. The breast of a woman.
Papilla. Any small nipple-like growth.
Papula [L.]. A pimple.
Peg. A wooden pin for fastening articles together.
Pilaster. A columnar projection.
Pimple. A small swelling of the skin.
Pock. A swelling in an eruptive disease.
Point of land. A cape.
Polypus. A tumor on the mucous membrane.
Proboscis. A prolonged flexible snout.
Process. A growth or swelling.

CONCAVITY—Denotations—*Continued.*

Arch. Any bow-like curve, structure, or object. See CURVATION.
Basin. A cavity like that of a basin.
Bay. The water between two projecting capes. See GULF.
Bottom. The ground beneath a body of water.
Cave. } An underground cavity, recess, or chamber.
Cavern. }
Cell. A small chamber, or enclosed cavity. See CONTENTS-RECEIVER.
Combe. A bowl-shaped valley.
Cove. A small bay, or bay-like recess.
Crater. A cup-shaped depression on the top of a volcano.
Cul-de-sac [F.]. A passage closed at one end.
Cup. A small drinking vessel.
Dale. A small valley.
Dell. A dale.
Dimple. A slight depression on the surface of the human body.
Dingle. A shady glen or hollow.
Follicle. A minute cavity or sac.
Glade. An open space in a wood.
Glen. A secluded hollow among the hills.
Grot. } A small cavern, or cavern-like retreat.
Grotto. }
Grove. A small wood cleared of underbrush.
Gully. A channel cut by running water. See INTERSPACE.
Honeycomb. Anything full of holes or cells.
Intaglio. Incised carving.
Lacuna. A small pit, hollow, or depression.
Punch-bowl. A large bowl in which punch is mixed.
Slade. A glade.
Socket. A hollow or depression into which something fits.
Strath. A wide, open valley.
Vale. A valley.
Valley. A depression of the earth's surface.

CONCAVITY—*Nouns of Agent.*

Excavator. One who or that which excavates.
Miner. One whose occupation is to excavate ore.
Sapper. A soldier employed in making trenches.

CONCAVITY—*Verbs.*

Burrow. To dig in the ground like an animal.
Delve. To dig.
Dent. To make a mark in by a blow.
Depress. To press below the surrounding surface.
Dig. To hollow out with a pick, etc.
Dint. Dent.
Excavate. To make a hole in something.
Gouge. To cut out with a gouge.
Hollow. To make a hole in.
Mine. To dig out ores.
Retire. To draw inward.
Sap. To weaken the support of.
Scoop. To hollow out with a scoop
Tunnel. To cut through.
Undermine. To make an excavation under.

CONCAVITY—*Verbal Expressions.*

Be concave, etc. (see *Adjectives*); **cave in; render concave,** etc. (see *Adjectives*); **scoop out.**

CONCAVITY—*Adjectives.*

Alveolar. Marked by alveoli.
Arched. Having an arch or arches.
Bell-shaped. Shaped like a bell.
Campaniform. Bell-shaped.
Capsular. Like a capsule.
Cavernous. Containing caverns.
Cellular. Containing cells.
Concave. Curved in.
Depressed. Lower than the surrounding surface.
Funnel-shaped. Shaped like a funnel.
Hollow. Having a vacant place in the interior.
Honeycombed. Having cells like a honeycomb.
Infundibular. } Funnel-shaped.
Infundibuliform. }
Porous, etc. Containing pores, etc. See APERTURE.
Retiring. } Bending towards the rear.
Retreating. }
Spongious. } Porous.
Spongy. }
Stove in. Dented.
Vaulted. Concaved below.

CONVEXITY—Denotations—Continued.

Promontory. A high cape.
Proud flesh. A growth resembling flesh in a wound
Pustule. A slight swelling of the outer skin.
Relief. Carving or engraving projecting from a background
Rib. One of the bony rods which encircle the body-cavity
Ridge. A lengthened elevation of land.
Rilievo [It.]. Relief.
Sarcoma. A tumor or group of tumors.
Shoulder. Part of the body between the neck and the free portion of the arm.
Snag. A jagged or stumpy knot.
Snout. The projecting part of a beast's head.
Spur. A projecting crag or ridge.
Stud. A knob; an ornamental button.

Sugar-loaf. Any conical growth or mass. See SHARPNESS.
Teat. A nipple.
Tongue. The organ situated in the mouth, anything resembling the tongue in shape.
Tooth. One of the hard structures projecting from the jaws of animals.
Trunnion. A cylindrical projection from the side of a cannon.
Tubercle. A small growth of bone or morbid granules.
Tuberosity. Any swelling or protuberance.
Tumor. A swelling from some morbid growth
Wale. A ridge made on the flesh by flogging.
Wart. A small outgrowth from the true skin.
Weal. See WALE.
Wen. A tumor on the scalp.
Withers. The highest part of the back of a horse.

CONVEXITY—*Verbs.*

Beetle. To jut out
Bouge. } To swell out.
Bulge. }
Bunch. To gather in groups.
Chase. To ornament by indenting.

Emboss. To ornament by raised-work.
Pout. To stick out the lips in anger.
Project. To stick out.
Protrude. To rise gradually above the surrounding surface.
Raise, etc. Emboss, etc. See ELEVATION.

CONVEXITY—*Verbal Expressions*

Bend over; be prominent (see *Adjectives*)**; bristle up; cock up; hang over; jut out; poke out; render prominent,** etc. (see *Adjectives*)**; shoot up; stand out; start up; stick out; swell over.**

CONVEXITY—*Adjectives.*

Arched. Shaped like, or provided with an arch.
Bellied. Having the shape of a belly.
Bloated, etc. Swollen from water or gas, etc. See ENLARGEMENT.
Bold. Projecting out prominently.
Bossed. Ornamented or strengthened with knobs or studs.
Bossy. Of a bossed nature.
Bowed. Bulged out.
Bulbous. Swelling like a bud.
Bunchy. Gathered in bunches.
Clavate. } Club- or nail-like in appearance.
Clavated. }
Convex. Curved.
Cornute. Horn-shaped.
Gibbous. Irregularly round.
Hemispheric. Like a hemisphere.
Hummocky. Rising up like a little hill.
In relief. Raised or projecting.

Lenticular. Like a lens.
Lentiform. Shaped like a double convex lens.
Maniform. Shaped like a hand.
Moutonné [F.]. Fleecy.
Nodular. Shaped like nodules
Odontoid. Tooth-like.
Papulose. } Marked by papulæ.
Papulous. }
Projecting, etc. Sticking out, etc. See *Verbs*
Prominent. Easily noticeable.
Protuberant. Rising up gradually.
Salient. Standing out.
Repoussé [F.]. Recoiling.
Raised. Higher than the surrounding surface.
Tuberculous. Having tubercles.
Tuberous. Bearing tubers.
Tumorous. Like a tumor.

con-vey'. To transmit; to communicate; to steal. ALIENATION, MEANING-JARGON, TRANSFER, **convey away,** THEFT; **convey the knowledge of,** ENLIGHTENMENT-SECRECY

con-vey'-ance. The act of conveying; that by which anything is conveyed. ALIENATION, CONVEYANCE-VESSEL, TRANSFER.

CONVEYANCE—VESSEL.

Carriage. A wheeled vehicle.
Conveyance. } That by which anything is carried
Vehicle. }

CONVEYANCE—*Denotations.*

Ambulance. A wagon for conveying wounded from a battle-field.
Araba. An ox-cart used in India and Turkey.
Automobile. A carriage moved by steam or some other force which it carries.
Barouche. A four-wheeled, low carriage with folding top.
Barrow. A support having handles, and with or without a wheel, on which things can be transported by hand.
Bath-chair. A chair on wheels, used by invalids at Bath, England.
Berlin. A four-wheeled carriage, having a sheltered seat behind the body.
Bicycle. A two-wheeled vehicle propelled by the feet
Brancard. A litter on which a person may be carried.
Break. A large four-wheeled carriage, with a driver's seat in front, and footman's behind.
Britzska. A long carriage, so made as to be changed into a kind of couch on wheels.
Brougham. A light, close carriage with seats for two or four.
Buggy. A light, four-wheeled vehicle, with or without a top.
Cab. A close carriage, usually a public vehicle.
Cabriolet. A one-horse carriage with two seats and calash top; named from its springy motion like that of a goat, *L. Capra.*
Calash. A light carriage with low wheels, having a top or hood that can be raised or lowered, and a movable front.
Calèche [F.]. A low carriage with folding top.
Car. A small vehicle moved on wheels; a vehicle adapted to the rails of a railroad.

Craft. Vessel of any kind.
Ship. Large sea-going vessel.
Vessel. Large craft designed to float on water.

VESSEL—*Denotations*

Aerostat. A balloon.
Air-balloon. A balloon for aerial navigation
Argosy. A ship of Venice, Italy.
Balloon. A bag of silk or other light material, filled with a gas, so as to float in the air.
Barcon. A Mediterranean freight vessel.
Bark. } A small sailing vessel or boat of any kind.
Barque. }
Barkentine. A three-masted sailing vessel
Bateau. A flat-bottomed boat.
Bilander. A two-masted vessel of Holland.
Boat. A small open vessel moved by oars, paddles, or sails.
Brig. A two-masted, square-rigged vessel.
Brigantine. A brig that does not carry a square mainsail.
Bucenteur. Once the state barge of Venice.
Bumboat. A clumsy boat.
Buss. A vessel used in the herring fishery
Caique. A sailing vessel of the Levant.
Canoe. A boat made of bark or skins.
Carack. A Spanish merchantman carrying cannon.
Caravel. } The sailing vessels of the fifteenth century.
Carvel. }
Cascoe. A freight boat used in the Philippines.
Catamaran. A raft used in the East and West Indies.
Chasse marée [F.]. A coasting vessel.

CONVEYANCE—Denotations—*Continued.*

Caravan. A large covered wagon, or train of such wagons.

Cariole. A small, light, open, one-horse carriage.

Cart. A two-wheeled vehicle for hauling earth, stone, etc.

Cattle-truck. A car for transporting cattle.

Chair. A movable seat with a back.

Chaise. A two-wheeled carriage for two persons.

Char-à-banc [F.]. A long carriage.

Chariot. A two-wheeled car or vehicle for war, racing, etc.

Clarence. A close carriage with glass front.

Coach. A large, close, four-wheeled carriage having doors in the sides.

Crate. A box or case whose sides are of wooden slats with interspaces.

Curricle. A two-wheeled chaise drawn by two horses abreast.

Désobligeant [F.]. A coach for two.

Diligence. A four-wheeled public stage-coach used in France.

Dog-cart. A light one-horse carriage.

Dormeuse. Heavy carriage.

Drag. A heavy coach with seats on top.

Dray. A strong low cart for heavy loads.

Droshki. } A low four-wheeled open carriage used in Russia.
Drosky. }

Equipage. A carriage of state or pleasure with all that accompanies it.

Express train. A train despatched with special speed.

Fiacre. A French hackney coach.

First class carriage. The best railroad car.

First class compartment. The best section of a railroad car.

First class train. A passenger train of the highest regular class.

Fly. A light carriage.

Four-in-hand. A vehicle drawn by four horses.

Four-wheeler. A vehicle having four wheels.

Glass-coach. A coach having glass windows.

Go-cart. A framework moving on casters to support children learning to walk.

Goods-train. A train which carries freight.

Growler. A four-wheeled cab.

Hackney-coach. A carriage kept for hire.

Hand-barrow. A frame or barrow without a wheel.

Hansom. A light, two-wheeled covered carriage with the driver's seat behind.

Hearse. A carriage for carrying the dead.

Hobby-horse. A frame in the form of a horse, on which a child makes believe to ride.

Hod. A wooden box with a long handle for carrying mortar, bricks, etc.

Hoe. A tool for loosening and gathering the earth.

Horse-box. A railroad car for transporting horses.

Hurdle. A sled for carrying criminals to the place of execution.

Jaunting-car. A low open vehicle, used in Ireland, in which the passengers ride sidewise, sitting back to back.

Kibitka. A Russian vehicle on wheels or on runners.

Ladle. A cup-like spoon with a long handle.

Limber. The fore part of a gun carriage.

Litter. A bed or stretcher for sick persons.

Locomobile. A carriage propelled by steam or electricity.

Luggage-train. A train that carries baggage.

Mail-coach. A car in which mail is transported.

Mail-phaeton. A light carriage for carrying the mail.

Omnibus. A four-wheeled carriage having seats for many people.

Outside car. A car having seats on the top.

Palankeen. } An enclosed litter used in China and India.
Palanquin. }

Parliamentary train. A train which, by act of Parliament, railroad companies must run for carrying third-class passengers at reduced rates.

Passenger-train. A train for conveying passengers.

Perambulator. A baby carriage.

Phaeton. A four-wheeled carriage open in front.

Pitch-fork. A tool with prongs for throwing straw, etc.

Post-chaise. A carriage for conveying travelers who travel post.

Pullman car. A passenger car fitted with all possible comforts.

Railroad. Parallel tracks of iron or steel for cars to run upon.

Random. A carriage.

Road-wagon. A small two-wheeled gig; also a light buggy; a chaise; a light two-wheeled vehicle.

Rolling stock. The locomotives and cars of a railway.

Second class carriage. See First class carriage.

Second class compartment. See First class compartment.

Second class train. See First class train.

Sedan chair. A chair or vehicle for carrying a single person.

VESSEL—Denotations—*Continued.*

Clipper. A vessel with a sharp bow, built for fast sailing.

Coaster. A vessel engaged in the coasting-trade.

Coble. A flat-floored fishing-boat.

Cockboat. A small river boat.

Cockleshell. A light boat.

Cog. A small fishing-boat moved by oars.

Collier. A ship for carrying coal.

Coracle. A boat of hide, anciently used in Europe.

Corvette. A flush-decked wooden war-vessel.

Cutter. A fast sailing vessel with one mast.

Dandy. A sloop or cutter carrying a lugsail.

Dhow. An Arabian coasting vessel.

Diabeah. A boat used on the Nile.

Dingy. A boat used in the East Indies.

Dogger. A Dutch fishing vessel.

Eight-oar. A rowboat propelled by eight oars.

Felucca. A Mediterranean coasting vessel.

Ferry-boat. A vessel for carrying passengers across narrow streams.

Fire-balloon. A balloon which is filled with heated air.

Fishing-boat. A boat used in the fishing-trade.

Foist. A light, swift galley.

Float. A number of timbers joined together forming a raft.

Fore-and-aft schooner. A vessel having only fore-and-aft sails.

Funny. A pleasure boat rowed with a pair of sculls.

Galleon. A Spanish or Mediterranean three-decker.

Galley. A seagoing vessel propelled wholly or partly by oars.

Galley-foist. A state barge.

Galliass. A Mediterranean armed galley.

Galliot. A two-masted Dutch or Flemish merchant vessel.

Gig. A commanding officer's boat on a ship.

Gondola. A flat-bottomed Venetian boat.

Hermaphrodite brig. A two-masted vessel, having its masts rigged differently.

Hooker. } A two-masted Dutch vessel.
Howker. }

Hoy. A single-masted coasting vessel.

Hulk. An old unseaworthy vessel.

Ice-boat. A framework with masts and sails and runners, for sailing over ice.

Ice-canoe. A boat with a broad flat keel fitted with runners, for use in water or on ice.

Jolly-boat. A small boat employed in doing a ship's marketing.

Junk. A large Chinese vessel.

Kayak. An Eskimo boat.

Ketch. A two-masted vessel sometimes mounting guns.

Kite. A device made of paper or other light material, to be flown in the air.

Launch. The largest of a man-of-war's boats.

Life-boat. A boat with a double hull, with the interspace filled with cork, by which it is rendered very buoyant.

Lighter. A barge used in loading and unloading ships.

Long-boat. A large ship's boat, often from thirty to forty feet long.

Lorcha. A Chinese coasting vessel.

Lugger. A small two- or three-masted fishing vessel.

Man-of-war. A warship.

Merchantman. } A trading vessel as distinguished from a warship.
Merchant ship. }

Montgolfier. A hot-air balloon.

Outrigger. A light racing boat.

Paddle steamer. A boat propelled by paddles.

Packet. A mail boat.

Pair-oar. A boat having an oar on each side.

Parachute. A basket attached to a balloon in which a person may be carried.

Pilot-balloon. A small balloon sent up before a larger one to show the direction and velocity of the wind.

Pilot-boat. A boat in which pilots cruise off shore to meet incoming vessels.

Pinnace. A six- or eight-oared boat of an English man-of-war.

Polacca. } A three-masted Mediterranean vessel.
Polacre. }

Pontoon. A vessel used in the construction of floating bridges.

Praam. A flat-bottomed boat of Holland.

Prahu. } A swift Malaysian vessel, sailing equally well in any direction.
Proa. }

Punt. A small flat-bottomed boat.

Quadrireme. A ship with four banks of oars.

Raft. A floating construction of logs or boards.

Randan. A four-oared boat rowed by three persons.

Saick. A sailing vessel of the Levant.

CONVEYANCE—VESSEL—*Continued.*

CONVEYANCE—Denotations—*Continued.*

Shandredhan. A depreciative name for a vehicle in Ireland.
Shofle. A cab.
Shovel. A broad-scooped implement for lifting and throwing earth, etc.
Skate. A metallic runner with a frame made to fit the sole of a shoe, used to move rapidly on ice.
Sled. A vehicle on runners for conveying loads over the snow.
Sledge. A vehicle which is made of a plank slightly turned up at one end.
Sleeping car. A car in which beds are arranged.
Sleigh. A vehicle on runners.
Sociable. A carriage having two double seats facing each other.
Spade. An implement for cutting and throwing earth.
Spatula. An implement shaped like a knife, used for spreading paints, etc.
Special train. A train run on some unusual occasion.
Spoon. An implement consisting of a small bowl with a handle, for dishing food, etc.
Spud. A sharp spade for digging up large-rooted weeds.
Stage. A large vehicle running from station to station.
Stage-coach. A coach that runs regularly from one station to another
Stage-wagon. A stage-coach.
Stretcher. A litter for carrying injured persons.
Sulky. A light two-wheeled carriage for a single person.
Tandem. A team of horses harnessed one before the other.
Third class carriage. See First class carriage.
Third class compartment. See First class compartment.
Third class train. See First class train.
Tilbury. A two-wheeled carriage without top or cover.
Toboggan. A sledge made of pliable boards turned up at one or both ends
Train. A connected line of cars.
Tram. A four-wheeled truck running on rails.
Trap. A wagon.
Tricycle. A three-wheeled vehicle propelled by the feet.
Truck. A low, wheeled vehicle for carrying goods.
Tumbrel. A rough cart.
Turnout. An equipage.
Unicorn. A coaching-team consisting of a pair of wheelers with a single leader.
Van. A light wagon for carrying goods.
Velocipede. A vehicle propelled by the feet.
Victoria. A four-wheeled carriage with a calash top.
Vis-à-vis [F.]. A carriage in which persons sit face to face.
Waggon. See Wagon.
Waggonette. A pleasure wagon with seats extending along the sides.
Wagon. A four-wheeled vehicle used for carrying goods.
Wagon-train. A line of wagons.
Wain. A wagon.
Wheel-barrow. A frame having two handles and one wheel, and rolled by a single person.
Wheel-chair. A chair on wheels.
Whisky. A light carriage built for rapid motion.
Whitechapel. A light two-wheeled spring cart used by grocers.

con-vey′-an-cer. One whose business is conveyancing. Advocate.
con-vey′-an-cing. The business of transferring titles. Alienation.
con-vey′-er. One who or that which conveys. Conveyer.

CONVEYER

Bearer. One who bears, either in motion or at rest.
Carrier. One who carries, always in motion.
Conveyer. One who carries from one place to another.

Conveyer—*Denotations.*

Arab. An Arabian horse.
Ass. An equine quadruped smaller than the horse, and distinguished by its harsh bray and long ears.
Barb. A Barbary horse.
Bayard. A bay horse; any horse.
Beast of burden. An animal used for carrying burdens.
Bidet. A small horse.

VESSEL—Denotations—*Continued.*

Sailer. ⎫
Sailing vessel. ⎭ A boat that is impelled by sails.
Sampan. A Chinese house-boat.
Schooner. A fore-and-aft rigged vessel having three or more sails.
Scow. A boat with flat bottom and square ends.
Screw vessel. A ship driven by screw propellers.
Shallop. A boat for two oarsmen.
Ship. A large seagoing vessel.
Skiff. A light canoe.
Slaver. A ship used in the slave-trade
Sloop. A single-masted vessel.
Smack. A fishing-boat.
Snow. A two-masted square-rigged vessel.
Steamboat. ⎫
Steamer. ⎭ A boat or vessel propelled by steam.
Store-ship. A ship for carrying supplies for a fleet.
Tartane. A Mediterranean vessel.
Tender. A vessel accompanying a large ship.
Three-masted schooner. A fore-and-aft rigged vessel with three masts.
Topsail schooner. A schooner fitted with a topsail.
Transport. A vessel used in carrying troops.
Trawler. A traveling vessel.
Trireme. A three-banked oar ship.
Tug. A steam vessel for towing other vessels.
Whaler. A boat used in whale fishery.
Wherry. A light rowboat for passengers.
Xebec. A three-masted vessel of Algiers.
Yacht. A light vessel for racing or pleasure.
Yawl. A small sailing vessel rigged like a sloop.

Vessel—*Figurative Nouns.*

Bottom. The bottom of a ship; hence, a ship.
Sail. Part of a ship; hence, a ship.

Vessel—*Collective Nouns.*

Fleet. Several vessels under one command.
Flotilla. A fleet of small vessels.
Marine. Shipping or shipping interests, generally.
Navy. The entire marine military force of a country.
Shipping. Ships of all kinds.

Vessel—*Parts of a Vessel.*

Gunwale. The uppermost wale.
Head sail. Sail set forward of the foremast.
Heel-post. Post supporting propeller shaft.
Kedge. Light anchor.
Mainsail. Large sail carried on the mainmast.
Spinnaker. Large sail carried opposite the mainsail on a racing vessel.
Thwarts. Seats in a small boat.
Topsail. A sail carried above the lowest sail.

Vessel—*Adverbs.*

Aboard. On the ship.
Afloat. In a floating condition.
On board. On the ship.
On shipboard. On the deck of a ship

Blood-horse. A horse of approved breed.
Bucephalus. A famous horse owned by Alexander the Great.
Camel. A large ruminant used in Eastern countries for carrying burdens.
Carriage. A wheeled vehicle. See Conveyance.
Carrier-pigeon. A domestic pigeon used to convey letters from one station to another.
Cattle. All domestic quadrupeds.
Cart-horse. A horse used to pull a cart.
Charger. A war-horse.
Cob. A short-legged and stout horse.
Colt. A young horse.
Conductor. A man in charge of a public conveyance.
Coolie. An East Indian porter or carrier.
Courser. A race-horse.
Donkey. An ass.
Draft-horse. A strong horse for pulling heavy burdens.
Dromedary. A camel having one hump on its back.
Elephant. A large animal having a long trunk and sometimes two ivory tusks the largest land animal in existence.
Filly. A female colt.
Foal. A young horse.
Galloway. A small horse raised at Galloway, Scotland.

Garran. } A galloway.
Garron. }
Gelding. A castrated horse.
Genet. A small Spanish horse.
Goer. A horse, considered in reference to his gait.
Hack. A horse who draws a hackney-coach.
Hinny. A hybrid between a stallion and an ass.
Horse. A solid-hoofed and one toed quadruped.
Hunter. A horse used in the chase.
Jackass. A male ass.
Jade. A mean or tired horse.
Jennet. A small Spanish horse.
Jument. A beast of burden.
Llama. A South American ruminant allied to the camel.
Locomotive. An engine propelled by steam.
Mare. The female horse.
Mule. A hybrid between an ass and a mare.
Nag. A small horse.
Packhorse. A horse employed in carrying packs.
Pad. An easy-paced horse.
Palfrey. A saddle-horse.
Pegasus. A fabled winged horse of the Muses.
Pony. A small horse.
Porter. One who carries baggage.
Post-horse. A horse stationed, intended to be used for the post.
Punch. A breed of large, heavy draft horses.
Race-horse. A horse bred for running races.
Racer. A race-horse.
Reindeer. A ruminant of the deer family found in northern regions.
Roadster. A horse suitable for use on ordinary roads.
Roan. A horse of bay, chestnut, brown, or black color, interspersed with gray or white.
Rozinante. The horse of Don Quixote.
Sheltie. A Shetland pony.
Ship. A seagoing vessel. See VESSEL.
Stallion. A male horse kept for breeding.
Steed. A horse for state or war.
Stud. A collection of breeding horses.
Sumpter-horse. } A horse or mule that carries burdens
Sumpter-mule. }
Tarpan. A wild horse found in the region of the Caspian Sea.
Thoroughbred. A horse of the best breed.
Tit. A small horse.
Tranter. A carrier.

CONVEYER—*Adjectives.*

Asinine. Having the qualities of an ass.
Equine. Pertaining to a horse.

con-vict'. To prove guilty. EXCULPATION-CONVICTION, FAITH-MISGIVING, GOOD MAN-BAD MAN.
con-vict'-ed. Condemned. **Self-convicted.** REPENTANCE-OBDURACY.
con-vic'-tion. The state of being convinced; condemnation; the state of being religiously convicted. EXCULPATION-CONVICTION, FAITH-MISGIVING, PROOF-DISPROOF.
con-vince'. To satisfy by evidence; to confute. EDUCATION-MISTEACHING, FAITH-MISGIVING.
con-vinced'. Persuaded. FAITH-MISGIVING.
con-vince'-ment. Proof. FAITH-MISGIVING.
con-viv'-i-al. Social. SOCIABILITY-PRIVACY.
con-viv''-i-al'-i-ty. Mirth. SOCIABILITY-PRIVACY.
con'-vo-cate. To summon to meet. GATHERING-SCATTERING.
con-vo-ca'-tion. An ecclesiastical body similar to a synod. CHURCH, COUNCIL.

con-voke'. Summon to meet. GATHERING-SCATTERING.
con'-vo-lu''-ted. Involved. CIRCLE-WINDING.
con''-vo-lu'-tion. A fold; whorl. AGITATION, CIRCLE-WINDING, CROSSING.
con'-voy. Escort for protection during transportation. SECURITY-INSECURITY, TRANSFER.
con-vulse'. To agitate violently. AGITATION, ORGANIZATION-DISORGANIZATION, PLEASURABLENESS-PAINFULNESS, SENSUALITY-SUFFERING, TURBULENCE-CALMNESS.
con-vulsed'. Agitated violently. **Convulsed with laughter,** ENTERTAINMENT-WEARINESS, JUBILATION-LAMENTATION; **convulsed with rage,** FAVORITE-ANGER.
con-vul'-sion. A spasm. AGITATION, REGULARITY-IRREGULARITY, REVOLUTION, SENSUALITY-SUFFERING, TURBULENCE-CALMNESS; **in convulsions,** AGITATION.
con-vul'-sive. Spasmodic. AGITATION, TURBULENCE-CALMNESS.
coo. A murmuring note. CRY-ULULATION.
cook. To prepare food by subjecting to the action of heat; one who does such work; to tamper with. BETTERMENT-DETERIORATION, CHIEF-UNDERLING, HEATING-COOLING, PREPARATION-NONPREPARATION, TRUTHFULNESS-FALSEHOOD; **cook accounts,** ACCOUNTS; **too many cooks,** SKILL-UNSKILFULNESS.
cook'-er-y. Place for cooking. PREPARATION-NONPREPARATION.
cook'-ing. Preparing food. PREPARATION-NONPREPARATION.
cool. To make less hot or less excited; lacking cordiality. AMITY-HOSTILITY, EXCITABILITY-INEXCITABILITY, GRAY-BROWN, HEAT-COLD, HEATING-COOLING, MOTIVE-CAPRICE, POLITENESS-IMPOLITENESS, RECKLESSNESS-CAUTION, SAGACITY-INCAPACITY, TURBULENCE-CALMNESS, UNCONCERN; **cool down,** EXCITABILITY-INEXCITABILITY; **cool one's heels,** ACTION-PASSIVENESS, EARLINESS-LATENESS; **look cool upon,** SOCIABILITY-PRIVACY; **take coolly,** EXCITABILITY-INEXCITABILITY.
cooled. Deprived of heat. HEATING-COOLING.
cool'-er. That which cools. OVEN-REFRIGERATOR.
cool'-head''-ed. Free from passion. EXCITABILITY-INEXCITABILITY, SAGACITY-INCAPACITY.
coo'-lie. A Chinese or East-Indian laborer employed under contract. BELLIGERENT, CONVEYER.
cool'-ing. Making cool. HEATING-COOLING.
cool'-ness. Absence of passion or feeling. EXCITABILITY-INEXCITABILITY, LOVE-HATE, RECKLESSNESS-CAUTION, SENSITIVENESS-APATHY.
coop. An enclosure for small animals. DWELLER-HABITATION, RELEASE-PRISON, RELEASE-RESTRAINT.
co-op'-er-ate. To work together. ANTAGONISM-CONCURRENCE.
co-op'-er-a''-ting. Working together. ANTAGONISM-CONCURRENCE.
co-op''-er-a'-tion. Joint action. ANTAGONISM-CONCURRENCE, ASSENT-DISSENT, COOPERATION-OPPOSITION, HARMONY-DISCORD, PARTICIPATION.

COOPERATION—OPPOSITION.

Agreement, etc. The state of being in accord, etc. See HARMONY.
Alliance. A combination or union for a common purpose.
Coagency. The condition of joint agency.
Concert, etc. An agreement together to a single purpose, etc. See ANTAGONISM-CONCURRENCE.
Concurrence. Agreement in mind or opinions.
Cooperation. The act of cooperating.
Consent, etc. Harmony in opinion, etc. See ASSENT.
Partnership, etc. Joint interest or ownership etc. See ASSOCIATION.
Union. Coalescence.

Antagonism. Opposition of persons or causes to each other.
Check, etc. Hindrance in the progress of something, etc. See OBSTRUCTION.
Clashing, etc. Violent meeting of two opposing things or interests, etc. See *Verbs.*
Collision. Meeting of two things in opposition.
Contrariety, etc. Repugnant opposition, etc. See SAMENESS-CONTRAST.
Counteraction. Hindrance.
Counterblast. Opposing argument.
Friction. Lack of harmony.

COOPERATION—OPPOSITION—*Continued.*

COOPERATION—*Verbs.*

Agree. To be of one mind or opinion.
Concur. To agree in opinion or action.
Conduce. To bring about.
Conspire. To combine secretly for a bad purpose.
Contribute. To share in effecting a result.
Go along with. Accompany.
Go hand in hand with. Combine with.
Go with. Accompany.
Hang together. To be associated.
Help to, etc. See OBSTRUCTION-HELP.
Keep pace with. Go as fast as.
Pull together, etc. See ANTAGONISM-CONCURRENCE.
Run parallel. Go together.
Unite. Combine.

COOPERATION—*Adjectives.*

At one with. Agreed.
Banded together. Confederated.
Concurrent. Occurring or acting together.
Concurring, etc. Coming together in opinion or action, etc. See *Verbs.*
In alliance with. In agreement with.
Of one mind. Agreed.

COOPERATION—*Adverb.*

With one consent. Altogether.

COOPERATION—*Phrase.*

Due teste valgono piu che una sola [It.]. "Two heads are better than one."

———

OPPOSITION—ADJECTIVES—*Continued from Column 2*

Contrary, etc. Opposing, etc. See CONTRAST.
Counteracting, etc. Action in opposition, etc. See *Verbs.*
Reactionary. Pertaining to, of the nature of, or favoring reaction.
Renitent. Offering resistance to an influence or force.
Retroactive. Having reverse action.

OPPOSITION—*Adverbs,* etc.

Against. In opposition to
Although, etc. In spite of the fact that, etc. See COMPENSATION.
In spite of, etc. Notwithstanding, etc. See ANTAGONISM.

Interference. Interposing; meddling.
Neutralization, etc. Act of counteracting, etc. See COMPENSATION.
Opposition. The thwarting of an action.
Polarity. Quality of having opposite poles.
Reaction. Return action.
Renitence. Quality of offering resistance.
Repression. A forcing back.
Resistance. The quality of acting the opposite direction.
Retroaction, etc. Reaction, etc. See IMPETUS-REACTION.
Vis inertiæ [L.]. Force of inertia; resistance against impetus.
Voluntary opposition, etc. See ANTAGONISM.
Voluntary resistance, etc. See REPRISAL-RESISTANCE.

OPPOSITION—*Verbs.*

Antagonize. To set one cause or person against another.
Beat against. Struggle against.
Clash. To come into noisy conflict.
Conflict with. To contend with.
Counteract. To act in opposition to.
Counterpoise, etc. To act against with equal power, etc. See COMPENSATION.
Cross. To obstruct or hinder.
Go against. To be in opposition to.
Hinder, etc. To be or act as an obstruction, etc. See OBSTRUCTION.
Interfere with. To disarrange.
Jostle. To push or crowd against.
Militate against. To have influence against.
Neutralize. To make of no effect.
Oppose, etc. To strive against, etc. See ANTAGONISM.
Overpoise. To outweigh.
React, etc. To act in an opposite manner, etc. See IMPETUS-REACTION.
Repress, etc. To keep under restraint, etc. See RELEASE-RESTRAINT.
Run against. To come into contact, collision, or antagonism with.
Run counter. To go, act, or operate contrary.
Stultify. To cause to appear absurdly inconsistent.
Undo. To annul the effect of.
Withstand, etc. To make resistance, etc. See REPRISAL-RESISTANCE.

OPPOSITION—*Adjectives.*

Antagonistic. Contending or acting against.
Conflicting. Contending.

(*Continued on Column* 1.)

---

co-op'-er-a''-tor. A joint laborer; a fellow worker. ANTAGONIST-ASSISTANT.
co''-op-ta'-tion. Choice. CHOICE-NEUTRALITY.
co-or'-di-nate. To put in the same rank, class, or order. EQUALITY-INEQUALITY, MENSURATION, ORGANIZATION-DISORGANIZATION.
co-or'-di-nates. A mathematical term. MENSURATION
co-or''-di-na'-tion. State of being coordinate. EQUALITY-INEQUALITY.
co'-pal. A resin used for varnishes. PULPINESS-ROSIN.
co-par'-cen-a-ry. An estate inherited conjointly. PARTICIPATION.
co-par'-cen-er. One of two or more coheirs. PARTICIPATION.
co-part'-ner. A sharer. COOPERATION-OPPOSITION, FRIEND-FOE, SOLITUDE-COMPANY.
co-part'-ner-ship. A joint interest in any matter. ASSOCIATION, OPPOSITION-CONCURRENCE, PARTICIPATION, SOLITUDE-COMPANY.
cope. To strive on equal terms; a long mantle worn by priests; a ceremonial vest worn by laymen. ANTAGONISM-CONCURRENCE, EQUALITY-INEQUALITY, STRIFE-PEACE.
co'-peck. Russian coin. VALUES.
copia verborum [L.] (co'-pi-a ver-bo'-rum). A rich supply of words. SPEECH-INARTICULATENESS, TALKATIVENESS-TACITURNITY, TERSENESS-PROLIXITY.
cop'-ied. Imitated. NATURE-ART.
cop'-ing-stone''. The top stone, as of a wall. COMPLETION-NONCOMPLETION, TOP-BOTTOM.

co'-pi-ous. Abundant. ENOUGH, TERSENESS-PROLIXITY.
co'-pi-ous-ness. Abundance. ENOUGH.
co-por'-tion. Equal share. PARTICIPATION.
cop'-per. Metal; coin made of copper. CHEMISTRY, MONEY.
cop'-per-col''-or-ed. Of the color of copper; reddish. BLUENESS-ORANGE.
cop'-per-plate''. Engraved on copper. ENGRAVING.
cop'-per-plate'' en-gra'-ving. Engraving cut into a copper plate. ENGRAVING.
cop'-per-plate'' print'-ing. Printing from copper plates. ENGRAVING.
cop'-pice. A thicket. FAUNA-FLORA.
cop'-ro-lite. Petrified dung of carnivorous reptiles. CLEANNESS-FILTHINESS.
copse. A coppice. FAUNA-FLORA.
cop'-u-la. A word that unites the subject and the predicate of a sentence. CONNECTIVE.
copula, felices ter et amplius, quos irrupta tenet [L.] (cop'-yu-la, fî-lai'-sîz ter et am'-pli-us, quos ir-rup'-ta ti'-net). Thrice happy, and more, those whom the marriage-bond unbroken holds. MATRIMONY-DIVORCE.
cop'-u-la-tive. Kind of verb or conjunction. PARTICLE, VERB.
cop'-y. A reproduction; a printed pamphlet, book, etc.; a pattern given for imitation. COPY-MODEL, DELINEATION-CARICATURE, DESIGN, IMITATION-ORIGINALITY, MARK-OBLITERATION, NATURE-ART, TRUTHFULNESS-FRAUD, WRITING-PRINTING

COPY—MODEL.

Adumbration. An indistinct shadow or outline.
Apograph. A copy written off.
Burlesque. Ludicrously exaggerated imitations.
Caricature. A distorted resemblance.
Cast. A molded form.
Chip of the old block. A son with his father's characteristics.
Copy. A reproduction after an original.
Counterfeit, etc. See TRUTHFULNESS-FRAUD.
Counterpart. One of two exactly similar things.
Duplicate. A reproduction of the original in its entirety.
Echo. A close imitation; a reverberation of sound.
Ectype. A type of some original.
Effigies [L.]. An effigy.
Effigy. A representation of the whole or part of a person.
Facsimile. A likeness exact in every detail.
Fair copy. Good reproduction.
Form. Similar appearance.
Hectograph. A contrivance for multiple copying.
Imitation. Something copied after an original.
Likeness. Semblance in appearance.
Model. An approximate reproduction; a pattern.
Paraphrase. A liberal translation of the thought in a passage or work.
Parody. A light and ludicrous imitation.
Portrait, etc. See DELINEATION.
Rechauffé [F.]. Something warmed over; a revision.
Reflex. An image; a retroaction.
Reflexion. A counterpart reflected.
Representation. Expressed likeness.
Reprint. A copied print.
Reproduction. Something brought forward in the likeness of an existing object.
Revise. Something reexamined.
Second edition, etc. See RECURRENCE.
Semblance. Similarity.
Servile copy.   ⎫
Servile imitation. ⎬ Ignoble reproduction.
Shadow. An indistinct representation.
Similitude. That which is likened to something else.
Study. A representation in art, designed for instruction,
Transcript. A rewritten original.
Transcription. The result of transcribing.
Travestie. See TRAVESTY.
Travesty. An ignoble rearrangement of a lofty theme.

COPY—Adjectives.

Faithful. Conformable.
Lifelike, etc. See LIKENESS.

Antitype. That after which the type is copied.
Archetype. The first model.
  opy. Something to be reproduced.
Design. An original scheme or plan.
Die. The mold from which the casts are made
Ensample. A model for imitation.
Example. Something which is to be followed in imitation.
Exemplar. A specimen for copying.
Fugleman. A soldier who displays his skill at arms for the purpose of instruction.
Intaglio. A sunken die for producing a relief design.
Keynote. The fundamental tone of a chord.
Last. A form for shaping shoes.
Lay-figure. A jointed model used by artists.
Model. That to which copies are referred.
Module. A unit of measure.
Mold. An object after which others are patterned.
Negative. A picture from which positives are made
Original. The first of its class.
Paradigm. Something set up as an example; as of verbs or nouns
Paragon. A model of beauty or eloquence.
Pattern. Something to be copied.
Plasm. A mold or matrix.
Precedent. A previous instance which may be authoritatively followed.
Protoplasm. The principal portion of an animal or vegetable cell.
Protoplast. The first formed of a class.
Prototype. A primitive form to which subsequent forms may be traced.
Scantling. An outline.
Standard. An established, authoritative type.
Text. The original words of an author.
Type. That which represents something to come.

MODEL—Nouns of Instrument.

Matrix. That which gives form or origin to anything
Proplasm. A mold.
Punch. A tool for stamping or perforating.
Seal. An engraved stamp used for making an impression in wax.

MODEL—Noun of Place.

Mint. A place where money is coined.

MODEL—Verbs.

Be an example. Be a model.
Set a copy. Make a model.
Set an example. Be a model.

MODEL—Phrase.

Exempla sunt odiosa [L.]. Examples are offensive. Comparisons are odious.

cop'-y-hold". A tenure of lands evidenced by copy of court roll. PROPERTY.
cop'-y-ist. One whose business it is to copy; an imitator. ARTIST, WRITING-PRINTING.
cop'-y-right". The exclusive right secured by law to authors and artists to publish and dispose of their works for a limited time. PROPERTY.
co-quet'. To trifle in love. ADULATION-DISPARAGEMENT, BIGOTRY-APOSTASY, BLANDISHMENT, DELINEATION-CARICATURE, PRESUMPTION-OBSEQUIOUSNESS; **coquet with,** DETERMINATION-VACILLATION.
co'-quet-ry. Flirtation. ADULATION-DISPARAGEMENT, BIGOTRY-APOSTASY, BLANDISHMENT, SOCIETY-AFFECTATION.
co-quette'. A flirt. LOVE-HATE, SOCIETY-AFFECTATION, SOCIETY-DANDY.
co-quet'-ting. Flirting. BIGOTRY-APOSTASY.
co"-quil-lage'. A form of ornamentation imitating shells. EMBELLISHMENT-DISFIGUREMENT.
cor'-a-cle. A small fishing-boat. CONVEYANCE-VESSEL.
cor'-al. The hard structures secreted by various marine zoophytes; something made of coral. EMBELLISHMENT-DISFIGUREMENT; GEOLOGY; **coral-reef,** SECURITY-PITFALL.
coram judice [L.] (co'-ram jiu'-di-sî). Before the judge. JUDICATURE, LITIGATION.
cor Anglais [F.] (cor an'-glê'). An English horn. MUSICAL INSTRUMENTS.

corbeille [F.] (cor-bey'). A basket. CONTENTS-RECEIVER.
cor'-bel. One of a series of brackets projecting from the wall. ARCHITECTURE, SUSPENSION-SUPPORT.
cord. A string or small rope; quantity of wood. CONNECTIVE, LAMINA-FIBER, MEASURE, RELEASE-PRISON; **cord foot,** MEASURE.
cord'-age. Ropes and cords in general. CONNECTIVE.
cor'-da-ted. Heart-shaped. CURVATION-RECTILINEARITY.
cor'-dial. Hearty; that which invigorates; a sweet and aromatic alcoholic liquor. AMITY-HOSTILITY, EMOTION, PLEASURABLENESS-PAINFULNESS, POLITENESS-IMPOLITENESS, PUNGENCY, READINESS-RELUCTANCE, REMEDY-BANE, SENSUALITY-SUFFERING.
cor-dial'-i-ty. Affection. AMITY-HOSTILITY, EMOTION, READINESS-RELUCTANCE.
cor'-di-form. Cordate. CURVATION-RECTILINEARITY.
cor"-dil-le'-ra. Mountain ranges. GEOLOGY.
cordon [F.] (cor-don"). A cord or ribbon used as a badge of honor; a line of military posts. CIRCLE-WINDING, ENCLOSURE, OUTLINE, TITLE.
cordon bleu [F.] (cor-don" blu). A first-rate cook. CHIEF-UNDERLING.
cordon sanitaire [F.] (cor-don" sa-ni-têr'). A line of sentries to prevent communication with an infected district. CONSERVATION, SECURITY-INSECURITY.

cor'-du-roy''. A cotton stuff, corded and ribbed. GROOVE.

cord'-wain-er. A shoemaker. AGENT, DRESS-UNDRESS.

core. The central or innermost part of anything. CENTER, CONSEQUENCE-INSIGNIFICANCE; **true to the core,** UPRIGHTNESS-DISHONESTY.

co''-ri-a'-ceous. Of a leathery texture. TOUGHNESS-BRITTLENESS.

Cor-in'-thi-an. Pertaining to an order of architecture. TASTE-VULGARITY; **Corinthian order,** ARCHITECTURE.

co-ri'-val. A rival. BELLIGERENT.

cork. The outer bark of the cork-oak; to stop with cork. HEAVINESS-LIGHTNESS, PERFORATOR-STOPPER; **cork jacket,** REFUGE-PITFALL; **cork up,** APERTURE-CLOSURE, RELEASE-RESTRAINT.

cork'-ing-pin''. A large pin. CONNECTIVE.

cork'-screw''. An instrument for drawing corks. CIRCLE-WINDING, CIRCUITION, INJECTION-EJECTION, PERFORATOR-STOPPER.

cor'-mo-rant. A voracious water-bird; greedy. DESIRE-DISTASTE, FASTING-GLUTTONY.

corn. A horny thickening of the cuticle. CONVEXITY-CONCAVITY.

Cor-na'-ro. A sumptuous painting. MODERATION-SELFINDULGENCE.

cor'-ne-a. The anterior, horny, transparent part of the outer coat of the eyeball. ANATOMY, SIGHT-BLINDNESS.

corned. Intoxicated. TEETOTALISM-INTEMPERANCE

cor'-ne-ous. Horny. HARDNESS-SOFTNESS.

cor'-ner. An angle; a nook. ANGULARITY, CONTENTS-RECEIVER, EXTENSION-PLACE; **corner stone,** ATTACK-DEFENSE, CONSEQUENCE-INSIGNIFICANCE, SUSPENSION-SUPPORT; **creep into a corner,** SOCIABILITY-PRIVACY; **drive into a corner,** ENLIGHTENMENT-SECRECY; **in a dark corner,** ENLIGHTENMENT-SECRECY, LIBERTY-SUBJECTION; **push into a corner,** OBSTRUCTION-HELP; **rub off corners,** CONVENTIONALITY-UNCONVENTIONALITY; **turn a corner,** CIRCUITION; **turn the corner,** BETTERMENT-DETERIORATION.

cor'-net. A small wind-instrument of the trumpet class. MUSICAL INSTRUMENTS.

cor'-net. The lowest commissioned cavalry officer. CHIEF-UNDERLING.

cornet-à-piston [F.] (cor-net'-a-pis-ton'). Key-bugle. MUSICAL INSTRUMENTS.

cor'-nice. The horizontal molded projection at the top of a building. ARCHITECTURE, TOP-BOTTOM.

cor-nic'-u-late. Horned. SHARPNESS-BLUNTNESS.

Corn'-ish hug. A hold in wrestling; deceitful dealing. TRUTHFULNESS-FRAUD.

corno [It.] (cor'-no). A horn. MUSICAL INSTRUMENTS.

corno di bassetto [It.] (cor'-no dî bas-set'-to). Basset-horn. MUSICAL INSTRUMENTS.

corno Inglese [It.] (cor'-no îng-lê'-zê). English horn. MUSICAL INSTRUMENTS.

cor-no'-pe-an. A wind-instrument of the trumpet class, with valves. MUSICAL INSTRUMENTS.

corn'-shuck''. The husk covering an ear of maize. COVER-LINING.

corn'-starch''. Starch made from maize, used for puddings, etc. NUTRIMENT-EXCRETION.

cor''-nu-co'-pi-a. The horn of plenty. ENOUGH.

cor-nute'. Having horns. CONVEXITY-CONCAVITY, SHARPNESS-BLUNTNESS.

cor'-ol-la-ry. A consequence. DECISION-MISJUDGMENT, INCREMENT-REMNANT.

co-ro'-na. A wreath; circle of light. ASTRONOMY, CIRCLE-WINDING.

cor'-o-nach. A dirge. JUBILATION-LAMENTATION.

cor''-o-na'-tion. The act or ceremony of crowning a monarch. COMMISSION-ABROGATION, SOLEMNIZATION.

cor'-o-ner. An officer whose duty it is to inquire into the cause of sudden or violent death. JUDICATURE.

cor'-o-net. An inferior crown, denoting various degrees of noble rank less than sovereign. CIRCLE-WINDING, SCEPTER, TITLE.

co-ro'-ni-form. Crown-shaped. CIRCLE-WINDING.

cor'-po-ral. Belonging or relating to the body as opposed to the mind; the lowest non-commissioned officer in a company of soldiers. CHIEF-UNDERLING, MATERIALITY-SPIRITUALITY; **corporal major,** CHIEF-UNDERLING.

cor''-po-ral'-i-ty. State of being corporal. MATERIALITY-SPIRITUALITY.

cor'-po-rate. Associated by legal enactment for the transaction of business. UNION-DISUNION; **corporate body,** ASSOCIATION.

cor''-po-ra'-tion. Corporate body. ASSOCIATION, CONVEXITY-CONCAVITY, GREATNESS-LITTLENESS, JUDICATURE, LABOR-CAPITAL.

cor-po'-re-al. Physical. MATERIALITY-SPIRITUALITY, **corporeal hereditaments,** PROPERTY.

cor''-po-re'-i-ty. Materiality. MATERIALITY-SPIRITUALITY.

corps. A number of persons in some way acting together. BELLIGERENT, GATHERING-SCATTERING.

corps d'armée [F.] (cor dar-mê'). An army corps. BELLIGERENT.

corps de réserve [F.] (cor de rê-zerv'). An army held in reserve. STORE.

corps perdu, à [F.] (cor per-dü', a). Headlong. HURRY-LEISURE, RECKLESSNESS-CAUTION.

corpse. A dead body. LIFE-CORPSE.

corpse'-like''. Like a dead body. LIFE-CORPSE.

cor'-pu-lence. An undue accumulation of fat in the body. BREADTH-NARROWNESS, GREATNESS-LITTLENESS.

cor'-pu-lent. Obese. GREATNESS-LITTLENESS.

corpus [L.] (cor'-pus). A body. MATERIALITY-SPIRITUALITY.

corpus delicti [L.] (cor'-pus dî-lic'-tai). The body of the crime. INNOCENCE-GUILT, LITIGATION.

corpus juris [L.] (cor'-pus jiu'-ris). The body of law. LAW-LAWLESSNESS, PRECEPT.

cor-pus'-cle. A minute particle of matter. MAGNITUDE-SMALLNESS.

cor'-pus'-cu-lar. Atomic. GREATNESS-LITTLENESS.

cor-ra''-di-a'-tion. A conjunction of rays in one point. ADMISSION-EXPULSION, GATHERING-SCATTERING.

cor-ral'. A pen for live stock. ENCLOSURE, RELEASE-RESTRAINT.

cor-rect'. Make right; to remedy; to punish. APPROVAL-DISAPPROVAL, BETTERMENT-DETERIORATION, DUENESS-UNDUENESS, ENLIGHTENMENT-SECRECY, EXCULPATION-PUNITION, EXPOSURE-HIDINGPLACE, REGULARITY-IRREGULARITY, RENOVATION-RELAPSE, TRUTH-ERROR, UPRIGHTNESS-DISHONESTY, VIRTUE-VICE; **correct ear,** HEARING-DEAFNESS, MUSICIAN; **correct memory,** REMEMBRANCE-FORGETFULNESS; **correct reasoning,** RATIOCINATION-INSTINCT; **correct style,** BETTERMENT-DETERIORATION, GRAMMAR-SOLECISM, PURITY-CRUDENESS.

cor-rec'-tion. Rectification. BETTERMENT-DETERIORATION, EXCULPATION-PUNITION, RECOMPENSE-PUNITION; **house of correction,** SUCCESS-FAILURE; **under correction,** SELFRESPECT-HUMBLENESS.

cor-rect'-ive. Adapted to correct. REMEDY-BANE.

cor-reg'-i-dor. The chief magistrate of a Spanish town. CHIEF-UNDERLING.

cor''-re-la'-tion. Reciprocal relation. CONNECTION-INDEPENDENCE, INTERDEPENDENCE.

cor-rel'-a-tive. Related. CONNECTION-INDEPENDENCE.

cor''-re-spond'. Agree; write. HARMONY-DISCORD, MISSIVE-PUBLICATION.

cor-re-spond′-ence. Agreement; the act of communicating by means of letters. HARMONY-DISCORD, MISSIVE-PUBLICATION.

cor-re-spond′-ent. One who communicates or transacts business by means of letters; similar. CONSIGNEE, HARMONY-DISCORD, INVESTIGATION-ANSWER, LITIGATION, MESSENGER, SYNONYM-ANTONYM.

cor′-ri-dor. A wide gallery or passage in a building. CONTENTS-RECEIVER, WAY.

cor-ri-gen′-dum. A thing or word to be corrected. TRUTH-ERROR.

cor′-ri-gi-ble. Capable of being corrected. BETTERMENT-DETERIORATION.

cor-ri′-val. A rival. BELLIGERENT.

cor-ri′-val-ship. State of being rivals. STRIFE-PEACE.

cor-ri′-val-ry. Competition. STRIFE-PEACE.

cor″-ri-va′-tion. The running together of different streams. RIVER-WIND.

cor-rob′-o-rant. Invigorating. REMEDY-BANE.

cor-rob′-o-rate. To confirm. ASSENT-DISSENT, EVIDENCE-COUNTEREVIDENCE.

cor-rob″-o-ra′-tion. Confirmation. ASSENT-DISSENT, EVIDENCE-COUNTEREVIDENCE.

cor-rob″-o-ra-tive. Verifying. EVIDENCE-COUNTEREVIDENCE.

cor-rode′. To eat away gradually. BETTERMENT-DETERIORATION, HEATING-COOLING, PLEASURABLENESS-PAINFULNESS.

cor-rod′-ing. Rusting. PLEASURABLENESS-PAINFULNESS.

cor-ro′-sion. Decay. BETTERMENT-DETERIORATION.

cor-ro′-sive. Having the power of corroding. GOODNESS-BADNESS, VIGOR-INERTIA.

cor′-ru-gate. Wrinkled. ENLARGEMENT - DIMINUTION, ORGANIZATION-DISORGANIZATION, PLICATURE, SMOOTHNESS-ROUGHNESS.

cor″-ru-ga′-tion. Wrinkle. ENLARGEMENT-DIMINUTION, ORGANIZATION-DISORGANIZATION.

cor-rupt′. Dishonest; tainted. BETTERMENT-DETERIORATION, CLEANNESS-FILTHINESS, PATRIOTISM-TREASON, UPRIGHTNESS-DISHONESTY, VIRTUE-VICE.

cor-rupt′-ing. Depraving. GOODNESS-BADNESS.

cor-rup′-tion. Destruction by reason of decomposition; depravity; departure from correct style. BETTERMENT - DETERIORATION, CLEANNESS - FILTHINESS, COMPOSITION - RESOLUTION, UPRIGHTNESS - DISHONESTY, VIRTUE-VICE, WORD-NEOLOGY.

cor′-sage. The bodice or waist of a woman's dress. DRESS-UNDRESS.

cor′-sair. A pirate. ROBBER.

corse. A corpse. LIFE-CORPSE.

corse′-let. The complete armor of a soldier. DRESS-UNDRESS.

cor′-set. A close-fitting, stiff bodice. DRESS-UNDRESS.

corso [Sp.] (cor′-so). A race-ground for horses. LISTS.

cortège [F.] (cor-têzh′). A train of attendants. CHIEF-UNDERLING, CONTINUITY-INTERRUPTION, INCREMENT-REMNANT, SOLITUDE-COMPANY, TRAVELING-NAVIGATION.

Cor′-tes. The national legislature of Spain or of Portugal. COUNCIL.

cor′-tex. The bark or rind. COVER-LINING.

cor′-ti-cal. External. COVERING-LINING.

cor′-us-cate. To sparkle. LIGHT-DARKNESS.

cor″-us-ca′-tion. Sparkling. LIGHT-DARKNESS.

cor″-vette′. A war-vessel. CONVEYANCE-VESSEL.

cor′-y-bant. A priest of the goddess Cybele. MINISTRY-LAITY.

cor″-y-ban′-tic. Madly excited. SANENESS-LUNACY.

cor″-y-phe′-us. The conductor, leader, or chief of a dramatic chorus. INSTRUCTOR-PUPIL, MANAGER.

cosa ben fatta è fatta due volte [It.] (co′-za bên fat′-ta ê fat′-ta du′-ê vol′-tê). A thing well done is twice done. COMPLETION-NONCOMPLETION, TOIL-RELAXATION.

cos-cin′-o-man″-cy. Divination by suspending a sieve, etc. PROPHECY.

co″-sig-nif′-i-ca-tive. Having the same signification. INTERPRETATION-MISINTERPRETATION.

co′-sine. The sine of the complement of an angle. PARALLELISM-INCLINATION.

cos-met′-ic. A compound applied to the skin to improve its appearance. EMBELLISHMENT-DISFIGUREMENT, REMEDY-BANE.

cos′-mic-al. Belonging to the material universe. UNIVERSE.

cos-mog′-o-ny. A doctrine or an account of the creation or of the system of the universe. UNIVERSE.

cos-mog′-ra-phy. Science of the universe. UNIVERSE.

cos-mol′-o-gy. Science of the universe. UNIVERSE.

cos″-mo-pol′-i-tan. Common to all the world; a citizen of the world. DWELLER-HABITATION, HUMANITARIANISM-MISANTHROPY, HUMANITY.

cos″-mo-pol′-i-tan-ism. A cosmopolitan character. HUMANITARIANISM-MISANTHROPY.

cos-mop′-o-lite. World-wide. HUMANITARIANISM-MISANTHROPY, HUMANITY.

cos″-mo-ra′-ma. An exhibition through a lens of drawings or paintings, like seeing the world. APPEARANCE-DISAPPEARANCE.

cos′-mos. The world or universe considered as a system. UNIVERSE.

Cos′-sack. A member of the race inhabiting the lower Don and Dnieper. BELLIGERENT.

cos′-set. To pet. BLANDISHMENT, FAVORITE-ANGER.

cost. The price. PRICE-DISCOUNT; **cost price,** COSTLINESS-CHEAPNESS; **cost what it may,** DETERMINATION-VACILLATION; **pay costs,** SETTLEMENT-DEFAULT; **to one's cost,** GOOD-EVIL, GOODNESS-BADNESS.

cos′-ter-mon″-ger. A street hawker of fruits, etc. DEALER.

cos′-tive. Constipated. TALKATIVENESS-TACITURNITY.

cos′-tive-ness. Uncommunicativeness. TALKATIVENESS-TACITURNITY.

cost′-less. Costing nothing. COSTLINESS-CHEAPNESS.

cost′-li-ness. Expensiveness. COSTLINESS-CHEAPNESS.

COSTLINESS—CHEAPNESS.

Costliness. The quality of being expensive.
Dearness, etc. Excessiveness in price, etc. See *Adjectives*.
Exorbitance. A going beyond proper limits in making charges.
Extortion. Overcharge.
Extravagance. Lavish expenditure.
Famine price. Price caused by scarcity.
Heavy pull upon the purse. Expensiveness.
High price. High valuation.
Overcharge. An excessive price.

COSTLINESS—*Verbs*.

Bleed. To draw money from one at a disadvantage.
Be dear, etc. To come high in price, etc. See *Adjectives*.

Bargain. An advantageous transaction.
Cheapness. The quality of being low in price.
Depreciation. Decrease in value.
Free admission. Allowed to enter without charges.
Free quarters. Place of abode free.
Free seats. Seats obtained gratis.
Good penny worth. Much for the money laid out or work done.
Gratuity. A free gift; a present.
Labor of love. Task undertaken without hope of compensation.
Low price. Cheapness.
Nominal price. Comparatively small price.
Peppercorn rent. A nominal rent.

COSTLINESS—CHEAPNESS—*Continued.*

COSTLINESS—Verbs—*Continued.*

Cost a pretty penny. To have cost an exorbitant amount.
Cost much. Be high in price.
Extort. To practise the charging of unreasonable prices.
Fleece. To strip of one's property
Look up. To examine the items of an account.
Overcharge. To charge too much.
Pay through the nose. Pay extravagantly.
Pay too dear for one's whistle. [Remember Franklin's story.]
Pay too much. Pay an exorbitant price.
Rise in price. To become more valuable.

COSTLINESS—Adjectives.

Costly. Paid for with a big price.
Dear. Sold for a high price.
Exorbitant. Marked by a desire to get more than is reasonable.
Expensive. Costing much.
Extortionate. Oppressive.
Extravagant. Immoderately high.
High. Costing more than usual.
Precious. Having great inherent value.
Priceless. Worth a great deal.
Unreasonable. Too high in price

COSTLINESS—Adverbial Expressions.

Above price; at a premium; beyond price; dearly bought; high priced; not to be had, hard to get; not to be had for love or money, not to be obtained at any price; **of great price; of priceless value; unreasonable; worth a Jew's eye,** exceedingly costly.

COSTLINESS—Adverbs.

À grand frais [F.].
At great cost. } At a great expense.
At heavy cost. }
Dear. } At a very high price.
Dearly. }

CHEAPNESS—Verbs.

Be cheap, etc. See *Adjectives.*
Buy for a mere nothing. Buy cheaply.
Buy for an old song. To buy for a mere trifle.
Come down in price. To lessen the cost.
Cost little. Be cheap.
Fall in price. A drop in the cost of an article.
Have one's money's worth. Get full value.

CHEAPNESS—Adjectives.

A drug in the market. Plenteous with lack of demand; hence, cheap.
Catchpenny. Cheap and showy.
Cheap. Low in price.
Cheap and nasty. Cheap and filthy; worthless.
Cheap as dirt; cheap at the price; costless.
Depreciated. Sunk in value.
Dirt cheap; dog cheap, very cheap; **expenseless; free; free of cost; free of expense; good price,** reasonable; **gratis, free of charge; gratuitous** (see *Nouns*); **half-price; honorary,** without any expenditure of energy, time, or money; **inexpensive,** without expense; **low; low priced;** *magnifique et pas cher* [F.], magnificent and not dear; **not charged; reasonable; rent-free; scot-free,** without payment; **shot-free,** same as SCOT-FREE; **unbought,** got without money; **unexpensive** (see INEXPENSIVE); **unpaid; well worth the money;** without charge; **worth the money.**

CHEAPNESS—Adverbial Phrases

À bon marché [F.], at a good bargain; **at a reduction; at cost price; at prime cost,** at first cost; **for a mere song.**

COSTLINESS—*Continued.*

COSTLINESS—Phrases.

Prices looking up. Exorbitant; extravagant.
Vel prece, vel pretio [L.]. Either with prayer or with price.

---

cost′-ly. Expensive. COSTLINESS-CHEAPNESS, GOODNESS-BADNESS.
cos′-tume. The garments, collectively, worn at one time. DRESS-UNDRESS; **theatrical costume,** ACTING, VESTMENTS.
costume [F.] (cos-tüm′). Characteristic dress. DRESS-UNDRESS.
costume bal [F.] (cos-tüm′ bɑl). A ball dress. ENTERTAINMENT-WEARINESS.
costumier [F.] (cos-tüm-mi-ê′). Property-man. ACTING, DRESS-UNDRESS.
cot. A small and humble house; a light bedstead. DWELLER-HABITATION, SUSPENSION-SUPPORT.
co-tan′-gent. One of the trigonometrical functions. ANGULARITY, PARALLELISM-INCLINATION.
cote. A sheepfold. DWELLER-HABITATION.
co-ten′-an-cy. Joint tenancy. PARTICIPATION.
co-ten′-ant. Landholder. PARTICIPATION.
co′′-te-rie′. A clique. ASSOCIATION, SOCIABILITY-PRIVACY.
co-thur′-nus. A buskin; a tragedy. ACTING.
co-ti′-dal. Indicating simultaneity in tides. OCEAN-LAND, SAMENESS-CONTRAST.
co-til′-lion. A quadrille. ENTERTAINMENT-WEARINESS.
cot′-tage. A small dwelling. COUNTRY, DWELLER-HABITATION.
cot′-ta-ger. The occupant of a cottage. DWELLER-HABITATION.
cot′-ter. A cottager. DWELLER-HABITATION.
cot′-tier. Cottager. DWELLER-HABITATION.
cot′-ton. A soft, woolly, fibrous material appended to the seeds of the cotton-plant. LAMINA-FIBER.
cot′-ton ex-change′. Place where cotton is sold LABOR-CAPITAL.
couch. To cause to lie; a bed; to lurk. ELEVATION-DEPRESSION, ENLIGHTENMENT-SECRECY, ERECTNESS-FLATNESS, SUSPENSION-SUPPORT; **couch in terms,** PHRASE; **couch one's lance,** STRIFE-PEACE.

couch′-ant. Lying down. ERECTNESS-FLATNESS.
couci-couci [F.] (cu-si′-cu-si′). Half-hearted. FAULTLESSNESS-FAULTINESS.
cough. A sudden, harsh expulsion of the breath. RIVER-WIND; **churchyard cough,** HEALTH-SICKNESS.
cou-lée′. A solidified stream of lava. RIVER-WIND.
couleur de rose [F.] (cu-lur′ de roz). Rose-color. GOODNESS-BADNESS, SANGUINENESS-HOPELESSNESS, WELFARE-MISFORTUNE; **view** *en couleur,* LIGHTHEARTEDNESS-DEJECTION.
couleur de rose, vin en [F.] (cu-lur′ de roz, van·an′). Rose-colored wine. SANGUINENESS-HOPELESSNESS.
coulisses [F.] (cu-lîs′). One of the side scenes of a stage in a theater. ACTING.
coul′-ter. A blade or disk on the beam of a plow. SHARPNESS-BLUNTNESS.
coun′-cil. An assembly of persons convened for consultation or deliberation. ADVICE, CHURCH, COUNCIL; **council of education,** SCHOOL; **hold a council,** ADVICE.

COUNCIL.

Amphictyonic Council. Council of delegates from the Greek states.
Assembly. A number of persons met for a particular purpose.
Bench. The corps of judges of a court.
Board of control. Board having control of school matters.
Board of works. A number of persons having charge of particular work.
Cabinet. The official advisers of the head of a government.
Caput. Formerly, the governing body at the University of Cambridge.
Caucus. Meeting of the members of a political party to nominate candidates and further the interests of the party.
Chamber. Assembly or association.
Chamber of Deputies. The popular branch of the French legislature.
Chapter. A branch of an association.
Clique. Association of a few for common interests

Cockpit. The government office-building opposite Whitehall, Westminster.

Comitia [L.]. Assembly of the Romans to elect officers and pass laws.

Committee. A portion of an assembly appointed to do certain work.

Conclave. The meeting of the cardinals of the Roman Catholic Church for electing a pope.

Conference. Meeting of persons having common or conflicting interests for settlement of some question.

Congress. The legislative body of the United States. Any large and important assembly.

Consistory. The governing body in some churches.

Conventicle. Meeting for religious worship.

Convention. A meeting of delegates to discuss religious, social, political, etc., questions.

Convocation. Assembly, especially of the clergy of the Church of England, or of the governing body of Oxford University

Cortes [Sp.]. The Spanish legislative body.

Council. Body of men summoned for consultation.

Court. Place for hearing cases at law; the judge or judges hearing a case.

Court of appeal, etc. A court to whom appeals from the decision of other courts may be taken, etc. See TRIBUNAL.

Diet. Legislative body in some European countries.

Directory. The governing body of the French from 1795–1799.

Divan. The privy council of the Sultan of Turkey.

Durbar [Hind.]. The court of a prince of India.

House. A branch of the legislative body.

Junta [Sp.]. A grand council of state.

Meeting. A gathering for any purpose.

Musnud [Ar.]. A Mussulman court

Palaver. An African conference.

Parliament. The legislative body of any country, especially of England.

Pourparler [F.]. Conference held before making a treaty.

Privy cabinet. The chief members of the privy council of the sovereign of England.

Privy council. The whole advisory body of the crown of England.

Quorum [L.]. The number of a body required to be present before business can be done.

Reichsrath [G.]. The Austrian parliament.

Rigsdag [Dan.]. The Danish parliament.

Sanhedrim [Heb.]. The highest court of the ancient Jews.

Séance [F.]. A sitting of some body of inquiry.

Senate. The upper house of the legislative body in some countries, especially in the United States and France.

Senatus [L.]. Senate.

Session. The whole period during which a body sits.

Sitting. Session.

Staff. The officers employed in carrying a superior officer's commands into execution.

States General. The legislative body of a country, especially of Holland.

Storthing [Norw.]. The parliament of Norway.

Subcommittee. A small committee appointed by a larger one.

Syndicate. An official or other body undertaking a business project.

Synod. A church council.

Vestry. A church governing body.

Witenagemote. The parliament of the Anglo-Saxons.

COUNCIL—*Constituent Nouns.*

Councilor. A member of a council.

Member. A person belonging to any deliberative body.

Member of Parliament. A member of either of the houses of the national legislatures of some countries.

M. P. Member of Parliament.

Representative of the people. A delegate sent by the people to a legislative body.

Senator. A member of the higher house of the legislature in the United States.

COUNCIL—*Adjectives.*

Curule. Pertaining to those Roman offices the incumbents of which sat in certain kind of a chair.

Senatorial. Pertaining to the Senate or Senators.

coun'-cil-man. Member of a council. PRESIDENT-MEMBER.

coun'-cil-or. A member of a council. ADVICE, COUNCIL.

coun'-sel. Advice; a lawyer. ADVICE, ADVOCATE; **keep one's own counsel,** ENLIGHTENMENT-SECRECY;

take counsel, INVESTIGATION-ANSWER, MIND-IMBECILITY.

coun'-sel-or. Adviser. ADVICE, ADVOCATE.

count. To enumerate; a distinct charge; a nobleman. DECISION-MISJUDGMENT, GENTILITY-DEMOCRACY, NUMBERING; **count the cost,** RECKLESSNESS-CAUTION; **count upon,** EXPECTATION-SURPRISE, FAITH-MISGIVING; **to be counted on one's fingers,** MULTIPLICITY-PAUCITY.

coun'-te-nance. To approve; the face. ANTERIORITY-POSTERIORITY, APPEARANCE-DISAPPEARANCE, APPROVAL-DISAPPROVAL, OBSTRUCTION-HELP; **countenance falling,** EXPECTATION-DISAPPOINTMENT, LIGHTHEARTEDNESS-DEJECTION; **keep in countenance,** APPROVAL-DISAPPROVAL, BRAVERY-COWARDICE, CONVENTIONALITY-UNCONVENTIONALITY, JUSTIFICATION-CHARGE, MOTIVE-CAPRICE, OBSTRUCTION-HELP; **keep one's countenance,** EXCITABILITY-INEXCITABILITY, LIGHTHEARTEDNESS-DEJECTION; **out of countenance,** CONCEIT-DIFFIDENCE, SELFRESPECT-HUMBLENESS; **put out of countenance,** REPUTATION-DISCREDIT, SELFRESPECT-HUMBLENESS; **stare out of countenance,** PRESUMPTION-OBSEQUIOUSNESS.

coun'-ter. Contrary; a calculator; a table from which goods are sold; a piece of wood, ivory, etc., used in games. MARKET, NUMBER, SAMENESS-CONTRAST, SIGN, SUSPENSION-SUPPORT; **counter to,** ANTAGONISM-CONCURRENCE; **over the counter,** BUYING, DEALER, EXCHANGE; **run counter,** COOPERATION-OPPOSITION.

coun''-ter-act'. To check by opposing. ANTAGONISM-CONCURRENCE, COMPENSATION, COOPERATION-OPPOSITION, OBSTRUCTION-HELP.

coun''-ter-act'-ing. Opposing. COOPERATION-OPPOSITION.

coun''-ter-ac'-tion. Hindrance. ANTAGONISM-CONCURRENCE, COOPERATION-OPPOSITION.

coun''-ter-bal'-ance. To offset. COMPENSATION.

coun'-ter-blast''. An opposing blast; an answering argument. COOPERATION-OPPOSITION, REPRISAL-RESISTANCE.

coun''-ter-change'. To interchange. COMMUTATION-PERMUTATION, INTERDEPENDENCE.

coun'-ter-charm''. An opposing charm. DEVOTION-CHARM.

coun''-ter-check''. A check for a check; a cross-demand alleged by a defendant against the plaintiff. OBSTRUCTION-HELP, SIGN.

coun'-ter-ev''-i-dence. Rebutting evidence. EVIDENCE-COUNTEREVIDENCE.

coun'-ter-feit. An imitation usually fraudulent. COPY-MODEL, IMITATION-ORIGINALITY, TRUTHFULNESS-FALSEHOOD, TRUTHFULNESS-FRAUD.

coun'-ter-foil''. A stub or coupon. SIGN.

coun''-ter-mand'. To order or command contrary to previous order or command. COMMISSION-ABROGATION.

coun''-ter-march'. To march back. ADVANCE-RETROGRESSION, TRAVELING-NAVIGATION.

coun'-ter-mark''. An added mark. SIGN.

coun''-ter-mine'. To mine counter to. ANTAGONISM-CONCURRENCE, DESIGN.

coun'-ter-mo''-tion. Movement in a contrary direction. ADVANCE-RETROGRESSION.

coun'-ter-move''-ment. Opposition. ADVANCE-RETROGRESSION.

coun'-ter-or''-der. An order contrary to a preceding order. COMMISSION-ABROGATION.

coun'-ter-pane''. An outside bed-cover. COVER-LINING.

coun'-ter-part''. A facsimile; an opposite. COPY-MODEL, LATERALITY-CONTRAPOSITION, LIKENESS-UNLIKENESS.

coun″-ter-plot′. To oppose plot to plot. ANTAGONISM-CONCURRENCE, DESIGN, REPRISAL-RESISTANCE.

coun′-ter-point″. Art of writing an accompaniment to a melody. MELODY-DISSONANCE.

coun″-ter-poise′. To counterbalance. COMPENSATION, HEAVINESS-LIGHTNESS, OBSTRUCTION-HELP.

coun′-ter-poi″-son. An antidote. REMEDY-BANE.

coun′e-tr-proj″-ect. A project given in opposition to another. REPRISAL-RESISTANCE.

coun′-ter-pro″-test. A protest against a protest. EVIDENCE-COUNTEREVIDENCE.

coun′-ter-rev-o-lu′-tion. A revolution opposed to a former one. CONVERSION-REVERSION.

coun′-ter-scarp″. The slope of a ditch opposite a parapet. ATTACK-DEFENSE.

coun′-ter-sign″. A watchword. ASSENT-DISSENT, EVIDENCE-COUNTEREVIDENCE, SIGN.

coun′-ter-stroke″. A stroke in retaliation. REPRISAL-RESISTANCE.

coun′-ter-term″. Antonym. SYNONYM-ANTONYM.

coun″-ter-vail′. To counterbalance. COMPENSATION, EQUALITY-INEQUALITY, EVIDENCE-COUNTEREVIDENCE.

coun″-ter-vail′-ing. Counteracting. COMPENSATION.

coun″-ter-work′. To work in opposition to. ANTAGONISM-CONCURRENCE.

count′-ess. The wife of an earl or a count. GENTILITY-DEMOCRACY.

count′-ing–house″. A business-office of an establishment. MARKET.

count′-less. Incapable of being counted. INFINITY.

coun′-tri-fied. Rustic. TASTE-VULGARITY.

coun′-try. A land under a particular government; a rural region. CITY-COUNTRY, DOMESTICATION-AGRICULTURE, DWELLER-HABITATION, EXTENSION-DISTRICT; **love of country,** HUMANITARIANISM-MISANTHROPY.

coun′-try–dance″. A dance in which the partners are ranged in opposite lines. ENTERTAINMENT-WEARINESS.

coun′-try church′-yard. Yard around a church. CITY-COUNTRY.

coun′-try-man. A rustic; an inhabitant of the same country with another. FRIEND-FOE, GENTILITY-DEMOCRACY.

coun′-try–seat″. A dwelling in the country. COUNTRY, DWELLER-HABITATION, SOCIABILITY-PRIVACY.

coun′-try-side″. District. CITY-COUNTRY.

coun′-try-wom″-an. Woman living in the country. CITY-COUNTRY.

counts. Things sold by the piece. UNIVERSALITY-PARTICULARITY.

coun′-ty. A civil division of a state or kingdom. EXTENSION-DISTRICT; **county court,** TRIBUNAL.

coup [F.] (cu). A master-stroke. ACTION-PASSIVENESS, DESIGN, ETERNITY-INSTANTANEITY.

coup sûr, à [F.] (cu sür, a). Certainly. CERTAINTY-DOUBT.

coup de bec [F.] (cu de bec). Slander. APPROVAL-DISAPPROVAL, ATTACK-DEFENSE.

coup de grâce [F.] (cu de gras). The finishing blow. BEGINNING-END, COMPLETION-NONCOMPLETION, EXCULPATION-PUNITION, LIFE-KILLING.

coup de l'épée dans l'eau [F.] (cu de lê-pê′ dan· lo). To strike a sword into the water. USEFULNESS-USELESSNESS.

coup de main [F.] (cu· de man·). A sudden attack. ACTION-PASSIVENESS, ATTACK-DEFENSE, TURBULENCE-CALMNESS.

coup de maître [F.] (cu de mêtr). A master-stroke. GOODNESS-BADNESS, SKILL-UNSKILFULNESS, SUCCESS-FAILURE.

coup d'œil [F.] (cu duy). First sight. APPEARANCE-DISAPPEARANCE, POMP, SIGHT-BLINDNESS.

coup de plume [F.] (cu de plüm). The stroke of a pen. WRITING-PRINTING.

coup de soleil [F.] (cu de so-lêy′). Sunstroke. HEATING-COOLING, SANENESS-LUNACY.

coup d'essai [F.] (cu de-sê′). A first attempt. VENTURE.

coup d'état [F.] (cu dê-ta′). A bold piece of statesmanship. ACTION-PASSIVENESS, DESIGN, LAW-LAWLESSNESS, REVOLUTION.

coup de théâtre [F.] (cu de tê-atr′). A theatrical hit. APPEARANCE-DISAPPEARANCE, POMP.

coup′-le. A pair. DUALITY, MATRIMONY-CELIBACY, UNION-DISUNION.

coup′-led. United in pairs. DUALITY; **coupled with,** ADDITION-SUBTRACTION, SOLITUDE-COMPANY.

coup′-let. Two lines of verse in immediate sequence and rhyming together. POETRY-PROSE.

cou′-pon″. A section or detachable portion of a bond, ticket, etc. MONEY.

cour′-age. Bravery. BRAVERY-COWARDICE; **courage oozing out,** BRAVERY-COWARDICE; **moral courage,** DETERMINATION-VACILLATION.

courage de ses convictione, il a le [F.] (cu-razh′ de sê con′-vic-si-on·′, îl a le). He has the courage of his convictions. BRAVERY-COWARDICE.

cou-ra′-geous. Brave. BRAVERY-COWARDICE.

courage sans peur [F.] (cu-razh′ san· pur). Courage without fear. BRAVERY-COWARDICE.

courant [F.] (cu′-ran·). Current. *au courant* [F.] (o curan·′), in the current; informed. KNOWLEDGE-IGNORANCE.

coureur, avant [F.] (cu-rur′, a-van·′). A herald. PREPARATION-NONPREPARATION.

cou′-ri-er. An emissary carrying messages. MESSENGER, WAYFARER-SEAFARER.

course. Career; line of motion; line of conduct; regular sequence; the portion of a meal served at one time; a charge or bout in a tournament. AIM-ABERRATION, CONDUCT, CONTINUITY-INTERRUPTION, DURATION-NEVERNESS, EDUCATION-MISTEACHING, LISTS, MOVEMENT-REST, NUTRIMENT-EXCRETION, PERIOD-PROGRESS, QUEST-EVASION, REGULARITY-IRREGULARITY, RIVER-WIND, TRAVELING-NAVIGATION, WAY; **bend one's course,** QUEST-EVASION, TRAVELING-NAVIGATION; **course of action,** CONDUCT; **course of business,** OCCUPATION; **course of events,** OCCURRENCE-DESTINY; **course of inquiry,** INVESTIGATION-ANSWER; **course of preparation,** PREPARATION-NONPREPARATION; **course of study,** EDUCATION-MISTEACHING; **course of things,** OCCURRENCE-DESTINY; **course of time,** FUTURE-PAST; **course runs smooth,** WELFARE-MISFORTUNE; **follow as of course,** PROOF-DISPROOF; **hold a course,** AIM-ABERRATION, QUEST-EVASION; **in course,** NATURE-ART; **in due course,** OPPORTUNENESS-UNSUITABLENESS; **in the course of,** DURATION-NEVERNESS, OCCURRENCE-DESTINY; **in the course of nature,** NATURE-ART; **keep one's course,** ADVANCE-RETROGRESSION, PERSISTENCE-WHIM; **let things take their course,** ACTION-PASSIVENESS, DISCONTINUANCE-CONTINUANCE; **mark out a course,** DESIGN; **of course,** ASSENT-DISSENT, ASTONISHMENT-EXPECTANCE, CAUSE-EFFECT, CERTAINTY-DOUBT, CONSENT, CONVENTIONALITY-UNCONVENTIONALITY, HABIT-DESUETUDE, PROOF-DISPROOF, VOLITION-OBLIGATION; **run its course,** BEGINNING-END, COMPLETION-NONCOMPLETION; **take a course,** QUEST-EVASION; **take its course,** OCCURRENCE-DESTINY.

cours′-er. A fleet and spirited horse. CONVEYER, SWIFTNESS-SLOWNESS.

cours′-ing. The sport of chasing and hunting hares with greyhounds. LIFE-KILLING, QUEST-EVASION.

court. To woo; solicit; a tribunal; the residence of a

sovereign; the council and retinue of a sovereign; a level space for playing games; flattering attention. ADULATION-DISPARAGEMENT, BLANDISHMENT, CHIEF-UNDERLING, CONTENTS-RECEIVER, COUNCIL, DESIRE-DISTASTE, DWELLER-HABITATION, EXTENSION-DISTRICT, JUDGE, MOTIVE-CAPRICE, PETITION-EXPOSTULATION, QUEST-EVASION, SOCIETY-LUDICROUSNESS, TRIBUNAL; **bring into court,** EVIDENCE-COUNTEREVIDENCE; **consistorial court,** CHURCH; **court card,** DESIGN; **court of common council,** TRIBUNAL; **court of final appeal,** CERTAINTY-DOUBT; **court of honor,** UPRIGHTNESS-DISHONESTY; **friend at court,** ANTAGONIST-ASSISTANT; **pay court to,** ADULATION-DISPARAGEMENT, BLANDISHMENT, LOVE-HATE, PRESUMPTION-OBSEQUIOUSNESS; **put out of court,** SUCCESS-FAILURE.

cour′-te-ous. Polite. POLITENESS-IMPOLITENESS.

cour′-te-ous-ly. Politely. POLITENESS-IMPOLITENESS.

cour′-te-sy. Politeness; a gesture of civility or respect. ELEVATION - DEPRESSION, POLITENESS - IMPOLITENESS, REGARD-DISRESPECT, VIBRATION, YIELDING; **show courtesy,** POLITENESS-IMPOLITENESS, REGARD-DISRESPECT.

cour′-te-zan. A prostitute. PURITY-RAKE.

court′-ier. A member of the court circle. FLATTERER-DEFAMER, PRESUMPTION-OBSEQUIOUSNESS.

court′-ier-like. ADULATION-DISPARAGEMENT.

court′-ier-ly. Like a courtier. ADULATION-DISPARAGEMENT.

court′-ly. Elegant in manners. SOCIETY-LUDICROUSNESS.

court′-ship. The time of wooing. BLANDISHMENT, LOVE-HATE.

cous′-in. One descended from a common ancestor, but not a brother or sister. RELATIONSHIP; **first cousin,** RELATIONSHIP; **second cousin,** RELATIONSHIP; **cousin once removed,** RELATIONSHIP; **cousin twice removed,** RELATIONSHIP.

cous′-in-hood. Relationship of cousins. RELATIONSHIP.

coûte-que-coûte [F.] (cut-ke-cut). Cost what it may. CERTAINTY-DOUBT, DETERMINATION-VACILLATION, VOLITION-OBLIGATION.

cove. A small bay or bay-like recess. CONTENTS - RECEIVER, CONVEXITY - CONCAVITY, GULF-PLAIN.

cov′-e-nant. A compact. CONTRACT, MODIFICATION, SECURITY, TERMS.

Cov′-en-try. A town of Warwickshire, England. Earl of Coventry, ENTERTAINMENT-WEARINESS; **send to Coventry,** ADMISSION-EXPULSION, REPUTATION-DISCREDIT, SOCIABILITY-PRIVACY.

cov′-er. To overspread; screen; compensate for; to accomplish; to put one's hat on; a defense. CLEANNESS-FILTHINESS, CONSERVATION, COMPENSATION, COVER-LINING, DRESS-UNDRESS, ENLIGHTENMENT-SECRECY, EXPOSURE-HIDINGPLACE, PERFORATOR-STOPPER, SECURITY-INSECURITY; **cover with dust,** CLEANNESS-FILTHINESS; **under cover,** ENLIGHTENMENT-SECRECY, SECURITY-INSECURITY, TRUTHFULNESS-FALSEHOOD.

COVER—LINING.

Cover.
Covering. } That which fits over, encloses, or protects anything.

Incrustation. A covering over with a crust.

Integument.
Tegument. } An inner lining; that which protects the inner parts, as against the outside.

COVER—*Denotations, etc.*

Anointing. The act of covering with oil, especially for consecration. See *Verbs*.

Awning. A roof-like cover for protection from the sun, or rain.

Bandage. A strip of woven material for binding up wounds.

Bark. The exterior covering of the trunk and branches of a tree.

Bed-quilt.
Blanket. } A bed-cover.

Canopy. A roof-like covering.

Capsule. A gelatinous envelope in which nauseous doses of medicine are enclosed.

Case. A box or covering.

Casing. An outside covering.

Ceiling. The inside lining of a roof overhead.

Cerement. A wrapping for the dead: was originally of wax cloth.

Clothing. Covering for the body. See DRESS.

Coat. An article of clothing covering the upper part of the body.

Coating. A layer of any substance, as a cover or protection.

Cod. A husk or pod.

Compo. Composition for plastering.

Cornshuck. The husk which covers the ear of corn.

Cortex. Bark, as of a tree.

Counterpane. A coverlet for a bed.

Covercle. A small cover.

Coverlet. The uppermost cover of a bed or any piece of furniture.

Crust. The hard external covering of anything.

Cuticle. The outer skin.

Door. A barrier by which an entrance into a house is closed and opened.

Dossil. A covering for a wound, originally a plug or spiggot.

Drugget. A coarse cloth used as a covering for carpets.

Egg-shell. The shell of an egg.

Eiderdown. The down of the eider, used as a stuffing for coverlets, etc.

Elytron. One of the broad dorsal scales of certain worms.

Enamel. A material applied to metals to form a surface for painting.

Engobe. A paste covering for inferior pottery.

Envelope. A paper case or wrapper.

Coating, etc. That with which anything is covered, etc. See COVER.

Filling. Something used to fill a hole.

Lining. The inside covering of a thing.

Padding. Any material used for stuffing.

Stuffing. A substance used for filling up empty space.

Wadding. Cotton put up in sheets; innercoating.

LINING—*Denotations.*

Parietes. The walls of the cavities of the body.

Stalactite. A conical formation projecting downward from the top of a cave.

Stalagmite. A conical formation projecting upward from the floor of a cave.

Wainscot. A lining for inner walls.

Wall. The partition between rooms of a house.

LINING—*Verbs.*

Fill. To make full.

Incrust. To cover with a crust or hard substance.

Line. To cover the inside.

Pad. To put padding in or on.

Wad. To stuff with wadding.

LINING—*Adjectives.*

Lined, etc. Covered with a lining, etc. See *Verbs*.

COVER—*Denotations—Continued.*

Epidermis. The outer skin.

Facing. The covering plate or layer for protection.

Fell. A growth of hair.

Finger-stall. A cover to protect a finger.

Fleece. The woolly covering of a sheep.

Fur. The soft, fine coat of many mammals.

Ground. The first coat or cover of paint on a surface.

Hide. The skin of a large animal.

Housing. Shelter from the weather.

Incrustation. A crust or coat of anything on the surface of a body.

Inunction. Anointment with oil.

Involucrum. A sheath at the base of a flower.

Leads. Leaden sheets for covering a roof.

Leather. The skin of an animal when tanned.

Lid. A cover for a vessel or utensil.

Linoleum. A canvas covered with a linseed-oil preparation, used as a floor covering.

COVER—Denotations—Continued.

Lint. A soft down used for covering wounds.
Marquee. An officer's field-tent.
Mask. A covering for the face. See Disclosure-Hidingplace.
Obduction. Act of drawing over, as a covering.
Ointment. Oil placed upon the head as a mark of consecration. See Pulpiness-Oil.
Operculum. A lid, or lid-like part of an organ of the body.
Paint. A solid color or pigment intended as a surface-coating.
Pantile. A tile.
Parasol. A small, light umbrella for protection against the sun's rays.
Pavement. A hard surface-covering for a floor or roadway
Peel. The natural coating of certain kinds of fruit.
Pellicle. A thin skin or film.
Pelt. An undressed fur-skin.
Peltry. Pelts collectively.
Pentile. See Pantile.
Plaister.}
Plaster.} A composition of lime and sand for coating walls.
Pod. A seed-vessel or capsule of a plant.
Purdah. A curtain or screen used in Eastern countries to seclude women of rank.
Quilt. A bed-covering.
Rind. The coating of certain kinds of fruit.
Roof. The cover of a house.
Rug. A heavy textile covering for a floor.
Scale. One of the thin, flat bony outgrowths from the skin of various vertebrates. See Lamina.
Scarf-skin. The outer skin.
Shagreen. The skin of various sharks, rays, and other fishes.
Sheath. A case into which a blade is thrust; the covering of the fruit of some plants.

Sheathing. That which forms a sheath or covering.
Shed. A slight temporary covering. See Dweller-Habitation.
Sheet. A bed-cover.
Shell. A hard structure encasing an animal, as the oyster.
Shield. A defensive covering for the body. See Defense.
Skin. The covering of an animal's body.
Slates.}
Slating.} Slate used for roofing purposes.
Sunshade. A light umbrella for protection against the sun.
Superposition. Act of placing one thing over or on top of another.
Stucco. A fine plaster.
Tarpaulin. A water-proof canvas for covering merchandise.
Tent. A shelter made of canvas supported on poles.
Tente d'abri [F.]. A shelter tent.
Thatch. A covering of reeds, flags, or straw.
Theca. A sheath or case.
Tile. A thin piece of baked clay for covering roofs, floors, etc.
Tiling. A roofing or flooring of tile.
Tilt. A canvas cover, as a tent or awning.
Top. The cover, as of a carriage.
Umbrella. A cloth supported on a frame of wires for protection against the rain.
Varnish. A resinous solution to produce a shining, hard coating on paints. See Pulpiness-Rosin.
Veil. A piece of light, thin cloth worn over the face. See Luminary-Shade.
Veneer. A thin layer or cover of rare material, as ivory, mother-of-pearl, etc.
Vesicle. A small bladder-like covering.
Whitewash. A coating of slaked-lime.
Wrapper.}
Wrapping.} Any case or covering.

COVER—Scientific Terms.

Conchology. The branch of zoology treating of mollusks in reference to their shells.

Dermatology. The science of the skin and its diseases.

COVER—Verbs.

Anoint. To put ointment on; to consecrate by pouring oil on.
Bedaub. To spot or splatter through carelessness or lack of skill.
Besmear. To spread a thick or viscous substance over.
Bind. To put covers on, as on a book.
Cap. To cover the top of.
Case. To put into a case.
Coat. To spread with something.
Conceal, etc. To put out of sight, etc. See Secrecy.
Cover. To put a lid or cover on.
Dab. To spread over by striking gently.
Do over. To spread on the surface.
Enamel. To cover with enamel.
Endome. To cover with a dome.
Face. To put an outer covering on for ornament or protection.
Gild. To cover with gold or gold-colored substance.
Incase. To put into a case.
Incrust. To cover with a crust or hard coat.
Japan. To cover with a hard brilliant varnish.
Lacker.}
Lacquer.} To cover or decorate with lacquer.
Lay it on thick. To apply a thick cover or coating.

Overarch. To put an arch over.
Overlay. To put a layer on.
Overlie. To lie upon.
Overspread. To spread upon or over.
Paint. To spread paint upon.
Paper. To fasten paper on.
Pave. To cover a walk or road with a hard surface.
Pay. To coat with water-proof composition.
Plaster. To cover with plaster.
Plate. To overlay with a thin layer of metal.
Stucco. To cover with fine plaster.
Superimpose.}
Superpose.} To lay on something else.
Tar. To coat with tar.
Tip. To cover the tip of anything with a substance.
Varnish. To apply varnish to.
Veneer. To overlay with some material for ornament or protection.
Wash. To overlay with a metal by use of a liquid.
Whitewash. To cover with some white liquid.
Wrap, etc. To enclose in paper, or other substance, etc. See Dress.

COVER—Adjectives.

Armor-plated. Faced with armor plate.
Cortical. Pertaining to the bark.
Covered, etc. See *Verbs*.
Covering, etc. See *Verbs*.
Cutaneous. Pertaining to the skin.
Cuticular. Pertaining to the outer coat of the skin.
Dermal. Pertaining to the lower layer of the skin.
Encuirassed. Covered with a hard surface or hard plates.

Imbricated. Covered with overlapping scales.
Ironclad. Covered with iron.
Loricated. Covered with a shell or plates.
Scaly. Covered with scales.
Skinny. Lacking in flesh to make the form plump; covered with skin.
Squamous. Covered with scales.
Tegumentary. Resembling a tegument.
Under cover. Covered.

cov′-er-cle. A lid. Cover-Lining.
cov′-ered. Enwrapped. Cover-Lining.
cov′-er-ing. That which covers. Cover-Lining.
cov′-er-let. A quilt. Cover-Lining.
Cov′-er-ley. The chief character in the club professing to write the *Spectator*. **Sir Roger de Coverley**, Entertainment-Weariness.
cov′-ert. Something that shelters or defends. Dweller-Habitation, Manifestation-Latency,

Refuge-Pitfall, Visibility-Invisibility; **covert way**, Way.
coverte, feme [F.] (cuv′-ert, fem). A married woman. Matrimony-Celibacy.
cov′-er-ture. Marriage. Matrimony-Celibacy.
cov′-et. To have inordinate or unlawful desire for. Desire-Distaste, Pardon-Envy.
cov-et-ing. Desiring. Desire-Distaste.
cov′-et-ous. Miserly. Extravagance-Avarice.

cov'-et-ous-ness. Avarice. DESIRE-DISTASTE.

cov'-ey. A flock. GATHERING-SCATTERING, MULTI-PLICITY-PAUCITY.

cov'-in. Swindle. TRUTHFULNESS-FALSEHOOD, TRUTH-FULNESS-FRAUD.

cov'-in-ous. Fraudulent. TRUTHFULNESS-FALSEHOOD, TRUTHFULNESS-FRAUD.

cow. To intimidate; the female of domestic cattle and other animals. FAUNA-FLORA, MALE-FEMALE, SAN-GUINENESS-TIMIDITY.

cow'-ard. One who shrinks from duty or danger. BRAVERY-COWARDICE.

cow'-ard-ice. The state or condition of being a coward. BRAVERY-COWARDICE.

cow'-ard-ly. Timid. BRAVERY-COWARDICE.

cow'-er. To quail. BRAVERY-COWARDICE, ELEVATION-DEPRESSION, PRESUMPTION-OBSEQUIOUSNESS, SAN-GUINENESS-TIMIDITY.

cow'-herd". A cow-tender. DOMESTICATION-AGRICUL-TURE.

cow'-hide". A coarse riding-whip. RECOMPENSE-SCOURGE.

cow'-house". A cow-stable. DWELLER-HABITATION.

cow'-keep"-er. A cowherd. DOMESTICATION-AGRI-CULTURE.

cowl. A monk's hood. VESTMENTS.

co"-work'-er. A fellow worker. AGENT.

cow'-shed". Place for cattle. DWELLER-HABITA-TION.

cox'-comb". A fop. CONCEIT-DIFFIDENCE, SOCIETY-DANDY.

cox'-comb"-ry. Foppishness. CONCEIT-DIFFIDENCE, SOCIETY-AFFECTATION.

cox'-swain. One who steers or has charge of a rowboat. WAYFARER-SEAFARER.

coy. Shy. CONCEIT-DIFFIDENCE, SANGUINENESS-TIMIDITY.

coz'-en. To cheat. TRUTHFULNESS-FRAUD.

coz'-en-age. Deceit. TRUTHFULNESS-FALSEHOOD.

cozy. Snugly comfortable. SENSUALITY-SUFFERING. SOCIABILITY-PRIVACY.

crab. Sour. SWEETNESS-ACIDITY; **crablike motion,** ADVANCE-RETROGRESSION.

crab'-bed. Sour-tempered; abstruse; cramped; sour. CLEARNESS-OBSCURITY, DIFFICULTY-FACILITY, FA-VORITE-MOROSENESS, PERSPICUITY-OBSCURITY, PO-LITENESS-IMPOLITENESS, SWEETNESS-ACIDITY.

crab'-like. Like a crab. AIM-ABERRATION.

crack. To split; snap; a peculiar tone of the voice; first-class; to boast. BETTERMENT-DETERIORATION, BRAGGING, CONTINUITY-INTERRUPTION, CRASH-DRUMMING, ETERNITY-INSTANTANEITY, GOODNESS-BADNESS, GROOVE, INTERSPACE-CONTACT, MANAGE-MENT, NUTRIMENT-EXCRETION, SOCIABILITY-PRIVACY, TEETOTALISM-INTEMPERANCE; **crack a joke,** WITTINESS-DULNESS; **crack of doom,** BEGINNING-END, CREATION-DESTRUCTION, FUTURE-PAST; **crack one's invention,** FANCY; **crack shot,** ADEPT-BUNGLER.

crack'-brained". Weak-minded. SANENESS-LUNACY.

cracked. Discordant; insane; broken. CACOPHONY, FAULTLESSNESS-FAULTINESS, SANENESS-LUNACY; **cracked bell,** RESONANCE-NONRESONANCE; **cracked voice,** VOCALIZATION-MUTENESS.

crack'-er. A person or thing that cracks. CRASH-DRUMMING.

crack'-le. To produce light cracking sounds. CRASH-DRUMMING.

cracks'-man. A burglar. ADEPT-BUNGLER, ROBBER.

cra'-dle. A rocking or swinging bed, for an infant; a place of birth. BEGINNING-END, CAUSE-EFFECT, CONTENTS-RECEIVER, ESTABLISHMENT-REMOVAL, IN-FANCY-AGE, OBSTRUCTION-HELP, PREPARATION-NON-PREPARATION, SUSPENSION-SUPPORT; **in the cradle,** INFANT-VETERAN.

craft. Cunning or skill; a vessel or vessels; a trade. CONVEYANCE-VESSEL, CRAFT-ARTLESSNESS, OCCUPA-TION, SKILL-UNSKILFULNESS.

CRAFT—ARTLESSNESS.

Archness. The quality of being cunning or sly.

Artful dodge. Act of evading by some skilful movement.

Artifice. An elaborate trick.

Artificiality. The quality of being cunning or artful.

Backstairs influence. Underhand scheming at court. [Burke, 1, 131.]

Chicane. Artifice to hide the truth.

Circumvention. Taking advantage of others' weakness in dealing with them.

Concealment, etc. Act of keeping unknown. See ENLIGHTEN-MENT-SECRECY.

Craft. } Skill employed to effect purposes by deceit or shrewd
Craftiness. } devices. See *Adjectives*.

Cunning. } Act of using stratagem to accomplish a purpose.
Cunningness. }

Device. Scheme.

Diplomacy. Dexterity or skill in securing advantages.

Dodge. A low trick.

Duplicity, etc. The habit of pretending to act from motives different from the real motives, etc. See TRUTHFULNESS-FALSEHOOD.

Espièglerie [F.]. Playful trick.

Evasion. The practise of avoiding something in a tricky way.

Finesse. Acute and unscrupulous artifice.

Foul play. Unfair means.

Go by. Artifice.

Guile. Disposition to defraud.

Jobbery. Low political intriguing.

Juggle. } Deception.
Jugglery. }

Knavery. The practise of fraud and artifice.

Machiavelism. Craftiness in statesmanship.

Machination, etc. Wicked plotting against the life and interests of another, etc. See DESIGN.

Maneuver, etc. Skilful management without the intention of de-ceiving, etc. See *Verbs*.

Maneuvering, etc. See *Verbs*.

Plot, etc. Union of men for purposes of mischief, etc. See DESIGN.

Abandon [F.]. Absence of conventionality.

Artlessness, etc. Freedom from artful practises, etc. See *Adjec-tives*.

Bonhomie [F.]. Pleasantness of manner.

Candor. Fairness of mind towards ourselves and others.

Épanchement [F.]. Effusion.

Honesty, etc. Straightforwardness of speech and conduct, etc. See UPRIGHTNESS.

Innocence, etc. The quality of not injuring, etc. See INNOCENCE.

Naïveté [F.]. Frankness of manner.

Nature. Quality or disposition of the mind.

Plain speaking. Openness of speech or dealings.

Simplicity. Freedom from cunning.

Sincerity. The quality of speaking only what we think.

Singleness of heart. } Freedom from duplicity.
Singleness of purpose. }

ARTLESSNESS—*Denotations.*

Enfant terrible [F.]. A child that asks ill-timed questions.

Le palais de vérité [F.]. The palace of truth.

Rough diamond. A rude but worthy person.

ARTLESSNESS—*Verbs.*

Be artless, etc. (see *Adjectives*); **be free with one,** to speak frankly to; **call a spade a spade,** to talk in unmistakable words; **look one in the face,** to act as if telling the truth; **speak one's mind; speak out; think aloud,** to tell everything one thinks; **wear one's heart upon his sleeves for the daws to peck at,** to be too frank.

ARTLESSNESS—*Adjectives.*

Arcadian. Simple, like the Arcadians.

Artless. Not given to the practise of artifices.

Blunt. Purposely rough in speech or conduct.

Candid. Characterized by candor.

Direct. Not ambiguous.

Downright. Undisguised.

CRAFT—ARTLESSNESS—*Continued.*

Ruse.   Petty artifice.
Ruse de guerre [F.].   Stratagem in war.
Shift.   An irregular but only temporary invasion.
Sideblow.   An unexpected or concealed blow.
Stratagem.   A plot or plan so disguised as to cause another to misjudge.
Subterfuge.   A tricky means of escaping from something.
Subtlety.   Craft added to an ability to analyze and use the advantageous.
Temporization.   Forbearance to act for fear of losing.
Thin edge of the wedge.   Small beginning which will have a great ending.
Tour de force [F].   A feat of strength.
Trick.   Deception of the senses for personal gain or for inconvenience of others.
Trickery, etc.   See TRUTHFULNESS-FRAUD.
Tricks of the trade.   Deception of business.
Tricks upon travelers.   Deception played on strangers.
White lie.   A lie which causes no injury.   See FALSEHOOD-FABRICATION.
Wile.   Guile.

CRAFT—*Figurative Terms.*

Net.   Complicated scheming.
Trap, etc.   Scheme for taking advantage of another, etc.   See TRUTHFULNESS-FRAUD.

CRAFT—*Denotations.*

Politics.   Political wire-pulling; trickery.
Sleuth.   Track of anything followed by the scent.

CRAFT—*Cunning Persons.*

Fox.   A sly animal; hence, figuratively, a crafty person.
Intrigant [F.].   One who intrigues.
Jew.   One of the Hebrew race, noted for craftiness in business; hence, any crafty person.
Machiavel.   An Italian author who advocated unscrupulous principles in a work, *Del Principe;* hence, any double-dealing person.
Reynard.   A fox; hence, a crafty person.
Scotchman.   A native of Scotland, noted for shrewdness; hence, a shrewd person.
Sly boots.   A roguish, sly person.
Ulysses.   A crafty Greek in the Trojan war; hence, a crafty person.
Yankee.   A native of New England, noted for his shrewdness; hence, anyone displaying this quality of the Yankee.
Yorkshireman.   An inhabitant of Yorkshire, noted for cunning; hence, any shrewd person.

CRAFT—*Verbs.*

Circumvent.   To take advantage of another's weakness or inexperience, etc., in dealing with him.
Contrive, etc.   To find a means to an end, etc.   See DESIGN.
Double.   To deal falsely.
Finesse.   To practise finesse.
Flatter.   To give excessive praise to.
Intrigue.   To plot or scheme.
Maneuver.   To plan or manage skilfully without trying to deceive.
Overreach, etc   To cheat, etc.   See TRUTHFULNESS-FRAUD.
Surprise, etc.   To lead one into something unawares, etc.   See EXPECTATION-SURPRISE.
Temporize.   To refrain from acting for fear of losing.
Undermine.   To ruin in an unfair way.
Waylay.   To lie in wait for.

CRAFT—*Verbal Expressions.*

Ambiguas in vulgum spargere voces [L.], to give doubtful reports to the people; **be cunning,** etc. (see *Adjectives*); **diamond cut diamond,** to contend with an equal; **have cut one's eyeteeth,** to have become knowing or crafty; **introduce the thin end of the wedge,** to make a beginning which shall lead to something greater; **live by one's wits,** to be without regular employment; **make things pleasant; play a deep game,** to deal very craftily; **play tricks with;** *reculer pour mieux sauter* [F.], to go back to take a better leap; **snatch a verdict,** to get a verdict by resorting to any available means; **steal a march upon,** to take an advantage unobserved; **stoop to conquer,** to condescend in order to make some gain; **throw off one's guard,** to cause to lose one's watchfulness.

CRAFT—*Adjectives.*

Acute.   Quick to see and understand.
Arch.   Roguish.
Artful.   Full of art.

ARTLESSNESS—ADJECTIVES—*Continued.*

Frank.   Free from restraint in expressing thoughts and feelings.
Guileless.   Free from guile.
Honest, etc.   Not exhibiting any deceit, etc.   See UPRIGHTNESS
Inartificial.   Natural.
Ingénu [F.].   Artless.
Ingenuous.   Not acting or speaking in disguise.
Innocent, etc.   Simple, etc.   See INNOCENCE.
Naive.   Frank.
Native.   Simple; sincere.
Natural.   Without affectation.
Open.   Not reserved.
Plain.   Free from anything which will hide the nature or meaning of anything.
Pure.   Perfect in moral cleanliness.
Simple.   Acting as without a knowledge of the world.
Sincere.   Marked by sincerity.
Straightforward.   Honest.
Unaffected.   Not affected.
Undesigning.   Not designing.
Unflattering.   Not flattering.
Unpoetical.   Plain.
Unreserved.   Frank.
Unsophisticated.   Simple.
Untutored.   Uneducated.

ARTLESSNESS—*Adjective Expressions.*

Above-board, open; **frank-hearted, free-spoken; matter-of-fact,** adhering to facts; **open as day; open-hearted; outspoken; plain-spoken; simple-hearted; simple-minded; single-hearted; single-minded.**

ARTLESSNESS—*Adverbs.*

In plain English; in plain words; not to mince the matter, etc. (see ASSERTION); **without mincing the matter,** to use plain language.

ARTLESSNESS—*Phrases.*

Davus sum non Œdipus [L.].   I am Davus, not Œdipus; plain man, not a guesser of Sphinx's riddles.   [Terence, *Andria*, I, ii, 23.]
Liberavi animam meam [L.].   I have freed my soul.

CRAFT—ADJECTIVES—*Continued.*

Artificial.   Affected; unnatural.
Astute.   Characterized by acuteness and finesse.
Canny.   Cautious.
Contriving.   Planning.
Crafty.   Displaying craft.
Crooked.   Deceitful and dishonest.
Cunning.   Possessing cunning.
Deceitful, etc.   Full of deceit, etc.   See TRUTHFULNESS-FRAUD.
Deep.   Not easily seen into.
Designing.   Laying artful plans for the future.
Diplomatic.   Marked by diplomacy.
Feline.   Sly like a cat.
Insidious.   Practising underhandedness while appearing friendly.
Intriguing, etc.   Practising intrigue, etc.   See *Verbs*.
Knowing.   Possessing more knowledge of some kinds than is desirable.
Leery.   Shrewd and sly.
Machiavelian.   Practising the principles of Machiavel.
Pawky.   Arch.
Politic.   Self-seeking.
Profound.   Deep.
Sharp.   Quickness to perceive.
Shrewd.   Slightly acute.
Skilful, etc.   Using skill, etc.   See SKILL.
Sly.   Observing and acting in a furtive manner.
Stealthy.   Sly.
Strategic.   Marked by stratagem.
Subdolous.   Somewhat crafty.
Subtle.   Exhibiting subtlety.
Tactical.   Strategic.
Tricksy. } Given to playing tricks.
Tricky. }
Underhand, etc.   Private, secret, etc.   See ENLIGHTENMENT. SECRECY.
Vulpine.   Foxlike.
Wily.   Showing guile.

CRAFT—*Continued.*

CRAFT—*Adjective Expressions.*

Cunning as a fox, cunning as a serpent, extremely cunning; deep laid; not to be caught with chaff, not to be easily deceived; sharp as a needle; time-serving, seeking personal advancement by sacrificing good moral principles; too clever by half; up to snuff, not imposed upon.

CRAFT—*Adverbs.*

Cunningly, etc. In a cunning manner, etc. See *Adjectives.*
By a side wind, indirectly; on the sly, slyly.

Slyly. In a sly manner.

CRAFT—*Phrases.*

À bis ou à blanc [F.]. In one way or another.

Fin contre fin [F.]. Cunning matched against cunning.

craft'-i-ness. Cunning. CRAFT-ARTLESSNESS, SKILL-UNSKILFULNESS.
crafts'-man. A member of a craft. AGENT.
craft'-y. Cunning. CRAFT-ARTLESSNESS.
crag. A rough, steep, or broken rock rising or jutting out prominently. HARDNESS-SOFTNESS, OCEAN-LAND, SHARPNESS-BLUNTNESS.
crag'-gy. Full of crags. ROUGHNESS-SMOOTHNESS, SHARPNESS-BLUNTNESS.
craig. A crag. HEIGHT-LOWNESS.
crake. A boast. BRAGGING.
cram. To crowd; to force into the mind; to eat with greediness. APERTURE-CLOSURE, EDUCATION-LEARNING, EDUCATION-MISTEACHING, ENLARGEMENT-DIMINUTION, FASTING-GLUTTONY, GATHERING-SCATTERING; cram down the throat, COERCION, FAITH-MISGIVING.
crambe repetita [L.] (cram'-bĭ rep-e-tai'-ta). Warmed over; an old story. DESIRE-REPLETION, ENTERTAINMENT-WEARINESS.
crammed. Stuffed. ENTIRETY-DEFICIENCY; crammed to overflowing, EXCESS-LACK.
cram'-mer. A lie. TRUTHFULNESS-FABRICATION.
cramp. To hold tightly; to restrain; an involuntary, painful, muscular contraction. CONNECTIVE, ENLARGEMENT-DIMINUTION, GREATNESS-LITTLENESS, MIGHT-IMPOTENCE, OBSTRUCTION-HELP, SENSUALITY-SUFFERING, STRENGTH-WEAKNESS.
cramped. Inelegant; crude. PURITY-CRUDENESS.
cran. A quantity equal to the contents of a barrel. CONTENTS-RECEIVER.

cranch. To crush or grind audibly. FRIABILITY, NUTRIMENT-EXCRETION, UNION-DISUNION.
crane. A hoisting-machine. ANGULARITY, ELEVATION-DEPRESSION; crane neck, CURVATION-RECTILINEARITY.
cra''-ni-ol'-o-gy. The science that treats of the characteristics of skulls. MIND-IMBECILITY.
cra''-ni-os'-co-py. Study of the form of the skull. MIND-IMBECILITY.
cra'-ni-um. The brain-box. MIND-IMBECILITY.
crank. A device for causing rotation of an axis; one who lacks mental balance. INSTRUMENT, RECOMPENSE-SCOURGE, WITTINESS-DULNESS.
cran'-kle. To crinkle. PLICATURE.
crank'-ling. Crinkled. SMOOTHNESS-ROUGHNESS.
cranks, quips and gibes. Jokes. WITTINESS-DULNESS.
crank'-y. Mentally unbalanced. HEALTH-SICKNESS, STRENGTH-WEAKNESS.
cran'-ny. A small, narrow opening. INTERSPACE-CONTACT.
crape. A thin gauze-like material. CIRCLE-WINDING, JUBILATION-LAMENTATION.
crap'-u-len-cy. Surfeit. FASTING-GLUTTONY, MODERATION-SELFINDULGENCE, TEETOTALISM-INTEMPERANCE.
crap'-u-lent. Drunken. FASTING-GLUTTONY.
crap'-u-lous. Drunken. CLEANNESS-FILTHINESS, MODERATION-SELFINDULGENCE, TEETOTALISM-INTEMPERANCE.
crash. To dash in pieces noisily. CRASH-DRUMMING, CREATION-DESTRUCTION, IMPETUS-REACTION.

CRASH—DRUMMING.

Burst. A sudden explosion.
Crepitation. Succession of quick sharp sounds.
Decrepitation. A crackling noise caused by heating.
Detonation. Explosion of gases.
Discharge. A firing, as of a gun.
Explosion. A bursting with violence and loud noise.
Firing. The discharge of firearms.
Rapping, etc. See *Verbs.*
Report. An explosive sound.
Salvo. Simultaneous discharge of artillery.
Snap, etc. See *Verbs.*
Thud. A dull heavy sound.
Volley. Simultaneous discharge of firearms.

CRASH—*Nouns of Agency.*

Cracker. Anything that cracks, as a Chinese fire-cracker.
Gun. A metal tube for firing projectiles by the force of powder.
Pop-gun. A toy gun in which the discharge is caused by compressed air.
Squib. A roll or case filled with powder, as for blasting.

CRASH—*Verbs.*

Bang. To hit roughly; to make a loud noise.
Brustle. To crackle; rustle.
Burst on the ear. Suddenly be heard.
Clap. Strike the hands together.
Clash. To collide with a loud noise.
Click. To produce or cause to make a short, sharp sound.

Charivari [F.]. An uproar.
Clutter. A confused chattering.
Cuckoo. An imitative sound.
Devil's tattoo. A drumming with the hands or feet.
Ding-dong. The peal of a bell.
Drumming, etc. See *Verbs.*
Peal of bells. A loud musical sounding of bells.
Pitapat. A succession of light taps or like sounds.
Quaver. A tremulous unsteady sound.
Racket. A clattering confused prolonged noise.
Rat-a-tat. Sound of repeated knocking or beating.
Repetition, etc. The rapid repercussion of a chord or tone. See RECURRENCE.
Reverberation, etc. A prolonged resounding or echo, etc. See RESONANCE.
Roll, etc. See *Verbs.*
Rubadub. The sound of a drum when beaten.
Tantara. Quick succession of notes upon a horn.
Tattoo. A continuous beating or drumming.
Whir. A trilling sound without musical quality.

DRUMMING—*Verbs.*

Beat. To strike repeatedly.
Chime. To ring in harmony.
Clack. To make a clapping, rattling noise.
Clatter. To make short repeated sounds.
Din in the ear. To disturb with a noise.
Drum. To beat repeatedly on or as on a drum; to beat a drum.
Drum in the ear. Sound persistently.
Hum. To make a low murmuring sound; to sing softly with lips closed

CRASH—DRUMMING—*Continued.*

CRASH—Verbs—*Continued.*

Crack.   To produce a forceful quick sound.
Crackle.   To crack slightly and repeatedly.
Crash.   To dash or fall in pieces with a violent broken sound.
Knock.   Hit with something hard; to strike a blow.
Pop.   'To give or cause to give forth a short explosive noise, to utter suddenly; as when one pops corn, or pops the question.
Rap.   To strike a short sharp blow upon; to knock.
Slam.   To strike or shut with violence.
Snap.   To make or cause to make a sharp quick sound, as by breaking.
Tap.   To hit lightly.

CRASH—*Adjectives.*

Rapping, etc.   See *Verbs.*

cra'-sis.   The mixture of the constituents of a fluid; the combination of two vowels; temperament.   COMPOSITION-RESOLUTION, INCLUSION-OMISSION, SUBJECTIVENESS-OBJECTIVENESS.
crass.   Dense.   MAGNITUDE-SMALLNESS; **crass ignorance,** KNOWLEDGE-IGNORANCE.
crass'-i-tude.   Grossness.   BREADTH-NARROWNESS, VISCIDITY-FOAM.
crate.   A large hamper of wickerwork or a protective framework.   CONTENTS-RECEIVER, CONVEYANCE-VESSEL.
cra'-ter.   The bowl-shaped vent of a volcano or hot-spring.   CONVEXITY-CONCAVITY, DEEPNESS-SHALLOWNESS.
craunch.   To crush audibly.   FRIABILITY, NUTRIMENT-EXCRETION, UNION-DISUNION.
cra-vat'.   A neckcloth.   DRESS-UNDRESS.
crave.   To importune.   DESIRE-DISTASTE, PETITION-EXPOSTULATION.
cra'-ven.   A base coward.   BRAVERY-COWARDICE, YIELDING.
cra'-ving.   Appetite.   DESIRE-DISTASTE.
craw.   The crop of a bird.   CONTENTS-RECEIVER.
crawl.   To creep; to insinuate oneself.   PRESUMPTION-OBSEQUIOUSNESS, SWIFTNESS-SLOWNESS.
cray'-ons.   Drawings executed with crayon.   PAINTING.

DRUMMING—Verbs—*Continued.*

Patter.   To make a succession of light quick sounds.
Peal.   To ring out in a loud prolonged tone.
Rattle.   To make a rapid succession of hard, sharp sounds.
Roll.   To give forth a deep, reverberating sound.
Rumble.   To make a low, heavy, rolling sound.
Shake.   To rattle.
Tick.   To make a light clicking sound.
Toll.   To ring with slow measured sounds.
Trill.   To give forth a tremulous vibrating sound.

DRUMMING—*Adjectives.*

Like a bee in a bottle.   Buzzing.
Monotonous, etc.   Repeated until tiresome, etc.   See RECURRENCE.
Rolling, etc.   See *Verbs.*

craze.   To make mad.   SANENESS-LUNACY
crazed.   Maddened.   SANENESS-LUNACY.
cra'-zy.   Insane.   SANENESS-LUNACY, STRENGTH-WEAKNESS.
creach'-y.   Liable to fall.   STRENGTH-WEAKNESS.
creak.   A sharp, squeaking sound.   CACOPHONY.
cream.   The light-yellow substance that gathers on milk; the best part of anything.   CONSEQUENCE-INSIGNIFICANCE, GOODNESS-BADNESS, PULPINESS-OIL, VISCIDITY-FOAM; **cream color,** WHITENESS-BLACKNESS, YELLOWNESS-PURPLE; **cream of the jest,** WITTINESS-DULNESS.
cream'-y.   Resembling or containing cream.   VISCIDITY-FOAM, WHITENESS-BLACKNESS, YELLOWNESS-PURPLE.
crease.   The mark of a wrinkle, fold, etc.   PLICATURE.
cre-ate'.   To cause to come into existence; to originate.   CAUSE-EFFECT, CREATION-DESTRUCTION, DIVINITY, FANCY.
cre-a'-ted.   Produced.   NATURE-ART.
cre-a'-ted be'-ing.   A living being regarded as created.   FAUNA-FLORA.
cre-a'-tion.   The act of God in bringing the universe into existence; production.   CAUSE-EFFECT, CREATION-DESTRUCTION, DIVINITY, NATURE-ART, UNIVERSE; **creation of beauty,** NATURE-ART.

CREATION—DESTRUCTION.

Achievement.   The act of successfully performing.
Architecture.   Construction in general; specifically, the art of building houses, churches, etc.
Authorship.   The act of being an author; origination.
Birth.   The act of being born; beginning.
Bringing forth, etc.   A production, etc.   See *Verbs.*
Building.   The act of erecting or establishing.
Childbirth.   Act of bringing forth a child.
Coinage.   The making of coins; a fabrication.
Construction.   The art of putting together materials with some end in view.
Creation.   A producing out of nothing or out of existing materials.
Delivery.   Act of giving birth to.
Development.   Growth or production.
Eccaleobion.   Machine for hatching eggs artificially.
Edification.   The act of edifying; a building up, as in religion, etc.
Erection.   A setting up and fixing in a given place.
Establishment.   Act of establishing, of fixing permanently.
Fabrication.   The art of building or fashioning in any way; also, a falsehood.
Fecundation.   The act of making fertile or productive.
Flowering.   Act of bringing forth flowers.
Formation.   Process of making or combining materials.
Fructification.   A making of fruit; a bringing to completion.
Generation.   The act of begetting or producing.
Genesis.   A birth.
Geniture.   Generation; creation.
Gestation.   Act of bearing offspring.   See PREPARATION.
Growth.   Production.
Impregnation.   Act of making pregnant.

Abolition.   The act of putting away, of putting an end to, **as of** institutions, customs, and conditions.   See COMMISSION-ABROGATION.
Annihilation.   Complete destruction, reduction to nothing.
Bouleversement [F.].   An overturn.
Break down.   A disabling by falling.
Breaking up.   } A dissolving; a scattering.
Break up.   }
Commencement de la fin [F.].   Beginning of the end.
Consumption.   Gradual destruction or waste.
Crash.   A ruin; a failure as of a commercial firm.
Débâcle [F.].   A breaking up.
Délabrement [F.].   An overthrow.
Demolishment.   The act of demolishing or destroying by **tearing** down.
Demolition.   The act or result of destroying by pulling down.
Desolation.   The state of being desolate, or deprived of inhabitants.
Destroying, etc.   See *Verbs.*
Destruction.   A bringing into ruin; a demolition
Destruction of life, etc.   See LIFE-KILLING.
Devastation.   Act of devastating; of laying waste by any means.
Dilapidation, etc.   State of being dilapidated; of falling into partial ruin through neglect or misuse, etc., as of stones falling away in a large wall.   See BETTERMENT-DETERIORATION.
Diruption.   A disruption.
Disorganization.   The act of disorganizing; destruction of the organic union of parts.
Disruption.   The act of bursting asunder; a breaking up into pieces.
Dissolution.   A breaking up; a melting; disintegration.
Doom.   Death or destruction.

CREATION—DESTRUCTION—*Continued.*

Incubation. Hatching.
Manufacture. A making by hand or machinery.
Organization. The act of bringing together in systematic connections for working purposes.
Parturition. Act of giving birth to.
Performance. The act of bringing to completion.
Procreation. Production by generation.
Production. The act of obtaining a result from a given work; of bringing into existence.
Progeneration. The act of begetting.
Propagation. The act of propagating; of causing to continue or multiply.
Publication. Bringing into public existence.
Putting together, etc. See *Verbs.*
Workmanship. The quality of work in respect to execution.

CREATION—*Associated Nouns.*

Birth throe. The pains attendant upon childbirth.
Confinement. Accouchement.
Labor. The pains of childbirth.
Midwifery. The practise of assisting at childbirth.
Nisus formativus [L.]. The formative labor.
Travail. The pains of childbirth.

CREATION—*Scientific Terms.*

Abiogenesis. Genesis of living matter without intervention of living organism.
Archebiosis. Origination of living matter from non-living.
Archegenesis. Spontaneous generation.
Biogenesis. Production of life from life.
Epigenesis. The theory of generation which holds that the germ is created entirely new; view opposed to evolution.
Evolution. The process of growth.
Homogenesis. The method of reproduction by which successive generations are alike and run through the same cycles.
Obstetrics. That branch of medicine which has to do with childbirth and the care of the mother.
Spontaneous generation. The theory that living matter is produced from non-living.
Xenogenesis. The production of one organism from another organism.

CREATION—*Nouns of Result.*

Building. That which is built.
Edifice. A structure distinguished for dignity and importance.
Fabric. Something that has been constructed or put together.
Flower. The blossom or bloom of a plant.
Fruit. The matured seed-vessel of a plant.
Pile. A massive building or group of buildings.
Publication. That whiah is published.
Structure. That which is built or constructed.
Tower. A building very high in proportion to its depth and width.

CREATION—*Verbs.*

Accomplish, etc. To bring to an issue by perseverance or skill, etc. See COMPLETION.
Achieve. To perform something worthy or honorable.
Acquire, etc. To get in one's possession by skill or purchase, etc. See GAIN.
Bear. To give birth to; to produce.
Bear fruit. Produce.
Be brought to bed. To give birth to a child.
Beget. To produce; to generate.
Breed. To produce young; to bring up.
Bring forth; bring into being; bring into existence; bring up.
Build. To construct, as a building; to put together by any process.
Call into being, call into existence. Create.
Carve. To accomplish or produce, as by cutting or carving.
Cause, etc. To be the cause of; to produce, etc. See CAUSE.
Chisel. To accomplish or achieve, as by carving or chiseling.
Coin. To make into coins; to fabricate.
Compose. To produce by putting together.
Constitute. To make up the substance of.
Construct. To bring together and put up as an edifice.
Contrive. To plan ingeniously; to design.
Create. To make come into existence either out of nothing or existing materials.
Develop. To cause to increase in power, strength, etc.
Do. Perform; make.
Drop. To bring forth; to give birth to, as young.
Ean. To bring forth young.
Edify. To build up as in morals, etc.
Engender. To cause to be in existence.

CREATION—DESTRUCTION

Downfall. The state of having fallen, or of being ruined.
Extinction. Act of extinguishing; a complete destruction.
Extirpation, etc. A destruction by taking up by the roots, etc. See INJECTION-EJECTION.
Fall. Destruction.
Havoc. A wild, general destruction; a carnage.
Incendiarism. An act of destruction by maliciously setting on fire.
Overthrow. The act of overthrowing; of throwing down into ruin.
Perdition. Utter destruction; in theology, utter loss of the soul in a future state.
Prostration. The act of prostrating; of causing to fall flat; an overthrow.
Ravage. A violent destruction by pillage or other destructive means; the results of such action.
Ruin. Any change that destroys or renders a thing useless; a destruction.
Sacrifice. Destruction or giving up for the good of something else.
Shipwreck. A destruction of a ship; the destruction of a thing so as to render it practically useless.
Smash. Act of smashing; of breaking up into pieces; a falling into pieces.
Subversion. A turning over; an overthrow.
Suppression. Act of putting down by force; a crushing.
Washout. Excavation made by rain and swollen streams.
Waste. Wanton destruction.
Wrack. State of being wrecked; destruction.
Wreck. The act of wrecking; the ruin of anything.

DESTRUCTION—*Nouns of Means.*

Cataclysm. A flood.
Crack of doom. The sound of the Judgment Day.
Razzia. A destructive raid.
Revolution. An overturning.
Road to ruin. A beginning of destruction by any means.

DESTRUCTION—*Verbs.*

Annihilate. To destroy completely; said of races or numbers of animals.
Annul, etc. To render void or null, etc. See COMMISSION-ABROGATION.
Batter. To beat with many blows; to deface.
Be all over with.
Be all up with. } To be in a ruined condition; to be at an end.
Beat down. Demolish.
Be destroyed. Be ruined.
Blast. To destroy as by an explosion; to destroy or shrivel as by wind; to bring to ruin in respect to reputation.
Blot out. To destroy by covering with spots; to obliterate.
Blow down. To throw down by a current of wind.
Blow up. To destroy by blowing up with an explosive.
Break down. To disable or be disabled.
Break up. To dissolve; to disperse.
Cast to the dogs. To let go to ruin.
Confound. To throw the mind into confusion; to perplex.
Consume. To destroy slowly, as by fire, eating, rust, etc.
Crash. To break into pieces with noise.
Crumble. To make into small pieces; disintegrate.
Crumble to dust; crumble utterly.
Crumple up. To wrinkle up.
Crush to pieces; crush to stones; crush under foot.
Cut down.
Cut short. } To be destroyed or killed.
Cut to pieces. Destroy.
Deal destruction. To ravage.
Demolish. To destroy by tearing down.
Desolate. To deprive of inhabitants; to make sorrowful.
Destroy. To lay waste; to bring to ruin.
Devastate. To desolate or destroy, as by war, famine, etc.
Devour. To eat with greediness; to lay waste.
Dish. To use up badly; to ruin.
Dismantle, etc. To ruin by stripping of defenses, etc. See USEFULNESS-USELESSNESS.
Disorganize. To destroy the organization f
Dispel. To scatter in many directions.
Dissipate. To scatter away; to waste.
Dissolve. To make liquid; to decompose; to make weak.
Do away with. To abolish.
Do for. To kill; to hurt fatally.
Engulf. To swallow up, as in a gulf.
Eradicate, etc. To destroy by tearing out by the roots; to cut out entirely, etc. See INJECTION-EJECTION.

CREATION—DESTRUCTION—*Continued.*

CREATION—Verbs—*Continued.*

Erect. To set up, as a building.
Establish. To fix firmly; to set up and secure firmly.
Evolve. To open; to develop.
Fabricate. To construct by art; to invent.
Farrow. To bring forth young; said of swine.
Fecundate. To make fruitful, as in children.
Flower. To produce flowers; to bloom.
Forge. To make or shape by hammering; to alter with fraudulent intentions.
Form. To take existing materials and give shape to; to put in a particular shape.
Frame. To put together for some specific end.
Fructify. To make fruitful.
Gar. To cause
Generate. To cause to be, to bring into being.
Get. To gain possession of; to come to be.
Give birth to. Bring forth in birth.
Hatch. To produce young from eggs by incubation.
Impregnate. To make pregnant or prolific.
Incubate. To hatch eggs by heating.
Induce. To produce by a course of reasoning.
Institute. To set up and put in operation.
Kindle. To light a fire; to arouse, to produce an effect.
Kitten. To bring forth, as kittens.
Lay. To construct by arranging in order, as bricks, etc.
Lie in. To be in childbirth.
Make. To cause in all its various senses.
Make productive, etc. See Fertility.
Manufacture. To make by hand or machinery.
Operate. To accomplish; to conduct or manage affairs.
Organize. To bring the parts into connection and working harmony; to establish with cooperative parts.
Perform. To carry out; to execute completely.
Procreate. To produce by generation.
Produce. To bring into existence, as by nature; to manufacture.
Progenerate. To beget.
Propagate. To multiply, as by natural generation.
Pullulate. To germinate; to bud.
Pup. To bring forth young; said of a female dog.
Put together. Compose; construct.
Raise. To put up in a place; to cause to grow; to breed.
Rear. To bring up as children; to build up.
Run up. To put up rapidly and hurriedly, as a building; to put in a prominent place, as a flag.
Set up. Put up.
Superinduce. To induce in addition.
Suscitate. To call into life or activity.
Teem. To produce, as offspring.
Usher into the world. To bring into existence.
Weave. To make by weaving; to construct with elaboration.
Yean. To bring forth young, as a sheep.

CREATION—*Adjectives.*

Big with. Pregnant.
Brought to bed with. Confined to bed with childbirth.
Creative. Having the power to create or produce.
Enascent. Being born.
Enceinte [F.]. Pregnant, big with child.
Formative. Having power to form, or shape.
Fraught with. Laden or charged with.
Genetic. Pertaining to creation or generation.
Genetical. Variant of genetic.
Genital. Pertaining to the reproductive organs of animals.
In the family way. Soon to give birth to a child.
In the straw. In childbed.
Parturient. Bringing forth young.
Pregnant. Big with child; fruitful.
Produced, etc. } See *Verbs.*
Producing, etc. }
Productive of. Having the power of producing.
Prolific, etc. Producing abundantly, etc. See Fertility.
Puerperal. Pertaining to childbirth.
Puerperous. Bearing children.
Teeming. Prolific; produced in abundance.

CREATION—*Phrases.*

Ex nihilo nihil fit [L.]. Out of nothing, nothing is made.
Fiat lux [L.]. Let there be light. [Bible. Genesis i, 3.].
Materiam superabat opus [L.]. The workmanship was better than the material. [Ovid, *Metamorphoses*, ii, 5.].

DESTRUCTION—Verbs—*Continued.*

Erase. To remove by rubbing or scraping.
Expunge. To wipe out completely.
Exterminate. To destroy absolutely; said of men or animals, **not** of individuals.
Extinguish. To put out of existence; to quench.
Fall; fall to pieces; fall to the ground.
Fell. To cause to fall; to cut down.
Fling to the winds. To scatter carelessly.
Go all to smash. Be utterly ruined.
Go by the board. To go to utter ruin.
Go to shivers. To fall to pieces.
Go to smash. Be ruined.
Go to the pot. To become worthless.
Go to the wall. To become bankrupt.
Go to wrack and ruin. Go utterly to destruction.
Gut. To take out; to remove, as guts or intestines.
Knock down; knock over; knock to atoms.
Lay in ashes. To destroy by fire.
Lay in ruins; lay in the dust; lay waste.
Level with the ground. To raze; to demolish.
Make a clean sweep of. To sweep away entirely; to remove encumbrances.
Make mince-meat of. Utterly destroy.
Make short work of. To injure; to ruin.
Make way with. To remove; to kill.
Mine. To undermine with intent of ruining.
Mow down. To cut down, as grass.
Nip. To cut the surface of; to bite.
Nullify. To make null and void.
Overthrow. To throw over; subvert.
Overturn. To upset; to bring to falling.
Overwhelm. To submerge or crush with a sudden onset, as of water.
Perish. To be destroyed.
Pick to pieces. To tear apart; to destroy.
Prostrate. To bring on one's back; to overthrow.
Pull down. To demolish.
Pull to pieces. To damage; to destroy.
Put an end to. To terminate.
Put down. To overcome by force; to crush.
Put out. To extinguish.
Quash. To make void or null; to put down forcibly.
Quell. To make yield by force; to subdue.
Quench. To extinguish, as fire with water.
Ravage. To lay waste by any means.
Ravage with fire and sword.
Raze. To demolish; to level to the ground.
Ruin. To subject to ruin; to change so as to make without value or service.
Sacrifice. To yield to another person or thing; to incur loss or suffering.
Sap. To withdraw gradually; to weaken.
Sap the strength of. To undermine slowly.
Scatter to the winds. To disperse utterly.
Scuttle. To sink a ship by putting holes in the bottom.
Seal the doom of. To consign to death.
Shake to pieces. To pull apart; to destroy.
Shatter. To break into pieces; to smash.
Shipwreck. To wreck a ship; to bring ruin to.
Shiver. To break suddenly into pieces.
Sink. To submerge; to bring to ruin; to waste.
Smash. To break in pieces suddenly.
Snuff out. To pinch the end of a candle; to put out, as a candle.
Spring a mine. To explode a mine or blast.
Squash. To beat into a pulp; to ruin.
Squelch. To put an end to; to defeat.
Stamp out. To crush or put down.
Strike at the root of. Destroy from the foundations.
Strike out. To run a pencil through; to expunge.
Submerge. To sink under water.
Subvert. To overturn; to destroy utterly.
Suppress. To put down by force; to crush.
Swallow up. To make disappear; to ruin.
Swamp. To founder as a boat; to be brought low by difficulties.
Sweep away. To destroy quickly.
Take off. To kill.
Tear to pieces; tear to rags; tear to tatters; tear up; tear up root and branch; throw over; throw overboard.
Topple. To fall from its own weight.
Totter to its fall. To waver till it falls.

DESTRUCTION—Verbs—*Continued.*

Trample in the dust.
Trample out. } To tread heavily on, to crush.
Trample under foot.
Tread under foot. Trample on.

Tumble. To throw about; to throw into confusion
Undo. To fail to do; to ruin, as in morals, etc.
Upset. To overturn or overset.
Wreck. To cause or have a shipwreck; to ruin in any way.

DESTRUCTION—*Adjectives.*

Deadly, etc. Causing death; sure to destroy, etc. See LIFE-KILLING.
Deletory. Blotting out.
Destroyed, etc. } See *Verbs.*
Destroying, etc.
Destructive. Causing destruction fitted to destroy.
Extinct. Being at an end; quenched.
Incendiary. Destroying by maliciously setting fire to.

In course of destruction, etc. See *Nouns.*
Nodding to its fall. Tottering.
Perishing, etc. See *Verbs.*
Ruinous. Tending to ruin; gone to decay.
Subversive. Tending to subvert or overturn.
Suicidal. Pertaining to suicide, destroying one's own interests.
Tottering to its fall. } About to fall.
Trembling to its fall.

DESTRUCTION—*Adverbs.*

With a sledge hammer, with crushing effect.

DESTRUCTION—*Phrases.*

Delenda est Carthago [L.] Carthage must be destroyed. [Cato the elder so closed every speech he made in the Roman Senate.]

Dum Roma deliberat, Saguntum perit [L.]. While Rome deliberates, Saguntum perishes.
Ecrasez l'infâme [F.]. Crush the wretch. [Voltaire, often.]

cre-a′-tive. Constructive. CREATION-DESTRUCTION, FANCY.
Cre-a′-tor. God, as Maker of the universe. DIVINITY.
crea′-ture. That which has been created; a dependent. CAUSE-EFFECT, CHIEF-UNDERLING, FAUNA-FLORA, HUMANITY, SUBSTANCE-NULLITY; **creature comforts,** NUTRIMENT-EXCRETION, SENSUALITY-SUFFERING.
crèche [F.] (crêsh). A day-nursery. SCHOOL.
credat Judæus Apella [L.] (crî′-dat jiu-dî′-us ap-pel′-la). Let Apella the Jew [Horace] believe it. ADAGE-NONSENSE, FAITH-MISGIVING.
cre′-dence. Belief. FAITH-MISGIVING, FANE.

cre-den′-da. Things to be believed. FAITH-MISGIVING.
cre-den′-tial. That which certifies one's authority or claim to confidence. EVIDENCE-COUNTEREVIDENCE.
cre-den′-tials. Certificate. SIGN.
cred″-i-bil′-i-ty. Worthiness of belief. FAITH-MISGIVING, LIKELIHOOD-UNLIKELIHOOD.
cred′-i-ble. Believable. FAITH-MISGIVING, LIKELIHOOD-UNLIKELIHOOD, POSSIBILITY-IMPOSSIBILITY.
cred′-it. Trust; belief; interest; a balance in one's favor. ACCOUNTS, APPROVAL-DISAPPROVAL, CREDIT-DEBT, FAITH-MISGIVING, LABOR-CAPITAL, PROPERTY, REPUTATION-DISCREDIT, RULE-LICENSE, VIRTUE-VICE; **to one's credit,** PROPERTY.

CREDIT—DEBT.

Account A list of debits and credits between two persons.
Acquit [F.] Discharge from debt.
Bond. A written agreement pledging assets.
Circular note. A note for public circulation.
Credit. Transference of property on promise of future payment.
Debenture, An instrument in the nature of a bond.
Duplicate. A paper having the force of an original.
Floating credit. Credit due at various times.
Letter of credit. A paper authorizing the bearer to draw money.
Lien. A legal claim on property.
Mortgage. A claim on property as security
Paper credit. Written promise to pay.
Score. An account kept by marks or notches; any account, usually of indebtedness.
Tally. An account kept in two corresponding parts.
Tick. Trust.
Trust, Credit

Arrears. The unpaid part of a debt overdue.
Debit. A debt recorded in an account.
Default. Lack of money.
Deficit. Excess of debits over credits, or of expenses over receipts.
Floating capital. Capital free to use when required.
Floating debt. Unfunded indebtedness.
Indebtment. The state of being in debt.
Insolvency, etc. Inability to pay one's debts when due, etc. See SETTLEMENT-DEFAULT.
Interest. Price paid for the use of money or for the non-payment of a debt.
Liability. Debt.
Obligation. A contract.
Score. An account, especially, a debt.
Usance. Period allowed for the payment of debt in foreign countries.
Usury. Interest above that which is allowed by law.

CREDIT—*Nouns of Agent.*

Creditor. A person to whom money is owing.
Dun. A troublesome creditor, who urges payment.
Lender. One who gives money to a person on security.
Lessor. One to whom a lease is made.
Mortgagee. One in whose favor a mortgage is made.
Usurer. A person who charges high or illegal rates of interest.

DEBT—*Nouns of Agent.*

Borrower. One who makes a practise of borrowing.
Debitor. } One who owes a debt.
Debtor.
Defaulter. One who fails to account for money with which he is entrusted. See SETTLEMENT-DEFAULT.
Mortgagor. One against whom a mortgage is made.

CREDIT—*Verbs*

Accredit. To credit with.
Credit To give credit for, as a sum of money paid.
Entrust To give as a charge.

DEBT—*Verbs.*

Borrow, etc. To get on promise of return, etc. See LOAN-BORROWING.
Owe. To be indebted to.

CREDIT—*Verbal Expressions*

Fly a kite, to issue fictitious commercial paper to obtain money; **give credit; keep an account with,** to have business relations with; **place to one's account,** to debit one with; **place to one's credit; run up an account with,** to become another's creditor or debtor, usually the latter in repeated business transactions; **take credit.**

DEBT—*Verbal Expressions.*

Answer for, to satisfy or make good, be in debt; **contract a debt,** etc. (see *Nouns*): **get into debt; go bail for,** act as bail for; **go on tick,** etc , to buy on credit; **incur a debt,** etc. (see *Nouns*); **outrun the constable,** to incur heavier debts than one can pay; **run into debt; run up a bill, run up an account, run up a score,** to increase one's indebtedness towards another.

CREDIT—DEBT—*Continued.*

CREDIT—*Adjectives.*

Accredited. Credited with.
Bailable. Admitting of bail.
Credited. Placed to one's credit.
Crediting. Giving credit.

CREDIT—*Adverbs.*

À compte [F.]. On account.
On credit, etc., by promising to pay in the future, etc. (see *Nouns*); **to the account of,** to the debit of; **to the credit of.**

DEBT—ADJECTIVE EXPRESSIONS—*Continued from Column 2.*

unable to meet debts promptly; **involved in debt; out of pocket,** lacking of the original capital; **over head and ears in debt; plunged in debt.**

DEBT—*Phrases.*

Aes alienum debitorem leve, gravius inimicum facit [L.]. A light sum owed makes a debtor; one too heavy, an enemy.

---

cred′-it-a-ble. Praiseworthy. APPROVAL-DISAPPROVAL, DUENESS-UNDUENESS. POSSIBILITY-IMPOSSIBILITY, REPUTATION-DISCREDIT, VIRTUE-VICE.
cred′-it-ed. Trusted. CREDIT-DEBT.
cred′-it-ing. Trusting. CREDIT-DEBT.
credit mobilier [F.] (crê-dî′ mo-bî-lyê′). A financial institution. TREASURY.
cred′-it-or. One to whom another is indebted. CREDIT-DEBT.

DEBT—*Adjectives.*

Chargeable. Liable to be made responsible for some debt.
Due. Payable because of the expiration of the time agreed upon.
Incumbered. Burdened with debts.
Indebted. Owing.
Insolvent, etc. Unable to pay debts when due, etc. See SETTLEMENT-DEFAULT.
Involved. Burdened, as with debt.
Liable. Responsible.
Minus. Lacking.
Outstanding. Unpaid.
Owing. To be paid.
Unpaid. Not paid.
Unrequited. Not repaid.
Unrewarded. Not rewarded.

DEBT—*Adjective Expressions.*

Deep in debt; deeply involved; fast tied up, much in debt; **in arrears,** in debt; **in debt; in difficulties; in embarrassed circumstances,**
(*Continued on Column* 1.)

---

credo quia impossibile [L.] (crî′-do quai′-a im-possi′-bi-lî). I believe it because it is impossible. CREDULOUSNESS-SKEPTICISM. [Tertullian.]
cre-du′-li-ty. The state or quality of being credulous. CREDULOUSNESS-SKEPTICISM.
cred′-u-lous-ness. Easiness of belief. CREDULOUSNESS-SKEPTICISM

CREDULOUSNESS—SKEPTICISM

Bigotry, etc. Stubborn and unreasoning attachment to an opinion, etc. See BIGOTRY.
Credulity. } Readiness to believe anything, etc. See *Adjectives.*
Credulousness, etc. }
Cullibility. } The state of being easily cheated.
Gullibility. }
Hyperorthodoxy, etc. Extremeness in interpreting a doctrine, etc. See ORTHODOXY-HETERODOXY.
Infatuation. The state of being excessively and unreasonably influenced by something.
Misjudgment, etc. Lack of judgment, etc. See DECISION-MISJUDGMENT.
Self-deception. Deception of oneself.
Self-delusion. Delusion of oneself.
Superstition. Ignorant and irrational belief in the supernatural.

CREDULOUSNESS—*Denotations.*

One's blind side. The weak part or point.
Credulous person, etc. See GULL.

CREDULOUSNESS—*Verb*

Swallow. To believe very readily.

CREDULOUSNESS—*Verbal Expressions.*

Be credulous, etc. (see *Adjectives*); **catch at straws,** over-credulous; **follow implicitly; gulp down,** to believe without good evidence; **impose upon,** etc., to deceive with low motives, etc. (see TRUTHFULNESS-DECEPTION); **jump to a conclusion,** to form an opinion without consideration; *jurare in verba magistri* [L.], to swear with the words of a master, to obey implicitly; **run away with an idea, run away with a notion,** to be overactive in some cause or take an extreme position in regard to something; **rush to a conclusion** (see JUMP TO A CONCLUSION); **take for gospel,** to accept as absolute truth; **take for granted,** to believe without questioning the truth of it; **take on trust; take the shadow for the substance; think the moon is made of green cheese,** to believe absurdities

CREDULOUSNESS—*Adjectives*

Childish. Believing like a child.
Confiding, etc. Trusting one's secrets or opinions to another, etc. See FAITH.
Credulous. Ready to believe.
Green. Inexperienced, so as to be easily imposed upon.
Gullible. Easily cheated.
Infatuous. Easily drawn to.
Overconfident. Too confident.
Overcredulous. Too credulous.
Silly. Acting so as to show lack of judgment or experience.
Simple. Trusting because of lack of knowledge.

Incredulity. } Lack of credulity
Incredulousness. }
Pyrrhonism. Universal doubt. Like that of the Greek philosopher, Pyrrho.
Scrupulosity. Excessive doubtfulness in action, for fear of doing wrong.
Skepticism. Disbelief in a God.
Suspicion, etc. Imagination or apprehension without sufficient evidence, etc. See FAITH-MISGIVING.
Suspiciousness, etc. The state or quality of being suspicious, etc. See *Adjectives.*
Want of faith, etc. See FAITH-MISGIVING.

SKEPTICISM—*Verbs.*

Distrust, etc. Not to have confidence in, etc. See FAITH-MISGIVING.
Ignore. To take no notice of purposely.

SKEPTICISM—*Verbal Expressions.*

Be incredulous, etc. (see *Adjectives*); **hold aloof,** to keep away from purposely· *nullius jurare in verba magistri* [L.], to swear by the words of no master, to be completely independent [Horace, *Epistles*, I, i, 14]; **refuse to believe; shut one's ears to, shut one's eyes, turn a deaf ear to,** not to wish to believe or become aware of something.

SKEPTICISM—*Adjectives.*

Distrustful. Lacking in confidence.
Inconvincible. Not capable of being convinced.
Incredulous. Not credulous.
Scrupulous. Inclined to hesitate for fear of doing wrong.
Skeptical. Disbelieving in a God.
Suspicious. Apt to be continually suspecting something.
Unbelieving. Not believing.

CREDULOUSNESS—ADJECTIVES—*Continued.*

Soft. Simple.
Stupid. Easily deceived.
Superstitious. Given to superstition.

CREDULOUSNESS—*Phrases.*

Credo quia impossibile [L.]. I believe it because it is impossible. [Tertullian, *De Carne Christi,* 5.]
No es oro todo lo que reluce [Sp.]. All is not gold that glitters.
Omne ignotum pro magnifico [L.]. Everything unknown is something magnificent. [Tacitus, *Agricola*, 30.]
The wish the father to the thought. One is overready to believe because of prejudices.

cred'-u-lous per'-son. A dupe. CREDULOUSNESS-SKEPTICISM, DECISION-MISJUDGMENT, FAITH-MISGIVING, GULL-DECEIVER.

creed. A confession of faith. FAITH-MISGIVING, THEOLOGY; **Apostles' Creed**, ORTHODOXY-HETERODOXY.

creek. A cove; a small stream. GULF-PLAIN, INTERSPACE-CONTACT.

creel. An angler's basket. CONTENTS-RECEIVER.

creep. To crawl. SWIFTNESS-SLOWNESS; **creep in**, ENTRANCE-EXIT; **creep into a corner**, SOCIABILITY-PRIVACY; **creep into the good graces of**, ADULATION-DISPARAGEMENT; **creep out**, EXPOSURE-HIDINGPLACE; **creep upon one**, EXPECTATION-SURPRISE; **creep with**, EXCESS-LACK, MULTIPLICITY-PAUCITY.

creep'-er. A plant growing upon a surface by sending out rootlets from the axis. FAUNA-FLORA.

creep'-ing. A nervous sensation as of insects moving on the flesh. SWIFTNESS-SLOWNESS; **creeping thing**, FAUNA-FLORA.

creese. A dagger or sword with a waved blade. WEAPON.

cre-ma'-tion. The act or practise of burning. HEATING-COOLING, LIFE-FUNERAL.

crème de la crême [F.] (crêm de la crêm). Cream of the cream. GOODNESS-BADNESS.

Cre-mo'-na. Any violin made at Cremona, from the 16th to the 18th century, by the Amati family or by Antonio Stradivari and Josef Guarnerius. MUSICAL INSTRUMENTS.

cre'-nate. Scalloped. INDENTATION.

cre'-na''-ted. Scalloped. INDENTATION.

cren'-el-a''-ted. Decorated with crenelles. **Crenelated molding**, ARCHITECTURE.

cre-nelle'. An indentation. INDENTATION.

cren'-u-late. Having the edge cut into small scallops. INDENTATION.

cre'-ole. A native of Spanish America or the West Indies, of European parentage. CONSTITUENT-ALIEN.

crêpe. Crape. CIRCLE-WINDING.

crepidam, ultra [L.] (crep'-i-dam, ul'-tra). Beyond the last. POSSIBILITY-IMPOSSIBILITY.

crep''-i-ta'-tion. The act of crackling. CRASH-DRUMMING.

cre-pus'-cule. Twilight. DIMNESS, MORNING-EVENING.

cres-cen'-do. Slowly increasing in loudness or power. INCREASE-DECREASE, MUSIC.

cres'-cent. Something having the shape of the new moon. CURVATION-RECTILINEARITY, DWELLER-HABITATION.

cres-cen'-tric. Crescent-shaped. CURVATION-RECTILINEARITY.

cres'-set. A frame or vessel mounted to hold a torch or beacon. SIGN.

crest. The top of anything. SELFRESPECT-HUMBLENESS, SHARPNESS-BLUNTNESS, SIGN, SMOOTHNESS-ROUGHNESS, TOP-BOTTOM.

crest'-fal''-len. Dejected. LIGHTHEARTEDNESS-DEJECTION, SELFRESPECT-HUMBLENESS.

cre-ta'-ceous. Chalky. GEOLOGY.

crev-asse'. A deep fissure in a glacier. INTERSPACE-CONTACT.

crev'-ice. A small fissure. INTERSPACE-CONTACT.

crew. A company of seamen belonging to one vessel; a crowd. ASSOCIATION, DWELLER-HABITATION, GATHERING-SCATTERING, WAYFARER-SEAFARER.

crib. A child's bedstead with side railings; a petty theft. EXTRAVAGANCE-AVARICE, SUSPENSION-SUPPORT, THEFT.

crib'-bage. A game of cards. ENTERTAINMENT-WEARINESS.

cribbed. Shut in. **Cabined, cribbed, confined**, RELEASE-RESTRAINT.

crib'-ble. To sift. APERTURE-CLOSURE.

crib'-ri-form. Resembling a sieve. APERTURE-CLOSURE.

Crich'-ton. A Scottish scholar and adventurer. **Admirable Crichton**, ADEPT-BUNGLER, FAULTLESSNESS-FAULTINESS, SCHOLAR-DUNCE.

crick. A spasmodic affection of the muscles. SENSUALITY-SUFFERING.

crick'-et. An outdoor game. ENTERTAINMENT-WEARINESS; **cricket-ground**, ENTERTAINMENT-WEARINESS, ERECTNESS-FLATNESS.

cri'-er. One who makes vocal public proclamation. MESSENGER; **send round the crier**, PUBLICITY.

crim. con. Criminal conversation. PURITY-IMPURITY.

crime. A grave offense against morality or social order or an offense that subjects the doer to legal punishment. INNOCENCE-GUILT, VIRTUE-VICE.

crim'-i-nal. Guilty of crime. GOOD MAN-BAD MAN, VIRTUE-VICE.

crim''-i-nal'-i-ty. Guilt. INNOCENCE-GUILT.

crim'-i-nate. To accuse of a crime. JUSTIFICATION-CHARGE.

crim''-i-na'-tion. Accusation. JUSTIFICATION-CHARGE.

crim'-i-na-to-ry. Accusing. JUSTIFICATION-CHARGE.

crim''-i-nol'-o-gist. A student of crime. SCHOLAR.

crim''-i-nol'-o-gy. Scientific study of crime and criminals. SCHOLAR.

crim'-i-nous-ness. Heinousness. INNOCENCE-GUILT.

crimp. To crinkle; one who decoys people to a place where they are robbed. CIRCLE-WINDING, GULL-DECEIVER, INDENTATION, TAKING-RESTITUTION, THEFT, TOUGHNESS-BRITTLENESS.

crim'-ple. To wrinkle. PLICATURE.

crim'-son. Deep-red. REDNESS-GREENNESS.

cringe. To crouch in servility or cowardice. PRESUMPTION-OBSEQUIOUSNESS, YIELDING.

crin'-ging. Wincing. PRESUMPTION-OBSEQUIOUSNESS.

cri'-nite. Bearded with long weak hairs. SMOOTHNESS-ROUGHNESS.

crin'-kle. To wrinkle. ANGULARITY, CIRCLE-WINDING, PLICATURE.

crin'-kled. Wrinkled. ANGULARITY.

crin'-o-line. A stiff elastic fabric. DRESS-UNDRESS.

cri'-nose. Hairy. SMOOTHNESS-ROUGHNESS.

crip'-ple. To impair or destroy the power of. BETTERMENT-DETERIORATION, HEALTH-SICKNESS, MIGHT-IMPOTENCE, OBSTRUCTION-HELP, STRENGTH-WEAKNESS, USEFULNESS-USELESSNESS.

crip'-pled. Impaired in power. HEALTH-SICKNESS, MIGHT-IMPOTENCE.

cri'-sis. A critical moment. CONDITION-SITUATION, DIFFICULTY-FACILITY, OCCURRENCE-DESTINY, OPPORTUNENESS-UNSUITABLENESS, TIME; **bring to a crisis**, DETERMINATION-VACILLATION; **come to a crisis**, COMPLETION-NONCOMPLETION.

crisp. To crinkle; to make brittle. CIRCLE-WINDING, SMOOTHNESS-ROUGHNESS, TERSENESS-PROLIXITY, TOUGHNESS-BRITTLENESS.

cris''-tal-lo-man''-ti-a. Divination by spirits seen in a magic lens. PROPHECY.

cri-te'-ri-on. A test. EVIDENCE-COUNTEREVIDENCE, SIGN, TRIAL.

crith'-o-man''-cy. Divination by dough of cakes. PROPHECY.

crit'-ic. A judge of the qualities of anything. DECISION-MISJUDGMENT, ESSAY, FLATTERER-DEFAMER, TASTE-VULGARITY.

crit'-ic-al. Judicious. APPROVAL-DISAPPROVAL, CONDITION-SITUATION, CONSEQUENCE-INSIGNIFICANCE, DIFFICULTY-FACILITY, OPPORTUNENESS-UNSUITABLENESS, SECURITY-INSECURITY.

crit'-i-cism. Judgment. ADULATION-DISPARAGE-MENT, APPROVAL-DISAPPROVAL, DECISION-MISJUDG-MENT, ESSAY.

crit'-i-cize. To examine critically. ADULATION-DIS-PARAGEMENT, APPROVAL-DISAPPROVAL, DECISION-MISJUDGMENT, TASTE-VULGARITY.

cri-tique'. A criticism. DECISION-MISJUDGMENT, DIFFERENTIATION-INDISCRIMINATION, ESSAY.

critique est aisée, et l'art est difficile [F.] (cri-tîc' êt ê-zê', ê lart ê di-fi-sil'). Criticism is easy and art is difficult. DECISION-MISJUDGMENT, DIFFERENTIA-TION-INDISCRIMINATION.

croak. A harsh guttural sound; to grumble. CONTENTEDNESS-DISCONTENTMENT, CRY-ULULATION, JUBILATION-LAMENTATION, SPEECH-INARTICULATE-NESS, WARNING.

croak'-er. A grumbler. CONTENTEDNESS-DISCONTENTMENT, LIGHTHEARTEDNESS-DEJECTION, VOCALIZA-TION-MUTENESS.

Cro'-at. Austrian light-cavalryman. BELLIGERENT.

croch'-et. A note in music; a whim. DECISION-MISJUDGMENT, MELODY-DISSONANCE, PERSISTENCE-WHIM.

crock. An earthen pot. CONTENTS-RECEIVER.

crock'-er-y. Earthenware. HEATING-COOLING MATERIALS.

crock'-et. Ornament. ARCHITECTURE.

croc'-o-dile tears. False tears. TRUTHFULNESS-FALSEHOOD.

cro'-cus. A genus of herbs of the iris family. YELLOWNESS-PURPLE.

Crœ'-sus. A king of Lydia. AFFLUENCE-PENURY.

croft. A small farm. DWELLER-HABITATION.

crom'-lech. A stone monument. LIFE-FUNERAL.

crone. A withered old woman, or man. INFANT-VETERAN, SAGE-FOOL.

cro'-ny. A familiar friend. FAVORITE-ANGER, FRIEND-FOE.

crook. A bend or curve. AIM-ABERRATION, CURVA-TION-RECTILINEARITY, PARALLELISM-INCLINATION.

crook'-backed''. Hunchbacked. PROPORTION-DE-FORMITY.

crook'-ed. Not straight; dishonest. ANGULARITY, BEAUTY-UGLINESS, CRAFT-ARTLESSNESS, MANIFES-TATION-LATENCY, PARALLELISM-INCLINATION, PRO-PORTION-DEFORMITY, UPRIGHTNESS-DISHONESTY; **crooked path,** DIFFICULTY-FACILITY; **crooked temper,** FAVORITE-QUARRELSOMENESS; **crooked ways,** AIM-ABERRATION.

crook'-ed-ness. Condition of being crooked. PARALLELISM-INCLINATION, PROPORTION-DEFORMITY.

crop. Harvest; craw; to cut or eat off stems or the ends of grasses; to reap. CAUSE-EFFECT, CON-TENTS-RECEIVER, GAIN-LOSS, LENGTH-SHORTNESS, NUTRIMENT-EXCRETION, STORE, TAKING-RESTITU-TION; **crop out,** EXPOSURE-HIDINGPLACE, VISIBIL-ITY-INVISIBILITY; **crop up,** BEGINNING-END. OCCUR-RENCE-DESTINY, RENEWAL, VISIBILITY-INVISIBILITY.

crop'-per. A fall headlong. ASCENT-DESCENT.

cro-quet'. A lawn-game. ENTERTAINMENT-WEARI-NESS; **croquet-grounds,** ERECTNESS-FLATNESS.

cro'-sier. A staff surmounted by a crook or cross borne by or before a bishop or an archbishop. VEST-MENTS.

cross. An ancient instrument of torture; a mixing of varieties; an ornament, in some form of the cross, worn as a distinction; across; to hinder; out of humor. ANTAGONISM-CONCURRENCE, CEREMONIAL, CROSS-ING, FAVORITE-ANGER, FAVORITE-QUARRELSOME-NESS, MIXTURE-HOMOGENEITY, PLEASURABLENESS-PAINFULNESS, PROFFER-REFUSAL, RECOMPENSE-SCOURGE, SUCCESS-FAILURE, TITLE, TRANSMISSION, WELFARE-MISFORTUNE; **cross and pile,** PURPOSE-LUCK; **cross-breed,** CONVENTIONALITY-UNCONVEN-

TIONALITY; **cross-cut,** MIDCOURSE-CIRCUIT; **crossed bayonets,** ANTAGONISM-CONCURRENCE; **crossed in love,** LOVE-HATE; **cross-fire,** ANTAGONISM-CONCUR-RENCE, ATTACK-DEFENSE, DIFFICULTY-FACILITY; **cross-purposes,** ANTAGONISM-CONCURRENCE, DIFFI-CULTY-FACILITY, INTERPRETATION-MISINTERPRETA-TION, REGULARITY-IRREGULARITY, SKILL-UNSKIL-FULNESS, TRUTH-ERROR, VARIANCE-ACCORD; **cross-questions,** ENTERTAINMENT-WEARINESS, INVESTIGA-TION-ANSWER, VARIANCE-ACCORD; **cross-road,** WAY; **cross sea,** RIVER-WIND; **cross swords,** FIGHTING-CONCILIATION; **cross the mind,** REFLECTION-VA-CANCY; **cross the path of,** OBSTRUCTION-HELP; **cross the Rubicon,** BEGINNING-END, CHOICE-NEUTRALITY; **fire cross,** FIGHTING-CONCILIATION; **red cross,** REM-EDY-BANE.

cross'-bow. A missile weapon consisting of a bow fixed transversely upon a stock. WEAPON.

crossed. Obstructed. CROSSING, SUCCESS-FAILURE.

cross'-ex-am-i-na''-tion. A questioning. INVESTIGA-TION-ANSWER.

cross'-ex-am''-ine. To cross-question. INVESTIGA-TION-ANSWER.

cross'-grained''. Perverse. BIGOTRY-APOSTASY, FA-VORITE-MOROSENESS.

cross'-ing. The act of going across; junction of roads. CITY-COUNTRY, CROSSING.

CROSSING.

Anastomosis. Communication between two or more vessels or nerves.

Convolution. A winding or crossing in and out.

Crossing, etc. Place where two things in different directions run by each other, etc. See *Verbs.*

Decussation. A crossing made at an acute angle.

Entanglement. The state of being entangled.

Inosculation. Intercommunication of tubes, as the veins of the body.

Interdigitation. A locking together, like the fingers.

Intersection. A meeting or cutting into each other, as lines.

Intertexture. The state of being interwoven.

Mortise. The joining of two pieces of timber, etc., made by putting the end of one into a cavity in the other.

Network. Mesh.

Reticulation. State of being netted.

Transversion. A crossing.

CROSSING—*Denotations.*

Braid. A tape or woven strip for binding the edges of fabrics.

Cat's cradle. A game played by means of a loop of string turned about the fingers and producing various figures.

Chain. A string of interlinked links or rings.

Cross. A structure made of a piece of timber, and a cross-piece.

Felt. A fabric made by interlocking wool, fur, or hair.

Filigree. Ornamental jewelry resembling lacework.

Fretwork. Ornamental work in relief done by carving.

Grating. An arrangement of parallel, crossed, or interlacing bars.

Gridiron. A hinged double grating of iron wires for broiling.

Grille [F.]. A grated gate.

Knot. An intertwining of the parts of one or more ropes, or cords

Lace. A delicate openwork fabric of threads of linen, silk, cotton, etc.

Lattice. Openwork of metal or wood formed by crossing strips or bars.

Mat. An article woven from fiber, rushes, wire, etc.

Mesh. A net or network.

Mokes. Nets.

Net. An open fabric of twine, woven or tied with meshes.

Netting. A fabric of openwork.

Plait. A braid as of straw or hair.

Plexus. A network or interlacement.

Reticle. A net of fine threads, connected with a telescope, to determine the position of an observed object.

Skein. A quantity of yarn or thread wound to a certain length, then doubled and knotted.

Sleeve. A short pipe receiving the ends of two other pipes.

Tracery. Foliated ornament or scrollwork of any kind.

Trellis. A cross-barred grating or lattice.

Twill. A fabric of woven threads.

Wattle. A frame made of interwoven twigs.
Web. A textile fabric woven in the loom.
Wicker. Ware made of interwoven young shoots or rods.
Wreath. A twisted band as of leaves or flowers.

CROSSING—Verbs.

Anastomose. To intercommunicate, as the blood-vessels.
Braid. To form into a braid.
Cross. To run through, over, or under anything.
Decussate. To cross at an acute angle.
Dishevel. To put into a disorderly state.
Dovetail. To join with dovetails.
Entangle. To complicate so as not to be easily separated.
Entwine. To twine.
Felt. To make into felt.
Inosculate. To connect, as tubes.
Interdigitate. To lock, like the fingers of the hands.
Interlace. To lace together.
Interlink. To link together.
Intersect. To cut into.
Intertwine. To twine together.
Intertwist. To twist several things together.
Interweave. To weave together.
Inweave. To weave in.
Knot. To tie into knots.
Link. To connect by links.
Mat. To twist or weave into a mat.
Net. To make into a net.
Plait. }
Plat. } To braid.
Raddle. To twist together.
Ravel. To pull apart or disentangle.
Splice. To unite two ends in some way.
Tangle. To mix or interweave in a disorderly manner.
Twill. To weave so as to produce diagonal lines on the surface.
Twine. To wind threads around each other or something else.
Twist. To wind threads, etc., together.
Weave. To fasten together so as to form a texture.
Wreath. To wind or fasten together in the form of a wreath.

CROSSING—Adjectives.

Areolar. Having interstices like the areolæ.
Barred. Marked with lines drawn across.
Cancellated. Like a lattice.
Cross. Not in the same direction.
Crossed. Placed crosswise.
Crossing, etc. Running in different directions through or near, etc. See *Verbs.*
Crucial. Intersecting.
Grated. Made like grates.
Matted, etc. Twined together, etc. See *Verbs.*
Reticular. }
Reticulated. } Like a net.
Retiform. }
Streaked. Marked with streaks.
Textile. Capable of being woven.
Transverse. Crosswise.

CROSSING—Adverbs.

Across. From side to side.
Athwart. Obliquely.
Thwart. Athwart.
Transversely. Crosswise.

cross'-ness. Ill-temper. FAVORITE-QUARRELSOME-NESS.
cross'-patch". An ill-natured person. POLITENESS-IMPOLITENESS.
crotch. A fork. ANGULARITY.
crotch'-et-y. Eccentric. DECISION-MISJUDGMENT, PERSISTENCE-WHIM.
crouch. To bend down; to fawn. ELEVATION-DEPRESSION, HEIGHT-LOWNESS, PRESUMPTION-OBSEQUIOUSNESS, SANGUINENESS-TIMIDITY; **crouch before,** YIELDING.
crouched. Stooped. HEIGHT-LOWNESS.
crouch'-ing. Stooping; cringing. PRESUMPTION-OBSEQUIOUSNESS.
croup. A disease of the throat; the buttocks of a quadruped. ANTERIORITY-POSTERIORITY.
crou'-pi-er. A stake-holder. MANAGER.

crow. A bird; boast. BRAGGING, CRY-ULULATION, INSTRUMENT, JUBILATION-LAMENTATION, WHITE-NESS-BLACKNESS; **as the crow flies,** AIM-ABERRATION; **crow's foot,** INFANCY-AGE; **crow's nest,** TOP-BOTTOM; **crows to pluck,** FAVORITE-ANGER, JUSTIFICATION-CHARGE, PARDON-VINDICTIVENESS, VARIANCE-ACCORD; **pluck a crow with,** APPROVAL-DISAPPROBATION.
crow'-bar". An iron lever. INSTRUMENT.
crowd. A large multitude. EXCESS-LACK, GATHER-ING-SCATTERING, GENTILITY-DEMOCRACY, MULTI-PLICITY-PAUCITY, REMOTENESS-NEARNESS; **in the crowd,** MIXTURE-HOMOGENEITY.
crowd'-ed. Pressed closely together. MULTIPLICITY-PAUCITY.
crown. The top; a royal ornament; a trophy; coin. CIRCLE-WINDING, COMMISSION-ABROGATION, COM-PLETION-NONCOMPLETION, RECOMPENSE-PUNITION, SCEPTER, TITLE, TOP-BOTTOM, TROPHY, VALUES; **crowned head,** CHIEF-UNDERLING; **crowned with laurel,** REPUTATION-DISCREDIT; **crowned with success,** SUCCESS-FAILURE; **to crown all,** CONSEQUENCE-INSIGNIFICANCE, SUPREMACY-SUBORDINACY.
crown'-ing. Highest. BEGINNING-END, COMPLETION-NONCOMPLETION, SUPREMACY-SUBORDINACY; **crowning point,** TOP-BOTTOM.
crow's'-foot". A wrinkle about the eye. PLICATURE.
cruche à l'eau qu'à la fin elle se casse, tant va la [F.] (crüsh a lo ka la fan· el se cas, tan· va la). The pitcher goes so often to the well that it comes home broken at last. WELFARE-MISFORTUNE.
cru'-cial. Crosswise; testing. CROSSING, PROOF-DIS-PROOF; **crucial test,** TRIAL.
cru'-ci-ate. To torture. PLEASURABLENESS-PAINFUL-NESS, SENSUALITY-SUFFERING.
cru"-ci-a'-tion. State of being crossed. SENSUALITY-SUFFERING.
cru'-ci-ble. A chemical vessel. CHEMISTRY, CON-TENTS-RECEIVER, CONVERSION, OVEN-REFRIGER-ATOR, SCHOLAR-DUNCE, WORKSHOP; **put into the crucible,** RENEWAL.
cru'-ci-fix. A small cross. CEREMONIAL.
cru"-ci-fix'-ion. Act of putting to death by nailing on a cross. RECOMPENSE-PUNITION, SENSUALITY-SUF-FERING.
cru'-ci-form. Cross-shaped. CROSSING.
cru'-ci-fy. Kill on the cross. PLEASURABLENESS-PAINFULNESS, RECOMPENSE-PUNITION, SENSUALITY-SUFFERING.
crucis experimentum [L.] (cru'-sis ex-per-i-men'-tum). Trial of the cross. TRIAL.
crude. Raw. COLOR-ACHROMATISM, ENTIRETY-DEFI-CIENCY, FAULTLESSNESS-FAULTINESS, PREPARATION-NONPREPARATION, PURITY-CRUDENESS.
cru'-di-ty. State of being crude. PREPARATION-NON-PREPARATION.
cruel. Inhuman. CHARITABLENESS-MALEVOLENCE, HARSHNESS-MILDNESS, PLEASURABLENESS-PAINFUL-NESS, TYRANNY-ANARCHY.
cruel'-ly. Inhumanly. MAGNITUDE-SMALLNESS.
cru'-el-ness. Quality of being cruel. CHARITABLENESS-MALEVOLENCE.
cru'-el-ty. Disposition to inflict pain. CHARITABLE-NESS-MALEVOLENCE.
cru'-et. A small glass bottle for holding vinegar. CONTENTS-RECEIVER.
cruise. To rove on the seas; a cruet. CONTENTS-RECEIVER, TRAVELING-NAVIGATION.
cruis'-er. A person or ship that cruises. BELLIGERENT.
crumb. A fragment. FRIABILITY, MAGNITUDE-SMALL-NESS; **crumb of comfort,** ALLEVIATION-AGGRAVA-TION.
crum'-ble. To break into small pieces. BETTERMENT-DETERIORATION, CREATION-DESTRUCTION, FRIABIL-

ITY, INCREASE-DECREASE, STRENGTH-WEAKNESS, TOUGHNESS-BRITTLENESS; **crumble into dust,** COMPOSITION-RESOLUTION, TOUGHNESS-BRITTLENESS; **crumble under one's feet,** WELFARE-MISFORTUNE.

crumb'-ling. Breaking into fragments. BETTERMENT-DETERIORATION, CREATION-DESTRUCTION, FRIABILITY, INCREASE-DECREASE, NOVELTY-ANTIQUITY, SECURITY-INSECURITY, STRENGTH-WEAKNESS, TOUGHNESS-BRITTLENESS.

crumb'-ly. Apt to crumble. FRIABILITY.

cru'-me-nal. A purse. MONEY. [Spenser.]

crump. Crooked. CURVATION-RECTILINEARITY, PROPORTION-DEFORMITY.

crum'-ple. To wrinkle. PLICATURE, SMOOTHNESS-ROUGHNESS; **crumple up,** CREATION-DESTRUCTION, ENLARGEMENT-DIMINUTION.

crunch. To grind noisily. NUTRIMENT-EXCRETION, UNION-DISUNION.

crup'-per. The rump of a horse. ANTERIORITY-POSTERIORITY.

cru-sade'. A religious expedition. FIGHTING-CONCILIATION.

crush. Break by pressure; humble. CREATION-DESTRUCTION, ENLARGEMENT-DIMINUTION, FRIABILITY, GATHERING-SCATTERING, SELFRESPECT-HUMBLENESS; **crush one's hopes,** EXPECTATION-DISAPPOINTMENT, SANGUINENESS-HOPELESSNESS; **crush under an iron heel,** HARSHNESS-MILDNESS.

crushed. Overcome. PLEASURE-PAIN.

crush'-ing. Overwhelming. PLEASURABLENESS-PAINFULNESS.

crust. The hard outside covering. COVER-LINING.

crus-ta'-ce-an. A family of arthropods having crust-like shells. FAUNA-FLORA.

crust'-y. Peevish. FAVORITE-MOROSENESS.

crutch. A staff for cripples. ANGULARITY, SUSPENSION-SUPPORT.

crux criticorum [L.] (crux cri-ti-co'-rum). The puzzle of critics. TIDINGS-MYSTERY.

crux, fidei coticula [L.] (crux, fai-di'-ai co-tic'-yu-la). The cross is the touchstone of faith. ATONEMENT.

cry. To weep; to proclaim; to beg. CRY-ULULATION, HABIT-DESUETUDE, JUBILATION-LAMENTATION, PUBLICITY, SIGN, TIDINGS-MYSTERY, VOCALIZATION-MUTENESS; **cry aloud,** PETITION-EXPOSTULATION; **cry and little wool,** BRAGGING, EXPECTATION-DISAPPOINTMENT, OVERVALUATION-UNDERVALUATION; **cry before hurt,** JUBILATION-LAMENTATION; **cry down,** ADULATION-DISPARAGEMENT, APPROVAL-DISAPPROBATION; **cry for,** DESIRE-DISTASTE; **cry for joy,** JUBILATION-LAMENTATION; **cry for vengeance,** RIGHT-WRONG; **cry out against,** APPROVAL-DISAPPROBATION, MOTIVE-DEHORTATION; **cry shame,** APPROVAL-DISAPPROBATION; **cry to,** PETITION-EXPOSTULATION; **cry up,** APPROVAL-DISAPPROBATION, POMP; **cry wolf,** ALARM, SANGUINENESS-TIMIDITY, TRUTHFULNESS-FALSEHOOD; **cry you mercy,** COMPASSION-RUTHLESSNESS, PARDON-VINDICTIVENESS, PETITION-EXPOSTULATION; **full cry,** LOUDNESS-FAINTNESS; **raise a cry,** SIGN.

CRY—ULULATION.

Bark. The cry ordinarily made by a dog.
Chorus. A company of singers.
Clamor. A great disorderly shouting.
Cry, etc. The noise made by animals in pain, etc. See *Verbs.*
Hullabaloo. Tumult.
Lungs. Organs of respiration, used to provide the air for speaking.
Outcry. A loud yell.
Plaint. Audible expression of sorrow.
Stentor. A person having a loud voice.
Vagitus. The first cry of a new-born infant.
Vociferation. A vehement use of the voice.
Voice. The sound made by the organs of speech.

CRY—*Verbs.*

Bawl. } To utter inarticulate words in a loud voice like some
Bellow. } lower animals.
Brawl. To quarrel in a noisy manner.
Cheer. To give applause with yells.
Cry. To make a sound, as if in pain or distress.
Exclaim. To speak out suddenly.
Groan. To utter an involuntary noise by breathing when in great pain.
Grumble. To complain in a surly tone of voice.
Grunt, etc. To give a short, rough sound like a pig, etc. See CRY-ULULATION.
Halloa. } To shout to call some one's attention.
Halloo. }
Hoop. To give a sudden shout.
Hoot. To give a contemptuous cry.
Howl. To utter a loud piercing cry.
Moan. To utter a low plaintive sound.
Pipe. To talk in a high shrill key.
Pule. To make a noise like a little chicken.
Roar. To utter a loud harsh utterance.
Screak. To give a harsh shrill sound.
Scream. To utter a prolonged shriek.
Screech. To utter a sharp shrill sound.
Shout. To give a loud, sonorous utterance of the voice.
Shriek. To utter a sound suddenly at the top of one's voice.
Snore. To make a rattling noise in the throat while sleeping.
Snort. To puff violently through the nose.
Squall. To cry vehemently.
Squeak. To make a small, sharp, disagreeable noise.
Vociferate. To utter any articulate sounds vehemently and continuously.
Whine. To utter a long plaintive sound.

Belling. Bellowing.
Bow-wow. Cry of a dog.
Cry, etc. Utterance of inarticulate sounds as in pain, joy, etc. See *Verbs.*
Crying. A prolonged, plaintive utterance as if in pain.
Drone. A low humming sound.
Fritinancy. A chirping like a cricket.
Latration. A barking.
Reboation. The echo of a bellow.
Ululation. A howling.
Wood-note. The voice of a wild bird.
Insect cry. The noise made by an insect.

ULULATION—*Nouns of Cause.*

Cuckoo. A small bird, which utters a cry represented by its name.
Screech-owl. An owl which utters a screech instead of hooting.

ULULATION—*Verbs.*

Bark. To snap out a sound like a dog.
Bay. To bark in a long, low, hoarse voice.
Bellow. To give forth a loud hollow sound.
Blare. To utter a loud harsh sound.
Blatter. To make a rattling or senseless noise.
Bleat. To make a noise like a lamb.
Bray. To utter a loud discordant noise, as an ass.
Buzz. To make a noise, as the bee does.
Cackle. To make a short, jerky noise, as a chicken.
Caterwaul. To cry, as a cat in rutting time.
Caw. To make a noise, as a crow does.
Cheep. To peep.
Chirp. To make a noise, as a robin does.
Chirrup. To chirp.
Chuck. } To utter a noise, as a hen does in calling her chickens.
Chuckle. }
Clack. To talk rapidly and continually.
Cluck. To call, as a hen does her chickens.
Coo. To make a noise, as a dove does.
Croak. To utter as if from the lower part of the throat, as a frog.
Crow. To make a noise, as a rooster does.
Cry. To utter a long, plaintive noise as if in pain.
Cuckoo. To make a sound, as the male cuckoo does during mating season.
Gaggle. To make a noise, as the goose.
Gobble. To make a sound, like the turkey-cock.
Growl. To utter a low angry sound.

CRY—ULULATION—*Continued.*

CRY—Verbs—*Continued.*

Whoop. To hoop.
Yaup. To utter a cry of distress like a child or young bird.
Yell. To give a loud cry.

CRY—*Verbal Expressions.*

Call out; cry out; give a cry; lift up the voice; raise the voice; rend the air; *s' égosiller* [F.], to make one's throat sore by shouting; shout at the pitch of one's breath; shout at the top of one's voice; sing out; strain the lungs; strain the throat; strain the voice; thunder at the pitch of one's breath; thunder at the top of one's voice.

CRY—*Adjectives.*

Clamant. Urgent in the call for help.
Clamorous. Making a great disorderly shouting.
Crying, etc. See *Verbs.*
Open-mouthed. Clamorous.
Stentorian, etc. Extremely loud, like Homer's Stentor, etc. See LOUDNESS.
Vociferous. Vehement in shouting.

ULULATION—Adjectives—*Continued from Column 2.*

Crying, etc. See *Verbs.*
Latrant. Barking.
Mugient. Lowing.
Remugient. Bellowing or lowing again.

ULULATION—*Adverb.*

In full cry. In full pursuit.

ULULATION—Verbs—*Continued*

Grunt. }
Gruntle. } To utter a low, short noise like the hog.
Guggle. To gurgle.
Hiss. To force air out between the teeth
Howl. To utter a loud mournful cry.
Hum. To make a buzzing noise.
Low. To make a noise like a cow.
Mew. To make a noise like a cat.
Mewl. To cry like a young child.
Moo. To low.
Neigh. To make a noise like a horse.
Pule. To cry like a chicken.
Purr. To make a humming noise like a cat when pleased or asleep.
Quack. To make a noise like a duck.
Rebellow. To bellow again.
Roar. To make a loud deep sound.
Screech. To make a high-keyed, harsh sound.
Snarl. To utter a vicious growl.
Snort. To blow the breath violently through the nose like a horse.
Squeak. To utter a sharp, short noise.
Troat. To make a noise like a male deer in rutting time.
Twitter. To make a noise like a sparrow.
Yap. To bark.
Yarr. To growl like a dog.
Yawl. To howl.
Yelp. To utter a short howl.

ULULATION—*Adjectives.*

Blatant. Bawling out like a beast.

(*Continued on Column 1.*)

---

cry'-ing. Weeping; notorious. CRY-ULULATION, JUBILATION-LAMENTATION, NEED; crying evil, GOOD-EVIL; **crying shame,** REPUTATION-DISCREDIT; **crying sin,** VIRTUE-VICE.
crypt. A cell. CONTENTS-RECEIVER, EXPOSURE-HIDINGPLACE, FANE, LIFE-DEATH.
crypt'-ic. Hidden. ENLIGHTENMENT-SECRECY.
crypt'-ic-al. Quality of being hidden. ENLIGHTENMENT-SECRECY.
cryp-tog'-ra-phy. Cipher-writing. ENLIGHTENMENT-SECRECY, WRITING-PRINTING.
crys'-tal. Transparent quartz. CHEMISTRY, DIAPHANEITY-OPAQUENESS, HARDNESS-SOFTNESS, MINERALOGY; **crystal oil,** PULPINESS-OIL; **snow crystal,** HEAT-COLD.
crys'-tal-line. Like crystal. DIAPHANEITY-OPAQUENESS, MINERALOGY, SOLIDITY-RARITY.
crys'-tal-li''-za-ble. Capable of being crystallized. SOLIDITY-RARITY.
crys''-tal-li-za'-tion. The process of forming crystals. CHEMISTRY, HARDNESS-SOFTNESS, SOLIDITY-RARITY.
crys'-tal-lize. To cause to form crystals. SOLIDITY-RARITY.
crys''-tal-lo-graph'-ic. Pertaining to crystallography. **Crystallographic axes,** MINERALOGY.
crys''-tal-log'-ra-phy. Science of crystals. MINERALOGY.
csa'-ko. A helmet. ATTACK-DEFENSE, DRESS-UNDRESS.
cuar'-to. Spanish coin. VALUES.
cub. A whelp; a rough youth. GENTILITY-DEMOCRACY, INFANT-VETERAN, TASTE-VULGARITY; **unlicked cub,** FORM-FORMLESSNESS, TASTE-VULGARITY.
cube. A hexahedron; the third power. ANGULARITY, TRIALITY, TRIPLICATION-TRISECTION.
cu'-bic-al. Pertaining to a cube. ANGULARITY.
cu'-bic foot. A unit volume. MEASURE.
cu'-bit. A measure of length. LENGTH-SHORTNESS.
cu'-bit-al. Part of a spider. ANATOMY.
cuck'-ing-stool''. A chair of punishment. RECOMPENSE-SCOURGE.
cuck'-old. The husband of an adulteress. MATRIMONY-DIVORCE, PURITY-IMPURITY.

cuck'-ol-dom. The state of a cuckold. PURITY-IMPURITY.
cuck'-oo. A bird. CRASH-DRUMMING, CRY-ULULATION, IMITATION-ORIGINALITY, RECURRENCE.
cud'-dle. To hug. BLANDISHMENT.
cudg'-el. A club. IMPETUS-REACTION, RECOMPENSE-SCOURGE, WEAPON; **cudgel one's brains,** FANCY, REFLECTION-VACANCY; **take up the cudgels,** ATTACK-DEFENSE, FIGHTING-CONCILIATION, OBSTRUCTION-HELP, STRIFE-PEACE.
cue. A hint; a watchword. ENLIGHTENMENT-SECRECY, OCCUPATION, PRETEXT, SIGN; **in proper cue,** SKILL-UNSKILFULNESS; **take one's cue from,** ADVICE.
cuff. A sleeve; a blow. DRESS-UNDRESS, EXCULPATION-PUNITION, IMPETUS-REACTION.
cui bono [L.] (cai bo'-no). For whose advantage. USEFULNESS-USELESSNESS.
cuique voluptas sui [L.] (cai'-quî vo-lup'-tas siu'-ai). To each one his own pleasure. DESIRE-DISTASTE.
cui-rass'. A breastplate. ATTACK-DEFENSE.
cui''-ras-sier'. A mounted soldier. BELLIGERENT.
cuisine [F.] (cwî-zîn'). A kitchen. NUTRIMENT-EXCRETION.
cuisine batterie [F.] (cwî-zîn' bat-rî'). Kitchen utensils. FASTING-GLUTTONY.
culbute [F.] (cül-büt'). A somersault. ASCENT-DESCENT, REVERSAL.
culbuter [F.] (cül-bü-tê'). To throw head over heels. REVERSAL.
cul'-de-lampe'. A fancy border of a page. EMBELLISHMENT-DISFIGUREMENT, ENGRAVING.
cul''-de-sac'. Blind alley. APERTURE-CLOSURE, DIFFICULTY-FACILITY, SHARPNESS-BLUNTNESS.
cu'-li-na-ry. Pertaining to cooking. NUTRIMENT-EXCRETION; **culinary art,** PREPARATION-NONPREPARATION.
cull. A dupe; to pick out. CHOICE-NEUTRALITY, GULL-DECEIVER, TAKING-RESTITUTION.
cul'-len-der. A sieve. APERTURE-CLOSURE.
cul''-li-bil'-i-ty. Credulity. CREDULOUSNESS-SKEPTICISM.
cul'-lion. A poltroon. GOOD MAN-BAD-MAN.

cul'-ly. A dupe. GULL-DECEIVER, TRUTHFULNESS-FRAUD.

culm. Coal-dust. COMBUSTIBLE.

cul'-mi-nate. To attain completion. COMPLETION-NONCOMPLETION, HEIGHT-LOWNESS, SUPREMACY-SUBORDINACY, TOP-BOTTOM.

cul''-mi-na'-ting. Resulting. SUPREMACY-SUBORDINACY, TOP-BOTTOM.

cul''-mi-na'-tion. The highest point. COMPLETION-NONCOMPLETION, HEIGHT-LOWNESS, SUPREMACY-SUBORDINACY.

cul''-pa-bil'-i-ty. Guiltiness. INNOCENCE-GUILT, VIRTUE-VICE.

cul'-pa-ble. Deserving blame. INNOCENCE-GUILT, VIRTUE-VICE.

culpam pœna premit comes [L.] (cul'-pam pî'-na prî-mit co'-mîz). Punishment presses close upon crime. INNOCENCE-GUILT, RECOMPENSE-PUNITION.

cul'-prit. A criminal. GOOD MAN-BAD MAN.

cul'-ti-vate. To till; to develop. BETTERMENT-DETERIORATION, DOMESTICATION-AGRICULTURE, FEELING-INSENSIBILITY, OBSTRUCTION-HELP, PREPARATION-NONPREPARATION.

cul'-ti-va''-ted. Courteous. POLITENESS-IMPOLITENESS; **cultivated taste,** TASTE-VULGARITY.

cul''-ti-va'-tion. Tillage. BETTERMENT-DETERIORATION, DOMESTICATION-AGRICULTURE, PREPARATION-NONPREPARATION, TASTE-VULGARITY.

cul'-ti-va''-tor. An agriculturist. DOMESTICATION-AGRICULTURE.

cul'-ture. Refinement. BETTERMENT-DETERIORATION, KNOWLEDGE-IGNORANCE, TASTE-VULGARITY.

cul'-ver-in. A cannon. WEAPON.

cul'-vert. An artificial water-course. WATERCOURSE-AIRPIPE.

cum'-ber. To hinder; to oppress. HEAVINESS-LIGHTNESS, OBSTRUCTION-HELP.

cum'-ber-some. Unwieldy. HEAVINESS-LIGHTNESS, PLEASURABLENESS-PAINFULNESS, PROPRIETY-IMPROPRIETY.

cum'-brous. Heavy. HEAVINESS-LIGHTNESS, OBSTRUCTION-HELP, PLEASURABLENESS-PAINFULNESS, PROPRIETY-IMPROPRIETY.

cum multis aliis [L.] (cum mul'-tis ê'-li-is). With many others. ADDITION-SUBTRACTION, MULTIPLICITY-PAUCITY.

cu''-mu-la'-tion. Process of massing together; a heap. GATHERING-SCATTERING.

cu'-mu-la-tive. Superadded. GATHERING-SCATTERING; **cumulative evidence,** EVIDENCE-COUNTEREVIDENCE; **cumulative vote,** CHOICE-NEUTRALITY.

cu'-mu-lo-stra''-tus. A form of cloud. VISCIDITY-FOAM.

cu'-mu-lus. A cloud. VISCIDITY-FOAM.

cunctando restituit rem [L.] (cunc-tan'-do rî-stit'-yu-it rem). By delaying he retarded the affair. ACTION-PASSIVENESS.

cunc-ta'-tion. Delay. EARLINESS-LATENESS.

cu'-ne-i-form. Wedge-shaped. ANGULARITY, WRITING-PRINTING; **cuneiform character,** WRITING-PRINTING.

cun'-ning. Artful. CRAFT-ARTLESSNESS, PREDETERMINATION-IMPULSE, SAGACITY-INCAPACITY, SKILL-UNSKILFULNESS, TRUTHFULNESS-FRAUD; **cunning fellow,** ADEPT-BUNGLER; **cunning man,** ADEPT-BUNGLER, DEVOTION-MAGICIAN.

cun'-ning-ly. Shrewdly. CRAFT-ARTLESSNESS.

cun'-ning-ness. Shrewdness. ADEPT-BUNGLER.

cup. A drinking vessel; strong drink; a surgical instrument. CONTENTS-RECEIVER, CONVEXITY-CONCAVITY, NUTRIMENT-EXCRETION, REMEDY-BANE, TEETOTALISM-INTEMPERANCE; **cup of humiliation,** SELF-RESPECT-HUMBLENESS; **cup that cheers,** NUTRIMENT-EXCRETION; **cup too low,** LIGHTHEARTEDNESS-DE-

JECTION; **dash the cup from one's lips,** EXPECTATION-DISAPPOINTMENT; **in one's cups,** TEETOTALISM-INTEMPERANCE.

cup'-bear''-er. One who serves the wine-cup. CHIEF-UNDERLING.

cup'-board. A closet. CONTENTS-RECEIVER.

Cu'-pid. The god of love. BEAUTY-UGLINESS, LOVE-HATE.

cu-pid'-i-ty. Avarice. DESIRE-DISTASTE, EXTRAVAGANCE-AVARICE.

cu'-po-la. A dome. ARCHITECTURE, CONVEXITY-CONCAVITY, HEIGHT-LOWNESS.

cup'-ping. An operation of blood-drawing. REMEDY-BANE.

cup'-toss''-ing. A game of chance. PURPOSE-LUCK.

cur. A dog; a sneak. FAUNA-FLORA, GOOD MAN-BAD MAN.

cur'-a-ble. Remediable. REMEDY-BANE, RENOVATION-RELAPSE.

cur'-a-ble-ness. Capability of being cured. RENOVATION-RELAPSE.

cu'-ra-cy. A charge. CHURCH.

curæ leves loquuntur, ingentes stupent [L.] (kiu'-rî lî'-vîz lo-quun'-tur, in-jen'-tîz stiu-pent), Trivial anxieties talk, great ones stand mute. BRAGGING, WELFARE-MISFORTUNE.

cura futuri, mihi [L.] (kiu'-ra fiu-tiu'-rai mai'-hai). My care is for the future. PREVISION.

cu'-rate. A minister. MINISTRY-LAITY.

cur'-a-tive. Able to cure. RENOVATION-RELAPSE.

cu-ra'-tor. Custodian. CONSIGNEE.

curb. To restrain. ARCHITECTURE, CASING, MOTIVE-DEHORTATION, RELEASE-PRISON, RELEASE-RESTRAINT, SWIFTNESS-SLOWNESS, TURBULENCE-CALMNESS.

curb'-stone''. Stone at the edge of a sidewalk. CITY-COUNTRY.

curd. Coagulated milk. PULPINESS-OILINESS, SOLIDITY-RARITY.

cur'-dle. To coagulate. SOLIDITY-RARITY; **make the blood curdle,** PLEASURABLENESS-PAINFULNESS.

cur'-dled. Coagulated. VISCIDITY-FOAM.

cure. To make well; to preserve; a remedy; a spiritual charge. ALLEVIATION-AGGRAVATION, CHURCH, CONSERVATION, HEALTH-SICKNESS, REMEDY-BANE, RENOVATION-RELAPSE.

cu''-ré. A parish priest. MINISTRY-LAITY.

cure'-less. Incurable. SANGUINENESS-HOPELESSNESS.

cur'-few. A bell-ringing at evening. CITY, MORNING-EVENING.

curiosa felicitas [L.] (kiu-ri-o'-sa fî-lis'-i-tas). A happy idea. SKILL-UNSKILFULNESS.

cu''-ri-os'-i-ty. Inquisitiveness; a strange object. CONVENTIONALITY-UNCONVENTIONALITY, EXPECTATION-SURPRISE, INQUISITIVENESS-INDIFFERENCE, PHENOMENON.

cu'-ri-ous. Exceptional; inquisitive. BEAUTY-UGLINESS, CONVENTIONALITY-UNCONVENTIONALITY, DESIRE-DISTASTE, EXPECTATION-SURPRISE, INQUISITIVENESS-INDIFFERENCE, TRUTH-ERROR.

cu'-ri-ous-ly. Unusually. MAGNITUDE-SMALLNESS.

cu'-ri-ous-ness. Eagerness. INQUISITIVENESS-INDIFFERENCE.

curl. A bend; to bend. CIRCLE-WINDING, CURVATION-RECTILINEARITY, PLICATURE, SMOOTHNESS-ROUGHNESS; **curl up one's lip,** REGARD-SCORN.

curl'-ing. A game. ENTERTAINMENT-WEARINESS.

cur-mud'-geon. A miserly churl. EXTRAVAGANCE-AVARICE, GENTILITY-DEMOCRACY.

cur'-ren-cy. Money; publicity. MONEY, PUBLICITY.

cur'-rent. Generally accepted; now present; common; a stream. ELECTRICITY, ENTITY-NONENTITY, HABIT-DESUETUDE, LANGUAGE, OCCURRENCE-DESTINY, PUBLICITY, RIVER-WIND, TIDINGS-MYSTERY, TIME;

account current, ACCOUNTS; **against the current,** AN-TAGONISM-CONCURRENCE; **current belief,** ASSENT-DISSENT; **current of events,** OCCURRENCE-DESTINY; **current of ideas,** REFLECTION-VACANCY; **current of time,** PERIOD-PROGRESS; **go with the current,** CONVENTIONALITY-UNCONVENTIONALITY; **pass current,** FAITH-MISGIVING, PUBLICITY, SOCIETY-LUDICROUSNESS.

currente calamo [L.] (cur-ren′-tî cal′-a-mo). With rapid pen. WRITING-PRINTING.

cur′-ri-cle. A two-wheeled vehicle. CONVEYANCE-VESSEL.

cur-ric′-u-lum. A course. EDUCATION-MISTEACHING.

cur′-ry. To rub; a sauce. CONDIMENT, FRICTION-LUBRICATION; **curry favor with,** ADULATION-DISAPPROVAL, LOVE-HATE.

curse. To execrate; calamity. CHARITABLENESS-CURSE, PLEASURABLENESS-PAINFULNESS, REMEDY-BANE, WELFARE-MISFORTUNE.

curs′-ed. Execrable. CHARITABLENESS-CURSE, GOODNESS-BADNESS.

curs′-ing. Blasphemy. CHARITABLENESS-CURSE.

cur′-si-tor. A law-clerk. ADVOCATE.

cur′-so-ry. Rapid and superficial. HEED-DISREGARD, HURRY-LEISURE, LASTINGNESS-TRANSIENTNESS; **take**

a cursory view of, CAREFULNESS-CARELESSNESS, HEED-DISREGARD.

curst. Peevish. FAVORITE-MOROSENESS.

curt. Concise. LENGTH-SHORTNESS, TALKATIVENESS-TACITURNITY, TERSENESS-PROLIXITY.

cur-tail′. To cut short. ADDITION-SUBTRACTION, LENGTH-SHORTNESS; **curtailed of its fair proportions,** BEAUTY-UGLINESS, LENGTH-SHORTNESS, PROPORTION-DEFORMITY.

cur-tail′-ment. A shortening. ADDITION-SUBTRACTION, LENGTH-SHORTNESS.

cur′-tain. A shade. ACTING, ATTACK-DEFENSE, ENLIGHTENMENT-SECRECY, EXPOSURE-HIDINGPLACE, LUMINARY-SHADE; **behind the curtain,** ENLIGHTENMENT-SECRECY, KNOWLEDGE-IGNORANCE, VISIBILITY-INVISIBILITY; **close the curtain,** ENLIGHTENMENT-SECRECY; **curtain lecture,** APPROVAL-DISAPPROVAL; **raise the curtain,** EXPOSURE-HIDINGPLACE; **rising of the curtain,** APPEARANCE-DISAPPEARANCE.

curt′-ness. Shortness. TALKATIVENESS-TACITURNITY.

curt′-sy. A bow. ELEVATION-DEPRESSION, POLITENESS-IMPOLITENESS, YIELDING, VIBRATION.

cu′-rule. Magisterial. COUNCIL.

cur-va′-tion. Act of curving. CURVATION-RECTILINEARITY.

CURVATION—RECTILINEARITY.

Arcuation. Bending.
Bend. A change of direction in a thing.
Bending. The act of causing to be bent.
Bought. Flexure.
Conflexure. Bending.
Crook. Deviation from a straight line.
Curl. Waviness in any object.
Curling. The act of putting into the form of curls.
Curvation.⎫
Curvature.⎬ The state of being slightly bent.
Curvity.⎭
Deflexion.⎫ A turning from the proper course.
Detour.⎭
Devexity. Downward curvature.
Deviation. Departure from the regular course.
Flexion.⎫
Flexure.⎪
Incurvation.⎬ State of being bent.
Incurvity.⎪
Inflexion.⎭
Recurvation.⎫ State of being bent back.
Recurvity.⎭
Sinuosity, etc. State of having deep folds, etc. See CIRCLE-WINDING.
Sweep. Departure of a curve, etc., from a rectilinear line.
Turn. Change of course.

CURVATION—Denotations.

Arc. Anything in the shape of an arch or curve.
Arcade. A vaulted passageway.
Arch. Any bow-like curve, structure, or object.
Bough. The limb of a tree, which usually hangs in a bow-like curve.
Bow. Something bent or curved.
Cardioid. A heart-shaped curve.
Caustic. A surface so curved as to give the greatest amount of heat in reflecting heat rays.
Catenary. The curve made by a chain hanging by both ends.
Conchoid. A geometrical curve of the fourth degree.
Festoon. A garland hanging in a curve between two points.
Half-moon. Anything in the shape of a half-moon.
Hook. A device consisting of a curved or bent piece of metal serving to hold an object.
Horseshoe. A U-shaped metal shoe for a horse.
Hyperbola. A curve composed of two branches which never meet.
Loop. A curve or bend of any kind.
Lunule. A crescent-shaped figure.
Parabola. A plane curve such that the distance of every point in it from the focus is equal to the distance of the same point from a fixed straight line called the directrix.
Tracery. A scrollwork of any kind.
Vault. An arched apartment or chamber.

Directness. The state of being direct.
Inflexibility, etc. The state of not bending easily, etc. See HARDNESS.
Rectilinearity. The state of being rectilinear.
Straightness. The state of being straight.

RECTILINEARITY—Denotations.

Direct line.⎫ A straight line.
Right line.⎭
Short cut. The straight line between two points.
Straight line. The shortest distance between two points.

RECTILINEARITY—Verbs.

Rectify. To set right again.
Straighten. To make straight.
Unbend. To take the bend out of.
Uncurl, etc. To cause something to lose its curl, etc. See CIRCLE-WINDING.
Unfold. To lay the folds open.
Unravel, etc. To disentangle, etc. See CROSSING.
Unwrap. To take the wrapper off.

RECTILINEARITY—Verbal Expressions.

Be straight, etc. (see *Adjectives*); go straight; have no turning; not bend to either side; not deviate to either side; not incline to either side; not turn to either side; put straight; render straight; set straight; steer for, etc. (see AIM).

RECTILINEARITY—Adjectives.

Direct. Leading only to one place.
Even. Free from abrupt changes in direction.
In a line. Straight.
Inflexible, etc. Not to be bent, etc. See HARDNESS.
Rectilineal.⎫ Straight.
Rectilinear.⎭
Right. Mathematically straight.
Straight. Not crooked.
Straight as an arrow. See AIM.
True. Exact.
Unbent, etc. Not bent, etc. See *Verbs*.
Undeviating. Not deviating.
Undistorted. Not distorted.
Unswerving. Not moving from the right course.
Unturned. Not turned.

CURVATION—Continued.
CURVATION—Verbs.

Arch. To make in the shape of an arch.
Arcuate. To make bow-shaped.

CURVATION—Verbs—*Continued.*

Bend. To change the direction in a thing.	**Incurvate.** } To turn from a straight course.
Bow. To bend over slightly.	**Inflect.** }
Concamerate. To arch over.	**Recurve.** To bend back.
Crook. To cause to deviate from a straight line.	**Reenter.** To turn in.
Curl. To make in the form of curls.	**Round.** To make round.
Curve. To bend slightly.	**Sag.** } To settle.
Deflect. } To turn from the proper or regular course, etc. See	**Swag.** }
Deviate, etc. } AIM-ABERRATION.	**Sweep.** To move with a swinging motion.
Frizzle. To curl.	**Turn.** To move in a different direction.

CURVATION—*Verbal Phrases.*

Arch over be curved, etc. (see *Adjectives*); **render curved,** etc. (see *Adjectives*).

CURVATION—*Adjectives.*

Bell-shaped. Shaped like a bell.	**Falcated.** } Bent like a sickle.
Bowed, etc. Bent over, etc. See *Verbs.*	**Falciform.** }
Bow-legged, etc. Having the legs bent in an outward curve, etc. See PROPORTION-DEFORMITY.	**Fig-shaped.** Shaped like a fig.
	Heart-shaped. Of the form of a heart.
Cardioid. Heart-shaped.	**Hooked.** Shaped like a hook.
Circular, etc. Like a circle, etc. See CIRCLE.	**Lenticular.** } In the form of a double convex lens.
Conchoidal. In the form of a conchoid.	**Lentiform.** }
Cordated. } Heart-shaped.	**Luniform.** } Moon-shaped.
Cordiform. }	**Lunular.** }
Crescentic. Crescent-shaped.	**Oblique,** etc. Slanting, etc. See PARALLELISM-INCLINATION.
Crump. Crooked.	**Pear-shaped.** Shaped like a pear.
Curved, etc. }	**Recurved.** } Curved back.
Curviform. } In the shape of a curve, etc. See *Adjectives*	**Recurvous.** }
Curvilineal. }	**Reniform.** Kidney-shaped.
Curvilinear. }	**Semicircular.** Of the form of a half-circle.
Devex. Bending down.	**Semilunar.** Of the form of a half-moon.
Devious. Departing from the regular course.	**Vaulted.** In the form of a vault.

curv′-a-ture. Act of bending. CURVATION-RECTILINEARITY.

curve. To bend; a line of which no portion is straight. AIM-ABERRATION, CURVATION-RECTILINEARITY.

curved. Bent. CURVATION-RECTILINEARITY, PARALLELISM-INCLINATION.

cur′-vet. To prance. AGITATION, CIRCUITION, CURVATION-RECTILINEARITY, SPRING-DIVE, VIBRATION.

cur′-vi-form. Curved. CURVATION-RECTILINEARITY.

cur″-vi-lin′-e-ar. Formed by curved lines. CURVATION-RECTILINEARITY.

curv′-i-ty. State of being curved. CURVATION-RECTILINEARITY.

cush′-ion. A pillow. ALLEVIATION-AGGRAVATION, HARDNESS-SOFTNESS, PLEASURE-PAIN, SUSPENSION-SUPPORT.

cusp. A point. ANGULARITY, SHARPNESS-BLUNTNESS.

cus′-pid. A canine tooth. SHARPNESS-BLUNTNESS.

cus′-pid-ate. Having a cusp. SHARPNESS-BLUNTNESS.

cus′-pi-da″-ted. Having cusps. SHARPNESS-BLUNTNESS.

custodes quis custodiet [L.] (cus-to′-dîz quis cus-to′-di-et). Who will watch the watchmen. CAREFULNESS-CARELESSNESS.

cus-to′-di-an. A guardian. GUARD-PRISONER, SECURITY-INSECURITY.

cus′-to-dy. Safe keeping. KEEPING-RELINQUISHMENT, RELEASE-RESTRAINT, SECURITY-INSECURITY; **in custody,** GUARD-PRISONER, JUSTIFICATION-CHARGE; **take into custody,** LIBERTY-SUBJECTION, RELEASE-RESTRAINT.

cus′-tom. Habit; tax; fashion; patronage. BUYING-SALE, EXCHANGE, HABIT-DESUETUDE, NOVELTY-ANTIQUITY, PRICE-DISCOUNT, SOCIETY-LUDICROUSNESS; **custom honored in breach,** HABIT-DESUETUDE, RIGHT-WRONG.

cus′-tom-a-ry. Habitual. HABIT-DESUETUDE, UNIFORMITY-MULTIFORMITY, SOCIETY-LUDICROUSNESS, UNIVERSALITY-PARTICULARITY.

cus′-tom-er. A purchaser. BUYING-SALE.

cus′-tom–house″. Toll-house. MARKET. **Custom-house officer,** JUDICATURE.

custos [L.] (cus′-tos). Guardian. GUARD-PRISONER.

custos rotulorum [L.] (cus′-tos rot″-yu-lo′-rum). Keeper of the records. RECORDER.

cut. To divide; to hew; to carve; to wound; a cleft; a gash; a division; a print; a way; a snub. ADMISSION-EXPULSION, ATTACK-DEFENSE, CAREFULNESS-CARELESSNESS, CONTINUITY-INTERRUPTION, DOMESTICATION-AGRICULTURE, ENGRAVING, EXCITATION, FEELING-INSENSIBILITY, FORM-FORMLESSNESS, HEATING-COOLING, IMPETUS-REACTION, INTERSPACE-CONTACT, LAMINA-FIBER, LENGTH-SHORTNESS, PLEASURABLENESS-PAINFULNESS, POLITENESS-IMPOLITENESS, SCULPTURE, SHARPNESS-BLUNTNESS, SOCIABILITY-PRIVACY, TEETOTALISM-INTEMPERANCE, UNION-DISUNION, WAY, WHOLE-PART; **cut according to the cloth,** GENEROSITY-FRUGALITY, RECKLESSNESS-CAUTION; **cut across,** TRANSMISSION; **cut adrift,** UNION-DISUNION; **cut a figure,** APPEARANCE-DISAPPEARANCE, POMP, REPUTATION-DISCREDIT, SOCIETY-LUDICROUSNESS; **cut along,** SWIFTNESS-SLOWNESS; **cut and come again,** ENOUGH, RECURRENCE; **cut and dried,** ORGANIZATION-DISORGANIZATION, PREPARATION-NONPREPARATION; **cut and run,** QUEST-EVASION; **cut and thrust,** ATTACK-DEFENSE; **cut a poor figure,** REPUTATION-DISCREDIT; **cut away,** SWIFTNESS-SLOWNESS; **cut blocks with a razor,** PROVISION-WASTE, RATIOCINATION-INSTINCT, USE-MISUSE; **cut both ways,** EVIDENCE-COUNTEREVIDENCE; **cut capers,** SPRING-DIVE; **cut dead,** SOCIABILITY-PRIVACY; **cut direct,** SOCIABILITY-PRIVACY; **cut down,** CREATION-DESTRUCTION, ELEVATION-DEPRESSION, LENGTH-SHORTNESS, LIFE-KILLING; **cut jokes,** WITTINESS-DULNESS; **cut in two,** DOUBLING-HALVING; **cut of one's jib,** APPEARANCE-DISAPPEARANCE; **cut off,** ADDITION-SUBTRACTION, GAIN-LOSS, LIFE-KILLING, OBSTRUCTION-HELP, UNION-DISUNION; **cut one's own throat,** SKILL-UNSKILFULNESS; **cut one's stick,** ARRIVAL-DEPARTURE, QUEST-EVASION; **cut one's way through,** TRANSMISSION; **cut out,** COMMUTATION-PERMUTATION, DESIGN, SUPREMACY-SUBORDINACY; **cut out for,** SKILL-UNSKILFULNESS; **cut out work,** MANAGEMENT, PREPARATION-NON-

PREPARATION; **cut the first turf,** BEGINNING-END; **cut the ground from under one,** CHARITABLENESS-MALEVOLENCE, PROOF-DISPROOF, SUCCESS-FAILURE; **cut to the heart,** EXCITATION, PLEASURABLENESS-PAINFULNESS; **cut to the quick,** EXCITATION, PLEASURABLENESS-PAINFULNESS; **cut up,** APPROVAL-DISAPPROVAL, CONTENTEDNESS-DISCONTENTMENT, CREATION-DESTRUCTION, JUBILATION-LAMENTATION, PLEASURABLENESS-PAINFULNESS, PLEASURE-PAIN, UNION-DISUNION; **cut up root and branch,** CREATION-DESTRUCTION; **cut up rough,** FAVORITE-ANGER; **what one will cut up for,** PROPERTY.

cu-ta′-ne-ous. Pertaining to the skin. COVER-LINING.

cu′-ti-cle. The outer skin. COVER-LINING.

cu-tic′-u-lar. Pertaining to the cuticle. COVER-LINING.

cut′-lass. A short sword. WEAPON.

cut′-ler-y. Cutting-instruments. SHARPNESS-BLUNTNESS.

cut′-purse″. A robber. ROBBER.

cut′-ter. A sloop. CONVEYANCE-VESSEL, SHARPNESS-BLUNTNESS.

cut′-throat″. A ruffian. BENEFACTOR-EVILDOER, LIFE-KILLING.

cut′-ting. Sharp; painful. APPROVAL-DISAPPROVAL, EMOTION, HEAT-COLD, PLEASURABLENESS-PAINFULNESS, SHARPNESS-BLUNTNESS, WHOLE-PART.

cut′-tings. Selections. CHOICE-REJECTION, DIGEST.

cut′-ty-stool. A seat of rebuke. REPENTANCE-OBDURACY.

cwt. A hundredweight. FIVE-QUINQUESECTION, HEAVINESS-LIGHTNESS.

cy-an′-o-gen. A gas with a purple flame. BLUENESS-ORANGE.

cy′-cle. A period; a loop. PERIODICITY-IRREGULARITY, REVOLUTION-EVOLUTION.

cy′-cloid. Like a circle. CIRCLE-WINDING.

cy-cloi′-dal. Shaped like a cycloid. CIRCLE-WINDING.

cy′-clone. A tornado. REVOLUTION-EVOLUTION, RIVER-WIND.

cy″-clo-pe′-di-a. An encyclopedia. KNOWLEDGE-IGNORANCE, MISSIVE-PUBLICATION.

cy″-clo-pe′-an. Huge and strong. GREATNESS-LITTLENESS, STRENGTH-WEAKNESS.

Cy′-clops. A huge and stupid monster; a one-eyed giant in the Homeric legends. CONVENTIONALITY-UNCONVENTIONALITY, GREATNESS-LITTLENESS, GULL-DECEIVER, STRENGTH-WEAKNESS.

cygne, chant du [F.] (cîny, shan· dü). The song of the swan. LIFE-DEATH.

cygne noir [F.] (cîny nwar). The black swan. FAULTLESSNESS-FAULTINESS.

cyl′-in-der. A solid body. ROUNDNESS.

cy-lin′-dric. Shaped like a cylinder. ROUNDNESS.

cy-lin′-dric-al. Shaped like a cylinder. ROUNDNESS.

cy-lin-dric′-i-ty. Quality of being cylindrical. ROUNDNESS.

cyl′-in-droid. A solid body. ROUNDNESS.

cy′-ma. Curved molding. ARCHITECTURE.

cym′-bal. A metallic instrument. MUSICAL INSTRUMENTS.

cy-moph′-a-nous. Opalescent. VARIEGATION.

cyn′-ic. A misanthrope. AUSTERITY, FLATTERER-DEFAMER, HUMANITARIANISM-MISANTHROPY; **closet cynic,** SOCIABILITY-PRIVACY.

cyn′-ic-al. Pessimistic. ADULATION-DISPARAGEMENT, APPROVAL-DISAPPROVAL, AUSTERITY, REGARD-SCORN, SOCIABILITY-PRIVACY.

cyn′-i-cism. Discourtesy. ADULATION-DISPARAGEMENT, AUSTERITY, HUMANITARIANISM-MISANTHROPY, POLITENESS-IMPOLITENESS.

cy′-no-sure. An object of interest. MANAGEMENT, REPUTATION-DISCREDIT, SIGN.

Cyn′-thi-a. The moon. MUTABILITY-STABILITY.

cy′-pher. Zero. NUMBER, NUMBERING, SUBSTANCE-NULLITY.

cy′-press. An evergreen tree. JUBILATION-LAMENTATION, LIFE-FUNERAL.

Cyp′-ri-an. A courtezan. PURITY-RAKE.

cyst. A membranous sac. CONTENTS-RECEIVER.

cyst′-ic. Having cysts. CONTENTS-RECEIVER.

czar. A supreme lord (Cæsar). The emperor of Russia. CHIEF-UNDERLING, TYRANNY-ANARCHY.

cza-ri′-na. The empress of Russia. CHIEF-UNDERLING.

Czol′-gosz. The assassin of President McKinley. TYRANNY-ANARCHY.

D

dab. An expert; a light blow. ADEPT-BUNGLER, COVER-LINING, IMPETUS-REACTION.

dab'-ble. To dip gently. ACTIVITY-INDOLENCE, CLEANNESS-FILTHINESS, WATER-AIR.

dab'-bled. Lightly splashed. DAMPNESS-DRYNESS.

dab'-bler. One who dabbles. SCHOLAR-DUNCE.

dab'-bling. Making a dab. ACTIVITY-INDOLENCE.

da capo [It.] (da ca'-po). From the (head) beginning. A direction to repeat a strain in music. RECURRENCE.

da-coit'. One of a band of robbers in India. ROBBER.

dac'-tyl. A foot with a long syllable followed by two short ones. POETRY-PROSE, RHETORIC.

dac-tyl'-ic. Pertaining to a dactyl. RHETORIC.

dac-tyl'-i-o-man''-cy. Divination with a finger-ring. PROPHECY.

dac''-tyl-ol'-o-gy. The art of talking with the fingers. SIGN.

dac''-tyl-on'-o-my. The art of counting on fingers. NUMBERING, SIGN.

dad. Father. PARENTAGE-PROGENY.

da'-do. A flat surface between a base and a surbase. TOP-BOTTOM.

dae'-dal. Artistic. SAMENESS-CONTRAST, VARIEGATION.

dae-da'-li-an. Cunningly wrought. CIRCLE-WINDING, SKILL-UNSKILFULNESS.

daft. Weak-minded. SANENESS-LUNACY.

dag'-ger. A weapon. PLEASURABLENESS-PAINFULNESS, WEAPON; **air drawn dagger,** FANCY; **at daggers drawn,** AMITY-HOSTILITY, ANTAGONISM-CONCURRENCE, LOVE-HATE, VARIANCE-ACCORD; **look daggers,** CHARITABLENESS-MENACE, FAVORITE-ANGER; **plant dagger in the breast,** PLEASURABLENESS-PAINFULNESS; **speak daggers,** APPROVAL-DISAPPROVAL.

dag'-gle. To draggle. CLEANNESS-FILTHINESS, SUSPENSION-SUPPORT.

dag'-o-ba. A Buddhist shrine. FANE.

Da'-gon. A Philistine god. REVELATION-PSEUDO-REVELATION.

da-guerre'-o-type. A kind of photograph. DELINEATION-CARICATURE, PAINTING.

dai'-ly. Every day. FREQUENCY-RARITY, PERIODICITY-IRREGULARITY; **daily occurrence,** CONVENTIONALITY-UNCONVENTIONALITY, HABIT-DESUETUDE.

dain'-ty. Fastidious. BEAUTY-UGLINESS, DESIRE-PARTICULARNESS, NUTRIMENT-EXCRETION, PALATABLENESS-UNPALATABLENESS, PLEASURABLENESS-PAINFULNESS, SENSUALITY-SUFFERING, TASTE-VULGARITY.

dai'-ry. A place where milk is made into butter. CONTENTS-RECEIVER.

da'-is. A platform. SCEPTER, SUSPENSION-SUPPORT.

dai'-sy. A flower. "Daisies pied and violets blue." [Shakespeare, *Love's Labor Lost*, V, ii.] EMBELLISHMENT-DISFIGUREMENT; **fresh as a daisy,** HEALTH-SICKNESS.

dale. A valley. CONVEXITY-CONCAVITY.

dal'-li-ance. The act of dallying. BLANDISHMENT.

dal'-ly. To trifle away time. ACTIVITY-INDOLENCE, BLANDISHMENT, DETERMINATION-VACILLATION, EARLINESS-LATENESS, ENTERTAINMENT-WEARINESS.

dal-mat'-ic. A tunic with wide sleeves. VESTMENTS.

dal'-ton-ism. Color-blindness. [Named after the chemist Dalton.] SIGHT-DIMSIGHTEDNESS.

Dal'-ton's the'-o-ry. A theory of chemistry. CHEMISTRY.

dam. A barrier; a female parent. APERTURE-CLOSURE, LAKE-PLAIN, OBSTRUCTION-HELP, PARENTAGE-PROGENY.

dam'-age. Destruction of value. BETTERMENT-DETERIORATION, GOOD-EVIL, PRICE-DISCOUNT.

dam'-ag-es. Legal compensation in money. RECOMPENSE-PENALTY.

dam''-as-cene'. To imitate Damascus work. VARIEGATION.

dam'-ask. A rich fabric. REDNESS-GREENNESS.

dame. A woman of high position. GENTILITY-DEMOCRACY, INSTRUCTOR-PUPIL, MALE-FEMALE.

damn. To condemn; to curse. EXCULPATION-CONVICTION, CURSE; **damn with faint praise.** [Pope.] ADULATION-DISPARAGEMENT, APPROVAL-DISAPPROVAL.

dam'-na-ble. Deserving condemnation. GOODNESS-BADNESS.

dam-na'-tion. The state of being damned. EXCULPATION-CONVICTION.

dam'-na-to-ry. Tending to condemn. APPROVAL-DISAPPROVAL, EXCULPATION-CONVICTION.

damned. Given to destruction. GOODNESS-BADNESS.

dam'-ni-fy. Cause damage to. BETTERMENT-DETERIORATION, GOODNESS-BADNESS.

damnosa hereditas [L.] (dam-no'-sa hî-red'-i-tas). Injurious inheritance. FRIEND-FOE.

Dam'-o-cles, sword of. The sword that hung by a single hair, at a feast, over Damocles, a parasite and courtier of Dionysius of Syracuse. REFUGE-PITFALL.

Da'-mon and Pyth'-i-as. Ancient ideal friends, of Syracuse. FRIEND-FOE.

damp. Moist. DAMPNESS-DRYNESS, HEATING-COOLING, LIGHTHEARTEDNESS-DEJECTION, MOTIVE-DEHORTATION, OBSTRUCTION-HELP, TURBULENCE-CALMNESS, WITTINESS-DULNESS; **damp the sound,** RESONANCE-NONRESONANCE.

damp'-er. That which damps or checks. LIGHTHEARTEDNESS-DEJECTION, MOTIVE-DEHORTATION, OBSTRUCTION-HELP, OVEN-REFRIGERATOR, RESONANCE-NONRESONANCE.

damp'-ness. Moisture. DAMPNESS-DRYNESS.

DAMPNESS—DRYNESS.

Dew. Moisture from the atmosphere condensed by cool bodies upon their surfaces.

Humectation. A moistening.

Humidity. Dampness or moisture, especially of the atmosphere.

Madefaction. The act of making wet.

Marsh. A tract of soft wet land. See SWAMP.

Moistness. See *Adjectives*.

Moisture. Slight wetness or that which makes wet.

Serein [F.]. The night dew.

Arefaction. Act of making dry.

Aridity. The state of being without moisture.

Desiccation. The act of becoming dry.

Drainage. A gradual flowing off of water.

Drought. Lack of rain or water.

Dryness. The state of being dry.

Exsiccation. State of being dried up.

Siccity. Dryness.

DAMPNESS—DRYNESS—*Continued*

Dampness—*Scientific Terms.*

Hygrometer. An instrument to measure the degree of moisture in the atmosphere.

Hygrometry. The branch of physics which treats of the determination of the humidity of various bodies, especially the atmosphere.

Dampness—*Verbs.*

Bedew. To wet with dew.

Be moist. See *Adjectives.*

Damp. To make damp or moderately wet.

Drench, etc. To wet thoroughly. See WATER.

Humect. }
Humectate. } To make wet; to moisten.

Imbrue. To moisten or wet, especially in blood.

Imbue. To cause to absorb or imbibe.

Infiltrate. To enter a substance by penetrating through the pores.

Moisten. To make slightly wet.

Not have a dry thread. To be thoroughly wet.

Perspire, etc. To emit the secretions of the sudoriferous glands through the pores of the skin; to sweat. See EGRESS.

Saturate. To cause to become thoroughly soaked or penetrated

Soak. To cause to take up wet or moisture.

Sponge. To dampen.

Wet. To moisten or fill with liquid.

Dampness—*Adjectives.*

Dabbled. Moistened by little dips.

Damp. Between dry and wet.

Dank. Damp and close.

Dewy. Moist with dew.

Dripping. Falling in drops.

Humid. Somewhat wet.

Irriguous. Watery; moist.

Juicy. Full of juice.

Moist. Slightly wet.

Muddy. Turbid with mud.

Muggy. Damp; moist.

Reeking. Emitting vapor.

Roral. Dewy.

Rorid. Bedewed.

Roscid. Containing dew.

Saturated. See *Verbs.*

Sloppy. Wet; muddy, especially wet so as to spatter easily.

Soaking. See *Verbs.*

Sodden. Saturated or heavy with moisture.

Soft. Made to yield to pressure by the presence of moisture

Soggy. Soaked with water.

Swampy, etc. Like a swamp; low and wet. See SWAMP.

Swashy. Soft, like overripe fruit.

Undried. Not dried.

Watery, etc. Full of water. See WATER.

Dryness—*Denotations.*

Ebb tide. The retiring or falling tide.

Low water. The sinking to the farthest ebb of the tide.

Dryness—*Nouns of Agent.*

Dephlegmation. In chemistry the process of separating water from spirits or acids.

Dryness—*Verbs.*

Be dry. See *Adjectives.*

Be fine. To be clear weather

Desiccate. To dry up or become dry.

Drain. To cause to flow off by degrees.

Dry. To free from moisture.

Dry up. To become dry.

Exsiccate. To exhaust the water from.

Hold up. To cease to rain

Parch. To dry by heat.

Render dry. See *Adjectives.*

Soak up. To take in by the pores.

Sponge. To imbibe as a sponge.

Swab. To dry with a mop.

Wipe. To remove moisture by rubbing.

Dryness—*Adjectives.*

Anhydrous. Lacking water.

Arid. Devoid of moisture.

Dried. See *Verbs.*

Dry. Not wet or moist.

Dry as a biscuit. }
Dry as a bone. }
Dry as a mummy. } Extremely dry.
Dry as a stick. }
Dry as dust. }

Fine. Clear and bright.

Husky. Dry and harsh.

Juiceless. Destitute of juice; dry.

Rainless. Devoid of rain.

Sapless. Without sap, hence dry, withered.

Sear. Dried up or withered, as leaves in autumn

Undamped. Not moistened or wet.

Water-proof. Impervious to water.

Water-tight. So close or tight as not to leak.

Without rain. Dry.

Dampness—*Adjectives—Continued.*

Wet. Moistened by water.

Wet through. }
Wet to the skin. } Thoroughly wet.
Wringing wet. }

---

dam'-sel. A maiden. INFANT-VETERAN, MALE-FEMALE.

Danaë [Gr.] (dan'-a-î). Mother of Perseus. AFFLUENCE-PENURY.

Danaos timeo [L.] (dan'-a-os tim'-î-o). I fear the Greeks. FAITH-MISGIVING, RECKLESSNESS-CAUTION.

dance. To move with measured steps. AGITATION, ENTERTAINMENT-WEARINESS, JUBILATION-LAMENTATION, SPRING-DIVE, VIBRATION; **dance attendance,** CHIEF-UNDERLING, EARLINESS-LATENESS, PETITION-EXPOSTULATION; **dance the back step,** ADVANCE-RETROGRESSION; **dance the war dance,** DEFIANCE; **dance upon nothing,** RECOMPENSE-PUNITION; **lead one a dance,** QUEST-EVASION, MIDCOURSE-CIRCUIT, REGARD-DISRESPECT; **lead the dance,** DOMINANCE-IMPOTENCE.

dance'-mu''-sic. Music for dancing. MUSIC.

dan'-der. Dandruff. [Slang.] Anger. FAVORITE-ANGER.

Dan'-die Din'-mont. A hardy hairy terrier with short legs. [John Brown, *Our Dogs.*] FAUNA-FLORA.

dan'-di-fied. Having the characteristics of a dandy. SOCIETY-AFFECTATION.

dan'-di-prat. A little fellow. SOCIETY-DANDY.

dan'-dle. To toss caressingly in the arms. BLANDISHMENT.

dan'-druff. Scurf from the head. CLEANNESS-FILTHINESS.

dan'-dy. A vessel; a man over-refined in dress and manners. CONVEYANCE-VESSEL, SOCIETY-DANDY.

dan'-dy-ism. Foppishness. SOCIETY-AFFECTATION.

dan'-ger. The state of being exposed to any evil. SECURITY-INSECURITY; **danger past,** SECURITY-INSECURITY; **danger signal,** ALARM; **in danger,** CONTINGENCY, HEALTH-SICKNESS.

dan'-ger-ous. Full of danger. SECURITY-INSECURITY; **dangerous classes,** BENEFACTOR-EVILDOER; **dangerous illness,** HEALTH-SICKNESS; **dangerous person,** REFUGE-PITFALL.

dan'-gle. To hang loosely. POMP, SUSPENSION-SUPPORT, VIBRATION.

dan'-gler. One who dangles. LEADING-FOLLOWING.

Dan'-iel come to judg'-ment, a. An upright judge. [Shakespeare, *Merchant of Venice,* IV, i.] JUDGE.

Dan'-iel, second. A second upright judge [Shakespeare, *Merchant of Venice,* IV, i.] SAGE-FOOL.

dank. Filled with cold moisture. DAMPNESS-DRYNESS.

Dan to Be-er'-she-ba. The two extreme points of Palestine; the whole length of the land. EXTENSION-DISTRICT.

dap'-per. Neat in appearance. BEAUTY-UGLINESS, GREATNESS-LITTLENESS.

dap'-per-ling. A little fellow. GREATNESS-LITTLENESS.

dap'-ple. To mark with spots. GRAY-BROWN.

dap'-pled. Marked with spots. VARIEGATION.

Dar'-by and Jo'-an. The characters in the ballad, *The Happy Couple.* MATRIMONY - CELIBACY, SO-CIABILITY-PRIVACY.

dare. To defy. DEFIANCE, BRAVERY-COWARDICE; **dare say,** FAITH-MISGIVING, HYPOTHESIS, LIKELI-HOOD-UNLIKELIHOOD.

dare'-dev''-il. A reckless person. BRAWLER, RECK-LESSNESS-CAUTION.

dar'-ing. Having courage. BRAVERY-COWARDICE, DEFIANCE; **daring imagination,** FANCY.

dark. Without light. CLEARNESS-OBSCURITY, EN-LIGHTENMENT-SECRECY, LIGHT-DARKNESS, LIGHT-HEARTEDNESS-DEJECTION, LUMINARY-SHADE, MANI-FESTATION-LATENCY, SIGHT-BLINDNESS, UPRIGHT-NESS-DISHONESTY, VISIBILITY-INVISIBILITY, WHITE-NESS-BLACKNESS; **dark ages,** KNOWLEDGE-IGNO-RANCE; **dark cloud,** WELFARE-MISFORTUNE; **dark lantern,** LUMINARY-SHADE; **dark retreat,** CITY-COUN-TRY; **in the dark,** ENLIGHTENMENT-SECRECY, KNOWL-EDGE-IGNORANCE; **keep dark,** ENLIGHTENMENT-SE-CRECY; **leap in the dark,** PURPOSE-LUCK, SECURITY-INSECURITY, TRIAL; **view with dark eyes,** APPROVAL-DISAPPROVAL.

dark'-en. To make dark. CLEARNESS-OBSCURITY.

dark'-ly. In a dark manner. SIGHT-BLINDNESS; **see through a glass darkly,** CLEARNESS-OBSCURITY, KNOWLEDGE-IGNORANCE, SIGHT-DIMSIGHTEDNESS.

dark'-ness. Absence of light. DIMNESS, KNOWL-EDGE-IGNORANCE, LIGHT-DARKNESS, MANIFESTA-TION-LATENCY, WHITENESS-BLACKNESS; **children of darkness,** GODLINESS-UNGODLINESS; **powers of darkness,** ANGEL-SATAN.

dark'-y. A negro. WHITENESS-BLACKNESS.

dar'-ling. A favorite. FAVORITE-ANGER, LOVE-HATE.

darn. To repair. RENOVATION-RELAPSE.

dart. To move quickly; a weapon. PUSH-PULL, SWIFTNESS-SLOWNESS, WEAPON; **dart to and fro,** HURRY-LEISURE.

dash. A sudden onset. ACTIVITY-INDOLENCE, BRAV-ERY-COWARDICE, HURRY-LEISURE, IMPETUS-RE-ACTION, MAGNITUDE-SMALLNESS, MIXTURE-HOMO-GENEITY, PUSH-PULL, SIGN, SWIFTNESS-SLOWNESS; **cut a dash,** POMP, REPUTATION-DISCREDIT; **dash at,** ATTACK-DEFENSE, DETERMINATION-VACILLATION; **dash cup from lips,** LEAVE-PROHIBITION; **dash down,** ELEVATION-DEPRESSION; **dash hopes,** EXPECTATION-DISAPPOINTMENT, LIGHTHEARTEDNESS-DEJECTION, SANGUINENESS-HOPELESSNESS, SUCCESS-FAILURE; **dash of the pen,** WRITING-PRINTING; **dash off,** AC-TIVITY-INDOLENCE, HURRY-LEISURE, PAINTING, SWIFTNESS-SLOWNESS, WRITING-PRINTING; **dash on,** HURRY-LEISURE, SWIFTNESS-SLOWNESS.

dashed. Suddenly and violently thrown. BRAVERY-COWARDICE, IMPETUS-REACTION, LIGHTHEARTED-NESS-DEJECTION, MAGNITUDE-SMALLNESS, MIXTURE-HOMOGENEITY, PUSH-PULL, SELFRESPECT-HUMBLE-NESS, SIGN, SUCCESS-FAILURE.

dash'-ing. Spirited. BRAVERY-COWARDICE, POMP, SOCIETY-LUDICROUSNESS.

das'-tard. One who meanly avoids danger. BRAVERY-COWARDICE.

das'-tard-ly. Sneaking. BRAVERY-COWARDICE.

das'-tard-ness. The quality of being a dastard. BRAVERY-COWARDICE.

das'-tard-y. Base cowardice. BRAVERY-COWARDICE.

da'-ta. Admitted facts. EVIDENCE-COUNTEREVI-DENCE, HYPOTHESIS, RATIOCINATION-INSTINCT.

date. Assigned time. CHRONOLOGY-ANACHRONISM, DURATION-NEVERNESS.

da'-tive. A grammatical case. NOUN.

daub. To smear with some soft material. CLEAN-NESS-FILTHINESS, COVER-LINING, DELINEATION-CARICATURE.

daub'-ing. The act of one who daubs. DELINEATION-CARICATURE.

daugh'-ter. A female child. PARENTAGE-PROGENY.

daunt. To subdue by fear. SANGUINENESS-TIMID-ITY.

daunt'-less. Not capable of being daunted. BRAV-ERY-COWARDICE.

dav'-en-port. A small writing-desk. CONTENTS-RE-CEIVER.

Davus sum, non Œdipus [L.] (dê'-vus sum, non ed'-i-pus). I am Davus [an ordinary man], not Œdipus [a wise man]. CRAFT-ARTLESSNESS, SAGACITY-IN-CAPACITY, WITTINESS-DULNESS.

Da'-vy lamp. A safety - lamp. [Humphry Davy.] CHEMISTRY.

daw'-dle. To waste by idling. ACTIVITY-INDOLENCE, DETERMINATION - VACILLATION, EARLINESS - LATE-NESS, SWIFTNESS-SLOWNESS.

daw'-dling. Wasting in idleness. ACTIVITY - INDO-LENCE.

dawk. An East-Indian runner. MESSENGER.

dawn. Daybreak. ANTECEDENCE-SEQUENCE, BE-GINNING-END, DIMNESS, KNOWLEDGE-IGNORANCE, MORNING-EVENING, PREDECESSOR-CONTINUATION.

daw'-pluck''-er. A calumniator. FLATTERER-DE-FAMER.

day. The time of sunlight. LIGHT-DARKNESS, MEAS-URE, PERIOD-PROGRESS, TIME; **all day,** LASTING-NESS-TRANSIENTNESS; **all in one's day's work,** OCCU-PATION; **clear as day,** CERTAINTY-DOUBT, CLEAR-NESS-OBSCURITY, MANIFESTATION-LATENCY; **close of day,** MORNING-EVENING; **day after day,** FRE-QUENCY - RARITY, LASTINGNESS - TRANSIENTNESS; **day after the fair,** OPPORTUNENESS-UNSUITABLE-NESS; **day after to-morrow,** FUTURE-PAST; **day and night,** FREQUENCY-RARITY; **day before yesterday,** FUTURE-PAST; **day by day,** DURATION-NEVERNESS, PERIODICITY-IRREGULARITY, RECURRENCE; **day of judgment,** FUTURE-PAST; **day of rest,** TOIL-RELAX-ATION; **day one's own,** SUCCESS-FAILURE; **days gone by,** FUTURE-PAST; **days numbered,** LASTING-NESS-TRANSIENTNESS, LIFE-DEATH; **days of week,** PERIODICITY-IRREGULARITY; **decline of day,** MORN-ING-EVENING; **denizens of the day,** FAUNA-FLORA; **happy as the day is long,** LIGHTHEARTEDNESS-DE-JECTION, PLEASURE-PAIN; **have had its day,** NOV-ELTY-ANTIQUITY; **labor day and night,** TOIL-RELAX-ATION; **open as day,** CRAFT-ARTLESSNESS; **order of the day,** HABIT-DESUETUDE; **red letter day,** CONSE-QUENCE-INSIGNIFICANCE; **see the light of day,** VISI-BILITY-INVISIBILITY; **to this day,** TIME.

day'-book. Journal of accounts. ACCOUNTS, MARK-OBLITERATION.

day'-break. Early dawn. DIMNESS, MORNING-EVENING.

day'-dream. A reverie. FANCY, SANGUINENESS-TIMIDITY.

day'-la''-bor-er. One who works by the day. AGENT.

day'-light''. Sunlight. LIGHT-DARKNESS; **see day-light,** CLEARNESS-OBSCURITY.

daze. To confuse. LIGHT-DARKNESS.

daz'-zle. To overcome with light. ASTONISHMENT-EXPECTATION, HEED-DISREGARD, LIGHT-DARKNESS, RIGHT-WRONG, SIGHT-BLINDNESS.

daz'-zle-ment. That which dazzles.

daz'-zling. Very bright. BEAUTY-UGLINESS.

de die in diem [L.] (dî dai'-î in dai'-em). From day to day. DURATION-NEVERNESS, PERIODICITY-IRREGU-LARITY.

de facto [L.] (dî fac'-to). In fact. ENTITY-NON-ENTITY.

de fond en comble [F.] (de fon· tan· con·bl). From the foundation. ENTIRETY-DEFICIENCY.

de novo [L.] (dî no′-vo) From the beginning. RE-CURRENCE.

de omnibus rebus [L.] (dî om′-ni-bus rî′-bus). Concerning all things. UNIFORMITY-MULTIFORMITY.

dea′-con. A church officer. MINISTRY-LAITY.

dea′-con-ess. A female deacon. MINISTRY-LAITY.

dea′-con-ry. The office of a deacon. CHURCH.

dea′-con-ship. The office of a deacon. CHURCH.

dead. Having ceased to live. COLOR-ACHROMATISM, FEELING-INSENSIBILITY, LIFE-DEATH, VIGOR-INERTIA; **dead against,** ANTAGONISM-CONCURRENCE, SAMENESS-CONTRAST; **dead asleep,** ACTIVITY-INDOLENCE; **dead beat,** MIGHT-IMPOTENCE, SUCCESS-FAILURE; **dead certainty,** CERTAINTY-DOUBT; **dead color,** PAINTING; **dead cut,** SOCIABILITY-PRIVACY; **dead drunk,** TEETOTALISM-INTEMPERANCE; **dead failure,** SUCCESS-FAILURE; **dead flat,** ERECTNESS-FLATNESS; **dead heat,** EQUALITY-INEQUALITY; **dead languages,** LANGUAGE; **dead letter,** DUTY-DERELICTION, LAW-LAWLESSNESS, MEANING-JARGON, MIGHT-IMPOTENCE, RULE-LICENSE, USEFULNESS-USELESSNESS; **dead lift,** TOIL-RELAXATION; **dead lock,** DIFFICULTY-FACILITY, DISCONTINUANCE-CONTINUANCE, MOVEMENT-REST; **dead march,** LIFE-FUNERAL; **dead of night,** LIGHT-DARKNESS, MORNING-EVENING; **dead reckoning,** MENSURATION, NUMBERING; **dead secret,** TIDINGS-MYSTERY; **dead set against,** ANTAGONISM-CONCURRENCE; **dead set at,** ATTACK-DEFENSE; **dead shot,** ADEPT-BUNGLER; **dead silence,** SOUND-SILENCE; **dead sound,** RESONANCE-NONRESONANCE; **dead stop,** DISCONTINUANCE-CONTINUANCE; **dead to,** SENSITIVENESS-APATHY; **dead wall,** ATTACK-DEFENSE, OBSTRUCTION-HELP; **dead water,** GULF-PLAIN; **dead weight,** OBSTRUCTION-HELP; **more dead than alive,** WEARINESS-REFRESHMENT.

dead′-en. To lessen the force of. MIGHT-IMPOTENCE, SENSITIVENESS-APATHY, TURBULENCE-CALMNESS.

dead′-house. A place where dead bodies are temporarily kept; a morgue. LIFE-FUNERAL.

dead′-ly. Able to cause death. GOODNESS-BADNESS, HEALTHINESS-UNHEALTHINESS, LIFE-KILLING; **deadly sin,** INNOCENCE-GUILT; **deadly weapon,** LIFE-KILLING, WEAPON.

dead′-ness. The state of being dead. SENSITIVENESS-APATHY.

deaf. Devoid of hearing. HEARING-DEAFNESS, HEED-DISREGARD; **deaf and dumb,** VOCALIZATION-MUTENESS; **deaf to,** SENSITIVENESS-APATHY; **deaf to advice,** BIGOTRY-APOSTASY; **deaf to reason,** FAVORITE-MOROSENESS; **turn deaf ear to,** CAREFULNESS-CARELESSNESS, CREDULOUSNESS-SKEPTICISM, HEARING-DEAFNESS, PROFFER-REFUSAL.

deaf′-en. Make deaf. HEARING-DEAFNESS, LOUDNESS-FAINTNESS.

deaf′-ened. Made deaf. HEARING-DEAFNESS.

deaf′-en-ing. Making incapable of hearing. LOUDNESS-FAINTNESS.

deaf′-ness. The state of being deaf. HEARING-DEAFNESS.

deal. To distribute. ASSIGNMENT, MAGNITUDE-SMALLNESS, ORGANIZATION-DISORGANIZATION; **deal a blow,** ATTACK-DEFENSE, BETTERMENT-DETERIORATION, RECOMPENSE-PUNITION; **deal board,** HARDNESS-SOFTNESS; **deal in,** EXCHANGE; **deal out,** GATHERING-SCATTERING, GIVING-RECEIVING; **deal with,** CONDUCT, ESSAY, EXCHANGE.

deal′-er. A trader. DEALER

DEALER

Banker. One engaged in the business of banking

Broker, etc. One who does business for another, as an agent who buys and sells on commission. See CONSIGNEE

Buyer, etc. One who buys. See PURCHASE.

Cadger. A traveling or itinerant huckster; a codger.

Cambist. A dealer in bills of exchange; a banker.

Chandler. One who makes and sells candles, also a dealer in other commodities.

Changer. One who changes, especially a money-changer.

Chapman. A dealer in small wares.

Colporteur. One who sells or gives away Bibles and religious literature.

Costerman. One who sells fruit, vegetables, etc.

Costermonger. A dealer in fruits or vegetables of any kind.

Dealer. One who deals or has to do with others; a trader.

Hawker. One who sells goods in the street by crying them.

Higgler. One who peddles provisions ; one who higgles or chaffers.

Huckster. A retailer of small wares, provisions, etc.

Jobber. A dealer in public stocks.

Mercer. A dealer in silks, cloths and laces.

Merchant. One who buys and sells commodities for a profit and as a business

Money broker. A broker who deals in money or bills of exchange.

Money changer. A broker.

Moneyer. ⎫ A dealer in money.
Money lender. ⎭

Monger. A dealer or trader.

Pedler. One who travels from house to house retailing small wares.

Regrater. One who buys corn or provisions at a fair or market with the view of selling them again in the community at a higher price.

Retailer. One who sells goods directly to the consumer.

Salesman. One who sells goods.

Seller, etc. A person who sells. See BUYING-SALE.

Shopkeeper. One who sells goods in a shop; a retailer.

Shopman. One who keeps a shop.

Sutler. A person who follows an army and is licensed to sell goods to the soldiers.

Tallyman. One who sells goods on the instalment plan.

Trader. One who trades or is engaged in trade or commerce.

Tradesfolk. People engaged in trade.

Tradesman. A person engaged in trade.

Tradespeople. People employed in trade.

Trust. Several concerns united to form a monopoly.

Usurer. One who lends money at interest above the legal rate.

Vintner. A wine-merchant.

Vivandière [F.]. A female sutler.

DEALER—*Denotations*.

Autolycus. A rogue in Shakespeare's *Winter's Tale*.

DEALER—*Collective Nouns*.

Concern. Persons associated in business.

Firm, etc. The union of two or more people for transacting business

deal′-ings. Business transactions. ACTION-PASSIVENESS; **have dealings with,** AMITY-HOSTILITY, EXCHANGE.

dean. A church officer. MINISTRY-LAITY.

dean′-er-y. The office of a dean. CHURCH, FANE.

dear. Expensive. COSTLINESS-CHEAPNESS, FAVORITE-ANGER, LOVE-HATE; **dear at any price,** PROPRIETY-IMPROPRIETY, USEFULNESS-USELESSNESS; **dear me!** ASTONISHMENT-EXPECTANCE; **O dear!** JUBILATION-LAMENTATION; **pay dear for whistle,** PROPRIETY-IMPROPRIETY, SKILL-UNSKILFULNESS.

dear′-ly. At high price. COSTLINESS-CHEAPNESS.

dear′-ness. High price. COSTLINESS-CHEAPNESS.

dearth. Scarcity. EXCESS-LACK.

death. Extinction of life. BEGINNING-END, DISCONTINUANCE-CONTINUANCE, LIFE-DEATH; **be the death of one,** ENTERTAINMENT-WEARINESS; **death in the pot,** HEALTHINESS-UNHEALTHINESS, REFUGE-PITFALL; **house of death,** LIFE-FUNERAL; **in at the death,** ARRIVAL-DEPARTURE, COMPLETION-NONCOMPLETION, LIFE-KILLING, PERSISTENCE-WHIM; **pale as death,** COLOR-ACHROMATISM, SANGUINENESS-TIMIDITY; **put to death,** LIFE-KILLING; **still as death,** MOVEMENT-REST; **violent death,** LIFE-KILLING.

death′-bed re-pent′-ance. Repentance while dying. REPENTANCE-OBDURACY.

death′-blow. Fatal blow. BEGINNING-END, LIFE-KILLING, SUCCESS-FAILURE.

death'-less. Undying. ETERNITY-INSTANTANEITY, REPUTATION-DISCREDIT.

death'-like. Resembling death. BEAUTY-UGLINESS, SOUND-SILENCE.

death'-song. A funeral hymn. JUBILATION-LAMENTATION, LIFE-DEATH.

death'-strug″-gle. A final effort. STRIFE-PEACE.

death'-war″-rant. An official order directing one's execution. EXCULPATION-CONVICTION, LIFE-DEATH.

death'-watch. The last vigil. WARNING.

de-bac'-le. A violent flood. ASCENT-DESCENT, CREATION-DESTRUCTION, RIVER-WIND.

de-bar'. To bar out. LEAVE-PROHIBITION, OBSTRUCTION-HELP, RELEASE-RESTRAINT.

de-bark'. To go ashore. ARRIVAL-DEPARTURE.

de″-bark-a'-tion. The act of going ashore. ARRIVAL-DEPARTURE.

de-base'. To lower morally. BETTERMENT-DETERIORATION, CLEANNESS-FILTHINESS, ELEVATION-DEPRESSION, REPUTATION-DISCREDIT.

de-based'. Lowered morally. HEIGHT-LOWNESS, UPRIGHTNESS-DISHONESTY.

de-base'-ment. A debased condition. BETTERMENT-DETERIORATION, HEIGHT-LOWNESS, UPRIGHTNESS-DISHONESTY.

de-ba'-ta-ble. Subject to debate. CERTAINTY-DOUBT, RATIOCINATION-INSTINCT.

de-bate'. To argue. CONVERSATION-MONOLOGUE, DETERMINATION-VACILLATION, PRESIDENT-MEMBER, RATIOCINATION-INSTINCT, STRIFE-PEACE.

de-ba'-ter. One who debates. RATIOCINATION-INSTINCT.

de-bauch'. To corrupt. BETTERMENT-DETERIORATION, MODERATION-SELFINDULGENCE, PURITY-IMPURITY.

de-bauched'. Corrupted. MODERATION-SELFINDULGENCE, PURITY-IMPURITY.

deb″-au-chee'. A libertine. PURITY-RAKE.

de-bauch'-er-y. Excessive indulgence in the passions. MODERATION-SELFINDULGENCE, PURITY-IMPURITY.

de-ben'-ture. A kind of bond. CREDIT-DEBT, MONEY, SECURITY.

deb'-ile. Weak. STRENGTH-WEAKNESS.

de-bil'-i-tate. To make weak. STRENGTH-WEAKNESS.

de-bil'-i-ty. Lack of vigor. STRENGTH-WEAKNESS.

deb'-it. A debt. ACCOUNTS, CREDIT-DEBT.

deb'-it-or. A debtor. CREDIT-DEBT.

deb″-o-nair'. Affable. LIGHTHEARTEDNESS-DEJECTION.

de-bouch'. Pass out. ARRIVAL-DEPARTURE, ENTRANCE-EXIT.

débouché [F.] (dê-bu-shê) An opening. ENTRANCE-EXIT.

dé″-bris'. Ruins. FRIABILITY, USEFULNESS-USELESSNESS, WHOLE-PART.

debt. An obligation. CREDIT-DEBT, PROPERTY; **debt of nature,** LIFE-DEATH; **get out of debt,** SETTLEMENT-DEFAULT; **out of debt,** AFFLUENCE-PENURY.

debt'-or. One who owes. CREDIT-DEBT, SETTLEMENT-DEFAULT; **debtor and creditor,** ACCOUNTS.

dé-but'. First attempt. BEGINNING-END, VENTURE.

dé″-bu-tant'. One who makes a début. ACTING, INSTRUCTOR-PUPIL.

dé″-bu-tante'. A female débutant. ACTING.

dec'-ade. A group of ten. DURATION-NEVERNESS, FIVE-QUINQUESECTION, PERIOD-PROGRESS.

de-ca'-dence. A decline in force. BETTERMENT-DETERIORATION.

de-ca'-den-cy. Decadence. BETTERMENT-DETERIORATION.

dec'-a-gon. A figure having ten sides and ten angles. ANGULARITY.

dec'-a-gram. A weight of ten grams. MEASURE.

dec'-a-li″-ter. A measure of ten liters capacity. MEASURE.

dec'-a-logue. The ten commandments. DUTY-DERELICTION.

dec'-a-me″-ter. A measure of ten meters of length. MEASURE.

de-camp'. To run away. ARRIVAL-DEPARTURE, QUEST-EVASION.

de-camp'-ment. Act of decamping. ARRIVAL-DEPARTURE.

de-cant'. To pour gently. TRANSFER.

de-cant'-er. A vessel for decanting. CONTENTS-RECEIVER.

de-cap'-i-tate. To behead. RECOMPENSE-PUNITION.

de-cap″-i-ta'-tion. The act of beheading. RECOMPENSE-PUNITION.

de-cay'. To deteriorate. BETTERMENT-DETERIORATION, CLEANNESS-FILTHINESS, ENLARGEMENT-DIMINUTION, HEALTH-SICKNESS, INCREASE-DECREASE, NOVELTY-ANTIQUITY, WELFARE-MISFORTUNE; **decay of memory,** REMEMBRANCE-FORGETFULNESS; **natural decay,** LIFE-DEATH.

de-cayed'. Gone into decay. BETTERMENT-DETERIORATION, HEALTH-SICKNESS, NOVELTY-ANTIQUITY, STRENGTH-WEAKNESS, WELFARE-MISFORTUNE.

de-cease'. Death. LIFE-DEATH.

de-ceased'. Dead. LIFE-DEATH.

de-ceit'. The act of deceiving. CRAFT-ARTLESSNESS, TRUTHFULNESS-FALSEHOOD, TRUTHFULNESS-FRAUD.

de-ceit'-ful. Tending to deceive. CRAFT-ARTLESSNESS, TRUTH-ERROR, TRUTHFULNESS-FALSEHOOD, TRUTHFULNESS-FRAUD.

de-ceive'. To mislead. EDUCATION-MISTEACHING, TRUTH-ERROR, TRUTHFULNESS-FALSEHOOD, TRUTHFULNESS-FRAUD.

de-ceived'. Misled. GULL-DECEIVER, TRUTH-ERROR, TRUTHFULNESS-FALSEHOOD, TRUTHFULNESS-FRAUD.

de-ceiv'-er. One who deceives. GULL-DECEIVER.

de-ceiv'-ing. Misleading. TRUTHFULNESS-FRAUD.

de'-cen-cy. The quality of being decent. PURITY-IMPURITY.

de-cen'-ni-um. A decade of years. PERIOD-PROGRESS.

de'-cent. Having propriety of conduct, speech, etc. FAULTLESSNESS-FAULTINESS, PURITY-IMPURITY.

de-cen'-tral-ize. To remove from the center. COMPOSITION-RESOLUTION.

deceptio visûs [L.] (dî-sep'-shi-o vai'-sus). Optical illusion. SIGHT-DIMSIGHTEDNESS.

de-cep'-tion. The act of deceiving. TRUTHFULNESS-FALSEHOOD, TRUTHFULNESS-FRAUD.

de-cep'-tive. Tending to deceive. RATIOCINATION-INSTINCT, TRUTHFULNESS-FRAUD; **deceptive reasoning,** RATIOCINATION-INSTINCT.

de-ces'-sion. Departure. ARRIVAL-DEPARTURE.

de-chris'-tian-ize. To turn from Christianity. GODLINESS-DISBELIEF.

de-cide'. Come to a decision. CAUSE-EFFECT, CERTAINTY-DOUBT, CHOICE-NEUTRALITY, DECISION-MISJUDGMENT, SECURITY-INSECURITY.

de-ci'-ded. Free from doubt. ASSERTION-DENIAL, BEGINNING-END, CERTAINTY-DOUBT, DETERMINATION-VACILLATION, MAGNITUDE-SMALLNESS; **take a decided step,** CHOICE-NEUTRALITY.

de-ci'-ded-ly. With decision. MAGNITUDE-SMALLNESS.

de-cid'-u-ous. Falling off in season. ASCENT-DESCENT, BETTERMENT-DETERIORATION, LASTINGNESS-TRANSIENTNESS.

decies repetita placebit [L.] (dî'-si-îz rep-i-tai'-ta pla-sî'-bit). Ten times repeated it will still please. PLEASURABLENESS-PAINFULNESS.

dec'-i-gram. A measure of weight equal to ten grams. MEASURE.

dec'-i-li″-ter. A measure of capacity equal to ten liters. MEASURE.

dec'-i-mal. Pertaining to decimals. FIVE-QUINQUESECTION, NUMBER.

dec'-i-mate. To kill one out of ten. ADDITION-SUB-TRACTION, BETTERMENT - DETERIORATION, FIVE-QUINQUESECTION, LIFE-KILLING, MULTIPLICITY-PAUCITY, RECOMPENSE-PUNITION, STRENGTH-WEAKNESS.

dec''-i-ma'-tion. The act of decimating. FIVE-QUINQUESECTION, MULTIPLICITY-PAUCITY.

dec-ime'. A French coin. VALUES.

dec'-i-me''-ter. One-tenth of a meter. MEASURE.

dec'-i-mo. A Spanish coin. VALUES.

de-ci'-pher. To make out the sense of. INTERPRETATION-MISINTERPRETATION.

de-ci'-sion. Act of deciding. CHOICE-NEUTRALITY, DECISION-MISJUDGMENT, DETERMINATION-VACILLATION, LITIGATION, PURPOSE-LUCK.

DECISION—MISJUDGMENT.

Adjudication. The act of rendering judgment.
Appreciation. True and adequate judgment or estimation.
Arbitrament. Act of judging by arbitration.
Arbitration. Hearing and judging a question by a party mutually agreed upon by the interested ones.
Arbitrement. See ARBITRAMENT.
Assessment. Apportionment, as taxes.
Award. A judgment, sentence, or final decision.
Casting vote. Decisive vote of a presiding officer.
Conclusion. The act of coming to a judgment.
Corollary. A consequence.
Criticism. Art of judging with knowledge and propriety.
Critique. Critical estimate of a work.
Decision. Act of settling by giving judgment on the matter at issue.
Decree. A decision or sentence given in an equity court.
Deduction. Act of judgment by deducing.
Determination. Result of deliberation.
Dijudication. Act of judgment by discerning or distinguishing.
Ergotism. A logical judgment.
Estimate. A rating by the mind without actually measuring.
Estimation. A judgment formed without precise data.
Finding. Result of a judicial examination or inquiry.
Good judgment. Coming to a just decision. See SAGACITY.
Illation. Judgment by inference; deduction.
Inference. That which is deduced by reason of something known.
Judication. Decision.
Judgment. Conclusion or result of judging.
Moral. The judgment to be inferred from a fable or the like.
Notice. An announcement.
Opinion. Conviction founded on probable evidence.
Plebiscite. Expression of will by popular vote.
Ponderation. Act of judging thoughtfully.
Porism. A corollary.
Report. Announcement of the result of an inquiry.
Res judicata [L.]. A decided point of law.
Result. The outcome of an action; effect; consequence.
Review. A critical examination.
Sentence. A judgment, especially one of an unfavorable nature.
Upshot. Final outcome; result.
Valuation. A judgment of worth.
Verdict. Decision of a jury.
Voice. Opinion or choice expressed.
Vote. Expression of will or choice. See CHOICE.

DECISION—*Nouns of Agent.*

Arbiter. One who arbitrates. See *Verbs.*
Arbitrator. See *Verbs.*
Assessor. One with special knowledge of the subject to be decided, appointed to assist a judge.
Censor. One empowered to judge critically.
Commentator. One who writes in annotation; an expounder.
Connoisseur. A competent judge of art.
Critic. One who judges anything by some standard.
Inspecting officer. An officer who examines and criticizes.
Inspector. A supervisor; overseer.
Judge. A judicial officer empowered to administer justice.
Referee. One to whom a thing is left for judgment.
Reviewer. One who examines for critical judgment.
Umpire. One chosen to decide a question, if arbitators shall disagree.

DECISION—*Verbs.*

Account. To give a reckoning.
Adjudge. To decide judicially.
Adjudicate. To act as a judge.
Appreciate. To judge the true worth of anything.
Arbitrate. To judge as an arbitrator. See ARBITRATION.
Arrive at a conclusion. To come to a decision.
Ascertain. To judge with certainty; define.
Assess. To charge with a tax, based on a judgment of property.
Award. To adjudge among contestants.
Bring in a verdict. To return a decision.

Fixed idea. An idea firmly established as by prejudice.
Fool's paradise. Misjudged happiness.
Foregone conclusion. A conclusion made up beforehand.
Hasty conclusion. A conclusion arrived at without due deliberation.
Idée fixe [F.]. Idea dominating the mind.
Mentis gratissimus error [L.]. A mistake that affords pleasure.
Miscalculation. Erroneous estimate.
Miscomputation. False reckoning.
Misconception. Wrong understanding.
Misjudgment. Wrong, or unjust determination.
Obliquity of judgment. Judgment deviating from moral rectitude.
Preapprehension. An apprehension formed before examination.
Preconceived idea. An idea formed beforehand.
Preconception. Opinion or conception formed beforehand.
Predilection. A previous liking.
Prejudgment. Judgment before due examination.
Prejudication. Act of judging without duly examining facts and evidence.
Prenotion. A notion preceding something else.
Prepossession. Preoccupation; preconceived opinion
Presentiment. An anticipation of future evil.
Presumption. Misjudged confidence.

MISJUDGMENT—*Nouns of Cause.*

Bias. Prejudice.
Bigotry. Obstinate attachment to a cause. See BIGOTRY.
Blind side. The side on which one is least able to see danger.
Clannishness. State of being actuated by the traditions of a clan.
Confined views. Views limited and mean.
Crotchet. A peculiar conceit.
Doctrinaire [F.]. A political theorist.
Esprit de corps [F.]. The animating spirit of a body.
Fad. A passing whim.
Hypercriticism. Excessive harshness of criticism; Zoilism.
Infatuation. State of being affected with folly.
Mote in the eye. Anything which causes imperfect judgment. [Bible.]
Narrow mind. A contracted intellect.
Narrow views. A contracted mental outlook.
Odium theologicum [L.]. The hatred which contending theologians bear each other.
Partiality. State of being partial.
Partial views. Views inclined to favor without principle.
Partizanship. Feelings appropriate to a partizan.
Party spirit. Devotion to party.
Pedantry A vulgar display of knowledge.
Prestige. Ascendancy based on known power.

MISJUDGMENT—*Verbs.*

Bias. To prejudice.
Dare pondus fumo [L.]. Give weight to smoke ; make much out of little.
Dogmatize. To express oneself in an arrogant manner.
Fly in the face of facts. To set facts at defiance.
Forejudge. To judge before hearing the facts or proofs.
Get the wrong sow by the ear. To happen upon the wrong thing or conclusion See ADEPT-BUNGLER.
Give a bias.
Give a twist. } To make prejudiced; misrepresent.
Have a bias. To be prejudiced.
Have only one idea. To be narrow-minded.
Jurare in verba magistri [L.]. To swear by the words of a master; to echo his sentiments.
Jump to a conclusion. To conclude hastily.
Look only at one side of the shield. Figurative for to take a narrow, one-sided view of a thing.
Miscalculate. To estimate wrongly.
Miscompute. To reckon wrongly.
Misconceive. To misunderstand.
Misconjecture. To guess wrong.
Misestimate. To estimate erroneously.
Misjudge. To pass wrong judgment. See TRUTH-ERROR.
Misreckon. To compute wrongly.
Misthink. To have a wrong idea of.

DECISION—MISJUDGMENT—*Continued.*

DECISION—Verbs—*Continued.*

Collect.   To gather together.
Come to a conclusion.   Arrive at a decision.
Comment.   To remark in explanation or criticism.
Conclude.   To come to a decision.
Confirm.   To verify; make certain.
Count.   To reckon; compute.
Criticize.   To examine and pass judgment.
Decide.   To determine; adjudge.
Deduce.   To judge by inference.
Deliver judgment.   To render a judicial decision.
Derive.   To obtain by regular process.
Determine.   To resolve; decide.
Doom.   To sentence to calamity or death.
Draw a conclusion.   To arrive at a determination.
Draw an inference.   To make a deduction.
Estimate.   To form an opinion; compute.
Find.   To arrive at judgment after judicial investigation.
Form an estimate.   Make a computation.
Gather.   To deduce mentally; infer.
Give an opinion.   Express a judgment.
Give judgment.   Return a decision.
Hear a cause.   Attend a case judicially.
Hold the scales.   Figurative for sit in judgment.
Investigate.   To inquire into.   See Investigation.
Judge.   To come to a conclusion; to decide authoritatively; to try judicially.
Make absolute.   To make certain.
Make a deduction.   Arrive at an inference.
Make up one's mind.   To decide absolutely.
Pass an opinion.   To express judgment.
Pass judgment.   To give a decision.
Pass sentence.   To grant judgment.
Pass under review.   To pass in examination.   See Heed.
Rank.   To place in order; estimate.
Rate.   To adjudge the relative value of.
Regard.   To give heed to.
Report.   To relate in detailed account.
Review.   To go over judicially.
Rule.   To control; govern; settle.
Sentence.   To condemn to punishment.
Set a question at rest.   To decide finally.
Sit in judgment.   To deliberate on the adjudication of a question.
Try.   To cause to pass through a trial; to investigate judicially.
Try a cause.   To investigate a cause judicially.
Value.   To estimate or judge the worth of.
Ween.   To guess; fancy.
Weet.   To know; to wit.

DECISION—*Adjectives.*

Conclusive.   Decisive; ending doubt.
Determinate.   Fixed or limited definitely.
Judging.   Inclined or disposed to judge.   See *Verbs.*
Judicious.   Acting with good judgment.   See Sagacity.

DECISION—*Adverbs.*

All things considered.   To consider the case in detail.
On the whole.   The subject in its entirety.

DECISION—*Phrases.*

La critique est aisée, et l'art est difficile [F.].   Criticism is easy and art is difficult.

MISJUDGMENT—Verbs—*Continued.*

Not see beyond one's nose.   To confine one's ideas too closely to self.
Overestimate.   To overvalue.
Prejudge.   To judge beforehand without hearing evidence.
Prejudicate.   To determine disadvantageously beforehand.
Prejudice.   To cause a prejudice; oftenest against.
Prepossess.   To preoccupy the opinion, generally in a good sense.
Presume.   To believe without examination.
Presuppose.   To take for granted.
Run away with the notion.   To depart without an adequate opinion being formed.
Rush to a conclusion.   To come to a conclusion overhastily.
Twist.   To pervert; turn from its true significance.
Underestimate.   To give not enough value to.
View through distorting spectacles.   Judge with a prejudice.
View with jaundiced eye.   View jealously.
Warp.   To turn in a wrong direction.

MISJUDGMENT—*Adjectives.*

Besotted.   Enslaved; infatuated.
Bigoted.   Stubbornly attached to an opinion.
Conceited.   Having a great opinion of self.
Confined.   Within limits; too narrow; mean.
Credulous.   Apt to believe without enough evidence
Crotchety.   Full of conceits or fancies.
Dogmatic.   Arrogant; overbearing.
Entêté. [F.].   Obstinate; headstrong.
Fanatical.   Moved by intemperate zeal.
Fussy.   Inclined to make much ado about nothing.
Illiberal.   Stingy; niggardly.
Ill judging.   Not judging well.
Impracticable.   Not to be practised; not to be managed.
Infatuated.   Excited to misjudged passion.
Intolerant.   Narrow-minded; bigoted.
Jaundiced.   Affected with prejudice or envy.
Misjudged.   Falsely judged.   See *Verbs.*
Misjudging.   Forming false opinions.   See *Verbs.*
Narrow-minded.   Bigoted; illiberal.
Opiniâtre [F.].   Obstinate; stubborn; headstrong.
Opinionated.   Too much attached to one's opinion.
Opinionative.   Opinionated.
Opinioned.   Conceited.
Partial.   Favoring one party.
Positive.   Overconfident; dictatorial.
Prejudiced.   Biased with a premature like or dislike.
Purblind.   Near-sighted.
Self-opinioned.   Self-conceited.
Short-sighted.   Unable to understand deep things.
Stupid.   Lacking understanding.   See Sagacity-Incapacity.
Superficial.   Comprehending only the obvious.
Unreasonable.   Beyond reason.
Unreasoning.   Lacking reason.
Wedded to an opinion.   Attached closely by prejudice to an opinion.
Wrong-headed.   Having the head filled with false notions.

MISJUDGMENT—*Adverb.*

Ex parte [L.].   Relating to one part only.

MISJUDGMENT—*Phrases.*

Nothing like leather.
The wish the father to the thought.   Desire originates thought.

---

de-ci'-sive.   Putting an end to uncertainty.   Certainty-Doubt, Proof-Disproof; **take a decisive step,** Choice-Neutrality, Determination-Vacillation.
deck.   To adorn; part of a ship.   Dress-Undress, Embellishment-Disfigurement, Top-Bottom.
de-claim'.   To harangue.   Speech-Inarticulateness; **declaim against,** Approval-Disapproval.
dec″-la-ma′-tion.   The act of declaiming.   Simplicity-Floridness, Speech-Inarticulateness.
de-clam'-a-to-ry.   Pertaining to declamation.   Simplicity-Floridness, Speech-Inarticulateness.
dec″-la-ra′-tion.   The act of declaring.   Assertion-Denial, Litigation; **declaration of faith,** Faith-Misgiving, Theology; **declaration of war,** Fighting-Conciliation, Variation-Accord.

de-clar'-a-to-ry.   Making a declaration.   Enlightenment-Secrecy, Meaning-Jargon.
de-clare'.   To make known.   Assertion-Denial, Meaning-Jargon.
de-clen'-sion.   Inflection of nouns, etc.; deterioration.   Ascent-Descent, Betterment-Deterioration, Godliness-Ungodliness, Grammar-Solecism, Increase-Decrease, Proffer-Refusal.
de-clen'-sions.   Paradigms.   Subjectiveness-Objectiveness.
dec″-li-na′-tion.   The state of bending downward.   Aim-Aberration, Ascent-Descent, Astronomy, Betterment-Deterioration, Mensuration.
de-cline'.   The act of declining.   Ascent-Descent, Betterment-Deterioration, Choice-Rejection, Health-Sickness, Increase-Decrease, Novelty-

ANTIQUITY, PARALLELISM-INCLINATION, PROFFER-REFUSAL, STRENGTH-WEAKNESS, WELFARE-MISFORTUNE; **decline of day,** MORNING-EVENING; **decline of life,** INFANCY-AGE.

de-clin'-ing. Bending downward. PARALLELISM-INCLINATION, PROFFER-REFUSAL.

de-cliv'-i-tous. Like a declivity. PARALLELISM-INCLINATION.

de-cliv'-i-ty. A slope. ASCENT-DESCENT, PARALLELISM-INCLINATION.

de-coc'-tion. The act of boiling anything. HEATING-COOLING.

de-col'-late. To behead. RECOMPENSE-PUNITION.

de-col''-or-a'-tion. The removal of color. COLOR-ACHROMATISM.

de-col'-or-ize. To free from color. COLOR-ACHROMATISM.

de''-com-pose'. To resolve into elements. CHEMISTRY, COMPOSITION-RESOLUTION, ORGANIZATION-DISORGANIZATION.

de''-com-posed'. Decayed. COMPOSITION-RESOLUTION.

de-com''-po-si'-tion. A separation into constituent parts. COMPOSITION-RESOLUTION, UNION-DISUNION.

de''-com-pound'. To decompose. COMPOSITION-RESOLUTION.

de-con'-se-crate. To secularize. COMMISSION-ABROGATION.

de-con''-se-cra'-tion. The act of deconsecrating. COMMISSION-ABROGATION.

dec'-o-rate. To adorn. EMBELLISHMENT-DISFIGUREMENT.

dec'-o-ra''-ted. Ornamented. EMBELLISHMENT-DISFIGUREMENT.

dec''-o-ra'-tion. The act of decorating. BEAUTY-UGLINESS, EMBELLISHMENT-DISFIGUREMENT, SCEPTER, TITLE, TROPHY.

de-co'-rous. Marked by decorum. DUENESS-UNDUENESS, PURITY-IMPURITY, REGARD-DISRESPECT.

de-cor'-ti-cate. To strip off bark. DRESS-UNDRESS.

de-cor''-ti-ca'-tion. The act of decorticating. DRESS-UNDRESS.

de-co'-rum. Propriety. DUTY-DERELICTION, PURITY-IMPURITY, SOCIETY-LUDICROUSNESS.

dé cousu [F.] (dê cu-sü'). Looseness. CONTINUITY-INTERRUPTION, SUCCESS-FAILURE.

de-coy'. To lead on by some inducement. GULL-DECEIVER, MOTIVE-CAPRICE, TRUTHFULNESS-FRAUD.

de-crease'. To make less. ADDITION-SUBTRACTION, BETTERMENT-DETERIORATION, ENLARGEMENT-DIMINUTION, INCREASE-DECREASE.

de-creased'. Made less. INCREASE-DECREASE.

de-creas'-ing. Becoming less. INCREASE-DECREASE.

de-cree'. A formal order. DECISION-MISJUDGMENT, LAW-LAWLESSNESS, ORDER.

dec'-re-ment. The act of decreasing. ENLARGEMENT-DIMINUTION, INCREASE-DECREASE, INCREMENT-DECREMENT.

de-crep'-id, de-crep'-it. Enfeebled. BETTERMENT-DETERIORATION, HEALTH-SICKNESS, INFANCY-AGE, STRENGTH-WEAKNESS.

de-cre'-tal. An authoritative decree. ORDER.

de-cre'-tive. Of a decree. ORDER.

dec'-re-to-ry. Of a decree. ORDER.

de-cry'. To cry down. ADULATION-DISPARAGEMENT, APPROVAL-DISAPPROVAL.

de-cum'-bence. A decumbent posture. ERECTNESS-FLATNESS.

de-cum'-ben-cy. A decumbent posture. ERECTNESS-FLATNESS.

de-cum'-bent. Lying down. ERECTNESS-FLATNESS.

dec'-u-ple. Tenfold. FIVE-QUINQUESECTION.

de-cur'-rent. Running downward. ASCENT-DESCENT.

de-cur'-sive. Running down. ASCENT-DESCENT.

de-cur-ta'-tion. A cutting short. LENGTH-SHORTNESS.

de-cus'-sate. To cross. CROSSING.

dec''-us-sa'-tion. The act of crossing. CROSSING.

de-dec''-o-ra'-tion. The act of disgracing. REPUTATION-DISCREDIT.

de-dec'-o-rous. Disgraceful. POLITENESS-IMPOLITENESS, REPUTATION-DISCREDIT.

ded'-i-cate. To consecrate. REPUTATION-DISCREDIT, USE-DISUSE.

ded''-i-ca'-tion. The act of dedicating. REPUTATION-DISCREDIT.

de-duce'. To conclude by a process of reasoning. ADDITION-SUBTRACTION, DECISION-MISJUDGMENT.

de-du'-ci-ble. Capable of being deduced. EVIDENCE-COUNTEREVIDENCE, PROOF-DISPROOF.

de-duct'. To take away. ADDITION-SUBTRACTION, TAKING-RESTITUTION.

de-duc'-tion. The act of deducing. ADDITION-SUBTRACTION, DECISION-MISJUDGMENT, INCREMENT-DECREMENT, RATIOCINATION-INSTINCT.

deed. An act. ACTION-PASSIVENESS, EVIDENCE-COUNTEREVIDENCE, MARK-OBLITERATION, SECURITY; **deeds of arms,** STRIFE-PEACE; **deed without a name,** INNOCENCE-GUILT.

deem. To think. FAITH-MISGIVING.

deep. Having depth. COLOR-ACHROMATISM, CRAFT-ARTLESSNESS, DEEPNESS-SHALLOWNESS, EMOTION, LOUDNESS-FAINTNESS, MAGNITUDE-SMALLNESS, OCEAN-LAND, SAGACITY-INCAPACITY; **deep color,** COLOR-ACHROMATISM; **deep game,** CRAFT-ARTLESSNESS; **deep in debt,** CREDIT-DEBT; **deep knowledge,** KNOWLEDGE-IGNORANCE; **deep mourning,** JUBILATION-LAMENTATION; **deep note,** RESONANCE-NONRESONANCE; **deep potations,** TEETOTALISM-INTEMPERANCE; **deep reflection,** REFLECTION-VACANCY; **deep sense,** EMOTION; **deep sigh,** JUBILATION-LAMENTATION; **deep study,** HEED-DISREGARD; **in deep water,** DIFFICULTY-FACILITY; **plow the deep,** TRAVELING-NAVIGATION.

deep'-en. To make deep. DEEPNESS-SHALLOWNESS, INCREASE-DECREASE.

deep'-dyed. Of a decided color. VIGOR-INERTIA, VIRTUE-VICE, WHITENESS-BLACKNESS.

deep'-felt. Felt deeply. EMOTION.

deep'-laid. Elaborately designed. DESIGN.

deep'-mouthed. Having a sonorous voice. CRY-ULULATION, EMOTION, RESONANCE-NONRESONANCE.

deep'-mu''-sing. Profound meditation. HEED-DISREGARD, REFLECTION-VACANCY.

deep'-ness. The state of being deep. DEEPNESS-SHALLOWNESS.

DEEPNESS—SHALLOWNESS.

Deepness. Depth; quality of being deep.
Depression. See CONVEXITY-CONCAVITY.
Depth. Extent downward or inward.
Profundity. Quality or state of being deep or profound.

DEEPNESS—*Denotations.*

Bottomless pit. A pit so deep that it cannot be measured; hell.
Bowels of the earth. The interior part of the earth.
Crater. The basin-like opening or mouth of a volcano.
Depth of water. The perpendicular measurement downward from the surface.

Mere scratch. Thin; not far from the surface.
Shallowness. Quality or state of being shallow. See *Adjectives.*
Shoals. Places where the water has little depth.

SHALLOWNESS—*Adjectives.*

Ankle-deep. Of a depth sufficient to cover the ankle
Just enough to wet one's feet. Shallow.
Knee-deep. Of a depth sufficient to cover the knee.
Shallow. Not deep.
Shoal. Shallow.

DEEPNESS—SHALLOWNESS—*Continued.*

DEEPNESS—Denotations—*Continued.*

Gulf. A deep land-locked body of water. See Gulf.
Hell. The place of punishment for the wicked after death, usually represented as a bottomless pit.
Hollow. A natural or artificial cavity.
Pit. A large cavity or hole in the ground.
Shaft. An excavation in the earth for raising ore, etc.
Sound. A narrow passage of water, usually deep.
Well. A pit or hole sunk in the earth to such a depth as to reach water.

DEEPNESS—*Associated Nouns.*

Draft. The depth of water necessary to float a ship.
Lead. A mass of lead used in sounding at sea.
Plummet. A lead attached to a string to find the depth of water.
Probe. An instrument for examining the depth of a wound.
Sounding line. A line having a plummet at the end used in making soundings.
Sounding rod. A rod used to ascertain the depth of water in a ship's hold.
Soundings. Measurements by soundings.

DEEPNESS—*Verbs.*

Be deep. See *Adjectives.*
Deepen. To increase the downward or inward distance.
Dig. See Convexity-Concavity.
Heave the lead. To take soundings with lead and line.
Plunge. See Spring-Dive.
Render deep. Make deep.
Sound. To try to find depth of water.
Take soundings. To find depths at different places.

DEEPNESS—*Adjectives.*

Abysmal. Deep; profound; pertaining to an abyss.

deep'–read''. Of much book-learning. Knowledge-Ignorance.
deep'–root''–ed. Reaching below the surface. Affections, Faith-Misgiving, Habit-Desuetude, Mutability-Stability.
deep'–seat''–ed. Deeply lodged. Deepness-Shallowness, Outside-Inside.
deer. A ruminant, Fauna-Flora; **in heart a deer**, Recklessness-Caution.
deev. An evil spirit. Jove-Fiend.
de-face'. To mar the face. Beauty-Ugliness, Betterment-Deterioration, Form-Formlessness, Mark-Obliteration.
de-face'-ment. Disfigurement. Form-Formlessness.
def''-al-ca'-tion. Embezzlement. Enlargement-Diminution, Entirety-Deficiency, Settlement-Default, Transcursion-Shortcoming.
def''-a-ma'-tion. The act of defaming. Adulation-Disparagement.
de-fam'-a-to-ry. Tending to defame. Adulation-Disparagement, Approval-Disapproval.
de-fame'. Injure a good name. Adulation-Disparagement, Approval-Disapproval, Reputation-Discredit.
de-fa'-mer. One who defames. Flatterer-Defamer.
de-fat''-i-ga'-tion. Weariness. Entertainment-Weariness.
de-fault'. A failure in the performance of an obligation. Carefulness-Carelessness, Credit-Debt, Entirety-Deficiency, Excess-Lack, Settlement-Default, Transcursion-Shortcoming; **in default of**, Presence-Absence; **judgment by default**, Yielding.
de-fault'-er. One who defaults. Credit-Debt, Good Man-Bad Man, Robber, Settlement-Default.
de-fea'-sance. Defeat. Commission-Abrogation.
de-feat. To overcome. Obstruction-Help, Proof-Disproof, Success-Failure; **defeat one's hope,** Expectation-Disappointment.
de-feat'-ed. Vanquished. Success-Failure.

SHALLOWNESS—Adjectives—*Continued.*

Shoaly. Full of shoals.
Skin-deep. Going only through the skin.
Superficial. Lying on the surface.

DEEPNESS—Adjectives—*Continued.*

Ankle-deep. Reaching to the ankle.
Bottomless. Without a bottom.
Buried. Covered up; deep in the earth.
Deep. Extending far below the surface.
Deep as a well. Having the same depth as a well.
Deep-seated. Having the seat far down.
Ebbless. Not decreasing in depth.
Fathomless. Not to be measured.
Knee-deep. Deep enough to extend to the knee.
Profound. Deep in meaning.
Soundless. That can not be sounded.
Subaqueous. Adapted for use under water.
Submarine. Relative to the lower part of the sea; like submarine divers.
Submerge. See Spring-Dive.
Submerged. Sunk down so as to be covered.
Subterranean. Under the surface of the earth.
Subterrene. See Subterranean.
Sunk. Fallen down; in.
Underground. Below the surface of the earth.
Unfathomable. Not to be measured for depth.
Unfathomed. Not measured.

DEEPNESS—*Adverbial Phrases.*

Beyond one's depth; out of one's depth; **over head and ears.**

def'-e-cate. To clear from dregs. Cleanness-Filthiness.
def''-e-ca'-tion. The act of defecating. Cleanness-Filthiness.
de-fect'. A fault. Embellishment-Disfigurement, Entirety-Deficiency, Faultlessness-Faultiness, Increment-Decrement, Virtue-Vice.
de-fec'-tion. The forsaking of duty. Bigotry-Apostasy, Insubordination-Obedience, Quest-Abandonment.
de-fect'-ive. Having a defect. Entirety-Deficiency, Faultlessness-Faultiness; **defective verb,** Verb.
def''-e-da'-tion. Pollution. Betterment-Deterioration, Cleanness-Filthiness.
de-fend'. To protect. Attack-Defense, Justification-Charge, Patriotism-Treason.
de-fend'-ant. One who is accused. Justification-Charge.
de-fend'-ed. Protected. Attack-Defense.
de-fend'-er. One who defends. Attack-Defense, Patriotism-Treason.
de-fend'-ing. Giving defense. Attack-Defense.
de-fense'. Protection. Attack-Defense, Justification-Charge.
de-fense'-less. Without defense. Might-Impotence, Security-Insecurity, Strength-Weakness.
de-fense'-less-ness. The state of having no defense. Security-Insecurity.
de-fen'-si-ble. Capable of defense. Justification-Charge, Security-Insecurity.
de-fen'-sive. Suitable for defense. Attack-Defense.
de-fen'-sive al-li'-ance. Association for defense. Association.
de-fen'-sive-ly. On the defense. Attack-Defense.
defensor, fidei [L.] (dî-fen'-sor, fai-dî'-ai). Defender of the faith. Attack-Defense.
de-fer'. To postpone; to yield. Earliness-Lateness; **defer to,** Assent-Dissent, Regard-Disrespect.
def'-er-ence. Respectful submission. Insubordination-Obedience, Regard-Disrespect, Self-respect-Humbleness.

def″-er-en′-tial. Respectful. REGARD-DISRESPECT.

de-fer′-ring. Postponing. EARLINESS-LATENESS.

de-fi′-ance. The act of defying. BRAVERY-COWARD-ICE, CHARITABLENESS-MALEVOLENCE, CURSE-MEN-ACE, DEFIANCE; **defiance of danger,** BRAVERY-COW-ARDICE; **in defiance,** ANTAGONISM-CONCURRENCE, HARMONY-DISCORD; **set at defiance,** INSUBORDINA-TION-OBEDIENCE.

DEFIANCE.

Challenge. An invitation to engage in a combat, duelistic or intellectual.

Daring. Defiance; challenge.

Defiance. A provocation to combat.

Threat. See CHARITABLENESS-MENACE

DEFIANCE—Denotation.

Cartel. A letter of defiance.

DEFIANCE—Associated Nouns.

War-cry. A cry or signal used in war.

War-whoop. A war-cry, especially of the American Indians.

DEFIANCE—Verbs.

Beard. To oppose openly.

Bid defiance to. To challenge.

Bluster. To storm with anger.

Brave. See BRAVERY.

Call out. To summon to battle.

Challenge. See *Nouns.*

Dance the war dance. Among savages, to dance as an incitive to battle; to prepare for war.

Dare. To have the courage to undertake some enterprise.

Defy. To provoke to combat.

Disobey. See sub DISOBEDIENCE.

Double the fist. To defy.

Fling down the gage.
Fling down the gauntlet. } To challenge.
Fling down the glove.

Hurl defiance at. To be ready to oppose vigorously.

Laugh to scorn. To deride; to hold in contempt.

Look big. Defiant; arrogant.

Threaten. See MENACE.

Throw down the gage
Throw down the gauntlet. } See FLING DOWN THE GAGE, etc.
Throw down the glove.

Set at defiance. To treat contemptuously.

Set at naught. To ignore.

Shake the fist. To defy.

Show a bold front. To exhibit no fear.

Show fight. To be brave; daring.

Show one's teeth. To threaten.

Snap the fingers at. To challenge; disdain.

Stand akimbo. To hold others in contempt, with arms crooked.

Threaten. To attempt to alarm with the promise of something evil

DEFIANCE—Adjectives.

Defiant. Bold; insolent.

Defying. See *Verbs.*

With arms akimbo. To have the elbows turned out; disdainful.

DEFIANCE—Adverbial Phrases.

In defiance of; in the teeth of; under one's very nose.

DEFIANCE—Interjections.

Come if you dare! come on! do your worst! marry come up!

DEFIANCE—Phrases.

Nemo me impune lacessit [L.]. No one assails me with impunity
Noli me tangere [L.]. Touch me not.

de-fi′-ant. Having defiance. CHARITABLENESS-MEN-ACE, DEFIANCE.

de-fi′-cien-cy. The state of being deficient. ENTIRETY-DEFICIENCY, EXCESS-LACK, FAULTLESSNESS-FAULTI-NESS, SUPREMACY-SUBORDINACY, VIRTUE-VICE.

de-fi′-cient. Without a proper amount. ENTIRETY-DEFICIENCY, EXCESS-LACK, FAULTLESSNESS-FAULTI-NESS, TRANSCURSION-SHORTCOMING.

def′-i-cit. Shortage. CREDIT-DEBT, ENTIRETY-DE-FICIENCY.

de-fig′-ure. To disfigure. BEAUTY-UGLINESS.

de-file′. To render filthy. BETTERMENT-DETERIO-RATION, CLEANNESS-FILTHINESS, PURITY-IMPURITY, REPUTATION-DISCREDIT.

de-file′. To march in a line. INTERSPACE-CONTACT, TRAVELING-NAVIGATION.

de-file′-ment. The act of defiling. CLEANNESS-FILTH-INESS, PURITY-IMPURITY, REPUTATION-DISCREDIT.

de-fine′. To state the exact meaning of. INTERPRE-TATION-MISINTERPRETATION, NAME-MISNOMER.

de-fined′. Having the meaning exactly stated. MANIFESTATION-LATENCY.

def′-i-nite. With fixed limits. BOUNDARY, CER-TAINTY-DOUBT, CLEARNESS-OBSCURITY, MANIFESTA-TION-LATENCY, PERSPICUITY-OBSCURITY, TRUTH-ERROR, UNIVERSALITY-PARTICULARITY, VISIBILITY-INVISIBILITY.

def″-i-ni′-tion. The act of defining. INTERPRETA-TION-MISINTERPRETATION, PERSPICUITY-OBSCURITY.

de-fin′-i-tive. Being a definition. ASSERTION-DENIAL, BEGINNING-END, DETERMINATION-VACILLATION.

def′-la-gra′-tion. A burning. HEATING-COOLING.

de-flect′. To turn aside. AIM-ABERRATION, CURVA-TION-RECTILINEARITY.

de-flec′-tion. A turning aside. CROSSING, CURVATION-RECTILINEARITY.

de-flex′-ure. Deflection. AIM-ABERRATION.

def″-lo-ra′-tion. The act of deflowering. PURITY-IMPURITY.

de-flow′-er. To rob of flowers; to despoil of purity. BETTERMENT-DETERIORATION, PURITY-IMPURITY.

de-flux′-ion. A flowing of humors. ENTRANCE-EXIT, RIVER-WIND.

de-form′. To mar the form. FORM-FORMLESSNESS, PROPORTION-DEFORMITY.

de-formed′. Deprived of form. PROPORTION-DE-FORMITY.

de-form′-i-ty. Lack of proper form. BEAUTY-UGLI-NESS, EMBELLISHMENT-DISFIGUREMENT, FORM-FORMLESSNESS, PROPORTION-DEFORMITY.

de-fraud′. To take anything by fraud. THEFT, TRUTHFULNESS-FRAUD.

de-fray′. To make payment for. SETTLEMENT-DE-FAULT.

de-fray′-ment. The act of defraying. SETTLEMENT-DEFAULT.

deft. Of neat and skilful action. HARMONY-DISCORD, SKILL-UNSKILFULNESS.

de-funct′. Having ceased to exist. ENTITY-NON-ENTITY, LIFE-CORPSE, LIFE-DEATH.

de-fy′. To challenge. BRAVERY-COWARDICE, CHARI-TABLENESS-MENACE, DEFIANCE, INSUBORDINATION-OBEDIENCE; **defy danger,** BRAVERY-COWARDICE.

de-fy′-ing. Showing defiance. DEFIANCE.

dégagé [F.] (dê-ga-zhê′). Free from constraint. LIB-ERTY-SUBJECTION, SOCIETY-LUDICROUSNESS.

de-gen′-er-a-cy. A growing worse. BETTERMENT-DE-TERIORATION.

de-gen′-er-ate. To grow worse. BETTERMENT-DE-TERIORATION.

de-gen′-er-ate-ness. The state of being degenerate. BETTERMENT-DETERIORATION.

de-gen″-er-a′-tion. The state of growing worse. BETTERMENT-DETERIORATION.

deg″-lu-ti′-tion. The act of swallowing. NUTRI-MENT-EXCRETION, TAKING-RESTITUTION.

deg″-ra-da′-tion. The act of degrading. BETTER-MENT-DETERIORATION.

de-grade′. To reduce in grade. BETTERMENT-DETE-RIORATION, REPUTATION-DISCREDIT.

de-gra′-ding. Reducing in grade. REPUTATION-DIS-CREDIT, UPRIGHTNESS-DISHONESTY, VIRTUE-VICE.

de-gree′. A stage in progression. ADMISSION-EXCLU-SION, QUANTITY-MEASURE, REPUTATION-DISCREDIT; **adverb of degree,** ADVERB; **by degrees,** QUANTITY-

Measure, Swiftness-Slowness; **by slow degrees,** Swiftness-Slowness.

de″-gus-ta′-tion. The act of tasting. Savor-Taste-lessness.

de-his′-cence. A gape. Aperture-Closure.

de-hort′. To dissuade. Motive-Dehortation, Warning.

de″-hor-ta′-tion. The act of dehorting. Motive-Dehortation, Warning.

de-hort′-a-to-ry. Of dissuasion. Motive-Dehortation.

Dei gratia [L.] (dî′-ai grê′-shi-ɑ). By the grace of God. Dueness-Undueness.

de″-i-fi-ca′-tion. The act of deifying. Devotion-Idolatry, Heaven-Hell.

de′-i-fy. To make a god of. Devotion-Idolatry, Reputation-Discredit.

deign. To allow condescendingly Consent, Self-respect-Humbleness.

de′-ism. The belief of a deist. Godliness-Disbelief, Orthodoxy-Heterodoxy.

de′-ist. One who believes in God, but not in revelation. Godliness-Disbelief, Orthodoxy-Heterodoxy.

de-is′-tic-al. Of deists. Godliness-Disbelief.

De′-i-ty. God. Divinity; **tutelary deity,** Security-Insecurity.

de-ject′. To make dejected. Lightheartedness-Dejection.

de-ject′-ed-ness. The state of being dejected. Lightheartedness-Dejection.

de-jec′-tion. Depression; excrement. Lightheartedness-Dejection, Nutriment-Excretion, Pleasure-Pain.

déjeuner [F.] (dê-zhu-nê′). Breakfast. Nutriment-Excretion.

délabrement [F.] (dê-lɑbr-mɑn·′). Dilapidation. Betterment-Deterioration, Creation-Destruction.

de-lac″-er-a′-tion. A tearing to pieces. Betterment-Deterioration.

de-la′-tion. An accusation. Earliness-Lateness, Justification-Charge.

de-la′-tor. An informer. Enlightenment-Secrecy.

de-lay′. Postponement. Earliness-Lateness, Lastingness-Transientness, Swiftness-Slowness.

de-layed′. Postponed. Earliness-Lateness.

dele [L.] (dî′-lî). Erase. Mark-Obliteration.

de-lec″-ta-bil′-i-ty. The quality of giving pleasure. Pleasurableness-Painfulness.

de″-lec-ta′-tion. Delight. Pleasure-Pain.

de-lec′-tus. A text-book for beginners in Greek and Latin. Word-Neology.

del′-e-gate. A representative. Commission-Abrogation, Consignee, President-Member, Representative, Transfer.

del″-e-ga′-tion. The act of delegating. Commission-Abrogation

delenda est Carthago [L.] (dî-len′-dɑ est cɑr-thê′-go). Carthage must be destroyed. [A saying of Cato.] Charitableness-Curse, Creation-Destruction.

del″-e-te′-ri-ous. Hurtful. Excitability-Inexcitability, Faultlessness-Faultiness, Goodness-Badness, Healthiness-Unhealthiness.

de-le′-tion. Extinction. Mark-Obliteration.

del′-e-to-ry. That which blots out. Creation-Destruction.

de-lib′-er-ate. To weigh in the mind. Advice, Heed-Disregard, Hurry-Leisure, Reflection-Vacancy, Swiftness-Slowness.

de-lib′-er-ate-ly. With deliberation. Earliness-Lateness, Predetermination-Impulse, Purpose-Luck.

de-lib″-er-a′-tion. The act of deliberating. Reflection-Vacancy.

de-lib′-er-a-tive. Of deliberation. Reflection-Vacancy; **deliberative assembly,** President-Member.

del′-i-ca-cy. The quality of being delicate. Beauty-Ugliness, Difficulty-Facility, Health-Sickness, Hearing-Deafness, Nutriment-Excretion, Palatableness-Unpalatableness, Pleasurableness-Painfulness, Purity-Impurity, Readiness-Reluctance, Strength-Weakness, Taste-Vulgarity, Uprightness-Dishonesty.

del′-i-cate. Pleasing to the senses. Beauty-Ugliness, Breadth-Narrowness, Difficulty-Facility, Palatableness-Unpalatableness, Pleasurableness-Painfulness, Purity-Impurity, Texture, Truth-Error.

délice [F.] (dê-lîs′). Delight. Sensuality-Suffering.

deliciæ humani generis [L.] (dî-lis′-i-î hiu-mê′-nai jen′-e-ris). The delights of the human race. Humanitarianism-Misanthropy.

de-li′-cious. Very pleasant. Palatableness-Unpalatableness, Pleasurableness-Painfulness.

delicti, corpus [L.] (dî-lic′-tai, cor′-pus). The body of the crime. Innocence-Guilt, Litigation.

delicto, ex [L.] (dî-lic′-to, ex). From the crime. Virtue-Vice.

delicto, flagrante [L.] (dî-lic′-to, flê-gran′-tî). While the crime was being done; in the very act. Innocence-Guilt.

de-light′. A high degree of pleasure. Lightheartedness-Dejection, Pleasurableness-Painfulness, Pleasure-Pain.

de-light′-ful. Giving delight. Pleasurableness-Painfulness.

De-li′-lah. A Philistine woman, the mistress of Samson. Purity-Rake.

de-lin′-e-ate. To outline. Delineation - Caricature.

de-lin″-e-a′-tion. The act of delineating. Delineation-Caricature.

DELINEATION—CARICATURE.

Delineation. A representation, either pictorial or in words

Depictment. A vivid delineation.

Designing. The act of giving visible expression to an original conception.

Iconography. The art of representing by pictures, images, etc.

Illustration. The act of illustrating. See *Verbs.*

Imagery. The act or art of representing the products of fancy and imagination.

Imitation. The act of making a copy or likeness of an original.

Impersonation. The act of impersonating. See *Verbs.*

Personation. See Impersonation.

Personification. A typical exemplification.

Portraiture. The act of portraying. See *Verbs.*

Representation. The act of representing. See *Verbs.*

Delineation—*Nouns of Means.*

Art. The application of skill to the production of the beautiful by imitation or design.

Anamorphosis. A deformed or distorted image.

Bad likeness. An imperfect or incorrect picture or portrait.

Caricatura [L.]. A caricature.

Caricature. An exaggerated or distorted picture, usually for **pur**poses of burlesque or ridicule.

Daub. A poor, coarse painting.

Daubing. Bad painting.

Distortion. False or incorrect representation.

Exaggeration. Representation with extravagant or untruthful additions.

Misrepresentation. Untrue representation, whether on purpose **or** by mistake.

Scratch. An outline made by scratching, or by rubbing with **any**thing pointed or rough.

Sign-painting. The business of painting signs and advertisements.

Caricature—*Verbs.*

Caricature. See Delineation-Caricature.

DELINEATION—CARICATURE—*Continued.*

DELINEATION—Nouns of Means—*Continued.*

Drama. A composition, in prose or poetry, intended to exhibit a picture of life.

Engraving. The art of producing upon hard material incised or raised patterns.

Fine arts. Those arts employed in the production of the beautiful.

Painting. The art of making a colored representation of any object or scene.

Photography. The art of producing pictures by the action of light on sensitive plates.

Sculpture. The art of carving wood, stone, metal, etc., into statues or figures.

DELINEATION—*Denotations.*

Aglet. A decoration representing a certain military rank.

Anaglyph. An ornament in relief, as a cameo.

Atlas. A collection of maps.

Bust. A piece of sculpture representing the upper portion of the human figure.

Chart. A paper or book exhibiting information; especially, geographical information.

Chartography. The art of drawing maps.

Copy. An imitation.

Daguerreotype. One of the earliest photographic processes.

Design. A visible representation of an original concept.

Diagram. A representation by means of lines.

Draft. A delineated figure; an outline sketch.

Drawing. The delineation of an object or conception; a design.

Effigy. A representation of a person, usually in sculpture or on coins.

Elevation. A drawing of an object on a vertical plane.

Facsimile. An exact copy or reproduction.

Fantoccini [It.]. A puppet-show.

Figure. A representation or likeness of the form of any object.

Figurehead. An ornamental image of any kind on the prow of a vessel.

Figurine [F.]. A small figure; a statuette.

Ground-plan. A horizontal drawing of the ground-floor of a building.

Hieroglyphs. Writing by means of pictures.

Icon. An image.

Image. A visible representation of a person or thing; especially, a sculptured or painted figure.

Lay-figure. A model for the use of an artist.

Likeness. An image or picture.

Manikin. A model of the human body.

Map. A representation of a portion of the earth's surface.

Marionette. A puppet moved by strings, as on a stage.

Maumet. An idol.

Model. An image or other representation to serve as a pattern.

Monogram. A character usually made up of several letters combined.

Outline. A brief drawing or sketch.

Picture. A surface representation.

Plan. A drawing or design.

Portrait. A likeness of a person, painted, drawn, or engraved.

Projection. A drawing on a perspective plane.

Puppet. A marionette.

Scheme. An outline drawing or sketch; less definite than plan.

Sketch. A rough suggestive drawing.

Speaking likeness. A likeness that is lifelike.

Statue. A plastic representation in some solid substance.

Statuette. A small statue.

Striking likeness. A representation strongly resembling the original.

Tracing. A reproduction of a drawing or plan by means of thin paper or the like.

delineavit [L.] (dĭ-lin-e-ê-vit'). He has drawn it. PAINTING.

de-lin'-quen-cy. Failure of duty. INNOCENCE-GUILT.

de-lin'-quent. One who commits a fault. GOOD MAN-BAD MAN.

del''-i-qua'-tion. The act of melting. LIQUEFACTION-VOLATILIZATION.

del''-i-ques'-cent. Able to become liquid. LIQUEFACTION-VOLATILIZATION.

de-liq'-ui-um. Liquefaction. MIGHT-IMPOTENCE, WEARINESS-REFRESHMENT.

delirant reges plectuntur Achivi [L.] (dĭ-lai'-rant rĭ-jĭz plec-tun'-tur a-kai'-vai). The kings commit follies, still the Greeks are punished. [Hor., *Epistle*, I, ii, 14.] HARSHNESS-MILDNESS.

CARICATURE—Verbs—*Continued.*

Daub. To paint coarsely.

Distort. To give a false or incorrect representation.

Exaggerate. See EXAGGERATION.

Misrepresent. To make a poor likeness of.

Overdraw. To give an exaggerated representation.

CARICATURE—*Adjectives.*

Misrepresented, etc. See *Verbs.*

DELINEATION—Denotations—*Continued.*

Very image. A likeness that seems real.

View. A representation of something that can be seen, as a view of the lake.

Waxwork. Figures made in wax.

DELINEATION—*Verbs.*

Act. To perform on the stage.

Adumbrate. To slightly sketch.

Assume a character. To act the part of another.

Body forth. To give definite form to, either mentally or bodily.

Carve. To represent by cutting or chiseling.

Catch a likeness. To make an exact copy of.

Copy. To make in imitation or duplicate.

Daguerreotype. See *Nouns.*

Delineate. To draw in outline, to represent by a sketch.

Depict. To represent vividly.

Depicture. To depict in words or colors.

Describe. To represent by words or drawings

Dress up. To dress lavishly.

Engrave. To represent by cutting in or upon; to carve artistically.

Figure. To represent by, or fashion, a figure. See *Nouns.*

Hit off. To represent by a few quick but exact strokes.

Hold the mirror up to nature. To draw, portray, or in any way represent things as they are.

Illustrate. To adorn or represent by means of pictures.

Impersonate. To appear or act in the character of another.

Mimic. To imitate or act as another, usually in ridicule.

Mold. To fashion after a model.

Paint. To represent in colors.

Personate. To play the part of.

Photograph. To take a picture by the action of light on films.

Play. To act; to impersonate.

Portray. To represent by drawing, painting, etc.

Pose as. To assume a certain character.

Represent. To portray or bring before the mind in any manner whatever.

Shadow forth. To indicate faintly or by a meager outline.

Shadow out. See SHADOW FORTH.

Symbolize. To represent by a symbol, type, or figure

Take a likeness. To make a picture, portrait, or photograph of.

Trace. To make a tracing. See TRACING.

DELINEATION—*Adjectives.*

Figurative. Representing by means of figures or symbols.

Graphic. Portraying vividly.

Illustrative. Designed or tending to adorn or make clear.

Imitative. See IMITATE.

Like. Similar.

Representative. See *Verbs.*

Represented. See *Verbs.*

Representing. See *Verbs.*

de-lir'-i-ous. Having delirium. SANENESS-LUNACY.

de-lir'-i-um. A disordered mental condition. EXCITABILITY-INEXCITABILITY, SANENESS-LUNACY; **delirium tremens,** TEETOTALISM-INTEMPERANCE.

del''-i-tes'-cence. The sudden disappearance of inflammation; concealment. SOCIABILITY-PRIVACY, VISIBILITY-INVISIBILITY.

del''-i-tes'-cent. Concealed. MANIFESTATION-LATENCY, SOCIABILITY-PRIVACY.

de-liv'-er. To release; transfer. GIVING-RECEIVING, RELEASE-RESTRAINT, RESCUER, SPEECH-INARTICULATENESS, TRANSFER, VOCALIZATION-MUTENESS; **deliver a judgment,** DECISION-MISJUDGMENT; **deliver a speech,** SPEECH-INARTICULATENESS; **deliver as one's act and deed,** EVIDENCE-COUNTEREVIDENCE.

de-liv'-er-ance. The act of delivering. ALLEVIATION-AGGRAVATION, RELEASE-RESTRAINT, RESCUE.

de-liv'-er-y. The act of setting free. CREATION-DESTRUCTION, SPEECH-INARTICULATENESS, VOCALIZATION-MUTENESS.

dell. A glen. CONVEXITY-CONCAVITY.

Del'-phic or'-a-cle. The oracle of Apollo, at Delphi. CLEARNESS-AMBIGUITY, MANIFESTATION-LATENCY, SOOTHSAYER.

del'-ta. A tract of land in the shape of the Greek letter of that name [Δ]. GEOLOGY, OCEAN-LAND.

de-lude'. To mislead. TRUTH-ERROR, TRUTHFULNESS-FRAUD.

del'-uge. A flood. EXCESS-LACK, GATHERING-SCATTERING, RIVER-WIND, WATER-AIR.

de-lu'-sion. The act of deluding. SANENESS-LUNACY, TRUTH-ERROR, TRUTHFULNESS-FRAUD; **self-delusion,** CREDULOUSNESS-SKEPTICISM.

de-lu'-sive. Misleading. TRUTH-ERROR, TRUTHFULNESS-FRAUD.

de-lu'-so-ry. Tending to mislead. TRUTHFULNESS-FRAUD.

delve. To dig. CONVEXITY-CONCAVITY, DOMESTICATION-AGRICULTURE; **delve into,** INVESTIGATION-ANSWER.

dem'-a-gogue. A leader of the people. ANTAGONIST-ASSISTANT, INSUBORDINATION-OBEDIENCE, MANAGER.

dem'-a-gog''-y. Demagogism. RULE-LICENSE.

de-mand'. A claim. DUENESS-UNDUENESS, INVESTIGATION-ANSWER, ORDER, PRICE-DISCOUNT, PROPERTY; **in demand,** DESIRE-DISTASTE, NEED.

de''-mar-ca'-tion. The act of marking limits. BOUNDARY.

de-mean' one-self'. To behave. CONDUCT, SELFRESPECT-HUMBLENESS, UPRIGHTNESS-DISHONESTY.

de-mean'-or. Deportment. APPEARANCE-DISAPPEARANCE, CONDUCT, SOCIETY-LUDICROUSNESS.

de-men'-cy. Insanity. SANENESS-LUNACY.

de-ment'-ate. Demented. SANENESS-LUNACY.

de''-men-ta'-tion. Madness. SANENESS-LUNACY.

de-ment'-ed. Insane. SANENESS-LUNACY.

de-men'-ti-a. Insanity. SANENESS-LUNACY.

de-mer'-it. Ill desert. VIRTUE-VICE.

de-mesne'. A manor-house with adjacent land. DWELLER-HABITATION, PROPERTY.

demi [F.] (de-mi'). A prefix meaning "half." DOUBLING-HALVING.

dem'-i-god. An inferior deity. BRAVERY-COWARDICE, GOOD MAN-BAD MAN.

dem''-i-gra'-tion. Emigration. TRAVELING-NAVIGATION.

dem'-i-john. A glass vessel. CONTENTS-RECEIVER.

demi-jour [F.] (de-mi-zhur'). Half-light; partial illumination. DIMNESS.

dem'-i-monde''. Women of doubtful reputation. GENTILITY-DEMOCRACY, PURITY-RAKE.

dem'-i-rep. A woman of suspected chastity. PURITY-RAKE.

de-mise'. Death. ALIENATION, LIFE-DEATH, LOANING-BORROWING.

de-mised'. Left by will. LIFE-DEATH.

dem'-i-sem''-i-qua'-ver. A thirty-second note in music. MELODY-DISSONANCE.

de-mis'-sion. Relinquishment. COMMISSION-ABROGATION.

dem'-i-urge. An imaginary supernal creator. AGENT, JOVE-FIEND.

dem'-i-volt. One of the movements of a horse. SPRING-DIVE.

de-moc'-ra-cy. Government by the people. GENTILITY-DEMOCRACY, RULE-LICENSE.

dem'-o-crat. One who adheres to democracy. GENTILITY-DEMOCRACY.

De-moc'-ri-tus. A so-called laughing Greek philosopher. JUBILATION-LAMENTATION.

dem''-oi-selle'. A damsel. INFANT-VETERAN.

de-mol'-ish. To destroy. CREATION-DESTRUCTION, PROOF-DISPROOF.

de-mol'-ish-ment. Demolition. CREATION-DESTRUCTION.

dem''-o-li'-tion. Destruction. CREATION-DESTRUCTION.

de'-mon. An evil spirit. ANGEL-SATAN, GOOD-EVIL, JOVE-FIEND, REMEDY-BANE, TURBULENCE-CALMNESS; **demon in human shape,** BENEFACTOR-EVILDOER, GOOD MAN-BAD MAN; **demon worship,** HEAVEN-HELL.

de''-mo-ni'-a-cal. Devilish. CHARITABLENESS-MALEVOLENCE, EXCITATION, JOVE-FIEND, VIRTUE-VICE.

de'-mon-ism. Belief in demons. DEVOTION-IDOLATRY.

de''-mon-ol'-a-try. Worship of demons. DEVOTION-IDOLATRY.

de''-mon-ol'-o-gy. The science of demons. DEVOTION-MAGIC, JOVE-FIEND.

de-mon'-o-my. Dominion of demons. DEVOTION-MAGIC.

de'-mon-ry. The influence of demons. JOVE-FIEND.

de'-mon-ship. The state of a demon. DEVOTION-MAGIC.

de-mon'-stra-ble. Capable of proof. PROOF-DISPROOF.

de-mon'-strate. To prove. PROOF-DISPROOF.

dem'-on-stra''-ted. Proved. PROOF-DISPROOF.

dem'-on-stra''-ting. The act of proving. PROOF-DISPROOF.

dem''-on-stra'-tion. Proof. MANIFESTATION-LATENCY, POMP, PROOF-DISPROOF; **ocular demonstration,** SIGHT-BLINDNESS, VISIBILITY-INVISIBILITY.

de-mon'-stra-tive. With the power of demonstration. EXCITABILITY-INEXCITABILITY, MANIFESTATION-LATENCY, PROOF-DISPROOF, SIGN.

de-mon'-stra-tive. A pronoun. PRONOUN.

dem'-on-stra''-tor. One who demonstrates. INTERPRETER.

de-mor''-al-i-za'-tion. Loss of morals. BETTERMENT-DETERIORATION, VIRTUE-VICE.

de-mor'-al-ize. To corrupt morals. BETTERMENT-DETERIORATION, VIRTUE-VICE.

de-mor'-al-ized. Corrupt in morals. VIRTUE-VICE.

de-mor'-al-iz''-ing. Tending to corrupt morals. VIRTUE-VICE.

demos [Gr.] (dī'-mos). The people. GENTILITY-DEMOCRACY.

De-mos'-the-nes. A celebrated Athenian orator and patriot, of the fourth century, B. C. SPEECH-INARTICULATENESS.

de-mul'-cent. Any soothing application. REMEDY-BANE, TURBULENCE-CALMNESS.

de-mur'. To take exception. ASSENT-DISSENT, DETERMINATION-VACILLATION, FAITH-MISGIVING, READINESS-RELUCTANCE.

de-mure'. With a modest demeanor. CONCEIT-DIFFIDENCE, EXCITABILITY-INEXCITABILITY, LIGHTHEARTEDNESS-DEJECTION, SOCIETY-LUDICROUSNESS.

de-mure'-ness. The state of being demure. CONCEIT-DIFFIDENCE, LIGHTHEARTEDNESS-DEJECTION, SOCIETY-AFFECTATION.

de-mur'-rer. One who demurs. LITIGATION.

de-mur'-ring. Taking exceptions. READINESS-RELUCTANCE.

den. A cave. CLEANNESS-FILTHINESS, CONTENTS-RECEIVER, DWELLER-HABITATION, RELEASE-PRISON; **den of thieves,** THEFT.

de-na'-ri-us. Roman coin. VALUES.

den'-a-ry. Tenfold. FIVE-QUINQUESECTION.

de-nat'-u-ral-ize. To make unnatural. BETTERMENT-DETERIORATION.

de-nat'-u-ral-ized. Made unnatural. CONVENTIONALITY-UNCONVENTIONALITY.

den'-dri-form. Shaped like a tree. PROPORTION-DEFORMITY.

den'-droid. Like a tree. PROPORTION-DEFORMITY.

den-drol'-o-gy. A discourse on trees. ZOOLOGY-BOTANY.

de-ni'-al. Contrary assertion. ASSERTION-DENIAL, PROFFER-REFUSAL; **self-denial,** MODERATION-SELFINDULGENCE.

de-nied'. Contradicted. ASSERTION-DENIAL.

den'-i-grate. To blacken. WHITENESS-BLACKNESS.

den''-i-za'-tion. The act of making one a citizen. LIBERTY-SUBJECTION.

den'-i-zen. A citizen; an inhabitant. DWELLER-HABITATION, LIBERTY-SUBJECTION; **denizens of the air,** JOVE-FIEND; **denizens of the day,** FAUNA-FLORA.

Den'-mark, something rot'-ten in the state of. Something wrong in any place. [Shakespeare, *Hamlet,* I, v.] MANIFESTATION-LATENCY.

de-nom'-i-nate. To name. NAME-MISNOMER.

de-nom''-i-na-tion. The act of denominating. ASSOCIATION, DIVISION, NAME-MISNOMER; **religious denomination,** THEOLOGY.

de-nom''-i-na'-tion-al. Pertaining to a denomination. ASSENT-DISSENT, THEOLOGY; **denominational education,** EDUCATION-MISTEACHING.

de-nom'-i-na''-tor. A unit or divisor. NUMBER.

de-no'-ta-ble. Able to be denoted. SIGN.

de-no'-ta-tive. Able to denote. SIGN.

de-note'. To represent. SIGN.

dé-noue'-ment. Outcome. BEGINNING-END, CAUSEEFFECT, COMPLETION-NONCOMPLETION, EXPOSUREHIDINGPLACE.

de-nounce'. To accuse publicly as deserving censure. APPROVAL-DISAPPROVAL, CHARITABLENESS-CURSE, JUSTIFICATION-CHARGE.

de-nounce'-ment. The act of denouncing. JUSTIFICATION-CHARGE.

dense. Thick. GATHERING-SCATTERING, SOLIDITYRARITY.

den'-si-ty. The quality of being dense. SOLIDITYRARITY.

dent. A hollow; a dint. CONVEXITY-CONCAVITY, INDENTATION.

den'-tal. One of a class of letters of the alphabet. LETTER.

den'-tate. Having teeth. INDENTATION.

den'-ta''-ted. Dentate. INDENTATION.

den-tic'-u-late. Finely dentate. INDENTATION.

den-tic'-u-la''-ted. Denticulate. INDENTATION, SHARPNESS-BLUNTNESS.

den'-ti-form'. Of the form of a tooth. SHARPNESSBLUNTNESS.

den'-tist-ry. The art of a dentist. REMEDY-BANE.

den''-u-da'-tion. The act of denuding. DRESS-UNDRESS.

de-nude'. To make nude. DRESS-UNDRESS.

de-nu'-ded. Made nude. GAIN-LOSS; **denuded of,** EXCESS-LACK.

de-nun''-ci-a'-tion. The act of denouncing. APPROVAL-DISAPPROVAL, CHARITABLENESS-CURSE, JUSTIFICATION-CHARGE.

de-nun'-ci-a-to-ry. Having denunciation. APPROVALDISAPPROVAL, CHARITABLENESS-CURSE, JUSTIFICATION-CHARGE.

de-ny'. To contradict. ASSERTION-DENIAL, COMMISSION-RETIREMENT, PROFFER-REFUSAL; **deny oneself,** DEVOTION, MODERATION-SELFINDULGENCE, QUEST-EVASION, SOCIABILITY-PRIVACY.

Deo volente [L.] (dī'-o vo-len'-tî). God willing. POSSIBILITY-IMPOSSIBILITY.

de''-ob-struct'. To clear away obstructions. DIFFICULTY-FACILITY.

de'-o-dand. A personal chattel given to God, that is, forfeited to the crown. RECOMPENSE-PENALTY.

de-o'-dor-ize. To destroy odor. CLEANNESS-FILTHINESS, ODOR-INODOROUSNESS.

de-o'-dor-ized. Free from odor. ODOR-INODOROUSNESS.

de-o'-dor-iz''-ing. Tending to free from odor. ODOR-INODOROUSNESS.

de''-on-tol'-o-gy. The science of duty. DUTY-DERELICTION.

de-op'-pi-late. To free from obstructions. DIFFICULTY-FACILITY.

de-op''-pi-la'-tion. Removal of obstructions. DIFFICULTY-FACILITY.

de-or''-gan-i-za'-tion. Loss of organic character. ORGANIZATION-DISORGANIZATION.

de-os''-cu-la'-tion. Kissing. BLANDISHMENT.

de-part'. To leave. APPROACH-WITHDRAWAL, ARRIVAL-DEPARTURE, ESTABLISHMENT-REMOVAL; **depart from,** AIM-ABERRATION, QUEST-ABANDONMENT; **depart this life,** LIFE-DEATH.

de-part'-ed. Dead. ENTITY-NONENTITY, LIFEDEATH.

de-part'-ing. Departure. ARRIVAL-DEPARTURE.

de-part'-ment. A separate part. DIVISION, EXTENSION-DISTRICT, OCCUPATION, WHOLE-PART.

de-part'-ure. A going away. APPROACH-WITHDRAWAL, ARRIVAL-DEPARTURE, ESTABLISHMENTREMOVAL, QUEST-EVASION; **new departure,** BEGINNING-END; **point of departure,** ARRIVAL-DEPARTURE.

de-pend'. To rely fully. CERTAINTY-DOUBT, SUSPENSION-SUPPORT; **depend on circumstances,** CERTAINTYDOUBT; **depend upon,** EVIDENCE-COUNTEREVIDENCE, FAITH-MISGIVING, LIBERTY-SUBJECTION.

de-pend'-ant. One who depends on another. CHIEFUNDERLING.

de-pend'-ed on, to be. Trustworthy. CERTAINTYDOUBT, FAITH-MISGIVING, UPRIGHTNESS-DISHONESTY.

de-pend'-ence. The act of depending. LIBERTY-SUBJECTION.

de-pend'-en-cy. The state of being dependent. HOLDING-EXEMPTION, LIBERTY-SUBJECTION, PROPERTY, SUSPENSION-SUPPORT.

de-pend'-ent. Subject to some exterior control. CAUSEEFFECT, CHIEF-UNDERLING, LIBERTY-SUBJECTION, SUSPENSION-SUPPORT.

de''-per-di'-tion. Destruction. GAIN-LOSS.

de''-phleg-ma'-tion. A freeing from water by evaporation. DAMPNESS-DRYNESS.

de-pict'. To represent vividly. DELINEATION-CARICATURE, PAINTING.

de-pict'-ing. Representing by a picture. PAINTING.

de-pict'-ment. The act of depicting. DELINEATIONCARICATURE.

de-pic'-ture. To depict in colors or words. DELINEATION-CARICATURE.

dep''-i-la'-tion. The act of removing hair. DRESSUNDRESS.

de-pil'-a-to-ry. Adapted to remove hair. REMEDYBANE.

de-ple'-tion. The act of depleting. EXCESS-LACK.

de-plor'-a-ble. Fit to be deplored. GOODNESS-BADNESS, PLEASURABLENESS-PAINFULNESS, WELFAREMISFORTUNE.

de-plore'. To regret. CONTENTEDNESS-DISCONTENTMENT, JUBILATION-LAMENTATION.

de-ploy'. To unfold. ENLARGEMENT-DIMINUTION.

de-pone'. To testify. ASSERTION-DENIAL.

de-po'-nent. One who deposes. EVIDENCE-COUNTEREVIDENCE.

de-pop'-u-late. To dispeople. ADMISSION-EXPULSION, SOCIABILITY-PRIVACY.

de-pop''-u-la'-tion. The act of depopulating. SOCIABILITY-PRIVACY.

de-port'. To transport. ADMISSION-EXPULSION.

de''-por-ta'-tion. Transportation. ADMISSION-EXPULSION, TRANSFER.

de-port'-ment. Conduct. CONDUCT.

de-po'-sal. The act of deposing. COMMISSION-ABROGATION.

de-pose'. To testify; to remove from office. ASSERTION-DENIAL, COMMISSION-ABROGATION, EVIDENCE-COUNTEREVIDENCE, RULE-LICENSE.

de-pos'-it. To place. ESTABLISHMENT-REMOVAL, OUTLAY-INCOME, SECURITY, SOLIDITY-RARITY, STORE.

de-pos'-i-ta-ry. A trustee. TREASURER.

dep''-o-si'-tion. The act of deposing. ASSERTION-DENIAL, COMMISSION-ABROGATION, ESTABLISHMENT-REMOVAL, EVIDENCE-COUNTEREVIDENCE, MARK-OBLITERATION, RULE-LICENSE.

de-pos'-i-to-ry. A place for storing. STORE, TREASURY.

de'-pot. A warehouse. GATHERINGPLACE, MARKET, STORE.

de-prave'. To make bad. BETTERMENT-DETERIORATION.

dep''-ra-va'-tion. The act of depraving. BETTERMENT-DETERIORATION.

de-praved'. Morally bad. BETTERMENT-DETERIORATION, GOODNESS-BADNESS, VIRTUE-VICE.

de-prave'-ment. Depravity. BETTERMENT-DETERIORATION.

de-prav'-i-ty. The state of being depraved. GOODNESS-BADNESS, VIRTUE-VICE.

dep'-re-cate. To pray against. COMPASSION-RUTHLESSNESS, JUBILATION-LAMENTATION, MOTIVE-DEHORTATION.

dep''-re-ca'-tion. Prayer. COMPASSION-RUTHLESSNESS, MOTIVE-DEHORTATION, PETITION-EXPOSTULATION.

de-pre'-ci-ate. To fall in esteem. ADULATION-DISPARAGEMENT, APPROVAL-DISAPPROVAL.

de-pre'-ci-a''-ted. Undervalued. COSTLINESS-CHEAPNESS, OVERVALUATION-UNDERVALUATION.

de-pre'-ci-a''-ting. Falling in value. OVERVALUATION-UNDERVALUATION.

de-pre''-ci-a'-tion. The act of depreciating. ADULATION-DISPARAGEMENT, APPROVAL-DISAPPROVAL, COSTLINESS-CHEAPNESS, INCREASE-DECREASE, JUSTIFICATION-CHARGE, OVERVALUATION-UNDERVALUATION, PRICE-DISCOUNT.

dep''-re-da'-tion. A plundering. THEFT.

dep'-re-da''-tor. A spoiler. ROBBER.

dep''-re-hen'-sion. A seizing. TAKING-RESTITUTION.

de-press'. To press down. CONTENTEDNESS-DISCONTENTMENT, CONVEXITY-CONCAVITY, ELEVATION-DEPRESSION, WITTINESS-DULNESS.

de-pressed'. Pressed down. ELEVATION-DEPRESSION.

de-press'-ing. Bringing down in spirits. LIGHTHEARTEDNESS-DEJECTION, PLEASURABLENESS-PAINFULNESS.

de-pres'-sion. The act of depressing. CONVEXITY-CONCAVITY, DEEPNESS-SHALLOWNESS, ELEVATION-DEPRESSION, HEIGHT-LOWNESS, LIGHTHEARTEDNESS-DEJECTION.

de-press'-ive. Tending to depress. PLEASURABLENESS-PAINFULNESS.

dep''-ri-va'-tion. The act of depriving. GAIN-LOSS, TAKING-RESTITUTION.

de-prive'. To take anything away from. ADDITION-SUBTRACTION, TAKING-RESTITUTION; **deprive of life,** LIFE-DEATH; **deprive of power,** MIGHT-IMPOTENCE; **deprive of strength,** STRENGTH-WEAKNESS.

de-prived' of. Dispossessed. GAIN-LOSS.

de-prive'-ment. Deprivation. TAKING-RESTITUTION.

depth. Deepness. DEEPNESS-SHALLOWNESS, SAGACITY-INCAPACITY; **depth of misery,** PLEASURE-PAIN; **depth of thought,** REFLECTION-VACANCY; **depth of winter,** HEAT-COLD; **out of one's depth,** DIFFICULTY-FACILITY, RECKLESSNESS-CAUTION.

dep'-u-rate. To purify. CLEANNESS-FILTHINESS.

dep'-u-ra-to-ry. Purifying. REMEDY-BANE.

dep''-u-ta'-tion. A delegation. COMMISSION-ABROGATION.

de-pute'. To delegate. COMMISSION-ABROGATION.

Dep'-u-ties, Cham'-ber of. One branch of the French legislature. COUNCIL.

dep'-u-ty. Delegate. REPRESENTATIVE, PRESIDENT-MEMBER, RULE-LICENSE.

de-quan'-ti-tate. To lessen the quantity. INCREASE-DECREASE.

de-range'-ment. Disorder. ORGANIZATION-DISORGANIZATION, REGULARITY-IRREGULARITY, SANENESS-LUNACY.

Der'-by day. The day of the Derby sweepstakes. STRIFE-PEACE.

der'-e-lict. Deserted. KEEPING-RELINQUISHMENT, OCEAN-LAND, SOCIABILITY-PRIVACY.

der''-e-lic'-tion. Failure in duty. INNOCENCE-GUILT, KEEPING-RELINQUISHMENT; **dereliction of duty,** DUTY-DERELICTION.

der'-ham [Ar.]. Arabic coin. VALUES.

de-ride'. To ridicule. REGARD-DISRESPECT, SOCIETY-DERISION.

de-ri'-sion. Ridicule. JUBILATION-LAMENTATION, REGARD-DISRESPECT, REGARD-SCORN, SOCIETY-DERISION.

de-ri'-sive. Showing derision. REGARD-DISRESPECT, SOCIETY-DERISION.

de-ri'-so-ry. Showing derision. SOCIETY-DERISION.

der''-i-va'-tion. The act of deriving. CAUSE-EFFECT, RATIONALE-LUCK, WORD-NEOLOGY.

de-riv'-a-tive. Derived. CAUSE-EFFECT, NOUN, WORD-NEOLOGY.

de-rive'. To obtain by regular process. DECISION-MISJUDGMENT, GAIN-LOSS, OUTLAY-INCOME, RATIONALE-LUCK.

de-rived' verb. Kind of verb. VERB.

der'-mal. Of the skin. COVER-LINING.

der''-ma-tol'-o-gy. The science of the skin. COVER-LINING.

dernier ressort [F.] (dêr-ni-ê' re-sor'). Last resort. VOLITION-OBLIGATION.

dérobée, à la [F.] (dê-ro-bê', à la). By stealth. ENLIGHTENMENT-SECRECY.

der'-o-gate. To disparage. ADULATION-DISPARAGEMENT, UPRIGHTNESS-DISHONESTY; **derogate from,** REPUTATION-DISCREDIT.

der''-o-ga'-tion. The act of derogating. REPUTATION-DISCREDIT.

de-rog'-a-to-ry. Lessening in repute. ADULATION-DISPARAGEMENT, REPUTATION-DISCREDIT, UPRIGHTNESS-DISHONESTY.

der'-rick. A machine for lifting and swinging heavy weights. ELEVATION-DEPRESSION.

der'-vish. A Mohammedan monk. MINISTRY-LAITY.

désagrément [F.] (dê-za-grê-man'). Something disagreeable. PLEASURABLENESS-PAINFULNESS.

des-cant'. To discourse at length. ESSAY, MUSIC, TERSENESS-PROLIXITY.

de-scend'. To go downward. ASCENT-DESCENT, INCREASE-DECREASE, PARALLELISM-INCLINATION; **descend to particulars,** ACCOUNT, UNIVERSALITY-PARTICULARITY.

de-scend'-ant. Offspring. PARENTAGE-PROGENY.

de-scen'-sion. Descent. ASCENT-DESCENT.

descensus Averni, facilis [L.] (dî-sen'-sus a-ver'-nai fas'-i-lis). The descent to Avernus is easy. [Virg., Æneid, vi, 126.] SECURITY-INSECURITY.

de-scent'. The act of descending. ASCENT-DESCENT, CAUSE-EFFECT, GAIN-LOSS, INCREASE-DECREASE, PARENTAGE-PROGENY.

de-scribe'. To give a description. ACCOUNT, DELINEATION-CARICATURE.

de-scribed'. Having the characteristics given. ACCOUNT.

de-scrip'-tion. The act of describing. ACCOUNT, DIVISION, NAME-MISNOMER, RHETORIC.

de-scrip'-tive. Having description. ACCOUNT, RHETORIC.

de-scry'. To discern. SIGHT-BLINDNESS.

des'-e-crate. To profane. GODLINESS-UNGODLINESS, REGARD-DISRESPECT, USE-DISUSE.

des'-e-cra"-ting. Profaning. GODLINESS-UNGODLINESS.

des'-e-cra"-tion. The act of desecrating. GODLINESS-UNGODLINESS, USE-MISUSE.

des'-ert. A waste; empty. FERTILITY - STERILITY, GULF-PLAIN, PRESENCE-ABSENCE; waste sweetness on the desert air, PROVISION-WASTE.

de-sert'. Abandon; what one deserves. COMMISSION-RETIREMENT, QUEST-ABANDONMENT, QUEST-EVASION, VIRTUE-VICE.

de-sert'-ed. Forsaken. OBSTRUCTION-HELP, PRESENCE-ABSENCE, SOCIABILITY-PRIVACY.

de-sert'-er. One who forsakes duty. BIGOTRY-APOSTASY, PATRIOTISM-TREASON.

de-sert'-ful. High in desert. VIRTUE-VICE.

de-sert'-ing. Forsaking. QUEST-ABANDONMENT.

de-ser'-tion. The act of deserting. SOCIABILITY-PRIVACY.

de-sert'-less. Undeserving. VIRTUE-VICE.

de-serve'. To merit. DUENESS-UNDUENESS; deserve belief, FAITH-MISGIVING; deserve notice, CONSEQUENCE-INSIGNIFICANCE.

de-served'. Merited. DUENESS-UNDUENESS, RIGHT-WRONG.

de-serv'-ing. Worthy of regard. DUENESS-UNDUENESS, VIRTUE-VICE.

désespoir, au [F.] (dê-zes-pwar', o). In despair. LIGHTHEARTEDNESS - DEJECTION, SANGUINENESS-HOPELESSNESS.

déshabillé, en [F.] (dê-za-bi-yê', an·). In undress. DRESS-UNDRESS, EMBELLISHMENT-DISFIGUREMENT, PREPARATION-NONPREPARATION.

des'-ic-cate. To dry. DAMPNESS-DRYNESS.

des"-ic-ca'-tion. The act of desiccating. DAMPNESS-DRYNESS.

de-sid'-er-ate. To desire. DESIRE-DISTASTE, NEED.

de-sid"-e-ra'-tum. Something desirable. DESIRE-DISTASTE, INVESTIGATION-ANSWER, NEED.

de-sign'. A drawing. COPY-MODEL, DELINEATION-CARICATURE, DESIGN, PAINTING, PURPOSE-LUCK.

DESIGN.

Deep-laid plan, etc. Cunningly formed plan. See PREDETERMINATION.

Design. A preliminary plan or sketch.

Germ, etc. The earliest form. See CAUSE.

Motion. A suggestion or proposal looking forward to action.

Organization, etc. A systematic arrangement, preparatory to action or use. See ORGANIZATION.

Plan. A formulated scheme of action or procedure.

Precaution, etc. A provision made in advance to ward off evil or secure success. See PREPARATION.

Project. An impracticable scheme.

Proposal. That which is offered for consideration; a scheme.

Proposition. Something presented for discussion or consideration.

Resolution. Something resolved or determined; a settled purpose.

Scheme. A design or plan of something to be done.

Suggestion. That which is suggested or intimated; a hint.

System, etc. Formal arrangement. See REGULARITY.

DESIGN—Denotations, etc.

Alternative. The course of action or the thing offered in place of another.

Artifice. An artful or crafty device.

Base of operations. A place from which the forward movements of an army are made, supplies drawn, etc.

Bill. Any paper containing a statement of particulars.

Bill of fare. An enumeration of the dishes served at a public table. See NUTRIMENT.

Bold hit. }
Bold move. } An unexpected or daring operation.
Bold stroke. }

Bright idea. } A brilliant, lively thought.
Bright thought. }

Brouillon [F.]. A rough draft.

Cabal. An intrigue.

Card. A piece of pasteboard or thick paper for various uses.

Carte du pays [F.]. A map of a country.

Cheval de bataille [F.]. A war-horse· the main dependence.

Clever hit. }
Clever move. } An act or movement showing skill.
Clever stroke. }

Complot. A conspiracy.

Conspiracy. An agreement between two or more persons to commit a crime.

Contrivance. A scheme or plan.

Copy. A reproduction of an original work.

Counterplot. A plot opposed to another.

Coup [F.]. A stroke.

Coup d'état [F.]. A bold stroke of policy.

Court card. A card bearing a coated figure.

Device. That which is formed by design.

Draft. }
Draught. } A plan drawn in outline.

Ébauche [F.]. A rough sketch.

Expedient. Suitable means to accomplish an end.

Forecast. A previous plan or determination.

Great gun. A plan or movement or person superior to others.

Intrigue. A plot or scheme intended to effect something secretly.

Invention. An original contrivance or construction.

Last shift. An expedient tried in a difficulty. See VOLITION-OBLIGATION.

List of *agenda*. List of things to be done.

Loophole. A means of escape or evasion.

Machination. A hostile or treacherous scheme.

Master stroke. A masterly deed.

Measure. An act designed for the accomplishment of an object.

Nostrum. A device of a quack.

Order of the day. The outline of business for the day, of a legislative or deliberative body.

Outline. A sketch having only the borders of a figure.

Platform. A declaration of principles.

Plot. Any scheme, or secret design.

Policy. Settled method by which affairs are conducted. See CONDUCT.

Program. An outline of the order to be followed.

Proof. A trial impression.

Prospectus. A summary or plan of something proposed.

Protocol. A preliminary treaty.

Receipt. A form according to the directions of which things are to be taken or combined.

Revise. A second proof-sheet.

Rôle [F.]. A part taken, as in a play

Rough cast. A rude model.

Rough draft. }
Rough draught. } A rude drawing or sketch.

Shift. A plan or method tried in a difficulty. See COMMUTATION.

Skeleton. The framework of anything.

Sketch. The first rough plan of anything.

Step. A measure or action.

Stratagem. A trick; especially of the leader of an army. See CRAFT.

Stroke. } A powerful or sudden effort by which something is
Stroke of policy. } done.

Trick. A sly procedure. See FRAUD.

Trump card. The winning card; the winning action.

Underplot. A secret scheme; a secondary plot in a play.

DESIGN—Nouns of Agent.

Artist. One skilled in a fine art.

Conspirator. One who engages in a conspiracy.

Designer. One who designs or plans.

Intrigant, etc. [F.]. An intriguing fellow. See CRAFT.

Machinator. One who forms evil designs; an artful schemer.

Projector. One who forms fanciful schemes.

Promoter. One who assists in setting a financial enterprise on foot.

Schematist. One given to forming schemes.

Schemist. A schemer.

Strategist. A person skilled in strategy.

DESIGN—Verbs.

Arrange, etc. To make ready or prepare, etc. See ORGANIZATION.

Cast. To fix or distribute, as the parts of a play.

Chalk out. To sketch, as with chalk; to plan.

DESIGN—Verbs—*Continued*.

Concert. To devise or arrange.
Concoct. To contrive or plan.
Contrive To devise by the exercise of ingenuity.
Countermine. To frustrate by clandestine measures.
Counterplot. To attempt to frustrate by stratagem.
Cut out To scheme or prepare.
Design. To sketch for a pattern or model.
Devise. To formulate in the mind; to contrive.
Dig a mine. Plot.
Digest. To arrange methodically.
Fall upon. To attempt; to hit upon.
Forecast. To plan beforehand.
Frame. To originate or plan.
Hatch. To originate or contrive.
Hatch a plot.
Hit upon. To come upon by chance.
Intrigue, etc. To form a scheme or plan, etc. See Craft.
Invent, etc. To contrive something not before known. See Fancy.
Lay a train. }
Lay down a plan. } To make preparations.
Lay out. To plan in detail.
Map out. }
Mark out a course. } To clearly indicate; to sketch.
Mature. To bring to maturity; complete.
Organize. To arrange the various parts of a plan for action or work.
Plan. To form a delineation or representation of.
Plot. To devise secretly; scheme.
Preconcert. To arrange beforehand.
Predetermine, etc. To determine beforehand. See Predetermination.
Preestablish. To establish beforehand.
Prepare, etc. To make ready. See Preparation
Project. To sketch out in the mind.
Recast. To shape anew or to compute a second time.
Scheme. To form a scheme; design.
Set one's wits to work, etc. See Fancy.
Shape out a course. Plan.
Sketch. To make a rough draft of.
Spring a project. See *Nouns*.
Strike out. To devise or contrive.
Systematize. To arrange or dispose methodically.
Take measures. }
Take steps. } To move in a matter.

DESIGN—*Adjectives*.

In course of preparation, etc. See Preparation.
On the carpet. Under consideration.
On the tapis. On the table or under consideration.
Planned. See *Verbs*.
Planning. See *Verbs*.
Strategic. }
Strategical. } Pertaining to strategy or effected by strategy.
Under consideration.

des'-ig-nate. To point out. Name-Misnomer, Universality-Particularity.
des''-ig-na'-tion. The act of designating. Division, Name-Misnomer.
de-signed'. Intentional. Predetermination-Impulse.
de-sign'-ed-ly. Purposely. Purpose-Luck.
de-sign'-er. One who designs. Artist, Design.
de-sign'-ing. Making a plan. Delineation-Caricature.
de-sign'-ing. Cunning. Craft-Artlessness.
de-sign'-less. Without intention. Purpose-Luck.
des'-i-nence. A termination. Beginning-End, Discontinuance-Continuance.
desipere in loco [L.] (dî-sip'-e-rî in lo'-co). To unbend on occasion. Jubilation-Lamentation.
de-sir''-a-bil'-i-ty. The state of being desirable. Propriety-Impropriety.
de-sir'-a-ble. Fit to be desired. Desire-Distaste, Propriety-Impropriety.
de-sir'-a-ble-ness. The quality of being desirable. Propriety-Impropriety.
de-sire'. A longing. Desire-Distaste, Love-Hate, Need, Purpose-Luck, Readiness-Reluctance, Sanguineness-Hopelessness; **have no desire for,** Sensitiveness-Apathy, Unconcern.

DESIRE—DISTASTE.

Allurement. Some attractive real or supposed good.
Ambition. The desire for advancement.
Animus. That animating spirit which impels one to achieve
Anxiety. Concern about some event not yet known.
Appetence. Eager desire.
Appetency. That natural desire in animals to seek that which is best suited to their nature and nourishment, as the duck takes to the water.
Appetite. A physical want.
Appetition. A seeking after something.
Ardor. The eagerness with which one follows his work.
Aspiration. High hope for attainment.
Attraction. The quality of drawing objects outside of itself to itself.
Avidity. Intense desire.
Bent. Inclination; tendency toward.
Breathless impatience. Overanxiety to attain one's end.
Cacoethes. A bad habit; desire for the worthless.
Canine appetite. A voracious appetite, like that of a dog.
Concupiscence. Sexual lust.
Coveting. Wrongfully seeking the property of others.
Covetousness. The quality of being covetous.
Craving. Eager desire.
Cupidity. Desire for wealth, gain, possessions.
Desire. A longing for some real or supposed good not possessed.
Dipsomania. Insatiable desire for alcoholic drinks.
Drought. Thirst for.
Eagerness. Earnest desire.
Edge of appetite. A sharp appetite.
Edge of hunger. A strong want of food.
Empressement. Assiduity; eagerness.
Exigency. Urgent want.
Fancy. Liking; inclination.
Fantasy. See Fancy.
Fascination. A charm; a spell.
Fondness. Attachment to, or liking for.
Furore. Excitement.
Grasping Seizing everything that can be gotten hold of.
Greed. An eager desire for something.

Abhorrence. Detestation.
Abomination. Extreme disgust.
Animosity. See Favorite-Anger.
Antipathy. Settled aversion.
Aversation. A turning away from in dislike
Averseness. Opposition.
Aversion. Dislike; disgust.
Backwardness. See Readiness-Reluctance.
Disgust. Repugnance.
Disinclination. Loathing; aversion
Detestation. Extreme hatred or dislike.
Dislike. Hate; antipathy.
Displacency. Envious displeasure.
Disrelish. Want of enjoyment.
Distaste. Disgust; displeasure.
Gall and wormwood. See Palatableness-Unpalatableness.
Hate. See Love-Hate.
Horror. Dread; that which excites fear.
Loathing. Distasteful.
Misrelish. Dislike.
Mortal antipathy. }
Mortal horror. } Deepest dislike.
Nausea. Squeamishness.
Queasiness. Qualmishness; delicate.
Reluctance. Unwillingness; hesitancy.
Repugnance. Antipathy; dislike.
Rooted antipathy. }
Rooted horror. } Deep dislike.
Shuddering. Horror; fear.
Sickener Anything that causes disgust.
Turn. Change of tendency or feeling, as from desire to dislike.

DISTASTE—*Associated Nouns*.

Cold sweat. Perspiration accompanied by chilliness, caused by fear.
Hydrophobia. A great dread of water, a symptom of canine madness.

DISTASTE—*Verbs*.

Abhor. Detest; shun.
Abominate. To feel great disgust.

Greediness. The quality of being greedy.

Hankering. A longing after.

Height of one's ambition. Having attained all that one ever desired.

Hobby. One's favorite object or pursuit.

Hobbyhorse. A specialty; some subject which appeals most strongly.

Hunger. The desire for food.

Inclination. Tendency; attraction.

Inextinguishable desire. A desire not to be satisfied.

Impetuosity. See EXCITABILITY.

Inkling. An intimation; a hint.

Itch. An irritating desire.

Itching. See ITCH.

Itching palm. A hand itching for money. [Shakespeare, *Julius Cæsar*, IV, iii.]

Keenness. Eagerness; ardentness.

Kleptomania. An irresistible mania to steal.

Leaning. A hankering for; a tendency toward.

Lickerish tooth. Eagerness to taste or enjoy.

Liking. Kindly disposition for.

Longing. Desire; wish.

Longing eye. Wistful eye.

Love. Affection; devotion.

Lust. Carnal appetite.

Maggot. An odd fancy.

Mania. A mad desire.

Manie. See MANIA.

Mind. Inclination; disposition.

Mouth-watering. Eager desire for something delightful to the taste.

Need. Want; necessity.

Overanxiety. Too much concern about the happening of some event.

Partiality. Special favor.

Passion. A desire intensified by the presence of the object.

Penchant. A bias; a decided taste.

Predilection. A predetermined affection for some one or something.

Prestige. Expectation of the future based on the experience of the past.

Propensity. See AFFECTIONS.

Prurience. Uneasy with a lustful desire.

Rage. Vehement desire; unreasonable passion.

Rapacity. Exorbitant greediness for gain.

Ravenousness. The quality of being eager for gratification.

Relish. Appetite; fondness.

Sharp appetite. Intense longing for.

Sheep's eye. A bashful or amorous glance.

Solicitude. Anxiety; concern.

Stomach. An appetite.

Sweet tooth. A special fondness for sweetmeats.

Thirst. Desire for drink.

Thirstiness. The state of being thirsty.

Twist. Turning from one's usual course to gain favor.

Vaulting ambition. Gaining of preferment, as by leaping upon a horse. [Shakespeare, *Macbeth*, I, vii.]

Voracity. See FASTING-GLUTTONY.

Want. Wish; desire. See NEED.

Whim. A capricious fancy.

Whimsey. A craze for.

Willingness. See READINESS.

Wish. Expression of desire.

Wistful eye. Expression of desire.

Yearning. A longing desire.

Zeal. Passionate ardor in the pursuit of anything.

DESIRE—*Nouns of Agent.*

Amateur. A lover of some pursuit or science for the pleasure he finds in following it.

Aspirant. One who hopes for honors, achievements.

Candidate. A seeker for office.

Cormorant. See FASTING-GLUTTONY.

Devotee. A person wholly given up to religion.

Lover. One who loves.

Magnet. Something which draws other objects to itself.

Solicitant. One who desires to obtain something.

Votary. One devoted to some particular state in life.

DESIRE—*Associated Nouns.*

Completion wished for. The end or satisfaction of desire.

Consummation devoutly to be wished. An earnest and heart-felt desire. [Shakespeare, *Hamlet*, III, i.]

Desideratum [L.]. Anything desired.

Fortunatus' cap. The cap of Fortune by which a person could secure anything desired.

Idol. That on which the affections are strongly set.

Avoid. See QUEST-EVASION.

Cause dislike. See *Nouns.*

Conceive a dislike. See *Nouns.*

Conceive an aversion to. See *Nouns.*

Detest. To abhor; to shun; to testify against.

Disgust. To offend one's taste.

Disincline. To turn away.

Dislike. To hate; to feel aversion.

Disrelish. To feel a distaste.

Entertain a dislike. See *Nouns.*

Entertain an aversion to. To tolerate a feeling of antipathy towards another.

Eschew. To steer clear of.

Excite a dislike. To provoke unfriendliness.

Go against the grain. To be distasteful.

Go against the stomach. To cause loathing.

Hate. See LOVE-HATE.

Have enough of. See DESIRE-REPLETION.

Have a dislike. ⎫

Have an aversion to. ⎬ Dislike.

Have no stomach for. ⎪

Have no taste for. ⎭

Have rather not. Object to.

Insouciance. Careless, indifferent unconcern.

Loathe. To feel disgust, or nausea; to hate.

Look askance at. Look at sidelong with contempt.

Make a grimace. To distort one's face.

Make a mouth. To distort the mouth.

Make a wry face. To draw up one's face.

Make faces. Show distaste.

Make one's blood run cold. See PLEASURABLENESS-PAINFULNESS.

Make sick. To nauseate.

Mind. To notice; to be displeased with.

Mislike. See DESIRE-DISTASTE.

Nauseate. To loathe; to disgust.

Not care for. Dislike.

Not to be able to abide. ⎫

Not to be able to bear. ⎬ Dislike extremely.

Not to be able to endure. ⎭

Object to. To oppose.

Pall. To lose spirit or taste for.

Recoil from. To withdraw from in disgust.

Render sick. To make sick.

Repel. To drive back.

Shock. To frighten; horrify.

Shrink from. To be horrified.

Shrug the shoulders at. To show contempt.

Shudder at. To be afraid of.

Shun. To avoid; to refuse the company of.

Sicken. To disgust.

Stick in the throat. Not to agree with one's liking.

Stink in the nostrils. To be an abomination to one.

Take a dislike. To hate.

Take amiss. See FAVORITE-ANGER.

Take an aversion to. To become offended.

Turn one's stomach. To produce vomiting; produce extreme disgust.

Turn up the nose at. To disdain.

Wamble. To cause the stomach to roll; disagree.

Withdraw from. Refuse to associate with.

DISTASTE—*Adjectives.*

Abhorrent. Detestable; repugnant.

Adverse. Opposed.

Adverse to. Turned from; hostile to.

Disagreeable. See PLEASURABLENESS-PAINFULNESS.

Disgusting. See *Verbs.*

Disinclined. Alienated; indisposed.

Dislike. See *Verbs.*

Disliking. See *Verbs.*

Dogsick. Very sick.

Fulsome. Offensive from excess.

Heartsick. Despondent; pained in mind.

Insufferable. Unendurable.

Loathful. Hating; abhorring.

Loathsome. Exciting disgust.

Loth. Odious; hateful.

Offensive. Distasteful.

Out of conceit with. Not having a favorable opinion of.

Queasy. Ticklish; squeamish.

Repellent. Tending to drive back.

Repugnant. Combative.

Repulsive. Bitter; arousing disgust.

Shy of. Afraid of.

DESIRE—Associated Nouns—*Continued.*

Seduction.　The act of leading to do wrong.
Temptation.　The act of being led to do wrong.
Torment of Tantalus.　The torment of a Phrygian king who was placed in the midst of a lake whose waters reached to his chin, but receded whenever he attempted to allay his thirst, while over his head hung branches of fruit which receded when he grasped for them.

DESIRE—*Verbs.*

Affect.　To aspire to or aim at.
Allure.　To attempt to draw to.
Appetize.　To excite an appetite.
Aspire after.　Strive to attain.
Attract.　To draw to.
Be bent upon.　Eager to follow.
Be desirous.　See *Adjectives.*
Be hungry.　See *Adjectives.*
Be on thorns for.　To be very anxious about.
Be ravenous.　See *Adjectives.*
Be wishful.　See *Adjectives.*
Burn to.　To have a strong desire.
Care for.　To be solicitous; concerned.
Cast a sheep's eye upon.　To look furtively on the object of affection.
Catch at.　To attempt to obtain.
Cause desire.　Awaken desire.
Cling to.　To hold on tenaciously.
Court.　To woo; make love to.
Covet.　See *Nouns.*
Crave after.　To long for earnestly.
Create desire.　Produce a desire which was lacking.
Cry for.　To want something earnestly.
Desiderate.　To miss; to want.
Desire.　See *Nouns.*
Die for.　To give up one's life in the interest of.
Excite desire.　To stir up a feeling of longing.
Faire venir l'eau à la bouche [F.].　To make the mouth water.
Fancy.　See *Nouns.*
Feel the want of.　To know the necessity.
Find it in one's heart.　See sub READINESS.
Fish for.　To seek for; to go in quest of.
Gape for.　To anxiously wait for something.
Gasp for.　To express eager desire for.
Grasp at.　To try to get hold of.
Gratify desire.　See PLEASURABLENESS.
Hanker after.　To have a vehement desire for.
Have a fancy for.　To take a liking to.
Have a good appetite.　To possess a proper desire for food.
Have a longing.　See *Nouns.*
Have a mind to.　To be kindly inclined to.
Have an eye to.　To watch with interest.
Have at heart.　To be much concerned about.
Hold out allurements.　To offer inducements; to draw on.
Hold out temptations.　To try to lead astray.
Hope.　See SANGUINENESS.
Hope for.　To expect to obtain.
Hunger after.　To desire with great eagerness.
Itch after.　To have an irritating desire for.
Jump at.　To be glad to accept.
Languish for.　To pine away for.
Like.　Love; favor; desire.
List.　To lean; to incline.
Long for.　To hanker after; to want.
Look sweet upon.　To regard; to woo.
Lust after.　Desire to seduce.
Make one's mouth water.　See *Nouns.*
Miss.　To notice the absence of; to care for
Need.　To be necessary to satisfy want.
Ogle.　To show a fondness for.
Pant for.　Earnestly long for.
Pine for.　To waste away with desire.
Play a good knife and fork.　To be a good eater.
Prefer.　See CHOICE.
Provoke desire.　To call forth desire.
Put up for.　To care for.
Raven for.　To display a devouring appetite.
Run mad after.　To have an uncontrollable passion.
Set one's cap at.　A phrase applied to the action of a woman who desires to win the love of a certain man.
Set one's eyes upon.　To have hope of attainment.
Set one's heart upon.　To determine to gain.
Set one's mind upon.　See SET ONE'S HEART UPON.
Sigh for.　To yearn for.
Solicit.　To manifest deep concern.

DISTASTE—Adjectives—*Continued.*

Sick.　Affected by disease.
Sick of.　Disgusted with.
Uncared for.　Neglected; unloved.
Unpopular.　Disliked; despised.

DISTASTE—*Adverbial Phrase.*

Usque ad nauseam [L.].　To disgust.

DISTASTE—*Interjections.*

Faugh! foh! ugh!

DISTASTE—*Phrase.*

Non libet [L.].　It does not please me.

DESIRE—Verbs—*Continued.*

Take a fancy to.　To take a liking to something.
Take into one's head.　To admit into favor.
Take one's fancy.　To have the quality of winning favor.
Take to.　To form a fascination for.
Tantalize.　To sharpen one's desire by presenting the desired object and not allowing one to have it, as was done to Tantalus.
Tempt.　To try to seduce to commit sin.
Thirst after.　A craving.
Titillate.　To arouse a pleasing tickling sensation.
Want.　To wish for; to desire.
Whet the appetite.　To stimulate; to excite.
Whistle for.　To desire to have some one answer to a call
Wish.　⎫
Wish for.　⎭ To express a desire to obtain.
Woo.　To court; to love.
Would be glad of.　Would be pleased at.
Would fain do.　Would do gladly.
Would fain have.　Would be glad to possess.
Yearn for.　To desire eagerly.

DESIRE—*Adjectives.*

Agog.　In eager desire.
Alieni appetens [L.].　Coveting the property of others.
All agog.　All eager.
Ambitious.　Desirous of power, honor, preferment.
Anxious.　Concern about the outcome of certain events.
Appetizable.　Able to excite an appetite.
Appetizing.　Exciting appetite.
Ardent.　Glowing; warm.
Aspiring.　Longing for; hoping.
At a loss for.　In need of.
Athirst.　In need of drink.
Avid.　Eagerly longing for.
Bent on.　⎫
Bent upon.　⎭ Inclined; leaning in that way.
Breathless.　Overanxious; very desirous.
Burning.　Earnest; eager.
Covetous.　Desiring the property of another.
Craving.　With an intense appetite for.
Curious.　Eager to find out.
Desirable.　Profitable to have.
Desired.　Wished for.
Desiring.　See *Verbs.*
Desirous.　Wanting something.
Devoured by desire.　Overcome with passion.
Drouthy.　Thirsty.
Dry.　Needing drink.
Dying for.　Giving up one's life for.
Eager.　Excited by desire in the pursuit of anything.
Enragé [F.].　Made furious.
Esurient.　Hungry.
Exacting.　Unreasonably severe in making demands.
Extortionate.　Oppressive; hard.
Fain.　Glad; willing.
Famished.　Overcome with hunger.
Fervent.　Hot; zealous.
Grasping.　Miserly; greedy.
Greedy.　Gluttonous; rapacious.
Greedy as a hog.　Very greedy.
Hungry.　Desirous for food.
Hungry as a churchmouse.　⎫
Hungry as a hawk.　⎪
Hungry as a horse.　⎬ Very hungry.
Hungry as a hunter.　⎭
Impatient.　See EXCITABILITY.
Inclined.　See READINESS.
In demand.　Desirous of possessing.

DESIRE—Adjectives—*Continued.*

Insatiable. Not able to be satisfied.
Intent on. }
Intent upon. } Eager in the pursuit of.
Keen. Eager.
Lickerish. Eager to taste; craving.
Mad after. Overcome by passion.
Omnivorous. Eating everything indiscriminately.
Open-mouthed. Gaping; clamorous.
Optative. Expressing desire.
Overeager. Too eager.
Parched with thirst. Very thirsty.
Partial to. Biased in favor of.
Peckish. Hungry.
Pinched with hunger. Very hungry.
Pleasing. See Pleasurableness.
Quenchless. Inextinguishable.
Rabid. Mad, as a mad dog.
Rapacious. Gluttonous; greedy.
Ravening. Greedily devouring.
Ravenous. Voracious.
Ravenous as a wolf. Very ravenous.
Sedulous. Constant in attendance to business.
Set on. }
Set upon. } Adhering to closely.
Sharp-set. Eager in appetite or desire of gratification.
Sky-aspiring. Extravagant in ambition.
Solicitous. Concerned; care for.
Sordid. Meanly avaricious.
Tantalizing. See *Verbs.*

Thirsty. In need of water.
Unquenchable. Inextinguishable.
Unsated. }
Unsatisfied. } Not satisfied.
Unslaked. Unquenched.
Vaulting. Leaping unrestrained.
Voracious. Rapacious; greedy.
Wishful. Having the desire to gain.
Wistful. Longing; desirous.
With an empty stomach. Grasping; hungry.

DESIRE—*Adverbs.*

Fain. Gladly.
Wistfully. See *Adjectives.*

DESIRE—*Interjections.*

Esto perpetua [L.]. Let it endure forever.
O for! would that! would that it were!

DESIRE—*Phrases.*

Aut Cæsar aut nullus [L.]. Either Cæsar or no one.
Hoc erat in votis [L.]. This was in my prayers.
I frutti proibiti sono i piu dolci [It.]. Forbidden fruits are the sweetest.
Sua cuique voluptas [L.]. Every man has his own pleasure.
The fingers itching. Desirous of grasping or seizing something
The mouth watering. Eager to have something.
The wish being father to the thought. Desire too strong becoming thought.
Ubi mel, ibi apes [L.]. Where the honey is, there are the bees.

DESIRE—PARTICULARNESS.

PARTICULARNESS.

Difficulty in being pleased. Fastidiousness.
Epicureanism. The philosophy which teaches that pleasure is the supreme good and the chief end of life. [Epicurus.]
Fastidiousness. The quality of being hard to please.
Friandise [F.]. Daintiness; delicacy.
Hypercriticism. Overnice or excessive criticism.
Nicety. Extreme delicacy or precision.
Omnia suspendens naso [L.]. Sniffing at everything; daintiness.
Particularness. The quality of giving careful and minute attention to.
Prudery. An extreme and often insincere display of delicacy and modesty.

PARTICULARNESS—*Agents.*

Epicure. One devoted to luxurious sensual enjoyments. [Epicurus.]
Gourmet [F.]. A person of great delicacy of taste in matters of eating and drinking.

PARTICULARNESS—*Verbs.*

Be fastidious. See *Adjectives.*
Have a smooth tooth. Have a taste for delicacies.
Look a gift horse in the mouth. To pick flaws or find fault with a gift or favor.
Mince the matter. To affect extreme delicacy.
See spots in the sun. To find imaginary faults.
Turn up one's nose at. Be hard to please by.

PARTICULARNESS—*Adjectives.*

Censorious. Given to censuring or faultfinding.
Dainty. Very refined or particular in taste.
Délicat [F.]. Delicate.
Delicate. Very refined; dainty.
Difficult to please. Fastidious.
Fastidious. Overdelicate; very hard to please.
Finical. Overnice or fastidious in matters of dress or manners.
Hard to please. Fastidious.
Hypercritical. See Hypercriticism.
Lickerish. Having a keen relish; lustful.
Nice. Very refined; overparticular in tastes or habits.
Particular. See Desire-Particularness.
Pleasing. Agreeable to the tastes or habits.
Queasy. Very particular in matters of eating; squeamish.
Querulous. Given to finding fault.
Scrupulous. Very particular and careful in matters of right and wrong.
Squeamish. Easily disgusted or shocked in matters of taste or conscience.
Squeasy. See Queasy.
Strait-laced. Strict in morals or manners.
Thin-skinned. Sensitive; easily offended.

PARTICULARNESS—*Phrase.*

Noli me tangere [L.]. Do not touch me.

DESIRE—REPLETION.

REPLETION.

Glut. An excessive supply or amount.
Repletion. Complete or excessive fulness; surfeit.
Satiety. The condition of being filled or gratified beyond desire.
Satisfaction. Gratification of desire within the limits of propriety.
Saturation. To make so full by absorption that it will hold no more.
Surfeit. Excess in eating or drinking.
Weariness. The condition produced by continued exertion.

REPLETION—*Associated Nouns.*

Crambe repetita [L.]. Cabbage warmed up and served again.
Enfant gâté [F.]. A spoiled child.
Spoiled child. A child permitted to gratify its every wish.
Too much of a good thing. Something desirable, made undesirable by overabundance.
Toujour perdrix [F.]. Partridge again; too much of a good thing.

REPLETION—*Verbs.*

Be satiated. See Satiety.
Bore. To make weary by persistently annoying, or by continued dulness.

Cloy. To satisfy until desire turns to loathing.
Glut. To fill to excess.
Gorge. To fill the throat or stomach to excess.
Have enough of. }
Have one's fill of. } Be satisfied.
Have quite enough of. }
Have too much of. Be sated.
Pall. To dull by satiety; to cloy.
Quench. To allay or cause to cease; as desire or passion.
Sate. To satisfy the appetite to excess.
Satiate. To gratify beyond natural desire.
Satisfy. To gratify desire or appetite, but not to excess.
Saturate. To fill to the full; usually said of a liquid taken up by absorption.
Slake. To quench.
Spoil. To impair by overindulgence.
Surfeit. See Surfeit.
Tire. To cause weariness; also, to bore.

DESIRE—REPLETION—*Continued.*

REPLETION—*Adjectives.*

Blasé [F.]. Surfeited; not capable of further enjoyment.
Heartsick. Extremely depressed in spirits; very despondent.
Overgorged. See GORGE.
Satiated. See *Verbs.*

Sick of. Cloyed.
Used up. Worn out.

REPLETION—*Interjections.*

Eheu! jam satis! [L.] Alas! now it is enough!
Enough!
Hold!

de-sired'. Longed for. DESIRE-DISTASTE.
de-sir'-ing. Longing for. DESIRE-DISTASTE.
de-sir'-ous. Having a desire. DESIRE-DISTASTE.
de-sist'. To cease from acting. ACTION-PASSIVENESS, DISCONTINUANCE-CONTINUANCE, QUEST-ABANDONMENT.
de-sist'-ance. A ceasing to act. DISCONTINUANCE-CONTINUANCE.
desk. A kind of table. CONTENTS-RECEIVER, FANE, SCHOOL, SUSPENSION-SUPPORT.
désobligeant [F.] (dê-zo-blî-zhan·'). Disobliging; a vehicle for one person only. CONVEYANCE-VESSEL.
désœuvré [F.] (dê-zu-vrê'). An idler. ACTION-PASSIVENESS.
des'-o-late. Deprived of inhabitants. CREATION-DESTRUCTION, LIGHTHEARTEDNESS-DEJECTION, SOCIABILITY-PRIVACY, SOLITUDE-COMPANY.
des'-o-la''-ting. Filling with sadness. PLEASURABLENESS-PAINFULNESS.
des''-o-la'-tion. The state of being desolate. CREATION-DESTRUCTION, PLEASURE-PAIN, SOCIABILITY-PRIVACY.
désolé [F.] (dê-zo-lê'). Disconsolate. LIGHTHEARTEDNESS-DEJECTION.
désorienté [F.] (dê-zo-ri-an·-tê'). Confused. CERTAINTY-DOUBT.
de-spair'. To give up all hope. LIGHTHEARTEDNESS-DEJECTION, PLEASURE-PAIN, SANGUINENESS-HOPELESSNESS.
de-spair'-ing. Giving up all hope. SANGUINENESS-HOPELESSNESS.
des-patch'. The act of despatching. ACTIVITY-INDOLENCE, ADMISSION-EXPULSION, COMPLETION-NONCOMPLETION, CONDUCT, HURRY-LEISURE, LIFE-KILLING, MISSIVE-PUBLICATION, NUTRIMENT-EXCRETION, ORDER, TIDINGS-MYSTERY; **happy despatch,** RECOMPENSE-PUNITION.
des''-per-a'-do. A reckless ruffian. BENEFACTOR-EVILDOER, BRAWLER, RECKLESSNESS-CAUTION.
des'-pe-rate. Having no care for danger or safety. DIFFICULTY-FACILITY, MAGNITUDE-SMALLNESS, POSSIBILITY-IMPOSSIBILITY, RECKLESSNESS-CAUTION, SANGUINENESS-HOPELESSNESS, TURBULENCE-CALMNESS.
des'-per-ate-ly. Recklessly. MAGNITUDE-SMALLNESS.
des''-per-a'-tion. A state of despair. DETERMINATION-VACILLATION, EXCITABILITY-INEXCITABILITY, FAVORITE-ANGER, RECKLESSNESS-CAUTION, SANGUINENESS-HOPELESSNESS, TURBULENCE-CALMNESS.
des'-pi-ca-ble. Worthy of being despised. REGARD-SCORN, REPUTATION-DISCREDIT.
de-spi'-cien-cy. Contempt. REGARD-DISRESPECT, REGARD-SCORN.
de-spi'-sal. Contempt. REGARD-SCORN.
de-spise'. Hold in contempt. REGARD-SCORN; **despise danger,** BRAVERY-COWARDICE.
de-spised'. Held in scorn. REGARD-SCORN.
de-spi'-sed-ness. The state of being despised. REGARD-SCORN.
de-spite'. Malice. CHARITABLENESS-MALEVOLENCE; **in despite,** ANTAGONISM-CONCURRENCE.
de-spite'-ful. Full of spite. GODLINESS-UNGODLINESS.
de-spoil'. To pillage. BETTERMENT-DETERIORATION, TAKING-RESTITUTION, THEFT.
des-pond'. To lose courage. LIGHTHEARTEDNESS-DEJECTION, SANGUINENESS-HOPELESSNESS.

des-pond'-en-cy. The loss of hope and courage. LIGHTHEARTEDNESS-DEJECTION, SANGUINENESS-HOPELESSNESS, SANGUINENESS-TIMIDITY.
des-pond'-ing. Giving up hope. LIGHTHEARTEDNESS-DEJECTION.
des'-pot. A tyrant. CHIEF-UNDERLING, HARSHNESS-MILDNESS, TYRANNY-ANARCHY.
des-pot'-ic. Of a despot. LAW-LAWLESSNESS, TYRANNY-ANARCHY.
des-pot'-ic-al. Despotic. LAW-LAWLESSNESS.
des-pot'-ic-al-ly. Tyrannically. TYRANNY-ANARCHY.
des'-pot-ism. The spirit of a despot. HARSHNESS-MILDNESS, LAW-LAWLESSNESS, RULE-LICENSE, TYRANNY-ANARCHY.
des'-pu-mate. To froth. CLEANNESS-FILTHINESS.
des''-qua-ma'-tion. Peeling off. DRESS-UNDRESS.
des-sert'. The last course at dinner. NUTRIMENT-EXCRETION.
dessous des cartes [F.] (de-su' de cart). The under side of the cards. The unknown element. CAUSE-EFFECT, MANIFESTATION-LATENCY, TIDINGS-MYSTERY.
dessous des cartes, connaître les [F.] (de-su' de cart, co-nêtr' le). To know the under side of the cards. KNOWLEDGE-IGNORANCE.
dessous dessus, sens [F.] (de-su' de-sü', san·s). Upside down. REVERSAL.
des'-ti-nate. Determined. PURPOSE-LUCK.
des''-ti-na'-tion. A place fixed for the end of a journey. ARRIVAL-DEPARTURE, BEGINNING-END, PURPOSE-LUCK, VOLITION-OBLIGATION.
des'-tine. To settle anything in advance. PURPOSE-LUCK, VOLITION-OBLIGATION.
des'-tined. Predetermined. OCCURRENCE-DESTINY, VOLITION-OBLIGATION.
des'-ti-ny. A predetermined lot. OCCURRENCE-DESTINY, VOLITION-OBLIGATION; **fight against destiny,** BIGOTRY-APOSTASY.
des'-ti-tute. Being in want. AFFLUENCE-PENURY, EXCESS-LACK, NEED; **refuge for destitute,** REFUGE-PITFALL.
des''-ti-tu'-tion. The state of being destitute. AFFLUENCE-PENURY.
des'-tri-er. A war-horse. BELLIGERENT.
des-troy'. To ruin. ACTION-PASSIVENESS, BETTERMENT-DETERIORATION, COMMISSION-ABROGATION, CREATION-DESTRUCTION, ENTITY-NONENTITY, GOODNESS-BADNESS; **destroy hopes,** SANGUINENESS-HOPELESSNESS.
des-troyed'. Ruined. CREATION-DESTRUCTION, SUCCESS-FAILURE.
des-troy'-er. One who destroys. BENEFACTOR-EVILDOER, MAKER-DESTROYER.
de-struc'-tion. Ruin. CREATION-DESTRUCTION, REVOLUTION.
de-struc'-tive. Ruinous. CREATION-DESTRUCTION, GOODNESS-BADNESS.
des'-ue-tude. A cessation of use. HABIT-DESUETUDE, QUEST-ABANDONMENT, USE-DISUSE.
des'-ul-to-ry. Suddenly passing from one thing to another. AGITATION, AIM-ABERRATION, CONTINUITY-INTERRUPTION, MUTABILITY-STABILITY, PERIODICITY-IRREGULARITY, UNIFORMITY-MULTIFORMITY.
de-sume'. To borrow. LOAN-BORROWING.
de-tach'. To sever. COHESION-LOOSENESS, UNION-DISUNION.

de-tached'. Severed. COHESION-LOOSENESS, CONNECTION-INDEPENDENCE.

de-tach'-ment. The act of detaching. BELLIGERENT, UNION-DISUNION, WHOLE-PART.

de-tail'. A single part. ACCOUNT, ASSIGNMENT, EMBELLISHMENT-DISFIGUREMENT, UNIVERSALITY-PARTICULARITY; **attention to detail,** CAREFULNESS-CARELESSNESS, HEED-DISREGARD; **in detail,** WHOLE-PART.

de-tailed' ac-count'. An account giving particulars. ACCOUNT.

de-tails'. Minute particulars. CONSEQUENCE-INSIGNIFICANCE, MAGNITUDE-SMALLNESS.

de-tain'. To keep back. KEEPING-RELINQUISHMENT.

de-tect'. To discover. DISCOVERY.

de-tec'-tion. Discovery. DISCOVERY.

de-tect'-ive. Skilled in detection. ENLIGHTENMENT-SECRECY.

de-ten'-tion. The act of detaining. KEEPING-RELINQUISHMENT; **house of detention,** RELEASE-PRISON; **in house of detention,** JUSTIFICATION-CHARGE.

détenu [F.] (dê-te-nü') One detained; a prisoner. GUARD-PRISONER.

de-ter'. To prevent. MOTIVE-DEHORTATION, SANGUINENESS-TIMIDITY.

de-terge'. To cleanse. CLEANNESS-FILTHINESS.

de-ter'-gent. Purging. CLEANNESS-FILTHINESS, REMEDY-BANE.

de-te'-ri-o-ra''-ted. Made worse. BETTERMENT-DETERIORATION, GOODNESS-BADNESS.

de-te''-ri-o-ra'-tion. The act of growing worse. BETTERMENT-DETERIORATION, RENOVATION-RELAPSE.

de-ter'-min-ate. Definitely settled. CERTAINTY-DOUBT, DECISION-MISJUDGMENT, PURPOSE-LUCK, UNIVERSALITY-PARTICULARITY.

de-ter''-min-a'-tion. The act of determining. DETERMINATION-VACILLATION.

DETERMINATION—VACILLATION.

Aplomb. Assurance resulting from self-confidence.

Decision. The quality of being positive and firm in judgment or action.

Desperation. The being' defiant of consequences, as being without hope.

Determination. The quality of being firm and decided; uninfluenced by the opinions of others.

Devotedness. Strong attachment.

Devotion. Ardent affection or zeal.

Energy. Force of character and readiness for action.

Firmness. The quality of not being easily moved.

Gameness. Endurance, as of a game-cock.

Iron will. A strong unyielding will.

Manliness. The quality of possessing those things which are characteristic of the true man; as firmness, resolution, etc.

Mastery over self. Self-control.

Moral courage. Determination to do one's duty in the face of opposition.

Moral strength. See MORAL COURAGE.

Obstinacy. Headstrong determination.

Perseverance. Persistence in following out a determination or resolution.

Pluck. Courage and perseverance in dangers and difficulties.

Resoluteness. See RESOLUTION.

Resolution. The quality of being firm and determined in the carrying out of some purpose or course of conduct.

Self-command. The state of having all the powers and faculties at command.

Self-conquest. } The act or habit of having one's faculties, especially
Self-control. } the inclinations and emotions, under control of the will

Self-denial. Forbearance or refusal to gratify one's own feelings or inclinations.

Self-government. The act of governing oneself.

Self-possession. The full control of one's powers or faculties.

Self-reliance. Dependence on one's own abilities, resources, or judgment.

Self-restraint. Restraint, as of the passions, by the force of one's own will.

Strength of mind. } Capability of acting or operating with effect;
Strength of will. } moral force.

Tenacity. The quality of clinging to an opinion or purpose persistently; extreme and even foolish resoluteness.

Unconquerable will. Moral force, or strength that cannot be overcome.

Vigor. See ENERGY.

Will. Strong determination; energy of character.

Will of one's own. Self-reliance; independence.

Will-power. Strength of will as shown in the face of opposition.

Zeal. Ardent and continued devotion.

DETERMINATION—*Figurative Nouns.*

British lion. The national emblem of Great Britain; hence, Great Britain.

Bull-dog. A large breed of dogs noted for courage and tenacity; hence, a stubborn or tenacious person.

New Year's Day. The day of making good resolutions.

Alternative. The condition or necessity of choosing between two things.

Caprice. A natural disposition to make sudden changes of mood or purpose without adequate motive, like a goat.

Changeableness. The condition of being of a wavering and inconstant disposition.

Cowardice. Want of courage.

Demur. Hesitation; lack of readiness to decide or act.

Fickleness. The quality of being inconstant in judgment or action.

Fluctuation. The condition of changing irregularly, like the waves.

Hesitancy. See HESITATION.

Hesitating. See *Verbs.*

Hesitation. The quality of acting with timidity and lack of promptness.

Indecision. Lack of settled purpose.

Indetermination. Lack of ability to consider all things and come to a conclusion.

Infirmity of purpose. Want of settled purpose or intention.

Irresolution. Lack of constancy in carrying out a purpose or course of action.

Légèreté [F.]. Lightness; levity.

Pliancy. The quality of being easily moved or influenced.

Suspense. The state of being hung up; uncertainty; indecision.

Timidity. Want of courage or boldness.

Uncertainty. Indecision.

Undetermination. See INDETERMINATION.

Unsettlement. The state of being unsettled or undecided.

Vacillation. The quality of changing from one opinion or mood to another; changeableness.

Weakness. The condition of lacking strength and decision of character.

VACILLATION—*Denotations.*

Ass between two bundles of hay. An ass unable to decide from which bundle of hay to eat; hence, an undecided and vacillating person. Buridan's ass, the typical doubter.

Butterfly. An insect that flits from flower to flower; hence, a person of unsettled notions.

Half-measure. A weak or indefinite step of policy.

Shuttlecock. A cork stuck with feathers, struck back and forth in play.

Waverer. A person who is unsettled in opinion.

VACILLATION—*Verbs.*

Alternate. To change back and forth, as between two opinions.

Balance. To weigh in the mind; be undecided.

Be afraid. Fear.

Be irresolute. See *Adjectives.*

Be thrown off one's balance. To be made uncertain.

Blink. To shut one's eyes to; to dodge.

Blow hot and cold. To vacillate; to be inconstant or inconsistent.

Boggle. To hesitate; to shrink back.

Change. To alternate in judgment or action.

Chasser-balancer [F.]. To hesitate; to be uncertain.

Compromise. To yield in part.

Coquet with. To trifle with; to flirt with.

Dally with. To delay.

Dawdle. To act in an undecided and uncertain manner.

Debate. To consider; to turn over in the mind before deciding.

DETERMINATION—VACILLATION—*Continued.*

DETERMINATION—*Verbs.*

Be resolved, etc. See *Adjectives.*
Bring to a crisis. To bring to a point where a decision must be made.
Buckle to. To apply oneself resolutely.
Come to a determination. ⎫
Come to a resolution. ⎬ Decide.
Come to a resolve. ⎭
Conclude. To come to a decision; to determine.
Decide. To settle in one's mind; to resolve.
Determine. To have a fixed intention to do.
Determine once for all. Determine finally
Devote oneself to. Persist.
Drive matters to an extremity. Go all lengths.
Fix. To decide definitely; to settle; to fasten down.
Form a determination. ⎫
Form a resolution. ⎬ Resolve.
Form a resolve. ⎭
Give oneself up to. To devote oneself to.
Go all lengths. To make every effort possible.
Go in for. To enter into with energy and determination.
Go the whole hog. ⎫
Go through fire and water. ⎬ To go to extremes
Have determination. See *Nouns.*
Insist upon. To hold to or maintain firmly.
Kick down the ladder. To resolutely determine to go through with a thing, casting aside all means of retreat.
Know one's own mind. To have decision of character.
Lay one's shoulder to the wheel. To set oneself to anything with a purpose, instead of calling on Hercules to help.
Make a dash at. To go at a thing with great vigor.
Make a point of. To carefully carry out some course of action or conduct.
Make short work of. To accomplish a thing resolutely and quickly.
Make up one's mind. To decide.
Nail one's colors to the mast. Decide finally.
Not listen to the voice of the charmer. Be unyielding.
Not stick at trifles. Be unscrupulous.
Persist. To cling to tenaciously.
Plunge *in medias res* [L.]. To plunge into the very midst of.
Put one's foot down. To determine finally; settle for good.
Put one's heart into. To be earnest about.
Put one's shoulder to the wheel. See LAY ONE'S SHOULDER TO THE WHEEL.
Resolve. To settle in the mind. To determine is more truly an act of the judgment; to resolve is an act of the will.
Ride the whirlwind and direct the storm. [Addison, *The Campaign*, 291.]
Run the gantlet. To go through difficulties.
Rush *in medias res* [L.]. See PLUNGE *in medias res.*
Seal. To determine or settle beyond question.
Set one's back against the wall. To resolutely determine to fight a thing out.
Set one's heart upon. To determine to accomplish or gain.
Set one's mind upon. See SET ONE'S HEART UPON.
Set one's shoulder to the wheel. See LAY ONE'S SHOULDER TO THE WHEEL.
Set one's teeth. To be firmly resolved.
Stand firm. Be unyielding.
Stand no nonsense. To be in great earnest.
Steel oneself. To harden oneself against difficulties and misfortunes
Stick at nothing. Be unscrupulous.
Take a decisive step. Put an end to uncertainty.
Take one's stand. Make up one's mind.
Take the bull by the horns. To meet dangers or difficulties resolutely and boldly.
Take upon oneself. To resolve to carry through.
Throw away the scabbard. To make up one's mind to act.
Will. To be determined to do.

DETERMINATION—*Adjectives.*

Bent upon. Determined.
Decided. Unwavering.
Definitive. Bringing to an end; conclusive.
Determined, etc. See *Verbs.*
Earnest. Serious in purpose.
Firm. Settled; unshaken.
Game to the backbone. Thoroughly resolved.
Indomitable. Unyielding.
Inexorable. Not to be moved by entreaty or prayer.
Inflexible. Not to be turned from a purpose; firm.
Intent upon. Having the mind set upon.
In utrumque paratus [L.]. Prepared for either alternative.

VACILLATION—VERBS—*Continued.*

Demur. See DEMUR.
Dilly-dally. To trifle with; to dally with.
Falter. To act with hesitancy and irresolution.
Fluctuate. To change irregularly.
Go half way. Compromise.
Gybe. To swing about, especially a sail on a mast.
Hang in suspense. To be undetermined.
Hang upon. To be undecided or in suspense.
Hesitate. See HESITATION.
Hover. To hesitate on the verge of action or decision.
Hum and haw. To be confused and undecided what to do.
Keep in suspense. Delay decision.
Keep off and on. To change back and forth; to vacillate.
Leave *ad referendum* [L.]. To leave to be further considered.
Let "I dare not" wait upon "I would." [Shakespeare, *Macbeth*, I,vii.]
Make a compromise. See COMPROMISE.
Not know one's own mind. Not be clear of purpose; not know one-self.
Pause. To hesitate.
Play fast and loose. Vacillate.
Remain neuter. To take neither side; to be undecided.
Retreat. To withdraw; fall or shrink back.
Shuffle. To shift this way and that; to waver.
Stagger like a drunken man. Sway back and forth.
Think twice about. Waver.
Trim. To avoid difficulty by time-serving methods.
Vacillate. See VACILLATION.
Waver. To be irresolute; to hesitate.
Will and will not. To hesitate.

VACILLATION—*Adjectives.*

At a loss. Doubtful.
Capricious. See *Nouns.*
Cowardly. Of a timid, faint-hearted disposition.
Double-minded. Unsettled; unstable.
Easy-going. Taking things without concern.
Facile. Easily moved or influenced.
Fast and loose. Inconstant; uncertain.
Feeble-minded. Of weak will; lacking decision.
Fickle. See FICKLENESS.
Fidgety. Changing about in a nervous fashion.
Frail. Easily influenced or led astray.
Frothy. Unsubstantial; trivial.
Giddy. Inconstant to foolishness; having the head swim.
Half-hearted. Timid; hesitating.
Hesitating. See HESITATION.
Infirm of purpose. See INFIRMITY OF PURPOSE.
Irresolute. Not fixed or constant in carrying out a purpose.
Light. Not serious or resolute.
Light-minded. Lacking seriousness or strength of mind.
Lightsome. Of a cheerful disposition.
Off one's balance. Uncertain.
Reversible. Capable of being changed.
Revocable. Capable of being repealed or reversed.
Shilly-shally. Of a vacillating, trifling nature.
Timid. See TIMIDITY.
Tremulous. Of a timid and irresolute nature; trembling.
Unable to say no. Like an *assentator* or *Jaherr;* easily persuaded.
Undecided. ⎫
Undetermined. ⎬ Not having the mind made up
Unresolved. ⎭
Unsteadfast. Not to be depended upon.
Unsteady. Inconstant.
Vacillating. See *Verbs.*
Volatile. Easily affected; changeable.
Weak. Lacking firmness and energy of character.
Without ballast. Unsteady, like an unballasted ship.

VACILLATION—*Adverbs.*

From pillar to post. From one thing to another
In flattering accents. Persuasively.
Irresolutely. In an inconstant manner.
Irresolvedly. In an unsettled and undecided manner.
Off and on. At one time or another.
Seesaw. In a vacillating or alternating manner; teetering.

VACILLATION—*Phrase*

How happy could I be with either, were t'other dear charmer away. [John Gay, *What d'Ye Call It,* II, ii.]

DETERMINATION—Adjectives—Continued.

Iron. Unyielding; not to be bent.
Not to be put down. }
Not to be shaken. } Immovable.
Obstinate. Stubborn: firm to the extreme.
Peremptory. Very positive in opinion or judgment; dogmatic.
Proof against. Capable of resisting successfully.
Relentless. Unmoved by pity.
Resolute. Having a fixed purpose and constant in carrying it out.
Resolved, etc. See *Verbs*.
Self-possessed. Full of self-control.
Serious. Earnest.
Set upon. Bent upon.
Steady. Constant; unwavering.
Steeled against. Immovable.
Strong-minded. Inflexible.
Strong-willed. Resolute.
Tenax propositi [L.]. Tenacious of purpose.
Trenchant. Effective.
Unflinching. Resolute.
Unhesitating. With readiness of judgment or action.
Unshrinking. Resolute.

DETERMINATION—Adverbs.

At all events. }
At all hazards. }
At all risks. }
At any cost. }
At any hazard. } Whatever happens.
At any price. }
At any rate. }
At any risk. }
At any sacrifice. }

À tort et à travers [F.]. Blindly; at random.
Cost what it may. At any price.
Coûte que coûte [F.]. Let it cost what it may.
Earnestly. See *Adjectives*.
Heart and soul. Thoroughly.
In earnest. }
In good earnest. } Seriously.
Joking apart. No nonsense.
Like a man. Manfully.
Manfully. Same as above.
Neck or nothing. At all risks.
Once for all. Finally.
On one's mettle. Aroused to one's utmost effort or endurance.
Resolutely. See *Adjectives*.
Seriously. See *Adjectives*.
With a high hand. With defiance of right, authority, or opposition.
With a strong hand. In a firm unyielding manner.

DETERMINATION—Phrases.

À bis ou à blanc [F.]. In one way or another; "by hook or crook."
Celui qui veut, celui-la peut [F.]. Who has the will, has the skill.
Chi non s'arrischia non guadagna [It.]. Nothing ventured, nothing have.
Fortis cadere, cedere non potest [L.]. The brave man may fall, yield he cannot.
Frangas, non flectes [L.]. You may break, you shall not bend.
J'y suis, et j'y reste [F.]. Here I am, and here I stay.
Manu forti [L.]. With the strong hand.
Spes sibi quisque [L.]. Each man must rely on himself.
Tentanda via est [L.]. A way must be attempted.

de-ter'-mine. To decide. Aim-Aberration, Beginning-End, Cause-Effect, Certainty-Doubt, Decision-Misjudgment, Determination-Vacillation, Discovery, Investigation-Answer, Universality-Particularity, Volition-Obligation.
de-ter'-mined. Resolute. Bravery-Cowardice, Determination-Vacillation.
de''-ter-ra'-tion. Unearthing. Exposure-Hidingplace.
de-ter'-sion The act of cleaning. Cleanness-Filthiness.
de-ter'-sive. Having power to cleanse. Remedy-Bane.
de-test'. To abhor. Desire-Distaste, Love-Hate.
de-test'-a-ble. Abominable. Goodness-Badness.
det''-es-ta'-tion. Abhorrence. Desire-Distaste, Politeness-Impoliteness.
de-throne'. To drive from a throne. Commission-Abrogation, Rule-License.
de-throne'-ment. Removal from regal power. Commission-Abrogation, Rule-License.
det'-o-nate. To explode. Turbulence-Calmness.
det''-o-na'-tion. An explosion. Crash-Drumming, Turbulence-Calmness.
det'-o-nize. To detonate. Turbulence-Calmness.
de-tort'. To pervert. Interpretation-Misinterpretation.
de-tor'-tion. A warping. Proportion-Deformity.
de''-tour'. A roundabout way. Aim-Aberration, Curvation-Rectilinearity, Midcourse-Circuit.
de-tract'. To take away. Addition-Subtraction, Adulation-Disparagement.
de-tract'-ing. Defaming. Adulation-Disparagement.
de-trac'-tion. Slander. Adulation-Disparagement, Approval-Disapproval.
de-tract'-or. A defamer. Adulation-Disparagement, Flatterer-Defamer.
de-tract'-o-ry. Defamatory. Adulation-Disparagement.
det'-ri-ment. An injury. Betterment-Deterioration, Good-Evil.
det''-ri-men'-tal. Hurtful. Goodness-Badness.
de-tri'-tion. A wearing down. Friability.
de-tri'-tus. Fragments of rock. Friability, Whole-Part.
de-trude'. To thrust out. Admission-Expulsion, Elevation-Depression.

de-trun'-cate. To cut off. Addition-Subtraction.
det''-run-ca'-tion. The act of cutting off. Addition-Subtraction.
deuce. Two; the devil. Angel-Satan, Duality; **the deuce is in him,** Persistence-Whim; **play the deuce,** Betterment-Deterioration, Excitability-Inexcitability.
deu'-ced. Devilish. Pleasurableness-Painfulness.
deu'-ced-ly. Exceedingly. Magnitude-Smallness.
deus ex machina [L.] (dī'-us ex mê'-ki'-na). A god from the machine; a mechanical device in a writer's plot. Antagonist-Assistant, Devotion-Magician, Divinity, Obstruction-Help.
deus nobis hæc otia fecit [L.] (dī'-us no'-bis hec o'-shi-a fī-sit). God has given us this ease. Entertainment-Weariness.
deus vindex, cernit omnia [L.] (dī'-us vin'-dex, ser'-nit om'-ni-a). God, the avenger, sees all things. Divinity, Prevision.
deus vult [L.] (dī'-us vult). God wills (it). Volition-Obligation.
deu''-te-rog'-a-my. A second marriage. Matrimony-Celibacy.
dev'-as-tate. To lay waste. Creation-Destruction.
dev''-as-ta'-tion. The act of devastating. Attack-Defense, Creation-Destruction.
de-vel'-op. To unfold. Creation-Destruction, Enlargement-Diminution, Revolution-Evolution.
de-vel'-op-ment. An unfolding. Cause-Effect, Creation-Destruction, Enlargement-Diminution, Increase-Decrease, Revolution-Evolution.
de-vex'. Bending down. Curvation-Rectilinearity, Parallelism-Inclination.
de-vex'-i-ty. A sloping. Curvation-Rectilinearity, Parallelism-Inclination.
de'-vi-ate. To wander. Aim-Aberration, Concentration-Radiation, Curvation-Rectilinearity, Deviation, Mutation-Permanence; **deviate from rectitude,** Uprightness-Dishonesty.
de'-vi-a''-ting. Turning aside. Aim-Aberration.
de''-vi-a'-tion. The act of deviating. Aim-Aberration, Concentration-Radiation, Curvation-Rectilinearity, Deviation, Mutation-Permanence.

DEVIATION.

Aberration. Variation from truth or right.
Alteration, etc. See MUTATION.
Deviation, etc. See AIM-ABERRATION.
Divergency. etc. See CONCENTRATION-RADIATION.
Innovation. Variation from what is old or established.
Modification. Slight alteration.
Moods and tenses. Variations in the form of a verb to denote difference in time or manner of action, or being.
Variation. Difference in the form, position or state of a thing at different times.

DEVIATION—*Verbs*

Deviate, etc. See AIM-ABERRATION.
Diverge, etc. See CONCENTRATION-RADIATION.
Vary, etc. See MUTATION.

DEVIATION—*Adjectives.*

Diversified, etc. See UNIFORMITY-DIVERSITY.
Modified. Slightly altered or varied.
Varied, etc. Made different in form, position, or state   See *Verbs.*

de-vice′. A contrivance. CRAFT-ARTLESSNESS, DESIGN-SIGN.
dev′-il. The evil one. ANGEL-SATAN, BENEFACTOR-EVILDOER, GOOD MAN-BAD MAN, JOVE-FIEND, PUNGENCY; **devil in one,** FAVORITE-QUARRELSOMENESS, RECKLESSNESS-CAUTION; **devil may care,** PRESUMPTION-OBSEQUIOUSNESS, RECKLESSNESS-CAUTION, UNCONCERN; **devil take,** CHARITABLENESS-CURSE; **devil take the hindmost,** BRAVERY-COWARDICE, HURRY-LEISURE, QUEST-EVASION; **devil to pay,** GOOD-EVIL, RECOMPENSE-PENALTY, REGULARITY-IRREGULARITY, SUCCESS-FAILURE, TURBULENCE-CALMNESS; **devil's tattoo,** CRASH-DRUMMING; **fight like devils,** FIGHTING-CONCILIATION; **give the devil his due,** JUSTIFICATION-CHARGE, RIGHT-WRONG, UPRIGHTNESS-DISHONESTY; **have a devil,** SANENESS-LUNACY; **machinations of the devil,** GOOD-EVIL; **play the devil with,** BETTERMENT - DETERIORATION, CHARITABLENESS-MALEVOLENCE; **printer's devil,** WRITING-PRINTING.
dev′-il-ish. With the qualities of the devil. ANGEL-SATAN, CHARITABLENESS-MALEVOLENCE.

dev′-il-ish-ly. Wickedly. MAGNITUDE-SMALLNESS
dev′-il-ism. The state of the devil. ANGEL-SATAN.
dev′-il-ship. The character of the devil. ANGEL-SATAN.
de′-vi-ous. Out of the usual track   AIM-ABERRATION, CURVATION-RECTILINEARITY.
de-vise′. To form in the mind; to give by will. DESIGN, FANCY, GIVING-RECEIVING.
de-vised′ by the en′-e-my. Contrived in a hostile manner. TRUTHFULNESS-FABRICATION.
dev″-i-see′. The recipient of a devise. GIVING-RECEIVING, HOLDER.
de-void′. Destitute. EXCESS-LACK, HOLDING-EXEMPTION, PRESENCE-ABSENCE.
devoir [F.] (de-vwar′) Duty POLITENESS-IMPOLITENESS, REGARD-DISRESPECT.
devoir, faire mon [F.] (de-vwar′, fêr mon·). To do my duty. DUTY-DERELICTION.
de-volve′. To transfer ALIENATION; **devolve on,** DUTY-DERELICTION
De-vo′-ni-an pe′-ri-od. A geologic period. GEOLOGY.
de-vote′. To direct special attention. REPUTATION-DISCREDIT, USE-DISUSE, VOLITION-OBLIGATION; **devote oneself to,** DETERMINATION-VACILLATION, ENTERPRISE; **devote the mind to,** HEED-DISREGARD; **devote to destruction,** CHARITABLENESS-CURSE.
de-vo′-ted. With strong attachment. GODLINESS-UNGODLINESS, HABIT-DESUETUDE, INSUBORDINATION - OBEDIENCE, LOVE-HATE, PLEASURE - PAIN, WELFARE-MISFORTUNE.
dev″-o-tee′. One entirely devoted. ACTIVITY-INDOLENCE, DESIRE-DISTASTE, GODLINESS-UNGODLINESS, PATRIOTISM-TREASON.
de-vo′-tion. The condition of being devoted. ACTIVITY-INDOLENCE, DETERMINATION-VACILLATION, DEVOTION-IDOLATRY, GODLINESS-UNGODLINESS, INSUBORDINATION-OBEDIENCE, LOVE-HATE, REGARD-DISRESPECT, UNSELFISHNESS-SELFISHNESS.

DEVOTION—IDOLATRY

Adoration. Service of the heart to a Supreme Being in which dependence and obedience are acknowledged.
Aspiration. Earnest longing for that which is noble, pure, and spiritual.
Ava Maria. Hail Mary; salutation and prayer to the Virgin.
Devotion. A yielding of the heart and affections to God, with reverence, faith, and piety.
Genuflexion. Reverential bending of the knee in worship.
Hierolatry. Worship of saints or sacred things.
Homage. Reverence directed to the Supreme Being.
Humiliation. A humbling or reducing to lowliness and submission before the Almighty.
Kneeling. Supplicatingly bending the knee in worship.
Latria. The highest kind of worship, or that paid to God.
Prostration. Falling down or bowing in humility or adoration
Service. Spiritual obedience, reverence, and love.
Worship. Service in the outward form of showing reverence to some supposed superior being.

DEVOTION—*Associated Nouns*

Allelujah. A song of praise.
Anthem. A selection from the Scriptures set to sacred music.
Antiphon. A hymn sung in parts by turns.
Antiphony. The alternate singing of two choirs.
Bead-roll. A list of those persons to be mentioned in prayers
Benediction. An expression of blessing or prayer.
Burnt offering. Something offered and burnt on an altar, as an atonement for sin.
Chant. A song arranged for chanting.
Collect. A short condensed prayer.
Discipline. The enforcement of methods of correction against one guilty of ecclesiastical offenses.
Divine service. Service in worship of God.
Doxology. A hymn expressing praise and honor to God.
Dulia. An inferior worship paid to saints.
Duty. Reverence toward a superior

Bibliolatry. Book-worship, extreme reverence for the Bible.
Demonism. Belief in the existence of demons.
Demonolatry. The worship of demons or evil spirits.
Demon-worship. See DEMONOLATRY.
Devil-worship. Worship paid to the devil by many savage tribes under the assumption that the powers of evil are as powerful as the powers of good.
Fetichism. The practise of worshiping any material object, living or dead, supposed to be the dwelling of a spirit.
Fire-worship. The worship of fire practised by the Parsees.
Heliolatry. Sun-worship.
Hero-worship. Extravagant admiration of great men.
Idolatry. The worship of idols, images, or anything that is not God.
Idolism. Idolatrous worship.
Idol-worship. See IDOLATRY.
Mariolatry. The worship of the Virgin Mary.
Zoolatry. The worship of animals, as in the religion of the ancient Egyptians.

IDOLATRY—*Denotations.*

Baal, etc. The sun-god among the Syro-Phenician nations   See REVELATION-PSEUDOREVELATION.
Fetich. A material object worshiped as the incarnation of a spirit
Golden calf.
Graven image. } An object of idolatrous worship.
Idol.
Juggernaut. A famous idol among the Hindus.
Lares et penates [L.]. The domestic and household gods of the Romans.
Sabian. One of an ancient Persian sect who worshiped God but also other supposed heavenly beings.

IDOLATRY—*Nouns of Action.*

Apotheosis. The act of exalting to divine honors.
Avatar. The descent of a Hindu deity.
Canonization. The act of ranking a deceased person in the catalogue of saints.

DEVOTION—IDOLATRY—Continued.

DEVOTION—Associated Nouns—Continued.

Evensong. The evening service or form of worship.
Giving thanks. A thanksgiving service.
Glorification. The act of glorifying.
Grace. The exercise of love, kindness, mercy, and favor.
Hallelujah. A song of praise.
Holy breathing. The blessing of the Holy Ghost
Hosanna. An invocation of blessings.
Hymn. A song of praise or adoration.
Hyperdulia. The worship paid to the Virgin Mary.
Incense. Odors exhaled from spices when burned in religious rites.
Invocation. Act of calling for the presence of some superior being.
Latria. The highest kind of worship, or that paid to God.
Libation. The act of pouring wine on a victim in sacrifice, in honor of some deity
Lord's Prayer. The prayer which Jesus taught His disciples.
Mass The sacrifice in the sacrament of the eucharist.
Matins. Morning prayers.
Morning Prayer. The early morning religious service.
Motet. A short piece of sacred music.
Non nobis Domine [L.]. The first words of the Latin version of the 115th Psalm.
Nunc dimittis [L.]. The canticle of Simeon from the first words in the Latin version [*Luke* ii, 29]. The sweetest canticle is *Nunc dimittis* when a man has obtained worthy ends [Bacon, *Essay on Death*].
Oblation. An offering.
Offertory. The Scripture sentences said or sung during the collection of the offerings.
Orison. A prayer.
Pæan. A song of triumph.
Paternoster. The Lord's Prayer.
Petition. A prayer. See Petition.
Plain song. A chant with tones of equal length and unvaried.
Praise. The tribute of gratitude rendered to the Divine Being.
Prayer. A supplication addressed to God
Psalm. A sacred song.
Psalmody. The practise of singing psalms or sacred songs.
Response. The answer of the congregation to the clergyman, in the litany and other parts of divine service.
Returning thanks. A service of thanksgiving.
Revival. A renewal of special interest and attention to religious services.
Rogation. The litany.
Sacrifice. The act of making an offering to God as a tribute of thanksgiving, or as an atonement for sin.
Self-denial. Forbearance to gratify one's own feelings or desires.
Self-discipline. Punishment or correction of oneself as an atonement for sin.
Self-examination. An inquiry or inspection of one's own conduct.
Stabat Mater. First words of a celebrated hymn.
Supplication. Any earnest request or petition.
Te Deum [L.]. A hymn of the early Christian Church.
Thanksgiving. A service of thanks to God.
Vespers. Evening services.
Vigils. Religious devotions on the eve of any holy day
Votive offering. An offering dedicated by a vow.

DEVOTION—Nouns of Agent.

Celebrant. The officiating priest in the eucharist.
Communicant. One who partakes of the sacrament of the Lord's Supper.
Congregation. A number of persons met for divine worship.
Eidoloclast. Iconoclast.
High-priest. Principal priest among the Jews.
Iconoclast. A breaker of idols.
Worshiper. One who pays divine honors to.

DEVOTION—Nouns of Time

Holy day, etc. A sacred day, or one set apart for religious uses. See Ceremonial

DEVOTION—Verbs

Adore. To speak to or address in worship; pay divine honor to
Aspire. To desire with eagerness; to pant after
Attend mass. To be present at mass for worship.
Attend service. To be present at religious worship
Bend the knee. To petition in a kneeling attitude.
Beseech, etc. To ask or pray with urgency. See Petition.
Bless. To set apart or consecrate to holy purposes.
Bow down and worship. To kneel in adoration
Bow the knee. To bend in token of reverence.
Communicate, etc. To administer to or partake of the Lord's Supper. See Ceremonial.

IDOLATRY—Nouns of Action—Continued.

Deification. The act of exalting to the rank of a god
Mactation. The killing of a sacrificial victim.

IDOLATRY—Nouns of Means.

Hecatomb. Among the ancients, the sacrifice of a hundred oxen at one time.
Holocaust. A sacrifice the whole of which was consumed by fire
Human sacrifices. Human beings offered in worship to a deity.
Immolation. That which is sacrificed.
Infanticide. The intentional sacrificing of infants.
Sacrifices. Victims offered to a deity as an expression of worship
Self-immolation. Sacrificing of self as an act of worship.
Suttee. In India, the sacrifice of a widow on the funeral pile of her husband.

IDOLATRY—Verbs.

Canonize. To declare to be or to regard as a saint.
Deify. To exalt to the rank of a god.
Worship idols. To do religious service to idols
Worship pictures. To idolize pictures.
Worship relics. To act towards or treat relics as if divine.

IDOLATRY—Adjective.

Idolatrous. Pertaining to idolatry; given to the worship of false gods.

IDOLATRY—Phrase.

Adorer le veau d'or [F.]. To worship the golden calf.

DEVOTION—Verbs—Continued.

Deny oneself. To decline the gratification of appetites or desires.
Do service. To do religious work.
Fall down. To prostrate oneself in worship
Fall down on one's knees. To supplicate in a prostrate condition.
Fast. To practise abstinence as a religious exercise or duty
Give alms. To help the poor and needy.
Give benediction. To pronounce a solemn or affectionate invocation
Give thanks. To make acknowledgments for kindness bestowed.
Glorify. To praise in worship; extol.
Go to church. To attend divine service.
Humble oneself. To make meek and submissive.
Intone. To chant.
Invoke. To address in prayer.
Kneel. To bend the knee in prayer.
Laud. To praise in words or song; extol.
Lead the choir. To direct and govern the singing.
Lift up the heart. To become joyful in praise and song; be reverent.
Magnify. To praise or extol highly
Offer sacrifices. ⎫
Offer up petitions. ⎬ To present as an act of worship; present devotionally
Offer up prayers. ⎪
Offer vows. ⎭
Pay homage. To do reverential worship.
Praise. To glorify in words or song, as God.
Pray. To address or petition the Supreme Being.
Propitiate. To appease and dispose to kindness or favor.
Prostrate oneself. To fall down in adoration.
Put up petitions. ⎫ To present or offer earnest entreaties.
Put up prayers. ⎭
Return thanks. To reply or make answer for kindness received.
Revere, etc. To regard with worshipful veneration. See Regard.
Say grace. To offer a short prayer before or after a meal.
Say one's prayers. To offer up one's petitions.
Sing praises. To worship in song.
Supplicate. To seek by earnest prayer; beseech.
Tell one's beads. To recite prayers, checking them off by the beads on a rosary.
Vow. To consecrate to God by solemn promise.
Work out one's salvation. To effect one's deliverance from the power of sin.
Worship. To perform religious service; pay divine honors to

DEVOTION—Adjectives.

Devotional. Of or pertaining to devotion.
Devout. Earnestly attentive to religious duties; pious.
Fervid, etc. Burning with religious zeal or eagerness. See Emotion
Prayerful. Given to prayers.
Pure. Free from everything that can debase or render unclean
Reverent. Expressing reverence; profoundly respectful
Solemn. Marked with religious gravity or pomp
Worshiping, etc Paying divine honors to; devout See *Verbs.*

DEVOTION—Interjections

Allelujah! **Glory be to God!** **God bless!** **God forbid!** **God grant!** **God save!** **Hallelujah!** **Hosanna!** **O Lord!** **Pray God that!** *Sursum corda!* [L.] Lift up your hearts!

DEVOTION—*Continued.*
DEVOTION—*Phrases.*

Bene orasse est bene studuisse [L.]. To have prayed well is to have studied well

Ex voto [L.]. According to one's vow.
Ore e sempre [It.]. Now and always.

DEVOTION—MAGIC.

MAGIC.

Animal magnetism. A force which is produced in animal tissues and passes from one body to another with or without actual contact.
Bedevilment. State of being brought under diabolical influence.
Bewitchery. Irresistible power possessed by any person or thing over a creature.
Clairvoyance [F.]. Ability to discern anything not present to the senses; second sight.
Conjuration. The act of invoking supernatural aid by the use of a magical form of words.
Divination, etc. Foretelling future events. See PROPHECY.
Electro-biology. That phase of mesmerism whose phenomena are supposed to be produced by a form of electricity.
Enchantment. Production of certain wonderful effects by the aid of supposed spirits.
Exorcism. Act of expelling evil spirits by conjurations.
Fetichism. The doctrine or practise of belief in fetiches.
Glamour. A charm on the eyes making them see things different from what they are. [Scotch for grammar, Anglicized by Walter Scott.]
Magic. The pretended art of working by the aid of spirits.
Mesmerism. The doctrine of animal magnetism. [Dr. Mesmer, Frenchman.]
Necromancy. Divination by the agency of the spirits of the dead or by devils.
Od force. } The supposed force that produces the phenomena of
Odylic force. } mesmerism.
Ordeal. A medieval form of judicial trial, as by fire, poison, or water.
Possessed. One under the influence of evil spirits.
Second sight. Supposed power of seeing things future or distant.
Shamanism. Idolatrous worship and practises of the Ostiaks of Siberia.
Sorcery. Divination by the aid of evil spirits.
Sortes Virgilianæ [L.]. A form of divination in which future events are determined by taking the first passage of Virgil upon which the eye fell.
Sortilege. Divination by drawing lots.
Spiritualism. The belief that departed spirits communicate with men, usually through a medium.
Thaumaturgy. The act of performing something wonderful.
Theurgy. The power of doing supernatural deeds by invoking God.
Vampirism. The practise of extortion or preying on others.
Witchcraft. } A supernatural power supposed to be obtained by
Witchery. } entering into compact with the devil.

MAGIC—*Associated Nouns.*

Demonomy. The science of demons; demon-worship.
Demonship. The character of a demon.
Diablerie [F.]. Devilry.
Hocus-pocus, etc. A conjurer's trick. See TRUTHFULNESS-FRAUD.
Mysticism. The quality of being remote from or obscure to human observation.

Occult art. The practise of magic.
Occult sciences. Certain medieval sciences, as alchemy and astrology.
Spirit rapping. The professed communication with departed spirits by means of raps.
Table turning. The act of causing a table to turn or move, apparently without the application of physical force, believed by some to be due to the agency of departed spirits.
The black art. Art practised by witches and conjurers.

MAGIC—*Scientific Noun.*

Demonology. The science or systematic study of demons.

MAGIC—*Verbs.*

Bedevil. To bring under diabolical influence.
Bewitch. To gain power over by charms or incantations.
Call up spirits. To summon spirits.
Call spirits from the vasty deep. [Shakespeare, *King Henry IV*, I, iii, 1.]
Cast a nativity. To find out and represent the position of the heavenly bodies at the time of a birth.
Cast a spell. To throw or exercise a magical influence over.
Charm. To subdue or control by incantation or supernatural influence.
Conjure. To call on or summon by a sacred name
Enchant. To subdue by charms or spells.
Entrance. To put into a state of ecstasy; make insensible to present objects.
Exorcise. To expel evil spirits by ceremonies or conjurations.
Fascinate, etc. To allure by some powerful influence. See MOTIVE.
Magnetize. To bring under the influence of animal magnetism.
Mesmerize. To influence by external agency so as to cause a state of insensibility or somnambulism.
Practise sorcery, etc. To be engaged in magic-working. See *Nouns.*
Raise spirits from the dead. Summon spirits of dead persons.
Rub the lamp. } To summon spirits as Aladdin did. [*Arabian Nights.*]
Rub the ring. }
Taboo. To forbid, or forbid the use of; render inviolable.
Vodoo. To bewitch.
Wave a wand. To do works of magic.

MAGIC—*Adjectives.*

Cabalistic. Containing or conveying an occult meaning.
Charmed, etc. Enchanted; protected by charms. See *Verbs.*
Incantatory. Dealing by enchantment; magical.
Magic. Possessing supernatural powers, like the *Magi* of the East.
Magical. Pertaining to magic.
Mystic. Remote from human observation; secret.
Phylacteric. Pertaining to any charm or amulet worn as a preservative against danger or disease.
Weird. Pertaining to the world of witches; supernatural.
Talismanic. Having the properties of a preservative against evils by occult influence.

DEVOTION—CHARM.

CHARM.

Charm. Words, figures, or things supposed to possess some hidden or mysterious power.
Spell. Any form of words which, when recited, were supposed to possess magical power.

CHARM—*Nouns of Means and Instrument.*

Abracadabra. A word or collocation of letters used in incantations.
Agnus Dei [L.]. A figure of a lamb bearing a cross, used in devotions.
Amulet. Something worn in the belief that it will ward off disease or evil.
Bell, book, and candle. A solemn formula of excommunication in the Roman Catholic Church.
Cabala. A secret science or knowledge by which the Jewish rabbins professed to explain all Scripture difficulties.
Caduceus. The wand of Mercury.
Cantrap. A magic charm; a mischievous trick.
Counter-charm. That by which a charm is destroyed or dissolved.
Divining rod. A forked branched rod used by those who pretend to discover water or metals under ground.
Ephesian letters. Magical symbols. [Shakespeare, *Merry Wives* IV, v.]
Evil eye. A hostile or envious look from certain persons was supposed to influence for injury.

Fee-faw-fum. Nonsensical mysterious utterances of the Giant in *Jack the Giant Killer.* [Shakespeare, *Lear*, III, iv, 188.]
Fortunatus' cap. A cap which will transport its wearer wherever he desires, or command fortune.
Fetich. } A material object worshiped among savages as the incar-
Fetish. } nation of a spirit.
Lamp of Aladdin. A magic lamp, the rubbing of which did wonders. [*Arabian Nights.*]
Mum-bo-jumbo. Any ridiculous object of superstitious homage.
Open sesame. A magical password. [*Arabian Nights.*]
Periapt. Something worn as a charm against evil or danger.
Philter. A potion intended to excite love.
Phylactery. Strips of parchment inscribed with Scriptural passages worn by devout Jews.
Rod. A staff used or worn by magicians.
Runes. Secret alphabet or system of writing
Talisman. Any object endowed with certain magical powers and which can be carried about the person.
Telesm. A kind of amulet or magical charm. See TALISMAN.
Veronica. A cloth said to have been miraculously impressed with the Saviour's image from being used to wipe the perspiration from His face.
Wand. A rod used by conjurers and diviners.

DEVOTION—CHARM—*Continued.*

CHARM—Nouns of Means and Instrument—*Continued*

Weird. A spell; a charm; an incantation.

Wishing cap. A cap fabled to give one whatever he wishes for when wearing it.

CHARM—*Nouns of Action.*

Exorcism. The act of expelling evil spirits by formulas or conjurations.

Exsufflation. A kind of exorcism, performed by blowing and spitting at the evil spirit.

Incantation. The act of enchanting by songs or words of sorcery.

DEVOTION—MAGICIAN.

MAGICIAN

Astrologer. One who foretells the future by reading the stars.

Banshee. A goblin supposed to give warnings of death.

Charmer. One who has the power of exerting a magical influence.

Clairvoyant [F.]. One who claims the power of seeing or knowing what is not present to the senses.

Conjurer. One who practises magic arts; sleight-of-hand performer.

Cunning man. One who exercises craft or shrewdness.

Deus ex machina [L.]. A mechanical device introduced into a writer's plot.

Ecstatica. A strongly emotional woman, subject to profound reveries or trances.

Exorcist. One who expels evil spirits by formulas or conjurations.

Fairy, etc. An imaginary good or bad being, said to influence the fate of men. See FIEND.

Figure-flinger. A pretender to astrology

Hag. A forbidding or malicious old woman; an ugly crone.

Lamia [L.]. A kind of a demon among the ancients under the form of a beautiful woman; a witch.

Mage. Contraction for magician.

Magician. One professedly skilled in magic or the black art.

Medicine man. Among savages, a witch doctor or exorciser.

Medium. A person believed to be possessed or controlled by the personality of some deceased person.

Mesmerist. One who practises or believes in personal magnetism.

Necromancer. One who practises divination by means of pretended communication with the dead

Seer. One who can foresee future events.

Shaman. A wizard or priest among those who profess Shamanism.

Sorcerer. A wizard who divines by the aid of magic or evil spirits.

Soothsayer, etc. One who undertakes to foretell future events. See SOOTHSAYER.

Thaumaturgist. One who works wonders.

Warlock. A male witch; wizard.

Witch. One who is supposed to have influence or dealings with evil spirits.

Wizard. One supposed to be in league with the devil.

MAGICIAN—*Figurative Nouns.*

Cagliostro. The assumed name of Joseph Balsamo of Palermo, one of the most impudent and successful of impostors; hence, a magician.

Circe. A fabled being who changed her enraptured victims into beasts; hence, a charmer. [Homer, *Odyssey.*]

Katerfelto. Assumed name of a magician.

Mesmer. A Frenchman who first brought into notice the doctrine of animal magnetism; hence, a magician or mesmerist.

Rosicrucian. A member of a secret sect of fanatic alchemists who claimed to know the secret of the philosopher's stone; hence, a magician.

Siren. One of the sweet-voiced mythological beings who enticed sailors to their destruction on the Italian coast; a charmer.

Weird Sisters. The fates who control human destinies.

Zamaliel. A prince of demons.

de-vo′-ted-ness. The state of being devoted. DE-TERMINATION-VACILLATION.

de-vo′-tion. Ardent love and affection DEVOTION-IDOLATRY.

de-vour′. To eat ravenously. CREATION-DESTRUCTION, FASTING-GLUTTONY, NUTRIMENT-EXCRETION.

de-voured. Eagerly eaten. DESIRE-DISTASTE, EMOTION

de-vour′-ing el′-e-ment. A destroying agent. HEAT-COLD.

de-vout′. Given to devotion. DEVOTION-IDOLATRY, GODLINESS-UNGODLINESS.

de-vout′-less. Without devotion GODLINESS-DISBELIEF.

de-vout′-ly. In a devout manner EMOTION.

dew Condensed moisture. DAMPNESS-DRYNESS, **shake as dewdrops from lion's mane,** OVERVALUATION-UNDERVALUATION

dew′-y. Like dew. DAMPNESS-DRYNESS.

dew′-y eve. An evening when the dew falls. MORNING-EVENING.

dex′-ter. To the right. RIGHT-LEFT.

dex-ter′-i-ty. Manual skill. SKILL-UNSKILFULNESS.

dex′-ter-ous. Being skilful. SKILL-UNSKILFULNESS

dex′-ter-ous-ness. Dexterity. SKILL-UNSKILFULNESS

dex′-tral. On the right side. RIGHT-LEFT

dex-tral′-i-ty. The state of being on the right side RIGHT-LEFT.

dey. A Turkish governor of Algiers. CHIEF-UNDERLING.

dhow. A coasting vessel. CONVEYANCE-VESSEL.

diable a quarte, le [F.] (di-abl′ a cart, le). A daredevil. EXCITABILITY - INEXCITABILITY, LOUDNESS - FAINTNESS, REGULARITY-IRREGULARITY, TURBULENCE-CALMNESS.

diable au corps, avoir le [F.] (di-abl′ o cor, a-vwar′ le) To be devilish. SANENESS-LUNACY.

diable par la queue, tirer le [F.] (di-abl′ par la ku, ti-rê′ le) To pull the devil's tail AFFLUENCE-PENURY.

di-a′-ble-rie. Doings with the devil. DEVOTION-MAGIC.

di″-a-bol′-ic. Devilish. ANGEL-SATAN, CHARITABLENESS-MALEVOLENCE, GOODNESS-BADNESS, VIRTUE-VICE.

di″-a-bol′-ic-al. Devilish CHARITABLENESS-MALEVOLENCE.

di-ab′-o-lism. Devilishness. ANGEL-SATAN.

di″-a-cous′-tics. The science of the refraction of sounds. SOUND-SILENCE.

di″-a-crit′-i-cal. Distinguishing. SIGN

di′-a-dem. A crown. SCEPTER.

di″-ag-no′-sis. The art of discriminating diseases DIFFERENTIATION-INDISCRIMINATION.

di″-ag-nos′-tic. Pertaining to a diagnosis SIGN TRIAL, UNIVERSALITY-PARTICULARITY.

di″-ag-nos′-tics. The science of diagnosis SUBJECTIVENESS-OBJECTIVENESS

di-ag′-o-nal. Extending from corner to corner PARALLELISM-INCLINATION.

di′-a-gram. A plan DELINEATION-CARICATURE.

di′-al. A device for showing time. CHRONOLOGY-ANACHRONISM; **as the dial to the sun,** OBSERVANCE-NONOBSERVANCE, TRUTHFULNESS-FALSEHOOD.

di′-a-lect. A mode of speech RHETORIC, SIGN, WORD-NEOLOGY

di″-a-lec′-tic. Pertaining to a dialect; logical LANGUAGE, RATIOCINATION-INSTINCT, RHETORIC.

di″-a-lec-ti′-cian. A logician RATIOCINATION-INSTINCT.

di-al′-o-gism. An imaginary discussion. ADDRESS-RESPONSE

di-al′-o-gist. One who speaks in a dialogue. CONVERSATION-MONOLOGUE.

di′-a-logue. A formal conversation between two or more persons. CONVERSATION-MONOLOGUE

di-al′-y-sis. Separation. CHEMISTRY.

di-am′-e-ter. A line through the center of a figure. BREADTH-NARROWNESS.

di″-a-met′-ric-al-ly op′-po-site. With the greatest degree of opposition. LATERALITY-CONTRAPOSITION, SAMENESS-CONTRAST.

di'-a-mond. A precious gem. ANGULARITY, EMBELLISHMENT-DISFIGUREMENT, GOODNESS-BADNESS; **diamond cut diamond**, CRAFT-ARTLESSNESS, REPRISAL-RESISTANCE; **rough diamond**, CRAFT-ARTLESSNESS.

Di-an'-a. A virgin goddess of the Romans, representing the moon. PURITY-IMPURITY, UNIVERSE.

di''-a-pa'-son. A stop in a pipe-organ. MELODY-DISSONANCE.

di'-a-per. A kind of surface-decoration. EMBELLISHMENT-DISFIGUREMENT.

di''-a-pha-ne'-i-ty. Transparency. DIAPHANEITY-OPAQUENESS.

DIAPHANEITY—OPAQUENESS.

Diaphaneity. Quality of being diaphanous; pellucid. See *Adjectives.*
Fluorescence. The property, possessed by some transparent bodies, of giving off, when illuminated, light differing in color from their own.
Limpidity. Marked by sparkling clearness.
Lucidity. State of being lucid; intellectual clearness.
Pellucidity. State or quality of being pellucid. See *Adjectives.*
Translucence.⎱ The property of permitting rays of light to pass
Translucency.⎰ through.
Transparence.⎱ Diaphaneity; state of being transparent. See
Transparency.⎰ *Adjectives.*

DIAPHANEITY—*Objects.*

Crystal. A material of quartz, in crystallization transparent or nearly so.
Glass. A hard, brittle, transparent substance, made by fusing together silica with lime, potash, soda, or lead oxid.
Glasswork. Any article made of glass.
Lymph. A colorless fluid contained in the lymphatic vessels of the body.
Transparent medium. Any substance through which light is transmitted.
Vitrite. A hard glass used for electrical appliances.
Water. A clear, transparent liquid consisting of hydrogen and oxygen.

DIAPHANEITY—*Verbs.*

Be transparent. See *Adjectives.*
Transmit. To cause to pass over or through.

DIAPHANEITY—*Adjectives.*

Clear. Free from opacity or obscurity.
Clear as crystal. Absolutely transparent.
Crystalline. Resembling crystal in clearness.
Diaphanous. Having power to transmit rays of light; clear; transparent.
Glassy. Resembling glass in transparency.
Hyaline. Glassy; crystalline.
Limpid. Marked by clearness or transparency.
Lucid.⎱ Clear; transparent.
Pellucid.⎰
Relucent. Throwing back light; clear; bright.
Serene. Clear; placid.

Opacity. The state or quality of being impervious to light.
Opaqueness. See sub *Adjectives.*

OPAQUENESS—*Denotations.*

Cloud. See VISCIDITY-FOAM.
Film. An opaque, membranous covering.

OPAQUENESS—*Verbs.*

Be opaque. To obstruct the light rays.
Obfuscate.⎱ To darken.
Offuscate.⎰
Obstruct the passage of light. Prevent light from passing.

OPAQUENESS—*Adjectives.*

Adiaphanous. Not to be seen through.
Cloudy. Obscure, as though by clouds.
Dim. Obscure from scarcity of light. See DIMNESS.
Dirty. Having the quality of dirt; unclean.
Foggy. Opaque through fog.
Fuliginous. Pertaining to soot or smoke; hence, opaque.
Fumid. Smoky; hence, opaque.
Hazy. Rendered opaque by reason of haze.
Impervious to light. Not permitting light to pass through.
Misty. Pervaded by mist; hence, opaque.
Muddy. Turbid; clouded; opaque as though by mud.
Muggy. Warm and moist; opaque by reason of moisture held in suspension.
Murky. Dark; obscure.
Nubiferous. Bringing clouds.
Obfuscated. Obscured; clouded.
Opacous. Impervious to the rays of light.
Opaque. Not transparent.
Smoky. Rendered opaque by reason of smoke.
Thick. Having considerable density; hence, turbid; opaque.
Turbid. Thick and cloudy.
Vaporous. Having the nature of vapors.

DIAPHANEITY—*Adjectives—Continued.*

Tralucent.⎱ Transmitting rays of light; transparent; clear.
Translucent.⎰
Transparent. Having the property of transmitting rays of light so that bodies can be seen through; diaphanous.
Transpicuous. Transparent; pervious to the sight.
Vitreous. Having the quality of glass.

DIAPHANEITY—OPALESCENCE.

OPALESCENCE.

Milkiness. State or quality of being milky.
Opalescence. The property of combined refraction and reflection of light.
Pearliness. State or quality of being pearly.
Semi-transparency. Partial transparency.

OPALESCENCE—*Denotations.*

Film. A membranous covering almost opaque.
Gauze. A very thin cloth or material.
Mist. See VISCIDITY-FOAM.
Muslin. A very thin cotton cloth.

OPALESCENCE—*Adjectives.*

Milky. Like milk; turbid.
Opalescent. Reflecting a milky or pearly light.
Opalescine. See OPALESCENT.
Pearly. Reflecting an almost clear light.
Semi-diaphanous. Half or imperfectly transparent.
Semi-opacous. Semi-opaque.
Semi-opaque. Half transparent.
Semi-pellucid. Imperfectly transparent.
Semi-transparent. Half or imperfectly transparent.

di-aph'-a-nous. Transparent. DIAPHANEITY-OPAQUENESS.

di''-a-phon'-ics. Diacoustics. SOUND-SILENCE.

di''-a-pho-re'-sis. Free perspiration. NUTRIMENT-EXCRETION.

di'-a-phragm. A muscle used in respiration. ENVIRONMENT-INTERPOSITION, MIDDLE.

di''-a-po-re'-sis. A figure in rhetoric representing a speaker as hesitating. CERTAINTY-DOUBT.

di''-ar-rhe'-a. A looseness of the bowels. NUTRIMENT-EXCRETION.

di'-a-ry. A daily record. CHRONOLOGY-ANACHRONISM, MARK-OBLITERATION.

di-as'-to-le. The regular expansion of the heart in beating. ENLARGEMENT-DIMINUTION.

di''-a-tes'-sa-ron. A perfect fourth in music. MELODY-DISSONANCE.

di''-a-ther'-mal. Permitting the passage of heat. HEATING-COOLING.

di''-a-ther'-man-cy. The property of transmitting heat. HEATING-COOLING.

di''-a-ther'-mous. Diathermal. HEATING-COOLING.

di-ath'-e-sis. A predisposition to any particular disease. AFFECTION, CONDITION-SITUATION, SUBJECTIVENESS-OBJECTIVENESS.

di″-a-ton′-ic. Designating the regular tones of a key in music. MELODY-DISSONANCE.

di′-a-tribe. An abusive discourse. APPROVAL-DISAPPROVAL.

dib′-ble. A gardener's pointed tool. DOMESTICATION-AGRICULTURE, PERFORATOR-STOPPER.

di-cac′-i-ty. Sauciness. PRESUMPTION-OBSEQUIOUSNESS.

dice. Marked cubes used in gaming. PURPOSE-LUCK, **on the dice,** POSSIBILITY-IMPOSSIBILITY.

di′-cer. One who plays dice. PURPOSE-LUCK, **false as dicer's oaths,** TRUTHFULNESS-FABRICATION.

di-chot′-o-mize. To cut in two. DOUBLING-HALVING.

di-chot′-o-my. A cutting into two parts. ANGULARITY, DOUBLING-HALVING.

di′-chro-ism. The property of exhibiting different colors when seen in different directions. VARIEGATION.

dichtung und wahrheit [G.] (diʜ′-tung unt var′-hait). Fiction and fact. POETRY-PROSE, TRUTHFULNESS-FALSEHOOD.

dic′-tate. To declare with authority. ADVICE, MOTIVE-CAPRICE, ORDER, PRESUMPTION-OBSEQUIOUSNESS, RULE-LICENSE, WRITING-PRINTING.

dic-ta′-tion. The act of dictating. ORDER, RULE-LICENSE.

dic-ta′-tor. One who dictates. CHIEF-UNDERLING, TYRANNY-ANARCHY.

dic″-ta-to′-ri-al. Disposed to dictate. PRESUMPTION-OBSEQUIOUSNESS.

dic-ta′-tor-ship. The office of a dictator. HARSHNESS-MILDNESS, RULE-LICENSE, TYRANNY-ANARCHY

dic′-tion. The choice and use of words. STYLE.

dic′-tion-a-ry. A book containing words arranged in a stated order. INTERPRETATION-MISINTERPRETATION, WORD-NEOLOGY.

dic′-tum. A positive utterance. ADAGE-NONSENSE, ASSERTION-DENIAL, ORDER.

dictum ac factum [L.] (dic′-tum ac fac′-tum). No sooner said than done. ACTIVITY-INDOLENCE.

dictum de dicto [L.] (dic′-tum dî dic′-to). Hearsay report. EVIDENCE-COUNTEREVIDENCE.

dictum quod non dictum sit prius, nullum est jam [L.] (dic′-tum quod non dic′-tum sit prai′-us, nul′-lum est jam). Nothing is said nowadays that has not been said before. NOVELTY-ANTIQUITY, RECURRENCE.

di-dac′-tic. Pertaining to teaching. EDUCATION-MISTEACHING.

did′-der. To shiver. HEAT-COLD.

did′-dle. To outwit. TRUTHFULNESS-FRAUD.

Did′-dler, Jer′-e-my. A character in James Kenney's play, entitled *Raising the Wind.* A term applied to a swindler. ROBBER.

di-duc′-tion. A separation. UNION-DISUNION.

die. To pass from life; to mold with a die. BEGINNING-END, BETTERMENT-DETERIORATION, COPY-MODEL, ENGRAVING, ENTITY-NONENTITY, LIFE-DEATH; **die a violent death,** LIFE-KILLING; **die and make no sign,** REPENTANCE-OBDURACY; **die away,** DISCONTINUANCE - CONTINUANCE, INCREASE - DECREASE; **die for,** DESIRE-DISTASTE; **die from the** memory, REMEMBRANCE-FORGETFULNESS; **die game,** REPENTANCE-OBDURACY; **die hard,** BIGOTRY-APOSTASY, REPRISAL-RESISTANCE; **die in harness,** DISCONTINUANCE-CONTINUANCE, PERSISTENCE-WHIM; **die in one's shoes,** RECOMPENSE-PUNITION; **die in the last ditch,** PERSISTENCE-WHIM; **die of a rose in aromatic pain,** SENSITIVENESS-APATHY; **die out,** ENTITY-NONENTITY; **die with ennui,** ENTERTAINMENT-WEARINESS; **die with laughter,** JUBILATION-LAMENTATION; **hazard of the die,** PURPOSE-LUCK; **never say die,** PERSISTENCE-WHIM; **not willingly let die,** CONSERVATION; **the die is cast,** CERTAINTY-DOUBT, VOLITION-OBLIGATION.

dies faustus [L.] (dai′-îz faus′-tus) Lucky day SUCCESS-FAILURE.

dies infaustus [L.] (dai-îz in-faus′-tus) Unlucky day SUCCESS-FAILURE.

dies iræ, dies illa [L.] (dai′-îz ai′-rî, dai-îz il′-la). Day of wrath, that day; the first words of a Latin hymn on the Day of Judgment. HEAVEN-HELL, PARDON, VINDICTIVENESS.

dies non [L.] (dai′-îz non). Abbreviation of *dies non juridicus,* a non-judicial day; a legal holiday. DURATION-NEVERNESS, TOIL-RELAXATION.

di′-et. Food; a legislative assembly. COUNCIL, NUTRIMENT-EXCRETION; **spare diet,** FASTING-GLUTTONY.

di′-et-a-ry. A system of diet. NUTRIMENT-EXCRETION, REMEDY-BANE.

di″-e-tet′-ic. Of diet. NUTRIMENT-EXCRETION.

di″-e-tet′-ics. The science of diet. REMEDY-BANE.

dieu avec nous [F.] (di-u′ a-vec′ nu). God with us. DIVINITY, PRESENCE-ABSENCE.

dieu défend le droit [F.] (di-u′ dê-fan·′ le drwa). God defend the right. ATTACK-DEFENSE, RIGHT-WRONG.

dieu est ma fiance, en [F.] (di-u′ ê ma fi-an-s′, an·). In God is my trust. DIVINITY, SANGUINENESS-HOPELESSNESS.

dieu et mon droit [F.] (di-u′ ê mon drwa). God and my right. DIVINITY, RIGHT-WRONG.

dieu vous garde [F.] (di-u′ vu gard). God guard you. DIVINITY, PETITION-EXPOSTULATION, SECURITY-INSECURITY.

dif′-fer. To be unlike. VARIANCE-ACCORD, VARIATION; **differ in opinion,** ASSENT-DISSENT; **differ** *toto cœlo,* ASSENT-DISSENT, LIKENESS-UNLIKENESS, SAMENESS-CONTRAST, VARIATION.

dif′-fer-ence. The quality of being unlike. EQUALITY-INEQUALITY, LIKENESS-UNLIKENESS, NUMBER, VARIANCE-ACCORD, VARIATION; **difference engine,** NUMBERING; **perception of difference,** DIFFERENTIATION-INDISCRIMINATION; **split the difference,** COMPOSITION.

dif′-fer-ent. Not the same. SYNONYM-ANTONYM, UNIFORMITY-MULTIFORMITY, VARIATION; **different time,** TIME.

dif″-fer-en′-tial. Pertaining to differentials. NUMBER; **differential calculus,** NUMBERING.

dif″-fer-en′-ti-a-tion. Act of noting specific differences in things. DIFFERENTIATION-INDISCRIMINATION

dif′-fer-ent-ly. Not the same way VARIATION.

DIFFERENTIATION—INDISCRIMINATION.

Appreciation of difference. The power of clearly understanding the various shades of meaning.

Critique. A careful and thorough analysis; critical examination.

Diagnosis. An accurate examination of facts; determining nature of disease from symptoms.

Differentiation. The act of noting specific differences in things.

Diorism. A thorough distinction; logical difference.

Discernment. The capability of forming true judgments. See SAGACITY.

Discrimination. The power to discern accurately; careful scrutiny

Distinction. Noting differences critically

Estimation. See MENSURATION.

Indiscrimination. Lacking the power of discernment or judgment.

Indistinction. Want of distinction; indefiniteness; confusion.

Indistinctness. The quality of vagueness; lacking clearness.

Uncertainty. See CERTAINTY-DOUBT

INDISCRIMINATION—*Verbs*

Confound. To mingle; pour together.

Confuse. To confound; intermingle.

Not discriminate. See DISCRIMINATION.

Overlook a distinction. See CAREFULNESS-CARELESSNESS

Judgment. The power of the mind to discriminate superior qualities of matter as well as operations of the mind.
Nice perception. Clear discernment.
Nicety. Exactness of perception.
Nuances [F.]. Shades of difference.
Perception of difference. Knowledge of difference.
Refinement. Elegance in making distinctions.
Tact. Nice perception or discernment.
Taste. See TASTE.

DIFFERENTIATION—*Verbs.*

Allow due weight. To give all the consideration a thing deserves.
Discriminate. See DISCRIMINATION.
Distinguish. To differentiate; to classify.
Draw a line. To separate; to discriminate.
Estimate. See MENSURATION.
Give due weight. See ALLOW DUE WEIGHT.
Know "a hawk from a hand-saw." To decide carefully. [Shakespeare, *Hamlet*, II, ii.]
Know what is what. To be wise in judgment.
Know which is which. To know one from the other.
Separate. To distinguish by judgment.
Separate the chaff from the wheat. To separate the bad from the good.
Severalize. To distinguish.
Sift. Winnow; to search out.
Split hairs. To divide with extreme accuracy.

dif'-fi-cult. Hard to do. DIFFICULTY-FACILITY; **difficult to please,** DESIRE-DISTASTE.
dif'-fi-cul-ties. Obstacles. AFFLUENCE-PENURY; **in**

DIFFICULTY—FACILITY.

Ado. Intricate business; fuss.
Augean task. A task of Hercules, to clean the Augean stables.
Awkwardness. Quality of being difficult to manage or effect.
Bone to pick. A dispute to be settled.
Brunt. The hardest part of a battle or task.
Coil. See CIRCLE-WINDING.
Crisis. The decisive period.
Critical situation. The point of supreme danger.
Crooked path. Hard to follow.
Cross-fire. Shot at from different places at the same time.
Crux. Difficulty of explanation.
Cul de sac [F.]. A maze; a snare.
Dead lift. One made without any mechanical device.
Dead lock. Impossibility of coming to an agreement; an obstruction.
Dead set. Unmovable difficulty.
Delicacy. That quality which requires great care in handling.
Delicate point. That period where greatest care and skill must be exercised to be successful.
Difficulty. That which is hard to solve, accomplish, master.
Dignus vindice nodus [L.]. A knot worthy to be unloosed.
Dilemma. A state of things where it is difficult (but necessary) to determine which of two courses to pursue.
Embarrassment. Impediment to freedom of action.
Emergency. Great need; a sudden occasion to be met.
Entanglement. See REGULARITY-IRREGULARITY.
Exigency. Pressing necessity; crisis.
False position. Occupying a place at a disadvantage.
Fix. A position from which it is difficult to escape.
Gordian knot. Almost impossible task; the knot cut by Alexander the Great.
Hardness. Difficulty; intricacy.
Hard task. See AUGEAN TASK.
Hard to crack. Difficulty of solving, understanding, or realizing.
Hard work. Some undertaking which is hard on mind or body to do.
Herculean task. An attempt which is like a labor of Hercules.
Hitch. A check; an obstacle.
Hobble. A device put on an animal to impede its progress.
Hornet's nest. Something hard to escape without being injured.
Horns of a dilemma. The two courses before one in a dilemma.
Hot water. A difficult position.
Imbroglio. A complicated position; a condition surrounded by difficulties.
Impracticability. Impossibility.
Intricacy. Perplexity; complexity.
Job. A difficult task.
Knot. Something not easily solved.
Knotty point. Most difficult to understand clearly.
Maze. An intertwined pathway.
Meshes. Nets; entanglements.

INDISCRIMINATION—*Adjectives.*

Indiscriminate. Not systematic.
Undistinguishable. Not able to be distinguished.
Undistinguished. Not recognized apart.
Unmeasured. Not measured.

INDISCRIMINATION—*Phrase.*

Valeat quantum valere potest [L.]. Let it pass for what it is worth.

DIFFERENTIATION—VERBS—*Continuea.*

Take into account.
Take into consideration. } To make allowance for.
Weigh carefully. To estimate deliberately and maturely.
Winnow the chaff from the wheat. Sift; thrash.

DIFFERENTIATION—*Adjectives.*

Dioristic. Distinguishing.
Discriminating. Making or seeing a difference.
Discriminative. Making a difference.
Distinctive. Expressing distinction or difference.
Nice. Apprehending slight differences or delicate distinctions.

DIFFERENTIATION—*Phrases.*

Il y a fagots et fagots [F.]. All men are not alike.
La critique est aisée, et l'art est difficile [F.]. Criticism is easy, and art is difficult.
Rem acu tetigisti [L.]. You have touched it with a needle; that is, exactly.

difficulties, CREDIT-DEBT.
dif'-fi-cul-ty. The state of being difficult. DIFFICULTY-FACILITY.

DIFFICULTY—FACILITY.

Capability. Capacity; power to do.
Deoppilation. Removal of all obstacles.
Disencumbrance. The state of being unburdened.
Disentanglement. Clearing of difficulties.
Ease. Rest; freedom from restraint.
Easiness. The state of being free.
Facility. Ease in the performance of anything.
Feasibility. See POSSIBILITY.
Flexibility. The quality of being bent easily.
Full play. See LIBERTY.
Permission. See LEAVE.
Pliancy. See HARDNESS-SOFTNESS.
Smoothness. See SMOOTHNESS.

FACILITY—*Denotations.*

Clear coast. A coast or pathway free from impediment or obstruction.
Clear stage. A portion of a road or course free from traveling difficulties.
Fair wind. A wind favorable for sailing.
Holiday task. A work in which no work, or little effort is required.
Mere child's play. A work or task requiring no exertion of strength
Plain sailing. Travel by water, free from dangers.
Royal road. A road used only by royalty.
Smooth road. A way on which travel is easy.
Smooth sailing.
Straight sailing. } Easy and safe sailing.
Smooth water. Surface of the water unbroken by waves.
Tabula rasa [L.]. A smooth tablet.

FACILITY—*Verbs.*

Be at home in. See SKILL.
Be easy. Be free from care; be tranquil.
Bridge over. To make easy the passage over difficulties.
Clear. To remove obstacles.
Clear the ground.
Clear the path.
Clear the road. } Open the way.
Clear the way.
Cut the knot. Remove an obstacle by force.
Deobstruct. To remove all hindrances.
Deoppilate. To take away obstructions
Disburden. To unburden; relieve oneself of care.
Disembarrass. To remove all embarrassment.
Disencumber. To remove impediments.
Disengage. To clear; to extricate.
Disentangle. To straighten out; to free.
Drift with the stream.
Drift with the tide. } Take things easy.
Ease. To make light or easy of accomplishment.

Mess. A mixture or confusion of things.
Net. Anything designed to entrap or catch.
Nice point. Intricate in the texture of the thoughts comprising it
Nonplus. Puzzle; quandary; unsurmountable difficulty
Nut to crack. Difficulty to solve.
Paradox. Something that seems contrary to the accepted opinion, yet may be true.
Pass. Predicament; crisis.
Peck of troubles. A very large amount of troubles.
Perplexity. See CERTAINTY-DOUBT.
Pickle. A disagreeable position; a difficult state to be in.
Pinch. A tight and crowded place.
Pons asinorum [L.]. The fifth proposition in the first book of Euclid; hence, difficulty.
Poser. A puzzler.
Pretty kettle of fish. A pretty mess to contend with.
Pretty pass. A pass hard to get through.
Puzzle. See ENLIGHTENMENT-SECRECY.
Quagmire. Boggy land which easily gives way when one walks over it; uncertain position.
Quandary. A maze of doubt; perplexity.
Rasper. A high fence difficult for game to get over.
Rub. Difficult task.
Scramble. A hard struggle for a rare thing.
Scrape. Trouble; difficulty.
Sea of troubles. Trouble resembling the sea in vastness. [Shakespeare, *Hamlet*, III. i.]
Set fast. Anything which brings one to a standstill.
Sisyphean labors. Labor impossible to be accomplished; like those of Sisyphus.
Slough. A miry place; a trap.
Stand. An opposition; a defense.
Stew. A pickle; a bog.
Strait. A narrow passage.
Stress. An urgent occasion; a pressing circumstance.
Stumbling block. See OBSTRUCTION
Subtle point. A delicate task.
Task of Sisyphus. Rolling an impossible stone up a hill. See SISYPHEAN LABORS.
Teaser. A provoking task.
Ticklish card to play. A perplexing task.
Tough job. Hard task.
Tough work. See TOUGH JOB.
Trial. Difficulty; a severe task.
Uphill work. A work with great disadvantages, as going up a hill.
Vexata quæstio [L.]. A vexed question.
Vexed question. A cause of trouble or disquiet.
Where the shoe pinches. In strait circumstances.

DIFFICULTY—*Verbs.*

Bear the brunt. To endure the hardest part of the battle.
Be difficult. See *Nouns.*
Be impossible. See IMPOSSIBILITY.
Be in difficulty. To try to overcome an obstacle.
Be in the way of. See OBSTRUCTION.
Be put to one's shifts. To try every expedient to get out of difficulty
Boggle. To anticipate difficulties.
Bother. To trouble; to throw obstacles in the way.
Bring a hornet's nest about one's ears. To arouse severe criticism.
Bring to a deadlock. To stop business.
Buffet the waves. To contend with repeatedly.
Come to a deadlock. To check proceedings, as a deadlock in a legislature.
Come to a stand. To become inactive; stand still
Come to the pinch. Arrive at the critical point.
Come to the push. To come to the difficult part.
Contend with difficulties. To strive against difficulties or obstacles.
Embarrass. To hinder; check freedom of thought, speech, and movement.
Encumber. To obstruct; impede.
Enmesh. To entangle.
Entangle. To complicate as to make escape difficult.
Fish in troubled waters. To labor amid difficulties.
Flounder. To struggle without success, as a fish on land.
Get into a scrape. }
Get into difficulties. } To get into trouble.
Go against the grain. To do anything under great obstacles; work against one's nature.
Go hard with one. To win one's way by undergoing hardships.
Grapple with difficulties. Contend with difficulties.
Gravel. To check; embarrass.
Grope in the dark. Struggle in vain
Have a hard time of it. See GO HARD WITH ONE.
Have much ado with. To experience great difficulty with.

Emancipate. To set at liberty.
Exonerate. To free from blame.
Extricate. To unravel; disentangle
Facilitate. To lessen the labor of
Flow with the stream. }
Flow with the tide. } Let things drift
Free. To set at liberty, remove every bar
Free from. Clear of
Give full play. }
Give full swing. } Give a good chance to
Give the reins to. }
Go on all fours. Agree with
Go on smoothly. }
Go with the stream. } Move smoothly
Go with the tide. }
Have full play. Have a good chance.
Have it all one's own way. }
Have the game in one's own hand. } Have no opposition
Humor. To indulge by skilful adaptation.
Leave a hole to creep out. To leave an opening for escape.
Leave the matter open. To submit for further discussion.
Lighten. To decrease the burden of.
Lighten the labor. To make the work easier
Lubricate. See FRICTION-LUBRICATION.
Make light of. To pay little attention to.
Make no bones of. To give only a passing notice
Make nothing of. To notice with indifference.
Make way for. To open a pass.
Obey the helm. To yield to power or influence
Open the door to. To allow to enter; to welcome
Open the way. Give freedom of passage.
Pave the way. To cover with stone or brick to smooth the way.
Permit. See LEAVE.
Popularize. To bring into favor with the people
Prepare the ground. }
Prepare the path. }
Prepare the road. } Get ready
Prepare the way. }
Relieve. See ALLEVIATION.
Render easy. To cause to become easy
Run on all fours. To go more easily.
Run smoothly. To go along without any hindrances.
See one's way. To find no obstructions ahead
Smooth. To gloss over.
Smooth the ground. }
Smooth the path. } To level; make easy.
Smooth the road. To rid of rough places.
Smooth the way. To remove objectionable places.
Swim with the stream. To swim with the current.
Swim with the tide. To be borne along with it.
Unclog. To disencumber.
Unload. To unburden; to remove the weight
Untie the knot. To open the knot.
Unravel. To unfold; to disentangle.
Walk over the course. To have full sway.
Win at a canter. To come off successful easily
Work well. Be successful in labor

FACILITY—*Adjectives.*

Accessible. Within reach.
At ease. Calm; composed
At home. Skilful.
Disburdened. Relieved.
Disembarrassed. See *Verbs*
Disencumbered. See *Verbs*
Ductile. Easily led; yielding.
Easily accomplished. Not hard to do
Easily managed. Not hard to manage
Easy. Not hard.
Easy of access. Not hard to get to
Exonerated. See *Verbs*
Facile. Not difficult.
Feasible. See POSSIBILITY
For the million. Any one can do the work.
Glib. Smooth-tongued.
In one's element. What one is best fitted to do.
In smooth water. No opposition
Light. Easily handled.
Manageable. Docile; able to be controlled.
On friction wheels. On smooth surfaces.
On velvet. Soft; pliable
Open to. Accessible.
Pliant. See HARDNESS-SOFTNESS.

DIFFICULTY—VERBS—*Continued.*

Hold the wolf by the ears. To be impracticable.
Labor under a disadvantage. Find drawbacks.
Lead a pretty dance. To go through the movements of a dance awkwardly.
Lose one's way. Be at a loss.
Meet with difficulties. Meet with troubles.
Nonplus. To puzzle.
Not know which way to turn. See UNCERTAINTY.
Perdre son Latin [F.]. To be at one's wit's end.
Perplex. See CERTAINTY-DOUBT.
Plunge into difficulties. To rush headlong into difficulties.
Pose. To puzzle; embarrass.
Put a spoke in the wheel. See OBSTRUCTION.
Put one out. To vex; displease; trouble.
Put to one's shifts. Be at a loss what to do.
Put to one's wit's end. To be outwitted; fail to know what to do.
Ravel. To ravel up; to tangle up.
Render difficult. To make hard.
Run one hard. To drive one hard.
Scud under bare poles. To sail without sails.
Stick at. To be brought to a stand by encountered difficulties.
Stick fast. To be incapable of going any further.
Stick in the mud. Come to a stand.
Struggle. To put forth every effort.
Struggle with difficulties. ⎱
Swim against the stream. ⎰ Contend with obstacles.
Try one. To put one to a test.
Try one's patience. To undertake an intricate task.
Walk among eggs. Walk with difficulty.
Weave a tangled web. To tangle ourselves up. "What a tangled web we weave when first we practise to deceive." [Walter Scott, *Marmion*, vi, 17.]

DIFFICULTY—*Adjectives.*

Accomplished with difficulty. Hard to do.
Aground. Checked.
Arduous. Laborious; toilsome.
At a loss. See CERTAINTY-DOUBT.
At a nonplus. In a fix: quandary.
At a standstill. Aground.
At bay. Cornered up, as a hunted boar.
At cross-purposes. Having different intentions.
At one's wit's end. Puzzled.
At the end of one's tether. Having come to the end of the rope or string.
Au bout de son Latin [F.] At one's wit's end.
Aux abois [F.]. At bay.
Awkward. Clumsy; unskilful.
Beset with difficulties. In trouble.
Between Scylla and Charybdis. Dangerous; difficult to pass without suffering destruction.
Between two stools. To try to do two things at once and fail in both.
Complicated. See REGULARITY-IRREGULARITY.
Crabbed. Perplexing; difficult.
Critical. Careful in passing judgments.
Delicate. See *Nouns.*
Desperate. See SANGUINENESS-HOPELESSNESS.
Difficult. See DIFFICULTY.
Difficult to deal with. Perplexing.
Driven from post to pillar. ⎫
Driven into a corner. ⎪
Driven to extremity. ⎬ Much embarrassed.
Driven to one's wit's end. ⎪
Driven to the wall. ⎭
Embarrassing. Obstructing; rendering difficult.
Encompassed with difficulties. ⎱ Perplexed.
Entangled by difficulties. ⎰
Formidable. Dreadful; fearful.
Full of difficulties. Difficult.
Graveled. Checked: run aground.
Hard. Difficult.
Hard-earned. Earned with difficulty.
Hard-fought. Contested vigorously.
Hard-pressed. Pressed vigorously.
Hard put to it. In straits.
Hard-set. Firmly resolved.
Hard to deal with. Difficult.
Hard up. Poor.
Herculean. Like Hercules, first in strength and labors for mankind.
Ill-conditioned. Not fit for the contest.
Impracticable. See POSSIBILITY-IMPOSSIBILITY.
In a clever stick. Caught.

FACILITY—ADJECTIVES—*Continued.*

Quite at home. Well acquainted with the work.
Slippery. Smooth; glossy.
Smooth. See SMOOTHNESS.
Submissive. Obedient.
Towardly. Willing to do or learn.
Tractable. Manageable.
Unburdened. Relieved of difficulty.
Unembarrassed. Free from difficulty.
Unencumbered. Not weighed down by difficulty.
Unloaded. See *Verbs.*
Unobstructed. Unimpeded.
Unrestrained. See LIBERTY.
Untrammeled. Not hampered.
Wieldy. Controllable.
Within reach. Attainable.
Yielding. To give in; docile.

FACILITY—*Adverbs.*

Easily; on easy terms; readily ; single-handed; smoothly; swimmingly.

FACILITY—*Phrase.*

Touch and go. Narrowly escaping.

DIFFICULTY—ADJECTIVES—*Continued.*

In a fine pickle. In a sorry plight; smarting in the acid of pickle.
In a fix. In trouble.
In a scrape. See GET INTO A SCRAPE.
In deep water. Puzzled.
In difficulty. In trouble.
In extremis [L.]. In the greatest difficulty.
In hot water. In trouble.
In the suds. In worry; in difficulty, as "my Kate, upon the washing-day."
In the wrong box. In a wrong position.
Intractable. Hard to govern.
Intricate. Difficult to understand, follow, or arrange.
Invious. Untrodden.
Irksome. Tiresome; burdensome.
Knotted. Made difficult.
Knotty. Intricate; complicated.
Laborious. Arduous.
Labyrinthine. See CIRCLE-WINDING.
More easily said than done. Hard to do.
Nonplussed. Confused; puzzled.
Not easy. Difficult.
Not feasible. See POSSIBILITY.
Not made with rose-water. Not easy.
Not out of the woods. More difficulties to be overcome.
Not to be handled with kid gloves. Not easily managed.
Onerous. Burdensome.
Operose. Wrought with labor.
Out of one's depth. Out too far to touch bottom.
Pathless. Without a way or guide to get out of.
Perplexing. See CERTAINTY-DOUBT.
Perverse. Intractable; obstinate.
Pinched. Put into a tight place.
Plaguy. Troublesome; tiresome.
Put to it. Tested; tried.
Put to one's shifts. Make use of every expedient.
Puzzled. Baffled; put in a quandary.
Reduced to straits. Pinched; pressed.
Refractory. Unruly; disobedient.
Rugged. Stiff; hard.
Run hard. Abused; overworked.
Set fast. Unmovable; unflinching.
Sooner said than done. Hard to do.
Sorely pressed. In narrow straits.
Straitened. Confined; hampered.
Stranded. Run aground.
Stubborn. See BIGOTRY.
Stuck fast. Caught.
Surrounded by breakers. ⎫
Surrounded by difficulties. ⎬ In difficulties.
Surrounded by quicksands. ⎪
Surrounded by shoals. ⎭
Thorny. Rough; hard to travel.
Thrown out. Disabled; disqualified.
Ticklish. Delicate; difficult.
Toilsome. Burdensome; cumbersome.
Tough. Very intricate; complicated.
Trackless. Untrodden.

DIFFICULTY—Adjectives—*Continued.*

Troublesome. Bringing trouble.
Trying. Straining.
Under a difficulty. In trouble.

Unmanageable. Hard to manage.
Unwieldy. Bulky; awkward.
Up a tree. In difficulty, from which the dogs prevent escape.

DIFFICULTY—*Adverbs.*

Against the grain; against the stream; *à rebours* [F.], reversed; **at a pinch; at long odds; hardly; in the teeth of,** not likely to escape; *invita Minerva* [L.], not endowed with mental capacity; **uphill; upon a pinch; with difficulty; with much ado.**

DIFFICULTY—*Phrases.*

Ab inconvenienti [L.]. From the inconvenience involved.
Ad astra per aspera [L.]. To the stars through difficulties.
Aucun chemin de fleurs ne conduit à la gloire [F.]. There is no pathway of flowers that leads to glory.
Ay, there's the rub. [Shakespeare, *Hamlet*, III, i.]

Chercher une aiguille dans une botte de foin [Fr.]. To look for a needle in a haystack.
Hic labor, hoc opus [L.]. This is labor, that is toil. [Virgil, *Æneid.*]
Things are come to a pretty pass.

dif-fide'. To distrust. FAITH-MISGIVING.
dif'-fi-dence. Timidity. CONCEIT-DIFFIDENCE, SANGUINENESS-TIMIDITY.
dif'-fi-dent. Having self-distrust. CONCEIT-DIFFIDENCE, SANGUINENESS-TIMIDITY.
dif'-flu-ent. Dissolving. RIVER-WIND.
dif-fuse'. To scatter widely. ANATOMY, GATHERING-SCATTERING, MIXTURE-HOMOGENEITY, PUBLICITY, TERSENESS-PROLIXITY.
dif-fuse'-ly. Copiously. TERSENESS-PROLIXITY.
dif-fuse'-ness. The quality of being diffuse. TERSENESS-PROLIXITY.
dif-fu'-sion. A scattering. GATHERING-SCATTERING, MIXTURE-HOMOGENEITY, PRESENCE-ABSENCE.
dig. To turn up with a spade. CONVEXITY-CONCAVITY, DEEPNESS-SHALLOWNESS, DOMESTICATION-AGRICULTURE; **dig the foundations,** PREPARATION-NONPREPARATION; **dig up,** DISCOVERY.
dig'-a-my. A second marriage. MATRIMONY-CELIBACY.
di-gest'. To assimilate; systematize. ANATOMY, DESIGN, DIGEST, EXCITABILITY-INEXCITABILITY, HEATING-COOLING, ORGANIZATION-DISORGANIZATION, PREPARATION-NONPREPARATION, REFLECTION-VACANCY.

DIGEST.

Abbreviation. A brief summary; an abridgment.
Abbreviature. An epitome; an abbreviation.
Abridgment. An epitome or compend of a book.
Abstract. An inventory, summary, or epitome.
Analysis. A table of the principal heads of a continued discourse.
Brief. A concise statement of the law and authorities.
Compend. A brief compilation.
Compendium. An abridgment or epitome.
Contents. A summary or index of the matter in a book.
Digest. That which is worked over, classified, and arranged.
Draft. A plan delineated.
Epitome. A compendium containing the substance or principal matters of a book.
Outlines. A sketch showing the principal characteristics of a work.
Summary. Giving the sum and substance of a document or statement.
Synopsis. A general view of a subject or its treatment.

DIGEST—*Denotations.*

Album. A printed compilation of selections.
Analecta [L.]. Selections or extracts from a literary work.
Anthology. A collection of choice extracts or flowers from books.
Aperçu [F.]. A short sketch.
Collectanea [L.]. Passages selected from various authors.
Common-place book. A memorandum book.
Compilation. A book or documents composed of materials selected from other books or documents.
Compression. Condensation of thought or language in writing.
Conspectus [L.]. A general sketch or outline of a sketch.
Contraction. An abbreviation of a writing.
Cuttings. Pieces cut out, as newspaper cuttings.
Excerpta. Passages extracted.
Extracts. Passages from a book or document.
Flowers. Choice extracts.
Fugitive pieces. } Extracts exciting only passing notice.
Fugitive writings. }
Heads. Titles used to characterize that which follows.

Memorandum book. A book containing a record of things to be remembered.
Minute. An official record of the proceedings of any deliberative body.
Multum in parvo [L.]. Much in little; an abbreviation containing the ideas of a passage.
Note. A brief comment appended to the text of a work; a brief record.
Note-book. A book for notes.
Pandect. The digest of Roman law made by Justinian.
Précis [F.]. A concise statement.
Prospectus. An outline of a proposed literary undertaking.
Recapitulation. A summing up.
Résumé [F.]. A summary.
Review. An article containing comments upon the characteristics of some work.
Scrap-book. A book containing clippings from books, newspapers, etc.
Shortening. An abbreviation of a writing.
Spicilegium [L.]. A gleaning.
Sum and substance. An epitome of the thought of a composition.
Syllabus. A compendium containing the heads of a discourse.
Text-book. A book so interspaced as to afford room for comment between the lines.
Variorum. Comments by different authors.

DIGEST—*Verbs.*

Abbreviate. To make briefer.
Abridge. To shorten or contract by using fewer words, yet retaining the substance.
Abstract. To epitomize.
Compile. To compose out of materials from other books and documents.
Compile an abstract. To make a summary.
Condense. To compress into a smaller compass.
Draw an abstract. To make a summary.
Epitomize. To abstract, in a summary, the principal matters of.
Make an abstract. To make a summary.
Prepare an abstract. To make an epitome.
Recapitulate. To repeat again the principal points.
Review. To go over again critically and deliberately to revise.
Run over. To go over hastily.
Skim. To pass over superficially.
Summarize. To express in concise form.
Sum up. To present in brief.

DIGEST—*Adjectives.*

Abridged. Shortened.
Analectic. Made up of selections.
Compendious. Containing the substance in a narrow compass.
Synoptic. Arranged for giving general view.

DIGEST—*Adverbs.*

In a few words. Briefly.
In epitome. In brief summary.
In short. Briefly.
In substance. Essentially.

DIGEST—*Phrase.*

It lies in a nutshell.

di-ges'-tion. Act of digesting. ANATOMY, ORGANIZATION-DISORGANIZATION, PREPARATION-NONPREPARATION.
dight. To dress. DRESS-UNDRESS, EMBELLISHMENT-DISFIGUREMENT.

dight'-ed. Dressed. DRESS-UNDRESS.

dig'-it. One of the ten numerals. NUMBER.

dig'-i-ta''-ted. With parts arranged like the fingers on the hand. SHARPNESS-BLUNTNESS.

di-gla''-di-a'-tion. A fight with swords. STRIFE-PEACE.

dig''-ni-fi-ca'-tion. Exaltation. REPUTATION-DISCREDIT.

dig'-ni-fied. Having dignity. REPUTATION-DISCREDIT, SELFRESPECT-HUMBLENESS.

dig'-ni-fy. To add dignity to. REPUTATION-DISCREDIT.

dig'-ni-ta-ry. One holding high official position. MINISTRY-LAITY.

dig'-ni-ty. The state of being worthy. REPUTATION-DISCREDIT, SELFRESPECT-HUMBLENESS, UPRIGHTNESS-DISHONESTY.

dignus vindice nodus [L.] (dig'-nus vin'-di-sî no'-dus). A knot worthy of being loosed. [Horace, *Art of Poetry*, 191.] CLEARNESS-OBSCURITY, DIFFICULTY-FACILITY, PHENOMENON.

di-gress'. To turn aside. AIM-ABERRATION, TERSENESS-PROLIXITY.

di-gres'-sion. The act of digressing. AIM-ABERRATION, MIDCOURSE-CIRCUIT.

di-gress'-ive. Tending to digression. TERSENESS-PROLIXITY.

di''-hex-ag'-o-nal. Twelve-sided. **Dihexagonal pyramid,** MINERALOGY.

diis aliter visum [L.] (dai-is al'-i-ter vai'-sum). To the gods it has seemed otherwise. [Virgil, *Æneid*, ii, 428.] EXPECTATION-DISAPPOINTMENT, VOLITION-OBLIGATION.

di-ju''-di-ca'-tion. The act of dijudicating. DECISION-MISJUDGMENT.

dike. A channel; embankment. ATTACK-DEFENSE, ENCLOSURE, GEOLOGY, GROOVE, GULF-PLAIN, INTERSPACE-CONTACT, WATERCOURSE-AIRPIPE.

di-lac''-er-a'-tion. A tearing asunder. UNION-DISUNION.

di-lap'-i-date. To bring to decay. BETTERMENT-DETERIORATION.

di-lap'-i-da''-ted. Fallen into decay. BETTERMENT-DETERIORATION.

di-lap''-i-da'-tion. The act of dilapidating. BETTERMENT-DETERIORATION, CREATION-DESTRUCTION.

di-la''-ta-bil'-i-ty. The quality of being dilatable. ENLARGEMENT-DIMINUTION.

dil''-a-ta'-tion. Expansion. SOLIDITY-RARITY.

di-late'. To expand. ENLARGEMENT-DIMINUTION, INCREASE-DECREASE, SOLIDITY-RARITY, TERSENESS-PROLIXITY.

di-la'-ting. Expanding. TERSENESS-PROLIXITY.

di-la'-tion. The act of dilating. BREADTH-NARROWNESS, ENLARGEMENT-DIMINUTION, INCREASE-DECREASE, SOLIDITY-RARITY.

dil'-a-to-ry. Tardy. ACTIVITY-INDOLENCE, EARLINESS-LATENESS, SWIFTNESS-SLOWNESS.

di-lec'-tion. A preference. LOVE-HATE.

di-lem'-ma. A perplexing situation. CERTAINTY-DOUBT, CHOICE-NEUTRALITY, DIFFICULTY-FACILITY, RATIOCINATION-INSTINCT.

dil''-et-tan'-te. A dabbler in art and letters. SCHOLAR-DUNCE, TASTE-VULGARITY.

dil''-et-tant'-ism. A dabbling in art and letters. KNOWLEDGE-IGNORANCE, TASTE-VULGARITY.

dil'-i-gence. Industry. ACTIVITY-INDOLENCE.

dil'-i-gence. A stage-coach. CONVEYANCE-VESSEL.

dil'-i-gent. Showing diligence. ACTIVITY-INDOLENCE; **diligent thought,** HEED-DISREGARD.

dil'-ly–dal'-ly. To trifle. ACTIVITY-INDOLENCE, DETERMINATION-VACILLATION.

di-lu''-ci-da'-tion. Clearness. INTERPRETATION-MISINTERPRETATION.

dil'-u-ent. Diluting. WATER-AIR.

di-lute'. To thin by mixing. STRENGTH-WEAKNESS, WATER-AIR.

di-lu'-ted. Made thin by mixing. WATER-AIR.

di-lu'-tion. A making thinner. WATER-AIR.

di-lu'-vi-an. Of a deluge. NOVELTY-ANTIQUITY.

dim. Not distinct. CLEARNESS-OBSCURITY, DIAPHANEITY-OPAQUENESS, DIMNESS, LIGHT-DARKNESS, VISIBILITY-INVISIBILITY.

dime. Coin. VALUES.

di-men'-sion. Extent in one direction. GREATNESS-LITTLENESS.

dim'-e-ter. Verse of two feet. RHETORIC.

di-mid'-i-ate. Cut in half. DOUBLING-HALVING.

di-mid''-i-a'-tion. The act of halving. DOUBLING-HALVING.

di-min'-ish. To make less. ADDITION-SUBTRACTION, ENLARGEMENT-DIMINUTION, INCREASE-DECREASE, MAGNITUDE-SMALLNESS; **diminish the number,** MULTIPLICITY-PAUCITY.

di-min'-ished. Made less. SUPREMACY-SUBORDINACY.

dim''-i-nu'-tion. Reduction. ENLARGEMENT-DIMINUTION, INCREASE-DECREASE.

di-min'-u-tive. Small. GREATNESS-LITTLENESS, MAGNITUDE-SMALLNESS.

di-min''-u-en'-do. Gradually diminishing in volume of sound. MUSIC.

dim'-ness. Lack of clearness. DIMNESS.

DIMNESS.

Darkness, etc. The state of being destitute of light. See LIGHT-DARKNESS.

Demi-jour [F.]. Faint light.

Dimness, etc. The state or quality of lacking luster or brilliancy. See *Adjectives.*

Glimmer. A faint or feeble light.

Glimmering. A faint beaming of light.

Half-light. An indistinct light.

Nebulosity. The state of having a faint, indistinct appearance.

Paleness, etc. The state or quality of being dim. See COLOR-ACHROMATISM.

DIMNESS—*Denotations.*

Aurora. The rising light or glow of early morning in the eastern sky.

Break of day. The beginning of daylight.

Candle-light. The light shed by a candle.

Cloud. See VISCIDITY-FOAM.

Cockshut time. Twilight.

Crepuscule. The twilight of morning or of evening.

Dawn.
Daybreak. } The beginning of day.

Dusk. The state between darkness and light, especially between day and night.

Eclipse. The obscuration of a heavenly body by its entering the shadow of another body.

Farthing candle. A cheap candle shedding a dim light.

Firelight. Light from an open fire.

Moonbeam. A ray of moonlight.

Moonlight.
Moonshine. } The light of the moon.

Owl's light. Twilight.

Partial eclipse. A partial cutting off of the light of a body by its coming into the shadow of another body.

Partial shadow. The cutting off of part of the light shed by a body.

Rush light. Light made by a rush candle.

Shades of evening. Twilight.

Shadow of a shade. A very dim light.

Starlight. Light shed by a star.

Twilight. Light diffused over the sky after sunset and before sunrise by the reflection of sunlight from the higher portions of the atmosphere.

DIMNESS—*Verbs.*

Be dim, etc. To be in a state of obscurity or semi-darkness. See *Adjectives.*

Bedim. To render dim or obscure.

Dim. To cause to become indistinct or obscure.

Fade. To lose brightness; become dim.

Flicker. To burn with a wavering motion.

Glimmer. To shine faintly.

DIMNESS—Verbs—*Continued*.

Grow dim, etc. To become dim. See *Adjectives*.
Loom. To shine; rise gradually into an impressive position.
Lower. To grow less; diminish.
Obscure. To render dim or indistinct.
Pale. To become faint; indistinct.
Pale its ineffectual fire. To grow dim, as the glowworm at dawn. [Shakespeare, *Hamlet*, I, v.]
Render dim, etc. To make dim. See *Adjectives*.
Twinkle. To shine faintly with unsteady light.

DIMNESS—*Adjectives*.

Cloudy. Lacking clearness or brightness.
Confused, etc. Rendered indistinct. See Visibility-Invisibility.
Crepuscular. Pertaining to the dawn.
Dark, etc. Not light; without brightness. See Light-Darkness.
Darkish. Somewhat dark.
Dim. Obscure; indistinct; not clear.
Dingy. Of a dark color.
Dirty. Not clean or clear; indistinct.
Dull. Not bright; indistinct.
Dun. Dark; obscure.
Fading. Becoming dim.
Faint. Not bright; dull.
Fuliginous. Dark; dusky.
Glassy. Having a fixed, staring appearance.
Lack luster. Wanting brightness.
Leaden. Of a dull appearance like lead.
Looming, etc. Shining. See *Verbs*.
Lurid. Gloomy; dismal.
Misty, etc. Obscure; dim. See Diaphaneity-Opaqueness.
Muddy. Turbid; dull; not clear.
Muggy. Moist and close.
Nebular. }
Nebulous. } Cloudy; hazy; dim.
Obnubilated. Clouded; obscure.
Overcast. Darkened; clouded.
Pale, etc. Faint or light in color. See Color-Achromatism.
Shadowed forth. Indicated dimly.
Shorn of its beams. Deprived of its light.

dim′-ple. A slight depression. Convexity-Concavity, Indentation.
dim′-sight″. Indistinct vision. Sight-Blindness.
dim′-sight″-ed. Having dim sight. Sagacity-Incapacity, Sight-Blindness.
dim′-sight″-ed-ness. The quality of having dim sight. Sight-Blindness, Sight-Dimsightedness.
din. A loud continuous noise. Loudness-Faintness; **din in the ear,** Crash-Drumming, Recurrence, Talkativeness-Taciturnity.
di′-nar [Ar.]. Coin. Values.
din′-arch-y. A form of government in which two persons rule jointly. Rule-License.
dine. To take dinner. Nutriment-Excrement; **dine with Duke Humphrey,** Solitude-Company.
di-ne′-ro [Peru]. Coin. Values.
ding′-dong″. The sound of a ringing bell. Crash-Drumming, Recurrence.
din′-gle. A small valley. Convexity-Concavity.
din′-gy. A small boat. Conveyance-Vessel.
din′-gy. Of a dusky color. Beauty-Ugliness, Color-Achromatism, Dimness, Gray-Brown, Light-Darkness, Whiteness-Blackness.
di′-ning-room. A room to dine in. Contents-Receiver.
din′-ner. The chief meal of the day. Nutriment-Excrement.
dint. A small depression; force. Convexity-Concavity, Impetus-Reaction, Might-Impotence; **by dint of,** Instrumentality, Might-Impotence.
dio, sub [L.]. (dai′-o, sub). In the open air. Outside-Inside, Water-Air.
di-oc′-e-san. Of a diocese. Ministry-Laity.
di′-o-cese. The territory under the jurisdiction of a bishop. Church.
Di-og′-e-nes. The Greek philosopher who lived in a tub. Humanitarianism-Misanthropy, Sociability-Privacy; **lantern of Diogenes,** Investigation-Answer.

di-op′-trics. The science of the refraction of light. Light-Darkness.
di″-o-ra′-ma. A painting for spectacular exhibition in a dark room. Appearance-Disappearance, Painting.
di′-o-rism. Definition. Differentiation-Indiscrimination.
di″-o-ris′-tic. Defining. Differentiation - Indiscrimination.
dios que da la llaga, da la medicina [Sp.] (dî-os′ kê da la lyá-ga da la mê-dith-î′-na). God, who sends the wound, sends the cure. Divinity, Remedy-Bane.
dip. The act of dipping. Admission-Expulsion, Aim-Aberration, Ascent-Descent, Ceremonial, Convexity - Concavity, Elevation - Depression, Geology, Parallelism - Inclination, Spring-Dive, Water-Air; **dip into,** Education-Learning, Heed-Disregard, Investigation - Answer: **dip one's hands into,** Taking-Restitution.
diph′-thong. A union of two vowels in sound. Letter.
dip′-loid. Form of crystal. Mineralogy.
di-plo′-ma. A letter granting some privilege or honor. Commission-Abrogation, Evidence-Counterevidence.
di-plo′-ma-cy. The art of conducting negotiations. Contract, Craft-Artlessness, Mediation.
dip′-lo-mate. A diplomat. Consignee.
dip″-lo-mat′-ic. Of diplomacy. Craft-Artlessness.
dip″-lo-mat′-ics. The science of diplomas. Mediation.
di-plo′-ma-tist. One skilled in diplomacy. Consignee, Mediation.
dip″-so-ma′-ni-a. A morbid craving for alcoholic drink. Desire-Distaste, Saneness-Lunacy, Teetotalism-Intemperance.
dip″-so-ma′-ni-ac. One having dipsomania. Saneness-Maniac.
dip′-tych. Anything with two folds. Mark-Obliteration, Record.
dire. Extremely dreadful. Goodness - Badness, Pleasurableness - Painfulness, Sanguineness - Timidity, Welfare-Misfortune.
di-rect′. Manage; being the straightest course. Aim-Aberration, Craft-Artlessness, Curvation-Rectilinearity, Education-Misteaching, Management, Order, President-Member; **direct attention to,** Education - Misteaching, Enlightenment-Secrecy, Heed-Disregard; **direct one's course,** Aim-Aberration, Quest-Evasion; **direct the eyes to,** Sight-Blindness.
di-rect′-ed. Having the direction pointed out. Aim-Aberration.
di-rect′-ing. Giving direction. Management.
di-rect′-ing post. A post giving direction. Sign.
di-rec′-tion. The position of one point in relation to another. Aim-Aberration, Education-Misteaching, Management, Order, Precept, Sign.
di-rect′-ly. In a direct line; at once. Earliness-Lateness.
di-rect′-ness. The quality of being direct. Curvation-Rectilinearity.
di-rect′-or. One who directs. Instructor-Pupil, Management, Manager.
di-rect′-or-ship. The office of director. Rule-License.
di-rect′-o-ry. Having directions. Council, Record.
dire′-ful. Very dire. Sanguineness-Timidity.
di-remp′-tion. A violent breaking. Union-Disunion.
di-rep′-tion. The act of plundering. Theft.
dirge. A funeral hymn. Jubilation-Lamentation, Life-Funeral, Music.
dirk. A dagger. Weapon.
dirt. Any unclean substance. Cleanness-Filthiness, Embellishment-Disfigurement; **dirt cheap,** Costliness-Cheapness; **throw dirt,** Regard-Disrespect, Reputation-Discredit.

dirt'-y. Not clean. CLEANNESS-FILTHINESS, DIAPHANEITY-OPAQUENESS, DIMNESS, REPUTATION-DISCREDIT, UPRIGHTNESS-DISHONESTY; **dirty end of stick,** SKILL-UNSKILFULNESS; **dirty sky,** RIVER-WIND, VISCIDITY-FOAM; **dirty weather,** RIVER-WIND; **do dirty work,** FLATTERER-DEFAMER, PRESUMPTION-OBSEQUIOUSNESS.

di-rup'-tion. A breaking asunder CREATION-DESTRUCTION.

dis''-a-bil'-i-ty. Want of ability. MIGHT-IMPOTENCE.

dis-a'-ble. To deprive of ability. MIGHT-IMPOTENCE, USEFULNESS-USELESSNESS.

dis-a'-bled. Deprived of power. MIGHT-IMPOTENCE.

dis-a'-ble-ment. Want of power. MIGHT-IMPOTENCE.

dis''-a-buse'. To undeceive. ENLIGHTENMENT-SECRECY, EXPOSURE-HIDINGPLACE.

dis''-ac-cord'. Lack of agreement. VARIANCE-ACCORD.

dis''-ad-van'-tage. That which hinders. GOOD-EVIL; **at a disadvantage,** SUPREMACY-SUBORDINACY; **lie under a disadvantage,** FAULTLESSNESS-FAULTINESS.

dis-ad''-van-ta'-geous. Detrimental. GOODNESS-BADNESS, PROPRIETY-IMPROPRIETY.

dis''-af-fect'-ed. Estranged. AMITY-HOSTILITY.

dis''-af-fec'-tion. Discontent. AMITY-HOSTILITY, ASSENT-DISSENT, LOVE-HATE.

dis''-af-firm'. To deny. ASSERTION-DENIAL.

dis''-a-gree'. To differ. ASSENT-DISSENT, HARMONY-DISCORD, VARIANCE-ACCORD.

dis''-a-gree'-a-ble. Not agreeable. DESIRE-DISTASTE, PLEASURABLENESS PAINFULNESS.

dis''-a-gree'-ing. Differing. HARMONY-DISCORD, VARIANCE-ACCORD.

dis''-a-gree'-ment. Lack of agreement. HARMONY-DISCORD, VARIANCE-ACCORD, VARIATION.

dis''-al-low'. To refuse to allow. LEAVE-PROHIBITION.

dis''-al-low'-ance. Refusal to allow. LEAVE-PROHIBITION.

dis''-an-nul'. To annul thoroughly. COMMISSION-ABROGATION.

dis''-ap-pear'. To pass from sight. APPEARANCE-DISAPPEARANCE, ENTITY-NONENTITY, SUBSTANCE-NULLITY.

dis''-ap-pear'-ance. A passing from sight. APPEARANCE-DISAPPEARANCE.

dis''-ap-pear'-ing. Passing from sight. APPEARANCE-DISAPPEARANCE.

dis''-ap-point'-ed. Defeated in expectation or hope. CONTENTEDNESS-DISCONTENTMENT, EXPECTATION-DISAPPOINTMENT.

dis''-ap-point'-ing. Defeating one's hopes. CONTENTEDNESS-DISCONTENTMENT.

dis''-ap-point'-ment. The state of being disappointed. CONTENTEDNESS-DISCONTENTMENT, EXPECTATION-DISAPPOINTMENT.

dis-ap''-pro-ba'-tion. The act of disapproving. APPROVAL-DISAPPROVAL, REPUTATION-DISCREDIT.

dis''-ap-prov'-al. The withholding of approval. APPROVAL-DISAPPROVAL.

dis''-ap-prove'. To regard with censure. APPROVAL-DISAPPROVAL, EXCULPATION-CONVICTION.

dis''-ap-proved'. Regarded with censure. APPROVAL-DISAPPROVAL.

dis''-ap-prov'-er. One who disapproves. FLATTERER-DEFAMER.

dis''-ap-prov'-ing. Regarding with censure. APPROVAL-DISAPPROVAL.

dis-arm'. To deprive of arms. COMPASSION-RUTHLESSNESS, CONTENTEDNESS-DISCONTENTMENT, MIGHT-IMPOTENCE, STRENGTH-WEAKNESS.

dis''-ar-range'. To disturb the arrangement. ORGANIZATION-DISORGANIZATION.

dis''-ar-ray'. Lack of array. DRESS-UNDRESS, REGULARITY-IRREGULARITY.

dis''-as-so''-ci-a'-tion. The act of disassociating. UNION-DISUNION.

dis-as'-ter. A calamity GOOD-EVIL, WELFARE-MISFORTUNE.

dis-as'-trous. Producing disaster. GOOD-EVIL, GOODNESS-BADNESS, PLEASURABLENESS-PAINFULNESS, WELFARE-MISFORTUNE.

dis''-a-vow'. To refuse to acknowledge. ASSERTION-DENIAL.

dis''-a-vow'-al. Denial. ASSERTION-DENIAL, BIGOTRY-APOSTASY.

dis-band'. To set free from bands. GATHERING-SCATTERING, RELEASE-RESTRAINT, UNION-DISUNION.

dis-bar'. To expel from the bar. COMMISSION-ABROGATION, RECOMPENSE-PUNITION.

dis''-be-lief'. The act of not believing. FAITH-MISGIVING, GODLINESS-UNGODLINESS.

dis''-be-lieve'. To refuse credence. FAITH-MISGIVING, GODLINESS-DISBELIEF.

dis-bench'. (Eng. Law.) To take away the privilege of a bencher. COMMISSION-ABROGATION, RECOMPENSE-PUNITION.

dis-bow'-el. To remove the bowels. ADMISSION-EXPULSION.

dis-branch'. To tear off branches. UNION-DISUNION.

dis-bur'-den. To get rid of a burden. ALLEVIATION-AGGRAVATION, DIFFICULTY-FACILITY; **disburden oneself of,** KEEPING-RELINQUISHMENT; **disburden one's mind,** EXPOSURE-HIDINGPLACE.

dis-burse'. To pay out. OUTLAY-INCOME.

dis-burse'-ment. The act of paying out. OUTLAY-INCOME.

dis-card'. To cast away. CHOICE-REJECTION, COMMISSION-ABROGATION, HEIGHT-LOWNESS, KEEPING-RELINQUISHMENT, OBSERVANCE-NONOBSERVANCE, PROFFER-REFUSAL, QUEST-RELINQUISHMENT, USE-DISUSE; **discard from one's thoughts,** HEED-DISREGARD.

dis''-cep-ta'-tion. Dispute. RATIOCINATION-INSTINCT.

dis-cern'. To see distinctly. KNOWLEDGE-IGNORANCE, SAGACITY-INCAPACITY, SIGHT-BLINDNESS.

dis-cern'-i-ble. Able to be discerned. VISIBILITY-INVISIBILITY.

dis-cern'-ing. Discriminating. SAGACITY-INCAPACITY.

dis-cern'-ment. Mental insight. DIFFERENTIATION-INDISCRIMINATION, SAGACITY-INCAPACITY, SIGHT-BLINDNESS.

dis-cerp'-tion. A separation. UNION-DISUNION.

dis-charge'. The act of discharging. ADMISSION-EXPULSION, COMMISSION-ABROGATION, COMPLETION-NONCOMPLETION, CONDUCT, CRASH-DRUMMING, DUTY-IMMUNITY, ELECTRICITY, EXCULPATION-CONVICTION, NUTRIMENT-EXCRETION, PUSH-PULL, RELEASE-RESTRAINT, SETTLEMENT-DEFAULT, TURBULENCE-CALMNESS; **discharge a duty,** DUTY-DERELICTION, VIRTUE-VICE; **discharge a function,** OCCUPATION, USEFULNESS-USELESSNESS; **discharge an obligation,** OBSERVANCE-NONOBSERVANCE; **discharge from the memory,** REMEMBRANCE-FORGETFULNESS; **discharge from the mind,** HEED-DISREGARD; **discharge itself,** RIVER-WIND.

dis-cind'. To cut in two. UNION-DISUNION.

dis-ci'-ple. A pupil. INSTRUCTOR-PUPIL, REVELATION-PSEUDOREVELATION.

dis'-ci-pli-nal. Of discipline. EDUCATION-MISTEACHING.

dis''-ci-pli-na'-ri-an. One who disciplines. HARSHNESS-MILDNESS, INSTRUCTOR-PUPIL.

dis'-ci-pline. Systematic training. DEVOTION-IDOLATRY, EDUCATION-MISTEACHING, RECOMPENSE-PUNITION, REGULARITY-IRREGULARITY, RELEASE-RESTRAINT.

dis-claim'. To disown. ASSERTION-DENIAL, CHOICE-REJECTION, COMMISSION-ABROGATION, COMMISSION-RETIREMENT, PROFFER-REFUSAL.

dis-claim'-er. One who disclaims. ASSERTION-DENIAL, PROFFER-REFUSAL.

dis-close'. To uncover. DISCOVERY, EXPOSURE-HIDINGPLACE; **disclose the secrets of,** PATRIOTISM-TREASON.

dis-closed'. Uncovered. ENLIGHTENMENT-SECRECY, EXPOSURE-HIDINGPLACE, MANIFESTATION-LATENCY.

dis-clo'-sure. The act of disclosing. EXPOSURE-HIDINGPLACE.

dis'-coid. With the form of a disk. LAMINA-FIBER, LEVELNESS, OUTSIDE-INSIDE.

dis-col'-or. To stain. BETTERMENT-DETERIORATION.

dis-col'-or-a'-tion. The act of discoloring. BETTERMENT-DETERIORATION, COLOR-ACHROMATISM.

dis-col'-ored. Stained. BEAUTY-UGLINESS, BETTERMENT-DETERIORATION, COLOR-ACHROMATISM, EMBELLISHMENT-DISFIGUREMENT.

dis-com'-fit. To frustrate. SUCCESS-FAILURE.

dis-com'-fi-ture. Failure. SUCCESS-FAILURE.

dis-com'-fort. A lack of comfort. PLEASURE-PAIN, SENSUALITY-SUFFERING.

dis''-com-mend'. To censure. APPROVAL-DISAPPROVAL.

dis-com''-men-da'-tion. Disapproval. APPROVAL-DISAPPROVAL.

dis''-com-mode'. To put to trouble. OBSTRUCTION-HELP.

dis''-com-mo'-di-ous. Troublesome. PROPRIETY-IMPROPRIETY.

dis''-com-mod'-i-ty. Inconvenience. PROPRIETY-IMPROPRIETY.

dis''-com-pose'. To render uneasy. FAVORITE-ANGER, HEED-DISREGARD, OBSTRUCTION-HELP, PLEASURABLENESS-PAINFULNESS, REPUTATION-DISCREDIT.

dis-com''-po-si'-tion. Discomposure. ORGANIZATION-DISORGANIZATION.

dis''-com-po'-sure. A disturbed condition. PLEASURE-PAIN.

dis''-con-cert'. To confuse. CONTENTEDNESS-DISCONTENTMENT, HEED-DISREGARD, OBSTRUCTION-HELP, ORGANIZATION-DISORGANIZATION, REPUTATION-DISCREDIT, SANGUINENESS-HOPELESSNESS.

dis''-con-cert'-ed. Confused. EXPECTATION-DISAPPOINTMENT, HEED-DISREGARD, SANGUINENESS-HOPELESSNESS.

dis''-con-form'-i-ty. Want of conformity. CONVENTIONALITY-UNCONVENTIONALITY.

dis''-con-gru'-i-ty. Want of congruity. HARMONY-DISCORD.

dis''-con-nect. To undo connection. CONTINUITY-INTERRUPTION, UNION-DISUNION.

dis''-con-nect'-ed. Having connection dissolved. CONNECTION-INDEPENDENCE, CONTINUITY-INTERRUPTION.

dis''-con-nec'-tion. The act of disconnecting. CONNECTION-INDEPENDENCE, CONTINUITY-INTERRUPTION, UNION-DISUNION.

dis-con'-so-late. Without consolation. LIGHTHEARTEDNESS-DEJECTION.

dis-con'-so-late-ness. The state of being disconsolate. LIGHTHEARTEDNESS-DEJECTION.

dis-con-tent'. A lack of content. CONTENTEDNESS-DISCONTENTMENT.

dis''-con-tent'-ed. Without content. ASSENT-DISSENT, CONTENTEDNESS-DISCONTENTMENT, PLEASURE-PAIN.

dis''-con-tent'-ment. The state of being discontented. CONTENTEDNESS-DISCONTENTMENT.

dis''-con-tin'-u-ance. The act of discontinuing. DISCONTINUANCE-CONTINUANCE, QUEST-ABANDONMENT.

DISCONTINUANCE—CONTINUANCE.

Abeyance. A state of temporary extinction.

Arrival. A coming to a stopping-place. See ARRIVAL.

Cessation. The act of discontinuing action or motion.

Dead lock.
Dead stand. }A block or stoppage of progress or business.
Dead stop.

Death. The ending of physical life.

Desinence. Conclusion.

Desistance. The act or state of forbearing, or ceasing from.

Discontinuance. A want of continued connection; a breaking off.

Drop. Stop.

End. The point in time at which some process ceases. See BEGINNING-END.

Full stop. An entire stoppage of motion or progress.

Halt. A stopping.

Intermission. Temporary abstinence from work or a pursuit.

Interregnum. Suspension of authority through a change of government.

Interruption. A breaking in upon.

Lull. An abatement of noise or violence.

Pause. A short rest, or stop.

Remission. Relaxation in application or study.

Respite. An interval of rest.

Rest. Cessation from labor, exertion, or motion of any kind.

Stop. The act of ceasing from any motion or course of action.

Stoppage. The act of arresting motion or progress; or the state of being stopped.

Stopping. See *Verbs*.

Suspense. Delay for a short time.

Suspension. A temporary withholding, interruption, or cessation.

Truce. A cessation of hostilities.

DISCONTINUANCE—*Associated Nouns*

Colon. A punctuation-mark used to denote a discontinuity in sense or grammatical construction.

Comma. A punctuation-mark indicating the slightest punctuated separation in ideas or construction.

Period. A punctuation-mark indicating the greatest separation in construction.

Semi-colon. A punctuation-mark indicating a separation in ideas or construction between that indicated by the comma and that indicated by the colon.

Continuance. Unbroken succession; permanence of condition, habits, etc.

Continuation. Unceasing extension, or succession.

Persistence. Staying or continuing quality. See PERSISTENCE.

Repetition. A doing or saying again. See RECURRENCE.

Run. Continuance in a certain course or series.

CONTINUANCE—*Verbs.*

Abide. To continue stable or fixed.

Carry on. To promote; to keep going.

Continue. To be constant; to remain as before; to keep up.

Die in harness. To die in the midst of one's ordinary labors.

Follow up. To persist in.

Go on. To progress; to hold out.

Harp upon. See RECURRENCE.

Hold on. To keep at it.

Hold on the even tenor of one's way. To be regular in one's course of life.

Hold up. To endure.

Jog on. To keep on slowly.

Keep. To continue in any position or state.

Keep alive. }
Keep going. } Keep efficient; to maintain.

Keep on. To continue.

Keep on foot. To continue to advance.

Keep the pot boiling. Keep in force or action.

Keep up. To prevent from decrease or diminution.

Keep up the ball. Continue.

Let be. To let alone.

Let things take their course. Let things continue their way.

Maintain. To hold or keep in any particular state or condition.

Maintain its course. Continue its way.

Perpetuate. To cause to endure forever.

Persist. To remain fixed; to continue obstinately.

Preserve. See PERSISTENCE.

Pursue. To stick to; to follow up.

Pursue the even tenor of one's way. To continue life in an easy, natural style or manner. [Gray, *Elegy*, 19.]

Quieta non movere [L.]. Things that are at rest not to move.

Run on. To be continued or kept up; to keep up.

Stare super antiquas vias [L.]. To keep up the old habits or customs. [Bacon, Bible, *Jeremiah*, vi, 16.]

DISCONTINUANCE—CONTINUANCE—*Continued.*

Discontinuance—*Verbs.*

Arrest. To put an end to the motion or action of.
Arrive. See ARRIVAL.
Be at an end. End.
Break off. To separate by rupture or violence.
Bring to a stand. } To bring to a halt; to impede.
Bring to a standstill. }
Cease. To put a stop to; to come to an end.
Come to a dead-lock. } Come to an end.
Come to a full stop. }
Come to a stand. } Come to a halt.
Come to a standstill. }
Cut short. To bring to an end.
Desist. To cease from action or progress.
Die away. To gradually decrease.
Discontinue. To break the continuity of.
Give over. To act no further.
Give up. See QUEST-ABANDONMENT.
Go out. To become extinguished.
Halt. To come to a stop.
Hang fire. To delay in discharging as a blast or gun.
Have done with. To have finished.
Hold. To keep in check.
Hold one's hand. To keep from action.
Intermit. To cease, or cause to cease temporarily.
Interpel. To break in upon.
Interrupt. To check by breaking in upon the course or progress of.
Intromit. To interfere with another's business.
Leave off. To forsake; desist from.
Pass away. See FUTURE-PAST.
Pause. To cease temporarily.
Pull the check-string. To signal to stop, as in a coach.
Pull up. To halt.
Put an end to. }
Put a period to. } To stop.
Put a stop to. }
Remit. To give up; to resign.
Repose on one's laurels. To rest satisfied with one's achievements.
Rest. To quit from motion or action temporarily.
Rest on one's oars. To be idle for a while.
Shut up shop. To give up any endeavor.
Stay. To restrain from proceeding.
Stay one's hand. To stop; to cease from.
Stem the tide. To check the course of.

dis''-con-tin'-ue. To bring to an end. CONTINUITY-INTERRUPTION, DISCONTINUANCE-CONTINUANCE.

dis''-con-ti-nu'-i-ty. Want of continuity. CONTINUITY-INTERRUPTION, UNION-DISUNION.

dis''-con-tin'-u-ous. Lacking continuity. CONTINUITY-INTERRUPTION.

dis'-cord. Strife. AMITY-HOSTILITY, CACOPHONY, HARMONY-DISCORD, MELODY-DISSONANCE, REGULARITY-IRREGULARITY, VARIANCE-ACCORD.

dis-cord'-ance. A discordant condition. ASSENT-DISSENT, HARMONY-DISCORD, MELODY-DISSONANCE.

dis-cord'-ant. Not agreeing. CACOPHONY, COLOR-ACHROMATISM, CONNECTION-INDEPENDENCE, HARMONY-DISCORD, MELODY-DISSONANCE, VARIATION-ACCORD.

dis-cord'-ant-ly. In a discordant way. HARMONY-DISCORD.

dis-count'. To deduct a portion. INCREASE-DECREASE, MONEY.

dis'-count. An amount deducted. INCREMENT-DECREMENT, MODIFICATION, PRICE-DISCOUNT; **at a discount,** APPROVAL-DISAPPROVAL, PRICE-DISCOUNT, REPUTATION-DISCREDIT.

dis-coun'-te-nance. To disapprove. OBSTRUCTION-HELP, PROFFER-REFUSAL.

dis-count'-ing. Counting off. PRICE-DISCOUNT.

dis-cour'-age. To destroy courage. LIGHTHEARTEDNESS-DEJECTION, MOTIVE-DEHORTATION, SANGUINENESS-TIMIDITY.

dis-cour'-aged. Deprived of courage. LIGHTHEARTEDNESS-DEJECTION.

dis-course'. A formal address. CEREMONIAL, CONVERSATION-MONOLOGUE, EDUCATION-MISTEACHING, ESSAY, SPEECH-INARTICULATENESS.

dis-cours'-ive. Of a conversational character. CONVERSATION-MONOLOGUE, ESSAY.

dis-cour'-te-ous. Lacking in courtesy. POLITENESS-IMPOLITENESS.

dis-cour'-te-ous-ly. In a discourteous manner.

dis-cour'-te-sy. Rude conduct. POLITENESS-IMPOLITENESS, REGARD-DISRESPECT.

dis'-cous. Like a disk. BREADTH-NARROWNESS.

dis-cov'-er. To have first knowledge of. DISCOVERY, EXPOSURE-HIDINGPLACE, INVESTIGATION-ANSWER, KNOWLEDGE-IGNORANCE, SIGHT-BLINDNESS; **discover itself,** EXPOSURE-HIDINGPLACE, VISIBILITY-INVISIBILITY.

dis-cov'-er-y. The act of discovering. DISCOVERY, INVESTIGATION-ANSWER, KNOWLEDGE-IGNORANCE.

CONTINUANCE—VERBS—*Continued.*

Stick to. To persevere.
Sustain. To maintain; to keep up.
Take its course. Pursue its way.
Uphold. To support.

CONTINUANCE—*Adjectives.*

Continuing, etc. See *Verbs.*
Inconvertible. Not capable of being changed into something else.
Sustained. Upheld; continued.
Undying. See ETERNITY.
Unintermitting. Unceasing.
Uninterrupted. Unbroken in connection.
Unreversed. Unchanged.
Unrevoked. Not annulled.
Unshifting. Stable.
Unstopped. Not checked.
Unvaried. Unaltered.
Unvarying. Constant.

CONTINUANCE—*Interjection.*

Right away! Immediately!

CONTINUANCE—*Phrases.*

Labitur, et labetur [L.]. It (a river and time) flows and it will flow. [Horace, *Epistles,* I, ii, 43.]
Nolumus leges Angliæ mutari [L.]. We do not wish the laws of England to be changed. [English peers in Parliament.]
Tenez [F.]. Hold; wait.
Vestigia nulla retrorsum [L.]. No footsteps backward. [Horace, *Epistles,* I, i, 74.]

DISCONTINUANCE—VERBS—*Continued.*

Stem the torrent. To restrain the force of.
Stick. To refrain from further motion; to be checked.
Stop. To leave off entirely; to hinder from acting or moving.
Stop short. To cease abruptly.
Surcease. To put at an end; or be at an end.
Suspend. To withhold temporarily; to cause to cease for a while.
Wear away. To diminish or impair by gradual attrition.
Wear off. To diminish by rubbing.

DISCONTINUANCE—*Interjections.*

A truce to! avast! enough! have done! hold! leave off! soft! stop!

DISCOVERY.

Detection. The laying open what was concealed or hidden.
Discovery. Act of exposing to view or finding out something previously unknown.
Disenchantment. Act of delivering from the power of charms and spells.
Trover. Gaining possession of anything by finding.

DISCOVERY—*Verbs.*

Burn. To approach near to a concealed object which is sought.
Catch. To come upon by surprise.
Detect. To find out; bring to light.
Determine. To find out the specific character or name of.
Disclose. To remove a cover or envelope from.
Discover. To obtain for the first time sight or knowledge of.
Disinter. To bring out, as from a grave or hiding-place.

Educe. To cause to appear.
Elicit. To bring to light.
Evolve. To open and expand.
Fathom. To penetrate; to get to the bottom of.
Find. To come upon by seeking.
Identify. To prove to be the same with something known.
Interpret. To explain or tell the meaning of.
Realize. To bring into concrete existence.
Recognize. To perceive the identity of, with a person or thing previously known.
Resolve. To clear up, or dispel, as doubt.
Scent. To perceive by the sense of smell.
Smoke. To smell out; to find out.
Snuff. To perceive by the nose.
Solve. To clear up what is obscure or difficult to be understood.
Trace. To find by footsteps, tracks or tokens.
Unearth. To bring out from concealment.
Unlock. To lay open.
Unravel. To clear from complication or difficulty.
Unriddle. To solve or explain.
Verify. To establish the truth of by examination.

DISCOVERY—*Verbal Expressions.*

Arrive at the truth; be near the truth; bring out; bring to light; catch tripping, to come upon unexpectedly; come across; dig up; draw out; fall in with; fall upon; find a clue; find a clue to; find out; fish up; fish up; fix upon; get at; get at the truth; grub up; have it; hit it; hit the right nail on the head; hit upon; hunt out; lay one's finger upon; lay one's hands upon; light upon; make certain of; meet with; open the eyes to; open the lock; pick the lock; pitch upon; pop upon; put the saddle on the right horse; root out; see daylight; see in its true colors; see the cloven foot; see through; smell a rat; stumble upon; trace out; worm out.

DISCOVERY—*Interjection.*

Eureka [Gr.] I have found it, [Archimedes. Motto of California.]

dis-cred'-it. The act of discrediting. FAITH-MIS-GIVING, REPUTATION-DISCREDIT.
dis-cred'-i-ta-ble. Harmful to credit. REPUTATION-DISCREDIT, VIRTUE-VICE.
dis-creet'. Having discernment. CAREFULNESS-CARELESSNESS, RECKLESSNESS-CAUTION.
dis-crep'-an-cy. Difference between contrasted things. HARMONY-DISCORD.
dis-crep'-ant. Discordant. HARMONY-DISCORD.
dis-crete'. Not connected with others. UNION-DISUNION.
dis-cre'-tion. Ability to act with prudence. CHOICE-NEUTRALITY, RECKLESSNESS-CAUTION, SKILL-UNSKILFULNESS, VOLITION-OBLIGATION; **surrender at discretion,** YIELDING; **years of discretion,** MANHOOD.
discrétion, à [F.] (dis-crê-si-on·', a). At discretion. VOLITION-OBLIGATION.
dis-cre'-tion-al. At discretion. CHOICE-NEUTRALITY, VOLITION-OBLIGATION.
dis-cre'-tion-a-ry. Left to discretion. LIBERTY-SUBJECTION, VOLITION-OBLIGATION.
dis-crim'-i-nate. To note differences. DIFFERENTIATION-INDISCRIMINATION, SAGACITY-INCAPACITY, TASTE-VULGARITY, VARIATION.
dis-crim'-i-na''-ting. Noting differences. DIFFERENTIATION-INDISCRIMINATION.
dis-crim''-i-na'-tion. The act of discriminating. DIFFERENTIATION-INDISCRIMINATION, SAGACITY-INCAPACITY, VARIATION.
dis-crim'-i-na-tive. Making distinctions. DIFFERENTIATION-INDISCRIMINATION, VARIATION.
dis-cul'-pate. To exonerate. JUSTIFICATION-CHARGE.
dis-cum'-bence. Discumbency. ERECTNESS-FLATNESS.
dis-cum'-ben-cy. The habit of reclining at meals. ERECTNESS-FLATNESS.
dis-cur'-sion. A running about. TRAVELING-NAVIGATION.
dis-cur'-sive. Wandering from the subject. AIM-ABERRATION, CONVERSATION-MONOLOGUE, ESSAY, RATIOCINATION-INSTINCT, TERSENESS-PROLIXITY, TRAVEL-NAVIGATION.

dis-cur'-so-ry. Argumentative. RATIOCINATION-INSTINCT.
dis'-cus. A quoit. ENTERTAINMENT-WEARINESS, PUSH-PULL.
dis-cuss'. To debate. ESSAY, INVESTIGATION-ANSWER, NUTRIMENT-EXCRETION, RATIOCINATION-INSTINCT, REFLECTION-VACANCY.
dis-cus'-sion. A debate. ESSAY, INVESTIGATION-ANSWER, RATIOCINATION-INSTINCT; **open to discussion,** CERTAINTY-DOUBT; **under discussion,** INVESTIGATION-ANSWER.
dis-dain'. To hold unworthy of regard. REGARD-SCORN, UNCONCERN.
dis-dain'-ful. Filled with disdain. SELFRESPECT-HUMBLENESS.
dis-ease'. A lack of health. HEALTH-SICKNESS; **diseased mind,** SANENESS-LUNACY.
dis-eased'. Having disease. HEALTH-SICKNESS.
dis-em-bark'. To land. ARRIVAL-DEPARTURE.
dis-em''-bar-ka'-tion. The act of landing. ARRIVAL-DEPARTURE.
dis''-em-bar'-rass. To relieve of embarrassment. DIFFICULTY-FACILITY.
dis''-em-bar'-rassed. Freed from embarrassment. DIFFICULTY-FACILITY.
dis''-em-bod'-ied. Freed from the body. MATERIALITY-SPIRITUALITY.
dis''-em-bod'-y. To free from the body. COMPOSITION-RESOLUTION, GATHERING-SCATTERING, MATERIALITY-SPIRITUALITY.
dis''-em-bogue'. To pour out. ENTRANCE-EXIT, RIVER-WIND.
dis''-em-bow'-el. To remove the bowels. ADMISSION-EXPULSION.
dis''-em-broil'. To relieve of confusion. ORGANIZATION-DISORGANIZATION.
dis''-en-a'-ble. To disable. MIGHT-IMPOTENCE.
dis''-en-chant'. To free from enchantment. MOTIVE-DEHORTATION, PLEASURABLENESS-PAINFULNESS.
dis''-en-chant'-ment. Freedom from enchantment. DISCOVERY.
dis''-en-cum'-ber. To disburden. DIFFICULTY-FACILITY.
dis''-en-cum'-bered. Freed from a burden. DIFFICULTY-FACILITY.
dis''-en-cum'-ber-ment. Freedom from encumbrance. DIFFICULTY-FACILITY.
dis''-en-cum'-brance. Freedom from encumbrance. DIFFICULTY-FACILITY.
dis''-en-dow'. To deprive of endowment. COMMISSION-ABROGATION.
dis''-en-dow'-ment. Deprivation of endowment. COMMISSION-ABROGATION.
dis''-en-gage'. To set free. DIFFICULTY-FACILITY, RELEASE-RESTRAINT, UNION-DISUNION.
dis''-en-gaged'. At liberty. PROFFER-REFUSAL.
dis''-en-gage'-ment. The act of disengaging. RELEASE-RESTRAINT, UNION-DISUNION.
dis''-en-tan'-gle. To free from tangles. DIFFICULTY-FACILITY, INTERPRETATION-MISINTERPRETATION, MIXTURE-HOMOGENEITY, ORGANIZATION-DISORGANIZATION, RELEASE-RESTRAINT, REVOLUTION-EVOLUTION, UNION-DISUNION.
dis''-en-tan'-gle-ment. Freedom from tangles. DIFFICULTY-FACILITY.
dis''-en-thrall'. To set free. RELEASE-RESTRAINT.
dis''-en-throne'. To dethrone. COMMISSION-ABROGATION.
dis''-en-ti'-tle. To deprive of title. DUENESS-UNDUENESS.
dis''-en-ti'-tled. Deprived of title. DUENESS-UNDUENESS.
dis''-es-pouse'. To divorce. MATRIMONY-DIVORCE.
dis''-es-tab'-lish. To deprive of a fixed state. COMMISSION-ABROGATION, ESTABLISHMENT-REMOVAL.

dis″-es-tab′-lish-ment. The act of disestablishing. COMMISSION-ABROGATION.

dis″-es-teem′. To dislike. APPROVAL-DISAPPROVAL REGARD-DISRESPECT.

dis″-es-ti-ma′-tion. Disesteem. REGARD-DISRESPECT.

diseur de bons mots [F.] (di-zur′ de bon′ mo). A sayer of good things. WAG.

dis-fa′-vor. To withdraw favor. ANTAGONISM-CONCURRENCE, LOVE-HATE; **view with disfavor,** APPROVAL-DISAPPROVAL.

dis-fig′-ure. To mar the figure. BEAUTY-UGLINESS, BETTERMENT - DETERIORATION, EMBELLISHMENT-DISFIGUREMENT, FORM-FORMLESSNESS.

dis-fig′-ured. Deformed. BEAUTY-UGLINESS.

dis-fig′-ure-ment. That which disfigures. BEAUTY-UGLINESS, EMBELLISHMENT-DISFIGUREMENT, FORM-FORMLESSNESS.

dis-fran′-chise. To take away a franchise. DUENESS-UNDUENESS.

dis-fran′-chised. Deprived of franchise. DUENESS-UNDUENESS.

dis-gorge′. To eject. ADMISSION-EXPULSION, SETTLEMENT-DEFAULT, TAKING-RESTITUTION.

dis-grace′. A loss of favor. REPUTATION-DISCREDIT, UPRIGHTNESS-DISHONESTY; **sense of disgrace,** SELFRESPECT-HUMBLENESS.

dis-graced′. Deprived of favor. REPUTATION-DISCREDIT.

dis-grace′-ful. Causing disgrace. REPUTATION-DISCREDIT, UPRIGHTNESS-DISHONESTY, VIRTUE-VICE.

dis-guise′. To alter the appearance of. ENLIGHTENMENT-SECRECY, EXPOSURE-HIDINGPLACE, TRUTHFULNESS-FABRICATION, TRUTHFULNESS-FALSEHOOD, TRUTHFULNESS-FRAUD.

dis-guised′. Changed in appearance. TEETOTALISM-INTEMPERANCE, TRUTHFULNESS-FRAUD.

dis-guise′-ment. Disguise. TRUTHFULNESS-FRAUD.

dis-gust′. Repugnance for anything offensive. DESIRE-DISTASTE, ENTERTAINMENT-WEARINESS, PALATABLENESS-UNPALATABLENESS, PLEASURABLENESS-PAINFULNESS; **disgust of life,** LIGHTHEARTEDNESS-DEJECTION, LOVE-HATE.

dis-gust′-ing. Serving to excite disgust. DESIRE-DISTASTE, LOVE-HATE, PLEASURABLENESS-PAINFULNESS.

dish. A vessel for serving food. CONTENTS-RECEIVER, CREATION-DESTRUCTION, NUTRIMENT-EXCRETION; **dish of tea,** SOCIABILITY-PRIVACY.

dis″-ha-bille′. Negligent dress. DRESS-UNDRESS, PREPARATION-NONPREPARATION.

dis-heart′-en. To discourage. CONTENTEDNESS-DISCONTENTMENT, LIGHTHEARTEDNESS - DEJECTION, MOTIVE-DEHORTATION.

dis-heart′-ened. Deprived of courage. LIGHTHEARTEDNESS-DEJECTION.

dis-heart′-en-ing. Discouraging. PLEASURABLENESS-PAINFULNESS.

dished. Badly used up. [Slang.] SUCCESS-FAILURE.

di-shev′-el. To disarrange. CROSSING, ORGANIZATION-DISORGANIZATION.

di-shev′-eled. Disarranged. COHESION-LOOSENESS, GATHERING-SCATTERING.

dis-hon′-est. Wanting in honesty. TRUTHFULNESS-FALSEHOOD, UPRIGHTNESS-DISHONESTY.

dis-hon′-est-ly. In a dishonest way. UPRIGHTNESS-DISHONESTY.

dis-hon′-es-ty. Lack of honesty. UPRIGHTNESS-DISHONESTY.

dis-hon′-or. Lack of honor. REGARD-DISRESPECT, REPUTATION-DISCREDIT, PATRIOTISM-TREASON, SETTLEMENT-DEFAULT.

dis-hon′-or-a-ble. Bringing dishonor. UPRIGHTNESS-DISHONESTY.

dish′-wat″-er. Water in which dishes have been washed. CLEANNESS-FILTHINESS.

dis-in″-cli-na′-tion. Lack of inclination. DESIRE-DISTASTE, READINESS-RELUCTANCE.

dis″-in-cline′. To render unwilling. DESIRE-DISTASTE, MOTIVE-DEHORTATION.

dis″-in-clined′. Indisposed. DESIRE-DISTASTE, READINESS-RELUCTANCE.

dis″-in-fect′. To free from infection. CLEANNESS-FILTHINESS, RENOVATION-RELAPSE.

dis″-in-fect′-ant. Anything that disinfects. CLEANNESS-FILTHINESS, REMEDY-BANE, RENOVATION-RELAPSE.

dis″-in-fec′-tion. The act of disinfecting. CLEANNESS-FILTHINESS.

dis″-in-gen′-u-ous. Not ingenuous. TRUTHFULNESS-FALSEHOOD, UPRIGHTNESS-DISHONESTY.

dis″-in-her′-it. To deprive of inheritance. ALIENATION.

dis-in′-te-grate. To break in pieces. FRIABILITY, UNION-DISUNION.

dis″-in-te-gra′-tion. The act of disintegrating. FRIABILITY, UNION-DISUNION.

dis-in-ter′. To dig up. DISCOVERY, LIFE-FUNERAL.

dis-in′-ter-est-ed. The quality of being free from self-interest. UNSELFISHNESS-SELFISHNESS.

dis″-in-ter′-ment. The act of disinterring. LIFE-FUNERAL.

disjecta membra [L.] (dis-jec′-ta mem′-bra). Scattered members. GATHERING-SCATTERING, REGULARITY-IRREGULARITY, UNION-DISUNION.

disjecta membra poetæ [L.] (dis-jec′-ta mem′ bra po-i′-ti). A poet's disjointed writings. POETRY-PROSE.

dis-join′. To sunder. UNION-DISUNION.

dis-joined′. Sundered. UNION-DISUNION.

dis-joint′. Out of joint. UNION-DISUNION.

dis-joint′-ed. Having the joints separated. MIGHT-IMPOTENCE, REGULARITY-IRREGULARITY.

dis-junc′-tion. Disunion. COHESION-LOOSENESS, COMPOSITION-RESOLUTION, CONTINUITY-INTERRUPTION, GATHERING-SCATTERING, UNION-DISUNION.

dis-junc′-tive. Tending to separate. PARTICLE, UNION-DISUNION.

disk. Any flat, round plane. ANTERIORITY-POSTERIORITY, OUTSIDE-INSIDE.

dis-kind′-ness. Lack of kindness. CHARITABLENESS-MALEVOLENCE.

dis-like′. Aversion. AMITY-HOSTILITY, APPROVAL-DISAPPROVAL, DESIRE-DISTASTE, READINESS-RELUCTANCE.

dis-liked′. Regarded with aversion. LOVE-HATE.

dis-li′-king. Having aversion for. DESIRE-DISTASTE.

dis′-lo-cate. To put out of joint. ORGANIZATION-DISORGANIZATION, UNION-DISUNION.

dis′-lo-ca″-ted. Out of joint. REGULARITY-IRREGULARITY.

dis″-lo-ca′-tion. The act of displacing. ESTABLISHMENT-REMOVAL, ORGANIZATION-DISORGANIZATION, UNION-DISUNION.

dis-lodge′. To eject. ADMISSION-EXPULSION, ESTABLISHMENT-REMOVAL.

dis-lodg′-ment. The act of dislodging. ADMISSION-EXPULSION.

dis-loy′-al. False to obligations. UPRIGHTNESS-DISHONESTY.

dis-loy′-al-ty. Lack of loyalty. UPRIGHTNESS-DISHONESTY.

dis′-mal. Cheerless. LIGHTHEARTEDNESS-DEJECTION, PLEASURABLENESS-PAINFULNESS.

dis-man′-tle. To deprive of furniture. BETTERMENT-DETERIORATION, CREATION-DESTRUCTION, DRESS-UNDRESS, PREPARATION-NONPREPARATION, USE-DISUSE, USEFULNESS-USELESSNESS.

dis-mask′. To unmask. EXPOSURE-HIDINGPLACE.

dis-mast′. To deprive of a mast. BETTERMENT-DETERIORATION, USEFULNESS-USELESSNESS.

dis-may'. To take away one's courage. SANGUINE-NESS-TIMIDITY.

dis-mem'-ber. To tear part from part. GATHERING-SCATTERING, UNION-DISUNION.

dis-mem'-ber-ment. The act of dismembering. UNION-DISUNION.

dis-miss'. To discharge. COMMISSION-ABROGATION, KEEPING-RELINQUISHMENT, RECOMPENSE-PUNITION, RELEASE-RESTRAINT, USE-DISUSE; dismiss from the mind, HEED-DISREGARD, REFLECTION-VACANCY.

dis-miss'-al. Discharge. COMMISSION-ABROGATION, RELEASE-RESTRAINT.

dis-mount'. To descend. ARRIVAL-DEPARTURE, ASCENT-DESCENT, USEFULNESS-USELESSNESS.

dis''-o-be'-di-ence. Lack of obedience. INSUBORDI-NATION-OBEDIENCE, LAW-LAWLESSNESS, OBSERV-ANCE-NONOBSERVANCE.

dis''-o-be'-di-ent. Not obedient. INSUBORDINATION-OBEDIENCE.

dis''-o-bey'. To fail to obey. DEFIANCE, INSUBOR-DINATION-OBEDIENCE.

dis''-o-blige'. To refuse to oblige. CHARITABLENESS-MALEVOLENCE.

dis''-o-bli'-ging. Not obliging. CHARITABLENESS-MALEVOLENCE.

dis-or'-der. Lack of order. FORM-FORMLESSNESS, HEALTH - SICKNESS, ORGANIZATION - DISORGANIZA-TION, REGULARITY-IRREGULARITY; disordered intel-lect, SANENESS-LUNACY.

dis-or'-der-ly. Disreputable. REGULARITY-IRREGU-LARITY, TURBULENCE-CALMNESS, VIRTUE-VICE.

dis-'or''-gan-i-za'-tion. The act of disorganizing. BET-TERMENT-DETERIORATION, CREATION-DESTRUCTION.

dis-or'-gan-ize. To destroy organization. BETTER-MENT - DETERIORATION, CREATION - DESTRUCTION, ORGANIZATION-DISORGANIZATION.

dis-own'. To refuse to own. ASSERTION-DENIAL.

dis-pair'. To separate. UNION-DISUNION.

dis-pan'-sion. A spreading out. ENLARGEMENT-DIMINUTION.

dis-par'-age. To regard slightingly. ADULATION-DISPARAGEMENT, APPROVAL-DISAPPROVAL, OVER-VALUATION-UNDERVALUATION, REGARD-DISRESPECT.

dis-par'-age-ment. The act of disparaging. ADULA-TION-DISPARAGEMENT, APPROVAL-DISAPPROVAL, RE-GARD-DISRESPECT.

dis-par'-a-ging. Regarding slightingly. ADULATION-DISPARAGEMENT, APPROVAL-DISAPPROVAL, REGARD-DISRESPECT.

dis'-pa-rate. Unlike. EQUALITY-INEQUALITY, LIKE-NESS-UNLIKENESS, UNION-DISUNION.

dis-par'-i-ty. Inequality. HARMONY-DISCORD, LIKE-NESS-UNLIKENESS, UNION-DISUNION, VARIATION.

dis-part'. To separate. UNION-DISUNION.

dis-pas'-sion. Freedom from passion. EXCITABILITY-INEXCITABILITY.

dis-pas'-sion-ate. Without passion. EXCITABILITY-INEXCITABILITY; dispassionate opinion, FAITH-MIS-GIVING.

dis-patch'. The act of dispatching. ACTIVITY-INDO-LENCE, CIRCLE-WINDING, COMPLETION-NONCOMPLE-TION, CONDUCT, LIFE-KILLING, MISSIVE-PUBLICA-TION, NUTRIMENT-EXCRETION, ORDER, TIDINGS-MYSTERY.

dis-pel'. To disperse. ATTRACTION-REPULSION, CREA-TION - DESTRUCTION, ESTABLISHMENT - REMOVAL, GATHERING-SCATTERING.

dis-pen'-sa-ble. Capable of being distributed. USE-FULNESS-USELESSNESS.

dis-pen'-sa-ry. A place where medicine is kept. REMEDY-BANE.

dis''-pen-sa'-tion. A distribution. ASSIGNMENT, DUTY-IMMUNITY, GIVING-RECEIVING, KEEPING-RE-LINQUISHMENT, LEAVE-PROHIBITION, ORDER; dis-pensations of Providence, DIVINITY.

dis-pense'. To distribute. ASSIGNMENT, BUYING-SALE, GATHERING-SCATTERING, GIVING-RECEIVING; dispense with, DUTY-IMMUNITY, LEAVE-PROHIBITION, USE-DISUSE; can not be dispensed with, NEED.

dis-peo'-ple. To depopulate. ADMISSION-EXCLUSION, SOCIABILITY-PRIVACY.

dis-perse'. To scatter. COMPOSITION-RESOLUTION, CONCENTRATION-RADIATION, GATHERING-SCATTER-ING, PROVISION-WASTE, UNION-DISUNION.

dis-per'-sion. The act of dispersing. COMPOSITION-RESOLUTION, CONCENTRATION-RADIATION, ENLARGE-MENT-DIMINUTION, GATHERING-SCATTERING, LIGHT-DARKNESS, PROVISION-WASTE, UNION-DISUNION; chromatic dispersion, COLOR-ACHROMATISM.

dis-pir'-it. To depress in spirits. LIGHTHEARTED-NESS-DEJECTION, MOTIVE-DEHORTATION.

dis-place'. To put out of place. CHEMISTRY, ESTAB-LISHMENT-REMOVAL, ORGANIZATION-DISORGANIZA-TION, SWIFTNESS-SLOWNESS.

dis-placed'. Out of place. ESTABLISHMENT-REMOVAL, ORGANIZATION-DISORGANIZATION, SWIFTNESS-SLOW-NESS.

dis-place'-ment. The act of displacing. ESTABLISH-MENT-REMOVAL, MUTATION-PERMANENCE, TRANS-FER.

dis-pla'cen-cy. The condition of being displeased. APPROVAL-DISAPPROVAL DESIRE-DISTASTE, POLITE-NESS-IMPOLITENESS.

dis-plant'. To root up. ESTABLISHMENT-REMOVAL.

dis-play'. A show. APPEARANCE-DISAPPEARANCE, MANIFESTATION-LATENCY, POMP.

dis-please'. To offend. PLEASURABLENESS-PAINFUL-NESS.

dis-pleased'. Offended. PLEASURE-PAIN.

dis-pleas'-ing. Offending. PLEASURABLENESS-PAIN-FULNESS.

dis-pleas'-ure. A feeling of anger. FAVORITE-ANGER, PLEASURE-PAIN.

dis-plo'-sion. An explosion. TURBULENCE-CALMNESS.

dis-plume'. To deprive of plumes. TAKING-RESTITU-TION.

dis-port'. To divert. ENTERTAINMENT-WEARINESS.

dis-po'-sal. The act of disposing. BUYING-SALE, ORGANIZATION-DISORGANIZATION, USE-DISUSE; at one's disposal, HOLDING-EXEMPTION, ORGANIZATION-DISORGANIZATION.

dis-pose'. To set in order. INCLINATION, MOTIVE-CAPRICE, ORGANIZATION-DISORGANIZATION; dispose of, BUYING-SALE, COMPLETION-NONCOMPLETION, GIVING - RECEIVING, KEEPING - RELINQUISHMENT, USE-DISUSE.

dis-posed'. With a particular disposition. AFFEC-TIONS, MOTIVE-CAPRICE, READINESS-RELUCTANCE.

dis''-po-si'-tion. The act of disposing. AFFECTIONS, ORGANIZATION-DISORGANIZATION, READINESS-RE-LUCTANCE, REGULARITY-IRREGULARITY.

dis''-pos-sess'. To deprive of possession. ALIEN-ATION, TAKING-RESTITUTION; dispossess oneself of, KEEPING-RELINQUISHMENT.

dis''-pos-sessed'. Deprived of self-possession. GAIN-LOSS.

dis''-pos-sess'-ion. The act of dispossessing. TAKING-RESTITUTION.

dis-praise'. To speak of with censure. APPROVAL-DISAPPROVAL.

dis-pread'. To expand. GATHERING-SCATTERING.

dis-prize'. To undervalue. OVERVALUATION-UNDER-VALUATION.

dis-proof'. Refutation. EVIDENCE-COUNTEREVI-DENCE, PROOF-DISPROOF.

dis''-pro-por'-tion. Lack of proportion. HARMONY-DISCORD.

dis''-pro-por'-tion-ate. Out of proportion. HARMONY-DISCORD.

dis''-pro-por'-tion-ate-ness. The state of being out of proportion. HARMONY-DISCORD.

dis''-pro-por'-tioned. Not matched. HARMONY-DISCORD.

dis-prove'. To refute. PROOF-DISPROOF.

dis'-pu-ta-ble. Liable to be disputed. FAITH-MISGIVING.

dis'-pu-tant. One who disputes. ANTAGONIST-ASSISTANT, BELLIGERENT, RATIOCINATION-INSTINCT, VARIANCE-ACCORD.

dis''-pu-ta'-tion. Controversy. RATIOCINATION-INSTINCT.

dis''-pu-ta'-tious. Given to controversy. FAVORITE-QUARRELSOMENESS, RATIOCINATION-INSTINCT, VARIANCE-ACCORD.

dis-pute'. A discussion. ASSERTION-DENIAL, FAITH-MISGIVING, LITIGATION, RATIOCINATION-INSTINCT, VARIANCE-ACCORD; **in dispute,** INVESTIGATION-ANSWER.

dis-qual''-i-fi-ca'-tion. Want of qualification. MIGHT-IMPOTENCE, PREPARATION-NONPREPARATION, SKILL-UNSKILFULNESS.

dis-qual'-i-fied. Made unfit. DUENESS-UNDUENESS, MIGHT-IMPOTENCE, PREPARATION-NONPREPARATION, SKILL-UNSKILFULNESS.

dis-qual'-i-fy. To make unfit. DUENESS-UNDUENESS, MIGHT-IMPOTENCE, USEFULNESS-USELESSNESS.

dis-qui'-et. Restlessness. AGITATION, EXCITABILITY-INEXCITABILITY, MUTABILITY-STABILITY, PLEASURABLENESS-PAINFULNESS, PLEASURE-PAIN, SANGUINENESS-TIMIDITY.

dis-qui'-e-tude. Want of quiet. EXCITABILITY-INEXCITABILITY, MUTABILITY-STABILITY, SANGUINENESS-TIMIDITY.

dis''-qui-si'-tion. A dissertation. ESSAY.

dis''-qui-si'-tion-a-ry. Of disquisition. ESSAY.

dis''-re-gard'. Lack of regard. CAREFULNESS-CARELESSNESS, EXCITABILITY-INEXCITABILITY, HEED-DISREGARD, OVERVALUATION-UNDERVALUATION, REGARD-DISRESPECT, REGARD-SCORN, SENSITIVENESS-APATHY; **disregard of time,** CHRONOLOGY-ANACHRONISM.

dis''-re-gard'-ed. Not regarded. REGARD-DISRESPECT.

dis''-re-gard'-ing. Not regarding. SENSITIVENESS-APATHY.

dis-rel'-ish. A feeling of repugnance. DESIRE-DISTASTE, LOVE-HATE.

dis-rep'-u-ta-ble. Being in disrepute. REPUTATION-DISCREDIT, VIRTUE-VICE.

dis''-re-pute'. Want of reputation. REPUTATION-DISCREDIT.

dis''-re-spect'. Lack of respect. POLITENESS-IMPOLITENESS, REGARD-DISRESPECT.

dis''-re-spect'-ful. Lacking in respect. REGARD-DISRESPECT.

dis''-re-spect'-ful-ly. In a disrespectful way. REGARD-DISRESPECT.

dis-robe'. To undress. DRESS-UNDRESS.

dis-rupt'. To break asunder. VARIANCE-ACCORD.

dis-rup'-tion. Rupture. CREATION-DESTRUCTION, UNION-DISUNION, VARIANCE-ACCORD.

dis-rup'-ture. Rupture. VARIANCE-ACCORD.

dis-sat''-is-fac'-tion. Discontent. CONTENTEDNESS-DISCONTENTMENT.

dis-sat'-is-fied. Discontented. CONTENTEDNESS-DISCONTENTMENT.

dis-sat'-is-fy. To render discontented. CONTENTEDNESS-DISCONTENTMENT.

dis-sect'. To cut to pieces. INVESTIGATION-ANSWER.

dis-sec'-tion. The act of dissecting. COMPOSITION-RESOLUTION, INVESTIGATION-ANSWER, UNION-DISUNION.

dis-sem'-blance. Lack of resemblance. LIKENESS-UNLIKENESS.

dis-sem'-ble. To conceal. TRUTHFULNESS-FALSEHOOD.

dis-sem'-bler. One who dissembles. GULL-DECEIVER.

dis-sem'-i-nate. To spread abroad. EDUCATION-MISTEACHING, GATHERING-SCATTERING, PUBLICITY.

dis-sem'-i-na''-ting. Promulgating. TRUTHFULNESS-FALSEHOOD.

dis-sem''-i-na'-tion. The act of disseminating. GATHERING-SCATTERING.

dis-sen'-sion. Discord. ASSENT-DISSENT, HARMONY-DISCORD, VARIANCE-ACCORD; **sow dissension,** LOVE-HATE.

dis-sent'. Disagreement. ASSENT-DISSENT, CONTENTEDNESS-DISCONTENTMENT, FAITH-MISGUIDANCE, ORTHODOXY-HETERODOXY, PROFFER-REFUSAL, READINESS-RELUCTANCE, VARIANCE-ACCORD.

dis-sent'-er. One who dissents. ASSENT-DISSENT, ORTHODOXY-HETERODOXY.

dis-sen'-tient. Dissenting. ASSENT-DISSENT, CONTENTEDNESS-DISCONTENTMENT, VARIANCE-ACCORD.

dis-sent'-ing. Withholding assent. ASSENT-DISSENT, ORTHODOXY-HETERODOXY.

dis''-ser-ta'-tion. Thesis. ESSAY, RHETORIC.

dis-serv'-ice. Bad service. GOOD-EVIL, USEFULNESS-USELESSNESS.

dis-serv'-ice-a-ble. Detrimental. GOODNESS-BADNESS.

dis-sev'-er. To sever. UNION-DISUNION.

dis-sev'-er-ance. Separation. UNION-DISUNION.

dis''-si-dence. Disagreement. CONTENTEDNESS-DISCONTENTMENT, HARMONY-DISCORD, VARIANCE-ACCORD.

dis''-si-dent. Dissenting. ASSENT-DISSENT, CONTENTEDNESS-DISCONTENTMENT.

dis-sil'-i-ence. The act of bursting. TURBULENCE-CALMNESS.

dis-sim'-i-lar. Unlike. LIKENESS-UNLIKENESS.

dis-sim''-i-lar'-i-ty. Unlikeness. LIKENESS-UNLIKENESS.

dis''-sim-il'-i-tude. Unlikeness. LIKENESS-UNLIKENESS.

dis-sim'-u-late. To feign. TRUTHFULNESS-FALSEHOOD.

dis-sim''-u-la'-tion. The act of dissimulating. TRUTHFULNESS-FALSEHOOD.

dis'-si-pate. To disperse. CREATION-DESTRUCTION, EXTRAVAGANCE-AVARICE, GATHERING-SCATTERING.

dis'-si-pa''-ted. Dissolute. EXTRAVAGANCE-AVARICE, PURITY-IMPURITY.

dis''-si-pa'-tion. The act of dissipating. ENTERTAINMENT-WEARINESS, MODERATION-SELFINDULGENCE, PURITY-IMPURITY.

dis-so''-cia-bil'-i-ty. Lack of sociability. SOCIABILITY-PRIVACY.

dis-so'-cial. Unsocial. SOCIABILITY-PRIVACY.

dis-so'-ci-ate. To separate. UNION-DISUNION.

dis-so''-ci-a'-tion. The act of dissociating. CONNECTION-INDEPENDENCE.

dis'-so-lute. Profligate. MODERATION-SELFINDULGENCE, PURITY-IMPURITY, VIRTUE-VICE.

dis''-so-lu'-tion. The act of separating into parts. COMMISSION-ABROGATION, COMPOSITION-RESOLUTION, CREATION-DESTRUCTION, LIFE-DEATH, LIQUEFACTION-VOLATILIZATION.

dis-solve'. To pass from a solid state to a fluid; **to break up.** APPEARANCE-DISAPPEARANCE, COMMISSION-ABROGATION, COMPOSITION-RESOLUTION, CREATION-DESTRUCTION, ENTITY-NONENTITY, LIQUEFACTION-VOLATILIZATION, SUBSTANCE-NULLITY.

dis-solv'-ing views. Gradually changing pictures. APPEARANCE-DISAPPEARANCE.

dis'-so-nance. Discord. HARMONY-DISCORD, MELODY-DISSONANCE, VARIANCE-ACCORD.

dis'-so-nant. Harsh in sound. MELODY-DISSONANCE.

dis-suade'. To give contrary advice. MOTIVE-DE-HORTATION.

dis-sua'-ded. Having purpose changed. MOTIVE-DE-HORTATION.

dis-sua'-ding. Changing purpose. MOTIVE-DEHORTA-TION.

dis-sua'-sion. The act of dissuading. MOTIVE-DE-HORTATION.

dis-sua'-sive. Tending to dissuade. MOTIVE-DEHOR-TATION.

dis-syl'-la-ble. A word of two syllables. LETTER.

dis-tain'. To discolor. CLEANNESS-FILTHINESS.

dis'-tal. Remote from the point of attachment. RE-MOTENESS-NEARNESS.

dis'-tance. Length in space. ADVANCE-RETROGRES-SION, REMOTENESS-NEARNESS, SUCCESS-FAILURE, TRANSCURSION-SHORTCOMING; **angular distance,** AN-GULARITY; **distance of time,** FUTURE-PAST, LASTING-NESS-TRANSIENTNESS; **keep at a distance,** POLITE-NESS-IMPOLITENESS; **keep one's distance,** CONCEIT-DIFFIDENCE, QUEST-EVASION, REGARD-DISRESPECT; **teach one his distance,** SELFRESPECT-HUMBLENESS.

dis'-tant. Remote. REMOTENESS-NEARNESS.

dis'-tant re-la'-tion. Remote connection. RELATION-SHIP.

dis'-tant-ly al-lied'. Remotely connected. RELATION-SHIP.

dis-taste'. Disrelish. DESIRE-DISTASTE.

dis-taste'-ful. Offensive to the taste. PLEASURABLE-NESS-PAINFULNESS.

dis-tem'-per. A disease. COLOR-ACHROMATISM, HEALTH-SICKNESS, PAINTING.

dis-tem'-per-a-ture. Indisposition. HEALTH-SICKNESS.

dis-tend'. To expand. ENLARGEMENT-DIMINUTION.

dis-tend'-ed. Expanded. ENLARGEMENT-DIMINUTION.

dis-ten'-tion. Inflation. ENLARGEMENT-DIMINUTION.

dis'-tich. A couplet. POETRY-PROSE.

dis-til'. To extract. CHEMISTRY, ENTRANCE-EXIT, LIQUEFACTION-VOLATILIZATION, RIVER-WIND.

dis''-til-la'-tion. Process of extraction. CHEMISTRY, ENTRANCE-EXIT, LIQUEFACTION-VOLATILIZATION.

dis-tilled'. Having impurities extracted. **Distilled water,** CHEMISTRY.

dis-tinct'. Clear to the mind or senses. ASSERTION-DENIAL, CLEARNESS-OBSCURITY, MANIFESTATION-LATENCY, SOUND-SILENCE, UNION-DISUNION, VISI-BILITY, VOCALIZATION-MUTENESS.

dis-tinc'-tion. The act of distinguishing. DIFFEREN-TIATION-INDISCRIMINATION, GENTILITY-DEMOCRACY, REPUTATION-DISCREDIT, VARIATION; **distinction without a difference,** EQUALITY-INEQUALITY.

dis-tinct'-ive. Characteristic. VARIATION; **distinctive feature,** UNIVERSALITY-PARTICULARITY.

dis-tinct'-ness. The state of being distinct. VISI-BILITY-INVISIBILITY, VOCALIZATION-MUTENESS.

distingué [F.] (dis-tan'-gê'). Distinguished. REPUTA-TION-DISCREDIT, SOCIETY-LUDICROUSNESS.

dis-tin'-guish. To discriminate. DIFFERENTIATION-INDISCRIMINATION, SIGHT-BLINDNESS; **distinguish by the name of,** NAME-MISNOMER.

dis-tin'-guish-a-ble. Able to be distinguished. VARI-ATION.

dis-tin'-guished. Eminent. REPUTATION-DISCREDIT, SUPREMACY-SUBORDINACY.

dis-tort'. To twist. BEAUTY-UGLINESS, DELINEA-TION-CARICATURE, INTERPRETATION-MISINTERPRE-TATION, PARALLELISM-INCLINATION, PROPORTION-DEFORMITY, TRUTHFULNESS-FALSEHOOD.

dis-tort'-ed. Twisted. PROPORTION-DEFORMITY.

dis-tor'-tion. The act of distorting. BEAUTY-UGLI-NESS, DELINEATION-CARICATURE, PARALLELISM-IN-CLINATION, PROPORTION-DEFORMITY, SIGHT-DIM-SIGHTEDNESS, TRUTHFULNESS-FALSEHOOD.

dis-tract'-ed. Bewildered. EXCITATION, SANENESS-LUNACY.

dis-trac'-tion. Excitement. EXCITABILITY-INEX-CITABILITY, HEED-DISREGARD; **love to distraction,** LOVE-HATE.

dis-train'. To take by distress. LITIGATION, PRICE-DISCOUNT, TAKING-RESTITUTION.

dis-traint'. Distress. TAKING-RESTITUTION.

dis-trait'. Absent-minded. HEED-DISREGARD.

dis-traught'. Bewildered. CERTAINTY-DOUBT, SANE-NESS-LUNACY.

dis-tress'. Great suffering. AFFLUENCE-PENURY, PLEASURABLENESS-PAINFULNESS, PLEASURE-PAIN, TAKING-RESTITUTION; **signal of distress,** ALARM.

dis-tressed'. Painfully agitated. AFFLUENCE-PEN-URY.

dis-tress'-ing. Painful. PLEASURABLENESS-PAINFUL-NESS.

dis-trib'-ute. To allot. ASSIGNMENT, GATHERING-SCATTERING, ORGANIZATION-DISORGANIZATION.

dis''-tri-bu'-tion. The act of distributing. GATHER-ING-SCATTERING.

dis-trib'-u-tive. Kind of pronoun. PRONOUN.

dis'-trict. A portion of territory. EXTENSION-DIS-TRICT.

dis-trust'. To doubt. CREDULOUSNESS-SKEPTICISM, FAITH-MISGIVING, SANGUINENESS-TIMIDITY.

dis-trust'-ful. Full of distrust. CREDULOUSNESS-SKEPTICISM.

dis-turb'. To agitate. AGITATION, EXCITATION, MUTATION-PERMANENCE, ORGANIZATION-DISORGAN-IZATION, PLEASURE-PAIN, PLEASURABLENESS-PAIN-FULNESS.

dis-turb'-ance. Disorder. AGITATION, ORGANIZA-TION-DISORGANIZATION, REGULARITY-IRREGULARITY, VARIANCE-ACCORD.

dis-turbed'. Disquieted. PLEASURE-PAIN.

dis-un'-ion. The state of being disunited. REGULAR-ITY-IRREGULARITY, UNION-DISUNION, VARIANCE-ACCORD.

dis''-u-nite'. To destroy union. UNION-DISUNION.

dis''-u-ni'-ted. Separated. GATHERING-SCATTERING.

dis-u'-ni-ty. Want of unity. UNION-DISUNION.

dis-u'-sage. Gradual neglect of use. HABIT-DESUE-TUDE.

dis-use'. To stop using. HABIT-DESUETUDE, USE-DISUSE.

dis-used'. Not used. HABIT-DESUETUDE.

dis-val'-ue. To undervalue. APPROVAL-DISAPPROVAL.

dis-val''-u-a'-tion. The state of being disvalued. AP-PROVAL-DISAPPROVAL.

ditch. A trench. ATTACK-DEFENSE, ENCLOSURE, GROOVE, GULF-PLAIN, WATERCOURSE-AIRPIPE.

ditch'-wa''-ter. The foul water in a ditch. CLEAN-NESS-FILTHINESS.

di''-tet-rag'-on-al. Twice tetragonal. **Ditetragonal pyramid,** MINERALOGY.

di'-the-ism. The belief in two coequal gods. ORTHO-DOXY-HETERODOXY.

dith'-y-ramb. A hymn in honor of Bacchus. MUSIC, POETRY-PROSE.

dith''-y-ram'-bic. Of the nature of the dithyramb. SANENESS-LUNACY.

dit'-to. The same thing. RECURRENCE; **say ditto to,** ASSENT-DISSENT.

dit'-ty. A little song. MUSIC.

di-ur'-nal. Daily. PERIODICITY-IRREGULARITY.

di''-u-tur'-nal. Lasting. LASTINGNESS-TRANSIENTNESS.

di''-u-tur'-ni-ty. Long duration. LASTINGNESS-TRAN-SIENTNESS.

di-van'. A council; a cushioned seat. COUNCIL, SCEPTER, SUSPENSION-SUPPORT, TRIBUNAL.

di-var'-i-cate. To spread apart. CONCENTRATION-RADIATION, DOUBLING-HALVING, VARIANCE.

di-var″-i-ca′-tion. The act of divaricating. CONCEN-TRATION-RADIATION, DOUBLING-HALVING.

dive. To plunge; den. CITY, SPRING-DIVE, TRAVEL-ING-NAVIGATION; **dive into,** INVESTIGATION-ANSWER.

di-vel′-li-cate. To tear in pieces. UNION-DISUNION.

di′-ver. One who dives. SPRING-DIVE.

di-verge′. To go in different directions. AIM-ABER-RATION, CONCENTRATION-RADIATION, DEVIATION.

di-ver′-gence. The act of diverging. AIM-ABERRA-TION, CONCENTRATION-RADIATION, HARMONY-DIS-CORD.

di-ver′-gen-cy. Divergence. CONCENTRATION-RADI-ATION, DEVIATION.

di-ver′-gent. Going farther apart. CONCENTRATION-RADIATION, HARMONY-DISCORD.

di-ver′-ging. Divergent. CONCENTRATION-RADI-ATION.

di′-vers. More than one. MULTIPLICITY-PAUCITY, UNIFORMITY-MULTIFORMITY, VARIATION; **divers colored,** VARIEGATION.

di-verse′. Different. VARIATION.

di-ver′-si-fied. Having various forms, etc. DEVI-ATION, LIKENESS-UNLIKENESS, RULE-MULTIFORM-ITY, UNIFORMITY-DIVERSITY, VARIATION.

di-ver′-si-fy. To make diverse. DEVIATION, MUTA-TION.

di-ver′-sion. Amusement. AIM-ABERRATION, ENTER-TAINMENT-WEARINESS, MUTATION.

di-ver′-si-ty. Variety. LIKENESS-UNLIKENESS, UNI-FORMITY - DIVERSITY, UNIFORMITY - MULTIFORMITY, VARIATION; **diversity of opinion,** ASSENT-DISSENT.

di-vert′. To turn aside. AIM-ABERRATION, ENTER-TAINMENT-WEARINESS, TRUTHFULNESS-FRAUD; **di-vert the mind,** HEED-DISREGARD.

di-vert′-ed. Turned aside. REFLECTION-VACANCY.

di-vert′-ing. Amusing. ENTERTAINMENT-WEARINESS.

divertissement [F.] (di-ver-tis-man′). A ballet between the acts of a play. ACTING, ENTERTAINMENT-WEARI-NESS.

Di′-ves. The rich man in the parable. [*Luke* xvi, 19.] AFFLUENCE-POVERTY.

di-vest′. To strip. DRESS-UNDRESS, TAKING-RESTI-TUTION; **divest oneself of,** COMMISSION-ABROGATION, KEEPING-RELINQUISHMENT.

di-vest′-ed. Stripped. DRESS-UNDRESS.

di-vest′-ment. A denuding. DRESS-UNDRESS, TAK-ING-RESTITUTION.

di-vide′. To sever into parts. ASSIGNMENT, CHOICE-NEUTRALITY, DOUBLING-HALVING, NUMBERING, ORGANIZATION-DISORGANIZATION, UNION-DISUNION, WHOLE-PART.

di-vi′-ded. Severed into parts. WHOLE-PART.

div′-i-dend. A share. ASSIGNMENT, NUMBER, WHOLE-PART.

divina particula auræ [L.] (di-vai′-na par-tic′-yu-la au′-ri). A gentle breeze. MIND-IMBECILITY.

div″-i-na′-tion. The act of divining. DEVOTION-MAGIC, HYPOTHESIS, PROPHECY.

di-vine′. Pertaining to God. DIVINITY, FAULTLESS-NESS-FAULTINESS, HYPOTHESIS, MINISTRY-LAITY, ORTHODOXY-HETERODOXY, PROPHECY, THEOLOGY; **divine right,** RULE-LICENSE; **divine service,** DEVO-TION-IDOLATRY.

di-vine′-ness. The quality of being divine. DIVINITY.

di-vi′-ning-rod″. A rod used in pretended discovery. DEVOTION-CHARM, SIGN.

di-vin′-i-ty. The quality of being divine. DIVINITY, THEOLOGY.

DIVINITY.

DIVINITY—*Appellations of God.*

Author of all things; Author of our being; Creator of all things; Deity; Divinity; El; *Ens Entium* [L.], Being of beings; God; God-head; Godship; God the Father; Jehovah; Lord; Omnipotence; Providence; the All-Holy; the All-Merciful; the All-Powerful; the All-Wise; the Almighty; the Creator; the Eternal; the First Cause; the Holy Trinity; the Infinite; the Maker; the Preserver; the Supreme Being; the Trinity; the Trinity in Unity; the Triune God; the Universal Intelligent Force.

DIVINITY—*Appellations of God the Son.*

Emmanuel; God the Son; Immanuel; Jesus Christ; the Advocate; the Anointed; the Bread of Life; the Good Shepherd; the Hypo-static Union; the Incarnation; the Intercessor; the Judge; the King of Glory; the King of kings and Lord of lords; the Lamb of God; the Life; the Light of the World; the Lord our Righteous-ness; the Mediator; the Messiah; the Prince of Peace; the Redeemer; the Saviour; the Son of David; the Son of God; the Son of Man; the Sun of Righteousness; the Truth; the Way; the Word.

DIVINITY—*Appellations of the Holy Spirit*

God the Holy Ghost; Paraclete; the Comforter; the Dove; the Holy Spirit; the Spirit of Truth.

DIVINITY—*Functions of God the Father.*

Creation. The act of God in bringing the universe into existence.

Dealings of Providence. The acts of God in relation to the human race.

Dispensations of Providence. The revelations of the mind and will of God to man.

Divine government. The direct control of God over man.

Preservation. The act of God in keeping or supporting creation.

Providence. The care, control, and guidance exercised by God over the universe, in all its parts and contents.

Thearchy. } The immediate sovereignty of God.
Theocracy. }

Visitations of Providence. Revelations of God to man.

Ways of Providence. The plan or line of action in the dealing of God with man.

DIVINITY—*Functions of God the Son.*

Atonement. The work of Christ in the reconciliation of God and man, making them at one.

Intercession. The mediation of Christ with God for the salvation of the redeemed.

Judgment. The final award or sentence of the human race.

Mediation. The interposition of Christ with the Father for the human race.

Propitiation. The work of Christ, as having justified the grace and removed the obstacles to man's salvation.

Redemption. Salvation from sin through the atonement of Christ.

Salvation. Deliverance from the penalty and power of sin.

DIVINITY—*Functions of God the Holy Spirit.*

Consolation. Alleviation or mitigation of sorrow.

Inspiration. Supernatural divine influence exerted upon the sacred teachers and writers by the Holy Spirit.

Regeneration. The being born again, so as to have the same spirit as Christ.

Sanctification. The work of the Holy Spirit whereby the believer is freed from sin and exalted to holiness of life.

Unction. Divine grace.

DIVINITY—*Attributes of Deity.*

Divineness. The possession of divine character or qualities.

Divinity. See DIVINENESS.

Eternity. Infinite existence.

Glory. The effulgence of the divine presence.

Holiness. Absolute moral purity, or perfect sanctity.

Immutability. The quality of being unchangeable.

Infinite goodness. Unbounded moral excellence.

Infinite justice. Everlasting conformity to the principles of right.

Infinite mercy. Disposition to treat even the worst offender with less severity than he deserves in strict justice.

Infinite power. The right, ability, and capacity to exercise boundless authority or control.

Infinite truth. Conformity to the ideal of God.

Infinite wisdom. Perfect insight into the divine law.

Infinity. The quality or state of being boundless, immeasurable, or perfect.

Majesty. The quality that inspires reverence or awe.

Omnipotence. Unlimited and universal power.

Omnipresence. The quality of being everywhere present at the same time.

Omniscience. Unlimited or infinite knowledge.

Sovereignty. The possession or exercise of supreme power.

Unity. The state of being indivisibly one.

DIVINITY—*Associated Nouns.*

Æon. Eon.
Avatar [Hind.]. Incarnation.
Deus ex machina.. A god from the machine.
Eon. Personification of a divine attribute.
Special Providence. Instance of God's care.

DIVINITY—*Verbs.*

Atone. To reconcile; make reparation.
Bless. To make happy; glorify.
Call. To summon divinely.
Create. To form out of nothing.
Elect. To separate as a special people or person.
Glorify. To make glorious.
Govern. To exercise authority.
Justify. To make just before the law.
Mediate. To intervene between two for reconciliation.
Ordain. To appoint; consecrate to the service of God.
Predestinate. Foreordain as brethren of Christ.
Preserve. Protect; keep in order.
Propitiate. To render favorable.
Redeem. Buy back from servitude to sin.
Sanctify. To make holy; free from sin.
Save. Make safe in union with Christ.
Uphold. To keep from sin.

DIVINITY—*Adjectives.*

Almighty; anointed; celestial; divine; ghostly; hallowed; heavenly; holy; hyperphysical, above physical laws; sacred; spiritual; superhuman; supernatural; theistic; theocratic; unearthly.

DIVINITY—*Adverbial Phrase.*

Jure divino [L.]. By divine right.

DIVINITY—*Phrases.*

Deus vindex cernit omnia [L.]. The avenging divinity sees all.
Dieu avec nous [F.]. God with us.
Dieu et mon droit [F.]. God and my right.
Dieu vous garde ! [F.] God guard you.
Dios que da la llaga, da la medicina [Sp.]. God who sends the wound sends the cure.
Domine, dirige nos [L.]. Lord, direct us.
En Dieu est ma fiance [F.] In God is my trust.
Notre Dame [F.]. Our Lady; the Blessed Virgin.

di-vis'-i-ble. Capable of being divided. NUMBER, UNION-DISUNION.

di-vi'-sion. The act of dividing. ASSIGNMENT, BELLIGERENT, DIVISION, NUMBERING, ORGANIZATION-DISORGANIZATION, PRESIDENT-MEMBER, UNION-DISUNION, VARIANCE-ACCORD, WHOLE-PART.

DIVISION.

Assortment. A class or group into which things are assorted.
Breed. A race or strain, especially of domestic animals, that maintains characteristics artificially acquired.
Caste. One of the classes into which society is divided in Hindustan.
Category. A comprehensive class.
Clan. A body of kindred having a class-name and tribal organization.
Class. A group with common characteristics.
Department. A part or portion as separate from a whole.
Division. One of the parts into which a thing has been divided.
Domain. A sphere of action or interest.
Family. A collection of persons forming a domestic household.
Gender. A distinction of words into classes as they agree in forms and syntax.
Genus. A group of animals or plants embracing one or more species.
Head. A set division of a discourse, sermon, or the like.
Kin. Persons of the same blood.
Kind. Essential or distinguishing quality; a genus.
Kit. An entire set of anything.
Order. A class of a common degree of excellence
Province. A sphere of knowledge or activity.
Race. A primary division of the human species.
Range. A series or chain.
Sect. A body of persons distinguished by peculiarities of faith from other bodies.
Section. A separate part or division.
Sept. A group of related persons claiming descent from a common ancestor.
Set. A number of persons or things associated in fact or in thought.
Sex. A division of the human species.

Sort. A number of persons or things characterized by similar qualities.
Species. A classificatory group of animals or plants.
Stamp. A kind or sort.
Suit. A group or series of things of like kind.
Tribe. A division, class, or distinct portion of people.
Type. A class or group that embodies particular characteristics.
Variety. A collection of various things in a group.

DIVISION—*Associated Nouns.*

Character. The combination of qualities distinguishing a person.
Denomination. A name.
Description. A group of characteristics.
Designation. A distinguishing mark.
Manner. Sort or kind.
Predicament. A class distinguished by definite marks.
Similarity. The quality or state of being similar.

DIVISION—*Figurative Nouns.*

Feather. Kind; class.
Kidney. Temperament.

DIVISION—*Scientific Term.*

Categorema. A category.

di-vi'-sor. A number that divides. NUMBER.
di-vorce'. The legal dissolution of the marriage relation. MATRIMONY-DIVORCE, UNION-DISUNION.
di-vorce' court. A court specially devoted to divorce cases. TRIBUNAL.
di-vor-cee'. A divorced woman. MATRIMONY-DIVORCE.
di-vorce'-ment. Divorce. MATRIMONY-DIVORCE.
di-vulge'. To disclose. EXPOSURE-HIDINGPLACE.
di-vul'-sion. The act of rending. UNION-DISUNION.
di-wa'-ni [Anglo-Ind.]. Coin. VALUES.
dixi [L.] (dix'-ai). I have said. ASSERTION-DENIAL.
Dix-ie. Popular American song. PATRIOTISM-TREASON.
diz'-en. To embellish. EMBELLISHMENT-DISFIGUREMENT.
diz'-zard. A blockhead. SAGE-FOOL.
diz'-zi-ness. Giddiness. SANENESS-LUNACY, SIGHT-DIMSIGHTEDNESS.
diz'-zy. Giddy. HEED-DISREGARD; **dizzy round**, REVOLUTION-EVOLUTION.
djer'-rid. A Persian javelin. WEAPON.
do. To accomplish. ACTION-PASSIVENESS, COMPLETION-NONCOMPLETION, CONDITION-SITUATION, CONTENTEDNESS-DISCONTENTMENT, CREATION-DESTRUCTION, ENOUGH, HARMONY-DISCORD, PETITION-EXPOSTULATION, SUCCESS-FAILURE, TRUTHFULNESS-FRAUD; **do a service**, USEFULNESS-USELESSNESS; **do as one pleases**, LIBERTY-SUBJECTION; **do as others do**, CONVENTIONALITY-UNCONVENTIONALITY; **do away with**, ADMISSION-EXPULSION, COMMISSION-ABROGATION, CREATION-DESTRUCTION; **do battle**, FIGHTING-CONCILIATION; **do business**, OCCUPATION; **do for**, CREATION-DESTRUCTION, LIFE-KILLING, SUCCESS-FAILURE; **do good**, CHARITABLENESS-MALEVOLENCE, GOODNESS-BADNESS; **do harm**, CHARITABLENESS-MALEVOLENCE, GOODNESS-BADNESS; **do honor to**, REPUTATION-DISCREDIT; **do into**, INTERPRETATION-MISINTERPRETATION; **do justice to**, APPROVAL-DISAPPROVAL, RIGHT-WRONG; **do like**, IMITATION-ORIGINALITY; **do little**, ACTIVITY-INDOLENCE; **do no harm to**, GOODNESS-BADNESS; **do nothing**, ACTION-PASSIVENESS, ACTIVITY-INDOLENCE; **do nothing but**, FREQUENCY-RARITY; **do one's bidding**, INSUBORDINATION-OBEDIENCE; **do one's office**, OBSERVANCE-NONOBSERVANCE; **do over**, COVER-LINING; **do the dirty work of**, PRESUMPTION-OBSEQUIOUSNESS; **do the work**, TOIL-RELAXATION; **do unto others as we would men should do unto us**, SELFISHNESS-UNSELFISHNESS; **do up**, RENOVATION-RELAPSE; **do without**, USE-DISUSE; **do wrong**, RIGHT-WRONG; **have to do with**, ACTION-PASSIVENESS, CONDUCT; **thing to do**, OCCUPATION.

docendo discimus [L.] (do-sen′-do dis′-si-mus). We learn by teaching. EDUCATION-LEARNING.

docent, quæ nocent [L.] (do′-sẹnt, quî no′-sent). Things that injure teach; we burn and learn. EDUCATION-LEARNING.

docere, pisces natare [L.] (do-se′-rî, pis′-sîz na-tê′-rî). To teach fish to swim. EDUCATION-MISTEACHING, EXCESS-LACK.

docet discit, qui [L.] (do′-set dis′-sit, quai). Who teaches learns. EDUCATION-LEARNING.

doc′-i-bil′-i-ty. Teachableness. READINESS-RELUCTANCE.

doc′-ile. Teachable. EDUCATION-LEARNING, READINESS-RELUCTANCE.

do-cil′-i-ty. The quality of being docile. EDUCATION-LEARNING, READINESS-RELUCTANCE.

dock. To shorten; an artificial basin for vessels; an enclosed space in court. DWELLER-HABITATION, LENGTH-SHORTNESS, STORE, TRIBUNAL, WORKSHOP.

docked. Shortened. ENTIRETY-DEFICIENCY.

dock′-et. A condensed statement. EVIDENCE-COUNTEREVIDENCE, MARK-OBLITERATION, SIGN.

dock′-yard. A yard for naval stores and timber. WORKSHOP.

doc′-tor. A physician; teacher. BETTERMENT-DETERIORATION, REMEDY-BANE, RENOVATION-RELAPSE, SCHOLAR-DUNCE; **after death the doctor,** OPPORTUNENESS-UNSUITABLENESS; **doctor accounts,** ACCOUNTS; **when doctors disagree,** RATIOCINATION-INSTINCT.

doc′-tri-naire′. A theorist. BRAWLER, CERTAINTY-DOUBT, DECISION-MISJUDGMENT, SCHOLAR-DUNCE, SOCIETY-AFFECTATION.

doc′-tri-nal. Pertaining to teaching. EDUCATION. MISTEACHING, FAITH-MISGIVING.

doc′-trine. That which is taught. FAITH-MISGIVING, KNOWLEDGE-IGNORANCE.

doc′-u-ment. A paper considered as evidence. EVIDENCE-COUNTEREVIDENCE, MARK-OBLITERATION.

doc″-u-ment′-a-ry ev′-i-dence. Evidence based on documents. EVIDENCE-COUNTEREVIDENCE.

do-dec″-a-he′-dron. A solid bounded by twelve plane faces. ANGULARITY.

dodge. To avoid. AIM-ABERRATION, CRAFT-ARTLESSNESS, INVESTIGATION-ANSWER, MOVEMENT-REST, QUEST-EVASION, VIBRATION.

Dodg′-er, Art′-ful. A character in Dickens's *Oliver Twist.* ROBBER, TRUTHFULNESS-FRAUD.

dodg′-ing. Avoiding. TRANSFER.

doe. A female deer. FAUNA-FLORA, MALE-FEMALE, SWIFTNESS-SLOWNESS.

do′-er. One who does. AGENT.

doff. To take off. DRESS-UNDRESS; **doff the cap,** POLITENESS-IMPOLITENESS.

dog. A domesticated carnivorous mammal. FAUNA-FLORA, GOOD MAN-BAD MAN, LEADING-FOLLOWING, MALE-FEMALE, QUEST-EVASION; **cast to the dogs,** CHOICE-REJECTION, COMMISSION-ABROGATION, CREATION - DESTRUCTION, KEEPING - RELINQUISHMENT, USE-DISUSE; **dog in the manger,** UNSELFISHNESS-SELFISHNESS; **dogs of war,** FIGHTING-CONCILIATION; **fire-dog,** OVEN-REFRIGERATOR; **go to the dogs,** AFFLUENCE-PENURY, CREATION-DESTRUCTION, SUCCESS-FAILURE, WELFARE-MISFORTUNE; **hair of the dog that bit you,** TEETOTALISM-INTEMPERANCE; **watchdog,** GUARD - PRISONER, SECURITY - INSECURITY, WARNING.

dog′-cart″. A two-wheeled one-horse carriage. CONVEYANCE-VESSEL.

dog″-cheap′. Absurdly cheap. COSTLINESS-CHEAPNESS.

dog′-days″. The sultry days of summer. HEAT-COLD.

doge. The chief magistrate of Venice and Genoa. CHIEF-UNDERLING.

dog′-ged. Sullenly stubborn. BIGOTRY-APOSTASY, BRAVERY-COWARDICE, FAVORITE-MOROSENESS.

dog′-ger. A kind of fishing-smack. CONVEYANCE-VESSEL.

dog′-gerel. Bad verse. EMBELLISHMENT-VULGARITY, POETRY-PROSE, SOCIETY-LUDICROUSNESS.

dog′-hole″. A place fit only for a dog. DWELLER-HABITATION.

dog′-Lat″-in. Mongrel Latin. WORD-NEOLOGY.

dog′-ma. A doctrine. FAITH-MISGIVING.

dog-mat′-ic. Inclined to make positive assertions. ASSERTION-DENIAL, BIGOTRY-APOSTASY, DECISION-MISJUDGMENT.

dog′-ma-tism. The quality of being dogmatic. ASSERTION-DENIAL, BIGOTRY-APOSTASY, CERTAINTY-DOUBT.

dog′-ma-tist. One who dogmatizes. ASSERTION-DENIAL, BIGOTRY-APOSTASY, BRAWLER, CERTAINTY-DOUBT.

dog′-ma-tize. To speak dogmatically. ASSERTION-DENIAL, DECISION-MISJUDGMENT.

dog′-ma-tiz″-er. One who dogmatizes. CERTAINTY-DOUBT.

dog's′-ear″. A turned down corner of a leaf in a book. PLICATURE.

dog′-sick″. Very sick. DESIRE-DISTASTE.

dog′-star″. The star Alpha of the constellation Canis Major. LUMINARY-SHADE.

dog′-trot″. A regular, easy trot. SWIFTNESS-SLOWNESS.

dog′-wea″-ry. Very weary. WEARINESS-REFRESHMENT.

doi′-ly. A small table napkin, named after its first maker. CLEANNESS-FILTHINESS.

do′-ing. Going on. OCCURRENCE-DESTINY; **up and doing,** ACTIVITY-INDOLENCE; **what one is doing,** OCCUPATION.

do′-ings. Conduct. ACTION-PASSIVENESS, OCCURRENCE-DESTINY.

doit. A small Dutch coin; a trifle. CONSEQUENCE-INSIGNIFICANCE, MONEY.

dolce far niente [It.] (dol′-chê far nî-en′-tê). Sweet doing nothing. ACTIVITY-INDOLENCE.

dol′-drums. Low spirits. FAVORITE-MOROSENESS, LIGHTHEARTEDNESS-DEJECTION.

dole. A gratuity. ASSIGNMENT, EXCESS-LACK, EXTRAVAGANCE-AVARICE, GIVING-RECEIVING, MAGNITUDE-SMALLNESS, PLEASURE-PAIN.

dole′-ful. Sorrowful. LIGHTHEARTEDNESS-DEJECTION.

doll. A toy baby. DELINEATION-CARICATURE, ENTERTAINMENT-WEARINESS, GREATNESS-LITTLENESS.

dol′-lar. A silver coin of the United States, equal to 100 cents. MONEY, VALUES.

do′-lor. Sorrow. PLEASURE-PAIN, SENSUALITY-SUFFERING.

dolore che ricordarsi del tempo felice nella miseria, nessun maggior [It.] (do-lo′-rê kê rî-cor-dar′-sî del têm′-po fê-lî′-chê nêl′-la mî-ser′-î-a, nês-sun′ madjî-or′). There is no greater sorrow than to recall happiness in misery. [Boethius, *De Consolatione Philosophiæ,* ii; Dante, *Inferno,* v, 121; Chaucer, *Troilus,* iii, 1626; Tennyson, *Locksley Hall.*] PLEASURE-PAIN.

dolorem, infandum renovare [L.] (do-lo′-rem, in-fan′-dum ren-o-vê′-rî). To revive unspeakable grief. [Virg. *Æneid,* ii, 3.] CONTENTEDNESS-REGRET.

dol″-o-rif′-ic. Causing grief. PLEASURABLENESS-PAINFULNESS.

dol′-o-rous. Causing sorrow PLEASURABLENESS-PAINFULNESS.

dol′-phin. A large fish of the open seas. OCEAN-LAND.

dolt. A dunce. SAGE-FOOL.

dolt′-ish. Stupid. SAGACITY-INCAPACITY.

do-main′. Province. DIVISION, EXTENSION-DISTRICT, PROPERTY.

dom-dan'-iel. A mythical submarine cave of Arabian magicians. HEAVEN-HELL.

dome. A cupola; shaft of a cavern. CONVEXITY-CONCAVITY, GEOLOGY, HEIGHT-LOWNESS.

domes'-day book. The record of the survey of England, made by William the Conqueror, in 1085–86. MARK-OBLITERATION, RECORD.

domes'-man. [Old Eng. Law.] A judge of an inferior court. JUDGE.

do-mes'-tic. Belonging to the house. CHIEF-UNDERLING, DOMESTICATION-AGRICULTURE, DWELLER-HABITATION, OUTSIDE-INSIDE, SOCIABILITY-PRIVACY; **domestic animals,** FAUNA-FLORA.

do-mes'-ti-cate. To render domestic. ESTABLISHMENT-REMOVAL; **domesticate animals,** DOMESTICATION-AGRICULTURE.

do-mes'-ti-ca''-ted. Made domestic. DWELLER-HABITATION, ESTABLISHMENT-REMOVAL.

do-mes''-ti-ca'-tion. The act of domesticating. DOMESTICATION-AGRICULTURE, ESTABLISHMENT-REMOVAL.

DOMESTICATION—AGRICULTURE.

Breeding. The process of bringing up and training the young.
Cicuration. The process of taming.
Domestication. The art of bringing under the control of man.
Domesticity. The state of being domestic.
Taming. Domesticating.

DOMESTICATION—*Denotations.*

Manège. The art of training horses.
Pisciculture. The art of raising fish artificially.
Veterinary art. The art of treating the diseases of cattle.

DOMESTICATION—*Nouns of Agent.*

Breeder. One who manages the breeding of animals.
Cowherd. One who tends cows as an occupation.
Cowkeeper. One who keeps cows.
Drover. One who drives animals.
Grazier. One who pastures cattle.
Neatherd. A cowkeeper or herdsman.
Shepherd. A keeper of sheep.
Trainer. One who trains animals or men.

DOMESTICATION—*Associated Nouns.*

Apiary. A place where bees are kept.
Aquarium. A tank, building or the like, for aquatic animals or plants.
Aviary. An enclosure in which live birds are kept.
Bear-pit. A place in a zoological garden in which bears are kept.
Bird-cage. A boxlike structure for keeping birds.
Cage. An enclosure for animals.
Cauf. A submerged perforated box for keeping fish.
Duck-pond. A pond for ducks.
Fishery. A place where fish and other aquatic animals may be captured.
Fish-pond. A pond for raising fish.
Hen-coop. A crib for confining fowls.
Menagery. An exhibition of wild animals.
Sheepfold. An enclosure where sheep are kept.
Vivarium. A place for keeping live animals.
Zoological garden. A park or garden in which animals are kept on exhibition.

DOMESTICATION—*Scientific Terms.*

Phthisozoics. The art of killing harmful animals.
Zoohygiantics. Science of curing animals.

DOMESTICATION—*Verbs.*

Acclimatize. To habituate to a new or foreign climate.
Break in. To reduce to discipline; to train.
Breed. To produce; to train.
Bridle. To put a bridle on.
Cage. To place in a cage.
Domesticate. To bring under the control of man.
Tame. To make tame.
Tend. To take care of.
Train. To bring to a standard by instruction and practise.

DOMESTICATION—*Adjectives.*

Bucolic. Pertaining to herdsmen or shepherds.
Domestic. Tame.
Home-made. Of domestic manufacture.
Pastoral. Pertaining to the life of shepherds and rustics.
Tame. Having lost native or ancestral wildness.

AGRICULTURE—ASSOCIATED NOUNS—*Continued.*

Vinery. A greenhouse for grapes.
Vineyard. A large collection of cultivated grape-vines.
Winter garden. An ornamental garden protected by glass from the cold of winter.

Agriculture. The science of cultivating the soil.
Agronomy. The art of cultivating the ground.
Cultivation. The working of ground for the purpose of raising crops.
Farming. The management of or labor on a farm.
Floriculture. The culture of flowers.
Gardening. The art of executing garden-work.
Geoponics. The art or science of cultivating the soil.
Horticulture. The art of cultivating gardens.
Husbandry. Agriculture.
Landscape gardening. Art of laying out grounds, planting trees, etc., to produce a picturesque effect
Spade husbandry. A system of cultivation in which spade-digging is used instead of plowing.
Tillage. The act or art of tilling.
Vintage. The cultivation of a vineyard.

AGRICULTURE—*Nouns of Agent.*

Agricultor. An agriculturist.
Agriculturist. One engaged in agriculture.
Backwoodsman. An inhabitant of the forest; a frontiersman.
Cultivator. One who cultivates.
Farmer. One who tills the soil.
Florist. One who cultivates flowers.
Gardener. One who makes or tends a garden.
Horticulturist. One who practises the art of cultivating gardens.
Husbandman. A cultivator or tiller of the soil.
Tiller of the soil. A husbandman.
Triptolemus. The inventor of the plow and patron of agriculture.
Wood-cutter. A person who cuts wood.
Yeoman. A man who owns and cultivates his own farm.

AGRICULTURE—*Associated Nouns.*

Abode. A habitation.
Arboretum. A botanical garden.
Avenue. A broad thoroughfare.
Bed. A level piece of ground in a garden.
Border. The edge of a garden.
Botanic garden. A garden for the culture of plants to illustrate the science of botany.
Conservatory. A greenhouse.
Farm. A tract of land enclosed for cultivation.
Field. Cleared land.
Flower garden. A garden in which flowers are cultivated
Garden. A piece of ground used for the cultivation of herbs or plants.
Georgics. A poem by Virgil on husbandry.
Grass-plat. A lawn.
Greenhouse. A house in which tender plants are sheltered and kept green through winter.
Hop-garden. A garden where hops are raised.
Hothouse. A house kept artificially warm for the production of flowers, fruits, etc.
Kitchen-garden. A vegetable garden.
Lawn. A piece of ground covered with grass, kept mown.
Market-garden. A garden in which vegetables and small fruits are cultivated for market.
Meadow. A tract of low and level grass-land.
Nursery. A place where trees, shrubs, etc., are raised for transplanting.
Orangery. A place for cultivating orange trees.
Orchard. A collection of fruit trees.
Ornamental garden. A garden used to adorn a place.
Park. A tract of land set apart for ornament or recreation.
Parterre. An ornamental arrangement of flower beds.
Pinetum. A plantation of pines.
Pinery. A pine forest or a hothouse for pineapples.
Plantation. A place that is planted.
Pleasure ground. Ground equipped for pleasure or recreation.
Seed-plot. A plot in which seeds are sown to raise plants for transplanting.
Shrubbery. A collection of shrubs.

DOMESTICATION—AGRICULTURE—*Continued.*

AGRICULTURE—*Verbs.*

Cultivate.   To raise by tillage.
Cut.   To remove by or as by a sharp edged tool.
Delve.   To turn over the ground, as with a spade.
Dibble.   To make holes in soil or plant with a dibble.
Dig.   To break up, as for cultivation.
Dress the ground.   To prepare the ground.
Farm.   To till the soil.
Garden.   To lay out or till a garden.
Harrow.   To work with a harrow.
Hoe.   To loosen, scrape, till, or spread with a hoe.
Lop and top.   To cut and bend the tops of small treees and shrubs.

Manure.   To apply fertilizing substance to.
Mow.   To cut off or down.
Plant.   To set in the ground for growth.
Plough.   Plow.
Plow.   To break up or turn up the surface of land with a plow.
Rake.   To scrape together or loosen with a rake.
Reap.   To cut down and gather in.
Sow.   To scatter over the earth.
Till.   To put and keep in order for the production of crops.
Till the soil.   To cultivate the soil.
Weed.   To pull up and root out weeds.

AGRICULTURE—*Adjectives.*

Agrarian.   Pertaining to land or its tenure.
Agrestic.   Rural.
Agriculture.   The cultivation of the soil for food-products.
Arable.   Capable of being plowed.
Country.   Pertaining to the country

Horticultural.   Pertaining to the culture of gardens.
Predial.   Consisting of land or farms.
Rural.   Pertaining or belonging to the country.
Rustic.   Pertaining to the country.

do″-mes-tic′-i-ty.   State of being domestic.   DOMESTICATION-AGRICULTURE, SOCIABILITY-PRIVACY.
dom′-i-cile.   Place of abode.   DWELLER - HABITATION.
dom′-i-ciled.   Provided with a home.   PRESENCE-ABSENCE.

dom″-i-cil′-i-a-ry.   Of a domicile.   DWELLER-HABITATION; **domiciliary visit,** INVESTIGATION-ANSWER.
dom″-i-cil′-i-a″-ted.   Provided with a domicile.   DWELLER-HABITATION.
dom′-i-nance.   Control; power.   DOMINANCE-IMPOTENCE.

DOMINANCE—IMPOTENCE.

Ascendancy.   Influence superior to all others.
Authority, etc.   Controlling influence.   See RULE.
Capability.   The state of having influence to direct or perform.   See MIGHT.
Dominance.   Governing influence.
Importance.   The quality of being of great influence.   See CONSEQUENCE.
Influence.   The exercising of control over others.
Interest.   Influence to produce favorable regard.
Predominance.}
Predominancy.}   Superiority over others in influence.
Preponderance.   The state of outweighing others in influence.
Pressure.   An impelling or constraining moral influence.
Prevalence.   Wide-spread and general influence.
Reign.   A dominant and prevalent influence.
Weight.   Practical influence.

DOMINANCE—*Associated Nouns.*

Auspices.   Favoring, protecting influence or guidance.
Footing.   Position or condition.
Leverage.   Increased power or advantage.
Patronage.   Favor, aid, protection, or care from a patron.
Play.   Room, condition, or situation for the exercise of powers or faculties.
Protection.   Preservation from harm or danger.
Purchase.   Any device that gives mechanical advantage; hence, any favoring act.   See SUSPENSION-SUPPORT.
Vantage-ground.   A favorable position.

DOMINANCE—*Figurative Expressions.*

Host in himself.}
Tower of strength.}   A powerful person.

DOMINANCE—*Verbs.*

Bear upon.   To use influence upon.
Be influential, etc.   See *Adjectives.*
Be listened to.   To have one's opinions regarded as influential.
Be recognized.   To be formally acknowledged as influential.
Be rife, etc.   See *Adjectives.*
Carry weight.   To have influence.
Dominate.   To rule over.
Gain a footing.}
Gain a hearing.}   Be listened to.
Gain full play.   Prevail.
Gain head.   To gain an influential advantage.
Gain the upper hand.}
Get the upper hand.}   To gain predominance.
Get full play.   Get a good chance.
Have a hold upon.   To exert influence upon.
Have full play.   To prevail.
Have influence, etc.   See *Nouns.*

Impotence, etc.   A lack of power or strength.   See MIGHT-IMPOTENCE.
Inertness, etc.   Lack of inherent power to act.   See VIGOR-INERTIA.
Irrelevancy, etc.   The condition of being not pertinent to the subject in question.   See CONNECTION-INDEPENDENCE.

IMPOTENCE—*Verb.*

Have no influence, etc.   See DOMINANCE.

IMPOTENCE—*Adjectives.*

Irrelevant, etc.   Not pertinent.   See CONNECTION-INDEPENDENCE.
Powerless, etc.   Lacking power.   See MIGHT-IMPOTENCE.
Unconducing.   Not tending to bring about as a result.
Unconducive.   Not contributing to an end.
Unconducting to.   Not leading to.
Uninfluential.   Not having the power of influence.

DOMINANCE—*Verbs—Continued.*

Have the upper hand.   To predominate.
Lead the dance.   To be ascendant.
Magnetize.   To draw to oneself by secret influence.
Make one's voice heard.   To gain recognition for one's ideas.
Outweigh.   To be of so great influence as to take everything else out of consideration.
Overbear.   To overpower.
Override.   To set aside by reason of greater influence.
Overweigh.   To exceed in influence.
Pervade.   To have influence through the whole of something.
Play a leading part in.   To be influentially concerned in.
Play a part.   To take part.
Play a part in.   To take part in.
Predominate.   To exercise governing influence.
Prevail.   To have effectual influence widely extended.
Pull the strings.   To exert a controlling influence without seeming to do so.
Rage.   To prevail without restraint.
Run through.   To overcome by power.
Set the fashion.   To influence others.
Spread like wild-fire.   To rage furiously.
Strike root in.   To have influence in.
Take hold.   To get control.
Take root.   To have an effect upon.
Take the lead.   To assume the direction of.
Tell.   To make one's influence count.
Throw one's weight into the scale.   To give one's influence towards some purpose.
Turn the scale.   To give the advantage to the other side.
Weigh.   To have influence.
Work upon.   To influence the passions.

Dominant. Exercising a ruling influence.
Hegemonical. Pertaining to leadership or supreme command.
Important, etc. Of great influence. See CONSEQUENCE.
Influential. Exercising control over others.
In the ascendant. Having influence superior to all others.
Predominance. Possessing superiority in influence.

Prevailing, etc. See *Verbs*.
Prevalent. Having widespread and effectual influence.
Rampant. Influential beyond all bounds.
Regnant. Influential as a ruler.
Rife. Abundant in number and quantity.
Weighty. Of great practical influence.

With telling effect. In a manner that influences.

Tel maître, tel valet [F.]. Like master, like man.

dom′-i-nant. Ruling. DOMINANCE-IMPOTENCE, MELODY-DISSONANCE, RULE-LICENSE.
dom′-i-nate. To control. DOMINANCE-IMPOTENCE, RULE-LICENSE.
dom″-i-na′-tion. The act of dominating. RULE-LICENSE.
Domine, dirige nos [L.] (dom′-i-nî, dir′-i-jî nos). Lord, direct us. [Motto of the city of London.] DIVINITY, ORDER.
dom″-i-neer′. To rule arbitrarily. HARSHNESS-MILD-NESS, PRESUMPTION-OBSEQUIOUSNESS, TYRANNY-ANARCHY.
dom″-i-neer′-ing. Overbearing. HARSHNESS-MILD-NESS, PRESUMPTION-OBSEQUIOUSNESS.
Domini, anno [L.] (dom′-i-nai, an′-no). In the year of the Lord. DURATION-NEVERNESS.
Do-min′-i-can. Of St. Dominic. MINISTRY-LAITY.
dom′-i-nie. A schoolmaster. INSTRUCTOR-PUPIL.
do-min′-ion. Supreme authority. RULE-LICENSE.
dom′-i-no. A mask. DRESS-UNDRESS, EXPOSURE-HIDINGPLACE.
dom′-i-noes. A game. ENTERTAINMENT-WEARINESS.
don. To put on. DRESS-UNDRESS, GENTILITY-DE-MOCRACY, SCHOLAR-DUNCE.
do-na′-tion. A gift. GIVING-RECEIVING, OUTLAY-INCOME.
don′-a-tive. A donation. GIVING-RECEIVING.
done. Completed. COMPLETION-NONCOMPLETION; **done for,** BETTERMENT-DETERIORATION, COMPLE-TION-NONCOMPLETION, SUCCESS-FAILURE; **done up,** BETTERMENT-DETERIORATION, COMPLETION-NON-COMPLETION, MIGHT-IMPOTENCE, WEARINESS-RE-FRESHMENT; **have done with,** DISCONTINUANCE-CON-TINUANCE, QUEST-ABANDONMENT, USE-DISUSE; **work done,** COMPLETION-NONCOMPLETION.
do-nee′. The receiver of a donation. GIVING-RE-CEIVING.
don′-jon. The chief tower of a castle. ATTACK-DE-FENSE, RELEASE-PRISON.
don′-key. An ass. CONVEYOR, SAGE-FOOL.
don′-na. Mistress. MALE-FEMALE.
Don′-ny-brook Fair. A famous annual fair in Ireland. REGULARITY-IRREGULARITY, VARIANCE-ACCORD.
dono, ex [L.] (do′-no, ex). By the gift. GIVING-RECEIVING.
do′-nor. One who gives a present. GIVING-RECEIV-ING.
don′-ship. The position of a don. GENTILITY-DEMOC-RACY.
don′-zel. A page. CHIEF-UNDERLING.
doo′-dle. A trifler. SAGE-FOOL.
doom. Destiny. BEGINNING-END, CREATION-DE-STRUCTION, DECISION-MISJUDGMENT, EXCULPATION-CONVICTION, LIFE-DEATH, OCCURRENCE-DESTINY, VOLITION-OBLIGATION; **doom sealed,** LIFE-DEATH, WELFARE-MISFORTUNE.
doomed. Destined to ruin or death. PLEASURE-PAIN.
dooms′-day″. The day of judgment. BEGINNING-END, FUTURE-PAST; **till doomsday,** ETERNITY-IN-STANTANEITY.
door. A passageway. APERTURE-CLOSURE, BEGINNING-END, BORDER, COVER-LINING, ENCLOSURE, EN-

TRANCE-EXIT, WAY; **at one's door,** REMOTENESS-NEARNESS; **beg from door to door,** PETITION-EXPOS-TULATION; **close the door upon,** RELEASE-RESTRAINT; **death's door,** LIFE-DEATH; **keep within doors,** MOVE-MENT-REST; **lie at one's door,** DUTY-DERELICTION; **open a door to,** CONTINGENCY; **open the door to,** AD-MISSION-EXPULSION, DIFFICULTY-FACILITY, LEAVE-PROHIBITION; **show the door to,** ADMISSION-EXPUL-SION, POLITENESS-IMPOLITENESS.
door′-keep″-er. One who guards the entrance. PER-FORATOR-STOPPER.
door′-way. The way of entrance and exit. APER-TURE-CLOSURE.
doq′-uet. Docket. EVIDENCE-COUNTEREVIDENCE, POSSIBILITY-IMPOSSIBILITY.
Do-ra′-do, El″. An imaginary country, rich in gold, so named by the Spaniards in the 16th century. AF-FLUENCE-PENURY.
Dor′-ic. Pertaining to a kind of architecture. **Doric capital,** ARCHITECTURE; **Doric order,** ARCHITECTURE.
dor′-mant. Torpid. ACTIVITY-INDOLENCE, MANI-FESTATION-LATENCY, VIGOR-INERTIA.
dor′-mer-win″-dow. Gable-window. ARCHITECTURE.
dormeuse [F.] (dor-muz′). A carriage adapted for sleeping. CONVEYANCE-VESSEL.
dormir debout, conte à [F.] (dor-mir′ de-bu′, con't a). Dull story. WITTINESS-DULNESS.
dor′-mi-to-ry. A building for students to study and sleep in. CONTENTS-RECEIVER.
dor′-mouse″. A small rodent. ACTIVITY-INDOLENCE.
dorp. A village. DWELLER-HABITATION.
dor′-sal. Of the back. ANTERIORITY-POSTERIORITY.
dor′-ser. A basket. CONTENTS-RECEIVER.
dor′-sum. The back. ANTERIORITY-POSTERIORITY, CONVEXITY-CONCAVITY.
dose. A portion of medicine. ASSIGNMENT, QUAN-TITY-MEASURE, REMEDY-BANE, WHOLE-PART.
dos′-ser. A basket; pannier. CONTENTS-RECEIVER.
dos′-sil. A plug. COVER-LINING, PERFORATOR-STOP-PER.
dot. A small round mark. EXTENSION-DISTRICT, MAGNITUDE-SMALLNESS, SIGN, VARIEGATION.
do′-tage. Senility. INFANCY-AGE, SAGACITY-INCA-PACITY, SANENESS-LUNACY.
do′-tard. One in his dotage. SAGE-FOOL.
do-ta′-tion. The act of making a dowry. GIVING-RECEIVING.
dote. To be silly. SAGACITY-INCAPACITY, SANENESS-LUNACY; **dote upon,** LOVE-HATE.
do′-ting. Excessively fond. SANENESS-LUNACY.
dot′-ting. Marking with a dot. MARK-OBLITERA-TION.
dou-an′-i-er. An officer of the French customs. JUDI-CATURE.
doub′-le. Anything twice as much. ADVANCE-RETRO-GRESSION, COMMUTATION-PERMUTATION, CRAFT-ART-LESSNESS, DOUBLING-HALVING, LIKENESS-UNLIKE-NESS, PLICATURE, UPRIGHTNESS-DISHONESTY; **double acrostic,** LETTER, WITTINESS-DULNESS; **double a point,** CIRCUITION; **double entry,** ACCOUNTS; **double meaning,** AMBIGUITY; **double reef topsails,** SECURITY-INSECURITY; **double sure,** CERTAINTY-

DOUBT; **double the fist**, CHARITABLENESS-MENACE; **double up**, MIGHT-IMPOTENCE; **in double quick time**, SWIFTNESS-SLOWNESS; **march in double time**, SWIFTNESS-SLOWNESS; **see double**, SIGHT-DIMSIGHTEDNESS, TEETOTALISM-INTEMPERANCE; **work double tides**, TOIL-RELAXATION.

doub'-le–bass. The largest instrument played with a bow. MUSICAL INSTRUMENTS.

doub'-led. Made as much again. DOUBLING-HALVING.

doub'-le–deal''-ing. Treachery. TRUTHFULNESS-FALSEHOOD, UPRIGHTNESS-DISHONESTY.

doub'-le–dis–tilled''. Twice distilled. VIGOR-INERTIA.

doub'-le–dyed''. Twice dyed. COLOR-ACHROMATISM.

doub'-le–edged''. Having two edges. VIGOR-INERTIA.

doub'-le en–ten'–dre. A word with a double meaning. CLEARNESS-AMBIGUITY, PURITY-IMPURITY.

doub'-le–faced''. Having two faces. DOUBLING-

HALVING, TRUTHFULNESS-FALSEHOOD, UPRIGHTNESS-DISHONESTY.

doub'-le–hand''-ed. Having two hands. TRUTHFULNESS-FALSEHOOD.

doub'-le–heart''-ed. False in heart. TRUTHFULNESS-FALSEHOOD.

doub'-le–mean''-ing. Having two meanings. AMBIGUITY.

doub'-le–mind''-ed. Unstable. DETERMINATION-VACILLATION, TRUTHFULNESS-FALSEHOOD.

doub'-le–shot''-ted. Loaded with twice the weight. VIGOR-INERTIA.

doub'-le–sight''. A seeing double. SIGHT-DIMSIGHTEDNESS.

doub'-let. A kind of garment. DRESS-UNDRESS.

doub'-le–tongued''. Having duplicity of speech. TRUTHFULNESS-FALSEHOOD, UPRIGHTNESS-DISHONESTY.

doub'-ling. Making as much again. DOUBLING-HALVING.

DOUBLING—HALVING.

Doubling. Making twice as much or as many.
Duplication. The act of folding twice.
Gemination. A repetition; a doubling.
Ingemination. Same as above.
Iteration. Going over again.
Reduplication. Repeating the same again and again.
Renewal. Beginning the same thing again, as if anew.

DOUBLING—*Verbs.*

Double. To increase by adding as much or as many.
Geminate. To bring forth in pairs; to double.
Redouble. To multiply; to increase by adding many times the original quantity.
Reduplicate. To augment greatly.
Renew. See *Nouns.*
Repeat. To say the same again; to recite from memory.

DOUBLING—*Adjectives.*

Bifacial. Having the opposite surfaces alike.
Bifarious. Arranged in two parallel rows.
Bifold. Twofold; of two kinds, degrees, etc.
Biform. Having two bodies, shapes, and forms.
Bilateral. Having two sides; relating to two sides, questions, parties.
Double. See *Verbs.*
Doubled. See *Verbs.*
Double-faced. Of two faces to perform the same work; deceitful; hypocritical.
Duplex. See *Verbs.*
Duplicate. See *Verbs.*
Second. Next to the first; subordinate; inferior in rank.
Twofold. Double.
Two-sided. Folded as to have two parts.

DOUBLING—*Adverbs.*

Again; as much again; in the second place; once more; over again; secondly; twice; twofold.

HALVING—ADJECTIVES—*Continued from Column 2.*

Cleft. Rent in two by force.
Cloven. Divided; pertaining to cloven feet.
Demi-⎫
Hemi-⎬Half.
Semi-⎭

Bifurcation. A forking or division into two parts.
Bipartition. Dividing into two parts, alike or unlike.
Bisection. Dividing into two equal parts.
Branching. Separating into two subordinate divisions.
Dichotomy. Distribution of genera into two species.
Dimidiation. The act of dividing into halves.
Divarication. Separation into two parts or branches.
Forking. Diverging into two branches.
Half. One of the two equal parts of a whole.
Halving. Separating into two equal parts.
Moiety. Dividing an estate, goods, or profits into two equal parts.
Ramification. A division into principal and subordinate branches.
Subdichotomy. Division into pairs.

HALVING—*Denotations.*

Fold. A part doubled over another.
Fork. A device consisting of a handle and two or more prongs.
Prong. The tine of a fork; branch of anything.

HALVING—*Verbs.*

Bifurcate. See *Nouns.*
Bisect. See *Nouns.*
Branch off. To diverge; deviate.
Branch out. To enlarge; expand.
Cleave. Divide by force; rive; break.
Cut in two. Separate into two, not necessarily equal.
Demidiate. See *Nouns.*
Dichotomize. See *Nouns.*
Divide. To apportion equally between two.
Divide with. To share equally with another.
Fork. To divide the main-rod; to branch off.
Go halves. See DIVIDE WITH.
Halve. To divide into equal or nearly equal parts; hence, to lessen.
Ramify. See *Nouns.*
Separate. To disconnect two; to sunder.

HALVING—*Adjectives.*

Biconjugate. Twice paired.
Bicuspid. Double pointed; like bicuspid teeth.
Bifid. Cleft to the middle.
Bifurcate. See sub *Noun.*
Bifurcous. Having two forks.
Bipartite. See *Nouns.*
Bisected. See *Nouns.*

(Continued on Column 1.)

doubt. Uncertainty. CERTAINTY-DOUBT, FAITH-MISGIVING, GODLINESS-DISBELIEF, LIGHT-DARKNESS, RHETORIC.

doubt'-ful. Subject to doubt. CERTAINTY-DOUBT, INVESTIGATION-ANSWER; **doubtful meaning**, CLEARNESS-OBSCURITY.

doubt'-ful-ness. A state of doubt. CERTAINTY-DOUBT.

doubt'-less. Confident. ASSENT-DISSENT, CERTAINTY-DOUBT, FAITH-MISGIVING.

dou''-ceur'. A small gift. GIVING-RECEIVING, RECOMPENSE-PUNITION.

douche. A current of water or vapor applied to some part of the body. WATER-AIR.

dough. A portion of soft moistened flour. HARDNESS-SOFTNESS, PULPINESS-OILINESS.

dough'-ty. Brave. BRAVERY-COWARDICE.

dough'-y. Like dough. HARDNESS-SOFTNESS.

dour. Hard. HARSHNESS-MILDNESS.

douse. To dip suddenly. RECOMPENSE-PUNITION, SPRING-DIVE, WATER-AIR.

dove. A pigeon; the symbol of the Holy Ghost. DIVINITY, INNOCENCE-GUILT; **roar like a sucking dove**, TURBULENCE-CALMNESS.

dove'-cote''. House for tame pigeons. DWELLER-HABITATION.

dove'-like. Like a dove. INNOCENCE-GUILT.

dove'-tail''. To join together with tenons shaped like a dove's spread tail. CROSSING, ENVIRONMENT-INTERPOSITION, HARMONY-DISCORD, INJECTION-EJECTION, UNION-DISUNION.

dove'-tailed''. Having the form of a dovetail joint. ANGULARITY.

dove'-tail''-ing. Making a dovetail joint. ENVIRONMENT-INTERPOSITION.

dow'-a-ger. A widow with dower. MALE-FEMALE, MATRIMONY-DIVORCE.

dow'-dy. A slovenly woman. CLEANNESS-FILTHINESS, TASTE-VULGARITY.

dow'-er. A widow's portion. PROPERTY.

dow'-er-less. Without dower. AFFLUENCE-PENURY.

down. To a lower level, place, etc. HEIGHT-LOWNESS; **bear down upon,** ATTACK-DEFENSE; **be down upon,** ATTACK-DEFENSE, HARSHNESS-MILDNESS; **come down,** ASCENT-DESCENT; **down in price,** COSTLINESS-CHEAPNESS; **down in the mouth,** CONTENTEDNESS-DISCONTENTMENT, LIGHTHEARTEDNESS-DEJECTION; **down on one's marrow-bones,** PRESUMPTION-OBSEQUIOUSNESS; **get down,** ASCENT-DESCENT; **go down,** ASCENT-DESCENT, BETTERMENT-DETERIORATION; **go down like a stone,** SPRING-DIVE; **money down,** SETTLEMENT-DEFAULT; **take down,** ELEVATION-DEPRESSION, MARK-OBLITERATION, SELFRESPECT-HUMBLENESS.

down. The fine soft feathers of birds. HARDNESS-SOFTNESS, HEAVINESS-LIGHTNESS, SMOOTHNESS-ROUGHNESS; **bed of down,** SENSUALITY-SUFFERING, TOIL-RELAXATION.

down'-cast''. Directed to the ground. LIGHTHEARTEDNESS-DEJECTION; **downcast eyes,** SELFRESPECT-HUMBLENESS.

down'-fall''. A falling downward. ASCENT-DESCENT, CREATION-DESTRUCTION, SUCCESS-FAILURE, WELFARE-MISFORTUNE.

down'-fall'-en. Fallen. LIGHTHEARTEDNESS-DEJECTION.

down'-heart''-ed. With the heart cast down. LIGHTHEARTEDNESS-DEJECTION.

down'-hill''. Sloping. ASCENT-DESCENT, PARALLELISM-INCLINATION; **go down-hill,** BETTERMENT-DETERIORATION, WELFARE-MISFORTUNE.

down'-pour''. The act of pouring down. RIVER-WIND.

down'-right''. Straight down. CRAFT-ARTLESSNESS, MAGNITUDE-SMALLNESS, MANIFESTATION-LATENCY.

downs. Undulating land covered with turf. GULF-PLAIN.

down'-trod''-den. Trodden under foot. LIBERTY-SUBJECTION, REGARD-SCORN, REPUTATION-DISCREDIT, SUCCESS-FAILURE, YIELDING.

down'-wards. To a lower level. ASCENT-DESCENT, DEEPNESS-SHALLOWNESS.

down'-y. Like down. HARDNESS-SOFTNESS, SMOOTHNESS-ROUGHNESS.

dow'-ry. The property a wife brings to her husband. AFFLUENCE-PENURY, PROPERTY.

dowse. To immerse. IMPETUS-REACTION.

dox-ol'-o-gy. A hymn of praise to God. DEVOTION-IDOLATRY.

dox'y. [Slang.] A mistress. PURITY-RAKE.

doy'-ley. A napkin. CLEANNESS-FILTHINESS.

doze. A light sleep. ACTIVITY-INDOLENCE.

doz'-en. Twelve of a kind. FIVE-QUINQUESECTION.

do'-zy. Inclined to doze. ACTIVITY-INDOLENCE.

drab. A yellowish-gray color. GRAY-BROWN.

drab. A slattern. CLEANNESS-FILTHINESS, PURITY-RAKE.

drab'-ble. To draggle. CLEANNESS-FILTHINESS.

drachm. A unit of weight. HEAVINESS-LIGHTNESS.

Dra'-co. An Athenian archon, about 621 B. C., noted for severity. HARSHNESS-MILDNESS, MANAGER.

Dra-co'-ni-an. Of Draco. HARSHNESS-MILDNESS.

draff. Refuse from breweries. CLEANNESS-FILTHINESS.

draft [Sometimes **draught**]. The act of drawing, in any sense; that which is drawn; a current; depth to which a vessel sinks; a levy. BELLIGERENT, DEEPNESS-SHALLOWNESS, DELINEATION-CARICATURE, DESIGN, DIGEST, MONEY, MULTIPLICITY-PAUCITY, NUTRIMENT-EXCRETION, PAINTING, PUSH-PULL, RIVER-WIND; **draft off,** ESTABLISHMENT-REMOVAL, GATHERING-SCATTERING, TRANSFER.

draft'-horse''. A horse fit for heavy loads. CONVEYOR.

drafts'-man [Sometimes **draughtsman**]. One who makes plans. ARTIST.

drag. Anything which drags. CONVEYANCE-VESSEL, MOTIVE-CAPRICE, OBSTRUCTION-HELP, PUSH-PULL, RELEASE-PRISON, SWIFTNESS-SLOWNESS; **drag a chain,** LASTINGNESS-TRANSIENTNESS, LIBERTY-SUBJECTION, TOIL-RELAXATION; **drag before the republic,** PUBLICITY; **drag into,** COERCION, INCLUSION-OMISSION; **drag into open day,** PUBLICITY; **drag on,** LASTINGNESS-TRANSIENTNESS; **drag slow length,** ENTERTAINMENT-WEARINESS; **drag through mire,** REPUTATION-DISCREDIT; **drag towards,** ATTRACTION-REPULSION; **put on the drag,** SWIFTNESS-SLOWNESS.

drag'-gle. To drag on the ground. CLEANNESS-FILTHINESS.

drag'-gle-tail''. A bedraggled person. CLEANNESS-FILTHINESS.

drag'-gle-tailed''. Bedraggled. CLEANNESS-FILTHINESS.

drag'-net''. A net drawn at the bottom of the water. UNIVERSALITY-PARTICULARITY.

drag'-o-man. An interpreter for foreign travelers in the East. INTERPRETER.

drag'-on. A fabulous monster. CONVENTIONALITY-UNCONVENTIONALITY, FAVORITE-QUARRELSOMENESS, TURBULENCE-CALMNESS.

drag''-on-nade'. Persecution by the use of troops, after the fashion of Louis XIV. ATTACK-DEFENSE, RECOMPENSE-PUNITION.

drag-oon'. A British cavalryman. BELLIGERENT, CHARITABLENESS-MALEVOLENCE, COERCION, PRESUMPTION-OBSEQUIOUSNESS.

drain. To draw off gradually. ADMISSION-EXPULSION, CLEANNESS-FILTHINESS, DAMPNESS-DRYNESS, ENTRANCE-EXIT, EXTRAVAGANCE-AVARICE, PROVISION-WASTE, TAKING-RESTITUTION, WATERCOURSE-AIRPIPE; **drain into,** RIVER-WIND; **drain of resources,** EXCESS-LACK; **drain the cup,** NUTRIMENT-EXCRETION, TEETOTALISM-INTEMPERANCE; **drain the cup of misery,** PLEASURE-PAIN.

drain'-age. The act of draining. ADMISSION-EXPULSION, CLEANNESS-FILTHINESS, DAMPNESS-DRYNESS, ENTRANCE-EXIT.

drake. A male duck. MALE-FEMALE; **firedrake,** LUMINARY-SHADE.

dram. A drink of liquor; unit of weight. MEASURE, MOTIVE-CAPRICE, NUTRIMENT-EXCRETION, PUNGENCY; **dram-drinking,** TEETOTALISM-INTEMPERANCE.

dra'-ma. A composition suited to action on the stage. ACTING.

dra-mat'-ic. Of the drama. ACTING, POMP; **dramatic author,** ACTING; **dramatic poetry,** POETRY-PROSE.

dramatis personæ [L.] (dram'-a-tis per-so'-nî). The characters in a play. ACTING, AGENT, ASSOCIATION, HUMANITY.

dram'-a-tist. A writer of dramas. ACTING.

dram'-a-tur''-gy. The art of dramatic composition and representation. ACTING.

drame [F.] (dram). Drama. ACTING.

drame, comédie [F.] (dram, co-mê-dî'). Comedy drama. ACTING.

drap d'or [F.] (dra dor). Cloth of gold. EMBELLISHMENT-DISFIGUREMENT.

drape. To cover or clothe. DRESS-UNDRESS.

dra'-per-y. That with which anything is draped. DRESS-UNDRESS.

dras'-tic. Acting with vigor. VIGOR-INERTIA.

draught. See DRAFT.

draughts. The game of checkers. ENTERTAINMENT-WEARINESS.

draughts'-man. See DRAFTSMAN.

draw. To make move. DELINEATION-CARICATURE, GAIN-LOSS, INJECTION-EJECTION, MONEY, MOTIVE-CAPRICE, PAINTING, PUSH-PULL, TAKING-RESTITUTION; **draw a curtain**, LUMINARY-SHADE; **draw a parallel**, CONNECTION-INDEPENDENCE; **draw a picture**, ACCOUNT; **draw an inference**, DECISION-MISJUDGMENT; **draw and quarter**, RECOMPENSE-PUNITION; **draw aside**, AIM-ABERRATION; **draw back**, ADVANCE-RETROGRESSION; **draw breath**, ALLEVIATION-AGGRAVATION, EMOTION, WEARINESS-REFRESHMENT; **draw down**, CAUSE-EFFECT; **draw forth**, USE-DISUSE; **draw from**, OUTLAY-INCOME; **draw in**, ENLARGEMENT-DIMINUTION; **draw in one's horns**, BIGOTRY-APOSTASY, CONCEIT-DIFFIDENCE, SELFRESPECT-HUMBLENESS, YIELDING; **draw lots**, PURPOSE-LUCK; **draw near**, APPROACH-WITHDRAWAL, FUTURE-PAST; **draw off**, ADMISSION-EXPULSION, OBSTRUCTION-HELP; **draw off the attention**, HEED-DISREGARD; **draw on**, FUTURE-PAST, MOTIVE-CAPRICE, OCCURRENCE-DESTINY; **draw on futurity**, EARLINESS-LATENESS; **draw out**, DISCOVERY, EARLINESS-LATENESS, INJECTION-EJECTION, LASTINGNESS-TRANSIENTNESS, MANIFESTATION-LATENCY, TERSENESS-PROLIXITY; **draw over**, MOTIVE-CAPRICE; **draw profit**, GAIN-LOSS; **draw the line**, DIFFERENTIATION-INDISCRIMINATION; **draw the pen through**, MARK-OBLITERATION; **draw the sword**, ATTACK-DEFENSE, FIGHTING-CONCILIATION; **draw the teeth of**, MIGHT-IMPOTENCE; **draw the veil**, ENLIGHTENMENT-SECRECY; **draw together**, ANTAGONISM-CONCURRENCE, GATHERING-SCATTERING; **draw towards**, ATTRACTION-REPULSION; **draw up**, MOVEMENT-REST, REGULARITY-IRREGULARITY, WRITING-PRINTING; **draw up a statement**, ACCOUNT; **draw upon**, MONEY.

draw'-back". A hindrance. FAULTLESSNESS-FAULTINESS, GOOD-EVIL, OBSTRUCTION-HELP, PRICE-DISCOUNT.

draw'-bridge". A bridge that may be drawn. ESCAPE, WAY.

draw'-can-sir. A bully. BRAWLER. [From a character in *The Rehearsal*.]

draw-ee'. One on whom a bill of exchange is drawn. MONEY.

draw'-er. One who draws. ARTIST, CONTENTS-RECEIVER, MONEY; **drawer of water**, AGENT.

draw'-ers. An undergarment. DRESS-UNDRESS.

draw'-ing. Delineating. DELINEATION-CARICATURE, PAINTING, PUSH-PULL.

draw'-ing-room". A room to receive company in. GATHERING-SCATTERING, GREATNESS-LITTLENESS, SOCIETY-LUDICROUSNESS.

drawl. A slow monotonous utterance. ACTIVITY-INDOLENCE, LENGTH-SHORTNESS, SPEECH-INARTICULATENESS. SWIFTNESS-SLOWNESS,

drawn. Not decided. EQUALITY-INEQUALITY; **drawn battle**, COMPLETION-NONCOMPLETION, FIGHTING-CONCILIATION.

dray. A low cart for heavy loads. CONVEYANCE-VESSEL.

dray'-man. One who drives a dray. WAYFARER-SEAFARER.

dread. To fear greatly. SANGUINENESS-TIMIDITY.

dread'-ful. Causing dread. BRAVERY-COWARDICE, GOODNESS-BADNESS, LIGHTHEARTEDNESS-DEJECTION, PLEASURABLENESS-PAINFULNESS, SANGUINENESS-TIMIDITY.

dread'-ful-ly. In a dreadful way. MAGNITUDE-SMALLNESS.

dread'-less. Without dread. BRAVERY-COWARDICE.

dread'-nought". A kind of garment. DRESS-UNDRESS.

dream. To have a vision while asleep. ACTIVITY-INDOLENCE, FANCY, HEED-DISREGARD, REFLECTION-VACANCY, SUBSTANCE-NULLITY, TRUTH-ERROR; **dream of**, PURPOSE-LUCK, REFLECTION-VACANCY; **golden dream**, SANGUINENESS-HOPELESSNESS.

dream'-er. One who dreams. FANCY, SANENESS-MANIAC.

dream'-ing. Thinking in sleep; indulging in fancy. FANCY; **dreaming on other things**, HEED-DISREGARD.

dream'-y. Of dreams. ACTIVITY-INDOLENCE, HEED-DISREGARD, SUBSTANCE-NULLITY.

drear'-y. Causing sadness. LIGHTHEARTEDNESS-DEJECTION, PLEASURABLENESS-PAINFULNESS, SOLITUDE-COMPANY.

dredge. An apparatus for raising something from under water. ELEVATION-DEPRESSION, GATHERING-SCATTERING, INJECTION-EJECTION.

dreg'-gy. Full of dregs. CLEANNESS-FILTHINESS.

dregs. Sediment. CLEANNESS-FILTHINESS, INCREMENT-REMNANT, USEFULNESS-USELESSNESS; **dregs of the people**, GENTILITY-DEMOCRACY; **dregs of vice**, VIRTUE-VICE.

drench. To saturate. DAMPNESS-DRYNESS, EXCESS-LACK, NUTRIMENT-EXCRETION, RIVER-WIND, WATER-AIR; **drench with physic**, REMEDY-BANE.

drenched. Thoroughly wet. EXCESS-LACK.

drench'-ing. Wetting thoroughly. WATER-AIR.

drench'-ing-rain". A rain that saturates. RIVER-WIND.

dress. That which is used to cover the body. DRESS-UNDRESS, EMBELLISHMENT-DISFIGUREMENT, EQUALITY-INEQUALITY, HARMONY-DISCORD, POMP, PREPARATION-NONPREPARATION, RECOMPENSE-PUNITION, SOCIETY-LUDICROUSNESS; **dress the ground**, DOMESTICATION-AGRICULTURE; **dress to advantage**, EMBELLISHMENT-DISFIGUREMENT; **dress up**, DELINEATION-CARICATURE, PREPARATION-NONPREPARATION, TRUTHFULNESS-FALSEHOOD; **dress wounds**, REMEDY-BANE; **full dress**, EMBELLISHMENT-DISFIGUREMENT, POMP, SOCIETY-LUDICROUSNESS.

DRESS—UNDRESS.

Accouterment. Equipment in general; apparel; dress.

Apparel. Raiment; garb; clothing.

Array. Clothing for the body.

Attire. Dress or clothing; garments.

Canonicals, etc. The robes prescribed by canon to be worn by the clergy when they officiate, etc. See VESTMENTS.

Caparison. Decorative trappings, as for a horse; showy or sumptuous apparel.

Clothes. Articles of raiment worn by human beings.

Clothing. Dress in general; garments.

Costume. The garments, collectively, worn at one time.

Bareness, etc. The state of being bare. See *Adjectives*.

Decortication. The act of stripping off the bark, rind, hull, or outer coat.

Denudation. The act of stripping off covering or removing the surface.

Depilation. Act of pulling out or removing the hair.

Desquamation. The separation or shedding of the cuticle or epidermis in the form of flakes or scales.

Dishabille, etc. A loose, negligent dress, etc. See DRESS.

Divestment. The act of divesting or unclothing.

Excoriation. Act of excoriating or flaying, or state of being excoriated or stripped of skin.

DRESS—UNDRESS—*Continued.*

Covering, etc. Anything which serves to cover, etc. See COVER.
Drapery. Loosely hanging attire on figures in painting and sculpture.
Dress. That which is worn as a covering for the body; clothes collectively; the outer garment of a woman or child; elegant or fashionable attire.
Equipment. Whatever constitutes an outfit for some special purpose.
Garb. The complete dress of a person; especially, a characteristic dress.
Garment. An article of clothing.
Gear. Equipment; clothing.
Guise. The external appearance as produced by garb or costume.
Habiliment. An article of clothing.
Harness. The equipment put upon a draft-animal in order to attach it for work to a wheeled vehicle or the like.
Ice-wool. A kind of fabric for wear.
Investment. A covering; the act of investing.
Livery. A uniform worn by servants; the distinguishing dress of any organization.
Outfit. A fitting out or equipment.
Palliament. A dress; a robe.
Raiment. Wearing-apparel.
Regimentals. Military uniform.
Rigging. Dress.
Sable. Black dress, indicating mourning.
Slops. Cheap, ready-made clothing.
Suit. A set of things having individual use, but together constituting an outfit.
Things. Clothes, especially, outer garments.
Toggery. Togs collectively; clothes.
Togs. Articles of clothing.
Toilet. A person's actual dress or style of dress.
Toilette [F.]. Attire; dress.
Trappings. Ornamental housing or harness for a horse.
Traps. Small or portable articles for dress.
Trim. Proper fashion, or becoming ornament; costume; dress.
Trousseau [F.]. A bride's outfit.
Turn-out. That which is prominently brought forward or exhibited; hence, an equipage.
Uniform. A dress of uniform style and appearance, worn by persons belonging to some body, organization, etc., for distinguishing them as members of that body.
Vestment. An article of dress; clothing; a garment or robe of state or office.
Vesture. Garments; clothing.
Wardrobe. Entire outfit in garments of any one person.
Wearing apparel. Apparel designed for wear.

DRESS—*Denotations.*

Antigropelos. Water-proof leggings.
Apron. An article of dress made of cloth or leather to protect the front of a person's clothes.
Baby-linen. A baby's clothing.
Balmoral. A petticoat made of striped woolen stuff; an ankle-boot. [Balmoral, Scotland.]
Bearskin. A cap made of the skin of a bear.
Beaver. A hat made of beaver-fur.
Bedgown. A night-dress.
Berretta. A head-dress for men.
Bib. A cloth worn under the chin for cleanliness.
Billy-cock. A low-crowned felt hat.
Birrus. A woolen cap or hood.
Blouse. A working shirt or frock.
Blucher boot. A half-boot. [German general.]
Boa. A long fur worn by women.
Bodice. A close-fitting waist of a woman's dress.
Body clothes. Clothing for the body.
Bonnet. A woman's head-dress.
Boot. A covering for the foot and lower leg.
Bornouse. See BURNOOSE.
Breeches. A man's garment extending from the waist to the feet.
Brogue. A rude shoe of untanned hide.
Burnoose. A white woolen mantle with a hood.
Burnous. See BURNOOSE.
Busby. A tall fur cap, with or without a plume.
Buskin. A shoe reaching half way to the knee, worn in tragedy.
Bustle. A pad or frame worn by women on the back below the waist.
Caftan. An Arab and Turkish undercoat.
Calash. A woman's hood having hoops like a calash-top.
Calico. Cotton cloth with a figured design printed on one side. [Calicut, India.]

Exfoliation. The scaling off of a bone, a rock, a mineral, etc.; the state of being exfoliated.
Molting. The act of casting, as the hair, skin, feathers, or the like.
Nudation. The act of stripping, or making bare or naked.
Nudity. The quality of state or being nude; nakedness.
Taking off, etc. Removing; divesting, etc. See *Verbs.*
Undress. A loose, negligent dress.

UNDRESS—*Verbs.*

Bare. Lay bare; uncover; strip.
Cast off. Throw off; shed in process of growth.
Cast the skin. Shed the skin.
Decorticate. Strip off the bark or outer cover of; peel.
Denude. Make naked.
Dismantle. Strip of furniture, equipments, or defenses; divest.
Disrobe, etc. Unclothe; undress; strip. See DRESS.
Divest. Strip, as of clothes.
Doff. Take off, as a hat or cloak; strip off.
Excoriate. Strip off the skin or covering of; abrade.
Exfoliate. Remove scales, flakes, etc., from; come off in scales or flakes.
Expose. Lay bare or open.
Flay. Strip off the skin from; skin.
Lay open. Uncover; expose; reveal.
Mew. Molt.
Molt. Cast off, as hair, feathers, etc.; shed the outside integument or its appendages.
Pare. Cut the outside part from apples and the like.
Peel. Strip off the bark or skin of trees, peaches, and the like.
Put off. Lay aside; discard, as a robe.
Scalp. Tear or remove the scalp from; hence, to remove the covering or top of anything.
Skin. Strip or peel the skin from.
Strip. Pull off the covering from; denude; remove one's clothing; undress.
Take off. Remove, as from the surface or outside.
Uncoif. Deprive of the coif or cap.
Uncover, etc. Take the cover from; divest of the hat or cap. etc. See COVER.
Undress. Divest of clothes; strip; disrobe.

UNDRESS—*Adjectives.*

Bald. Destitute of hair or natural clothing.
Bald as a coot. Figurative for very bald, the common coot having a bald forehead.
Bare. Devoid of covering or dress; naked.
Bare as the back of one's hand. Figurative for bare.
Barefoot. With feet bare.
Callow. Not yet feathered out; unfledged; hairless.
Divested. Stripped, as of clothes.
Exposed. Laid bare or open.
Hairless. Without hair; bald.
In a state of nature. Naked as when born.
In birthday suit. Nude.
In buff. Naked.
In dishabille. Having on a loose, negligent dress.
In native buff. Naked as when born.
In nature's garb. Naked.
In puris naturalibus [L]. Quite naked.
Leafless. Having no leafage.
Naked. Having no clothes on; bare; stripped.
Napless Made without a nap; threadbare.
Nude. Destitute of clothing or covering; naked.
Out at elbows. With coat worn through at the elbows; shabby.
Ragged. Worn out; wearing frayed or shabby garments.
Roofless. Having no roof; destitute of shelter.
Stark naked. Wholly naked; quite bare.
Threadbare. Worn so that the threads show; clad in garments worn so that the threads show.
Undraped. Stripped of drapery; uncovered.
Undressed. Divested of clothes; stripped; disrobed.
With nothing on. Naked; nude; stripped.

DRESS—DENOTATIONS—*Continued.*

Cambric. A fine white linen fabric.
Camisole [F.]. A short night-dress.
Cap. A covering for the head.
Cape. A sleeveless garment worn over the shoulders.
Capote. A hooded coat or cloak.
Cardinal. A short hooded cloak.
Cashmere. A fine, soft woolen dress fabric.
Casque. A helmet.

DRESS—Denotations—*Continued*.

Cassock. A close-fitting priests' garment.
Castor. Hat or cap.
Chapeau [F.]. A hat.
Chemise. A woman's undergarment.
Chignon [F.]. A roll of hair worn on the back of the head by women.
Chlamys. A loose outer garment worn by the ancient Greeks.
Cloak. A loose outer garment for men or women.
Clog. A shoe with thick wooden sole and heel.
Coat. An outer garment for the upper part of the body.
Coif. Any close-fitting cap or head-dress.
Coiffure [F.]. Head-dress.
Collar. A band worn around the throat.
Comforter. A long woolen scarf.
Corsage. The waist of a woman's dress.
Corselet. The complete armor of a soldier.
Corset. A close-fitting bodice stiffened by strips of steel or whale-bone, worn for the purpose of giving shape to the figure.
Cravat. A neckcloth. [Croats.]
Crinoline. A hoop-skirt.
Crown. A decorative circlet for the head. See CIRCLE.
Csako. A stiff high military cap.
Cuff. A band worn about the wrist.
Dishabille. A loose-fitting dress.
Domino. A loose flowing hooded garment worn by priests.
Doublet. A close-fitting outer garment belted at the waist.
Drawers. An undergarment.
Dreadnought. A garment made of heavy cloth.
Dress coat. A coat for evening wear.
Dressing-gown. A loose gown worn while dressing.
Faille. A soft silk.
Farthingale. A hoop-skirt of the 16th and 17th centuries.
Ferrandine. A stuff of silk and wool.
Fez. A brimless felt cap worn by the Turks.
Filibeg. A kilt.
Finery, etc. Ornamental dress. See EMBELLISHMENT.
Forage cap. A small low cap worn by soldiers.
Foreskirt. The front part of a skirt.
Foresleeve. The sleeve below the elbow.
Frock. The outer garment of a woman.
Frock coat. A coat for men's wear having long skirts.
Front. False hair for the fore part of the head.
Full dress, etc. The dress required to be worn at formal social gatherings. See POMP.
Gabardine. A long loose cloak.
Gaiter. A cloth or leather covering for the ankle and lower leg.
Galligaskins. Long loose hose worn in the 16th century.
Galoche. A wooden shoe.
Gamache [F.]. A high boot.
Gambado. A bootlike stirrup.
Garniture. Ornamental clothing.
Gaskins. Packing of hemp or the like.
Gauntlet. A glove with a long wrist-extension.
Girdle. A belt worn about the waist. See CIRCLE.
Glove. A covering for the hand.
Goloshes. Overshoes.
Gown. A woman's dress or outer garment.
Greatcoat. An overcoat.
Greave. Armor for the upper leg.
Habit. An outer garment or garments.
Haik. An Oriental outside garment.
Handkerchief. A piece of cloth for wiping the face or nose.
Hat. A covering for the head.
Head.
Head-dress. } Something worn on the head.
Head-gear.
Helmet. Armor for the head.
Hessian boot. High boots worn early in the 19th century.
High-low. A laced boot ankle-high.
Hood. A head cover.
Horse-cloth. A cloth to cover a horse.
Hose. A covering for the foot and lower leg.
Hosiery. See HOSE.
Houppelande [F.]. A greatcoat.
Housing. A leather cover attached to a horse-collar.
Huke. An outer garment worn in the middle ages.
Inexpressibles. Trousers.
Jack-boot. A heavy top-boot reaching above the knee.
Jacket. A short garment for the upper part of the body.
Jerkin. A waistcoat.
Jersey. A thick knit shirt.
Jupe. A sleeveless jacket worn over the armor in the 14th century.
Képi [F.]. A military cap.

Kerchief. A covering for the neck; a handkerchief.
Kilt. The skirt worn by the Scotch Highlanders.
Kirtle. A garment with a skirt.
Knickerbockers. Wide knee-breeches gathered below the knee. [Dutch New Yorkers.]
Layette [F.]. Baby-linen.
Legging. A covering for the lower leg.
Linen. Fabric woven from the fibers of flax; clothing made of linen.
Mackintosh. A water-proof outer garment. [Man's name.]
Mantelet. A small mantle worn by women.
Mantilla. A lady's light cloak or cape.
Mantle. A loose garment without sleeves worn over the other garments.
Mantua. A woman's cloak or gown. [Place name.]
Mask. A covering for the face.
Millinery. Women's bonnets, hats, and the like. [Milan, Italy.]
Mitten. A covering for the hand.
Mobcap. A woman's or girl's cap.
Moccasin. A shoe made of soft leather, worn by North American Indians.
Morion. An open helmet.
Morning dress. Dress suitable for the morning hours.
Mourning. Clothing suitable to be worn as a manifestation of grief.
Muff. A covering into which the hands are thrust from opposite ends.
Muffler. A scarf worn about the throat.
Mufti. A citizen's dress when worn by a naval or military officer.
Murrion. An open helmet.
Neckcloth. A covering for the neck.
Neckerchief. A kerchief for the neck.
Négligé [F.]. Undress.
Nightcap. A covering for the head, worn during sleep.
Nightgown. }
Nightshirt. } A night-dress.
Old clothes. Clothes the worse for wear.
Overalls. High loose trousers worn over the clothing.
Overcoat. An outer coat worn over the other clothing.
Paletot [F.]. An overcoat.
Pall. A cover thrown over a coffin.
Panier [F.]. A hoop-petticoat.
Pantaloons. Trousers.
Patten. A thick-soled wooden shoe.
P-coat. }
Pea-coat. } A pea-jacket.
Pea-jacket. A thick coat worn by sailors.
Pelerine. A woman's cape.
Pelisse [F.]. An outer garment for men or women.
Pelt. An undressed fur-skin.
Periwig. A head-dress of false hair.
Peruke. A wig.
Petticoat. A woman's undergarment.
Philibeg. A kilt.
Pickelhaube [G.]. A helmet.
Pinafore. A sleeveless apron.
Plaid. A woolen garment worn by Scotch Highlanders of both sexes.
Pocket-handkerchief. A handkerchief.
Poncho. A blanket worn by Spanish Americans as an outer garment.
Pump. A low shoe with a thin sole.
Rags. Wornout clothes.
Robe. A long, loose, flowing garment worn over the other dress.
Roquelaure [F.]. A cloak reaching a little below the knees.
Ruff. A high fluted collar worn in the 16th century by both men and women.
Sandal. A shoe consisting only of sole and heel held to the foot by cords.
Sark. A shirt or chemise.
Scarf. A long knitted sash worn around the neck.
Scullcap. A cap closely fitting the skull.
Shako. A military cap.
Shawl. A wrap worn on the upper part of the body.
Shift. A chemise.
Shirt. A garment for the arms and upper part of the body.
Shoe. A covering for the foot and ankle.
Shooting coat. A canvas coat worn by gunners.
Skirts. That part of the dress that hangs below the waist.
Skullcap. A tight-fitting cap.
Sleeve. The part of a garment that covers the arm.
Slipper. A low, light shoe.
Small-clothes. A man's undergarments for the hips and thighs.
Smalls. Small-clothes.
Smock. A woman's undergarment.

DRESS—Denotations—*Continued.*

Smockfrock. A frock resembling a shirt worn over the other clothes, by field-laborers in England.
Snood. A fillet for binding the hair.
Snow-shoe. A broad long frame attached to the shoe, for walking on snow.
Sock. A half hose.
Sontag. A woman's knitted cape.
Spatter-dash. A legging reaching to the knee.
Spencer. A short jacket for men and women.
Stays. Corsets.
Stock. A band worn around the neck.
Stocking. A covering for the foot and lower leg.
Stomacher. An article of dress for the breast and stomach worn by men and women in the 15th century.
Surcoat. An outer coat or garment.
Surtout [F.]. An overcoat
Swaddling cloth. A cloth used to bandage an infant.
Tabard. A tunic or mantle.
Tablier. An apron-like part of a woman's dress.
Taffeta. A silk and linen, or silk and wool fabric.
Taglioni. A style of overcoat.
Tail-coat. A coat with tails.
Tailoring. Articles of dress.
Taj. A head-dress. [Persian.]
Talaria. Winged boots.
Talma. A long cape or cloak.
Tam-o'-shanter. A tight-fitting woolen cap.
Tarboosh. A red cap with a tassel worn in Moslem countries.
Tarlatan. A fine muslin.
Tatters. Wornout clothes.
Theatrical properties. Dramatic costumes

Tie. A band worn around the neck.
Tights. A skin-fitting garment.
Tile. A high, stiff silk hat.
Tippet. A scarflike garment for the neck.
Toga. A loose outer garment worn by the Romans.
Top-boot. A boot with a high top.
Trousers. A man's garment covering the body from the waist to the feet.
Trowsers. See TROUSERS.
Trunk hose. A breeches extending from the waist to the middle of the thigh.
Tucker. A lace garment covering the neck and shoulders.
Tunic. A body-garment with short sleeves and reaching about to the knees, worn by the Romans.
Turban. A head-dress worn in Eastern countries.
Ulster. A very long, loose overcoat.
Under-clothing. Clothing worn next to the skin.
Under waistcoat. A waistcoat worn over the shirt.
Undress. Ordinary attire.
Veil. A covering of thin material for the face.
Vest. A jacket without sleeves.
Waistcoat. A sleeveless garment worn under the coat.
Waterproof. A heavy outer garment, impervious to water.
Weeds. Mourning garments.
Wellington boot. A kind of long-legged boot.
Wide-awake. A broad-brimmed, low-crowned felt hat.
Wig. A false hair covering for the head.
Wimple. A covering for the chin.
Wrapper. A loose flowing garment.
Wraprascal. A coarse upper coat, or overcoat.
Wristband. A band worn around the wrist.

DRESS—*Nouns of Agent.*

Breeches maker. One who makes breeches.
Clothier. One who makes or sells cloths or clothing.
Cobbler. One who cobbles or mends boots and shoes.
Cordwainer. A worker in cordwain; a shoemaker.
Costumier [F.]. One who deals in costumes or fancy dresses
Dressmaker. One who makes dresses.
Habit maker. One who makes habits or dresses.
Hatter. One who manufactures or deals in hats.
Hosier. One who deals in hose.

Milliner. A person employed in making, trimming, or selling bonnets, women's hats, and the like; in England one who furnishes complete costumes for women.
Sempstress. A seamstress; a woman whose occupation is sewing.
Shoemaker. One who manufactures boots and shoes.
Snip. A tailor.
Tailor. One who makes to order or repairs men's outer garments, or makes cloaks, gowns, etc., for women.

DRESS—*Verbs.*

Accouter. Furnish with accouterments; array; dress; equip.
Apparel. Cover, clothe, or invest with attire.
Array. Clothe; dress.
Attire. Dress; array; adorn.
Caparison. Clothe richly.
Circumvest. Cover round, as with a garment.
Clothe. Cover with clothing; dress.
Cover, etc. Overspread or overlay with something so as to protect or hide, etc. See COVER.
Deck, etc. Array; clothe or dress elegantly, etc. See EMBELLISHMENT.
Dight. Dress; adorn; equip.
Don. Put on.
Drape. Cover or clothe, as with hanging cloth.
Dress. Attire suitably; clothe; array
Enclothe. To clothe.
Enrobe. Invest with a robe; attire.
Envelop. Put a covering about; wrap up or in.
Enwrap. Enfold in a wrapper; wrap up.
Equip. Dress or attire, as for a special purpose.
Fit out. Furnish or equip.
Fold up. Cover or wrap up.
Harness. Put harness on; attach by means of harness.
Huddle on. Put on hastily or roughly.
Invest. Put a covering or garment upon; clothe.
Involve. Inwrap; infold.
Inwrap. Surround or cover by wrapping; infold.
Lap. Wrap around; infold.
Lap up. Involve; infold.

Mantle. Cover with a mantle; overspread the surface of something.
Muffle up. Wrap up so as to conceal.
Overlap. Lie or be folded partly upon.
Perk. Make trim or smart.
Put on. Invest oneself with, as clothes.
Rig. Dress; equip; clothe, especially in an odd or fanciful manner
Robe. Put a robe or robes upon; array.
Roll up in. Infold; inwrap.
Sheathe. Put into a sheath; cover with a protecting substance.
Slip on. Put on in haste or loosely.
Swaddle. Bind as with a bandage; bind or wrap tightly with clothes.
Swathe. Bind with a swathe, band, bandage, or rollers.
Vest. Clothe with a vestment; dress.
Wear. Carry on the person, as a garment.
Wrap. Cover by winding or folding; infold.
Wrap up. Cover; infold.

DRESS—*Adjectives.*

Chaussé [F.]. Having shoes on; booted.
Clad. Dressed; covered with clothing.
Costume [F.]. Dressed up.
Dight. Dressed; arrayed; adorned.
Dighted. Same as DIGHT.
En grande tenue, etc. [F.]. In full dress. See POMP.
Habited. Clothed; dressed.
Invested, etc. Covered with a garment; clothed. See *Versb.*
Sartorial. Of or pertaining to a tailor or his work
Shod. Furnished with a shoe or shoes.

---

dress coat. A coat for full-dress occasions. DRESS-UNDRESS.
dress'-er. A kitchen table. SUSPENSION-SUPPORT.
dress'-er. One who dresses wounds. REMEDY-BANE.
dress'-ing. [Colloq.] A flogging. APPROVAL-DISAPPROVAL.
dress'-ing-gown". A gown worn while dressing. DRESS-UNDRESS.

drib'-ble. To fall in drops. ENTRANCE-EXIT, RIVER-WIND.
drib'-let. Small part of anything. MAGNITUDE-SMALLNESS.
drib'-lets. Small parts of anything. WHOLE-PART.
drib'-bling. Falling in drops. ENTRANCE-EXIT.
dried. Made dry. DAMPNESS-DRYNESS.
drift. To float or be driven along. AIM-ABERRATION,

APPROACH-WITHDRAWAL, GATHERING-SCATTERING, INCLINATION, MEANING-JARGON, MOVEMENT-REST, PURPOSE-LUCK, RIVER-WIND, TRANSFER, TRAVELING-NAVIGATION; **snow drift,** GATHERING-SCATTERING, HEAT-COLD.

drift'-ed. Driven at random. TRANSFER.

drift'-less. Without direction. PURPOSE-LUCK.

drill. A tool for cutting; the act of teaching by repetition. APERTURE-CLOSURE, EDUCATION-MISTEACHING, PERFORATOR-STOPPER.

drink. Any liquid taken by swallowing. ADMISSION-EXPULSION, NUTRIMENT-EXCRETION, TEETOTALISM-INTEMPERANCE; **drink in,** NUTRIMENT-EXCRETION; **drink in learning,** EDUCATION-LEARNING; **drink one's full,** ENOUGH, NUTRIMENT-EXCRETION; **drink to,** POLITENESS-IMPOLITENESS, SOLEMNIZATION.

drink'-ing. The act of swallowing fluids. ADMISSION-EXPULSION, NUTRIMENT-EXCRETION; **drinking song,** POETRY-PROSE; **take to drinking,** TEETOTALISM-INTEMPERANCE.

drink'-ing-bout''. A season of drinking. MODERATION-SELFINDULGENCE.

drink'-mon''-ey. Money to buy drink. GIVING-RECEIVING.

drip. To fall in drops. RIVER-WIND.

drip'-ping. That which drips. DAMPNESS-DRYNESS, PULPINESS-OIL.

drive. To impel with force. COERCION, HURRY-LEISURE, IMPETUS-REACTION, MANAGEMENT, PUSH-PULL, TRAVELING-NAVIGATION; **drive a bargain,** EXCHANGE, EXTRAVAGANCE-AVARICE; **drive a coach and six through,** CONVENTIONALITY-UNCONVENTIONALITY, OBSERVANCE-NONOBSERVANCE; **drive at,** MEANING-JARGON, PURPOSE-LUCK; **drive dull care away,** LIGHTHEARTEDNESS-DEJECTION; **drive from,** ATTRACTION-REPULSION; **drive in,** INJECTION-EJECTION; **drive into a corner,** DIFFICULTY-FACILITY, LIBERTY-SUBJECTION, OBSTRUCTION-HELP, SUCCESS-FAILURE; **drive matters to an extremity,** DETERMINATION-VACILLATION; **drive one hand,** ATTACK-DEFENSE; **drive to despair,** SANGUINENESS-HOPELESSNESS; **drive to the last,** EARLINESS-LATENESS; **drive trade,** EXCHANGE, OCCUPATION.

driv'-el. Involuntary flow of spittle; twaddle. ADMISSION-EXPULSION, SAGACITY-INCAPACITY, SANENESS-LUNACY.

driv'-el-er. One who drivels. SAGE-FOOL, TALKATIVENESS-TACITURNITY.

driv'-el-ing. Letting spittle flow from the mouth. SAGACITY-INCAPACITY.

dri'-ver. One who drives. MANAGER, WAYFARER-SEAFARER.

dri'-ving-rain''. A rain of great force. RIVER-WIND.

driz'-zle. A light rain. RIVER-WIND.

droil. Drudgery. ACTIVITY-INDOLENCE.

droit, au bon [F.] (drwa, o bon·). Of good right. RIGHT-WRONG.

droit au travail [F.] (drwat o tra-vaiy'). Right of labor. DUENESS-UNDUENESS.

droit des gens [F.] (drwa de zhan·). Law of nations. LAW-LAWLESSNESS.

droit du plus fort [F.] (drwa dü plü for). The law of the stronger. COERCION.

drole. Game of cards. ENTERTAINMENT-WEARINESS.

drôle [F.] (drol). Droll. GOOD MAN-BAD MAN.

drôle de corps [F.] (drol de cor). A droll fellow. WAG.

droll. Comical. SOCIETY-LUDICROUSNESS.

droll'-er-y. Comical speech. ENTERTAINMENT-WEARINESS, SOCIETY-LUDICROUSNESS, WITTINESS-DULNESS.

droll'-ish. Somewhat droll. SOCIETY-LUDICROUSNESS.

drom'-e-da-ry. An Arabian camel. CONVEYER.

drone. A dull, monotonous sound. ACTIVITY-INDO-

LENCE, CRY-ULULATION, MELODY-DISSONANCE, SWIFTNESS-SLOWNESS.

dro'-nish. Like a drone. ACTIVITY-INDOLENCE.

dro'-ny. Dronish. ACTIVITY-INDOLENCE.

droop. A sinking down. ASCENT-DESCENT, BETTERMENT-DETERIORATION, HEALTH-SICKNESS, LIGHTHEARTEDNESS-DEJECTION, PLEASURE-PAIN, WEARINESS-REFRESHMENT.

droop'-ing. Bending downward. HEALTH-SICKNESS, STRENGTH-WEAKNESS, WEARINESS-REFRESHMENT; **drooping spirits,** LIGHTHEARTEDNESS-DEJECTION.

drop. To let fall in drops. ACTING, ADDITION-SUBTRACTION, ASCENT-DESCENT, CREATION-DESTRUCTION, KEEPING-RELEASING, MIGHT-IMPOTENCE, QUEST-ABANDONMENT, RECOMPENSE-SCOURGE, RIVER-WIND, ROUNDNESS, STRENGTH-WEAKNESS, TEETOTALISM-INTEMPERANCE, WEARINESS-REFRESHMENT; **drop a hint,** ENLIGHTENMENT-SECRECY; **drop all idea of,** QUEST-ABANDONMENT; **drop astern,** ADVANCE-RETROGRESSION; **drop by drop,** QUANTITY-MEASURE, WHOLE-PART; **drop dead,** LIFE-DEATH; **drop from the clouds,** EXPECTATION-SURPRISE; **drop in,** ARRIVAL-DEPARTURE, INJECTION-EJECTION, SOCIABILITY-PRIVACY; **drop in the ocean,** CONSEQUENCE-INSIGNIFICANCE, MAGNITUDE-SMALLNESS; **drop into a good thing,** WELFARE-MISFORTUNE; **drop into the grave,** LIFE-DEATH; **drop off,** INCREASE-DECREASE, LIFE-DEATH; **drop the mask,** EXPOSURE-HIDINGPLACE; **drop the subject,** HEED-DISREGARD; **drop too much,** TEETOTALISM-INTEMPERANCE; **let drop,** ELEVATION-DEPRESSION; **ready to drop,** WEARINESS-REFRESHMENT.

drop'-let. A small drop. MAGNITUDE-SMALLNESS.

drop'-ping. Falling in drops. RIVER-WIND.

drop'-ping fire. A continuous irregular firing of guns. CONTINUITY-INTERRUPTION.

drop'-scene''. A drop-curtain with a scene painted on it. ACTING.

drop'-si-cal. Relating to dropsy. ENLARGEMENT-DIMINUTION, EXCESS-LACK.

drop'-sy. An unnatural accumulation of serous fluid in some part of the body. ENLARGEMENT-DIMINUTION.

drosh'-ki, dros'-ky. An open four-wheeled Russian carriage. CONVEYANCE-VESSEL.

dross. Waste matter. CLEANNESS-FILTHINESS.

dross'-i-ness. The quality of being dross. CLEANNESS-FILTHINESS.

drought. Dry weather. DAMPNESS-DRYNESS, EXCESS-LACK.

drought'-y. Dry. DESIRE-DISTASTE.

drouth. Thirst. DESIRE-DISTASTE.

drove. A number of animals in a body. GATHERING-SCATTERING, MULTIPLICITY-PAUCITY.

dro'-ver. One who drives animals in droves. DOMESTICATION-AGRICULTURE.

drown. To die by suffocation in water or other liquid. LIFE-KILLING, SUCCESS-FAILURE, WATER-AIR; **drown care,** ENTERTAINMENT-WEARINESS; **drown the voice,** VOCALIZATION-MUTENESS.

drowse. To be dull with sleepiness. ACTIVITY-INDOLENCE.

drow'-si-ness. The state of being drowsy. ACTIVITY-INDOLENCE, WEARINESS-REFRESHMENT.

drow'-sy. Heavy with sleepiness. ACTIVITY-INDOLENCE, WEARINESS-REFRESHMENT.

drub. To beat with a stick. RECOMPENSE-PUNITION, SUCCESS-FAILURE.

drub'-bing. A sound beating. SUCCESS-FAILURE.

drudge. To work hard at slavish tasks. AGENT, TOIL-RELAXATION.

drudg'-er-y. The act of drudging. ACTIVITY-INDOLENCE, WEARINESS-REFRESHMENT.

drug. Anything used as medicine, or in chemical

operations. Consequence - Insignificance, Excess-Lack, Remedy-Bane; **drug in the market,** Costliness-Cheapness, Excess-Lack.

drug'-get. A coarse woolen fabric. Cleanness-Filthiness, Cover-Lining, Conservation.

drug'-gist. One who deals in drugs. Remedy-Bane.

dru'-id. One of an order of priests of the ancient Gauls and Britons. Ministry-Laity.

drum. A musical instrument. Crash-Drumming, Musical Instruments, Recurrence, Roundness, Sociability-Privacy; **beat of drum,** Alarm, Fighting-Conciliation, Order, Pomp, Sign; **drum out,** Recompense-Punition; **ear drum,** Hearing-Deafness; **muffled drum,** Life-Funeral, Resonance-Nonresonance.

drum'-head". The membrane at the end of a drum. Law-Lawlessness, Tribunal.

drum'-ma"-jor. The leader of a drum-corps. Chief-Underling.

drum'-mer. One who drums. Musician.

drum'-ming. The act of beating a drum. Crash-Drumming, Recurrence.

drunk. Intoxicated with liquor. Teetotalism-Intemperance.

drunk'-en. Given to drunkenness. Teetotalism-Intemperance; **reel like a drunken man,** Agitation.

drunk'-en-ness. The state of being drunk. Nutriment-Excretion, Teetotalism-Intemperance.

dry. Not wet. Approval-Disapproval, Conservation, Dampness-Dryness, Desire-Distaste, Entertainment-Weariness, Excess-Lack, Force-Weakness, Purity-Crudeness, Simplicity-Floridness, Taking-Restitution, Vocalization-Muteness; **dry joke,** Wittiness-Dulness; **dry land,** Ocean-Land; **dry the tears,** Alleviation-Aggravation; **dry up,** Dampness-Dryness, Provision-Waste; **run dry,** Excess-Lack; **with dry eyes,** Provision-Waste, Sensitiveness-Apathy.

dry'-ad. A wood-nymph. Jove-Fiend.

dry'-as-dust". Dull and prosy. Future-Past, Wittiness-Dulness.

dry'-land". Land free from water. Ocean-Land.

dry'-ness. The quality of being dry. Dampness-Dryness.

dry'-nurse". A nurse that rears a child without suckling it. Education-Misteaching, Instructor-Pupil, Obstruction-Help.

dry'-point". An engraving made with a needle. Engraving.

dry'-rot" A disease in timber. Betterment-Deterioration, Cleanness-Filthiness, Remedy-Bane.

du'-al. Denoting two. Duality, Noun.

du'-al-ism. The state of being dual. Duality, Orthodoxy-Heterodoxy.

du"-al-is'-tic. Of dualism. Duality.

du-al'-i-ty. The state of being two. Duality.

DUALITY.

Biformity. A double form.
Biplicity. State of being twofold.
Conjugation. A union of two or more.
Dualism. State of being dual or twofold; any system founded on a twofold distinction.
Duality. State or quality of being two or twofold.
Duplicity. Doubleness; doubleness of heart or speech.
Polarity. Quality of a body in virtue of which it exhibits contrary or opposite powers; as attraction, repulsion, etc.

Duality—*Denotations.*

Brace. A pair. [Arms.]
Castor and Pollux. The two brightest stars in the constellation Gemini, named after twin sons of Jupiter; Dioscuri, as the brothers Grim in the German galaxy of philologists.

Cheeks. The sides of the face.
Couple. Two connected things of a kind.
Deuce. Two; a card having two spots.
Fellows. Persons joined in action, location, or position.
Gemini. The constellation containing the twin-stars Castor and Pollux.
Pair. Two of a kind.
Siamese twins. Two Siamese children whose bodies were joined together.
Twins. Two children born at one birth.
Two. Consisting of a unit taken once again.
Yoke. A pair of draft-animals.

DUALITY—*Verbs.*

Bracket. To enclose with two braces; couple.
Conduplicate. To fold lengthwise
Couple. To pair; unite two.
Pair. Combine two, like or unlike.
Yoke. To join two with a frame.

DUALITY—*Adjectives.*

Binary. Found in pairs
Binomial. An expression of two terms.
Biparous. Bringing forth two at the same birth.
Both. Including two at the same time.
Conduplicate. State of being folded lengthwise; twofold.
Conjugate. Joined together; combined in pairs.
Couple. United.
Dual Composed of two.
Dualistic. Consisting of two.
Duplex. Having two folds.
Dyadic. Relative to two parts.
Tête-à-tête [F.]. Face to face; in confidence; familiarly.
Twain. Two; a couple; a pair.
Twin. See *Nouns.*
Two. See *Nouns.*

du'-arch-y. Government by two equal rulers. Rule-License.

dub. To name. Name-Misnomer.

dub'-belt-je. [Du.] Coin. Values.

du-bi'-e-ty. The state of being doubtful. Certainty-Doubt.

du'-bi-ous. Doubtful in opinion. Certainty-Doubt.

du'-bi-ous-ness. The state of being dubious. Certainty-Doubt.

du'-bi-tan-cy. Doubt. Certainty-Doubt.

du"-bi-ta'-tion. Doubt. Certainty-Doubt.

duc'-at. Coin. Values.

duch'-ess. The wife or widow of a duke; a woman having the sovereignty of a duchy. Chief-Underling, Gentility-Democracy.

duch'-y. The territory of a duke. Extension-District.

duck. To dip suddenly under water. Elevation-Depression, Spring-Dive, Water-Air.

duck. A short-legged, web-footed water-bird; [colloq.] a pet. Favorite-Anger; **like a duck in thunder,** Astonishment-Expectance; **play ducks and drakes,** Extravagance-Avarice, Impetus-Reaction.

duck'-ing. The act of plunging into water. Spring-Dive.

duck'-ing-stool". A stool for ducking scolds. Recompense-Scourge.

duck'-pond". A pond for ducks. Domestication-Agriculture.

duct. A passage for conveying fluid. Watercourse-Airpipe.

duc'-tile. Capable of being drawn out. Bigotry-Apostasy, Difficulty-Facility, Hardness-Softness.

duc-til'-i-ty. The quality of being ductile. Hardness-Softness, Insubordination-Obedience.

dudg'-eon. (1) Sullen displeasure. Contentedness-Discontentment, Favorite-Anger, Favorite-Moroseness, Love-Hate.

dudg'-eon. (2) Kind of dagger. Weapon.

due. Owing. Credit-Debt, Dueness-Undueness, Duty-Dereliction, Propriety-Impropriety; **due**

sense of, Sagacity-Incapacity; **due time,** Earli-ness-Lateness; **due to,** Cause-Effect, Dueness-Undueness, Rationale-Luck; **give due weight,** Differentiation-Indiscrimination; **give his due to,** Justification-Charge, Right-Wrong, Up-rightness-Dishonesty; **in due course,** Opportune-ness-Unsuitableness, Period-Progress.

du′-el. A fight between two persons. Strife-Peace.

du′-el-ist. One who fights duels. Belligerent.

duello [It.] (du-el′-lo). The art of dueling. Strife-Peace.

due′-ness. The state of being due. Dueness-Undue-ness, Duty-Dereliction.

DUENESS—UNDUENESS.

Authority. Independence of action belonging to a person.
Birthright. An inherited privilege.
Bond. See Security.
Charter. A special privilege; a formal instrument granting special rights.
Claim. A demand on the ground of right.
Constitution. See Law.
Demand. A request as by right.
Due. Something owed.
Dueness. Quality of being due; what is due or coming.
Franchise. Freedom; liberty; a freeman′s right, as the elective franchise.
Immunity. Exemption from obligation.
Liberty. Freedom; privilege.
License. A special grant; permission.
Prerogative. Unquestionable right.
Prescription. First claim by length of possession; authoritative direction.
Pretension. Any claim, lawful or unlawful.
Privilege. A special favor; advantage.
Right. A just claim; privilege of enjoyment.
Sanction. Act which ratifies and gives validity.
Tenure. The right to hold office or property, especially real estate.
Title. A just cause for possession.
Vested interest.⎰ Right or interest not in a state of contingency or
Vested right. ⎱ suspension.
Warrant. That which vouches for or insures anything.
Warranty. Security.

Dueness—*Associated Nouns.*

Appellant. One who appeals to a higher court of law for the settlement of his cause.
Claimant. Any person who presents a claim.
Plaintiff. Beginner of a lawsuit. See Justification-Charge.

Dueness—*Verbs.*

Allot. To appoint; grant.
Appeal to for. To vindicate; to earnestly ask for.
Arrogate. To make presumptuous claims.
Assert. To maintain; defend.
Assume. To take upon oneself.
Authorize. See Leave.
Be due to. See *Adjectives.*
Be entitled to. To have legal claims.
Belong to. See Property.
Be the due of. See *Nouns.*
Be worthy of. To deserve.
Call upon for. To appeal to.
Challenge. To settle claim by combat.
Claim. To assert.
Come upon for. To demand.
Confer a right. Bestow a privilege.
Demand. Claim; to ask for.
Deserve. To be worthy of.
Enforce. To strengthen; assert one′s claim.
Entitle. To qualify.
Exact. To require authoritatively.
Give a right. To grant a privilege.
Give everyone his due. See Right.
Have claim to. Be entitled to.
Have claim upon. Have a right to ask from.
Have one′s due. ⎰ Obtain what is just.
Have one′s rights.⎱
Have right to. Be entitled to.
Have title to. Have legal claim to.
Insist on. To compel; to enforce.
Insist upon. Same as above.
Lay claim to. To demand as a right.
Lay under contribution. To subject to make contribution.
Legalize. To make legal.
Make a point of. To lay special importance upon.
Make good. To enforce; to vindicate.
Make out a case. To establish.
Merit. To deserve.

Breach. Violation; infraction.
Disfranchisement. Deprivation of the privileges of citizenship.
Emptiness of title. A title bearing no significance.
Encroachment. Unlawful intrusion on the rights of others.
Exaction. An unjust claim.
Falseness. Underhandedness; untruthfulness.
Forfeiture. Loss of some right, claim, privilege, etc., by some offense.
Illegality. See Law-Lawlessness.
Illegitimacy. Unlawfulness; impropriety; bastardy.
Imposition. An arbitrary exaction.
Impropriety. Unsuitableness; the quality of being out of place.
Invalidity of title. Want of legal force.
Lion′s share. An improper share in the distribution of something; the whole. [Æsop′s Fable of the lion′s part.]
Loss of right. Forfeiture.
Malum prohibitum [L.]. An act made criminal by prohibition of civil law.
Presumption. Strong probability; arrogant conduct.
Stretch. A strain of power.
Tort. Mischief; calamity.
Undueness. The quality of not conforming to fixed law or rule.
Usurpation. An unauthorized seizure of power.
Violation. A breach of law.

Undueness—*Nouns of Agent.*

Pretender. An apparent claimant.
Usurper. One who appropriates power and authority to himself.

Undueness—*Verbs.*

Arrogate. To presume; make exorbitant claims.
Arrogate to oneself. To assume as one′s own.
Be undue. See *Adjectives.*
Disentitle. To deprive of right.
Disfranchise. To take away the right of citizenship.
Disqualify. To disable.
Do violence to. To harm; to outrage.
Encroach. To go beyond proper limits.
Exact. To wrest from.
Give an inch and take an ell. To take more than rightfully belongs.
Infringe. To transgress on the rights of others.
Invalidate. To erase the authority; make null.
Misbecome. To be unbefitting.
Misbehave. To conduct oneself improperly.
Not be due. See Dueness.
Relax. To make less rigid.
Strain a point. ⎰ Go too far.
Stretch a point. ⎱
Trench on. To encroach; to overreach.
Usurp. To seize control unlawfully.
Violate. To infringe upon the rights of.

Undueness—*Adjectives.*

Bastard. Not genuine; illegitimate.
Contra bonos mores [L.]. Against good custom.
Disentitled. Deprived of right or title.
Disfranchised. Deprived of citizenship.
False. Not genuine or real.
Forfeited. Lost by default.
Illegitimate. Unlawful.
Illicit. Not legal.
Improper. Not suitable.
Misbecoming. Unbecoming.
Not the thing. Unsuited; out of place.
Not to be thought of. Contrary to reason.
Out of the question. Not to be asked for.
Preposterous. Absurd; monstrous.
Pretentious. Claiming to be more than one′s true value.
Seemless. Unseemly.
Spurious. Not legitimate; not genuine.
Tortious. Injurious; wrongful.
Unallowed; unauthorized; unbecoming; unbefitting; unchartered; unconstitutional; undeserved; undue; unearned; unentitled; unfit; unfulfilled; unjustified; unlawful; unmeet; unmerited;

DUENESS—UNDUENESS—*Continued.*

DUENESS—Verbs—*Continued.*

Ordain. To install; set in authority.
Pay one's dues. To give what one owes.
Prescribe. See *Nouns.*
Put in force. To enforce; carry out.
Require. To request authoritatively.
Revendicate. To claim the restoration of.
Revendicate a claim. To revive a claim.
Richly deserve. To be worthy of in the highest degree.
Sanctify. To consecrate by holy rites.
Substantiate. To verify; establish the truth of.
Take one's stand. To be determined.
Use a right. To take possession of.
Vindicate a claim. To show the reasonableness of.
Vindicate a right. To assert.

DUENESS—*Adjectives.*

Absolute. Free from control.
Allowable. See Leave.
Allowed. Permitted; granted.
Authorized. Given power to act.
Becoming. Fit; appropriate.
Befitting. Seemly; in place.
Chartered. Having written legal authority.
Claiming. Asserting a right to.
Condign. Worthy; suitable.
Constitutional. Consistent with the supreme law of the land.
Correct. Right; legal.
Creditable. Worthy of commendation.
Decorous. Becoming; fit.
Deserved. Merited; worthy.
Deserving. Worthy of praise or honor.
Due. Owed.
Due to. Owed to.
Enfranchised. Given free citizenship.
En règle [F.]. In order.
Entitled to. Earned; won.
Equitable. See Right.
Fit. Adequate.
Fitting. Becoming.
Having a right to. See *Verbs.*
Imprescriptible. Not capable of being lost or acquired by usage.
Inalienable. Not able to be alienated.

DUENESS—*Adverbial Phrases.*

By divine right. By the authority of God.
By right. Rightly.
Dei gratia [L.]. By the grace of God.
De jure [L.]. From the law.

DUENESS—*Phrases.*

À chaque saint sa chandelle [F.]. To every saint his candle.
Civis Romanus sum [L.]. I am a Roman citizen. [Cicero *Against Verres.*]

UNDUENESS—Adjectives—*Continued.*

unprivileged; unqualified; unsanctioned; unseemly; unwarranted. Not allowed, authorized, etc.
Usurped. Seized unlawfully.
Would-be. Pretentious; presumptuous.

UNDUENESS—*Phrase.*

Filius nullius [L.]. Son of nobody

DUENESS—Adjectives—*Continued.*

Indefeasible. Not able to be defeated, or set aside.
Inviolable. Intact; not to be injured.
Just. Rendering what is due.
Just the thing. Exactly right.
Lawful. } According to law.
Legal. }
Legalized. See Law.
Legitimate. Authorized; lawful.
Licit. Lawful.
Meet. Appropriate; becoming.
Merited. Deserved.
Meriting. Deserving.
Ordained. Appointed; set apart.
Prescribed. Appointed; directed.
Prescriptive. Gained by long possession.
Presumptive. Giving ground for belief.
Privileged. Accorded special rights.
Proper. Decent; becoming.
Quite the thing. See Just the thing.
Richly deserved. See *Verbs.*
Right. Correct; consistent.
Right as a trivet. Not unstable.
Sanctioned. Approved of.
Seemly. Becoming; befitting.
Selon les règles [F.]. According to rules.
Square. Upright; honest.
Unalienable. See Inalienable.
Unchallenged. Exercising authority without opposition.
Unexceptionable. Choice; select.
Unimpeachable. Not to be questioned.
Up to the mark. Meeting with approval; superior.
Warranted. Given authority or power to do.
Worthy of. Meriting.

Duly. Properly; in a becoming manner.
Ex officio [L.]. By virtue of an office.
In the name of. As representative of.
Jure divino [L.]. By divine right.

Droit au travail [F.]. Right of labor.

---

du-en′-na. An elderly woman who keeps careful guard of a young woman. Guard-Prisoner, Instructor-Pupil, Security-Insecurity.
dues. Anything owed. Price-Discount.
du-et′. A composition for two voices. Music.
duf′-fer. A pedler of cheap articles. Adept-Bungler, Robber.
dug. A teat. Convexity-Concavity.
duke. An English peer of the highest rank. Chief-Underling, Gentility-Democracy.
dulce domum [L.] (dŭl′-sî do′-mum). Sweet home. Dweller-Habitation.
dulce et decorum est pro patria mori [L.] (dŭl′-sî′ et dî-co′-rum est pro pê′-tri-α mo′-raī). It is sweet and decorous to die for one's country. [Horace, *Odes*, III, ii, 13.] Patriotism-Treason.
dul′-cet. Sweet to the sense. Loudness-Faintness, Melody-Discord, Pleasurableness-Painfulness, Sweetness-Acidity.
dul′-ci-fi-ca′-tion. The act of dulcifying. Sweetness-Acidity.
dul′-ci-fy. To sweeten. Sweetness-Acidity.
dul′-ci-mer. A stringed instrument. Musical Instruments.
dul-cin′-e-a. A lady-love. From a character in *Don Quixote.* Love-Hate.

dul′-ci-tude. Sweetness. Sweetness-Acidity.
dul′-co-rate. To sweeten. Sweetness-Acidity.
dul″-co ra′-tion. The act of dulcorating. Sweetness-Acidity.
du-li′-a. The worship of saints and angels. Devotion-Idolatry.
dull. Not sharp or keen. Activity-Indolence, Color-Achromatism, Dimness, Embellishment-Simplicity, Entertainment-Weariness, Feeling-Insensibility, Force-Weakness, Lighthearted-ness-Dejection, Loudness-Faintness, Sensitive-ness-Apathy, Sharpness-Bluntness, Skill-Un-skilfulness, Strength-Weakness, Turbulence-Calmness, Vigor-Inertia; **dull of hearing,** Hearing-Deafness; **dull sight,** Sight-Dimsightedness.
dull′-ard. A stupid person. Sage-Fool.
dul′-ness. The state of being dull. Activity-Indolence, Sensitiveness-Apathy, Vigor-Inertia, Wittiness-Dulness.
du′-ly. In a due time or manner. Dueness-Undueness.
dumb. Without power of speech. Talkativeness-Taciturnity, Vocalization-Muteness; **dumb animal,** Fauna-Flora; **dumb show,** Sign; **strike dumb,** Astonishment-Expectance, Selfrespect-Humbleness, Vocalization-Muteness.

dum″-found′. To strike dumb. Astonishment-Expectance.

dum″-found′-ed. Struck dumb. Selfrespect-Humbleness.

dum″-found′er. To strike dumb. Astonishment-Expectance, Expectation-Disappointment, Vocalization-Muteness.

dummodo sit dives, barbarus ipse placet [L.] (dŭm′-mo-do sit dai′-vîz, bar′-bar-us ip′-sî plê′-set). Provided only he is rich, a very barbarian pleases. [Ovid, *Ars Amatoria*, II, 276.] Gentility-Democracy, Money.

dum′-my. A silent person. Activity-Indolence, Commutation-Permutation, Might-Impotence, Vocalization-Muteness.

dump. Melancholy. Jubilation-Lamentation, Music.

dump′-ish. Morose. Lightheartedness-Dejection.

dumps. Low spirits. Contentedness-Discontentment, Favorite-Moroseness, Lightheartedness-Dejection.

dump′-y. Short and thick. Beauty-Ugliness, Breadth-Narrowness, Greatness-Littleness, Length-Shortness.

dum spiro, spero [L.] (dŭm spai′-ro, spî′-ro). While I breathe, I hope. [Part of the motto of South Carolina.] Sanguineness-Hopelessness.

dum vivimus, vivamus [L.] (dŭm viv′-im-us, vi-vê′-mus). While we live, let us live. [From an ancient inscription.] Entertainment-Weariness.

dun. Of a dull color; to press for payment of a debt. Color-Achromatism, Credit-Debt, Dimness, Petition-Expostulation, White-Black.

dunce. A dull-witted person. [A follower of Duns Scotus, brightest of the Schoolmen, but out of fashion.] Sage-Fool, Scholar-Dunce.

dun′-der-head″. A dunce. Sage-Fool.

dun′-der-pate″. A dunce. Sage-Fool.

dune. A hill of loose sand. Height-Lowness.

dung. Animal excrement. Cleanness-Filthiness.

dun′-geon. An underground prison. Release-Prison.

dung′-hill. A heap of dung. Bravery-Cowardice, Cleanness-Filthiness, Gentility-Democracy; **dunghill cock,** Bravery-Cowardice, Fauna-Flora.

du′-o. A duet. Music.

du″-o-dec′-i-mal. Denoting by twelves. Five-Quinquesection.

du″-o-dec″-i-mo. A book with twelve leaves to the sheet. Greatness-Littleness, Missive-Publication.

du″-o-de′-nal. Of a duodene. Five-Quinquesection.

du″-o-den′-a-ry. Pertaining to the number twelve. Five-Quinquesection.

du′-o-logue. Dialogue. Acting, Conversation-Monologue.

dupe. One who is deceived. Gull-Deceiver, Truthfulness-Fraud.

du′-plex. Twofold. Doubling-Halving, Duality, Luminary-Shade.

du′-pli-cate. Made like a copy. Copy-Model, Credit-Debt, Doubling-Halving, Excess-Lack, Mark-Obliteration, Sign.

du″-pli-ca′-tion. The act of duplicating. Doubling-Halving, Imitation-Originality.

du′-pli-ca-ture. A folding. Plicature.

du-plic′-i-ty. Deceitfulness. Craft-Artlessness, Duality, Truthfulness-Falsehood.

du″-ra-bil′-i-ty. The quality of being durable. Lastingness-Transientness.

du′-ra-ble. Able to endure. Lastingness-Transientness, Mutability-Stability.

du′-ra-ble-ness. The power of lasting. Lastingness-Transientness.

dura lex sed lex [L.] (diu′-ra lɛx sed lex). Hard law but law. Duty-Dereliction.

du′-rance. Imprisonment. Release-Restraint; **in durance,** Guard-Prisoner.

du-ra′-tion. Continuance in time. Duration-Neverness; **contingent duration,** Contingent-Duration.

DURATION—NEVERNESS.

Age. The whole duration of a being.

Course. The period occupied by a revolution of the moon, or of the earth round the sun, marking a month or a year. See Period-Progress.

Date. Point of time at which an event or transaction takes place.

Decade. A period of ten years. See Period-Progress.

Duration. Continuance in time.

Epoch. A period of time remarkable for influential events.

Era. A period of time reckoned from some particular date.

Interim [L.]. The mean time; intervening time.

Interlude. Time between the acts of a play.

Intermediate time. Intervening time.

Intermission. An intervening period of time.

Intermittence. Act of intermitting, or causing to cease for a time.

Interregnum. The time during which a government is changed.

Interval. The time intervening between two periods.

Intervention. Space of time between points of time or events

Moment. A minute portion of time. See Eternity-Instantaneity.

Pendency. State of being undecided.

Period. A specified portion of time.

Respite. To relieve for a period of time.

Season. A period of time.

Space. An interval of time.

Span. A brief portion of time.

Spell. A short or limited space of time

Stage. A period of time in any development.

Term. Prescribed or actual duration.

The whole period. The entire space of time.

The whole time. The entire portion of duration.

Time. A definite portion of duration; the measure of duration.

Time of life. An age.

While. A period of time, or time in general.

Year. A period of 365 days.

Duration—*Figurative Expressions.*

Glass of time. A glass for measuring time by the passage of sand through an orifice; hence, time itself.

Absence of time. Lack of time.

Dies non [L.]. A day on which judges do not sit.

Greek kalends. As the Greeks had no kalends, Greek kalends means a time that never occurred.

Neverness. Beyond time, or without time.

No time. A time which never comes.

Tib's eve. A possible or impossible future occurrence.

Neverness—*Adverbs.*

At no period. } Never.
At no time. }

Never. Not at any time.

Never in all one's born days. Never in one's life.

Nevermore. Never again; at no time in the future.

On no occasion. Never at any event.

Sine die [L.]. Without a day appointed.

Duration—Figurative Expressions—*Continued.*

Noiseless foot of time. The representation of time as a person; hence, the passing of time.

Ravages of time. The wear or wasting away of old age.

Scythe. The implement carried by time represented by an old man; hence, time itself.

Whirligig of time. A merry-go-round, representing time by its rapid passage and re-passage over the same place.

Duration—*Verbs.*

Consume time. To waste time.

Continue. To abide for any time indefinitely.

Elapse. To slip silently away as time.

Employ time. To make use of time.

Endure. To have duration.

Fill time. To make full use of time.

Go on. To continue.

Intervene. To occur between points of time.

Last. To continue in time.

DURATION—Verbs—Continued.

Occupy time. ⎫
Pass away time. ⎬ To take up time.
Pass time. ⎭
Persist. To endure against opposition.
Remain. To continue on in time.
Seize an opportunity. See OPPORTUNENESS.
Spend time. Occupy time

Take time. ⎫
Take up time. ⎭ Occupy time.
Talk against time. To get as much talk as possible in a prescribed time.
Tide over. Surmount.
Waste time. See ACTIVITY-INDOLENCE.
While away time. To pass away time pleasantly.

DURATION—Adjectives.

Continuing. See *Verbs*.
On foot. Originated; started.

Permanent. Durable. See LASTINGNESS-TRANSIENTNESS

DURATION—Adverbs, etc.

A. C. *Ante Christum.* Before Christ.
A D. *Anno Domini.* In the year of our Lord.
Ad interim [L.]. In the mean time.
All along. The whole duration.
All the time. Unceasingly.
Always. For all time.
Anno [L.]. Within a year.
Anno Domini [L.]. In the year of our Lord.
Anno regni [L.]. In the year of the reign.
Anno urbis conditæ [L.]. In the year since the founding of the city, *i. e.*, Rome.
Ante Christum [L.]. Before Christ.
A. R. *Anno regni.* See above.
A. U. C. *Anno urbis conditæ.* See above.
B. C. Before Christ.
Before Christ. Before the Christian era.
Day by day. Continually; without intermission of a day.
De die in diem [L.]. From day to day.
During. In the time of.
During the interval. Within the time between any two events.
During the time. Within the time.
For a season. ⎫
For a time. ⎭ For a limited time.
For good. See LASTINGNESS.
For the time being. For the present time.
From day to day. As time passes.

From hour to hour. In the course of time.
Hereupon. At this time; hereon.
Hourly. Every hour.
In the course of. At some time during.
In the *interim.* See *Adverbs.*
In the meantime. In the interval between two given times.
In the time of. At some time during a certain event.
In the time when. Coincident time.
Meantime. In the interval between two given times.
Meanwhile. In the intervening time.
Once upon a time. Formerly.
One fine morning. Some indefinite time.
Pendente lite [L]. Pending or during suit.
Pending. During the time intervening before.
Then. Being at that time.
Thereupon. Upon that, or this.
The whole time. The entire time; continually.
Throughout. See ENTIRETY.
Till. Unto; up to: used in respect to time.
Until. Up to; till; before: used of time.
Up to. See UNTIL.
Whereupon. Upon which; after which.
While. See UNTIL.
Whilst. Same as WHILE.
Yet. At the same time; up to the present time; before some future time.

DURATION—Phrases.

Ad calendas Græcas [L.]. To the Greek calends; never.
Time runs. Time passes quickly.

Time, runs against. To run as rapidly as possible to ascertain the greatest speed attainable or the greatest distance which can be traveled in a given time.

dur'-bar. An official reception in British India, given by a native ruler. CONVERSATION-MONOLOGUE, COUNCIL, TRIBUNAL.

du'-ress. Imprisonment. COERCION, RELEASE-RESTRAINT.

dur'-ing. In the time of. DURATION-NEVERNESS; **during pleasure,** CONTINGENT-DURATION.

du'-ri-ty. Hardness. HARDNESS-SOFTNESS.

dusk. Twilight. LIGHT-DARKNESS, LUMINARY-SHADE, MORNING-EVENING.

dusk'-y. Dim. LIGHT-DARKNESS, WHITENESS-BLACKNESS.

dust. Anything pulverized. CLEANNESS-FILTHINESS, CONSEQUENCE-INSIGNIFICANCE, FRIABILITY, HEAVINESS-LIGHTNESS, LIFE-CORPSE, MONEY; **come down with the dust,** FRIABILITY, SETTLEMENT-DEFAULT; **come to dust,** LIFE-DEATH; **dust in the balance,** CONSEQUENCE-INSIGNIFICANCE; **dust one's jacket,** RECOMPENSE-PUNITION; **humbled in the dust,** SELF-RESPECT-HUMBLENESS; **kick up a dust,** ACTIVITY-INDOLENCE, PRESUMPTION-OBSEQUIOUSNESS; **level with the dust,** CREATION-DESTRUCTION; **lick the dust,** SUCCESS-FAILURE, YIELDING; **make to bite the dust,** SUCCESS-FAILURE; **throw dust in the eyes,** PRETEXT, SIGHT-BLINDNESS, TRUTHFULNESS-FRAUD; **turn to dust,** LIFE-DEATH, ORGANIZATION-INORGANIZATION.

dust'-er. That which removes dust. CLEANNESS-FILTHINESS.

dust'-hole''. A receptacle for dust. CLEANNESS-FILTHINESS, USEFULNESS-USELESSNESS; **fit for the dust-hole,** BETTERMENT-DETERIORATION, CLEANNESS-FILTHINESS, USEFULNESS-USELESSNESS.

dust'-man. One who removes dust and ashes. CLEANNESS-FILTHINESS.

dust'-storm''. A storm of dust. FRIABILITY.

dust'-y. Covered with dust. CLEANNESS-FILTHINESS, FRIABILITY.

Dutch. Pertaining to the Dutch. **Dutch auction,** BUYING, SALE; **Dutch courage,** BRAVERY-COWARDICE; **high Dutch,** CLEARNESS-OBSCURITY.

Dutch'-man, fly'-ing. A legendary spectral ship. FANCY.

du'-te-ous. Giving due respect and obedience. VIRTUE-VICE.

du'-ti-ful. Performing one's duty. VIRTUE-VICE.

du'-ty. That which one ought to do. CEREMONIAL, DEVOTION-IDOLATRY, DUTY-DERELICTION, OCCUPATION, POLITENESS-IMPOLITENESS, PRICE-DISCOUNT, REGARD-DISRESPECT, TOIL-RELAXATION; **do one's duty,** UPRIGHTNESS-DISHONESTY, VIRTUE-VICE; **on duty,** ACTION-PASSIVENESS, ACTIVITY-INDOLENCE.

DUTY—DERELICTION.

Accountableness. The quality or state of being accountable.
Acquittal. Performance of one's part.
Allegiance. Obligation owed.
Bounden duty. Compulsory duty.
Call. An appeal to duty.
Calling. See OCCUPATION.

Dead letter. An obligation which has lost its force or power.
Dereliction of duty. A wilful neglect or omission of duty.
Evasion. Act of eluding or shirking
Failure. Non-performance of duty.
Fault. See INNOCENCE-GUILT.
Infraction. A breaking; non-observance.

DUTY—DERELICTION—*Continued.*

Call of duty. Felt obligation.
Case of conscience. A duty felt to be imposed upon one by conscience.
Conscience. The mind's faculty to discern between right and wrong
Consciousness. See UPRIGHTNESS.
Decalogue. The Ten Commandments; duty to God.
Decorum. Propriety of conduct.
Discharge. The act of removing an obligation, debt, etc.
Dueness. See DUENESS.
Duty. That which a person is bound by moral obligation to do or refrain from doing.
Engagement. See ENGAGEMENT.
Fealty. Fidelity to a superior.
Fitness. The quality of being fit.
Fulfilment. Accomplishment; completion.
Function. The performance of any duty.
Good behavior. Mode of conducting oneself.
Imperative duty. See BOUNDEN DUTY.
Inward monitor. Conscience which points out duty.
Liability. Obligation to pay.
Morality. Conformity to the right.
Moral obligation. Duty to morality.
Morals. A system of rules formulated to guide conduct.
Observance. Adherence to rule.
Onus [L.]. An obligation.
Part. The share of duty falling to one's lot.
Performance. The act of accomplishing.
Polity. Principles regulating public affairs.
Propriety. Suitableness of manner.
Redemption. Act of delivering; rescue.
Responsibility. Accountableness for a trust.
Satisfaction. The settlement of a claim.
Seemliness. Comeliness.
Sense of duty. Feeling of duty.
Still small voice within. Conscience.

Neglect. Failure to attend to.
Non-observance. Neglect.
Non-performance. Failure to perform.
Relaxation. Withdrawal of effort.
Sin. See VIRTUE-VICE.
Transgression. Violation of law or principle.
Violation. Infringement; breach of law.

DERELICTION—*Verbs.*

Break. To violate; transgress.
Break through. To overstep proper bounds.
Call to account. See APPROVAL-DISAPPROVAL.
Escape. To avoid; evade.
Evade. To go out of the way for.
Fail. To want; come short.
Forswear. To break an oath.
Infringe. To encroach upon.
Neglect. Non-observe.
Renounce. To disclaim; declare against bitterly.
Repudiate. To cast off; refuse to pay.
Set aside. To ignore; pay little attention to.
Set at naught. To regard as nothing.
Slight. Neglect; overlook.
Trample on. Transgress; infringe.
Trample under foot. To tread on.
Transgress. To violate; to break.
Wash one's hands of. To renounce interest in.

DUTY—*Continued.*

The proper thing.
The proper thing to do.
The right thing to do. } What duty demands.
The thing.
What ought to be done.
To prepon [Gr.]. Fitness.

DUTY—*Scientific Terms.*

Aretology. That part of moral philosophy which treats of virtue and the means of attaining to it.
Casuistry. That part of moral philosophy which deals with particular cases of conscience.
Deontology. The science which relates to moral obligation.

Ethical philosophy. Philosophy pertaining to ethics.
Ethics. Science of human duty.
Ethology. The science of character.
Moral philosophy. The science of duty and the relations springing from duty.

DUTY—*Verbs.*

Acquit oneself of an obligation. To clear oneself of an obligation.
Act one's part. Live up to one's duty.
Adhere to an obligation. Hold fast to an obligation.
Assign. To point out some duty to perform.
Be at one's post. To attend to duty's call.
Be bound to. To be constrained.
Become. To be suitable.
Become bound to. To be compelled.
Become sponsor for. To take another's obligations
Befit. To be in accord with.
Behoove. To fall to one's lot.
Be incumbent on. See *Adjectives.*
Be responsible. See *Adjectives.*
Beseem. To be befitting.
Be sponsor for. See BECOME SPONSOR FOR.
Be the duty of. To owe something, as an obligation.
Be under an obligation. Be bound to fulfil a vow, contract, etc.
Bind. To force.
Bind over. To subject to the course of law.
Call upon. To appeal to for the performance of duty.
Discharge a duty. To carry out a duty.
Discharge an obligation. To perform an obligation.
Do duty. To do what is right.
Do justice to. To reward fully.
Do one's duty. See VIRTUE.
Enjoin. To order; to charge.
Enter upon a duty. To take a duty upon oneself.
Enter upon an obligation. See ENTER UPON A DUTY.

Exact. To make a demand.
Fall to one's lot. Be assigned to one.
Fulfil a duty. Do what one ought.
Fulfil an obligation. Do what one feels bound to.
Impose a duty. To force upon arbitrarily.
Incur a responsibility. To become liable to.
Lie at one's door. }
Lie on one's head. } To be an obligation.
Lie under an obligation. Be bound.
Lie upon one's head. Be an obligation.
Look to. Attend to.
Mind one's P's and Q's. To be extremely accurate.
Oblige. To put another under obligation for a favor rendered.
Observe a duty. }
Observe an obligation. } Do what one ought.
Owe it to oneself. Feel personally bound.
Perform an obligation. Do one's duty.
Pertain to. To belong to.
Prescribe. To command; to order.
Redeem one's pledge. To live up to one's promise.
Require. To demand.
Rest on the shoulders. Be a burden.
Rest with. Belong to.
Saddle with. To put on a burden.
Satisfy a duty. }
Satisfy an obligation. } Do what one ought.
Take upon oneself. See ENGAGEMENT.

DUTY—*Adjectives.*

Accountable. Answerable.
Amenable Liable to be punished.
Answerable. Able to be replied to.
Beholden to. Indebted.
Behooving. See *Verbs.*
Binding. Holding firmly.
Bound by. Held by.
Bound to. Under obligation to.

Casuistical. Pertaining to casuistry.
Chargeable on. Liable to be laid at one's door.
Compromised. See ENGAGEMENT.
Conscientious. Bound by conscience.
Due to. Owing to.
Ethical. Pertaining to ethics.
Ethological. Pertaining to the science of character.
Imperative. Mandatory.

DUTY—Adjectives—*Continued.*

Incumbent on. Falling to one's lot.
Indebted to. Beholden.
In duty bound. Held by duty.
Liable. Responsible; answerable
Meet. See Dueness.
Moral. Bound to exercise right conduct.
Obligatory. Imposing duty or obligation.
Obliged to. Put under obligation to do.
Peremptory. Positive; decisive.

Saddled with. Under a burden, as a horse.
Stringent. See Harshness.
Responsible. Answerable; liable to requite.
Right. Conformable to the will of God.
Stringent. Binding strongly.
Tied by. ⎱ Bound to do.
Tied down. ⎰
Under obligation. Bound.

Duty—*Adverbial Phrases.*

As in duty bound.
At one's own risk.
In foro conscientiæ [L.]. Before the tribunal of conscience.
On one's own responsibility.

Quamdiu se bene gesserit [L.]. During good behavior.
Suo periculo [L.]. At one's own peril
With a safe conscience.

Duty—*Phrases.*

Devoir, faire mon [F.]. To do my duty.
Dulce et decorum est pro patria mori [L.]. It is sweet and seemly to die for one's fatherland.
Dura lex sed lex [L.]. It is a hard law, but it must be observed because it is a law.

Hodie mihi, cras tibi [L]. To-day for me to-morrow for you.
Honos habet onus [L.]. Honor is onerous, *i. e*, has its responsibility.
Loyauté m'oblige [F.]. Loyalty binds me.

DUTY—IMMUNITY.

Immunity.

Absolution. Freedom from guilt.
Discharge. Removal of load.
Dispensation. Privilege to do something forbidden.
Exculpation. See Exculpation.
Excuse. Release; pardon.
Exemption. Release from the operations of the law.
Exoneration. A disburdening.
Franchise. Exemption from constraint, a freeman's right.

Freedom. Liberty; independence.
Immunity. A particular privilege.
Irresponsibility. Want of responsibility.
Liberty. Exemption from subjection to the authority of another.
License. A permit.
Release. Freedom; pardon.
Renunciation. A cutting loose; repudiation.

Immunity—*Verbs.*

Absolve. See Pardon.
Acquit. To release from an obligation.
Be exempt. See *Adjectives.*
Discharge. See *Nouns.*
Dispense with. To suspend the operations of.
Excuse. To pardon; release from obligation.
Exempt. To give special freedom to.
Exonerate. See Exculpation.
Free. To relieve from the constraint of.
Give dispensation. See Dispensation.
Let off. Excuse; release.

License. To permit or authorize by license.
Pass over. To overlook; fail to execute judgment.
Quit-claim. Give up a claim to.
Release. See *Nouns.*
Remise. Surrender by deed.
Remit. Give up.
Save the necessity. Prevent the necessity.
Set at liberty. Free.
Spare. Excuse; remit; dispense with.
Stretch a point. Exaggerate; strain one's conscience.

Immunity—*Adjectives.*

At liberty; excusable; exempt; free; irresponsible; not answerable; released (see *Verbs*); scot-free, clear; unaccountable; unbound; unencumbered.

Immunity—*Phrase.*

Bonis nocet, si quis malis pepercerit [L.]. If any one spares the bad, he injures the good

du-um′-vi-rate. The joint office of duumviri, two magistrates holding an office jointly. Rule-License.
Du-val′, Claude. A highway robber. Robber.
D. V. Abbreviation of *Deo volente* [L.]. (Di′-o vo-len′-tî.) God willing. Possibility-Impossibility.
dwarf. Any thing unnaturally small. Enlargement-Diminution, Greatness-Littleness, Increase-Decrease, Jove-Fiend.

dwarfed. Kept small. Greatness-Littleness.
dwarf′-ish. Like a dwarf. Greatness-Littleness.
dwell. To have a fixed habitation; to linger. Movement-Rest, Presence-Absence; **dwell upon,** Terseness-Prolixity.
dwell′-er. A permanent resident. Dweller-Habitation.

DWELLER—HABITATION.

Aborigines. The original inhabitants of a country.
Autochthones. Inhabitants claiming origin from the land they live in.
Back settler. A backwoodsman.
Backwoodsman. A dweller in the backwoods.
Burgess. A freeman living in a borough.
Burgher. A dweller in a burgh.
Cit. Familiar name for citizen.
Citizen. A resident of a city or town.
Cockney. A dweller in that part of London near Bow-bells.
Colonist. A dweller in a colony.
Commorant. The legal term for dweller.
Compatriot. A fellow countryman.
Cottager. ⎫
Cotter. ⎬ A dweller in a cottage.
Cottier. ⎭
Denizen. One not a native, but made a citizen.
Dweller. One who lives in a place as his home.

Abode. A permanent habitation.
Acropolis. An elevated citadel.
Address. The direction to the residence of any person.
Aerie. The nest of any predatory bird.
Ale-house. A house where liquors are sold.
Arbor, etc. See Contents-Receiver
Ark. A shelter.
Assembly-room. A room in which assemblies are held.
Atrium. An ancient entrance hall.
Barn. A shelter for horses or cattle.
Barrack. A permanent building for the lodgment of soldiers.
Bawn. A large house with all its appurtenances.
Beadhouse. An almshouse.
Berth. A lodging place.
Bivouac. A temporary encampment of soldiers without tents.
Booth. A stall at a public market.
Bothie. A hut for laborers.
Bothy. A shepherd's or hunter's hut.

DWELLER—HABITATION—Continued.

Habitant [F.]. A dweller.
House-holder. A dweller in a house.
Incumbent. A person in possession of an office.
Indigene. One dwelling in his native country.
Indweller. A poetic name for inhabitant.
Inhabitant. One who lives permanently in a place.
Inmate. One who dwells in a place with others.
Innkeeper. One who manages an inn.
Islander. A dweller on an island.
Locum tenens [L.]. Holding a place; an inhabitant.
Lodger. One who lives in another's house.
Marchman. A man dwelling on a march or border.
Native. One who dwells in the country in which he was born. See CONSTITUENT-ALIEN.
Newcomer, etc. See CONSTITUENT-ALIEN.
Occupant. }
Occupier. } A tenant in possession.
Resident. }
Residentiary. } One who dwells in a place for some time.
Settler. A dweller in a new country.
Sojourner. A temporary resident.
Squatter. One who occupies land without right or permission.
Tenant. One who dwells in a house or on lands owned by another.
Townsman. A dweller in a town.
Villager. A dweller in a village.

DWELLER—*Denotations.*

American. A native or inhabitant of the American continent.
Brother Jonathan. The people of the United States, collectively, or a typical specimen of them.
Englishman. A native or citizen of England.
John Bull. The people of England, or a typical specimen of them.
Hoosier. An inhabitant of the State of Indiana.

DWELLER—*Collective Nouns.*

Colony. A body of emigrants settling in a remote country.
Crew. The seamen belonging to one ship or boat.
Garrison. The soldiers stationed in a fort or town.
Household. A number of persons dwelling under the same roof and composing a family.
Mir. A Russian community holding land in common.
People. The whole body of persons comprising a state or nation. See HUMANITY.
Population. The whole number of people in a place.
Settlement. The body of people having their abode in the same definite region.

DWELLER—*Verbs.*

Indenizen, etc. See ESTABLISHMENT.
Inhabit, etc. See PRESENCE.

DWELLER—*Adjectives.*

American. Dwelling in America.
Autochthonous. See AUTOCHTHONES.
British. Dwelling in Great Britain.
Domestic Pertaining to the household.
Domesticated. Made domestic.
Domiciled. Provided with a home.
Domiciliated. Settled in a home.
English. Dwelling in England.
Garrisoned by. Manned with troops.
Indigenous. Originating in a place or country.
In the occupation of. Holding in possession.
Natal. Pertaining to one's birth.
Native. Pertaining to the place of one's birth.
Naturalized. Having obtained the rights and privileges of citizenship.
Occupied by. Held in possession by a tenant.
Vernacular. Originating in one's native land.

HABITATION—*Continued from Column 2.*

Hutch. A small, dark room.
Inn. A public place of lodging and entertainment.
Kennel. A small house for a dog or dogs.
Khan. An Oriental inn.
Kiosk. A fanciful pavilion built in Oriental style.
Lair. The den of a wild animal.
Lap. A place for supporting or fostering.
Lares et penates [L.]. Household gods.
Lean-to. A shed placed against another building and having a single-pitched roof.
Livery stable. A place where horses are stabled and where they can be hired.

Bower, etc. A retired dwelling in a wood. See CONTENTS-RECEIVER.
Box. A building with some resemblance to a box.
Building. Any structure intended for occupation. See CREATION.
Bungalow. An East Indian country house.
Byre. A cow-house.
Cabaret. A wineshop.
Cabin. A small, rudely constructed house
Café [F.]. A restaurant.
Camp. The temporary stopping place of an army or expedition.
Canteen. A shop where liquors are sold to soldiers.
Cantonment. A section of a town reserved for lodging soldiers.
Capital. A chief city.
Caravansary. A resting-place for caravans.
Casemate. A chamber in a fortification.
Casern. A barrack in a garrison town.
Castle. A strong, fortified building.
Castrametation. The plan of a camp.
Cave. A natural cavity under the surface of the earth.
Cell. A small chamber.
Châlet [F.]. A Swiss peasant's cottage.
Chamber, etc. A room in a dwelling-house. See CONTENTS-RECEIVER.
Château [F]. A French country mansion.
Club. The apartments occupied by a social organization.
Club-house. Meeting-place for clubs.
Coffee-house. A restaurant.
Coop. A very small building for keeping small animals.
Cot. A small and unpretentious house.
Cote. A place of shelter.
Cottage. A small house.
Country-seat. A mansion in the country.
Court. The residence of a sovereign.
Court-house. Judicial building of a county.
Covert. A sheltering place.
Cow-house. A barn used entirely for cattle.
Cow-shed. A small building used to shelter cattle.
Croft. A very small farm.
Den. An underground retreat.
Dog-hole. A hole in the ground used as a shelter by a dog.
Domicile. A fixed place of abode.
Dove-cote. A small house for tame pigeons.
Dulce domum [L.]. Sweet home.
Dwelling. A house in which people reside.
Eating-house. A public house where food is served.
Encampment. A camp and the persons occupying it.
Enodochium. Lodging-room of a monastery.
Estaminet [F.]. A smoking-room.
Eyry. See AERIE.
Farm. A piece of property devoted to agriculture.
Farm-house. A dwelling-house on a farm.
Fatherland. The land of one's birth.
Fireside. Home and its tender associations.
Folly. A costly and ruinous structure.
Gin-palace. A drinking-saloon.
Grange. A farm and farm-house with all appurtenances.
Habitat. The region where some species of plant or animal is usually found.
Habitation. A dwelling-place.
Hacienda [Sp.]. A large country estate.
Hall. A large building for public use.
Haunt. A place of frequent resort for some person.
Headquarters. The lodging-place of the chief persons in an event.
Hearth. }
Hearthstone. } The domestic fireside.
Hermitage. The dwelling-place of a hermit.
Hive. The dwelling-place of bees.
Hole. A low and dirty place of abode.
Home. One's family residence.
Homestead. The home and the adjacent land occupied with it.
Hospice. A place of refuge for travelers in difficulty.
Hostel. }
Hostelry. } An inn.
Hotel. A public place of sojourning for travelers.
Hôtel de ville [F.]. A city hall.
House. A building intended for habitation.
Household. The persons in a house composing a family.
Household goods. Movable property connected with a household.
Housing. A shelter from the weather.
Hovel. A poor and miserable dwelling.
Hut. A small and rude dwelling.

(*Continued on Column* 1.)

HABITATION—*Continued.*

Local habitation. A dwelling-place confined to a definite region.

Lodge. A small house for temporary shelter.

Lodging. A temporary habitation.

Maison de campagne [F.]. A country seat.

Manor-house. The house of a nobleman on his landed estate.

Mansion. A place of residence of some size and pretension.

Meeting-house. A house used as a place of public worship.

Messuage. The legal term for a house and the adjacent buildings and lands used by the household.

Motherland. The land of one's ancestors.

Mug-house. A public house where liquors are sold.

Native land. The land in which one was born.

Native soil. The soil on which one was born.

Nest. The habitation made by a bird for its young

Nidification. The act of making a nest.

Nidus. A place for laying eggs.

Odeon. In ancient Greece, a roofed temple in which trial performances were held.

Palace. A splendid and stately residence.

Paternal domicile. The home of one's father.

Pavilion. An open building for entertainment.

Pen, etc. A small enclosure for animals. See ENCLOSURE.

Perch. A pole used as a roost for birds.

Posada [Sp.]. An inn.

Pot-house. An ale-house.

Public-house. A house where all proper comers have lodging and entertainment.

Pump-room. A public room at a mineral spring.

Quarters. A place of temporary residence.

Quincunx. An arrangement of houses by fives in a square or rectangle.

Resiance. A residence.

Residence. The place of one's abode.

Resort. A place much used as a temporary habitation for pleasure.

Restaurant. A public eating-house.

Retreat. A place of seclusion and safety.

Roof. A home.

Rookery. An overcrowded, rickety building.

Roost. A perch upon which birds rest at night.

Rotunda. A round building.

Rus in urbe [L.]. Country in city.

Sanctum sanctorum [L.]. The holy of holies; a place of great privacy.

Seat. A mansion and the estate connected with it.

Shanty. A rough and rickety wooden house.

Shed. A small building with open sides.

Shippen. A stable.

Snuggery. A cozy room.

Sojourn. Temporary residence.

Spa. A watering-place with mineral springs.

Stable. A building to keep horses and cattle in.

Stall. A compartment in which a horse or bovine animal is kept.

Sty. An enclosure for swine.

Taberna. A tent; booth.

Tabernacle. A tentlike structure for temporary habitation.

Tavern. A public house where guests are entertained for pay.

Teepee. One of the conical lodges of the North American Indians.

Temple, etc. A house of worship. See FANE.

Tenement. A building having apartments to be let.

Tent. A movable shelter of canvas. See COVER.

Throne. The seat of a monarch.

Tower. A very tall structure.

Villa. A beautiful country residence.

Watering-place. A pleasure resort near a lake or by the sea.

Where one's lot is cast. The place of one's residence.

Wigwam. A tent of the North American Indians.

Zenana. An East Indian harem.

HABITATION—*Collective Nouns.*

Borough.
Burgh. } An incorporated village or town.

Capital. A chief city or town; the seat of government.

City. A municipality of the first class, governed by a mayor and created by charter.

Country. A land under a particular government, inhabited by a certain people, within definite geographical limits.

Dorp. A small village.

Ham. The old Anglo-Saxon village or town.

Hamlet. A little village.

Kraal. An African village.

Metropolis. The chief city of a state or country.

Province. Any large administrative division of a country.

Suburb. A region or place adjacent to a city.

Thorp. A small village.

Town. A collection of dwelling-houses as distinguished from the adjacent country.

Village. A collection of houses larger than a hamlet and smaller than a town.

HABITATION—*Associated Nouns.*

Alley. A narrow walk or street.

Arcade. A covered street.

Block of buildings. The buildings enclosed in a single square bounded by streets.

Circus. A circle formed by bow-shaped rows of houses.

Close. A narrow lane.

Colonnade. A walk bordered by columns.

Court. A yard or space surrounded wholly by buildings or walls.

Crescent. An arc-shaped row of houses, or street.

Demesne. A manor-house and the adjoining lands.

Embankment. A bank or dike along a river forming a level driveway.

Esplanade. A level place for promenading.

Garden. A place set apart for the cultivation of flowers.

Ghetto. The Jewish quarter in a city.

Grove. A group of cultivated trees.

Lane. A narrow way or path, confined between fences, walls, or the like.

Mall. A public walk.

Market-place. A place where merchandise is exposed for sale.

Mews. A range of buildings used as stables.

Parade. The ground where military reviews are held; a public walk.

Parish, etc. See EXTENSION-DISTRICT.

Park. A tract of land set apart for ornament and recreation.

Passage. A narrow walk between buildings.

Piazza. An open area or public square in a city.

Place. An open space or square in a city.

Plaisance [F.]. A retired pleasure-ground.

Pleasure-ground. A place devoted to recreation.

Polygon. A space laid out in the form of a polygon.

Quad. A quadrangular court.

Quadrangle. A court, square or oblong, almost or entirely surrounded by buildings.

Quarter. A particular part, division, or district, as of a town.

Rents. Certain periodical profits from the use of lands and tenements.

Residences. Dwelling-places.

Road. A way or street.

Row. A line of houses.

Square. An open space in a city.

Terrace. A level area on the side of a sloping bank.

Wynd. A lane or alley.

Yard. The grounds about a house.

HABITATION—*Nautical Terms.*

Anchorage. A place where ships may lie at anchor.

Basin. A dock.

Dock. The space between two adjoining piers.

Harbor. A sheltered place where ships may find protection from storms.

Port. Any bay or inlet where a ship may be sheltered from storms.

Quay. An artificial landing place where vessels may discharge their cargoes.

Roads.
Roadstead. } An open place some distance from the shore where ships may ride at anchor.

Wharf. A landing-place for vessels and their cargoes.

HABITATION—*Verbs.*

Inhabit, etc. To live in as a home. See PRESENCE.

Take up one's abode, etc. See ESTABLISHMENT.

HABITATION—ADJECTIVES—*Continued.*

Cosmopolitan.   Common to the whole world.
Domestic.   Pertaining to the home.
Habitable.   That may be dwelt in.
Metropolitan.   Pertaining to a chief city.
Palatial.   Pertaining to or becoming a palace; grand in style.

Provincial.   Pertaining to a province.
Rural.   Pertaining to the country.
Rustic.   Belonging to the country.
Suburban.   Pertaining to the suburbs of a city.
Urban.   Belonging to a city.

HABITATION—*Phrases.*

Eigner Herd ist Goldes werth [G.].   One's own hearth has golden worth.

Ubi libertas, ibi patria [L.].   Where liberty is, there is my fatherland.

dwell'-ing.   A house occupied as an abode.   DWELLER-HABITATION, ESTABLISHMENT-REMOVAL.

dwerg'-er.   A sprite.   JOVE-FIEND.

dwin'-dle.   To become less.   ENLARGEMENT-DIMINUTION.

dy-ad'-ic.   Consisting of two parts.   DUALITY.

dye.   To fix a color in.   COLOR-ACHROMATISM.

dy'-ing.   Ceasing to live.   LIFE-DEATH.

dy-nam'-ic.   Of forces not in equilibrium.   IMPETUS-REACTION.

dy-nam'-i-cal.   Of forces not in equilibrium.   IMPETUS-REACTION; **dynamical geology,** GEOLOGY.

dy-nam'-ic en'-er-gy.   Energy pertaining to mechanical force.   MIGHT-IMPOTENCE, STRENGTH-WEAKNESS.

dy-nam'-ics.   The science that treats of the laws of force.   IMPETUS-REACTION.

dy-nas'-tic.   Of a dynasty.   RULE-LICENSE.

dy'-nas-ty.   A succession of kings in one line of descent.   RULE-LICENSE.

dys-pep'-si-a.   Bad digestion.   HEALTH-SICKNESS.

dys-pep'-tic.   Relating to dyspepsia.   HEALTH-SICKNESS.

dys'-pho-ny.   Enfeebled voice.   VOCALIZATION-MUTENESS.

E

each. One of several. UNIVERSALITY-PARTICULAR-ITY; **each in his turn,** COMMUTATION-PERMUTATION; **each other,** INTERDEPENDENCE; **each to each,** ASSIGNMENT, UNIVERSALITY-PARTICULARITY.

ea'-ger. Earnest. ACTIVITY-INDOLENCE, DESIRE-DISTASTE, EMOTION, READINESS - RELUCTANCE; **eager expectation,** EXPECTATION-SURPRISE; **eager glance,** SAGACITY-INCAPACITY.

ea'-ger-ness. Earnestness. ACTIVITY-INDOLENCE, DESIRE-DISTASTE, EMOTION, READINESS - RELUCTANCE.

ea'-gle. Coin; a vicious bird of prey. SIGN, SWIFTNESS-SLOWNESS, VALUES; **eagle eye,** SAGACITY-INCAPACITY, SIGHT-BLINDNESS; **eagle speed,** SWIFTNESS-SLOWNESS; **eagle-winged,** SWIFTNESS-SLOWNESS; **eagle-wood,** CEREMONIAL.

ea'-gly. Eagle-like. SWIFTNESS-SLOWNESS.

ea'-gre. A tidal wave. RIVER-WIND.

ean. To bring forth young. CREATION-DESTRUCTION.

ear. The organ of hearing. HEARING-DEAFNESS; **all ears,** HEARING-DEAFNESS; **come to one's ears,** ENLIGHTENMENT-SECRECY; **din in the ears,** CRASH-DRUMMING, LOUDNESS-FAINTNESS; **ear for music,** HEARING-DEAFNESS, MUSICIAN; **have the ears of,** AMITY-HOSTILITY, FAITH-MISGIVING; **in at one ear, out at the other,** HEED-DISREGARD, REMEMBRANCE-

FORGETFULNESS; **lend an ear,** HEARING-DEAFNESS, HEED-DISREGARD; **make the ears tingle,** FAVORITE-ANGER; **meet the ears,** HEARING-DEAFNESS; **nice ears,** HEARING-DEAFNESS; **no ears,** HEARING-DEAFNESS; **not for ears polite,** PURITY-IMPURITY; **offend the ears,** CACOPHONY; **prick up the ears,** EXPECTATION-SURPRISE, HEED-DISREGARD; **pull about one's ears,** ELEVATION-DEPRESSION; **quick ears,** HEARING-DEAFNESS; **reach one's ears,** ENLIGHTENMENT-SECRECY; **ring in the ears,** LOUDNESS-FAINTNESS, RESONANCE-NONRESONANCE; **set by the ears,** FAVORITE-ANGER, LOVE-HATE, VARIANCE-ACCORD; **split the ears,** LOUDNESS-FAINTNESS; **together by the ears,** STRIFE-PEACE, VARIANCE-ACCORD; **up to one's ears,** ACTIVITY-INDOLENCE, EXCESS-LACK; **willing ears,** READINESS-RELUCTANCE; **word in the ear,** ADDRESS-RESPONSE.

ear'-drum. The tympanum. HEARING-DEAFNESS.

earl. A member of the British nobility. GENTILITY-DEMOCRACY.

earl''-dom. The dignity of an earl. GENTILITY-DEMOCRACY.

ear'-less. Having no ears. HEARING-DEAFNESS.

ear'-li-er. Sooner. ANTECEDENCE-SEQUENCE.

ear'-li-ness. The state of being early. EARLINESS-LATENESS.

EARLINESS—LATENESS.

Anticipation. Foreseeing expectancy.
A stitch in time. A stitch taken early, which " saves nine."
Earliness, etc. The state of being early. See *Adjectives.*
Haste, etc. Speed of action. See SWIFTNESS.
Morning. Early part of the day; earliness of time. See MORNING.
Precipitation. The act of rushing headforemost, or heedlessly.
Precocity. Earliness of growth.
Prematurity. Being full-grown before the natural period.
Promptitude, etc. Readiness for action at the call. See ACTIVITY.
Punctuality. Exactness of time in keeping appointments or doing work.
Suddenness, etc. Unexpected happening. See ETERNITY-INSTANTANEITY.

EARLINESS—*Verbs.*

Accelerate. To increase the velocity.
Anticipate. To act before.
Be beforehand, etc. Be earlier than necessary. See *Adverbs.*
Be early, etc. Be in good time. See *Adjectives.*
Bespeak. To speak or ask for early.
Draw on futurity. To do now so as to save time later.
Engage. To fix upon a time for doing.
Expedite, etc. To hasten or push ahead. See SWIFTNESS.
Forestall. `To prevent by taking care in time; to buy goods on the way to market to raise the price in market.
Gain the start. To be farther ahead or have more done than another.
Gain time. To do so as not to require as much time.
Have the start. To be ahead.
Keep time. To do at the right moment.
Make haste, etc. To hasten. See HURRY.
Preengage. To bargain for beforehand.
Secure. To make certain by early action.
Steal a march upon. To act quietly before another so as to deceive him.
Take time by the forelock. To do early so as to save time or labor later.

EARLINESS—*Adjectives.*

Anticipatory. Acting beforehand, or in expectation of something.
Early. In good time; soon.
Forward. In the lead.
Immediate. At the same instant.
In time. Not too late.
Near. }
Near at hand. } Not far off.

Adjournment. Suspending the session of a body till a later time.
Chancery suit. A long delayed trial in the Chancellor's Court.
Cunctation. Cautious slowness.
Deferring, etc. Putting off from one time to another. See *Verbs.*
Delation. }
Delay. } Loss of time.
Fabian policy. The tendency to put off till a more favorable opportunity, as Fabius did with Hannibal.
High time. The end of the time for doing something.
Lateness, etc. The state of much time having passed. See *Adjectives.*
Leeway. Lost time.
Médecine expectante [F.]. The system of giving remedies only when the disease has had time to develop.
Postponement. A putting off for a time.
Procrastination. Blamable deferring.
Prolongation. Deferring.
Prorogation. A putting off to another time.
Protraction. Delaying of the termination of a thing.
Respite. Rest from effort or labor.
Retardation. Lessening of the movement of a thing.
Tardiness, etc. Not being present at the appointed time See SWIFTNESS-SLOWNESS.

LATENESS—*Verbs.*

Adjourn. To discontinue the session of a body at intervals.
Await. To be ready for. See EXPECTATION.
Be kept waiting. To be delayed in going forward.
Be late. To come after the appointed time. See sub *Adjectives.*
Bide. To wait.
Bide one's time. Not to be hasty.
Consult one's pillow. To sleep before acting further.
Cool one's heels. To wait long.
Dally. To lose time by playing or loitering.
Dance attendance. Wait upon another continually.
Dawdle. To act lazily. See INACTIVITY.
Defer. To put off.
Delay. To hinder progress.
Draw out. To lengthen.
Drive to the last. Continue to the very end.
Faire antichambre [F.]. To wait in the anteroom.
Gain time. To do so as to save time in the action.
Hang fire. To be slow in taking effect.

EARLINESS—LATENESS—*Continued.*

EARLINESS—Adjectives—*Continued.*

Precipitate. Without due forethought; headforemost.
Precocious. Developed before the usual time.
Premature. Ripened or done before the proper time.
Prevenient. Previous.
Prime. Of the best quality; being in the best period of growth or strength.
Prompt, etc. Ready at short notice. See ACTIVITY.
Punctual. Observing exactly appointed times of action.
Rath. Early.
Sudden, etc. Coming without warning. See ETERNITY-INSTANTANEITY.
Summary. Regardless of the usual methods; quickly.
Timely. Happening at right time.
Unexpected, etc. Not foreseen. See EXPECTATION-SURPRISE.

EARLINESS—*Adverbs.*

Almost immediately. In the next instant.
Anon. Immediately; soon; at once.
Apace. Rapidly.
At once. Without waiting; anon.
At short notice. In a short time; almost immediately.
At sight. Immediately upon looking.
At the first opportunity. The first time that chance is given.
Beforehand. Previous to the time of action.
Before its time. Sooner than was proper.
Before long. Soon.
Before one can say "Jack Robinson." In the shortest possible time. [A work it is as easy to be done, as 'tis to say Jack! robes on! *Old Play.*]
Before one's time. Before the person was born.
Before the ink is dry. In a very few minutes.
Betimes. Soon enough.
Briefly. In a few words.
By and by. After a short time.
Directly. Without delay.
Early. Ahead of the required or usual time.
Eft. Again.
Eftsoons. Soon afterward.
Ere long. Before a long time has passed.
Extempore. Without preparation.
Forthwith. Immediately.
Immediately. Without any delay.
In anticipation. For preventing.
In a while. After a short lapse of time.
Incontinently. At the same instant.
In due time. Requiring only as much time as is proper.
In good time. Before the last moment.
In military time. With promptness and punctuality.
In no long time. Soon.
In no time. In a very short space of time.
In pudding time. At the last minute.
In time. Before or at the required instant.
Offhand. Without preparation.
On the instant. At the same point of time.
On the spot. At that very place, without hesitation.
On the spur of the moment. Following the emotions of a critical instant.
On the spur of the occasion. [His laws were not made on the spur of a particular occasion for the present, but out of providence for the future. Bacon, *History of Henry VII.*]
Out of hand. Immediately.
Precipitately. Without due deliberation. See HURRY.
Prematurely. Before the proper time. See *Adjectives.*
Presently. Soon.
Punctually, etc. Exactly at the appointed or fixed time. See *Adjectives.*
Quickly. With haste.
Rath. Early. Rather, sooner.
Shortly. After the lapse of a short time.
Soon. After a short time.
Speedily. Quickly.
Straight.
Straightforth. } Without loss of time.
Straightway.
Suddenly, etc. Without warning. See ETERNITY-INSTANTANEITY.
Summarily. Not going through the usual forms.
Time enough. Time sufficiently long for the purpose.
Too soon. Earlier than was necessary or right.
To the minute. Through the full limit of the time.
Unexpectedly. Without being previously thought of or seen. See EXPECTATION-SURPRISE.

LATENESS—Verbs—*Continued.*

Keep back. To hold away from.
Kick one's heels. To wait impatiently.
Lay.
Lay over. } To wait or delay.
Lengthen out. To extend.
Let the matter stand over. To defer further action for a time.
Lie over. To be left for consideration later.
Linger. To move slowly.
Loiter. To spend time idly.
Lose an opportunity, etc. To miss a chance, etc. See OPPORTUNENESS-UNSUITABLENESS.
Postpone. To put off for a time.
Procrastinate. To defer without cause.
Prolong. To continue.
Prorogue. To end a session.
Protract. To be slow to conclude.
Push to the last. To do everything else first.
Put off. To delay in doing.
Remand. To send back.
Reserve, etc. To keep back. See STORE.
Retard. To make go slower.
Shift off. To defer artfully.
Sit up.
Sit up at night. } To work late at night.
Sleep upon it. To think deeply during resting hours. [Webster, *Reply to Hayne.*]
Spin. To draw out at great length.
Stand over. To leave for later consideration.
Stave off. To ward off or drive off.
Stay. To tarry.
Suspend. To stop or quit for a time.
Take one's time. To act slowly.
Take time. To plan to have time to do something.
Tarry. To linger.
Temporize. To delay by yielding to adverse circumstances.
Tide over. To pass through or over safely.
Wait. To stay for something.
Wait impatiently. To remain unwillingly.
Waive. To let go for the present.

LATENESS—*Adjectives.*

Backward. Retiring.
Behindhand. Late.
Belated. Kept back past the proper time.
Delayed, etc. Hindered so as to arrive late. See *Verbs.*
Dilatory, etc. Acting slowly. See SWIFTNESS-SLOWNESS.
In abeyance. Not in force; not vested, as the title to land wanting its heir.
Late. After the usual or appointed time for something.
Posthumous. Occurring after death.
Postliminous. Contrived, done, or existing subsequently.
Slow. Backward.
Tardy. Late.
Unpunctual. Not observant of the exact time.

LATENESS—*Adverbs.*

After time. Past a certain hour.
At last. Finally.
At length. After a long while.
At one's leisure. Whenever one cares to.
At sunset. } When the time or opportunity was almost
At the eleventh hour. } gone.
Backward. Slowly; tardily.
Behind time. Late.
Deliberately. Using plenty of time.
Late. Not early enough.
Late in the day. After 3 or 4 o'clock p. m.
Lateward. A little late.
Leisurely. Taking plenty of time.
Slowly. Without haste.
Too late. Not early enough.
Too late for. Not early enough for. See OPPORTUNENESS-UNSUITABLENESS.
Ultimately. Finally.

LATENESS—*Phrases.*

È meglio tardi che mai [It.]. It is better late than never.
Ex post facto [L.]. After the doing of a deed. [Law.]
Nonum prematur in annum [L.]. Let it (a poem) be kept for nine years. [Horace, *Ars Poetica*, 388.]
Sine die [L.]. Without date; indefinitely.

À vue d'œil [F.]. Visibly.
No sooner said than done. Acted upon (as a suggestion) at once.
Touch and go. Barely done.

Tout vient à temps pour qui sait attendre [F.]. Everything comes in time to him who knows how to wait.

earl'-ship. The office of an earl. Gentility-Democracy.

ear'-ly. In good season. Earliness-Lateness; **get up early,** Activity-Indolence.

ear'-mark". A mark of identification. Sign.

earn. To gain as a just return. Gain-Loss.

ear'-nest. Zealous and determined; a pledge. Consequence-Insignificance, Determination-Vacillation, Emotion, Outlay-Income, Readiness-Reluctance, Security; **in earnest,** Activity-Indolence, Assertion-Denial, Determination-Vacillation, Truthfulness-Falsehood.

ear'-nest-ly. With determination. Determination-Vacillation.

ear'-nest-ness. State of being earnest. Activity-Indolence, Emotion, Readiness-Reluctance.

earn'-ings. Wages. Affluence-Penury, Gain-Loss, Money, Outlay-Income.

ear'-pier"-cing. Shrill. Cacophony.

ear'-ring". A ring or hook passed through the ear. Embellishment-Disfigurement.

ear'-shot. Ear-reach. Remoteness-Nearness; **out of ear-shot,** Loudness-Faintness.

ear'-split"-ting. Deafening. Loudness-Faintness.

earth. The world; soil. Astronomy, Life-Corpse, Ocean-Land, Top-Bottom, Universe; **what on earth,** Astonishment-Expectance, Investigation-Answer.

earth'-born". Of earthly origin. Gentility-Democracy.

earth'-en-ware". Vessels, etc., made of baked clay. Heating-Cooling, Sculpture.

earth'-li-ness. Worldliness. Humanity.

earth'-ling. A worldling. Humanity.

earth'-ly. Worldly. Godliness-Disbelief, Ocean-Land, Universe, Unselfishness-Selfishness; **end one's earthly career,** Life-Death; **of no earthly use,** Usefulness-Uselessness.

earth'-ly-mind"-ed. Worldly-minded. Unselfishness-Selfishness.

earth'-quake". A shaking of the ground. Geology, Revolution, Turbulence-Calmness.

earth'-ward". Toward the earth. Universe.

earth'-work". A fortification made of earth. Attack-Defense.

ear'-wig". A secret informer; to influence by secret counsel. Adulation-Disparagement, Flatterer-Defamer.

ear'-wise. Through the ear. Hearing-Deafness.

ear'-wit"-ness. One who testifies from hearing. Evidence-Counterevidence.

ease. Rest; facility. Alleviation-Aggravation, Contentedness-Discontentment, Difficulty-Facility, Hurry-Leisure, Pleasure-Pain, Purity-Crudeness, Sensuality-Suffering; **at ease,** Sensuality-Suffering; **at one's ease,** Hurry-Leisure, Liberty-Subjection, Sensuality-Suffering, Welfare-Misfortune; **ease off,** Admission-Expulsion; **ease one of,** Taking-Restitution; **mind at ease,** Contentedness-Discontentment, Lightheartedness-Dejection; **set at ease,** Alleviation-Aggravation; **take one's ease,** Contentedness-Discontentment, Hurry-Leisure, Toil-Relaxation.

ea'-sel. A frame for supporting a picture, etc. Painting, Suspension-Support; **easel-picture,** Suspension-Support.

ease'-ment. A certain incorporeal right; convenience. Alleviation-Aggravation, Property.

eas'-i-ly. Readily. Difficulty-Facility, Purity-Crudeness, Swiftness-Slowness; **easily accom-**plished, Difficulty-Facility; **easily deceived,** Credulousness-Skepticism; **easily persuaded,** Readiness-Reluctance; **let one down easily,** Pardon-Vindictiveness.

eas'-i-ness. State of being easy. Difficulty-Facility.

eas'-ing. Eaves. Architecture.

east. A cardinal point of the compass. Aim-Aberration, Laterality-Contraposition.

east'-a-bout". In an easterly direction. Aim-Aberration.

East'-er. A Christian festival. Ceremonial, Periodicity-Irregularity; **Easter Monday,** Entertainment-Weariness; **Easter offering,** Giving-Receiving.

east'-er. To shift to the east. Aim-Aberration.

east'-er-ly. Eastward. Aim-Aberration.

east'-ern. Of the east. Laterality-Contraposition.

East'-ern-er. One who dwells in the eastern part of the United States. Constituent-Alien.

east'-ward. Toward the east. Aim-Aberration.

easy. Tranquil; facile. Difficulty-Facility, Purity-Crudeness, Swiftness-Slowness; **easy ascent,** Parallelism-Inclination; **easy chair,** Suspension-Support, Toil-Relaxation; **easy circumstances,** Affluence-Penury; **easy going,** Contentedness-Discontentment, Determination-Vacillation, Excitability-Inexcitability, Harshness-Mildness, Readiness-Reluctance, Unconcern; **easy of belief,** Likelihood-Unlikelihood; **easy sail,** Swiftness-Slowness; **easy temper,** Politeness-Impoliteness; **easy terms,** Difficulty-Facility; **easy to understand,** Clearness-Obscurity; **easy virtue,** Purity-Impurity; **make oneself easy about,** Faith-Misgiving; **take it easy,** Activity-Indolence, Excitability-Inexcitability; **woman of easy virtue,** Purity-Rake.

eat. To consume. Admission-Expulsion, Excitability-Inexcitability, Nutriment-Excretion; **eat dirt,** Yielding; **eat heartily,** Nutriment-Excretion; **eat off the same trencher,** Sociability-Privacy; **eat one's fill,** Enough, Fasting-Gluttony; **eat one's words,** Bigotry-Apostasy; **eat out of house and home,** Extravagance-Avarice, Fasting-Gluttony, Taking-Restitution.

eat'-a-ble. Fit to be eaten. Nutriment-Excretion.

eat'-a-bles. Edibles. Nutriment-Excretion.

eat'-age. Pasturage. Nutriment-Excretion.

eat-en up with. Imbued with. Affections.

eat'-er. One who eats. Nutriment-Excretion.

eat'-ing. Taking sustenance. Admission-Expulsion, Nutriment-Excretion.

eat'-ing-house". A restaurant. Dweller-Habitation, Nutriment-Excretion.

eau à la bouche, faire venir l' [F.] (lo a la bush, fêr venîr'). To make one's mouth water. Desire-Distaste.

eau, battre l' [F.] (lo, batr). To beat the water; to labor in vain. Usefulness-Uselessness.

eau bénite de cour [F.] (o bê-nit' de cur). Court holy water; fair empty words. Ceremonial.

eau dans son vin, mettre de l' [F.] (lo dan· son· van·, metr de). To put water in his wine; to cool one's passion. Turbulence-Calmness.

eau de Cologne [F.] (o de co-lony'). Cologne water. Perfume-Stench.

eau sucrée [F.] (o sü-crê'). Sweetened water. Sweetness-Acidity.

eaves. The projecting edge of a roof. Architecture, Convexity-Concavity.

eaves'-drop". To listen secretly to. Enlightenment-Secrecy.

eaves'-drop''-per. A listener. ENLIGHTENMENT-SECRECY, HEARING-DEAFNESS, INQUISITIVENESS-INDIFFERENCE.

eaves'-drop''-ping. Listening secretly. HEARING-DEAFNESS, TIDINGS-MYSTERY.

ébauche [F.] (ê-bosh'). Sketch. DESIGN.

e''-bau'-choir'. A broad chisel used by sculptors. SCULPTURE.

ebb. Decrease. ADVANCE-RETROGRESSION, BETTERMENT-DETERIORATION, ENLARGEMENT-DIMINUTION, ENOUGH, INCREASE-DECREASE; **ebb and flow,** VIBRATION; **ebb of life,** LIFE-DEATH; **low ebb,** DEEPNESS-SHALLOWNESS, ELEVATION-DEPRESSION, EXCESS-LACK, INCREASE-DECREASE.

ebb'-less. Having no ebb. ADVANCE-RETROGRESSION, DEEPNESS-SHALLOWNESS, INCREASE-DECREASE.

ebb'-tide. Low tide. DAMPNESS-DRYNESS, DEEPNESS-SHALLOWNESS, EXCESS-LACK.

eb''-do-ma'-ri-us. An officer in a cathedral. MINISTRY-LAITY.

Eb'-en-e'-zer. Any memorial of divine help. CHURCH.

Eb'-i-on-ite. A member of an early Church party characterized by Jewish tendencies. ORTHODOXY-HETERODOXY.

Eb'-lis. The chief of the jinus who was cast out of heaven. JOVE-FIEND.

eb'-on. Very black. WHITENESS-BLACKNESS.

eb'-on-y. A hard, heavy, dark wood. WHITENESS-BLACKNESS.

éboulement [F.] (ê-bul-man·'). The falling of a fortress wall. ATTACK-DEFENSE.

e-bri'-et-y. Drunkenness. TEETOTALISM-INTEMPERANCE.

e''-bri-os'-i-ty. Habitual intoxication. TEETOTALISM-INTEMPERANCE.

e'-bri-ous. Drunken. TEETOTALISM-INTEMPERANCE.

e-bul'-lient. Boiling. EXCITATION, HEAT-COLD, TURBULENCE-CALMNESS.

e-bul'-lio-scope. An instrument for ascertaining the amount of alcohol in a mixture by its boiling-point. HEATING-COOLING.

eb''-ul-li'-tion. A boiling; an outburst. AGITATION, EXCITABILITY-INEXCITABILITY, FAVORITE-ANGER, HEATING-COOLING, TURBULENCE-CALMNESS, VIGOR-INERTIA.

eb'-ur-in. An imitation ivory. WHITENESS-BLACKNESS.

écarté [F.] (ê-car-tê'). A game of cards. ENTERTAINMENT-WEARINESS.

ec-bat'-ic. Telling the possible results of an event. CONSEQUENCE-INSIGNIFICANCE.

ec-cal''-e-o'-bi-on. An artificial egg-hatcher. CREATION-DESTRUCTION.

ecce iterum Crispinus [L.] (ec'-sî ai'-ter-um cris-pai'-nus). Here he is again. RECURRENCE.

ecce signum [L.] (ec'-sî sig'-num). Behold the signal. SIGN.

ec-cen'-tric. Erratic. CONVENTIONALITY-UNCONVENTIONALITY, PERSISTENCE-WHIM, SAGACITY-INCAPACITY, SANENESS-LUNACY.

ec''-cen-tric'-i-ty. The state of being eccentric. CONVENTIONALITY-UNCONVENTIONALITY, SAGACITY-INCAPACITY, SANENESS-LUNACY.

ec-chy-mo'-sis. A discoloration. NUTRIMENT-EXCRETION.

ec-cle'-si-arc. A church officer. MINISTRY-LAITY.

ec-cle'-si-ast. The preacher. MINISTRY-LAITY.

Ec-cle''-si-as'-tes. One of the books of the Bible. REVELATION-PSEUDOREVELATION.

ec-cle''-si-as'-tic. A cleric; clerical. CHURCH, MINISTRY-LAITY.

ec-cle''-si-as'-tic-al. Not secular. CHURCH, REVELATION-PSEUDOREVELATION; **ecclesiastical courts,** CHURCH; **ecclesiastical law,** LAW-LAWLESSNESS.

ec-cle''-si-og''-ra-phy. The descriptive history of the Church. CHURCH.

ec-cle''-si-o-log'-ic-al. Belonging to ecclesiology. CHURCH.

ec-cle''-si-ol'-o-gist. One versed in ecclesiology. CHURCH.

ec-cle''-si-ol'-o-gy. Science of organic Christianity. CHURCH.

ecco [It.] (êc'-co). Look here. HEED-DISREGARD.

écervelé [F.] (ê-sêr-ve-lê'). Hare-brained. HEED-DISREGARD.

échafaudage [F.] (ê-sha-fo-dazh'). Scaffolding. PREPARATION-NONPREPARATION.

échappée [F.] (ê-sha-pê'). A prank. ENTERTAINMENT-WEARINESS.

échapper belle [F.] (ê-sha-pê' bel). To escape narrowly. ESCAPE.

ech'-e-lon. An arrangement of troops in the form of steps. ATTACK-DEFENSE.

e-che'-um. Bell-shaped vase. ARCHITECTURE.

e-chi'-nus. Part of a column. ARCHITECTURE.

ech'-o. A repetition; to repeat. ASSENT-DISSENT, COPY-MODEL, IMITATION-ORIGINALITY, INVESTIGATION-ANSWER, RECURRENCE, RESONANCE-NONRESONANCE; **applaud to the echo,** APPROVAL-DISAPPROVAL.

éclaircissement [F.] (ê-clêr-sîs-man·'). A full explanation. INTERPRETATION-MISINTERPRETATION.

éclat [F.] (ê-cla'). Splendor. REPUTATION-DISCREDIT.

ec-lec'-tic. Selecting. CHOICE-NEUTRALITY.

ec-lec'-ti-cism. An eclectic method. CHOICE-NEUTRALITY.

ec-lim'-e-ter. An instrument for measuring zenith distances of objects near the horizon. REMOTENESS-NEARNESS.

e-clipse'. An obscuration; to hide. APPEARANCE-DISAPPEARANCE, DIMNESS, ENLIGHTENMENT-SECRECY, LIGHT-DARKNESS, REPUTATION-DISCREDIT, SUPREMACY-SUBORDINACY; **partial eclipse,** DIMNESS; **total eclipse,** LIGHT-DARKNESS; **under an eclipse,** COLOR-ACHROMATISM, REPUTATION-DISCREDIT, VISIBILITY-INVISIBILITY.

e-clipsed'. Darkened or hidden. APPEARANCE-DISAPPEARANCE.

e-clip'-tic. The sun's path. ASTRONOMY, UNIVERSE.

ec'-logue. A pastoral poem. POETRY-PROSE.

ec''-o-nom'-ic. Pertaining to money matters. GENEROSITY-FRUGALITY, MONEY.

ec''-o-nom'-ic-al. Frugal. GENEROSITY-FRUGALITY.

ec''-o-nom'-ics. Political economy. CONDUCT.

e-con'-o-mist. One who is careful in money matters. GENEROSITY-FRUGALITY, MONEY.

e-con'-o-mize. To be frugal. GENEROSITY-FRUGALITY.

e-con'-o-my. Frugality. CONDUCT, GENEROSITY-FRUGALITY, REGULARITY-IRREGULARITY; **animal economy,** LIFE-DEATH.

écorcheé les oreilles [F.] (ê-cor-shê' lez o-rêîy'). To grate on the ears. CACOPHONY.

écrasez l' infâme [F.] (ê-cra-zê' lan·-fam'). Crush the wretch. CREATION-DESTRUCTION, GOOD MAN-BAD MAN.

ec'-sta-sis. A trance. ACTIVITY-INDOLENCE.

ec'-sta-sy. Excessive emotion. EMOTION, FANCY, PLEASURE-PAIN.

ec-stat'-ic. Entrancing. EMOTION, PLEASURABLENESS-PAINFULNESS, PLEASURE-PAIN.

ec-stat'-i-ca. An emotional woman. DEVOTION-MAGICIAN.

ec'-type. A reproduction. COPY-MODEL.

ec''-u-men'-ic-al. Universal. UNIVERSALITY-PARTICULARITY.

e-da'-cious. Given to eating. FASTING-GLUTTONY.

e-dac'-i-ty. Voracity. FASTING-GLUTTONY.

Ed'-da. Icelandic literature. REVELATION-PSEUDO-REVELATION.

ed'-dy. A whirlpool. REVOLUTION-EVOLUTION, RIVER-WIND.

E'-den. Paradise. HEAVEN-HELL, PLEASURE-PAIN.

e-den'-tate. Having no teeth. ZOOLOGY-BOTANY.

edge. Margin; acuteness. BORDER, HEIGHT-LOWNESS, VIGOR-INERTIA; **blunt the edge of,** STRENGTH-WEAKNESS; **cutting edge,** SHARPNESS-BLUNTNESS; **edge in,** ENVIRONMENT-INTERPOSITION; **edge of hunger,** DESIRE-DISTASTE; **edge one's way,** ADVANCE-RETROGRESSION; **set on edge,** SMOOTHNESS-ROUGHNESS; **take off the edge,** SHARPNESS-BLUNTNESS; **take the edge off,** TURBULENCE-CALMNESS.

edge'-tools". Tools having a sharp edge. SHARPNESS-BLUNTNESS; **to play with edge tools,** RECKLESSNESS-CAUTION.

edge'-wise. With the edge forward. PARALLELISM-INCLINATION.

edg'-ing. A border. BORDER, EMBELLISHMENT-DISFIGUREMENT.

edg'-ing-ly. With a cautious action. RECKLESSNESS-CAUTION.

ed'-i-ble. Eatable. NUTRIMENT-EXCRETION.

ed'-i-bles. Things edible. NUTRIMENT-EXCRETION.

e'-dict. An authoritative proclamation. ORDER.

ed"-i-fi-ca'-tion. Instruction. CREATION-DESTRUCTION, EDUCATION-LEARNING, EDUCATION-MISTEACHING, GODLINESS-UNGODLINESS.

ed'-i-fice. A building. CREATION-DESTRUCTION.

ed'-i-fy. To build up. CREATION-DESTRUCTION, EDUCATION-MISTEACHING, GODLINESS-UNGODLINESS.

ed'-i-fy-ing. Improving. GOODNESS-BADNESS.

e'-dile. A Roman magistrate. JUDICATURE.

ed'-it. To prepare for publication. PUBLICITY.

e-di'-tion. Publication. PUBLICITY; **new edition,** BETTERMENT-DETERIORATION, RENEWAL.

editio princeps [L.] (î-dish'-i-o prin'-seps). First edition. APPEARANCE-DISAPPEARANCE.

ed'-i-tor. One who edits. MISSIVE-PUBLICATION.

ed"-i-to'-ri-al. An article by an editor. MISSIVE-PUBLICATION.

ed'-i-tor-ship. The office of an editor. MISSIVE-PUBLICATION.

ed'-i-tress. A female editor. MISSIVE-PUBLICATION.

ed'-u-ca-ble. Capable of being educated. EDUCATION-MISTEACHING.

ed'-u-cate. To train, EDUCATION-MISTEACHING.

ed"-u-ca'-ted. Trained. KNOWLEDGE-IGNORANCE.

ed"-u-ca'-tion. Training; culture. EDUCATION-MISTEACHING, EDUCATION - LEARNING, KNOWELDGE-IGNORANCE; **man of education,** SCHOLAR-DUNCE.

EDUCATION—MISTEACHING.

A B C, etc. The first three letters of the alphabet, used generally for the whole; also a primer for teaching elementary reading. See BEGINNING.

Apologue. A fable used to teach a moral.

Calisthenics. A course of exercise which teaches grace and strength.

Classical education. An education founded on the Greek and Roman languages and literatures.

Course. A systematized order of teaching the arts or sciences.

Course of study. A systematized order of study.

Curriculum. A fixed course of study in a school.

Denominational education. An education controlled by some religious denomination.

Direction. The act of administrating.

Discipline. The teaching of the mind and manners.

Discourse. Connected communication of thought.

Drill. The act of teaching military or other exercises.

Edification. Improvement of the mind.

Education. Teaching and training.

Educator. Teacher.

Elementary education. Education embracing but the first rudiments.

Exercise. Activity for the training of body or mind.

Exercitation. Exercise; practise.

Explanation, etc. The meaning assigned to explain anything. See CONTINUITY-INTERPRETATION.

Grammar. A treatise for teaching the principles of any science.

Guidance. The act of guiding; direction.

Gymnastics. Disciplinary exercises of body or mind.

Inculcation. Teaching by repeated and emphatic admonitions.

Indoctrination. Teaching in doctrines or principles.

Initiation. Teaching the rudiments.

Inoculation. Teaching harmful principles.

Instruction. The act of teaching.

Lecture. Teaching by discourse.

Lesson. Instruction conveyed by a teacher.

Liberal education. A refined education.

Moral education. Education which treats of the moral obligations.

Moral tuition. Ethical teaching.

Parable. A story based on probable events of life and nature, and teaching a moral.

Persuasion. Teaching by argument and reason.

Physical education. Training the body by exercise

Practise. Teaching by frequent action.

Preachment. Teaching by discourse or sermon.

Prelection. A lecture read in public.

Preparation. Qualification.

Primary education. Teaching of the first rudiments.

Propædeutics. Preliminary learning.

Propaganda [L.] A system for teaching a peculiar doctrine.

Propagandism. The act of spreading by certain system a peculiar doctrine.

College of Laputa. A college on the flying island of Laputa in *Gulliver's Travels,* wherein was taught the folly of human wisdom.

False teaching. Teaching contrary to truth.

Misdirection. A wrong direction.

Misguidance. Direction into error.

Misinformation. Wrong information.

Misinstruction. Wrong teaching.

Misintelligence. Misunderstanding.

Misleading, etc. See *Verbs.*

Mispersuasion. A wrong opinion.

Misteaching. Wrong instruction.

Perversion. A turning from truth.

Sophistry. False and deceptive reasoning. See RATIOCINATION-CASUISTRY.

The blind leading the blind. Ignorant teachers trying to teach ignorant pupils.

MISTEACHING—*Verbs.*

Ambiguas in vulgum spargere voces [L.]. To spread doubtful reports among the people. [Virgil, *Æneid,* ii, 98.]

Bewilder, etc. To confuse. See CERTAINTY-DOUBT.

Deceive, etc. To mislead; to impose upon. See TRUTHFULNESS-FRAUD.

Lie. To utter a wilful falsehood.

Miscorrect. To correct wrongly.

Misdirect. To direct wrongly.

Misguide. To lead into error.

Misinform. To give false information.

Misinstruct. To teach wrongly.

Mislead, etc. See TRUTH-ERROR.

Misrepresent. To represent falsely.

Misteach. To instruct wrongly.

Mystify. To perplex; to treat obscurely. See ENLIGHTENMENT-SECRECY.

Pervert. To turn to a wrong use.

Preach to the wise. To preach below an audience's mental capacity.

Put on a false scent. To deceive.

Render unintelligible, etc. See CLEARNESS-OBSCURITY.

Teach one's grandmother to suck eggs. To teach an experienced person something he already knows.

Throw off the scent. To put off the track.

Unteach. To cause to give up what has been taught.

MISTEACHING—*Adjectives.*

Misteaching, etc. See *Verbs.*

Unedifying. Not improving the mind.

MISTEACHING—*Phrase.*

Piscem natare doces [L.]. Teach a fish to swim. Figurative for teaching an experienced person what he knows already.

EDUCATION—*Continued.*

Proselytism. The act of converting to a religious sect.
Qualification. An acquirement or trait which fits a person for a place.
Religious education. An education conducted along the lines of religion.
Schooling, etc. See *Verbs.*
Secondary education. An education of secondary rank.
Secular education. An education disassociated with religious teaching.
Sermon. A discourse upon a religious topic.
Sophomore. The second year of study in American colleges; a foolish sophister.

Task. A portion of study assigned by a teacher.
Teaching, etc. See *Verbs.*
Technical education. An education comprising the study of some particular art, science or trade.
Three R's. Reading, Writing, and Arithmetic.
Training. The process of teaching.
Tuition. The act of teaching.
Tutelage. State of being under a guardian.
Tutorage. The office of a private teacher.

EDUCATION—*Verbs.*

Beat into.
Beat into the head. } To teach by repetition.
Break.
Break in. } To make tractable by teaching.
Breed. To form by teaching.
Bring forward. To cause to advance; to adduce.
Bring to. To recall the forgotten.
Bring up. To educate; to teach manners to.
Coach. To prepare, as for an examination, by private teaching.
Convince, etc. To satisfy by evidence. See FAITH.
Cram. To qualify for examination by hurried teaching of the subjects thereof.
Direct. To instruct; to teach.
Direct attention to. See HEED.
Discipline. To prepare by teaching.
Disseminate. To sow broadcast, as education.
Drill. To teach by frequent repetition.
Dry-nurse. To teach his duties to an officer of superior rank.
Edify. To teach and improve.
Educate. To instruct; to teach.
Enlarge the mind. To increase the capacity of the mind for learning.
Enlighten, etc. See ENLIGHTENMENT.
Exercise. To teach by training or practise.
Expound. To teach by interpretation.
Familiarize with. To make conversant with, as by study or practise.
Form. To model by teaching and discipline.
Give a discourse, etc. See *Nouns.*
Give a lecture, etc. See *Nouns.*
Give a lesson, etc. See *Nouns.*
Give a sermon, etc. See *Nouns.*
Give an idea of. To give a general impression of.
Give new ideas, etc. See *Nouns.*
Graft. To unite vitally, as new ideas.
Ground. To teach thoroughly the first principles.
Guide. To instruct and direct.
Habituate. To familiarize by repetition or use.
Hold forth. To teach by haranguing or preaching.
Imbue. To pervade thoroughly with knowledge.
Implant. To infix instruction for growth.
Impregnate. To imbue with an active principle.
Impress upon the memory. To stamp deeply on the memory.
Impress upon the mind. To stamp deeply on the mind.
Improve. To make better by instruction. See BETTERMENT.
Inculcate. To teach by frequent repetitions.

Indoctrinate. To teach in any doctrine.
Infiltrate. To let learning in slowly, as water slowly filters through sand.
Infix. To implant instruction in the mind.
Infuse. To instil, as instruction.
Ingraft. To set deep and firm, as instruction.
Initiate. To guide by instruction in rudiments.
Inoculate. To introduce into the mind.
Instil. To infuse instruction slowly.
Instruct. To teach by systematic method.
Inure. To habituate.
Lecture. To deliver a discourse for instruction.
Moralize. To furnish with moral lessons.
Nurture. To educate.
Open the eyes. To make known to.
Point a moral. To teach a moral lesson.
Practise. To teach by practise. See *Nouns.*
Preach. To teach by sermon or other earnest discourse.
Preinstruct. To teach beforehand.
Prepare. To make ready.
Prime. To teach one beforehand what he is to do.
Put in the way of.
Put to nurse. } To give the first elements of learning to.
Put up to.
Qualify. To furnish with the knowledge or skill for any particular place.
Read a discourse.
Read a lecture.
Read a lesson. } To teach in a formal way.
Read a sermon.
Rear. To bring up; to train and educate.
School. To teach, as in a school.
Send to school. To place under instruction.
Sermonize. To advise.
Set right. To correct; to put in order.
Sharpen the wits. To render the wits more acute.
Sow the seeds of. Implant the beginning of.
Take in hand. To undertake to execute.
Tame. To reclaim from wildness.
Teach. To give instruction to.
Teach the young idea how to shoot. To teach the youth to think. [Thomson, *The Seasons, Spring,* 1149.]
Train. To educate; to rear and to teach.
Tutor. To instruct; to teach.

EDUCATION—*Adjectives.*

Academic. Belonging to an academy.
Didactic. Intended to teach.
Disciplinal. Pertaining to discipline.
Doctrinal. Pertaining to teaching, or to doctrine.
Educable. Capable of being educated.
Educational. Pertaining to education.

Educative. Imparting education.
Instructive. Serving to teach.
Scholastic. Scholarlike
Taught, etc. } See *Verbs.*
Teaching, etc.

EDUCATION—*Phrases.*

A bove majori discit arare minor [L.]. From the older ox the younger learns to plow.
Adeo in teneris consuescere multum est [L.]. So important is it to become trained at a tender age. [Virgil, *Georgics,* ii, 272.]
Docendo discimus [L.]. By teaching we learn.
Experientia docet stultos [L.]. Experience teaches fools. [Seneca, *Epistles.*]

Quæ nocent docent [L.]. Things that injure teach; we burn and learn.
Qui docet discit [L.]. Who teaches learns.
The schoolmaster abroad. A phrase first used by Lord Brougham to express the diffusion of education.

EDUCATION—LEARNING.

LEARNING.

Acquirement. An attainment, as of learning.
Acquisition of knowledge, etc. See KNOWLEDGE.
Acquisition of skill, etc. See SKILL.
Apprenticeship. The state of being bound to a master for the sake of learning a profession or trade.

Aptitude, etc. Natural fitness. See SKILL.
Attainment. Mental acquirements.
Docility, etc. Readiness to learn. See READINESS.
Edification. Improvement and progress in learning or morals.
Erudition. Learning particularly in literature.

LEARNING—*Continued.*

Inquiry, etc. Search for learning by interrogation. See INVESTI-GATION-ANSWER.
Learning. Acquired knowledge.
Matriculation. Act of registering in a society of learning.
Novitiate. Apprenticeship.
Perusal. A careful examination for the purpose of learning.
Prenticeship. Apprenticeship.
Pupilage. } State of being a pupil; a learner.
Pupilarity. }
Reading. Study of books.
Scholarship. Erudition or learning.
Self-instruction. Teaching oneself.
Study. State or act of learning by means of mental application.
Tutelage. State of being under a guardian or instructor.

LEARNING—*Verbs.*

Acquaint oneself with. To familiarize oneself with.
Acquire information. }
Acquire knowledge. } To obtain learning.
Acquire learning. }
Be informed, etc. See ENLIGHTENMENT.
Be studious, etc. See *Adjectives.*
Be taught, etc. See EDUCATION.
Coach up. To privately prepare for examination.
Collect information. }
Collect knowledge. } To learn from many sources.
Collect learning. }
Con over. To study in order to know.
Consume the midnight oil. To study through midnight.
Cram. To prepare hurriedly for examination.
Dip into. To study cursorily.
Drink in information. }
Drink in knowledge. } To learn rapidly.
Drink in learning. }
Gain information.
Gain knowledge.
Gain learning.
Gather information.
Gather knowledge.
Gather learning. } To learn from all sources.
Get information.
Get knowledge.
Get learning.
Glean information.
Glean knowledge.
Glean learning.
Get up. To prepare, as a lesson.
Go to college. }
Go to school. } To go to an institution for instruction.
Go to the university. }

Grind. To instruct; to teach.
Imbibe information. To learn.
Imbibe knowledge. To drink in learning eagerly.
Imbibe learning. To learn.
Learn. To receive instruction.
Learn by heart. To commit to memory.
Learn by rote. To learn by mere effort of memory.
Learn one's trade.. To learn a particular kind of work.
Make oneself acquainted with. To learn well.
Make oneself master of. To learn perfectly.
Master. To learn understandingly.
Mind one's book. To apply oneself to study.
Obtain information. }
Obtain knowledge. } To learn.
Obtain learning. }
Peruse. To read carefully.
Pick up information. }
Pick up knowledge. } To learn.
Pick up learning. }
Pore over. To study thoroughly.
Read. To go over and learn the meaning.
Receive information. }
Receive knowledge. } To learn.
Receive learning. }
Run the eye over. To look over hastily.
Run the eye through. To look through hastily.
Serve an apprenticeship. To be an apprentice.
Serve one's time. To undergo apprenticeship.
Spell. To study by noting characters.
Study. To apply the mind to learning.
Take in information. }
Take in knowledge. } To learn.
Take in learning. }
Thumb over. To wear out by frequent handling.
Turn over the leaves. To look over hastily.
Wade through. To study or read with labor.

LEARNING—*Adjectives.*

Apt. Quick to learn. See SKILL.
Docile. Easily taught. See READINESS.
Industrious. Zealous in laboring. See ACTIVITY.
Scholarly. Like a scholar.
Scholastic. Pertaining to education or schools.
Studious. Given to learning.
Teachable. Capable of learning.

LEARNING—*Adverbs.*

At one's books. While one studies.
In statu pupillari [L.] In a state of learning.

ed″-u-ca′-tion-al. Pertaining to education. EDUCATION-MISTEACHING, SCHOOL.
ed′-u-ca-tive. Imparting education. EDUCATION-MISTEACHING.
ed′-u-ca″-tor. A teacher. EDUCATION-MISTEACHING.
e-duce′. To draw out. DISCOVERY, INJECTION-EJECTION.
e′-duct. Outcome. INCREMENT-REMNANT.
e-duc′-tion. Deduction. INCREMENT-REMNANT.
e-dul′-co-rant. Sweetening. SWEETNESS-ACIDITY.
e-dul′-co-rate. To sweeten. CLEANNESS-FILTHINESS, SWEETNESS-ACIDITY.
e-dul″-co-ra′-tor. That which sweetens or cleanses. SWEETNESS-ACIDITY.
eel. A certain fish. CIRCLE-WINDING; **wriggle like an eel,** AGITATION.
ef-face′. To wipe out. APPEARANCE-DISAPPEARANCE, MARK-OBLITERATION; **efface from the memory,** REMEMBRANCE-FORGETFULNESS.
ef-fect′. To accomplish; the result. CAUSE-EFFECT, COMPLETION-NONCOMPLETION; **carry into effect,** CONDUCT; **good effect,** BEAUTY-UGLINESS; **in effect,** SUBJECTIVENESS-OBJECTIVENESS, TRUTH-ERROR; **take effect,** SUCCESS-FAILURE; **to that effect,** MEANING-JARGON; **with crushing effect,** CREATION-DESTRUCTION.

ef-fect′-ive. Efficient. MIGHT-IMPOTENCE, SUCCESS-FAILURE, USEFULNESS-USELESSNESS.
ef-fects′. Movable property. MERCHANDISE, PROPERTY.
ef-fec′-tu-al. Efficacious. AGENCY, MIGHT-IMPOTENCE, SUCCESS-FAILURE, USEFULNESS-USELESSNESS.
ef-fec′-tu-al-ly. With effect. ENTIRETY-DEFICIENCY.
ef-fec′-tu-ate. To accomplish. COMPLETION-NONCOMPLETION.
ef-fem′-i-na-cy. Womanishness. BRAVERY-COWARDICE, MODERATION-SELFINDULGENCE, STRENGTH-WEAKNESS.
ef-fem′-i-nate. Like a woman. BRAVERY-COWARDICE, MALE-FEMALE, STRENGTH-WEAKNESS.
ef-fen′-di. A Turkish title. GENTILITY-DEMOCRACY.
ef′-fer-ent. Carrying outward. TRANSFER.
ef″-fer-vesce′. To bubble up. AGITATION, EXCITABILITY-INEXCITABILITY, TURBULENCE-CALMNESS, VISCIDITY-FOAM.
ef″-fer-ves′-cence. Excitement; bubbling up. AGITATION, TURBULENCE-CALMNESS, VIGOR-INERTIA, VISCIDITY-FOAM.
ef″-fer-ves′-cent. Gently bubbling. WATER-AIR, VISCIDITY-FOAM.
ef-fete′. Worn out. BETTERMENT-DETERIORATION,

Cleanness-Filthiness, Infancy-Age, Strength-Weakness, Usefulness-Uselessness.

ef″-fi-ca′-cious. Effective. Agency, Usefulness-Uselessness.

ef′-fi-ca-cy. Effective energy. Might-Impotence, Usefulness-Uselessness.

ef-fi′-cien-cy. Effectiveness. Might-Impotence, Usefulness-Uselessness.

ef-fi′-cient. Competent. Agency, Might-Impotence, Skill-Unskilfulness, Usefulness-Uselessness.

ef′-fi-gy. A figure or image. Copy-Model, Delineation-Caricature.

ef-fla′-tion. An emanation. River-Wind.

effleurer [F.] (e-flu-rê′). To graze. Carefulness-Neglect, Traveling-Navigation.

ef″-flo-resce′. To become powdery. Chemistry.

ef″-flo-res′-cence. The act of flowering. Friability.

ef″-flo-res′-cent. Liable to effloresce. Friability.

ef′-flu-ence. Emanation. Entrance-Exit, River-Wind.

ef-flu′-sion. A flowing forth. Entrance-Exit.

ef-flu′-vi-um. An invisible emanation. Liquid-Gas, Odor-Inodorousness.

ef′-flux. An outflow. Entrance-Exit.

ef-flux′-ion. A flowing forth. Entrance-Exit.

ef-form′. To shape. Form-Formlessness.

ef″-for-ma′-tion. The act of giving shape or form. Form-Formlessness.

ef′-fort. Strenuous endeavor. Toil-Relaxation.

ef-front′-ery. Insolent assurance. Presumption-Obsequiousness.

ef-fulge′. Radiate. Light-Darkness.

ef-ful′-gence. Splendor. Light-Darkness.

ef-ful′-gent. Bright. Light-Darkness.

ef-fuse′. To pour forth. Admission-Expulsion, Entrance-Exit, Nutriment-Excretion, Speech-Inarticulateness.

ef-fused′. Poured forth. Entrance-Exit.

ef-fu′-sion. A shedding. Admission-Expulsion, Nutriment-Excretion, Speech-Inarticulateness; **effusion of blood,** Life-Killing.

ef-reet′. A powerful evil genie. Jove-Fiend.

eft. A newt. Earliness-Lateness, Fauna-Flora.

eft-soons′. Speedily. Antecedence-Sequence, Earliness-Lateness.

e. g., exempli gratia [L.], (ex-em′-plai grê′-shi-a). For example. Conventionality-Unconventionality.

e-gad′. By God. Assertion-Denial.

égards [F.] (ê-gar′). Regards. Regard-Disrespect.

egesta [L.] (î-jes′-ta). Excreta. Nutriment-Excretion.

e-ges′-tion. Defecation. Admission-Expulsion.

egg. The oval or roundish body laid by birds, and certain other animals. Cause-Effect, Continuity-Interruption; **egg and dart,** Embellishment-Disfigurement; **egg and tongue,** Embellishment-Disfigurement; **egg on,** Motive-Caprice; **too many eggs in one basket,** Recklessness-Caution, Skill-Unskilfulness; **walk among eggs,** Difficulty-Facility.

egg′-shaped″. Ovoid. Circle-Winding, Roundness.

egg′-shell″. The hard covering of an egg. Cover-Lining.

eg′-o. Self. Materiality-Spirituality, Subjectiveness-Objectiveness; **non-ego,** Subjectiveness-Objectiveness.

eg′-o-hood. Personality. Subjectiveness-Objectiveness.

eg′-o-ism. Selfishness. Unselfishness-Selfishness.

eg′-o-tism. Self-conceit. Conceit-Diffidence, Humanitarianism-Misanthropy, Unselfishness-Selfishness.

eg′-o-tist. One having self-conceit. Humanitarianism-Misanthropy, Unselfishness-Selfishness.

eg″-o-tis′-tic. Characterized by egotism. Conceit-Diffidence, Unselfishness-Selfishness.

eg″-o-tis′-tic-al. Egotistic. Conceit-Diffidence, Humanitarianism-Misanthropy, Unselfishness-Selfishness.

e-gre′-gious. Extreme. Adage-Nonsense, Conventionality-Unconventionality, Goodness-Badness, Gull-Hyperbole.

e-gre′-gious-ly. Extremely. Magnitude-Smallness, Supremacy-Subordinacy.

e′-gress. Departure. Entrance-Exit, Transmission.

e-gur′-gi-tate. To vomit out. Entrance-Exit.

eheu! fugaces labuntur anni [L.] (î′-hiu! fiu-gê′-sîz lê-bun′-tur an′-nai). Alas! the fleeting years slip away. Lastingness-Transientness.

ei′-der—down″. The down of the eider, used largely for stuffing pillows. Cover-Lining.

ei-dol′-o-clast. An idol-breaker. Devotion-Idolatry.

eidolon [Gr.] (ai-do′-lon). Image. Conception-Theme.

ei″-dou-ra′-ni-on. A representation of the heavens. Universe.

eight. A cardinal number. Five-Quinquesection.

eighth. An ordinal numeral. Five-Quinquesection.

eight′-oar″. A vessel. Conveyance-Vessel.

eight′-y. A cardinal number. Five-Quinquesection.

eile mit weile [G.] (ai′-le mit vai′-le). Make haste slowly. Hurry-Leisure.

ei″-le-ton′. A cloth on which the eucharistic elements are laid to be consecrated. Ceremonial.

ei″-se-ge′-sis. A mode of interpretation in which the commentator introduces his own thoughts as those of the author. Interpretation-Misinterpretation.

ei′-ther. One or the other of two. Choice-Neutrality; **happy with either,** Determination-Vacillation.

e-jac′-u-late. To utter suddenly; to eject. Push-Pull, Vocalization-Muteness.

e-jac″-u-la′-tion. Emission; exclamation. Push-Pull, Vocalization-Muteness.

e-jac′-u-la-to-ry. Exclamatory. Vocalization-Muteness.

e-ject′. To expel. Admission-Expulsion.

e-jec′-ta. Matter cast out. Nutriment-Excretion.

e-jec′-tion. Expulsion. Admission-Expulsion, Injection-Ejection, Push-Pull.

e-ject′-ment. A casting out. Admission-Expulsion.

eke. To add to. Addition-Subtraction; **to eke out,** Entirety-Deficiency, Lastingness-Transientness.

El. God, the Almighty. Divinity.

e-lab″-or-ate. To work up; carefully wrought out. Betterment-Deterioration, Completion-Noncompletion, Preparation-Nonpreparation, Toil-Relaxation.

e-lab″-o-ra′-tion. State or quality of being elaborate. Betterment-Deterioration, Completion-Noncompletion, Preparation-Nonpreparation.

el-a′-in. Olein. Pulpiness-Rosin.

élan [F.] (ê-lan′). Ardor. Impetus-Reaction.

e-lapse′. To pass away. Duration-Neverness, Period-Progress.

e-lapsed′. Passed away. Future-Past.

e-laps′-ing. Passing away. Period-Progress.

e-las′-tic. Springy. Elasticity-Inelasticity; **elastic fluid,** Liquid-Gas.

el″-as-tic′-i-ty. Springiness. Elasticity-Inelasticity, Impetus-Reaction, Might-Impotence, Strength-Weakness, Vigor-Inertia.

ELASTICITY—INELASTICITY.

Buoyancy. The tendency to rise to the surface of a liquid.

Elasticity.
Renitency.
Resilience. } Tendency to recover the former condition when forced out of it by pressure, twisting, etc.
Spring.
Springiness.

ELASTICITY—Denotations.

Caoutchouc. India-rubber
Gum elastic. India-rubber.
India-rubber. A soft, very elastic substance, derived from the milky sap of various tropical plants.
Whalebone. A horny substance developed in the form of flattened horny plates from the palate of the whalebone whales.

ELASTICITY—Verbs.

Be elastic, etc. To have the quality of elasticity. See *Adjectives.*
Spring back. To return to former condition because of elasticity.

e-late'. To puff up; exultant. BRAGGING, LIGHT-HEARTEDNESS-DEJECTION.
e-la'-ted. Exultant; puffed up. BRAGGING, JUBILATION-LAMENTATION, LIGHTHEARTEDNESS-DEJECTION, SANGUINENESS-HOPELESSNESS.
e-la'-tion. Exaltation. CONCEIT-DIFFIDENCE.
el'-bow. A joint of the arm; an angle. ANATOMY, ANGULARITY, CONVEXITY-CONCAVITY, IMPETUS-REACTION, PLICATURE; **at one's elbow,** ADVICE, REMOTENESS-NEARNESS; **elbow one's way,** ACTIVITY-INDOLENCE, ADVANCE-RETROGRESSION, QUEST-EVASION; **out at elbows,** AFFLUENCE-PENURY, DRESS-UNDRESS, REPUTATION-DISCREDIT.
el'-bow–chair". An armchair. SUSPENSION-SUPPORT.
el'-bow–grease". Exertion of the arms. FRICTION-LUBRICATION.
el'-bow–room". Scope for activity. EXTENSION-INEXTENSION, LIBERTY-SUBJECTION.
el'-der. Senior; a church officer. INFANCY-AGE, INFANT-VETERAN, MINISTRY-LAITY, NOVELTY-ANTIQUITY.
eld'-er-ly. Somewhat old. INFANCY-AGE.
eld'-er-ship. Seniority. NOVELTY-ANTIQUITY.
eld'-est. Oldest. NOVELTY-ANTIQUITY.
El Do-ra'-do. Any region rich in gold. AFFLUENCE-PENURY.
e-lect'. To choose; chosen. CHOICE-NEUTRALITY, DIVINITY, GODLINESS-UNGODLINESS, GOODNESS-BADNESS, VOLITION-OBLIGATION.
e-lect'-ed. Chosen. GODLINESS-UNGODLINESS.
e-lec'-tion. The act of selecting. CHOICE-NEUTRALITY, NUMBER, VOLITION-OBLIGATION.
e-lec"-tion-eer'-ing. Canvassing for votes. CHOICE-NEUTRALITY.
e-lec'-tor. One who elects. CHIEF-UNDERLING.
e-lec'-tor-ate. The rank or territory of an elector. RULE-LICENSE.
e-lec'-tric. Relating to electricity; easily excited. ELECTRICITY, EMOTION, EXCITABILITY-INEXCITABILITY, SWIFTNESS-SLOWNESS; **electric bell,** ELECTRICITY; **electric light,** ELECTRICITY; **electric motor,** ELECTRICITY; **electric railway,** ELECTRICITY; **electric telegraph,** ELECTRICITY.
e-lec"-tric'-i-ty. A force or power in nature exhibiting itself in light, heat, etc. ELECTRICITY, MIGHT-IMPOTENCE, SWIFTNESS-SLOWNESS.

ELECTRICITY.

Electricity. A non-material form of energy in nature exhibiting itself in lightning, in attraction or repulsion of certain substances, in the production of heat, light, concussion, chemical changes, etc.

ELECTRICITY—Associated Words.

Ampere. Unit of strength of electric current. [French scientist.]
Anion. The portion of an electrically decomposed compound deposited at the anode.
Anode. The positive pole of a battery.

Absence of elasticity. See ELASTICITY.
Inelasticity, etc. Want of elasticity. See HARDNESS-SOFTNESS.
Want of elasticity. See ELASTICITY.

INELASTICITY—Adjectives.

Inelastic, etc. Not elastic. See HARDNESS-SOFTNESS.

ELASTICITY—Continued.

ELASTICITY—Adjectives.

Buoyant. Not sinking in a liquid.
Elastic.
Renitent. } Having the quality of returning to the former condition when forced from it.
Resilient.
Springy.
Tensile. Able to be drawn out.

ELECTRICITY—Associated Words—Continued.

Arc lights. Electric light in which the current gives light while passing over a small break in the circuit.
Armature. Coil of conducting wire rotated near the magnet of a dynamo; piece of soft iron connecting the poles of a horseshoe magnet.
Battery. A number of electric cells, dynamos, etc., coupled so as to give a single current.
Cathode. The negative pole of a battery.
Cell. One element of a voltaic battery.
Charge. Quantity of electricity produced or used in something.
Chronograph. Electrical instrument for measuring time.
Circuit. Course passed through by an electric current.
Conductor. Medium for conveying electricity.
Current. Flow of electricity.
Dielectric. Substance transmitting electricity by induction rather than by conduction.
Discharge. The flow of electricity from one pole to another when connected by a conductor.
Dynamo. Machine for producing an electric current.
Electric bell. Bell rung by an electrical appliance.
Electric light. Light produced by an electric current.
Electric motor. Motor run by electricity.
Electric railway. Railway on which electricity is used as the motive force.
Electric telegraph. Apparatus for transmitting messages, run by electricity.
Electrication. Execution by means of electricity.
Electrification. Process of electrifying.
Electrobiology. Science of electric currents in living organisms.
Electrocution. See ELECTRICATION.
Electrode. A pole of a cell or battery.
Electrodynamics. Study of induction of electric currents.
Electrokinetics. Study of motion of electricity and the forces producing it.
Electrolysis. Decomposition of a compound by passing through it an electric current.
Electroplating. Process of plating by use of an electric current.
Electroscope. Instrument for detecting the presence of electricity.
Electrostatics. Science treating of electrity at rest.
Electrotype. Printing plate covered with a hard metal by electroplating.
Galvanic cell. See CELL.
Galvanometer. Instrument used in measuring strength of an electric current.
Generator. Machine used in generating electricity.
Helix. Wire wound around in the form of a cylinder.
Hoop. An electric conductor in the shape of a hoop.
Hysteresis. Friction of molecules caused by magnetic changes.
Incandescent light. Light formed by a current passing through a fine filament in an air-tight chamber
Inductor. Any part of an electrical apparatus which induces a current in another part.
Insulator. Substance through which electricity does not readily pass.
Kathode. Negative pole of a cell.
Kinetoscope. A device by which the motion of a figure is produced on a picture.
Lodestone. Magnetic iron ore.
Long distance telephone. Telephone operating for many miles.
Magnetic flux. The flow of electricity.
Magnetic whirls. Lines of force around an electrical conductor.
Magnetism. The property shown in some substance of attraction and repulsion of others, etc.
Magnetization. State of being magnetized

ELECTRICITY—ASSOCIATED WORDS—Continued.

Motor. That which communicates motion.

Ohm. The unit measure of electrical resistance.

Ohm's law. Law of electrification discovered by Ohm.

Polarization. Inactivity of a cell caused by gas collecting on the negative plate.

Pole. Point of greatest magnetic or electric force.

Radiograph. An instrument for photographing objects through opaque substances; the X ray.

Rheotome. Contrivance for rapidly making and breaking a circuit.

Solenoid. Helix with one of the wires extending back lengthwise through the inside.

Tasimeter. Instrument for measuring changes in electromotive force.

Trolley. Grooved wheel forming the connection between a car and the wire carrying the current.

Volt. The unit of electric force.

Voltaic pile. Kind of cell invented by Volta.

Volt-ampere. Rate of working in a circuit of one ampere having one volt potential.

Volt-columb. The energy necessary to raise the potential of one columb one volt.

Volt-meter. Instrument for measuring the electromotive force in volts.

Watt. See VOLT-AMPERE.

Wireless telegraphy. Sending of messages without the use of wire conductors.

ELECTRICITY—Verbs.

Break the circuit. To disconnect a conductor.

Make the circuit. To make connections in a conductor.

e-lec″-tri-cu′-tion. Electric execution of criminals. ELECTRICITY.

e-lec″-tri-fi-ca′-tion. Process of electrifying. ELECTRICITY.

e-lec′-tri-fy. To thrill, as with electricity. ASTONISHMENT-EXPECTANCE, EXCITATION, EXPECTATION-SURPRISE.

e-lec″-tro-bi-ol′-o-gy. Mesmerism. ELECTRICITY, DEVOTION-MAGIC.

e-lec″-tro-chem′-is-try. Science of chemical action induced by electricity. ELECTRICITY.

e-lec″-tro-cu′-tion. Electrication. ELECTRICITY.

e-lec′-trode. Pole of a dynamo, etc. ELECTRICITY.

e-lec″-tro-dy-nam′-ics. Science of electric currents. ELECTRICITY.

e-lec″-tro-ki-net′-ics. Science of electricity in motion. ELECTRICITY.

e-lec″-trol′-y-sis. Decomposition by electricity. ELECTRICITY.

e-lec′-tro-lyze. To decompose by electricity. CHEMISTRY, COMPOSITION-RESOLUTION.

e-lec″-tro-mag′-net-ism. Magnetism developed by electricity. MIGHT-IMPOTENCE.

e-lec″-tro-pla′-ting. Plating by electricity ELECTRICITY.

e-lec′-tro-scope. Instrument for detecting electricity. ELECTRICITY.

e-lec′-tro-type. A metallic copy made by electrodeposition. CHEMISTRY, ELECTRICITY, WRITING-PRINTING.

e-lec′-tu-a-ry. A confection. REMEDY-BANE.

el″-e-e-mos′-y-na-ry. Charitable. GIVING-RECEIVING.

el′-e-gance. Gracefulness. BEAUTY-UGLINESS, PURITY-CRUDENESS, RHETORIC, SIMPLICITY-FLORIDNESS, TASTE-VULGARITY.

el′-e-gant. Marked by grace; exhibiting refined taste. BEAUTY-UGLINESS, PURITY-CRUDENESS, TASTE-VULGARITY.

elegantiarum, arbiter [L.] (el″-e-gan-shi-ê′-rum, ar′-bi-ter). An umpire in matters of taste. SOCIETY-LUDICROUSNESS, TASTE-VULGARITY.

el′-e-gant-ly. In good taste. TASTE-VULGARITY.

el-e′-gi-ac. Pertaining to elegies. JUBILATION-LAMENTATION, LIFE-FUNERAL, POETRY-PROSE.

el-e′-gi-acs. Elegies. POETRY-PROSE.

el′-e-gy. Plaintive poetry. JUBILATION-LAMENTATION, LIFE-FUNERAL, POETRY-PROSE.

el′-e-ment. A component part. CAUSE-EFFECT, CONSTITUENT-ALIEN, MATERIALITY-SPIRITUALITY; **devouring element,** HEAT-COLD; **in one's element,** CONTENTEDNESS-DISCONTENTMENT, DIFFICULTY-FACILITY; **out of its element,** ESTABLISHMENT-REMOVAL, HARMONY-DISCORD.

el″-e-men′-ta-ry. Incomplete state of development. MIXTURE-HOMOGENEITY; **elementary education,** EDUCATION-MISTEACHING.

el′-e-ments. The bread and wine of the Lord's Supper. BEGINNING-END, CEREMONIAL.

e-lench′. A refutation. RATIOCINATION-INSTINCT.

elenchus [L.] (e-len′-cus). A refutation. RATIOCINATION-INSTINCT.

el′-e-phant. A large animal. CONVEYER, GREATNESS-LITTLENESS; **white elephant,** REMEDY-BANE.

elephantus non capit murem [L.] (el-e-fan′-tus non kê′-pit miu′-rem). Elephants do not catch mice. CONSEQUENCE-INSIGNIFICANCE.

el′-e-vate. To raise up. ELEVATION-DEPRESSION, REPUTATION-DISCREDIT.

el′-e-va″-ted. Raised up; selfish; slightly intoxicated. ELEVATION-DEPRESSION, FORCE-WEAKNESS, HEIGHT-LOWNESS, TEETOTALISM-INTEMPERANCE, UNSELFISHNESS-SELFISHNESS.

el″-e-va′-tion. The act of raising up. DELINEATION-CARICATURE, ELEVATION-DEPRESSION, ERECTNESS-FLATNESS, FORCE-WEAKNESS, HEIGHT-LOWNESS, UNSELFISHNESS-SELFISHNESS; **angular elevation,** ANGULARITY; **elevation of style,** BETTERMENT-DETERIORATION, REPUTATION-DISCREDIT.

ELEVATION—DEPRESSION.

Elevation. The act of raising up.

Elevator. Machine for raising weights.

Erection. The act of standing up straight.

Exaltation. The raising to a superior condition.

Lift. The act of moving upward by direct force.

Prominence, etc. The condition of being noticeable.

Raising. The act of making higher.

Sublevation. Elev tion.

Sublimation. Changing to a vapor by heating.

Upheaval. The process of heaving up.

ELEVATION—Nouns of Agency.

Capstan. An apparatus for hoisting anchors or other weights.

Crane. A hoisting-machine having the capacity of moving a load in a horizontal or longitudinal direction.

Derrick. An apparatus for hoisting and swinging great weights.

Heaver. One who or that which heaves or lifts.

Lever. A mechanical device consisting of a rigid structure turning freely on a fixed point or fulcrum, and serving to impart pressure or motion from a source of power.

Winch. A windlass used for hoisting.

Windlass. A horizontal drum for hoisting by winding.

Abasement. Humiliation.

Depression. The state of being put or held down.

Detrusion. The state of being thrust down.

Dip, etc. Inclination downward. See CONCAVITY.

Lowering. Becoming lower.

Overset. To throw down.

Overthrow. To overturn; destroy.

Precipitation. The act of throwing headforemost downward.

Prostration. The state of lying flat.

Reduction. The state of being brought lower, or ruined.

Subversion. Overturning; utter destruction.

Upset. State or act of being upset.

DEPRESSION—Denotations.

Bow. A salutation by an inclination of the body or head forward and downward.

Courtesy. A gesture of respect made by bending the knees so as to drop the body slowly a short distance and raise it again.

Curtsy. See COURTESY.

Genuflexion. A bending of the knees, especially in worship.

ELEVATION—DEPRESSION—*Continued.*

ELEVATION—*Verbs.*

Buoy. To keep from sinking in a liquid.
Dredge. To dig up from the bottom of a stream.
Elevate. To bring from a lower to a higher level.
Erect. To raise perpendicularly on a base.
Exalt. To elevate in dignity.
Give a lift. To raise.
Heave. To impel a heavy body upward.
Heighten. To make higher.
Hoist. To raise a heavy body with mechanical means or by great effort.
Lift. To bring up higher by direct exertion
Mount. To ascend by climbing.
Place on a pedestal. To elevate.
Raise. To make the base higher.
Rear. To erect.
Set on a pedestal. To raise up.
Sublimate. To make a vapor of by raising the temperature.
Upbear. To bear up.
Upcast. To cast up.
Upheave. To heave up.
Uphoist. To hoist up.
Uplift. To lift up.
Upraise. To raise up.
Uprear. To rear up.
Weigh. To lift, as an anchor.

ELEVATION—*Verbal Expressions.*

Drag up; draw oneself to his full height; fish up; get up; hold oneself up; hold one's head up; jump up; perch up; perk up; rise up; set up· spring to one's feet; stand up; stick up; take up; tilt up.

ELEVATION—*Adjectives.*

Attolent. Lifting.
Elevated, etc. Raised from a lower to a higher level. See *Verbs.*
Rampant. Leaping.
Stilted. Bombastic.

ELEVATION—*Adverbs, etc.*

On one's hind legs. To one's full height.
On one's legs. Standing up.
On stilts. ⎫
On the shoulders of. ⎬ Raised up.

DEPRESSION—*Continued from Column 2.*

DEPRESSION—*Phrase.*

Facinus quos inquinat æquat [L.]. Crime reduces those whom it stains to one level.

élève [F.] (ê-lev′). A pupil. INSTRUCTOR-PUPIL.
e-lev′-en. A cardinal number. FIVE-QUINQUESECTION.
e-lev′-enth. An ordinal numeral. FIVE-QUINQUE-SECTION; **eleventh hour,** EARLINESS-LATENESS, MORNING-EVENING, OPPORTUNENESS-UNSUITABLE-NESS.
elf. A sprite. GREATNESS-LITTLENESS, INFANT-VETERAN, JOVE-FIEND, MALE-FEMALE.
elf′-in. An elf. JOVE-FIEND.
elf′-like″. Like an elf. JOVE-FIEND.
e-lic′-it To draw out gradually. CAUSE-EFFECT, DISCOVERY, INJECTION-EJECTION, MANIFESTATION-LATENCY.
el′-i-gi-ble. Suitable. PROPRIETY-IMPROPRIETY.
e-lim′-i-nate To remove. ADDITION-SUBTRACTION, ADMISSION-EXPULSION, INCLUSION-OMISSION, INJECTION-EJECTION, MIXTURE-HOMOGENEITY, MULTIPLICITY-PAUCITY.
e-lim″-i-na′-tion. The act of eliminating. INCLUSION-OMISSION, INJECTION-EJECTION, MIXTURE-HOMOGENEITY, MULTIPLICITY-PAUCITY.
e-li′-sion. The omission of a part of a word. LENGTH-SHORTNESS, UNION-DISUNION

DEPRESSION—DENOTATIONS—*Continued.*

Kowtow. A Chinese form of obeisance in which an inferior kneels and touches the ground with his forehead.
Obeisance. An act of courtesy or reverence made by an inclination of the body or the bending of the knee.

DEPRESSION—*Verbs.*

Abase. To humiliate.
Bend. To crook.
Bob. To move up and down in a quick, restless manner.
Bow. To nod the head.
Cast. To throw down.
Courtesy. Bow.
Cower. To crouch down as if in fear.
Crouch. To cringe in fear.
Curtsy. Bow.
Debase. To lower in value, character.
Depress. To hold down.
Detrude. To thrust down forcibly.
Dip. To sink or let down for an instant.
Duck. To plunge under water for an instant.
Fell. To cause to fall.
Kneel. To rest on the knees.
Level. To make parallel to horizon.
Lower. To cause to take a lower position.
Overset. ⎫
Overthrow. ⎬ To destroy.
Overturn. ⎭
Pitch. To plunge downward.
Precipitate. To hurl headfirst from a height.
Prostrate. To knock down.
Raze. To tear down.
Recline, etc. To lean. See ERECTNESS-FLATNESS.
Reduce. To bring from a higher to a lower position.
Sink. To go down through a lighter medium.
Squat. To rest on the haunches.
Stoop. To bend the body down.
Subvert. To turn upside down.
Upset. To overturn.

DEPRESSION—*Verbal Expressions.*

Bend the head, bend the knee, bow down, bow the head, bow the knee, submit; bring low; cast down; cut down; dash down; fling down; hew down; knock down; let down; let down a peg, let down a little; let drop; let fall; pull about one's ears, to annoy; pull down; raze to the ground; sit down; take down; take down a peg, to humiliate somewhat; throw down; trample in the dust, to treat with the greatest insult.

DEPRESSION—*Adjectives.*

At a low ebb. In the lowest or weakest condition.
Depressed. Held down. See sub *Verbs.*
Prostrate, etc. Stretched out; helpless. See ERECTNESS-FLATNESS.

(Continued on Column 1.)

élite [F.] (ê-lît′). The choicest part. GENTILITY-DEMOCRACY, GOODNESS-BADNESS, REPUTATION-DISCREDIT, SOCIETY-LUDICROUSNESS.
e″-lix-a′-tion. Extracting by steeping or boiling. HEATING-COOLING.
el-ix′-ir. A cordial or invigorator. REMEDY-BANE.
ell. A measure of length. LENGTH-SHORTNESS; **take an ell,** DUENESS-UNDUENESS, PRESUMPTION-OBSEQUIOUSNESS, RIGHT-WRONG, UNSELFISHNESS-SELFISHNESS.
el-lipse′. A certain plane curve. CIRCLE-WINDING.
el-lip′-sis. The omission of words obviously understood. LENGTH-SHORTNESS, RHETORIC, TERSENESS-PROLIXITY.
el-lip′-soid. A solid, every plane section of which is either a circle or an ellipse. CIRCLE-WINDING, ROUNDNESS.
el-lip′-tic. Shaped like an ellipse. CIRCLE-WINDING.
el-lip′-tic-al. Shaped like an ellipse. CIRCLE-WINDING, RHETORIC, TERSENESS-PROLIXITY.
el″-o-ca′-tion. Removal from one's control. ESTABLISHMENT-REMOVAL, TRANSFER.

el″-o-cu′-tion. The art of correct speaking. Speech-Inarticulateness.

el″-o-cu′-tion-a-ry. Pertaining to elocution. Speech-Inarticulateness.

éloge [F.] (ê-lozh′). A biographical and eulogistic memoir. Approval-Disapproval.

e-lon′-gate. To make longer. Length-Shortness.

e-lon″-ga′-tion. Extension. Astronomy, Remoteness-Nearness.

e-lope′. To run away. Quest-Evasion.

e-lope′-ment. A running off. Escape.

el′-o-quence. Lofty, impassioned, and fluent utterance. Force-Weakness, Speech-Inarticulateness.

el′-o-quent. Having remarkable power in public speaking. Force-Weakness, Speech-Inarticulateness.

else. Besides; otherwise. Addition-Subtraction.

else′-where″. Somewhere else. Presence-Absence.

e-lu′-ci-date. To make plain. Clearness-Obscurity, Interpretation-Misinterpretation.

e-lude′. To escape from. Escape, Observance-Nonobservance, Quest-Evasion, Ratiocination-Casuistry, Success-Failure.

e-lu′-sion. The act of eluding. Quest-Evasion.

e-lu′-sive. Hard to grasp or keep. Truthfulness-Fraud.

e-lu′-so-ry. Intangible. Truthfulness-Fraud.

e-lu′-tri-ate. To purify by washing. Cleanness-Filthiness.

e-lu′-vi-um. Wind-drift. River-Wind.

E-lys′-ian. Blissful. Heaven-Hell, Pleasurableness-Painfulness; **Elysian fields,** Heaven-Hell.

E-lys′-i-um. The Greek paradise. Heaven-Hell, Pleasure-Pain.

el′-y-tron. One of the thickened forewings of beetles, etc. Cover-Lining.

El′-ze-vir. Relating to the Elzevirs, publishers of Amsterdam and Leyden. **Elzevir edition,** Greatness-Littleness.

e-ma″-ci-a″-ted. Thin. Breadth-Narrowness.

e-ma″-ci-a′-tion. Excessive leanness. Breadth-Narrowness, Enlargement-Diminution.

em′-a-nant. Issuing from a source. Entrance-Exit.

em′-a-nate. To originate. Entrance-Exit, Nutriment-Excretion; **emanate from,** Cause-Effect, Truthfulness-Falsehood.

em″-a-na′-tion. Effluence. Entrance-Exit, Nutriment-Excretion, Odor-Inodorousness.

em′-a-na″-tist. One who maintains that all things are produced by an evolution from the Divine Being. Revelation-Pseudorevelation.

e-man′-ci-pate. To liberate. Difficulty-Facility, Release-Restraint.

e-man″-ci-pa′-tion. The act of setting free. Liberty-Subjection, Release-Restraint.

e-mas′-cu-late. To weaken. Cleanness-Filthiness, Might-Impotence.

e-mas″-cu-la′-tion. Removal of strength. Might-Impotence.

em-balm′. To keep from decay. Conservation, Life-Funeral, Perfume-Stench; **embalm in the memory,** Remembrance-Forgetfulness.

em-bank′-ment. Any artificial bank. Attack-Defense, Dweller-Habitation, Refuge-Pitfall.

em″-bar-ca′-tion. Act of embarking. Arrival-Departure, Beginning-End.

em-bar′-go. To prohibit; an authoritative stoppage of foreign commerce. Leave-Prohibition, Movement-Rest.

em-bark′. To venture. Arrival-Departure, Transfer; **embark in,** Beginning-End, Enterprise.

embarquer sans biscuits, s' [F.] (san′-bar-kê′ san· biscwi′). To begin without sufficient preparation. Preparation-Nonpreparation.

embarras de choix [F.] (an′-bar-ra′ de shwa). The difficulty of choosing. Choice-Neutrality.

embarras de richesses [F.] (an′-bar-ra′ de ri-shes′). The plague of riches. Affluence-Penury, Excess-Lack.

em-bar′-rass. To disconcert. Certainty-Doubt, Difficulty-Facility, Obstruction-Help, Propriety-Impropriety.

em-bar′-rassed. Involved in difficulties. Affluence-Penury, Credit-Debt.

em-bar′-rass-ing. Confusing. Difficulty-Facility.

em-bar′-rass-ment. Difficulty. Certainty-Doubt, Difficulty-Facility, Obstruction-Help.

em-base′. To vitiate. Betterment-Deterioration.

em-bas′-sa-dor. A state agent. Consignee.

em′-bas-sy. The person, mission, or office of an ambassador. Commission-Abrogation, Consignee, Tidings-Mystery.

em-bat′-tled. Ready for battle; crenulated. Association, Fighting-Conciliation, Organization-Disorganization.

em-bay′. Enclose. Keeping-Relinquishment.

em-bed′. To lay, as in a bed. Establishment-Removal, Injection-Ejection, Outside-Inside, Suspension-Support.

em-bed′-ded. Sunk or laid. Confinement, Establishment-Removal.

em-bel′-lish. To decorate. Embellishment-Disfigurement.

em-bel′-lish-ment. Decoration. Embellishment-Disfigurement.

EMBELLISHMENT—DISFIGUREMENT.

Adornment. That which beautifies or adorns.

Decoration. A state of being decked or ornamented in order to beautify.

Excess of ornament, etc. See Taste-Vulgarity.

Embellishment. Artificial, showy decoration.

Ornament. Anything added to a thing to increase its beauty or elegance.

Ornamental art. The art of ornamenting or decorating.

Ornamentation. The state of being adorned or made beautiful.

Ornateness. The state of being highly and artistically finished.

Ornature. Decoration; embellishment.

Richness. State of being luxuriant.

Blemish. A defacing mark.

Blot. A stain or a blemish.

Blur. A blemish.

Defect, etc. Want of something necessary for completeness, etc. See Faultlessness-Faultiness.

Deformity. } Anything that destroys beauty, grace, or propriety.
Disfigurement. }

Flaw. A natural defect.

Spot. A stain or blemish.

Spottiness. The state of being full of spots.

Stain. A defective mark, tarnish.

Tarnish. Soil

EMBELLISHMENT—*Denotations.*

Acanthus. A decoration in the shape of the acanthus leaf.

Agate. A variety of quartz, presenting various tints in the same specimen.

Aigrette [F.]. A plume.

Aiglet. A tag of lace formerly used in dress.

Amethyst. A violet blue gem.

DISFIGUREMENT—*Denotations.*

Birthmark. Some peculiar mark or blemish on the body at birth.

Blain. A blister.

Blotch. A spot or daub.

Dirt, etc. See Cleanness-Filthiness.

Excrescence. An unnatural growth, as a wart or tumor.

Eyesore. Something offensive to the eye or sight.

EMBELLISHMENT—DISFIGUREMENT—*Continued.*

EMBELLISHMENT—Denotations—*Continued.*

Anklet.   A ring for the ankle.
Anthemion.   A floral ornament.
Arabesque.   A fanciful ornament of plant and animal forms.
Architecture.   The science or art of constructing or building.
Arras.   A figured ornamental tapestry.
Astragal.   A small convex molding.
Balais [F.].   A rose-colored ruby.
Beau-catcher.   A curl worn by women over the temple.
Beryl.   A bluish yellowish variety of green emerald.
Bijou [F.].   Anything small and of elegant workmanship.
Bijouterie.   Jewels.
Bijoutry.   Small articles, as jewelry, trinkets, etc.
Border.   A strip arranged along the edge as an ornament or finish.
Bouquet.   A bunch of flowers.
Bow.   An ornamental knot formed by doubling a ribbon.
Bracelet.   An ornamental ring or band for the wrist or arm.
Brilliant.   A fine diamond.
Brocade.   A fabric woven with raised figures.
Brocatelle [F.].   A figured fabric.
Broidery.   Ornamental needlework.
Brooch.   An ornament, in various forms, with a pin or loop for attaching it to a garment.
Calcedony.   A colored, waxy quartz.
Carbuncle.   A gem of a brilliant deep red color.
Carcanet.   A jeweled necklace of gold.
Cartouche.   An inscribed ornamental scroll.
Chain.   A series of links or rings, usually of metal, used for ornament.
Chaplet.   A garland worn on the head.
Chatelaine.   An ornament hanging from a woman's belt.
Chrysolite.   A mineral of a yellow or green color.
Clinquant [F.].   Tinsel.
Coquillage [F.].   Ornamentation in imitation of shells.
Coral.   The hard parts of the skeleton of various small sea animals, used for ornamentation.
Cosmetics   A compound applied to the skin to beautify it.
Cul-de-lampe [F.].   Ornamental design to fill out a page.
Detail.   A minor ornamental part.
Diamond.   The most precious of gems
Diaper.   A fine silk or linen cloth with interwoven figures.
Drap d'or [F.].   Cloth of gold.
Earring.   An ornament consisting of a ring passed through the lobe of the ear.
Edging   That which forms an edge or border.
Embroidery.   Needlework used to enrich textile fabrics.
Emerald.   A precious stone of a deep green color.
Enamel.   A glassy hard coating used for ornamental purposes.
Epaulet. } A shoulder ornament or badge worn by military and
Épaulette. } naval officers.
Ermine.   A white fur used to ornament certain robes of office.
Feather.   A dermal appendage of birds, much used for ornament
Festoon.   A garland of decorative material.
Fillet.   A narrow band to encircle the head.
Finery.   Ornament or decoration.
Fleur-de-lis [F.].   A conventional flower suggested by the iris, and having a form which fits it for the terminal decoration of a scepter, the ornaments of a crown, etc.
Fleuron [F.].   A rose-like ornament surrounded by leaves.
Flourish.   A decorative mark.
Flower.   The bloom or blossom of a plant.
French polish.   A varnish for woodwork.
Fret.   An ornamental relief work.
Fringe.   An ornamental appendage to a piece of stuff.
Frippery.   Cheap and tawdry decoration.
Frog.   An ornamental button with a loop to fasten a cloak.
Galloon.   A dress trimming.
Garland.   A wreath made of branches, flowers, or feathers.
Garnet.   A variously colored precious stone.
Garnish.   Something added for embellishment.
Gaud.   Vulgar finery.
Geegaw.   A useless gaudy ornament.
Gem.   A precious stone of any kind.
Gilding.   Any superficial coating or appearance.
Gimcrack.   A cheap gaudy ornament.
Girasol. } An opal with reddish reflections.
Girasole. }
Graining.   Painting or staining, in imitation of the grain of wood, stone, etc.
Hanging.   That which is hung, as lining or drapery for the walls of a room.
Headpiece.   An engraved ornament at the head of a chapter or page.

DISFIGUREMENT—Denotations—*Continued.*

Freckle.   A small yellowish or brownish spot on the skin.
Injury, etc.   See Betterment-Deterioration.
Macula.   A spot on the skin.
Maculation.   The act of spotting; a blemish.
Mole.   A small permanent spot on the skin.
Patch.   A piece of anything used to repair a breach, or hide a defect.
Pimple, etc.   See Convexity.
Pustule.   An elevation of the upper skin containing pus.
Scar.   A mark remaining in the skin or flesh after a wound is healed.
Smudge.   A stain or blot.
Speck. } A spot or stain.
Speckle. }
Spots on the sun.   Dark spots that appear on the sun's disk.
Wen.   An encysted tumor.

DISFIGUREMENT—*Verbs.*

Begrease.   To cover with grease.
Disfigure, etc.   To render unsightly or destroy the beauty of, etc. See Betterment-Deterioration.
Speckle.   To cover with spots.

DISFIGUREMENT—*Adjectives.*

Bloodshot.   Red and inflamed.
Bobtailed.   Having a short tail or a tail cut off.
Discolored.   Having an unnatural color.
Freckled.   Covered with spots.
Imperfect, etc.   Not complete, etc.   See Faultlessness-Faultiness.
Injured, etc.   Hurt, not perfect, etc.   See Betterment-Deterioration.
Pitted.   Marked with hollows.

EMBELLISHMENT—Denotations—*Continued.*

Heliotrope.   A green calcedony; a fragrant flower, named as if it turned with the sun.
Hyacinth.   A brown, orange, or red precious stone.
Illumination.   Adornment of books and manuscripts with colored illustrations.
Jacinth.   Hyacinth.
Japanning lacquer.   A hard, black varnish.
Jasper.   An opaque variety of quartz, of red, yellow, and other dull colors.
Jewel.   An ornament of dress usually made of a precious metal.
Jewellery. } Jewels, collectively.
Jewelry. }
Knot.   An intricately interwoven piece of embroidery.
Lace.   A fabric of fine threads of linen, silk, or cotton, etc.
Lapis-lazuli.   A mineral of a rich blue color.
Lazuli.   See Lapis-lazuli.
Listel.   A fillet.
Locket.   A little case for holding a miniature or lock of hair.
Millinery.   Articles made by a milliner, as head-dresses, hats, laces, etc. [Milan, Italy.]
Molding.   Grooved or ornamental bars of wood or metal.
Necklace.   A string of beads, etc., worn around the neck.
Nosegay   A bunch of odorous and showy flowers.
Onyx.   A variously colored variety of quartz.
Opal.   A gem of peculiarly changing colors.
Oriental topaz.   A very hard, dark-colored mineral used in polishing.
Panache.   A plume of feathers. [French from Latin *penna.*]
Paneling.   Woodwork with raised margins, molded or otherwise.
Parure.   A set of ornaments, as of trimmings for a costume.
Paste.   False jewelry.
Pattern.   Figure or style of decoration.
Pearl.   A shelly concretion, usually rounded and having a brilliant luster, found in the shell of the pearl oyster.
Peridot.   Chrysolite.
Pilaster.   A column-like projection from a wall.
Pinchbeck.   A cheap imitation of gold.
Plasma.   A greenish quartz used as a gem.
Plume.   A feather, or group of feathers, used as an ornament.
Polish.   Anything used to produce a gloss.
Posy.   A small bouquet. [Poesy.]
Powdering.   The act of employing powder to make the complexion more beautiful.
Precious stone.   A gem or jewel.
Rosette.   A rose-like ornament.
Ruby.   A precious stone of a deep red color.

EMBELLISHMENT—Denotations—*Continued.*

Sapphire. A blue gem.
Sard. A deep blood-red gem.
Sardonyx. A variety of onyx.
Shoulder-knot. An ornament worn by military or naval officers.
Spangle. Something brilliant used as an ornament.
Spinel. }
Spinelle. } A variously colored very hard mineral.
Star. A device of star-shape to distinguish rank.
Strapwork. An ornament.
Tailpiece. An ornament placed at the bottom of a short page to fill up the space.
Tapestry. A fabric worked with pictorial designs.
Tassel. A pendent ornament.
Texture. A woven fabric.
Tinsel. A shining material used for ornamental purposes.
Topaz. A yellowish and pellucid mineral.
Topknot. An ornamental knot worn on top of the head.
Torque. A necklace of wire.
Tracery. Ornamental work with ramified lines.
Trapping. Ornamental harness for a horse.
Trimming. That which serves to ornament.
Trinket. A small ornament.
Turquoise. A blue or green gem.
Varnish. A resinous liquid used for imparting a smooth, glossy surface.
Vignette. An ornament of leaves and tendrils.
Wreath. Something twisted, intertwined, or curled.
Zigzag. A series of short, sharp angles.
Zircon. A hard colored mineral cut into gems.

Embellishment—*Figurative Nouns and Expressions.*

"Daisies pied and violets blue." [Shakespeare, *L. L. L.*, V, ii, 904.]
Egg and dart. }
Egg and tongue. } Alternate egg and dart-shaped decorations
Flowers of rhetoric, etc. See Simplicity-Floridness.
Pride. The most ornamented or beautiful part of anything
Work of art. A production or work requiring the application of the highest skill.

Embellishment—*Verbs.*

Adonize. To beautify; dainty oneself, like Adonis.
Adorn. To enhance the beauty of in the most tasteful manner.

EMBELLISHMENT—Verbs—*Continued.*

Array. To decorate, dress.
Beautify. To make beautiful or more pleasing.
Become, etc. See Harmony.
Bedeck. To cover with.
Bedight. To array, adorn.
Bedizen. To dress or adorn vulgarly or in bad taste.
Bespangle. To cover or adorn with spangles.
Chase. To ornament a metal by embossing.
Deck. To cover.
Decorate. To improve the appearance of by additions.
Dight. To dress or adorn.
Dizen. To dress or ornament.
Dress up. To put on elaborate clothing.
Embellish. To decorate showily.
Emblazon. To adorn.
Emboss. To cover with raised ornaments.
Embroider. To work designs with a needle.
Enamel. To cover with a hard varnish.
Fig out. To dress.
Fret. To decorate with ornamental work.
Furbish. To make bright by rubbing.
Garnish. To surround with ornaments.
Gild. To cover with gold plate.
Grain. To paint or stain like the grain of wood or marble.
Illuminate. To adorn with colored figures.
Illustrate. To adorn with pictures.
Japan. To cover with lacquer.
Lacquer. To cover with a varnish; enamel.
Ornament. To affix separate and distinct decorations.
Paint. To decorate with colors.
Polish. To make bright by rubbing.
Powder. To improve the appearance by means of powder.
Prank. To adorn in a showy manner.
Prink. To adorn oneself with great care and nicety.
Smarten. To improve one's appearance.
Spangle. To decorate with spangles.
Trick out. To dress or ornament with something showy and cheap.
Trim. To dress.
Varnish. To cover with a lustrous polish.
Whitewash. To coat with a mixture of slaked lime and water.
Work. To embroider.

Embellishment—*Adjectives.*

Beautified. Embellished; made beautiful.
Becoming, etc. Suitable, etc. See Harmony.
Bedight. Adorned, covered, dressed.
Begilt. Covered with gilt.
Decorative. Ornamental; pertaining to a decoration.
Dressed to advantage. Well dressed.
Endimanché [F.]. Dressed in Sunday clothes.
En grande tenue [F.]. }
En grande toilette [F.]. } In full dress.
Festooned. Decorated.
Fine as a carrot fresh scraped. }
Fine as a Mayday queen. } Very splendid.
Fine as fivepence. }
Flashy. Having a cheap and showy appearance.
Flowery. Overadorned.
Gairish. }
Garish. } Having a gaudy effect.
Gaudy, etc. Flashy, etc. See Taste-Vulgarity.
Gay. Brilliant in appearance.

Gilt. Golden.
Glittering. Shining, sparkling.
Gorgeous. Conspicuous on account of brilliant colors.
In best bib and tucker. In best appearance.
In full dress, etc. See Society.
In Sunday best. In best dress.
New gilt. Newly covered with gold.
New spangled. Newly decorated with spangles.
Ornamental. Decorative.
Ornamented, etc. Having ornaments added, etc. See *Verbs.*
Ornate. Highly decorated.
Pranked out. Dressed with showy ornaments.
Rich. Composed of precious materials.
Showy. Gaudy; dressed in cheap ornaments.
Smart. Well and carefully dressed.
Tasselated. Adorned with tassels.
Tricksy. Neat; like Ariel [*Tempest*, V, i, 226]; quaint [*Merchant of Venice*, III, v, 74].

EMBELLISHMENT—SIMPLICITY.

Simplicity.

Chastity. Purity.
Homeliness. The state or quality of being simple.
Plainness. A simple and unaffected state.
Simplicity. The state of being free from artificiality.
Undress. The habitual dress of a soldier, not his full uniform.

Simplicity—*Verbs.*

Be simple, etc. To be plain, unaffected, etc. See *Adjectives.*
Render simple, etc. To make plain, etc. See *Adjectives.*
Simplify. To make plain or easy to understand.

Simplicity—*Adjectives.*

Bald. Free from all adornment.
Chaste. Pure.

Dull. Not bright; obscure.
Flat. Without gloss.
Free from affectation. }
Free from ornament. } Without artificiality or decoration.
Homely. Not pretentious; plain.
Homespun. Plain and simple in character.
Inornate. Not decorated or embellished.
Ordinary. Usual; common
Plain. Unpretentious; unadorned. Plain in thy neatness [Milton], *simplex munditiis.*
Severe. Free from all useless ornament.
Simple. Free from affectation; natural.
Unadorned. Not embellished; when unadorned, adorned the most [Thomson, *Seasons, Autumn*, 204].
Unaffected. Simple and unpretentious in manner.

EMBELLISHMENT—SIMPLICITY—*Continued.*

Unarrayed.
Undecked.
Ungarnished.
Unornamented. } Without decoration.
Untrimmed.
Unvarnished.

En déshabillé [F.]. In undress.
Sans façon [F.] Informally
Simplex munditiis [L.]. Of simple elegance. [Horace, *Odes*, 1, 2, 5.]

SIMPLICITY—*Phrase.*

Veritatis simplex oratio est [L.]. The language of truth is simple.

em′-bers. Smoldering remnants of fire. HEATING-COOLING.

em-bez′-zle. To appropriate by breach of trust. THEFT.

em-bez′-zle-ment. Fraudulent appropriation. THEFT.

em-bit′-ter. To render bitter. ALLEVIATION-AGGRAVATION, BETTERMENT-DETERIORATION, FAVORITE-ANGER.

em-bla′-zon. To adorn with armorial ensigns; to extol. COLOR-ACHROMATISM, EMBELLISHMENT-DISFIGUREMENT, POMP.

em′-blem. Symbol. SIGN; **emblem of authority,** SCEPTER.

em′′-blem-at′-ic. Symbolic. SIGN.

em-bod′-ied. Clothed. **Embodied beauty,** NATURE-ART.

em-bod′-i-ment. The act of embodying. COMPOSITION-RESOLUTION, WHOLE-PART.

em-bod′-y. To incorporate. COMPOSITION-RESOLUTION, INCLUSION-OMISSION, UNION-DISUNION, WHOLE-PART.

em-bold′-en. To encourage. BRAVERY-COWARDICE, SANGUINENESS-TIMIDITY.

em′-bo-lism. Interrelation. ENVIRONMENT-INTERPOSITION.

em′′-bo-lis′-mal. Pertaining to embolism. ENVIRONMENT-INTERPOSITION.

embonpoint [F.] (an′-bon′-pwan′). Stoutness. GREATNESS-LITTLENESS.

em-bos′-omed. Enclosed. CONFINEMENT, ENVIRONMENT-INTERPOSITION, ESTABLISHMENT-REMOVAL.

em-boss′. To ornament in relief. CONVEXITY-CONCAVITY, EMBELLISHMENT-DISFIGUREMENT.

em-boss′-ment. Figure in relief. CONVEXITY-CONCAVITY.

embouchure [F.] (an′-bu-shür′). Point of discharge. APERTURE-CLOSURE.

em-bow′-el. To disembowel; to bury. ADMISSION-EXPULSION.

em-brace′. To hug; to accept; to enclose. ADMISSION-EXCLUSION, AMITY-HOSTILITY, BLANDISHMENT, CENTER, CHOICE-NEUTRALITY, INCLUSION-OMISSION, POLITENESS-IMPOLITENESS, SOCIABILITY-PRIVACY, TAKING-RESTITUTION; **embrace an offer,** CONSENT.

em-bran′-gle. To entangle. ORGANIZATION-DISORGANIZATION.

em-bran′-gle-ment. Entanglement. VARIANCE-ACCORD.

em-bra′-sure. A splayed opening in a wall. APERTURE-CLOSURE, INDENTATION.

em-breast′-ment. A swelling in the surface of the ground. CONVEXITY-CONCAVITY.

em′-bro-cate. To moisten and rub. REMEDY-BANE.

em′′-bro-ca′-tion. A liniment. REMEDY-BANE.

em-broid′-er. To ornament. EMBELLISHMENT-DISFIGUREMENT, TRUTHFULNESS-FALSEHOOD, VARIEGATION.

em-broid′-ered. Ornamented. VARIEGATION.

em-broid′-er-y. Ornamental work done with the needle. EMBELLISHMENT-DISFIGUREMENT, GULL-HYPERBOLE, INCREMENT-REMNANT.

em-broil′. To involve in strife. ORGANIZATION-DISORGANIZATION, VARIANCE-ACCORD.

em-broiled′. Mixed up. VARIANCE-ACCORD.

em-broil′-ment. Contention. REGULARITY-IRREGULARITY, VARIANCE-ACCORD.

em-brown′. To darken. GRAY-BROWN.

em′-bry-o. The germ of anything. BIOLOGY, CAUSE-EFFECT; **in embryo,** BEGINNING-END, CAUSE-EFFECT, OCCURRENCE-DESTINY, PREPARATION-NONPREPARATION.

em′′-bry-on′-ic. Rudimentary. BEGINNING-END, CAUSE-EFFECT, GREATNESS-LITTLENESS, PREPARATION-NONPREPARATION.

em′′-bry-ot′-ic. Pertaining to the embryo. CAUSE-EFFECT.

em′′-en-da′-tion. Correction. BETTERMENT-DETERIORATION.

e-mend′-a-to-ry. Pertaining to emending. BETTERMENT-DETERIORATION.

em′-er-ald. Green; a gem. EMBELLISHMENT-DISFIGUREMENT, REDNESS-GREENNESS.

e-merge′. To issue from. ENTRANCE-EXIT.

e-mer′-gence. Process of emerging. CONDITION-SITUATION, ENTRANCE-EXIT.

e-mer′-gen-cy. An unexpected occurrence. CONDITION-SITUATION, DIFFICULTY-FACILITY, OCCURRENCE-DESTINY.

em′-er-il. A glazier's diamond. WORKSHOP.

e-mer′-i-tus. Retired from active service. REGARD-DISRESPECT, SAGE-FOOL.

e-mer′-sion. The act of coming forth. ENTRANCE-EXIT.

em′-er-y. A variety of corundum. SHARPNESS-BLUNTNESS; **emery paper,** SMOOTHNESS-ROUGHNESS.

em′-e-sis. Vomiting. ADMISSION-EXPULSION.

e-met′-ic. A medicine to induce vomiting. REMEDY-BANE.

émeute [F.] (ê-mut′). A riot. INSUBORDINATION-OBEDIENCE.

em′′-i-ca′-tion. A scintillation. LIGHT-DARKNESS.

em′-i-grant. Migrating; a person going from one country to another. CONSTITUENT-ALIEN, ENTRANCE-EXIT, WAYFARER-SEAFARER.

em′-i-grate. To remove permanently from native land. TRAVELING-NAVIGATION.

em′′-i-gra′-tion. A going from one's native land. ENTRANCE-EXIT, TRAVELING-NAVIGATION.

em′-i-nence. HEIGHT-LOWNESS, MINISTRY-LAITY, REPUTATION-DISCREDIT.

em′-i-nent. High; distinguished. HEIGHT-LOWNESS, REPUTATION-DISCREDIT.

em′-i-nent-ly. In an eminent degree. SUPREMACY-SUBORDINACY.

e-mir′. A high Turkish official. CHIEF-UNDERLING, GENTILITY-DEMOCRACY.

em′-is-sa-ry. A secret agent. CONSIGNEE, MESSENGER.

e-mis′-sion. A throwing out. ADMISSION-EXPULSION.

e-mit′. To discharge. ADMISSION-EXPULSION, PUBLICITY; **emit vapor,** LIQUEFACTION-VAPORIZATION.

e-mit′-ted. Put forth. ADMISSION-EXPULSION.

e-mit′-ting. Putting forth. ADMISSION-EXPULSION.

Em-man′-u-el. Immanuel. DIVINITY.

em′′-me-le′-ia. Perfect harmony. MELODY-DISCORD.

em′-met. An ant. GREATNESS-LITTLENESS.

em′′-ol-les′-cence. The act of becoming soft. HARDNESS-SOFTNESS.

e-mol′-li-ent. Softening. REMEDY-BANE.

e-mol′-u-ment. Compensation. GAIN-LOSS, OUTLAY-INCOME, RECOMPENSE-PUNITION.

e-mo′-tion. An act or state of excited feeling. AFFECTIONS.

EMOTION

Affection. Strong attachment
Agitation. Strong, confused feelings, aroused by fear, etc.
Ardor. Intensity of passion.
Cordiality. Warmth of manner.
Deep sense. Strong and intelligent idea.
Eagerness. Impatient desire to accomplish.
Earnestness. Deep, resolute desire to accomplish.
Ecstasy. Extreme delight.
Emotion. Excited feeling of any kind.
Empressement [F.]. Demonstrative cordiality.
Endurance. Power to bear pain.
Enthusiasm. Extraordinary fervor.
Excitation of feeling. Production of feeling.
Experience. Something undergone or enjoyed.
Fanaticism. Extravagant zeal.
Feeling. Mental stirring.
Ferment. Intense excitement.
Fervency.}
Fervor. } Intensity of feeling.
Flurry. Sudden, confused state of the mind.
Flush. Sudden elation or excitement.
Fluster.}
Flutter.} Confused state of the mind.
Fulness of the heart. Generosity.
Furore. Overmastering passion for.
Glow. Fervency or intensity of feeling.
Gusto. Keen enjoyment; relish.
Heartiness. Earnestness and sincerity.
Hectic. An habitual flush.
Hurry of spirits. Excitement.
Impression. The effect produced on the mind, feelings, etc.
Inspiration. Divine influence; elevating influence of genius or occasion.
Passion. Overpowering feeling.
Pathos. Tender or sorrowful feeling.
Perturbation. Agitation of mind.
Pother. Continued confusion.
Pulsation. A beating or throbbing of the heart.
Response. Act or feeling as a result of an appeal.
Ruffle. State of slight vexation.
Sensation. An impression made on the mind through the senses.
Shock. Startling emotion; violence to the feelings.
Stew. A state of agitating excitement.
Sufferance. Experience of pain or evil.
Suffering. Severe pain.
Supportance. Assistance to an infirm person.
Sympathy. Fellow feeling for one in pain or trouble.
Thrill. A tremor of feeling or excitement.
Tolerance. Allowing what is not altogether approved
Trepidation. Trembling with fear.
Turn. A shock, as from alarm.
Unction. That quality in language or address which excites emotion.
Vehemence. Strength or impetuosity of feeling or passion.
Verve. The enthusiasm of a poet or artist.
Warmth. Slight passion.
Zeal. Enthusiastic devotion.

EMOTION—*Associated Nouns.*

Blush. A reddening of the face or cheeks, indicating modesty, shame, or confusion.
Flush. A heightened color or reddening, indicative of some sudden emotion.
Glow. A flush or blush.
Heaving. A rising and falling alternately of the bosom in labored breathing or excitement.
Palpitation. A rapid throbbing of the heart, excited by fear, fright, etc.
Panting. Short, labored breathing, as from agitation.
Quiver. A shuddering or trembling.
Suffusion. A covering, as with color.
Throb. A strong beating of the heart, as from great excitement.
Throbbing. See THROB.
Tingling. A prickly, stinging sensation.
Tremor. An involuntary trembling or shivering, as from emotion.
Twitter. An agitated, excited state.

EMOTION—*Verbs.*

Abide. To endure or bear: said usually of consequences.
Aby. To pay the penalty for.
Be agitated. Be in a state of agitation.
Bear. To continue under with patience.
Bear the brunt of. Bear the main shock, or the severest part of.

Be excited. Be influenced by passion.
Be impressed with, etc. See *Adjectives.*
Blush. To redden in the face from shame, etc.
Brave. To meet with courage.
Catch the contagion.}
Catch the flame. } Partake of another's enthusiasm.
Catch the infection. To be influenced by the emotion of others.
Change color. To blush.
Cherish feeling. To hold a feeling continually: said of good feelings.
Draw a deep breath. Indication of relief.
Endure. To bear: said of great pain or trouble.
Entertain feeling. To hold a feeling continually.
Enter the spirit of. To be enthusiastic.
Experience. To feel.
Feel. To be conscious of.
Flush. Grow red suddenly.
Flutter. To move about quickly and nervously.
Glow. To be animated with emotion.
Go pit-a-pat. To flutter: said of the heart.
Harbor feeling. To continually hold a feeling: said of bad feelings.
Heave. To breathe hard and deep.
Impress. To fix in the mind.
Labor under. To be hindered by.
Look black. To appear displeased.
Look blue. To appear distressed in spirits.
Mantle. To become suffused with blood, as the face.
Palpitate. To beat unusually fast, as the heart.
Pant. To breathe rapidly; to desire ardently.
Prove. To show to be correct; to verify.
Quiver. To shake; tremble.
Receive an impression, etc. See *Nouns.*
Respond. To act in answer to a feeling or appeal.
Shake. To tremble violently
Smart under. To feel sharp, mental pain.
Stand. To endure; to suffer.
Suffer. To bear pain passively; be in pain.
Support. To buoy up, as in trouble.
Sustain. To endure without yielding.
Swell. To be puffed up with some feeling.
Taste. To have a slight experience of.
Thrill. To cause a tremor of feeling.
Throb. To beat rapidly or strongly, as the heart.
Tingle. To produce a prickly, stinging sensation.
Tremble. To have a vibratory motion.
Turn black in the face. To show anger.
Turn color. To show a sudden change of feeling
Turn pale. To show fear or surprise.
Turn red. To show modesty, shame, etc.
Twitter. To be excited.
Warm. To develop interest, passion, or enthusiasm.
Wince. Be restive under pain or reproof.

EMOTION—*Adjectives.*

Absorbing. Engrossing.
Acute. Keenly affecting the senses or sensibilities.
Affected with. Somewhat influenced by.
Ardent. Intensely passionate.
Boiling. }
Boiling over.} Raging.
Breathless. Indicative of fear, surprise.
Burning. Vehement
Caustic. Bitterly sarcastic.
Cordial. Warm in feeling.
Cutting. Sharp; sarcastic.
Deep. Profound; heartfelt.
Deep-felt. Heartfelt.
Deep-mouthed. Ready to express feeling.
Devoured by. Completely absorbed by.
Eager. Impatiently desirous for action
Earnest. Having a deep, resolute desire to accomplish.
Ecstatic. Extremely delightful.
Electric. Spirited; thrilling.
Emotional. Of, having, or pertaining to emotion.
Emotive. Tending to excite emotion.
Enraptured, etc. Filled with rapture, etc.
Enthusiastic. Filled with enthusiasm.
Fanatical. Extravagantly zealous.
Feeling, etc. See *Verbs.*
Fervent.}
Fervid. } Showing intensity of feeling.
Feverish. Excitable and uncertain.
Fiery. Vehement; passionate.
Flaming. Intensely excited; vehement.
Glowing. Fervent; intense.

Gushing. Exuberant; abundant.
Heart-expanding. Large-hearted; generous in praise, etc.
Heartfelt. Most sincere.
Hearty. Warm and sincere.
Home-felt. Inward; private.
Hysterical. Fitfully emotional.
Imbued with. Filled with.
Impetuous. Acting with great vehemence or violence.
Impressed with. Very sensible of.
Impressive. Likely to fix on the mind.
In a quiver, etc. See *Nouns*.
Incisive. Cutting; penetrating.
Indelible. Not able to be blotted out or forgotten.
Keen. Sharp like a knife.
Keen as a razor. Extremely keen.
Lively. Gay; animated; brisk.
Moved with. Roused to action by.
Of feeling, etc. See *Nouns*.
Passionate. Characterized by passion.
Penetrating. Powerful to pierce or sink deep.
Penetrated with. Deeply affected by.
Pervading. Permeating every part.
Piercing. Sharp and penetrating like a needle.
Piquant. Agreeably sharp or severe.
Poignant. Severely painful, cutting, or severe.
Profound. Deep and intense.
Pungent. Very piquant.
Quick. Irritable; hasty; easily angered; alive.
Rabid. Raging mad, like a mad dog.
Racy. Strikingly and vigorously original.
Rapt. Carried away from oneself into raptures.
Rapturous. Extremely and deeply joyful.
Raving. Pertaining to irrational or furious talk.
Red-hot. Raging; furious; fiery.
Seized with. Entirely overcome by.
Sensorial.⎫
Sensory.⎬ Pertaining to the nervous system.
Sensuous. Keenly alive to pleasures derived through the senses.
Sentient. Having sensation or feeling.
Sharp. Affecting the feelings as if cut by a knife.
Sincere. In reality what it appears to be.
Smart. Emphatic and sharp.
Soul-stirring. Passionate and profoundly impressive.
Strong. Marked by force or strength.
Struck all of a heap. Affected suddenly.
Swelling. Pompous; increasing in intensity.
Thrilling. Causing a thrill.
Touched with. Moved to compassion.
Trenchant. Cutting deeply and quickly.
Warm. Slightly passionate.
Warmhearted. Cordial.
Wistful. With longing or desire.
With feeling, etc. See *Nouns*.
Wrought up. Roused into a passion.
Zealous. Enthusiastically devoted.

EMOTION—*Adverbs.*

Ab imo pectore [L.]. From the bottom of one's heart.
At heart. With deep earnestness.
Con amore [It.]. With love; earnestly.
Devoutly. With earnest, religious feelings.
From bottom of one's heart. Profoundly.
Heart and soul. With all might and spirit.
Heartily. Earnestly and cordially.
Over head and ears. Completely.

EMOTION—*Phrases.*

The heart beating; the heart beating high; the heart big; the heart breaking; the heart bursting; the heart flowing; the heart full; the heart melting; the heart overflowing; the heart pulsating; the heart swelling; the heart throbbing; the heart thumping.

e-mo′-tion-al. Pertaining to emotion. EMOTION.
e-mo′-tive. Tending to excite emotion. EMOTION.
em-pale′. To thrust a sharp stake through. RECOMPENSE-PUNITION.
em-pale′-ment. The act of empaling. APERTURE-CLOSURE.
em-pan′-el. To enroll on a list for jury duty. LITIGATION.
em′-per-or. The sovereign of an empire. CHIEF-UNDERLING.

em′-per-y. Authority. RULE-LICENSE.
em′-pha-sis. Special force of voice. ASSERTION-DENIAL, CONSEQUENCE-INSIGNIFICANCE, RHETORIC, VOCALIZATION-MUTENESS.
em′-pha-size. To put stress on. ASSERTION-DENIAL, CONSEQUENCE-INSIGNIFICANCE.
em-phat′-ic. Forcible; a form of the verb in grammar. ASSERTION-DENIAL, CONSEQUENCE-INSIGNIFICANCE; emphatic form, NOUN.
em-phat′-ic-al-ly. Decidedly. MAGNITUDE-SMALLNESS.
em-pierce′. To pierce into. APERTURE-CLOSURE, INJECTION-EJECTION.
em′-pire. A territory governed by an emperor. PROPERTY, RULE-LICENSE.
em″-pi-re′-ma. Proposition based on experience. RATIOCINATION-INSTINCT.
em-pir′-ic. Charlatanic. GULL-DECEIVER.
em-pir′-ic-al. Based on experience. GULL-DECEIVER, TRIAL, VENTURE.
em-pir′-i-cism. The empirical character or method. TRIAL.
em-ploy′. To use. COMMISSION-ABROGATION, LIBERTY-SUBJECTION, OCCUPATION, USE-DISUSE; employ one's capital in, EXCHANGE; employ oneself, ACTION-PASSIVENESS; employ one's time in, OCCUPATION; in one's employ, CHIEF-UNDERLING.
em″-ploy-é′. A person employed. CHIEF-UNDERLING, CONSIGNEE.
em-ploy′-er. One who employs. BUYING-SALE.
em-ploy′-ment. Service; act of using. OCCUPATION, USE-DISUSE.
em-poi′-son. To envenom. BETTERMENT-DETERIORATION.
em-po′-ri-um. An important trading-place. MARKET.
em-pow′-er. To authorize. COMMISSION-ABROGATION, LEAVE-PROHIBITION, MIGHT-IMPOTENCE.
em′-press. A woman who rules an empire. CHIEF-UNDERLING.
empressement [F.] (an′-pres-man′). Demonstrative cordiality. ACTIVITY-INDOLENCE, DESIRE-DISTASTE, EMOTION.
em-prise′. Adventure. ENTERPRISE.
empta dolore docet experientia [L.] (emp′-ta do-lo′-rî do′-set ex-pî-ri-en′-shi-a). Experience bought with pain teaches. KNOWLEDGE-IGNORANCE, PLEASURE-PAIN.
emp′-ti-ness. State of being empty. PRESENCE-ABSENCE.
emp′-tion. The act of buying. BUYING-SALE.
emp′-tor. A buyer. BUYING-SALE.
emptor, caveat [L.] (emp′-tor, kê′-vî-at). Let the buyer beware. CONTRACT.
emp′-ty. Vacant. ADMISSION-EXPULSION, ESTABLISHMENT-REMOVAL, EXCESS-LACK, KNOWLEDGE-IGNORANCE, PRESENCE-ABSENCE, PROVISION-WASTE, SUBSTANCE-NULLITY, USEFULNESS-USELESSNESS; beggarly account of empty boxes, AFFLUENCE-PENURY; empty one's glass, NUTRIMENT-EXCRETION; empty pocket, AFFLUENCE-PENURY; empty purse, AFFLUENCE-PENURY; empty sound, MEANING-JARGON; empty stomach, DESIRE-DISTASTE; empty title, DUENESS-UNDUENESS; NAME-MISNOMER; empty words, TRUTHFULNESS-FABRICATION.
emp′-ty-hand″-ed. Not prepared to give. EXCESS-LACK.
emp′-ty-head″-ed. Foolish. KNOWLEDGE-IGNORANCE.
em-pur′-ple. To make purple. YELLOWNESS-PURPLE.
em-pyr′-e-al. Celestial. HEAVEN-HELL.
em″-py-re′-an. Highest heaven. PLEASURABLENESS-PAINFULNESS, UNIVERSE.
em″-py-reu′-ma. The peculiar taste or odor of animal or vegetable substances, burnt in close vessels. MIXTURE-HOMOGENEITY, PERFUME-STENCH.

em″-py-reu-mat′-ic. Pertaining to empyreuma. PER-FUME-STENCH.

em″-py-ro′-sis. A general conflagration. HEATING-COOLING.

em′-u-late. To vie with. ANTAGONISM-CONCUR-RENCE, GOODNESS-BADNESS, IMITATION-ORIGINAL-ITY, REPUTATION-DISCREDIT, STRIFE-PEACE.

em″-u-la′-tion. Rivalry. ANTAGONISM-CONCUR-RENCE.

em′-u-lous. Rivaling. ANTAGONISM-CONCURRENCE.

e-mul′-sion. A liquid mixture in which a fatty or resinous substance is suspended in minute globules. VISCIDITY-FOAM.

e-mul′-sive. Milklike. VISCIDITY-FOAM.

e-munc′-to-ry. Excretory. WATERCOURSE-AIRPIPE.

en bloc [F.] (an· bloc). In a lump. WHOLE-PART.

en effet [F.] (an· e-fê′). In effect. SUBJECTIVENESS-OBJECTIVENESS.

en grand tenue [F.] (an· gran· te-nü′). In full dress. EMBELLISHMENT-DISFIGUREMENT, SOCIETY-LUDI-CROUSNESS.

en grand toilette [F.] (an· gran· twa-let′). In grand costume. EMBELLISHMENT-DISFIGUREMENT.

en masse [F.] (an· mas). In a mass. WHOLE-PART.

en passant [F.] (an· pa-san·′). By the way. CONNEC-TION-INDEPENDENCE, LASTINGNESS-TRANSIENTNESS, OPPORTUNENESS-UNSUITABLENESS, PURPOSE-LUCK.

en rapport [F.] (an· ra-por′). In harmony with. CON-NECTION-INDEPENDENCE.

en règle [F.] (an· rêgl). According to rule. CONVEN-TIONALITY-UNCONVENTIONALITY, REGULARITY-IR-REGULARITY.

en route [F.] (an· rut). On the way. ADVANCE-RETROGRESSION, TRAVELING-NAVIGATION.

en-a′-ble. To make able. MIGHT-IMPOTENCE.

en-a′-ble-ment. Ability. MIGHT-IMPOTENCE.

en-act′. To carry out. ACTING, ACTION-PASSIVE-NESS, COMPLETION-NONCOMPLETION, CONDUCT, LAW-LAWLESSNESS, ORDER.

en-act′-ment. A statute. LAW-LAWLESSNESS, ORDER.

en-al′-la-ge. The use of one part of speech or inflection for another. TROPE.

en-am′-el. A glossy lacquer; to cover with enamel. COVER-LINING, EMBELLISHMENT-DISFIGUREMENT, PAINTING.

en-am′-el-er. One who enamels. ARTIST.

en-am′-el-ist. One who enamels. ARTIST.

en-am′-or. To inspire with ardent love. LOVE-HATE.

e-nas′-cent. Being born. CREATION-DESTRUCTION.

e-nate′. Related on the mother's side. RELATION-SHIP.

en avant [F.] (an· a-van·′). Forward. AIM-ABERRA-TION.

en-cage′. To imprison. RELEASE-RESTRAINT.

en-camp′. To form a camp. DWELLER-HABITATION, ESTABLISHMENT-REMOVAL.

en-camp′-ment. A camp. ESTABLISHMENT-REMOVAL.

en-caus′-tic paint′-ing. A method of painting used by the ancients. PAINTING.

en″-ceinte′. A close or precinct; pregnant. CRE-ATION-DESTRUCTION, ENCLOSURE.

en-ce′-ni-a. A church wake. CEREMONIAL.

en-chafe′. To chafe or irritate. PLEASURABLENESS-PAINFULNESS.

en-chain′. To attach firmly. RELEASE-RESTRAINT.

en-chant′. To bewitch. DEVOTION-MAGIC, PLEAS-URABLENESS-PAINFULNESS.

en-chant′-ed. Fascinated. PLEASURE-PAIN.

en-chant′-ing. Charming. BEAUTY-UGLINESS, LOVE-HATE, MELODY-DISSONANCE, PLEASURABLENESS-PAINFULNESS.

en-chant′-ment. Incantation. DEVOTION-MAGIC, LOVE-HATE, PLEASURABLENESS-PAINFULNESS, PLEASURE-PAIN.

en-chase′. To incase in a setting. UNION-DISUNION.

en″-chi-rid′-i-on. A hand-book. MISSIVE-PUBLICA-TION.

enciente [Sp.] (en-thi-en′-tê). A fortified region. EX-TENSION-DISTRICT.

en-cinc′-ture. To encircle with a girdle. ENVIRON-MENT-INTERPOSITION.

en-cir′-cle. To encompass. CIRCLE-WINDING, EN-VIRONMENT-INTERPOSITION.

en-clave′. To enclose; a territory surrounded by pos-sessions of another government. EXTENSION-DIS-TRICT, BOUNDARY.

en-close′. To surround; to fence in. ADMISSION-EXCLUSION, CONFINEMENT, ENVIRONMENT-INTER-POSITION, OUTSIDE-INSIDE.

en-closed′. Fenced in. OUTSIDE-INSIDE.

en-clo′-sure. An enclosed space, or object. CONFINE-MENT, CONTENTS-RECEIVER, ENVIRONMENT-INTER-POSITION, ENCLOSURE, INCLUSION-OMISSION, RE-LEASE-RESTRAINT.

ENCLOSURE.

Balustrade. An enclosure made up of a row of balusters supporting a hand rail and used to inclose a balcony, staircase,etc.

Barricade. An enclosure that obstructs, as a waterway.

Barrier. Anything which stops progress, as a fence.

Case, etc. See CONTENTS-RECEIVER.

Circumvallation; An inclosure of military works.

Cordon [F.]. A line of sentinels or military posts guarding any place or thing.

Corral. Space enclosed for livestock.

Dike. An embankment made to prevent inundation.

Ditch. A narrow enclosure in the ground, used for drainage.

Door. A frame, generally of wood, used to close the entrance to a house, etc.

Dyke. See DIKE.

Enceinte [F.]. The line of works forming the enclosure of a fortress.

Enclosure. Anything that encompasses or encloses.

Envelope. A paper wrapper used to enclose letters and the like.

Espalier [F.]. A railing or trellis.

Fence, etc. A structure of rails, wires, etc., used to enclose an area. See ATTACK-DEFENSE.

Fold. An enclosure for certain domestic animals, as sheep.

Fosse. A ditch used to enclose and protect a fortification.

Gate. A movable barrier used to close the entrance to a garden, mountain gap, etc.

Gateway. Whatever is regarded as a means of entrance or egress.

Girdle, etc. See OUTLINE.

Hatch. The cover to an opening in a deck, floor, etc.

Hedge. A fence made of shrubs or bushes.

Hedgerow. An orderly row of shrubs or trees planted to serve as a fence.

Hogpen. An inclosure for keeping hogs.

Incasement. Anything that incases.

Infold. A fold or enclosure.

Moat. A trench outside the wall of a fortress.

Net. A fabric of twine or the like for enclosing fish.

Paddock. An enclosure for pasturing or exercising horses.

Pale. A fence enclosing an area; hence any boundary.

Paling. A fence made of upright sticks.

Park paling. Paling enclosing a park.

Pen. An enclosure, as for pigs.

Penfold. An enclosure for stray cattle or domestic animals.

Pound. An enclosure set apart by authority for keeping stray cattle.

Prison, etc. See RELEASE-PRISON.

Quickset hedge. A hedge made of living shrubs or trees.

Rail. A wooden or metal bar stretching from one post to another, as in a fence.

Railing. A series of rails or bars forming a fence.

Ring fence. A fence encircling a large piece of land or a whole estate.

Seine net. A large fish-net provided with weights and floats.

Sheepfold. A pen or fold for keeping sheep.

Wall. A brick or stone fence.

Wrapper. That in which anything is enclosed.

ENCLOSURE—Verbs

Circumscribe, etc. See CONFINEMENT.

Enclose. Fence in; encircle.

en-clothe'. To clothe. DRESS-UNDRESS.

en-co'-mi-ast. A eulogist. FLATTERER-DEFAMER.

en-co''-mi-as'-tic. Eulogistic. APPROVAL-DISAPPROVAL.

en-co'-mi-um. A eulogy. APPROVAL-DISAPPROVAL, RHETORIC.

en-com'-pass. To encircle. ENVIRONMENT-INTERPOSITION; **encompassed with difficulties,** DIFFICULTY-FACILITY.

en-com'-pass-ment. The act of surrounding. ENVIRONMENT-INTERPOSITION.

en''-core'. Once more; to call for repetition; the repetition. APPROVAL-DISAPPROVAL, RECURRENCE.

en-coun'-ter. To meet with; a meeting. ANTAGONISM-CONCURRENCE, ARRIVAL-DEPARTURE, IMPETUS-REACTION, OCCURRENCE-DESTINY, STRIFE-PEACE; **encounter danger,** SECURITY-INSECURITY; **encounter risk,** PURPOSE-LUCK; **encounter the chance,** PURPOSE-LUCK.

en-cour'-age. To stimulate. ALLEVIATION-AGGRAVATION, BRAVERY-COWARDICE, MOTIVE-CAPRICE, OBSTRUCTION-HELP, SANGUINENESS-HOPELESSNESS.

en-cour'-age-ment. The act of encouraging. ALLEVIATION-AGGRAVATION, MOTIVE-CAPRICE.

en-cour'-a-ging. Cheering. SANGUINENESS-HOPELESSNESS.

En'-cra-tism. Abstinence. MODERATION-SELFINDULGENCE.

en-croach'. To infringe. DUENESS-UNDUENESS, RIGHT-WRONG, TRANSCURSION-SHORTCOMING.

en-croach'-ment. Gradual intrusion. DUENESS-UNDUENESS, TRANSCURSION-SHORTCOMING.

en''-cui-rassed'. Having a cuirass-like covering. COVER-LINING.

en-cum'-ber. To embarrass. DIFFICULTY-FACILITY, OBSTRUCTION-HELP.

en-cum'-bered. Loaded with debts. CREDIT-HELP.

en-cum'-brance. Impediment. CREDIT-DEBT, OBSTRUCTION-HELP.

en-cyc'-li-cal. A circular letter. MISSIVE-PUBLICATION.

en-cy''-clo-pe'-di-a. A work treating the whole circle of the sciences in order. KNOWLEDGE-IGNORANCE, MISSIVE-PUBLICATION.

en-cy''-clo-pe'-dic-al. Possessing extensive knowledge. UNIVERSALITY-PARTICULARITY; **encyclopedical knowledge,** KNOWLEDGE-IGNORANCE; **encyclopedical learning,** KNOWLEDGE-IGNORANCE.

en-cyst'-ed. Enclosed in a membranous sac or cyst. CONFINEMENT.

end. The extreme limit. BEGINNING-END, CAUSE-EFFECT, DISCONTINUANCE-CONTINUANCE, PURPOSE-LUCK, TOP-BOTTOM; **at an end,** BEGINNING-END, DISCONTINUANCE-CONTINUANCE; **begin at the wrong end,** SKILL-UNSKILFULNESS; **come to its end,** COMPLETION-NONCOMPLETION; **end in smoke,** MIGHT-IMPOTENCE, SUCCESS-FAILURE, TRANSCURSION-SHORTCOMING; **end of life,** LIFE-DEATH; **end of one's tether,** DIFFICULTY-FACILITY, EXCESS-LACK, KNOWLEDGE-IGNORANCE, RATIOCINATION-CASUISTRY; **end one's days,** LIFE-DEATH; **ends of the earth,** REMOTENESS-NEARNESS; **end to end,** EXTENSION-INEXTENSION, INTERSPACE-CONTACT, LENGTH-SHORTNESS; **on end,** ERECTNESS-FLATNESS; **one's journey's end,** ARRIVAL-DEPARTURE; **put an end to,** CREATION-DESTRUCTION, LIFE-KILLING.

en-dam'-age. To injure. GOODNESS-BADNESS.

en-dan'-ger. To expose to peril. SECURITY-INSECURITY.

en-dear'. To cause to be loved. LOVE-HATE.

en-dear'-ment. A caress; love. BLANDISHMENT.

en-deav'-or. To try. QUEST-EVASION, VENTURE; **endeavor after,** PURPOSE-LUCK; **use one's best endeavor,** TOIL-RELAXATION, VENTURE.

end'-ed. Finished. BEGINNING-END.

en-dem'-ic. Peculiar to a country or people; a local disease. HEALTH-SICKNESS, OUTSIDE-INSIDE, UNIVERSALITY-PARTICULARITY.

endimanché [F.] (an·-di-man·-shê'). Dressed in one's Sunday clothes. EMBELLISHMENT-DISFIGUREMENT, POMP.

end'-ing. Terminating. BEGINNING-END.

end'-less. Eternal; infinite. ETERNITY-INSTANTANEITY, INFINITY, MULTIPLICITY-PAUCITY.

end'-long. Lengthwise. LENGTH-SHORTNESS.

en-dog'-a-my. The custom of some uncivilized tribes of marrying only within the group. MATRIMONY-CELIBACY.

en-dog'-e-nous. Growing from within. FAUNA-FLORA.

en-dome'. To cover with a dome. COVER-LINING.

en-dorse'. To write upon the back of; to approve. APPROVAL-DISAPPROVAL, ASSENT-DISSENT, CONTRACT, EVIDENCE-COUNTEREVIDENCE, MONEY; **endorsed with reason,** MIND-IMBECILITY.

en-dorse'-ment. Superscription; approval. SIGN.

en'-dos''-mose. Osmose from an outer vessel to one contained within it. TRANSMISSION.

en-dow'. To furnish. GIVING-RECEIVING, MIGHT-IMPOTENCE.

en-dowed'. Furnished with gifts. SKILL-UNSKILFULNESS; **endowed with,** HOLDING-EXEMPTION.

en-dow'-ment. A gift; act of endowing. GIVING-RECEIVING, MIGHT-IMPOTENCE, SKILL-UNSKILFULNESS, SUBJECTIVENESS-OBJECTIVENESS.

en-due'. To put in possession of. MIGHT-IMPOTENCE.

en-dur'-ance. Durability; duration. EMOTION, EXCITABILITY-INEXCITABILITY, MUTATION-PERMANENCE.

en-dure'. To withstand; to suffer. DURATION-NEVERNESS, EMOTION, EXCITABILITY-INEXCITABILITY, LASTINGNESS-TRANSIENTNESS, MUTATION-PERMANENCE, OCCURRENCE-DESTINY; **endure for ever,** ETERNITY-INSTANTANEITY; **endure pain,** PLEASURE-PAIN.

en-dur'-ing. Bearing with patience. EXCITABILITY-INEXCITABILITY.

end'-wise. On end. ERECTNESS-FLATNESS.

E. N. E. East-northeast. AIM-ABERRATION.

en'-e-my. An adversary. ANTAGONIST-ASSISTANT, ENTERTAINMENT-WEARINESS, FRIEND-FOE; **enemy to society,** FRIEND-FOE; **the common enemy,** ANGEL-SATAN; **thing devised by the enemy,** TRUTHFULNESS-FABRICATION.

en''-er-get'-ic. Strenuous; forceful. DETERMINATION-VACILLATION, TOIL-RELAXATION, VIGOR-INERTIA.

en'-er-gize. To make energetic. VIGOR-INERTIA.

en''-er-gu'-men. A demoniac. SANENESS-LUNACY.

en'-er-gy. Force. ACTIVITY-INDOLENCE, DETERMINATION-VACILLATION, MIGHT-IMPOTENCE, STRENGTH-WEAKNESS, VIGOR-INERTIA.

e-ner'-vate. To weaken. MIGHT-IMPOTENCE, STRENGTH-WEAKNESS, TOIL-RELAXATION.

en'-er-va'-tion. Debility. STRENGTH-WEAKNESS.

en-face'. To write on the face of. WRITING-PRINTING.

enfant, bon [F.] (an·-fan·', bon·). A good fellow. CHARITABLENESS-MALEVOLENCE.

enfant gâté [F.] (an·-fan·' ga-tê'). A spoiled child. DESIRE-REPLETION, FAVORITE-ANGER, WELFARE-MISFORTUNE.

enfants perdus [F.] (an·-fan·' per-dü'). Lost children; a forlorn hope. RECKLESSNESS-CAUTION, SANGUINENESS-HOPELESSNESS.

enfant terrible [F.] (an·-fan·' ter-ribl'). A torment. CRAFT-ARTLESSNESS, SANGUINENESS-TIMIDITY.

en-fee'-ble. To weaken. STRENGTH-WEAKNESS.

en-feoff'-ment. The act or the instrument by which the title and possessions of an estate in fee are transferred. STRENGTH-WEAKNESS.

En'-field ri'-fle. A muzzle-loading rifle formerly used by the English government. WEAPON.

en'-fi-lade''. To rake lengthwise with shot or missiles. APERTURE-CLOSURE, LENGTH-SHORTNESS, TRANSMISSION.

en-fold'. To fold within. CONFINEMENT.

en-force'. To put into execution; to compel. ADVICE, COERCION, DUENESS-UNDUENESS, MOTIVE-CAPRICE.

en-force'-ment. Compulsion. COERCION.

en-fran'-chise. To endow with political privilege. LEAVE-PROHIBITION, LIBERTY-SUBJECTION, RELEASE-RESTRAINT.

en-fran'-chised. Invested with citizen's or freeman's rights. DUENESS-UNDUENESS.

en-fran'-chise-ment. Act of enfranchising. LIBERTY-SUBJECTION, RELEASE-RESTRAINT.

en-gage'. To pledge; to hire; to encounter in battle. COMMISSION-ABROGATION, CONTRACT, EARLINESS-LATENESS, ENGAGEMENT-RELEASE, ENTERPRISE, FIGHTING-CONCILIATION, MOTIVE-CAPRICE, QUEST-EVASION; **engage the attention,** HEED-DISREGARD; **engage the thoughts,** HEED-DISREGARD; **engage with,** STRIFE-PEACE; **ill engage,** ASSERTION-DENIAL.

en-gaged'. Built into a structure. **Engaged column,** ARCHITECTURE.

en-gage'-ment. The act of engaging. DUTY-DERELICTION, ENGAGEMENT-RELEASE, ENTERPRISE, PURPOSE-LUCK, STRIFE-PEACE.

ENGAGEMENT—RELEASE.

Affiance. A marriage contract or engagement.

Assurance. Something that inspires confidence, a promise.

Betroth.
Betrothal. } An engagement to marry.
Betrothment.

Contract. An agreement between two or more parties having a consideration. See CONTRACT.

Engagement. The act of binding by a promise.

Guarantee. An agreement whereby one person is to stand for the performance of some obligation by another.

Insurance. A system by which one party is guaranteed indemnity for loss or damage, by another party.

Oath. A solemn affirmation with an appeal to God in support of its truth. See ASSERTION.

Obligation. A binding by a legal or moral requirement.

Parole. A pledge of honor given by captured soldiers in consideration of indulgences or that they will not take arms against the captor.

Pledge. A promise solemnly given.

Plight. A solemn engagement or pledge.

Preengagement. A prior engagement.

Profession. The act of professing, of openly declaring one's purposes.

Promise. A declaration, oral or written, that a person will do or not do a given act.

Troth. A pledging.

Undertaking. In law, an engagement; the act of undertaking.

Vow. A solemn promise to God to do or not do something.

Warranty. A guarantee that a given thing is as represented.

Word. A promise.

Word of honor. A promise to which one's honor is pledged.

ENGAGEMENT—Verbs.

Adjure. To entreat earnestly as if under oath.

Administer an oath. To have one promise upon the witness of a high or holy personage.

Answer for. To be responsible for.

Assure. To make confident, to give surety to.

Attest, etc. To declare as accurate, to vouch for. See EVIDENCE.

Be answerable for. Responsible.

Become bound to. To be apprenticed to

Become sponsor for. To stand good for.

Betroth. To engage to marry.

Bind oneself. To be obligated.

Commit oneself. To pledge oneself.

Contract an obligation. Bind oneself.

Covenant, etc. To bind oneself to do a single act, etc. See CONTRACT.

Engage. To bind by promise; to pledge.

Enter into an engagement.
Enter on an engagement. } To promise or bind oneself to do something.
Form an engagement.

Guarantee. To engage to stand for another.

Give a promise, etc. See Nouns.

Give one's credit.
Give one's honor.
Give one's troth. } Pledge oneself.
Give one's word.

Give security. See SECURITY.

Hold out an expectation. To offer reasonable hopes.

en-ga'-ging. Attractive. LOVE-HATE, PLEASURABLENESS-PAINFULNESS.

en-gar'-ri-son. To supply with a garrison. ATTACK-DEFENSE.

Release, etc. Liberation from a promise or obligation. See RELEASE.

RELEASE—Adjectives.

Absolute. Without limitation or condition.

Unconditional, etc. Limited by no conditions. See LIBERTY.

ENGAGEMENT—VERBS—Continued.

Make a form. To take a promise.

Make an engagement. To promise.

Pass one's credit.
Pass one's honor.
Pass one's troth. } To promise formally.
Pass one's word.

Pledge one's credit.
Pledge oneself.
Pledge one's honor.
Pledge one's troth.
Pledge one's word.
Plight faith. } Bind oneself in honor.
Plight one's credit.
Plight one's honor.
Plight one's troth.
Plight one's word.

Promise. To engage to do or not to do something.

Put to one's oath. To exact an oath.

Secure. To make safe; to guarantee against loss.

Swear, etc. To affirm solemnly with an appeal to God in support of its accuracy and truth, etc. See ASSERTION.

Swear a witness. To take oath of.

Take upon oneself. To be answerable for.

Tie oneself. Bind oneself.

Undertake. To guarantee the performance of.

Underwrite. To engage to buy all stock not bought by the public.

Vow. To promise solemnly to God.

Warrant. To guarantee that the article is as represented.

ENGAGEMENT—Adjectives.

Affianced. Engaged to marry.

Bound. Constrained by a legal or moral obligation.

Committed. Devoted; pledged; bound.

Compromised. Pledged to.

In for it. Committed to a given course.

Pledged. Deposited as a security.

Promised, etc. }
Promising, etc. } See Verbs.

Promissory. Of the nature of a promise.

Under hand and seal. Under one's signature and certification of legality.

Upon oath. Upon the most sacred promise.

Votive. Dedicated or given on account of a vow.

ENGAGEMENT—Adverbs, etc.

As one's head shall answer for.

Ex voto [L.]. According to one's vow.

Gage d'amour [F.]. Pledge of love.

In for a penny, in for a pound.

en-gen'-der. To produce. CREATION-DESTRUCTION.

en'-gine. A machine or contrivance for producing mechanical effect. INSTRUMENT.

en'-gine–dri'-ver. The engineer of a locomotive. Way-farer-Seafarer.

en''-gi-neer'. One versed in any branch of engineering; to manage skilfully. Agent, Belligerent.

en''-gi-neer' ing. The science and art of making, building, or using engines and machines. Instrument.

en-gird'. To encompass. Environment-Interposition.

en-gla'-ci-al. Embedded with glacier-ice. Geology.

Eng'-lish. Relating to England or its inhabitants; the language of the people of England, America, etc. Dweller-Habitation; broken English, Word-Neology; king's English, Language; murder the king's English, Grammar-Solecism, Speech-Inarticulateness; plain English, Clearness-Obscurity, Interpretation-Misinterpretation, Simplicity-Floridness.

Eng'-lish-men. Citizens of England. Dweller-Habitation.

en-gobe'. A substance used to cover coarse pottery. Cover-Lining.

en-gorge'. To gorge; to swallow food greedily. Admission-Expulsion, Fasting-Gluttony.

en-gorge'-ment. The condition of being engorged. Excess-Lack.

en-grail'. To make indented. Variegation.

en-grave'. To carve upon some surface. Delineation-Caricature, Engraving, Groove, Sign; engrave in the memory, Remembrance-Forgetfulness.

en-graved'. Carved. Engraving.

en-gra'-ver. A person who engraves. Artist.

en-gra'-ving. An engraved plate; the act, process, or art of producing by cutting on metal, stone, or wood. Delineation-Caricature, Engraving.

ENGRAVING.

Anastatic printing. Printing from a raised surface.

Aquatinta. A process of etching in which spaces as well as lines are bitten by an acid.

Cerography. The art of engraving on wax.

Chalcography. The art of engraving on copper or brass.

Chalk-engraving. Imitating chalk-drawings by stipple-engravings.

Chromolithography. The method of making pictures by the use of a number of stones, each having a portion of the picture drawn upon it.

Copperplate engraving. The art of engraving on copper plates by incised lines.

Copperplate printing. Printing from a copper plate.

Decalcomania. Art of transferring pictures to glass or china.

Dry-point. Method of etching on copper plate with a fine needle without the use of acids.

Engraving. The process of cutting designs in metal, wood, etc.

Etching. The process of engraving lines by the use of an acid.

Glyphography. The engraving of a design in relief on a copper plate.

Glypography. Engraving on gems.

Heliogravure. The art of photographic engraving.

Lignography. Engraving on wood.

Line-engraving. Reproducing of designs by lines cut in copper plate.

Lithographic printing. The art of printing from a stone treated with various colors of ink.

Lithography. Lithographic printing.

Mezzotint engraving. A process of engraving in which, after a uniformly black surface is produced by minute incisions, the design is engraved and the lighter parts of the design brought out by scraping.

Photolithography. The process of reproducing photographs on prepared stone.

Plate-engraving. The art of cutting designs on any metal or stone plate.

Plate-printing. The art of producing printed characters on metal plates.

Printing. The art of making impressions on paper, etc., by the use of inked type and plates.

Steel-engraving. The art of cutting designs into steel plate.

Stipple-engraving. A process of engraving in which dots and not lines are used to produce shadings.

ype-printing, etc. See Printing.

Wood-engraving. The cutting of a design in wood in relief.

Xylography. The art of engraving in colors in wood.

Zincography. Making of zinc type by marking the letters on a zinc plate with ink and cutting away the unprotected part with acid.

Engraving—Denotations, etc.

Aquatint. An engraving in which spaces are bitten by the use of aqua fortis, resembling a drawing in water-colors.

Autotype. A facsimile.

Bur. The thin edge left by a tool in cutting or shaping metal, as in turning, engraving, etc.

Cerograph. A writing on wax.

Chromolithograph. A picture printed in tints and colors by repeated impressions from a series of stones prepared by the lithographic process.

Copperplate. A plate of polished copper on which a design or writing is engraved.

Cul-de-lampe [F.]. Ornamental work to fill out a page.

Cut. An engraved block or plate.

Engraving. An impression from an engraved plate, block of wood, or other material.

Etching. A design carried out by means of acid which eats away lines or surfaces left unprotected in metal, glass, or the like.

Glyphograph. A plate made by a process in which, by means of voltaic electricity a raised copy of a drawing is made.

Glyptograph. An engraving on precious stones.

Graphotype. A process for producing a design upon a surface in relief so that it can be printed from.

Heliotype. A picture obtained by the process of heliotypy.

Illumination. Adornment of books and manuscripts with colored illustrations.

Illustration. A picture designed to decorate a volume.

Impression. A print on paper from a wood block, metal plate, or the like.

Initial letter. The first letter of a chapter, division of a chapter, or verse; often elaborately painted and gilded.

Lignograph. A print made by lignography.

Lithograph. A print made by lithography.

Lithotint. A kind of lithography by which the effect of a tinted drawing is produced.

Mezzotint. An engraving by mezzotint.

Mordant. Biting; caustic.

Photogravure. A photoengraving.

Photolithograph. A lithographic picture or copy from a stone prepared by the aid of photography.

Plate. A piece of metal on which anything is engraved.

Print. Stamp or die for molding or impressing an ornamental design.

Steelplate. A plate used for engraving.

Stereotype. A plate forming an exact facsimile of a page of type or an engraving.

Tailpiece. An ornament placed at the bottom of a short page to fill up the space.

Vignette. Any picture, as an engraving, a photograph, or the like, which vanishes gradually at the edge.

Woodcut. An engraving on wood.

Xylograph. An engraving on wood.

Zincograph. An engraving on zinc.

Engraving—Nouns of Instrument.

Burin. A tool used in engraving.

Die. A stamp of hard substance used to form coins, etc

Etching-point. A kind of needle used in tracing lines.

Graver. A tool used for incising by engravers.

Negative. A picture having the lights and shades reversed, from which ordinary photographs are made.

Plate. An engraved piece of metal from which prints are made.

Punch. A steel tool used in making holes.

Stamp. A tool used for marking by impressions.

Stone. A stone (or metal) used in printing.

Style. An etching-needle.

Wood-block. A block of wood prepared for engraving

Engraving—Verbs.

Bite. To corrode with an acid.

Bite in. To cut in with a mordant.

Engrave. To cut a design into something.

Etch. To engrave by the use of a mordant.

Grave. To cut out with an instrument.

Imprimit [L.]. He engraved it.

Lithograph, etc. To print by the lithographic method. See *Nouns.*

Print. To make impressions by the use of inked type or plates.

Scrape. To rub the surface of with a hard instrument.

Sculpsit [L.]. He sculptured.

Stipple. To engrave with dots instead of lines.

ENGRAVING—*Adjectives.*

Engraved. Having a design cut upon it.
Insculptured. Having incised or raised designs cut into.

en-gross'. To transcribe; to absorb. HOLDING-EXEMPTION, WRITING-PRINTING; **engross the thought,** HEED-DISREGARD, REFLECTION-VACANCY.
en-gulf'. To overwhelm completely. ADMISSION-EXPULSION, CREATION-DESTRUCTION, SPRING-DIVE.
en-hance'. To augment; to elevate. BETTERMENT-DETERIORATION, INCREASE-DECREASE.
en''-har-mon'-ic. Having intervals less than a half-step. MELODY-DISSONANCE; **enharmonic scale,** MELODY-DISSONANCE.
e-nig'-ma. A riddle. INVESTIGATION-ANSWER, TIDINGS-MYSTERY.
e''-nig-mat'-ic. Obscure; puzzling. CERTAINTY-DOUBT, CLEARNESS-OBSCURITY.
e''-nig-mat'-ic-al. Obscure. CLEARNESS-OBSCURITY.
énigme, mot d' [F.] (ê-nigm', mo d'). The answer to a puzzle. INTERPRETATION-MISINTERPRETATION.

en-join'. To command; to urge. ADVICE, DUTY-DERELICTION, ORDER.
en-joy'. To delight in. HOLDING-EXEMPTION, SENSUALITY-SUFFERING; **enjoy a state,** CONDITION-SITUATION; **enjoy health,** HEALTH-SICKNESS.
en-joy'-ing. Delighting in. PLEASURE-PAIN, SENSUALITY-SUFFERING.
en-joy'-ment. Delight. PLEASURE-PAIN.
en-kin'-dle. To set on fire. EXCITATION, HEATING-COOLING.
en-large'. To increase. ENLARGEMENT-DIMINUTION, INCREASE-DECREASE, MAGNITUDE-SMALLNESS, RELEASE-RESTRAINT, TERSENESS-PROLIXITY; **enlarge the mind,** EDUCATION-MISTEACHING.
en-larged'. Expanded. SUPREMACY-SUBORDINACY; **enlarged views,** SAGACITY-INCAPACITY.
en-large'-ment. The act of enlarging; expansion. ENLARGEMENT-DIMINUTION, INCREASE-DECREASE, RELEASE-RESTRAINT.

ENLARGEMENT—DIMINUTION.

Accretion. Growth by the addition of new matter.
Aggrandizement. Increase of wealth, power, etc.
Ampliation. Diffuseness.
Amplification. Elaboration.
Augmentation. Mode of increasing.
Development. The unwrapping of what has been entirely shut out from view.
Dilatability. Act of widening out.
Dilation. Act of expanding.
Dispansion. A spreading out.
Distention. A spreading out in every direction.
Enlargement. The act of becoming greater in extent.
Expansibility. Ability to be spread out by unfolding.
Expansion. Process of spreading out by unfolding.
Extension. The act of stretching out to include a greater space.
Germination. The beginning of growth in the seed.
Growth. Natural and gradual increase.
Growth upward. Increase in height.
Increase of size, etc. See INCREASE.
Increment. Act or process of increasing.
Inflation. Undue swelling as if by air being blown in.
Intumescence. Act or process of enlarging.
Overdistension. Excessive distension.
Overgrowth. Excessive growth.
Puffiness. State of being puffy.
Puffing. Strong breathing.
Pullulation. Sprouting.
Rarefaction. Increase of volume without increase of mass.
Spread. Widening in any sense or way.
Superiority of size. Greatness as compared with some other object.
Swell. } Enlargement in volume.
Swelling. }
Tumefaction. Act or process of swelling or raising into a tumor.
Turgescence. Bombast.
Turgidity. State of being puffed or swollen.
Turgidness. State of being swollen.
Upgrowth. An enlargement upward.

ENLARGEMENT—*Denotations.*

Bulb. The enlarged part of a root. See CONVEXITY.
Diastole. The expansion or dilation of the heart and arteries.
Dropsy. A swelling of the body caused by an unnatural collection of serous fluid.
Hypertrophy. The excessive development of an organ or part of the body.
Obesity. The state of being excessively corpulent. See GREATNESS.
Pandiculation. A stretching of the trunk and extremities.
Plumper. One who, or that which, plumps or swells out something else.
Tumor. A morbid swelling or growth on any part of the body.
Tympany. A flatulent distention of the belly.

ENLARGEMENT—*Verbs.*

Aggrandize. To increase in power and influence.
Amplify. To elaborate.

Astringency. The quality or power of drawing together organic tissues.
Attenuation. Thinness.
Collapse. A falling together.
Compactness. The condition of being close together.
Compendium. A short introduction into a subject.
Compressibility. Ability to be pressed into a smaller volume.
Compression. The state of being pressed into a smaller compass.
Condensation. The state of being reduced to a smaller volume.
Contractility. The quality of drawing together.
Contraction. The state of being drawn together.
Corrugation. Contraction into alternate ridges and furrows.
Decrease of size, etc. See INCREASE-DECREASE.
Decrement. That which is taken away.
Defalcation. Reduction of a claim by subtracting a counter claim.
Diminution. Becoming less.
Inferiority in size.
Lessening. Becoming less.
Reduction. The state of having come to a lower from a higher position or plane.
Shrinking. Drawing together.
Squeezing. A contraction by weight or force.

DIMINUTION—*Denotations.*

Astringents. Medicines or other substances that produce contraction in the soft organic textures.
Atrophy. A wasting away from want of nourishment.
Coarctation. A stricture or narrowing, as of a canal or orifice.
Consumption. A pulmonary disease which causes a wasting away of the body.
Emaciation. The state of being reduced to excessive leanness.
Hour-glass. A glass vessel having two compartments, from the uppermost of which a quantity of sand occupies an hour in running through a small opening into the lower.
Marasmus. A wasting of flesh without apparent disease.
Neck. A reduction in size near the end of an object.
Sclerotics. What pertains to sclerosis.
Strangulation. Inordinate compression or constriction of a tube, as of the throat.
Systole. The contraction of the heart and arteries.
Tabefaction. A gradual losing of flesh by disease.

DIMINUTION—*Verbs.*

Attenuate. To become thin.
Become small; become smaller. Diminish.
Bedwarf. To hinder the growth of.
Be smaller than. To be less than another thing.
Chip. To diminish by breaking off small pieces.
Circumscribe, etc. To set bounds to, etc. See CONFINEMENT.
Coarctate. Contract.
Collapse. To fall together.
Compress. To press together.
Condense. To bring to occupy a smaller volume.
Constrict. } To draw together at a point.
Constringe. }
Contract. To draw together as a body.

ENLARGEMENT—DIMINUTION—*Continued.*

ENLARGEMENT—Verbs—*Continued.*

Become larger, etc.
Be larger than. } See GREATNESS.
Blow up. To praise excessively.
Bourgeon. To bud.
Bud. To grow, as a bud does.
Burst. To expand so much as to fly apart into pieces.
Cram. To fill forcibly.
Deploy. To extend in front of an army by decreasing the depth.
Develop. To bring forth what has been entirely hidden.
Dilate. To widen out.
Distend. To spread out in every direction.
Enlarge. To make greater in extent.
Exaggerate. To make or represent in undue proportions.
Expand. To spread out by unfolding.
Extend. To stretch or reach out.
Fatten. To lay on fat.
Fill out.
Gain flesh. } To become plump.
Gather. To come together.
Germinate. To sprout.
Grow. To increase naturally and gradually.
Grow flesh.
Grow up. } To increase in weight and size.
Incrassate. To become thicker.
Increase. To add to.
Inflate. To swell by blowing air in.
Magnify. To increase magnitude of.
Mantle. To spread out in a graceful manner.
Open. To disclose.
Outgrow. To grow too large for something.
Overrun. To become of such volume as to flow over the boundaries.
Pad. To increase for the sake of appearance.
Puff. To give exaggerated praise.
Pullulate. To multiply by sprouting.
Put forth. To grow.
Rarefy. To increase the volume, but not the mass.
Render larger, etc. See GREATNESS.
Shoot. To increase in length.
Spread. To extend the surface of.
Spread like wild-fire. To spread very fast.
Spread out. To become larger in breadth.
Spring up. To increase in height.
Sprout. To burst forth from the stem.
Stretch. To reach out.
Stuff. To cram.
Surpass. To excel in quality, etc. See sub SUPERIORITY.
Swell. To increase in size.
Take open order. To take a position at a certain distance from another.
Vegetate. To grow.
Wax. To grow.
Widen. To broaden.

ENLARGEMENT—*Adjectives.*

Big. Of great size.
Bigswoln. Swelled to a great size.
Bloated. Distended by fluid or gas.
Blowzy. Having a fat, red face.
Bulbous, etc. Having bulbs. See CONVEXITY.
Distended. Spread out in every direction.
Dropsical. Affected with dropsy.
Exaggerated. Represented in undue proportions.
Expanded, etc. Unfolded. See *Verbs.*
Expansive. Stretching out to a great distance.
Fat. Fleshy.
Flabelliform. Spread out like a fan.
Full-blown.
Full-formed. } Completely expanded.
Full-grown.
Hypertrophied. Having an excessive growth.
Larger, etc. Of greater size. See GREATNESS.
Obese. Large in body.
Oedematous. Dropsical.
Overgrown. Larger than normal growth.

DIMINUTION—Verbs—*Continued.*

Corrugate. To contract into alternate ridges and furrows.
Cramp. To restrain the action.
Crumple up. To crush into a mass.
Crush. To mash.
Decay. To decompose. See sub DETERIORATION.
Decrease, etc.
Diminish. } To become less. See INCREASE-DECREASE.
Draw in. To make less.
Dwarf. To stunt the growth of.
Dwindle. To decrease gradually.
Ebb. To fail.
Fall away. To decrease in size.
Fall short of. To be below a required size.
File. To wear away with a file.
Grind. To wear away with a grindstone.
Grow less. To become smaller.
Lessen. To cause to become less.
Lose flesh. To become thin.
Narrow. To make less wide.
Not come up to. See SUPREMACY-SUBORDINACY.
Pack. To place together tightly.
Pare. To take off from the outside.
Pinch. To squeeze tightly.
Purse up. To wrinkle.
Reduce. To bring from a higher to a lower level.
Render smaller. Cause to decrease.
Restrain. To hold within bounds.
Rub down. To make smooth by rubbing.
Scrape. To rub off from the surface.
Shave.
Shear. } To reduce by cutting off.
Shorten. To decrease the length of.
Shrink. To contract.
Shrivel. To form wrinkles.
Squeeze. To press tightly.
Stow. To cut off.
Strangle. To compress the neck.
Tighten. To make tight.
Wane. To decrease.
Warp. To decrease in size.
Waste. To diminish by needless use.
Wither. To shrink and become limp.
Wizen. To wither.

DIMINUTION—*Adjectives.*

Astringent. Causing flesh to draw together.
Compact. Placed close together.
Compressible. Able to be compressed.
Contracted, etc. Drawn together. See *Verbs.*
Contractile. Having the quality of contraction.
Contracting. Drawing together. See *Verbs.*
Neap. Low.
Shrunk. Drawn up into wrinkles.
Smaller, etc. Of less size. See GREATNESS-LITTLENESS.
Strangulated. Constricted.
Stunted. Checked in growth.
Tabid. Wasted by disease.
Unexpanded, etc. Undeveloped. See ENLARGEMENT.
Waning. Decreasing.
Wizened. To be shriveled.

ENLARGEMENT—Adjectives—*Continued.*

Patulous. Spreading slightly.
Pot-bellied. Having a protuberant belly.
Puffy. Distended by air or something soft.
Pursy. Fat
Swag-bellied. Having a protuberant belly.
Swollen. Increased in bulk.
Tumid. Swollen by an alteration of the internal structure.
Turgid. Swollen by something put in.
Wide-open.
Wide-spread. } Expanded.

---

en-league'. To unite in a league. ASSOCIATION.
en-light'-en. To instruct; to brighten. EDUCATION-MISTEACHING, ENLIGHTENMENT-SECRECY.
en-light'-ened. Highly civilized; possessing knowl-

edge. KNOWLEDGE-IGNORANCE.
en-light'-en-ment. Moral and intellectual advancement. ENLIGHTENMENT-SECRECY, KNOWLEDGE-IGNORANCE.

ENLIGHTENMENT—SECRECY.

Acquaintance. Information about a person or thing acquired from experience.
Acquainting, etc. See *Verbs.*
Announcement. The public proclamation of a piece of information.
Annunciation. The act of announcing.
Broad hint. A very slight mention or allusion.
Communication. Message.
Communicativeness. Tendency to talk.
Enlightenment. The state of being supplied with morally useful information.
Enunciation. An announcement.
Hint. An indirect allusion.
Information. Knowledge gained.
Instruction, etc. Teaching. See EDUCATION
Intercommunication. Correspondence.
Intimation. Information given in an indirect way.
Knowledge, etc. All acquired information. See KNOWLEDGE.
Mention. Calling of attention to indirectly,
Notice. Formal public information.
Notification. The act of giving information.
Presentment. The act of presenting information.
Publicity, etc. The state of being a piece of common information. See PUBLICITY.
Representation. An assertion of fact.
Word in the ear. Secret information.

ENLIGHTENMENT—*Denotations.*

Account, etc. See ACCOUNT.
Advice. An opinion recommended or offered, as worthy to be followed.
Byplay. Action carried on aside, while the main action proceeds.
Case. That which befalls, comes, or happens.
Cue. A hint or intimation.
Estimate. An opinion or judgment formed without using precise data.
Gentle hint. A slight mention.
Gesture, etc. See SIGN.
Inkling. A hint.
Innuendo. A remote allusion or reference, usually derogatory.
Insinuation. A suggestion by distant allusion.
Monition. Instruction or advice given by way of caution.
News, etc. See TIDINGS.
Passing word. A word spoken in passing.
Report. A story or statement circulating by common talk.
Return. Formal report on an action performed. See MARK.
Round-robin. A written petition, protest, etc., the signatures to which are written in a circle so as not to indicate who signed first.
Gazetteer. A geographical dictionary.
Guide. One who, or that which, directs another.
Guide-book. A book of directions and information for travelers.
Informant. }
Informer. } One who imparts information.
Intelligencer. One who, or that which, conveys news.
Itinerary. A register of places and distances. See TRAVELING.
Manual. A handbook.
Map. A representation of some portion of the earth's surface.
Messenger, etc. See MESSENGER.
Mouchard [F.]. A police-spy.
Mouthpiece. One who delivers the opinion of others.
Newsmonger. One who is active in hearing and telling news.
Pilot. A guide, especially of a vessel.
Plan. A representation drawn on a plane, as a map or chart.
Reporter. One who collects news for a newspaper.
Specification. The designation of particulars.
Statement, etc. See ASSERTION.
Subaudition. The act of understanding or supplying something not expressed.
Suggestion. A hint.
Verbum sapienti [L.]. A word to the wise; a sufficient hint.
Whisper. Something communicated in secret or by whispering.
Word in the end. A suggestion.
Word to the wise. A sufficient hint.

ENLIGHTENMENT—*Nouns of Agent.*

Amicus curiæ [L.]. A friend of the court.
Authority. A person whose opinion is worthy to be taken as a precedent.
Chart. A paper on which information is exhibited.
Cicerone [It.]. One who shows strangers the curiosities of a place, and orates like Cicero.
Delator. An informer.

Arrière pensée [F.]. Mental reservation.
Closeness. State of being close or secret.
Concealment. The act or state of keeping out of sight.
Disguise. Artificial language or manner assumed for secrecy or deception. See HIDINGPLACE.
Evasion. Artful means of avoiding discovery.
Hiding. The act of putting out of sight.
Incognita [L.]. The assumption of disguise or of a feigned character.
Latency, etc. The state of not being visible or apparent. See MANIFESTATION-LATENCY.
Latitancy. The state of lying in concealment.
Latitation. A lying in concealment.
Mental reservation. The failure to disclose something that affects a statement, promise, etc., which would change its import.
Misprision. Concealment.
Mystery. Something kept cautiously concealed.
Mystification. Concealing by confusing designedly.
Obreption. The act of creeping upon secretly.
Occultation. The concealing of one heavenly body by the intervention of another.
Privacy. The condition of being in a concealed position.
Reserve. The act of keeping back, or out of sight.
Reticence. The state of keeping silence.
Seclusion. Separation from society.
Secrecy. The condition or quality of being concealed.
Secret. Something concealed from view or knowledge.
Secretiveness. Disposition or tendency to conceal. See *Adjectives.*
Secretness. The state of being concealed.
Silence. Secrecy, etc. See TALKATIVENESS-TACITURNITY.
Slyness. The state of being marked by cunning secrecy. See CRAFT.
Stealth. A concealed manner of acting.
Stealthiness. The state of acting secretly.
Suppression. } Act of suppressing. See TRUTHFULNESS-
Suppression of truth. } FALSEHOOD.
Underhand dealing. Secret or unfair dealing.
White lie. A lie one finds it convenient to tell and excuses himself for telling.

SECRECY—*Nouns of Agency.*

Cryptography. A system of cipher-writing.
Free-masonry. The rites or practises of a secret organization.
Hiding-place, etc. A place of concealment See EXPOSURE-HIDING-PLACE.
Masked battery. A battery so placed as not to be seen by an enemy until it opens fire.
Masquerade. An assembly of persons wearing masks, and amusing themselves with dancing, etc.
Screen. Anything that hides or conceals. See EXPOSURE-HIDING-PLACE.
Steganography. The art of writing in concealed characters.

SECRECY—*Figurative Expressions.*

Seal of secrecy. Agreement to be concealed.
Snake in the grass. A concealed danger; a deceptive person.

SECRECY—*Verbs.*

Bamboozle, etc. To impose upon. See TRUTHFULNESS-FRAUD.
Becloud. To conceal by obscuring.
Be concealed, etc. See *Verbs.*
Befog. To conceal as by a fog.
Bemask. To conceal by disguising.
Blindfold. To conceal by covering the eyes.
Blind the eyes. To conceal by deception.
Bottle up. To conceal by enclosing.
Bury. To conceal by covering up.
Bury one's talents in a napkin. To hide one's natural ability. [Bible.]
Cloak. To disguise.
Close the curtain. To conceal by covering.
Conceal. To keep out of sight.
Couch. To conceal in a form of words.
Cover. To overlay with something so as to conceal.
Curtain. To conceal by hanging something in front of.
Disguise. To conceal by changing the appearance of.
Draw the curtain. } To hide or conceal in any way.
Draw the veil. }
Eclipse. To conceal by casting a shadow.
Ensconce. To conceal securely.
Fence with a question. To conceal one's own position by asking questions.

ENLIGHTENMENT—SECRECY—*Continued.*

ENLIGHTENMENT—Nouns of Agent—*Continued.*

Detective. One whose business is to detect criminals or discover matters of secrecy.

Eavesdropper. A secret listener.

Exponent. One who stands as a representative or upholder of principles.

Spy. One who is sent secretly into an enemy's camp to inspect his works, etc.

Teller. One who tells or communicates; or keeps tally and counts, as money.

Valet de place [F.]. A stranger's guide.

Vade mecum [L.]. Go with me; a constant companion

ENLIGHTENMENT—*Verbs.*

Acquaint with. To inform in all details.

Advise. To inform in a formal manner.

Allude to. To refer to indirectly.

Announce. To inform in a public manner.

Annunciate. To bring tidings.

Apprise. To inform of something of personal interest.

Awaken. To begin to learn.

Awaken to. To become aware of.

Become alive to. } To become aware of.
Become awake to. }

Be informed of, etc. To know from information, etc. See KNOWLEDGE.

Breathe. To inform by a mere suggestion.

Bring word. To inform by a message.

Come to one's ears. } To receive information in an indirect
Come to one's knowledge. } manner.

Communicate. To impart information to others.

Convey the knowledge to. To inform.

Correct. To rectify error.

Direct the attention to, etc. See HEED.

Disabuse. To remove a false idea from.

Disclose, etc. To inform of something before concealed, etc. See EXPOSURE.

Drop a hint. Suggest.

Eavesdrop. To pry into or overhear private conversation.

Enlighten. To impart useful information to.

Explain, etc. To make plain, etc. See INTERPRETATION.

Express. To set forth a piece of information.

Gather from. To form an idea from.

Get scent of. To learn a secret.

Give a bit of one's mind. To express one's own opinions, generally as a reproof.

Give a hint. Suggest.

Give an account, etc. See ACCOUNT.

Give an inkling of. To inform in an indirect manner by a hint.

Give notice. To announce.

Give one to understand. To inform in a threatening or reproving manner.

Give the cue. To intimate.

Glance at. To make a slight intimation.

Have one to know. See GIVE ONE TO UNDERSTAND.

Hear. To be informed by hearing.

Hint. To suggest indirectly.

Impart. To share a piece of information with another.

Impart to. To give information to.

Inform. To tell a matter of fact to one who did not know it before.

Inform of. To impart information about.

Insinuate. To inform by indirect means as an artifice.

Instruct, etc. See EDUCATION.

Intimate. To inform indirectly because of indecision.

Know, etc. See KNOWLEDGE.

Lay before. To present to view.

Learn, etc. See LEARNING.

Leave word. To leave a message.

Let fall. To inform as if by accident.

Let one know. To inform one.

Make acquainted with. See ACQUAINT WITH.

Make an allusion to. See ALLUDE TO.

Make known. To tell or announce to.

Mention. To inform of without describing.

Notify. To inform by any means.

Open one's eyes to. To become aware of.

Open the eyes of. To make aware of.

Overhear. To hear accidentally or intentionally words not intended for the hearer.

Point out. To inform of by pointing.

Prompt. To mention what is next to be said.

SECRECY—Verbs—*Continued.*

Hide. To put out of sight.

Hide in holes and corners. To put in unusual places.

Hide oneself. To get out of sight.

Hide one's light under a bushel. To conceal one's own ability. [Bible.]

Hold one's tongue, etc. See TALKATIVENESS-TACITURNITY.

Hoodwink. To conceal from, as if by blinding.

Hush up. To make silent.

Ignore, etc. To pass as unworthy of notice. See CAREFULNESS-CARELESSNESS.

Keep a secret. To keep something concealed.

Keep back. To hold back from general knowledge.

Keep close. } To keep secret.
Keep dark. }

Keep from. To withhold from.

Keep from view. To withhold from view.

Keep in ignorance. Not to tell to some one.

Keep in the background. To conceal by putting in an unimportant position.

Keep in the dark. To conceal.

Keep in the shade. To conceal.

Keep one's own counsel. To conceal one's own plans.

Keep out of sight. }
Keep out of view. }
Keep secret. } To conceal.
Keep snug. }
Keep to oneself. }

Leave in ignorance. } To withhold from.
Leave in the dark. }

Lie close. To lie in a concealed position.

Lie hid. To be out of sight.

Lie in ambush. To lie in wait for.

Lie perdu. To lie in concealment.

Lock up. To withhold.

Lurk. To lie hidden, as in ambush.

Make no sign. To wish to remain unknown.

Mask. To cover by way of concealment.

Muffle. To prevent seeing or hearing by wraps bound around the head.

Mystify. To make secret.

Not breathe a syllable about.

Not breathe a word. To keep entirely secret.

Not let it go further. To conceal it for the future.

Not let the right hand know what the left is doing. To do or act with the greatest secrecy. [Bible.]

Play at bopeep. } To conceal oneself.
Play at hide and seek. }

Prowl. To go about secretly.

Put out of sight. To hide.

Puzzle, etc. To keep in ignorance by perplexing. See CERTAINTY-DOUBT.

Reserve. To withhold for the present.

Retire from sight. To withdraw from sight.

Screen. To conceal by something that cuts off the view.

Screen from observation. } To hide.
Screen from sight. }

Seal. To conceal securely.

Seclude oneself. To conceal oneself from company.

Secrete. To conceal from observation, or from the knowledge of others.

Shade. To hide so as not to be injured.

Shroud. To conceal by covering completely.

Sink. To put out of observation.

Skulk. To keep hidden from an evil motive.

Slink. To creep away secretly as a result of meanness.

Smother. To conceal by suppressing.

Sneak. To move in a fearful manner as a result of shame

Steal along. To move in a concealed manner.

Steal by. }
Steal into. } To move quietly and without being observed.
Steal out of. }

Stifle. To conceal from public knowledge by suppressing.

Suffer an eclipse. To be temporarily obscured.

Suppress. To prevent from being made public.

Throw a veil over. To conceal by covering.

Throw in the background. See KEEP IN THE BACKGROUND.

Throw into the shade. To conceal in an obscure position.

Veil. To conceal as by a covering.

Whisper. To speak in a low voice as not to be heard.

Withhold. To keep from sight or hearing.

ENLIGHTENMENT—SECRECY—*Continued.*

ENLIGHTENMENT—Verbs—*Continued.*

Publish, etc. See PUBLICITY.
Put before. See LAY BEFORE.
Put into one's head. To suggest an idea.
Put one in possession of. To give information to.
Reach one's ears. To hear indirectly.
Render an account. See GIVE AN ACCOUNT.
Report.⎫
Report progress.⎬ To give information obtained by investigation.
Represent. To bring before the mind.
Retail. To inform as a matter of gossip.
Send word. To give knowledge of.
Set before. State.
Set right. To correct.
Show cause. To give the reason.
Signify. To make known by signs or words.
Speak volumes. To say or mean a great deal.
Specify. To give particulars.
State. To make known; to repeat. See ASSERTION.
Suggest. To impart indirectly.
Tell. To inform in detail.
Tell once for all. To give an only warning.
Tell one plainly. To speak that one cannot be misunderstood.
Throw out a hint. To give secret or indirect information to.
Tip the wink, etc. See SIGN.
Unbeguile. To free from the influences of deceit.
Undeceive. To free from deception.
Understand. To be informed from some creditable source.
Whisper. To scatter information abroad secretly.
Whisper in the ear. To give a hint to.
Write word. To inform by a written message.

ENLIGHTENMENT—*Adjectives.*

Communicative. Inclined to be talkative.
Communicatory. Imparting information.
Communiqué [F.]. Communicated.
Declaratory. Making clear or manifest.
Enunciative. Definite in statement.
Explicit, etc. See MANIFESTATION.
Expository. Serving to explain.
Expressive, etc. See MEANING.
Informed. Made known. See *Verbs.*
Nuncupatory. Oral.
Plain-spoken, etc. See CRAFT-ARTLESSNESS.
Published. Announced to the public. See PUBLICITY.
Reported. Publicly known. See *Verbs.*

ENLIGHTENMENT—*Phrases.*

A little bird told me. I will not tell where I got the information.
From information received.

SECRECY—Adverbs—*Continued from Column 2.*

Confidentially. Secretly.
En tapinois [F.]. Stealthily.
Entre nous [F.]. Between ourselves.
Hugger-mugger. In a clandestine manner.
In a whisper. In a low tone not to be generally heard.
In camera [L.]. In secret.
Incognito. In a secret manner under an assumed name or character.
In confidence. In secret.
In holes and corners. Out of sight.
In one's sleeve. Out of sight.
In private.⎫
In secret.⎬ Not to be made known.
In strict confidence.⎭
Inter nos [L.]. Between ourselves.
In the background. Out of sight.
In the dark, etc. See *Adjectives.*
Januis clausis [L.]. With closed doors.
Like a thief in the night. Stealthily.
On the sly. Without being seen.
Secretly, etc. See *Adjectives*
Sotto voce [It.]. In an undertone.
Stealthily, etc. See *Adjectives.*
Sub rosa [L.]. Under the rose; privately.
Underhand. In a mean and secret manner.
Under the cloak of. Underhanded.

SECRECY—*Adjectives.*

Auricular. Spoken secretly so as to be heard only by the ears intended for.
Behind a screen, etc. See EXPOSURE-HIDINGPLACE.
Buried. Concealed by being covered.
Buttoned up. Concealed by closing up.
Cabalistic. Concealed under mystery.
Clandestine. Kept secret.
Close. Hidden by being enclosed.
Close as wax.
Clouded. Hidden by being obscured.
Concealed, etc. See *Verbs.*
Confidential. Secret.
Covert, etc. Concealed for an evil purpose, etc. See MANIFESTATION-LATENCY.
Cryptic.⎫
Cryptical.⎬ Not plainly evident.
Dark. Hidden by a lack of light.
Esoteric. Understood by, or designed only for a few.
Evasive. Escaping ready apprehension.
Feline. Stealthy like a cat.
Furtive. Slinking like a thief.
Hidden. Put out of sight.
Hole and corner. Hiding to promote evil.
In a cloud. Beclouded.
In a dark corner.⎫
In a fog.⎬ Out of sight.
In a haze. Indistinctly visible.
In ambush. Hidden in order to attack without warning.
In a mist. Hidden.
In disguise. Hidden under an unusual costume.
In hiding. In an unknown place.
In petto [L.]. Within the breast; in reserve.
In the dark. Out of sight.
In the shade.
Inviolable. Not capable of being broken.
Inviolate. Not broken, as to be seen.
Invisible, etc. That cannot be seen. See VISIBILITY-INVISIBILITY.
Irrevealable. That may not be brought from concealment.
Mysterious, etc. Hidden in mystery. See CLEARNESS-OBSCURITY.
Mystic. Hidden from human observation.
Not to be spoken of. Out of mind.
Obreptitious. With secrecy or by concealment of the truth.
Occult. Hidden from observation or knowledge
Perdu [F.]. Hidden from sight.
Private. Hidden from publicity.
Privy. Hidden in seclusion.
Recondite. Hidden from easy perception.
Reserved. Kept back for the present.
Reticent. Habitually concealing by silence.
Secluded, etc. Hidden from others. See SOCIABILITY-PRIVACY.
Secret. Hidden from view or knowledge.
Secretive. Having a tendency to hide.
Skulking. Hiding from an evil motive.
Sly, etc. Clever in doing things in a hidden manner. See CRAFT
Stealthy. Acting in a hidden manner.
Surreptitious. Accomplished by secret means.
Taciturn, etc. Habitually silent. See TALKATIVENESS-TACITURNITY.
Uncommunicative. Not inclined to talk.
Under an eclipse.
Under cover. In hiding.
Underground. Deeply hidden.
Underhand. Done in a treacherous and hidden manner.
Undisclosed, etc. See EXPOSURE.
Untold, etc. See ENLIGHTENMENT.
Wrapt in clouds. Clouded.

SECRECY—*Adverbs.*

À huis clos [F.]. With closed doors.
À la dérobée [F.]. By stealth.
À la sourdine [F.]. Suddenly; stealthily.
Aside. Apart from the rest.
Behind a screen, etc. See EXPOSURE-HIDINGPLACE.
Behind one's back.⎫
Behind the curtain.⎬ In secret.
Behind the scenes.⎭
Between ourselves.⎫
Between you and me.⎬ Quietly or secretly
By stealth.⎭

(*Continued on Column 1.*)

SECRECY—Adverbs—*Continued.*

Under the rose. Privately.
Under the seal of secrecy. Confidentially.
Under the table. Out of sight.

With bated breath. In a whisper.
With closed doors. Secretly.
Without beat of drum. Quietly.

SECRECY—*Phrases.*

À couverts [F.]. Under cover.
Alitur vitium vivitque tegendo [L.]. Vice is nourished and lives by concealment.

It must go no further. }
It will go no further. } No one else dare know.
Nobody the wiser. Kept secret.
Tell it not in Gath. Keep it secret.

---

en-link'. To join by links; connect closely. UNION-DISUNION.
en-list'. To engage the service of. COMMISSION-ABROGATION, FIGHTING-CONCILIATION, MOTIVE-CAPRICE; enlist into the service, USE-DISUSE; enlist under the banners of, OBSTRUCTION-HELP.
en-li'-ven. To animate. ENTERTAINMENT-WEARINESS, LIGHTHEARTEDNESS-DEJECTION, PLEASURABLENESS-PAINFULNESS.
en-mesh'. To entangle in meshes. DIFFICULTY-FACILITY.
en'-mi-ty. Hostility. AMITY-HOSTILITY, CHARITABLE-NESS-MALEVOLENCE, LOVE-HATE, VARIANCE-ACCORD.
en-no'-ble. To dignify. REPUTATION-DISCREDIT.
en''-nui'. Mental weariness produced by satiety. ENTERTAINMENT-WEARINESS.
e-nor'-mi-ty. Outrageous wickedness. GREATNESS-LITTLENESS, INNOCENCE-GUILT, MAGNITUDE-SMALLNESS.
e-nor'-mous. Very great. GREATNESS-LITTLENESS, MAGNITUDE-SMALLNESS; enormous number, MULTIPLICITY-PAUCITY.
e-nor'-mous-ly. Greatly. MAGNITUDE-SMALLNESS.
e-nough'. Sufficient. DISCONTINUANCE-CONTINUANCE, ENOUGH, FAULTLESSNESS-FAULTINESS, MAGNITUDE-SMALLNESS, OUTLAY-INCOME; enough and to spare, ENOUGH; enough in all conscience, EXCESS-LACK; enough to drive one mad, PLEASURABLENESS-PAINFULNESS; know when one has had enough, MODERATION-SELFINDULGENCE.

ENOUGH.

Abundance. Great excess above what is necessary.
Adequacy. The quality of being equal to what is required.
Affluence, etc. See AFFLUENCE.
A land flowing with milk and honey. A land of great productiveness.
Amplitude. Quality of being somewhat more than necessary.
Competence. Adequate ability; applied mostly to mental endowments.
Copiousness, etc. See *Adjectives.*
Cornucopia. The horn of plenty, symbolizing peace and prosperity.
Enough. A quantity or number that will satisfy the need, demand, or purpose.
Fat of the land. The rich products of the land.
Fill. A full supply.
Flood. An abundant supply of anything.
Full measure. Measure that is amply correct.
Fulness. Great quantity.
Galore. Abundance. [Sent off proofs and copy galore, before breakfast. Walter Scott, *Journal*, 12, *April.*]
"Good measure pressed down and running over." [*Luke* vi, 38.]
Horn of Amalthæa. } A horn filled with fruits, symbolizing peace
Horn of plenty. } and prosperity.
Lots. A great quantity or amount.
Luxuriance. See FERTILITY.
Mediocrity. A moderate degree or rate.
Mine. A rich source of supply.
No less. A sufficient quantity.
Outpouring. A copious effusion.
Plenitude. Great quantity; applied more to moral or abstract things.
Plenty. More than enough; applied usually to supplies of food, water, etc.
Profusion. Rich abundance.

Quantum sufficit [L.] A sufficient quantity.
Repletion. The quality of being lavishly stocked or supplied.
Satiety, etc. See DESIRE-REPLETION.
Satisfaction. Full gratification of desire, need, or want.
Sufficiency. All that is needful to serve a purpose.
Tide. A quantity as irresistible as a tide.

ENOUGH—*Verbs.*

Abound. To be plentifully supplied with.
Be sufficient, etc. See *Adjectives.*
Bristle with. To be thickset with difficulties, as a wild boar with bristles.
Do. To be sufficient for.
Drink one's fill. To drink all one feels like.
Eat one's fill. To eat all one likes.
Exuberate. To exist in great abundance.
Flow. To be as abundant as the waters of a river.
Have enough, etc. See *Nouns.*
Have one's fill. To eat or drink or enjoy all one feels like.
Just do. To be exactly sufficient.
Pass muster To be good enough to be approved
Pour. To expend or shed lavishly.
Pour in. To come in in great numbers.
Rain. To pour down like rain.
Render sufficient, etc. See *Adjectives.*
Replenish. Fill up afresh; stock with abundance.
Roll in. To be in such abundance that one might roll in it.
Satisfy. To fully gratify desire, need, or want.
Shower down. To be as plentiful as if come down in a rain.
Stream. To move or come in continued succession of parts.
Suffice. To be sufficient.
Swarm. To be in swarms.
Swim in. To be in such abundance that one might swim in it.
Teem. To abound exceedingly.
Wallow in. To revel in in an indecent manner.

ENOUGH—*Adjectives.*

Abounding, etc. See *Verbs.*
Abundant. In great excess above what is necessary.
Adequate. Equal to what is required, morally, intellectually, or materially.
Affluent. See AFFLUENCE.
Ample. Somewhat more than necessary.
Big with. Fruitful with; teeming with.
Choke full. Completely full.
Commensurate. Corresponding in amount or degree.
Competent. Adequate in ability; applied to mental endowments.
Copious. In great quantities, as if from a rich source.
Enough. Having a quantity that will satisfy the purpose or demand.
Enough and to spare. More than enough.
Exhaustless. Inexhaustible.
Flush. Quite full.
Full. Abounding in; containing all that it can hold.
Inexhaustible. Impossible to be used up, or consumed.
Lavish. Bestowed or given in profusion.
Liberal. Large in quantity, as a gift, or supply.
Luxuriant, etc. See FERTILITY.
Measured. Regulated; restrained within bounds
Moderate. Limited in quantity.
Plenteous. Plentiful.
Plentiful. More than enough; applied to supplies of food, water, etc.
Plenty. Plentiful.
Plenty as blackberries. Very plentiful.
Replete. Filled again; completely filled.
Rich. Yielding great quantities.
Satisfactory. Answering all desires and requirements.
Stintless. Without bounds or limits.
Sufficient. What is needful to serve a purpose; applied to what is to be used or employed.
Tangible. Capable of being handled or touched
Unexhausted. Not exhausted.

Unmeasured. Not measured
Unsparing. Not sparing.
Unstinted. Not stinted.
Unstinting. Not stinting.
Unwasted. Not wasted.
Up to the mark. Up to the standard.
Valid. Having sufficient soundness: said of arguments, etc.
Wantless. Having no want; abundant.
Well provided. } Having a sufficient supply.
Well stocked. }
Wholesale. Done on a large scale.
Without stint. Lavish; without limit.

ENOUGH—*Adverbs.*

Ad libitum [L.]. As much as one pleases.
Amply, etc. See *Adjectives.*
Full. Very.
In abundance. See *Nouns.*
Sufficiently, etc. See *Adjectives.*
To one's heart's content. As much as one pleases.
Withal. In addition.
With no sparing hand. Given plentifully.
Without stint. Without bound or limit.

ENOUGH—*Phrases.*

Cut and come again.
Das Beste ist gut genug [G.]. The best is good enough.
Dictum sapienti sat est [L.]. A word to the wise is sufficient.

en-rage′. To exasperate. FAVORITE-ANGER, PLEAS-URABLENESS-PAINFULNESS.
enragé [F.] (an′-ra-zhê′). Mad; rabid. DESIRE-DIS-TASTE.
en-rap′-ture. To transport with pleasure. EXCITA-TION, LOVE-HATE, PLEASURABLENESS-PAINFULNESS.
en-rap′-tured. Extravagantly delighted. EMOTION, PLEASURE-PAIN.
en-rav′-ish. To enrapture. PLEASURABLENESS-PAIN-FULNESS.
en-rav′-ished. Delighted. PLEASURE-PAIN.
en-rav′-ish-ing. Delighting extremely. PLEASURABLE-NESS-PAINFULNESS.
en-rav′-ish-ment. Ecstasy. EXCITATION.
en-rich′. To make rich. AFFLUENCE-PENURY, BET-TERMENT-DETERIORATION.
en-robe′. To attire. DRESS-UNDRESS.
en-roll′. To record; to enlist. COMMISSION-ABROGA-TION, FIGHTING-CONCILIATION, MARK-OBLITERATION.
en-rol′-ment. A record. MARK-OBLITERATION.
ens [L.] (enz). An existence, entity, or being. ENTITY-NONENTITY.
Ens entium [L.] (enz en′-she-um). The Being of beings. DIVINITY.
ens, non [L.] (enz, non). Not a being. ENTITY-NONENTITY.
ens rationis [L.] (enz rê″-she-o′-nis). A rational being. ENTITY-NONENTITY, MIND-IMBECILITY.
en-sam′-ple. An example to follow or avoid. COPY-MODEL.
en-san′-guined. To dye or steep with blood. LIFE-KILLING.
en-sconce′. To settle. ENLIGHTENMENT-SECRECY, SECURITY-INSECURITY.
en-sconced′. Situated. ESTABLISHMENT-REMOVAL.
en″-sem′-ble. The general appearance and effect. WHOLE-PART.
en-shrine′. To cherish. CONFINEMENT, GODLINESS-DISBELIEF, REPUTATION-DISCREDIT; **enshrine in the memory,** REMEMBRANCE-FORGETFULNESS.
en-shrine′-ment. Act of enshrining. REPUTATION-DISCREDIT.
en′-si-form. Sword-shaped. SHARPNESS-BLUNTNESS.
en′-sign. A standard; a symbol; an officer, naval or military. BELLIGERENT, CHIEF-UNDERLING, SIGN; **ensign of authority,** SCEPTER.
en-slave′. To enthrall. LIBERTY-SUBJECTION.

en-slaved′. In bondage. LIBERTY-SUBJECTION.
en-slave′-ment. State of being in bondage. LIBERTY-SUBJECTION.
en-snare′. To entrap. PATRIOTISM-TREASON, TRUTH-FULNESS-FRAUD.
en-sue′. To follow. OCCURRENCE-DESTINY, PRE-CEDENCE-SUCCESSION.
en-sure′. To secure against possible loss. CERTAINTY-DOUBT.
en-tab′-la-ture. The uppermost member of a columnar system. TOP-BOTTOM.
en-tail′. To involve; to restrict the inheritance of to a particular class of heirs. CAUSE-EFFECT, KEEPING-RELINQUISHMENT.
en-tan′-gle. To perplex; to tangle. CROSSING, DIFFI-CULTY-FACILITY, MIXTURE-HOMOGENEITY, ORGAN-IZATION-DISORGANIZATION, TRUTHFULNESS-FRAUD, UNION-DISUNION, VARIANCE-ACCORD.
en-tan′-gled. Twisted into a tangle. REGULARITY-IRREGULARITY; **entangled by difficulties,** DIFFICULTY-FACILITY.
en-tan′-gle-ment. State of being entangled. CROSS-ING, DIFFICULTY-FACILITY, REGULARITY-IRREGU-LARITY.
entbehre gern was du nicht hast [G.] (ent‑bê′-re gêrn vas du niнt hast). Willingly renounce what you do not possess. HOLDING-EXEMPTION, QUEST-ABAN-DONMENT.
entend, cela s' [F.] (san′-tan″, se-la′). That is under-stood. HABIT-DESUETUDE.
entendre, double [F.] (an′-tan·dr′, dubl). Double meaning: an idiom not used in French. WITTINESS-DULNESS.
entente cordiale [F.] (an′-tan·t′ cor-di-al′). A cordial understanding. AMITY-HOSTILITY, VARIANCE-ACCORD.
en′-ter. To go in; to join. ACCOUNTS, BEGINNING-END, ENTRANCE-EXIT, MARK-OBLITERATION; **enter a profession,** OCCUPATION; **enter in,** CONCENTRATION-RADIATION; **enter into an engagement,** ENGAGE-MENT-RELEASE; **enter into collision,** IMPETUS-RE-ACTION; **enter into details,** ACCOUNT, UNIVERSALITY-PARTICULARITY; **enter into one's views,** ASSENT-DIS-SENT; **enter into the composition of,** CONSTITUENT-ALIEN, INCLUSION-OMISSION; **enter into the feelings of,** CHARITABLENESS-MALEVOLENCE, COMPASSION-RUTHLESSNESS; **enter into the ideas of,** CLEARNESS-OBSCURITY; **enter into the spirit of,** EMOTION; **enter the lists,** ATTACK-DEFENSE, STRIFE-PEACE; **enter the mind,** MIND-IMBECILITY; **enter upon,** BEGINNING-END.
en′-ter-prise. Energy; a bold undertaking. BRAVERY-COWARDICE, ENTERPRISE, QUEST-EVASION; **com-mercial enterprise,** EXCHANGE.

ENTERPRISE.

Compact. An agreement binding a number of persons entering into an undertaking. See CONTRACT.
Emprise. An undertaking of an adventurous or chivalrous nature.
Engagement, etc. A formal and mutual promise. See ENGAGE-MENT.
Enterprise. A dangerous or hazardous undertaking.
First move, etc. The very beginning of an undertaking. See BEGINNING.
Matter in hand, etc. The undertaking now being carried out. See OCCUPATION.
Move. An act in the carrying out of an undertaking.
Undertaking. The act of engaging to perform a project.

ENTERPRISE—*Verbs.*

Apprentice oneself to. To enter upon an undertaking as a learner.
Be in for. To undertake with some object in view.
Begin, etc. To commence an undertaking. See BEGINNING.
Betake oneself to. To undertake to engage in.

Break the neck of a business. To overcome the principal difficulty of an undertaking.
Broach. To open an undertaking.
Contract. To form an agreement about an undertaking.
Devote oneself to. To undertake in an earnest manner.
Embark in. To enter upon an undertaking.
Engage, etc. To bind by mutual and formal promises. See ENGAGEMENT.
Engage in. To take part in an undertaking.
Fall to. To undertake hastily and eagerly.
Fall to work. To enter upon an undertaking hastily and eagerly.
Go about. To set oneself to business.
Go to do. To begin to undertake.
Have in hand, etc. To be engaged in something. See OCCUPATION.
Have many irons in the fire. To be engaged in many undertakings.
Institute, etc. To set an undertaking in operation. See CAUSE.
Launch forth. To start a new undertaking.
Launch into. To start into a new undertaking.
Lay one's hand to the plow. } To undertake with great determination.
Lay one's shoulder to the wheel. }
Plunge into. To rush into an undertaking.
Put in execution. To start an undertaking in operation.
Put in hand. To undertake.
Put one's foot in. To get into difficulty with an undertaking; to blunder.
Put one's hand to. To enter upon an undertaking.
Put one's hand to the plow. To undertake with earnestness.
Set about. To take the first steps in an undertaking.
Set forward. To promote an undertaking.
Set to. To cause to commence an undertaking.
Set up shop. To commence a business undertaking.
Tackle. To undertake something difficult.
Take in hand. To attempt to execute.
Take up. To carry on or manage.

Take upon oneself. To undertake upon one's own responsibility.
Take upon one's shoulders. To undertake something alone.
Turn one's hand to. To apply oneself to an undertaking.
Undertake. To engage upon the performance of something.
Volunteer. To voluntarily offer to undertake.

ENTERPRISE—*Adjectives.*

On the anvil. In a state of formation.
Undertaking. Engaging in.

ENTERPRISE—*Phrase.*

There goes. An undertaking begins.

en'-ter-pri''-sing. Energetic and progressive. ACTIVITY-INDOLENCE, BRAVERY-COWARDICE.
en''-ter-tain'. To extend hospitality to; to divert. ENTERTAINMENT-WEARINESS, HEED-DISREGARD, OBSTRUCTION-HELP, REGARD-DISRESPECT, SOCIABILITY-PRIVACY; **entertain an idea,** MIND-IMBECILITY; **entertain an opinion,** FAITH-MISGIVING; **entertain doubts,** FAITH-MISGIVING; **entertain feeling,** EMOTION; **entertain hope,** SANGUINENESS-HOPELESSNESS.
en''-ter-tained'. Treated hospitably. SOCIABILITY-PRIVACY.
en''-ter-tain'-ing. Diverting. ENTERTAINMENT-WEARINESS.
en''-ter-tain'-ment. Amusement; a social party; hospitable accommodation. ENTERTAINMENT-WEARINESS.

ENTERTAINMENT—WEARINESS.

Amusement. An employment or occupation which gives ease to the mind whether purposely sought or not.
Diversion. That which turns or draws the mind from care and study.
Divertissement [F.]. Amusement; sport.
Entertainment. A species of amusement which is always more or less of an intellectual nature.
Festivity. Social joy or gaiety of spirits at an entertainment.
Fredaine [F.]. A frolic.
Frolic. A noisy merrymaking.
Fun. Noisy amusement.
Gala. Show or festivity.
Gambade [F.] Gambol.
Gambol. A skipping or leaping about in frolic.
Game. A contest, physical o. mental, for amusement or recreation.
Heyday. High spirits or frolicsomeness.
Holiday making. Exemption from labor for amusement and gaiety.
Jocoseness. } A merry or sportive act or saying.
Jocosity. }
Jollification. A merrymaking or noisy festivity.
Jollity. Noisy enjoyment.
Joviality } Noisy mirth.
Jovialness. }
Labor of love. A labor undertaken through pleasure in the work itself, without expectation of reward.
Laughter, etc. Expression of cheerfulness, gaiety, or mirth. See JUBILATION.
Merriment. Gaiety with laughter.
Merrymaking. That which produces amusement.
Passetemps [F.] Agreeable pastime.
Pastime. That which amuses, and makes time pass agreeably.
Play. Exercise intended for amusement.
Pleasantry. That which promotes good humor or cheerfulness.
Pleasure, etc. An occurrence in which the mind finds satisfaction or diversion. See PLEASURE.
Prank. A gay or sportive action.
Reaction. Effect produced upon the body by diversion.
Rejoicing, etc. Expression of delight or gladness. See JUBILATION.
Relaxation. Remission from attention and labor.
Round of pleasures. Continuous amusement or entertainment
Solace. That which cheers or consoles.
Sport. That which diverts, and causes pleasure.
Sporting, etc. Engaging in sports. See QUEST.
Tomfoolery. An amusing trifle.
Wit. Sudden and ingenious association of ideas and words causing surprise and exhilaration.

Defatigation. Fatigue; weariness.
Disgust. Repugnance for what is offensive.
Drowsiness, etc. State of being heavy with sleepiness. See ACTIVITY-INDOLENCE.
Ennui. Mental weariness.
Lassitude, etc. Chronic fatigue.
Loathing. Extreme disgust or dislike.
Nausea. Sickness of the stomach, accompanied by an impulse to vomit; also disgust.
Satiety, etc. Gratification to excess which produces wearisomeness or loathing. See DESIRE–REPLETION.
Sickness. Wearisome dislike, as of flattery; nausea.
Tædium vitæ [L.]. Weariness of life.
Tediousness, etc. Wearisomeness from slowness or continuance of some action. See *Adjectives.*
Tedium. Wearisomeness; irksomeness.

WEARINESS—*Associated Nouns.*

Bore. A person or thing that wearies one through lack of interest.
Buttonhole. A person who bores one with his talk.
Dull work. Anything that wearies one.
Heavy hours. Hours of idleness or weariness.
Monotony. Irksome uniformity of any kind.
Proser. A dull or tedious writer or talker.
The enemy. Time, especially unoccupied time.
Twice-told tale. A story that wearies a person by its repetition.
Wet blanket. A discouragement, or one who discourages.

WEARINESS—*Verbs.*

Be tired of, etc. } Be jaded or wearied. See *Adjectives.*
Be tired with, etc. }
Bore. Annoy or weary.
Bore out of all patience. }
Bore out of one's life. } Weary extremely.
Bore to death. }
Die with ennui. Die of mental weariness.
Disgust. Excite loathing or aversion in.
Drag its slow length along. Be tedious or wearisome.
Drag its weary length along. Be wearisome.
Harp on the same string. Dwell on the same subject with wearisome persistence.
Nauseate. Affect with a feeling of disgust.
Never hear the last of.
Pall. Make or become insipid or uninteresting.
Send to sleep. } Make tired or weary because of lack of interest.
Set to sleep. }

ENTERTAINMENT—WEARINESS—*Continued.*

ENTERTAINMENT—*Denotations, etc.*

American bowls. The game of tenpins or bowling.

Antic. A grotesque trick.

Aquatics. Sports or exercises practised on the water.

Arbiter elegantiarum [L.]. Master of ceremonies.

Archery. The practise of shooting with bow and arrows.

A short life and a merry one. Life of pleasure.

Athletic sports. The games and sports of athletes.

Backgammon. A game played by two persons on a board marked off into twenty-four spaces called points. The movements from point to point are determined by throwing dice.

Bagatelle. A game played on an oblong board, having at one end cups or arches into or through which balls are to be driven by a rod held in the hand.

Banquet. A feast. See NUTRIMENT.

Baseball. A game of ball, so called from the four bases which designate the circuit which each player endeavors to make after striking the ball.

Battledore and shuttlecock. A game which consists of striking a cork stuck with feathers, with a racket.

Bauble. A cheap, showy plaything.

Billiards. A game played with ivory balls on a cloth-covered, rectangular table, bounded by elastic cushions.

Blindman's buff. A game in which one person is blindfolded, and tries to catch some one and tell who it is.

Bonfire. A large fire built in the open air for amusement.

Bout. A contest or trial.

Bowls The game of tenpins

Buffoonery. Ridiculous pranks.

Carnival. A festival celebrated with merriment and revelry.

Carousal.⎫ A jovial feast or drunken revel.
Carouse.⎭

Cricket. A game played with ball, bats, and wickets, the players being in two contesting parties.

Croquet. A game in which the players endeavor to drive wooden balls, by means of mallets, through a series of hoops or arches.

Cross questions and crooked answers. A game of question and answer.

Curling. A Scottish game in which heavy weights of stone are propelled by hand over the ice.

Discus. Exercise with a heavy plate intended to be pitched as a trial of strength and skill.

Dissipation. A dissolute course of life in pursuit of pleasure.

Doll. A child's toy baby. [A pet name for *Dorothy*, Gr. *Dorothea*, gift of God.]

Dominoes. A game played with twenty-eight blocks left blank or dotted after the manner of dice.

Draughts. The game of checkers.

Échappée [F.]. A prank.

Escapade [F.]. A trick.

Espièglerie [F.]. A playful trick.

Feast. A festive or joyous meal.

Festival. A time of feasting or celebration.

Fête. A festival.

Fête champêtre [F.] A rustic feast.

Feu-de-joie [F.]. A bonfire.

Fireworks. A device for producing a display of light, or figures, by the combustion of materials that burn in some peculiar manner.

Fives. A game resembling tennis.

Football. The game of kicking and carrying the football by opposing parties of players between goals.

French and English. An out-door game in which the players are divided into contesting parties.

Gala. Festivity.

Gallanty-show. A peep show.

Gambling. Playing for money, or other stake.

Game. A contest for amusement, recreation, or winning a stake.

Game at romps. Noisy, exciting play.

Game of chance. A game played for a stake, not decided by skill.

Game of fox and goose. A game in which one person tries to catch another as he runs from goal to goal.

Game of skill. Any game which requires skill in playing.

Gamester. A person who plays for a stake.

Go-bang. A game played on a checker board, usually of 256 squares with fifty colored counters.

Golf. A game played with a small ball and a bat or club crooked at the lower end.

Greasy pole. The contest of climbing a slippery pole.

Gymnastics. Athletic exercises.

Hide and seek. A play of children, in which some hide themselves and others seek them.

High jinks. An old Scottish pastime; wild sport.

WEARINESS—VERBS—*Continued.*

Sicken. Disgust.

Tire. Weary; fatigue.

Tire out of all patience.⎫
Tire out of one's life.⎬ Figurative degrees of weariness.
Tire to death.⎭

Weary. To grow tired in body and depressed in spirits.

Weary out of all patience.⎫
Weary out of one's life.⎬ Degrees of weariness.
Weary to death.⎭

Yawn. Open the mouth involuntarily with a long, full inspiration of the breath as a result of drowsiness, fatigue, or dulness.

WEARINESS—*Adjectives.*

Arid. Dry; uninteresting; wearisome.

Bald. Bare; literal; wearisome.

Blasé [F.]. Cloyed.

Devoid of interest. Lacking interest; wearisome.

Disgusting, etc. Exciting aversion or loathing, etc. See *Verbs.*

Drowsy, etc. Heavy with sleepiness; dull, etc. See ACTIVITY-INDOLENCE.

Dry. Lacking interest.

Dull. Depressing; sad; wearisome; not active or bright.

Flagging. Becoming spiritless or tired; growing uninteresting.

Flat. Uninteresting; monotonous.

Humdrum. Tedious; uninteresting.

Irksome. Wearisome; tiresome; vexatious.

Life-weary. Weary of life.

Monotonous. Wearisomely uniform.

Mortal. Long and wearisome.

Prosing. Speaking or writing in a wearisome or prosy way.

Prosy. Dull; tiresome.

Sick of. Tired of; disgusted with.

Slow. Dull; tedious.

Somniferous. Producing sleep; wearisome.

Soporific. Causing sleep; tiresome.

Stupid. Lacking apprehension or understanding dull.

Tedious. Producing weariness; slow.

Tired, etc. Wearied; fatigued; jaded, etc. See *Verbs.*

Tiresome. Wearisome; tedious.

Unenjoyed. Unsatisfying; not affording enjoyment; wearisome.

Uninterested. Having no interest in; bored; wearied.

Uninteresting. Not of interest; not engaging the attention.

Used up. Tired out; exhausted to weariness.

Weariness. Weakness of body with flagging of the spirits.

Wearing. Exhausting; wearying.

Wearisome. Causing weariness.

Wearisomeness. The quality of causing weariness or fatigue.

Weary. Worn out by toil, endurance, or vexation.

Wearying, etc. Tiring; making weary, etc. See *Verbs.*

Weary of life. Tired of living, life-weary.

Worn out. Exhausted; wearied.

WEARINESS—*Adverbs.*

Usque ad nauseam [L.]. To the point of disgust.

Wearily, etc. In a weary manner, etc. See *Adjectives.*

WEARINESS—*Phrases.*

Crambe repetita [L.]. Cabbage warmed over; the same old story.

Time hanging heavily on one's hands.

Toujours perdrix [F.]. Always partridges; the same thing over and over.

ENTERTAINMENT—*Denotations—Continued.*

Hockey. A game in which two parties of players, armed with curved or hooked sticks, attempt to drive a ball or block of wood toward opposite goals.

Hopscotch. A child's game, in which a player, hopping on one foot, drives a stone or block from one compartment to another of a figure traced or scotched on the ground.

Hop, skip, and jump. An exercise which consists of a hop, a skip, and a jump.

Horse racing. The practise of racing with horses.

Hunt the slipper. A game in which a slipper or anything is hidden by a person and others look for it.

Jubilee. A season of general joy.

Junket. A feast or entertainment.

Kail. A game played by rolling an iron ball among nine holes made in the ground.

Kiss in the ring. A children's game in which one of the players attempts to kiss another before he can enter a line formed by the other players.

ENTERTAINMENT—Denotations—*Continued.*

Knickknack. A trifle; a toy. See Consequence-Insignificance.

Knur and spell. A game played in Northern England in which the players bat a wooden ball or knur as it is thrown from a trap or spell.

Lacrosse. A game of ball, originating among the North American Indians, in which each player carries a long-handled racket called a crosse, and with this catches and tosses a ball through one of the goals placed at opposite ends of the field.

La grâce [F.]. A game played with hoops.

Lark. A frolic.

Lawn-tennis. A variety of the game of tennis.

Leap-frog. A boy's game in which one stoops down and another leaps over him by placing his hands on the shoulders of the former.

Lotto. A game of chance, played with cards, on which numbers are inscribed and any contrivance, as a wheel containing numbered balls, for determining a set of numbers by chance.

Magic lantern, etc An optical instrument for throwing upon a screen greatly magnified pictures from slides. See Appearance.

Master of ceremonies. One who presides at a feast or entertainment.

Master of the revels. One who presides over a feast.

Merelles. Nine-men's-morris.

Monkey-trick. A mischievous prank.

Morra. A game in which the object is to guess the number of fingers held out by one or more players.

Mummery. Frolic in disguise.

Nine-men's-morris. A game played with counters, or men, which are placed at the angles of a figure drawn on a board or on the ground.

Ninepins. A game played with nine pins or pieces of wood, set on end, at which a wooden ball is bowled to knock them down.

Pall-mall. A game in which a wooden ball is driven with a mallet, through a hoop or ring of iron.

Pallone [It.]. An Italian game played with a large leather ball.

Party. A gathering for amusement. See Sociability.

Peep-show. A small show, or object exhibited, which is viewed through an orifice or magnifying glass.

Picnic. An excursion or pleasure party.

Ping-pong. An indoor game resembling lawn tennis.

Plaything. A thing to play with.

Polo. A game resembling hockey, with the players on horseback.

Pool. A game which consists in pocketing the balls on a pool table.

Practical joke. See Society-Derision.

Prank. A trick.

Puppet-show. A mock drama performed by puppets moved by wires.

Pyramids. The game of pool in which the balls are placed in the form of a triangle at spot.

Quintain. An object to be tilted at.

Quip. A smart, sarcastic turn or jest.

"Quips and cranks and wanton wiles, nods and becks and wreathed smiles."

Quirk. A twist or turn of the fancy.

Quoits. A game played with flattened ring-shaped pieces of iron to be pitched at a fixed stake.

Racketing. A clattering, confused noise of play.

Rackets. A variety of the game of tennis.

Raree-show. A show carried about in a box.

Regale. A banquet.

Regatta. Originally, a gondola race in Venice; now, a rowing or sailing race or a series of such races anywhere.

Reveler. One who revels.

Revels. Riotous festivity or merrymaking.

Rifle shooting. A trial of skill in the use of the rifle.

Rig. A frolic.

Romp. Noisy play.

Saturnalia. The festival of Saturn; a feast of riotous enjoyment.

Skating. The exercise of moving on the ice on skates.

Skittles. A game resembling ninepins, but played by throwing wooden disks instead of rolling balls.

Skylarking. Frolicking.

Sliding. Exercise of gliding over a smooth or inclined surface.

Snapdragon. A play in which raisins are snapped from a vessel of burning brandy, and eaten.

Sportsman. One who engages in sports.

Spree. A drinking frolic.

Symposium. A banquet.

Teetotum. A child's toy resembling a top.

Tennis. A play in which a ball is driven from player to player by a racket.

Tenpins. Ninepins played with ten pins.

Tent-pegging. A cavalry exercise in which a horseman, while at full speed, attempts to uproot a tent-peg with his lance.

Tilting at the ring. An exercise with the lance.

Tip-cat. A game in which a small piece of wood, pointed at both ends, is tipped or struck with a bat, so as to fly into the air.

Tivoli. A game resembling bagatelle.

Tournament. A mock fight or warlike game; any contest of skill in which there are many contestants.

Toy. A plaything.

Toy-shop. A shop where toys are sold.

Trap-ball. An old game of ball, played with a trap, which consists of a pivoted arm on one end of which is placed the ball to be thrown into the air by striking the other end.

Treat. That which affords entertainment.

Tug-of-war. A contest in which two opposing parties try to pull each other from their positions.

Turfman. A follower of the race-course.

Vagary. A wild or fanciful freak.

Wake. The pastimes connected with a wake.

Wassail. A drinking bout.

Yule log. A large log of wood put on the hearth on Christmas eve and brought in with much ceremony.

ENTERTAINMENT—*Card Games.*

All fours. A game at cards called "High, Low, Jack, and the Game."

Baccarat [F.]. A French game of cards, played by a banker and punters.

Beggar my neighbor. A game of cards in which the object is to win the cards of all the players.

Besique [F.]. A game of cards in which various combinations of cards in the hand, when declared, score points.

Blind hookey. A game of cards in gambling.

Boaston. } A game of cards played by four persons, with two packs of

Boston. } fifty-two cards each; so called from Boston, Massachusetts.

Brag. A card game similar to poker.

Cards. Pieces of thick paper, etc., for playing games of chance, and having each pack divided into four suits of hearts, diamonds, clubs, and spades.

Casino. A game of cards played by two or more persons.

Commerce. A round game at cards, in which the cards are subject to exchange, barter, or trade.

Commit. A card game.

Connexions. A card game.

Cribbage. A game of cards characterized by a great variety of chances.

Écarté [F.]. A game of cards, played usually by two persons, in which the players may discard any or all the cards dealt and receive others from the pack.

Euchre. A game of cards in which the highest card is the knave of the same suit as trump, the lowest card being the seven spot.

Hearts. A game in which the heart suit alone counts.

Lift smoke. A nonsensical card game.

Loo. Old game played with five, or three, cards dealt to each player.

Lottery. A gaming scheme in which one or more tickets bearing particular numbers draw prizes, and the rest of the tickets are blanks.

Monte. A game played with three cards, one of which is marked.

Napoleon. Six-handed euchre.

Old maid. A game with picture cards.

Ombre. A Spanish card game played by three persons.

Pairs. A card game.

Patience. The game of cards played by one person.

Penny-ante. A poker game.

Picquet. A game of cards played by two persons, with thirty-two cards, all the deuces, threes, fours, fives, and sixes being set aside.

Poker. The American game of brag or bluff.

Polish bank. A game of cards.

Pope Joan. A game of cards played on a round board with compartments.

Quadrille. A game played by four persons with forty cards the tens, nines, and eights being discarded.

Quinze [F.]. A game of cards in which the object is to make fifteen points.

Pinocle. A game played with two packs, the cards below the nine spot being left out.

Reverse. } A certain game of cards in which the player wins who

Reversis. } takes the fewest tricks.

Round game. A game of cards in which each plays on his own account.

Rubber. The odd game when there is a tie between the players.

Snip-snap-snorem. A humorous card game.

Solitaire. A card game played by one person.

ENTERTAINMENT—Card Games—Continued.

Speculation. A game of cards in which the players buy from one another trumps or whole hands, upon a chance of getting the highest trump dealt, which entitles the holder to the pool or stakes.

Thirty-one. A game in which exactly or nearest to thirty-one points are sought to be scored.

Vingt-un [F.]. A game of cards in which the object is to get cards. the sum of whose spots is twenty-one.

Whist. A game of cards, so called because it requires silence and close attention. It is played by four persons, those who sit opposite each other being partners. Points are scored for the tricks taken in excess of six and for the honors held.

ENTERTAINMENT—Dancing.

Allemande [F.]. A dance in moderate twofold time.

Bal [F.] A ball.

Bal costumé [F.]. Fancy-ball.

Ball. A social assembly for the purpose of dancing.

Ballet [F.]. An artistic dance performed as a theatrical entertainment.

Bal masqué [F.]. A mask-ball.

Bayadere. A female dancer in the East Indies.

Brawl. A kind of sprightly dance.

Cotillon [F.]. A brisk dance, performed by eight persons.

Country-dance. A dance in which the dancers are arranged in opposite lines.

Dance. An amusement, in which the movements of the persons are regulated by music.

Fling. A kind of dance.

Galop.
Galopade. } A lively dance.

Gavot.
Gavotte. } A dance to a brisk and lively tune.

Hop. An informal dance or ball.

Hornpipe. A dance performed by one person, to music on a hornpipe.

Jig. A lively dance.

Masquerade. A mask-ball.

Mazurka. A Polish dance.

Minuet. A slow graceful dance.

Morisco.
Morris-dance. } A dance in which the performers take the parts of various characters.

Pas-seul. A dance without a partner.

Polka. A dance by two persons in common time.

Quadrille. A dance having five figures, in common time, four couples of dancers being in each set.

Redowa. Bohemian dance either in triple time, or in two-four time

Reel. A lively dance of the Scotch Highlanders.

Ridotto [It.]. A favorite Italian public entertainment, consisting of music and dancing.

Rigadoon. A gay, lively dance for one couple.

Saraband. A slow Spanish dance.

Sir Roger de Coverley. A formal graceful dance.

Skirt-dance. A dance in which the performer wears a skirt made very full, so that it may be gracefully waved with the motions of the body.

Strathspey. A lively Scottish dance.

Terpsichore. The muse who presided over the dance.

Waltz. A dance by two persons in circular figures with a whirling motion.

ENTERTAINMENT—Times of Amusement.

Bairam [Turk.]. A great Mohammedan festival

Bank-holiday. A day observed in England as a legal holiday.

Derby day. The day of the annual race for the Derby stakes,—Wednesday of the week before Whitsuntide.

Easter Monday. The next day after Easter.

Field-day. A day of unusual display.

Gala-day. A day of festivity.

High-day. A holy or feast day.

High-days and holidays. Feast days.

Holiday. A day of amusement.

Labor-day. First Monday of September.

May-day. The first day of May; celebrated by dancing about a May pole.

Play-day. A holiday.

Red-letter day. A holy or feast day; a day that is auspicious.

Saint-Monday. Easter Monday.

Whit-Monday. The day following Whitsunday.

Yule. Christmas.

ENTERTAINMENT—Places of Amusement.

Arbor. A shaded retreat.

Archery ground. The place where archery is practised.

Assembly-room. The room where dances are held.

Ballroom. Place for dancing.

Bowling-alley. A long narrow lane or passage where bowls is played.

Bowling-green. A level piece of greensward for bowling.

Concert-hall. A place where entertainments are given.

Cricket-ground. The place where cricket is played.

Croquet-ground. A level space suitable for playing croquet.

Croquet-lawn. See CROQUET-GROUND.

Garden. A place for amusements.

Hunting-ground. An enclosed lodge for keeping game.

Merry-go-round. A ring of flying hobbyhorses.

Montagne Russe [F.]. Russian mountain; artificial slide.

Music-hall. A place for entertainments.

Park. A public playground.

Place of amusement. A place suitable for games or amusements

Plaisance [F.]. A pleasure-house.

Playground. A place fitted for children's games.

Pleasure-ground. A place of amusement.

Racket-court. A level space for playing tennis and the like.

Rink. An artificial sheet of ice, used for skating.

Round-about. A merry-go-round.

Skating-rink. See RINK.

Swing. An apparatus for recreation, consisting of a rope tied by both ends, and a seat placed on the loop.

Tennis-court. A place fitted for playing tennis

Theater. A place for public entertainments.

The turf. The race-course.

ENTERTAINMENT—Verbs.

Amuse. To entertain or occupy in a pleasant manner

Banquet. To gratify oneself with good eating and drinking.

Caper. To leap about in a sprightly manner.

Carouse. To take part in a jovial feast or drunken revel.

Cheer. To make cheerful or joyous.

Dally. To waste time in pleasures.

Dance, etc. To move nimbly or merrily. See SPRING.

Disport. To carry oneself away from work.

Divert. To turn away from business or study to amusement

Enliven. To give spirit or vivacity to.

Entertain. To engage the attention agreeably

Feast. To entertain with costly provisions.

Frisk. To leap or dance in frolic and gaiety.

Frolic. To play wild pranks.

Gambol. To dance and skip about in sport.

Game. To play at any sport or amusement.

Interest. To excite pleasant emotions.

Junket. To feast.

Play. To exercise for the sake of amusement.

Please. To afford or impart pleasure.

Recreate. To refresh with amusement after toil or anxiety.

Regale. To entertain with something that delights.

Rejoice. To experience gladness in a high degree.

Revel. To feast in a riotous manner.

Romp. To leap and frisk about in play.

Solace. To cheer or console.

Sport. To play or make merry.

Tickle. To please or gratify.

Titillate. To excite pleasurably.

Toy. To trifle or play with.

Treat. To entertain with food and drink.

Wanton. To frolic in an unseemly manner.

ENTERTAINMENT—Verbal Expressions

Amuse oneself; beguile the time; be the death of one; cause laughter; convulse with laughter; create laughter; *desipere in loco* [L.], to jest at the proper time; drive dull care away; drown care; excite laughter; go a Maying; have one's fling; keep holiday; keep up the ball; kill time; make holiday; make merry; occasion laughter; play a game; play pranks; play the fool; play tricks; produce laughter; put in good humor; raise a smile; raise laughter; run a rig; see life; set the table in a roar; sow one's wild oats; take one's pleasures; tickle the fancy; while away the time.

ENTERTAINMENT—*Continued.*

ENTERTAINMENT—*Adjectives.*

Amused, etc. See *Verbs.*
Amusing. Entertaining.
Festal.⎫
Festive.⎭ Joyous, gay.
Jocund. Cheerful.
Jolly. Full of life and mirth.
Jovial. Mirth-inspiring.
Laughable, etc. See SOCIETY-LUDICROUSNESS.
Ludibrious. Ridiculous.

Diverting, etc. See *Verbs.*
Entertaining. Pleasing.
Lusory. Playful.
Playful. Sportive.
Pleasant, etc. See PLEASURABLENESS.
Recreative. Giving relief after labor.
Rompish. Given to rude play.
Witty, etc. See WITTINESS.

ENTERTAINMENT—*Adverbs.*

At play.⎫
In sport.⎭ Frolicking.

ENTERTAINMENT—*Interjections.*

Vive la bagatelle! [F.] Success to trifles!

Vogue la galère! [F.] Let the world wag!

ENTERTAINMENT—*Phrases.*

Arbiter bibendi [L.]. Toast-master.
Deus nobis hæc otia fecit [L.]. God has given us this ease.
Dum vivimus vivamus [L.]. While we live, let us live.
"On the light fantastic toe." Dancing. [Milton, *L'Allegro*, 34.]

Playful as a kitten.
"Pleased with a feather, tickled with a straw." ["The child, by nature's kindly law, Pleased with a rattle, tickled with a straw." Pope, *Essay on Man*, ii, 275.]

entêté [F.] (an·-tê-tê′). Obstinate. BIGOTRY-APOSTASY, CONCEIT-DIFFIDENCE, DECISION-MISJUDGMENT.
en-thrall′. To enslave; to bring the mind under any overmastering influence. LIBERTY-SUBJECTION, RELEASE-RESTRAINT.
en-thral′-ment. Enslavement. LIBERTY-SUBJECTION.
en-throne′. To invest with authority. REPUTATION-DISCREDIT.
en-throne′-ment. The act of placing on a throne. COMMISSION-ABROGATION, REPUTATION-DISCREDIT.
en-thu′-si-asm. Fervor. EMOTION, LOVE-HATE, SANGUINENESS-HOPELESSNESS.
en-thu′-si-ast. An ardent adherent. ACTIVITY-INDOLENCE, BIGOTRY-APOSTASY, SANENESS-MANIAC.
en-thu′-si-as-tic. Full of zeal and fervor. EMOTION,

EXCITABILITY-INEXCITABILITY, FANCY, SANGUINENESS-HOPELESSNESS, SENSITIVENESS-APATHY.
en′-thy-meme. An argument in which one of the premises of the syllogism is suppressed. RATIOCINATION-CASUISTRY.
en-tice′. ·To persuade. MOTIVE-CAPRICE.
en-tice′-ment. Inducement. MOTIVE-CAPRICE.
en-ti′-cing. Alluring. PLEASURABLENESS-PAINFULNESS.
en-tire′. Whole. CONTINUITY-INTERRUPTION, ENTIRETY-DEFICIENCY, WHOLE-PART; **entire** horse, MALE-FEMALE.
en-tire′-ly. Completely. MAGNITUDE-SMALLNESS, WHOLE-PART.
en-tire′-ty. Entireness; a complete thing. ENTIRETY-DEFICIENCY, WHOLE-PART.

ENTIRETY–DEFICIENCY.

All. The entire number.
Allness. Completeness.
Completeness. The state of lacking nothing.
Entirety. The state of being uninjured or unmarred.
Fill. That which fills or is sufficient to fill.
Perfection, etc. The state of having completeness with highest excellence of parts, etc. See FAULTLESSNESS.
Replete. Completely filled; abounding.
Sufficiency. The state of being enough for a specific purpose.

ENTIRETY—*Denotations.*

Bellyful. All that the stomach will hold; hence, one's fill; more than enough
Brimmer.⎫
Bumper.⎭ A glass or cup filled to the brim.
Flood-tide.⎫
High-tide.⎬ The coming in of the tide; the tide at its height.
High-water.⎭
Load. As much as can be carried.
Spring-tide The high-tide that occurs twice every month, at the times of new and full moon.

ENTIRETY—*Nouns of Cause.*

Complement. Something that fills up or completes what any number, quantity, etc., lacks of completeness.
Completion, etc. See COMPLETION.
Filling-up. That which fills up.
Ideal. The highest degree of perfection.
Impletion. The act of filling.
Integration. The collection of parts into a whole.
Limit. Boundary.
Make weight. Something added to give weight.
Ne plus ultra [L.]. The farthest point; perfection.

Defect. Lack or absence of something essential to the completeness of a thing.
Deficiency. A state of being wanting in completeness.
Immaturity. Imperfection in development.
Imperfection, etc. Want of perfection. See FAULTLESSNESS-FAULTINESS.
Incompleteness. An unfinished state.
Insufficiency, etc. Inadequateness. See EXCESS-LACK.
Non-completion. See COMPLETION-NONCOMPLETION.
Omission. Act of omitting or leaving out.
Shortcoming, etc. The act of failing. See TRANSCURSION-SHORTCOMING.
Short measure. Quantity below the standard measurement.

DEFICIENCY—*Denotations.*

Baldhead. One whose head is bald.
Break. An opening or breach made as by breaking
Caret. A sign (∧) placed below a line, indicating where omitted words, letters, etc., should be inserted.
Defalcation. Embezzlement.
Deficit. A falling short in amount.
Half-measures. An imperfect or inadequate measure, plan or effort.
Interval. A break in space. See INTERSPACE.
Part wanting. Incompleteness

DEFICIENCY—*Verbs.*

Be incomplete. To be unfinished.
Caret [L.]. It is wanting.
Fall short of, etc. To be incomplete. See TRANSCURSION-SHORTCOMING.
Lack. To be in want.
Neglect, etc. To omit. See CAREFULNESS-CARELESSNESS.

ENTIRETY—DEFICIENCY—*Continued.*

ENTIRETY—Nouns of Cause—*Continued.*

Saturation. }
Saturity. } The state of being completely permeated.
Solidarity. An entire union.
Solidity. State of being full.
Supplement. Something added that supplies a deficiency.
Unity. State of being complete.

ENTIRETY—*Verbs.*

Be complete. To lack nothing.
Charge. To fill.
Come to a head. To come to an issue or climax.
Complete. To fill up or fill out.
Eke out. To make barely sufficient
Fill. To cause the whole space to be occupied.
Fill in. To insert something in a vacant place.
Fill to the brim. }
Fill the measure of. } To complete.
Fill up. To make full.
Go all lengths. To use every effort.
Go the whole hog. To go to the utmost limit.
Go the whole length. To go as far as possible.
Load. To heap up; to fill.
Make good. To supply a deficit.
Make up. To supply a deficiency.
Piece out. To complete by adding to.
Render complete. To make lacking nothing.
Replenish. To fill again.
Saturate. To fill by absorption.
Supply deficiencies. To make up for a want.

ENTIRETY—*Adjectives.*

Absolute. Free from limitations.
Abundant. Fully sufficient.
All-sided. Developed on all sides.
Ascititious. Not essential; added from without.
As full as an egg is of meat. Filled to the shell.
As full as a vetch. As full as a pea-pod.
Brimful. Filled to the point of overflowing.
Brimming. Full or filling to the brim.
Chock-full. Choke-full.
Choke-full. Completely full.
Complete. Having all the needed or usual parts.
Completing. Making complete.
Consummate. Finished; complete.
Crammed. Filled.
Entire. Complete in all its parts
Exhaustive. Thorough and complete.
Fraught. Filled; loaded.
Free. Not under restraint
Full. With as much in as possible.
Full-charged. Carrying as much as possible.
Full-fraught. Fully laden.
Full-laden. With a full load.
Good. Full or complete in measure.
Heavy laden. Carrying much.
Laden. Filled up.
Perfect, etc. Without defect or lack. See FAULTLESSNESS.
Plenary. Full in all respects; entire; absolute.
Radical. Carried to the fullest limit.
Regular. Thoroughgoing; complete.
Replete. Full to the uttermost.
Saturated. Filled by absorption.
Sheer. Utter.
Solid. Completely filled.
Supplemental. Like, or pertaining to a supplement.
Supplementary. Supplemental.
Sweeping. Carrying all before it.
Thorough. Complete; going through and through.
Thoroughgoing. Going to the bottom of things.
Topful. Brimful.
Unconditional. Not limited in any way.
Undivided. Entire.
Unmitigated. Having full force.
Unqualified. Without limitations or restrictions.
Whole, etc. Having all the parts See FAULTLESSNESS.
With all its parts. Whole.

ENTIRETY—*Adverbs.*

Ab ovo usque ad mala [L.]. From egg to apples. [A Roman meal.]
A capite ad calcem [L.]. From head to heel.
À fond [F.]. To the bottom.

DEFICIENCY—*Adjectives.*

Crude. Unfinished.
Defective. Lacking a part.
Deficient. Not meeting certain requirements.
Docked. Curtailed.
Failing. Wanting.
Garbled. To pick out parts to serve a purpose.
Going on. In process of completion.
Half-and-half.
Hollow. Containing an empty space.
Imperfect, etc. Not complete in all its parts. See FAULTLESSNESS-FAULTINESS.
In arrear. Unpaid though due.
Incomplete. Not finished.
In default. Incompleted.
In hand. In process of being made.
In progress. Unfinished.
Lame. Imperfect; unsatisfactory.
Lopped. Cut off.
Meager. Defective in quantity or poor in quality.
Mutilated. Crippled.
Perfunctory. Done without interest or zeal.
Proceeding. In the process.
Short. Defective.
Short of. Incomplete.
Sketchy. Containing only an outline.
Truncated. Cut short.
Uncompleted, etc. See COMPLETION.
Unfinished. Incomplete.
Wanting. Deficient.

DEFICIENCY—*Adverbs.*

By halves. Incompletely.
Incompletely. Inadequately.

DEFICIENCY—*Phrase.*

Cetera desunt [L.]. The rest is wanting.

ENTIRETY—Adverbs—*Continued.*

Altogether. Completely.
À outrance [F.]. To the last extremity; to the bitter end.
As ... as can be. Altogether.
As far as possible. To the end.
At all points. Completely.
Cap-à-pie [F.]. From head to foot.
Clean. As much as possible.
Clean as a whistle. Faultlessly.
Completely. Fully; entirely.
De fond en comble [F.]. From bottom to top.
Effectually. Thoroughly.
Every inch. }
Every whit. } Completely.
Fore and aft. From one end of a vessel to the other.
For good and all. Always.
From beginning to end.]
From end to end. |
From first to last. |
From head to foot. } Completely.
From one end to the other. |
From top to bottom. |
From top to toe.]
Fully. As much as possible.
Head and shoulders. Altogether.
Heart and soul. With all one's might.
Hollow. Utterly; completely.
In all respects. }
In every respect. } Completely.
In toto [L.]. In the whole; totally.
Neck and crop. Altogether and at once.
Neck and heel. With full speed.
Nicely. Very well.
On all accounts. For every reason.
Out and out. Completely.
Outright. Completely.
Over head and ears. Altogether.
Quite. Without limitation.
Root and branch. In a thorough manner; completely.
Sous tous les rapports [F.]. In all respects.
Stark. In the greatest degree.
Throughout. From beginning to end.

ENTIRETY—Adverbs—*Continued.*

Through thick and thin. Through all obstacles.
To all intents and purposes. Seemingly.
Totally. Entirely.
To the backbone. To the utmost.
To the end of the chapter. To the last.
To the full. }
To the top of one's bent. } Completely.
To the utmost. To the highest degree.

Toto cælo [L.]. By the whole heaven; as far apart as possible.
Up to the brim. }
Up to the ears. } Completely.
Up to the eyes. }
Utterly. To the highest degree.
Wholly. Entirely.
With a vengeance. Extremely.
With a witness. [Arch. and Colloq.]. With demonstrative force.

ENTIRETY—*Phrases.*

Falsus in uno, falsus in omnibus [L.]. False in one point, false in all.

Omnem movere lapidem [L.]. To leave no stone unturned.
Una scopa nuova spazza bene [It]. "A new broom sweeps clean."

en-ti'-tle. To designate; to give a right to receive or require. Dueness-Undueness, Name-Misnomer.

en-ti'-tled to. Having a right to. Dueness-Undueness.
en'-ti-ty. Being. Entity-Nonentity.

ENTITY—NONENTITY.

Actual existence. Indisputable being.
Actualism. The doctrine that all existence is active
Actuality. State of being actual.
Being. Having form in either mind or matter.
Coexistence, etc. State of existing at the same time. See Coexistence
Ens [L.]. Entity, being, or existence.
Entity. Essence of a thing regardless of its properties.
Esse [L.]. Essence.
Existence. Continuance of being.
Fact. Reality.
Matter of fact. Something not imaginary.
No joke. Really the truth
Not a dream, etc. Truth; not a figment of the imagination. See Fancy.
Ontology. The science of being.
Positiveness, etc. Certainty. See *Adjectives.*
Presence, etc. State of being present. See Presence.
Reality. Actual existence.
Sober reality. Serious or undeniable truth.
Stubborn fact. A reality.
Subsistence. Process of living.
Truth. That which is according to facts. See Truth.

ENTITY—*Verbs.*

Arise. To happen. See Beginning.
Be. To exist.
Become. To change or pass from one state to another. See Conversion.
Be the case. Facts to be as given.
Breathe. To have life.
Bring into existence. To make something grand out of disconnected or conflicting parts. See Creation.
Come forth. To issue from. See Visibility.
Come into existence. To commence, to exist.
Consist in. To be marked by; to depend on.
Exist. To have being.
Find oneself. To become aware of being.
Have being. To exist.
Have place. To belong; have room.
Lie in. To depend on for existence.
Live. To have life.
Obtain. To be true; to prevail.
Occur, etc. To come to pass; to happen. See Occurrence.
Pass the time. To do something while the time passes.
Prevail. To be widely in force.
Stand. To be firm or unalterable.
Subsist. To retain existence.
Vegetate. To live in idleness.

ENTITY—*Adjectives.*

Absolute. Unconditional.
Actual. Existing as the result of antecedents.
Afloat. Not having disappeared.
Current. In vogue.
Existent. }
Existing. } Having being. See *Verbs.*
Extant. Not lost or destroyed.
In existence. Not lost.
Not potential. Real. See Entity-Nonentity.
On foot. In action.

Abeyance. Inaction.
Absence, etc. State of not being present. See Presence-Absence.
Annihilation. Complete destruction.
Blank. Unoccupied surface, space, or time.
Extinction, etc. State of being quenched or suppressed, as life, light. See Creation-Destruction.
Inexistence. State of not having existence.
Negativeness. State of lacking activity. See *Adjectives.*
Nihilism. The doctrine that nothing exists.
Nihility. Nothingness.
Nil. Nothing.
Nonentity. Not a reality.
Non-existence. Inexistence.
Non-subsistence. State of not having life.
No such thing. etc. That is not true. See Substance-Nullity
Nullity. State of not being a reality.
Tabula rasa [L.]. A blank tablet

NONENTITY—*Verbs.*

Abrogate, etc. To abolish or repeal with authority See Commission-Abrogation.
Annihilate. To totally destroy.
Become extinct, etc. To lose existence. See *Adjectives.*
Be extinct. To have lost former existence.
Be no more. To be dead; to have lost its identity.
Be null and void. To be invalid.
Cease to exist, etc. To leave the state of being or of living. See Entity.
Destroy, etc. To ruin; to kill. See Creation-Destruction.
Die, etc. To stop living. See Life-Death.
Disappear, etc. To pass from sight. See Appearance-Disappearance.
Dissolve. To melt or separate into parts in a liquid.
Go. To depart from this state of existence.
Have no existence, etc. Not to be a reality. See Entity.
Leave not a track behind. To disappear in its entirety.
Melt away. To be dissipated.
Not exist, etc. Not to be. See Entity.
Nullify. To make of no effect.
Pass away. To lose existence.
Perish. To become nothing; to decay.
Remove, etc. To change from this state to another. See Establishment-Removal.
Render null. To make worthless.
Take away. To move from.

NONENTITY—*Adjectives.*

Absent. Not present. See Presence-Absence.
Annihilated, etc. Entirely destroyed, etc. See Verbs.
Baseless. Without foundation.
Blank. Free from writing or printing.
Defunct. Dead; extinct. See Life-Death.
Departed. Dead.
Exhausted. Having lost its vital force.
Extinct. Quenched; put out.
Fabulous. Unreal.
Gone. Ruined; deceased.
Ideal. Not practical. See Fancy.
Lost. Gone beyond recovery.

ENTITY—NONENTITY—*Continued*

ENTITY—ADJECTIVES—*Continued.*

Positive. Not admitting of doubt.
Prevalent. Superior; customary.
Real. In its true essence.
Self-existent. } Having being by its own power.
Self-existing. }
Substantial. Having or pertaining to the real existence.
Substantive. Pertaining to what is essential.
True, etc According to facts. See TRUTH.
Under the sun. In existence.
Undestroyed. Not destroyed.
Unideal. Not ideal.
Unimagined. Not merely fanciful.
Well-founded. Originated with good reasons or grounds.

ENTITY—*Adverbs.*

Actually. Truly; in the present state. See under *Adjectives.*
Indeed. In truth.
In fact. As a matter of truth.
In point of fact. As regards the fact.
In reality. Really.
De facto [L.]. From the fact.
Ipso facto [L.]. By the very fact.

ENTITY—*Phrases.*

Ens rationis [L.]. A creature of reason.
Ergo sum, cogito [L.]. I think, therefore I am.

en-tomb′. To bury. LIFE-FUNERAL RELEASE-RESTRAINT.
en′′-to-mol′-o-gy. The branch of zoology that treats of insects. ZOOLOGY-BOTANY.
en′′-tou′′-rage′. Associates; surroundings. ENVIRONMENT-INTERPOSITION.

NONENTITY—ADJECTIVES—*Continued.*

Missing. Not to be found; departed
Negative. Not active; tending to go in the opposite direction.
Omitted. Left out.
Perished. Decayed; passed from life.
Potential. Possible, but not yet existing.
Supposititious. Only imagined. See HYPOTHESIS.
Unbegotten. Not yet brought forth.
Unborn. Not yet born.
Unconceived. Not yet conceived or thought of.
Uncreated. Not yet created.
Unmade. Not yet made.
Unproduced. Not yet produced.
Unreal. Not having reality.
Unsubstantial. Without substance. See SUBSTANCE-NULLITY.
Vain. Profitless; unreal.
Virtual. Efficacious without the agency of the material

NONENTITY—*Adverbs.*

Negatively. In a manner implying the lack of something.
Virtually In effect, but not in reality. See *Adjectives.*

NONENTITY—*Phrase.*

Non ens [L.] Nonentity.

en′′-to-zo′-on. One of the entozoa. GREATNESS-LITTLENESS.
en′-trails. Viscera. OUTSIDE-INSIDE.
en-tram′-mel. To hamper. RELEASE-RESTRAINT.
en′-trance. The act or place of entering. BEGINNING-END, ENTRANCE-EXIT; **give entrance to,** ADMISSION-EXPULSION, ENTRANCE-EXIT.

ENTRANCE—EXIT.

Admission, etc. The act of entering with some one's consent. See ADMISSION.
Entrance. The act of passing into a place or condition.
Entry. The act of coming or going in.
Illapse. A sliding into.
Immigration. Going into a country for permanent residence.
Import. That which is brought from one country into another.
Incursion. A hostile entrance into a land.
Infiltration. Entrance of a liquid or gas by passing through small openings.
Influx. Entrance by flowing in.
Ingress. The act or right of entering.
Inroad. A forcible encroachment.
Insertion, etc. The act of putting between or among other things. See INJECTION.
Insinuation, etc. The act of introducing gradually. See ENVIRONMENT-INTERPOSITION.
Interpenetration. The act of penetrating deeply.
Introgression. The act of going into.
Intrusion. The act of coming into without permission.
Invasion. A hostile entrance.
Irruption. A breaking or rushing in.
Penetration. The act of entering deeply.

ENTRANCE—*Denotations, etc.*

Barway. A way closed by bars.
Conduit. A tube, pipe, or passageway for a fluid. See WATERCOURSE.
Door. The entrance to a house. See APERTURE.
Immigrant. A foreigner who enters a country to settle there.
Inlet. A small body of water leading into a larger.
Mouth. The orifice in the face through which food is taken into the body.
Path. A way or narrow road. See WAY.
Way in. A passage.

ENTRANCE—*Verbs.*

Break in. } To force an entrance.
Break into. }
Break in upon. To come upon suddenly.
Burst in. }
Burst into. } To break in with violence.
Burst in upon. }

Débouché [F.]. An outlet for goods.
Defluxion. The flowing off of liquids.
Discharge, etc. The issuing out of a liquid. See NUTRIMENT-EXCRETION.
Distillation. An emission by drops.
Drain. The act of drawing a fluid off gradually.
Drainage. The gradual flowing off of any liquid.
Dribbling, etc. A falling by drops. See *Verbs.*
Effluence. A flowing out.
Efflux. The act or process of flowing forth in a stream.
Effluxion. A flowing forth.
Effusion. The act or process of pouring forth.
Egress. A going or passing out.
Emanation. The act of proceeding from a source.
Emergence. The process of coming forth, as from a fluid.
Emersion. The act or process of rising out of something.
Emigrant. One who leaves his country.
Emigration. Removal from one country to another.
Eruption. A breaking forth with violence.
Evacuation. A discharge of fluids.
Exit. Departure; passage out of a place.
Exodus. A going out. See ARRIVAL-DEPARTURE.
Expatriation. Leaving and forsaking of one's country.
Export. Act of sending out of a country.
Extravasation. The act of escaping from the proper vessel.
Exudation. Discharge, as through pores or incisions.
Gush, etc. A sudden outpouring. See RIVER.
Issue. The act of passing or flowing out.
Leakage. The act of oozing out through a containing vessel.
Oozing. To flow out slowly and imperceptibly.
Outbreak. A sudden and violent issuing forth
Outburst. A violent breaking forth.
Outcome. The visible result.
Outpour. A free and steady outflow.
Outpouring. The act of flowing out freely.
Output. The quantity produced ready for use in a specified time.
Percolation. The act of passing through fine interstices.
Perspiration. The secretion of sweat by pores of the skin.
Proruption. A bursting forth or out.
Remigration. Return to the place from which one came.
Sweating. The act of exuding moisture in drops.
Transudation. The act of passing through the pores or interstices of a membranous substance.

ENTRANCE—EXIT—*Continued.*

ENTRANCE—Verbs—*Continued.*

Come in.
Come into. } Enter.

Creep in.
Creep into. } To enter stealthily.

Enter.   To pass into.

Find one's way into.   Find entrance.

Flow in.
Flow into. } To enter in a steady stream.

Give entrance to, etc.   See ADMISSION.

Go in.
Go into. } Enter.

Have the *entrée.*   To have a privilege of entering as a visitor.

Infiltrate.   To enter through small openings.

Insert, etc.   To enter among.   See INJECTION.

Insinuate itself.   To enter gradually.

Interpenetrate.   To penetrate within or between.

Intrude.   To enter without invitation.

Invade.   To enter a land with a hostile army.

Penetrate.   To enter into the interior.

Pop in.
Pop into. } To enter suddenly.

Pour in.
Pour into. } To enter with rapid flow.

Set foot on.   To enter upon a new shore.

Slip in.
Slip into. } To go in stealthily.

Worm oneself into.
Wriggle into. } To enter with difficulty.

ENTRANCE—*Adjectives*

Entrant.   Going in.

Incoming.   Entering.

Penetrable.   That which may be pierced by **any** force.

EXIT—Verbs—*Continued from Column 2.*

Pour out.   To send forth continuously and abundantly.

Pour out of.   To flow from in a continuous and copious stream.

Run.   To give forth a discharge or flow.

Run out.   To become empty from continual draining off.

Run through.   To get rid of by squandering.

Spout.   To pour out copiously and forcibly.

Strain.   To pass through some porous substance so as to be purified.

Sweat.   To exude moisture in drops.

Transcolate.   To cause to pass through a sieve.

Transude.   To pass through a membranous substance.

Trickle, etc.   To flow slowly by drops, etc.   See RIVER.

Well.   To pour forth as from a spring.

Well out.   To issue forth.

EXIT—*Adjectives.*

Effused, etc.   See *Verbs.*

Emanant.   Flowing from a source.

Outgoing.   Issuing out.

EXIT—*Nouns of Means.*

Air-pipe, etc.   See WATERCOURSE-AIRPIPE.

Conduit, etc.   See WATERCOURSE-AIRPIPE.

Door, etc.   See APERTURE-CLOSURE.

Floodgate.   A gate for regulating the flow of water.

Mouth.   The entrance of the alimentary canal.

Outgate.   A way out.

Outlet.   A passage for escape or discharge.

Path, etc.   See WAY.

Pour.   A heavy flow.

Sally-port.   A gate or passage in a fortification.

Sluice.   An artificial water-channel.

Spout.   A tube for the discharge of a liquid.

Tap.   An arrangement for drawing liquid from a cask.

Vent.   A small hole for the passage of something.

Vomitory.   The principal entrance to a Roman theater.

Way out.   A passage or means of exit.

EXIT—*Verbs.*

Break forth.
Burst out. } To issue forth violently.
Burst through.

Come forth.
Come out of. } To come into view.

Debouch.   To march out of a narrow place.

Discharge itself.   To send forth the contents of.

Disembogue.   To flow out at the mouth, as a river.

Distil.   To give forth in drops.

Drain.   To flow away gradually.

Dribble.   To flow in a scanty and broken stream.

Effuse.   To pour forth widely.

Egurgitate.   To gush out.

Emanate.   To flow forth from a source.

Emerge.   To come forth from concealment.

Escape.   To slip out or away from.

Evacuate.   To discharge through the excretory passages.

Extravasate.   To escape from the proper vessel.

Exude.   To discharge gradually through small openings.

Filter.   To pass through a porous substance.

Filtrate.   To purify by straining.

Find vent.   To find an outlet.

Flow.
Flow out of. } To proceed from a source in a steady stream.

Go out of.   To depart.

Gush.   To pour out suddenly and in volume.

Issue.   To pass from any enclosed place.

Leak.   To escape through a defective part of the containing vessel.

Move out of.   To leave.

Ooze.   To discharge slowly.

Pass off.   To be thrown off as an exhalation.

Pass out of.   To issue from.

Percolate.   To pass through interstices.

Perspire.   To emit through the pores of the skin.

Pour.   To cause to flow out in a stream.

(Continued on Column 1)

---

en-trance .   To ravish with delight.   DEVOTION-MAGIC, PLEASURABLENESS-PAINFULNESS.

en-tranced'.   Ravished with delight.   PLEASURE-PAIN.

en-trance'-ment.   The act of entrancing.   EXCITATION.

en-tran'-cing.   Very delightful.   PLEASURABLENESS-PAINFULNESS.

en'-trant.   Entering; admitting.   ADMISSION-EXPULSION, ENTRANCE-EXIT.

en-trap'.   To ensnare.   TRUTHFULNESS-FRAUD.

en-treat'.   To beseech.   PETITION-EXPOSTULATION.

en-treat'-y.   An earnest request.   PETITION-EXPOSTULATION.

entrée [F.] (ɑn·-trê').   Entry; a side-dish.   ADMISSION-EXPULSION, NUTRIMENT-EXCRETION; **give the entrée,** ADMISSION-EXPULSION; **have the entrée,** ENTRANCE-EXIT.

entremet [F.]. (ɑn·''tr-mê').   A side dish or dishes.   NUTRIMENT-EXCRETION.

entre nous [F.] (ɑn·tr nu).   Between us.   ENLIGHTENMENT-SECRECY.

entrepreneur [F.] (ɑn·'''tr-prɛ-nur')   One who starts and conducts extensive industrial enterprises.   ACTING.

entrepôt [F.] (ɑn·'tr-po'').   A distributing commercial center; a depot.   MARKET, STORE.

entresol [F.] (ɑn·'tr-sol'').   A half story.   CONTENTS-RECEIVER.

en-trust'.   To confide.   CREDIT-DEBT, COMMISSION-ABROGATION, GIVING-RECEIVING, LEAVE-PROHIBITION.

en'-try.   Entrance.   BEGINNING-END, ENTRANCE-EXIT, MARK-OBLITERATION.

en-twine'.   To twine round; to interweave.   CIRCLE-WINDING, CROSSING, UNION-DISUNION

e-nu'-cle-ate.   To disclose.   INTERPRETATION-MISINTERPRETATION.

e-nu'-mer-ate.   To specify singly.   NUMBERING; **enumerate among,** ADMISSION-EXCLUSION.

e-nu''-mer-a'-tion.   Act of enumerating.   NUMBERING.

e-nun'-ci-ate.   To articulate; to speak.   ASSERTION-DENIAL, VOCALIZATION-MUTENESS.

e-nun''-ci-a'-tion.   Definite statement.   ENLIGHTENMENT-SECRECY, VOCALIZATION-MUTENESS.

e-nun'-ci-a-tive. Declarative. ENLIGHTENMENT-SE-CRECY.

en-vel'-op. To wrap up. DRESS-UNDRESS.

en-vel'-ope. A wrapper. CONFINEMENT, COVER-LINING, ENCLOSURE.

en-ven'-om. To infuse venom into. ALLEVIATION-AGGRAVATION, BETTERMENT-DETERIORATION, FAVORITE-ANGER, LOVE-HATE.

en-ven'-omed. Malignant. CHARITABLENESS-MALEV-OLENCE, GOODNESS-BADNESS, HEALTHINESS-UN-HEALTHINESS, PLEASURABLENESS-PAINFULNESS.

en'-vious. Spiteful. PARDON-ENVY.

en'-vi-ous-ness. Spitefulness. PARDON-ENVY.

en-vi'-ron. To encompass. ENVIRONMENT - INTERPO-SITION.

en-vi'-ron-ment. Surroundings. ENVIRONMENT-INTER-POSITION.

ENVIRONMENT—INTERPOSITION.

Circumambience. A going around or surrounding.
Circumjacence. The condition or state of lying on all sides.
Encompassment. The act of surrounding.
Entourage [F.]. Surroundings; adjuncts.
Environment. That which surrounds; the act of surrounding.
Surroundings. That which environs.

ENVIRONMENT—*Denotations.*

Atmosphere. The body of air that surrounds the earth.
Banlieue [F.]. Outskirts.
Border. The outer portion or limit.
Boulevard. Originally, a rampart; now a broad city avenue.
Encincture. A girdle.
Environs. The surrounding regions.
Faubourgs [F.]. A quarter of a city outside the old walls.
Girdle. A band that encircles the waist.
Medium. Anything that serves or acts intermediately between two bodies; hence, something surrounding or bordering on these bodies.
Outpost. A line of defense held by a body of troops stationed at a distance from the main body.
Outskirts. Border regions.
Precincts. A place definitely marked out by boundaries.
Purlieus. } Outlying districts.
Suburbs. }

ENVIRONMENT—*Verbs.*

Begird. To surround with a band.
Beset. To hem in on all sides.
Circumvent. To gain advantage over.
Compass. To go about or around.
Embrace. To clasp or enclose in the arms.
Encircle. To form a circle about.
Enclose. To inclose.
Encompass. To describe a circle about.
Engird. To surround, as with a girdle.
Environ. To surround.
Gird. To surround with a band.
Hem in. To surround.
Inclose. To confine on all sides.
Lap. To enfold or involve.
Lie around. To be situated around.
Skirt. To border.
Surround. To shut in on all sides.
Twine around. To encircle or coil around.

ENVIRONMENT—*Adjectives.*

Ambient. Encompassing on all sides.
Circumambient. Being on all sides.
Circumfluent. Flowing round.
Circumjacent. Bordering on all sides.
Circumferential. Pertaining to the circumference.
Suburban. Of or pertaining to a suburb.
Surrounding. Going completely around.

ENVIRONMENT—*Adverbs.*

About. } On all sides.
All round. }
Around. In a circle.
On all sides. } Everywhere around.
On every side. }
Right and left. On all sides.
Round about. Surrounded.
Without. In or on the outer part.

INTERPOSITION—VERBS—*Continued from Column 2.*

Interleave. To insert a leaf into.
Interline. To write between lines.
Interpenetrate. To penetrate between substances.
Interpolate. To add a spurious word to a manuscript.

Dovetailing. A fitting by means of mortise and socket.
Embolism. Insertion of time in an account of time to produce regularity.
Infiltration. The process of causing to pass through pores.
Insertion. The act of throwing between.
Insinuation. Gradual introduction.
Intercalation. Irregular interpolation.
Intercurrence. A running between.
Interference. A taking part in the affairs of others.
Interjacence. A lying between.
Interjection. The act of throwing between.
Interlineation. Insertion of words between lines.
Interlocation. A placing between.
Interpenetration. A passing into each other reciprocally.
Interpolation. The act of putting words into passages to which they do not belong.
Interposition. The state of being between.
Interspersion. Act of putting between or among in a scattering fashion.
Intervenience. } Act of coming between.
Intervention. }
Intrusion. Act of entering into a place without right or invitation.
Obtrusion. Act of interrupting something by its presence.
Partition. Act of dividing.
Permeation. The act of passing through pores.

INTERPOSITION—*Denotations, etc.*

Bodkin. An instrument for piercing holes in cloth.
Diaphragm. A muscle situated between the thoracic and abdominal cavities.
Episode. An incident connected with some important occasion or event.
Fly-leaf. Blank leaf at beginning or end of a book.
Half-way house. House midway between two places.
Indigitation. The space between fingers.
Intermediary. Something acting or lying between things.
Intermedium. Space lying between.
Midriff. The diaphragm.
Obiter dictum [L.]. A thing said by the way.
Panel. Part of a door or of a fence.
Parenthesis. Curved lines which enclose a parenthetic word or phrase.
Party-wall. A wall placed between two properties and used in common.
Septum. A dividing membrane.
Veil. Cloth hung so as to conceal something.

INTERPOSITION—*Nouns of Agency.*

Go-between. One who acts as an agent or assistant to another in intrigues.
Interloper. One who thrusts himself into a place without right.
Intruder. One who makes himself felt where he is not desired.

INTERPOSITION—*Verbs.*

Come between. To interpose.
Dovetail. To fasten by dovetailing.
Edge in. To get in slyly.
Foist in. To thrust in wrongfully.
Get between. To arrive between.
Have a finger in the pie. To be concerned in.
Import. To introduce from without.
Infiltrate. To enter by penetrating the pores.
Ingrain. To impregnate the whole matter.
Insinuate. To creep, wind, or flow in.
Intercalate. To insert between others.
Interdigitate. To interweave.
Interfere. To intermeddle.
Interject. To throw in between.
Interlard. To diversify by mixture.

(*Continued on Column 1.*)

INTERPOSITION—Verbs—*Continued.*

Interpose. To place between.
Intersperse. To scatter or set here and there.
Intervene. To come or be between persons or things.
Interweave. To intermix.
Introduce. To lead or bring in.
Introduce the thin end of the wedge. To start something in a small way.
Intrude. To thrust in.
Jam in. To press into a tight place.
Let in. To give leave to come in.
Lie between. To be situated between.
Mortise. To cut a mortise in.
Obtrude. To push into some place.
Permeate. To pass through the pores.

Plow in. To cover by plowing.
Put between. Insert.
Put in an oar. To intrude remarks into other people's conversation.
Run in. To insert without making a break.
Slide in. To fit smoothly.
Smuggle. To take into or out of a country illegally.
Splice. To unite by overlapping or interweaving.
Throw in. To inject.
Thrust in. To intrude. See *Injection.*
Thrust one's nose in. To meddle officiously in.
Wedge in. To force in, as a wedge.
Work in. To mix or combine with something.
Worm in. To insinuate into.

INTERPOSITION—*Adjectives.*

Embolismal. Pertaining to intercalation.
Embosomed. Taken to the bosom.
Episodic. Pertaining to an episode.
Intercalary. Inserted or intruded into the midst of others.
Intercurrent. Running between or among.
Interjacent. Lying or being between.
Interlinear. Situated between lines.
Intermediary. That which lies between

Intermediate. Lying or being in the middle place.
Interstitial. Pertaining to interstices.
Intervenient. Coming or being between.
Intervening. Separating.
Intrusive. Entering without right or welcome.
Mediterranean. Enclosed by land.
Merged. To cause to disappear into.
Parenthetical. Thrown in.

INTERPOSITION—*Adverbs.*

Amid. In the midst of.
Amidst. In the center of.
Among. In or into the midst of.
Amongst. Among.
Between. In the intervening space.
Betwixt. Between.
Betwixt and between. Between.

In the thick of. When anything is most intense.
'Mid. Amid.
Midst. Amidst.
Parenthetically. By insertion.
Sandwich-wise. In the way of a sandwich.
'Twixt. Betwixt.

en-vi′-rons. Outskirts. ENVIRONMENT-INTERPOSITION, REMOTENESS-NEARNESS; in such and such environs, POSITION.
en′-voy. A diplomatic agent. CONSIGNEE, MESSENGER, SECURITY-INSECURITY.
en′-vy. To regard with discontent; vexation at another's success. PARDON-ENVY.
en-wrap′. To wrap up. DRESS-UNDRESS.
E-o′-li-an harp. A stringed instrument so constructed as to produce musical sounds when exposed to a current of air. MUSICAL INSTRUMENTS.
E′-o-lus. The god of the winds. RIVER-WIND.
e′-on. The personification of a divine attribute. DIVINITY.
ep′-act. The excess of the solar days over twelve lunar months. EXCESS-LACK.
ep″-a-go′-ge. Inductive reasoning. RATIOCINATION-INSTINCT.
épanchement [F.] (ê-pan·sh-man·′). Outpouring. BLANDISHMENT, CRAFT-ARTLESSNESS, MANIFESTATION-LATENCY.
ep′-arch. The manager of a Grecian eparchy. MANAGER.
ep′-au-let. An ornamental badge of rank. EMBELLISHMENT-DISFIGUREMENT, SIGN, TITLE.
ep-en′-the-sis. Insertion of a letter into a word. RHETORIC.
éperdu [F.] (ê-pêr-dŭ′). Bewildered. EXCITATION.
e-pergne′. An ornamental centerpiece for a dinner-table. CONTENTS-RECEIVER.
eph-em′-er-al. Living but a day. LASTINGNESS-TRANSIENTNESS.
eph-em′-er-is. A publication giving the positions of the heavenly bodies for each day in the year. CHRONOLOGY-ANACHRONISM, MARK-OBLITERATION, MISSIVE-PUBLICATION.
Eph-e′-sian. Relating to Ephesus. Ephesian letters, DEVOTION-CHARM.
eph″-i-al′-tes. Incubus. OBSTRUCTION-HELP, PLEASURE-PAIN, SENSUALITY-SUFFERING.

eph′-or. One of the magistrates of certain Doric towns. JUDGE.
ep′-ic. Stately verse reciting the deeds of great personages, heroes, demigods. ACCOUNT, POETRY-PROSE.
ep″-i-ce′-di-um. A dirge. JUBILATION-LAMENTATION.
ep′-i-cene. Of common gender. CONVENTIONALITY-UNCONVENTIONALITY, UNIFORMITY-MULTIFORMITY.
épicier [F.] (ê-pis-i-ê′). Grocer. GENTILITY-DEMOCRACY.
ep′-i-cure. A glutton; one who cultivates a delicate taste for eating or drinking. DESIRE-PARTICULARNESS, FASTING-GLUTTONY, MODERATION-VOLUPTUARY.
ep″-i-cu-re′-an. Given to the pleasures of the table. MODERATION-SELFINDULGENCE, MODERATION-VOLUPTUARY.
ep″-i-cu-re′-an-ism. Luxurious living. MODERATION-SELFINDULGENCE
ep′-i-cur-ism. Luxury. FASTING-GLUTTONY, MODERATION-SELFINDULGENCE.
Ep-i-cu′-rus. A Greek philosopher. System of Epicurus, MODERATION-SELFINDULGENCE.
ep′-i-cy″-cle. A circle that rolls upon the external or internal circumference of another circle. ASTRONOMY, CIRCLE-WINDING.
ep″-i-cy′-cloid. A curve traced by a point on the circumference of a circle which rolls upon the convex circumference of another circle. CIRCLE-WINDING.
ep″-i-dem″-ic. Widespread occurrence of a disease in a certain region. GATHERING-SCATTERING, HEALTH-SICKNESS, HEALTHINESS-UNHEALTHINESS, UNIVERSALITY-PARTICULARITY.
ep″-i-der′-mis. The cuticle. COVER-LINING.
ep″-i-gas′-tric. Pertaining to the abdomen. ANATOMY.
ep″-i-gen′-e-sis. The theory that the germ is created by union of the fecundating principles of the male and female. CREATION-DESTRUCTION.
ep′-i-gram. A pithy or antithetical phrasing of a shrewd observation. WITTINESS-DULNESS.

ep″-i-gram-mat′-ic. Witty. Terseness-Prolixity, Wittiness-Dulness.

ep″-i-gram′-ma-tist. A writer of epigrams. Wag.

ep′-i-graph. An inscription on a tomb, etc. Sign.

ep′-i-lep-sy. A chronic nervous disease. Agitation.

ep′-i-logue. The conclusion of an argument, speech, etc. Acting, Predecessor-Continuation.

épingles, tiré à quatre [F.] (ê-pɑn·gl′, ti-rê′ ɑ kɑtr). To look as if one came from a bandbox. Society-Affectation.

E-piph′-a-ny. A festival of the Christian Church. Ceremonial.

e-pis′-co-pa-cy. Office of a bishop. Church.

e-pis′-co-pal. Governed by bishops. Church.

E-pis″-co-pa′-lian. A member of the Protestant Episcopal Church. Church, Orthodoxy-Heterodoxy.

E pis″-co-pa′-lian-ism. The doctrines and usages of Episcopalians. Church.

e-pis′-co-pate. A bishopric. Church.

ep′-i-sode. An incidental narrative. Admission-Exclusion, Environment-Interposition, Increment-Remnant, Terseness-Prolixity.

ep″-i-sod′-ic. Adventitious. Connection-Independence, Environment-Interposition, Terseness-Prolixity.

e-pis′-tle. A letter. Missive-Publication.

E-pis′-tles. Ancient epistolary writings of sacred character. Revelation-Pseudorevelation.

e-pis′-to-la-ry. Belonging to correspondence by letter. Missive-Publication.

ep′-i-taph. An inscription on a tomb or monument. Life-Funeral.

ep″-i-tha-la′-mi-um. A nuptial poem or song. Marriage-Celibacy.

ep″-i-them. Any external application, as a fomentation. Remedy-Bane.

ep′-i-thet. An appellation. Name-Misnomer.

e-pit′-o-me. A summary; a compendium. Digest, Greatness-Littleness, Length-Shortness, Terseness-Prolixity.

e-pit′-o-mize. To curtail. Digest, Length-Shortness.

ep″-i-zo-ot′-ic. Epidemic among animals. Healthiness-Unhealthiness.

ep′-och. A fixed point of time; age. Chronology-Anachronism, Duration-Neverness, Eternity-Instantaneity, Time.

ep′-ode. An after-song. Poetry-Prose.

ep″-o-pee′. } An epic poem. Poetry-Prose.
ep″-o-poe′-a. }

eppur si muove [It.] (êp′-pur sî mu-o′-vê). And yet it (the earth) does move. [Galileo.] Movement-Rest.

Ep″-som salts. A purgative. Remedy-Bane.

ep″-u-la′-tion. A feasting.

ep″-u-lot′-ic. Having power to cicatrize and heal. Remedy-Bane.

ep″-u-ra′-tion. The act of purifying. Cleanness-Filthiness.

e′-qua-ble. Even; steady. Right-Wrong.

e′-qual. Of the same value with another; to be or become equal to. Equality-Inequality, Proportion-Deformity, Right-Wrong; **equal chance,** Rationale-Luck; **equal times,** Coexistence; **equal to,** Might-Impotence.

e-qual′-i-ty. The state or quality of being equal. Equality-Inequality, Sameness-Contrast.

EQUALITY—INEQUALITY.

Adjustment. The state of being settled in regard to points of difference.

Balance. The state of equality of opposing forces or interests.

Coextension. The condition of being extended equally far.

Co-ordination. Act of putting in the same order, class, or rank.

Equality. The state of being of the same value.

Equalization. The state of being made alike.

Equation. A making equal.

Equilibration. }
Equilibrium. } State of balance.
Equipoise. }

Equipollence. } The state of being of equal weight, significance, ect.
Equivalence. }

Evenness. The quality of being even.

Identity, etc. The state of being exactly the same. See Sameness.

Monotony. The quality of lacking variation.

Par. Equality of real and nominal values.

Parity. Equality of rank or condition.

Poise. State of self-balance.

Ponderance. Weight of opinion.

Quits. The condition of being even with all obligations.

Readjustment. Considering and settling again.

Similarity. The state of having same parts and in equal proportions.

Symmetry. Balance of like parts.

Tie. An equality in numbers.

EQUALITY—Denotations.

Brother. A male person having the same parents as another.

Compeer. One having equal rank or standing.

Dead heat. A race in which two or more contestants come out even.

Distinction without a difference. A separation or classification not caused by a difference in the objects.

Drawn battle. A battle in which neither side has gained an advantage.

Drawn game. A game in which the contestants prove equal in skill, etc.

Equal. A person or thing equal to another.

Equator. The imaginary line which divides the earth into two equal parts.

Match. One's equal.

Mate. One that is paired with another; an equal in a contest.

Casting weight. A weight that turns a balance.

Difference, etc. Unlikeness. See Variation.

Disparity. Inequality in reference to a common standard.

Imparity. Inequality.

Inclination of the balance. Tendency to one side or another.

Inequality. Absolute difference.

Inferiority, etc. The state of being lower in rank, excellence. See Supremacy-Subordinacy.

Makeweight. Anything that is used to fill up a deficiency.

Odds. Advantages over others.

Partiality. Tendency to favor one rather than another.

Shortcoming. A falling away from a standard.

Superiority, etc. The state of being above in rank, excellence. See Supremacy.

Unevenness. The state of being uneven.

INEQUALITY—*Verb.*

Countervail. To oppose with equal force.

INEQUALITY—*Verbal Expressions.*

Be unequal (see *Adjectives*); **give the advantage; have the advantage; kick the beam,** to be light in weight; **not come up to; overmatch,** to match unevenly (see Supremacy); **topple over,** to fall over; **turn the scale,** to incline the balance to one side.

INEQUALITY—*Adjectives.*

Disparate. Not conforming to the common standard.

Lop-sided. Heavier on one side than on the other.

Over-balanced. Heavier on one side than on the other.

Partial. Favoring one more than another.

Top-heavy. Too heavy in the upper parts in proportion to the remaining part.

Unbalanced. Not in a state of balance.

Unequal. Not equal.

Uneven. Not even.

INEQUALITY—*Adverb.*

Haud passibus æquis [L.]. Not with equal steps, [Virgil, *Æneid,* ii, 724.]

EQUALITY—Denotations—*Continued.*

Neck and neck race. A dead heat.
Not a pin to choose. A difference smaller than a pin.

Peer. An equal.
Six of one and half a dozen of the other. Absence of difference.

EQUALITY—*Verbs.*

Accommodate. To make to agree by mutual or willing sacrifice.
Adapt, etc. To join properly by exercise of judgment. See HARMONY.
Adjust. To set right.
Amount to. Equal to.
Balance. To have equal weight on each side.
Be equal, etc. See *Adjectives.*
Be on a level with. Equal in height.
Come to.
Come to the same thing. } Equal.
Come up to.
Cope with. To strive with on equal terms.
Dress. To set right.
Equal. To be or become of the same degree.
Equalize. To make of equal value.
Equate. To represent as equal.
Establish equality. } To balance.
Establish equilibrium.

Fit. To be or make just right for the purpose.
Keep pace with. To equal in any sense.
Level. To make even.
Lie on a level with.
Match. To select something similar or equal.
Poise. To balance without help.
Reach. To come up to.
Readjust. To set right again.
Render equal, etc. See *Adjectives.*
Restore equality. } To make equal.
Restore equilibrium.
Run abreast. Keep even with.
Stretch on the bed of Procrustes. To suit to conditions by force.
Strike a balance.
Trim. To be in a state of equilibrium.

EQUALITY—*Adjectives.*

All one. The same.
All the same. Equal.
As broad as long. Equal in all directions.
As good as. Equal in quality.
Balanced. Having equal weight on each side.
Coequal. Of the same rank, value, etc.
Convertible. Easily made equal to; exchangeable with.
Co-ordinate. Of the same order.
Drawn. Indeterminable.
Equal. Exactly the same as.
Equalized. Made equal to. See sub *Verbs.*
Equipollent. }
Equivalent. } Of the same significance as.
Equiponderant. }
Equiponderous. } Having equal weight.
Even. Equally distributed, etc.
Half and half.

Homologous. Existing in the same relation in corresponding objects.
Level. Parallel to the horizon.
Monotonous. The quality of being all or much alike
Much at one. } Alike.
Much the same as.
Neither more nor less. Exactly alike.
On a footing with. }
On a level with. } Like; equal to.
On a par with. }
Quits. On even terms.
Resolvable into. Capable of being made into, or like something else.
Symmetrical. Having parts arranged so as to balance.
Synonymous. Having nearly the same meaning.
Tantamount. Equal in our own estimation.
The same thing as. Like; identical.
Up to the mark. Up to the standard.

EQUALITY—*Adverbs.*

Ad eundem [L.]. To the same.
Cæteris paribus [L.]. Other things being equal.
Equally, etc. In the same degree, etc. See *Adjectives.*

In equilibrio [L.]. Equally balanced.
Pari passu [L.]. With an equal pace.
To all intents and purposes. Practically the same as.

EQUALITY—*Phrases.*

It amounts to the same thing.

It comes to the same thing.

e″-qual-i-za′-tion. An equal state. EQUALITY-INEQUALITY.
e′-qual-ize. To make equal. COMPENSATION.
e′-qual-ized. Made equal. EQUALITY-INEQUALITY.
e′-qual-ly. In equal measure. EQUALITY-INEQUALITY.
e″-qua-nim′-i-ty. Composure of spirit. EXCITABILITY-INEXCITABILITY.
e-quate′. To make or regard equal. EQUALITY-INEQUALITY.
e-qua′-tion. A proposition expressing the equality of two quantities. COMPENSATION, EQUALITY-INEQUALITY.
e-qua′-tions. Propositions expressing the equality of two quantities. NUMBERING.
e-qua′-tor. A great circle equally distant from the poles and dividing a sphere into hemispheres. MIDDLE, UNIVERSE.
e′-qua-tor′-i-al. Relating to the equator. MIDDLE.
eq′-uer-ry. An officer having charge of the horses of a prince or nobleman. CHIEF-UNDERLING.
e-ques′-tri-an. A horseman. WAYFARER-SEAFARER.
e″-qui-bal′-anced. Counterpoised. EQUALITY-INEQUALITY.
e″-qui-dis′-tance. Equal distance. MIDDLE.
e″-qui-dis′-tant. Situated at the same distance from the same point. MIDDLE.
e″-qui-li-bra′-tion. Equipoise. EQUALITY-INEQUALITY.

e″-qui-lib′-ri-um. Equipoise. EQUALITY-INEQUALITY.
e′-quine. Pertaining to, or like, a horse. CONVEYER, FAUNA-FLORA.
e′-qui-nox. Time when the sun enters the equinoctial points. MORNING-EVENING.
e-quip′. To fit out with all requirements. DRESS-UNDRESS, PREPARATION-NONPREPARATION.
eq′-ui-page. Equipment; retinue. CONVEYANCE-VESSEL, INSTRUMENT, POMP, PROPERTY.
e-quip′-ment. The act of equipping; whatever is used in equipping. DRESS-UNDRESS, INSTRUMENT, PREPARATION-NONPREPARATION.
e′-qui-poise. Even balance. EQUALITY-INEQUALITY.
e″-qui-pol′-lence. Equality of power, etc. EQUALITY-INEQUALITY.
e″-qui-pol′-lent. Equivalent. EQUALITY-INEQUALITY, SYNONYM-ANTONYM.
e″-qui-pon′-der-ant. Of the same weight. EQUALITY-INEQUALITY.
e″-qui-pon′-der-ous. Having equal weight. EQUALITY-INEQUALITY.
eq′-ui-ta-ble. Impartial; conformable to right and justice. DUENESS-UNDUENESS, RIGHT-WRONG, SAGACITY-INCAPACITY, UPRIGHTNESS-DISHONESTY; **equitable interest,** PROPERTY.
eq′-ui-ta-ble-ness. The quality of being equitable. RIGHT-WRONG.

eq″-ui-ta′-tion. Horsemanship. Traveling-Navigation.

eq′-ui-ty. Fairness and impartiality. Law-Lawlessness, Right-Wrong, Uprightness-Dishonesty;
equity draftsman, Advocate; **in equity,** Right-
Wrong.

e-quiv′-a-lence. State of being equivalent. Equality-
Inequality.

e-quiv′-a-lent. Equal in value; that which is equal in
value. Commutation-Permutation, Compensa-
tion, Equality-Inequality, Interpretation-Misinterpretation, Sameness-Contrast, Synonym-
Antonym; **equivalent term,** Synonym-Antonym;
equivalent word, Synonym-Antonym.

e-quiv′-o-cal. Of doubtful meaning; suspicious. Certainty-Doubt, Purity-Impurity.

e-quiv′-o-cal-ness. Ambiguity. Ambiguity, Purity-
Impurity.

e-quiv′-o-cate. To prevaricate. Ambiguity, Ratiocination-Casuistry, Truthfulness-Falsehood.

e-quiv″-o-ca′-tion. Prevarication. Ambiguity,
Ratiocination-Casuistry, Truthfulness-Falsehood; **without equivocation,** Truthfulness-Falsehood.

eq′-ui-voque. An equivocal word or phrase. Ambiguity.

e′-ra. An epoch. Chronology-Anachronism, Duration-Neverness.

e-rad′-i-cate. To root out. Creation-Destruction,
Injection-Ejection.

e-rad″-i-ca′-tion. Extirpation. Injection-Ejection.

e-rase′. To expunge. Creation-Destruction,
Mark-Obliteration.

E-ras′-ti-an. An adherent of the doctrine of Erastus.
Orthodoxy-Heterodoxy.

E-ras′-ti-an-ism. The principles of the Erastians.
Orthodoxy-Heterodoxy.

e-ra′-sure. Obliteration. Mark-Obliteration.

Er′-a-to. The muse of erotic and other lyric poetry.
Musician.

erba mala presto cresco [It.] (êr′-ba ma′-la pres′-to
cres′-co). An ill weed grows fast. Goodness-Badness.

ere. Before. Antecedence-Sequence; **ere long,**
Earliness-Lateness; **ere now,** Antecedence-
Sequence, Future-Past.

Er′-e-bus. The abode of the subterranean powers.
Heaven-Hell, Light-Darkness.

e-rect′. Vertical; to set up. Creation-Destruction,
Elevation-Depression, Erectness-Flatness;
erect the scaffolding, Preparation-Nonpreparation; **with head erect,** Selfrespect-Humbleness.

e-rec′-tion. The act of erecting. Creation-Destruction, Elevation-Depression, Erectness-
Flatness.

e-rect′-ness. Uprightness of form. Erectness-Flatness.

ERECTNESS—FLATNESS.

Elevation. The state of being raised up.
Erection. A setting of something in an upright position.
Erectness. Uprightness of posture or form.
Perpendicularity. The state of being straight up and down.
Verticality. The state of being at right angles to the horizon.

ERECTNESS—*Denotations.*

Azimuth circles. Great circles of a sphere intersecting each other in
the zenith and nadir and cutting the horizon at right angles.
Cliff. A high perpendicular rock.
Plumb line.⎫ An instrument used for adjusting erections to a perpen-
Plummet. ⎭ dicular line.
Precipice. A high and very steep cliff.
Right angle. The angle formed by two lines intersecting each other
at 90 degrees.
Square. A portion of a surface whose bounding lines form angles of
90 degrees with each other.
Wall. A piece of masonry built vertically.

ERECTNESS—*Verbs.*

Be vertical. Be upright in position.
Cock up. To set erect.
Erect. To raise and place in an upright or perpendicular position.
Raise on its legs. To cause to stand erect
Raise up. To cause to rise up.
Rear. To raise.
Render vertical. To place upright.
Set up. To elevate.
Stand erect. To stand not bowed over.
Stand on end. To rise resting upon an extremity.
Stand up. To rise from sitting.
Stand upright. To stand in an erect position.
Stick up. To rise vertically.

ERECTNESS—*Adjectives.*

Bolt upright. Boldly erect.
Erect. In a perpendicular posture.
Normal. Forming a right angle.
Orthogonal. Rectangular.
Perpendicular. Exactly upright.
Rampant. Standing upright upon his hind legs.
Rectangular. Right-angled.
Standing up. Being erect.
Straight. Direct.
Upright. In an erect position.
Vertical. Perpendicular to the plane of the horizon.

Dead flat. Perfect flatness.
Dead level. Absolute uniformity of flatness.
Flatness. Evenness of surface.
Horizontality. The state of being horizontal.

FLATNESS—*Denotations, etc.*

Azimuth. An astronomical circle used in determining levels.
Billiard table. A table having an oblong rectangular surface for
playing billiards.
Bowling green. A level lawn for playing bowls.
Campus. Originally, the level ground marked out for contestants in
trial by battle; now, the grounds of a college.
Cricket-ground. A level space fitted for playing cricket.
Croquet-ground. A level court for playing croquet.
Croquet-lawn. See Croquet-ground.
Dead flat. ⎫ A perfectly level piece of ground or floor.
Dead level. ⎭
Esplanade. A level space for promenading.
Estrade. A slightly raised platform.
Floor. The bottom surface in a room or building.
Ledge. A shelf.
Level. A surface, or extent of land approximately horizontal.
Level plane. A flat surface.
Parterre. A level plot or space.
Plain. A level, or nearly level, tract of land.
Plateau. An elevated plain.
Platform. A raised floor.
Table-land. A tract of land resembling a table in flatness.
Terrace. A raised level space having one or more sloping sides.

FLATNESS—*Nouns of Action.*

Accubation. A reclining on a couch, as by the ancients at meals.
Decumbence.⎫ The act or state of lying down.
Decumbency.⎭
Discumbency. Practise of reclining at meals, as among the ancients.
Lying down. The act of laying the body down.
Proneness. The state of lying with the front or face down.
Prostration. A lying flat.
Reclination. Act or state of leaning back.
Recumbency. State of leaning.
Resupination.⎫ Act or state of lying on the back.
Supination. ⎭

FLATNESS—*Verbs.*

Be horizontal.⎫ To lie down or recline.
Couch. ⎭
Fell. To prostrate.

ERECTNESS—FLATNESS—*Continued.*

ERECTNESS—*Adverbs.*

À plomb [F.]. Perpendicularly.
At right angles. Perpendicularly.
Endwise. Erectly.
On end. In an erect position.
On one's legs. Erectly.
Right on end. In a position perpendicular to the horizon.
Up. In or to a vertical or nearly vertical position.
Up on end. With erectness.
Vertically. In a vertical manner.

FLATNESS—ADJECTIVES—*Continued from Column 2.*

Horizontal. Parallel to the horizon.
Jacent. Lying at length.
Level. Not having one part higher than another.
Lying. Being prostrate
Plane. Without elevations or depressions.
Procumbent. Lying down or on the face.
Prone. Flat on the face.
Prostrate. Lying on the ground.
Recumbent. Leaning.
Smooth. Having an even surface.
Smooth as glass. Having a polished surface.
Supine. Lying on the back, or with the face upward.

FLATNESS—*Adverbs.*

Horizontally. On a level.
On all fours. On hands and knees.
On its beam ends. On its side.
On one's back. With the back down.

FLATNESS—VERBS—*Continued.*

Flatten. To reduce to an equal or even surface.
Floor. To strike down or lay level with the floor.
Knock down. To prostrate by a blow or blows.
Lay down. To place horizontally.
Lay out. To place in a decent position, as a corpse.
Level. To make smooth or even.
Lie. To rest extended on the ground.
Lie down. To lay the body on the ground or level place.
Lie flat. To recline upon the back.
Lie prostrate. To lie with the body extended on the ground or other flat surface.
Loll. To lie at ease.
Prostrate. To lay flat.
Recline. To take a recumbent position.
Render horizontal. To make parallel to the horizon.
Sit down. To place oneself on a chair or other seat.
Sprawl. To spread or stretch the body carelessly in a horizontal position.

FLATNESS—*Adjectives.*

Accumbent. Leaning or reclining; as the ancients at meals.
Alluvial. Relating to the deposits of sand, clay, or gravel made by river action.
Calm. Undisturbed.
Calm as a mill pond. Perfectly serene.
Couchant. Lying down.
Decumbent. Bending or lying down.
Even. Level, smooth, or equal in surface.
Flat, etc. Having an even and horizontal surface, etc. See LEVELNESS.
Flat as a billiard table. Level.
Flat as a bowling-green. Even.

(*Continued on Column 1.*)

ere'-while''. Recent; heretofore. ANTECEDENCE-SEQUENCE, FUTURE-PAST.
er'-go. Therefore. RATIOCINATION-CASUISTRY.
er'-got-ism. Arguing. DISCOVERY.
er'-got-ize. To wrangle. FAITH-MISGIVING.
er''-i-om''-e-ter. An apparatus for measuring small diameters. OPTICAL INSTRUMENTS.
er'-mine. The stoat; the fur of the ermine. EMBELLISHMENT-DISFIGUREMENT, SCEPTER.
e-rode'. To wear away. BETTERMENT-DETERIORATION.
eros [Gr.] (î'-ros). Love. LOVE-HATE.
e-ro'-sion. Act of eroding. BETTERMENT-DETERIORATION, GEOLOGY.
er-ot'-ic. Amorous. LOVE-HATE, PURITY-IMPURITY.
err. To be incorrect; to sin. TRUTH-ERROR, VIRTUE-VICE.
er'-rand. Business intrusted to a messenger. COMMISSION-ABROGATION, OCCUPATION, TIDINGS-MYSTERY.
er'-rand–boy. A boy who does small errands. MESSENGER.
er'-rant. Roving. AIM-ABERRATION.
errare humanum est [L.] (er-rê'-rî hiu-mê'-num est). To err is human. TRUTH-ERROR.
er-rat'-ic. Eccentric. AIM-ABERRATION, MOVEMENT-REST, MUTABILITY-STABILITY, PERSISTENCE-WHIM.
er-ra'-tum. An error. TRUTH-ERROR.
er-ro'-ne-ous. Mistaken. TRUTH-ERROR.
er'-ror. False belief; inaccuracy. INNOCENCE-GUILT, ORTHODOXY-HETERODOXY, TRUTH-ERROR, VIRTUE-VICE; **court of error,** TRIBUNAL; **writ of error,** LITIGATION.
erst. Formerly. FUTURE-PAST.
er''-u-bes'-cence. Redness. REDNESS-GREENNESS.
er''-u-bes'-cent. Reddening. REDNESS-GREENNESS.
erubuit, salva res est [L.] (î-ru'-biu-it, sal'-va rîz est). Where there is shame, there is virtue. REPENTANCE-OBDURACY.
e-ruct'-ate. To give vent to. ADMISSION-EXPULSION.

e''-ruc-ta'-tion. Act of belching. ADMISSION-EXPULSION.
er'-u-dite. Scholarly. KNOWLEDGE-IGNORANCE.
er''-u-di'-tion. A high degree of knowledge. EDUCATION-LEARNING, KNOWLEDGE-IGNORANCE.
e-rup'-tion. A bursting forth; a disease of the skin. ENTRANCE-EXIT, GEOLOGY, HEALTH-SICKNESS, TURBULENCE-CALMNESS; **volcanic eruption,** PHENOMENON.
es''-ca-lade'. An attack by means of ladders; to scale, as a wall. ASCENT-DESCENT, ATTACK-DEFENSE.
es-cal'-lop. To shape the edge of into lobes or rounded projections. CIRCLE-WINDING.
escamoter [F.] (es-ca-mo-tê'). To juggle. TRUTHFULNESS-FRAUD.
es'-ca-pade. A prank. ADAGE-NONSENSE, ENTERTAINMENT-WEARINESS, PERSISTENCE-WHIM.
es-cape'. To get away from; flight. DUTY-DERELICTION, ENTRANCE-EXIT, ESCAPE, QUEST-EVASION, RELEASE-RESTRAINT, SECURITY-INSECURITY, USEFULNESS-USELESSNESS; **escape the lips,** EXPOSURE-HIDINGPLACE; **escape the memory,** REMEMBRANCE-FORGETFULNESS; **escape the notice,** HEED-DISREGARD, VISIBILITY-INVISIBILITY; **means of escape,** REFUGE-PITFALL, SECURITY-INSECURITY.

ESCAPE.

Avolation. Flight.
Come off. Departure or passing off from.
Elopement. A running away of lovers to be married.
Escape. Successful flight from any annoyance.
Evasion. Artful means of eluding.
Flight. Hasty departure.
Hair-breadth escape. A very narrow escape.
Impunity. Freedom from the ordinary consequences of an act.
Liberation. The act of being made free. See sub LIBERATION.
Narrow escape.
Refugee, etc. One who seeks shelter from disaster. See QUEST-EVASION.
Reprieve, etc. Temporary suspension of punishment. See RESCUE.
Retreat. A going back to a place of safety.
Scape. Escape.

Escape—*Nouns of Means.*

Drawbridge. A small bridge raised and let down at one end like a hinge.

Fire-escape. A ladder or stair-case bolted on the outside of buildings for use in case of fire.

Loophole, etc. A small opening affording a means of escape. See APERTURE.

Path. A walk or way, especially one beaten by the foot. See WAY.

Refuge, etc. A place where one is protected or sheltered. See REFUGE.

Safety-valve. A valve so arranged as to relieve pressure or strain above a certain limit.

Vent. An outlet for the passage of something from a confined space.

Vent-peg. A peg for stopping a vent, as in a barrel.

Escape—*Verbs.*

Elude. To keep away from by tricks.

Escape. To get away from annoyance.

Scape. Escape.

Escape—*Verbal Expressions.*

Break away; break from prison; break loose; *echapper belle* [F.], to escape entirely; **effect one's escape; escape scot-free,** to escape altogether; **find a hole to creep out of; find vent,** find a means of escape; **get away; get clear off; get off; get well out of; give one the slip,** to escape from one; **make good one's escape; make off,** etc. (see QUEST-EVASION); **make one's escape; march off,** etc. (see ARRIVAL-DEPARTURE); **save one's bacon,** to keep from harm; **slip away,** go away without notice; **slip the collar; slip through the fingers; slip through the hands; weather the storm,** to pass through danger safely; **wriggle out of,** to free with difficulty.

Escape—*Adjectives.*

Escaped, etc. Fled from. See *Verbs.*

Escaping. In the act of getting away.

Fled. Having departed suddenly.

Stolen away. Having departed stealthily.

Escape—*Phrase.*

The bird has flown. The object searched for has taken its flight.

es-caped′. Gotten away. ESCAPE.

es-ca′-ping. Fleeing; leaking. ESCAPE.

es-carp′. The side of the ditch next the parapet. ATTACK-DEFENSE.

es-carp′-ment. A steep slope. HEIGHT-LOWNESS, LAMINA-FIBER, PARALLELISM-INCLINATION.

es″ char-ot′-ic. Capable of destroying living tissue and forming an eschar. PUNGENCY, VIGOR-INERTIA.

es-cheat′. To take possession of, as lapsed or forfeited. RECOMPENSE-PENALTY.

es-chew′. To avoid with care. DESIRE-DISTASTE, QUEST-EVASION.

esclandre. [F.] (es-clan·dr′). Unpleasant notoriety. PLEASURE-PAIN, PLEASURABLENESS-PAINFULNESS.

es-cort′. To safeguard on a journey. SOLITUDE-COMPANY.

es′-cort. Body-guard. KEEPER-PRISONER, SECURITY-INSECURITY.

es′-cu-lent. Eatable. NUTRIMENT-EXCRETION.

es-cutch′-eon. The heraldic shield. SIGN.

e-soph′-a-gus. Gullet. ANATOMY.

es′-o-ter′-ic. Recondite. ENLIGHTENMENT-SECRECY, UNIVERSALITY-PARTICULARITY

Espagne, château en [F.] (es-pany′, sha-to′ an·). A castle in Spain ; castle in the air. FANCY, SANGUINENESS-HOPELESSNESS.

es-pal′-ier. A trellis; to train upon an espalier, as small trees. ENCLOSURE.

es-pe′-cial. Eminent. UNIVERSALITY-PARTICULARITY.

es-pe′-cial-ly. Particularly. SUPREMACY-SUBORDINACY.

es-pi′-al. Concealed observation. SIGHT-BLINDNESS.

espièglerie [F.] (es″-pi-egl-ri′). Roguish bantering. CRAFT-ARTLESSNESS, ENTERTAINMENT-WEARINESS, WITTINESS-DULNESS.

es′-pi-o-nage. Excessive surveillance. INVESTIGATION-ANSWER, SIGHT-BLINDNESS.

es″-pla-nade′. A level open place, for promenading or driving. CITY-COUNTRY, DWELLER-HABITATION, ERECTNESS-FLATNESS.

es-pou′-sals. Betrothal. MATRIMONY-CELIBACY.

es-pouse′. To promise in marriage. CHOICE-NEUTRALITY, MATRIMONY-CELIBACY; **espouse a cause,** ANTAGONISM-CONCURRENCE, OBSTRUCTION-HELP.

esprit [F.] (es-prî′). Spirit; wit. SAGACITY-INCAPACITY, WITTINESS-DULNESS.

esprit, bel [F.] (es-prî′, bel). A fine wit. WAG.

esprit de corps [F.] (es-prî′ de cor). Comradeship. ANTAGONISM-CONCURRENCE, DECISION-MISJUDGMENT, SOCIABILITY-PRIVACY.

esprit fort [F.] (es-prî′ for). A free-thinker. GODLINESS-DISBELIEF, SAGE-FOOL.

es-py′. To discover. SIGHT-BLINDNESS.

es-quire′. A title of dignity, office, courtesy. GENTILITY-DEMOCRACY, TITLE.

es-say′. To attempt. TRIAL, VENTURE.

es′-say. A composition on some special subject; an attempt. ESSAY, NATURE-ART, TRIAL, VENTURE.

ESSAY.

Article. A treatise on some topic, like a magazine article.

Commentary. An annotation or exposition of the abstruse points of some literary work.

Commentator. One who writes commentaries; an expounder.

Critic. One skilled in judging the merits of literary works.

Criticism. An article giving a critical examination of some subject.

Critique. A critical examination or estimate of any subject.

Discourse. An oral treatise of some topic in a logical order of thought.

Discussion, etc. See RATIOCINATION.

Disquisition. A complete investigation and treatise of some subject.

Dissertation. An argumentative discussion or discourse.

Essay. A short composition treating of any particular subject.

Essayist. One who writes essays.

Exposition, etc. See INTERPRETATION.

Homily. An exhortation on some moral point.

Investigation, etc. See INVESTIGATION.

Leader. The main editorial article.

Leading article. The principal article in a newspaper or a book.

Lecture. A formal and methodical discourse.

Memoir. A record of something deemed worthy.

Pamphlet. A booklet not bound.

Pamphleteer. A writer of pamphlets.

Pandect. A comprehensive treatise of some science; with special reference to law.

Review. A critical examination of an article or book.

Running commentary. A hasty annotation.

Sermon. A discourse delivered by a clergyman for religious instruction.

Study. See REFLECTION.

Theme. A subject or topic for discussion.

Thesis. A position or proposition set forth and maintained by arguments.

Tract. A short treatise on practical religion.

Tractate. A treatise; an essay.

Tractation. The act of treating or discussing a topic.

Treatise. A formal, scientific exposition of some subject.

Essay—*Verbs.*

Canvass a subject. To thoroughly investigate a subject.

Deal with a subject. To treat in any manner.

Descant upon a subject. To comment fully upon a subject.

Discuss a subject. To treat; to reason about.

Dissert upon a subject. To discourse or discuss a subject.

Do justice to a subject. To bring out all that is contained in a subject.

Go into a subject. To find out its primary significance.

Handle a subject. To treat skilfully.

Take up a subject. To start; to treat.

Touch upon a subject. To give some notice to.

Treat of a subject. To discourse upon; to handle.

Ventilate a subject. To throw light on a subject; to clarify.

Write upon a subject. To give one's ideas upon a matter.

Essay—*Adjectives.*

Discoursive. Passing from one judgment to another.

Discursive. Wandering, drawing conclusions from premises.

Disquisitionary, etc. See ESSAY.

Expository. Set forth; explain, propound.

es-say'-ing. Attempting. Venture.
es'-say-ist. A writer of essays. Essay, Missive-Publication.
esse [L.] (es'-sĭ). To be. Entity-Nonentity.
es'-sence. Constituent qualities of a thing; odor. Odor-Inodorousness, Subjectiveness-Objectiveness.
Es-sene'. One of a party of the ancient Jews. Austerity, Orthodoxy-Heterodoxy.
es-sen'-tial. Characteristic; a necessary element. Consequence-Insignificance, Magnitude-Smallness, Nature-Art, Need, Subjectiveness-Objectiveness.
es-sen''-ti-al'-i-ty. The essential part. Nature-Art, Need.

es-sen'-tial-ly. Inherently. Magnitude-Smallness, Substance-Nullity.
es-sen'-tial-ness. The quality of being essential. Subjectiveness-Objectiveness.
es-tab'-lish. To institute; to substantiate. Creation-Destruction, Establishment-Removal, Evidence-Counterevidence, Mutability-Stability, Proof-Disproof; **establish equality,** Equality-Inequality; **establish equilibrium,** Equality-Inequality.
es-tab'-lished. Rendered valid. Habit-Desuetude, Mutability-Stability, Mutation-Permanence; **established church,** Orthodoxy-Heterodoxy.
es-tab'-lish-ment. The act of establishing; the thing established. Association, Creation-Destruction, Establishment-Removal, Market, Mutability-Stability.

ESTABLISHMENT—REMOVAL.

A local habitation and a name." A definite place and existence. [The poet's pen gives to airy nothing a local, etc. Shakespeare, *Midsummer Night's Dream,* V, i.]
Anchorage. A place where ships are anchored.
Cantonment. Temporary shelter for an army.
Cohabitation. The act of living together.
Collocation. The act of placing together, arranging, or stationing.
Colony. A settlement.
Deposition. The act of setting down or placing.
Domestication. The process of making accustomed to new conditions.
Establishment. The act of fixing or locating; settlement.
Fixation. The act of making firm or establishing.
Habitation. A place of abode. See Dweller-Habitation.
Indenization. The act of naturalizing.
Insertion, etc. The act of fixing or fastening in between other things, etc. See Injection.
Installation. The act of giving a place to.
Lading. Process of loading.
Localization. The act of fixing in a definite place.
Location. The act of placing or fixing in a definite spot.
Lodgment. The act of placing or fixing anything permanently.
Mooring. A place for anchoring ships.
Naturalization. The act of making an alien a citizen of a country.
Package.} Act of stowing away.
Packing.}
Plantation. A settlement in a new country.
Reposition. The act of laying up or placing for permanence or safety.
Settlement. The act of fixing or placing, or the state of being fixed or settled.
Situation. A location in reference to other places.
Stowage. The process of placing in a compact mass.

ESTABLISHMENT—*Verbs.*

Adopt. To take up and receive as one's own.
Anchor. To fix or fasten firmly, as with an anchor.
Bag. To capture.
Billet on. To quarter, as soldiers.
Bivouac. An encampment for the night without tents.
Burrow. To lodge in any deep or concealed place
Camp. To rest or lodge at a place.
Cast anchor. To moor a ship.
Colonize. To plant or establish a colony.
Come to an anchor. To become fixed.
Cradle. To lie or lodge as in a cradle.
Deposit. To lodge; lay down; place.
Domesticate. To accustom to live near habitated places.
Embed. To lay or place in surrounding matter.
Encamp. To settle down for a temporary stay, as soldiers.
Establish. To make stable or fix firmly; settle.
Establish oneself. To make oneself secure.
Fit. To adjust; put in a state of readiness.
Fix. To place in a definite position.
Freight. To load or burden with.
Get a footing. To gain a firm position.
Graft. To implant or propagate by inserting.
Hive. To lay up in store: get bees into a hive.
House. To shelter, protect.
Indenizen. To naturalize.
Inhabit, etc. To dwell in, etc. See Presence.
Install. To give a place to.
Invest in. To place in a safe condition, enclose.
Keep house. To maintain a house.

Dislocation, etc. The act of displacing, etc. See Organization-Disorganization.
Displacement. The act of removing or putting out of place.
Ejectment, etc. The act of expelling or casting out, etc. See Admission-Expulsion.
Elocation. Removal from a customary place of abode.
Exile, etc. The state of forced separation from one's country, etc. See Sociability-Privacy.
Misplacement. The act of putting in the wrong place.
Removal, etc. The act of taking from one place to another, etc. See Transfer.
Transposition. Change of place.

REMOVAL—*Figurative Expression.*

Fish out of water. A person in an unaccustomed position.

REMOVAL—*Verbs.*

Ablegate. To send abroad.
Cart away. To carry away in a cart.
Depart, etc. To go away, etc. See Arrival-Departure.
Disestablish. To unsettle; break up.
Dislodge. To remove from a place or position of quiet and rest.
Dispel. To drive away.
Displace. To remove; change the place of.
Displant. To remove from a place in which it was planted.
Draw off. To take away.
Empty, etc. To exhaust; make void; draw off the contents, etc. See Admission-Expulsion.
Exile, etc. To banish from one's country, etc. See Sociability-Privacy.
Lade, etc. To throw out or in, as water, etc. See Establishment.
Remove. To take from a place formerly occupied.
Set aside. To put aside.
Take away. To carry to another place.
Take draft off. To shut off a current of air.
Take off. To remove from the outside or surface.
Transfer, etc. To remove from one place to another, etc. See Transfer.
Unload. To discharge from a burden.
Vacate. To leave; go away from.

REMOVAL—*Adjectives.*

Displaced, etc. Put out of place, etc. See *Verbs.*
Homeless. Without a home.
Houseless. Without a house.
Misplaced. Put in a wrong place.
Out of a situation. Without a place.
Out of its element. Out of its proper sphere or condition.
Out of place. Displaced.
Unestablished. Not settled or fixed.
Unharbored. Unprotected; unsheltered.
Unhoused. Deprived of shelter.
Unplaced. Undetermined as to place.
Unsettled. Not fixed or firm.

ESTABLISHMENT—Verbs—*Continued*

Lade. To burden or weigh down with.
Lay. To place in a low, flat position.
Lay down. To deposit or place.
Load. To put on burdens, weigh down.
Localize. To fix or place in a definite position or place
Locate. To set in some definite spot or place.

ESTABLISHMENT—Verbs—*Continued.*

Locate oneself. To establish oneself in some particular place.
Lodge. To set or fix firmly.
Make a place for. Make room.
Moor. To secure a ship in some definite station by means of anchors and cables.
Naturalize. To adopt; confer the rights of citizenship upon.
Pack. To load; stow away in, as a trunk.
Perch. To settle or light on a fixed body.
Picket. To fasten to a sharpened stake.
Pin. To fasten with a pin; enclose.
Pitch. To fix firmly.
Pitch one's tent. To set up one's tent.
Place. To put into a particular spot.
Plant, etc. To set firmly; establish. See Injection.
Plant oneself. To establish oneself firmly.
Pocket. To put into a pocket; conceal.
Post. To set; place; assign to a station.
Put. To lay down; place.
Put at. To place in a certain position.
Put back. To delay; hinder; obstruct.
Put up. To place out of sight, as a letter.
Put up one's horses at. To stay.
Quarter. To furnish with temporary shelter.
Quarter upon. To cause to lodge with by compulsion.

Replace, etc. To restore to a former place or condition, etc. See Renovation.
Reposit. To lay up; lodge for safety.
Root. To fasten firmly.
Saddle with. To burden down with.
Seat. To rest.
Se nicher [F.]. To hide oneself.
Set. To make assume a specified position; seat.
Settle. To place in a fixed or permanent position; determine; colonize.
Settle down. Settle permanently.
Shelve. To place on a shelf.
Sit down. To settle; fix a permanent abode.
Situate. To fix permanently.
Squat. To crouch on the hams, close to the ground.
Station. To place; set.
Stow. To place or arrange in a compact mass.
Strike root. } To begin to grow.
Take root. }
Take up one's abode. To settle; take up one's dwelling-place.
Take up one's quarters. To lodge.
Tether. To confine as with ropes.
Tuck in. To close in.
Vest. To furnish; endow.

Establishment—*Adjectives.*

At anchor. Fastened with an anchor.
Domesticated. Made domestic.
Embosomed. Hidden or half concealed.
Ensconced. Sheltered; protected.
Imbedded. Deposited, as in a bed.
Moored, etc. Fastened, as a vessel, etc. See *Verbs.*

Placed. To set or put in a particular position.
Posited. Firmly placed.
Rooted. Firmly fixed.
Situate. Permanently fixed.
Unremoved. Not taken away.
Vested in. Placed in.

es″-ta-fet′. A courier. Messenger.
estaminet [F.] (es-ta-mî-nê′). A coffee-house where smoking is permitted. Dweller-Habitation.
es-tate′. Landed property; rank. Condition-Situation, Property; **come to man's estate,** Manhood.
es-teem′. To value; respect. Approval-Disapproval, Faith-Misgiving, Regard-Disrespect; **in high esteem,** Approval-Disapproval, Regard-Disrespect.
es-thet′-ic. Relating to beauty or taste. Taste-Vulgarity.
es-thet′-ics. Science of beauty or taste. Taste-Vulgarity.
es′-ti-ma-ble. Worthy of respect. Approval-Disapproval, Goodness-Badness.
es′-ti-mate. To compute; appraisement. Decision-Misjudgment, Differentiation-Indiscrimination, Enlightenment-Secrecy, Mensuration; **estimate too highly,** Overvaluation-Undervaluation.
es″-ti-ma′-tion. Estimate; esteem. Decision-Misjudgment, Differentiation-Indiscrimination, Mensuration, Regard-Disrespect.
es′-ti-val. Relating to summer. Heat-Cold.
esto perpetua [L.] (es′-to per-pet′-iu-a). May it last forever. Approval-Disapproval, Desire-Distaste, Eternity-Instantaneity, Mutation-Permanence, Regard-Disrespect.
esto quod esse videris [L.] (es′-to quod es′-sî vid-î′-ris). Be what you seem to be. Truthfulness-Falsehood.
es-top′. To preclude from averring in an action what is contrary to prior acts or admissions. Obstruction-Help.
es-topped′. Impeded. Obstruction-Help.

es-trade′. A dais. Erectness-Flatness.
es-trange′. To alienate. Amity-Hostility, Love-Hate.
es-tranged′. Disaffected. Amity-Hostility, Sociability-Privacy.
es-trange′-ment. Alienation. Amity-Hostility, Love-Hate.
estrapade [F.] (ês-tra-pad′). A rearing and kicking. Attack-Defense, Recompense-Punition.
es-treat′. To take from the rolls or record of a court. Recompense-Penalty.
es″-tu-a′-ry. A wide mouth of a tidal river. Gulf-Plain.
es″-tu-a′-tion. Boiling; agitation. Heating-Cooling.
e-su′-ri-ent. Greedily covetous. Desire-Distaste.
et cetera [L.] (et set′-e-ra). And other things. Addition-Subtraction, Admission-Exclusion, Plurality-Fraction.
et hoc genus omne [L.] (et hoc jî′-nus om′-nî). And all that sort of thing. Addition-Subtraction, Admission-Exclusion, Uniformity-Multiformity.
e′-tal-age. Show of goods. Pomp.
état-major [F.] (ê-ta′-ma-zhor′). The staff of an army. Chief-Underling.
etch. To engrave by means of a corrosive fluid. Engraving, Furrow.
etch′-ing. An engraving. Engraving.
e-ter′-nal. Everlasting. Eternity-Instantaneity; **eternal home,** Heaven-Hell.
E-ter′-nal. God. Divinity.
e-ter′-ni-ty. Time without beginning. Divinity, Eternity-Instantaneity; **an eternity,** Lastingness-Transientness; **launch into eternity,** Life-Death, Life-Killing.

ETERNITY—INSTANTANEITY.

Athanasia. Deathlessness.
Aye. Eternity.
Eternity. Infinite duration, having no beginning and no end.
Everlastingness. Endless duration.

Abruptness. The state of being abrupt or sudden.
Instantaneity. } The quality of happening after the loss of only
Instantaneousness. } an imperceptible period of time.
Suddenness. The state of being sudden.

ETERNITY—INSTANTANEITY—*Continued*

Everness. Eternity.
Immortality. The state of not being subject to death.
Perpetuation. The act of making everlasting.
Perpetuity. The state of being perpetual or everlasting; endless time.
Sempiternity. Endless future duration.

ETERNITY—*Verbal Expressions.*

Endure forever.
Go on forever. } Be eternal; *esto perpetua.* [Father Paul to his
Have no end.   country, *Blackstone*, I, i.]
Last forever.

ETERNITY—*Adjectives.*

Amaranthine. Never fading.
Ceaseless. Without a stop or end.
Coeternal. Equally eternal.
Continual. Without interruption; unceasing.
Deathless. Not subject to death; immortal.
Endless. Without end.
Eternal. Having neither beginning nor end.
Ever-flowing. Unceasing.
Evergreen. Remaining unwithered throughout the year.
Everlasting. Having no end.
Ever-living. Living always.
Having no end. Continuing forever.
Immortal. Not subject to death; undying.
Imperishable. Exempt from liability to decay; not destructible.
Incessant. Going on without interruption.
Indesinent. Perpetual.
Interminable. Having no termination or limit; endless.
Never dying.
Never ending. } Continuing always.
Never fading.
Perpetual. Continuing without intermission; everlasting.
Sempiternal. With a beginning, but without end; everlasting.
Unceasing. Never ceasing.
Undying. Imperishable; immortal.
Unending. Having no end.
Unfading. Not fading; everlasting
Uninterrupted. Ceaseless.

ETERNITY—*Adverbs.*

Always. Throughout all time.
Aye. Continually.
Constantly, etc. Without ceasing. See FREQUENCY.
Ever. Without cessation.
Evermore. For an indefinite period.
For aye. Forever.
Forever. Throughout eternity.
Forever and a day.
Forever and ever. } Forever (emphatic).
For evermore.
From age to age. Through all time.
In all ages. Always.
In secula seculorum [L.]. For ages on ages.
Perpetually, etc See *Adjectives.*
Till doomsday. Till the end of time.
Time without end. Forever.
To the crack of doom. To the end of time.
To the end of time.
"To the last syllable of recorded time." [*Macbeth*, V, v.] } Forever.
Without end. Endlessly.
World without end. Forever.

ETERNITY—*Phrases.*

Esto perpetua [L.]. Let it endure forever. See above.
Labitur, et labetur, in omne volubilis ævum [L.]. It flows, and it will flow, rolling on forever. [Horace, *Epistles*, 1, 2, 43.]
Ohne Hast, aber ohne Rast [G.]. Unhasting, but unresting. [Goethe's motto, at first said of the sun.]
Ore e sempre [It.]. Now and always.

e-ter'-nize. To make eternal. ETERNITY-INSTANTA-NEITY.
e'-ther. A colorless, volatile liquid compound; a subtle substance supposed to pervade space. HEAVINESS-LIGHTNESS, LIQUID-GAS, SENSIBILITY-INSENSIBILITY, SOLIDITY-RARITY.
e-the'-re-al. Airy; exquisite. HEAVINESS-LIGHTNESS, LIQUID-GAS, SUBSTANTIALITY-NULLITY.

INSTANTANEITY—*Denotations, etc.*

Breath. A single act of respiration; the time of a single respiration; an instant.
Burst. A sudden breaking forth.
Correct time. The exact time.
Coup [F.]. A sudden stroke; hence, the time in which the stroke is heard.
Crack. A sudden sound; hence, the time in which the sound is heard.
Epoch. An interval of time; a moment of time when a varying quantity had a certain given value.
Exact time. Time conformed as nearly as possible to a standard.
Flash. A sudden and transient blaze; hence, the time in which such a blaze is seen.
Flash of lightning. A sudden blaze of light caused by the discharge of electricity between two electrified clouds; hence, the time occupied by such a flash.
Hour. One-twenty-fourth part of a day.
Instant. A very brief portion of time.
Jiffy. A moment.
Minute. One-sixtieth part of an hour.
Moment. A period of time too short to be taken into account.
Present time. The passing moment.
Right time. Time conforming to some standard.
Second. One-sixtieth part of a minute.
Stroke of time. The time indicated by a blow made by a striking instrument.
Time. A definite portion of duration.
Time of day. The precise or appointed moment, instant, or hour from sunrise to sunset.
Time of night. The precise moment, instant, or hour from sunset to sunrise.
Trice. A very short time.
True time. Time conformable to a standard regulated by the sun.
Twinkling. The time occupied in a twinkling of light.
Very hour. }
Very time. } The precise moment.

INSTANTANEITY—*Verbs.*

Be instantaneous. See *Adjectives.*
Flash. To come or pass suddenly.
Twinkle. To flash at short intervals.

INSTANTANEITY—*Adjectives.*

Abrupt. Without notice to prepare the mind for the event.
Hasty. Done in a hurry; quick.
Instant. Closely pressing in time.
Instantaneous. Happening after an imperceptible period of time.
Momentary. Lasting a very short time.
Quick as lightning.
Quick as thought. } As quickly as possible.
Rapid as electricity.
Subitaneous. Hasty.
Sudden. Happening unexpectedly.

INSTANTANEITY—*Adverbs.*

All at once; at a stroke; at once; "at one fell swoop," at an instant; at one jump; at the same instant (see *Nouns*); *ex tempore* [L.], **without premeditation; immediately, etc., without delay** (see EARLINESS); **in a moment, etc.** (see *Nouns*); **in less than no time; in no time; instantaneously, etc.** (see *Adjectives*); *instanter* [L.], **at once; in the same breath; in the twinkling of a bed-post; in the twinkling of an eye; just then; like a shot; on the spot; on the spur of the moment;** *per saltum* [L.], **by a leap; plump, suddenly;** *presto* [It.], **quickly; slap, instantly; slapdash, etc., all at once** (see HURRY); *subito* [It.], **rapidly; suddenly** (see *Adjectives*); *uno saltu* [L], **at one leap.**

INSTANTANEITY—*Phrases.*

No sooner said than done.
Touch and go.
Tout-à-l' heure [F.]. Instantly.

eth'-ic-al. Pertaining to ethics or morals. DUTY-DERELICTION.
eth'-i-cism. Ethics. ORTHODOXY-HETERODOXY.
eth'-ics. The science of human duty. DUTY-DERELICTION, VIRTUE-VICE.
E'-thi-op. Ethiopian; black. WHITENESS-BLACKNESS.
E''-thi-o'-pi-an. A negro. Ethiopian's skin, ETHNOLOGY, MUTABILITY-STABILITY.

E″-thi-op′-ic. Relating to Ethiopians. WHITENESS-BLACKNESS.

eth′-nic. Racial. ORTHODOXY-HETERODOXY.

eth′-nic-al. Belonging to races or nations. OR-THODOXY-HETERODOXY.

eth′-nog′-ra-pher. Student of ethnography. ETH-NOLOGY.

eth-nog′-ra-phy. A science treating of man geographically and descriptively. ETHNOLOGY, HUMANITY.

eth″-no-log′-ic-al. Pertaining to ethnology. ETH-NOLOGY.

eth-nol′-o-gy. The science of the races and families of men. ETHNOLOGY, HUMANITY, KNOWLEDGE-IGNO-RANCE.

ETHNOLOGY.

Anthropography. The branch of anthropology which treats of the distribution of the human race in its different divisions.
Anthropologist. One versed in anthropology.
Anthropology. The science of man.
Anthroposophy. Knowledge of the nature of man.
Ethnographer. One who investigates ethnography.
Ethnography. The branch of knowledge which treats of the characteristics of the human family.
Ethnology. The science which treats of the division of mankind into races, their origin, distribution and relation.
Genealogy. Regular descent, of a person from progenitor.
Human race. } Mankind collectively.
Human species. }
Mankind. The human race.
Race. A tribe or nation belonging to the same stock.
Science of races.
Sociologist. One versed in sociology.
Sociology. That branch of philosophy which treats of the constitution and development of human society.
Tribe. A family or race descending from the same progenitor.

ETHNOLOGY—Nouns of Classification.

Aryan. One of the ethnological divisions of mankind called also the Indo-European.
Caucasian. A member of any of the white races of mankind.
Celtic. One of the divisions of the Caucasian race.
Ethiop. A member of the black race of mankind.
Hamitic. The black race of mankind.
Indo-European. One of the great ethnological divisions of mankind, distinguished by its white skin.
Mongolian. One of the great divisions of the human race distinguished by its copper-colored skin.
Negro. A member of the black race of mankind.
Semitic. A division of the Caucasian race.
Slavonic. A division of the Caucasian race.
Teutonic. A division of the Caucasian race.
Turanian. A race closely related to the Mongolian.

ETHNOLOGY—Adjectives.

Ethnological. Pertaining to the divisions of mankind.
Genealogical. Showing the descent from a common ancestor.
Sociological. Pertaining to the origin and history of human society.

eth″-o-log′-ic-al. Pertaining to ethics. DUTY-DERE-LICTION.

eth-ol′-o-gy. Ethics. DUTY-DERELICTION, KNOWL-EDGE-IGNORANCE.

e′-ti-o-late. To blanch; to become white. COLOR-ACHROMATISM, WHITENESS-BLACKNESS.

e″-ti-o-la′-tion. Paleness. COLOR-ACHROMATISM, WHITENESS-BLACKNESS.

e″-ti-ol′-o-gy. The science of efficient causes. KNOWL-EDGE-IGNORANCE, RATIONALE-LUCK.

et′-i-quette″. The conventional ceremonial of polite society. HABIT-DESUETUDE, POMP, SOCIETY-LUDI-CROUSNESS.

étoile, à la belle [F.] (ê-twal′, a la bel). In the open air. OUTSIDE-INSIDE, WATER-AIR.

étoile du nord [F.] (ê-twal′ dŭ nor). North star. LUMINARY-SHADE.

étourderie [F.] (ê-turd-rî′). Thoughtlessness. HEED-DISREGARD, SKILL-UNSKILFULNESS.

et″-y-mol′-o-gy. The science of the origin and derivation of words. WORD-NEOLOGY.

et′-y-mon. The root form of a word. CAUSE-EFFECT, WORD-NEOLOGY.

eu′-cha-rist. The Lord's Supper. CEREMONIAL.

eu″-cha-ris′-tic-al. Pertaining to the eucharist. CER-EMONIAL.

eu-chol′-o-gy. A liturgy or prayer-book. CEREMONIAL.

eu′-chre. A game of cards. ENTERTAINMENT-WEARI-NESS.

eu″-di-om′-e-ter. A graduated glass vessel used in the volumetric analysis of gases. HEALTHINESS-UN-HEALTHINESS, WATER-AIR.

euge [Gr.] (yu′-gî). Excellent. APPROVAL-DISAPPROVAL.

eu′-lo-gist. One who praises. FLATTERER-DEFAMER.

eu″-lo-gis′-tic. Expressing high praise. APPROVAL-DISAPPROVAL.

eu-lo′-gi-um. A formal eulogy. APPROVAL-DISAP-PROVAL.

eu′-lo-gize. To speak a eulogy upon. APPROVAL-DIS-APPROVAL.

eu′-lo-gy. A laudation. APPROVAL-DISAPPROVAL, RHETORIC.

Eu-men′-i-des. The furies. BENEFACTOR-EVILDOER, FAVORITE-ANGER, PARDON-REVENGE.

eu′-phe-mism. A figure of speech by which a more agreeable word or phrase is substituted for a more accurate one. ADULATION-DISPARAGEMENT, RHET-ORIC, SIMPLICITY-FLORIDNESS.

eu′-phe-mist. A user of euphemisms. FLATTERER-DEFAMER, SUBJECTIVENESS-OBJECTIVENESS, TASTE-VULGARITY.

eu″-phe-mis′-tic. Characterized by euphemism. FORCE-WEAKNESS, PURITY-CRUDENESS, TASTE-VUL-GARITY.

eu-phon′-ic. Pertaining to euphony. MELODY-DIS-SONANCE.

eu-phon′-ic-al. Euphonic. MELODY-DISSONANCE.

eu-pho′-ni-ous. Well-sounding. MELODY-DISSONANCE, PURITY-CRUDENESS, VOCALIZATION-MUTENESS.

eu′-pho-nism. Euphony. MELODY-DISSONANCE.

eu′-pho-ny. Agreeableness of sound. MELODY-DISSO-NANCE, PURITY-CRUDENESS, VOCALIZATION-MUTE-NESS.

Eu-phros′-y-ne. One of the Graces. LIGHTHEARTED-NESS-DEJECTION.

eu′-phu-ism. A high-flown periphrastic style. PUR-ITY-CRUDENESS, RHETORIC, SIMPLICITY-FLORIDNESS, SOCIETY-AFFECTATION.

eu′-phu-ist. One who affects refinement of language. SIMPLICITY-FLORIDNESS, SOCIETY-AFFECTATION.

eu″-phu-is′-tic. Affectedly refined. PURITY-CRUDE-NESS, SIMPLICITY-FLORIDNESS, SOCIETY-AFFECTA-TION.

eureka [Gr.] (yu-rî′-ka). I have found it. [Archimedes, in his bath.] DISCOVERY, INVESTIGATION-ANSWER.

Eu-ri′-pus. The narrow channel between Euboea and Boeotia, opposite Chalcis. GULF-PLAIN.

eu-ryth′-my. Harmony and just proportion. PRO-PORTION-DEFORMITY.

Eu-se′-bi-an. A follower of Eusebius. ORTHODOXY-HETERODOXY.

Eu-ter′-pe. One of the muses, who presided over lyric song. MUSIC.

eu-tha-na′-si-a. A painless, peaceful death. LIFE-DEATH.

e-vac′-u-ate. To abandon possession of; to discharge. ADMISSION-EXPULSION, ARRIVAL-DEPARTURE, EN-TRANCE-EXIT.

e-vac″-u-a′-tion. The act of emptying. ADMISSION-EXPULSION, ENTRANCE-EXIT, NUTRIMENT-EXCRE-TION.

e-vade′. To elude or baffle. DUTY-DERELICTION, OBSERVANCE-NONOBSERVANCE, QUEST-EVASION, RATIOCINATION-CASUISTRY.

e″-va-ga′-tion. A rambling. AIM-ABERRATION.

ev″-a-nes′-cence. Disappearance. APPEARANCE-DIS-APPEARANCE, LASTINGNESS-TRANSIENTNESS.

ev″-a-nes′-cent. Fading; fleeting. APPEARANCE-DISAPPEARANCE, GREATNESS-LITTLENESS, LASTINGNESS-TRANSIENTNESS, MAGNITUDE-SMALLNESS.

ev″-an-gel′-ic-al. Pertaining to the Gospels; orthodox. ORTHODOXY-HETERODOXY, REVELATION-PSEUDOREVELATION.

E-van′-gel-ist. A writer of one of the Gospels; a preacher. REVELATION-PSEUDOREVELATION.

e-van″-gel-is′-tic. Pertaining to the Evangelists. REVELATION-PSEUDOREVELATION.

E-van′-gel-ists. The writers of the Gospels. REVELATION-PSEUDOREVELATION.

e-van′-id. Evanescent. STRENGTH-WEAKNESS.

e-vap′-or-a-ble. Disposed to vaporize. LIQUEFACTION-VOLATILIZATION, LIQUID-GAS.

e-vap′-or-ate. To vaporize; to pass away. LASTINGNESS-TRANSIENTNESS, LIQUEFACTION-VOLATILIZATION, SUBSTANCE-NULLITY.

e-vap″-o-ra′-tion. The act of evaporating. CHEMISTRY, LIQUEFACTION-VOLATILIZATION.

e-va′-sion. The act, means, or result of eluding; escape. CRAFT-ARTLESSNESS, DUTY-DERELICTION, ENLIGHTENMENT-SECRECY, OBSERVANCE-NONOBSERVANCE, QUEST-EVASION, RATIOCINATION-CASUISTRY, TRUTHFULNESS-FABRICATION, TRUTHFULNESS-FALSEHOOD.

e-va′-sive. Elusive. ENLIGHTENMENT-SECRECY, OBSERVANCE-NONOBSERVANCE, RATIOCINATION-INSTINCT, TRUTHFULNESS-FALSEHOOD.

eve. The evening preceding some particular day. MORNING-EVENING; **on the eve of,** ANTECEDENCE-SEQUENCE, FUTURE-PAST, LASTINGNESS-TRANSIENTNESS.

e-vec′-tion. The largest inequality in the motion of the moon. ORGANIZATION-DISORGANIZATION.

e′-ven. Level; uniform; to equalize. ANTAGONISM-CONCURRENCE, CURVATION-RECTILINEARITY, EQUALITY-INEQUALITY, ERECTNESS-FLATNESS, LEVELNESS, MODIFICATION, SMOOTHNESS-ROUGHNESS, SUPREMACY-SUBORDINACY, UNIFORMITY-DIVERSITY; **be even with,** REPRISAL-RESISTANCE, SETTLEMENT-DEFAULT; **even course,** MIDCOURSE-CIRCUIT; **even now,** TIME; **even so,** ASSENT-DISSENT, COMPENSATION; **even temper,** EXCITABILITY-INEXCITABILITY; **even terms,** RIGHT-WRONG; **even tenor,** REGULARITY-IRREGULARITY, UNIFORMITY-DIVERSITY; **pursue the even tenor,** DISCONTINUANCE-CONTINUANCE, OCCUPATION, QUEST-EVASION.

e′-ven–hand′-ed. Impartial. RIGHT-WRONG, UPRIGHTNESS-DISHONESTY.

eve′-ning. The closing part of the day. MORNING-EVENING; **evening dress,** POMP, SOCIETY-LUDICROUSNESS; **evening party,** SOCIABILITY-PRIVACY; **shades of evening,** DIMNESS.

e′-ven-ness. The state of being even. EQUALITY-INEQUALITY.

E′-ven–song″. Evening Prayer DEVOTION-IDOLATRY.

e-vent′. Occurrence; outcome. OCCURRENCE-DESTINY, STRIFE-PEACE; **in the event of,** CONDITION-SITUATION, HYPOTHESIS, OCCURRENCE-DESTINY; **justified by the event,** JUSTIFICATION-CHARGE.

e-vent′-ful. Momentous. ACTIVITY-INDOLENCE, CONSEQUENCE - INSIGNIFICANCE, OCCURRENCE - DESTINY.

e′-ven-tide″. Evening. MORNING-EVENING.

e-vents′. Happenings. OCCURRENCE-DESTINY.

e-ven′-tu-al. Final. FUTURE-PAST.

e-ven″-tu-al′-i-ty. A consequential event or issue. FUTURE-PAST, OCCURRENCE-DESTINY.

e-ven′-tu-al-ly. Ultimately. CAUSE-EFFECT, FUTURE-PAST, OCCURRENCE-DESTINY.

e-ven′-tu-ate. To happen. OCCURRENCE-DESTINY

ev′-er. At all times. ETERNITY-INSTANTANEITY; **ever and anon,** FREQUENCY-RARITY; **ever changing,** MUTABILITY-STABILITY; **ever recurring,** RECURRENCE.

ev′-er so. In or to whatever conceivable degree or extent. MAGNITUDE-SMALLNESS; **ever so little,** MAGNITUDE-SMALLNESS; **ever so long,** LASTINGNESS-TRANSIENTNESS; **ever so many,** MULTIPLICITY-PAUCITY; **ever so much,** MAGNITUDE-SMALLNESS.

ev′-er-green″. Always fresh; a plant which retains its leaves all the year. CONTINUITY-INTERRUPTION, ETERNITY - INSTANTANEITY, LASTINGNESS - TRANSIENTNESS, NOVELTY-ANTIQUITY.

ev″-er-last′-ing. Infinite in duration. ETERNITY-INSTANTANEITY; **everlasting fire,** HEAVEN-HELL; **everlasting life,** OCCURRENCE-DESTINY; **everlasting torment,** HEAVEN-HELL.

ev″-er-last′-ing-ness. Infinite duration. ETERNITY-INSTANTANEITY.

ev′-er-more″. Eternally. ETERNITY-INSTANTANEITY.

e′-ver-ness. Everlastingness. ETERNITY - INSTANTANEITY.

e-ver′-sion. The act of everting. REVERSAL, REVOLUTION-EVOLUTION.

e-vert′. To turn inside out. MUTATION-PERMANENCE.

ev′-er-y. All, taken one by one. UNIVERSALITY-PARTICULARITY; **at every turn,** PRESENCE-ABSENCE; **every day,** CONVENTIONALITY-UNCONVENTIONALITY, FREQUENCY-RARITY, HABIT-DESUETUDE; **every description,** UNIFORMITY-MULTIFORMITY; **every hand against one,** FRIEND-FOE; **every inch,** ENTIRETY-DEFICIENCY, WHOLE-PART; **every other,** PERIODICITY-IRREGULARITY; **every whit,** ENTIRETY-DEFICIENCY; **in every mouth,** ASSENT-DISSENT, REPUTATION-DISCREDIT, TIDINGS-MYSTERY; **in every quarter,** EXTENSION-INEXTENSION; **in every respect,** ENTIRETY-DEFICIENCY, TRUTH-ERROR; **on every side,** ENVIRONMENT-INTERPOSITION; **every body,** UNIVERSALITY-PARTICULARITY; **every one,** UNIVERSALITY-PARTICULARITY; **every one his due,** RIGHT-WRONG; **every one in his turn,** COMMUTATION-PERMUTATION; **every where,** EXTENSION - INEXTENSION, PRESENCE-ABSENCE.

e-vict′. To expel forcibly. ADMISSION-EXPULSION.

e-vic′-tion. The act of evicting. ADMISSION-EXPULSION, ORGANIZATION-DISORGANIZATION, TAKING-RESTITUTION.

ev′-i-dence. Ground of belief. EVIDENCE-COUNTEREVIDENCE; **ocular evidence,** VISIBILITY-INVISIBILITY.

EVIDENCE—COUNTEREVIDENCE.

Admission. A conceding, acknowledging, or confessing.

Attestation. The statement made in certifying to anything as accurate or true.

Authentification. The showing of anything to be true.

Authority. That which may be appealed to in support of an action or opinion.

Certificate. A writing so signed and authenticated as to be legal evidence.

Circumstantial evidence. Evidence consisting of circumstances which furnish reasonable ground for believing as to the existence of fact.

Citation. An authority quoted.

Conflicting evidence.} Testimony in opposition to evidence already
Counterevidence. } presented.

Counterprotest. A formal objection or declaration in opposition.

Disproof. Refutation.

Evidence on the other hand.} Testimony to support an opposing side
Evidence on the other side. } or case.

Negation. Denial. See DENIAL.

Other side of the shield. Other side of a question.

Plea. An argument in favor of something desired. See PRETEXT.

Refutation. Proof of the baselessness of a charge. See PROOF-DISPROOF.

EVIDENCE—COUNTEREVIDENCE—*Continued*.

Collateral evidence. Evidence which tends to the same conclusion as direct evidence.

Comprobation. A joint attestation.

Compurgation. Act of clearing an accused person by the oaths of several others.

Confirmation. The establishment of a statement as true.

Constructive evidence. Evidence that is assumed or inferred to bear upon the question at issue.

Corroboration. The strengthening of a statement or evidence.

Credential. That which certifies one's authority.

Criterion. A standard by which to determine the correctness of a judgment or conclusion.

Cumulative evidence. Evidence that consists of portions gathered or collected one after another.

Data. Something assumed, conceded, or known as the basis of an argument.

Deed. A written instrument containing a grant signed and sealed by the grantor.

Deponent. A person who, as a witness, gives testimony in writing.

Deposition, etc. The statement of a deponent. See ASSERTION.

Diploma. A writing granting some privilege or authority.

Docket. Abstract; calendar of cases.

Document. A manuscript regarded as conveying information or evidence.

Documentary evidence. Evidence based upon documents.

Doquet. A warrant.

Ear-witness. One who testifies what he has heard.

Evidence. That which helps to bring out the truth or falsity of something.

Evidence in chief. The best evidence which the nature of the case admits.

Examination. Testimony reduced to writing.

Ex-parte evidence. Evidence relating to one side only.

External evidence. Evidence from outside sources.

Extrinsic evidence. External evidence.

Eye-witness. One who testifies to what he has seen.

Facts. True or correct statements.

Grounds. That which furnishes the basis of a judgment or conclusion.

Hearsay evidence. Testimony concerning what a witness has heard.

Indication. Anything which points out. See SIGN.

Indicator. Something which helps to prove.

Internal evidence. } The evidence of the genuineness of a document
Intrinsic evidence. } or work of literature, as furnished by its structure, contents, etc.

Oral evidence. Evidence of spoken words.

Pièce justicative [F.]. A justifying statement.

Præcognita [L.]. That which must be known in order to comprehend something else.

Premises. The basis of a judgment or conclusion.

Presumptive evidence. Evidence from which, in the absence of direct proof, a fact is presumed to exist.

Proof. Evidence establishing a point.

Ratification. Confirmation.

Record. A writing for the purpose of preserving authentic evidence of facts. See RECORD.

Reference. A note referring to some book or passage.

Seal, etc. See SIGN.

Secondary evidence. Evidence which is used when the primary evidence is not obtainable.

Signature. The name of a person, or something representing his name, written by himself as a sign of acknowledgment.

Sponsor. One who makes himself responsible for a statement of another.

Testamur. A certificate that one has passed an examination in an English university.

Testification. Testimony.

Testimony. Evidence given by a person or adduced from anything.

Voucher. Anything that serves to attest an alleged act.

Warrant. That which gives authority for some act or course.

Witness. A person who has seen or known something, and is therefore competent to give evidence concerning it.

EVIDENCE—*Verbs*.

Argue. To try to prove.

Attest. To bear witness.

Authenticate. To show to be true.

Bespeak. To give evidence of.

Betoken. To be a sign of.

Breathe. To indicate.

Certify. To give testimony of.

Cite. To refer to in support of an argument.

Confirm. To strengthen.

Reverse of the shield. Counterevidence. [The shield on one side gold, on the other silvery, as to the color of which knights fought.]

Tu quoque **argument.** "Thou also" argument; an argument in which a person assailed retorts with a similar charge.

Vindication. Successful defense.

COUNTEREVIDENCE—*Verbs*.

Check. To injure the effectiveness of an argument.

Contradict. To speak in opposition to. See DENIAL.

Contravene. To conflict with.

Countervail. To be of equal value in opposition.

Oppose. To set against.

Rebut. To repel. See DISPROOF.

Subvert. To overthrow. See sub DESTROY.

Weaken. To impair the strength of.

COUNTEREVIDENCE—*Verbal Phrases*.

Alter the case; *audire alteram partem* [L.], to hear the other side; **cut both ways; prove a negative; tell another story; turn the scale.**

COUNTEREVIDENCE—*Adjectives*

Contradictory. Tending to deny.

Countervailing. Acting to an equal extent in the opposite direction. See *Verbs*.

Unattested. Unsupported by evidence.

Unauthenticated. Not shown to be trustworthy.

Unsupported by evidence. Seemingly untrue.

COUNTEREVIDENCE—*Adverb*

Per contra [L.]. On the contrary.

EVIDENCE—VERBS—*Continued*.

Corroborate. To agree with.

Countersign. To authenticate by an additional signature.

Depose. To testify under oath.

Endorse. To approve.

Establish. To prove by a line of evidence.

Evince. To show plainly.

Imply. Contain or point to by logical inference

Indicate. To point out.

Involve. To include by necessity.

Quote. To use another's words in support of an argument.

Ratify. To confirm.

Seal. To settle beyond doubt.

Show. To make plain.

Sign. To point out.

Substantiate. To establish as true.

Support. To vindicate.

Testify. To give evidence.

Undersign. To bear witness to.

Uphold. To support or justify.

Verify. To prove the truth of.

EVIDENCE—*Verbal Expressions*.

Appeal to, to refer to in proof of; **bear out,** confirm; **bear witness; be evidence; bring forward; bring home to,** to prove conclusively to; **bring into court; bring to book,** to call to account; **bring together evidence; call forward; call into court; call to witness; carry weight,** be important; **collect evidence; confront witnesses; deliver as one's act and deed; depend upon; give evidence** (see *Nouns*); **have a case; have weight; make absolute; make good; produce witnesses; quote chapter and verse; rake up evidence; refer to witnesses; repose on; rest upon; set one's hand and seal; sign and seal; speak for itself** (see MANIFESTATION); **speak volumes.**

EVIDENCE—*Adjectives*.

Based on. Having as a foundation.

Corroborative. } Strengthening.
Confirmatory. }

Deducible. Capable of being inferred. See PROOF.

Founded on. } Based on.
Grounded on. }

Indicative. } Serving to show.
Indicatory. }

Showing. Pointing out. See *Verbs*.

EVIDENCE—*Adverbs, etc.*

According to. In agreement with.

A fortiori [L.]. With stronger reason.

By inference. To judge from,

EVIDENCE—Adverbs—*Continued.*

In corroboration of, etc. See *Nouns.*
Raison de plus [F.]. Greater reason.
Still less. With less reasons.
Still more. For greater reasons.

Under one's hand and seal.⎫ Authenticated by the signature and seal.
Under seal. ⎭
Valeat quantum [L.]. This may be taken for what it is worth.
Witness. According to.

Evidence—*Phrase.*

Dictum de dicto [L.]. Hearsay report.

e'-vi-dence. Obviousness. In evidence, VISIBILITY-INVISIBILITY.
ev'-i-dent. Plain or manifest. CERTAINTY-DOUBT, MANIFESTATION-LATENCY, PROOF-DISPROOF.
e'-vil. Morally bad. GODLINESS-UNGODLINESS, GOOD-EVIL, GOODNESS-BADNESS; evil courses, VIRTUE-VICE; evil day, PREPARATION-NONPREPARATION, WELFARE-MISFORTUNE; evil eye, APPROVAL-DISAPPROVAL, CHARITABLENESS-MALEVOLENCE, DEVOTION-CHARM, JOVE-FIEND, SIGHT-BLINDNESS; evil favored, BEAUTY-UGLINESS; evil fortune, WELFARE-MISFORTUNE; evil genius, JOVE-FIEND, WELFARE-MISFORTUNE; evil hap, WELFARE-MISFORTUNE; evil hour, OPPORTUNENESS-UNSUITABLENESS; evil lot, WELFARE-MISFORTUNE; evil one, ANGEL-SATAN; evil plight, WELFARE-MISFORTUNE; evil star, GOODNESS-BADNESS, WELFARE-MISFORTUNE; through evil report, PERSISTENCE-WHIM.
e'-vil-dis-posed''. Malicious. CHARITABLENESS-MALEVOLENCE, VIRTUE-VICE.
e'-vil-do''-er. One who does evil. BENEFACTOR-EVILDOER, GOOD-EVIL, GOODNESS-BADNESS, GOOD MAN-BAD MAN.
e'-vil-do''-ing. Wicked conduct. VIRTUE-VICE.
e'-vil-mind''-ed. Malicious. CHARITABLENESS-MALEVOLENCE, VIRTUE-VICE.
e'-vil-speak''-ing. Defamation. ADULATION-DISPARAGEMENT, APPROVAL-DISAPPROVAL, CHARITABLENESS-CURSE.
e'-vil-work''-er. A wicked person. BENEFACTOR-EVILDOER.
e-vince'. To make manifest. EVIDENCE-COUNTEREVIDENCE, PROOF-DISPROOF.
e-vis'-cer-ate. To disembowel. ADMISSION-EXPULSION, INJECTION-EXTRACTION.
e-vis'-cer-a-ted. Disemboweled. SUBSTANCE-NULLITY.
e-voke'. To call out. CAUSE-EFFECT, EXCITATION, REQUEST-EXPOSTULATION.
ev''-o-lu'-tion. Development; a mathematical process. ACTION-PASSIVENESS, CIRCUITION, CREATION-DESTRUCTION, INJECTION-EJECTION, MOVEMENT-REST, NUMBERING, PREPARATION-NONPREPARATION, REVOLUTION-EVOLUTION; military evolutions, FIGHTING-CONCILIATION.
e-volve'. To develop. CREATION-DESTRUCTION, DISCOVERY, INJECTION-EJECTION, REVOLUTION-EVOLUTION.
e-volved'. Produced by evolution. REVOLUTION-EVOLUTION.
e-volved' from. Expanded from. CAUSE-EFFECT.
e-volv'-ing. Unfolding. REVOLUTION-EVOLUTION.
e-vul'-gate. To divulge. PUBLICATION.
e-vul'-sion. Forcible extraction. INJECTION-EJECTION.
evviva [It.] (êv-vî'-va). Hurrah. APPROVAL-DISAPPROVAL.
ewe. A female sheep. FAUNA-FLORA, MALE-FEMALE.
ew'-er. A water pitcher. CONTENTS-RECEIVER.
ex animo [L.] (ex an'-i-mo). Willingly. READINESS-RELUCTANCE.
ex hypothesis [L.] (ex hai-poth'-e-sis). From the hypothesis. FORCE-WEAKNESS.
ex officio [L.] (ex of-fish'-i-o). By virtue of office. RULE-LICENSE, TRUTH-ERROR.

ex parte [L.] (ex par'-tî). Relating to one side only. DECISION-MISJUDGMENT, EVIDENCE-COUNTEREVIDENCE, SIGN.
ex pede Herculem [L.] (ex pî'-dî her'-kiu-lem). From the foot, Hercules; from a part, the whole. CONVENTIONALITY-UNCONVENTIONALITY.
ex post facto [L.] (ex post fac'-to). After the deed. EARLINESS-LATENESS, FUTURE-PAST.
ex tempore [L.] (cx tem-po'-rî). Without preparation. OPPORTUNENESS-UNSUITABLENESS, PERPETUITY-INSTANTANEITY.
ex-ac'-er-bate. To exasperate. ALLEVIATION-AGGRAVATION, INCREASE-DECREASE, TURBULENCE-CALMNESS.
ex-ac''-er-ba'-tion. The act of making more violent. FLATTERER-DEFAMER, INCREASE-DECREASE.
ex-act'. To enforce; to demand; precise. DUENESS-UNDUENESS, DUTY-DERELICTION, LIKENESS-UNLIKENESS, ORDER, PERSPICUITY-OBSCURITY, PRESUMPTION-SERVILITY, PRICE-DISCOUNT, TERSENESS-PROLIXITY, TRUTH-ERROR; exact meaning, MEANING-JARGON; exact observance, OBSERVANCE-NONOBSERVANCE; exact truth, TRUTH-ERROR.
ex-ac'-ting. Oppressive. CONTENTEDNESS-DISCONTENTMENT, DESIRE-DISTASTE.
ex-ac'-tion. The act of compelling to pay; extortion. DUENESS-UNDUENESS, ORDER.
ex-act'-i-tude. Exactness. TRUTH-ERROR.
ex-act'-ly. Accurately. ASSENT-DISSENT, TRUTH-ERROR.
ex-act'-ment. Exaction. PRICE-DISCOUNT.
ex-act'-ness. Accuracy; precision. PERSPICUITY-OBSCURITY, SIGHT-BLINDNESS.
ex-ag'-ger-ate. To increase immoderately; to magnify. ADULATION-DISPARAGEMENT, DELINEATION-CARICATURE, EXCESS-LACK, GULL-HYPERBOLE, INCREASE-DECREASE, OVERVALUATION-UNDERVALUATION.
ex-ag'-ger-a''-ted. Overstatement; hyperbole. ENLARGEMENT-DIMINUTION, GULL-HYPERBOLE.
ex-ag''-ger-a'-tion. Overstatement. ADAGE, NONSENSE, ALLEVIATION-AGGRAVATION, BRAGGING, DELINEATION-CARICATURE, GULL-HYPERBOLE, INCREASE-DECREASE, OVERVALUATION-UNDERVALUATION, TRUTHFULNESS-FABRICATION.
ex-alt'. To promote; to extol. APPROVAL-DISAPPROVAL, ELEVATION-DEPRESSION, INCREASE-DECREASE; exalt one's horn, REPUTATION-DISCREDIT.
ex''-al-ta'-tion. Act of exalting. ELEVATION-DEPRESSION, UNSELFISHNESS-SELFISHNESS.
exaltée, tête [F.] (eg-zal-tê', têt). Crazy. SANENESS-MANIAC.
ex-alt'-ed. Dignified. GENTILITY-DEMOCRACY, HEIGHT-LOWNESS, REPUTATION-DISCREDIT, UNSELFISHNESS-SELFISHNESS.
ex-am''-in-a'-tion. Investigation. EVIDENCE-COUNTEREVIDENCE, INVESTIGATION-ANSWER, REFLECTION-VACANCY; post-mortem examination, LIFE-FUNERAL; undergo examination, INVESTIGATION-ANSWER.
ex-am'-ine. To investigate critically. HEED-DISREGARD, INVESTIGATION-ANSWER.
ex-am'-in-er. One who examines. INVESTIGATION-ANSWER.
ex-am'-ple. A pattern. CONVENTIONALITY-UNCON-

VENTIONALITY; **bad example**, GOOD MAN-BAD MAN, INSTRUCTOR-PUPIL; **good example**, GOOD MAN-BAD MAN; **make an example of**, RECOMPENSE-PENALTY; **set a good example**, VIRTUE-VICE.

ex-an′-i-mate. Inanimate. ACTIVITY-INDOLENCE, LIFE-DEATH.

ex′-arch″. A provincial governor of the Byzantine emperor. CHIEF-UNDERLING.

ex-as′-per-ate. To irritate exceedingly. ALLEVIATION-AGGRAVATION, FAVORITE-ANGER, INCREASE-DECREASE, TURBULENCE-CALMNESS.

ex-as″-per-a′-tion. Extreme anger. ALLEVIATION-AGGRAVATION, FAVORITE-ANGER.

ex′-ca-vate. To hollow out. CONVEXITY-CONCAVITY.

ex″-ca-va′-tion. A cavity. CONVEXITY-CONCAVITY.

ex″-ce-ca′-tion. Act of making blind. CONVEXITY-CONCAVITY, SIGHT-BLINDNESS.

ex-ceed′. To surpass. INCREMENT-DECREMENT, MODERATION-SELFINDULGENCE, SUPREMACY-SUBORDINACY, TRANSCURSION-SHORTCOMING.

ex-ceed′-ing. Surpassing. INCREASE-DECREASE, INCREMENT-REMNANT.

ex-ceed′-ing-ly. To an unusual degree. MAGNITUDE-SMALLNESS.

ex-cel′. To outdo. SUPREMACY-SUBORDINACY; **excel in**, SKILL-UNSKILFULNESS.

ex′-cel-lence. Superiority. GOODNESS-BADNESS, SKILL-UNSKILFULNESS, VIRTUE-VICE.

excellence, par [F.] (ek-sel-ɑn′s′, par). Surpassing all. CONSEQUENCE-INSIGNIFICANCE.

ex′-cel-len-cy. A title of honor. TITLE.

ex′-cel-lent. Having very good qualities. GOODNESS-BADNESS, VIRTUE-VICE.

ex-cen′-tric. Out of the center. OUTSIDE-INSIDE.

ex″-cen-tric′-i-ty. Distance between center and focus of an ellipse or hyperbola. OUTSIDE-INSIDE.

ex-cept′. To exclude; leaving out. ADDITION-SUBTRACTION, CHOICE-REJECTION, CONVENTIONALITY-UNCONVENTIONALITY, INCLUSION-OMISSION.

ex-cept′-ing. Leaving out. ADDITION-SUBTRACTION.

ex-cep′-tion. That which is omitted. APPROVAL-DISAPPROVAL, CONVENTIONALITY-UNCONVENTIONALITY, INCLUSION-OMISSION, MODIFICATION; **take exception**, APPROVAL-DISAPPROVAL, FAVORITE-ANGER, MODIFICATION.

ex-cep′-tion-a-ble. Objectionable. APPROVAL-DISAPPROVAL, GOODNESS-BADNESS, INNOCENCE-GUILT.

ex-cep′-tion-al. Unusual. CONSTITUENT-ALIEN, CONVENTIONALITY-UNCONVENTIONALITY, HARMONY-DISCORD, MODIFICATION.

ex-cep′-tions. Fault-finding. FAVORITE-MOROSENESS, FAVORITE-QUARRELSOMENESS.

exceptis excipiendis [L.] (ex-sep′-tis ex-sip-i-en′-dis). Proper exceptions having been made. MODIFICATION.

ex-cern′. To excrete. ADMISSION-EXPULSION.

ex-cerp′-ta. Passages extracted. CHOICE-NEUTRALITY, DIGEST, MARK-OBLITERATION, WHOLE-PART.

ex-cerp′-tion. The act of making excerpts. CHOICE-NEUTRALITY.

ex-cess′. Unwonted degree or abundance. EXCESS-LACK, INCREMENT-REMNANT, MODERATION-SELFINDULGENCE, SUPREMACY-SUBORDINACY; **in excess**, EXCESS-LACK.

EXCESS—LACK.

Accumulation. The result of repeated additions.

Avalanche. A great or overwhelming influx of anything.

Bonanza. A very profitable investment.

Bonus. An amount given in excess of the stipulation.

Burden. A heavy load; something often repeated or dwelt upon.

Congestion. An excessive and unhealthy accumulation.

Crowd. A large number of persons close together.

Drug. An article of slow sale, or of no demand.

Drug in the market. A commodity unsalable, usually from oversupply.

Duplicate. An exact copy or reproduction.

Embarras de richesse [F.]. Oversupply of material.

Engorgement. Condition of being filled to excess, as an organ of the body.

Enough in all conscience. Quite enough.

Epact. Excess of the solar year over twelve lunar months.

Excess. That which passes beyond what is ordinary, required, allowed, proper, fit, etc.

Exorbitance. Quality of being excessive in degree or amount: applied to demands or requirements.

Expletive. An interjection used for emphasis only.

Extravagance, etc. See EXTRAVAGANCE.

Exuberance. Quality resulting from a fertile or sometimes excessive source.

Glut. Full supply; supply to loathing.

Heap. A large number of things piled up together.

Intemperance. See MODERATION-SELFINDULGENCE.

Inundation. An overflowing abundance.

Lavishment. Expenditure in a profuse manner.

Lion's share. The greater part.

Load. As much as can be carried, often with difficulty.

Luxury. Free indulgence in rich food, clothing, furniture, etc.

Margin. A border, edge; difference between cost and selling price.

More than enough. Excess.

Nimiety. State of being in excess.

Overdose.

Overflow. } Greater quantity than is necessary

Overmeasure.

Overplus.

Oversupply. } That which remains above the quantity needed.

Pleonasm. See TERSENESS-PROLIXITY.

Plethora. Superabundance of blood.

Profuseness. Rich abundance, in relation to conscious agents.

A beggarly account of empty boxes. Poverty.

Banyan day. A day of poor fare.

Bare subsistence. Hardly enough to live on.

Dearth. Great scarcity of provisions, etc.

Deficiency. State of being below the standard, or less than there ought to be.

Depletion. A state of reduction from use, waste, etc.

Dole. That which is doled out as a charitable gift.

Drought. Dry weather continued till it injures vegetation.

Ebb-tide. The tide when it is out.

Emptiness. State of containing nothing.

Exigency. State of, or a case requiring immediate attention.

Famine. A grievous dearth.

Flaccidity. Want of firmness or elasticity

Half rations. Scarcity of food.

Imperfection, etc. See FAULTINESS.

Inadequacy.

Inadequateness. } State of not being adequate.

Inanition. Exhaustion from lack of nourishment.

Incompetence. State of being not competent. See ENOUGH.

Indigence. See AFFLUENCE-PENURY.

Insolvency. See SETTLEMENT-DEFAULT.

Insufficiency. State of not being sufficient. See ENOUGH.

Lack. Need.

Low water. The lowest point of ebb-tide; the lowest condition.

Need. Condition of being without that which is necessary.

None to spare. Just enough.

Paucity. Fewness of number.

Pittance. A meager allowance.

Poorness. The condition of lacking the means of a comfortable subsistence.

Poverty. Condition of being without means of support.

Scantiness. Condition of being scarcely enough.

Scarcity. State of being not abundant enough for the need or demand.

Short allowance. Scant rations, etc.

Shortcoming. See TRANSCURSION-SHORTCOMING.

Short commons. Scant fare.

Starvation. State of suffering or dying from lack of food.

Stint. A fixed or allotted amount.

Vacancy. State of being unoccupied.

Want. State of being without that which is very desirable.

EXCESS—LACK—*Continued.*

Profusion. Rich abundance, in relation to unconscious objects.
Redundance. A superfluous abundance.
Remainder. See INCREMENT-REMNANT.
Repletion. State of being completely full or supplied.
Satis superque [L.]. Enough and more than enough.
Sickener. Something that tends to sicken, nauseate, or disgust.
Superabundance. An abundance above what can be used, controlled, etc.
Supererogation. Performance of more than duty or necessity requires.
Superfluence.⎫ Superabundance: applied to materials, supplies, etc.
Superfluity.⎭
Supersaturation. State of the air when it contains more moisture than sufficient to saturate it.
Surfeit. Indulgence to satiety.
Surplus. Excess beyond what is prescribed.
Surplusage. Surplus; overplus.
Too many. More in number than enough.
Too many irons in the fire. Too many projects on hand.
Too much. More in quantity than enough.
Transcendency. Superiority of excellence.
Turgescence. State of being swollen.
Work of supererogation. See SUPEREROGATION.

EXCESS—*Verbs.*

Accloy. To fill to satiety.
Brim over. To be full to overflowing.
Bristle with. To be covered as with bristles.
Choke. To have the breathing hindered by an obstruction in the throat.
Cloy. To satiate, as with richness or sweetness.
Creep with. To be covered with beings so that the surface seems to be moving.
Deluge. To cover with vast quantities of water by heavy rains.
Drench. To wet thoroughly by pouring or sprinkling.
Drug. To oversupply.
Drug the market. To oversupply the market.
Exaggerate. See GULL-HYPERBOLE.
Flood. To cover with water, as by overflow of a river's banks, etc.
Flow over. To be more than full.
Glut. To fill or supply to excess.
Go a begging. Be without market value.
Gorge. To fill the stomach greedily.
Hang heavy on hand. To have more than one can use; said of time.
Inundate. To cover by overflowing.
Kill the slain. To do what is already done.
Know no bounds. To have no bounds.
Lay on thick. To use extravagantly, as flattery.
Lavish. See EXTRAVAGANCE.
Load. To put on all one can carry.
Meet one at every turn. To see very frequently.
Overabound. Be too plentiful.
Overburden. Overtask.
Overcharge. To charge too much.
Overdo. To do or use too often
Overdose. To give too much, as of a medicine.
Overfeed. To feed too much.
Overflow. To run over.
Overlay. To put a new surface on, as to overlay with silver; to occupy fully.
Overload. To place too heavy a load upon.
Overrun. To run over.
Overshoot the mark. See TRANSCURSION.
Overstock. To have too much of any article
Overwhelm. To overcome completely.
Pile up. To accumulate.
Remain on one's hands. To be unsalable on account of oversupply.
Roll in. See ENOUGH.
Run over. To flow over.
Run riot. To act or move without restraint.
Suffocate. To abound exceedingly.
Superabound. To abound in larger quantities than can be used.
Supersaturate. To fill with moisture so as to contain more than sufficient to saturate it.
Surcharge. Overload; overburden.
Swarm. To be in great numbers, like bees.
Wallow in. See ENOUGH.
Well over. To flow over, as water from a spring.
Whelm. To immerse deeply; cover completely.

EXCESS—*Verbal Expressions.*

Butter one's bread on both sides. To go to excess.
Carry coals to Newcastle. To do anything unnecessary.

LACK—*Verbs.*

Be insufficient. See *Adjectives.*
Be in want. See *Verbs.*
Caret [L.]. It lacks.
Come short of. See TRANSCURSION-SHORTCOMING.
Do insufficiently, etc. See *Adverbs.*
Drain of resources. Exhaust the means of support or revenue.
Impoverish. See PROVISION-WASTE.
Lack. To be without; usually limited to one thing.
Live from hand to mouth. To incur expenses to the limit of one's wages.
Need. To be without what is necessary.
Not suffice. Not be sufficient.
Put on short allowance. To give less food or money than usual.
Render insufficient, etc. See *Adjectives.*
Require. To claim on the ground of necessity or right.
Run dry. To become dry; as a stream.
Scotch the snake. Do incompletely; wound slightly.
Stint. To limit or bound.
Want. To be without what is very desirable.

LACK—*Adjectives.*

At a low ebb. In a low condition.
At the end of one's tether. At the end of one's resources.
Bare. Without ornament, as bare walls.
Deficient. Below the standard, or less than there ought to be.
Denuded of. Stripped of its covering or appendages.
Destitute of. Without that which is necessary or desirable.
Devoid of. Without that which naturally does or may belong there.
Drained. Empty of wealth, resources, etc.
Dry. Free from moisture; lacking interest
Empty. Containing nothing.
Empty-handed. Without help or resources.
Famine-stricken. Suffering from famine; said of a people or land.
Famished. Suffering or dead from lack of nourishment, especially water.
Half-starved. Deprived of food.
Ill-furnished. Not well fitted out.
Ill-off. Poor or unfortunate.
Ill-provided. Not having much on hand, or not in a state of readiness.
Ill-stored. Poorly supplied.
Imperfect. See FAULTLESSNESS-FAULTINESS.
Inadequate. Not adequate. See ENOUGH.
Incompetent. Not competent. See ENOUGH.
In debt. Owing something.
Insufficient. Not sufficient. See ENOUGH.
In want. See *Nouns.*
Jejune. Devoid of life, point, or interest.
Meager. Deficient in quantity or quality.
Not enough, etc. See ENOUGH.
Not to be had. Scarce.
Not to be had at any price.⎫ Very scarce.
Not to be had for love or money.⎭
Out of. Without.
Perfunctory. See CAREFULNESS-CARELESSNESS.
Poor. Lacking the means of a comfortable subsistence.
Scant. Scarcely enough.
Scarce. Not abundant enough for the need or demand.
Scrimp. Short; scanty.
Scurvy. Vile; mean; low; vulgar.
Short of. Lacking.
Slack. Lacking diligence, promptness, speed, etc.
Spare. Scanty; thin; lean.
Sparing. Slight.
Starved. Suffering or dead from hunger.
Starveling. Failing to meet the needs or requirements.
Stingy. Meanly ungenerous.
Stinted. Limited.
Thin. Not crowded, abundant, or thick.
Too little. Not enough.
Unequal to. Inadequate for the purpose.
Unfed. Unprovided with food.
Unfurnished. Not fitted up.
Unprovided. Not in a state of readiness; with nothing on hand.
Unreplenished. Without being filled up again.
Unstored. Not collected together.
Unsupplied. Without supplies.
Untreasured. Despoiled of treasure.
Vacant. To be unoccupied.
Wanting, etc. See *Verbs.*

EXCESS—LACK—*Continued.*

EXCESS—Verbal Expressions—*Continued.*

Employ a steam engine to crack a nut. To use great efforts to do a small thing.
Gild refined gold. To do what is already done.
Paint the lily. To attempt to beautify what is as beautiful as possible. "To gild refined gold, to paint the lily, is wasteful and ridiculous excess." [Shakespeare, *King John*, IV, ii.]
Pisces natare docere [L.]. To teach fishes to swim.
Put butter upon bacon. To do anything unnecessary.
Send coals to Newcastle. See Carry coals to Newcastle.
Teach one's grandmother to suck eggs. To teach one what one already knows.

EXCESS—*Adjectives.*

Adscititious. Supplemental; additional. See Addition.
Crammed to overflowing. Gorged.
De trop [F.]. Too much.
Drenched. Wet from being poured or sprinkled on.
Dropsical. Resembling dropsy.
Duplicate. Exactly copied.
Excessive. Passing beyond what is ordinary, required, fit, etc.
Exorbitant. Excessive in degree or amount; applied to demands.
Expletive. Inserted or added for emphasis.
Extravagant. See Extravagance.
Exuberant. Copious and rich. See *Nouns.*
Filled to overflowing. Gorged.
Gorged. Filled by eating greedily.
In excess. More than sufficient.
Inordinate. Not limited; said of human desires.
Lavish. See Extravagance.
Needless. Unnecessary.
Obese. Encumbered with flesh or fat.
On one's hands. Not to be used or sold.
Over and above. Being more than required.
Overcharged, etc. See *Verbs.*
Overflowing. Running over.
Overfond. Fond to excess.
Overmuch. More than necessary.
Overweening. Arrogant in one's thoughts or claims.
Plethoric. Evincing plethora.
Prodigal. See Extravagance.
Profuse. Richly abundant.
Ready to burst. Gorged.
Redundant. Abundant to superfluity.

ex-ces'-sive. Extreme. Magnitude-Smallness, Supremacy-Subordinacy.
ex-cess'-ive-ly. Immoderately. Magnitude-Smallness.
ex-change'. To barter; traffic. Alienation, City-Country, Commutation-Permutation, Exchange, Interdependence, Market; **bill of exchange,** Security; **exchange blows,** Strife-Peace.

EXCHANGE.

Agiotage. The maneuvering of men in changing the prices in the stock market.
A Roland for an Oliver. Tit for tat; to give in return as good as you receive; one hero of romance for another.
Bargain. An agreement between parties concerning the sale of anything.
Bargain and sale. A contract for the sale and conveyance of valuable property, the operative words of such contract.
Barter. The exchanging of goods.
Brokery. The work or business of a broker.
Business. Mercantile or commercial enterprise.
Buying and selling. Acquiring property and disposing of it.
Commerce. The buying and selling of commodities, especially when carried on on a large scale and between distant places.
Commercial enterprise. The carrying on of commerce.
Commutation. An exchange of commodities.
Composition. The settling of a debt or other disagreement by a money consideration.
Custom. Frequenting a place of business to make purchases.
Dealing. Carrying on business transactions.
Exchange. The act of giving one thing for another.
Free trade. Commerce not restricted by any duties.
Interchange, etc. The mutual exchange of property between persons. See Commutation-Permutation.

LACK—Adjectives—*Continued.*

"**Weighed in the balances and found wanting.**" Lacking a necessary qualification; *Tekel.* [*Daniel* v, 27.]
Without resources, etc. Without that which can be turned to aid. See Means.

LACK—*Adverbs.*

Failing. Lacking.
For want of. Because of the lack of.
In default of. Owing to lack or failure of.
Insufficiently. See *Adjectives.*

EXCESS—Adjectives—*Continued.*

Replete. Completely full or supplied.
Running down. Going to waste.
Running over. More than full.
Running to waste. Having more than is sufficient.
Spare. Over and above what is necessary.
Superabundant. More than can be used or controlled.
Supererogatory. Not required by duty.
Superfluous. Superabundant; said of things material.
Supernumerary. Beyond the number stated. See Store.
Supersaturated. See *Verbs.*
Supervacaneous. Needless.
Too many.
Too much. } More than enough.
To spare. More than enough.
Turgid. Swollen.
Uncalled for. Unnecessary.
Unnecessary. Needless.

EXCESS—*Adverbs.*

Aburst; beyond measure; beyond the mark (See Transcursion)**; extra; out of measure; over; over and above; over head and ears; overmuch; too; too far; too much; up to one's ears; up to one's eyes; without measure; with . . . to spare.**

EXCESS—*Phrases.*

Acervatim [L.]. In heaps.
Fortuna multis dat nimium, nulli satis [L.]. Fortune to many gives too much, to none enough. [Martial, 10, 12, 2.]
It never rains but it pours.

Jobbing. The business of buying goods from importers and manufacturers and selling to retailers.
Mercature. Traffic; commerce.
Negotiation. Business transaction between different countries.
Nundination. Buying and selling at fairs.
Quid pro quo [L.]. Something for something; an exchange.
Scorse. Exchange; trade.
Shopping. Visiting of shops or stores to buy goods.
Speculation. A risky investment of money with the expectation of great gain.
Stockjobbing. The business of dealing in stocks.
Trade. Business of exchanging commodities by buying and selling for money.
Traffic. The interchange of goods.
Transaction. The doing of any business.
Truck system. The giving of goods instead of money as wages.

EXCHANGE—*Verbs.*

Ask. To demand as a price.
Bargain. To make a contract for the sale or exchange of goods.
Barter. To exchange one commodity for another without using money.
Beat down. To contend for a lower price.
Be in business. To be engaged in some method of exchange.
Be in the city. To be in business.
Bid for. To make an offer for anything.
Buy and sell. To engage in trade.
Buy in the cheapest and sell in the dearest market. To trade advantageously.
Carry on a trade. To buy and sell.
Chaffer. To haggle about a price.
Charge. To ask a price.
Cheapen. To lower the price.
Commutate, etc. To exchange one thing for another. See Commutation.
Compound for. To settle for less than the sum due.
Deal in. To exchange a particular commodity.

Deal with. To trade with.
Do business with. To trade with.
Drive a bargain. To make a bargain after persistent effort
Drive a trade. To make a trade after much haggling.
Employ one's capital in. To do business in.
Exchange. To give in consideration of something received as an equivalent.
Give and take. To average gains and losses.
Give a sprat to catch a herring. To give up something of little value to get something of great value.
Haggle. To quibble about the terms of a bargain
Have dealings with. To do business with.
Higgle. To dispute for a small advantage in buying and selling.
Huckster. To deal in articles of little value.
Interchange, etc. To give and take. See COMMUTATION-PERMUTATION.
Keep an account with. To do business with.
Keep a shop. To be engaged in a mercantile business on a small scale.
Make a bargain. To trade to advantage.
Negotiate. To treat with another concerning a business transaction.
Nundinate. To traffic at fairs.
Open an account with. To begin a protracted business relationship.
Outbid. To bid higher than somebody else.
Ply a trade. To practise a trade.
Rig the market. To change the market price by fraud.
Scorse. To trade.
Speculate. To make risky purchases or investments with the hope of large gain.
Stickle. To contend over small matters.
Stickle for. To contend for a small advantage.
Strike a bargain, etc. To obtain a bargain. See CONTRACT.
Swop. To exchange.
Trade. To buy and sell or engage in business.
Trade with. To have business relations with.
Traffic. To carry on business.
Transact business with. To do business.
Truck. To barter; peddle.
Underbid. To bid less than somebody else.

EXCHANGE—*Adjectives.*

Commercial. Pertaining to commerce.
For sale. Offered to those who want to buy.
Interchangeable. Capable of being exchanged
In the market. Offered for sale.
Marketable. Fit to be sold; in demand
Mercantile. Pertaining to buying and selling.
Retail. Concerned in selling goods in small quantities.
Staple. Established in trade, as an article of commerce
Trading. Employed in commerce.
Wholesale. Concerned in selling goods in large quantities.

EXCHANGE—*Adverb.*

Across the counter. In a business manner.

EXCHANGE—*Phrases.*

Cambio non è furto [It.]. Exchange is no robbery.
Lettre de créance [F.] Letter of credit.

ex-cheq'-uer. The treasury of a state. TREASURY; **baron of exchequer,** JUDGE; **court of exchequer,** TRIBUNAL; **exchequer bill,** MONEY.
ex-cise'. An internal revenue tax. ADDITION-SUBTRACTION, PRICE-DISCOUNT.
ex-cise'-man. An officer who collects duties, and guards against violation of the excise law. JUDICATURE.
ex-ci'-sion. Pruning. ADDITION-SUBTRACTION.
ex-ci'-ta-ble. Easily excited. FAVORITE-QUARRELSOMENESS.
ex-ci"-ta-bil'-i-ty. Susceptibility to excitement. EXCITABILITY - INEXCITABILITY, FAVORITE - QUARRELSOMENESS, SENSITIVENESS-APATHY.

EXCITABILITY—INEXCITABILITY.

Agitation. Disturbance of thoughts or feelings. See AGITATION.
Agony. Intense mental suffering, shown like that of a wrestler in the games.
Anger. Keen displeasure felt at a wrong, real or supposed. See ANGER.
Boiling. State of being violently aroused.
Boisterousness. Unchecked merriment. See *Adjectives.*
Burst Sudden outbreak.
Delirium. Frantic condition of the mind.
Desperation. Utter hopelessness.
Disquiet. } Uneasiness of mind.
Disquietude. }
Distraction. Lack of unity of mind in action because of pain, etc.
Ebullition. Boiling.
Effervescence. Lively exhibition of feeling.
Fascination. Charm.
Ferment. State of unrest, as in fermentation.
Fever. State of great unrest, as in heat.
Fidgetiness. Tendency of the mind to change from one thing to another.
Fidgets. Condition of restless nervousness.
Fierceness. Savageness of mood. See *Adjectives.*
Fieriness. Irritability.
Fire. Liveliness of feeling.
Fit. Impulsive activity.
Flame. Outburst.
Flurry. }
Flush. }
Fluster. } Sudden disturbance.
Flutter. }
Fume. Fretful anger.
Furor. } Unbounded excitement.
Furore. }
Fury. Fierceness.
Fuss. Much ado about nothing.
Gust. A sudden violent outburst of feeling, as from wind.
Heat. Excitement.
Hurry. Injurious haste
Hysterics. Uncontrolled excitement.
Impatience. Fretfulness.
Impetuosity. Absence of reserve

Calmness. State of being unruffled.
Composure. State of having the emotions completely controlled.
Coolness. Absence of passion.
Dispassion. Display of indifference.
Endurance. Power to bear.
Equanimity. Evenness of temper in trying circumstances.
Forbearance. Endurance of offenses without retaliation.
Fortitude. A calm and unfaltering strength in all dangers.
Gravity. Seriousness of character; weight.
Hebetation. } Stupidity.
Hebetude. }
Impassibility. Inability to feel. See SENSITIVENESS-APATHY.
Imperturbability. Quality of not being moved.
Imperturbation. State of not being moved.
Indisturbance. Freedom from disturbance.
Inexcitability. Quality of not being easily excited.
Inirritability. Quality of not being easily provoked.
Longanimity. Disposition to endure offenses.
Long-sufferance. Passive allowance.
Moderation. The habit of staying within bounds.
Passiveness. Inaction; placidity. See VIGOR-INERTIA.
Patience. The quality of enduring without complaint.
Patience of Job. Great patience, like that shown by the Biblical character Job.
Patience on a monument, smiling at grief. [Shakespeare, *Twelfth Night*, II, iv.]
Patience sovereign o'er transmuted ills. Patience that overcomes all evils. [Samuel Johnson, *Vanity of Human Wishes*, 362.]
Peace of mind. Calmness or freedom from excitement.
Philosophy. Fortitude.
Placidity. Evenness of temper.
Quakerism. Affected seriousness
Quiet. } Absence of excitement.
Quietude. }
Repression of feeling. Control of one's emotions.
Resignation. Unconcern for results.
Restraint. Bridling of the emotions. See RELEASE-RESTRAINT
Sang froid [F.]. Cold blood; indifference.
Self-command. }
Self-control. } Calm control of one's powers under trying circumstances.
Self-possession. }

EXCITABILITY—INEXCITABILITY—*Continued.*

Self-restraint. Control of one's passions.
Infatuation. Passion weakening the judgment.
Intolerance. Unwillingness to endure.
Intoxication. High degree of excitement, as from drink or a poisoned arrow.
Irritability. The quality of being easily provoked. See FAVORITE-QUARRELSOMENESS.
Itching. Teasing uneasiness, allayed by rubbing, as an "itching palm" to be rubbed with gold [Shakespeare, *Julius Cæsar*, IV, iii]; "itching ears" [II *Timothy* iv, 3]. See DESIRE.
Non-endurance. Lack of power of endurance.
Outbreak. } Demonstration.
Outburst. }
Paroxysm. Sudden and violent activity.
Passion. Overpowering agitation of mind, in which reason suffers.
Perturbation. Thorough disquiet.
Phrenzy. Irrational excitement.
Pother. Confused excitement continuing for a long time.
Quixotism. Chivalry or philanthropy run mad with amiable madness, as in *Don Quixote.*
Rage. Raving anger.
Raving. Wild, incoherent talk.
Restlessness. Disturbance of mind.
Ruffle. Tumult.
Scene. Show of excitement.
Stew. A state of worry.
Storm. } A furious commotion.
Tempest. }
Tête montée [F.]. The head raised.
Thrill. A quiver running through the body See EMOTION.
Trepidation. Excited alarm.
Tumult. High excitement.
Turbulence. State of great disorder.
Vehemence. Excessive passion.
Violence. State of being furious. See TURBULENCE.
Whiff. Puff; outbreak.
Wincing. Trembling from excitement.

EXCITABILITY—*Verbs.*

Chafe. To be provoked.
Fidget. To be in a state of nervousness.
Foam. } To be furious.
Fume. }
Fuss. To make much ado about nothing.
Rage. To be violent in anger.
Rant. To utter high-sounding but meaningless language.
Rave. To speak wildly.
Tear. To distress violently.
Toss. To make or be restless.
Wince. To twist or give way under pain.

EXCITABILITY—*Verbal Expressions.*

Battre la campagne [F], to talk at random; **bear ill,** to suffer unwillingly; **be impatient; be in a stew,** to worry; **be out of all patience; boil over, break out, burst into a flame, burst out, champ the bit;** *faire le diable à quatre* [F.], to play the devil; **fire up, flame up, flare up, fly off, fly off at a tangent, fly out; go into hysterics, go mad, go off, go wild, lose one's temper,** etc. (see FAVORITE-ANGER), to be restless or excited; **not be able to bear** (see INEXCITABILITY); **play the deuce, run amuck, run mad, run riot, run wild,** to be uncontrolled; **take fire,** to become aroused; **toss on one's pillow,** to have something disturbing the mind.

EXCITABILITY—*Adjectives.*

Boisterous. Noisy.
Burning. Producing an intense feeling.
Chafing. Fretful. See sub *Verbs.*
Clamorous. Making a great outcry.
Delirious. Raving.
Demonstrative. Making a great show.
Electric. Thrilling.
Enthusiastic. Filled with enthusiasm.
Excitable. Easily roused up.
Excited. Stirred up.
Exciting. Producing excitement. See EXCITATION.
Fanatical. Showing unreasonable enthusiasm.
Febrile. Feverish.
Feverish. Highly excited.
Fidgety. Nervous.
Fierce. Unrestrained.
Fiery. Easily wrought up.
Furious. Raging.
Fussy. Paying too much attention to trifles.

Serenity. Freedom from anxiety.
Sobriety. Habitual freedom from inebriation.
Staidness. Absence of flightiness. See *Adjectives.*
Stoicism. Indifference to pleasure and pain. [A stoic of the woods, a man without a tear. Campbell, *Gertrude of Wyoming*, i, 23.]
Stupefaction. A state of dulness.
Subjugation of feeling. Bringing feeling under the yoke of reason
Submission. Spirit of humility. See YIELDING.
Sufferance. Passive allowance.
Supportance. Submission.
Tolerance. Endurance of opinions differing from one's own.
Tranquillity. } Freedom from agitation, etc. See TURBULENCE-
Tranquillization. } CALMNESS.

INEXCITABILITY—*Verbs.*

Abide. To endure.
Abide with. To have patience with.
Aby. To endure.
Acquiesce. To agree without opposition.
Æquam servare mentem [L.]. To preserve an even temper.
Allay one's excitability. See EXCITABILITY.
Appease. To allay anger. See TURBULENCE-CALMNESS.
Bear. To put up with.
Bear the brunt. To endure; to sustain the heaviest part.
Bear well. } Have patience with.
Bear with. }
Be borne. } Endured patiently
Be endured. }
Bide. To endure.
Brave. To meet with courage.
Brook. Tolerate.
Calm down. To grow calm.
Check oneself. } To restrain one's passions.
Cool down. }
Digest. To submit to. [You shall digest the venom of your spleen though it do split you. Shakespeare, *Julius Cæsar*, IV, iii, 47.]
Disregard. To pay no attention to.
Eat. To endure submissively
Endure. To suffer; to bear.
Faire aller [F.]. To allow to do as it pleases.
Go down. } To endure.
Go through. }
Grow cool. To overcome excitement.
Keep one's countenance. To appear unaffected.
Laisser aller [F.]. To let go as it will.
Live and let live. To have regard for others.
Make a virtue of necessity. To seem to do willingly what is done by compulsion. [Chaucer, *Knight's Tale*, 3044.]
Make light of. To treat with contempt.
Make oneself easy. } To drive away some care.
Make one's mind easy. }
Make the most of. To interpret in the best or worst possible meaning.
Master one's feelings. To exercise self-control.
Overcome one's excitability. See EXCITABILITY
Pocket. To put up with.
Propitiate. To give satisfaction for an offense.
Put a good face on. To assume an indifferent air.
Put up with. To endure.
Reconcile oneself to. To yield to.
Render insensible. See SENSITIVENESS-APATHY.
Repress. To keep checked. See RELEASE-RESTRAINT.
Repress one's excitability.
Resign oneself to. To yield to willingly
Rub on. To live on in spite of difficulty.
Set one's mind at ease. } To cease to have care about something.
Set one's mind at rest. }
Stand. } To endure quietly.
Stomach. }
Submit. To yield.
Submit with a good grace. To yield calmly.
Suffer. To allow.
Support. To undergo.
Swallow. To put up with.
Take coolly. Not to be affected by.
Take easily. To be not much concerned about.
Take in good part. Take with good grace.
Take it easy.
Take things as they come. } To make little attempt to control.
Take things easily. }
Take up with. To become familiar with; to enjoy.

EXCITABILITY—INEXCITABILITY—*Continued.*

EXCITABILITY—Adjectives—*Continued.*

Hasty. Quickly aroused to anger.
Hurried. Excited.
Hurry-skurry. Confused; in a bustle.
Hysterical. Fitfully emotional.
Impassioned. Expressing great emotion.
Impatient. Restless.
Impetuous. Acting spontaneously.
Impulsive. Acting without forethought.
Inextinguishable. Uncontrollable, like the laughter of the gods at Vulcan. [Homer, *Iliad*, 1, 763.]
Intolerant. Not enduring difference of opinions, etc.
Irrepressible. Not to be checked.
Irritable. Easily provoked. See FAVORITE-QUARRELSOMENESS.
Mad. Raging.
Madcap. Acting in a rash or giddy manner.
Mercurial. Sprightly; lighthearted; like the god Mercury, or quicksilver.
Mettlesome. High-spirited.
Moody. Variable in humor.
Passionate. Subject to suffering from overpowering feeling.
Rabid. Inordinately excited. See DESIRE.
Rampant. Unbridled.
Restless. Fidgety.
Simmering. Gently moved by emotion.
Skittish. Easily frightened.
Stanchless. Not able to be stopped.
Startlish. Timid.
Tempestuous. Stormy.
Tumultuous. Disorderly.
Turbulent. In great commotion.
Uncontrollable. Not to be controlled.
Ungovernable. Not to be governed.
Unquiet. Disturbed.
Uproarious. Making a great disturbance.
Vehement. Marked by impetuous animation.
Violent. Intense.
Volcanic. Bursting out with violence, like the chimney of the forge of Vulcan.
Wild. Greatly excited.

EXCITABILITY—*Adjective Expressions.*

In an excited state; maggoty-headed, whimsical; *noli me tangere* [L.], touch me not, **irritable; over-zealous.**

EXCITABILITY—*Interjections.*

Pish! An exclamation of contempt.
Pshaw! An exclamation of disgust.

EXCITABILITY—*Phrase.*

Maggiore fretta, minore atto [It.]. "The more haste, the less speed."

INEXCITABILITY—*Continued from Column 2.*

INEXCITABILITY—*Adverbs, etc.*

Æquo modo [L.]. In just measure.
In cold blood. Deliberately.
"Like patience on a monument smiling at grief." See page 372, 2.
Patience! and shuffle the cards.

INEXCITABILITY—*Phrase.*

Mens æqua in arduis [L.]. An equal mind in circumstances of difficulty. [Warren Hastings, on his portrait at Calcutta.]

ex″-ci-ta′-tion. The act of exciting; excitement.
ASSERTION-DENIAL, EXCITATION, VIGOR-INERTIA.

EXCITATION.

Agitation. Uncontrolled feeling.
Calling forth. A drawing out, or excitation, as of emotion.
Casus belli [L.]. A cause of war.
Enravishment. } Ecstasy of delight.
Entrancement. }
Excitation of feeling. Act of exciting; excitement.

INEXCITABILITY—Verbs—*Continued.*

Thaw. To make more lively or interesting.
Tolerate. To allow.

INEXCITABILITY—*Adjectives*

Armed with patience. Patient.
Bearing with. Enduring.
Calm. Unmoved.
Chastened. Subdued; softened.
Clement. Lenient.
Cold-blooded. Heartless.
Collected. Having all powers awake and at command.
Cool. Not excited.
Cool as a cucumber. } Not agitated.
Cool as a custard. }
Cool-headed. Not easily excited.
Demure. Grave, modest, quiet looking, like pussy.
Dispassionate. Unprejudiced.
Easygoing. Not easily aroused.
Enduring. Long-suffering. See *Verbs*.
Gentle. Mild in disposition.
Gentle as a lamb. Very gentle.
Grave. Serious in manner.
Grave as a judge. Very grave.
Imperturbable. Not easily agitated.
Inexcitable. Not easily excited.
Inirritable. Not easily provoked.
Lamb-like. Gentle; unoffending.
Long-suffering. Very patient.
Meek. Not resisting.
Mild. Showing no unpleasantness.
Mild as mother's milk. Very mild.
Patient. Bearing uncomplainingly.
Patient as Job. Very patient.
Peaceful. Not given to agitation.
Philosophic. Showing great fortitude.
Placid. Naturally calm.
Platonic. Ideal; devoid of sensual feeling.
Quiet. Temporarily at peace.
Quiet as a mouse. Very quiet.
Resigned. Submissive.
Sedate. Not buoyant.
Serene. Calm, like the night of stars.
Sober. Even-tempered; free from the wine cup.
Sober-minded.
Soft as peppermint. Very soft.
Staid. } Not fanciful.
Stayed. }
Stoical. Looking with indifference on pleasure and pain. See above.
Suaviter in modo [L.]. In a gentle manner.
Subdued. Having all excitement or passion conquered.
Submissive. Passive. See YIELDING.
Tame. Lacking in spirit.
Temperate. Not passionate.
Tolerant. Enduring cheerfully the opinions of others.
Tranquil. At peace.
Undemonstrative. Not expressing emotions by actions, etc.
Undisturbed. Not disturbed.
Unexcited. Not excited.
Unimpassioned. Not working on the emotions.
Unoffending. Harmless.
Unpassionate. Lacking in passion.
Unperturbed. Unmoved by passion.
Unresisting. Humble.
Unruffled. Not disturbed.
Unstirred. Unmoved.
Unsusceptible. Not yielding to influence easily.

(*Continued on Column* 1.)

Excitement. State of aroused feeling.
Fascination. State of being charmed.
Galvanism. Animal electricity. [Galvani.]
High pressure. The condition in which it is difficult to keep one's emotions in check.
Impressiveness, etc. Quality of exciting emotion. See *Adjectives.*
Inspiration. Influence arousing to action.
Intoxication. Excessive mental excitement. [Shot by a poisoned arrow.]
Irritation, etc. Excitement of ill-temper. See FAVORITE-ANGER.
Mental excitement. A stirring up of the nervous forces.

Passion, etc.   Intense feeling.   [Suffering.]   See EXCITABILITY.
Perturbation.   Temporary disturbance.
Piquancy.   Quality of arousing interest.
Provocation.   Conduct exciting resentment.
Ravishment.   State of being seized by intense emotion.
Repression of feeling.   A keeping of one's emotions under control.
Stimulation.   State of being spurred on.
Subjugation.   Act of subduing; bringing under the yoke.
Suscitation.   The act of exciting.
Thrill.   Quiver of excitement running through the body.
Trial of temper.   Anything which tends to stir up heat of mind or passion.
Unction.   Affected emotion, as of one anointed.

EXCITATION—*Verbs.*

Absorb.   To engross completely.
Affect.   Arouse emotions.
Agitate.   To disturb the feelings of.
Animate.   To instil life or vigor.
Arouse.   To stir up.
Astound.   To astonish; to strike with thunder.
Awake. } To stir into activity.
Awaken. }
Boil.   To be in a state of violent agitation.
Bouleverser [F.].   To upset.
Disturb.   To destroy the quiet of.
Electrify.   To startle; to give an electric shock.
Enkindle.   To inflame.
Enrapture, etc.   To delight very much.   See PLEASURABLENESS.
Evoke.   To bring or cause to come forth.
Excite.   To stir up.
Exsuscitate.   [Obs.]   To rouse up.
Fan.   Stimulate a flame.
Fascinate.   To have an irresistible influence over.
Fire.   To work up the feelings.
Flame.   To become excited.
Fluster.   To disturb the calmness of.
Foam.   To utter with rage and violence.
Foment.   To stir up strife.
Foster.   Encourage.
Fume.   To rage.
Galvanize.   To inspire with fictitious life.
Heat.   To inflame.
Impassion.   To affect with strong feeling.
Impress.   To make a deep mark on the mind.
Infect.   To imbue through sympathy.
Inflame.   To arouse.
Infuriate.   To make mad or raging.
Inspire.   To influence in a subtle manner.
Inspirit.   To impart encouragement.
Interest.   To arouse the curiosity.
Intoxicate.   To inspire with frenzy.
Irritate.   To stir up ill-temper.
Kindle.   To start excitement.
Madden.   To infuriate violently.
Mantle.   To excite or provoke.
Move.   To affect.
Overpower. } To gain control of emotions.
Overwhelm. }
Penetrate.   Affect.
Perturb.   To disturb temporarily.
Petrify.   To turn to stone; to dumfound.
Pierce.   To touch the emotions.
Pique.   To anger slightly.
Provoke.   To act so as to arouse resentment; to call forth as a challenge.
Quicken.   To enliven.
Rage.   To be moved with violent passion; to be rabid.
Raise.   To incite to action.
Rave.   To act as if mad.
Rekindle.   To stir up again.
Revive.   To give new enthusiasm to.
Rouse.   To waken or startle.
Ruffle.   Disturb.
Seethe.   To be violently excited.
Shake.   To excite suddenly.
Sharpen.   To make more intense.
Shock.   To astonish and fill with disgust.
Simmer.   To be ready to burst out with passion.
Smite.   To affect deeply.
Stagger.   To overcome by surprise.
Startle.   To excite suddenly.
Stimulate.   To arouse to action.

Sting.   To give acute pain.
Stir.   To move the spirits of.
Strike.   Surprise.
Stun.   To deprive of power from astonishment.
Suscitate.   [Obs.]   To excite.
Touch.   To affect the feelings.
Upset.   To deprive of self-possession.
Wake. } To stir up.
Waken. }
Warm.   To work up enthusiasm.
Whet.   To stimulate.

EXCITATION—*Verbal Expressions.*

Absorb the soul, take full possession of; **affect the soul; apply the torch,** start excitement; **be excited; blow the coals,** revive something; **blow up; bring new blood; call forth; call up; catch the infection,** to be influenced by; **come home to the feelings; cut to the heart, cut to the quick,** to hurt the feelings; **disturb the soul; fan into a flame,** encourage; **fan the fire,** to help keep up excitement; **fire the blood,** arouse the feelings; **flare up,** to fly into a passion; **flash up; fool to the top of one's bent,** to fool as much as one's inclination will allow; **get up,** stir up; **get up the steam, give a fillip,** arouse; **give new life to; give one a shock; give one a turn,** to frighten; **go through one,** to cause a thrilling sensation in one; **go to one's heart,** to feel deeply; **hurry on,** to hasten; **imbrue the soul; infuse life into; introduce new blood; keep the pot boiling,** to keep agitating; **keep up; lash into fury; light up; make one's blood boil,** to arouse anger or strong feeling; **penetrate the soul,** affect the soul; **pervade the soul; play on the feelings,** to move by arousing the emotions; **possess the soul; prey on the mind,** to have an injurious effect upon; **put on one's mettle,** to arouse one's utmost powers; **raise to a fever heat,** excite to the highest degree; **raise up,** to rouse up; **rake up,** to revive; **rip up,** reopen; **rivet the attention,** to hold attentive; **run mad,** to become suddenly insane, etc. (see EXCITABILITY); **set astir,** to arouse into activity; **set on fire,** to move the passions; **sink into the heart, sink into the mind,** to affect deeply; **spirit up,** to animate; **stir the blood,** to arouse; **stir the embers,** encourage; **stir the feelings; stir up,** to enliven; **strike all of a heap,** to disconcert; **summon up; touch a chord, touch a string,** to work on the feelings; **touch the heart, touch the soul,** to call forth sympathy; **touch to the quick,** to pain; **try one's temper,** to vex grievously; **turn one's head,** to deprive of good judgment; **wake up,** to become active; **warm the blood,** stir up; **work oneself up,** to give in to the emotions; **work up; work upon,** to stir up the feelings of.

EXCITATION—*Adjectives.*

Agonizing.   Causing agony; wrestling.
Appetizing.   Stimulating desire.
Astir.   Active.
Boiling.   In a state of intense emotion.
Bouleversé [F.].   Upset.
Demoniacal.   Devilish; crazy.
Distracted.   Mentally disordered; torn asunder.
Ebullient.   Boiling.
Éperdu [F.].   Bewildered.
Excited, etc.   Temporarily nervous.   See *Nouns.*
Exciting, etc.   Stirring up the spirits.   See *Verbs.*
Fervid.   Burning with zeal.
Feverish.   Restless.
Flaming.   Bursting forth with passion.
Flushed.   To be overcome by excitement.
Foaming.   Furious.
Fuming.   Exhibiting fretful passion.
Glowing.   Hot.
Haggard.   Desperate.
Hot.   Highly excited.
Hysterical.   Liable to uncontrollable outbursts of emotion.
Imposing.   Impressive.
Lost.   Bewildered.
Mad.   Raving; crazy, as with wrath.
Overpowering. } Depriving of self-control.
Overwhelming. }
Piquant.   Hurting the feelings.
Provocative.   Arousing ill-temper.
Provoquant [F.].   Provoking.
Raging.   In a violent state of emotion.
Raving.   Speaking in a frenzied manner.
Seething.   Violently agitated.
Sensational.   Stirring up excitement.
Sparkling.   Lively.
Spicy.   Marked by zest.
Swelling.   Stirred up by anger.

Tantalizing. Teasing by disappointing continually, as Tantalus.
Telling. Effective.
Thrilling. Sending quivers through the body.
Up. Excited.
Warm. Stirred by passion or excitement.
Wild. In a state of frenzy.

EXCITATION—*Adjective Expressions.*

All in a pucker, all of a twitter, much confused; **beside oneself,** crazy; **black in the face,** dejected; **boiling over,** full to overflowing; **carried away by passion; foaming at the mouth,** raging; **heart swelling,** causing the heart to swell; **high wrought,** highly excited; **in a blaze,** bursting out with emotion; **in a ferment,** in commotion; **in a fever,** in a state of great excitement; **in a quiver; in a state of excitement; in hysterics,** in an uncontrollable outburst of emotion; **more than flesh and blood can bear; on one's high ropes,** in high spirits; **on the** *qui vive,* on the alert; **out of one's wits,** crazy; **ready to burst,** violently agitated; **ready to sink,** hopeless; **red hot,** very much moved by passion; **soul-stirring; soul-subduing; soul-thrilling; spirit stirring; stung to the quick,** hurt; **with quivering lips; with tears in one's eyes; wrought up,** stirred.

EXCITATION—*Adverbs.*

Till one is black in the face. To the limit of one's powers.

EXCITATION—*Phrases.*

The blood being up, the blood boiling in one's veins, the eye glistening, the eye "in a fine frenzy rolling," the head turned, the heart beating high, the heart going pit-a-pat, the heart leaping into one's mouth, excited

ex-cite′. To rouse. EXCITATION, TURBULENCE-CALMNESS, VIGOR-INERTIA; **excite an impression,** FAVORITE-ANGER, SENSIBILITY-INSENSIBILITY; **excite attention,** HEED-DISREGARD; **excite desire,** DESIRE-DISTASTE; **excite hope,** PROPHECY; **excite fancy,** FANCY; **excite laughter,** ENTERTAINMENT-WEARINESS.

ex-ci′-ted. Agitated in feeling; stimulated. EXCITABILITY-INEXCITABILITY, EXCITATION, TURBULENCE-CALMNESS.

ex-cite′-ment. The state of being agitated; stimulation. EXCITABILITY-INEXCITABILITY, EXCITATION, FAVORITE-ANGER.

ex-ci′-ting. Stimulating. EXCITATION.

ex-claim′. To cry out abruptly. CRY-ULULATION; **exclaim against,** APPROVAL-DISAPPROVAL.

ex″-cla-ma′-tion. Interjection. VOCALIZATION-MUTENESS.

ex-clude′ To debar, to reject. CHOICE-REJECTION,

INCLUSION-OMISSION, LEAVE-PROHIBITION, SOCIABILITY-PRIVACY.

ex-clu′-ded. Debarred. INCLUSION-OMISSION.
ex-clu′-ding. Debarring. INCLUSION-OMISSION.
ex-clu′-sion. Rejection; debarment. ADMISSION-EXCLUSION, CHOICE-REJECTION, INCLUSION-OMISSION, SOCIABILITY-PRIVACY.
ex-clu′-sive. Existing alone; disposed to limit social arrangements. CONVENTIONALITY-UNCONVENTIONALITY, INCLUSION-OMISSION, LEAVE-PROHIBITION, MIXTURE-HOMOGENEITY, UNIVERSALITY-PARTICULARITY; **exclusive of,** ADDITION-SUBTRACTION, INCLUSION-OMISSION; **exclusive possession,** HOLDING-EXEMPTION; **exclusive thought,** HEED-DISREGARD.
ex-cog′-i-tate. To devise. FANCY, REFLECTION-VACANCY.
ex-cog″-i-ta′-tion. Invention. FANCY, REFLECTION-VACANCY.
ex″-com-mu′-ni-cate. To exclude from communion, or from any organization. CEREMONIAL, CHARITABLENESS-CURSE, SOCIABILITY-PRIVACY.
ex″-com-mu″-ni-ca′-tion. Exclusion from communion. CEREMONIAL, CHARITABLENESS-CURSE, SOCIABILITY-PRIVACY.
ex-co′-ri-ate. To flay. DRESS-UNDRESS.
ex-co″-ri-a′-tion. The act of excoriating. DRESS-UNDRESS.
ex′-cre-ment. Ordure. CLEANNESS-FILTHINESS, NUTRIMENT-EXCRETION.
ex-cres′-cence. Any unnatural outgrowth. CONVEXITY-CONCAVITY, EMBELLISHMENT-DISFIGUREMENT.
ex-cre′-ta. All useless matter eliminated from the bodily system. CLEANNESS-FILTHINESS, NUTRIMENT-EXCRETION.
ex-crete′. To throw off. ADMISSION-EXPULSION, NUTRIMENT-EXCRETION.
ex-cre′-tion. The act of excreting. BIOLOGY, NUTRIMENT-EXCRETION.
ex-cru′-ci-ate. To torture. SENSUALITY-SUFFERING.
ex-cru′-ci-a″-ting. Agonizing. PLEASURABLENESS-PAINFULNESS, SENSUALITY-SUFFERING.
ex-cul′-pate. To justify; to excuse. EXCULPATION-CONVICTION, INNOCENCE-GUILT, JUSTIFICATION-CHARGE, PARDON-REVENGE.
ex″-cul-pa′-tion. Vindication. DUTY-IMMUNITY, EXCULPATION-CONVICTION, JUSTIFICATION-CHARGE, PARDON-VINDICTIVENESS.

EXCULPATION—CONVICTION.

Absolution. Releasing from a transgression or sin.
Acquitment. Acquittal.
Acquittal. A clearance of blame or guilt.
Clearance. The showing of the innocence of a man by fact or argument.
Compurgation. Clearing an accused by the testimony of twelve men who swore to his innocence, he being one. [Early English laws.]
Discharge. Relief from a debt or release from confinement. See RELEASE.
Exculpation. Rescue from guilt or blame.
Impunity. Freedom from punishment.
Pardon. Remission of punishment after having been convicted of guilt. See PARDON.
Quietus. Final release from a debt or obligation; quit claim.
Reprieve. Temporary suspension of a sentence of condemnation.
Respite. A temporary relief from any pressure, or execution of sentence.

EXCULPATION—*Verbs*

Absolve. To remit from guilt or crime.
Acquit. To declare the innocence of an accused.
Assoil. To clear of, to absolve.
Clear. To free from the imputation of guilt.
Discharge. To set free from anything that threatens.
Exculpate. To free from the blame of.
Exonerate. To free from the burden of a charge.

Attainder. Condemnation of a person by legislative decree.
Attainment. An attainder; a conviction.
Attainture. State of being attainted.
Condemnation. The act of declaring one guilty.
Conviction. Finding guilty of a sin by proof.
Damnation. Condemnation.
Death-warrant. An order by the magistrate for execution of a criminal.
Proscription. Dooming to death; putting outside of the pale of law.

CONVICTION—*Verbs.*

Accuse, etc. To formally declare of having committed a crime, etc. See JUSTIFICATION-CHARGE.
Attaint. To deprive of all civil rights.
Bring home to. To lay upon with proof.
Cast. To defeat in a lawsuit, to put damages on.
Condemn. To pronounce judicial sentence upon.
Confiscate. To appropriate to the public treasury.
Convict. To prove guilty.
Damn. To condemn to everlasting punishment.
Disapprove. To regard unfavorably. See APPROVAL-DISAPPROVAL.
Doom. To sentence.
Find guilty. To publicly declare one guilty after trial.
Non-suit. To order the dismissal of a suit.
Pass sentence on. To punish.
Proscribe. To make outlaws of.

EXCULPATION—CONVICTION—*Continued.*

EXCULPATION—Verbs—*Continued.*

Let off. Not to inflict all the punishment; not to inflict any punishment; to let go free.
Let scot-free. To let go free of scot or tax.
Liberate. To free from restraint. See Release.
Pardon. To let pass without punishment a crime or transgression; to forgive. See Pardon.
Release. To let loose from confinement or obligation.
Reprieve. To temporarily withhold punishment.
Respite. To grant a respite.
Whitewash. To free from debts, as a bankrupt.

EXCULPATION—*Adjectives.*

Acquitted, etc. Freed from the charge of crime. See *Verbs.*
Unchastised. Not punished.
Uncondemned. Not found guilty.
Unpunished. Not having a penalty inflicted.

EXCULPATION—*Phrase.*

Nemo bis punitur pro eodem delicto [L.]. No one is twice punished for the same offense.

ex-cul′-pa-to-ry. Excusing. Justification-Charge.
ex-cur′-sion. A pleasure trip; digression. Circuition, Traveling-Navigation.
ex-cur′-sion-ist. One who makes an excursion. Wayfarer-Seafarer.
ex-cur′-sive. Erratic. Aim-Aberration; **excursive style,** Terseness-Prolixity.
ex-cu′-sa-ble. Justifiable. Duty-Immunity, Justification-Charge.
ex-cuse′. To exculpate; to forgive; a justification. Duty-Immunity, Justification-Charge, Pardon-Revenge, Pretext.
ex′-e-cra-ble. Accursed. Goodness-Badness, Pleasurableness-Painfulness.
ex′-e-crate. To curse. Approval-Disapproval, Charitableness-Curse, Love-Hate.
ex″-e-cra′-tion. The act of execrating. Approval-Disapproval, Charitableness-Curse.
ex′-e-cute. To carry out a work, or a sentence, as of death. Action-Passiveness, Completion-Noncompletion, Conduct, Musician, Observance-Nonobservance, Recompense-Punition, Security.
ex″-e-cu′-tion. Performance; carrying out sentence of death. Action-Passiveness, Completion-Noncompletion, Conduct, Life-Killing, Musician, Recompense-Punition, Security; **carry into execution,** Action-Passiveness, Completion-Noncompletion, Observance-Nonobservance; **put in execution,** Enterprise.
ex″-e-cu′-tion-er. One who carries into effect a death sentence. Life-Killing, Maker-Destroyer, Recompense-Scourge.
ex-ec′-u-tive. Administrative; an official charged with administering government. Conduct, Judicature, Rule-License.
ex-ec′-u-tor. A person appointed in and by a will to carry the will into effect. Agent; **to one and his executor,** Property.
ex-ec′-u-trix. A woman executor. Agent.
ex″-e-ge′-sis. Explanation of a literary work. Interpretation-Misinterpretation.
ex″-e-get′-ic-al. Interpretative. Interpretation-Misinterpretation.
ex-em′-plar. A model to be copied. Copy-Model.
ex′-em-pla-ry. Worthy of imitation. Conventionality-Unconventionality, Virtue-Vice.
exempla sunt odiosa [L.] (ex-em′-pla sunt o-di-o′-sa). Examples are offensive. Copy-Model.
exempli, moli [L.] (ex-em′-plai, mo′-lai). Of bad example. Good Man-Bad Man.

CONVICTION—Verbs—*Continued.*

Sentence. To pass penalty or sentence.
Sequestrate. To seize for the use of the government.
Sign the death-warrant. To condemn to death.
Stand condemned. Convicted after trial.

CONVICTION—*Adjectives.*

Condemnatory. Containing disapproval or censure.
Condemned. Pronounced guilty. See *Verbs.*
Damnatory. Dooming to damnation.
Non-suited. Adjudged to have abandoned his suit. See Success-Failure.
Self-convicted. Convicted by one's own self.

CONVICTION—*Phrases.*

Gibier de potence [F.]. Game for the gibbet.
Mutato nomine de te fabula narratur [L.]. Changing the name, the story is told about you.

ex-em″-pli-fi-ca′-tion. The act of exemplifying. Conventionality-Unconventionality, Interpretation-Misinterpretation.
ex-em′-pli-fy. To illustrate. Conventionality-Unconventionality, Interpretation-Misinterpretation.
exemplum, transeat in [L.] (ex-em′-plum, trans′-î-at in). Let it pass into precedent. Litigation.
ex-empt′. To grant immunity to; released from some liability. Duty-Immunity, Liberty-Subjection; **exempt from,** Holding-Exemption, Mixture-Homogeneity, Presence-Absence.
ex-emp′-tion. Immunity from some liability, requirement, or evil. Conventionality-Unconventionality, Duty-Immunity, Holding-Exemption, Leave-Prohibition, Liberty-Subjection, Modification, Presence-Absence.
ex″-e-qua′-tur. An official warrant or permission given by the executive of the government. Commission-Abrogation.
ex′-e-quies. Funeral ceremonies. Life-Funeral.
ex′-er-cise. To employ actively; to take exercise; a practising; activity for the sake of health of mind or body; occupation. Action-Passiveness, Agency, Education-Misteaching, Occupation, Toil-Relaxation, Use-Disuse; **exercise authority,** Rule-License; **exercise discretion,** Volition-Obligation, Weariness-Refreshment; **exercise oppression,** Tyranny-Anarchy; **exercise power,** Might-Impotence; **exercise the intellect,** Reflection-Vacancy.
ex″-er-ci-ta′-tion. An exercise; practise. Action-Passiveness, Toil-Relaxation, Use-Disuse.
ex-ert′. To put forth strength or ability. Enterprise; **exert authority,** Rule-License; **exert oneself,** Toil-Relaxation, Vigor-Inertia.
ex-er′-tion. Strong effort; labor. Activity-Indolence, Toil-Relaxation, Vigor-Inertia.
ex-fo′-li-ate. To scale off; to peel off. Dress-Undress.
ex-fo″-li-a′-tion. A scaling off. Dress-Undress.
ex″-ha-la′-tion. A breathing out; effluvium; emanation. Liquefaction-Vaporization, Nutriment-Excretion, Odor-Inodorousness.
ex-hale′. To breathe forth. Admission-Expulsion, Anatomy.
ex-haust′. To draw out or drain off entirely; to wear out; to weary. Completion-Noncompletion, Extravagance-Avarice, Might-Impotence, Provision-Waste, Weariness-Refreshment.
ex-haust′-ed. Used up; spent. Entity-Nonentity, Might-Impotence, Weariness-Refreshment.

ex-haus'-tion. Act of exhausting; state of being exhausted. MIGHT-IMPOTENCE, PROVISION-WASTE, WEARINESS-REFRESHMENT.

ex-haust'-ive. Thorough and complete in execution. COMPLETION - NONCOMPLETION, ENTIRETY - DEFICIENCY; **exhaustive inquiry,** INVESTIGATION-ANSWER.

ex-haust'-less. Inexhaustible. ENOUGH, INFINITY.

ex-hib'-it. To display; anything exhibited. MANIFESTATION-LATENCY, POMP.

ex''-hi-bi'-tion. The act of exhibiting. MANIFESTATION-LATENCY.

ex-hil'-a-rate. To stimulate; to cheer. LIGHTHEARTEDNESS-DEJECTION.

ex-hil'-a-ra''-ting. Enlivening. LIGHTHEARTEDNESS-DEJECTION.

ex-hort'. To importune; to advise. ADVICE, MOTIVE-CAPRICE.

ex''-hor-ta'-tion. The act of exhorting; earnest advice. ADVICE, MOTIVE-CAPRICE.

ex-hume'. To disinter. FUTURE-PAST, LIFE-FUNERAL.

ex''-hu-ma'-tion. The act of exhuming. LIFE-FUNERAL.

ex''-i-geant'. Exacting. HARSHNESS-MILDNESS.

ex'-i-gen-cy. Pressing need; distress; emergency. CONDITION-SITUATION, DESIRE-DISTASTE, DIFFICULTY-FACILITY, EXCESS-LACK, NEED.

ex'-i-gent. Urgent; exacting. CONTENTEDNESS-DISCONTENTMENT, HARSHNESS-MILDNESS, NEED.

ex''-i-gu'-i-ty. Slenderness; diminutiveness. BREADTH-NARROWNESS, GREATNESS-LITTLENESS.

ex-ig'-u-ous. Slender; minute. GREATNESS-LITTLENESS.

ex'-ile. To banish; banishment; a subject of banishment. ESTABLISHMENT-REMOVAL, EXCULPATION-PUNITION, INCLUSION-OMISSION, SOCIABILITY-PRIVACY; **voluntary exile,** SOCIABILITY-PRIVACY.

ex-il'-i-ty. Smallness. BREADTH-NARROWNESS.

ex-ist'. To be. ENTITY-NONENTITY.

ex-ist'-ence. Being, or the state of being; actuality. ENTITY-NONENTITY, LIFE-DEATH, PRESENCE-ABSENCE, SUBSTANCE-NULLITY; **come into existence,** OCCURRENCE-DESTINY.

ex-ist'-ent. Having being. ENTITY-NONENTITY.

ex-ist'-ing. Being. ENTITY-NONENTITY, TIME.

ex'-it. Place of egress; any departure; death. APPEARANCE-DISAPPEARANCE, ARRIVAL-DEPARTURE, ENTRANCE-EXIT; **give exit to,** ADMISSION-EXPULSION; **make one's exit,** ADMISSION-EXPULSION.

exitus acta probat [L.] (ex'-i-tus ac'-ta pro'-bat). The event approves the acts. PROOF-DISPROOF.

exochên, kat' [Gr.] (ex-o-kên', kat). Par excellence; preeminently. CONSEQUENCE - INSIGNIFICANCE, SUPREMACY-SUBORDINACY.

ex'-ode. A tragical conclusion. ACTING.

ex'-o-dus. A departure. ARRIVAL-DEPARTURE, ENTRANCE-EXIT.

ex-og'-e-nous. Growing by external additions. FAUNA-FLORA.

ex-on'-er-ate. To acquit; to relieve from a responsibility. DIFFICULTY-FACILITY, DUTY-IMMUNITY, EXCULPATION - CONVICTION, JUSTIFICATION - CHARGE, LEAVE-PROHIBITION, PARDON-REVENGE.

ex-on'-er-a-ted. Absolved. DIFFICULTY-FACILITY.

ex-on''-er-a'-tion. The act of exonerating. DUTY-IMMUNITY, JUSTIFICATION-CHARGE.

ex'-or-a-ble. Capable of relenting. COMPASSION-RUTHLESSNESS.

ex-or'-bi-tance. Excessiveness; extravagance. COSTLINESS-CHEAPNESS, EXCESS-LACK.

ex-or'-bi-tant. Excessive. COSTLINESS-CHEAPNESS, EXCESS-LACK, MAGNITUDE-SMALLNESS.

ex-or'-bi-tant-ly. Excessively. MAGNITUDE-SMALLNESS.

ex'-or-cise. To expel by magic. DEVOTION-MAGIC.

ex'-or-cism. The act or ceremony of expelling evil spirits. DEVOTION-CHARM, DEVOTION-MAGIC.

ex'-or-cist. One who drives out evil spirits. DEVOTION-MAGICIAN.

ex-or'-di-um. Introduction. PREDECESSOR-CONTINUATION.

ex'-os''-mose. Osmose from an inner to an outer vessel. TRANSMISSION.

ex''-os-to'-sis. A morbid bony outgrowth on the surface of a bone or cartilage. CONVEXITY-CONCAVITY.

ex''-o-ter'-ic. Belonging to the outside or to the uninitiated. MANIFESTATION-LATENCY, PUBLICITY.

ex-ot'-ic. Foreign; strange; a foreign flower. CONNECTION-INDEPENDENCE, CONVENTIONALITY-UNCONVENTIONALITY, FAUNA-FLORA.

ex-pand'. To distend; to dilate; to display. BREADTH-NARROWNESS, ENLARGEMENT-DIMINUTION, SOLIDITY-RARITY.

ex-pand'-ed. Enlarged. ENLARGEMENT-DIMINUTION, SUPREMACY-SUBORDINACY.

ex-panse'. A continuous area or stretch; expansion. EXTENSION-INEXTENSION, GREATNESS-LITTLENESS.

ex-pan''-si-bil'-i-ty. Capacity of being expanded. ENLARGEMENT-DIMINUTION.

ex-pan'-sion. Enlargement; immensity. ENLARGEMENT-DIMINUTION, EXTENSION-INEXTENSION, SOLIDITY-RARITY.

ex-pan'-sive. Capable of enlarging. ENLARGEMENT-DIMINUTION, EXTENSION-INEXTENSION.

ex-pa'-ti-ate. To diffuse; to enlarge in statement; to roam at large. SPEECH-INARTICULATENESS, TALKATIVENESS - TACITURNITY, TERSENESS - PROLIXITY, TRAVELING-NAVIGATION.

ex-pa'-tri-ate. To exile; to change citizenship from one country to another. ENTRANCE-EXIT, SOCIABILITY-PRIVACY.

ex-pa''-tri-a'-tion. Act of banishing. ENTRANCE-EXIT.

ex-pect'. To look forward to as certain or probable; to require. ASTONISHMENT-EXPECTANCE, EXPECTATION-SURPRISE, LIKELIHOOD-UNLIKELIHOOD, PREVISION, SANGUINENESS-HOPELESSNESS; **reason to expect,** LIKELIHOOD-UNLIKELIHOOD.

ex-pect'-ance. Expectation. ASTONISHMENT-EXPECTANCE, EXPECTATION-SURPRISE.

ex-pect'-an-cy. Abeyance. EXPECTATION-SURPRISE, PROPERTY.

ex-pect'-ant. Waiting in expectation. EXPECTATION-SURPRISE.

expectante médecine [F.] (ex-pec-tan't' méd-sîn'). Expectant medicine. EARLINESS-LATENESS, REMEDY-BANE.

ex''-pec-ta'-tion. Advantage hoped for. EXPECTATION-SURPRISE; **beyond expectation,** EXPECTATION-SURPRISE; **hold out an expectation,** ENGAGEMENT-RELEASE.

EXPECTATION—SURPRISE.

Abeyance. State of inoperation.

Anticipation. A looking forward to a possible event as most probable, and acting accordingly.

Anxious expectation. } Intense desire.
Ardent expectation. }

Auspices, etc. Indications of success or failure. See PROPHECY.

Blow. A sudden calamity.

False expectation. See EXPECTATION-DISAPPOINTMENT.

Inexpectation. Absence of expectation.

Miscalculation. Something that does not occur as expected.

Non-expectation. Inexpectation.

Shock. Any great sudden surprise, as of joy or sorrow.

EXPECTATION—SURPRISE—*Continued*.

Breathless expectation. A desire so intense or eager, as if holding the breath.

Calculation. Prediction made after carefully. working out the chances for and against.

Contemplation. The act of thinking indefinitely of something to be done.

Curiosity, etc. A keen eagerness to understand the mysterious. See INQUISITIVENESS.

Destiny, etc. Predetermined lot. See OCCURRENCE-DESTINY.

Eager expectation. An expectation or desire which one is impatiently anxious to obtain.

Expectance. }
Expectancy. } The state of waiting for the future.

Expectation. The act of looking to a future event as certain.

Foresight, etc. The calculation of future experiences See PREVISION.

Hope, etc. A welcome expectation. See SANGUINENESS.

Prospect. Hopeful indications.

Prospection. Care for future welfare.

Reckoning. Calculation.

Sanguine expectation. An expectation which one is confident of realizing.

Suspense. Anxiety for the outcome of some event.

Torment of Tantalus. A hope or expectation impossible to be realized.

Trust, etc. Absence of anxiety. See FAITH.

Waiting. State of delay for a certain time.

EXPECTATION—*Associated Nouns*.

Horizon. The line of apparent junction of the earth and sky; hence, figuratively, the bounds of one's expectation.

Perspective. A picture giving the illusion of a scene of nature; hence, a picture of one's hopes.

Vista. A mental view of future events.

EXPECTATION—*Verbs*.

Abide. To wait for a time.

Anticipate. To look at a possible event as sure to happen.

Contemplate. To have an indefinite idea of something to be done.

Expect. To look for.

Foresee. To anticipate future experiences.

Forestall, etc. To anticipate and prevent the effects of something. See EARLINESS.

Prepare for. To get ready for future purposes.

Watch. To expect something.

EXPECTATION—*Verbal Expressions*.

Bargain for; bide one's time; count upon, etc., to expect certain conditions (see FAITH); **have in contemplation; have in prospect; have in store for**, etc. (see OCCURRENCE-DESTINY); **hold one's breath**, to be in a state of suspense or expectation; **hope for; keep a good lookout for; keep a sharp lookout for; keep in view; lead one to expect** (see PROPHECY); **lie in wait for**, to be prepared to harm some one at a convenient time; **look for; look forward to; look out for; not wonder at** (see ASTONISHMENT); **not wonder if; nous verrons** [F.], we shall see; **prick up one's ears**, to be in a state of slight surprise or expectancy; **promise oneself; stand at "attention"; tarry for; think likely** (see LIKELIHOOD); **wait for; watch for; we shall see.**

EXPECTATION—*Adjectives*.

Abeyant. Being in suspense.

Agape. Having the mouth open, showing a state of expectancy.

Curious. Eager to examine everything. See INQUISITIVENESS.

Expectant. }
Expecting. } Waiting for something.

Gaping. Holding the mouth open, expressive of expectancy

Impending Likely to happen. See OCCURRENCE-DESTINY.

Prospective. Looking towards the future.

Ready. At hand.

EXPECTATION—*Adjective Expressions*.

All agog, in a state of expectancy and curiosity; **aux aguets** [F.], on the lookout; **in expectation** (see *Nouns*); **in the horizon; in one's eye**, in imagination; **in prospect** (see *Nouns*); **in view; long expected; on tenter-hooks; on the watch** (see CAREFULNESS); **on the tiptoe of expectation; on tiptoe; open-eyed; open-mouthed.**

EXPECTATION—SURPRISE—*Continued*.

Sudden burst. A sudden breaking or shattering, as of one's hopes or expectations.

Surprise. The feeling felt when anything is different than was expected.

Thunder-clap. A sharp violent detonation of thunder; hence, figuratively, a shock.

Wonder, etc. Surprise arising from ignorance. See ASTONISHMENT.

SURPRISE—*Verbs*.

Astonish. To strike with great surprise, awe, etc.

Electrify. To thrill with excitement.

Miscalculate. No mistake.

Pop. To come or go suddenly.

Stagger. To nearly deprive one of senses.

Start. To move or jerk suddenly from fear.

Startle. To cause one to start.

Stun. Suddenly to deprive one completely of his powers.

Surprise. To come upon, or do something to, unawares.

SURPRISE—*Verbal Expressions*.

Be taken by surprise; be unexpected, etc. (see *Adjectives*); **bounce upon one; burst like a thunder-bolt; burst like a thunder-clap; catch by surprise; catch unawares; come like a thunder-bolt; come like a thunder-clap; come unawares** (see *Adverbs*); **come upon; come upon one; creep upon one; drop from the clouds, fall upon, come upon suddenly; flash upon one; not bargain for, not to expect; not expect** (see EXPECTATION); **pounce upon; spring a mine upon**, to astonish; **steal upon one**, to come upon one quietly; **take aback**, to surprise greatly; **take away one's breath**, to be so surprised as to hold the breath; **take by surprise; take unawares; throw off one's guard**, to mislead so as to be easily surprised; **turn up**, to appear unexpectedly.

SURPRISE—*Adjectives*.

Inattentive. Not on the lookout.

Startling. Causing one to start.

Sudden. Coming at an unexpected time. See INSTANTANEITY.

Surprised. Affected with surprise. See *Verbs*.

Unanticipated. Not anticipated.

Unaware. Not aware.

Unexpected. Not expected.

Unforeseen. Not seen beforehand.

Unwarned. Not warned.

SURPRISE—*Adjective Phrases*.

Against expectation; beyond expectation; contrary to expectation; dropped from the clouds, unexpected; non-expectant; off one's guard, to be not watching; **out of one's reckoning**, in an unexpected position; **unheard of** (see CONVENTIONALITY-UNCONVENTIONALITY); **unhoped for; unlooked for.**

SURPRISE—*Adverbs*.

Abruptly. Beginning or ending suddenly.

Plump. With sudden and forcible action.

Pop. With a sudden appearance or disappearance.

Suddenly. In a sudden manner.

Unawares. Unexpectedly.

Unexpectedly. Without being thought of.

SURPRISE—*Adverbs, etc.*

À l'improviste [F.], suddenly; **in an unguarded moment**, while one is not watching; **like a thief in the night, like a thunder-bolt**, unexpectedly; **without notice; without saying "by your leave"; without warning.**

SURPRISE—*Interjection*.

Heydey! An exclamation of cheerfulness, surprise, etc. See ASTONISHMENT.

SURPRISE—*Phrases*.

Little did one expect, little did one think, it was not foreseen; **nobody would ever expect, nobody would ever suppose, nobody would ever think**, it is not easily foreseen or thought of; **who would have thought?**

EXPECTATION—*Continued*.

EXPECTATION—*Adverbs, etc.*

Arrectis auribus [L.], with ears erect; **on the watch** (see *Adjectives*); **with bated breath**, with the breathing checked, expressive of fear; **with breathless expectation** (see *Nouns*).

EXPECTATION—DISAPPOINTMENT.

DISAPPOINTMENT.

Afterclap. An unpleasant happening after an affair was supposed to have ended, as a thunder-storm.

Baik. A check in the progress of some plan.

Bitter disappointment. A disappointment that causes pain or suffering.

Blighted hope. A withering of prospects, or a prevention of progress or prosperity.

Blow. A sudden misfortune.

Disappointment. Miscarriage of one's expectations.

False expectation. Hope or expectation that cannot be realized.

Fool's paradise. Any state of happiness founded on vain hopes.

Miscalculation. A false reckoning of one's expectations. See DECISION-MISJUDGMENT.

Much cry and little wool. Great promises with little results; shearing hogs, A. D. 1579. [*Hudibras*, I, i, 851.]

Non-fulfilment of one's hopes. Disappointment.

Sad disappointment. A disappointment that causes sorrow.

Slip 'twixt cup and lip. A check to one's expectations. [Erasmus, *Proverbs*, A. D. 1552 Sheridan, 1777.]

Trick of fortune. An unexpected turn of either good or bad fortune.

Vain expectation. An expectation that cannot be realized.

DISAPPOINTMENT—*Verbs*

Balk. To check one in his plans.

Bilk. To disappoint in an engagement.

Disappoint. Not to happen as expected.

Dumfounder. To confuse.

Jilt. To disappoint intentionally in love.

Tantalize. To tease.

DISAPPOINTMENT—*Verbal Expressions.*

Balk one's expectation; balk one's hopes; be disappointed, blight one's expectation; blight one's hopes; crush one's expectations; crush one's hopes; dash one's expectations; dash one's hope; dash the cup from the lips, to refrain at the point of doing; defeat one's expectations; defeat one's hope; disappoint one's expectations; disappoint one's hope; falsify one's expectations; falsify one's hope; find one a false prophet, to find one who does not predict rightly; find to one's cost, to learn by unpleasant experience; laugh on the wrong side of one's mouth, to grieve or weep just after a period of hilarity; look aghast (see ASTONISHMENT); look blank, look blue, to look disappointed; not realize one's expectations; not realize one's hope; play one a trick; play one false, to disappoint or deceive; stand aghast, etc. (see sub ASTONISHMENT).

DISAPPOINTMENT—*Adjectives.*

Aghast. Terrified.

Disappointed. See *Verbs*.

Disconcerted. Confused.

Out of one's reckoning. Not to find conditions just as expected.

DISAPPOINTMENT—*Phrases.*

Diis aliter visum [L.]. The gods have judged otherwise.

Nascitur ridiculus mus, parturiunt montes [L.]. The mountains are in travail, a ridiculous mouse is born.

One's countenance falling. Showing disappointment.

The bubble burst. The scheme came to an abrupt end.

The mountain brought forth a mouse. The results were small in proportion to the promises.

---

ex-pect'-ed. Looked for. ASTONISHMENT-EXPECTANCE, EXPECTATION-SURPRISE; **as well as can be expected,** HEALTH-SICKNESS.

ex-pect'-ing. Waiting. ASTONISHMENT-EXPECTANCE, EXPECTATION-SURPRISE.

ex-pec'-to-rate. To spit out. ADMISSION-EXPULSION.

ex-pe'-di-ence. Advisability. PROPRIETY-IMPROPRIETY.

ex-pe'-di-en-cy. Quality of being proper. PROPRIETY-IMPROPRIETY.

ex-pe'-di-ent. Advisable; suitable. DESIGN, INSTRUMENTALITY, MEANS, PROPRIETY-IMPROPRIETY, SAGACITY-INCAPACITY, USEFULNESS-USELESSNESS.

ex-pe'-di-ents. Means. MEANS.

ex'-pe-dite. To hasten; to facilitate. EARLINESS-LATENESS, HURRY-LEISURE, OBSTRUCTION-HELP, SWIFTNESS-SLOWNESS.

ex''-pe-di'-tion. A journey, etc., for a definite purpose; the equipment of such a journey; despatch. ACTIVITY-INDOLENCE, EARLINESS-LATENESS, FIGHTING-CONCILIATION, HURRY-LEISURE, OBSTRUCTION-HELP, SWIFTNESS-SLOWNESS, TRAVELING-NAVIGATION.

ex-pe-di'-tious. Speedy ACTIVITY-INDOLENCE, SWIFTNESS-SLOWNESS.

ex-pel'. To force out; to eject. ADMISSION-EXPULSION, PUSH-PULL, RECOMPENSE-PUNITION, REPUTATION-DISCREDIT.

ex-pend'. To use up; to disburse. ADMISSION-EXPULSION, OUTLAY-INCOME, PROVISION-WASTE, SETTLEMENT-DEFAULT, USE-DISUSE; **expend itself,** ACTIVITY-INDOLENCE.

ex-pend'-ed. Spent. OUTLAY-INCOME.

ex-pend'-ing. Invested. OUTLAY-INCOME.

ex-pend'-i-ture. The act of expending anything, as money or time; disbursement. OUTLAY-INCOME, PROVISION-WASTE.

ex-pense'. Disbursement; loss; charge. PRICE-DISCOUNT; **joke at one's expense,** WITTINESS-DULNESS; **spare no expense,** GENEROSITY-FRUGALITY.

ex-pense'-less. Without cost. COSTLINESS-CHEAPNESS.

ex-pen'-ses. Money expended. OUTLAY-INCOME.

ex-pen'-sive. Costly. COSTLINESS-CHEAPNESS.

ex-pe'-ri-ence. To undergo personally; experimental knowledge. EMOTION, KNOWLEDGE-EXPERIENCE, OCCURRENCE-DESTINY, SENSUALITY-SUFFERING; **learn by experience,** REPENTANCE-OBDURACY.

ex-pe'-ri-enced. Taught by experience; skilled. SKILL-UNSKILFULNESS; **experienced eye,** ADEPT-BUNGLER.

ex-pe'-ri-en-ces. Instances of experimental knowledge. ACCOUNT.

experientia docet stultos [L.] (ex-pî-ri-en'-shi-a do'-set stul'-tos). Experience teaches fools. EDUCATION-LEARNING.

ex-per'-i-ment. To make a test or trial; a trial. TRIAL, VENTURE.

ex-per''-i-men'-tal. Based on experiment. CERTAINTY-DOUBT, TRIAL; **experimental philosophy,** MATERIALITY-SPIRITUALITY.

ex-per''-i-men'-tal-ly. By trial. VENTURE.

ex-per''-i-men'-ter. One who experiments. TRIAL.

experimentum crucis [L.] (ex-per-i-men'-tum cru'-sis). A crucial test. PROOF-DISPROOF, TRIAL, VENTURE.

ex'-pert. Adroit; a specialist. ADEPT-BUNGLER, SAGE-FOOL, SKILL-UNSKILFULNESS.

ex-pert'-ness. Skilfulness. SKILL-UNSKILFULNESS.

experto credite [L.] (ex-per'-to cred'-i-tî). Believe one who speaks from experience. FAITH-MISGIVING.

expertus, metuit [L.] (ex-per'-tus, met'-yu-it). Having experience, he fears. SANGUINENESS-TIMIDITY.

ex'-pi-ate. To atone for. ATONEMENT.

ex''-pi-a'-tion. Atonement. ATONEMENT.

ex'-pi-a-to''-ry. Having the character of an atonement. ATONEMENT.

ex-pire'. To exhale; to die. BEGINNING-END, LIFE-DEATH, PERIOD-PROGRESS.

ex-pired'. Extinct. FUTURE-PAST.

ex'-pi-ry. A coming to an end. BEGINNING-END.

ex-plain'. To make clear; interpret. INVESTIGATION-ANSWER, INTERPRETATION-MISINTERPRETATION; **explain away,** INTERPRETATION-MISINTERPRETATION.

ex-plain'-er. One who interprets. INTERPRETER.

ex''-pla-na'-tion. Sense. EDUCATION-MISTEACHING, INTERPRETATION-MISINTERPRETATION, RATIONALE-LUCK.

ex'-ple-tive. An exclamatory oath; something serving to fill out. EXCESS-LACK, TERSENESS-PROLIXITY.

ex''-pli-ca'-tion. Explanation. INTERPRETATION-MISINTERPRETATION.

ex'-pli-ca-tive. Explanatory. INTERPRETATION-MISINTERPRETATION.

ex'-pli-ca-to-ry. Explanatory. INTERPRETATION-MISINTERPRETATION.

ex-plic'-it. Definite; unreserved. ASSERTION-DENIAL, CLEARNESS-OBSCURITY, ENLIGHTENMENT-SECRECY, MANIFESTATION-LATENCY, PERSPICUITY-OBSCURITY.

ex-plic'-it-ness. Clearness. MEANING-JARGON.

ex-plode'. To cause to burst in pieces by force from within; to refute; to destroy. CHEMISTRY, EXCITABILITY-INEXCITABILITY, PROOF-DISPROOF, SUCCESS-FAILURE, TURBULENCE-CALMNESS.

ex-plo'-ded. Refuted; destroyed; antiquated. APPROVAL-DISAPPROVAL, CRASH-DRUMMING, FAVORITE-ANGER, FUTURE-PAST, NOVELTY-ANTIQUITY, REVOLUTION, TRUTH-ERROR, TURBULENCE-CALMNESS.

ex-ploit'. To employ in selfish schemes; a deed, especially one of daring. ACTION-PASSIVENESS, BRAVERY-COWARDICE.

ex''-ploi-ta'-tion. The act or process of exploiting. INVESTIGATION-ANSWER.

ex-plore'. To search through the parts of. INVESTIGATION-ANSWER, TRIAL.

ex-plor'-er. One who explores. WAYFARER-SEAFARER.

ex-plo'-sion. The act of exploding; a sudden and violent outbreak. APPROVAL-DISAPPROVAL, CRASH-DRUMMING, EXCITABILITY-INEXCITABILITY, FAVORITE-ANGER, FUTURE-PAST, IMPETUS-REACTION, NOVELTY-ANTIQUITY, PROOF-DISPROOF, REVOLUTION, SUCCESS-FAILURE, TRUTH-ERROR, TURBULENCE-CALMNESS.

ex-plo'-sive. Any substance that may cause an explosion. SECURITY-INSECURITY, TURBULENCE-CALMNESS.

ex-po'-nent. An authoritative exemplifier; an index; one who explains. ENLIGHTENMENT-SECRECY, INTERPRETER, NUMBER, SIGN.

ex-po-nen'-tial. Having an explanatory character NUMBER, SIGN.

ex'-port, n.; **ex-port',** v. To send out of a country; something exported. ENTRANCE-EXIT, INJECTION-EJECTION.

ex-pose'. To show plainly; to leave open to any influence; to abandon. APPROVAL-DISAPPROVAL, DRESS-UNDRESS, ENLIGHTENMENT-SECRECY, EXPOSURE-HIDINGPLACE, PROOF-DISPROOF; **expose oneself,** REPUTATION-DISCREDIT; **expose to danger,** SECURITY-INSECURITY; **expose to view,** MANIFESTATION-LATENCY, VISIBILITY-INVISIBILITY.

expose [F.] (ex-po-zê'). An undesirable or embarrassing disclosure or exposure. ACCOUNT, EXPOSURE-HIDINGPLACE.

ex-posed'. Laid bare. DRESS-UNDRESS, SECURITY-INSECURITY.

ex-posed' to. Put under certain influences. CONTINGENCY.

ex-po-si'-tion. Act of exposing; explanation or interpretation; commentary; a public exhibition. APPROVAL-DISAPPROVAL, DRESS-UNDRESS, EXPOSURE-HIDINGPLACE, INTERPRETATION-MISINTERPRETATION, PROOF-DISPROOF.

ex-pos'-i-tor. One who expounds. INSTRUCTOR-PUPIL, INTERPRETER.

ex-pos'-i-to-ry. Conveying, containing, or pertaining to exposition. ENLIGHTENMENT-SECRECY, ESSAY, INTERPRETATION-MISINTERPRETATION.

ex-pos'-tu-late. To represent earnestly the impropriety of a course of conduct. ADVICE, APPROVAL-DISAPPROVAL, MOTIVE-DEHORTATION, PETITION-EXPOSTULATION.

ex-pos''-tu-la'-tion. Earnest reasoning. ADVICE, APPROVAL-DISAPPROVAL, MOTIVE-DEHORTATION, PETITION-EXPOSTULATION.

ex-pos'-tu-la-to-ry. Reasoning. MOTIVE-DEHORTATION, PETITION-EXPOSTULATION.

ex-po'-sure. The state of being laid open; aspect; open situation or position. APPEARANCE-DISAPPEARANCE, APPROVAL-DISAPPROVAL, DRESS-UNDRESS, EXPOSURE-HIDINGPLACE, PROOF-DISPROOF; **exposure to weather,** WATER-AIR.

EXPOSURE—HIDINGPLACE.

Acknowledgment. Confession; owning up.
Avowal. Open declaration; outright acknowledgment.
Confession. Admission of personal doings, obligations, etc.
Dénouement [F.]. The discovery of a plot; catastrophe.
Deterration. The act of uncovering something buried under ground.
Disclosure. The act of revealing; bringing to the light.
Exposé [F.]. Undesirable disclosures.
Exposition. The act of displaying something to public view.
Exposure. The state of being laid open.
Retection. The act of uncovering some concealed thing.
Revealment. The act of making known; unveiling.
Revelation. The act of disclosing what was before unknown.
Unveiling. The act of uncovering; removing obstructions.

EXPOSURE—Associated Nouns.

Bursting of a bubble. Collapse of a fraud.
Confessional. Priest's stall for hearing confessions.
Shrift. The act of hearing confession and giving absolution.
Tell-tale. See TIDINGS.
Whole truth. The truth with nothing concealed.

EXPOSURE—Verbs.

Acknowledge. To admit the truth of.
Admit. To concede as true; to own the fact of.
Allow. To permit; to accept.
Avow. To make strong declaration; to acknowledge.
Bare. To lay open; to expose.
Become known. Be disclosed.
Be disclosed. To be laid open; to be made known.
Betray. To give a secret away; to give into the hands of the enemy.
Blab. To tattle; to talk thoughtlessly.
Blurt out. To burst out unexpectedly with.

Ambuscade.
Ambush. } Place where men are hidden to surprise an enemy.
Coverture. Place of concealment.
Hiding-place. Refuge; place of concealment.
Lurking-hole.
Lurking-place. } Place from which unexpected attacks can be made.
Retreat. Place of shelter. See REFUGE.

HIDINGPLACE—Nouns of Means.

Blind. Any means of keeping out the light.
Blinker. Piece of leather fastened to a bridle to keep the horse from looking back.
Cloak. A means of concealment.
Cloud. A shelter.
Cover. Means of defense or shelter.
Curtain. That which hides or separates.
Disguise. That which changes the appearance of something so as to be unrecognizable.
Domino. A mark for the upper part of the face.
Mask. A covering for the face.
Masquerade dress. A dress or costume to conceal one's identity.
Pitfall. See REFUGE-PITFALL.
Screen. That which shelters or protects.
Shade. That which cuts off the light.
Stalking-horse. A horse behind which the rider hides to stalk his game.
Trap. See TRUTHFULNESS-FRAUD.
Visor. The shield on a cap to protect the eyes from the sun's rays.

HIDINGPLACE—Denotations.

Abditory. A place to store valuables.
Adytum. The innermost recess of ancient temples where the oracles were interpreted.

EXPOSURE—HIDINGPLACE—*Continued.*

EXPOSURE—Verbs—*Continued.*

Break the seal. To disclose; to make known.
Break through the clouds. To become known.
Breathe. To tell; to impart.
Bring to light. To publish; to open.
Come in sight. See Visibility.
Come out. To become known.
Come out with. To tell; to give away the secret.
Come to light. To appear.
Concede. Grant; acknowledge.
Confess. To admit as true; to own.
Correct. To rectify falsehoods by stating the truth; to amend.
Creep out. To leak out in spite of any effort to prevent it.
Crop out. To appear above the surface; to be manifest.
Désillusionner [F.]. To destroy the illusions of.
Disabuse. To rectify mistakes; to eradicate fallacies.
Disburden one's conscience.
Disburden one's heart. } To impart to others what no longer can
Disburden one's mind. } be kept secret.
Disclose. To make known; to tell.
Discover. To uncover; to find.
Discover itself. Come to light.
Dismask. To unmask; to take off the mask.
Divulge. To disclose; to make known.
Draw the veil. } Uncover; to permit things to be seen in their
Draw the veil aside. } true light.
Drop the mask. Speak frankly.
Escape. To steal away.
Expose. To exhibit; to display.
Flash on the mind. To dawn on the mind quickly.
Give utterance to. To express.
Give vent to. To make known.
Grant. Admit; concede as true.
Lay bare. To expose; exhibit.
Lay bare a piece of one's mind. Expose one's thought.
Lay open. To disclose.
Leak out. To become known gradually.
Let drop. } To make public inadvertently.
Let fall. }
Let into the secret. To share a secret with another.
Let out. To let a secret escape.
Lift the mask. }
Lift the veil. } To disclose.
Lift up the veil. }
Make a clean breast. To make a full confession.
Make public. To expose; to exhibit.
Ooze out. To escape gradually.
Open a piece of one's mind. To tell what one thinks.
Open the eyes of. To make aware of something.
Open the lips. To tell, as a secret.
Open up. To unfasten; disclose.
Own to the soft impeachment. To confess to a charge.
Peach. To testify against some one else.
Peep out. To look out; to become visible at times.
Raise the mask. To declare one's real purposes.
Raise up the curtain. } To remove obstructions to seeing.
Raise up the veil. }
Remove the curtain. } To divest oneself of all obstructions to get a
Remove the veil. } good view.
Reveal the secrets of the prison-house. To disclose; to communicate
to others. [Shakespeare, *Hamlet*, I, v.]
Say the truth. To relate facts.
Set right. To correct; to rectify.

HIDINGPLACE—Denotations—*Continued*

Back-stairs. An approach from behind.
Closet. A room where one is shut off from the rest of the world.
Crypt. An underground vault.
Hole. An out-of-the-way place.
Holes and corners. Unusual places.
Oubliette [F.]. A trap dungeon.
Secret drawer. A private place to store trinkets and business papers.
Secret path. Concealed path.
Secret place. A retreat; a removed corner.

HIDINGPLACE—Verbs.

Lie in ambush, etc. See Enlightenment-Secrecy.
Lie in wait for. Eagerly watching for.
Set a trap for. See Truthfulness-Fraud.

HIDINGPLACE—Adverbs.

Aux aguets [F.]. To the watches.

EXPOSURE—Verbs—*Continued.*

Show its color. To disclose its true nature.
Show one's cards. }
Show one's hand. } To divulge one's intentions.
Speak out, etc. See Manifestation.
Speak the truth. Say what is true.
Tear the curtain. }
Tear the veil. } To remove a cover, etc.
Tell, etc. See Enlightenment.
Tell a piece of one's mind. To let know what one thinks of other
people.
Tell tales out of school. To tattle what others have no right to know.
Throw off all disguise. To conceal nothing.
Throw off the mask. Same as Raise the mask.
Transpire. To become public.
Turn King's or Queen's evidence. To confess a crime and testify
against an accomplice.
Unbeguile. To undeceive.
Unbosom oneself. To share one's secrets with another.
Uncover. To unfold; disclose.
Undeceive. To tell the truth.
Unfold. To reveal.
Unkennel. To discover; to drive out of a hole or hiding-place.
Unmask. See Dismask.
Unriddle. See Discovery.
Unseal. Unfold.
Unveil. To make known; disclose.
Utter. To express.
Vent. To let out; to pour forth.

EXPOSURE—Adjectives.

Disclosed. See *Verbs.*
Discovered. See *Verbs.*

EXPOSURE—Interjections.

Out with it!
Tell it!
Speak!

EXPOSURE—Phrases.

A light breaks in upon one; the murder is out; the scales fall from
one's eyes [Bible]; the eyes are opened.

---

ex-pound'. To interpret; to elucidate. Instructor-
Pupil, Interpretation-Misinterpretation.
ex-pound'-er. An expositor. Interpreter.
ex-pound'-ing. Interpreting. Interpretation-Misinterpretation.
ex-press'. To utter; to press out; to send by express;
explicit; a quick conveyance; a despatch. Assertion-Denial, Enlightenment-Secrecy, Injection-
Ejection, Manifestation-Latency, Meaning-Jargon, Phrase, Purpose-Luck, Swiftness-Slow-
ness; **by express,** Hurry-Leisure; **express by words,**
Language, Phrase, Style; **express train,** Conveyance-Vessel.
ex-pressed'. Uttered. **Well expressed,** Phrase, Purity-Crudeness.

ex-press'-ion. The act of uttering; a saying; look;
expressiveness; in music, the mode of executing.
Appearance-Disappearance, Injection-Ejection,
Manifestation-Latency, Meaning-Jargon, Musician, Name-Misnomer, Phrase; **mode of expression,**
Style; **new-fangled expression,** Word-Neology.
ex-press'-ive. Full of meaning. Clearness-Obscurity, Enlightenment-Secrecy, Meaning-Jargon,
Sensitiveness-Apathy.
ex-pro'-brate. To censure. Approval-Disapproval.
ex-pro-bra'-tion. Censure. Approval-Disapproval,
Justification-Charge.
ex-pro'-pri-ate. To deprive of rights. Keeping-Relinquishment.
ex-pro''-pri-a'-tion. The exclusion of the small owner

from the ownership of land and other property through their centralization in the hands of monopolists. Keeping-Relinquishment.

ex-pug'-na-ble. Capable of being taken by storm. Security-Insecurity.

ex"-pug-na'-tion. The act of taking by storm. Success-Failure.

ex-pul'-sion. A driving out; forcible ejection. Admission-Expulsion, Push-Pull, Recompense-Punition.

ex-punge'. To erase; to destroy. Creation-Destruction, Mark-Obliteration.

ex'-pur-gate. To purify. Cleanness-Filthiness.

expurgatorius, index [L.] (ex-pur-ga-to'-ri-us, in'-dex). A list of books which may be read in expurgated editions. Leave-Prohibition.

ex'-qui-site. Delicately beautiful; refined; fastidious; poignant; a fop. Goodness-Badness, Palatableness-Unpalatableness, Pleasurableness-Painfulness, Society-Dandy.

ex'-qui-site-ly. Extremely. Magnitude-Smallness.

ex'-sic-cate. To dry up or out. Dampness-Dryness.

ex"-sic-ca'-tion. Act of drying. Dampness-Dryness.

exspectat rusticus dum defluit amnis [L.] (ex-pec'-tat rus'-ti-cus dum di'-flu-it am'-nis). The rustic waits while the river flows by. Sanguineness-Hopelessness.

ex"-su-da'-tion. The act or process of exuding slowly. Nutriment-Excretion.

ex"-suf-fla'-tion. Exorcism by blowing. Devotion-Charm.

ex-sus'-ci-tate. To rouse up. ·Excitation.

ex'-tant. Still existing. Entity-Nonentity.

ex'-ta-sy. Excess of gladness or of grief; ecstasy Emotion, Fancy, Pleasure-Pain.

ex-tem"-po-ra'-ne-ous. Unpremeditated; given to speaking without preparation. Earliness-Lateness, Eternity-Instantaneity, Opportuneness-Unsuitableness, Predetermination - Impulse, Preparation-Nonpreparation.

ex-tem"-po-ra'-ne-ous-ly. Done without preparation. Predetermination-Impulse.

ex-tem'-po-re. Extemporaneous; extemporaneously; extemporaneous composition. Earliness-Lateness, Eternity-Instantaneity, Opportuneness-Unsuitableness, Predetermination - Impulse. Preparation-Nonpreparation.

ex-tem'-po-rize. To compose without preparation. Predetermination - Impulse, Preparation-Nonpreparation.

ex-tend'. To lengthen; to enlarge; to advance; to offer. Enlargement - Diminution, Length - Shortness; **extend to,** Length-Shortness, Remoteness-Nearness.

ex-tend'-ed. Extensive. Breadth-Narrowness.

ex-tend'-i-bil"-i-ty. Capability of being stretched. Hardness-Softness.

ex-ten"-si-bil'-i-ty. Capability of extension. Hardness-Softness.

ex-ten'-sile. Capable of extension. Hardness-Softness.

ex-ten'-sion. Prolongation; addition; that property of matter by which it has dimensions. Enlargement-Diminution, Extension-Inextension, Increase-Decrease, Length-Shortness; **extension of time,** Lastingness-Transientness.

EXTENSION-INEXTENSION.

Compass. An enclosed space or limit.
Expanse. A wide extent of space.
Expansion. An extended space; expanse.
Extension. The state of being stretched out.
Extent. The space to which a thing is stretched out.
Field. An open space of any kind.
Free space. An open unrestrained space.
Infinity, etc. Unlimited extent of space. See Infinity.
Latitude. Space; room; freedom from confinement.
Open space. Unrestrained space.
Play. Scope; room for movement.
Range. Compass; extent; scope.
Room. Compass; space which can be occupied.
Scope. Free space for action.
Space. Extension independent of anything it may contain.
Spread. Extent; compass.
Superficial extent. Surface extent.
Sweep. The compass of a stroke.
Swing. Free course.
Unlimited space. Space without limit.
Void, etc. An empty space. See Presence-Absence.

Extension—Denotations.

Abyss, etc. A bottomless gulf. See Interspace.
Acreage. Area in acres; quantity or extent of cultivated land.
Acres. A field; lands.
Acres, roods, and perches. Quantity or extent of land.
Arena. A scene or sphere of action or contest.
Campagna [It.] An open plain.
Elbow-room. Room for action.
House-room. Room or lodging, as in a house.
Length and breadth of the land. Extent of land.
Margin. A space along an edge.
Moor. }
Moorland. } A tract of waste land, marshy and abounding in peat
Opening. A tract of land where trees are thinly scattered.
Proportions. Dimensions or extent of surface.
Roomage. Extent of room or space.
Spare room. Room or space above what is necessary.
Sphere. Field of operations.
Square inches. Extent of surface measured in inches.
Square yards. Extent of surface measured in yards.
Stowage. Room or space in which things may be stowed.

Atom, etc. An ultimate, indivisible particle of matter. See Magnitude-Smallness.
Inextension. Want of extension.
Nonextension. The state of not occupying space.
Point. That which has neither length, breadth, nor thickness.

Extension—Denotations—*Continued*.

Ubiquity, etc. Whereabouts; region. See Presence.
Waste. Land not under cultivation.
Way. Length of space passed over.
Wilderness. An uncultivated or barren region.
Wildness. A wilderness.
World. The earth.

Extension—*Adjectives*.

Ample. Great in extent.
Boundless, etc. Limitless; unbounded. See Infinity.
Capacious. Spacious; extended.
Expansive. Wide-extending.
Extensive. Having a wide extent.
Pathless. Untrodden; having no path.
Roomy. Spacious; wide.
Shoreless. Of unlimited extent.
Spacious. Vast in extent.
Trackless. Untrodden.
Uncircumscribed. Not circumscribed.
Vast. Immense; very great.
Wide. Having great extent.
Widespread. Spread over great extent.
World-wide. Extended through the whole world.

Extension—*Adverbs*

All over. Over a great extent.
All the world over. Over the whole world.
Everywhere. At all places.
Extensively, etc. In an extensive manner. See *Adjectives*.
Far and near. }
Far and wide. } Over a great extent.
From all points of the compass. Everywhere.

EXTENSION—ADVERBS—*Continued.*

From China to Peru. [Johnson, *Vanity of Human Wishes.*] }
From Dan to Beersheba. [Bible.] }
From end to end. }
From Indus to the Pole. ["Waft a Sigh." Pope, *Eloisa.*] } Over a great distance; extensively.
From pole to pole. }

Here, there, and everywhere. }
In all lands. } Everywhere.
In all quarters. }

In every quarter. }
In the wide world. }
On the face of the earth. } Everywhere.
Right and left. }
Throughout the length and breadth of the land.
Throughout the world. Over the whole world.
To the four winds. In all directions.
To the uttermost parts of the earth.
Under the sun. Everywhere.
Wherever. At whatever place.

EXTENSION—*Phrase.*

Lex loci [L.]. The law of the place.

EXTENSION—DISTRICT.

DISTRICT.

Area. The surface included between lines; any plane surface.
Beat. A round or course frequently traveled over.
Canton. A district.
Circuit. A space included between certain definite limits.
District. A portion of territory of undefined extent.
Ground. A portion of the earth's surface set apart.
Hemisphere. Half of the surface of the terrestrial globe.
Orb. A circle, orbit, or anything circular.
Quarter. Specific place.
Realm. A region or country.
Region. A portion of space of indefinite extent.
Soil. Land; country.
Sphere. Circuit; province; compass.

DISTRICT—*Denotations.*

Arena. An enclosed space where exhibitions are held.
Arrondissement [F.]. A subdivision of a French department.
Circle. An enclosure.
Climate. A region of the earth considered in relation to its temperature.
Clime. A portion or region of the earth.
Close. Any place shut in or enclosed.
Commune. A local government district in European countries.
Compartment. A room.
Country. A land within definite geographical limits.
County. A civil division of a state.
Court. A space enclosed on three sides.
Department. A civil division of a state.
Domain. A territory or region over which dominion is exercised by a sovereign.
Duchy. The territory or dominion of a duke.
Enceinte [F.] A circuit.

Enclave [F.]. A piece of land enclosed within another.
Enclosure. An enclosed space.
Field. A piece of land under cultivation.
Hundred. A subdivision of a county.
Kingdom. The territory ruled by a king.
Latitude. A region or place with reference to its distance north or south of the equator.
March. The region or district lying along a boundary-line.
Meridian. Situation, especially as marking local conditions.
Pale. That which is enclosed within bounds. See COVER.
Parish. A religious or ecclesiastical district; a civil division of a county.
Patch. A small piece of ground.
Plot. A fenced piece of ground.
Precinct. An election district.
Principality. The territory of a reigning prince.
Province. A civil division of an empire.
Riding. A division of an English county.
Shire. A county.
Street. A public way. See DWELLER-HABITATION.
Territory. The domain of a sovereign state.
Township. A civil division of a county.
Tract. An extent of land.
Walk. A piece of ground set apart for the exercise of sporting animals.
Wapentake. A division of an English county.
Ward. A territorial division of cities.
Zone. A region of the earth enclosed between two parallels of latitude.

DISTRICT—*Adjectives.*

Local. Pertaining to some particular or definite place.
Parochial. Pertaining to or relating to a parish.
Provincial. Pertaining to or relating to a province.
Territorial. Pertaining to a territory.

EXTENSION—PLACE.

PLACE.

Abode, etc. A place of habitation. See DWELLER HABITATION.
Locality, etc. Situation in a place. See POSITION.
Place. A portion of space measured off and regarded as distinct from all other space.
Point. An indefinitely small space clearly indicated
Precinct. A district within certain definite limits.
Premises. A distinct portion of real estate.
Spot. A small extent of space.
Station. A spot or place where anything stands.

PLACE—*Denotations.*

Compartment. A room.
Dot. A small spot.

Every hole and corner. Everywhere.
Ins and outs. Windings of a place.
Lien. A legal claim on property.
Niche. A recessed space or hollow.
Nook, etc. A corner. See ANGULARITY.
Pigeon-hole, etc. A small compartment in a desk for holding letters, etc. See CONTENTS-RECEIVER.

PLACE—*Adverbs.*

Here and there; in some place; in various places; *passim* [L.], here and there; somewhere; wherever it may be.

---

ex-ten′-sive. Great; wide. EXTENSION-INEXTENSION, MAGNITUDE - SMALLNESS; extensive knowledge, KNOWLEDGE-IGNORANCE.
ex-ten′-sive-ly. Widely. EXTENSION-INEXTENSION.
extenso, in [L.] (ex-ten′-so, in). In full. TERSENESS-PROLIXITY, WHOLE-PART.
ex-tent′. Compass; bulk. EXTENSION-INEXTENSION, QUANTITY-MEASURE.
ex-ten′-u-ate. To mitigate; to attenuate; to depreciate. INCREASE-DECREASE, JUSTIFICATION-CHARGE, STRENGTH-WEAKNESS.

ex-ten′-u-a-ted. Slender. BREADTH - NARROWNESS.
ex-ten′-u-a-ting. Mitigating. **Extenuating circumstances,** JUSTIFICATION-CHARGE, MODIFICATION.
ex-ten″-u-a′-tion. Palliation. JUSTIFICATION-CHARGE.
ex-te′-ri-or. Outside. OUTSIDE-INSIDE.
ex″-te-ri-or′-i-ty. The state or quality of being outside. OUTSIDE-INSIDE.
ex-ter′-mi-nate. To annihilate. CREATION-DESTRUCTION.
ex-ter″-min-a′-tion. Eradication. INJECTION-EXTRACTION.

ex-ter'-nal. Outside; superficial. Outside-Inside; **external evidence,** Evidence-Counterevidence; **external senses,** Sensibility-Insensibility.

ex-tinct'. Quenched; worn out; exterminated. Creation-Destruction, Entity-Nonentity, Future-Past, Light-Darkness.

ex-tinc'-teur. A portable fire-extinguisher. Heating-Cooling.

ex-tinc'-tion. Complete destruction. Creation-Destruction, Entity-Nonentity; **extinction of life,** Life-Death.

ex-tin'-guish. To quench; to put out; to destroy. Creation-Destruction, Heating-Cooling, Light-Darkness.

ex-tin'-guish-er. One who or that which destroys. Maker-Destroyer; **put an extinguisher upon,** Obstruction-Help, Success-Failure.

ex'-tir-pate. To eradicate. Injection-Ejection.

ex''-tir-pa'-tion. Act of taking out by the roots. Creation-Destruction, Injection-Ejection.

ex''-ti-spi'-cious. Pertaining to the inspection of entrails by a haruspex. Prophecy.

ex-tol'. To praise highly; to elevate. Approval-Disapproval, Overvaluation-Undervaluation.

ex-tort'. To wrest away; to exact without legal right. Compulsion, Costliness-Cheapness, Injection-Ejection, Taking-Restitution.

ex-tort'-ed. Secured unwillingly. Assent-Dissent.

ex-tor'-tion. An extortionate charge; the act or practise of extorting. Costliness-Cheapness, Extravagance-Avarice, Taking-Restitution.

ex-tor'-tion-ate. Unreasonable. Costliness-Cheapness, Desire-Distaste, Extravagance-Avarice, Harshness-Mildness.

ex-tor'-tion-er. One who takes illegally. Extravagance-Avarice, Harshness-Mildness.

ex'-tra. Additional; something additional. Addition-Subtraction, Excess-Lack, Missive-Publication.

extra, ab [L.] (ex'-tra, ab). From without. Outside-Inside.

ex'-tract. A quotation; an essential extracted or drawn out. Digest, Injection-Ejection.

ex-trac'-tion. Extract; the act of extracting; lineage. Injection-Ejection, Parentage-Progeny; **extraction of roots,** Numbering.

ex-tract'-or. One who or that which extracts. Injection-Ejection.

ex'-tracts. Selections from writings. Digest.

ex''-tra-di'-tion. The surrender by a government of a person accused or convicted to another government. Admission-Expulsion, Transfer.

ex''-tra-ju-di'-cial. Happening out of court or out of the proper court. Law-Lawlessness.

ex''-tra-mun'-dane. Existing outside the limits of the world or of the material universe. Universe.

ex''-tra-mu'-ral. Outside the wall. Outside-Inside.

extra muros [L.] (ex'-tra miu'-ros). Without the walls. Outside-Inside.

ex-tra'-ne-ous. External; foreign. Connection-Independence, Constituent-Alien, Subjectiveness-Objectiveness.

ex-tra'-ne-ous-ness. The state of being extraneous. Constituent-Alien.

ex''-traor'-di-na-ry. Unusual. Conventionality-Unconventionality, Magnitude-Smallness.

ex''-tra-re-gard'-ing. Looking outward. Outside-Inside.

ex-trav'-a-gance. Excess. Adage-Nonsense, Costliness-Cheapness, Excess-Lack, Extravagance-Avarice, Gull-Hyperbole, Sagacity-Incapacity, Society-Ludicrousness.

EXTRAVAGANCE—AVARICE.

Extravagance. Needless freedom in the expenditure of money.
Prodigality. Excessive and wasteful expenditure of money.
Prodigence. Waste; extravagance.
Profuseness. Characteristic of being extravagant.
Profusion. ⎱ Lavish liberality; over-supply.
Squandering. ⎰
Unthriftiness. Carelessness and imprudence in the management of one's resources.
Waste. The act of wasting or squandering gradually and thoughtlessly.

Extravagance—*Associated Nouns.*

Locust. Anything that destroys or devours like the locust.
Losel. A person inclined to idleness and waste.
Malversation. Fraudulent conduct in public office or places of trust.
Prodigal. One wasteful or extravagant in the use of money or property.
Spendthrift. ⎱ One who spends beyond his means or reasonable requirements.
Wastethrift. ⎰

Extravagance—*Verbs.*

Be prodigal. See *Adjectives.*
Burn the candle at both ends. To be foolishly extravagant.
Dissipate. To squander by spending in a reckless manner.
Drain. To draw off slowly; to spend or cause to spend to exhaustion.
Eat out of house and home. Impoverish another by depending upon him for support.
Exhaust. To lessen greatly or entirely withdraw the supply of.
Fool away one's money. ⎱ To spend without any returns.
Fritter away one's money. ⎰
Kill the goose that lays the golden eggs. To destroy foolishly one's resources. Fable.
Lavish. To expend wastefully and liberally.
Make ducks and drakes of one's money. To squander.
Manger son blé en herbe [F.]. To eat the calf in the cow's belly.
Misspend. To spend wrongfully.
Muddle away one's money. Spend foolishly.
Outrun the constable. To run into debt.
Overdraw. To draw excessively.

Auri sacra fames [L]. The accursed hunger for gold.
Avarice. A passion for the acquisition of money.
Avidity. A strong desire for money, food, etc.
Extortion. Acquiring or obtaining by violence.
Illiberality. Want of liberality; ungenerosity.
Parcity. Sparingness.
Parsimoniousness. State of being frugal to excess.
Parsimony. Closeness in expenditure often with a bad sense.
Rapacity. Quality of being rapacious or given to plundering and extorting.
Selfishness. Condition of being selfish, of caring only for oneself. See Selfishness.
Stinginess. Quality of being stingy. See *Adjectives.*
Stint. The act of stinting, of being sparing, of prescribing limits.
Tenacity. The quality of holding fast to what is in one's possession.
Venality. Prostitution of offices, etc., for money.

Avarice—*Nouns of Agent, etc.*

Churl. A sordid or stingy person.
Codger. A niggardly or miserly man.
Crib. Piracy or plagiarism.
Curmudgeon. One who is miserly or grasping.
Harpagon. An iron grappling hook; hence, a grasping person.
Harpy. Any rapacious person; like the harpies in Virgil.
Hunks. A person who grasps everything.
Jew. A crafty dealer or grasping money-lender.
Luck-penny. A trifle returned "for luck" by the vendor to a purchaser.
Miser. A person given to saving and hoarding unduly.
Muckworm. A miser.
Niggard. A stingy person.
Screw. An extortioner or miser.
Scrimp. A pinching miser.
Skinflint. A hard, close money-getter.
Usurer. One who loans money at an exorbitant rate.

Avarice—*Verbs.*

Beat down. To lessen the price of by haggling.
Begrudge. To envy the possession of.

EXTRAVAGANCE—AVARICE—*Continued.*

EXTRAVAGANCE—Verbs—*Continued*

Pay through the nose. To pay excessively.
Potter away one's money. To be extravagant.
Pour forth like water. To spend money too freely.
Pour water into a sieve. To spend without a purpose or without a result.
Run out. ⎫
Run through. ⎭ To waste.
Sow broadcast. Spend without any attention.
Spill. To cause to pour out or to waste.
Squander. To spend recklessly.
Throw away one's money. To waste one's resources.
Throw good money after bad. To act foolishly in spending.
Throw the helve after the hatchet. To squander principal as well as income.
Waste. To spend gradually.

EXTRAVAGANCE—*Adjectives.*

Dissipated. Scattered, squandered.
Extravagant. Carelessly expending in excess of income.
Fullhanded. Having hands full.
Improvident. Lacking foresight; careless.
Lavish. Bountifully extravagant.
Losel. Slothful and wasteful.
Overliberal. More generous than one can afford.
Penny-wise and pound-foolish. Economical in small matters, extravagant in large things.
Prodigal. Given to extravagant expenditures.
Profuse. Liberal or abundant to excess.
Thriftless. Having no foresight or prudence in management of resources.
Unthrifty. Not thrifty or careful in management of money affairs.
Wasteful. Full of waste; prodigal.

EXTRAVAGANCE—*Adverbs.*

Money burning one's pocket.
With an unsparing hand.

EXTRAVAGANCE—*Phrases.*

Amor nummi [L.]. Love of the dollar.
Facile largiri de alieno [L.]. It is easy to be lavish with what is not your own.
Les fous font les festins, et les sages les mangent [F.]. Fools make feasts and wise men eat them.
Wie gewonnen, so zerronnen [G.]. As won, so flown; light come, light go.

AVARICE—Adjectives—*Continued from Column 2.*

Tight-fisted. Stingy.
Ungenerous. Not generous; illiberal.
Usurious. Practising usury; eager to increase one's wealth rapidly even though illegally.
Venal. Purchasable or purchased; working for money without principle.

AVARICIOUS—*Adverb.*

With a sparing hand. Frugal.

AVARICE—Verbs—*Continued.*

Be parsimonious. See *Adjectives.*
Cheapen. To make less in price.
Dole out. To give sparingly.
Drive a bargain. ⎫
Drive a hard bargain. ⎭ To trade with advantage to oneself.
Famish. To faint or die from hunger.
Grab. To get possession of dishonestly or greedily.
Grasp. To be greedy of gain.
Gripe. To get money by exaction.
Grudge. To envy the possession of.
Have an itching palm. To be greedy. [Shakespeare, *J. Cæsar*, IV, iii.]
Hold back. Retain.
Live upon nothing. To be very stingy.
Pinch. To be close in money affairs.
Screw. To act in money matters as an extortioner.
Skin a flint. To get money in a mean, contemptible way.
Starve. To die from lack of food.
Stint. To provide scantily.
Stop one hole in a sieve. Be stingy.
Withhold. To keep back.

AVARICE—*Adjectives.*

Avaricious. Eagerly craving for money.
Chary. Very careful and cautious.
Churlish. Like a churl; sordid.
Close. Not open or liberal; stingy.
Closefisted. Not inclined to give; mean.
Closehanded. Mean; illiberal.
Covetous. Desirous of getting something from its possessor.
Extortionate. Oppressive.
Fasthanded. Parsimonious.
Greedy. Wishing to have or enjoy everything oneself.
Griping. See *Verbs.*
Grudging. Envying one the possession of.
Hardfisted. Avaricious in disposition; closefisted.
Hidebound. Narrow-minded; penurious.
Illiberal. Not liberal; ungenerous.
Mean. Miserly in expenditure.
Mercenary. Governed by a sordid love of gain; able to be hired.
Miserly. Like a miser; given to hoarding.
Near. Inclined to be penurious; close.
Niggardly. Acquiring by mean and petty savings.
Parsimonious. Close in the expenditure of one's money.
Peddling. Occupying oneself in small affairs.
Penny-wise. Economical in small matters.
Penurious. Very sparing in the expenditure of money.
Rapacious. Acquiring by violence, as a robber; eagerly grasping.
Scrubby. Like a scrub; stunted; sordid.
Shabby. Dressed in rags; paltry.
Sordid. Meanly avaricious.
Sparing. Refraining from using; illiberal.
Stingy. Extremely close and desirous of keeping others from getting.
Straithanded. Closehanded.
Tight. Close and careful in expending.

(Continued on Column 1.)

---

ex-trav'-a-gant. Immoderate; visionary; wasteful. ADAGE-NONSENSE, COSTLINESS-CHEAPNESS, EXCESS-LACK, EXTRAVAGANCE-AVARICE, FANCY, MAGNITUDE-SMALLNESS, SAGACITY-INCAPACITY, SOCIETY-LUDICROUSNESS, TASTE-VULGARITY, TURBULENCE-CALMNESS.
ex-trav''-a-gan'-za. An extravagant or fantastic composition. ESSAY, FANCY.
ex-trav''-a-ga'-tion. A roaming beyond proper bounds. TRANSCURSION-SHORTCOMING.
ex-trav'-a-sate. To escape from the proper vessel. ADMISSION-EXPULSION, ENTRANCE-EXIT.
ex-trav''-a-sa'-tion. Act of escaping from the proper vessel. ENTRANCE-EXIT, INJECTION-EJECTION.
ex-treme'. Of the highest degree; last; exacting. BEGINNING-END, MAGNITUDE-SMALLNESS; **extreme unction,** CEREMONIAL.
ex-treme'-ly. To the utmost. MAGNITUDE-SMALLNESS.
extremis, in [L.] (ex-tri'-mis, in). In extremity. DIFFICULTY-FACILITY, LIFE-DEATH.

ex-trem'-i-ty. Termination; the greatest degree; a state of want or misery. BEGINNING-END, PLEASURE-PAIN, WELFARE-MISFORTUNE; **at the last extremity,** SECURITY-INSECURITY; **drive matters to an extremity,** DETERMINATION-VACILLATION.
ex'-tri-ca-ble. Able to be untangled. RESCUE.
ex'-tri-cate. To disentangle; to disembarrass. DIFFICULTY-FACILITY, INJECTION-EJECTION, RELEASE-RESTRAINT, RESCUE.
ex''-tri-ca'-tion. Act of liberating. INJECTION-EJECTION, RELEASE-RESTRAINT, RESCUE.
ex-trin'-sic. Foreign. OUTSIDE-INSIDE, SUBJECTIVENESS-OBJECTIVENESS.
ex-trin'-sic-al. Quality of being foreign. SUBJECTIVENESS-OBJECTIVENESS.
ex-trin''-si-cal'-i-ty. The state of being non-inherent. CONSTITUENT-ALIEN, SUBJECTIVENESS-OBJECTIVENESS.
ex-trin'-sic-al-ly. Foreign to. SUBJECTIVENESS-OBJECTIVENESS.

ex-trin′-sic ev′-i-dence. Evidence from outside circumstances. EVIDENCE-COUNTEREVIDENCE.

ex-tru′-sion. Expulsion. ADMISSION-EXPULSION, ENTRANCE-EXIT.

ex-u′-ber-ance. Copiousness. EXCESS-LACK, TERSENESS-PROLIXITY.

ex-u′-ber-ant. Producing plenteously; copious. ENOUGH, EXCESS-LACK, TERSENESS-PROLIXITY.

ex-u′-ber-ate. To abound. ENOUGH.

ex″-u-da′-tion. The act or process of exuding; that which is exuded. ENTRANCE-EXIT, NUTRIMENT-EXCRETION.

ex-ude′. To trickle forth. ENTRANCE-EXIT, MEDIUM.

ex-ul′-cer-ate. To cause ulcers to grow upon; to irritate. BETTERMENT-DETERIORATION.

ex-ult′. To feel or manifest delight. BRAGGING, JUBILATION-LAMENTATION, REPUTATION-DISCREDIT.

ex-ult′-ant. Rejoicing greatly. BRAGGING, JUBILATION-LAMENTATION, SANGUINENESS-HOPELESSNESS.

ex-ult′-ing. Rejoicing in. LIGHTHEARTEDNESS-DEJECTION.

ex′-unge. Ointment. PULPINESS-OILINESS.

ex-u′-vi-æ. Parts cast off or shed by animals. CLEANNESS-FILTHINESS, NUTRIMENT-EXCRETION.

eye. The organ of vision; sight; ability to see; inspection; mien. APERTURE-CLOSURE, CIRCLE-WINDING, SIGHT-BLINDNESS, VISIBILITY-INVISIBILITY; **appear to one's eye,** VISIBILITY-INVISIBILITY; **before one's eyes,** ANTERIORITY-POSTERIORITY, MANIFESTATION-LATENCY, VISIBILITY-INVISIBILITY; **cast the eyes on,** SIGHT-BLINDNESS; **cast the eyes over,** HEED-DISREGARD; **catch the eye,** HEED-DISREGARD; **close the eyes,** ACTIVITY-INDOLENCE, LIFE-DEATH, SIGHT-BLINDNESS; **dry eyes,** SENSITIVENESS-APATHY; **eye askance,** SANGUINENESS-TIMIDITY; **eye glistening,** EXCITATION; **eye of a needle,** APERTURE-CLOSURE; **eye of the master,** MANAGEMENT; **eyes draw straws,** ACTIVITY-INDOLENCE; **eyes open,** CAREFULNESS-CARELESSNESS, HEED-DISREGARD, PURPOSE-LUCK; **eyes opened,** EXPOSURE-HIDINGPLACE; **eyes out,** SIGHT-BLINDNESS; **fix the eyes on,** HEED-DISREGARD; **have an eye to,** DESIRE-DISTASTE, HEED-DISREGARD, PURPOSE-LUCK; **have one's eyes about one,** CAREFULNESS-CARELESSNESS; **in one's eyes,** VISIBILITY-INVISIBILITY; **in the eye of the law,** LAW-LAWLESSNESS; **in the eyes of,** APPEARANCE-DISAPPEARANCE, FAITH-MISGIVING; **keep an eye upon,** CAREFULNESS-CARELESSNESS; **look with one's own eyes,** CAREFULNESS-CARELESSNESS; **mind's eye,** FANCY; **open the eyes to,** DISCOVERY; **set one's eyes upon,** DESIRE-DISTASTE; **shut one's eyes to,** HEED-DISREGARD, LEAVE-PROHIBITION; **to the eyes,** APPEARANCE-DISAPPEARANCE; **under the eyes of,** PRESENCE-ABSENCE; **up to one's eyes,** EXCESS-LACK; **with moistened eyes,** JUBILATION-LAMENTATION; **with open eyes,** ASTONISHMENT-EXPECTANCE.

eye′-glass″. A pair of glasses resembling spectacles without bows; the glass nearest the eye in a telescope, or similar instrument. OPTICAL INSTRUMENTS.

eye′-less. Deprived of sight. SIGHT-BLINDNESS.

eye′-let. A little aperture. APERTURE-CLOSURE.

eye′-piece″. The lens in a telescope nearest the eye. OPTICAL INSTRUMENTS.

eye′-sight″. The sense of sight; extent of sight. SIGHT-BLINDNESS.

eye′-sore″. A diseased place on or near the eye; anything that offends the eye. BEAUTY-UGLINESS, EMBELLISHMENT-DISFIGUREMENT.

eye′-teeth″. The upper canine teeth. **Have cut one's eyeteeth,** CRAFT-ARTLESSNESS, MANHOOD, SKILL-UNSKILFULNESS.

eye′-wit″-ness. One who sees a thing with his own eyes. EVIDENCE-COUNTEREVIDENCE, ONLOOKER.

ey′-ot. A little island. SWAMP-ISLAND.

eyre. A court of circuit judges. TRIBUNAL.

ey′-ry. The nest of any predatory bird, especially the eagle. DWELLER-HABITATION.

F

faber est quisque fortunæ suæ [L.] (fê'-ber est quis'-quî for-tiu'-nî siu'-î). Every man is the architect of his own fortune. SUCCESS-FAILURE, WELFARE-MIS-FORTUNE.

Fa'-bi-an. Delaying. **Fabian policy,** ACTION-PAS-SIVENESS, EARLINESS-LATENESS, RECKLESSNESS-CAUTION.

fa'-ble. Fiction. ACCOUNT, RHETORIC, TROPE, TRUTH-ERROR, TRUTHFULNESS-FABRICATION.

fab'-ric. Texture. CAUSE-EFFECT, CONDITION-SITU-ATION, CREATION-DESTRUCTION, ELASTICITY-INELAS-TICITY.

fab'-ri-cate. Construct. CREATION - DESTRUCTION, FANCY, TRUTHFULNESS-FALSEHOOD.

fab'-ri-ca-ted. Made up in the imagination. TRUTH-FULNESS-FRAUD.

fab''-ri-ca'-tion. A falsehood. CREATION - DESTRUC-TION, TRUTHFULNESS-FABRICATION, TRUTHFULNESS-FALSEHOOD.

fabula narratur, de te [L.] (fab'-yu-la nar-rê'-tur, dî tî). The story is told of you. EXCULPATION-CON-VICTION, REPRISAL-RESISTANCE.

fab'-u-list. A falsifier. ACCOUNT.

fab'-u-lous. Fictitious; incredible. GULL-HYPER-BOLE, FANCY, MAGNITUDE-SMALLNESS, TRUTHFUL-NESS-FABRICATION.

fab'-ur-den. A refrain. MELODY-DISSONANCE.

fa''-çade'. An elevation of a building. ANTERIORITY-POSTERIORITY.

face. Oppose; visage. ANATOMY, ANTAGONISM-CON-CURRENCE, ANTERIORITY-POSTERIORITY, APPEAR-ANCE-DISAPPEARANCE, BRAVERY-COWARDICE, COV-ER-LINING, MINERALOGY, OUTSIDE-INSIDE, PRE-SUMPTION-OBSEQUIOUSNESS, REPRISAL-RESISTANCE; **change the face of,** REVOLUTION; **face about,** AIM-ABERRATION; **face to face,** ANTERIORITY-POSTERI-ORITY; **face of the country,** GULF-PLAIN; **face to the thing,** APPEARANCE-DISAPPEARANCE; **fly in the face of,** INSUBORDINATION-OBEDIENCE, PRESUMP-TION-OBSEQUIOUSNESS, REPRISAL-RESISTANCE; **in the face of,** ANTAGONISM-CONCURRENCE, PRESENCE-ABSENCE; **look in the face,** SIGHT-BLINDNESS, BRAV-ERY-COWARDICE; **make faces,** BEAUTY-UGLINESS, DESIRE-DISTASTE, PROPORTION-DEFORMITY, REGARD-DISRESPECT; **not show face,** REPUTATION-DISCREDIT, SELFRESPECT-HUMBLENESS; **on the face of,** AP-PEARANCE-DISAPPEARANCE, MANIFESTATION-LATEN-CY; **on the face of the earth,** EXTENSION-DISTRICT; **put a good face upon,** EXCITABILITY-INEXCITABILITY, JUSTIFICATION-CHARGE, LIGHTHEARTEDNESS-DEJEC-TION, POMP, SANGUINENESS-HOPELESSNESS, SELF-RESPECT-HUMBLENESS, TRUTHFULNESS-FRAUD; **set one's face against,** ANTAGONISM-CONCURRENCE, QUEST-EVASION; **show face,** PRESENCE-ABSENCE, VISIBILITY-INVISIBILITY; **to one's face,** MANIFESTA-TION-LATENCY; **wry face,** BEAUTY-UGLINESS, SEN-SUALITY-SUFFERING.

fac'-et. A small face. OUTSIDE-INSIDE.

facetiæ [L.] (fa-sî'-shi-î). Witty sayings. WITTI-NESS-DULNESS.

fa-ce'-tious. Witty. WITTINESS-DULNESS.

fa-ce'-tious-ness. Drollness. WITTINESS-DULNESS.

fac'-ile. Easy; skilful. DETERMINATION-VACILLA-TION, DIFFICULTY-FACILITY, READINESS-RELUCT-ANCE.

facile princeps [L.] (fas'-i-lî prin'-seps). Easily first. SUPREMACY-SUBORDINACY.

facilis descensus Averni [L.] (fas'-i-lis dî-sen'-sus a-ver'-nai). The road to hell is easy. PARALLELISM-INCLINATION, SECURITY-INSECURITY.

fa-cil'-i-tate. To make easier. DIFFICULTY-FACIL-ITY.

fa-cil'-i-ty. Readiness; affability. DIFFICULTY-FA-CILITY, LIBERTY-SUBJECTION, SKILL-UNSKILFULNESS.

fa'-cing. Covering. COVER-LINING, LATERALITY-CONTRAPOSITION.

fa-cin'-o-rous. Atrociously wicked. VIRTUE-VICE.

facinus quos inquinat æquat [L.] (fas'-i-nus quos in'-qui-nat î'-quat). Crime reduces those whom it stains to one level. ELEVATION-DEPRESSION, INNOCENCE-GUILT.

façon de parler [F.] (fa-son' de par-lê'). Manner of speaking. GULL-HYPERBOLE, TROPE.

façon, sans [F.] (fa-son', san'). Without fashion. EMBELLISHMENT-SIMPLICITY.

fac-sim'-i-le. An exact copy. COPY-MODEL, DE-LINEATION-CARICATURE, SAMENESS-CONTRAST.

fact. An act; a truth. CERTAINTY-DOUBT, ENTITY-NONENTITY, TRUTH-ERROR, VARIATION; **in fact,** ENTITY-NONENTITY.

facta non verba [L.] (fac'-ta non ver'-ba). Deeds, not words. BRAGGING.

fac'-tion. A party; dissension. ASSOCIATION, VA-RIANCE-ACCORD.

fac'-tious. Partizan. VARIANCE-ACCORD.

fac-ti'-tious. Artificial. TRUTHFULNESS-FABRICATION, TRUTHFULNESS-FRAUD.

fac'-tor. An agent; one of two or more quantities which, when multiplied together, produce a given quantity. CONSIGNEE, DEALER, MANAGER, NUMBER.

fac-to'-ri-al. A continued product of factors differing by unity. NUMBERING.

fac'-tor-ing. Resolving into factors. NUMBERING.

fac'-to-ry. Manufactory. WORKSHOP.

fac-to'-tum. A man of all work. AGENT, CONSIGNEE, MANAGER.

facts. Things stated or assumed as true. **A summary of facts,** EVIDENCE-COUNTEREVIDENCE.

facula [L.] (fac'-yu-la). A small spot on the sun brighter than the rest of the photosphere. ASTRONO-MY, LIGHT-DARKNESS.

fac'-ul-ties. The powers of the mind. MIND-IMBE-CILITY; **in possession of one's faculties,** SANENESS-LUNACY.

fac'-ul-ty. A special power of mind or body; a body of instructors. OCCUPATION, MIGHT-IMPOTENCE, SKILL-UNSKILFULNESS.

fac-un'-di-ty. Eloquence. SPEECH-INARTICULATENESS.

fad. A hobby. DECISION-MISJUDGMENT, PERSIST-ENCE-WHIM.

fad'-dle. To trifle. ACTIVITY-INDOLENCE.

fade. To disappear gradually; to lose freshness. AP-PEARANCE-DISAPPEARANCE, BETTERMENT-DETERI-ORATION, COLOR-ACHROMATISM, DIMNESS, LAST-INGNESS-TRANSIENTNESS, NOVELTY-ANTIQUITY, STRENGTH-WEAKNESS, SUBSTANCE-NULLITY; **fade from memory,** REMEMBRANCE-FORGETFULNESS.

fade. Insipid. SAVOR-TASTELESSNESS.

fa'-ded. Without vigor or energy. STYLE.

fade'-less. Unfading. MUTABILITY-STABILITY.

fadge. To suit; succeed. HARMONY-DISCORD.

fa'-ding. Losing its color. APPEARANCE-DISAPPEARANCE.

fæces [L.] (fî'-sîz). Excrement. BETTERMENT - DETERIORATION, NUTRIMENT-EXCRETION.

fæx populi [L.] (fex pop'-yu-lai). The dregs of the people. GENTILITY-DEMOCRACY.

fag. A drudge; a rough spot in goods. AGENT, TOIL-RELAXATION; **fag-end,** BEGINNING-END, INCREMENT-REMNANT.

fag'-ging. Drudging. TOIL-RELAXATION.

fag'-ot. A bundle. COMBUSTIBLE, GATHERING-SCATTERING.

fa-got'-to. The bassoon. MUSICAL INSTRUMENTS.

fagots et fagots [F.] (fa-goz' ê fa-go'). All men are not alike. DIFFERENTIATION - INDISCRIMINATION, VARIATION.

Fah'-ren-heit. Pertaining to that thermometer-scale in which the boiling point is 212° and the freezing point 32°. THERMOMETER.

fa''-ience'. Highly decorated earthenware. BEAUTY-UGLINESS, CONTENTS-RECEIVER.

fail. To forsake; to prove defective; to become insolvent. DUTY - DERELICTION, GOODNESS - BADNESS, OBSERVANCE - NONOBSERVANCE, PROOF - DISPROOF, SETTLEMENT - DEFAULT, SKILL - UNSKILFULNESS, STRENGTH - WEAKNESS, SUCCESS - FAILURE, TRANSCURSION-SHORTCOMING, TRUTH-ERROR.

fail'-ing. A minor fault; the act of becoming bankrupt. DUTY-DERELICTION, ENTIRETY-DEFICIENCY, EXCESS - LACK, INNOCENCE - GUILT, OBSERVANCE-NONOBSERVANCE, PROOF-DISPROOF, SETTLEMENT-DEFAULT, STRENGTH-WEAKNESS, SUCCESS-FAILURE, TRANSCURSION-SHORTCOMING, VIRTUE-VICE; **failing heart,** LIGHTHEARTEDNESS-DEJECTION; **failing luck,** WELFARE-MISFORTUNE; **failing memory,** REMEMBRANCE-FORGETFULNESS; **failing sight,** SIGHT-DIMSIGHTEDNESS; **failing strength,** STRENGTH-WEAKNESS.

faille. A nun's hood. DRESS-UNDRESS.

fail'-ure. The act of failing; bankruptcy. DUTY-DERELICTION, INNOCENCE-GUILT, OBSERVANCE-NONOBSERVANCE, RATIONALE-LUCK,SETTLEMENT-DEFAULT, SKILL-UNSKILFULNESS, SUCCESS-FAILURE, TRANSCURSION-SHORTCOMING, VIRTUE-VICE, WELFARE-MISFORTUNE.

fain. Willing. COERCION, DESIRE-DISTASTE, READINESS-RELUCTANCE.

fainéant [F.] (fê-nê-an'). Lazy. ACTIVITY-INDOLENCE.

faint. To swoon; to despond; to vanish. COERCION, COLOR - ACHROMATISM, DESIRE - DISTASTE, DIMNESS, INCREMENT - REMNANT, LOUDNESS - FAINTNESS, MIGHT-IMPOTENCE, READINESS-RELUCTANCE, STRENGTH-WEAKNESS, WEARINESS-REFRESHMENT; **faint heart,** BRAVERY-COWARDICE; SANGUINENESS-TIMIDITY, **damn with faint praise,** ADULATION - DISPARAGEMENT, APPROVAL - DISAPPROVAL, REGARD-SCORN.

faint'-ing. Swooning. WEARINESS-REFRESHMENT.

faint'-ish. Rather faint. STRENGTH - WEAKNESS.

faint'-ly. Not distinctly. MAGNITUDE - SMALLNESS.

faint'-ness. Want of vigor. FAINTNESS, LOUDNESS, WEARINESS-REFRESHMENT.

fair. Clear; equitable; not dark; beautiful; moderately satisfactory. BEAUTY-UGLINESS, COLOR-ACHROMATISM, CONSEQUENCE - INSIGNIFICANCE, FAULTLESSNESS-FAULTINESS, GOODNESS-BADNESS, MAGNITUDE-SMALLNESS, MARKET, RIGHT-WRONG, SAGACITY-INCAPACITY, UPRIGHTNESS-DISHONESTY, WHITENESS-BLACKNESS; **by fair means or foul,** INSTRUMENTALITY; **fair chance,** LIKELIHOOD-UNLIKELIHOOD; **fair copy,** COPY-MODEL, WRITING-PRINTING; **fair field,** OPPORTUNENESS-UNSUITABLENESS, RIGHT-WRONG; **fair game,** SOCIETY-LAUGHINGSTOCK; **fair name,** REPUTATION-DISCREDIT; **fair play,** RIGHT-WRONG, UPRIGHTNESS-DISHONESTY; **fair question,** INVESTIGATION-ANSWER; **fair sex,** MALE-FEMALE; **fair weather,** WELFARE-MISFORTUNE; **fair wind,** DIFFICULTY-FACILITY, WELFARE-MISFORTUNE; **fair words,** POLITENESS-IMPOLITENESS; **in a fair way,** CONSERVATION, INCLINATION, LIKELIHOOD-UNLIKELIHOOD, SANGUINENESS-HOPELESSNESS, WELFARE-MISFORTUNE; **Vanity Fair,** SOCIETY-LUDICROUSNESS.

faire l'aimable [F.] (fêr lê-mabl'). To do the elegant talking. ACTION-PASSIVENESS.

faire sans dire [F.] (fêr san' dîre). To act without speaking.

faire, savoir [F.] (fêr, sa-vwar'). To know just what to do. SOCIETY-LUDICROUSNESS.

fair'-ing. A present. GIVING-RECEIVING.

fair'-ly. Equitably; reasonably; beautifully. SUBJECTIVENESS-OBJECTIVENESS; **get on fairly,** MEDIOCRITY.

fair'-ness. Honesty; free from spots or stains. BEAUTY-UGLINESS, UPRIGHTNESS-DISHONESTY.

fair'-spo''-ken. Plausible. ADULATION-DISPARAGEMENT, POLITENESS-IMPOLITENESS.

fair'-way''. The proper course through a channel. TRAVELING-NAVIGATION.

fair'-weath''-er. Clear weather, especially for traveling. PLEASURABLENESS-PAINFULNESS, TRAVELING-NAVIGATION.

fair'y. An imaginary being supposed to change the form at will. DEVOTION-MAGICIAN, FANCY, JOVE-FIEND; **fairy tale,** ACCOUNT.

fair'-y-land''. The fancied abode of the fairies. FANCY.

fair'-y-like''. Resembling a fairy. FANCY, JOVE-FIEND.

fait, au [F.] (fe, o). In fact. KNOWLEDGE-IGNORANCE, SKILL-UNSKILFULNESS.

fait accompli [F.] (fet a-con'-plî'). An accomplished fact. CERTAINTY-DOUBT.

fait à peindre [F.] (fet a pan·dr). A model for a painter. BEAUTY-UGLINESS.

faith. Belief; a religious creed or article; fidelity. FAITH-MISGIVING, GODLINESS-UNGODLINESS, SANGUINENESS-HOPELESSNESS, UPRIGHTNESS-DISHONESTY; **declaration of faith,** THEOLOGY; **i' faith,** ASSERTION-DENIAL; **keep faith with,** OBSERVANCE-NONOBSERVANCE, UPRIGHTNESS-DISHONESTY; **plight faith,** ENGAGEMENT-RELEASE; **true faith,** ORTHODOXY-HETERODOXY; **want of faith,** CREDULOUSNESS-SKEPTICISM, GODLINESS-DISBELIEF.

FAITH—MISGIVING.

Assent. Concurrence in opinion.

Assurance. Freedom from doubt.

Belief. Assent to the truth of reasons.

Calm belief. } A belief or opinion arrived at without passion or
Calm opinion. } emotion.

Certainty. Infallible proof or accuracy.

Conception. An idea formed in the mind on any subject.

Conclusion. Anything believed as a result of reasoning. See DECISION.

Confidence. Implicit belief in anything.

Change of opinion. See FAITH.

Demur. Hesitation in deciding.

Disbelief. Positive rejection of truth.

Discredit. State of being disbelieved.

Dissent. Refusal to accept something proposed, etc. See ASSENT-DISSENT.

Distrust. Lack of confidence or reliance.

Doubt. Unsettled opinion concerning anything, etc. See CERTAINTY-DOUBT.

Incredibility. State of being difficult to believe.

FAITH—MISGIVING—*Continued.*

Conviction. Belief or persuasion concerning our most important duties.
Convincement. State of being convinced.
Credence. Reliance on evidence other than personal knowledge.
Credenda [L.]. Things to be believed.
Credibility. Worthiness of belief. See LIKELIHOOD
Credit. Belief; trust.
Declaration of faith. A distinct statement of one's judgment upon a matter.
Deep-rooted belief.
Deep-rooted opinion. } A settled belief which is difficult to change.
Dependence on. Confidence or trust in.
Dispassionate belief. A belief not influenced by passion.
Dispassionate opinion. An opinion unaffected by passion.
Doctrine. That which is held as true, particularly speculative belief.
Dogma. Something held as an opinion.
Expectation. Prospect of something to come. See SANGUINENESS.
Faith. An earnest, practical belief.
Firm belief.
Firm opinion. } A belief or opinion not easily changed or excited.
Fixed belief.
Fixed opinion. } An unalterable belief or opinion.
Impartial belief.
Impartial opinion. } A belief or opinion not favoring one thing more than another.
Implicit belief.
Implicit opinion. } A belief or opinion without doubt or reserve.
Impression. An indistinct belief.
Inveterate belief.
Inveterate opinion. } A belief firmly established.
Mind. An opinion or belief.
Opinion. A conclusion held as probable.
Persuasion. Belief, resulting from the action of the will and leading to action.
Plerophory. Full conviction.
Popular belief. See ASSENT.
Presumption. A judgment of whose truth there is a probability.
Principle. A fundamental belief.
Profession of faith. Open acknowledgment of faith.
Reliance on. Trust on or confidence in.
Rooted belief.
Rooted opinion. } A belief or opinion growing from one's character and circumstances.
Sanguine expectation. Confident hope or belief.
School. The body of the beliefs of a particular class or age.
Self-conviction. Persuasion of the truth of something through oneself or of oneself.
Settled belief.
Settled opinion. } A judgment not easily changed.
Sober belief.
Sober opinion. } A judgment unaffected by passion.
Staunch belief.
Staunch opinion. } A constant and zealous belief or opinion.
Steadfast belief.
Steadfast opinion. } A firm belief or opinion.
Surmise. A belief based on scanty evidence. See HYPOTHESIS.
Tenet. A belief or doctrine.
Thinking. Opinion formed in judgments.
Troth. Belief or faith.
Trust. Confident belief.
Uberrima fides [L.]. Abounding faith.
Unshaken belief.
Unshaken opinion. } A judgment which cannot be changed.
View. Manner of looking at anything; opinion.
Way of thinking. A judgment expressed on any subject.
Well-founded belief.
Well-founded opinion. } A judgment based on good authority or evidence.

FAITH—*Associated Nouns.*

Articles. See ORTHODOXY.
Canons. Codes of belief.
Catechism. A short treatise giving in catechetical form an outline of the fundamental principles of a religious creed.
Creed. A formal summary of fundamental points of religious belief.
Propaganda. A plan for spreading some particular doctrine.
System of opinions. A statement of one's convictions on religious subjects.
Thirty-nine Articles. The articles of belief of the Church of England.

FAITH—*Verbs.*

Account as. To regard.
Adopt a belief. See *Nouns.*
Adopt an opinion. See *Nouns.*
Allow some weight to. To have some confidence in

Incredibleness. Incredibility.
Incredulity. Refusal to believe.
Infidelity. Lack of faith in the inspiration of the Scriptures, etc. See GODLINESS-DISBELIEF.
Jealousy. A painful apprehension of rivalry in cases touching our own interest.
Misbelief. False belief.
Miscreance. Adherence to a false faith.
Misdoubt. Hesitation.
Misgiving. Evil apprehension.
Mistrust. Lack of confidence.
Onus probandi [L.]. The burden of proving.
Qualm. Unrest of conscience.
Retractation. The act of taking back what has been said, etc. See BIGOTRY-APOSTASY.
Scruple. Doubt concerning a question of morality.
Skepticism. Doubt concerning the doctrines of Christianity.
Suspicion. Act of mistrusting.
Unbelief. Lack of belief, especially in divine revelation.

MISGIVING—*Agent.*

Unbeliever. One who has no religious faith.

MISGIVING—*Verbs.*

Awake a doubt.
Awake suspicion. } To cause distrust.
Be doubtful. See CERTAINTY-DOUBT.
Be skeptical as to. See *Adjectives.*
Bring in question.
Call in question. } To doubt.
Cause a doubt.
Cause suspicion. } To cause distrust.
Cavil. To raise objections without sufficient reason.
Challenge. To call in question.
Demur. To hesitate.
Deny. To declare untrue, etc. See ASSERTION-DENIAL.
Diffide. To distrust.
Disbelieve. To hold to be untrue.
Discredit. Not to believe.
Dispute. To deny the truth of.
Distrust. Not to put confidence in.
Doubt. To hesitate to believe; to stand between two.
Doubt the truth of. To disbelieve.
Entertain doubts.
Entertain suspicions. } To be uncertain.
Ergotize. To dispute.
Hang in doubt.
Hang in suspense. } To be unsettled.
Harbor doubts.
Harbor suspicions. } To mistrust.
Have doubts.
Have one's doubts. } To be uncertain of.
Have suspicions.
Hesitate. To be in suspense.
Misbelieve. To believe wrongly.
Mistrust. To look upon with suspicion.
Not believe. See FAITH.
Pause. To hesitate.
Question. To doubt.
Raise a doubt.
Raise a question. } To regard as doubtful.
Raise suspicion.
Refuse to admit. See ASSENT-DISSENT.
Refuse to believe. See CREDULOUSNESS-SKEPTICISM.
Scent. To have a suspicion of.
Scruple. To hesitate.
Shake one's belief.
Shake one's faith. } To cause a doubt.
Smell a rat. To have reason to suspect.
Smoke. To ferret out.
Stagger. To cause to hesitate.
Stagger one's belief.
Stagger one's faith. } To cause one to disbelieve or waver
Start a doubt. To make one distrustful.
Startle. To take by surprise.
Start suspicion. To cause doubt.
Stick at. To hesitate.
Suggest a doubt.
Suggest suspicion. } To do something which makes one doubtful.
Suspect. To view with doubt.
Throw doubt upon. To mistrust.

FAITH—MISGIVING—*Continued.*

FAITH—Verbs—*Continued.*

Apprehend. To lay hold of mentally.
Assume. To receive without evidence.
Assure oneself. To make oneself certain.
Attach some weight to. To believe to some extent.
Be assured. See *Adjectives.*
Be current. To have general acceptance.
Believe. To give credence to.
Believe in. To accept as true.
Be of opinion. To have a judgment on a question.
Be received. See *Verbs.*
Bring home to. To prove beyond a doubt.
Bring over. To convert to one's opinion.
Bring round. To bring to a desired belief.
Build upon. To confidently expect.
Calculate upon. To study to arrive at an opinion or judgment.
Carry conviction. To make others have the same opinion.
Cause to be believed. To convince.
Cherish a belief. } To have a judgment of one's own.
Cherish an opinion. }
Come round to an opinion. To accept the judgment of another.
Conceive. To formulate in the mind.
Conceive as. To have an opinion of.
Confide in. To put confidence in.
Consider. To weigh carefully in the mind.
Count upon. To place faith in.
Convert. To change from one belief to another.
Convict. To arouse to the consciousness of sin or guilt.
Convince. To overcome the understanding by argument.
Cram down the throat. To force an opinion on any one.
Credit. To put confidence in
Deem as. To think of as.
Depend upon. To have faith in.
Doubt not. To believe.
Drive home to. To impress.
Embrace a belief. } To accept the judgment of another.
Embrace an opinion. }
Entertain a belief. } To have a judgment upon anything.
Entertain an opinion. }
Esteem. To have a favorable opinion of.
Esteem as. To consider as.
Fancy. To believe without good evidence.
Find credence. See *Nouns.*
Foster a belief. } To encourage a belief or opinion.
Foster an opinion. }
Gain the confidence of. To get one's good opinion.
Get hold of a belief. } To understand.
Get hold of an opinion. }
Get it into one's head. To understand.
Give credence to. }
Give credit to. } To accept as worthy of belief.
Give faith to. }
Give one credit for. To ascribe a judgment to a person.
Go down. To be received as true.
Have a belief. } To have reached a conclusion by the exercise of
Have an opinion. } judgment.
Have it. To understand anything.
Have no doubt. To believe entirely.
Have the ear of. To gain the confidence of.
Hazard a belief. } To express an opinion upon a doubtful ques-
Hazard an opinion. } tion.
Hold To receive, as an opinion.
Hold a belief. } To have a view of one's own.
Hold an opinion. }
Hold as. To consider as.
Imbibe a belief. } To accept the conclusion of another; swallow.
Imbibe an opinion. }
Indoctrinate. To instruct in principles or doctrines. See EDUCATION.
Know. To be fully convinced of.
Know for certain. To regard as true.
Lay one's account for. To trust.
Lean upon. To rest upon the opinion of another.
Look upon as. To consider as.
Make no doubt. To believe fully.
Make oneself easy about. To be certain of.
Make oneself easy on that score. To have no doubt of a matter
Make sure of. To discover the truth of.
Make up one's mind. To come to a conclusion by the exercise of judgment.
Nurture a belief. } To continue to hold an opinion.
Nurture an opinion. }
Opine. To hold an opinion.
Pass current. To be generally accepted as true.

MISGIVING—*Adjectives.*

Controvertible. Admitting of debate. See TRUTH-ERROR.
Disputable. That may be called in question.
Distrustful of. Uncertain about.
Doubtful. Subject to doubt. See CERTAINTY-DOUBT.
Doubting. See *Verbs*
Fallible. Capable of being in error. See CERTAINTY-DOUBT.
Hard to believe. Seemingly doubtful.
Inconceivable. Not capable of being explained by the human intellect.
Incredible. Not admitting of belief.
Incredulous as to. Doubtful about.
Not to be believed. Seeming false or impossible.
Open to doubt. } Uncertain.
Open to suspicion. }
Questionable. Admitting of question or suspicion.
Skeptical as to. Doubtful about.
Shy of. Avoiding with suspicion.
Staggering. See *Verbs.*
Suspect. Doubtful.
Suspicious. Admitting of mistrust.
Suspicious of. Distrustful.
Unbelieving. Doubtful.
Undemonstrable. Not admitting of demonstration or proof.
Undeserving of belief. See FAITH.
Unworthy of belief. False; incredible.

MISGIVING—*Phrases.*

Credat Judæus Apella [L.]. Let Apella, the Jew, believe it (*i. e.* only a superstitious person will). [Horace, *Satires*, 4, 5, 106.]
Cum grano salis [L.]. With a grain of salt.
Fronti nulla fides [L.]. No reliance on appearances. [Juvenal, 2, 8.]
Let those believe who may.
Nimium ne crede colori [L.]. Do not trust too much to looks. [Virgil, *Eclogues*, 2, 19.]
Timeo Danaos et dona ferentes [L.]. I fear the Greeks even when they bring gifts. [Virgil, *Æneid*, 2, 492.]
With grains of allowance. With some degree of doubt.

FAITH—Verbs—*Continued.*

Persuade. To bring the will of another to a desired decision.
Persuade oneself. To make oneself agree to a certain opinion or view.
Pin one's faith upon. } To rely upon.
Place implicit confidence in. }
Place reliance on. To have faith in.
Possess a belief. See *Nouns.*
Possess an opinion. See *Nouns.*
Possess the mind. To have entire control of a person's judgment.
Presume. To take as true without examination or proof.
Produce conviction. See *Nouns.*
Put one's trust in. To have full faith in.
Realize. To impress upon the mind as real.
Receive. To accept as true.
Reckon upon. To depend upon.
Regard as. To consider
Regard to. To relate to.
Rely upon. To have faith in.
Repose implicit confidence in. To trust fully.
Rest assured. To be without a doubt.
Rest upon. To trust.
Satisfy. To rid of doubt.
Satisfy oneself. To be satisfied as far as one's own judgment is concerned.
See. To perceive with the mind.
Set down as. } To consider as.
Set down for. }
Surmise. To infer on scanty evidence. See HYPOTHESIS.
Swallow. To accept a belief without scruple. See CREDULOUSNESS.
Swear by. To place implicit confidence in.
Take as. To consider as.
Take at one's word. To trust.
Take for. Consider as.
Take for gospel. To accept as true.
Take for granted. To accept as true without proof.
Take hold of the mind. To influence strongly.
Take it. To understand.
Take it into one's head. To adopt a certain belief.
Take on credit. To accept without proof.
Take one's word for. To trust.
Take on trust. To accept without proof or evidence.
Take possession of the mind. To impress.

FAITH—Verbs—*Continued.*

Think. To arrive at a conclusion.
Trow. To believe or suppose.
View as. To consider in a certain light.

Wean.
Ween. } To think; to fancy.
Win over. To have an opponent accept one's belief.

Faith—*Adjectives.*

Accredited. Having trust reposed in.
Assured. Made certain.
Believed. See *Verbs.*
Believing. See *Verbs.*
Certain. Not admitting of doubt.
Cocksure. Very certain.
Commanding belief. Producing belief.
Confident. Fully assured.
Confiding. Having faith in.
Convinced. Fully satisfied by proof.
Credible. Worthy of being believed.
Credulous. Apt to believe on slight proof, etc. See CREDULOUSNESS.
Deserving of belief. Worthy of belief.
Doctrinal. Pertaining to doctrine.
Fiducial. Indicative of faith.
Fiduciary. Pertaining to one in a position of trust.
Imbued with. Deeply impressed with.
Impressed with. Strongly influenced by.
Impressive. Touching the conscience.
Penetrated with. Believing thoroughly in.

Persuasive. Having power to persuade.
Positive. Very decided in opinion.
Probable. With more evidence for than against. See LIKELIHOOD.
Putative. Commonly supposed.
Relating to belief. Doctrinal.
Reliable. Worthy of confidence.
Satisfactory. Removing doubt from the mind.
Satisfied. See *Verbs.*
Secure. Firm in opinion; free from care.
Sure. Deserving to be depended on; free from doubt.
Suspectless. Not having any suspicion.
To be depended upon. Worthy of belief.
Trustworthy. Worthy of confidence.
Under the impression. Having a particular judgment.
Unhesitating. Without hesitation.
Unsuspected. Not suspected.
Unsuspecting. Not mistrusting.
Unsuspicious. Not inclined to suspect.
Void of suspicion. Satisfied.
Wedded to. Firmly attached to.
Worthy of belief. Credible.

Faith—*Adverbs, etc.*

Be assured; depend upon it; I am sure; I dare say; I doubt not; I have no doubt; I'll warrant you (see ASSERTION), in the eyes of; in the opinion of; *me judice* [L.], in my opinion; meseems; methinks; rely upon it; rest assured; sure enough (see CERTAINTY); to the best of one's belief.

Faith—*Phrases.*

Experto credite [L.]. Believe one who speaks from experience.
Fata viam invenient [L.]. The Fates will discover a way.

Justitiæ soror incorrupta Fides [L.]. Uncorrupt Faith, sister of Justice.
Vide et crede [L.]. See and believe.

faith'-ful. Trustworthy in the performance of duty, in the fulfilment of promises, etc.; true in detail; truthful; firm in faith. COPY-MODEL, FAITH-MISGIVING, GODLINESS-UNGODLINESS, INSUBORDINATION-OBEDIENCE, LIKENESS-UNLIKENESS, OBSERVANCE-NONOBSERVANCE, SANGUINENESS-HOPELESSNESS, THEOLOGY, TRUTH-ERROR, UPRIGHTNESS-DISHONESTY.
faith'-ful-ly. In a faithful manner. OBSERVANCE-NONOBSERVANCE.
faith'-ful-ness. Uprightness; trustworthiness. UPRIGHTNESS-DISHONESTY.
faith'-less. Unfaithful; untrustworthy; unbelieving. TRUTHFULNESS-FALSEHOOD, UPRIGHTNESS-DISHONESTY, GODLINESS-DISBELIEF.
faith'-less-ness. Lack of faithfulness. PATRIOTISM-TREASON, UPRIGHTNESS-DISHONESTY.
fake. A deception. TRUTHFULNESS-FRAUD.
fa'-kir. A Mohammedan or Hindu ascetic or mendicant devotee. MINISTRY-LAITY.
fal-cade'. The leaping action of a frisky horse. SPRING-DIVE.
fal'-cate. Sickle-shaped. ANGULARITY, CURVATION-RECTILINEARITY.
fal'-ca-ted. Sickle-shaped. ANGULARITY, CURVATION-RECTILINEARITY.
fal'-chion. A broad, curved sword. WEAPON.
Fal-cid'-i-an law. A law enacted at Rome in 40 B. C., making it compulsory for a testator to leave one-fourth of his property to his natural heir. PROPERTY.
fal'-ci-form. Curved like a sickle. ANGULARITY, CURVATION-RECTILINEARITY.
fal'-con. A bird of prey used in hunting. ROBBER.
fal'-con-er. One who hunts with falcons. QUEST-EVASION.
fal'-co-net. A small cannon. WEAPON.
fald'-stool''. A desk at which the litany is read. FANE, SUSPENSION-SUPPORT.
fall. To drop; to befall; to be slain; to go down; to

sin. ASCENT-DESCENT, CREATION-DESTRUCTION, LIFE-DEATH, MORNING-EVENING, OCCURRENCE-DESTINY, PARALLELISM-INCLINATION, PROGRESSION-RETROGRESSION, RIVER-WIND, SUCCESS-FAILURE, VIRTUE-VICE, WELFARE-MISFORTUNE; **fall a cursing,** CHARITABLENESS-CURSE; **fall a prey to,** LIBERTY-SUBJECTION, SUCCESS-FAILURE; **fall asleep,** ACTIVITY-INDOLENCE; **fall astern,** ANTERIORITY-POSTERIORITY; **fall at one's feet,** YIELDING; **fall away,** ENLARGEMENT-DIMINUTION, INCREASE-DECREASE; **fall back,** ADVANCE-RETROGRESSION, APPROACH-WITHDRAWAL, RENOVATION-RELAPSE; **fall back upon,** ATTACK-DEFENSE, USE-DISUSE; **fall dead,** LIFE-DEATH; **fall down,** DEVOTION-IDOLATRY; **fall down before,** REGARD-DISRESPECT; **fall flat on the ear,** WITTINESS-DULNESS; **fall foul of,** IMPETUS-REACTION; **fall from one's high estate,** REPUTATION-DISCREDIT, WELFARE-MISFORTUNE; **fall from the lips,** SPEECH-INARTICULATENESS; **fall in,** CONTINUITY-INTERRUPTION, OCCURRENCE-DESTINY, REGULARITY-IRREGULARITY; **fall in love with,** BLANDISHMENT, LOVE-HATE; **fall in price,** COSTLINESS-CHEAPNESS; **fall in the way of,** PRESENCE-ABSENCE; **fall into,** CONVERSION-REVERSION, RIVER-WIND; **fall into a custom,** CONVENTIONALITY-UNCONVENTIONALITY, HABIT-DESUETUDE; **fall into a habit,** HABIT-DESUETUDE; **fall into a passion,** FAVORITE-ANGER; **fall into a trap,** GULL-DECEIVER, SKILL-UNSKILFULNESS; **fall into decay,** BETTERMENT-DETERIORATION; **fall into oblivion,** REMEMBRANCE-FORGETFULNESS; **fall into raptures,** PLEASURE-PAIN; **fall in with,** CONCENTRATION-RADIATION, CONSENT, CONVENTIONALITY-UNCONVENTIONALITY, DISCOVERY, HARMONY-DISCORD, VARIANCE-ACCORD; **fall of day,** MORNING-EVENING; **fall off,** BETTERMENT-DETERIORATION, INCREASE-DECREASE, RENOVATION-RELAPSE, UNION-DISUNION; **fall off again,** RENOVATION-RELAPSE; **fall of curtain,** BEGINNING-END; **fall**

of snow, HEAT-COLD; **fall of the leaf,** MORNING-EVENING; **fall on one's knees,** DEVOTION-IDOLATRY, PETITION-EXPOSTULATION, PRESUMPTION-OBSEQUIOUSNESS, THANKFULNESS-THANKLESSNESS, YIELDING; **fall out,** AMITY-HOSTILITY, OCCURRENCE-DESTINY, VARIANCE-ACCORD; **fall short,** ENLARGEMENT-DIMINUTION, ENTIRETY-DEFICIENCY, SUCCESS-FAILURE, SUPREMACY-SUBORDINACY, TRANSCURSION-SHORTCOMING; **fall through,** SUCCESS-FAILURE, TRANSCURSION-SHORTCOMING; **fall to one's lot,** DUTY-DERELICTION, GIVING-RECEIVING, OCCURRENCE-DESTINY, RATIONALE-LUCK; **fall to pieces,** CREATION-DESTRUCTION, TOUGHNESS-BRITTLENESS, UNION-DISUNION; **fall to the ground,** CREATION-DESTRUCTION, PROOF-DISPROOF, SUCCESS-FAILURE, TRANSCURSION-SHORTCOMING; **fall under,** ADMISSION-EXCLUSION, LIBERTY-SUBJECTION; **fall under one's notice,** HEED-DISREGARD; **fall upon,** ATTACK-DEFENSE, DESIGN, DISCOVERY, EXPECTATION-SURPRISE; **fall upon the ear,** HEARING-DEAFNESS; **have to fall back upon,** PROVISION-WASTE; **let fall,** ELEVATION-DEPRESSION, ENLIGHTENMENT-SECRECY, SPEECH-INARTICULATION; **waterfall,** RIVER-WIND.

fal-la'-cious. Illogical; fitted to deceive. RATIOCINATION-INSTINCT, TRUTH-ERROR.

fal'-la-cy. Error; any unsound reasoning. RATIOCINATION-INSTINCT, TRUTH-ERROR.

fall'-en an'-gel. An evil spirit; a bad man. ANGEL-SATAN, GOOD MAN-BAD MAN.

fal''-li-bil'-i-ty. The state of being fallible. CERTAINTY-DOUBT.

fal'-li-ble. Liable to error. CERTAINTY-DOUBT, FAITH-MISGIVING, RATIOCINATION-INSTINCT.

fall'-ing. Descending; dropping. ASCENT-DESCENT, WELFARE-MISFORTUNE.

fall'-ing star. A shooting star. UNIVERSE.

fal'-low. Left unseeded after tilling; sallow. ACTION-PASSIVENESS, FERTILITY-STERILITY, PREPARATION-NONPREPARATION, YELLOWNESS-PURPLE.

false. Contrary to truth or fact; dishonest; temporary. DUENESS-UNDUENESS, PATRIOTISM-TREASON, RATIOCINATION-CASUISTRY, TRUTH-ERROR, TRUTHFULNESS-FALSEHOOD, TRUTHFULNESS-FABRICATION, UPRIGHTNESS-DISHONESTY; **false alarm,** ALARM; **false coloring,** GULL-HYPERBOLE, INTERPRETATION-MISINTERPRETATION, TRUTHFULNESS-FALSEHOOD; **false construction,** INTERPRETATION-MISINTERPRETATION, TRUTHFULNESS-FALSEHOOD; **false doctrine,** ORTHODOXY-HETERODOXY; **false expectation,** EXPECTATION-DISAPPOINTMENT, EXPECTATION-SURPRISE; **false-hearted,** UPRIGHTNESS-DISHONESTY; **false impression,** TRUTH-ERROR; **false light,** SIGHT-DIMSIGHTEDNESS, TRUTH-ERROR; **false money,** MONEY; **false ornament,** TASTE-VULGARITY; **false plea,** PRETEXT, TRUTHFULNESS-FABRICATION; **false position,** DIFFICULTY-FACILITY; **false pretenses,** THEFT; **false prophet,** EXPECTATION-DISAPPOINTMENT; **false reasoning,** RATIOCINATION-CASUISTRY; **false scent,** EDUCATION-MISTEACHING, TRUTH-ERROR; **false shame,** SOCIETY-AFFECTATION; **false statement,** TRUTHFULNESS-FABRICATION; **false step,** SUCCESS-FAILURE; **false teaching,** EDUCATION-MISTEACHING; **false witness,** ADULATION-DISPARAGEMENT, GULL-DECEIVER.

false'-faced''. Hypocritical. UPRIGHTNESS-DISHONESTY.

false'-hood. An intentional untruth; fallacy. TRUTHFULNESS-FABRICATION, TRUTHFULNESS-FALSEHOOD.

false'-ly. In a false manner. TRUTHFULNESS-FALSEHOOD.

false'-ness. The state of being false. TRUTHFULNESS-FRAUD, VIRTUE-VICE.

fal-set'-to. Shrill; the tones higher than the chest-voice. CACOPHONY, SPEECH-INARTICULATION, VOCALIZATION-MUTENESS.

falsi crimen [L.] (fal'-sai crai'-men). The crime of forgery. TRUTHFULNESS-FRAUD.

fal''-si-fi-ca'-tion. The act of falsifying. TIDINGS, TRUTHFULNESS - FABRICATION, TRUTHFULNESS-FALSEHOOD.

fal'-si-fied. Made false. TRUTHFULNESS-FALSEHOOD.

fal'-si-fy. To make deceptive; to disprove. TRUTH-ERROR, TRUTHFULNESS-FALSEHOOD; **falsify accounts,** ACCOUNTS; **falsify one's hope,** EXPECTATION-DISAPPOINTMENT.

fals'-ism. A self-evident falsity. TRUTH-ERROR, TRUTHFULNESS-FALSEHOOD

fal'-si-ty. The quality of being false. TRUTHFULNESS-FRAUD.

falsus in uno, falsus in omnibus [L.] (fal'-sus in yu'-no, fal'-sus in om'-ni-bus). False in one point, false in all. ENTIRETY-DEFICIENCY, TRUTHFULNESS-FRAUD.

fal'-ter. To speak with broken utterance or act with weakness. DETERMINATION - VACILLATION, SANGUINENESS-HOPELESSNESS, SANGUINENESS-TIMIDITY, SPEECH - INARTICULATENESS, SUCCESS - FAILURE, SWIFTNESS-SLOWNESS.

fal'-ter-ing ac'-cents. Broken or undecided utterance. DETERMINATION-VACILLATION.

fama semper vivat [L.] (fê'-ma sem'-per vai'-vat). May his fame live forever. REPUTATION-DISCREDIT.

fame. Renown; report. REPUTATION-DISCREDIT, TIDINGS-MYSTERY.

famed. Renowned. REPUTATION-DISCREDIT.

fa-mil'-iar. Well known; free from affectation. AMITY-HOSTILITY, HABIT-DESUETUDE, KNOWLEDGE-IGNORANCE, POLITENESS-IMPOLITENESS, SOCIABILITY-PRIVACY; **familiar spirit,** JOVE-FIEND; **on familiar terms,** AMITY-HOSTILITY.

fa-mil''-i-ar'-i-ty. Intimacy. AMITY - HOSTILITY, KNOWLEDGE-IGNORANCE, SOCIABILITY-PRIVACY.

fa-mil'-iar-ize. To make familiar. EDUCATION-MISTEACHING, HABIT-DESUETUDE.

Fam'-i-list. One of a sect called the Family of Love, which rose in the sixteenth century. LOVE-HATE, ORTHODOXY-HETERODOXY.

fam''-i-lis'-te-ry. A family in which all things are common. ASSOCIATION.

famille [F.] (fa-mîy'). Family. SOCIABILITY-PRIVACY.

fam'-i-ly. A group of persons consisting of a father, mother, and their children; a number of persons sprung from one ancestor; a clan, tribe, or nation. ASSOCIATION, DIVISION, PARENTAGE-PROGENY, RELATIONSHIP; **family circle,** SOCIABILITY-PRIVACY; **family jars,** VARIANCE-ACCORD; **family likeness,** LIKENESS-UNLIKENESS; **family tie,** RELATIONSHIP; **happy family,** VARIANCE-ACCORD; **in the bosom of one's family,** OUTSIDE-INSIDE; **in the family way,** CREATION-DESTRUCTION.

fam'-ine. Great scarcity of anything, especially food. EXCESS-LACK; **famine price,** COSTLINESS-CHEAPNESS.

fam'-ine-strick'-en. Afflicted by famine. EXCESS-LACK.

fam'-ish. To starve; to suffer extremity of hunger or thirst. EXTRAVAGANCE-AVARICE, FASTING-GLUTTONY.

fam'-ished. Starved; in extremity of hunger or thirst. DESIRE-DISTASTE, EXCESS-LACK.

fam'-ish-ment. State of being famished. AUSTERITY.

fa'-mous. Renowned. REPUTATION-DISCREDIT.

fa'-mous-ly. In a famous manner. MAGNITUDE-SMALLNESS.

fa'-mous-ness. The state of being famous. REPUTATION-DISCREDIT.

fam'-u-list. In Oxford University, an attendant. INSTRUCTOR-PUPIL.

fan. To agitate the air round or upon by any device; to excite. EXCITATION, HEATING-COOLING, RIVER-WIND, WEARINESS-REFRESHMENT; **fan into a flame,**

EXCITATION, FAVORITE-ANGER; **fan the embers,** REMEMBRANCE-FORGETFULNESS; **fan the flame,** AL-LEVIATION-AGGRAVATION, EXCITATION, HEATING-COOLING, OBSTRUCTION-HELP; **flirt a fan,** SOCIETY-AFFECTATION.

fa-nat'-ic. One who is actuated by intemperate zeal, usually in religious matters. BIGOTRY-APOSTASY, CONVERSATION-MONOLOGUE, FANCY, ORTHODOXY-HETERODOXY, PATRIOTISM-TREASON, SANENESS-MANIAC.

fa-nat'-ic-al. Actuated by extravagant zeal. DE-CISION-MISJUDGMENT, EMOTION, EXCITABILITY-INEX-CITABILITY, GODLINESS-UNGODLINESS, PATRIOTISM-TREASON, SANENESS-LUNACY.

fa-nat'-i-cism. The spirit or conduct characteristic of a fanatic; irrational zeal. BIGOTRY-APOSTASY, EMO-TION, EXCITABILITY-INEXCITABILITY, ORTHODOXY-HETERODOXY, SANENESS-LUNACY.

fan'-ci-ful. Produced by fancy; unreal; whimsical. FANCY, PERSISTENCE-WHIM, SOCIETY-LUDICROUS-NESS.

fan'-cy. To suppose or believe without substantial grounds; to take pleasure in; have a notion; extrava-gant. BELLIGERENT, BIGOTRY-APOSTASY, CHOICE-NEUTRALITY, CONCEPTION-THEME, DESIRE-DIS-TASTE, FAITH-MISGIVING, FANCY, HYPOTHESIS, LOVE-HATE, MIND-IMBECILITY, REFLECTION-VACANCY, WITTINESS-DULNESS; **after one's fancy,** LOVE-HATE, TASTE-VULGARITY; **fancy dog,** FAUNA-FLORA; **in-dulge one's fancy,** CHOICE-NEUTRALITY; **take a fancy to,** DESIRE-DISTASTE, LOVE-HATE, PLEASURE-PAIN; **take one's fancy,** PLEASURABLENESS-PAINFULNESS.

FANCY.

Castle-building. Forming imaginary schemes.
Conceit. Flattering imagination of one's own worth.
Conception. The faculty of forming an idea in the mind.
Dreaming. Imagining.
Ecstasy. Rapturous imaginations.
Excogitation. Invention; contrivance.
Fancy. Combination of mental images without regard to reason. **Ardent—, boiling—, bold—, daring—, excited—, fertile—, fiery—, heated—, lively—, playful—, sanguine—, warm—, wild—fancy.**
Fantasy. Grotesque imagination; a mental caprice.
Frenzy. Violent imagination.
Idealism. The quality or state of being imaginary.
Ideality. The condition or character of being imaginary.
Illusion. An unreal imagination.
Imagery. Collection of images.
Imagination. The power of producing mental images. **Ardent—, boiling—, bold—, daring—, excited—, fertile—, fiery—, heated—, lively—, playful—, sanguine—, warm—, wild—imagination.**
Inspiration. A kindling influence. "And still He breatheth and in-spireth light into the face of His chosen." [Bacon, *Essay on Truth.*]
Invention. The act of discovering something new; the creative faculty in art, especially useful art.
Originality. The quality or power of being able to imagine some-thing new.
Phrensy. See FRENZY.
Reverie. Listless fancy or musing.
Romanticism. An imaginative or visionary style, like that of the tales written in the Romance languages, and in contrast with the classic writings of Greece and Rome.
Somnambulism. The act of walking in one's sleep.
Utopianism. The imaginings of a Utopian; optimism. [More, *Utopia.*]
Verve [F.]. Animation; spirit.
Vorstellung [G.]. Idea; image.

FANCY—*Associated Nouns.*

"A fine frenzy." A violent agitation approaching temporary deliri-um. [Shakespeare, *Midsummer Night's Dream,* V, i.]
Air-drawn dagger. An imaginary dagger. [*Macbeth,* III, iv.]
Arabian Nights. A collection of stories of the Eastern countries.
Atlantis. A mythical island, located by Plato and ancient writers in the far West. [Bacon, *New Atlantis.*]
Bugbear. An imaginary object of terror.
Calenture. A delirious fever causing vivid and dangerous halluci-nations.
Castle in the air. A day-dream.

Château en Espagne [F.]. A castle in Spain, a boasted castle of a Spanish adventurer; a baseless vision.
Chimera. An absurd creation of the imagination.
Cloudland. The realm of imagination.
Coinage of the brain. ⎫
Creation of the brain. ⎬ Imaginings.
Day-dream. An idle exercise of the imagination.
Dream. A train of thoughts, or images passing through the mind during sleep.
Dreamland. The realm of dreams.
Dreams of Alnaschar. Day-dreams, from the dreams of the Barber's brother in the *Arabian Nights.*
Extravaganza [It.]. A fantastic composition in music or drama.
Fairyland. An imaginative land.
Fata Morgana. The fairy Morgana, sister of King Arthur
Figment. Something invented or imagined. See LUMINARY.
Flight of fancy. Exercise of the imagination.
Flying Dutchman. A legendary spectral ship supposed to be seen near the Cape of Good Hope, in stormy weather.
Fumes of fancy. Anything unsubstantial or evanescent.
Golden dream. Imagination of a condition of great happiness and prosperity.
Great sea-serpent. An animal of snake-like form and monstrous size, believed by many to inhabit the ocean.
Happy valley. The realm of fancy.
Kingdom of Micomicon. Imaginary kingdom.
Land of Prester John. A fabulous empire in Asia.
Le pot au lait [F.]. The milk pot.
Maggot The larva of a fly; figuratively, a whim or fancy.
Man in the moon. The fancied appearance of a face in the disk of the full moon.
Millennium. A period of a thousand years; the thousand years of the kingdom of Christ on earth.
Mind's eye. The imagination.
Myth. An imaginary person, object, or event believed real by old nations.
Nightmare. A condition in sleep, giving the sense of a difficulty or danger from which one cannot escape.
Phantasm. An apparition or optical illusion.
Phantom. Something that exists only in appearance. See SIGHT-DIMSIGHTEDNESS.
Rhapsody. A series of sentences without natural connection, com-posed under excitement, often characterized by extravagance.
Romance. A form of prose fiction which gives scope to the imagina-tion.
Shadow. An image produced by reflected light.
Stretch of the imagination. See GULL-HYPERBOLE.
"Such stuff as dreams are made of." Visionary objects. [Shake-speare, *Tempest,* IV, i.]
Thick-coming fancies. Objects presented to the imagination. [Shakespeare, *Macbeth,* V, iii.]
Trance. A state in which the soul seems to have passed into another condition or to be rapt into visions.
Utopia. An imaginary island having a perfect social and political system, described by Sir Thomas More.
Vagary. A wandering of the thoughts.
Vapor. That which is fleeting and unsubstantial. See VISCIDITY-FOAM.
Vision. A mental representation of external objects or scenes, hence a dream.
Whim. A peculiar fancy, purpose, or notion.
Whimsey. A whim or freak.
Work of fiction. A picture of feigned life. See ACCOUNT.

FANCY—*Nouns of Agent.*

Dreamer. One who dreams or imagines.
Idealist. One who forms ideas that exist only in the imagination.
Mopus. A spiritless, dreamy person.
Rhapsodist. One who speaks or writes disconnectedly, etc. See MANIAC.
Romancer. An extravagantly imaginative story-teller.
Romanticist. One who favors the wonderful and fantastic in modern literature.
Somnambulist. One who walks or does other acts during sleep.
Visionary. An imaginative schemer.

FANCY—*Verbs.*

Coin. To invent.
Conceive. To form an image in the mind.
Conjure up a vision. To imagine.
Crack one's invention. To exert one's imaginative faculty to the utmost.
Create. To form in the mind.

Cudgel one's brains. ⎫
Rack one's brains. ⎬ To exercise one's wits.
Ransack one's brains. ⎭
Devise. To invent; imagine.
Dream. ⎫
Dream of. ⎬ To go through in imagination.
Excogitate. To contrive; devise.
Fabricate. To concoct; invent.
Fancy. ⎫
Fancy to oneself. ⎪
Figure to oneself. ⎬ To imagine lightly
Picture to oneself. ⎪
Represent to oneself. ⎭
Float in the mind. To be vaguely under consideration.
Give a loose to fancy. ⎫
Give play to fancy. ⎬ To use the fancy freely
Give reins to fancy. ⎭
Give a loose to the imagination. ⎫
Give play to the imagination. ⎬ To use the imagination freely
Give reins to the imagination. ⎭
"Give to airy nothing a local habitation and a name." To describe pictures of the imagination. [Shakespeare, *Midsummer Night's Dream.* V, i.]
Idealize. To make imaginary.
Imagine. To form an image.
Improvise. To compose or invent offhand.
Indulge in reverie. To yield without constraint to the imagination
Invent. To devise first; contrive by ingenuity
Originate. To be the origin of; create.
Realize. To cause to seem real.
Set one's wits to work. To be actively imaginative.
Strain one's invention. To exert one's imaginative faculty to the utmost.
Strike out something new. To imagine and produce something new
Suggest itself. See REFLECTION.
Vorstellen [G.]. To imagine; conceive.

FANCY—*Adjectives*

Air-built. Chimerical; fanciful.
Air-drawn. Imaginary.
Bon trovato [It.]. Happily invented.
Chimerical. Merely fanciful.
Creative. Having the imaginative faculty.
Enthusiastic. Filled with enthusiasm; highly imaginative.
Extravagant. Immoderate in imagination; fantastic.
Fabulous. Imagined; not real.
Fairy. Produced by the fairies, as fairy rings, fairy gold.
Fairylike. Like a fairy.
Fanatic. Extravagant in opinions.
Fanciful. Imaginative.
Fancy. Extravagant; imagined.
Fantastical. Imagined; unreal.
Fertile. Inventive.
Flighty. Given to flights of fancy.
High-flown. Extravagant.
Ideal. Reaching an idea above the forms of the senses
Illusory. Deceiving. See TRUTH-ERROR.
Imaginary. Existing only in imagination
Imaginative. Creative or constructive.
Imagined. Fancied, etc. See *Verbs.*
Imagining, etc. Supposing, etc. See *Verbs*
In nubibus [L.] In the clouds.
In the clouds. In the realm of fancy
Inventive. Imaginative.
Legendary. Consisting of legends.
Mythic. Imaginary.
Mythological. Pertaining to the myths. See *Nouns* above.
Notional. Existing only in imagination.
Original. Imagined for the first time; not imitated.
Quixotic. Like Don Quixote; romantically mad.
Romantic. Imaginative.
Unreal. Existing in imagination only.
Unsubstantial. Lacking in substance; visionary.
Utopian. Pertaining to Utopia or imaginary perfection.
Visionary. Existing in imagination only
Whimsical. Fanciful; freakish.

FANCY—*Phrases.*

Ægri somnia vana [L.]. A sick man's empty dreams.
Tous songes sont mensonges [F.]. Dreams all are lies all.
Wahrheit und Dichtung [G.]. Fact and fable.

fan-dan'-go. A Spanish dance. ENTERTAINMENT-WEARINESS.

fandi mollia tempora [L.] (fan'-dai, mol'-li-a tem'-por-a). Favorable opportunities for speaking. CONVERSATION-MONOLOGUE
fane. A temple. FANE.

FANE.

Abbey. The buildings of a monastery or nunnery.
Basilica [L.]. A Roman building of rectangular form used as a temple.
Bethel. A dissenting church of England.
Bishop's palace. The house in which a bishop resides.
Calvary. A kind of chapel.
Cathedral. The church of a bishop.
Chantry. A church endowed for maintaining masses.
Chapel. A small place of worship.
Church. A building dedicated to Christian worship.
Cloister. A monastery; a convent.
Convent. The house occupied by monks or nuns.
Conventicle. A meeting of dissenters from the established Church
Dagoba. A Buddhist building containing religious relics.
Deanery. The residence of a dean.
Fane. A temple; a church.
Friary. A convent of friars.
Golgotha. A burial house.
House of God. ⎫
House of prayer. ⎬ A church, a temple.
Joss-house. A Chinese temple.
Kiosk. A Turkish temple
Kirk. A Scotch church.
Manse. The dwelling-house of a clergyman.
Meeting-house. A place of worship.
Minster. A cathedral church.
Monastery. A house of religious seclusion.
Mosque. A Mohammedan temple.
Nunnery. The residence of nuns.
Pagoda. A Hindu temple for idol worship
Pantheon. A temple dedicated to all the gods.
Parsonage. The residence of a parson.
Place of worship. A house given up to religious services.
Priory. A religious house in dignity below an abbey presided over by a prior or prioress.
Rectory. A parish church, or mansion of a rector
Sacrarium. The sanctuary of a church.
Sanctuary. A house consecrated to the worship of God
Sanctum sanctorum [L.] The Holy of Holies.
Synagogue. The house of Jewish worship.
Tabernacle. A movable temple used by the Jews when wandering in the wilderness.
Temple. A building dedicated to religious worship.
Tope. A Buddhist monument in which relics are preserved.
Vatican. The Roman palace which is the residence of the Pope
Vicarage. The residence of a vicar.
Vihara. A Buddhist idol-house and monastery.

FANE—*Associated Words*

Aisle. A passageway in a church.
Altar. A raised place in a temple on which sacrifices are burned or communion offered.
Ambo. A desk or pulpit in a church.
Apse. The vaulted end of a church in which the altar is generally placed.
Baldacchino [It.]. ⎫
Baldachin. ⎬ A canopy used in church services.
Baptistery. That part of a church in which baptism is given.
Belfry. A bell tower attached to a church.
Chancel. That part of a church in which the altar is placed.
Choir. The part of a church occupied by the singers.
Churchyard. The ground adjoining a church, used as a cemetery
Cloisters. The arched ways running around monastic walls.
Communion table. The table in a church at which the communicants sit or kneel.
Confessional. A compartment in a church in which the priests hear confession.
Credence. A small table in a church beside the communion table on which the bread and wine are placed before they are consecrated.
Crypt. That part of a church below the floor, sometimes used as a chapel.
Faldstool. A bishop's chair.
Font. The vessel used in churches for holding the baptismal water.
Glebe. The land belonging to a parish church.
Holy of Holies. The innermost apartment of the Jewish tabernacle
Holy-place. A place set apart and consecrated to a sacred use.

Holy-table. The table of the sacrament.

Jesse. A large candlestick used in a church.

Jubé [F.] A gallery from which part of the church-service was read.

Lectern. A church reading-desk.

Lord's table. The sacrament of the Lord's Supper.

Marabout. A North African sorcerer, held in high esteem because of his miracle working.

Nave. The part of a church between the aisles.

Oratory. A place for private devotions.

Oriel. A private chamber in a church.

Pew. A seat in a church.

Prothesis. The place in a church on which the elements of the sacrament are placed before consecration.

Pulpit. An elevated place in a church in which the preacher stands.

Pyx. In the Roman Catholic Church, a covered vessel used as a repository for the consecrated host.

Quire. That part of a church set apart for the singers; a choir.

Reading-desk. A desk at which reading is done; a pulpit.

Sacristy. A church apartment for storing the sacred utensils and vestments.

Shrine. A box for holding the remains of departed saints· later, any sacred place.

Stall. A fixed seat in the choir or chancel, of a cathedral.

Synagogue. The Jewish house of worship.

Table of the Lord. The sacrament of the Lord's Supper.

Transept. The transverse part of a church built in the form of a cross.

Vestry. A room appendant to a church where the vestments are kept and the clergy robe themselves.

FANE—*Adjectives.*

Claustral. Pertaining to a cloister. See *Nouns*.

Cloistered. Furnished with cloisters.

Conventual. Monastic.

Monasterial. }
Monastic. } Pertaining to monks or nuns; ascetic.

FANE—*Phrases*

Ne vile fano [L.] Let there be nothing vile in the temple.

fan′-fare. A flourish of trumpets; a noisy or showy parade. LOUDNESS-FAINTNESS, SOLEMNIZATION.

fan″-fa-ron′. A bully. BRAGGING-BRAWLER.

fan-far″-o-nade′. A boastful or bullying manner. BRAGGING.

fangs. A long pointed tooth; the root of a tooth. KEEPING-RELINQUISHMENT, REMEDY-BANE, RULE-LICENSE.

fan′-light″. A fan-shaped window over a door. APERTURE-CLOSURE.

fan′-like. Resembling a fan. BREADTH-NARROWNESS.

fan′-nel. A peculiar striped scarf worn at mass by the pope or Eastern bishops. VESTMENTS.

fan′-ning. Wafting; producing air currents. RIVER-WIND.

fan′-on. A FANNEL.

fan″-ta-si′-a. A fanciful musical composition of peculiar form. MUSIC.

fan-tas′-tic. Odd; capricious; fanciful. BIGOTRY-APOSTASY, CONVENTIONALITY-UNCONVENTIONALITY, FANCY, SOCIETY-LUDICROUSNESS.

fan-tas′-tic-al. Fanciful. FANCY.

fan′-ta-sy. A fantastic design; the form of representation that brings before the mind images as such, severed from their ordinary relations. DESIRE-DISTASTE, FANCY.

fantoccini [It.] (fan″-to-chî′-nî). Puppets run by machinery, often to represent dramatic scenes. ACTING, DELINEATION-CARICATURE.

fa-quir′. Fakir.

far. Remote. **Far and near,** EXTENSION-DISTRICT; **far and wide,** EXTENSION-DISTRICT, MAGNITUDE-SMALLNESS, REMOTENESS-NEARNESS; **far away,** REMOTENESS-NEARNESS; **far be it from,** PETITION-EXPOSTULATION, READINESS-RELUCTANCE; **far between,** INTERSPACE-CONTACT, MULTIPLICITY-PAUCITY, UNION-DISUNION; **far from it,** ASSERTION-DENIAL, LIKENESS-UNLIKENESS, TRANSCURSION-

SHORTCOMING; **far from the truth,** TRUTHFULNESS-FABRICATION; **far off,** REMOTENESS-NEARNESS.

farce. A short comedy with exaggerated effects and incidents; a ridiculous proceeding. ACTING, ADAGE-NONSENSE, SOCIETY-DERISION, SOCIETY-LUDICROUSNESS, TRUTHFULNESS-FRAUD, WITTINESS-DULNESS; **mere farce,** CONSEQUENCE-INSIGNIFICANCE, USEFULNESS-USELESSNESS.

farceur [F.] (far-sur′). A farce-player. ACTING, SOCIETY-LUDICROUSNESS, WAG.

far′-ci-cal. Ludicrous. ACTING, CONSEQUENCE-INSIGNIFICANCE, SOCIETY-LUDICROUSNESS.

far′-del. A bundle. GATHERING-SCATTERING, OBSTRUCTION-HELP.

fare. To be in any state, good or bad; food and drink; passage-money. CONDITION-SITUATION, NUTRIMENT-EXCRETION, PRICE-DISCOUNT; **bill of fare,** RECORD.

fare, fac [L.] (fê′-rî, fac). Speak, do. ACTION-PASSIVENESS.

fare′-well′. A parting salutation; a taking leave. ARRIVAL-DEPARTURE, GAIN-LOSS, QUEST-ABANDONMENT; **farewell to greatness,** REPUTATION-DISCREDIT.

far′-famed″. Widely known. REPUTATION-DISCREDIT.

far′-fetched″. Brought in only by laborious effort. CONNECTION-INDEPENDENCE.

far′-gone″. Advanced. BETTERMENT-DETERIORATION, MAGNITUDE-SMALLNESS, SANENESS-LUNACY.

fa-ri′-na. A meal or flour obtained from cereals, potatoes, etc. FRIABILITY.

far″-i-na′-ceous. Consisting of meal or flour. FRIABILITY.

fari quæ sentiat [L.] (fê′-rai quî sen′-shi-at). To speak what one thinks. MANIFESTATION-LATENCY.

farm. A tract forming a single property devoted to agriculture; to cultivate; to take on lease. DOMESTICATION-AGRICULTURE, EXTENSION-PLACE, LOAN-BORROWING, PROPERTY.

farm′-er. An agriculturist; one who collects revenues for a percentage. DOMESTICATION-AGRICULTURE; **afternoon farmer,** ACTIVITY-INDOLENCE.

farm′-house″. The principal dwelling on a farm. DWELLER-HABITATION.

farm′-ing. The business of cultivating land. DOMESTICATION-AGRICULTURE.

far′-ness. Remoteness. REMOTENESS-NEARNESS.

far′-o. A game of cards. PURPOSE-LUCK.

far′-o-bank″. The proprietor's risk on the game. PURPOSE-LUCK.

far-ra′-go. A jumble. ADAGE-NONSENSE, REGULARITY-IRREGULARITY.

far′-ri-er. One who shoes horses. AGENT.

far′-row. To give birth to; little pig or pigs. CREATION-DESTRUCTION, MULTIPLICITY-PAUCITY, PARENTAGE-PROGENY.

farse. To lengthen the church service by insertion. CEREMONIAL.

far′-see″-ing. Having foresight. PREVISION.

far′-sight″-ed. Long-sighted; prescient. PREVISION, SAGACITY-INCAPACITY.

far′-ther. More distant. REMOTENESS-NEARNESS.

far′-thing. The smallest English monetary unit. CONSEQUENCE-INSIGNIFICANCE, MONEY, QUADRUPLICATION-QUADRISECTION, VALUES; **farthing candle,** DIMNESS.

far′-thin-gale. A woman's hoop-skirt. DRESS-UNDRESS.

fas′-ces. A bundle of rods enclosing an ax, borne by lictors as a symbol of power. SCEPTER.

fas′-ci-a. Condensed connective tissue forming bands; a fillet. CIRCLE-WINDING, LAMINA-FIBER.

fas-cic′u-la″-ted. Grouped in a fascicle. GATHERING-SCATTERING.

fas-cic'-u-lus. A little bundle. GATHERING-SCATTERING.

fas'-ci-nate. To enchant; captivate. ASTONISHMENT-EXPECTANCE, DESIRE-DISTASTE, DEVOTION-MAGIC, EXCITATION, LOVE-HATE, MOTIVE-CAPRICE, PLEASURABLENESS-PAINFULNESS.

fas'-ci-na''-ted. Captivated. PLEASURE-PAIN.

fas'-ci-nat''-ing. Bewitching; enchanting. LOVE-HATE, MOTIVE-CAPRICE, PLEASURABLENESS-PAINFULNESS.

fas''-ci-na'-tion. Enchantment. ASTONISHMENT-EXPECTANCE, DEVOTION-MAGIC, EXCITABILITY-INEXCITABILITY, EXCITATION, LOVE-HATE, MOTIVE-CAPRICE, PLEASURABLENESS-PAINFULNESS.

fas''-cine'. A fagot, as used in earthworks. GATHERING-SCATTERING.

fas et nefas, per [L.] (fas et nî'-fas, per). Through right and wrong. DETERMINATION-VACILLATION, INSTRUMENTALITY.

fash. Worry. PLEASURABLENESS-PAINFULNESS.

fash'-ion. To shape; usage. CONDITION-SITUATION, FORM-FORMLESSNESS, HABIT-DESUETUDE, SOCIETY-LUDICROUSNESS, WAY; **after a fashion,** MAGNITUDE-SMALLNESS; **after this fashion,** WAY; **be in the fashion,** ASSENT-DISSENT; **follow the fashion,** CONVENTIONALITY-UNCONVENTIONALITY, SOCIETY-LUDICROUSNESS; **for fashion's sake,** SOCIETY-LUDICROUSNESS; **height of fashion,** SOCIETY-LUDICROUSNESS; **man of fashion,** SOCIETY-LUDICROUSNESS; **set the fashion,** DOMINANCE-IMPOTENCE, MOTIVE-CAPRICE, RULE-LICENSE.

fash'-ion-a-ble. According to the prevailing form or style. HABIT-DESUETUDE, REPUTATION-DISCREDIT, SOCIETY-LUDICROUSNESS.

fash'-ion-a-bly. In a manner according to the prevailing practise. SOCIETY-LUDICROUSNESS.

fast. To abstain from food beyond the usual time; firm; steadfast; lasting; swift; dissolute. BRAVERY-COWARDICE, CEREMONIAL, DEVOTION-IDOLATRY, FASTING-GLUTTONY, MODERATION-VOLUPTUARY, MUTABILITY-STABILITY, PERIODICITY-IRREGULARITY, SOCIETY-LUDICROUSNESS, SWIFTNESS-SLOWNESS, UNION-DISUNION; **fast and loose,** BIGOTRY-APOSTASY, DETERMINATION-VACILLATION, PERSISTENCE-WHIM, RATIOCINATION-INSTINCT, TRUTHFULNESS-FALSEHOOD; **fast asleep,** ACTIVITY-INDOLENCE; **fast by,** REMOTENESS-NEARNESS; **fast day,** FASTING-GLUTTONY; **fast friend,** FRIEND-FOE; **fast man,** PURITY-RAKE, SOCIETY-DANDY; **stand fast,** MUTATION-PERMANENCE; **stick fast,** DIFFICULTY-FACILITY.

fast'-en. To make fast; to affix; to cling. MUTABILITY-STABILITY, RELEASE-RESTRAINT, SUSPENSION-SUPPORT, UNION-DISUNION; **fasten a quarrel upon,** VARIANCE-ACCORD; **fasten on the mind,** MIND-IMBECILITY; **fasten upon,** TAKING-RESTITUTION.

fast'-en-ing. The act of making fast; that which fastens. CONNECTIVE, SUSPENSION-SUPPORT.

fast'-hand''-ed. Miserly. EXTRAVAGANCE-AVARICE.

fas-tid'-i-ous. Hard to please. APPROVAL-DISAPPROVAL, SENSITIVENESS-APATHY.

fas-tid'-i-ous-ness. Overniceness. PARTICULARNESS, SENSITIVENESS-APATHY.

fast'-ing. The act of abstaining from food. ATONEMENT, AUSTERITY, DEVOTION-IDOLATRY, FASTING-GLUTTONY, READINESS-RELUCTANCE.

FASTING—GLUTTONY.

Banyan-day. A day of poor fare.
Barmecide feast. An imaginary or illusive feast.
Famishment. Extreme want.
Fast. The time of abstaining from food, or from certain foods.
Fast-day. A day on which a fast is kept.
Fasting. The act of abstaining partly or altogether from food for a time.
Jour maigre [F.]. Fast-day.
Lent. A fast of forty days kept in the spring.
Lenten diet. Sparing diet.
Lenten entertainment. Plain entertainment.
Meager diet. Diet deficient either in quantity or quality.
Quadragesima. A fast of forty days.
Ramadan.⎱ Annual Mohammedan feast of thirty days.
Ramazan.⎰
Short commons. Sparing fare.
Soupe maigre [F.]. Thin soup.
Spare diet. Diet deficient in quantity.
Starvation. Suffering or perishing from hunger.
Xerogaphy. Eating of dry food.

FASTING—Verbs.

Clem. To starve.
Dine with Duke Humphrey. To be dinnerless; to spend the hour in St. Paul's Church, with the memories of the Duke, A.D 1592.
Famish. To suffer or die from hunger or thirst.
Fast. To abstain partly or altogether from food for a time.
Make two bites of a cherry. To make a dinner on very little food.
Perish with hunger. To starve.
Starve. To suffer or die from hunger.

FASTING—Adjectives.

Fasting. See *Verbs*.
Half-starved. Reduced by hunger.
Hungry. Feeling pain from want of food.
Lenten. Pertaining to Lent; sparing.
Quadragesimal. Pertaining to the number forty; pertaining to Lent.
Starved. See *Verbs*.
Unfed. Without proper nourishment.

GLUTTONY—Verbs—*Continued from Column 2.*

Gulp. To swallow eagerly and in large drafts.
Guttle. To devour greedily.
Guzzle. To drink immoderately or hastily.
Have the stomach of an ostrich. To be a voracious eater.

Crapulence. Sickness from intemperance in eating or drinking.
Edacity. Excess in eating.
Epicurism. Refined indulgence in food.
Gastronomy. Art of preparing and serving appetizing food.
Gluttony. Gross indulgence in eating.
Good cheer. Provisions for a meal or feast.
Good living. Rich and costly food.
Greed. Excessive appetite for food.
Greediness. See *Adjectives*.
Gulosity. Excessive fondness for the pleasures of the table.
Guttling. Gormandizing.
Guzzling. Swallowing liquor greedily.
High living. Very good living.
Voracity. Habit of eating much and hastily.

GLUTTONY—*Denotations.*

Apicius. A notorious Roman epicure; hence, whatever is peculiarly dainty and expensive in cookery.
Batterie de cuisine [F.]. Kitchen utensils.
Belly-god. A glutton.
Blow-out. A jovial feast.
Bon-vivant [F.] A high liver.
Cormorant. Having the nature of a cormorant; hence, a greedy, rapacious person.
Epicure. One who cultivates a delicate taste for eating and drinking. Epicurus held pleasure to be the highest good, his followers chose the pleasures of the senses.
Feast. An abundant and sumptuous repast.
Gastronome. A judge of good eating.
Glutton. One who gluts himself with food and drink.
Gourmand. A greedy or ravenous feeder.
Hog. A gluttonous or grasping person.

GLUTTONY—*Verbs.*

Bolt. To swallow hurriedly without chewing.
Cram. To eat beyond satiety.
Devour. To eat ravenously.
Eat one's fill. To eat to satiety.
Eat out of house and home. To consume all the provisions.
Engorge. To gorge.
Fill. To satisfy; eat to satiety.
Gobble up. To swallow eagerly or in large mouthfuls.
Gorge. To fill the stomach with food.
Gormandize. To eat greedily and ravenously.

(Continued on Column 1.)

FASTING—GLUTTONY—*Continued.*
GLUTTONY—VERBS—*Continued.*

Overeat oneself. } To eat to excess.
Overgorge oneself. }
Pamper. To indulge in luxurious living.

Play a good knife and fork. To eat a good hearty meal.
Raven. To prey upon like a beast of prey.
Stuff. To feed gluttonously.

GLUTTONY—*Adjectives.*

Crapulent. Sick from intemperance in eating or drinking.
Edacious. Eating to excess.
Gluttonous. Grossly indulging in eating.
Gormandizing. See *Verbs.*
Greedy. Having an excessive appetite for food or drink.

Omnivorous. Eating food of all kinds.
Overfed. Fed to excess.
Overgorged. Having eaten excessively.
Pampered. Reared on luxurious food.
Swinish. Like a swine; greedy; beastly.

fast'-ness. A stronghold; security. ATTACK-DEFENSE, REFUGE-PITFALL.
fat. Corpulent; containing much oil; broad. ENLARGEMENT-DIMINUTION, GREATNESS-LITTLENESS, PULPINESS-OILINESS; **fat in the fire,** REGULARITY-IRREGULARITY, TURBULENCE-CALMNESS; **fat of the land,** ENOUGH, MODERATION-SELFINDULGENCE, SENSUALITY-SUFFERING, OPPORTUNENESS-MISFORTUNE; **kill the fatted calf,** SOCIABILITY-PRIVACY, SOLEMNIZATION.
fata morgana [It.] (fa'-ta mor-ga'-na). A mirage, attributed to the fairy Morgana. FANCY, LUMINARY-SHADE, OPPORTUNENESS-UNSUITABLENESS.
Fata obstant [L.] (fa'-ta ob'-stant). The Fates oppose. VOLITION-OBLIGATION.
fa'-tal. Destructive. LIFE-DEATH, LIFE-KILLING; **fatal disease,** HEALTH-SICKNESS.
fa'-tal-ism. The doctrine that every event is predetermined and inevitable. VOLITION-OBLIGATION.
fa'-tal-ist. One who maintains that all things happen by inevitable necessity. VOLITION-OBLIGATION.
fa'-tal-i-ty. Destiny. VOLITION-OBLIGATION.
Fata viam invenient [L.] (fē'-ta vai'-am in-vi'-ni-ent). The Fates will discover a way. FAITH-MISGIVING.
fat'-brained". Dull. WITTINESS-DULNESS.
fate. Predetermined and inevitable necessity; lot. BEGINNING-END, PURPOSE-LUCK, RATIONALE-LUCK, VOLITION-OBLIGATION; **be one's fate,** RATIONALE-LUCK; **sure as fate,** CERTAINTY-DOUBT, VOLITION-OBLIGATION.
fa'-ted. Destined. VOLITION-OBLIGATION.
Fates. The three goddesses who were supposed to control all destinies. VOLITION-OBLIGATION.
fat'-head"-ed. Stupid. SAGACITY-INCAPACITY.
Fa'-ther. God. God the Father, DIVINITY.
fa'-ther. The male parent of a child; one looked upon or acting as a father. MINISTRY-LAITY, PARENTAGE-PROGENY; **Apostolical fathers,** REVELATION-PSEUDOREVELATION; **Father of His Country,** PATRIOTISM-TREASON; **father upon,** RATIONALE-LUCK; **gathered to one's fathers,** LIFE-DEATH; **heavy father,** ACTING.
fa'-ther-land". The land of one's birth. DWELLER-HABITATION.
fa'-ther-less. Not having a living father. MIGHT-IMPOTENCE.

fa'-ther-ly. Of or pertaining to a father; paternal. CHARITABLENESS-MALEVOLENCE.
fath'-om. To sound; to discover the hidden meaning; a measure of length. DISCOVERY, INVESTIGATION-ANSWER, KNOWLEDGE-IGNORANCE, LENGTH-SHORTNESS, MEASURE, MENSURATION.
fath'-om-less. Unfathomable. DEEPNESS-SHALLOWNESS.
fa-tid'-ic-al. Able to prophesy. PROPHECY.
fat"-i-ga'-tion. Weariness. WEARINESS-REFRESHMENT.
fa-tigue'. To tire out; weariness. WEARINESS-REFRESHMENT.
fa-tigued'. Wearied. ACTION-PASSIVENESS, GOODNESS-BADNESS.
fa-tigu'-ing. Wearying. WEARINESS-REFRESHMENT.
fat'-ling. A young animal fattened for slaughter. NUTRIMENT-EXCRETION.
fatras [F.] (fa-tra'). A jumble. CONSEQUENCE-INSIGNIFICANCE.
fat'-ten. To make or become fat, plump, or productive; to grow rich. BETTERMENT-DETERIORATION, ENLARGEMENT-DIMINUTION, WELFARE-MISFORTUNE; **fatten on,** PRESUMPTION-OBSEQUIOUSNESS; **fatten upon,** NUTRIMENT-EXCRETION.
fat'-ty. Greasy. PULPINESS-OILINESS.
fa-tu'-i-ty. Foolishness combined with obstinacy or conceit; imbecility. REFLECTION-VACANCY, SAGACITY-INCAPACITY.
fat'-u-ous. Feeble in mind. SAGACITY-INCAPACITY.
fat'-wit"-ted. Of a dull wit. SAGACITY-INCAPACITY.
faubourg [F.] (fo-burg'). A suburb. ENVIRONMENT-INTERPOSITION.
fau'-ces. The throat. BORDER.
faugh. An exclamation of disgust. DESIRE-DISTASTE.
fault. A slight offense; defect. CONTINUITY-INTERRUPTION, DUTY-DERELICTION, FAULTLESSNESS-FAULTINESS, GEOLOGY, INNOCENCE-GUILT, SUCCESS-FAILURE, TRUTH-ERROR, VIRTUE-VICE; **at fault,** CERTAINTY-DOUBT, KNOWLEDGE-IGNORANCE, SKILL-UNSKILFULNESS, SUCCESS-FAILURE; **find fault with,** APPROVAL-DISAPPROVAL; **in fault,** INNOCENCE-GUILT.
fault'-less. Without fault. FAULTLESSNESS-FAULTINESS, INNOCENCE-GUILT.
fault'-less-ness. Perfection. FAULTLESSNESS-FAULTINESS.

FAULTLESSNESS—FAULTINESS.

Acme of perfection. The highest point of perfection.
Faultlessness. Condition or state of being without fault, blemish, or defect.
Impeccability. The quality of being exempt from sin or error.
Impecancy. Sinlessness.
Indefectibility. The quality of not being liable to failure or neglect.
Ne plus ultra [L.]. Nothing further; hence, perfection.
Perfection. The highest attainable degree of development.
Perfectness. See *Adjectives.*
Pink. The embodiment or perfection of something.
Pink of perfection. The embodiment of perfection.
Standard. A criterion set by common consent.
Summit. The highest degree, etc. See TOP
Superexcellence. Extraordinary excellence, etc. See GOODNESS.
Transcendence Superior excellence, etc. See SUPREMACY.
Very prince of. The best of the kind.

FAULTLESSNESS—*Denotations, etc.*

Admirable Crichton. A Scottish gentleman of the 16th century, who

Attainder. The state of being in dishonor; extinction of civil rights.
Defect. Want of something necessary to perfectness or completeness.
Deficiency. The state or quality of not having a proper or adequate supply.
Drawback. A loss of advantage; a hindrance.
Faultiness. State of being imperfect or defective.
Immaturity. The state of being unripe or not fully developed. See PREPARATION-NONPREPARATION.
Imperfection. Want of the highest degree of development.
Imperfectness. See *Adjectives.*
Inadequacy. The state of being unequal to the purpose. See EXCESS-LACK.
Mediocrity. The state of being ordinary or of a middle quality.
No great catch. Of little importance.
No great shakes. Of no great importance.
Not much to boast of. Something or some person not worthy of being spoken highly of.

FAULTLESSNESS—FAULTINESS—*Continued.*

FAULTLESSNESS—Denotations, etc.—*Continued*

was very precocious and took his degree of Master of Arts at the age of 14.

Beau idéal [F.]. A perfect model of beauty

Chrysolite. A yellow topaz used as a gem

Cygne noir [F.]. The black swan.

Kohinoor. The largest diamond belonging to the British crown.

Master-piece. A work showing the hand of a master.

Mirror. Whatever reflects or clearly represents a pattern

Model. Something to be imitated or patterned after

Paragon. A model or pattern.

Pattern. Something to be imitated.

Philosopher's stone. A fabled stone, formerly sought by alchemists, which was supposed to turn baser metals into gold.

Phenix. A bird fabled to be consumed by fire at its own wish, and to rise again from its ashes more beautiful than before.

Trump. The most attractive article.

FAULTLESSNESS—*Verbs*

Be perfect. See *Adjectives.*

Bring to perfection. See *Nouns.*

Complete. To finish or perfect. See COMPLETION

Mature. To arrive at the state of full development; complete.

Perfect. To raise to a perfect state.

Put in trim. To thoroughly prepare. See PREPARATION.

Ripen. To bring to completeness or perfection.

Transcend. To surpass: to excel. See SUPREMACY

FAULTLESSNESS—*Adjectives.*

Best. Having the highest degree of excellence, etc. See GOODNESS.

Beyond all praise. See APPROVAL.

Consummate. Of the highest quality, etc. See ENTIRETY.

Divine. Godlike; excellent in the highest degree.

Faultless. Free from blemish.

Finished. Polished in the highest degree, etc. See COMPLETION

Free from imperfection. See FAULTLESSNESS-FAULTINESS.

Harmless. Free from the disposition to harm; innocent.

Immaculate. Without spot or blemish.

Impeccable. Not liable or subject to sin.

Indefectible. Not liable to defect or failure.

Indefective. Not wanting in anything.

Indeficient. Full.

Inimitable. Surpassingly excellent.

In perfect condition. Faultless

In seipso totus teres atquo rotundus [L.] All smooth and round in itself. [Horace, *Satires*, 2, 7, 86.]

Intact. Untouched by anything harmful.

Model. Worthy to be imitated.

Perfect. Having all that is needful to its nature and kind.

Right as a trivet. Standing firm.

Sans peur et sans reproche [F]. Without fear and without reproach.

Scatheless. Unharmed.

Seaworthy. In condition to go on a voyage, etc. See USEFULNESS.

Sound. Perfect of its kind.

Sound as a roach. Perfectly sound.

Spotless. Free from spots, pure.

Standard. Having a permanent value.

Superhuman. Above that which is human.

Unblemished. Without blemish or defect.

Uninjured. Not injured or harmed. See BETTERMENT-DETERIORATION.

Unparagoned. Without an equal.

Unparalleled. Having no parallel or equal. See SUPREMACY.

FAULTLESSNESS—*Adverbs.*

Ad unguem [L.]. To the nail; exactly.

Clean. Entirely

Clean as a whistle. The highest degree of cleanness or perfection.

Perfectly. See *Adjectives.*

To perfection. Exactly.

FAULTLESSNESS—*Phrase.*

Das Beste ist gut genug [G]. The best is good enough.

FAULTINESS—Adjectives—*Continued from Column 2.*

Second-rate. Of the second class, rank, quality, or value.

Short-handed. Lacking in the regular number of helpers.

So-so. Neither very good nor very bad.

Sprung. Said of a spar that has been cracked or strained.

Tainted. Corrupted.

Tolerable. Moderately good.

Peccancy. The quality of being guilty of sin or transgression. See GOODNESS-BADNESS.

Screw loose. Something out of order, so that work doesn't go along smoothly

Shortcoming. The act of falling short. See TRANSCURSION-SHORTCOMING.

Weakness. The quality of being lacking in strength, power, or force. See FORCE-WEAKNESS.

FAULTINESS—*Denotations.*

Bar sinister. A mark of illegitimacy

Blemish. A disfiguring mark See EMBELLISHMENT-DISFIGUREMENT

Fault. An imperfection or defect in a person or thing.

Flaw. An inherent defect. See CONTINUITY-INTERRUPTION.

Gap. A vacant space. See INTERSPACE.

Half-blood. One whose parents are of different races.

Hole in one's coat. An imperfection.

Taint. A spot or stain.

Twist. A pulling or pushing out of shape or place. See PROPORTION. DEFORMITY.

Weak point. An imperfection.

FAULTINESS—*Verbs.*

Barely pass muster. To pass through inspection with difficulty.

Be imperfect. See *Adjectives.*

Fall short. To be deficient. See TRANSCURSION-SHORTCOMING.

Have a defect. See *Nouns.*

Lie under a disadvantage. See *Nouns.*

Not pass muster. Not to pass through inspection.

Spring a leak. To begin to leak.

FAULTINESS—*Adjectives.*

Admissible. Worthy of being admitted; allowable.

Average. Of middle size, quality, or ability. See MEDIUM.

Bearable. That can be endured.

Below its full complement. Deficient in quantity, number, or amount.

Below its full strength. Imperfect.

Below par. At a discount.

Couci-couci [F.]. Indifferent; so-so.

Cracked. Having a crack, broken.

Crude. Not mature or perfect, etc. See PREPARATION-NONPREPARATION.

Decent. Moderate; fairly good.

Defective. Lacking something.

Deficient. Wanting, incomplete.

Fair. Middling; average.

Faulty. Having faults or defects.

Found wanting. Deficient.

Frail. Easily broken or destroyed, etc. See FORCE-WEAKNESS.

Good enough. Passable.

Imperfect. Wanting in some of its parts.

Inadequate, etc. Not equal to the purpose, etc. See EXCESS-LACK.

Incomplete, etc. Deficient in some of its parts, etc. See ENTIRETY-DEFICIENCY.

Indifferent. Neither very good, nor very bad.

Inferior. Poor or mediocre.

Injured, etc. Impaired in excellence or quality; damaged, etc. See BETTERMENT-DETERIORATION.

Inobjectionable. Not deserving of disapproval; not offensive.

Lame. Disabled in limb; crippled.

Leaky. Allowing water or other fluid to leak in or out.

Mediocre. Having a middle quality.

Middling. Of middle rank or quality.

Milk and water. Weak and vacillating.

Moderately good. Of the average.

Not amiss. Not wrong or out of order.

Not bad. A little below the average.

Not perfect. See FAULTLESSNESS.

Only better than nothing. Faulty.

Ordinary. Of common rank or ability; inferior.

Out of order. Disarranged; in confusion.

Out of tune. Discordant; not in agreeing temper.

Passable. Such as may be allowed to pass; mediocre.

Peccant. Guilty of sin or transmission. See GOODNESS-BADNESS.

Pretty good.

Pretty well. } In some degree good

Rather good.

Secondary. Not of the first order or rate

Second best. Next to the best.

(Continued on Column 1.)

FAULTINESS—Adjectives—Continued.

Under its full complement. Deficient in number.
Under its full strength. Imperfect.
Unsound. Not sound.

Warped. Twisted out of its true shape. See Proportion-Deformity.
Well enough. In a tolerable degree.

Faultiness—Adverbs.

All things considered. In the circumstances.
Almost. Nearly; well-nigh.
Considering. After all.
Enough. In a tolerable degree.
Moderately. To a moderate extent.

Only. Merely; simply; barely.
Pretty. In a moderate degree.
Rather, etc. Somewhat; in some degree, etc. See Magnitude-Smallness.
To a limited extent. To some degree.

Faultiness—Phrase.

Surgit amari aliquid [L.]. Something bitter rises.

fault'-y. Having faults. Faultlessness-Faultiness, Grammar-Solecism.
faun. A deity of the woods and herds. Jove-Fiend.

fau'-na. The animals inhabiting a given area or existing within a given period. Fauna-Flora.

FAUNA—FLORA.

Animal. An organized living body possessing sensation and power of motion; a sentient being lower than man.
Animalcule. A very minute animal. See Greatness-Littleness.
Beast. Any irrational animal governed by animal appetite.
Brute. An animal being characterized by absence of intelligence.
Created being. A being that is brought into existence.
Creature. A living being or animal regarded as created.
Creeping thing. Any animal that creeps.
Dumb animal.
Dumb creature. } Any animal lower than man.
Fauna. The animals occupying a section of country.
Insect. A small animal whose body appears almost divided into parts.
Living thing. Any being endowed with life.
Worm. A creeping or crawling animal.

Fauna—Denotations.

Asp. A venomous serpent.
Badger-dog. A dog with a small body and short crooked legs.
Barndoor fowl. The ordinary domestic fowl.
Beagle. A small short-coated hound.
Bloodhound. A hound remarkable for its keen sense of smell and ability to keep on the same scent.
Boar. The native hog of continental Europe, with shorter body and longer snout and tusks than the domestic hog.
Buck. The male of various animals, as of deer, rabbits, and goats.
Bull. The male of domestic cattle.
Bulldog. A dog remarkable for the tenacity of its hold.
Bullock. An ox, especially a beef-ox, over four years old.
Calf. The young of the cow.
Canary. A finch, now a common cage-bird, from the Canary Islands.
Cat. A domestic carnivorous animal, kept to kill mice and rats.
Cattle. Domesticated bovine animals.
Chanticleer. A cock.
Chicken. The common domestic fowl.
Cock. The male of the domestic fowl.
Collie. A Scottish sheep-dog.
Cow. The female of domestic cattle.
Cur. A mongrel, worthless, or ugly dog.
Deer. A ruminant having antlers.
Deerhound. A dog trained to track deer.
Dicky-bird. A small bird.
Doe. The female of the deer.
Dog. A domesticated carnivorous animal, remarkable for its intelligence and attachment to man.
Dunghill cock. A domestic fowl of mongrel breed.
Eft. A European lizard.
Ewe. A female sheep.
Fancy dog. A pet dog of high breed.
Finch. A small seed-eating bird, as the canary.
Fowl. The common domestic cock or hen.
Fox. A canine mammal having a long bushy tail.
Foxhound. A breed of dogs trained for fox-hunting.
Fox-terrier. A white terrier used to drive foxes from their holes.
Gib-cat. A castrated cat.
Greyhound. A tall, very slender hunting-dog, remarkable for its keen sight and swiftness.
Grimalkin. A cat.
Harrier. A buzzard-like bird which preys on poultry.
Hart. The male of the red deer.
Heifer. A young cow.
Hen. The female of domestic fowl.

Annual. A plant that lives but one year.
Biennial. A plant that lives for two years.
Bush. A shrub with branches near the foot.
Creeper. A plant that runs on the ground.
Exotic. A plant not indigenous.
Flora. All the plants of a given section of country.
Grass. A plant on which horses and cattle feed.
Herb. A plant that does not have a woody stem.
Herbage. The vegetable growth upon which animals feed.
Perennial. A plant that lives continuously.
Plant. A completely organized vegetable.
Shrub. A woody plant smaller than a tree.
Tree. A woody plant growing to considerable height and perennial.
Triennial. A plant that lives three years.
Vegetable. A plant; a plant used for food.
Vegetable kingdom. Plant life in general.
Verdure. Freshness of vegetation.

Flora—Denotations.

Bine. A climbing stem of a plant.
Blossom. The flower of fruit trees, etc.
Bough. A branch of a tree.
Bracken. The brake or other large fern of temperate regions.
Branch. A subordinate stem of a plant or tree.
Conferva. A genus of fresh-water plants.
Fern. A flowerless cryptogamous plant.
Flower. The blossom or bloom of a plant.
Flowering plant. A plant raised for its flowers.
Foliage. Any growth of leaves.
Fruit-tree. A tree producing an edible fruit.
Fungus. A cryptogamous plant deriving nourishment almost wholly from organic compounds.
Furze. A spiny shrub of the bean family.
Gorse. The furze.
Grass. The green plant on which cattle feed.
Heather. A variety of shrub.
Leaf. An appendage growing out of the stems of plants.
Legume. The fruit of the bean family.
Lichen. A low flowerless plant.
Mold. A fungous growth on food, clothing, walls, etc.
Moss. A delicate cryptogamous plant.
Mushroom. A large rapidly-growing fungus.
Pasture. The grass or herbage that cattle eat.
Pulse. Plants of the bean family.
Ramage. Branches, as of a tree or shrub.
Rush. A grass-like herb.
Sedge. A coarse grass-like plant.
Timber-tree. A well-grown tree suitable for timber.
Toadstool. An umbrella-shaped fungus.
Turf. A mass of matted roots of grass, etc.
Weed. A useless herbaceous plant.
Whin. Furze.
Yam. A fleshy edible root.
Yew. An evergreen tree or shrub.
Zinnia. An American herb of the aster family.

Flora—Associated Nouns.

Arboretum. A collection of rare trees and shrubs. See Domestication-Agriculture.
Bocage [F.]. A woodland.
Broke. Land broken up for plants.
Brushwood. A thicket of small trees or shrubs.

FAUNA—FLORA—Continued.

FAUNA—Denotations—Continued

Hog. A domestic variety of the wild boar, kept for its meat.
Honey-bee. A bee that collects honey.
Horse. A solid-hoofed and odd-toed quadruped having mane and tail of long, coarse hair.
Hound. A dog used in the chase.
House dog. A pet dog.
Kine. Cows.
Lamb. A young sheep.
Lambkin. A little lamb.
Lapdog. A small dog fondled in the lap.
Mastiff. A large breed of dogs, valued as watch-dogs.
Milch cow. A cow yielding milk.
Mollusk. A shell-fish.
Mongrel. The progeny resulting from the crossing of different breeds.
Newfoundland dog. A large breed of dogs noted for their swimming powers.
Otter-hound. A hound used for hunting otters.
Ox. A castrated male of the domestic bovine quadruped.
Partlet. A hen.
Pig. A hog or hog-like animal.
Pointer. A breed of dogs trained to point out game to sportsmen.
Poodle. A breed of curly-haired dogs.
Poultry. Domesticated fowls.
Pug. A small short-haired dog resembling a bulldog, having a wrinkled face and upturned nose.
Pup.
Puppy. } A young dog.
Puss.
Pussy. } A cat.
Ram. The male of the sheep.
Retriever. A dog trained to retrieve game.
Roe. A variety of deer.
Rooster. A cock.
Serpent. A scaly, limbless reptile.
Setter. A breed of dogs trained to indicate the presence of game birds.
Sheep-dog.
Shepherd's dog. } A dog trained to guard and control sheep.
Sheep. An animal kept for its wool and flesh.
Short-horn. A breed of cattle with short horns.
Singing-bird. Any bird that sings
Skye-terrier. A small active dog.
Snake. A serpent.
Sow. A female hog.
Spaniel. A breed of small dogs having long ears and long silky hair.
Sporting dog. A dog used in the chase.
Stag. The male of the red deer.
Staghound. A hound trained to hunt deer
Swine. The domesticated hog
Terrier. A small dog that burrows after its prey.
Tomcat. The male cat.
Toydog. A small dog, usually a terrier or spaniel, bred to extreme smallness.
Tup. A male sheep.
Turnspit. A small dog, formerly used in a treadmill to turn a roasting spit.
Vam.
Vermin. A noxious or troublesome insect.
Viper. A venomous Old World snake.
Vixen. A female fox
Watch-dog. A large breed of dogs used for watching or guarding homes.
Water-dog.
Water-spaniel. } A dog habituated to the water.
Whelp. A young dog.
Yak. A bovine intermediate between the bison and ox.
Zebu. The Indian ox.

Fauna—Associated Words.

Animal kingdom. One of the divisions of nature embracing all animals.
Beast of the field. Cattle.
Birds. Small feathered animals that fly.
Brute creation. The animals lower than man.
Domestic animals. Animals trained for use.
Feathered songsters.
Feathered tribes. } The birds.
Feræ naturæ [L]. Wild animals.
Fish. Animals that swim or live in water.
Flocks and herds. Cattle.

FLORA—Associated Nouns—Continued.

Clump of trees. A group of trees.
Chase. An open hunting-ground.
Coppice. A thicket of brushwood.
Copse. A grove of small growth.
Forest. A collection of trees.
Frith. A park.
Greenwood. A forest when green.
Grove. A piece of land clear of underbrush and covered with trees.
Growth. Anything grown; a wild underbrush.
Heath. Open land covered with coarse herbage.
Holt. A piece of woodland.
Hurst. A wood or grove.
Jungle. A thicket almost impenetrable because of underbrush.
Park. A piece of land well kept, having trees, flowers, and walks.
Pasturage. A place of pasture.
Prairie. A piece of land, fertile, treeless, and covered with coarse grass.
Spinet. A small wood or thicket.
Spinney. A clump of trees and underbrush.
Thicket. A thick growth of anything.
Timber. Any wood fit for building purposes.
Tope. A grove.
Turburary. A place where turf is gathered.
Underwood. Growth low down to the ground
Weald. A wood or forest.
Wood. A growth of trees.
Woodlands. Land occupied by or given up to growing trees.

Flora—Adjectives.

Arborary. Pertaining to trees.
Arboreous. Belonging to trees.
Arborescent. Resembling a tree.
Arborical. Arboreal; living or situated among trees.
Botanic. Pertaining to plants.
Endogenous. Growing from within outward.
Exogenous. Opposite of endogenous.
Floral. Pertaining to flowers.
Grassy. Having grass; resembling grass.
Herbaceous.
Herbal. } Having the character of an herb.
Leguminous. Having a pod.
Ligneous. Like wood, woody.
Lignous. See Ligneous.
Mossy. Covered with moss; of moss.
Silvan.
Sylvan. } Woody, like a plant.
Vegetable. Having the nature of plants or vegetables.
Vegetal.
Vegetous. } Pertaining to plants.
Verdant. Green, like foliage.
Verdurous. Of or pertaining to greenness or green foliage
Wooden Made of wood.
Woody. Of the nature of wood; covered with wood.

FAUNA—Associated Words—Continued.

Fowls of the air. Birds.
Game. Any hunted animals.
Live stock. Domestic animals of a farm.
Shell-fish. All aquatic animals covered with a shell.
Wild animals. Untamed animals.

Fauna—Figurative.

Dandie Dinmont. A breed of hairy, short-legged terriers.
Denizens of the air.
Denizens of the day. } Birds.
Reynard. The fox

Fauna—Scientific.

Carnivora. Flesh-eating animals.
Crustacean. A division of arthropods.
Mammal. A class of vertebrates whose females have milch sacks.
Quadruped. Four-footed animals.
Reptile. Any cold-blooded animal crawling on the stomach.
Zoophyte. An invertebrate animal.

Fauna—Adjectives.

Animals. Having the nature of a brute.
Bovine. Related to a cow or ox.

FAUNA—Adjectives—Continued.

Canine. Of a dog, relating to a dog.
Equine. Of or pertaining to a horse.
Feline. Like a cat; characteristic of cats.
Fishy. Like a fish.
Molluscous. Of or pertaining to a mollusk.

faut bien, il s'en [F.] (fo bi-an'', il san·). It is far from being so. ASSENT-DISSENT.

faut, comme il [F.] (fo, com il). As it should be. SOCIETY-LUDICROUSNESS, TASTE-VULGARITY.

faut considérer le fin, en toute chose il [F.] (fo con'-si-dê-rê' le fan·, an· tut shoz il). It is necessary to consider the end in all things. BEGINNING-END, REFLECTION-VACANCY.

faut, tant s'en [F.] (fo, tan· san·). So far from it. ASSERTION-DENIAL.

faute [F.] (fot). A fault. SUCCESS-FAILURE.

faute de mieux [F.] (fot de mi-v'). For want of something better. COMMUTATION-PERMUTATION, VOLITION-OBLIGATION.

fauteuil [F.] (fo-tu-y'). An upholstered arm-chair. SUSPENSION-SUPPORT.

fau'-tor. A favorer. FRIEND-FOE.

faux pas [F.] (fo pa). A mistake; a breach of good breeding. INNOCENCE-GUILT, PURITY-IMPURITY, SUCCESS-FAILURE.

fa'-vor. An act or course of generosity; kindness bestowed on one to the exclusion of others; kind permission; something given as a token; a letter.

Piscatorial. }
Piscatory. } Pertaining to fishes.
Vaccine. Relating to cows; pertaining to cow-pox.
Vermicular. Pertaining to a worm.
Zoological. Of the animal kingdom; pertaining to zoology.

GIVING-RECEIVING, HARSHNESS-MILDNESS, LEAVE-PROHIBITION, MISSIVE-PUBLICATION, OBSTRUCTION-HELP, RIGHT-WRONG, SIGN; **appearances in favor of,** LIKELIHOOD-UNLIKELIHOOD; **favor with,** GIVING-RECEIVING; **get into favor,** AMITY-HOSTILITY, LOVE-HATE; **in favor,** APPROVAL-DISAPPROVAL, REPUTATION-DISCREDIT; **in favor of,** APPROVAL-DISAPPROVAL, OBSTRUCTION-HELP; **under favor of,** LEAVE-PROHIBITION; **view with favor,** CHARITABLENESS-MALEVOLENCE.

fa'-vor-a-ble. Advantageous; propitious. DETERMINATION-VACILLATION, GOODNESS-BADNESS, OBSTRUCTION-HELP, OPPORTUNENESS-UNSUITABLENESS; **favorable opportunity,** EARLINESS-LATENESS; **favorable prospect,** LIKELIHOOD-UNLIKELIHOOD; **favorable to,** ANTAGONISM-CONCURRENCE; **take a favorable turn,** BETTERMENT-DETERIORATION, WELFARE-MISFORTUNE.

fa'-vor-a-bly. In a favorable manner. GOOD-EVIL.

fa'-vor-er. One who or that which favors. FRIEND-FOE.

fa'-vor-ite. Preferred. FAVORITE-ANGER, LOVE-HATE, PLEASURABLENESS-PAINFULNESS.

FAVORITE—ANGER.

Apple of one's eye. A favorite.
Cosset. A pet lamb; a pet.
Crony. A familiar friend.
Darling. One very dear.
Dear. One much beloved.
Duck. An endearing expression for a person.
Enfant gâté [F.]. A spoiled child.
Favorite. Person or thing very much liked.
Fondling. One much caressed.
General favorite. One liked by most people.
Honey. Pet name for dear.
Idol. Person extravagantly loved.
Idol of the people. A man dear to the people.
Jewel. Pet name for one beloved.
Led captain. An humble, obsequious follower.
Love. The object of affection.
Man of one's own heart. A man who suits one's tastes exactly.
Minion. A servile favorite.
Moppet. }
Mopsey. } Terms of fondness applied to little girls.
Pet. Some one loved and fondled.
Spoiled child. A poorly trained child, due to indulgence.
Sweetheart. A female lover.
Universal favorite. One loved by all.

ANGER—Continued from Column 2.

Passion. Intense feeling, especially anger.
Pet. A fit of peevishness.
Pique. Slight, transient feeling of anger.
Pucker. A state of confusion or agitation.
Rage. Anger that carries one beyond discretion.
Rankling. Deep and active irritation of the mind.
Resentment. Persistent anger, from brooding over injuries.
Revenge. See PARDON-REVENGE.
Scowl. An expression of displeasure or sullenness. See POLITENESS-IMPOLITENESS.
Slap in the face. A direct blow or expression of one's enmity.
Soreness. State of having the feelings galled.
Spleen. Melancholy, and latent spite.
Storm. An ebullition of passion.
Sulks. Fit of sullenness. See FAVORITE-MOROSENESS.
Taking. Trouble; perplexity.
Tantrums. Petulant fit of passion.
Tiff. Peevish display of irritation.
Towering passion. Rage.
Umbrage. Sense of injury.
Violence. Conduct characterized by intensity.

Acerbity. Sharpness of temper and manners.
Acharnement [F.]. Fury; passion.
Acrimony. Deep-seated bitterness in language or speech.
Affront. Demonstrative disrespect, less bitter than an insult.
Anger. Sudden, brief ill-will.
Angry mood. Temporary state of anger.
Animosity. Active, vehement, transitory dislike.
Asperity. Roughness in manner or disposition.
Bad humor. Unpleasant frame of mind.
Bad temper. State of a mind habitually passionate.
Bile. Peevishness.
Bitterness. Sharpness and severity.
Bitter resentment. Sharp and severe resentment.
Burst. Sudden, violent expression, as of passion.
Casus belli [L.]. Cause for war.
Choler. A still anger, shown in the countenance and gestures.
Crow to pluck. See PARDON-REVENGE.
Dander. Anger.
Desperation. Recklessness of despair.
Displeasure. A slight feeling of anger.
Dudgeon. Sullen displeasure.
Ebullition. Violent display, as of the feelings.
Exasperation. Anger, greatly increased.
Excitement. The state of being roused into action.
Explosion. Sudden, violent outbreak.
Ferment. Intense excitement.
Fire and fury. A most violent outburst of passion.
Fit. A violent mood which masters one for a time.
Fume. Confusing or stupefying anger.
Fury. Ungovernable rage.
Gall. Bitterness; rancor.
Gnashing of teeth. Rage; anguish.
Grudge. An old cause of quarrel.
Heartburning. }
Heartswelling. } Deep-seated, secret enmity.
High words. Quarrel.
Hot blood. Passion; irascibility.
Huff. Sudden rise of anger.
Ill blood. Hostile feeling.
Ill humor. Unpleasant frame of mind.
Ill temper. State of a mind habitually passionate.
Indignation. Strong, unselfish displeasure at wrong.
Irascibility. Proneness to anger.
Ire. Quiet, persistent anger.
Irritation. Show of displeasure on slight provocation.
Miff. A feeling of slight vexation.
Paroxysm. Fit of rage

(Continued on Column 1.)

ANGER—*Continued.*

Virulence. Extreme bitterness and hostility
Warmth. A slight amount of passion.

Wrath. Deep, determined, lasting anger.
Wrathful indignation. Indignation that is severe and persistent

ANGER—*Associated Words.*

Box on the ears. A slap on the ears.
Buffet. A blow, especially with the hand
Eumenides. The Furies.
Furies. The avenging deities
Indignity. Unmerited and contemptuous treatment.
Offense. That which wounds the feelings or causes displeasure.

Provocation. Action that excites vindictive feelings.
Rap on the knuckles. A blow, as a mark of displeasure.
Sore subject. A disagreeable subject; a subject that may stir up a quarrel.
Vials of wrath. Stored-up anger.

ANGER—*Verbs.*

Add fuel to the flame. To aggravate.
Affront. To treat with insolence or indignity
Aggravate. To make matters worse.
Anger. To cause to smart; irritate.
Bear malice. To have feelings of revenge
Bite one's thumb. To be angry
Boil. }
Boil over. } To be greatly angered.
Boil with indignation. To fume with indignation.
Boil with rage. To fume with rage.
Breathe revenge. To be full of revenge.
Bridle up. To show vexation by raising the head and drawing in the chin.
Bring a hornet's nest about one's ears. To stir up a quarrel.
Bristle up. To arouse greatly.
Burst with anger. To rage fiercely.
Cause anger. To anger from its frequence.
Chafe. To provoke with a disagreeable subject.
Champ the bit. To be angrily impatient.
Color. To change color of the face during emotion.
Cut up rough. To act passionately.
Discompose. To confuse.
Drive one mad. To make very angry.
Embitter. To make sour or unhappy; intensify in angry feeling.
Enrage. To throw into a rage.
Envenom. To imbue with malice or bitter hatred.
Exasperate. To provoke to unrestrained anger.
Excite. To awaken passion
Fall into a passion. }
Fall into a rage. } To become infuriated suddenly.
Fan into a flame. To aggravate.
Fire up. }
Flare up. } To become angered quickly.
Fly into a passion. }
Fly into a rage. } To suddenly get into a rage.
Fly out. To flare up.
Foam. To express with rage or violence.
Foam with rage. To rage so as to foam at the mouth.
Fool to top of one's bent. To trifle or provoke to anger.
Fret. To irritate continually.
Froth up. To give vent to, as anger.
Frown. To contract the forehead in disapproval.
Fume. To be confused or stupefied with anger.
Get into a passion. }
Get into a rage. } To become enraged.
Give offense. To offend.
Give umbrage. To give sense of injury.
Gnarl. To snarl.
Gnash To snap the teeth in rage.
Grind one's teeth.
Growl. To murmur.
Have a fling at. To have opportunity to nettle.
Huff. To give sudden offense.
Hurt the feelings. To give displeasure to.
Incense. To arouse to violent anger.
Inflame. To arouse to unnatural activity.
Infuriate. To become furious.
Insult. To attack insolently.
Irritate. To cause ill temper.
Kindle. To excite the feelings or passions.
Knit the brow. To show displeasure or anger by wrinkles in the brow
Lash into fury. }
Lash into madness. } To make furious by some means.
Look black. To appear angry.

Look black as thunder. To appear very angry.
Look daggers. To look severely.
Lose one's temper. To be so angry as to be unable to control oneself.
Lower. To look sullen.
Madden. To violently enrage.
Make one's blood boil. To arouse.
Make one's ears tingle. To anger.
Mantle. To conceal anger.
Ne pas entendre raillerie [F.]. Not to be trifled with.
Nettle. To anger slightly.
Offend. To cause displeasure.
Open the vials of one's wrath. To vent stored-up anger.
Pique. To give a slight, transient feeling of anger.
Pour out vials of one's wrath. To give forth pent-up anger.
Pout. To stick the lips out in ill humor.
Provoke. To arouse vindictive feelings.
Put one's back up. }
Put one's monkey up. } To make angry.
Put out of humor. To put into an unpleasant frame of mind.
Quiver with rage. To rage so as to tremble.
Rage. To be so angry as to go beyond discretion.
Raise anger. To cause to become angry
Raise one's choler. }
Raise one's dander. } To rouse one's wrath.
Raise one's gorge. }
Rankle. To cause lingering pain.
Redden. To become flushed with anger.
Resent. To be indignant at, as an injury or insult
Rile. To make slightly angry.
Roil. To vex or irritate.
Ruffle. To vex; disturb.
Scowl. To frown angrily.
Set by the ears. To drive to anger.
Show one's teeth. To be angry.
Snap. To utter sharp, quick words.
Snarl. To speak in surly terms
Stamp the foot. }
Stamp with rage. } To rage so as to stamp.
Stand on one's hind legs. To rise as if in anger.
Stick in one's gizzard. To rankle.
Sting. To give a sharp pain.
Sting to the quick. To sting deeply.
Stir the blood. To arouse.
Stir up bile. To arouse evil passions.
Storm. To give vent boisterously to rage.
Swell with rage. To be so angry as to seem puffed up.
Take amiss. To think of as unkind.
Take exception to. To have a dislike for
Take fire. To become angry.
Take huff. To feel offended; be angry.
Take ill. To think of as unkind.
Take in bad part. }
Take in dudgeon. } To take unkindly; be offended at.
Take in ill part. }
Take offense. To be offended.
Take to heart. To be too sensitive to injury; worry over.
Take umbrage. To have a sense of injury.
Throw into a ferment. To throw into a violent commotion.
Vent one's rage. } To give expression of one's anger in words or
Vent one's spleen. } actions.
Widen the breach. To aggravate.
Work up into a passion. To enrage.
Wound. To seriously injure pride, vanity, or honor.

ANGER—*Adjectives.*

Acharné [F.]. Furious; passionate.
Acrimonious. Full of bitterness or virulence.
Angry. Moved by violent indignation.
Bitter. Feel as showing enmity, hate, etc.

Boiling. } Greatly angered.
Boiling over. }
Burning. Extremely sharp.
Cantankerous. Given to wrangling and fault-finding.

ANGER—Adjectives—*Continued*.

Convulsed with rage. In a fit of rage.
Cross. Peevish and angry.
Fierce. Intensely excited.
Fiery. Easily provoked; passionate.
Flushed with anger. Red with wrath.
Flushed with rage. Inflamed with rage.
Foaming. Raging.
Foaming at the mouth. Raging, so as to foam.
Fuming. Confused or stupefied with anger.
Furious. In uncontrollable anger.
Hurt. Offended; grieved.
In a fume; in a fury; in a huff; in a passion; in a pucker; in a rage; in a stew; in a taking; in a way; in high dudgeon.
Indignant. Having such anger and scorn as is aroused by meanness or wickedness.
Infuriate. Furious.
Irate. Wrathful.
Ireful. Full of strong resentment.
Mad with rage. Furious.
Offended. Sorely displeased.

On one's high ropes. Haughty.
Rabid. Unreasonably excited.
Rageful. }
Raging. } Furious.
Relentless. Pitiless.
Savage. Brutal and unfeeling.
Set against. Opposed to.
Sore. Aggrieved.
Sulky. Showing ill feeling by keeping aloof.
Up in arms. Very angry.
Violent. Marked by force and rapidity.
Virulent. Extremely bitter and hostile.
Warm. Slightly passionate.
Waxy. Enraged.
Wild. Roused to fury.
Worked up. Excited.
Wrath. }
Wrathful. } Being in a state of anger.
Wrought. Stirred up by anger.

ANGER—*Adverbs*.

Angrily. See *Adjectives*.
In the heat of passion.

In the heat of the moment.
In the height of passion.

ANGER—*Absolute Constructions*.

Eyes flashing fire; one's back,—blood,—monkey being up; the blood boiling,—rising; the gorge rising.

ANGER—*Interjections*.

Marry come up!
'Sdeath! God's death!

Tantæne animis cœlestibus iræ! [L.] Can such anger dwell in heavenly minds! [Virgil, *Æneid*, 1, 2.]
Zounds!

ANGER—*Phrases, etc*

Chi t'ha offeso, non ti perdona mai [It.]. Who has wronged you never forgives you.
Fervens difficili bile jecur [L.]. The soul raging with fierce anger.
Gravis ira regum est semper [L.]. Heavy is ever the ire of kings [Seneca, *Meditation*, 474.]

Hæret lateri letalis arundo [L.] The fatal arrow clings fast in her side. [Virgil, *Æneid*, 4, 73.]
Ira furor brevis est [L.]. Anger is a brief madness. [Horace, *Epistles*, 1, 2, 62.]
Quem Jupiter vult perdere, dementat prius [L.]. Whom Jupiter wishes to destroy, he first makes mad.

FAVORITE—MOROSENESS.

MOROSENESS.

Bad humor. }
Bad temper. } See FAVORITE-ANGER.
Bearishness. }
Black looks. } Ill temper.
Bouderie [F.]. (Rare.) Pouting; sulks.
Churlishness. See POLITENESS.
Crabbedness. Sour temper.
Doldrums. Low spirits.
Dumps. Sullenness; low spirits.
Dudgeon. See FAVORITE-ANGER.
Fit of the sulks. Fit of sullenness.
Huff. See FAVORITE-ANGER.
Ill humor. }
Ill temper. } See FAVORITE-ANGER.
Irascibility. }
Moodiness. Gloominess.
Moroseness. }
Morosity. } Bitter dissatisfaction with the world in general.
Mumps. Sulkiness.
Obstinacy. Stubborn adherence to purpose.
Perversity. Quality or habit of doing the contrary.
Scowl. A deep frown, indicative of sullenness.
Spinosity. Quality of being sharp or cutting.
Spleen. See FAVORITE-ANGER.
Sulks. Fits of sullenness.
Sullenness. Gloomy, angry silence.
Torvity. Sourness of countenance.

MOROSENESS—*Verbs*.

Be sullen, etc. See *Adjectives*.
Frown. To wear a disapproving look.
Gloam. To be gloomy or threatening in appearance.
Glower. To stare frowningly.
Have a hang-dog look. To be sullen.
Lower. To look angry or sullen.
Pout. }
Scowl. } See ANGER.
Sulk. To have fits of sullenness.

Deaf to reason. Stubborn.
Dogged. Sullenly obstinate.
Exceptious. Captious; faultfinding.
Froward. Reluctant to comply with requirements
Frumpish. Ill-tempered.
Glowering. Staring frowningly.
Glum. Gloomy and silent.
Grim. Stern and forbidding.
Growling. Murmuring angrily.
Grum. Severe of countenance.
Grumpy. Surly; morose.
Humorsome. Full of whims or humors.
Ill-affected. Not favorably inclined.
Ill-disposed. Habitually ill-affected.
Ill-humored. In an unpleasant frame of mind.
Ill-tempered. Having a tendency to be passionate.
In a bad humor. }
In an ill humor. } Ill-humored.
In a shocking humor. }
In a bad temper. }
In an ill temper. } Ill-tempered.
In a shocking temper. }
In the sulks. In a fit of sullenness.
Intractable. Indisposed to be governed.
Knaggy. Rough in temper.
Moody. Out of humor; gloomy.
Morose. Bitterly dissatisfied with the world in general.
Out of humor. }
Out of sorts. } In a bad humor.
Out of temper. In a bad temper.
Peevish. Feebly fretful; petulant. See FAVORITE-QUARRELSOMENESS.
Perverse. Tending to do the contrary.
Restiff. } Chafing under restraint or control. See FAVORITE-QUAR-
Restive. } RELSOMENESS.
Rusty. Surly.
Scowling. Wearing a gloomy aspect.
Sinister. }
Sinistrous. } Boding evil or harm.

FAVORITE—MOROSENESS—*Continued*.

MOROSENESS—*Adjectives*.

Bearish.   Like a bear; ill-tempered.
Black-browed.   Sullen.
Cankered.   Embittered.
Cantankerous.   Ill-natured; contrary.
Crabbed.   Sour-tempered.
Cross.   Unkind in speech or manner.
Cross-grained.   Hard to please.
Crusty.   Curt in manner or speech.
Curst.   Ill-tempered; cross-grained.

Spleenish.
Spleenly. } Irritable and melancholy.
Splenetic.
Sour.   Crabbed and morose.
Sour as a crab.
Sulky.   See FAVORITE-ANGER.
Sullen.   Habitually sulky.
Surly.   Rude and snarling.
Torvous.   Of a severe countenance.
Unaccommodating.   Not disposed to do a favor.
Wayward.   Wickedly froward.

FAVORITE—QUARRELSOMENESS.

QUARRELSOMENESS.

Acerbity.
Asperity. } Harshness or roughness of temper. See FAVORITE-ANGER.
A word and a blow.   Quickness of resentment.
Bad temper.   See FAVORITE-ANGER.
Churlishness.   Rudeness in manner and speech.
Crooked temper, etc.   See *Adjectives*.
Crossness.   Peevishness mixed with anger.
Crossness.   See *Adjectives*.
Excitability.   Quality of being easily moved.
Fiery temper.   See *Adjectives*.
Genus irritable [L].   The irritable class.
Hot blood.
Huff. } See FAVORITE-ANGER.
Ill humor, etc.   See FAVORITE-MOROSENESS.
Irascibility.   See FAVORITE-ANGER.
Irritability.   Extreme sensibility to offense.
Irritable temper.   See *Adjectives*.
Petulance.   Capricious passion unrestrained.
Procacity.   Impudence.
Protervity.   Petulance.
Pugnacity.   Disposition to fight or quarrel.
Susceptibility.   Capacity for emotional excitement.
Tartness.   Slight asperity with intellectual readiness.
Temper.   Heat of mind or passion.

QUARRELSOMENESS—*Nouns of Agent*.

Brabbler.   A quarrelsome fellow.
Dragon.   An overbearing person.
Fire-eater.   A pugnacious person.
Fury.   A violent woman.
Porcupine.   A quadruped covered with quills; an easily irritated person.
Scold.   A rude, clamorous woman.
Shrew.   A peevish, scolding woman.
Sir Fretful Plagiary.   A peevish character in Sheridan's play, *The Critic*.
Spitfire.   Violent, passionate person.
Tartar.   A person of an irritable temper.
Termagant.   Bold, ranting woman.
Virago.   Impudent, turbulent woman.
Vixen.   A quarrelsome woman.
Xantippe.   A scold; from the wife of Socrates.

QUARRELSOMENESS—*Verbs*.

Be irascible, etc.   See *Adjectives*.
Fire up   To become excited.   See ANGER.
Have a devil in one.   To be full of malicious mischief.
Have a temper.   To be easily irritated.

QUARRELSOMENESS—*Adjectives*.

Acariâtre [F.].   Ill-natured.
Angry.   See ANGER.
Bad-tempered.   Liable to be passionate.
Cantankerous.   Perverse or malicious.
Captious.   Disposed to find fault.
Choleric.   Quick to anger.
Churlish.   Rude in manners and speech.
Contentious.   Fond of contention.

Cross.   Angrily peevish.
Cross as a cat.
Cross as a crab.
Cross as a dog. } Very cross.
Cross as the tongs.
Cross as two sticks.
Disputatious.   Inclined to dispute.
Exceptious.   (Obs.) Captious.
Excitable.   Easily aroused.
Fidgety.   Unable to sit still.
Fiery.   Easily provoked; passionate.
Fretful.   Complaining of small grievances.
Fractious.   Inclined to be rebellious.
Hasty.   Quick-tempered.
Hot.   Passionate; vehement.
Huffy.   Easily offended.
Ill-tempered.   Liable to be passionate.
In a bad temper.   In an angry mood.
Irascible.   Prone to anger.
Irritable.   Easily excited to anger.
Like tinder.
Like touchwood. } Fiery.
Moodish.   Apt to have sullen moods.
On the fret.   Showing vexation.
Overhasty.   Very hot-tempered.
Passionate.   Inclined to strong passion.
Peevish.   Feebly fretful and irritable.
Peppery.   Quick-tempered.
Petulant.   Capriciously passionate.
Pettish.   Subject to fits of ill temper.
Pugnacious.   Prone to quarrel or fight.
Quarrelsome.   Showing a contentious disposition.
Querulous.   Habitually complaining
Quick.   Quick-tempered.
Resentful.
Resentive. } Susceptible to offense.
Restiff.
Restive. } Showing restlessness and impatience of control.
Shrewish.   Inclined to nag and scold.
Snappish.   Sharp and surly.
"Sudden and quick in quarrel."   Quick-tempered. [Shakespeare, *As You Like It*, II, vii.]
Sulky.   Sullenly cross.
Susceptible.   Capable of emotional impression.
Techy.   Peevishly sensitive.
Testy.   Irritable and quick-tempered.
Tetchy.   Same as TECHY.
Thin-skinned.   Sensitive to wrong.
Touchy.   Irascible.
Vindictive.   Having a tendency to revenge.
Warm.   Slightly passionate.
Waspish.   Resentful of trifles.

QUARRELSOMENESS—*Interjection*.

Pish!

QUARRELSOMENESS—*Phrase*

A vieux comptes nouvelles disputes [F.].   Old accounts breed new disputes.

fa'-vor-it-ism.   A disposition to favor.   AMITY-HOSTILITY, RIGHT-WRONG.
fawn.   To show affection by cringing before; to seek favor by subserviency.   ADULATION-DISPARAGEMENT, PRESUMPTION-OBSEQUIOUSNESS.
fawn'-col''-ored.   Colored like a fawn, light yellowish brown.   GRAY-BROWN.
fawn'-ing.   Cringing.   ADULATION-DISPARAGEMENT, PRESUMPTION-OBSEQUIOUSNESS.

fay.   Fairy.   JOVE-FIEND.
fe'-al-ty.   Fidelity.   DUTY-DERELICTION, INSUBORDINATION-OBEDIENCE, REGARD-DISRESPECT.
fear.   Uneasiness attended with alarm.   BRAVERY-COWARDICE, SANGUINENESS-TIMIDITY.
fear'-ful.   Afraid.   BRAVERY-COWARDICE, PLEASURABLENESS-PAINFULNESS, SANGUINENESS-TIMIDITY.
fear'-ful-ly.   Apprehensively.   ASTONISHMENT-EXPECTANCE, MAGNITUDE-SMALLNESS.

fear'-ful-ness. Timidity. SANGUINENESS-TIMIDITY

fear'-ing. Dreading. SANGUINENESS-TIMIDITY.

fear'-less. Being without fear. BRAVERY-COWARDICE, SANGUINENESS-HOPELESSNESS.

fear'-some. Causing fear. SANGUINENESS-TIMIDITY.

fea''-si-bil'-i-ty. Practicability. DIFFICULTY-FACILITY, POSSIBILITY-IMPOSSIBILITY.

fea'-si-ble. Practicable. DIFFICULTY-FACILITY, POSSIBILITY-IMPOSSIBILITY

feast. To delight; a banquet ENTERTAINMENT-WEARINESS, FASTING-GLUTTONY, GODLINESS-UNGODLINESS, NUTRIMENT-EXCRETION, PERIODICITY-IRREGULARITY, SENSUALITY-SUFFERING; **feast one's eyes,** LOVE-HATE.

feast of rea'-son. An entertainment, conversation, etc., delighting the mind. CONVERSATION-MONOLOGUE; **feast of reason and flow of the soul,** CONVERSATION-MONOLOGUE, SOCIABILITY-PRIVACY.

feat. A notable act. ACTION-PASSIVENESS, BRAVERY-COWARDICE; **feat of arms,** STRIFE-PEACE; **feat of strength,** STRENGTH-WEAKNESS.

feath'-er. One of the appendages growing out of the skin of a bird; something like a feather; kind; to adorn. CONSEQUENCE-INSIGNIFICANCE, DIVISION, HEAVINESS-LIGHTNESS, SMOOTHNESS-ROUGHNESS, SOCIETY-LAUGHINGSTOCK, TITLE; **feather in one's cap,** REPUTATION-DISCREDIT, TITLE, TROPHY; **feather in the scale,** CONSEQUENCE-INSIGNIFICANCE; **feather one's nest,** AFFLUENCE-PENURY, GENEROSITY-FRUGALITY, PREPARATION-NONPREPARATION, UNSELFISHNESS-SELFISHNESS, WELFARE-MISFORTUNE; **feather the oar,** SKILL-UNSKILFULNESS; **hear a feather drop,** SOUND-SILENCE; **in full feather,** AFFLUENCE - PENURY, PREPARATION - NONPREPARATION, WELFARE-MISFORTUNE; **in high feather,** BRAGGING, HEALTH-SICKNESS, LIGHTHEARTEDNESS-DEJECTION, STRENGTH - WEAKNESS, WELFARE - MISFORTUNE; **pleased with a feather,** ENTERTAINMENT-WEARINESS

feath'-er-bed''. A bed filled with feathers. HARDNESS-SOFTNESS.

feath'-er-brained'' Light - headed. SAGACITY - INCAPACITY.

feath'-ered tribes. The birds. FAUNA-FLORA.

feath'-er-y. Covered with feathers. SMOOTHNESS-ROUGHNESS.

feat'-ly. Skilfully. ACTIVITY-INDOLENCE

fea'-ture. Any part of the human face. APPEARANCE-DISAPPEARANCE, CONSTITUENT-ALIEN, FORM-FORMLESSNESS, SIGN, SUBJECTIVENESS-OBJECTIVENESS.

fea'-ture-less. Without features. FORM-FORMLESSNESS.

feb-rif'-u-gal. Antifebrile. REMEDY-BANE.

feb'-ri-fuge. A medicine that is efficacious against fever. REMEDY-BANE.

feb'-rile. Pertaining to fever. EXCITABILITY-INEXCITABILITY.

Feb'-ru-a-ry. The second month of the year. PERIODICITY-IRREGULARITY.

fe'-cal. Pertaining to refuse. CLEANNESS-FILTHINESS.

fecit [L.] (fī'-sit). He made it. PAINTING.

fec'-u-la. Starch. CLEANNESS-FILTHINESS.

fec'-u-lence. Foulness. CLEANNESS-FILTHINESS.

fec'-u-lent. Foul; muddy. CLEANNESS-FILTHINESS.

fec'-und. Prolific. FERTILITY-STERILITY.

fec'-un-date. To render fruitful. CREATION-DESTRUCTION, FERTILITY-STERILITY.

fec''-un-da'-tion. Impregnation. CREATION-DESTRUCTION.

fec-un'-di-ty. Fruitfulness. FERTILITY-STERILITY.

fed'-er-al-ist. A supporter of federalism. ASSOCIATION.

fed''-er-a'-tion. A league. ASSOCIATION.

fed'-er-a-tive. Federal. ASSOCIATION.

fee. Payment for services; a charge for a privilege; an estate of inheritance. GIVING-RECEIVING, HOLDING-EXEMPTION, OUTLAY-INCOME, PROPERTY, RECOMPENSE-PUNITION.

fee'-ble. Weak. FORCE-WEAKNESS, RATIOCINATION-INSTINCT, STRENGTH-WEAKNESS.

fee'-ble-mind''-ed. Imbecile. DETERMINATION-VACILLATION, SAGACITY-INCAPACITY.

fee'-ble-ness. Weakness. FORCE-WEAKNESS.

feed. To give food to; to supply. NUTRIMENT-EXCRETION, PROVISION-WASTE; **feed the flame,** OBSTRUCTION-HELP.

feed'-er. A steward. PROVISION-WASTE

fee'-fa'-fum'. Jargon to awe the foolish or ignorant. DEVOTION-CHARM, SANGUINENESS-TIMIDITY.

feel. To perceive, as by touch; to have a sensation or emotion. EMOTION, FEELING-INSENSIBILITY, SENSUALITY-SUFFERING, TOUCH; **feel for,** CHARITABLENESS-MALEVOLENCE, COMPASSION-RUTHLESSNESS, INVESTIGATION-ANSWER, TRIAL; **feel one's way,** RECKLESSNESS-CAUTION, TRIAL, VENTURE; **feel the pulse,** INVESTIGATION-ANSWER; **feel the want of,** DESIRE-DISTASTE.

feel'-er. One who or that which feels; something put forth indirectly to gain information. INVESTIGATION-ANSWER, TOUCH, TRIAL.

feel'-ing. Possessed of warm sensibilities. EMOTION, FEELING-INSENSIBILITY, TOUCH.

FEELING—INSENSIBILITY

Consciousness. The state of being conscious. See KNOWLEDGE.

Esthetics. That branch of knowledge which treats of taste and beauty.

External senses. The faculties by which we perceive external objects.

Feeling. The power by which the mind apprehends impressions from without or changes within the body.

Impression. Influence or effect on the senses or intellect.

Moral sensibility. See SENSITIVENESS.

Perceptivity. Power or tendency to perceive.

Physical sensibility. The state or quality of being sensible of physical impressions.

Sensation. The consciousness of action or influence upon some organ of sense.

Sensibility. Acuteness of feeling.

Sensitiveness. The state or quality of being easily and acutely affected

FEELING—*Verbs*

Be sensible of. See *Adjectives*.

Cause sensation. To cause to be felt.

Cultivate. To develop by study; cherish.

Excite an impression. To excite.

Feel. To become aware of by touch; to have a feeling.

Impress. To fix by forcible or continued presentation

Anesthesia. Loss of the sensation of feeling from disease or a drug.

Insensibility. The state of being blunted in feeling.

Moral insensibility. See SENSITIVENESS-APATHY.

Obtuseness. The state or quality of being dull in feeling.

Palsy. Any weakening of power of sensation.

Paralysis. Loss or diminution of power of perceiving sensations.

Physical insensibility. The state or quality of being destitute of the power of feeling.

Sleep. A period of inactivity of sensible emotions.

INSENSIBILITY—*Nouns of Cause.*

Anesthetic agent. A drug or anything that produces insensibility.

Chloral. A colorless oily liquid obtained by the action of chlorin upon ethal alcohol; a strong anesthetic agent.

Chloroform. A liquid anesthetic produced by the action of chlorin and an alkali upon alcohol.

Ether. An anesthetic obtained by the distillation of alcohol with sulphuric acid.

Laudanum. Tincture of opium, used as an anesthetic.

Laughing-gas. An anesthetic agent, so called from the laughter it sometimes produces when inhaled.

Nitrous oxid. Laughing-gas.

Opium. The juice of the white poppy; a strong narcotic poison, producing deep sleep.

Refrigeration. Act or process of cooling.

FEELING—INSENSIBILITY—*Continued.*

FEELING—Verbs—*Continued.*

Perceive. To have knowledge of through the senses.
Produce an impression. To affect the senses.
Render sensible. To make perceptible by the senses
Sharpen. To render more acute, as the senses.
Tutor. To train or cultivate.

FEELING—*Adjectives.*

Acute. Having senses that act or respond quickly.
Conscious. Aware of an action, influence, or effect upon the organs of sense; knowing any state of mind.
Esthetic. With the artistic sense well cultivated.
Impressive. Adapted to excite solemn attention and feeling.
Keen. Quick to perceive or apprehend; eager and sharp.
Lively. Making a striking effect upon the sense or perception.
Perceptive. Having power to become aware of through the medium of the senses.
Sensible. Capable of being affected by outside influences.
Sensitive. Easily affected by outside influences; relating to the senses.
Sensuous. Known through the senses. Poetry is "Simple, sensuous, and passionate." [Milton.]
Sentient. Having powers of sense, or of causing sensation.
Sharp. Having strong or quick powers of sensibility; keen.
Thin-skinned. Easily affected.
Vivid. Producing a lively effect.

FEELING—*Adverb.*

To the quick. With very great effect; to the life.

INSENSIBILITY—Adjectives—*Continued from Column 2.*

Thick-skinned. Incapable of being sensibly affected by external action or influence.
Unfeeling. Destitute of power of sensation.

fee–sim′–ple. An absolute fee. PROPERTY.
feet. The plural of foot. HEIGHT-LOWNESS, TRAVELING-NAVIGATION; **at one′s feet,** LIBERTY-SUBJECTION, REMOTENESS - NEARNESS, SELFRESPECT - HUMBLENESS; **fall at one′s feet,** YIELDING; **fall on one′s feet,** WELFARE-MISFORTUNE; **lick the feet of,** PRESUMPTION-OBSEQUIOUSNESS; **light upon one′s feet,** SECURITY-INSECURITY; **spring to one′s feet,** ELEVATION-DEPRESSION; **throw oneself at the feet of,** PETITION-EXPOSTULATION.
feetail. An estate of inheritance limited and restrained to some particular heirs. PROPERTY.
feign. To pretend. TRUTHFULNESS-FALSEHOOD.
feigned. Pretended. TRUTHFULNESS-FRAUD.
feint. A deceptive movement. TRUTHFULNESS-FRAUD.
felicitas, curiosa [L.] (fî-lis′-i-tas, kiu-ri-o′-sɑ). Studied felicity. SKILL-UNSKILFULNESS.
felicitas multos habet amicos [L.] (fî-lis′-i-tas mul′-tos hê-bet ɑ-mai′-cos). Prosperity has many friends. WELFARE-MISFORTUNE.
fe-lic′-i-tate. To wish happiness to. FELICITATION.
fe-lic″-i-ta′-tion. Congratulation. FELICITATION.

FELICITATION.

Compliments of the season. Good wishes given at different occasions.
Condolence. Expression of sympathy in another's sorrow. See CONDOLENCE.
Congratulation. An expression of joy at the good fortune of another.
Felicitation. A wishing of happiness.
Gratulation. A feeling of gratification.
Salute. A sign of respect or honor. See CONDOLENCE.

FELICITATION—*Verbs.*

Congratulate. To express sympathy and pleasure to on account of a happy event.
Felicitate. To wish joy or happiness to.
Gratulate. Same as CONGRATULATE.

FELICITATION—*Verbal Expressions.*

Congratulate oneself; give one joy; offer one's congratulations; tender one's congratulations; wish a Merry Christmas and a Happy New Year; wish many happy returns of the day; wish one joy.

FELICITATION—*Adverbs.*

Congratulatory.
Gratulatory.
} Expressive of congratulations.

INSENSIBILITY—*Verbs.*

Be insensible. See *Adjectives.*
Benumb. To deprive of sensation.
Blunt. To make less keen.
Have a rhinoceros hide. To have a thick skin.
Have a thick skin. To be insensitive.
Obtund. To render dull or insensible to pain.
Pall. To make dull by satiety.
Paralyze. To stupefy.
Put under the influence of chloroform.
Render insensible. Take away sensation.
Stun. To render senseless by a blow.
Stupefy. To deprive of perception or sensibility.

INSENSIBILITY—*Adjectives.*

Anesthetic. Relating to anesthesia.
Callous. Hardened as to sensation or feeling.
Case-hardened. Rendered hardened to external influences.
Dead. Wholly incapable of sensation in any sense.
Dull. Not keenly felt; lacking in lively sensation.
Hard. Having no feeling.
Hardened. Rendered callous or insensible to feeling.
Impercipient. Not being able to perceive.
Insensible. Blunted in feeling.
Numb. Lacking the power of sensation or of motion.
Obtuse. Dull in feeling and sensibility.
Pachydermatous. Thick-skinned.
Palsied. Affected with loss of sensation.
Paralytic. Pertaining to or affected with paralysis.
Proof. Impenetrable, as to sensation or impression.
Senseless. Lacking the power of sense.

(Continued on Column 1.)

fe-lic′-i-tous. Producing felicity; appropriate. HARMONY-DISCORD; **felicitous style,** PLEASURABLENESS-PAINFULNESS, PURITY-CRUDENESS, SKILL-UNSKILFULNESS, SUCCESS-FAILURE.
fe-lic′-i-ty. Well-founded happiness. PLEASURE-PAIN, SKILL-UNSKILFULNESS.
fe′-line. Cat-like; sly. CRAFT-ARTLESSNESS, ENLIGHTENMENT-SECRECY, FAUNA-FLORA.
fell. To cause to fall; inhuman; a barren hill; a pelt. CHARITABLENESS - MALEVOLENCE, COVER - LINING, CREATION-DESTRUCTION, ELEVATION-DEPRESSION, ERECTNESS-FLATNESS, HEIGHT-LOWNESS, SANGUINENESS-TIMIDITY.
fel′-lah. A peasant. GENTILITY-DEMOCRACY.
fel′-low. Associated; a companion; equal. DUALITY, EQUALITY - INEQUALITY, LIKENESS - UNLIKENESS, MALE-FEMALE, SOLITUDE-COMPANY.
fel′-low com″-mon-er. One of a class of Oxford students. INSTRUCTOR-PUPIL.
fel′-low com-pan′-ion. An associate. FRIEND-FOE.
fel′-low coun″-try-man. One of the same country. FRIEND-FOE.
fel′-low crea′-ture. A man; one of the same race or kind. HUMANITY.
fel′-low feel″-ing. Sympathy. AMITY - HOSTILITY, CHARITABLENESS-MALEVOLENCE, COMPANION-RUTHLESSNESS, LOVE-HATE.
fel′-low man″. A human being as belonging to the same race with any other human being. FRIEND-FOE.
fel′-low-ship. The state of being a companion; community of interest. AMITY-HOSTILITY, ASSOCIATION.
fel′-low stu″-dent. A student of the same institution. INSTRUCTOR-PUPIL.
felo de se [L.] (fî′-lo de sî). A suicide. LIFE-KILLING.
fel′-on. A criminal. GOOD MAN-BAD MAN.
fe-lo′-ni-ous. Criminal in intent. VIRTUE-VICE.
fel′-o-ny. A grave crime. INNOCENCE-GUILT.
felt. A fabric made by interlocking wool, fur, hair, etc. CROSSING; **deep felt,** EMOTION.
fe-luc′-ca. A small coasting vessel. CONVEYANCE-VESSEL.

fe′-male. Characterized by organs for bringing forth young or producing ova. MALE-FEMALE.

feme cov′-ert. A married woman. MATRIMONY-CELIBACY.

feme sole. A woman unmarried. MATRIMONY-CELIBACY.

femina, varium et mutabile semper [L.] (fem′-i-na, vê′-ri-um et miu-tab′-i-lî sem′-per). A thing inconstant and changeable ever is woman. MUTABILITY-STABILITY.

fem″-i-nal′-i-ty. The female nature. MALE-FEMALE, STRENGTH-WEAKNESS.

fem′-i-nate. Feminine. STRENGTH-WEAKNESS.

fem′-i-nine. Belonging to or characteristic of womankind. MALE-FEMALE.

femme de chambre [F.] (fam de shan·′-br′). A chambermaid. CHIEF-UNDERLING.

fem′-o-ral. Pertaining to the femur. ANATOMY.

fe′-mur. Thigh-bone. ANATOMY.

fen. A marsh. SWAMP-ISLAND.

fence. A structure enclosing some space; to practise with a foil or sword; a receiver of stolen goods. ATTACK-DEFENSE, ENCLOSURE, RELEASE-PRISON, ROBBER, STRIFE-PEACE, TRUTHFULNESS-FALSEHOOD; **fence round,** ATTACK-DEFENSE, CONFINEMENT, SECURITY-INSECURITY; **fence with a question,** ENLIGHTENMENT-SECRECY.

fenced. Concluded. TERMS.

fence′-less. Without a fence. SECURITY-INSECURITY.

fen′-ci-ble. Capable of defending or being defended. BELLIGERENT.

fen′-cing. Warding off; evading. TRUTHFULNESS-FRAUD.

fen-er-a′-tion. Interest. LOAN-BORROWING

fend. To ward off. ATTACK-DEFENSE.

fend′-er. One who or that which fends. ATTACK-DEFENSE.

Fe′-ni-an. A member of the Irish society called the Fenian Brotherhood. ANTAGONIST-ASSISTANT, INSUBORDINATION-OBEDIENCE.

fen′-ny. Swampy. SWAMP-ISLAND.

feod′-al. Feudal.

feo-dal′-i-ty. Feudal tenure. HOLDING-EXEMPTION, RULE-LICENSE.

feoff. To invest with a fee or feud. PROPERTY.

feoff-ee′. One to whom a feoffment is made. GIVING-RECEIVING, HOLDER.

feoff′-er. One who grants a feoffment. GIVING-RECEIVING.

feræ naturæ [L.] (fî′-rî na-tiu′-rî). Of a wild nature. FAUNA-FLORA.

fe′-rine. Wild; malignant. CHARITABLENESS-MALEVOLENCE.

fer′-i-ty. Wildness. CHARITABLENESS-MALEVOLENCE.

fer′-ment. To produce fermentation; agitate; a substance capable of producing fermentation. AGITATION, EMOTION, EXCITABILITY-INEXCITABILITY, FAVORITE-ANGER, HEAVINESS-LIGHTNESS, REGULARITY-IRREGULARITY, TURBULENCE-CALMNESS, VIGOR-INERTIA, VISCIDITY-FOAM, **in a ferment,** EXCITATION, REGULARITY-IRREGULARITY.

fer″-men-ta′-tion. A chemical decomposition of an organic compound. BIOLOGY, VIGOR-INERTIA, VISCIDITY-FOAM; **acetous fermentation,** SWEETNESS-ACIDITY.

fern. A flowerless plant of the order Filices. FAUNA-FLORA.

fe-ro′-cious. Fierce. AGITATION, CHARITABLENESS-MALEVOLENCE, TURBULENCE-CALMNESS.

fe-roc′-i-ty. Fierce cruelty. CHARITABLENESS-MALEVOLENCE, TURBULENCE-CALMNESS.

fer′-ran-dine. A seventeenth century fabric. DRESS-UNDRESS.

Fer-ra′-ra. A sword made by one of the family of Ferrara. WEAPON.

fer′-ret out. To search out. DISCOVERY, INVESTIGATION-ANSWER.

fer′-ric. Pertaining to iron. CHEMISTRY.

fer′-ry. To cross a body of water in a boat or float; the place where boats cross regularly. TRANSFER, WAY.

fer′-ry–boat″. A boat for conveying persons and things across a body of water. CONVEYANCE-VESSEL.

fer′-ry–man. One who has charge of a ferry. WAYFARER-SEAFARER.

fer′-tile. Producing or capable of producing. FANCY, FERTILITY-STERILITY; **fertile imagination,** FANCY.

fer-til′-i-ty. Fruitfulness. FERTILITY-STERILITY.

FERTILITY—STERILITY.

Fecundity. Productiveness in general; specifically reproductive power.

Fertility. The state of being fertile, of producing vegetation in abundance.

Fertilization. The act or process of rendering fertile.

Fructification. The forming of fruit; a rendering productive of fruit.

Luxuriance. State of being superabundant in growth.

Multiplication. The act of multiplying; of making more numerous.

Pregnancy. Fruitfulness in bearing children.

Procreation. Generation and production of young.

Productiveness. A yielding in abundance; fertility. See *Adjectives.*

Propagation. The spreading abroad; the multiplying and disseminating.

Pullulation. A budding.

Superfetation. Double fetation.

Uberty. Fruitfulness.

FERTILITY—*Associated Nouns.*

Hydra. A small fresh-water animal, the pieces or parts of whose body grow into complete hydra.

Land flowing with milk and honey. A very productive land. [*Joshua* v, 6.]

Milch cow. A cow that gives milk.

Protoplasm. The original cell substances of vegetable and animal life.

Rabbit. A small, remarkably prolific animal.

Seed-plot. A place where plants are cultivated for the seed.

Warren. A place for keeping animals, as hares, pheasants, etc.

Impotence. A lack of the power of reproduction; barrenness. See MIGHT-IMPOTENCE.

Infecundity. Want of fecundity; sterility.

Infertility. Want of fertility; unproductiveness.

Sterility. Want of reproductive power.

Unproductiveness. Want of productiveness. See *Adjectives.*

Unprofitableness. Want of profitableness. See USEFULNESS-USELESSNESS.

STERILITY—*Associated Nouns.*

Desert. A barren tract incapable of supporting population.

Howling wilderness. A wild country. [*Deuteronomy* xxxii, 10.]

Sahara. A great desert in Northern Africa.

Waste. An unproductive tract of land.

Wild. A forest or desert.

Wilderness. A region uncultivated and uninhabited by human beings.

STERILITY—*Verbs.*

Be unproductive. See *Adjectives.*

Come to nothing. To have no result.

Flash in the pan. To discharge the powder in the pan without discharging the load; hence, to be an abortive, unproductive attempt.

Hang fire. To fail to explode; come to nothing.

STERILITY—*Adjectives.*

Addled. Spoiled and unproductive, as addled eggs.

Arid. Parched and dry; barren.

Barren. Incapable of producing anything; sterile.

Fallow. Plowed and unseeded; uncultivated.

Fruitless. Without fruit or result.

Infecund. Not producing young.

FERTILITY—STERILITY—*Continued.*

FERTILITY—*Verbs.*

Conceive. To become pregnant with.
Fecundate. To make fruitful; impregnate.
Fecundify. To make fruitful.
Fertilize. To render fruitful; enrich.
Fructify. To render fruitful.
Generate. To produce; beget.
Impregnate. To make pregnant or productive.
Make productive. See *Adjectives.*
Multiply. To increase in numbers.
Procreate. To generate and produce.
Produce. To bring into being. See CREATION.
Spermatize. To yield seed.
Teem. To bring forth; be full or abundant.

FERTILITY—*Adjectives.*

Fecund. Fruitful, as in children.
Fertile. Producing in abundance; capable of productiveness.
Frugiferous. Fruit-bearing.
Fruit-bearing. Having fruit in distinction from vegetables.
Fruitful. Fertile; productive.
Generative. Having power to generate or produce.
Life-giving. Giving life or animation.
Luxuriant. Producing in superabundance.
Multiparous. Producing many at one birth.
Omnific. All-creating.
Parturient. Giving birth to a child. See CREATION.

fer″-ti-li-za′-tion. The act or process of rendering fertile. BIOLOGY, FERTILITY-STERILITY.

fer′-ti-lize. To make fruitful or productive. FERTILITY-STERILITY.

fer″-til-i′-zer. Manure, etc. CHEMISTRY.

fer′-ule. A flat stick for striking on the hand. RECOMPENSE-SCOURGE; **come under the ferule,** APPROVAL-DISAPPROVAL.

fer′-ven-cy. Heat of mind. EMOTION.

fer′-vent. Ardent in feeling; very hot. DESIRE-DISTASTE, EMOTION, HEAT-COLD; **fervent hope,** SANGUINENESS-HOPELESSNESS.

fer′-vid. Burning with zeal; fiery. DEVOTION-IDOLATRY, EMOTION, EXCITATION, HEAT-COLD.

fer′-vor. Ardor; heat. EMOTION, HEAT-COLD, LOVE-HATE.

Fes′-cen-nine. Indelicate. PURITY-IMPURITY.

fes′-tal. Pertaining to a festival, feast, or holiday. SOCIABILITY-PRIVACY.

fes′-ter. To ulcerate. CLEANNESS-FILTHINESS, HEALTH-SICKNESS.

festina lente [L.] (fes-tai′-na len′-tî). Hasten slowly. RECKLESSNESS-CAUTION.

fes′-ti-val. A time of feasting or celebration. ENTERTAINMENT-WEARINESS, SOCIABILITY-PRIVACY.

fes′-tive. Festal. ENTERTAINMENT-WEARINESS, SOCIABILITY-PRIVACY.

fes-tiv′-i-ty. Gaiety, as at a feast. ENTERTAINMENT-WEARINESS, SOCIABILITY-PRIVACY.

fes-toon′. A length of any decorative material hanging in a curve between two points. ARCHITECTURE, CURVATION-RECTILINEARITY, EMBELLISHMENT-DISFIGUREMENT.

fes-tooned′. Ornamented with festoons. EMBELLISHMENT-DISFIGUREMENT.

fetch. To go after and bring; to bring as a price; a stratagem. ARRIVAL-DEPARTURE, PRICE-DISCOUNT, TRANSFER, TRUTHFULNESS-FRAUD; **fetch and carry,** AIM-ABERRATION, PRESUMPTION-OBSEQUIOUSNESS; **fetch a sigh,** JUBILATION-LAMENTATION; **fetch one a blow,** ATTACK-DEFENSE, IMPETUS-REACTION.

fête [F.] (fêt). A festival. ENTERTAINMENT-WEARINESS, POMP.

fêté [F.] (fê-tê′). Feasted. SOCIABILITY-PRIVACY, SOLEMNIZATION.

fe′-tich. Fetish.

fet′-id. Emitting an offensive odor. ANIMALITY-VEGETABILITY, PERFUME-STENCH.

STERILITY—*Adjectives—Continued.*

Inoperative. Producing no effect; not active.
Issueless. Without issue; unable to have issue.
Null and void. }
Of no effect. } Inoperative.
Sine prole [L.]. Without offspring.
Sterile. Having no productive power; barren.
Teemless. Barren.
Unfertile. Not-rich or productive.
Unfruitful. Not producing abundant results.
Unproductive. Not productive.
Unprofitable. Not profitable. See USELESSNESS.
Unprolific. Not producing offspring or fruit.

FERTILITY—*Adjectives—Continued.*

Pregnant. Being with young; big with child.
Procreant. Generative; productive.
Procreative. Having power to generate.
Productive. Having the power of producing; yielding in abundance.
Profitable. Bringing profit; lucrative. See USEFULNESS.
Prolific. Producing young, with the idea of frequency and numbers.
Propagable. Capable of being spread, continued, or multiplied.
Spermatic. Relating or pertaining to semen.
Teemful. Prolific.
Teeming. Productive.
Uberous. Abundantly fruitful.

fe-tish. A material object worshiped among savages. DEVOTION-CHARM, DEVOTION-IDOLATRY, DEVOTION-MAGIC.

fe′-tish-ism. The worship of fetishes. DEVOTION-IDOLATRY, DEVOTION-MAGIC.

fe′-tor. Stench. CLEANNESS-FILTHINESS, PERFUME-STENCH.

fet′-ter. To shackle. RELEASE-PRISON, RELEASE-RESTRAINT, UNION-DISUNION.

fet′-tle. To repair. PREPARATION-NONPREPARATION.

fe′-tus. Embryo. ANATOMY.

feu d'enfer [F.] (fu dan·-fer′). A devil of a fire. ATTACK-DEFENSE.

feu de joie [F.] (fu de zhwa). A bonfire. ENTERTAINMENT-WEARINESS, SOLEMNIZATION.

feud. Vindictive strife between persons or parties; land held on condition of rendering service. PROPERTY, VARIANCE-ACCORD.

feu′-dal. Relating to a feud, or fee. LIBERTY-SUBJECTION, PROPERTY, SUCCESS-FAILURE.

feud′-al-ism. The feudal system. LIBERTY-SUBJECTION, RULE-LICENSE.

feud-al′-i-ty. The state or quality of being feudal. LIBERTY-SUBJECTION.

feu′-da-to-ry. Held by feudal tenure. LIBERTY-SUBJECTION.

fe′-ver. A high temperature of the body; extreme emotional excitement. EXCITABILITY-INEXCITABILITY, HEALTH-SICKNESS, HEAT-COLD; **fever heat,** EXCITABILITY-INEXCITABILITY.

fe′-ver-ish. Affected with fever; impatient. EMOTION, EXCITABILITY-INEXCITABILITY, EXCITATION, HURRY-LEISURE.

few. Not many. FREQUENCY-RARITY, MAGNITUDE-SMALLNESS, MULTIPLICITY-PAUCITY; **a few,** PLURALITY-FRACTION; **few and far between,** CONTINUITY-INTERRUPTION, MULTIPLICITY-PAUCITY; **few words,** DIGEST, TALKATIVENESS-TACITURNITY, TERSENESS-PROLIXITY.

few′-ness. Smallness of number. FREQUENCY-RARITY, MAGNITUDE-SMALLNESS, MULTIPLICITY-PAUCITY.

fez. A brimless hat. DRESS-UNDRESS.

fiancée. A betrothed person. LOVE-HATE.

fi-as′-co. A complete failure. SUCCESS-FAILURE.

fi′-at. An authoritative command. ORDER.

fib. An untruth told without evil intent. STRIFE-PEACE, TRUTHFULNESS-FABRICATION, TRUTHFULNESS-FALSEHOOD.

fi′-ber. A fine filament. CONNECTIVE, LAMINA-FIBER.

fi′-bril-lous. Pertaining to fibers. LAMINA-FIBER.

fi′-brous. Containing, or consisting of fibers. LAMINA-FIBER.

fib′-u-la. Bone in lower leg. ANATOMY.

fick′-le. Unduly changeable. DETERMINATION-VACILLATION, MUTABILITY-STABILITY, PERSISTENCE-WHIM.

fick′-le-ness. Inconstancy. DETERMINATION-VACILLATION.

fic′-tile. Plastic. FORM-FORMLESSNESS.

fic′-tion. That which is feigned or imagined. TRUTHFULNESS-FABRICATION; **work of fiction,** ACCOUNT, FANCY.

fic-ti′-tious. Belonging to fiction. TRUTHFULNESS-FABRICATION.

fid′-dle. A violin; to play a fiddle. MUSICAL INSTRUMENTS, MUSICIAN.

fid″-dle–de-dee′. Nonsense. ADAGE-NONSENSE, CONSEQUENCE-INSIGNIFICANCE, REGARD-SCORN.

fid′-dle–fad″-dle. Idle talk. ACTIVITY-INDOLENCE, CONSEQUENCE-INSIGNIFICANCE, MEANING-JARGON.

fid′-dler. One who plays a fiddle. MUSICIAN; **drunk as a fiddler,** TEETOTALISM-INTEMPERANCE.

fid′-dle-stick″. A fiddle-bow. CONSEQUENCE-INSIGNIFICANCE, MUSICAL INSTRUMENTS· **fiddlestick-end,** CONSEQUENCE-INSIGNIFICANCE.

fi-del′-i-ty. Faithfulness in the discharge of duty; reliability. OBSERVANCE-NONOBSERVANCE, PATRIOTISM-TREASON, TRUTHFULNESS-FALSEHOOD, UPRIGHTNESS-DISHONESTY.

Fides, Justitiæ soror incorrupta [L.] (fai′-dîz, jus-ti′-shi-î so′-ror in-cor-rup′-ta). Uncorrupt Faith, sister of Justice. FAITH-MISGIVING, RIGHT-WRONG.

fidg′-et. Nervous restlessness. ACTIVITY-INDOLENCE, EXCITABILITY - INEXCITABILITY, HURRY - LEISURE, MUTABILITY-STABILITY.

fid′-get-i-ness. Restlessness. ACTIVITY-INDOLENCE, EXCITABILITY-INEXCITABILITY.

fidg′-et-y. Restless. ACTIVITY-INDOLENCE, DETERMINATION - VACILLATION, EXCITABILITY - INEXCITABILITY, FAVORITE-QUARRELSOMENESS, SANGUINENESS-TIMIDITY.

fi-du′-cial. Undoubting. FAITH-MISGIVING.

fi-du′-ci-a-ry. Pertaining to a guardian or trustee; trustful. FAITH-MISGIVING.

fidus Achates [L.] (fai′-dus a-kê′-tîz). A true friend. ANTAGONIST-ASSISTANT, FRIEND-FOE, UPRIGHTNESS-DISHONESTY

fie. An expression of impatience or disapproval. APPROVAL-DISAPPROVAL, REPUTATION-DISCREDIT; **fie upon it,** APPROVAL-DISAPPROVAL.

fief. A fee; feud. PROPERTY.

fiel, pero desdichado [Sp.] (fî-el′, per′-o des-dî-tcha′-do). Faithful, but unfortunate. WELFARE-MISFORTUNE.

field. A piece of land larger than a garden or plot; a region; a sphere of action; the open country. DOMESTICATION-AGRICULTURE, EXTENSION-DISTRICT, GULF-PLAIN, LISTS, OCCUPATION, PROPERTY; **beasts of the field,** FAUNA-FLORA; **field of inquiry,** CONCEPTION-THEME, INVESTIGATION-ANSWER; **field of investigation,** INVESTIGATION-ANSWER; **field of view,** CONCEPTION-THEME, SIGHT-BLINDNESS, VISIBILITY-INVISIBILITY; **take the field,** FIGHTING-CONCILIATION.

field′-day″. A day of military display; a college holiday devoted to athletic sports. ENTERTAINMENT-WEARINESS, POMP, STRIFE-PEACE.

field′-glass″. A spy-glass. OPTICAL INSTRUMENTS.

field′-mar″-shal. A general officer of the highest rank in the armies of several European nations. CHIEF-UNDERLING.

field′-piece″. A cannon mounted on wheels for rapid movement. WEAPON.

field′-preach″-er. An open-air preacher. MINISTRY-LAITY.

field′-work″. A temporary fortification. ATTACK-DEFENSE.

fiend. An evil spirit; a very wicked person. BENEFACTOR-EVILDOER, JOVE-FIEND.

fiend′-ish. Like a fiend, malignant. CHARITABLENESS-MALEVOLENCE, JOVE-FIEND.

fiend′-like. Fiendish. CHARITABLENESS-MALEVOLENCE, JOVE-FIEND, VIRTUE-VICE.

fierce. Having a cruel or violent nature; ferocious. BRAVERY-COWARDICE, EXCITABILITY-INEXCITABILITY, FAVORITE-ANGER, TURBULENCE-CALMNESS.

fierce′-ness. Violence. EXCITABILITY-INEXCITABILITY.

fieri facias [L.] (fai′-e-rai fê′-shi-as). A writ ordering a judgment to be satisfied by levy on the personal property of the defendant. LAW-LAWLESSNESS, SETTLEMENT-DEFAULT.

fier′-i-ness. Spiritedness. EXCITABILITY-INEXCITABILITY.

fier′-y. Like fire; impetuous. EMOTION, EXCITABILITY-INEXCITABILITY, FAVORITE-ANGER, FAVORITE-QUARRELSOMENESS, HEAT - COLD, TURBULENCE-CALMNESS; **fiery cross,** SIGN; **fiery furnace,** OVEN-REFRIGERATOR; **fiery imagination,** FANCY; **fiery ordeal,** PLEASURE-PAIN.

fife. A small flute-like wind instrument. MUSICAL INSTRUMENTS.

fi′-fer. One who plays on a fife. MUSICIAN.

fifth. Next in order after the fourth; one of the five equal parts of a unit. FIVE-QUINQUESECTION.

fif′-ty. Five times ten. FIVE-QUINQUESECTION.

fig. A fruit of any one of the species Ficus; a trifle. CONSEQUENCE-INSIGNIFICANCE; **fig out,** EMBELLISHMENT-DISFIGUREMENT; **in the name of the prophet, figs,** ADAGE-NONSENSE.

fight. To contend. FIGHTING-CONCILIATION, STRIFE-PEACE; **fight against destiny,** BIGOTRY - APOSTASY; **fight it out,** FIGHTING-CONCILIATION; **fight one's battles again,** ACCOUNT; **fight one's way,** ACTIVITY-INDOLENCE, QUEST - EVASION, TOIL - RELAXATION; **fight shy,** BRAVERY-COWARDICE, QUEST-EVASION; **fight the good fight,** FIGHTING-CONCILIATION, VIRTUE-VICE.

fight′-er. A combatant. BELLIGERENT.

fight′-ing. Ready or disposed to fight. FIGHTING-CONCILIATION.

FIGHTING—CONCILIATION.

Active service. Military duty.

Battle. A fight between armies.

Campaign. An organized action or movement for carrying on a contest; a taking the field.

Campaigning. Act of engaging in military operations.

Civil war. A war between different sections or parties of the same country.

Crusade. A concerted movement or enterprise, undertaken enthusiastically; especially that of Europeans to recover Jerusalem for the holy cross.

Expedition. A military enterprise or march of an army for a hostile purpose.

Accommodation. Adjustment of differences; agreement.

Adjustment. The act of settling or making right.

Amnesty. General pardon of past offenses by a government.

Arrangement. A settling of differences by agreement.

Compromise. Agreement to settle differences by mutual concessions.

Conciliation. The act of bringing to a friendly state those formerly at enmity or variance.

Pacification. The act of peacemaking.

Pax in bello [L.]. Peace in war.

Reconcilement. } Restoration to a state of harmony.
Reconciliation. }

FIGHTING—CONCILIATION—*Continued.*

Fighting. A contest for advantage or superiority. See *Verbs.*
Guerre à mort [F.]. War to the death.
Guerre à outrance [F.]. War to the uttermost.
Hostilities. Open warfare; attacks of an enemy.
Internecine war. War to the death.
Mobilization. Calling out and preparing troops for active service.
Open war. War carried on to the knowledge of all.
Ordeal of battle. See WAGER OF BATTLE.
Service. Active military duty.
State of siege. The condition of a fortified place subject to a continued attempt to gain possession of it.
Tug-of-war. An athletic contest in which two opposing parties try to pull each other out of certain positions.
Wager. The settling of a cause by single combat between accuser and accused, or their substitutes. See STRIFE-PEACE.
War. An armed contest between nations or states.
Warfare. The waging or carrying on of war.
War to the death.⎫ War carried on until one or both of the parties
War to the knife.⎭ engaged are killed.

FIGHTING—*Nouns of Means.*

Arms. Weapons of war, collectively.
Gunpowder. A chemical composition used in guns.
Shot. Balls or bullets for firearms.

FIGHTING—*Nouns of Instrument, etc.*

Battle-cry. A cry to rally men in battle.
Beat of drum. Beats on a drum to call to arms or to quarters.
Bugle. A military musical instrument used to convey the commands of officers.
Cælumet of war. An Indian pipe whose rejection means war.
Clarion. A clear shrill trumpet used in warfare.
Fire-cross. A Scottish signal summoning men to arms within a limited time.
Foot-guards. Infantry soldiers.
Password. That which upon utterance entitles one to pass war fortifications, etc.
Pibroch. The wild martial music of the bagpipe.
Rappel. Beat of drum to call soldiers to arms.
Slogan. A Highland war-cry or gathering cry.
Tom-tom. A sonorous drum of the East Indies used in war-dances.
Trumpet. A wind instrument used in giving military orders.
War-cry. A national cry made in charging the enemy in battle.
War-whoop. Yell uttered by savages in advancing to battle.
Watchword. An identifying word given to sentinels.
Word of command. An injunction; an order.

FIGHTING—*Associated Words.*

Art of war. Principles underlying warfare.
Ballistics. The science or art of hurling projectiles.
Battle array. A regular arrangement of troops; order of battle.
Castrametation. The art or practise of encamping.
Chivalry. The system of knighthood.
Generalship. Military skill.
Gunnery. The science and art of managing guns, mortars, etc.
Kriegspiel. Game of military maneuvers, used for training officers.
Military evolutions. Various evolutions and maneuvers that troops go through in practise drilling.
Soldiership. Martial skill.
Strategy. The science of carrying on complicated military movements; the art of leading an army.
Tactics. The science and art of disposing land and naval forces for attack and defense.

FIGHTING—*Nouns of Place.*

Battle-field. A place where a battle has been fought. See LISTS.
Tented-field. A field covered with tents for military purposes.

FIGHTING—*Figurative Nouns.*

Appeal to arms. Resort to war, as to a supreme court.
Appeal to the sword. Resort to war to obtain a country's claims.
Arbitrament of the sword. Settlement by war.
Bellona. Roman goddess of war; personified, war.
Grim-visaged war. Stern, relentless, cruel war.
Horrida bella [L.] Severe and frightful war. "Hath smoothed his wrinkled front." [Shakespeare, *King Henry VI*, V, vi.]
Mars. Roman god of war; figuratively, war.
The sword. Destruction by war; justice.
Ultima ratio regum [L.]. The last resource of kings; war.

Shaking of hands. Agreement to forget past differences.
Terms. Conditions of settlement which the contracting parties agree upon.

CONCILIATION—*Denotations, etc.*

Armistice. A cessation from war for a short time.
Breathing time. Pause; relaxation.
Cartel. A written agreement between belligerents for an exchange of prisoners; the cessation of hostilities during such exchange.
Convention. An agreement preliminary to a treaty.
Deed of release. A writing or instrument by which one person gives up to another person his rights in any property.
Drawn battle. A battle in which neither side has gained an advantage.
Flag of truce. A white flag displayed as an invitation to conference.
Hollow truce. A truce not to be depended on.
Parlementaire [F.]. A flag of truce.
Suspension of arms. ⎰ A short truce or cessation of operations,
Suspension of hostilities. ⎱ agreed on by the commanders, as for burying the dead, surrender, etc.
White flag. A flag of truce, or a flag denoting surrender.
Truce. A temporary cessation of hostilities.

CONCILIATION—*Nouns of Means.*

Peace offering. An offering for the sake of reconciliation.
Preliminaries of peace. Introductory arrangements for peace.

CONCILIATION—*Figurative Nouns.*

Calumet of peace. A North American Indian pipe whose acceptance denotes peace.
Olive-branch. Emblem of peace.

CONCILIATION—*Verbs.*

Accommodate differences. To adjust; settle.
Accommodate matters. To adapt things one to the other.
Allay. To make quiet; pacify. See CALMNESS.
Arrange differences. To come to an agreement or settlement.
Arrange matters. To agree as to the details of.
Be pacified. To be appeased; be restored to a condition of peace.
Bridge over. To cause to change sides in a dispute or contest.
Bring to terms. To compel to agree, or assent.
Bury the hatchet. To forget injuries and make peace.
Close the temple of Janus. To enter upon a period of peace.
Come round. To assent or agree after some opposition.
Come to an understanding. To arrive at an intelligent settlement or agreement.
Come to terms. To settle terms of agreement.
Compose. To adjust or settle, as a dispute.
Conciliate. To bring to a state of friendliness; pacify.
Heal the breach. To reconcile; make whole.
Hold out the olive-branch. To promise or offer peace.
Hush up. To become silent; suppress.
Keep the peace. To avoid or prevent a breach of the peace. See VARIANCE-ACCORD.
Lay down one's arms. To give up hostilities; relinquish.
Make it up. To arrange a settlement; become peaceful.
Make matters up. To come to a settlement about past differences.
Make peace. To agree to be peaceful.
Make up a quarrel. To renew peaceful relations.
Meet half-way. To make mutual concession.
Pacify. To bring into a peaceful state.
Placate. To bring from a state of variance into one of friendliness; appease.
Propitiate. To appease one who is offended.
Put up the sword. To lay aside all differences.
Raise a siege. To relinquish the attempt to take a place.
Reconcile. To adjust, as differences; reunite after estrangement.
Restore harmony. To renew or reestablish good feeling.
Shake hands. To become reconciled, as friends.
Set straight. To adjust; arrange.
Settle differences. To wipe out all differences; come to a final settlement.
Settle matters. To agree about matters at issue, even to the details.
Sheathe the sword. To make peace; cease the struggle.
Smoke the calumet of peace. To enter into peace negotiations.
Tantas componere lites [L.]. To adjust all disputes.
Tranquilize. To make calm or peaceful.
Turn swords into plowshares. To return to peaceful times.

CONCILIATION—*Adjectives.*

Composing. Being in a state of adjusting or settling. See *Verbs.*
Conciliatory. Tending to placate or mollify.
Pacified. Restored to peace. See *Verbs.*

FIGHTING—CONCILIATION—Continued.

FIGHTING—Verbs.

Appeal to arms. To settle a difference by war.
Appeal to the sword. To obtain claims by recourse to arms.
Arm. To provide with arms.
Battle with. To contend or strive with.
Be on active service. To be employed in actual warfare.
Be on service. To be on employment in the army or navy.
Be under fire. To be in an engagement.
Break a lance with. To enter the lists with; oppose oneself to.
Campaign. To serve or operate in a campaign.
Carry on hostilities. To keep up a contest or struggle.
Carry on war. To maintain war.
Combat. To fight; struggle with.
Come to blows. To engage in combat; fight.
Come to close quarters. To get into immediate contact.
Contend. To contest, as in battle. See STRIFE.
Cross swords. To engage in a combat.
Cry havoc. To set up a signal cry for indiscriminate slaughter.
Declare war. To announce a state of war as existing.
Dig up the hatchet. To enter upon hostilities anew.
Do battle. To engage in battle.
Draw the sword. To enter a contest.
Draw the trigger. To take up a fight.
Engage. To encounter; bring to conflict.
Engage in battle. To enter into conflict; join battle.
Enlist. To engage for military service; register.
Enroll. To enter in an army or naval register.
Fall to. To begin, as battle.
Fight. To contend for victory
Fight hand to hand. To combat at close quarters.
Fight it out. To contend until a decisive result is reached.
Fight like devils. To combat as if endowed with superhuman power.
Fight one's way. To gain or win by continuous struggling.
Fight the good fight. To contend in a noble cause.
Flesh one's sword. To use or bury one's weapon into flesh for the first time.
Fling away the scabbard. To engage in a conflict to the death.
Fly to arms. To rush to arms suddenly.
Give battle. To attack an enemy.
Go to battle. To come or move into the conflict.
Go to war. To start for the seat of the war.

CONCILIATION—Phrase.

Requiescat in pace [L.] R. I. P. May he or she rest in peace.

FIGHTING—Verbs—Continued.

Hoist the black flag. To show a desire for a conflict; express defiance.
Imbrue the hands in blood. To engage in a murderous struggle; spill blood.
Join battle. To engage in battle; meet the attack.
Keep the field. To continue a campaign; hold one's ground against all comers.
Kindle the torch of war. To excite or arouse to warlike action.
Let slip the dogs of war. To begin or start a conflict.
Light the torch of war. To declare war.
Measure swords with. To match one's abilities with an antagonist.
Mobilize troops. To put troops in a state of readiness for active service.
Raise one's banner. To announce one's side in a conflict.
Raise the fire-cross. To summon men to arms.
Raise troops. To collect or obtain troops.
Rise up in arms. To commence war.
See active service. } To do duty in an actual war.
See service. }
Sell one's life dearly. To cause great damage or loss to those who are seeking one's life.
Serve. To do service, as in an army.
Set-to. To apply oneself, as in an encounter.
Shoulder a musket. To take part in hostilities.
Smell powder. To be in a battle.
Spill blood. To shed blood, or suffer it to be shed, as in battle.
Take the field. To enter upon a campaign.
Take the law into one's own hands. To administer punishment without a previous trial.
Take up arms. To commence hostilities.
Take up the cudgels. To engage in a contest. See STRIFE.
Take up the sword. To begin war.
Throw away the scabbard. To enter actively and unfettered into a struggle.
Unsheathe the sword. To make war.
Wage war. To carry on war.
Wield the sword. To challenge or defy.

FIGHTING—Adjectives.

Armed. Furnished with weapons for fighting.
Armed *cap-à-pie.* Covered with armor; totally sheathed
Armed to the teeth. Entirely equipped with arms.
Armigerous. Bearing arms.
At war with. Fighting; contending.
Bellicose. Inclined to war.
Belligerent. Carrying on war; waging war.
Bristling with arms. Conspicuously covered with arms.
Chivalrous. Pertaining to chivalry, warlike.
Combative. Disposed to fight.
Contending. Defending; fighting.
Contentious. Relating to strife, fond of contention. See STRIFE.
Embattled. Furnished with embattlements; ready for battle.
In arms. Ready or prepared to fight.
In battle array. Equipped and waiting for battle.

In open arms. At war.
Internecine. Seeking mutual destruction.
In the field. Out for warlike purposes; looking for battle.
Martial. Pertaining to war; military.
Militant. Of a warlike disposition; engaged in warfare.
Military. Relating to soldiers, arms, or warfare.
Soldier-like. Brave.
Soldierly. Like or characteristic of a real soldier; heroic.
Strategical. Effected by artifice.
Sword in hand. Ready for the fray.
Under arms. Drawn up fully armed and equipped.
Unpacific. Not inclined to conciliation.
Unpeaceful. Unquiet.
Up in arms. Eager for war; in a warlike attitude.
Warlike. Disposed for war; menacing war.

FIGHTING—Adverbs.

At the point of the bayonet. } Under compulsion.
At the sword's point. }
Flagrante bello [L.] During hostilities.

In the cannon's mouth } In the center of active fighting during a
In the thick of the fray. } combat.

FIGHTING—Interjections.

To arms!
To your tents, O Israel!

Væ victis! [L.] Woe to the vanquished!

FIGHTING—Phrases.

Bis peccare in bello non licet [L.]. To blunder twice in war is not permitted.
Jus gladii [L.]. Law of the sword.

Mars gravior sub pace latet [L.]. More serious war lurks under the peace [Claudius, *IV Honorius,* 307.]
Si vis pacem, para bellum [L.]. If you wish peace, prepare for war
The battle rages.

---

fight'-ing-cock". A game-cock. BELLIGERENT, BRAVERY-COWARDICE.
fight'-ing-man". A man, able, qualified, or ready to fight. BELLIGERENT.
fig'-ment. Something imagined. FANCY
fig'-u-rante'. A ballet-dancer. ACTING.
fig'-ur-ate. Of a certain determinate figure. NUMBER.
fig'-u-rate num'-ber. One of a series of numbers begin-

ning with unity, and so formed that if each be subtracted from the following, and the series so formed be treated in the same way, by a continuation of the process, equal differences will be obtained. NUMBER.
fig"-ur-a'-tion. The process of shaping or marking anything. FORM-FORMLESSNESS.
fig'-ur-a-tive. Metaphorical. TROPE, TRUTHFULNESS-

FALSEHOOD; **figurative style**, SIMPLICITY-FLORID-NESS.

fig'-ur-a-tive-ness. The state of being figurative. SIMPLICITY-FLORIDNESS, TROPE.

fig'-ure. Shape; a drawing; distinction; a character representing a number; price. APPEARANCE-DIS-APPEARANCE, BEAUTY-UGLINESS, DELINEATION-CARICATURE, FORM-FORMLESSNESS, NUMBER, PRICE-DISCOUNT, REPUTATION-DISCREDIT, RHETORIC, SIGN, TROPE; **cut a figure**, POMP, REPUTATION-DISCREDIT; **figure of speech**, GULL-HYPERBOLE, MEANING-JARGON, PAINTING, TROPE; **figure to oneself**, FANCY; **poor figure**, REPUTATION-DISCREDIT.

fig'-ure-fling"-er. An astrologer. DEVOTION-MAGICIAN.

fig'-ure-head". An ornamental image on the prow of a vessel; a nominal head or chief. DELINEATION-CARICATURE, SIGN.

fig"-ur-ine'. A small figure or attached group of figures. DELINEATION-CARICATURE.

fig'-ur-ist. One who uses or explains figures of speech. ARTIST.

fi-la'-ceous. Filamentous. LAMINA-FIBER.

fil'-a-ment. A fine thread or fiber. LAMINA-FIBER.

fil"-a-men'-tous. Threadlike. LAMINA-FIBER, SMOOTHNESS-ROUGHNESS.

filch. To pilfer. THEFT.

filch'-er. A thief. ROBBER.

file. A hard steel abrading or smoothing instrument; any device to keep papers or documents arranged systematically; any orderly succession or line. ADDITION-SUBTRACTION, BELLIGERENT, CHEMISTRY, CONTINUITY-INTERRUPTION, ENLARGEMENT-DIMINUTION, FRIABILITY, FRICTION-LUBRICATION, GATHERING-SCATTERING, ORGANIZATION-DISORGANIZATION, RECORD, SMOOTHNESS-ROUGHNESS, STORE, TRAVELING-NAVIGATION; **file a claim**, LITIGATION, MARK-OBLITERATION; **file off**, CONCENTRATION-RADIATION, TRAVELING-NAVIGATION.

file'-fire". The fire of small arms by files. ATTACK-DEFENSE.

fil'-ial. Due to parents. PARENTAGE-PROGENY.

fil"-i-a'-tion. The relation of a child to a parent; the judicial determination of parentage. CONNECTION-INDEPENDENCE, PARENTAGE-PROGENY, RATIONALE-LUCK, RELATIONSHIP.

fil'-i-bus"-ter. A freebooter; one engaged in an unlawful military expedition into a foreign country. ROBBER.

fil'-i-bus"-ter-ing. Acting the part of a filibuster. THEFT.

fil'-i-bus"-ter-ism. The acts or practises of filibusters. THEFT.

fil'-i-form. Threadlike. LAMINA-FIBER.

fil'-i-gree. Ornamental openwork. CROSSING.

fi'-lings. The particles removed by a file. FRIABILITY.

filius nullius [L.] (fil'-i-us nul'-li-us). Son of nobody. WELFARE-MISFORTUNE.

filius terræ [L.] (fil'-i-us ter'-r'). Son of the soil. GENTILITY-DEMOCRACY.

fill. To make full. CONTENTS-RECEIVER, COVER-LINING, ENOUGH, ENTIRETY-DEFICIENCY, PRESENCE-ABSENCE, PROVISION-WASTE; **eat one's fill**, FASTING-GLUTTONY; **fill an office**, OCCUPATION, RULE-LICENSE; **filled to overflowing**, EXCESS-LACK; **fill one's pocket**, AFFLUENCE-POVERTY, GAIN-LOSS; **fill time**, DURATION-NEVERNESS; **fill to the brim**, ENTIRETY-DEFICIENCY; **fill up**, APERTURE-CLOSURE, COMPENSATION, ENTIRETY-DEFICIENCY, INCLUSION-OMISSION, RENOVATION-RELAPSE; **fill up the time**, ACTION-PASSIVENESS; **have one's fill**, DESIRE-REPLETION, ENOUGH.

filled. Having no empty space. **Filled to overflowing**, EXCESS-LACK.

fille de chambre [F.] (fiy de shan·br). A chambermaid. CHIEF-UNDERLING.

fille de joie [F.] (fiy de zhwa). A woman of pleasure; a prostitute. PURITY-RAKE.

fil'-let. A narrow band or ribbon for encircling the head; a strip, slice, or band of flesh, metal, etc. CIRCLE-WINDING, CONNECTION, EMBELLISHMENT-DISFIGUREMENT, LAMINA-FIBER.

fil'-li-beg. A kilt. DRESS-UNDRESS.

fill'-ing. That which fills. COVER-LINING.

fil'-lip. A snap or blow with the end of the finger; an incitement. **Give a fillip**, EXCITATION, IMPETUS-REACTION, MOTIVE-CAPRICE, PUSH-PULL.

fil'-ly. A young mare. CONVEYER.

film. A thin membrane or coating. DIAPHANEITY-OPALESCENCE, DIAPHANEITY-OPAQUENESS, LAMINA-FIBER; **film over the eyes**, KNOWLEDGE-IGNORANCE, SIGHT-DIMSIGHTEDNESS.

film'-y. Like a film. LAMINA-FIBER, TEXTURE.

fils [F.] (fîs). Son. PARENTAGE-PROGENY.

fil'-ter. Any device or porous substance arranged or used for straining. CHEMISTRY, CLEANLINESS-FILTHINESS, ENTRANCE-EXIT.

fil'-ter-pa"-per. Paper used in filtering. CHEMISTRY.

filth. That which is foul, dirty, or obscene. CLEANNESS-FILTHINESS.

filth'-y. Defiled with filth. CLEANNESS-FILTHINESS.

fil'-trate. To filter. CLEANNESS-FILTHINESS, ENTRANCE-EXIT.

fimbriæ [L.] (fim'-bri-î). Fringes or fringed borders. SMOOTHNESS-ROUGHNESS.

fim'-bri-a"-ted. Having a fringe. SMOOTHNESS-ROUGHNESS.

fin. A membranous extension from the body of a fish or other aquatic animal, serving to propel, balance or steer. TRAVELING-NAVIGATION.

fi'-nal. Last. BEGINNING-END, COMPLETION-NONCOMPLETION; **court of final appeal**, CERTAINTY-DOUBT; **final cause**, CAUSE-EFFECT, PURPOSE-LUCK; **final stroke**, COMPLETION-NONCOMPLETION; **final touch**, COMPLETION-NONCOMPLETION.

fi-na'-le. The end. BEGINNING-END, COMPLETION-NONCOMPLETION.

fi-nal'-i-ty. That which is final; the doctrine of final causes. BEGINNING-END, COMPLETION-NONCOMPLETION.

fi'-nal-ly. Ultimately. BEGINNING-END, CASUISTRY, MUTATION-PERMANENCE, RATIOCINATION-INSTINCT.

fi-nance'. The science of monetary affairs. ACCOUNTS, MONEY; **minister of finance**, TREASURER.

fi-nan'-cial. Pertaining to finance. MONEY.

fin"-an-cier'. One skilled in or occupied with financial affairs. ACCOUNTS, TREASURER.

finch. A small seed-eating bird. FAUNA-FLORA.

fin contre fin [F.] (fan· con·tr fan·). Cunning matched against cunning. CRAFT-ARTLESSNESS.

find. To discover; to ascertain; to furnish; to arrive at and express in form a judicial conclusion. DECISION-MISJUDGMENT, DISCOVERY, GAIN-LOSS, OCCURRENCE-DESTINY, PROVISION-WASTE; **find a clue to**, DISCOVERY; **find credence**, FAITH-MISGIVING; **find in**, PROVISION-WASTE; **find means**, MEANS; **find one's account in**, SUCCESS-FAILURE, USEFULNESS-USELESSNESS; **find oneself**, ENTITY-NONENTITY; **find one's way**, SUCCESS-FAILURE, TRAVELING-NAVIGATION; **find one's way into**, ENTRANCE-EXIT; **find out**, DISCOVERY; **find the cause of**, INTERPRETATION-MISINTERPRETATION; **find the key of**, INTERPRETATION-MISINTERPRETATION; **find the meaning of**, INTERPRETATION-MISINTERPRETATION; **find to one's cost**, EXPECTATION-DISAPPOINTMENT; **find vent**, ESCAPE, PUBLICITY.

find'-ing. Discovery; a verdict as to matters of fact. DECISION-MISJUDGMENT.

fine. Excellent; thin; showy; refined; pleasant. ADULATION-DISPARAGEMENT, BEAUTY-UGLINESS, BREADTH-

NARROWNESS, DAMPNESS-DRYNESS, EMBELLISH-MENT-DISFIGUREMENT, GOODNESS-BADNESS, GREAT-NESS-LITTLENESS, RECOMPENSE-PENALTY, SELFRE-SPECT-HUMBLENESS, SOLIDITY-RARITY, TEXTURE, TRUTH-ERROR; **fine air**, HEALTHINESS-UNHEALTHI-NESS; **fine arts**, DELINEATION-CARICATURE, NATURE-ART; **fine feather**, HEALTH-SICKNESS, STRENGTH-WEAKNESS; **fine frenzy**, FANCY; **fine gentleman**, SELF-RESPECT-HUMBLENESS, SOCIETY-DANDY; **fine grain**, TEXTURE; **fine lady**, SELFRESPECT-HUMBLENESS, SOCIETY-DANDY; **fine powder**, FRIABILITY; **fine talk-ing**, BRAGGING, OVERVALUATION-UNDERVALUATION; **fine time of it**, WELFARE-MISFORTUNE; **fine voice**, VOCALIZATION-MUTENESS; **fine writing**, RHETORIC, SIMPLICITY-FLORIDNESS; **in fine**, BEGINNING-END, RATIOCINATION-INSTINCT; **one fine morning**, DURA-TION-NEVERNESS; **some fine morning**, TIME.

fine'-draw''. To sew or close up with fine thread or delicate workmanship. RENOVATION-RELAPSE.

fine'-fin''-gered. Expert in the work that requires delicate touch.

finem respice [L.] (fai'-nem res'-pi-sî). Regard the end. BEGINNING-END, HEED-DISREGARD.

fi'-ner-y. Ornament. DRESS-UNDRESS, EMBELLISH-MENT-DISFIGUREMENT, TASTE-VULGARITY.

'fine'-spo''-ken. Speaking politely or fairly. ADULA-TION-DISPARAGEMENT, POLITENESS-IMPOLITENESS.

fine'-spun''. Drawn or spun out to the finest degree of tenuity; subtle. BREADTH-NARROWNESS, RATIOCI-NATION-INSTINCT.

fi-nesse'. Subtle contrivance used to gain a point. CRAFT-ARTLESSNESS, SKILL-UNSKILFULNESS, TASTE-VULGARITY.

fine'-still''. To distil liquor from fermented molasses, etc. LIQUEFACTION-VOLATILIZATION.

fin'-ger. To touch or handle with the fingers; digit of the hand. ANATOMY, KEEPING-RELINQUISHMENT, TOUCH; **at one's fingers' ends**, KNOWLEDGE-IGNO-RANCE, REMEMBRANCE-FORGETFULNESS, REMOTE-NESS-NEARNESS; **finger in the pie**, ACTION-PASSIVE-NESS, ACTIVITY-INDOLENCE, ANTAGONISM-CONCUR-RENCE, CAUSE-EFFECT, ENVIRONMENT-INTERPOSI-TION; **finger on the lips**, TALKATIVENESS-TACITURN-ITY, VOCALIZATION-MUTENESS; **finger's breadth**, BREADTH-NARROWNESS; **lay the finger on**, DISCOVERY, HEED-DISREGARD; **lift a finger**, ACTION-PASSIVENESS; **not lift a finger**, ACTION-PASSIVENESS; **point the finger at**, HEED-DISREGARD; **turn round one's little finger**, RULE-LICENSE.

fin'-ger-post''. A post bearing finger-boards. SIGN.

fin'-ger-stall'' A cover to protect a finger. COVER-LINING.

fin'-gle-fan''-gle. A mere trifle. CONSEQUENCE-IN-SIGNIFICANCE.

fin'-i-al. Ornament. ARCHITECTURE.

fin'-i-cal. Overnice. CONSEQUENCE-INSIGNIFICANCE, PARTICULARNESS, SOCIETY-AFFECTATION.

fin'-i-kin. Overnice. CONSEQUENCE-INSIGNIFICANCE, SOCIETY-AFFECTATION.

finis [L.] (fai'-nis). The end. BEGINNING-END.

finis coronat opus [L.] (fai'-nis co-ro'-nat o'-pus). The end crowns the work. COMPLETION-NONCOMPLETION.

fin'-ish. To complete. BEGINNING-END, COMPLETION-NONCOMPLETION, PROPORTION-DEFORMITY.

fin'-ished. Completed; carried to a high degree of per-fection. FAULTINESS-FAULTLESSNESS, MAGNITUDE-SMALLNESS, PROPORTION-DEFORMITY, SKILL-UN-SKILFULNESS.

fin'-ish-ing. Completing. **Finishing stroke**, COMPLE-TION-NONCOMPLETION, LIFE-KILLING; **finishing touch**, COMPLETION-NONCOMPLETION.

fi'-nite. Limited. MAGNITUDE-SMALLNESS.

fi'-nite-ness. The state of being finite. MAGNITUDE-SMALLNESS.

fiord. A long, narrow arm of the sea. GULF-PLAIN.

fire. Combustion; to set on fire; to excite. ATTACK-DEFENSE, EXCITABILITY-INEXCITABILITY, EXCITA-TION, HEAT-COLD, HEATING-COOLING; **between two fires**, SECURITY-INSECURITY; **catch fire**, HEATING-COOLING; **fire and fury**, FAVORITE-ANGER; **fire and sword**, CREATION-DESTRUCTION; **fire at**, ATTACK-DEFENSE; **fire a volley**, ATTACK-DEFENSE; **fire dis-trict**, CITY; **fire of genius**, SAGACITY-INCAPACITY; **fire off**, PUSH-PULL; **fire the blood**, EXCITATION; **fire up**, EXCITABILITY-INEXCITABILITY, FAVORITE-ANGER; **go through fire and water**, BRAVERY-COW-ARDICE, DETERMINATION-VACILLATION, PERSIST-ENCE-WHIM, TOIL-RELAXATION; **hell fire**, HEAVEN-HELL; **on fire**, HEAT-COLD; **open fire**, BEGINNING-END; **play with fire**, RECKLESSNESS-CAUTION; **set on fire**, EXCITATION; **take fire**, EXCITABILITY-INEXCITA-BILITY, FAVORITE-ANGER, HEATING-COOLING; **under fire**, FIGHTING-CONCILIATION, SECURITY-INSECURITY.

fire'-an-ni'-hi-la''-tor. A chemical fire-extinguisher. HEATING-COOLING.

fire'-arms''. A weapon in which an explosive is used. WEAPON.

fire'-ball''. A ball filled with powder or combustibles intended to be thrown among enemies; a luminous meteor. COMBUSTIBLE, WEAPON.

fire'-bal-loon''. A hot-air balloon. CONVEYANCE-VESSEL.

fire'-bar''-rel. A cylinder for carrying combustibles on a fire-ship. COMBUSTIBLE.

fire'-brand''. A burning piece of wood or other sub-stance; an incendiary. BENEFACTOR-EVILDOER, COMBUSTIBLE, MOTIVE-CAPRICE, REFUGE-PITFALL.

fire'-bri-gade''. An organized body of men for extin-guishing fires. HEATING-COOLING.

fire'-cross''. A cross made of two firebrands used as a signal to take up arms. ALARM, FIGHTING-CONCILI-ATION.

fire'-drake.'' A fiery dragon; a fiery meteor. LUMI-NARY-SHADE.

fire'-eat''-er. An irascible person. BELLIGERENT, BRAVERY-COWARDICE, BRAWLER, FAVORITE-QUAR-RELSOMENESS, RECKLESSNESS-CAUTION, TURBU-LENCE-VIOLENCE.

fire'-eat''-ing. Irascible. PRESUMPTION-OBSEQUIOUS-NESS, RECKLESSNESS-CAUTION.

fire'-es-cape''. Any device to enable a person to leave or be taken from a burning building. ESCAPE.

fire'-fly''. Any luminous winged insect. LUMINARY-SHADE.

fire'-light''. Light from a fire. DIMNESS.

fire'-lock''. An old form of musket. WEAPON.

fire'-man. One who aids in extinguishing fires; a stoker. HEATING-COOLING, WAYFARER-SEAFARER.

fire'-place''. A structure in which or on which a fire may be built. OVEN-REFRIGERATOR.

fire'-proof''. Incombustible. HEATING-COOLING, SECURITY-INSECURITY.

fire'-side''. A hearth. DWELLER-HABITATION.

fire'-wood''. Wood used or fit to use as fuel. COMBUS-TIBLE.

fire'-work''. Any device containing combustibles or explosives for producing brilliant or colored light. COMBUSTIBLE, ENTERTAINMENT-WEARINESS, HEAT-COLD, LUMINARY-SHADE.

fire'-wor''-ship. The worship of fire. DEVOTION-IDOLATRY.

fire'-wor''-ship-er. One who worships fire. ORTHO-DOXY-HETERODOXY.

fir'-ing. The act of discharging firearms; fuel. COM-BUSTIBLE, CRASH-DRUMMING.

fir'-kin. A wooden hooped vessel for lard, butter, etc. CONTENTS-RECEIVER.

firm. Close-knit; stable; resolute; a business partnership. ASSOCIATION, BRAVERY-COWARDICE, DEALER, DETERMINATON-VACILLATION, HARDNESS-SOFTNESS, MUTABILITY - STABILITY, UNION - DISUNION; **firm belief**, FAITH-MISGIVING; **firm hold**, KEEPING-RELINQUISHMENT; **stand firm**, DETERMINATION-VACILLATION, REPRISAL-RESISTANCE.

fir'-ma-ment. The sky or heavens. UNIVERSE.

fir'-man. A decree granting a privilege; a license. LEAVE-PROHIBITION, ORDER.

firm'-ly. Closely. UNION-DISUNION.

firm'-ness. The state of being firm. BRAVERY-COWARDICE, DETERMINATION - VACILLATION, PERSISTENCE-WHIM.

first. Preceding all others. BEGINNING-END; **at first sight,** APPEARANCE-DISAPPEARANCE, SIGHT-BLINDNESS; **come back to first love,** BIGOTRY-APOSTASY; **first and foremost,** BEGINNING-END; **first and last,** SOLITUDE-COMPANY; **first blow,** ATTACK-DEFENSE; **first blush,** APPEARANCE-DISAPPEARANCE, BEGINNING-END, MANIFESTATION-LATENCY, MORNING-EVENING, SIGHT-BLINDNESS; **first cause,** DIVINITY; **first come first served,** CHOICE-NEUTRALITY; **first fiddle,** ADEPT-BUNGLER, CONSEQUENCE-INSIGNIFICANCE, REPUTATION-DISCREDIT, RULE-LICENSE; **first impression,** BEGINNING-END; **first in war, first in peace, first in the hearts of his countrymen,** PATRIOTISM-TREASON; **first move,** BEGINNING-END, ENTERPRISE; **first opportunity,** EARLINESS-LATENESS; **first stage,** BEGINNING-END; **first stone,** ATTACK-DEFENSE; PREPARATION-NONPREPARATION; **first that comes,** CHOICE-NEUTRALITY; **of the first water,** GOODNESS-BADNESS; **on the first summons,** ORDER.

first'-born". The first brought forth. INFANCY-AGE, NOVELTY-ANTIQUITY.

first'-class". Of the first rank or quality. GOODNESS-BADNESS.

first'-fruits". The first rewards or results of anything. CAUSE-EFFECT.

first'-lings. Those born first. CAUSE-EFFECT, INFANCY-AGE.

first'-rate". Of the first class, quality, or character. COMBATANT, CONSEQUENCE-INSIGNIFICANCE, GOODNESS-BADNESS, SUPREMACY-SUBORDINACY.

firth. An arm of the sea. GULF-PLAIN.

fisc [F.] (fisc). A treasury. MONEY.

fish. A vertebrate, aquatic animal with gills; to catch or try to catch fish. FAUNA-FLORA, LIFE-KILLING, QUEST-EVASION; **drink like a fish,** TEETOTALISM-INTEMPERANCE; **fish for,** DESIRE-DISTASTE, INVESTIGATION-ANSWER, QUEST-EVASION, TRIAL; **fish for compliments,** CONCEIT-DIFFIDENCE; **fish in the air,** USEFULNESS-USELESSNESS; **fish in troubled waters,** DIFFICULTY-FACILITY, VARIANCE-ACCORD; **fish out,** DISCOVERY, INVESTIGATION-ANSWER; **fish out of water,** ADEPT-BUNGLER, CONVENTIONALITY-UNCONVENTIONALITY, ESTABLISHMENT-REMOVAL, HARMONY-DISCORD; **fish up,** DISCOVERY, ELEVATION-DEPRESSION; **other fish to fry,** ACTIVITY-INACTIVITY, OPPORTUNENESS-UNSUITABLENESS; **queer fish,** CONVENTIONALITY - UNCONVENTIONALITY, SOCIETY-LAUGHINGSTOCK.

fish'-er-man. A fisher. LIFE-KILLING.

fish'-er-y. The fishing industry; fishing-grounds. DOMESTICATION-AGRICULTURE.

fish'-ing. Pertaining to fishery; used in fishing. LIFE-KILLING, QUEST-EVASION.

fish'-ing-boat". A boat used in fishing. CONVEYANCE-VESSEL.

fish'-pond". A pool containing fish. DOMESTICATION-AGRICULTURE, GULF-PLAIN.

fish'-tail". The tail of a fish; like the tail of a fish. TRAVELING-NAVIGATION.

fish'-y. Fishlike; improbable. FAUNA-FLORA, KNOWLEDGE-IGNORANCE.

fish'-y trans-ac'-tion. A dishonest dealing, usually concealed. UPRIGHTNESS-DISHONESTY.

fisk. To frisk. SWIFTNESS-SLOWNESS, TRAVELING-NAVIGATION.

fis'-sile. That may be split. TOUGHNESS-BRITTLENESS.

fis-sil'-i-ty. The quality of being fissile. GEOLOGY, TOUGHNESS-BRITTLENESS.

fis'-sure. A cleft. GEOLOGY, INTERSPACE-CONTACT, UNION-DISUNION.

fist. The hand closed tightly. KEEPING-RELINQUISHMENT,. WRITING-PRINTING; **shake the fist,** CHARITABLENESS-MENACE, DEFIANCE.

fist'-i-cuffs". A pugilistic encounter. STRIFE-PEACE.

fis'-tu-la. Any abnormal opening into a natural canal or hollow organ. APERTURE-CLOSURE.

fist'-u-lous. Having the form or nature of a fistula. APERTURE-CLOSURE.

fit. Adapted to an end; suitable; ready; to prepare; a convulsion; a sudden overmastering emotion. AGITATION, CONDITION-SITUATION, DUENESS-UNDUENESS, EQUALITY-INEQUALITY, EXCITABILITY-INEXCITABILITY, FAVORITE-ANGER, HARMONY-DISCORD, HEALTH-SICKNESS, PERSISTENCE-WHIM, PROPRIETY-IMPROPRIETY, RIGHT-WRONG, TURBULENCE-CALMNESS; **by fits and starts,** AGITATION, CONTINUITY-INTERRUPTION, HURRY-LEISURE, PERIODICITY-IRREGULARITY, PERSISTENCE-WHIM, REGULARITY-IRREGULARITY; **fit for,** SKILL-UNSKILFULNESS; **fit of abstraction,** HEED-DISREGARD, ORGANIZATION-DISORGANIZATION; **fit of crying,** JUBILATION-LAMENTATION; **fit of laughter,** JUBILATION-LAMENTATION; **fit out,** DRESS-UNDRESS, PREPARATION-NONPREPARATION; **fit to be seen,** BEAUTY-UGLINESS; **in fits,** AGITATION; **think fit,** VOLITION-OBLIGATION.

fit'-ful. Occurring in fits. CONTINUITY-INTERRUPTION, MUTABILITY-STABILITY, PERIODICITY-IRREGULARITY, PERSISTENCE-WHIM.

fit'-ness. Suitableness. DUTY-DERELICTION, HARMONY-DISCORD, PROPRIETY-IMPROPRIETY, RIGHT-WRONG.

fit'-ted. Well adapted. SKILL-UNSKILFULNESS.

fit'-ting. Suitable. DUENESS-UNDUENESS, PROPRIETY-IMPROPRIETY.

fit'-tings. Articles of equipment or adjustment. INSTRUMENT.

five. The sum of four and one. FIVE-QUINQUESECTION; **division by five,** FIVE-QUINQUESECTION: **five-act play,** ACTING; **five and twenty,** FIVE-QUINQUESECTION.

FIVE—QUINQUESECTION.

Cinque [F.]. Five.
Five. Four and one.

FIVE—*Associated Words, etc.*

Baker's dozen. Thirteen.
Billion. One thousand millions.
Centenary. A hundredth anniversary.
Century. A hundred; a hundred years.
Chiliad. A thousand; a thousand years.
Cwt. Abbreviation for hundredweight.
Decade. A division of ten; ten years.

Decimation. Destruction of one-tenth; destruction of a large part.
Division by five. Quinquesection.
Fifth. Last of five equal parts.
Quinquesection. Act of cutting into five parts.

QUINQUESECTION, ETC.—*Verb.*

Decimate. To destroy one-tenth; destroy a large part.

QUINQUESECTION, ETC.—*Adjectives.*

Centesimal. Based on hundredths.
Decimal. Based on ten.

FIVE—QUINQUESECTION—*Continued.*

FIVE—Associated Words, etc.—*Continued.*

Dozen. Twelve units.
Eight. A number greater by three units than five.
Eighty. Eight times ten.
Eleven. A number greater by one than ten.
Fifty. Ten times five.
Five and twenty. Five times five.
Forty. Eight times five.
Four and twenty. A number greater by four than twenty.
Four score. Eighty.
Four score and ten. Ninety.
Gross. Twelve times twelve.
Half a dozen. Six.
Hecatomb. A sacrifice of a hundred oxen.
Hundred. Twenty times five.
Hundredweight. A weight of one hundred pounds.
Lac. One hundred thousand.
Long dozen. Thirteen.
Milliard. A thousand millions.
Million. Ten hundred thousand.
Myriad. Ten thousand.
Nine. A number greater by four than five.
One hundred and forty-four. A gross.
One hundred thousand. A thousand taken a hundred times.
Plum. £100,000 sterling; $500,000.
Quarter of a hundred. Twenty-five.
Quincunx. An arrangement of five things.
Quint. A set or sequence of five.
Score. Twenty.
Seven. A number greater by two than five.
Seventy. Seven times ten.
Six. A number greater by one than five.
Sixty. Six times ten.
Ten. Two times five.
Ten thousand. A thousand taken ten times.
Thirteen. Three more than ten.
Thousand. Ten hundred.
Thousand millions. One billion.
Three score. Sixty.
Three score and ten. Seventy.
Three times three. Nine.
Trillion. A million millions.
Twelve. A number greater by two than ten.
Twenty. Two times ten.
Twenty-five. Five times five.
Twenty-four. A number greater by four than twenty.
Two dozen. Twenty-four.
Two score. Forty.

FIVE, etc.—*Verb.*

Centuriate. To divide into hundreds.

QUINQUESECTION, etc.—Adjectives—*Continued.*

Duodecimal. Based on twelve.
Hundredth. Pertaining to one of a hundred parts.
Millesimal. Pertaining to thousandths.
Octifid. Eighth.
Quinquarticular. Consisting of five articles.
Quinquefid. Five-cleft.
Quinquepartite. Consisting of five parts.
Sexagenary. Composed of sixty parts.
Sexagesimal. Based on the number sixty.
Tenth. Last in a series of ten.
Tithe. A tenth.
Twelfth. Last in a series of twelve.

FIVE, etc.—Adjectives—*Continued.*

Centenary. Pertaining to a hundred.
Centennial. Pertaining to a hundred years.
Centuple. Increased a hundredfold.
Centuplicate. A hundredfold.
Centurial. Pertaining to a century.
Decimal. Founded upon ten.
Decuple. Tenfold.
Denary. Containing ten.
Duodenal. Relating to musical groups of twelves.
Duodenary. Relating to twelve; twelvefold.
Eighth. Next after seventh.
Eleventh. Next after tenth.
Fifth. Next after fourth.
Five. See *Nouns.*
Hundredth. Next after ninety-ninth.
In one's 'teens. But a youth. Thirteen through nineteen years old.
Ninefold. Nine times.
Ninth. Next after eighth.
Octuple. Multiplied by eight.
Quinary. Arranged in fives.
Quintuple. Fivefold.
Secular. Observed once in a century.
Senary. Containing six.
Seventh. Next after sixth.
Sextuple. Sixfold; multiplied by six.
Sixth. Next after fifth.
Tenfold. Ten times.
Tenth. Next after ninth.
Thirteenth. Next after twelfth.
Thousandth. Last in a series of one thousand.
Twelfth. Next after eleventh.
Twentieth. Next after nineteenth.
Twenty-fourth, etc. Next after twenty-third, etc.
Vicesimal. Twentieth.
Vigesimal. Pertaining to twenty.

---

fives. A game similar to court-tennis. ENTERTAINMENT-WEARINESS.
fix. To fasten; to set; to adjust. DETERMINATION-VACILLATION, DIFFICULTY-FACILITY, ESTABLISHMENT-REMOVAL, MOVEMENT-REST, MUTABILITY-STABILITY, ORGANIZATION-DISORGANIZATION, SOLIDITY-RARITY, UNION-DISUNION; **fix a price,** PRICE-DISCOUNT; **fix the attention,** HEED-DISREGARD; **fix the eyes upon,** SIGHT-BLINDNESS; **fix the foundations,** PREPARATION-NONPREPARATION; **fix the memory,** REMEMBRANCE-FORGETFULNESS; **fix the thoughts,** HEED-DISREGARD; **fix the time,** CHRONOLOGY-ANACHRONISM; **fix upon,** CHOICE-NEUTRALITY, DISCOVERY.
fix-a'-tion. The act of establishing. ESTABLISHMENT-REMOVAL.
fixed. Established. MOVEMENT-REST, MUTABILITY-STABILITY, SUBJECTIVENESS-OBJECTIVENESS; **fixed belief,** FAITH-MISGIVING; **fixed idea,** BIGOTRY-APOSTASY, DECISION-MISJUDGMENT; **fixed opinion,** FAITH-MISGIVING; **fixed periods,** PERIODICITY-IRREGULARITY.
fix'-i-ty. Fixedness. MOVEMENT-REST.
fix'-ture. One who or that which is expected to remain permanently in its position. MUTABILITY-STABILITY, ORDER, PROPERTY.

fiz'-gig". A gadding, flirting girl. LUMINARY-SHADE.
fizz. A hissing noise. RESONANCE-SIBILATION.
fiz'-zle. To make a hissing sound. RESONANCE-SIBILATION.
flab'-ber-gast. To astonish. ASTONISHMENT-EXPECTANCE.
flab"-ber-gas-ta'-tion. Astonishment. ASTONISHMENT-EXPECTANCE.
flab'-ber-gas"-ted. Confounded. SELFRESPECT-HUMBLENESS.
fla-bel'-li-form. Fan-shaped. ENLARGEMENT-DIMINUTION.
flab'-by. Wanting firmness. HARDNESS-SOFTNESS.
flac'-cid. Flabby. EXCESS-LACK, HARDNESS-SOFTNESS, STRENGTH-WEAKNESS.
flac-cid'-i-ty. Flabbiness. EXCESS-LACK, HARDNESS-SOFTNESS, STRENGTH-WEAKNESS.
flag. To droop; a piece of cloth used as a standard, symbol, or signal; a flagstone. ACTIVITY-INDOLENCE, ENTERTAINMENT-WEARINESS, HEALTH-SICKNESS, LAMINA-FIBER, SCEPTER, SIGN, SMOOTHNESS-ROUGHNESS, STRENGTH-WEAKNESS, SWIFTNESS-SLOWNESS, TOP-BOTTOM, WAY, WEARINESS-REFRESHMENT; **flag of truce,** FIGHTING-CONCILIATION, MEDIATION; **flagship,** BELLIGERENT; **black flag,** FIGHTING-CONCILIATION; **lower one's flag,** YIELDING; **red flag,** ALARM;

yellow flag, ALARM, WARNING; **white flag,** FIGHTING-CONCILIATION.

flag′ bear″er. One who carries a flag. MESSENGER

flag′-el-late. To scourge. RECOMPENSE-PUNITION.

flag″-el-la′-tion. A beating. ATONEMENT, AUSTERITY, CEREMONIAL, EXCULPATION-PUNITION.

fla-gel′-li-form. Like a whip-lash. LAMINA-FIBER.

flage′-o-let′. A musical instrument resembling a flute. MUSICAL INSTRUMENTS.

flag′-ging. Weakening. ACTIVITY-INDOLENCE, HEALTH-SICKNESS.

fla-gi′-tious. Flagrantly wicked. VIRTUE-VICE.

flag′-on. A vessel with a narrow mouth used for holding liquors. CONTENTS-RECEIVER.

fla′-gran-cy. The condition or quality of being flagrant. PUBLICITY, VIRTUE-VICE.

fla′-grant. Openly scandalous. MAGNITUDE-SMALLNESS, MANIFESTATION-LATENCY, PUBLICITY, VIRTUE-VICE.

flagrante bello [L.] (flê-gran′-tî bel′-lo). During hostilities. FIGHTING-CONCILIATION.

flagrante delicto [L.] (flê-gran′-tî di-lic′-to). In the very act. ACTION-PASSIVENESS, CERTAINTY-DOUBT, INNOCENCE-GUILT.

fla-gra′-tion. A conflagration. HEATING-COOLING.

flag′-staff. A staff on which a flag is hoisted. HEIGHT-LOWNESS, SIGN.

flail. An implement for separating grain by beating. IMPETUS-REACTION.

flake. A thin piece or chip of anything. LAMINA-FIBER; **snowflake,** HEAT-COLD.

fla′-ky. Consisting of flakes or locks. LAMINA-FIBER.

flam. A deception. TRUTHFULNESS-FALSEHOOD.

flambé [F.] (flan-bê′) Singed; ruined. SUCCESS-FAILURE.

flam′-beau. A torch. DIAPHANEITY-OPAQUENESS.

flame. A stream of vapor or gas made luminous by heat. EXCITABILITY-INEXCITABILITY, EXCITATION, HEAT-COLD, LIGHT-DARKNESS, LOVE-HATE, LUMINARY-SHADE; **add fuel to the flames,** TURBULENCE-CALMNESS; **catch the flame,** CONTENTEDNESS-DISCONTENTMENT; **consign to the flames,** HEATING-COOLING; **flame-colored,** BLUENESS-ORANGE, REDNESS-GREENNESS; **flame up,** EXCITABILITY-INEXCITABILITY; **in flames,** HEAT-COLD.

fla′-men. A priest. MINISTRY-LAITY.

fla′-ming. Blazing; passionate. BRAGGING, EMOTION, EXCITATION, POMP, SIMPLICITY-FLORIDNESS, TURBULENCE-CALMNESS.

flaneur [F.] (fla-nur′). A lounger. FLATTERER-DEFAMER.

flange. A projecting rim for keeping something in place. BORDER, CONVEXITY-CONCAVITY, SUSPENSION-SUPPORT.

flank. Side. LATERALITY-CONTRAPOSITION, SECURITY-INSECURITY.

flanked. Attacked on the flank. LATERALITY-CONTRAPOSITION.

flank′-ing. Bordering. LATERALITY-CONTRAPOSITION.

flan′-nel. A loosely woven woolen stuff. HEATING-COOLING.

flap. A broad, limber, and loosely hanging part. AGITATION, IMPETUS-REACTION, INCREMENT-REMNANT, SUSPENSION-SUPPORT; **flap the memory,** REMEMBRANCE-FORGETFULNESS.

flap′-per. One who, or that which, flaps or jogs the memory. REMEMBRANCE-FORGETFULNESS.

flap′-ping. Swinging to and fro COHESION-LOOSENESS.

flare. An unsteady glare. LIGHT-DARKNESS, TURBULENCE-CALMNESS; **flare up,** EXCITABILITY-INEXCITABILITY, EXCITATION, FAVORITE-ANGER, LIGHT-DARKNESS.

flar′-ing. Flaming. COLOR-ACHROMATISM.

flash. A sudden burst of light. ETERNITY-INSTANTANEITY, HEAT-COLD, LIGHT-DARKNESS, PREDETERMINATION-IMPULSE, TURBULENCE-CALMNESS; **eyes flash fire,** FAVORITE-ANGER; **flash across the memory,** REMEMBRANCE-FORGETFULNESS; **flash in the pan,** CONSEQUENCE-INSIGNIFICANCE, FERTILITY-STERILITY, MIGHT-IMPOTENCE, SUBSTANCE-NULLITY, SUCCESS-FAILURE; **flash note,** MONEY; **flash of wit,** WITTINESS-DULNESS; **flash on the mind,** EXPOSURE-HIDINGPLACE, PREDETERMINATION-IMPULSE, REFLECTION-VACANCY, REMEMBRANCE-FORGETFULNESS; **flash tongue,** WORD-NEOLOGY; **flash up,** EXCITATION; **flash upon,** EXPECTATION-SURPRISE.

flash′-ing. Bursting forth suddenly. POMP.

flash′-y. Pretentious. COLOR-ACHROMATISM; **flashy style,** EMBELLISHMENT-DISFIGUREMENT, SIMPLICITY-FLORIDNESS.

flask. A small bottle. CHEMISTRY, CONTENTS-RECEIVER.

flask′-et. A long, shallow basket CONTENTS-RECEIVER.

flat. Level; positive; dull; below pitch; apartment. ACTING, ADEPT-BUNGLER, ASSERTION-DENIAL, CONCENTRATION-RADIATION, CONTENTS-RECEIVER, EMBELLISHMENT-SIMPLICITY, ENTERTAINMENT-WEARINESS, ERECTNESS-FLATNESS, GULL-DECEIVER, HEIGHT-LOWNESS, LEVELNESS, LIGHTHEARTEDNESS-DEJECTION, MELODY-DISSONANCE, REFUGE-PITFALL, SENSITIVENESS-APATHY, VIGOR-INERTIA, WITTINESS-DULNESS; **fall flat,** SUCCESS-FAILURE; **flat contradiction,** ASSERTION-DENIAL; **flat refusal,** PROFFER-REFUSAL.

flat′-ness. Evenness of surface. ERECTNESS-FLATNESS, LEVELNESS, WITTINESS-DULNESS.

flat′-ten. To level. ERECTNESS-FLATNESS, LEVELNESS.

flat′-ter. To praise unduly, obsequiously, or insincerely. ADULATION-DISPARAGEMENT, APPROVAL-DISAPPROVAL, CRAFT-ARTLESSNESS, PLEASURABLENESS-PAINFULNESS, SANGUINENESS-HOPELESSNESS, TRUTHFULNESS-FRAUD; **flatter oneself,** LIKELIHOOD-UNLIKELIHOOD, SANGUINENESS-HOPELESSNESS; **flatter the palate,** PALATABLENESS-UNPALATABLENESS.

flat′-ter-er. One who flatters. FLATTERER-DEFAMER, PRESUMPTION-OBSEQUIOUSNESS, SOCIETY-AFFECTATION

FLATTERER—DEFAMER

Adulator. A user of servile flattery

Claqueur [F.] A hired applauder.

Clawback. One who curries favor, as who strokes the cat's back

Courtier. To attempt to gain favor by attentions and address.

Doer of dirty work. One who does base acts to obtain favor.

Earwig. One who gains favor by telling tales about others

Encomiast. One who pronounces encomiums.

Eulogist. One who speaks in high praise.

Euphemist. One who uses fair words for ugly things

Flaneur [F.] Lounger.

Flatterer. One who praises unduly or insincerely

Hanger on. Parasite.

Laudator [L.] One who praises highly

Backbiter. One who speaks secretly to one's injury.

Calumniator. Inventor and propagator of evil reports.

Carper. An unreasonable faultfinder.

Castigator. To punish with or as with a rod.

Caviler. One who raises frivolous objections.

Censor. An officer who examines all manuscripts before they are permitted to be published; one given to faultfinding.

Censurer. One who expresses disapprobation of a person.

Critic. One who passes rigorous judgment.

Cynic. One who holds others in contempt; a surly dog.

Dawplucker. A plucker of jackdaws or simpletons.

Defamer. One who injures another's reputation.

Detractor. One who depreciates.

FLATTERER—DEFAMER—*Continued.*

Optimist. One who looks on the brightest side of things, saying "this is the best of all possible worlds."

Parasite. One who basely lives at another's expense.

Prôneur [F.]. Puffer.

Puffer. One who gives fulsome or interested praise.

Sir Pertinax MacSycophant. A worldly old man in Macklin's *Man of the World*.

Sycophant. One who flatters servilely in the hope of ingratiating himself, originally a tale-bearer about violations of the export laws of Athens about figs.

Toad-eater.⎫ An obsequious flatterer.
Toady. ⎭

Touter. One who seeks customers for inns, public conveyances, etc.

Whitewasher. One who attempts to render reputable a person of doubtful reputation.

Disapprover. One who does not approve.

Frondeur [F.] A political opponent.

Good-natured friend. A rival; opponent; enemy.

Lampooner. One who writes pasquinades.

Laudator temporis acti [L.]. A praiser of time past. [Horace, *Ars Poetica*, 1, 73.]

Libeler. One who writes defamatory accounts.

Reprover. One who administers strong, personal censure.

Reviler. A user of opprobrious and contemptuous language.

Satirist. A user of satire.

Shrew. A brawling, vexatious woman.

Sir Benjamin Backbite. A slanderer in Sheridan's *School for Scandal*.

Slanderer. A speaker of defamatory remarks.

Traducer. One who odiously misrepresents character or reputation.

Vituperator. An abusive censurer.

Wordcatcher. One who cavils at or misrepresents others' words.

DEFAMER—*Denotations.*

Thersites. The ugliest and most scurrilous of the Greeks before Troy.

Zoilus. Critic of Homer, in 4th century.

(*Continued on Column* 1.)

DEFAMER—*Continued from Column* 2.

DEFAMER—*Adjective.*

Black-mouthed. Foul and abusive.

---

flat'-ter-ing. That flatters. **Flattering tale,** SANGUINENESS-HOPELESSNESS; **flattering unction to one's soul,** ADULATION-DISPARAGEMENT, CONCEIT-DIFFIDENCE, CONTENTEDNESS-DISCONTENTMENT.

flat'-ter-y. Adulation. ADULATION-DISPARAGEMENT, TRUTHFULNESS-FALSEHOOD.

flat'-u-lence. The state of being flatulent. LIQUID-GAS.

flat'-u-len-cy. Affected with an accumulation of gas in the alimentary canal. LIQUID-GAS.

flat'-u-lent. Affected with gas in the stomach and bowels. LIQUID-GAS, RIVER-WIND, WATER-AIR; **flatulent style,** FORCE-WEAKNESS, TERSENESS-PROLIXITY.

fla'-tus. Windiness. LIQUID-GAS, RIVER-WIND.

flaunt. To display ostentatiously. POMP, REPUTATION-DISCREDIT.

flaunt'-ing. Gaudy. COLOR-ACHROMATISM, POMP.

flaut'-ist. A flutist. MUSICIAN.

Fla'-vi-an Am''-phi-the'-a-ter. The Colosseum. LISTS.

fla'-vor. The peculiar taste of a thing. SAVOR-TASTELESSNESS.

fla'-vous. Yellow. YELLOWNESS-PURPLE.

flaw. An inherent defect. CONTINUITY-INTERRUPTION, EMBELLISHMENT-DISFIGUREMENT, FAULTLESSNESS-FAULTINESS, INNOCENCE-GUILT, INTERSPACE-CONTACT, TRUTH-ERROR; **flaw in an argument,** RATIOCINATION-CASUISTRY.

flay. To skin. DRESS-UNDRESS, EXCULPATION-PUNITION.

flea. A parasitic insect. CLEANNESS-FILTHINESS, SPRING-DIVE; **flea in one's ear,** ADMISSION-EXPULSION, ATTRACTION-REPULSION, POLITENESS-IMPOLITENESS, PROFFER-REFUSAL, REGARD-SCORN, REPUTATION-DISCREDIT, SELFRESPECT-HUMBLENESS.

flea'-bite''. The bite of a flea. CONSEQUENCE-INSIGNIFICANCE.

flea'-bit''-ten. Bitten by a flea. VARIEGATION.

flecked. Spotted. VARIEGATION.

fleck'-ered. Spotted. VARIEGATION.

flecti, non frangi [L.] (flec'-tai, non fran'-jai). To be bent, not to be broken. STRENGTH-WEAKNESS.

flec'-tion. A curved part. AIM-ABERRATION.

fled. Escaped. ESCAPE.

fledge. To furnish with feathers. PREPARATION-NONPREPARATION.

flee. To run away. QUEST-EVASION.

fleece. The woolly covering of a sheep or similar animal; to shear off the fleece. AFFLUENCE-PENURY, COSTLINESS-CHEAPNESS, COVER-LINING, TAKING-RESTITUTION, THEFT.

fleeced. Stripped of money or property. AFFLUENCE-PENURY.

fleer. To jeer at. REGARD-DISRESPECT, SOCIETY-DERISION.

Fleet. A debtors' prison in London. RELEASE-PRISON.

fleet. Swift; several vessels in company or under one command. BELLIGERENT, FIGHTING-CONCILIATION, MEDIATION.

fleet'-ing. Transitory. LASTINGNESS-TRANSIENTNESS.

flesh. The portion of an animal body that consists of the softer tissues; meat; human nature. ANATOMY, ANIMALITY-VEGETABILITY, GREATNESS-LITTLENESS, HUMANITY, PURITY-IMPURITY; **flesh and blood,** ANIMALITY-VEGETABILITY, GREATNESS-LITTLENESS, MATERIALITY-SPIRITUALITY, SUBSTANCE-NULLITY; **gain flesh,** ENLARGEMENT-DIMINUTION; **ills that flesh is heir to,** GOOD-EVIL, HEALTH-SICKNESS; **in the flesh,** LIFE-DEATH; **one flesh,** MATRIMONY-CELIBACY; **make the flesh creep,** PLEASURABLENESS-PAINFULNESS, SANGUINENESS-TIMIDITY; **way of all flesh,** LIFE-DEATH; **weakness of the flesh,** VIRTUE-VICE.

flesh'-col''-or. A light pink. REDNESS-GREENNESS.

flesh'-pots''. Plenty. NUTRIMENT-EXCRETION.

flesh'-y. Corpulent. ANIMALITY-VEGETABILITY, GREATNESS-LITTLENESS.

fleur d'eau [F.] (flur do). Even with the surface of the water. TOP-BOTTOM.

fleur de lis [F.] (flur de lî). An heraldic device. EMBELLISHMENT-DISFIGUREMENT, PATRIOTISM-TREASON.

fleu-ron'. A rose-like flower or ornament in the abacus of Corinthian capitals. EMBELLISHMENT-DISFIGUREMENT.

flex''-i-bil'-i-ty. Pliancy. HARDNESS-SOFTNESS, YIELDING.

flex'-i-ble. Pliant. HARDNESS-SOFTNESS, YIELDING.

flex'-ile. Pliant. HARDNESS-SOFTNESS.

flex'-ion. A curved or bent part. AIM-ABERRATION, CURVATURE-RECTILINEARITY, PLICATURE.

flex'-u-ous. Having bends. CIRCLE-WINDING.

flex'-ure. A bent part. CURVATION-RECTILINEARITY, PLICATURE.

fib'-ber-ti-gib''-bet. An imp. JOVE-FIEND.

flick'-er. To be unsteady. AGITATION, DIMNESS, LIGHT-DARKNESS, MUTABILITY-STABILITY, VIBRATION.

flick'-er-ing. Wavering. PERIODICITY-IRREGULARITY.

flies. The space over and on both sides of the stage of a theater. ACTING.

flight. The act of fleeing or escaping; a number of flying creatures moving together. APPROVAL-DIS-

APPROVAL, ARRIVAL-DEPARTURE, ESCAPE, MULTI-PLICITY - PAUCITY, QUEST - EVASION, SWIFTNESS-SLOWNESS, TRAVELING-NAVIGATION; **flight of fancy,** FANCY, GULL-HYPERBOLE; **flight of stairs,** ASCENT-DESCENT, WAY; **flight of time,** PERIOD-PROGRESS, **put to flight,** ATTACK-DEFENSE, PUSH-PULL, SUC-CESS-FAILURE.

flight'-y. Capricious. FANCY, SANENESS-LUNACY.

flim'-flam'. A freak, a lie. PERSISTENCE-WHIM, TRUTHFULNESS-FALSEHOOD.

flim'-sy. Weak; ineffective. CONSEQUENCE-INSIGNIFI-CANCE, HARDNESS-SOFTNESS, RATIOCINATION-IN-STINCT, SOLIDITY-RARITY, STRENGTH-WEAKNESS.

flinch. To shrink. BIGOTRY-APOSTASY, QUEST-EVA-SION, REMEDY-BANE, SANGUINENESS-TIMIDITY

flin'-ders. Splinters. MAGNITUDE-SMALLNESS.

fling. A sling; a jibe; a lively dance. ENTERTAINMENT-WEARINESS, PUSH-PULL, REGARD-DISRESPECT; **fling aside,** KEEPING-RELINQUISHMENT; **fling away,** CHOICE-NEUTRALITY, KEEPING-RELINQUISHMENT, PROVISION-WASTE; **fling down,** ELEVATION-DEPRES-SION; **fling to the winds,** CHOICE-REJECTION, CREA-TION-DESTRUCTION, OBSERVANCE-NONOBSERVANCE, REGARD-SCORN; **have a fling at,** ATTACK-DEFENSE, FAVORITE-ANGER, MEANS, REGARD-DISRESPECT; **have one's fling,** ACTIVITY-INDOLENCE, ENTERTAIN-MENT-WEARINESS, LIBERTY-SUBJECTION, RULE-LI-CENSE.

flint. A variety of quartz. HARDNESS-SOFTNESS

flint glass. Glass containing lead. CHEMISTRY

flint'-heart''-ed. Hard-hearted. CHARITABLENESS-MALEVOLENCE.

flip. A hot drink spiced and sugared. NUTRIMENT-EXCRETION.

flip'-pan-cy. Fluency of speech. TALKATIVENESS-TACITURNITY.

flip'-pant. Shallow and impertinent. PRESUMPTION-OBSEQUIOUSNESS, TALKATIVENESS-TACITURNITY.

flip'-per. A limb used to swim with. TRAVELING-NAVI-GATION.

flirt. A coquette; a sudden toss. BLANDISHMENT, LOVE-HATE, PUSH-PULL; **flirt a fan,** SOCIETY-AFFEC-TATION.

flir-ta'-tion. Coquetry. BLANDISHMENT

flirt'-ing. A flirtation. BLANDISHMENT.

flit. To move rapidly from place to place. ARRIVAL-DEPARTURE, LASTINGNESS-TRANSIENTNESS, MOVE-MENT-REST, MUTABILITY-STABILITY, PERIOD-PROG-RESS, QUEST - EVASION, SWIFTNESS - SLOWNESS, TRAVELING-NAVIGATION.

flit'-ter. A shred; to flutter. AGITATION, MAGNITUDE-SMALLNESS, MUTABILITY-STABILITY.

flit'-ting. A fluttering. LASTINGNESS-TRANSIENTNESS, TRAVELING-NAVIGATION.

float. To be supported or carried along by a liquid or gas. ASCENT-DESCENT, CONVEYANCE-VESSEL, HEAVINESS-LIGHTNESS, TRAVELING - NAVIGATION; **float a bond issue,** LABOR-CAPITAL; **float a loan,** LA-BOR-CAPITAL; **float before the eyes,** VISIBILITY-IN-VISIBILITY; **float in the mind,** CONCEPTION-THEME, FANCY, MIND-IMBECILITY; **float on the air,** LOUD-NESS-FAINTNESS.

float'-ing. Afloat. ASCENT-DESCENT, CONVEYANCE-VESSEL, HEAVINESS-LIGHTNESS, LOUDNESS-FAINT-NESS, TIDINGS-MYSTERY, TRAVELING-NAVIGATION; **floating battery,** BELLIGERENT; **floating capital,** CREDIT-DEBT; **floating debt,** CREDIT-DEBT.

floats. Mechanical contrivances for elevating the players above the stage in spectacular plays. ACT-ING; **before the floats,** ACTING

Flo'-bert. A rifle. WEAPON.

floc'-cule. A loose tuft, like wool. FRIABILITY.

floc'-cu-lent. Woolly. FRIABILITY, HARDNESS-SOFT-NESS, SMOOTHNESS-ROUGHNESS

flock. A herd of animals; a congregation. GATHERING-SCATTERING, MINISTRY-LAITY, MULTIPLICITY-PAU-CITY; **flocks and herds,** FAUNA-FLORA; **flock together,** GATHERING-SCATTERING. •

floe. A tabular mass. HEAT-COLD.

floe'-berg''. Floe ice in large masses. HEAT-COLD.

flog. To whip RECOMPENSE-PUNITION, SENSUALITY-SUFFERING.

flood. A copious flow or stream; an abundant supply. ENOUGH, EXCESS-LACK, GATHERING-SCATTERING, MAGNITUDE-SMALLNESS, RIVER-WIND, WELFARE-MISFORTUNE; **flood of light,** LIGHT-DARKNESS; **flood of tears,** JUBILATION-LAMENTATION; **stem the flood,** ANTAGONISM-CONCURRENCE.

flood'-gate''. A gate for regulating the flow of water. BOUNDARY, ENTRANCE-EXIT, WATERCOURSE-AIR-PIPE; **open the flood-gates,** ADMISSION-EXPULSION, LEAVE-PROHIBITION.

flood'-mark''. A high-water mark. MENSURATION.

flood'-tide''. The rising tide. ADVANCE-RETROGRES-SION, ENTIRETY-DEFICIENCY, HEIGHT-LOWNESS, IN-CREASE-DECREASE, WATER-AIR.

floor. The lower part of any room; a horizontal surface; to strike down. ERECTNESS-FLATNESS, LAMINA-FIBER, SUCCESS-FAILURE, TOP-BOTTOM; **ground floor,** CONTENTS-RECEIVER.

flop. To flap. AGITATION.

Flo'-ra. The goddess of flowers. FAUNA-FLORA, ZOOLOGY-BOTANY.

flo'-ral. Pertaining to flowers. FAUNA-FLORA.

flo'-ri-cul''-ture. The cultivation of flowers. DOMESTI-CATION-AGRICULTURE.

flor'-id. Of a lively reddish hue. COLOR-ACHROMA-TISM, REDNESS-GREENNESS; **florid style,** HEALTH-SICKNESS, SIMPLICITY-FLORIDNESS.

flor'-id-ness. Excessive embellishment. SIMPLICITY-FLORIDNESS.

flor'-in. Coin. VALUES.

flo'-rist. A grower or dealer in flowers. DOMESTICA-TION-AGRICULTURE.

flosculi sententiarum [L.] (flos'-kiu-lai sen-ten''-shi-ê'-rum). Flowers of wisdom. SAGACITY-INCAPACITY.

floss. Floss-silk. SMOOTHNESS-ROUGHNESS.

flo-til'-la. A small fleet. BELLIGERENT, CONVEYANCE-VESSEL.

flot'-sam and jet'-sam. Goods thrown up by the tide from wrecked vessels or vessels lightened in time of danger. GATHERING-SCATTERING.

flounce. A gathered or plaited strip sewed by its upper edge to a skirt; a fling. AGITATION, BORDER, PLICA-TURE, SPRING-DIVE.

floun'-der. To stumble or struggle. AGITATION, CER-TAINTY-DOUBT, DIFFICULTY-FACILITY, MUTABILITY-STABILITY, SKILL-UNSKILFULNESS, SUCCESS-FAIL-URE, VIBRATION.

flour. Any finely powdered substance. FRIABILITY.

flour'-ish. To brandish; an ornamental design; to be prosperous; to boast. AGITATION, BRAGGING, EM-BELLISHMENT-DISFIGUREMENT, GULL-HYPERBOLE, HEALTH-SICKNESS, POMP, REPUTATION-DISCREDIT, SIMPLICITY-FLORIDNESS, SPEECH-INARTICULATENESS, VIBRATION, WELFARE-MISFORTUNE; **flourish of trum-pets,** BRAGGING, LOUDNESS-FAINTNESS, POMP, PUB-LICITY, SOLEMNIZATION.

flour'-y. Of or resembling flour. FRIABILITY.

flout. To scoff at. REGARD-DISRESPECT, REGARD-SCORN.

flow. To overflow; to glide. ENOUGH, HARDNESS-SOFTNESS, LOUDNESS-FAINTNESS, MOVEMENT-REST, PERIOD-PROGRESS, RIVER-WIND, STREAM, SUSPEN-SION-SUPPORT, TALKATIVENESS-TACITURNITY; **flow from,** CAUSE-EFFECT; **flow in,** ENTRANCE-EXIT; **flow into,** ENTRANCE-EXIT, RIVER-WIND; **flow of ideas,** REFLECTION-VACANCY; **flow of soul,** CONVERSATION-MONOLOGUE, SOCIABILITY-PRIVACY; **flow of spirits,**

LIGHTHEARTEDNESS - DEJECTION; **flow of thoughts,** MIND-IMBECILITY; **flow of time,** PERIOD-PROGRESS; **flow of words,** SPEECH-INARTICULATENESS, TALKATIVENESS - TACITURNITY, TERSENESS - PROLIXITY; **flow out,** ENTRANCE-EXIT, RIVER-WIND; **flow over,** EXCESS-LACK, RIVER-WIND; **flow with the tide,** DIFFICULTY-FACILITY.

flow'-er. The organ or organs of reproduction in a plant; the choicest part of anything; any flower-like ornament. BEAUTY-UGLINESS, CREATION-DESTRUCTION, EMBELLISHMENT-DISFIGUREMENT, FAUNA-FLORA, GOODNESS - BADNESS, REPUTATION - DISCREDIT, WELFARE-MISFORTUNE; **flower of age,** MANHOOD; **flower of flock,** GOODNESS-BADNESS; **flower of life,** INFANCY-AGE; **flower painting,** SPEECH-INARTICULATENESS, TALKATIVENESS-TACITURNITY.

flow'-er-ing. Blossoming. CREATION-DESTRUCTION.

flow'-er-ing plant. A plant which has pistils and stamens and produces true seeds. FAUNA-FLORA.

flow'-ers. Anthology. DIGEST; **flowers of rhetoric,** SIMPLICITY-FLORIDNESS.

flow'-er-y. Full of flowers; florid. EMBELLISHMENT-DISFIGUREMENT, SIMPLICITY-FLORIDNESS.

flow'-ing. Gliding along smoothly. LOUDNESS-FAINTNESS, PURITY-CRUDENESS, RIVER-WIND, SUSPENSION-SUPPORT; **flowing periods,** PURITY-CRUDENESS.

fluc'-tu-ate. To pass forward and backward irregularly. DETERMINATION-VACILLATION, MUTABILITY-STABILITY, VIBRATION.

fluct''-u-a'-tion. Unsteadiness; sudden rise and fall. DETERMINATION-VACILLATION, VIBRATION.

flue. A channel for smoke or air or gases of combustion. APERTURE-CLOSURE, CLEANNESS-FILTHINESS, HEAVINESS-LIGHTNESS, WATERCOURSE-AIRPIPE.

flu'-en-cy. Volubility. TALKATIVENESS-TACITURNITY.

flu'-ent. Having readiness in speaking or writing; a stream; a variable quantity. LIQUID-GAS, NUMBER, RIVER-WIND; **fluent language,** PURITY-CRUDENESS, TALKATIVENESS-TACITURNITY.

flu'-id. A liquid or gas. LIQUID-GAS; **fluid in motion,** STREAM.

flu-id'-i-ty. The state or quality of being fluid. LIQUID-GAS.

fluke. A harpoon barb; an accidental or unexpected advantage. ANGULARITY, PURPOSE-LUCK.

flum'-mer-y. Empty compliment. ADULATION-DISPARAGEMENT, MEANING-JARGON.

flunk'-y. A servant in livery. CHIEF - UNDERLING, PRESUMPTION-OBSEQUIOUSNESS.

flunk'-y-ism. Toadyism. ADULATION-DISPARAGEMENT.

flu''-o-res'-cence. The property, possessed by some transparent bodies, of giving off light differing from their own. DIAPHANEITY-OPALESCENCE.

flur'-ry. Perturbation. ACTIVITY-INDOLENCE, EMOTION, EXCITABILITY-INEXCITABILITY, HURRY-LEISURE.

flush. To redden suddenly; to wash out with water; even; quite full. CLEANNESS-FILTHINESS, COLOR-ACHROMATISM, EMOTION, ENOUGH, EXCITABILITY-INEXCITABILITY, HEALTH-SICKNESS, HEAT-COLD, JUBILATION - LAMENTATION, LEVELNESS, LIGHT-DARKNESS, REDNESS - GREENNESS, RIVER - WIND, TEETOTALISM-INTEMPERANCE; **flush of cash,** AFFLUENCE-PENURY.

flushed. Reddened. BRAGGING, CONCEIT-DIFFIDENCE, EXCITATION, JUBILATION - LAMENTATION, LIGHTHEARTEDNESS - DEJECTION, SANGUINENESS-HOPELESSNESS, SELFRESPECT-HUMBLENESS, TEETOTALISM-INTEMPERANCE; **flushed with rage,** FAVORITE-ANGER; **flushed with success,** SUCCESS-FAILURE; **flushed with victory,** BRAGGING.

flus'-ter. A confused state of mind. EMOTION, EXCITABILITY-INEXCITABILITY, EXCITATION, HEED-DISREGARD.

flus'-tered. Intoxicated. TEETOTALISM-INTEMPERANCE.

flute. A small tubular wind-instrument; a concave groove. GROOVE, MUSICAL INSTRUMENTS.

flûte, en [F.] (flüt, an'). With guns on the upper deck only. TOP-BOTTOM, WEAPONS.

flu'-ted. Formed with flutes. GROOVE.

flu'-ting. A channel or furrow in a column or in the goods of a lady's ruffle. PLICATURE.

flut'-ter. To shake; to fluster. AGITATION, EMOTION, EXCITABILITY - INEXCITABILITY, HURRY - LEISURE, MUTABILITY-STABILITY, SANGUINENESS-TIMIDITY.

flu'-vi-al. Of or pertaining to rivers. RIVER-WIND.

flu'-vi-a-tile. Fluvial. RIVER-WIND.

flux. A flowing; to melt; chemical promoting melting. CHEMISTRY, CONVERSION-REVERSION, LIQUEFACTION - VOLATILIZATION, MOVEMENT - REST, RIVER-WIND.

flux de bouche [F.] (flü de bush). An inordinate flow of words. TALKATIVENESS-TACITURNITY.

flux'-ion. The rate of variation of a changing quantity. NUMBER.

flux'-ion-al. Variable. NUMBER.

flux'-ions. Calculus as developed by Newton. NUMBERING.

fly. To use wings, to flee; to explode; an insect; a carriage. ARRIVAL-DEPARTURE, COLOR-ACHROMATISM, CONVEYANCE - VESSEL, GREATNESS - LITTLINESS, LASTINGNESS-TRANSIENTNESS, PERIOD-PROGRESS, QUEST - EVASION, SANGUINENESS - TIMIDITY, SWIFTNESS - SLOWNESS, TOUGHNESS - BRITTLENESS, TRAVELING-NAVIGATION, TURBULENCE-CALMNESS; **fly at,** ATTACK-DEFENSE; **fly back,** IMPETUS-REACTION; **fly from,** QUEST-EVASION; **fly in the face of,** ANTAGONISM - CONCURRENCE, INSUBORDINATION-OBEDIENCE, REPRISAL-RESISTANCE; **fly in the face of facts,** ANTAGONISM-CONCURRENCE, BIGOTRY-APOSTASY, DECISION-MISJUDGMENT, REPRISAL-RESISTANCE; **fly kites,** CREDIT-DEBT, LOAN-BORROWING, SETTLEMENT-DEFAULT; **fly off,** CONCENTRATION-RADIATION, PUSH-PULL; **fly open,** APERTURE-CLOSURE; **fly out,** EXCITABILITY-INEXCITABILITY, FAVORITE-ANGER, TURBULENCE-CALMNESS; **fly to arms,** FIGHTING-CONCILIATION.

fly'-blown''. Tainted with the eggs or larvæ of a fly. CLEANNESS-FILTHINESS.

fly'-boat''. A flat-bottomed boat for canal or coasting. CONVEYANCE-VESSEL.

fly'-ing. The act of flight. ARRIVAL-DEPARTURE, COLOR-ACHROMATISM, CONVEYANCE-VESSEL, LASTINGNESS-TRANSIENTNESS, QUEST-EVASION, SWIFTNESS-SLOWNESS, TOUGHNESS-BRITTLENESS, TRAVELING-NAVIGATION, TROPHY; **flying buttress,** ARCHITECTURE; **flying colors,** POMP, SOLEMNIZATION, SUCCESS-FAILURE; **flying column,** BELLIGERENT; **flyingfish,** CONVENTIONALITY-UNCONVENTIONALITY; **flying rumor,** TIDINGS-MYSTERY.

fly'-leaf''. A blank leaf at the beginning or end of a book. ENVIRONMENT-INTERPOSITION, MISSIVE-PUBLICATION.

fly'-trap''. A fly-catcher. REFUGE-PITFALL.

fly'-wheel''. A heavy wheel used in machinery to assist in securing uniform motion. REVOLUTION-EVOLUTION.

foal. To bring forth a colt or filly. CONVEYER, INFANT-VETERAN.

foam. A collection of minute bubbles; rage. AGITATION, EXCITABILITY-INEXCITABILITY, EXCITATION, FAVORITE - ANGER, TURBULENCE - CALMNESS, VISCIDITY-FOAM; **foam with rage,** FAVORITE-ANGER.

foam'-ing. Present participle of foam. EXCITATION.

fob. A watch-pocket in the waistband of trousers. CONTENTS - RECEIVER; **fob off,** TRUTHFULNESS-FRAUD.

fo'-cal. Of, pertaining to, situated at, or constituting a focus. CENTER.

focis, pro aris et [L.] (fo'-sis, pro ê'-ris et). For our firesides and altars. ATTACK-DEFENSE.

fo'-cus. A point of meeting of a system of rays after passing through a lens or being reflected from a mirror. CENTER, GATHERINGPLACE, OVEN-REFRIGERATOR; **bring into a focus,** CONCENTRATION-RADIATION, GATHERINGPLACE, GATHERING-SCATTERING; **in focus,** VISIBILITY-INVISIBILITY; **out of focus,** VISIBILITY-INVISIBILITY.

fod'-der. Coarse feed for animals. NUTRIMENT-EXCRETION.

foe. An enemy. FRIEND-FOE.

fœderis, casus [L.] (fed'-er-is, kê'-sus). The cause of union. TERMS.

foe'-man. An enemy in war. FRIEND-FOE.

fœnum habet in cornu [L.] (fî'-num hê'-bet in cor'-niu). He has hay upon his horn. BENEFACTOR-EVILDOER, WARNING.

fœtor [L.] (fî'-tor). A stench. PERFUME-STENCH.

fœ'-tus. The young in the womb or in the egg. INFANT-VETERAN.

fog. Condensed watery vapor suspended in the atmosphere; bewilderment. CERTAINTY-DOUBT, VISCIDITY-FOAM; **in a fog,** ENLIGHTENMENT-SECRECY; **London fog,** YELLOWNESS-PURPLE.

fog'-gy. Full of fog; obscure. DIAPHANEITY-OPAQUENESS.

fog-horn. A horn for sounding warning during a fog on the water. ALARM, WARNING.

fog'-sig"-nal. A horn, whistle, etc., for sounding a warning during a fog on the water. ALARM, WARNING.

fo'-gy. An old-fashioned fellow. SAGE-FOOL, SOCIETY-LAUGHINGSTOCK.

foh. An exclamation of disgust. DESIRE-DISTASTE.

Foh'-ist. A Chinese worshiper of Foh. MINISTRY-LAITY.

foi, bonne [F.] (fwa, bon). Good faith. UPRIGHTNESS-DISHONESTY.

foi, gardez la [F.] (fwa, gar-dê' la). Keep the faith. OBSERVANCE-NONOBSERVANCE.

foi'-ble. A personal weakness; the middle portion of a sword- or foil-blade. VIRTUE-VICE.

foil. To frustrate; metal in very thin sheets. ARCHITECTURE, LAMINA-FIBER, OBSTRUCTION-HELP, SAMENESS-CONTRAST, SUCCESS-FAILURE, WEAPON.

foiled. Baffled. SUCCESS-FAILURE.

foin. To run through, as with a sword. IMPETUS-REACTION.

foist. A light, swift galley. CONVEYANCE-VESSEL; **foist in,** ENVIRONMENT-INTERPOSITION; **foist upon,** TRUTHFULNESS-FRAUD.

folâtre [F.] (fo-latr'). Frolicsome. LIGHTHEARTEDNESS-DEJECTION.

fold. One part doubled over another; a plait; a pen; a church; ANGULARITY, COUNTRY, DOUBLING-HALVING, ENCLOSURE, GEOLOGY, MINISTRY-LAITY, PLICATURE, RELEASE-PRISON; **fold in one's arms,** BLANDISHMENT; **fold one's arms,** ACTION-PASSIVENESS; **fold up,** DRESS-UNDRESS.

fold'-ed. Doubled. PLICATURE.

fo"-li-a'-ceous. Of the nature or form of a leaf. LAMINA-FIBER.

fo'-li-age. Any growth of leaves. FAUNA-FLORA.

fo'-li-a"-ted. Beaten into a leaf, as metal. LAMINA-FIBER.

fo"-li-a'-tion. Decoration. ARCHITECTURE.

fo'-li-o. A book or the like composed of sheets folded but once. MISSIVE-PUBLICATION, WRITING-PRINTING.

folk. People collectively. HUMANITY.

folk'-lore". The traditions, beliefs, and customs of the common people. JOVE-FIEND.

fol'-li-cle. A minute cavity, sac, or tube. CONTENTS-RECEIVER, CONVEXITY-CONCAVITY.

fol-lic'-u-lar. Like a follicle. APERTURE-CLOSURE.

fol'-low. To go or come after and in the same direction; to succeed in time; to keep the thread of thought; to act under the leadership of. ANTECEDENCE-SEQUENCE, CLEARNESS-OBSCURITY, CONVENTIONALITY-UNCONVENTIONALITY, INSUBORDINATION-OBEDIENCE, LEADING-FOLLOWING, PRECEDENCE-SUCCESSION, PROOF-DISPROOF, QUEST-EVASION; **follow advice,** ADVICE, MOTIVE-CAPRICE; **follow from,** CAUSE-EFFECT, RATIOCINATION-INSTINCT; **follow implicitly,** CREDULOUSNESS-SKEPTICISM; **follow suit,** IMITATION-ORIGINALITY; **follow the dictates of,** MOTIVE-CAPRICE; **follow the example of,** IMITATION-ORIGINALITY; **follow the lead of,** ANTAGONISM-CONCURRENCE, INSUBORDINATION-OBEDIENCE; **follow the trail,** INVESTIGATION-ANSWER, QUEST-EVASION; **follow up,** DISCONTINUANCE-CONTINUANCE, PERSISTENCE-WHIM, QUEST-EVASION.

fol'-low-er. One who follows; an admirer. CHIEF-UNDERLING, CLEARNESS-OBSCURITY, CONVENTIONALITY-UNCONVENTIONALITY, INSTRUCTOR-PUPIL, INSUBORDINATION-OBEDIENCE, LEADING-FOLLOWING, LOVE-HATE, PRECEDENCE-SUCCESSION, QUEST-EVASION.

fol'-low-ing. Succeeding. ANTECEDENCE-SEQUENCE, LEADING-FOLLOWING, PROOF-DISPROOF.

fol'-ly. Foolish conduct; the result of a ruinous enterprise. DWELLER-HABITATION, SAGACITY-INCAPACITY, SKILL-UNSKILFULNESS; **act of folly,** SAGACITY-INCAPACITY, SKILL-UNSKILFULNESS.

fo"-ment'. To bathe with warm or medicated lotions; to stir up to heat or violence. ALLEVIATION-AGGRAVATION, EXCITATION, HEATING-COOLING, OBSTRUCTION-HELP, TURBULENCE-CALMNESS.

fonctionnaire [F.] (fon·c"-si-on-êr'). Public officer. CHIEF-UNDERLING.

fond. Disposed to love. LOVE-HATE; **fond hope,** SANGUINENESS-HOPELESSNESS.

fon'-dle. To caress. BLANDISHMENT.

fon'-dling. One who or that which is fondled. FAVORITE-ANGER, LOVE-HATE.

fond'-ness. Strong preference. DESIRE-DISTASTE, FELICITATION.

fondre en larmes [F.] (fon·dr an· larm). To dissolve in tears. JUBILATION-LAMENTATION.

fons et origo [L.] (fonz et orai'-go). The source and origin. CAUSE-EFFECT.

font. A receptacle for water used in baptizing; a fountain; a complete assortment of type of one kind. CAUSE-EFFECT, CEREMONIAL, FANE, WRITING-PRINTING.

food. Nutriment. NUTRIMENT-EXCRETION, OBSTRUCTION-HELP; **food for powder,** BELLIGERENT; **food for the mind,** CONCEPTION-THEME; **preparation of food,** PREPARATION-NONPREPARATION.

fool. An idiot; to gull. GULL-DECEIVER, HEALTHINESS-UNHEALTHINESS, REGARD-DISRESPECT, SAGE-FOOL, SCHOLAR-DUNCE, TRUTHFULNESS-FRAUD; **April fool,** SOCIETY-LAUGHINGSTOCK; **fool away money,** EXTRAVAGANCE-AVARICE; **fool away time,** ACTIVITY-INDOLENCE; **fool's errand,** SKILL-UNSKILFULNESS, TRUTHFULNESS-FRAUD; **fool's mate,** SUCCESS-FAILURE; **fool's paradise,** DECISION-MISJUDGMENT, EXPECTATION-DISAPPOINTMENT, RECKLESSNESS-CAUTION, SANGUINENESS-HOPELESSNESS, SUBSTANCE-NULLITY; **fool to the top of one's bent,** ADULATION-DISPARAGEMENT, EXCITATION, FAVORITE-ANGER, SOCIETY-DERISION; **make a fool of oneself,** SKILL-UNSKILFULNESS, SOCIETY-LUDICROUS-

NESS; **motley fool**, SOCIETY-DERISION, WAG; **play the fool**, ENTERTAINMENT-WEARINESS, SAGACITY-INCAPACITY, SOCIETY - DERISION, SOCIETY - LUDICROUSNESS.

fool'-hard''-i-hood. Mad rashness. RECKLESSNESS-CAUTION.

fool'-hard''-i-ness. Courage without sense or judgment. RECKLESSNESS-CAUTION.

fool'-har''-dy. Reckless. RECKLESSNESS-CAUTION.

fool'-ing. Jesting. WITTINESS-DULNESS.

fool'-ish. Like a fool. ADAGE-NONSENSE, RATIOCINATION-CASUISTRY, SAGACITY-INCAPACITY, SKILL-UNSKILFULNESS; **act foolishly**, SKILL-UNSKILFULNESS; **look foolish**, REPUTATION - DISCREDIT, SELFRESPECT-HUMBLENESS.

fool'-ish-ness. Folly. SAGACITY-INCAPACITY.

fools'-cap''. Writing-paper folded to make pages about thirteen by eight inches. SIGN, WRITING-PRINTING.

foot. The part below the ankle in man; twelve inches; a succession of long and short or accented and unaccented syllables. ANATOMY, LENGTH-SHORTNESS, MEASURE, POETRY-PROSE, TOP-BOTTOM; **at foot's pace**, SWIFTNESS-SLOWNESS; **at the foot of**, HEIGHT-LOWNESS; **foot by foot**, WHOLE-PART; **foot it**, SPRING-DIVE, TRAVELING-NAVIGATION; **keep on foot**, DISCONTINUANCE - CONTINUANCE, PREPARATION - NONPREPARATION, PROVISION-WASTE, SUSPENSION-SUPPORT; **not stir a foot**, ACTION-PASSIVENESS; **one foot in the grave**, INFANCY-AGE, LIFE-DEATH; **on foot**, ACTIVITY-INDOLENCE, AGENCY, CONCEPTION-THEME, DURATION - NEVERNESS, ENTITY - NONENTITY, OCCURRENCE-DESTINY, OCCUPATION, PREPARATION-NONPREPARATION, TRAVELING-NAVIGATION; **put one's foot down**, PERSISTENCE-WHIM; **put one's foot in**, ENTERPRISE, SKILL-UNSKILFULNESS; **set foot on land**, OCEAN-LAND; **trample under foot**, REGARD-SCORN, REPUTATION-DISCREDIT.

foot'-ball''. A game in which two contesting parties try to kick or carry a large inflated ball past an opposite goal. ENTERTAINMENT-WEARINESS, LIBERTY-SUBJECTION.

foot'-boy''. A page. CHIEF-UNDERLING.

foot'-bridge''. A bridge for pedestrians only. WAY.

foot'-fall'. The sound of a footstep. MOVEMENT-REST, SIGN, SUCCESS-FAILURE.

Foot-Guards. The English king's palace guards. FIGHTING-CONCILIATION.

foot'-ing. A place to walk or stand on; a recognized condition of social relations; a footstep; the adding of a column of figures or the sum so obtained. CONDITION-SITUATION, DOMINANCE-IMPOTENCE, OUTLAY-INCOME, POSITION, STATION, SUSPENSION-SUPPORT, TOP-BOTTOM; **be on a footing**, CONDITION-SITUATION; **friendly footing**, AMITY-HOSTILITY; **get a footing**, ESTABLISHMENT-REMOVAL; **pay one's footing**, RECOMPENSE-PUNITION, SETTLEMENT-DEFAULT.

foot'-lights''. A row of lights in front of the stage of a theater. ACTING.

foot'-man. A man-servant who attends a carriage. CHIEF-UNDERLING.

foot'-mark''. The impression of a foot. MARK-OBLITERATION.

foot'-pad''. A highwayman. ROBBER.

foot'-pas''-sen-ger. One who passes or travels on foot. WAYFARER-SEAFARER.

foot'-path''. A path for persons walking. WAY.

foot'-print''. A footmark. MARK-OBLITERATION.

foot'-sol''-dier. An infantryman. BELLIGERENT.

foot'-sore''. Having sore feet. WEARINESS-REFRESHMENT.

foot'-step''. A footprint. MARK-OBLITERATION.

foot'-stool''. A stool for the feet; a down-trodden person or thing. SUSPENSION-SUPPORT.

fop. A dandy. POMP, SOCIETY-DANDY.

fop'-per-y. Dandyism. POMP.

fop'-pish. Characteristic of a fop. SOCIETY-AFFECTATION.

for. Since; because. INCLINATION, MOTIVE-CAPRICE, PREPARATION - NONPREPARATION, PURPOSE - LUCK, RATIOCINATION-INSTINCT; **as for**, CONNECTION-INDEPENDENCE; **for all that**, COMPENSATION, MODIFICATION; **for all the world like**, LIKENESS-UNLIKENESS; **for a season**, DURATION-NEVERNESS; **for a time**, DURATION-NEVERNESS; LASTINGNESS-TRANSIENTNESS; **for aught one knows**, RATIONALE-LUCK; **for better for worse**, UNIVERSALITY-PARTICULARITY; **forever**, ETERNITY-INSTANTANEITY; **for example**, CONVENTIONALITY-UNCONVENTIONALITY; **for form's sake**, CONVENTIONALITY-UNCONVENTIONALITY; **for good**, DURATION - NEVERNESS, ENTIRETY - DEFICIENCY, LASTINGNESS - TRANSIENTNESS, MUTATION-PERMANENCE; **for nothing**, COSTLINESS - CHEAPNESS; **for the most part**, MAGNITUDE-SMALLNESS, UNIVERSALITY-PARTICULARITY; **for the nonce**, TIME; **for the time being**, DURATION-NEVERNESS, TIME; **have for**, PRICE-DISCOUNT.

for'-age. Fodder; to collect food by roving search. NUTRIMENT-EXCRETION, PROVISION-WASTE, THEFT.

for'-age-cap''. A low cap worn by officers when not in full-dress uniform. DRESS-UNDRESS.

fo-ra'-men. An opening. APERTURE-CLOSURE.

fo-ram'-i-nous. Full of holes. APERTURE-CLOSURE.

for''-as-much'' as. Seeing or considering that. CONNECTION-INDEPENDENCE, MOTIVE-CAPRICE, RATIOCINATION-INSTINCT, RATIONALE-LUCK.

for'-ay. A raid. ATTACK-DEFENSE, THEFT.

for-bear'. To refrain from; to be patient. COMPASSION-RUTHLESSNESS, EXCITABILITY-INEXCITABILITY, HARSHNESS - MILDNESS, MODERATION - SELFINDULGENCE, QUEST-EVASION, USE-DISUSE.

for-bear'-ance. The exercise of patience. COMPASSION-RUTHLESSNESS, EXCITABILITY-INEXCITABILITY, MODERATION - SELFINDULGENCE, QUEST - EVASION, USE-DISUSE.

for-bear'-ing. Patient. COMPASSION-RUTHLESSNESS.

for-bid'. To prohibit. LEAVE-PROHIBITION; **God forbid**, APPROVAL-DISAPPROVAL, ASSENT-DISSENT, DEVOTION-IDOLATRY, PETITION-EXPOSTULATION.

for-bid'-den fruit. The fruit of the tree of knowledge of good and evil in the garden of Eden; unlawful pleasure. LEAVE-PROHIBITION, MOTIVE-CAPRICE.

for-bid'-ding. Repulsive. BEAUTY-UGLINESS, LEAVE-PROHIBITION.

force. Any operating energy; an army; vigor. AGENCY, COERCION, FORCE-WEAKNESS, MIGHT-IMPOTENCE, MOTIVE-CAPRICE, RHETORIC, STRENGTH-WEAKNESS, TURBULENCE-CALMNESS, VIGOR-INERTIA; **armed force**, BELLIGERENT; **brute force**, LAW-LAWLESSNESS, STRENGTH-WEAKNESS; **force down the throat**, COERCION, HARSHNESS - MILDNESS; **force majeure**, COERCION, **force of argument**, COERCION, RATIOCINATION-INSTINCT; **force of arms**, COERCION; **force one's way**, ADVANCE-RETROGRESSION, TRANSMISSION; **put in force**, COMPLETION - NONCOMPLETION, DUENESS-UNDUENESS.

FORCE—WEAKNESS.

Force. The capacity to convince, convict, or move.

Power. Great or telling force.

Vigor. Capacity for energetic action or exertion, physical, intellectual, or moral.

Feebleness. The quality of lacking force, energy, or vigor.

Weakness. A want of strength or vigor.

WEAKNESS—*Adjectives.*

Bald. Without embellishments or elegance; pointless.

FORCE—WEAKNESS—*Continued.*

FORCE—*Denotations, etc.*

Antithesis. A strong contrast.
Boldness. State of being bold.
Command of language. } Power to use language to express its strong-
Command of words. } est meaning.
Elevation. Exaltation of thought.
Eloquence. The power of expressing strong emotions in striking and appropriate language.
Glow. Intense excitement or earnestness.
Gravity. Importance or dignity.
Loftiness. State or character of being elevated or noble.
Piquancy. Agreeable intellectual keenness.
Point. That to which especial importance is attached.
Raciness. The quality of being exciting to the mental taste by a distinctive character of thought or language.
Sententiousness. The quality of giving terse expression to thought.
Spirit. Energy or vivacity.
Strong language. Language adapted to make an effectual impression on the mind.
Sublimity. The quality of awakening of awe, etc.
Verve. Excitement of imagination.
Warmth. A state of lively and excited interest.

FORCE—*Adjectives.*

Antithetical. Strongly contrasted.
Bold. Audacious; striking.
Elevated. Lofty in character; sublime.
Eloquent. Powerfully expressive; stirring; convincing
Forcible. Vigorous; energetic.
Full of point. Cogent.
Glowing. Burning; showing intense feeling.
Impassioned. Greatly animated or excited.
Impressive. Holding the attention; exciting admiration.
Incisive. Cutting; penetrating; trenchant.
Lively. Vivid; spirited.
Lofty. Stately; noble; elevated.
Nervous. Manifesting terseness, vigor, and crispness.
Petulant. Fretful; peevish; snappish.
Piquant. Racy; sparkling; lively.
Pithy. Forcible; sententious.
Poetic. Having regard to beauty.
Pointed. Pungent; epigrammatic.
Powerful. Having great effect on the mind; convincing.
Pungent. Piercing; caustic.
Racy. Lively; piquant; tasting of the stock or family, like certain choice wines.
Sensational. Causing strong feeling.
Sententious. Pithy; axiomatic.
Slashing. Striking or cutting at random.
Sparkling. Brilliant; vivacious.
Spirited. Full of spirit, life, or vigor.
Sublime. Lofty, mighty; grand; majestic; solemn.
Trenchant. Effective; penetrating; biting.

WEAKNESS—*Adjectives—Continued.*

Careless. Not carefully done or performed.
Childish. Immature.
Cold. Having little or no liveliness, ardor, or enthusiasm.
Diffuse. Characterized by redundance or prolixity.
Dry. Lacking interest.
Dull. Not pleasing, bright, or spirited.
Feeble. Lacking force, energy, or vigor.
Flatulent. Full of pretense without substance or reality.
Frigid. Lacking in warmth of feeling.
Inexact. Not exact, accurate, or true.
Jejune. Devoid of life, point, or interest.
Languid. Wanting in interest or animation.
Lax. Wanting preciseness of meaning or application.
Loose. Not precise or exact; vague; indefinite.
Meager. Deficient in or destitute of quantity or quality.
Monotonous. Tiresomely unvarying in any respect.
Poor. Lacking in good qualities, or the qualities that render a thing valuable.
Prosaic. Lacking in those qualities that impart animation or interest.
Prosing. Dull and tedious in minuteness of writing or speaking.
Prosy. Commonplace; tiresome; prosaic.
Puerile. Childish; immature; juvenile.
Rambling. Showing absence of plan or system.
Sketchy. Given roughly or suggestively without detail or finish.
Slight. Of small importance or significance.
Slip-shod. Slovenly.
Slip-shop. Slouchy; slip-shod.
Tame. Lacking in interest or animation; vapid.
Trashy. Consisting of or like trash; worthless.
Unvaried. Monotonous.
Vapid. Lacking life and animation; dull; mawkish.
Washy. Feeble; wanting in force; savoring like dishwater.
Weak. Lacking in power or force.
Wishy-washy. Lacking in solidity or vigor; forceless; unsubstantial.

FORCE—*Adjectives—Continued.*

Vehement. Carrying all before it; impetuous; passionate; fiery.
Vigorous. Powerful; forcible.

FORCE—*Adverbs.*

In glowing terms.
In good set terms. In good established sentences. A fool who railed in good set terms. [Shakespeare, *As You Like It*, II, vii.]
In no measured terms. In a style unrestrained or unmoderated.

FORCE—*Phrase.*

"Thoughts that breathe and words that burn." [Gray, *Progress of Poesy*, 3, 3²]

---

force, à toute [F.] (fors, a tut). With all one's might. MIGHT-IMPOTENCE.
forced. Strained; unnatural. CONNECTION - INDEPENDENCE, PURITY-CRUDENESS.
for'-ceps. Pincers. KEEPING - RELINQUISHMENT, TRANSCURSION-SHORTCOMING.
force'-pump". A pump for delivering liquids at a great pressure. RIVER-WIND, WATERCOURSE-AIRPIPE.
for'-ces. An army; troop. BELLIGERENT.
for'-ci-ble. Cogent. AGENCY, COERCION, CONVERSION-REVERSION, FORCE-WEAKNESS, MIGHT-IMPOTENCE, MOTIVE-CAPRICE, STRENGTH-WEAKNESS, TURBULENCE-CALMNESS, VIGOR-INERTIA.
ford. To wade across. TRANSMISSION, WAY.
fore. The foremost part. ANTERIORITY-POSTERIORITY.
fore'-and-aft'. Lying or going in the direction of the ship's length. ENTIRETY-DEFICIENCY, LENGTH-SHORTNESS; **fore-and-aft schooner,** CONVEYANCE-VESSEL.
fore-arm'. To arm beforehand. PREPARATION-NONPREPARATION.
fore-bode'. Presage. PROPHECY.

fore-bo'-ding. Foretelling. PROPHECY.
fore-cast'. To plan in advance; to predict. DESIGN, PREVISION, PROPHECY.
fore-close'. To shut out or bar. OBSTRUCTION.
fore-doom'. To doom in advance. VOLITION-OBLIGATION.
fore'-fa"-ther. An ancestor. PARENTAGE-PROGENY.
fore'-fin"-ger. The digit next to the thumb. TOUCH.
fore-go'. To relinquish. COMMISSION-RETIREMENT, KEEPING-RELINQUISHMENT, QUEST-ABANDONMENT.
fore-go'-ing. Occurring previously. ANTECEDENCE-SEQUENCE, FUTURE-PAST, PRECEDENCE-SUCCESSION.
fore-gone'. Determined already. ANTECEDENCE-SEQUENCE, FUTURE-PAST; **foregone conclusion,** DECISION-MISJUDGMENT, PREDETERMINATION-IMPULSE, PREVISION.
fore'-ground". That part of the landscape or picture nearest the spectator. ANTERIORITY-POSTERIORITY; **in the foreground,** ANTERIORITY-POSTERIORITY, MANIFESTATION-LATENCY.
fore'-head. The upper part of the face between the eyes and the hair. ANATOMY, ANTERIORITY-POSTERIORITY.

for'-eign. Alien; not belonging to the place or body in which it is found. CONNECTION-INDEPENDENCE, CONSTITUENT-ALIEN; **foreign accent,** VOCALIZATION-MUTENESS; **foreign parts,** CONSTITUENT-ALIEN, REMOTENESS-NEARNESS.

for'-eign-er. A citizen of a foreign country. CONSTITUENT-ALIEN.

fore-judge'. To judge beforehand. DECISION-MISJUDGMENT, PREVISION.

fore-know'. To know beforehand. PREVISION.

fore-knowl'-edge. Knowledge of a thing before it happens. PREVISION.

fore-land'. A projecting point of land. CONVEXITY-CONCAVITY, HEIGHT-LOWNESS.

fore-lay'. To waylay. TRUTHFULNESS-FRAUD.

fore'-lock''. A lock of hair growing over the forehead. **Take time by the forelock,** EARLINESS-LATENESS, OPPORTUNENESS-UNSUITABLENESS.

fore'-man. The head man. MANAGER.

fore'-most''. First in place, time, rank, or order. ANTERIORITY-POSTERIORITY, BEGINNING-END, CONSEQUENCE-INSIGNIFICANCE, LEADING-FOLLOWING, REPUTATION-DISCREDIT, SUPREMACY-SUBORDINACY.

fore-noon'. The morning. MORNING-EVENING.

fo-ren'-sic. Pertaining to courts of justice. ADVOCATE.

forensis strepitus [L.] (fo-ren'-sis strep'-i-tus). The clamor of the forum. SOUND-SILENCE.

fore''-or-dain'. To predestinate. OCCURRENCE-DESTINY.

fore-or''-di-na'-tion. Predestination. VOLITION-OBLIGATION.

fore'-part''. The fore part. ANTERIORITY-POSTERIORITY.

fore'-rank''. The front. ANTERIORITY-POSTERIORITY.

fore-run'. To run in advance of. ANTECEDENCE-SEQUENCE, LEADING-FOLLOWING.

fore-run'-ner. A precursor. PREDECESSOR-CONTINUATION.

fore-see''. To see or discern beforehand. EXPECTATION-SURPRISE, FUTURE-PAST, PREVISION, SAGACITY-INCAPACITY.

fore-see'-ing. Seeing or knowing before occurrence. PREVISION.

fore-seen'. Foreknown. ASTONISHMENT-EXPECTANCE, EXPECTATION-SURPRISE.

fore-shad'-ow. To suggest, indicate, or typify beforehand. PROPHECY.

fore-short'-en. To shorten parts of a representation on a surface so as to give the proper impression concerning form and proportion. LENGTH-SHORTNESS.

fore-show'. To prophesy. PROPHECY.

fore'-sight''. Foreknowledge. EXPECTATION-SURPRISE, PREVISION, RECKLESSNESS-CAUTION, SAGACITY-INCAPACITY.

fore'-skirt''. The front of a skirt. DRESS-UNDRESS.

fore'-sleeve''. The part of the sleeve below the elbow. DRESS-UNDRESS.

for'-est. A wooded tract of land. COUNTRY, FAUNA-FLORA.

fore-stall'. To hinder or guard against by preparation; to preoccupy. ANTECEDENCE-SEQUENCE, EARLINESS-LATENESS, FUTURE-PAST, HOLDING-EXEMPTION.

fore'-taste''. Enjoyment by anticipation. PREVISION

fore-tell'. To predict. PROPHECY.

fore'-thought''. Foresight. CAREFULNESS-CARELESSNESS, PREVISION.

fore'-to''-ken. A token in advance. PROPHECY.

for-ev'-er. To the end of time. ETERNITY-INSTANTANEITY.

fore-warn'. To admonish or caution previously. PREVISION, PROPHECY, WARNING.

for'-feit. To lose title to or possession of through failure to fulfil some obligation or condition. GAIN-LOSS, OBSERVANCE-NONOBSERVANCE, RECOMPENSE-PUNITION; **forfeit one's good opinion,** APPROVAL-DISAPPROVAL.

for'-feit-ed. Past participle of forfeit. DUENESS-UNDUENESS.

for'-fei-ture. The act of forfeiting, or that which is forfeited. DUENESS-UNDUENESS, GAIN-LOSS, OBSERVANCE-NONOBSERVANCE, RECOMPENSE-PENALTY.

for-fend'. To ward off. ATTACK-DEFENSE, LEAVE-PROHIBITION, OBSTRUCTION-HELP.

for-gath'-er. To associate. GATHERING-SCATTERING.

forge. An open fireplace or hearth with forced draft for heating metals; to fashion or form in any way. CREATION-DESTRUCTION, OVEN-REFRIGERATOR, TRUTHFULNESS-FALSEHOOD, WORKSHOP; **forge fetters,** RELEASE-RESTRAINT.

forged. Fraudulently imitated. TRUTHFULNESS-FABRICATION.

for'-ger. One who makes a false imitation of anything. AGENT, ROBBER.

for'-ger-y. The act of forging. TRUTHFULNESS-FABRICATION, TRUTHFULNESS-FRAUD.

for-get'. To be unable to recall to the mind. CAREFULNESS-CARELESSNESS, HEED-DISREGARD, REMEMBRANCE-FORGETFULNESS; **forget benefits,** THANKFULNESS-THANKLESSNESS; **forget injury,** PARDON-VINDICTIVENESS; **forget oneself,** VIRTUE-VICE; **hand forget cunning,** SKILL-UNSKILFULNESS.

for-get'-ful. Apt to forget. REMEMBRANCE-FORGETFULNESS.

for-get'-ful-ness. The quality of being forgetful. REMEMBRANCE-FORGETFULNESS.

for-give'. To pardon. PARDON-VINDICTIVENESS.

for-giv'-en. Pardoned. PARDON-VINDICTIVENESS.

for-give'-ness. The act of forgiving. PARDON-VINDICTIVENESS.

for-giv'-ing. Disposed to forgive. PARDON-VINDICTIVENESS.

for-go'. To forego.

for-got'-ten. Lost from memory. FUTURE-PAST, REMEMBRANCE-FORGETFULNESS, THANKFULNESS-THANKLESSNESS; **forgotten by the world,** SOCIABILITY-PRIVACY.

fork. A pronged implement. ANGULARITY, DOUBLING-HALVING; **forked lightning,** LUMINARY-SHADE; **fork out,** GIVING-RECEIVING, OUTLAY-INCOME, SETTLEMENT-DEFAULT.

forked. Diverged into two branches. DOUBLING-HALVING.

fork'-ing. Branching. ANGULARITY.

for-lorn'. Abandoned; lonely; wretched. LIGHTHEARTEDNESS-DEJECTION, SANGUINENESS-HOPELESSNESS, SOCIABILITY-PRIVACY; **forlorn hope,** RECKLESSNESS-CAUTION, SECURITY-INSECURITY.

form. To make; to shape; to shape by mental or moral influences; a bench; a class in school, or in social life. BEAUTY-UGLINESS, CEREMONIAL, CONDITION-SITUATION, CONSTITUENT-ALIEN, CONVERSION-REVERSION, COPY-MODEL, CREATION-DESTRUCTION, EDUCATION-MISTEACHING, FORM-FORMLESSNESS, INCLUSION-OMISSION, INSTRUCTOR-PUPIL, LAW-LAWLESSNESS, ORGANIZATION-DISORGANIZATION, POMP, PRECEPT, REGULARITY-IRREGULARITY, SOCIETY-LUDICROUSNESS, SUSPENSION-SUPPORT, WAY; **form a part of,** CONSTITUENT-ALIEN; **form a party,** ASSOCIATION; **form a resolution,** DETERMINATION-VACILLATION.

FORM—FORMLESSNESS.

Build. General figure, as of a man.
Cast. An object run in a mold.

Amorphism. State of being without determinate shape.
Defacement. Injury to the surface.

FORM—FORMLESSNESS—*Continued*.

Configuration. External form or shape.
Conformation. Particular structure of a body.
Construction. Act of building; that which is built.
Contour. The line that defines a body.
Cut. A block upon which something is engraved.
Cut of one's jib. One's general appearance. [Sailor's metaphor.]
Efformation. Act of giving form.
Fashion. Shape.
Feature. Any part or lineament of the face.
Figuration. The act of giving definite form.
Figure. Visible form of a person or thing.
Form. Appearance, as distinguished from the materials.
Formation. That which is made by a combination of materials.
Forming. The exact shaping.
Frame. Main timbers of a structure; skeleton.
Isomorphism. A similarity of crystalline form.
Lineament. Outline of a figure, usually of the face.
Make. Constitution, structure, as a man's physical make.
Mold. That after which something else is patterned.
Morphology. Science of form.
Sculpture. A work produced by the chisel.
Shape. External appearance.
Stamp. Cast or form.
Structure. Manner of building.
Trim. Order or condition.
Turn. Form or fashion.
Type. Form or character impressed.

FORM—*Associated Nouns*.

Attitude. Position appropriate to expression of feeling.
Phase. An aspect of that which presents various aspects.
Pose. Position for artistic effect.
Posture. Position without reference to expression of feeling.
Set. Carriage; an acquired bend.

FORM—*Verbs*.

Block out. To mark out roughly.
Build. To make or raise anything, as a house.
Carve. To cut raised or incised figures.
Cast. To form into a particular shape by pouring liquid metal into a mold.
Chisel. To form by cutting away with a chisel.
Cut. To separate; notch with an edged tool.
Efform. To give form to.
Fashion. To mold; shape.
Figure. To form an image or likeness of.
Form. To make from given materials.
Hammer out. To form by persistent mental labor.
Hew. To dress with an edged tool.
Knead. To work and press ingredients into a mass.
Lick into shape. To bring gradually into shape, as the kitten or the unlicked cub.
Model. To form after a pattern.

Deformity. Something detrimental to the shape of an entire thing.
Disfigurement. That which mars the general appearance.
Disorder. Want of any order or method.
Featureless. Having no distinctive features.
Informity. Shapelessness.
Mutilation. Cutting off an essential part.
Rudis indigestaque moles [L.]. A rude and undigested mass.
Unlicked cub. An untrained person.

FORMLESSNESS—*Verbs*.

Deface. To destroy or mar the face or external appearance of.
Deform. To spoil the form of.
Derange. To put out of proper arrangement. See ORGANIZATION-DISORGANIZATION.
Disfigure. To mar the shape or figure of.
Mutilate. To destroy or remove a material part of.
Truncate. To cut off.

FORMLESSNESS—*Adjectives*.

Amorphous. Having no determinate shape.
Barbarous. Rude, as if done by a barbarian.
Formless. Without due order of parts.
Gothic. Rude; barbaric.
Rough. Lacking the finish of art.
Rude. Exhibiting but the least of art.
Rugged. Steep and rocky.
Shapeless. Without shape or form.
Unfashioned. Not shaped.
Unformed. Not molded or fashioned.
Unhewn. In its virgin state.
Unshapen. Not shaped; misshapen.

FORM—VERBS—*Continued*.

Mold. To form into a particular shape, as in or by a mold.
Put into shape. To put into working order.
Rough cast. Arrange in the rough.
Rough hew. To dress roughly with an edged tool.
Sculpture. To cut out images with the chisel.
Set. To fix in position.
Shape. To reduce to particular form.
Sketch. To make a hasty and incomplete presentation.
Stamp. To impress with a mark or figure.
Trim. To dress or decorate; cut or lop off.
Work up into. To make out of partially spoiled material

FORM—*Adjectives*.

Fictile. Relating to pottery.
Formed. See *Verbs*.
Isomorphous. Similar in form.
Plasmic. }
Plastic. } Giving form; capable of being molded.

---

formæ, spretæ injuria [L.] (for'-mî, sprî'-tî in-jiu'-ri-α). The insult to her despised beauty. BEAUTY-UGLINESS.

form'-al. Made, framed, or done in accordance with regular and established forms and methods. ASSERTION-DENIAL, BEAUTY-UGLINESS, CEREMONIAL, CONDITION-SITUATION, CONVENTIONALITY-UNCONVENTIONALITY, EDUCATION-MISTEACHING, FORM-FORMLESSNESS, INSTRUCTOR-PUPIL, LAW-LAWLESSNESS, POMP, PURITY-CRUDENESS, SOCIETY-AFFECTATION, SOCIETY-LUDICROUSNESS, WAY; **formal speech**, SPEECH-INARTICULATENESS.

form'-al-ism. Scrupulous and critical observance of forms. CEREMONIAL.

form'-al-ist. One who is over-attentive to forms. CEREMONIAL.

form-al'-i-ty. Conventionality. ASSERTION-DENIAL, LAW, POMP, SOCIETY-AFFECTATION, SOCIETY-LUDICROUSNESS.

for-ma'-tion. The act or process of forming by the combination of materials. CREATION-DESTRUCTION, FORM-FORMLESSNESS.

form'-a-tive. Giving form. CREATION-DESTRUCTION.

formed. Shaping. AFFECTIONS, FORM-FORMLESSNESS.

for'-mer. Preceding in the order of time. ANTECEDENCE-SEQUENCE, FUTURE-PAST, PRECEDENCE-SUCCESSION.

for'-mer-ly. In time past. FUTURE-PAST.

for"-mi-ca'-tion. An itching sensation like the creeping of ants. TINGLING-NUMBNESS.

for'-mi-da-ble. Dangerous to encounter. DIFFICULTY-FACILITY, SANGUINENESS-TIMIDITY.

form'-ing. Shaping. CONSTITUENT-ALIEN, FORM-FORMLESSNESS.

form'-less. Shapeless. FORM-FORMLESSNESS.

for'-mu-la. A fixed rule or set form. ADAGE-NONSENSE, LAW, NUMBER, PRECEPT, UNIFORMITY-MULTIFORMITY.

for'-mu-la-ry. A church ritual. CEREMONIAL, PRECEPT.

for'-mu-late. To reduce to a formula. LAW-LAWLESSNESS.

for"-ni-ca'-tion. Illicit sexual intercourse between unmarried persons. PURITY-IMPURITY.

for'-ni-ca"-tor. One who fornicates. PURITY-RAKE.

for'-ni-ca"-tress. A harlot. PURITY-RAKE.

foro conscientiæ [L.] (fo'-ro con"-shi-en'-shi-î). Before the tribunal of conscience. DUTY-DERELICTION,

TRUTHFULNESS-FALSEHOOD, UPRIGHTNESS-DISHONESTY.

for-sake'. To desert. QUEST-ABANDONMENT.

for-sa'-ken. Deserted. LOVE-HATE.

for-sooth'. In truth. ASSERTION-DENIAL.

for-swear'. To abjure; to swear falsely. BIGOTRY-APOSTASY, DUTY-DERELICTION, PROFFER-REFUSAL, TRUTHFULNESS-FALSEHOOD, UPRIGHTNESS-DISHONESTY.

for-sworn'. Perjured. TRUTHFULNESS-FALSEHOOD.

fort. A single enclosed work capable of independent defense. ATTACK-DEFENSE, REFUGE-PITFALL.

fort, du . . . au faible [F.] (dü-fort o fêbl). Strong and weak take together. SOLITUDE-COMPANY, STRENGTH-WEAKNESS.

fort, le droit de plus [F.] (for, le drwa de plü). Club law. COERCION, LAW-LAWLESSNESS.

fort'-a-lice. An outwork of a fortification. ATTACK-DEFENSE.

forte. Chief excellence. SKILL-UNSKILFULNESS.

fort'-e-lage. A fortalice. ATTACK-DEFENSE.

fortes fortuna adjuvat [L.] (for'-tîz for-tiu'-na ad'-jiuvat). Fortune favors the brave. BRAVERY-COWARDICE, RATIONALE-LUCK.

forth. Forward. ADVANCE-RETROGRESSION; **and so forth,** ADDITION-SUBTRACTION; **come forth,** ENTRANCE-EXIT, VISIBILITY-INVISIBILITY; **go forth,** ARRIVAL-DEPARTURE; **the decree has gone forth,** ORDER.

forth'-com''-ing. Coming forth. OCCURRENCE-DESTINY, PREPARATION-NONPREPARATION.

forth''-with'. Immediately. EARLINESS-LATENESS.

for''-ti-fi-ca'-tion. Any military defensive work. ATTACK-DEFENSE.

for'-ti-fy. To strengthen. STRENGTH-WEAKNESS.

fortiori, a [L.] (for''-shi-o'-rai, ê). With stronger reason. EVIDENCE-COUNTEREVIDENCE, RATIOCINATION-INSTINCT.

fortis cadere, cedere non potest [L.] (for'-tis cad'-er-î, sed'-er-î non po'-test). The brave man may fall, yield he cannot. DETERMINATION-VACILLATION, MIGHT-IMPOTENCE.

fortiter in re [L.] (for'-ti-ter in rî). Firmly in the act. VIGOR-INERTIA.

for'-ti-tude. Patient courage. BRAVERY-COWARDICE, EXCITABILITY-INEXCITABILITY.

fort'-night''-ly. Occurring, coming, or issued every fortnight. PERIODICITY-IRREGULARITY.

fort'-ress. A stronghold. ATTACK-DEFENSE, RELEASE-PRISON.

for-tu'-i-tous. Occurring by chance. PURPOSE-LUCK, RATIONALE-LUCK; **fortuitous concourse of atoms,** REGULARITY-IRREGULARITY.

fortuna, magna servitus est magna [L.] (for-tiu'-na, mag'-na ser'-vi-tus est mag'-na). Great fortune is great slavery. AFFLUENCE-PENURY.

fortuna favet fatuis [L.] (for-tiu'-na fê'-vet fat'-yu-is). Fortune favors fools. RATIONALE-LUCK, SAGE-FOOL.

fortuna multis dat nimium, nulli satis [L.] (for-tiu'-na mul'-tis dat nim'-i-um, nul'-lai sê'-tis). Fortune to many gives too much, to none enough. EXCESS-LACK.

for'-tu-nate. Lucky; prosperous. OPPORTUNENESS-UNSUITABLENESS, SUCCESS-FAILURE, WELFARE-MISFORTUNE.

For-tu-na'-tus's cap. A cap given to Fortunatus, the hero of a drama, by the gods. It rendered the wearer invisible. DESIRE-DISTASTE, DEVOTION-CHARM; **Fortunatus's purse,** AFFLUENCE-PENURY.

for'-tune. Chance; wealth; the forecast of one's future. ACCOUNT, AFFLUENCE-PENURY, RATIONALE-LUCK, VOLITION-OBLIGATION; **be one's fortune,** OCCURRENCE-DESTINY; **evil fortune,** WELFARE-MIS-

FORTUNE; **good fortune,** SUCCESS-FAILURE, WELFARE-MISFORTUNE; **make one's fortune,** PURPOSE-LUCK, VENTURE; **tempt fortune,** AFFLUENCE-PENURY, SUCCESS-FAILURE; **trick of fortune,** EXPECTATION-DISAPPOINTMENT; **try one's fortune,** TRIAL, VENTURE; **wheel of fortune,** VOLITION-OBLIGATION.

for'-tune-hunt''-er. One who seeks to marry a fortune. PRESUMPTION-OBSEQUIOUSNESS, UNSELFISHNESS-SELFISHNESS.

for'-tune-less. Without a fortune or inheritance. AFFLUENCE-PENURY.

for'-tunes of. The events of one's life. ACCOUNTING.

for'-tune-tel''-ler. One who pretends to a knowledge of futurity and foretells the events of one's life. SOOTHSAYER.

for'-tune-tel''-ling. The foretelling of the future events of one's life. PROPHECY.

for'-ty. Four times ten. FIVE-QUINQUESECTION; **forty winks,** ACTIVITY-INDOLENCE.

fo'-rum. A court. SCHOOL, TRIBUNAL.

for'-ward. To send on ahead; to advance the growth of; located at or near the front; bold. ACTIVITY-INDOLENCE, ADVANCE-RETROGRESSION, BETTERMENT-DETERIORATION, CONCEIT-DIFFIDENCE, EARLINESS-LATENESS, FELICITATION, OBSTRUCTION-HELP, PRESUMPTION-OBSEQUIOUSNESS, READINESS-RELUCTANCE, TRANSFER; **bend forward,** ANTERIORITY-POSTERIORITY; **come forward,** POMP, PROFFER-REFUSAL, VISIBILITY-INVISIBILITY; **forward in,** KNOWLEDGE-IGNORANCE; **move forward,** ADVANCE-RETROGRESSION; **press forward,** HURRY-LEISURE; **put forward,** ASSERTION-DENIAL, HELP; **put oneself forward,** CONCEIT-DIFFIDENCE, POMP; **set forward,** ENTERPRISE.

for'-ward-ness. Promptness. READINESS-RELUCTANCE.

fosse. A ditch or moat. ATTACK-DEFENSE, ENCLOSURE, GROOVE.

fos'-sil. An organic body so situated in the earth as to be capable of indefinite preservation. GEOLOGY, HARDNESS-SOFTNESS, LIFE-CORPSE, NOVELTY-ANTIQUITY, ORGANIZATION-INORGANIZATION.

fos'-ter. To provide with nourishment. BETTERMENT-DETERIORATION, BLANDISHMENT, EXCITATION, OBSTRUCTION-HELP, PATRIOTISM-TYRANNY; **foster a belief,** FAITH-MISGIVING.

fou [F.] (fu). Mad. TEETOTALISM-INTEMPERANCE.

foul. Filthy; unfair; ugly; to collide. BEAUTY-UGLINESS, CLEANNESS-FILTHINESS, GOODNESS-BADNESS, IMPETUS-REACTION, UPRIGHTNESS-ROGUE, VIRTUE-VICE; **fall foul of,** ANTAGONISM-CONCURRENCE, APPROVAL-DISAPPROVAL, ATTACK-DEFENSE, OBSTRUCTION-HELP, STRIFE-PEACE, VARIANCE-ACCORD; **foul fiend,** ANGEL-SATAN; **foul language,** CHARITABLENESS-CURSE; **foul odor,** PERFUME-STENCH; **foul play,** CRAFT-ARTLESSNESS, GOOD-EVIL, RIGHT-WRONG, UPRIGHTNESS-DISHONESTY; **run foul of,** IMPETUS-REACTION, OBSTRUCTION-HELP.

foule, en [F.] (ful, an·). In a crowd. MULTIPLICITY-PAUCITY.

foul'-mouthed''. Using vile language. ADULATION-DISPARAGEMENT, POLITENESS-IMPOLITENESS.

foul'-ness. Filthiness. PERFUME-STENCH.

foul'-spok''-en. Foul-mouthed. ADULATION-DISPARAGEMENT, POLITENESS-IMPOLITENESS.

foul'-tongued''. Abusive. ADULATION-DISPARAGEMENT.

found. To establish. BEGINNING-END, CAUSE-EFFECT, SUSPENSION-SUPPORT.

foun-da'-tion. The act of establishing; the base upon which a building or machine is erected. CAUSE-EFFECT, MUTABILITY-STABILITY, PREPARATION-NONPREPARATION, SUSPENSION-SUPPORT, TOP-BOTTOM; **lay the foundations,** PREPARATION-NONPREPARATION;

sandy foundation, REFUGE-PITFALL; **shake to its foundations,** AGITATION.

found'-ed. Established. **Founded on,** EVIDENCE-COUNTEREVIDENCE, TOP-BOTTOM; **well founded,** LIKELIHOOD-UNLIKELIHOOD.

found'-er. One who founds or endows. MAKER-DESTROYER, SPRING-DIVE, SUCCESS-FAILURE; **religious founders,** REVELATION-PSEUDOREVELATION.

found'-ered. Failed; miscarried. SUCCESS-FAILURE.

found'-ling. A deserted infant of unknown parentage. GAIN-LOSS, KEEPING-RELINQUISHMENT, WAYFARER-SEAFARER.

foun'-dry. An establishment where metals are cast. WORKSHOP.

fount. A complete collection of a particular kind of type. RIVER-WIND, STORE, WRITING-PRINTING.

foun'-tain. A spring of water; a supply-vessel. CAUSE-EFFECT, RIVER-WIND, STORE; **fountain head,** CAUSE-EFFECT, TOP-BOTTOM.

four. Twice two. QUATERNITY; **four-in-hand,** CONVEYANCE-VESSEL; **fourscore,** etc., FIVE-QUINQUE-SECTION; **four times,** QUADRUPLICATION-QUADRISECTION; **from the four winds,** AIM-ABERRATION; **on all fours,** DIFFICULTY-FACILITY, ERECTNESS-FLATNESS, HARMONY-DISCORD, SAMENESS-CONTRAST, SELFRESPECT-HUMBLENESS, WELFARE-MISFORTUNE.

four'-fold''. Quadruple. QUADRUPLICATION-QUADRISECTION.

four'-oar''. A boat with four oars. CONVEYANCE-VESSEL.

fourth. Next in order after the third; one of four equal parts; the interval between any note and the fourth note above it. MELODY-DISSONANCE, QUADRUPLICATION-QUADRISECTION.

fourth'-ly. In the fourth place. QUADRUPLICATION-QUADRISECTION.

four'-wheel''-er. A vehicle having four wheels. CONVEYANCE-VESSEL.

fous, les ...font les festins et les sages les mangent [F.] (lê fu:fon· lê fes-tan· ê lê sazh lê man·zh). Fools make feasts and wise men eat them. EXTRAVAGANCE-AVARICE, SAGE-FOOL.

fowl. Any bird. FAUNA-FLORA.

fowl'-ing-piece''. A light smooth-bore shotgun for bird-shooting. WEAPON.

fox. A burrowing canine mammal having an elongated pointed muzzle and long bushy tail; a crafty person. CRAFT-ARTLESSNESS, FAUNA-FLORA; **fox-chase,** QUEST-EVASION.

fox'-hound''. A superior variety of hound for chasing foxes. FAUNA-FLORA.

fox'-ter''-ri-er. A dog of the terrier breed resembling a fox in the shape of his head. FAUNA-FLORA.

fox'-y. Reddish-brown. GRAY-BROWN, REDNESS-GREENNESS.

Fox'-y Quil'-ler. A braggart; from a character in *The Highwayman,* BRAGGING.

fra'-cas. A noisy fight; an uproar. LOUDNESS-FAINTNESS, REGULARITY-IRREGULARITY, STRIFE-PEACE, VARIANCE-ACCORD.

frac'-tion. A quantity less than a unit. MAGNITUDE-SMALLNESS, NUMBER, PLURALITY-FRACTION, WHOLE-PART.

frac'-tion-al. Pertaining to fractions. NUMBER, WHOLE-PART; **fractional distillation,** CHEMISTRY.

frac'-tious. Unruly. FAVORITE-QUARRELSOMENESS.

frac'-ture. To separate the parts of with violence. CONTINUITY-INTERRUPTION, UNION-DISUNION.

frag'-ile. Frail. STRENGTH-WEAKNESS, TOUGHNESS-BRITTLENESS.

fra-gil'-i-ty. Brittleness. STRENGTH-WEAKNESS, TOUGHNESS-BRITTLENESS.

frag'-ment. A part broken off. GREATNESS-LITTLENESS, MAGNITUDE-SMALLNESS, WHOLE-PART.

frag'-ment-a-ry. Broken up; not entire. WHOLE-PART.

fra'-grance. The state or quality of being fragrant. PERFUME-STENCH.

fra'-grant. Sweet-smelling. PERFUME-STENCH.

fra'-grant weed. A sweet-smelling weed. PUNGENCY.

frail. Easily broken or destroyed; deficient in moral strength. DETERMINATION-VACILLATION, FAULTLESSNESS-FAULTINESS, PURITY-IMPURITY, STRENGTH-WEAKNESS, TOUGHNESS-BRITTLENESS, VIRTUE-VICE; **frail sisterhood,** PURITY-RAKE.

frail'-ty. Sin of infirmity. VIRTUE-VICE.

frais, à grands [F.] (frê, a gran·). A great expense. COSTLINESS-CHEAPNESS.

frame. The general arrangement or constitution of a thing; a case or border; to put together. BORDER, CONDITION-SITUATION, CREATION-DESTRUCTION, DESIGN, FORM-FORMLESSNESS, MATERIALITY-SPIRITUALITY, TEXTURE; **frame of mind,** AFFECTIONS, READINESS-RELUCTANCE, VOLITION-OBLIGATION; **have framed and glazed,** POMP.

framed. Formed. AFFECTIONS.

frame'-work''. A skeleton structure or frame for supporting something. SUSPENSION-SUPPORT, TEXTURE.

franc. Coin. VALUES.

française, à la [F.] (fran·-sêz', a la). In French style. SOCIETY-LUDICROUSNESS.

fran'-chise. A special privilege or exemption vested in a person or body. DUENESS-UNDUENESS, DUTY-IMMUNITY, LIBERTY-SUBJECTION.

Fran-cis'-can. A member of a mendicant order founded by St. Francis. MINISTRY-LAITY.

franc-tireur [F.] (fran·-tî-rur'). A French sharpshooter. BELLIGERENT.

franges, non flectes [L.] (fran'-jîz, non flec'-tîz). You may break, you shall not bend. DETERMINATION-VACILLATION.

fran''-gi-bil'-i-ty. The state or quality of being frangible. TOUGHNESS-BRITTLENESS.

fran'-gi-ble. Easily broken. TOUGHNESS-BRITTLENESS.

frank. Candid and open in manner and disposition. CRAFT-ARTLESSNESS, MANIFESTATION-LATENCY, TRUTHFULNESS-FALSEHOOD.

frank''-al-moigne'. A tenure by which a religious corporation holds lands given to them and their successors forever. LIBERTY-SUBJECTION.

Fran'-ken-stein. The hero of a novel named after him, who created a monster. BENEFACTOR-EVILDOER, JOVE-FIEND; **Frankenstein's monster,** BENEFACTOR-EVIL-DOER, JOVE-FIEND.

frank'-in-cense. An aromatic substance produced by the Norway spruce. PERFUME-STENCH.

Frank'-lin-stove''. A stove invented by Benjamin Franklin. OVEN-REFRIGERATOR.

frank'-ness. Candor. TRUTHFULNESS-FALSEHOOD.

fran'-tic. Frenzied. EXCITATION, SANENESS-LUNACY, TURBULENCE-CALMNESS.

fra-ter'-nal. Brotherly. AMITY-HOSTILITY, RELATIONSHIP, VARIANCE-ACCORD.

fra-ter'-ni-ty. A brotherhood. AMITY-HOSTILITY, ASSOCIATION, RELATIONSHIP.

frat''-er-ni-za'-tion. The act of uniting as brothers. AMITY-HOSTILITY.

fra-ter-nize. To bring into brotherly relations. AMITY-HOSTILITY, ANTAGONISM-CONCURRENCE, CHARITABLENESS-MALEVOLENCE, SOCIABILITY-PRIVACY, VARIANCE-ACCORD.

frat'-ri-cide. One who kills a brother. LIFE-KILLING.

fraud. An act of deliberate deception practised with the object of gaining something to the prejudice of another. THEFT, TRUTHFULNESS-FALSEHOOD, TRUTHFULNESS-FRAUD, UPRIGHTNESS-DISHONESTY; **pious fraud,** PIETY-UNGODLINESS.

fraude, ab ulla [L.] (frau'-dî, ab ul'-la). Without any fraud. UPRIGHTNESS-DISHONESTY.

fraud'-u-lence. Deceitfulness. TRUTHFULNESS-FALSEHOOD.

fraud'-u-len-cy. The quality of being fraudulent. TRUTHFULNESS-FRAUD.

fraud'-u-lent. Obtained or performed by fraud. TRUTHFULNESS-FALSEHOOD, TRUTHFULNESS-FRAUD, UPRIGHTNESS-DISHONESTY.

fraught. Freighted or laden. CREATION-DESTRUCTION, ENTIRETY-DEFICIENCY, HOLDING-EXEMPTION; **fraught with danger,** SECURITY-INSECURITY.

fray. To wear the surface or margin off; a combat FRICTION-LUBRICATION, STRIFE-PEACE; **in the thick of the fray,** FIGHTING-CONCILIATION.

frayed. Raveled. BETTERMENT-DETERIORATION.

freak. A whim. PERSISTENCE-WHIM.

freak'-ish. Capricious. PERSISTENCE-WHIM.

freck'-le. A small spot on the skin. EMBELLISHMENT-DISFIGUREMENT.

freck'-led. Marked with freckles. EMBELLISHMENT-DISFIGUREMENT, VARIEGATION.

fredaine [F.] (fre-dên'). A frolic. ENTERTAINMENT-WEARINESS.

free. Independent; frank; immodest; unobstructed; without fee; liberal; not attached. COHESION-LOOSENESS, COSTLINESS-CHEAPNESS, DIFFICULTY-FACILITY, DUTY-IMMUNITY, ENTIRETY-DEFICIENCY, GENEROSITY-FRUGALITY, LIBERTY-SUBJECTION, PURITY-IMPURITY, RELEASE-RESTRAINT, UNION-DISUNION, VOLITION-OBLIGATION; **free and easy,** AMITY-HOSTILITY, CONCEIT-DIFFIDENCE, LIBERTY-SUBJECTION, LIGHTHEARTEDNESS-DEJECTION, PRESUMPTION-OBSEQUIOUSNESS, RECKLESSNESS-CAUTION, SOCIABILITY-PRIVACY; **free fight,** STRIFE-PEACE; **free from,** MIXTURE-HOMOGENEITY, OBSTRUCTION-HELP; **free from imperfection,** FAULTLESSNESS-FAULTINESS; **free gift,** GIVING-RECEIVING; **free land,** GIVING-RECEIVING; **free liver,** MODERATION-VOLUPTUARY; **free play,** AGENCY, LIBERTY-SUBJECTION; **free quarters,** COSTLINESS-CHEAPNESS, SOCIABILITY-PRIVACY; **free seats,** COSTLINESS-CHEAPNESS; **free space,** EXTENSION-DISTRICT; **free stage,** LIBERTY-SUBJECTION; **free trade,** EXCHANGE, LIBERTY-SUBJECTION; **free translation,** INTERPRETATION-MISINTERPRETATION; **free will,** VOLITION-OBLIGATION; **make free of,** LIBERTY-SUBJECTION; **make free with,** CRAFT-ARTLESSNESS, LIBERTY-SUBJECTION, POLITENESS-IMPOLITENESS, SOCIABILITY-PRIVACY, TAKING.

free'-boot"-er. A robber. ROBBER.

free'-born". Not born in servitude. LIBERTY-SUBJECTION.

freed'-man. An emancipated slave. LIBERTY-SUBJECTION.

free'-dom. Liberty. COHESION-LOOSENESS, DUTY-IMMUNITY, LIBERTY-SUBJECTION, RULE-LICENSE, VOLITION-OBLIGATION.

free'-hand"-ed. Generous. GENEROSITY-FRUGALITY.

free'-heart"-ed. Generous. GENEROSITY-FRUGALITY, MANIFESTATION-LATENCY.

free-hold". An estate in lands. LIBERTY-SUBJECTION, PROPERTY.

free'-liv"-er. One who gratifies his appetite. MODERATION-VOLUPTUARY.

free'-liv"-ing. Living without restraint. MODERATION-SELFINDULGENCE.

free'-love". The doctrine of unrestrained choice in sexual relations. LOVE-HATE, MATRIMONY-CELIBACY, PURITY-IMPURITY.

free'-ly. Willingly. LIBERTY-SUBJECTION, READINESS-RELUCTANCE.

free'-man. One not a slave. LIBERTY-SUBJECTION.

Free'-ma"-son-ry. The institutions and principles of Freemasons. ANTAGONISM-CONCURRENCE, ASSOCIATION, CLEARNESS-OBSCURITY, ENLIGHTENMENT-SECRECY, SIGN.

Free'-soil"-er. A member of the Free-soil political party in the United States. ASSOCIATION.

free'-spo"-ken. Accustomed to speak without reserve. CRAFT-ARTLESSNESS.

free'-think"-er. One unbiased by authority or dogma. GODLINESS-DISBELIEF.

Free'-will" Bap'-tist. An open communion Baptist. ORTHODOXY-HETERODOXY.

freeze. To harden with cold. HEATING-COOLING.

freeze the blood, PLEASURABLENESS-PAINFULNESS.

freez'-ing. Hardening with cold. HEAT-COLD; **freezing mixture,** OVEN-REFRIGERATOR.

freight. To lade with goods for transportation. CONTENTS-RECEIVER, ESTABLISHMENT-REMOVAL, TRANSFER.

freight'-age. The price for carrying goods. PRICING-DISCOUNT.

French. Pertaining to France. **French and English,** ENTERTAINMENT-WEARINESS; **French horn,** MUSICAL INSTRUMENTS; **French leave,** LIBERTY-SUBJECTION, QUEST-EVASION; **French polish,** EMBELLISHMENT-DISFIGUREMENT; **pedler's French,** WORD-NEOLOGY.

fre-net'-ic. Relating to mental disorder. SANENESS-LUNACY.

fren'-zied. Distracted. SANENESS-LUNACY, TURBULENCE-CALMNESS.

fren'-zy. Frantic excitement. EXCITABILITY-INEXCITABILITY, FANCY, SANENESS-LUNACY.

fre'-quen-cy. Occurrence oft repeated. FREQUENCY-RARITY.

FREQUENCY—RARITY.

Frequency. Occurrence of a thing often, at short intervals.
Oftenness. Property of happening many times.
Repetition. An action done again.

FREQUENCY—*Verbs.*

Do nothing but. To do continually.
Frequent. To visit often.
Keep. }
Keep on. } To happen continually; continue.
Recur. To occur again according to an established rule. See RECURRENCE.

FREQUENCY—*Adjectives.*

Constant. Without irregularity.
Continual. Long continued.
Frequent. Occurring often at short intervals.
Habitual. Constant.
Incessant. Without perceptible pause.
Many times. }
Not rare. } Occurring often.
Perpetual. Never ceasing.
Repeated. Done or said more than once.
Thickcoming. Coming close together.

Fewness. Smallness of number.
Infrequency. Quality of not happening often.
Rareness. }
Rarity } Quality of being uncommon.
Seldomness. Quality of happening only at great intervals.

RARITY—*Verbs.*

Be rare. etc. See *Adjectives.*

RARITY—*Adjectives.*

Infrequent. Not often.
Few. Small in number.
Rare. Occurring but seldom.
Rare as a blue diamond. Exceedingly rare.
Scarce. Rarely occurring.
Unfrequent. Not happening often.
Unprecedented. Unlike anything that goes before.

RARITY—*Adverbs.*

Almost unheard of.
Hardly. Scarcely ever.
Hardly ever. Seldom.
Not often. Rarely.

FREQUENCY—RARITY—*Continued.*

FREQUENCY—*Adverbs.*

Again and again. Repeatedly.
At all times. Continually.
At times. Occasionally.
Commonly. Frequently.
Constantly. Steadily.
Continually. Without cessation.
Daily. Occurring every day.
Daily and hourly. Frequently.
Day after day. Daily.
Day and night. Continually.
Ever and anon. Occasionally.
Every day. Daily.
Every hour. Hourly.
Every moment. Very frequently.
Frequently. Happening often at short intervals.
From time to time. At intervals.
Hourly. Occurring every hour.
Incessantly. Without perceptible pause.
In quick succession. } Very frequently.
In rapid succession. }
Many a time and oft. Very often. [Shakespeare, *Julius Cæsar*, I, i.]
Morning, noon, and night. Continually.
Most often. Very frequently.
Night and day. Continually.
Now and then. Occasionally.
Not unfrequently. Quite often.
Not unseldom. Occasionally.
Occasionally. Every once in a while.
Oft. } Many times.
Often. }

FREQUENCY—*Phrase.*

Ein mal, kein mal [G.]. Just once, nothing counts; one time, no time.

RARITY—*Adverbs—Continued.*

Not within one's previous experience.
Not within the memory of the oldest inhabitant.
Once. Occurring one time.
Once for all. The last and only time.
Once in a blue moon. Very seldom.
Once in a way. Once, somehow.
Pro hac vice [L.]. For this occasion.
Rarely. Not often.
Scarcely. Hardly.
Scarcely ever. Not often.
Seldom. Once in a great while.
Unfrequently. Not very often.
Unoften. Not often.

RARITY—*Phrase.*

Ein mal, kein mal [G.]. Just once, nothing counts.

FREQUENCY—*Adverbs—Continued.*

Often enough. Quite frequently.
Oftentimes. } At frequent intervals.
Ofttimes. }
Perpetually. Never ceasing.
Repeatedly. More than once.
Sometimes. Occasionally.
There being times when. Upon occasion.
Toties quoties [L.]. As often as.
Unseldom. Often.
Without ceasing. Continually.

---

fre′-quent. Occurring often; to resort to habitually. FREQUENCY-RARITY, HABIT-DESUETUDE, PRESENCE-ABSENCE, RECURRENCE.

fre′-quent-ly. Often. FREQUENCY-RARITY, RECURRENCE.

fres′-co. A picture painted on plaster. HEAT-COLD, PAINTING; **al fresco,** OUTSIDE-INSIDE, WATER-AIR.

fresh. Newly prepared; refreshing; new; sober; without frost. BEGINNING-END, COLOR-ACHROMATISM, GOODNESS-BADNESS, HEALTH-SICKNESS, HEAT-COLD, NOVELTY-ANTIQUITY, REMEMBRANCE-FORGETFULNESS, RIVER-WIND, TEETOTALISM-INTEMPERANCE; **fresh breeze,** RIVER-WIND; **fresh color,** REDNESS-GREENNESS; **fresh news,** TIDINGS-MYSTERY.

fresh′-en up. To revive. WEARINESS-REFRESHMENT.

fresh′-et. A sudden flood. RIVER-WIND.

fresh′-man. A college student in the first year of the course. INSTRUCTOR-PUPIL.

fresh′-water–sail′-or. Unskilled. ADEPT-BUNGLER.

fret. To worry; tetter; ornamental work in relief. ARCHITECTURE, CONTENTEDNESS-DISCONTENTMENT, EMBELLISHMENT-DISFIGUREMENT, FAVORITE-ANGER, JUBILATION-LAMENTATION, LIGHTHEARTEDNESS-DEJECTION, PLEASURABLENESS - PAINFULNESS, PLEASURE-PAIN, SENSUALITY-SUFFERING; **fret and fume,** PLEASURE-PAIN.

fret′-ful. Peevish. FAVORITE-QUARRELSOMENESS.

fretta, maggiore . . . minore atto [It.] (ma - chi - o′ - rê frêt′-ta, mi-no′-rê at′-to). The more haste, the less speed. EXCITABILITY-INEXCITABILITY, HURRY-LEISURE.

fret′-work″. Ornamental work composed of frets. CROSSING.

fri″-a-bil′-i-ty. Friableness. FRIABILITY.

FRIABILITY.

Efflorescence. In chemistry, the act or process of becoming powdery, wholly or in part.

Friability. The quality of being easily crumbled, or reduced to powder.

Pulverulence. The state of being covered with fine powder or dust.

Sandiness. The quality or state of being sandy. See *Adjectives.*

FRIABILITY—*Associated Nouns.*

Bran. The coat of the seed of grain separated from the flour or meal by sifting or bolting.
Cloud of dust. A mass of flying dust resembling vapor.
Cloud of sand. A mass of flying sand.
Cloud of smoke. A volume of smoke resembling vapor.
Crumb. A small fragment; especially, a small piece of bread.
Débris [F.]. Fragments.
Detritus. A mass of earthy matter worn off from solid portions, and reduced to small portions.
Dust. Fine, dry particles of earth or other matter, wafted by the wind.
Dust-storm. A great volume of flying particles of earth.
Farina [L.]. Ground corn.
Filings. Particles rubbed off by the act of filing.
Fine powder. Anything ground very fine.
Flocculi [L.]. Little locks of wool.
Flour. Finely ground meal of wheat.
Grain. A single small hard seed; any small hard particle.
Grit. Sand or gravel.
Limature. That which is filed off; filings.
Magistery. A precipitate.
Meal. Coarsely ground grain.
Particle. A minute portion of matter. See MAGNITUDE-SMALLNESS.
Powder. The fine particles to which any dry substance is reduced by pounding, grinding, etc.
Puff of smoke. A sudden emission of smoke.
Sand. Fine particles of stone.
Sand-storm. A great volume of sand wafted in the air.
Sawdust. Small fragments of wood made by the cutting of a saw.
Scobs. Raspings of ivory, hartshorn, etc.
Seed. The ripened ovule of a plant.
Shingle. A piece of wood sawed thin and small, with one end thinner than the other.
Smoke. The visible vapor from a burning substance.
Spore. A minute grain of flowerless plants, analogous to seed.
Sporule. A small spore.
Volumes of smoke. Great masses of vapor.

FRIABILITY—*Nouns of Means.*

Abrasion. The act of wearing or rubbing off.
Attenuation. The act or process of making slender.

Comminution. The act of reducing to a fine powder.
Contusion. The act or process of beating, bruising, or pounding
Detrition. The act or process of wearing away.
Disintegration. The process of wearing away or falling to pieces.
Filing. The process of reducing to small particles with a file. See *Verbs.*
Granulation. The act or process of forming into grains.
Levigation. The act of reducing to the finest powder
Limation. Filing.
Multure. The portion of grain taken as a toll for grinding.
Pulverization. The act of reducing to dust.
Subaction. The act of reducing to any state.
Trituration. Pulverization by grinding, rubbing, etc.

FRIABILITY—*Nouns of Instrument.*

File. A steel instrument having cutting ridges or teeth, used in abrading or smoothing.
Grater. An instrument with a rough indented surface, for rubbing off small particles of any substance.
Grinder. Any instrument for grinding.
Grindstone. A flat, circular stone, revolving on an axis, for grinding or sharpening tools.
Kern. A hand mill; a quern.
Mill. A machine for grinding.
Nutmeg-grater. A small instrument with a rough indented surface used for grating nutmegs.
Pestle and mortar. Two instruments, one for pounding, and the other for holding the substance to be reduced to a powder.
Quern. A mill for grinding grain, the upper stone of which was turned by hand.
Rasp. A coarse file.
Teeth The hard bony appendages in the jaws for grinding food; anything resembling the teeth.

FRIABILITY—*Verbs.*

Abrade. To rub or wear away.
Attenuate. To pulverize etc. See DIMINUTION.
Beat. To strike; batter; strike repeatedly.
Be disintegrated. To be reduced to fragments or powder.
Be reduced to powder. To be ground fine.
Bray. To bruise or pound with a pestle; grind to powder.
Bruise. To pound small, crush in a mortar.
Come to dust. "Golden lads and girls all must, as chimney sweepers, come to dust." [Shakespeare, *Cymbeline*, IV, ii.]
Comminute. To reduce to minute particles; crush.
Contund. To beat; bruise by beating.
Contuse. To bruise by a blow.
Cranch. }
Craunch. } To crunch.
Crumble. To cause to fall into small pieces.
Crunch. To crush with the teeth, especially with noise; crush or grind audibly.
Crush. To break into bits by pressure.
Disintegrate. To break into pieces or particles; crumble.
File. To pulverize by rubbing or cutting with a file.
Granulate. To form into grains; become granular.
Grate. To wear away in minute particles by rubbing.
Grind. To reduce to fine particles by crushing and friction or like process.
Grind to powder. To grind fine.
Levigate. To reduce to a fine powder.

Pound. To break to pieces.
Pulverize. To reduce to powder, as by grinding, crushing, etc.; crush; become reduced to powder.
Rasp. To grate with a rasp; file down.
Reduce to powder. To grind.
Rub down. To reduce or remove by rubbing.
Scranch. To grind with the teeth and with a crackling sound.
Scrape. To scratch with a hard surface or edge.
Triturate. To reduce to a fine powder or pulp.

FRIABILITY—*Adjectives.*

Arenaceous. Made up of sandy particles.
Arenarious. Sandy.
Arenose. Full of fine sand or grit; gritty.
Attrite. Rubbed; worn by friction.
Branny. Resembling or consisting of bran.
Crumbly. Easily crumbled; friable; brittle.
Dusty. Filled with dust; clouded with dust.
Efflorescent. Forming into white threads or powder.
Farinaceous. Mealy; consisting of meal.
Flocculent. Coalescing in small flocks or flakes.
Floury. Resembling flour; mealy.
Friable. Easily crumbled or pulverized.
Furfuraceous. Made of bran; like bran; scurfy.
Granular. Consisting of, or resembling grains.
Gritty. Containing sand or grit; full of hard particles.
Impalpable. Extremely fine, so that no grit can be perceived by touch.
In pieces. Broken up.
Mealy. Soft, dry, and friable.
Powdery. Easily crumbling to pieces; dusty.
Pulverizable. That can be reduced to powder.
Pulverized. Reduced to powder, etc. See *Verbs.*
Pulverulent. Powdery; dusty; easily reduced to powder.
Sabulous. Sandy, gritty.
Sandy. Consisting of, abounding with, grains of sand.
Shivery. Easily broken; brittle.

fri'-a-ble. Easily crumbled. FRIABILITY, TOUGHNESS-BRITTLENESS.
friandise [F.] (fri-an'-dîz'). Daintiness; delicacy. DESIRE-PARTICULARNESS.
fri'-ar. A member of one of the mendicant monastic orders. MINISTRY-LAITY; **Blackfriars,** MINISTRY-LAITY; **friar's-lantern,** LUMINARY-SHADE.
fri'-ar-y. A monastery of a mendicant order. FANE.
frib'-ble. To fritter; a trifler. ACTIVITY-INDOLENCE, CAREFULNESS-CARELESSNESS, CONSEQUENCE-INSIGNIFICANCE, SOCIETY-DANDY.
fric''-as-see'. A dish of meat cut into small pieces, stewed or fried, and served with gravy. NUTRIMENT-EXCRETION.
fri-ca'-tion. Friction. FRICTION-LUBRICATION.
fric'-tion. The rubbing together of two bodies; resistance to motion due to the contact of surfaces. CO-OPERATION-OPPOSITION, FRICTION-LUBRICATION, MIGHT-IMPOTENCE; **on friction wheels,** DIFFICULTY-FACILITY.

FRICTION—LUBRICATION.

Abrasion. Wearing away by friction.
Affriction. Rubbing together of two bodies.
Arrosion. A gnawing at.
Attrition. Wearing down by friction.
Confrication. Rubbing together.
Contrition. Grinding to powder.
Elbow-grease. Continuous arm labor, as rubbing; energy.
Frication. Friction; rubbing.
Limature. Act of filing or polishing.
Rub. Act of passing one surface over another with friction and pressure.
Rubbing. Friction with pressure. See *Verbs.*

FRICTION—*Noun of Agent.*

Rosin. Substance put on gliding surfaces to cause friction.

FRICTION—*Verbs.*

Curry. To clean by rubbing with a currycomb.
File. To wear off with a file.
Fray. To break the surface or margin.

Anointment. The state of pouring oil upon.
Lubricant. A substance used to diminish friction.
Lubrication. }
Lubrification. } Act of making slippery or smooth.
Oiling. Act of lubricating with oil. See *Verbs.*
Smoothness. See SMOOTHNESS.
Unctuousness. Quality of being oily to the touch. See PULPINESS-OILINESS.

LUBRICATION—*Means.*

Glycerine. An oily, viscous liquid, used as a lubricant.
Lather. Foam made by soap moistened with water.
Oil, etc. One of a great variety of unctuous combustible substances, not miscible with water. See PULPINESS-OILINESS. [Olive-oil.]
Saliva. A fluid secreted in the glands of the mouth, for moistening the food.
Synovia. A fluid secreted by the membranes about the joints of the body.

LUBRICATION—*Verbs.*

Grease. To smear with fat.

FRICTION—LUBRICATION—*Continued.*

FRICTION—Verbs—*Continued.*

Gnaw. To eat away little by little.
Graze. To rub lightly in passing.
Grind. To give shape to by abrasion.
Polish. To make smooth or bright by friction.
Rasp. To scrape with a rasp.
Rosin. To make rough or sticky with rosin.
Rub. To pass over the surface with friction and pressure.
Rub out. To erase.
Scour. To cleanse by rubbing an abrasive substance.
Scrape. To rub the surface with a hard edge.
Scratch. To mark or tear the surface.
Scrub. To cleanse by rubbing with an instrument.
Set one's teeth on edge. To feel a nervous shock on hearing the noise of friction.

friend. One who entertains regard for another and takes active interest in his welfare. ANTAGONIST-

LUBRICATION—Verbs—*Continued.*

Lather. } To cover with suds.
Lubricate. }
Lubricitate. To supply moving parts of machinery with oil.
Oil. To cover with oil.
Soap. To rub or cover with soap.
Wax. To make smooth with wax.

LUBRICATION—*Adjective.*

Lubricated. See *Verbs.*

FRICTION—*Continued.*

FRICTION—*Adjective.*

Anatriptic. Pertaining to rubbing as a remedy for disease.

ASSISTANT, FRIEND-FOE; **be friends,** AMITY-HOSTILITY; **next friend,** REPRESENTATIVE.

FRIEND—FOE.

Acquaintance. A person well known.
Advocate. One called to plead another's cause.
Ally. Associate in national or military affairs.
Alter ego [L.]. Another self.
Amicus usque ad aras [L.]. A friend to the last extremity.
Amphitryon. A host at dinner. [From Molière.]
Arcades ambo [L.]. Arcadians both.
Associate. Habitual companion.
Bedfellow. } A sleeping companion.
Bedmate. }
Boniface. An innkeeper.
Boon-companion. Jovial or merry companion.
Bosom friend. Very intimate friend.
Camarade [F.]. Comrade.
Chum. A room-mate, as at college; an intimate associate.
Classman. One of a class in college.
Classmate. Member of the same class.
Companion. A person frequently with another.
Compatriot. Patriot of the same country.
Compeer. One of equal rank; an associate.
Comrade. An intimate companion.
Confidante [F.]. One to whom secrets are entrusted.
Confrère [F.]. A professional, political, or scientific associate.
Co-partner. One jointly associated in business.
Countryman. Citizen of the same country.
Crony. A familiar friend.
Fast friend. A constant friend.
Fautor. A patron; a favorer.
Favorer. One who assists or promotes success.
Fellow companion. A close friend.
Fellow countryman. A person from the same country.
Fidus Achates [L.]. A true friend. [Virgil, *Æneid.*]
Friend. One attached to another by affection, esteem, or respect.
Friend in need. A friend to the last extremity.
Friend of one's bosom. A most intimate friend.
Good genius. Good tutelary deity.
Guest. One entertained in the house of another.
Host. One who entertains another.
Maid of honor. Lady of high birth in attendance upon a queen.
Mate. One who customarily associates with another.
Messmate. One who eats at same table.
Neighbor. A person who lives near one.
Old crony. A companion of long standing.
Pal. A confederate.

Back friend. Secret enemy.
Bitter enemy. A very hostile enemy.
Enemy. One who hates, and wishes injury; no lover.
Enemy to society. One who is a harm to good government and morals.
Foe. A deadly enemy; one hated.
Foeman. An enemy in war.
Open enemy. One who does not conceal his enmity.
Opponent. One who opposes in debate or argument.
Public enemy. An enemy to the community or state.

FOE—*Phrase.*

Every hand being against one. Being opposed on all sides.

FRIEND—*Continued.*

Par nobile fratrum [L.]. Two just alike; literally, a noble pair of brothers.
Partizan. One of the same party or faction.
Partner. An associate in business.
Patron. One who protects, supports, or lends aid.
Playfellow. } Companion at play.
Playmate. }
Pot-companion. A drinking associate.
Protégé [F.]. One under the protection of another.
Schoolfellow. An associate at school.
Shipmate. One who shipped on the same ship.
Shopmate. One who worked in the same shop.
Sympathizer. One who sympathizes with you or your cause.
Tutelary saint. A guardian saint.
Visitor. One who comes to see another in friendship.
Well-wisher. One friendly inclined.

FRIEND—*Denotations.*

Castor and Pollux. The twin sons of Jupiter and Leda.
Damon and Pythias. Legendary friends of Syracuse.
Mæcenas. The friend and patron of Horace, the Roman poet.
Nisus and Euryalus. A famous pair of friends in Virgil's *Æneid.*
Pylades and Orestes. Two faithful friends in a tragedy by Euripides.

FRIEND—*Phrase.*

Amici probantur rebus adversis [L.]. Friends are tested by adversity.

friend'-less. Having no friends. SOCIABILITY-PRIVACY.
friend'-li-ness. The condition or quality of being friendly. AMITY-HOSTILITY.
friend'-ly. Befitting friendship. AMITY-HOSTILITY, CHARITABLENESS-MALEVOLENCE, OBSTRUCTION-HELP, VARIANCE-ACCORD.
friend'-ship. Mutual regard cherished by kindred minds. AMITY-HOSTILITY, CHARITABLENESS-MALEVOLENCE.
frieze. The middle division of an entablature. TOP-BOTTOM.

frig'-ate. An old-style war-vessel. BELLIGERENT.
fright. Sudden and violent alarm; a game of cards. ENTERTAINMENT-WEARINESS, SANGUINENESS-TIMIDITY.
fright'-en. To disturb with fear. SANGUINENESS-TIMIDITY.
fright'-ened. Disturbed with fear. BRAVERY-COWARDICE, SANGUINENESS-TIMIDITY.
fright'-ful-ly. Terribly. MAGNITUDE-SMALLNESS.
frig'-id. Cold; lacking in warmth of feeling. FORCE-WEAKNESS, HEAT-COLD, SENSITIVENESS-APATHY, UNCONCERN.

frig″-i-da′-ri-um. A room kept at a low temperature to preserve fruits, etc. OVEN-REFRIGERATOR.

fri-gid′-i-ty. Coldness. HEAT-COLD, SENSITIVENESS-APATHY.

frig″-o-rif′ic. Producing cold. HEATING-COOLING.

frill. A flounce; a ruffle. BORDER, CIRCLE-WINDING.

fringe. An ornamental border or trimming of pendant cords, threads, etc. BORDER, EMBELLISHMENT-DISFIGUREMENT, GULL-HYPERBOLE, SMOOTHNESS-ROUGHNESS.

fringed. Bordered. SMOOTHNESS-ROUGHNESS.

frip′-per-y. Worthless things. CONSEQUENCE-INSIGNIFICANCE, EMBELLISHMENT-DISFIGUREMENT, POMP, SOCIETY-LUDICROUSNESS, TASTE-VULGARITY.

frisk. To leap about playfully. ENTERTAINMENT-WEARINESS, LIGHTHEARTEDNESS-DEJECTION, SPRING-DIVE, TRAVELING-NAVIGATION.

frisk′y. Lively in action. ACTIVITY-INDOLENCE, LIGHTHEARTEDNESS-DEJECTION.

frith. An arm of the sea; a forest. FAUNA-FLORA, GULF-PLAIN, INTERSPACE-CONTACT.

frit′-i-nan-cy. A chirping or creaking. CRY-ULULATION.

frit′-ter. To waste little by little. MAGNITUDE-SMALLNESS; **fritter away,** INCREASE-DECREASE, PROVISION-WASTE; **fritter away time,** ACTIVITY-INDOLENCE.

fri-vol′-i-ty. Triflingness. CONSEQUENCE-INSIGNIFICANCE, SAGACITY-INCAPACITY.

friv′-o-lous. Lacking in seriousness. CONSEQUENCE-INSIGNIFICANCE, PERSISTENCE-WHIM, RATIOCINATION-INSTINCT, SAGACITY-INCAPACITY.

frizz. To give a crinkled appearance to. CIRCLE-WINDING, CURVATION-RECTILINEARITY, PLICATURE.

friz′-zle. To curl or crisp. CIRCLE-WINDING, CURVATION-RECTILINEARITY, PLICATURE.

friz′-zy. Curled or crisped. CIRCLE-WINDING.

frock. A gown; a monk's robe. DRESS-UNDRESS, VESTMENTS; **frock coat,** DRESS-UNDRESS.

frog. A small, tailless, amphibious, web-footed animal; an ornamental spindle-shaped button with a loop. EMBELLISHMENT-DISFIGUREMENT, SPRING-DIVE.

frol′-ic. Sport. ENTERTAINMENT-WEARINESS.

frol′-ic-some. Playful. LIGHTHEARTEDNESS-DEJECTION.

from. A word indicating removal, separation, source. MOTIVE-CAPRICE; **from day to day,** DURATION-NEVERNESS, PERIODICITY-IRREGULARITY; **from end to end,** ENTIRETY-DEFICIENCY, LENGTH-SHORTNESS; **from nature,** NATURE-ART; **from that time,** ANTECEDENCE-SEQUENCE; **from this cause,** RATIONALE-LUCK; **from time immemorial,** FUTURE-PAST; **from time to time,** FREQUENCY-RARITY.

fronder [F.] (fron-dê′). To carp at. APPROVAL-DISAPPROVAL.

frondeur [F.] (fron-dur′). A faultfinder. FLATTERER-DEFAMER, INSUBORDINATION-OBEDIENCE.

front. The foremost part of anything; false hair on the fore part of the head; effrontery. ANTERIORITY-POSTERIORITY, DRESS-UNDRESS, PRESUMPTION-OBSEQUIOUSNESS, REPRISAL-RESISTANCE; **bring to the front,** MANIFESTATION-LATENCY; **come to the front,** ANTERIORITY-POSTERIORITY, CONSEQUENCE-INSIGNIFICANCE, REPUTATION-DISCREDIT, TRANSCURSION-SHORTCOMING; **front danger,** BRAVERY-COWARDICE; **front of the house,** ACTING; **front rank,** ANTERIORITY-POSTERIORITY; **front to front,** ANTAGONISM-CONCURRENCE; **in front,** ANTERIORITY-POSTERIORITY, LEADING-FOLLOWING; **in the front rank,** CONSEQUENCE-INSIGNIFICANCE, REPUTATION-DISCREDIT; **present a front,** REPRISAL-RESISTANCE.

front à front [F.] (fron·t a fron·). Front to front. ANTERIORITY-POSTERIORITY.

front′-age. Linear extent of front. ANTERIORITY-POSTERIORITY.

fron′-tal. Pertaining to the front. ANATOMY, ANTERIORITY-POSTERIORITY, OUTSIDE-INSIDE.

fron″-tier′. The border. BOUNDARY, INTERSPACE-CONTACT.

front′-ing. Facing. LATERALITY-CONTRAPOSITION.

fronti nulla fides [L.] (fron′-tai nul′-la fai′-dîz). There is no trusting to appearances. FAITH-MISGIVING, TRUTHFULNESS-FRAUD.

fron′-tis-piece″. An illustration in the front of a book. ANTERIORITY-POSTERIORITY, PREDECESSOR-CONTINUATION.

frost. Minute crystals of ice formed from atmospheric water-vapor. HEAT-COLD.

frost′-y. Attended with or producing frost. HEAT-COLD.

froth. Bubbles; unsubstantial matter. CLEANNESS-FILTHINESS, CONSEQUENCE-INSIGNIFICANCE, VISCIDITY-FOAM; **froth up,** FAVORITE-ANGER.

froth′-y. Foamy; not firm; pretentious. CONSEQUENCE-INSIGNIFICANCE, DETERMINATION-VACILLATION, SIMPLICITY-FLORIDNESS, TERSENESS-PROLIXITY, VISCIDITY-FOAM.

frounce. A flounce. PLICATURE.

fro′-ward. Perverse. FAVORITE-MOROSENESS.

frown. To rebuke by look or word with manifest displeasure; to scowl. APPROVAL-DISAPPROVAL, FAVORITE-ANGER, FAVORITE-MOROSENESS, PLEASURABLENESS-PAINFULNESS, PLEASURE-PAIN, POLITENESS-IMPOLITENESS; **frown down,** APPROVAL-DISAPPROVAL, SELFRESPECT-HUMBLENESS; **frowns of fortune,** WELFARE-MISFORTUNE.

frown′-ing. Looking stern. LIGHTHEARTEDNESS-DEJECTION.

frow′-zy. Unkempt. PERFUME-STENCH.

fro′-zen. Solidified, benumbed or killed by cold. HEAT-COLD, HEATING-COOLING.

fruc″-ti-fi-ca′-tion. Fecundation. CREATION-DESTRUCTION, FERTILITY-STERILITY.

fruc′-ti-fy. To render fruitful. BETTERMENT-DETERIORATION, CREATION-DESTRUCTION, FERTILITY-STERILITY, WELFARE-MISFORTUNE.

fru′-gal. Exercising economy. GENEROSITY-FRUGALITY, MODERATION-SELFINDULGENCE.

fru-gal′-i-ty. Prudent economy. GENEROSITY-FRUGALITY, MODERATION-SELFINDULGENCE.

fruges consumere natus [L.] (fru′-jîz con-sum′-er-î nê′-tus). Born only to eat. ACTIVITY-INDOLENCE, GENTILITY-DEMOCRACY, USEFULNESS-USELESSNESS.

fru-gif′-er-ous. Fruitful. FERTILITY-STERILITY.

fruit. Any vegetable product used as food; any result or effect. CAUSE-EFFECT, CREATION-DESTRUCTION, GAIN-LOSS; **forbidden fruit,** MOTIVE-CAPRICE; **fruit-tree,** FAUNA-FLORA; **reap the fruits,** RECOMPENSE-PUNITION, SUCCESS-FAILURE.

fruit′-ful. Producing abundant results. FERTILITY-STERILITY.

fru-i′-tion. The bearing of fruit. PLEASURE-PAIN.

fruit′-less. Barren. FERTILITY-STERILITY, SUCCESS-FAILURE, USEFULNESS-USELESSNESS.

frump. A frowzyish, ill-tempered woman. POLITENESS-IMPOLITENESS, TASTE-VULGARITY.

frump′-ish. Ill-tempered. FAVORITE-MOROSENESS.

frus′-trate. To baffle. SUCCESS-FAILURE.

frus-tra′-tion. Disappointment. SUCCESS-FAILURE.

frus′-tum. That which is left of a solid after cutting off the upper part by a plane parallel to the base. WHOLE-PART.

frutti, i . . . proibiti sono i piu dolci [It.] (î frut′-tî pro-î-bî′-tî so′-no î pî′u dol′-chî). The forbidden fruits are sweetest. DESIRE-DISTASTE, VIRTUE-VICE.

fry. To cook in grease; a multitude or quantity of persons or objects of small importance. HEATING-COOLING, INFANT-VETERAN, MULTIPLICITY-PAUCITY; **small fry,** CONSEQUENCE-INSIGNIFICANCE, GENTILITY-DEMOCRACY.

fry'-ing-pan". A shallow pan for frying food. HEAT-ING-COOLING; **out of the frying-pan into the fire,** ALLEVIATION-AGGRAVATION, BETTERMENT-DETERIORATION, SKILL-UNSKILFULNESS, SUCCESS-FAILURE, WELFARE-MISFORTUNE.

fuch'-sin. A crystalline coal-tar product. REDNESS-GREENNESS.

fud'-dle. To drink to excess. TEETOTALISM-INTEMPERANCE.

fud'-dled. Stupid with drink. TEETOTALISM-INTEMPERANCE.

fudge. Humbug; an interjection of contempt. CONSEQUENCE-INSIGNIFICANCE, MEANING-JARGON.

fu'-el. Combustible material used to feed a fire. COMBUSTIBLE, MATERIALS; **add fuel to the flame,** ALLEVIATION-AGGRAVATION, FAVORITE-ANGER, HEAT-COLD, INCREASE-DECREASE.

fugaces labuntur anni [L.] (fiu-gê'-sîz la-bun'-tur an'-nai). The fleeting years glide by. LASTINGNESS-TRANSIENTNESS, PERIOD-PROGRESS.

fu-ga'-cious. Transitory. LASTINGNESS-TRANSIENTNESS.

fu-gac'-i-ty. Instability. LASTINGNESS-TRANSIENTNESS.

fu'-gi-tive. Escaping; evanescent. LASTINGNESS-TRANSIENTNESS, QUEST-EVASION, WAYFARER-SEAFARER; **fugitive writings,** DIGEST.

fu'-gle-man. A file-leader; one who sets an example. COPY-MODEL, MANAGER.

fugue. A musical composition in which the theme is repeated in the several parts. MUSIC.

ful'-ci-ment. A fulcrum. SUSPENSION-SUPPORT.

ful'-crum. The support on or against which a lever rests. SUSPENSION-SUPPORT.

ful-fil'. To complete the time, course, or purport of. COMPLETION-NONCOMPLETION, OBSERVANCE-NONOBSERVANCE; **fulfil a duty,** DUTY-DERELICTION; **fulfil an obligation,** OBSERVANCE-NONOBSERVANCE.

ful-fil'-ment. Accomplishment. COMPLETION-NONCOMPLETION, DUTY-DERELICTION, OBSERVANCE-NONOBSERVANCE.

ful'-gent. Beaming or shining brightly. LIGHT-DARKNESS.

ful'-gid. Shining. LIGHT-DARKNESS.

ful-gid'-i-ty. Splendor. LIGHT-DARKNESS.

ful'-gor. Dazzling brightness. LIGHT-DARKNESS.

fu-lig'-i-nous. Like soot; dark, as if shrouded in smoke. DIMNESS, DIAPHANEITY-OPAQUENESS, WHITENESS-BLACKNESS.

full. Having no empty or vacant space; abounding in something; complete; filled with food or drink; to scour. CLEANNESS-FILTHINESS, ENOUGH, ENTIRETY-DEFICIENCY, GREATNESS-LITTLENESS, LOUDNESS-FAINTNESS, MAGNITUDE-SMALLNESS; **full age,** MANHOOD; **full bloom,** BEAUTY-UGLINESS, HEALTH-SICKNESS; **full-blown,** ENLARGEMENT-DIMINUTION, REPUTATION-DISCREDIT; **full-colored,** COLOR-ACHROMATISM; **full cry,** CRY-ULULATION, LOUDNESS-FAINTNESS, QUEST-EVASION; **full-dress,** DRESS-UNDRESS, EMBELLISHMENT-DISFIGUREMENT, POMP, SOCIETY-LUDICROUSNESS; **full drive,** HURRY-LEISURE, SWIFTNESS-SLOWNESS; **full feather,** AFFLUENCE-PENURY, PREPARATION-NONPREPARATION; **full force,** STRENGTH-WEAKNESS; **full gallop,** SWIFTNESS-SLOWNESS; **full heart,** AFFECTIONS; **full many,** MULTIPLICITY-PAUCITY; **full measure,** ENOUGH; **full of business,** ACTIVITY-INDOLENCE; **full of incident,** OCCURRENCE-DESTINY; **full of meaning,** MEANING-JARGON; **full of people,** PRESENCE-ABSENCE; **full of point,** FORCE-WEAKNESS, WITTINESS-DULNESS; **full of sound and fury,** etc., MEANING-JARGON, PRESUMPTION-OBSEQUIOUSNESS; **full of whims,** PERSISTENCE-WHIM; **full play,** DIFFICULTY-FACILITY, LIBERTY-SUBJECTION; **full scope,** LIBERTY-SUBJECTION; **full score,** MUSIC; **full size,** GREATNESS-LITTLENESS; **full speed,** SWIFTNESS-SLOWNESS; **full stop,** DISCONTINUANCE-CONTINUANCE, MOVEMENT-REST; **full swing,** ACTIVITY-INDOLENCE, DIFFICULTY-FACILITY, LIBERTY-SUBJECTION, STRENGTH-WEAKNESS, SUCCESS-FAILURE; **full tide,** RIVER-WIND; **full tilt,** ACTIVITY-INDOLENCE, HURRY-LEISURE; **full view,** VISIBILITY-INVISIBILITY.

full'-fed". Fed to the full. MODERATION-SELFINDULGENCE.

full'-fla"-vored. Of strong flavor. PUNGENCY.

full'-grown". Having the completed growth; adult. GREATNESS-LITTLENESS, MANHOOD.

full'-hand"-ed. Liberal. EXTRAVAGANCE-AVARICE, GENEROSITY-FRUGALITY.

full'-length". Entire length; life size. PAINTING.

full'-mouthed". With wide open mouth. CRY-ULULATION.

full'-toned". Rich in tone. MELODY-DISSONANCE.

ful'-ly. Entirely. ENTIRETY-DEFICIENCY, MAGNITUDE-SMALLNESS.

fulmen, eripuit cælo . . ., sceptrumque tyrannis [L.] (î-rip'-yu-it sî'-lo ful'-men, sep-trum'-quî tir-ran'-nis). He snatched from heaven the thunderbolt and the scepter from tyrants. MIGHT-IMPOTENCE.

ful'-min-ate. To explode; to utter a threat; to detonate. CHARITABLENESS-CURSE, CHARITABLENESS-MENACE, LOUDNESS-FAINTNESS, PUSH-PULL, TURBULENCE-CALMNESS; **fulminate against,** APPROVAL-DISAPPROVAL.

ful"-mi-na'-tion. The act of fulminating. CHARITABLENESS-CURSE, CHARITABLENESS-MENACE.

ful'-ness. Completeness; abundance. CLEANNESS-FILTHINESS, ENOUGH, ENTIRETY-DEFICIENCY, GREATNESS-LITTLENESS, LOUDNESS-FAINTNESS, MAGNITUDE-SMALLNESS; **fulness of heart,** EMOTION; **in the fulness of time,** PERIOD-PROGRESS.

ful'-some. Offensive from excess of praise; indelicate. ADULATION-DISPARAGEMENT, DESIRE-DISTASTE, GOODNESS-BADNESS, PALATABLENESS-UNPALATABLENESS, PERFUME-STENCH, PLEASURABLENESS-PAINFULNESS, PURITY-IMPURITY.

ful'-vid. Reddish-yellow. YELLOWNESS-PURPLE.

ful'-vous. Reddish-yellow. YELLOWNESS-PURPLE.

fum'-ble. To handle clumsily. ORGANIZATION-DISORGANIZATION, SKILL-UNSKILFULNESS, TOUCH, TRIAL.

fum'-bler. One who fumbles. ADEPT-BUNGLER.

fume. Vapor; rage. EXCITABILITY-INEXCITABILITY, EXCITATION, FAVORITE-ANGER, HEAT-COLD, LIQUEFACTION-VOLATILIZATION, LIQUID-GAS, ODOR-INODOROUSNESS, TURBULENCE-CALMNESS; **fumes of fancy,** FANCY, FAVORITE-ANGER; **in a fume,** CONTENTEDNESS-DISCONTENTMENT.

fu'-mid. Smoky. DIAPHANEITY-OPAQUENESS.

fu'-mi-gate. To expose to the action of fumes or smoke. CLEANNESS-FILTHINESS, LIQUEFACTION-VOLATILIZATION.

fu"-mi-ga'-tion. The act of fumigating. LIQUEFACTION-VOLATILIZATION.

fu'-ming. Raging. EXCITATION, FAVORITE-ANGER.

fumo, dare pondus [L.] (fiu'-mo, dê'-rî pon'-dus). To give importance to trifles. DECISION-MISJUDGMENT.

fun. That which excites merriment. ENTERTAINMENT-WEARINESS, WITTINESS-DULNESS; **make fun of,** SOCIETY-DERISION, WITTINESS-DULNESS.

fu-nam'-bu-list. A tight- or slack-rope performer. ADEPT-BUNGLER.

func'-tion. Any specific power of acting or operating that belongs to an agent; a quantity whose value is dependent on the value of some other quantity. AGENCY, BIOLOGY, DUTY-DERELICTION, NUMBER, OCCUPATION, USEFULNESS-USELESSNESS.

func'-tion-al. Pertaining to functions. OCCUPATION.

func′-tion-a-ry. An official. CONSIGNEE, MANAGER.

functus officio [L.] (func′-tus of-fish′-i-o). Out of office. COMMISSION-ABROGATION.

fund. A sum of money. STORE; **sinking fund,** TREASURY.

fun″-da-men′-tal. Relating to or constituting a foundation; essential. SUBJECTIVENESS-OBJECTIVENESS, SUSPENSION-SUPPORT, TOP-BOTTOM; **fundamental bass,** MELODY-DISSONANCE; **fundamental tone,** MELODY-DISSONANCE.

fun″-da-men′-tal-ly. Primarily. GREATNESS-SMALLNESS.

funds. Money. MONEY; **in funds,** AFFLUENCE-PENURY; **public funds,** TREASURY.

fu-ne′-bri-al. Funereal. LIFE-FUNERAL.

fu′-ner-al. The formal conveyance of a dead person to the grave. LIFE-FUNERAL; **funeral pace,** SWIFTNESS-SLOWNESS.

fu-ne′-re-al. Mournful; pertaining to a funeral. LIFE-FUNERAL, LIGHTHEARTEDNESS-DEJECTION.

fun′-gi-form. Having a termination similar to the head of a fungus. ROUNDNESS.

fun-gol′-o-gy. The science or study of fungi. ZOOLOGY-BOTANY.

fun-gos′-i-ty. A fungous growth. CONVEXITY-CONCAVITY.

fun′-gus. A cryptogamous plant deriving nourishment from organic compounds. CONVEXITY-CONCAVITY, FAUNA-FLORA, PERFUME-STENCH, REMEDY-BANE.

fu′-ni-cle. A small cord. LAMINA-FIBER.

fu-nic′-u-lar. Consisting of a small cord or fiber. LAMINA-FIBER.

funk. To frighten. BRAVERY-COWARDICE, SANGUINENESS-TIMIDITY.

fun′-nel. A tunnel; a chimney. APERTURE-CLOSURE, WATERCOURSE-AIRPIPE.

fun′-nel-shaped″. Having the form of a funnel; conical. CONVEXITY-CONCAVITY.

fun′-ny. Comical; a long, light rowboat. CONVEYANCE-VESSEL, SOCIETY-LUDICROUSNESS, WITTINESS-DULNESS.

fur. The hairy covering of many mammals; to remove scale from. CLEANNESS-FILTHINESS, COVER-LINING, HEATING-COOLING, SMOOTHNESS-ROUGHNESS

fu-ra′-cious. Thievish. THEFT.

fur′-be-low. A plaited or puckered flounce. BORDER.

fur′-bish. To brighten by rubbing. BETTERMENT-DETERIORATION, EMBELLISHMENT-DISFIGUREMENT, PREPARATION-NONPREPARATION.

fur′-cated. Forked. ANGULARITY.

fur′-fur. A dandruff. CLEANNESS-FILTHINESS.

fur′-fur-a′-ceous. Of the nature of bran or scurf. FRIABILITY.

Fu′-ries. The Fates. BENEFACTOR-EVILDOER, FAVORITE-ANGER.

fu′-ri-ous. Raging. EXCITABILITY-INEXCITABILITY, FAVORITE-ANGER, HURRY-LEISURE, TURBULENCE-CALMNESS.

fu′-ri-ous-ly. Violently. MAGNITUDE-SMALLNESS.

furl. To gather in a roll and secure to something. REVOLUTION-EVOLUTION.

fur′-long. One-eighth of a mile. LENGTH-SHORTNESS, MEASURE.

fur′-lough. Leave of absence granted to a soldier or sailor. LEAVE-PROHIBITION.

fur′-nace. A structure or apparatus containing a chamber for heating. HEATING-COOLING, OVEN-REFRIGERATOR, WORKSHOP; **like a furnace,** HEAT-COLD; **sighing like a furnace,** BLANDISHMENT, JUBILATION-LAMENTATION

fur′-nish. To equip. GIVING-RECEIVING, PREPARATION-NONPREPARATION, PROVISION-WASTE; **furnish a handle,** JUSTIFICATION-CHARGE, PRETEXT; **furnish aid,** OBSTRUCTION-HELP; **furnish its quota,** GIVING-RECEIVING

fur′-ni-ture. Equipment; household articles. INSTRUMENT.

fu′-ror. Rage; excitement. AFFECTIONS, DESIRE-DISTASTE, EMOTION, EXCITABILITY-INEXCITABILITY, SANENESS-LUNACY.

furor, ira . . . brevis est [L.] (ai′-ra fiu′-ror bri′-vis est). Anger is a brief madness. FAVORITE-ANGER, SANENESS-LUNACY.

furor arma ministrat [L.] (fiu′-ror ar′-ma min-is′-trat). Rage supplies arms. TURBULENCE-CALMNESS.

furor loquendi [L.] (fiu′-ror lo-quen′-dai). Rage for speaking. TALKATIVENESS-TACITURNITY.

furor poeticus [L.] (fiu′-ror po-et′-i-cus). Poetic rage. POETRY-PROSE.

furor scribendi [L.] (fiu′-ror scri-ben′-dai). Rage for writing. ACCOUNT, MISSIVE-PUBLICATION.

fu′-rore. Furor.

fur′-row. Any long depression in the earth. GROOVE, INTERSPACE-CONTACT.

fur′-rowed. Grooved. GROOVE.

Fürst ist der erste Diener seines Staats, der [G.] (fürst ist der êrst-e dî′-ner sai′-nes stats, der). The prince is the first servant of his state. CHIEF-UNDERLING.

fur′-ther. To help; more remotely; in addition. ADDITION-SUBTRACTION, OBSTRUCTION-HELP, REMOTELESS-NEARNESS; **go further and fare worse,** BETTERMENT-DETERIORATION, SKILL-UNSKILFULNESS; **not let it go further,** ENLIGHTENMENT-SECRECY.

fur′-ther-more″. Besides. ADDITION-SUBTRACTION.

fur′-tive. Stealthy; gained by theft. ENLIGHTENMENT-SECRECY, KEEPING-RELINQUISHMENT.

fu′-run″-cle. A boil. CONVEXITY-CONCAVITY.

fu′-ry. Frenzy. BRAWLER, EXCITABILITY-INEXCITABILITY, FAVORITE-ANGER, FAVORITE-QUARRELSOMENESS, JOVE-FIEND, TURBULENCE-VIOLENCE.

furze. A spiny shrub having many branches and a yellow flower. FAUNA-FLORA.

fus′-cous. Grayish-brown. SIGHT-DIMSIGHTEDNESS.

fuse. To melt; to unite or blend by melting; cord or tube which fires gun, blast, bomb, mine, etc. COMBUSTIBLE, COMPOSITION-RESOLUTION HEATING-COOLING.

fu-see′. A fuse. COMBUSTIBLE.

fu′-si-form. Tapering from the middle toward the end. ANGULARITY, SHARPNESS-BLUNTNESS.

fu′-sil. A flint-lock musket. WEAPON.

fu″-si-lade′. A simultaneous discharge of firearms. ATTACK-DEFENSE, LIFE-KILLING.

fu″-si-leer′. An infantryman. BELLIGERENT.

fu′-sion. Melting; coalescence. ANTAGONISM-CONCURRENCE, COMPOSITION-RESOLUTION, HEATING-COOLING.

fuss. To trouble with trifles. ACTIVITY-INDOLENCE, AGITATION, EXCITABILITY-INEXCITABILITY, HURRY-LEISURE, POMP; **make a fuss about,** APPROVAL-DISAPPROVAL, CONSEQUENCE-INSIGNIFICANCE, JUBILATION-LAMENTATION.

fus′-sy. Making a great ado about small matters. ACTIVITY-INDOLENCE, DECISION-MISJUDGMENT, EXCITABILITY-INEXCITABILITY, HURRY-LEISURE.

fus′-tian. Bombast. ADAGE-NONSENSE, MEANING-JARGON, PURITY-CRUDENESS, SIMPLICITY-FLORIDNESS.

fus′-ti-gate. To cudgel. EXCULPATION-PUNITION.

fus″-ti-ga′-tion. Cudgeling. RECOMPENSE-PUNITION.

fust′-y. Musty. CLEANNESS-FILTHINESS, PERFUME-STENCH.

fu′-tile. Of no avail. USEFULNESS-USELESSNESS.

fu-til′-i-ty. Uselessness. USEFULNESS-USELESSNESS.

fu′-ture. The time yet to come. ANTECEDENCE-SEQUENCE, FUTURE-PAST, **eye to the future,** PREVISION; **future possession,** HOLDING-EXEMPTION; **future state,** HEAVEN-HELL, OCCURRENCE-DESTINY.

FUTURE—PAST.

After -age, -ages, -days, -hours, -life, -time, -years. Time to come.
Approaching -age, -ages, -days, -hours, -life, -time, -years. The future.
Approach of time. The coming of time.
Coming -age, -ages, -days, -hours, -life, -time, -years. The future.
Destiny. Future condition appointed by divine will.
Eventuality. Character of happening contingently.
Foresight. See PREVISION.
Future. The time yet to come.
Futurition. Actualization in the future of something proposed or prophesied.
Futurity. State or quality of being yet to come.
Hereafter. A future state or existence.
Morrow. First day after the present; the future.
Prospect. What the future seems to hold in store. See EXPECTATION.
Remote future. Distant future.
Tempi passati [It.]. Times gone by.
Time drawing on. } The future.
Time to come. }
Womb of time. Great extent of time. "There are many events in the womb of time, which will be delivered." [Shakespeare *Othello*, I, iii, 364.]

FUTURE—*Associated Nouns.*

Advent. The second coming of Christ.
Crack of doom. The end of time.
Day of judgment. The general judgment day at the end of the world.
Doomsday. The day of judgment; *dies iræ.*
Heirs. Those who are entitled to succeed to the possessions of another after his death.
Heritage. That which passes from heir to heir.
Millennium. The thousand years of Revelation, during which holiness shall rule in the world.
Posterity. Offspring to the furthest generation.

FUTURE—*Verbs.*

Anticipate. See EXPECTATION.
Approach. To come near.
Await. To look forward to as a certainty.
Come on. }
Draw near. } Approach
Draw on. }
Forestall. To anticipate and hinder.
Impend. To hang over threateningly.
Look forwards. Anticipate.
Threaten. To be indicative of harm or evil.

FUTURE—*Adjectives*

Close at hand. Near.
Coming. Approaching.
Eventual. Happening as a final or remote consequence.
Future. That is to be or come hereafter
In prospect. Likely to happen.
Near. }
Near at hand. } Approaching.
Next. The one following
To come. Of the future.
Ulterior. Later in time.

FUTURE—*Adverbs.*

About to. Going to immediately.
After a time. } Hereafter.
After a while. }
Close upon. Soon after.
Eventually. As a final consequence.
From this time. }
Henceforth. } Beginning at this time.
Henceforwards. }
Hereafter. } In time to come.
In after time. }
In future. Hereafter.
In the course of time. } After sufficient lapse of time.
In the fulness of time. }
In the process of time. As time goes by.
One of these days. Sometime.
On the brink of. Close to.
On the eve of. Just before.
On the point of. About to.
Paulo post futurum [L.]. About to be shortly.
Prospectively. With reference to the future.
Proximo [L.]. Of the next month.
Soon. After a short elapse of time.
Sooner or later. Sometime.
The day after to-morrow. Two days from the present

Ancestry. See PARENTAGE.
Ancient times. Times of long ago, generally before Christ.
Antiquarianism. The taste for collecting and examining ancient objects.
Antiqueness. The quality or nature of being antique.
Antiquity. Former ages.
Archæology. The study of history from remains and relics of antiquity.
Bygone days. Times past.
Days gone by. }
Days of old. } Days past.
Days of yore. }
Days past. Time past.
Distance of time. Lapse of time.
Foretime. Earlier time.
Former times. Times past.
Good old time. Time past.
Lang syne [Scot.]. Long ago.
Looking back. Recollections.
Medievalism. Spirit of the Middle Ages.
Memory. See REMEMBRANCE.
Old times. Times long ago.
Paleography. Science of deciphering ancient documents.
Paleology. Science of antiquities.
Paleontology. Science of fossil plants and animals.
Paletiology. Science of explaining past conditions by reasoning upon present conditions.
Past time. Time gone by.
Pre-Rafaelitism. A theory in painting giving preference to the style prevailing before Rafael.
Preterition. State of being past.
Priority. State of being antecedent in time.
Remote age. }
Remote past } Time long past.
Remote time. }
Retrospection. Act or faculty of looking back on things past.
Rust of antiquity. Marks of antiquity.
Status quo [L.]. In the same state as before.
The olden time. The past.
The past. Time gone by.
Time immemorial. Ancient times.
Times gone by. The past.
Times of old. } Long ago in the past.
Times of yore. }
Times past. Times gone by.

PAST—*Associated Nouns.*

Antiquarian. } One who searches for and studies the relics of antiquity.
Antiquary. }
Archæologist. One versed in the science of antiquities.
Archaism. A word or expression no longer in common use.
Dryasdust. An imaginary personage who serves as an introducer of some of Sir Walter Scott's novels.
Laudator temporis acti [L.]. One who praises old times.
Medievalist. One versed in the history of the Middle Ages.
Oldbuck. A character in Sir Walter Scott's *Antiquary*, devoted to the study and collection of old coins and medals.
Pre-Rafaelite. One who favors or practises art as it was before Rafael.

PAST—*Verbs.*

Be past. To have happened in some past time.
Blow over. To drop and be forgotten.
Cast the eyes back. Look back.
Exhume. Unbury.
Go away. Depart.
Go by. Pass
Go off. To take place, as a celebration.
Have expired. See *Adjectives.*
Have had its day. To have become old or of little use.
Have run its course. To have become old or useless.
Lapse. To pass entirely away by degrees.
Look back. To think of the past.
Pass. To occur.
Pass away. To disappear.
Pass by. To go near and beyond a certain place.
Pass off. To occur, as a celebration.
Trace back. To go back in time, step by step.

PAST—*Adjectives.*

Ancestral. Pertaining to ancestors.
Archæological. See *Nouns.*
Blown over. Dropped and forgotten

FUTURE—PAST—*Continued.*

FUTURE—Adverbs—*Continued.*

Thence. }
Thenceforth. } From that time forward.
Thenceforward. }
To-morrow. The day after this one.
Ultimately. Final in purpose.
Upon which. } Then; after which.
Whereupon. }

PAST—Adjectives—*Continued from Column 2.*

Overnight. During the night.
Passed away. Elapsed.
Past. Gone.
Preterlapsed. Past and gone.
Preterperfect. The perfect tense in grammar.
Preterpluperfect. Pluperfect.
Pristine. Belonging to the earliest period or state.
Quondam [L.]. Former.
Recent. Happened lately.
Retroactive. Affecting past acts, etc.
Retrospective. Looking back.
Run out. Expired; worn out; ended.
That has been. Now no longer existing.

Ages ago. Very long ago.
Ago. Past.
A long time ago. } Long ago.
A long while ago. }
Already. In the near past.
Anciently. In ancient times.
Before now. In the past.
Ere now. Before now.
Erewhile. A little while ago.
Erst. Once; long ago.
Ex post facto [L.]. Arising or enacted after the fact or deed.
Formerly. In the past.
From time immemorial. Time out of mind.
Heretofore. } Up to this time.
Hitherto. }
In the memory of man. Since history began
In the olden time. See *Nouns.*
Last month. In the month just gone by.
Last season. In the season just gone by.
Last year. In the year just gone by.
Lately. In the near past.

PAST—Adjectives—*Continued.*

Bygone. Past.
Cidevant [F.] Of the past.
Elapsed. Passed away
Expired. Terminated.
Exploded. Suddenly come to an end.
Extinct. No longer existing, said of species of animals, etc
Foregoing. Preceding.
Foregone. Decided beforehand.
Forgotten. Not held in mind any more.
Former. Past.
Gone. } Past.
Gone by. }
Irrecoverable. Not to be regained or restored.
Lapsed. Passed away slowly.
Last. Final in order of time.
Late. Recent; coming after the appointed time
Latter. The following of two things mentioned.
Looking back. See *Verbs*
Never to return.
No more. Past.
Obsolete. Gone out of use.
Over. Past.

(Continued on Column 1)

PAST—Adverbs.

Long ago. In the remote past
Long since. Some time ago.
No longer. No more.
Of old. } Anciently.
Of yore. }
Once. At a former time.
Once upon a time. At a certain former time.
Over. Past.
Retrospectively. In a retrospective manner.
Some time ago. }
Some time back. } In the near past.
Some time since. }
The day before yesterday. Two days ago.
Till now. To the present.
Time out of mind. For a very long time.
Ultimo [L.]. Last month.
Up to this time. Up to the present.
Whilom. Formerly.
Years ago. Long ago.
Yesterday. The day before the present.
Yet. Up to the present time.

PAST—Phrases

Fuit Ilium [L.]. Ilium has been. }
Fuimus Troës [L.]. We Trojans have been. } [Virgil, Æneid, 3, 25.]
Hoc erat in more majorum [L.]. This was in the custom of our fathers.

Tempi passati [L.] Time gone by
The time has been. }
The time hath been. } There was a time.
Time was. }
Ultimus Romanorum [L.]. Last of the Romans.

fut″-u-ri′-tion. The state of being future. Future-Past.
fu-tu′-ri-ty. The future. Antecedence-Sequence, Future-Past, Occurrence-Destiny

fuz′-zle. To intoxicate. Teetotalism - Intemper-ance.
fy. Fie, an expression of disapproval. Approval-Disapproval

G

gab. Idle talk. Talkativeness-Taciturnity; **gift of gab,** Speech-Inarticulateness.

gab″-ar-dine. A loose coarse gown. Dress-Undress.

gab′-ble. To jabber. Talkativeness-Taciturnity

ga-bel′.
ga-belle′. } Tax. Price-Discount.

gab′-er-lun″-zie. A beggar's pouch. Gentility-Democracy.

ga′-ble. The end wall of a building. Architecture, Laterality-Contraposition; **gable end,** Beginning-End, Laterality-Contraposition.

ga′-by. A dunce. Sage-Fool.

gad. To roam idly. Traveling-Navigation, Wayfarer-Seafarer.

gad′-ding. Roving. Traveling-Navigation.

gad′-ling. A tramp. Traveling-Navigation.

gad″-so′. An oath, "God's hooks." Astonishment-Expectation, Expectance.

gaff. A game-cock's steel spur. Weapon.

gaf′-fer. An old man. Gentility-Democracy, Male-Female.

gag. To silence forcibly. Acting, Release-Prison, Release-Restraint, Vocalization-Muteness.

gage. (1) A pledge. Security; **throw down the gage,** Defiance. (2) A measure. Mensuration; **rain gage,** Sign, River-Wind; **wind gage,** River-Wind.

gage d'amour [F.] (gazh da-mur′). Pledge of love. Engagement-Release, Love-Hate.

ga′-ger. One who measures. Judicature.

gag′-gle. To cackle like a goose. Cry-Ululation.

ga′-ging. Measuring. Mensuration.

gaieté de cœur [F.] (gê-e-tê′ de cur). Gaiety of heart. Lightheartedness-Dejection.

gai′-e-ty. State of being gay. Lightheartedness-Dejection.

gail″-lard′. A spry person. Wag.

gain. To make profit. Gain-Loss, Good-Evil, Skill-Unskilfulness; **gain a point,** Success-Failure; **gain a victory,** Success-Failure; **gain credit,** Approval-Disapproval; **gain ground,** Advance-Retrogression, Swiftness-Slowness; **gain head,** Dominance-Impotence; **gain laurels,** Reputation-Discredit; **gain learning,** Education-Learning; **gain one's ends,** Success-Failure; **gain over,** Motive-Caprice; **gain private ends,** Unselfishness-Selfishness; **gain strength,** Increase-Decrease; **gain the confidence of,** Faith-Misgiving; **gain the start,** Antecedence-Sequence, Earliness-Lateness; **gain time,** Earliness-Lateness, Lastingness-Transientness; **gain upon,** Approach-Withdrawal, Habit-Desuetude.

GAIN—LOSS.

Acquisition. Anything gained, or made one's own.

Benefit. Whatever is for the good or advantage of a person. See Good.

Crop. The gain from what is planted.

Descent. The transmission of property by inheritance.

Earnings. Wages gained by service.

Emolument. The profit or gain arising from office, employment, or labor. See Recompense.

Find. Something valuable discovered.

Foundling. A child found without a parent or owner.

Fruit. Anything produced either from the earth or by industry.

Gain. That which is obtained as an advantage.

Gaining, etc. See *Verbs.*

Gift. Anything received without compensation. See Giving.

Harvest. The gathering of a crop of any kind; the product of any toil or effort.

Income. The gain which comes from labor, business, property, or capital of any kind.

Inheritance. A possession which is derived by an heir from an ancestor or other person.

Innings. The ingathering of grain.

Loaves and fishes. Symbols of resources or plenty.

Lucre. Gain in money or goods, as the object of greed.

Money-grubbing. The process of making money by contemptible methods.

Money-making. The process of gaining wealth.

Net profit. The difference in favor of the seller between the selling price and the original cost after deducting all charges.

Obtainment. That which is brought into one's possession.

Outcome. The visible result or gain.

Output. The quantity produced or ready for use.

Pelf. Wealth; often implying ill-gotten gains.

Pickings. That which is picked or gleaned.

Pool. A collective stake.

Prize. An honor or reward striven for in a competitive contest.

Proceeds. That which comes forth or results; sum accruing from a sale.

Procuration. } That which is gained, or the act of gaining or
Procurement. } obtaining.

Produce. That which is produced, brought forth, or yielded.

Bereavement. Anything taken away from, especially the loss of a relative by death.

Deperdition. Anything taken from by destruction.

Deprivation. The act of taking something possessed or enjoyed. See Taking.

Forfeiture. The loss of some right, privilege, estate, honor, or the like, for an offense or crime.

Lapse. An unobserved or gradual diminution in strength.

Loss. The act of parting with unintentionally.

Perdition. Entire loss or destruction.

Privation. The act of taking away something necessary or required.

Riddance. Deliverance from something undesirable.

Loss—*Verbs.*

Allow to slip through the fingers. To lose by negligence.

Be lost. Parted with unwillingly.

Be without. Lacking. See Holding-Exemption.

Experience a loss. To have a loss befall one.

Forfeit. To lose by some error or fault.

Get rid of. To part with something not wanted. See Keeping-Relinquishment.

Incur a loss. Lose.

Lapse. To fall away gradually.

Let slip. To lose by neglect.

Lose. To part with unintentionally or unwillingly

Meet with a loss. Lose.

Mislay. To lay in a place not recollected.

Miss. To fail to obtain, learn, or find.

Waste. To part with carelessly or unnecessarily.

Loss—*Adjectives.*

Bereaved. Deprived of something highly valued

Bereft. Poetical form for bereaved.

Cut off. Parted from.

Denuded. Deprived of all covering.

Deprived of. Divested of.

Dispossessed. To be put out of possession See Taking.

Irretrievable. Not to be recovered. See Sanguineness-Hopelessness.

GAIN—LOSS—*Continued*

Product. Anything that is produced as the result of labor, growth, thought, or involuntary causes.

Profit Gain in any transaction or occupation.

Purchase. The acquisition of title to, or property in, anything for a price.

Recovery. That which is regained; the act of regaining.

Redemption. The act of regaining possession of by purchase

Replevin. An action at law to recover goods or chattels wrongfully withheld.

Retrieval. The act of restoring from loss or injury.

Return. That which is gained from labor or investment.

Revendication. The act of reclaiming.

Salvage. Compensation gained for aiding a ship in distress.

Stealing. The act of taking the personal property of another without his consent or knowledge. See STEALING.

Subreption. The act of obtaining a gain or favor through fraudulent concealment of facts.

Sweepstakes. A prize in a sporting contest comprising several stakes.

The main chance. The most favorable opportunity for increasing one's resources.

Thrift. Care and prudence in the management of one's resources.

Trick. A device for getting an advantage by deception.

Trouvaille [F.]. Anything that is found.

Trover. Gaining possession of any goods whether by finding or any other means.

Wealth. A great abundance of anything valuable or desirable See AFFLUENCE.

Winnings. Anything that is won, as money.

GAIN—*Verbs*

Accrue. Arise as an addition or advantage. See GIVING-RECEIVING.

Acquire. Get as one's own.

Answer. Pay or atone

Bag. Catch or take.

Be profitable. To be of advantage.

Bring grist to the mill. To gather one's earnings.

Bring home. To take into one's ownership.

Clear To gain over and above expenses.

Coin money. To make great gains in business.

Collect. Gather together. See sub ASSEMBLE.

Come by. To obtain, gain, or acquire.

Come by one's own. To receive one's rightful possessions.

Come in for. To claim or receive.

Come into possession. To gain or win.

Come upon. To have a claim upon.

Derive. To obtain by regular and orderly process

Draw. To call for and receive, as from a fund.

Draw profit. To reap gain from.

Earn. To gain as a just return by service.

Enter into possession. To take into one's ownership.

Fill one's pockets. To make money.

Find. To discover or meet with accidentally

Gain. To secure as profit or earnings.

Gain an advantage. To be placed in the way of getting something desirable.

Gather. To acquire in increasing amount.

Get. To secure as one's own.

Get at. To reach.

Get back. To get what one had before.

Get between one's thumb and finger. To secure certain possession of.

Get hold of. ⎫

Get in. ⎬ To get into one's ownership

Get into one's hand. ⎭

Get in the harvest. To gather one's earnings.

Glean To collect or gather anything.

GAIN—*Adjectives.*

Acquired. Gained; won.

Acquiring. Gaining by one's own exertions.

Acquisitive. Having the power to acquire.

Advantageous. Gainful; profitable.

Gainful. Producing gain

GAIN—*Phrase*

Lucri causa [L.] For the sake of gain

LOSS—ADJECTIVES—*Continued.*

Long lost. ⎫

Losing. ⎬ See *Verbs*

Lost. ⎭

Minus. Without positive value.

Not having. See sub EXEMPTION.

Off one's hands. Out of one's possession or care.

Out of pocket. Having expended more money than one has received.

Quit of. Deprived of the care of.

LOSS—*Interjections.*

Adieu to! Farewell to!

GAIN—VERBS—*Continued*

Inherit. To receive from one's ancestors.

Light upon. To find.

Make capital out of. To use for a personal advantage.

Make money. ⎫

Make money by. ⎬ Add to one's fortune.

Make profit. ⎭

Make the pot boil. To do something which yields a good return.

Net. To earn or yield as clear profit.

Obtain. To get hold of by effort.

Obtain a return. Obtain a reward for labor or expenditure.

Pay. To be profitable.

Pick. ⎫

Pick up. ⎬ To improve by degrees.

Pitch upon. To lay hold of.

Procure. To bring into possession.

Produce. To bring forth as a natural product or growth See CREATION.

Profit. To gain.

Raise funds. ⎫

Raise money. ⎬ To collect or bring together for use or service.

Raise the wind. To make very much money.

Realize. To convert any kind of property into money.

Reap an advantage. To receive as the fruit of labor or works.

Reap and carry. To gain and enjoy.

Reap the fruits of. To obtain the gain or advantage.

Receive. To take, as something that is offered. See GIVING-RECEIVING.

Recover. To win or gain back.

Redeem. To regain possession by payment of a fixed sum.

Regain. To gain or come to anew.

Replevy. To take or get back under a writ, goods and chattels, upon security to try the right to them in a suit at law.

Retrieve. To restore to an improved condition.

Revendicate. To demand the restoration of.

Sack. To plunder.

Scrape together. ⎫

Scrape up. ⎬ To gather in small portions by laborious effort.

Secure. To put beyond risk of losing.

Step into. ⎫

Step into a fortune. ⎬ To fall heir to.

Step into the shoes of. ⎪

Succeed to. ⎭

Take. ⎫

Take possession. ⎬ To acquire the ownership of.

Treasure up. To store up one's gains. See STORE

Turn a penny. ⎫

Turn an honest penny. ⎬ To earn by labor.

Turn to account. ⎫

Turn to profit. ⎬ To use to one's own advantage.

Win. To gain at play.

GAIN—*Adjectives.*

Lucrative. Making increase of money or goods.

Paying. Yielding a return for money expended.

Profitable. Bringing profit or gain.

Remunerative. Affording an ample return for industry or an investment

gain'-ful. Profitable. GAIN-LOSS, USEFULNESS-USELESSNESS.

gain'-less. Profitless. USEFULNESS-USELESSNESS.

gain''-say'. To contradict ASSERTION-DENIAL

gair'-ish. Gaudy. COLOR-ACHROMATISM, EMBELLISHMENT-DISFIGUREMENT, LIGHT-DARKNESS, POMP.

gait. Manner of walking. MOVEMENT-REST, WAY

gait'-er. Covering for the leg. DRESS-UNDRESS.

ga'-la. Festivity. ENTERTAINMENT-WEARINESS, POMP.

ga'-la–day''. A holiday. ENTERTAINMENT-WEARINESS.

ga-lac'-tic. Pertaining to the galaxy. **Galactic circle,** UNIVERSE.

galantuómo [It.] (ga-lan-tu-o'-mo). An honest man. UPRIGHTNESS-DISHONESTY.

gal''-a-vant. Gallivant. BLANDISHMENT.

gal'-ax-y. Any brilliant group. GATHERING-SCATTERING, LUMINARY-SHADE, MULTIPLICITY-PAUCITY, REPUTATION-DISCREDIT, UNIVERSE.

gale. Storm. RIVER-WIND.

Ga'-len. Greek physician of second century. REMEDY-BANE.

ga-len'-ic-als. Poison antidote. REMEDY-BANE.

gal''-i-ma'-tias. Nonsense. ADAGE-NONSENSE.

gal'-i-ot. A small galley. CONVEYANCE-VESSEL.

gal'-i-pot. Gallipot.

gall. An abrasion of the skin caused by rubbing; bitter feeling. CHARITABLENESS-MALEVOLENCE, FAVORITE-ANGER, PALATABLENESS-UNPALATABLENESS, PLEASURABLENESS-PAINFULNESS, SENSUALITY-SUFFERING; **dip the pen in gall,** ADULATION-DISPARAGEMENT.

gal'-lant. Brave. BRAVERY-COWARDICE, LOVE-HATE, POLITENESS-IMPOLITENESS, PURITY-IMPURITY, PURITY-RAKE.

gal'-lant-ry. Undue attention to women. BLANDISHMENT, BRAVERY-COWARDICE, IMPURITY, LOVE-HATE, POLITENESS-IMPOLITENESS.

gal''-lant-y–show'. A miniature shadow-pantomime. APPEARANCE-DISAPPEARANCE, ENTERTAINMENT-WEARINESS.

galled. Having some skin rubbed off. **Let the galled jade wince,** BRAGGING.

gal'-le-on. A large sailing vessel. CONVEYANCE-VESSEL.

gal'-ler-y. Room for displaying things; hall; seating space above the main floor of churches, etc. ACTING, APERTURE-CLOSURE, CONTENTS-RECEIVER, STORE.

gal'-ley. Seagoing vessel fitted with oars. CONVEYANCE-VESSEL, RECOMPENSE-PUNITION, RECOMPENSE-SCOURGE; **work like a galley-slave,** TOIL-RELAXATION.

gal''-ley–foist'. A state barge. CONVEYANCE-VESSEL.

gal'-leys. Prison boats. RECOMPENSE-PUNITION, RECOMPENSE-SCOURGE.

gal'-li-ass. A large galley. CONVEYANCE-VESSEL.

Gal'-li-cism. French mode of speaking. WORD-NEOLOGY.

gal''-li-gas'-kins. Long loose hose. DRESS-UNDRESS.

gal''-li-mau'-frey. Harsh. MIXTURE-HOMOGENEITY.

gall'-ing. Chafing. PLEASURABLENESS-PAINFULNESS.

gal'-li-pot. A glazed pot for medicine. RECEIVER-RECEPTACLE.

gal''-li-vant'. To gad about. BLANDISHMENT.

gal'-lon. Unit of measure. MEASURE.

gal-loon'. Kind of lace. EMBELLISHMENT-DISFIGUREMENT.

gal'-lop. To move with a swift leaping motion, as a horse. LASTINGNESS-TRANSIENTNESS, SWIFTNESS-SLOWNESS, TRAVELING-NAVIGATION.

gal'-lop-ing. Moving in a gallop. SWIFTNESS-SLOWNESS; **galloping consumption,** HEALTH-SICKNESS.

gal'-lo-way. A small horse. CONVEYER.

gal'-lows. A framework on which to execute criminals. LIFE-KILLING, RECOMPENSE-SCOURGE; **bring to the gallows,** RECOMPENSE-PUNITION; **come to the gallows,** RECOMPENSE-PUNITION.

gal'-op. A lively dance. ENTERTAINMENT-WEARINESS.

gal''-o-pade'. Galop. ENTERTAINMENT-WEARINESS.

ga-lore'. Abundant. ENOUGH.

ga-losh'. To cover with strong water-proof material. DRESS-UNDRESS.

gal-van'-ic. Excitable. EXCITABILITY-INEXCITABILITY; **galvanic cell,** ELECTRICITY.

gal'-van-ism. Electricity produced by chemical action. EXCITATION, MIGHT-IMPOTENCE.

gal'-van-ize. To excite. EXCITATION.

gal''-va-nom'-e-ter. Electrical instrument. ELECTRICITY.

Ga-ma'-li-el. A learned Jew of the first century. **Brought up at the feet of Gamaliel,** SCHOLAR-DUNCE.

ga-mash'-es. High boots. DRESS-UNDRESS.

gam-bade'. Prank. ENTERTAINMENT-WEARINESS, SPRING-DIVE.

gam-ba'-do. Legging; prank. DRESS-UNDRESS, SPRING-DIVE.

gam'-bler. One who gambles. PURPOSE-LUCK.

gam'-bling. Risking value in a game. ENTERTAINMENT-WEARINESS, PURPOSE-LUCK, RECKLESSNESS-CAUTION.

gam'-bling–house''. Place where gambling is done. PURPOSE-LUCK.

gam-boge'. Kind of resin. YELLOWNESS-PURPLE.

gam'-bol. To skip sportively. ENTERTAINMENT-WEARINESS.

game. Wild animals; sport; unflinching; to gamble. BRAVERY-COWARDICE, CONDUCT, DETERMINATION-VACILLATION, ENTERTAINMENT-WEARINESS, FAUNA-FLORA, PALATABLENESS-UNPALATABLENESS, PERSISTENCE-WHIM, PURPOSE-LUCK, QUEST-EVASION, SOCIETY-LAUGHINGSTOCK; **game at romps,** ENTERTAINMENT-WEARINESS; **game at which two can play,** REPRISAL-RESISTANCE; **game in one's hands,** DIFFICULTY-FACILITY, RULE-LICENSE, SUCCESS-FAILURE; **game to the last,** PERSISTENCE-WHIM; **game up,** SUCCESS-FAILURE; **drawn game,** SUCCESS-FAILURE; **make game of,** REGARD-DISRESPECT, SOCIETY-DERISION, TRUTHFULNESS-FRAUD; **play a desperate game,** RECKLESSNESS-CAUTION; **play the game of,** ANTAGONISM-CONCURRENCE.

game'-cock''. Cock trained for fighting. BELLIGERENT, BRAVERY-COWARDICE.

game'-keep''-er. One who cares for the game. GUARD-PRISONER.

game'-some. Playful. LIGHTHEARTEDNESS-DEJECTION.

game'-ster. Gambler. ENTERTAINMENT-WEARINESS, PURPOSE-LUCK, RECKLESSNESS-CAUTION.

gam'-in. Street arab. CITY-COUNTRY, GENTILITY-DEMOCRACY.

ga'-ming. Playing for money. PURPOSE-LUCK, RECKLESSNESS-CAUTION.

ga'-ming–house''. Gambling-house. PURPOSE-LUCK.

gam'-mer. An old woman. INFANT-VETERAN, MALE-FEMALE.

gam'-mon. Hoax. TRUTHFULNESS-FALSEHOOD, TRUTHFULNESS-FRAUD.

ga'-my. High-flavored. PUNGENCY.

gam'-ut. The diatonic scale. MELODY-DISSONANCE.

gan'-der. Male goose. MALE-FEMALE.

gang. Group; to go. ASSOCIATION, GATHERING-SCATTERING, MOVEMENT-REST.

gan'-grene. First stage of mortification. HEALTH-SICKNESS.

gang'-way''. Passageway. LENGTH-SHORTNESS, WAY.

gant'-let. Punishment inflicted by running between two lines of men who strike the runner with whips, etc. RECOMPENSE-PUNITION; **run the gantlet,** BRAVERY-COWARDICE, DETERMINATION-VACILLATION.

gaol. Jail. RELEASE-PRISON; **gaol delivery,** RESCUE.

gaol'-er. Keeper of a jail. GUARD-PRISONER, RECOMPENSE-SCOURGE.

gap. Fissure. APERTURE-CLOSURE, ASTONISHMENT-EXPECTANCE, INQUISITIVENESS-INDIFFERENCE, INTERSPACE-CONTACT; **stand in the gap,** ATTACK-DEFENSE.

gape. Opening. CONTINUITY-INTERRUPTION, FAULTLESSNESS-FAULTINESS, INTERSPACE-CONTACT; **gape for,** DESIRE-DISTASTE.

ga'-ping. Yawning. APERTURE-CLOSURE, EXPECTATION-SURPRISE.

G. A. R. Grand Army of the Republic. PATRIOTISM-TREASON.

gar. To make. CREATION-DESTRUCTION.

garb. Clothing. DRESS-UNDRESS; **under the garb of,** TRUTHFULNESS-FRAUD.

gar'-bage. Refuse. CLEANNESS-FILTHINESS.

gar'-ble. To alter. ADDITION-SUBTRACTION, INCLUSION-OMISSION, INTERPRETATION-MISINTERPRETATION, TRUTHFULNESS-FALSEHOOD; **garble accounts,** ACCOUNTS.

gar'-bled. Changed. ENTIRETY-DEFICIENCY.

gar'-bling. A picking or sorting. ADDITION-SUBTRACTION.

garde meurt, et ne se rend pas, la [F.] (gard mur, ê ne se ran· pa, la). The guard dies, it does not surrender. BRAVERY-COWARDICE, PERSISTENCE-WHIM.

garde nationale [F.] (gard na-si-o-nal'). National guard. BELLIGERENT.

garde royale [F.] (gard rwa-yal'). Royal guard. ATTACK-DEFENSE, BELLIGERENT.

gar'-den. A small piece of cultivated land. BEAUTY-UGLINESS, DOMESTICATION-AGRICULTURE, DWELLER-HABITATION, ENTERTAINMENT-WEARINESS; **botanic garden,** DOMESTICATION-AGRICULTURE, ZOOLOGY-BOTANY; **garden party,** SOCIABILITY-PRIVACY; **zoological garden,** DOMESTICATION-AGRICULTURE.

gar'-den-er. One who tends a garden. DOMESTICATION-AGRICULTURE.

gar'-dens. Place of amusement ornamented with flowers. DWELLER-HABITATION.

gardez [F.] (gar-dê'). Take care. RECKLESSNESS-CAUTION, WARNING.

gardez bien [F.] (gar-dê' bi-an·'). Take good care. RECKLESSNESS-CAUTION.

gardez la foi [F.] (gar-dê' la fwa). Keep the faith. OBSERVANCE-NONOBSERVANCE.

Gar-gan'-tu-a. Giant of fiction who could drink a river dry. [Rabelais.]

Gar-gan'-tu-an. Enormous. GREATNESS-LITTLENESS.

gar'-gle. Liquid used to cleanse the throat. WATER-AIR.

gar'-goyle. Projecting spout. ARCHITECTURE, WATERCOURSE-AIRPIPE.

gar'-ish. Gaudy. COLOR-ACHROMATISM, EMBELLISHMENT-DISFIGUREMENT, LIGHT-DARKNESS, POMP.

gar'-land. Wreath. CIRCLE-WINDING, EMBELLISHMENT-DISFIGUREMENT, SIGN, TITLE, TROPHY.

gar'-lic. A kind of herb. CONDIMENT, PERFUME-STENCH.

gar'-ment. Clothing. DRESS-UNDRESS.

gar'-ner. Granary; to store. STORE; **garner up,** STORE.

gar'-net. A shade of red. EMBELLISHMENT-DISFIGUREMENT.

gar'-nish. To ornament. EMBELLISHMENT-DISFIGUREMENT, INCREMENT-REMNANT, OUTLAY-INCOME, PREPARATION-NONPREPARATION.

gar'-ni-ture. Anything used for garnishing. DRESS-UNDRESS.

gar'-ran. A Galloway horse. CONVEYER.

gar'-ret. The room immediately under the roof. CONTENTS-RECEIVER, TOP-BOTTOM.

gar'-ri-son. Military station. ATTACK-DEFENSE, BELLIGERENT, DWELLER-HABITATION, SECURITY-INSECURITY.

gar'-ri-soned by. Protected by. DWELLER-HABITATION.

gar-rote'. To kill by strangling with a garrote; an instrument for capital punishment. LIFE-KILLING, MIGHT-IMPOTENCE, RECOMPENSE-PUNITION.

gar-ro'-ter. A strangler. LIFE-KILLING.

gar-ru'-li-ty. Talkativeness. TALKATIVENESS-TACITURNITY.

gar'-ru-lous. Talkative. TALKATIVENESS-TACITURNITY.

gar'-ter. Band used to hold up a stocking. CONNECTIVE, TITLE; **garter blue,** BLUENESS-ORANGE.

gas. Matter in the aeriform state. CHEMISTRY, LIQUID-GAS, LUMINARY-SHADE.

gas'-con. A boaster. BRAGGING.

gas''-con-ade.' To boast. BRAGGING.

gas''-con-a'-ding. Boasting. BRAGGING.

gas-e'-i-ty. State of being gaseous. LIQUID-GAS.

gash. To cut. GOOD-EVIL, INTERSPACE-CONTACT, UNION-DISUNION.

gas''-i-fi-ca'-tion. The process of changing into a gas. WATER-AIR.

gas'-kins. Leather leggings. DRESS-UNDRESS.

gas'-light''. Light made by burning gas. LUMINARY-SHADE.

gas''-o-lier'. A gas chandelier. LUMINARY-SHADE.

gas-om'-e-ter. Tank for storing gas. LUMINARY-SHADE, STORE.

gasp. To breathe or talk with difficulty. HEALTH-SICKNESS, RIVER-WIND, WEARINESS-REFRESHMENT; **at the last gasp,** LIFE-DEATH; **gasp for,** DESIRE-DISTASTE.

gas'-ping. Struggling for breath. HEALTH-SICKNESS.

gas'-tro-man''-cy. A kind of divination. PROPHECY

gas'-tro-nome. An epicure. FASTING-GLUTTONY.

gas-tron'-o-my. The art of preparing appetizing food. FASTING-GLUTTONY.

gate. Small movable part of a fence. APERTURE, BEGINNING-END, ENCLOSURE, OBSTRUCTION-HELP; **gateway,** APERTURE-CLOSURE, BEGINNING-END, ENCLOSURE, WAY; **water gate,** WATERCOURSE-AIRPIPE.

gâté enfant [F.] (ga-tê' an·-fan·') A spoiled child. WELFARE-MISFORTUNE.

Gath. A Philistine city; **tell it not in Gath,** APPROVAL-DISAPPROVAL, ENLIGHTENMENT-SECRECY.

gath'-er. To collect. DECISION-MISJUDGMENT, ENLARGEMENT-DIMINUTION, GAIN-LOSS, GATHERING-SCATTERING, PLICATURE, TAKING-RESTITUTION; **gather breath,** WEARINESS-REFRESHMENT; **gather flesh,** ENLARGEMENT-DIMINUTION; **gather from one,** ENLIGHTENMENT-SECRECY; **gather fruits,** SUCCESS-FAILURE.

gath'-ered. Gotten together, **gathered to one's fathers,** LIFE-DEATH.

gath'-er-ing. Meeting; collection of anything. GATHERING-SCATTERING, HEALTH-SICKNESS; **gathering clouds,** CHARITABLENESS-MENACE, LIGHT-DARKNESS, LUMINARY-SHADE, PORTENT, SECURITY-INSECURITY, WANDERING, WELFARE-MISFORTUNE.

GATHERING—SCATTERING.

Accumulation. Collection in a heap. See STORE.

Acervation. A heaping up, a collection.

Agglomeration. Heaping together in a disordered mass.

Aggregation. Collection or assemblage into one whole or mass.

Assemblage. A bringing together of persons, generally conspicuous.

Assembly. A coming together of persons with one object

Association. A voluntary union of persons in a society

Assortment. A great number of many kinds.

Apportionment. Separation into portions.

Circumfusion. Act of spreading abroad.

Diffusion. A spreading out in all directions

Disjunction. A parting of what was joined. See UNION-DISUNION.

Dispersion. The act of scattering.

Dissemination. The act of spreading like seed.

Dissipation. State of being dispersed or scattered.

Distribution. A separation into parts.

GATHERING—SCATTERING—*Continued.*

Attroupement [F.]. A riotous assembly.
Brotherhood. An association for a purpose, fraternity.
Coacervation. The act of heaping up.
Coagmentation. The act of joining together.
Collection. Any act of gathering of anything or persons.
Colligation. A gathering together of isolated facts.
Collocation. The act of placing side by side.
Compilation. A selected collection of matters.
Concentration. The act of drawing to a common place.
Concourse. A coming together; an assembly.
Conflux. A flowing together; confluence.
Congeries. A collection of particles; heap.
Conglobation. Collection into a mass.
Conglomerate. A collection of things massed without any order.
Conglomeration. Collection of heterogeneous material in a mass.
Congregation. To collect into a flock or body.
Contesseration. An assemblage of those holding tesseræ as tickets of admission; a mosaic.
Convergence. Approaching to a point. See CONCENTRATION.
Cumulation. Act of heaping together.
Gathering. An assemblage, a collection.
Glomeration. The act of collecting into a ball.
Ingathering. The drawing or collecting together.
Levy. A calling together; collection.
Meeting. A coming together, a joining.
Muster. An assemblage of people or soldiers for review.
Omnium-gatherum. An assembly of all.
Populousness. The state of the country in regard to the number of people collected thereon.
Quantity. A considerable amount without regard to form or shape.
Reunion. A gathering together after separation.

GATHERING—*Nouns of Place.*

Drawing-room. A room used for the assembling of company.
Menagery. A place where various wild animals are kept for show.
Museum. A place where collections of curiosities are kept.

GATHERING—*Associated Words.*

At home. In preparation for reception of company.
Black hole of Calcutta. A dark hole in which 123 prisoners were suffocated in Calcutta.
Noah's ark. A child's toy in which all kinds of animals are put.
Pleiades. A group of stars in Taurus; seven stars, of which one is lost.
Spicilegium [L.]. A gathering in, as of corn.

GATHERING—*Special Assemblage of Persons.*

Conclave. A secret assembly, a council. See COUNCIL.
Congress. A formal assembly of deputies, representatives, or legislators.
Conventicle. A secret religious assembly.
Convention. A coming together of minds for arrangement or settlement of difficulties.
Gemot. An assembly of the English barons.
Posse. A squad of men deputized by a sheriff.
Posse comitatus [L.]. Citizens summoned by a sheriff to his assistance.

GATHERING—*Scientific Nouns.*

Collectanea. A collection of passages from many authors.
Congestion. Accumulation of too much blood in the veins.
Fascine. A bundle of sticks used in making ramparts, etc.
Miscellany. A collection of compositions on various subjects.

GATHERING—*Denotations.*

Army. A collection or body of men armed for war.
Array. A body of persons drawn up in regular lines.
Bale. A bundle or package of anything in a cloth cover, or corded for storage or transportation.
Band. A company of persons united in any common design.
Batch. A quantity of anything produced at one operation.
Bevy. An assembly of persons, especially of ladies.
Body. A number of individuals spoken of collectively, usually organized for some purpose.
Budget. A bag with its contents; hence, an accumulation.
Bunch. A collection of things of the same kind.
Bundle. A number of things bound together.
Clan. A tribe, or collection of families regarded as having the same common ancestor.
Cloud. A collection of visible vapor; a great crowd or multitude.
Clump. A growth of small trees.
Cluster. A number of similar things collected together.
Company. An assemblage of persons.
Conversazione. A meeting for conversation on some special topic. See SOCIABILITY.

Divergence. Separation from one point. See CONCENTRATION-RADIATION.
Interspersion. The act of scattering here and there.
Respersion. Sprinkling or scattering.
Scattering. A throwing about without regard to order.
Spargefaction. The act of sprinkling.
Spread. An extending in all directions.

SCATTERING—*Denotations.*

Disjecta membra [L.]. Scattered parts. [Horace, *Satires*, 1, 4, 62.].
Flotsam and jetsam. Goods lost by shipwreck and floating on the sea, or sunk to the bottom.
Hand-bill. A loose, printed sheet, to be distributed by hand.
Waifs and estrays. Goods found of which the owner is not known, or an animal wandering from its owner; waifs are thrown away by a thief in his flight.

SCATTERING—*Verbs.*

Apportion. To divide up into portions. See ASSIGNMENT.
Blow off. To cause to leave some place.
Cast. To throw away with force.
Cast adrift. } To throw away.
Cast forth. }
Circumfuse. To pour around as a liquid.
Deal out. To give out in portions.
Diffuse. To spread abroad.
Disband. To break up an organization.
Disembody. To discharge from a military organization.
Dismember. To separate limb from limb.
Dispel. To drive away by scattering.
Dispense. To divide into portions.
Disperse. To scatter away.
Disperse themselves. To scatter.
Disseminate. To scatter as seed.
Distribute. To apportion among a number.
Draft off. To draw off.
Intersperse. To scatter here and there.
Issue. To send forth for distribution.
Let out. To permit to scatter.
Overspread. To be scattered over.
Resperse. To scatter.
Retail. To distribute in small portions.
Scatter. To throw about in different directions.
Scatter to the winds. To scatter in all directions.
Set abroach. To set in a state of diffusion.
Shed. To separate in weaving.
Sow. To scatter as seed.
Sow broadcast. To throw all over.
Spirtle. To issue in a scattering manner.
Spread. To stretch over an extent.
Spread like wildfire. To spread or be scattered very widely and rapidly.
Sprinkle. To scatter as drops of water.
Straw. To spread.
Strew. To cast about loosely.
Strow. See STREW.
Ted. To stir up and scatter, as for drying.
Turn adrift. To let go at random.
Utter. To send out; to put in circulation.

SCATTERING—*Adjectives.*

Adrift. Floating about.
Broadcast. Scattered widely.
Disheveled. Thrown into disorder, as the hair.
Dispersed. See *Verbs.*
Dispread. Widely diffused.
Epidemic. Affecting great numbers. See UNIVERSALITY.
Sparse. Thinly scattered.
Sporadic. Occurring irregularly.
Stray. Having wandered from the way.
Streaming. Flowing abundantly.
Unassembled. Not called into same place. See GATHERING.
Widespread. Very generally distributed.

SCATTERING—*Adverbs.*

Here and there. Scattered.
Passim [L.]. In various places.
Sparsim [L.]. Scatteredly.

———

GATHERING—DENOTATIONS—*Continued.*

Shower. That which resembles a shower in falling through the air; a copious supply.

GATHERING—Denotations—*Continued*.

Corps. An organized division of a military establishment.
Covey. A flock of quails or partridges.
Crew. A company of people associated together; a company of seamen who man a ship.
Crowd. A number of persons collected in a close body without order.
Drift. A collection of loose earth and rocks, or boulders.
Drove. A collection of cattle.
Fagot. A bundle of sticks or small branches of trees used for fuel.
Fardel. A bundle or little pack.
Fasciculus [L.]. A small bundle.
Flock. A company of living creatures, especially of sheep or birds.
Galaxy. Clusters of stars.
Gang. A number of persons associated for a particular purpose.
Group. An assemblage of either persons or things collected without any form.
Haycock. A heap of hay in the field.
Heap. A collection of things thrown together so as to form an elevation.
Herd. A number of beasts assembled together.
Horde. Any gathered multitude of human beings.
Host. Any great number of men.
Knot. A small group of persons.
Levee. A morning assembly of visitors.
Lot. A large quantity or number.
Lump. A mass or aggregate of things.
Mob. An unlawful or riotous assembly; *mobile vulgus*.
Pack. A bundle; a number of dogs kept for hunting; a number of connected or similar things.
Package. A small bundle.
Parcel. A number of things put up together.
Party. A number of persons united in opinion, action, or entertainment.

Pencil. A collection of rays of light.
Pile. A mass of things heaped together.
Pyramid. A collection of things in the shape of a pyramid.
Rabble. A noisy crowd of people.
Regiment. A body of soldiers consisting of ten companies, or about one thousand men.
Rick. A stack or pile, as of grain, straw, or hay.
Rouleau [F.]. A roll.
School. An assemblage of scholars; a multitude, as a school of fish.
Seron. }
Seroon. } A bale or package covered with wood bound with hide.
Set. A number of things of the same kind, ordinarily classed together.
Sheaf. A quantity of the stalks of grain bound together.
Shoal. A great multitude assembled, especially of fish.
Shock. A pile of sheaves of grain, set up in a field.
Snowball. A round mass of snow pressed or rolled together.
Snowdrift. A great pile of snow driven together by the wind.
Squad. A small party of men assembled for drill, etc.
Stack. A pile of unthrashed grain.
Stock. A supply or accumulation of goods or resources.
Storm. A heavy shower or fall.
Swarm. A large number of small animals or insects.
Throng. A multitude of persons pressed into a close body.
Tissue. A web or texture.
Tribe. A collection of families having the same ancestor.
Troop. A collection of people; soldiers.
Troupe. The company of performers in a play or opera.
Truss. A bundle or package.
Tuft. A collection of small, flexible, or soft things in a knot or bunch.
Volley. A great number of missiles discharged at the same time.
Wisp. A small bundle, as of straw.

GATHERING—*Nouns of Cause*.

Cohue [F.]. A riot.
Crush. A jamming together of a crowd of persons.
Deluge. A great flood.

Flood. An excessive amount of water.
Press. A jam made by a big crowd.
Rush. A tumultuous movement of a large number of persons

GATHERING—*Verbs*.

Accumulate. To collect together by slow accessions.
Acervate. To heap up.
Agglomerate. To collect in a mass.
Aggregate. To collect into a gross lump.
Aggroup. To bring together in groups.
Amass. To gather much into a heap.
Assemble. To bring together at the same place.
Associate. To combine in some enterprise, to bring into close relation.
Bring to a focus. To bring to a central point; to concentrate.
Bring together. To gather.
Center around. To collect about; to cluster.
Cluster. To collect together in a close group.
Collect. To gather from different places into the same place.
Collect in a focus. To collect at one point.
Collect in a drag net. Drawn together by force.
Colligate. To bind together for comparison.
Collocate. To set in its place; to arrange.
Come together. Gather.
Compile. To draw together from various sources.
Complete. To supply all needed parts.
Concentrate. To bring to a central point; to unite more solidly.
Conglomerate. To bring together in a ball.
Congregate. To collect persons in a crowd.
Convene. To come together in one place.
Convocate. To call together.
Convoke. To summon to one place.
Cram. To force together in a small compass.
Crowd. To press together; be numerous.
Draw together. Collected.
Dredge. To gather by a dredge.
Flock. To gather in crowds.
Flock together. To meet.
Foregather. To meet accidentally; forgather.

Gather. To bring together.
Get in. To bring together.
Get together. To collect.
Group. To make into groups or classes.
Heap. To put together in a pile.
Heap Ossa on Pelion. To pile up mountains.
Herd. To gather or keep together as a flock of sheep
Hold a meeting. To come together in one place.
Huddle. To throw together in confusion.
Join. To add, combine, unite together.
Lump together. To heap together heterogeneously.
Mass. To put together in a mass.
Meet. To come to and together.
Muster. To call together for review.
Pack. To collect for transportation.
Pig together. To huddle together like pigs.
Pile. }
Pile up. } To gather into a heap.
Put. To place in a certain place.
Put together. To join.
Put up. Put together.
Rake up. To gather in one place.
Reassemble. To assemble again.
Rejoin. To join again.
Rendezvous. To meet at an appointed place.
Resort. To repair to; to assemble.
Scrape together. To draw together indiscriminately into a heap.
Stream. To flow along abundantly.
Surge. To swell and to roll.
Swarm. To collect like bees.
Throng. To gather in a crowd.
Truss. To pack together.
Unite. To bring together into an integral whole.

GATHERING—*Adjectives*.

All of a heap. Piled together without any arrangement.
Assembled. Brought or called together. See *Verbs*.
As thick as hops. As thick as possible.
Closely packed. Gathered in a mass.
Crowded to suffocation. So dense as to have little air for breathing.
Cumulative. Piled up; gathering volume by addition.

Dense. Having its parts close together.
Fasciculated. Grouped in a fascicle or bunch.
Populous. Thickly inhabited.
Serried. Crowded in rows; compact.
Swarming. Thick like a hive of bees.
Teeming. Produced in great numbers.

GATHERING—*Phrases*.

Acervatim [L.]. In heaps.
The plot thickens. The affair becomes more intricate.

Tibi seris, tibi metis [L.]. For yourself you sow, for yourself you reap.

gath'-er-ing–place". Place where people come together. GATHERINGPLACE.

GATHERINGPLACE.

Center. The point equally distant from a number of given points.
Club. The meeting-place of a society.
Corradiation. A concentration of rays at one point.
Depot. A central warehouse for the transfer of goods.
Focus. Meeting point of converging lines.
Gathering-place. Place for coming together.
Haunt. Place of frequent resort.
Headquarters. Place from which orders are issued.
Home. House in which a family lives.
Issue. Point in debate or dispute.
Place of assignation. A meeting-place for lovers.
Place of meeting. A spot agreed upon for coming together.
Place of resort. A much frequented place.
Point de réunion [F.]. Point of reunion.
Point of convergence. Focus.
Rallying point. A place where a rally can be made.
Rendezvous. Prearranged meeting-place.
Resort. A place frequently visited.
Trysting-place. A place agreed upon for an interview.

GATHERINGPLACE—*Verbs.*

Bring to a focus. To gather at one point, as rays of light.
Bring to an issue. To bring different views to a common conclusion.
Bring to a point. To gather at one place.

gauche. Clumsy. SKILL-UNSKILFULNESS.
gauche"-rie'. Awkwardness. SKILL-UNSKILFULNESS, TASTE-VULGARITY.
gaud. Showy finery. EMBELLISHMENT-DISFIGUREMENT.
gaud'-er-y. Finery. CONCEIT-DIFFIDENCE.
gaud'-i-ness. Showiness. TASTE-VULGARITY.
gaud'-y. Showy. BEAUTY-UGLINESS; COLOR-ACHROMATISM, EMBELLISHMENT - DISFIGUREMENT, POMP, TASTE-VULGARITY.
gauge, etc. See GAGE, ETC.
gaunt. Lank. BEAUTY-UGLINESS, BREADTH - NARROWNESS, GREATNESS - LITTLENESS, PROPORTION-DEFORMITY.
gaunt'-let. Iron glove. ATTACK-DEFENSE, DRESS-UNDRESS; **fling down the gauntlet,** DEFIANCE; **take up the gauntlet,** STRIFE-PEACE.
Gau'-ta-ma. An old Vedic race. REVELATION-PSEUDOREVELATION.
gauze. Open-woven cloth. DIAPHANEITY-OPALESCENCE, LUMINARY-SHADE.
gav'-el. A small hammer used by a presiding officer. PRICE-DISCOUNT.
gav'-el-kind". Peculiar tenure of land. PARTICIPATION.
gav'-el-ock. Crowbar. INSTRUMENT.
gav'-ot. ⎰ Lively French dance. ENTERTAINMENT-
ga-votte'. ⎱ WEARINESS.
gawk'-y. Awkward. BEAUTY-UGLINESS, SKILL-UNSKILFULNESS.
gay. Bright; merry. COLOR-ACHROMATISM, EMBELLISHMENT-DISFIGUREMENT, LIGHTHEARTEDNESS-DEJECTION, POMP, PURITY-IMPURITY; **gay as a lark,** LIGHTHEARTEDNESS-DEJECTION; **gay world,** SOCIETY-LUDICROUSNESS.
gaze. To look attentively. SIGHT-BLINDNESS.
ga-ze'-bo. Summer-house having an extended view. SIGHT-BLINDNESS.
ga-zelle'. A kind of antelope. SWIFTNESS-SLOWNESS.
ga-zette'. Newspaper. MARK - OBLITERATION, PUBLICITY-MYSTERY; **in the gazette,** SETTLEMENT-DEFAULT.
ga"-zet'-ted. Published in the gazette. SETTLEMENT-DEFAULT.
gaz-et-teer'. Geographical dictionary; news - writer. ENLIGHTENMENT - SECRECY, MARK - OBLITERATION, RECORD.

ga'-zing–stock". Something gazed at. PHENOMENON, SOCIETY-LAUGHINGSTOCK.
géant, à pas de [F.] (zhê-an", a pa de). With the stride of a giant. SWIFTNESS-SLOWNESS.
ge-an"-ti-cli'-nal. Upheaval of earth. GEOLOGY.
gear. Clothes; implements. DRESS - UNDRESS, INSTRUMENT; **in gear,** PREPARATION-NONPREPARATION; **out of gear,** ORGANIZATION-DISORGANIZATION, PREPARATION-NONPREPARATION, REGULARITY-IRREGULARITY, UNION-DISUNION, USEFULNESS-USELESSNESS.
geese. Plural of goose. **All his geese are swans,** OVERVALUATION-UNDERVALUATION.
Ge-hen'-na. Hell. HEAVEN-HELL.
geist [G.] (gaist). Spirit. SAGACITY-INCAPACITY.
gelasma, anerithmon [Gr.] (gel'-as-ma, a-nê'-rithmon). Innumerable laughter, said of the waves of the ocean. [Æschylus, *Prometheus Vinctus,* 90.] RIVER-WIND.
gel'-a-tin. Substance obtained from animal tissue. VISCIDITY-FOAM.
gel-at'-i-nous. Like gelatin. VISCIDITY-FOAM.
geld. To castrate. ADDITION-SUBTRACTION, MIGHT-IMPOTENCE.
geld'-ing. A castrated horse. CONVEYER, MALE-FEMALE.
gel'-id. Coldness. HEAT-COLD.
ge-los'-co-py. Divination by the laugh. PROPHECY.
gem. Precious stone. GOODNESS-BADNESS, EMBELLISHMENT-DISFIGUREMENT.
gem'-i-nate. Coming in pairs. DOUBLING-HALVING.
gem"-i-na'-tion. The act of doubling. ASTRONOMY, BIOLOGY, DOUBLING-HALVING.
Gem'-i-ni. A constellation; the Twins. DUALITY; **O Gemini!** ASTONISHMENT-EXPECTANCE.
ge-mot'. Public meeting. GATHERING-SCATTERING.
gendarme [F.] (zhan-darm'). Uniformed and armed policeman. BELLIGERENT, JUDICATURE.
gen'-der. A grammatical distinction expressing the natural distinction of sex. DIVISION, NOUN; **feminine gender,** NOUN; **masculine gender,** NOUN; **neuter gender,** NOUN.
gen"-e-a-log'-ic-al. Pertaining to genealogy. ETHNOLOGY.
gen"-e-al'-o-gy. Pedigree. CONTINUITY-INTERRUPTION, PARENTAGE-PROGENY.
gen'-er-al. Common; the highest army officer. CHIEF-UNDERLING, HABIT-DESUETUDE, UNIVERSALITY-PARTICULARITY; **caviare to the general,** TASTE-VULGARITY; **general breaking up,** HEALTH-SICKNESS; **general favorite,** FAVORITE-ANGER; **general information,** KNOWLEDGE-IGNORANCE; **general meaning,** MEANING-JARGON; **general public,** HUMANITY; **general run,** HABIT-DESUETUDE.
gen"-er-al-is'-si-mo. Commander-in-chief. CHIEF-UNDERLING.
gen"-er-al'-i-ty. Majority. MEDIUM, UNIVERSALITY-PARTICULARITY.
gen'-er-al-i-za"-tion. The act of grouping particulars into a class. ADMISSION-EXCLUSION, RATIOCINATION-INSTINCT.
gen'-er-al-ize. To make general. UNIVERSALITY-PARTICULARITY.
gen'-er-al"-ly. Without detail. HABIT-DESUETUDE.
gen'-er-al-ship. Ability as a military commander. CONDUCT, FIGHTING.
gen'-er-ate. To produce. CREATION-DESTRUCTION, FERTILITY-STERILITY.
gen"-er-a'-tion. The process of producing. CREATION-DESTRUCTION, HUMANITY, PERIOD-PROGRESS, RELATIONSHIP-RENEWAL; **rising generation,** PARENTAGE-PROGENY; **spontaneous generation,** CREATION-DESTRUCTION; **wise in one's generation,** SAGACITY-INCAPACITY.

gen'-er-a-tive. Possessing power to produce. FER-TILITY-STERILITY.

gen'-er-a''-tor. That which generates. ELECTRICITY, MAKER-DESTROYER.

ge-ner'-ic. Wide in application. UNIVERSALITY-PARTICULARITY.

gen''-er-os'-i-ty. Liberality. BENEFACTOR-EVILDOER, CHARITABLENESS-MALEVOLENCE, GENEROSITY-FRUGALITY, GIVING-RECEIVING, UNSELFISHNESS-SELFISHNESS.

GENEROSITY—FRUGALITY.

Bounteousness.
Bountifulness. } Liberality in bestowing gifts or favors.

Bounty. Liberal and generous giving.

Charity, etc. Liberality in bestowing gratuitously. See CHARITABLENESS.

Generosity. The quality of giving freely, heartily, and self-sacrificingly.

Hospitality. Reception and entertainment of guests or strangers with kind and generous liberality.

Liberality. The quality of being generous, bounteous, and open-handed.

Munificence. Giving or bestowing with extraordinary liberality.

GENEROSITY—Verbs.

Be liberal, etc. See *Adjectives.*

Bleed freely. To induce to pay or draw money from.

Give *carte blanche.* To give unlimited authority.

Open one's purse-strings, etc. To disburse. See OUTLAY.

Shower down upon. To bestow upon freely.

Spare no expense. Grudge nothing.

Spend freely. Be liberal.

GENEROSITY—Adjectives.

Bounteous.
Bountiful. } Liberal in bestowing gifts or favors.

Charitable, etc. Generous; liberal in giving to the poor. See CHARITABLENESS.

Free. Liberal.

Free-handed.
Free-hearted. } Liberal; generous.

Full-handed. Liberal.

Generous. Giving freely and abundantly.

Handsome. Large and liberal, of a gift.

Hospitable. Treating strangers with kindness and without reward.

Large-hearted. Generous.

Liberal. Bestowing with a free hand.

Munificent. Very liberal in giving or bestowing.

Open-handed. Giving freely.

Open-hearted. Frank; generous.

Overpaid. Paid very generously.

Princely. Munificent.

Ungrudging. Freely giving; liberal.

Unsparing. Liberal.

FRUGALITY—ADJECTIVES—*Continued from Column 2.*

Sparing. Parsimonious; chary.

Thrifty. Thriving by industry and frugality.

Underpaid. Paid too little.

FRUGALITY—Adverbs.

Ne quid nimis [L.]. Wisely moderate.

Sparingly, etc. In a sparing manner. See *Adjectives.*

FRUGALITY—Phrase.

Adde parum parvo, magnus acervus erit [L.]. Add little to little, a great heap will be.

Care. Watchful regard or attention with a view to safety or prosperity.

Economy. Avoidance of all waste and extravagance in the management of affairs; household law.

Frugality. A system of habitual saving, cutting off all indulgences.

Good housewifery. Careful management of domestic affairs.

Husbandry. Domestic economy.

Parsimony. Excessive and unreasonable saving for the sake of saving.

Prevention of waste. Economy.

Retrenchment. The act of lessening expenses.

Savingness. The quality of being frugal.

Thrift. Economical management seeking to earn and save.

Thriftiness. The quality of being thrifty.

FRUGALITY—Associated Nouns.

Cheese parings and candle ends. Crumbs from cheese cutting, and small ends of candles, not generally used, but used by frugal persons.

Economist. One who manages concerns with frugality.

Saveall. Anything which saves fragments, or prevents waste or loss; a device for holding the ends of candles.

Savings. Something kept from being expended.

FRUGALITY—Verbs.

Be economical, etc. To be careful in management.

Cut one's coat according to one's cloth. To live within one's means.

Economize. To expend frugally.

Feather one's nest. To provide for oneself.

Husband. To manage with frugality.

Invest money. To put money in a place where it yields profit.

Keep within compass. To keep within one's limits.

Look after the main chance. To seek for that direction in which profit seems most readily obtainable.

Make both ends meet. To make one's income suffice without running into debt.

Meet one's expenses. To be able to pay for what one buys.

Pay one's way. To pay one's expenses.

Provide against a rainy day.
Provide for a rainy day. } To get ready for a day of adversity.

Put out to interest. To loan money for a fixed price.

Retrench. To lessen, as one's expenses.

Save. To be economical.

Save against a rainy day.
Save for a rainy day. } To make preparations for a day of adversity.

Save money. To put aside money.

FRUGALITY—Adjectives.

Careful. Provident; giving good heed.

Chary. Not liberal.

Economic.
Economical. } Managing with frugality.

Frugal. Saving unnecessary expense.

Parsimonious, etc. Excessively frugal. See EXTRAVAGANCE-AVARICE.

Saving.
Spare. } Frugal; economical.

(Continued on Column 1.)

---

gen'-er-ous. Kind; plentiful. GENEROSITY-FRUGALITY, HUMANITARIANISM-MISANTHROPY, UNSELFISHNESS-SELFISHNESS.

gen'-e-sis. Beginning. BEGINNING-END, CREATION-DESTRUCTION, RATIONALE-LUCK.

gen'-et. A small Spanish horse. CONVEYER.

ge-net'-ic. Pertaining to creation. CREATION-DESTRUCTION.

ge'-ni-al. Pleasant. CREATION-DESTRUCTION, HEAT-COLD, PLEASURABLENESS-PAINFULNESS, READINESS-RELUCTANCE, SENSUALITY-SUFFERING.

ge''-ni-al'-i-ty. State of being genial. LIGHTHEARTEDNESS-DEJECTION, READINESS-RELUCTANCE.

ge-nic'-u-la''-ted. Having knee-like protuberances. ANGULARITY.

gen'-i-tal. Pertaining to animal-generation. CREATION-DESTRUCTION.

gen'-i-tive. Case in grammar denoting the relation indicated in English by the possessive, or the preposition *of.* NOUN.

gen'-i-tor. Progenitor. PARENTAGE-PROGENY.

gen'-i-ture. Birth. CREATION-DESTRUCTION.

ge'-nius. Exceptional ability. ADEPT-BUNGLER, MIND-IMBECILITY, SAGACITY-INCAPACITY, SKILL-UNSKILFULNESS; **evil genius,** JOVE-FIEND; **genius for,** SKILL-UNSKILFULNESS; **genius loci,** SECURITY-IN-

SECURITY; **genius of a language**, LANGUAGE; **good genius**, BENEFACTOR - EVILDOER, FRIEND - FOE, JOVE-FIEND; **tutelary genius**, ANTAGONIST-ASSIST-ANT.

genossen ich habe, das irdische Glück, ich habe gelebt und geliebet [G.] (ge-nos'-sen iH ha'-be, das ir-dish'-e glük, iH ha'-be ge-lêbt' unt ge-lî'-bet). I have tasted the good of earth, I have lived and loved. CONTENTEDNESS-DISCONTENTMENT.

genre [F.] (zhan·r). Any art illustrating common life. PAINTING.

gens de même famille [F.] (zhan· de mêm fa-mîy'). "Birds of a feather." LIKENESS-UNLIKENESS.

gent. Gentleman. GENTILITY-COMMONALTY, TASTE-VULGARITY.

gen-teel'. Well-bred. CITY, GENTILITY-COMMONALTY, SOCIETY-LUDICROUSNESS; **genteel comedian**, ACTING; **genteel comedy**, ACTING.

gen'-tile. A person not a Jew. GODLINESS-DISBELIEF, ORTHODOXY-HETERODOXY.

gentilhomme [F.] (zhan'-ti-yom'). Gentleman. MALE-FEMALE, UPRIGHTNESS-DISHONESTY.

gen'-til-ism. Paganism. ORTHODOXY-HETERODOXY.

gen-til'-i-ty. State of being genteel. GENTILITY-COMMONALTY, POLITENESS-IMPOLITENESS, SOCIETY-LUDICROUSNESS.

GENTILITY—COMMONALTY.

Aristocracy. A government of the best; a privileged order controlling a State.
Baronetcy. The title and dignity of a baronet.
Birth. Inherited rank or social standing; good family.
Condition. Grade or rank; high or comparatively high social standing.
Dignity. Elevated office, giving a high rank in society; title of a nobleman.
Distinction. Eminence; elevation of rank in society.
Donship. The quality or rank of a gentleman or knight.
Gentility. Good extraction; dignity of birth.
Haut monde [F.]. The high world; the upper ranks of society.
High descent. Noble extraction; lofty lineage.
High life. Upper position in society; high social state.
Knighthood. The order or fraternity of knights.
Marquisate. The dignity or lordship of a marquis.
Nobility. Those who hold patents of peerage.
Noblesse [F.]. Persons of noble rank collectively.
Optimacy. A noble or privileged class.
Order. Social position as a basis of distinction; a class of persons.
Peerage. The body of peers; the rank of a peer.
Quality. Social status; persons of rank collectively.
Queenhood. The state, character, or dignity suitable for a queen.
Queenliness. Stateliness; the quality of having the bearing of a queen.
Rank. Station in society; high degree or position.

GENTILITY—*Figurative.*

Blood. High birth; good extraction.
"Every inch a king." Noble and stately. [Shakespeare, *Lear*, IV, vi.]
Magni nominis umbra [L.]. The shadow of a great name, Pompey [Lucian, 1, 135.]
Pur sang [F.]. Pure blood; of noble birth.

GENTILITY—*Denotations.*

Better sort. Superiors in social rank.
Élite [F.]. The select circle.
Fashionable world. The people of polite society.
Gentlefolk. } Persons of good family.
Great folks. }
House of Lords. { One of the legislative bodies of the British Government, composed of members who have an heredi-
House of Peers. { tary title to their seats.
Lords spiritual and temporal. The House of Lords of England, made up of members holding seats by virtue of their clerical offices, and those holding by hereditary title.
Magnates. Men of high rank and wealth.
Notabilities. Persons of note.
Notables. Members of the nobility.
Optimates [L.]. Persons of highest rank and importance.
Primates. Persons of highest rank and importance.
Squirearchy. English country gentlemen collectively.
Upper classes. } Persons of the higher ranks of society.
Upper ten thousand. }

GENTILITY—*Associated Nouns.*

Aristocrat. One of a select governing class.
Big-wig. A person of importance, like judges who wore official wigs.
Celebrity. A distinguished or famous person.
Don. Spanish title of nobility; a general title of respect.
Gentleman. A well-bred and honorable man.
Gentry. Persons possessed of landed property.
Grandee [Sp.]. A Spanish nobleman; a man of great rank.
Great man. A man of eminence.
Hidalgo [Sp.]. A nobleman of the lowest class.

Bourgeoisie [F.]. The middle classes of a country.
Commonalty. The common people; the lower classes.
Democracy. A government in which the people collectively rule.
Demos [Gr.]. The people; the mass.
Hoi polloi [Gr.]. The commonalty; multitude.
Obscurity. State of being unknown to fame; common existence.
Proletariat [F.]. The laboring classes; the workingmen.

COMMONALTY—*Associated Nouns.*

Barbarism. Rudeness of manner.
Barbarity. The conduct or breeding of uncivilized persons.
Barbarousness. State of being rude and uncultivated.
Canaille [F.]. The rabble.
Chaff. The lowest, worthless class of people.
Common herd. People outside the ranks of polite society.
Dregs of society. } The coarse, untrained class of people.
Dregs of the people. }
Fæx populi [L.]. The dregs of the people.
Great unwashed. The careless, unrefined class of people.
Hesterni Quirites [L.]. Romans of yesterday.
Hoc genus omne [L.]. All of this sort.
Horde. The great mass of people.
Humbler classes. } The mass of people below the ranks of wealth and
Humbler orders. } polite society.
Ignobile vulgus [L.]. The rude multitude.
Low company. }
Low condition. }
Low life. } The common people.
Low society. }
Lower classes. } The mass of people below the ranks of polite society.
Lower orders. }
Mass of society. } The ordinary class of people.
Mass of the people. }
Mob. The lowest classes of people.
No one knows. } People of little account.
No one knows who. }
Pantisocracy. The government of all by all.
Pessoribus orti [L.]. People of low birth.
Profanum vulgus [L.]. The common people.
Rabble. } The lower class of people.
Rabblerout. }
Rank and file. The whole body of common people.
Residuum of society. } The people below the ranks of polite society.
Residuum of the people. }
Riffraff. The common people: used contemptuously.
Rout. A miscellaneous crowd of people.
Scum of society. } The lowest classes of the people.
Scum of the people. }
Small fry. People not considered in polite society.
Swinish multitude. The uneducated, unrefined class of people.
Tag, rag, and bobtail. The rabble.
The crowd. }
The general. }
The many. }
The masses. }
The million. } The main body of people as distinguished from the
The mobility. } rulers or influential classes.
The multitude. }
The peasantry. }
The people. }
The populace. }
Vermin. Low, disreputable persons.
Vulgar herd. The unrefined people.

GENTILITY—COMMONALTY—*Continued.*

GENTILITY—Associated Nouns—*Continued.*

Laureate. A poet publicly crowned with laurel in recognition of merit; the royal poet in England.

Lord. A general title of nobility in Great Britain.

Magnate. A man of rank and wealth.

Magnifico [It.]. A noble of Venice.

Man of distinction. A man who has attained eminence.

Man of mark. A notable man.

Man of rank. A man of lofty position.

Noble. A person of rank above a commoner.

Nobleman. A titled gentleman.

Patrician. In ancient Rome, one of the nobility.

Peer. A nobleman; a member of the House of Lords.

Personage of distinction. ⎫
Personage of mark. ⎬ A distinguished person; a conspicuous character.
Personage of rank. ⎭

Squire. An English landed proprietor of long standing.

Star. One who is conspicuous in a calling or profession.

Swell. A foppish fellow; a dandy.

Three-tailed bashaw. One of the highest Turkish dignitaries who is distinguished by three horse-tails waving from his lance.

GENTILITY—*Diminutive Nouns.*

Lordling. A little lord; a would-be lord.

Squireen. A small proprietor, or somewhat independent tenant, with a long lease.

GENTILITY—*Nouns of Titles.*

Ameer. The sovereign of Afghanistan.

Armiger. An armor-bearer.

Atheling. A young Saxon noble.

Banneret. A knight, because of a display of valor, permitted to use his pennon as a banner.

Baron. A rank of nobility next to a viscount.

Baroness. The wife of a baron.

Baronet. The title next below a baron.

Begum. A woman of rank in India.

Boyar. A Russian nobleman.

Count. A foreign title of nobility answering to English earl.

Countess, etc. Wife of a count, and in some cases the daughter of one.

Dame. A woman of high social position; a married or mature woman.

Duchess. Wife or widow of a duke, or the sovereign of a duchy.

Duke. An English peer of the highest rank above a marquis or a bishop.

Earl. A member of the British nobility next above a viscount and below a marquis.

Earldom. Dignity or lands of an earl.

Earlship. Office of an earl.

Effendi. A Turkish title of respect corresponding to *Sir* or *Mr.*

Emir. A title of dignity among the Turks and Arabs; a descendant of Mohammed.

Esquire. Armor-bearer of a knight; a title of dignity.

King, etc. The male ruler of a kingdom; a sovereign. See Chief.

Knight. A title next below that of a baronet; a young man admitted to the privilege of bearing arms.

Lady. Wife of a titled gentleman; the title of the daughters of peers of the first three grades.

Laird [Scot.]. A lord; a proprietor of a landed estate.

Marchioness. Wife of a marquis.

Margrave. Formerly a governor of a German border, now a nobleman corresponding to the English marquis.

Marquis. A titled nobleman next in rank below a duke.

Prince. A sovereign of a state or territory; son of a king or emperor.

Princess. Wife of a prince; daughter of a king.

Sahib. Master; lord; in India, a white man.

Scherif. Title given to descendants of Mohammed through Ali and Fatima; given also to chiefs of Mecca and Medina.

Seignior. A lord, used in countries of Southern Europe.

Signor. An Italian title equivalent to *Sir* or *Mr.*

Thane. Originally a warrior companion of a king or chief; later a freeman possessed of some property.

Vavasour. The rank of a principal vassal next below a baron.

Viscount. A titled nobleman below an earl and above a baron.

Waldgrave. A title of German nobility.

GENTILITY—*Verbs.*

Be noble, etc. To be high in excellence or worth; be exalted in rank. See *Adjectives.*

GENTILITY—*Adjectives.*

Aristocratic. Very dignified; haughty; connected with the upper classes

COMMONALTY—*Figurative Nouns.*

Bœotian. Dull fellow. [From Bœotia, despised at Athens.]

Brown, Jones, and Robinson. Middle class people.

Cinderella. Down-trodden worth; the heroine of a fairy tale.

Goth. One destitute of taste for the fine arts.

Hewers of wood and drawers of water. Laborers of the lowest class.

Hottentot. A savage or brutal man.

King Mob. The common crowd.

Mr. Snooks. Typical name of a man of the middle class in England.

Philistine. According to Matthew Arnold, the middle class of England who are ignorant and narrow-minded. [Bible.]

Rough diamond. A person of intrinsic worth under a rude exterior.

Tony Lumpkin. In Goldsmith's *She Stoops to Conquer,* an ignorant and noisy country squire.

Vandal. Ruthless plunderer; one who wilfully destroys monuments of art and literature.

Yahoo. A person of low and vicious instincts. [Swift, *Gulliver's Travels.*]

Zulu. An uneducated, unrefined person; a South African native.

COMMONALTY—*Representative Nouns.*

Adventurer. One who takes risks; an unprincipled schemer.

Barbarian. Rude, uncultured person.

Beggar. One who is poor and asks charity.

Bog-trotter. One who trots over bogs; contemptuously applied to Irish peasantry.

Boor. A rustic; an ill-mannered, coarse man.

Boots. An under-servant in a hotel; youngest officer at a regimental mess.

Bourgeois [F.]. A townsman; a tradesman.

Bourgeois gentilhomme [F.]. Burgher turned gentleman. [Molière.]

Bumpkin. Awkward country fellow; stupid peasant.

Cad. A snob or vulgar person.

Caitiff. A base, mean, wicked wretch.

Carle. A bondman; a rude, rough man.

Chawbacon. A country lout; a bumpkin.

Chiffonnier [F.]. A rag-picker.

Chuff. A surly man; a coarse, fat-cheeked fellow.

Churl. A low-bred, surly fellow; a rustic.

Cinder-wench. A woman who rakes into heaps of ashes for cinders.

Clod. A dull, stupid fellow.

Clod-hopper. A plowman; rustic; lout.

Clown. A fool or jester; a countryman.

Cockney. One having certain peculiarities of uneducated Londoners; a milksop.

Commoner. One under the rank of nobility.

Countryman. One living in the country; a rustic.

Cub. A boy or girl, in contempt; ill-mannered youth.

Curmudgeon. One who is miserly or churlish.

Demi-monde [F.]. A genteel name for the select class of prostitutes.

Democrat. A friend to popular government.

Epicier [F.]. Grocer; chandler.

Fellah. In Egypt, Syria, etc., a peasant.

Gaberlunzie. A privileged beggar. [Scot.]

Gaffer. An old countryman; a foreman of laborers.

Gamin [F.]. An idle street-boy.

Gent. One who has the vulgar show but not the qualifications of a gentleman.

Gossoon. In Ireland, a big, clumsy boy.

Grisette [F.]. Tradesman's wife or daughter; a Parisian working-girl.

Groundling. A spectator in a theater pit; a base person.

Hind. A servant; husbandman; peasant.

Hobnail. A clownish person; in contempt.

Jade. A vicious woman; hussy; wench.

Kern. An idle person or vagabond; a cateran.

Longshoreman. A stevedore; one who lives near water, existing by fishing, etc.

Looby. A dull, lazy fellow; a clumsy person.

Loon. A stupid person; good-for-nothing fellow.

Lout. An awkward, ungainly fellow.

Low fellow. A coarse, uneducated, vicious person

Man of straw. One employed as an irresponsible tool or as a fraudulent surety.

Muckworm. A miser.

Moujik. A Russian peasant.

Mudlark. One who cleans sewers; a dirty child.

Mushroom. An upstart; one of low origin who suddenly becomes prominent.

Nobody. A person of no importance.

Novus homo [L.]. Among Romans one who has come into prominence from obscurity.

GENTILITY—COMMONALTY—*Continued.*

GENTILITY—Adjectives—*Continued.*

Comme il faut [F.]. As it should be.
Courtly, etc. Elegant in manners; befitting a court. See SOCIETY.
Exalted. Elevated in position or rank.
Genteel. Well-bred or refined.
Gentlemanlike. Befitting a gentleman; courteous.
High-born. Of lofty descent.
High caste. One of patrician birth.
Highly respectable. Worthy of esteem and honor.
Noble. Exalted in rank; most worthy.
Of gentle blood. Descended from noble stock.
Of rank, etc. Of eminence or dignity. See *Nouns.*
Patrician. Of noble or aristocratic lineage.
Princely. Like a prince; royal; dignified.
Titled. Having a title, as of nobility.
Well-born. Not of mean or common birth.

GENTILITY—*Adverb.*

In high quarters. In aristocratic circles.

GENTILITY—*Phrase.*

Ich dien [G.]. I serve. [Motto of the Prince of Wales.]

COMMONALTY—Adjectives—*Continued from Column 2*

Homely. Plain; not polished.
Homespun. Plain in manner or style; not elegant.
Ignoble. Of low birth or family; base.
Loutish. Clumsy; awkward.
Low. Mean or humble in rank; unrefined.
Low-born. Born in humble life.
Low-minded. Mean in mind or disposition.
Mean. Of humble antecedents; worthy of no respect.
Menial. Pertaining to servants; servile.
Mushroom. Resembling a mushroom; upstarting.
No great shakes, etc. Nothing extraordinary; of little worth. See CONSEQUENCE-INSIGNIFICANCE.
Obscure. Of humble condition; lowly.
Of low extraction.
Of low origin.
Of low parentage.
Of mean extraction. } Of low and humble birth.
Of mean origin.
Of mean parentage.
Plebeian. Relating to the common people.
Proletarian. Pertaining to the lower or lowest classes of society.
Raffish. Resembling the rabble; worthless.
Risen from the ranks. Ascended into prominence from among the lowly.
Rude. Coarse in manners or behavior.
Rustic. Pertaining to the country; plain; untaught.
Scrubby. Small and mean; inferior.
Snobbish. Pertaining to a snob.
Sorry. Poor; mean; worthless.
Subaltern. Inferior; subordinate.
Uncivilized. Lacking refinement; coarse.
Underling. Low; inferior.
Unknown to fame. Not known to the world.
Unlicked. Rough; uncultured.
Untitled. Not having a name of distinction or dignity.
Vile. Of little worth; base; depraved.
Vulgar. Pertaining to common people; inelegant.

COMMONALTY—Representative Nouns—*Continued*

One of the people. One who sympathizes with the masses.
Pariah. An outcast; one despised by society.
Parvenu [F.]. One newly risen into notice or power.
Peasant. Rural laborer; a rustic; a swain.
Plebeian. One of the common people.
Plowboy. One who assists in plowing; a country boy.
Plowman. One who manages a plow; a rustic.
Pot-walloper. One who cleans kitchen vessels, etc.; scullion.
Prolétaire [F.]. One whose only capital is his labor.
Proletary. A common person; one of the lower orders.
Put. A rustic; a clown.
Raff. A rowdyish person.
Ragamuffin. A worthless or ragged fellow; a vagabond.
Republican. One of the great community of persons.
Roturier [F.]. A person without rank; a plebeian.
Rough. A rude and violent person; a ruffian.
Rustic. An inhabitant of the country.
Ryot. In India, a farmer; peasant.
Sans culotte [F.]. A revolutionary anarchist; a communist.
Savage. An uncivilized person; a fierce, merciless being.
Scrub. One who labors hard and lives meanly; a sorry fellow.
Serf. One attached to the soil and transferred with it; loosely a peasant.
Skip-jack. An upstart; a lackey.
Slubberdegullion. A mean, base wretch.
Snob. One who apes gentility; a scab, said of a workingman.
Swain. A rustic gallant; a lover.
Tatterdemalion. A ragged, dirty fellow; a ragamuffin.
Tike. An uncouth fellow.
Tiller of the soil. A farmer; a hard-working man.
Tramp. An idle wanderer; a vagrant.
Tyke. A selfish, snarling fellow; a vulgar person.
Underling. An inferior person or agent; a mean fellow.
Unlicked cub. Unmannerly or uncultivated person; raw.
Upstart. One who puts on an arrogant tone or bearing.
Vagabond. One without a settled home; a wanderer; a vagrant.
Villain. }
Villein. } A member of the lowest order of persons who were not free
Vulgar fellow. One of the common people.
Yokel. A countryman; a bumpkin.

COMMONALTY—*Adjectives.*

Barbaresque. Barbaric in form or style.
Barbarian. Uncivilized and cruel.
Barbaric. Destitute of refinement.
Barbarous. Wild; brutal; savage.
Base. Of humble or ignoble birth; of low station
Base-born. Born out of wedlock.
Beggarly. Miserably poor; mean; sordid.
Below par. Inferior in position or rank.
Boorish. Awkward and rude in manners.
Born within sound of Bow-bells. Having the characteristics of a cockney.
Brutish. Like a beast; ferocious.
Churlish. Like a churl; rude; sordid.
Clownish. Coarse and ill-bred.
Cockney. Related to or like a vulgar Londoner.
Common. Commonplace; vulgar; coarse; low.
Dunghill. Sprung from the dunghill; base; mean.
Earth-born. Mean or ignoble.

(*Continued on Column* 1.)

COMMONALTY—*Verbs.*

Barbarize. To make barbarous.
Be ignoble, etc. Be unworthy or degraded in character or purpose;
be low-born. See *Adjectives.*
Be nobody, etc. Be a person of no importance. See *Nouns.*

COMMONALTY—*Adverb.*

Below the salt. Those beyond the saltcellar at table; interior in rank.

COMMONALTY—*Phrases.*

Dummode sit dives Barbarus ipse placet [L.]. Provided only he is rich, a very barbarian pleases. [Ovid, *Art of Love*, 2, 276.]
Filius terræ [L.]. Son of the soil. [Perseus, 6, 57]
Fruges consumere nati [L.]. Born to consume the fruits. [Horace, *Epistles*, 1, 2, 27.]
Giuoco di mano, giuoco di villano [It.]. Practical jokes are the jokes of low folks.

---

gentium, jus [L.] (jen'-shi-um, jus). The law of nations. LAW-LAWLESSNESS.
gen'-tle. Mild. EXCITABILITY-INEXCITABILITY, HARSHNESS - MILDNESS, LOUDNESS - FAINTNESS; SWIFTNESS - SLOWNESS, TURBULENCE - CALMNESS,

gentle blood, EXCITABILITY-INEXCITABILITY; **gentle hint,** ENLIGHTENMENT-SECRECY; **gentle slope,** PARALLELISM-INCLINATION.
gen'-tle-folk". Well-bred people. GENTILITY-COMMONALTY.

gen'-tle-man. A well-bred man. GENTILITY-COMMON-ALTY, MALE-FEMALE, UPRIGHTNESS-DISHONESTY; **gentleman of the press,** MISSIVE-PUBLICATION; **the old gentleman,** ANGEL-SATAN; **walking gentleman,** ACTING.

gen'-tle-man-like. Gentlemanly. GENTILITY-COMMON-ALTY, POLITENESS-IMPOLITENESS, UPRIGHTNESS-DISHONESTY.

gen'-tle-man-li-ness. The conduct or character of a gentleman. SOCIETY-LUDICROUSNESS.

gen'-tle-man-ly. Acting like a gentleman. SOCIETY-LUDICROUSNESS.

Gen-too'. A Hindu. ORTHODOXY-HETERODOXY.

gen'-try. People of good birth. GENTILITY-COMMON-ALTY; **landed gentry,** HOLDER.

gen''-u-flec'-tion. Bending of the knee. DEVOTION-IDOLATRY, ELEVATION-DEPRESSION, POLITENESS-IMPOLITENESS, PRESUMPTION-OBSEQUIOUSNESS, RE-GARD-DISRESPECT, YIELDING.

gen'-u-ine. Not counterfeit. GOODNESS-BADNESS, NATURE-ART, TRUTH-ERROR.

gen'-u-ine-ness. Quality of being genuine. NATURE-ART.

genus irritabile vatum [L.] (jĭ'-nus ir-ri-tab'-i-lî vê'-tum). The irritable tribe of bards. POETRY-PROSE.

ge'-o-de'-sia. Same as geodesy. MENSURATION.

ge-od'-e-sy. Determination of size and figure of the earth. MENSURATION, UNIVERSE.

ge''-o-det'-i-cal. Pertaining to geodesy. MENSURATION.

ge''-o-det'-ics. Same as geodesy. MENSURATION.

ge-og'-e-ny. The study of the formation of the earth. MENSURATION.

ge-og'-ra-phy. Description of the earth. ETHNOLOGY, POSITION.

ge-ol'-o-gy. Science of the structure of the earth. GEOLOGY, ORGANIZATION-INORGANIZATION.

GEOLOGY.

Geology. The science that treats of the structure and constitution of the globe, of the action of its physical forces, and the history of its structural development.

GEOLOGY—*Associated Words.*

Algonkian. A stratum of the earth's crust.
Anticline. Bend in stratified rock with the convex side upward.
Argillaceous. Of the nature of clay.
Bad lands. Waste lands of horizontal strata curiously eroded.
Basin. Oval or round depression in the land.
Breccia. Angular fragments of rock cemented together.
Cambrian period. Period during which some of the lowest strata of rock were formed.
Carboniferous period. Period characterized by luxuriant land-vegetation.
Cleavage. Division of rock into layers parallel or transverse to the plane of bedding.
Conglomerate. Rocks composed of rounded fragments cemented together.
Coral. The solid secretion of certain small forms of animal life.
Cordillera. The entire system of sub-parallel mountain ranges that borders a continent.
Cretaceous period. Period marked by its chalk formations.
Delta. Deposit at the mouth of a river.
Devonian period. Period characterized by its fish-life.
Dike. Mass of igneous rock which has intruded into and fills a fissure in other rocks.
Dip. Angle which a stratum makes with the horizon.
Dome. Large vertical shaft of a cavern.
Dynamical geology. The study of the laws and actions of agencies that have produced geologic changes.
Earthquake. Shaking of the ground.
Erosion. The wearing away of rocks by water, wind, etc.
Eruption. Emission of smoke, etc., through the crust of the earth, as by a volcano.
Fault. A fracture of strata.
Ferruginous. Impregnated or coated with oxide of iron.
Fissility. Quality of being easily split in the direction of the grain.
Fissure. Cleft; a narrow opening.
Fold. Bend in a stratum with steeply inclined sides.
Fossil. Organic body preserved in solid rock.
Geanticlinal. Extensive upward flexure of the earth's crust.
Geyser. Hot spring throwing up water at intervals.

Glacier. Field of ice moving slowly down a slope.
Ground-moraine. A deposit of sand gravel under a glacier.
Igneous rock. Rock formed from a molten state.
Joint. Plane dividing a rock transverse to the bedding-plane.
Jurassic period. The period next preceding the Cretaceous.
Laccolith. Lava intruding between strata and lifting the overlying part into domes.
Lava. Melted rock intruding between strata or ejected from the crust of the earth.
Lithology. The science of the microscopic characters of rocks.
Loess. Deposit of loam in the Quaternary period.
Mesozoic period. Period remarkable for the production of reptiles.
Metamorphism. Recrystallization of the constituents of rocks.
Mountain range. Series of connected mountains.
Obsidian. An acid glassy volcanic rock.
Outcrop. Stratum sticking out of the surface of the ground.
Overlap. The condition when a stratum rests on rock older than a stratum immediately beneath the first stratum.
Paleontology. Science of fossil organisms.
Paleozoic period. The period next beyond the Mesozoic, including the ages of amphibians, fishes, and invertebrates.
Paragenesis. Branch of chemical geology treating of the order of succession of the formation of mineral species.
Permian period. The most recent division of the Paleozoic period.
Petrology. Science of rocks.
Physiographical geography. Description of nature.
Plication. The folding of a stratum.
Precambrian period. The most remote of the geologic periods.
Pyroclastic rocks. Rocks formed from the fragmentary ejecta of volcanoes.
Quaternary period. The last of the geologic periods.
Schistosity. Quality of splitting easily.
Scoria. Lava of coarse, cellular structure.
Sedimentary rocks. Rocks formed by deposits of sediment from water.
Shale. Kind of clayey rock easily split with the grain.
Stratification. The deposit of sediments in layers.
Stratified rocks. Rocks formed in layers.
Stratum. Layer of rock, etc.
Strike. The compass-course of any horizontal line in the bedding-plane of a dipping stratum and at right angles to the dip.
Structural geology. Study of the formation and arrangement of rock-masses.
Talus. Sloping mass of fallen fragments at the base of a cliff.
Terminal moraine. Debris left by a glacier at its lower terminus.
Tertiary period. Period between the Mesozoic and Quaternary periods.
Thrust. Crushing of the pillars in a mine by the weight of the roof.
Topography. The most important physical features of a region.
Triassic period. The most remote division of the Mesozoic period.
Volcano. Opening in the earth's surface throwing out lava.

ge'-o-man''-cer. One skilled in geomancy. SOOTH-SAYER.

ge-om'-e-try. Study of space and its relations. MEN-SURATION, NATURE-ART.

ge''-o-pon'-ics. The science of agriculture. DOMESTI-CATION-AGRICULTURE.

ge''-o-ra'-ma. A hollow sphere, on the inside of which is a representation of the earth. APPEARANCE-DIS-APPEARANCE.

ge''-or'-gics. Poems treating of husbandry. DOMESTI-CATION-AGRICULTURE.

ge-ot'-ic. Belonging to earth. UNIVERSE.

ger'-fal''-con. A large northern falcon. BENEFACTOR-EVILDOER.

germ. Embryo. BEGINNING-END, CAUSE-EFFECT, DE-SIGN, PREPARATION-NONPREPARATION.

ger'-man. Having the same grandparents. RELATION-SHIP; **cousin german,** RELATIONSHIP.

ger-mane'. Pertinent. HARMONY-DISCORD.

ger'-mi-nal. Pertaining to a germ. CAUSE-EFFECT.

ger'-mi-nate. To begin to grow. ENLARGEMENT-DIMI-NUTION; **germinate from,** CAUSE-EFFECT.

ger''-mi-na'-tion. The act of sprouting. BIOLOGY, ENLARGEMENT-DIMINUTION.

ger''-ry-man'-der. To redistrict unfairly; from Gov. Gerry, Mass. RULE-LICENSE, TRUTHFULNESS-FRAUD.

gest. Joke. ACTION-PASSIVENESS.

ges-ta'-tion. Pregnancy. CREATION-DESTRUCTION, PREPARATION-NONPREPARATION, TRANSFER.

ges-tic′-u-late. To use gestures in speaking. SIGN.

ges-tic″-u-la′-tion. A motion of the body or limbs intended to illustrate speech. SIGN.

ges′-ture. Action in speaking. ACTING, ENLIGHTEN-MENT-SECRECY, SIGN.

get. To become; to obtain. CONVERSION, CREATION-DESTRUCTION, GAIN; **get ahead,** ADVANCE-RETRO-GRESSION, INCREASE-DECREASE, LEADING-FOLLOW-ING; **get a head of,** SUPREMACY-SUBORDINACY; **get along,** ADMISSION-EXPULSION, ADVANCE-RETROGRES-SION; **get along with you,** ADMISSION-EXPULSION, COMMISSION-ABROGATION; **get a sight of,** KNOWL-EDGE-IGNORANCE, SIGHT-BLINDNESS; **get at,** DIS-COVERY, GAIN-LOSS; **get away,** ADMISSION-EXPUL-SION, APPROACH-WITHDRAWAL; **get back,** ADVANCE-RETROGRESSION, ARRIVAL-DEPARTURE, GAIN-LOSS; **get better,** BETTERMENT-DETERIORATION, HEALTH-SICKNESS, WEARINESS-REFRESHMENT; **get by heart,** REMEMBRANCE-FORGETFULNESS; **get down,** ASCENT-DESCENT, NUTRIMENT-EXCRETION; **get for one's pains,** RECOMPENSE-PUNITION; **get home,** ARRIVAL-DEPARTURE; **get in,** GATHERING-SCATTERING, GAIN-LOSS; **get into harness,** PREPARATION-NONPREPARA-TION; **get into the way of,** HABIT-DESUETUDE; **get into trouble,** SUCCESS-FAILURE; **get loose,** UNION-DIS-UNION; **get near,** APPROACH-WITHDRAWAL; **get off,** ARRIVAL-DEPARTURE, ESCAPE; **get on,** ADVANCE-RETROGRESSION, WELFARE-MISFORTUNE; **get out,** ADMISSION-EXPULSION, INJECTION-EJECTION, PUB-LICITY; **get over,** CONTENTEDNESS-DISCONTENTMENT, RENOVATION-RELAPSE, SUCCESS-FAILURE; **get over the ground,** ADVANCE-RETROGRESSION, SWIFTNESS-SLOWNESS; **get ready,** PREPARATION-NONPREPARA-TION; **get rid of,** COMMISSION-ABROGATION, COMMIS-SION-RETIREMENT, GAIN-LOSS, RELEASE-RESTRAINT, RESCUE; **get the best of,** SUCCESS-FAILURE; **get through,** BEGINNING-END, COMPLETION-NONCOMPLE-TION, CONDUCT, OUTLAY-INCOME; **get to,** ARRIVAL-DEPARTURE, REMOTENESS-NEARNESS; **get together,** GATHERING-SCATTERING; **get up,** ACTIVITY-INDO-LENCE, ASCENT-DESCENT, EDUCATION-LEARNING, ELEVATION-DEPRESSION, EXCITATION, PREPARATION-NONPREPARATION, TRUTHFULNESS-FALSEHOOD; **get you gone,** ADMISSION-EXPULSION.

gew′-gaw. Bauble. CONSEQUENCE-INSIGNIFICANCE, EMBELLISHMENT-DISFIGUREMENT, TASTE-VULGAR-ITY.

gewonnen, so zeronnen, wie [G.] (ge-von′-nen, zo tser-on′-nen, vî). As won, so flown; "light come, light go." AFFLUENCE-PENURY, EXTRAVAGANCE-AVA-RICE.

gey′-ser. A spouting, hot spring. GEOLOGY, RIVER-WIND.

ghast′-ly. Hideous. BEAUTY-UGLINESS, COLOR-ACHROMATISM, SANGUINENESS-TIMIDITY.

ghat. A mountain pass. BREADTH-NARROWNESS.

Ghet′-to. The Jews' quarter of a city. CITY, DWELLER-HABITATION.

ghost. Demon. JOVE-FIEND, LIFE-CORPSE, MIND-IMBECILITY, SIGHT-DIMSIGHTEDNESS; **give up the ghost,** LIFE-DEATH; **Holy Ghost,** DIVINITY; **needs no ghost to tell us,** MANIFESTATION-LATENCY; **pale as a ghost,** COLOR-ACHROMATISM, SANGUINENESS-TIMID-ITY.

ghost′-like″. Like a ghost. BEAUTY-UGLINESS, JOVE-FIEND.

ghost′-ly. Relating to specters. DIVINITY, JOVE-FIEND, MIND-IMBECILITY.

ghoul. Grave robber. BENEFACTOR-EVILDOER, JOVE-FIEND.

ghyll. Gully. RIVER-WIND.

gi′-ant. Person of great size. GREATNESS-LITTLENESS, HEIGHT-LOWNESS; **giant-like,** GREATNESS-LITTLE-NESS; **giant refreshed,** STRENGTH-WEAKNESS, WEARI-NESS-REFRESHMENT; **giant's strides,** REMOTENESS-NEARNESS, SWIFTNESS-SLOWNESS.

giaour. Infidel. GODLINESS-DISBELIEF, ORTHODOXY-HETERODOXY.

gib′-ber. To talk disconnectedly. SPEECH-INARTICU-LATENESS.

gib′-ber-ish. Senseless talk. MEANING-JARGON, WORD-NEOLOGY.

gib′-bet. Gallows. RECOMPENSE-PUNITION, RECOM-PENSE-SCOURGE.

gib′-bet–gab″-ble. Gabble. TALKATIVENESS-TACI-TURNITY.

gib-bos′-i-ty. A round prominence. CONVEXITY-CON-CAVITY.

gib′-bous. Irregularly round. ROUNDNESS, CON-VEXITY-CONCAVITY; **gibbous phase,** ASTRONOMY.

gib′-cat″. Castrated cat. FAUNA-FLORA, MALE-FEMALE.

gibe. To mock. REGARD-DISRESPECT.

gibier de potence [F.] (zhi-bi-ê′ de po-tan·s′). Game for the gibbet. EXCULPATION-PUNITION, GOOD MAN-BAD MAN.

gid′-di-ness. Dizziness; levity. SAGACITY-INCAPACITY.

gid′-dy. Foolish. BIGOTRY-APOSTASY, DETERMINA-TION-VACILLATION, HEED-DISREGARD, SANENESS-LUNACY, RECKLESSNESS-CAUTION, SAGACITY-INCA-PACITY, SKILL-UNSKILFULNESS.

gid′-dy-brained′. Light-headed; silly. HEED-DISRE-GARD.

gid′-dy-head″. Foolish person. SAGE-FOOL.

gid′-dy-paced″. Reeling. AGITATION.

gift. Something given. GIVING-RECEIVING, HOLDING-EXEMPTION, MIGHT-IMPOTENCE, SKILL-UNSKILFUL-NESS; **gift of the gab,** SPEECH-INARTICULATENESS, TALKATIVENESS-TACITURNITY; **look a gift-horse in the mouth,** DESIRE-PARTICULARNESS, THANKFUL-NESS-THANKLESSNESS

gift′-ed. Having special endowments. SKILL-UN-SKILFULNESS.

gig. Boat. CONVEYANCE-VESSEL.

gi-gan′-tic. Very large. GREATNESS-LITTLENESS, HEIGHT-LOWNESS, REGULARITY-IRREGULARITY.

gig′-gle. To titter. JUBILATION-LAMENTATION.

gild. To cover with yellow substance; an association. ASSOCIATION, BEAUTY-UGLINESS, BLUENESS-ORANGE, COVER-LINING, EMBELLISHMENT-DISFIG-UREMENT, TRIBUNAL.

gild′-hall″. Meeting-place of a gild. MARKET.

gild′-ing. Adorning. EMBELLISHMENT-DISFIGURE-MENT.

Gil′-e-ad. Region east of the river Jordan. **Balm in Gilead,** ALLEVIATION-AGGRAVATION, SANGUINENESS-HOPELESSNESS.

Giles's Greek. St. Giles's Greek. WORD-NEOLOGY.

gill. Ravine. RIVER-WIND.

gil′-lie. Man-servant. CHIEF-UNDERLING.

gilt. Gilding material. EMBELLISHMENT-DISFIGURE-MENT.

gim′-bals. Mechanism allowing something to be hori-zontal under all conditions. REVOLUTION-EVOLU-TION.

gim′-crack″. Something cheap. CONSEQUENCE-IN-SIGNIFICANCE, EMBELLISHMENT-DISFIGUREMENT, SOCIETY-LUDICROUSNESS, STRENGTH-WEAKNESS, TOUGHNESS-BRITTLENESS.

gim′-let. Small tool for boring. PERFORATOR-STOP-PER.

gimp. Decorative trimming. BEAUTY-UGLINESS, CLEANNESS-FILTHINESS.

gin. A trap; a machine; alcoholic drink. JOVE-FIEND, INSTRUMENT, NUTRIMENT-EXCRETION, TEE-TOTALISM-INTEMPERANCE, TRUTHFULNESS-FRAUD.

gin′-drink″-er. One who drinks gin. TEETOTALISM-IN-TEMPERANCE.

gin'-ger-bread''. Cake flavored with ginger. STRENGTH-WEAKNESS, TASTE-VULGARITY.

gin'-ger-ly. Cautiously. CAREFULNESS-CARELESSNESS, TURBULENCE-CALMNESS.

ging'-ham. A cotton dress-goods. MATERIALS.

gin'-gle. See JINGLE.

gin'-pal''-ace. Gaudily furnished barroom. DWELLER HABITATION.

giovine santo, diavolo vecchio [It.] (jo-vĭ'-nè san'-to, dĭ-a-vo'-lo vech'-o). Young saint, old devil. GODLINESS-UNGODLINESS.

gip'-sy. One of a certain wandering tribe. GULL-DECEIVER, WAG, WAYFARER-SEAFARER; **gipsy lingo,** WORD-NEOLOGY.

gi-raffe'. A long-necked animal. HEIGHT-LOWNESS.

gir'-an-dole. Bracket-light. LUMINARY-SHADE.

gir'-a-sol. Opal. EMBELLISHMENT-DISFIGUREMENT.

gird. To surround. ENVIRONMENT-INTERPOSITION, REGARD-DISRESPECT, STRENGTH-WEAKNESS, UNION-DISUNION; **gird up one's loins,** PREPARATION-NONPREPARATION, STRENGTH-WEAKNESS.

gird'-er. Supporting-beam. CONNECTIVE, SUSPENSION-SUPPORT.

gir'-dle. That which encompasses. CIRCLE-WINDING, CONNECTIVE, DRESS-UNDRESS, ENCLOSURE, ENVIRONMENT-INTERPOSITION, OUTLINE; **put a girdle round the earth,** CIRCUITION.

girl. Female child. INFANT-VETERAN, MALE-FEMALE.

girl'-hood. Time of being a girl. INFANCY-AGE.

girl'-ish. Youthful. INFANT-VETERAN.

girt. To gird; encircled. OUTLINE.

girth. Strap. CONNECTIVE, OUTLINE.

gis-arm'. Armor. WEAPON.

gist. The principal part. CONDITION-SITUATION, CONSEQUENCE-INSIGNIFICANCE, MEANING-JARGON.

gît, ci [F.] (zhî, sî) Here lies. LIFE-FUNERAL.

git'-tern. Zither. MUSICAL INSTRUMENTS.

giuoco di mano, giuoco di villano [It.] (ju-o'-co dî ma'-no, ju-o'-co dî vîl-la'-no). Practical jokes are the jokes of low folks. GENTILITY-DEMOCRACY, REPUTATION-DISCREDIT.

give. To transfer from one to another. GIVING-RECEIVING, HARDNESS-SOFTNESS, HEAT-COLD, PRICE-DISCOUNT; **give a black eye,** RECOMPENSE-PUNITION; **give advice,** ADVICE; **give aid,** OBSTRUCTION-HELP; **give a dressing,** RECOMPENSE-PUNITION; **give a horse his head,** LIBERTY-SUBJECTION; **give a loose to mirth,** LIGHTHEARTEDNESS-DEJECTION; **give and take,** COMMUTATION-PERMUTATION, COMPENSATION, COMPOSITION, EXCHANGE, REPRISAL-RESISTANCE, RIGHT-WRONG; **give a sigh,** JUBILATION-LAMENTATION; **give a turn to,** MUTATION-PERMANENCE; **give away,** GIVING-RECEIVING, KEEPING-RELINQUISHMENT, MATRIMONY-CELIBACY; **give back,** TAKING-RESTITUTION; **give bail,** SECURITY; **give birth to,** CREATION-DESTRUCTION, LIFE-DEATH; **give** *carte blanche,* LEAVE-PROHIBITION; **give chase,** QUEST-EVASION; **give consent,** CONSENT; **give expression to,** PHRASE; **give forth,** PUBLICITY; **give in,** LITIGATION-YIELDING; **give in charge,** RELEASE-RESTRAINT; **give in custody,** RELEASE-RESTRAINT; **give into,** CONSENT; **give it one,** APPROVAL-DISAPPROVAL; **give light,** LIGHT-DARKNESS; **give notice,** ENLIGHTENMENT-SECRECY, SIGN, WARNING; **give one credit,** FAITH-MISGIVING; **give one the slip,** ESCAPE; **give one to understand,** ENLIGHTENMENT-SECRECY; **give out,** ADMISSION-EXPULSION, GIVING-RECEIVING, PUBLICITY; **give over,** DISCONTINUANCE-CONTINUANCE, QUEST-ABANDONMENT, SANGUINENESS-HOPELESSNESS; **give over to the foe,** PATRIOTISM-TREASON; **give place to,** COMMUTATION-PERMUTATION, QUEST-EVASION; **give play to the imagination,** FANCY; **give quarter,** COMPASSION-RUTHLESSNESS, HARSHNESS-MILDNESS; **give rise to,** CAUSE-EFFECT; **give security,** SECURITY; **give the advantage,** EQUALITY-INEQUALITY; **give the go by,** OBSERVANCE-NONOBSERVANCE, QUEST-EVASION, TRUTHFULNESS-FRAUD; **give the mind to,** HEED-DISREGARD; **give the sacrament,** CEREMONIAL; **give tongue,** PUBLICITY, SPEECH-INARTICULATENESS, VOCALIZATION-MUTENESS; **give up,** CHOICE-REJECTION, CLEARNESS-OBSCURITY, COMMISSION-RETIREMENT, KEEPING-RELINQUISHMENT, QUEST-ABANDONMENT, SANGUINENESS-HOPELESSNESS, TAKING-RESTITUTION, YIELDING; **give up the ghost,** LIFE-DEATH; **give way,** CONCEIT-DIFFIDENCE, LIGHTHEARTEDNESS-DEJECTION, PLEASURE-PAIN, STRENGTH-WEAKNESS, TOUGHNESS-BRITTLENESS, YIELDING.

giv'-en. Stated. CONDITION-SITUATION, GIVING-RECEIVING, HYPOTHESIS; **given over,** LIFE-DEATH; **given time,** OPPORTUNENESS-UNSUITABLENESS; **given to,** HABIT-DESUETUDE.

giv'-er. One who gives. GIVING-RECEIVING.

giv'-ing. The act of transferring from one to another. GIVING-RECEIVING; **giving thanks,** DEVOTION-IDOLATRY.

GIVING—RECEIVING.

Accordance. The act of giving something due and appropriate.
Award. A decision by judges as to the giving of something.
Bestowal. The act of conferring as a gift.
Cession. The act of giving away.
Communication. Something given in a message.
Concession. The act of giving something up.
Consignment. The act of sending to be given.
Delivery. The act of giving from one person to another.
Dispensation. A divine giving.
Donation. A giving for some public purpose.
Endowment. A giving for the support of some public institution.
Giving. The act of bestowing voluntarily without expectation of return.
Investiture. The act of giving legal possession.
Investment. The act of laying out money productively.
Presentation. A public giving.
Presentment. A giving in a formal or ceremonious manner.

GIVING—*Nouns of Cause.*

Act of grace. The act of giving something not earned.
Almsgiving. Giving to the poor.
Charity. Giving to supply the bodily wants of the needy.
Generosity. Giving with self-sacrificing heartiness.
Grace. Giving unmerited favor.
Liberality. The act of being very free in giving.

Acceptance. The act of receiving what is offered.
Acquisition. Anything received as a result of effort or labor. See GAIN.
Admission. The state of being received into something. See ADMISSION.
Income. That gain which proceeds from labor, business, capital, etc.
Receiving. Obtaining from another in any manner.
Reception. The act of being received.
Recipiency The state of having received something.
Suspiciency. The state of having received an influence.

RECEIVING—*Nouns of Agent.*

Accipient. One who receives a gift.
Almsman. One who receives alms.
Assignee. One who has received property in trust or for himself.
Beneficiary. One who receives a gift, benefit, or advantage.
Devisee. One who receives something transmitted by a will.
Donee. One who receives a donation.
Feofee. One who receives a corporeal hereditament by delivery.
Grantee. One who receives a grant.
Legatee. One who receives a legacy.
Legatary. One who receives a bequest.
Lessee. The person to whom a lease is granted.
Pensionary. One who receives a pension.
Pensioner. One who lives on or receives a pension.

GIVING—RECEIVING—*Continued.*

GIVING—*Denotations, etc.*

Allowance. A portion or amount granted for some particular purpose.

Alms. A gift for the relief of the poor.

Amortization. The act of conveying lands and tenements to a corporation having perpetual succession.

Appanage. A portion of land given by a king for the support of his younger sons.

Backshish. The Oriental term for a tip or gratuity.

Bait. A gift given as a bribe.

Benefaction. A charitable deed.

Bequest. A legacy of personal property.

Bonanza. A lucky operation, or profitable investment.

Bonus. An allowance additional to what is usual or stipulated.

Boon. A good thing bestowed.

Bounty. The gifts bestowed by a generous giver.

Bribe. Any gift or advantage, given or promised, for the purpose of influencing one's conduct or judgment.

Cadeau [F.]. A present.

Christmas box. A Christmas present in England.

Consideration. The thing given or done by a party to a contract.

Contribution. That which is given.

Devise. A gift of lands by a last will and testament.

Dole. That which is shared in portions.

Donation. That which is given as a gift.

Donative. A benefice bestowed by a patron or founder.

Dotation. The act of making or sharing a dowry.

Douceur [F.]. A small present.

Drink-money. A gift used to buy drink.

Easter-offering. A gift given in commemoration of the Easter festival.

Fairing. A present.

Favor. An act or course of kindness; a small gift.

Fee. A payment for services done. See RECOMPENSE.

Free gift. A gift given without any obligation to give.

Gift. Something voluntarily given without expectation of return.

Grant. Anything given or bestowed.

Gratuity. That which is given without demand or claim.

Ground-bait. Bait strewn on the ground to attract fish to the place.

Handsel. A gift to secure favor or good luck.

Help. Assistance given.

Honorarium. A voluntary fee for professional services.

Immolation. A sacrificial offering.

Largess. A generous gift.

Legacy. Property, especially personal property, given by will.

Oblation. Anything offered in worship.

Offering. That which is given.

Offertory. A contribution to aid church-work.

Peace-offering. Any gift given voluntarily as a pledge of peace and good-will.

Pour boire [F.]. Drink-money.

Present. That which is presented or given.

Sacrifice. A tribute or gift to God as an expression of thanksgiving.

Sportule. A small alms.

Subscription. A written promise to give.

Subsidy. Aid granted by the government to some enterprise productive of public benefit.

Subvention. A grant in aid of something.

Tribute. Money given as an acknowledgment of submission.

Trink-geld [G.]. Drink-money.

Vail. Money given to servants as a gratuity.

Voluntary conveyance. A voluntary grant of land. See ALIENATION.

Voluntary settlement. A payment of any charge or debt without compulsion.

Will. The instrument by which a person makes a disposition of his property to take effect after his death.

GIVING—*Nouns of Agent.*

Donor. One who makes a donation.

Feoffor. One who makes a grant of land by deed and delivery.

Giver. One who gives.

Grantor, etc. One who grants. See *Verbs*.

Settlor. One who settles estates.

GIVING—*Verbs.*

Accommodate with. To give as a favor.

Accord. To give as due and appropriate.

Administer. } To give something necessary or required.
Administer to. }

Afford. To yield.

Allow. To give as an allowance.

Assign. To give a special designation to.

RECEIVING—NOUNS OF AGENT—*Continued*

Recipient. One who receives something.

Relessee. One to whom an instrument of release has been given.

Sportulary. One living on alms or charitable institutions.

Stipendiary. One who receives wages or salary.

RECEIVING—*Verbs.*

Accept. To receive something offered.

Accrue. To receive as a natural growth.

Acquire. To receive as a result of effort or labor. See GAIN.

Admit. To receive into.

Be received. Be accepted; be obtained in any way.

Catch. To receive as the result of a temporary effort.

Come in. To be received.

Come to hand. To be received by one himself.

Come to one. To become one's property.

Fall into one's hand. To be received with no especial effort on the part of the receiver.

Fall to one. To come into one's possession.

Fall to one's lot. To receive as one's fate in life.

Fall to one's share. To receive as one's portion.

Go into one's pockets. To accrue to one's financial benefit.

Have given. To receive without a return being expected.

Have given to. To be received by any one without a return being expected.

Pass into one's hand. To be received by one person from another.

Pocket. To receive into the pocket.

Put into one's purse. } To give.
Put into one's pocket. }

Receive. To obtain from another in any manner.

Take. To receive by putting forth exertion. See TAKING.

Take in. To receive into.

Take off one's hands. To rid another of something by receiving it from him.

Touch. To take by force.

RECEIVING—*Adjectives.*

Given. See GIVING.

Not given. Not receive as a gift.

Received. See *Verbs*.

Receiving. See *Verbs*.

Recipient. Ready to receive.

Second-hand. Received after use by another.

Suscipient. Receiving as an effect or influence.

Unbestowed. Not given.

GIVING—*Verbs—Continued.*

Award. To give for merit or excellence in a competition.

Bequeath. To give as a legacy.

Bestow. To confer as a gift.

Bribe. To make a gift to corrupt a public officer.

Cast. To throw away as a gift.

Cede. To give up.

Communicate. To give by intercourse.

Concede. To give up in consequence of a command.

Confer. To give as a benefit.

Consign. To give into the care of another.

Contribute. To give in aid of some object.

Deal out. To give out in a number of portions.

Deliver. } To give into the power or possession of another.
Deliver over. }

Devise. To give by a last will.

Dispense. To give out in a diffuse manner.

Dispose of. To make over.

Dole out. To give in shares.

Endow. To give a permanent fund or income to.

Entrust. To give in trust.

Favor with. To give as a favor.

Fork out. To give over, as hay, manure, etc.

Furnish. To give a supply of.

Furnish its quota. To give its due share.

Give. To bestow without expecting a return.

Give away. To confer on without an equivalent.

Give out. To distribute.

Grant. To give in a formal manner.

Grease the palm. To bribe.

Hand. To give with the hand.

Hand over. To give over with the hand.

Help. To give means towards.

Immolate. To give as a sacrifice.

GIVING—Verbs—*Continued*

Impart. To give part of.
Indulge with. To give way unduly to the inclinations of
Invest. To give out money in investments
Lavish. To give prodigally.
Leave. To give by will.
Make a present. To bestow a gift
Make over. To transfer.
Mete out. To give out by measure.
Minister to. To give necessities to.
Offer. To give with solemnity or in worship See Proffer
Part with. To give away with reluctance.
Pass. To give from one person to another
Pass over. To give over.
Pay. To give as payment. See Settlement.
Pour on. To give freely.
Present. To give formally.
Put into the hands of. To give into the control of

Render. To give what is due.
Sacrifice. To give as a religious offering.
Settle upon. To give by permanent grant.
Shed. To give freely and diffusely.
Shower down upon. To give as freely as rain
Spare. To give as something saved.
Spend. To give out money for things bought. See Outlay.
Squeeze out. To give in grudgingly.
Subscribe. To promise to give by writing one's name beneath a pledge.
Supply. To give something needful or desirable.
Thrust upon. To force a gift upon.
Tickle the palm. To bribe.
Tip. To give to a servant as a favor
Turn over. To hand over.
Vest in. To give ownership of, as property, to a person.
Yield. To give as the result of labor or investment.

Giving—*Adjectives*

Allowable. That may be given.
Allowed. That is given.
Charitable. In the habit of giving out of charity.
Communicable. That may be given by intercourse.
Concessional. Yielding.
Eleemosynary. Relating to giving alms.

Given. Bestowed without expectation of return.
Giving. Bestowing without expectation of return.
Gratis. Given absolutely for nothing.
Sportulary. Pertaining to giving small alms.
Tributary. Pertaining to giving tribute.

Giving—*Phrases.*

Auctor pretiosa facit [L.]. The giver adds value to the gift.

Ex dono [L.]. By the gift.

giz′-zard. The second stomach of birds. Contents-Receiver; **stick in one's gizzard,** Favorite-Anger.
gla′-brous. Without hair. Smoothness-Roughness
gla′-cial. Pertaining to glaciers. Heat-Cold.
gla′-ci-ate. To change to ice. Heating-Cooling.
gla′-ci-er. Ice-mass. Geology, Heat-Cold.
gla′-cis. Sloping ground in front of a fort. Attack-Defense.
glad. Pleased. Pleasurableness-Painfulness, Pleasure-Pain; **glad tidings,** Tidings-Mystery; **would be glad of,** Desire-Distaste.
glade. Open tract in the woods. Aperture-Closure, Convexity-Concavity, Luminary-Shade.
glad′-den. To make glad. Alleviation-Aggravation, Lightheartedness-Dejection.
glad′-i-a″-tor. Professional fighter in the days of Rome. Belligerent.
glad″-i-a-to′-ri-al. Pertaining to gladiators. Strife-Peace, Variance-Accord.
glad′-ness. Pleasure of mind. Pleasure-Pain.
glad′-some. Pleasing. Pleasure-Pain, Pleasurableness-Painfulness.
glair. White of an egg. Viscidity-Foam.
glaive. See Glave.
glam′-our. Charm. Devotion-Magic.
glance. To look quickly. Sight-Blindness, Sign; **glance at,** Approval-Disapproval, Enlightenment-Secrecy, Heed-Disregard; **glance off,** Aim-Aberration, Concentration-Radiation; **see at a glance,** Onlooker, Sagacity-Incapacity.
gland. An organ. Anatomy.
glare. Dazzle. Light-Darkness, Sight-Blindness, Sight-Dimsightedness, Visibility-Invisibility.
glar′-ing. Shining. Color-Achromatism, Magnitude-Smallness, Manifestation-Latency, Visibility-Invisibility.
glar′-ing-ly. Openly. Magnitude-Smallness.
glass. Hard transparent substance, formed by fusing silica with a metal. Contents-Receiver, Diaphaneity-Opaqueness, Dress-Undress, Optical Instruments, Toughness-Brittleness, **glass of fashion,** Society-Ludicrousness; **glass too much,** Teetotalism-Intemperance; **live in a glass house,** Security-Insecurity, Toughness-Brittleness, Visibility-Invisibility; **musical glasses,** Cohesion-Looseness, Musical Instruments; **see through a glass darkly,** Knowledge-Ignorance.

glass′-coach″. Coach with glass windows in it. Conveyance-Vessel.
glas′-ses. Spectacles. Optical Instruments.
Glass′-ite. A Christian of the Glassite sect. Orthodoxy-Heterodoxy.
glass tub′-ing. Tubes of glass. Chemistry.
glass′-ware″. Articles made of glass. Diaphaneity, Heating-Cooling.
glass′-y. Like glass. Color-Achromatism, Diaphaneity-Opaqueness, Light-Darkness, Light-Dimness, Smoothness-Roughness.
glau′-cous. Sea-green. Redness-Greenness.
glave. A kind of sword. Weapon.
glav′-er. To flatter. Adulation-Disparagement.
glaze. To give a glassy appearance. Smoothness-Roughness.
gla′-zier. One who applies glaze to pottery. Agent.
gleam. To emit light. Light-Darkness, Magnitude-Smallness.
glean. To collect; a collection. Choice-Rejection, Gain-Loss.
glean′-ings. That which has been collected with much labor. Choice-Rejection.
glebe. Land belonging to a church; land containing ore. Church, Fane, Ocean-Land.
glee. Gaiety. Lightheartedness-Dejection, Music, Pleasure-Pain.
gleek. To gibe. Regard-Disrespect.
glee′-some. Happy; joyous. Lightheartedness-Dejection.
glen. Small valley. Convexity-Concavity.
glib. Flippant. Difficulty-Facility, Faith-Misgiving.
glib′-ly. Smoothly. Talkativeness-Taciturnity.
glide. To move smoothly. Movement-Rest, Period-Progress, Traveling-Navigation; **glide into,** Conversion-Reversion
glim′-mer. To shine feebly. Knowledge-Ignorance, Light-Darkness, Light-Dimness, Visibility-Invisibility.
glim′-mer-ing. A faint view; shining faintly. Knowledge-Ignorance
glimpse. Glance. Knowledge-Ignorance, Sight-Blindness.
glint. To gleam. Light-Darkness.
glis′-ten. To shine. Light-Darkness.
glit′-ter. Sparkle. Light-Darkness, Pomp, Reputation-Discredit.

glit'-ter-ing. Sparkling. BRAWLER, POMP.

gloam. To become dark. FAVORITE-MOROSENESS.

gloar. To look at fiercely. ASTONISHMENT-EXPECTANCE, SIGHT-BLINDNESS.

gloat. To look at with malignant satisfaction. **Gloat on,** SENSUALITY-SUFFERING, SIGHT-BLINDNESS; **gloat over,** PLEASURE-PAIN, SENSUALITY-SUFFERING

glo'-ba''-ted. Globe-shaped. ROUNDNESS.

globe. Sphere. ROUNDNESS, UNIVERSE; **on the face of the globe,** UNIVERSE.

glo-bose'. Round. ROUNDNESS.

glo-bos'-i-ty. The quality of being round. ROUNDNESS.

glo'-bous. Spherical. ROUNDNESS.

glob'-u-lar. Round, like a ball. ROUNDNESS.

glob'-ule. A small globe. MAGNITUDE-SMALLNESS, ROUNDNESS.

glom''-er-a'-tion. State of being densely clustered. GATHERING-SCATTERING.

gloom. Duskiness. LIGHT-DARKNESS, LIGHTHEARTEDNESS-DEJECTION.

gloom'-y. Sad; dismal. LIGHTHEARTEDNESS-DEJECTION.

gloom'-y ho-ri'-zon. SANGUINENESS-HOPELESSNESS.

gloriæ incendium fax mentis [L.] (glo'-ri-î in-sen'-di-um, fax men'-tis). A burning desire for glory is a torch to the mind. MOTIVE-CAPRICE.

glo''-ri-a'-tion. Boasting. BRAGGING.

glo''-ri-fi-ca'-tion. The act of giving honor; state of being glorified. BRAGGING, DEVOTION-IDOLATRY, REPUTATION-DISCREDIT.

glo'-ri-fy. To honor; to praise. APPROVAL-DISAPPROVAL, DEVOTION-IDOLATRY, DIVINITY, REPUTATION-DISCREDIT.

glo'-ri-ous. Grand. REPUTATION-DISCREDIT, TEETOTALISM-INTEMPERANCE.

glo'-ry. Praise; brightness. DIVINITY, HEAVEN-HELL, LIGHT-DARKNESS, REPUTATION-DISCREDIT; **glory be to God,** DEVOTION-IDOLATRY; **glory in,** SELFRESPECT-HUMBLENESS; **King of Glory,** DIVINITY.

gloss. Brightness of surface. BEAUTY-UGLINESS, INTERPRETATION-MISINTERPRETATION, JUSTIFICATION-CHARGE, LIGHT-DARKNESS, PRETEXT, SMOOTHNESS-ROUGHNESS, TRUTHFULNESS-FABRICATION; **gloss of novelty,** NOVELTY-ANTIQUITY; **gloss over,** CAREFULNESS-CARELESSNESS, JUSTIFICATION-CHARGE, RATIOCINATION-INSTINCT, TRUTHFULNESS-FALSEHOOD.

glos'-sa-ry. Lexicon. WORD-NEOLOGY.

glos-sog'-ra-pher. Writer of explanatory notes. SCHOLAR-DUNCE, WORD-NEOLOGY.

glos-sol'-o-gist. Glossographer. SCHOLAR-DUNCE.

glos-sol'-o-gy. Comparative philology. LANGUAGE, WORD-NEOLOGY.

gloss'-y. See GLOSS. BEAUTY-UGLINESS, SMOOTHNESS-ROUGHNESS.

glot-tol'-o-gy. Philology. LANGUAGE.

glove. Covering for the hand. DRESS-UNDRESS; **take up the glove,** STRIFE-PEACE; **throw down the glove,** DEFIANCE.

glow. To give off light and heat. COLOR-ACHROMATISM, EMOTION, FORCE-WEAKNESS, HEAT-COLD, LIGHT-DARKNESS.

glow'-er. To scowl. FAVORITE-MOROSENESS, POLITENESS-IMPOLITENESS, SIGHT-DIMSIGHTEDNESS.

glow'-er-ing. Scowling. FAVORITE-MOROSENESS.

glow'-ing. Shining. BEAUTY-UGLINESS, BLUENESS-ORANGE, EXCITATION, FORCE-WEAKNESS, HEAT-COLD; **glowing terms,** FORCE-WEAKNESS.

glow'-worm''. Beetle displaying a phosphorescent light. LUMINARY-SHADE.

gloze. To flatter. ADULATION-DISPARAGEMENT, JUSTIFICATION-CHARGE.

glue. A sticky substance. COHESION-LOOSENESS, CONNECTIVE, VISCIDITY-FOAM.

glum. Sullen. CONTENTEDNESS-DISCONTENTMENT, FAVORITE-MOROSENESS, LIGHTHEARTEDNESS-DEJECTION.

glut. Oversupply. DESIRE-REPLETION, EXCESS-LACK.

glu'-ten. A tough substance made from wheat and similar grains. VISCIDITY-FOAM.

glu''-tin-os'-i-ty. Tenacity. VISCIDITY-FOAM.

glu'-ti-nous. Sticky. VISCIDITY-FOAM.

glut'-ton. An excessive eater. FASTING-GLUTTONY.

glut'-ton-ous. Given to excessive eating. FASTING-GLUTTONY.

glut'-ton-y. Habit of eating too much. FASTING-GLUTTONY, NUTRIMENT-EXCRETION.

glyc'-er-in. A sweet, oily liquid. FRICTION-LUBRICATION, PULPINESS-OIL.

glyph'-o-graph. To make impressions by glyphography; an impression so made. ENGRAVING.

glyph-og'-ra-phy. Process of making relief plates for printing. ENGRAVING.

glyp'-to-graph. A design cut on a gem. ENGRAVING.

glyp-tog'-ra-phy. Design cut on a gem. ENGRAVING.

glyp''-to-the'-ca. A collection of engravings. SCULPTURE.

gnarl. To snarl. CHARITABLENESS-MENACE, FAVORITE-ANGER.

gnarled. Knotted. SMOOTHNESS-ROUGHNESS, SOLIDITY-RARITY.

gnash. To snap the jaws together. **Gnash one's teeth,** FAVORITE-ANGER, JUBILATION-LAMENTATION.

gnat. A small fly. GREATNESS-LITTLENESS; **strain at a gnat,** BIGOTRY-APOSTASY.

gnaw. To bite off little by little. BETTERMENT-DETERIORATION, FRICTION-LUBRICATION, NUTRIMENT-EXCRETION, PLEASURABLENESS-PAINFULNESS.

gnaw'-ing. Constant biting; consuming. PLEASURE-PAIN; **gnawing pain,** SENSUALITY-SUFFERING.

gnome. Dwarf. JOVE-FIEND.

gno'-mon. A pin the shadow of which indicates the time on a dial. CHRONOLOGY-ANACHRONISM.

Gnos'-tic. An adherent of Gnosticism. ORTHODOXY-HETERODOXY.

Gnos'-ti-cism. The doctrines of the Gnostics. ORTHODOXY-HETERODOXY, THEOLOGY.

gnothi seauton [Gr.] (gno'-thi se-au-ton'). Know thyself. KNOWLEDGE-IGNORANCE, SAGACITY-INCAPACITY.

go. To depart. ADMISSION-EXPULSION, APPEARANCE-DISAPPEARANCE, APPROACH-WITHDRAWAL, ARRIVAL-DEPARTURE, COLOR-ACHROMATISM, ENTITY-NONENTITY, MOVEMENT-REST, SOCIETY-LUDICROUSNESS, VIGOR-INERTIA; **as things go,** HABIT-DESUETUDE; **come and go,** VIBRATION; **give the go by to,** CAREFULNESS-CARELESSNESS, OBSERVANCE-NONOBSERVANCE, QUEST-EVASION, TRUTHFULNESS-FRAUD; **go about,** CIRCUITION, ENTERPRISE, PUBLICITY; **go about your business,** ADMISSION-EXPULSION, COMMISSION-ABROGATION; **go across,** TRANSMISSION; **go after,** ANTECEDENCE-SEQUENCE, LEADING-FOLLOWING; **go against,** ANTAGONISM-CONCURRENCE, COOPERATION-OPPOSITION; **go ahead,** ACTIVITY-INDOLENCE, LEADING-FOLLOWING, PUSH-PULL, SWIFTNESS-SLOWNESS; **go all lengths,** DETERMINATION-VACILLATION, ENTIRETY-DEFICIENCY, TOIL-RELAXATION; **go astray,** TRUTH-ERROR, VIRTUE-VICE; **go away,** ADMISSION-EXPULSION, APPROACH-WITHDRAWAL, ARRIVAL-DEPARTURE, FUTURE-PAST; **go bad,** BETTERMENT-DETERIORATION; **go back,** ADVANCE-RETROGRESSION, FUTURE-PAST; **go bail,** SECURITY-INSECURITY; **go before,** ANTECEDENCE-SEQUENCE, LEADING-FOLLOWING; **go between,** ENVIRONMENT-INTERPOSITION, INSTRUMENT, MEDIATION; **go beyond,** TRANSCURSION-SHORTCOMING; **go by,** CONVENTIONALITY-UNCONVENTIONALITY, CRAFT-ARTLESSNESS, FUTURE-PAST, PERIOD-PROGRESS, TRANSCURSION-SHORTCOMING;

go by the board, MIGHT-IMPOTENCE; **go by the name of,** NAME-MISNOMER; **go deep into,** INVESTIGATION-ANSWER; **go down,** ASCENT-DESCENT, BETTERMENT-DETERIORATION, CONTENTEDNESS-DISCONTENT, EXCITABILITY-INEXCITABILITY; **go down with,** CONTENTEDNESS-DISCONTENTMENT, EXCITABILITY-INEXCITABILITY, FAITH-MISGIVING; **go farther and fare worse,** BETTERMENT-DETERIORATION, SKILL-UNSKILFULNESS; **go for nothing,** CONSEQUENCE-INSIGNIFICANCE, RATIOCINATION-INSTINCT; **go forth,** ARRIVAL-DEPARTURE, PUBLICITY; **go from one's word,** OBSERVANCE-NONOBSERVANCE; **go halves,** DOUBLING-HALVING, PARTICIPATION; **go hand in hand,** COEXISTENCE, SOLITUDE-COMPANY, VARIANCE-ACCORD; **go hard,** DIFFICULTY-FACILITY; **go in,** ENTRANCE-EXIT; **go in for,** DETERMINATION-VACILLATION, QUEST-EVASION; **go into,** ENTRANCE-EXIT, ESSAY, LETTER; **go mad,** SANENESS-LUNACY; **go near,** APPROACH-WITHDRAWAL; **go no further,** ENLIGHTENMENT-SECRECY; **go off,** ARRIVAL-DEPARTURE, BETTERMENT-DETERIORATION, LIFE-DEATH, MATRIMONY-CELIBACY, TURBULENCE-CALMNESS; **go on,** ADVANCE-RETROGRESSION, DISCONTINUANCE-CONTINUANCE, DURATION-NEVERNESS, PUSH-PULL; **go on forever,** ETERNITY-INSTANTANEITY, INFINITY; **go on ill,** WELFARE-MISFORTUNE; **go out of one's head,** REMEMBRANCE-FORGETFULNESS; **go over,** INVESTIGATION-ANSWER, PERSISTENCE-APOSTASY, REVERSAL, TRANSMISSION, UPRIGHTNESS-DISHONESTY; **go round,** CIRCUITION, REVERSAL; **go shares,** PARTICIPATION; **go smoothly,** DIFFICULTY-FACILITY; **go through,** ACTING, CIRCUITION, COMPLETION-NONCOMPLETION, CONDUCT, EXCITABILITY-INEXCITABILITY, INVESTIGATION-ANSWER, OCCURRENCE-DESTINY, TRANSMISSION; **go to,** ADVICE, AIM-ABERRATION, REMOTENESS-NEARNESS, TRAVELING-NAVIGATION; **go to pieces,** CREATION-DESTRUCTION; **go to sleep,** ACTIVITY-INDOLENCE, TOIL-RELAXATION; **go to war,** FIGHTING-CONCILIATION; **go up,** ASCENT-DESCENT; **go with,** ASSENT-DISSENT, VARIANCE-ACCORD; **go with the stream,** ASSENT-DISSENT, CONVENTIONALITY-UNCONVENTIONALITY, DIFFICULTY-FACILITY, PRESUMPTION-OBSEQUIOUSNESS.

goad. A pointed stick. MOTIVE-CAPRICE.

goal. Something aimed at. ARRIVAL-DEPARTURE, BEGINNING-END, MOVEMENT-REST, PURPOSE-LUCK; **reach the goal,** COMPLETION-NONCOMPLETION.

goat. A small horned animal. PURITY-RAKE, ZOOLOGY-BOTANY; **he goat,** MALE-FEMALE.

go-bang'. A game played on a checker-board. ENTERTAINMENT-WEARINESS.

gob'-bet. Mouthful. MAGNITUDE-SMALLNESS, NUTRIMENT-EXCRETION.

gob'-ble. Make a noise like a turkey; to eat too much CRY-ULULATION, FASTING-GLUTTONY.

gobemouche [F.] (gob-mush'). Silly person. GULL-DECEIVER, SAGE-FOOL.

go'-be-tween''. A middle-man. CONSIGNEE, INSTRUMENTALITY, MEDIATION.

gob'-let. Drinking vessel. CONTENTS-RECEIVER.

gob'-lin. Kobold. JOVE-FIEND.

go'-cart''. Hand-cart. CONVEYANCE-VESSEL.

God. The Creator of the universe. DIVINITY; **for God's sake,** PETITION-EXPOSTULATION; **God bless me,** ASTONISHMENT-EXPECTANCE; **God bless you,** ARRIVAL-DEPARTURE; **God forbid,** ASSENT-DISSENT, GAIN-LOSS; **God grant,** DEVOTION-IDOLATRY; **God knows,** KNOWLEDGE-IGNORANCE; **God's acre,** LIFE-FUNERAL; **God save the King,** PATRIOTISM-TREASON; **God's grace,** CHARITABLENESS-MALEVOLENCE; **God's love,** CHARITABLENESS-MALEVOLENCE; **God's will,** VOLITION-OBLIGATION; **God willing,** POSSIBILITY-IMPOSSIBILITY; **house of God,** FANE; **kingdom of God,** HEAVEN-HELL; **sons of God,** ANGEL-SATAN.

god. That which is worshiped. JOVE-FIEND; **household gods,** DWELLER-HABITATION; **tutelary gods,** SECURITY-INSECURITY.

god'-child''. A child for whom a person becomes sponsor at baptism. PARENTAGE-PROGENY.

god'-dess. Female deity; good or beautiful woman. JOVE-FIEND, LOVE-HATE.

god'-fa''-ther. A man who becomes sponsor for a child at baptism. PARENTAGE-PROGENY.

God'-fear''-ing. Having reverence for God and his laws. GODLINESS-UNGODLINESS.

God'-head The Trinity. DIVINITY

god'-like. Like God. VIRTUE-VICE.

god'-less. Ungodly. GODLINESS-DISBELIEF.

god'-li-ness. The character of being godly. GODLINESS-UNGODLINESS.

GODLINESS—UNGODLINESS.

Anointed. Consecrated to divine service.
Beauty of holiness. Godliness.
Consecration. The state of being set apart to the service and worship of God.
Devotion. Zealous application to religious duties.
Edification. The state of being built up or instructed in moral and religious knowledge.
Faith. Operative belief in the truths of religion.
Godliness. Character or state of being pious or godly.
Grace. The exercise of love, mercy and kindness.
Holiness. See *Adjectives*.
Humility. Lowliness of mind.
Odor of sanctity. Godliness.
Piety. Reverence of God and loving obedience to his will.
Prostration, etc. The act of kneeling or bowing in reverence and worship. See DEVOTION.
Religion. The reverent acknowledgment in both heart and act of the Supreme Being.
Religionism. Intense piety.
Religiousness. Deep devotion to the practise of godliness.
Reverence, etc. Profound respect, mingled with fear and affection for the Supreme Being. See REGARD.
Saintship. The qualities of a saint or godly person.
Sanctimony, etc. Scrupulous devoutness, especially outward or pretended holiness. See GODLINESS-UNGODLINESS.
Sanctitude. Holiness; sanctity.
Sanctity. The state of being morally pure.
Spiritual existence. Heavenly-mindedness.
Theism. The belief in God as both immanent and transcendent.

Austerity. Harsh discipline.
Backsliding. A falling away from faith or duty.
Bigotry, etc. Blind enthusiasm in favor of something. See BIGOTRY and MISJUDGMENT.
Blasphemy. Irreverence in speaking or writing of God.
Cant. Insincere use of religious phraseology.
Declension. A falling toward a worse state.
Desecration. The act of desecrating or profaning.
Formalism. Dependence on external forms in matters of religion.
Hardening. Confirming in wickedness or shame.
Hypocrisy, etc. The assumption of a false appearance of religion or virtue. See TRUTHFULNESS-FALSEHOOD.
Impiety. Disregard for the Supreme Being and his laws.
Irreverence. Want of respect for God and religion.
Lip-devotion. Prayer coming from the lips and not the heart.
Lip-reverence. Veneration consisting of words only.
Lip-service. Profession unaccompanied by practise.
Misdevotion. Mistaken devotion.
Odium theologicum [L.]. The hatred of theologians.
Perversion. Diversion from truth or right.
Pharisaism. Strict adherence to external forms of religion.
Pietism. Affectation of devotion.
Pious fraud. Religious pretension.
Precisianism. The state of being overprecise or ceremoniously exact in religious rites.
Profanation. Irreverent and disrespectful treatment of that which is sacred.
Profaneness. See *Adjectives*.
Profanity. The state of being profane; blasphemy.

GODLINESS—UNGODLINESS—*Continued.*

Unction. Religious fervor and tenderness.
Veneration. Respect for holy things mingled with awe.

GODLINESS—*Associated Nouns.*

Believer. One who gives credit to the truth of the Scriptures, as a revelation from God.
Christian. One who believes in Jesus Christ, and the truth as taught by Him.
Convert. A person who is won over to a creed or religious system in which he has not previously believed.
Devotee. One given wholly to religion.
Madonna. A picture of the Virgin Mary.
Notre Dame [F.]. Our Lady; the Blessed Virgin.
Pietist. One who makes a display of religious feeling.
Saint. A holy or godly person.
The believing.
The children of God.
The children of light. } The whole body of Christian believers.
The children of the kingdom.
The elect. Persons chosen as the objects of mercy or divine favor
The good. Those having admirable moral qualities.
Theist. One who believes in a personal God.
The just.
The righteous. } Persons free from wrong, guilt, or sin.

GODLINESS—*Theological Terms.*

Adoption. The state of being incorporated into God's family as a child.
Beatification. In the Roman Catholic Church, the pronouncing of a deceased person to be blessed.
Body and Blood of Christ. [*Matthew* xxvi, 26–28.]
Bread of Life. The Body of Christ.
Conversion. A change of heart evidenced by a new course of life and love to God.
Inspiration. A supernatural influence enabling men to receive and communicate divine truth.
Justification. The act of justifying or treating a sinful person as if righteous in the sight of God, for the sake of the merits of Jesus Christ.
Regeneration. The entering into a new spiritual life through the action of the Holy Spirit.
Salvation. The redemption of man by Jesus Christ from sin and condemnation and the bestowal on him of everlasting life and happiness.
Sanctification. The act of purifying one's thoughts and affections through the instrumentality of the Holy Spirit.
Theopathy. Capacity for religious worship or affections.

GODLINESS—*Verbs.*

Beatify. To make happy or supremely blessed.
Be converted. To have experienced conversion.
Believe. To be fully persuaded of the truths of religion.
Be pious. See *Adjectives.*
Consecrate. To set apart to the service or worship of God.
Convert. To produce conversion in.
Edify. To instruct or build up in moral or religious knowledge.
Enshrine. To cherish or preserve as sacred.
Have faith. See *Nouns.*
Inspire. To communicate by divine influence.
Receive Christ. To believe in Christ.
Regenerate. To produce regeneration.
Revere, etc. To look upon with reverence or profound respect and affection. See REGARD.
Sanctify. To make pure or cleanse from moral and spiritual corruption.

GODLINESS—*Adjectives.*

Adopted. Taken by adoption.
Believing. See *Verbs.*
Catholic. Universal.
Christian. Pertaining to Christ or Christianity.
Consecrated. See *Verbs.*
Converted. See *Verbs.*
Devoted. Showing strong attachment to religion.
Devout. Devoted to religion or religious duties.
Elected. Selected as an object of special mercy and favor.
Faithful. Strong in faith or belief.
Godfearing. Devout.
Godly. Pious; conformed to the law of God.
Heavenly-minded. Devout.
Holy. Morally excellent; pure in heart.

Reprobation. State of being abandoned to punishment without hope of pardon.
Sabbatarianism.
Sabbatism. } Strained observance of the Jewish Sabbath.
Sacerdotalism. Devotion to the interests of the priestly order.
Sacrilege. The crime of violating sacred things.
Sanctimoniousness. See *Adjectives.*
Sanctimony. Outward or assumed holiness.
Scoffing. See *Verbs.*
Sin, etc. The transgression of or want of conformity to the law of God. See VIRTUE-VICE.
Ungodliness. The character of having no reverence for God.

UNGODLINESS—*Associated Nouns.*

Bigot. A person who regards his own faith and views in matters of religion as unquestionably right.
Blasphemer. One who speaks with impious irreverence.
Children of darkness. People in a state of ignorance or error on religious subjects.
Devotee. A bigot.
Fanatic. A person who indulges in wild and extravagant notions of religion.
Formalist. One who rests in external religious forms, without the life and spirit of religion.
Hypocrite. One who feigns to be other and better than he is. See GULL-DECEIVER.
Mawworm. A hypocritical ranter in Bickerstaff's comedy of *The Hypocrite.*
Pharisee. A sect of Jews noted for their strict and formal observance of the rites and ceremonies of the elders; a person pretending to superior sanctity.
Pietist. One who makes a show of religious feeling; a hypocrite.
Precisian. One rigid or ceremonious in the observance of rules and forms; hence, one not religious at heart.
Purist. One who pretends to excessive purity.
Puritan. Members of the English Church who advocated simpler forms of faith and worship than those established by law; one strict in his religious life; originally, a term of ridicule.
Ranter. A raving declaimer on religious matters.
Religionist. One too zealously attached to a religion.
Sabbatarian. A strict observer of the Jewish Sabbath.
Sabbath-breaker. One who violates the law of the Sabbath.
Sacrilegist. One guilty of violating or profaning sacred things.
Saint. An ironical expression for an over-pious person.
Scoffer. One who speaks of religious subjects in derision.
Sinner, etc. One condemned by the law of God. See GOOD MAN-BAD MAN.
Sons of Belial.
Sons of men. } Wicked and depraved persons.
Sons of the wicked one.
Tartufe. A hypocritical priest, the hero of Molière's comedy of that name.
The evil.
The reprobate.
The unjust. } Sinners.
The wicked.
Worldling. One neglectful of his spiritual life, in his devotion to temporal pursuits and enjoyments.

UNGODLINESS—*Verbs.*

Be impious. See *Adjectives.*
Blaspheme. To utter blasphemy.
Commit sacrilege. See *Nouns.*
Desecrate. To violate the sanctity of.
Idolize. To worship an image as the representative of God.
Profane. To violate anything sacred, as the temple by money changers.
Revile. To abuse with contemptuous language.
Scoff. To manifest ridicule or contempt for.
Snuffle. To take offense; to talk through the nose sanctimoniously.
Swear, etc. To use profane language. See CHARITABLENESS-CURSE.
Turn up the whites of one's eyes. To get very angry, sanctimoniously

UNGODLINESS—*Adjectives.*

Bigoted. Unreasonably devoted to a creed, opinion, or party.
Blasphemous. Sacrilegious in the use of God's name.
Canting. Affectedly pious.
Desecrating. See *Verbs.*
Fanatical. Moved by intemperate zeal.
Hardened. Fixed in error or vice.
Hypocritical, etc. False in religious pretensions. See TRUTHFULNESS-FALSEHOOD.

GODLINESS—UNGODLINESS—*Continued.*

GODLINESS—Adjectives—*Continued.*

Humble.　Thinking lowly of oneself.
Inspired.　See *Verbs.*
Justified.　See *Verbs.*
Not of the earth.　Heavenly.
Pietistic.　Making an ostentatious display of religion.
Pious.　Having piety; religious.
Pure.　Free from moral defilement or guilt; innocent.
Regenerated.　See *Verbs.*
Religious.　Having religion, godly.
Reverent.　Showing due respect to religion.
Sacred.　Pertaining to religion or religious services.
Saintlike.　Resembling a saint.
Saintly.　Like a saint.
Sanctified.　See *Verbs.*
Seraphic.　Becoming a seraph; pure, sublime.
Solemn.　Connected with religion; characterized by seriousness.
Spiritual.　Controlled by the Divine Spirit; holy.
Unearthly.　Supernatural.

GODLINESS—*Phrase.*

Ne vile fano [L.].　Let there be nothing vile in the temple.

UNGODLINESS—*Continued from Column 2.*

UNGODLINESS—*Phrases.*

Giovine santo, diavolo vecchio [It.].　Young saint, old devil.
Ludere cum sacris [L]　To sport with things sacred.

DISBELIEF.

Antichristianity.　Opposition to the Christian religion.
Atheism.　Disbelief in the existence of God.
Deism.　The belief in God as transcendent only.
Disbelief.　The conviction that a statement or doctrine is false.
Doubt, etc.　Want of conviction referring either to matters of belief or practise.　See FAITH-MISGIVING.
Freethinking.　Disbelief in inspired religion.
Hylotheism.　The doctrine that identifies God with the material universe; pantheism.
Incredulity.　A withholding of belief; disbelief.
Incredulousness.　See *Adjectives*
Indevotion.　Lack of devotion.
Infidelity.　Want of belief in some religious system.
Irreligion.　Want of religion.
Laxity.　The state of lacking firmness and strictness in religion.
Materialism.　The doctrine of those who deny the existence of any object but matter.
Nihilism.　The doctrine that nothing can be known.
Pantheism.　The doctrine that nature is God.
Positivism.　A system of philosophy which excludes from philosophy everything except the natural phenomena and properties of knowable things.
Pyrrhonism.　Universal doubt.　[Pyrrho, a Greek philosopher.]
Quietism.　The doctrine that religion consists in the withdrawal of the mind from all worldly thoughts and interests and its constant employment in religious contemplation.
Rationalism.　The doctrine of those who deduce their religious beliefs from reason, as opposed to revelation.
Skepticism.　The doctrine that all knowledge is uncertain.
Unbelief.　Failure to admit or believe.
Ungodliness.　The quality or state of having no reverence for God.　See *Adjectives.*
Want of belief. }
Want of faith. }　Irreverence for God.

DISBELIEF—*Nouns of Agent.*

Alien.　One estranged from truth or the favor of God.
Atheist.　One who denies the existence of a God.
Deist.　One who believes in the existence of a God, but denies revealed religion.
Esprit fort [F.].　A freethinker.
Freethinker.　One who forms opinions independent of the authority of revelation or of the Church.
Gentile.　One neither a Jew nor a Christian; a worshiper of false gods.
Giaour.　An infidel, especially one who does not believe in the faith of the Mohammedans.
Heathen.　One who worships idols and denies the true God
Infidel.　One who does not believe in the inspiration of the Scriptures and the supernatural origin of Christianity.
Latitudinarian.　One who indulges unwarranted freedom in religious opinions.
Materialist.　One who denies the existence of spiritual substances.
Nazarene.　In the first and second centuries of Christianity, a Juda-

UNGODLINESS—Adjectives—*Continued.*

Impious.　Wickedly and boldly defiant of God and his law.
Irreligious, etc.　Wanting faith and godliness.　See GODLINESS-DISBELIEF.
Irreverent.　Lacking in due regard for the Supreme Being.
Mammon worship.　Devoted to money-getting.
Overrighteous.　Affectedly righteous.
Perverted.　Corrupted; led astray.
Pharisaical.　Resembling the Pharisees, hence hypocritical; self-righteous.
Pietistical.　Ostentatiously religious.
Priest-ridden.　Governed or controlled by priests.
Profane.　Not sacred; given to swearing.
Reprobate.　Morally depraved.
Righteous overmuch.　Overrighteous.
Sacrilegious.　Violating or profaning sacred things.
Sanctimonious.　Hypocritically or affectedly pious or saintly
Unctuous.　Insincerely fervid.
Unhallowed,　Not consecrated; unholy.
Unregenerate.　Not renewed in heart.
Unsanctified.　Not sanctified or made pure.

UNGODLINESS—*Adverbs.*

Under the cloak of religion; under the form of religion; under the guise of religion; under the mask of religion; under the pretense of religion.

(*Continued on Column 1.*)

GODLINESS—DISBELIEF

izing Christian who observed the law of Moses and held to certain heresies.
Nihilist.　One who believes that nothing can be known, or asserted to exist.
Positivist.　A believer in a system of philosophy which excluded everything but the natural phenomena or properties of knowable things.
Pyrrhonist.　An absolute skeptic.
Rationalist.　One who deduces his religious opinions from reason or the understanding as opposed to revelation.
Skeptic.　A person who doubts the existence or perfection of God, or the truth of revelation.
Unbeliever.　One who does not believe that the Bible is a divine revelation

DISBELIEF—*Verbs.*

Be irreligious.　See *Adjectives.*
Dechristianize.　To turn from Christianity.
Disbelieve.　To refuse to believe.
Doubt.　To be undecided as to belief.
Lack faith.　To be infidel.
Question, etc.　To raise a doubt concerning, etc　See FAITH-MISGIVING

DISBELIEF—*Adjectives*

Antichristian.　Opposed to Christianity.
Atheistic.　Denying the existence of God.
Carnal.　Relating to the body or its appetites.
Deistical.　Pertaining to deism.
Devoutless.　Wanting devotion.
Earthly.　Belonging to this world; not spiritual.
Faithless.　Not believing in God or religion
Freethinking.　Denying revealed religion.
Godless.　Without belief in the existence of God.
Graceless.　Gone away from divine grace.
Incredulous.　Not disposed to admit or believe
Indevout.　Not attentive to religion.
Irreligious.　Indifferent to things sacred
Lacking faith.　Not believing in.
Mundane.　Worldly as opposed to spiritual.
Skeptical.　Inclined to question the grounds for belief.
Unbelieving.　Not believing.
Unchristian.　Not believing in Christ
Unconverted.　Not turned to God.
Undevout.　Irreligious.
Ungodly.　Without faith in God.
Unhallowed. }
Unholy. }　Without reverence for God.
Unsanctified.　Not cleansed from sin.
Without God.　Irreligious.
Worldly.　Relating to this world or life; temporal.
Worldly-minded.　Ungodly

DISBELIEF—*Adverb.*

Irreligiously.　See *Adjectives.*

god'-ly. Pious. GODLINESS-UNGODLINESS, VIRTUE-VICE.

god'-moth"-er. A female sponsor. PARENTAGE-PROGENY.

god'-send". Good fortune looked upon as coming from God. GOOD-EVIL, WELFARE-MISFORTUNE

god'-ship. Deity. DIVINITY

God'-speed". Success. APPROVAL-DISAPPROVAL, ARRIVAL-DEPARTURE, CHARITABLENESS-MALEVOLENCE, POLITENESS - IMPOLITENESS, SANGUINENESS - HOPELESSNESS.

go'-er. Something swift. CONVEYER.

goes. See Go. As one goes, TRANSFER; here goes, ENTERPRISE.

Gog and Ma'-gog. Two effigies in the Guildhall, London. GREATNESS-LITTLENESS.

gog'-gle. To stare. SIGHT-BLINDNESS; goggle eyes, SIGHT-DIMSIGHTEDNESS.

gog'-gle-eyed". Having large prominent eyes. SIGHT-DIMSIGHTEDNESS.

gog'-gles. Kind of eye-protectors. OPTICAL INSTRUMENTS.

go'-ing. See Go. LIFE-DEATH, MOVEMENT-REST, TIDINGS-MYSTERY, UNIVERSALITY-PARTICULARITY; going on, COMPLETION-NONCOMPLETION, ENTIRETY-DEFICIENCY, OCCUPATION, OCCURRENCE-DESTINY.

Gol-con'-da. Mine of great city in India, famous for diamonds. AFFLUENCE-PENURY.

gold. A yellow metal. BLUENESS-ORANGE, CHEMISTRY, MONEY, YELLOWNESS-PURPLE; worth its weight in gold, GOODNESS-BADNESS; write in letters of gold, CONSEQUENCE-INSIGNIFICANCE.

gold'-en. Made of gold; valuable; best. YELLOWNESS-PURPLE; golden age, PLEASURE-PAIN, WELFARE-MISFORTUNE; golden apple, MOTIVE-CAPRICE; golden calf, AFFLUENCE-PENURY, DEVOTION-IDOLATRY, REVELATION-PSEUDOREVELATION; golden dream, FANCY, SANGUINENESS-HOPELESSNESS; golden mean, MEDIOCRITY, MEDIUM, MIDCOURSE-CIRCUIT, TURBULENCE-CALMNESS; golden opinions, APPROVAL-DISAPPROVAL, REPUTATION-DISCREDIT; golden rule, PRECEPT; golden season of life, INFANCY-AGE.

golf. An out-door game. ENTERTAINMENT-WEARINESS.

Gol'-go-tha. Place of Christ's crucifixion. FANE, LIFE-FUNERAL.

Go-li'-ath. A Philistine giant. GREATNESS-LITTLENESS, STRENGTH-WEAKNESS.

golondrina no hace verano, una [Sp.]. (go-lon-dri'-na no ath'-ê ver-a'-no, u'-na). One swallow does not make a summer. COMPLETION-NONCOMPLETION.

go-losh'-es. See GALOSH.

gon'-do-la. Long, narrow boat. CONVEYANCE-VESSEL.

gon"-do-lier'. A gondola-rower. WAYFARER-SEAFARER.

gone. See Go. APPEARANCE-DISAPPEARANCE, ENTITY-NONENTITY, FUTURE-PAST, LIFE-DEATH, PRESENCE-ABSENCE; gone bad, CLEANNESS-FILTHINESS; gone by, FUTURE-PAST, NOVELTY-ANTIQUITY; gone out of one's recollection, REMEMBRANCE-FORGETFULNESS.

gon'-fa-lon. Ensign. SIGN.

gong. Bell. MUSICAL INSTRUMENTS.

go"-ni-om'-e-ter. Instrument for measuring angles. ANGULARITY, MENSURATION, MINERALOGY.

go"-ni-om'-e-try. Art of measuring angles. ANGULARITY.

good. Excellent. APPROVAL-DISAPPROVAL, ASSENT-DISSENT, ENTIRETY-DEFICIENCY, GODLINESS-UNGODLINESS, GOOD-EVIL, GOOD MAN-BAD MAN, PALATABLENESS-UNPALATABLENESS, PLEASURABLENESS-PAINFULNESS, RIGHT-WRONG, VIRTUE-VICE; as good as, REMOTENESS-NEARNESS; be good enough, PETITION-EXPOSTULATION; be so good as, PETITION-EXPOSTULATION; do good, CHARITABLENESS-MALEVOLENCE, GOODNESS-BADNESS; for good, CONVERSION, HEALTH-SICKNESS, LASTINGNESS-TRANSIENTNESS, USEFULNESS-USELESSNESS; good actions, VIRTUE-VICE; good as one's word, OBSERVANCE-NONOBSERVANCE, TRUTHFULNESS-FALSEHOOD, UPRIGHTNESS-DISHONESTY; good at, SKILL-UNSKILFULNESS; good at the price, COSTLINESS-CHEAPNESS; good auspices, SANGUINENESS-HOPELESSNESS; good behavior, CONTINGENT-DURATION, DEVOTION-MAGICIAN, DUTY-DERELICTION, VIRTUE-VICE; good-bye, ARRIVAL-DEPARTURE; good chance, LIKELIHOOD-UNLIKELIHOOD; good cheer, LIGHTHEARTEDNESS-DEJECTION, NUTRIMENT-EXCRETION; good circumstances, AFFLUENCE-PENURY, good condition, GREATNESS-LITTLENESS; good day, ARRIVAL-DEPARTURE, POLITENESS-IMPOLITENESS; good effect, BEAUTY-UGLINESS, GOODNESS-BADNESS; good enough, FAULTLESSNESS-FAULTINESS; good fellow, SOCIABILITY-PRIVACY; good fellowship, FRIEND-FOE; good fight, FIGHTING-CONCILIATION, VIRTUE-VICE; good for, HEALTHINESS-UNHEALTHINESS, USEFULNESS-USELESSNESS; good for nothing, MIGHT-IMPOTENCE, USEFULNESS-USELESSNESS; good fortune, GOOD-EVIL, SUCCESS-FAILURE, WELFARE-MISFORTUNE; good genius, BENEFACTOR-EVILDOER, FRIEND-FOE, JOVE-FIEND; good hand, ADEPT-BUNGLER, WRITING-PRINTING; good humor, CHARITABLENESS-MALEVOLENCE, ENTERTAINMENT-WEARINESS, LIGHTHEARTEDNESS-DEJECTION, POLITENESS-IMPOLITENESS, VARIANCE-ACCORD; good intention, CHARITABLENESS-MALEVOLENCE; good judgment, DISCOVERY, SAGACITY-INCAPACITY; good lack, ASTONISHMENT-EXPECTANCE; good living, FASTING-GLUTTONY, NUTRIMENT-EXCRETION; good lookout, CAREFULNESS-CARELESSNESS; good looks, BEAUTY-UGLINESS; good luck, PURPOSE-LUCK, WELFARE-MISFORTUNE, good man, GOOD MAN-BAD MAN, GOODNESS-BADNESS, MATRIMONY-CELIBACY, MALE-FEMALE; good manners, POLITENESS-IMPOLITENESS; good morrow, ARRIVAL-DEPARTURE, POLITENESS-IMPOLITENESS; good name, REPUTATION-DISCREDIT; good nature, CHARITABLENESS-MALEVOLENCE; good offices, AMITY-HOSTILITY, CHARITABLENESS-MALEVOLENCE, MEDIATION; good old time, FUTURE-PAST; good omen, SANGUINENESS-HELPLESSNESS; good opinion, APPROVAL-DISAPPROVAL; good pennyworth, COSTLINESS-CHEAPNESS; good repute, REPUTATION-DISCREDIT; good sense, SAGACITY-INCAPACITY; good society, VULGARITY-LUDICROUSNESS; good taste, TASTE-VULGARITY; good temper, POLITENESS-IMPOLITENESS; good thing, GOODNESS-BADNESS; good time, EARLINESS-LATENESS, OPPORTUNENESS, UNSUITABLENESS, WELFARE-MISFORTUNE; good turn, CHARITABLENESS-MALEVOLENCE, GOOD-EVIL; good understanding, AMITY-HOSTILITY, VARIANCE-ACCORD; good wife, MALE-FEMALE, MATRIMONY-CELIBACY; good-will, CHARITABLENESS-MALEVOLENCE, PRESUMPTION-OBSEQUIOUSNESS, READINESS-RELUCTANCE; good word, APPROVAL-DISAPPROVAL, JUSTIFICATION-CHARGE; good works, CHARITABLENESS-MALEVOLENCE; in good case, GREATNESS-LITTLENESS; in good odor, APPROVAL-DISAPPROVAL, REPUTATION-DISCREDIT; in one's good books, AMITY-HOSTILITY; in one's good graces, AMITY-HOSTILITY; make good, ATONEMENT, COMPLETION-NONCOMPLETION, DUENESS-UNDUENESS, EVIDENCE-COUNTEREVIDENCE, JUSTIFICATION-CHARGE, MUTABILITY-STABILITY, RENOVATION-RELAPSE; much good may it do, CHARITABLENESS-MALEVOLENCE; put a good face upon, JUSTIFICATION-CHARGE, LIGHTHEARTEDNESS-DEJECTION, POMP, SELFRESPECT-HUMBLENESS; so far so good, APPROVAL-DISAPPROVAL, GOOD-EVIL;

take in good part, Charitableness-Malevolence, Pleasure-Pain, Politeness-Impoliteness; think good, Approval-Disapproval, Readiness-Reluctance; to good purpose, Success-Failure; to the good, Property; turn to good account, Success-Failure; what's the good, Usefulness-Uselessness.

GOOD—EVIL.

Advantage. Something serving for good.
Behalf. The best interests of any one.
Behoof. That which is of good to any one.
Benefit. Anything tending to the good of some one.
Boot. That which is of great good to any one.
Commonweal. The general good.
Consummation devoutly to be wished. An end greatly to be desired.
Gain. That which is acquired as an advantage.
Good. The quality of being morally excellent.
Improvement. The act of making better See Betterment
Interest. That which serves for good.
Profit. Any accession of good.
Service. Any act done for the good of another.
Summum bonum [L.] The highest good.
Weal. Prosperity, happiness, or welfare of human beings.
World of good. The greatest possible good.

Good—Concrete Nouns

Boon. That which is asked or granted as a benefit or favor.
Godsend. An unexpected acquisition or piece of good fortune.
Harvest. Gain or reward as the product of any exertion or labor
Nuts. An unexpected piece of good luck.
Prize. A valuable possession held or in prospect.
Treasure trove. Any money, bullion, or the like found hidden, the owner of which is not known.
Waif. Property found without an owner; thrown away by a thief.
Windfall. An unexpected legacy or other gain.

Good—Associated Nouns

Good fortune. An advantage coming from chance
Goodness. The quality of being good. See Goodness.
Good luck. See Good fortune.
Good turn A good action.
Happiness. Pleasure coming from the possession of goodness. See Pleasure.
Luck. Fortunate dealings.
Main chance. That which brings prosperity.
Piece of good fortune. } Something which brings unexpected success
Piece of good luck } or prosperity.
Pleasure-giving. Making happy by doing good. See Pleasurableness.
Remedy. That which makes better. See Remedy.
Utility. Fitness for doing good. See Usefulness.

Good—Adjectives.

Beneficial, etc. Affording good. See Goodness.
Commendable, etc. To be praised for goodness. See Approval.
Good, etc. Possessing moral excellence. See Goodness.
Useful, etc. Serving a good purpose. See Usefulness.

Good—Adverbs.

All for the best. In every respect favorable.
Aright. In a good manner.
Favorably. Propitiously.
In one's favor. } To one's advantage or good.
In one's interest. }
Not amiss. Quite well.
Satisfactorily. Answering all desires.
To one's advantage. Beneficially.
Well. In a successful manner.

Good—Phrases.

Magnum bonum [L.]. A great good.
So far so good.

EVIL—Continued from Column 2.

Evil—Adverbs.

Amiss. Out of the proper and usual order.
Ill. Not well; unfortunately.
To one's cost. Causing evil to oneself.
Wrong. In an evil or incorrect manner.

Crying evil. A great and distressing evil.
Evil. Something of an injurious or morally bad nature.
Harm. An evil which inflicts injury or loss.
Hurt. An evil causing pain either physical or mental.
Ill. Anything that prevents or diminishes what is good.
Ills that flesh is heir to. Evils inherent in the body.
Machinations of the devil. Evil contrivances of Satan.
Mischief. Malicious evil.
Nuisance. Anything that works evil.

Evil—Denotations.

Accident. An undesigned and unforeseen occurrence of an afflictive) or unfortunate character.
Adversity. A state of adverse fortune.
Bad job. }
Bad turn. } An affair or event which affects one unfortunately
Bale. That which causes ruin.
Bane. Any cause of ruin or lasting injury.
Calamity. Any great misfortune or cause of misery.
Casualty. An unforeseen injury of the body.
Catastrophe. A final event of a calamitous or disastrous nature.
Damage. Injury or harm to person, property, or reputation.
Devil to pay. Trouble.
Disaster. A sudden and extraordinary misfortune.
Disservice. Injury, harm, or mischief.
Foul play. Any conduct that is intended to take another at an unfair advantage.
Grievance. A wrong done and suffered.
Ill turn. Any action or conduct calculated to injure another
Immedicabile vulnus [L.]. An incurable wound.
Injury. Any damage or hurt done to a person or thing.
Loss. The act of losing; destruction.
Misfortune. Unhappy conditions; adventures that fail.
Mishap. Evil accident; misfortune. See Welfare-Misfortune
Outrage. Injurious violence or wrong done to persons or things.
Pandora's box. Source of evil; from the box of Pandora, whence escaped all human ills.
Ruin. Such a change of anything as destroys it. See Creation-Destruction.
Spoliation. Robbery or plunder. See Theft.
Tragedy. Any event in which human lives are lost by violence
Wrong. An act which inflicts injury on a person.

Evil—Nouns of Cause.

Badness. Anything that produces or causes evil.
Bane. That which causes evil.
Blow. A sudden and violent infliction of injury.
Bruise. The evil effects of a blow upon the skin.
Buffet. A blow, especially with the hand.
Demon. An evil spirit. See Jove-Fiend.
Disadvantage. That which is prejudicial to success.
Drawback. A hindrance.
Evil-doer. One who makes a practise of acting maliciously. See Benefactor-Evildoer.
Gash. A long, deep flesh-wound.
Mental suffering. Evil suffered in the mind. See Pleasure-Pain.
Mortal blow. A blow inflicting death.
Mortal wound. A wound resulting in death.
Mutilation. The act of depriving of an essential part of the body.
Painfulness. The state of being full of suffering. See Pleasurableness-Painfulness.
Prejudice. Detriment, as arising from a hasty and unfair judgment.
Scratch. A slight skin-wound.
Stroke. Any sudden attack of evil.
Wound. A hurt or injury to the body

Evil—Verb.

Be in trouble. See Welfare-Misfortune.

Evil—Adjectives.

Awry. In an evil course
Bad. Marked by evil.
Disastrous. Occasioning or accompanied by evil.
Out of joint. Gone wrong.

(Continued on Column 1.)

good'-ly. Well-built; beautiful. Beauty-Ugliness, Good-Evil, Greatness-Littleness, Magnitude-Smallness.

good man. An upright person. Good Man-Bad Man.

GOOD MAN—BAD MAN.

Angel. A person good to a superhuman degree.
Aristides. A Grecian eminently good in public life, called the Just.
Benefactor. One who helps his fellow man. See Benefactor.
Brick. A man good to be depended upon.
Church-goer. A regular attendant at religious service.
Demi-god. A good man with the attributes of a god.
Good example. A type of a good man.
Good man. A morally or spiritually excellent man.
Hero. A good man distinguished for valor; a demi-god.
Innocent. A good man distinguished for innocence. See Innocence.
Model. One whose goodness may be used as a pattern.
Paragon. A perfectly good man. See Faultlessness.
Philanthropist. One who loves his fellow man and acts accordingly. See Humanitarianism.
Rough diamond. A good, but unpolished man.
Saint. A holy person. See Godliness.
Seraph. A person of the highest goodness.
Trump. A very agreeable good man; a trump card.
Worthy. A man of eminent goodness and worth.

Good Man—Phrases.

One in ten thousand. An exceptionally good man.
Salt of the earth. The best people of the earth. [Bible.]
Si sic omnes [L.]. If all were so good.

BAD MAN—Continued from Column 2.

Reptile. A sneaking and treacherous person.
Riffraff. The scum of society.
Rip. A thoroughly worthless and vicious fellow.
Rogue. An idle, disreputable person. See Uprightness-Rogue.
Roué [F.]. A profligate.
Rough. A low and violent bad man.
Rowdy. A bad man distinguished for engaging in rows.
Ruffian. A lawless or brutal fellow.
Runagate.}
Renegade.} One who deserts a cause· a fugitive.
Runnion. A scurvy person.
Sad dog. A miserable wretch.
Scamp. A confirmed rogue.
Scapegrace. A worthless creature.
Scoundrel. A low, petty villain.
Scum of the earth. The lowest and worst class of people.
Serpent. An insinuating and treacherous person, like the old serpent.
Sinner. A person who violates the moral law.
Sneak. A cowardly fellow with an underhand manner.
The wicked. People who are bad in principle and practise.
Thief. A bad man who steals.
Ticket-of-leave man. A convict who is allowed to leave prison before the end of his term on condition of good behavior.
Tiger. A dissolute bully.
Ugly customer. A bad-tempered man who is hard to handle.
Urchin. A mischievous bad boy.
Vagabond. A worthless fellow with no definite residence.
Varlet. A scoundrel.
Varmin. Any person or animal considered as troublesome.
Vaurien [F.]. A good-for-nothing scamp.
Villain. A very bad man capable or guilty of great wickedness.
Viper. A person with an evil disposition towards others.
Whelp. A contemptible young man or boy.
Workers of iniquity. Those who strive to bring about evil.
Wretch. One sunk in the deepest unhappiness and vice.
Wrong-doer. An offender against the moral law.

Bad Man—Phrases.

Acherontis pabulum [L.]. Food for Acheron.
Arcades ambo [L.]. Arcadians both; "Blackguards both." [Byron.] Pastoral poets. [Virgil, *Bucolics*, 7, 4.]
Écrasez l'infâme [F.]. Crush the wretch.
Gibier de potence [F.]. Game for the gibbet.
Mali exempli [L.]. Of bad example.
Sirrah! Fellow: an expression of contempt.

Ame damnée [F.]. A damned soul.
Ame de boue [F.]. A base-minded person.
Bad example. A type which bad men pattern after.
Bad man. An immoral man.
Bad woman. An immoral woman.
Basilisk. A fabled creature whose breath and look were fatal.
Blackguard. A low, bad man.
Black sheep. A bad outcast.
Bully. A quarrelsome, threatening, cowardly fellow.
Caitiff. A cowardly bad man.
Castaway. One who has been cast adrift in the world because of his badness.
Cockatrice. A beautiful and fascinating bad woman.
Convict. A bad man found guilty of crime.
Criminal. One who has done a crime.
Cullion. A mean-spirited and cowardly bad man.
Culprit. One charged directly with crime.
Cur. A mean or malicious bad man.
Defaulter. One who embezzles money held in trust.
Delinquent. One who neglects to perform his duties.
Demon in human shape. A very wicked and cruel bad man.
Devil. A wicked or malignant bad man. See Jove-Fiend.
Devil incarnate. An exceedingly wicked man.
Dog. A despicable bad man.
Drôle [F.]. A low, saucy fellow.
Evil-doer. One who does wicked acts. See Evildoer.
Fallen angel. A bad person who was once very good.
Felon. A bad man who has committed an atrocious violation of the law.
Hangman. A bad man of the lowest order.
Hell-cat. A furious or spiteful woman.
Hell-hound. A diabolical and savage bad man.
Hound. A dastardly bad man.
Incendiary. A bad man who maliciously sets buildings on fire.
Jade. A vicious woman of a low order.
Jail-bird. A bad man who has been imprisoned.
Jezebel. A bold and contriving bad woman. [Bible.]
Jonathan Wild. A notorious highwayman. Hero of a novel of De-Foe and a life by Fielding.
Kern. A country lout.
Law-breaker. One who disobeys the law
Loafer. One who lounges about.
Loon. A stupid good-for-nothing.
Loose fish. A dangerous or good-for-nothing person.
Lost sheep. One wandering from the paths of righteousness. [Bible.]
Lown. Lout.
Malefactor. One who violates the law in a flagrant manner.
Mauvais sujet [F.]. A worthless scamp.
Mean wretch. A bad man with a contemptible spirit.
Misanthrope. One who hates and mistrusts all mankind.
Miscreant. A vile and unprincipled bad man; unbeliever; infidel.
Misdemeanant. One who commits any offense less than felony.
Mongrel. One who represents an incongruous mixture of badness.
Monster. An unnatural and inhuman bad man.
Mucker. A low, rough fellow.
Murderer. One who kills another with malice prepense.
Nana Sahib. A cruel, petty tyrant.
Ne'er do well. A hopeless good-for-nothing.
Nihilist. One devoted to the destruction of political, religious, and social institutions.
One who has sold himself to the devil. A slave to Satan.
Outcast. One cast out of decent society because of immorality.
Outlaw. A bad person deprived of the benefit of the law.
Pollison [F.]. A scapegrace.
Prodigal. A spendthrift
Rake. A man addicted to lewd acts.
Rake-hell. A debauchee.
Rapscallion. A man too bad to have social recognition.
Rascal. A tricking, dishonest fellow.
Rascallion. A low and mean bad man.
Recreant. A cowardly and mean-spirited bad man.
Reprobate. A person given up wholly to sin.

(Continued on Column 1.)

good'-ness. State of being good. Goodness-Badness; **goodness gracious,** Astonishment-Expect-ANCE; goodness of heart, Charitableness-Malevolence; **have the goodness,** Petition-Expostulation

GOODNESS—BADNESS.

A1. The very best.
Beneficence. The practise of doing good
Bijou. A jewel wrought in gold.
Brilliant. A diamond of the finest cut.
Chef d'œuvre [F.]. A masterpiece.
Cock of the walk. A pompous superior
Cock of the roost. A haughty chief.
Coup de maître [F.] A master-stroke
Cream. The choice of anything.
Crême de la crême [F.]. Cream of the cream; the very choicest
Diamond. A costly gem.
Élite [F.]. The select company.
Excellence. Superiority in anything.
Flower. The best and finest part.
Flower of the flock. The best one.
Gem. A precious stone; a small and perfect work.
Gem of the first water. The most precious gem
Good man. A morally excellent man.
Goodness. The state or quality of being good.
Good thing. Anything giving pleasure or value to its possessor.
Jewel. Anything of value and merit.
Merit. That which demands consideration.
Masterpiece. A production of supreme excellence.
Nonesuch. Unmatched excellence.
Nonpareil. Unqualified superiority.
One in a thousand. A person or thing whose equal is rarely met.
Pearl. Something highly esteemed.
Perfection. Supreme excellence; transcendent merit.
Pick. The best
Precious stone. A stone highly prized for beauty or value.
Price. Great worth.
Prime. The foremost in rank, merit, ability, or excellence.
Rara avis [L.]. Rare bird; a thing of exceptional value.
Ruby. A deep red gem-stone; anything prized.
Salt of the earth. Those of weight, stability, and influence.   [Bible.]
Supereminence. Excessive superiority.
Superexcellence. Merit in a surpassing degree.
Superiority. The state of surpassing in merit, morality, ability, or excellence
Tidbit. A choice morsel.
Treasure. Something kept or cherished, as money, jewels, and wealth.
Value. Anything that has power in exchange.
Virtue. Moral goodness.
Worth. The property of anything which makes it desirable and useful.

Goodness—Verbs.

Benefit. To do good to; to be useful.
Emulate. To strive to equal or excel another
Excel. To surpass another.
Improve. To make better; to increase in value
Profit. To be of use or advantage to.
Rival. To strive to equal.
Transcend. To surpass all
Vie. To contend for success with another

Goodness—Verbal Expressions.

Be A1; bear away the bell; be beneficial; be good; be the making of; break no bones; challenge comparison; confer a benefit; confer an obligation; do a good turn; do a world of good; do good; do no harm; make a man of; pass an examination; pass muster; produce a benefit; produce a good effect; produce good; stand the proof; stand the test.

Goodness —Adjectives.

Above par. Better than the usual quality.
Admirable. Excellent in a high degree.
Advantageous. Affording advantage; favorable.
Beneficial. Tending to help
Best. Of the highest degree of excellence.
Better. Of a higher degree of excellence than usual.
Capital. Of the first quality.
Cardinal. Of prime or special importance.
Choice. Having special excellence.
Costly, etc. Of great value. See Costliness
Couleur de rose [F.]. Of the color of the rose; pleasant
Crack. Of superior excellence, first-class.
Edifying. Tending to moral or spiritual improvement.
Elect. Deserving to be chosen among many.
Estimable. Deserving of good opinion.
Excellent. Having good qualities in a high degree.
Exquisite. Fitted to excite great pleasure.
Fair. Pleasing to the eye or mind.

Abomination. An object of intense dislike; anything hateful or loathsome.
Abuse. A corrupt or immoral practise.
Amari aliquid [L.]. Something bitter.
Annoyance. Something continually troublesome.
Badness. The quality of lacking moral excellence.
Bane. A deadly poison; hence anything pernicious or fatal.
Depravity. Moral degeneracy.
Evil-doer. A worker of badness.
Evil star. A star having an evil influence on one's destiny.
Guilt. The state of one who violates the law.
Hurtfulness. The state of being injurious.
Ill-treatment. Mistreatment by another.
Ill wind. Any misfortune, calamity, or disaster.
Injury. Molestation of one's rights; damage to a man's person or property.
Malevolence. An evil disposition towards others.
Malignity. The state of having excessive hatred for another; virulent envy.
Misanthropy. Hatred for mankind.
Misusage. Improper use.
Molestation. The interference with one to injuriously disturb him.
Oppression. Requirement of unreasonable exactions; severity in intercourse with men.
Outrage. Open violence; wanton abuse.
Painfulness. State of uneasiness, distress, or mental suffering.
Peccancy. State of being guilty of transgression.
Persecution. The persistent harassing or molesting of one hated.
Pestilence. Any mortal disease sweepingly destructive; any fatal or harmful power.
Plague-spot. A center of moral evil; a deadly sign.
Rotgut. Bad whisky.
Skeleton in the closet. An humiliating family secret.
Snake in the grass. A concealed or treacherous enemy.
Thorn in the side. A bodily defect that incapacitates and mortifies.
Tender mercies. [Ironically.] Kindness
Virulence. Extreme bitterness.

Badness—Verbs.

Abuse. To put to a bad use.
Aggrieve. To afflict one.
Bear down. To weigh down upon heavily.
Bear hard upon. To press on one with violence.
Be hurtful. To do harm.
Bring into trouble. To put into a position of distress or injury.
Bruise. To injure.
Buffet. To strike a blow with the fist.
Cause evil, etc. See Good-Evil.
Cause hurt. To do damage.
Damnify. To inflict damage on any one; injure at law.
Destroy. To damage by pulling down.
Do a mischief. To injure.
Do evil. To do wrong; act badly; work corruption.
Do harm. To injure.
Do mischief. To do malicious evil.
Do violence. To injure
Endamage. To cause injury to
Harm. To injure by causing trouble, inconvenience, or unpleasantness.
Hurt. To cause pain.
Inflict evil, etc. See Good-Evil.
Inflict hurt. To injure.
Injure. To infringe upon one's rights of person or property.
Ill-treat. To disregard one's obligations toward others.
Ill-use. To use badly; abuse; maltreat.
Make mischief. To harm or interfere with.
Maltreat. To treat unkindly or abusively
Maul. To rudely buffet.
Molest. To harm by interference.
Oppress. To press hard upon; to impose unreasonable burdens
Outrage. To openly and recklessly injure.
Overburden. To impose unreasonable burdens.
Pain. To hurt one's feelings by physical or mental injury.
Persecute. To incessantly injure; to systematically oppress.
Pierce. To enter forcibly.
Produce evil, etc. See Good-Evil.
Put upon. To oppress.
Run down. To weaken in health.
Scratch. To lacerate and hurt the skin.
Smite. To strike with the hand or weapon.
Stab. To inflict a wound by a pointed weapon.
Trample upon. To crush down under foot.
Tread upon. To press under foot.
Victimize. To make a dupe of.

GOODNESS—BADNESS—*Continued.*

GOODNESS—Adjectives—*Continued.*

Favorable. Affording means to aid or benefit.
Fine. Excellent or superior in character, form, or appearance.
First-class. } Of the best quality.
First-rate. }
Fresh. Having undiminished excellence.
Genuine, etc. Not false or spurious. See Truth.
Good. Desirable, or excellent in any respect.
Good as gold. Of high value.
Harmless. Without hurt or loss.
High-wrought. Skilfully or finely made.
Hurtless. Harmless.
Inestimable. Above price; very excellent.
In fair condition. Moderately good.
In good condition. Unimpaired.
Inimitable. Surpassingly excellent.
Innocent. Free from qualities that can harm or injure.
Innocuous. Producing no bad effects.
Inoffensive. Not displeasing.
Invaluable. Beyond price; very excellent.
Nice. Pleasing to the senses.
Of great price. Valuable, or desirable.
Of the first water. Of the highest excellence or purity.
Of value. Desirable.
Picked. Highest-rated.
Pleasing. Agreeable to the senses.
Praiseworthy, etc. Deserving of praise. See Approval.
Precious. Highly prized.
Precious as the apple of the eye. Of the highest value to a person.
Priceless. Above price; very excellent.
Prime. Of the first quality.
Profitable. Yielding gain or benefit.
Propitious. Attended by favorable prospects or circumstances. See Sanguineness.
Rare. Highly valued because of infrequency.
Recherché [F.]. Much sought after.
Salutary, etc. Tending to promote good. See Healthiness.
Satisfactory. Fulfilling every desire.
Select. Taken as being most excellent.
Serviceable, etc. Such as does serve a useful purpose. See Usefulness.
Sound, etc. Free from defect or injury. See Faultlessness.
Standard, etc. Of a very high type or kind. See Faultlessness.
Superexcellent. Of superior excellence.
Superfine. Of the very best quality.
Superlatively good, etc. Of the very highest degree of goodness. See Supremacy.
Tidy. Fairly well and comfortable.
Tip-top. Best of its kind.
Tolerable, etc. Passably or moderately good. See Faultlessness-Faultiness.
Unexceptionable. As good as any.
Unobjectionable. Without defect.
Unobnoxious. Without harmful qualities.
Unparagoned. Matchless.
Unparalleled, etc. Without an equal. See Supremacy.
Up to the mark. Satisfactory.
Valuable. Costly.
Very best. Of the highest degree of excellence.
Worth a Jew's eye. } Of the highest value.
Worth its weight in gold. }

GOODNESS—Adverbs.

Beneficially, etc. See *Adjectives.*
Well, etc. See Good.

GOODNESS—Phrase.

Eigner Herd ist Goldes werth [G.]. One's own hearth has golden worth.

BADNESS—Adjectives—*Continued from Column 2.*

Pernicious. Thoroughly destructive.
Pitiable. Meriting compassion.
Pitiful. Calling forth compassion.
Poisonous. Deadly in effects.
Prejudicial. Characterized by bias.
Rank. Strong in a bad sense.
Reprehensible. Deserving reproof.
Rotten. Having become putrid.
Rotten to the core. Morally depraved in every respect.
Sad. Afflicted with grief.
Scathful. Inflicting severe injury

BADNESS—Verbs—*Continued.*

Weigh down. } To bear heavily on one.
Weigh heavy on. }
Work evil, etc. See Good-Evil.
Work hurt. To do injury; to do wrong.
Wrong. To turn aside from the right; to injure; to do injustice

BADNESS—*Adjectives.*

Abominable. Very hateful.
Accursed. Doomed to utter destruction; detestable.
Arrant. Thoroughly bad.
As bad as bad can be. Very bad.
Bad. Opposed to good; morally perverted.
Baleful. Full of malignity.
Baneful. Having deadly qualities.
Base. Morally mean.
Below par. Lower than the standard.
Burdensome. Harmfully oppressive.
Confounded. Mingled together in confusion.
Corrosive. Eating away.
Corrupting. Turning from good to bad.
Cursed. Execrated, or deserving execration.
Damnable. Meriting punishment.
Damned. Declared guilty; adjudged worthy of sentence.
Deadly. Causing death.
Deleterious. Harmful, morally or physically.
Deplorable. That should be lamented.
Depraved. Morally corrupt.
Destructive. Causing ruin.
Deteriorated. Reduced in quality or value.
Detestable. Deserving abhorrence.
Detrimental. Involving or producing loss.
Diabolic. Having the attributes of the devil; malicious; infernal; nefarious.
Dire. Terribly evil.
Disadvantageous. Not suited to the promotion of success.
Disastrous. Occasioning or accompanied by terrible and ruinous effects.
Disserviceable. Incapable of being used to advantage.
Dreadful. Causing terror and fear.
Envenomed. Infected with poison or malice.
Evil. Contrary to divine law; having morally injurious qualities.
Exceptionable. Liable to objection.
Execrable. Worthy of hate.
Foul. Offensive to the moral sense.
Full of mischief. Full of small pranks; inclined to tease and cut capers.
Fulsome. Offensive from excessive flattery.
Grievous. Hard to bear.
Harmful. Tending to bring about permanent injury.
Hateful. Exciting dislike.
Hateful as a toad. Regarded as an object of scorn, aversion, and contempt.
Horrible. Causing terror.
Horrid. Suited to arouse terror.
Hurtful. Tending to cause physical or mental pain.
Ill. Productive of harm.
Ill-conditioned. Badly or weakly conditioned.
Ill-contrived. Badly put together; weakly conceived.
Inauspicious. Lacking favorable omens.
Incompetent, etc. Not capable. See Skill-Unskilfulness.
Indifferent. Without any preference, neither good nor bad.
Infernal. Evil enough for hell.
Injured. Wronged; deprived of just and natural rights.
Injurious. That which tends to harm or wrong.
Irremediable, etc. Not to be reclaimed or replaced. See Sanguineness-Hopelessness.
Lamentable. Causing sorrow and regret.
Malefic. Occasioning evil or disaster.
Malign. Having an ill disposition toward others.
Malignant. Animated by excessive hatred.
Mean. Low-minded; low in rank; low in character.
Mischief-making. Making trouble or disturbance.
Mischievous. Given to the doing of pranks that injure or harm.
Nocuous. Pertaining to poison.
Noisome. Very offensive.
Noxious. Productive of harm.
Obnoxious. Liable to censure.
Onerous. Having weight; burdensome.
Oppressive. Pressing on one heavily.
Peccant. Guilty of transgression.

(*Continued on Column 1.*)

BADNESS—Adjectives—Continued.

Shocking. Causing surprise and horror.
Sinister. Left-handed; ill-omened; dishon
Unadvisable. That which could not be done after deliberation; imprudent.
Unlucky. Not having fortune; ill-omened.
Unprofitable. Producing no gain; making no improvement; not conducive to progress.
Unsatisfactory. Causing dissatisfaction; failing to gratify.
Untoward. Not easily taught; not docile; perverse; awkward.

Venomous. Having a malign spirit.
Vile. Base in morals.
Villainous. Capable of great wickedness.
Virulent. Strongly poisonous; extremely bitter; malignant.
Wide-wasting. Destroying to a great distance; ravaging far and wide.
Woful. Afflicted with grief or calamity; causing sorrow or grief.
Wretched. Very unhappy; fallen deep in disaster.
Wrong. Going aside from right; falling in error.

BADNESS—Adverbs, etc.

Badly, etc. See *Adjectives.*
Ill. In a bad manner.
To one's cost. Injuriously.

Where the shoe pinches. At the point of difficulty.
Wrong. In a wrong manner.

BADNESS—Phrases.

Bad is the best.
Erba mala presto cresco [It.]. An ill weed grows fast.

The worst come to the worst.

---

goods. Possessions. MERCHANDISE-PROPERTY.
Good'-win Sands. Dangerous shoals in Strait of Dover, near Tenterden Steeple. REFUGE-PITFALL.
good'-y. A poor, old woman. MALE-FEMALE.
Goo-roo'. Hindu spiritual teacher. MINISTRY-LAITY.
goose. A bird of the web-footed family. RESONANCE-NONRESONANCE, SAGE-FOOL; **game of goose,** ENTERTAINMENT-WEARINESS; **giddy as a goose,** HEED-DISREGARD; **kill the goose with golden eggs,** EXTRAVAGANCE-AVARICE, SKILL-UNSKILFULNESS.
goose'-ber"-ry. A silly person. **Gooseberry eyes,** SIGHT-BLINDNESS; **old gooseberry,** ANGEL-SATAN.
goose'-ber"-ry-eyed". Eyes like gooseberries. SIGHT-DIMSIGHTEDNESS.
goose'-cap". A silly person. SAGE-FOOL.
goose'-quill". Quill of a goose, used in writing. WRITING-PRINTING.
goose"-skin'. Rough skin. HEAT-COLD.
Gor'-di-an knot. Difficulty. [Cut by Alexander.] DIFFICULTY-FACILITY, REGULARITY-IRREGULARITY.
gore. Blood; to hook. APERTURE-CLOSURE, LIFE-KILLING.
gorge. Ravine; to stuff. DESIRE-REPLETION, EXCESS-LACK, FASTING-GLUTTONY, INTERSPACE-CONTACT; **gorge the hook,** READINESS-RELUCTANCE; **raise one's gorge,** FAVORITE-ANGER.
gorged. Stuffed. EXCESS-LACK.
gorge de pigeon [F.] (gorzh de pi-zhon') Shot-colored. VARIEGATION.
gor'-geous. Pompous. BEAUTY-UGLINESS, COLOR-ACHROMATISM, EMBELLISHMENT-DISFIGUREMENT.
gor'-geous-ness. Magnificence. BEAUTY-UGLINESS.
gor'-gon. Ugly object. SANGUINENESS-HOPELESSNESS.
go-ril'-la. Animal of the ape family. BENEFACTOR-EVILDOER.
gor'-mand. A voracious eater. FASTING-GLUTTONY, MODERATION-VOLUPTUARY.
gor'-mand-ize. To eat greedily. FASTING-GLUTTONY, NUTRIMENT-EXCRETION.
gor'-man-diz-ing. Devouring greedily. FASTING-GLUTTONY.
gorse. Furze. FAUNA-FLORA.
gor'-y. Bloody. CLEANNESS-FILTHINESS, LIFE-KILLING.
gos'-pel. God's message. CERTAINTY-DOUBT, REVELATION-PSEUDOREVELATION, TRUTH-ERROR; **take for gospel,** FAITH-MISGIVING.
Gos'-pels. The first four books of the New Testament. REVELATION-PSEUDOREVELATION.
gos'-sa-mer. Gauze. HEAVINESS-LIGHTNESS, LAMINA-FIBER.
gos'-sa-mer-y. Flimsy. TEXTURE.
gos'-sip. Idle talk. CONVERSATION-MONOLOGUE, TALKATIVENESS-TACITURNITY, TIDINGS-MYSTERY.
gos-soon'. Servant boy. GENTILITY-DEMOCRACY.

Go'-ta-ma. An early Hindu philosopher. REVELATION-PSEUDOREVELATION.
Goth. One of an old Germanic tribe. GENTILITY-DEMOCRACY, TASTE-VULGARITY.
Go'-tham. City of England. **Wise men of Gotham.** SAGE-FOOL.
Goth'-ic. Pertaining to the Goths. FORM-FORMLESSNESS, TASTE-VULGARITY.
Goth'-i-cism. Barbarousness. TASTE-VULGARITY.
gouache [F.] (gwach). Kind of water-color painting. PAINTING.
gouge. Chisel having a curved edge. CONVEXITY-CONCAVITY, PERFORATOR-STOPPER.
gour"-met'. An epicure. DESIRE-PARTICULARNESS, MODERATION-VOLUPTUARY.
goût, chacun à son [F.] (gu, sha-kun' a son'). Every man to his taste. TASTE-VULGARITY.
goût, haut [F.] (gu, ho). High flavor. PUNGENCY.
goutte d'eau, il se noyerait dans une [F.] (gut do, il se nwa-ye-rê' dan·z ün). He would drown in a drop of water. SKILL-UNSKILFULNESS.
gov'-ern. To rule. DIVINITY, MANAGEMENT, PRESIDENT-MEMBER, RULE-LICENSE.
gov'-ern-ess. Instructress. GUARD-PRISONER, INSTRUCTOR-PUPIL.
gov'-ern-ment. Rule or power. CHIEF-UNDERLING, CONDUCT, RULE-LICENSE; **divine government,** DIVINITY; **petticoat government,** MANAGEMENT, SKILL-UNSKILFULNESS.
gov'-ern-or. One who governs. CHIEF-UNDERLING, GUARD-PRISONER, INSTRUCTOR-PUPIL, MANAGER, PRESIDENT-MEMBER.
gowk. Fool. SAGE-FOOL.
gown. Dress. DRESS-UNDRESS, VESTMENTS.
gowns'-man. Student. SCHOLAR-DUNCE.
grab. To seize. EXTRAVAGANCE-AVARICE, TAKING-RESTITUTION.
grab'-ble. To sprawl. TOUCH.
grace. Elegance; kindness. BEAUTY-UGLINESS, COMPASSION-RUTHLESSNESS, GIVING-RECEIVING, GODLINESS-UNGODLINESS, LEAVE-PROHIBITION, PARDON-REVENGE, PURITY-CRUDENESS, TASTE-VULGARITY, THANKFULNESS-THANKLESSNESS, TITLE, UPRIGHTNESS-DISHONESTY, WORSHIP-IDOLATRY; **act of grace,** GIVING-RECEIVING; **grace before meat,** THANKFULNESS-THANKLESSNESS; **God's grace,** CHARITABLENESS-MALEVOLENCE; **heart of grace,** BRAVERY-COWARDICE; **in one's good graces,** AMITY-HOSTILITY; **say grace,** DEVOTION-IDOLATRY; **submit with a good grace,** EXCITABILITY-INEXCITABILITY, SELFRESPECT-HUMBLENESS, YIELDING; **with a bad grace,** READINESS-RELUCTANCE; **with a good grace,** POLITENESS-IMPOLITENESS, READINESS-RELUCTANCE.

grâce, coup de [F.] (gras, cu de). The finishing blow. COMPASSION-RUTHLESSNESS.

grace'-ful. Becoming. BEAUTY-UGLINESS, PURITY-CRUDENESS.

grace'-ful-ness. Elegance of manner. BEAUTY-UGLINESS.

grâce, la [F.] (gras, la). An outdoor game. ENTERTAINMENT-WEARINESS.

grace'-less. Wanting grace. BEAUTY-UGLINESS, GODLINESS-DISBELIEF, PURITY-CRUDENESS, REPENTANCE-OBDURACY, VIRTUE-VICE.

Gra'-ces. Three mythological goddesses. BEAUTY-UGLINESS.

gra'-cious. Favorable. CHARITABLENESS-MALEVOLENCE, POLITENESS-IMPOLITENESS, READINESS-RELUCTANCE; **good gracious,** ASTONISHMENT-EXPECTANCE.

gra'-cious-ly. In a kindly manner. READINESS-RELUCTANCE.

gra-da'-tim. Gradually. CONTINUITY-INTERRUPTION, REGULARITY-IRREGULARITY, SWIFTNESS-SLOWNESS.

gra-da'-tion. Grade. CONTINUITY-INTERRUPTION, QUANTITY-MEASURE, REGULARITY-IRREGULARITY.

grade. Rank. QUANTITY-MEASURE, STATION.

gra'-di-ent. Rising by steps. PARALLELISM-INCLINATION.

grado in grado, di [It.] (gra'-do in gra'-do, di). By degrees. QUANTITY-MEASURE.

grad'-u-al. Proceeding regularly. CONTINUITY-INTERRUPTION, QUANTITY-MEASURE, SWIFTNESS-SLOWNESS.

grad'-u-al-ly. In a slow and regular manner. CONTINUITY, CONVERSION-REVERSION.

grad'-u-ate. To grade; give a degree to. CHEMISTRY, CONTINUITY-INTERRUPTION, HARMONY-DISCORD, MENSURATION, ORGANIZATION-DISORGANIZATION, SCHOLAR-DUNCE.

grad'-u-ated. Graded. **Graduated scale,** MENSURATION.

grad''-u-a'-tion. Act of gradually modifying. MENSURATION, ORGANIZATION-DISORGANIZATION.

gra'-dus. Dictionary of prosody. WORD-NEOLOGY.

Græculus esuriens [L.] (grî'-kiu-lus î-sur'-i-ens). The hungry Greekling. PRESUMPTION-OBSEQUIOUSNESS.

graft. Shoot. EDUCATION-MISTEACHING, ESTABLISHMENT-REMOVAL, INJECTION-EJECTION, UNION-DISUNION.

Gra'-ham's law. Important law of chemistry. CHEMISTRY.

grain. Small, hard body; a small weight, arrangement of particles of anything. AFFECTIONS, COLOR-ACHROMATISM, EMBELLISHMENT-DISFIGUREMENT, FRIABILITY, GREATNESS-LITTLENESS, HEAVINESS-LIGHTNESS, INCLINATION, MAGNITUDE-SMALLNESS, MEASURE, SMOOTHNESS-ROUGHNESS, SUBJECTIVENESS-OBJECTIVENESS, TEXTURE; **against the grain,** ANTAGONISM-CONCURRENCE, PLEASURABLENESS-PAINFULNESS, READINESS-RELUCTANCE, SMOOTHNESS-ROUGHNESS; **grains of allowance,** ALARM, HURRY-LEISURE; **like grains of sand,** COHESION-LOOSENESS.

gra-mer'-cy. Many thanks. THANKFULNESS-THANKLESSNESS.

gram''-i-niv'-o-rous. Grass-eating. NUTRIMENT-EXCRETION.

gram'-mar. Science of correct usage of language. BEGINNING-END, EDUCATION-MISTEACHING, GRAMMAR-SOLECISM, NATURE-ART, SCHOOL; **bad grammar,** GRAMMAR-SOLECISM; **comparative grammar,** GRAMMAR-SOLECISM; **grammar-school,** SCHOOL.

GRAMMAR—SOLECISM.

Grammar. The science which treats of the principles of language.

Jus et norma loquendi [L.]. The laws and rules of speaking.

Philology. The science of words and language. See LANGUAGE.

GRAMMAR—*Associated Nouns.*

Ablative. The instrumental case.

Accidence. A book containing the declensions and conjugations of verbs

Conjugation. The exhibition of the inflections of a verb.

Correct style. The quality of writing according to the rules of grammar.

Declension. The exhibition of the inflections of a noun, pronoun, or adjective.

Inflection. The changes undergone by words to express the relations of case, number, gender, tense, etc.

Lindley Murray. The name of an American writer of an English grammar once very common in use. See SCHOOL.

Parataxis. Arrangement of clauses without connectives.

Parathesis. Apposition.

Parts of speech. The classes of words into which language is grouped.

Praxis. The part of grammar containing exercises to be studied.

Punctuation. The use of marks for the division of written matter into its due parts.

Syntax. The part of grammar that treats of the sentence and its construction.

GRAMMAR—*Verbs.*

Parse. To describe a word by giving its grammatical value.

Punctuate. To use marks to divide sentences in writing.

GRAMMAR—*Adjective.*

Syntactic. Pertaining to syntax.

Bad grammar. Incorrect usage of language.

Bull. A ridiculous contradiction in terms.

False grammar. The mistaken use of language.

Faulty grammar. The use of language with violation of many rules.

Lapsus linguæ [L.]. A slip of the tongue.

Slip of the pen. An accidental mistake in writing.

Slip of the tongue. An accidental mistake in speaking.

Slipslop. A slovenly blunder in speaking.

Solecism. A violation of the rules of grammar.

SOLECISM—*Verbs.*

Break Priscian's head. To make a bad blunder in grammar. [A Latin grammarian.]

Commit a solecism. To commit a violation of the rules of grammar.

Murder the king's English. } To persistently violate the rules of
Murder the queen's English. } English grammar.

Solecize. To violate the rules of grammar.

Use bad grammar. To speak and write according to incorrect usage.

Use faulty grammar. To commit many solecisms in speaking and writing.

SOLECISM—*Adjectives.*

Faulty. Characterized by solecisms.

Inaccurate. Not exact in grammar.

Incorrect. Not according to the rules of grammar

Ungrammatical. Marked by solecisms.

gram-ma'-ri-an. One learned in grammar. SCHOLAR-DUNCE.

gran'-a-ry. Storeroom for grain. STORE.

grand. Magnificent; preeminent. BEAUTY-UGLINESS, CONSEQUENCE-INSIGNIFICANCE, POMP, REPUTATION-DISCREDIT, SELFRESPECT-HUMBLENESS; **grand climacteric,** INFANCY-AGE; **grand doings,** POMP; **grand master,** PRESIDENT-MEMBER; **grand style,** PAINTING; **grand tour,** TRAVELING-NAVIGATION; **grand Turk,** CHIEF-UNDERLING; **grand vizier,** MANAGER.

grand, en [F.] (gran', an'). Of full size. GREATNESS-LITTLENESS.

grand seigneur, en [F.] (gran' sen-yur', an'). In lordly fashion. PRESUMPTION-OBSEQUIOUSNESS.

grande tenue, en [F.] (gran'd te-nü', an'). In full dress.

EMBELLISHMENT - DISFIGUREMENT, SOCIETY - LUDI-CROUSNESS.

gran'-dam. A grandmother. INFANT-VETERAN.

grand'-child"-ren. Children of one's son or daughter. PARENTAGE-PROGENY.

gran-dee'. Spanish nobleman. GENTILITY-DEMOCRACY.

gran'-deur. Grandness. REPUTATION-DISCREDIT.

grand'-fa"-ther. The father of one's father or mother. INFANT-VETERAN, PARENTAGE-PROGENY.

gran-dil'-o-quent. Bombastic. SIMPLICITY-FLORIDNESS.

gran'-di-ose. Pompous. SIMPLICITY-FLORIDNESS.

grand'-moth"-er. The mother of one's father or mother. PARENTAGE-PROGENY; **teach grandmother,** EDUCATION-MISTEACHING.

grand'-sire". Forefather. INFANT-VETERAN, PARENTAGE-PROGENY.

grange. Farm. DWELLER-HABITATION.

gran'-ite. A kind of rock. HARDNESS-SOFTNESS.

gra-nit'-ic. Like granite. HARDNESS-SOFTNESS.

gra-niv'-o-rous. Grain-eating. NUTRIMENT-EXCRETION.

grano salis, cum [L.] (grê'-no sê'-lis, cum). With a grain of allowance. FAITH-MISGIVING, MODIFICATION.

grant. Allow. ALIENATION, CONSENT, EXPOSURE-HIDINGPLACE, GIVING-RECEIVING, LEAVE-PROHIBITION; **God grant,** DEVOTION-IDOLATRY; **grant a lease,** SECURITY.

grant'-ed. Allowed. ASSENT-DISSENT; **take for granted,** FAITH-MISGIVING, FANCY.

grant-ee'. Receiver of a grant. GIVING-RECEIVING, HOLDER.

grant'-or. Maker of a grant. GIVING.

gran'-u-lar. Grainlike. FRIABILITY.

gran'-u-late. To become or make granular. FRIABILITY.

gran"-u-la'-tion. Forming into grains. FRIABILITY.

gran'-ule. Small grain. MAGNITUDE-SMALLNESS.

grape. Grape-shot. WEAPON.

grapes. The fruit of a certain vine. **Sour grapes,** POSSIBILITY-IMPOSSIBILITY, PRETEXT, TRUTHFULNESS-FALSEHOOD.

grape'-shot". Small shot. ATTACK, WEAPON.

graph'-ic. Pertaining to writing. ACCOUNT, CLEARNESS-OBSCURITY, DELINEATION-CARICATURE, PAINTING; **graphic symbols,** CHEMISTRY.

graph'-ite. Black lead. CHEMISTRY.

graphoideophrenoia. Writing mania, combined with marked perversion of ideas.

graph-ol'-o-gy. The science of estimating character by the handwriting. WRITING-PRINTING.

graph-om'-e-ter. Instrument for measuring angles. ANGULARITY.

graph'-o-scope. An instrument for magnifying pictures. OPTICAL INSTRUMENTS.

graph'-o-type. A kind of engraving. ENGRAVING.

grap'-nel. Grappling-iron. REFUGE-PITFALL.

grap'-ple. To seize. TAKING-RESTITUTION, UNION-DISUNION; **grapple with,** ANTAGONISM-CONCURRENCE, DIFFICULTY-FACILITY, INVESTIGATION-ANSWER, REPRISAL-RESISTANCE, STRIFE-PEACE.

grap'-pling-i"-ron. Hook used in seizing an object. CONNECTIVE, REFUGE-PITFALL.

grasp. To seize; to understand. CLEARNESS-OBSCURITY, EXTRAVAGANCE-AVARICE, KEEPING-RELINQUISHMENT, RULE-LICENSE, TAKING-RESTITUTION; **grasp at,** DESIRE-DISTASTE; **grasp of intellect,** SAGACITY-INCAPACITY; **in one's grasp,** RULE-LICENSE; **tight grasp,** HARSHNESS-MILDNESS.

grasp'-ing. Greedy. DESIRE-DISTASTE.

grass. Herbage. FAUNA-FLORA; **let the grass grow under one's feet,** CAREFULNESS-CARELESSNESS, RECK-LESSNESS-CAUTION; **not let the grass,** etc., ACTIVITY-INDOLENCE.

grass'-hop"-per. A long-legged insect. SPRING-DIVE.

grass'-plot". Lawn. DOMESTICATION-AGRICULTURE, GULF-PLAIN.

grass'-y. Abounding in grass. FAUNA-FLORA.

grate. Framework of iron bars; to make a harsh noise. FRIABILITY, OVEN-REFRIGERATOR, SENSUALITY-SUFFERING; **grate on the ear,** CACOPHONY, PLEASURABLENESS-PAINFULNESS, SENSUALITY-SUFFERING; **grate on the feelings,** PLEASURABLENESS-PAINFULNESS

gra'-ted. Barred. CROSSING.

grate'-ful. Thankful. PLEASURABLENESS-PAINFULNESS, SENSUALITY-SUFFERING, THANKFULNESS-THANKLESSNESS.

gra'-ter. That which grates. FRIABILITY.

gratia, exempli [L.] (grê'-shi-a, ex-em'-plai). For the sake of example. CONVENTIONALITY-UNCONVENTIONALITY.

grat"-i-fi-ca'-tion. That which pleases. PLEASURE-PAIN, SENSUALITY-SUFFERING.

grat'-i-fy. To please. CONTENTEDNESS-DISCONTENTMENT, PLEASURABLENESS-PAINFULNESS.

gra'-ting. See GRATE. CROSSING, PLEASURABLENESS-PAINFULNESS.

gra'-tis. Free. COSTLINESS-CHEAPNESS, LIBERTY-SUBJECTION, SETTLEMENT-DEFAULT.

grat'-i-tude. Thankfulness. THANKFULNESS-THANKLESSNESS.

gra-tu'-i-tous. Free. HYPOTHESIS, RATIOCINATION-INSTINCT, READINESS-RELUCTANCE, THANKFULNESS-THANKLESSNESS.

gra-tu'-i-ty. Present. GIVING-RECEIVING, THANKFULNESS-THANKLESSNESS.

grat'-u-late. Congratulate. FELICITATION.

grat"-u-la'-tion. Congratulation. FELICITATION.

grat'-u-la-to-ry. Expressive of gratulation. FELICITATION.

gra-va'-men. Complaint. CONSEQUENCE-INSIGNIFICANCE; **gravamen of a charge,** JUSTIFICATION-CHARGE.

grave. Tomb; serious. CONSEQUENCE-INSIGNIFICANCE, ENGRAVING, EXCITABILITY-INEXCITABILITY, LIFE-FUNERAL, LIGHTHEARTEDNESS-DEJECTION, MAGNITUDE-SMALLNESS, PLEASURABLENESS-PAINFULNESS, VIRTUE-VICE; **look grave,** APPROVAL-DISAPPROVAL, LIGHTHEARTEDNESS-DEJECTION; **grave in the memory,** REMEMBRANCE-FORGETFULNESS; **grave note,** RESONANCE-NONRESONANCE; **look grave,** APPROVAL-DISAPPROVAL; **on this side of the grave,** LIFE-DEATH; **rise from the grave,** RENOVATION-RELAPSE; **silent as the grave,** SOUND-SILENCE, TALKATIVENESS-TACITURNITY; **sink into the grave,** LIFE-DEATH.

grav'-el. Sand and pebbles. DIFFICULTY-FACILITY.

grav'-eled. Embarrassed; perplexed. DIFFICULTY-FACILITY.

gra'-ven. Carved. **Graven image.** DEVOTION-IDOLATRY.

grav'-e-o-lent. Offensive smell. ODOR-INODOROUSNESS.

gra'-ver. Engraver's chisel. ENGRAVING.

grave'-yard". A cemetery. LIFE-FUNERAL.

grav'-i-tate. To come together. ASCENT-DESCENT, HEAVINESS-LIGHTNESS; **gravitate towards,** INCLINATION.

grav'-i-ty. Attraction of bodies for each other; seriousness. ATTRACTION-REPULSION, CONSEQUENCE-INSIGNIFICANCE, EXCITABILITY-INEXCITABILITY, FORCE-WEAKNESS, HEAVINESS-LIGHTNESS, LIGHTHEARTEDNESS-DEJECTION, MIGHT-IMPOTENCE, PLEASURE-PAIN; **center of gravity,** CENTER; **specific gravity,** HEAVINESS-LIGHTNESS, SOLIDITY-RARITY.

gra'-vy. Juice of cooked meat. LIQUID-GAS.

gray. Mixed black and white in color. GRAY-BROWN,

Infancy-Age, Whiteness-Blackness; **bring gray hairs to the grave**, Pleasurableness-Painfulness, Welfare-Misfortune; **gray beard**, Infant-Vet- ERAN, **gray hairs**, Infancy-Age; grayhound, Fauna-Flora; Swiftness-Slowness.

GRAY—BROWN.

Black, etc. See Whiteness-Blackness.
Gray. A dull color consisting of white and black mixed.
Neutral tint. An artificial tint with no decided color, but predominantly grayish.
Pepper and salt. A color of mixed gray and black.
Silver. A soft gray luster.

Gray—*Associated Nouns.*

Chiaroscuro. The art of mingling light and shadow in painting.
Grisaille [F.] Grizzly hair.
Payne's gray. A gray pigment.

Gray—*Adjectives.*

Ash-colored. Gray as ashes.
Ashen.⎱ Gray like ashes.
Ashy.⎰
Cineritious.⎱ Of a gray resembling ashes
Cinerous.⎰
Cool. Of a dull color.
Dingy. Of a soiled gray color.
Drab. A yellowish-gray.
Dun. Of a dull, dark-gray color.
Gray.⎱ Of the color of white and black mixed
Grey.⎰
Grizzled. Gray as the hair of an old man.
Grizzly. Grayish.
Iron-gray. Gray like iron.
Leaden. Gray like lead.
Livid. Gray like bruised flesh.
Mouse-colored. Gray as a mouse.
Pearly. Having a gray luster, like a pearl.
Roan. Dark with spots of gray thickly interspersed
Russet. Reddish or yellowish gray.
Sad. Of a dark color.
Silver.⎱
Silvered.⎬ Gray as silver.
Silvery.⎰
Slate-colored. Dark gray like slate.
Somber. Dusky gray.
Stone-colored. Gray as stone.

Bister. A brown pigment prepared from wood-soot.
Brown, etc. A dark color shading towards red, yellow, or black See *Adjectives.*
Hazel. Brown like the hazel-nut.
Ocher. A brown pigment made from clay.
Sepia. A brown pigment made from the secretion of the cuttle-fish.
Vandyke brown. A pigment of a semi-transparent brown color

Brown—*Adjectives*

Auburn. Reddish-brown.
Bay. Red-brown, inclining to a chestnut color
Brown. Of a dark color, inclining to redness.
Brown as a berry. Of the color of a berry.
Brown as mahogany. Of the color of mahogany
Brunette. Of a brownish complexion.
Chestnut. Of the same color as a chestnut
Chocolate. Dark-brown as chocolate.
Cinnamon. Yellowish-brown as cinnamon.
Dapple. Variegated brown.
Fawn-colored. Of a light-brown color, like a young deer.
Foxy. Reddish-brown like a fox.
Fuscous. Grayish-brown.
Liver-colored. Of a dark-brown color; dark or brownish-red, like the liver.
Mahogany. Dark reddish-brown, like mahogany.
Maroon. Brownish crimson.
Nut-brown. Brown as the shell of a dried hazel-nut.
Russet. Reddish or yellowish-brown, like a russet apple.
Snuff-colored. Of a dark yellowish-brown color.
Sunburnt. Burnt brown by the sun.
Tan. Of a yellowish brown color tinged with red
Tanned. Turned to a tan by the sun.
Tawny. Yellowish-brown in color, like tanned leather.
Whity-brown. Brownish with a white tinge.

Brown—*Verbs.*

Bronze. To make the color of brass.
Embrown. To color brown.
Render brown, etc. To make brown. See *Adjectives.*
Tan. To make the color of bark.

graze. To rub slightly; to eat grass. Friction-Lubrication, Interspace-Contact, Nutriment-Excretion.
gra′-zier. Stock-raiser. Domestication-Agriculture.
gré, savoir [F.] (grê, sɑ-vwɑr′). To take kindly. Thankfulness-Thanklessness.
grease. Fat. Friction-Lubrication, Pulpiness-Oil; **grease the palm,** Giving-Receiving, Motive-Caprice, Settlement-Default.
greas′-y. Fatty. Pulpiness-Oiliness.
great. Large, grand. Friction-Lubrication, Greatness-Littleness, Magnitude-Smallness, Reputation - Discredit, Unselfishness - Selfishness; **great bear,** Universe; **great circle sailing,** Midcourse-Circuit; **greatcoat,** Dress -Undress; **great doings,** Activity-Indolence, Consequence-Insig-

nificance; **great folks,** Gentility-Democracy; **great gun,** Design; **great man,** Gentility-Democracy; **great mogul,** Chief-Underling; **great number,** Multiplicity-Fewness; **great quantity,** Magnitude-Smallness.
great′-er. Having more of greatness. Supremacy-Subordinacy; **greater number,** Multiplicity-Paucity; **greater part,** Magnitude-Smallness, Whole-Part.
great′-est. Great in the highest degree. Supremacy-Subordinacy.
great′-ly. Largely. Magnitude-Smallness.
great′-ness. State of being great. Consequence-Insignificance, Magnitude-Smallness, Reputation-Discredit, Supremacy-Subordinacy.

GREATNESS—LITTLENESS.

Amplitude. The state or quality of being great in extent.
Bigness. State of being of great or of considerable size.
Bulk. Substance in reference to magnitude; the majority.
Caliber. Internal dimension of a tube.
Capacity. Amount of space for holding or carrying.
Corporation. The human body, especially if large and unwieldy
Corpulence. Large accumulation of fat on the body.
Dimension. Measurable extent or magnitude.
Embonpoint [F.]. Moderate corpulence.
Enormity. The state or quality of being excessively great.
Expanse, etc. Anything lying spread out in space, especially an extensive surface. See Extension.
Flesh and blood. A real substance or personage.
Full size. The limit of growth.
Greatness, etc. The state or quality of being relatively large. See *Adjectives.*

Exiguity. The state of being small and scanty
Inextension. Lack of extent in dimensions.
Littleness, etc. The state or quality of being below normal size. See *Adjectives.*
Parvitude. The state of being small and scanty.
Parvity. See Parvitude.
Smallness, etc. The state or quality of being comparatively less than another. See *Adjectives.*
Thinness, etc. The state or quality of lacking breadth or thickness. See Breadth-Narrowness.

Littleness—*Associated Nouns.*

Animalcule. A small animal, as a fly.
Atom. The smallest particle of matter that can enter into combination; indivisible. See Magnitude-Smallness.
Bacteria. Microscopic vegetable organisms.

GREATNESS—LITTLENESS—*Continued.*

Hugeness. The state or quality of being great in bulk.
Immensity. The state or quality of being very great in size.
Largeness. The state or quality of being greater than most of the same kind
Largest portion. The greatest part of anything. See WHOLE-PART.
Lustihood. Vigor of body.
Magnitude. Amount of measurable extent.
Mass. Several quantities regarded as a whole.
Monstrosity. The state or quality of being extraordinary in size.
Obesity. Excessive fatness.
Plumpness. The state of being well-rounded.
Proportions. Relative magnitude.
Scantling. Dimensions of a timber in length and breadth; a set of fixed measures.
Size. Measure of a thing in reference to a standard; sometimes relative largeness as opposed to smallness.
Tonnage. Internal cubic capacity expressed in tons.
Tunnage. Same as TONNAGE.
Turgidity, etc. The state or quality of being unnaturally distended or swollen. See ENLARGEMENT.
Volume. A large quantity.

GREATNESS—*Associated Nouns.*

Antæus. A giant athlete slain by Hercules.
Behemoth. An animal, probably the hippopotamus, described in the Book of Job.
Block. A piece of wood more or less bulky.
Brobdingnagian. One of a race of giants in *Gulliver's Travels.*
Bulk. Magnitude of material substance.
Bushel. A dry measure of thirty-two quarts.
Clod. A lump or mass of earth, turf, etc.
Colossus. A statue of gigantic size. [Colossus at Rhodes, said to bestride the harbor entrance.]
Cyclops. One of a race of giants, sons of Neptune and Amphitrite, having but one eye in the middle of the forehead.
Elephant. The largest land animal in existence.
Gargantua. A gigantic, wonderful personage of Rabelais.
Giant. A man of extraordinary bulk and stature.
Gog and Magog. Popular names for two colossal wooden statues in the Guildhall, London.
Goliath. A Philistine giant. [Bible.]
Heap, etc. A great number or large quantity of things not placed in a pile. See GATHERING.
Hippopotamus. A large amphibious mammal common to the rivers of Africa.
Leviathan. An aquatic animal described in the Book of Job.
Life-size. The natural size.
Loaf. Any thick lump, mass, or cake.
Lump. A solid mass of matter of irregular shape.
Mammoth. An extinct, hairy, maned elephant whose remains are found in the northern parts of both continents.
Mass. A large quantity.
Monster. Something of unnatural size.
Mound. An artificial hill or elevation of earth.
Mountain. A portion of land rising above the level of the earth
Nugget. A mass of precious metal.
Porpoise. The true dolphin, a fish about five feet in length.
Spanker. Something larger than common.
Strapper. A person or thing of uncommon size.
Thumper. That which causes a heavy sound when falling.
Triton among the minnows. A marine deity among small fish. [Shakespeare, *Coriolanus*, III, i.]
Tun. A large cask.
Whale. A large aquatic mammal, which sometimes grows to be one hundred feet long
Whopper. Something uncommonly large of the kind.

GREATNESS—*Verbs.*

Become large, etc. See ENLARGEMENT.
Be large, etc See *Adjectives.*

GREATNESS—*Adjectives.*

Ample. Of great dimensions or capacity.
Amplitudinous. Of great extent.
Big. Of great or considerable size or amount, relatively or absolutely.
Bouncing. Large and active.
Brawny. Having or characterized by great muscular strength
Brobdingnagian. Gigantic. [*Gulliver's Travels.*]
Bulky. Of great magnitude and unwieldy.
Burly. Large of body.
Capacious. Able to contain much

LITTLENESS—ASSOCIATED NOUNS—*Continued.*

Barleycorn. A grain of barley.
Bubble. A thin film of liquid inflated with air or gas.
Button. A globule of metal remaining in an assay cup after fusion.
Chit. A child or babe.
Cock-sparrow. The male of a very common small bird.
Dapperling. A dwarf.
Doll. A toy baby; Dolly; Dorothy
Duodecimo. A book consisting of sheets, each of which is folded into twelve leaves.
Dwarf. An animal or plant which is much below the ordinary size of its kind or species.
Elf. A small imaginary supernatural being.
Elzevir edition. Books published by the Elzevir family at Amsterdam, from about 1592 to 1680, noted for their neatness and elegant small type.
Emmet. An ant.
Entozoon. One of the species of worms which live parasitically in the interior of other animals.
Epitome. A brief abridgment of a writing.
Fly. A small winged insect.
Fragment, etc. A small, detached portion. See WHOLE-PART.
Gnat. A small blood-sucking fly.
Grain of sand. A single small particle of earth or rock.
Grub. The larva of an insect, especially of a beetle.
Homunculus. A little man; a dwarf.
Hop-o'-my-thumb. Anything very small; a dwarf.
Infusoria. One of the class of the lowest divisions of the animal kingdom.
Insect. A very small animal.
Liliputian. A person or thing of very small size. [Swift, *Gulliver's Travels.*]
Maggot. The footless larva of any fly.
Manikin. } A little man; a model of the human body.
Mannikin. }
Mathematical point. A point so small that it cannot be seen.
Microcosm. A little world; man, as a supposed epitome of the exterior universe.
Midge. A very small fly.
Millet-seed. The seed of several species of grasses.
Minnow. A small fresh-water fish.
Minutiæ. Very small particles. See CONSEQUENCE-INSIGNIFICANCE.
Mite. A small coin; a small weight; a minute insect.
Molehill. A little hillock of earth thrown up by moles.
Monad. Something ultimate and indivisible.
Mouse. A small rodent.
Mustard-seed. The very fine seed of the mustard plant.
Pebble. A small roundish stone.
Pigmy. A short, insignificant person; a race known to the Greeks.
Pigwidgeon. A cant word for anything petty or small.
Point. An indefinitely small spot.
Point of a pin. The sharp end of a pin.
Powder, etc. The fine particles to which any dry substance is reduced by pounding, etc. See FRIABILITY.
Puppet. A small image in the human form.
Rudiment. That which lies at the bottom of any development.
Runt. An unusually small animal compared with others of its kind.
Shrimp. A small shell-fish.
Small fry. Young or small things in general.
Tit. A small horse; a morsel.
Tom Thumb. A diminutive personage celebrated in the legendary history of England; the name assumed by Charles Sherwood Stratton, a famous American dwarf, who exhibited himself in public for many years, 1838-1883.
Tomtit. The titmouse.
Urchin. A child.
Vanishing-point. The point to which all parallel lines in the same plane tend in the representation.
Worm. A small creeping or crawling animal.

LITTLENESS—*Scientific Terms.*

Micography. The description of microscopic objects.
Micrometer. An instrument for measuring very small distances.
Microscope. An instrument to aid in seeing very minute objects.
Scale. Anything marked by lines for use in measurement.
Vernier. A small movable auxiliary scale for obtaining fractional parts of a scale. [P. Vernier, French inventor.]

LITTLENESS—*Verbs.*

Become small, etc. See INCREASE-DECREASE, ENLARGEMENT-DIMINUTION.

GREATNESS—LITTLENESS—*Continued.*

GREATNESS—Adjectives—*Continued.*

Chopping.   Strong and active.
Chubby-faced.   Having a full, round face.
Chub-faced.   See Chubby-faced.
Colossal.   Of immense size. ["He doth bestride the narrow world like a Colossus." Shakespeare, *Julius Cæsar*, I, ii.]
Comprehensive.   Large in scope.
Considerable.   Somewhat large
Corpulent.   Very fleshy.
Cyclopean.   Gigantic.
Enormous.   Far exceeding the usual size.
Fat.   Having excessive flesh.
Fat as a pig.
Fat as a quail.
Fat as bacon.   } Very fat.
Fat as brawn.
Fat as butter.
Fine.   Of good size.
Fleshy.   Of much flesh.
Full.   Ample in extent or volume; well filled.
Fullgrown.   As large as it is likely to become.
Gargantuan.   Incredibly big. [Gargantua, Rabelais.]
Gaunt.   Tall and thin.
Giant.   Of very great size.
Giantlike.   Like a giant.
Gigantic.   Unusually great in dimensions.
Goodly.   Rather large.
Great, etc.   Relatively or unusually large.   See Magnitude.
Huge.   Having great bulk or unusual size.
Hulking.   Unwieldy; bulky.
Hulky.   See Hulking.
Immeasurable.   Indefinitely extensive.
Immense.   Very great in size.
In condition.   Ready for service.
Infinite, etc.   So great as to be immeasurable.   See Infinity
In good case.   In good condition.
In good condition.   Strong.
Jolly.   Most remarkable
Large.   Exceeding most other things of like kind in bulk or size.
Large as life.   Of life-size.
Lubberly.   Big and clumsy.
Lumpish.   Large and inert.
Lusty.   Big and strong.
Magnificent.   Imposing in appearance.
Massive.   Of great bulk and weight.
Massy.   Having much bulk or weight.
Mighty.   Of unusual size or power.
Monster.   Extraordinary in size.
Monstrous.   Of extraordinary and unnatural size.
Overgrown.   Grown beyond the fit or natural size
Plump.   Extended to the full.
Plump as a dumpling.   } Degrees of size.
Plump as a partridge.
Portly.   Somewhat stout or corpulent.
Puffy.   Swelled with air or anything soft.
Spacious, etc.   Of very great extent.   See Extension.
Spanking.   Uncommonly large.
Squab.   Fat and thick.
Stalwart.   Large and powerful.
Stout.   Having full measure.
Strapping.   Large and strong.
Stupendous.   Astonishing in magnitude.
Thumping.   Of extraordinary size
Thundering.   Very great.
Towering.   Very high.
Unwieldy.   Difficult to handle on account of size.
Vast.   Of great or immeasurable extent
Vasty.   See Vast.
Voluminous.   Of great bulk or size.
Well-fed.   Fat.
Whacking.   Very large.
Whopping.   Unusually large.

LITTLENESS—Verbs—*Continued.*

Be little, etc.   See *Adjectives.*
Lie in a nutshell.   Be very small.

LITTLENESS—*Adjectives.*

Atomic.   Extremely minute.
Corpuscular.   Small and insignificant in size.
Cramp.   Contracted in form.
Cramped.   Contracted in form and action.
Dapper.   Little and active.
Diminutive.   Of relatively small size.
Dumpy.   Short and thick.
Duodecimo.   Of twelve pages of small size, as a book.
Dwarf.   Smaller than others of its species.
Dwarfed.   Kept or made to become smaller.
Dwarfish.   Below the normal size.
Embryonic.   Not yet developed.
Evanescent.   Gradually passing away.
Exiguous.   Small and slender.
Granular, etc.   Small and fine, like grains.   See Friability.
Homeopathic.   Very small in quantity.
Impalpable.   Too small to be felt by the touch.
Imperceptible.   Too small to be perceived.
Inappreciable.   Too small to be taken into account.
Inconsiderable, etc.   Small in quantity or importance.   See Conse-quence-Insignificance.
Infinitesimal.   Infinitely small.
Intangible.   Imperceptible to the touch.
Invisible.   Incapable of being seen.
Liliputian.   Abnormally and ridiculously small. [*Gulliver's Travels.*]
Limited.   Confined to certain bounds.
Little.   Below normal size; smaller than other like things.
Microscopic.   Visible only under a microscope.
Miniature.   Much smaller than reality.
Minikin.   Of small size and delicate form.
Minute.   Exceedingly small.
Molecular.   Of or pertaining to extremely small particles.
Petty.   Of little importance.
Pigmy.   Very small for its kind.
Pocket.   Small enough to go into a pocket.
Pollard.   Shorn of the head.
Portable.   Small enough to carry.
Portative.   Easily carried.
  uny.   Small and weak.
Rudimental.   Only partially developed.
Rudimentary.   In an incomplete state of development.
Scant.   Scarcely enough.
Scraggy.   Lean and bony.
Scrubby.   Of stunted growth.
Short, etc.   Of little stature or length.   See Length-Shortness.
Shrunk, etc.   Made smaller by contraction.   See Enlargement-Diminution.
Small, etc.   Comparatively less than another or than a standard.   See Magnitude-Smallness.
Squat.   Short and thick.
Stunted.   Checked in growth.
Thin, etc.   Lacking plumpness of figure.   See Breadth-Narrow-ness.
Tiny.   Very small.
Undersized.   Below normal size.
Weazened.   Shrunken and withered.
Wee.   Very small.

LITTLENESS—*Adverbs.*

In a nutshell.   Briefly.
In a small compass.   Diminutively.
On a small scale.   In miniature.

greave.   Armor for the lower leg.   Dress-Undress.
greed.   Excessive desire.   Desire-Distaste, Fasting-Gluttony.
greed'-i-ness.   Ardent and selfish desire.   Desire-Distaste, Fasting-Gluttony.
greed'-y.   Avaricious.   Desire-Distaste, Extrava-gance-Avarice, Fasting-Gluttony.

Greek.   The language of the Greeks; belonging to Greece.   Clearness-Obscurity, Robber; **Greek Church,** Orthodoxy-Heterodoxy; **Greek Kalends,** Duration-Neverness; **St. Giles's Greek,** Word-Neology.
green.   Unripe; inexperienced; new.   Credulousness-Skepticism,   Gulf-Plain,   Habit-Desuetude,

HEALTH-SICKNESS, INFANCY-AGE, KNOWLEDGE-IGNORANCE, PREPARATION-NONPREPARATION, NOVELTY-ANTIQUITY, REDNESS-GREENNESS, REMEMBRANCE-FORGETFULNESS, SKILL-UNSKILFULNESS; **board of green cloth,** TRIBUNAL; **green fields and pastures new,** CITY-COUNTRY; **green memory,** REMEMBRANCE-FORGETFULNESS; **green old age,** INFANCY-AGE.

green'-back". Paper money. MONEY.

green'-eyed" mon'-ster. Jealousy. PARDON-JEALOUSY.

green'-horn". Novice. ADEPT-BUNGLER, GULL-DECEIVER, SAGE-FOOL, SCHOLAR-DUNCE.

green'-house". House for sheltering tender plants. CONTENTS-RECEIVER, DOMESTICATION-AGRICULTURE.

green'-ish. Somewhat green. REDNESS-GREENNESS.

green'-ness. The state of being green. REDNESS-GREENNESS.

green'-room". Waiting room for actors in a theater. ACTING.

green'-sward". Green turf. GULF-PLAIN.

greet. To address on meeting. JUBILATION-LAMENTATION, POLITENESS-IMPOLITENESS.

greet'-ing. Welcome. POLITENESS-IMPOLITENESS, SOCIABILITY-PRIVACY.

gre-ga'-ri-ous. Flocking together. SOCIABILITY-PRIVACY.

gre-nade'. Explosive shell. WEAPON.

gren"-a-dier'. One of a regiment of big soldiers. BELLIGERENT, HEIGHT-LOWNESS.

grey. See GRAY.

grid'-e-lin. Gray violet. YELLOWNESS-PURPLE.

grid'-i"-ron. Broiling-grate. CROSSING, OVEN-REFRIGERATOR.

grief. Sorrow. PLEASURE-PAIN; **come to grief,** PLEASURE-PAIN, WELFARE-MISFORTUNE.

griev'-ance. Wrong done. GOOD-EVIL, PLEASURABLENESS-PAINFULNESS, RIGHT-WRONG, SUCCESS-FAILURE.

grieve. To sorrow. JUBILATION-LAMENTATION, LIGHTHEARTEDNESS-DEJECTION, PLEASURABLENESS-PAINFULNESS, PLEASURE-PAIN, RIGHT-WRONG.

griev'-ous. Causing grief. GOODNESS-BADNESS, PLEASURABLENESS-PAINFULNESS.

griev'-ous-ly. Heavily. MAGNITUDE-SMALLNESS.

grif'-fin. Vulture. CONVENTIONALITY-UNCONVENTIONALITY.

griff'-fin-age. Greenness. WRITING-PRINTING.

griffo [It.] (grîf'-fo). Frizzled. MIXTURE-HOMOGENEITY.

grig. Cricket. LIGHTHEARTEDNESS-DEJECTION.

grill. Gridiron. HEATING-COOLING.

grille. Grated gate. CROSSING.

grim. Disagreeable. BEAUTY-UGLINESS, FAVORITE-MOROSENESS, LIGHTHEARTEDNESS-DEJECTION, PLEASURABLENESS-PAINFULNESS, POLITENESS-IMPOLITENESS; **grim-faced,** BEAUTY-UGLINESS, LIGHTHEARTEDNESS; **grim-visaged war,** BEAUTY-UGLINESS, FIGHTING-CONCILIATION, LIGHTHEARTEDNESS-DEJECTION.

gri-mace'. Smirk. PROPORTION-DEFORMITY, SOCIETY-AFFECTATION.

grimacier [F.] (gri-mɑ-si-ê'). Grinner. ACTING, BEAUTY-UGLINESS, WAG.

gri-mal'-kin. Old female cat. FAUNA-FLORA.

grime. Make dirty. CLEANNESS-FILTHINESS.

gri'-my. Dirty. CLEANNESS-FILTHINESS.

grin. Smile. JUBILATION-LAMENTATION, SOCIETY-DERISION; **grin a ghastly smile,** BEAUTY-UGLINESS, LIGHTHEARTEDNESS-DEJECTION.

grind'. To rub. CHARITABLENESS-MALEVOLENCE, EDUCATION-LEARNING, ENLARGEMENT-DIMINUTION, FRIABILITY, FRICTION-LUBRICATION, SHARPNESS, BLUNTNESS; **grind one's teeth,** FAVORITE-ANGER; **grind the organ,** MUSICIAN.

grind'-er. That which grinds. FRIABILITY, INSTRUCTOR-PUPIL.

grind'-ing. See GRIND. CHARITABLENESS-MALEVOLENCE, HARSHNESS-MILDNESS, PLEASURABLENESS-PAINFULNESS.

grind'-stone". Stone used in sharpening tools. FRIABILITY, SHARPNESS-BLUNTNESS.

grip. Hold. KEEPING-RELINQUISHMENT, RULE-LICENSE, TAKING-RECEIVING; **grip of the hand,** POLITENESS-IMPOLITENESS.

gripe. See GRIP. EXTRAVAGANCE-AVARICE, SENSUALITY-SUFFERING, PLEASURABLENESS-PAINFULNESS, RULE-LICENSE.

griped. Grasped. PLEASURE-PAIN.

gri'-ping. Avaricious. EXTRAVAGANCE-AVARICE.

grisaille [F.] (gri-zêl'). A style of painting. GRAY-BROWN, PAINTING.

grisette [F.] (gri-zet'). Working-girl of Paris. GENTILITY-DEMOCRACY, MALE-FEMALE, PURITY-RAKE.

gris'-ly. Savage. BEAUTY-UGLINESS.

grist. Grain to be ground. MATERIALS, PROVISION-WASTE; **grist to the mill,** GAIN-LOSS, PROVISION-WASTE, USEFULNESS-USELESSNESS.

gris'-tle. Cartilage. SOLIDITY-RARITY, TOUGHNESS-BRITTLENESS.

gris'-tly. Consisting of gristle. TOUGHNESS-BRITTLENESS.

grist'-mill". A mill for grinding grain. FRIABILITY.

grit. Sand. FRIABILITY; **grit in the oil,** OBSTRUCTION-HELP.

grit'-ty. Containing grit. FRIABILITY, HARDNESS-SOFTNESS.

griz'-zled. Gray. GRAY-BROWN, VARIEGATION.

griz'-zly. Grayish. GRAY-BROWN.

groan. Moan. CRY-ULULATION, JUBILATION-LAMENTATION.

groat. Old English coin. MONEY.

gro'-cer. Dealer in groceries. PROVISION-WASTE.

gro'-cer-y. Grocer's store. SWEETNESS-ACIDITY.

grog. Drink of water and spirits. NUTRIMENT-EXCRETION, TEETOTALISM-INTEMPERANCE.

grog'-gy. Tipsy. See TEETOTALISM-INTEMPERANCE.

groin. Junction of thigh and abdomen. ANGULARITY.

groom. One who cares for horses. CHIEF-UNDERLING; **groom of the chambers,** CHIEF-UNDERLING.

groove. Furrow. GROOVE, HABIT-DESUETUDE; **move in a groove,** CONVENTIONALITY-UNCONVENTIONALITY; **put in a groove for,** PREPARATION-NONPREPARATION.

GROOVE.

Chamber. A groove or channel.
Channel. Bed of a long body of water.
Crack. A partial break.
Dike. } A ditch.
Dyke. }
Ditch. A trench dug in the ground.
Fluting. A groove cut spirally.
Fosse. A ditch around a fortified place.
Furrow. Any long depression.
Groove. A furrow for something to fit in.
Gutter. A channel for carrying off rain-water.
Incision. An opening made with a cutting instrument.
Kennel. The gutter of a street.
Moat. A ditch on the outside of a fortress wall.
Ravine. A deep gorge or hollow.
Rut. A groove forming a path for anything.
Score. Notch; incised line.
Scratch. A slight linear incision.
Slit. A long, deep incision.
Streak. A long, irregular line.
Stria. Minute grooves.
Sulcus. A long, narrow furrow.
Trench. A long, narrow excavation in the ground.
Trough. A long open receptacle for water.

Groove—Verbs.

Bite in. To make an indentation mark in.
Furrow, etc. See *Nouns*.
Engrave. To carve upon a surface.
Etch. To engrave by means of a needle and mordant.
Flute. To form parallel grooves.
Incise. To cut with a sharp instrument.
Plow. To furrow with a plow.

Groove—Adjectives.

Bisulcate.
Bisulcous. } Having the hoof divided by two grooves.
Canaliculated. Furrowed longitudinally.
Corduroy. A kind of ribbed cotton cloth.
Fluted. Ornamented with parallel grooves.
Furrowed, etc. Marked with grooves or furrows. See *Verbs*.
Ribbed. Having ridges.
Striated. Covered with minute grooves.
Sulcated. Having a deep furrowed surface.
Trisulcate. Having the hoof divided by three grooves.

grope. To feel about in the dark. TOUCH, TRIAL; **grope in the dark,** DIFFICULTY-FACILITY.
gro'-schen. A coin. VALUES.
gross. Coarse; large. BEAUTY-UGLINESS, CLEANNESS-FILTHINESS, FIVE-QUINQUESECTION, MAGNITUDE-SMALLNESS, PURITY-IMPURITY, REPENTANCE-OBDURACY, VIRTUE-VICE, WHOLE-PART; **gross credulity,** CREDULOUSNESS-SKEPTICISM; **gross receipts,** OUTLAY-INCOME.
gross'-ly. Greatly. MAGNITUDE-SMALLNESS.
gross'-head". Stupid person. SAGE-FOOL.
gross'-head-ed. Stupid. SAGACITY-INCAPACITY
grossiereté, [F.] (gro-si-êr-tê'). Coarseness. POLITENESS-IMPOLITENESS.
gross'-ness. Rudeness. PURITY-IMPURITY.
grot. A small cave. CONVEXITY-CONCAVITY.
gro-tesque'. Fantastic. CONVENTIONALITY-UNCONVENTIONALITY, PROPORTION-DEFORMITY, PURITY-CRUDENESS, SOCIETY-LUDICROUSNESS.
grot'-to. Small cavern. CONTENTS-RECEIVER, CONVEXITY-CONCAVITY.
ground. Soil; base, important part, or beginning of anything. CAUSE-EFFECT, COVER-LINING, EDUCATION-MISTEACHING, EVIDENCE-COUNTEREVIDENCE, EXTENSION-DISTRICT, GULF-PLAIN, MOTIVE-CAPRICE, OCEAN-LAND, PROPERTY, SUSPENSION-SUPPORT, TOP-BOTTOM; **above ground,** LIFE-DEATH; **dress the ground,** DOMESTICATION-AGRICULTURE; **fall to the ground,** SUCCESS-FAILURE; **get over the ground,** SWIFTNESS-SLOWNESS; **go over the ground,** TRANSMISSION; **ground bait,** GIVING-RECEIVING; **ground cut from under one,** SUCCESS-FAILURE; **ground floor,** CONTENTS-RECEIVER, HEIGHT-LOWNESS, TOP-BOTTOM; **ground of quarrel,** VARIANCE-ACCORD; **ground on,** RATIONALE-LUCK; **ground plan,** DELINEATION-CARICATURE; **ground sliding from under one,** SECURITY-INSECURITY; **ground swell,** AGITATION, RIVER-WIND; **level with the ground,** CREATION-DESTRUCTION; **maintain one's ground,** ATTACK-DEFENSE, PERSISTENCE-WHIM; **prepare the ground,** PREPARATION-NONPREPARATION; **stand one's ground,** ATTACK-DEFENSE, CONSERVATION, REPRISAL-RESISTANCE.
ground'-age. A toll levied on vessels importing grain into the port of London. PRICE-DISCOUNT.
ground'-ed. Stuck in the ground. SUCCESS-FAILURE; **grounded on,** EVIDENCE-COUNTEREVIDENCE, TOP-BOTTOM; **well grounded,** KNOWLEDGE-IGNORANCE.
ground'-less. Without foundation or cause. RATIOCINATION-INSTINCT, SUBSTANCE-NULLITY, TRUTH-ERROR.
ground'-ling. One standing in the pit of a theater. GENTILITY-DEMOCRACY.
ground"-mo-raine'. A till under an iceberg. GEOLOGY.

grounds. Settlings. CLEANNESS-FILTHINESS, GULF-PLAIN.
ground'-work". Basis. CAUSE-EFFECT, PREDECESSOR-CONTINUATION, PREPARATION-NONPREPARATION, SUSPENSION-SUPPORT, TOP-BOTTOM.
group. Gathering. GATHERING-SCATTERING, ORGANIZATION-DISORGANIZATION.
grout. Cement. CONNECTIVE.
grove. Woods free from underbrush. CONVEXITY-CONCAVITY, DWELLER-HABITATION, FAUNA-FLORA.
grov'-el. To creep. HEIGHT-LOWNESS, PRESUMPTION-OBSEQUIOUSNESS, SWIFTNESS-SLOWNESS, UPRIGHTNESS-DISHONESTY.
grov'el-ling. Mean; sordid. PRESUMPTION-OBSEQUIOUSNESS, UPRIGHTNESS-DISHONESTY.
grow. To increase. CONVERSION, ENLARGEMENT-DIMINUTION, INCREASE-DECREASE; **grow from,** CAUSE-EFFECT; **grow into,** CONVERSION-REVERSION; **grow less,** ENLARGEMENT-DIMINUTION; **grow taller,** HEIGHT-LOWNESS; **grow together,** COHESION-LOOSENESS; **grow up,** ENLARGEMENT-DIMINUTION; **grow upon one,** HABIT-DESUETUDE.
growl. To talk in a surly manner. CHARITABLENESS-MENACE, CRY-ULULATION, FAVORITE-ANGER, JUBILATION-LAMENTATION, POLITENESS-IMPOLITENESS.
growl'-er. One who growls; vessel for carrying beer. CONTENTEDNESS-DISCONTENTMENT, CONVEYANCE-VESSEL.
growl'-ing. Angry faultfinding. FAVORITE-MOROSENESS.
grown. Increased. **Grown up,** MANHOOD.
growth. That which has grown. CONVERSION-REVERSION, CONVEXITY-CONCAVITY, CREATION-DESTRUCTION, ENLARGEMENT-DIMINUTION, FAUNA-FLORA, INCREASE-DECREASE.
grub. Kind of worm; food. GREATNESS-LITTLENESS, NUTRIMENT-EXCRETION; **grub up,** DISCOVERY, INJECTION-EJECTION.
Grub'-street". Center for literary hacks in London. **Grub-street writer,** MISSIVE-PUBLICATION.
grudge. To begrudge. EXTRAVAGANCE-AVARICE, FAVORITE-ANGER, LOVE-HATE, PROFFER-REFUSAL, READINESS-RELUCTANCE; **bear a grudge,** CHARITABLENESS-MALEVOLENCE, LOVE-HATE; **owe a grudge,** LOVE-HATE.
grudg'-ing. Reluctant. EXTRAVAGANCE-AVARICE. READINESS-RELUCTANCE; **grudging praise,** APPROVAL-DISAPPROVAL.
grudg'-ing-ly. Reluctantly. READINESS-RELUCTANCE.
grue'-some. Horrid. BEAUTY-UGLINESS.
gruff. Surly. CACOPHONY, POLITENESS-IMPOLITENESS, RESONANCE-NONRESONANCE.
grum. Sour. CACOPHONY, FAVORITE-MOROSENESS.
grum'-ble. To find fault. CONTENTEDNESS-DISCONTENTMENT, CRY-ULULATION.
grum'-bler. One who complains. APPROVAL-DISAPPROVAL, JUBILATION-LAMENTATION.
grume. Clot. PULPINESS-OILINESS.
gru'-mous. Clotted. PULPINESS-OILINESS, SOLIDITY-RARITY.
grump'-y. Gruff. FAVORITE-MOROSENESS.
grunt. To make a noise like a pig. CRY-ULULATION, JUBILATION-LAMENTATION.
grun'-tle. To grunt. CRY-ULULATION.
gua'-no. Kind of fertilizer. CLEANNESS-FILTHINESS.
guar"-an-tee'. Promise; security. ENGAGEMENT-RELEASE, SECURITY.
guar'-an-ty. A pledge. SECURITY.
guard. One who watches; that which protects. ATTACK-DEFENSE, BELLIGERENT, CONSERVATION, GUARD-PRISONER, SECURITY-INSECURITY, WAYFARER-SEAFARER; **advanced guard,** WARNING; **guard against,** ATTACK-DEFENSE, PREPARATION-NONPREP-

ARATION; **guard ship,** BELLIGERENT; **off one's guard,** CAREFULNESS-CARELESSNESS, EXPECTATION-SURPRISE, HEED-DISREGARD, SECURITY-INSECURITY; **on one's guard,** CAREFULNESS-CARELESSNESS, RECK-LESSNESS-CAUTION, WARNING; **rear guard,** ANTERIORITY-POSTERIORITY, WARNING; **throw off one's guard,** CAREFULNESS-CARELESSNESS, CRAFT-ARTLESSNESS.

GUARD—PRISONER.

Ayah. A nurse or waiting-maid.
Body-guard. A number of persons maintained for the purpose of personal protection.
Bonne [F.]. A nurse-maid.
Castellan. The keeper of a castle.
Charley. A name given to a night watchman.
Coast-guard. Police stationed along a coast.
Concierge [F.]. A janitor or doorkeeper.
Custodian. One having the care of anything.
Custos (L.]. A guardian or custodian.
Duenna. An elderly woman who keeps watch over a young woman.
Escort. A guard which accompanies a person when traveling.
Gamekeeper. One having the care of game.
Gaoler. Jailer.
Governess. A female governor; especially, over children.
Governor. One who governs or controls; especially, one having executive authority.
Guard. A person who or thing which protects or defends.
Guarda costa [It.]. A coast-guard.
Guardian. One having legal power over person or property, or both, of another.
Jailer. The keeper of a jail.
Keeper. A person or thing that keeps or has possession of anything.
Nurse. One who cares for children or invalids.
Protector. One who guards from injury.
Ranger. One who protects large tracts of land.
Sentinel. A soldier stationed at some point for protection.
Sentry. A sentinel.
Turnkey. One having the keys of a prison.
Warder. One who wards or keeps.
Watch. One or more persons set to guard against danger.

guarda costa [It.] (gwar'-da cos'-ta). Coast-guard. GUARD-PRISONER.
guard'-ed. Protected; cautious. CAREFULNESS-CARELESSNESS, RECKLESSNESS-CAUTION, TERMS.
guard'-i-an. Protector. ATTACK-DEFENSE, GUARD-PRISONER, SECURITY-INSECURITY; **guardian angel,** ANTAGONIST-ASSISTANT, BENEFACTOR-EVILDOER, SECURITY-INSECURITY.
guard'-less. Lacking defense. SECURITY-INSECURITY.
guard'-room". Prisoner's cell. RELEASE-PRISONER.
gu"-ber-na'-tion. Government. MANAGEMENT.
gu"-ber-na-to'-ri-al. Pertaining to a governor. RULE-LICENSE.
gudg'-eon. Simpleton. GULL-DECEIVER.
guer'-don. Reward. RECOMPENSE-PUNITION.
guerre à outrance [F.] (gêr a u-tran·s'). War to extermination. FIGHTING-CONCILIATION.
guerre, nom de [F.] (gêr, non· de). A nickname. NAME-MISNOMER.
guerre, ruse de [F.] (gêr, rüz de). Stratagem of war. CRAFT-ARTLESSNESS.
guer-ril'-la. One of an irregular band of soldiers. BELLIGERENT.
guess. To conjecture. HYPOTHESIS.
guess'-work". Guess. HYPOTHESIS.
guest. Visitor. FRIEND-FOE.
guet-apens [F.] (gê-ta-pan'). An ambush. LIFE-KILLING, TRUTHFULNESS-FRAUD.
guet, mot du [F.] (gê, mo dü). A watchword. SIGN.
guf-faw'. Noisy laughter. JUBILATION-LAMENTATION.
gug'-gle. To gurgle. CRY-ULULATION, RESONANCE-NONRESONANCE, RIVER-WIND, VISCIDITY-FOAM.
guid'-ance. A leading. ADVICE, EDUCATION-MISTEACHING, MANAGEMENT.
guide. Director. ADVICE, EDUCATION-MISTEACHING, ENLIGHTENMENT-SECRECY, INSTRUCTOR-PUPIL, MANAGEMENT, MANAGER, SIGN, TRAVELING-NAVIGATION.
guide'-board". A board bearing direction for travelers. SIGN, WARNING.
guide'-book". Hand-book of maps, etc. ENLIGHTENMENT-SECRECY.

PRISONER.

Captive. One captured and held in confinement.
Close prisoner. One held in strict confinement.
Détenu [F.]. A prisoner.
Jail-bird. One who has frequently been imprisoned
Prisoner. One who is confined in a prison.
Ticket-of-leave man. A prisoner having a permit to be at large.

PRISONER—*Verbs*.

Be imprisoned. See *Adjectives*.
Stand committed. To be held for trial.

PRISONER—*Adjectives*.

Imprisoned. Confined in a prison.
In chains. Held in captivity by chains.
In charge. Under the care of.
In custody. In the safe-keeping of.
In durance vile. Kept as a prisoner.
In limbo. In prison.
In prison. Confined within the walls of a prison.
In quod. In prison.
On parole. Released on word of honor not to escape.
Under hatches. Confined under the deck of a ship.
Under lock and key. Restrained by lock and key.

GUARD—*Continued*.

Watch and ward. Continuous watch for the purpose of guarding.
Watchdog. A dog which watches or protects.
Watchman. One who watches or guards, as at night.

guid'-ed. Directed; guided by. CONVENTIONALITY-UNCONVENTIONALITY.
guide'-less. Lacking a guide. SECURITY-INSECURITY.
guide'-post". Post to which is nailed the guide-board. SIGN.
guid'-ing. Showing the way. **Guiding star,** MANAGEMENT, MANAGER.
gui'-don. A guide-flag carried by a mounted cavalry-man. SIGN, WARNING.
guild. See GILD.
guild'-hall". See GILDHALL.
guile. Deceit. CRAFT-ARTLESSNESS, TRUTHFULNESS-FRAUD.
guile'-less. Frank. CRAFT-ARTLESSNESS, TRUTHFULNESS-FALSEHOOD.
guil-loche'. Ornament. Architecture.
guil"-lo-tine'. To behead; an instrument for beheading. RECOMPENSE-PUNITION, RECOMPENSE-SCOURGE.
guilt. State of one who has done wrong. GOODNESS-BADNESS, INNOCENCE-GUILT.
guil'-ti-ness. INNOCENCE-GUILT.
guilt'-less. Innocent. INNOCENCE-GUILT.
guilt'-less-ness. State of being guiltless. INNOCENCE-GUILT.
guilt'-sick". Sick with guilt. INNOCENCE-GUILT.
guilt'-y. Having done wrong. **Find guilty,** EXCULPATION-CONVICTION; **plead guilty,** REPENTANCE-OBDURACY.
guindé [F.] (gan·-dê'). Bombastic. PURITY-CRUDENESS.
guin'-ea. An English coin. MONEY, VALUES.
guis'-ard. A clown. ACTING.
guise. Pretense; dress. APPEARANCE-DISAPPEARANCE, CONDITION-SITUATION, CONDUCT, DRESS-UNDRESS, PRETEXT, WAY.
guis'-er. Masker. ACTING.
gui-tar'. Musical instrument. MUSICAL INSTRUMENTS.
gules. Red color. REDNESS-GREENNESS.
gulf. Body of water extending into the land. DEEPNESS-SHALLOWNESS, GULF-PLAIN, INTERSPACE-CONTACT,

GULF—PLAIN.

Armlet. A little arm of the sea.

Arm of the sea. A body of water projecting into the land from the sea.

Bay. The water between two projecting headlands

Belt. A long, narrow strait of water.

Bight. A slightly receding bay.

Cove. A small recess in the seashore.

Creek. A narrow inlet of water from the sea into the land.

Estuary. The mouth of a tidal river.

Euripus. The narrowest portion of the channel which separates Euboea from the mainland.

Fiord. A long and narrow arm of the sea with high rocky banks.

Firth. } The opening of a river into the sea.
Frith. }

Gulf. } A large body of water lying within a curve of the general
Gulph. } coast-line of a country.

Gut. A narrow passage of water.

Indraft. A small body of water leading into a larger.

Inlet. A small sheltered body of water.

Kyles. A strait.

Land covered with water. A pond, etc.

Lagoon. } A shallow inlet of the sea.
Lagune. }

Mouth. The part of a river where its waters join those of a larger body.

Natural harbor. An inlet of the sea so protected by nature as to afford safety for ships.

Ostiary. The opening by which a river empties its waters into the sea.

Roads. A place of anchorage off shore.

Sound. A long and proportionately narrow passage of water, more extensive than a strait.

Strait. A narrow passage of water. See LAKE.

GULF.—*Associated Nouns.*

Artesian well. A deep bored well receiving its water from an underground lake.

Broad. A lake formed by the expansion of a river.

Dead-water. Eddy-water.

Fish-pond. A small lake in which fish are kept.

Lake. A inland body of water.

Lin. A waterfall.

Loch. The Scottish word for lake.

Lough. The Irish word for lake.

Mere. A small lake.

Mill-pond. A pond formed by the water held back by the mill-dam.

Plash. A small collection of standing water.

Pond. A body of still water.

Pool. A collection of water in a natural depression.

Puddle. A small and dirty pool.

Reservoir. A basin, either natural or artificial, containing water to be used for some specific purpose. See STORE.

Sheet of water. A broad extent of water.

Slab. A puddle.

Standing water. Stagnant water.

Tarn. A small mountain lake.

Well. A spring.

GULF—*Nouns of Means.*

Dam. A barrier to stop the flow of a stream so as to form a small lake.

Ditch. A narrow trench in the ground in connection with a dike.

Dike. } An embankment thrown up to form an artificial body of
Dyke. } water.

Basin. A whole tract of country drained by a river and its tributaries.

Bush. Flat country covered by a scrubby growth.

Campagna [It.]. The flat country about Rome.

Campus. College grounds. [American.]

Champaign country. Level and open ground.

Common. A flat piece of ground owned in common by a town.

Desert. A barren plain.

Downs. Broad ridges of elevated land near the sea, covered with fine turf.

Face of the country. The open, level part of the country.

Field. A cultivated piece of flat land.

Grass-plat. A small, even piece of ground covered with grass.

Green. A small grassy plain.

Greensward. Turf on which grass grows.

Grounds. A level tract of land put to a special use.

Haugh. Low-lying rich lands.

Heath. } A plain covered with coarse herbage, especially heather.
Heather. }

Lawn. A flat grassy space.

Lay. See LEA.

Lea. } A plain used for pasturage.
Ley. }

Llano. An extensive plain with or without grass.

Mead. A poetic form for meadow.

Meadow. A plain producing grass, generally mown for hay.

Moor. An extensive tract of waste land.

Moorland. See MOOR.

Open country. Country level and free from growth.

Pampas. The great treeless plains of South America.

Park An enclosed and partly wooded plain used for recreation.

Pasturage. A plain used for grazing.

Plain. An expanse of level land.

Plat. A small, flat piece of ground.

Plateau, etc. An elevated plain. See ERECTNESS-FLATNESS.

Plot. A piece of ground set apart.

Prairie. A treeless plain covered with rolling grass, especially as in the western part of the United States.

Savanna. A plain covered with low vegetation in a tropical region.

Sod. A small extent of grassy surface-soil.

Steppe. A vast, treeless plain, as in Russia and Siberia.

Sward. Land thickly covered with grass.

Table-land. An elevated plain.

Tundra. A rolling plain of Russia and Siberia, covered with moss

Turf. A flat piece of ground covered with grass.

Vega. An open and usually fruitful plain.

Veldt. An open plain used generally for pasturage.

Waste. An uncultivated plain.

Weary waste. A desolate and uncultivated plain.

Wild. An uninhabited or uncultivated plain.

Wold. A gently sloping plain.

PLAIN—*Adjectives.*

Alluvial. Pertaining to earth laid down by means of water.

Campestrian. Growing in or pertaining to plains.

Champaign. Pertaining to level country.

GULF—*Continued.*

GULF—*Adjective.*

Lacustrine. Pertaining to a lake.

---

gull. One easily duped. GULL-DECEIVER, HYPERBOLE, TRUTHFULNESS-FALSEHOOD.

GULL—DECEIVER.

April fool. One who is sportively imposed upon by others on the first day of April.

Cat's-paw. One who is used by another to accomplish his purposes.

Cull. } A person easily deceived tricked, or imposed upon.
Cully. }

Cyclops. The one-eyed giants cunningly deceived by Ulysses.

Dupe. One who has been, or is easily deceived.

Flat. A dull fellow; a simpleton.

Fool. One destitute of reason or the powers of understanding. See SAGE-FOOL.

Gobemouche [F.]. A silly and credulous person.

Greenhorn. A raw, inexperienced person.

Gudgeon. A simpleton.

Gull. A person who is easily taken advantage of.

Actor. See ACTING.

Charlatan. A pretender; a quack.

Cheat. An impostor; a deceiver.

Cockatrice. A serpent.

Conjuror. A juggler.

Crimp. One who entraps men into military or naval service.

Deceiver. One who leads into error.

Decoy-duck. A person who lures others into danger.

Dissembler. A cheat; a pretender.

Empiric. A charlatan.

False witness. One who gives untrue testimony.

Gipsy. A deceiver by magic arts.

Humbug. A swindler; a trickster.

Hypocrite. One who feigns to be something which he is not.

GULL—DECEIVER—*Continued*.

Laughing-stock. A person who is an object of ridicule. See Society-Laughingstock.
Pigeon. An unsuspecting victim of sharpers.
Puppet. One controlled in his actions by the will of another.
Simple Simon. An artless person. [Nursery rhyme.]
Victim. One who is duped or cheated.

GULL—*Verbs*.

Be deceived. See Truthfulness-Fraud.
Be the dupe of. To be the tool of; the laughing-stock.
Bite. To be trapped.
Catch a Tartar. To assail one whom you cannot conquer.
Fall into a trap. Get caught unawares.
Nibble at the bait. Play with fire and not to know it.
Swallow the bait. Ensnared; entrapped.

GULL—*Adjectives*.

Credulous. See Credulousness.
Mistaken. See Truth-Error.

DECEIVER—Denotations—*Continued from Column 2*.

Joseph Surface. A hypocrite in Sheridan's comedy, *The School for Scandal*.
Judas. The disciple who betrayed Christ; a treacherous wretch.
Mawworm. A hypocritical ranter in Bickerstaff's comedy of *The Hypocrite*.
Pecksniff. A hypocrite in Dickens's *Martin Chuzzlewit*.
Pharisee. A censorious or self-righteous person in matters of morals, etc.
Rosicrucian. A Knight of the Rosy Cross.
Scapin. A knavish valet in Molière's comedy, *Les Fourberies de Scapin*.
Tartufe. A hypocritical priest in Molière's comedy of the same name; hence, a hypocritical pretender.
Zingaro. A gipsy.

Impostor. A faker; a fraud.
Jilt. A coquette; one who deceives her lover.
Jobber. An intriguer.
Jockey. One who cheats in horse-trading.
Juggler. One who deceives by legerdemain or sleight-of-hand.
Knave. A rogue; a dishonest servant.
Liar. See sub Falsehood.
Medicaster. A quack.
Menteur à triple étage [F.]. A deceiver by eminence.
Mountebank. A quack doctor; a deceiver.
Opossum. An animal that plays dead when seen or caught.
Perjurer. False witness under oath.
Prestidigitator. A sleight-of-hand performer; a juggler.
Pretender. A false claimant.
Quack. A charlatan; a fake doctor.
Quacksalver. A mountebank; a pretending healer.
Rogue. A knave; an impostor.
Saltimbanco. See Saltimbanque.
Saltimbanque [F.]. A mountebank; a quack.
Serpent. An intriguing person.
Shuffler. A crafty artificer; one who changes his position.
Snake in the grass. A deceitful person; a copperhead.
Soi-disant [F.]. A pretender; self-presumptive.
Sophist. An impostor in argument.
Story-teller. A teller of fictitious stories; a liar.
Swindler. A cheat; a rascal.
Trickster. A deceiver.
Wolf in sheep's clothing. A hypocrite; a angerous personage.

DECEIVER—*Denotations*.

Ass in lion's skin. See Adept-Bungler. [Old fable.]
Cagliostro. One of the most prominent impostors of modern times.
Fernão Mendez Pinto. Portuguese adventurer.
Janus. The Roman deity with two faces; hence, a deceitful person.
Jesuit. An intriguer; a casuist; one of the Society of Jesus.

(Continued on Column 1.)

GULL—HYPERBOLE.

HYPERBOLE.

Aggravation. See Alleviation-Aggravation.
Caricatura. [It.]. Something overdone or exaggerated.
Caricature. See Delineation-Caricature.
Coloring. The act of making a thing unnatural; false
Embroidery. Ornamentation by adding figures and colors.
Exaggeration. The act of overdrawing; an extravagant statement.
Expansion. See Enlargement.
Extravagance. See Extravagance.
Façon de parler [F.]. Manner of speaking.
False coloring. See Truthfulness-Falsehood.
Figure of speech. A beautiful expression employed to embellish one's language.
Flight of fancy. See Fancy.
Fringe. Ornamental goods sewed on a piece of cloth to add to its beauty.
High coloring. Richly toned; decorated.
Hyperbole. An exaggeration; an overdrawn statement.
Men in buckram. Men in stiff, ornamented suits.
Much ado about nothing. See Overvaluation.
Puffery. See Bragging.
Rant. See Embellishment.
Storm in a teacup. See Much ado about nothing.
Strain. Drawn too tightly; a violent tension.
Stretch. Extending over more than it naturally would.
Stretch of fancy. Fancy drawn out.
Stretch of the imagination. Flight of the imagination.
Traveler's tale. A fictitious story.
Yarn. A manufactured lie.

HYPERBOLE—*Noun of Agent*.

Baron Munchausen. A German army officer who is credited with impossible adventures.

HYPERBOLE—*Verbs*.

Aggravate. See sub Aggravation.
Amplify. See Enlargement.
Border. To ornament a garment or garden.
Color. See Truthfulness-Falsehood.
Color highly. To paint in rich colors; to adorn.
Color too highly. To overdraw; to stretch.
Deal in the marvelous. To talk about the impossible, the marvelous.
Draw a long bow. To tell exaggerated stories.
Exaggerate. To make statements that are overdrawn.

Flourish. To boast; brag.
Go great lengths. To overdraw; to go to great extremes.
Heighten. To make lofty and transcendental statements.
Hyperbolize. To express oneself with manifest exaggeration.
Magnify. To laud too highly; exaggerate.
Make much of. To make much ado about an insignificant thing.
Make the most of. To exhaust of all its possibilities.
Out-Herod Herod. To exceed in wickedness and violence. [Bible.]
Overcharge. To overload; charge too heavily.
Overcolor. To exaggerate.
Overdraw. To magnify; exaggerate.
Overestimate. See Overvaluation.
Overlay. To spread on excessively.
Overpraise. To praise too highly.
Overshoot. To go wide of the mark.
Overshoot the mark. To go beyond.
Overstate. To exaggerate; make extravagant statements.
Pile up. To exaggerate.
Puff. See Bragging.
Run riot. To go to excess.
Shoot with a long bow. To tell exaggerated stories.
Spin a long yarn. To tell a long, fictitious story.
Strain To injure by exerting something too violently.
Strain a point. To stretch a point; often too extensively.
Stretch. To draw out.
Stretch a point. See Strain a point.
Talk at random. To talk thoughtlessly.

HYPERBOLE—*Adjectives*.

Bombastic. See Embellishment.
Egregious. Surpassing in rascality.
Exaggerated. Beyond what is strictly true.
Extravagant. Going beyond proper bounds.
Fabulous. Not true; invented.
High-flying. Lofty; extravagant.
Hyperbolical. Given to exaggeration.
On stilts. Above people's heads.
Outré [F.]. Beyond; extravagant.
Overwrought. Overworked; overdone.
Preposterous. Absurd; monstrous.

HYPERBOLE—*Adverbs*.

Hyperbolically, etc. See *Adjectives*.

gull'-er-y. Trickery. TRUTHFULNESS-FRAUD.
gul''-li-bil'-i-ty. Unsuspecting credulity. CREDU-LOUSNESS-SKEPTICISM.
gul'-li-ble. Easily deceived. CREDULOUSNESS-SKEPTICISM.
gul'-let. Esophagus; channel. APERTURE-CLOSURE, RIVER-WIND.
gul'-ly. Ravine. APERTURE-CLOSURE, CONVEXITY-CONCAVITY, INTERSPACE-CONTACT, WATERCOURSE-AIRPIPE.
gu-los'-i-ty. Greediness. FASTING-GLUTTONY.
gulp. To swallow hastily. ADMISSION-EXPULSION, FASTING-GLUTTONY, NUTRIMENT-EXCRETION; **gulp down,** CREDULOUSNESS-SKEPTICISM, NUTRIMENT-EXCRETION, YIELDING.
gulph. See GULF.
gum. India-rubber; solidified excretion from some trees. COHESION-LOOSENESS, CONNECTIVE, PULPINESS-ROSIN, VISCIDITY-FOAM; **gum elastic,** ELASTICITY-INELASTICITY.
gum-mos'-i-ty. The nature of gum. VISCIDITY-FOAM.
gump'-tion. Shrewdness. SAGACITY-INCAPACITY.
gun. Firearm. CRASH-DRUMMING, PUSH-PULL, WEAPON; **blow great guns,** RIVER-WIND; **great guns,** DESIGN; **sure as a gun,** CERTAINTY-DOUBT.
gun'-boat''. Kind of war-vessel. BELLIGERENT.
gun'-flint''. A piece of flint put on the hammer of a musket. WEAPON.
gun'-lock''. The device for discharging a gun. WEAPON.
gun'-ner. One who fires a gun. BELLIGERENT.
gun'-ner-y. Use of artillery. FIGHTING-CONCILIATION, WEAPON.
gun'-pow''-der. Explosive, used in shooting guns. FIGHTING-CONCILIATION, WEAPON; **not invent gunpowder,** SAGE-FOOL; **sit on a barrel of gunpowder,** SECURITY-INSECURITY.
gun'-shot''. Distance a gun will shoot. REMOTENESS-NEARNESS.
gun'-wale''. The upper part of a ship's side. CONVEYANCE-VESSEL.
gurge. Whirlpool. REVOLUTION-EVOLUTION, RIVER-WIND.
gur'-gle. Babble. LOUDNESS-FAINTNESS, RESONANCE-NONRESONANCE, RIVER-WIND, VISCIDITY-FOAM.
gur'-goyle. See GARGOYLE.
gush. Sudden emersion. ENTRANCE-EXIT, RIVER-WIND.
gush'-ing. Flowing freely. EMOTION, SENSITIVENESS-APATHY.
gust. Squall. EXCITABILITY-INEXCITABILITY, RIVER-WIND, SAVOR-TASTELESSNESS, TASTE-VULGARITY.
gus-ta-tion. Act of tasting. SAVOR-TASTELESSNESS.
gust'-ful. Tasteful. PALATABLENESS-UNPALATABLENESS.
gust'-less. Tasteless. SAVOR-TASTELESSNESS.

gus'-to. Feeling or taste. EMOTION, PLEASURE-PAIN, SAVOR-TASTELESSNESS, SENSUALITY-SUFFERING.
gut. To plunder; to eviscerate; intestines; strait. ADMISSION-EXPULSION, APERTURE-CLOSURE, CREATION-DESTRUCTION, GULF-PLAIN, TAKING-RESTITUTION, THEFT.
guts. Entrails. OUTSIDE-INSIDE.
gut'-ta. Ornament. ARCHITECTURE.
gut'-ter. Ditch at side of road; trough around the eaves of a house. CITY-COUNTRY, GROOVE, WATERCOURSE-AIRPIPE.
gut'-ti-form''. Drop-shaped. CIRCLE-WINDING.
gut'-tle. To eat voraciously. FASTING-GLUTTONY.
gut'-tling. Gormandizer. FASTING-GLUTTONY.
gut'-tur-al. Pertaining to the throat. LETTER, SPEECH-INARTICULATENESS.
guy. Rod or chain for steadying. CONNECTIVE, RELEASE-PRISON.
guz'-zle. To drink much. FASTING-GLUTTONY, INTEMPERANCE.
guz'-zling. Pouring down. FASTING-GLUTTONY.
gybe. To shift from one side of a vessel to the other. DETERMINATION-VACILLATION.
gym-na'-si-um. Building for physical exercise; higher school, as in Germany. LISTS, SCHOOL.
gym'-nast. Athlete. STRENGTH-WEAKNESS.
gym-nas'-tic. Relating to bodily exercise. TOIL-RELAXATION.
gym-nas'-tics. Art of exercising the body. EDUCATION-MISTEACHING, ENTERTAINMENT-WEARINESS, STRENGTH-WEAKNESS, STRIFE-PEACE, TOIL-RELAXATION.
gym-nos'-o-phist. Hindu hermit-philosopher. MODERATION-SELFINDULGENCE, ORTHODOXY-HETERODOXY, VOLUPTUARY.
gyn'-ar-chy. Government by a woman. RULE-LICENSE.
gyn''-e-ce'-um. Part of a Greek house reserved for women. MALE-FEMALE.
gyn''-e-coc'-ra-sy. Female rule. RULE-LICENSE.
gyn''-e-ol'-a-try. Woman-worship. BLANDISHMENT, LOVE-HATE.
gyn''-e-pho'-bi-a. Dislike of woman's society. LOVE-HATE.
gyp. Servant at Cambridge University, England. CHIEF-UNDERLING.
gy'-rate. To rotate. REVOLUTION-EVOLUTION.
gy-ra'-tion. Any rotating. REVOLUTION-EVOLUTION.
gy'-ra-to-ry. Having a circular motion. REVOLUTION-EVOLUTION.
gyre. A gyration. REVOLUTION-EVOLUTION.
gyr'-fal''-con. See GERFALCON.
gy-roi'-dal. Non-symmetrical. MINERALOGY.
gyr'-o-man''-cy. Kind of divination. PROPHECY.
gy'-sart. Guiser; a masker. ACTING.
gyve. Shackles. RELEASE-PRISON.

H

habeas corpus [L.] (hē′-be-as cor′-pus). A writ to produce a prisoner before a court or judge. LAW-LAWLESSNESS.

hab′-er-dash″-er. A dealer in gentlemen's furnishings. BUYING-SALE.

hab′-er-geon. A coat of mail. ATTACK-DEFENSE.

habiles gens, *en* [F.] (ɑ-bil′ zhɑn·, ɑn·). Like able men. STRENGTH-WEAKNESS.

ha-bil′-i-ment. Clothing. DRESS-UNDRESS.

ha-bil″-i-ta′-tion. Equipment. SKILL-UNSKILFULNESS.

hab′-it. Physical temperament; dress; custom. DRESS-UNDRESS, HABIT-DESUETUDE, SUBJECTIVE-NESS-OBJECTIVENESS; habit of mind, AFFECTIONS; habits of business, POMP; want of habit, HABIT-DES-UETUDE.

HABIT—DESUETUDE.

Acclimatization. The process of becoming habituated to a new climate.

Addiction. The state of being devoted or accustomed.

Assuefaction. The act of becoming used to.

Assuetude. Habit or habitual use.

Bad habit. Fixed or established usage which is injurious to health, morals, etc.

Cacoëthes [Gr.]. A bad habit.

Common course.
Common run. } Ordinary usage, or peculiar ways of acting.
Common state of things.

Confirmed habit. Tendency to perform certain actions.

Conformity. Compliance with some custom or practise.

Conventionalism. Accordance with fashion, tradition, or usage.

Conventionality. Adherence to social formalities.

Cry. A word or phrase caught up by a party or faction and repeated for effect.

Custom. Established practise.

Fashion. The prevailing mode or style.

General course.
General run. } Method or procedure in use by a great number.
General state of things.

Habit. Involuntary tendency to perform certain actions which is acquired by their frequent repetition.

Habitude. Usual or accustomed state with reference to something else.

Hardening. The act of becoming confirmed in any act.

Immemorial usage. A practise whose beginning is lost to memory.

Intrinsic habit. A practise which is inherited.

Inurement. The process of becoming accustomed to.

Inveterate habit. A habit firmly established by long continuance.

Knack. Aptness at doing something, gained by practise.

Matter of course. Anything done by habit.

Mode. Regular manner of doing or acting.

Natural course.
Natural run. } Operation or usage in conformity to the order or laws of nature.
Natural state of things.

Observance. A customary act or service of attention.

One's old way. A course of acting established by habit.

Ordinary course.
Ordinary run. } Settled or regular method or course of action.
Ordinary state of things.

Practise. Frequently repeated or customary action.

Precedent. Something done or said that may serve as an example for a subsequent act.

Prescription. A title or claim established by immemorial use or enjoyment.

Prevalence. The quality of being received or accepted generally.

Radication. The process of taking root deeply.

Routine. Regular sequence of duties or acts.

Run. Continuation in a certain course.

Seasoning. The process of becoming accustomed to.

Second nature. Very strong habit.

Training, etc. Systematic instruction, etc. See EDUCATION.

Trick. A particular habit or manner.

Usage. Long practise of some custom by many.

Use. One's habitual employment of anything.

Vogue. Popular and temporary fashion.

Way. Habitual method of life or action.

Wont. Custom.

HABIT—*Associated Nouns.*

Laudator temporis acti [L.]. One who praises the past.

Old school. Persons believing in the manners or methods of the past.

Order of the day. Plan of a day's work in a deliberative body

Desuetude. Cessation of a practise.

Disusage. Gradual cessation of use or custom.

Disuse. Cessation of use.

Infraction of usage. The act of breaking a habit or practise.

Inusitation. Want of use.

Newness to. The quality of being unfamiliar with.

Non-prevalence. Want of prevalence.

Want of habit. } State of being without a regular method or
Want of practise. } course of doing or acting.

DESUETUDE—*Associated Words.*

A custom more honored in the breach than in the observance. A bad custom which one opposes by not observing. [*Hamlet*, I, iv.]

New brooms. Figuratively, a person who does his work well, because he has just been appointed to his position.

DESUETUDE—*Verb.*

Disuse. Not to use.

DESUETUDE—*Verbal Expressions.*

Be unaccustomed; break off a custom; break off a habit; break through a custom; break through a habit; cast off a custom; cast off a habit; leave off a custom; leave off a habit; infringe a custom; infringe a habit; violate a custom; violate a habit; wean oneself of a custom; wean oneself of a habit; wear off.

DESUETUDE—*Adjectives.*

Disused, etc. Not used, etc. See USE-DISUSE.

Green, etc. Inexperienced, etc. See SKILL-UNSKILFULNESS.

New. Not old.

Non-observant. Not observant.

Unaccustomed.
Unhabituated.
Unhackneyed.
Uninured.
Unseasoned. } Not accustomed, etc. See HABIT.
Untrained.
Unused.
Unusual.
Unwonted.

HABIT—ASSOCIATED NOUNS—*Continued*

Pipe-clay. A white clay used in whitening military accouterments; hence, military formality.

Red-tape. Official formality.

Red-tapism. The practise of red-tape.

Standing order. A regular method of procedure.

Veteris vestigia flammæ [L.]. The vestiges of an old flame; mark of an old habit.

HABIT—*Figurative Nouns.*

Beaten ground. Ground beaten by travel; hence, an often repeated course.

Beaten path. A path made by much walking; hence, frequent repetition of anything.

Beaten track. See BEATEN PATH.

Groove. A furrow or channel formed by steady grinding, etc.; hence, the habitual course of life, work, or affairs.

Rut. A track worn by a wheel; hence, a method of doing established by frequent repetition.

HABIT—*Verbs.*

Acclimatize. To become accustomed to a climate.

Accustom. To make familiar by use.

Case-harden. To make insensible to influences.

Familiarize. To get a thorough knowledge of.
Habituate. To make accustomed to.
Harden. To accustom to endure.
Inure. To train.
Learn, etc. To acquire skill in, etc. See EDUCATION.

Naturalize. To acclimate.
Prevail. To be in general use.
Repeat, etc. To do again, etc. See RECURRENCE.
Season. To habituate.
Train. To develop.

HABIT—*Verbal Expressions*.

Acquire a habit; acquire a trick; addict oneself to; adhere to; become a habit; be habitual (see *Adjectives*); cling to; come into use; contract a habit; contract a trick; fall into a custom (see CONVENTIONALITY); fall into a habit; fall into a trick; follow the beaten path; follow the beaten track; gain upon one; get into the knack of; get into the way of; go around like a horse in a mill; go on in the old jog-trot way; grow upon one; keep one's hand in; move in a rut; run in a groove; *stare super antiquas vias* [L.], to stand upon the old ways; take to; take root; tread the beaten path; tread the beaten track.

HABIT—*Adjectives*.

Accredited. Given credit for.
Accustomary. Customary.
Accustomed. Used to a state or action.
Acknowledged. Admitted as genuine.
Admitted. Accepted as true.
Besetting. Constantly troubling.
Common. General.
Commonplace. Ordinary
Conformable. Showing external agreement with anything.
Conventional. Agreeing with any arbitrary standard.
Current. Generally accepted.
Customary. According to custom.
Devoted. Strongly attached to.
Established. Made stable or constant.
Every-day. Usual.
Familiar. Well known.
Fashionable. According to some arbitrary and temporary way. See SOCIETY.
Fixed. Established.
Frequent. Happening often.
General. Found widely practised.
Habitual. Done involuntarily because of frequent repetition.
Habitué [F] Habitual.
Hackneyed. Worn out.
Household. Commonly known.

Ingrafted. Developed by training.
Ingrained. Firmly set by instinct.
Inveterate. Addicted to a certain habit.
Jog-trot. Commonplace.
Naturalized. Made familiar by custom.
Ordinary. Not exceptional.
Permanent. Enduring.
Prescriptive. Acquired by immemorial use.
Prevailing. Most generally found.
Prevalent. Widely spread, as a disease.
Received. Accepted
Recognized. Acquainted with.
Regular. According to law or custom.
Rooted. Deep-seated.
Seasoned. Adapted.
Set. Fixed.
Stereotyped. Distinctly marked off.
Stock. Continually used.
Trite. Worn out from frequent use.
Understood. Established by belief.
Usual. Ordinary.
Vernacular. Native.
Wont. Using or doing habitually.
Wonted. Accustomed.

HABIT—*Adjective Expressions*.

According to custom; according to routine; according to use; addicted to; at home in; attuned to; deep-rooted; devoted to; given to; habituated to; imbued with; in fashion; in the habit of; in vogue; of course; of daily occurrence; of every-day occurrence; used to; wedded to; well known; well trodden.

HABIT—*Adverbs*.

Always, etc. Every time See UNIFORMITY.
Generally. In most but not all cases. See *Adjectives*.

Habitually. From force of habit. See *Adjectives*.

HABIT—*Adverbial Expressions*.

As a rule; as is one's wont; as the sparks fly upward; as the world goes; as things go; as usual; for the most part; *more solito* [L.], according to custom; *more suo* [L.], according to his custom; most frequently; most often.

HABIT—*Phrases*.

Abeunt studia in mores [L]. One's habitual pursuits pass over into character.
Adeo in teneris consuescere multum est [L.]. So important is it to become wonted at a tender age.
Cela s'entend [F.]. That is understood.

Ex more [L.]. According to custom.
Hoc erat in more majorum [L.]. This was in the custom of the fathers.
Magna est vis consuetudinis [L.]. Great is the power of habit.

hab′-it-a-ble. Fit to dwell in. DWELLER-HABITATION.
ha′′-bi-tan′. A small rural proprietor. DWELLER-HABITATION.
hab′-i-tat. The natural abode of a plant or animal. DWELLER-HABITATION.
hab′′-i-ta′-tion. A place of abode. DWELLER-HABITATION, ESTABLISHMENT-REMOVAL.
hab′-it-ed. Clothed. DRESS-UNDRESS.
hab′′-it-ma′-ker. One who makes habits or dresses. DRESS-UNDRESS.
ha-bit′-u-al. Common; customary. CONVENTIONALITY-UNCONVENTIONALITY, FREQUENCY-RARITY, HABIT-DESUETUDE, RECURRENCE.
ha-bit′-u-al-ly. Customarily. HABIT-DESUETUDE.
ha-bit′-u-ate. To render familiar; accustom. EDUCATION-MISTEACHING, HABIT-DESUETUDE.

hab′-i-tude. State of living or acting; habit. HABIT-DESUETUDE.
habitué [F.] (a-bi′′-tü-ê′). An habitual frequenter. HABIT-DESUETUDE.
hacienda [Sp.] (ath-i-en′-da). A landed estate; a plantation on which the owner resides. DWELLER-HABITATION, PROPERTY.
hack. To cut irregularly; a horse kept for hire; a writer who writes anything for pay; a drudge. AGENT, CONVEYER, LENGTH-SHORTNESS, UNION-DISUNION; literary hack, MISSIVE-PUBLICATION.
hack′-a-more. A kind of halter. RELEASE-RESTRAINT.
hack′-but. A firearm of the fifteenth century. WEAPON.
hack′-le. To tear to pieces. UNION-DISUNION.
hack′-man. The driver of a hack. CONVEYER.

hack'-ney–coach''. A coach kept for hire. CONVEY-ANCE-VESSEL.

hack'-neyed. Trite; well-known; threadbare; habitual ADAGE-NONSENSE, HABIT-DESUETUDE, KNOWLEDGE-IGNORANCE, SKILL-UNSKILFULNESS.

hack'-ster. A ruffian. BELLIGERENT, BRAWLER.

Ha'-des. The abode of the souls of the dead. HEAVEN-HELL.

hadji [Ar.] (haj'-i). A Mohammedan who has made the pilgrimage to Mecca; a title of respect. MINISTRY-LAITY, WAYFARER-SEAFARER.

hæ tibi erunt artes [L.] (hî ti'-bi i'-runt ɑr'-tîz). These were thy methods. WAY.

hæret lateri lethalis arundo [L.] (hî'-ret lat'-er-ɑi leth-ê'-lis ɑ-run'-do). The deadly arrow sticks in his side. FAVORITE-ANGER, PLEASURE-PAIN.

haft. A handle. INSTRUMENT.

hag. An ugly old woman; a witch. BEAUTY-UGLINESS, BENEFACTOR-EVILDOER, ᵭEVOTION-MAGICIAN.

hag'-gard. Worn out; wild; ugly. BEAUTY-UGLINESS, EXCITATION, SANENESS-LUNACY; WEARINESS-REFRESHMENT.

hag'-gle. To cut unskilfully; dispute about price. EXCHANGE, UNION-DISUNION.

Ha''-gi-og'-ra-pha. The books of the Old Testament not reckoned in the Law or Prophets. REVELATION-PSEUDOREVELATION.

Ha''-gi-og'-ra-phy. Sacred writings. THEOLOGY.

Ha''-gi-ol'-o-gy. A treatise on sacred writings. REVELATION-PSEUDOREVELATION, THEOLOGY.

hague'-but. An old species of firearm. WEAPON.

ha'-ha''. A sunk fence; escarpment. ANTAGONIST-ASSISTANCE, INTERSPACE-CONTACT.

haik [Ar.] (ha'-îk). An Oriental outside garment. DRESS-UNDRESS.

hail. A familiar greeting; a salutation; frozen rain. ADDRESS-RESPONSE, APPROVAL-DISAPPROVAL, ARRIVAL-DEPARTURE, HEAT-COLD, JUBILATION-LAMENTATION, POLITENESS-IMPOLITENESS, REGARD-DISRESPECT, REPUTATION-DISCREDIT, SOLEMNIZATION; **hail, all hail,** SOLEMNIZATION; **hail fellow well met,** AMITY-HOSTILITY, SOCIABILITY-PRIVACY.

hail'-stone''. A pellet of hail. HEAT-COLD.

hair. One of the filaments on the skin of animals; anything very small; roughness caused by hair. ANATOMY, GREATNESS-SMALLNESS, LAMINA-FIBER, SMOOTHNESS-ROUGHNESS; **hair-breadth escape,** ESCAPE, SECURITY-INSECURITY; **hair's breadth,** BREADTH-NARROWNESS, REMOTENESS-NEARNESS; **hairs on the head,** MULTIPLICITY-PAUCITY; **hair-splitting,** RATIOCINATION-INSTINCT; **make one's hair stand on end,** ASTONISHMENT - EXPECTANCE, PLEASURABLENESS-PAINFULNESS, SANGUINENESS-TIMIDITY; **to a hair,** TRUTH-ERROR.

hair'-less. Deprived of hair. DRESS-UNDRESS.

hair'-y. Covered with hair. SMOOTHNESS-ROUGHNESS.

hal'-berd. A weapon in the form of a battle-ax and pike. WEAPON.

hal''-ber-dier'. One armed with a halberd. BELLIGERENT.

hal'-cy-on. Calm; peaceful; happy. PLEASURABLENESS-PAINFULNESS, STRIFE-PEACE, TURBULENCE-CALMNESS, WELFARE-MISFORTUNE; **halcyon days,** PLEASURE-PAIN, WELFARE-MISFORTUNE.

hale. Of sound health. HEALTH-SICKNESS.

half. One of the two equal parts of a whole. DOUBLING-HALVING; **half a dozen,** FIVE-QUINQUESECTION, MULTIPLICITY-PAUCITY; **half a gale,** RIVER-WIND; **half a hundred,** FIVE-QUINQUESECTION; **half-and-half,** ENTIRETY-DEFICIENCY, EQUALITY-INEQUALITY, MIXTURE - HOMOGENEITY; **half-and-half measure,** MIDCOURSE-CIRCUIT; **half-breed,** CONVENTIONALITY-UNCONVENTIONALITY; **half-caste,** CONVENTIONALITY-UNCONVENTIONALITY, MIXTURE-HOMOGENEITY;

half-distance, MIDDLE; **half-length,** PAINTING; **half-light,** LUMINARY-SHADE; **half-measure,** DETERMINATION - VACILLATION, ENTIRETY - DEFICIENCY, QUEST-EVASION; **half-moon,** CURVATURE-RECTILINEARITY; **half-price,** COSTLINESS-CHEAPNESS; **half-rations,** EXCESS-LACK; **half-scholar,** SCHOLAR-DUNCE; **half-seas-over,** TEETOTALISM - INTEMPERANCE; **half-sight,** SIGHT-DIMSIGHTEDNESS; **half-speed,** TURBULENCE-CALMNESS; **half the battle,** CONSEQUENCE-INSIGNIFICANCE, SUCCESS-FAILURE; **half-truth,** TRUTHFULNESS-FABRICATION; **see with half an eye,** CLEARNESS-OBSCURITY, ENLIGHTENMENT - SECRECY, SAGACITY-INCAPACITY.

half'-blind''. Not entirely blind. SIGHT-DIMSIGHTEDNESS.

half'-blood''. A half-breed; of mixed blood. CONVENTIONALITY-UNCONVENTIONALITY, MIXTURE-HOMOGENEITY, FAULTLESSNESS-FAULTINESS.

half'-froz''-en. Not quite frozen. VISCIDITY-FOAM.

half'-heart''-ed. Wanting in affection; unkind; indifferent. DETERMINATION-VACILLATION, SENSITIVENESS-APATHY, UNCONCERN.

half'-learned''. Imperfectly learned. KNOWLEDGE-IGNORANCE.

half'-melt''-ed. Partly melted. VISCIDITY-FOAM.

half'-pen''-ny. An English coin of small value. CONSEQUENCE-INSIGNIFICANCE.

half'-starved''. Nearly starved. EXCESS-LACK, FASTING-GLUTTONY.

half'-way''. In the middle; partially. ENVIRONMENT-INTERPOSITION, MAGNITUDE-SMALLNESS, MIDDLE; **go half-way,** DETERMINATION-VACILLATION, MIDCOURSE-CIRCUIT; **half-way house,** PRECEDENCE-SUCCESSION; **meet half-way,** COMPOSITION, FIGHTING-CONCILIATION, READINESS-RELUCTANCE.

half'-wit. A person of weak mind. SAGE-FOOL.

half'-wit''-ted. Feeble-minded. SAGACITY-INCAPACITY, SAGE-FOOL.

hall. A large room for public use; the part of a house first entered. CONTENTS-RECEIVER, DWELLER-HABITATION, MARKET; **hall-mark,** SIGN; **hall of audience,** CONVERSATION-MONOLOGUE; **music-hall,** ACTING.

hal''-le-lu'-iah. Praise be to God. DEVOTION-IDOLATRY.

hal-loa'. An exclamation to attract the attention. CRY-ULULATION.

hal-loo'. To call loudly; shout; an interjection calling the attention. ADDRESS-RESPONSE, ASTONISHMENT-EXPECTANCE, CRY-ULULATION, HEED-DISREGARD.

hal'-low. To make holy; reverence. REGARD-DISRESPECT, SOLEMNIZATION.

hal'-lowed. Made holy. DIVINITY.

Hal'-low-e'en'. The evening before All Saints' Day. PERIODICITY-IRREGULARITY.

hal-lu''-ci-na'-tion. A delusion; a kind of insanity. SANENESS-LUNACY, TRUTH-ERROR.

ha'-lo. A luminous circle; a nimbus; ideal brightness. LIGHT-DARKNESS, REPUTATION-DISCREDIT.

ha'-lo-man''-cy. Divination with salt. PROPHECY.

hal'-ser. A large and heavy rope. CONNECTIVE.

halt. To walk lamely; be in doubt; stop; be imperfect. DISCONTINUANCE - CONTINUANCE, HEALTH-SICKNESS, MOVEMENT-REST, STRENGTH-WEAKNESS, SUCCESS - FAILURE, SWIFTNESS - SLOWNESS; TOIL-RELAXATION; **at the halt,** MOVEMENT-REST.

hal'-ter. A rope to restrain; a hangman's rope. CONNECTIVE, RECOMPENSE-SCOURGE, RELEASE-PRISON; **wear a halter,** REPUTATION-DISCREDIT; **with a halter round one's neck,** SECURITY-INSECURITY.

halt'-ing. Stopping. HEALTH-SICKNESS, PURITY-CRUDENESS, REPUTATION - DISCREDIT; **halting ground,** ARRIVAL-DEPARTURE; **halting place,** ARRIVAL-DEPARTURE.

halve. To divide into two equal portions. DOUBLING-HALVING.

halves. The plural of half. **Do by halves,** CAREFULNESS-CARELESSNESS, COMPLETION-NONCOMPLETION, SKILL-UNSKILFULNESS, SUCCESS-FAILURE; **go halves,** PARTICIPATION; **not do by halves,** COMPLETION-NONCOMPLETION.

halv′-ing. The act of dividing into two equal parts. DOUBLING-HALVING.

ham. A house; home. DWELLER-HABITATION.

ham′-a-dry″-ad. A fabled wood-nymph. JOVE-FIEND.

Ha-mit′-ic. Pertaining to descendants of Ham. ETHNOLOGY.

ham′-let. A small village. CITY-COUNTRY, DWELLER-HABITATION.

ham′-mer. To work constantly; to beat; to talk continually. IMPETUS-REACTION, INSTRUMENT, RECURRENCE, TALKATIVENESS-TACITURNITY; **between the hammer and anvil,** REFUGE-PITFALL; **hammer at,** REFLECTION-VACANCY, TOIL-RELAXATION; **hammer out,** COMPLETION-NONCOMPLETION, FORM-FORMLESSNESS, PREPARATION-NONPREPARATION; **under the hammer,** BUYING-SALE.

ham′-mer-beam″ roof. A roof without a tie-beam at the top of the wall. ARCHITECTURE.

ham′-mer-ing. The act of striking with a hammer. TOIL-RELAXATION.

ham′-mock. A swinging couch hung by the ends. SUSPENSION-SUPPORT.

ham′-per. A fetter; a basket of wickerwork. CONTENTS-RECEIVER, OBSTRUCTION-HELP.

ham′-string″. To cut the hamstring so as to cripple. BETTERMENT-DETERIORATION, MIGHT-IMPOTENCE.

han′-a-per. A basket made of wickerwork. TREASURY.

hance. Haunch of an arch. ARCHITECTURE.

hand. To transmit; assist; the organ of apprehension; dexterity; a person; a form of penmanship; a measure; the width of the hand; control; one who toils with the hands; agent; side. AGENT, ALIENATION, ANATOMY, HUMANITY, INSTRUMENTALITY, KEEPING-RELINQUISHMENT, LATERALITY-CONTRAPOSITION, LENGTH-SHORTNESS, SIGN, TOUCH, TRANSFERENCE, WRITING-PRINTING; **at hand,** FUTURE-PAST, OCCURRENCE-DESTINY, REMOTENESS-NEARNESS, USEFULNESS-USELESSNESS; **bad hand,** WRITING-PRINTING; **bird in hand,** KEEPING-RELINQUISHMENT; **come to hand,** ARRIVAL-DEPARTURE, GIVING-RECEIVING; **fold one's hands,** ACTION-PASSIVENESS; **give one's hand to,** MATRIMONY-CELIBACY; **good hand,** ADEPT-BUNGLER, SKILL-UNSKILFULNESS, WRITING-PRINTING; **hand and glove,** AMITY-HOSTILITY; **hand down,** ALIENATION, MARK-OBLITERATION; **hand gallop,** SWIFTNESS-SLOWNESS; **hand in hand,** AMITY-HOSTILITY, ANTAGONISM-CONCURRENCE, ASSOCIATION, SOLITUDE-COMPANY, UNION-DISUNION; **hand of death,** LIFE-DEATH; **hand over,** ALIENATION, GIVING-RECEIVING; **hand over head,** CAREFULNESS-CARELESSNESS, HEED-DISREGARD, RECKLESSNESS-CAUTION; **hands off,** ACTION-PASSIVENESS, LEAVE-PROHIBITION, QUEST-EVASION, REPRISAL-RESISTANCE; **hand to hand,** INTERSPACE-CONTACT; **have a hand in,** ACTION-PASSIVENESS, ACTIVITY-INDOLENCE, ANTAGONISM-CONCURRENCE, CAUSE-EFFECT, PARTICIPATION; **have one's hand in,** SKILL-UNSKILFULNESS; **have one's hands full,** ACTIVITY-INDOLENCE, OCCUPATION; **helping hand,** ANTAGONIST-ASSISTANT, OBSTRUCTION-HELP; **hold in hand,** RULE-LICENSE; **hold out the hand,** POLITENESS-IMPOLITENESS; **hold up the hand,** CHOICE-NEUTRALITY; **in hand,** COMPLETION-NONCOMPLETION, ENTIRETY-DEFICIENCY, HOLDING-EXEMPTION, MONEY, OCCUPATION, PREPARATION-NONPREPARATION; **in the hands of,** LIBERTY-SUBJECTION, RULE-LICENSE; **keep one's hand in,** HABIT-DESUETUDE; **lay**

hands on, CEREMONIAL, DISCOVERY, TAKING-RESTITUTION, USE-DISUSE; **live from hand to mouth,** AFFLUENCE-PENURY, EXCESS-LACK, PREPARATION-NONPREPARATION; **much on one's hands,** ACTIVITY-INDOLENCE; **no hands in,** QUEST-EVASION; **old hand,** ADEPT-BUNGLER; **on one's hands,** BUYING-SALE, COMPLETION-NONCOMPLETION, EXCESS-LACK, HOLDING-EXEMPTION, OCCUPATION; **poor hand,** ADEPT-BUNGLER; **put into one's hands,** GIVING-RECEIVING; **put one's hands to,** ENTERPRISE; **ready to one's hand,** PREPARATION-NONPREPARATION; **shake hands,** FIGHTING-CONCILIATION, PARDON-VINDICTIVENESS; **stretch forth one's hand,** ACTION-PASSIVENESS; **take by the hand,** OBSTRUCTION-HELP; **take in hand,** EDUCATION-MISTEACHING, ENTERPRISE; **time hanging on one's hands,** ACTION-INACTION, ENTERTAINMENT-WEARINESS, HURRY-LEISURE; **try one's hand,** VENTURE; **turn one's hand to,** OCCUPATION; **under one's hand,** WRITING-PRINTING; **with one's hands in the pockets,** ACTION-PASSIVENESS.

hand′-bar″-row. A stretcher. CONVEYANCE-VESSEL.

hand′-bill″. An advertising sheet circulated by hand. GATHERING-SCATTERING.

hand′-book″. A small guide-book or manual. ENLIGHTENMENT-SECRECY, MISSIVE-PUBLICATION, TRAVELING-NAVIGATION.

hand′-breadth″. A space equal to the breadth of the palm. LENGTH-SHORTNESS.

hand′-cuff″. A manacle for the hands. RELEASE-PRISON, RELEASE-RESTRAINT.

hand′-fast″. To pledge; betroth. MATRIMONY-CELIBACY.

hand′-ful. A small quantity. MAGNITUDE-SMALLNESS, MULTIPLICITY-PAUCITY, QUANTITY-MEASURE.

hand′-i-cap. To impose impediments to offset advantages. STRIFE-PEACE.

hand′-i-craft″. A mechanical or manual trade. ACTION-PASSIVENESS, OCCUPATION.

hand′-i-crafts″-man. An artisan. AGENT, LABOR-CAPITAL.

hand′-i-work″. Work done by the hands. AGENT, CAUSE-EFFECT.

hand′-ker-chief. A neckerchief; a kerchief for wiping the face or nose. CLEANNESS-FILTHINESS, DRESS-UNDRESS.

han′-dle. To touch; treat upon; manipulate; that part of an instrument intended to be grasped by the hand. ESSAY, MANAGEMENT, MEANS, PRETEXT, TOUCH, USE-DISUSE; **furnish a handle,** JUSTIFICATION-CHARGE, PRETEXT; **handle a case,** CONDUCT; **handle to one's name,** NAME-MISNOMER, TITLE; **make a handle of,** PRETEXT, USE-DISUSE.

hand′-maid″. A female servant. ANTAGONIST-ASSISTANT, CHIEF-UNDERLING, INSTRUMENTALITY.

hand′-or″-gan. A musical instrument worked by a hand-crank. MUSICAL INSTRUMENTS.

hand′-post″. A guide-post. SIGN.

hand′-sel. A gift to secure good luck; earnest money on a contract; the first money received in a new shop. BEGINNING-END, GIVING-RECEIVING, OUTLAY-INCOME, SECURITY.

hand′-some. Liberal in size; beautiful; suitable in action. BEAUTY-UGLINESS, GENEROSITY-FRUGALITY, UNSELFISHNESS-SELFISHNESS; **handsome fortune,** AFFLUENCE-PENURY.

hand′-spike″. A lever used to lift heavy weights. INSTRUMENT.

hand′-staff″. A javelin. WEAPON.

hand′-wri″-ting. The form of writing peculiar to a person. SIGN, WRITING-PRINTING; **handwriting on the wall,** WARNING.

hand′-y. Skilful; convenient; near by. PREPARATION-NONPREPARATION, REMOTENESS-NEARNESS, SKILL-UNSKILFULNESS, USEFULNESS-USELESSNESS.

hang. To be suspended and have a free motion; kill;

execute on the gallows; a curse. CHARITABLENESS-CURSE, CONNECTIVE, LIFE-KILLING, RECOMPENSE-PUNITION, SUSPENSION-SUPPORT; **hang about,** ACTIVITY-INDOLENCE, QUEST-EVASION; **hang back,** ACTIVITY-INDOLENCE, QUEST-EVASION; **hang by a thread,** SECURITY-INSECURITY; **hang down the head,** LIGHTHEARTEDNESS-DEJECTION; **hang fire,** ACTIVITY-INDOLENCE, COMPLETION - NONCOMPLETION, DISCONTINUANCE - CONTINUANCE, EARLINESS-LATENESS, FERTILITY-STERILITY, PROFFER-REFUSAL, READINESS-RELUCTANCE, SUCCESS-FAILURE, SWIFTNESS-SLOWNESS, VIGOR-INERTIA; **hang in doubt,** FAITH-MISGIVING; **hang in suspense,** DETERMINATION-VACILLATION, FAITH-MISGIVING; **hang it,** CONTENTEDNESS-DISCONTENTMENT, REGARD-SCORN; **hang on,** SOLITUDE-COMPANY; **hang on hand,** EXCESS-LACK; **hang on the sleeve of,** ADULATION-DISPARAGEMENT, CHIEF-UNDERLING, PRESUMPTION-OBSEQUIOUSNESS; **hang out,** POMP, SOCIABILITY-PRIVACY; **hang out a light,** LIGHT-DARKNESS; **hang out a signal,** SIGN; **hang over,** CONVEXITY-CONCAVITY, HEIGHT-LOWNESS, OCCURRENCE-DESTINY; **hang together,** ANTAGONISM-CONCURRENCE, COHESION-LOOSENESS, COOPERATION-OPPOSITION, UNION-DISUNION; **hang upon,** CAUSE-EFFECT, LIBERTY-SUBJECTION; **hang upon the lips of,** HEARING-DEAFNESS.

hang'-dog" look. A skulking appearance. FAVORITE-MOROSENESS.

hanged if, I'll be. I will not. ASSENT-DISSENT.

hang'-er. A short cut-and-thrust sword. WEAPON; **hanger-on,** CHIEF-UNDERLING, PRESUMPTION-OBSEQUIOUSNESS, SOLITUDE-COMPANY, **pothooks and hangers,** WRITING-PRINTING.

hang'-ing. Killing by strangling; drapery for a room. CHARITABLENESS - CURSE, EMBELLISHMENT - DISFIGUREMENT, EXCULPATION-PUNITION, HEIGHT-LOWNESS, LIFE-KILLING, RECOMPENSE-PUNITION, SUSPENSION-SUPPORT; **hanging look,** BEAUTY - UGLINESS.

hang'-man. A public executioner; a term of reproach. BENEFACTOR-EVILDOER, GOOD MAN-BAD MAN, RECOMPENSE-SCOURGE.

hang'-nail". An agnail. SUSPENSION-SUPPORT.

hank. A rope, coil, or tie. CONNECTIVE.

hank'-er. To have an incessant appetite for. DESIRE-DISTASTE.

hank'-er-ing. A craving for. DESIRE-DISTASTE.

Hannibalem, expende [L.] (han-nib'-α-lem, ex-pen'-di). Weigh Hannibal. CONSEQUENCE-INSIGNIFICANCE.

han'-sard. A printed record of the proceedings of the British Parliament. MARK.

han'-som. A low, two-wheeled, one-horse cab. CONVEYANCE-VESSEL.

hap. Chance; luck. RATIONALE-LUCK.

hap'-haz"-ard. Mere chance. PURPOSE-LUCK, RATIONALE-LUCK.

hap'-less. Having no luck. WELFARE-MISFORTUNE.

hap'-ly. By chance; perhaps. POSSIBILITY-IMPOSSIBILITY.

hap'-pen. To come to pass. OCCURRENCE-DESTINY; **happen as it may,** PURPOSE-LUCK; **happen what may,** RATIOCINATION-INSTINCT, RECKLESSNESS-CAUTION.

hap'-pen-ing. An occurrence. OCCURRENCE-DESTINY.

hap'-pi-ly. Fortunately. PLEASURE-PAIN.

hap'-pi-ness. Good fortune; blessedness; unstudied grace. LIGHTHEARTEDNESS-DEJECTION, OPPORTUNENESS - UNSUITABLENESS, PLEASURE - PAIN, PURITY-CRUDENESS; **the greatest happiness of the greatest number,** HUMANITARIANISM-MISANTHROPY.

hap'-py. Joyous; blessed; dexterous; opportune. LIGHTHEARTEDNESS-DEJECTION, OPPORTUNENESS-UNSUITABLENESS, PLEASURE-PAIN, PURITY-CRUDENESS; **happy despatch,** RECOMPENSE-PUNITION; **happy go lucky,** PREPARATION-NONPREPARATION; **happy returns of the day,** FELICITATION; **happy**

thought, WITTINESS-DULNESS; **happy valley,** FANCY, PLEASURE-PAIN.

ha'-ra–ki'-ri. A Japanese method of committing suicide by ripping open the bowels. EXCULPATION-PUNITION.

ha-rangue'. An oration. SPEECH-INARTICULATENESS.

har'-ass. To vex; annoy; tire out. CHARITABLENESS-MALEVOLENCE, PLEASURABLENESS-PAINFULNESS, WEARINESS-REFRESHMENT.

har'-ass-ing. Worriment. PLEASURABLENESS-PAINFULNESS.

har'-bin-ger. An omen; a courier who rides in advance to make arrangements. PORTENT, PREDECESSOR-CONTINUATION.

har'-bor. To give protection; a haven; a place of refuge. ARRIVAL-DEPARTURE, DWELLER-HABITATION, EMOTION, REFUGE-PITFALL; **harbor a design,** PURPOSE-LUCK; **harbor an idea,** REFLECTION-VACANCY; **harbor revenge,** PARDON-VINDICTIVENESS; **natural harbor,** GULF-PLAIN.

har'-bor-less. Without a harbor. SECURITY-INSECURITY.

hard. Unyielding; unsparing; coarse; wicked; vigorous; sound; offensive. DIFFICULTY-FACILITY, HARDNESS-SOFTNESS, HARSHNESS-MILDNESS, PLEASURABLENESS-PAIN, REPENTANCE-OBDURACY, SENSIBILITY - INSENSIBILITY, SENSITIVENESS - APATHY, STRENGTH-WEAKNESS, SWEETNESS-ACIDITY; **blow hard,** RIVER-WIND; **go hard,** DIFFICULTY-FACILITY, PLEASURE-PAIN, SUCCESS-FAILURE, WELFARE-MISFORTUNE; **hard at it,** ACTIVITY-INDOLENCE; **hard at work,** ACTIVITY-INDOLENCE; **hard bargain,** EXTRAVAGANCE-AVARICE; **hard by,** REMOTENESS-NEARNESS; **hard case,** WELFARE-MISFORTUNE; **hard cash,** MONEY; **hard drinker,** TEETOTALISM-INTEMPERANCE; **hard earned,** PROFFER-REFUSAL; **hard fortune,** WELFARE-MISFORTUNE; **hard fought,** DIFFICULTY-FACILITY; **hard frost,** HEAT-COLD; **hard hap,** WELFARE-MISFORTUNE; **hard heart,** REPENTANCE-OBDURACY; **hard knocks,** STRIFE-PEACE; **hard life,** WELFARE-MISFORTUNE; **hard lines,** HARSHNESS-MILDNESS, WELFARE-MISFORTUNE; **hard liver,** MODERATION-VOLUPTUARY; **hard lot,** WELFARE-MISFORTUNE; **hard luck,** COMMISSION-ABROGATION; **hard master,** RULE-LICENSE; **hard measure,** RULE-LICENSE; **hard names,** APPROVAL-DISAPPROVAL; **hard necessity,** VOLITION-OBLIGATION; **hard nut to crack,** DIFFICULTY-FACILITY; **hard of belief,** CREDULOUSNESS-SKEPTICISM; **hard of hearing,** CRY-ULULATION; **hard pressed,** DIFFICULTY-FACILITY, HURRY-LEISURE, OBSTRUCTION-HELP; **hard put to it,** DIFFICULTY-FACILITY; **hard time,** DIFFICULTY-FACILITY; **hard to believe,** FAITH-MISGIVING; **hard to please,** DESIRE-PARTICULARNESS; **hard up,** AFFLUENCE-PENURY, DIFFICULTY-FACILITY; **hard upon,** APPROVAL-DISAPPROVAL; **hard water,** CHEMISTRY; **hard winter,** HEAT-COLD; **hard words,** APPROVAL-DISAPPROVAL, CLEARNESS-OBSCURITY, POLITENESS-IMPOLITENESS; **hard work,** DIFFICULTY-FACILITY, TOIL-RELAXATION; **hit hard,** IMPETUS-REACTION; **look hard at,** SIGHT-BLINDNESS; **not to be too hard upon,** PARDON-VINDICTIVENESS; **strike hard,** IMPETUS-REACTION, VIGOR-INERTIA; **try hard,** TOIL-RELAXATION.

hard'-en. To make unyielding, hard, wicked, coarse, sound, offensive, unsparing. DIFFICULTY-FACILITY, HARDNESS-SOFTNESS, HARSHNESS-MILDNESS, PLEASURABLENESS-PAINFULNESS, REPENTANCE-OBDURACY, SENSIBILITY-INSENSIBILITY, SENSITIVENESS-APATHY, STRENGTH-WEAKNESS, SWEETNESS-ACIDITY; **harden the heart,** AMITY-HOSTILITY, REPENTANCE - OBDURACY, SENSITIVENESS-APATHY.

hard'-ened. Confirmed in error or vice. FEELING-INSENSIBILITY, GODLINESS-UNGODLINESS, SENSITIVENESS-APATHY; **hardened front,** PRESUMPTION-OBSEQUIOUSNESS.

hard'-en-ing. The state of being made indifferent or insensible. GODLINESS-UNGODLINESS, HABIT-DESUETUDE.

hard'-fa"-vored. Having coarse features. PROPRIETY. IMPROPRIETY.

hard'-feat"-ured. Having coarse features. BEAUTY-UGLINESS.

hard'-fist"-ed. Covetous. EXTRAVAGANCE-AVARICE.

hard'-head"-ed. Obstinate; stubborn. SAGACITY-INCAPACITY.

hard'-heart"-ed. Unfeeling. CHARITABLENESS-MALEVOLENCE.

har'-di-hood. Persistent courage; presumptuous boldness. BRAVERY-COWARDICE, PRESUMPTION-OBSEQUIOUSNESS.

hard'-ly. Almost not; scarcely; harshly. DIFFICULTY-FACILITY, FREQUENCY-RARITY, MAGNITUDE-SMALLNESS; **deal hardly with,** HARSHNESS-MILDNESS; **hardly any,** MULTIPLICITY-PAUCITY; **hardly anything,** CONSEQUENCE-INSIGNIFICANCE, MAGNITUDE-SMALLNESS; **hardly ever,** FREQUENCY-RARITY.

hard'-mouthed". Not easily controlled. BIGOTRY-APOSTASY.

hard'-ness. The state of being hard. HARDNESS-SOFTNESS; **hardness of heart,** REPENTANCE-OBDURACY, VIRTUE-VICE.

HARDNESS—SOFTNESS.

Callosity. A hardening of the skin as a result of continued pressure.

Crystallization. The process by which a substance in solidifying assumes the form and structure of a crystal.

Durity. Hardness.

Hardness, etc. The state of being hard, etc. See *Adjectives.*

Induration. The process of growing hard.

Inflexibility. The state of being rigid.

Lapidescence. A changing into stone.

Lapidification. The state of turning into stone.

Ossification. The state of turning into bone.

Petrifaction. The process of changing into stone.

Renitence. The quality of being able to resist pressure.

Rigidity. The quality of being stiff or unyielding.

Temper. The state of a substance, especially as to its hardness, produced by some process of heating or cooling.

Vitrification. The process of turning into glass.

HARDNESS—*Concrete Nouns.*

Adamant. A stone supposed by some to be of impenetrable hardness.

Block. A solid mass of wood, stone, etc.

Board. A piece of timber, long and broad as compared with its thickness.

Bone. The hard, calcified tissue of the skeleton of vertebrate animals.

Brick. A block of clay tempered with water, sand, etc., and sundried, or burnt in a kiln.

Cartilage. A translucent, elastic tissue of the body.

Cast iron. Highly carbonized iron, brittle and very hard.

Cement. A mixture of clay and lime, for making mortar which will harden under water.

Concrete. A mixture of broken stone with cement.

Crag. A compacted bed of gravel mixed with shells.

Crystal. The material of quartz.

Deal board. A board or plank.

Flint. An impure variety of quartz.

Fossil. The remains of an animal or plant found in stratified rocks.

Granite. A very hard rock consisting of quartz, felspar, and mica.

Hardware. Ware made of metal.

Heart of oak. Firmness of spirit.

Iron. The most common metallic element.

Marble. A massive compact limestone.

Nail. A piece of metal used for fastening pieces of wood together.

Pebble. A small roundish stone.

Quartz. A form of silica, very hard and brittle.

Rock. A large concrete mass of stony material.

Steel. A variety of iron between wrought iron and cast iron.

Stone. Concreted earthy or mineral matter.

Wrought iron. The purest form of iron, containing very little carbon

HARDNESS—*Verbs.*

Accrust. To make hard into a crust.

Harden. To make or render hard.

Indurate. To harden.

Ossify. To turn into bone.

Petrify. To turn into stone.

Render hard, etc. To make hard, etc. See *Adjectives.*

Stiffen. To make rigid.

Temper. To make hard.

Vitrify. To turn into glass.

HARDNESS—*Adjectives.*

Adamantean. Hard as adamant.

Adamantine. Adamantean.

Bony. Like bone; consisting of bone.

Cartilaginous. Consisting of cartilage.

Ductility. The property of a metal which allows it to be drawn into wires.

Emollescence. Process of becoming soft.

Extendibility. A condition of softness possessing the power of extension.

Extensibility. Extendibility.

Flaccidity. The state of lacking firmness.

Flexibility. The power of being bent without breaking.

Inelasticity. The inability of a body to return to its original form.

Laxity. Want of strictness or exactness.

Malleability. Capacity to be hammered without breaking.

Mollification. A softening.

Plasticity. The property of being molded.

Pliability. Pliableness.

Pliableness, etc. Flexibility, etc. See *Adjectives.*

Pliancy. The state of being flexible.

Sequacity. The state of being ductile.

Softness. The state of being yielding; not hard.

Tractility. The capacity of being drawn out.

SOFTNESS—*Concrete Nouns.*

Butter. The oily, unctuous substance obtained from cream or milk by churning.

Clay. Soft earth.

Cushion. A case or bag stuffed with feathers or some soft substance,

Dough. A soft mass of moistened flour or meal, not yet baked.

Down. The soft under-feathers of birds.

Feather-bed. A bed filled with feathers.

Padding. The material with which anything is filled to render it soft and bulky.

Pillow. A bag or case filled with feathers, etc., used for a head-rest.

Pudding. A species of food of a soft consistence.

Wadding. Any soft substance of which wads may be made.

Wax. A soft, fatty substance produced by bees.

SOFTNESS—*Verbs.*

Bend. To turn from a straight line.

Give. To yield on account of pressure.

Knead. To work by repeated pressure with the knuckles.

Mash. To reduce to a soft state by bruising.

Mellow. To make soft; friable.

Mollify. To render soft.

Relax. To loosen; ease.

Relent. To yield; grow soft.

Render soft, etc. To make soft or yielding. See *Adjectives.*

Soften. To make yielding.

Squash. To mash; beat into a pulp.

Temper. To soften; mollify.

Yield. To give to pressure.

SOFTNESS—*Adjectives.*

Argillaceous. Clayey; of the nature of clay.

Doughy. Like dough.

Downy. Like down.

Ductile. Capable of being drawn out.

Edematous. Like the puffiness of the skin arising from dropsy.

Extensile. Capable of being extended.

Flabby. Lacking firmness.

Flaccid. Flabby.

Flexible. Capable of being bent.

Flexile. Flexible.

Flimsy. Of thin texture.

HARDNESS—SOFTNESS—*Continued.*

HARDNESS—Adjectives—*Continued.*

Concrete. Forming a hard mass.
Corneous. Horny; hard.
Firm. Solid; unyielding.
Granitic. Composed of granite.
Gritty. Consisting of grains or grit.
Hard. Solid; inflexible.
Hard as stone. Denoting a degree of hardness.
Horny. Like horn.
Indurate. }
Indurated. } Hardened.
Inflexible. Not capable of being bent.
Osseous. Bony; like bone.
Ossific. Forming bone.
Proof. Impenetrable; able to resist pressure.
Rigid. Stiff; unbending.
Starch. Stiff.
Starched, etc. Stiff with starch. See *Verbs.*
Stark. Inflexible; stiff; rigid.
Stiff. Not easily bent.
Stiff as buckram. }
Stiff as a poker. } Degrees of hardness or stiffness.
Stony. Hard; like a stone.
Stubborn. Intractable; unyielding.
Tense. Drawn; stretched; rigid.
Unbending. Not deflected.
Unlimber. Not pliant; stiff.
Unyielding. Unpliant.
Vitreous. Like glass in hardness.

SOFTNESS—Adjectives—*Continued.*

Flocculent. Like flakes; woolly.
Inelastic. Not elastic.
Limber. Limp; without stiffness.
Limbered, etc. In a condition of limberness, etc. See *Verbs.*
Limp. Limber.
Lissom. Limber; flexible.
Lithe. Supple; bending easily.
Lithesome. Somewhat lithe.
Malleable. Capable of being rolled or hammered into a thin plate.
Medullary. Pertaining to the marrow.
Mellow. Soft; friable.
Plastic. Capable of being molded.
Pliable. Capable of being bent.
Pliant. Pliable.
Remollient. Softening.
Sequacious. Ductile; pliable.
Soft. Not hard; impressible.
Soft as butter. }
Soft as down. } Very soft.
Soft as silk. }
Spongy. Of sponge-like consistency
Supple. Flexible; easily bent.
Tender. Soft, not tough, delicate.
Tender as a chicken. Having softness or gentleness of spirit.
Tractable. Not showing a refractory spirit.
Tractile. Ductile.
Yielding. Pliable; bending.
Yielding as wax. As soft as wax.

hard'-ship. Adversity. Welfare-Misfortune.
hard'–vis"-aged. Hard-featured. Beauty-Ugliness.
hard'-ware". Ware made from hard metals. Hardness-Softness.
har'-dy. Bold; strong; robust. Bravery-Cowardice, Health-Sickness, Strength-Weakness.
hare. A long-eared rodent of genus *Lepus.* Swiftness-Slowness; **hold with the hare and run with the hounds,** Presumption-Obsequiousness, Volition-Obligation.
hare'-brained". Foolish; giddy Heed-Disregard, Recklessness-Caution.
hare'-lip". A lip having a hare-like division. Proportion-Deformity.
ha'-rem. The collection of wives and concubines of one man. Purity-Impurity.
har"-i-o-la'-tion. Soothsaying. Prophecy.
hark. To listen; hear. Hearing-Deafness, Heed-Disregard; **hark back,** Advance-Retrogression; **hark ye,** Heed-Disregard.
hark'-en. To hear by listening. Hearing-Deafness
har'-le-quin. One who plays tricks; a character in pantomime. Acting, Mutability-Stability, Swiftness-Slowness, Variegation, Wag.
har"-le-quin-ade'. Pantomime. Acting, Wittiness-Dulness.
har'-lot. A prostitute. Purity-Rake.
har'-lot-ry. Habitual lewdness. Purity-Impurity.
harm. Injury; evil; loss. Betterment-Deterioration, Charitableness-Malevolence, Good-Evil, Goodness-Badness.
har-mat'-tan. A hot, dry wind on the west coast of Africa. River-Wind.

harm'-ful. Detrimental. Carefulness-Carelessness.
harm'-less. Not harmful; without hurt or loss. Faultlessness-Faultiness, Goodness-Badness, Healthiness-Unhealthiness, Innocence-Guilt, Might-Impotence, Security-Insecurity, Melody-Dissonance; **bear harmless,** Attack-Defense.
har-mon'-i-ca. A musical instrument. Musical Instruments.
har-mon'-i-cal. Harmonious. **Harmonical progression,** Number.
har-mon'-i-con. A musical instrument. Musical Instruments.
har-mon'-ics. The science of musical sounds. Melody-Dissonance.
har-mo'-ni-ous. Concordant in sound; free from discord; having parts proportioned. Amity-Hostility, Beauty-Ugliness, Color-Achromatism, Harmony-Discord, Music, Variance-Accord.
har-mo'-ni-ous-ly. In an harmonious manner. Melody-Dissonance.
har-mon'-i-phone. A reed instrument. Musical Instruments.
har'-mo-nist. A master of musical harmony. Melody-Dissonance.
har-mo'-ni-um. A reed-organ. Musical Instruments.
har'-mo-nize. To agree. Harmony-Discord, Melody-Dissonance.
har'-mo-ny. A fit adaptation of parts; the science which treats of chords; concord; friendship. Amity-Hostility, Harmony-Discord, Melody-Dissonance, Strife-Peace, Variance-Accord.

HARMONY—DISCORD.

Accommodation. The act of adjusting or obliging; compromise; adaptation.
Accord. The making to agree; harmony.
Accordance. Agreement of sentiments or actions.
Adaptation. The act of making fit; fitness.
Adjustment. Arrangement of parts to a systematic whole.
Admissibility. The quality of being entitled to be allowed or conceded.
Agreement. Harmony of sentiments, action, or character.
Applicability. The quality of being fit to be applied.
Apposition. The putting of things side by side.

Concordia discors [L.]. Discordant harmony. [Horace, *Epistles,* i, 12, 19.]
Conflict, etc. Violent collision, disagreement, etc. See Antagonism.
Disagreement. Difference of opinion; failure to agree.
Discongruity. Want of congruity; unsuitableness.
Discord. Want of agreement; strife.
Discordance. Opposition; incongruity
Discrepancy. Difference; discordance.
Disparity. Want of equality; dissimilarity.
Disproportion. Lack of symmetry; unsuitableness.
Disproportionateness. Inadequacy to something else.

HARMONY—DISCORD—*Continued.*

Aptitude. Fitness or suitableness; readiness.
Aptness. Suitableness or appropriateness.
Assimilation. The transformation of anything into a homogeneous part.
Case in point. An example as near as can be to a question or subject discussed.
Coaptation. The act of adjusting or fitting together
Cognation. Agreement in ancestry.
Commensurability. The capacity of being reducible to a common measure.
Compatibility. Suitableness.
Concert. Agreement in carrying out a scheme.
Concord. Agreement between persons or things
Concordance. Harmony; agreement.
Concurrence. Agreement of plan or action.
Conformance. The state of being in accord or harmony.
Conformity. Agreement in form.
Congeniality. Similarity or agreement of disposition.
Congruence. Fitness, agreement, harmony of things.
Congruity. Logical harmoniousness.
Consent. Agreement to the proposals of another
Consentaneousness. Mutual acquiescence.
Consistency. Harmony of character and action.
Consonance. Agreement of sound.
Cooperation. Working together in harmony.
Correspondence. A general likeness; a resemblance.
Emmeleia. Perfect harmony.
Fitness. Adaptation; meetness; suitability.
Graduation. Slow adjustment.
Harmony. Agreement in all its parts.
Just the thing. Something agreeing with anything in the mind.
Keeping. Just proportion; harmony.
Parallelism. State of being similar, resemblance.
Pertinence. Close relation to the subject; relevantness.
Pertinency. Suitableness; appositeness.
Propriety. Fitness; conformity to customs.
Quite the thing. Entirely suitable; something entirely suitable to a purpose.
Reconcilement. Agreement of things once held at variance.
Reconciliation. Agreement of things seemingly contradictory or incompatible.
Relevancy. The quality of being relevant; pertinency.
Right man in right place. A person having all the qualifications for a position.
Sortance. Suitableness; agreement.
Uniformity. Constant, unvaried resemblance to itself.
Union. Joining together two or more things in harmony.
Unison. Sameness of sound; agreement; concord.
Very thing. Something agreeing in all points with a model or idea.

HARMONY—*Verbs.*

Accommodate. To adjust; adapt; compromise.
Accord. To make to agree; to agree to grant.
Adapt. To adjust or fit.
Adapt itself to. To adjust to circumstances.
Adjust. To make corresponding to something.
Agree. To come into one mind; to concur.
Assimilate. To become similar or like something else
Be accordant. To be like in thought or sympathy. See *Adjectives.*
Become one. To be suited to one's character or condition.
Befit. To be suitable to.
Chime in with. To fall in with; to agree.
Comport with. To carry in accordance with; to be compatible.
Consent. To yield to a proposal; acquiesce. See ASSENT.
Consort with. To unite or join, as in harmony, company, etc.
Correspond. To suit; to be proportioned or congruous.
Do. To make ready or suitable for an object or use.
Dovetail. To fit nicely and strongly.
Dress. To arrange or put in good order.
Fadge. To suit; to agree.
Fall in with. To concur in; to comply with.
Fit. To shape and adjust one thing to another.
Fit like a glove. ⎱
Fit to a T. ⎰ To nicely and closely adapt one thing to another
Fit to a tittle. ⎰
Graduate. To divide into spaces; to advance gradually
Harmonize. To make agree throughout; to be in peace.
Match. To make equal or similar; to suit. See LIKENESS
Meet. To come together by mutual concessions
Quadrate with. To square with; to agree.
Readjust. To adjust or settle again.
Reconcile. To bring in accord what was incompatible or unlike.

Dissension. Violent disagreement in opinion.
Dissidence. Dissent; disagreement.
Dissonance. Disagreeing of sounds; inharmoniousness.
Divergence. Deviation from agreement.
Fish out of water. A person out of his natural sphere of work, etc.
Inapplicability, etc. Unfitness, etc. See *Adjectives.*
Inaptitude. Want of general fitness.
Inconcinnity. Want of congruousness.
Incongruence. Want of suitableness or propriety.
Incongruity. Lack of harmony or fitness.
Inconsistency. Want of consistency; capriciousness.
Interference. Intervention.
Intrusion. Act of thrusting in without invitation.
Irrelevancy, etc. The quality of being inapplicable, etc. See CON-NECTION-INDEPENDENCE.
Jarring. Discord; a clashing of interests. See *Verbs.*
Mésalliance [F.]. Improper relation.
Misjoinder. An incorrect union of parties or of causes in a lawsuit.
Misjoining. Unsuitable connection.
Mismatch. Bad joining or match.
Repugnance. Resistance; dislike.
Syncretism. Attempted union of many systems of philosophy or religions.
Unconformity, etc. Absence of conformity, etc. See CONVENTION-ALITY-UNCONVENTIONALITY.
Unfitness, etc. Lack of fitness, etc. See *Adjectives.*
Variance. Difference resulting in controversy; discord.

DISCORD—*Verbs.*

Clash. To collide; to conflict or disagree.
Come amiss. To go astray; to go wrong.
Disagree, etc. Not to cooperate; not to be of the same kind or opinion, etc. See *Nouns.*
Humano capiti cervicem jungere equinam [L.]. To join a horse's neck to a human head. [Horace, *Art of Poetry,* i.]
Interfere. To interpose; to intermeddle.
Intrude. To enter without permission or right.
Jar, etc. To act in opposition; to clash. See VARIANCE
Mismatch. To badly match or join.
Not concern. Not to be related or affected.

DISCORD—*Adjectives.*

At odds. ⎫
At variance. ⎬ In disagreement; at enmity.
At variance with. ⎪
At war. ⎭
Disagreeing. Lacking harmony.
Discordant. Clashing.
Discrepant. Different.
Disproportionate. ⎱ Unsuitable to something else in bulk, form, etc.
Disproportionated. ⎰
Divergent. Receding farther and farther from each other.
Exceptional. Unusual; anomalous; unconformable.
Hostile. Repugnant; disagreeing strongly.
Ill-assorted. Badly arranged
Ill-sorted. Badly selected; ill fitted.
Ill-timed. Done at an unsuitable time.
Improper. Not proper; not fit.
Inadmissible. Not allowable.
Inapplicable. Not fit.
Inapposite. Not suitable or pertinent. See IRRELATION, super.
Inappropriate. Not suited; not fitted.
Inapt. Unfit.
Incompatible. Not consistent; not consonant.
Incongruous. Not well mated; having dissimilar natures.
Inconsistent with. Not agreeing at all times with itself.
Intrusive. Forcing itself in without permission.
Irreconcilable. Not being made able to agree.
Irreducible. Not resolvable into something else.
Mal à propos [F.]. Ill-timed.
Misjoined. ⎫
Mismatched. ⎬ Not fittingly united, and suited.
Mismated. ⎪
Misplaced. ⎭
Out of character. ⎫
Out of its element. ⎪
Out of joint. ⎪
Out of keeping. ⎬ Unfitted for, or disagreeing with.
Out of place. ⎪
Out of proportion. ⎪
Out of season. ⎪
Out of tune. ⎭

HARMONY—DISCORD—*Continued.*

HARMONY—Verbs—*Continued.*

Regulate. To adjust with respect to some thing or person.
Render accordant. To cause to be accordant. See *Adjectives*
Respond. To act in sympathy or harmony; agree; suit.
Square. To shape or fit.
Square with. To mold, fit, adjust, or shape to an agreement.
Suit. To fit; to adapt; to agree.
Tally. To make to correspond; conform.

HARMONY—*Adjectives.*

Accordant. Agreeing in a purpose.
Ad rem [L.]. To the purpose.
Agreeing, etc. Concurring, etc. See *Verbs*.
Apt. Quick at understanding; pertinent.
At home. In the proper place.
At one with. Concurring in a given proposition.
Becoming. Suited to character, position, or disposition.
Commensurate. Commensurable.
Compatible. Not repugnant; agreeing.
Concordant. Agreeing; consonant.
Conformable. Agreeing in form; correspondent.
Congenial. Suited in temperament or character.
Congruous. Characterized by suitability.
Consentaneous. Reciprocally acquiescent.
Consistent. Agreeing in reality with profession.
Consonant. Likeness of sound; according.
Correspondent. Having suitability; fit.
Harmonious. Concordant; peaceable.
In accord.
In accordance with.
In harmony with. } Having the idea of agreement, similarity, or harmony.
In keeping with.
In loco [L.]. In place; in the right place.
In one's proper element. Suitable to.
In point. Under discussion.
In unison with. Agreeing with.
Of a piece. Of same sort; like.
Of one mind. Agreeing.
On all fours. To correspond with exactly.
Pat. Exactly fitting.
Pertinent. Applicable; relevant; suited.
Proportionate. Adjusted in a due proportion.
Reconciled. Brought in harmony; harmonized.
Suiting, etc. Adapting; befitting; agreeing, etc. See *Verbs*.
To the point.
To the purpose. } Suitable.

HARMONY—*Associated Adjectives.*

Adapted. Accommodated to a situation.
Admissible. Allowable; requiring assent.
Applicable. Suitable.
Appropriate. Limited to a particular use.
Àpropos [F.]. In this connection.

har'-ness. To make ready for draft; equipment for a draft animal; equipment for any business. Connective, Dress-Undress, Instrument, Release-Prison, Union-Disunion; **in harness,** Action-Passiveness, Activity-Indolence, Enclosure, Liberty-Subjection, Preparation-Nonpreparation.

harp. To revert to some subject continually; play on the harp. Discontinuance-Continuance, Musical Instruments, Recurrence.

har'-pa-gon. An iron grappling-hook. Extravagance-Avarice.

harp'-er. One who plays the harp. Musician.

harp'-ing. Dwelling upon one subject. Recurrence.

har-poon'. A missile weapon to capture whales and other large fish. Weapon.

harp'-si-chord. An old-fashioned keyed and stringed instrument. Musical Instruments.

har'-py. Any rapacious person; a fabulous winged monster. Benefactor-Evildoer, Harshness-Mildness, Jove-Fiend, Robber.

har'-que-bus. An antique form of musket. Weapon.

DISCORD—Adjectives—*Continued.*

Repugnant to. Opposed; antagonistic.
Unaccommodating. Not suiting and fitting.
Unapt. Inapt; unsuited.
Unbecoming. Not suited to rank or character.
Unbefitting. Unsuited.
Uncommensurable. Unproportionate.
Unconformable. Not correspondent; not compliant
Uncongenial. Having a similar nature.
Unconsonant. Inharmonious.
Unfit. Not fit; incompetent.
Unfitting. Making unsuitable.
Unharmonious. Not the same; discordant.
Unsuitable. Improper; incongruous.
Unsuited. Unfitted; discordant.

DISCORD—*Adverbs, etc.*

À tort et à travers [F.]. Without settled purpose.
Discordantly. Out of harmony. See *Adjectives*.
In contempt of.
In defiance of. } Contrary to; disagreeing with. See *Adjectives*.
In spite of.

DISCORD—*Phrase.*

Asinus ad lyram [L.]. The ass at the lyre; hence, anything altogether out of place.

HARMONY—Associated Adjectives—*Continued.*

Bearing upon. Situated so as to affect; related to the subject in hand.
Deft. Handy; clever; apt.
Felicitous. Well applied; appropriate.
Fit. Adapted to an end or object.
Germane. Closely allied; relevant; pertinent.
Happy. Felicitous; appropriate.
Idoneous. Proper; suitable.
Meet. Fitting; suitable.
Opposite. Placed over against.
Relevant. Pertaining to the case in hand.
Seasonable. Done at the proper time; opportune.
Sortable. Suitable; befitting.
Suitable. Fitting; accordant.

HARMONY—*Adverbs.*

Àpropos. Relevantly.
Pertinently, etc. Appropriately. See *Adjectives*.

HARMONY—*Phrases.*

Auxilia humilia firma consensus facit [L.]. Concord makes feeble assistance strong.
It is appropriate. It is in harmony with.
Rem acu tetigisti [L.]. You have touched it with a needle-point.
The cap fits. It is pat.

har'-ri-dan. A hag; a strumpet. Beauty-Ugliness, Purity-Rake.

har'-ri-er. A small hound used to hunt hares. Fauna-Flora.

har'-row. To pulverize plowed ground with a harrow. Domestication-Agriculture, Pleasurableness-Painfulness; **harrow up the soul,** Sanguineness-Timidity.

har'-row-ing. Lacerating the feelings. Pleasurableness-Painfulness.

har'-ry. To annoy; pillage; harass. Attack-Defense, Charitableness-Malevolence, Pleasurableness-Painfulness.

harsh. Rough; disagreeable; offensive; grating; abusive; austere. Cacophony, Charitableness-Malevolence, Compassion-Ruthlessness, Harshness-Mildness, Melody-Dissonance, Pleasurableness-Painfulness, Politeness-Impoliteness, Purity-Crudeness, Vigor-Inertia; **harsh voice,** Vocalization-Muteness.

harsh'-ness. The quality or state of being harsh. Harshness-Mildness, Melody-Dissonance, Vigor-Inertia.

HARSHNESS—MILDNESS.

Absolutism. The doctrine of unlimited power and control of the sovereign.
Arbitrary power. Despotic power.

Clemency. A disposition to forgive.
Compassion, etc. A sympathizing feeling for the misfortunes of others, etc. See Compassion.

HARSHNESS—MILDNESS—*Continued*.

Arrogance, etc. The state or quality of being arrogant, etc. See PRESUMPTION.
Assumption. The act of assuming: disposition to assume too much.
Austerity. The state or quality of being austere.
Autocracy. The rule of one having unrestricted and irresponsible authority.
Brute force. }
Brute strength. } Physical exertion; cruel power.
Coercion. Forcible constraint or restraint.
Despotism. Unlimited and severe rule in which those ruled have no part.
Dictatorship. The office of one who has obtained absolute power generally in an emergency, as in ancient Rome.
Domineering. Arbitrary exercise of power.
Hard lines. A difficult or distressing situation. [Walter Scott, *Redgauntlet*; *Psalms* xvi, 8.]
Hard measure. Oppressive treatment.
Harshness, etc. The quality of being harsh, etc. See COMPASSION-RUTHLESSNESS.
Inclemency. Severity.
Inquisition. A severe, critical examination.
Iron hand. }
Iron heel. }
Iron rule. } Firm, relentless control or government.
Iron sway. }
Martial law. Arbitrary law proceeding from military authority.
Officialism. Strict adherence to rule or form.
Oppression. The act of oppressing; the state of being oppressed; that which oppresses.
Pipe-clay. A settling up accounts, as soldiers' equipments are rubbed up for parade with white clay.
Reign of Terror. A period of anarchy and great bloodshed in France; any similar period or situation.
Rigor. Relentless temper or sternness.
Severity. Cruel treatment; harshness.
Sharp practise. Cunning stratagem.
Strictness. The state or quality of adhering to a fixed rule.
Stringency. The state or quality of being stringent.
Strong hand. Violence; force.
Tender mercies. Entire lack of compassion or pity.
Tight grasp. }
Tight hand. } Relentless, harsh control.
Tyranny. Government of a tyrant.
Usurpation. Unlawful and arbitrary seizure of power.

HARSHNESS—*Nouns of Agency*.

Bashaw. Turkish title of honor; a powerful ruler.
Despot. One who rules regardless of law or right.
Disciplinarian. One who enforces rigid discipline.
Draco. Famous law-giver of Athens; any severe, rigorous ruler or governor.
Extortioner. One who takes something from another by force or the unlawful exercise of power.
Hard master. One who uses harsh or cruel measures over his subordinates.
Harpy. A ravenous extortioner. [Virgil, *Æneid*.]
Inquisitor. A severe questioner or investigator.
Jingo. One favoring an aggressive foreign policy.
Martinet. One laying great stress on strict adherence to discipline in detail.
Oppressor. One who oppresses.
Stickler. One who persistently contends for some trifling point.
Tyrant. One who exercises power or authority, unlawfully and cruelly.
Vulture. A rapacious bird; hence, figuratively, a greedy and exacting person.]

HARSHNESS—*Verbs*.

Arrogate. To claim a right to presumptuously.
Assume. To take unjustly.
Bear a heavy hand upon. Exercise oppression over.
Be down upon. To dislike and treat harshly.
Be hard upon. Treat in a cruel, unpleasant manner.
Be severe, etc. See *Adjectives*.
Bully, etc. To coerce by threats, etc. See PRESUMPTION.
Chastise with scorpions. To treat or punish with great cruelty.
Coerce, etc. To compel or restrain by force, etc. See COERCION.
Come down upon. To reprimand.
Crush under an iron heel. To forcibly suppress.
Deal hardly with. Treat roughly.
Deal hard measure to. To be oppressive or harsh toward.
Domineer. To assume haughty, insolent rule over.
Dye with blood. Treat or punish with brutal cruelty.

Favor. A kind act; an inclination to mildness.
Forbearance. The exercise of patience.
Gentleness. The quality or state of being gentle.
Indulgence. } The quality of allowing self or others too much freedom
Indulgency. } in any direction.
Lenience. }
Leniency. } The state or quality of being lenient.
Lenity. Lenience.
Mercy. Compassionate treatment of an offender.
Mildness. The quality or state of being mild.
Moderation. The state or quality of being temperate.
Quarter. Compassionate treatment by an enemy, as in sparing life.
Tolerance. Capacity to endure or act of enduring that which is objectionable or unpleasant.
Toleration. The quality of allowing when one has power or influence to prevent.

MILDNESS—*Verbs*.

Allow one to have his own way. To be lenient or gentle with.
Bear with. To show forbearance.
Be lenient, etc. See *Adjectives*.
Give quarter. To spare; to assign quarters to a foe.
Indulge. To forbear from controlling.
Parcere subjectis [L.]. To spare the conquered.
Spoil. Impair, as in disposition, by overindulgence.
Tolerate. To allow to be or to be done without opposition.

MILDNESS—*Adjectives*.

Clement, etc. Characterized by clemency, etc. See COMPASSION.
Easygoing. Mild-tempered.
Forbearing. Treating with consideration and indulgence.
Gentle. Refined; amiable; tender.
Indulgent. Prone to indulge.
Lenient. Not severe in punishment.
Mild. Not harsh in disposition.
Mild as milk. Very mild.
Soft. Expressing gentleness or sympathy.
Tolerant. Allowing what one has the power to prevent.

HARSHNESS—*Verbs—Continued*.

Force down the throat. Compel to do unwillingly.
Hold a tight hand. Keep control.
Ill-treat. To treat cruelly or improperly.
Inflict. To cause another to suffer.
Keep a tight hand. Maintain severe control.
Lay a heavy hand on. Be very severe or oppressive.
Oppress. To overburden unjustly.
Override. To supersede or suppress.
Put on the screw. To use extortion upon; to coerce.
Ride roughshod over. To cause pain to others in an inconsiderate manner.
Rivet the yoke. To bind in servitude or oppression.
Rule with a rod of iron. To rule with severe, rigid authority.
Stretch a point. To go beyond one's rightful authority.
Take liberties. To do more than is proper or right.
Trample down. }
Trample under foot. }
Trample upon. } Oppress; overwhelm.
Tread down. }
Tread under foot. }
Tread upon. } To oppress.
Tyrannize. To act as a tyrant.
Usurp. To appropriate, as authority, without proper right or by force.
Wreak. To inflict, as a punishment.

HARSHNESS—*Adjectives*.

Absolute. With no restriction.
Arbitrary. Unreasonable; harsh.
Arrogant, etc. Assuming too much authority, etc. See PRESUMPTION.
Austere. Severe or grave in manner or judgment.
Coercive, etc. Serving or intending to coerce, etc. See COERCION.
Cruel. Fitted to cause pain or grief.
Dour. Obstinate; hard.
Draconian. Relentless; severe.
Exigeant [F.]. Requiring too much.
Exigent. Demanding immediate action; exacting.
Extortionate. Given to extortion; oppressive.
Grinding. Oppressing by exactions, as in a mill or with a grindstone.

HARSHNESS—Adjectives—Continued.

Hard. Stern and unsympathetic.
Harsh. Severe and abusive.
Haughty. Contemptuously overbearing and oppressive
Imperative. Demanding obedience.
Inclement. Lacking mildness or kindliness.
Inexorable. Not to be moved from adherence to a rule.
Inflexible. Firm in will; unchangeable; inexorable.
Inquisitorial. Like an inquisitor.
Iron-handed. Rude; harsh.
Obdurate. Opposing all sympathetic influences.
Oppressive. Unreasonably severe.
Peremptory. Not admitting of remonstrance.
Positive. Confident and overbearing.
Relentless. Insensible or unyielding to appeals.

Rigid. Not indulgent or yielding; severe
Rigorous. Characterized by rigor.
Searching. Severe and critical in investigation
Severe. Characterized by severity.
Stern. Severe in aspect and judgment, or manner.
Stiff. Unyielding; harsh.
Straitlaced. Rigid in opinion and manners.
Strict. Governing or governed by rigid rules.
Stringent. Making rigid; severe requirements
Tyrannical. Like a tyrant.
Uncompromising. Making no concessions.
Unsparing. Not considerate.
Withering. Causing to shrink or be abashed

HARSHNESS—Adverbs

At the point of the bayonet. In a cruel, barbarous manner
At the point of the sword. By compulsion or force.
Severely, etc. In a severe manner, etc. See *Adjectives*

With a heavy hand.
With a high hand.
With a strong hand. } Oppressively and overbearingly
With a tight hand.

HARSHNESS—Phrases

Bonis nocet si quis malis pepercerit [L.]. If any one spares the bad he injures the good.

Delirant reges plectuntur Achivi [L.]. The kings rage and the Greeks suffer: the people must pay for the folly of their rulers.
Manu forti [L.]. With the strong hand

hart. The male of the red deer. FAUNA-FLORA, MALE-FEMALE.
har'-um-scar'-um. Marked by extreme haste or disorder. HEED-DISREGARD, REGULARITY-IRREGULARITY.
ha-rus'-pice. A soothsayer. SOOTHSAYER.
har'-vest. The product of any toil; a crop stored up. ASSIGNMENT, CAUSE-EFFECT, GOOD-EVIL, STORE; **get in the harvest,** COMPLETION-NONCOMPLETION, GAIN-LOSS, SUCCESS-FAILURE; **harvest home,** SOLEMNIZATION; **harvest time,** TOIL-RELAXATION.
has'-been''. A person or thing out of date. FUTURE-PAST.
hash. To cut into small pieces; mix; a dish of chopped and cooked meat. MIXTURE-HOMOGENEITY, NUTRIMENT-EXCRETION, REGULARITY-IRREGULARITY; **make a hash,** SKILL-UNSKILFULNESS.
hash'-ish. An intoxicating substance made from the Indian hemp MODERATION-SELFINDULGENCE, REMEDY-BANE.
hasp. To fasten; a fastening. UNION-DISUNION, CONNECTIVE.
has'-sock. A thick mat used as a footstool SUSPENSION-SUPPORT.
Hast, aber ohne Rast, ohne [G.] (hast, ab'-er o'-nê rast, o'-nê). Unhasting, but unresting. ETERNITY-INSTANTANEITY, HURRY-LEISURE.
haste. Speed; hurry. ACTIVITY-INDOLENCE, HURRY-LEISURE, SWIFTNESS.
ha'-sten. To expedite. OBSTRUCTION-HELP, SWIFTNESS-SLOWNESS.
ha'-sti-ly. Speedily. HURRY-LEISURE.
ha'-sty. Rash; quick-tempered; done with celerity. ETERNITY-INSTANTANEITY, EXCITABILITY-INEXCITABILITY, FAVORITE-QUARRELSOMENESS, HURRY-LEISURE.
hat. A covering for the head. DRESS-UNDRESS; **cardinal's hat,** VESTMENTS; **hat in hand,** PRESUMPTION-OBSEQUIOUSNESS; **send round the hat,** PETITION-EXPOSTULATION; **shovel-hat,** VESTMENTS.
hatch. To develop in and come forth from an egg; plan; evolve in the mind; a door with an opening over it; to mark with lime. APERTURE-CLOSURE, CREATION-DESTRUCTION, DESIGN, ENCLOSURE, PAINTING, PREPARATION-NONPREPARATION, TRUTHFULNESS-FALSEHOOD; **hatch a plot,** DESIGN.
hatch'-es, un'-der. In confinement; in distress. AFFLUENCE-PENURY, GUARD-PRISONER, RELEASE-RESTRAINT

hatch'-et. A small, short-handled ax. SHARPNESS-BLUNTNESS; **dig up the hatchet,** FIGHTING-CONCILIATION; **throw the helve after the hatchet,** EXTRAVAGANCE-AVARICE.
hatch'-et-faced''. Thin and narrow-featured. BREADTH-NARROWNESS.
hatch'-ing. Evolving by long meditation. PREPARATION-NONPREPARATION.
hatch'-ment. The armorial bearings of a deceased person; an ornament on the hilt of the sword. LIFE-FUNERAL, MARK-OBLITERATION, SIGN.
hatch'-way. An opening in a deck, floor, roof, or the like. APERTURE-CLOSURE.
hate. Intense aversion, with animosity and malignity. AMITY-HOSTILITY, CHARITABLENESS-MALEVOLENCE, DESIRE-DISTASTE, LOVE-HATE, VARIANCE-ACCORD.
hate'-ful. Manifesting hatred; odious. GOODNESS-BADNESS, PLEASURABLENESS-PAINFULNESS.
hath been, the time. FUTURE-PAST.
ha'-ting. Filled with hatred. LOVE-HATE.
hat'-rack''. A rack for hanging hats on. HOLDER.
ha'-tred. A sustained feeling of bitter aversion. AMITY-HOSTILITY, CHARITABLENESS-MALEVOLENCE, DESIRE-DISTASTE, LOVE-HATE, VARIANCE-ACCORD; **object of hatred,** CEREMONIAL.
hat'-ter. One who makes or deals in hats. DRESS-UNDRESS.
hat'-ti-sher-if''. An imperial decree of the highest authority, in Turkey. ORDER.
hau'-berk. A medieval coat of mail. ATTACK-DEFENSE.
haud passibus æquis [L.] (haud pas'-si-bus î'-quis), Not with equal steps. EQUALITY-INEQUALITY, SWIFTNESS-SLOWNESS.
haugh. Low-lying, rich land. GULF-PLAIN.
haugh'-ti-ness. Pride. PRESUMPTION-OBSEQUIOUSNESS, SELFRESPECT-HUMBLENESS.
haugh'-ty. Proud; disdainful; arrogant. HARSHNESS-MILDNESS, PRESUMPTION-OBSEQUIOUSNESS, REGARD-SCORN, SELFRESPECT-HUMBLENESS.
haul. To drag or pull with force. PUSH-PULL, TAKING-RESTITUTION; **haul down one's flag,** YIELDING.
haul'-age. The process of hauling. PUSH-PULL.
haunch. The fleshy part of the hip; anything hip-shaped. ARCHITECTURE, LATERALITY-CONTRAPOSITION.
haunt. To visit in the form of a ghost; resort much to; a place to which one resorts frequently. CHARITABLENESS-MALEVOLENCE, DWELLER-HABITATION,

GATHERINGPLACE, PRESENCE-ABSENCE; **haunt the memory**, PLEASURABLENESS-PAINFULNESS, REMEMBRANCE-FORGETFULNESS.

haunt'-ed. Frequently visited by ghosts or apparitions. JOVE-FIEND.

haut'-boy. A wooden wind instrument. MUSICAL INSTRUMENTS.

haut, en [F.] (o, an·). Above. HEIGHT-LOWNESS.

haut en bas, regarder de [F.] (o an· ba, re-gar-dê' de). To look high and low. PRESUMPTION-OBSEQUIOUSNESS.

haut en bas, traiter de [F.] (o an· ba, trê-tê' de). To treat with contempt. PRESUMPTION-OBSEQUIOUSNESS, REGARD-SCORN.

hau''-teur'. Disdainful pride. SELFRESPECT-HUMBLENESS.

hâut''-gout' [F.] (o''-gu'). High flavor. PUNGENCY.

haut-monde [F.] (o''-mon·d'). The high world. GENTILITY-DEMOCRACY.

have. To own; hold in the mind. HOLDING-EXEMPTION, KNOWLEDGE-IGNORANCE, PROOF-DISPROOF; **have at,** ATTACK-DEFENSE; **have done,** DISCONTINUANCE-CONTINUANCE; **have for one's own,** PROPERTY; **have** *in petto,* INSTRUMENTALITY; **have in store,** OCCURRENCE-DESTINY, PROVISION-WASTE; **have it,** DISCOVERY, FAITH-MISGIVING; **have it your own way,** YIELDING; **have no choice,** CHOICE-NEUTRALITY; **have no end,** ETERNITY-INSTANTANEITY; **have nothing to do with,** CONNECTION-INDEPENDENCE, FIGHTING-CONCILIATION; **have one's rights,** DUENESS-UNDUENESS; **have one to know,** ENLIGHTENMENT-SECRECY; **have other fish to fry,** OPPORTUNENESS-UNSUITABLENESS; **have rather,** CHOICE-NEUTRALITY; **have some knowledge,** KNOWLEDGE-IGNORANCE; **have the advantage,** EQUALITY-INEQUALITY, SUPREMACY-SUBORDINACY; **have the chair,** PRESIDENT-MEMBER; **have the start,** ANTECEDENCE-SEQUENCE; **have to,** PURPOSE-LUCK; **have up,** JUSTIFICATION-CHARGE.

ha'-ven. A port; a place of anchorage for ships. ARRIVAL-DEPARTURE, MOVEMENT-REST, REFUGE-PITFALL.

hav'-er-sack. A soldier's ration-bag. CONTENTS-RECEIVER.

hav'-oc. General destruction. BETTERMENT-DETERIORATION, CREATION-DESTRUCTION; **cry havoc,** FIGHTING-CONCILIATION; **play havoc,** BETTERMENT-DETERIORATION.

haw. To hesitate in speaking. SPEECH-INARTICULATENESS.

hawk. To clear the throat of phlegm; to peddle; a bird of prey. ADMISSION-EXPULSION, BUYING-SALE, SIGHT-BLINDNESS; **between hawk and buzzard,** AGITATION, PLEASURE-PAIN; **eye of a hawk,** SAGACITY-INCAPACITY; **hawk about,** BUYING-SALE, PROFFER-REFUSAL, PUBLICITY; **know a hawk from a hand-saw,** DIFFERENTIATION-INDISCRIMINATION.

hawk'-er. A pedler. DEALER.

hawk'-eyed''. Having keen, piercing eyes. SIGHT-BLINDNESS.

hawk'-ing. Hunting with hawks. QUEST-EVASION.

haw'-ser. A large and heavy rope. CONNECTIVE.

hay'-cock''. A conical pile of hay in the field. GATHERING-SCATTERING.

hay'-fe''-ver. Nasal catarrh. HEALTH-SICKNESS.

Hay'-mar''-ket. District in Chicago. **Haymarket gang,** TYRANNY-ANARCHY.

hay'-mow''. A mass of hay laid up in a barn. QUANTITY-MEASURE.

hay while the sun shines, make. OPPORTUNENESS-UNSUITABLENESS.

haz'-ard. Risk; chance. PURPOSE-LUCK, RATIONALE-LUCK, SECURITY-INSECURITY; **at all hazards,** DETERMINATION-VACILLATION; **hazard a conjecture,** HYPOTHESIS; **hazard a proposition,** RATIOCINATION-INSTINCT.

haz'-ard-ed. Exposed to danger. RATIOCINATION-INSTINCT.

haz'-ard-ous. Perilous; dangerous. SECURITY-INSECURITY.

haze. Vapor which renders the air thick; dimness of perception. CERTAINTY-DOUBT, VISCIDITY-FOAM; **in a haze,** ENLIGHTENMENT-SECRECY.

ha'-zel. Dark-brown. GRAY-BROWN.

ha'-zy. Lacking clearness. DIAPHANEITY-OPAQUENESS.

he. The man or male person before named. HUMANITY.

head. The uppermost; foremost; leader; an individual; the understanding; a chapter; climax; a head-dress; title; director; master; the rounded mass of foam which rises on the top of any effervescing liquor. BEGINNING-END, CHIEF-UNDERLING, CONCEPTION-THEME, DIVISION, DRESS-UNDRESS, HUMANITY, LEADING-FOLLOWING, MANAGEMENT, MANAGER, MIND-IMBECILITY, MISSIVE-PUBLICATION, NAME-MISNOMER, PAINTING, PRECEDENCE-SUCCESSION, SAGACITY-INCAPACITY, TOP-BOTTOM, VISCIDITY-FOAM; **as one's head shall answer for,** ENGAGEMENT-RELEASE; **at the head of,** MISSIVE-PUBLICATION, REPUTATION-DISCREDIT, RULE-LICENSE; **bow the head,** ELEVATION-DEPRESSION; **can't get out of one's head,** REMEMBRANCE-FORGETFULNESS; **come into one's head,** REFLECTION-VACANCY; **from head to foot,** ENTIRETY-DEFICIENCY, LENGTH-SHORTNESS; **gain head,** DOMINANCE-IMPOTENCE; **get into one's head,** FAITH-MISGIVING, REFLECTION-VACANCY, TEETOTALISM-INTEMPERANCE; **give a horse his head,** LIBERTY-SUBJECTION; **hang one's head,** SELFRESPECT-HUMBLENESS; **have in one's head,** KNOWLEDGE-IGNORANCE, **have no head,** REMEMBRANCE-FORGETFULNESS, SAGACITY-INCAPACITY; **head above water,** AFFLUENCE-PENURY, SECURITY-INSECURITY, WELFARE-MISFORTUNE; **head and front,** CONSEQUENCE-INSIGNIFICANCE; **head and front of one's offending,** JUSTIFICATION-CHARGE, PLEASURABLENESS-PAINFULNESS; **head and shoulders,** ENTIRETY-DEFICIENCY, HURRY-LEISURE; **head over heels,** REVERSAL, REVOLUTION-EVOLUTION; **hold one's head up,** ELEVATION-DEPRESSION; **knock one's head against,** IMPETUS-REACTION, SKILL-UNSKILFULNESS; **knock on the head,** LIFE-KILLING; **lie on one's head,** DUTY-DERELICTION; **lift up one's head,** SELFRESPECT-HUMBLENESS; **make head against,** ANTAGONISM-CONCURRENCE, REPRISAL-RESISTANCE, SUCCESS-FAILURE; **make neither head nor tail,** CLEARNESS-OBSCURITY; **master head,** ADEPT-BUNGLER; **never entered into one's head,** HEED-DISREGARD; **not know whether one stands on head or heels,** ASTONISHMENT-EXPECTANCE, CERTAINTY-DOUBT; **on one's head,** REVERSAL; **over head and ears,** CREDIT-DEBT, EXCESS-LACK, LOVE-HATE; **put into one's head,** ENLIGHTENMENT-SECRECY, HYPOTHESIS; **put out of one's head,** HEED-DISREGARD; **run in the head,** HYPOTHESIS, REMEMBRANCE-FORGETFULNESS; **take into one's head,** DESIRE-DISTASTE, MIND-IMBECILITY, PERSISTENCE-WHIM, PURPOSE-LUCK; **trouble one's head about,** HEED-DISREGARD; **turn the head,** SENSITIVENESS; **with head erect,** SELFRESPECT-HUMBLENESS.

head'-ache''. A pain in the head. SENSUALITY-SUFFERING.

head'-cen''-ter. A chief manager. MANAGER.

head'-dress''. A covering or ornament for the head. DRESS-UNDRESS.

head'-er. A plunge or fall head foremost. SPRING-DIVE.

head'' fore'-most. Rash; violent. RECKLESSNESS-CAUTION, TURBULENCE-CALMNESS.

head'-gear''. A head-dress. DRESS-UNDRESS, LEADING-FOLLOWING.

head'-ing. A caption, title, or the like. BEGINNING-END, NAME-MISNOMER, PREDECESSOR-CONTINUATION, SIGN.

head'-land". A cliff projecting into the sea. CONVEXITY-CONCAVITY, HEIGHT-LOWNESS.

head'-light". A light in front of a car to light the track. ALARM, SIGN.

head'-line". A line printed above some article as a title. WRITING-PRINTING.

head'-long". Impetuous; rash. HURRY-LEISURE, RECKLESSNESS-CAUTION; **rush headlong,** TURBULENCE-CALMNESS.

head'-man". A leader. MANAGER.

head'-most. The most advanced. ANTERIORITY-POSTERIORITY, LEADING-FOLLOWING.

head'-piece". A decorative design at the top of a printed page; the intellect. EMBELLISHMENT-DISFIGUREMENT, MIND-IMBECILITY, SAGACITY-INCAPACITY.

head'-quar"-ters. The location of the commanding officer, in camp; the center of authority. DWELLER-HABITATION, GATHERINGPLACE, RULE-LICENSE.

head'-race". The channel by which water is led to a water-wheel. WATERCOURSE-AIRPIPE.

heads. Topics. DIGEST; **heads I win, tails you lose,** UPRIGHTNESS-DISHONESTY; **heads or tails,** PURPOSE-LUCK, RATIONALE-LUCK; **lay heads together,** ADVICE, ANTAGONISM-CONCURRENCE.

head'-sail". A sail set forward on the foremast. CONVEYANCE-VESSEL.

head'-ship. The chief place. RULE-LICENSE.

heads'-man. A public executioner who beheads the condemned. RECOMPENSE-SCOURGE.

head'-strong". Ungovernable; obstinate. BIGOTRY-APOSTASY, RECKLESSNESS-CAUTION, TURBULENCE-CALMNESS.

head'-tone". In singing, a tone coming from the head. MUSIC.

head'-way. Forward motion, especially of a vessel. ADVANCE-RETROGRESSION, TRAVELING-NAVIGATION.

head'-wind". An opposing wind. ANTAGONISM-CONCURRENCE, OBSTRUCTION-HELP.

head'-work". Mental labor. MIND-IMBECILITY.

head'-y. Headstrong. BIGOTRY-APOSTASY.

heal. To restore to health or soundness. RENOVATION-RELAPSE; **heal the breach,** FIGHTING-CONCILIATION; **let the wound heal,** PARDON-VINDICTIVENESS.

heal'-ing art. The art of medicine. RENOVATION-RELAPSE.

health. The state of being sound and well. HEALTH-SICKNESS.

HEALTH—SICKNESS.

Bloom. A state of healthful youth and vigor.

Excellent health.
Good health. } A high degree of freedom from physical disease or pain.
Good state of nealth.

Health. The state of being hale, whole, free from disease.

Incorruptibility. The quality of being incapable of decay or corruption.

Incorruption. The condition of being free from corruption.

Perfect health. Complete freedom from disease.

Robust health.
Rude health. } State of being strong and vigorous.

Sanity. Soundness of mind or body.

Soundness, etc. The state of being sound, firm, not diseased, etc. See *Adjectives.*

Vigor. Active force or strength of mind or body.

Virile. Mature; strong; physically capable.

HEALTH—*Denotations.*

Clean bill of health. A statement indicating freedom from disease or sickness.

Hygeia. The goddess of health.

HEALTH—*Verbs.*

Be in health, etc. To be in a sound, healthy condition. See *Nouns*

Bloom. To be in a state of healthful growth and vigor.

Cure, etc. To restore to health, etc. See RENOVATION.

Enjoy a good state of health. } To be in good health; to be free from
Enjoy good health. } sickness.

Flourish. To be in a thriving state.

Get better, etc. To be in the process of becoming well or free from disease, etc. See BETTERMENT.

Have a clean bill of health. To be free from all disease or sickness.

Keep body and soul together. To keep alive.

Keep on one's legs. To keep healthy.

Recover, etc. To return to health, etc. See RENOVATION

Recruit. To renew in strength or health.

Restore to health. To bring back to health.

Return to health. To come back to health.

Take a fresh lease of life. } To become healthy, as after a serious ill-
Take a new lease of life. } ness

Tinker. To mend in body

HEALTH—*Adjectives.*

As well as can be expected. As healthy as possible under the circumstances.

Brave. Splendid in appearance.

Florid. Blooming; in a healthy condition.

Flush. Full of vigor.

Fresh. Full of original vigor and health.

Fresh as a daisy.
Fresh as April. } In good health; blooming.
Fresh as a rose.

Ailing, etc. Mental or physical illness, etc. See *Verbs*

Ailment. Morbid affection of the body

Attack. A fit of sickness.

Break-up of the system. A general weakness and wearing away of the body through long disease.

Complaint. The cause of pain or uneasiness of body

Dangerous illness. An illness that may cause death.

Disease. Deep-rooted disorder.

Disorder. A slightly unhealthy condition of the system for a short time.

Distemper. A virulent disorder.

Distemperature. A slight illness.

Fatal disease. A sickness that causes death See SANGUINENESS-HOPELESSNESS.

General breaking up. Derangement of all the functions of the body through prolonged sickness.

Illness. Disorder of health; sickness.

Indisposition. A slight disorder of the system.

Infirmity. Local weakness resulting from sickness or age.

Invalidation. The process of rendering invalid.

Loss of health. Continued weakness or sickness.

Malady. A lingering disorder or abnormal condition in any part of the body.

Morbidity. Tendency of a disorder to show itself in disease

Morbosity. A diseased state

Sickness, etc. Any derangement of the constitution, etc See *Adjectives*

SICKNESS—*Denotations*

Abscess. A collection of pus in any tissue or organ of the body, the result of a morbid process.

"All the ills that flesh is heir to." Every kind of mental or physical disease. "The thousand natural shocks," etc [*Hamlet*, III, i.]

Atrophy. A wasting away from want of nourishment.

Black death. A pestilence which ravaged Europe and Asia in the fourteenth century.

Blood-stroke. Loss of sensation and motion from hemorrhage or congestion of the brain.

Bloody flux. A disease in which the discharge from the bowels has a mixture of blood.

Boil. A hard, painful, inflamed tumor

Brash.
Breaking out. } A rash or eruption on the skin.

Cachexia. } A condition of ill-health and impairment of nutrition
Cachexy. } due to impoverishment of the blood.

Calenture. A delirium caused by the heat of the sun.

Cancer. Any malignant growth attended with great pain and ulceration.

Canker. A corroding ulcer

Carbuncle. A very painful inflammation of the subcutaneous tissue, especially of the back of the neck.

HEALTH—SICKNESS—*Continued.*

HEALTH—Adjectives—*Continued.*

Green. Full of vigor and life.
Hale. Sound; robust; healthy.
Hardy. Strong; firm.
Healthful. Wholesome; tending to produce health.
Healthy. Enjoying health.
Hearty. Firm; sound; not weak.
Hearty as a buck. Figurative expression for perfection of health.
In fine feather. In good health.
In full bloom. In entire strength and vigor.
In good case. In good health.
In health, etc. Not ill; well, etc. See *Nouns.*
In high feather. In good health.
On one's legs. Well; recovering.
Pretty bobbish. In good spirits.
Robust. Strong, sound, and vigorous in health.
Safe and sound. Perfectly unharmed.
Sanatory, etc. Conducive to health. See Renovation.
Sanitary, etc. Relating to the preservation of health, etc. See Healthiness.
Sound. Free from imperfections or decay
Sound as a bell. } Figurative expressions for healthiness.
Sound as a roach. }
Sound of mind and body. Well in soul and body.
Sound of wind. Free from weakness of breathing.
Stanch. } Sound and firm.
Staunch. }
Tolerably well. Fairly well.
Uninjured. Unharmed; whole; sound.
Unmaimed. Not disabled.
Unmarred. Not hurt, injured, or spoiled.
Unscathed. Not harmed or damaged.
Untainted. Not corrupted or diseased.
Vigorous. Strong and healthy.
Weather-proof. Proof against rough weather.
Well. Healthy; sound in body.
Whole. Well; sound.

HEALTH—*Phrases.*

Hôtel des Invalides [F.]. Home for invalids (*i. e.*, invalid soldiers).
Mens sana in corpore sano [L.]. A sound mind in a sound body [Juvenal, *Satires*, x, 356.]
Non est vivere, sed valere, vita [L.]. Not to live, but to be well, is life. [Martial, vi, 7015.]

SICKNESS—Denotations—*Continued from Column 2.*

Ulcer. A sore discharging pus.
Varicose. An irregular swelling of parts of the body, as a vein.
Variola. Smallpox.
Virus. The contagion by which a disease is introduced into the organism.
Visitation. An attack of sickness.

SICKNESS—*Nouns of Result.*

Case. A patient under treatment; an instance of sickness or injury.
Cripple. One who has lost, or never had, the use of a limb.
Invalid. A person who is weak and infirm.
Leper. A person affected with leprosy.
Martyr to disease. A person suffering from long-protracted illness.
Patient. A person under medical treatment.
Sick-chamber. } A room in which a person is confined by sickness.
Sick-room. }
Valetudinarian. } A person of a weak or sickly constitution
Valetudinary. }

SICKNESS—*Scientific Nouns.*

Diagnosis. The art of distinguishing a disease.
Etiology. That branch of medical science which treats of the causes of diseases.
Nosology. A systematic classification of diseases.
Pathology. The science which treats of the nature, causes, symptoms, etc., of diseases.

SICKNESS—*Verbs.*

Ail. To be affected with pain or trouble either in mind or body
Be affected with. Acted on by.
Be ill, etc. To be unwell, etc. See *Adjectives.*
Break out. To appear suddenly.
Catch a disease, etc. To take a disease as by infection, etc.
Catch an infection. To become infected.
Complain of. To express pain or distress.

SICKNESS—Denotations—*Continued.*

Carcinoma. An indolent tumor or cancer.
Caries. A process in which bone disintegrates and is carried away piecemeal.
Chicken-pox. A mild eruptive disease.
Churchyard cough. A consumptive cough which seems likely to end fatally.
Consumption. A wasting away of the body caused by pulmonary phthisis, and associated with cough, spitting of blood, etc.
Corruption. } Decomposition. See Betterment-Deterioration
Decay. }
Decline. A gradual wasting away of the physical faculties.
Delicacy. Weakness of body.
Dyspepsia. A kind of indigestion.
Endemic. A disease constantly present in a place.
Epidemic. A disease which prevails widely at some one time or periodically.
Fester. A small inflamed sore.
Fever. A diseased state of the system, marked by increased heat, quickening of the pulse, and a general derangement of the functions.
Galloping consumption. Pulmonary disease whose progress is very rapid.
Gangrene. Mortification of the soft tissues of the body
Gathering. A tumor or boil.
Hay-fever. A catarrhal affection of the mucous membrane of the eyes and air-passages, characterized by its annual recurrence at the same time in the same person.
Hypochondria. Melancholy; the blues.
Idiocy. Absence, or marked deficiency, of sense and intelligence. See Sagacity-Incapacity. [In Greek, one in private life.]
Imposthume. A collection of pus in any part of the body.
Indigestion. Failure of the normal changes which food should undergo in the alimentary tract.
Infection. The communication of disease.
Inflammation. A morbid condition of any part of the body, with obstruction of the blood-current, and growth of morbid tissue.
Influenza. An epidemic affection, characterized by acute nasal catarrh.
Insanity. Unsoundness or derangement of mind. See Saneness-Lunacy.
Issue. An artificial ulcer, made to secure the discharge of pus.
La grippe [F.]. Influenza; the grip.
Lockjaw. A contraction of the muscles of the jaw by which its motion is suspended.
Lyssa. Hydrophobia.
Marasmus. Consumption.
Measles. A contagious eruptive disease.
Meningitis. Inflammation of the membranes of the brain.
Mortification. The death or decaying of one part of an animal body, while the rest continues to live.
Murrain. An infectious and fatal disease among cattle.
Necrosis. Mortification or gangrene.
Neuralgia. A disease accompanied by a very acute pain along the course of a nervous branch.
Palsy. Paralysis.
Paralysis. Loss of the power of voluntary motion.
Peccant humor. Morbid or corrupt animal fluid. [Bacon.]
Pestilence. A contagious or infectious epidemic disease.
Pimple, etc. A small elevation of the cuticle. See Convexity-Concavity.
Plague. A fever that often prevails in Egypt, Syria, and Turkey.
Pollution. Foulness or uncleanness.
Pox. A disease characterized by eruptions of any kind.
Prostration. Great oppression of natural strength or vigor.
Rash. A fine eruption on the body.
Rickets. Children's disease, characterized by overgrowth of bones.
Rot. Decay.
Scrofula. A disease, generally hereditary, marked by chronic enlargement and cheesy degeneration of the lymphatic glands.
Seizure. Sudden or violent gripe of a disease
Septicity. Tendency to putrefaction.
Smallpox. A contagious disease, characterized by a peculiar pustular eruption.
Sore. A rupture of the skin and flesh
Sphacelus. The death of a bone.
Sporadic. A disease which manifests itself occasionally.
Stroke. A sudden attack of disease.
Taint. Infection or corruption.
Typhoid. A disease characterized by high fever, great prostration and muscular debility.

(*Continued on Column* 1.)

Droop. To grow weak.
Feign sickness, etc. To pretend illness, etc. See Truthfulness-Falsehood.
Flag. To grow weak or spiritless.
Gasp. To labor for breath; respire with difficulty
Halt. To stop from proceeding.
Keep one's bed. To be ill or unwell in bed.
Labor under. To be oppressed with difficulties or disease.
Languish. To become weak; lose strength or animation.

Lay by. To discard.
Lay up. To confine in bed.
Peak. To look thin and ill.
Pine. To grow weak and thin from disease or anxiety
Sicken. To become ill.
Suffer. To endure or undergo pain, illness, or the like.
Take a disease, etc. To become infected with a disease, etc. See Nouns.
Take an infection. To become infected with a disease.

SICKNESS—*Adjectives.*

Affected with illness. Acted upon by illness; sick.
Afflicted with illness. Stricken with illness.
Ailing, etc. Affected with pain or illness, etc. See *Verbs.*
Bedridden. Confined to bed by disease or age.
Broken-winded. Disordered respiration.
Cankered. Having an unkind or malignant temper.
Chlorotic. Affected with or like to the disease which causes the skin to become of a greenish hue.
Confined. Kept in bed by sickness.
Contaminated. Corrupted; tarnished
Cranky. Rickety.
Crippled. Deprived of limbs, strength, or activity.
Decayed, etc. Having become weak, corrupted, or disintegrated, etc. See Betterment-Deterioration.
Decrepit. Broken down and weakened by old age.
Diseased. Ill; not well.
Drooping. Growing weak or faint.
Dyspeptic. Afflicted with or pertaining to dyspepsia.
Endemic. Pertaining to a disease peculiar to a locality.
Epidemic. Contagious and afflicting great numbers.
Flagging. Growing weak or faint.
Gasping. Laboring for breath or respiring convulsively.
Halting. Tending to stop the progress.
Healthless. Without health.
Hors de combat [F.]. Disabled from fighting; wounded.
Ill. Not well; not in a normal condition of health.
Ill of. Sick of.
In a bad way. Seriously ill.
Incurable, etc. Not to be made well. See Sanguineness-Hopelessness.
In danger. In a state of exposure to injury, pain, or disease.
In declining health. In failing health.
Indisposed. Slightly out of health.
Infirm. Weak; not strong.
In hospital. Sick; ill.
Invalided. Made like an invalid.
Laid up. Unable to work or be about.
Lame. Crippled or disabled in limb.
Leprous. Afflicted with or pertaining to leprosy

Mangy. Infected with mange, a skin disease.
Morbid. Not sound or healthful; abnormal.
Morbific, etc. Causing disease, etc. See Refuge-Pitfall.
Moribund, etc. At the point of death, etc. See Life-Death.
Morose. Of a sour, ill-natured temper.
On the sick list. Among the sick.
Out of health. Ill; not well.
Out of sorts. Unwell.
Palsied. Affected with palsy.
Paralytic. Afflicted with paralysis.
Peccant. Morbid; not healthy.
Poisoned. Infected with poison; made corrupt.
Poorly. Indisposed; slightly unwell.
Prostrate. Deprived of strength.
Rotten. Decaying; unsound.
Rotten at the core. Unsound at the most important part.
Rotten to the core. Completely unsound.
Seasick. Sick from the motion of a ship.
Seedy. Old and worn out.
Seized with. Invaded with suddenly.
Sick. Affected with disease; ill.
Sickly. Unhealthy; not well.
Spavin. A hard tumor or swelling in the hough of a horse
Squeamish. Having a stomach that is easily turned.
Tabid. Pertaining to progressive emaciation of the body.
Tainted. Corrupted; spoiled.
Taken ill. Become ill.
Touched in the wind. Short of breath.
Unbraced. Loosened; relaxed.
Unhealthy. Sickly; not well.
Unsound. Not strong.
Unwell. Somewhat ill; indisposed.
Valetudinary. Infirm; weak; sickly.
Vitiated. Injured; spoiled.
Weakened, etc. Made less in strength, etc. See Strength-Weakness.
Weakly, etc. With little strength, etc. See Strength-Weakness.
Withered. Dried up; passing away.
Zymotic. Pertaining to disease caused by a morbific principle acting like a ferment.

health'-ful. Salubrious. Health-Sickness, Healthiness-Unhealthiness.

health'-i-ness. The state of being sound and well. Healthiness-Unhealthiness.

HEALTHINESS—UNHEALTHINESS.

Fine air. Healthful air.
Fine climate. Climate conducive to good health.
Healthiness, etc. The state or quality of being healthy.
Hygiene. The science of health.
Salubrity. The quality of being salubrious.
Sanitarian. One who promotes laws for sanitary reform.
Valetudinarian. One who is seeking to get well.
Valetudinarianism. The state of being a valetudinarian

HEALTHINESS—*Associated Nouns.*

Endiometer. An instrument for testing purity of air
Sanitarium. A place where sick people are treated.

HEALTHINESS—*Verbs*

Agree with. To have a good effect upon.
Assimilate, etc. To transform, as food, into bodily tissue See Harmony.
Be salubrious, etc. See *Adjectives.*

HEALTHINESS—*Adjectives.*

Benign. Propitious; mild.
Bracing. Giving strength or vigor
Good for. Beneficial to.
Harmless. Incapable of doing harm.
Healthful. Conducive to good health.

Contagion. The communication of disease from one person to another.
Death in the pot. A hidden cause of death, as a poison.
Insalubrity. The quality of being unhealthy.
Malaria, etc. A condition of unwholesomeness; unhealthy air, etc. See Remedy-Bane.
Non-naturals. Things not constituting being, but necessary to existence.
Plague spot. A mark denoting a person having the plague.
Unhealthiness, etc. The condition or quality of being unhealthy, etc. See *Adjectives.*

UNHEALTHINESS—*Adjectives*

Azotic. Incapable of supporting life.
Catching. Infectious.
Contagious. Liable to be communicated by contact.
Deadly, etc. Causing death. See Life-Killing.
Deleterious. Destructive or unwholesome.
Envenomed. Infused with venom.
Epidemic. Affecting a large number of people.
Epizootic. Affecting a large number of animals.
Indigestible. Incapable of being converted into food.
Infectious. Easily communicable by contact or otherwise; liable to transmit disease.
Innutritious. Not nourishing.
Insalubrious. Not conducive to good health.

HEALTHINESS—UNHEALTHINESS—*Continued*.

HEALTHINESS—Adjectives—*Continued*

Healthy. Having good health.
Hygeian. Relating to health or hygiene.
Hygienic. Pertaining to hygiene.
Innocent. Harmless.
Innocuous. Having no injurious qualities.
Innoxious. Not liable to injure.
Invigorating. Imparting vigor.
Nutritious. Able to build up animal tissue.
Prophylactic. Having power to prevent disease.
Restorative, etc. Having power to restore. See Renovation.
Salubrious. Contributing to health and bodily strength.
Salutary. Promoting health.
Salutiferous. Producing good health.
Sanative. Tending to heal or cure.
Sanitary. Pertaining to the preservation of health; also sanative.
Tonic. Having power to give bodily strength.
Uninfectious. } Not able to cause disease.
Uninjurious. }
Useful, etc. Producing good, etc. See Usefulness.
Wholesome. Producing and advancing good health.

UNHEALTHINESS—Adjectives—*Continued*.

Mephitic. Having the quality of mephitis; exhaling poison.
Morbiferous. Developing disease.
Morbific. See Morbiferous.
Narcotic. Producing insensibility or stupor.
Noisome. Offensive and injurious.
Noxious. Liable to cause injury to health.
Pestiferous. Bringing pestilence or disease.
Pestilent. Engendering malignant diseases.
Pestilential. Having the nature of a pestilence.
Poisonous. Containing or having the effect of poison.
Septic. Causing putrefaction.
Taking. Catching.
Toxic. Poisonous.
Uncongenial. Not suited to one's temperament.
Ungenial. Not imparting life and health.
Unhealthy. Not in good health; not productive of good health.
Unwholesome. Not producing or promoting good health.
Venomous. Containing or having effect of venom; poisonous.
Virulent. Exceedingly poisonous.
Zymotic. Pertaining to morbific fermentation.

health´-less. Without health. Health-Sickness.
health´-y. Well; having health. Health-Sickness, Healthiness-Unhealthiness.
heap. A collection of things thrown together in a pile; a great number. Excess-Lack, Gathering-Scattering, Magnitude-Smallness, Store; rubbish heap, Usefulness-Uselessness.
hear. To perceive sound; receive tidings. Enlightenment-Secrecy, Hearing-Deafness; hear a cause, Decision-Misjudgment, Litication; hear, hear,

Approval-Disapproval; hear out, Heed-Disregard; not hear of, Proffer-Refusal.
hear´-er. One who hears. Hearing-Deafness.
hear´-ing. The capacity to hear. Enlightenment-Secrecy, Hearing-Deafness, Litigation; gain a hearing, Dominance-Impotence; give a hearing, Hearing-Deafness; hard of hearing, Hearing-Deafness; out of hearing, Remoteness-Nearness; within hearing, Remoteness-Nearness.

HEARING—DEAFNESS.

Audibility. The quality of being capable to be heard.
Audition. The sense of hearing.
Auscultation. An audition; a listening.
Eavesdropping. Secret listening.
Hearing, etc. The capacity to perceive sound, etc. See *Verbs.*

Hearing—*Nouns of Agent.*

Audience. An assemblage of listeners.
Auditor. One who hears; who has the capacity to perceive sound.
Eavesdropper. One who listens by stealth.
Hearer. One who listens.
Listener. One who hears.

Hearing—*Nouns of Instrument.*

Acute ear. An ear that hears well.
Auditory. An auditorium; an audience room.
Correct ear. } An ear that can distinguish slight differences in
Delicate ear. } sounds.
Ear for music. A musical ear.
Ear-trumpet. An instrument made to collect sound, for the deaf.
Microphone. An instrument used for reproducing and vastly increasing a slight sound.
Musical ear. An ear that can observe distinctions of musical sounds.
Nice ear. An ear that is able to distinguish distinctions of sound.
Phonograph. An instrument for recording and reproducing sounds.
Quick ear. } An ear that is able to detect slight sounds.
Sharp ear. }
Speaking trumpet. A trumpet-like instrument by which sound can be projected great distances.
Telephone. An instrument for transmitting sound.

Hearing—*Organs of Hearing.*

Acoustic organs. Organs for hearing.
Auditory apparatus. The device for hearing.
Auricle. The prima; the external ear.
Ear. The organ of hearing.
Ear-drum. The membrane separating the outer from the middle ear; the tympanum.
Lug. The lobe of the ear.
Tympanum. The ear-drum.

Hearing—*Verbs.*

Be all ear. To pay very close attention.
Become audible. To get into a state to be heard.
Be heard. To be audible.
Bend an ear. To listen; to pay attention.

Deaf-mute. One lacking the power of hearing and speaking.
Deafness. Inability to hear.
Hardness of hearing. Difficulty to perceive sound.
Inaudibility. The state or quality of not being heard.
Surdity. Deafness.

Deafness—*Verbs.*

Be deaf, etc. To be unable to hear, etc. See *Adjectives.*
Close one's ears to. Pay no attention to.
Deafen. To render deaf.
Have no ear. Not to have the ability to hear.
Render deaf. To make deaf.
Shut one's ears to. } Pay no attention to.
Stop one's ears to. }
Stun. To deaden the sense of hearing.
Turn a deaf ear to. To pay no attention to.

Deafness—*Adjectives.*

Deaf. Lacking the sense of hearing.
Deaf as a beetle. }
Deaf as an adder. } Entirely deaf.
Deaf as a post. }
Deaf as a trunk-maker. }
Deafened. Made deaf.
Dull of hearing. Lacking some power of hearing.
Earless. Without ears; deaf.
Hard of hearing. Having one's hearing powers impaired.
Inaudible. Without sound.
Out of hearing. Too far away to be heard.
Stone deaf. Totally deaf.
Stunned. Overpowered as to one's sense of hearing.
Surd. Deaf.

Hearing—Verbs—*Continued.*

Catch a sound. To hear a sound.
Catch the ear. To become audible.
Fall upon the ear. To be heard.
Give a hearing. To grant permission to speak to.
Give an ear. To listen.
Give audience. To grant permission to speak to.
Hang upon the lips of. To pay very close attention.
Hark. } Listen.
Harken. }
Hear. To be able to perceive sound.
Lend an ear. To listen.

HEARING—VERBS—*Continued.*

List. To hear; harken.
Listen. To pay close attention; to harken.
Listen with both ears. To listen closely; sharply.
Meet the ear. To be heard.

Overhear. To hear words not intended for the hearer.
Prick up one's ears. To endeavor to hear.
Reach the ear. To be heard.
Ring in the ears, etc. To resound, etc. See RESONANCE.

HEARING—*Adjectives.*

Acoustic. Pertaining to the sense of hearing.
Auditory. Relating to hearing.

Auricular. Aural; pertaining to the ear.
Hearing, etc. Pertaining to the sense of hearing. See *Verbs.*

HEARING—*Adverbs.*

Arrectis auribus [L.]. With pricked up ears, with attentive ears.

Earwise. Through the ear; by hearing.

HEARING—*Interjections.*

Hark! hark ye! hear! listen! Oyez! oyez! A call commanding attention to a proclamation.

hear'-say". Common talk. TIDINGS-MYSTERY.
hearse. A vehicle for carrying the dead to the grave. CONVEYANCE-VESSEL.
heart. Courage; love; the essential or vital part of anything; the seat of the affections and passions. AFFECTIONS, ANATOMY, BRAVERY-COWARDICE, CENTER, CONSEQUENCE-INSIGNIFICANCE, LOVE-HATE, MIND-IMBECILITY, OUTSIDE-INSIDE, READINESS-RELUCTANCE, SUBJECTIVENESS-OBJECTIVENESS; **at heart,** AFFECTIONS, EMOTION; **beating heart,** EMOTION, EXCITATION; **break the heart,** PLEASURABLENESS-PAINFULNESS; **by heart,** REMEMBRANCE-FORGETFULNESS; **do one's heart good,** AFFECTIONS, PLEASURABLENESS-PAINFULNESS; **from bottom of heart,** TRUTHFULNESS-FALSEHOOD; **go to one's heart,** EXCITATION; **have a place in the heart,** LOVE-HATE; **heart and soul,** AFFECTIONS, DETERMINATION-VACILLATION, EMOTION, ENTIRETY-DEFICIENCY, READINESS-RELUCTANCE, TOIL-RELAXATION; **heart bleeding for,** COMPASSION-RUTHLESSNESS; **heart expanding,** EMOTION; **heart failing one,** LIGHTHEARTEDNESS-DEJECTION, SANGUINENESS-TIMIDITY; **heart in hand,** READINESS-RELUCTANCE; **heart in the right place,** CHARITABLENESS-MALEVOLENCE; **heart leaping into one's mouth,** EXCITATION; **heart leaping with joy,** JUBILATION-LAMENTATION, PLEASURE-PAIN; **heart of grace,** SANGUINENESS-HOPELESSNESS; **heart of hearts,** PLEASURABLENESS-PAINFULNESS; **heart of oak,** BRAVERY-COWARDICE, HARDNESS-SOFTNESS, STRENGTH-WEAKNESS; **heart of stone,** EXCITATION, FAVORITE-QUARRELSOMENESS; **heart's core,** AFFECTIONS, MIND-IMBECILITY; **heart sinking,** SANGUINENESS-TIMIDITY; **heart swelling,** EMOTION, EXCITATION; **in good heart,** SANGUINENESS-HOPELESSNESS; **know by heart,** KNOWLEDGE-IGNORANCE, REMEMBRANCE-FORGETFULNESS; **lay to heart,** LIGHTHEARTEDNESS-DEJECTION; **learn by heart,** EDUCATION-MISTEACHING; **lift up the heart,** DEVOTION-IDOLATRY; **lose heart,** LIGHTHEARTEDNESS-DEJECTION; **lose one's heart,** LOVE-HATE; **man after one's own heart,** AMITY-HOSTILITY; **nearest to one's heart,** LOVE-HATE; **not find it in one's heart,** READINESS-RELUCTANCE; **put one's heart into,** DETERMINATION-VACILLATION; **set one's heart upon,** DESIRE-DISTASTE, DETERMINATION-VACILLATION; **take heart,** BRAVERY-COWARDICE, CONTENTEDNESS-DISCONTENTMENT, SANGUINENESS-HOPELESSNESS; **take to heart,** CONTENTEDNESS-DISCONTENTMENT, FAVORITE-ANGER, LIGHTHEARTEDNESS-DEJECTION, SENSITIVENESS-APATHY; **to one's heart's content,** CONTENTEDNESS-DISCONTENTMENT, ENOUGH, READINESS-RELUCTANCE, **warm heart,** SENSITIVENESS; **wind around the heart,** LOVE-HATE; **with a heavy heart,** READINESS-RELUCTANCE; **with all one's heart,** READINESS-RELUCTANCE.
heart'-ache". Mental anguish. PLEASURE-PAIN

heart'-break"-ing. Extremely distressing. EMOTION, PLEASURABLENESS-PAINFULNESS.
heart'-brok"-en. Deeply affected. PLEASURE-PAIN.
heart'-burn"-ing. Discontent; secret enmity. AMITY-HOSTILITY, CONTENTEDNESS-DISCONTENTMENT, CONTENTEDNESS-REGRET, FAVORITE-ANGER.
heart'-cor-rod"-ing. Affecting by injurious influences. PLEASURABLENESS-PAINFULNESS.
heart'-felt". Very sincere. EMOTION, PLEASURABLENESS-PAINFULNESS.
heart'-har"-row-ing. Preying on the feelings. PLEASURABLENESS-PAINFULNESS.
hearth. A fireplace; the home. DWELLER-HABITATION, OVEN-REFRIGERATOR.
hearth'-stone". A stone laid to form a hearth. DWELLER-HABITATION.
heart'-i-ly. With the whole heart. EMOTION.
heart'-i-ness. Cordiality. EMOTION, SOCIABILITY-PRIVACY.
heart'-less. Destitute of sympathy; pitiless. SENSITIVENESS-APATHY, VIRTUE-VICE.
heart'-quake". Nervousness from fear. SANGUINENESS-TIMIDITY.
heart'-rend"-ing. Very distressing. PLEASURABLENESS-PAINFULNESS.
hearts'-ease". The pansy. CONTENTEDNESS-DISCONTENTMENT.
heart'-shaped". Like the heart in form. CURVATURE-RECTILINEARITY.
heart'-sick". Sick of; deeply grieved. DESIRE-DISTASTE, DESIRE-REPLETION.
heart'-sick"-en-ing. Causing deep grief. PLEASURABLENESS-PAINFULNESS.
heart'-sink"-ing. Depression of mind. SANGUINENESS-TIMIDITY.
heart'-some". Merry. SANGUINENESS-TIMIDITY.
heart'-strick"-en. Overwhelmed with grief. PLEASURE-PAIN.
heart'-strings", tear the. To lacerate the feelings. PLEASURABLENESS-PAINFULNESS.
heart'-swell"-ing. Causing the heart to swell. FAVORITE-ANGER.
heart'-wound"-ing. Affecting the feelings. PLEASURABLENESS-PAINFULNESS.
heart'-y. Cordial; full of health. AMITY-HOSTILITY, EMOTION, HEALTH-SICKNESS, LIGHTHEARTEDNESS-DEJECTION, READINESS-RELUCTANCE; **hearty laugh,** JUBILATION-LAMENTATION; **hearty meal,** NUTRIMENT-EXCRETION; **hearty reception,** SOCIABILITY-PRIVACY.
heat. A form of energy manifested by a rise of temperature; a single course of a race; excitement; to make hot. EXCITATION, EXCITABILITY-INEXCITABILITY, HEAT-COLD, HEATING-COOLING, STRIFE-PEACE; **dead heat,** EQUALITY-INEQUALITY; **heat of passion,** FAVORITE-ANGER.

HEAT—COLD.

Afric heat. Great heat, like that in Africa.
Bengal heat. Great heat, like that in Bengal.
Bloodheat. Heat equal to the temperature of human blood, or about 98½°.
Calidity. Heat; state of warmth.

Chill.
Chilliness. } Moderate degree of coldness.
Cold. The absence of heat or warmth.
Coldness, etc. The state or quality of being cold, etc. See *Adjectives.*

HEAT—COLD—*Continued.*

Calorescence. A kind of generation of heat.
Caloric. A general term for heat.
Fervor. Excessive warmth; heat.
Fever. A diseased condition marked by increased heat.
Flush. A rush of blood to the face.
Glow. White or red heat.
Heat. A form of energy manifested by a rise of temperature and expansion.
Hectic. Fever heat.
Incalescence. Increasing heat.
Incandescence. White heat.
Summer heat. The heat of the warmest part of the year.
Temperature. Degree of heat or cold.
Tropical heat. Heat characteristic of tropical regions.
Warmth. The state of possessing gentle heat.
White heat. The heat given off by anything heated to whiteness.

HEAT—*Scientific Nouns.*

Phlogiston. The supposed principle of inflammability.
Pyrology. A treatise on heat.
Pyrotechny. The art of making fireworks.
Thermology. A treatise on heat.
Thermometer, etc. An instrument to measure rise or fall of temperature, etc. See THERMOMETER.
Thermotics. The science of heat.

HEAT—*Nouns of Cause.*

Baking, etc. The act of cooking in a dry heat. See HEATING.
Blaze. Intense direct light accompanied with heat.
Bonfire. A large fire built in the open air; a glad fire.
Broiling sun. A condition in which so much heat comes from the sun as to seem to broil things.
Devouring element. Fire.
Fire. The evolution of light and heat in the combustion of bodies.
Firework. A device for producing a display of light, or figures in colored fire, by the combustion of materials that burn in a peculiar manner.
Flame. A stream of burning vapor or gas, emitting light and heat.
Flash. A sudden burst of light.
Insolation. The process of exposing to the rays of the sun for the purpose of drying.
Lambent flame. A flame playing lightly on the surface.
Scintillation. A spark or flash.
Sheet of fire. }
Sheet of flame. } Fire that occurs in thin broad portions.
Simoom. A hot, dry wind that blows in Arabia and Syria and the neighboring countries.
Sirocco. A hot, oppressive wind blowing from the Libyan deserts.
Spark. A flash of fire.
Summer. The warmest portion of the year.
Sun. The universe's source of light and heat.
Warming, etc. The act of heating gradually. See HEATING.
Wildfire. A composition of inflammable materials which when kindled is very hard to quench.

HEAT—*Verbs:*

Bask. To lie in genial warmth.
Be hot, etc. To be in a state of heat, etc. See *Adjectives.*
Blaze. To burn with a bright flame.
Boil. To heat a liquid until it bubbles and vaporizes.
Broil. To cook by being placed directly over hot coals.
Burn. To consume with fire.
Flame. To burn so as to cause illumination.
Flush. To make or become red and glowing.
Fume. To smoke or throw off vapor.
Give. To yield or emit sparks.
Glow. To shine with intense heat.
Heat, etc. To cause to become hot, etc. See HEATING.
Pant. To beat or throb with unnatural violence.
Parch. To burn or dry up the surface of.
Reek. To steam; emit a warm, moist vapor.
Seethe. To be hot; boil.
Simmer. To boil gently.
Smoke. To emit a visible vapor as a result of combustion
Smolder. To burn by slow combustion.
Stew. To boil slowly.
Sweat. To excrete moisture from the pores of the skin, to perspire.
Swelter. To be faint with heat.
Thaw. To melt.

HEAT—*Adjectives.*

Ablaze. On fire.
Afire. Burning.

Fresco [It.]. A cool and refreshing state of air.
Frigidity. The condition or quality of lacking warmth.
Inclemency. Severe coldness; want of warmth.

COLD—*Denotations.*

Chattering of teeth. Noise made by collision of the teeth in shivering.
Depth of winter. The coldest part of the year.
Fall of snow. Descent of snow.
Floe-berg. A large mass of floating ice.
Frost. Frozen dew.
Glacier. A large field or stream of ice.
Goose-skin. A roughness of the skin produced by cold.
Hail. Frozen rain.
Hailstone. A single particle of ice falling from a cloud.
Hard frost. Very thick frost.
Hard winter. A winter of severe cold.
Heavy fall. Fall of much snow.
Hoarfrost. The white particles formed by the freezing of dew.
Horripilation. A bristling of the hair resulting from chilliness.
Ice. Water reduced to a solid state by cold.
Iceberg. A large mass of ice floating in the ocean
Ice-floe. A mass of floating ice.
Icicle. A pendent mass of ice formed by the freezing of dripping water.
Nevée [F.]. The upper part of a glacier.
Nova Zembla. Two islands in the Arctic Ocean, north of Russia
Rigor. A sense of chilliness, with contraction of the skin.
Rime. Frozen dew or vapor.
Serac [F.]. A large block into which a glacier breaks.
Sharp frost. A severe frost.
Shivering. A trembling or shaking from cold.
Siberia. A country of Northern Russia in Asia, marked by its extreme coldness.
Sleet. Hail or snow, mingled and driven by the wind.
Snow. Watery particles frozen into white or transparent crystals in the air.
Snow-crystal. A single particle of snow.
Snowdrift. A bank of drifted snow.
Snowflake. A small filmy mass of snow.
Thick-ribbed ice. Thick ice. "Thrilling region of," etc. [*Measure for Measure*, III, i.]
White frost. Hoarfrost.
Winter. The coldest season of the year.

COLD—*Verbs.*

Be cold, etc. To be deprived of warmth, etc. See *Adjectives.*
Chill, etc. To affect with cold, etc. See HEATING-COOLING.
Didder. To shiver with cold.
Perish with cold. To die of cold.
Quake. To tremble with cold.
Quiver. To shake with cold.
Shake. To tremble with cold.
Shiver. To shake with cold.
Shudder. To tremble or quake.
Starve. To perish or die with cold.
Tremble. To shake or shiver.

COLD—*Adjectives.*

Aguish. Somewhat cold.
Algid. Very cold.
Arctic. Cold; frigid; pertaining to the northern regions.
Biting. Sharp; severe.
Bitter. Characterized by severity.
Bleak. Cold and sweeping.
Boreal. Pertaining to the north or north wind.
Brumal. Pertaining to the winter.
Chill. Moderately cold.
Chilly. Disagreeably cold.
Clay-cold. Cold as clay or earth
Cold. Deprived of heat; frigid; not warm.
Cold as a frog. }
Cold as a stone. }
Cold as charity. }
Cold as Christmas. } Very cold.
Cold as iron. }
Cold as lead. }
Cold as marble. }
Cool. Moderately cold.
Cool as a cucumber. } Expressions for moderate coldness.
Cool as a custard. }
Cutting. Chilling.
Freezing. Becoming congealed by cold.

HEAT—COLD—*Continued.*

HEAT—Adjectives—*Continued.*

Alight. Lighted up.
Ardent. Burning, having the appearance of fire.
Baking, etc. Being heated and dry, etc. See Heating.
Blazing, etc. Emitting flame or light, etc. See *Verbs.*
Blood-hot. ⎫
Blood-warm. ⎬ Of the temperature of normal blood, about 98½°.
Burning-hot, etc. See *Verbs.*
Calorific. Causing or producing heat.
Candênt. Glowing white with heat.
Canicular. Pertaining to the dog-days.
Close. Oppressive and stifling.
Ebullient. Boiling over.
Estival. Pertaining to the summer.
Fervent. Hot; glowing.
Fervid. Very hot; burning.
Fiery. Like fire; burning.
Genial. Comfortably warm.
Glowing. Shining with intense heat.
Hot. Having sensible heat; excessively warm.
Hot as fire. ⎫
Hot as pepper. ⎬ Degrees of heat.
Hot enough to roast an ox. ⎭
Igneous. Pertaining to or resembling fire.
In a blaze. ⎫
In a fever. ⎪
In a glow. ⎬ Hot.
In a heat. ⎪
In a perspiration. ⎪
In a sweat. ⎭
Incalescent. Increasing in heat.
Incandescent. White with heat.
In flames. On fire; burning.
Isotheral. Running through places of equal summer heat.
Isothermal. Pertaining to an isotherm, or line of equal heat.
Isothermic Having the nature of an isotherm.
Like a furnace. ⎫
Like an oven. ⎬ Very hot.
Lukewarm. Moderately warm.
Mild. Neither hot nor cold.
On fire. Burning.
Oppressive. Overwhelming; heavy.
Piping-hot. Boiling; simmering.
Plutonic. Burning; fiery.
Red hot. Heated to redness.
Reeking, etc. Emitting a warm, moist vapor, etc. See *Verbs.*
Smoking. Emitting a visible vapor as a result of combustion.
Smoking-hot, etc. See *Verbs.*
Smoldering. Burning slowly.
Stifling. Very hot and close so as to make breathing difficult.
Stuffy. Close; ill-ventilated; stifling.
Sudorific. Causing sweat.
Suffocating. Stopping respiration; stifling.
Sultry. Hot and moist.
Sunny. Exposed to the rays of the sun.
Sweltered. Oppressed with heat.
Sweltering. Oppressively hot.
Tepid. Moderately warm.

COLD—Adjectives—*Continued.*

Fresh. Cool; brisk.
Frigid. Cold; wanting heat
Frost-bitten. ⎫
Frost-bound. ⎬ Injured by freezing.
Frost-nipped. ⎭
Frosty. Cold enough to congeal water.
Frozen out. Affected by freezing.
Gelid. Very cold.
Glacial. Pertaining to a glacier.
Hibernal. Wintry; cold.
Hyemal. Belonging to winter.
Hyperboreal. ⎫
Hyperborean. ⎬ Very cold.
Icy. Cold like ice; frigid.
Ice-bound. Totally surrounded by ice.
Inclement. Severe; rigorously cold.
Isocheimal. ⎫ Pertaining to an imaginary line connecting all places
Isocheimenal. ⎬ of an equal winter temperature.
Keen. Sharp; biting.
Lukewarm. Neither hot nor cold.
Nipping. Checking the growth of, as by frost.
Niveous. Resembling snow.
Piercing. Penetrating.
Pinching. Biting.
Raw. Piercingly cold and damp.
Shivering, etc. Trembling. See *Verbs.*
Siberian. Pertaining to or like Siberia.
Starved, etc. Made cold. See Heating-Cooling.
Tepid. Lukewarm.
Transi de froid [F.]. Chilled with cold.
Unthawed. Not melted.
Unwarmed. Not warmed; chilly.
Wintry. Like winter; chilly.

COLD—*Adverbs, etc.*

A pierre fendre [F.]. Cold enough to break stone.
Bitterly, etc. In a cold and chilly manner. See *Adjectives.*
Coldly. In a cold manner.

HEAT—Adjectives—*Continued.*

Thermal. ⎫
Thermic. ⎬ Pertaining to heat.
Torrid. Violently hot.
Tropical. Pertaining to the tropics.
Unextinguished. Not put out.
Unfrozen. Not frozen.
Unquenched. Not extinguished.
Volcanic. Pertaining to a volcano.
Warm. Possessing a moderate degree of heat.
Warm as toast. Hot.
Warm as wool. Moderately warm.
White-hot. Incandescent.

HEAT—*Phrase.*

Not a breath of air. A stifling hotness.

---

heat′-ed. Made hot. Heating-Cooling; **heated fancy,** Fancy; **heated imagination,** Fancy.
heat′-er. One who or that which heats. Oven-Refrigerator.
heath. An uncultivated tract covered with coarse herbage; a plant. Fauna-Flora, Gulf-Plain.
hea′-then. Pagan; irreligion. Godliness-Ungodliness, Orthodoxy-Heterodoxy; **heathen mythology,** Jove-Fiend.

heath′-en-dom. Heathenism. Orthodoxy - Heterodoxy.
hea′-then-ish. Rude. Orthodoxy-Heterodoxy, Taste-Vulgarity.
hea′-then-ism. Paganism. Orthodoxy-Heterodoxy.
heath′-er. Heath; a moor. Fauna-Flora, Gulf-Plain.
heat′-ing. The act of making hot. Heating-Cooling.

HEATING—COOLING.

Accension. The act of kindling or the state of being ignited.
Adustion. The act or process of burning or parching.
Arson. Malicious destruction of buildings by burning.
Boiling. See *Verbs.*
Burning. See *Verbs.*
Calcination. The process of rendering a substance friable by the action of heat.
Calefaction. The process of warming or heating or the state of being heated.
Carbonization. Reducing to carbon as by the action of fire.

Congelation. The act or process of becoming a solid by reason of cold.
Conglaciation. The act or process of freezing solid.
Cooling, etc. See *Verbs.*
Extincteur [F.]. A portable fire-extinguisher.
Fire-annihilator. Fire annihilator.
Fire-brigade. The whole number of firemen of a town or district.
Fireman. One whose business is to extinguish fire.
Freezing, etc. See *Verbs.*
Ice, etc. Frozen water, etc. See Heat-Cold.

Cauterization. Burning or searing with a caustic or hot iron.

Cautery. The burning of the flesh to prevent bleeding or the spread of a disease.

Cineration. The reducing of anything to ashes by burning.

Coction. The process of boiling.

Combustibility. The quality of being capable of being burned.

Combustion. The operation of burning.

Concremation. The burning of different things together.

Conflagration. An extensive fire.

Cremation. The process of burning dead bodies.

Decoction. The process of boiling anything, generally in water.

Deflagration. The act of causing to burn suddenly.

Ebullition. The boiling of a liquid.

Elixation. Extracting or cooking by boiling or steeping.

Empyrosis. A general burning.

Estuation. A boiling.

Flagration. Same as conflagration.

Furnace. To heat or smelt in a furnace.

Fusion. The changing of a solid into a liquid by heating.

Heating, etc. See sub *Verbs.*

Ignition. The act of setting afire or being afire.

Incension. State of being kindled or on fire.

Incineration. The reducing to ashes by burning.

Increase of temperature. A growing hotter.

Inflammability. The state or quality of being easily set on fire.

Inflammation. A setting afire.

Insolation. An exposure to the sun's rays.

Scorification. The process of reducing to a slag.

Sunburn. Redness of skin caused by the heat of the sun.

Tepefaction. The act of making a thing moderately warm.

Torrefaction. The operation of scorching or drying; the state of being roasted or dried.

Transcalency. The state of permitting the passage of heat.

Ustulation. The roasting or drying of moist substances.

HEATING—*Associated Nouns.*

Ambustian. A scald or burn.

Apozem. A medicated decoction; a decoction.

Ash. The residue remaining after the burning of a combustible substance.

Auto da fé [Pg.]. A burning at the stake.

Brick. A block of clay with proper ingredients of sand and water, heated in a kiln.

Carbon. An abundant, non-metallic element combustible in some forms which are used for heating.

Ceramics. Work made of baked clay.

Charcoal. A mixture of carbon and inorganic ash used as a fuel, an absorbent, a filter, etc.

China. A delicate porcelain-ware made in China by baking.

Cinder. A partly burned combustible substance in which the fire is extinct.

Clinker. A shapeless mass of incombustible material remaining after the combustion of coal.

Coke. A coal deprived of its volatile matter by roasting in a kiln or by distillation.

Crockery. Earthenware made of clay burned in kilns.

Diathermancy. The capacity for allowing the free transmission of heat rays.

Earthenware. Utensils and ornaments of baked clay.

Ebullioscope. Instrument to determine the alcohol in a mixture by its boiling point.

Embers. Burning coals smoldering in ashes.

Glassware. Utensils made of glass.

Incendiarism. The act or practise of maliciously destroying buildings by fire.

Incubator. A machine for hatching eggs by artificial heat.

Liquefaction. The conversion of a solid into a liquid by the influence of heat.

Melting. The act of causing to change to a liquid from a solid as a result of heating.

Mug. An earthenware cup made from baked clay.

Porcelain. A fine translucent kind of earthenware.

Pot. A round vessel generally of baked clay.

Pottery. Clayware shaped when plastic, then baked in a kiln, or in the sun.

Products of combustion. Heat, ashes, etc.

Scoriæ. The slag of fused metals.

Slag. The refuse of fused substances

Stoneware. Pottery characterized by hardness and infusibility.

Terra-cotta. A kind of hard unglazed pottery.

Waffle-irons. Iron forms used in baking waffles.

Ice-box. Small refrigerator.

Incombustibility. The quality of being fire-proof.

Incombustibleness, etc. See *Adjectives.*

Infrigidation. Coldness.

Reduction of temperature. Process of cooling.

Refrigeration. The act of causing to become cold; or the state of being cold.

Solidification. The passage of a body from a gaseous or liquid state to a solid, produced by the action of cold.

COOLING—*Verbs.*

Benumb. To make stiff from cold.

Bite. To be extremely cold: said of weather or winds.

Burn out. To cease to be afire.

Chill. To unpleasantly reduce the temperature of.

Chill to the marrow. To affect with great cold.

Congeal. To harden or to become hardened as by freezing.

Cool. To lower the temperature of, or to become less hot.

Cut. To pierce, as with cold.

Damp. To cool, as with a wet cloth or sponge.

Extinguish. To put out; to destroy.

Fan. To cool by agitating the air with a flat surface.

Freeze. To solidify, or become solidified from cold.

Glaciate. To change or become changed into ice.

Go out. To cease burning.

Ice. To chill or freeze with ice.

Make one's teeth chatter. To affect with cold.

Nip. To bite or sting as by extreme cold.

Petrify. To become as hard as stone, or to make a substance rock-like in hardness.

Pierce. To penetrate: said of a cold, sharp wind.

Pinch. To sting as with cold.

Put out. To extinguish, as a fire.

Quench. To put out a fire, especially with water.

Refresh. To reinvigorate, as by cooling.

Refrigerate. To make cold.

Regelate. To unite again by freezing.

Slack. To cool by dipping in water.

Stamp out. To extinguish a fire by stamping it.

Starve. To kill with cold, or to perish from cold.

COOLING—*Adjectives.*

Cooled, etc. See *Verbs.*

Cooling, etc. See *Verbs.*

Fire-proof. Not burnable.

Frigorific. Cold-producing.

Frozen out. Ostracized.

Iced, etc. See *Verbs.*

Icing, etc. See *Verbs.*

Incombustible. Not destructible by fire.

Nipped, etc. Affected by the cold. See *Verbs.*

Nipping, etc. Biting; piercing. See *Verbs.*

Unflammable [Obs.].⎫
Uninflammable. ⎭ Not capable of being ignited.

HEATING—*Continued.*

HEATING—*Nouns of Means.*

Blanket. A thick, heavy piece of cloth used for warmth.

Caustic. Any substance or means used medicinally to burn animal tissues.

Clothing. Any woven stuff used for warming the body.

Coup de soleil [F.]. A sunstroke.

Flannel. A soft woolen cloth loosely woven, used as a garment.

Fur. The fine, soft hair of certain animals who need its protection from the cold.

Insolation. Process of drying by exposing to the heat of the sun.

Lunar caustic. Nitrate of silver used by surgeons for burning animal tissues.

Match. A small strip of soft wood having one end tipped with an easily inflammable substance and used for starting a fire.

Moxa. A soft woolly material prepared in China and Japan, used as a cautery by burning it on the skin.

Sunstroke. Acute prostration from excessive heat of the sun.

Wadding. Carded cotton used for padding bed-covers and garments.

HEATING—*Nouns of Agent.*

Baker. One who bakes food.

Incendiary. A person who maliciously sets fire to a building.

Pétroleuse. [F.]. One who uses petroleum for incendiary purposes.

HEATING—COOLING—*Continued*.

HEATING—*Verbs*.

Add fuel to the flames. To cause to become hotter.
Apply the match.
Apply the torch to. } To set on fire.
Bake. To expose to intense dry heat.
Blaze. To make a flame.
Blow the fire. To make hotter.
Boil. To subject to the action of a boiling liquid; to be in a state of ebullition.
Brand. To mark with a hot iron.
Burn. To expose to fire or heat.
Burn in. To eat in, as fire.
Burn to a cinder. To burn completely.
Calcine. To render friable by expelling volatile matter by heat.
Catch fire. To begin to burn; to take or conceive fire.
Cauterize. To burn organic tissue for a medicinal purpose.
Chafe. To burn by rubbing.
Char. To burn the surface of; to make charcoal of.
Commit to the flames.
Consign to the flames. } To burn.
Cook. To subject to the action of heat, generally; to prepare for food.
Corrode. To eat away as by a caustic.
Digest. To soften by heat and moisture.
Do to rags. To burn to dust.
Enkindle. To set afire.
Fan the flame. To make hotter.
Fire. To subject to combustion.
Foment. To bathe with hot lotions.
Fry. To cook in a pan containing butter, fat, or olive-oil.
Fuse. To unite by heating to the melting point.
Grill. To cook on a gridiron.
Heat. To impart warmth to or subject to the action of fire.
Ignite. To kindle; to make luminous.
Incinerate. To burn to ashes.
Inflame. To cause to glow.
Kindle. To set ablaze.

Light. To apply a flame to.
Liquefy, etc. See LIQUEFACTION.
Make a bonfire of. To burn.
Make hot, etc. See HEAT.
Melt. To reduce a solid substance to a liquid by the influence of heat.
Parboil. To boil partly; once, to boil thoroughly.
Parch. To make extremely dry by heating.
Poke the fire. To push into the fire to cause to burn brighter.
Reduce to ashes. To burn completely.
Rekindle. To kindle again.
Relume. To light again. ["I know not where is that Promethean heat that can thy light relume." Shakespeare, *Othello*, V, ii. 13.]
Roast. To subject to the action of radiant heat; also to cook in a closed oven.
Scald. To burn with boiling water or other liquid.
Scorch. To burn the surface of.
Scorify. To reduce to slag.
Sear. To burn the surface to dryness and hardness
Seethe. To place in a boiling liquid; or to be in a state of violent ebullition.
Set fire to.
Set on fire. } To start to burn.
Simmer. To cause to boil moderately, or to boil in that manner.
Singe. To parch.
Smelt. To melt or fuse for the purpose of refining.
Stew. To boil with simmering heat.
Stir the fire. To cause to burn hotter.
Stive. To stew.
Strike a light. To cause light by burning something.
Sun oneself. To warm oneself in the heat of the sun.
Take fire. To become ignited.
Thaw. To change from a frozen state because of being heated.
Toast. To make brown by heating.
Torrefy. To subject to heat.
Warm. To increase the temperature of by contact with heat.

HEATING—*Adjectives*.

Burnt, etc. See *Verbs*.
Combustible. Easily destroyed by fire.
Diathermal. Easily permeable by radiant heat.
Diathermanous. Possessing the property of transmitting radiant heat.
Heated.
Inflamed, etc. } See *Verbs*.

Heating.
Kindling. } See *Verbs*.
Inflammable. Easy to become kindled.
Molten. Changed to a fluid state by heat.
Rechauffé [F.]. Warmed over.
Sodden. Poorly baked.
Volcanic. Of or pertaining to a volcano.

heauton timoroumenos [Gr.] he-au-ton' ti-mo-ru'-me-nos). *The Self-Tormentor;* a play by Menander. AUSTERITY, LIGHTHEARTEDNESS-DEJECTION.
heave. To raise with an effort; make mighty efforts. ELEVATION - DEPRESSION, EMOTION, PUSH-PULL; heave a sigh, JUBILATION-LAMENTATION; heave in sight, VISIBILITY - INVISIBILITY; heave the lead, DEEPNESS-SHALLOWNESS, MENSURATION; heave to, MOVEMENT-REST.
heave'-of''-fer-ing. An offering of the Jewish service. *Numbers* xv, 20. DEVOTION-IDOLATRY.

heav'-en. A place or condition of supreme happiness. HEAVEN-HELL; call heaven to witness, ASSERTION-DENIAL; for heaven's sake, PETITION-EXPOSTULATION; heaven be praised, JUBILATION-LAMENTATION, THANKFULNESS-THANKLESSNESS; heaven forfend, PETITION - EXPOSTULATION; heaven knows, CERTAINTY-DOUBT, KNOWLEDGE-IGNORANCE; in the face of heaven, MANIFESTATION-LATENCY; light of heaven, LIGHT-DARKNESS; move heaven and earth, TOIL-RELAXATION; will of heaven, VOLITION-OBLIGATION.

HEAVEN—HELL.

Abode of the blessed. Heaven.
Arcadia. A picturesque district of the Peloponnesus; a place of ideal simplicity and contentment.
Bowers of bliss. A place of happiness, especially heaven. "Plucks amaranthine joys from." [Cowper, *Hope*, 164.]
Celestial bliss. Heavenly joy or happiness.
Eden. Paradise; first abode of the human race.
Elysian Fields. In Greek mythology, the abode of the blessed dead.
Elysium. The Greek paradise; a place of supreme delight.
Empyreal. Abode of God and the angels.
Eternal home. The Christian heaven.
Future state. An existence in heaven.
Garden of the Hesperides. The beautiful garden of the gods containing the golden apples of Juno.
Glory. Radiancy; the bliss of heaven; the home of the glorified.
Heaven. The dwelling-place of righteous souls after death.
Heavenly kingdom. The realm of heaven.
Inheritance of the saints in light. Heaven.

Abaddon. The bottomless pit; the depth of hell.
Abyss. A bottomless gulf.
Avernus. A lake in Italy represented to be the entrance to hell.
Bottomless pit. Hell.
Cocytus. The river of lamentation; one of the five rivers in Hades.
Domdaniel. A cave under the ocean where magicians worshiped their lord once a year.
Erebus. The region of the dead.
Everlasting fire.
Everlasting torment. } Hell.
Fire that is never quenched. The fire of hell; fire that never dies.
Gehenna. A place outside of Jerusalem where the refuse of the city was burned; hell.
Habitation of the fallen angels. Hell.
Hades. The lower world; the Greek hell.
Hell. The infernal regions; the place where the wicked are punished.
Hell-fire. The fire of hell.
Infernal regions. Hell; the lower regions.

HEAVEN—HELL—*Continued*.

Kingdom of God. } The Christian heaven.
Kingdom of heaven. }
Nirvana. The Buddhist heaven; a state of utter annihilation, or extinction of the finite in union with the infinite.
Olympus. A mountain in Thessaly, the dwelling-place of the Greek gods.
Paradise. Heaven; the garden of Eden.
Presence of God. The state of being in company with God.
Third heaven. A heaven spoken of by Paul, *II Cor.* xii. 2.
Throne of God. The royal seat of God.
Valhalla. The Norse heaven.
Walhalla. Valhalla.
Zion. The heavenly Jerusalem.

HEAVEN—*Adjectives*.

Beatific. Happy; blessed; heavenly.
Celestial. Heavenly; beatific.
Elysian. Like Elysium; happy.
From on high. From heaven; from above.
Heavenly. Like heaven; blessed.
Paradisiacal. Like Paradise; supremely blissful.
Supernal. From above; heavenly.
Unearthy. Unlike the earth; heavenly.

HEAVEN—*Phrases*.

Champs Elysées [F.]. Elysian Fields; a parkway in Paris.
Vigeur de dessus [F.]. Strength from on high.

heav'-en—born''. Born of heaven. REPUTATION-DISCREDIT, SAGACITY-INCAPACITY, VIRTUE-VICE.
heav'-en—di—rect''-ed. Directed by divine powers. SAGACITY-INCAPACITY.
heav'-en—kiss''-ing. Very high. HEIGHT-LOWNESS.
heav'-en—ly. Celestial; divine. DIVINITY, HEAVEN-HELL, UNIVERSE; **heavenly bodies,** UNIVERSE; **heavenly host,** ANGEL-SATAN; **heavenly kingdom,** HEAVEN-HELL.

Inferno. The title of a poem by Dante; hell.
Lake of fire and brimstone. Hell.
Limbo. The border region between heaven and hell; **a place of** neither pain nor pleasure.
Pandemonium. The abode of demons.
Pit of Acheron. The infernal regions, in Greek mythology.
Place of torment. Hell.
Pluto. The god of the lower regions, in Greek mythology.
Purgatory. Region where souls are purged from the sins of this world.
Realms of Pluto. The infernal regions.
Rhadamanthus. In Greek mythology, one of the three judges of the lower regions.
Shades below. The spirits of the departed.
Sheol. The grave; place of departed spirits.
Stygian Creek. In Greek mythology, the river over which the spirits of the dead must pass to go to their final abode; Styx.
Styx. A river of the infernal regions; hell.
Tartarus. The mythological hell.
Tophet. A place outside of Jerusalem where fire was continually kept burning; hell. [Hebr. Topheth.]
Worm that never dies. Eternal punishment.

HELL—*Adjectives*.

Hellish. Like hell, fiendish.
Infernal. Pertaining to the lower regions.
Stygian. Pertaining to Styx or hell.

HELL—*Phrase*.

Dies iræ, dies illa [L.]. Day of wrath, that day. [*Zephaniah* i 15, *Latin Hymns*.]

heav'-en—ly—mind''-ed. Having the thoughts turned to heaven. GODLINESS-UNGODLINESS.
heav'-ens. The universe. UNIVERSE; **heavens and earth,** ASTONISHMENT-EXPECTANCE.
heav'-er. One who lifts. ELEVATION-DEPRESSION.
heaves. An asthmatic disease. HEALTH-SICKNESS.
heav'-i—ness. The quality of being heavy. ACTIVITY-INDOLENCE, HEAVINESS-LIGHTNESS, WITTINESS-DULNESS; **heaviness of heart,** LIGHTHEARTEDNESS-DEJECTION.

HEAVINESS—LIGHTNESS.

Burden. } Something borne or carried, usually of considerable weight.
Burthen. } weight.
Counterpoise. A weight that balances another weight.
Gravitation. The force with which all bodies attract each other.
Gravity. The quality of possessing weight.
Heaviness, etc. The quality of possessing gravity, etc. See *Adjectives*.
Load. Quantity of material to be transported.
Lump of. } Principal part of anything.
Mass of. }
Ponderosity. The quality of possessing great weight.
Pressure. The weight one body brings to bear upon another.
Specific gravity. Comparative weight of anything with an equal bulk of water.
Weight. The downward pressure of a body.
Weight of. The amount of downward pressure of.

HEAVINESS—*Associated Nouns*.

Ballast. Any heavy substance, put into the hold of a vessel to sink it to such a depth as to prevent capsizing.
Lead. One of the heaviest of the elements.
Millstone. A heavy circular stone used for grinding grain.
Mountain. A large mass of earth and rock rising above the common level of the earth; something of great bulk.
Ossa on Pelion. Two mountains in Thessaly, fabled to have been piled on top of each other by the giants to scale Olympus.
Trutination. Act of weighing.
Weighing. The act of measuring weight.

HEAVINESS—*Nouns of Measure*.

Apothecaries' weight. The system of weights used by druggists.
Avoirdupois weight. The ordinary system of determining weight.
Carat. A unit of weight for precious stones.
Cwt. The abbreviation for a hundred (*centum*) weight.
Dram. A unit in apothecaries' weight.
Grain. The smallest weight in troy and in avoirdupois weight.
Hundredweight. Weight of a hundred pounds.

Buoyancy. Tendency or power to float.
Imponderability. Having no weight.
Levity. The quality of relative lightness.
Lightness. The condition or quality of having little weight.
Volatility. The property of a substance which causes it to be quickly dissipated on account of its levity.

LIGHTNESS—*Denotations*.

Air. The invisible fluid which surrounds the earth.
Bubble. A thin film of liquid inflated with air or gas.
Buoy. A floating object moored to the bottom, to mark out a channel.
Cobweb. The very fine network spread by a spider.
Down. The hairy crown or envelope of the seeds of certain plants.
Dust. Fine, dry particles of earth or other matter, raised and wafted by the wind.
Ether. Supposed matter above the air; the air.
Feather. The dermal appendage of a bird.
Float. Anything which floats or rests on the surface of a liquid.
Flue. Dust-like stuff scraped from cloth.
Gossamer. A thin, filmy substance, like cobwebs, floating in the air.
Mote. A small particle, as of floating dust.
Straw. The stalk of grains.
Thistle-down. The hairy crown of the flower of the thistle.

LIGHTNESS—*Nouns of Agent*.

Barm. Brewer's yeast, used as a leaven.
Ferment. That which causes to grow light by means of yeast.
Leaven. Anything that sets up fermentation so as to make lighter.
Yeast. A fungous growth used to make dough lighter.

LIGHTNESS—*Verbs*.

Be buoyed up. To be kept afloat.
Be light, etc. To have little weight. See *Adjectives*.
Float. To remain on the surface of a liquid.
Leaven. To make light by the action of leaven.
Lighten. } To make light. See *Adjectives*.
Render light. }
Swim. Not to sink.

HEAVINESS—LIGHTNESS—*Continued.*

HEAVINESS—Nouns of Measure—*Continued.*

Lb. The abbreviation for pound. [*L, libra.*]
Load. A customary weight of various amounts.
Ounce. A weight of 437½ grains.
Pennyweight. A weight of 24 grains.
Ponderation. Act of weighing.
Pound. A weight of 7000 grains.
Quintal. A unit of weight in the metric system; 100 kilograms.
Scruple. A unit in apothecaries' weight; 20 grains.
Stone. An English measure of weight, usually 14 pounds.
Tod. A measure of weight of about 28 pounds.
Ton. A measure of gravity in the avoirdupois system
Troy weight. A system of weighing used by goldsmiths and jewelers.

HEAVINESS—*Instruments of Measure.*

Balance. An instrument for weighing, consisting of a dish suspended from each end of a lever.
Beam. The bar of a balance.
Scales. The dishes of a balance.
Spring balance. A contrivance for weighing by the elasticity of a spiral spring.
Steelyard. A device for weighing, consisting of a movable weight on a graduated beam.
Weighbridge. A weighing machine on which loaded carts may be weighed.

HEAVINESS—*Scientific Term.*

Statics. The science of the equilibrium of forces, or of bodies at rest.

HEAVINESS—*Verbs.*

Be heavy, etc. See *Adjectives.*
Cumber. To weigh down.
Gravitate. To tend toward another body by gravity
Load. To place a quantity of material upon.
Poise. To determine the weight of by balancing.
Press. To act upon by weight.
Weigh. To measure the mass of.

LIGHTNESS—*Adjectives.*

Airy. Light as air.
Astatic. Under the influence of no directive agent.
Buoyant. So light as to float.
Ethereal. Light as ether.
Floating. Hanging free in the air or on the top of some liquid.
Imponderable.⎫
Imponderous.⎭ So light as to have no perceptible weight.
Light. Having little weight.
Light as a feather.⎫
Light as air.⎬ Degrees of lightness.
Light as thistle-down.⎭
Portable. Light enough to be easily carried.
Sublimated. Vaporized by heat.
Subtile. Delicately constituted.
Uncompressible. Impossible to be compressed on account of levity.
Volatile. So light as to be easily vaporized.
Weightless. Extremely light.

HEAVINESS—*Adjectives.*

Beefy. Heavy and ponderous.
Burdensome. Hard to bear on account of weight.
Cumbersome. Moving heavily.
Cumbrous. Unwieldy.
Heavy as lead. Of great gravity.
Incumbent. Weighing upon something.
Lumpish. Heavy like a lump.
Lumpishy. Heavy.
Massive. Of great weight and bulk.
Ponderable. Having appreciable weight.
Ponderous. Having unusually great weight and mass.
Superincumbent. Lying upon something else.
Unwieldy. Not easily handled on account of great weight and bulk.
Weighing. That may be used to measure gravity.
Weighty. Having great gravity.

---

heav′-ing. An upward lift; a sigh. JUBILATION-LAMENTATION.
heav′-y. Burdensome; not light; weighed down; violent; great; slow; powerful. ACTIVITY-INDOLENCE, BELLIGERENT, HEAVINESS-LIGHTNESS, MAGNITUDE-SMALLNESS, SAGACITY-INCAPACITY, TASTE-VULGARITY, VIGOR-INERTIA, WITTINESS-DULNESS; **heavy affliction,** PLEASURE-PAIN; **heavy-armed,** WEAPON; **heavy book,** WITTINESS-DULNESS; **heavy cost,** COSTLINESS-CHEAPNESS; **heavy dragoon,** BELLIGERENT; **heavy father,** ACTING; **heavy gun,** WEAPON; **heavy-handed,** SKILL-UNSKILFULNESS; **heavy heart,** PLEASURE-PAIN, READINESS-RELUCTANCE; **heavy-hearted,** LIGHTHEARTEDNESS-DEJECTION; **heavy hours,** ENTERTAINMENT-WEARINESS; **heavy news,** PLEASURABLENESS-PAINFULNESS; **heavy on hand,** EXCESS-LACK; **heavy on the mind,** LIGHTHEARTEDNESS-DEJECTION; **heavy sea,** AGITATION, RIVER-WIND; **heavy sleep,** ACTIVITY-INDOLENCE; **heavy-wet,** NUTRIMENT-EXCRETION.
heav′y-la″den. Weighed down; troubled. OBSTRUCTION-HELP, PLEASURE-PAIN.
heav′-y-weight″. A boxer weighing over 154 pounds. BELLIGERENT.
heb-dom′-a-dal. Occurring weekly. PERIODICITY-IRREGULARITY.
heb-dom′-a-da-ry. Weekly. PERIODICITY-IRREGULARITY.
He′-be. The goddess of youth. BEAUTY-UGLINESS.
heb′-e-tate. To render dull or blunt. SENSITIVENESS-APATHY.
heb′-e-tude. Stupidity. EXCITABILITY-INEXCITABILITY, SAGACITY-INCAPACITY, SENSITIVENESS-APATHY.

He′-brew. A Jew; jargon. CLEARNESS-OBSCURITY, ORTHODOXY-HETERODOXY.
hec′-a-tomb. A sacrifice of a hundred oxen; a great slaughter. DEVOTION-IDOLATRY, FIVE-QUINQUESECTION.
hec′-tare. Unit of square measure. MEASURE.
hec′-tic. The bright pink-red spot, on the cheek, in hectic fever. EMOTION, HEAT-COLD.
hec′-to-gram. Unit of weight. MEASURE.
hec′-to-graph. A contrivance for multiple copying. COPY-MODEL.
hec′-to-li″-ter. Unit of capacity. MEASURE.
hec′-to-me″-ter. Unit of length. MEASURE.
hec′-tor. To bully; domineer over. BRAVERY-COWARDICE, BRAWLER, PRESUMPTION-OBSEQUIOUSNESS, RECKLESSNESS-CAUTION.
hec′-tor-ing. Boasting. PRESUMPTION-OBSEQUIOUSNESS.
hedge. To bet on both sides; a fence of bushes, shrubs, and the like growing close together. COMPENSATION, ENCLOSURE; **hedge in,** CONFINEMENT, OBSTRUCTION-HELP, TERMS.
hedge′-grown″. Overgrown with hedges. ENCLOSURE.
hedge′-hog″. A small spiny-skinned mammal.
hedge′-row″. A fence of low shrubs. BOUNDARY, CONTINUITY-INTERRUPTION, SHARPNESS-BLUNTNESS.
hedge′-wri″-ter. A low writer. MISSIVE-PUBLICATION.
hed′-on-ism. The doctrine that pleasure is the only good. PLEASURABLENESS-PAINFULNESS.
hed′-on-ist. One who holds the doctrine of hedonism. PLEASURABLENESS-PAINFULNESS.
heed. To take notice; pay attention. CAREFULNESS-CARELESSNESS, HEED-DISREGARD, RECKLESSNESS-CAUTION.

HEED—DISREGARD.

Advertence. The act of turning the mind or attention to.
Advertency. The state of giving attention to.
Attention. Steady application of the mind to a specific object.

Absence of mind. Want of attention to surroundings.
Absorption of mind. State of being wholly engrossed in one subject to the exclusion of all others.

HEED—DISREGARD—*Continued.*

HEED—Synonymous Phrases—*Continued.*

Circumspection, etc. Cautious watchfulness, etc. See CAREFUL-NESS.
Consideration. The act of closely observing.
Heed. Careful attention or consideration.
Indication. The act of indicating, of pointing out.
Inspection. Careful investigation.
Intentiveness. Closeness of attention or application of mind.
Intentness. The act of having the mind firmly fixed upon anything.
Introspection. Examination within.
Mindfulness, etc. The state of having in mind; observation. etc. See *Adjectives.*
Minuteness. The attending to small things.
Notice. Act of making observations.
Observance. The act of observing.
Observation. Careful scrutiny.
Particularity. The state or quality of being attentive to small matters.
Perpension. Act of weighing carefully.
Reflection. Act of thinking long upon experiences.
Regard. Paying attention to; notice. See *Verbs.*
Revisal. Result of revision.
Revision. Act of looking over for corrections
Scrutiny. Close investigation.
Study. Application of the mind to anything.
Thought. The act of thinking; result of thinking.

Heed—*Synonymous Phrases.*

Absorption of mind; abstract application; abstract attention; abstract study; abstract thought; active application; active attention; active study; active thought; attention to detail; calling attention to; close application; close attention; close study; close thought; deep application; deep attention; deep study; deep thought; deliberate application; deliberate attention; deliberate study; deliberate thought; diligent application; diligent attention; diligent study; diligent thought; exclusive application; exclusive attention; exclusive study; exclusive thought; intense application; intense attention; intense study; intense thought; labored application; labored attention; labored study; labored thought; minute application; minute attention; minute study; minute thought; profound application; profound attention; profound study; profound thought.

Heed—*Verbs.*

Attend. To fix the mind upon.
Consider. To reflect upon, or think about.
Contemplate. To consider attentively. See REFLECTION.
Entertain. To receive and hold in the mind.
Heed. To attend and obey.
Indicate. To point out something.
Indigitate. To point out with the finger.
Inspect. To examine closely.
Look. To direct the attention to
Mark. To pay attention to.
Note. To make a note of.
Notice. To observe closely.
Observe. To watch closely.
Overhaul. To examine carefully.
Perstringe. To glance at.
Recognize. To take knowledge of.
Regard. To attend with respect and attention.
Remark. To make an observation.
Revise. To go over again to make corrections.
Scan. To examine critically.
Scrutinize. To search closely.
See. To turn the attention to.
Show. To point out.
Skim. To pass over without much attention.
View. To inspect mentally.
Watch, etc. To observe with care, etc. See EXPECTATION, MIND.

Heed—*Verbal Expressions.*

Absorb the attention; absorb the mind; absorb the thoughts; advert to; animadvert to; apply attention to; apply the eye to; apply the mind to; arrest the attention; arrest the mind; arrest the thoughts; attract notice; attract the attention; attract the mind; attract the thoughts; awaken the attention; awaken the mind; awaken the thoughts; bear in mind; be attentive; bend one's mind to; bend the attention to; bend the eye to; bend the mind to; be present to the mind; be under consideration; be uppermost in the mind; bring forward; bring under one's notice; call attention to; call

DISREGARD—Verbs—*Continued.*

Abstraction. Act of withdrawing, or of inattention to objects.
Brown study. Deep thought resulting in absent-mindedness.
Deep musing. Abstract thought.
Disregard. Want of regard or attention.
Distraction. A separating of the attention of the mind in many directions.
Étourderie [F.]. Heedlessness.
Fit of abstraction. A sudden mood of mental inattention.
Heedlessness, etc. Want of care or attentiveness, etc. See CAREFULNESS-CARELESSNESS.
Inadvertence. Unintentional heedlessness.
Inadvertency. State of being heedless.
Inattention. Failure to give heed to what is directly before one.
Inconsiderateness, etc. The quality of being inconsiderate, etc. See *Adjectives.*
Inconsideration. Want of giving thought or consideration.
Insouciance [F.], etc. Heedlessness; carelessness; etc. See UNCONCERN.
Non-observance. Failure to observe or to take notice.
Oversight. A mistake or wrong coming from inattention.
Preoccupation. Act of preoccupying or of engrossing the mind.
Reverie. Inattentive thinking; a purposeless train of thought.
Supineness, etc. State of lying on the back; hence, careless. See ACTIVITY-INDOLENCE.
Want of thought. Thoughtlessness.

Disregard—*Verbs.*

Bewilder. To bring into mental confusion.
Confuse. To perplex.
Dazzle. To be confused by excessive brightness.
Discompose. To throw into disorder.
Disconcert. To confuse the faculties of.
Disregard. To pay no attention to.
Dream. To be as in a dream.
Fluster. To confuse the mind.
Forget, etc. To have no remembrance. See REMEMBRANCE-FORGETFULNESS.
Meddle. To turn the attention to the affairs of others.
Moider. To confuse.
Muddle. To mix up in the mind.
Overlook. To examine very slightly.
Perplex. To involve the mind in confusion.

Disregard—*Verbal Expressions.*

Abstract oneself; be inattentive; call away the attention; call away the mind; call away the thoughts; call off the attention; call off the mind; call off the thoughts; close one's eyes to; come in one ear and go out at the other; discard from one's mind; discard from one's thoughts; discharge from one's mind; discharge from one's thoughts; draw off the attention; draw off the mind; draw off the thoughts; distract the attention; distract the mind; distract the thoughts; divert the attention; divert the mind; divert the thoughts; drop the subject; escape attention; escape notice; indulge in reverie; not observe; pass by; pay no attention to; put aside; put out; put out of one's head; set aside; shut one's eyes to; think little of; think no more of; throw a sop to Cerberus; turn a deaf ear to; turn aside; turn away from; turn one's attention; turn one's back upon.

Disregard—*Adjectives*

Absent. Inattentive; tending to wander from present surroundings.
Absent-minded. Having the mind away from the present.
Abstracted. Drawn off for a time by the consideration of weightier matters.
Bemused. Dazed or muddled as with liquor.
Blind. Incapable of seeing; unwilling to attend or understand.
Brainsick. Mentally deranged.
Careless, etc. Having no concern; thoughtless; etc See CAREFULNESS-CARELESSNESS.
Cursory. Rapid; superficial; careless.
Deaf. Incapable of hearing; obstinately inattentive.
Disconcerted. Deranged as to mind; thrown into confusion.
Distrait. Lost in thought.
Dizzy. Thoughtless, heedless.
Dreaming on other things. Not attentive to the subject in hand.
Dreamy. Characteristic of dreams, absent-minded.
Écervelé [F.]. Harebrained.
Engrossed, etc. Wholly absorbed, etc. See HEED.
Giddy. Thoughtless.
Giddy as a goose. Very unsteady and flighty.
Giddy-brained. Without thoughtfulness or stability.

HEED—DISREGARD—*Continued.*

HEED—Verbal Expressions—*Continued.*

soldiers to "attention"; cast the eyes over; catch the attention; catch the eye; catch the mind; catch the thoughts; claim the attention; claim the mind; claim the thoughts; come to the point; devote the attention to; devote the eye to; devote the mind to; dip into; direct the attention to; direct the eye to; direct the mind to; engage the attention; engage the mind; engage the thoughts; engross the attention; engross the mind; engross the thoughts; examine closely; examine curiously; examine intently; excite the attention; excite the mind; excite the thoughts; fall under one's notice; fall under one's observation; fix the attention; fix the eye; fix the mind; fix the thoughts; give a thought to; give heed to; give one's mind to; give the attention to; give the eye to; give the mind to; glance at; glance over; glance upon; have an eye to; have in one's eye; have regard to; have the ears open; have the eyes open; hearken to; hear out; incline an ear to; invite the attention; invite the mind; invite the thoughts; keep in sight; keep in view; keep the eyes open; lay the finger on; lend an ear to; listen to; look after; look at; look into; look over; look to; make note of; meet with attention; mind one's business; occupy oneself with; occupy the attention; occupy the mind; occupy the thoughts; pass under review; pay attention to; pay heed to; point at; point out; point the finger at; point to; pore over; prick up the ears; put a mark upon; revert to; rivet the attention on; rivet the eye on; rivet the mind on; rivet the thoughts on; run over; see to; solicit the attention; solicit the mind; solicit the thoughts; strike the attention; strike the eye; strike the mind; strike the thoughts; take a cursory view of; take cognizance of; take into account; take into consideration; take note of; take notice of; take stock of; think out; trouble one's head about; turn over the leaves; turn the eye to; turn the mind to; turn the 'attention to; wake the attention; wake the mind; wake the thoughts.

HEED—*Adjectives.*

Absorbed. Having the attention wholly engaged.
Alive to. In full action; attentive to.
Attentive. Having the mind firmly fixed on one object.
Awake to. Attentive.
Breathless. Not breathing from excitement or interest.
Engaged in. Earnestly employed in.
Engrossed in. Absorbed in.
Intent on. Bending the mind to a purpose.
Mindful. Attentive.
Observant. Watchful; careful in viewing.
Observing, etc. See *Verbs.*
Occupied with. Busy with; employed in.
On the watch, etc. Watchful, etc. See Expectation.
Open-eyed. Having open eyes, watchful.
Preoccupied, etc. Absorbed in thought, etc. See Heed-Disregard.
Rapt. Wholly absorbed.
Regardful. Having regard or respect for.
Steadfast. Fixed on one place.
Taken up with. Engrossed in.
Undistracted. Not drawn aside from the pursued object.
Upon the stretch. Making a persistent effort.
Watchful. On the watch; vigilant. See Carefulness.
Wrapped in. So attentive as to disregard all other things.

HEED—*Interjections, etc.*

Attention! behold! halloo! hark! hark ye! I'd have you to know; lo! lo and behold! look here! look to it! look you! mark! mind! **N. B.;** *nota bene* [L], note well! notice! observe! oh yes! *oyez!* [F.], hear! see! soho! yoho!
* ,†. Marks or signs calling attention to something.

DISREGARD—Adjectives—*Continued.*

Hand over head. Without thinking.
Harebrained. Reckless and foolish.
Harum-scarum. In careless haste.
Heedless. Having no heed or care.
High-flying. Having extravagant aims or views.
Inadvertent. Careless and heedless.
Inattentive. Not fixing the mind upon a thing.
Inconsiderate. Having no consideration or thought.
In a reverie. In a musing mood.
In the clouds. In the place of the unreal or superficial.
Listless, etc. Having no activity, etc. See Unconcern.
Lost. Wandered away; bewildered.
Lost in thought. Inattentive to everything save his mental operation.
Mindless. Not regarding with attention; heedless.
Musing on other things. Careless of what one is doing.
Muzzy. Absent-minded.
Napping. Careless.
Offhand. Without preparation or attention.
Off one's guard, etc. Unawares; incautious, etc, See Expectation-Surprise.
Percursory. Very cursory.
Preoccupied. Having the attention occupied before.
Put out, etc. See *Verbs.*
Rantipole. Rakish; reckless.
Rapt. Carried out of oneself, as with love or admiration.
Regardless. Having no regard or respect.
Respectless. Without regard.
Scatter-brained. Giddy; careless.
Thoughtless. Wanting thought; rash.
Undiscerning. Lacking power to discriminate.
Unheeding. Not heeding.
Unmindful. Not keeping in mind; inattentive.
Unobservant. Neglect of observance; careless.
Unreflecting. Not thinking or considering.
Wild. Not cultivated; reckless.
Wrapped in thought. Wholly absorbed in thought.

DISREGARD—*Adverbs.*

Inadvertently, etc. See *Adjectives.*
Inattentively. Without attention.
Per incuriam [L.]. Through carelessness.
Sub silentio [L.]. In silence.

DISREGARD—*Interjections.*

Stand at ease! stand easy!

DISREGARD—*Phrases.*

Had it been a bear it would have bitten you; it never entered into one's head; one's thoughts being elsewhere; one's wits gone a bird's-nesting; one's wits gone a wool-gathering; the attention wanders; the mind running on other things.

HEED—*Continued.*

HEED—*Phrases.*

Absence d'esprit [F.]. Absence of mind.
Dictum sapienti sat est [L.]. A word to the wise is sufficient.
Ecco [It.]. Look here.
Finem respice [L.]. Regard the end.
These are to give notice.
This is to give notice.

---

heed'-ful. Vigilant; careful. Carefulness-Carelessness, Recklessness-Caution.
heed'-ful-ness. Carefulness. Carefulness-Carelessness.
heed'-less. Careless; inattentive. Carefulness-Carelessness, Heed-Disregard, Recklessness-Caution.
heed'-less-ness. Carelessness. Carefulness-Carelessness, Recklessness-Caution.
heel. The hinder part of the foot; to lean; move around on the heel. Aim-Aberration, Circuition, Parallelism-Inclination, Suspension-Support; **heel of Achilles,** Security-Insecurity; **iron heel,** Recompense-Scourge; **turn on one's heel,** Advance-Retrogression, Circuition, Quest-Evasion.
heel'-piece". To put a piece of leather on the heel of a shoe; the rear of anything; the end. Anteriority-Posteriority, Predecessor-Continuation, Renovation-Relapse.
heel'-post". A post, as the heel of a steam-vessel, supporting the outer end of the propeller-shaft. Conveyance-Vessel.
heel'-tap". A small piece of leather for the heel of a shoe; a small quantity of liquor left in a glass. Cleanness-Filthiness, Increment-Remnant.

heels. The bottom of the feet. HEIGHT-LOWNESS; **at the heels of,** ANTERIORITY-POSTERIORITY, HEIGHT-LOWNESS, REMOTENESS-NEARNESS; **cool one's heels,** ACTION-PASSIVENESS; **follow on the heels of,** LEADING-FOLLOWING, QUEST-EVASION; **heels over head,** HURRY-LEISURE, RECKLESSNESS-CAUTION, REVERSAL; **laid by the heels,** RELEASE-RESTRAINT; **lay by the heels,** TAKING-RESTITUTION; **show a light pair of heels,** QUEST-EVASION; **take to one's heels,** QUEST-EVASION; **tread on the heels of,** APPROACH-WITHDRAWAL, LEADING-FOLLOWING, QUEST-EVASION, REMOTENESS-NEARNESS.

heft. To lift up; a handle. INSTRUMENT, TOIL-RELAXATION.

he''-ge-mon -ic. Dominant; chief. RULE-LICENSE.

he''-ge-mon'-ic-al-ly. In a hegemonic manner DOMINANCE-IMPOTENCE, RULE-LICENSE.

he'-ge-mo-ny. Leadership. RULE-LICENSE.

heif'-er. A young cow. FAUNA-FLORA.

heigh'-ho''. An exclamation. LIGHTHEARTEDNESS-DEJECTION.

height. The highest degree; altitude; summit. HEIGHT-LOWNESS, PRICE-DISCOUNT, QUANTITY-MEASURE, TOP-BOTTOM; **at its height,** MAGNITUDE-SMALLNESS; **draw oneself up to one's full height,** ELEVATION-DEPRESSION.

HEIGHT—LOWNESS.

Altitude. Extent of space from a base up to something.
Elevation. State of being considerably above something else.
Eminence. Elevation of position.
Height. Distance from some natural base up to something.
Loftiness, etc. The state of being large and high, etc. See *Adjectives*.
Pitch. The degree or rate of ascent or slope.
Procerity. Tallness; stature.
Prominence, etc. The quality or state of standing out from or above something else. See CONVEXITY.
Stature. The height of man
Sublimity. Extreme highness.
Tallness. Quality or state of being tall.

HEIGHT—*Denotations, etc.*

Aerie. A lofty nest of a bird of prey.
Alp. A very high mountain. "O'er many a frozen, many a fiery alp." [Milton's *Paradise Lost*, ii, 620.]
Alpland. A portion of the earth higher than the common level.
Alps. A range of lofty mountains in Europe.
Altimetry. The art of measuring altitudes or heights.
Barrow. The raised earth over a burial place.
Bluff. A high, steep bank
Brae. A hillside.
Butte. A detached low mountain.
Campanile. A bell-tower.
Cape. A point of land rising above the sea's level.
Ceiling. The inside lining of a room overhead.
Cliff. A high, steep rock.
Clough. A cleft in a hill.
Colossus. An immense statue, one of the Seven Wonders of the World.
Column. A cylindrical support for a roof, ceiling, etc.
Craig. A cliff.
Cupola. A dome rising above the roof of a building.
Dome. A hemispherical or inverted cup-shaped roof.
Down. A treeless hill, having a broad level top.
Dune. An elevation of loose drifting sand.
Edge. A sharp terminating border.
Escarpment. A steep slope about a fortified place.
Fell. A barren hill.
Flagstaff. A staff on which a flag is hoisted.
Flood-tide. The high or rising tide.
Foreland. A high cape.
Giant. A man of extraordinary bulk and stature. [*Genesis* vi, 4.]
Giraffe. The tallest of living animals, a camelopard
Grenadier. A soldier of a regiment of men of great stature.
Headland. A high point of land extending into the water.
Heights. A hill or mountain.
Highland. An elevated region or country.
High tide. The rising of the water along the seashore
Hill. An elevation of land lower than a mountain.
Hillock. A small hill.
High water. The rising of the water above some common mark.
Hog's back. A ridge-like structure of alternate hills and valleys.
Hummock. A rise of ground of no great extent.
Knap. A knob-like hill.
Knoll. A small, round hill.
Ledge. A ridge or reef of rocks.
Maypole. A decorated pole around which dancing takes place on May Day.
Minaret. A slender tower in Turkish architecture.
Mole. A tower-like tomb.
Monticle. A little mountain.
Monument. A building, pillar, stone, or the like to preserve the remembrance of a person, event, etc.

Debasement. A making lower.
Depression, etc. The state of being low, etc. See CONVEXITY-CONCAVITY.
Lowness, etc. The quality of being below the level of something else, etc. See *Adjectives*.
Prostration. The state of being laid flat.

LOWNESS—*Denotations.*

Basement floor. The ground floor of a house.
Ebb-tide. The low tide.
Feet. The parts of the body below the ankles; the lowest part of anything
Ground floor. The floor of a building beneath the principal story; the floor on a level with the ground.
Heels. The back part of the feet.
Hold. The lowest part of a ship.
Lowlands. A tract of land lower than the adjacent country.
Low tide. The falling, or the recession of the water to the ocean.
Low water. The height of the water below a fixed mark.
Mole-hill. A little heap or ridge of earth thrown up by a mole in burrowing.
Neap tide. The low tide occurring after the first and third quarters of the moon.
Rez de chaussée [F.]. The ground floor.
Spring tide. The high tide occurring after the new and full moon

LOWNESS—*Verbs.*

Below, etc. To be depressed, etc. See *Adjectives*.
Crouch. To stoop low.
Grovel. To lie prostrate
Lie flat. } To be low.
Lie low. }
Lower, etc. To make low, etc. See ELEVATION-DEPRESSION.
Slouch. To hang down carelessly.
Underlie. To lie beneath.
Wallow. To roll about, as in mire.

LOWNESS—*Adjectives.*

Be low. In a low condition.
Crouched. In a cringing condition.
Debased. Lowered.
Flat. Not elevated.
Level with the ground. In the same plane as the ground.
Low. Having little upward elevation.
Lying low, etc. Resting in a low condition, etc. See *Verbs.*
Neap. Low or lowest.
Nether. Lower.
Nethermost. Lowest.
Prostrate, etc. Fallen low or flat, etc. See ERECTNESS-FLATNESS.
Squat. Crouching; short and low.
Subjacent. Lying underneath.

LOWNESS—*Adverbs.*

Adown. Downward; down.
At a low ebb. At low tide.
At the foot of. At the bottom of.
Below. Underneath; under.
Below par. Below face value.
Below stairs. At the foot of the stairs. [*High Life Below Stairs.*]
Down. From higher to lower level.
Downstairs. Below the stairs.
Downward. From higher to lower position.
Under. Situated below.
Under foot. Beneath the feet.
Under ground. Beneath or below the ground.
Underneath. Below.

Moor. An extensive waste covered with patches of heath.
Moorland. Land consisting of moors.
Mound. An artificial hill or elevation of earth,
Mount. A mountain
Mountain. A portion of the earth's surface rising considerably above the common level.
Obelisk. An upright, four-sided pillao, tapering to a point.
Peak. The top of a hill or mountain.
Pike. A pointed or peaked hill
Pikestaff. A long staff with a spike in the lower end, to guard against slipping.
Pillar. A firm, upright support for a structure.
Pole. A long, slender piece of wood.
Promontory. A high cape.
Ridge. A range of hills or mountains.

Rising ground. Ground higher than the common level.
Spire. The roof of a tower, of a pyramidal form and very high in proportion to its width.
Spring tide. The high tide.
Steeple. A spire.
Steeps. A precipitous hill, mountain, or rock.
Top. The highest point of anything.
Topgallant mast. The mast next above the topmast.
Topmast. The second mast, or that next above the lower mast.
Tor. A high hill or peak.
Tower. A building standing alone, and high in proportion to its diameter.
Turret. A little tower.
Upland. High land.
Vantage ground. Elevated position which gives one an advantage.

HEIGHT—*Verbs.*

Become high, etc. To grow elevated, etc. See *Adjectives.*
Be high, etc. See *Adjectives.*
Beetle. To project out.
Bestride. To step over; to surpass.
Cap. To surmount; surpass
Command. To overlook.
Cover, etc. To cap; overspread. See COVER.
Culminate. To reach the highest point.
Grow.
Grow higher. } To increase in height.
Grow taller. }
Hang over. To be greater in height.
Heighten, etc. To make higher, etc See ELEVATION.
Hover. To hang over.

Impend. Overhang.
Mount. To rise higher; go up.
Overhang. To be higher than.
Overtop, etc. To be higher than, etc. See SUPREMACY.
Perch. To fix on an elevated place.
Render high, etc. See *Adjectives.*
Ride. To be seated on top of, as on a horse.
Rise, etc. To go upward, etc. See ASCENT.
Soar. To float through the air; to fly upward.
Stand on tiptoe. To stretch oneself out to his full height.
Surmount. To rise above; mount above.
Tower. To rise to a great height.
Upgrow. To grow up.

HEIGHT—*Adjectives.*

Aerial. Pertaining to the upper air.
Alpine. Like the Alps.
Beetling. Jutting; prominent.
Cloud-capped. }
Cloud-topped. } High as the clouds
Cloud-touching. }
Elevated, etc. Raised up; made high, etc See ELEVATION
Eminent. Surpassing; very high.
Exalted. Raised to a position of prominence.
Gigantic, etc. Of great size, etc. See GREATNESS
Hanging. Suspended in the air.
Heaven-kissing. As high as heaven; very high [Hamlet, III, iv.]
High. Elevated; lofty; tall.
Highest, etc. Topmost; crowning, etc. See TOP
Hilly. Rugged; like hills.
Incumbent. Placed above, or leaning upon something.
Lanky, etc. Thin and tall, etc. See BREADTH-NARROWNESS.
Lofty. Very high.
Moorland. Like the moorland.

Mountainous. Hilly; elevated; like the region of mountains.
Overhanging, etc. Jutting out over, or appearing to, as rocky cliffs, etc. See *Verbs.*
Overlying. Placed above.
Patagonian. Like an inhabitant of Patagonia; very tall
Prominent, etc. In bold relief, etc. See CONVEXITY.
Soaring. Floating on high.
Sub-Alpine. Under the Alps.
Superimposed. Placed above.
Superincumbent. Resting on something.
Supernatant. Floating or swimming above.
Tall. Of great height
Tall as a Maypole. }
Tall as a poplar. } Very tall
Tall as a steeple. }
Towering. Very high.
Upper. Above.
Upland. High in situation

HEIGHT—*Adverbs, etc.*

Above. Higher up; overhead; over the surrounding surface.
Above stairs. At the top of the steps.
Airward. Up in the air.
Aloft. On high; in a high place.
Aloof. Apart; at a distance; above.
Breast high. As high as the breast.
En haut [F.]. Above.
From top to bottom, etc. Along its full height. See ENTIRETY
High up. Above; aloft.
In the clouds. On high

On high. Above; aloft; high up.
On stilts. }
On tiptoe. } Raised up.
On the shoulders of. As high as a person.
Over. Above.
Overhead. Above the head.
Over head and ears. Above the height of a person.
Up. Above.
Upstairs. In the higher part of a building.
Upwards. Toward a higher place.

HEIGHT—*Phrase.*

È meglio cader dalle finestre che dal tetto [It.]. It is better to fall from the window than from the roof.

height'-en. To exaggerate; intensify; elevate. ALLE-VIATION-AGGRAVATION, GULL-HYPERBOLE, INCREASE-DECREASE, INJECTION-EJECTION.
height'-en-ing. A raising up; an elevation. ALLEVIA-TION-AGGRAVATION.
heights. That which is high. HEIGHT-LOWNESS, TOP-BOTTOM.
hei'-nous. Extremely wicked. VIRTUE-VICE.
heir. One who becomes entitled to a deceased person's estate. FUTURE-PAST, HOLDER, PARENTAGE-PROG-ENY.

heir'-ess. A female heir. HOLDER, PARENTAGE-PROG-ENY.
heir'-loom''. A piece of personal property or a quality, endowment, or the like, that is inherited. PROPERTY.
heir'-ship. The right of inheriting. HOLDING-EX-EMPTION.
heg'-i-ra. A flight. ARRIVAL-DEPARTURE.
he-li'-ac-al. Pertaining to the sun. UNIVERSE.
hel'-i-cal. Having a spiral shape. CIRCLE-WINDING.
Hel'-i-con. A mountain in Bœotia, the residence of Apollo and the Muses. POETRY.

he'-li-o-chrome. A photograph in natural colors. LIGHT-DARKNESS.

He''-li-o-ga'-ba-lus. A Roman emperor killed by his soldiers. MODERATION-VOLUPTUARY.

he'-li-o-graph. A photograph taken by sunlight. PAINTING.

he''-li-o-graph'-ic. Of or pertaining to heliography. LIGHT-DARKNESS.

he''-li-og'-ra-phy. The operation of transmitting signals with a heliograph; photography. LIGHT-DARKNESS, PAINTING.

he''-li-o-gra'-vure. Photo-engraving. ENGRAVING.

he''-li-ol'-a-try. Sun-worship. DEVOTION-IDOLATRY.

he''-li-om'-e-ter. An instrument for measuring small angles in the heavens. MENSURATION.

he'-li-o-scope''. A telescope in which the eyes are protected while looking at the sun. MENSURATION.

he'-li-o-trope''. A green chalcedony. EMBELLISHMENT-DISFIGUREMENT.

he'-li-o-type''. A picture obtained by a process similar to lithography. ENGRAVING, PAINTING.

he'-li-um. An element. CHEMISTRY.

he'-lix. A spiral. ANATOMY, ARCHITECTURE, CIRCLE-WINDING, ELECTRICITY.

hell. The infernal regions; a place of evil; the abode of evil spirits. DEEPNESS-SHALLOWNESS, HEAVEN-HELL, PURPOSE-LUCK; **hell broke loose,** REGULARITY-IRREGULARITY; **hell upon earth,** PLEASURE-PAIN, WELFARE-MISFORTUNE.

hell'-born''. Born in hell. ANGEL-SATAN, VIRTUE-VICE.

hell'-cat''. Spiteful woman. GOOD MAN-BAD MAN.

hel'-ler. Coin. VALUES.

hell'-hag''. An evil old woman. BENEFACTOR-EVIL-DOER.

hell'-ish. Pertaining to hell; diabolical. CHARITABLE-NESS-MALEVOLENCE, HEAVEN-HELL, VIRTUE-VICE.

helluo librorum [L.] (hel'-liu-o lai-bro'-rum). A bookworm. SCHOLAR-DUNCE.

helm. A place of control or responsibility; the steering apparatus of a vessel. INSTRUMENT, SCEPTER; **answer the helm,** INSUBORDINATION-OBEDIENCE; **at the helm,** MANAGEMENT; **obey the helm,** DIFFICULTY-FACILITY; **take the helm,** MANAGEMENT.

hel'-met. A defensive armor for the head; a dome-like hat. DEFIANCE, DRESS-UNDRESS.

hel''-min-thol'-o-gy. The science of worms. ZOOLOGY-BOTANY.

helms'-man''. A steersman. MANAGER.

hel'-ot. A slave. CHIEF-UNDERLING.

help. Aid; a servant; remedy. CHIEF-UNDERLING, GIVING-RECEIVING, OBSTRUCTION-HELP, REMEDY-BANE, USEFULNESS-USELESSNESS; **God help you,** COMPASSION-RUTHLESSNESS; **help oneself to,** TAKING-RESTITUTION; **it can't be helped,** CONTENTEDNESS-DISCONTENTMENT, SENSITIVENESS-APATHY, YIELDING; **so help me God,** ASSERTION-DENIAL.

help'-er. One who assists. ANTAGONIST-ASSISTANT.

help'-ful. Affording aid. OBSTRUCTION-HELP.

help'-less. Unable to help oneself; destitute. MIGHT-IMPOTENCE, SECURITY-INSECURITY.

help'-less-ness. Inability to help oneself. MIGHT-IMPOTENCE.

help'-mate''. A coworker; a wife. ANTAGONIST-ASSISTANT, MATRIMONY-CELIBACY.

hel'-ter-skel'-ter. Confused hurry. HURRY-LEISURE, REGULARITY-IRREGULARITY.

helve af'-ter the hatch'-et, throw the. EXTRAVAGANCE-AVARICE.

hem. A fold made in the edge of a cloth; an interjection. ASTONISHMENT-EXPECTANCE, BORDER, PLICATURE; **hem in,** RELEASE-RESTRAINT; **kiss the hem of one's garment,** PRESUMPTION-OBSEQUIOUSNESS.

hem'-i. Half. DOUBLING-HALVING.

hem''-i-he'-drism. One-half the parts crystalized. MINERALOGY.

hem''-i-mor'-phism. A crystal whose two ends have unlike planes. MINERALOGY.

hem'-i-sphere. A half-sphere. EXTENSION-DISTRICT.

hem''-i-spher'-ic. Pertaining to a hemisphere. CONVEXITY-CONCAVITY.

hem'-lock. A poisonous biennial herb. REMEDY-BANE.

hem'-or-rhage. A discharge of blood. NUTRIMENT-EXCRETION.

hemp. A strong fiber obtained from a plant. LAMINA-FIBER.

hen. A female fowl. FAUNA-FLORA, MALE-FEMALE; **hen with one chicken,** ACTIVITY-INDOLENCE.

hen'-bane''. A poisonous coarse herb. REMEDY-BANE.

hence. Away from this place; from this cause; therefore. ARRIVAL-DEPARTURE, RATIOCINATION-INSTINCT, RATIONALE-LUCK; **hence loathed melancholy,** LIGHTHEARTEDNESS-DEJECTION.

hence''-forth'. From this time on. FUTURE-PAST.

hence''-for'-ward. From this time forward. FUTURE-PAST.

hench'-man. A male servant. CHIEF-UNDERLING.

hen'-coop''. A place for confining hens. DOMESTICATION-AGRICULTURE.

hen'-pecked''. Domineered over by one's wife. INSUBORDINATION-OBEDIENCE, LIBERTY-SUBJECTION.

hep'-ta-gon. A plane figure of seven sides. ANGULARITY.

Her''-a-cli'-tus. A Greek philosopher. JUBILATION-LAMENTATION.

Heraclitus rideret [L.] (her-a-clai'-tus rai-di''-ret). Heraclitus would smile. SOCIETY-LUDICROUSNESS.

her'-ald. To proclaim; a proclaimer; a forerunner. LEADING-FOLLOWING, MESSENGER, PREDECESSOR-CONTINUATION, PROPHECY, PUBLICITY.

her'-ald-ry. The science which treats of the explanation of coats of arms. SIGN.

herb. A plant not possessing a woody stem. FAUNA-FLORA.

her-ba'-ceous. Having the character of an herb. FAUNA-FLORA.

herb'-age. Herbs, collectively. FAUNA-FLORA.

herb'-al. An herbarium. ZOOLOGY-BOTANY.

her-ba'-ri-um. A collection of dried plants. ZOOLOGY-BOTANY.

her-biv'-o-rous. Feeding on vegetable matter. NUTRIMENT-EXCRETION.

her''-bo-ri-za'-tion. Botanical research. ZOOLOGY-BOTANY.

herb'-o-rize. To search for new plants. ZOOLOGY-BOTANY.

Her-cu'-le-an. Requiring much labor; very strong; very difficult. DIFFICULTY-FACILITY, STRENGTH-WEAKNESS, TOIL-RELAXATION.

Herculem, ex pede [L.] (her'-kiu-lem, ex pi'-di). We judge the whole from the specimen. CONVENTIONALITY-UNCONVENTIONALITY, SIGN.

Her'-cu-les. A man of great size and strength. STRENGTH-WEAKNESS, SUSPENSION-SUPPORT; **pillars of Hercules,** BOUNDARY, SIGN.

herd. A crowd. GATHERING-SCATTERING, MULTIPLICITY-PAUCITY.

Herd ist Goldes werth, eigner [G.] (hērd ist gol'-des vērt, aiH-ner). One's own hearth has golden worth. DWELLER-HABITATION, GOODNESS-BADNESS.

herds'-man''. One who owns or tends a herd. CHIEF-UNDERLING.

here. At this place; hither; in the present life. APPROACH-WITHDRAWAL, ARRIVAL-DEPARTURE, POSITION, PRESENCE-ABSENCE; **here and there,** EXTENSION-PLACE, GATHERING-SCATTERING, MULTIPLICITY-PAUCITY, POSITION; **here below,** universe; **here goes,** ENTERPRISE; **here, there, and everywhere,** Ex-

TENSION-INEXTENSION, PRESENCE-ABSENCE, UNI-FORMITY-DIVERSITY; **here to-day and gone to-morrow,** LASTINGNESS-TRANSIENTNESS.

here'-a-bouts". In this neighborhood. POSITION, RE-MOTENESS-NEARNESS.

here-aft'-er. At some future time. FUTURE-PAST.

here-by'. By means of this. PURPOSE-LUCK.

her"-e-dit'-a-ment. Anything capable of being inheri-ted. PROPERTY.

he-red'-i-ta-ry. Endowed naturally with certain traits and tendencies; deriving by inheritance. CAUSE-EFFECT, SUBJECTIVENESS-OBJECTIVENESS.

here-in'. In this. OUTSIDE-INSIDE.

her'-e-sy. Opposition to established doctrine. OR-THODOXY-HETERODOXY, TRUTH-ERROR.

her'-e-tic. One who denies commonly accepted views. ORTHODOXY-HETERODOXY, PATRIOTISM-TREASON.

he-ret'-ic-al. At variance with accepted beliefs. OR-THODOXY-HETERODOXY, TRUTH-ERROR.

here"-to-fore'. Previously. CREDULOUSNESS-SKEP-TICISM, FUTURE-PAST.

here"-up-on'. Upon this. DURATION-NEVERNESS.

here-with'. With this. MEANS, SOLITUDE-COMPANY.

her'-it-age. That which is inherited. FUTURE-PAST, HOLDING-EXEMPTION, PROPERTY.

her'-i-tor. A holder in a parish. HOLDER.

her-maph'-ro-dite. Having the sexual characteristics of both sexes. BIOLOGY, CONVENTIONALITY-UNCON-VENTIONALITY; **hermaphrodite brig,** CONVEYANCE-VESSEL.

her"-me-neu'-tics. The interpretation of literary works. INTERPRETATION-MISINTERPRETATION.

Her'-mes. The herald of the gods. SPEECH-INARTICU-LATENESS.

her-met'-ic-al-ly. Sealed by hermetic process. AP-ERTURE-CLOSURE.

her'-mit. One who abandons society and lives alone; an anchorite. AUSTERITY, SOCIABILITY-PRIVACY.

her'-mit-age. A retreat; cell. CONTENTS-RECEIVER, DWELLER-HABITATION, SOCIABILITY-PRIVACY.

he'-ro. A man distinguished for valor, bravery, and the like. BRAVERY-COWARDICE, GOOD MAN-BAD MAN, REPUTATION-DISCREDIT; **hero worship,** APPROVAL-DISAPPROVAL, DEVOTION-IDOLATRY.

Her'-od, out"-Her'-od. To surpass in violence and cru-elty. GULL-HYPERBOLE.

he-ro'-ic. Having the characteristics of a hero. BRA-VERY-COWARDICE, GOOD MAN-BAD MAN, REPUTA-TION - DISCREDIT, UNSELFISHNESS - SELFISHNESS; **mock-heroic,** SOCIETY-LUDICROUSNESS.

he-ro'-ics. Bombastic language. BRAGGING.

her'-o-ism. Heroic character. BRAVERY-COWARDICE.

her"-pe-tol'-o-gy. The science which treats of reptiles and amphibians. ZOOLOGY-BOTANY.

her'-ring. Pungent and salty as a herring. PUN-GENCY; **trail of a herring,** MOTIVE-CAPRICE.

her'-ring-gut'-ted. Very slender. BREADTH-NARROW-NESS.

hes'-i-tan-cy. A pausing to consider. DETERMINATION-VACILLATION.

hes'-i-tate. To be doubtful as to action or decision; fal-ter in speech. CERTAINTY-DOUBT, DETERMINATION-VACILLATION, FAITH-MISGIVING, READINESS-RELUC-TANCE, SANGUINENESS-TIMIDITY, SPEECH-INARTICU-LATENESS.

hes'-i-ta"-ting. In doubt. DETERMINATION-VACILLA-TION.

hes"-i-ta'-tion. Vacillation; doubt; uncertainty; slow-ness of speech. CERTAINTY-DOUBT, DETERMINA-TION-VACILLATION, READINESS-RELUCTANCE, SAN-GUINENESS-HOPELESSNESS, SPEECH-INARTICULATE-NESS.

Hes-pe'-ri-an. In the West. LATERALITY-CONTRAPO-SITION.

Hes-per'-i-des, Gar'-den of the. The delightful garden where the golden apples of Juno were kept. HEAVEN-HELL.

Hes'-sian boot. A boot worn by Hessian soldiers. DRESS-UNDRESS.

hest. A command. ORDER.

hesterni quirites [L.] (hes-ter'-nai qui-rai'-tîz). Slaves recently set free. GENTILITY-DEMOCRACY.

het'-er-arch"-y. The government of an alien. RULE-LICENSE.

het'-er-o-clite. Inflected irregularly. CONVENTIONAL-ITY-UNCONVENTIONALITY.

het'-er-o-dox. At variance with commonly accepted doctrine. ORTHODOXY-HETERODOXY.

het'-er-o-dox"-y. Doctrine at variance with an accep-ted standard. ORTHODOXY-HETERODOXY.

het"-er-o-ge-ne'-i-ty. Unlikeness of constituent parts. CONNECTION-INDEPENDENCE.

het"-er-o-ge'-ne-ous. Composed of dissimilar elements mixed. CONNECTION-INDEPENDENCE, CONVENTION-ALITY-UNCONVENTIONALITY, MINERALOGY, MIXTURE-HOMOGENEITY, UNIFORMITY-MULTIFORMITY, VARIA-TION.

het"-er-on'-o-my. Subjected to the authority of another. RULE-LICENSE.

het'-man. A general of the Cossacks. CHIEF-UNDER-LING.

hew. To cut with a sharp instrument; fashion. FORM-FORMLESSNESS, LENGTH-SHORTNESS, UNION-DIS-UNION; **hew down,** ELEVATION-DEPRESSION.

hew'-ers of wood. Wood-cutters. AGENT, GENTILITY-DEMOCRACY.

hex'-a-gon. A plane figure of six sides. ANGULAR-ITY.

hex-ag'-on-al. Having six sides; **hexagonal system,** MINERALOGY.

hex"-a-he'-dron. A solid bounded by six plane faces. ANGULARITY, MINERALOGY.

hex-am'-e-ter. A verse of six feet. POETRY-PROSE, RHETORIC.

hex-oc"-ta-he'-dron. Form of crystal. MINERALOGY.

hey. An exclamation to attract attention. ADDRESS-RESPONSE.

hey'-day". An expression of joy or wonder. ASTON-ISHMENT-EXPECTANCE, ENTERTAINMENT-WEARINESS, EXPECTATION-SURPRISE, JUBILATION-LAMENTATION, LIGHTHEARTEDNESS-DEJECTION; **heydey of the blood,** AFFECTIONS; **heydey of youth,** INFANCY-AGE.

hi-a'-tion. The act of gaping. APERTURE - CLO-SURE.

hi-a'-tus. A break or interruption. INTERSPACE-CON-TACT, PRESENCE-ABSENCE.

hiatus maxime deflendus [L.] (hai-ê'-tus max -i-mî dî-flen'-dus). A deficiency much to be regretted. IN-TERSPACE-CONTACT.

hi-ber'-nal. Pertaining to winter. HEAT-COLD.

Hi-ber'-ni-cism. An Irish idiom or peculiarity of speech. ADAGE-NONSENSE, WORD-NEOLOGY.

hic'-cup. A short inspiratory movement, attended by a convulsive contraction of the diaphragm. APPEAR-ANCE-DISAPPEARANCE.

hic jacet [L.] (hic jê'-set). Here lies. LIFE-FUNERAL.

hic labor, hoc opus [L.] (hic lê'-bor, hoc o'-pus). This is labor, this is work. DIFFICULTY-FACILITY.

hid. Concealed. **Hid under a bushel,** CAREFULNESS-CARELESSNESS.

hi-dal'-go. Coin; Spanish nobleman of the lower classes. GENTILITY-DEMOCRACY, VALUES.

hid'-den. Secreted. CLEARNESS-OBSCURITY, ENLIGHT-ENMENT-SECRECY; **hidden meaning,** MANIFESTATION-LATENCY.

hide. To conceal; the skin of a large animal. COVER-LINING, ENLIGHTENMENT - SECRECY; **hide and seek.** ENTERTAINMENT-WEARINESS, TRUTHFULNESS-FRAUD; **hide diminished head,** EXTRAVAGANCE-AVA-

RICE, INCREASE-DECREASE, SUPREMACY-SUBORDINA-
CY; **hide one's face**, CONCEIT-DIFFIDENCE.

hide'-bound". Narrow-minded; niggardly. BIGOTRY-
APOSTASY, EXTRAVAGANCE - AVARICE, RELEASE-
RESTRAINT.

hid'-e-ous. Exciting terror. BEAUTY-UGLINESS.

hi'-ding–place". A place of concealment; a refuge.
DWELLER-HABITATION, ENLIGHTENMENT-SECRECY,
EXPOSURE-HIDINGPLACE, REFUGE-PITFALL.

hie. To go; hurry. MOVEMENT-REST, SWIFTNESS-
SLOWNESS; **hie to**, TRAVELING-NAVIGATION.

hi'-er-arch. The chief of a sacred order. MINISTRY-
LAITY.

hi"-er-arch'-ic-al. Pertaining to an ecclesiastical rule.
CHURCH.

hi'-er-arch"-y. A body of ecclesiastical rulers. CHURCH.

hi"-er-o-glyph'-ic. Sacred writing; Egyptian picture-
writing. DELINEATION-CARICATURE, LETTER, WRIT-
ING-PRINTING.

hi"-er-o-glyph'-ic-al. Pertaining to picture-writing.
WRITING-PRINTING.

hi"-e-rog'-ra-pha. Sacred writings. REVELATION-
PSEUDOREVELATION.

hi"-er-ol'-a-try. The scientific study of religions. DE-
VOTION-IDOLATRY.

hi'-er-o-man"-cy. Divination by observing things offered in sacrifice. PROPHECY.

hi-er'-o-phant. The chief priest of the Eleusinian mysteries. MINISTRY-LAITY.

hi"-er-os'-co-py. Divination by examining the entrails
of sacrificed victims. PROPHECY.

hig'-gle. To be difficult in making a bargain. EX-
CHANGE.

hig'-gle-dy–pig'-gle-dy. In a disordered state. REGU-
LARITY-IRREGULARITY.

hig'-gler. One who peddles. BUYING-SALE.

high. Elevated; expensive; intense; prominent; proud.
CACOPHONY, CLEANNESS-FILTHINESS, COSTLINESS-
CHEAPNESS, HEIGHT-LOWNESS, MAGNITUDE-SMALL-
NESS, PERFUME-STENCH, REPUTATION-DISCREDIT,
SELFRESPECT - HUMBLENESS, UNSELFISHNESS-SELF-
ISHNESS; **from on high**, HEAVEN-HELL; **high and dry**,
MUTABILITY-STABILITY, SECURITY-INSECURITY; **high
and mighty**, GENTILITY-DEMOCRACY, PRESUMPTION-
OBSEQUIOUSNESS; **high art**, PAINTING; **high celebra-
tion**, CEREMONIAL; **high color**, ARTIST, COLOR-
ACHROMATISM; **high days and holidays**, ENTERTAIN-
MENT-WEARINESS; **high descent**, GENTILITY-DEMOC-
RACY; **high flood**, ENTIRETY-DEFICIENCY; **high glee**,
LIGHTHEARTEDNESS-DEJECTION; **high hand**, DETER-
MINATION-VACILLATION, HARSHNESS-MILDNESS, LAW-
LAWLESSNESS, RULE-LICENSE, TURBULENCE-CALM-
NESS; **high holiday**, ENTERTAINMENT-WEARINESS;
high in tone, WHITENESS-BLACKNESS; **high life**, GEN-
TILITY-DEMOCRACY, SOCIETY-LUDICROUSNESS; **high
living**, MODERATION-SELFINDULGENCE; **highly respec-
table**, GENTILITY-DEMOCRACY; **high mass**, CEREMO-
NIAL; **high mightiness**, REPUTATION-DISCREDIT; **high
note**, CACOPHONY, RESONANCE-SIBILATION; **high
notions**, SELFRESPECT-HUMBLENESS; **high places**,
TOP-BOTTOM; **high pressure**, EXCITATION, VIGOR-
INERTIA; **high price**, COSTLINESS-CHEAPNESS; **high
priest**, MINISTRY-LAITY; **high relief**, CONVEXITY-CON-
CAVITY; **high repute**, REPUTATION-DISCREDIT; **high
seas**, OCEAN-LAND; **high spirits**, LIGHTHEARTEDNESS-
DEJECTION; **high tide**, RIVER-WIND, WELFARE-MIS-
FORTUNE; **high time**, EARLINESS-LATENESS, OPPOR-
TUNENESS-UNSUITABLENESS; **high treason**, INSUB-
ORDINATION-OBEDIENCE, UPRIGHTNESS-DISHONESTY;
high words, FAVORITE-ANGER, STRIFE-PEACE, VARI-
ANCE-ACCORD; **in a high degree**, MAGNITUDE-SMALL-
NESS; **in high esteem**, REGARD-DISRESPECT; **in high
feather**, BRAGGING, HEALTH-SICKNESS, LIGHTHEART-
EDNESS-DEJECTION, STRENGTH-WEAKNESS, WEL-

FARE-MISFORTUNE; **in high quarters**, GENTILITY-DE-
MOCRACY; **in high spirits**, LIGHTHEARTEDNESS-DEJEC-
TION; **on high**, HEIGHT-LOWNESS; **on one's high ropes**,
BRAWLER, EXCITATION, FAVORITE-ANGER; **on the
high road to**, SANGUINENESS-HOPELESSNESS, WAY;
ride the high horse, SELFRESPECT-HUMBLENESS; **think
highly of**, APPROVAL-DISAPPROVAL.

high'-born". Of noble birth. GENTILITY-DEMOCRACY.

high'-er. More high. SUPREMACY-SUBORDINACY.

high'-est. Topmost. HEIGHT-LOWNESS, TOP-BOTTOM.

high'-fla"-vored. Highly spiced. PUNGENCY.

high'-fli"-er. One who is extreme in his opinions or
pretensions. SANENESS-MANIAC, SELFRESPECT-HUM-
BLENESS.

high'-flow"-ing. Extravagant in style. SIMPLICITY-
FLORIDNESS.

high'-flown". Extravagant in style; proud; puffed up.
CONCEIT-DIFFIDENCE, FANCY, PRESUMPTION-OBSE-
QUIOUSNESS, SELFRESPECT-HUMBLENESS, SIMPLICITY-
FLORIDNESS.

high'-fly"-ing. Ostentatious; high-flown. GULL-HY-
PERBOLE, HEED-DISREGARD, SENSITIVENESS.

high'-hand"-ed. Arbitrary. PRESUMPTION-OBSEQUI-
OUSNESS, SELFRESPECT-HUMBLENESS, TYRANNY-AN-
ARCHY.

high'-lands. An elevation of land. HEIGHT-LOWNESS,
OCEAN-LAND.

high'-low". A high-laced shoe. DRESS-UNDRESS.

high'-met"-tled. High-spirited. BRAVERY-COWARDICE,
EXCITABILITY-INEXCITABILITY, SELFRESPECT-HUM-
BLENESS.

high'-mind"-ed. Magnanimous; noble. SELFRESPECT-
HUMBLENESS, UNSELFISHNESS - SELFISHNESS, UP-
RIGHTNESS-DISHONESTY.

high'-ness. A title belonging to persons of princely
rank. TITLE.

high'-plumed". Proud; dignified. SELFRESPECT-HUM-
BLENESS.

high'-priced." Costly; dear. COSTLINESS-CHEAPNESS.

high'-priest". A chief priest. CHIEF-UNDERLING, DE-
VOTION-IDOLATRY.

high'-sea"-soned. Highly spiced. PUNGENCY.

high'-souled". Showing high principles. SELFRESPECT-
HUMBLENESS.

high'-sound"-ing. Ostentatious; loud. LOUDNESS-
FAINTNESS, POMP, SIMPLICITY-FLORIDNESS; **high-
sounding words**, SIMPLICITY-FLORIDNESS.

high'-spir"-it-ed. Full of spirit; impetuous. BRAVERY-
COWARDICE, UPRIGHTNESS-DISHONESTY.

hight. To call; name. NAME-MISNOMER.

high'-toned". Aristocratic; of high principles. SELF-
RESPECT-HUMBLENESS.

high'-wa"-ter. The time when the tide has reached its
height. ENTIRETY-DEFICIENCY, FRICTION-LUBRICA-
TION, HEIGHT-LOWNESS, WATER-AIR; **high-water
mark**, MENSURATION.

high'-way". A specified line of travel. WAY; **highways
and byways**, WAY.

high'-way"-man. A robber who plunders on public
roads. ROBBER.

high'-wrought". Finely and skilfully worked; of
strained emotions. EXCITATION, GOODNESS-BAD-
NESS, PREPARATION-NONPREPARATION.

hi-la'-ri-ous. In high spirits. LIGHTHEARTEDNESS-
DEJECTION.

hi-lar'-i-ty. Noisy merriment. LIGHTHEARTEDNESS-
DEJECTION.

hill. A natural elevation of land. ASCENT-DESCENT,
CONVEXITY-CONCAVITY, HEIGHT-LOWNESS, PARAL-
LELISM-INCLINATION; **old as the hills**, NOVELTY-AN-
TIQUITY.

hill'-ock. A little hill. HEIGHT-LOWNESS.

hilt. The handle and guard of a sword or similar
weapon. INSTRUMENT.

hinc illæ lachrymæ [L.] (hinc il'-lî lac'-ri-mî). Hence these tears. PLEASURABLENESS-PAINFULNESS, RATIONALE-LUCK.

hind. Belonging to the rear; a farm laborer. ANTERIORITY-POSTERIORITY, GENTILITY-DEMOCRACY; **on one's hind legs,** ELEVATION-DEPRESSION, FAVORITE-ANGER.

hin'-der. To impede the progress, action, or the like. ATTACK-DEFENSE, OBSTRUCTION-HELP.

hin'-der-er. One who hinders. OBSTRUCTION-HELP.

hin'-der-ing. Checking. OBSTRUCTION-AID.

hind'-er-most''. The farthest from the front. ANTERIORITY-POSTERIORITY, BEGINNING-END.

hind'-most''. In the extreme rear. ANTERIORITY-POSTERIORITY.

hin'-drance. The act of hindering or that which hinders. ANTAGONISM-CONCURRENCE, LEAVE-PROHIBITION, OBSTRUCTION-HELP, RELEASE-RESTRAINT.

Hin'-du-ism. The religious beliefs of the Hindus. ORTHODOXY-HETERODOXY.

hinge. The joint or fastening upon which a door, or the like, swings; that upon which anything depends. CAUSE-EFFECT, CONNECTIVE, REVOLUTION-EVOLUTION, UNION-DISUNION.

hin'-ny. The offspring of a stallion and a she ass. CONVEYER.

hint. To suggest indirectly; a covert or indirect allusion. ENLIGHTENMENT-SECRECY, HYPOTHESIS, REMEMBRANCE-FORGETFULNESS, SIGN; **hint a fault,** etc., APPROVAL-DISAPPROVAL; **take a hint,** SAGACITY-INCAPACITY.

hip. The lateral part of the body between the brim of the pelvis and the free part of the thigh. ANATOMY, LATERALITY-CONTRAPOSITION; **have on the hip,** LIBERTY-SUBJECTION, PROOF-DISPROOF, RULE-LICENSE, SUCCESS-FAILURE.

hip'-knob''. Finial. ARCHITECTURE.

hip''-po-cen'-taur. A centaur. UNIFORMITY-MULTIFORMITY.

Hip-poc'-ra-tes. A famous Greek physician (fifth century, B. C.). REMEDY-BANE.

hip''-po-crat'-ic. Having pale, sunken, and contracted features in disease. LIFE-DEATH.

hip'-po-drome. A race-course for horses and chariots; a modern circus. ACTING, LISTS.

hip'-po-grif. A fabulous animal, half horse and half griffin. CONVENTIONALITY-UNCONVENTIONALITY.

Hip-pol'-y-tus. A Greek bishop and martyr. PURITY-IMPURITY.

hip-poph'-a-gy. The practise of eating horse-flesh. NUTRIMENT-EXCRETION.

hip''-po-pot'-a-mus. A large, thick-skinned, short-legged, amphibious animal; a river-horse. GREATNESS-LITTLENESS.

hir'-die-gir'-die. Topsyturvy. REVERSAL.

hire. To grant the use of for pay. COMMISSION-ABROGATION, LOAN-BORROWING, PHENOMENON, RECOMPENSE-PUNITION; **on hire,** PROFFER-REFUSAL.

hire'-ling. A person serving for hire. CHIEF-UNDERLING.

hir'-sute. Having a hairy covering. SMOOTHNESS-ROUGHNESS.

his'-pid. Rough with stiff hairs. SMOOTHNESS-ROUGHNESS.

hiss. To make a sibilant sound; utter a hiss in contempt or disapprobation. APPROVAL-DISAPPROVAL, CRY-ULULATION, REGARD-DISRESPECT, REGARD-SCORN, RESONANCE-NONRESONANCE.

hiss'-ing. A hiss. APPROVAL-DISAPPROVAL, RESONANCE-SIBILATION.

hist. Be silent. TALKATIVENESS-TACITURNITY, ADDRESS-RESPONSE.

his-tol'-o-gy. That branch of biology which treats of the microscopic structure of organic tissues. BIOLOGY, TEXTURE.

his-to'-ri-an. One who writes, compiles, or relates a history. ACCOUNT, RECORDER.

his-tor'-ic. Mentioned or celebrated in history. ACCOUNT.

his-tor'-ic-al. Of or pertaining to history. ARTIST, PAINTING.

his-to''-ri-ette'. A short history. ACCOUNT.

his-to''-ri-og'-ra-pher. One who writes history. RECORDER.

his-to''-ri-og'-ra-phy. The art or occupation of an historian. ACCOUNT.

his'-to-ry. A systematic account of past events. ACCOUNT, MARK-OBLITERATION; **natural history,** ORGANIZATION-INORGANIZATION.

his''-tri-on'-ic. Pertaining to the stage or actors. ACTING.

hit. To arrive by chance; strike; attain one's aim; a stroke of luck; success. APPROVAL-DISAPPROVAL, ARRIVAL-DEPARTURE, IMPETUS-REACTION, RATIONALE-LUCK, SUCCESS-FAILURE; **good hit,** DESIGN; **hit one's fancy,** PLEASURABLENESS-PAINFULNESS; **hit off,** DELINEATION-CARICATURE; **hit the mark,** SUCCESS-FAILURE; **hit upon,** DISCOVERY, DESIGN; **make a hit,** SKILL-UNSKILFULNESS, SUCCESS-FAILURE.

hitch. To jerk along; fasten; an obstruction; a slight difficulty. AGITATION, DIFFICULTY-FACILITY, OBSTRUCTION-HELP, SUSPENSION-SUPPORT, UNION-DISUNION.

hith'-er. In this direction. ADVANCE-RETROGRESSION, AIM-ABERRATION.

hith''-er-to'. To this time. FUTURE-PAST.

hive. A hollow structure in which bees live; a place filled with life and activity; a great multitude. ESTABLISHMENT-REMOVAL, INTERSPACE-CONTACT, MULTIPLICITY-PAUCITY, WORKSHOP.

H. M. S. His (or Her) Majesty's Ship. BELLIGERENT.

hoar. White with age; frosty. INFANCY-AGE, WHITENESS-BLACKNESS; **hoarfrost,** HEAT-COLD.

hoard. That which has been accumulated and stored away. STORE.

hoarse. Harsh or grating in sound. CACOPHONY, LOUDNESS-FAINTNESS, VOCALIZATION-MUTENESS.

hoarse'-ness. State or quality of being harsh and rough in sound. LOUDNESS-FAINTNESS.

hoar'-y. White; aged. INFANCY-AGE, WHITENESS-BLACKNESS; **hoary age,** INFANCY-AGE.

hoax. A practical joke. TRUTHFULNESS-FRAUD.

hob. A projection on the side of a fireplace. OVEN-REFRIGERATOR, SUSPENSION-SUPPORT; **hob and nob,** POLITENESS-IMPOLITENESS.

hob'-ble. A halting or limping motion; an embarrassment; a fetter for the legs of an animal. DIFFICULTY-FACILITY, RELEASE-RESTRAINT, SKILL-UNSKILFULNESS, SUCCESS-FAILURE, SWIFTNESS-SLOWNESS.

hob'-ble-de-hoy''. A youth between manhood and boyhood. INFANT-VETERAN.

hob'-bling. Limping. SUCCESS-FAILURE.

hob'-by. A favorite object or pursuit of any one. DECISION-MISJUDGMENT, DESIRE-DISTASTE, QUEST-EVASION.

hob'-by-horse''. A rocking-horse. CONVEYANCE-VESSEL, DESIRE-DISTASTE.

hob-gob'-lin. A mischievous imp; a horrible apparition. JOVE-FIEND, SANGUINENESS-TIMIDITY.

hob'-nail''. A lout or clodhopper. GENTILITY-DEMOCRACY.

Hob'-son's choice. A choice without an alternative. CHOICE-NEUTRALITY, COERCION, VOLITION-OBLIGATION.

hoc erat in more majorum [L.] (hoc i'-rat in mo'-rî majo'-rum). This was in the custom of the fathers. FUTURE-PAST, HABIT-DESUETUDE.

hoc genus omne [L.] (hoc jî-'nus om'-nî). All this race. GENTILITY-DEMOCRACY.

hock'-ey. An outdoor game. ENTERTAINMENT-WEARINESS.

ho'-cus. A conjurer; impostor. TRUTHFULNESS-FRAUD.

ho'-cus-po'-cus. A conjurer's trick; cheat. COMMUTATION-PERMUTATION, DEVOTION-MAGIC, MEANING-JARGON, TRUTHFULNESS-FALSEHOOD.

hod. A trough-like receptacle for carrying bricks or mortar. CONTENTS-RECEIVER, CONVEYANCE-VESSEL.

hod'-dy-dod'-dy. A foolish, awkward person. SAGE-FOOL.

hodge'-podge". A confused mixture. REGULARITY-IRREGULARITY.

hodie mihi, cras tibi [L.] (ho'-dai-î mai'-hai, cras tib'-i). To-day for me, to-morrow for thee. DUTY-DERELICTION.

hoe. A common garden or field tool. CONVEYANCE-VESSEL, DOMESTICATION-AGRICULTURE.

hoe'-cake". A thin cake of Indian meal, water, and salt. NUTRIMENT-EXCRETION.

hog. A swine; a gluttonous or grasping person. FASTING-GLUTTONY, FAUNA-FLORA, MODERATION-VOLUPTUARY; **go the whole hog,** COMPLETION-NONCOMPLETION, DETERMINATION-VACILLATION, ENTIRETY-DEFICIENCY; **greedy as a hog,** DESIRE-DISTASTE.

hog'-pen". A pigsty. ENCLOSURE.

hogs'-back". A ridgy structure. HEIGHT-LOWNESS.

hogs'-head. Cask. MEASURE.

hog'-wash". Kitchen refuse and the like. CLEANNESS-FILTHINESS.

hoist. To raise to a higher position. ELEVATION-DEPRESSION; **hoist a flag,** SIGN; **hoist on one's own petard,** REPRISAL-RESISTANCE, SUCCESS-FAILURE; **hoist the black flag,** FIGHTING-CONCILIATION; **hoist the blue peter,** ARRIVAL-DEPARTURE.

hoi'-ty-toi'-ty. An interjection rebuking impetuosity. ASTONISHMENT-EXPECTANCE.

hold. To retain; prevent from falling; possess; stop; adhere to; believe; continue on one's way; endure; a controlling influence; the part of a ship below deck; a place of security; stop. ACTION-PASSIVENESS, ATTACK-DEFENSE, COHESION-LOOSENESS, CONTENTS-RECEIVER, DISCONTINUANCE-CONTINUANCE, DESIRE-REPLETION, FAITH-MISGIVING, HEIGHT-LOWNESS, HOLDING-EXEMPTION, INCLUSION-OMISSION, KEEPING-RELINQUISHMENT, LEAVE-PROHIBITION, MOVEMENT-REST, MUTATION-PERMANENCE, OCCURRENCE-DESTINY, RELEASE-PRISON, RELEASE-RESTRAINT, RULE-LICENSE, SUSPENSION-SUPPORT, TOP-BOTTOM; **gain a hold upon,** KEEPING-RELINQUISHMENT; **get hold of,** GAIN-LOSS, TAKING-RESTITUTION; **have a firm hold,** HOLDING-EXEMPTION, KEEPING-RELINQUISHMENT; **have a hold upon,** DOMINANCE-IMPOTENCE; **hold a council,** ADVICE; **hold a fast,** RULE-LICENSE; **hold a lease,** SECURITY; **hold aloof,** CREDULOUSNESS-SKEPTICISM, QUEST-EVASION; **hold a meeting,** GATHERING-SCATTERING; **hold an argument,** RATIOCINATION-INSTINCT; **hold a situation,** OCCUPATION; **hold at arm's length,** ATTACK-DEFENSE; **hold authority,** RULE-LICENSE; **hold back,** EXTRAVAGANCE-AVARICE, KEEPING-RELINQUISHMENT, MOTIVE-DEHORTATION, OBSTRUCTION-HELP, QUEST-EVASION, RELEASE-RESTRAINT, STORE; **hold both one's sides,** JUBILATION-LAMENTATION; **hold converse,** CONVERSATION-MONOLOGUE; **hold fast,** COHESION-LOOSENESS, KEEPING-RELINQUISHMENT, RELEASE-RESTRAINT; **hold forth,** EDUCATION-MISTEACHING, SPEECH-INARTICULATENESS; **hold good,** MUTATION-PERMANENCE, PROOF-DISPROOF, TRUTH-ERROR; **hold hard,** MOVEMENT-REST; **hold in hand,** RULE-LICENSE; **hold in remembrance,** REMEMBRANCE-FORGETFULNESS; **hold in solution,** LIQUEFACTION-VOLATILIZATION; **hold off,** OCCUPATION, QUEST-EVASION; **hold office,** MANAGEMENT, RULE-LICENSE; **hold on,** DISCONTINUANCE-CONTINUANCE; **MUTATION-PERMANENCE, PERSISTENCE-WHIM; hold one's breath,** ASTONISHMENT-EXPECTANCE, EXPECTATION-SURPRISE; **hold one's ground,** MUTATION-PERMANENCE, REPRISAL-RESISTANCE; **hold one's hand,** DISCONTINUANCE-CONTINUANCE, QUEST-ABANDONMENT; **hold one's head above water,** WELFARE-MISFORTUNE; **hold one's own,** ATTACK-DEFENSE, CONSERVATION, KEEPING-RELINQUISHMENT, REPRISAL-RESISTANCE, RULE-LICENSE; **hold one's tongue,** TALKATIVENESS-TACITURNITY; **hold oneself in readiness,** PREPARATION-NONPREPARATION; **hold oneself up,** ELEVATION-DEPRESSION; **hold out,** ASSERTION-DENIAL, BRAVERY-COWARDICE, PERSISTENCE-WHIM, PROFFER-REFUSAL, REPRISAL-RESISTANCE; **hold to,** READINESS-RELUCTANCE; **hold together,** ANTAGONISM-CONCURRENCE, UNION-DISUNION; **hold up,** APPROVAL-DISAPPROVAL, DAMPNESS-DRYNESS, DISCONTINUANCE-CONTINUANCE, OBSTRUCTION-HELP, POMP, SUSPENSION-SUPPORT; **hold up one's head,** BRAVERY-COWARDICE; **quit one's hold,** KEEPING-RELINQUISHMENT; **take hold,** DOMINANCE-IMPOTENCE.

hold'-er. One who or that which holds. HOLDER.

HOLDER.

Beneficiary. One who receives anything as a gift; the holder of a benefice or the profits of an estate.

Cestui-que-trust [F.]. A person who has the equitable and beneficial interest in property, the legal interest in which is vested in a trustee.

Devisee. One who receives a gift of lands by a will.

Feoffee. A person who is feoffed.

Grantee. One to whom a grant of any kind is made.

Heir. One entitled to receive the estates of a deceased person.

Heir apparent. One who is bound to become heir if he outlives his ancestor.

Heir presumptive. One who is an heir at present, but whose claims may be invalidated by the birth of another.

Heiress. A female inheritor.

Heritor. A holder of a heritable estate.

Holder. One who has in possession by any means or title.

Holder of the legal estate. A legal holder.

Impropriator. A lay holder of church property.

Inheritor. One who will inherit; a male heir.

Inheritress. A female heir.

Inheritrix. Variant of inheritress.

Laird. Scottish for lord or landlord.

Landed gentry. A class of people of good social position having estates in lands.

Landholder. An owner of land.

Landlady. A female holder of land; the wife of a landlord.

Landlord. } The owner of lands or houses which he leases to a
Landowner. } tenant or tenants.

Legatary. A legatee.

Legatee. One who receives a legacy.

Lessee. One who leases or rents land.

Lodger. One who holds rooms in a house.

Lord. The person to whom military service was due in return for the land; a landlord; a title given to a superior; Anglo-Saxon *hlaford* (loaf keeper), correlative with *hlafaeter* (loaf eater), a servant, a laborer.

Lord of the manor. Landholder.

Lord paramount. The king.

Man in possession. The apparent owner.

Master. One who has possession or control of.

Mesne lord. An intermediate lord.

Mistress. A female owner or proprietor; wife of master.

Mortgagee. One to whom the mortgage is given.

Mortgagor. One who gives mortgages.

Occupant. One who has possession.

Occupier. Variant of occupant.

Owner. One who has possession of the legal title.

Person in possession. A person who holds property by ownership or by lease.

Possessor. One who has the right of property in actual exercise.

Proprietary. A proprietor.

Proprietor. A person having legal title to anything.

Proprietress. A female proprietor.

Relessee. A releasee; one to whom a release is made.

Remainder-man. One to whom an estate is left in remainder.

Renter. One who receives possession of land in return for a compensation.
Reversioner. One having a right to an estate in reversion.
Right owner. } Legal owner.
Rightful owner. } Legal owner.
Ryot. A tenant: used in India.
Tenant. One who holds lands or tenements of a superior.
Tenant at will. One who holds during the will of the lord.
Tenant for life. One who holds during his own or another's life.

Tenant for years. One who holds for a certain, determinate period.
Tenant from year to year. A tenant who holds yearly.
Tenant on sufferance. One who held by legal right, but continues to hold after the expiration of the right.
Trustee. Any one who holds property in trust for another
Underlessee. An underleaser.
Vavasour. One who holds under a baron.
Zemindar. A landowner.

hold'-fast". A contrivance by which something is held in its place. CONNECTIVE.

hold'-ing. The act of possessing; that which is held by legal title. HOLDING-EXEMPTION, PROPERTY

HOLDING—EXEMPTION.

Chivalry. A tenure of land by knight's service.
Dependency. That which is attached to something else.
Exclusive possession. Right to hold to the exclusion of everybody else.
Fee. Property; possession.
Feodality. Feudal tenure.
Future possession. Ownership to become legal at some future time.
Heirship. The right of inheriting.
Heritage. An inheritance; a possession.
Hold. The act of holding.
Holding. The act or state of retaining; a tenure.
Impropriation. The act of putting an ecclesiastical benefice in the hands of a layman or lay corporation.
Inheritance. The act of inheriting; that which is or may be inherited.
Knight service. A tenure of land held by knights on condition of military service.
Monopoly. Exclusive possession.
Occupancy. The act of holding possession
Ownership, etc. The state of being an owner or possessor, etc. See PROPERTY.
Possession. The state of possessing or holding as one's own; the thing possessed.
Preoccupancy. The right of taking possession before another.
Prepossession. Prior possession.
Retention, etc. The act of retaining; the right of retaining property until the debt due the party be duly paid, etc. See KEEPING.
Reversion. A right to future possession or enjoyment.
Seigniority. The right by which a lord holds possession of his estates.
Seisin. Possession; possession of an estate of freehold.
Socage. A tenure of lands and tenements by a certain service.
Tenancy. A holding; tenure.
Tenure. The right of holding, as property.
Uti possidetis [L.]. The state of present possession.
Villanage. Tenure on condition of doing the meanest services for the lord.
Villenage. Villanage.

HOLDING—*Denotations.*

Bird in hand. A holding or possession to which one's right is certain.
Chose in possession. The object held.

HOLDING—*Noun of Cause.*

Nine points of the law. The holding of anything which gives a person strong ground for permanent possession.

HOLDING—*Verbs.*

Appertain to. To belong or relate to.
Be in one's possession. To be owned by one.
Belong to. To be the property of.
Be possessed of, etc. See *Adjectives.*
Come in for. To receive.
Come to. To be received by, as a fortune.
Command. To have within a sphere of control; to receive as a right.
Engross. To take or assume in undue quantity.
Enjoy. To possess and use with satisfaction.
Forestall. To take possession of in advance of somebody else.
Get into one's hand, etc. See GAIN.
Have. To possess or hold.
Have a firm hold of, etc. See KEEPING.
Have all to oneself. To be sole owner.
Have in hand, etc. See *Adjectives.*
Hold. To have or possess.
Impropriate. To place the profits of ecclesiastical property in the hands of laymen for distribution.

hold out. To affirm; promise; persevere in resistance, opposition, or the like; keep up exertions. ASSERTION-DENIAL, BRAVERY-COWARDICE, PERSISTENCE-

Absence, etc. Lack. See PRESENCE-ABSENCE.
Exemption. Freedom from any charge, burden, etc., to which others are subject.

EXEMPTION—*Verbs.*

Be without. See *Adjectives.*
Not have, etc. See HOLDING.

EXEMPTION—*Adjectives.*

Devoid of. Wanting; lacking.
Exempt from. Free from.
Not having, etc. See HOLDING.
Unacquired. Not having possession of.
Unblest with. Not endowed with.
Unobtained. Not having gained possession of.
Unpossessed. } Not owning.
Unpossessed of. } Not owning.
Untenanted, etc. See PRESENCE-ABSENCE.
Without. Devoid of; wanting.
Without an owner. Belonging to nobody.

HOLDING—*Verbs—Continued.*

Inherit. To take by descent from an ancestor.
Monopolize. To obtain exclusive possession of.
Occupy. To hold possession of.
Own, etc. To be the possessor of, etc. See PROPERTY
Pertain to. To belong or to to have relation to.
Possess. To have or hold as property.
Regrate. To buy in large quantities with a view to selling again near the same place at a higher price.
Vest in. To clothe with possession.

HOLDING—*Adjectives.*

At one's command. } In one's ownership or control.
At one's disposal. } In one's ownership or control.
Blest with. In possession of.
By one. In one's possession.
Charged with. Entrusted with or having the care of.
Endowed with. Enriched or furnished with something of the nature of a gift.
Fraught with. Laden or filled with.
In hand. }
In one's hand. }
In one's grasp. } Holding.
In one's possession. }
In possession of. }
Instinct with. Imbued or alive with.
In stock. } In hand.
In store. } In hand.
Laden with. Loaded or burdened with.
Master of. In control of.
One's own, etc. See PROPERTY
On hand. Ready.
Possessed, etc. See *Verbs.*
Possessed of. Having in possession.
Possessing. Owning.
Seized of. Possessed of.
Unshared. Not shared.
Unsold. Still in possession.
Worth. Having possessions or wealth equal to.

HOLDING—*Phrases.*

Entbehre gern was du nicht hast [G.]. Willingly renounce what you do not possess.
Meum et tuum [L.] Mine and thine.
Tuum est [L.]. It is thine.

WHIM, PROFFER-REFUSAL, REPRISAL-RESISTANCE; **hold out expectation,** ENGAGEMENT-RELEASE, PROPHECY; **hold out temptation,** DESIRE-DISTASTE.

hold up. To stop; cease; display. APPROVAL-DISAP-PROVAL, DAMPNESS-DRYNESS, DISCONTINUANCE-CONTINUANCE, OBSTRUCTION-HELP, PERSISTENCE-WHIM, POMP, SUSPENSION-SUPPORT; **hold up one's hand,** CHOICE-NEUTRALITY, SIGN; **hold up the mirror,** MANIFESTATION-LATENCY; **hold up to execration,** APPROVAL-DISAPPROVAL, CHARITABLENESS-CURSE; **hold up to scorn,** REGARD-SCORN; **hold up to shame,** REPUTATION-DISCREDIT; **hold up to view,** MANIFESTATION-LATENCY.

hole. A cavity extending into a solid mass; an aperture; a vile or squalid habitation; an opening. APERTURE-CLOSURE, CONTENTS-RECEIVER, DWELLER-HABITATION, EXPOSURE-HIDINGPLACE, EXTENSION-PLACE, INTERSPACE-CONTACT; **dust hole,** SECURITY-INSECURITY; **hole and corner,** APPROVAL-DISAPPROVAL, ENLIGHTENMENT-SECRECY, EXPOSURE-HIDINGPLACE, EXTENSION-PLACE, INVESTIGATION-ANSWER; **hole in one's coat,** ADULATION-DISPARAGEMENT, MARK-OBLITERATION; **hole to creep out of,** DIFFICULTY-FACILITY, ESCAPE, PRETEXT.

hol'-i-day. A day of exemption from labor; a day set apart for any celebration. DEVOTION-IDOLATRY, ENTERTAINMENT-WEARINESS, HURRY-LEISURE, TOIL-RELAXATION; **holiday task,** DIFFICULTY-FACILITY.

ho'-li-ness. Moral and spiritual purity and perfection. DIVINITY, GODLINESS-UNGODLINESS; **beauty of holiness,** GODLINESS-UNGODLINESS.

hol-loa'. An interjection used to attract attention. CRY-ULULATION; **holloa before one is out of the wood,** PRESUMPTION-OBSEQUIOUSNESS.

hol'-low. Having an empty space within; sunken; complete; deep and low in sound; insincere. CONVEXITY-CONCAVITY, DEEPNESS-SHALLOWNESS, ENTIRETY-DEFICIENCY, RESONANCE-NONRESONANCE, SUBSTANCE-NULLITY, TRUTHFULNESS-FALSEHOOD, VOCALIZATION-MUTENESS; **beat hollow,** SUCCESS-FAILURE; **hollow truce,** FIGHTING-CONCILIATION.

hol'-low-ness. The state of being hollow; deceitfulness. CONVEXITY-CONCAVITY, SUBSTANCE-NULLITY, TRUTHFULNESS-FRAUD.

hol'-ly. A shrub bearing glossy leaves and bright red berries, which are used for decorations. ENTERTAINMENT-WEARINESS.

holm. A small island in a river. SWAMP-ISLAND.

hol'-o-caust. Wholesale slaughter; a sacrifice, the whole of which is consumed by fire. DEVOTION-IDOLATRY, LIFE-KILLING.

hol'-o-graph. A document written wholly by the person in whose name it appears. WRITING-PRINTING.

hol''-o-he'-dral. Symmetrical. MINERALOGY.

hol''-o-he'-dron. Form of crystal. MINERALOGY.

holt. A group of trees. FAUNA-FLORA.

ho'-ly. Preeminently and absolutely good; pious; free from sin. DIVINITY, GODLINESS-UNGODLINESS; **holy breathing,** DEVOTION-IDOLATRY; **holy day,** CEREMONIAL; **Holy Ghost,** DIVINITY; **holy men of old,** REVELATION-PSEUDOREVELATION; **holy of holies,** FANE; **holy orders,** CHURCH; **holy place,** FANE; **Holy Scriptures,** REVELATION-PSEUDOREVELATION; **Holy Spirit,** DIVINITY; **holy table,** FANE; **holy water,** CEREMONIAL; **Holy Week,** CEREMONIAL; **temple of the Holy Ghost,** ORTHODOXY-HETERODOXY.

hom'-age. Deference; worship; submission. APPROVAL-DISAPPROVAL, DEVOTION-IDOLATRY, INSUBORDINATION-OBEDIENCE, REGARD-DISRESPECT, YIELDING.

hombre bueno no le busquen abolengo, al [Sp.] (om'-brê bu-en'-o no lê bus-quen' a-bol-en'-go, al). No one explores a good man's pedigree. PARENTAGE-PROGENY, REPUTATION-DISCREDIT.

home. One's fixed place of abode; a place of refuge;

closely. ARRIVAL-DEPARTURE, CONTENTEDNESS-DISCONTENTMENT, GATHERINGPLACE, OUTSIDE-INSIDE, REFUGE-PITFALL, REMOTENESS-NEARNESS, SUSPENSION-SUPPORT; **at home,** DIFFICULTY-FACILITY, GATHERING-SCATTERING, HARMONY-DISCORD, OUTSIDE-INSIDE, PRESENCE-ABSENCE, SOCIABILITY-PRIVACY; **at home in,** HABIT-DESUETUDE, KNOWLEDGE-IGNORANCE, SKILL-UNSKILFULNESS; **at home with,** AMITY-HOSTILITY; **be at home,** SOCIABILITY-PRIVACY; **bring home to,** EVIDENCE-COUNTEREVIDENCE, EXCULPATION-CONVICTION, FAITH-MISGIVING, JUSTIFICATION-CHARGE, RATIONALE-LUCK; **come home,** ARRIVAL-DEPARTURE; **eternal home,** HEAVEN-HELL; **feel at home,** CONTENTEDNESS-DISCONTENTMENT, LIBERTY-SUBJECTION, PLEASURE-PAIN, SOCIABILITY-PRIVACY; **from home,** PRESENCE-ABSENCE; **get home,** ARRIVAL-DEPARTURE; **go from home,** ARRIVAL-DEPARTURE; **go home,** ADVANCE-RETROGRESSION; **home stroke,** AGENCY; **home thrust,** ATTACK-DEFENSE, APPROVAL-DISAPPROVAL; **look at home,** JUSTIFICATION-CHARGE; **make oneself at home,** LIBERTY-SUBJECTION, SOCIABILITY-PRIVACY; **not be at home,** PROFFER-REFUSAL; **stay at home,** MOVEMENT-REST; **strike home,** VIGOR-INERTIA.

home'-bred''. Simple or uncultivated. TASTE-VULGARITY.

home'-felt''. Private; experienced inwardly. EMOTION, EXCITATION.

home'-less. Having no home. ESTABLISHMENT-REMOVAL, SOCIABILITY-PRIVACY.

home'-li-ness. Plainness. EMBELLISHMENT-SIMPLICITY, TASTE-VULGARITY.

home'-ly. Plain and simple; rude. BEAUTY-UGLINESS, EMBELLISHMENT-SIMPLICITY, GENTILITY-DEMOCRACY, SIMPLICITY-FLORIDNESS, TASTE-VULGARITY.

home'-made''. Of domestic manufacture. DOMESTICATION-AGRICULTURE.

ho'-me-o-path'-ic. Extremely small in quantity. GREATNESS-LITTLENESS, MAGNITUDE-SMALLNESS.

ho''-me-op'-a-thy. A system of medicine founded on the principle that "like cures like." REMEDY-BANE.

home'-sick''. Pining for home. CONTENTEDNESS-REGRET.

home'-sick''-en. To make homesick. CONTENTEDNESS-REGRET.

home'-spun''. Cloth or fabric woven at home. EMBELLISHMENT-SIMPLICITY, GENTILITY-DEMOCRACY, SIMPLICITY-FLORIDNESS, TASTE-VULGARITY, TEXTURE.

home'-stall'. A homestead. DWELLER-HABITATION.

home'-stead. The place of a home. DWELLER-HABITATION.

home'-ward-bound''. Returning home from abroad. ARRIVAL-DEPARTURE.

hom'-i-ci''-dal. Relating to homicide. LIFE-KILLING.

hom'-i-cide. The killing of or one who kills another person. LIFE-KILLING.

hom''-i-let'-ic-al. Pertaining to familiar discourse. SOCIABILITY-PRIVACY.

hom'-i-ly. A serious admonition; a textual discourse. CEREMONIAL, ESSAY.

hominem, argumentum ad [L.] (hom'-i-nem, ar-giu-men'-tum ad). An argument to the man. JUSTIFICATION-CHARGE.

homme propose et Dieu dispose [F.] (om pro-poz' ê diu dis-poz'). Man proposes and God disposes. RULE-LICENSE.

hom'-mock. A hummock. HEIGHT-LOWNESS.

ho''-mo-cen'-tric. Having a common center. CENTER.

ho''-mo-ge-ne'-i-ty. Identity or similarity of structure, kind, or composition. CONNECTION-INDEPENDENCE, MIXTURE-HOMOGENEITY, UNIFORMITY-DIVERSITY.

ho''-mo-ge'-ne-ous. Made up of similar elements. MINERALOGY, MIXTURE-HOMOGENEITY, UNIFORMITY-DIVERSITY.

ho″-mo-ge′-ne-ous-ness. The state of being uniform. UNIFORMITY-DIVERSITY.

ho″-mo-gen′-e-sis. A mode of reproduction in which the offspring is like the parent and passes through the same cycle of existence. CREATION-DESTRUCTION.

ho-mol′-o-gous. Similar. EQUALITY-INEQUALITY, UNIFORMITY-DIVERSITY.

ho-mol′-o-gy. Affinity dependent on structure or the essential correspondence of parts. CONNECTION-INDEPENDENCE, UNIFORMITY-DIVERSITY.

ho′-mo-nym. A word agreeing in sound but different in meaning from another. AMBIGUITY, SYNONYM-ANTONYM, VOCALIZATION-MUTENESS.

ho-mon′-y-mous. Of the same sound but a different sense. AMBIGUITY.

ho-mon′-y-my. Ambiguity. AMBIGUITY, SYNONYM-ANTONYM.

ho-moph′-o-nous. Single-voiced. MELODY-DISSONANCE.

ho-moph′-o-ny. Sameness of sound. MELODY-DISSONANCE.

ho-mun′-cu-lus. An undersized man. GREATNESS-LITTLENESS.

hone. An instrument for sharpening edged tools. SHARPNESS-BLUNTNESS.

hon′-est. Sincere; truthful; genuine. CRAFT-ARTLESSNESS, PURITY-IMPURITY, TRUTHFULNESS-FALSEHOOD, UPRIGHTNESS-DISHONESTY; honest meaning, MEANING-JARGON; honest truth, TRUTH-ERROR, TRUTHFULNESS-FALSEHOOD; turn an honest penny, GAIN-LOSS.

hon′-es-ty. Uprightness of conduct. CRAFT-ARTLESSNESS, TRUTHFULNESS-FALSEHOOD, UPRIGHTNESS-DISHONESTY.

hon′-ey. Sweetness in general; the dearest one. FAVORITE-ANGER, SWEETNESS-ACIDITY; milk and honey, WELFARE-MISFORTUNE.

hon′-ey–bee″. A bee that collects honey. FAUNA-FLORA.

hon′-ey-comb″. Anything full of holes or flaws; the wax cells containing the honey of bees, which have a concave bottom. APERTURE-CLOSURE, BETTERMENT-DETERIORATION, CONVEXITY-CONCAVITY.

hon′-ey-combed. Full of cells or perforations. APERTURE-CLOSURE, CONVEXITY-CONCAVITY.

hon′-eyed. Very sweet. SWEETNESS-ACIDITY.

hon′-eyed phra′-ses. Flattering words. ADULATION-DISPARAGEMENT, POLITENESS-IMPOLITENESS.

hon′-eyed words. Flattery ADULATION-DISPARAGEMENT, MOTIVE-CAPRICE.

hon′-ey-moon″. The first month after marriage; a period of enjoyment. BLANDISHMENT, MATRIMONY-CELIBACY, PLEASURE-PAIN.

hon′-ey–mouthed″. Persuasive; flattering. ADULATION-DISPARAGEMENT, POLITENESS-IMPOLITENESS.

hon′-ey-suck″-le. A sweet-scented flower. SWEETNESS-ACIDITY.

hon′-or. The esteem paid or due to worth; high rank or place; uprightness; glory; respect. APPROVAL-DISAPPROVAL, PATRIOTISM-TREASON, PROPERTY, REGARD-DISRESPECT, REPUTATION-DISCREDIT, TITLE, UPRIGHTNESS-DISHONESTY; affair of honor, STRIFE-PEACE; do honor to, SOLEMNIZATION; do the honors, POLITENESS-IMPOLITENESS, REGARD-DISRESPECT, SOCIABILITY-PRIVACY; his honor, JUDGE, TITLE; honor a bill, SETTLEMENT-DEFAULT; honor be to, REPUTATION-DISCREDIT; honor bright, TRUTHFULNESS-FALSEHOOD, UPRIGHTNESS-DISHONESTY; in honor of, SOLEMNIZATION; man of honor, UPRIGHTNESS-DISHONESTY; upon my honor, ASSERTION-DENIAL; word of honor, ENGAGEMENT-RELEASE; your honor, TITLE.

hon′-or-a-ble. Estimable; worthy of honor. OBSERVANCE-NONOBSERVANCE, REPUTATION-DISCREDIT, UPRIGHTNESS-DISHONESTY.

hon′-or-a-bly. In an honorable manner. UPRIGHTNESS-DISHONESTY.

hon″-o-ra′-ri-um. A voluntary fee paid to a professional man. GIVING-RECEIVING, RECOMPENSE-PUNITION.

hon′-or-a-ry. Given or conferred as an honor. COSTLINESS-CHEAPNESS.

honore, avito viret [L.] (ho-no′-rî, a-vai′-to vai′-ret). He flourishes in ancestral honor. REPUTATION-DISCREDIT.

hon′-ored. Regarded with esteem. REPUTATION-DISCREDIT.

honores mutant mores [L.] (ho-no′-rîz miu′-tant mo′-rîz). Honors change (men's) customs. MUTABILITY-STABILITY, OSTENTATION.

honor habet onus [L.] (ho′-nor hê′-bet o′-nus). Honor is onerous (i. e., has its responsibilities). DUTY-IMMUNITY.

hon″-or-if′-ic. Conferring honor. REPUTATION-DISCREDIT.

honor virtutis præmium [L.] (ho′-nor vir-tiu′-tis prî′-mi-um). Honor is the reward of virtue. RECOMPENSE-PUNITION, REPUTATION-DISCREDIT.

honte, mauvaise [F.] (hon·t, mo-vêz′). False modesty. CONCEIT-DIFFIDENCE.

hood. A covering for the head and shoulders. DRESS-UNDRESS, VESTMENTS.

hood′-lum. A ruffian. SAGE-FOOL.

hood′-wink. To impose upon; deceive; conceal; blindfold. ENLIGHTENMENT-SECRECY, KNOWLEDGE-IGNORANCE, SIGHT-BLINDNESS, TRUTHFULNESS-FRAUD.

hoof. The horny substance which encases the digits or foot in many mammals. ERECTNESS-FLATNESS; cloven hoof, SIGN.

hook. A piece of metal so bent as to fasten, sustain, or catch; to entrap; pilfer. CONNECTIVE, CURVATION-RECTILINEARITY, KEEPING-RELINQUISHMENT, SUSPENSION-SUPPORT, TAKING-RESTITUTION, TRUTHFULNESS-FRAUD, UNION-DISUNION; by hook or by crook, INSTRUMENTALITY.

hooked. Bent like a hook. CURVATION-RECTILINEARITY.

hook′-er. A two-masted Dutch vessel. CONVEYANCE-VESSEL.

hook′-ey, blind. A game of cards, in gambling. ENTERTAINMENT-WEARINESS.

hooks, go off the. To die. LIFE-DEATH.

hoop. A circular band of wood or metal; a shout. CIRCLE-WINDING, CRY-ULULATION, ELECTRICITY.

Hoo′-sier. A native of the State of Indiana. DWELLER-HABITATION, NAME-MISNOMER.

hoot. To utter contemptuous cries; jeer; mock. APPROVAL-DISAPPROVAL, CRY-ULULATION, REGARD-DISRESPECT, REGARD-SCORN.

hop. To move by short leaps. ENTERTAINMENT-WEARINESS, SPRING-DIVE; hop, skip, and jump, AGITATION, ENTERTAINMENT-WEARINESS, HURRY-LEISURE, SPRING-DIVE; hop the twig, LIFE-DEATH.

hope. Desire accompanied by expectation. DESIRE-DISTASTE, EXPECTATION-SURPRISE, SANGUINENESS-HOPELESSNESS; band of hope, TEETOTALISM-INTEMPERANCE; beyond all hope, WELFARE-MISFORTUNE; dash one's hopes, EXPECTATION-DISAPPOINTMENT, LIGHTHEARTEDNESS-DEJECTION; excite hope, PROPHECY; foster hope, SANGUINENESS-HOPELESSNESS; hope against hope, SANGUINENESS-HOPELESSNESS; hope deferred, LIGHTHEARTEDNESS-DEJECTION, SANGUINENESS-HOPELESSNESS; hope for, DESIRE-DISTASTE, EXPECTATION-SURPRISE; hope for the best, SANGUINENESS-HOPELESSNESS; well-grounded hope, LIKELIHOOD-UNLIKELIHOOD.

hope'-ful. Full of hope; promising success; a son or daughter. INFANT-VETERAN, LIGHTHEARTEDNESS-DEJECTION, LIKELIHOOD-UNLIKELIHOOD, SANGUINE-NESS-HOPELESSNESS.

hope'-ful-ly. In a hopeful manner. SANGUINENESS-HOPELESSNESS.

hope'-ful-ness. The state of being hopeful. SANGUINENESS-HOPELESSNESS.

hope'-less. Without hope. SANGUINENESS-HOPELESSNESS.

hope'-less-ness. The state of being without hope. POSSIBILITY-IMPOSSIBILITY, SANGUINENESS-HOPELESSNESS.

hop'-gar''-den. A hop-yard. DOMESTICATION-AGRICULTURE.

ho'-ping. Desiring for fulfilment. SANGUINENESS-HOPELESSNESS.

hop'-o'-my-thumb'. A dwarfish person. GREATNESS-LITTLENESS.

hop'-per. A funnel-shaped receiver. CONTENTS-RECEIVER.

hop'-scotch''. A game in which the players hop on one foot. ENTERTAINMENT-WEARINESS.

hora fugit [L.] (ho'-ra fiu'-jit). The hour flies. LASTINGNESS-TRANSIENTNESS.

ho'-ra-ry. Occurring hourly. PERIOD-PROGRESS.

horde. A gathered multitude. ASSOCIATION, GATHERING-SCATTERING, GENTILITY-DEMOCRACY.

ho-ri'-zon. The circular line where the earth and sky seem to meet; the bounds of observation. EXPECTATION-SURPRISE, REMOTENESS-NEARNESS, SIGHT-BLINDNESS; **gloomy horizon,** SANGUINENESS-HOPELESSNESS.

hor''-i-zon'-tal. On a level. ERECTNESS-FLATNESS.

hor''-i-zon-tal'-i-ty. The state or quality of being horizontal. ERECTNESS-FLATNESS.

hor''-i-zon'-tal-ly. In a horizontal manner. ERECTNESS-FLATNESS.

horn. The hard substance projecting from the heads of certain animals; a drinking-cup; a wind musical instrument. CONTENTS-RECEIVER, MUSICAL INSTRUMENTS, SHARPNESS-DULNESS; **draw in one's horns,** BIGOTRY-APOSTASY, SELFRESPECT-HUMBLENESS, YIELDING; **exalt one's horns,** REPUTATION-DISCREDIT; **horn-mad,** PARDON-JEALOUSY; **horn of plenty,** ENOUGH; **horns of a dilemma,** DIFFICULTY-FACILITY, RATIOCINATION-INSTINCT; **wear the horns,** MATRIMONY-DIVORCE.

horn'-book''. A single-leafed primer for children. SCHOOL.

hor'-net. One who gives constant annoyance. BENEFACTOR-EVILDOER; **hornet's nest,** APPROVAL-DISAPPROVAL, DIFFICULTY-FACILITY, PLEASURABLENESS-PAINFULNESS, REFUGE-PITFALL.

horn'-pipe''. A very lively English dance. ENTERTAINMENT-WEARINESS.

horn'-work''. A single-fronted work before a fortification. ATTACK-DEFENSE.

horn'-y. Like or of horn. HARDNESS-SOFTNESS.

hor'-o-loge. A timepiece. CHRONOLOGY-ANACHRONISM.

ho-rol'-o-gy. The science of measuring time. CHRONOLOGY-ANACHRONISM.

ho-rom'-e-try. The art of measuring time by hours. CHRONOLOGY-ANACHRONISM.

hor'-o-scope. A representation of the aspect of the heavens at a given time as a means to foretell future events. PROPHECY.

ho-ros'-co-py. The art of casting horoscopes. PROPHECY.

horrendum, informe, ingens, cui lumen ademptum, monstrum [L.] (hor-ren'-dum, in-for'-mî, in'-jens, quai lu'-men ad-emp'-tum, mons'-trum). A horrid monster, misshapen, gigantic, blind. BEAUTY-UGLINESS.

horresco referens [L.] (hor-res'-co ref'-er-enz). I shudder to relate. SANGUINENESS-TIMIDITY.

hor'-ri-ble. Causing terror; terrible; exciting abhorrence; huge; hideous. BEAUTY-UGLINESS, GOODNESS-BADNESS, PLEASURABLENESS-PAINFULNESS, SANGUINENESS-TIMIDITY.

hor'-ri-bly. So as to cause horror. MAGNITUDE-SMALLNESS.

hor'-rid. Causing horror; dreadful; very obnoxious; huge; terrible. BEAUTY-UGLINESS, GOODNESS-BADNESS, MAGNITUDE-SMALLNESS, PLEASURABLENESS-PAINFULNESS, SANGUINENESS-TIMIDITY.

horrida bella [L.] (hor'-ri-da bel'-la). Horrible wars. FIGHTING-CONCILIATION.

hor-rif'-ic. Causing horror; terrible; dreadful; huge; obnoxious. BEAUTY-UGLINESS, GOODNESS-BADNESS, MAGNITUDE-SMALLNESS, PLEASURABLENESS-PAINFULNESS, SANGUINENESS-TIMIDITY.

hor'-ri-fied. Frightened; filled with horror. PLEASURE-PAIN.

hor'-ri-fy. To fill with horror. LOVE-HATE, PLEASURABLENESS-PAINFULNESS, SANGUINENESS-HOPELESSNESS.

hor-ri''-pi-la'-tion. The peculiar shuddering sensation, resulting chiefly from sudden fright or horror. HEAT-COLD.

hor-ris'-o-nous. Sounding terribly. CACOPHONY.

hor'-ror. Extreme fear; dislike. DESIRE-DISTASTE, SANGUINENESS-TIMIDITY; **view with horror,** LOVE-HATE.

hor'-rors. The blues. LIGHTHEARTEDNESS-DEJECTION; **cup full of horrors,** PLEASURE-PAIN.

hor'-ror-strick''-en. Overcome with horror. PLEASURE-PAIN.

hors de combat [F.] (or de con'-ba'). Out of the struggle; disabled. HEALTH-SICKNESS, MIGHT-IMPOTENCE, USEFULNESS-USELESSNESS, WEARINESS-REFRESHMENT; **put *hors de combat*,** SUCCESS-FAILURE.

hors-d'oeuvre [F.] (or''-duvr'). A dish not forming a part of the regular course. NUTRIMENT-EXCRETION.

horse. A well-known domestic animal; a wooden frame with legs; cavalry; the male of a horse. BELLIGERENT, CONVEYER, FAUNA-FLORA, MALE-FEMALE, SUSPENSION-SUPPORT; **horse and foot,** BELLIGERENT; **horse artillery,** BELLIGERENT; **horse laugh,** JUBILATION-LAMENTATION; **horse marine,** ADEPT-BUNGLER; **horse soldier,** BELLIGERENT; **horse track,** WEAPON; **like a horse in a mill,** ENTERTAINMENT-WEARINESS, HABIT-DESUETUDE, STRIFE-PEACE; **put the horses to,** PREPARATION-NONPREPARATION; **put up one's horses at,** ESTABLISHMENT-REMOVAL; **put up one's horses together,** AMITY-HOSTILITY, VARIANCE-ACCORD; **ride the high horse,** PRESUMPTION-OBSEQUIOUSNESS; **take horse,** TRAVELING-NAVIGATION; **war-horse,** BELLIGERENT; **work like a horse,** TOIL-RELAXATION.

horse'-back''. The state of being on a horse. TRAVELING-NAVIGATION.

horse'-box''. A padded car for transporting horses. CONVEYANCE-VESSEL.

horse'-cloth''. A cloth to cover a horse. DRESS-UNDRESS.

horse'-man''. One who rides a horse. WAYFARER-SEAFARER.

horse'-man-ship. Equestrian skill. SKILL-UNSKILFULNESS, TRAVELING-NAVIGATION.

horse'-path''. A tow-path. WAY.

horse'-road''. A road for horses. WAY.

horse'-play''. Rough, boisterous play. SOCIETY-DERISION.

horse'-shoe''. A metal shoe for a horse's hoof. CURVATION-RECTILINEARITY.

hors l'honneur, tout est perdu [F.] (or lo-nur', tut e per-dü'). All is lost save honor. REPUTATION-DISCREDIT, SUCCESS-FAILURE.

hor-ta'-tion. Exhortation. MOTIVE-CAPRICE.

hor'-ta-tive. Encouraging. ADVICE, MOTIVE-CAPRICE.

hor'-ta-to-ry. Inciting. ADVICE, MOTIVE-CAPRICE.

hor''-ti-cul'-tur-al. Pertaining to gardening. DOMESTICATION-AGRICULTURE.

hor'-ti-cul''-ture. The art of cultivating gardens. DOMESTICATION-AGRICULTURE.

hor''-ti-cul'-tur-ist. A professional gardener. DOMESTICATION-AGRICULTURE.

hortus siccus [L.] (hor'-tus sic'-cus). An herbarium. ZOOLOGY-BOTANY.

ho-san'-na. An exclamation of praise to God. APPROVAL-DISAPPROVAL, DEVOTION-IDOLATRY.

hose. A stocking; a flexible tube or pipe. DRESS-UNDRESS, WATERCOURSE-AIRPIPE.

ho'-sier. One who deals in hose. DRESS-UNDRESS.

ho'-sier-y. Hosiers' wares. DRESS-UNDRESS.

hos'-pice. A place of entertainment or shelter. DWELLER-HABITATION, REMEDY-BANE.

hos'-pi-ta-ble. Ready with warm welcome; social. GENEROSITY-FRUGALITY, SOCIABILITY-PRIVACY.

hos'-pi-tal. A house for the reception and aid of the sick. REMEDY-BANE; in hospital, HEALTH-SICKNESS.

hos''-pi-tal'-i-ty. The state or quality of being hospitable. GENEROSITY-FRUGALITY, SOCIABILITY-PRIVACY.

hos'-po-dar. A title of dignity borne by the Emperor of Russia. CHIEF-UNDERLING.

host. A great number; an army; one who entertains a guest; the consecrated wafer used in the sacrament of the Lord's Supper. BELLIGERENT, CEREMONIAL, FRIEND-FOE, GATHERING-SCATTERING, MULTIPLICITY-PAUCITY; host in himself, DOMINANCE-IMPOTENCE; host of heaven, ANGEL-SATAN; reckon without one's host, RECKLESSNESS-CAUTION, SKILL-UNSKILFULNESS, SUCCESS-FAILURE, TRUTH-ERROR.

hos'-tage. A person left in the hands of the enemy as a pledge. SECURITY.

hos'-tel. A hostelry. DWELLER-HABITATION.

hos'-tel-ry. A house of lodging and entertainment. DWELLER-HABITATION.

host'-ess. A female host. MALE-FEMALE.

hos'-tile. Antagonistic; having a spirit of enmity. AMITY-HOSTILITY, ANTAGONISM-CONCURRENCE, HARMONY-DISCORD, SAMENESS-CONTRAST; hostile meeting, STRIFE-PEACE; in hostile array, ANTAGONISM-CONCURRENCE.

hos-til'-i-ties. Warlike measures. FIGHTING-CONCILIATION.

hos-til'-i-ty. Enmity. AMITY-HOSTILITY.

hos'-tler. A man who takes care of horses. CHIEF-UNDERLING.

hot. High in temperature; pungent; marked by passion; violent; fiery. BLUENESS-ORANGE, EXCITATION, FAVORITE-MOROSENESS, HEAT-COLD, PUNGENCY, REDNESS-GREENNESS, TURBULENCE-CALMNESS; blood-hot, HEAT-COLD; blow hot and cold, BIGOTRY-APOSTASY, DETERMINATION-VACILLATION, PERSISTENCE-WHIM, RATIOCINATION-INSTINCT, TRUTHFULNESS-FALSEHOOD; hot blast, CHEMISTRY; hot blood, FAVORITE-ANGER, FAVORITE-QUARRELSOMENESS; hot water, DIFFICULTY-FACILITY, PLEASURABLENESS-PAINFULNESS, VARIANCE-ACCORD; in hot haste, HURRY-LEISURE; in hot pursuit, QUEST-EVASION; make hot, HEATING-COOLING.

hot'-bed''. A place which favors rapid growth and development. CAUSE-EFFECT, CENTER, WORKSHOP.

hot'-blood''-ed. Easily angered. RECKLESSNESS-CAUTION.

hot'-brained''. Having a violent temper. RECKLESSNESS-CAUTION.

hotch'-pot''. A confused mixture. MIXTURE-HOMOGENEITY, PARTICIPATION, REGULARITY-IRREGULARITY.

hotch'-potch''. A confused mixture. REGULARITY-IRREGULARITY.

ho-tel'. A house for the entertainment of travelers and others. DWELLER-HABITATION.

Hôtel des Invalides [F.] (o-tel' dez an'-va-lîd'). Home for invalids (*i. e.*, invalid soldiers). BELLIGERENT, HEALTH-SICKNESS.

hôtel de ville [F.] (o-tel' de vîl). Town-hall. DWELLER-HABITATION.

hot'-head''-ed. Of violent or hasty temper. EXCITABILITY-INEXCITABILITY, HURRY-LEISURE, RECKLESSNESS-CAUTION.

hot'-house''. A covered building heated for rearing plants. DOMESTICATION-AGRICULTURE, OVEN-REFRIGERATOR, WORKSHOP.

hot'-press'. To iron. SMOOTHNESS-ROUGHNESS.

hot'-spur. A hot-headed fellow. RECKLESSNESS-CAUTION.

Hot'-ten-tot. A South African native. GENTILITY-DEMOCRACY.

hough. To disable by cutting the sinews of the ham. BETTERMENT-DETERIORATION.

hound. A dog used in the chase; a dastardly fellow; to hunt; pursue relentlessly and persistently. CHARITABLENESS-MALEVOLENCE, FAUNA-FLORA, GOOD MAN-BAD MAN, QUEST-EVASION; hold with the hare but run with the hounds, BIGOTRY-APOSTASY; hound on, MOTIVE-CAPRICE.

houppelande [F.] (hup-lan·d'). A greatcoat. DRESS-UNDRESS.

hour. One twenty-fourth of a civil day; a set or appointed time. ETERNITY-INSTANTANEITY, MEASURE, PERIOD-PROGRESS, TIME; hour after hour, LASTINGNESS-TRANSIENTNESS; improve the shining hour, ACTIVITY-INDOLENCE; one's hour is come, LIFE-DEATH, OPPORTUNENESS-INOPPORTUNENESS.

hour'-an''-gle. Term used in astronomy. ASTRONOMY.

hour'-cir''-cle. Astronomical term. ASTRONOMY.

hour'-glass''. An instrument for measuring time. BREADTH-NARROWNESS, CHRONOLOGY-ANACHRONISM, ENLARGEMENT-DIMINUTION.

hou'-ri. A nymph of Paradise in Moslem belief. BEAUTY-UGLINESS.

hour'-ly. Frequently; occurring every hour. DURATION-NEVERNESS, FREQUENCY-RARITY, PERIODICITY-IRREGULARITY, RECURRENCE.

house. A place of abode; a family of kindred; one of the divisions of a legislative body; the body of people constituting an audience; to shelter. ACTING, ASSOCIATION, COUNCIL, DWELLER-HABITATION, ESTABLISHMENT-REMOVAL, PARENTAGE-PROGENY, SECURITY-INSECURITY; bring the house about one's ears, SKILL-UNSKILFULNESS; eat out of house and home, EXTRAVAGANCE-AVARICE, FASTING-GLUTTONY; house divided against itself, VARIANCE-ACCORD; house of cards, STRENGTH-WEAKNESS, TOUGHNESS-BRITTLENESS; house of correction, RECOMPENSE-SCOURGE, RELEASE-PRISON; house of death, LIFE-FUNERAL; house of detention, RELEASE-PRISON; house of God, FANE; House of Lords, GENTILITY-DEMOCRACY; House of Peers, GENTILITY-DEMOCRACY; house of prayer, FANE; keep house, ESTABLISHMENT-REMOVAL; set one's house in order, ATONEMENT, PREPARATION-NONPREPARATION; turn house out of windows, VARIANCE-ACCORD.

house'-break''-er. One who breaks into a house with felonious intent. ROBBER.

house'-break''-ing. The act of breaking into a house. THEFT.

house'-dog''. A watch-dog. FAUNA-FLORA, WARNING.

house'-hold''. A family living together. DWELLER-HABITATION, HABIT-DESUETUDE; household gods, DWELLER-HABITATION; household stuff, MATERIALS; household troops, BELLIGERENT; household words, KNOWLEDGE-IGNORANCE, LANGUAGE, SIMPLICITY-FLORIDNESS.

house'-hold''-er. One who occupies a house. DWELL-ER-HABITATION.

house'-keep''-er. One who has the chief care over a house or family. MANAGER.

house'-keep''-ing. The management of household affairs. CONDUCT.

house'-less. Without a house. ESTABLISHMENT-REMOVAL.

house'-maid''. A girl or woman who does housework. CHIEF-UNDERLING.

house'-room''. Room in a house. EXTENSION-INEXTENSION.

house'-top''. The roof of a house. TOP-BOTTOM; **proclaim from the housetop,** PUBLICITY.

house'-warm''-ing. An entertainment on the occasion of taking possession of a new house. SOCIABILITY-PRIVACY.

house'-wife''. The mistress of a household. ACTIVITY-INDOLENCE.

house'-wife''-ry. Female management of domestic affairs. CONDUCT, GENEROSITY-FRUGALITY.

hous'-ing. The act of providing with a house; a short mantle worn about the head and shoulders; the ornamental trappings of a horse. COVER-LINING, DRESS-UNDRESS, DWELLER-HABITATION.

hov'-el. A wretched dwelling. DWELLER-HABITATION.

hov'-er. To hang fluttering over; move about threateningly; remain in an irresolute state. ASCENT-DESCENT, DETERMINATION-VACILLATION, HEIGHT-LOWNESS, TRAVELING-NAVIGATION; **hover about,** MOVEMENT-REST; **hover over,** REMOTENESS-NEARNESS.

how. In what way; by what means. MEANS, WAY; **how comes it,** INVESTIGATION-ANSWER, RATIONALE-LUCK; **how now,** ASTONISHMENT-EXPECTANCE.

how-be'-it. Be it as it may. COMPENSATION.

how-ev'-er. To whatever degree; nevertheless. COMPENSATION, CONVENTIONALITY-UNCONVENTIONALITY, QUANTITY-MEASURE.

how'-itz-er. A short, light cannon. WEAPON.

how'-ker. A two-masted Dutch vessel; a hooker. CONVEYANCE-VESSEL.

howl. The cry of a dog, wolf, or similar animal; a cry of pain or grief. CRY-ULULATION, JUBILATION-LAMENTATION.

howl'-ing wil'-der-ness. A desert region filled with wild beasts. FERTILITY-STERILITY, SOCIABILITY-PRIVACY.

how''-so-ev'-er. In what manner. QUANTITY-MEASURE.

hoy. A heavy coasting-vessel. CONVEYANCE-VESSEL.

hoy'-den. A romping or bold girl. INFANT-VETERAN, TASTE-VULGARITY.

hub'-bub. A confused noise or noisy disorder. AGITATION, LOUDNESS-FAINTNESS, VARIANCE-ACCORD.

huck'-ster. A small retailer. DEALER, EXCHANGE.

hud'-dle. To throng or crowd in a disorderly manner; embrace; throw into disorder. GATHERING-SCATTERING, ORGANIZATION-DISORGANIZATION, REGULARITY-IRREGULARITY, REMOTENESS-NEARNESS; **huddle on,** DRESS-UNDRESS.

Hu''-di-bras'-tic. Verse in the style of *Hudibras;* burlesque, heroic and satirical. POETRY-PROSE, SOCIETY-DERISION.

hue. The particular shade of a color. COLOR-ACHROMATISM; **hue and cry,** ALARM, APPROVAL-DISAPPROVAL, CRY-ULULATION, PUBLICITY, QUEST-EVASION; **raise a hue and cry,** APPROVAL-DISAPPROVAL, PUBLICITY.

hue'-less. Without hue. COLOR-ACHROMATISM.

huff. A sudden rise of anger; a fit of arrogance. FAVORITE-ANGER, PRESUMPTION-OBSEQUIOUSNESS.

huff'-y. Marked by petulance. FAVORITE-QUARRELSOMENESS.

hug. To press in close embrace; hold fast with affection; cling to; keep close to the shore. BLANDISHMENT, COHESION-LOOSENESS, KEEPING-RELINQUISHMENT, LOVE-HATE, POLITENESS-IMPOLITENESS, REMOTENESS-NEARNESS; **hug a belief,** BIGOTRY-APOSTASY; **hug a sin,** VIRTUE-VICE; **hug oneself,** CONTENTEDNESS-DISCONTENTMENT, JUBILATION-LAMENTATION, PLEASURE-PAIN, SELFRESPECT-HUMBLENESS; **hug the shore,** APPROACH-WITHDRAWAL, TRAVELING-NAVIGATION.

huge. Enormous in size or degree. GREATNESS-LITTLENESS, MAGNITUDE-SMALLNESS.

huge'-ness. Magnitude. GREATNESS-LITTLENESS.

hug'-ger-mug'-ger. To proceed secretly. ENLIGHTENMENT-SECRECY.

Hu'-gue-not. A French Protestant of the 16th and 17th centuries. ORTHODOXY-HETERODOXY.

huis clos, à [F.] (üî clo, a). With closed doors. ENLIGHTENMENT-SECRECY.

huissier [F.] (uî-siê'). An usher. JUDICATURE.

huke. A 15th century garment. DRESS-UNDRESS.

hulk. The body of a ship unfit for service; a large ship of clumsy make. CONVEYANCE-VESSEL, WHOLE-PART.

hulk'-ing. Bulky; unwieldy. BEAUTY-UGLINESS, GREATNESS-LITTLENESS.

hulk'-y. Bulky; unwieldy; clumsy. BEAUTY-UGLINESS, GREATNESS-LITTLENESS, PROPRIETY-IMPROPRIETY.

hull. The body of a vessel. WHOLE-PART.

hul''-la-ba-loo'. A loud and confused noise. CRY-ULULATION, LOUDNESS-FAINTNESS.

hum. A low, monotonous, buzzing sound; to sing with the mouth closed; impose upon. CRASH-DRUMMING, CRY-ULULATION, LOUDNESS-FAINTNESS, MUSICIAN, TRUTHFULNESS-FABRICATION, TRUTHFULNESS-FRAUD; **busy hum of men,** ACTIVITY-INDOLENCE; **hum and haw,** DETERMINATION-VACILLATION, SPEECH-INARTICULATENESS.

hu'-man. Belonging or pertaining to man. HUMANITY; **human race,** ETHNOLOGY, HUMANITY; **human sacrifice,** DEVOTION-IDOLATRY; **human species,** ETHNOLOGY.

hu-mane'. Kind, tender, and compassionate. CHARITABLENESS-MALEVOLENCE, COMPASSION-RUTHLESSNESS, HUMANITARIANISM-MISANTHROPY.

hu-man''-i-ta'-ri-an. Pertaining to humanitarianism; a philanthropist. COMPASSION-RUTHLESSNESS, HUMANITARIANISM-MISANTHROPY, HUMANITY.

hu-man''-i-ta'-ri-an-ism. The doctrines or principles of the humanitarians. HUMANITARIANISM-MISANTHROPY.

HUMANITARIANISM—MISANTHROPY.

Amor patriæ [L.]. Love of country.

Benevolence. Love of mankind; a desire to promote happiness.

Chivalry. The character of knights; disinterested courtesy.

Civism. The state of citizenship.

Commonweal. The state or people of the state.

Communism. A scheme for equalizing social conditions.

Cosmopolitanism. The system of one whose interests and affections are world-wide.

Cynicism. Contempt for the opinions of others and of what others value.

Egotism, etc. A speaking or writing too much of oneself; self-conceit, etc. See UNSELFISHNESS-SELFISHNESS.

Incivism. Lack of patriotism or love for one's country.

Misanthropy. Dislike or hatred of mankind; opposed to philanthropy.

Moroseness, etc. Sourness of temper or disposition, etc. See FAVORITE-MOROSENESS.

HUMANITARIANISM—MISANTHROPY—*Continued,*

Deliciæ humani generis [L.]. The delight of the human race. [The appellation of the Roman Emperor Titus.]

Generosity, etc. Self-forgetful kindness in disposition and action, etc. See UNSELFISHNESS.

Humanitarianism. The system holding that one's duty is limited to the advancement of the human race.

Humanity. The state of being humane or compassionate.

Knight-errantry. The customs and actions of knights errant; chivalry.

Love of country. Disposition to do everything for the best interests of one's country.

Nationality. The state of being strongly attached to one's country.

Patriotism. Devotion to one's country and its welfare.

Philanthropy. Love of mankind accompanied by a disposition to promote happiness.

Public spirit. Devotion to the interests of the community or public.

Socialism. A system of social reform contemplating the complete reconstruction of society, with a more equal distribution of labor and property.

Social science. The science treating of social problems and conditions.

The greatest happiness of the greatest number. [The motto of a prominent party in English politics.]

Universal benevolence. All-pervading love of mankind.

Utilitarianism. The doctrine which makes the greatest good to the greatest number the end and criterion of action and basis of morality

HUMANITARIANISM—*Nouns of Agent.*

Amicus humani generis [L.]. A friend of the human race.

Benthamite. A believer in the utilitarian doctrines taught by Jeremy Bentham.

Citizen of the world. One who is at home and claims his rights everywhere.

Communist. One who advocates the theory or practise of communism.

Cosmopolite. One who is at home in all parts of the world; a citizen of the world.

Knight errant. A wandering knight in search of adventures connected with the safety of others.

Patriot. One who is devoted to his country.

Philanthropist. One who seeks to promote the welfare of others.

Socialist. An adherent to the doctrines of socialism.

Utilitarian. One who believes in utilitarianism.

HUMANITARIANISM—*Adjectives.*

Chivalric. Pertaining to chivalry; knightly

Cosmopolitan. Free from local prejudices.

hu-man′-i-ties. Learning and literature concerned with human culture; the classical branches of study. LANGUAGE.

hu-man′-i-ty. The human race; mankind. CHARITABLENESS - MALEVOLENCE, COMPASSION - RUTHLESSNESS, HUMANITARIANISM-MISANTHROPY, HUMANITY.

HUMANITY

Cosmopolite. A person at home everywhere; one familiar with all parts of the world.

Creature. A living being regarded as created.

Dramatis personæ [L.]. The characters in a play; hence, the characters in the play of life.

Earthling. A dweller on the earth.

Fellow creature. A created being.

Folk. People in general.

Generation. The body of persons existing at the same time or period.

Human being. One of the human race

Humanity.
Human nature. } The character of mankind.

Human race.
Human species. } Mankind collectively.

Individual. A human being.

Lords of creation. The race of man.

Man. A representative of the human race.

Mankind. The whole human species.

Mortal. A living person.

Mortality. The world of human beings subject to death.

One. A single person.

Ourselves. We human beings.

People. The human race.

MISANTHROPY—*Nouns of Agent.*

Cynic. One of a group of philosophers who despised riches, the arts, the sciences, and the usages of society.

Diogenes. A Greek cynic philosopher. [412?–323 B. C.]

Egotist. One caring only for himself and his own opinions.

Man-hater. A hater of mankind; a misanthrope.

Misanthrope. One who hates mankind.

Misogynist. A woman-hater.

Timon. The cynical hero of Shakespeare's *Timon of Athens;* also a hater of mankind described by Plutarch and Lucian.

Woman-hater. A hater of womankind; a misogynist.

MISANTHROPY—*Adjectives.*

Antisocial. Hostile or averse to society.

Egotistical, etc. Referring to self often, etc. See UNSELFISHNESS-SELFISHNESS.

Inhumane. Hard-hearted.

Misanthropic. Hating mankind.

Morose, etc. Having a sour temper or sullen disposition, etc. See FAVORITE-MOROSENESS.

Unpatriotic. Not patriotic; having no love of country.

HUMANITARIANISM—ADJECTIVES—*Continued.*

Generous, etc. Having nobleness of mind or kindness in disposition and action, etc. See UNSELFISHNESS.

Humane. Disposed to treat other human beings or animals with kindness.

Humanitarian. Relating to humanitarianism.

Large-hearted, etc. Kind; generous, etc. See CHARITABLENESS.

Patriotic. Unselfishly devoted to one's country and its interests.

Philanthropic. Characterized by philanthropy.

Public-spirited. Disposed to advance the public interests or those of the community.

Utilitarian. Pertaining to utilitarianism.

HUMANITARIANISM—*Phrases.*

Ducit amor patriæ [L.]. Love of country leads (me).

Humani nihil a me alienum puto [L.]. I believe that nothing human is foreign to me. [Terence, *Heauton*, 1, 1, 25.]

Omne solum forti patria [L.]. Every soil is fatherland to the brave man. [Ovid, *Fasti*, 1, 493.]

Pro aris et focis [L.]. For our altars and firesides. [Cicero, *N. D.*,3, 40.]

Pro bono publico [L.]. For the public welfare.

Un bien fait n'est jamais perdu [F.]. A kind act is never lost.

Vincet amor patriæ [L.]. Love of country will conquer. [Virgil, *Æneid*, 6, 823.]

Person. A human being

Personage. An individual being.

Persons. The human race.

Society. The collective body of the human race.

HUMANITY—*Collective Nouns.*

Body politic. The body of citizens constituting the state.

Commonweal. The community or commonwealth.

Commonwealth. The whole people of a state as united under a government for the common good.

Community. The people who reside in one locality and are subject to the same laws, etc.

Community at large. The body of people constituting a state

General public. The people collectively.

Million. The mass of people. See GENTILITY-DEMOCRACY

Nation. The people associated together and organized under one civil government.

Nationality. A people who possess national independence and unity.

Party. A number or company of persons joined by common interests.

Population. The whole number of people in a place. See DWELLER.

Public. The people collectively.

Realm. The people under the rule of a sovereign.

Republic. A representative democracy; a community of persons devoted to the same cause.

State. The political community organized under a distinct government.

HUMANITY—*Figurative Nouns.*

Body. The entire physical part of man; hence, a man.

Flesh. The muscular part of the body; hence, the human race

Hand. A part of the fore limb in man; hence, a person.

Head. The part of an animal that contains the brain and the organs of special sense; hence, a person.

Living soul. The incorporeal or indestructible nature of man; hence, a person.

Soul. See LIVING SOUL.

World. The created universe; hence, the human race

HUMANITY—*Scientific Nouns*

Anthropogeny. The science of the origin and development of man.

Anthropography. The study of the physical characteristics, language, institutions, and customs of the human race.

Anthropology. The science of the physical facts concerning man and his development and history.

Anthroposophy. Knowledge of the anatomy and physiology of man.

Ethnography. The science which treats of man geographically, of the causes of migration, etc.

Ethnology. The science of the natural races and families of man.

Humanitarian. One who studies the interests of the human race, for philanthropic and humane reasons.

HUMANITY—*Adjectives.*

Anthropoid. Manlike.

Civic. Pertaining to a city, citizen, or citizenship.

Cosmopolitan. Common to all the world.

Human. Having the qualities or attributes of man.

Individual. Characteristic of a single person.

Mortal. Belonging to man.

National. Common to a whole people or race.

Personal. Pertaining to a particular person.

Public. Belonging to the people.

Social. Relating to the public as an aggregate body

hu′-man-ize. To render capable of humane actions. POLITENESS-IMPOLITENESS.

humano capiti cervicem jungere equinam [L.] (hiu-mê′-no cap′-i-tai ser′-vi-sem jun′-jer-î î-quai′-nam). To join a horse's neck to a human head. HARMONY-DISCORD.

hum′-ble. Modest; meek; unobtrusive. CONCEIT-DIFFIDENCE, HEAVEN-HELL, SELFRESPECT-HUMBLENESS, YIELDING; **eat humble pie,** YIELDING; **humble oneself,** DEVOTION-IDOLATRY, REPENTANCE-OBDURACY, SELFRESPECT-HUMBLENESS; **your humble servant,** ASSENT-DISSENT, PROFFER-REFUSAL.

hum′-bled. Reduced in pride. SELFRESPECT-HUMBLENESS.

hum′-ble-mind″-ed. Lowly in mind. SELFRESPECT-HUMBLENESS.

hum′-ble-ness. The state or quality of being humbled. SELFRESPECT-HUMBLENESS.

hum′-bler class′-es. Lower orders. GENTILITY-DEMOCRACY.

hum′-bly. In a humble manner. CONCEIT-DIFFIDENCE.

hum′-bug″. A sham; fraud; one who deceives. CONSEQUENCE, INSIGNIFICANCE, GULL-DECEIVER, TRUTHFULNESS-FALSEHOOD, TRUTHFULNESS-FRAUD.

hum′-drum″. Monotonous; listless. ENTERTAINMENT-WEARINESS, WITTINESS-DULNESS.

hu′-mect. To moisten. DAMPNESS-DRYNESS.

hu-mec′-tate. To moisten. DAMPNESS-DRYNESS.

hu″-mec-ta′-tion. The act of moistening. DAMPNESS-DRYNESS, WATER-AIR.

hu′-me-rus. Upper arm-bone. ANATOMY.

hu′-mid. Containing sensible moisture. DAMPNESS-DRYNESS.

hu-mil′-i-ate. To lower in esteem. SELFRESPECT-HUMBLENESS.

hu-mil′-i-a″-ting. Mortifying. REPUTATION-DISCREDIT.

hu-mil″-i-a′-tion. A low or humble condition; shame; the act of lowering in esteem. DEVOTION-IDOLATRY, REPUTATION-DISCREDIT, SELFRESPECT-HUMBLENESS; **self-humiliation,** REPENTANCE-OBDURACY.

hu-mil′-i-ty. Freedom from pride. CONCEIT-DIFFIDENCE, GODLINESS-UNGODLINESS, PRESUMPTION-OBSEQUIOUSNESS, SELFRESPECT-HUMBLENESS.

hum′-ming-top″. A toy that hums while rotating on a point. MUSICAL INSTRUMENTS.

hum′-mock. A small elevation. CONVEXITY-CONCAVITY, HEIGHT-LOWNESS.

hum′-mock-y. Hilly CONVEXITY-CONCAVITY

hu′-mor. Disposition of mind or feeling; an animal fluid; a facetious turn of mind; playful fancy; to adapt oneself to; manage by concession. ADULATION-DISPARAGEMENT, AFFECTIONS, DIFFICULTY-FACILITY, DOMINANCE-IMPOTENCE, LEAVE-PROHIBITION, LIQUID-GAS, OBSTRUCTION-HELP, PERSISTENCE-WHIM, PLEASURABLENESS-PAINFULNESS, READINESS-RELUCTANCE, RHETORIC, SUBJECTIVENESS-OBJECTIVENESS, WITTINESS-DULNESS; **in the humor,** READINESS-RELUCTANCE; **out of humor,** FAVORITE-MOROSENESS; **peccant humor,** CLEANNESS-FILTHINESS, HEALTH-SICKNESS.

hu′-mor-ist. One who has a playful fancy. WAG.

hu′-mor-ous. Adapted to excite laughter. RHETORIC, WITTINESS-DULNESS.

hu′-mor-some. Full of whims; capricious. FAVORITE-MOROSENESS, PERSISTENCE-WHIM.

hump. The protuberance formed by a crooked back. CONVEXITY-CONCAVITY.

hump′-backed″. Having a crooked back. PROPORTION-DEFORMITY.

humph. An exclamation of doubt or dissatisfaction. ASTONISHMENT-EXPECTANCE.

Hum′-phrey, dine with Duke. To go without dinner. FASTING-GLUTTONY, SOLITUDE-COMPANY.

hunch. A hump. CONVEXITY-CONCAVITY.

hunch′-backed″. Humpbacked. PROPORTION-DEFORMITY.

hun′-dred. A number; a subdivision of a county. EXTENSION-DISTRICT, FIVE-QUINQUESECTION, MULTIPLICITY-PAUCITY.

hun′-dredth. One of a hundred equal parts. FIVE-QUINQUESECTION.

hun′-dred-weight″. A hundred pounds. HEAVINESS-LIGHTNESS, MEASURE.

hun′-ger. A craving or strong desire for food. DESIRE-DISTASTE; **hunger after,** DESIRE-DISTASTE.

hun′-gry. Suffering for want of food. DESIRE-DISTASTE, FASTING-GLUTTONY.

hunks. A covetous man. EXTRAVAGANCE-AVARICE.

hunt. To make a close search; pursuit for the purpose of killing. INVESTIGATION-ANSWER, LIFE-KILLING, QUEST-EVASION; **hunt after,** QUEST-EVASION; **hunt down,** CHARITABLENESS-MALEVOLENCE; **hunt in couples,** ANTAGONISM-CONCURRENCE; **hunt out,** DISCOVERY, INVESTIGATION-ANSWER; **hunt the slipper,** ENTERTAINMENT-WEARINESS.

hunt′-er. An animal used in hunting; a person who hunts. CONVEYER, LIFE-KILLING, QUEST-EVASION; **place-hunter,** PETITIONER; **pot-hunter,** PETITIONER.

hunt′-ing. Pursuit of game for sport and with intent to kill. LIFE-KILLING, QUEST-EVASION.

hunt′-ing-ground″. A place where hunting is carried on. ENTERTAINMENT-WEARINESS.

hunts′-man. One who hunts. LIFE-KILLING, QUEST-EVASION.

hur′-dle. A framework on which criminals were dragged to the place of execution. CONVEYANCE-VESSEL.

hur′-dy-gur″-dy. A stringed musical instrument. MUSICAL INSTRUMENTS.

hurl. To throw with violence. PUSH-PULL; **hurl defiance at,** DEFIANCE.

hurler avec les loups [F.] (hür-lê′ a-vec′ lê lu). To howl with the wolves. CONVENTIONALITY-UNCONVENTIONALITY, VARIANCE-ACCORD.

Hur-lo-thrum′-bo. A burlesque opera by Samuel Johnson; absurdity and nonsense. SANGUINENESS-TIMIDITY.

hur′-ly-bur″-ly. Tumult. AGITATION.

hur-rah′. A shout of joy or triumph. JUBILATION-LAMENTATION, LIGHTHEARTEDNESS-DEJECTION.

hur′-ri-cane. A violent gale. RIVER-WIND; **hurricane deck,** TOP-BOTTOM.

hur'-ried. Showing haste; urged on. Excitability-Inexcitability, Hurry-Leisure.

hur'-ry. To hasten; haste. Excitability-Inexcitability, Hurry-Leisure, Swiftness-Slowness;

hurry forward, Hurry-Leisure; **hurry of spirits,** Emotion; **hurry off with,** Taking-Restitution; **hurry on,** Motive-Caprice.

HURRY—LEISURE.

Acceleration. The act of increasing speed.
Brusquerie [F.]. The quality of being rough or rude in manner or speech.
Bustle. Activity with excitement and hurry.
Dash. Quickness of execution.
Despatch. The act of doing anything promptly and quickly.
Dispatch. Despatch.
Drive. Pressure demanding prompt action or attention.
Fidget. Restlessness.
Flurry. Sudden commotion or excitement.
Flutter. Rapid irregular motion.
Forced march. A quick march by great exertion.
Fuss. Annoying display of activity.
Haste. Quickness of motion.
Hurry. Confused haste.
Impetuosity. Want of reflection; driving or rushing with violence.
Precipitancy. The quality of being rash or headlong.
Precipitation. Headlong haste or hurry.
Precipitousness, etc. A moving onward rapidly and hurriedly. See *Adjectives.*
Rush. A moving forward with haste.
Scramble. Any disorderly or hurried performance.
Spirt. See Spurt.
Splutter. Hastiness.
Spurt. An increase of speed or energy for a short time.
Urgency. Condition of demanding immediate action.
Velocity, etc. Swiftness; celerity, etc. See Swiftness.

Hurry—Verbs.

Accelerate. To quicken the motion of anything; to hasten.
Be in a hurry. See *Nouns.*
Be in haste. See *Nouns.*
Be precipitate, etc. To be in a hurry, etc. See *Adjectives.*
Bestir oneself, etc. To quicken one's movements. See Activity.
Bundle on. To dispose of in a hurried manner.
Bustle. To hurry; hustle.
Dash forward. To hasten ahead.
Dash off. To hurry away.
Dash onward. To hasten in advance.
Dart to and fro. To move quickly from place to place
Expedite. To hasten the process of.
Flutter. To move with quick vibrating motion.
Hasten. To act so as to take less time.
Have not a moment to lose. ⎫
Have not a moment to spare. ⎬ To be in a hurry.
Have no time to lose. ⎪
Have no time to spare. ⎭
Hurry. To hasten with some confusion.
Hurry forward. To hasten ahead.
Hurry onward. To hasten in advance.
Jump at. To be eager after.
Lose no time. To squander no time; to hurry.
Lose not a moment. ⎫ To hurry.
Lose not an instant. ⎭
Make a dash. ⎫ See *Nouns.*
Make haste. ⎭
Make short work of. To do away with quickly.
Make the best of one's time. To do as much as possible in a short time.
Make the best of one's way. To go as far as possible in a certain time.
Plunge. To rush or hurry into a state or action.
Plunge headlong. To rush into without delay.
Precipitate. To hasten, to hurry.
Press forward. ⎫ To hasten.
Press onward. ⎭
Push forward. ⎫ To urge by persistent effort.
Push onward. ⎭
Put on. To apply force, as steam; to urge forward.
Quicken, etc. To hasten, to precipitate, etc. See Swiftness.
Rush, etc. To move in a hurry, etc. See Swiftness.
Scramble. To run or climb hurriedly.
Scuttle along. To scamper; run in great haste.
Skurry. To move in confused haste.
Urge. To drive onward, press hard.
Whip. To urge ahead by force.
Whip forward. ⎫ To turn suddenly and run ahead.
Whip onward. ⎭

Ease. Freedom from labor or effort.
Holiday. A day of exemption from labor.
Leisure. Freedom from necessary occupation.
Otium cum dignitate [L.]. Leisure with honor. Cicero, *Sextius*, 45.]
Spare hours. ⎫
Spare moments. ⎬ Time not employed in labor, care, or attention.
Spare time. ⎭
Time. Leisure.
Time on one's hands. ⎫ Time not employed in labor.
Time to spare. ⎭
Vacant hour. Unemployed time; leisure.

Leisure—Verbs.

Be an idle man. To have one's time unemployed.
Be master of one's time. To be able to go or act when one chooses.
Have leisure, etc. To have spare time, etc. See *Nouns.*
Move slowly, etc. See Swiftness-Slowness.
Repose, etc. To rest. See Toil-Relaxation.
Take one's ease. ⎫
Take one's leisure. ⎬ To be unemployed.
Take one's time. ⎭
While away the time, etc. To spend time pleasantly, etc. See Action-Passiveness.

Leisure—Adjectives.

At a loose end. ⎫
At leisure. ⎬ Free from labor and care.
At one's ease. ⎭
Calm. Unmoved; at rest.
Deliberate. Slow; leisurely.
Leisurely. Not hasty.
Quiet. At rest; unmoving.
Slow, etc. Not quick; undisturbed, etc. See Swiftness-Slowness.
Undisturbed. Not disturbed; inactive.

Leisure—Phrases.

Eile mit weile [G.]. Make haste slowly.
Time hanging heavily on one's hands. Time passing slowly.

HURRY—Verbs—Continued.

Work against time. To attempt to do in a shorter time than is really necessary.

Hurry—Adjectives.

Boisterous. Rough; blustery.
Breathless. So quickly as to be unable to breathe.
Brusque. Short; sharp; quick.
Cursory. Rapid; hasty.
Feverish. Impatient; very desirous.
Furious. Frantic; very great, as furious speed,
Fussy. Fidgety.
Hard-pressed. Chased.
Hasty. With haste.
Headlong. Hasty; precipitous.
Hot-headed. Quick-tempered.
Hurried. In haste.
Impetuous. Doing without thought.
In a hurry. ⎫ Hasty; speedy, etc. See *Nouns.*
In haste. ⎭
In all haste. ⎫ Hurriedly.
In hot haste. ⎭
Precipitate. Rash; quick.
Pressed for time. In need of time.
Pushing, etc. Hasty, etc. See *Verbs.*
Scrambling. Hurriedly.
Urgent. Demanding immediate action.

Hurry—Adverbs, etc.

À corps perdu [F.]. Headlong; precipitously.
All at once, etc. Suddenly, etc. See Eternity-Instantaneity.
All haste. Hastily.
Amain. Without delay.
Apace, etc. Rapidly; quickly, etc. See Swiftness.
At short notice, etc. See Earliness.

HURRY—*Continued.*

HURRY—*Adverbs, etc.*

By express.
By forced marches. } As quickly as possible
By telegraph.
By fits and starts. } In short, irregular, quick movements.
By spurts.
Full drive. } With entire speed.
Full tilt.
Hastily. With haste.
Headlong. Precipitately.
Head over heels. }
Head over shoulders. } After a tumbling and overturned manner
Heels over head.

Helter-skelter. In a disorderly and hurried manner.
Hop, skip, and jump. In a reckless manner.
Immediately, etc. In a short time.
In haste, etc. See *Adjectives.*
Post haste. With speed; with relays of horses.
Slap bang. Hurriedly; without care and with noise
Slap dash. Recklessly.
With all haste. As quickly as possible.
With breathless speed. So quickly as to be unable to breathe.
With haste. Quickly.

HURRY—*Phrases.*

A word and a blow.
Devil take the hindmost.
Eile mit weile [G.]. Make haste slowly.
Maggiore fretta, minore atto [It.]. The more haste, the less speed.
No sooner said than done, etc. Something done very quickly, etc.
See EARLINESS.

No time to be lost.
Ohne Hast, aber ohne Rast [G.]. Unhasting but unresting (like the sun). [Goethe's motto.]
Sauve qui peut [F.]. Save himself who can.

hur'-ry-skur"-ry. Confused, hasty movements. EXCITABILITY-INEXCITABILITY.
hurst. A group of trees. FAUNA-FLORA.
hurt. To injure; maltreat; physical pain; detriment. BETTERMENT-DETERIORATION, GOOD-EVIL, GOODNESS-BADNESS, PLEASURABLENESS-PAINFULNESS, SENSUALITY-SUFFERING; hurt the feelings, FAVORITE-ANGER, PLEASURABLENESS-PAINFULNESS; more frightened than hurt, SANGUINENESS-TIMIDITY.
hurt'-ful. Injurious. GOODNESS-BADNESS, PLEASURABLENESS-PAINFULNESS.
hurt'-ful-ness. The state of being hurtful. CLEANNESS-FILTHINESS, GOODNESS-BADNESS.
hurt'-ing. Causing pain. PLEASURABLENESS-PAINFULNESS.
hur'-tle. To move with violence. IMPETUS-REACTION.
hurt'-less. Harmless. GOODNESS-BADNESS.
hus'-band. To save for a future emergency; a married man; a manager. CONSERVATION, GENEROSITY-FRUGALITY, MALE-FEMALE, MANAGER, MATRIMONY-CELIBACY, STORE.
hus'-band-man. One who tills the soil. DOMESTICATION-AGRICULTURE.
hus'-band-ry. Agriculture; economical management. CONDUCT, DOMESTICATION-AGRICULTURE, GENEROSITY-FRUGALITY.
hush. To make silent; restrain; stillness. MOVEMENT-REST, SOUND-SILENCE, TALKATIVENESS-TACITURNITY, TURBULENCE-CALMNESS; hush up, ENLIGHTENMENT-SECRECY, FIGHTING-CONCILIATION.
hush'-mon"-ey. A bribe to secure silence. COMPENSATION, RECOMPENSE-PUNITION.
husk. The outer cover of anything. COVER-LINING.
husk'-y. Dry; not clear; hoarse. DAMPNESS-DRYNESS, LOUDNESS-FAINTNESS, VOCALIZATION-MUTENESS.
hus-sar'. A light-horse trooper. BELLIGERENT.
hus'-sy. A forward girl. PURITY-RAKE.
hust'-ings. A council; a platform for making speeches. LISTS, SCHOOL, TRIBUNAL.
hus'-tle. To jostle roughly; move with difficulty; shuffle together in confusion. AGITATION, IMPETUS-REACTION, OBSTRUCTION-HELP, ORGANIZATION-DISORGANIZATION.
hut. A small, mean dwelling. DWELLER-HABITATION.
hutch. A place for storing anything. DWELLER-HABITATION.
huzz. To hum. RESONANCE-SIBILATION.
huz-za. Hurrah. JUBILATION-LAMENTATION.
hy'-a-cinth. A precious stone. EMBELLISHMENT-DISFIGUREMENT.

hy'-a-line. Something transparent. DIAPHANEITY-OPAQUENESS.
hy'-ber-nate. To pass the winter. ACTIVITY-INDOLENCE.
hy"-ber-na'-tion. The act of passing the winter in seclusion or sleep. ACTIVITY-INDOLENCE.
hy'-brid. The produce of different kinds or species. CONVENTIONALITY-UNCONVENTIONALITY, MIXTURE-HOMOGENEITY.
hy'-dra. A many-headed monster. CONVENTIONALITY-UNCONVENTIONALITY, FERTILITY-STERILITY.
hy'-drant. A discharge-pipe connected with a water-main. RIVER-WIND.
hy-drau'-lics. The science of liquid in motion. RIVER-WIND.
hy"-dro-chlo'-ric. Containing hydrogen and chlorin. Hydrochloric acid, CHEMISTRY.
hy"-dro-dy-nam'-ics. The dynamics of fluids. LIQUID-GAS, WATER-AIR.
hy'-dro-gen. An element. CHEMISTRY.
hy-drog'-ra-pher. One versed in hydrography. OCEAN-LAND.
hy"-dro-graph'-ic. Relating to hydrography. OCEAN-LAND.
hy-drol'-o-gy. The science which treats of the waters of the earth. OCEAN-LAND.
hy'-dro-mel. Honey mixed with water SWEETNESS-ACIDITY.
hy-drom'-e-ter. An instrument for obtaining the strength, density, etc., of liquids. SOLIDITY-RARITY.
hy-drop'-a-thy. Water-cure. REMEDY-BANE.
hy"-dro-pho'-bi-a. A disease caused by the bite of a rabid dog. DESIRE-DISTASTE.
hy"-dro-stat'-ics. The science which treats of fluids at rest. OCEAN-LAND.
hy-drox'-id. A compound. CHEMISTRY.
hy-e'-mal. Pertaining or belonging to winter. HEAT-COLD.
hy-e'-na. A fierce untamable quadruped. BENEFACTOR-EVILDOER.
hy"-et-og'-ra-phy. The science treating of the distribution of rainfall and the graphical exhibition of it on charts. RIVER-WIND.
hy"-et-ol'-o-gy. That branch of meteorology which treats of rain. RIVER-WIND.
Hy-ge'-ia. The goddess of health. HEALTH-SICKNESS.
hy-ge'-ian. Pertaining to health. HEALTHINESS-UNHEALTHINESS.
hy-gi-an'-tics. Science of curing disease. CONSERVATION
hy'-gi-ene. The science which treats of the laws of health. HEALTHINESS-UNHEALTHINESS.

hy″-gi-en′-ic. Promotive of health; wholesome. CONSERVATION, HEALTHINESS-UNHEALTHINESS.

hy′-gre. A sudden flood of tide in an estuary. RIVER-WIND.

hy-grom′-e-ter. An instrument for ascertaining the humidity of the atmosphere. DAMPNESS-DRYNESS.

hy-grom′-e-try. The science which treats of the measurement of moisture in bodies. DAMPNESS-DRYNESS.

hy′-le. A Greek term meaning matter in general. MATERIALITY-SPIRITUALITY.

hy′-lo-the″-ism. Material pantheism. GODLINESS-UNGODLINESS, ORTHODOXY-HETERODOXY.

Hy′-men. The god of marriage. MATRIMONY-CELIBACY.

hy″-men-e′-al. Nuptial. MATRIMONY-CELIBACY; **hymeneal altar,** MATRIMONY-CELIBACY.

hymn. A song of praise or worship. DEVOTION-IDOLATRY, MUSICIAN.

hym′-nal. A book or collection of hymns. CEREMONIAL.

hymn′-book″. A hymnal. CEREMONIAL.

hym-nol′-o-gy. The study or science of hymns. CEREMONIAL.

hy-pal′-la-ge. A figure of speech by which one grammatical form, or one construction, is substituted for another. REVERSAL, RHETORIC.

hy-per′-ba-ton. The transposition of words from their grammatical order. REVERSAL, RHETORIC.

hy-per′-bo-la. A plane curve such that the difference of the distances from any point of the curve to two fixed points is constant. CURVATION-RECTILINEARITY.

hy-per′-bo-le. An exaggeration. GULL-HYPERBOLE, RHETORIC.

hy″-per-bol′-ic. Exaggerating. RHETORIC.

hy″-per-bol′-ic-al. Exaggerating. GULL-HYPERBOLE.

hy″-per-bol′-ic-al-ly. In an exaggerating manner. GULL-HYPERBOLE.

hy-per′-bo-lize. To exaggerate. GULL-HYPERBOLE.

hy″-per-bo′-re-al. Very cold. HEAT-COLD.

Hy″-per-bo′-re-an. A dweller in the extreme north. HEAT-COLD, REMOTENESS-NEARNESS.

hy″-per-crit′-i-cism. Excessive or ungenerous criticism. APPROVAL-DISAPPROVAL, CONTENTEDNESS-DISCONTENTMENT, DECISION-MISJUDGMENT, DESIRE-PARTICULARNESS.

hy″-per-du′-li-a. A kind of superior devotion paid to the Virgin Mary. DEVOTION-IDOLATRY.

Hy-pe′-ri-on. A model of manly beauty. BEAUTY-UGLINESS; **Hyperion to a satyr,** SAMENESS-CONTRAST.

hy″-per-or′-tho-dox-y. Excessive orthodoxy. CREDULOUSNESS-SKEPTICISM, ORTHODOXY-HETERODOXY.

hy″-per-phy′-si-cal. Supernatural. DIVINITY.

hy-per′-tro-phied. Excessively developed. ENLARGEMENT-DIMINUTION.

hy-per′-tro-phy. An excessive development. ENLARGEMENT-DIMINUTION.

hy′-phen. The mark connecting the parts of a compound word. CONNECTIVE.

hyp-nol′-o-gy. The science of the phenomena of sleep. ACTIVITY-INDOLENCE.

hyp-not′-ic. Tending to produce sleep. ACTIVITY-INDOLENCE, REMEDY-BANE, TURBULENCE-CALMNESS.

hyp′-no-tism. An artificially induced somnambulistic state of mind. ACTIVITY-INDOLENCE.

hyp′-o-caust. A furnace for heating baths or dwelling-rooms. OVEN-REFRIGERATOR.

hyp″-o-chon′-dri-ac. A person tormented by gloomy fancies. ANATOMY, LIGHTHEARTEDNESS-DEJECTION, SANENESS-MANIAC.

hyp″-o-chon-dri′-ac-al. Pertaining to hypochondria. LIGHTHEARTEDNESS-DEJECTION.

hyp″-o-chon-dri′-a-sis. Hypochondria. LIGHTHEARTEDNESS-DEJECTION.

hypocrisie est un hommage que le vice rend à la vertu [F.]

(i-poc-ri-zi′ êt un˙o-mazh′ ke le vis rɑn˙t ɑ lɑ ver-tü′). Hypocrisy is a homage which vice pays to virtue. SAGE-FOOL, VIRTUE-VICE.

hyp-oc′-ri-sy. Assuming a false appearance of virtue or religion. GODLINESS-UNGODLINESS, TRUTHFULNESS-FALSEHOOD.

hyp′-o-crite. One who feigns to be what he is not. GODLINESS-UNGODLINESS, GULL-DECEIVER; **play the hypocrite,** TRUTHFULNESS-FALSEHOOD.

hyp″-o-crit′-i-cal. Of or pertaining to hypocrisy. APPROVAL-DISAPPROVAL, CONTENTEDNESS-DISCONTENTMENT, GODLINESS-UNGODLINESS, TRUTHFULNESS-FALSEHOOD.

hyp″-o-gas′-tric. Pertaining to the hypogastrium. ANATOMY.

hy-pos′-ta-sis. A common nature or essence. SUBSTANCE-NULLITY.

hy″-po-stat′-ic. Elemental; constitutive. SUBSTANCE-NULLITY.

hy″-po-stat′-ic un′-ion. The union of two natures in one body. DIVINITY.

hy-poth′-e-cate. To assign in pledge, as security. SECURITY.

hy-poth″-e-ca′-tion. The pledging of personal property as collateral security. SECURITY.

hy-poth′-e-nuse. Hypotenuse, the longest side of a right-angled triangle. PARALLELISM-INCLINATION.

hy-poth′-e-sis. Something assumed for the purpose of argument. HYPOTHESIS.

HYPOTHESIS.

Association of ideas. Connection of one idea or thought with another, so that one will follow the other.

Assumption. Something taken for granted as a basis for reasoning.

Bare suggestion. A slight mention or hint.

Bare supposition. Nothing but a supposition.

Conceit. A vain conception of one's own abilities or accomplishments.

Condition. Something necessary to an occurrence.

Conjecturality. Quality of being conjectural.

Conjecture. An opinion based on defective or presumptive evidence.

Data. Grounds for inference or deduction; facts known or conceded.

Divination. A forecast of future events.

Guess. An attempt to hit upon truth without certain evidence.

Guesswork. Work performed by guesses or based upon guesses

Hint. Something slight or covert to call attention to something.

Hypothesis. A principle taken for granted in order to prove the point in question. A working hypothesis is a theorem not yet proved.

Inkling. Faint notion.

Loose suggestion. A suggestion given without much thought.

Loose supposition. Supposition made without much thought.

Position. Attitude assumed with reference to a subject.

Postulate. } A basis of argument laid down as too plain to
Postulatum [L.]. } require proof.

Postulation. The act of postulating.

Presumption. Belief based on strong but not conclusive evidence.

Presupposition. Something implied as a necessary condition; something previously supposed.

Proposal. That which is offered for acceptation.

Proposition. That which is offered for consideration.

Rough guess. A guess hastily made.

Shot. A guess.

Speculation. Opinions resulting from mental examination.

Suggestion. Words intended to furnish some assistance or directions.

Supposition. An opinion based on several reasons.

Surmise. An opinion based on none or the slightest evidence.

Suspicion. Imagination of the existence of something upon little or no evidence.

Theorem. A proposition, not self-evident, but demonstrably true.

Theory. A rational explanation that agrees with all the facts.

Thesis. A proposition that requires explanation or proof.

Vague suggestion. } A suggestion or supposition of uncertain source
Vague supposition. } or authority.

HYPOTHESIS—*Verbs.*

Allude to. To make mention of in an indirect manner.

Assume. To take for granted as a basis for reasoning.

Believe. To accept as true on the authority of others.

Conjecture. To give an opinion or explanation from defective or presumptive evidence.

Dare say. To venture a guess.

Divine. To foretell by supernatural aid.

Fancy. To believe without substantial grounds.

Give a guess. To make a guess.

Guess. To hit upon the truth at random.

Hazard a conjecture. To venture to make a conjecture.

Hazard a suggestion. To venture to make a suggestion.

Hint. To make a slight mention of, or covertly to call attention to something.

Make a motion. To make a proposition to an assembly.

Marvel if. ⎫
Marvel whether. ⎬ To wonder greatly whether.

Move. To put before an assembly.

Presume. To consider as very likely, though not certain.

Presuppose. To consider as a necessary condition; to suppose previously.

Presurmise. To surmise beforehand.

Propose. To offer for consideration or acceptation.

Propound. To state for consideration or solution.

Put a case. To state a case.

Put forth. To present to notice.

Put forward a conjecture. To present a conjecture to notice.

Put forward a suggestion. To present a suggestion to notice.

Put it into one's head. To suggest it to one.

Run in one's head. To be continually in one's thoughts.

Speculate. To subject to mental examination.

Start. To send forth.

Suggest. To give directions or words of assistance in a modest or quiet way.

Suppose. To think a thing likely for several reasons.

Surmise. To form an opinion on none or the slightest evidence.

Suspect. To have a vague idea of the existence of, without grounds or proof.

Take it. To consider as fact or truth.

Take it for granted. To hold as true.

Take it into one's head. To be seized with a sudden notion.

Theorize. To formulate theories.

Throw out a conjecture. To conjecture carelessly or loosely.

Throw out a suggestion. To suggest carelessly or loosely.

Wis. To suppose or think.

Wonder if. ⎫
Wonder whether. ⎬ To be desirous of knowing.

Hypothesis—*Adjectives.*

Allusive. Mentioning in an obscure or indirect manner; suggesting something similar in another book.

Assumed, etc. See *Verbs.*

Conjectural. Consisting of conjectures.

Given. Stated; admitted as a fact.

Gratuitous. Given without claim or consideration, as money advice

Hypothetical. Of the nature of, or based on hypotheses.

Mooted. Under consideration.

Postulatory. Assumed without proof.

Presumptive. Founded on presumption.

Putative. Commonly thought or supposed.

Speculative. Consisting of speculation.

Suggestive. Fitted or likely to suggest.

Supposable. Likely or possible to suppose.

Supposing, etc. See *Verbs.*

Supposititious. Supposed.

Suppositive. Consisting of or implying supposition.

Theoretical. Consisting of theory.

Hypothesis—*Adverbs, etc*

An. And if.

As if. Like.

Ex hypothesi [L.]. According to the hypothesis.

For aught one knows. It may be.

If. On the supposition that.

If so be. Provided.

In case. ⎫
In the event of. ⎬ If so be.

On the supposition, etc. See *Nouns.*

Perhaps. It may be.

Provided. On condition.

Quasi. Appearing as if.

hy″-po-thet′-ic-al. Assumed; conditional. HYPOTHESIS, MODIFICATION, RATIOCINATION-INSTINCT.

hypped. Hypochondriacal; insane. LIGHTHEARTEDNESS-DEJECTION, SANENESS-MANIAC.

hyp-som′-e-try. The art of measuring the heights of points above the earth's surface. MENSURATION.

Hyr-ca′-ni-an Wood. A forest in an ancient province in Asia. TIDINGS-MYSTERY.

hy′-son. A grade of green tea. NUTRIMENT-EXCRETION.

hys″-ter-e′-sis. A state of magnetism. ELECTRICITY

hys-te′-ri-a. A nervous disease. SANENESS-MANIAC.

hys-ter′-ic. Violently emotional. TURBULENCE-CALMNESS.

hys-ter′-ic-al. Emotional; excitable. EMOTION, EXCITABILITY-INEXCITABILITY, EXCITATION, PERSISTENCE-WHIM.

hys-ter′-ics. Hysteria. EXCITABILITY-INEXCITABILITY, TURBULENCE-CALMNESS; in hysterics, EXCITATION, SANGUINENESS-TIMIDITY, TURBULENCE-CALMNESS.

hys″-te-ron–prot′-e-ron. The cart before the horse. A figure of speech that inverts the natural order of words or clauses. REVERSAL, RHETORIC.

I

I. Self - designating pronoun. MATERIALITY - SPIRITUALITY, UNIVERSALITY-PARTICULARITY.

i-am′-bic. Pertaining to the iambus. POETRY-PROSE, RHETORIC.

i-am′-bus. A foot composed of a short syllable followed by a long one, or an unaccented syllable followed by an accented. POETRY-PROSE.

I-ap′-et-us. Satellite of Saturn. ASTRONOMY.

I-ca′-ri-an. Venturesome. RECKLESSNESS-CAUTION.

Ic′-a-rus. Greek mythological character. RECKLESSNESS-CAUTION, WAYFARER-SEAFARER; **fate of Icarus,** ASCENT-DESCENT.

ice. Frozen water. HEAT-COLD, HEATING-COOLING, SMOOTHNESS-ROUGHNESS.

ice′-berg″. A floating mass of ice. HEAT-COLD.

ice′-boat″. A boat for sailing on ice. CONVEYANCE-VESSEL.

ice′-bound″. Obstructed by ice. HEAT-COLD, RELEASE-RESTRAINT.

ice′-box″. A refrigerator. HEATING-COOLING.

ice′-ca-noe″. A canoe for traveling on ice. CONVEYANCE-VESSEL.

ice′-cream″. Cream or milk sweetened, flavored, and frozen. NUTRIMENT-EXCRETION.

ice′-floe″. A large mass of floating ice. HEAT-COLD.

ice′-house″. A building for storing ice. OVEN-REFRIGERATOR.

ice′-wa″-ter. Water chilled by ice. NUTRIMENT-EXCRETION.

ice′-wool″. A fine wool for shawls. DRESS-UNDRESS.

Ich′-a-bod. A son of Phinehas. [The glory has departed.] REPUTATION-DISCREDIT.

ich dien [G.] (iH dîn). I serve. (The motto of the Prince of Wales.) GENTILITY-DEMOCRACY.

ich-nog′-ra-phy. Art of tracing plans. DELINEATION-CARICATURE.

i′-chor. Ethereal fluid in veins of the gods; discharge from an ulcer. LIQUID-GAS.

ich″-thy-ol′-o-gy. The science of fishes. ZOOLOGY-BOTANY.

ich′-thy-o-man″-cy. Divination by the heads or entrails of fishes. PROPHECY.

ich″-thy-oph′-a-gous. Fish-eating. NUTRIMENT-EXCRETION.

ich″-thy-oph′-a-gy. The practise of eating fish. NUTRIMENT-EXCRETION.

ich″-thy-ot′-o-my. Dissection of fishes. NUTRIMENT-EXCRETION.

i′-con. An image. DELINEATION-CARICATURE.

i-con′-o-clasm. Image-breaking. ORTHODOXY-HETERODOXY.

i-con′-o-clast. An image-breaker. BENEFACTOR-EVILDOER, MAKER-DESTROYER, ORTHODOXY-HETERODOXY.

i-con″-o-clast′-ic. Breaking images. ORTHODOXY-HETERODOXY.

i″-co-nog′-ra-phy. Art of representation by pictures. DELINEATION-CARICATURE.

i″-co-sa-he′-dron. A solid with 20 plane faces. ANGULARITY.

i″-co-si-tet″-ra-he′-dron. Form of crystal. MINERALOGY.

ic′-tus. A metrical accent on a word or syllable. POETRY-PROSE.

id est [L.] (id est). That is. CLEARNESS-OBSCURITY, INTERPRETATION-MISINTERPRETATION.

i-de′-a. Conception. CONCEPTION-THEME, MAGNITUDE-SMALLNESS; **give an idea of,** EDUCATION-MISTEACHING.

i-de′-al. A model of excellence; unreal. ENTIRETY-DEFICIENCY, ENTITY-NONENTITY, FANCY, TRUTH-ERROR.

idéal, beau [F.] (i-dê-al′, bo). A perfect model of beauty. BEAUTY-UGLINESS.

i-de′-al-ism. The system or theory that makes all immediate knowledge ideas. FANCY.

i-de′-al-ist. One who holds the doctrine of idealism. FANCY.

i″-de-al′-i-ty. Quality or state of being ideal; power to form ideals. FANCY, MIND-IMBECILITY.

i-de′-al-ize. To form ideas. FANCY.

idée fixe [F.] (i-dê′ fix). A fixed idea. DECISION-MISJUDGMENT.

i′-dem. The same. SAMENESS-CONTRAST.

i-den′-ti-cal. The same. SAMENESS-CONTRAST, SYNONYM-ANTONYM.

i-den′-ti-cal-ly. In an identical manner. SAMENESS-CONTRAST.

i-den″-ti-fi-ca′-tion. Act of identifying; state of being identified. COMPARISON-DISCOVERY, SAMENESS-CONTRAST.

i-den′-ti-fy. To make to be the same. DISCOVERY, SAMENESS-CONTRAST.

i-den′-ti-ty. Sameness. EQUALITY-INEQUALITY, SAMENESS-CONTRAST.

i″-de-ol′-o-gy. Science of the evolution of human ideas. MIND-IMBECILITY.

ides. The 15th of March, May, July, and October, and the 13th of the other months. **Ides of March,** VOLITION-OBLIGATION.

id″-i-oc′-ra-sy. Peculiarity of constitution. INCLINATION, SUBJECTIVENESS-OBJECTIVENESS.

id′-i-o-cy. State of being idiotic. SAGACITY-INCAPACITY.

id′-i-om. Peculiar mode of expression of a language. PHRASE, UNIVERSALITY-PARTICULARITY.

id″-i-o-mat′-ic. Peculiar to a certain language. PHRASE.

id″-i-o-syn′-cra-sy. Constitutional peculiarity; distinctive mental quality. AFFECTIONS, CONVENTIONALITY-UNCONVENTIONALITY, INCLINATION, SUBJECTIVENESS-OBJECTIVENESS, UNIVERSALITY-PARTICULARITY.

id′-i-ot. An imbecile. SAGE-FOOL, SANENESS-LUNACY; **tale told by an idiot,** MEANING-JARGON.

id″-i-ot′-ic. Like an idiot. SAGACITY-INCAPACITY.

id′-i-ot-ism. An idiom; idiocy. PHRASE, SAGACITY-INCAPACITY.

i′-dle. Vain; doing nothing; slothful; spend in idleness. ACTIVITY-INDOLENCE, CONSEQUENCE-INSIGNIFICANCE, SAGACITY-INCAPACITY; **be an idle man,** HURRY-LEISURE; **idle conceit,** WITTINESS-DULNESS; **idle hours,** ACTION-PASSIVENESS; **idle talk,** CONVERSATION-MONOLOGUE; **idle time away,** ACTIVITY-INDOLENCE; **lie idle,** ACTION-PASSIVENESS.

i′-dle-ness. Inactivity. ACTIVITY-INDOLENCE.

i′-dler. One who idles. ACTIVITY-INDOLENCE.

i′-dol. Object of passionate affection; image of a heathen god. DESIRE-DISTASTE, DEVOTION-IDOLA-

TRY, FAVORITE-ANGER; **idol of the people,** FAVORITE-ANGER.

i-dol'-a-ter. A worshiper of idols. ORTHODOXY-HETERODOXY

i-dol'-a-trous. Worshiping idols. DEVOTION - IDOLATRY, ORTHODOXY-HETERODOXY.

i-dol'-a-try. Worship of idols; idolatrous love. DEVOTION-IDOLATRY, FAVORITE-ANGER, ORTHODOXY-HETERODOXY.

i'-dol-ism. Idolatry. DEVOTION-IDOLATRY.

i'-dol-ize. Regard with love; worship idolatrously. GODLINESS-UNGODLINESS, LOVE-HATE.

i-do'-ne-ous. Suitable. HARMONY-DISCORD.

i'-dyl. A short pastoral poem; a narrative poem. POETRY-PROSE.

i'-dyl-ist. A pastoral poet or painter. POETRY-PROSE.

i-dyl'-lic. Having a rural quality. POETRY-PROSE.

if. In case that; granting that; whether. CONDITION-SITUATION, HYPOTHESIS, MODIFICATION; **if possible,** MODIFICATION, POSSIBILITY-IMPOSSIBILITY; **if you please,** PETITION-EXPOSTULATION.

ig'-ne-ous. Pertaining to or like fire. HEAT-COLD; **igneous rock,** GEOLOGY.

ignis fatuus [L.] (ig'-nis fat'-yu-us). Will-o'-the-wisp; a misleading influence. LIGHT-DARKNESS, LUMINARY-SHADE, SIGHT-DIMSIGHTEDNESS, SUBSTANCE-NULLITY, TRUTHFULNESS-FRAUD.

ig-nite'. To kindle. CHEMISTRY, HEATING-COOLING.

ig-ni'-tion. Act of kindling. HEATING-COOLING.

ig-no'-ble. Base; shameful; low-born. GENTILITY-DEMOCRACY.

ig''-no-min'-i-ous. Disgraceful. REPUTATION-DISCREDIT, UPRIGHTNESS-DISHONESTY.

ig'-no-min''-y. Public disgrace; shame. REPUTATION-DISCREDIT.

ig''-no-ra'-mus. An ignorant person. SCHOLAR-DUNCE.

ig'-no-rance. Want of knowledge. KNOWLEDGE-IGNORANCE; **keep in ignorance,** ENLIGHTENMENT-SECRECY; **plead ignorance,** JUSTIFICATION-CHARGE.

ignorance crasse [F.] (i-nyo-rans' cras). Gross ignorance. KNOWLEDGE-IGNORANCE.

ig'-no-rant. Illiterate; unknowing. CERTAINTY-DOUBT, KNOWLEDGE-IGNORANCE, SCHOLAR-DUNCE.

ignorantia legis neminem excusat [L.] (ig-no-ran'-shi-a li'-jis nem'-i-nem ex-kiu'-zat). Ignorance of the law excuses no one. LAW-LAWLESSNESS.

ig'-no-rant-ly. Without knowing. KNOWLEDGE-IGNORANCE.

ignoratio elenchi [L.] (ig-no-rê'-shi-o î-len'-kai). Ignorance of the refutation. RATIOCINATION-CASUISTRY.

ig-nore'. Disregard; be ignorant of; reject. ASSERTION-DENIAL, CAREFULNESS-CARELESSNESS, COMMISSION-ABROGATION, CREDULOUSNESS-SKEPTICISM, ENLIGHTENMENT-SECRECY, KNOWLEDGE-IGNORANCE, OBSERVANCE-NONOBSERVANCE.

ignoscito sæpe alteri, nunquam tibi [L.] (ig-nos'-si-to sî'-pî al'-ter-ai, nun'-quam tib'-i). Pardon another often, never thyself. OBSERVANCE-NONOBSERVANCE, PARDON-VINDICTIVENESS.

ignotum, omne . . . pro magnifico [L.] (om'-nî ig-no'-tum pro mag-nif'-i-co). Everything unknown [is assumed to be] something magnificent. CREDULOUSNESS-SKEPTICISM.

ignotum per ignotius [L.] (ig-no'-tum per ig-no'-shi-us). A thing unknown by a thing more unknown. RATIOCINATION-CASUISTRY.

il'-e-um. Part of the intestines. ANATOMY.

il'-i-ac. Pertaining to the ileum. ANATOMY.

Ilium fuit [L.] (il'-i-um fiu'-it). Ilium [Troy] has been. FUTURE-PAST.

ilk. Same. SAMENESS-CONTRAST.

ill. Badness; misfortune; sickness; sick. GOOD-EVIL, GOODNESS-BADNESS, HEALTH-SICKNESS; **as ill luck**

would have it, OPPORTUNENESS-UNSUITABLENESS; WELFARE - MISFORTUNE, **bird of ill omen,** WARNING; **do an ill office to,** CHARITABLENESS-MALEVOLENCE; **go on ill,** SUCCESS-FAILURE, WELFARE-MISFORTUNE; **house of ill fame,** PURITY-IMPURITY; **ill at ease,** LIGHTHEARTEDNESS-DEJECTION, PLEASURE-PAIN; **ill betide,** CHARITABLENESS-CURSE; **ill blood,** CHARITABLENESS - MALEVOLENCE, LOVE - HATE; **ill humor,** FAVORITE-ANGER, FAVORITE-MOROSENESS, FAVORITE-QUARRELSOMENESS; **ill luck,** WELFARE-MISFORTUNE; **ill off,** AFFLUENCE-PENURY, EXCESS-LACK, WELFARE-MISFORTUNE; **ill repute,** REPUTATION-DISCREDIT; **ills that flesh is heir to,** GOOD-EVIL, HEALTH-SICKNESS, PLEASURE-PAIN; **ill turn,** CHARITABLENESS - MALEVOLENCE, GOOD - EVIL; **ill usage,** CHARITABLENESS - MALEVOLENCE; **ill will,** CHARITABLENESS - MALEVOLENCE, GOODNESS-BADNESS, OBSTRUCTION-HELP, WELFARE-MISFORTUNE; **look ill,** BEAUTY-UGLINESS; **take ill,** CONTENTEDNESS-DISCONTENTMENT, FAVORITE-ANGER.

ill'-ad-vised''. Badly advised. PROPRIETY-IMPROPRIETY, SAGACITY-INCAPACITY, SKILL-UNSKILFULNESS.

ill'-af-fect''-ed. Badly affected. FAVORITE-MOROSENESS.

il-lapse'. Fall or glide. CONVERSION-REVERSION, ENTRANCE-EXIT.

il-la'-que-ate. Insnare. TRUTHFULNESS-FRAUD.

ill'-as-sort''-ed. Badly assorted. HARMONY-DISCORD

il-la'-tion. Inference. DECISION-MISJUDGMENT.

il-laud'-a-ble. Not praiseworthy. INNOCENCE-GUILT.

ill'-be-haved''. Discourteous. POLITENESS-IMPOLITENESS.

ill'-bo''-ding. Threatening. PORTENT.

ill'-bred''. Badly taught or reared. POLITENESS-IMPOLITENESS, TASTE-VULGARITY.

ill-breed'-ing. Poor training. POLITENESS-IMPOLITENESS.

ill'-con-di''-tion-ed. Having bad qualities; being in bad state. CHARITABLENESS-MALEVOLENCE, DIFFICULTY-FACILITY, GOODNESS-BADNESS, POLITENESS-IMPOLITENESS, VIRTUE-VICE.

ill'-con-duct''-ed. Badly managed SKILL-UNSKILFULNESS.

ill'-con-trived''. Badly devised or schemed. CHARITABLENESS-MALEVOLENCE, GOODNESS-BADNESS, PROPRIETY-IMPROPRIETY, SKILL-UNSKILFULNESS.

ill'-de-fined''. Badly marked out. VISIBILITY-INVISIBILITY.

ill'-de-vised''. Badly contrived SAGACITY-INCAPACITY, SKILL-UNSKILFULNESS.

ill'-di-gest''-ed. Badly arranged in the mind. PREPARATION-NONPREPARATION.

ill'-dis-posed''. Maliciously inclined. CHARITABLENESS-MALEVOLENCE, DUENESS-UNDUENESS, FAVORITE-MOROSENESS.

il-le'-gal. Unlawful. LAW-LAWLESSNESS, LEAVE-PROHIBITION, RIGHT-WRONG.

il''-le-gal'-i-ty. State of being illegal DUENESS-UNDUENESS, LAW-LAWLESSNESS.

il-le'-gal-ly. Unlawfully. LAW-LAWLESSNESS.

il-leg'-i-ble. Not easily read. CLEARNESS-OBSCURITY; **illegible hand,** WRITING-PRINTING; **render illegible,** MARK-OBLITERATION.

il''-le-git'-i-ma-cy. Unlawfulness DUENESS-UNDUENESS, LAW-LAWLESSNESS.

il''-le-git'-i-mate. Illegal; illogical. DUENESS-UNDUENESS, LAW-LAWLESSNESS, TRUTHFULNESS-FRAUD.

ill'-fa''-ted. Unfortunate. WELFARE-MISFORTUNE.

ill'-fa''-vored. Ugly. BEAUTY-UGLINESS.

ill'-fla''-vored. Tasting badly. PALATABLENESS-UNPALATABLENESS.

ill'-fur''-nished. Badly provided. EXCESS-LACK.

ill'-hu''-mored. Crabbed. FAVORITE-MOROSENESS.

il-lib'-er-al. Not generous; mean; lacking culture. DECISION-MISJUDGMENT, EXTRAVAGANCE-AVARICE, UNSELFISHNESS-SELFISHNESS.

il-lib''-er-al'-i-ty. Bigotry. EXTRAVAGANCE-AVARICE, POLITENESS-IMPOLITENESS, UNSELFISHNESS-SELFISHNESS.

il-lic'-it. Illegal. DUENESS-UNDUENESS, LAW-LAWLESSNESS.

ill''-im-ag'-ined. Badly fancied or devised. SAGACITY-INCAPACITY, SKILL-UNSKILFULNESS.

il-lim'-it-a-ble. Boundless. INFINITY.

il-lim'-it-ed. Not bounded. INFINITY.

ill'-in-ten''-tioned. Malevolent. CHARITABLENESS-MALEVOLENCE.

il-lit'-er-ate. Uneducated. KNOWLEDGE-IGNORANCE.

ill'-judged''. Foolish; injudicious. SAGACITY-INCAPACITY, SKILL-UNSKILFULNESS.

ill'-judg''-ing. Estimating badly. DECISION-MISJUDGMENT.

ill'-made''. Badly formed. BEAUTY-UGLINESS, PROPORTION-DEFORMITY.

ill'-man''-nered. Rude; impolite. POLITENESS-IMPOLITENESS, TASTE-VULGARITY.

ill' man'-ners. Poor breeding POLITENESS-IMPOLITENESS.

ill'-marked''. Ill-defined. VISIBILITY-INVISIBILITY.

ill name. Bad repute. REPUTATION-DISCREDIT.

ill na'-ture. Peevishness. CHARITABLENESS-MALEVOLENCE.

ill'-na''-tured. Peevish. CHARITABLENESS-MALEVOLENCE.

ill'-ness. Sickness. HEALTH-SICKNESS.

il-log'-ic-al. Contrary to the rules of logic. RATIOCINATION-CASUISTRY, TRUTH-ERROR.

il-log'-ic-al-ly. Inconsistently. RATIOCINATION-INSTINCT.

ill'-o''-mened. Inauspicious. SANGUINENESS-HOPELESSNESS, SECURITY-INSECURITY, WELFARE-MISFORTUNE.

ill'-pro-por''-tioned. Unsymmetric. PROPORTION-DEFORMITY.

ill'-pro-vid''-ed. Not well supplied. EXCESS-LACK.

ill'-qual''-i-fied. Badly fitted. SKILL-UNSKILFULNESS.

ill'-re-qui''-ted. Ill-repaid. THANKFULNESS-THANKLESSNESS.

ill'-spent''. Unprofitable. USEFULNESS-USELESSNESS.

ill tem'-per. Irritability. FAVORITE-QUARRELSOMENESS, FAVORITE-MOROSENESS.

ill'-tem''-pered. Sullen; irascible. FAVORITE-MOROSENESS, FAVORITE-QUARRELSOMENESS.

ill'-timed''. Inopportune. HARMONY-DISCORD, OPPORTUNENESS-UNSUITABLENESS.

ill'-treat''. Treat badly. CHARITABLENESS-MALEVOLENCE, GOODNESS-BADNESS, HARSHNESS-MILDNESS.

ill'-treat''-ment. Unkindness. GOODNESS-BADNESS.

il-lume'. To throw light upon. LIGHT-DARKNESS.

il-lu'-mi-nate. Enlighten; decorate with colors. COLOR-ACHROMATISM, EMBELLISHMENT-DISFIGUREMENT, LIGHT-DARKNESS, LUMINARY-SHADE.

illuminati [L.] (il-lu-min-ê'-tai). Those who are enlightened. SCHOLAR-DUNCE.

il-lu''-mi-na'-tion. Enlightenment: coloring: celebration. EMBELLISHMENT-DISFIGUREMENT, ENGRAVING, LIGHT-DARKNESS, SOLEMNIZATION.

il-lu'-mine. Enlighten. LIGHT-DARKNESS.

ill'-use''. Bad treatment. CHARITABLENESS-MALEVOLENCE, GOODNESS-BADNESS.

ill'-used''. Treated badly. PLEASURE-PAIN

il-lu'-sion. Any misleading appearance. FANCY, TRUTH-ERROR, TRUTHFULNESS-FRAUD, VISION-DIMSIGHTEDNESS.

il-lu'-sive. Fallacious; deceitful. FANCY, RATIOCINATION-CASUISTRY, TRUTH-ERROR, TRUTHFULNESS-FABRICATION, TRUTHFULNESS-FRAUD.

il-lu'-so-ry. Deceiving. FANCY, RATIOCINATION-CASUISTRY, TRUTH - ERROR, TRUTHFULNESS - FABRICATION, TRUTHFULNESS-FRAUD.

il-lus'-trate. Explain; elucidate; adorn. CONVENTIONALITY-UNCONVENTIONALITY, DELINEATION-CARICATURE, EMBELLISHMENT-DISFIGUREMENT, INTERPRETATION-MISINTERPRETATION.

il-lus'-tra''-ted. Adorned. NATURE-ART.

il''-lus-tra'-tion. An example; a picture. CONVENTIONALITY-UNCONVENTIONALITY, DELINEATION-CARICATURE, EMBELLISHMENT-DISFIGUREMENT, ENGRAVING, INTERPRETATION-MISINTERPRETATION, NATURE-ART, RHETORIC.

il-lus'-tra-tive. Explanatory. CONVENTIONALITY-UNCONVENTIONALITY, DELINEATION-CARICATURE.

il-lus'-tri-ous. Renowned. REPUTATION-DISCREDIT.

il-lus'-tri-ous-ness. Fame. REPUTATION-DISCREDIT.

im'-age. Likeness; representation; metaphor or simile. APPEARANCE-DISAPPEARANCE, CONCEPTION-THEME, DELINEATION-CARICATURE, LIKENESS-UNLIKENESS, RHETORIC, TROPE; **graven image,** DEVOTION-IDOLATRY.

im'-age-ry. Formation of images; figurative description. DELINEATION-CARICATURE, FANCY, TROPE.

im-ag'-i-na-ry. Non-existing; fancied. FANCY; **imaginary quantity,** NUMBER.

im-ag''-i-na'-tion. Power to create mental images. FANCY.

im-ag'-i-na-tive. Fanciful. FANCY.

im-ag'-ine. To fancy. FANCY.

im-ag'-ined. Fancied. FANCY.

im-ag'-in-ing. Fancying. FANCY.

i-mam'. Officer in Mohammedan mosques; title of Mohammed. CHIEF-UNDERLING, MINISTRY-LAITY.

im-bec-ile. Incapable; silly. MIGHT-IMPOTENCE, SAGACITY-INCAPACITY, SANENESS-LUNACY.

imbécile [F.] (an'-bê-sil'). Fool. SAGE-FOOL.

im''-bec-il'-i-ty. Feebleness. ADAGE-NONSENSE, MIND-IMBECILITY, REGULARITY-IRREGULARITY, SAGACITY-INCAPACITY.

im-bibe'. Drink or take in. ADMISSION-EXPULSION; **imbibe learning,** EDUCATION-LEARNING.

im''-bi-bi'-tion. Drinking in. ADMISSION-EXPULSION.

im-bran'-gle. Mix confusedly. ORGANIZATION-DISORGANIZATION.

im'-bri-ca''-ted. Lying regularly over one another. COVER-LINING.

im-bro'-glio. Troublesome complication; intricate plot. DIFFICULTY-FACILITY, REGULARITY-IRREGULARITY, VARIANCE-ACCORD.

im-brue'. Wet or moisten; impregnate. DAMPNESS-DRYNESS, INJECTION-EJECTION; **imbrue one's hands in blood,** CHARITABLENESS-MALEVOLENCE, FIGHTING-CONCILIATION, LIFE-KILLING; **imbrue the soul,** EXCITATION.

im-bue'. Cause to become thoroughly pervaded. COLOR-ACHROMATISM, DAMPNESS-DRYNESS, EDUCATION-MISTEACHING, INJECTION-EJECTION, MIXTURE-HOMOGENEITY.

im-bued'. Thoroughly pervaded. AFFECTIONS; **imbued with,** AFFECTIONS, EMOTIONS, FAITH-MISGIVING, HABIT-DESUETUDE.

im-burse'. Supply with money. AFFLUENCE-PENURY

im'-i-ta-ble. Possible to imitate. IMITATION-ORIGINALITY.

im'-i-tate. To copy. IMITATION-ORIGINALITY, LIKENESS-UNLIKENESS.

im'-i-ta''-ted. Copied. IMITATION-ORIGINALITY.

im''-i-ta'-tion. Faculty of imitating; copying; likeness. COPY-MODEL, DELINEATION-CARICATURE, IMITATION-ORIGINALITY, NATURE-ART.

IMITATION—ORIGINALITY.

Assimilation. The act of bringing to a resemblance, likeness, or identity.
Copy, etc. An imitation or reproduction of an original work.
Copying, etc. The act of imitating or reproducing. See *Verbs*.
Duplication. Exact imitation or copying.
Echo. Repeated sound.
Forgery. False imitation with fraudulent intention
Imitation. Copying which is inferior to the original.
Mimicry. Ludicrous imitation for sport or ridicule.
Mockery. Act of exposing to contempt by insincere imitation.
Paraphrase. Reproduction in different terms of the sense, as of an author's words.
Parody. Burlesque imitation.
Personation. The act of counterfeiting the person or character of another.
Plagiarism. Quoting without giving credit to the source.
Quotation. Repetition of the words, as of an author.
Reduplication. Duplication again and again.
Repetition. The act of doing or saying something over.
Representation. The act of re-presenting.
Reproduction. The act of bringing forward again, as of a play; repetition of living organisms.
Semblance. Actual or apparent resemblance.
Simulation. The act of assuming a feigned or untrue appearance.
Transcription. The act of copying; a copy.

IMITATION—*Nouns of Agent.*

Ape. An animal that imitates human actions.
Cuckoo. A small bird whose cry gives it its name.
Imitator. One who imitates.
Mimic. One who imitates for sport.
Mocking-bird. A bird which imitates the notes of other birds.
Monkey. An animal which imitates human actions.
Parrot. A bird which imitates human speech.

IMITATION—*Verbs.*

Act, etc. See ACTING.
Ape. To imitate like an ape or servilely.
Burlesque. To represent ridiculously.
Caricature. To exaggerate ridiculously.
Catch. To become affected with, as a disease.
Copy. To reproduce.
Counterfeit. To imitate; pretend; coin money without lawful authority.
Do like. To imitate.
Echo. To reflect in sound.
Emulate. Strive to be like.
Follow in the footsteps of.
Follow in the steps of. } To imitate.
Follow in the wake of.
Follow suit. To play a card of the same suit as the leading one; hence, to do like.
Follow the example of. Set up the deeds of for imitation.
Imitate. To make a copy of.
Match. To be of the same character, form, size, or quality.
Mimic. To imitate for sport or ridicule.
Mirror. To reflect, as a mirror reflects.
Mock. To imitate in derision or sport.
Model after. To plan or form after.
Parody. To produce a parody on.
Parallel. To make to be like something else in character; to be like.

No imitation.
Non-imitation. Something original or uncopied.
Originality. The power of being original or inventive.

ORIGINALITY—*Adjectives.*

Inimitable. That cannot be copied.
Original. Not imitated or copied
Uncopied. Not imitated.
Unimitated. Not copied.
Unique. Without a like.
Unmatched. Not of the same character, form, size, or quality.
Unparalleled. Having no equal; unmatched.

IMITATION—VERBS—*Continued.*

Personate. To take the character of.
Reecho. To reflect again in sound.
Reflect. To turn back an image of.
Repeat. To say or do something over.
Represent, etc. To form a representation of, etc. See DELINEATION.
Reproduce. To bring forth offspring; to make a copy of.
Simulate. To take or have only the appearance or form of.
Strike in with. To conform with; to side with.
Take after. To attempt to imitate.
Take a leaf out of another's book. To copy or imitate exactly.
Take off. To imitate and mimic.
Take pattern by. Follow the example of.
Transcribe. To reproduce in the same words
Travesty. To imitate so as to make ridiculous or ludicrous.
Tread in the footsteps of.
Tread in the steps of. } To imitate.
Tread in the wake of.
Walk in the shoes of. To copy after.

IMITATION—*Adjectives.*

Imitable. That can be imitated.
Imitated. Copied.
Imitative. Inclined to copy.
Literal. Exactly translated or transcribed; unimaginative.
Mimic. Inclined to imitate for sport or ridicule.
Mock. Merely imitative.
Modeled after. Copied after; imitating.
Molded on. Shaped or formed after.
Paraphrastic. Of the nature of a paraphrase. See *Nouns*.
Second-hand. Not from the original source; being a poor imitation.

IMITATION—*Adverbs, etc.*

Literally. Word by word; unimaginatively.
Literatim [L.]. Letter for letter.
Mot à mot [F.]. Word for word.
Sic [L.]. Thus.
To the letter. Letter by letter.
Totidem verbis [L.]. In so many words.
Verbatim [L.]. In the same words.
Word for word. Exactly.

IMITATION—*Phrase.*

Like master, like man. The servant will be what his master is.

---

im'-i-ta"-tive. Inclined to imitate. DELINEATION-CARICATURE, IMITATION-ORIGINALITY.
im'-i-ta"-tor. A copyist. IMITATION-ORIGINALITY.
im-mac'-u-late. Without spot; pure. CLEANNESS-FILTHINESS, FAULTLESSNESS-FAULTINESS, INNOCENCE-GUILT.
im'-ma-nent. Inherent. SUBJECTIVENESS-OBJECTIVENESS.
im-man'-i-ty. Barbarity. CHARITABLENESS-MALEVOLENCE.
Im-man'-u-el. God with us; a name given to Christ. DIVINITY.
im"-ma-te'-ri-al. Unimportant; spiritual. CONSEQUENCE-INSIGNIFICANCE, MATERIALITY-SPIRITUALITY.

im-ma-te'-ri-al-ism. Spirituality. MATERIALITY-SPIRITUALITY.
im"-ma-te"-ri-al'-i-ty. Spirituality; unimportance. CONSEQUENCE-INSIGNIFICANCE, MATERIALITY-SPIRITUALITY, MIND-IMBECILITY.
im"-ma-te'-ri-al-ness. Spirituality MATERIALITY-SPIRITUALITY.
im"-ma-te'-ri-ate. Incorporeal. MATERIALITY-SPIRITUALITY.
im"-ma-ture'. Undeveloped; imperfect. NOVELTY-ANTIQUITY, PREPARATION-NONPREPARATION.
im"-ma-tu'-ri-ty. Incompletion. ENTIRETY-DEFICIENCY, FAULTLESSNESS-FAULTINESS, NOVELTY-ANTIQUITY, PREPARATION-NONPREPARATION.

im-meas'-u-ra-ble. Illimitable; vast. INFINITY, MAGNITUDE-SMALLNESS.

im-meas'-u-ra-bly. Infinitely. MAGNITUDE-SMALLNESS.

im-me'-di-ate. Instant. CONTINUITY-INTERRUPTION, EARLINESS-LATENESS.

im-me'-di-ate-ly. Instantly; forthwith. EARLINESS-LATENESS, ETERNITY - INSTANTANEITY, HURRY-LEISURE.

immedicabile vulnus [L.] (im-med-i-cab'-il-î vul'-nus) Irreparable injury. GOOD-EVIL.

im-med'-i-ca-ble. Incurable. SANGUINENESS-HOPELESSNESS.

im-mel-o'-di-ous. Inharmonious. MELODY - DISSONANCE.

im''-me-mo'-ri-al. Reaching back beyond memory. NOVELTY-ANTIQUITY; **from time immemorial,** FUTURE-PAST; **immemorial usage,** HABIT-DESUETUDE, NOVELTY-ANTIQUITY.

im-mense'. Vast; very great. GREATNESS-LITTLENESS, INFINITY, MAGNITUDE-SMALLNESS.

im-men'-si-ty. Greatness. GREATNESS-LITTLENESS, MAGNITUDE-SMALLNESS.

im-merge'. Plunge; disappear. INJECTION-EJECTION, WATER-AIR.

im-merse'. Dip entirely under water or other liquid. INJECTION-EJECTION, WATER-AIR.

im-mersed'. Dipped. **Immersed in,** CONFINEMENT.

im-mer'-sion. Dipping; baptism. INJECTION-EJECTION, MATERIALITY-SPIRITUALITY.

im''-meth-od'-ic-al. Lacking method. REGULARITY-IRREGULARITY.

im'-mi-grant. One who immigrates. CONSTITUENT-ALIEN, ENTRANCE-EXIT.

im''-mi-gra'-tion. An immigrating. ENTRANCE-EXIT, TRAVELING-NAVIGATION.

im'-mi-nent. Impending. APPROACH-WITHDRAWAL, OCCURRENCE-DESTINY.

im-mis''-ci-bil'-i-ty. Quality of not mixing. COHESION-LOOSENESS.

im-mis'-ci-ble. Not capable of mixing. COHESION-LOOSENESS.

im-mis'-sion. A sending in. ADMISSION-EXPULSION.

im-mit'-i-ga-ble. Not capable of being softened. PARDON - VINDICTIVENESS, SANGUINENESS - HOPELESSNESS.

im-mix'. Mingle together. MIXTURE-HOMOGENEITY.

im''-mo-bil'-i-ty. Fixedness. MOVEMENT-REST, MUTABILITY-STABILITY.

im-mod'-er-ate-ly. Excessively. MAGNITUDE-SMALLNESS.

im-mod'-est. Impure. PURITY-IMPURITY.

im-mod'-est-ly. Indelicately. PURITY-IMPURITY.

im-mod'-es-ty. Forwardness. PURITY-IMPURITY.

im'-mo-late. To sacrifice. GIVING-RECEIVING, LIFE-KILLING.

im''-mo-la'-tion. Killing; sacrificing; giving. DEVOTION-IDOLATRY, GIVING-RECEIVING, LIFE-KILLING.

im-mor'-al. Wrong; licentious. RIGHT-WRONG, VIRTUE-VICE.

im''-mo-ral'-i-ty. Vice. VIRTUE-VICE.

im-mor'-tal. Deathless; worthy to endure. ETERNITY-INSTANTANEITY, REPUTATION-DISCREDIT, SOLEMNIZATION.

im''-mor-tal'-i-ty. Fame; eternal life. ETERNITY-INSTANTANEITY, REPUTATION-DISCREDIT.

im-mor'-tal-ize. Confer fame. REPUTATION-DISCREDIT.

im-mov''-a-bil'-i-ty. Stability. BIGOTRY-APOSTASY.

im-mov'-a-ble. Firm; quiescent; obstinate. BIGOTRY-APOSTASY, MOVEMENT-REST, MUTABILITY-STABILITY.

im''-mun-dic'-i-ty. Uncleanness. CLEANNESS-FILTHINESS.

im'-mun'-di-ty. Uncleanness. CLEANNESS-FILTHINESS.

im-mu'-ni-ty. Freedom; exemption; privilege. DUENESS-UNDUENESS, DUTY-IMMUNITY, LIBERTY-SUBJECTION.

im-mure'. Shut up within walls. RELEASE-RESTRAINT.

im-mu''-ta-bil'-i-ty. Unchangeableness. DIVINITY, MUTABILITY-STABILITY.

im-mu'-ta-ble. Unchangeable. MUTABILITY-STABILITY.

imo pectore, ab [L.] (ai'-mo pec'-to-ri, ab). From the bottom of the heart. EMOTION.

imp. A little devil. JOVE-FIEND.

im'-pact. Contact; collision; insertion. IMPETUS-REACTION, INJECTION-EJECTION, UNION-DISUNION.

im-pair'. Injure. BETTERMENT-DETERIORATION.

im-pair'-ment. Deterioration. BETTERMENT-DETERIORATION.

im-pale'. Execute; fix on a pale. APERTURE-CLOSURE, RECOMPENSE-PUNITION.

im-pale'-ment. Execution. RECOMPENSE-PUNITION.

im-pal'-pa-ble. Intangible. FRIABILITY, GREATNESS-LITTLENESS, TINGLING-NUMBNESS.

im''-pa-na'-tion. Embodiment in bread. CEREMONIAL.

impar sibi [L.] (im'-par sib'-i). Unequal to itself. PERSISTENCE-WHIM.

im-par'-i-ty. Inequality. EQUALITY-INEQUALITY.

im-part'. Give; make known. ENLIGHTENMENT-SECRECY, GIVING-RECEIVING.

im-par'-tial. Unbiased. RIGHT-WRONG, SAGACITY-INCAPACITY, UPRIGHTNESS-DISHONESTY; **impartial opinion,** FAITH-MISGIVING.

im-par''-ti-al'-i-ty. Fairness. UPRIGHTNESS-DISHONESTY.

im-pass'-a-ble. Not passable; impossible. APERTURE-CLOSURE, POSSIBILITY-IMPOSSIBILITY.

im-pas''-si-bil'-i-ty. Apathy. EXCITABILITY-INEXCITABILITY, SENSITIVENESS-APATHY.

im-pas'-si-ble. Apathetic. POSSIBILITY-IMPOSSIBILITY, SENSITIVENESS-APATHY.

im-pas'-si-ble-ness. Apathy. SENSITIVENESS-APATHY.

im-pas'-sion. Affect with passion. EXCITATION.

im-pas'-sion-a-ble. Excitable. SENSITIVENESS-APATHY.

im-pas'-sioned. Stirring; excited. EXCITABILITY-INEXCITABILITY.

im-pas'-sive. Apathetic. INQUISITIVENESS-INDIFFERENCE, SENSITIVENESS-APATHY.

im-pa'-tience. Intolerance. EXCITABILITY-INEXCITABILITY.

im-pa'-tient. Restless. EXCITABILITY-INEXCITABILITY; **impatient of control,** DESIRE-DISTASTE, INSUBORDINATION-OBEDIENCE.

im-pawn'. Pledge. SECURITY.

im-peach'. Accuse; censure. APPROVAL-DISAPPROVAL, JUSTIFICATION-CHARGE, LITIGATION.

im-peach'-ment. Accusation. JUSTIFICATION-CHARGE; **soft impeachment,** BLANDISHMENT.

im-pec''-ca-bil'-i-ty. Faultlessness; innocence. FAULTLESSNESS-FAULTINESS, INNOCENCE-GUILT.

im''-pe-cu''-ni-os'-i-ty. Penury. AFFLUENCE-PENURY.

im''-pe-cu'-ni-ous. Poor. AFFLUENCE-PENURY.

im-pede'. Obstruct. OBSTRUCTION-HELP.

im-ped'-i-ment. Hindrance. OBSTRUCTION - HELP; **impediment in speech,** SPEECH-INARTICULATENESS.

impedimenta [L.] (im-ped-i-men'-ta). Obstructions; baggage. PROPERTY.

im'-pe-dite. Hinder. OBSTRUCTION-HELP.

im-pe-di'-tion. Hindrance. OBSTRUCTION-HELP.

im-pel'. Drive; urge. IMPETUS-REACTION, MOTIVE-CAPRICE.

im-pelled'. Forced. IMPETUS-REACTION.

im-pel'-lent. Moving. IMPETUS-REACTION.

im-pel'-ling. Moving. IMPETUS-REACTION.

im-pend'. Overhang; threaten; be imminent. FUTURE-PAST, HEIGHT-LOWNESS, OCCURRENCE-DESTINY.

im-pend'-ing. Near; threatening. APPROACH-WITHDRAWAL, EXPECTATION-SURPRISE, OCCURRENCE-DESTINY.

im-pen''-e-tra-bil'-i-ty. Imperviousness. SOLIDITY-RARITY.

i n-pen'-e-tra-ble. Impervious; inaccessible. APERTURE-CLOSURE, CLEARNESS-OBSCURITY, MANIFESTATION-LATENCY, SOLIDITY-RARITY.

im-pen'-i-tence. Hardness of heart. REPENTANCE-OBDURACY.

im-pen'-i-tent. Obdurate. REPENTANCE-OBDURACY.

im-per'-a-tive. Required; binding; authoritative. DUTY-DERELICTION, HARSHNESS-MILDNESS, NEED, RULE-LICENSE; **imperative mode,** VERB.

imperator [L.] (im-per-ē'-tor) Commander. CHIEF-UNDERLING.

im-per'-a-to''-ri-al. Commanding. RULE-LICENSE.

im''-per-cep'-ti-ble. Not perceptible; inappreciable; indiscernible. GREATNESS-LITTLENESS, SWIFTNESS-SLOWNESS, VISIBILITY-INVISIBILITY.

im-per-cep'-ti-bly. Unnoticeably. MAGNITUDE-SMALLNESS, MANIFESTATION-LATENCY, VISIBILITY-INVISIBILITY.

im''-per-cip'-i-ent. Not perceiving. FEELING-INSENSIBILITY.

im-per'-di-ble. Indestructible. SECURITY-INSECURITY.

im-per'-fect. Incomplete; defective. BETTERMENT-DETERIORATION, EMBELLISHMENT-DISFIGUREMENT, ENTIRETY-DEFICIENCY, EXCESS-LACK, FAULTLESSNESS-FAULTINESS, VIRTUE-VICE; **imperfect tense,** VERB.

im''-per-fec'-tion. Lack of perfection; faultiness. ENTIRETY-DEFICIENCY, EXCESS-LACK, FAULTLESSNESS-FAULTINESS, TRANSCURSION-SHORTCOMING, VIRTUE-VICE.

im-per'-fect-ly. Defectively. MAGNITUDE-SMALLNESS.

im-per'-fo-rate. Without perforations. APERTURE-CLOSURE.

im-per''-fo-ra'-tion. Condition of being without aperture. APERTURE-CLOSURE.

im-pe'-ri-al. Predominant; a beard; a luggage case. CONTENTS-RECEIVER, RULE-LICENSE, SMOOTHNESS-ROUGHNESS.

im-pe'-ri-al-ism. A kind of government. TYRANNY-ANARCHY.

im-per'-il. Endanger. SECURITY-INSECURITY.

im-pe'-ri-ous. Domineering; imperative. PRESUMPTION-OBSEQUIOUSNESS, RULE - LICENSE, SELFRESPECT-HUMBLENESS, TYRANNY-ANARCHY; **imperious necessity,** VOLITION-OBLIGATION.

im-per'-ish-a-ble. Enduring; eternal. ETERNITY-INSTANTANEITY, MUTABILITY-STABILITY, REPUTATION-DISCREDIT.

imperium in imperio [L.] (im-pī'-ri-um in im-pī'-ri-o) A government within a government. RULE-LICENSE.

im-per'-ma-nence. Transientness. LASTINGNESS-TRANSIENTNESS.

im-per'-ma-nent. Not lasting. LASTINGNESS-TRANSIENTNESS.

im-per'-me-a-bil'-i-ty. Imperviousness. APERTURE-CLOSURE, SOLIDITY-RARITY.

im-per'-me-a-ble. Impenetrable. APERTURE - CLOSURE, SOLIDITY-RARITY.

im-per'-son-al. Not personal; general. MATERIALITY-SPIRITUALITY, UNIVERSALITY-PARTICULARITY; **impersonal verb,** VERB.

im-per'-son-ate. Personify. DELINEATION-CARICATURE.

im-per''-son-a'-tion. Mocking. ACTING, DELINEATION-CARICATURE.

im-per''-spi-cu'-i-ty. Vagueness. CLEARNESS-OBSCURITY.

im''-per-sua'-si-ble. Inflexible. BIGOTRY-APOSTASY.

im-per'-ti-nence. Irrelevance; impudence. CONNECTION-INDEPENDENCE, PRESUMPTION-OBSEQUIOUSNESS.

im-per'-ti-nent. Irrelevant, insolent. CONNECTION-INDEPENDENCE, PRESUMPTION-OBSEQUIOUSNESS.

im''-per-turb''-a-bil'-i-ty. Calmness. EXCITABILITY-INEXCITABILITY.

im''-per-turb'-a-ble. Calm. EXCITABILITY-INEXCITABILITY, PLEASURE-PAIN, SENSITIVENESS-APATHY.

im-per''-tur-ba'-tion. Calmness. EXCITABILITY-INEXCITABILITY, SENSITIVENESS-APATHY.

im-per'-vi-ous. Impenetrable; pathless; impassable. APERTURE-CLOSURE, BIGOTRY-APOSTASY, POSSIBILITY-IMPOSSIBILITY, SENSITIVENESS-APATHY; **impervious to light,** DIAPHANEITY-OPAQUENESS; **impervious to reason,** BIGOTRY-APOSTASY.

im-per'-vi-ous-ness. Density. APERTURE-CLOSURE.

im''-pe-tig'-i-nous. Like impetigo, a skin-disease. CLEANNESS-FILTHINESS.

im'-pe-trate. Gain by entreaty PETITION-EXPOSTULATION.

im''-pe-tra'-tion. Entreaty. PETITION-EXPOSTULATION.

im-pet''-u-os'-i-ty. Rashness. DESIRE-DISTASTE, EXCITABILITY-INEXCITABILITY, HURRY-LEISURE, RECKLESSNESS-CAUTION, TURBULENCE-CALMNESS.

im-pet'-u-ous. Hasty; precipitate; passionate. EMOTION, EXCITABILITY-INEXCITABILITY, HURRY-LEISURE, TURBULENCE-CALMNESS.

im'-pe-tus. Impulse. IMPETUS-REACTION.

IMPETUS—REACTION

Appulse. A driving toward impulse; act of coming into conjunction.

Arietation. A battering with a battering-ram

Bang. A heavy blow.

Beating, etc. See RECOMPENSE-PUNITION.

Blow. A forcible stroke with the hand, fist or some instrument.

Booming. Violent rushing.

Brunt. Severest shock or stress.

Bump. Violent collision.

Calcitration. The act of kicking.

Cannon. In billiards, the impact of one cue-ball on two or more balls in succession.

Carambole [F.]. In billiards, the impact of the cue-ball against two balls in succession.

Carom. A cannon in billiards.

Charge, etc. See ATTACK.

Clash. Noisy collision.

Collision. Act of striking together with violence.

Concussion. Act of agitating violently; shock.

Contrecoup [F.] A rebound or recoil.

Elasticity, etc. See ELASTICITY.

Kick. Recoil of a gun or other firearm.

Reaction. Act of recoiling; reverse action.

Rebound. Recoil from something that has been struck.

Rebuff. Unexpected and sudden repulse.

Recalcitration. A kicking back, recoil; repugnance.

Recoil. A moving back; rebound.

Reflection. Reflex; the recoil of the mind upon itself.

Reflex. Reflection; an image made by reflection.

Reflux. Recoil of a fluid; flowing back.

Repercussion. The act of driving back, or the state of being driven back; rebound.

Repulse. The act of beating back, or the state of being driven back

Retroaction. Backward action; recoil on something past or preceding.

Return. The act, process, or result of coming back or sending back.

Reverberation, etc. See RESONANCE.

Revulsion. A sudden change or strong reaction.

IMPETUS—REACTION—*Continued.*

Crash. A loud noise resulting from the breakage of things suddenly and violently.
Cuff. A blow with the open hand. See RECOMPENSE-PUNITION.
Cut. A stroke or blow with an edged instrument or whip.
Dab. A gentle blow with the hand.
Dint. A blow.
Dowse. A sudden fall into the water.
Elan [F.]. A jerk or start.
Encounter. A running against or coming together.
Explosion, etc. See TURBULENCE.
Fillip. A smart blow.
Hit. A striking against.
Impact. Forcible collision or contact.
Impetus. The force with which a body is impelled; momentum.
Impulse. Effect of an impelling force; motion resulting from a sudden force acting for a short time.
Impulsion. The act of driving onward or the state of being so driven.
Jog. A slight shake or impulse.
Jolt. A sudden shock.
Kick. A blow with the foot.
Knock. A blow with something hard or heavy.
Lunge. A sudden thrust, as with a sword.
Momentum. The quantity of motion in a body, as determined by multiplying the mass by the velocity.
Occursion. Collision; clash.
Pat. A light, quick blow with the fingers.
Pelt. A blow or stroke from something thrown.
Percussion. Forcible striking of one body against another.
Propulsion, etc. Act of driving forward or backward. See PUSH.
Pulsion. Propulsion.
Punce. } A blow with the fist.
Punch. }
Push. A propelling pressure.
Rap. A quick, smart blow.
Ruade [F.]. A kick.
Shock. Violent collision.
Shove. A strong push.
Slam. A blow with some implement with force.
Slap. A blow with the open hand.
Smack. A quick, smart blow; a kiss.
Squash. A sudden fall of a heavy, soft body.
Stroke. A blow.
Swap. A stroke.
Tap. A light blow with the fingers.
Throw. A driving from the hand or machine.
Thrust. A sudden and violent push.
Thump. A blow with something blunt or heavy.
Thwack. A heavy blow with something flat.
Whack. A smart, resounding blow.
Whap. A blow, or quick, smart stroke.
Yerk. A sudden thrust or motion.

IMPETUS—*Nouns of Cause.*

Ax, etc. See SHARPNESS.
Bat. A stick used to strike a ball.
Battering-ram. An engine used by the ancients to batter down walls; a hammer used by a blacksmith.
Cudgel, etc. See WEAPON.
Flail. An implement used for separating grain by beating.
Hammer. An implement used for driving nails, pounding, etc.
Mall. An implement consisting of a hammer and pick used by the horse-soldiers of the middle ages to break armor.
Mallet. A wooden hammer
Maul. A heavy mallet.
Monkey. A heavy metal hammer worked by pulleys used for driving piles.
Pile-driving engine. An apparatus used for driving piles.
Punch. A tool for driving in or out an object, as a nail, inserted in a hole.
Ram. A steel or iron projection from the bow of a war-vessel, used to cut into or crush the vessel of an enemy.
Rammer. One who or that which rams or batters.
Sledge-hammer. A heavy hammer used by blacksmiths, by road builders, etc.

IMPETUS—*Scientific Terms.*

Dynamics. The science that treats of the laws of mechanical forces.
Seismometer. An instrument for measuring the intensity, duration, etc., of earthquakes and like phenomena.

Ricochet [F.]. A rebound.
Springing back, etc. Recoil; rebound, etc. See *Verbs.*

REACTION—*Denotations.*

Boomerang. A weapon used by the natives of Australia, which has the peculiar property of returning to the thrower.
Ducks and drakes. Rebounding of flat stones thrown on the surface of water.
Reactionist. One who favors reaction.
Spring. An elastic body used in mechanics to cause a recoiling of doors, etc., to their proper position.

REACTION—*Verbs.*

Bound back. Move back with a sudden spring.
Fly back. Move back violently or suddenly.
React. Act in an opposite way; tend toward a former condition.
Rebound. Recoil from something struck.
Recalcitrate. Kick against.
Recoil. Move back; rebound; spring back.
Repercuss. Drive back; reverberate; reflect.
Reverberate. Echo; reflect; repel.
Spring back. Recoil; rebound.

REACTION—*Adjectives.*

Reactionary. Relating to or having the nature of reaction or reverse action.
Recalcitrant. Kicking back or against; repugnant.
Recoiling, etc. Moving back, etc. See *Verbs.*
Refluent. Flowing back; ebbing.
Repercussive. Reverberated; repellent.
Retroactive. Having reverse action; retrospective.

REACTION—*Adverbs.*

On the recoil, etc. While recoiling or rebounding. See *Nouns.*

IMPETUS—*Continued.*

IMPETUS—*Verbs.*

Bang. Knock; beat with a noise.
Baste. Thrash; cudgel.
Batter. Beat with successive blows.
Beat. Strike repeatedly.
Belabor. Beat soundly; thrash.
Boom. Push with a boom or pole, as to boom out a sail; to impel with a rush.
Buffet. Strike with the hand or fist; thump.
Bump against. Collide.
Butt. Strike with the head or horns.
Butt against. Impel the head against.
Calcitrate. To kick.
Cant. Throw suddenly; jerk; tilt up.
Collide. Meet and strike with violence.
Come into collision. Collide.
Dab. Strike quickly; thrust; pat.
Dash. Throw suddenly and forcibly.
Dowse. Strike.
Drive. Push forward; impel.
Elbow. Push with the elbows.
Encounter. Come against suddenly or deliberately.
Enter into collision. Collide.
Fall foul of. Collide with; attack.
Fetch one a blow. Strike one.
Flap. Strike with a flap.
Foin. Thrust with, as with a sword-stab.
Foul. Collide so as to impede or entangle.
Give an impetus to, etc. Impel, etc. See *Nouns.*
Give a start to. Originate motion in, especially with a sudden impulse.
Hit. Strike; administer a blow to.
Hit hard. Strike with a heavy blow
Hurtle. Move violently; hurl.
Hustle. Push roughly.
Impel. Drive forward.
Impinge. Dash against; clash with.
Jog. Push with a jog; nudge.
Jolt. Shake or cause to shake with a sudden up-and-down motion.

IMPETUS—Verbs—*Continued.*

Jostle. Crowd against; elbow.
Justle. See Jostle.
Kick. Give a blow to with the foot.
Knock. Give a blow to or with.
Knock one's head against. Bump with the head.
Lunge. Make a long, sudden thrust.
Pat. Strike lightly or gently, as with the hand.
Patter. Strike with a quick succession of pats.
Pelt. Throw something at; come down violently.
Pink. Stab with a pointed weapon.
Poke at. Thrust against.
Prod. Poke some pointed instrument into.
Punch. Make a hole in; beat with the fists.
Push. Impel by pressure.
Rap. Hit sharply and quickly
Run against. Collide with.
Run foul of. Come into collision.
Run one's head against. To strike with the head.
Set going. Cause to go; give an impulse to.

Shoulder. Push with the shoulders.
Shove. Impel along, as on a surface.
Slam. Impel with violence; close violently.
Slap. Strike with something flat, as the palm of the hand.
Start. Begin motion by a sudden impulse.
Strike. Touch or hit forcibly; come into collision with.
Strike at. See Attack.
Strike hard. Hit hard or violently.
Swap. Fall with violence; beat the air; flap.
Tap. Strike gently or lightly.
Throw, etc. See Push.
Thump. Strike with a heavy, dull sound.
Thrust. Push or shove forcibly; pierce.
Thwack. Strike with something flat or weighty.
Urge. Drive; impel.
Whack. Strike with heavy, resounding blows.
Whip, etc. See Recompense-Punition.
Yerk. Jerk; throw with a sudden movement.

IMPETUS—*Adjectives.*

Booming. Rushing violently.
Dynamic. } Pertaining to dynamics; characterized by mechanical
Dynamical. } force.
Impelled, etc. Driven; urged, etc. See *Verbs.*

Impellent. Having the power to impel.
Impelling, etc. Driving; urging, etc. See *Verbs.*
Impulsive. Having the power of driving or impelling.

im-pi'-e-ty. Ungodliness. Godliness-Ungodliness.
im-pig'-no-rate. Pledge. Security.
im-pinge'. Strike. Impetus-Reaction.
im'-pi-ous. Ungodly. Godliness-Ungodliness.
imp'-ish. Like an imp. Jove-Fiend.
im-pla''-ca-bil'-i-ty. Relentlessness. Love-Hate, Pardon-Vindictiveness.
im-pla'-ca-ble. Cruel; unforgiving. Love-Hate, Pardon-Vindictiveness.
im-plant'. Insert; inculcate. Education-Misteaching, Injection-Ejection.
im''-plan-ta'-tion. Insertion. Injection-Ejection.
im-plant'-ed. Ingrained. Subjectiveness-Objectiveness.
im-plead'. Sue at law. Litigation.
im'-ple-ment. Tool. Instrument.
im-ple'-tion. Filling. Entirety-Deficiency.
im'-plex. Intricate. Mixture-Homogeneity.
im'-pli-cate. Involve; accuse. Inclusion-Omission, Justification-Charge.
im'-pli-ca''-ted. Involved; constituent. Connection-Independence, Constituent-Alien.
im''-pli-ca'-tion. Entanglement; deduction. Manifestation-Latency, Regularity-Irregularity.
im-plic'-it. Implied. Manifestation-Latency; **implicit belief,** Faith-Misgiving.
im-plied'. Understood. Manifestation-Latency, Meaning-Jargon.
im''-plo-ra'-tion. Entreaty. Petition-Expostulation.
im-plore'. Entreat. Petition-Expostulation.
im-ply'. Involve; signify. Evidence-Counterevidence, Likelihood-Unlikelihood, Manifestation-Latency, Meaning-Jargon.
im-pol'-i-cy. Unsuitableness. Skill-Unskilfulness.
im''-po-lite'. Discourteous. Politeness-Impoliteness.
im-pon''-der-a-bil'-i-ty. Lightness. Heaviness-Lightness.
im-pon'-der-a-ble. Without weight. Heaviness-Lightness.
im-po-ros'-i-ty. Imperviousness. Solidity-Rarity.
im-po'-rous. Dense; very close. Aperture-Closure, Solidity-Rarity.
im-port'. Take in; mean; concern. Admission-Expulsion, Consequence-Insignificance, Entrance-Exit, Environment-Interposition, Injection-Ejection, Meaning-Jargon.

im-por'-tance. Consequence. Consequence-Insignificance, Dominance-Impotence, Magnitude-Smallness, Precedence-Succession, Reputation-Discredit; **attach importance to,** Consequence-Insignificance; **attach too much importance to,** Overvaluation-Undervaluation; **of no importance,** Consequence-Insignificance.
im-por'-tant. Consequential. Consequence-Insignificance, Dominance-Impotence, Magnitude-Smallness.
im''-por-ta'-tion. Introduction. Entrance-Exit.
im-por'-tu-nate. Urgent. Petition-Expostulation, Pleasurableness-Painfulness.
im''-por-tune'. Beg; pester. Petition-Expostulation, Pleasurableness-Painfulness.
im''-por-tun'-i-ty. Urgency. Petition-Expostulation.
im-pose'. Lay on; awe. Order, Regard-Disrespect; **impose upon,** Credulousness-Skepticism, Right-Wrong, Truthfulness-Fraud.
im-pos'-ing. Impressive. Consequence-Insignificance, Excitation, Reputation-Discredit.
im-po-si'-tion. A laying on; command; injustice; fraud. Dueness-Undueness, Order, Truthfulness-Fraud; **imposition of hands,** Ceremonial.
impossibile, credo quia [L.] (im-pos-sib'-i-lî, crî'-do quai'-a). I believe because it is impossible. Credulousness-Skepticism.
im-pos''-si-bil'-i-ties. Things that cannot be done. **Seek after impossibilities,** Usefulness-Uselessness.
im-pos''-si-bil'-i-ty. Impracticability. Possibility-Impossibility.
im-pos'-si-ble. Impracticable. Number, Possibility-Impossibility, Proffer-Refusal.
im'-post. Plane of base of an arch; a tax. Architecture, Price-Discount.
im-pos'-thume. An abscess. Health-Sickness.
im-pos'-tor. A deceiver. Gull-Deceiver.
im-pos'-ture. Cheat. Truthfulness-Fraud.
im'-po-tence. Feebleness. Might-Impotence, Strength-Weakness.
im'-po-tent. Without strength. Might-Impotence, Strength-Weakness; **impotent conclusion,** Success-Failure.
im-pound'. Shut up. Release-Restraint.
im-pov'-er-ish. Make poor; exhaust; weaken. Affluence-Penury, Excess-Lack, Property, Provision-Waste, Strength-Weakness.

im-prac'-ti-ca-bil"-i-ty. Uselessness. DIFFICULTY - FACILITY.

im-prac'-ti-ca-ble. Impossible; not easily managed; misjudging. BIGOTRY - APOSTASY, DIFFICULTY-FACILITY, JUDGMENT-MISJUDGMENT, POSSIBILITY-IMPOSSIBILITY, SANGUINENESS-HOPELESSNESS.

im'-pre-cate. Curse. CHARITABLENESS-CURSE, PETITION-EXPOSTULATION.

im"-pre-ca'-tion. Curse. CHARITABLENESS - CURSE, PETITION-EXPOSTULATION.

im-preg'-na-ble. Safe from attack. SECURITY-INSECURITY, STRENGTH-WEAKNESS.

im-preg'-nate. Make pregnant; fertilize; insert; imbue. COMPOSITION - RESOLUTION, CREATION - DESTRUCTION, EDUCATION-MISTEACHING, FERTILITY-STERILITY, INJECTION-EJECTION, MIXTURE-HOMOGENEITY.

im"-preg-na'-tion. Mixture; fecundation. COMPOSITION-RESOLUTION, CREATION-DESTRUCTION, MIXTURE-HOMOGENEITY.

impresario [It.] (îm"-prê-sa'-rî-o). Opera manager. ACTING.

im"-pre-scrip'-ti-ble. Incapable of being either lost or acquired by usage or prescription. DUENESS-UNDUENESS.

im-press'. Influence; fix; indent. EMOTION, EXCITATION, FEELING-INSENSIBILITY, SIGN; **impress upon the mind,** EDUCATION-MISTEACHING, REMEMBRANCE-FORGETFULNESS.

im-pressed'. Influenced. **Impressed with,** EMOTION, FAITH-MISGIVING.

im-press"-i-bil'-i-ty. Susceptibility. MOTIVE-CAPRICE, SECURITY-INSECURITY, SENSITIVENESS-APATHY.

im-press'-i-ble. Susceptible. SENSITIVENESS-APATHY.

im-pres'-sion. Stamp; mark; print; effect. CONCEPTION-THEME, EMOTION, ENGRAVING, FAITH-MISGIVING, FEELING-INSENSIBILITY, KNOWLEDGE-IGNORANCE, SIGN, WRITING-PRINTING; **make an impression,** REFLECTION-VACANCY, VIGOR-INERTIA.

im-pres'-sion-a-ble. Susceptible of impression. SENSITIVENESS-APATHY.

im-press'-ive. Making an impression; effective. CONSEQUENCE-INSIGNIFICANCE, EMOTION, EXCITATION, FAITH-MISGIVING, FEELING-INSENSIBILITY, FORCE-WEAKNESS.

im-press'-ive-ness. The quality of being impressive. EXCITATION.

imprimis [L.] (im-prai'-mis). Chiefly. BEGINNING-END.

imprimit [L.] (im'-prim-it). It imprints. ENGRAVING.

im-print'. Print; make an impression. PUBLICITY, SIGN; **imprint in the memory,** REMEMBRANCE-FORGETFULNESS.

im-pris'-on. Put into prison. CONFINEMENT, RELEASE-RESTRAINT.

im-pris'-oned. Put in prison. CONFINEMENT, GUARD-PRISONER, RELEASE-RESTRAINT.

im-pris'-on-ment. Restraint of liberty. ATONEMENT, LAW-LAWLESSNESS, RELEASE-RESTRAINT.

im-prob"-a-bil'-i-ty. Unlikelihood. LIKELIHOOD-UNLIKELIHOOD.

im-prob'-a-ble. Unlikely. LIKELIHOOD-UNLIKELIHOOD.

im'-pro-bate. Disapprove of. APPROVAL - DISAPPROVAL.

im"-pro-ba'-tion. The act of disapproving. APPROVAL-DISAPPROVAL.

im-prob'-i-ty. Dishonesty. UPRIGHTNESS-DISHONESTY.

im-promp'-tu. Anything done on the impulse of the moment. PREDETERMINATION-IMPULSE.

impromptu fait à loisir [F.] (an'-pron'p-tü' fêt a lwazir'). Anything done at leisure. PREPARATION-NONPREPARATION.

im-prop'-er. Not proper; unfit; indecent. DUENESS-UNDUENESS, HARMONY-DISCORD, PROPRIETY-IMPROPRIETY, RIGHT-WRONG, SAGACITY-INCAPACITY, VIRTUE-VICE, WELFARE-MISFORTUNE; **improper time,** OPPORTUNENESS-UNSUITABLENESS.

im-pro'-pri-ate. Appropriate. HOLDING-EXEMPTION, TAKING-RESTITUTION.

im-pro"-pri-a'-tion. The act of impropriating. HOLDING-EXEMPTION.

im-pro'-pri-a"-tor. One who impropriates. HOLDER.

im-pro-pri'-e-ty. Unsuitableness. HARMONY - DISCORD, PROPRIETY-IMPROPRIETY, VIRTUE-VICE.

im-prov'-a-ble. Capable of being improved. BETTERMENT-DETERIORATION.

im-prove'. Make better. BETTERMENT - DETERIORATION, EDUCATION-MISTEACHING, GOODNESS-BADNESS; **improve the occasion,** OPPORTUNENESS-UNSUITABLENESS; **improve the shining hour,** ACTIVITY-INDOLENCE; **improve upon,** BETTERMENT-DETERIORATION.

im-prove'-ment. Betterment. ADVANCE-RETROGRESSION, BETTERMENT-DETERIORATION, GOOD-EVIL.

im-prov'-i-dence. Want of providence. CAREFULNESS-CARELESSNESS, PREPARATION-NONPREPARATION.

im-prov'-i-dent. Lacking foresight. CAREFULNESS-CARELESSNESS, EXTRAVAGANCE-AVARICE, PREPARATION-NONPREPARATION, RECKLESSNESS-CAUTION.

im-prov'-i-sate. To improvise. PREDETERMINATION-IMPULSE.

im-prov"-i-sa'-tion. An impromptu. PREDETERMINATION-IMPULSE, PREPARATION-NONPREPARATION.

improvisatore [It.] (îm-pro-vi-za-to'-rê). One who composes and sings extemporaneously. POETRY-PROSE, PREDETERMINATION-IMPULSE, SPEECH-INARTICULATENESS.

im-prov'-i-sa-to-ry. Relating to extempory composition of rhymes. PREDETERMINATION-IMPULSE.

im-pro-vise'. Compose, sing, etc., without previous study or preparation. FANCY, PREDETERMINATION-IMPULSE, PREPARATION-NONPREPARATION.

improvisé [F.] (an'-pro-vi-zê'). Done extempore. PREDETERMINATION-IMPULSE.

im-pro-vised'. Done off-hand. PREDETERMINATION-IMPULSE.

im-pro-vi'-so. Impromptu. PREDETERMINATION-IMPULSE.

improviste, à l' [F.] (an'-pro-vist', al). Unexpectedly. EXPECTATION - SURPRISE, PREDETERMINATION - IMPULSE.

im-pru'-dence. Want of prudence. RECKLESSNESS-CAUTION.

im-pru'-dent. Lacking discretion. CAREFULNESS-CARELESSNESS, RECKLESSNESS-CAUTION.

im'-pu-dence. Rudeness. POLITENESS - IMPOLITENESS, PRESUMPTION-OBSEQUIOUSNESS.

im'-pu-dent. Insolent; rude. POLITENESS-IMPOLITENESS, PRESUMPTION-OBSEQUIOUSNESS.

im"-pu-dic'-i-ty. Immodesty. PURITY-IMPURITY.

im-pugn'. Assail; oppose; blame. APPROVAL-DISAPPROVAL, ASSERTION-DENIAL, ATTACK-DEFENSE.

im"-pug-na'-tion. Act of impugning. ANTAGONISM-CONCURRENCE.

im-pu'-is-sance. Inability. MIGHT-IMPOTENCE.

im'-pulse. Impetus; push; sudden feeling. IMPETUS-REACTION, MOTIVE-CAPRICE, PREDETERMINATION-IMPULSE; **blind impulse,** VOLITION-OBLIGATION; **creature of impulse,** PREDETERMINATION-IMPULSE; **give an impulse to,** MOTIVE-CAPRICE, OBSTRUCTION-HELP, PUSH-PULL.

im-pul'-sion. The act of impelling or driving onward. IMPETUS-REACTION, MOTIVE-CAPRICE.

im-pul'-sive. Actuated by impulse; having power of impelling. EXCITABILITY-INEXCITABILITY, IMPETUS-REACTION, MOTIVE - CAPRICE, PREDETERMINATION-

IMPULSE, RATIOCINATION-INSTINCT, RECKLESSNESS-CAUTION, VOLITION-OBLIGATION.

im-pu'-ni-ty. Freedom from punishment. ESCAPE, EXCULPATION-CONVICTION; **with impunity,** SECURITY-INSECURITY.

im-pure'. Defiled. CLEANNESS-FILTHINESS, PURITY-IMPURITY.

im-pu'-ri-ty. Foulness; licentiousness. CLEANNESS-FILTHINESS, PURITY-IMPURITY.

im-pu'-ta-ble. Chargeable. JUSTIFICATION-CHARGE.

im''-pu-ta'-tion. Ascription; censure. JUSTIFICATION-CHARGE, RATIONALE-LUCK, REPUTATION-DISCREDIT.

im-pu'-ta-tive. Insinuating. JUSTIFICATION-CHARGE.

im-pute'. Charge. JUSTIFICATION-CHARGE.

in. Within. OUTSIDE-INSIDE; **go in,** ENTRANCE-EXIT; **in and out,** CIRCLE-WINDING, VIBRATION; **in as much as,** CONNECTION-INDEPENDENCE, QUANTITY-MEASURE; **in doors,** OUTSIDE-INSIDE; **in for,** ENGAGEMENT-RELEASE, ENTERPRISE; **ins and outs,** EXTENSION-PLACE.

in articulo [L.] (in ar-tic'-yu-lo). At the moment. LASTINGNESS-TRANSIENTNESS.

in extenso [L.] (in ex-ten'-so). At full length. TERSENESS-PROLIXITY, WHOLE-PART.

in forma pauperis [L.] (in for'-ma pau'-per-is). As a poor man. AFFLUENCE-PENURY.

in limine [L.] (in lim'-i-nî). At the threshold. BEGINNING-END.

in loco [L.] (in lo'-co). In the place. HARMONY-DISCORD, USEFULNESS-USELESSNESS.

in medias res [L.] (in mî'-di-as rîz) In the midst of affairs. MIDDLE.

in propria persona [L.] (in pro'-pri-a per-so'-na). In person. UNIVERSALITY-PARTICULARITY.

in statu pupillari [L.] (in stê'-tiu piu-pil-lê'-rai). In an orphan condition. INFANCY-AGE.

in statu quo [L.] (in stê'-tiu quo). In the former state. MUTATION-PERMANENCE.

in toto [L.] (in to'-to). Entirely. ENTIRETY-DEFICIENCY.

in transitu [L.] (in tran'-si-tiu). In passing. CONVERSION-REVERSION, LASTINGNESS-TRANSIENTNESS, TRANSFER.

in''-a-bil'-i-ty. Want of power or skill. MIGHT-IMPOTENCE, SKILL-UNSKILFULNESS.

in-ab'-sti-nence. Indulgence. MODERATION-SELFINDULGENCE.

in-ab'-sti-nent. Not refraining from indulgence. MODERATION-SELFINDULGENCE.

in''-ac-ces'-si-ble. Not to be reached. POSSIBILITY-IMPOSSIBILITY, REMOTENESS-NEARNESS.

in-ac'-cu-rate. Incorrect. GRAMMAR-SOLECISM, TRUTH-ERROR.

in-ac'-tion. Idleness. ACTION-PASSIVENESS, ACTIVITY-INDOLENCE, VIGOR-INERTIA.

in-act'-ive. Idle. ACTIVITY-INDOLENCE, SKILL-UNSKILFULNESS, VIGOR-INERTIA.

in-act'-ive-ly. Idly. ACTIVITY-INDOLENCE, VIGOR-INERTIA.

in''-ac-tiv'-i-ty. Idleness. ACTION-PASSIVENESS, ACTIVITY-INDOLENCE, STRENGTH-WEAKNESS, VIGOR-INERTIA.

in-ad'-e-qua-cy. Insufficiency. EXCESS-LACK, PROVISION-WASTE, USEFULNESS-USELESSNESS.

in-ad'-e-quate. Insufficient; imperfect. EXCESS-LACK, MIGHT-IMPOTENCE, FAULTLESSNESS-FAULTINESS, USEFULNESS-USELESSNESS; **inadequate adversative,** PARTICLE.

in''-ad-mis'-si-ble. Requiring rejection. CONSTITUENT-ALIEN, HARMONY-DISCORD, INCLUSION-OMISSION, PROPRIETY-IMPROPRIETY.

in''-ad-vert'-ence. Heedlessness. HEED-DISREGARD.

in''-ad-vert'-en-cy. Heedlessness. HEED-DISREGARD.

in''-ad-vert'-ent. Heedless. HEED-DISREGARD.

in''-ad-vert'-ent-ly. Heedlessly. HEED-DISREGARD.

in''-ad-vi'-sa-ble. Not advisable. PROPRIETY-IMPROPRIETY.

in-af'-fa-ble. Reserved. POLITENESS-IMPOLITENESS.

in-a'-lien-a-ble. Not transferable. HARMONY-DISCORD, KEEPING-RELINQUISHMENT.

in-a''-mo-ra'-ta. A sweetheart. LOVE-HATE.

in-ane'. Senseless; void; vacant. CONSEQUENCE-INSIGNIFICANCE, MEANING-JARGON, SUBSTANCE-NULLITY, USEFULNESS-USELESSNESS.

in-an'-i-mate. Lifeless. LIFE-DEATH, ORGANIZATION-INORGANIZATION; **inanimate matter,** ORGANIZATION-INORGANIZATION.

in''-a-ni'-tion. Exhaustion. EXCESS-LACK.

in-an'-i-ty. Senselessness; vacancy. CONSEQUENCE-INSIGNIFICANCE, MEANING-JARGON, SUBSTANCE-NULLITY, USEFULNESS-USELESSNESS.

in-ap'-pe-ten-cy. Want of desire. SENSITIVENESS-APATHY, UNCONCERN.

in-ap''-pli-ca-bil'-i-ty. Unfitness. HARMONY-DISCORD.

in-ap''-pli-ca-ble. Unsuitable. CONNECTION-INDEPENDENCE, HARMONY-DISCORD.

in-ap'-po-site. Not pertinent; unfit. CONNECTION-INDEPENDENCE, HARMONY-DISCORD.

in''-ap-pre'-ci-a-ble. Too small to be perceived. GREATNESS-LITTLENESS, MAGNITUDE-SMALLNESS.

in-ap''-pre-hen'-si-ble. Unintelligible. CLEARNESS-OBSCURITY, SAGACITY-INCAPACITY.

in''-ap-pro'-pri-ate. Unbecoming. HARMONY-DISCORD, PROPRIETY-IMPROPRIETY.

in-apt'. Unsuitable; unskilful. HARMONY-DISCORD, MIGHT-IMPOTENCE, PROPRIETY-IMPROPRIETY, SAGACITY-INCAPACITY, SKILL-UNSKILFULNESS, USEFULNESS-USELESSNESS.

in-apt'-i-tude. Unreadiness. HARMONY-DISCORD, MIGHT-IMPOTENCE, USEFULNESS-USELESSNESS.

in''-ar-tic'-u-late. Not uttered with distinctness. SPEECH-INARTICULATENESS, VOCALIZATION-MUTENESS.

in''-ar-tic'-u-late-ness. Indistinctness. SPEECH-INARTICULATENESS.

in-ar''-ti-fi'-cial. Natural. CRAFT-ARTLESSNESS.

in''-ar-tis'-tic. Not tastefully executed. BEAUTY-UGLINESS.

in''-as-much'. Since. CONNECTION-INDEPENDENCE, QUANTITY-MEASURE, RATIOCINATION-INSTINCT.

in''-at-ten'-tion. Disregard. CAREFULNESS-CARELESSNESS, HEED-DISREGARD, UNCONCERN.

in''-at-ten'-tive. Listless. CAREFULNESS-CARELESSNESS, EXPECTATION-SURPRISE, HEED-DISREGARD, SENSITIVENESS-APATHY.

in''-at-ten'-tive-ly. Listlessly. HEED-DISREGARD.

in-au''-di-bil'-i-ty. Incapability to be heard.

in-au'-di-ble. Silent; incapable of being heard. HEARING-DEAFNESS, LOUDNESS-FAINTNESS, SOUND-SILENCE, VOCALIZATION-MUTENESS.

in-au'-gu-ral. Pertaining to an inauguration. BEGINNING-END, PREDECESSOR-CONTINUATION.

in-au'-gu-rate. Begin; install. BEGINNING-END, COMMISSION-ABROGATION, SOLEMNIZATION.

in-au''-gu-ra'-tion. Beginning; installation. BEGINNING-END, COMMISSION-ABROGATION, SOLEMNIZATION.

in''-aus-pi'-cious. Ill-omened; unlucky. GOODNESS-BADNESS, OPPORTUNENESS-UNSUITABLENESS, SANGUINENESS-HOPELESSNESS.

in'-be''-ing. Inherent existence. SUBJECTIVENESS-OBJECTIVENESS.

in'-born''. Innate. AFFECTIONS, SUBJECTIVENESS-OBJECTIVENESS.

in'-bred''. Bred within; innate. AFFECTIONS, SUBJECTIVENESS-OBJECTIVENESS.

in'-ca. Peruvian chief. CHIEF-UNDERLING.

in-cage'. Confine in a cage. RELEASE-RESTRAINT.

in-cal′-cu-la-ble. Beyond calculation. INFINITY.

in″-ca-les′-cence. Increase in heat. HEAT-COLD.

in″-can-des′-cence. A white heat. HEAT-COLD.

in″-can-des′-cent. White. **Incandescent light,** ELECTRICITY.

in″-can-ta′-tion. Singing or reciting of formulas; enchantment. DEVOTION-CHARM, PETITION-EXPOSTULATION.

in-can′-ta-to-ry. Magical. DEVOTION-MAGIC.

in-ca″-pa-bil′-i-ty. Incapacity. MIGHT-IMPOTENCE.

in-ca′-pa-ble. Impotent. MIGHT-IMPOTENCE.

in″-ca-pa′-cious. Narrow; small. BREADTH-NARROWNESS.

in″-ca-pac′-i-tate. Render incapable. MIGHT-IMPOTENCE.

in″-ca-pac′-i-ty. Incapability. KNOWLEDGE-IGNORANCE, MIGHT-IMPOTENCE, SAGACITY-INCAPACITY.

in-car′-cer-ate. Imprison. RELEASE-RESTRAINT.

in-car″-cer-a′-tion. Imprisonment. RELEASE-RESTRAINT.

in-car′-na-dine. Dye red or flesh-color. REDNESS-GREENNESS.

in-car′-nate. Embodied in flesh. SUBJECTIVENESS-OBJECTIVENESS, VIRTUE-VICE; **devil incarnate,** ANGEL-FIEND, GOOD MAN-BAD MAN, UNSELFISHNESS-SELFISHNESS.

In″-car-na′-tion. Assumption of the human nature by Jesus Christ. DIVINITY.

in-case′. Enclose in a case. CONFINEMENT, COVER-LINING.

in-case′-ment. To enclose in a case. ENCLOSURE.

in-cau′-tious. Rash. RECKLESSNESS-CAUTION.

in-cen′-di-a-rism. An incendiary act. CREATION-DESTRUCTION, HEATING-COOLING.

in-cen′-di-a-ry. Pertaining to malicious setting on fire; tending to inflame passion; one who commits arson. BENEFACTOR-EVILDOER, CHARITABLENESS-MALEVOLENCE, CREATION-DESTRUCTION, GOOD MAN-BAD MAN, HEATING-COOLING, MOTIVE-CAPRICE.

in-cense′. Enrage. FAVORITE-ANGER, LOVE-HATE.

in′-cense. Perfume exhaled by burning spices. ADULATION-DISPARAGEMENT, CEREMONIAL, COMBUSTIBLE, DEVOTION-IDOLATRY, PERFUME-STENCH.

in-cen′-sion. Kindling. HEATING-COOLING.

in-cen′-tive. Motive. BEGINNING-END, MOTIVE-CAPRICE.

in-cep′-tion. Beginning. BEGINNING-END.

in-cep′-tor. A beginner. INSTRUCTOR-PUPIL.

in-cer′-ti-tude. Doubt. CERTAINTY-DOUBT.

in-ces′-sant. Unceasing; repeated. ETERNITY-INSTANTANEITY, FREQUENCY-RARITY, RECURRENCE.

in-ces′-sant-ly. In an unceasing manner. FREQUENCY-RARITY.

in′-cest. Coition between persons too nearly related to marry. PURITY-IMPURITY.

in-ces′-tu-ous. Guilty of incest. PURITY-IMPURITY.

inch. One-twelfth of a foot. LENGTH-SHORTNESS, MAGNITUDE-SMALLNESS, MEASURE; **by inches,** QUANTITY-MEASURE, SWIFTNESS-SLOWNESS, WHOLE-PART; **give an inch and take an ell,** DUENESS-UNDUENESS, PRESUMPTION-OBSEQUIOUSNESS, RIGHT-WRONG, TAKING-RESTITUTION; **inch by inch,** QUANTITY-MEASURE, SWIFTNESS-SLOWNESS, WHOLE-PART; **not see an inch beyond one's nose,** SKILL-UNSKILFULNESS; **not yield an inch,** BIGOTRY-APOSTASY; **to an inch,** TRUTH-ERROR.

in′-cho-ate. Incipient. BEGINNING-END, PREPARATION-NONPREPARATION.

in″-cho-a′-tion. Commencement. BEGINNING-END.

in-cho′-a-tive. Inceptive. BEGINNING-END.

in-cide′. Cut. UNION-DISUNION.

in′-ci-dence. A falling on or upon. AIM-ABERRATION

in′-ci-dent. A happening. OCCURRENCE-DESTINY; **full of incident,** OCCURRENCE-DESTINY.

in″-ci-den′-tal. Contingent; concomitant; casual. CONDITION-SITUATION, CONNECTION-INDEPENDENCE, CONTINGENCY, OCCURRENCE-DESTINY, PURPOSE-LUCK, RATIONALE-LUCK, SUBJECTIVENESS-OBJECTIVENESS.

in″-ci-den′-tal-ly. Casually. CONNECTION-INDEPENDENCE, PURPOSE-LUCK.

incidit in Scyllum qui vult vitare Charybdin [L.] (in′-si-dit in sil′-lam quai vult vai-tê′-rî kar-ib′-din·). He falls into Scylla who seeks to avoid Charybdis. SECURITY-INSECURITY.

in-cin′-er-ate. Reduce to ashes. HEATING-COOLING.

in-cip′-i-ence. Inception. BEGINNING-END.

in-cip′-i-ent. Initial. BEGINNING-END.

in-cir′-cum-spect. Heedless. CAREFULNESS-CARELESSNESS.

in-cise′. To cut. GROOVE, UNION-DISUNION.

in-ci′-sion. Cut. GROOVE, UNION-DISUNION.

in-ci′-sive. Penetrating. EMOTION, FORCE-WEAKNESS, VIGOR-INERTIA.

in″-ci-ta′-tion. Incitement. MOTIVE-CAPRICE.

in-cite′. Urge. MOTIVE-CAPRICE, TURBULENCE-CALMNESS.

in-cite′-ment. Arousal. MOTIVE-CAPRICE.

in″-ci-vil′-i-ty. Impoliteness. POLITENESS-IMPOLITENESS.

in-civ′-ism. Want of patriotism. HUMANITARIANISM-MISANTHROPY.

in-clasp′. Encircle. CONFINEMENT.

in-clave′. Dovetailed. ARCHITECTURE.

in-clem′-en-cy. Severity of weather. HARSHNESS-MILDNESS, HEAT-COLD, TURBULENCE-CALMNESS.

in-clem′-ent. Harsh; severe. COMPASSION-RUTHLESSNESS, HARSHNESS-MILDNESS, HEAT-COLD.

in″-cli-na′-tion. Tendency; slope. AIM-ABERRATION, DESIRE-DISTASTE, INCLINATION, LOVE-HATE, MOTIVE-CAPRICE, PARALLELISM-INCLINATION, READINESS-RELUCTANCE.

INCLINATION.

Applicability. Quality of being fit to be applied.

Aptitude. A natural tendency for anything.

Aptness. See APTITUDE.

Bent. A tendency or propensity of the mind.

Bias. A tendency.

Cast. Tendency of manner or mien.

Conducement. A tendency.

Conduciveness. The state of tending to advance or promote.

Drift. See AIM.

Grain. An essential tendency of disposition.

Humor. A tendency to excite mirth.

Idiocrasy. A tendency peculiar to oneself.

Idiosyncrasy. See IDIOCRASY.

Inclination. A tendency of the mind or will.

Leaning to. A tendency toward.

Liability. See CONTINGENCY.

Mood. A tendency of the mind.

Nature. The essential inherent tendencies peculiar to one's body or mind.

Predisposition. Previous inclination or tendency.

Proclivity. A propensity or tendency.

Proneness. Inclination of mind or heart

Propensity. A natural tendency.

Quality. A characteristic tendency.

Set. An attitude, position, or tendency.

Subservience. See INSTRUMENTALITY.

Susceptibility. Capability of being affected.

Temperament. Constitutional tendency.

Tendency. The character of tending towards some end; inclination.

Tone. The prevailing character or tendency.

Turn. New tendency.

Vein. Peculiar tendency or turn of mind.

View. Tendency in looking at things.

INCLINATION—*Verbs.*

Affect. To give a tendency to.
Bend to. To direct a tendency toward.
Bid fair to. Show a tendency toward.
Carry. To urge, effect, accomplish.
Conduce. To tend toward a result.
Contribute. To give in aid for something.
Dispose. To give a tendency to.
Gravitate toward. To have a strong tendency toward.
Incline. To give a tendency to.
Lead. To tend toward.
Promote. See OBSTRUCTION-HELP.
Redound to. To contribute; conduce.
Tend. To have a tendency toward; to exert an influence in a certain way.
Trend. To have a general tendency.
Verge. To approach.

INCLINATION—*Adjectives.*

Calculated to. Intended to produce a certain effect.
Conducive. Tending toward a result.
In a fair way to. Tending fairly toward.
Liable. See LIABILITY.
Subservient. Tending toward some end or purpose. See INSTRUMENTALITY.

Subsidiary. See OBSTRUCTION-HELP.
Tending. See *Verbs.*
Useful. See USEFULNESS.
Working toward. Tending toward.

INCLINATION—*Adverbs.*

For. Tending toward.
Whither. Tending to what or which place.

in-cline'. Tend; slope. AIM-ABERRATION, INCLINATION, MOTIVE-CAPRICE, PARALLELISM-INCLINATION, READINESS-RELUCTANCE; **incline an ear to,** HEED-DISREGARD.
in-clined'. Sloped. **Inclined plane,** AFFECTIONS, DESIRE-DISTASTE, INSTRUMENT, READINESS-RELUCTANCE.
in-clude'. Comprise. INCLUSION-OMISSION, **include in a class,** ADMISSION-EXCLUSION.
in-clu'-ded. Comprised. ADMISSION-EXCLUSION.
in-clu'-ding. Embracing. ADDITION-SUBTRACTION, ADMISSION-EXCLUSION.
in-clu'-sion. Act of including. ADMISSION-EXCLUSION, INCLUSION-OMISSION.

INCLUSION—OMISSION.

Admission. The state of allowing to enter.
Combination. A joining together so as to form a whole. See COMPOSITION.
Composition. The act of putting together of parts.
Comprehension. The act or state of including.
Constitution. The established system of parts.
Inclusion. The act of including or the state of being included.
Reception. The act of admitting.

INCLUSION—*Scientific Noun.*

Crasis. The joining two vowels into one long vowel.

INCLUSION—*Verbs.*

Admit. To afford entrance to.
Be composed of. Made up of.
Be formed of. ⎫
Be made of. ⎬ Made of.
Be made up of. ⎭
Be resolved into. To be combined into a harmony.
Build up. To increase and strengthen.
Compose. To form by uniting two or more things.
Comprehend. To include or take in.
Consist of. To be composed of.
Constitute. To form the substance of.
Contain. To have for its contents.
Drag into. To bring in needlessly.
Embody. To put into.
Embrace. To take in the arms.
Enter into the composition of. To form a part of.
Fill up. To bring all parts together into a whole.
Form. To go to make up.
Hold. To receive and retain.
Implicate. To entangle.
Include. To enclose within.
Involve. To draw into entanglement.
Made of. To have in composition.
Made up of. To be composed of.
Make. To form out of materials.
Make up. To compose.
Resolved into. To separate into constituent parts.
Take in. To give entrance to.

INCLUSION—*Adjectives.*

Constituting. Serving to form, compose, or make up.
Containing. Being able to hold.

———

OMISSION—ADJECTIVES—*Continued from Column 2.*

Not included in. Not embraced in.
Unrecounted. Not considered.

Elimination. The act of casting out or getting rid of.
Exception. The act of omitting from mention.
Exclusion. The act of shutting out.
Exile, etc. Forced separation from one's country. See SOCIABILITY-PRIVACY.
Non-admission. The act of being kept out.
Omission. The act of leaving out.
Rejection. The act of casting away as worthless.
Repudiation. The process of putting away.
Segregation. A placing or grouping apart from others.
Separation. The act or process of disconnecting.
Seposition. A setting apart.

OMISSION—*Denotation.*

Coffer-dam. A temporary dam to keep water from men at work.

OMISSION—*Verbs.*

Banish. To compel to leave one's country.
Bar. To close to entrance.
Bar out. To shut out, from a school-room or class-room.
Be excluded from. Shut out of, or kept away from.
Black-ball. To bar out by the use of the black ball.
Eliminate. To cut out or get rid of.
Exclude. To shut out.
Excluded from. To be kept away from.
Garble. To take good from a document, perverting it.
Lay apart. To place to one side.
Lay aside. To abandon.
Leave out. To omit.
Neglect. To leave out purposely See CAREFULNESS-CARELESSNESS.
Omit. To leave out.
Pass over. To overlook.
Put apart. To separate from.
Put aside. Put away from something.
Reject. To send away, or discard.
Relegate. To put back or away.
Repudiate. To reject.
Segregate. To place apart from others or the rest.
Separate. To take apart.
Set apart. ⎫
Set aside. ⎬ To place alone.
Shut out. To exclude from, as from scoring in a game.
Strike off. To take off a list, etc.
Strike out. To make one's strike without hitting.
Throw overboard. To discard.
Weed. To take out and eradicate.
Winnow. To separate good from bad.

OMISSION—*Adjectives.*

Excluded. Kept out.
Excluding. Debarring.
Exclusive. Shutting out or desiring to shut out.
Inadmissible. Such as should be rejected.

(*Continued on Column* 1.)

OMISSION—*Continued.*

OMISSION—*Adverbs.*

Barring. Apart from; excepting.
Except. With the exclusion of.
Exclusive of. Without.

Save. Unless.
With the exception of. Leaving out.

in-clu′-sive. Embracing. ADDITION-SUBTRACTION, ADMISSION-EXCLUSION, CONSTITUENT-ALIEN.

in-cog′-i-ta-ble. Thoughtless. REFLECTION-VACANCY.

in-cog′-i-tan-cy. Thoughtlessness. REFLECTION-VACANCY.

incognita [It.] (in-cog′-ni-ta). Unknown. ENLIGHTENMENT-SECRECY.

incognita terra [L.] (in-cog′-ni-ta ter′-ra). An unknown country. KNOWLEDGE-IGNORANCE.

incognito [It.] (in-cog′-ni-to). Without being known. ENLIGHTENMENT-SECRECY.

in-cog′-ni-za-ble. Incapable of being known. CLEARNESS-OBSCURITY.

in″-co-he′-rence. Looseness. COHESION-LOOSENESS.

in-co-he′-rent. Incongruous. COHESION-LOOSENESS, SANENESS-LUNACY.

in″-co-he′-sion. Lack of cohesion. COHESION-LOOSENESS.

in″-com-bus″-ti-bil′-i-ty. State of being incombustible. HEATING-COOLING.

in″-com-bus′-ti-ble. Uninflammable. HEATING-COOLING.

in″-com-bus′-ti-ble-ness. Want of flammability. HEATING-COOLING.

in′-come. Amount of money coming in. AFFLUENCE-PENURY, GAIN-LOSS, GIVING-RECEIVING, KEEPING-RELINQUISHMENT, OUTLAY-INCOME.

in′-com″-ing. Coming in. ENTRANCE-EXIT, OUTLAY-INCOME.

in″-com-men″-su-ra-bil′-i-ty. No measurement. CONNECTION-INDEPENDENCE.

in″-com-men′-su-ra-ble. Having no common standard of comparison. CONNECTION-INDEPENDENCE; **incommensurable quantity,** NUMBER, NUMBERING.

in-com-men′-su-rate. Not to be measured. NUMBERING.

in″-com-mode′. Disturb. OBSTRUCTION-HELP, PLEASURABLENESS-PAINFULNESS.

in″-com-mo′-di-ous. Unsuitable. OBSTRUCTION-HELP.

in″-com-mu′-ni-ca-ble. Incapable of being imparted to others. CLEARNESS-OBSCURITY, KEEPING-RELINQUISHMENT, MEANING-JARGON.

in″-com-mu′-ni-ca-tive. Reserved. SOCIETY-PRIVACY.

in″-com-mu′-ta-ble. Incapable of being exchanged for another. MUTABILITY-STABILITY.

in-com′-pa-ra-ble. Matchless. SUPREMACY-SUBORDINACY.

in″-com-pas′-sion-ate. Void of pity. COMPASSION-RUTHLESSNESS.

in″-com-pas′-sion-ate-ness. Want of pity. COMPASSION-RUTHLESSNESS.

in″-com-pat′-i-ble. Discordant. HARMONY-DISCORD, POSSIBILITY-IMPOSSIBILITY.

in-com′-pe-tence. Inability; want of fitness. MIGHT-IMPOTENCE, SAGACITY-INCAPACITY, SKILL-UNSKILFULNESS.

in-com′-pe-tent. Unfit. EXCESS-LACK, MIGHT-IMPOTENCE, SKILL-UNSKILFULNESS, USEFULNESS-USELESSNESS.

in-com-plete′. Not complete. FAULTLESSNESS-FAULTINESS, PREPARATION-NONPREPARATION, WHOLE-PART.

in″-com-plete′-ly. Imperfectly. SKILL-UNSKILFULNESS, WHOLE-PART.

in″-com-plete′-ness. Imperfection; non-completion. COMPLETION-NONCOMPLETION, ENTIRETY-DEFICIENCY, TRANSCURSION-SHORTCOMING.

in″-com-pli′-ance. Obstinacy. PROFFER-REFUSAL.

in-com″-pre-hen″-si-bil′-i-ty. Unintelligibility. CLEARNESS-OBSCURITY.

in-com″-pre-hen′-si-ble. Infinite; unintelligible. CLEARNESS-OBSCURITY, INFINITY.

in-com″-pre-hen′-sion. Want of understanding. KNOWLEDGE-IGNORANCE.

in″-com-press′-i-ble. Resisting compression. SOLIDITY-RARITY.

in″-con-ceal′-a-ble. Not concealable. MANIFESTATION-LATENCY.

in″-con-ceiv′-a-ble. Incomprehensible. ASTONISHMENT-EXPECTANCE, CLEARNESS-OBSCURITY, FAITH-MISGIVING, LIKELIHOOD-UNLIKELIHOOD, POSSIBILITY-IMPOSSIBILITY.

in″-con-ceiv′-a-ble-ness. Incomprehensibility. CLEARNESS-OBSCURITY.

in″-con-cep′-ti-ble. Inconceivable. CLEARNESS-OBSCURITY.

in″-con-cin′-ni-ty. Unsuitableness. BEAUTY-UGLINESS, HARMONY-DISCORD.

in″-con-clu′-sive. Leading to no conclusion. RATIOCINATION-CASUISTRY.

in″-con-coc′-tion. Immaturity. MALE-FEMALE.

in-con′-dite. Badly constructed. TASTE-VULGARITY.

in-con′-gru-ence. Lack of harmony. HARMONY-DISCORD.

in-con-gru′-i-ty. Unsuitableness. ADAGE-NONSENSE, HARMONY-DISCORD, RATIOCINATION-CASUISTRY, SAGACITY-INCAPACITY.

in-con′-gru-ous. Not fitting. HARMONY-DISCORD.

in″-con-nec′-tion. Disconnection. CONNECTION-INDEPENDENCE, UNION-DISUNION.

in-con′-se-quence. State or quality of being inconsequent. CONNECTION-INDEPENDENCE.

in-con′-se-quent. Not consequent. RATIOCINATION-CASUISTRY.

in-con″-se-quen′-tial. Irrelevant. RATIOCINATION-CASUISTRY.

in″-con-sid′-er-a-ble. Not worth considering. CONSEQUENCE-INSIGNIFICANCE, GREATNESS-LITTLENESS, MAGNITUDE-SMALLNESS.

in″-con-sid′-er-ate. Thoughtless; heedless. CAREFULNESS-CARELESSNESS, HEED-DISREGARD, REFLECTION-VACANCY, SKILL-UNSKILFULNESS.

in″-con-sid′-er-ate-ness. Thoughtlessness. HEED-DISREGARD.

in″-con-sid″-er-a′-tion. Thoughtlessness. HEED-DISREGARD.

in″-con-sist′-ent. Discordant; contradictory. ADAGE-NONSENSE, HARMONY-DISCORD, RATIOCINATION-CASUISTRY, SAGACITY-INCAPACITY, SAMENESS-CONTRAST.

in″-con-so′-la-ble. Grieved beyond solace. LIGHTHEARTEDNESS-DEJECTION.

in-con′-so-nant. Disagreeing. HARMONY-DISCORD, MUTABILITY-STABILITY.

in″-con-spic′-u-ous. Not noticeable. VISIBILITY-INVISIBILITY.

in-con′-stan-cy. Changeableness. MUTABILITY-STABILITY.

in-con′-stant. Not stable. MUTABILITY-STABILITY.

in″-con-test′-a-ble. Clear beyond dispute. CERTAINTY-DOUBT, STRENGTH-WEAKNESS.

in″-con-tig′-u-ous. Not in contact. REMOTENESS-NEARNESS.

in-con'-ti-nence. Immoderation. Purity-Impurity

in-con'-ti-nent. Unchaste. Purity-Impurity.

in-con'-ti-nent-ly. Immediately. Earliness-Lateness.

in''-con-trol'-la-ble. Not controllable. Turbulence-Calmness.

in-con''-tro-vert'-i-ble. Indisputable. Certainty-Doubt, Mutability-Stability.

in''-con-ve'-nience. Inexpediency. **Put to inconvenience,** Obstruction-Help, Propriety-Impropriety.

in''-con-ve'-nient. Unsuitable. Propriety-Impropriety.

in''-con-vers'-a-ble. Reserved. Sociability-Privacy, Talkativeness-Taciturnity.

in''-con-vert'-i-ble. Unchangeable. Discontinuance-Continuance.

in''-con-vin'-ci-ble. Not convincible. Credulousness-Skepticism.

in-cor'-po-rate. Embodied. Composition-Resolution.

in''-cor-por'-al. Immaterial. Materiality-Spirituality.

in-cor''-po-ra'-tion. Organization. Association.

in''-cor-po'-re-al. Immaterial. Materiality-Spirituality; **incorporeal hereditaments,** Property.

in-cor''-po-re'-i-ty. State of being not material. Materiality-Spirituality.

in''-cor-rect'. Inaccurate; faulty. Grammar-Solecism, Ratiocination-Casuistry, Truth-Error, Virtue-Vice.

in''-cor'-ri-gi-ble. Bad beyond correction. Bigotry-Apostasy, Repentance-Obduracy, Sanguineness-Hopelessness, Virtue-Vice.

in''-cor-rupt'-i-bil'-i-ty. The character of the incorruptible. Uprightness-Dishonesty.

in''-cor-rupt'-i-ble. That cannot be morally corrupted. Uprightness-Dishonesty.

in''-cor-rup'-tion. Freedom from corruption. Innocence-Guilt, Uprightness-Dishonesty.

in-cras'-sate. Make or become thick. Enlargement-Diminution, Solidity-Rarity; **incrassate fluids,** Viscidity-Foam.

in''-cras-sa'-tion. Thickness. Viscidity-Foam.

in'-crease. Augmentation. Enlargement-Diminution, Increase-Decrease.

INCREASE—DECREASE.

Accession, etc See Addition.

Accretion. Increase by external additions.

Aggrandizement. Increase and exaltation.

Aggravation. A being made worse or heavier.

Ascent, etc. See Ascent.

Augmentation. Increase and enlargement.

Development. Gradual increase or evolution.

Dilatation, etc. See Enlargement.

Enlargement. Increase in range, scope, or capacity.

Exacerbation. Increase in the violence of the symptoms of a disease.

Exaggeration. Overstatement.

Extension. Increase in time, space, or scope.

Flood-tide. Rising or increasing tide.

Growth. The gradual and natural increase of a living creature.

Increase. Enlargement.

Increment. The amount of increase of a variable as it passes from one of its values to another.

Rise. Ascent; increase, as in price.

Spread, etc. See Gathering-Scattering.

Increase—Verbs.

Add fuel to the flame. Increase the intensity of.

Add to. Increase.

Advance. Increase; elevate; promote.

Aggrandize. Increase in greatness.

Aggravate. Increase in weight or intensity.

Ascend, etc. See Ascent.

Augment. Increase in any way.

Deepen. Increase in depth in any sense.

Dilate, etc. See Enlargement.

Enhance. Increase in measure or importance.

Enlarge. Increase or expand.

Exacerbate. Increase in severity or sharpness.

Exaggerate. Increase unduly or extravagantly.

Exalt. Increase in rank or position.

Exasperate. Increase the anger of; make worse.

Gain strength. Increase in strength.

Get ahead. Surpass.

Grow. Increase in mass by natural methods.

Heighten. Increase in import or intensity.

Increase. Make or become greater or larger

Intensify. Increase in intensity.

Magnify. Increase the size or importance of.

Oleum addere camino [L.]. To add oil to the fire.

Raise. Increase in amount, rank, or elevation.

Redouble. Increase fourfold or greatly.

Rise. Advance; from one to a higher position.

Run up. Increase; get large.

Shoot up. Advance or increase rapidly.

Spread, etc. See Gathering-Scattering.

Sprout, etc. See Enlargement.

Strengthen. Increase in strength.

Abatement. Decrease in force, value, or quantity.

Abridgment, etc. See Length-Shortness.

Anticlimax. A sentence in which the ideas decrease in importance or impressiveness toward the close.

Coarctation. Contraction.

Declension. Decline; deterioration.

Decline. Gradual deterioration.

Decrease. Diminution.

Decrement. A decreasing; loss by decrease.

Depreciation. Decrease in worth.

Descent, etc. See Ascent-Descent.

Deterioration, etc. See Betterment-Deterioration.

Diminution. Decrease in size, rank, or authority.

Extenuation. Decrease in gravity or importance.

Lessening, etc. Decrease, etc. See *Verbs.*

Mitigation, etc. Decrease in painfulness or severity, etc. See Turbulence-Calmness.

Reduction. Decrease in size, condition, value, etc.

Reflux. Decrease in the height of the tide; flowing back.

Shrinking, etc. See Enlargement-Diminution.

Subsidence. Decrease in violence, as of passions.

Subtraction, etc. See Addition-Subtraction.

Wane. Decrease, as of influence, fame, or prosperity.

Decrease—Verbs.

Abate. Decrease in value, quantity, or force.

Abridge, etc. See Length-Shortness.

Attenuate. Decrease in size, force, or intensity.

Bate. Decrease the amount, force, or intensity of.

Crumble. Fall or cause to fall to pieces; decrease in density

Decay. Deteriorate; rot.

Decline. Diminish; decrease.

Decrease. Lessen or cause to lessen; diminish

Depreciate. Decrease in value or estimation.

Dequantate. Decrease the quantity of.

Descend, etc. See Ascent-Descent.

Die away. Decrease gradually.

Diminish. Decrease; make smaller.

Discount. Decrease the face value of anything; discredit.

Drop off. Gradually decrease in numbers, as an audience; fall asleep gently.

Dwarf. Decrease in size; stunt.

Ebb. Decrease in height, as the tide; decline.

Extenuate. Decrease the importance or seriousness of.

Fall away. Decrease gradually, as the body; fade, as color.

Fall off. Decrease in abundance, value, or interest.

Fall to a low ebb. Decrease seriously in vitality.

Fritter away. Decrease to nothing little by little.

Hide its diminished head. To disappear.

Languish. Decrease in animation or activity

Lessen. Diminish; make smaller.

Lower. Decrease, as in height or quality; abase.

Melt away. Gradually decrease by melting

INCREASE—DECREASE—*Continued.*

INCREASE—VERBS—*Continued.*

Superadd, etc. Increase what has been added. See ADDITION.
Wax. Grow; increase gradually.

INCREASE—*Adjectives.*

Accrual. Increasing.
Additional, etc. See ADDITION.
Ebbless. Not flowing back.
Increased, etc. Made larger; augmented, etc. See *Verbs.*
On the increase. Increasing.
Undiminished. Not decreased.

INCREASE—*Adverb.*

Crescendo [It.]. Increasing gradually and slowly in loudness or power.

INCREASE—*Phrase.*

Vires acquirit eundo [L.]. She (Rumor) increases in strength as she goes. [Virgil, *Æneid,* 4, 175.]

DECREASE—ADJECTIVES—*Continued from Column 2.*

"**Small by degrees and beautifully less.**" Fine by, etc. [Prior, *Henry and Emma.*]
Unincreased, etc. See INCREASE.

DECREASE—VERBS—*Continued.*

Mitigate, etc. See TURBULENCE-CALMNESS.
Reduce, etc. See ENLARGEMENT-DIMINUTION.
Retire into the shade. Decrease in importance.
Run low. Be in a low or decreased condition.
Shorten, etc. See LENGTH-SHORTNESS.
Shrink, etc. See ENLARGEMENT-DIMINUTION.
Subside. Decrease in violence; fall to a lower level.
Subtract, etc. See ADDITION-SUBTRACTION.
Tail off. Fall behind, a sporting term.
Throw into the shade. Decrease the brightness of; obscure.
Wane. Decrease in size and brightness, as the moon; decrease in importance.
Waste. Decrease by unnecessary expenditure.
Weaken. Diminish the strength of.
Wear. Decrease and consume away by use.

DECREASE—*Adjectives.*

Decreased, etc. Lessened; diminished, etc. See *Verbs.*
Decreasing, etc. Diminishing; lessening, etc. See *Verbs.*
On the wane, etc. Waning; decreasing in size, brightness, or importance, etc. See *Nouns.*

(*Continued on Column* 1.)

---

in-creased'. Made greater. INCREASE-DECREASE, SUPREMACY-SUBORDINACY.
in-cred″-i-bil'-i-ty. Incredibleness. FAITH-MISGIVING, LIKELIHOOD-UNLIKELIHOOD, MAGNITUDE-SMALLNESS.
in-cred'-i-ble. Surpassing belief. ASTONISHMENT-EXPECTANCE, FAITH-MISGIVING, LIKELIHOOD-UNLIKELIHOOD, MAGNITUDE-SMALLNESS, POSSIBILITY-IMPOSSIBILITY.
in-cred'-i-ble-ness. Not to be believed. FAITH-MISGIVING.

in″-cre-du'-li-ty. Skepticism. CREDULOUSNESS-SKEPTICISM, FAITH-MISGIVING, GODLINESS-DISBELIEF.
in-cred'-u-lous. Skeptical. CREDULOUSNESS-SKEPTICISM, GODLINESS-DISBELIEF.
in-cred'-u-lous-ness. Skepticism. GODLINESS-DISBELIEF.
in'-cre-ment. Enlargement. ADDITION-SUBTRACTION, ENLARGEMENT-DIMINUTION, INCREASE-DECREASE, INCREMENT-REMNANT.

INCREMENT—REMNANT.

Accession. Addition; attainment.
Accompaniment. Something attendant.
Addendum [L.]. Something added; appendix.
Addition. An increase; augmentation.
Additament. An addition.
Additum [L.]. Something to be added.
Adjective. An accessory.
Adjunct. Something joined or added.
Affix. An appendage; a suffix.
Annexe [F.]. Something annexed and appended.
Appendage. A subordinate adjunct.
Augment. Enlargement by addition.
Augmentation. The act of increasing.
Complement. An adjunct required to supply a deficiency
Continuation. That which carries on; supplement.
Increment. Growth in any relation; augmentation.
Item. A paragraph in a newspaper.
Reinforcement. An addition of strength.
Suffix. A letter or syllable appended. See PREDECESSOR-CONTINUATION.
Supernumerary. Exceeding the required number.
Supplement. That which serves to make complete.

INCREMENT—*Denotations, etc.*

Corollary. That which is given beyond what is actually due; an additional deduction from a demonstration.
Cortege. A train of attendants.
Embroidery. Diversified ornamental work.
Episode. A separate incident, story, or action, introduced for the purpose of giving a greater variety.
Flap. Anything broad and limber that hangs loose.
Garnish. Something added for embellishment.
Lappet. A small decorative fold or flap on a garment.
Off-shoot. That which shoots off or separates from a main stem.
Rider. An addition or amendment to a manuscript or other document.
Sauce. Appetizing ingredients eaten with food as a relish.
Skirt. A loose edging to any part of a dress.

Balance. Difference between totals; a surplus.
Complement. A filling up; an addition.
Educt. That which is drawn out; outcome.
Excess. Amount of difference between unequals; surplus.
Overplus. Surplus; excess.
Relic. That which remains; a small portion left over
Remainder. Something left over; residue.
Remains. That left behind.
Remanet [L.]. It remains.
Remnant. A small remainder.
Residue. A remainder left after being acted upon.
Rest. The remainder; the balance.
Result. That which is an outcome, effect, consequence.
Superfluity. The being of more than is needed; a superabundance. See EXCESS.
Surplus. The excess of what is needful.
Survival. What is left over alive.
Survivancy. The state of being a survivorship.

REMNANT—*Denotations.*

Alluvium. Deposits of earth, sand, gravel, etc., carried down by streams of water.
Candle ends. Small bits of candle.
Cheese parings. The particles that fall off in cutting cheese.
Dregs. Matter precipitated from a liquid. See CLEANNESS-FILTHINESS.
Fag end. An end of poorer quality, or in a spoiled condition.
Heel-tap. A small portion of liquor left in a glass after drinking.
Leavings. Things left over.
Odds and ends. That which is left; fragments.
Orts. Morsels left at a meal.
Refuse. Waste or worthless matter. See USEFULNESS.
Residuum. That which is left over after any process of purification.
Ruins. That which is fallen down and becomes worthless from injury or decay.
Skeleton. The framework of anything.
Stump. The part of a tree remaining after the trunk is cut off.

INCREMENT—REMNANT—*Continued.*

INCREMENT—Denotations, etc.—*Continued.*

Tail. The terminal posterior appendage of an animal.
Trappings. Superficial decorations.

INCREMENT—*Adjective.*

Additional. Supplementary See ADDITION.

INCREMENT—*Adverb.*

In addition. See ADDITION.

REMNANT—ADJECTIVES—*Continued from Column 2*

Residual. Left over after part is taken.
Residuary. Pertaining to a residue
Remaining. Continuing after others have been removed.
Sedimentary. Characterized by sediment; left over.
Superfluous. More than is required. See EXCESS.
Surviving. Left over alive.
Unconsumed. Left over after a conflagration.

REMNANT—Denotations—*Continued.*

Stubble. The stumps of wheat or grains left in the ground.
Wreck. The remains of anything ruined.

REMNANT—*Verbs.*

Be left. To remain. See *Adjectives.*
Exceed. To go beyond; surpass.
Leave. To withdraw; quit; depart.
Survive. To be left over alive.

REMNANT—*Adjectives.*

Cast off. Thrown off; discarded.
Exceeding. Going beyond; excelling.
Left.
Left behind. } Remaining after something has been taken away.
Left over.
Net. Clear of all charges; having no remainder.
Odd. Having a remainder when divided by 2.
Outlying. Situated outside; extrinsic.
Outstanding. Standing still; projecting.
Over and above. Left over.

(*Continued on Column* 1.)

INCREMENT—DECREMENT.

DECREMENT.

After-glow. The light left over after sunset.
Decrement. The state of falling off; decreasing.
Deduction. The act of taking away from.

Defect. Want of something essential; deficiency.
Discount. Amount rebated on a given sum.
Eduction. Exhaustion, as of steam from a cylinder.
Loss. The act of being deprived of or the state of being deprived of.

in″-cre-pa′-tion. A chiding. APPROVAL-DISAPPROVAL.
in-crim′-i-nate. Charge with a crime. JUSTIFICATION-CHARGE.
in-crim″-i-na′-tion. A charge. JUSTIFICATION-CHARGE.
in-crust′. Cover with a crust. COVER-LINING.
in″-crus-ta′-tion. A crust. COVER-LINING.
in′-cu-bate. To hatch by sitting. CREATION-DESTRUCTION.
in″-cu-ba′-tion. Hatching. PREPARATION-NONPREPARATION.
in′-cu-ba″-tor. An apparatus, artificially warmed, for hatching eggs. CREATION-DESTRUCTION, HEATING-COOLING.
in′-cu-bus. Mental burden; a demon. JOVE-FIEND, OBSTRUCTION-HELP, PLEASURE-PAIN.
in-cul′-cate. Teach. EDUCATION-MISTEACHING.
in″-cul-ca′-tion. Teaching. EDUCATION-MISTEACHING.
in-cul′-pa-ble. Blameless. INNOCENCE-GUILT.
in-cul-pa′-tion. Blamelessness. INNOCENCE-GUILT.
in-cul′-ture. Want of culture. PREPARATION-NONPREPARATION.
in-cum′-ben-cy. Full possession and exercise of any office. CHURCH, OCCUPATION.
in-cum′-bent. Lying; resting; a person in present possession of an office. DUTY-DERELICTION, DWELLER-HABITATION, HEAVINESS-LIGHTNESS, HEIGHT-LOWNESS, MINISTRY-LAITY.
incunabula [L.] (in″-kiu-nab′-yu-la). Swaddling-clothes. INFANCY-AGE.
incunabulis, ab [L.] (in″-kiu-nab′-yu-lis, ab) From the cradle. BEGINNING-END.
in-cur′. Bring upon oneself. CONTINGENCY; **incur a debt,** CREDIT-DEBT; **incur a loss,** GAIN-LOSS; **incur blame,** APPROVAL-DISAPPROVAL; **incur danger,** SECURITY-INSECURITY; **incur disgrace,** REPUTATION-DISCREDIT; **incur the risk,** PURPOSE-LUCK.
in-cur′-a-ble. Irremediable. HEALTH-SICKNESS, SANGUINENESS-HOPELESSNESS, SUBJECTIVENESS-OBJECTIVENESS.
incuriam, per [L.] (in-kiu′-ri-am, per). Through carelessness. CAREFULNESS-CARELESSNESS, HEED-DISREGARD.

in-cu″-ri-os′-i-ty. Want of curiosity. INQUISITIVENESS-INDIFFERENCE.
in-cu′-ri-ous. Not inquisitive. INQUISITIVENESS-INDIFFERENCE.
in-cu′-ri-ous-ness. Unconcernedness. INQUISITIVENESS-INDIFFERENCE.
in-cur′-sion. Inroad; ingress. ATTACK-DEFENSE, ENTRANCE-EXIT.
in-curv′-ate. Curved. CURVATION-RECTILINEARITY.
in″-cur-va′-tion. A bending. CURVATION-RECTILINEARITY.
in″-da-ga′-tion. Search. INVESTIGATION-ANSWER.
in-debt′-ed. Owing. CREDIT-DEBT, DUTY-DERELICTION, THANKFULNESS-THANKLESSNESS.
in-debt′-ment. Indebtedness. CREDIT-DEBT.
in-de′-cen-cy. Indecorum. PURITY-IMPURITY.
in-de′-cent. Immodest. PURITY-IMPURITY.
in″-de-cid′-u-ous. Permanent. MUTABILITY-STABILITY.
in″-de-ci′-sion. Wavering of mind. CHOICE-NEUTRALITY, DETERMINATION-VACILLATION.
in″-de-ci′-sive. Inconclusive. CERTAINTY-DOUBT.
in″-de-cli′-na-ble. Not varied by inflection. MUTABILITY-STABILITY.
in″-de-co′-rous. Improper. PURITY-IMPURITY, TASTE-VULGARITY, VIRTUE-VICE.
in″-de-co′-rum. Lack of decorum. TASTE-VULGARITY, VIRTUE-VICE.
in-deed′. In truth. ASSENT-DISSENT, ASSERTION-DENIAL, ASTONISHMENT-EXPECTANCE, ENTITY-NONENTITY, MAGNITUDE-SMALLNESS, TRUTH-ERROR.
in″-de-fat″-i-ga-bil′-i-ty. The state of being indefatigable. PERSISTENCE-WHIM.
in″-de-fat′-i-ga-ble. Unwearied. ACTIVITY-INDOLENCE, PERSISTENCE-WHIM.
in″-de-fat′-i-ga-ble-ness. The quality of being unwearied. PERSISTENCE-WHIM.
in″-de-fat′-i-ga-tion. Unweariedness. ACTIVITY-INDOLENCE.
in″-de-fea′-si-ble. Not to be defeated. DUENESS-UNDUENESS, MUTABILITY-STABILITY.
in″-de-fect′-i-ble. Not subject to defect. FAULTLESSNESS-FAULTINESS.

in″-de-fect′-i-bly. Unfailingly. FAULTLESSNESS-FAULTI-
NESS.

in″-de-fec′-tive. Perfect. FAULTLESSNESS-FAULTI-
NESS.

in″-de-fen′-si-ble. Untenable; unjustifiable. JUSTIFI-
CATION-CHARGE, MIGHT-IMPOTENCE, VIRTUE-VICE,
YIELDING.

in″-de-fi′-cient. Not deficient. FAULTLESSNESS-FAULTI-
NESS.

in″-de-fi′-na-ble. That cannot be defined. CERTAINTY-
DOUBT.

in-def′-i-nite. Uncertain; unbounded. CERTAINTY-
DOUBT, CLEARNESS-OBSCURITY, INFINITY, TRUTH-
ERROR, VISIBILITY-INVISIBILITY.

in-def′-i-nite-ly. Vaguely. MAGNITUDE-SMALLNESS.

in″-de-lib′-er-ate. Unpremeditated. PREDETERMINA-
TION-IMPULSE.

in-del′-i-ble. Ineffaceable. EMOTION, MUTABILITY-
STABILITY, REMEMBRANCE-FORGETFULNESS, SIGN.

in-del′-i-ca-cy. The quality of being indelicate. PURITY-
IMPURITY.

in-del′-i-cate. Offensive to refined taste. PURITY-IM-
PURITY.

in-dem″-ni-fi-ca′-tion. Preserving against loss. COM-
PENSATION, RECOMPENSE-PUNITION.

in-dem′-ni-fy. To compensate for loss or damage. COM-
PENSATION, RECOMPENSE-PUNITION.

in-dem′-ni-ty. Compensation for damages; amnesty.
COMPENSATION, PARDON-VINDICTIVENESS, RECOM-
PENSE-PUNITION; deed of indemnity, SECURITY.

in-den″-i-za′-tion. Act of naturalizing. ESTABLISH-
MENT-REMOVAL.

in-den′-i-zen. Naturalize. ESTABLISHMENT - REMO-
VAL.

in-dent′. Notch. CIRCLE-WINDING, CONTRACT, OR-
GANIZATION-INORGANIZATION.

in″-den-ta′-tion. Notching; a notch. CONVEXITY-
CONCAVITY, INDENTATION.

INDENTATION.

Cut. Opening made by an edged instrument.
Dent. A small hollow in a body or mass.
Dimple. Depression in the face.
Indent. An incision; a stamp.
Indentation. A cut in an edge or border.
Nick. A slight cut in anything.
Notch. A mark or nick cut in anything.

INDENTATION—*Denotations*.

Battlement. A notch-like wall used for military protection.
Crenelle. A loophole in a fortress.
Embrasure. An opening in the walls of a fortification through
which cannon are pointed.
Machicolation. An opening in a floor for shooting or dropping
missiles.
Saw. A thin blade of steel with a series of sharp teeth for cutting.
Scallop. The shell of a species of fish, radially ribbed and undu-
lated.
Scollop. See SCALLOP.
Tooth. Any projection like the tooth of an animal.
Vandyke. A collar or edge furnished with scallops, as in the paintings
of Vandyke.

INDENTATION—*Verbs*.

Crenulate. To make a notch in a wall.
Crimp. To pinch up in small ridges.
Cut. To make an incision; to divide with a sharp tool.
Dent. To make a small hollow.
Indent. To notch the edge of.
Jag. To cut like the teeth of a saw.
Nick. To chip; to notch.
Notch. To cut in small hollows.
Scarify. To scratch, as in the skin in surgery.
Scollop. To cut the border of a thing into segments of a circle.
Scotch. To lash; to cut slightly.
Vandyke. To slash or cut out.

INDENTATION—*Adjectives*.

Crenate. }
Crenated.} Toothed with even, rounded notches, as a leaf.

Dentate. }
Dentated.} Having short triangular divisions of the margin.

Denticulate. }
Denticulated.} Finely toothed.

Notched, etc. Cut into small hollows. See *Verbs*.
Palmated. Having the shape of a hand, as in some leaves; webbed.
Serrated. Notched on the edge like a saw.
Toothed. Having teeth or jags.

in-den′-ture. An instrument of contract under seal.
CONTRACT, SECURITY.

in″-de-pend′-ence. Irrelation; freedom; competency.
AFFLUENCE-PENURY, CONNECTION-INDEPENDENCE,
LIBERTY-SUBJECTION.

In″-de-pend′-ent. An English Congregationalist. CON-
NECTION-INDEPENDENCE, LIBERTY-SUBJECTION, OR-
THODOXY-HETERODOXY.

in″-de-scri′-ba-ble. Not to be described. ASTONISH-
MENT-EXPECTANCE, MAGNITUDE-SMALLNESS.

in-des′-i-nent. Unceasing. ETERNITY-INSTANTANEITY.

in″-de-struc′-ti-ble. That cannot be destroyed. MU-
TABILITY-STABILITY.

in″-de-ter′-min-ate. Uncertain; not fixed. RATIOCI-
NATION-CASUISTRY, RATIONALE-LUCK.

in-de-ter″-min-a′-tion. Want of determination. DE-
TERMINATION-VACILLATION, RATIONALE-LUCK.

in″-de-vo′-tion. Impiety. GODLINESS-DISBELIEF.

in-de-vout′. Not devout. GODLINESS-DISBELIEF.

in-′dex. That which points out. NUMBER, ORGANI-
ZATION-DISORGANIZATION, RECORD, SIGN, WORD-
NEOLOGY.

index expurgatorius [L.] (in′-dex ex-pur-ga-to′-ri-us).
A list of books which must not be read by Roman
Catholics, except in expurgated editions. LEAVE-
PROHIBITION.

in″-dex-ter′-i-ty. Clumsiness. SKILL-UNSKILFULNESS.

In′-di-an. Pertaining to India or the East Indies. **Indian file,** PREDECESSOR-CONTINUATION; **Indian rubber,** ELASTICITY-INELASTICITY; **Indian weed,** PUN-
GENCY.

in′-di-cate. Point out; mean. HEED-DISREGARD,
MANIFESTATION-LATENCY, MEANING-JARGON, SIGN.

in′-di-ca″-ted. Pointed out; suggested. SIGN.

in′-di-ca″-ting. Pointing out. SIGN.

in″-di-ca′-tion. Sign. HEED-DISREGARD, MANIFESTA-
TION-LATENCY, SIGN.

in-dic′-a-tive. Bringing to notice. EVIDENCE-COUN-
TEREVIDENCE, SIGN; indicative mode, VERB.

in′-di-ca″-tor. One who or that which points out. EVI-
DENCE-COUNTEREVIDENCE, SIGN.

in′-di-ca-to-ry. Serving to show. EVIDENCE-COUNTER-
EVIDENCE, SIGN.

in′-dice. Index. SIGN.

in-dict′. Charge with crime. JUSTIFICATION-CHARGE,
LITIGATION.

in-dic′-tion. A proclamation. PUBLICITY.

in-dict′-ment. A formal charge of crime, preferred by a
grand jury. JUSTIFICATION-CHARGE, LITIGATION.

in-dif′-fer-ence. Lack of interest or concern. CHOICE-
NEUTRALITY, DESIRE-DISTASTE, INQUISITIVENESS-
INDIFFERENCE, READINESS-RELUCTANCE; **matter of
indifference,** CONSEQUENCE-INSIGNIFICANCE.

in-dif′-fer-ent. Lacking interest; apathetic. CHOICE-
NEUTRALITY, CONSEQUENCE-INSIGNIFICANCE, DE-
SIRE-DISTASTE, FAULTLESSNESS-FAULTINESS, GOOD-
NESS - BADNESS, INQUISITIVENESS - INDIFFERENCE,
READINESS-RELUCTANCE, SENSITIVENESS-APATHY.

in′-di-gence. Poverty. AFFLUENCE-PENURY, EXCESS-
LACK.

in′-di-gene. One born in a country. DWELLER-HABI-
TATION.

in-dig'-e-nous. Native; inherent. DWELLER-HABITA-TION, NATURE-ART, SUBJECTIVENESS-OBJECTIVE-NESS.

in'-di-gent. Poor. AFFLUENCE-PENURY.

in''-di-gest'-ed. Not digested. PREPARATION-NON-PREPARATION.

in''-di-gest'-i-ble. Not digestible. HEALTHINESS-UN-HEALTHINESS.

in''-di-ges'-tion. Dyspepsia. HEALTH-SICKNESS.

in-dig'-i-tate. Point out. HEED-DISREGARD.

in-dign'. Unworthy. UPRIGHTNESS-DISHONESTY.

in-dig'-nant. Feeling wrath. FAVORITE-ANGER.

in''-dig-na'-tion. Anger. FAVORITE-ANGER; indignation meeting, CONTENTEDNESS-DISCONTENTMENT.

in-dig'-ni-ty. Insult; contumely. FAVORITE-ANGER, REGARD-DISRESPECT.

in'-di-go. A deep violet-blue. BLUENESS-ORANGE.

in-dil'-i-gence. Want of diligence. ACTIVITY-INDO-LENCE.

in-di-rect'. Circuitous; devious. AIM-ABERRATION, MANIFESTATION-LATENCY, MIDCOURSE-CIRCUIT, PAR-ALLELISM-INCLINATION.

in-dis-cern'-i-ble. Invisible. VISIBILITY-INVISIBILITY.

in''-dis-cerpt'-i-bil-i-ty. State of being indiscerptible. SOLIDITY-RARITY.

in''-dis-cerpt'-i-ble. Exempt from dissolution. SOLID-ITY-RARITY, WHOLE-PART.

in''-dis-cov'-er-a-ble. Undiscoverable. MANIFESTA-TION-LATENCY.

in''-dis-creet'. Imprudent. RECKLESSNESS-CAUTION, VIRTUE-VICE.

in''-dis-cre'-tion. Imprudence. INNOCENCE-GUILT, RECKLESSNESS-CAUTION, SKILL-UNSKILFULNESS.

in''-dis-crim'-i-nate. Confused. DIFFERENTIATION-INDISCRIMINATION, MIXTURE-HOMOGENEITY, PUR-POSE-LUCK, REGULARITY-IRREGULARITY, UNIFORMI-TY-MULTIFORMITY.

in''-dis-crim''-i-na'-tion. Lack of discrimination. DIF-FERENTIATION-INDISCRIMINATION.

in''-dis-pen''-sa-bil'-i-ty. The state of being absolutely necessary. NEED.

in''-dis-pen'-sa-ble. Absolutely necessary. NEED.

in''-dis-pose'. Disincline. MOTIVE-CAPRICE.

in''-dis-posed'. Disinclined; slightly sick. HEALTH-SICKNESS, READINESS-RELUCTANCE.

in''-dis-po'-sed-ness. Unfitness; unsuitableness. READ-INESS-RELUCTANCE.

in-dis''-po-si'-tion. Disinclination. HEALTH-SICK-NESS, READINESS-RELUCTANCE.

in-dis'-pu-ta-ble. Incontrovertible. CERTAINTY-DOUBT.

in-dis'-so-lu-ble. Not to be melted; stable. MUTA-BILITY-STABILITY, SOLIDITY-RARITY, UNION-DIS-UNION, WHOLE-PART.

in''-dis-solv'-a-ble-ness. The state of being indissoluble. SOLIDITY-RARITY.

in''-dis-tinct'. Dim. VISIBILITY-INVISIBILITY.

in''-dis-tinct'-ness. Indefiniteness; dimness. DIFFER-ENTIATION-INDISCRIMINATION, RATIOCINATION-IN-STINCT.

in''-dis-tinc'-tion. Uncertainty. DIFFERENTIATION-IN-DISCRIMINATION.

in''-dis-tin'-guish-a-ble. Inseparable; invisible. SAME-NESS-CONTRAST, VISIBILITY-INVISIBILITY.

in''-dis-turb'-ance. Calmness. EXCITABILITY-INEXCI-TABILITY, MOVEMENT-REST.

in-dite'. Compose. WRITING-PRINTING.

in''-di-vid'-u-al. Single; person. HUMANITY, SIGN, SOLITUDE-COMPANY, UNIVERSALITY-PARTICULARITY, WHOLE-PART.

in''-di-vid''-u-al'-i-ty. Separate nature or existence. CONVENTIONALITY-UNCONVENTIONALITY, SOLITUDE-COMPANY, UNIVERSALITY-PARTICULARITY.

in''-di-vid'-u-al-ize. To confer personal characteristics upon. UNIVERSALITY-PARTICULARITY.

in''-di-vi-du'-i-ty. Separate existence. UNIVERSALITY-PARTICULARITY.

in''-di-vis''-i-bil'-i-ty. The state of being indivisible. SOLIDITY-RARITY, WHOLE-PART.

in''-di-vis'-i-ble. Not separable into parts. SOLIDITY-RARITY, WHOLE-PART.

in''-do-cil'-i-ty. Unteachableness. BIGOTRY-APOSTASY, MIGHT-IMPOTENCE, READINESS-RELUCTANCE, SIGN.

in-doc'-tri-nate. Instruct. EDUCATION-MISTEACHING, FAITH-MISGIVING.

in-doc''-tri-na'-tion. Information. EDUCATION-MIS-TEACHING.

in'-do-lence. Laziness. ACTIVITY-INDOLENCE.

In''-do-Eu-ro-pe'-an. Pertaining to certain languages; Aryan. ETHNOLOGY.

In''-do-I-ran'-ic. The Indo-European languages of India and Persia. ETHNOLOGY.

in'-do-lent. Habitually idle. ACTIVITY-INDOLENCE.

in-dom'-i-ta-ble. Unconquerable. BRAVERY-COWARD-ICE, DETERMINATION-VACILLATION, PERSISTENCE-WHIM, REPRISAL-RESISTANCE, STRENGTH-WEAK-NESS.

in'-door''. Performed within doors. OUTSIDE-IN-SIDE.

in-dorse'. Sanction; ratify. CONTRACT, SECURITY.

in-dors'-er. One who indorses. SECURITY.

in-dorse'-ment. Superscription. ASSENT-DISSENT, MARK-OBLITERATION, SECURITY, SIGN.

in'-draft''. Inward suction or flow. GULF-PLAIN, RIVER-WIND.

in-du'-bi-ous. Certain. CERTAINTY-DOUBT.

in-du'-bi-ta-ble. Unquestionably true. CERTAINTY-DOUBT.

in-duce'. Prevail on. CAUSE-EFFECT, CREATION-DE-STRUCTION, MOTIVE-CAPRICE.

in-duced'. Prevailed on. MOTIVE-CAPRICE.

in-duce'-ment. Incentive; motive. MOTIVE-CAPRICE.

in-duct'. Install; initiate. CHURCH, COMMISSION-ABROGATION.

in-duc'-tion. Inference drawn from particulars; intro-duction; prologue. ACTING, CHURCH, INVESTIGA-TION-ANSWER, RATIOCINATION-INSTINCT.

in-duct'-or. An electrical apparatus. ELECTRIC-ITY.

in-due'. Endow. MIGHT-IMPOTENCE.

in-dulge'. Give way to; humor. HARSHNESS-MILD-NESS, LEAVE-PROHIBITION, PLEASURABLENESS-PAIN-FULNESS, SOCIETY-DANDY; indulge in, PLEASURE-PAIN; indulge in reverie, FANCY, HEED-DISREGARD, REFLECTION-VACANCY; indulge oneself, UNSELFISH-NESS-SELFISHNESS; indulge one's fancy, CHOICE-NEU-TRALITY; indulge with, GIVING-RECEIVING.

in-dulged'. Humored; gratified. MODERATION-SELF-INDULGENCE.

in-dul'-gence. Humoring; absolution; forbearance of restraint. HARSHNESS-MILDNESS, LEAVE-PROHIBI-TION, PARDON-VINDICTIVENESS, PLEASURABLENESS-PAINFULNESS, SOCIETY-DANDY.

in-dul'-gen-cy. Indulgence. HARSHNESS-MILDNESS.

in-dul'-gent. Mild. CHARITABLENESS-MALEVOLENCE, HARSHNESS-MILDNESS, LEAVE-PROHIBITION.

in'-du-rate. To make hard. HARDNESS-SOFTNESS.

in'-du-ra''-ted. Made hard. HARDNESS-SOFTNESS.

in''-du-ra''-tion. Hardening; impenitence. HARDNESS-SOFTNESS, REPENTANCE-OBDURACY.

In'-dus. River in Asia. From Indus to the pole, EX-TENSION-DISTRICT.

in-dus'-tri-al. Pertaining to the arts of industry LABOR-CAPITAL, OCCUPATION.

in-dus'-tri-ous. Laborious; diligent. ACTIVITY-INDO-LENCE, EDUCATION-LEARNING.

in'-dus-try. Habitual diligence; any department of business. ACTIVITY-INDOLENCE, LABOR-CAPITAL, OCCUPATION; hive of industry, WORKSHOP.

in'-dwell''-er. An inhabitant. DWELLER-HABITATION.

in-e'-bri-ate. To make drunk. TEETOTALISM-INTEMPERANCE.

in-e'-bri-a''-ted. Drunk. TEETOTALISM-INTEMPERANCE.

in-e''-bri-a'-tion. Drunkenness. TEETOTALISM-INTEMPERANCE.

in''-e-bri'-e-ty. Drunkenness. TEETOTALISM-INTEMPERANCE.

in-e'-bri-ous. Drunken. TEETOTALISM-INTEMPERANCE.

in-ef'-fa-ble. Unutterable. ASTONISHMENT-EXPECTANCE, MAGNITUDE-SMALLNESS.

in''-ef-face'-a-ble. Indelible. AFFECTIONS.

in''-ef-fec'-tive. Futile. MIGHT-IMPOTENCE, SUCCESS-FAILURE.

in-ef-fec'-tu-al. Inefficient; useless. MIGHT-IMPOTENCE, SUCCESS-FAILURE, USEFULNESS-USELESSNESS; **ineffectual attempt,** SUCCESS-FAILURE; **pale its ineffectual fire,** DIMNESS, REPUTATION-DISCREDIT.

in-ef''-fi-ca'-cious. Not efficacious. MIGHT-IMPOTENCE, SUCCESS-FAILURE, USEFULNESS-USELESSNESS.

in-ef''-fi-ca'-cious-ness. Inefficacy. GATHERING-SCATTERING.

in-ef''-fi-ca'-cy. Futility. KEEPING-RELINQUISHMENT, MIGHT-IMPOTENCE, USEFULNESS-USELESSNESS.

in''-ef-fi'-cien-cy. Incapacity. MIGHT-IMPOTENCE.

in''-ef-fi'-cient. Not efficient. MIGHT-IMPOTENCE.

in''-e-las'-tic. Lacking elasticity. ELASTICITY-INELASTICITY, HARDNESS-SOFTNESS, LIQUID-GAS; **inelastic fluid,** LIQUID-GAS.

in''-e-las-tic'-i-ty. Want of elasticity. ELASTICITY-INELASTICITY, HARDNESS-SOFTNESS.

in-el'-e-gance. Want of elegance or grace. BEAUTY-UGLINESS, PURITY-CRUDENESS.

in-el'-e-gant. Not elegant. BEAUTY-UGLINESS, PURITY-CRUDENESS.

in-el'-i-gi-ble. Not qualified. PROPRIETY-IMPROPRIETY.

in-ept'. Unfit; useless. MIGHT-IMPOTENCE, SAGACITY-INCAPACITY, USEFULNESS-USELESSNESS.

in-ept'-i-tude. Unfitness. SAGACITY-INCAPACITY, USEFULNESS-USELESSNESS.

in''-e-qual'-i-ty. Want of equality. EQUALITY-INEQUALITY.

in-eq'-ui-ta-ble. Unfair. RIGHT-WRONG.

in''-e-rad'-i-ca-ble. Not to be rooted out. MUTABILITY-STABILITY, SUBJECTIVENESS-OBJECTIVENESS.

in-err'-a-ble. Infallible. INNOCENCE-GUILT.

in-ert'. Sluggish. ACTIVITY-INDOLENCE, BIGOTRY-APOSTASY, SENSITIVENESS-APATHY, VIGOR-INERTIA.

in-er'-tia. Indisposition to move or act. SENSITIVENESS-APATHY, VIGOR-INERTIA.

in-er'-tion. Quietude. VIGOR-INERTIA.

in-ert'-ness. Sluggishness. ACTIVITY-INDOLENCE, DOMINANCE-IMPOTENCE, SENSITIVENESS-APATHY, VIGOR-INERTIA.

in-es'-ti-ma-ble. Above price. GOODNESS-BADNESS.

in-ev'-i-ta-ble. Unavoidable. CERTAINTY-DOUBT, VOLITION-OBLIGATION.

in-ev'-i-ta-ble-ness. Certain to happen. VOLITION-OBLIGATION.

in-ex-act'. Inaccurate. CAREFULNESS-NEGLECT, FORCE-WEAKNESS, TRUTH-ERROR.

in-ex-act'-ness. Inaccurateness. CAREFULNESS-NEGLECT, CLEARNESS-OBSCURITY, TRUTH-ERROR.

in''-ex-cit''-a-bil'-i-ty. Insusceptibility to excitement. EXCITABILITY-INEXCITABILITY, VIGOR-INERTIA.

in''-ex-cit'-a-ble. Not easily excited. EXCITABILITY-INEXCITABILITY.

in''-ex-cu'-sa-ble. Not to be justified. JUSTIFICATION-CHARGE, VIRTUE-VICE.

in-ex''-e-cu'-tion. Nonperformance. COMPLETION-NONCOMPLETION.

in''-ex-haust'-i-ble. Unfailing. ENOUGH.

in''-ex-ist'-ence. Want of being. ENTITY-NONENTITY, PRESENCE-ABSENCE.

in''-ex-ist'-ent. Innate. ENTITY-NONENTITY, PRESENCE-ABSENCE.

in-ex'-o-ra-ble. Unyielding; relentless; unavoidable. BIGOTRY-APOSTASY, COERCION, COMPASSION-RUTHLESSNESS, DETERMINATION-VACILLATION, HARSHNESS-MILDNESS, PARDON-VINDICTIVENESS, VOLITION-OBLIGATION.

in-ex''-pec-ta'-tion. Absence of expectation. EXPECTATION-SURPRISE.

in''-ex-pe'-di-ence. Want of fitness. PROPRIETY-IMPROPRIETY.

in''-ex-pe'-di-en-cy. Impropriety. PROPRIETY-IMPROPRIETY.

in''-ex-pe'-di-ent. Improper. OPPORTUNENESS-UNSUITABLENESS, PROPRIETY-IMPROPRIETY, SAGACITY-INCAPACITY.

in''-ex-pen'-sive. Costing little. COSTLINESS-CHEAPNESS.

in''-ex-pe'-ri-ence. Lack of personal and experimental knowledge. KNOWLEDGE-IGNORANCE, SKILL-UNSKILFULNESS.

in''-ex-pert'. Unskilled. SKILL-UNSKILFULNESS.

in-ex'-pi-a-ble. So heinous as not to be atoned for. VIRTUE-VICE.

in-ex'-pli-ca-ble. Not to be explained. CLEARNESS-OBSCURITY.

in''-ex-press'-i-ble. Unutterable; unintelligible. ASTONISHMENT-EXPECTANCE, CLEARNESS-OBSCURITY, MAGNITUDE-SMALLNESS, MEANING-JARGON.

in''-ex-press'-i-bles. Trousers. DRESS-UNDRESS.

in''-ex-pres'-sion. Lack of expression. MANIFESTATION-LATENCY.

in''-ex-press'-ive. Lacking expression; incompletely expressing. MEANING-JARGON.

in''-ex-pug'-na-ble. Unconquerable. SECURITY-INSECURITY.

in''-ex-ten'-sion. Want of extension. EXTENSION-INEXTENSION, GREATNESS-LITTLENESS, MATERIALITY-SPIRITUALITY.

in''-ex-tin'-guish-a-ble. Unquenchable. EXCITABILITY-INEXCITABILITY, MUTABILITY-STABILITY, STRENGTH-WEAKNESS; **inextinguishable desire,** DESIRE-DISTASTE.

in-ex'-tri-ca-ble. Hopelessly entangled. COHESION-LOOSENESS, POSSIBILITY-IMPOSSIBILITY, REGULARITY-IRREGULARITY.

in-fal''-li-bil'-i-ty. Incapability of error. CERTAINTY-DOUBT; **assumption of infallibility,** PRESUMPTION-OBSEQUIOUSNESS.

in-fal'-li-bly. Without fail. CERTAINTY-DOUBT.

in'-fa-mous. Notorious. REPUTATION-DISCREDIT, UPRIGHTNESS-DISHONESTY, VIRTUE-VICE.

in'-fa-my. Dishonor; vileness. REPUTATION-DISCREDIT, UPRIGHTNESS-DISHONESTY, VIRTUE-VICE.

in'-fan-cy. Early childhood. BEGINNING-END, INFANCY-AGE.

INFANCY—AGE.

Babyhood. The state of being a very young child.
Bloom. The flower of youth or manhood.
Boyhood. The period of life in a male between childhood and puberty.

Advanced age. Old age.
Age. The closing period of life.
Anility. The state of being imbecile in old age; like an old woman
Caducity. The state of failing in old age.

INFANCY—AGE—*Continued.*

Childhood. The time from infancy to near puberty.
Girlhood. The state of being a female child.
Incunabula [L.]. Things of the cradle of a race, or an art ; specimens of printing A. D. 1500 or thereabouts.
Infancy. The state of being too young to speak.
Juniority. The state of being younger.
Juvenescence. A growing young.
Juvenility. Youthfulness.
Minority. The condition of being under age.
Nonage. The condition of being under age.
Puberty. The age at which persons are capable of begetting children.
Pucelage. Virginity.
Pupilage. The state or period of being a pupil.
Teens. The years of one's age designated by the numbers ending in teen.
Tender age. The period of early childhood.
Youth.
Youthhood. } The period of life between childhood and manhood.

INFANCY—*Associated Nouns.*

Cradle. A bed or cot for a baby swinging or rocking.
Leading strings. Strings by which children are supported when beginning to walk.
Nursery. An apartment in a house appropriated to the care of children.

INFANCY—*Figurative Expressions.*

Flower of life.
Golden season of life.
Heyday of youth.
Prime of life.
Rising generation. } Youth.
School days.
Seed-time of life.
Spring-tide of life.

INFANCY—*Adjectives.*

Beardless. Too young to have a beard.
Budding. Developing during youth.
Callow. Without experience in the world.
Green. Of an unripe youth.
In one's teens. See TEENS.
In statu pupilari [L.]. In the condition of ward.
Junior. Belonging to youth or earlier life.
Juvenile. Characteristic of youth.
Puisné [F.]. Junior as to rank.
Sappy. Immature in age.
Under age. In one's nonage.
Young. Pertaining to youth.
Youngster. A young person.
Youthful. Having youth.

INFANCY—*Phrase.*

Bis pueri senes [L.]. Old men are children twice.

AGE—ADJECTIVES—*Continued from Column 2.*

Senior. Older in years or office.
Stricken in years. Infirm from age.
Superannuated. Incapacitated by age.
Time-worn. Feeble from age.
Turned of. Having passed beyond a certain age.
Venerable. Meriting esteem on account of age.
Waning. Gradually declining, like the old moon.
Wrinkled. Having furrows in the skin from age.
Years old. Of age.

AGE—*Phrase.*

Bis pueri senes [L.]. Old men are children twice.

Climacteric. One of the critical ages in man's life.
Decline of life. The period in which man begins to age.
Declining years. Advancing old age.
Decrepitude. The state of being broken down by old age.
Dotage. Feebleness of mind. due to old age.
Elders. Those who are of greater age.
Eldership. Seniority.
Grand climacteric. The age of 63 years.
Gray hairs. Figurative expression for old age.
Green old age. A happy and hearty old age.
Hoary age. Great age, with white hair.
Longevity. Tendency to live to a great age.
Old age. The advanced period of life.
Oldness. The state or quality of being old.
Ripe age. Having advanced to a perfectly developed age.
Primogeniture. The state of being the first born of a family
Second childhood.
Second childishness. } Senility.
Senescence. The state of growing old.
Senility. The state of being old.
Seniority. The state of being older than another.
Sere and yellow leaf. Old age. [Shakespeare, *Macbeth*, V, i.]
Superannuation. State of being too old for office or business.
Three score years and ten. The allotted years of man.
Time of life. The age of man.
Vale of years. Old age; the Valley of Baca, the vale of tears. [*Psalm* 84, 6.]
Years. Advanced age.

AGE—*Verbs.*

Age. To grow old.
Be aged, etc. See *Adjectives.*
Decline. To become impaired by age.
Get old, etc. See *Adjectives.*
Grow old, etc. See *Adjectives.*
Wane. To decline gradually.

AGE—*Adjectives.*

Advanced in life.
Advanced in years. } Old.
Aged. Approaching the term of existence.
Ancestral. Pertaining to an ancestor.
Anile. Enfeebled in the intellect by age.
Antiquated. Of an old and obsolete style.
Declining. Weakening from age.
Decrepit. Enfeebled by age.
Effete. Worn out by age and incapable of further production.
Elder. Having lived more years than another.
Elderly. Having passed the prime of life.
Eldest. First-born.
First-born. Eldest.
Firstling. The first-born.
Gray.
Gray-headed. } Old.
Having one foot in the grave. Having lived to an advanced age.
Hoar.
Hoary. } White from age.
In years. Elderly.
Marked with a crow's foot. Marked with a wrinkle under the eye, as a sign of age.
Matronly. Advanced in years.
Mellow. Ripened by age.
No chicken. Having advanced beyond the years of youth.
Of a certain age.
Old. Advanced far in years or life. See NOVELTY-ANTIQUITY.
Old as Methuselah. Old as the oldest man. [*Genesis* v, 27.]
Older. More advanced in years than another.
Oldest. Born first.
Passé [F.]. Past the prime of life.
Past one's prime. Going toward old age.
Patriarchal. Old and venerable.
Ripe. Fully matured.
Run to seed. Grown old and useless.
Senile. Affected by old age.

(*Continued on Column* 1.)

infandum renovare dolorem [L.] (in-fan'-dum ren''-o-vê'-rî do-lo'-rem). To revive unspeakable grief. CONTENTEDNESS - DISCONTENTMENT, JUBILATION LAMENTATION, REMEMBRANCE - FORGETFULNESS.

[Virgil, *Æneid*, 2, 1.]
in'-fant. Babe. INFANT - VETERAN, SAGE - FOOL, STRENGTH-WEAKNESS.

INFANT—VETERAN.

Babe.⎫
Baby.⎭ A very young child of either sex.
Bairn. A child of either sex
Bambino. A little child.
Bantling. A young child
Boy. A male child.
Brat. A contemptuous term for child.
Bratling. Diminutive of brat.
Cadet. A younger or the youngest son.
Calf. The young of the bovine species.
Callant. A young man.
Callow. An unfledged bird.
Chicken. The young of the common fowl.
Child. The young of the human race.
Chit. A lively child.
Chrysalis. The undeveloped young of an insect in the pupa state.
Cocoon. One of the stages of insect life
Codlin. An immature apple
Codling. A young cod.
Colt. A young horse.
Cub. A young bear.
Damsel.⎫
Demoiselle [F.]⎭ A young unmarried woman
Elf. A fairy.
Enfants terribles [F.]. Terrible children.
Fetus. The young in the womb or the egg
Foal. The young of an equine animal
Fry. Very young fish.
Girl. A female child.
Hobbledehoy. An awkward youth.
Hopeful. A young son or daughter ironically spoken of as the hope of the house.
Hoyden. A romping or bold girl.
Infant. A child too young to speak
Kitten. A young cat.
Lad. A youth.
Lamb. A young sheep
Lambkin. A little lamb.
Larva. The young of insects after leaving the egg.
Lass. A young woman
Lassie. A little lass
Lionel. A small lion.
Lionet. A young lion.
Little one. A young child.
Maid.⎫
Maiden.⎭ A young unmarried woman.
Master. A young gentleman
Minor. A person under age.
Miss. A young girl.
Nestling. A bird too young to leave the nest.
Nursling. A child still under the care of a nurse.
Olive-branch. A humorous term for offspring. [Bible.]
Orphan. A child deprived of its parents by death
Papoose. A North American Indian infant
Piccaninny. A little negro child.
Pullet. A young hen.
Pup. The young of various carnivoræ.
Quab. A squab or nestling.
Sapling. A young tree.
School-boy. A boy attending a school.
Scion. A child of a noble family.
Seedling. A young tree or plant.
Squab. A nestling pigeon.
Stripling. A mere youth.

Centenarian. A person one hundred years old
Crone. A withered old woman.
Elders. Those who have lived longer
Forefathers, etc. Remote ancestors See CREATION
Gaffer. An old man.
Gammer. An old woman
Grandam. A grandmother
Grandfather. The father of either of one's parents.
Grandsire. A grandfather.
Graybeard. An old man with a gray beard.
Methuselah. A Biblical character said to have lived 969 years; a very old person; "the oldest man."
Nestor. An old and very wise man. [Homer.]
Nonagenarian. A person ninety years old.
Octogenarian. A person eighty years old.
Old man. A person advanced in years, usually above fifty years.
Old Pan. A quite old man. [Pan himself, the simple shepherd's awe-inspiring god. Wordsworth, *Excursion*, iv.]
Old stager. One who has resided in a place or filled a position for a long time.
Pantaloon. An old dotard.
Patriarch. An aged and venerable man
Preadamite. Existing before Adam.
Seer. An old and prophetic man.
Sexagenarian. A person sixty years old.
Veteran. A person old in any service.

INFANT—*Continued.*

Suckling. An unweaned mammal.
Tadpole. A young frog or toad.
Tendril. A young shoot.
Urchin. A mischievous boy.
Vagitus. The first cry of a new-born babe.
Virgin. A pure young woman.
Weanling. A child or animal just weaned.
Wench. A young woman of lowly condition.
Whelp. The young of the carnivoræ.
Whipper-snapper. An insignificant young person.
Whipster. A young and nimble fellow.
Yearling. A young animal in its second year
Youngster.⎫
Younker.⎭ A young person
Youth. A young man

INFANT—*Adjectives.*

At the breast. Nursing
Baby. Young or little.
Babyish. Without discretion, like a baby.
Boyish. Full of mischief and sport, like a boy.
Callow. Wanting experience in the world.
Childish. Silly and trifling, like a child.
Girlish. Frivolous, like a girl.
In arms. That has to be carried about in the arms.
Infantile. Childish.
Infantine. Pertaining to infants.
In long clothes. In an infant state
In one's teens. In the years ending with teen
In swaddling clothes.⎫
In the cradle.⎭ In an infant state
Kittenish. Playful and thoughtless, like a kitten
New-born. Recently born.
New-fledged. Having just acquired feathers.
Puerile. Immature and weak, like a child.
Unfledged. Not having attained to full growth

---

in-fan'-ta. Any royal princess of Spain or Portugal CHIEF-UNDERLING.
in-fan'-ti-cide. Killing of a child before, at, or after birth. DEVOTION-IDOLATRY, LIFE-KILLING.
in'-fan-tile. Pertaining to infants. INFANT-VETERAN SAGACITY-INCAPACITY.
in'-fan-tine. Pertaining to infants; foolish. INFANT-VETERAN, SAGACITY-INCAPACITY.
in'-fan-try. Foot-soldiers with small arms. BELLIGERENT.
in'-fan-try-man. A foot-soldier. BELLIGERENT.
in-farc'-tion. Stoppage of a channel. APERTURE-CLOSURE.
in-fat''-u-a'-ted. Misled. BIGOTRY-APOSTASY, CREDU-

LOUSNESS - SKEPTICISM. DECISION - MISJUDGMENT, SANENESS-LUNACY.
in-fat''-u-a'-tion. Extravagant passion. BIGOTRY-APOSTASY, CREDULOUSNESS-SKEPTICISM, DECISION-MISJUDGMENT, EXCITABILITY-INEXCITABILITY, LOVE-HATE, SAGACITY-INCAPACITY, SANENESS-LUNACY.
in-fea'-si-ble. Impracticable. POSSIBILITY-IMPOSSIBILITY.
in-fect'. Contaminate; imbue. BETTERMENT-DETERIORATION, EXCITATION, MIXTURE-HOMOGENEITY.
infecta, re [L.] (in-fec'-ta, rî). The business being unfinished. ACTION-PASSIVENESS, COMPLETION-NONCOMPLETION, SKILL-UNSKILFULNESS, SUCCESS-FAILURE, TRANSCURSION-SHORTCOMING

in-fec'-tion. Communication of disease. EXCITATION, HEALTH-SICKNESS.

in-fec'-tious. Catching. HEALTHINESS-UNHEALTHINESS.

in-fec'-und. Unfruitful. FERTILITY-STERILITY.

in''-fe-cun'-di-ty. Sterility. FERTILITY-STERILITY.

in''-fe-lic'-i-tous. Not happy. PLEASURE-PAIN.

in''-fe-lic'-i-ty. Unhappiness; unsuitableness. PLEASURE-PAIN, SKILL-UNSKILFULNESS.

in'-fer-ence. Illation. DECISION-MISJUDGMENT, INTERPRETATION-MISINTERPRETATION, RATIOCINATION-INSTINCT; **by inference,** MANIFESTATION-LATENCY, RATIOCINATION-INSTINCT.

in''-fer-en'-tial. Deducible by inference. MANIFESTATION-LATENCY, PROOF-DISPROOF.

in-fe'-ri-or. Unequal to. FAULTLESSNESS-FAULTINESS, SUPREMACY-SUBORDINACY.

in-fe''-ri-or'-i-ty. Lower state or condition. ENLARGEMENT-DIMINUTION, EQUALITY-INEQUALITY, SUPREMACY-SUBORDINACY; **personal inferiority,** SUPREMACY-SUBORDINACY.

in-fer'-nal. Hellish. ANGEL-FIEND, CHARITABLENESS-MALEVOLENCE, GOODNESS-BADNESS, HEAVEN-HELL, VIRTUE-VICE; **infernal machine,** WEAPON; **infernal regions,** HEAVEN-HELL.

in-fer'-no. Hell. HEAVEN-HELL.

in''-fer-til'-i-ty. Sterility. FERTILITY-STERILITY.

in-fest'. Overrun. PLEASURABLENESS-PAINFULNESS.

in''-fes-ta'-tion. Vexation. PLEASURABLENESS-PAINFULNESS.

in''-fes-tiv'-i-ty. Cheerfulness. LIGHTHEARTEDNESS-DEJECTION, WITTINESS-DULNESS.

in-fib''-u-la'-tion. Clasping. UNION-DISUNION.

in'-fi-del. A skeptic. GODLINESS-DISBELIEF.

in''-fi-del'-i-ty. Disbelief; unfaithfulness. FAITH-MISGIVING, GODLINESS-DISBELIEF, UPRIGHTNESS-DISHONESTY.

in-fil'-trate. Penetrate gradually. DAMPNESS-DRYNESS, EDUCATION-MISTEACHING, ENTRANCE-EXIT, ENVIRONMENT-INTERPOSITION, MIXTURE-HOMOGENEITY, WATER-AIR.

in''-fil-tra'-tion. Act of infiltrating. ENTRANCE-EXIT, ENVIRONMENT-INTERPOSITION, MIXTURE-HOMOGENEITY, TRANSMISSION, WATER-AIR.

In'-fi-nite. God. DIVINITY.

in'-fi-nite. Boundless. INFINITY, **infinite goodness,** DIVINITY, GREATNESS-LITTLENESS.

in'-fi-nite-ly. Greatly. INFINITY, MAGNITUDE-SMALLNESS.

in'-fi-nite-ness. Greatness. INFINITY.

in-fin''-i-tes'-i-mal. Infinitely small. GREATNESS-LITTLENESS, MAGNITUDE-SMALLNESS; **infinitesimal calculus,** NUMBERING.

in-fin'-i-tive. The mode of a verb used as a noun. VERB.

in-fin'-i-tude. The quality of being infinite. INFINITY.

in-fin'-i-ty. Boundlessness. EXTENSION - DISTRICT, INFINITY, MAGNITUDE-SMALLNESS.

INFINITY.

Infiniteness, etc. The state or condition of being infinite. See *Adjectives.*

Infinitude, etc. The state of being without limits. See *Adjectives.*

Infinity, etc. The quality or state of being immeasurable and unbounded; absolute and unconditioned. See *Adjectives.*

Perpetuity, etc. The quality or state of being infinite in duration. See DURATION-NEVERNESS.

INFINITY—*Verbs*

Be infinite etc. See *Adjectives.*
Go on forever. To be perpetual.
Have no bounds. } To go on without end
Have no limits. }
Know no bounds. } To be without end.
Know no limits }

INFINITY—*Adjectives.*

Boundless. Having no bounds.
Countless. That cannot be counted.
Endless. Without end.
Exhaustless. That cannot be exhausted.
Illimitable. That cannot be limited.
Illimited. Not limited or bounded.
Immeasurable. That cannot be estimated by comparison with something else.
Immense. Incapable of measurement.
Incalculable. So great that an estimate cannot be formed.
Incomprehensible. That cannot be grasped mentally.
Indefinite. So large as to have no precise limits.
Infinite. Having no bounds or limits; absolute and unconditioned
Innumerable. So numerous as not to be counted.
Interminable. Having no limit or end.
Limitless. Without limits.
Measureless. Having no standard great enough to be measured by.
Numberless. Not to be counted.
Perpetual, etc. Infinite in duration. See DURATION-NEVERNESS.
Sumless. Not to be computed.
Termless. Boundless.
Unapproachable. That may not be reached
Unbounded. Having no known bounds.
Unfathomable. Infinite in depth.
Unlimited. Having no limits.
Unmeasured. Not measured.
Unnumbered. Indefinitely numerous.
Untold. Not numbered.
Without end. }
Without limit. } Infinite.
Without measure. }
Without number. }

INFINITY—*Adverbs.*

Ad infinitum [L.]. To an infinite degree or extent; endlessly.
Infinitely, etc. See *Adjectives.*

in-firm'. Lacking strength. HEALTH-SICKNESS, STRENGTH-WEAKNESS, VIRTUE-VICE; **infirm of purpose,** BRAVERY-COWARDICE, DETERMINATION-VACILLATION.

in-fir'-ma-ry. A place for treatment of the sick. REMEDY-BANE.

in-fir'-mi-ty. Weakness; enfeebling disease. HEALTH-SICKNESS, STRENGTH-WEAKNESS, VIRTUE-VICE.

in-fix'. Fasten in. EDUCATION-MISTEACHING.

in-flame'. Excite flame or passion in. EXCITATION, FAVORITE-ANGER, HEATING-COOLING, TURBULENCE-CALMNESS, VIGOR-INERTIA.

in-flam''-ma-bil'-i-ty. Capable of being set on fire. HEATING-COOLING.

in-flam'-ma-ble. Easily set on fire. CHEMISTRY, COMBUSTIBLE, HEATING-COOLING.

in''-flam-ma'-tion. Setting on fire; morbid process in the body.

in-flate'. Swell. CONCEIT-DIFFIDENCE, ENLARGEMENT-DIMINUTION, RIVER-WIND, TERSENESS-PROLIXITY.

in-fla'-ted. Bombastic; puffed up. CONCEIT-DIFFIDENCE, SIMPLICITY - FLORIDNESS, SOCIETY - LUDICROUSNESS.

in-fla'-tion. Expansion. ENLARGEMENT-DIMINUTION, RIVER-WIND, SIMPLICITY-FLORIDNESS, SOLIDITY-RARITY.

in-flect'. Vary the form of. CURVATION-RECTILINEARITY.

in-flec'-tion. The changes undergone by words to express their relations and attributes. VERB.

in-flex''-i-bil'-i-ty. Firmness. BIGOTRY-APOSTASY, CURVATION-RECTILINEARITY, HARDNESS-SOFTNESS.

in-flex'-i-ble. Unyielding; rigid. BIGOTRY-APOSTASY, CURVATION-RECTILINEARITY, DETERMINATION-VACILLATION HARDNESS-SOFTNESS, HARSHNESS-MILDNESS.

in-flex'-ion. A bending; changes in form of words. CURVATION-RECTILINEARITY, GRAMMAR-SOLECISM,

in-flict'. Lay on; cause to suffer. ACTION-PASSIVE-NESS, HARSHNESS-MILDNESS; **inflict evil,** GOODNESS-BADNESS; **inflict pain,** PLEASURABLENESS - PAIN-FULNESS, SENSUALITY-SUFFERING; **inflict punishment,** EXCULPATION-PUNITION.

in-flic'-tion. Pain; punishment. PLEASURE-PAIN, PLEASURABLENESS-PAINFULNESS, RECOMPENSE-PUNITION, WELFARE-MISFORTUNE.

in-flic'-tive. Conveying an infliction. EXCULPATION-PUNITION.

in'-flu-ence. Affect; induce; sway. AGENCY, DOMINANCE - IMPOTENCE, MIGHT - IMPOTENCE, MOTIVE-CAPRICE, MUTATION-PERMANENCE, RULE-LICENSE

in''-flu-en'-tial. Having the power of influence. MIGHT-IMPOTENCE, RULE-LICENSE.

in''-flu-en'-za. Violent catarrh. HEALTH-SICKNESS.

in'-flux. Continuous coming or flowing in. ENTRANCE-EXIT.

in-fold'. Enclose. ENCLOSURE.

in-form'. Impart information. ENLIGHTENMENT-SECRECY; **inform against,** JUSTIFICATION-CHARGE, LITIGATION.

in-form'-al. Irregular. CONVENTIONALITY-UNCONVENTIONALITY, LAW-LAWLESSNESS.

in''-for-mal'-i-ty. Want of regular form. CONVENTIONALITY - UNCONVENTIONALITY, LAW-LAWLESSNESS, OBSERVANCE-NONOBSERVANCE.

in-form'-ant. An informer. ENLIGHTENMENT-SECRECY.

in''-for-ma'-tion. Knowledge acquired; a complaint ENLIGHTENMENT-SECRECY, KNOWLEDGE-IGNORANCE, LITIGATION, TIDINGS-MYSTERY; **pick up information,** EDUCATION-LEARNING.

in-formed'. Given information. ENLIGHTENMENT-SECRECY.

in-form'-er. One who informs against others. ENLIGHTENMENT - SECRECY, JUSTIFICATION - CHARGE, MESSENGER.

in-form'-i-ty. Shapelessness. FORM-FORMLESSNESS.

infra dignitatem [L.] (in'-fra dig-ni-tê'-tem). Beneath dignity. REPUTATION - DISCREDIT, UPRIGHTNESS-DISHONESTY.

in-frac'-tion. Infringement. DUTY-DERELICTION, INSUBORDINATION-OBEDIENCE, OBSERVANCE-NONOBSERVANCE; **infraction of usage,** etc., CONVENTIONALITY-UNCONVENTIONALITY, HABIT-DESUETUDE.

in-fran'-gi-ble. Not breakable. COHESION-LOOSENESS, SOLIDITY-RARITY.

in-fre'-quen-cy. Rareness. FREQUENCY-RARITY, MULTIPLICITY-PAUCITY.

in-fre'-quent. Not often. MULTIPLICITY-PAUCITY.

in-frig''-i-da'-tion. A chilling. HEATING-COOLING.

in-fringe'. Transgress; violate. DUENESS-UNDUENESS, DUTY-DERELICTION, INSUBORDINATION-OBEDIENCE, OBSERVANCE - NONOBSERVANCE, TRANSCURSION-SHORTCOMING; **infringe a law,** etc., CONVENTIONALITY-UNCONVENTIONALITY.

in-fringe'-ment. Violation. INSUBORDINATION-OBEDIENCE, OBSERVANCE-NONOBSERVANCE, TRANSCURSION-SHORTCOMING.

in'-fu-mate. To cure or dry by smoking. PREPARATION-NONPREPARATION.

in''-fun-dib'-u-lar. Infundibuliform. APERTURE-CLOSURE, CONVEXITY-CONCAVITY.

in''-fun-dib'-u-li-form''. Funnel-shaped. CONVEXITY-CONCAVITY.

in-fu'-ri-ate. Enrage. EXCITATION, FAVORITE-ANGER, TURBULENCE-CALMNESS.

in-fus'-cate. Darken. WHITENESS-BLACKNESS.

in''-fus-ca'-tion. Darkness. WHITENESS-BLACKNESS.

in-fuse'. Instil; pour in. EDUCATION-MISTEACHING, INJECTION-EJECTION, MIXTURE-HOMOGENEITY; **infuse courage,** BRAVERY-COWARDICE; **infuse life into,** EXCITATION; **infuse new blood,** BETTERMENT-DETERIORATION.

in-fu'-si-ble. Incapable of being melted. SOLIDITY-RARITY.

in-fu'-sion. Instillation; steeping. EDUCATION-MISTEACHING, INJECTION-EJECTION, LIQUEFACTION-VOLATILIZATION, MIXTURE-HOMOGENEITY.

in''-fu-so'-ri-a. A division of the animal kingdom. GREATNESS-LITTLENESS.

in''-gan-na'-tion. Deception. TRUTHFULNESS-FRAUD.

in-gath'-er-ing. Act of gathering in. GATHERING-SCATTERING.

in-gem'-i-nate. To repeat. DOUBLING-HALVING.

in-gem''-i-na'-tion. Repetition. DOUBLING-HALVING.

in-gen'-er-ate. Inborn. SUBJECTIVENESS-OBJECTIVENESS.

in-ge'-nious. Evincing skill or cleverness. SKILL-UNSKILFULNESS.

in-ge'-nite. Innate. SUBJECTIVENESS-OBJECTIVENESS.

ingenium, perfervidum [L.] (in-jî'-ni-um per-fer'-vid-um). Overheated genius. ACTIVITY-INDOLENCE.

ingenium sine mixtura dementiæ fuit, nullum magnum [L.] (in-jî'-ni-um saî'-nî mix-tiu'-ra dî-men'-shi-î fiu'-it, nul'-lum mag'-num). No great genius was ever without a mixture of madness. SAGACITY-INCAPACITY.

ingénu [F.] (an·-zhê-nü') Frank. CRAFT-ARTLESSNESS.

ingénue [F.] (an·-zhê-nü'). Representation of an artless character. ACTING.

in''-ge-nu'-i-ty. Cleverness. NATURE-ART, SKILL-UNSKILFULNESS.

in-gen'-u-ous. Candid. CRAFT-ARTLESSNESS, NATURE-ART, SKILL-UNSKILFULNESS.

in-gen'-u-ous-ness. Candor. TRUTHFULNESS-FALSEHOOD.

in-gest'. To take in. ADMISSION-EXPULSION.

in-ges'-ta. Things taken into the body as food. NUTRIMENT-EXCRETION.

in-ges'-tion. Act of taking in. ADMISSION-EXPULSION, BIOLOGY.

in'-gle. A fire or fireplace. COMBUSTIBLE.

in-glo'-ri-ous. Shameful. REPUTATION-DISCREDIT, UPRIGHTNESS-DISHONESTY.

in-glo'-ri-ous-ness. Shamefulness. REPUTATION-DISCREDIT.

in'-got. A bar of gold or silver for coining. MONEY.

in-graft'. Insert for propagation; implant. ADDITION-SUBTRACTION, EDUCATION-MISTEACHING, INJECTION-EJECTION, UNION-DISUNION.

in-graft'-ed. Implanted. HABIT-DESUETUDE, SUBJECTIVENESS-OBJECTIVENESS.

in-grain'. Dye; fix deeply. COLOR-ACHROMATISM, ENVIRONMENT-INTERPOSITION.

in-grained'. Fixed deeply. AFFECTIONS, COMPOSITION-RESOLUTION, HABIT-DESUETUDE, SUBJECTIVENESS-OBJECTIVENESS.

in'-grate''. Ungrateful. THANKFULNESS-THANKLESSNESS.

in-gra'-ti-ate. Bring into favor. LOVE-HATE.

in-gra'-ti-a-ting. Rendering pleasant. POLITENESS-IMPOLITENESS.

in-grat'-i-tude. Lack of gratitude. THANKFULNESS-THANKLESSNESS.

in-gre'-di-ent. Component. CONSTITUENT-ALIEN.

in'-gress. Going in. ENTRANCE-EXIT, TRANSMISSION.

in-gur'-gi-tate. Swallow greedily. ADMISSION-EXPULSION.

in-gur''-gi-ta'-tion. Greedy swallowing. ADMISSION-EXPULSION.

in-gus'-ta-ble. Tasteless. SAVOR-TASTELESSNESS.

in-hab'-ile. Incompetent. SKILL-UNSKILFULNESS.

in-hab'-it. Live in. DWELLER-HABITATION, ESTABLISHMENT-REMOVAL, PRESENCE-ABSENCE.

in-hab''-i-ta'-tion. Indwelling. PRESENCE-ABSENCE.

in-hab'-it-ant. A resident. DWELLER-HABITATION.

in-hab'-it-ed. Populated. DWELLER-HABITATION.

in-hab'-it-ing. Living in. DWELLER-HABITATION.

in''-ha-la'-tion. Act of inhaling. ADMISSION-EXPULSION.

in-hale'. Inspire. ANATOMY, ODOR-INODOROUSNESS, SWEETNESS-ACIDITY.

in''-har-mo'-ni-ous. Disagreeing; discordant. MELODY-DISSONANCE; **inharmonious color,** COLOR-ACHROMATISM; **inharmonious sound,** MELODY-DISSONANCE.

in-her'-ence. Permanent existence in something. SUBJECTIVENESS-OBJECTIVENESS.

in-her'-ent. Intrinsic. SUBJECTIVENESS-OBJECTIVENESS.

in-her'-it. Receive by nature from ancestors. GAIN-LOSS, HOLDING-EXEMPTION, PROPERTY.

in-her'-it-ance. That which is inherited. GAIN-LOSS, HOLDING-EXEMPTION, PROPERTY; **inheritance of the saints,** HEAVEN-HELL.

in-her'-it-ed. Received by nature from ancestors. SUBJECTIVENESS-OBJECTIVENESS.

in-her'-it-or. One who inherits. HOLDER.

in-her'-it-ress. One who inherits (a female). HOLDER.

in-her'-it-rix. A female inheritor. HOLDER.

in-he'-sion. Inherence. SUBJECTIVENESS-OBJECTIVENESS.

in-hib'-it. Restrain; prohibit. LEAVE-PROHIBITION, OBSTRUCTION-HELP, RELEASE-RESTRAINT.

in''-hi-bi'-tion. Restriction. LEAVE-PROHIBITION, OBSTRUCTION-HELP.

in-hos'-pi-ta-ble. Not hospitable. SOCIABILITY-PRIVACY.

in-hos'-pi-ta-ble-ness. Want of sociability. SOCIABILITY-PRIVACY.

in-hos''-pi-tal'-i-ty. Want of hospitality. SOCIABILITY-PRIVACY.

in-hu'-man. Cruel. CHARITABLENESS-MALEVOLENCE.

in''-hu-mane'. Disposed to cruelty. CHARITABLENESS-MALEVOLENCE, HUMANITARIANISM-MISANTHROPY.

in-hu-man'-i-ty. Want of humanity. CHARITABLENESS-MALEVOLENCE.

in''-hu-ma'-tion. A burial. LIFE-FUNERAL.

in-hume'. Inter. LIFE-FUNERAL.

in''-im-ag'-i-na-ble. Inconceivable. ASTONISHMENT-EXPECTANCE, LIKELIHOOD-UNLIKELIHOOD, POSSIBILITY-IMPOSSIBILITY.

in-im'-i-cal. Adverse. AMITY-HOSTILITY, ANTAGONISM-CONCURRENCE.

in-im'-i-ta-ble. Matchless; surpassingly excellent. FAULTLESSNESS-FAULTINESS, GOODNESS-BADNESS, IMITATION-ORIGINALITY, SUPREMACY-SUBORDINACY.

in-iq'-ui-tous. Characterized by iniquity RIGHT-WRONG, VIRTUE-VICE.

in-iq'-ui-ty. Wickedness. RIGHT-WRONG, VIRTUE-VICE; **worker of iniquity,** GOOD MAN-BAD MAN.

in-ir''-ri-ta-bil'-i-ty. Lack of irritableness. EXCITABILITY-INEXCITABILITY.

in-ir'-ri-ta-ble. Lacking irritableness. EXCITABILITY-INEXCITABILITY.

in-i'-tial. Standing at the beginning. BEGINNING-END; **initial letter,** ENGRAVING.

in-i'-ti-ate. Begin; instruct in rudiments. BEGINNING-END, EDUCATION-MISTEACHING.

in-i'-ti-a''-ted. Instructed in rudiments. SKILL-UNSKILFULNESS.

in-i''-ti-a'-tion. Admission into a society. BEGINNING-END.

in-i'-ti-a-tive. Serving to initiate. BEGINNING-END

in-i'-ti-a-to''-ry. Introductory. BEGINNING-END.

in-ject'. Force in. INJECTION-EJECTION, WATER-AIR.

in-jec'-tion. Act of injecting. INJECTION-EJECTION.

INJECTION—EJECTION.

Bath. The act of plunging into, or exposing the body to water, etc., for purposes of cleanliness, etc. See WATER.

Dip. The action of dipping or plunging for a moment into a liquid.

Forcible ingress. The act of making entrance by main force.

Immersion. The act of dipping entirely under water.

Implantation. The act of planting for the purpose of growth.

Importation. The act of bringing in from abroad.

Infusion. The act of pouring in.

Ingress, etc. The act of entering.

Injection. The act of throwing or forcing in.

Inoculation. The insertion of virus through the skin.

Insertion. The act of placing between or among other things.

Insinuation, etc. The act of introducing gradually. See ENVIRONMENT-INTERPOSITION.

Interment, etc. The act of depositing a dead body in the earth. See LIFE-FUNERAL.

Introduction. The act of leading or bringing in.

Planting, etc. See *Verbs.*

Plunge. The act of thrusting into or submerging.

Submersion. The act of placing under water.

INJECTION—*Verbs.*

Bathe. To put into water to wash.

Bud. To graft by inserting a bud into the slit bark.

Bury, etc. To place under the earth. See LIFE-FUNERAL.

Dip. To immerse temporarily.

Dove-tail. To fix together by interlocking the joints.

Drive in. To push in forcibly.

Drop in. To let fall in.

Embed. To sink or lay in.

Empierce. To make a hole into.

Graft. To insert a shoot from one tree or plant into another.

Imbrue. To soak into.

Imbue. To cause to become pervaded with.

Immerge. To plunge into or under.

Immerse. To place entirely under some fluid.

Impact. To drive firmly together.

Implant. To plant for the purpose of growth.

Avulsion. A forcible tearing away.

Ejection, etc. The act of putting out suddenly and violently. See ADMISSION-EXPULSION.

Eliminating. The getting rid of something.

Elimination. The removal of some useless or offensive feature.

Eradication. The act of removing entirely.

Evolution. The act of unfolding or unrolling.

Evulsion. The act of plucking out.

Export. The act of carrying or sending abroad.

Expression. The act of pressing out by force.

Extermination. The act of removing by destroying utterly.

Extirpation. The act of getting rid of something undesirable by totally destroying it.

Extract. That which is drawn out.

Extracting. A drawing out.

Extraction. The act of drawing out.

Removal. The act of moving from one position to another

Squeezing. The act of forcing out by pressing.

Wrench. The act of removing by twisting suddenly and with force.

EJECTION—*Nouns of Agent.*

Corkscrew. An instrument with a spiral for drawing corks from bottles.

Extractor. A forceps or instrument for extracting substances.

Forceps. An instrument for grasping, holding firmly, or extracting substances.

Pliers. A small pincers with long jaws, used for bending or cutting metal rods.

EJECTION—*Verbs.*

Averruncate. } To root up.
Draw.

Draw out. To remove by pulling.

Dredge. To clean out, as the bottom of a river, with a machine adapted for that purpose.

Educe. To draw out.

Elicit. To draw out by some inducement.

Eliminate. To remove as undesirable.

Eradicate. To remove entirely.

Eviscerate. To disembowel.

Evolve. To unfold or unroll.

INJECTION—EJECTION—*Continued.*

INJECTION—Verbs—*Continued.*

Import. To bring or carry in.
Impregnate. To saturate thoroughly with another substance.
Infuse. To pour in.
Ingraft. To insert a graft.
Inject. To put into by force.
Inoculate. To communicate by inserting.
Insert. To put between or among other things.
Insert itself. To fix in a certain place
Instil. To imbue drop by drop.
Interject. To throw in among other things.
Introduce. To bring or lead in
Intromit. To send into.
Merge. To cause to be swallowed up in something else.
Obtrude. To thrust in or upon in an unwarranted manner.
Plant. To set in the ground for growth.
Plunge, etc. To thrust suddenly into. See Spring-Dive.
Plunge *in medias res* [L.]. To leap into the middle of things.
Pop in. To enter suddenly and unexpectedly
Press in. To enter in by exerting weight.
Put in. } To fix in a certain place or position
Put into. }
Ram in. To drive in with great force.
Run into. To insert suddenly and forcibly.
Soak, etc. To penetrate thoroughly. See Water.
Stick in. To fix in place by inserting.
Stuff in. To crowd into.
Thrust in. To shove in with force.
Tuck in. To fold under

INJECTION—*Adjectives.*

Inserted, etc. See *Verbs*

in″-ju-di′-cial. Not judicial. Law-Lawlessness.
in″-ju-di′-cious. Indiscreet. Sagacity-Incapacity.
in-junc′-tion. Mandate; precept; prohibition. Advice, Leave-Prohibition, Order.
in′-jure. Inflict harm. Betterment-Deterioration, Charitableness-Malevolence, Goodness-Badness.
in′-jured. Damaged. Betterment-Deterioration, Embellishment - Disfigurement, Faultiness-Faultlessness, Propriety-Impropriety.
injuria formæ spretæ [L.] (in-ju′-ri-a for′-mî sprî′-tî). The wrong of slighted beauty. Beauty-Ugliness.
in′-ju-ry. Damage; harm. Betterment-Deterioration, Embellishment-Disfigurement, Good-Evil, Goodness-Badness
in-jus′-tice. Wrong. Right-Wrong.
ink. A writing fluid. Whiteness-Blackness; **before the ink is dry,** Earliness-Lateness; **pen and ink,** Writing-Printing.
ink′-bot″-tle. A bottle for holding ink. Writing-Printing.
in′-kle. Broad linen tape. Connective.
ink′-ling. Slight intimation. Desire-Distaste, Enlightenment-Secrecy, Hypothesis, Knowledge-Ignorance.
ink′-plant″. A plant whose fruit contains a reddish fluid used as ink. Writing-Printing.
ink′-y. Black. Whiteness-Blackness

EJECTION—Verbs—*Continued.*

Exculpate. To free from unjust blame.
Express. To send out by special messenger
Extirpate. To get rid of by destroying.
Extort. To take from by violence; to twist out.
Extract. To pull out by a steady exertion of force
Extricate. To free from entanglement.
Get out. To procure from.
Grub out. } To dig up by the roots.
Grub up. }
Pick out. To take from by selection.
Pluck out. To remove by quick jerks.
Pluck up by the roots. To eradicate by a sudden effort
Pull out. } To draw out by force.
Pull up. }
Pull up by the roots. To eradicate forcibly.
Rake out. } To scratch out and up together
Rake up. }
Remove. To move from one position to another
Root out. } To eradicate.
Root up. }
Squeeze out. To force out by pressing.
Take out. To carry off.
Tear out. To pull out violently.
Unroot. To remove by destroying utterly.
Uproot. To eradicate.
Weed out. } To free from some harmful element, any one pulling
Weed up. } weeds out or up.
Wrench. To remove by twisting suddenly and forcibly
Wring from. To twist out by pressing.

EJECTION—*Adjectives.*

Extracted, etc. See *Verbs.*

in′-land. The interior of a country. Outside-Inside
in-lay′. Decorate. Variegation.
in′-let″. Small body of water leading to a larger, an opening. Aperture-Closure, Beginning-End, Entrance-Exit, Gulf-Plain, Interspace-Contact
in′-ly. Inwardly. Outside-Inside.
in′-mate. One who occupies a place with others. Dweller-Habitation.
in′-most″. Deepest within. Outside-Inside; **inmost soul,** Affections; **inmost thoughts,** Mind-Imbecility; **to the inmost core,** Sensitiveness-Apathy
inn. Public house for entertainment of travelers. Dweller-Habitation.
in′-nate″. Inborn. Subjectiveness-Objectiveness.
in-nav′-i-ga-ble. Impassable by ships. Possibility-Impossibility.
in′-ner. Interior. Outside-Inside; **inner coating,** Cover-Lining; **inner man,** Affections, Mind-Imbecility.
in′-ner-most″. Deepest within. Outside-Inside; **innermost recesses,** Outside-Inside.
in′-nings. A tract of land reclaimed from the sea; a turn at the bat; an ingathering. Gain-Loss, Ocean-Land, Outlay-Income.
inn′-keep″-er. The manager of an inn. Dweller-Habitation.
in′-no-cence. Freedom from guilt. Craft-Artlessness, Innocence-Guilt, Virtue-Vice.

INNOCENCE—GUILT

Guiltlessness, etc. The state of being free from guilt See *Adjectives.*
Impeccability. The state of being incapable of sinning
Incorruption. Freedom from moral depravity.
Innocence. The state of having no harmful influence

INNOCENCE—*Associated Nouns*

Clean hands. Hands not stained with guilt.
Clear conscience. One not troubled by remorse for evil done.
Mens sibi consica recti [L.]. A mind conscious of uprightness. [Virgil, *Æneid,* 1, 604.]

Atrocity. Extreme wickedness.
Blot. A cause of reproach.
Corpus delicti [L.]. The body of the crime.
Crime. An offense against some human or divine law
Criminality. That which constitutes a crime.
Criminousness. The state of being very wicked.
Culpability. The state of deserving blame.
Deadly sin. A crime punishable with death.
Deed without a name. An act of the greatest heinousness or wickedness. [Shakespeare, *Macbeth,* IV, i.]
Delinquency. A neglect of duty.

INNOCENCE—GUILT—*Continued.*

INNOCENCE—*Nouns of Agent.*

Dove. A bird, the symbol of innocence and gentleness.
Innocent. A person free from guilt or sin.
Lamb. A person innocent or gentle as a lamb.

INNOCENCE—*Verbs.*

Acquit, etc. To declare innocent. See EXCULPATION.
Be innocent, etc. See *Adjectives.*
Exculpate, etc. To clear from an unjust charge of guilt. See JUSTIFICATION.
Nil conscire sibi nulla palescere culpa [L.]. To be conscious of no fault. [Horace, *Epistles*, i, i, 61.]

INNOCENCE—*Adjectives.*

Above suspicion. Too innocent to be suspected.
Arcadian, etc. Simple and innocent. See CRAFT-ARTLESSNESS.
Blameless. Free from anything worthy of censure.
Clear. Free from guilt.
Dove-like. Inoffensive and innocent.
Faultless. Free from even a slight offense.
Guiltless. Free from wrong-doing.
Harmless. Not inflicting injury.
Harmless as doves. Harmless in an extreme degree. [*Matthew* x, 16.]
Immaculate. Without moral blemish.
Inculpable. That cannot be charged with wrong-doing.
Inerrable. Not able to go astray morally.
Innocent. Not having done wrong.
Innocent as a lamb. Very gentle and innocent.
Innocent as the babe unborn. Incapable of doing wrong.
Innocuous.⎫ Having no injurious qualities.
Innoxious.⎭
Inoffensive. Doing no harm.
Irreprehensible. That cannot justly be blamed.
Irreproachable. That cannot be found fault with.
Irreprovable. That cannot be censured with justice.
Lamb-like. Gentle and innocent.
More sinned against than sinning. [Shakespeare, *Lear*, III, ii.]
Not guilty. Having done nothing wrong.
Pure. Free from moral corruption.
Rectus in curia [L.]. Upright in the court: with clean hands.
Salvable. Capable of being saved.
Saturnian. Marked by simple innocence, as in the golden age, when Saturn ruled the gods and men.
Sinless. Perfectly innocent.
Spotless. Free from any blemish on moral character.
Stainless. Free from every moral taint.
Unblamable. That cannot be found fault with.
Unblamed. Free from censure.
Unblemished. Not marred by guilt.
Unculpable. That cannot be censured.
Undefiled, etc. Not made impure. See UPRIGHTNESS.
Unerring. Not going astray morally.
Unexceptionable. That cannot be taken exception to.
Unguilty. Not guilty.
Unhardened. Not made indifferent to sin.
Unimpeachable. Faultless.
Unimpeached. Not accused of guilt.
Unobjectionable. That cannot be found fault with.
Unreproached. Not found fault with.
Unreproved. Not censured.
Unspotted. Not tainted with guilt.
Venial, etc. Excusable. See JUSTIFICATION.
Virtuous. Characterized by moral excellence.

INNOCENCE—*Adverbs.*

Innocently, etc. See *Adjectives.*
With a clear conscience.⎫
With a safe conscience.⎬ Blameless.
With clean hands.⎭

---

in′-no-cent. Guiltless; naive; foolish. CRAFT-ARTLESSNESS, GOOD MAN-BAD MAN, GOODNESS-BADNESS, HEALTHINESS-UNHEALTHINESS, INNOCENCE-GUILT, SAGE-FOOL, UPRIGHTNESS-DISHONESTY, VIRTUE-VICE.
in′-no-cent-ly. Guiltlessly. INNOCENCE-GUILT.
in-noc′-u-ous. Harmless. GOODNESS-BADNESS, HEALTHINESS-UNHEALTHINESS, INNOCENCE-GUILT.

Dereliction. Wilful omission of duty.
Deviation from rectitude, etc. A turning aside from uprightness in principles and conduct. See UPRIGHTNESS-DISHONESTY.
Enormity. An exceeding offense against order, right, or decency
Error. The condition of going astray morally
Failing. A small fault, perhaps.
Failure. A slight fault.
Fault. A neglect of duty.
Faux pas [F.]. A false step; a breach of good breeding.
Felony. A crime punishable by death or imprisonment.
Flaw. A moral defect.
Guilt. The state of being liable to punishment on account of wrong-doing.
Guiltiness. The state of being conscious of wrong-doing.
Indiscretion. An imprudent act.
Lapse. A falling away from virtue.
Malefaction. A flagrant offense against the law.
Malfeasance. Evil conduct in general.
Malpractice. Improper conduct.
Malversation. Corrupt practises, especially in office.
Misbehavior. A guilty manner of conducting oneself.
Misconduct. Improper behavior.
Misdeed. A wrong act.
Misdemeanor. A wrong-doing.
Misdoing. A wrong done.
Misfeasance. The improper doing of a lawful act.
Misprision. The concealment of a high offense.
Mortal sin. A sin worthy of death; a deadly sin.
Offense. An open violation of law.
Omission. Neglect to perform a duty.
Outrage. A gross violation of right or decency.
Peccadillo. A trifling offense.
Sin. A violation of divine law.
Sinfulness, etc. The state of being prone to violate the divine law. See VIRTUE-VICE.
Slip. An unintentional error.
Transgression. The act of violating a law.
Trespass. To violate the rights of another.
Trip. A false step in conduct.

GUILT—*Adjectives.*

Blameworthy. Worthy of being treated with disapproval.
Censurable. Deserving to be found fault with.
Culpable. Deserving of censure or blame.
Exceptionable. Open to objection.
Guilt-sick. Sick with guilt.
Guilty. Conscious of wrong-doing.
Illaudable. Worthy of disparagement.
In fault. In the wrong.
Peccable. Liable to sin.
Reprehensible. Worthy of reproof.
To blame. To be found fault with.
Uncommendable. Not worthy of praise.
Weighed in the balance and found wanting. Guilty; "tekel." [*Daniel* v, 27.]

GUILT—*Adverbs.*

In flagrante delicto [L.].⎫
In the very act.　　　⎬ In the very act of committing a crime
Red-handed.　　　　　⎭

GUILT—*Phrases.*

Culpam pœna premit comes [L.]. Punishment presses close upon crime. [Horace, *Odes*, 4, 5, 25.]
Facinus quos inquinat æquat [L.]. Crime reduces those whom it stains to one level. [Lucan, 5, 290.]

INNOCENCE—*Continued.*

INNOCENCE—*Phrases.*

Ein Mal, kein Mal [G.]. Just once, nothing counts.
Murus æneus conscientia sana [L.]. A sound conscience is a wall of brass. [Horace, *Epistles*, i, i, 607.]
Notre Dame [F.]. Our Lady; the Blessed Virgin.

---

in-nom′-i-nate. Without specific name. NAME-MISNOMER.
in′-no-vate. To make innovations. MUTATION-PERMANENCE.
in″-no-va′-tion. Introduction of something new. DEVIATION, MUTATION-PERMANENCE, NOVELTY-ANTIQUITY.
in-nox′-ious. Innocuous. HEALTHINESS-UNHEALTHINESS, INNOCENCE-GUILT.

in″-nu-en′-do. Hint. Approval-Disapproval, Enlightenment-Secrecy, Manifestation-Latency.

in-nu′-mer-a-ble. Countless. Infinity.

in-nu-tri′-tious. Not nourishing. Healthiness-Unhealthiness.

in-ob-jec′-tion-a-ble. Not objectionable. Faultiness-Faultlessness.

in″-ob-serv′-ance. Non-observance. Observance-Nonobservance.

in-oc″-cu-pa′-tion. Want of occupation. Action-Passiveness.

in-oc′-u-late. Communicate disease; insert; imbue. Education-Misteaching, Injection-Ejection, Motive-Caprice.

in-oc″-u-la′-tion. Insertion of a virus. Education-Misteaching, Injection-Ejection.

in-o′-dor-ate. To make odors. Odor-Inodorousness.

in-o′-dor-ous. Having no odor. Odor-Inodorousness.

in″-of-fen′-sive. Giving no offense. Goodness-Badness, Innocence-Guilt.

in″-of-fi′-cious. Not civil. Charitableness-Malevolence.

in-op′-er-a-tive. Ineffectual. Fertility-Sterility, Might-Impotence, Usefulness-Uselessness.

in-op″-por-tune′. Unseasonable. Opportuneness-Unsuitableness, Propriety-Impropriety.

in-op″-por-tune′-ly. Unseasonably. Opportuneness-Unsuitableness.

in-or′-di-nate. Excessive. Excess-Lack, Magnitude-Smallness.

in-or′-di-nate-ly. Immoderately. Magnitude-Smallness.

in″-or-gan′-ic. Not organic. Inorganic chemistry, Chemistry.

in-or″-gan-i-za′-tion. Condition of being unorganized. Organization-Inorganization.

in″-or-nate′. Unadorned. Embellishment-Simplicity.

in-os′-cu-late. Unite by contact of openings. Circle-Winding, Crossing, Union-Disunion.

in-os″-cu-la′-tion. Union by contact of openings. Circle-Winding, Crossing, Union-Disunion.

in′-quest. Judicial inquiry. Investigation-Answer.

in-qui′-e-tude. Restlessness; apprehension. Contentedness-Discontentment, Mutability-Stability, Pleasure-Pain, Sanguineness-Timidity.

in′-qui-nate. To pollute. Betterment-Deterioration.

in″-qui-na′-tion. Pollution. Betterment-Deterioration.

in-quire′. Seek information. Investigation-Answer.

in-quir′-er. One who inquires. Investigation-Answer.

in-quir′-ing. Investigating. Inquiring mind, Inquisitiveness-Indifference.

in-quir′-y. Research. Investigation-Answer, Ratiocination-Instinct.

in″-qui-si′-tion. Inquiry; a tribunal. Harshness-Mildness, Investigation-Answer, Tribunal.

in-quis′-i-tive. Prying. Inquisitiveness-Indifference, Investigation-Answer.

in-quis′-i-tive-ness. Curiosity. Inquisitiveness-Indifference.

INQUISITIVENESS—INDIFFERENCE.

Curiosity. }
Curiousness. } Eagerness to obtain information.
Inquiring mind. Disposition to investigate causes.
Inquisitiveness. The inclination to ask many questions.
Interest. Concern.
Thirst for knowledge. Desire to know

INQUISITIVENESS—Nouns of Agent.

Eavesdropper. One who stands under the eaves to listen; a secret listener.
Gossip. One who runs from house to house tattling and telling news. See Tidings.
Inquisitive person. One who attempts to discover everything by a searching curiosity.
Newsmonger. One who is active in hearing and telling news.
Paul Pry. A curious, inquisitive person. [A character in John Poole's Paul Pry.]
Quid nunc [L.]. What now; a busybody.
Sight-seer. One eager for novelties or curiosities.

INQUISITIVENESS—Verbs.

Gape. To open the mouth unconsciously in curiosity.
Lionize. To pay much attention to.
Pry. To try to discover by personal observation.
Stare. To look with fixed eyes wide open, as through surprise.

INQUISITIVENESS—Verbal Expressions.

Be curious (see Adjectives); prick up the ears, to become aware of something; see sights; take an interest in.

Incuriosity. }
Incuriousness. } Absence of curiosity. See Adjectives.
Indifference. Lack of concern about a thing.
Insouciance [F.]. Thoughtlessness. See Unconcern.

INDIFFERENCE—Verbal Expressions.

Be incurious (see Adjectives); have no curiosity (see Inquisitiveness); mind one's own business, not to meddle in the affairs of others; take no interest in (see Sensitiveness-Apathy).

INDIFFERENCE—Adjectives.

Impassive. In a state of apathy. See Sensitiveness-Apathy
Incurious. Not curious.
Indifferent. Not concerned.
Uninquisitive. Not inquisitive.

INQUISITIVENESS—Continued.

INQUISITIVENESS—Adjectives.

Agape. Gaping. See Expectation.
Burning with curiosity. Very curious.
Curious. Showing curiosity.
Inquiring. Seeking the truth.
Inquisitive. Given to ask many questions.
Inquisitorial. Inclined to ask cruel and rigorous questions.
Overcurious. Too curious.
Prying. Disposed to pry.

INQUISITIVENESS—Phrases.

What next? what's the matter?

in-quis″-i-to′-ri-al. Like an inquisitor; severe. Harshness-Mildness, Inquisitiveness-Indifference, Investigation-Answer, Judicature.

in′-road. Hostile entrance. Attack-Defense, Betterment-Deterioration, Entrance-Exit.

in″-sa-lu′-bri-ous. Not salubrious. Healthiness-Unhealthiness.

in″-sa-lu′-bri-ty. Unhealthfulness. Healthiness-Unhealthiness.

in-sane′. Unsound in mind. Saneness-Lunacy.

in-san′-i-ty. Unsoundness of mind. Saneness-Lunacy.

in-sa′-tia-ble. Not to be satisfied Desire-Distaste.

in-sa′-tiate. Insatiable. Desire-Distaste.

in-scribe′. Write; blazon. Reputation-Discredit, Writing-Printing.

in-scrip′-tion. Entry in a roll, etc. Mark-Obliteration, Writing-Printing.

in-scroll′. Write on a scroll. Mark-Obliteration.

in-scru'-ta-ble. Incomprehensible. CLEARNESS-OBSCURITY.

in-sculp'-ture. Carved inscription. SCULPTURE.

in-sculp'-tured. Engraved. ENGRAVING.

in-sec'-a-ble. Indivisible. SOLITUDE-COMPANY, UNION-DISUNION.

in'-sect. Six-legged arthropod. FAUNA-FLORA, GREATNESS-LITTLENESS; **insect cry,** CRY-ULULATION.

in''-se-cure'. Not safe. SECURITY-INSECURITY.

in''-se-cu'-ri-ty. Instability. SECURITY-INSECURITY.

in-sen'-sate. Foolish; insane. SAGACITY-INCAPACITY, SANENESS-LUNACY.

in-sen''-si-bil'-i-ty. Loss of perception or feeling. FEELING-INSENSIBILITY, SENSITIVENESS-APATHY; **insensibility of benefits,** THANKFULNESS-THANKLESSNESS; **insensibility to the past,** REMEMBRANCE-FORGETFULNESS.

in-sen'-si-ble. Not able to perceive; callous; that cannot be perceived. FEELING-INSENSIBILITY, QUEST-EVASION.

in-sen'-si-ble-ness. FEELING-INSENSIBILITY.

in-sen'-si-bly. Very gradually. FEELING-INSENSIBILITY, QUEST-EVASION.

in-sep''-a-ra-bil'-i-ty. State of being inseparable. COHESION-LOOSENESS.

in-sep'-a-ra-ble. Not separable. COHESION-LOOSENESS, UNION-DISUNION; **inseparable prefix,** VERB.

in-sep'-a-ra-ble-ness. State of being inseparable. COHESION-LOOSENESS.

in-sert'. Place in; record. ENTRANCE-EXIT, INJECTION-EJECTION, MARK-OBLITERATION; **insert itself,** INJECTION-EJECTION.

in-ser'-tion. Act of inserting. ADDITION-SUBTRACTION, ADMISSION-EXPULSION, ENTRANCE-EXIT, ESTABLISHMENT-REMOVAL, INJECTION-EJECTION.

in-serv'-i-ent. Useful. USEFULNESS-USELESSNESS.

in-sev'-er-a-ble. Inseparable. SOLITUDE-COMPANY, UNION-DISUNION.

in'-side''. Interior surface or space; interior. CONTENTS-RECEIVER, OUTSIDE-INSIDE; **inside out,** REVERSAL; **turn inside out,** EXPOSURE-HIDINGPLACE.

in-sid'-i-ous. Treacherous. CRAFT-ARTLESSNESS, INNOCENCE-GUILT, TRUTHFULNESS-FRAUD.

in'-sight''. Penetration. APPEARANCE-DISAPPEARANCE, KNOWLEDGE-IGNORANCE.

in-sig'-ni-a. Marks of distinction. SIGN, TROPHY; **insignia of authority,** SCEPTER.

in''-sig-nif'-i-cance. No importance. CONSEQUENCE-INSIGNIFICANCE, MAGNITUDE-SMALLNESS.

in''-sig-nif'-i-cant. Without import or meaning. CONSEQUENCE-INSIGNIFICANCE, MEANING-JARGON.

in''-sin-cere'. Deceitful. TRUTHFULNESS-FALSEHOOD.

in''-sin-cere'-ly. Not sincerely. TRUTHFULNESS-FALSEHOOD.

in-sin'-u-ate. Worm in; hint; imply. APPROVAL-DISAPPROVAL, ENLIGHTENMENT-SECRECY, ENTRANCE-EXIT, ENVIRONMENT-INTERPOSITION, LOVE-HATE.

in-sin''-u-a'-tion. A hint; an implication. APPROVAL-DISAPPROVAL, ENLIGHTENMENT-SECRECY, ENTRANCE-EXIT, ENVIRONMENT-INTERPOSITION, MANIFESTATION-LATENCY, NUTRIMENT-EXCRETION.

in-sip'-id. Without flavor. SAVOR-TASTELESSNESS, UNCONCERN.

in''-si-pid'-i-ty. Tastelessness. SAVOR-TASTELESSNESS.

in-sist''. Demand; repeat with emphasis. ORDER, RATIOCINATION-INSTINCT; **insist upon,** ASSERTION-DENIAL, COERCION, DETERMINATION-VACILLATION, DUENESS-UNDUENESS, STRIFE-PEACE, TERMS, TERSENESS-PROLIXITY.

in''-so-bri'-e-ty. Intemperance. TEETOTALISM-INTEMPERANCE.

in''-so-la'-tion. Exposure to the rays of the sun. HEAT-COLD, HEATING-COOLING.

in'-so-lence. Haughtiness. PRESUMPTION-OBSEQUIOUSNESS.

in'-so-lent. Haughty. PRESUMPTION-OBSEQUIOUSNESS.

in-sol'-u-ble. Inexplicable; not soluble. CHEMISTRY, CLEARNESS-OBSCURITY, SOLIDITY-RARITY.

in-solv'-a-ble. Inexplicable. CLEARNESS-OBSCURITY.

in-solv'-en-cy. Bankruptcy. AFFLUENCE-PENURY, CREDIT-DEBT, EXCESS-LACK, SETTLEMENT-DEFAULT.

in-solv'-ent. Bankrupt. AFFLUENCE-PENURY, CREDIT-DEBT, SETTLEMENT-DEFAULT.

in-som'-ni-a. Sleeplessness. ACTIVITY-INDOLENCE.

insomnium [L.] (in-som'-ni-um). A dream. ACTIVITY-INDOLENCE.

insouciance [F.] (an'-su-si-an's'). Indifference. DESIRE-DISTASTE, HEED-DISREGARD, SENSITIVENESS-APATHY.

insouciant [F.] (an'-su-si-an'). Without care or concern. CAREFULNESS-CARELESSNESS, PRESUMPTION-OBSEQUIOUSNESS, SENSITIVENESS-APATHY.

in-spect'. Examine; make inquiry. HEED-DISREGARD, SIGHT-BLINDNESS.

in-spec'-tion. Close examination. HEED-DISREGARD, SIGHT-BLINDNESS.

in-spect'-or. One who inspects. DECISION-MISJUDGMENT, INVESTIGATION-ANSWER, MANAGER.

in''-spi-ra'-tion. Influence which quickens; supernatural divine influence. DIVINITY, EMOTION, EXCITATION, FANCY, GODLINESS-UNGODLINESS, MOTIVE-CAPRICE, PREDETERMINATION-IMPULSE, REVELATION-PSEUDOREVELATION, SAGACITY-INCAPACITY.

in-spire'. Prompt; animate; cheer. EXCITATION, GODLINESS-UNGODLINESS, LIGHTHEARTEDNESS-DEJECTION, MOTIVE-CAPRICE; **inspire courage,** BRAVERY-COWARDICE; **inspire hope,** SANGUINENESS-HOPELESSNESS; **inspire respect,** REGARD-DISRESPECT.

in-spired'. Animated by the Spirit. GODLINESS-UNGODLINESS, MOTIVE-CAPRICE, REVELATION-PSEUDOREVELATION.

in-spir'-it. Animate; encourage. BRAVERY-COWARDICE, EXCITATION, LIGHTHEARTEDNESS-DEJECTION, MOTIVE-CAPRICE.

in-spir'-it-ing. Cheering. LIGHTHEARTEDNESS-DEJECTION, SANGUINENESS-HOPELESSNESS.

in-spis'-sate. Thickened. SOLIDITY-RARITY, VISCIDITY-FOAM.

in''-spis-sa'-tion. Thickening. SOLIDITY-RARITY, VISCIDITY-FOAM.

in''-sta-bil'-i-ty. Want of firmness. MUTABILITY-STABILITY.

in-stall'. Induct into an office. COMMISSION-ABROGATION, ESTABLISHMENT-REMOVAL, SOLEMNIZATION.

in''-stal-la'-tion. Introduction into office. COMMISSION-ABROGATION, ESTABLISHMENT-REMOVAL, RULE-LICENSE, SOLEMNIZATION.

in-stal'-ment. Partial payment. OUTLAY-INCOME, SETTLEMENT-DEFAULT, WHOLE-PART.

in'-stance. Example; notion. CONVENTIONALITY-UNCONVENTIONALITY, ETERNITY-INSTANTANEITY, MOTIVE-CAPRICE, PETITION-EXPOSTULATION.

in'-stant. Urgent; moment. ACTIVITY-INDOLENCE, CONSEQUENCE-INSIGNIFICANCE, ETERNITY-INSTANTANEITY, NEED, OCCURRENCE-DESTINY, TIME; **lose not an instant,** HURRY-LEISURE; **on the instant,** EARLINESS-LATENESS.

in''-stan-ta-ne'-i-ty. Instantaneousness. ETERNITY-INSTANTANEITY.

in''-stan-ta'-ne-ous. Occurring instantly. ETERNITY-INSTANTANEITY.

in''-stan-ta'-ne-ous-ly. In an instantaneous manner. ETERNITY-INSTANTANEITY, SWIFTNESS-SLOWNESS.

in''-stan-ta'-ne-ous-ness. State of being instantaneous. ETERNITY-INSTANTANEITY.

instanter [L.] (in-stan'-ter). Instantly. ETERNITY-INSTANTANEITY.

instar omnium [L.] (in'-star om'-ni-um). An example to others. CONVENTIONALITY-UNCONVENTIONALITY, LIKENESS-UNLIKENESS.

in''-stau-ra'-tion. Repair. RENOVATION-RELAPSE.

in-stead'. In place. COMMUTATION-PERMUTATION.

in'-sti-gate. Provoke. MOTIVE-CAPRICE.

in''-sti-ga'-tion. Stimulation to action. MOTIVE-CA-PRICE.

in'-sti-ga''-tor. One who incites. MOTIVE-CAPRICE.

in-stil'. Inculcate; pour in by drops. EDUCATION-MISTEACHING, INJECTION-EJECTION, MIXTURE-HO-MOGENEITY.

in'-stinct. Natural aptitude or tendency. MIND-IM-BECILITY, RATIOCINATION-INSTINCT, WILL-OBLIGA-TION; brute instinct, MIND-IMBECILITY; instinct with, HOLDING-EXEMPTION, MOTIVE-CAPRICE.

in-stinct'-ive. Not due to forethought. PREDETER-MINATION-IMPULSE, RATIOCINATION-CASUISTRY, SUBJECTIVENESS-OBJECTIVENESS, VOLITION-OBLIGA-TION.

in'-sti-tute. Originate; an institution. ASSOCIATION, CAUSE-EFFECT, CREATION-DESTRUCTION, ENTER-PRISE, SCHOOL; institute an inquiry, INVESTIGATION-ANSWER.

in''-sti-tu'-tion. An established principle; a corporate body; words of Christ in instituting the euchar-ist. ASSOCIATION, CHURCH, LAW-LAWLESSNESS, SCHOOL.

in'-sti-tu''-tor. A founder. INSTRUCTOR-PUPIL.

in-struct'. Teach; order. ADVICE, EDUCATION-MIS-TEACHING, ENLIGHTENMENT-SECRECY, ORDER.

in-struct'-ed. Taught. KNOWLEDGE-IGNORANCE.

in-struc'-tion. Act of instructing; knowledge. ADVICE, EDUCATION-MISTEACHING, ENLIGHTENMENT-SECRE-CY, ORDER, SKILL-UNSKILFULNESS.

in-struc'-tive. Serving to instruct. ENLIGHTENMENT-SECRECY.

in-struct'-or. Teacher. INSTRUCTOR-PUPIL.

INSTRUCTOR—PUPIL.

Abecedarian. One who teaches the letters of the alphabet.
Apostle. Any person zealously teaching any doctrine or cause.
Bear-leader. One who exhibits a trained bear; hence, a tutor to a youth of rank on his travels.
Coach. A private teacher generally employed to fit a person for a particular examination.
Corypheus. The leader or teacher of a chorus.
Dame. The mistress of a primary school.
Director. One who teaches others by virtue of authority.
Disciplinarian. One versed in principles and practises who teaches them with precision.
Dominie. A schoolmaster.
Dry-nurse. A nurse who feeds the child without the breast; hence, an inferior who teaches his superior his duties.
Duenna. An older lady employed to guard and teach young girls.
Example. Instance serving to teach a rule or precept. See MODEL FOR IMITATION.
Expositor. One who teaches or explains.
Governess. A lady who teaches children in their homes.
Governor. One who teaches a pupil and trains his manners.
Grinder. One who teaches students hurriedly for examinations.
Guide. One who teaches a way or course.
Institutor. One who teaches.
Instructor. One who teaches by precept or information.
Lecturer. One who discourses to teach others.
Master. The one in authority over a corps of teachers.
Mentor. A wise and elderly teacher and guide. See ADVICE.
Missionary. A person sent somewhere to teach and do charitable work.
Monitor. One who teaches by way of reproof or caution.
Moonshe. A teacher of languages.
Pastor. A teacher of the Gospel. See MINISTRY
Pedagogue. A teacher of children.
Pioneer. One who teaches the way and removes obstacles from it.
Preacher. One who teaches religious topics.
Preceptor. A teacher.
Prelector. A teacher by the reading of lectures.
Professor. One who teaches an art, science, or any of the higher branches of learning, particularly in the colleges.
Professorship. The state or office of a public teacher. See SCHOOL.
Prolocutor. The presiding officer of a convocation.
Propagandist. One who teaches any system of principles with a view to making them widespread.
Pupil-teacher. One who is both a pupil and a teacher.
Reader. One who teaches by reading.
Schoolmaster. The teacher of a school.
Schoolmistress. The female who teaches a school.
Teacher. One who teaches.
Trainer. One who trains up.
Tutelage. State of being under the guardianship of a teacher. See EDUCATION.
Tutor. A teacher in anything.
Usher. An under teacher who has charge of the junior classes

Abecedarian. A learner of the letters of the alphabet.
Alphabetarian. A learner of the alphabet.
Alumnus. A foster son; a graduate of a school or college.
Apostle. One to whom a commission to teach is given
Apprentice. One learning a trade.
Articled clerk. An apprenticed clerk.
Beginner. One first entering a course of study, the arts or sciences
Catechumen. A learner in any kind of doctrines or principles.
Class. A number of learners.
Condisciple. A learner in the same school.
Débutant [F.]. One who makes a first appearance.
Disciple. A learner.
Élève [F.]. A learner; pupil.
Famulist. A collegian of inferior rank.
Fellow commoner. A student at Cambridge who dines at the fel-lows' table.
Fellow student. An associate in learning.
Follower. A disciple; an attendant in learning
Form. A rank of students in a school
Freshman. A student in his first college year.
Inceptor. A beginner in the rudiments of learning.
Junior soph. A student in his second college year at Cambridge, England.
Learner. One who is taught.
Neophyte. A beginner in learning.
Novice. A learner in any occupation
Probationer. A novice.
Proselyte. A learner in some religious sect.
Pupil. A learner; disciple.
Pupilage. The state of being a pupil. See EDUCATION-LEARNING.
Questionist. A student at Cambridge University.
Recruit. One newly enlisted, as a soldier, and hence having all to learn.
Remove. A class in a school.
Scholar. One who learns anything.
Schoolboy. A boy learning at a school.
Senior soph. A student in his third college year at Cambridge Uni-versity, England.
Sophister. A student advanced beyond his first college year.
Tyro. A beginner in learning anything.
Undergraduate. A student who has not taken his first degree.

PUPIL—*Adjectives.*

In leading strings. Figurative for having much to learn.
In statu pupillari [L.]. In a state of learning.

— — · —

INSTRUCTOR—*Continued.*

INSTRUCTOR—*Adjective.*
Professorial. Pertaining to a professor.

INSTRUCTOR—*Phrase.*
Qui docet discit [L.]. He who teaches learns.

in'-stru-ment. An implement; written acknowledg-ment. INSTRUMENT, INSTRUMENTALITY, MEANS, SE-CURITY; musical instrument, MUSICAL INSTRUMENTS; optical instrument, OPTICAL INSTRUMENTS.

INSTRUMENT

Accouterments. All the devices by which a soldier carries his arms ammunition, etc.

Apparatus. Any device or machine prepared for the accomplishment of a special purpose.

Appliances. Anything through or by which something is effected or accomplished.

Appointments. Equipment or furnishing.

Chattels. Any article of personal property.

Engine. A machine by which power is applied to the doing of work.

Engineering. The science and art of making, building, and using engines.

Equipage. The outfit necessary for a given purpose.

Equipment. Whatever constitutes an outfit or preparation for a special purpose.

Fittings. Any articles of permanent equipment and adjustment.

Furniture. Equipment or outfit; especially, household articles.

Gear. The moving parts or appliances that constitute some mechanical power.

Gin. A machine by which some mechanical power is employed.

Harness. The equipment put upon a draft-animal in order to attach it for work.

Implement. An instrument used in manual labor.

Jenny. A mechanism for spinning more than one strand of yarn at a time.

Lathe. A machine for cutting or turning a material to some circular form.

Machine. Any instrument used for utilizing power.

Machinery. A combination of machines working together.

Matériel [F.] Apparatus.

Mechanism. The structure of a machine.

Mill. A machine for transforming raw material.

Organ. An instrument for performing an important, special action.

Paraphernalia. Miscellaneous articles of equipment.

Plant. A set of machines, tools, etc., for a mechanical business.

Recapper. A tool for fixing fresh percussion caps in cartridges.

Rigging. A mechanism of ropes, pulley-blocks, hooks, etc.

Skimmer. A flat ladle for skimming liquids.

Snow-plow. A large plow-like structure for clearing railway-tracks of snow.

Sprag. A short wooden billet for chocking the wheels of a coal-car.

Tackle. } A mechanical contrivance for obtaining a satisfactory
Tackling. } hold over anything with a view to hoisting or moving it.

Tenpenny. A long nail, 1000 of which weigh 10 pounds.

Tool. A simple mechanism or instrument.

Trappings. Ornamental harness.

Upholstery. Goods or materials used in upholstering.

Utensil. An implement for domestic use.

Voting-machine. A contrivance to assist the accurate recording, counting, etc., of votes.

Votograph. A vote-recording machine.

INSTRUMENT—*Mechanical Powers.*

Arm. Any part of a machine used as a support or lever.

Calipers. A compass-like instrument for measuring diameters.

Cam. A rotating piece of machinery used to change a rotary into alternate motion.

Can-hook. A short rope with a broad flat hook at each end, used in slinging barrels.

Capstan. An apparatus for hoisting anchors or other weights. See ELEVATION.

Clock-work. Mechanism like the machinery of a clock.

Crank. A device for causing rotation of an axis.

Crow. An apparatus for keeping a street main pipe in place while being drilled.

Crowbar. A straight iron bar used as a lever

Gavelock. An iron crowbar.

Handspike. A bar used as a lever in lifting weights.

Inclined plane. An artificial slope used in mechanics for transferring heavy articles from one level to another.

Jimmy. A crowbar made in sections to avoid detection in carrying.

Knocker. A hinged metal striker fastened to a door and used for knocking to gain admittance.

Lever. A mechanical device consisting of a straight bar turning freely on a fixed point or fulcrum.

Leverage. The mechanical advantage or power gained by use of a lever.

Limb. An elementary piece of the mechanism of a lock.

Mainspring. The principal or most important spring in a piece of mechanism.

Mechanical advantage. The useful work exerted by any machine.

Oar. An implement for impelling a boat, used like a lever.

Paddle. An implement with a broad blade, which is used without a fixed fulcrum in propelling and steering boats.

Pedal. A lever acted on by the foot.

Pinion. A small cog-wheel driven by a larger one.

Pulley. A wheel with a broad or grooved rim for transmitting power.

Screw. A cylinder, having a continuous thread winding round it spirally, used for producing motion or pressure in the direction of its axis, by the sliding of the threads of the cylinder in grooves adapted to them.

Spring. An elastic body of any kind, as steel, etc., used for receiving or imparting power.

Water-wheel. A wheel for propelling machinery, that is made to rotate by the direct action of water.

Wedge. A piece of metal, etc., thick at one end and tapering to a thin edge, used in splitting wood, raising heavy bodies, etc.

Wheel, etc. A circular frame having handles on the circumference, used as a means of controlling the rudder for the purpose of steering a ship.

Wheel and axle. A wheel fixed to an axle, used for raising weights by applying power to the circumference of the wheel. See REVOLUTION.

Wheels within wheels. Complicated machinery.

Wheelwork. A combination of wheels and their connection in a machine.

Winch. The crank used in turning a wheel or axle.

Wing. Any means of flight or rapid motion

INSTRUMENT—*Parts.*

Blade. The cutting part of an instrument.

Haft. That part of an instrument by which it is held and used

Handle. That part of an instrument held in the hand.

Heft. A handle.

Helm. The tiller or wheel of the apparatus by which a ship is steered.

Hilt. A handle, as of a sword.

Key. That part of an instrument or machine which serves as a means of operating it.

Screw-driver. A tool for turning screws for driving them into their place.

Shaft. The long handle of a spear; that which resembles the handle of a spear.

Shank. That part of an instrument which connects the acting part with the handle.

Tiller. The lever for turning the rudder of a boat.

Treadle. A part of a machine which is pressed or moved by the foot.

Trigger. A piece, as a lever, which is connected with a catch or detent as a means of releasing it.

Turnscrew. A screw-driver.

INSTRUMENT.—*Appliances.*

Arms, etc. A soldier's equipment. See WEAPON.

Borer, etc. An instrument for boring. See PERFORATOR.

Edge-tool, etc. A tool with a sharp edge for cutting. See SHARPNESS.

Hammer, etc. An instrument for driving nails, beating metals, etc., consisting of a head of iron or steel, fixed cross-wise to a handle See IMPETUS.

Nail, etc. A piece of wood or metal for holding timbers together See CONNECTIVE.

Oar, etc. A long blade for propelling a boat. See TRAVELING-NAVIGATION.

Peg, etc. A small wooden nail. See SUSPENSION.

Rope, etc. A large, stout cord, made of strands twisted or braided together See CONNECTIVE.

Spoon, etc. An implement consisting of a small bowl with a handle See CONVEYANCE.

Support, etc. A strong beam or anything used to support weight See SUSPENSION-SUPPORT.

Teeth, etc. Any projection corresponding to the tooth of an animal. See KEEPING.

Vise, etc. An instrument for holding a material worked upon See KEEPING.

INSTRUMENT—*Adjectives.*

Brachial. Pertaining to the arm.

Instrumental, etc. Serving as an instrument. See INSTRUMENTALITY.

Machinal. Relating to machines.

Mechanical. Pertaining to mechanics

in″-stru-men′-tal. Serviceable; an instrument played on. AGENCY, INSTRUMENT, INSTRUMENTALITY, MEANS, MUSIC; **instrumental music,** MUSIC.

in″-stru-men′-tal-ist. One who plays upon an instrument. MUSICIAN.

in″-stru-men-tal′-i-ty. Subordinate agency INSTRUMENTALITY

INSTRUMENTALITY.

Agency, etc. The quality of exerting power. See AGENCY.
Aid, etc. Anything that is favorable to progress. See OBSTRUCTION-HELP.
Expedient. Suitable means to accomplish an end. See DESIGN.
Hand. Agency in doing.
Instrument, etc. That by which some work is accomplished. See INSTRUMENT.
Instrumentality. The condition of being a means for doing work.
Intermedium. An intervening agent.
Intervention. The act of coming between.
Means. That through which, or by the help of which, an end is attained. See MEANS.
Mediation. The act of interposing, often to reconcile.
Medium. An intervening agency.
Stepping-stone. A means of progress, as in crossing shallow water.
Subservience. The state of serving in a subordinate capacity.
Subserviency. Use that promotes some purpose.
Vehicle. An agent for the transmission of something else.

INSTRUMENTALITY—*Associated Nouns.*

Accoucheur [F.]. A male professional obstetrician.
Cat's-paw. A person used by another to accomplish his object, as taking chestnuts from the fire in the fable.
Go-between. A person who acts as an agent; usually in a disparaging sense.
Handmaid. A maid that waits at hand.
Key. An instrument by which a lock is opened.
Latch-key. A key used to raise, or throw back the latch of a door.
Master-key. A key that opens many different locks.
Midwife. A woman attendant in childbirth.
Minister. One who ministers to, or serves others.
Obstetrician. One who assists in childbirth.
Open sesame. The magical command which opened the door of the robbers' den in the *Arabian Nights'* tale of *The Forty Thieves.*
Passe partout [F.]. A safe conduct; a master-key.
Pass-key. A key for opening more than one lock.
Passport. A document giving its owner permission to pass from place to place.
Safe-conduct. A writing or pass, given to a person to enable him to travel safely.

INSTRUMENTALITY—*Verbs.*

Be instrumental, etc. See *Adjectives.*
Intervene. To come between for some purpose.
Mediate. To act as an intervening agency.
Minister. To perform a service for.

Pander to. To minister to the evil emotions of others, like Pandarus in the story of *Troilus and Cressida.* [Homer, Chaucer, Shakespeare.]
Subserve. To help forward.

INSTRUMENTALITY—*Adjectives.*

Instrumental. Serving as a means to an end.
Intermediate. Occupying a middle place in some action.
Intervening. Coming between other influences in the course of action.
Mediatorial. Pertaining to intervening for the purpose of reconciling.
Ministerial. Pertaining to ministering to.
Subservient. Serving some purpose.
Useful, etc. That can be made to serve a purpose. See USEFULNESS.

INSTRUMENTALITY—*Adverbs.*

Along with. Accompanying.
By. In the vicinity of.
By dint of. By the power of.
By fair means or foul. By any means.
By hook or crook. By any possible means.
By means of, etc. See MEANS.
By virtue of. By the inherent power of.
By the agency, etc. }
By the agency of, etc. } See AGENCY.
By the aid of, etc. See OBSTRUCTION-HELP
Hereby. By this.
In virtue of. By authority of.
On the shoulders of. By the aid of.
Per [L.]. By.
Per fas et nefas [L.]. Justly or unjustly, through right and wrong.
Somehow. In some way not yet determined.
Somehow or other. In one way or another.
Thereby. By that.
Through. By means of.
Through the medium, etc. }
Through the medium of, etc. } See AGENCY.
Whereby. By what.
With the aid of. By the help of.

in-suav'-i-ty. Impoliteness. POLITENESS-IMPOLITENESS.
in''-sub-or'-di-nate. Disobedient. INSUBORDINATION-OBEDIENCE.
in''-sub-or''-di-na'-tion. Disobedience. INSUBORDINATION-OBEDIENCE.

INSUBORDINATION—OBEDIENCE.

Contumacy. Stubbornness.
Defection. Abandoning; desertion.
Defiance. See DEFIANCE.
Disobedience. Disregard for authority.
Émeute [F.]. A seditious outbreak.
High treason. Treason or treachery against the sovereign or the state.
Infraction. A violation of a law or rule.
Infringement. An encroachment on rights and privileges.
Insubordination. The state of not being subject to the proper authorities.
Insurgent. Fighting against the established government.
Insurrection. A rising against civil or political authority.
Lese-majesty. A crime against the sovereign power.
Misprision of treason. The failure of the person cognizant of the committal of the crime to inform the proper authorities.
Mutineering. The act of disobeying superior naval or military officers.
Mutinousness. The quality of being guilty of mutiny.
Mutiny. Insurrection against military or naval authority.
Non-compliance. Refusal to surrender one's wishes.
Non-observance. Neglect to observe.
Outbreak. An open revolt.
Petty treason. The crime of killing a person to whom the offender owed obedience.
Præmunire. The offense of introducing a foreign authority into England.
Rebel. To take up arms against the established government.
Rebellion. Open defiance to law and authority.
Revolt. Resistance; a desertion.
Riot. An outbreak by a mob.
Rising. A revolt; an upheaval.
Secession. Withdrawal from an organization or government.
Sedition. Dissatisfaction; dissension.

Allegiance. Loyalty to a ruler or government for protection in return.
Compliance. A yielding to others.
Deference. Due respect for the wishes and opinions of another.
Devotion. Attachment; strong feeling toward God, amounting to worship.
Ductility. See HARSHNESS-MILDNESS.
Fealty. Fidelity; obligation of a tenant to his lord in feudal times.
Homage. Deference; respect; a promise to be another person's man.
Loyalty. Fidelity to duty, obligation.
Non-resistance. Ready obedience; submission.
Obedience. Compliance with the wishes of another
Obsequiousness. See PRESUMPTION-OBSEQUIOUSNESS.
Observance. Servile attention; the keeping of some celebration.
Passiveness. The quality of being unresisting; submissive.
Resignation. A giving up; a surrender.
Subjection. See LIBERTY-SUBJECTION.
Submissiveness. Acquiescence; obedience.
Submission. See YIELDING.
Submissness. See SUBMISSIVENESS.

OBEDIENCE—*Verbs.*

Answer the helm. Yield to a guiding power, as a ship does.
Attend to orders. To be obedient; strict in obedience.
Bear obedience to. To render obedience to; to submit.
Be obedient, etc. See *Adjectives.*
Come at one's call. To be obedient.
Comply. To respect the wishes and opinions of others.
Do one's bidding. To obey orders.
Do suit and service. To perform the duty of feudatories to attend the courts of their lords in time of peace, and to render military service in time of war.

INSUBORDINATION—OBEDIENCE—*Continued.*

Strike. See Reprisal-Resistance.
Treason. Treachery against a government or sovereign.
Tumult. The commotion or agitation of a multitude.
Uprising. Rebellion; insurrection.
Violation of the law. See Law-Lawlessness.

Insubordination—*Nouns of Agent.*

Anarchist. One who favors the overthrow of civil government.
Brawler. One who causes brawls in a neighborhood; a nuisance.
Carbonaro. A member of a secret political organization in Italy in the 19th century, whose purpose was to set up a republican form of government.
Communist. One who favors the equalization of property, social privileges etc.
Fenian. A member of an Irish secret organization which had for its object the overthrow of English rule.
Frondeur [F]. A member of the Fronde in France, an organization which opposed the government and attacked the royal party during the minority of Louis XIV.
Insurgent. One who rebels against civil authority.
Jack Cade. An Irishman who was leader of Cade's Rebellion in England, in 1450.
Masaniello. A Neapolitan insurrectionist.
Mutineer. One who refuses to obey his superior officer in the army or navy.
Rebel. A member of a rebellion.
Red republican. An extremely radical republican in France who wore a red cap as a badge of his party.
Revolter. One who withdraws his allegiance.
Ringleader. A person who is at the head of a company who are banded together to violate the law.
Rioter. One who takes part in a riot.
Runagate. A fugitive; a renegade.
Sansculottes. Members of the extreme republican party in France at the time of the Revolution. They refused to wear breeches because the nobles wore them.
Seceder. One who withdraws, as from the Union of the U. S. A
Spartacus. The leader of the slave insurgents in Italy, in the 1st century, B. C.
Traitor. One guilty of treason.
Wat Tyler. Leader of the peasant revolt in England, 1381.

Insubordination—*Verbs.*

Champ the bit. To chew noisily, a mark of impatience.
Disobey. To violate commands.
Fly in the face of. To insult; to resist.
Infringe. To neglect to fulfil or obey.
Kick over the traces. To become unruly.
Mutiny. To rebel against superior officers in the army or navy.
Rebel. See *Nouns.*
Rise in arms. To start an armed insurrection.
Run restive. To become refractory.
Run riot. To go to excess.
Secede. To withdraw, as from a union.
Set at defiance. See Defiance.
Set authority at naught. To revolt, rebel.
Shirk. To neglect; to escape.
Strike. See Reprisal-Resistance.
Take the law into one's own hands. To disregard law; to set law aside.
Turn restive. To become stubborn, unruly; to resist.
Violate. To break the bonds of.

Insubordination—*Adjectives.*

Contumacious. Perverse; refractory.
Disobedient. See *Nouns*

OBEDIENCE—Verbs—*Continued.*

Do what one is told. To carry out orders.
Follow the lead of. To yield; to submit.
Follow to the world's end. Follow everywhere.
Obey. To give ear to; to comply.
Play second fiddle. To allow another to lead.
Serve. See Chief-Underling.
Serve faithfully. To be obedient
Submit. See Yielding.

Obedience—*Adjectives.*

At one's beck and call. Ready to respond to a nod of the head and call.
At one's call. Ready to come without previous notice.
At one's commands. } Ready to obey.
At one's orders. }
Compliant. See *Nouns.*
Complying. Assenting; agreeing.
Devoted. Closely attached; worshiping God.
Faithful. Attendant; true to duty.
Henpecked. Dominated by some petty authority, as the husband by the wife.
Loyal. Faithful to one's government or trust.
Obedient. Disposed to obey.
Passive. Inactive; unresisting; indifferent.
Pliant. See Harshness-Mildness.
Resigned. Submissive; compliant.
Restrainable. Able to be held in check; to be controlled.
Submissive. See Yielding.
Under beck and call. Ready to cringe to the biddings of authority.
Under control. Obedient; docile.
Unresisted. Unopposed.

Obedience—*Adverbs.*

In compliance with. } Obedient to.
In obedience to. }
Obediently. Dutifully.

Obedience—*Phrases.*

As you please; *ich dien* [G.], I serve; **if you please; to hear is to obey.**

INSUBORDINATION—Adjectives—*Continued.*

Impatient of control. Hard to govern.
Insubordinate. Disobedient.
Insurgent. See *Nouns.*
Lawless. Not subject to law
Mutinous. Revolting.
Recalcitrant. Kicking; opposing.
Recusant. See Proffer-Refusal.
Refractory. Unruly; unmanageable.
Resisting. See Reprisal-Resistance
Restiff. Obstinate; stubborn.
Restive. See Restiff.
Riotous. Wanton; unrestrained.
Seditious. Stirring up contention; tending to turbulence.
Unbidden. Uncommanded; unrequested.
Uncompliant. Not submit to established laws, rules, etc.
Uncomplying. See Uncompliant.
Ungovernable. Not able to be controlled.
Unobeyed. Not obeyed.
Unruly. Factious; disobedient.
Unsubmissive. Not subjective; not compliant.

---

in″-sub-stan′-tial. Unreal. Substance-Nullity; **insubstantial pageant,** Pomp.
in-suf′-fer-a-ble. Intolerable. Desire - Distaste, Pleasurableness-Painfulness.
in″-suf-fi′-cien-cy. Inadequacy. Excess-Lack, Transcursion-Shortcoming.
in″-suf-fi′-cient. Not sufficient. Excess-Lack, Success-Failure.
in″-suf-fi′-cient-ly. In no sufficient manner. Excess-Lack, Success-Failure.
in″-suf-fla′-tion. A breathing or blowing into or upon. River-Wind.
in′-su-lar. Isolated; pertaining to an island. Connec-

tion-Independence, Solitude-Company, Swamp-Island, Union-Disunion.
in″-su-lar′-i-ty. Narrowness. Union-Disunion.
in′-su-late. Place in a detached situation. Union-Disunion.
in″-su-la″-tion. Separation. Union-Disunion.
in′-su-la″-tor. A substance that is a non-conductor. Electricity, Sound-Silence.
in-sulse′. Stupid. Sagacity-Incapacity, Wittiness-Dulness.
in′-sult. Indignity. Favorite-Anger, Politeness-Impoliteness, Regard-Disregard

in-sult'-ing. Insolent. LOVE-HATE, REGARD-DISRE-SPECT.

in''-su'-per-a-ble. Insurmountable. POSSIBILITY-IM-POSSIBILITY; **insuperable obstacle,** OBSTRUCTION-HELP.

in''-sup-port'-a-ble. Intolerable. PLEASURABLENESS-PAINFULNESS.

in''-sup-press'-i-ble. That cannot be suppressed. TUR-BULENCE-CALMNESS.

in-sur'-a-ble. Capable of being insured. SECURITY-IN-SECURITY.

in-sur'-ance. System of insuring against loss. EN-GAGEMENT-RELEASE.

in-sure'. Make sure; secure insurance. CERTAINTY-DOUBT, SECURITY.

in-sur'-gent. A rebel. INSUBORDINATION-OBEDIENCE.

in''-sur-mount'-a-ble. Insuperable. POSSIBILITY-IM-POSSIBILITY.

in''-sur-rec'-tion. Rebellion in its initial stage. INSUB-ORDINATION-OBEDIENCE, REPRISAL-RESISTANCE.

in''-sus-cep'-ti-ble. Incapable of being moved. MUTA-BILITY-STABILITY, SENSITIVENESS-APATHY; **insus-ceptible of change,** MUTABILITY-STABILITY.

in-tact'. Unimpaired. CONSERVATION, FAULTLESS-NESS-FAULTINESS, MUTATION-PERMANENCE.

in-ta'-glio. Incised carving. CONVEXITY-CONCAVITY, COPY-MODEL, SCULPTURE.

in-tan'-gi-ble. Imperceptible to the touch. GREAT-NESS-LITTLENESS, TINGLING-NUMBNESS.

in'-te-ger. Complete person or thing. NUMBER, WHOLE-PART.

integer vitæ scelerisque purus [L.] (in'-te-jer vai'-tî scl-er-is'-quî' piu'-rus). Unimpaired in vigor and free from crime. UPRIGHTNESS-DISHONESTY.

in'-te-gral. Whole. NUMBER, WHOLE-PART; **integral calculus,** NUMBERING; **integral part,** CONSTITUENT-ALIEN.

in'-te-grate. Make into a whole. WHOLE-PART.

in''-te-gra'-tion. Making whole. ENTIRETY-DEFI-CIENCY, NUMBERING, WHOLE-PART.

in-teg'-ri-ty. Whole; probity. UPRIGHTNESS-DISHON-ESTY, VIRTUE-VICE, WHOLE-PART.

in-teg'-u-ment. Outer covering. COVER-LINING, LAMINA-FIBER.

in'-tel-lect. Mind. MIND-IMBECILITY; **absence of in-tellect,** MIND-IMBECILITY; **exercise of the intellect,** REFLECTION-VACANCY.

in''-tel-lec'-tion. Exercise of the intellect MIND-IMBECILITY.

in''-tel-lec'-tu-al. Possessing intellect. MIND-IMBECIL-ITY.

in''-tel-lec''-tu-al'-i-ty. State of being intellectual. MIND-IMBECILITY.

in-tel'-li-gence. Mind; news. MIND-IMBECILITY, SA-GACITY-INCAPACITY, TIDINGS-MYSTERY.

in-tel'-li-gen-cer. Messenger. ENLIGHTENMENT-SE-CRECY.

in-tel'-li-gent. Discerning. SAGACITY-INCAPACITY.

in-tel''-li-gi-bil'-i-ty. Comprehensibility. CLEARNESS-OBSCURITY.

in-tel'-li-gi-ble. Comprehensible. MEANING-JARGON.

in-tem'-per-ance. Lack of moderation. EXCESS-LACK, MODERATION-SELFINDULGENCE, TEETOTALISM-IN-TEMPERANCE.

in-tem'-per-ate. Without moderation. MODERATION-SELFINDULGENCE.

in-tem''-pes-tiv'-i-ty. Unseasonableness. CHRONOLOGY-ANACHRONISM, OPPORTUNENESS-UNSUITABLENESS.

in-tend'. Design. DESIGN.

in-tend'-ant. Superintendent. MANAGER.

in-tend'-ed. Purposed. PREDETERMINATION-IM-PULSE, PURPOSE-LUCK, VOLITION-OBLIGATION

in-tend'-ing. Designing. DESIGN.

in-tense'. Extreme in degree; ardent. MAGNITUDE-

SMALLNESS, VIGOR-INERTIA; **intense color,** COLOR-ACHROMATISM; **intense thought,** HEED-DISREGARD.

in-tense'-ly. In an extreme degree. MAGNITUDE-SMALL-NESS.

in-ten'-si-fy. Heighten. INCREASE-DECREASE, VIGOR-INERTIA.

in-ten'-si-ty. Intenseness; current-strength. MAGNI-TUDE-SMALLNESS, QUANTITY-MEASURE, VIGOR-IN-ERTIA.

in-tent'. Attentive; intention. ACTIVITY-INDOLENCE, HEED-DISREGARD, MOTIVE-CAPRICE, PREDETERMINA-TION-IMPULSE, PURPOSE, LUCK; **intent upon,** DESIRE-DISTASTE, DETERMINATION-VACILLATION.

in-ten'-tion. Purpose. PURPOSE-LUCK; **bad intention,** CHARITABLENESS-MALEVOLENCE; **good intention.** CHARITABLENESS-MALEVOLENCE.

in-ten'-tion-al. Designed. PURPOSE-LUCK.

in-ten''-tion-al'-i-ty. Designedness. PURPOSE-LUCK.

in-ten'-tion-al-ly. Designedly. PREDETERMINATION-IMPULSE, PURPOSE-LUCK.

in-ten'-tive-ness. State of being intentive. HEED-DIS-REGARD.

in-tent'-ly. Attentively **Look intently,** SIGHT-BLIND-NESS.

in-tent'-ness. Attention. ACTIVITY-INDOLENCE, HEED-DISREGARD.

in-tents' and pur'-po-ses, to all. Practically. ENTIRETY-DEFICIENCY, EQUALITY-INEQUALITY

in-ter'. Bury. LIFE-FUNERAL.

inter alia [L.] (in'-ter ê'-li-a). Among other things. CONVENTIONALITY-UNCONVENTIONALITY.

inter nos [L.] (in'-ter nos). Between ourselves. EN-LIGHTENMENT-SECRECY.

in''-ter-ac'-tion. Reciprocal action. AGENCY.

in-ter'-ca-lary. Inserted. ENVIRONMENT-INTERPOSI-TION.

in-ter'-ca-late. Insert. ENVIRONMENT-INTERPOSITION

in-ter''-ca-la'-tion. An insertion. ENVIRONMENT-IN-TERPOSITION.

in''-ter-cede'. Mediate between two persons. MEDIA-TION, PETITION-EXPOSTULATION.

in''-ter-cept'. Stop. OBSTRUCTION-HELP, TAKING-RESTITUTION.

in''-ter-cep'-tion. A stoppage. OBSTRUCTION-HELP

in''-ter-ces'-sion. Mediation between persons; prayer. DEVOTION-IDOLATRY, DIVINITY, MEDIATION, PETI-TION-EXPOSTULATION

In''-ter-ces'-sor. Christ. DIVINITY, MEDIATION.

in''-ter-ces'-so-ry. Interceding. PETITION-EXPOSTU-LATION.

in''-ter-change'. Give and take. COMMUTATION-PER-MUTATION, EXCHANGE; **interchange visits,** etc., SO-CIABILITY-PRIVACY.

in''-ter-change''-a-bil'-i-ty. Allowance of change. COM-MUTATION-PERMUTATION.

in''-ter-change'-a-ble. Permitting transposition. COM-MUTATION-PERMUTATION, EXCHANGE, INTERDEPEND-ENCE, SYNONYM-ANTONYM.

in''-ter-change'-a-ble-ness. Alternation. COMMUTA-TION-PERMUTATION.

in'-ter-changed. Changed about. COMMUTATION-PER-MUTATION.

in''-ter-cip'-i-ent. Intercepting. OBSTRUCTION-HELP

in''-ter-clude'. Cut off. OBSTRUCTION-HELP.

in''-ter-clu'-sion. A cutting off. OBSTRUCTION-HELP.

in''-ter-com-mu''-ni-ca'-tion. Mutual intercourse. ENLIGHTENMENT-SECRECY.

in''-ter-com-mu'-ni-ty. Mutual communication. SO-CIABILITY-PRIVACY.

in''-ter-cos'-tal. Between the ribs. ANATOMY.

in'-ter-course. Frequent association. AMITY-HOS-TILITY, SOCIABILITY-PRIVACY; **verbal intercourse,** CONVERSATION-MONOLOGUE, SPEECH-INARTICULATE-NESS.

in″-ter-cur′-rence. A passing between; an intervening occurrence. COMMUTATION-PERMUTATION, ENVIRONMENT-INTERPOSITION, TRANSMISSION.

in″-ter-cur′-rent. Coming between or among. COMMUTATION - PERMUTATION, ENVIRONMENT - INTERPOSITION, TRANSMISSION.

in″-ter-de-pend′-ence. Mutual dependence. INTERDEPENDENCE.

INTERDEPENDENCE.

Barter. An exchange of commodities or services.
Correlation. Reciprocal relation between two or more objects.
Exchange. A transfer of equivalents.
Interchange. Alternate transposition. See COMMUTATION-PERMUTATION.
Interdependence. The dependence of one upon the other.
Mutuality. The quality of being mutual.
Mutualness. See *Adjectives.*
Reciprocalness, etc. Quality or condition of being effected equally. See *Adjectives.*
Reciprocation. A mutual giving and returning.
Reciprocity. Mutual action and reaction.

INTERDEPENDENCE—*Verbs.*

Alternate. To vary successively.
Counter-change. To exchange positions.
Exchange. To give for an equivalent return.
Interchange. See COMMUTATION-PERMUTATION.
Reciprocate. To give up and receive mutually.

INTERDEPENDENCE—*Adjectives.*

Alternate. One following the other in turn.
Commutual. Mutual.
Correlative. Reciprocally related.
Interchangeable. Capable of being transposed.
International. Pertaining to the mutual relations of nations.
Mutual. Affecting both of two persons, parties, or objects.
Reciprocal. Done or given by one, to or for the other in turn.

INTERDEPENDENCE—*Adverbs.*

By turns, etc. See COMMUTATION-PERMUTATION.
Each other. Each one the other.
Mutatis mutandis [L.] The necessary changes having been made.
Reciprocally. See *Adjectives.*
Vice versâ [L.] The order or relation being reversed.

in′-ter-dict″. A prohibitive order. LEAVE-PROHIBITION.

in″-ter-dic′-tion. Prohibition. LEAVE-PROHIBITION.

in″-ter-dig′-i-tate. Place between the fingers. CROSSING, ENVIRONMENT-INTERPOSITION.

in″-ter-dig″-i-ta′-tion. An interlocking. CROSSING, ENVIRONMENT-INTERPOSITION.

in′-ter-est. Personal concern; curiosity; payment for use of money; importance; share; excite; please; amuse. CONNECTION-INDEPENDENCE, CONSEQUENCE-INSIGNIFICANCE, CREDIT-DEBT, DOMINANCE-IMPOTENCE, ENTERTAINMENT-WEARINESS, EXCITATION, GOOD-EVIL, INQUISITIVENESS-INDIFFERENCE, PLEASURABLENESS-PAINFULNESS, PROPERTY; **devoid of interest,** ENTERTAINMENT-WEARINESS; **feel an interest in,** CHARITABLENESS-MALEVOLENCE; **make interest for,** OBSTRUCTION-HELP; **not know one's own interest,** SKILL-UNSKILFULNESS; **place out at interest,** LOAN-BORROWING; **take an interest in,** CHARITABLENESS - MALEVOLENCE, INQUISITIVENESS - INDIFFERENCE, LOVE-HATE; **take no interest in,** SENSITIVENESS-APATHY, UNCONCERN; **want of interest,** UNCONCERN.

in′-ter-est-ed. Biased. UNSELFISHNESS-SELFISHNESS.

in′-ter-est-ing. Engaging the attention. LOVE-HATE.

in″-ter-fa′-cial. Formed by two faces of a polyhedron. MINERALOGY.

in-ter-fere′. Intervene; thwart. COOPERATION-OPPOSITION, ENVIRONMENT-INTERPOSITION, HARMONY-DISCORD, MEDIATION, OBSTRUCTION-HELP, QUEST-EVASION.

in″-ter-fer′-ence. Act of interfering. COOPERATION-OPPOSITION, ENVIRONMENT-INTERPOSITION.

interim [L.] (in′-ter-im). Mean time. COEXISTENCE, DURATION-NEVERNESS.

in-te′-ri-or. Inside. OUTSIDE-INSIDE.

in-te″-ri-or′-i-ty. State of being interior. OUTSIDE-INSIDE.

in″-ter-ja′-cence. State of being between. ENVIRONMENT-INTERPOSITION, MIDDLE.

in″-ter-ja′-cent. Lying between. ENVIRONMENT-INTERPOSITION.

in″-ter-ject′. Introduce abruptly. ADMISSION-EXPULSION, ENVIRONMENT-INTERPOSITION, INJECTION-EJECTION.

in″-ter-jec′-tion. Interpolation. ENVIRONMENT-INTERPOSITION, PARTICLE.

in″-ter-lace′. Weave or twine together. CROSSING, UNION-DISUNION.

in″-ter-la′-cing. Twining together. **Interlacing arches,** ARCHITECTURE.

in″-ter-lard′. Insert frequently. ENVIRONMENT-INTERPOSITION, MIXTURE-HOMOGENEITY.

in″-ter-lard′-ing. Intermixing. MIXTURE-HOMOGENEITY.

in″-ter-leave′. Supply with additional leaves. ENVIRONMENT-INTERPOSITION.

in″-ter-line′. Write between the lines of; write in alternate lines. ENVIRONMENT-INTERPOSITION, WRITING-PRINTING.

in″-ter-lin′-e-ar. Having translations inserted between the lines of a text. ENVIRONMENT-INTERPOSITION.

in″-ter-lin″-e-a′-tion. Act of interlining. ENVIRONMENT-INTERSPACE.

in″-ter-link′. Join together. CROSSING, UNION-DISUNION.

in″-ter-lo-ca′-tion. A placing between. ENVIRONMENT-INTERPOSITION.

in″-ter-lock′. Lock together. UNION-DISUNION.

in″-ter-lo-cu′-tion. Conference. CONVERSATION-MONOLOGUE, SPEECH-INARTICULATENESS.

in″-ter-loc′-u-tor. One who takes part in a conversation. CONVERSATION-MONOLOGUE, SPEECH-INARTICULATENESS.

in″-ter-loc′-u-to-ry. Conversational. CONVERSATION-MONOLOGUE.

in′-ter-lo″-per. One who intrudes into an office, possession, etc., of another. CONSTITUENT-ALIEN, ENVIRONMENT-INTERPOSITION, OBSTRUCTION-HELP.

in′-ter-lude. A brief farcical comedy; an action coming between others of greater importance. ACTING, DURATION-NEVERNESS.

in″-ter-mar′-riage. Marriage between persons of different families, races, classes, or tribes. MATRIMONY-CELIBACY.

in″-ter-mar′-ry. Marriage between blood-kindred. MATRIMONY-DIVORCE.

in″-ter-med′-dle. Interfere. ACTIVITY-INDOLENCE, OBSTRUCTION-HELP.

in″-ter-med′-dling. Interfering. MEDIATION.

in″-ter-me′-di-a-ry. Located between. ENVIRONMENT-INTERPOSITION.

in″-ter-me′-di-ate. Interposed; interfering. ACTIVITY-INDOLENCE, ENVIRONMENT-INTERPOSITION, INSTRUMENTALITY, MEDIUM, MIDDLE; **intermediate time,** DURATION-NEVERNESS.

in″-ter-me′-di-um. Something that is intermediate. CONNECTIVE, ENVIRONMENT-INTERPOSITION, INSTRUMENTALITY, MEDIUM.

in-ter′-ment. Burial. INJECTION-EJECTION, LIFE-FUNERAL.

in″-ter-mi-gra′-tion. Reciprocal migration. TRAVELER-NAVIGATION.

in-ter′-mi-na-ble. Having no limit. ETERNITY-INSTANTANEITY, INFINITY, LENGTH-SHORTNESS.

in″-ter-min′-gle. Mingle together. MIXTURE-HOMO-GENEITY.

in″-ter-mis′-sion. Interruption; recess. CONTINUITY-INTERRUPTION, DISCONTINUANCE-CONTINUANCE, DURATION-NEVERNESS, MIXTURE-HOMOGENEITY.

in″-ter-mit′. Interrupt; suspend. CONTINUITY-INTERRUPTION, DISCONTINUANCE-CONTINUANCE, PERIODICITY-IRREGULARITY.

in″-ter-mit′-tence. An intermittent state. DURATION-NEVERNESS, PERIODICITY-IRREGULARITY.

in″-ter-mit′-tent. Periodic. CONTINUITY-INTERRUPTION, PERIODICITY-IRREGULARITY; **intermittent sand-filtration,** CHEMISTRY.

in″-ter-mit′-ting. Having intermissions. CONTINUITY-INTERRUPTION.

in″-ter-mix′. Mingle. MIXTURE-HOMOGENEITY.

in″-ter-mu-ta′-tion. Mutual change. COMMUTATION-PERMUTATION.

in-tern′. Internal. OUTSIDE-INSIDE.

in-ter′-nal. Situated within; essential. OUTSIDE-INSIDE, SUBJECTIVENESS-OBJECTIVENESS; **internal evidence,** EVIDENCE-COUNTEREVIDENCE.

in-ter′-nal-ly. On the inside. OUTSIDE-INSIDE.

in″-ter-na′-tion-al. Affecting nations generally. RELATIONSHIP, SOCIABILITY-PRIVACY; **international law,** LAW-LAWLESSNESS.

in″-ter-ne′-cine. Mutually destructive. FIGHTING-CONCILIATION, LIFE-KILLING; **internecine war,** FIGHTING-CONCILIATION.

in″-ter-nun′-ci-o. Envoy; papal minister at minor courts. CONSIGNEE, MESSENGER.

in″-ter-pel′. Break in on. DISCONTINUANCE-CONTINUANCE.

in″-ter-pel-la′-tion. Demand for an official statement; summons. ADDRESS-RESPONSE, INVESTIGATION-ANSWER, ORDER, PETITION-EXPOSTULATION.

in″-ter-pen′-e-trate. Permeate. ENTRANCE-EXIT.

in″-ter-pen″-e-tra′-tion. Mutual penetration. ENTRANCE-EXIT, ENVIRONMENT-INTERPOSITION, TRANSMISSION.

in-ter′-po-late. To insert. ENVIRONMENT-INTERPOSITION.

in″-ter″-po-la′-tion. Derivation of intermediate values of a quantity; insertion. ENVIRONMENT-INTERPOSITION, NUMBERING.

in″-ter-pose′. Place between; intercede. ACTIVITY-INDOLENCE, ENVIRONMENT-INTERPOSITION, MEDIATION, OBSTRUCTION-HELP.

in″-ter-pos′-it. Common commercial depot. MARKET.

in″-ter-po-si′-tion. Mediation. ACTIVITY-INDOLENCE, ADDITION-SUBTRACTION, OBSTRUCTION-HELP.

in-ter′-pret. Translate. DECISION-MISJUDGMENT, INTERPRETATION-MISINTERPRETATION.

in-ter″-pre-ta′-tion. Explanation. INTERPRETATION-MISINTERPRETATION.

INTERPRETATION—MISINTERPRETATION.

Acceptance. Meaning; acceptation.

Acceptation. The accepted meaning of a word or phrase.

Acception. The received meaning; acceptation

Annotation. A note, added by way of interpretation or comment.

Answer. Something said or written in reply to a question, a call, an argument, or the like.

Apposition. A placing or being in juxtaposition.

Clue, etc. A thread that guides through a maze; something that leads to or suggests the solution of a puzzle or mystery, etc. See SIGN.

Comment. A note or remark in explanation or criticism.

Commentary. A treatise in annotation or explanation, as of the Scriptures.

Construction. The act of construing; interpretation.

Convertible terms. Interchangeable terms.

Definition. Such a description or explanation of a word or thing as serves to distinguish it from all others.

Dictionary, etc. A book containing the words of any language, or of any department of knowledge, arranged alphabetically, and usually also with the spelling, pronunciation, etymology, and definitions of the words, together with other explanatory or illustrative features. See WORD.

Dilucidation. The act of making clear.

Éclaircissement [F.]. Clearing up; explanation.

Eisegesis. The giving of one's own thoughts as if they were another's.

Elucidation. A making clear; explanation; exposition.

Equivalent. That which is equivalent or equal in force.

Equivalent meaning, etc. Meaning that is equal in force. See MEANING.

Exegesis. Explanation; exposition.

Exemplification. The act of illustrating by examples.

Explanation. The act of explaining, expounding or interpreting.

Explication. Explanation, as of a text.

Exposition. Interpretation of the meaning of something, as of a passage; a commentary.

Expounding. The act of explaining the points, principles, or meanings of.

Free translation. Rendition of a work into another language without closely adhering to the original.

Gloss. A note or comment explanatory of something obscure.

Illustration. The act of making clear and distinct; elucidation; that which illustrates.

Inference, etc. Conclusion; deduction, etc. See DECISION.

Interpretation. Explanation of what is obscure; the sense given by an interpreter; exposition.

Key. That which serves to unlock something unknown, or difficult; as, the key to a problem; an explanation.

Lection. A variation in the text of an author; a reading.

Abuse of terms. Improper use or application of terms.

Catachresis. Faulty or mixed use of metaphors; strained use of a word; use of a false form under a misunderstanding of its origin.

Cross-purposes. Purposes which antagonize one another.

Cross-reading. The reading of the lines of a newspaper, etc., directly across the page through the adjoining columns, thus confounding the sense.

Exaggeration, etc. Overstatement. See GULL-HYPERBOLE.

False coloring. False or specious appearance; misrepresentation.

False construction. Erroneous interpretation or understanding; an act of misconstruing.

Falsification, etc. The representing of anything to be what it is not; in law, the intentional alteration of any document so as to render it untrue. See TRUTHFULNESS-FALSEHOOD.

Misacceptation. Wrongly accepted meaning; wrong sense in which a word, phrase, etc., is accepted or received.

Misapplication. A wrong or false application.

Misapprehension. Misunderstanding of a fact, sense, or meaning; mistake.

Misconstruction. Error in understanding or interpreting; an act of misconstruing, as of a meaning.

Misinterpretation. The act of interpreting or understanding wrongly or falsely.

Misrepresentation. Wrong or false representation; incorrect, unfair, or false statement.

Mistake, etc. Wrong apprehension or opinion. See TRUTH-ERROR.

Misunderstanding. A mistake as to meaning or motive; misapprehension.

Parody. A trivial or comical imitation, especially of a poem; any burlesque imitation of something serious.

Perversion. Diversion from the true meaning; distorted construction; misapplication.

Travesty. Burlesque treatment of a subject originally treated in a serious or lofty style.

MISINTERPRETATION—*Verbs.*

Be at cross purposes. Have conflicting or antagonistic purposes.

Detort. Pervert; distort.

Distort. Give a strained meaning to; interpret falsely.

Explain away. Get rid of by explanation.

Garble, etc. Change, as a document, usually with evil intent, by suppression or elision, etc. See TRUTHFULNESS-FALSEHOOD.

Give a false coloring. Misrepresent.

Misapply. Apply wrongly; devote to an improper purpose.

Misapprehend. Take in a wrong sense; misunderstand.

Misconceive. Understand erroneously.

Misconstrue. Interpret erroneously; put a false meaning to.

Misinterpret. Interpret wrongly or falsely.

Misrepresent. Make false or wrong representations concerning.

INTERPRETATION—MISINTERPRETATION—*Continued.*

Light. That which illuminates or makes clear to the mind; enlightenment.

Literal translation. Rendition of a work into a different language, adhering closely to the original.

Meaning, etc. Signification; sense, etc. See MEANING.

Metaphrase. Translation word for word from one language into another.

Mot d'énigme [F.]. Key to an enigma or riddle.

Note. A marginal comment or explanation; a critical, explanatory or illustrative observation.

Paraphrase. Any free translation or reproduction, commonly explanatory, of the sense of a passage or work.

Plain interpretation. Plain explanation.

Polyglot. A book giving versions of the same subject-matter in several different languages.

Rationale. An explanation or exposition of the principles of some opinion, action, phenomenon, or the like.

Reading. An interpretation, as of a riddle, or of any latent or hidden meaning.

Rendering. A version; translation; in art, the presentation, expression, or interpretation of an idea, theme, or part.

Rendition. Translation; rendering; version.

Scholium. A marginal annotation; an explanatory remark or comment.

Secret. That which, when known, furnishes an explanation of something that was before unexplained or inexplicable; a key.

Simple interpretation. The plainest or clearest explanation.

Solution. The act or process of explaining, settling, or disposing, as of a difficulty or doubt.

Strict interpretation. Exact, accurate, or precise interpretation.

Synonym. A word having the same or almost the same meaning as some other; the equivalent of a word in another language.

Thesaurus. A treasury; a repository of knowledge or groups of words.

Translation. Rendition into another language; interpretation.

Version. A translation, or the act of translating, from one language into another.

INTERPRETATION—*Scientific Terms.*

Hermeneutics. The science of interpretation and explanation; especially, that branch of theology which defines the laws whereby the meaning of the Scriptures is to be ascertained.

Metoposcopy. The study of physiognomy; art of discovering the character of persons by their features, or the lines of the face.

Paleography, etc. Art or science of deciphering ancient writings. See LANGUAGE.

Physiognomy. The art of reading character by the lineaments of the face or form of the body.

Semeiology. The science of signs, especially of the symptoms of disease.

Symptomatology. Semeiology.

INTERPRETATION—*Verbs.*

Accept in a particular sense. Receive as having a special meaning.

Account for. Give a rational explanation of.

Annotate. Make explanatory notes upon.

Be given to understand. To be explained to.

Clear up. Make lucid or clear.

Comment upon. Make expository or critical notes or observations upon.

Construe. Translate word by word; interpret; explain.

Decipher. Make out the sense or the meaning of.

Define. State the meaning of; explain.

Disentangle. Free from perplexities or complications.

Do into. Translate or transform into.

Elucidate. Make clear by explanation or interpretation.

Enucleate. Bring to light; make clear.

Exemplify. Illustrate or show by example.

Explain. Make plain, manifest, or intelligible.

Expound. Interpret; lay open the meaning of.

Find out the meaning of, etc. See MEANING.

Find the cause of. Make out the cause of.

Find the key of. Find the explanation of.

Illustrate. Explain by means of figures, comparisons, etc.

Interpret. Unfold the meaning of; construe; translate orally.

Make out. Explain.

Popularize, etc. Interpret so as to be clear and acceptable to the people.

Put a construction on. To give an explanation.

Read. Interpret; explain.

Read between the lines. Comment upon as one reads.

Receive in a particular sense. Receive as having a special meaning.

Render. Interpret; express; represent.

Resolve. Reduce to elementary principles; explain.

MISINTERPRETATION—VERBS—*Continued.*

Misspell. Spell incorrectly; decipher wrongly.

Mistake, etc. Understand wrongly, etc. See TRUTH-ERROR.

Mistranslate. Translate or interpret wrongly.

Misunderstand. Take in a wrong sense; mistake.

Pervert. Turn from its right purpose; misinterpret.

Play at cross purposes. Have conflicting or antagonistic purposes.

Play upon words. Give an ingenious or witty turn to words.

Put a bad construction upon. }
Put a false construction upon. } Misconstrue.

Strain the meaning.
Strain the sense. } Force beyond proper construction or true
Stretch the meaning. { intent.
Stretch the sense. }

Travesty. Treat so as to render ridiculous; imitate grotesquely.

Wrest the meaning. } Turn from the true meaning.
Wrest the sense. }

MISINTERPRETATION—*Adjectives.*

Misinterpreted, etc. Interpreted wrongly or falsely, etc. See *Verbs.*

Untranslatable. That cannot be translated.

Untranslated. Not translated.

INTERPRETATION—VERBS—*Continued.*

Shed a fresh light upon. }
Shed light upon. } To explain or interpret.
Shed new light upon. }

Solve. Free from perplexing difficulties.

Spell out. Discover by characters or marks; decipher.

Take in a particular sense. To give a special meaning to.

Tell the cause of, etc. See CAUSE.

Throw a fresh light upon. } Figurative expressions for explain or
Throw light upon. } interpret.
Throw new light upon. }

Transfuse the sense of. Cause the sense of to be instilled or imbibed.

Translate. Give the sense or equivalent of in another language; interpret; explain in other words.

Turn into. Convert into; change the form of; as, to turn prose into verse.

Understand by. To put a construction on.

Understand in a particular sense. Understand as having a special meaning.

Unfold. Make manifest; reveal.

Unravel. Explain; become disentangled.

INTERPRETATION—*Adjectives.*

Cosignificative. Having the same signification.

Equivalent, etc. Equal in force or meaning, etc. See EQUALITY

Exegetical. Serving to explain or interpret.

Explanatory. Serving or tending to explain.

Explicative. Explanatory.

Explicatory. Explicative.

Expository. Pertaining to, or containing, exposition; explanatory; illustrative.

Literal. According to the letter; following the exact words, as translation.

Metaphrastic. Close, or literal.

Paraphrastic. Of the nature of a paraphrase; explaining, or translating; not literal.

Polyglot. Containing several languages.

Synonymous. Having the character of a synonym; expressing the same thing.

INTERPRETATION—*Adverbs.*

Id est [L.]. That is; namely.

In explanation, etc. See *Nouns*

In other words.
In plain English.
In plainer English.
In plainer terms. } To speak plainly in explanation.
In plainer words.
In plain terms.
In plain words.

Literally. According to the primary and natural import of words; word for word.

More simply. More plainly.

Namely. That is to say;—introducing a particular or specific designation.

Strictly speaking. Speaking in a strict manner; precisely.

That is to say. That means; in other words.

To wit. Namely; that is to say;—used especially in legal language, to call attention to a particular thing.

Videlicet [L.]. To wit; namely.

in-ter'-pret-er. Explainer. INTERPRETER, SOOTH-SAYER.

INTERPRETER.

Annotator. One who annotates; a commentator; scholiast.
Cicerone [It.]. An Italian guide who explains the antiquities and curiosities of a place to travelers.
Commentator. One who writes commentaries, or makes explanatory notes on a text.
Demonstrator. One who exhibits and explains something or some process, as a teacher.
Diseur de bons mots [F.]. A sayer of good things.
Dragoman. An interpreter for foreign travelers in the East; especially, the interpreter to an embassy or consulate.
Explainer. One who explains or interprets.
Exponent. One who explains or expounds, as the exponent of philosophy.
Expositor. One who expounds; one who makes an exposition of any work.
Expounder. One who explains the points, principles, or meaning of.
Interpreter. One who or that which interprets; a person who makes intelligible the speech of a foreigner by oral translation.
Metaphrast. One who translates closely or word for word.
Mouthpiece. One who speaks for or on behalf of another.
Œdipus. In Greek legend, a king of Thebes, son of Laius and Jocaste. He explained the riddle of and slew the Sphinx.
Oneirocritic. One who interprets dreams.
Oracle, etc. See SOOTHSAYER.
Paraphrast. One who paraphrases or reproduces the sense of in other terms; one who translates freely.
Scholiast. A maker of scholia; especially, an annotator of classical texts.
Showman. One who exhibits, aids in exhibiting, or owns a show.

Speaker. One who speaks, one who engages in public speaking; an orator.
Spokesman. One who speaks in the name and behalf of another or others.
Valet de place [F.]. A person who serves as a guide for tourists.

in"-ter-reg'-num. Time during which a throne is vacant. DISCONTINUANCE-CONTINUANCE, DURATION-NEVERNESS, INTERSPACE-CONTACT, LASTINGNESS-TRANSIENTNESS, RULE-LICENSE.
in-ter'-ro-gate. Question. INVESTIGATION-ANSWER.
in-ter"-ro-ga'-tion. Question. INVESTIGATION-ANSWER, RHETORIC.
in"-ter-rog'-a-tive. Denoting inquiry RHETORIC; **interrogative pronoun,** PRONOUN.
in"-ter-rog'-a-to-ry. Questioning. INVESTIGATION-ANSWER.
in"-ter-rupt'. Obstruct; stop while in progress. CONTINUITY-INTERRUPTION, DISCONTINUANCE-CONTINUANCE, OBSTRUCTION-HELP.
in"-ter-rupt'-ed. Irregular. CONTINUITY-INTERRUPTION.
in"-ter-rup'-tion. Abrupt disturbance; interval. CONTINUITY-INTERRUPTION, DISCONTINUANCE-CONTINUANCE, INTERSPACE-CONTACT, OBSTRUCTION-HELP, ORGANIZATION-DISORGANIZATION.
in"-ter-sect'. Cut through. CROSSING.
in"-ter-sec'-tion. Crossing. CROSSING.
in'-ter-space". Interval of space. INTERSPACE-CONTACT, OUTSIDE-INSIDE.

INTERSPACE—CONTACT

Incompleteness, etc. State of being empty or open. See ENTIRETY-DEFICIENCY.
Interruption. The act of interrupting; a breaking in or cutting off.
Interspace. Interval of space; space between.
Interval. An opening space between two objects; distance between points or objects.
Separation, etc. The act or process of separating or the condition of being separated; division or parting. See UNION-DISUNION.

INTERSPACE—*Denotations.*

Abysm. } A bottomless or unfathomed depth.
Abyss. }
Breach. A gap or opening made by breaking or battering.
Break. An opening made by a fracture.
Cañon. A deep gulch worn by water-courses.
Cesura. A break or pause in a metrical foot.
Chap. A cleft or crack.
Chasm. A deep opening made by disruption.
Chink. A small fissure of greater length than breadth.
Cleft. A space or opening made by splitting.
Crack. A little separation of parts, with or without a perceptible opening.
Cranny. A small narrow opening.
Creek. A recess in the shore of the sea, or of a river.
Crevasse. A deep crack in the ice of a glacier.
Crevice. A narrow opening resulting from a split or crack.
Cut. An opening made with an edged instrument.
Defile. A narrow passage in which troops can march only in file.
Dike. A ditch.
Fissure. A narrow opening made by the parting of any substance.
Flaw. A crack or breach.
Frith. The opening of a river into the sea.
Furrow, etc. A trench in the earth made by, or as by, a plow. See GROOVE.
Gap. An opening in anything made by breaking or parting.
Gash. A deep and long cut.
Gorge. A narrow passage or entrance.
Gulf. A hollow place in the earth.
Gully. A channel or hollow worn in the earth by a current of water.
Ha-ha. A ditch not visible until one is close upon it.
Hiatus. An opening or gap; a defect in a manuscript where some part is lost.
Hiatus maxime deflendus. } [L.]. A gap greatly to be deplored.
Hiatus valde deflendus. }
Hole. An opening in or through a solid body.
Inlet. A passage by which an enclosed place may be entered.
Interregnum. The time during which a throne is vacant.

Abutment. The act or state of abutting; that which abuts or is abutted upon.
Adhesion, etc. The act of adhering or sticking to anything; the state of being attached or joined. See COHESION.
Apposition. The act of placing side by side, together, or in contact.
Appulse. An approach or impact of one moving body toward or upon another.
Coexistence. Concurrent existence.
Coincidence. The act or state of coinciding, or that which coincides.
Contact. The coming together of two bodies in space; meeting.
Contiguity. The relation of being contiguous or in actual contact.
Juxtaposition. A placing close together, side by side; contiguity.
Meeting. A coming together; an assembling.
Osculation. The act of kissing; in geometry, the contact between any given curve and another curve of the same curvature at the point of contact.
Proximity. The state of being near or next in time, place, etc.; nearness.
Rencontre [F.]. Meeting.
Rencounter. A sudden hostile collision, as with an enemy; an unexpected meeting, as of travelers.
Syzygy. One of the pair of opposite points of an orbit where the moving body is in conjunction with or opposition to the sun; in biology, an immovable union between two brachials of a crinoid; in zoology, the conjunction of two organisms without loss of identity.
Touching, etc The act of one who touches. See *Verbs.*

CONTACT—*Denotations.*

Border-land. Land lying along the limits or boundary.
Frontier, etc. That part of a country which fronts or faces another country. See BOUNDARY.
Tangent. The portion of a straight line, or the straight line which touches a curve.

CONTACT—*Verbs.*

Abut on. Touch at the end or boundary-line, be contiguous.
Adhere, etc. Stick fast or together, etc. See COHESION
Adjoin. Lie next or contiguous to, border on.
Be contiguous, etc. See *Adjectives.*
Coexist. Exist together at the same time or in the same place or conditions.
Coincide. Fall in together; collapse; have the same relations in any respect.
Come in contact. Touch.
Graze. Touch, brush, or rub lightly the surface of in passing.
Join. Set or bring together or into connection; be next to each other.

INTERSPACE—CONTACT—*Continued.*

INTERSPACE—Denotations—*Continued.*

Interstice. A crevice; an interval.
Lacuna [L.]. A space from which something has been omitted, lost, or removed.
Leak. A crack which admits water.
Mesh. The opening enclosed by the threads of a net.
Opening. A vacant place; a hole.
Parenthesis, etc. A word, phrase, or sentence inserted in another sentence. See Environment-Interposition.
Pass. An opening through a dangerous or otherwise impassable barrier.
Ravine. A deep and narrow hollow.
Rent. A break or breach made by force.
Rift. An opening made by riving or splitting.
Rime. A fissure or chink.
Scissure. A long opening in a body made by cutting.
Slit. A long cut or narrow opening.
Strait. A narrow pass or passage.
Void. An empty space.
Yawning gulf. A deep chasm.

INTERSPACE—Verbs.

Gape, etc. Open the mouth wide; split or crack open wide. See Aperture.

INTERSPACE—Adjectives.

Far between. Occurring at long intervals.
With an interval. Being open.

in″-ter-sperse′. Distribute scatteringly. Environment-Interposition, Gathering-Scattering.
in′-ter-sper′-sion. A scattering. Environment-Interposition, Gathering-Scattering.
in′-ter-stice. Crevice. Interspace-Contact.
in″-ter-sti′-tial. Pertaining to interstices. Environment-Interposition, Outside-Inside.
in″-ter-tex′-ture. Act of interweaving. Crossing, Texture.
in″-ter-twine′. Twine together. Crossing, Mixture-Homogeneity, Union-Disunion.
in″-ter-twist′. Twist together. Crossing, Union-Disunion.
in′-ter-val. Open space between two objects; intervening time. Duration-Neverness, Interspace-Contact, Melody-Dissonance; **at intervals,** Continuity-Interruption, Interspace-Contact; **at regular intervals,** Periodicity-Irregularity.
in″-ter-vene′. Divide by coming between; interpose. Continuity-Interruption, Duration-Neverness, Environment-Interposition, Instrumentality, Mediation.
in″-ter-ve′-nience. State of intervening. Environment-Interposition.
in″-ter-ve′-ning. Coming between. Environment-Interposition.
in″-ter-ven′-tion. Interposition. Difficulty-Facility, Duration-Neverness, Environment-Interposition, Instrument.
in″-ter-vert′. Change about; divert. Aim-Aberration, Mutation-Permanence.
in′-ter-view. Formal conference. Conversation-Monologue, Sociability-Privacy.
in″-ter-volved′. Coiled into each other. Union-Disunion.
in″-ter-weave′. Weave together. Crossing, Environment-Interposition, Mixture-Homogeneity, Union-Disunion.
in″-ter-work′-ing. Working together. Agency.
in-tes′-tate. Not having made a valid will. Mark-Obliteration.
in-tes′-ti-nal. Internal. Outside-Inside.
in-tes′-tine. Internal. Outside-Inside.
in-tes′-tines. Bowels. Outside-Inside.
in-thrall′. Enslave. Liberty-Subjection, Release-Restraint.

CONTACT—Verbs—*Continued.*

Meet. Come to and touch or unite with; become contiguous to or joined with.
Osculate. Kiss; in geometry, touch by osculation.
Touch. Be in or come into contact with.

CONTACT—Adjectives.

Close to, etc. In contact with. See Remoteness-Nearness.
Conterminous. Having common limits or boundaries.
Contiguous. Touching or joining at the edge or boundary.
End to end. Contiguous.
Hand to hand. In close union; within touch.
In contact, etc. See *Nouns.*
Osculatory. Of or pertaining to kissing; having the property of coinciding.
Pertingent. Touching.
Tangential. Of, pertaining to, or moving in the direction of a tangent.
Touching, etc. See *Verbs.*
With no interval, etc. Having no space between. See Interspace.

INTERSPACE—*Continued.*

INTERSPACE—Adverbs.

At intervals, etc. With intervening periods or spaces, etc. See Continuity-Interruption.
Longo intervallo [L.]. With a long interval.

in′-ti-ma-cy. Close friendship. Amity-Hostility.
in′-ti-mate. Familiarly acquainted. Amity-Hostility, Enlightenment-Secrecy, Remoteness-Nearness.
in′-tim-ate-ly. In an intimate manner. Union-Disunion.
in″-ti-ma′-tion. Hint. Enlightenment-Secrecy.
in-tim′-i-date. Make afraid. Charitableness-Menace, Presumption-Obsequiousness, Sanguineness-Timidity.
in-tim″-i-da′-tion. A scaring. Charitableness-Menace, Sanguineness-Hopelessness.
in′-to. To the inside of. Go into, Entrance-Exit, **put into,** Injection-Ejection; **run into,** Injection-Ejection.
in-tol′-er-a-ble. Insufferable. Pleasurableness-Painfulness.
in-tol′-er-ance. Bigotry; insolence. Bigotry-Apostasy, Charitableness-Malevolence, Excitability-Inexcitability.
in-tol′-er-ant. Illiberal. Decision-Misjudgment, Excitability-Inexcitability.
in-tomb′. Bury. Life-Funeral.
in″-to-na′-tion. Modulation of the voice in speaking. Melody-Dissonance, Sound-Silence, Vocalization-Muteness.
in-tone′. Recite in a musical monotone. Devotion-Idolatry, Musician.
in-tort′. Wind in and out. Circle-Winding.
in-tox′-i-cate. To overcome with wine, or excitement. Excitation.
in-tox′-i-ca″-ted. Drunk. Teetotalism-Intemperance.
in-tox″-i-ca′-tion. Drunkenness; excitement. Excitability-Inexcitability, Excitation, Teetotalism-Intemperance.
intra, ab [L.] (in′-tra, ab). From within. Outside-Inside.
in-trac′-ta-ble. Unruly. Bigotry-Apostasy, Difficulty-Facility, Favorite-Moroseness.
in″-tra-mu′-ral. Within the wall. Outside-Inside.
in-tran′-sient. Not passing away quickly. Lastingness-Transientness.
in-tran′-si-tive. Not passing farther. Lastingness-Transientness; **intransitive verb,** Verb

in″-trans-mu′-ta-ble. Not capable of being changed into another substance. LASTINGNESS-TRANSIENT-NESS, MUTABILITY-STABILITY.

in-trap′. Catch in a trap. TRUTHFULNESS-FRAUD.

in″-tra-re-gard′-ing. Looking into. OUTSIDE-INSIDE.

in-trench′. Throw up breastworks. ATTACK-DEFENSE, SECURITY-INSECURITY; **intrench on,** TRANSCURSION-SHORTCOMING.

in-trench′-ment. Breastwork. ATTACK-DEFENSE.

in-trep′-id. Fearless and bold. BRAVERY-COWARDICE.

in′-tre-pid′-i-ty. Bravery. BRAVERY-COWARDICE.

in′-tri-ca-cy. Perplexity. DIFFICULTY-FACILITY.

in′-tri-cate. Entangled; difficult to follow. CIRCLE-WINDING, DIFFICULTY-FACILITY, REGULARITY-IRREGULARITY.

in′-tri-gant″. A man given to intrigue. ACTIVITY-INDOLENCE, CRAFT-ARTLESSNESS, DESIGN, PURITY-RAKE.

in-trigue′. Plot; liaison. ACTIVITY-INDOLENCE, CRAFT-ARTLESSNESS, MIDCOURSE-CIRCUIT, PURITY-IMPURITY.

in-trigu′-er. Schemer. CRAFT-ARTLESSNESS.

in-trigu′-ing. Scheming. CRAFT-ARTLESSNESS.

in-trin′-sic. Inherent. NATURE-ART, SUBJECTIVE-NESS-OBJECTIVENESS; **intrinsic evidence,** EVIDENCE-COUNTEREVIDENCE; **intrinsic habit,** HABIT-DESUETUDE; **intrinsic truth,** TRUTH-ERROR.

in-trin′-sic-al. Inherent. SUBJECTIVENESS-OBJECTIVENESS.

in-trin″-si-cal′-i-ty. Quality of being intrinsic. SUBJECTIVENESS-OBJECTIVENESS.

in-trin′-si-cal-ly. Inherently SUBJECTIVENESS-OBJECTIVENESS.

in″-tro-duce′. Bring, lead or put in. ADDITION-SUBTRACTION, ADMISSION-EXPULSION, ENVIRONMENT-INTERPOSITION, INJECTION-EJECTION, LEADING-FOLLOWING, PRECEDENCE-SUCCESSION; **introduce new blood,** EXCITATION, MUTATION-PERMANENCE; **introduce new conditions,** MODIFICATION; **introduce to,** AMITY-HOSTILITY.

in″-tro-duc′-tion. Act of introducing. ADMISSION-EXPULSION, ACTING, AMITY-HOSTILITY, ENVIRONMENT-INTERPOSITION, INJECTION-EJECTION, LEADING-FOLLOWING, POLITENESS-IMPOLITENESS, PRECEDENCE-SUCCESSION, PREDECESSOR-CONTINUATION.

in″-tro-duc′-to-ry. Prefatory. ANTECEDENCE-SEQUENCE, BEGINNING-END, PRECEDENCE-SUCCESSION, PREDECESSOR-CONTINUATION.

in″-tro-gres′-sion. Entrance. ENTRANCE-EXIT.

in-tro′-it. The entrance. CEREMONIAL.

in″-tro-mis′-sion. Introduction. ADMISSION-EXPULSION.

in″-tro-mit′. Insert; intermeddle. ADMISSION-EXPULSION, DISCONTINUANCE-CONTINUANCE, INJECTION-EJECTION.

in″-tro-spec′-tion. Looking within. HEED-DISREGARD, SIGHT-BLINDNESS.

in″-tro-spec′-tive. Looking within. REFLECTION-VACANCY.

in″-tro-ver′-sion. A turning in. REVERSAL.

in″-tro-vert′. Turn within. REVERSAL.

in-trude′. Interfere; encroach. CONNECTION-INDEPENDENCE, ENTRANCE-EXIT, ENVIRONMENT-INTERPOSITION, HARMONY-DISCORD, OPPORTUNENESS-UNSUITABLENESS.

in-tru′-der. One who enters without leave or welcome. CONSTITUENT-ALIEN, ENVIRONMENT-INTERPOSITION.

in-tru′-sion. Encroachment. CONNECTION-INDEPENDENCE, ENTRANCE-EXIT, ENVIRONMENT-INTERPOSITION, HARMONY-DISCORD, OPPORTUNENESS-UNSUITABLENESS.

in-tru′-sive. Coming without warrant. ENVIRONMENT-INTERPOSITION, HARMONY-DISCORD, OPPORTUNENESS-UNSUITABLENESS.

in-trust′. Commit; confide. COMMISSION-ABROGATION, LOAN-BORROWING.

in″-tu-i′-tion. Instinctive knowledge. KNOWLEDGE-IGNORANCE, MIND-IMBECILITY, RATIOCINATION-INSTINCT.

in-tu′-i-tive. Perceived by the mind immediately. RATIOCINATION-INSTINCT.

in-tu′-i-tive-ly. Learned immediately RATIOCINATION-INSTINCT.

in″-tu-mes′-cence. A swelling. CONVEXITY-CONCAVITY, ENLARGEMENT-DIMINUTION.

in-twine′. Twist into or together. CIRCLE-WINDING, UNION-DISUNION.

in-unc′-tion. Act of anointing. COVER-LINING.

in-un′-date. Deluge. EXCESS-LACK, RIVER-WIND, WATER-AIR.

in″-un-da′-tion. Overflow EXCESS-LACK, RIVER-WIND.

in-un″-der-stand′-ing. Unintelligent. REFLECTION-VACANCY.

in″-ur-ban′-i-ty. Rudeness. POLITENESS-IMPOLITENESS.

in-ure′. Harden by use. EDUCATION-MISTEACHING, HABIT-DESUETUDE, PREPARATION-NONPREPARATION, SENSITIVENESS-APATHY.

in-ured′. Hardened. SENSITIVENESS-APATHY.

in-ure′-ment. Habit; practise. HABIT-DESUETUDE, PREPARATION-NONPREPARATION.

in-u″-si-ta′-tion. Disuse. HABIT-DESUETUDE.

in-u′-tile. Useless. USEFULNESS-USELESSNESS.

in″-u-til′-i-ty. Unprofitableness. PROPRIETY-IMPROPRIETY, USEFULNESS-USELESSNESS.

in-vade′. Enter with hostile intent. ATTACK-DEFENSE, ENTRANCE-EXIT.

in-va′-der. One who invades. ATTACK-DEFENSE.

in′-val-id. A sickly person. HEALTH-SICKNESS.

in-val′-id. Having no force or weight. RATIOCINATION-INSTINCT.

in-val′-i-date. Weaken; confute. DUENESS-UNDUENESS, MIGHT-IMPOTENCE, PROOF-DISPROOF, STRENGTH-WEAKNESS

in-val″-i-da′-tion. State of being invalidated. HEALTH-SICKNESS, PROOF-DISPROOF, STRENGTH-WEAKNESS.

in′-va-lid″-ed. Rendered infirm. HEALTH-SICKNESS.

in″-va-lid′-i-ty. Want of cogency. MIGHT-IMPOTENCE.

in-val′-u-a-ble. Inestimable. GOODNESS-BADNESS.

in-va″-ri-a-bil′-i-ty. Constancy. CONVENTIONALITY-UNCONVENTIONALITY.

in-va′-ri-a-ble. Unchangeable. MUTABILITY-STABILITY, SUBJECTIVENESS-OBJECTIVENESS, UNIFORMITY-DIVERSITY.

in-va′-ri-a-bly. Uniformly. UNIFORMITY-DIVERSITY.

in-va′-sion. Hostile entrance. ATTACK-DEFENSE, ENTRANCE-EXIT.

in-vec′-tive. Railing accusation. ADULATION-DISPARAGEMENT, APPROVAL-DISAPPROVAL, CHARITABLENESS-CURSE, JUSTIFICATION-CHARGE.

in-veigh′. Utter vehement censure. APPROVAL-DISAPPROVAL.

in-vei′-gle. Entice; hoodwink. MOTIVE-CAPRICE, PATRIOTISM-TREASON, TRUTHFULNESS-FRAUD.

in-vent′. Fabricate; devise. DESIGN, FANCY, TRUTHFULNESS-FALSEHOOD.

in-vent′-ed. Fabricated. TRUTHFULNESS-FABRICATION.

in-ven′-tion. Device; idea; skill in contriving; lie. DESIGN, FANCY, SKILL-UNSKILFULNESS, TRUTHFULNESS-FABRICATION, TRUTHFULNESS-FALSEHOOD.

in-vent′-ive. Quick at contrivance. FANCY, SKILL-UNSKILFULNESS.

in-vent′-or. One who invents. MAKER-DESTROYER.

in′-ven-to″-ry. A detailed account. RECORD.

in-verse′. Opposed; inverted. LATERALITY-CONTRAPOSITION, REVERSAL, SAMENESS-CONTRAST.

in-verse′-ly. In an inverse order. REVERSAL.

in-ver′-sion. Act of inverting. CONVERSION-REVERSION, LATERALITY-CONTRAPOSITION, MUTATION-PERMANENCE, ORGANIZATION-DISORGANIZATION, REVERSAL, RHETORIC, SAMENESS-CONTRAST, SIMPLICITY-FLORIDNESS.

in-vert′. Reverse. CHEMISTRY, REVERSAL, SAMENESS-CONTRAST.

in-vert′-ed. Reversed. ARCHITECTURE, REVERSAL.

in-vest′. Clothe; expend; lay out; besiege. ATTACK-DEFENSE, COMMISSION-ABROGATION, DRESS-UNDRESS, GIVING - RECEIVING, LOAN - BORROWING, MIGHT-IMPOTENCE, OUTLAY-INCOME; **invest in,** BUYING-SALE, ESTABLISHMENT-REMOVAL; **invest money,** GENEROSITY-FRUGALITY; **invest with,** RATIONALE-LUCK.

in-vest′-ed. Clothed. DRESS-UNDRESS.

in-ves′-ti-gate. Inquire. DECISION-MISJUDGMENT, INVESTIGATION-ANSWER.

in-ves′′-ti-ga′-tion. Careful inquiry or search. INVESTIGATION-ANSWER.

INVESTIGATION—ANSWER.

Analysis. An examination of anything by resolving it into its original or constituent elements.

Calculation. The act of determining or ascertaining by mathematical processes.

Catechism. A form of investigation or instruction by means of questions and answers.

Challenge. An invitation to engage in a contest or controversy of any kind.

Close inquiry. A thorough search for information by asking questions.

Cross-examination. The questioning of a witness by the party against whom he has been called and examined.

Discussion. Examination by argument. See RATIOCINATION.

Dissection. The act of separating or dividing for the purpose of close examination.

Domiciliary visit. A visit to a private residence for the purpose of searching it.

Espionage. The practise of watching the conduct of others.

Examination. A critical investigation.

Exhaustive inquiry. A search for information which embraces all sources.

Exploitation. A careful investigation undertaken for a special purpose; bringing into use and public knowledge.

Indagation. The act of searching out.

Inquest. A judicial investigation into the causes of death.

Inquiry. A seeking for information by asking questions.

Inquisition. An official examination.

Interpellation. The act of demanding of an official an explanation.

Interrogation. An examination by questions.

Interrogatory. A formal question or inquiry.

Investigation. A systematic search for a cause or for truth.

Narrow search. A search covering small ground or few sources.

Peep behind the curtain. A secret investigation.

Perquisition. A thorough inquiry or search.

Perscrutation. An investigation covering the minutest points.

Pervestigation. A diligent and thorough investigation.

Prying questioning, etc. A close and impertinent inspection. See Verbs.

Pursuit, etc. An earnest endeavor to attain. See QUEST.

Query. A question.

Quest. Attempt to find or obtain. See QUEST.

Question. Examination with reference to a decisive result.

Reconnaissance. ⎱ A preliminary examination, or survey.
Reconnoitering. ⎰

Request. An asking for something. See PETITION.

Research. Continued and diligent investigation.

Resolution. An investigation made by resolving into parts.

Review. An investigation repeated with a view to improvement.

Scrutiny. A close investigation.

Search. A thorough investigation with a specific object in view.

Searching inquiry. An examination embracing all sources of information.

Sifting. A critical and minute examination.

Strict inquiry. ⎱ A thorough examination.
Strict search. ⎰

Trial. Examination by a test; judicial examination.

Ventilation. The act of bringing to view or examination.

INVESTIGATION—Denotations.

Ad referendum [L.]. Question for further consideration.

Bone of contention, etc. An unsettled controversy. See VARIANCE-ACCORD.

Desideratum [L.]. That which is desired; the end of an investigation.

Enigma. A dark or obscure saying. See TIDINGS-MYSTERY.

Fair question. A proper question to ask in an investigation.

Feeler. A question put forth to ascertain the views of others.

Field of controversy. ⎱ The entire subject of investigation
Field of inquiry. ⎰

Acknowledgment. The act of admitting the truth of.

Answer. Something said in return to a question.

Antiphon. Any fitting answer.

Antiphony. An anthem sung responsively.

Echo. A sound thrown back by a reflecting surface.

Password. A prearranged answer to a sentry's challenge.

Rationale. An explanation of the principles of some opinion. See CAUSE.

Rebutter. A defendant's answer to a plaintiff's surrejoinder.

Rejoinder. An answer to a reply.

Repartee. A ready and witty retort.

Replication. A plaintiff's reply to a defendant's plea.

Reply. Something given as an answer in return for something that calls for it.

Rescript. An answer in writing.

Rescription. The answering of a letter.

Response. A reply to an objection in formal disputation.

Retort. A keen rejoinder.

Return. An answer. See MARK.

Riposte [F.]. Repartee.

Solution. An answer to a problem. See INTERPRETATION.

Surrebutter. The plaintiff's reply to a defendant's rebutter.

Surrejoinder. The answer of a plaintiff to a defendant's rejoinder

ANSWER—Associated Nouns.

Clue, etc. The thread leading through the labyrinth; a means of guidance. See SIGN.

Discovery, etc. Act of bringing to light. See DISCOVERY.

Œdipus. A character in Grecian story, who solved the riddle of the Sphinx; hence, one clever at solving riddles.

Oracle. A person reputed uncommonly wise. See SOOTHSAYER.

ANSWER—Verbs.

Acknowledge. To admit to be true.

Answer. To speak in return to a question.

Determine. To bring a question or controversy to an end.

Discover, etc. To make known. See DISCOVERY.

Echo. To repeat with assent.

Explain, etc. To make intelligible. See INTERPRETATION.

Fathom. To make the hidden meaning known.

Give answer. To respond.

Hunt out, etc. To search for. See INVESTIGATION.

Rebut. To contradict by counter-proof.

Rejoin. To answer to a reply.

Reply. To make a return in words or writing to some statement made by another.

Respond. To make a reply in words.

Retort. To make a keen rejoinder.

Return answer for. To answer in some one's stead.

Satisfy. To give a gratifying answer.

Set at rest. To remove all doubts or suspicions.

Solve, etc. To give a clear explanation which removes all perplexities; to untie the knot. See INTERPRETATION.

ANSWER—Adjectives.

Answering, etc. See Verbs.

Conclusive. Deciding the question in dispute.

Respondent. Giving response.

Responsive. Ready or inclined to answer.

ANSWER—Adverbs.

Because, etc. By reason of. See CAUSE.

On the right scent. Following up the correct clue.

On the scent. Following up a clue.

ANSWER—Interjection.

Eureka! [Gr.] I have found it! [Archimedes.]

INVESTIGATION—Denotations—*Continued.*

Issue. The result of an investigation.
Knotty point, etc. A question, the solution of which requires much investigation. See DIFFICULTY-FACILITY.
Matter in dispute.⎫
Moot point.   ⎬ The subject under investigation.
Open question. A subject not settled by an investigation.
Plain question. A question bearing directly on the matter under investigation.
Point in dispute.   ⎫
Point to be solved. ⎬ Matter of investigation.

Porism. A proposition affirming the possibility of finding such conditions as will render a determinate problem indeterminate.
Problem. A matter to be investigated.
Question at issue. The subject of investigation.
Quod libet [L.]. A debatable point.
Subject of controversy. ⎫ Matter for investigation.
Subject of inquiry.   ⎬
Threshold of inquiry. A question not entirely solved.

INVESTIGATION—*Nouns of Means.*

Baconian method. Induction.
Induction. The process of reasoning from a part to the whole, from particulars to generals, or from the individual to the universal.
Socratic method. Reasoning by a series of questions leading the one

to whom they were addressed to perceive and admit what was true or false.
Zetetic philosophy. A method of finding the value of unknown quantities by direct search.

INVESTIGATION—*Nouns of Agent.*

Analyst. One skilled in analysis.
Catechist. One who instructs by question and answer.
Correspondent. One who communicates information.
Examiner. One who examines.
Inquirer. One who makes an investigation.
Inquisitor. A judicial examiner

Inspector. One charged to make investigations.
Investigator. One who investigates.
Querist. One who asks questions.
Quid nunc [L.]. An inquisitive person. See INQUISITIVENESS.
Scrutator. One who makes careful investigation.
Scrutineer. An examiner of votes at an election.

INVESTIGATION—*Verbs.*

Agitate. To examine and discuss with heat.
Analyze. To make a critical and minute examination.
Anatomize. To cut in pieces for the purpose of examining the structure.
Ask. To seek information.
Audit. To examine an account with a view to correctness.
Beat up one's quarters. To make a careful investigation for a clue.
Be in question. To be under investigation.
Bring in question. To subject to an investigation concerning the truth of.
Calculate. To investigate by thinking out.
Canvass. To make a detailed examination.
Carry on an inquiry. To prosecute an inquiry.
Catechize. To inquire into conduct or belief by questioning.
Conduct an inquiry. To take direction of an inquiry.
Consider. To examine mentally.
Cross-examine. ⎫ To examine the reliability of evidence by question-
Cross-question.⎬ ing.
Delve into. To make a laborious investigation into.
Demand. To inquire urgently.
Dip into. To engage temporarily in an investigation.
Discuss. To make a question clearer by arguing it.
Dissect. To examine the structure by cutting apart.
Dive into. To make a deep investigation.
Dodge. To investigate with dexterous trickery.
Examine. To investigate critically; to weigh.
Explore. To make a close and strict investigation.
Fathom. To investigate to the very bottom.
Feel for, etc. To investigate by putting forth something indirectly. See TRIAL.
Feel the pulse. To test one's feelings.
Ferret out. To discover by a sharp and persevering search.
Fish for. ⎫ To investigate by artifice.
Fish out. ⎬
Follow the scent. To carry on an investigation by following clues.
Follow the trail. To conduct an investigation by following indications.
Follow up an inquiry. To search closely.
Go deep into. To conduct a serious and thorough investigation.
Go into a question. To study a question.
Go over. To make an investigation covering the whole ground.
Go through. To examine carefully.
Grapple with a question. To attempt to solve a question.
Hunt. To search diligently for.
Hunt out. To make a close search for one thing among other things
Inquire. To investigate by asking questions.
Institute an inquiry. To establish an inquiry.
Interrogate. To put questions to.
Investigate. To make a systematic search; to follow tracks.
Leave no stone unturned. To make a thorough examination.
Look about for. To search.
Look at. ⎫
Look for. ⎬To examine.
Look into.⎭
Look into every hole and corner. To examine thoroughly.

Look out for. ⎫
Look over.   ⎬ To investigate.
Look round.   ⎬
Look through. ⎭
Make inquiry, etc. See *Nouns.*
Make sure of. To find out certainly.
Moot a question. To present a subject for discussion.
Mouse. To investigate slyly and patiently.
Overhaul. To examine carefully.
Parse. To resolve into its grammatical elements.
Pass in review. To examine critically and deliberately.
Peer. To look into attentively and inquiringly.
Peer into every hole and corner. To examine thoroughly.
Pick the brains of. To examine one very thoroughly.
Pop a question. To ask a question unexpectedly.
Preexamine. To examine beforehand.
Probe. To investigate into the causes and circumstances thoroughly.
Probe to the bottom.⎫ To investigate into the most concealed
Probe to the quick. ⎬ causes.
Propose a question. To offer a question for consideration.
Propound a question. To state a question formally for consideration or solution.
Prosecute an inquiry. To begin and carry on an inquiry.
Pry. To investigate with sly curiosity.
Pry into every hole and corner. To pry into every hiding-place.
Pump. To elicit information by artful questions.
Pursue, etc. To make a persistent attempt to gain some piece of information. See QUEST.
Put a question. To bring a question into notice for discussion.
Put forth a question. To investigate.
Put to the proof. To test the truth of by examining the proof.
Put to the question. To put to a vote to find out the opinions of the people voting.
Question. To seek information.
Raise a question. To suggest a question.
Ransack. To make a thorough search through every part of.
Reconnoiter. To examine by the eye.
Require an answer. To need an answer.
Resolve. To examine by separating into the constituent parts.
Rummage. To make a thorough but disorderly search.
Scan. To examine with critical care.
Scratch the head. To seek ideas.
Scrutinize. To examine closely and in detail.
Search. To investigate thoroughly with a specific object in view.
Seek. To go in search of.
Seek a clew.⎫ To try to find an indication that may solve a
Seek a clue. ⎬ mystery.
Sift. To examine minutely.
Slap the forehead. To awaken thought.
Sound. To try to discover something hidden.
Spy. To investigate by secret methods.
Start a question. To bring up a question.
Stir a question. To agitate a question.
Study. To inquire into by means of mental application.
Subject to examination. To examine.

INVESTIGATION—Verbs—Continued.

Suck the brains of. See Pick the brains of
Suggest a question. To question.
Take counsel. To listen to the advice of others.
Take into consideration. To investigate.
Take up. To make a subject of inquiry.
Tax. To question closely.
Thresh out. To beat the wheat free from chaff.
Trace. }
Trace up. } To follow by questioning.

Track. }
Trail. } To endeavor to discover by following footprints.
Try in all its phases. To examine thoroughly.
Undergo examination.
Unearth. To bring out from concealment.
Ventilate a question. To expose a question to discussion.
View in all its phases. To examine thoroughly.
Winnow. To examine by blowing away chaff.

INVESTIGATION—Adjectives.

All-searching. Thorough.
Analytic. Resolving into first principles.
Catechetical. Pertaining to instructions by questions and answers.
Doubtful, etc. Open to question. See Doubt. Certainty-Doubt.
In course of inquiry. Under investigation.
In dispute. }
In issue. } Debated about.
In question. Under investigation.
In quest of. Seeking for something.
Inquiring, etc. Disposed to investigate. See Verbs.
Inquisitive, etc. Inclined to pry. See Inquisitiveness.
Inquisitorial. Pertaining to inquisition.
In search of. Seeking after something.
Interrogative. Denoting inquiry.

Moot. Open to discussion.
On the lookout for. Searching.
Proposed. Offered for consideration.
Requisitive. Expressing demand.
Requisitory. Sought for or demanded
Sub judice [L.]. Under consideration.
Undecided. Not yet adjudged.
Under consideration. }
Under discussion. } Subject to investigation.
Under investigation. Being tracked up.
Undetermined. Not settled by investigation.
Untried. Not yet found out by being tested.
Zetetic. That proceeds by inquiry.

INVESTIGATION—Interrogatives.

How? how comes it? how happens it? how is it? *Nicht wahr?* [G.] not true? what? what is the reason? what on earth? what's in the wind? what's the matter? when? whence? where? wherefore? whither? who? why?

---

in-ves'-ti-ture. A giving possession of any office. Commission-Abrogation.
in-vest'-ment. Clothing. Attack-Defense, Dress-Undress, Giving-Receiving, Loan-Borrowing, Outlay-Income; **make investments,** Preparation-Nonpreparation.
in-vest'-or. One who invests money. Labor-Capital.
in-ves'-ture. To clothe; to invest. Giving-Receiving.
in-vet'-er-ate. Habitual; deep-rooted. Affections, Mutability-Stability, Novelty-Antiquity; **inveterate belief,** Faith-Misgiving; **inveterate habit,** Habit-Desuetude.
invidia est cæca [L.] (in-vid'-i-a est sí'-ca). Envy is blind. Pardon-Envy.
in-vid'-i-ous. Disagreeable; envious. Charitableness-Malevolence, Love-Hate, Pardon-Envy, Pleasurableness-Painfulness.
in-vig'-or-ate. Strengthen. Betterment-Deterioration, Strength-Weakness.
in-vig'-or-a''-ting. Imparting vigor. Healthiness-Unhealthiness.
in-vig''-or-a'-tion. Making strong. Strength-Weakness.
in-vin' ci-ble. Unconquerable. Strength-Weakness.
in-vi'-o-la-ble. Not to be profaned or dishonored. Dueness-Undueness, Enlightenment-Secrecy, Uprightness-Dishonesty.
in-vi'-o-late. Unprofaned. Enlightenment-Secrecy, Mutation-Permanence,. Uprightness-Dishonesty.
in'-vi-ous. Impassable. Aperture-Closure, Difficulty-Facility.
in-vis''-i-bil'-i-ty. State or quality of being invisible. Manifestation-Latency, Visibility-Invisibility.
in-vis'-i-ble. That cannot be seen. Enlightenment-Secrecy, Greatness-Littleness, Manifestation-Latency, Visibility-Invisibility.
invita Minerva [L.] (in-vai'-ta mi-ner'-va). Without genius. Difficulty-Facility, Readiness-Reluctance.
in''-vi-ta'-tion. A requesting one's company Petition-Expostulation, Proffer-Refusal.
in-vite'. Give invitation; ask. Motive-Caprice, Petition-Expostulation, Proffer-Refusal; **invite the attention,** Heed-Disregard.
in-vi'-ting. That invites or allures. Motive-Cap-

rice, Petition-Expostulation, Pleasurableness-Painfulness, Proffer-Refusal.
in-vo-ca'-tion. A prayer for divine blessing. Address-Response, Devotion-Idolatry, Petition-Expostulation.
in'-voice''. A list. Record.
in-voke'. Implore. Address-Response, Devotion-Idolatry, Petition-Expostulation; **invoke curses,** Charitableness-Curse.
in''-vo-lu'-crum. An involucre. Cover-Lining.
in-vol'-un-ta-ri-ness. Unwillingness. Volition-Obligation.
in-vol'-un-ta-ry. Unwilling; resulting from necessity. Readiness-Reluctance, Will-Obligation; **involuntary servitude,** Liberty-Subjection.
in''-vo-lu'-tion. Inclusion; involved construction; multiplication of a quantity by itself. Dress-Undress, Evidence-Counterevidence, Inclusion-Omission, Manifestation-Latency, Meaning-Jargon, Numbering, Organization-Disorganization.
in-volve'. Inwrap; implicate; complicate; include; mean. Dress-Undress, Evidence-Counterevidence, Inclusion-Omission, Manifestation-Latency, Meaning-Jargon, Organization-Disorganization.
in-volved'. Obscure; embarrassed; convoluted. Affluence-Penury, Circle-Winding, Credit-Debt, Perspicuity-Obscurity, Regularity-Irregularity.
in-vul''-ner-a-bil'-i-ty. State of being invulnerable. Renovation-Relapse.
in-vul'-ner-a-ble. That cannot be wounded. Security-Insecurity.
in'-ward. Situated within. Outside-Inside, Subjectiveness-Objectiveness; **inward monitor,** Duty-Dereliction.
in-weave'. Weave together. Crossing, Environment-Interposition.
in-wrap'. Infold. Dress-Undress.
in-wrought'. Worked into. Outside-Inside, Subjectiveness-Objectiveness.
io triumphe [L.] (ai'-o trai-um'-fi). An exclamation of gladness; the Roman soldiers' hurrah. Jubilation-Lamentation, Solemnization.

i'-o-din. One of the elements. CHEMISTRY.

I-on'-ic. Pertaining to or composed of the Ionic foot; pertaining to a kind of Greek architecture. ARCHITECTURE, POETRY-PROSE.

i-o'-ta. A small or insignificant mark. MAGNITUDE-SMALLNESS.

I. O. U. Promise to pay. MONEY, SECURITY.

ipse dixit [L.] (ip'-sî dix'-it). He himself has said. ASSERTION-DENIAL, CERTAINTY-DOUBT.

ipsissima verba [L.] (ip-sis'-si-ma ver'-ba). The exact words. SAMENESS-CONTRAST, TRUTH-ERROR.

ipso facto [L.] (ip'-so fac'-to). By the fact itself. ENTITY-NONENTITY.

ira regum est semper, gravis [L.] (ai'-ra rî'-gum est sem'-per, grê'-vis). Heavy is ever the ire of kings. FAVORITE-ANGER, RECOMPENSE-PUNITION.

iræ amantium [L.] (ai'-rî ê-man'-shi-um). Lovers' quarrels. PARDON-VINDICTIVENESS.

iræ, tantæne animis cælestibus [L.] (ai'-rî, tan-tî'-nî an'-i-mis sî-les'-ti-bus). Can such anger dwell in heavenly minds. FAVORITE-ANGER.

i-ras''-ci-bil'-i-ty. Proneness to anger. FAVORITE-ANGER, FAVORITE-MOROSENESS, FAVORITE-QUARRELSOMENESS.

i-rate'. Wrathful. FAVORITE-ANGER.

ire. Wrath. FAVORITE-ANGER.

ir''-i-des'-cence. A many colored appearance. VARIEGATION.

ir''-i-des'-cent. Exhibiting changing rainbow colors. VARIEGATION.

I'-ris. Rainbow personified as the messenger of Juno. MESSENGER, WAYFARER-SEAFARER.

i'-ris. Rainbow; a curtain of the eye. SIGHT-BLINDNESS, VARIEGATION.

I'-rish-ism. An Hibernicism. ADAGE-NONSENSE.

irk. Weary. PLEASURABLENESS-PAINFULNESS, WEARINESS-REFRESHMENT.

irk'-some. Wearisome; annoying. DIFFICULTY-FACILITY, ENTERTAINMENT-WEARINESS, PLEASURABLENESS-PAINFULNESS, WEARINESS-REFRESHMENT.

i'-ron. Most important metal; like iron. CHEMISTRY, DETERMINATION-VACILLATION, HARDNESS-SOFTNESS; SMOOTHNESS-ROUGHNESS, STRENGTH-WEAKNESS; **iron age,** PLEASURE-PAIN, WELFARE-MISFORTUNE; **Iron Cross,** PATRIOTISM-TREASON; **iron entering into the soul,** PLEASURABLENESS-PAINFULNESS, PLEASURE-PAIN; **iron gray,** GRAY-BROWN; **iron grip,** STRENGTH-WEAKNESS; **iron gripe,** KEEPING-RELINQUISHMENT; **iron heel,** HARSHNESS-MILDNESS; **iron necessity,** VOLITION-OBLIGATION; **iron rule,** HARSHNESS-MILDNESS; **iron sway,** HARSHNESS-MILDNESS, RULE-LICENSE; **iron will,** DETERMINATION-VACILLATION; **rule with a rod of iron,** HARSHNESS-MILDNESS, RULE-LICENSE, WELFARE-MISFORTUNE.

i'-ron-bound''. Bound with iron. **Iron-bound coast,** OCEAN-LAND, REFUGE-PITFALL.

i'-ron-clad''. Covered or clad with iron. ATTACK-DEFENSE, BELLIGERENT, COVER-LINING.

i'-ron-hand''-ed. Despotic. HARSHNESS-MILDNESS.

i'-ron-heart''-ed. Brave. BRAVERY-COWARDICE.

i-ron'-ic-al. Covertly sarcastic. RHETORIC, SOCIETY-DERISION, SOCIETY-LUDICROUSNESS, TROPE, TRUTHFULNESS-FABRICATION.

i'-ron-mold''. Stain of iron-rust. REDNESS-GREENNESS.

i'-rons. Fetters. RELEASE-PRISON; **fire irons,** OVEN-REFRIGERATOR; **irons in the fire,** ACTIVITY-INDOLENCE, ENTERPRISE, EXCESS-LACK, OCCUPATION, SKILL-UNSKILFULNESS; **put in irons,** RELEASE-RESTRAINT.

i'-ro-ny. Use of words designed to convey a meaning opposite to the literal sense; feigning of ignorance. REGARD-DISRESPECT, RHETORIC, SOCIETY-DERISION, TROPE, TRUTHFULNESS-FABRICATION.

ir-ra'-di-ate. Illuminate. LIGHT-DARKNESS.

ir-ra''-di-a'-tion. Illumination. LIGHT-DARKNESS.

ir-ra'-tion-al. Absurd; silly; not expressible by a whole number or common fraction. NUMBER, RATIOCINATION-CASUISTRY, SAGACITY-INCAPACITY.

ir-ra''-tion-al'-i-ty. The state of lacking reason. SAGACITY-INCAPACITY.

ir''-re-claim'-a-ble. That cannot be redeemed. REPENTANCE-OBDURACY, SANGUINENESS-HOPELESSNESS, VIRTUE-VICE.

ir-rec'-on-ci''-la-ble. That cannot be reconciled. AMITY-HOSTILITY, HARMONY-DISCORD.

ir-rec'-on-ci''-la-ble-ness. Incompatibleness. CONNECTION-INDEPENDENCE.

ir''-re-cov'-er-a-ble. Irredeemable. FUTURE-PAST, SANGUINENESS-HOPELESSNESS.

ir-re-deem'-a-ble. Beyond reclaim. SANGUINENESS-HOPELESSNESS.

ir''-re-du'-ci-ble. Not to be arranged or brought into the desired condition. HARMONY-DISCORD, MUTABILITY-STABILITY, REGULARITY-IRREGULARITY.

ir-ref'-ra-ga-ble. Incontestable. PROOF-DISPROOF.

ir''-re-fu'-ta-ble. That cannot be disproved. CERTAINTY-DOUBT, PROOF-DISPROOF.

ir-reg'-u-lar. Out of the usual form, method, etc. BELLIGERENT, CONVENTIONALITY-UNCONVENTIONALITY, PERIODICITY-IRREGULARITY, PROPORTION-DEFORMITY, REGULARITY-IRREGULARITY, UNIFORMITY-DIVERSITY, UNIFORMITY-MULTIFORMITY; **irregular verb,** VERB.

ir-reg''-u-lar'-i-ty. Divergence from what is customary or fit. PERIODICITY-IRREGULARITY.

ir-reg'-u-lar-ly. In an irregular manner. PERIODICITY-IRREGULARITY, REGULARITY-IRREGULARITY.

ir''-re-la'-tion. Lack of relation. CONNECTION-INDEPENDENCE.

ir-rel'-a-tive. Unconnected. CONNECTION-INDEPENDENCE.

ir-rel'-e-van-cy. The condition of being irrelevant. CONNECTION-INDEPENDENCE, DOMINANCE-IMPOTENCE, HARMONY-DISCORD.

ir-rel'-e-vant. Impertinent. CONNECTION-INDEPENDENCE, DOMINANCE-IMPOTENCE, HARMONY-DISCORD, RATIOCINATION-INSTINCT.

ir''-re-lig'-ion. Ungodliness. GODLINESS-DISBELIEF.

ir''-re-lig'-ious. Not religious. GODLINESS-DISBELIEF, GODLINESS-UNGODLINESS.

ir''-re-me'-di-a-ble. Incurable. GOODNESS-BADNESS, SANGUINENESS-HOPELESSNESS.

ir''-re-mis'-si-ble. Unpardonable. VIRTUE-VICE.

ir''-re-mov'-a-ble. Immovable. MUTABILITY-STABILITY.

ir-rep'-a-ra-ble. That cannot be rectified. SANGUINENESS-HOPELESSNESS.

ir''-re-pent'-ance. Impenitence. REPENTANCE-OBDURACY.

ir-rep''-re-hen'-si-ble. Not blamable. INNOCENCE-GUILT.

ir''-re-press'-i-ble. That cannot be restrained. EXCITABILITY-INEXCITABILITY, LIBERTY-SUBJECTION, TURBULENCE-CALMNESS.

ir''-re-proach'-a-ble. Blameless. INNOCENCE-GUILT.

ir''-re-prov'-a-ble. Blameless. INNOCENCE-GUILT.

ir''-re-sist'-i-ble. That cannot be withstood or opposed. COERCION, EXCITABILITY-INEXCITABILITY, PROOF-DISPROOF, STRENGTH-WEAKNESS, VOLITION-OBLIGATION.

ir-res'-o-lu-ble. Not to be resolved. MUTABILITY-STABILITY.

ir-res'-o-lute. Wavering. BIGOTRY-APOSTASY, DETERMINATION-VACILLATION, MUTABILITY-STABILITY.

ir-res'-o-lute-ly. Without resolution. DETERMINATION-VACILLATION.

ir-res''-o-lu'-tion. Want of decision. DETERMINATION-VACILLATION.

ir″-re-solv′-a-ble. Not separable into parts. Soli-tude-Company.

ir″-re-solv′-ed-ly. In an irresolute manner. Deter-mination-Vacillation.

ir″-re-spec′-tive. Regardless. Connection-Inde-pendence.

ir-re-spec′-tive-ly. Without regard to. Connection-Independence.

ir″-re-spon′-si-ble. Not answerable. Duty-Immunity, Law-Lawlessness, Tyranny-Anarchy.

ir″-re-triev′-a-ble. Remediless; irreparable. Gain-Loss, Mutability-Stability, Sanguineness-Hope-lessness.

ir″-re-veal′-a-ble. That cannot be revealed. En-lightenment-Secrecy.

ir-rev′-er-ence. Deficiency of veneration. Godli-ness-Ungodliness, Regard-Disrespect.

ir-rev′-er-ent. Not reverent. Godliness-Ungodli-ness, Regard-Disrespect.

ir″-re-vers′-i-ble. That cannot be annulled. Muta-bility-Stability, Sanguineness-Hopelessness.

ir-rev′-o-ca-ble. Unalterable. Mutability-Sta-bility, Sanguineness-Hopelessness, Volition-Obligation.

ir′-ri-gate. Water. Water-Air.

ir″-ri-ga′-tion. The act of watering. River-Wind, Water-Air.

ir-rig′-u-ous. Watered. Dampness-Dryness, River-Wind.

ir-ri′-sion. Derision. Regard-Disrespect, Society-Derision.

irritabile genus [L.] (ir-ri-tab′-i-lî jî′-nus). The irrita-ble race. Favorite-Quarrelsomeness.

ir″-ri-ta-bil′-i-ty. Fretfulness. Excitability-Inex-citability.

ir′-ri-ta-ble. Petulant. Excitability-Inexcita-bility, Favorite-Quarrelsomeness.

ir′-ri-tate. Make petulant; fret. Excitation, Favor-ite-Anger, Love-Hate, Pleasurableness-Pain-fulness, Turbulence-Calmness.

ir″-ri-ta′-tion. Vexation; ill temper. Excitation, Favorite-Anger, Love-Hate, Pleasurableness-Painfulness, Pleasure - Pain, Turbulence-Calmness; **source of irritation**, Pleasurableness-Painfulness.

ir′-ri-ta″-ting. Fretting; exasperating. Excitation, Favorite-Anger, Love-Hate, Pleasurableness-Painfulness, Turbulence-Calmness, Vigor-Iner-tia.

ir-rup′-tion. Violent incursion. Attack-Defense, Entrance-Exit.

Ir′-ving-ite. A follower of Rev. Edward Irving. Ortho-doxy-Heterodoxy.

is. Present indicative, 3d person, singular number, of the verb *be*. **Is to be,** Occurrence-Destiny; **that is,** Time.

I′-sis. Principal goddess of Egyptian mythology. Jove-Fiend.

Is′-lam-ism. Mohammedanism. Orthodoxy-Het-erodoxy.

is′-land. A tract of land surrounded by water. Swamp-Island.

is′-lan-der. An inhabitant of an island. Dweller-Habitation, Swamp-Island.

isle. An island. Swamp-Island.

is′-let. A little isle. Swamp-Island.

i′-so-bar. A line joining points at which the barometric pressure is the same. Water-Air.

i″-so-chei′-mal. Relating to isocheims. Heat-Cold.

i″-so-chi′-me-nal. Isocheimal. Heat-Cold.

i-soch′-ro-nism. The state or quality of being isochro-nous. Coexistence.

i-soch′-ro-nous. Denoting equal intervals of time. Co-existence.

i″-so-cy′-a-nid. A compound of cyanic acid. Chemis-try.

is′-o-late. Place alone. Sociability-Privacy, Soli-tude-Company, Union-Disunion.

is′-o-la″-ted. Placed alone; unrelated. Connection-Independence, Solitude-Company, Union-Dis-union.

is″-o-la′-tion. State of being isolated. Solitude-Company, Union-Disunion.

i″-so-met′-ric. Of equal measure. **Isometric system,** Mineralogy.

i″-so-mor′-phism. Crystallization in identical or nearly identical forms. Form-Formlessness.

i″-so-mor′-phous. Having the quality of isomorphism. Form-Formlessness, Mineralogy.

i″-so-ther′-mal. Having equality of temperature. Heat-Cold.

i″-so-ther′-mic. Isothermal. Heat-Cold.

i″-so-ton′-ic. Having equal tones. Melody-Disso-nance.

is′-sue. Emission; egress; progeny; publication; ulcer; outcome; place of egress. Arrival-Departure, Cause-Effect, Completion-Noncompletion, En-trance-Exit, Gathering-Place, Gathering-Scat-tering, Health-Sickness, Investigation-Answer, Missive-Publication, Money, Occurrence-Desti-ny, Parentage-Progeny, Publicity, River-Wind; **at issue,** Antagonism-Concurrence, Assent-Dis-sent, Assertion-Denial, Occurrence-Destiny, Ratiocination-Instinct, Strife-Peace, Variance-Accord; **in issue,** Investigation-Answer; **issue a command,** Order; **join issue,** Litigation.

is′-sue-less. Having no offspring. Fertility-Ster-ility.

isth′-mus. A neck of land connecting two larger bod-ies. Breadth-Narrowness, Connective, Ocean-Land.

I-tal′-ics. Italic type. Sign; **put in Italics,** Conse-quence-Insignificance.

itch. Irritation of the skin; propensity. Desire-Distaste, Tingling-Numbness.

itch′-ing. Feeling irritated. Excitability-Inexcita-bility, Tingling-Numbness.

itch′-ing palm. Desire for a bribe. Desire-Distaste, Extravagance-Avarice.

i′-tem. Separate entry in an account. Addition-Sub-traction, Increment-Remnant, Universality-Particularity, Whole-Part.

it″-er-a′-tion. Repetition. Determination-Resolu-tion, Doubling-Halving, Recurrence.

i-tin′-er-ant. Wayfaring; a traveler. Traveling-Navigation, Wayfarer-Seafarer.

i-tin′-er-a-ry. Detailed account or plan of a tour. Enlightenment-Secrecy, Traveling-Navigation.

itur ad astra, sic [L.] (ai′-tur ad as′-tra, sic). Thus is the way to immortality. Life-Death.

i′-vo-ry. A hard, white substance constituting the tusks of elephants. Whiteness-Blackness.

Ix-i′-on. King of the Lapithæ, bound in hell to an endlessly revolving wheel. Revolution-Evolu-tion.

J

jab'-ber. To chatter. MEANING-JARGON, PORTENT, SPEECH-INARTICULATENESS.

ja'-cent. Lying at length. ERECTNESS-FLATNESS.

jacet, hic [L.] (jê'-set, hic). Here lies. LIFE-FUNERAL.

ja'-cinth. A hyacinth. EMBELLISHMENT-DISFIGUREMENT.

jack. A mechanical device. REVOLUTION-EVOLUTION, SIGN.

Jack. A nickname for John; from its frequency, a man. **Before one can say "Jack Robinson,"** EARLINESS-LATENESS; **Jack at a pinch,** ANTAGONIST-ASSISTANT; **Jack Cade,** INSUBORDINATION-OBEDIENCE; **jack in office,** BRAWLER, MANAGER; **Jack Ketch,** RECOMPENSE-SCOURGE; **jack of all trades,** ADEPT-BUNGLER; **jack-o'-lantern,** LUMINARY-SHADE; **Jack Pudding,** ACTING, BRAGGING, WAG; **jack-tar,** WAYFARER-SEAFARER.

jack''-a-dan'-dy. A ridiculous fop. SOCIETY-DANDY, WAG.

jack'-al. A dog-like animal. ANTAGONIST-ASSISTANT, PROVISION-WASTE.

jack'-a-napes''. An impertinent fellow. BRAWLER, SOCIETY-DANDY.

jack'-ass''. The male ass. CONVEYER.

jack'-boot''. A heavy hip boot. DRESS-UNDRESS.

jack'-daw''. A small crow-like bird. **Jackdaw in peacock's feathers,** ADEPT-BUNGLER.

jack'-et. A short coat. DRESS-UNDRESS; **cork-jacket,** REFUGE-PITFALL.

Jac'-o-bin. A friar; a member of a revolutionary party. ANTAGONIST-ASSISTANT.

Jacque''-rie'. A revolt. ATTACK-DEFENSE, REPRISAL-RESISTANCE.

jacta est alea [L.] (jac'-ta est ê'-lê-a). The die is cast. VOLITION-OBLIGATION.

jac''-ti-ta'-tion. A tossing about. AGITATION, BRAGGING.

jac'-u-late. To throw out. PUSH-PULL.

jac''-u-la'-tion. A throwing out. PUSH-PULL.

jade. An old horse; a low person. CONVEYER, GENTILITY-COMMONALTY, GOOD MAN-BAD MAN, PURITY-RAKE, WEARINESS-REFRESHMENT.

jag. A notch. INDENTATION.

jag'-ged. Having jags. ANGULARITY.

jail. A place of confinement. RELEASE-PRISON; **jailbird,** GOOD MAN-BAD MAN, GUARD-PRISONER.

jail'-er. One in charge of a jail. GUARD-PRISONER, RECOMPENSE-SCOURGE.

jakes. A privy. CLEANNESS-FILTHINESS.

jalousie de métier [F.] (zha-lu-zi' de mê-tiê') Professional jealousy. PARDON-ENVY.

jam. To crush; to fill up by crowding; a sweet conserve of fruit. ENVIRONMENT-INTERPOSITION, PULPINESS-OILINESS, SWEETNESS-ACIDITY, UNION-DISUNION.

jamb. A side-post. SUSPENSION-SUPPORT.

jammed in. Pressed into a tight place. RELEASE-RESTRAINT.

jan'-gle. Discordant sound; wrangling. CACOPHONY, VARIANCE-ACCORD.

jan'-i-tor. A building keeper. PERFORATOR-STOPPER.

jan'-i-za-ry. A member of a Mohammedan military force. BELLIGERENT.

Jan'-sen-ism. A system holding the doctrines of irresistible grace and of total depravity. ORTHODOXY-HETERODOXY.

jan'-ty. See JAUNTY.

Jan'-u-a-ry. A month, the first of the year. PERIODICITY-IRREGULARITY.

januis clausis [L.] (jan'-yu-is clau'-sis). With closed doors. ENLIGHTENMENT-SECRECY.

Ja'-nus. An ancient Italic deity. PERSISTENCE-WHIM; **close the temple of Janus,** FIGHTING-CONCILIATION.

Ja'-nus-faced''. Deceitful. TRUTHFULNESS-FALSEHOOD.

ja-pan'. Lacquered Japanese work; a varnish. COVER-LINING, EMBELLISHMENT-DISFIGUREMENT, PULPINESS-ROSIN.

jar. A shaking; a discord; a vessel. AGITATION, CACOPHONY, CONTENTS-RECEIVER, HARMONY-DISCORD, MELODY-DISSONANCE, VARIANCE-ACCORD; **jar upon the feelings,** PLEASURABLENESS-PAINFULNESS.

jar''-di''-nière'. A stand for flowers or plants. CONTENTS-RECEIVER.

jar'-gon. Unintelligible speech. ADAGE-NONSENSE, CLEARNESS-OBSCURITY, MEANING-JARGON, WORD-NEOLOGY.

jas'-per. An impure variety of quartz. EMBELLISHMENT-DISFIGUREMENT.

jaun'-dice. Yellowness of the skin. YELLOWNESS-PURPLE.

jaun'-diced. Jealous; prejudiced. CONTENTEDNESS-DISCONTENTMENT, PARDON-JEALOUSY, PROOF-DISPROOF, YELLOWNESS-PURPLE; **view with jaundiced eyes,** APPROVAL-DISAPPROVAL, DECISION-MISJUDGMENT.

jaunt. An excursion. TRAVELING-NAVIGATION.

jaun'-ting-car''. A vehicle. CONVEYANCE-VESSEL.

jaun'-ty. Sprightly; flippant. BEAUTY-UGLINESS, LIGHTHEARTEDNESS-DEJECTION, POMP, PRESUMPTION-OBSEQUIOUSNESS, RECKLESSNESS-CAUTION, SOCIETY-LUDICROUSNESS.

jave'-lin. A spear. WEAPON.

jaw. To scold; talk much; part of the head. ANATOMY, APPROVAL-DISAPPROVAL, TALKATIVENESS-TACITURNITY.

jaw''-fall'-en. Dejected. LIGHTHEARTEDNESS-DEJECTION.

jaws. A pair of members between which something is held, crushed, or cut. BORDER, NUTRIMENT-EXCRETION; **jaws of death,** LIFE-DEATH.

jay. A bird. TALKATIVENESS-TACITURNITY.

jeal'-ous. Fervid as to slight of love. **Jealous of honor,** UPRIGHTNESS-DISHONESTY.

jeal'-ous-y. State of being jealous. FAITH-MISGIVING, PARDON-JEALOUSY.

jecur, fervens difficili bile tumet [L.] (jî'-kur, fer'-venz dif-fis'-ci-lai bai'-lî tiu'-met). My heated liver swells with bile. FAVORITE-ANGER.

jeer. A taunt; mock. REGARD-DISRESPECT.

Je-ho'-vah. Lord. DIVINITY.

je'-hu. A fast driver; a coachman. WAYFARER-SEAFARER.

je-june'. Dry STRENGTH-WEAKNESS, EXCESS-LACK.

jel'-ly. A semisolid glutinous substance. VISCIDITY-FOAM; **beat to a jelly,** RECOMPENSE-PUNITION.

jem'-i-dar" An Indian lieutenant, or overseer CHIEF-UNDERLING.

jem'-my. A crowbar, neat INSTRUMENT, SOCIETY-DANDY.

je ne sais quoi [F.] (zhe ne sê kwa). I know not what. BEAUTY - UGLINESS, CONVENTIONALITY - UNCONVENTIONALITY, WORD-NEOLOGY.

jen'-net. A small Spanish horse. CONVEYER.

jen'-ny. A spinning-jenny. INSTRUMENT

jeop'-ard.
jeop'-ard-ize.} To imperil. SECURITY-INSECURITY.

jeop'-ar-dy. Exposure; danger SECURITY-INSECURITY.

jer'-bo-a. A mouse-like rodent. SPRING-DIVE.

jer'-e-mi"-ad. A tale of woe. JUBILATION-LAMENTATION, APPROVAL-DISAPPROVAL. [Bible, *Jeremiah*.]

Jer'-i-cho. A city in Palestine destroyed by the Jews. **Send to Jericho,** ADMISSION-EXPULSION.

jerk. A short, sharp pull. AGITATION, PUSH-PULL, REVOLUTION.

jer'-kin. A waistcoat. DRESS-UNDRESS.

jerks. Short, sharp pulls. **By jerks,** CONTINUITY-INTERRUPTION.

Jer'-ry Sneak. A thief; a henpecked husband. [Foote, *The Mayor of Garratt*.] BRAVERY-COWARDICE, UPRIGHTNESS-ROGUE.

jer'-sey. A shirt. DRESS-UNDRESS.

Jess'-a-my. Colloquial for jessamine. **Jemmy Jess-amy,** SOCIETY-DANDY.

jes'-se. A candlestick. FANE.

jest. A joke; exploit. CONSEQUENCE-INSIGNIFICANCE, WITTINESS-DULNESS.

jest'-book". A book of jokes. WITTINESS-DULNESS.

jest'-er. One who jests. WAG.

jest'-ing-stock". A butt. SOCIETY-LAUGHINGSTOCK.

Jes'-u-it. A member of the Society of Jesus; an intriguer. GULL-DECEIVER, MINISTRY-LAITY.

Jes"-u-it'-ic-al. Given to Jesuitism. RATIOCINATION-CASUISTRY, TRUTHFULNESS-FALSEHOOD.

Jes'-u-it-ry. The policy of the Jesuits. RATIOCINATION-CASUISTRY.

Je'-sus. The Savior. DIVINITY

jet. A spurt; the color of jet. RIVER-WIND; **jet black,** WHITENESS-BLACKNESS.

jet'-ty. A projecting part of a building; a wharf. CONVEXITY-CONCAVITY, REFUGE-PITFALL, WHITENESS-BLACKNESS.

jeu, beau retour, à beau [F.] (zhu, bo re-tur', a bo) Tit for tat. REPRISAL-RESISTANCE.

jeu d'esprit [F.] (zhu des-prî'). A witty remark. WITTINESS-DULNESS.

jeu de mots [F.] (zhu de mo). A play on words. WITTINESS-DULNESS.

jeu de théâtre [F.] (zhu de tê-atr'). A stage trick. ACTING.

jeu ne vaut pas la chandelle, le [F.] (zhu ne vo pa la shan'del', le). The game is not worth the candle. CONSEQUENCE-INSIGNIFICANCE, PROVISION-WASTE.

jeune premier [F.] (zhun pre-mi-ê'). The leading young gentleman in a play. ACTING.

jeune veuve [F.] (zhun vuv). A young widow in a play. ACTING.

Jew. An Israelite. AFFLUENCE-PENURY, CRAFT-ARTLESSNESS, EXTRAVAGANCE-AVARICE, ORTHODOXY-HETERODOXY; **Jew's harp,** MUSICAL INSTRUMENTS; **worth a Jew's eye,** COSTLINESS-CHEAPNESS, GOODNESS-BADNESS.

jew'-el. Something of rare value; precious stone. EMBELLISHMENT - DISFIGUREMENT, FAVORITE - ANGER, GOODNESS-BADNESS.

jew'-el-ry. Jewels taken collectively. **False jewelry,** TRUTHFULNESS-FRAUD.

Jez'-e-bel. A bold, vicious woman. BENEFACTOR-EVILDOER, GULL-DECEIVER, PURITY-RAKE. [Bible.]

jib. To move sidewise or backward. ADVANCE-RETROGRESSION; **cut of one's jib,** APPEARANCE-DISAPPEARANCE, FORM-FORMLESSNESS.

jif'-fy. An instant. ETERNITY-INSTANTANEITY.

jig. A dance. ENTERTAINMENT-WEARINESS.

jilt. To discard. EXPECTATION-SURPRISE, GULL-DECEIVER, TRUTHFULNESS-FRAUD, UPRIGHTNESS-DISHONESTY.

jilt'-ed. State of being discarded. LOVE-HATE.

jimp. Neat. BEAUTY-UGLINESS.

jin'-gal. A musket. WEAPON.

jin'-gle. To tinkle. RESONANCE-NONRESONANCE.

Jin'-go. One of a party in England favoring an aggressive foreign policy. HARSHNESS-MILDNESS.

Jin'-go-ism. Jingo spirit. PATRIOTISM-TREASON.

jinks. Loud sport **High jinks,** ENTERTAINMENT-WEARINESS.

jinn. A spirit. JOVE-FIEND.

Job. The hero of an Old Testament book **Job's comforter,** LIGHTHEARTEDNESS-DEJECTION, SANGUINENESS-HOPELESSNESS; **patience of Job,** EXCITABILITY-INEXCITABILITY; **poor as Job,** AFFLUENCE-PENURY.

job. Work done. ACTION-PASSIVENESS, OCCUPATION, UPRIGHTNESS-DISHONESTY; **tough job,** DIFFICULTY-FACILITY.

jo-ba'-tion. Scolding. APPROVAL-DISAPPROVAL.

job'-ber. A merchant; intriguer. ADEPT-BUNGLER, DEALER, GULL-DECEIVER, UNSELFISHNESS-SELFISHNESS.

job'-ber-nole. A blockhead. SAGE-FOOL.

job'-ber-y. Low intriguing. CRAFT-ARTLESSNESS, UPRIGHTNESS-DISHONESTY.

job'-bing. Act of performing jobs. EXCHANGE.

jock'-ey. A horse-rider or horse-dealer; a cheat. CHIEF-UNDERLING, GULL - DECEIVER, TRUTHFULNESS-FRAUD, WAYFARER-SEAFARER.

jo-cose'. Sportive. LIGHTHEARTEDNESS-DEJECTION, WITTINESS-DULNESS.

jo-cose'-ness. The quality of being jocose. ENTERTAINMENT-WEARINESS.

jo-cos'-i-ty. Jocularity. LIGHTHEARTEDNESS-DEJECTION.

joc'-u-lar. Jocose. LIGHTHEARTEDNESS-DEJECTION, WITTINESS-DULNESS.

joc"-u-lar'-i-ty. Light-heartedness. LIGHTHEARTEDNESS-DEJECTION.

joc'-und. Jovial. ENTERTAINMENT-WEARINESS, LIGHTHEARTEDNESS-DEJECTION.

jo-cun'-di-ty. Joviality LIGHTHEARTEDNESS-DEJECTION.

Joe" Mil'-ler. A stale joke. WITTINESS - DULNESS, WAG.

jog. To push or shake slightly. AGITATION, IMPETUS-REACTION; **jog on,** ADVANCE-RETROGRESSION, DISCONTINUANCE-CONTINUANCE, MEDIOCRITY, TRAVELING-NAVIGATION; **jog the memory,** REMEMBRANCE-FORGETFULNESS.

jog'-gle. To shake slightly. AGITATION.

jog'-trot". A slow trot. HABIT-DESUETUDE, SWIFTNESS-SLOWNESS, TRAVELING-NAVIGATION.

John Doe and Rich'-ard Roe. Fictitious names for plaintiff and defendant used in old law pleadings. SUBSTANCE-NULLITY.

John-so'-ni-an. Pompous. SIMPLICITY-FLORIDNESS.

joie, feu de [F.] (zhwa, fu de) A bonfire. SOLEMNIZATION.

join. To connect; unite. ARRIVAL-DEPARTURE, ASSOCIATION, CONVEYANCE-VESSEL, GATHERING-SCATTERING, INTERSPACE-CONTACT, MATRIMONY-CELIBACY, SOCIABILITY-PRIVACY, UNION-DISUNION; **join battle,** FIGHTING-CONCILIATION; **join forces,** ANTAGONISM-CONCURRENCE; **join hands,** ANTAGONISM-CONCURRENCE; **join in,** PARTICIPATION; **join in the chorus,**

ASSENT-DISSENT; **join issue,** ASSERTION-DENIAL, LITIGATION, RATIOCINATION-INSTINCT, STRIFE-PEACE, VARIANCE-ACCORD; **join with,** ANTAGONISM-CONCURRENCE.

joint. A junction. GEOLOGY, NUTRIMENT-EXCRETION, PLICATURE, SOLITUDE-COMPANY, UNION-DISUNION, WHOLE-PART; **joint concern,** ASSOCIATION.

joint'-stock". Pertaining to stock held jointly. ANTAGONISM-CONCURRENCE, PARTICIPATION.

joint'-ten"-an-cy. Tenure by more than one person. PARTICIPATION.

join'-ture. A marriage settlement. PROPERTY.

joist. A building timber. SUSPENSION-SUPPORT.

joke. A jest. CONSEQUENCE-INSIGNIFICANCE, SOCIETY-DERISION, WITTINESS-DULNESS; **in joke,** WITTINESS-DULNESS; **mere joke,** CONSEQUENCE - INSIGNIFI-CANCE; **no joke,** CONSEQUENCE-INSIGNIFICANCE, ENTITY-NONENTITY; **practical joke,** ENTERTAINMENT-WEARINESS, REGARD-DISRESPECT, SOCIETY-DERISION, TRUTHFULNESS - FRAUD; **take a joke,** SAGACITY-INCAPACITY.

jo'-ker. One who jests. WAG.

jo'-king a-part'. In fact. ASSERTION-DENIAL, DETERMINATION-VACILLATION.

jole. The jaw. LATERALITY-CONTRAPOSITION.

jol"-li-fi-ca'-tion. A merrymaking. ENTERTAINMENT-WEARINESS, MODERATION-SELFINDULGENCE.

jol'-li-ty. State of being jolly. ENTERTAINMENT-WEARINESS, LIGHTHEARTEDNESS-DEJECTION, SOCIABILITY-PRIVACY.

jol'-ly. Gay. GREATNESS-LITTLENESS, LIGHTHEARTEDNESS-DEJECTION; **jolly-boat,** CONVEYANCE-VESSEL; **jolly fellow,** SOCIABILITY-PRIVACY.

jolt. A shock. AGITATION, IMPETUS-REACTION.

jolt'-head". A dunce. SAGE-FOOL.

Jones. A proper name. **Davy Jones's locker,** LIFE-DEATH; **Paul Jones,** ROBBER.

jon'-quil. The juice of a plant used as an emetic. REMEDY-BANE.

jo'-rum. A bowl. CONTENTS-RECEIVER.

Jo'-seph. A Jewish hero. PURITY-IMPURITY; **Joseph's coat,** VARIEGATION.

joss. A Chinese idol. **Joss-house,** FANE.

jos'-tle. To hustle. AGITATION, IMPETUS-REACTION, VARIANCE-ACCORD.

jot. The least bit. CONSEQUENCE-INSIGNIFICANCE, GREATNESS-SMALLNESS.

jot'-ting. A memorandum. SIGN.

jounce. To jolt. AGITATION.

jour, bon [F.] (zhur, bon˙). Good-day. POLITENESS-IMPOLITENESS.

jour, bonne œuvre, bon [F.] (zhur, bon uvr, bon˙). The better the day the better the deed. GOOD-EVIL.

jour maigre [F.] (zhur mêgr). Fast day. FASTING-GLUTTONY.

jour'-nal. A record of proceedings. ACCOUNT, ACCOUNTS, CHRONOLOGY-ANACHRONISM, MARK-OBLITERATION, MISSIVE-PUBLICATION, PUBLICITY.

jour'-nal-ist. A newspaper man. MISSIVE-PUBLICATION, RECORDER.

jour'-ney. Passage from place to place. MOVEMENT-REST, TRANSMISSION, TRAVELING-NAVIGATION.

jour'-ney-man. A mechanic. AGENT, CHIEF-UNDERLING, LABOR-CAPITAL.

joust. A tilting match. STRIFE-PEACE.

Jove. A Latin deity. JOVE-FIEND.

JOVE—FIEND

Allah. The one supreme being; the true god of the Arabs.

Ariel. A spirit of the air or water; a tricky spirit. [Shakespeare, *Tempest;* Bible; Milton; Pope, *Rape of the Lock*.]

Astoreth. The moon-goddess of Syria and Phenicia; the same as Artemis and Diana of classical mythology.

Baal. The sun-god; the supreme male divinity of Syrians and Phenicians.

Banshee. A visiting fairy or wailing forerunner of death. [Scotch and Irish.]

Bel. The chief god of the Babylonians; it is the Chaldaic form of Baal; Belus.

Benshie. See BANSHEE.

Brahma. The supreme god of the Hindus

Buddha. Founder of Buddhist religion; a great religious teacher and reformer; to the Buddhist he is intelligence and wisdom incarnated.

Demiurge. According to Plato, he was the creator of the material universe; according to the Gnostics, Jehovah of the Jews, an emanation from the Supreme Being.

Denizens of the air. Beings inhabiting the air.

Dryad. A fairy or spirit presiding over the woods.

Fairy. A supernatural being, supposed to be of human form but capable of assuming different forms and of working good or ill to mankind.

Fairy mythology. The whole body of the stories and legends of the fairies.

Familiar. A familiar spirit, supposed to be summoned by soothsayers to serve them.

Fay. A fairy.

Folk-lore. The tales, legends, and beliefs current among the common people.

God. A supernatural being made the object of adoration and worship; a divinity; a male deity.

Goddess. A female divinity.

Good-genius. A kindly disposed spirit supposed to accompany one throughout life.

Hamadryad. A nymph of the woods supposed to live and die with the tree it inhabits.

Heathen gods and goddesses. Idols.

Heathen mythology. The whole body of the legends of the heathen world.

Isis. The principal Egyptian goddess.

Affreet. A demon; a powerful evil genie.

Afrite. Another form of AFFREET.

Ahriman. The evil principle of the Persians; the prince of darkness.

Asmodeus. The demon of matrimonial unhappiness and vanity.

Apparition. A supposed visible spirit; a ghost; a specter.

Bad fairy. A fairy working evil.

Bad spirit. A spirit working evil.

Banshee. A visiting fairy, often assuming the form of an old woman whose wailing under the windows of a house foretold the death of some of its occupants.

Belial. A wicked spirit; the Hebrew personification of lawlessness or recklessness.

Boggart. A local goblin.

Bogie. A goblin; a specter.

Bogle. Something terrifying; a bugbear; a hobgoblin.

Bogy. A fiend.

Brownie. A good-natured sprite in Scotland supposed to haunt farmhouses and do chores at night.

Cacodemon. An evil spirit; one possessed with an evil spirit; the nightmare.

Cluri-chaune. An Irish fairy corresponding to Puck of England.

Deev. In Persian and Hindu mythology a bad spirit, the servant of Ahriman.

Demon. An evil spirit holding a middle place between the gods and men in ancient mythology.

Demonology. The science of demons

Demonry. Demoniacal possession.

Devil. The evil one, who tempts mankind seeking their spiritual ruin; the ruler of the kingdom of evil. [Greek *diabolos,* accuser.]

Dwarf. A being much under the normal size.

Dwerger. Dwarfish sprite.

Eblis. A refractory spirit fabled to have been created two thousand years before Adam.

Effreet. See AFFREET.

Elf. A Saxon angel; a fairy haunting unfrequented places and delighting in tricks.

Evil eye. The supposed power that some people possess of communicating evil by a glance; the eye of envy which blighted good fortune.

Evil genius. A bad spirit presiding over a man's destiny.

Fairy. An imaginary being, small and graceful, with a human form but having power to change its form and work good or ill to mankind.

JOVE—FIEND—*Continued.*

Jove. See JUPITER.

Juggernaut. A name under which Vishnu is worshiped by the Hindus.

Jupiter. The great god of the Romans; god of the sky, thunder, and lightning.

Kelpie. An imaginary water-spirit, supposed to haunt fords in the form of a horse.

Krishna. One of the most celebrated of modern Hindu divinities.

Lemprière. The name of a current dictionary of mythology.

Mab. Spoken of in English folk-lore as queen of the fairies. See OBERON.

Mermaid. A mythological creature inhabiting the sea, having the head and body of a woman to the waist and ending like a fish.

Mumbo Jumbo. An imaginary demon in the western part of Africa, much feared by the natives.

Mythology. The body of the myths or legends of a people extending back to prehistoric times.

Naiad. A water-nymph, fabled to preside over fountains, lakes, wells, etc.

Nereid. A sea-nymph, a daughter of Nereus and an attendant upon Neptune.

Nix. } One of the water-spirits having a mischievous disposition.
Nixie. }

Nymph. A female divinity of lower order inhabiting a wood, lake, fountain, or the like.

Oberon. King of the fairies and husband of Queen Mab. [Shakespeare, *Midsummer Night's Dream.*]

Odin. The chief deity of the Scandinavians; same as Woden in German mythology.

Ondine. A female water-spirit, not having a soul; the only condition on which she could have a soul was that she marry a mortal and bear a son. [Le Motte Fouqué, *Undine.*]

Ormuzd. The good principle in the Persian religion.

Osiris. The most popular of the Egyptian divinities, husband of Isis, identified with the sun and the Nile, the god of light, verdure, agriculture, etc.; he has undergone many incarnations in the sacred bull Apis.

Pantheon. All the deities of a people taken together; a treatise on the gods; a temple of the gods at Rome.

Peri. An elf or fairy, fabled to be descended from a fallen angel and doing penance till it could be admitted to Paradise. [Tom Moore, *Lalla Rookh.*]

Pixy. A kind of fairy or elf of English folk-lore.

Sea-maid. Same as mermaid.

Shiva. The deity known as the destroyer; he with Brahma and Vishnu forms the Hindu trinity.

Sibyl. A prophetess under the inspiration of a deity; a fortune-teller.

Siva. See SHIVA.

Sprite. An imaginary being of the air; a fairy or goblin.

Sylph. An imaginary being or fairy inhabiting the air, so called by Paracelsus.

Sylphid. Diminutive of sylph.

Thor. In Norse mythology, the god of thunder and war. [Thursday.]

Tutelary genius. A guardian deity supposed to accompany one through life.

Undine. See ONDINE.

Vishnu. The second god of the Hindu triad. He impersonates protection.

Yama. The Hindu god of the dead.

Zeus. The great god of the Greeks; Jupiter.

JOVE—*Adjectives.*

Fairy-like. Having the qualities of a fairy.

Sylphic. Like a sylph or fairy.

Sylph-like. With qualities suggesting a sylph.

JOVE—*Phrase.*

Di il vero e affronterai il diavolo [It.]. Speak the truth and you will shame the devil.

FIEND—*Continued from Column 2.*

Troll. An imaginary being of Scandinavian mythology, sometimes represented as a giant and sometimes as a dwarf.

Unclean spirit. A morally impure supernatural being; a devil.

Urchin. A mischievous spirit which sometimes assumed the form of a hedgehog.

Vampire. A fabled being that sucks blood from persons when they sleep.

Vision. A supernatural appearance; an apparition.

Familiar. An evil spirit or demon attending upon one.

Faun. A deity of the woods or herds, usually represented with the legs of a goat.

Fiend. A wicked spirit; a devil; a demon; one hating.

Flibbertigibbet. An impulsive, flighty person; an imp or fiend.

Frankenstein's monster. A monster constructed by a student of physiology out of the remnants of the churchyard and dissecting-room, with a kind of convulsive life infused into it by galvanism. Life grew intolerable for it for the lack of sympathy, so it wreaked vengeance on its maker. It has become a proverb for one destroyed by his own works. [Godwin, Poe.]

Fury. One of the three avenging deities; they are Tesiphone, Alecto, and Megæra.

Ghost. The spirit apart from the body; the returned spirit of a deceased person; an apparition.

Ghoul. A wicked spirit fabled to rob graves.

Gin. One of the fabled good or evil spirits of Arabian mythology, supposed to be the children of fire and to have power to change their forms at will.

Gnome. One of the fabled dwarf goblins.

Goblin. A fancied spirit, supposed to reside in the woods and grottoes, frightful in appearance and of a malicious disposition.

Harpy. Originally a goddess of the storm; later, a winged demon with the head and body of a woman and the lower extremities of a bird. [Virgil, *Æneid.*]

Hobgoblin. A frightful imp or goblin, sometimes identified with the household spirit or Robin Goodfellow.

Imp. A fanciful evil spirit of low rank.

Incubus. An evil spirit supposed to have sexual intercourse with women by night.

Jinn. See GIN.

Kobold. The household spirit of German mythology.

Lamia. A monster with the form of a woman, who is said to have destroyed human beings by sucking their blood.

Lemures. Ghosts of the departed who could not find rest on account of their sins or the manner of their death.

Lepre-chaune. A fairy in Irish mythology supposed to help housewives.

Loki. The god of strife and spirit of evil.

Loup-garou. One who became a wolf and practised cannibalism; a werwolf.

Lycanthrope. A human being said to have been changed into a wolf.

Mephistopheles. One of the seven devils of old demonology, the second of the fallen archangels; he ranked next to Satan in power. [Goethe, *Faust.*]

Merfolk. The whole tribe of mermaids and mermen.

Mermaid. A mythological creature, represented as having the head and body of a beautiful woman and being from the waist down of the form of a fish.

Merman. The male corresponding to the mermaid.

Moloch. The fire-god or sun-god of the Ammonites, to whom human sacrifices were offered, especially children. [Bible.]

Necks. In Norse folk-lore, water-sprites.

Nis. A water-sprite.

Nix. In Teutonic mythology, a female water-spirit of mischievous disposition.

Oceanus. The god of the sea.

Ogre. An imaginary monster, supposed to devour human beings.

Ogress. A female ogre.

Oufe. Elf.

Pigwidgeon. Anything especially small.

Pixy. A kind of fairy, in English folk-lore, that danced in the "pixy rings."

Puck. A mischievous fairy of English folk-lore, also known as Robin Goodfellow. [Shakespeare, *Midsummer Night's Dream.*]

Robin Goodfellow. A mischievous elf. See PUCK.

Satyr. A cunning Sylvan deity, represented as half man and half goat.

Shade. A departed spirit; a ghost.

Shadow. A spirit or ghost.

Shedim. A devil.

Siren. A sea-nymph, represented as half woman and half bird, who by her sweet songs lured passersby to destruction.

Specter. An imaginary appearance of a departed spirit.

Spirit. A supernatural being.

Spook. An apparition, or ghost.

Sprite. A spirit; an elf; a shade.

Succuba. A fabled female demon, supposed to have sexual intercourse with men in their sleep.

Succubus. Male demon corresponding to Succuba.

Titan. Any one of the children of Uranus and Gæa. They are of great strength and incarnate the natural forces.

(Continued on Column 1.)

FIEND—*Continued.*

Will-o'-the-wisp. A phosphorescent light, appearing over marshy places, occasioned by gases arising from decaying animal and vegetable matter; hence, a misleading influence.

Wraith. An apparition of a living person, supposed to be ominous of his death

FIEND—*Adjectives.*

Demoniacal. Like a demon.
Elfin. Pertaining to elves.
Elf-like. Having the characteristics of an elf.
Fiendish. Like a fiend.
Fiend-like. With the qualities of a fiend; devilish.
Ghost-like.⎱ Like a ghost; spectral.
Ghostly. ⎰
Haunted. Frequented by ghosts or apparitions.

Impish. Like an imp.
Spectral. Having the appearance of a ghost or specter.
Supernatural. Beyond nature; miraculous.
Uncanny. Strange; weird.
Unearthly. Supernatural; alarming.
Weird. Caused by magical influence and awakening superstitious fear.

Jove, sub [L.] (jo'-vî, sub). In the open air. OUTSIDE-INSIDE, WATER-AIR.
jo'-vi-al. Joyous. ENTERTAINMENT - WEARINESS, LIGHTHEARTEDNESS - DEJECTION, SOCIABILITY - PRIVACY.
jo'-vi-al-ness. Jovial nature. ENTERTAINMENT-WEARINESS.
Jo-vin'-i-an-ist. A follower of Jovinian of Milan. ORTHODOXY-HETERODOXY.
jowl. The jaw. LATERALITY-CONTRAPOSITION.
joy. Gladness. PLEASURE-PAIN; **give one joy,** FELICITATION.
joy'-ful. Full of joy. LIGHTHEARTEDNESS-DEJECTION.

joy'-less. Destitute of joy. LIGHTHEARTEDNESS-DEJECTION.
joy'-ous-ness. Gladness. LIGHTHEARTEDNESS-DEJECTION.
J. P. Justice of the peace. JUDGE.
Juan. John. **Don Juan,** PURITY-RAKE.
ju'-be. A rood-loft at the entrance of the choir of a church. FANE.
jubeo, sic volo sic [L.] (ju'-bî-o, sic vo'-lo sic). As I wish, thus I command. ORDER.
ju'-bi-lant. Exultingly glad. BRAGGING, JUBILATION-LAMENTATION, LIGHTHEARTEDNESS-DEJECTION.
ju''-bil-a'-tion. Exultation. JUBILATION-LAMENTATION.

JUBILATION—LAMENTATION.

Congratulation. See CONGRATULATE.
Derision, etc. Contempt shown by laughter.
Exultation. Triumphant joy.
Jubilation. The act of rejoicing or exulting.
Jubilee. A season or occasion of rejoicing and festivity.
Laughter. Convulsive merriment.
Laughter holding both his sides. Great laughter. [Milton, *L'Allegro.*]
Merrymaking. An occasion of jollity and merriment.
Rejoicing. The expression of joy or gladness in any manner.
Reveling. Disorderly or drunken festivity.
Risibility. Tendency to laughter.
Rollicker. One who spends his time in frolic and reveling.
Triumph. Rejoicing and exultation because of great success.

JUBILATION—*Associated Nouns.*

Democritus the Abderite. The so-called laughing philosopher.
Heyday. A time of frolic and exultation.
Momus. The Grecian god of censure and mockery.
Pæan. A song of triumph.
Te Deum [L.]. A celebrated Christian hymn.

JUBILATION—*Nouns of Manner.*

Broad grin. A grin extending over the entire face.
Burst of laughter. A sudden fit of laughing.
Cachination. Loud hysterical laughter.
Cheer. A shout of applause.
Chuckle. Suppressed or broken laughter.
Crow. A triumphant shout.
Fit of laughter. Continued laughter which overpowers one for the time being.
Flush. The color which overspreads the face in time of exultation.
Giggle. A convulsive laugh. See *Verbs.*
Grin. A broad smile in which the teeth are exposed.
Guffaw. A burst of boisterous laughter.
Hearty laugh. A sincere vigorous laugh.
Horse-laugh. A guffaw.
Peal of laughter. Loud prolonged laughter.
Roar of laughter. Continued boisterous laughter.
Sardonic grin. A derisive or bitterly sarcastic grin.
Shout. A sudden outcry of joy.
Shout of laughter. A loud outburst of laughing.
Simper. A silly, conceited smile.
Smile. A joyful or pleasing expression of the face.
Smirk. A silly, self-complacent smile; a simper.
Snicker. A suppressed, broken laugh; a giggle.
Titter. A restrained laugh. See *Verbs.*

Condolence. Expressions of sympathy with one in grief.
Lachrimation. A weeping.
Lament. Grief or sorrow expressed in complaints or cries.
Lamentation. The act of lamenting. See LAMENT.
Languishment. The condition of pining away in sorrow.
Plaintiveness. Subdued sadness.
Suspiration. The act of sighing.
Wail of woe. A wild cry of overwhelming sorrow.
Weeping. Expression of sorrow by tears.
Weeping and gnashing of teeth. A figurative expression of great pain or grief. [Bible.]

LAMENTATION—*Associated Nouns.*

Coronach. A dirge formerly sung in the Highlands of Scotland on the death of a chieftain.
Death-song. A hymn sung at a funeral.
Dirge. A song expressing grief and mourning.
Elegy. A mournful poem.
Epicedium. A dirge.
Grumbler. One who continually speaks complainingly.
Heraclitus. The weeping philosopher.
Jeremiad. A tale of grief or woe. [Bible, *Jeremiah.*]
Monody. A melancholy literary composition.
Mourner. One who mourns.
Nenia. A funeral song.
Niobe. A woman of Grecian mythology, who was changed into a weeping stone, weeping for her children, slain by the gods.
Rachel. In Bible history the wife of Jacob, represented as weeping for her children.
Requiem. A hymn or service for the dead.
Threne. ⎱ An ode or song of lamentation.
Threnody. ⎰
Ulla-lulla. A lament for the dead.

LAMENTATION—*Nouns of Expression.*

Complaint. The expression of sorrow, pain, etc.
Cry. See CRY.
Deep sigh. See SIGH.
Dumps. A gloomy state of mind, the "doleful dumps," of *Chevy Chase.*
Fit of crying. Uncontrollable weeping.
Flood of tears. Great grief.
Frown. An expression of the face indicating displeasure.
Groan. See *Verbs.*
Grumble. See *Verbs.*
Heaving. A moving of the chest as in great grief.
Howl. A wail; a prolonged and mournful cry.

JUBILATION—LAMENTATION—*Continued.*

JUBILATION—*Verbs.*

Bless one's stars. To be thankful for one's good fortune.
Burst into a fit of laughter. See FIT OF LAUGHTER.
Burst out. To break out into laughter.
Cackle. To laugh in a broken, silly manner; to giggle.
Carol. To sing in a joyful strain.
Chirp. To give a quick, shrill cry of delight.
Chirrup. See CHIRP.
Chuckle. To laugh in a suppressed or broken manner, often in derision or mockery.
Clap one's hands. To applaud.
Congratulate oneself. To feel happiness over success, etc.
Crow. See CROW.
Cry for joy. To be so affected by feelings of joy as to cry.
Dance. To express joy by dancing.
Die with laughter. To be convulsed with laughter.
Exult. To rejoice exceedingly.
Fling up one's cap. To express joy by tossing up the cap.
Giggle. To laugh in a restrained and broken fashion, often sillily; to titter.
Grin. See *Nouns.*
Grin like a Cheshire cat. To show the teeth and gums in laughing.
Hold both one's sides. To laugh very heartily.
Hold jubilee. To rejoice or make merry.
Hug oneself. To congratulate oneself.
Hurrah. To give a shout of joy; to cheer.
Laugh. To give vent to laughter.
Laugh in one's sleeve. To be full of laughter without openly expressing it.
Laugh outright. To laugh openly and without restraint.
Leap with joy. To express joy by leaping.
Make merry. To rejoice or make merry.
Mock. To express pleasure at another's misfortune; to laugh in derision; to imitate.
Raise laughter, etc. To cause merriment.
Rejoice. To express pleasure or joy in any manner whatever.
Roar. To laugh noisily.
Roar with laughter. To laugh loudly.
Rub one's hands. To express satisfaction by the hands.
Shake one's sides. To be convulsed with great laughter.
Shout. To exult by shouting.
Simper. To smile in a silly, conceited manner.
Sing. To celebrate in song.
Skip. To leap about in a dancing fashion.
Smack the lips. To express relish or satisfaction by movements of the lips.
Smicker. To look amorously.
Smile. To give a joyous or pleasing expression to the countenance.
Smirk. To simper.
Snicker.
Snigger. } To laugh in a suppressed and often silly fashion.
Split. See SPLIT ONE'S SIDES.
Split one's sides. To laugh immoderately and uncontrollably.
Thank one's stars. See BLESS ONE'S STARS.
Titter. See GIGGLE.
Triumph. To rejoice or exult because of great success.

JUBILATION—*Adjectives.*

Convulsed with laughter. Moved by uncontrollable laughter.
Elated. Having the spirits raised by success.
Exultant. Rejoicing greatly.
Flushed. See FLUSH.
Jubilant. Manifesting or ready to manifest joy in shouts and songs.
Laughable. Tending to cause laughter.
Laughing, etc. See *Verbs.*
Ready to burst with laughter.
Ready to die with laughter. } Extremely amused.
Ready to split with laughter.
Rejoicing, etc. Expressing joy.
Risible. Prone to laugh.
Triumphant. Full of rejoicing because of success.

JUBILATION—*Interjections.*

Aha! An exclamation of triumph or mockery.
Hail! An exclamation of greeting or reverent salutation.
Heaven be praised! An exclamation of thanksgiving.
Hurrah! An exclamation of triumph.
Huzza! Same as hurrah.
Io triumphe! [L.] Hurrah!
So much the better! An expression of satisfaction.
Tant mieux! [F.] So much the better!
Tolderolloll! An exclamation of pleasure.

LAMENTATION—NOUNS OF EXPRESSION—*Continued.*

Knell. The tolling of a bell announcing a death or funeral.
Melting mood. A state of mind in which the feelings are easily affected.
Moan. A low mournful sound.
Murmur. A complaint uttered in a subdued voice.
Mutter. A complaining remark.
Outcry of wo. A loud wail of distress.
Plaint. A mournful expression of sorrow.
Scowl. An expression of the face indicating anger or extreme displeasure.
Scream. An expression of extreme fear or pain.
Sigh. A deep breath expressive of some distressing emotion. See *Verbs.*
Sob. A convulsive inhalation of air under the impulse of hysterical emotion. See *Verbs.*
Tear. A drop of the saline liquid which flows from the eyes in weeping.
Wail. A long-drawn sound of lamentation. See *Verbs.*
Whimper. A low, broken cry of complaint. See *Verbs.*
Whine. A plaintive cry, as of an animal in distress.

LAMENTATION—*Associated Words.*

Crape. Black material much worn in mourning.
Cypress. Any plant used as an emblem of mourning.
Deep mourning. Ordinary mourning intensified both as to garments and social intercourse. See MOURNING.
Lachrymatory. A small glass bottle to contain the tears of mourners.
Mourning. The black garments and crape worn in deep bereavement; also the condition of refraining from social intercourse.
Sackcloth and ashes. An expression of penitence or great grief.
Weeds. A token of mourning.
Willow. An emblem of sorrow.

LAMENTATION—*Verbs.*

Beat one's breast. To express great sorrow by striking the bosom.
Bellow like a bull. To roar with pain or grief.
Bemoan. To mourn for.
Bewail. To express grief in passionate utterance.
Bibber. To weep like a child.
Blubber. To sob in a childish, broken manner.
Burst into tears. To begin weeping suddenly.
Burst with grief. To be overcome with grief.
Clamor. To cry out repeatedly and in a noisy fashion.
Complain. To give expression to grief; also to find fault.
Complain without cause. To make useless objection.
Condole with. To express sympathy with.
Croak. To talk in a complaining manner; to grumble.
Cry. To express one's grief in tears; to weep.
Cry oneself blind. To weep excessively.
Cry one's eyes out. To weep continuously.
Cry out before one is hurt. Cry without cause.
Cry out lustily. To cry out in a strong, vigorous fashion.
Deplore. To regard some event of the past with regret or sorrow.
Deprecate. To express deep regret for.
Drop a tear. To have the feelings slightly moved; usually said of one not wont to shed tears.
Drop tears. To weep; usually said of one trying to repress his feelings.
Fetch a sigh. See HEAVE A SIGH.
Fondre en larmes [F.]. To melt in tears.
Fret. To worry; to express oneself peevishly.
Frown. To express displeasure. See *Nouns.*
Give a sigh. To sigh.
Give sorrow words. To give expression to one's sorrow.
Gnash one's teeth. To strike the teeth together as in rage or anguish.
Go into mourning. To wear emblems of mourning. See *Nouns.*
Greet. To weep.
Grieve. To sorrow over, often silently.
Groan. To utter a low moaning sound.
Growl. To give an angry guttural sound.
Grumble. To find fault.
Grunt. To give a short groan.
Heave a sigh. To sigh as with an effort.
Infandum renovare dolorem [L.]. To revive unspeakable grief. [Virgil, Æneid, 2, 1.]
Lament. To feel or express sorrow.
Make a fuss about. To grieve too much about trivial matters.
Make a wry face. To show displeasure by a distortion of the face.
Maunder. To complain in a broken, foolish manner.

JUBILATION—LAMENTATION—*Continued.*

JUBILATION—*Phrases.*

Le roi est mort, vive le roi ! [F.]   The king is dead, long live the king!
Thalatta ! thalatta ! [Gr.]   The sea! the sea!   The cry of the Greeks marching home from Persia, when they sighted the Mediterranean.
The heart leaping with joy.

LAMENTATION—ADJECTIVES—*Continued from Column 2.*

Lachrimose.   Given to shedding tears.
Lamenting, etc.   See *Verbs.*
"Like Niobe all tears."   Shedding tears profusely, like the stone into which Niobe was turned.   [*Hamlet,* I, ii.]
Mournful.   Oppressed with grief.
Plaintful.   Given to expressing sorrow.
Plaintive.   Given to, or characterized by, expressions of subdued sadness.
Querimonious.   Querulous.
Querulous.   Given to complaining.
Sorrowful.   Expressing deep sorrow.
Sorrowing, etc.   See *Verbs.*
Tearful.   Shedding tears.
With moisture in one's eyes.⎫
With moistened eyes.   ⎬ Ready to cry.
With tears in one's eyes.   Weeping.
With watery eyes.   Crying.

LAMENTATION—*Adverbs.*

De profundis [L.].   Out of the depths.
Les larmes aux yeux [F.].   Tears in the eyes.

LAMENTATION—*Interjections.*

Ah me!   An exclamation of sorrow.
Alack!   An exclamation of regret or sorrow.
Alackaday!   See ALACK.
Alas!   An exclamation of sorrow.
Alas the day!   Oh, unfortunate day.
Heigh-ho!   An exclamation of either joy or disappointment.
Lackadaisy!   See ALACK.
Lackaday!   See ALACKADAY.
Miserabile dictu ! [L.]   Sorrowful to tell!
O dear!   An exclamation of either surprise or disappointment.
O lud lud!   Vulgar form of O Lord Lord.
O tempora ! O mores !   O the times! O the manners!
Too true!
Welladay!   See WELLAWAY.
Wellaway!   Wo is me.
What a pity!⎫
Wo is me!   ⎬ Exclamation of regret.

LAMENTATION—*Phrases.*

Eyes brimming with tears; eyes overflowing with tears; eyes suffused with tears; eyes swimming with tears; tears standing in the eyes; tears starting from the eyes.

LAMENTATION—VERBS—*Continued.*

Melt in tears.   To be so moved in feeling that tears flow freely.
Mew.   To give the plaintive cry of a cat.
Moan.   To give a low mournful sound, more plaintive than a groan.
Mourn.   To weep.
Murmur.   To find fault in a low subdued tone
Mutter.   To complain in indistinct tones.
Pipe.   To weep.
Pipe one's eye.   To weep.
Pule.   To cry complainingly, as a child.
Put on mourning.   To wear emblems of sorrow.
Rend the air.   To cause the air to vibrate with cries of pain or anguish.
Roar.   To express one's grief in a loud boisterous manner.
Roar like a bull.   See BELLOW LIKE A BULL.
Roll on the ground.   To express great grief by throwing oneself on the earth.
Scream.   To give a shrill loud cry.
Scowl.   To express displeasure by contortion of the face.   See *Nouns.*
Shed a tear.   See DROP A TEAR.
Shed tears.   See DROP TEARS.
Sigh.   To take a deep, long-drawn, and audible respiration, expressive of some emotion, as grief.
Sigh like a furnace.   To sigh deeply and continuously.   [Shakespeare, *As You Like It.*]
Snivel.   To cry whiningly; also, to affect crying.
Sob.   To utter or weep convulsively.
Tear one's hair.   To pull one's hair; an expression of great grief.
"Waft a sigh from Indus to the pole."   To give forth a deep mournful sigh.   [Pope, *Eloisa to Abelard.*]
Wail.   To cry loudly.
Wear mourning.   To wear emblems of sorrow.   See *Nouns.*
Wear sackcloth and ashes.   To wear garments expressive of grief or sorrow.
Wear the willow.   To be in mourning because of the absence, death, or broken plight of a lover.
Weep.   To shed tears.
Weep over.   To weep because of.
Whimper.   To cry in low broken tones.
Whine.   See WHINE.
Wring one's hands.   To clasp the hands and twist them in great anguish or grief.

LAMENTATION—*Adjectives.*

Bathed in tears.   Shedding tears profusely.
Dissolved in tears.   Entirely overcome with grief.
Elegiac.   Sad or plaintive.
In mourning.   Wearing visible signs of mourning.
In tears.   Weeping.
In sackcloth and ashes.   Wearing sackcloth and ashes.
In the melting mood.   See MELTING MOOD.

(*Continued on Column* 1.)

---

ju′-bi-lee.   A season of festivity.   ENTERTAINMENT-WEARINESS, JUBILATION-LAMENTATION, PERIODIC-ITY-IRREGULARITY, SOLEMNIZATION.
ju-cund′-i-ty.   Pleasantness.   PLEASURABLENESS-PAIN-FULNESS.
Judæus Apella credat [L.] (jiu-dê′-e-ʋs ɑ-pel′-lɑ crî′-dat).   Let Apella, the superstitious Jew, believe it.   ADAGE-NONSENSE, FAITH-MISGIVING.
Ju-da′-i-cal.   Pertaining to the Jewish polity.   OR-THODOXY-HETERODOXY.
Ju′-da-ism.   Jewish polity.   ORTHODOXY-HETERODOXY.
Ju′-das.   The false disciple.   GULL-DECEIVER, PATRI-OTISM-TREASON, UPRIGHTNESS-ROGUE;   **Judas kiss,** TRUTHFULNESS-FALSEHOOD, UPRIGHTNESS-DISHON-ESTY.
judge.   A judicial officer; a connoisseur.   ADVOCATE, CHIEF-UNDERLING, DECISION-MISJUDGMENT, JUDGE, JUDICATURE, PRESIDENT-MEMBER, TASTE-VULGAR-ITY.

JUDGE.

Arbiter.   One chosen or appointed to settle matters in dispute.
Arbitrator.   One who has appointed power to judge disputes.
Archon.   A judge of ancient Athens.

Assessor.   An officer often in association with a judge to assess taxes.
Assistant judge.   A judge whose office is to assist the chief judge.
Barmaster.   A judge.
Beak.   [Slang.]   A magistrate.
Cadi.   A Turkish chief judge.
Censor.   A judge of ancient Rome.
Chancellor.   A judge in a court of equity.
Common sergeant.   An English court officer.
County-court judge.   The magistrate presiding over county courts.
Domesman.   A judge in the old English courts.
Ephor.   An ancient Spartan magistrate.
J. P.   Justice of the peace.
Judge.   A judicial officer with invested power to administer justice.
Judge of assize.   An English court judge.
Jurat.   An English municipal officer resembling an alderman.
Jury.   A body of men sworn to try a cause.
Justice.   A judge.
Justice of assize.   An English court judge.
Justice of the peace.   A judge of minor cases.
Justiciar.   A judge; formerly chief justice.
Justiciary.   A high judicial officer.
Kadi.   A Turkish judge.
Magistrate.   Usually, a minor local justice.
Mollah.   A Mohammedan judge.
Mufti.   A Turkish court officer.
Podesta.   An Italian magistrate.
Police magistrate.   A judge of a police court.

Prætor. A Roman judge ranking next to the consul

Puisne judge. An inferior judge.

Recorder. A criminal magistrate in a city or borough.

Referee. One appointed by a court to decide matters between litigants.

Referendary. One to whose decision some case is referred.

Revising barrister. One of a board appointed annually to revise the list of Parliamentary electors.

Rhadamanthus. A very just judge in Hades.

Syndic. Head of a university, college, or corporation.

Ulema. The body of Moslem doctors of the law who interpret the Koran.

Umpire. Person chosen to pass judgment on a case in controversy

JUDGE—*Nouns of Place.*

Court. A place where justice is administered. See TRIBUNAL

Tribune. A rostrum; platform.

JUDGE—*Nouns of Title.*

Attorney-General. Chief law officer of a state or the nation.

Baron. A noble of the lower order.

Baron of the Exchequer. A judge of the Court of Exchequer.

Chancellor. Chief justice of a court of equity.

His honor. The honorary title addressed to a judge.

His lordship. }
His worship. } Forms of address to a judge.

Judge Advocate. Person appointed to act as prosecutor at a court martial

Lord Chancellor. The title of England's chief magistrate.

Lord Chief Baron. The highest rank of the barons.

Lord Chief Justice. The highest rank of the justices of Court of Queen's Bench.

Lord Justice. The justice ranking after the Lord President.

Master in Chancery. Officer of a court of equity who assists the judge.

Master of the Rolls. One of the judges of the chancery division of the High Court of Justice, the keeper of the rolls of all patents and grants that pass the great seal, and all records of the Court of Chancery.

Mr. Justice. Honorary title addressed to a justice.

Prothonotary. A chief notary, or clerk.

Vice-Chancellor. A judge next in rank to a chancellor.

JUDGE—*Associated Noun.*

Litigant. A party to a lawsuit. See JUSTIFICATION-CHARGE.

JUDGE—*Verbs.*

Adjudge. To pass judgment upon. See DECISION

Try a case. To bring a case to trial.

Try a prisoner. To bring a prisoner to trial.

JUDGE—*Adjective.*

Judicial. Pertaining to a court or judge.

JUDGE—*Phrases.*

"A Daniel come to judgment." A just judge. Shakespeare, *Merchant of Venice.*

Twelve men in a box. Figurative for jury.

Judge. God, the Judge of the world. DEITY.

Judg'-ment. The final award or sentence of the human race. **Day of Judgment,** BEGINNING-END.

judg'-ment. The act or faculty of judging. DECISION-MISJUDGMENT, DIFFERENTIATION-INDISCRIMINATION, EXCULPATION-PUNITION, MIND-IMBECILITY, SAGACITY-INCAPACITY. .

judg'-ment–seat". The seat from which judgment is delivered. TRIBUNAL.

judicata, res [L.] (jiu-di-kê'-ta, rîz). An adjudged case. CERTAINTY-DOUBT, DECISION-MISJUDGMENT.

ju''-di-ca'-tion. Act of passing judgment DECISION-MISJUDGMENT.

ju'-di-ca-to-ry. Juridical; tribunal JUDICATURE, TRIBUNAL

ju'-di-ca-ture. The jurisdiction of a court. JUDICATURE

JUDICATURE.

Administration of justice. Act of administering or managing public affairs

Commission of the peace. A commission for the appointment of justices of the peace.

Executive. The officer who superintends the execution of the laws

Judicature. The administration of justice by trial and judgment

Jurisdiction. Lawful exercise of official authority.

Magistracy. The office of a magistrate. See RULE

Soc. The power of holding court in a district. [Anglo-Saxon.]

Tribunal. A court of justice.

JUDICATURE—*Nouns of Agent.*

Alcalde [Sp.]. Chief magistrate of a city of Spain.

Alguazil [Sp.]. A constable.

Bailiff. A court officer.

Beadle. An under officer in a parish.

Bedel. See BEADLE.

Bumbailiff. An under bailiff.

Bumbledom. Sarcastic for the petty pomposity of minor officials.

Catchpoll. A sheriff's officer to make arrests.

Constable. A civil officer appointed to make arrests.

Constabulary. The body of constables.

Coroner. An officer to inquire into sudden deaths.

Custom-house officer. A person authorized to do custom-house business.

Douanier. A customs officer.

Edile. A magistrate of Rome who superintended public buildings

Exciseman. An officer who collects excise duties.

Gager. An officer who ascertains the contents of casks.

Gendarme [F.]. A French policeman.

Hussar [G.]. A light cavalryman of the Hungarian police.

Judge. A civil officer who hears causes and administers justice.

Kavass. A Turkish police officer.

Lictor [L.]. A Roman officer in attendance upon a consul.

Lord lieutenant. A high official representing the sovereign.

Mace-bearer. An officer who carries a mace on public occasions.

Officer. A person authorized to fill a public position.

Paritor. A beadle.

Police constable. A member of the police force.

Police force. An organized body of police.

Policeman. An officer whose duty is the preservation of order, and the prevention and detection of crime.

Police sergeant. A superior police officer.

Portreeve. The chief magistrate in a maritime town.

Posse comitatus [L.]. The power of a county.

Press-gang. A party of seamen under an officer with power to impress men into naval service.

Sbirro [It.]. An Italian police officer.

Sheriff. The chief county officer who executes court decrees.

Tipstaff. An officer who bears a staff tipped with metal; a sheriff's attendant.

JUDICATURE—*Associated Nouns.*

Bailiwick. The jurisdiction of a bailiff.

Corporation. A body of persons empowered to transact business as one person

Municipality. An incorporated town possessing a charter conferring local self-government.

Shrievalty. The jurisdiction of a sheriff.

JUDICATURE—*Verbs*

Judge. To try judicially.

Sit in judgment. To deliberate for a judicial decision.

JUDICATURE—*Adjectives.*

Administrative. Administrating; executive.

Causidical. Pertaining to an advocate or the maintenance and defense of suits.

Executive. Pertaining to the execution of the laws or the conduct of affairs.

Inquisitorial. Pertaining to inquisition.

Judicatory. Pertaining to the administration of justice.

Judicial. Pertaining to courts of justice or to a judge.

Judiciary. Of or pertaining to courts of judicature, or legal tribunals.

Juridical. Pertaining to a judge or to jurisprudence.

Municipal. Of or pertaining to a city or corporation having the right of administering local government.

JUDICATURE—*Adverb*

Coram judice [L.] Before the judge.

judg'-ing. Deciding. DECISION-MISJUDGMENT.

Ju'-di-ca-ture. A court. **High Court of Judicature,** TRIBUNAL.

judice, coram [L.] (jiu'-di-sî, cor'-am). In the presence of a judge. JUDICATURE, LITIGATION.

judice, me [L.] (jiu'-di-sî, mî) In my judgment. DECISION-MISJUDGMENT.

judice, sub [L.] (jiu'-di-sî, sub). On trial. INVESTIGATION-ANSWER, LITIGATION.

ju-di'-cial. Pertaining to a court or judge. JUDGE, JUDICATURE, TRIBUNAL; **judicial astrology,** PROPHECY; **judicial murder,** LIFE-KILLING; **judicial separation,** MATRIMONY-DIVORCE.

ju-di'-ci-a-ry. Judges taken collectively. JUDICATURE.

ju-di'-cious. Prudent. DECISION-MISJUDGMENT, SAGACITY-INCAPACITY.

jug. A vessel. CONTENTS-RECEIVER.

Jug'-ger-naut. The lord of the world. [Hind.] DEVOTION-IDOLATRY, JOVE-FIEND, LIFE-KILLING.

jug'-gle. To trick. CRAFT-ARTLESSNESS, TRUTHFULNESS-FRAUD.

jug'-gler. A trickster. GULL-DECEIVER.

ju'-gu-lar. A vein. ANATOMY.

ju'-gu-late. To cut the throat of. LIFE-KILLING.

juice. The fluid part of vegetable or animal matter. LIQUID-GAS.

juice'-less. Devoid of juice. DAMPNESS-DRYNESS.

jui'-cy. Full of juice. DAMPNESS-DRYNESS, LIQUID-GAS.

ju'-jube A sweetmeat. SWEETNESS-ACIDITY.

ju'-lep. A sweetened drink. SWEETNESS-ACIDITY.

Ju'-li-an. Pertaining to Julius Cæsar. **Julian calendar,** ASTRONOMY.

jum'-ble. A confused mixture. MIXTURE-HOMOGENEITY, ORGANIZATION-DISORGANIZATION, REGULARITY-IRREGULARITY.

ju'-ment. A beast. CONVEYER.

jump. To leap over. CAREFULNESS-CARELESSNESS, REVOLUTION, SPRING-DIVE; **at one jump,** ETERNITY-INSTANTANEITY; **jump about,** AGITATION; **jump at,** CONSENT, DESIRE-DISTASTE, HURRY-LEISURE, QUEST-EVASION, READINESS-RELUCTANCE, TAKING-RESTITUTION; **jump over,** CAREFULNESS-CARELESSNESS; **jump to a conclusion,** CREDULOUSNESS-SKEPTICISM, DECISION-MISJUDGMENT; **jump up,** ELEVATION-DEPRESSION, SPRING-DIVE.

junc'-tion. The act of joining or condition of being joined. UNION-DISUNION.

junc'-ture. A joint. CONDITION-SITUATION, OPPORTUNENESS-UNSUITABLENESS, UNION-DISUNION.

jun'-gle. A thicket. FAUNA-FLORA, REGULARITY-IRREGULARITY.

jun'-ior. Younger, or lower in rank. INFANCY-AGE.

junk. A large vessel. CONVEYANCE-VESSEL.

jun'-ket. A delicacy; a picnic. ENTERTAINMENT-WEARINESS, NUTRIMENT-EXCRETION.

Ju'-no. A Latin goddess PARDON-VINDICTIVENESS.

junta [Sp.]. A council. COUNCIL.

jun'-to. A faction. ASSOCIATION.

jupe. A petticoat, or skirt. DRESS-UNDRESS.

Ju'-pi-ter. The supreme Roman god. JOVE-FIEND.

Jupiter ne quidem omnibus placet [L.] (jiu'-pi-ter nî quai'-dem om'-ni-bus plê'-set). Not even Jupiter pleases all. CONTENTEDNESS-DISCONTENTMENT.

Jupiter, quem .. vult perdere, dementat prius [L.] (quem jiu'-pi-ter vult per'-der-î, dî-men'-tat prai'-us). Whom Jupiter wishes to destroy he first makes mad. FAVORITE-ANGER, LOVE-HATE.

jurare in verba magistri [L.] (jiu-rê'-rî in ver'-ba majis'-trai) To swear with the words of a master. CREDULOUSNESS-SKEPTICISM, DECISION-MISJUDGMENT

Ju-ras'-sic pe'-ri-od. A period in geology. GEOLOGY.

ju'-rat. A sworn officer. JUDGE.

jure, de [L.] (jiu'-rî, dî). By law. DUENESS-UNDUENESS, LAW-LAWLESSNESS.

jure divino [L.] (jiu'-rî di-vai'-no). By divine right. DIVINITY, DUENESS-UNDUENESS.

ju-rid'-ic-al. Relating to law. JUDICATURE.

ju''-ris-con'-sult. A jurist. ADVOCATE.

ju''-ris-dic'-tion. Lawful power. JUDICATURE, RULE-LICENSE.

ju''-ris-pru'-dence. The science of law. LAW-LAWLESSNESS.

ju'-rist. One versed in the science of law.

ju'-ry. A body of men chosen and sworn to try a cause. JUDGE; **empanel a jury,** LITIGATION; **jury-box,** TRIBUNAL; **jury-mast,** COMMUTATION-PERMUTATION.

jus civile [L.] (jus si-vai'-li). The civil law. LAW-LAWLESSNESS.

jus et norma loquendi [L.] (jus et nor'-ma lo-quen'-dai). The law and rule of speaking. GRAMMAR-SOLECISM.

jus gentium [L.] (jus jen'-shi-um). The law of nations. LAW-LAWLESSNESS.

jus nocendi [L.] (jus no-sen'-dai). The law of retaliation. RULE-LICENSE.

jus oritur, ex facto [L.] (jus or'-i-tur, ex fac'-to). The law arises out of fact. TRUTH-ERROR.

jus, summum [L.] (jus, sum'-mum). The highest law RIGHT-WRONG.

just. Fair; upright. GODLINESS-UNGODLINESS, NOVELTY-ANTIQUITY, RIGHT-WRONG, TRUTH-ERROR, UPRIGHTNESS-DISHONESTY; **just as,** COEXISTENCE, LIKENESS-UNLIKENESS; **just do,** ENOUGH; **just in time,** OPPORTUNENESS - UNSUITABLENESS; **just now,** TIME; **just out,** NOVELTY-ANTIQUITY; **just reasoning,** RATIOCINATION-INSTINCT; **just so,** ASSENT-DISSENT; **just then,** ETERNITY-INSTANTANEITY; **just the thing,** HARMONY-DISCORD, TRUTH-ERROR.

juste milieu [F.] (zhůst mi-liu'). The golden mean. MIDCOURSE-CIRCUIT, MIDDLE, TURBULENCE-CALMNESS.

jus'-tice. Rectitude; impartiality. JUDGE, LAW-LAWLESSNESS, RIGHT - WRONG; UPRIGHTNESS - DISHONESTY; **administration of justice,** JUDICATURE; **bring to justice,** LITIGATION; **court of justice,** TRIBUNAL; **do justice to,** APPROVAL-DISAPPROVAL, DUTY-DERELICTION, JUSTIFICATION-CHARGE, NUTRIMENT-EXCRETION; **justice seat,** TRIBUNAL; **not do justice to,** OVERVALUATION-UNDERVALUATION; **retributive justice,** EXCULPATION-PUNITION.

justice, main de [F.] (zhůs-ts', man· de). The hand of justice. LAW-LAWLESSNESS.

jus-ti'-ci-ar. A chief justice. JUDGE.

jus-ti'-ci-a-ry. A judge. JUDGE.

jus'-ti-fi''-a-ble. Vindicated. JUSTIFICATION-CHARGE, RIGHT-WRONG.

jus''-ti-fi-ca'-tion. The act of justifying. GODLINESS-UNGODLINESS, JUSTIFICATION-CHARGE.

JUSTIFICATION—CHARGE

Acquittal. A discharge from accusation by judicial action.

Exculpation. The state of being freed from blame.

Exoneration. The state of being freed from a charge, accusation, imputation, obligation, or the like.

Extenuation. Palliation.

Justification. Vindication; defense.

Mitigation. The state of making less severe.

Palliation. The making to appear less guilty or offensive.

Softening. A making soft; mitigating.

Vindication. The state or act of proving true, right, or correct against denial, censure, or objection.

Whitewashing. An attempt to render fair and reputable what is doubtful or corrupt

Accrimination. An accusation.

Accusation. A charge of crime or misconduct.

Charge. What is alleged or brought forward by way of accusation.

Crimination. The act of accusing.

Denouncement. The act of accusing publicly.

Denunciation. The act of declaring a person worthy of reprobation or punishment.

Detraction. The act of taking away from the good name of another.

Exprobation. The act of censuring.

Gravamen of a charge. The burden of complaint against a person.

Head and front of one's offending. The special cause of offense.

Impeachment. A discrediting or calling in question of motives or conduct.

JUSTIFICATION—CHARGE—Continued

JUSTIFICATION—*Nouns of Agent, etc.*

Apologist. One who argues in defense of a person or cause.
Defendant. A person against whom a suit is brought.
Justifier. One who justifies; a vindicator.
Vindicator. A defender.

JUSTIFICATION—*Nouns of Means.*

Allowance. Toleration; sanction.
Allowance to be made. Recognition of modifying circumstances.
Apology. A justification or defense for what appears to others to be wrong.
Defense. A plea in justification, vindication, or support.
Excuse. A plea or reason exonerating one from a seeming fault.
Extenuating circumstances. Circumstances that serve to diminish the gravity or importance of an act.
Justifiable charge. A charge which is justified.
Locus pænitentiæ [L.]. Place for repentance.
Palliative. That which serves to palliate or extenuate.
Plea. Something urged in defense or justification of a course, past or proposed
Recrimination. A charge made by the accused against the accuser.
Reply. A plaintiff's answer to a defendant's plea or answer.
Salvo. A saving clause; proviso.
True bill. The indorsement by a grand jury on a bill of indictment which they find to be sustained by the evidence.
Varnish. A favorable representation, evil or false.
Warrant. A judicial writ or order authorizing officers to make arrests, searches, or seizures.

JUSTIFICATION—*Verbs.*

Acquit. To free or clear from an accusation.
Advocate. To defend in argument before a tribunal.
Apologize. To acknowledge with regret a delinquency.
Be an excuse for. To acquit of blame.
Bear out. To support; confirm; justify.
Be justified by the event. Shown to be just by the final outcome.
Bolster up. To give countenance to.
Clear. To purge from the imputation of guilt.
Confess and avoid. To set up new matter in defense without denying the plaintiff's plea.
Contend for. To maintain by argument.
Defend. To uphold by argument.
Disculpate. To exculpate.
Do justice to. To vindicate.
Exculpate. To vindicate from unjust charge or reproach.
Excuse. To absolve or free from imputation of fault.
Exonerate. To relieve or vindicate from accusation.
Extenuate. To diminish the gravity or importance of.
Furnish a handle. To give an excuse.
Give one his due. To give one the benefit of fair consideration.
Give the devil his due. To do justice to one hated or despised.
Gloss over. To palliate by specious explanation; to use fair words for ugly things.
Gloze. To palliate by specious representation.
Help a lame dog over a stile. To offer excuse for one.
Justify. To show to be just.
Keep in countenance. To give approval.
Lend a color. To afford a justification.
Make allowance for. To give recognition to modifying circumstances.
Make good. To defend successfully.
Mince. To diminish the strength or importance of.
Palliate. To cause to appear less guilty or offensive; to cloak.
Plead. To adduce in extenuation or vindication.
Plead ignorance. To ask for palliation on account of an absence of information.
Plead one's cause. To allege as an excuse or defense or as a reason for concession or favor; to adduce in extenuation or vindication.
Propugn. To contend or fight for.
Prove one's case. To establish one's position by argument.
Prove the truth of. To make clear that something is a fact.
Put a gloss upon. To palliate by specious explanation.
Put a good face upon. To make to appear at the best.
Put in a good word for. Take the part of.
Say in defense. To say in justification.
Set right. To rectify; make right; correct.
Slur. To pass over lightly.
Soften. To make less harsh; to mitigate.
Speak for. To argue or plead for.
Speak up for. To speak in one's favor.
Stand up for. To side with and defend.
Stick up for. To defend or uphold.

Imputation. Accusation, reproach, or censure.
Incrimination. The act of charging with a crime or fault.
Inculpation. The act of charging with wrong-doing.
Libel. Slander written or published in print.
Recrimination. A charge made by the accused against the accuser.
Scandal. Malicious repetition and spreading of evil reports against a person.
Scandalum magnatum [L.]. Defamation of persons of rank and dignity.
Slur. A slighting or contemptuous remark or accusation.
Tu quoque **argument.** A retort in which the person assailed answers with a similar charge against the accuser.

CHARGE—*Nouns of Agent, etc*

Accused. One against whom a charge is made.
Accuser. One who accuses.
Appellant. One who appeals or removes a cause from a lower to a higher tribunal.
Defendant. A person against whom a suit is brought.
Informer. One who informs against others.
Litigant. A party to a lawsuit.
Plaintiff. The party that begins an action at law.
Prisoner. One who is confined in a prison.
Prosecutor. One who institutes and carries on a suit.
Relator. A complainant or petitioner in chancery.
Respondent. The party called upon to answer an appeal or petition

CHARGE—*Nouns of Means, etc.*

Appeachment. Making information against; impeachment.
Argumentum ad hominem [L.]. An argument to the man.
Arraignment. The act of calling and setting a prisoner before a court to answer to an accusation.
Bill of indictment. A declaration in writing expressing some wrong the complainant has suffered.
Challenge. An exception taken.
Citation. A judicial summons to appear and answer.
Condemnation. The act of condemning.
Delation. An accusation, especially by an informer.
Indictment. A formal charge or accusation.
Invective. Utterance intended to cast opprobrium, censure, or reproach.
Lawsuit. An action in a court of law, equity, or admiralty, for enforcement of a claim or right.
Panel. The body of persons composing a jury.
True bill. The indorsement by a grand jury on a bill of indictment which they find to be sustained by the evidence.

CHARGE—*Verbs.*

Accuse. To charge with crime, misconduct, or culpable error.
Appeach. To censure; to reproach.
Arraign. To call or set at the bar of the court to plead guilty or not guilty, to the charge in the indictment.
Brand with reproach. To fix the character of infamy upon.
Bring an action against. To bring suit against to demand a right.
Bring home to. To prove conclusively.
Call to account. To demand explanation of.
Cast a slur on. To make a slighting or contemptuous remark about
Cast a stone at. To stigmatize.
Cast in one's teeth. To make a reproach.
Cast the first stone at. To bring the first charge against.
Challenge. To call in question.
Charge. To allege or bring forward by way of accusation
Charge with. To lay or impute something to.
Cite. To summon to appear before a tribunal.
Criminate. To accuse of a crime.
Denounce. To point out or publicly accuse.
Have a crow to pluck with. To have a quarrel to settle.
Have a rod in pickle for. To have a punishment in reserve.
Have up. To call before a court.
Impeach. To charge with a crime or misdemeanor.
Implicate. To bring into connection with.
Impute. To charge to one as the author, responsible originator, or possessor of.
Incriminate. To charge with a crime or fault
Inculpate. To bring or expose to blame.
Indict. To find or declare chargeable with crime.
Inform against. To communicate a knowledge of facts to any one, as by way of accusation.
Keep a rod in pickle for. To keep an argument in reserve
Lay the blame on. To blame.
Lay to one's charge. To charge with.
Lay to one's door. To accuse of a fault.

JUSTIFICATION—CHARGE—*Continued.*

JUSTIFICATION—Verbs—*Continued*

Support. To show to be true or trustworthy.
Take the will for the deed. To make good intentions an excuse for want of action.
Varnish. To disguise or palliate.
Vindicate. To support as right, true, or correct against denial, censure, or objection.
Warrant. To assure or guarantee the quality, accuracy, certainty, or sufficiency of.
Whitewash. To attempt to render fair and reputable what is doubtful or corrupt; especially in politics.

JUSTIFICATION—*Adjectives.*

Apologetic. Expressing regret for fault or failure.
Defensible. Capable of being defended, maintained, or justified.
Exculpatory. Tending to or resulting in exculpation.
Excusable. Admitting of excuse or pardon.
Justifiable. Capable of being justified.
Palliative. Extenuating.
Pardonable. That may be pardoned or shown clemency or indulgence.
Plausible. Seeming likely to be true though open to doubt.
Specious. Appearing right or correct at first sight.
Veniable. Excusable.
Venial. That may be pardoned, forgiven, overlooked, or tolerated.
Vindicated. Justified.
Vindicating. That proves true, right, or real.
Vindicative. Contributing to vindication.
Vindicatory. Bringing vindication.

JUSTIFICATION—*Phrases.*

Al buon vino non bisogna frasca [It.]. "Good wine needs no bush.
"*Honi soit qui mal y pense*" [F.]. Evil to him who evil thinks. [The motto of Great Britain.]

CHARGE—Adjectives—*Continued from Column 2.*

Vicious. Corrupt in conduct or habits.
In the watch-house. Imprisoned in the building occupied by the watch or guard.

CHARGE—*Interjections.*

Look at home!
Tu quoque! [L.] Thou, also! See REPRISAL.

CHARGE—*Phrase.*

Gli assenti hanno torti [It.]. The absent are in the wrong.

----

jus'-ti-fied. Saved by faith. GODLINESS-UNGODLINESS.
Justitia soror incorrupta Fides [L.] (jus-tish'-i-a so'-ror in-cor-rup'-ta fai'-dîz). Uncorruptible Faith, sister of Justice. FAITH-MISGIVING, RIGHT-WRONG.
justitia virtutum regina [L.] (jus-tish'-i-a vir-tiu'-tum rî-jai'-na). Justice is the queen of the virtues. RIGHT-WRONG, VIRTUE-VICE.
jus'-tle. To hustle. IMPETUS-REACTION, STRIFE-PEACE.

CHARGE—Verbs—*Continued.*

Lodge a complaint. To make a formal presentation of the commission of an offense.
Prosecute. To bring suit against for redress of wrong or punishment of crime.
Pull up. To extirpate; to eradicate.
Put in the black book. To charge with wrong.
Reproach. To charge with or blame for something wrong or disgraceful.
Saddle with. To load with a burden of blame.
Show up. To expose, as a fraud.
Slur. To treat with slighting contempt.
Stigmatize. To fix a mark of infamy upon.
Take to blame. To accuse of fault.
Take to task. To charge with a fault.
Taunt with. To remind spitefully or contemptuously of **one's** doings or condition.
Tax. To censure.
Throw in one's teeth. To fling a taunt at one.
Trump up a charge. To make up or invent a charge.
Twit. To tease by reminding of something discreditable.

CHARGE—*Adjectives.*

Accusable. Chargeable with crime.
Accusative. Producing accusations.
Accusatory. Pertaining to or containing an accusation.
Accused. Charged with crime or wrong.
Accusing. Censuring.
Criminatory. Involving accusation.
Denunciatory. Threatening.
Imputable. Chargeable with a fault.
Imputative. Transferred or transmitted by imputation.
In custody. Under guard.
Indefensible. Not capable of being defended or maintained.
In detention. Kept confined or detained.
Inexcusable. Not admitting excuse or justification.
In the house of detention. In prison.
In the lockup. In the place where persons are temporarily **confined** when under arrest.
Recriminatory. Accusing in return.
Suspected. Under surveillance as a suspicious character.
Under a cloud. Overshadowed by difficulties; having one's reputation injuriously affected.
Under suspicion. Mistrusted.
Under surveillance. Watched or guarded.
Unjustifiable. Not able to be proved to be just.
Unpardonable. That may not be shown clemency or pardoned.

(*Continued on Column 1.*)

----

jute. A vegetable fiber. LAMINA-FIBER.
jut out. To project. CONVEXITY-CONCAVITY.
jut'-ty. Jetty. CONVEXITY-CONCAVITY.
ju''-ve-nes'-cence. A growing youthful. INFANCY-AGE.
ju'-ve-nile. Youthful. INFANCY-AGE.
ju''-ve-nil'-i-ty. Youthfulness. INFANCY-AGE.
jux''-ta-po-si'-tion. Contiguity. INTERSPACE-CONTACT.

K

ka'-di. An Oriental magistrate. JUDGE.

kail. A ninepin. AMUSEMENT-WEARINESS.

kai'-ser. The title of the German Emperor. CHIEF-UNDERLING.

ka-lei'-do-scope. A kind of optical instrument. OPTICAL INSTRUMENTS, VARIEGATION.

kalon, to [Gr.] (ka-lon', to). The beautiful. BEAUTY-UGLINESS.

kan''-ga-roo'. An Australian animal. SPRING-DIVE.

kat' exochen [Gr.] (kat ex-o-hên'). Par excellence. CONSEQUENCE-INSIGNIFICANCE, MAGNITUDE-SMALLNESS, SUPREMACY-SUBORDINACY.

Kat-er-fel'-to. A noted sorcerer. MAGICIAN.

kath'-ode. A pole of a battery. ELECTRICITY.

ka-vass'. A Turkish police officer. JUDICATURE.

kay'-ak. A light canoe made of skin. CONVEYANCE-VESSEL.

ka''-zi-as-kier'. A title given in Turkey to two of the principal officers of the Ulema. MINISTRY-LAITY.

K. C. King's Counsel. ADVOCATE.

keck. To vomit. ADMISSION-EXPULSION.

kedge. A light anchor; to move by means of a grounded anchor. CONVEYANCE-VESSEL, REFUGE-PITFALL, TRAVELING-NAVIGATION.

keel. The principal timber in a ship. TOP-BOTTOM; **keel upwards,** REVERSAL.

keel'-haul''. A kind of punishment. RECOMPENSE-PUNITION.

keen. Sharp; cold; sensitive; active; eager. DESIRE-DISTASTE, FEELING-INSENSIBILITY, HEAT-COLD, SAGACITY-INCAPACITY, SHARPNESS-BLUNTNESS, VIGOR-INERTIA; **keen blast,** RIVER-WIND.

keen'-eyed''. Sharp-sighted. SAGACITY-INCAPACITY, SIGHT-BLINDNESS.

keen'-ness. Sharpness. DESIRE-DISTASTE, VIGOR-INERTIA.

keen''-sight'-ed. With penetrating sight. SAGACITY-INCAPACITY.

keen''-wit'-ted. With a sharp wit. SAGACITY-INCAPACITY.

keep. To hold; preserve; withhold; observe; support; guard; store up. ATTACK-DEFENSE, CONSERVATION, DISCONTINUANCE-CONTINUANCE, FREQUENCY - RARITY, KEEPING-RELINQUISHMENT, MUTATION-PERMANENCE, NUTRIMENT-EXCRETION, OBSERVANCE-NONOBSERVANCE, PROVISION-WASTE, REFUGE-PITFALL, RELEASE-PRISON, RELEASE-RESTRAINT, SOLEMNIZATION, STORE; **keep accounts,** ACCOUNTS; **keep a good lookout for,** EXPECTATION - SURPRISE; **keep alive,** CONSERVATION, LIFE-DEATH; **keep aloof,** QUEST-EVASION, REMOTENESS-NEARNESS, SOCIABILITY-PRIVACY; **keep an account with,** CREDIT-DEBT; **keep an eye upon,** CAREFULNESS-CARELESSNESS; **keep apart,** UNION-DISUNION; **keep a secret,** ENLIGHTENMENT-SECRECY, TALKATIVENESS-TACITURNITY; **keep a shop,** OCCUPATION; **keep away,** PRESENCE-ABSENCE; **keep back,** EARLINESS - LATENESS, ENLIGHTENMENT-SECRECY, KEEPING-RELINQUISHMENT, MANIFESTATION-LATENCY, MOTIVE-DEHORTATION, RELEASE-RESTRAINT, STORE, USE-DISUSE; **keep body and soul together,** HEALTH-SICKNESS, LIFE-DEATH; **keep close,** ENLIGHTENMENT - SECRECY, KEEPING - RELINQUISHMENT; **keep company,** SOLITUDE-COMPANY; **keep firm,** MUTABILITY-STABILITY; **keep from,** ACTION-PASSIVENESS, ENLIGHTENMENT-SECRECY, QUEST-EVASION, RELEASE-RESTRAINT; **keep going,** DISCONTINUANCE-CONTINUANCE, MOVEMENT-REST; **keep hold,** MUTABILITY-STABILITY; **keep house,** ESTABLISHMENT-REMOVAL; **keep in ignorance,** ENLIGHTENMENT-SECRECY, KNOWLEDGE-IGNORANCE; **keep in mind,** REMEMBRANCE - FORGETFULNESS; **keep in order,** MANAGEMENT; **keep in restraint,** LEAVE-PROHIBITION. RELEASE-RESTRAINT; **keep in sight,** CAREFULNESS-CARELESSNESS; **keep in suspense,** CERTAINTY-DOUBT, DETERMINATION-VACILLATION; **keep in the thoughts,** REMEMBRANCE-FORGETFULNESS; **keep in view,** EXPECTATION-SURPRISE, HEED-DISREGARD, REMEMBRANCE-FORGETFULNESS; **keep moving,** ACTIVITY-INDOLENCE, MOVEMENT-REST; **keep off,** ATTACK-DEFENSE, LEAVE-PROHIBITION, OBSTRUCTION-HELP, QUEST-EVASION, REPRISAL-RESISTANCE; **keep on,** DISCONTINUANCE-CONTINUANCE, FREQUENCY-RARITY, PERSISTENCE; **keep one in countenance,** EXCITABILITY-INEXCITABILITY, LIGHTHEARTEDNESS - DEJECTION; **keep one's bed,** HEALTH-SICKNESS; **keep one's course,** ADVANCE-RETROGRESSION; **keep one's ground,** MUTATION-PERMANENCE, PERSISTENCE-WHIM; **keep one's hand in,** SUCCESS-FAILURE; **keep one's head above water,** SECURITY-INSECURITY, SUCCESS-FAILURE, WELFARE-MISFORTUNE; **keep one's promise,** OBSERVANCE-NONOBSERVANCE; **keep one's word,** UPRIGHTNESS-DISHONESTY; **keep on foot,** DISCONTINUANCE-CONTINUANCE, PREPARATION-NONPREPARATION, PROVISION-WASTE, SUSPENSION-SUPPORT; **keep on one's legs,** HEALTH-SICKNESS; **keep out of harm's way,** PRESENCE-ABSENCE, RECKLESSNESS-CAUTION; **keep out of the way,** PRESENCE-ABSENCE, QUEST-EVASION; **keep pace with,** COEXISTENCE, EQUALITY-INEQUALITY; **keep quiet,** MOVEMENT-REST; **keep silence,** TALKATIVENESS-TACITURNITY, VOCALIZATION-MUTENESS; **keep the field,** FIGHTING-CONCILIATION; **keep the peace,** STRIFE-PEACE, VARIANCE-ACCORD; **keep time,** EARLINESS-LATENESS; **keep to,** PERSISTENCE; **keep together,** ANTAGONISM-CONCURRENCE; **keep to oneself,** ENLIGHTENMENT-SECRECY; **keep under,** LIBERTY-SUBJECTION, RETIREMENT, RULE-LICENSE; **keep up,** CONSERVATION, DISCONTINUANCE - CONTINUANCE, EXCITATION, PERSISTENCE-WHIM; **keep up a correspondence,** MISSIVE-PUBLICATION; **keep up appearances,** SOCIETY-LUDICROUSNESS; **keep up one's spirits,** LIGHTHEARTEDNESS-DEJECTION, SANGUINENESS-HOPELESSNESS; **keep up the ball,** ACTIVITY - INDOLENCE, ENTERTAINMENT-WEARINESS; **keep up the memory of,** MARK-OBLITERATION, REMEMBRANCE-FORGETFULNESS; **keep up with,** SWIFTNESS - SLOWNESS; **keep waiting,** EARLINESS - LATENESS; **keep watch,** CAREFULNESS-CARELESSNESS; **keep within bounds,** LEAVE-PROHIBITION, RELEASE-RESTRAINT, TRANSCURSION-SHORTCOMING.

keep'-er. One who has charge of. GUARD-PRISONER.

keep'-ing. Congruity. HARMONY-DISCORD; **in keeping,** COLOR-ACHROMATISM, CONVENTIONALITY-UNCONVENTIONALITY; **safe keeping,** CONSERVATION, SECURITY-INSECURITY.

KEEPING—RELINQUISHMENT.

Custody. The state of being held in keeping.
Detention. The act of keeping, or state of being kept.
Firm hold. The act of keeping with a tight grasp.
Grasp. Possession taken and kept by force.
Grip. Ability to seize and keep physically or mentally.
Gripe. A fast or firm hold.
Iron gripe. A gripe as inflexible as iron.
Keep. To have and retain in one's possession.
Keeping. Custody, charge, or possession.
Retaining. See *Verbs*.
Retention. The keeping within one's power or possession.
Tenacity. Persistency; retentiveness.

KEEPING—*Associated Nouns.*

Bird in hand. A figurative expression for a certain possession.
Captive. A prisoner taken by force or stratagem. See GUARD-PRISONER.

KEEPING—*Nouns of Means.*

Bond. That which binds two objects or parts together. See CONNECTIVE.
Claw. The sharp hooked nail of a quadruped, bird, or other animal.
Clutches. Talons, paws, hands.
Fangs. Long pointed teeth or roots of claws.
Finger. One of the terminal members of the hand.
Fist. The clenched hand.
Forceps. Pincers for grasping small objects.
Hand. Extremity of the arm with its fingers adapted for grasping.
Hook. A hard material bent into a curve for catching anything.
Nail. Horny scale at the ends of fingers and toes; claw or talon of a bird.
Neaf.
Neif. } The fist or hand.
Nippers. Pincers.
Paw. Foot of a beast having claws.
Pincers. A two-handled instrument with grasping jaws, for griping objects.
Pliers. Pincers for holding and bending small objects.
Talons. The claws of a bird of prey.
Teeth. The small bones attached to the jaws for chewing food.
Tentacle.
Tentaculum [L.]. } A slender organ of feeling or motion attached to the head of certain insects; polyps.
Tongs. A two-legged instrument for handling objects.
Vise. A clamping device consisting of two jaws closing together by a screw.
Wrist The joint uniting the hand and arm.

KEEPING—*Verbs.*

Clench.
Clinch. } To grasp firmly; to secure.
Clutch. To seize eagerly; to grasp and hold firmly.
Detain. To keep back.
Embay. To enclose, as a bay.
Entail. To leave or fix, as if by entail, upon another who comes after.
Grasp. To take and keep in possession.
Grip. To take firm hold of.
Have a firm hold of. To keep.
Have in stock. To have among the goods kept for sale. See HOLDING.
Hold back. To detain; restrain.
Hold fast. To keep in place securely.
Hold one's ground. To keep one's position.
Hold one's own. To keep possession of one's rights.
Hold tight. To keep in a secure grasp.
Hug. To keep close to.
Husband. To keep for a future emergency.
Keep. To have and retain in one's possession
Keep back. To withhold; restrain.
Keep close. To retain in secrecy.
Keep in stock. To hold as one's possessions.
Reserve. To keep back; to keep as one's own.
Retain. To keep in possession.
Secure. To make safe; to get safely in possession
Settle. To cause to become fixed.
Tie up. To fasten securely.
Withhold. To keep from action.

KEEPING—*Adjectives*

Inalienable. That cannot be rightfully taken away
Incommunicable. That cannot be revealed to others.

Abandonment. A giving up or relinquishment. See QUEST-ABANDONMENT.
Cession. A relinquishment of possessions or rights.
Dereliction. The act of voluntarily relinquishing all connection or concern with something.
Dispensation. The act of dispensing; a dealing out.
Expropriation. The act of putting out of one's possession.
Relinquishment. A recession or withdrawal from.
Renunciation. The act of renouncing. See *Verbs*.
Resignation. The act of resigning or giving up. See COMMISSION-RETIREMENT.
Riddance.
Surrender. The act of resigning possession of to another upon compulsion or demand; relinquishment.

RELINQUISHMENT—*Associated Nouns.*

Derelict. A thing voluntarily abandoned or wilfully cast away by its proper owner. See *Adjectives*.
Foundling. A child found without a parent or owner.

RELINQUISHMENT—*Verbs.*

Abandon. To forsake or relinquish wholly.
Be quit of.
Be rid of. } To be freed from that which is burdensome.
Cast aside. To throw away.
Cast away. To relinquish as worthless; to wreck, as a ship.
Cast behind. To reject.
Cast off. To discard; disown.
Cast overboard.
Cast to the dogs. } To throw away as useless.
Cast to the winds. To relinquish utterly.
Cede. To relinquish; yield.
Disburden oneself of. To remove a burden from.
Discard. To relinquish as worthless.
Dismiss. To discharge; reject.
Dispose of. To make final disposition of.
Dispossess. To eject from possession.
Dispossess oneself of. To deprive oneself of possession.
Divest oneself of. To deprive; dispossess.
Drop. To have done with; relinquish.
Eject. To cast forth or out; expel. See ADMISSION-EXPULSION.
Expropriate. To put out of one's possession.
Fling aside. To discard.
Fling away. To throw away; discard.
Fling overboard. Figurative for discard, renounce, betray.
Fling to the dogs. Figurative for abandon to ruin.
Forego. To give up; relinquish.
Get quit of.
Get rid of. } To get free of that which is troublesome.
Give away. To relinquish the ownership by gift.
Give notice to quit. To notify of dismissal.
Give warning. To notify to quit service or vacate premises.
Give up. To relinquish as hopeless; to yield.
Lay apart. To put away; to reject.
Lay aside. To put off or away; to abandon.
Lay down. To quit or relinquish.
Lay on the shelf. To relinquish for a season. See USE-DISUSE.
Let go. To relax hold of anything.
Let slip. To let go; to omit.
Make away with. To put out of the way; to remove; to kill.
Part with. To quit with; to take leave.
Pitch aside. To throw away.
Pitch away. To throw away; to discard.
Pitch overboard.
Pitch to the dogs. } To throw away as useless.
Put aside. To abandon.
Put away. To renounce; to discard.
Quit one's hold. To relinquish one's grasp.
Relinquish. To recede or withdraw from; forsake, abandon.
Renounce. To relinquish explicitly.
Resign. To give up or back; to relinquish the use or enjoyment of.
Rid oneself of. To free, as from a burden.
Set aside. To abandon; renounce.
Spare. To refrain from using, spending, or giving.
Supersede. To take the place of as by reason of superior worth.
Surrender. To relinquish possession of to another upon compulsion or demand.
Sweep away. To drive, destroy, or carry off with celerity or violence.
Sweep to the winds. To drive entirely away.
Throw aside. To have no use for.
Throw away. To discard as worthless; to waste.
Throw overboard.
Throw to the dogs. } To rid oneself of.

KEEPING—RELINQUISHMENT—*Continued.*

KEEPING—Adjectives—*Continued.*

In mortmain. In that state of lands and tenements held by a "dead hand," that is one that cannot alienate them; in inalienable possession.

In strict settlement. In limitation of lands to the parent for life, and after his death to his several children successively in tail with trustees interposed to preserve contingent remainders, thus tying up the descent to the utmost limit permitted by law.

Retaining.⎫ See *Verbs.*
Retentive.⎭

Tenacious. Strongly disposed to keep what is in possession.
Uncommunicated. Not communicated, or bestowed.
Undeprived. Not dispossessed of anything.
Undisposed. Not disposed; not appropriated.
Unforfeited. Not forfeited; kept

KEEPING—*Phrase.*

Uti possidetis [L.]. As you are in possession.

---

keep'-sake''. A token of friendship. REMEMBRANCE-FORGETFULNESS.
keg. A small barrel. CONTENTS-RECEIVER.
kel'-pie. An imaginary water-sprite. JOVE-FIEND.
kempt. Combed. CLEANNESS-FILTHINESS.
ken. Extent of sight or knowledge. KNOWLEDGE-IGNORANCE, SIGHT-BLINDNESS.
ken'-nel. A shelter for a dog; a hovel; a ditch. DWELLER-HABITATION, GROOVE, WATERCOURSE-AIRPIPE.
kep'-i. A kind of military cap. DRESS-UNDRESS.
kerb'-stone''. A stone on the outer edge of a sidewalk. BOUNDARY.
ker'-chief. A cloth covering for the head DRESS-UNDRESS; **wave a kerchief,** SIGN.
kern. A handmill; a rogue. FRIABILITY, GENTILITY-COMMONALTY, GOOD MAN-BAD MAN.
ker'-nel. The essential part. CENTER, CONSEQUENCE-INSIGNIFICANCE.
ketch. A kind of ship. CONVEYANCE-VESSEL.
Ketch, Jack. A hangman. RECOMPENSE-SCOURGE.
ket'-tle. A metallic cooking vessel. CONTENTS-RECEIVER, OVEN-REFRIGERATOR; **kettle-drum,** MUSICAL INSTRUMENTS, SOCIABILITY-PRIVACY; **kettle of fish,** DIFFICULTY-FACILITY, REGULARITY-IRREGULARITY.
key. An opener; solution; key-note; color; sign; authority. APERTURE-CLOSURE, CAUSE-EFFECT, COLOR-ACHROMATISM, CONSEQUENCE-INSIGNIFICANCE, INSTRUMENT, INSTRUMENTALITY, INTERPRETATION-MISINTERPRETATION, MELODY-DISSONANCE, SCEPTER, SIGN.
key'-hole''. A hole for a key. APERTURE-CLOSURE.
key'-note''. A fundamental tone; the main idea. CONSEQUENCE-INSIGNIFICANCE, COPY-MODEL, MELODY-DISSONANCE, UNIFORMITY-MULTIFORMITY.
key'-stone''. A support; an essential principle. ARCHITECTURE, COMPLETION-NONCOMPLETION, MOTIVE-CAPRICE, SUSPENSION-SUPPORT, USEFULNESS-USELESSNESS.
khan. An inn; an official. CHIEF-UNDERLING, DWELLER-HABITATION.
khed-ive'. A viceroy. CHIEF-UNDERLING.
ki-bit'-ka. A cart. CONVEYANCE-VESSEL.
kick. An impulse or recoil; an act of assault or scorn. ATTACK-DEFENSE, IMPETUS-REACTION, RECOMPENSE-PUNITION, REGARD-SCORN, REPRISAL-RESISTANCE; **kick against,** ANTAGONISM-CONCURRENCE, REPRISAL-RESISTANCE; **kick against the pricks,** ANTAGONISM-CONCURRENCE, RECKLESSNESS-CAUTION, REPRISAL-RESISTANCE, USEFULNESS-USELESSNESS; **kick one's heels,** ACTION-PASSIVENESS, EARLINESS-LATENESS; **kick over the traces,** INSUBORDINATION-OBEDIENCE; **kick the beam,** EQUALITY-INEQUALITY, SUPREMACY-SUBORDINACY; **kick up a dust,** ACTIVITY-

RELINQUISHMENT—Verbs—*Continued*

Throw to the winds. To discard utterly; to waste recklessly.
Turn away. To dismiss from service; discharge; discard.
Wash one's hands of. To disclaim or renounce interest in, or responsibility for an action, person, or thing.
Yield. To give up; to relinquish.

RELINQUISHMENT—*Adjectives.*

Cast off. Thrown or laid aside; discarded.
Derelict. Deserted or abandoned.
Left. See INCREMENT-REMNANT.
Relinquished. See *Verbs.*
Unappropriated. Having no particular application.
Unculled. Not gathered; not selected.
Unowned. Not owned; not acknowledged as one's own.

RELINQUISHMENT—*Interjection.*

Away with!

INDOLENCE, PRESUMPTION-OBSEQUIOUSNESS, VARIANCE-ACCORD; **kick up a row,** DOMINANCE-IMPOTENCE, VARIANCE-ACCORD.
kick'-ing. A sign of life. REPRISAL-RESISTANCE; **alive and kicking,** ACTIVITY-INDOLENCE, LIFE-DEATH.
kick'-shaw''. A trifle; a food. NUTRIMENT-EXCRETION, USEFULNESS-USELESSNESS.
kid'-gloves''. Gloves made from the skin of a kid. **Not to be handled with kid-gloves,** CLEANNESS-FILTHINESS, DIFFICULTY-FACILITY.
kid'-nap''. To deceive; abduct. TAKING-RESTITUTION, THEFT, TRUTHFULNESS-FRAUD.
kid'-nap''-er. One who abducts. TAKING-RESTITUTION, THEFT.
kid'-ney. Kind or disposition; organ of the body. ADMISSION-EXCLUSION, ANATOMY.
kil'-der-kin. A measure. CONTENTS-RECEIVER.
Kil-ken'-ny cats. Cats fabled to have fought to the death. VARIANCE-ACCORD.
kill. To destroy life. LIFE-KILLING; **kill the fatted calf,** SOCIABILITY-PRIVACY, SOLEMNIZATION; **kill the goose with golden eggs,** SKILL-UNSKILFULNESS; **kill the slain,** EXCESS-LACK; **kill time,** ACTIVITY-INDOLENCE, WITTINESS-DULNESS; **kill two birds with one stone,** ACTIVITY-INDOLENCE; **kill with kindness,** BLANDISHMENT.
kill'-ing. Captivating. PLEASURABLENESS-PAINFULNESS.
kill'-joy''. A gloomy person. OBSTRUCTION-HELP.
kiln. A kind of oven. OVEN-REFRIGERATOR.
kil'-o-gram. Unit of weight. MEASURE.
kil'-o-li''-ter. One thousand liters. MAGNITUDE-SMALLNESS, MEASURE.
kil'-o-me''-ter. A length of one thousand meters. LENGTH-SHORTNESS, MEASURE.
kilt. A skirt. DRESS-UNDRESS.
kim'-bo. Crooked. ANGULARITY.
kin. Those related. DIVISION.
kind. Class; of a generous nature. CHARITABLENESS-MALEVOLENCE, DIVISION; **kind regards,** POLITENESS-IMPOLITENESS.
kin'-der-gar''-ten. A school for small children. SCHOOL.
kind'-heart''-ed. Having a kind nature. CHARITABLENESS-MALEVOLENCE.
kind'-heart''-ed-ness. Benevolence. CHARITABLENESS-MALEVOLENCE.
kin'-dle. To set fire to; stir up; cause; intensify feeling. CAUSE-EFFECT, CREATION-DESTRUCTION, EXCITATION, FAVORITE-ANGER, HEATING-COOLING, LIGHT-DARKNESS, TURBULENCE-CALMNESS, VIGOR-INERTIA.
kind'-li-ness. Benignity CHARITABLENESS-MALEVOLENCE

kind'-ly. Generously. CHARITABLENESS - MALEVO-LENCE.

kind'-ness. Benignity. CHARITABLENESS-MALEVO-LENCE.

kin'-dred. Relatives by birth. RELATIONSHIP.

kine. Cows. FAUNA-FLORA.

kin''-e-mat'-ics. The science of pure motion. MOVE-MENT-REST.

ki-ne'-to-scope. Scientific instrument. ELECTRICITY.

king. A chief ruler. CHIEF-UNDERLING; **every inch a king,** GENTILITY-COMMONALTY, RULE-LICENSE; **King Death,** LIFE-DEATH; **King of kings,** DIVINITY; **King's Bench,** RELEASE-PRISON, TRIBUNAL; **King's Counsel,** ADVOCATE; **King's English,** LANGUAGE; **King's evidence,** EXPOSURE - HIDINGPLACE; **King's highway,** WAY.

king'-craft''. The art of governing. MANAGEMENT.

king'-dom. A territory; sovereign power. EXTENSION-DISTRICT, PROPERTY; **animal kingdom,** FAUNA-FLORA; **kingdom of heaven,** HEAVEN-HELL; **mineral kingdom,** ORGANIZATION-INORGANIZATION.

king'-hood. The state of being a king. RULE-LICENSE.

king'-ly. Worthy of a king. RULE-LICENSE.

king'-post''. A strut in a building; a middle-post. ARCHITECTURE.

king'-ship. Royalty. RULE-LICENSE.

kins'-folk. Relatives. RELATIONSHIP.

kins'-man. One related by blood. RELATIONSHIP.

ki-osk'. A kind of pavilion. DWELLER-HABITATION, FANE.

kirk. A church. FANE.

kir'-tle. A frock or mantle. DRESS-UNDRESS.

kis'-met. Fate. VOLITION-OBLIGATION.

kiss. To salute with the lips. BLANDISHMENT, POLITE-NESS-IMPOLITENESS; **kiss in the ring,** ENTERTAIN-MENT-WEARINESS; **kiss the book,** ASSERTION-DENIAL; **kiss the hem of one's garment,** PRESUMPTION-OBSE-QUIOUSNESS, REGARD-DISRESPECT; **kiss the rod,** YIELDING.

kit. An entire set; a basket or bottle; a violin. DIVI-SION, GREATNESS-LITTLENESS, MUSICAL INSTRU-MENTS.

kit'-cat''. A portrait. PAINTING.

kitch'-en. A room for cooking. CONTENTS-RECEIVER, WORKSHOP.

kitch'-en-er. A cook-stove. OVEN-REFRIGERATOR.

kitch'-en-gar''-den. A vegetable-garden. DOMESTICA-TION-AGRICULTURE.

kitch'-en-maid''. A maid that works in the kitchen. CHIEF-UNDERLING.

kite. A paper toy; a kind of money. CONVEYANCE-VESSEL, MONEY; **fly a kite,** CREDIT-DEBT, LOAN-BOR-ROWING, SETTLEMENT-DEFAULT.

kith. One's kindred. **Kith and kin,** RELATIONSHIP.

kith'-less. Without friends. SOCIABILITY-PRIVACY, SOLITUDE-COMPANY.

kit'-ten. Something young; to bring forth; a young cat. CREATION - DESTRUCTION, INFANT - VETERAN; **playful as a kitten,** ENTERTAINMENT-WEARINESS, LIGHTHEARTEDNESS-DEJECTION.

kit'-ten-ish. Playful. INFANT-VETERAN.

klep''-to-ma'-ni-a. An insane desire to steal. DESIRE-DISTASTE, SANENESS-LUNACY, THEFT.

klep''-to-ma'-ni-ac. One with an insane desire to steal. SANENESS-MANIAC, THEFT.

knack. A peculiar aptness. HABIT-DESUETUDE, SKILL: **get into the knack,** HABIT-DESUETUDE.

knag. A knot or knob. OBSTRUCTION-HELP.

knag'-gy. Of surly temper. FAVORITE-MOROSENESS.

knap. A summit. HEIGHT-LOWNESS.

knap'-sack''. A provision-sack. CONTENTS-RECEIVER.

knave. An impostor. GULL - DECEIVER, UPRIGHT-NESS-ROGUE.

kna'-ver-y. Deception. CRAFT-ARTLESSNESS, TRUTH-

FULNESS-FRAUD, UPRIGHTNESS-DISHONESTY, VIR-TUE-VICE.

knav'-ish. Trickish. UPRIGHTNESS-DISHONESTY.

knead. To mix; to mold. FORM - FORMLESSNESS, HARDNESS-SOFTNESS, MIXTURE-HOMOGENEITY.

knee. A joint of the leg. ANATOMY, ANGULARITY; **bend the knee,** ELEVATION-DEPRESSION, YIELDING; **down on one's knees,** DEVOTION-IDOLATRY, SELFRESPECT-HUMBLENESS; **fall on one's knees,** ATONEMENT, PETI-TION-EXPOSTULATION, PRESUMPTION-OBSEQUIOUS-NESS, YIELDING; **on one's knees,** PETITION-EXPOS-TULATION, REGARD-DISRESPECT.

knee'-deep''. Rising to the knee. DEEPNESS-SHALLOW-NESS.

kneel. To bow in devotion or to ask mercy. COMPAS-SION-RUTHLESSNESS, DEVOTION-IDOLATRY, ELEVA-TION-DEPRESSION, PETITION-EXPOSTULATION, PO-LITENESS-IMPOLITENESS, PRESUMPTION-OBSEQUIOUS-NESS, REGARD-DISRESPECT, YIELDING.

kneel'-ing. Resting on the knees. DEVOTION-IDOLA-TRY, POLITENESS-IMPOLITENESS, REGARD-DISRE-SPECT, YIELDING.

knell. A funeral bell. LIFE-FUNERAL, LIGHTHEARTED-NESS-DEJECTION; **strike the death-knell,** LIFE-KILL-ING.

knick'-er-bock''-ers. Knee-breeches. DRESS-UNDRESS.

knick'-knack''. Any trifling article. ENTERTAINMENT-WEARINESS, USEFULNESS-USELESSNESS.

knife. A sharp-edged instrument. SHARPNESS-BLUNT-NESS; **play a good knife and fork,** DESIRE, FASTING-GLUTTONY, NUTRIMENT-EXCRETION.

knight. A person of rank. GENTILITY-COMMONALTY; **carpet-knight,** SOCIETY-DANDY; **knight errant,** AT-TACK-DEFENSE, HUMANITARIANISM-MISANTHROPY, RECKLESSNESS-CAUTION, SANENESS-MANIAC; **knight-service,** HOLDING-EXEMPTION; **knight's-move,** AIM-ABERRATION.

knight'-er''-rant-ry. Chivalry. HUMANITARIANISM-MISANTHROPY, RECKLESSNESS-CAUTION

knight'-hood. The condition of a knight. GENTILITY-COMMONALTY, TITLE.

knight'-mar'-shal. An officer in the English sovereign's household. CHIEF-UNDERLING.

Knights of La'-bor. Organization of laborers. LABOR-CAPITAL.

Knight' Tem'-plar. One belonging to a certain order among Freemasons. ASSOCIATION.

knit. To weave with needles. CONTENTS - RECEIVER, UNION-DISUNION; **well knit,** STRENGTH-WEAKNESS; **knit the brow,** APPROVAL-DISAPPROVAL, CONTENTED-NESS-DISCONTENTEDNESS, FAVORITE-ANGER.

knob. A rounded protuberance. CONVEXITY-LEVEL-NESS, ROUNDNESS, SUSPENSION-SUPPORT.

knock. A blow; a harsh sound. CRASH-DRUMMING, IMPETUS-REACTION; **hard knocks,** STRIFE-PEACE; **knock at the door,** LIFE-DEATH, PETITION-EXPOSTU-LATION; **knock down,** BETTERMENT-DETERIORATION, CREATION-DESTRUCTION, ELEVATION-DEPRESSION, ERECTNESS-FLATNESS, LIGHTHEARTEDNESS-DEJEC-TION; **knock off,** COMPLETION-NONCOMPLETION; **knock one's head against,** SKILL-UNSKILFULNESS; **knock on the head,** LIFE-KILLING; **knock over,** CREA-TION-DESTRUCTION; **knock under,** REPENTANCE-OB-DURACY, YIELDING; **knock up,** WEARINESS-REFRESH-MENT.

knock'-down''. Having force to overthrow. **Knock-down argument,** PROOF-DISPROOF; **knock-down blow,** CREATION-DESTRUCTION.

knocked. Heavily hit. **Knocked on the head,** SUCCESS-FAILURE; **knocked to atoms,** CREATION-DESTRUC-TION; **knocked up,** WEARINESS-REFRESHMENT.

knock'-er. A metal hammer fastened to a door as a means of signaling for admission. INSTRUMENT, SIGN.

knock'–kneed". With deformity of the legs. ANGU-LARITY, PARALLELISM-INCLINATION, PROPORTION-DEFORMITY.

knoll. A small round hill. HEIGHT-LOWNESS.

knot. A bond of union; group; difficulty; knoll; ornament. ASSOCIATION, CONNECTIVE, CROSSING, DIFFICULTY-FACILITY, EMBELLISHMENT-DISFIGUREMENT, GATHERING-SCATTERING, OBSTRUCTION-HELP, REGULARITY-IRREGULARITY, ROUNDNESS, SOLIDITY-RARITY; **tie the nuptial knot,** MATRIMONY-CELIBACY; **true lover's knot,** BLANDISHMENT, LOVE-HATE.

knot'–ted. Full of knots. REGULARITY-IRREGULARITY, SMOOTHNESS-ROUGHNESS, SOLIDITY-RARITY.

knot'–ty. Full of knots. SOLIDITY-RARITY.

knout. A Russian scourge. RECOMPENSE-SCOURGE.

know. To be certain of; be acquainted with. AMITY-HOSTILITY, CERTAINTY-DOUBT, ENLIGHTENMENT-SECRECY, FAITH-MISGIVING, KNOWLEDGE-IGNORANCE, SOCIABILITY-PRIVACY; **I'd have you to know,** ASSERTION-DENIAL, HEED-DISREGARD; **I know bet-** ter, ASSERTION-DENIAL; **know by heart,** REMEMBRANCE-FORGETFULNESS; **know for certain,** FAITH-MISGIVING; **know no bounds,** EXCESS-LACK, INFINITY, MAGNITUDE-SMALLNESS; **know nothing of,** KNOWLEDGE-IGNORANCE; **know one's own mind,** DETERMINATION-VACILLATION; **know what one is about,** SKILL-UNSKILFULNESS; **know what's what,** DIFFERENTIATION - INDISCRIMINATION, KNOWLEDGE-IGNORANCE, SAGACITY-INCAPACITY, SKILL-UNSKILFULNESS; **know which is which,** DIFFERENTIATION-INDISCRIMINATION.

know'–ing. Of penetrating mind. CRAFT-ARTLESSNESS, KNOWLEDGE-IGNORANCE.

know'–ing–ly. Intelligently. PURPOSE-LUCK.

knowl'–edge. That which is known. ENLIGHTENMENT-SECRECY, KNOWLEDGE-IGNORANCE; **acquire knowledge,** EDUCATION-LEARNING; **come to one's knowledge,** ENLIGHTENMENT-SECRECY; **knowledge of the world,** SKILL-UNSKILFULNESS; **practical knowledge,** SKILL-UNSKILFULNESS.

KNOWLEDGE—IGNORANCE.

Accomplishment. An attainment that lends dignity or charm; the act of accomplishing.

Accurate knowledge.⎫ Knowledge derived from the best reliable
Accurate learning.⎭ sources.

Acquaintance. Familiar knowledge.

Acquirements. The act of acquiring; a faculty acquired and not natural.

Acquisitions. The act of acquiring; an acquirement obtained by effort.

Acroamatic knowledge.⎫ Knowledge acquired by hearing.
Acroamatic learning.⎭

Acroamatism. Quality of being oral.

Acroatic knowledge.⎫ See ACROAMATIC KNOWLEDGE.
Acroatic learning.⎭

Advance of learning.⎫ Progress of knowledge.
Advance of science.⎭

Appreciation, etc. Right estimate of value. See JUDGMENT.

Apprehension. The state or result of apprehending.

Attainment. The act of gaining, especially of mental or moral faculties.

Bibliolatry. The worship of books, especially of the Bible.

Bibliomania. A passion for books.

Body of doctrine. The entirety of what is taught.

Body of knowledge. All that one knows.

Bookishness. A liking for books.

Book-learning. Learning derived from studying books.

Circle of sciences. A particular field of learning.

Cognition. The act or power of understanding facts.

Cognizance. Knowledge of facts.

Cognoscence. Cognizance.

Comprehension. Power or act of grasping with the mind in detail.

Conscience. Power to distinguish between right and wrong.

Consciousness. The state of being conscious.

Culture. Development of mental faculties

Cyclopedia. The range of human knowledge.

Dawn. The beginning of understanding.

Deep knowledge.⎫ Profound learning.
Deep learning.⎭

Dilettantism. Superficial knowledge.

Discovery, etc. The act of discovering; that which is discovered. See JUDGMENT.

Doctrine. A system of beliefs.

Education. The development of mental powers; knowledge acquired by such means. See TEACHING.

Encyclopedia. The whole range of human knowledge.

Encyclopedical knowledge.⎫ Comprehensive knowledge.
Encyclopedical learning.⎭

Enlightenment. The state of being enlightened.

Erudition. Knowledge of things hard to understand, acquired by education.

Etiology. The science of causes.

Extensive knowledge.⎫ Wide information.
Extensive learning.⎭

Familiarity. Intimate knowledge.

General information. Knowledge of a general kind.

Glimmer. Momentary knowledge.

Glimmering. Same as glimmer.

Glimpse. Slight understanding.

Bewilderment, etc. Perplexity; condition caused by confusion of ideas. See CERTAINTY-DOUBT.

Blindness. The state of being blind.

Charlatanism. False pretension of knowledge.

Charlatanry. See CHARLATANISM.

Crass ignorance. Total ignorance.

Darkness. Total absence of intellectual enlightenment.

Glimmering. Momentary ineffectual knowledge.

Ignorance. The state of being ignorant.

Ignorance crasse [F.]. Gross ignorance.

Incapacity. Inability to retain knowledge.

Incomprehension. Lack of comprehension.

Inexperience. A lack of experience, or of knowledge gained by experience.

Nescience. The condition of not knowing.

Pedantry. Pretentious show of knowledge.

Sciolism. Pretension to knowledge.

Simplicity. The condition of knowing very little.

Smattering. Superficial knowledge.

Unacquaintance. Want of acquaintance.

Unconsciousness. The state of being unconscious.

IGNORANCE—*Time*.

Dark ages. A period of stagnation and obscurity in literature and art, from about 500 to about 1500 A. D.

IGNORANCE—*Figurative Nouns*.

Sealed book. That which is unknown or unknowable.

Tabula rasa [L.]. Emptiness; want of intellect.

Terra incognita [L.]. An unknown subject.

Unexplored ground. A topic or line of thought that has not been studied.

Unknown quantities. X, Y, Z; subjects not yet made known by research.

Virgin soil. A matter still to be investigated.

IGNORANCE—*Verbs*.

Be blind to. To be unable to understand.

Be ignorant, etc. See *Adjectives*.

Have a glimmering. Have a slight knowledge.

Have no conception.⎫
Have no idea.⎬ Be absolutely ignorant.
Have no notion.⎭

Ignore. To be ignorant.

Keep in ignorance, etc. See ENLIGHTENMENT-SECRECY.

Know not.⎫ Be ignorant.
Know nothing of.⎭

Know not what. To be uncertain about.

Not have the remotest idea. Have no notion.

Not know, etc. See KNOWLEDGE.

Not know what to make of. Not to be able to fully comprehend the meaning of.

Not pretend to say.⎫ Not know enough to say.
Not take upon oneself to say.⎭

Wonder whether. To be in doubt.

KNOWLEDGE—IGNORANCE *Continued.*

Impression. Effect produced by knowing.
Information. Knowledge acquired and retained; important or particular knowledge.
Inkling. A hint.
Insight. Knowledge of that which is within.
Intuition. Natural power of knowing.
Ken. Extent of knowledge.
Knowledge. That which is known; the state or act of knowing.
Learning. That knowledge which is acquired by study, the act of learning.
Letters. Learning in general.
Liberal education. Education in noble and refined thought and action.
Light. Knowledge in the sense of making clear or plain.
Literature. Knowledge in writing; acquaintance with writings.
Lore. The learning of a class or people.
March of intellect. The progress of mind.
Omniscience. Knowledge of all things.
Pandect. A compendium of some branch of knowledge.
Pansophy. A system or scheme of universal knowledge.
Pantology. A science including all branches of knowledge.
Perception. The act or result of perceiving.
Philosophy. The science that treats of the laws that govern facts or phenomena.
Practical knowledge, etc. Knowledge applicable to use. See Skill.
Precognition. Cognition beforehand.
Privity. Knowledge of something secret.
Proficiency. The state of being proficient.
Profound knowledge.
Profound learning. } Knowledge of abstruse subjects.
Progress of learning.
Progress of science. } Advance in knowledge.
Reading. The study of books.
Recognition. The act or result of recognizing.
Republic of letters, etc. The field of knowledge covered by literature. See Language.
Rudiments. The beginnings or first principles of understanding.
Scent. Limited knowledge which makes more extended knowledge possible.
Scholarship. The sum of acquired knowledge.
School, etc. A system of knowledge. See sub Belief.
Schoolmaster abroad. Dispersed knowledge.
Science. Systematized knowledge.
Solid knowledge.
Solid learning. } Reliable knowledge.
Store of knowledge. Amount of knowledge.
Suspicion. Knowledge sustained by little evidence.
System of knowledge. Orderly arrangement of knowledge.
Theory. Knowledge as distinguished from practise; the principle of a science.
Tree of knowledge. Power to distinguish good and evil.
Vast knowledge.
Vast learning. } Widely extended knowledge.

Knowledge—*Verbs.*

Appreciate. To form a right estimate of.
Apprehend. To know of as existing.
Be *au courant*, etc. To have present knowledge. See *Adverbs.*
Be aware of, etc. See *Adjectives.*
Be master of. To understand minutely.
Come to one's knowledge. To be discovered.
Comprehend. To fully understand the meaning of; to have a clear idea of.
Conceive. To form an idea of.
Connaître le dessous des cartes [F.]. To know the ins and outs of a thing; comprehend.
Discern. To distinguish a thing as separate from something else.
Discover, etc. To come to know first. See Discovery.
Experience. To know by experience.
Fathom. To find out all that can be known about anything.
Get a sight of. Perceive.
Have. To retain in the mind.
Have at one's fingers' ends.
Have in one's head. } To have ready for use.
Have some knowledge of. To know in some degree.
Ken. To understand.
Know. To comprehend anything with certainty; to have conviction that a thing is true; to be familiar with.
Know by heart. To know through the feelings.
Know by rote. To know by frequent repetition.
Know full well. To know very well.
Know what's what, etc. To thoroughly understand the situation. See Skill.

Have a film over the eyes. To be hindered from clearly understanding.
Not know chalk from cheese. To be unable to distinguish.
See through a glass darkly. To be in partial ignorance.

Ignorance—*Adjectives.*

A stranger to. Ignorant of.
At fault. Mistaken and worthy of blame.
At sea, etc. In a quandary. See Certainty-Doubt.
At the end of his tether. Having exhausted his stock of knowledge.
Au bout de son Latin [F.]. To the extent of his knowledge.
Behind the age. Not versed in present knowledge.
Belated. Slow of intellect.
Benighted. Kept in mental darkness.
Blinded. Prevented from knowing.
Blindfold. Having the intellect darkened; heedless.
Caught tripping. Found blundering.
Concealed etc. Hidden from investigation. See Concealment.
Empty. Having no intelligence.
Empty-headed. Senseless; foolish.
Green. Having no knowledge from experience, and hence liable to blunder.
Half-learned. Partially educated.
Hoodwinked. Easily deceived.
Ignorant. Not knowing; having no development in intellectual power.
Illiterate. Knowing nothing of literature; unable to read.
In the dark. Uncertain.
Misinformed. Wrongly informed.
Novel. Not previously known; strange.
Pedantic. Given to pedantry.
Philistine. Narrow-minded; from the Philistines of the Bible.
Rude. Uncultured, and hence lacking in manners.
Shallow. Having no depth of intellect.
Superficial. Able to know or characterized by only what is very easily understood.
Unacquainted, unapprehended, unapprized, unascertained, unaware, unbookish, unconscious, unconversant, uncultivated, uneducated, unenlightened, unexplained, unexplored, unguided, unheard of, uninformed, uninitiated, uninstructed, uninvestigated, unknowing, unknown, unlearned, unlettered, unperceived, unread, unschooled, untaught, untutored, unversed, unweeting, unwitting. Not acquainted, etc.
Weetless. Witless.
Witless. Without thoughtfulness; foolish.

Ignorance—*Adverbs.*

For anything one knows.
For aught one knows. } As far as one's knowledge goes.
Ignorantly, etc. In an ignorant manner. See *Adjectives.*
Not that one knows. Not as far as one's knowledge goes.
Unawares. Without knowing; unconsciously.

Ignorance—*Interjections.*

God knows! heaven knows! the Lord knows! nobody knows!

Knowledge—Verbs—*Continued.*

Make out. To know by examining.
Perceive. To know of existence through impression of the senses; to understand.
Possess. To have in mind an idea of.
Possess some knowledge of. Know in part.
Realize. To think of as real; to comprehend the meaning of.
Recognize. To perceive as something known before.
Scan. To examine hurriedly.
See. To perceive with the mind; to understand.
See one's way. To know what to do.
Take. To accept as true; to regard.
Trow. To suppose.
Understand. To know after having considered.
Ween. To make a guess.
Wit. To find out; learn.
Wot. Same as wit.
Wot of. To know of.

Knowledge—*Adjectives.*

Accomplished. Endowed with accomplishments.
Acquainted with. Having familiar knowledge of.

KNOWLEDGE—Adjectives—*Continued.*

Acroamatic. Difficult to understand.
Alive to. In a position to know; readily understanding.
Apprized of. Possessed of information concerning.
Ascertained. Investigated and understood with certainty
At home in. Thoroughly familiar with.
Au courant [F.]. Versed in up-to-date learning.
Au fait [F.]. Well educated.
Aware of. Knowing about.
Behind the curtain. } Having knowledge of things generally hidden.
Behind the scenes. }
Blue. Very much devoted to literature.
Bookish. Fond of books.
Book-learned. Possessed of knowledge obtained from books.
Cognitive. Having the power to understand a fact or truth.
Cognizable. Capable of being perceived or known.
Cognizant of. Having apprehension of.
Cognoscible. Capable of being ascertained.
Commonplace. Easily understood by all.
Conscious of. Knowing that anything exists.
Conversant with. Familiar with.
Deep-read. Versed in literature.
Educated. Having the benefits of an education.
Enlightened. Possessed of knowledge that enables to see clearly.
Erudite. Characterized by erudition.
Familiar. Characterized by intimate knowledge.
Familiar as household words. } Very familiar.
Familiar to every schoolboy. }
Familiar with. Having intimate knowledge of.
Forward in. Advanced in an understanding of.
Hackneyed. Oft repeated, and hence common, known to everybody.
Informed of. Having information concerning.
Instructed. Put in possession of knowledge.
In the secret. Having an insight into.

Knowing. Characterized by knowledge; shrewd.
Known. Recognized as the truth.
Learned. Possessed of much learning.
Let into. Permitted to know about, as a secret.
Lettered. Versed in literature.
Made acquainted with. } Informed of.
No stranger to. }
Noted. Famous on account of some accomplishment, as learning or wisdom.
Notorious. Famous; renowned.
Omniscient. Characterized by omniscience.
Privy to. Sharing a secret knowledge of.
Proficient in. Knowing well how to do; expert in.
Profound. Characterized by deep, exhaustive knowledge.
Proverbial. Having the characteristics of a proverb.
Read in. Versed in the literature of.
Received. Perceived; understood.
Recognized. Accepted as the truth.
Savant [F.]. Exceptionally learned.
Scholastic. Pertaining to or characterized by schools or scholars.
Self-taught. Educated by private study.
Shrewd. Quick to comprehend; artful.
Solid. Characterized by sound learning or judgment.
Strong in. Having especially thorough knowledge of.
Trite. Frequently repeated; commonplace.
Undeceived. Informed of the truth
Up to. Thoroughly conversant with; equipped with knowledge of.
Versed in. Educated in; knowing considerable about.
Well conned. Carefully studied.
Well educated. Having a good education.
Well grounded. Having a good fundamental knowledge.
Well informed. Having a good general knowledge of things.
Well known. Famous.
Well read. Having a good knowledge from reading.

KNOWLEDGE—*Adverbs.*

To one's knowledge. One knowing it to be the truth from personal evidence.

To the best of one's knowledge. As far as one knows.

KNOWLEDGE—*Phrases.*

Comprendre c'est tout pardonner [F.]. To understand all is to pardon all.
Empta dolore docet experientia [L.]. Experience wrought with pain teaches.
Gnothi seauton [Gr.]. Know thyself. [In the temple at Delphi.]
Les affaires font les hommes [F.]. Experience of affairs makes men.

Nec scire fas est omnia [L.]. To know all things is not permitted.
One's eyes being opened, etc. Having learned from experience. See DISCLOSURE.
Was ich nicht weiss, macht mich nicht heiss [G.]. What I do not know does not make me glow.

known. Understood; famous. KNOWLEDGE-IGNORANCE; **become known,** EXPOSURE-HIDINGPLACE; **known as,** NAME-MISNOMER; **known by,** SIGN; **make known,** ENLIGHTENMENT-SECRECY, PUBLICITY; **well known,** KNOWLEDGE-IGNORANCE.
knuck′-le. A joint in the hand. ANGULARITY; **knuckle down,** YIELDING.
knuck′-le-dus″-ter. A weapon. WEAPON.
knur′-and-spell″. A kind of game. ENTERTAINMENT-WEARINESS.
ko′-bold. A kind of goblin. JOVE-FIEND.
Koh″-i-noor′. A famous diamond. FAULTLESSNESS-FAULTINESS.
korakas, es [Gr.] (ko-ra′-kas, ês). To the crows. ASSENT-DISSENT.
Ko-ran′. The Mohammedan scriptures. REVELATION-PSEUDOREVELATION.
ko-tow′. A form of obeisance. ELEVATION-DEPRES-

SION, POLITENESS-IMPOLITENESS, REGARD-DISRESPECT, YIELDING.
kraal. A village. DWELLER-HABITATION.
kra′-ken. A fabled sea-monster. CONVENTIONALITY-UNCONVENTIONALITY.
kriegs′-spiel″. A game of war, played for practise, on maps. FIGHTING-CONCILIATION.
kris. A short sword. WEAPON.
Krish′-na. A Hindu deity. JOVE-FIEND.
kro′-ne. Coin. VALUES.
Krupp. A German founder. **Krupp gun,** WEAPON.
kudos [Gr.] (kiu′-dos). Glory. APPROVAL-DISAPPROVAL.
Ku′-klux″. The name of an old Southern secret political party. ASSOCIATION.
ky′-an-ize. To prevent decay by using mercuric chlorid. CONSERVATION.
kyle. A sound or strait. GULF-PLAIN.

L

Lab'-a-dist. A member of an old sect of Christian communists. ORTHODOXY-HETERODOXY.

lab'-a-rum. A Roman military standard; a certain ecclesiastical banner. SIGN.

lab'-e-fy. To weaken or impair. BETTERMENT-DETERIORATION.

la'-bel. A tag of paper or other material attached to something, telling its character, etc. NAME-MISNOMER, SIGN.

la'-bent. Slipping. ASCENT-DESCENT.

la'-bi-al. Pertaining to, formed, or articulated by the lips; one of the lip-sounds or letters. BORDER, LETTER.

la'-bi-a"-ted. Lipped. BORDER.

labitur et labetur [L.] (lab'-i-tur et lê-bî'-tur). It flows and it will flow. DISCONTINUANCE-CONTINUANCE, ETERNITY-INSTANTANEITY, PERIOD-PROGRESS.

la'-bor. Toil; a task; pain; travail. ACTION-PASSIVENESS, CREATION-DESTRUCTION, TOIL-RELAXATION; **hard labor,** RECOMPENSE-PUNITION; **labor for,** PURPOSE-LUCK; **labor in one's vocation,** OCCUPATION; **labor in vain,** PROVISION-WASTE, SUCCESS-FAILURE, TRANSCURSION-SHORTCOMING, USEFULNESS-USELESSNESS; **labor lost,** USEFULNESS-USELESSNESS; **labor of love,** COSTLINESS-CHEAPNESS, ENTERTAINMENT-WEARINESS, READINESS-RELUCTANCE, UNSELFISHNESS-SELFISHNESS; **labor under,** CONDITION-SITUATION, DIFFICULTY-FACILITY, EMOTION, HEALTH-SICKNESS, PLEASURE-PAIN; **mountain in labor,** PROVISION-WASTE; **Sisyphean labor,** DIFFICULTY-FACILITY.

LABOR—CAPITAL.

Industry. Useful labor; trade.
Labor. Physical toil or bodily exertion.

LABOR—*Nouns of Agent.*

Artificer. An artistic manufacturer; soldier-mechanic.
Artisan. One skilled in any mechanical art.
Breadwinner. One who works for his living.
Consumer. One who consumes.
Craftsman. } Skilled mechanic.
Handicraftsman. }
Journeyman. Mechanic who has completed his apprenticeship.
Laborer. One who does work requiring no skill.
Mechanic. One who uses tools other than agricultural.
Operative. One who tends machinery.
Producer. One who manufactures crude materials into articles of use.
Proletariat. The wage-workers of a state collectively.
Skilled workman. One skilled in a particular branch of industry.
The masses. The great body of the people.
Toiler. Laborer; hard worker.

LABOR—*Associated Nouns.*

American Federation of Labor. An open organization whose purpose is to advance the cause of laboring men.
Blacklist. A list of persons who are for some reason thought undeserving of employment.
Boycott. A combining to withhold or prevent dealings or social intercourse with.
Knights of Labor. A secret organization whose professed purpose is to secure and maintain the rights of workingmen.
Lockout. The closing of a factory or workshop by an employer, in order to bring the workmen to satisfactory terms by a suspension of wages.
Salary. Fixed regular wages.
Strike. Act of quitting work by a body of workmen, as a means of enforcing compliance with demands.
Union. A league of workmen engaged in a particular trade.
Wages. A compensation given to a hired person for services.

LABOR—*Verbs.*

Boycott. To refrain from any intercourse with some one.
Labor. To work.
Manufacture. To make.
Produce. To make; to yield.
Strike. To quit work, to compel an agreement with the employer.

LABOR—*Adjectives.*

Industrial. Pertaining to industries or trade.
Proletariat. Pertaining to the rabble.

labor, hoc opus, hic [L.] (lê'-bor, hoc o'-pus, hic). This is labor, this is work. DIFFICULTY-FACILITY.

Capital. Wealth employed in production.
Corporation. One or more persons empowered to engage in business under certain conditions.
Monopoly. The complete control of any branch of business.
Stock. Capital of an incorporated company represented by transferable shares.
Trust. A combination of corporations under one management.
Watered stock. Stock not in proportion to the paid-in capital.

CAPITAL—*Nouns of Agent.*

Bank. An establishment for the custody, loan, exchange, or issue of money.
Bank of England. The greatest financial establishment of England.
Bear. One who attempts to depress the value of stocks.
Bloated bondholder. A contemptuous expression for a wealthy person.
Bondholder. One who holds bonds.
Bull. One who attempts to raise the price of stocks.
Capitalist. One who has money invested.
Investor. One who invests money.
Long. One who buys stocks expecting to sell at a higher price.
Magnate. A person of influence in the financial or industrial world.
Man of means. A wealthy person.
Manufacturer. One who manufactures.
Monopolist. One who has complete control of anything.
Napoleon of finance. A leader in the financial world.
Operator. One who carries on an industry.
Rothschild. Figuratively, a leader in the financial world.
Short. One who sells stock for future delivery which he does not at present own.
Speculator. One who buys and sells goods or stocks, etc., with the expectation of deriving profits from the changing prices.

CAPITAL—*Nouns of Place.*

Cotton exchange. A place where cotton is bought and sold.
Exchange. The place where the bankers, merchants, and brokers meet at certain hours to transact business.
Lombard Street. The commercial and financial center of London.
Stock exchange. The place where stocks are bought and sold.
Wall Street. The principal financial center of New York.

CAPITAL—*Associated Nouns.*

Credit. Mercantile reputation entitling one to be trusted.
Plutocracy. A form of government in which the supreme power is in the hands of the wealthy.
Single tax. A tax upon land, held by some theorists to be the only tax which should be levied.

CAPITAL—*Verbs.*

Combine. To unite under one management.
Float a bond issue. To find purchasers for bonds.
Float a loan. To borrow money in exchange for bonds.

lab'-o-ra-to"-ry. A building or room fitted up for conducting scientific experiments. WORKSHOP.

la'-bored. Done with care; elaborate. PREPARATION-NONPREPARATION, PURITY-CRUDENESS; labored study, HEED-DISREGARD.

la'-bor-er. One who performs physical or manual labor. AGENT, LABOR-CAPITAL.

la'-bor-ing. Of or pertaining to labor. TOIL-RELAXATION; laboring man, AGENT; laboring oar, TOIL-RELAXATION.

la-bo'-ri-ous. Toilsome; arduous. DIFFICULTY-FACILITY, TOIL-RELAXATION.

la-bo'-ri-ous-ly. Arduously. TOIL-RELAXATION.

la-bo'-ri-ous-ness. State of being laborious. ACTIVITY-INDOLENCE.

lab'-y-rinth. A maze. CIRCLE-WINDING, REGULARITY-IRREGULARITY, TIDINGS-MYSTERY.

lab''-y-rin'-thi-an. Mazy. CIRCLE-WINDING.

lab''-y-rin'-thic. Complicated. CIRCLE-WINDING.

lab''-y-rin'-thine. Mazy. CIRCLE-WINDING.

lac. A resinous substance; the sum of 100,000. FIVE-QUINQUESECTION, PULPINESS-ROSIN; lac of rupees, MONEY.

lac'-co-lith. Lava. GEOLOGY.

lace. A delicate open network made of threads of various materials. CROSSING, EMBELLISHMENT-DISFIGUREMENT, UNION-DISUNION; lace one's jacket, RECOMPENSE-PUNITION.

lac'-er-a-ble. Capable of being lacerated. TOUGHNESS-BRITTLENESS.

lac'-er-ate. To tear rudely or raggedly. UNION-DISUNION; lacerate the heart, PLEASURABLENESS-PAINFULNESS..

lac''-er-a'-tion. The act of tearing. UNION-DISUNION.

lach'-es. Neglect. CAREFULNESS-NEGLECT, OBSERVANCE-NONOBSERVANCE.

lachrymæ, hinc illæ [L.] (lac'-ri-mî, hinc il'-lî). Hence these tears. PLEASURABLENESS-PAINFULNESS.

lack. To need; to want; to fail. AFFLUENCE-PENURY, ENOUGH, ENTIRETY-DEFICIENCY, NEED; lack faith, GODLINESS-DISBELIEF; lack preparation, PREPARATION-NONPREPARATION; lack wit, SAGE-FOOL.

lack'-a-dai'-si-cal. Affectedly pensive. ACTIVITY-INDOLENCE, DESIRE-DISTASTE, LIGHTHEARTEDNESS-DEJECTION.

lack'-a-dai''-sy. An exclamation denoting grief, regret, or surprise. ASTONISHMENT-EXPECTANCE, JUBILATION-LAMENTATION.

lack'-a-day''. An exclamation of grief, regret, etc. JUBILATION-LAMENTATION.

lack'-brain''. One deficient in understanding. SAGACITY-INCAPACITY, SAGE-FOOL.

lack'-er. A kind of varnish; to varnish. COVER-LINING, EMBELLISHMENT-DISFIGUREMENT, PULPINESS-ROSIN.

lack'-ey. An attending servant. CHIEF-UNDERLING.

lack'-lus''-ter. Want of luster; wanting brightness. COLOR-ACHROMATISM, DIMNESS.

la-con'-ic. Brief. TERSENESS-PROLIXITY.

lac'-o-nism. A brief expression. TERSENESS-PROLIXITY.

lac'-quer. A kind of varnish; to varnish. COVER-LINING, EMBELLISHMENT-DISFIGUREMENT, PULPINESS-ROSIN.

lac''-ri-ma'-tion. The act of shedding tears. JUBILATION-LAMENTATION.

lac'-ri-ma-to''-ry. A small narrow-necked glass bottle, of a type found in ancient tombs. JUBILATION-LAMENTATION.

lacrimis, quis temperet a [L.] (lac'-ri-mis, quis tem'-per-et ê). Who can refrain from tears? COMPASSION-RUTHLESSNESS.

lac'-ri-mose. Shedding tears. LIGHTHEARTEDNESS-DEJECTION.

la-crosse'. A game of ball. ENTERTAINMENT-WEARINESS.

lac'-te-al. Pertaining to milk. VISCIDITY-FOAM.

lac'-te-an. Milky. VISCIDITY-FOAM.

lac'-te-ous. Milk-like. VISCIDITY-FOAM.

lac-tes'-cent. Becoming milky. VISCIDITY-FOAM.

lac-tif''-e-rous. Containing milk. VISCIDITY-FOAM.

la-cu'-na. A small blank space. CONVEXITY-CONCAVITY, INTERSPACE-CONTACT.

la-cus'-trine. Pertaining to a lake. GULF-PLAIN.

lad. A boy or youth. INFANT-VETERAN.

lad'-der. A device for climbing and descending; means of ascent. ASCENT-DESCENT, WAY; kick down the ladder, DETERMINATION-VACILLATION.

lade. To load; to oppress. CONTENTS-RECEIVER, ESTABLISHMENT-REMOVAL; lade out, ADMISSION-EXPULSION.

la'-den. Loaded; weighed down. ENTIRETY-DEFICIENCY; heavy laden, AFFECTIONS; laden with, HOLDING-EXEMPTION.

la'-ding. The act of loading; burden. CONTENTS-RECEIVER, ESTABLISHMENT-REMOVAL, PROPERTY; bill of lading, RECORD.

la'-dle. A cup-shaped vessel intended for dipping and pouring; to use such a vessel. CONTENTS-RECEIVER, CONVEYANCE-VESSEL, TRANSFER.

la'-dy. A gentlewoman. GENTILITY-COMMONALTY, MALE-FEMALE, MATRIMONY-CELIBACY; lady help, CHIEF-UNDERLING; lady's maid, CHIEF-UNDERLING.

la'-dy-like''. Refined; gentle. MALE-FEMALE, SOCIETY-LUDICROUSNESS.

la'-dy-love''. A sweetheart. LOVE-HATE.

lag. To move slowly; to loiter. ACTIVITY-INDOLENCE, LEADING-FOLLOWING, SWIFTNESS-SLOWNESS.

lag'-gard. Slow; a loiterer. ACTIVITY-INDOLENCE, READINESS-RELUCTANCE.

lag'-ging. Loitering. ACTIVITY-INDOLENCE.

la-goon'. A pool or lake; a marshy place. GULF-PLAIN.

la-gune'. A lagoon. GULF-PLAIN.

la grippe [F.] (la grîp). Influenza. HEALTH-SICKNESS.

la'-ic-al. Lay. MINISTRY-LAITY.

laid. Put; stored; taken; placed. Laid by the heels, RELEASE-RESTRAINT; laid low, STRENGTH-WEAKNESS; laid on one's back, MIGHT-IMPOTENCE; laid up, HEALTH-SICKNESS.

lair. The den of a wild animal. CLEANNESS-FILTHINESS, DWELLER-HABITATION.

laird. A lord; a landlord. CHIEF-UNDERLING, GENTILITY-COMMONALTY, HOLDER.

La'-is. The name of two Greek courtezans. PURITY-RAKE.

laisse manger, cela se [F.] (lês man'-zhê', se-la' se). That is eatable. PALATABLENESS-UNPALATABLENESS.

laisser aller [F.] (lê-sê' al-lê'). To let alone. ACTION-PASSIVENESS, EXCITABILITY-INEXCITABILITY, LIBERTY-SUBJECTION, RULE-LICENSE.

laisser faire [F.] (lê-sê' fêr). To let alone. ACTION-PASSIVENESS, EXCITABILITY-INEXCITABILITY, LIBERTY-SUBJECTION, RULE-LICENSE.

la'-i-ty. The people as distinguished from the clergy. MINISTRY-LAITY.

lake. An inland body of water; a certain pigment. GULF-PLAIN, REDNESS-GREENNESS; lake of fire and brimstone, HEAVEN-HELL.

la'-ma. A priest, monk, or nun of the branch of Buddhism called Lamaism. CHIEF-UNDERLING, MINISTRY-LAITY.

La Marseillaise [F.] (la mar''-sê-lyêz'). French national hymn. PATRIOTISM-TREASON.

lamb. A young sheep; any gentle or innocent person. FAUNA-FLORA, INFANT-VETERAN, INNOCENCE-GUILT; go out like a lamb, TURBULENCE-CALMNESS; lion lies down with lamb, STRIFE-PEACE.

Lamb of God. Jesus Christ. DIVINITY.

lam'-bent. Playing with a licking movement; gently radiant. Touch; **lambent flame,** Heat-Cold, Light-Darkness.

lamb'-kin. A little lamb. Fauna-Flora, Infant-Veteran.

lamb'-like''. Gentle; innocent. Excitability-Inexcitability, Innocence-Guilt.

lame. Crippled; halting; to disable. Betterment-Deterioration, Entirety-Deficiency, Faultless-ness-Faultiness, Might-Impotence, Strength-Weakness, Success-Failure, Usefulness-Use-lessness; **help a lame dog over a stile,** Justification-Charge, Obstruction-Help; **lame conclusion,** Ratiocination-Casuistry, Success-Failure; **lame duck,** Settlement-Default; **lame excuse,** Pretext.

la-mel'-la. A thin scale, plate, or lamina. Lamina-Fiber.

lam'-el-lar. Scale-like. Lamina-Fiber.

lam'-el-la''-ted. Composed of or having thin plates, or lamellæ. Lamina-Fiber.

la-mel'-li-form. Scale-like. Lamina-Fiber.

la-ment'. To mourn for; to grieve; a loud complaint. Approval-Disapproval, Contentedness-Discontentment, Jubilation-Lamentation.

lam'-en-ta-ble. Grievous; mournful; causing dissatisfaction. Goodness-Badness, Lightheartedness-Dejection, Pleasurableness-Painfulness.

lam'-en-ta-bly. In a lamentable manner. Magnitude-Smallness.

lam''-en-ta'-tion. Utterance of profound grief. Jubilation-Lamentation.

la-ment'-ing. Bewailing. Jubilation-Lamentation.

La'-mi-a. A female demon that enticed youths and fed upon their flesh and blood. Devotion-Magician, Jove-Fiend.

lam'-i-na. A thin scale or sheet; a layer or coat lying over another. Lamina-Fiber, Whole-Part.

LAMINA—FIBER.

Bed. A layer or seam, or a horizontal stratum between layers.

Board. A piece of timber sawed thin.

Coat. A layer of any substance covering another.

Coats of an onion. The concentric layers of an onion.

Cut. A portion severed or cut off.

Escarpment. Ground about a fortified place cut nearly vertical to prevent hostile approach.

Film. A thin membranous covering.

Flag. A flat layer of stone used for paving.

Floor. The surface or platform of a structure on which we walk.

Foil. A leaf or very thin sheet of metal.

Integument. That which naturally covers another thing. See Cover.

Lamina. A layer or coat lying over another.

Laminella [L.]. A small layer.

Layer. A single thickness of anything.

Leaf. Something like a leaf in being wide and thin.

Membrane. A thin layer or fold of tissue.

Nest of boxes. A set of boxes fitting one into another.

Peel. The skin or rind.

Pellicle. A thin skin or film.

Plank. A piece of sawed timber, comparatively thin in proportion to its length and breadth.

Plate. A flat piece of metal, the thickness of which is small in comparison with the other dimensions.

Platter. A large plate or shallow dish.

Rasher. A thin slice of bacon.

Scale. A layer or leaf of metal or other material.

Scaliness. The condition of being scaly.

Shaving. A thin slice or strip pared off with a shave.

Sheet. A broad, thinly expanded portion of metal or other substance.

Shive. A thin piece or fragment of anything.

Slab. A thin piece of anything, especially of stone.

Slice. A thin, broad piece cut off.

Stage. A floor.

Story. A floor of a house.

Stratification. The act of placing in layers.

Stratum. A bed of earth or rock.

Substratum. A layer of earth underlying another.

Table. A broad flat surface.

Tablet. A flat surface.

Trencher. A large wooden plate.

Wafer. A thin cake.

Zone. A portion of a surface of a sphere.

Lamina—Verbs.

Coat. Cover with a layer.

Cover. Overlay with something. See Cover.

Pare. Cut off a layer.

Peel. Strip off a layer.

Plate. Cover with a thin layer.

Shave. Take from the surface by paring or scraping.

Slice. Cut into thin pieces.

Veneer. Cover with veneer.

Lamina—Adjectives.

Discoid. Like a disk in form.

Filmy. Like a film.

Band. A narrow ligament with which a thing is encircled.

Beard, etc. The hair that grows on the face of adult males. See Smoothness-Roughness.

Capillament. A very fine filament or thread.

Cilium [L.]. A slender thread.

Cord. A string or small rope, composed of several strands twisted together.

Cotton. A soft downy substance that grows in long fibers on the cotton plant.

Fascia [L.]. A band.

Fiber. A very fine and slender thread.

Filament. A hair-like thread.

Fillet. A little band used to encircle the head.

Flax. A plant whose fiber is used for making thread and cloth.

Funicle. A small cord or fiber.

Gossamer. A thin, filmy substance, like cobwebs, floating in the air.

Hair. The collection of filaments growing from the skin of an animal.

Hair-stroke. A fine stroke.

Hemp. A plant, the fibrous bark of which is used for making cloth and cordage.

Jute. A strong, coarse fiber of a plant used for making mats, cordage, etc.

Lath. A thin, narrow strip of wood.

Line. A linen thread or string; a more or less threadlike mark of a pen, pencil, etc.

List. A strip forming the woven border or selvage of cloth.

Oakum. The material obtained by untwisting and picking into loose fibers old hemp ropes.

Pack-thread. Strong thread or small twine used for tying parcels.

Ramification. A small branch or offshoot proceeding from a main stock.

Riband.⎫
Ribbon.⎭ A narrow strip or shred.

Roll. A quantity of cloth wound into a cylindrical form.

Rope. A large, stout cord made of strands twisted or braided together.

Sewing silk. Silk thread.

Shaving. A thin slice or strip pared off with a shave.

Shiver. One of the small pieces or splinters into which a brittle thing is broken.

Shred. A long, narrow piece cut or torn off.

Slip. A slender piece of any material.

Spill. A slender piece of anything.

Splinter. A thin piece split or rent off lengthwise.

String. A small cord, a line, or twine.

Strip. A narrow piece of any material.

Tape. A narrow fillet or band of cotton or linen.

Tendril. A slender, leafless portion of a plant by which it becomes attached to a supporting body.

Twine. A small thread composed of smaller threads braided together.

Twist. A closely twisted, strong sewing silk.

Vein. A narrow mass of rocks intersecting other rocks.

Whipcord. A kind of hard-twisted or braided cord, used for making whip-lashes.

Wire. A thread or slender rod of metal.

Yarn. Woolen thread.

LAMINA—FIBER—*Continued.*

LAMINA—Adjectives—*Continued.*

Flaky. Like flakes.
Foliaceous. Like a leaf.
Foliated. Reduced to a leaf.
Lamellar. ⎫
Lamellated. ⎬ Having thin plates.
Laminated. ⎭
Lamelliform. Like a thin plate in form.
Laminiferous. Bearing laminæ.
Membranous. Like membrane.
Micaceous. Of the nature of mica.
Scaly. With a covering of scales.
Schistose. Of the nature of schist.
Schistous. With the quality of being schistose.
Squamous. Coated with scales.
Stratified. Arranged in strata.
Stratiform. Of the form of a stratum.
Tabular. Of the nature of a table.

Fiber—*Adjectives.*

Anguilliform. Having the form of an eel.
Capillary. Hair-like; threadlike; very fine and slender.
Capilliform. Formed like a thread or filament.
Fibrillous. Pertaining to fibers.
Fibrous. Like or pertaining to a fiber.
Filaceous. Consisting of threads.
Filamentous. Like a filament or thread.
Filiform. Formed like a filament.
Flagelliform. Formed like a flagellum, long, narrow, and slender.
Funicular. Consisting of or pertaining to a fiber.
Hairy, etc. Covered with hairs; like hair. See SMOOTHNESS-ROUGHNESS.
Ropy. Having the capability to be drawn out into a thread.
Stringy. Having an appearance like a string.
Threadlike. Having the form of a thread.
Wire-drawn. Drawn out into a wire.
Wiry. Thin and flexible, like a wire.

lam'-i-na"-ted. Laminar; scaled. LAMINA-FIBER.
lam"-i-nif'-er-ous. Bearing or composed of laminæ. LAMINA-FIBER.
Lam'-mas. The feast of Peter's chains. CEREMONIAL.
lamp. Any device for furnishing a light; also, one for heating. LUMINARY-SHADE; **rub the lamp,** DEVOTION-MAGIC; **safety lamp,** REFUGE-PITFALL; **smell of the lamp,** PREPARATION-NONPREPARATION, SIMPLICITY-FLORIDNESS.
lamp'-light"-er. A person who lights lamps. ACTIVITY-INDOLENCE.
lam-poon'. A personal, sarcastic, and malicious publication. ADULATION-DISPARAGEMENT, APPROVAL-DISAPPROVAL.
lam-poon'-er. One who lampoons. FLATTERER-DEFAMER.
lana caprina, de [L.] (lē'-na cap-rai'-na, di). About goat's wool. [Something non-existent.] CONSEQUENCE-INSIGNIFICANCE.
la'-nate. Woolly. SMOOTHNESS-ROUGHNESS.
la'-na"-ted. Woolly. SMOOTHNESS-ROUGHNESS.
lance. A long shaft with a spear-head; to cut open; to pierce with a lance. APERTURE-CLOSURE, PUSH-PULL, WEAPON; **break a lance with,** ATTACK-DEFENSE, FIGHTING-CONCILIATION; **couch one's lance,** STRIFE-PEACE; **lance corporal,** CHIEF-UNDERLING.
lan'-cer. A cavalry soldier, carrying a lance. BELLIGERENT.
lan'-cet. A surgical instrument with small sharp blades. PERFORATOR-STOPPER, SHARPNESS-BLUNTNESS.
lan'-ci-nate. To shoot through, as a pain. PLEASURABLENESS-PAINFULNESS, SENSUALITY-SUFFERING.
land. The exposed surface of the earth; real estate; to come or bring to land. ARRIVAL-DEPARTURE, OCEAN-LAND, PROPERTY; **how the land lies,** CONDITION-SITUATION, PREVISION, RECKLESSNESS-CAUTION, TRIAL; **hug the land,** APPROACH-WITHDRAWAL, TRAVELING-NAVIGATION; **in the land of the living,** LIFE-DEATH; **land covered with water,** GULF-PLAIN; **land flowing with milk and honey,** FERTILITY-STERILITY, PLEASURABLENESS-PAINFULNESS; **make the land,** APPROACH-WITHDRAWAL; **on land,** OCEAN-LAND; **see land,** SANGUINENESS-HOPELESSNESS.
lan'-dam-man. The president of the Swiss republic. CHIEF-UNDERLING.
lan'-dau. A two-seated carriage with movable top. CONVEYANCE-VESSEL.
land'-ed. Having an estate in land; consisting in land. OCEAN-LAND, PROPERTY; **landed estate,** PROPERTY; **landed gentry,** HOLDER.
land'-grave". A title of nobility in the old German empire. CHIEF-UNDERLING.
land'-hold"-er. A landowner. HOLDER.

land'-ing. The act of going or placing ashore; a wharf; the head of a staircase, or a platform in it. ARRIVAL-DEPARTURE, SUSPENSION-SUPPORT.
land'-ing-place". A wharf; head of a stairs. ARRIVAL-DEPARTURE, SUSPENSION-SUPPORT.
land'-ing-stage". A float. ARRIVAL-DEPARTURE, SUSPENSION-SUPPORT.
land'-la"-dy. A woman who keeps an inn or boarding-place. HOLDER.
land'-locked". Well surrounded and protected by land. CONFINEMENT.
land'-lo"-per. A vagabond. WAYFARER-SEAFARER.
land'-lord". An innkeeper; one who owns and lets land. HOLDER.
land'-lub"-ber. A raw sailor. ADEPT-BUNGLER.
land'-mark". A fixed mark serving as a boundary mark; a distinguishing fact, event, era, or limit. BOUNDARY, MENSURATION, SIGN.
land'-own"-er. One who owns real estate. HOLDER.
land'-reeve". An assistant land-steward. MANAGER.
land'-scape. A stretch of country. APPEARANCE-DISAPPEARANCE, PAINTING; **landscape gardening,** BEAUTY-UGLINESS, DOMESTICATION-AGRICULTURE; **landscape painting,** PAINTING; **landscape painter,** ARTIST.
land'-shark". A land-grabber. ROBBER.
land'-slip". The slipping of a mass of earth to a lower level. ASCENT-DESCENT.
lands'-man. One who lives on land. OCEAN-LAND.
landsturm [G.] (lant'-sturm"). A general levy in time of war. BELLIGERENT.
land'-sur-vey"-ing. The locating of boundaries, areas, etc., of tracts of lands. MENSURATION.
land'-sur-vey"-or. A land-measurer. MENSURATION.
landwehr [G.] (lant'-vêr"). An emergency militia of Germany and certain other countries. BELLIGERENT.
lane. A narrow way or path. DWELLER-HABITATION, WAY.
lan'-grage shot. A langrel. WEAPON.
lan'-grel. A missile used to destroy the enemy's rigging. WEAPON.
lang'-syne'. Happy days gone by. FUTURE-PAST.
lan'-guage. Speech. LANGUAGE; **command of language,** FORCE-WEAKNESS, SPEECH-INARTICULATENESS, STYLE; **murder the language,** SPEECH-INARTICULATENESS; **strong language,** CHARITABLENESS-CURSE, FORCE-WEAKNESS.

LANGUAGE.

Babel. The tower at whose building there was confusion of tongues; hence, confused speech.
Dialect. The form of speech of a limited region of people.
Household words. Speech used most frequently in ordinary conversation.

King's English. Correct or current language of good speakers.

Language. A means of expressing ideas.

Lingo. Language rendered slightly unintelligible by peculiar expression.

Mother tongue. The language of one's native land.

Native tongue. The language born with one.

Pantomime. A dramatic representation in mute actions. See SIGN.

Pasigraphy. A universal sign language.

Phraseology. Manner of expression. See STYLE.

Queen's English. Correct English.

Speech. A particular language as distinct from others

Tongue. A language.

Vernacular. The common form of expression in a particular locality.

Vulgar tongue. The language of the common people.

LANGUAGE—*Literary Terms.*

Belles-lettres. Polite or elegant literature.

Classics. Literary works regarded as models; particularly those of ancient Greece and Rome.

Dead languages. Languages no longer in use except as models for study.

Genius of a language. The peculiar character of a language.

Humanities. Collectively the branches of classical literature.

Letters. Literary culture.

Literæ humaniores [L.] Polite literature.

Literature. Written appointed works.

Muses. The mythical goddesses of literary pursuits.

Polite literature. Refined literature.

Republic of letters. The collective body of literary men.

Scholarship, etc. A scholar's mental attainments. See KNOWLEDGE.

LANGUAGE—*Scientific Terms.*

Chrestomathy. Extracts compiled for instruction in a language.

Comparative grammar. Comparison of the grammatical forms of different languages.

Glossology.⎫ Study of the phenomena and classification of languages.
Glottology.⎭

Linguist. One learned in different languages. See SCHOLAR.

Linguistics. Comparative study of languages

Onomatopœia [Gr.] The formation of words by imitation of natural sounds.

Paleography. The study of ancient manuscripts.

Paleology. The study of antiquities.

Philology. The historical and literary study of language.

LANGUAGE—*Verbs.*

Express by words, etc. See PHRASES.

LANGUAGE—*Adjectives.*

Current. Passing from mouth to mouth.

Dialectic. Pertaining to a dialect.

Lingual. Pertaining to the tongue in speech.

Linguistic. Pertaining to language.

Literary. Pertaining to literature.

Polyglot. Expressed in many languages.

Vernacular. Belonging to one's native land.

LANGUAGE—*Phrases.*

Belles-lettres [F.]. Beautiful letters; polite literature.

Genius of a language. The dominant influence of a language.

Literæ humaniores [L.]. Studies especially adapted to humanize; polite literature.

Polite literature. Highly finished, elegant literature.

Republic of letters. The whole community of those devoted to literature.

lan'-guid. Devoid of energy; listless. ACTIVITY-INDOLENCE, FORCE-WEAKNESS, SENSITIVENESS-APATHY, STRENGTH-WEAKNESS, SWIFTNESS-SLOWNESS.

lan'-guish. To lose strength or animation; to fall off; to fade; to affect sentimental tenderness. ACTIVITY-INDOLENCE, HEALTH-SICKNESS, INCREASE-DECREASE, PLEASURE-PAIN, STRENGTH-WEAKNESS; **languish for,** DESIRE-DISTASTE.

lan'-guish-ing. Failing. STRENGTH-WEAKNESS.

lan'-guish-ment. The condition of drooping or pining. JUBILATION-LAMENTATION.

lan'-guor. Dulness or heaviness; languidness; inertness; lassitude of body. ACTIVITY-INDOLENCE, STRENGTH-WEAKNESS, SWIFTNESS-SLOWNESS, VIGOR-INERTIA.

lank. Lean. BREADTH-NARROWNESS.

lank'-y. Tall; somewhat shrunken. BREADTH-NARROWNESS, HEIGHT-LOWNESS.

lan'-tern. A transparent or translucent case, enclosing a lamp or light. LUMINARY-SHADE; **lantern jaws,** BREADTH-NARROWNESS; **lantern of Diogenes,** INVESTIGATION-ANSWER; **magic lantern,** APPEARANCE-DISAPPEARANCE, SIGHT-DIMSIGHTEDNESS.

lanterne, à la [F.] (lan'-tern, a la). To the lamp-post; hang him. RECOMPENSE-PUNITION.

lan'-tern-jawed''. Having a thin visage. BREADTH-NARROWNESS.

la-nu'-gi-nose''.⎫ Woolly or downy SMOOTHNESS-
la-nu'-gi-nous.⎭ ROUGHNESS.

La-oc'-o-on. A statue representing the death of the Trojan priest Laocoon and his two sons. SCULPTURE.

lap. To wrap around; to overlap; to lick up; to ripple against; the front surface of the thighs; a place of supporting; part of the dress covering the lap. CENTER, CONFINEMENT, DRESS-UNDRESS, DWELLER-HABITATION, ENVIRONMENT-INTERPOSITION, NUTRIMENT-EXCRETION, SUSPENSION-SUPPORT; **lap of luxury,** ACTIVITY-INDOLENCE, MODERATION-SELFINDULGENCE, SENSUALITY-SUFFERING; **lap up,** DRESS-UNDRESS.

lap'-dog''. A small dog fondled in the lap; an obsequious person. FAUNA-FLORA, PRESUMPTION-OBSEQUIOUSNESS.

la-pel'. Part of a garment which is made to turn back or fold over. PLICATURE.

lap'-i-date. To cut and polish precious stones; to stone. ATTACK-DEFENSE, LIFE-KILLING, RECOMPENSE-PUNITION.

lapidem, omnem movere [L.] (lap'-id-em, om'-nem mo-vî'-rî). To leave no stone unturned. ENTIRETY-DEFICIENCY.

lap''-i-des'-cence. A hardening into stone. HARDNESS-SOFTNESS.

la-pid''-i-fi-ca'-tion. The act of becoming stone, or like stone. HARDNESS-SOFTNESS.

lapis lazuli [L.] (lê'-pis laz'-yu-lai). A rich blue complex mixture of minerals. BLUENESS-ORANGE, EMBELLISHMENT-DISFIGUREMENT.

lap'-pet. A small flap used for ornamenting a head-dress or garment. INCREMENT-REMNANT.

lapse. To slip; to slip away; to become void; to deviate from rectitude; imperceptible movement; a mistake through lack of care or attention. ASCENT-DESCENT, BETTERMENT-DETERIORATION, CONVERSION, FUTURE-PAST, GAIN-LOSS, INNOCENCE-GUILT, PERIOD-PROGRESS, RENOVATION-RELAPSE, VIRTUE-VICE; **lapse of memory,** REMEMBRANCE-FORGETFULNESS; **lapse of time,** PERIOD-PROGRESS.

lapsed. Fallen; passed away. FUTURE-PAST.

lapsus linguæ [L.] (lap'-sus lin'-gwî). A slip of the tongue. GRAMMAR-SOLECISM, SPEECH-INARTICULATENESS, TRUTH-ERROR.

lapt. Wrapped around. CONFINEMENT.

La-pu'-ta. In *Gulliver's Travels,* a flying island peopled with philosophers. **College of Laputa,** EDUCATION-MISTEACHING.

lar'-board. The left-hand side of a vessel. RIGHT-LEFT.

lar'-ce-ny. Theft. THEFT.

lard. The semisolid oil of hog's fat. PULPINESS-OILINESS.

lar-da'-ceous. Of the nature of lard; fatty. PULPINESS-OILINESS.

lar'-der. Pantry. STORE; **contents of the larder,** NUTRIMENT-EXCRETION.

Lares et Penates [L.] (lê'-rîz et pen-ê'-tîz). Household gods. DEVOTION-IDOLATRY, DWELLER-HABITATION.

large. Great; extensive. GREATNESS-LITTLENESS, MAGNITUDE-SMALLNESS; **at large,** LIBERTY-SUBJECTION, TERSENESS-PROLIXITY; **become large,** GREATness-Littleness; **large as life,** Greatness-Little-ness; **large number,** Multiplicity-Paucity; **large type,** Consequence-Insignificance.

large'–heart''-ed. Sympathetic; generous. Charita-bleness - Malevolence, Generosity - Frugality, Humanitarianism-Misanthropy, Unselfishness-Selfishness.

large'-ness. Bigness. Greatness-Littleness.

larg'-er. Greater. Enlargement-Diminution.

larg''-ess. Bounty bestowed. Giving-Receiving.

larg'-est. Greatest. **Largest portion,** Greatness-Littleness.

larghetto [It.] (lar-get'-to). Slow: a direction to a musician. Music, Swiftness-Slowness.

lar-gil'-o-quent. Pompous; grandiloquent. Talkative-ness-Taciturnity, Terseness-Prolixity.

largiri de alieno, facile [L.] (lar-jai'-rai dî a-li-î'-no, fas'-i-lî). It is easy to be lavish with what is not your own. Extravagance-Avarice.

largo [It.] (lar'-go). A grave piece. Music, Swiftness-Slowness.

lark. A singing bird; a frolic. Ascent-Descent, En-tertainment-Weariness; **with the lark,** Morning-Evening.

larmes aux yeux [F.] (larm zoz yu). Tears in the eyes. Jubilation-Lamentation.

larmes, fondre en [F.] (larm, fon·dr an·). To burst into tears. Jubilation-Lamentation.

larmoyante, comédie [F.] (lar-mwa-yan·t', co-mê-dî'). Pathetic comedy. Acting.

lar'-rup. To thrash. Recompense-Punition.

lar'-um. An alarm. Alarm, Loudness-Faintness.

lar'-va. An insect in the caterpillar, or grub state. Biology, Infant-Veteran.

lar'-ynx. The special organ of voice. Watercourse-Airpipe.

lasciate ogni speranza [It.] (las-cha'-tê ony'-i spêr-an'-tsa). All hope abandon. Sanguineness-Hopeless-ness.

las-civ'-i-en-cy. Lewdness. Purity-Impurity.

las-civ'-i-ous. Lustful. Purity-Impurity.

lash. To scourge; to dash against; to berate; a whip; a stroke with a whip; a sarcastic fling; to tie together. Approval-Disapproval, Motive-Caprice, Recom-pense-Punition, Recompense-Scourge, Turbu-lence-Calmness, Union-Disunion; **lash into fury,** Excitation, Favorite-Anger, Turbulence-Calm-ness; **lash the waves,** Usefulness-Uselessness; **under the lash,** Coercion, Liberty-Subjection.

lass. A young woman. Infant-Veteran.

las'-sie. A little lass. Infant-Veteran.

las'-si-tude. Languor; debility. Entertainment-Weariness, Weariness-Refreshment.

las'-so. A long line with running noose; to capture with a lasso. Circle-Winding, Connective.

last. Final; to endure; to hold out; most remote from; utmost; a wooden form, on which to make a boot or shoe. Beginning-End, Copy-Model, Duration-Neverness, Future-Past, Lastingness-Tran-sientness, Mutation-Permanence; **at last,** Begin-ning-End, Earliness-Lateness; **at the last extrem-ity,** Security-Insecurity; **breathe one's last,** Life-Death; **die in the last ditch,** Persistence-Whim; **game to the last,** Persistence-Whim; **go to one's last home,** Life-Death; **last but one,** Beginning-End; **last finish,** Completion-Noncompletion; **last for-ever,** Eternity-Instantaneity; **last gasp,** Life-Death, Sanguineness-Hopelessness; **last resort,** Refuge-Pitfall, Volition-Obligation; **last shift,** Volition-Obligation; **last sleep,** Life-Death; **last stage,** Beginning-End; **last straw that breaks the camel's back,** Cause-Effect; **last stroke,** Comple-tion-Noncompletion; **last syllable of recorded time,** Eternity-Instantaneity; **last touch,** Completion-Noncompletion; **last word,** Assertion - Denial, Bigotry-Apostasy; **last year,** etc., Future-Past; **never hear the last of,** Recurrence; **on last legs,** Betterment-Deterioration, Life-Death, Strength-Weakness, Weariness-Refreshment, Welfare-Misfortune.

last'-ing. Durable. Lastingness-Transientness; **lasting friendship,** Amity-Hostility.

last'-ing-ness. Durableness. Lastingness-Tran-sientness.

LASTINGNESS—TRANSIENTNESS.

A century. A period of 100 years.

A length of time. } Considerable duration.
A long time. }

An age. A long time.

An eternity. Infinite duration.

Continuance. Duration; repetition of the same.

Delay. See Earliness-Lateness.

Distance of time. Time long past.

Diuturnity. Lastingness.

Durability. Power to remain the same for a long time.

Durableness. Quality of preventing decay.

Extension of time. A making to continue during a longer time.

Lastingness. Quality of continuing or remaining a long time.

Longevity, etc. Long duration of life. See Infancy-Age.

Permanence. See Stability.

Perpetuity. See Eternity.

Persistence. Continuing in the same line.

Prolongation. Extending the time; lengthening.

Protraction. Drawing out the time beyond the time set.

Slowness. Long duration. See Swiftness-Slowness.

Standing. Long continuance.

Survival. } Living or continuing longer than another person, thing.
Survivance. } or event.

LASTINGNESS—*Verbs.*

Abide. Stay; remain; tarry.

Brave a thousand years. To face a millennium. "Has braved a thou-sand years the battle and the breeze." [Campbell, *Ye Mariners of England.*]

Continue. To be permanent; persist.

Drag a lengthening chain. Drawing something increasing in weight. [Goldsmith, *The Traveler,* 7.]

Drag its slow length along. Draw along with difficulty, like a snail.

Caducity. Tendency to fall; feebleness of old age.

Changeableness. See Mutability.

Evanescence. The state or act of vanishing away.

Fugacity. Tendency to last but a short time.

Impermanence. Want of lastingness.

Interchange. Alternate succession.

Mortality. Subjection to death or the necessity of dying.

Suddenness. See Instantaneity.

Transientness. See *Adjectives.*

TRANSIENTNESS—*Associated Nouns.*

Bubble. A thin film of liquid inflated with air or gas; anything want-ing firmness or solidity.

Interregnum. The time during which a throne is vacant between the death or abdication of a sovereign and the accession of his suc-cessor.

May-fly. An insect which appears in May.

Nine days' wonder. Anything exciting wonder or admiration for a short time.

Span. A small space or brief portion of time.

Spurt. An increased exertion for a brief space.

Temporary arrangement. An arrangement for a short time.

Velocity. Quickness of motion. See Swiftness.

TRANSIENTNESS—*Verbs.*

Evaporate. Disappear; pass away.

Fade. To lose vitality; freshness.

Flit. To pass over rapidly.

Fly. To move quickly; hasten.

Gallop. To hurry, like a horse.

Vanish. Disappear.

LASTINGNESS—TRANSIENTNESS—*Continued.*

LASTINGNESS—Verbs—*Continued.*

Drag on. Pull along; trail.
Draw out. Lengthen; prolong.
Eke out. To piece out; obtain with difficulty.
Endure. To continue; be firm.
Gain time. Improve; progress; take a nearer course.
Lengthen out. Stretch; extend; prolong.
Live to fight again. Survive; be victorious.
Outlast. Surpass; excel.
Outlive. Endure longer; last longer than.
Prolong. See *Nouns.*
Protract. To draw out beyond the time set
Remain. Left over; continue.
Stand. To last; to endure; unchanged.
Survive. Outlive; outlast; exist.
Tarry. Abide; stay; remain. See LATENESS.
Temporize. To procrastinate; delay; time-serving.
Talk against time. Fill in a period with nothing to say.

LASTINGNESS—*Adjectives.*

Abiding. Continuing.
Chronic. Lingering; lasting.
Diuturnal. See *Nouns.*
Evergreen. Always green; fresh.
Intransient. Remaining; permanent.
Intransitive. Not passing over; constant.
Intransmutable. Unchangeable.
Lasting. Enduring; perpetual.
Life-long. Lasting for life.
Lingering. Protracted.
Livelong. Entire.
Longeval. } Capable of living long.
Long-lived. }
Long-pending. Lingering.
Long-standing. Enduring.
Long-winded. Prolonged.
Macrobiotic. Long-lived.
Perennial. Unfailing; unceasing.
Permanent. See sub *Nouns.*
Perpetual. See ETERNITY.
Prolonged. See *Nouns.*
Protracted. See *Nouns.*
Slow. See SLOWNESS.
Spun out. Greatly extended.

LASTINGNESS—*Adverbial Phrases.*

All the day long; all the year round; as the day is long; day after day; for ages; for a long time; for an age; for ever so long; for good; for many a long day; hour after hour; long ago (see PAST); *longo intervallo* [L.], by or with a long interval; **morning, noon, and night; permanently; the livelong day.**

TRANSIENTNESS—PHRASES—*Continued from Column 2.*

One's days are numbered.
Sic transit gloria mundi [L.]. Thus the glory of this world passeth away.
The time is up.

TRANSIENTNESS—*Verbal Expressions.*

Be transient; pass away; pass away like a cloud; pass away like a dream; pass away like a shadow; pass away like a summer cloud.

TRANSIENTNESS—*Adjectives.*

Brief. Short; transitory.
Brisk. Quick; lively; active.
Cursory. Hasty; desultory.
Deciduous. Falling off; shedding yearly.
Ephemeral. Beginning and ending in a day.
Evanescent. See *Nouns.*
Extemporaneous. On the spur of the moment; impromptu.
Fleeting. Swift; rapid; quick.
Flying. To pass through the air, as a bird.
Fugacious. Transitory; temporary; tendency to flee.
Fugitive. Escape by stealth; especially, from justice.
Impermanent. Not lasting; changeable; unstable.
Momentary. See ETERNITY-INSTANTANEITY.
Mortal. See *Nouns.*
Passing. Relating to the act of passing or going.
Perishable. Subject to decay.
Precarious. Uncertain; risky.
Pressed for time. See HURRY.
Provisional. Suited for the time being; set up for the present.
Provisory. Conditional; dependent.
Quick. Speedy; swift; hasty; alive.
Shifting. Moving from place to place.
Short-lived. Of short duration.
Slippery. Liable to fall away.
Spasmodic. Impulsive; transitory.
Sudden. Quickly; unexpected.
Summary. Rapidly performed.
Temporal. Pertaining to the present.
Temporary. Limited; not permanent.
Transient. Passing before the sight or perception and then disappearing.
Transitive. Not lasting or durable.
Transitory. Continuing only for a short time.

TRANSIENTNESS—*Adverbs.*

A while. For a short time.
Briefly. Quickly.
Pro tempore [L.]. For a time.
Temporarily. For the time being.

TRANSIENTNESS—*Adverbial Expressions.*

At short notice *en passant* [F.], in passing; **for a time; for the moment;** *in articulo* [L.], instantly; **in a short time;** *in transitu* [L.], in passing; **on the eve of; on the point of.**

TRANSIENTNESS—*Phrases.*

Dum loquimur jugerit invidia ætas [L.]. While we talk envious lifetime has been flying.
Eheu! jugaces labuntur anni [L.]. Alas! the fleeting years flow by.
Fugit hora [L.]. The hour flies.
Here to-day and gone to-morrow. Ephemeral.
Non semper erit æstas [L]. Time will not aways be.

(Continued on Column 1.)

---

latch. To fasten with a latch; a catch for a door or other hinged covering. CONNECTIVE, UNION-DISUNION.

latch'-et. The string that fastens a shoe. CONNECTIVE.

latch'-key''. A key for a spring-lock. INSTRUMENTALITY.

late. Tardy; recent; recently deceased; after delay; recently. EARLINESS-LATENESS, FUTURE-PAST, LIFE-DEATH, NOVELTY-ANTIQUITY; **late in the day,** EARLINESS-LATENESS; **too late,** OPPORTUNENESS-UNSUITABLENESS.

late'-ly. Not long ago. FUTURE-PAST, NOVELTY-ANTIQUITY.

la'-ten-cy. The state of being latent. CLEARNESS-OBSCURITY, ENLIGHTENMENT-SECRECY, MANIFESTATION-LATENCY, TIDINGS-MYSTERY, VIGOR-INERTIA, VISIBILITY-INVISIBILITY.

late'-ness. State of being late. EARLINESS-LATENESS.

la'-tent. Hidden; dormant; having potential activity. CLEARNESS-OBSCURITY, MANIFESTATION-LATENCY, VIGOR-INERTIA.

la'-ter. At a subsequent time. ANTECEDENCE-SEQUENCE.

lat'-er-al. Pertaining to, or proceeding from, a side. LATERALITY-CONTRAPOSITION.

lat''-er-al'-i-ty. The state of being lateral, or having sides. LATERALITY-CONTRAPOSITION.

LATERALITY—CONTRAPOSITION.

Laterality. The state of being lateral or having sides.

LATERALITY—*Associated Nouns.*

Broadside. The side of a ship above the water-line, from the bow to the quarter.

Contraposition. Opposite position.
Counterpart. Anything exactly like another; facsimile.
Polarity. The quality of having opposite sides.

LATERALITY—CONTRAPOSITION—*Continued.*

LATERALITY—Associated Nouns—*Continued.*

Cheek. The side of the face below the eye.
East. The direction toward the rising sun.
Flank. The muscular part of the side of an animal.
Gable. The vertical triangular portion of the end of a building, from the level of the cornice to the ridge of the roof.
Gable-end. See Gable.
Hand. Direction, either right or left.
Haunch. The hip or hind part.
Hip. The projecting region of the lateral parts of the leg.
Jole. } The cheek.
Jowl. }
Lee. } The side sheltered from the wind.
Leeside. }
Levant. The East.
Loin. That part of a human being which extends between the hip-bone and the false ribs.
Orient. The East.
Orientation. Determination of the east point of the compass.
Parietes. The sides of the human body.
Points of the compass. The thirty-two points of division on the compass card of the mariner's compass.
Profile. A human head represented sidewise.
Quarter. One limb of a quadruped with the adjacent parts.
Side. One of the halves of the body.
Temple. The part on either side of the head back of the eyes and forehead.
West. The direction toward the setting sun.
Wing. One of the two anterior limbs of a bird.

LATERALITY—Verbs.

Be on one side, etc. See *Adverbs.*
Flank. Be on the side of.
Outflank. Go round the side of.
Sidle. Put oneself on the side of.
Skirt. Be on or move along a side.

LATERALITY—Adjectives.

Bilateral. Having two sides.
Collateral. Being alongside.
Eastern. Toward the east.
Flanked. Having a pair of flanches.
Flanking. Posted on the side.
Hesperian. Of the west.
Lateral. On a side.
Levantine. Of the east.
Many-sided. } Having many sides.
Multilateral. }
Occidental. Western.
Orient. } Eastern.
Oriental. }
Parietal. Pertaining to a wall.
Quadrilateral. Having four sides.
Sideling. With a sidelong position.
Sidelong. Tending to one side.
Skirting. Being on a side or border.
Trilateral. Having three sides.
Western. Toward the west.

LATERALITY—Adverbs.

Abreast. Breast to breast.
Alongside. Close to the side.

CONTRAPOSITION—Associated Nouns.

Antipodes. The country of those who live on the opposite side of the globe.
Inverse. That which is opposite in order, relation, or effect. See *Adjectives.*
Inversion. The act of placing opposite. See Reversal.
North and south. Two opposite points of direction.
Opposite poles. Two points opposite to each other.
Opposite sides. Sides placed over against.
Opposition. The state of being placed over against.
Reverse. That which is directly opposite.

CONTRAPOSITION—Verbs.

Be opposite, etc. See *Adjectives.*
Subtend. To extend opposite to.

CONTRAPOSITION—Adjectives.

Antarctic. Pertaining to the south.
Antipodal. On the opposite side of the earth.
Arctic. Northern.
Austral. Southern.
Boreal. Northern.
Diametrically opposite. Extremely opposed.
Facing. } With the face or front in a given direction.
Fronting. }
Inverse. Opposite in order.
Northern. Toward the north.
Opposite. In front of.
Reverse. Turned backward.
Septentrional. To the north.
Southern. Toward the south.
Subcontrary. Somewhat contrary.

CONTRAPOSITION—Adverbs.

Against. Opposite.
As poles asunder. Opposite as far as the poles.
Face to face. Directly opposite.
Over. From one side.
Over against. In front of.
Over the way. Across.
Vis-à-vis [F.]. Visage to visage; face to face.

LATERALITY—Adverbs—*Continued.*

Aside. On one side.
Beside. Close by.
Broadside on. With the broadside presented.
By. Alongside.
By the side of. Near.
Cheek by jowl. With cheeks close.
Laterally. Sidewise.
On her beam ends. Tilted sidewise, as of a ship.
On one side. One-sidedly.
Right and left. In every direction.
Side by side. With sides close or touching.
Sidelong. } In a lateral direction.
Sideways. }
To leeward. In the direction the wind blows.
To windward. In the direction from which the wind blows.

---

lat'-er-al-ly. Toward the side; sidewise. Laterality-Contraposition.
lat''-e-ri'-ceous. Resembling brick. Redness-Greenness.
lateat scintillula forsan [L.] (lĕ'-tĭ-at sin-til'-lu-la for'-san). A little spark may perhaps be hidden. Sanguineness-Hopelessness.
lateritiam, urbem . . . invenit, marmoream reliquit [L.]. (ur'-bem lat-er-i'-shi-am in-vī'-nit, mar-mo'-re-am rī-lai'-quit). He found the city brick, he left it marble. Betterment-Deterioration.
latet anguis in herbâ [L.] (lĕ'-tet an'-gwis in her'-ba). There lurks a snake in the grass. Refuge-Pitfall.
late'-ward. Somewhat late; backward. Earliness-Lateness.
lath. A thin strip of wood. Lamina-Fiber; **thin as a lath,** Breadth-Narrowness.

lathe'. A machine by which wood and other materials are rounded. Instrument.
lath'-er. Foam or froth made by soap moistened with water; to cover with foam of soap. Friction-Lubrication, Viscidity-Foam.
Lat'-in. The language of the Romans. **Thieves' Latin,** Word-Neology.
Latin, au bout de son [F.] (la-tan·', o bu de son·). At the end of his Latin. Difficulty-Facility.
Latin, perdre son [F.] (la-tan·', perdr son·). To be at one's wits' end. Difficulty-Facility.
lat'-i-tan-cy. The act of lurking. Enlightenment-Secrecy.
lat'-i-tat. A writ by which a person is summoned to the King's Bench to answer, as supposing he lies concealed. Litigation.

lat″-i-ta′-tion. The act of lurking. ENLIGHTENMENT-SECRECY.

lat′-i-tude. Distance on the earth's surface from the equator; the distance of a heavenly body from the ecliptic; laxity; comprehensiveness. BREADTH-NARROWNESS, EXTENSION-DISTRICT, EXTENSION-INEXTENSION, LIBERTY-SUBJECTION, MENSURATION; **latitude and longitude,** MENSURATION, POSITION.

lat″-i-tu″-di-na′-ri-an. Broad in scope; tolerance; somewhat unorthodox. GODLINESS-DISBELIEF, ORTHODOXY-HETERODOXY.

la″-ti-tu″-di-na′-ri-an-ism. Freedom of thought. ORTHODOXY-HETERODOXY.

la′-trant. Barking. CRY-ULULATION.

la-tra′-tion. Barking. CRY-ULULATION.

la-tri′-a. That supreme worship given to God alone. DEVOTION-IDOLATRY.

la-trine′. A privy or water-closet. CLEANNESS-FILTHINESS.

lat′-ro-ci-ny. Robbery. THEFT.

lat′-ter. Of more recent date; modern. FUTURE-PAST, PRECEDENCE-SUCCESSION.

Lat′-ter-day″ Saints. The Mormons. ORTHODOXY-HETERODOXY.

lat′-ter-ly. Recently. NOVELTY-ANTIQUITY.

lat′-tice. Wooden or metal open-work, formed by crossing strips or bars. APERTURE-CLOSURE, CROSSING; **lattice window,** ARCHITECTURE.

lat′-tice-work″. Work formed of cross-strips. ARCHITECTURE.

latuit bene vixit, bene qui [L.] (lat′-yu-it bĭ′-nĭ vix′-it, bĭ′-nĭ quai). He who has kept hidden has lived well; who lived obscure has lived well. UPRIGHTNESS-DISHONESTY.

laud. To extol; a song of praise or honor. APPROVAL-DISAPPROVAL, DEVOTION-IDOLATRY.

laud′-a-ble. Praiseworthy. VIRTUE-VICE.

lau′-da-num. Tincture of opium. FEELING-INSENSIBILITY.

laudari a laudato viro [L.] (lau-dê′-rai ê lau-dê′-to vai′-ro). To be praised by a man that is praised. APPROVAL-DISAPPROVAL.

laudator temporis acti [L.] (lau-dê′-tor tem′-po-ris ac′-tai). Lauder of time gone by. CONTENTEDNESS-DISCONTENTMENT, CONTENTEDNESS-REGRET, FLATTERER-DEFAMER, FUTURE-PAST, HABIT-DESUETUDE.

lau′-da-to-ry. Eulogizing; a panegyric. APPROVAL-DISAPPROVAL.

laugh. To give vent to laughter. JUBILATION-LAMENTATION; **laugh at,** REGARD-DISRESPECT, REGARD-SCORN, SOCIETY-DERISION; **laugh in one's sleeve,** MANIFESTATION-LATENCY, REGARD-DISRESPECT, REGARD-SCORN, SOCIETY-DERISION; **laugh on the wrong side of one's mouth,** EXPECTATION-DISAPPOINTMENT, LIGHTHEARTEDNESS-DEJECTION, REPUTATION-DISCREDIT; **laugh outright,** JUBILATION-LAMENTATION; **laugh to scorn,** DEFIANCE, REGARD-DISRESPECT, REGARD-SCORN; **make one laugh,** SOCIETY-LUDICROUSNESS; **raise a laugh,** SOCIETY-DERISION.

laugh′-a-ble. Fitted to provoke laughter. ENTERTAINMENT-WEARINESS, JUBILATION-LAMENTATION, SOCIETY-LUDICROUSNESS.

laugh′-ing. Moving to laughter. JUBILATION-LAMENTATION; **laughing-gas,** SENSIBILITY-INSENSIBILITY; **no laughing matter,** CONSEQUENCE-INSIGNIFICANCE.

laugh′-ing-stock″. A fit object of laughter. GULL-DECEIVER, SOCIETY-LAUGHINGSTOCK, SOCIETY-LUDICROUSNESS.

laugh′-ter. Cachinnation. ENTERTAINMENT-WEARINESS, JUBILATION-LAMENTATION, LIGHTHEARTEDNESS-DEJECTION; **laughter holding both his sides,** JUBILATION-LAMENTATION.

laugh′-ter-lov″-ing. Desiring to laugh. LIGHTHEARTEDNESS-DEJECTION.

launch. To put into the water; to set out; a large, open boat. BEGINNING-END, CONVEYANCE-VESSEL, PUSH-PULL; **launch forth,** ENTERPRISE; **launch into,** ENTERPRISE; **launch into eternity,** LIFE-DEATH, LIFE-KILLING; **launch out,** TERSENESS-PROLIXITY; **launch out against,** ATTACK-DEFENSE.

laun′-dress. A washerwoman. CHIEF-UNDERLING, CLEANNESS-FILTHINESS.

laun′-dry. An establishment or room for washing clothes. CLEANNESS-FILTHINESS, CONTENTS-RECEIVER, OVEN-REFRIGERATOR.

lau′-re-ate. Crowned with laurel, as a mark of distinction. GENTILITY-COMMONALTY, POETRY-PROSE; **poet laureate,** POETRY-PROSE.

lau′-rel. An evergreen shrub; a crown or wreath of laurel; marks of distinction or honor. REPUTATION-DISCREDIT, TITLE, TROPHY; **repose on one's laurels,** MOVEMENT-REST.

la′-va. Melted rock; the same when cooled. GEOLOGY, NUTRIMENT-EXCRETION, VISCIDITY-FOAM.

la-va′-tion. Ablution. CLEANNESS-FILTHINESS.

lav′-a-to″-ry. A place for washing. CLEANNESS-FILTHINESS.

lave. To wash or bathe. CLEANNESS-FILTHINESS, WATER-AIR.

lav′-en-der. An aromatic shrub; its perfume; its color. YELLOWNESS-PURPLE.

la′-ver. One who or that which bathes. CLEANNESS-FILTHINESS.

laver la tête [F.] (la-vê′ la têt). To give it to a person. APPROVAL-DISAPPROVAL.

lav′-ish. To give or spend profusely; to squander; prodigal; superabundant. ENOUGH, EXCESS-LACK, EXTRAVAGANCE-AVARICE, GIVING-RECEIVING; **lavish of praise,** APPROVAL-DISAPPROVAL.

La″-voi″-sier′. French chemist. CHEMISTRY.

law. A rule of action established by recognized authority to enforce justice and direct duty; a rule established by custom or precedent. LAW-LAWLESSNESS, LEAVE-PROHIBITION, PRECEPT, RIGHT-WRONG, UNIFORMITY-MULTIFORMITY; **court of law,** TRIBUNAL; **give the law,** ORDER, RULE-LICENSE; **go to law,** LITIGATION; **Jewish law,** REVELATION-PSEUDOREVELATION; **law of Medes and Persians,** UNIFORMITY-MULTIFORMITY; **lay down the law,** ASSERTION-DENIAL, CERTAINTY-DOUBT, ORDER, PRESUMPTION-OBSEQUIOUSNESS, RULE-LICENSE; **learned in the law,** ADVOCATE; **make the law a dead letter,** LAW-LAWLESSNESS; **set the law at defiance,** LAW-LAWLESSNESS; **take the law into one's own hands,** FIGHTING-CONCILIATION, INSUBORDINATION-OBEDIENCE, LAW-LAWLESSNESS, VOLITION-OBLIGATION; **take the law of,** LITIGATION.

LAW—LAWLESSNESS.

By-law. }
Bye-law. } A local, subordinate, or private rule or regulation.

Canon, etc. A law or standard of judgment. See PRECEPT.

Canon law. A rule or regulation in religious matters.

Charter. An instrument bestowing rights or privileges.

Civil law. The Roman law.

Antinomy. The opposition of one rule or law to another rule or law.

Arbitrariness, etc. The quality of being despotic. See *Adjectives*.

Argumentum baculinum [L.]. Club-law; appeal to force instead of law.

Bar sinister. A mark of illegitimacy.

Breach of law. Infringement of law.

LAW—LAWLESSNESS—*Continued.*

Code. A system of laws.
Common law. A system of law developed by the courts.
Constitution. The organic law, or principles of government of a nation.
Corpus juris [L.]. The body of the law. See Right.
Decree, etc. An authoritative law or command. See Order.
Ecclesiastical law. Law governing religious affairs.
Enactment. A bill which has become a law.
Equity. Law developed by courts, supplemental to statutes.
Fieri facias [L.]. A law ordering an execution against the goods of a debtor.
Form. An established way of proceeding.
Formality. An established rule of procedure.
Formula. A fixed and established method in which something is to be done.
Habeas corpus [L.]. A writ commanding an officer to bring a prisoner before the court.
Institution. Permanent form of law or polity.
International law. Law by which nations are governed.
Jus civile [L.]. The civil law; the laws of Rome.
Jus gentium [L.]. The law of the nations.
Justice. Conformity to the principles of righteousness.
Law. A statement of a principle of right in the form of a command and sustained by the proper authority.
Law of nations. International law.
Legality. The state of conforming to law.
Legitimacy.
Legitimateness. } The state of being lawful.
Lex mercatoria [L.]. Mercantile law.
Lex non scripta [L.]. The unwritten law; the common law.
Lex scripta [L.]. Written law; statute law.
Ordinance.
Ordonance. } A permanent rule of action established by authority.
Plebiscite. A law enacted by a direct vote of the people. See Choice.
Regulation. A rule or order prescribed for management or government.
Rite. An established custom of religious observance.
Rule. A practise laid down by authority or habit.
Standing order. A continuing regulation for the conduct of parliamentary business.
Statute. A positive law laid down as the will of the legislative body of a land.
Statute law. An act of a legislative body.

Law—*Associated Nouns.*

Arm of the law. The power of the law.
Codification. The process of reducing laws to a system.
Constitutionalism. The theory, principles, or authority of constitutional government.
Constitutionality. The state of being in accordance with the principles or fundamental laws which govern a state.
Jurisprudence. The knowledge of the laws, customs, and rights of men in a community.
Legal process. The whole course of proceedings of a suit at law.
Legislation. The act of enacting laws.
Legislature. The body of men in a state having the power to enact or repeal laws.
Nomology. The science of law.
Pandect. A brief summary or treatise embracing all law.

Law—*Verbs.*

Codify. To arrange in a code or system.
Decree, etc. A formal authoritative declaration or decision. See Order.
Enact. To establish by a legal and authoritative act.
Formulate. To put into a formula.
Legalize. To make lawful.
Legislate. To make or enact a law.
Ordain. To arrange or establish according to rule.
Pass a law. To enact a law.

Law—*Adjectives.*

According to law. Lawful; legal.
Chartered. Enjoying the privileges of a charter.
Constitutional. According to the constitution.
Law-abiding. Observing law.
Lawful, etc. Permitted by law See Leave.
Legal. According to law.
Legalized. Made lawful.
Legislative. Pertaining to the enactment of laws.
Legislatorial. Of or pertaining to a legislature.

Brute force. Appeal to force instead of law.
Club-law. Appeal to force.
Coup d'état [F.]. A sudden exercise of power whereby the government is subverted without the consent of the people.
Despotism. The spirit, principles, or power of one who exercises complete control over another.
Disobedience, etc. Neglect or refusal to obey. See Insubordination.
Drumhead law. The decision or decree of a court martial.
Illegality. Unlawfulness; the state of being not in accordance with law.
Illegitimacy. The state of being not in accordance with law.
Informality. Want of regular proceedings or course.
Lawbreaker. One who disobeys the law.
Lawlessness. The state or quality of being unlawful.
Le droit du plus fort [F.]. The right of might.
Lidford law. Punishment without trial.
Lynch law. The infliction of punishment without the forms of law.
Martial law. The law of war as adopted by civilized belligerents.
Mob law. Law administered by a mob.
Nihilism. The doctrine of a secret organization, devoted to the destruction of political, religious, and social institutions.
Outlawry. The act of putting a man out of the protection of the law.
Poaching. Killing game contrary to law.
Simony. The crime of buying or selling ecclesiastical preferment.
Smuggling. Secret importation of goods contrary to law.
Trover and conversion. The gaining possession of goods by finding.
Unconformity, etc. Non-conformity. See Conventionality-Unconventionality.
Unlawfulness. The state of being not in accordance with the law.
Violation of law. Transgression of law.
Violence. Infringement of something that should be respected.

Lawlessness—*Verbs.*

Drive a coach and six through a statute. To violate or break a law
Make the law a dead letter. To cause a law to fall into disuse.
Offend against the law. To transgress the law.
Poach. To kill or destroy game contrary to the law.
Ride rough-shod over a statute. To transgress a statute.
Run. To be unrestrained by law.
Set the law at defiance. To defy the law.
Smuggle. To import or export secretly, contrary to the law, and without the payment of duty.
Take the law into one's own hands. To inflict punishment without due course of law.
Violate the law. To break the law.

Lawlessness—*Adjectives.*

Actionable. Admitting a suit.
A dead letter. A law which has fallen into disusage.
Arbitrary. Despotic; absolute in control.
Contraband. Prohibited by law or treaty.
Despotic.
Despotical. } Unrestrained by laws or constitution.
Extrajudicial. Out of the course of ordinary legal process.
Illegal. Unlawful.
Illegitimate. Not according to law.
Illicit. Unlawful.
Informal. Not according to established forms.
Injudicial. Not according to the forms of law.
Irresponsible. Not to be relied on.
Lawless. Without regard for law.
Not allowed. Forbidden.
Null and void. Having no legal binding force.
Prohibited, etc. Forbidden by authority. See Leave-Prohibition.
Summary. Quickly executed.
Unaccountable. Not responsible.
Unanswerable. Not to be answered.
Unauthorized. Not made legal.
Unchartered. Not chartered.
Unconstitutional. Not according to the constitution.
Unlawful. Contrary to law.
Unofficial. Not authorized by official action.
Unwarrantable. Not justifiable.
Unwarranted. Not justified.

Lawlessness—*Adverbs.*

Illegally, etc. In an unlawful manner. See *Adjectives.*
In violation of the law. Unlawfully.
With a high hand. In an oppressive or overbearing manner.

LAW—ADJECTIVES—*Continued.*

Legitimate. Lawful.
Statutable. Proceeding from a legislative act.

Statutory. Enacted by statute.
Vested. Given the right of present and future enjoyment.

LAW—*Adverbs.*

De jure [L.]. According to law.
In the eye of the law. From a legal point of view.

Legally, etc. In a lawful manner. See *Adjectives.*

LAW—*Phrases.*

Æquitas sequitur legem [L.]. Equity follows law.
Droit des gens [F.]. Law of nations.

Ignorantia legis neminem excusat [L.]. Ignorance of the law excuses no one.
Mens legis [L.] The spirit of the law.

law'-a-bi"-ding. Obedient to the law. LAW-LAW-LESSNESS.

law'-break"-er. One who violates the law. GOOD MAN-BAD MAN, LAW-LAWLESSNESS.

law'-ful. Conformable to law; rightful; permitted by law. DUENESS-UNDUENESS, LAW-LAWLESSNESS, LEAVE-PROHIBITION, RIGHT-WRONG.

law'-giv"-er. A legislator. MANAGER.

law'-less. Not subject or obedient to law; disobedient; illegal; outlawed. CONVENTIONALITY-UNCONVENTIONALITY, INSUBORDINATION-OBEDIENCE, LAW-LAWLESSNESS, OBSERVANCE-NONOBSERVANCE, VIRTUE-VICE.

law'-less-ness. Illegality; disobedience. LAW-LAWLESSNESS, OBSERVANCE-NONOBSERVANCE.

law'-ma"-ker. A legislator. MANAGER.

law'-mon"-ger. A pettifogger. ADVOCATE.

lawn. A space of ground covered with closely cut grass; an open space among woods. DOMESTICATION-AGRICULTURE, GULF-PLAIN; **lawn sleeves,** VESTMENTS; **lawn-tennis,** ENTERTAINMENT-WEARINESS.

law'-suit". An action in a court of law for enforcement of a claim. JUSTIFICATION-CHARGE, LITIGATION.

law'-yer. One who is versed in or practises law. ADVOCATE.

lax. Loose or slack; yielding; negligent; remiss; vague; not strict. COHESION-LOOSENESS, FORCE-WEAKNESS, RULE-LICENSE, TRUTH-ERROR, VIRTUE VICE.

lax'-i-ty. The state or quality of being lax, loose, or open; want of firmness, strictness, or exactness. COHESION-LOOSENESS, GODLINESS-DISBELIEF, HARDNESS-SOFTNESS, OBSERVANCE-NONOBSERVANCE, RULE-LICENSE, TRUTH-ERROR, UPRIGHTNESS-DISHONESTY, VIRTUE-VICE.

lax'-ness. The state of being lax. RULE-LICENSE.

lay. To cause to lie; to put in proper position; to devise; to impose; to inflict; to put up money; to allay; not clerical; a song; a lyric poem; a lake. CREATION-DESTRUCTION, ERECTNESS-FLATNESS, ESTABLISHMENT-REMOVAL, GULF-PLAIN, MINISTRY-LAITY, MUSIC, POETRY-PROSE, PURPOSE-LUCK, TURBULENCE-CALMNESS; **lay about one,** ACTIVITY-INDOLENCE, ATTACK-DEFENSE, RECOMPENSE-PUNITION, STRIFE-PEACE, TOIL-RELAXATION; **lay apart,** INCLUSION-OMISSION, KEEPING-RELINQUISHMENT, STORE; **lay aside,** CAREFULNESS-NEGLECT, CHOICE-REJECTION, INCLUSION-OMISSION, KEEPING-RELINQUISHMENT, USE-DISUSE; **lay at the door of,** RATIONALE-LUCK; **lay at one's feet,** PROFFER-REFUSAL; **lay bare one's mind,** EXPOSURE-HIDINGPLACE; **lay before one,** ENLIGHTENMENT-SECRECY, MANIFESTATION-LATENCY; **lay brother,** MINISTRY-LAITY, **lay by,** HEALTH-SICKNESS, STORE, USE-DISUSE; **lay claim to,** DUENESS-UNDUENESS, ORDER; **lay down,** ASSERTION-DENIAL, COMMISSION-RETIREMENT, ERECTNESS-FLATNESS, ESTABLISHMENT-REMOVAL, KEEPING-RELINQUISHMENT, SETTLEMENT-DEFAULT; **lay down a plan,** DESIGN; **lay down one's arms,** FIGHTING-CONCILIATION, YIELDING; **lay down one's life,** LIFE-DEATH; **lay down one's life for one's country,** PATRIOTISM-TREASON; **lay down the law,** ASSERTION-DENIAL, CERTAINTY-DOUBT, ORDER, PRESUMPTION-SERVILITY, RULE-LICENSE; **lay fast hold on,** TAKING-RESTITUTION; **lay-figure,** COPY-MODEL, DELINEATION-CARICATURE; **lay hands on,** CEREMONIAL, HARSHNESS-MILDNESS, TAKING-RESTITUTION, USE-DISUSE; **lay heads together,** ADVICE, ANTAGONISM-CONCURRENCE; **lay in,** NUTRIMENT-EXCRETION, PROVISION-WASTE, STORE; **lay in ruins,** CREATION-DESTRUCTION; **lay in the dust,** CREATION-DESTRUCTION; **lay it on thick,** ADULATION-DISPARAGEMENT, COVER-LINING, EXCESS-LACK; **lay on,** RECOMPENSE-PUNITION; **lay one's account for,** FAITH-MISGIVING; **lay oneself open to,** CONTINGENCY, SECURITY-INSECURITY; **lay oneself out for,** PREPARATION-NONPREPARATION; **lay one's finger upon,** DISCOVERY; **lay one's head on the block,** UNSELFISHNESS-SELFISHNESS; **lay one's life on the altar of one's country,** PATRIOTISM-TREASON; **lay on the shelf,** KEEPING-RELINQUISHMENT, USE-DISUSE; **lay on the table,** PRESIDENT-MEMBER; **lay open,** APERTURE-CLOSURE, DRESS-UNDRESS, EXPOSURE-HIDINGPLACE, MANIFESTATION-LATENCY; **lay out,** DESIGN, ERECTNESS-FLATNESS, LIFE-FUNERAL, OUTLAY-INCOME; **lay over,** EARLINESS-LATENESS; **lay siege to,** ATTACK-DEFENSE; **lay stress on,** ASSERTION-DENIAL, CONSEQUENCE-INSIGNIFICANCE; **lay the ax at the root of,** CREATION-DESTRUCTION; **lay the first stone,** BEGINNING-END, PREPARATION-NONPREPARATION; **lay the flattering unction to one's soul,** ALLEVIATION-AGGRAVATION, CONTENTEDNESS-DISCONTENTMENT; SANGUINENESS-HOPELESSNESS; **lay the foundations of,** BEGINNING-END, CAUSE-EFFECT, PREPARATION-NONPREPARATION; **lay to,** MOVEMENT-REST, RATIONALE-LUCK; **lay to one's charge,** JUSTIFICATION-CHARGE; **lay together,** UNION-DISUNION; **lay train,** DESIGN, PREPARATION-NONPREPARATION; **lay under hatches,** RELEASE-RESTRAINT; **lay under restraint,** RELEASE-RESTRAINT; **lay up,** HEALTH-SICKNESS, STORE, USE-DISUSE; **lay waste,** CREATION-DESTRUCTION.

lay'-er. A course or stratum. LAMINA-FIBER.

la-yette'. An outfit for a newly born child. DRESS-UNDRESS.

lay'-man. One of the laity. MINISTRY-LAITY.

lay'-stall". A place where offal is deposited. CLEANNESS-FILTHINESS.

laz"-a-ret'-to. A pest-house. REMEDY-BANE.

la'-zar-house". A pest-house. REMEDY-BANE.

laz'-u-li. A mixture of minerals used by the ancients for decoration. EMBELLISHMENT-DISFIGUREMENT.

la'-zy. Averse to labor. ACTIVITY-INDOLENCE; **lazy as Ludlam's dog,** ACTIVITY-INDOLENCE.

laz"-za-ro'-ni. In Naples, idlers who have no homes and live by odd jobs and begging. ACTIVITY-INDOLENCE.

lb. Abbreviation for *libra* (pound). HEAVINESS-LIGHTNESS.

lea. A grassy field or plain. COUNTRY, GULF-PLAIN, OCEAN-LAND.

lead. A soft, heavy metal; a mass of lead used in sounding. CHEMISTRY, DEEPNESS-SHALLOWNESS, HEAVINESS-LIGHTNESS; **heave the lead,** MENSURATION; **heavy as lead,** HEAVINESS-LIGHTNESS; **red lead,** REDNESS-GREENNESS.

lead. To guide; to control; to conduct; precedence. INCLINATION, LEADING-FOLLOWING, MANAGEMENT, MOTIVE-CAPRICE, PRECEDENCE-SUCCESSION, RULE-LICENSE; **take the lead,** CONSEQUENCE-INSIGNIFICANCE, DOMINANCE-IMPOTENCE, LEADING-FOLLOWING, MANAGEMENT, RULE-LICENSE; **lead a dance,** DIFFICULTY-FACILITY, MIDCOURSE-CIRCUIT, QUEST-EVASION, REGARD-DISRESPECT; **lead a life,** CONDUCT; **lead astray,** PATRIOTISM-TREASON, TRUTH-ERROR; **lead by the nose,** LIBERTY-SUBJECTION, RULE-LICENSE; **lead captive,** LIBERTY-SUBJECTION, RELEASE-RESTRAINT; **lead on,** MANAGEMENT; **lead one to expect,** EXPECTATION-SURPRISE, PROPHECY; **lead the choir,** WORSHIP-IDOLATRY; **lead the dance,** LEADING-FOLLOWING, PRECEDENCE-SUCCESSION; **lead the way,** BEGINNING-END, CONSEQUENCE-INSIGNIFICANCE, LEADING-FOLLOWING, MANAGEMENT, PRECEDENCE-SUCCESSION, REPUTATION-DISCREDIT; **lead to no end,** USEFULNESS-USELESSNESS; **lead to the altar,** MATRIMONY-CELIBACY.

lead'-en. Of the color of lead; heavy; dull or sluggish. ACTIVITY-INDOLENCE, COLOR-ACHROMATISM, DIMNESS, GRAY-BROWN.

lead'-er. One who leads or conducts; a commander; a chief editorial article. ADVOCATE, CHIEF-UNDERLING, ESSAY, MANAGER, PREDECESSOR-CONTINUATION.

lead'-ing. Chief; drawing attention, desire, or custom. BEGINNING-END, CONSEQUENCE-INSIGNIFICANCE; **leading article,** ESSAY; **leading note,** MELODY-DISSONANCE; **leading part,** DOMINANCE-IMPOTENCE; **leading question,** INVESTIGATION-ANSWER; **leading strings,** INFANCY-AGE, INFANT-VETERAN, INSTRUCTOR-PUPIL, LIBERTY-SUBJECTION, RELEASE-GUARD, RELEASE-RESTRAINT; **leading to no end,** USEFULNESS-USELESSNESS.

LEADING—FOLLOWING.

Heading. Something placed first or at the head.
Leading. Guiding, controlling influence.
Le pas [F.]. The step.
Precedence. A going before; superiority. See PRECEDENCE.
Precession. The act of preceding others.
Precursor. A running before; a warning. See PRELECESSOR.
Priority. Condition of being prior or antecedent. See ANTECEDENCE.
The lead. Superiority.
Van. Head; especially, head of an army. See ANTERIORITY

LEADING—*Verbs.*

Forerun. To run before; go before for announcing.
Head. To lead; be the first.
Herald. To announce; to usher in.
Introduce. To make acquainted with; **to usher in.**
Lead. To be ahead.
Outstrip. To go beyond; to outrun. See TRANSCURSION.
Precede. To go before.

LEADING—*Verbal Expressions.*

Get ahead; get before; get in front of; get the start; go ahead; go before; go in advance; go in the van; have the start; lead the dance; lead the way; steal a march; take precedence (see PRECEDENCE); take the lead; usher in.

LEADING—*Adjectives.*

Leading, etc. Going ahead. See *Verbs.*

LEADING—*Adverbs.*

Ahead. At the head.
Before. In advance.
Foremost. }
Headmost. } First.
In advance. Before.
In front. In the lead.
In the van. Ahead.

LEADING—*Phrase.*

Seniores priores [L.]. Elders first.

Coming after. See SUCCESSION. See SEQUENCE.
Following. A going after; those who go after; adherents.
Pursuit. A persistent following to seize; following out. See QUEST.
Sequence. That which follows; a succession.

FOLLOWING—*Nouns of Agency.*

Attendant. One who follows in an inferior capacity.
Dangler. One who follows persistently or besets another.
Follower. One who follows; imitator.
Satellite. An obsequious follower.
Shadow. An inseparable attendant.
Train. A body of attendants; a retinue

FOLLOWING—*Verbs.*

Attend. To go along as an attendant or companion.
Beset. To set about; to surround.
Dog. To follow as a dog; to follow continually.
Follow. To come after.
Lag. To fall behind.
Pursue. To follow with a view to seize. See QUEST.

FOLLOWING—*Verbal Expressions.*

Be in the rear of; be in the trail of; be in the wake of; dance attendance upon; fly after; follow as a shadow; follow in the rear of; follow in the trail of; follow in the wake of; follow on the heels of; get behind; go after; go in the rear of; go in the trail of; go in the wake of; hang on the skirts of; tread close upon; tread in the steps of; tread on the heels of.

FOLLOWING—*Adjectives.*

Following, etc. Going ahead. See *Verbs.*

FOLLOWING—*Adverbs.*

After. Coming or occurring behind. See ANTECEDENCE, PRECEDENCE-SUCCESSION.
Behind. Toward the back.
In the rear of. }
In the train of. } See FRONT-REAR.
In the wake of. }

leads. Leaden sheets used for covering roofs. COVER-LINING.

leaf. The organs of plants which shoot from the sides of the stem or branches; division of a sheet of paper; a thin sheet; an ornament. ARCHITECTURE, FAUNA-FLORA, LAMINA-FIBER, MISSIVE-PUBLICATION, WHOLE-PART; **turn over a new leaf,** BETTERMENT-DETERIORATION.

leaf'-less. Having no leafage. DRESS-UNDRESS.

leaf'-let. A little leaf. MISSIVE-PUBLICATION, WHOLE-PART.

leaf'-y. Full of leaves. SMOOTHNESS-ROUGHNESS.

league. A measure of distance; an alliance of persons, parties, states, etc. ANTAGONISM-CONCURRENCE, ASSOCIATION, LENGTH-SHORTNESS, MEASURE, VARIANCE-ACCORD; **be in league with,** ANTAGONISM-CONCURRENCE.

leak. A crack or crevice through which a liquid flows; the oozing of the liquid from this; any waste. ENTRANCE-EXIT, INTERSPACE-CONTACT, PROVISION-WASTE; **leak out,** EXPOSURE-HIDINGPLACE; **spring a leak,** BETTERMENT-DETERIORATION, FAULTLESSNESS-FAULTINESS.

leak'-age. The act or process of leaking; that which is wasted by leaking. ENTRANCE-EXIT, PROVISION-WASTE.

leak'-y. Having a leak or leaks. FAULTLESSNESS-FAULTINESS.

lean. To incline from an erect position; thin. BREADTH-NARROWNESS, PARALLELISM-OBLIQUITY; **lean on,**

SUSPENSION-SUPPORT; **lean-to**, CONTENTS-RECEIVER, READINESS - RELUCTANCE; **lean toward**, RIGHT-WRONG; **lean upon**, FAITH-MISGIVING, LIBERTY-SUBJECTION, SANGUINENESS-HOPELESSNESS.

lean'-ing. Inclination; bias; inclination from the perpendicular. DESIRE-DISTASTE, INCLINATION, PARALLELISM - INCLINATION, READINESS - RELUCTANCE, RIGHT-WRONG; **have a leaning to**, AMITY-HOSTILITY.

lean'-to''. A shed. ARCHITECTURE, DWELLER-HABITATION.

lean'-wit''-ted. Lacking in wit. SAGACITY-INCAPACITY.

leap. To spring over; to jump or vault; the act of leaping. ASCENT-DESCENT, REVOLUTION, SPRING-DIVE; **leap in the dark**, CERTAINTY-DOUBT, PURPOSE-LUCK, RECKLESSNESS - CAUTION, SECURITY - INSECURITY, TRIAL; **leap with joy**, JUBILATION-LAMENTATION; **make a leap at**, QUEST-EVASION.

leap'-frog''. A boy's game. ENTERTAINMENT-WEARINESS.

leap'-ing. Springing. SPRING-DIVE.

leap'-year''. A year of 366 days. PERIODICITY-IRREGULARITY.

learn. To gain knowledge. EDUCATION-LEARNING, ENLIGHTENMENT-SECRECY, HABIT-DESUETUDE; **learn by experience**, REPENTANCE-OBDURACY; **learn by heart**, REMEMBRANCE-FORGETFULNESS.

learn'-ed. Erudite. KNOWLEDGE-IGNORANCE, SCHOLAR-DUNCE; **learned man**, SCHOLAR-DUNCE.

learn'-er. A pupil. INSTRUCTOR-PUPIL.

learn'-ing. Erudition. EDUCATION-LEARNING, KNOWLEDGE-IGNORANCE; **drink in, imbibe, pick up, learning**, EDUCATION-LEARNING; **man of learning**, SAGE-FOOL, SCHOLAR-DUNCE.

leas'-a-ble. That may be let. LOAN-BORROWING, PROPERTY.

lease. A contract for the possession and profits of lands, etc., for a determinate period; the document for this. LOAN-BORROWING, PROPERTY; **grant a lease**, SECURITY; **lease and release**, ALIENATION; **take a new lease of life**, HEALTH-SICKNESS.

lease'-hold''. A tenure held by lease; held by lease. PROPERTY.

leash. A line, thong, or cord; to bind, hold, or secure by a leash; a brace and a half. TRIALITY, UNION-DISUNION.

least. Less than all others. SUPREMACY-SUBORDINACY; **at the least**, MAGNITUDE-SMALLNESS.

leath'-er. The tanned hide of an animal; to change into leather; to beat. COVER-LINING, RECOMPENSE-PUNITION, TOUGHNESS-BRITTLENESS; **leather or prunello**, CONSEQUENCE-INSIGNIFICANCE; **nothing like leather**, DECISION-MISJUDGMENT.

leath'-er-y. Resembling leather; tough. TOUGHNESS-BRITTLENESS.

leave. To depart; to allow to continue; to abandon, to allow; to cease; to bequeath; permission. ADJUNCT-REMNANT, GIVING-RECEIVING, LEAVE-PROHIBITION, QUEST-ABANDONMENT, UNION-DISUNION; **French leave**, QUEST-EVASION; **give me leave to say**, ASSERTION-DENIAL; **leave ad referendum**, DETERMINATION-VACILLATION; **leave alone**, ACTION-PASSIVENESS, LEAVE-PROHIBITION, LIBERTY-SUBJECTION; **leave an inference**, MANIFESTATION-LATENCY; **leave a place**, ARRIVAL-DEPARTURE; **leave a void**, CONTENTEDNESS-REGRET; **leave in the lurch**, QUEST-ABANDONMENT, TRANSCURSION - SHORTCOMING, TRUTHFULNESS-FRAUD; **leave it to one**, LEAVE-PROHIBITION; **leave not a rack behind**, APPEARANCE-DISAPPEARANCE, ENTITY-NONENTITY; **leave no trace**, APPEARANCE-DISAPPEARANCE, MARK-OBLITERATION; **leave off**, DISCONTINUANCE-CONTINUANCE, HABIT-DESUETUDE, QUEST-ABANDONMENT, USE-DISUSE; **leave out**, INCLUSION-OMISSION; **leave out of one's calculations**, CAREFULNESS-NEGLECT; **leave the beaten track**, CONVENTIONALITY-UNCONVENTIONALITY; **leave to chance**, PURPOSE-LUCK; **leave to oneself**, LIBERTY - SUBJECTION; **leave undecided**, CHOICE-NEUTRALITY; **leave undone**, COMPLETION-NONCOMPLETION; **leave unfinished**, COMPLETION-NONCOMPLETION; **leave word**, ENLIGHTENMENT-SECRECY; **take leave**, ARRIVAL-DEPARTURE, LIBERTY-SUBJECTION; **take leave of one's senses**, SAGACITY-INCAPACITY.

LEAVE—PROHIBITION.

Accordance. Agreement.

Admission. Permission to enter.

Allowance. The act of granting or permitting.

Authority. Legal right to exercise power of any sort.

Authorization. The act of empowering.

Concession. The act of yielding or conceding.

Congé [F.]. The act of taking leave.

Connivance. Passive consent.

Dispensation. The relaxation of the law for a special case.

Exemption. The act of releasing or state of being released from some obligation to which others are subject.

Favor. A kind act; mitigation of punishment.

Grace. Privilege conferred or favor bestowed.

Indulgence, etc. The act of bestowing as a concession, etc. See HARSHNESS-MILDNESS.

Law. A rule which is laid down by God or a government.

Leave. A grant of liberty.

Liberty. The state of one who is free.

License. Authority to do or forbear any act.

Permission. The act of permitting; leave.

Release. The act of setting free or state of being free.

Sanction. Ratification; authority.

Sufferance. Permission: leave.

Tolerance. The character or state of being tolerant or indulgent.

Toleration. The act of tolerating or the permission of that which is not wholly approved.

Vouchsafement. A grant in condescension.

Warranty. The assurance that property will be as represented.

LEAVE—*Nouns of Instrument.*

Brevet. A warrant from a government, granting a privilege, title, or dignity.

Ban. A prohibitory or mandatory public order.

Disallowance. Refusal to allow or permit.

Embargo. An order of the government prohibiting the departure of ships of commerce from some or all of its ports.

Forbidden fruit. A coveted unlawful pleasure. [Bible.]

Hindrance, etc. That which hinders. See OBSTRUCTION.

Index expurgatorius [L.]. A list of prohibited books unexpurgated.

Inhibition. The act of holding back or restraining, also a prohibition.

Injunction. That which is enjoined; an order prohibiting the doing of something.

Interdict. A prohibitive order or decree.

Interdiction. A prohibiting decree.

Prohibition. An injunction forbidding some action: an interdiction.

Proscription. A dooming to exile or destruction.

Restriction, etc. Confinement within bounds or limits. See RELEASE-RESTRAINT.

Taboo. A prohibition of intercourse with, or access to, some person or thing under pain of death.

Veto. An official communication containing a refusal to approve a bill.

PROHIBITION—*Verbs.*

Bar. To restrict or prohibit.

Bolt the door. To shut out.

Circumscribe. To confine within a certain limit.

Clip the wings of. To check the ambitions of.

Cohibit. To restrain.

Dash the cup from one's lips. To prohibit at the point of doing.

Debar, etc. To shut out from approach or entry, etc. See OBSTRUCTION.

Disallow. To refuse to permit.

LEAVE—PROHIBITION—*Continued.*

LEAVE—Nouns of Instrument—*Continued.*

Carte blanche [F.]. A blank paper, with a person's signature at the bottom, given to another person, with permission to put down whatever conditions he pleases.

Charter. A written evidence in due form of things done or granted.

Firman. A royal order or mandate in Turkey and other Oriental countries.

Furlough. A leave of absence.

Grant. A transfer of property.

License. A formal permission from the proper authorities to perform certain acts, or to carry on a certain business.

Pass. Permission to go and come.

Passport. A document given to a person permitting him to travel from place to place.

Patent. An official document conferring some right or privilege on a person or party.

Permit. A written permission given by a person having authority.

Precept. A command in writing.

Ticket of leave. A license or permit given to a convict or prisoner, to go at large.

Warrant. A commission giving authority or justifying the doing of anything.

LEAVE—*Verbs.*

Absolve, etc. To pronounce free, etc. See Exculpation.

Accord. To grant or allow as suitable or proper.

Admit. To allow to enter.

Allow. To grant or concede.

Ask leave. See *Nouns.*

Ask permission. See *Nouns.*

Authorize. To give legal power to.

Bear with. To be indulgent to.

Beg leave. See *Nouns.*

Beg permission. See *Nouns.*

Charter. To hire by charter or written agreement.

Concede, etc. To grant as a privilege. See Consent.

Confer a privilege. See *Nouns.*

Connive at. To permit something, as if not aware of it.

Dispense with. To allow by dispensation.

Empower. To grant authority to.

Enfranchise. To endow with the power to vote.

Entrust, etc. To give into the care of another. See Commission.

Exonerate. To relieve of a charge or obligation.

Favor. To look upon with kindness; aid.

Give a loose to. To be indulgent to or to yield to.

Give *carte blanche*. See *Nouns.*

Give permission. See *Nouns.*

Give power. See *Nouns.*

Give scope to. See Liberty.

Grant. To bestow or confer something which cannot be claimed by right.

Humor. To indulge the moods or caprices of.

Indulge. To yield or submit to the desire of.

Leave alone. To refrain from having to do with.

Leave it to one. To let alone or to cease to care for.

Leave the door open. To grant free access.

Let. To permit or allow.

Let off. To release, as from an obligation.

License. To permit by license.

Open the door to. To admit.

Open the flood-gates. To give unrestricted sway

Permit. To allow to be done.

Privilege. To invest with a particular right or immunity.

Recognize. To consent to admit.

Release. To set free from restraint.

Request leave. See *Nouns.*

Request permission. See *Nouns.*

Sanction. To grant approval.

Shut one's eyes to. To give tacit consent.

Stretch a point. To make a special concession against one's conscience or judgment.

Suffer. To permit or allow.

Tolerate. To permit or allow negatively.

Vouchsafe. To yield or concede.

Warrant. To give authority or power to do or forbear.

Wink at. To pretend not to see.

LEAVE—*Adjectives.*

Allowable. Not forbidden; permissible.

Chartered. Established by charter.

Indulgent. Yielding to the wishes or humor of those under one's care.

Lawful. Permitted by law.

PROHIBITION—Verbs—*Continued.*

Exclude. To shut out.

Forbid. To exclude from; to hinder.

Forbid the banns. To formally forbid an intended marriage.

Forefend. To prevent the approach of.

Inhibit. To prohibit or forbid.

Interdict. To forbid or debar.

Keep in. To restrain.

Keep within bounds. To restrain.

Limit. To set a limit to or restrict.

Place under an interdiction. See Interdiction.

Place under the ban. See Ban.

Prohibit. To forbid by authority.

Proscribe. To doom to destruction or exile

Put one's veto upon. See Veto.

Put under an interdiction. See *Nouns.*

Put under the ban. See *Nouns.*

Restrain, etc. To hold in check, etc. See Release-Restraint.

Restrict. To confine within certain bounds.

Show the door. To invite to leave.

Shut out. To exclude.

Shut the door. To exclude.

Taboo. To put under taboo.

Warn off. To give notice to leave.

Withhold. To restrain or hold back.

PROHIBITION—*Adjectives*

Contraband. Forbidden by law or treaty.

Exclusive. Having power to shut out: enjoyed to the exclusion of others.

Forbidding. See *Verbs.*

Illegal, etc. Not legal. See Law-Lawlessness

Not permitted, etc. See Leave.

Not to be thought of. Out of the question

Prohibited, etc. Forbidden. See *Verbs*

Prohibitive. That prohibits or forbids.

Prohibitory. Tending to prohibit.

Proscriptive. Relating to proscription.

Restrictive. Tending to restrict or limit.

Unauthorized. Not authorized.

Under the ban of. See Ban

Unlicensed. Not licensed

PROHIBITION—*Adverbs.*

On no account, etc. See Assertion-Denial.

PROHIBITION—*Interjections.*

Avast! forbid it heaven, etc. (see Petition-Expostulation), **hands off! hold! keep off! stop!**

PROHIBITION—*Phrase.*

That will never do.

LEAVE—*Adjectives*—*Continued.*

Legal. Relating to law.

Legalized. Made legal.

Legitimate. According to law.

Licit. Lawful.

Patent. Protected by a special privilege.

Permissible. That may be permitted or allowed.

Permissive. Granting leave.

Permitted. See *Verbs.*

Permitting. See *Verbs.*

Unconditional. Made without conditions; absolute.

Unforbid. } Not forbidden; allowable.
Unforbidden. }

LEAVE—*Adverbs.*

Ad libitum, etc. [L.]. At will or at pleasure. See Liberty; Volition.

By all means. See Readiness.

By leave. See *Nouns.*

On leave. See *Nouns.*

Speciali gratia [L.]. By special favor.

Under favor of.

With leave. See *Nouns.*

Yes, etc. A word expressing affirmation or consent. See Assent.

LEAVE—*Phrases.*

Avec permission [F.]. With permission.

Brevet d'invention [F.]. A patent.

leav'-en. To produce fermentation in; to taint; fermenting dough to lighten other dough; anything which produces a general change in the mass. BETTERMENT-DETERIORATION, CAUSE-EFFECT, CLEANNESS-FILTHINESS, CONSTITUENT-ALIEN, HEAVINESS-LIGHTNESS, MODIFICATION, REMEDY-BANE.

leave'-tak''-ing. A parting. ARRIVAL-DEPARTURE.

leav'-ings. Remnants; refuse. ADJUNCT-REMNANT, USEFULNESS-USELESSNESS.

lech'-er. An habitually lewd man. PURITY-RAKE.

lech'-er-ous. Lustful. PURITY-IMPURITY.

lech'-er-y. Gross lewdness. PURITY-IMPURITY.

lec'-tern. A reading-desk from which the Scripture lessons are chanted or read. FANE.

lec'-tion. A difference in copies of a manuscript or book; a reading. INTERPRETATION-MISINTERPRETATION, UNIVERSALITY-PARTICULARITY.

lec'-tion-a-ry. A service-book. CEREMONIAL.

lec'-ture. A formal discourse for instruction; a reprimand; to instruct by lectures; to read or deliver a formal discourse; a sermon. ADDRESS-RESPONSE, APPROVAL-DISAPPROVAL, CEREMONIAL, EDUCATION-MISTEACHING, ESSAY, SPEECH-INARTICULATENESS; **lecture-room**, SCHOOL.

lec'-tur-er. An instructor who delivers formal discourses; a preacher, hired to assist the regular incumbent. INSTRUCTOR-PUPIL, MINISTRY-LAITY.

lec'-ture-ship. A foundation for, or office of, lecturing. SCHOOL.

led. Under leading or control. **Led by the nose,** LIBERTY-SUBJECTION; **led captain,** CHIEF-UNDERLING, FAVORITE-ANGER, PRESUMPTION-SERVILITY.

ledge. A shelf; a shelf-like projection; a reef. CONVEXITY-CONCAVITY, ERECTNESS-FLATNESS, HEIGHT-LOWNESS, SUSPENSION-SUPPORT.

ledg'-er. The principal book of accounts of a business establishment. ACCOUNTS, MARK-OBLITERATION, RECORD.

lee. A calm or sheltered place; opposite the side from which the wind comes. LATERALITY-CONTRAPOSITION; **in the lee of,** ANTERIORITY-POSTERIORITY.

leech. A physician; an animal of the genus Hirudo,— a blood-sucker. ADVICE, REMEDY-BANE.

leech'-craft''. The art of healing. REMEDY-BANE.

leef. Lief; pleasing; willing. PLEASURABLENESS-PAINFULNESS.

leek. A culinary herb, resembling the onion. **Eat the leek,** BIGOTRY-APOSTASY, YIELDING.

leer. A look expressive of malicious thought; an affected cast of countenance. SIGHT-BLINDNESS, SIGN.

leer'-y. Shrewd and sly. CRAFT-ARTLESSNESS.

lees. Dregs. CLEANNESS-FILTHINESS.

lee shore. The shore on the lee side of a ship; a dangerous shore. REFUGE-PITFALL; **on a lee shore,** SECURITY-INSECURITY.

lee side. In geology, that side of glaciated rocks which looks away from the quarter whence the ice moved. LATERALITY-CONTRAPOSITION.

leet. A former court of England. **Court-leet,** TRIBUNAL.

lee'-wall''. A sheltering wall. REFUGE-PITFALL.

lee'-ward. That side or direction toward which the wind blows. LATERALITY-CONTRAPOSITION.

lee'-way''. The lateral drift of a vessel in the direction in which the wind blows; a general falling behind or away from a course. EARLINESS-LATENESS, TRANSCURSION-SHORTCOMING, TRAVELING-NAVIGATION; **make up leeway,** ADVANCE-RETROGRESSION, COMPENSATION.

left. That part or half of the body opposed to the right; discontinued; remaining. ADJUNCT-REMNANT, RIGHT-LEFT; **left alone,** LIBERTY-SUBJECTION; **left behind,** ADJUNCT-REMNANT; **left hand,** RIGHT-LEFT; **left in the lurch,** SUCCESS-FAILURE; **left to shift for oneself,** SOCIABILITY-PRIVACY; **over the left,** TRUTHFULNESS-FRAUD; **pay over the left shoulder,** SETTLEMENT-DEFAULT.

left'-hand''-ed. Using the left rather than the right hand habitually; clumsy. RIGHT-LEFT, SKILL-UNSKILFULNESS; **left-handed compliment,** APPROVAL-DISAPPROVAL; **left-handed marriage,** MATRIMONY-CELIBACY.

leg. A limb of an animal body used for support and locomotion; a swindler. ANATOMY, ROBBER, SUSPENSION-SUPPORT, TRAVELING-NAVIGATION; **best leg foremost,** TOIL-RELAXATION; **carry one off one's legs,** PUSH-PULL; **fast as legs will carry,** SWIFTNESS-SLOWNESS; **keep on one's legs,** HEALTH-SICKNESS; **last legs,** BETTERMENT-DETERIORATION, WEARINESS-REFRESHMENT; **leg bail,** QUEST-EVASION; **light on one's legs,** WELFARE-MISFORTUNE; **make a leg,** POLITENESS-IMPOLITENESS; **not a leg to stand on,** MIGHT-IMPOTENCE, PROOF-DISPROOF, RATIOCINATION-CASUISTRY, SUCCESS-FAILURE; **on one's legs,** ACTIVITY-INDOLENCE, ELEVATION-DEPRESSION, ERECTNESS-FLATNESS, HEALTH-SICKNESS, LIBERTY-SUBJECTION, SPEECH-INARTICULATENESS; **set on one's legs,** RENOVATION-RELAPSE.

leg'-a-cy. A bequest. GIVING-RECEIVING, PROPERTY.

le'-gal. Pertaining to law; lawful; permitted by law. DUENESS-UNDUENESS, LAW-LAWLESSNESS, LEAVE-PROHIBITION; **legal adviser,** ADVOCATE; **legal estate,** PROPERTY; **legal process,** LAW-LAWLESSNESS; **legal profession,** ADVOCATE.

le-gal'-i-ty. Lawfulness. LAW-LAWLESSNESS.

le'-gal-ize. To make lawful; to sanction. DUENESS-UNDUENESS, LAW-LAWLESSNESS.

le'-gal-ized. Made lawful; sanctioned; permitted. DUENESS-UNDUENESS, LAW-LAWLESSNESS, LEAVE-PROHIBITION.

le'-gal-ly. Lawfully. LAW-LAWLESSNESS.

leg'-a-ta-ry. A legatee. GIVING-RECEIVING, HOLDER.

leg'-ate. An envoy. CONSIGNEE, MESSENGER.

leg'-a-tee. The recipient of a legacy. GIVING-RECEIVING, HOLDER.

le-ga'-tion. A diplomatic mission. COMMISSION-ABROGATION.

le-ga'-to. A smooth, connected style of performance. MUSIC.

leg'-end. A narrative based on tradition; a brief inscription. ACCOUNT, MARK-OBLITERATION.

leg'-end-a-ry. Fabulous. ACCOUNT, FANCY.

leg'-er-de-main''. Sleight of hand. REVOLUTION, TRUTHFULNESS-FRAUD.

légèreté [F.] (lê-zhêr-tê'). Lightness; levity. DETERMINATION-VACILLATION.

leg'-gings. Coverings for the legs. DRESS-UNDRESS.

leg''-i-bil'-i-ty. The quality of being legible. CLEARNESS-OBSCURITY.

leg'-i-ble. That may be read. CLEARNESS-OBSCURITY; **legible hand,** WRITING-PRINTING.

le'-gion. A Roman body of infantry; army; multitude. BELLIGERENT, MULTIPLICITY-PAUCITY; **their "name is legion,"** MULTIPLICITY-FEWNESS.

le'-gion-a-ry. A soldier of a legion. BELLIGERENT.

légionnaire [F.] (lê-zhi-o-nêr'). A member of a legion. BELLIGERENT.

leg'-is-late. To enact laws. LAW-LAWLESSNESS; **legislate for,** MANAGEMENT.

leg''-is-la'-tion. Enactment of laws; a part or the whole body of laws. LAW-LAWLESSNESS, MANAGEMENT.

leg'-is-la''-tor. A lawmaker. MANAGER.

leg''-is-la-tor'-i-al. Pertaining to legislation; enacting laws. LAW-LAWLESSNESS.

leg'-is-la''-ture. A lawmaking body. LAW-LAWLESSNESS, MANAGEMENT.

le'-gist. One learned or skilled in the law. ADVO-CATE.

le-git'-i-ma-cy. Accordance with law. LAW-LAW-LESSNESS, NATURE-ART.

le-git'-i-mate. To render lawful; lawful; regular; proper; lawfully begotten. DUENESS-UNDUENESS, LAW-LAWLESSNESS, LEAVE-PROHIBITION, NATURE-ART, RIGHT-WRONG, TRUTH-ERROR.

le-git'-i-mate-ness. The state of being lawful. LAW-LAWLESSNESS.

leg'-ume. The fruit of the bean family. FAUNA-FLORA.

le-gu'-mi-nous. Producing legumes. FAUNA-FLORA.

lei'-sure. Spare time. HURRY-LEISURE; **at leisure,** ACTIVITY-INDOLENCE, HURRY-LEISURE; **at one's leisure,** EARLINESS-LATENESS.

lei'-sure-ly. Deliberate; deliberately. EARLINESS-LATENESS, HURRY-LEISURE, SWIFTNESS-SLOWNESS.

le'-man. A sweetheart. LOVE-HATE.

lem'-ma. A proposition assumed to be true. RATIOCINATION-CASUISTRY.

lem'-on. The color of the lemon. YELLOWNESS-PURPLE.

Lem-pri-ére. The author of a classical dictionary, for many years the standard work of its class. JOVE-FIEND.

Lem'-u-res. Spirits who could not find rest. JOVE-FIEND.

lend. To give the temporary use of. LOAN-BORROWING; **lend a color to,** PRETEXT; **lend a hand,** ACTION-PASSIVENESS, READINESS-RELUCTANCE; **lend aid,** OBSTRUCTION-HELP; **lend countenance,** OBSTRUCTION-HELP; **lend oneself to,** ANTAGONISM-CONCURRENCE, ASSENT-DISSENT, OBSTRUCTION-HELP; **lend on security,** LOAN-BORROWING; **lend wings to,** OBSTRUCTION-HELP.

lend'-er. One who lends. CREDIT-DEBT, LOAN-BORROWING; **money-lender,** DEALER, LOAN-BORROWING

lend'-ing. A loan. LOAN-BORROWING.

length. Longitudinal extent. LENGTH-SHORTNESS, **at length,** EARLINESS-LATENESS, LENGTH-SHORTNESS; **full length,** PAINTING; **go all lengths,** ACTIVITY-INDOLENCE, DETERMINATION-VACILLATION, ENTIRETY-DEFICIENCY, TOIL-RELAXATION; **go great lengths,** GULL-HYPERBOLE; **length and breadth of,** WHOLE-PART; **length and breadth of the land,** EXTENSION-INEXTENSION, PUBLICITY; **length of time,** LASTINGNESS-TRANSIENTNESS.

LENGTH—SHORTNESS

Extension. The state of being drawn out or protracted.
Length. A portion of space of definite extent.
Lengthening, etc. The act of stretching out. See *Verbs.*
Longitude. Measure of distance along the longest line.
Production. A lengthening.
Prolongation. The act of lengthening in space.
Protraction. The act of drawing out.
Span. Spread or extent.
Tension. } The state of being stretched out.
Tensure. }

LENGTH—*Associated Nouns.*

Bar. A piece of wood, metal, or other material, long in proportion to its breadth or thickness.
Line. That which has length, but not breadth or thickness.
Radius. The semidiameter of a circle or sphere.
Rule. A straight strip of metal, wood, or the like, which serves as a guide in drawing a straight line.
Spoke. The radius or ray of a wheel.
Streak. A long mark of a different color from the ground.
Strife. A line or long narrow division of anything.

LENGTH—*Measures of Length.*

Chain. A measure of 66 feet.
Cubit. A measure of length, being the distance from the elbow to the extremity of the middle finger.
Ell. A measure of cloth of 45 inches; an arm.
Fathom. A measure of length containing 6 feet.
Foot. A measure of length of 12 inches.
Furlong. The eighth part of a mile.
Hand. } A measure equal to a hand's breadth.
Hand-breadth. }
Inch. A measure of length, the twelfth part of a foot.
Kilometer. A measure of length, being a thousand meters.
League. A measure of length, being about three miles.
Line. A measure of length, one-twelfth of an inch.
Mile. A measure of length containing 5280 feet.
Nail. A measure of length of two inches and a quarter.
Palm. A lineal measure equal to the breadth of a hand.
Pole. } A measure of length equal to 5½ yards.
Rod. }
Rood. One-fourth of an acre.
Yard. A measure of 3 feet.

LENGTH—*Nouns of Instrument.*

Pedometer. An instrument for measuring distance by indicating the number of steps taken.
Perambulator. A surveyor's instrument for measuring distances.
Scale, etc. A series of spaces marked by lines, and representing proportionately larger distances. See MENSURATION.

Abbreviature. The act of shortening.
Brevity. Shortness.
Conciseness, etc. Brevity in speaking and writing. See TERSENESS
Concision. Act of making shorter.
Curtailment. Act of shortening by cutting off the end.
Decuration. The act of shortening.
Littleness, etc. The state of being small. See GREATNESS-LITTLENESS.
Reduction, etc. The act of making smaller. See ENLARGEMENT-DIMINUTION.
Retrenchment. The act of lessening or shortening.
Shortening, etc. Act of making shorter. See *Verbs.*
Shortness, etc. The state of being not long. See *Adjectives*

SHORTNESS—*Associated Nouns.*

Abbreviation. The form to which a word or phrase is reduced by contraction or omission.
Abridgment. A shortened or abridged form, as of a book.
Elision. The cutting off or suppression of a vowel or syllable for the sake of meter.
Ellipsis. The omission of one or more words in writing, which are obviously understood.
Epitome, etc. A work in which the contents of a former work are reduced within a smaller space. See DIGEST.
Span. A small space or a brief portion of time.

SHORTNESS—*Verbs.*

Abbreviate. To make short.
Abridge. To shorten.
Be short, etc. To be limited in extent. See *Adjectives.*
Check the growth of. To prevent or hinder the increase in size of.
Chop up. To cut to pieces.
Clip. To cut short as with scissors.
Compress, etc. To force into a smaller space. See ENLARGEMENT-DIMINUTION.
Crop. To cut off closely.
Curtail. To cut off the end; shorten.
Cut. To separate into parts.
Cut down. To cause to make shorter.
Cut short. To abridge.
Dock. To cut off a part of.
Epitomize, etc. To make an abstract; shorten. See DIGEST.
Foreshorten. To represent as seen obliquely.
Hack. To cut to pieces.
Hew. To cut off.
Lop. To shorten by cutting off the extremities.
Mow. To cut down with a scythe.
Nip. To cut off the ends.
Obtruncate. To deprive of a limb
Pare down. To cut down little by little.
Pollard. To lop the tops of.
Prune. To cut off anything superfluous.
Reap. To cut with a sickle, as grain.
Reduce. To diminish.

LENGTH—SHORTNESS—*Continued.*

LENGTH—*Verbs.*

Be long, etc. To be extended or drawn out. See *Adjectives.*
Drag its slow length along.
Drawl. To draw out to a tiresome length.
Draw out. To stretch out.
Elongate. To make long; extend.
Enfilade. To rake lengthwise with shot or missiles.
Extend. To prolong in a single direction; stretch out.
Extend to. To stretch out to
Lengthen. To make long.
Let out. To extend.
Look along. To estimate the length by sight.
Make a long arm. To reach out.
Produce. To lengthen out.
Prolong. To extend in length or space.
Protract. To draw out; lengthen.
Reach to. To extend to.
Render long. To make long.
Spin out. To draw out to a great length.
Sprawl. To lie with the limbs stretched out.
Stretch. ⎫
Stretch out. ⎬ To extend.
Stretch to. To reach to; extend to.
View in perspective. To view so that objects appear extended, while they really are in a plane.

LENGTH—*Adjectives.*

As long as my arm. ⎫
As long as to-day and to-morrow. ⎬ Comparative degrees of length.
Interminable. Without limit or end.
Lengthened, etc. Made long; extended. See *Verbs.*
Lengthy. Having length; very long.
Lineal. ⎫
Linear. ⎬ Pertaining to a line or measure of length.
Long. Extended; stretched out.
Longitudinal. Pertaining to or extending in length.
Longsome. Extended in length.
No end of. Without limit.
Oblong. Having one principal axis longer than the other.
Outstretched. Expanded.
Sesquipedalian, etc. A foot and one-half long, said especially of long words. See SIMPLICITY-FLORIDNESS.
Unshortened, etc. Not shortened. See LENGTH-SHORTNESS.
Wiredrawn. Stretched out like wire.

LENGTH—*Adverbs.*

Along. In a line with the length.
At length. In a long or protracted manner.
Endlong. In a line.
Fore-and-aft. From one end of a vessel to the other.

SHORTNESS—VERBS—*Continued.*

Render short, etc. To make short. See *Adjectives.*
Retrench. To lessen; curtail.
Scrimp. To shorten.
Shave. To cut off from the surface of a body with a keen-edged instrument.
Shear. To cut off with scissors or a similar instrument.
Shorten. To make less in length.
Snub. To clip the ends of.
Stunt. To confine or hinder the growth of.
Take in. To draw into a smaller compass.
Truncate. To cut off.

SHORTNESS—*Adjectives.*

Brief. Short; not long.
Compact. Brief; not diffuse.
Compendious. Abridged; shortened.
Concise, etc. Short; brief; compendious. See TERSENESS.
Curt. Short.
Curtailed of its fair proportion. Having part broken off.
Dumpy. Short and thick.
Little, etc. Not large; small. See GREATNESS-LITTLENESS.
Oblate. Flattened at the poles.
Pug. Short and thickset.
Scrimp. Short.
Shorn. Cut off by shears.
Short. Not long; limited in extent.
Short by. Not sufficiently long.
Squab. ⎫
Squabby. ⎬ Fat and thick.
Squat. Short and thick.
Stubbed. ⎫
Stubby. ⎬ Short and thick.
Stumpy. Short and thickset.
Summary. Reduced into a narrow compass.
Thickset. Having a short, thick body.

SHORTNESS—*Adverbs.*

In short, etc. Concisely; briefly. See TERSENESS.
Shortly, etc. In a short, brief manner. See *Adjectives.*

LENGTH—*Adverbs—Continued.*

From end to end. ⎫
From head to foot. ⎬
From stem to stern. ⎬ Throughout the whole distance.
From the crown of the head to the sole of the foot. ⎬
From top to toe. ⎭
In a line. Lengthwise.
In perspective. In the appearance of a solid while, in fact, in a plane.
Lengthwise. In the direction of the length.
Longitudinally. In the direction of length.
Tandem. One behind the other, as horses in harness.

---

length'-en. To elongate. LENGTH-SHORTNESS; **lengthen out,** EARLINESS-LATENESS, LASTINGNESS-TRANSIENTNESS.
length'-ened. Elongated. LENGTH-SHORTNESS.
length'-en-ing. Making longer. LENGTH-SHORTNESS.
length'-wise. In a longitudinal direction. LENGTH-SHORTNESS.
length'-y. Unduly long; protracted. LENGTH-SHORTNESS, TERSENESS-PROLIXITY.
le'-nience. Forbearance. HARSHNESS-MILDNESS.
le'-nien-cy. Mildness. COMPASSION-RUTHLESSNESS, HARSHNESS-MILDNESS.
le'-nient. Merciful; mild. COMPASSION-PITILESSNESS, HARSHNESS-MILDNESS, TURBULENCE-CALMNESS.
len'-i-fy. To assuage. TURBULENCE-CALMNESS.
len'-i-tive. An application that tends to allay pain; soothing. ALLEVIATION-AGGRAVATION, REMEDY-BANE, TURBULENCE-CALMNESS.
len'-i-ty. Forbearance. HARSHNESS-MILDNESS, TURBULENCE-CALMNESS.
lens. A piece of glass, or other transparent substance, one of whose two surfaces is a surface of revolution. OPTICAL INSTRUMENTS, SIGHT-DIMSIGHTEDNESS.

Lent. A fast of forty days observed as a period of penance and self-denial. CEREMONIAL, FASTING-GLUTTONY.
len'-ten. Spare. FASTING-GLUTTONY, PERIODICITY-IRREGULARITY; **lenten diet,** FASTING-GLUTTONY; **lenten entertainment,** FASTING-GLUTTONY.
len-tic'-u-lar. Lentiform. CONVEXITY-CONCAVITY, CURVATION-RECTILINEARITY.
len'-ti-form. Lenticular. CONVEXITY-CONCAVITY, CURVATION-RECTILINEARITY.
len'-tor. Viscidity; slowness. ACTIVITY-INDOLENCE, SWIFTNESS-SLOWNESS, VISCIDITY-FOAM.
len'-tous. Tenacious. VISCIDITY-FOAM.
leonem ex ungue [L.] (lî-o'-nem ex un'-gwî). From his claw [we may recognize] the lion. SIGN.
leones, noli irritare [L.] (lî-o'-nîz, no'-lai ir-ri-tê'-rî). Avoid irritating the lions. RECKLESSNESS-CAUTION.
le'-o-nine ver'-ses. Latin verses in which the syllable ending the verse has assonance with the syllable just before the cesural pause. POETRY-PROSE.
leop'-ard. The panther, a carnivorous mammal usually spotted over with dark brown or black. VARIEGATION; **leopard's spots,** MUTABILITY-STABILITY.

lep'-er. One afflicted with leprosy. HEALTH-SICKNESS.

lep'-re-chawn. A fairy fabled to help housewives. JOVE-FIEND.

lep'-ro-sy. A chronic skin-disease. HEALTH-SICKNESS.

lep'-rous. Having leprosy. HEALTH-SICKNESS.

lese"-maj'-es-ty. Any crime against the sovereign power. INSUBORDINATION-OBEDIENCE.

less. Smaller; inferior, not so much. ADDITION-SUBTRACTION, SUPREMACY-SUBORDINACY; **less than no time,** ETERNITY-INSTANTANEITY.

less'-ee. A person to whom a lease is granted. GIVING-RECEIVING, HOLDER.

less'-en. To lower; to decrease. ENLARGEMENT-DIMINUTION, INCREASE-DECREASE, TURBULENCE-CALMNESS; **lessen an evil,** BETTERMENT-DETERIORATION.

less'-en-ing. The act of becoming or making less. ENLARGEMENT-DIMINUTION, INCREASE-DECREASE.

less'-er. Less. SUPREMACY-SUBORDINACY.

les'-son. The thing taught or learned; a warning. EDUCATION-LEARNING, WARNING; **give a lesson to,** RECOMPENSE-PUNITION; **read a lesson to,** APPROVAL-DISAPPROVAL; **say one's lesson,** REMEMBRANCE-FORGETFULNESS.

les'-sor. The person who grants a lease. CREDIT-DEBT.

lest. For fear that. QUEST-EVASION.

let. (1) To permit; to give leave to; to lease; BUYING-SALE, LEAVE-PROHIBITION, LOAN-BORROWING, SECURITY; **apartments to let,** SAGACITY-INCAPACITY; **let alone,** ACTION-PASSIVENESS, ADDITION-SUBTRACTION, COMPLETION-NONCOMPLETION, CONVENTIONALITY-UNCONVENTIONALITY, LIBERTY-SUBJECTION, MOVEMENT-REST, MUTATION-PERMANENCE, QUEST-EVASION, USE-DISUSE; **let be,** ACTION-PASSIVENESS, DISCONTINUANCE-CONTINUANCE, MUTATION-PERMANENCE; **let blood,** ADMISSION-EXPULSION, REMEDY-BANE; **let down,** ELEVATION-DEPRESSION, SELFRESPECT-HUMBLENESS; **let down easily,** PARDON-REVENGE; **let fall,** ASCENT-DESCENT, ELEVATION-DEPRESSION, ENLIGHTENMENT-SECRECY, EXPOSURE-HIDINGPLACE, SPEECH-INARTICULATENESS; **let fly,** PUSH-PULL, TURBULENCE-CALMNESS; **let fly at,** ATTACK-DEFENSE; **let go,** CAREFULNESS-NEGLECT, KEEPING-RELINQUISHMENT, RELEASE-RESTRAINT, TAKING-RESTITUTION; **let I dare not, wait upon I would,** DETERMINATION-VACILLATION, SANGUINENESS-TIMIDITY; **let in,** ADMISSION-EXPULSION, ENVIRONMENT-INTERPOSITION, TRUTH-ERROR; **let into,** EXPOSURE-HIDINGPLACE, KNOWLEDGE-IGNORANCE; **let off,** DUTY-IMMUNITY, EXCULPATION-CONVICTION, LEAVE-PROHIBITION, PARDON-REVENGE, PUSH-PULL, TURBULENCE-CALMNESS; **let one know,** ENLIGHTENMENT-SECRECY; **let out,** ADMISSION-EXPULSION, CONCENTRATION-RADIATION, ENLIGHTENMENT-SECRECY, GATHERING-SCATTERING, RELEASE-RESTRAINT; **let out at,** ATTACK-DEFENSE; **let pass,** ACTION-PASSIVENESS, CAREFULNESS-NEGLECT; **let slip,** CAREFULNESS-NEGLECT, COMPLETION-NONCOMPLETION, GAIN-LOSS, KEEPING-RELINQUISHMENT, OPPORTUNENESS-UNSUITABLENESS, RELEASE-RESTRAINT; **let the matter stand over,** EARLINESS-LATENESS; **let things take their course,** ACTION-PASSIVENESS, DISCONTINUANCE-CONTINUANCE; **let well alone,** ACTION-PASSIVENESS, CONTENTEDNESS-DISCONTENTMENT, MOVEMENT-REST, RECKLESSNESS-CAUTION; **to let,** PROFFER-REFUSAL.

let. (2) To hinder. OBSTRUCTION-HELP.

le'-thal. Deadly; fatal. LIFE-KILLING.

lethalis arundo, hæret lateri [L.] (leth-ê'-lis a-run'-do, hî'-ret lat'-er-ai). The fatal arrow clings fast in her side. FAVORITE-ANGER.

le-thar'-gic. Drowsy, languid, or apathetic. ACTIVITY-INDOLENCE.

leth'-ar-gy. Inaction, indifference, or dulness; apathy. ACTIVITY-INDOLENCE, SENSITIVENESS-APATHY.

Le'-the. The stream of Oblivion in the lower world. **Waters of Lethe,** REMEMBRANCE-FORGETFULNESS.

Le-the'-an. Inducing oblivion. REMEMBRANCE-FORGETFULNESS.

le-thif'-er-ous. Inducing sleep; deadly LIFE-KILLING.

let'-ter. A character of the alphabet; an epistle. LETTER, MISSIVE-PUBLICATION, SIGN, WRITING-PRINTING; **letter of credit,** CREDIT-DEBT; **to the letter,** IMITATION-ORIGINALITY, TRUTH-ERROR.

LETTER.

Character. The peculiar form of letters used by a particular person or people.

Hieroglyphic, etc. A character used in Egyptian picture-writing. See WRITING.

Letter. A mark used to represent an articulate or other sound.

LETTER—*Denotations.*

A-B-C. The first three letters of the alphabet used for the whole alphabet.

Abecedary. A hymn or psalm in which the verses begin with the successive letters of the alphabet.

Acrostic. A composition usually in verse in which the first or last letters of the lines, or of words, taken in their order, one in each line, form a word or sentence.

Affix. One or more letters or syllables added to a word.

Alphabet. The letters of a language arranged in a customary order. *Alpha* is the Greek name of *a*, *beta* of *b*.

Anagram. A transposition of the letters of a name by which a new word is formed.

Anagrammatism. The act or practise of making anagrams.

Capital. A leading or heading letter used at the beginning of a sentence.

Christ-cross-row. The alphabet; so called either from the cross usually set before it, or from a custom of writing it in the form of a cross.

Cipher. A private alphabet, system of characters, or other mode of writing, contrived for the safe transmission of secrets.

Consonant. A letter representing an articulate sound which in utterance is combined with a vowel.

Dental. An articulation or letter formed by the aid of the teeth.

Diphthong. A union of two vowels pronounced in one syllable.

Dissyllable. A word of two syllables.

Double acrostic. An enigma in which words are to be guessed whose initial and final letters form other words.

Guttural. A sound formed in the throat.

Labial. A sound formed by the lips.

Lingual. A sound formed by the tongue.

Liquid. A letter which has a smooth, flowing sound.

Majusculæ [L.]. Capital letters, as found in the early Latin manuscripts.

Metagrammatism. The practise of making anagrams.

Minusculæ [L.]. Small letters, as found in the early Latin manuscripts.

Monogram. A character composed of two or more letters interwoven or combined so as to represent a name.

Monosyllable. A word of one syllable.

Mute. A letter which represents no sound.

Orthography. The art or practise of writing words with the proper letters according to standard usage.

Phonetic spelling. Spelling in sound characters, each representing one sound only.

Phonography. A representation of sounds by distinctive characters.

Polysyllable. A word of four or more syllables.

Prefix. An affix before the root of a word.

Spelling. The formation of words by letters.

Suffix. A letter, letters, syllable, or syllables added to the end of a word.

Syllable. An elementary sound, or a combination of elementary sounds uttered together.

Triphthong. A combination of three vowels.

Type. A raised letter or character, cast in metal or cut in wood, used for printing. See WRITING-PRINTING.

Vowel. A letter or character which represents a distinct vocal sound.

LETTER—*Adjectives.*

Abecedarian. Formed of or pertaining to the letters of the alphabet.
Alphabetical. Arranged in the order of, pertaining to, or furnished with the letters of the alphabet.
Cuneiform. Wedge-shaped: used to describe a kind of letter used in Mesopotamia.
Hieratic. Priestly: used to describe a kind of hieroglyph.
Literal. Consisting of letters.
Syllabic. According to or pertaining to syllables.
Uncial, etc. Pertaining to a species of large letters in form, some like the capitals, some like the small letters. See WRITING.

let'-ter–bag''. A bag in which letters are contained or carried. MESSENGER.
let'-tered. Learned. KNOWLEDGE-IGNORANCE.
let'-ter-press''. Letters and words printed. WRITING-PRINTING.
let'-ters. Literary culture, literature. KNOWLEDGE-IGNORANCE, LANGUAGE; **in large letters,** CONSEQUENCE-INSIGNIFICANCE; **letters of marque,** THEFT; **man of letters,** SCHOLAR-DUNCE.
lettres de cachet [F.] (letr de ca-shê'). Secret letters, sealed by the royal cachet, containing orders for arrest and imprisonment without trial. RELEASE-RESTRAINT.
lettre de créance [F.] (letr de crêan·s'). Letter of credit. EXCHANGE.
let'-tuce. A kitchen herb. NUTRIMENT-EXCRETION.
leu''-co-phleg-mat'-ic. Having a dropsical condition, with a white, bloated skin. SENSITIVENESS-APATHY.
Le-vant'. The Eastern Mediterranean and adjacent countries. LATERALITY-CONTRAPOSITION.
le-vant'. To abscond. QUEST-EVASION.
le-vant'-er. (1) An easterly gale in the Mediterranean. RIVER-WIND.
le-vant'-er. (2) An absconder. SETTLEMENT-DEFAULT.
le-vant'-ine. Eastern; Oriental. LATERALITY-CONTRAPOSITION.
lev-ee'. A morning reception, concourse, or assembly; a general reception. SCATTERING-GATHERING, SOCIABILITY-PRIVACY.
levée en masse [F.] (le-vê' an· mas). A rising in a body. REPRISAL-RESISTANCE.
lev'-el. Without inequalities, straight; even; to remove irregularities; to prostrate; to take aim. CREATION-DESTRUCTION, ELEVATION-DEPRESSION, EQUALITY-INEQUALITY, ERECTNESS-FLATNESS, LEVELNESS, SMOOTHNESS-ROUGHNESS, UNIFORMITY-DIVERSITY; **dead level,** ERECTNESS-FLATNESS; **level at,** AIM-ABERRATION, ATTACK-DEFENSE, PURPOSE-LUCK; **level with the ground,** CREATION-DESTRUCTION, HEIGHT-LOWNESS.
lev'-el-ness. The state of being level. LEVELNESS.

LEVELNESS

Flatness, etc. The state of being flat. See *Adjectives.*
Smoothness, etc. Freedom from roughness. See SMOOTHNESS.

LEVELNESS—*Denotations.*

Plate. A flat, or nearly flat, piece of metal or crockery for table use.
Platter. A large circular vessel of metal, wood, or earth, glazed and baked.
Slab. A thin piece of anything having plane surfaces.
Table. An article of furniture, consisting of a flat slab, board, or the like, having a smooth surface, fixed horizontally on legs.
Tablet. A small table or flat surface.

LEVELNESS—*Nouns of Instrument.*

Level. An instrument by which levelness is determined.
Plane. An instrument for leveling surfaces.

LEVELNESS—*Verbs.*

Flatten. To make flat.
Level, etc. To make level. See ERECTNESS-FLATNESS.
Render flat. To make level.

LEVELNESS—*Adjectives.*

Discoid. Disk-like.
Even. Free from great irregularities or roughness.
Flat. Free from projections or roundness.
Flat as a board.
Flat as a flounder.
Flat as a fluke. } Expressions for degrees of flatness or levelness.
Flat as a pancake.
Flat as my hand.
Flush. On the same level.
Level, etc. Free from rises or falls. See ERECTNESS-FLATNESS.
Plane. Exactly flat.
Scutiform. Shaped like a shield.

lev'-er. A mechanical device; that which exerts great power. CAUSE-EFFECT, ELEVATION-DEPRESSION, INSTRUMENT.
lever de rideau [F.] (le-vê' de ri-do'). The rise of the curtain. ACTING.
lev'-er-age. Increased power or advantage. DOMINANCE-IMPOTENCE, INSTRUMENT.
le-vi'-a-than. A large animal mentioned in the Scriptures. GREATNESS-LITTLENESS.
lev'-i-gate. To reduce to a powder. FRIABILITY.
lev''-i-ga'-tion. The grinding of a solid substance to a fine, impalpable powder. FRIABILITY.
lev'-i-rate. The custom of marriage between a man and the widow of his brother. MATRIMONY-CELIBACY.
Le'-vite. One of the tribe of Levi. MINISTRY-LAITY.
Le-vit'-i-cus. The third book of the Pentateuch. REVELATION-PSEUDOREVELATION.
lev'-i-ty. Lightness of humor or temperament; frivolity; cheerfulness. CONSEQUENCE-INSIGNIFICANCE, DETERMINATION-VACILLATION, HEAVINESS-LIGHTNESS, LIGHTHEARTEDNESS-DEJECTION, RECKLESSNESS-CAUTION.
lev'-y. To exact by compulsion; to impose or assess a tax; to collect, as troops; that which is levied. BELLIGERENT, GATHERING-SCATTERING, PRICE-DISCOUNT, TAKING-RESTITUTION; **levy blackmail,** THEFT.
lewd. Libidinous. PURITY-IMPURITY.
lex loci [L.] (lex lo'-sai). The law of the place. EXTENSION-PLACE, LAW-LAWLESSNESS.
lex mercatoria [L.] (lex mer-kê-to'-ri-a). Mercantile law. LAW-LAWLESSNESS.
lex non scripta [L.] (lex non scrip'-ta). Unwritten law; the common law of England. LAW-LAWLESSNESS.
lex scripta [L.] (lex scrip'-ta). Written law. LAW-LAWLESSNESS, PRECEPT.
lex talionis [L.] (lex tal-i-o'-nis). The law of retaliation. REPRISAL-RESISTANCE, RIGHT-WRONG.
lex''-i-cog'-ra-pher. One skilled in lexicography. SCHOLAR-DUNCE.
lex''-i-cog'-ra-phy. The making of dictionaries. WORD-NEOLOGY.
lex'-i-con. A dictionary. WORD-NEOLOGY.
ley. A meadow-land. GULF-PLAIN.
li'-a-bil'-i-ty. The state of being liable; that for which one is liable. CONTINGENCY, CREDIT-DEBT, DUTY-DERELICTION, LIBERTY-SUBJECTION, MONEY.
li'-a-ble. Exposed, as to damage, penalty, expense, burden, or anything unpleasant or dangerous. CONTINGENCY, CREDIT-DEBT, DUTY-DERELICTION, INCLINATION, LIBERTY-SUBJECTION.
li'-a-ble-ness. The state of being liable. CONTINGENCY.
li''-ai-son'. An illicit intimacy between two persons of opposite sex. PURITY-IMPURITY.
li'-ar. One who tells a falsehood or falsehoods. GULL-DECEIVER.
li-ba'-tion. The act of pouring wine in honor of a deity; that which is poured either as an honor to a deity, or to drink. NUTRIMENT-EXCRETION, SOBRIETY-INTEMPERANCE, WORSHIP-IDOLATRY.
li'-bel. Defamation; slander written or published. ADULATION-DISPARAGEMENT, JUSTIFICATION-CHARGE,

li'-bel-ler. One who libels another. FLATTERER-DEFAMER.

li'-bel-ous. Of the nature of a libel. ADULATION-DISPARAGEMENT.

lib'-er-al. Open-handed; plentiful. ENOUGH, GENEROSITY-FRUGALITY, UNSELFISHNESS-SELFISHNESS; **liberal arts,** NATURE-ARTS; **liberal education,** EDUCATION-MISTEACHING, KNOWLEDGE-IGNORANCE; **over liberal,** EXTRAVAGANCE-AVARICE.

lib'-er-al-ism. Opposite of conservatism. • LIBERTY-SUBJECTION, UNSELFISHNESS-SELFISHNESS.

lib''-er-al'-i-ty. Bountifulness; catholicity. GENEROSITY-FRUGALITY, GIVING-RECEIVING, UNSELFISHNESS-SELFISHNESS.

lib'-er-ate. To free; to disengage. CHEMISTRY, EXCULPATION-CONVICTION, RELEASE-RESTRAINT.

lib''-er-a''-ted. Freed. RELEASE-RESTRAINT.

lib''-er-a'-tion. The act of delivering from restraint. ESCAPE, RELEASE-RESTRAINT, RESCUE.

liberavi animam meam [L.] (lib-er-ê'-vai an'-im-am mi'-am). I have freed my mind. CRAFT-ARTLESSNESS.

lib'-er-tin-age. Debauchery. PURITY-IMPURITY.

lib'-er-tine. Licentious; a debauchee. PURITY-RAKE.

lib'-er-tin-ism. Debauchery. PURITY-IMPURITY.

libertas, ubi patria, ubi [L.] (lib-er'-tas, yu'-bai pê'-tri-a, yu'-bai). Where liberty is, there is my fatherland. DWELLER-HABITATION, LIBERTY-SUBJECTION.

libertatem est vendere, beneficium accipere [L.] (lib-er-tê'-tem est ven'-der-î, ben-î-fi'-shi-um ac-sip'-er-î). To accept a favor is to sell your liberty. VOLITION-OBLIGATION.

lib'-er-ty. Freedom; privilege; freedom from necessity. DUENESS-UNDUENESS, DUTY-IMMUNITY, LEAVE-PROHIBITION, LIBERTY-SUBJECTION; **gain one's liberty,** RELEASE-RESTRAINT; **liberty-hall,** LIBERTY-SUBJECTION; **set at liberty,** DUTY-IMMUNITY, RELEASE-RESTRAINT; **take a liberty,** HARSHNESS-MILDNESS, LIBERTY-SUBJECTION, POLITENESS-IMPOLITENESS, PRESUMPTION-OBSEQUIOUSNESS.

LIBERTY—SUBJECTION.

Affranchisement. Enfranchisement.

Allodium. Absolutely free tenure of land.

Autonomy. Self-government in a tributary state.

Denization. Act of making one a denizen.

Denizen. An alien made a citizen by letters-patent from the sovereign.

Elbow-room. Room for activity.

Emancipation. Release from bondage.

Enfranchisement. Endowment with political privileges.

Exemption. Freedom from that to which others are subject.

Facility. Freedom from difficulty.

Franchise. A privilege granted by a government.

Frankalmoigne. An ancient religious tenure of land upon distributing free alms.

Freedom. State of not being subject to any restraint.

Free play.
Free scope. } Plenty of room for activity.
Free stage and no favor.

Free trade. Trade unrestricted by protective tariffs.

Full play.
Full scope. } Plenty of room for activity

Full swing. Unrestrained liberty.

Immunity. Exemption based on title, position, or the nature of things.

Independence. Freedom from dependence upon or restraint by others.

Latitude. Undue liberty.

Liberalism. Principles of those opposed to aristocracy, monarchy, or narrowness in thought or religion.

Liberty. Power of putting one's will into action.

License. Unbounded liberty; lack of all due restraint.

Margin. Range of action.

Mortmain. Inalienable tenure of land held by religious corporations.

Non-interference. Freedom from outside restraint.

Play.
Range.
Rope. } Room for activity.
Scope.

Self-government. Government of an individual or state by itself.

Swing. Full liberty.

Wide berth. Room for activity.

LIBERTY—Associated Nouns.

Denizen. One who is admitted to all or parts of the rights of citizenship, where he did not possess them by birth.

Freedman. A man who has been a slave, and has been set free.

Freehold. An estate in real property, of inheritance or for life.

Freeland. A land in which its citizens enjoy full personal and political liberties.

Freeman. One who is not subject to the will of another.

Liberty Hall. [This is Liberty Hall. You may do just as you please. Goldsmith, *She Stoops to Conquer*, II, i.]

Liveryman. A freeman of the city, in London, who, having paid certain fees, is entitled to wear the distinguishing dress of the company to which he belongs.

LIBERTY—Verbs

Affranchise. To enfranchise.

Allow scope, etc. See *Nouns.*

Bondage. The lowest form of slavery.

Clientship. State of a plebeian under the protection of a patrician.

Constraint. Restrictions upon the movements.

Dependance.
Dependence. } State of being subject to the control of another.
Dependency.

Employ. Voluntary service.

Enslavement. Act of making one a slave.

Enthrallment. Enslavement; especially of the mind or senses.

Feudalism. } System of land tenure conditioned upon military
Feudality. } service.

Involuntary servitude. Slavery, as that of Slavs to Germans.

Liability. State of being bound in law.

Obedience. Submission to authority.

Oppression. Imposition of unreasonable hardships.

Serfdom. Condition of one belonging to the soil.

Service. Work for another.

Servitorship. Condition of a servitor.

Servitude. Compulsory service.

Slavery. Condition of a man owned by another, as Slavs were by the Germans.

Subjection. State of being under the power of another

Subjugation. Act of reducing to subjection.

Submission. Compliance with law or commands.

Subordination. Subjection to a superior.

Tendence. Care and attention; service.

Thrall.
Thralldom. } Slavery; especially of the mind

Tutelage. State of being under training and instruction.

Vassalage. Condition of a feudal tenant.

Villenage. State of a villain or serf.

Yoke. Slavery; servitude.

SUBJECTION—Verbs.

Be a football.
Be a mere machine. } Be slavishly subject to the will of another
Be a puppet.

Be at the mercy of. Be in the power of. [*Mercy* meant *ransom.*]

Bethrall. See ENTHRALL.

Break in. Teach the rudiments.

Depend upon. To be unable to get along without.

Drag a chain. To be in bondage.

Drag at one's chariot wheels. To triumph over. [" What tributaries follow him to Rome to grace in captive bonds his chariot wheels?" Shakespeare, *Julius Cæsar*, I, i.]

Drive into a corner. To have one almost conquered.

Enthrall. To enslave; especially the mind.

Enslave. To put one into the complete ownership and control of another.

Fall a prey to.
Fall under. } To become conquered by.

Hang upon. To depend upon.

Hold at the sword's point. To hold in one's power.

Hold in bondage. Hold in abject slavery.

Hold in leading strings. To have another under the power of one's will.

Hold in swaddling clothes. To control as a child.

Inthrall. To enthrall.

LIBERTY—SUBJECTION—*Continued.*

LIBERTY—Verbs—*Continued.*

Be free, etc. See *Adjectives.*
Do what one chooses.
Do what one likes.
Do what one pleases. } To have freedom.
Do what one wishes.
Enfranchise. To grant political privileges.
Feel at home. Free to act as one likes.
Give a horse his head. To allow him to choose his gait and course.
Give a loose to. To give free vent.
Give scope, etc. See *Nouns.*
Give the franchise. To give the right to vote.
Give the freedom of. Give all the privileges of.
Go at large. To be free.
Have a will of one's own. To be independent in thought and action.
Have one's own fling. To enjoy oneself to the full.
Have one's own way. To be free to act.
Have scope, etc. See *Nouns.*
Have the run of. Have full enjoyment of.
Laisser aller [F.].
Laisser faire [F.].
Leave alone. } Not to molest or restrain.
Leave to oneself.
Let alone.
Live and let live. To be happy and allow others to be happy.
Make free of. Allow all the privileges of.
Make free with. To be liberal or lavish with.
Make oneself at home. To be free to act as one likes.
Paddle one's own canoe. To be free to choose and act. "To yourself be true, And where'er you be, Paddle your own canoe." [S. J. Bolton, *Canoe,* I.]
Set free. To make free.
Shift for oneself. To think and act for oneself.
Stand on one's legs. To take care of oneself.
Stand on one's rights. To insist upon one's rights.
Take a liberty. To be unduly free.
Take French leave. Take secret departure. Leaving a reception without taking leave of the host was a French custom in the eighteenth century.
Take leave. To take permission.
Use a freedom. Take advantage of a privilege.

LIBERTY—*Adjectives.*

Absolute. Free from any limitation.
Allodial. Absolutely free of rent or service.
At ease. Free from pain or discomfort.
At large. At liberty.
At one's ease. Unembarrassed.
Autonomous. Pertaining to autonomy.
Dégagé [F.]. Free from constraint; easy.
Discretionary. Left to one's own judgment.
Exempt. Free from that to which others are subject.
Free. Not under restraint.
Free and easy. Having little regard for conventionality.
Free as air. Absolutely free.
Freeborn. Free by birth.
Freed. Set at liberty.
Freehold. Of full legal tenure.
Going a begging. Without an owner.
Gratis. Without reward.
Independent. Without restraint by or dependence upon others.
In full swing. In unrestrained liberty.
Irrepressible. Not to be kept back.
Left alone. } Unmolested; forsaken.
Left to oneself.
Loose. Not confined; dissolute.
Out of harness. Free from restraint.
Quite at home. Free to act.
Rampant. Wild; excessively prevalent.
Scot-free. Free from payment; unhurt.
Spontaneous. Acting of one's own accord.
Unassailed; unbiased; unbound; unbridled; unbuttoned; uncaught; unchained; unchecked; unclaimed; uncompelled; unconditional; unconfined; unconstrained; uncontrolled; uncurbed; unenslaved; unenthralled; unfettered; unforced; ungoverned; unhindered; unlimited; unmuzzled; unobstructed; unprevented; unreined;

SUBJECTION—Verbs—*Continued.*

Keep under. Keep in one's control.
Lead captive. To capture; overcome.
Lean upon. To rely greatly upon for support.
Lie at the mercy of. Be in the power of.
Master. To rule or manage.
Not dare to say one's soul is his own. To be in fearful bondage.
Obey. To carry out orders; to comply with commands.
Play second fiddle. To take a subordinate part.
Reduce to slavery. } To obtain complete power over.
Reduce to subjection.
Rule. To exercise authority over.
Serve. To work for another.
Subject. To make subjects of.
Subjugate. To bring under military control, under the yoke.
Submit. To cease to resist.
Take into custody. Put into safe-keeping.
Tame. To make docile.
Tread down.
Tread under foot. } To oppress.
Weigh down.

SUBJECTION—*Adjectives.*

A slave to. Under complete control of, as a Slav to a German master.
At one's beck and call. Servilely obedient.
At the feet of. In submission of.
At the mercy of. In the power of.
Constrained. Hindered in movement.
Dependent. Subject to.
Downtrodden. Oppressed.
Enslaved, etc. See *Verbs.*
Feudal. } Pertaining to feudalism.
Feudatory.
Henpecked. Domineered over by a wife.
In harness. In subjection.
In leading strings. Under control of another's will.
In subjection to. Under the power of.
In the clutches of.
In the hands of. } To be controlled by.
In the power of.
Led by the nose. Controlled by the will of another, like a bull or boar.
Liable. Bound in law.
On the hip. In one's power, as the wrestler's.
Overborne. } Crushed.
Overwhelmed.
Parasitical. Living upon another.
Stipendiary. Receiving a stipend.
Subject. Yielding obedience to an authority.
Subjected. Under the authority of.
Subordinate. Inferior in classification.
The plaything of.
The puppet of. } Completely controlled by.
The sport of.
Under control. In a manageable condition.
Under one's command. } Subordinate to.
Under one's orders.
Under one's thumb. Completely in one's power.
Under the lash. In slavery.

SUBJECTION—*Adverb.*

Under. In subjection; overpowered.

———

LIBERTY—ADJECTIVES—*Continued.*

unrestrained; unrestricted; unshackled; unsubject; untrammeled; unvanquished. Not assailed; not biased, etc.
Wanton. Without proper moral restraints.

LIBERTY—*Adverbs.*

Ad libitum [L.]. At will.
Freely, etc. See *Adjectives.*

LIBERTY—*Phrases.*

Regnant populi [L.]. The people rule. [Motto of Arkansas.]
Ubi libertas, ibi patria [L.]. Where liberty is, there is my fatherland.

libet, non [L.] (lai'-bet, non). It does not please me. DESIRE-DISTASTE.
li-bid'-i-nous. Full of sexual desire. PURITY-IMPURITY.

libitum, ad [L.] (lib'-i-tum, ad). As often as you please. ENOUGH, LEAVE-PROHIBITION, LIBERTY-SUBJECTION, VOLITION-OBLIGATION.

Li'-bra. Constellation. ASTRONOMY.

li-bra'-ri-an. One who has charge of a library MISSIVE-PUBLICATION.

li'-bra-ry. A collection of books, etc.; the place where such a collection is kept. CONTENTS-RECEIVER, MISSIVE-PUBLICATION.

li'-brate. To balance; to oscillate. VIBRATION.

li-bra'-tion. Equipoise. ASTRONOMY, VIBRATION.

li'-bra-to-ry. Oscillating. VIBRATION.

li-bret'-to. A book containing the text of an opera. ACTING, MISSIVE-PUBLICATION.

li'-cense. Permission; legal permission; unrestrained liberty of action. DUENESS-UNDUENESS, DUTY-IMMUNITY, LEAVE-PROHIBITION, LIBERTY-SUBJECTION, RULE-LICENSE; **license to plunder,** THEFT.

li'-censed. Permitted. RULE-LICENSE.

licentia vatum [L.] (li-sen'-shi-α vē'-tum). Poetic license. POETRY-PROSE, RULE-LICENSE.

li-cen'-ti-ate. A person licensed to preach or practise a profession. SCHOLAR-DUNCE.

li-cen'-tious. Wanton; loose. MODERATION-SELFINDULGENCE, PURITY-IMPURITY.

li-cen'-tious-ness. Lewdness. MODERATION-SELFINDULGENCE, RULE-LICENSE.

li'-chen. A low cryptogamic plant. FAUNA-FLORA.

lic'-it. Lawful. DUENESS-UNDUENESS, LEAVE-PROHIBITION.

lick. To lap; to overcome; a stroke of the tongue. NUTRIMENT-EXCRETION, RECOMPENSE-PUNITION, SUCCESS-FAILURE; **lick into shape,** FORM-FORMLESSNESS, PREPARATION-NONPREPARATION; **lick the dust,** ADULATION-DISPARAGEMENT, SUCCESS-FAILURE.

lick'-er-ish. Tempting the appetite; greedy; lustful. DESIRE-DISTASTE, DESIRE-PARTICULARNESS, PALATABLENESS-UNPALATABLENESS, PURITY-IMPURITY.

lick'-pen"-ny. A miser. EXTRAVAGANCE-AVARICE.

lick'-spit"-tle. Vulgar parasite. PRESUMPTION-OBSEQUIOUSNESS.

lic'-o-rice. The juice of the root of a tree of the same name, used for colds. REMEDY-BANE.

lic'-tor. One of a body of Roman public officers. JUDICATURE.

lid. The cover of an aperture. COVER-LINING.

Lid'-ford law. Lynch law. LAW-LAWLESSNESS.

lie. To recline; to rest; to have a location. EDUCATION-MISTEACHING, ERECTNESS-FLATNESS, POSITION, PRESENCE-ABSENCE; **lie at one's door,** DUTY-DERELICTION; **lie at the mercy of,** LIBERTY-SUBJECTION; **lie at the root of,** CAUSE-EFFECT, CONSEQUENCE-INSIGNIFICANCE; **lie by,** ACTION-PASSIVENESS; **lie down,** ERECTNESS-FLATNESS, TOIL-RELAXATION; **lie fallow,** PREPARATION-NONPREPARATION, TOIL-RELAXATION; **lie hid,** ENLIGHTENMENT-SECRECY, MANIFESTATION-LATENCY; **lie in,** CREATION-DESTRUCTION, ENTITY-NONENTITY; **lie in ambush,** ENLIGHTENMENT-SECRECY, EXPOSURE-HIDINGPLACE; **lie in a nutshell,** DIGEST, MAGNITUDE-SMALLNESS; **lie in one's power,** MIGHT-IMPOTENCE; **lie in wait for,** ACTION-PASSIVENESS, EXPECTATION-SURPRISE, EXPOSURE-HIDINGPLACE; **lie on,** SUSPENSION-SUPPORT; **lie over,** EARLINESS-LATENESS, OCCURRENCE-DESTINY; **lie perdu,** ENLIGHTENMENT-SECRECY; **lie still,** MOVEMENT-REST; **lie to,** ACTION-PASSIVENESS, MOVEMENT-REST; **lie under,** CONTINGENCY; **lie under a necessity,** VOLITION-OBLIGATION; **lie under error,** TRUTH-ERROR; **lie upon,** DUTY-DERELICTION.

lie. To utter falsehood; a fabrication. TRUTHFULNESS-FABRICATION, TRUTHFULNESS-FALSEHOOD, TRUTHFULNESS-FRAUD; **give the lie to,** ASSERTION-DENIAL; **lie like a trooper,** TRUTHFULNESS-FALSEHOOD; **white lie,** AMBIGUITY, CRAFT-ARTLESSNESS, PRETEXT.

liedertafel [G.] (lî'-der-ta'-fel). A singing society composed of men. MUSICIAN.

lief. Pleasing. PLEASURABLENESS-PAINFULNESS; **as lief,** CHOICE-NEUTRALITY, READINESS-RELUCTANCE.

liege. Sovereign; a sovereign. CHIEF-UNDERLING; **liege lord,** CHIEF-UNDERLING.

liege'-man. A vassal. CHIEF-UNDERLING.

li'-en. A legal claim on property; an imperative obligation. CREDIT-DEBT, SECURITY.

li'-en-ter-y. Diarrhea. CLEANNESS-FILTHINESS.

lieu. Place; stead. EXTENSION-PLACE; **in lieu of,** COMMUTATION-PERMUTATION.

lieu-ten'-ant. An officer who takes the place of another in his absence; a commissioned officer. CHIEF-UNDERLING, REPRESENTATIVE; **lord lieutenant,** JUDICATURE.

life. The state of being alive; animation; spirit; a biography; the actual character; period of efficient force. ACCOUNT, ACTIVITY-INDOLENCE, CONDUCT, LIFE-DEATH, LIGHTHEARTEDNESS-DEJECTION, OCCURRENCE-DESTINY; **animal life,** ANIMALITY-VEGETABILITY; **battle of life,** ACTIVITY-INDOLENCE; **breath of life,** LIFE-DEATH; **civilized life,** SOCIETY-LUDICROUSNESS; **come to life,** RENOVATION-RELAPSE; **estate for life,** PROPERTY; **infuse life into,** EXCITATION; **life and spirit,** ACTIVITY-INDOLENCE; **life or death,** CONSEQUENCE-INSIGNIFICANCE, NEED, STRIFE-PEACE; **life to come,** LIFE-DEATH; **put life into,** LIFE-DEATH; **recall to life,** RENOVATION-RELAPSE; **see life,** ENTERTAINMENT-WEARINESS; **support life,** LIFE-DEATH; **take away life,** LIFE-KILLING; **tenant for life,** HOLDER.

LIFE—DEATH.

Animal economy. The system of animal life in which means are adjusted to the ends of animal creation.

Animation. State or condition of being alive.

Archeus. The vital principle which presides over the growth and continuation of living beings.

Biology. That branch of knowledge which treats of living matter as distinct from that which is not living.

Breath of life. Figuratively, that which gives and strengthens life.

Breath of one's nostrils. Figuratively, life.

Existence, etc. The state of being or existing. See ENTITY.

Life. The state of an animal or plant in which any or all of its organs are capable of performing any or all their functions.

Life-blood. The blood necessary to life.

Life to come, etc. Immortality. See OCCURRENCE-DESTINY

Nourishment. That which serves to keep up life.

Physiology. The study of the processes incidental to, and characteristic of, life.

Prometheus. The demi-god who saved men and gave them fire.

Respiration. The act of taking and giving out air.

Revivification, etc. The act of recalling to life. See RENEWAL.

Staff of life. Bread, the principal article of food.

Asphyxia. Apparent death from suffocation.

Bereavement. The loss of a relative by death.

Break-up of the system. Death.

Cessation of life. Death.

Death. Extinction of life of all forms, human, animal, or vegetable.

Decease. Departure; especially, departure from this life.

Demise. The death of an illustrious person.

Departure. Death.

Dissolution. The extinction of human life.

Doom, etc. Death. See VOLITION-OBLIGATION.

Ebb of life, etc. The approach of death. See LIFE.

End of life, etc. Death. See BEGINNING-END.

Euthanasia. An easy or agreeable death.

Extinction of life. Death.

Mortality. Subjection to death or to the necessity of dying; death.

Natural death. } Death in accordance with the laws which govern
Natural decay. } human life; death not caused by accident.

Obit. Death.

Quietus. Figuratively, death. "For who would bear the whips and scorns of time . . . when he himself might his quietus make with a bare bodkin?" [*Hamlet*, III, iv.]

LIFE—DEATH—*Continued.*

Viability. The state of being capable to maintain existence.
Vital flame. The life-giving principle.
Vitality. The state of being alive.
Vital spark. The essential of life.
Vivification. Restoration of life.
Wind. Air we breathe.

LIFE—*Verbs.*

Be alive, etc. To be in a state of animation. See *Adjectives.*
Be born. To be brought into life.
Be spared. To be kept from danger or death.
Breathe. To inhale and exhale air.
Bring to life. To make alive
Come into the world. To be born.
Come to. To recover as from a faint.
Come to life. Return to life.
Draw breath. To breathe.
Draw the breath of life. To be living.
Fetch breath. To draw breath.
Fetch the breath of life. To live.
Give birth to, etc. To produce; bring to life. See CREATION.
Have nine lives like a cat. To have great vitality.
Keep alive. To maintain life.
Keep body and soul together. To keep alive.
Keep the wolf from the door. To keep out hunger
Live. To have life; be animated.
Put into life. To bring into life.
Quicken. To make alive.
Reanimate, etc. To make alive again. See RENOVATION.
Respire. To exhale and inhale air; breathe.
Revive. To make alive again.
See the light. To be born.
Strut and fret one's hour upon the stage. To live one's life. [Shakespeare, *Macbeth,* V, v.]
Subsist, etc. To have existence; be. See ENTITY.
Support life. To maintain life.
Vitalize. To make alive.
Vivificate. To give life to; animate.
Vivify. To endue with life; make alive.
Walk the earth. Live.

LIFE—*Adjectives.*

Above ground. Unburied; alive.
Alive. Filled or imbued with life; not dead.
All alive and kicking. Full of life.
Animated. Having the vital principle.
Breathing. Respiring.
In life. Alive.
In the flesh. Alive.
In the land of the living. Alive.
Lively, etc. Quick; active; animated. See ACTIVITY.
Living. Having life.
On this side of the grave. Living.
Promethean. Having a life-giving quality. ["I know not where is that Promethean heat that can thy light relume." Shakespeare, *Othello,* V, ii.]
Quick. Alive; animated; living.
Tenacious of life. Hard to kill.
Vital. Relating or belonging to life.
Vivified, etc. Made alive. See *Verbs.*
Vivifying. Making alive.

LIFE—*Adverb.*

Vivendi causa [L.]. The cause of living

LIFE—*Phrase.*

Non est vivere, sed valere, vita [L.] Not to live, but to be well, is life.

DEATH—VERBS—*Continued from Column 2.*

Meet one's death.
Meet one's end. } To die.
Pass away.
Pay the debt to nature. To expire, as all must in the course of nature.
Perish. To be destroyed; die; lose one's life.
Pop off. To die suddenly or unexpectedly.
Receive one's death-warrant. To receive the order for one's death.
Relinquish one's life. To give up one's life.
Resign one's being.
Resign one's breath. } To die without resistance.
Resign one's life.
Shuffle off this mortal coil. To die. [Shakespeare, *Hamlet,* III, i.]
Sink into the grave. To die.

Release. Deliverance from life.
Sudden death. Death happening unexpectedly.
Suffocation. Death caused by smothering or choking.
Untimely end. Sudden death.
Violent death. A death by accident or physical force.

DEATH—*Associated Nouns.*

Agonies of death. The last struggle of life.
Bill of mortality. An official statement of the number of deaths in a place in a given time.
Death-bed. The bed in which a person dies.
Death-blow. A stroke or blow which causes death. See LIFE-KILLING.
Death-rattle. A gurgling in the throat of a dying person.
Death-song, etc. A song in mourning for the dead. See JUBILATION-LAMENTATION.
Death-warrant. An order from the proper authority for the execution of a criminal.
Death-watch. A guard placed over a person to be executed.
Dying agonies. The last struggle of life.
Dying breath. The last breath of life.
Dying day. The day when one dies.
Fatal disease, etc. A disease that causes death. See HEALTH-SICKNESS.
Last agonies. The last struggle of life.
Last breath. }
Last gasp. } The end of life.
Necrology. A register of deaths.
Obituary. An account of a dead person.
Rigor mortis [L.]. The stiffness of death.

DEATH—*Figurative Nouns.*

Chant de cygne [F.], the song of the dying swan; **fall; hand of death; jaws of death; King Death; King of Terrors; rest; shades of death; stroke of death; Stygian shore; Valley of the Shadow of Death; watery grave.**

DEATH—*Verbs.*

Be all over with one. To die.
Be no more, etc. To be dead. See *Adjectives.*
Be taken. To die. [Euphemism.]
Break one's neck. To die a violent death.
Breathe one's last. To expire; die.
Catch one's death.
Cease to breathe.
Cease to live. } To die
Close one's eyes.
Come to an untimely end. To die prematurely or unseasonably.
Come to dust. To die. "Golden lads and girls all must, as chimney sweepers, come to dust." [Shakespeare, *Cymbeline* IV, ii.]
Cross the Stygian ferry. To cross the Styx; die
Depart this life. To decease; die.
Die. To pass from an animate to an inanimate state.
Die a natural death. To die from natural causes.
Die a violent death, etc. To die from unnatural causes. See LIFE-KILLING.
Drop dead.
Drop down dead. } To die.
Drop into the grave.
Drop off. To come to an end.
End one's days.
End one's earthly career. } To die
End one's life.
Expire. To come to an end; die; perish.
Fall dead.
Fall down dead. } To die.
Give up the ghost. To expire; die.
Go off.
Go off the hooks. } To die.
Go out like the snuff of a candle. To die easily.
Go the way of all flesh. To die.
Go to Davy Jones's locker. To drown.
Go to one's last home. }
Go to one's long account. } To die.
Go to the wall. To be pressed to extremes.
Hop the twig. To die.
Kick the bucket. To lose one's life; die.
Lay down one's life. To die usually for some cause or person.
Lose one's life. To meet death.
Make one's will. To make a legal declaration as to what is to become of a person's property after his death.

(*Continued on Column* 1.)

DEATH—Verbs—*Continued*.

Surrender one's life. To give up one's life.
Take one's last sleep.⎫
Turn to dust.⎭ To die.

Turn up one's toes.⎫
Yield one's breath. ⎬To die.
Yield the ghost.⎭

DEATH—*Adjectives*.

At death's door.
At the last gasp.⎫Close to death
At the point of death.⎭
Aux abois [F.]. At bay.
Booked. Doomed to die.
Dead. Deprived of life; inanimate; not living.
Dead and gone.
Dead as a door-nail; dead as a door-post; dead as a herring; dead as mutton; dead as nits.
Deadly, etc. Causing death; fatal; likely to cause death. See KILLING.
Deceased. Dead; departed from this life.
Defunct. Dead; deceased.
Demised. Pertaining to the death of a distinguished person.
Departed. Having left; gone; dead.
Departed this life, etc. See *Verbs*.
Dying, etc. Pertaining to death; perishing. See *Verbs*.
Exanimate. Deprived of animation.
Gathered to one's fathers. Dead.
Given over. Given to death.
Going.⎫
Going off.⎭ Dying
Gone. Departed; dead.
Hippocratic. Pertaining to the change produced in the face by death, long illness, or the like.

Inanimate. Not living; deprived of animation.
In articulo mortis [L.]. At the point of death.
In extremis [L.]. At the last moments.
In the agony of death. In the death-struggle.
In the jaws of death. At the point of death.
Late. Recently expired.
Launched into eternity. Suddenly killed; dead.
Lifeless. Without life; deprived of life.
Moribund. Dying; at the point of death.
Morient. Dying.
Mortuary. Belonging or pertaining to the burial of the dead.
Near one's end. Close to death.
No more. Dead; departed.
Numbered with the dead. Dead.
On one's death-bed. Dying.
On one's last legs. Near death.
Out of the world. Dead.
Released. Dead; freed from life.
Still-born. Dead at birth.
Taken off. Having died.
Tottering on the brink of the grave. At the point of death
With one foot in the grave. Close to death.

DEATH—*Adverbs*

Post mortem [L.]. After death.

Post obitum [L.]. After death.

DEATH—*Phrases*.

Death knocks at the door.⎫
Death stares one in the face.⎭ Death is near.
De mortuis nil nisi bonum [L.]. Of the dead say nothing but good.
Dulce et decorum est pro patria mori [L.]. It is sweet and glorious to die for one's country. [Horace, *Odes*, III, ii, 13.]
Honesta mors turpi vitâ potior [L.]. Honorable death is better than base life. [Tacitus *Agricola*, 33, 25.]
Life ebbs.⎫
Life fails.⎭ Life is going.

Life hangs by a thread. Life is in danger.
One's days are numbered.⎫
One's doom is sealed.⎬ Death is near.
One's hour is come.⎪
One's race is run.⎭
The breath is out of the body.⎫
The grave closes over one.⎭ Death has come
Sic itur ad astra [L.]. So one goes to the stars. [Virgil, *Æneid*, IX, 641.]

LIFE—KILLING.

KILLING.

Assassination. The act of killing by sudden violence or secret assault.
Bloodshed. The act of shedding human blood, or taking life.
Butchery. Murder or manslaughter when committed with unusual barbarity.
Carnage. Great destruction of life, as in battle.
Effusion of blood. The act of shedding human blood.
Execution, etc. The act of putting to death as a legal penalty See RECOMPENSE-PUNITION.
Felo de se [F.]. The killing of oneself.
Fratricide. The killing of one's brother.
Guet-apens [F.]. Killing by lying in ambush.
Homicide. The killing of a person.
Immolation. Killing as a sacrificial victim
Infanticide. The killing of an infant.
Judicial murder. A putting to death as a legal penalty.
Killing, etc. The act of depriving of life. See *Verbs*.
Manslaughter. The unlawful killing of a man, either in negligence or incidentally to the commission of some unlawful act.
Massacre. Indiscriminate killing of human beings.
Matricide. The killing of one's mother.
Murder. The act of killing a human being with malicious forethought.
Noyade [F.]. Killing by drowning.
Occision. The act of killing
Parricide. The killing of one's father.
Phthiozoics. The killing of harmful animals.
Regicide. The killing of a king.
Slaughter.⎫
Slaughtering.⎭ Extensive and unnecessary destruction of human life.
Sororicide. The killing of one's sister
Suicide. The killing of oneself.
Trucidation. The act of killing.
Vaticide. The killing of a prophet.

KILLING—*Nouns of Means*.

Casualty. Killing by an accident.
Coup de grâce [F.]. The death-blow

Coursing. Chasing game.
Deadly weapon. A weapon whose blow causes death. See WEAPON.
Death-blow. A blow which causes death.
Fatal accident. An accident that caused death.
Finishing stroke. A death-blow.
Fusilade. A simultaneous discharge of firearms.
Gallows. A frame from which is suspended the rope by which criminals are executed.
Garrote. An instrument for executing criminals by strangulation.
Hanging. Execution by strangulation.
Holocaust. The killing of many people, as by fire, etc.
Hunting. The pursuit of game or wild animals. See *Verbs*.
Pig-sticking. Killing by stabbing.
Quietus [L.]. Death-blow.
Shooting. The killing with a firearm.
Sport.⎫
Sporting.⎭ Fowling; hunting; fishing, etc.
Strangulation. Killing by choking.
Suffocation. Killing by smothering or choking.
Venery. The practise of hunting.

KILLING—*Nouns of Agent*.

Assassin. One who kills by surprise or secret assault.
Bravo [It]. An assassin or murderer.
Butcher. One who slays in an unusually bloody or cruel manner.
Cain. The first murderer, who slew his brother Abel; a murderer
Cut-throat. A murderer who cuts throats.
Executioner. One who inflicts capital punishment.
Felo de se [F.]. One who kills himself.
Fisherman. One who catches fish.
Fratricide. One who kills his brother.
Garroter. One who executes with the garrote.
Hunter.⎫
Huntsman.⎭ One who hunts game animals
Infanticide. One who kills an infant.
Man-eater. A ferocious tiger; a shark.
Matador [Sp.]. The man appointed to kill the bull in bull-fights,
Matricide. One who kills his mother.

LIFE—KILLING—*Continued*.

Murderer. One who murders.

Nimrod. The grandson of Ham, famous as a hunter; a hunter.

Parricide. One who kills his father or mother.

Regicide. One who kills a king.

Sabreur [F.]. A slasher.

Slayer. One who kills.

Sororicide. One who kills his sister.

Sportsman. A hunter.

Suicide. One who kills himself.

Suttee. In India, a widow who sacrifices herself on the funeral pile of her husband.

Thug. One of a band of murderers which existed in India and killed from religious motives.

Vaticide. One who kills a prophet.

KILLING—*Associated Nouns*.

Abattoir. A public slaughter-house in a city.

Aceldama. The field purchased with the money which Judas received for betraying his Master; a bloody field.

Blood. The fluid which carries nourishment to all parts of the body.

Gore. Shed blood.

Juggernaut. An Indian idol to which pilgrims formerly sacrificed themselves.

Martyrdom. Suffering death on account of adherence to the Christian faith.

Moloch. An Ammonite deity to whom human sacrifices were offered.

Shambles. A place where butcher's meat is sold.

Slaughter-house. A house where beasts are butchered for the market.

Thuggism. The practises of the Thugs of India.

KILLING—*Verbs*.

Asphyxiate. To suspend respiration; suffocate.

Assassinate. To kill or slay treacherously.

Bayonet. To stab or kill with the bayonet.

Behead. To take off the head.

Blow one's brains out. } To commit suicide.
Blow out one's brains. }

Bowstring, etc. To strangle with a bowstring. See RECOMPENSE-PUNITION.

Brain. To blow out the brains.

Burke. To smother.

Butcher. To murder in an unusually bloody manner.

Choke. To render unable to breathe; suffocate.

Commit suicide. To kill oneself.

Cut down. To fell; slay.

Cut off. To destroy.

Cut the throat. To kill by severing the throat.

Cut to pieces. To scatter and slaughter.

Dash out one's brains. To kill by a blow on the head.

Deal a death-blow. To give a finishing blow.

Decimate. To slay or kill in great numbers.

Deprive of life. To take away life from.

Despatch. To put to death quickly.

Die a violent death. To meet death by accident.

Dispatch. Despatch.

Do for. To put an end to.

Drown. To put to an end by immersion in any liquid.

Garrote. To kill by means of a garrote.

Give a *coup de grâce*. To give a finishing stroke.

Give a death-blow. To give a stroke which will kill.

Give a quietus. To put to an end

Give no quarter. To show no merciful treatment to an enemy.

Hang. To put to death by suspending with a rope around the neck.

Hunt. To pursue with the purpose of killing

Imbrue one's hands in blood. To drench one's hands in blood; kill excessively and with unusual cruelty.

Immolate. To kill as a victim.

Jugulate. To cut the throat.

Kill. To deprive of life.

Kill oneself. To commit suicide.

Knock on the head. To give a blow on the head.

Lapidate. To stone

Launch into eternity. To kill.

Make away with. To put out of the way.

Make away with oneself. To commit suicide.

Massacre. To kill with indiscriminate violence and contrary to the usage of nations.

Murder. To kill with malicious forethought.

Nip in the bud. To kill in the beginning.

Pour out blood like water. To massacre.

Put an end to. To slay; kill.

Put an end to oneself. To commit suicide.

Put to death. To kill.

Put to the edge of the sword. } To kill with the sword.
Put to the sword. }

Run amuck. To rush through the streets frantically attacking everything that comes in the way.

Run through the body. To pierce the body.

Sabre. To kill with a sabre.

Send to one's last account. To kill.

Settle. To make quiet; kill.

Shed blood. To kill indiscriminately.

Shoot, etc. To hit with firearms. See *Nouns*.

Shoot dead. To kill by shooting.

Sign one's death-warrant. To sign the order for one's death.

Slaughter. To kill extensively and unnecessarily.

Slay. To kill by violence.

Smother. To destroy life by suffocation.

Stab. To wound or kill with a pointed weapon.

Stifle. To suffocate by crowding something into the windpipe.

Stone. To kill with stones.

Stop the breath. } To destroy life by stopping the respiration.
Strangle. }

Strike the death-knell of. To give the death-signal.

Suffocate. To kill by stopping respiration.

Take away life. To kill.

Throttle. To strangle.

Victimize. To make a victim of.

Wade knee-deep in blood. To revel in bloodshed.

Welter in one's blood. To roll in one's blood.

KILLING—*Adjectives*.

Bloodstained. Marked with blood; guilty of murder.

Bloodthirsty. Cruel; murderous.

Bloody. Having a cruel disposition.

Bloody-minded. Cruel in disposition; inclined to shed blood.

Deadly } Causing or liable to cause death.
Deathly. }

Ensanguined. Bloody; covered with blood.

Fatal. Causing death; deadly; mortal.

Gory. Bloody.

Homicidal. Pertaining to homicide; murderous.

Internecine. Mutually destructive; deadly.

Killing, etc. Slaying; murdering. See *Verbs*.

Lethal. Deadly; mortal.

Lethiferous. Bearing oblivion; deadly.

Mortal. Causing death; deadly.

Mortiferous. Death-bearing; deadly.

Murderous. Bloody; sanguinary; fond of murder.

Piscatorial. } Pertaining to fishing.
Piscatory. }

Red-handed. Taken in the act of homicide.

Sanguinary. Bloodthirsty; eager to shed blood.

Sanguinolent. Bloody.

Slaughterous. Murderous.

Sporting. Pertaining to sport.

Suicidal. Partaking of the nature of suicide.

Unhealthy, etc. Not healthy. See HEALTHINESS.

KILLING—*Adverb*.

In at the death. Present at the end of a chase.

LIFE—CORPSE.

CORPSE.

Ashes. The remains of the human body when burnt or returned to dust by natural decay.

Bones. The skeleton of the human body.

Carcass. The dead body of an animal or human being.

Carrion. The dead and putrefying body of an animal.

Clay. The human body as formed from particles of earth.

Corpse. } The dead body of a human being.
Corse. }

Defunct. A dead person.

Dry bones. The skeleton or bony framework of the body.

Dust. The remains of the human body.

Earth. The remains of the human body when turned to dust by natural decay.

LIFE—CORPSE—*Continued.*

Food for worms. A dead body.
Fossils. The remains of animals or plants found in stratified rocks.
Ghost. The spirit appearing after death.
Manes [L.]. Shades or ghosts of the departed.
Mortal remains. The dead body of a human being or animal.
Mummy. The dead body embalmed and dried after the manner of the ancient Egyptians.
Relics. The body from which the soul has departed.
Reliquiæ [L.] The remains of the dead.

Shade. The spirit of the dead
Skeleton. The bony framework of the body
Tenement of clay. The body.
This mortal coil. Mortal life. [Shakespeare, *Hamlet*, III, i.]

CORPSE—*Adjectives.*

Cadaverous. Pertaining to or having the appearance of a dead body.
Corpse-like. Like a corpse in appearance.
Unburied, etc. Not buried. See LIFE-FUNERAL.

LIFE—FUNERAL.

FUNERAL.

Burial. The act of depositing a dead body in a grave or tomb or final resting-place.
Cremation. The burning of a dead body.
Funeral. The formal conveyance of a dead person to his grave and the final disposal of the body.
Humation. Burial.
Inhumation. The act of burying.
Interment. The act of placing a dead person in his grave or tomb.
Sepulture. The act of depositing a dead body of a human being in a grave.
Zoothapsis. Premature burial.

FUNERAL—*Associated Nouns.*

Autopsy. The examination of a dead body by dissection to ascertain the cause of death.
Barrow. A heap of earth or stones over a burial-place.
Bier. A horizontal framework with two handles at each end, for carrying the corpse to the grave.
Bone-house. A place where the bones of the dead are deposited.
Burial-ground. }
Burial-place. } A graveyard.
Cairn. A conical heap of stones erected by the early Britons as a sepulchral monument.
Catacomb. A long underground gallery with excavations in its sides for tombs.
Catafalque. A temporary decorated structure, representing a tomb
Cemetery. A place for burial. [Gr. A sleeping place.]
Cenotaph. A monument erected to the dead but not containing the remains.
Cerecloth. A cloth used as a winding-sheet for the dead ; wax-cloth
Cerement. A garment, covering, or wrapping for the dead.
Charnel-house. A depository under or near churches for dead men's bones
Churchyard. The enclosure about a church, especially when used as a graveyard.
Cinerary urn. An urn to hold the ashes of the cremated dead
Coffin. The case in which a corpse is buried; a casket.
Cromlech. A high monument consisting of a circle of standing stones, erected by the early Britons.
Crypt. A secret recess or vault used for burial
Cypress. A plant used as an emblem of mourning.
Dead-house. A place in which dead bodies are temporarily kept.
Dead-march. A piece of solemn music played at a funeral.
Dirge, etc. A song or tune expressing grief or mourning. See JUBILATION-LAMENTATION.
Disinterment. The act of taking out of the grave.
Elegy. A lyric poem lamenting the dead.
Epitaph. An inscription on a tomb or monument.
Exequies. Funeral ceremonies.
Exhumation. The taking up of that which has been buried.
Funeral oration. A funeral discourse or sermon.
Funeral pile. A mass of combustible material on which a corpse is burned
Funeral rite. The ceremonies at the burial of a person.
Funeral sermon. The discourse delivered at a funeral.
Funeral solemnity. The ceremonies at a funeral.
God's acre. [G.] God's field, where spiritual bodies are raised [I *Corinthians* xv, 44]; a graveyard.
Golgotha. The scene of the Saviour's crucifixion; a burial-place.
Grave. A pit or excavation in the earth for the burial of a dead body.
Grave-clothes. The clothes or wrappings in which a dead person is interred
Grave-digger. One whose occupation is to dig graves.
Gravestone. A stone bearing an inscription, placed at a grave to mark the spot.
Graveyard. An enclosure devoted to the burial of the dead.
Hatchment. The armorial bearings of a deceased person, usually placed on the house, hearse, tomb, or in church

Hearse. A vehicle for carrying the bodies of the dead to the place of burial.
House of death. A house in which a death has occurred.
Knell. The sound of a bell when tolled slowly and solemnly as to announce a death or a funeral.
Mausoleum. A grand monumental tomb, like that of Mausolus, one of the Seven Wonders of the World.
Memento mori [L.]. Be mindful of death; a monument
Monument. Anything erected to perpetuate the memory of a person.
Morgue. A place where the corpses of persons found dead are exposed for identification.
Mortuary. A place for the temporary reception of the dead.
Muffled drum. A drum whose sound is deadened by wraps "Our hearts, though stout and brave, still like muffled drums are beating funeral marches to the grave." [Longfellow, *Psalm of Life.*]
Mute. A person employed by undertakers at a funeral to guard the house-door and to precede the procession on foot.
Narrow house. The grave.
Necropolis. A city of the dead; a cemetery.
Necropsy. An examination of a dead body to ascertain the cause of death.
Obit. A funeral ceremony.
Obsequies. The burial service.
Ossuary. A place for holding the bones of the dead.
Pall. A cover of black cloth thrown over a coffin or over a tomb
Passing bell. The tolling of a bell at the time when one is dying.
Pit. A grave.
Post-mortem **examination.** An examination of a dead body to ascertain the cause of death.
Pyre. A heap of combustibles arranged for burning a dead body.
Sarcophagus. A stone coffin having elaborate carvings and decorations, originally of flesh-consuming stone.
Sepulcher. A burial-place; especially, one made in a rock or solidly built of stone.
Sexton. A church officer who superintends burials.
Shell. A coffin.
Shrine. A box or chest in which sacred relics are kept.
Shroud. A dress or garment for the dead.
Stone. A gravestone.
Tolling. The solemn and slow ringing of a bell at a funeral.
Tomb. A place for the deposit of the dead.
Tombstone. A stone marking a place of burial.
Tope. A Buddhist relic-shrine, dome, or tower, constructed to contain relics of the Buddhas.
Tumulus. A large, artificial mound containing burial-places.
Undertaker. One whose business is to arrange for burying the dead.
Urn. Something in which a dead body or its ashes are preserved.
Vault. A place of burial enclosed with masonry.
Wake. A watch over the dead body of a person all night, just before the burial.
Winding-sheet. The sheet that wraps a corpse.

FUNERAL—*Verbs.*

Bury. To cover out of sight the body of a dead person.
Consign to the grave. }
Consign to the tomb. } To bury.
Disinter. To take out of a grave or tomb.
Embalm. To preserve a dead body from decay by means of balm or other aromatic oils or spices.
Entomb. To put into the tomb.
Exhume. To disinter.
Inhume. To deposit in the earth, as a dead body.
Inter. To bury.
Intomb. To put into the tomb.
Lay in the grave. }
Lay in the tomb. } To bury.
Lay out. To dress in grave-clothes and place in a decent posture.
Mummify. To embalm and dry, as a mummy.
Perform a funeral. To carry out the funeral ceremonies.

LIFE—FUNERAL—*Continued*

Put to bed with a shovel. To bury.
Toll the knell. To ring a bell with the strokes slowly and uniformly repeated
Unearth. To bring out of the earth.

FUNERAL—*Adjectives.*

Buried, etc. Interred , put into the grave. See *Verbs.*
Burial. Pertaining to a funeral or burial.
Cinerary. Pertaining to ashes.
Elegiac. Expressing sorrow or lamentation.
Funebrial.}
Funereal.} Pertaining to burial ; mournful.
Mortuary. Belonging to the burial of the dead.

Necroscopic. Relating to post-mortem examinations.
Sepulchral. Pertaining to burial or the grave.

FUNERAL—*Adverbs.*

Beneath the sod. Under the ground
In memoriam [L] In memory
Post mortem [L]. After death.
Post obit [L.]. After death

FUNERAL—*Phrases.*

Ci-git [F] Here lies
Hic jacet [L] Here lies.
R. I P., *requiescat in pace.* Let him rest in peace.

Life, the. God. DIVINITY.
life′–blood″. Vital blood. LIFE-DEATH, SUBJECTIVENESS-OBJECTIVENESS.
life′–boat″. A carefully constructed boat for preserving life. CONVEYANCE-VESSEL, REFUGE-PITFALL.
life′–giv″-ing. Inspiriting. FERTILITY-STERILITY.
life′–guards″. Body-guards. BELLIGERENT.
life′–less. Dead; torpid. LIFE-DEATH, VIGOR-INERTIA.
life′–like. Realistic. LIKENESS-UNLIKENESS, NATURE-ART.
life′–long. Lasting through life. LASTINGNESS-TRANSIENTNESS.
life′–pre-serv″-er. An apparatus for saving the lives of persons in case of shipwreck, etc.; a loaded cane, etc. WEAPON.
life′–size″. Of the size of life. GREATNESS-LITTLENESS.
life′–time″. The time that life continues. PERIOD-PROGRESS.
life′–wear-y. Tired of life. ENTERTAINMENT-WEARINESS.
lift. To raise; assistance. ELEVATION-DEPRESSION, OBSTRUCTION-HELP; **dead lift,** DIFFICULTY-FACILITY; **give a lift,** ELEVATION-DEPRESSION, OBSTRUCTION-HELP; **lift a finger,** ACTION-PASSIVENESS; **lift cattle,** THEFT; **lift hand against,** ATTACK-DEFENSE, REPRISAL-RESISTANCE; **lift one's head,** WELFARE-MISFORTUNE; **lift the mask,** EXPOSURE-HIDINGPLACE; **lift the voice,** CRY-ULULATION, SPEECH-INARTICULATENESS; **lift up the eyes,** SIGHT-BLINDNESS; **lift up the heart,** WORSHIP-IDOLATRY.
lift′–smoke″. A game of cards. ENTERTAINMENT-WEARINESS.
lig′-a-ment. A strong substance binding related structures together. CONNECTIVE.
li-ga′-tion. The act of tying or binding up. UNION-DISUNION.
lig′-a-ture. Anything that serves for tying or binding. CONNECTIVE.
light. (1) To ignite; to illuminate; bright; clear; the agent which produces vision; a window: a source of light. APERTURE-CLOSURE, APPEARANCE-DISAPPEARANCE, COMBUSTIBLE, CONDITION-SITUATION, HEATING-COOLING, INTERPRETATION-MISINTERPRETATION, KNOWLEDGE-IGNORANCE, LIGHT-DARKNESS, LUMINARY-SHADE, WHITENESS-BLACKNESS; **a light breaks in on one,** EXPOSURE-HIDINGPLACE; **blue light,** SIGN; **bring to light,** DISCOVERY, EXPOSURE-HIDINGPLACE, MANIFESTATION-LATENCY; **children of light,** GODLINESS-UNGODLINESS; **come to light,** EXPOSURE-HIDINGPLACE; **false light,** SIGHT-DIMSIGHTEDNESS; **footlights,** ACTING; **half lights,** DIMNESS; **in one's own light,** SKILL-UNSKILFULNESS; **light and shade,** LIGHT-DARKNESS; **light purse,** AFFLUENCE-PENURY; **light under a bushel,** ENLIGHTENMENT-SECRECY, SELFRESPECT-HUMBLENESS, VANITY-DIFFIDENCE; **light up,** EXCITATION, LIGHT-DARKNESS. LIGHTHEARTEDNESS-DEJECTION; **obstruct the light,** DIAPHANEITY-OPAQUENESS; **see the light,** LIFE-DEATH, PUBLICITY; **throw light upon,** INTERPRETATION-MISINTERPRETATION; **transmit light,** DIAPHANEITY-OPAQUENESS.
light. (2) To settle down after flight; to happen upon; dismount; not heavy; not burdensome; trivial; cheerful; loose in morals; gay. ARRIVAL-DEPARTURE, ASCENT-DESCENT, CONSEQUENCE-INSIGNIFICANCE, DETERMINATION-VACILLATION, DIFFICULTY-FACILITY, HEAVINESS-LIGHTNESS, LIGHTHEARTEDNESS-DEJECTION, MAGNITUDE-SMALLNESS, PURITY-IMPURITY, SOLIDITY-RARITY, SWIFTNESS-SLOWNESS; **light comedy,** ACTING; **light fantastic toe,** ENTERTAINMENT-WEARINESS, SPRING-DIVE; **light heart,** LIGHTHEARTEDNESS-DEJECTION; **light horse,** BELLIGERENT; **light infantry,** BELLIGERENT; **light of heel,** SWIFTNESS-SLOWNESS; **light upon,** ARRIVAL-DEPARTURE, DISCOVERY, GAIN-LOSS, RATIONALE-LUCK; **light upon one's feet,** SECURITY-INSECURITY, WELFARE-MISFORTUNE; **make light of,** CONSEQUENCE-INSIGNIFICANCE, DIFFICULTY-FACILITY, EXCITABILITY-INEXCITABILITY, OVERVALUATION-UNDERVALUATION, REGARD-SCORN.

LIGHT—DARKNESS.

Aureola [L]. A halo of light.
Aurora. The rising light of the morning.
Beam. A ray of light from a luminous body.
Black and white. A succession of light and darkness.
Blaze. Intense direct light.
Brightness. The quality or state of being bright.
Brilliancy. Great brightness.
Broad daylight. The brightest light of the day.
Coruscation. A sudden, brilliant flash of light.
Day. The time of light.
Daylight. The light of day as opposed to the darkness of night.
Dazzlement. Dazzling flash or glare of light.
Effulgence. Brilliant light; extreme brightness.
Emication. A sparkling.
Facula [L.] A shining spot on the surface of the sun.
Flame, etc. A luminous and hot stream of burning gas or vapor.
Flash. A sudden and brilliant burst of light.

Adumbration. The act of casting a faint shadow.
Blackness. Total darkness.
Blind man's holiday. The period between daylight and lamplight.
Caligation. A state of darkness or dimness.
Chiaroscuro [It.]. The harmonious blending of light and darkness See LIGHT
Cimmerian darkness. Perpetual and profound darkness. "Melt and dispel, ye specter doubts, that roll Cimmerian darkness o'er the parting soul." [Campbell, *Pleasures of Hope*, I, 263.]
Darkness, etc. Total absence of light. See *Adjectives.*
Darkness that can be felt. Intense darkness.
Darkness visible. Darkness in which objects are visible. [Milton, *Paradise Lost*, i, 62.]
Dead of night. The darkest part of the night.
Distribution of shade. The scattering of darkness.
Dusk, etc. A state between light and darkness. See DIMNESS.

LIGHT—DARKNESS—*Continued.*

Flood of light. A great stream of light.
Flush. A tinge of red color.
Fulgidity. Brightness.
Fulgor. Dazzling brightness.
Fulguration. The act of lightening.
Gleam. A small stream of light.
Glimmering, etc. A wavering, somewhat dim light. See *Verbs.*
Glint. A glimpse, or gleam of light.
Glory. An emanation of light supposed to proceed from beings of peculiar sanctity.
Gloss. Brightness of a smooth surface.
Glow. A steady, clear light.
Halo. A luminous circle of light.
Ignis fatuus [L.]. The will-o'-the-wisp. See LUMINARY.
Illumination. Brightness or splendor.
Irradiation. Illumination; the act of emitting beams of light.
Lambent flame. A flame playing on the surface.
Light. A form of radiant energy which affects the retina of the eye and renders visible that from which it comes.
Light and shade. A succession of light and darkness.
Lightning. A discharge of atmospheric electricity accompanied by a flash of light.
Light of day. } Daylight or light given by the sun.
Light of heaven. }
Lucidity. The state of being bright or clear.
Luminosity. Quality or state of being luminous.
Luminousness, etc. The state of being luminous. See *Adjectives*
Luster. Brightness.
Moonbeam. A ray of light given by the moon.
Nimbus. A circle of light or halo around the heads of divinities.
Nitency. Brightness.
Noonday. }
Noontide. } The light of the brightest part of the day.
Noontide light. }
Phosphorescence. The quality or state of being phosphorescent.
Play of light. A succession of rays of light falling upon an object.
Radiance. The quality of being radiant or brilliant.
Ray. A line of light.
Refulgence. The quality of being bright and shining.
Renitency. Brightness.
Resplendence. The quality of having a brilliant luster.
Scintilla. A spark of light
Scintillation. The act of giving off sparks.
Sheen. Brightness.
Shimmer. A wavering light.
Spangle. A sparkling.
Spark. A small particle of fire emitted by a burning body.
Sparkling, etc. The act of emitting sparks of light. See *Verbs.*
Splendor. Great brightness.
Streak. A long line of light.
Stream. A beam or ray of light.
Sun, etc. The earth's great source of light. See LUMINARY.
Sunbeam. A ray of light from the sun.
Sunshine. The light given by the sun.
Tinsel. A shining.
Transplendence. Extraordinary brilliancy

LIGHT—*Associated Nouns.*

Breadth. The quality of having the lights and colors of a painting broad and massive.
Chiaroscuro [It.]. The art of arranging the light and dark parts of a picture harmoniously.
Clair-obscur [F.]. See *Chiaroscuro.*
Clear obscure. Light and shade in painting.
Dispersion. The separation of light into its different colored rays.
Heliochrome. A painting in colors.
Pencil. A collection of rays of light diverging from or converging to a point.
Radiation. The shooting forth of rays of light from a point or surface.
Reflection. } The return of rays of light from a surface.
Reflexion. }
Refraction. The change in the direction of a ray of light.
Tonality. The general color scheme of a picture.

LIGHT—*Scientific Nouns.*

Actinic rays. Rays of light which produce chemical changes.
Actinism. That power which the sun's rays have to produce chemical changes.
Calorescence. The conversion of obscure radiant heat into light.
Catoptrics. That branch of optics which treats of the properties and phenomena of reflected light.

Eclipse. The cutting off of light, especially of the light of a heavenly body.
Egyptian darkness. Intense darkness, like that which prevailed in Egypt during the plagues.
Erebus. A place of utter darkness, through which souls pass to Hades.
Extinction. The cutting off of light.
Gathering of the clouds. The act of becoming dark.
Gloom. Partial darkness, where is only a gleam of light.
Midnight. The period of greatest darkness.
Murk. Darkness.
Night. That part of the natural day when the sun is beneath the horizon, and darkness prevails; the noxious time.
Noctivigation. A roving or going about in the dark.
Obfuscation. The act of darkening.
Obscuration. The act of making dark.
Obscurity. Darkness.
Obtenebration. The act of making dark; darkness.
Obumbration. The act of darkening or obscuring.
Penumbra. An incomplete or partial shadow.
Sciagraphy. The act or science of drawing shades as they fall in nature.
Shade. Comparative obscurity owing to the interception of the rays of light.
Shading. Act or process of making a shade.
Shadow. Obscurity or deprivation of light within defined limits.
Stygian darkness. Intense darkness, like that which prevails about the fabled river Styx.
The palpable obscure. The abyss between earth and hell. [Milton, *Paradise Lost*, ii, 406.]
Total eclipse. A total deprivation of light.
Umbra. A perfect shadow.
Witching time of night. The time of greatest darkness.

DARKNESS—*Verbs.*

Adumbrate. To give a faint shadow.
Becloud. To obscure with clouds.
Be dark, etc. To be not light. See *Adjectives.*
Bedarken. To make dark.
Bedim. To make obscure or dim.
Blow out. To extinguish with a current of air.
Cast a gloom. }
Cast a shade. } To become slightly dark.
Cast a shadow. }
Cast into the shade. To darken.
Darken. To make dark.
Dim. To make obscure or dim.
Doubt. To be in intellectual darkness.
Eclipse. To obscure or darken.
Extinguish. To put out.
Lower. To make less light; darken.
Obfuscate. To darken or obscure.
Obscure. To make dark or indistinct.
Obumbrate. To darken; cloud.
Overcast. To cover with gloom or darkness.
Overshadow. To throw a shadow over.
Put out. To extinguish.
Shade. To intercept the waves of light with a screen.
Snuff out. To put out by snuffing.
Spread a gloom. }
Spread a shade. }
Spread a shadow. } To darken
Throw a gloom. }
Throw a shade. }
Throw a shadow. }
Tone down. To bring the colors of a picture into harmonious relations as to light and shade.

DARKNESS—*Adjectives.*

Benighted. Shrouded in darkness. See WHITENESS-BLACKNESS.
Black, etc. Destitute of light.
Caliginous. Obscure; dark.
Cloudy, etc. Dim; not clear. See DIAPHANEITY-OPAQUENESS.
Dark. Destitute of or not radiating or reflecting light.
Dark as a pit. }
Dark as Erebus. } Very dark.
Dark as pitch. }
Darkened, etc. Made dark. See *Verbs.*
Darkling. Without light.
Darksome. Gloomy; obscure.
Dingy. Of a dark or dusky color.

LIGHT—Scientific Nouns—*Continued.*

Dioptrics. That branch of optics which treats of the laws of refracted light

Heliography. Photography.

Optics. The science which treats of the properties and laws of light.

Photography. The science which relates to the action of light on sensitive bodies in the production of pictures.

Photology. The science of the nature and phenomena of light.

Photometer, etc. An instrument for measuring the relative intensities of light. See Optical instruments.

Photometry. The science which treats of the relative intensity of lights.

LIGHT—*Verbs.*

Beam. To emit light.

Be bright, etc. To be lighted up. See *Adjectives.*

Bedazzle. To dazzle with strong light.

Blaze. To burn with an extensive, brilliant flame.

Brighten. To make clear or bright.

Cast a light upon. To lighten; make brilliant.

Cast a luster upon. To cause to shine.

Clear up. To become bright or free from obscurity.

Coruscate. To throw off brilliant flashes of light

Daze. To dim or overpower by too strong a light.

Dazzle. To overpower by too strong a light.

Effulge. To beam with a luster.

Enlighten. To supply with light.

Flare. To burn with a glaring unsteady flame.

Flare up. To blaze up.

Flash. To shine suddenly and then disappear

Flicker. To burn with a wavering motion.

Give out a light.
Give out a luster. } To shine.

Glare. To shine with a painfully bright, steady light.

Gleam. To shine with a steady but transient or intermittent light.

Glimmer. To shine with a wavering light.

Glisten. To shine with a mild, subdued luster.

Glister. To be bright; shine with a sparkling light.

Glitter. To shine with a brilliant, cold, wavering light

Glow. To shine with a steady, subdued light.

Hang out a light.
Hang out a luster. } To give forth light or brightness.

Illume.
Illuminate. } To supply with light; enlighten.
Illumine.

Irradiate. To cast a bright light upon.

Kindle, etc. To set on fire; cause to burn. See Heating.

Light. To give light to.

Lighten. To fill with light; illuminate.

Light up. To illumine.

Radiate. To issue in rays.

Reflect light. To bend or throw back light.

Relume. To light again. [Shakespeare, *Othello*, V, ii.]

Scintillate. To emit sparks.

Shed light upon.
Shed luster upon. } To throw light upon.

Shimmer. To shine with a wavering light.

Shine. To emit rays of light; beam with a steady light.

Shine upon. To cast light upon.

Shoot out beams. To emit light.

Sparkle. A sudden light, as sparks emit.

Strike a light. To produce a light by striking.

Throw a light upon. To lighten.

Throw a luster upon. To make bright.

Twinkle. To shine with an unsteady, somewhat dim light.

LIGHT—*Adjectives.*

Ablaze. In a blaze; on fire.

Actinic. Pertaining to that power of the sun's rays which produces chemical changes.

Beaming. Emitting light.

Beamy. Shining.

Blazing. Burning with a brilliant flame.

Bright. Shedding much light; luminous.

Bright as day.
Bright as noonday.
Bright as silver. } Light; very bright.
Bright as the sun at noonday.

Burnished. Rendered bright or resplendent.

Clear. Undimmed; free from obscurity.

DARKNESS—Adjectives—*Continued.*

Dusky. Dark; gloomy; almost black.

Gloomy. Dark.

Lightless, etc. Without light. See Luminary.

Lurid. Gloomy; dismal.

Murksome. Dark, obscure, and gloomy.

Murky. Gloomy, dark, and obscure.

Noctivigant.
Noctivigous. } Wandering about at night.

Nocturnal. Pertaining to the night.

Obscure. Darkened; imperfectly illuminated.

Overcast, etc. Covered with gloom; darkened. See Dimness.

Pitch-dark. Very dark.

Pitchy. Black; dark; dismal.

Shady. Abounding with shade; overspread with shade.

Sombre.
Sombrous. } Dull; gloomy; dark; under a shade.

Sunless, etc. Shaded; destitute of the sun's rays. See Luminary

Tenebrious. Gloomy; dark.

Umbrageous. Shady; obscure.

Unilluminated, etc. Not lighted up. See Light.

DARKNESS—*Adverbs, etc.*

In the dark.
In the shade. } Cut off from light.

LIGHT—Adjectives—*Continued.*

Cloudless. Clear; free from clouds.

Effulgent. Diffusing a flood of light.

Fulgent.
Fulgid. } Shining; dazzling.

Gairish.
Garish. } Gaudy; showy; vulgarly bright.

Glassy. Having a fixed, staring appearance.

Glossy. Smooth and shining.

Heliographic. Pertaining to the art of taking pictures on any prepared material by means of the rays of the sun and a camera obscura.

In a blaze. Blazing.

Lambent. Licking, softly waving, as flame.

Light. Not dark; clear; bright.

Light as day.
Light as noonday. } Very bright
Light as the sun at noonday.

Lightsome. Luminous; not dark.

Lucent. Shining; resplendent.

Lucid. Bright; clear.

Luciferous. Giving light.

Lucific. Producing light.

Luculent. Clear; luminous.

Luminiferous. Producing light.

Luminous. Emitting light; bright.

Lustrous. Shining; luminous.

Meridian. Pertaining to noonday.

Meteoric. Pertaining to or consisting of meteors.

Nitid. Bright; lustrous; shining.

Noonday.
Noontide. } Pertaining to midday. "Still as night or summer's noontide air." [Milton, *Paradise Lost*, ii 309.]

Orient. Rising; east; bright; glittering; shining.

Phosphorescent. Shining with a faint light.

Photogenic. Producing light.

Photographic. Pertaining to photography.

Radiant. Emitting light.

Refulgent. Casting a bright light.

Relucent. Clear; shining.

Resplendent. Shining very brightly.

Rutilant. Shining.

Scintillant. Sparkling.

Sheen. Shining; glistening.

Sheeny. Shiny.

Shining, etc. Emitting a strong light; bright. See *Verbs.*

Shiny. Bright; luminous.

Splendent. Glossy; beaming with light

Splendid. Very bright.

Sunny. Pertaining to the sun or exposed to its rays.

Transplendent. Exceedingly bright.

Unclouded. Free from obscurity.

Unobscured. Clear; bright.

Vivid. Brilliant; bright; clear.

Light of the World. Jesus Christ. DIVINITY.

light'-en. To illumine; to enlighten; to relieve of weight; to alleviate. DIFFICULTY-FACILITY, HEAVINESS-LIGHTNESS, LIGHT-DARKNESS.

light'-er. A barge. CONVEYANCE-VESSEL.

light'-er-man. A man employed on a lighter. WAYFARER-SEAFARER.

light'-fin''-gered. Thievish. THEFT; **light-fingered gentry,** ROBBER.

light'-foot''-ed. Nimble in running or dancing. ACTIVITY-INDOLENCE, SWIFTNESS-SLOWNESS.

light'-head''-ed. Thoughtless. SANENESS-LUNACY.

light'-heart''-ed. Cheerful. LIGHTHEARTEDNESS-DEJECTION.

light'-heart''-ed-ness. The state of being free from care. LIGHTHEARTEDNESS-DEJECTION.

LIGHTHEARTEDNESS—DEJECTION.

Alacrity. Cheerful quickness of movement.

Allegresse [F.]. Light-heartedness.

Animation. Intellectual or spiritual brightness, usually shown in the aspect.

Bon naturel [F.]. Good nature.

Cheer. A buoyant mood.

Cheerfulness, etc. See *Adjectives.*

Euphrosyne. One of the Graces, who presided over the influences that make life cheerful.

Exhilaration. A feeling of liveliness, both mental and physical.

Flow of spirits. Generous quantity of spirits.

Gaieté de cœur [F.]. High animal spirits.

Gaiety. Cheerfulness combined with showiness.

Geniality. Warmth and kindness of disposition.

Glee. Expression of mirth or gaiety.

Good humor. A pleasant frame of mind.

Hey-day. The time of greatest vitality and ardor.

High glee. Great glee.

High spirits. The most pleasant spirits. See SPIRITS.

Hilarity. Mirth excited by social pleasure.

Jocularity. See WITTINESS.

Jocundity. Quality of being merry or lively.

Jollity. Life and mirth.

Joviality. Good-natured mirth or gaiety.

L'allegro [It.]. The cheerful man. [Milton.]

Laughter. See JUBILATION.

Levity. Lack of mental gravity.

Life. Animation; spirit; vivacity.

Light heart. A cheerful disposition.

Light-heartedness. Cheerfulness; freedom from care.

Liveliness, etc. See *Adjectives.*

Merriment. Gaiety, with laughter and noise.

Merrymaking. See ENTERTAINMENT.

Mirth. Pleasurable feelings, manifested by jesting and laughing.

Nepenthe. A drug reputed to banish pain and sorrow. [Homer.]

Optimism. Disposition to take the most hopeful or to look on the brightest side of things. See SANGUINENESS.

Rejoicing. See JUBILATION.

Self-complacency. Self-satisfaction.

Spirits. State of temper or mind.

Sunshine of the breast. Light-heartedness.

Sunshine of the mind. Cheerfulness.

Vivacity. Brightness shown in manner, movement, or speech.

LIGHTHEARTEDNESS—*Verbs.*

Animate. To impart life or vigor to.

Bear up. To keep up spirits.

Be cheerful, etc. See *Adjectives.*

Brighten up. To become cheerful.

Carol. To sing in a cheerful or joyous strain.

Cast away care. To be cheerful.

Cheer. To brighten; to gladden.

Cheer the heart. To brighten up.

Cheer up. To become cheerful.

Chirp. To express cheerful feelings.

Chirrup. To cheer up.

Delight. See PLEASURABLENESS.

Drive dull care away. To brighten up.

Elate. To cause to feel exultant.

Enliven. To infuse life or animation.

Exhilarate. To cause both mental and physical liveliness.

Frisk. To leap or skip about playfully.

Give a loose to mirth. To be mirthful without restraint.

Gladden. To make very cheerful.

Have the mind at ease. To feel at rest.

Inspire. To give ideas or emotions to.

Inspirit. To give spirit, animation, or vigor to.

Keep up one's spirits. To keep cheerful.

Lighten up. To cheer; gladden.

Perk up. To straighten up.

Put a good face upon. To bear with composure.

Put in good humor. To enliven.

Bad spirits. The condition of being disheartened.

Blank despondency. Absolute, downright despondency.

Blue devils. Extreme depression of spirits.

Broken heart. A crushing in feeling or spirit, by misfortune or sorrow.

Cave of despair. State of utter hopelessness and despondency.

Cave of Trophonius. The cave of the oracle consulted by the Greek architect Trophonius in his despair.

Damp on the spirits. Anything that dispirits or casts down.

Dejectedness. The condition of being dejected or cast down.

Dejection. The condition of being greatly cast down in spirits.

Demureness. Gravity of aspect or demeanor, affected or sincere.

Depressed spirits. A condition of hopelessness or sadness.

Depression. The condition of being downcast.

Depression of spirits. A failing of the spirits.

Despair, etc. Utter hopelessness and despondency. See SANGUINENESS-HOPELESSNESS.

Despondency. Depression or dejection accompanied by loss of hope for the future.

Disconsolateness. The condition of refusing or being unable to be consoled or comforted.

Disgust of life. Strong aversion to living.

Dismals. Gloomy feelings; bad days.

Doldrums. A gloomy state of mind.

Drooping spirits. Loss of vigor and spirit.

Dumps. See DOLDRUMS.

Failure of heart. Loss of spirit or courage.

Gloom. Low spirits; slight despondency.

Grave face. A mark of pain or trouble.

Gravity. Seriousness of demeanor; heaviness.

Heart-sinking. Loss of spirits.

Heaviness. Depression.

Heaviness of heart. A condition of trouble or worry.

Hope deferred. Disappointment.

Horrors. The blues; also, the delirium tremens.

Hypochondria. A morbid melancholy and extreme depression of mind.

Il penseroso [It.]. The pensive man. [Milton.]

Infestivity. The condition of not being festive or gay.

Long face. A mark of gloom or disappointment

Lowness of spirits. Dejection.

Low spirits. Hopelessness.

Malade imaginaire [F.]. Sick in imagination

Maladie du pays [F.]. Homesickness.

Megrims. Dulness; gloominess.

Melancholia. Melancholy.

Melancholy. An extremely gloomy and despondent condition especially, when such condition is chronic.

Mumps. Moroseness; ill temper.

Oppression on the spirits. Worry or trouble.

Pessimism. A disposition to take a gloomy view of affairs.

Prosternation. Dejection.

Prostration. The condition of being entirely overcome by grief.

Prostration of soul. Utter hopelessness or despair.

Sadness. Subdued and unexpressed sorrow.

Slough of despond. A condition of despondency. [Bunyan, *Pilgrim's Progress.*]

Solemnity. A condition of extreme seriousness or gravity.

Spleen. Ill humor.

Tædium vitæ [L.]. Weariness of life.

Vapors. Temporary depression of the spirits.

Weariness. The fatigued condition of mind and body resulting from continued exertion.

Weight on the spirits. Trouble or worry.

DEJECTION—*Nouns of Agent.*

Croaker. One always finding fault.

Heauton timoroumenos [Gr.] *The Self-Tormentor;* a play by Menander.

Hypochondriac. One subject to hypochondria. See HYPOCHONDRIA.

Médecin tant pis [F.]. A physician who makes worse

LIGHTHEARTEDNESS—Verbs—*Continued.*

Raise the spirits. To cheer.
Rejoice. See JUBILATION.
Rejoice the heart. To be cheerful.
Ridentem dicere verum [L.]. To speak the truth though laughing.
Rollick. To act mirthfully or with a frolicsome air.
Smile. To express joy with the features.
Take heart. To begin to cheer up.
View the bright side of the picture. To be affected more by the joy than by the sorrow of life.
View things *en couleur de rose.* To put the best construction upon things; to see things rose-colored.

LIGHTHEARTEDNESS—*Adjectives.*

Airy. Buoyant; as light as air
All alive. Full of life.
Allegro. Cheerful; lively.
Animated. See ANIMATION.
Blithe. Characterized by gladness and mirth.
Blithesome. Imparting gladness and mirth; blithe.
Bonny. Sweet and fair; comely.
Bright. Full of happiness, gladness, etc.
Brisk. Acting or moving quickly.
Brisk as a bee. Lively.
Buoyant. Resisting or easily recovering from depression.
Buxom. Having health and vigor combined with gaiety and liveliness.
Canty. Brisk; glad; lively.
Cardiac. }
Cardiacal. } Invigorating the spirits, giving strength and cheerfulness.
Cheering. Tending to cheer.
Cheerful. Full of cheer.
Cheerly. Cheerful.
Cheery. Spontaneously cheerful.
Cock-a-hoop. Elated; on the high horse.
Débonnaire [F.]. Courteous and affable.
Elate. }
Elated. } Exalted in spirit.
Exhilarating. Causing mental and physical liveliness.
Exulting. Feeling delight on account of victory.
Flushed. Slightly excited.
Folatre [F.]. Sportive.
Free and easy. Having little regard for conventionality.
Frisky. Playful in action.
Frolicsome. Full of prankish sport.
Full of play. }
Full of spirit. } Frolicsome.
Gamesome. Playful; sportive.
Gay. Cheerful and showy.
Gay as a lark.
Gleesome. Marked by glee.
Happy. See PLEASURE.
Happy as a king. }
Happy as the day is long. } Very happy.
Heartsome. Merry; lively.
Hearty. Full of health and strength.
Hilarious. Mirthful from social pleasure.
Hopeful. See SANGUINENESS.
In good spirits. Lively.
In high spirits. }
In high feather. } In very good spirits.
Inspiriting. See *Verbs.*
In spirits. In a favorable frame of mind.
Janty. }
Jaunty. } Gay, easy, and showy; affecting a careless ease.
Jocose. Done or said in jest; in the nature of a joke.
Jocular. See WITTINESS.
Jocund. Merry or lively.
Jolly. Mirthful and lively.
Jolly as a sand boy. Merry.
Jolly as a thrush. Lively.
Jovial. Good-naturedly mirthful and gay, as one born under the planet Jupiter.
Joyful. Very glad, especially at a particular thing.
Joyous. Joyful, but as a general or continued feeling.
Jubilant. Manifesting joy with shouts or songs.
Laughter-loving. Light-hearted.
Light. Cheerful.
Light-hearted. Cheerful; free from care.
Lightsome. Light, gay, or cheerful in character or mood.
Lively. Full of energetic action.
Merry. Noisily and laughingly gay

DEJECTION—Nouns of Agent—*Continued.*

Mope. One who is gloomy or stupid.
Mopus. A mope.
Pessimist. One who looks always on the dark side of things. See PESSIMISM.
Seek-sorrow. One who torments himself.
Self-tormentor. One who causes himself unnecessary worry.

DEJECTION—*Nouns of Cause.*

Affliction. Distress of body or mind.
Damper. Anything that depresses the mind.
Job's comforter. One who pretends to comfort, but does the opposite. [Bible.]
Memento mori [L.]. A remembrance of death.
Sorry sight. A case of utter hopelessness.
Wet blanket. A discouragement.

DEJECTION—*Verbs.*

Be dejected, etc. See *Adjectives.*
Be grave. To be serious in disposition or manner.
Break one's heart. To cause one sorrow.
Brood over. To think over despondently.
Cast a gloom on. }
Cast a shadow on. } To dishearten.
Damp. To discourage.
Damp one's hope. }
Damp the spirits. } To discourage.
Dash. To cast down in spirit or hope.
Dash one's hope. To discourage.
Deject. To cause to be greatly cast down. See DEJECTION.
Depress. To make gloomy or slightly despondent. See DEPRESSION.
Depress the spirits. To dishearten.
Despair. To give up hope.
Despond. To be in a gloomy state of mind. See DESPONDENCY.
Discourage. To take away the confidence; dishearten.
Dishearten. To depress the spirits of; stronger than discourage.
Dispirit. To dishearten.
Droop. To lose courage or heart.
Dull. To render less keen and active.
Fret. To worry; be peevish.
Frown. To be displeased.
Frown upon. To express displeasure.
Give way. To give up; to be overcome.
Grieve. To be gloomy and sad because of some misfortune.
Grin a ghastly smile. Death [highly pleased] grinned horrible a ghastly smile. [Milton, *Paradise Lost*, ii 846.]
Hang down the head. To be dejected.
Keep one's countenance. To refrain from smiling.
Knock down. To discourage.
Laugh on the wrong side of the face. To be cast down in spirit; especially, directly after one has been elated.
Lay to heart. To feel sorely.
Lie heavy on the mind. }
Lie heavy on the spirits. } To worry or brood over.
Look blue. To look discouraged; bilious.
Look downcast. To be disheartened.
Look grave. To be serious.
Look like a drowned man. To be hopeless.
Lose heart. To become discouraged.
Lower. To appear gloomy or threatening.
Make a long face. To express disapproval or disappointment.
Mope. See MOPE.
Mourn. To be in great grief or sorrow.
Pine. To grieve secretly; languish with longing.
Pine away. To waste away with longing or grief.
Pout. To be sullen.
Prey on the mind. To make despondent.
Prey on the spirits. See PREY ON THE MIND.
Prostrate. To cause to be completely overcome, as with grief.
Pull a long face. To express disappointment.
Refrain from laughter. To be serious or grave.
Repine. To be unhappy; to murmur.
Repress a smile. To be cheerless.
Sadden. To grow sad or despondent; also, to make sad.
Sink. To depress or discourage.
Sulk. To be sullen and ill-tempered.
Take on. To sorrow or grieve.
Take to heart. See LAY TO HEART.
Unman. To take away the courage; dishearten.
Weigh on the mind. }
Weigh on the spirits. } To be a cause of trouble or worry.

LIGHTHEARTEDNESS—DEJECTION—*Continued.*

LIGHTHEARTEDNESS—Adjectives—*Continued*

Merry as a cricket. ⎫
Merry as a grig. ⎬ Cheerful.
Merry as a marriage-bell.   Very cheerful.
Mirthful.   Full of mirth.
Mirthloving.   Gay.
Of good cheer.   Cheerful.
Palmy.   Marked by prosperity or triumph.
Playful.   Fond of play.
Playful as a kitten.   Frolicsome.
Playsome.   Playful.
Pleasing.   See PLEASURABLENESS.
Rattling.   Lively; surprising.
Rejoicing.   See JUBILATION.
Rollicking.   Mirthful and frolicsome.
Smiling.   See *Verbs*.
Sparkling.   Brilliant; vivacious.
Spirited.   Full of spirit, life, or vigor.
Spiritful.   Spirited.
Sportive.   Fond of play; having a playful habit.
Sprightful.   Sprightly.
Sprightly.   Cheerful in disposition and brisk in manner.
Spry.   Quick and active in movement.
Sunny.   Bright; genial.
Tricksy.   Fond of tricks or pranks.   [Shakespeare, *Tempest*, V, 1]
Vivacious.   Having vivacity.
Waggish.   Given to tricks or witty hits.
Winsome.   Having a winning appearance or manner.

LIGHTHEARTEDNESS—*Adverbs.*

Cheerfully, etc.   See *Adjectives*

LIGHTHEARTEDNESS—*Interjections.*

Away with melancholy! begone dull care! cheer up! come! hence, loathed melancholy! hurrah! never say die!

———

DEJECTION—Adjectives—*Continued from Column 2*

Lost.   Bewildered; perplexed.
Lowering.   Sullen; angry.
Low-spirited.   Depressed.
Lugubrious.   Mournful; doleful.
Melancholic.   Given to melancholy.   See MELANCHOLY.
Melancholy.   See MELANCHOLY.
Melancholy as a gib-cat.   Despondent.
Moody.   Out of humor; sullen.
Moping.   See MOPE.
Mopish.   Given to gloomy feelings.
Mournful.   Calling forth sorrow or grief
Mumpish.   See MUMPS.
Oppressed with melancholy.   Melancholy.
Out of heart.   Discouraged.
Out of humor.   Angry.
Out of sorts.   Not feeling good.
Out of spirits.   See OUT OF HEART.
Overcome.   Crushed; prostrated; as with grief.
Penseroso [It.].   Pensive.
Pensive.   Thoughtful; sad.
Rueful.   Causing sorrow or regret.
Sad.   In a condition of subdued sorrow.
Saturnine.   Having a gloomy or morose disposition.
Sedate.   Sober; serious.
Serious.   Of a sober, earnest disposition.
Sick at heart.   Disappointed.
Sober.   Not given to jesting.
Solemn.   Of an extremely serious and grave disposition.
Somber.   Somewhat melancholy.
Soul-sick.   Hopeless.
Spiritless.   Without life or spirit.
Splenetic.   Fretful and ill-tempered.
Staid. ⎫
Stayed. ⎬ Of a steady, sober disposition.
Sulky.   See SULK.
Sullen.   Of a gloomy, obstinate disposition.
Triste.   Sorrowful.
Tristful.   Sad; gloomy.
Uncheerful. ⎫
Uncheery. ⎬ Not bright or lively.
Unconsolable.   See INCONSOLABLE.
Unhappy.   Sorrowful.

DEJECTION—Verbs—*Continued.*

Wither one's hopes.   To disappoint.
Yearn.   To long for with a feeling of sadness.

DEJECTION—*Adjectives.*

A cup too low.   Not to have drunk enough to be in good spirits.
A prey to melancholy.   Melancholy.
Atrabilious.   Disposed to be melancholy.
Au désespoir [F.].   In despair.
Bilious.   Ill-natured.
Borne down.   Oppressed by sorrow or disappointment.
Bowed down. ⎫
Broken down. ⎬ Overcome by sorrow or disappointment.
Broken-hearted. ⎭
Careworn.   Tired and worn with care.
Cheerless.   Without cheer or comfort.
Chopfallen.   Disheartened; discouraged.
Clouded.   Gloomy.
Comfortless.   In want or distress.
Crestfallen.   Dispirited.
Cut up.   Badly used; broken in spirit.
Dark.   Gloomy.
Dashed.   Disappointed.
Demure.   Having a grave or sober bearing.
Depressing.   See *Verbs*.
Desolate.   Forsaken; sad and lonely.
Désolé [F.].   Desolate.
Desponding.   Gloomy.   See DESPOND.
Disconsolate.   Not to be comforted or consoled.
Discouraged.   Having lost heart.
Disheartened.   Having lost all spirit and courage.
Dismal.   Very gloomy.
Doleful.   Mournful.
Dolesome.   See DOLEFUL.
Downcast.   Downhearted.
Downfallen.   Dejected.
Downhearted.   Somewhat discouraged.
Down in the mouth.   Dejected.
Down on one's luck.   Disappointed.
Downtrodden.   Entirely disheartened.
Dreadful.   Full of fear or dread.
Dreary.   Lonely and cheerless.
Dull as a beetle. ⎫
Dull as ditchwater. ⎬ Cheerless and gloomy.
Dumpish.   Given to have the dumps.   See DUMPS.
Flat.   Dull; spiritless.
Forlorn.   Without help or friends in time of need.
Frowning.   See FROWN.
Funereal.   Sad; mournful.
Gloomy.   Taking a sad view of matters.
Glum.   Sullen and silent.
Grave as a judge.   Sober.
Grave as a mustard pot. ⎫
Grave as an undertaker. ⎬ Serious and solemn.
Grim.   Of stern countenance.
Grim-faced. ⎫
Grim-visaged. ⎬ Stern and forbidding in aspect.
Heart-sick.   Deeply grieved or sorrowful.
Heart-stricken.   Overwhelmed with grief.
Heavy-hearted.   Sad; despondent.
Hipped.   Offended; cross.
Hypochondriacal.   See HYPOCHONDRIA.
Ill at ease.   Restless.
In bad humor.   In an ill temper.
Inconsolable.   Not to be comforted.
In despair.   Utterly hopeless.
In doleful dumps.   Like Witherington in *Chevy-Chase* who "when his legs were smitten off, fought upon his stumps."
In low spirits.   Disheartened.
In tears.   Weeping.
In the doldrums.   Gloomy.
In the dumps.   See DUMPS.
In the suds.   In trouble or distress, as on washing day.
In the sulks.   See SULK.
Jaundiced.   Envious.
Jawfallen.   See CHOPFALLEN.
Joyless.   Dull and solemn.
Lackadaisical.   Listless.
Lacrymose.   Sad; ready to shed tears.
Lamentable.   Sorrowful.
Long-faced.   Despondent.

(Continued on Column 1.)

DEJECTION—Adjectives—Continued

Unlively. Not spirited.
Unmanned. See UNMAN.
Unnerved. Discouraged.

Wan. Haggard; pale.
Weary. Worn; tired.
Wobegone. Wretched.

DEJECTION—Adverbs, etc

Sadly. See SAD.
With a long face. Disappointedly or sorrowfully.

With tears in one's eyes. Weeping.

DEJECTION—Phrases.

The countenance falling; the heart failing one; the heart sinking within one.

---

light'-house''. A tower bearing at the top a lamp for guiding sailors at points of danger. LUMINARY-SHADE, SIGN, WARNING.
light'-leg''-ged. Swift-footed. SWIFTNESS-SLOWNESS
light'-less. Dark. LIGHT-DARKNESS.
light'-mind''-ed. Frivolous. DETERMINATION-VACILLATION.
light'-ness. The condition or quality of being light. HEAVINESS-LIGHTNESS.
light'-ning. A discharge of atmospheric electricity, accompanied by a vivid flash of light. LIGHT-DARKNESS, LUMINARY-SHADE, SWIFTNESS-SLOWNESS; **flash of lightning,** ETERNITY-INSTANTANEITY; **quick as lightning,** ETERNITY-INSTANTANEITY.
light'-some. Blithesome; luminous; playful. DETERMINATION-VACILLATION, LIGHT-DARKNESS, LIGHT-HEARTEDNESS-DEJECTION.
lig'-ne-ous. Woody. FAUNA-FLORA.
lig'-no-graph. A wood-cut. ENGRAVING.

lig-nog'-ra-phy. The art of engraving on wood. ENGRAVING.
lig'-nous. Ligneous. FAUNA-FLORA.
like. To have a taste for; to enjoy; to choose; having resemblance. APPROVAL-DISAPPROVAL, DELINEATION-CARICATURE, DESIRE-DISTASTE, IMITATION-ORIGINALITY, LIKENESS-UNLIKENESS, LOVE-HATE, PALATABLENESS - UNPALATABLENESS, PLEASURE-PAIN; **as like a dock as a daisy,** LIKENESS-UNLIKENESS; **do what one likes,** LIBERTY-SUBJECTION; **like enough,** LIKELIHOOD-UNLIKELIHOOD; **like master, like man,** IMITATION-ORIGINALITY; **look like,** APPEARANCE-DISAPPEARANCE; **the like,** LIKENESS-UNLIKENESS; **very like a whale,** LIKENESS-UNLIKENESS; **we shall not look upon his like again,** SUPREMACY-SUBORDINACY.
like'-li-hood. A probability; verisimilitude. LIKELIHOOD-UNLIKELIHOOD.

LIKELIHOOD—UNLIKELIHOOD.

Chance. Undetermined probability or likelihood. See PURPOSE-LUCK.
Circumstantial evidence. Evidence of an indirect nature, or dependent on circumstances.
Color. That which hides the reality; a plausible appearance.
Credibility. State of being worthy of one's confidence or belief.
Fair chance. A moderate probability.
Fair prospect. A reasonable expectation of.
Favorable prospect. An anticipation that seems sure.
Good chance. Favorable prospect.
Good prospect. An indication justifying hope or expectation.
Likelihood. Appearance of reality.
Likeliness. State of being likely. See Adjectives.
Plausibility. State of being plausible; a seeming of truth though uncertain.
Presumption. Strong probability.
Presumptive evidence. Evidence affording reasonable ground of belief.
Probability. The state of being probable, of being likely to happen.
Prospect. Anticipation; expectation.
Reasonable chance. } A hopeful indication.
Reasonable prospect. }
Semblance. An appearance; a likeness.
Show of. An external appearance; unreal exhibition.
Verisimilitude. Appearance of truth or reality.
Vraisemblance [F.]. A likelihood.
Well-grounded hope. Strong likelihood

LIKELIHOOD—Verbs.

Be probable. See Adjectives
Bid fair. To be likely; promise success. See PROPHECY.
Count upon. To rely; have confidence in. See FAITH.
Dare say. To have courage to say.
Expect. To look for as probable. See EXPECTATION
Flatter oneself. To persuade with visionary hopes
Give color to. To give appearance of.
Imply. To include by inference without being expressed in words. See EVIDENCE.
Lend color to. To make it very probable.
Point to. To indicate as probable.
Run a good chance. } To be a strong likelihood of occurring, etc
Stand a good chance. }
Stand fair for. To promise success.
Think likely. Probably

Bad chance. Slight probability.
Bare possibility. A very remote probability.
Improbability. That which is naturally unexpected to happen.
Incredibility. Quality of being untrustworthy or incredible. See FAITH-MISGIVING.
Little chance. Unfavorable conjunction of circumstances.
Long odds. A great deal.
No chance. }
Scarcely any chance. } Unlikelihood.
Small chance. }
Unfavorable chance. }
Unlikelihood. Want of likelihood.

UNLIKELIHOOD—Verbs.

Be improbable. See Adjectives.
Have a small chance. See Nouns.

UNLIKELIHOOD—Adjectives.

Contrary to all reasonable expectations. Improbable
Improbable. Not likely to happen.
Inconceivable. Not conceivable; contrary to reason.
Incredible. Unbelievable. See FAITH-MISGIVING.
Inimaginable. Unimaginable.
Rare. Infrequently occurring. See FREQUENCY-RARITY.
Unheard of. Improbable; obscure.
Unimaginable. Not capable of being imagined.
Unlikely. Not likely; not probable.

UNLIKELIHOOD—Phrases.

Aquila non capit muscas [L.]. An eagle does not catch flies.
Pedir peras al olmo [Sp.]. To look for pears on the elm.
The chances are against one. One is likely to lose.

LIKELIHOOD—Continued.

LIKELIHOOD—Adjectives.

Apparent. Plain to sight; seeming in distinction from real.
Ben trovato [It.]. Well found; reasonable.
Colorable. Having an appearance of right or fact.
Credible. Able to be believed.
Easy of belief. Very probable.
Hopeful. Promising success.
In a fair way. Of great likelihood.
Likely. Having probability; plausible.
Ostensible. Offered as a reason, real or professed.

LIKELIHOOD—Adjectives—Continued

Plausible. Apparently true though it may be false.
Presumable. Capable of being presumed; reasonable.
Presumptive. Offering grounds for belief.
Probable. Having more evidence for than against.
Reasonable. Based on reason; just.

Specious. Having the appearance of truth, ofttimes without **the** reality.
To be expected. Having strong likelihood of occurring.
Well founded. Supported by good evidence.

LIKELIHOOD—Adverbs.

According to every reasonable expectation; apparently; belike; in all likelihood; in all probabilities; like enough; most likely; *prima facie* [L.], at first appearance; **probably** (see *Adjectives*); seem-ingly; ten to one; to all appearances (see APPEARANCE); very likely.

LIKELIHOOD—Phrases

All Lombard Street to a china orange ; appearances are in favor of; chances are in favor of; I dare say; the chances are; the odds are; there is reason to believe; there is reason to expect; there is reason to think.

like'-li-ness. Probability. LIKELIHOOD - UNLIKELI-HOOD.
like'-ly. Plausible; probably. LIKELIHOOD-UNLIKELI-HOOD; **think likely,** EXPECTATION-SURPRISE, LIKELI-HOOD-UNLIKELIHOOD.

like'-ness. A resemblance; a portrait. COPY-MODEL, DELINEATION-CARICATURE, LIKENESS-UNLIKENESS, NATURE-ART; **bad likeness,** DELINEATION-CARICA-TURE.

LIKENESS—UNLIKENESS.

Affinity. Close resemblance or relationship.
Agreement, etc. The state of agreeing or of being conformable. See HARMONY.
Analogicalness. The quality of being analogical.
Analogy. A resemblance of relations.
Approximation. The act of approximating or state of being approxi-mated.
Brotherhood. The state of being a brother.
Close likeness. }
Close resemblance. } An exact or literal similarity.
Connaturality. The state or quality of being connatural.
Connaturalness. See CONNATURALITY.
Faithful likeness. }
Faithful resemblance. } Likeness in detail.
Family likeness. Likeness of features in members of a family.
Likeness. The state or quality of being like.
Parallelism. The state or quality of being parallel.
Repetition, etc. The act of repeating. See RECURRENCE.
Resemblance. The quality or state of resembling.
Sameness, etc. Absence of difference. See SAMENESS.
Semblance Outward likeness, imaginary or real.
Similarity. The state or quality of being similar.
Similitude. Similarity.
Speaking likeness. }
Speaking resemblance. } A lively likeness.
Striking likeness. }
Striking resemblance. } Likeness easily noted, impressive.
Uniformity. The state or quality of having sameness of form.

LIKENESS—Associated Nouns.

Alliteration. The recurrence of the same initial letter or sound in the first accented syllables of two or more words.
Alter ego [L.]. Another self; a friend.
Analogue. A word in one language corresponding to one in another
Arcades ambo [L.]. Arcadians both.
Birds of a feather. Persons of like traits.
Brother. A male person having the same parents as another.
Chip of the old block. A person resembling his father.
Counterpart. A person or thing precisely similar to another.
Double. A person or thing that closely resembles another.
Et hoc genus omne [L.]. And everything of this kind.
Fellow. A person joined to another in action, location, or position
Image, etc. A visible representation of a person or thing. See DELINEATION.
Match. One similar or equal in appearance, position, quality, or character.
Mate. One that is paired with another.
One's second self. A person exactly resembling another.
Pair. Two persons or things of a kind.
Parallel. Anything that corresponds in all important features with another.
Par nobile fratrum [L.]. A noble pair of brothers.
Pendant [F.]. A counterpart,
Photograph. A picture taken by light.
Pun. The witty use of a word in two senses.
Rhyme. A correspondence of sounds in two or more words.
Simile. A formal comparison, which directs the mind to the repre-sentative object itself, likening one thing to another.
Sister. A female person who has the same parents as another.

Difference, etc. The state or quality of being separate or unlike in any respect. See VARIATION.
Disparity. The state of being disparate.
Dissemblance. Lack of resemblance.
Dissimilarity. The state or quality of being dissimilar.
Dissimilitude. Dissimilarity.
Diversity. The state of differing in some essential characteristic.
Novelty. The quality of being new or novel.
Originality. The quality of being original.
Unlikeness. The state or quality of being unlike.

UNLIKENESS—Verbs.

Bear no resemblance. Be wholly unlike.
Be unlike, etc. See *Adjectives*.
Differ *toto cælo*. To be as different as possible.
Render unlike, etc. See MUTATION.
Vary, etc. To change or be changed partially; to be somewhat dif-ferent in one or more characteristics. See VARIATION.

UNLIKENESS—Adjectives.

As different as chalk from cheese. }
As different as Macedon and Monmouth. } Wholly unlike.
As like a dock as a daisy. }
Cast in a different mold. } Very different.
Disparate. That cannot be compared; entirely different.
Dissimilar. Not similar.
Diversified, etc. Made essentially different in various parts or characteristics.
Far from it. Very different.
Lucus a non lucendo [L.]. A grove, from not being light, given a name which means just the opposite.
New. Having no counterpart; recently come into existence.
No such thing. }
Nothing of the kind. } Very different.
Novel. Of recent origin; strange and unusual.
Of a different kind. See DIVISION.
Original. Not produced by imitation; able to produce without imitating.
Quite another thing. Different.
Tertium quid [L.]. A third something; a thing not yet known
Unique. The only one of its kind.
Unlike. Not like.
Unmatched. With an equal or similar one either not found or not in existence.
Unprecedented. Preceded by no similar case or example.
"Very like a whale." Like anything you please. [Shakespeare, *Hamlet*, III, iii.]

UNLIKENESS—Adverb.

Otherwise. In another way or manner

UNLIKENESS—Phrase.

Diis aliter visum [L.]. The gods have judged otherwise

LIKENESS—Associated Nouns—*Continued*.

The like. A like person, thing, or event.
Twin. One of two young produced at the same birth

Type, etc. One of a class or group of objects that embodies the characteristics of the group or class. See TROPE.

LIKENESS—*Verbs*.

Approximate. To make or become very nearly but not exactly alike
Assimilate. To become or cause to become more harmonious or conformable.
Bear resemblance. To be like unto.
Be similar, etc. See *Adjectives*.
Bring near. See *Adjectives*.
Connaturalize. To make connatural.
Imitate, etc. To produce a likeness of. See IMITATION
Look alike. To have resemblance
Make alike. To make similar.

Match. To make similar to something; obtain that which is exactly similar to.
Parallel. To make parallel.
Pun. To use a word in a double sense.
Render similar. To make alike.
Resemble. To be the same in nature, appearance, quality or operation.
Rhyme. Similarity of sound.
Savor of. Have certain characteristics of.
Smack of. To have a faint resemblance.
Take after. To resemble, as in habits or character.

LIKENESS—*Adjectives*.

Akin to. Related by blood to; of similar nature with.
Alike Differing either not at all or not in a marked degree; of the same essential form.
Allied to. Morphologically related.
Analogical. Containing or involving analogy.
Analogous. Bearing analogy or resemblance, as to form, relation, etc.
Approximate. Nearly resembling.
A show of. Make a real or fanciful appearance of
As like as it can stare. }
As like as two peas. } Exactly alike.
Cast in the same mold. Alike in form or disposition
Close. Very similar.
Comme deux gouttes d'eau [F.]. As like as two drops of water.
Congener. Of the same stock, group, kind, etc.
Connatural. Having the same nature.
Exact, etc. Precisely and perfectly conformed to a certain standard See TRUTH.
Faithful. True in detail or representation.
For all the world like. Having a very close resemblance.
Instar omnium [L.]. Worth them all.
Lifelike. Having the exact appearance of a living being.
Like. Nearly identical in appearance and characteristics.

Mock. Merely imitating the real.
Much the same. Having many characteristics in common.
Near. Closely related or similar.
Of a piece. Of the same kind.
Parallel. Conforming to something in character and form.
Pseudo [Gr.]. Exhibiting deceptive appearance of likeness.
Representing. To present a likeness of.
Resembling, etc. See *Verbs*.
Ridiculously like. So much alike that not to see the difference were ridiculous.
Similar. Bearing resemblance to each other or to something else; like, but not completely identical.
Simulating. Have a mere appearance of without reality.
So. Of a like degree or manner.
Something like. Bearing only a partial resemblance.
Such as. }
Such like. } Similar to.
The picture of. }
The very image of. } Very like.
True to nature. }
True to the life. } Exactly portraying.
Twin. Resembling, like twins; being one of twins.

LIKENESS—*Adverbs*.

As if; as if it were; as it were; just as; *quasi* [L.], appearing as if; **so to speak;** *veluti in speculum* [L.], as if into a mirror.

LIKENESS—*Phrases*

Et sic de similibus [L.]. And so of the like.
Gens de même famille [F.]. Birds of a feather

Tel maître, tel valet [F.]. Like master, like man.
Tel père, tel fils [F.]. Like father, like son.

---

like'-wise. In like manner; also; too. ADDITION-SUBTRACTION.
lik'-ing. Kindly feeling; fondness. DESIRE-DISTASTE, LOVE-HATE; **have a liking for,** PLEASURE-PAIN; **to one's liking,** PLEASURABLENESS-PAINFULNESS.
li'-lac. The color of the lilac flower. YELLOWNESS-PURPLE.
Lil'-ies of France. Emblem of France. PATRIOTISM-TREASON.
Lil''-li-pu'-tian. Very small. [Swift, *Gulliver's Travels*.] GREATNESS-LITTLENESS.
lil'-y. White and soft. BEAUTY-UGLINESS, WHITENESS-BLACKNESS.
lil'-y-heart''-ed. Cowardly. BRAVERY-COWARDICE.
lil'-y-liv''-ered. Cowardly. BRAVERY-COWARDICE.
limæ labor [L.] (laɪ'-mî lê'-bor). Labor of the file; painstaking literary work. BETTERMENT-DETERIORATION, TOIL-RELAXATION.
li-ma'-tion. The act of filing or polishing. FRIABILITY.
li'-ma-ture. Limation; filings. FRIABILITY, FRICTION-LUBRICATION.
limb. Edge or border; one of the members of the body. ASTRONOMY, INSTRUMENT, WHOLE-PART; **limb of the law,** ADVOCATE.
lim'-ber. Easily bent; limp; a hole cut through the floor timbers of a ship. CONVEYANCE-VESSEL, HARDNESS-SOFTNESS.
lim'-bo. A region bordering on hell; a prison. HEAVEN-

HELL, RELEASE-PRISON, RELEASE-RESTRAINT; **in limbo,** KEEPER-PRISONER, PLEASURE-PAIN.
lime. To ensnare. TRUTHFULNESS-FRAUD; **lime light,** LUMINARY-SHADE.
lime'-kiln''. A kiln for burning lime from limestone. OVEN-REFRIGERATOR.
lim'-it. To bound; to check. BEGINNING-END, BOUNDARY, CONFINEMENT, LEAVE-PROHIBITION, MODIFICATION.
lim''-i-ta'-tion. The act of limiting; that which limits. ALIENATION, CONFINEMENT, MODIFICATION, PROPERTY, RELEASE-RESTRAINT.
lim'-it-ed. Circumscribed. GREATNESS-LITTLENESS, MAGNITUDE-SMALLNESS; **to a limited extent,** FAULTLESSNESS-FAULTINESS.
lim'-it-less. Illimitable. INFINITY.
limn. To delineate. PAINTING.
lim'-ner. Illuminator. ARTIST.
limp. To walk lamely; soft or pliable; limber; weak. HARDNESS-SOFTNESS, STRENGTH-WEAKNESS, SUCCESS-FAILURE, SWIFTNESS-SLOWNESS.
lim'-pid. Crystal-clear. DIAPHANEITY-OPAQUENESS.
lim-pid'-i-ty. The quality of being limpid. DIAPHANEITY-OPAQUENESS.
lin. A pool; a waterfall. GULF-PLAIN, RIVER-WIND
linc'-ture. A syrup-like medicine. REMEDY-BANE.
linc'-tus. Medicine taken by licking with the tongue. REMEDY-BANE.

line. To make lines upon; to outline; to form in line; to cover the inside of; a string or cord; a stroke; outline; limit; route; kinship in direct descent; regular troops; rule; that which has but one dimension. AIM-ABERRATION, APPEARANCE-DISAPPEARANCE, BELLIGERENT, BREADTH-NARROWNESS, CONNECTIVE, CONTINUITY-INTERRUPTION, COVER-LINING, CURVATION-RECTILINEARITY, LENGTH-SHORTNESS, MELODY-DISSONANCE, MENSURATION, OCCUPATION, OUTLINE, PARENTAGE-PROGENY, POETRY-PROSE, SIGN, WRITING-PRINTING; **boundary line,** BOUNDARY; **draw the line,** DIFFERENTIATION-INDISCRIMINATION; **in a line,** CONTINUITY-INTERRUPTION, CURVATION-RECTILINEARITY; **in a line with,** AIM-ABERRATION; **line engraving,** ENGRAVING; **line of action,** CONDUCT; **line of battle,** CONTINUITY-INTERRUPTION; **line-of-battle ship,** BELLIGERENT; **line of march,** AIM-ABERRATION; **line of road,** WAY; **read between the lines,** INTERPRETATION-MISINTERPRETATION; **sounding line,** DEEPNESS-SHALLOWNESS; **straight line,** CURVATION-RECTILINEARITY; **troops of the line,** BELLIGERENT.

lin'-e-age. Ancestral line of consanguinity; pedigree; family. CONTINUITY-INTERRUPTION, PARENTAGE-PROGENY, RELATIONSHIP.

lin'-e-a-ment. Feature; outline. APPEARANCE-DISAPPEARANCE, FORM-FORMLESSNESS, SIGN.

lin'-e-ar. Of the nature of a line; involving measurement in one direction; in a straight line. CONTINUITY-INTERRUPTION, LENGTH-SHORTNESS, PARENTAGE-PROGENY.

lined. Fitted out on the inside. COVER-LINING.

lin'-en. A fabric woven from the fibers of flax. DRESS-UNDRESS.

lin'-en-scroll". Ornament. ARCHITECTURE.

lines. A row of fortifications. APPEARANCE-DISAPPEARANCE, ATTACK-DEFENSE, OUTLINE; **hard lines,** HARSHNESS-MILDNESS, WELFARE-MISFORTUNE.

lin'-ger. To drag; to hesitate; to tarry. EARLINESS-LATENESS, SWIFTNESS-SLOWNESS.

lin'-ger-ing. Remaining or continuing long. LASTINGNESS-TRANSIENTNESS.

lin'-go. Language; a dialect. LANGUAGE, WORD-NEOLOGY.

lingua franca [L.] (lin'-gwɑ fran'-cɑ). A mixture of Italian with Arabic, Turkish, Greek, etc.; a jargon. WORD-NEOLOGY.

lin-gua'-cious. Loquacious. TALKATIVENESS-TACITURNITY.

lin'-gual. Pertaining to or formed by the tongue. LANGUAGE, SPEECH-INARTICULATENESS.

lin'-guist. An adept in languages; a philologist. LANGUAGE, SCHOLAR-DUNCE.

lin-guis'-tic. Pertaining to language. LANGUAGE.

lin-guis'-tics. Comparative philology. LANGUAGE.

lin'-i-ment. A liquid or oily preparation for rubbing on the skin. PULPINESS-OILINESS, REMEDY-BANE.

li'-ning. A cover for the inner surface of a thing. COVER-LINING.

link. To interlock; to couple; part of a chain; a constituent part of a series; a torch. CONNECTION-INDEPENDENCE, CONNECTIVE, CROSSING, LUMINARY-SHADE, STATION, UNION-DISUNION, WHOLE-PART.

link'-boy". A torch-boy. MANAGER.

linked. Joined. **Linked together,** ASSOCIATION.

li-no'-le-um. A material used as floor-cloth. COVER-LINING, MATERIAL.

lin'-seed"-oil". Oil expressed from flaxseed. PULPINESS-OILINESS.

lin'-sey-wol'-sey. Made of linen and wool mixed. MIXTURE-HOMOGENEITY.

lin'-stock. A pointed staff with a crotch at one end to hold a lighted match. COMBUSTIBILITY.

lint. The soft down of raveled or scraped linen. COVER-LINING.

lin'-tel. The head-piece of a door, or window-frame. ARCHITECTURE, SUSPENSION-SUPPORT.

li'-on. A large animal of Africa and Asia; a courageous person; a prominent person; an object of interest. BRAVERY-COWARDICE, PHENOMENON, REPUTATION-DISCREDIT; **as dewdrops from the lion's mane,** OVERVALUATION-UNDERVALUATION; **come in like a lion,** TURBULENCE-CALMNESS; **in the lion's den,** SECURITY-INSECURITY; **lion in the path,** OBSTRUCTION-HELP; **lion lies down with the lamb,** STRIFE-PEACE; **lion's share,** DUENESS-UNDUENESS, EXCESS-LACK, SUPREMACY-SUBORDINACY, WHOLE-PART.

li'-on-el. A young lion. INFANT-VETERAN

li'-on-ess. A female lion. MALE-FEMALE.

li'-on-et. A small lion. INFANT-VETERAN.

li'-on-heart"-ed. Brave. BRAVERY-COWARDICE.

li'-on-ize. To pay great attention to socially. INQUISITIVENESS-INDIFFERENCE, REPUTATION-DISCREDIT.

li'-on-like". Resembling the lion in strength or courage. BRAVERY-COWARDICE.

lip. The edge or border of the mouth; a margin, edge, or border. BEGINNING-END, BORDER, CONVEXITY-CONCAVITY, LATERALITY-CONTRAPOSITION; **finger on the lips,** TALKATIVENESS-TACITURNITY, VOCALIZATION-MUTENESS; **hang on the lips of,** HEARING-DEAFNESS; **lip homage,** ADULATION-DISPARAGEMENT, TRUTHFULNESS-FALSEHOOD; **lip service,** GODLINESS-UNGODLINESS, TRUTHFULNESS-FALSEHOOD; **lip wisdom,** SAGACITY-INCAPACITY; **open one's lips,** SPEECH-INARTICULATENESS; **seal the lips,** TALKATIVENESS-TACITURNITY; **smack the lips,** PALATABLENESS-UNPALATABLENESS, SAVOR-TASTELESSNESS, SENSUALITY-SUFFERING.

li-poth'-y-my. Fainting; syncope. WEARINESS-REFRESHMENT.

lip'-pi-tude. Chronic ophthalmia. SIGHT-DIMSIGHTEDNESS.

li'-quate. Melt. LIQUEFACTION-VOLATILIZATION.

liq"-ue-fac'-tion. Conversion into or existence as a liquid. HEATING-COOLING, LIQUEFACTION-VOLATILIZATION.

LIQUEFACTION—VOLATILIZATION.

Alkahest. An imaginary universal solvent.

Apozem. A decoction.

Colliquation.
Colliquefaction.} The act of fusing different bodies into one mass.

Deliquation. Act of dissolving or melting.

Dissolution. Change from a solid to a liquid form.

Flux. The process of melting.

Infusion. The act of pouring in.

Liquefaction. The act of converting into liquid.

Liquescence.}
Liquescency.} The state of being liquescent.

Lixiviation. The process of lixiviating; leeching.

Lixivium. A solution obtained by lixiviation.

Melting, etc. The act of reducing from a solid to a liquid state by heat. See HEATING.

Menstruum. A solvent.

Cohobation. The act of cohobating.

Distillation. The act of distilling.

Evaporation. The act of becoming vapor.

Exhalation. The act of exhaling.

Fumigation. The act of fumigating.

Gasification. The act of changing into gas.

Steaming. The act of making steam.

Sublimation. The act of subliming.

Vaporization. The act of converting into vapor.

Volatility. The state of being volatile.

Volatilization. The act of volatilizing.

VOLATILIZATION—*Nouns of Agent*

Retort. A vessel used in distillation.

Still. An apparatus used in changing a substance by heat into vapor

Vaporizer. An instrument used in vaporization.

LIQUEFACTION—VOLATILIZATION—*Continued.*

Solution. The change of matter from a solid or gaseous into a liquid state by combination with a liquid.
Solvent. That which is suitable for dissolving.
Thaw. Changing from a frozen to an unfrozen state by heat.

LIQUEFACTION—*Verbs*

Dissolve. To change from a solid to a liquid condition.
Fine still. To distil from fermented molasses.
Hold in solution. Keep in a fluid state.
Liquate. } To convert into a liquid or liquid form
Liquefy. }
Melt. Become liquid by heat.
Render liquid. To convert into a liquid. See LIQUID.
Resolve. To separate into constituent parts.
Run. Become fluid.
Solve. To dissolve.

LIQUEFACTION—*Adjectives*

Colliquative. Melting.
Deliquescent. Becoming liquid in the air.
Liquefiable. Capable of being liquefied.
Liquefied. Made liquid.
Liquescent. Inclined to liquefy.
Soluble. Capable of liquefying.

liq'-ue-fi''-a-ble. Capable of being changed to a liquid. LIQUEFACTION-VOLATILIZATION.
liq'-ue-fied. Made like liquid. LIQUEFACTION-VOLATILIZATION, LIQUID-GAS.
liq'-ue-fy. Convert into a liquid. HEATING-COOLING, LIQUEFACTION-VOLATILIZATION, LIQUID-GAS.

VOLATILIZATION—*Verbs.*

Cohobate. Distil again.
Distil. To fall in drops.
Emit vapor. Give out vapor.
Evaporate. To pass off in vapor.
Exhale. To send out as vapor.
Fume. To pass off in vapor.
Fumigate. To expose to smoke.
Reek. To emit vapor.
Render gaseous, etc. See LIQUID-GAS.
Smoke. To emit smoke.
Steam. Give off steam.
Sublime. To turn a solid to vapor by heat.
Transpire. To pass off in the form of vapor.
Vaporize. To turn into vapor.
Volatilize. To make volatile.

VOLATILIZATION—*Adjectives*

Evaporable. Capable of being made into vapor.
Reeking, etc. See *Verbs.*
Vaporizable. Capable of being turned into vapor.
Volatile. Easily passing into vapor.
Volatilized, etc. See *Verbs.*

li-ques'-cence. The quality of being liquescent. LIQUEFACTION-VOLATILIZATION.
li-ques'-cent. Melting. LIQUEFACTION-VOLATILIZATION.
li-queur'. An alcoholic cordial sweetened and flavored. NUTRIMENT-EXCRETION, SWEETNESS-ACIDITY

LIQUID—GAS.

Fluid. Any substance that flows.
Fluidity. State of being fluid.
Gaseity, etc. State of being a gas.
Humor. Any moisture of the body.
Hydrodynamics. Dynamics of fluids.
Hydrology. Science of the waters of the earth.
Hydrostatics. Science of liquids at rest.
Inelastic liquid. A fluid that does not tend to expand to the limits of containing space.
Juice. Liquid part of animal or vegetable matter.
Liquid. A body in that state in which the particles move freely among themselves.
Liquidity. } State of being a liquid
Liquidness. }
Liquor. An alcoholic liquid.
Sap. The juice of plants.
Serosity. } A thin, watery, animal fluid.
Serum. }
Solubility. } Having the quality of being soluble.
Solubleness. }

LIQUID—*Denotations.*

Blood. The fluid that circulates in the heart, arteries, veins, and capillaries.
Champagne. A highly effervescent wine.
Chyle. A milky fluid contained in the lacteals of the small intestines during digestion.
Cider. The juice of apples, used as a beverage.
Gravy. The juice from meats in roasting.
Ichor. The ethereal fluid, answering to human blood, supposed to flow in the veins of the gods.
Lymph. A transparent, colorless fluid of the lymphatic vessels of the body.
Rheum. Thin watery fluid from the mucous membrane of the head
Sanies. A fluid of offensive smell discharged from ulcers.
Whisky. An alcoholic liquor obtained by the distillation of a fermented starchy compound.

LIQUID—*Verbs.*

Be fluid, etc. See *Adjectives.*
Flow. To move along by force of gravity. See RIVER-WIND.
Liquefy. To change to a liquid. See LIQUEFACTION-VOLATILIZATION

LIQUID—*Adjectives.*

Fluent. Capable of flowing.
Fluid. Having properties of a fluid.
Liquefied. Changed to a liquid state.
Liquid. Having properties of a liquid.
Juicy. Full of juice.
Sappy. Full of sap.

Aerodynamics. Dynamics of gases.
Aerostatics. Sciences of gases at rest.
Air. The mixture of gases that forms the envelope of the earth
Cloud. Visible vapor.
Effluvium. Exhalation perceived by smell.
Elastic fluid. One that tends to expand to the limits of the containing space.
Ether. A medium supposed to pervade all space.
Flatulence. } Property of generating wind.
Flatulency. }
Flatus. Puff of wind.
Fumarole. A hole in a volcano from which fumes issue.
Fume. Narcotic, choking vapor.
Gas. An aeriform fluid.
Gaseity. Having form of gas.
Gas-meter. An apparatus for measuring the quantity of gas consumed.
Gasometer. An apparatus for measuring and holding gas.
Pneumatics. } Science of elastic fluids.
Pneumostatics. }
Reek. Vapor.
Steam. Water in vaporous form.
Vapor. Gaseous state of a substance, ordinarily a solid or liquid.
Vaporousness. Having the properties of vapor.
Volatility. Disposition to evaporate.

GAS—*Verb.*

To emit vapor, etc. To give off vapor, etc. See LIQUEFACTION-VOLATILIZATION.

GAS—*Adjectives.*

Aerial. Consisting of air; found in the air.
Aeriform. Of the nature of air.
Airy. Consisting of air.
Ethereal. Pertaining to ether.
Evaporable. Capable of evaporating.
Flatulent. Tending to generate wind.
Gaseous. Having the state or properties of gas.
Vaporous. Of or like vapor.
Volatile. Disposed to evaporate.

LIQUID—*Adjectives*—*Continued.*

Serous. Watery, like serum.
Soluble. Capable of being dissolved, usually in water
Succulent. Having a juicy and soft pulp.
Uncongealed. In a liquid state.

LIQUID—*Phrase.*

Blut und Eisen [G.]. Blood and iron

liq'-uid. An inelastic fluid; one of the four consonants l, m, n, and r; mellifluous. LETTER, LIQUID-GAS, LOUDNESS-FAINTNESS.

liq'-ui-date. To settle; to arrange. SETTLEMENT-DEFAULT.

liq''-ui-da'-tor. A receiver. SETTLEMENT-DEFAULT TREASURER.

li-quid'-i-ty. Fluidity. LIQUID-GAS.

liq'-uid-ness. The state of being liquid. LIQUID-GAS.

liq'-uor. An alcoholic or intoxicating fluid. LIQUID-GAS, NUTRIMENT-EXCRETION; **in liquor,** TEETOTALISM-INTEMPERANCE; **liquor up,** TEETOTALISM-INTEMPERANCE.

liq'-uor-ice. An herb of the genus Glycyrrhiza. SWEETNESS-ACIDITY.

liq'-uor-ish. Tempting the appetite; greedy; lustful. DESIRE-DISTASTE, DESIRE-PARTICULARNESS, PALATABLENESS-UNPALATABLENESS, PURITY-IMPURITY.

li''-ra. Coin. VALUES.

lis litem generat [L.] (lis lai'-tem jen'-er at). Strife breeds strife. STRIFE-PEACE.

Lis'-bon. A light-colored wine. NUTRIMENT-EXCRETION.

lisp. An imperfect or timid utterance. SPEECH-INARTICULATENESS.

lis'-som. Lithesome. HARDNESS-SOFTNESS.

list. To enroll; to enlist; to gratify; to choose; to listen to; a catalogue or roll; a border or selvage; a narrow strip; desire; field of contest. BORDER, CHOICE-NEUTRALITY, DESIRE-DISTASTE, HEARING-DEAFNESS, LAMINA-FIBER, LISTS, PARALLELISM-INCLINATION, RECORD, VOLITION-OBLIGATION; **enter the lists,** ATTACK-DEFENSE, STRIFE-PEACE.

list'-ed. Sewed together, as strips of cloth, forming a party-colored appearance. VARIEGATION.

lis'-ten. To harken. HEARING-DEAFNESS; **be listened to,** DOMINANCE-IMPOTENCE; **listen to,** HEED-DISREGARD; **listen to reason,** SAGACITY-INCAPACITY.

list'-less. Inattentive; indifference to; inanimate. ACTIVITY-INDOLENCE, DESIRE-DISTASTE, HEED-DISREGARD.

lists. The barriers enclosing a jousting-field; the field itself. LISTS.

LISTS.

Aceldama. The potter's field, purchased with the bribe which Judas took for betraying his Master; a field of bloodshed.

Amphitheater. A circular building in which the seats rise upward and backward from a center pit or arena.

Arena. Any sandy plain, surrounded by seats, for public exhibitions.

Battle-field.
Battle-ground. } A field of battle.

Bear-garden. A place where bears are kept for exhibition.

Boards. The stage in a theater.

Camp. The ground occupied by an army.

Campus Martius. The field of Mars; the assembling place of the Roman legions.

Champ de Mars [F.]. The field of Mars; a large square in Paris, used for military exercises.

Circus. A circular spot in which feats of horses are exhibited.

Cockpit. An arena for cock-fighting.

Colosseum. The amphitheater of Vespasian in Rome, the largest in the world.

Corso [L.]. A race-course.

Course. An arena on which horses are raced.

Field. A place where a battle is fought.

Field of battle.
Field of slaughter. } Where armies fight.

Flavian amphitheater. The Colosseum.

Gymnasium. An arena for taking exercise.

Hippodrome. A place where horses are raced.

Hustings. A platform used in making political speeches.

Lists. A field enclosed for a race or combat.

Palæstra. A place for athletic exercises of any kind.

Platform. A raised surface for the use of speakers.

Playground. A piece of ground used for amusements.

Race-course. A place where races are held.

Ring. A circular arena in which races are conducted.

Seat of war. Place of operations of war.

Scene of action. Place or time of action.

Stage. The platform of a theater.

Theater. An edifice for spectacular representations.

Theater of war. A region in which operations of war are conducted.

The enemy's camp. A battle-field.

Tilting-ground.
Tilting-yard. } A place where the exercise of thrusting with a lance is practised.

Turf. A race-course.

Trysting-place. A place of meeting according to appointment. See GATHERINGPLACE.

Walk. A piece of land laid off for walking.

lit'-a-ny. A liturgical prayer. CEREMONIAL, WORSHIP-IDOLATRY.

lite pendente [L.] (lai'-tî pen-den'-tî). During the trial. LITIGATION.

litem, lite resolvit [L.] (lai'-tem, lai'-tî rî-sol'-vit). He settles strife by strife. REPRISAL-RESISTANCE, STRIFE-PEACE.

literæ humaniores [L.] (lit'-er-î hiu-mê''-ni-o'-rîz). Polite literature. LANGUAGE.

literæ scriptæ [L.] (lit'-er-î scrip'-tî). The written word. WRITING-PRINTING.

lit'-er-al. Primitive; following the exact words; expressed by letters; matter-of-fact; documentary. IMITATION-ORIGINALITY, INTERPRETATION-MISINTERPRETATION, LETTER, MANIFESTATION-LATENCY, MEANING-JARGON, OBSERVANCE-NONOBSERVANCE, TRUTH-ERROR, WORD-NEOLOGY; **literal meaning,** MEANING-JARGON; **literal translation,** INTERPRETATION-MISINTERPRETATION.

lit''-er-al'-i-ty. The state of being literal. INTERPRETATION-MISINTERPRETATION.

lit'-er-al-ly. Word by word. IMITATION-ORIGINALITY, INTERPRETATION-MISINTERPRETATION, TRUTH-ERROR.

literarum, homo multarum [L.] (lit-er-ê'-rum, ho'-mo mul-tê'-rum). Man of much literary accomplishment. SCHOLAR-DUNCE.

literarum, homo trium [L.] (lit-er-ê'-rum, ho'-mo trai'-um). A man of three letters; *i. e., fur* [L.], a thief. ROBBER.

lit'-er-a-ry. Pertaining to literature. LANGUAGE; **literary hack,** MISSIVE-PUBLICATION; **literary man,** SCHOLAR-DUNCE; **literary power,** STYLE.

lit''-er-a'-ti. Men of letters. SCHOLAR-DUNCE.

lit''-e-ra'-tim. Literally. IMITATION-ORIGINALITY, LETTER, MANIFESTATION-LATENCY, TRUTH-ERROR, WORD-NEOLOGY.

lit'-er-a-ture. The written or printed productions of the human mind collectively. KNOWLEDGE-IGNORANCE, LANGUAGE, NATURE-ART.

lith'-a-gogue. A medicine for expelling calculi. REMEDY-BANE.

lithe. Supple. HARDNESS-SOFTNESS.

lithe'-some. Somewhat lithe. HARDNESS-SOFTNESS

lith'-i-um. An element. CHEMISTRY.

lith'-o-graph. A lithographic print. ENGRAVING.

lith-og'-ra-phy. An art used in printing. ENGRAVING.

lith-ol'-o-gy. The natural history of stones. GEOLOGY, ORGANIZATION-INORGANIZATION.

lith'-o-man''-cy. Divination by stones. PROPHECY.

lith'-o-tint. The art or process of producing colored pictures from lithographic stones. ENGRAVING.

lit'-i-gant. Litigious; a party to a lawsuit. BELLIGERENT, JUDGE, JUSTIFICATION-CHARGE, LITIGATION, VARIANCE-ACCORD.

lit'-i-gate. To bring into litigation. VARIANCE-ACCORD.

lit''-i-ga'-tion. A judicial contest; a contest that depends upon evidence. LITIGATION, STRIFE-PEACE, UNION-DISUNION, VARIANCE-ACCORD.

LITIGATION.

Action. Lawful demand of rights through judicial proceedings.
Case. Cause of action.
Cause. An entire judicial proceeding.
Lawsuit. An action at law.
Litigation. A judicial contest.
Suit. A judicial action for the recovery of a right or the redress of a wrong.

LITIGATION—*Nouns of Means, etc.*

Accusation. The act of accusing. See JUSTIFICATION-CHARGE.
Affidavit. A sworn voluntary declaration in writing.
Answer. A denial of a charge.
Appeal. The carrying of a cause to a higher court.
Apprehension. Legal arrest.
Arraignment. Presenting in court on a criminal charge.
Arrest. Seizure by legal authority.
Bill. A paper filed in court.
Certiorari [L.]. To be certified; a writ from a superior court to a lower one requiring a certified record of its proceedings in a given case.
Citation. A legal summons to appear in court.
Claim. The assertion of a right.
Cojuror. One who confirms another's testimony.
Committal. The state of being committed.
Corespondent. One of several defendants.
Decision. A judgment. See DECISION.
Declaration. A paper filed by a plaintiff.
Demurrer. An issue on a point of law.
Dispute. A discussion over a point of law.
Hearing. A judicial investigation.
Impeachment. The act of accusing for crime.
Imprisonment. Confinement in prison. See RELEASE-RESTRAINT.
Indictment. A formal written accusation.
Information. An accusation in the nature of an indictment.
Latitat [L.]. He lies hid; a summons with supposition that the defendant lies hid.
Litigant. One engaged in a suit.
Motion. An application to a court for an order directing some act to be done.
Plea. An allegation of either party in a suit.
Pleadings. Pleas taken collectively.
Precedent. A decision taken as a rule for subsequent decisions.
Presentment. A grand jury's report to the court.
Prosecution. The act of prosecuting. See *Verbs.*
Rebutter. A defendant's answer to the plaintiff's reply to a previous rejoinder.
Rejoinder. The answer filed by a defendant to a plaintiff's replication.
Replication. A plaintiff's reply to a defendant's answer.
Reports. A published narration of judicial decisions.
Reseizer. One who takes into custody goods or lands unlawfully taken possession of.
Subpœna. A writ commanding one's appearance in court.
Suitor. A party to a suit.
Summons. See SUBPŒNA.
Surrebutter. A plaintiff's reply to a defendant's rebutter.
Surrejoinder. A plaintiff's reply to a defendant's rejoinder.
Talesman. A person summoned to make up a jury when the regular panel is deficient.
Trial. A judicial examination and determination of a suit.
True bill. A bill indorsed by a grand jury.
Venire. A writ issued to a sheriff for summoning a jury.
Verdict. The decision of a jury.
Writ. A mandatory precept of a court, under seal, commanding one to do or not to do a particular act. See DECISION.

LITIGATION—*Verbs.*

Accuse. Charge with crime, etc. See JUSTIFICATION-CHARGE.
Adjudicate. Determine judicially. See DECISION.
Appeal to the law. Appeal to the court.
Apprehend. Take into legal custody.
Arraign. Cause to come before the court for trial.
Arrest. To take into legal custody.
Attach. Take and hold in the name of the law.
Bring an action against. Institute legal proceedings against.
Bring to justice. } To compel to answer charges in a suit at law.
Bring to trial. }
Cite. Command to appear in court.
Close the pleadings. Bring pleadings to an end.
Commit. Place in custody.
Distrain. Hold as security.
Empanel a jury. Enroll on a list for jury duty.
File a claim. Deposit in court a written claim.

Give in charge, etc. Hand over for custody. See RELEASE-RESTRAINT.
Go to law. To bring suit in court.
Hear a cause. Try a case in court.
Impeach. Charge with wrong-doing in office.
Implead. Proceed against one legally.
Indict. Prefer a criminal charge.
Inform against. Give knowledge of facts against.
Join issue. Take opposite sides.
Prefer a claim. Lay a claim before a court in a formal manner.
Prosecute. Conduct legal proceedings on a criminal charge.
Pull up. To arrest.
Put on trial. To compel to answer charges in a court.
Serve with a writ. Deliver a writ to a designated person.
Set down for a hearing. Place in order for trial.
Sit in judgment. Exercise judicial authority.
Sue. To proceed legally to recover a right or redress a wrong.
Summon. } To notify or command to appear in court.
Summons. }
Try. Make a judicial investigation.

LITIGATION—*Adjectives.*

Coram judice [L.]. Before the judge; still under consideration.
Litigious, etc. Given to litigation. See FAVORITE-QUARRELSOMENESS.
Qui tam [L.]. Who so; a term applied to an action for a penalty given by statute to the person who sues for it.
Sub judice [L.]. Before the judge.

LITIGATION—*Adverb.*

Pendente lite [L.]. Suit pending; while suit is in progress.

LITIGATION—*Phrases.*

Accedas ad curiam [L.]. You may go to the court.
Accusare nemo se debet [L.]. No one is bound to accuse himself.
Ad huc sub judice [L.]. The dispute is still before the judge; the case is not yet decided.
Bill of rights. A declaration of the rights of individuals in both their absolute and related conditions.
Corpus delicti [L.]. The body of crime; the fundamental fact necessary for conviction.
Decided case. A trial brought to a decision.
Nisi prius [L.]. Unless sooner; a term suggesting the trial of civil causes before a judge and jury.
Party to a suit. One engaged in litigation.
Procès verbal [F.]. Verbal process; in French law, a written statement in detail of an official act.
Reo absente [L.]. In the absence of the defendant.
State of facts. A mutual statement of facts by the parties to a suit.
Take the law of. Bring action against.
Transeat in exemplum [L.]. Let it pass into precedent.
Writ of error. A judicial writ by which an appellate court may review the proceedings of an inferior court on matters of law.

li-tig'-ious. Inclined to litigation; quarrelsome. LITIGATION, VARIANCE-ACCORD.

lit'-ter. To scatter things carelessly; a number of young at a birth; waste materials; a stretcher; a couch. CONVEYANCE-VESSEL, MULTIPLICITY-FEWNESS, ORGANIZATION - DISORGANIZATION, PARENTAGE - PROGENY, REGULARITY-IRREGULARITY, SUSPENSION-SUPPORT, USEFULNESS-USELESSNESS.

littera scripta manet [L.] (lit'-ter-a scrip'-ta mě'-net). The written word remains. MUTABILITY-STABILITY, REMEMBRANCE-FORGETFULNESS.

littéraire, la morgue [F.] (li-tê-rêr', la morg). A lofty literary style. STYLE.

lit''-ter-a-teur'. A literary man. MISSIVE-PUBLICATION, SCHOLAR-DUNCE.

lit'-tle. Not large; not much; restricted; narrow; mean. GREATNESS-LITTLENESS, LENGTH-SHORTNESS, LOVEHATE, MAGNITUDE-SMALLNESS, UPRIGHTNESS-DISHONESTY; cost little, COSTLINESS-CHEAPNESS; do little, ACTIVITY-INDOLENCE; little by little, QUANTITYMEASURE, SWIFTNESS-SLOWNESS; little did one think, EXPECTATION-SURPRISE; little one, INFANT-VETERAN, little red school-house, CITY-COUNTRY; make little of, OVERVALUATION - UNDERVALUATION; signify little, CONSEQUENCE-INSIGNIFICANCE; think little of, HEEDDISREGARD; to little purpose, SUCCESS-FAILURE, USEFULNESS-USELESSNESS

lit'-tle-ness. The state of being little. GREAT-NESS-LITTLENESS, LENGTH-SHORTNESS, MAGNITUDE-SMALLNESS.

lit'-to-ral. Pertaining to or living on the shore. OCEAN-LAND.

lit'-ur-gy. Ritual. CEREMONIAL.

live. To have the vital principle; to pass life; to abide; alive; energetic. ENTITY-NONENTITY, LIFE-DEATH, MUTATION-PERMANENCE, REPUTATION-DISCREDIT; **live and let live,** ACTION-PASSIVENESS, EXCITABILITY-INEXCITABILITY, LIBERTY-SUBJECTION; **live by one's wits,** SKILL-UNSKILFULNESS, STRIFE-PEACE, THEFT, TRUTHFULNESS-FRAUD; **live from hand to mouth,** AFFLUENCE-PENURY, PREPARATION-NONPREPARATION; **live hard,** MODERATION-SELFINDULGENCE; **live in hope,** SANGUINENESS-HOPELESSNESS; **live in the memory,** REMEMBRANCE-FORGETFULNESS; **live on,** NUTRIMENT-EXCRETION; **live to fight again,** LASTINGNESS-TRANSIENTNESS; **live upon nothing,** EXTRAVAGANCE-AVARICE.

live'-li-hood. Means of subsistence. AFFLUENCE-PENURY.

live'-li-ness. Full of spirit. ACTIVITY-INDOLENCE, LIGHTHEARTEDNESS-DEJECTION.

live'-long". Entire. LASTINGNESS-TRANSIENTNESS.

live'-ly. Spirited; vigorous; intensely active in mind; keen; vivid; bright; briskly. ACTIVITY-INDOLENCE, EMOTION, FORCE-WEAKNESS, LIFE-DEATH, LIGHTHEARTEDNESS-DEJECTION, SENSIBILITY-INSENSIBILITY, SENSITIVENESS-APATHY; **lively imagination,** FANCY; **lively pace,** SWIFTNESS-SLOWNESS.

liv'-er. One who lives; an organ of the body. **Hard liver,** MODERATION-VOLUPTUARY; **white liver,** BRAVERY-COWARDICE.

liv'-er-col"-ored. Reddish-brown. GRAY-BROWN.

liv'-er-y. A peculiar uniform worn by servants; a distinctive dress. COLOR-ACHROMATISM, DRESS-UNDRESS, SIGN, TITLE; **livery servant,** CHIEF-UNDERLING.

liv'-er-y-man. A London voter. LIBERTY-SUBJECTION.

liv'-er-y-sta"-ble. A stable where horses are boarded or hired. DWELLER-HABITATION.

liv'-id. Black-and-blue; lead-colored. GRAY-BROWN, WHITENESS-BLACKNESS, YELLOWNESS-PURPLE.

li-vid'-i-ty. The state of being livid. MELODY-DISSONANCE, YELLOWNESS-PURPLE.

liv'-id-ness. Livid color. YELLOWNESS-PURPLE.

liv'-ing. Live; livelihood; a benefice. CHURCH, LIFE-DEATH, OCCUPATION; **good living,** FASTING-GLUTTONY; **living beings,** ORGANIZATION-DISORGANIZATION; **living soul,** HUMANITY; **living thing,** FAUNA-FLORA.

li"-vrai"-son'. A fascicle. MISSIVE-PUBLICATION.

lix-iv'-i-ate. To leach. CLEANNESS-FILTHINESS.

lix-iv"-i-a'-tion. Leaching. LIQUEFACTION-VOLATILIZATION.

lix-iv'-i-um. A solution of alkaline salts. LIQUEFACTION-VOLATILIZATION.

lla'-ma. A South-American ruminant. CONVEYER.

lla'-no. A flat, treeless plain. GULF-PLAIN.

lo. Behold. ASTONISHMENT-EXPECTANCE, HEED-DISREGARD.

load. To lade; to encumber; to make heavy; a burden; a customary weight; a grievous mental burden. CONTENTS-RECEIVER, ENTIRETY-DEFICIENCY, ESTABLISHMENT-REMOVAL, EXCESS-LACK, HEAVINESS-LIGHTNESS, MAGNITUDE-SMALLNESS, OBSTRUCTION-HELP, PLEASURABLENESS-PAINFULNESS, PLEASURE-PAIN, STORE, WELFARE-MISFORTUNE; **load the memory,** REMEMBRANCE-FORGETFULNESS; **load with,** OBSTRUCTION-HELP; **load with reproaches,** APPROVAL-DISAPPROVAL; **prime and load,** PREPARATION-NONPREPARATION; **take off a load of care,** ALLEVIATION-AGGRAVATION.

loaf. To lounge; a shaped mass of bread or cake. ACTIVITY-INDOLENCE, GREATNESS-LITTLENESS.

loaf'-er. An idle man; a vagrant. ACTIVITY-INDOLENCE, GOOD MAN-BAD MAN, WAYFARER-SEAFARER.

loam. A sort of earth. OCEAN-LAND.

loan. Something lent. LOAN-BORROWING.

LOAN—BORROWING.

Accommodation. The act of furnishing with something needed or desired.

Advance. The act of furnishing beforehand or on credit.

Feneration. The act of lending money on interest.

Investment. The lending or laying out of money where it is secure and yields profit.

Lending, etc. The act of loaning. See *Verbs.*

Loan. Something furnished to another on condition that it will be returned itself in an equivalent of its kind.

Mortgage, etc. A conveyance of property, on condition, as security for a debt, to become void on payment of the debt. See SECURITY.

LOAN—*Nouns of Agent, etc.*

Lender. One who lends.

Money-lender. One whose business is to lend money at interest.

Mont de piété [F.]. A pawnshop.

My uncle's. A pawnbroker's.

Pawnbroker. One engaged in the business of lending money on interest, on the security of personal property pledged in pawn.

Pawnshop. The place of business of a pawnbroker.

Usurer. One who loans money at an exorbitant or illegal rate.

LOAN—*Verbs.*

Accommodate. To furnish with something needed or desired.

Advance. To furnish on credit or beforehand.

Demise. To grant or bestow by will; give.

Entrust. To give to another with confidence in his fidelity.

Invest. To place money so that it will be safe and yield profit

Lease. To grant the temporary possession of lands or the like for rent

Lend. To give to another upon condition of receiving the same again or its equivalent.

Lend on security. To lend on the assurance that it will be paid.

Let. To put to hire or rent.

Pawn, etc. To give as a pledge or security that borrowed money will be repaid. See SECURITY.

Borrowed plumes. A dressing out in something not one's own.

Borrowing. The act of receiving from another on trust, with a promise of returning or giving something of equal value.

Plagiarism, etc. To take from the works of another and give out as one's own. See THEFT.

Pledging. To engage for by promise.

Replevin. A personal action to recover possession of goods wrongfully held or detained.

BORROWING—*Verbs.*

Borrow. To receive something of another on trust with the intention of paying him back.

Borrow of Peter to pay Paul. To borrow of one person to pay what one owes another.

Desume. To borrow.

Farm. To lease or let for an equivalent.

Fly a kite. To raise money or sustain one's credit by means of mercantile papers whose value is fictitious.

Hire. To procure for temporary use by paying for this use.

Hire by the hour. ⎫
Hire by the mile. ⎬ To borrow for a certain time.
Hire by the year. ⎭

Raise money. To procure or manage to get money.

Raise the wind. To procure ready money.

Rent. To procure by paying for the temporary possession of.

Replevy. To get back property which has been wrongfully detained.

Run into debt, etc. To enter into debt. See CREDIT-DEBT.

Take a demise. To take the transfer or conveyance of an estate in fee for life or a number of years.

Take a lease. To take a contract for a letting.

Take by the hour. ⎫
Take by the mile. ⎬ To borrow for a fixed time.
Take by the year. ⎭

Take up money. To borrow money.

BORROWING—*Phrase.*

Borgen macht Sorgen [G.]. Borrowing makes sorrow.

LOAN—Verbs—*Continued.*

Place out to interest.
Put out to interest. } To invest money where it will yield interest.

Sett. To let, as houses or lands.
Underlet. To lease at second hand.

Loan—*Adjectives.*

Lending, etc. Giving as a loan. See *Verbs.*
Lent, etc. Given as or pertaining to a loan. See *Verbs.*

Unborrowed, etc. Not borrowed. See Loan-Borrowing.

Loan—*Adverbs.*

In advance. Beforehand; on credit.

On loan.
On security. } Loaned.

---

loathe. To abhor; to abominate. Desire-Distaste, Love-Hate, Palatableness-Unpalatableness.

loath'-ful. Hating. Pleasurableness-Painfulness.

loath'-ing. Aversion; disgust. Desire-Distaste, Entertainment-Weariness, Love-Hate.

loath'-some. Producing loathing; detestable. Desire-Distaste, Palatableness-Unpalatableness, Pleasurableness-Painfulness.

loaves. Plural of loaf. **Loaves and fishes,** Affluence-Penury, Gain-Loss, Welfare-Misfortune.

lob. A beggar; *in lobspound,* held playfully between the legs or feet. Release-Restraint.

lob'-by. A hall, vestibule, or corridor. Contents-Receiver, Way.

lob'-by-ist. One who tries to influence legislators so as to procure certain pet laws or enactments. Manager.

lobe. A projecting part. Anatomy, Whole-Part.

lob'-ule. A small lobe. Whole-Part.

lo'-cal. Pertaining to place. Extension-District, Position; **local habitation,** Dweller-Habitation, Establishment-Removal.

lo-cal'-i-ty. A definite spot. Extension-Place, Position.

lo''-cal-i-za'-tion. Act of localizing. Establishment-Removal.

lo'-cal-ize. To assign a definite place to. Establishment-Removal.

lo'-cate. To settle. Establishment-Removal.

lo-ca'-tion. Place; the act of placing. Establishment-Removal.

loch. A lake. Gulf-Plain.

Loch'-a-ber ax. A kind of Scotch battle-ax. Weapon.

loci, genus [L.] (lo'-sai, ji'-nus). Guardian deity of a place. Security-Insecurity.

lock. A device for fastening a door, etc.; the barrier which confines water in a canal; a lockup; a tress; to join immovably. Connective, Movement-Rest, Obstruction-Help, Release-Prison, Smoothness-Roughness, Union-Disunion, Watercourse-Airpipe; **dead lock,** Movement-Rest; **in the lockup,** Justification-Charge; **lock hospital,** Remedy-Bane; **lock out,** Reprisal-Resistance; **lock the stable door,** Opportuneness-Unsuitableness, Skill-Unskilfulness, Usefulness-Uselessness; **lock up,** Enlightenment-Secrecy, Release-Restraint; **under lock and key,** Keeper-Prisoner, Release-Restraint, Security-Insecurity.

lock'-er. A receptacle that may be locked. Contents-Receiver.

lock'-et. A small ornamental case. Embellishment-Disfigurement.

lock'-jaw''. Contraction of the jaw-muscles, stopping mastication. Health-Sickness.

lock'-smith''. A lock-maker or repairer. Agent.

lock'-up. A prison. Release-Guard.

lock'-weir''. The weir of a lock. Watercourse-Airpipe.

loco, in [L.] (lo'-co, in). In its place. Harmony-Discord, Position, Propriety-Impropriety.

lo''-co-fo'-co. A friction match; an old section of the Democratic party. Association, Combustible.

lo''-co-mo'-tion. Movement from place to place. Movement-Rest.

lo''-co-mo'-tive. Having power to move; a self-propelling steam-engine. Conveyer, Traveling-Navigation.

locos y niños dicen la verdad [Sp.] (lo'-cos î nin-yos' dith-en' la ver-dad'). Children and fools speak the truth. Mind-Imbecility, Sage-Fool, Truth-Error.

loc'-u-lar. Having loculi or cells. Contents-Receiver.

locum tenens [L.] (lo'-cum tî'-nenz). Holding the place; a substitute; a representative. Commutation-Permutation, Dweller-Habitation, Representative.

locus penitentiæ [L.] (lo'-cus pen-i-ten'-shi-î). Place for, chance of, repentance. Justification-Charge, Pardon-Revenge, Repentance-Obduracy.

locus standi [L.] (lo'-cus stan'-dai). Standing-place. Pretext, Reputation-Discredit, Suspension-Support.

lo'-cust. Figuratively, a prodigal; an evil-doer. Benefactor-Evildoer, Extravagance-Avarice; **swarm like locusts,** Multiplicity-Paucity.

lo-cu'-tion. Phraseology. Speech-Inarticulateness.

lode'. A metal-bearing vein. Store.

lode'-star. A guiding star. Attraction-Repulsion, Management, Sign.

lode'-stone. Magnetic iron ore; any attraction. Attraction-Repulsion, Electricity, Motive-Caprice.

lodge. A rude hut; local subdivision of a society; to entertain; to harbor. Dweller-Habitation, Establishment-Removal, Presence-Absence; **lodge a complaint,** Justification-Charge.

lodg'-er. One who lodges or lives in lodgings. Dweller-Habitation, Holder.

lodg'-ing. Place of temporary abode. Contents-Receiver, Dweller-Habitation.

lodg'-ment. State of being lodged. Establishment-Removal.

loess. Deposit of loam. Geology.

loft. An attic; any upper floor. Contents-Receiver, Top-Bottom.

loft'-i-ness. State of being lofty Force-Weakness, Height-Lowness.

loft'-y. Very high; sublime; dignified; haughty. Force-Weakness, Height-Lowness, Presumption-Servility, Selfrespect-Humbleness, Unselfishness-Selfishness.

log. A piece of timber; a record-book; a device for showing the speed of a vessel. Combustible, Mark-Obliteration, Swiftness-Slowness.

log'-a-rithm. A mathematical quantity. Number.

log'-ger-head''. A blockhead. Sage-Fool; **at loggerheads,** Strife-Peace, Variance-Accord.

log'-gia. Gallery. Architecture.

log'-ic. The science of correct thinking. Nature-Art, Ratiocination-Casuistry.

log'-ic-al. Characterized by clear reasoning. Ratiocination-Instinct.

lo-gi'-cian. An expert reasoner. Ratiocination-Casuistry.

log′–line″. A line measured in equal parts used in paying out a log. Swiftness-Slowness.

log-og′-ra-phy. The art of reporting speeches in long hand. Writing-Printing.

log′-o-griph. A word-riddle. Tidings-Mystery.

log-om′-a-chy. A strife about words; a wordy contest; a game of word-matching. Conversation-Monologue, Ratiocination-Casuistry, Strife-Peace.

log-om′-e-ter. A logarithmic scale. Numbering.

log″-o-met′-ric. Referring to a logometer. Number.

Log′-os. The divine creative Word. Divinity.

log′–roll″-er. One who rolls logs. Manager.

log′–roll″-ing. A political combination. Antagonism-Concurrence.

log′-wood″. A Central-American tree used in making dye. Color-Achromatism.

loin. A part of the body. Anteriority-Posteriority; **gird up one's loins,** Preparation-Nonpreparation, Strength-Weakness.

loisir, impromptu fait à [F.] (lwɑ-zir′, an·-pron′p-tü′ fêt ɑ). A premeditated impromptu. Preparation-Nonpreparation.

loi′-ter. To consume idly; to delay; to linger. Activity-Indolence, Earliness-Lateness, Swiftness-Slowness.

Lo′-ki. An evil giant god. Jove-Fiend.

loll. To waste in idleness; to recline languidly. Activity-Indolence, Erectness-Flatness, Suspension-Support.

lol′-ly-pop. Bonbons. Sweetness-Acidity.

Lom′-bard Street. A street in. London, the business place of bankers and brokers. Labor-Capital; **Lombard Street to a china orange,** Likelihood-Unlikelihood.

lone. Solitary. Solitude-Company.

lone′-li-ness. The state of being lonely. Sociability-Privacy.

lone′-ly. Alone; sequestered from company. Sociability-Privacy, Solitude-Company.

lone′-some. Solitary and depressed. Sociability-Privacy.

long. Extended; lasting; diffuse; dealer in stocks. Labor-Capital, Lastingness-Transientness, Length-Shortness, Terseness-Prolixity; **draw the long bow,** Gull-Hyperbole; **go to one's long account,** Life-Death; **long ago,** Future-Past; **long and the short,** Terseness-Prolixity, Whole-Part; **long boat,** Conveyance-Vessel; **long clothes,** Infant-Veteran; **long distance telephone,** Electricity; **long drawn out,** Terseness-Prolixity; **long duration,** Lastingness-Transientness; **long expected,** Expectation-Surprise; **long face,** Contentedness-Discontentment, Lightheartedness-Dejection; **long for,** Desire-Distaste; **long-headed,** Sagacity-Incapacity; **long life to,** Approval-Disapproval, Reputation-Discredit; **long-lived,** Lastingness-Transientness; **long odds,** Difficulty-Facility, Likelihood-Unlikelihood, Rationale-Luck; **long pending,** Lastingness-Transientness; **long pull and strong pull,** Push-Pull; **long range,** Remoteness-Nearness; **long run,** Medium, Terseness-Prolixity, Whole-Part; **long sea,** River-Wind; **long-sighted,** Clearness-Obscurity, Sagacity-Incapacity, Sight-Dimsightedness; **long since,** Future-Past; **long spun,** Terseness-Prolixity; **long standing,** Lastingness-Transientness, Novelty-Antiquity; **long suffering,** Compassion-Ruthlessness, Excitability-Inexcitability; **long time,** Lastingness-Transientness; **long-winded,** Lastingness-Transientness, Talkativeness-Taciturnity, Terseness-Prolixity; **make a long arm,** Taking-Restitution, Toil-Relaxation; **take a long breath,** Alleviation-Aggravation, Weariness-Refreshment.

lon″-ga-nim′-i-ty. Endurance. Excitability-Inexcitability, Pardon-Revenge.

longe absit [L.] (lon′-jî ab′-sit). Far be it. Petition-Expostulation, Readiness-Reluctance.

lon-ge′-val. Long-lived. Lastingness-Transientness.

lon-gev′-i-ty. Tendency to live long. Infancy-Age, Lastingness-Transientness.

long′–head″. A wise man. Sage-Fool.

long′-ing. Craving. Desire-Distaste; **longing lingering look behind,** Contentedness-Regret.

lon-gin′-qui-ty. Greatness of extent. Remoteness-Nearness.

lon′-gi-tude. Length; distance east or west of a standard meridian. Length-Shortness, Mensuration, Position.

lon″-gi-tu′-di-nal. Consisting in length. Length-Shortness.

lon″-gi-tu′-di-nal-ly. Lengthwise. Length-Shortness.

long me′-ter. Kind of stanza. Rhetoric.

longo intervallo [L.] (lon′-go in-ter-val′-lo). With a long interval. Continuity-Interruption, Interspace-Contact, Lastingness-Transientness, Remoteness-Nearness, Variation.

long′–shore″-man. A stevedore; a waterman. Gentility-Commonalty, Wayfarer-Seafarer.

long′-some. Extended in length. Length-Shortness, Terseness-Prolixity.

long′-suf′-fer-ance. Patience. Excitability-Inexcitability.

loo. A game of cards. Entertainment-Weariness.

loo′-by. A lubber; a bungler. Adept-Bungler, Gentility-Commonalty, Sage-Fool.

look. To direct the gaze; to consider; to seem; to watch; a glance. Appearance-Disappearance, Heed-Disregard, Magnitude-Smallness, Sight-Blindness; **look about,** Carefulness-Neglect, Investigation-Answer; **look after,** Carefulness-Neglect, Heed-Disregard, Management; **look ahead,** Prevision; **look another way,** Sight-Blindness; **look back,** Future-Past, Remembrance-Forgetfulness; **look before one leaps,** Recklessness-Caution; **look beyond,** Prevision; **look black,** Approval-Disapproval, Contentedness-Discontentment, Emotion, Lightheartedness-Dejection; **look blue,** Approval-Disapproval, Contentedness-Discontentment, Emotion, Lightheartedness-Dejection; **look down upon,** Regard-Scorn; **look foolish,** Reputation-Discredit; **look for,** Expectation-Surprise, Investigation-Answer; **look forward to,** Expectation-Surprise, Future-Past, Prevision; **look here,** Heed-Disregard; **look in the face,** Bravery-Cowardice, Craft-Artlessness, Selfrespect-Humbleness; **look into,** Heed-Disregard, Investigation-Answer; **look like,** Appearance-Disappearance, Likeness-Unlikeness; **look on,** Onlooker, Presence-Absence, Sight-Blindness; **look out,** Appearance-Disappearance, Carefulness-Carelessness, Expectation-Surprise, Investigation-Answer, Occupation, Purpose-Luck; **look over,** Heed-Disregard, Investigation-Answer; **look round,** Investigation-Answer; **look sharp,** Activity-Indolence; **look through,** Investigation-Answer; **look to,** Carefulness-Carelessness, Duty-Dereliction; **look up,** Costliness-Cheapness, Sanguineness-Hopelessness, Sociability-Privacy, Welfare-Misfortune; **look upon as,** Faith-Misgiving; **look up to,** Approval-Disapproval, Regard-Disrespect, Reputation-Discredit.

look′-er-on″. A spectator. Onlooker.

look′-ing-glass″. A mirror. Optical Instruments.

loom. To shine; to appear gradually into a prominent position; a weaving machine; a coming dimly into view. DIMNESS, OCCURRENCE-DESTINY, SIGHT-DIMSIGHTEDNESS, VISIBILITY-INVISIBILITY, WORKSHOP; **loom of the land,** OCEAN-LAND.

loom'-ing. The indistinct appearance of objects seen in certain states of atmosphere. DIMNESS, SIGHT-DIMSIGHTEDNESS.

loon. A dull, stupid person; a rogue. GENTILITY-COMMONALTY, GOOD MAN-BAD MAN, SAGE-FOOL.

loop. A noose; a curve of any kind; crook. CIRCLE-WINDING, CURVATION-RECTILINEARITY, MIDCOURSE-CIRCUIT.

loop'-hole". A narrow aperture used for observation, light, and firing small arms through; any opening that may be used as a means of escape. APERTURE-CLOSURE, ATTACK-DEFENSE, DESIGN, ESCAPE, PRETEXT, SIGHT-BLINDNESS.

loose. To free from; to disengage; to dismiss; to relax; unbound; slovenly; wanton; indefinite; unconnected. AIM-ABERRATION, CLEARNESS-OBSCURITY, COHESION-LOOSENESS, FORCE-WEAKNESS, LIBERTY-SUBJECTION, PURITY-IMPURITY, RATIOCINATION-CASUISTRY, RULE-LICENSE, SUSPENSION-SUPPORT, UNION-DISUNION; **at a loose end,** HURRY-LEISURE; **give a loose to,** FANCY, LEAVE-PROHIBITION, LIBERTY-SUBJECTION, MODERATION-SELF-INDULGENCE, RULE-LICENSE; **leave a loose thread,** CAREFULNESS-NEGLECT; **let loose,** RELEASE-RESTRAINT; **loose character,** PURITY-IMPURITY; **loose fish,** GOOD MAN-BAD MAN, PURITY-RAKE; **loose rein,** RULE-LICENSE; **loose sentence,** RHETORIC; **loose suggestion,** HYPOTHESIS; **loose thread,** TRUTH-ERROR; **on the loose,** PURITY-IMPURITY; **screw loose,** FAULTLESSNESS-FAULTINESS, SANENESS-LUNACY, VARIANCE-ACCORD; **take up a loose thread,** SECURITY-INSECURITY.

loos'-en. To make loose; to become loose. COHESION-LOOSENESS, RELEASE-RESTRAINT.

loose'-ness. The state of being loose. COHESION-LOOSENESS, RULE-LICENSE.

loos'-en-ing. Making loose. COHESION-LOOSENESS, RULE-LICENSE.

loot. To pillage; plunder. PLUNDER, THEFT.

lop. To shorten. LENGTH-SHORTNESS; **lop and top,** DOMESTICATION-AGRICULTURE.

lopped. Cut off. ENTIRETY-DEFICIENCY.

lop'-sid"-ed. Heavier on one side. EQUALITY-INEQUALITY.

lo-qua'-cious. Given to continual talking. TALKATIVENESS-TACITURNITY.

lo-qua'-cious-ness. Talkativeness. TALKATIVENESS-TACITURNITY.

lo-quac'-i-ty. Talkativeness. TALKATIVENESS-TACITURNITY.

loquendi, cacoethes [L.] (lo-quen'-dai, cac"-o-i'-thîz). A passion for talking. TALKATIVENESS-TACITURNITY.

loquendi, jus et norma [L.] (lo-quen'-dai, jus et nor'-ma). Law and rule of speech. GRAMMAR-SOLECISM.

loquendi usus [L.] (lo-quen'-dai yu'-sus). Usage in speaking. SPEECH-INARTICULATENESS.

lor'-cha. A vessel rigged like a Chinese junk. CONVEYANCE-VESSEL.

lord. A ruler; a nobleman; to rule. CHIEF-UNDERLING, GENTILITY-COMMONALTY, TYRANNY-ANARCHY; **lord chancellor,** JUDGE; **lord it over,** PRESUMPTION-OBSEQUIOUSNESS, RULE-LICENSE, TYRANNY-ANARCHY; **lord justices,** JUDGE, TRIBUNAL; **lord lieutenant,** JUDICATURE; **lord of the creation,** HUMANITY; **lord of the manor,** HOLDER.

Lord. Jehovah; Jesus Christ. DIVINITY; **Lord of lords,** DIVINITY; **Lord's Day,** TOIL-RELAXATION;

Lord's Prayer, WORSHIP-IDOLATRY; **Lord's Supper,** CEREMONIAL; **Lord's Table,** FANE; **O Lord,** WORSHIP-IDOLATRY; **the Lord knows,** KNOWLEDGE-IGNORANCE.

lord'-ling. A little lord. GENTILITY-COMMONALTY.

lord'-ly. Lofty; noble; imperious. REPUTATION-DISCREDIT, SELFRESPECT-HUMBLENESS.

Lord May'-or. The mayor of London. CHIEF-UNDERLING; **Lord Mayor's show,** SOLEMNIZATION.

lord'-ship. The state or quality of a lord; a seigniory; supremacy; the title of address of lords and judges. JUDGE, PROPERTY, RULE-LICENSE, TITLE.

lore. Erudition. KNOWLEDGE-IGNORANCE.

lorette [F.] (lo-ret'). A member of the demi-monde. PURITY-RAKE.

Lo"-ret-tine'. A member of a Kentucky order of nuns. MINISTRY-LAITY.

lor"-gnette'. A pair of eye-glasses on a long handle. OPTICAL INSTRUMENTS.

lor"-i-ca'-ted. Encrusted. COVER-LINING.

lor"-i-ca'-tion. A defensive covering. ATTACK-DEFENSE.

lorn. Forsaken. SOCIABILITY-PRIVACY.

lose. To part from; to let slip; to be separated from; to waste; to miss. CLEARNESS-OBSCURITY, GAIN-LOSS, REMEMBRANCE-FORGETFULNESS, SUCCESS-FAILURE; **lose an opportunity,** OPPORTUNENESS-UNSUITABLENESS; **lose breath,** WEARINESS-REFRESHMENT; **lose caste,** REPUTATION-DISCREDIT, UPRIGHTNESS-DISHONESTY; **lose color,** COLOR-ACHROMATISM; **lose flesh,** ENLARGEMENT-DIMINUTION; **lose ground,** ADVANCE-RETROGRESSION, SUCCESS-FAILURE, SWIFTNESS-SLOWNESS, TRANSCURSION-SHORTCOMING; **lose heart,** LIGHTHEARTEDNESS-DEJECTION; **lose hope,** SANGUINENESS-HOPELESSNESS; **lose labor,** SUCCESS-FAILURE; **lose no time,** ACTIVITY-INDOLENCE, HURRY-LEISURE; **lose one's balance,** SUCCESS-FAILURE; **lose one's cunning,** SKILL-UNSKILFULNESS; **lose oneself,** CERTAINTY-DOUBT, TRUTH-ERROR; **lose one's head,** CERTAINTY-DOUBT, SKILL-UNSKILFULNESS; **lose one's heart,** LOVE-HATE; **lose one's life,** LIFE-DEATH; **lose one's reason,** SANENESS-LUNACY; **lose one's temper,** EXCITABILITY-INEXCITABILITY, FAVORITE-ANGER, POLITENESS-IMPOLITENESS; **lose one's way,** AIM-ABERRATION, DIFFICULTY-FACILITY, SKILL-UNSKILFULNESS; **lose sight of,** APPEARANCE-DISAPPEARANCE, CAREFULNESS-NEGLECT, COMPLETION-NONCOMPLETION, REMEMBRANCE-FORGETFULNESS, SIGHT-BLINDNESS, VISIBILITY-INVISIBILITY; **lose the clue,** CERTAINTY-DOUBT, CLEARNESS-OBSCURITY; **lose the day,** SUCCESS-FAILURE; **lose time,** ACTIVITY-INDOLENCE; **no time to lose,** HURRY-LEISURE.

lo'-sel. Inclined to idleness and waste. EXTRAVAGANCE-AVARICE.

los'-ing. That brings loss. GAIN-LOSS; **losing game,** SUCCESS-FAILURE, WELFARE-MISFORTUNE.

loss. Privation; that which is lost; state of being lost; waste; destruction. ADJUNCT-DECREMENT, BETTERMENT-DETERIORATION, GAIN-LOSS, GOOD-EVIL, LIFE-DEATH, PROVISION-WASTE; **at a loss,** CERTAINTY-DOUBT, DETERMINATION-VACILLATION, DIFFICULTY-FACILITY; **at a loss for,** DESIRE-DISTASTE; **loss of fortune,** AFFLUENCE-PENURY; **loss of health,** HEALTH-SICKNESS; **loss of life,** LIFE-DEATH; **loss of right,** DUENESS-UNDUENESS; **loss of strength,** STRENGTH-WEAKNESS.

lost. Not to be found or recovered; missed; ruined physically, morally, or spiritually; bewildered; not won, gained, used, or enjoyed. APPEARANCE-DISAPPEARANCE, CERTAINTY-DOUBT, ENTITY-NONENTITY, EXCITATION, GAIN-LOSS, HEED-DISREGARD, LIGHTHEARTEDNESS-DEJECTION, PLEASURE-PAIN, PRESENCE-ABSENCE, REPENTANCE-OBDURACY, SUCCESS-

FAILURE; **lost in admiration,** APPROVAL-DISAP-PROVAL; **lost in astonishment,** ASTONISHMENT-EX-PECTANCE; **lost in iniquity,** VIRTUE-VICE; **lost in thought,** HEED-DISREGARD, REFLECTION-VACANCY; **lost labor,** USEFULNESS-USELESSNESS; **lost to shame,** PRESUMPTION-OBSEQUIOUSNESS, UPRIGHTNESS-DIS-HONESTY; **lost to sight,** APPEARANCE-DISAPPEARANCE; **lost to virtue,** VIRTUE-VICE.

lot. Anything used in determining by chance; share, chance, or fortune; fate; allotment; a collection or parcel of things taken together. ASSIGNMENT, CON-DITION-SITUATION, GATHERING-SCATTERING, PUR-POSE-LUCK, QUANTITY-MEASURE, VOLITION-OBLIGA-TION; **be one's lot,** OCCURRENCE-DESTINY; **cast in one's lot with,** CHOICE-NEUTRALITY, DUTY-DERELIC-TION; **cast lots,** PURPOSE-LUCK; **fall to one's lot,** RATIONALE-LUCK; **in lots,** WHOLE-PART; **where one's lot is cast,** DWELLER-HABITATION.

loth. Loath. DESIRE-DISTASTE, READINESS-RELUC-TANCE.

Lo-tha'-ri-o. A gay deceiver; libertine. [Rowe, *The Fair Penitent.*] LOVE-HATE, PURITY-RAKE.

lo'-tion. A liquid preparation for healing or cleansing the skin. CLEANNESS-FILTHINESS, REMEDY-BANE, WATER-AIR.

lots. Great plenty. ENOUGH, MULTIPLICITY-PAUCITY.

lot'-ter-y. Allotment; any chance distribution of matter. ENTERTAINMENT-WEARINESS, RATIONALE-LUCK; **put into a lottery,** PURPOSE-LUCK.

lot'-to. Game of chance. ENTERTAINMENT-WEARINESS.

lo'-tus. An ornament. ARCHITECTURE.

lo'-tus-eat''-er. One of the Lotophagi; a voluptuary. ACTIVITY-INDOLENCE.

loud'-ly. In a loud manner. LOUDNESS-FAINTNESS.

loud'-ness. The state of being loud; clamor. LOUD-NESS-FAINTNESS.

LOUDNESS—FAINTNESS.

Blast. A loud or penetrating sound.
Bombilation. A buzzing or humming sound.
Boom. A deep, reverberating sound.
Charivari [F.]. A mock serenade of discordant music.
Clang. }
Clangor. } A sharp, ringing sound.
Clatter. A repeated rattling noise.
Din. A loud, stunning noise.
Fanfare [F.]. A flourish of trumpets.
Flourish of trumpets. A call sounded by trumpets.
Fracas. Noisy disturbance.
Hubbub. A confused noise, as of many voices.
Hullaballoo. A loud and confused noise. See CRY.
Larum. A noise giving warning of danger.
Loudness. The quality of producing a great sound.
Loud noise. A great noise.
Noise. Sound of any kind; noxious.
Peal. A loud musical sounding.
Power. Loudness of sound.
Racket. A confused clattering noise.
Resonance. The quality of prolonging sound. See RESONANCE.
Roar. A deep, prolonged cry.
Swell. Increase of intensity of sound.
Thunder. Any loud, rumbling roar.
Tintamarre [F.]. A hideous and confused noise.
Trumpet-blast. The sound made by blowing a trumpet.
Uproar. Violent disturbance and noise.
Vociferation. A shouting with a loud noise.

LOUDNESS—*Associated Nouns.*

Artillery. Guns borne on wheeled carriages.
Cannon. A heavy mounted gun.
Fanfare [F.]. A flourish or call sounded by trumpets.
Flourish of trumpets. A call sounded by trumpets.
Lungs. The organs of respiration; figuratively, sound.
Stentor. A person of uncommonly strong voice. [Homer, *Iliad.*]

LOUDNESS—*Verbs.*

Bellow, etc. To make a hollow, loud noise. See CRY-ULULATION.
Be loud, etc. To be making a great sound. See *Adjectives.*
Boom. To make a hollow sound or roar.
Clang. To sound in a sharp and ringing manner
Deafen. To deprive of the ability to hear.
Din in the ear. To cause a ringing in the ears.
Faire le diable à quatre [F.]. To play the devil.
Fill the air. To make the air full of sound.
Fulminate. To make a sudden, loud noise, as thunder; " fulmined over Greece." [Milton, *Paradise Regained,* iv, 270.]
Make one's windows shake. To make a great noise.
Peal. To cause to ring or sound.
Pierce the ears. }
Pierce the head. } To affect with a sharp, shrill sound.
Rend the air. ⎫
Rend the ears. ⎪
Rend the head. ⎬ To make a great noise.
Rend the skies. ⎭
Resound, etc. To sound loudly. See RESONANCE.
Ring in the ear. To cause a ringing sound.
Roar. To make a loud, confused sound.
Shout, etc. To utter a sudden, loud noise. See CRY.
Speak up. To speak loud or unreservedly.

Faintness. The state of being scarcely perceptible to the ear.
Faint sound. A low, almost imperceptible sound.

FAINTNESS—*Denotations.*

Breath. The act of respiration; something resembling breath, as a gentle sound or movement.
Hoarseness etc. Roughness or harshness of the voice, as from a cold or fatigue. See *Adjectives.*
Hum. A low monotonous buzzing or whirring sound.
Murmur. A low sound continually repeated.
Raucity. The quality of being rough of sound.
Still small voice. Conscience.
Susurration. A soft murmuring or whispering sound.
Tinkle. A succession of slight, sharp, clear sounds.
Underbreath. A low whispered sound.
Undertone. The tone of a subdued voice.
Whisper. A low, soft, sibilant voice.

FAINTNESS—*Verbs.*

Babble. To make a constant murmuring noise, as a little brook.
Breathe. To utter softly.
Float on the ear. To come to the ear gently.
Flow. To glide gently or smoothly.
Gurgle. To make a noise as a small stream on a stony bottom.
Hum. To make a dull, prolonged, nasal sound.
Melt on the ear. To strike with a low, pleasing sound.
Murmur. To make a low, continued noise.
Mutter, etc. To utter words with a low voice and compressed lips. See SPEECH-INARTICULATENESS.
Purl. To make a murmuring sound.
Ripple. To give forth a low murmuring sound, as water flowing over a rough bottom.
Steal on the ear. To come with a low, gentle sound.
Tinkle. To sound in a sharp, clear manner.
Whisper. To speak softly or under the breath.

FAINTNESS—*Adjectives*

Dulcet, etc. Sweet to the ear; melodious. See MELODY.
Dull. Low; not clear.
Faint. Scarcely audible.
Floating. Sounding quietly and gently.
Flowing, etc. Sounding smoothly. See *Verbs*
Gentle. Low; soft; not loud.
Hoarse. Having a rough or grating voice.
Husky. Rough in tone.
Inaudible. Incapable of being heard.
Just audible. Almost inaudible.
Liquid. Flowing smoothly.
Low. Not loud.
Muffled. Wrapped with something that renders sound inaudible.
Purling. Softly murmuring.
Scarcely audible. Hardly audible.
Soft. Gentle; not loud.
Soothing. Tending to calm or console.
Stifled. Deadened.
Whispered, etc. Lowly spoken. See *Verbs.*

FAINTNESS—*Adverbs.*

À la sourdine [F.]. In the manner of a low-stop on the organ
Aside. So as not to be overheard.

LOUDNESS—FAINTNESS— *Continued.*

LOUDNESS—Verbs—*Continued*

Split the ears. }
Split the head. } To affect with a piercing sound.
Stun. To overwhelm with sound.
Swell. To increase the sound of.
Thunder. To make a loud roaring noise.
Thunder in the ear. To affect with a deep heavy sound.

LOUDNESS—*Adjectives.*

Big sounding. Having a pompous sound.
Clamorous, etc. Noisy; loud; turbulent. See Cry.
Clangorous. Sharp or harsh in sound.
Deafening, etc. Very loud in sound. See *Verbs.*
Deep. Low in sound.
Ear-deafening. }
Ear-rending. } Loud; sharp in sound.
Ear-splitting. }
Enough to wake the dead. }
Enough to wake the seven sleepers. } Loud to an excessive degree.
Full. Abundant in quantity.
High-sounding. Noisy.
Loud. Making a great sound.
Multisonous. Sounding much.
Noisy. Making a loud sound.
Obstreperous. Loud; clamorous.
Piercing. Shrill.
Powerful. Having a full, loud sound.

FAINTNESS—Adverbs—*Continued.*

Between the teeth. In a whisper.
Inaudibly, etc. In a manner not to be heard. See *Adjectives.*
In a whisper. In a low voice.
Out of earshot. Out of the distance at which words can be heard.
Piano [It.]. In a soft manner.
Pianissimo [It.]. In a very low and soft manner.
Sotto voce [It.]. In a low voice.
With bated breath. With lowered voice.

LOUDNESS—Adjectives—*Continued.*

Rackety. Making a tumultuous noise.
Shrill, etc. Sharp and piercing in sound. See Cacophony.
Sonorous. Loud-sounding.
Stentophonic. }
Stentorian. } Extremely loud.
Thundering. Loud and full in sound.
Trumpet-tongued. Having a tongue as vociferous as a trumpet.
Uproarious. Making a great noise or tumult.

LOUDNESS—*Adverbs.*

Aloud. Loudly.
At the top of one's voice. As loudly as possible.
In full cry. Loudly.
Loudly, etc. In an audible or noisy manner. See *Adjectives.*
Lustily. In a vigorous, strong manner.

---

lough. A lake. Gulf-Plain.
louis d'or [F.] (lu-î′ dor). A French gold coin. Money.
lounge. To loaf. Activity-Indolence.
loun′-ger. An idler. Activity-Indolence.
loup-garou [F.] (lu″-ga-ru′). A werewolf. Jove-Fiend.
loups, hurler avec les [F.] (lu, hür-lê′ a-vec′ lê). To howl with the wolves. Variance-Accord.
louse. A parasitic insect. Cleanness-Filthiness.
lout. An awkward fellow; clown. Gentility-Commonalty, Sage-Fool.
lout′-ish. Clumsy. Gentility-Commonalty.
lou′-ver. A louver-window; a chimney-flue. Watercourse-Airpipe; **louver-window,** Architecture.

lov′-a-ble. Amiable. Love-Hate.
love. To be strongly attached to; to be in love with; devoted affection for; a sweetheart. Amity-Hostility, Approval-Disapproval, Charitableness-Malevolence, Desire-Distaste, Favorite-Anger, Love-Hate, Pleasure-Pain, Politeness-Impoliteness; **abode of love,** Love-Hate; **God's love,** Charitableness-Malevolence; **labor of love,** Costliness-Cheapness, Entertainment-Weariness, Readiness-Reluctance, Unselfishness-Selfishness; **love-affair,** Love-Hate; **love of country,** Humanitarianism-Misanthropy; **make love,** Endearment; **no love lost,** Variance-Accord; **not for love or money,** Costliness-Cheapness, Excess-Lack.

LOVE—HATE.

Admiration. An emotion of pleasure and approbation in view of anything excellent, beautiful, or sublime.
Adoration. Love in the highest degree.
Affection. That kind, constant, and tender feeling that goes out from one person to another.
Amor [L.]. Love.
Attachment. The state of being bound by strong and lasting ties.
Attractiveness. The power of pleasing, winning, or engaging.
Benevolence. Love to mankind. See Charitableness
Brotherly love. Love of the nature of love toward a brother.
Devotion. The state of feeling in which a person gives himself up entirely to some person or cause.
Dilection. A loving.
Enchantment. The state of being filled with delight by anything.
Enthusiasm. Ardent zeal for a person or cause.
Eros [Gr.]. Same as Cupid. God of love.
Fellow-feeling. A feeling of interest in the affairs of another.
Fervor. Ardor or intensity of feeling.
Flame. The passion of love.
Fondness, etc. Strong liking or preference; extravagant affection. See *Adjectives.*
Free love. The doctrine or custom of unrestrained choice in sexual relations.
Gallantry. Courtesy and deferential attention shown to women
Gyneolatry. Worship of woman.
Idolatry. Inordinate love or admiration.
Inclination, etc. Liking for one thing rather than another.
Infatuation. Extravagant or unreasonable love.
Liking. Inclination due to some attractive quality.
Love. The personal, strong, and tender affection between the sexes.
Maternal love. The love of a mother for her children.
Passion. Intense affection.
Plighted love. Engagement to be married.
Popularity. The character or condition of possessing the confidence or favor of the people.

Abomination. Extreme hatred.
Acrimony. A biting sharpness produced by a bitter spirit.
Alienation. Estrangement; a withdrawal of the affections.
Animosity, etc. Spiritedness in hatred. See Favorite-Anger.
Antipathy. Aversion to; repugnance.
Aversion. A fixed and habitual dislike not necessarily strong.
Bitterness. }
Bitterness of feeling. } A feeling of enmity, hate, or severe resentment.
Coolness. Indifference; the state of manifesting dislike
Detestation. The act of hating or disliking extremely.
Disaffection. Unfriendliness; dislike.
Disfavor. The state of being not in favor.
Dudgeon. Anger; resentment; ill will.
Enemy. One who is no friend; antagonist. See Friend-Foe.
Enmity, etc. Animosity; continued hatred. See Amity-Hostility.
Estrangement. The state of having ceased to be friendly towards.
Grudge. Hatred; secret enmity; ill will.
Gynephobia. Dislike of woman.
Hate. Strong aversion for a person and a desire to injure him.
Hatred. Extreme dislike; hate; ill will; aversion.
Implacability, etc. Irreconcilable anger. See Pardon-Vindictiveness.
Ingrate. An ungrateful person.
Malevolence. Evil disposition towards another.
Malice, etc. A natural desire to injure others without cause. See Charitableness-Malevolence.
Object of execration. Anything greatly hated.
Object of hatred. Anything that causes great displeasure.
Odium. Hatred; the quality which produces hatred.
Pique. A quick sense of resentment, usually not permanent.
Reprobate. To disapprove with strong dislike.
Repugnance, etc. That from which a man instinctively draws back. See Desire-Distaste.
Source of annoyance. Anything that causes trouble. See Painfulness.

LOVE—HATE—*Continued.*

Rapture. Act or expression of excessive delight.
Regard. That feeling which springs from any thing that excites esteem, affection, or the like.
Storge [Gr.]. Maternal love.
Sympathy. A feeling of compassion for another's sufferings or evils
Tenderness. Love.
Tender passion. Love.
The old story. Love.
Transport of love. The passion of love which carries one beyond the bounds of moderation.
Yearning. A strong emotion of longing or desire, especially with tenderness.

LOVE—*Associated Nouns.*

Abode of love. A lovers' meeting-place.
Agapemone [Gr.]. The abode of love.
Amour [F.]. A love intrigue.
Courtship. The attention of a man to a woman whom he desires to marry. See BLANDISHMENT.
Cupid. The god of love; figuratively, love.
Love-affair. All that happens in a love experience with a particular person.
Love-story. A story recounting experiences of love.
Love-suit. Courtship.
Love-tale. A story expressing love.
Love-token. A gift in token of love.
Myrtle. A plant considered sacred to Venus, goddess of love.
True-lover's knot. A knot tied in pledge of loyalty and love.
Venus. The goddess of love; figuratively, love.

LOVE—*Nouns of Agent*

Admirer. One who has special regard for another.
Adorer. A lover.
Affianced. A person engaged to be married.
Amoret. A sweetheart; a wanton.
Amoretto [It.]. A lover.
Amoroso [It.]. In a soft, amatory style. Music.
Amourette [F.]. A pretty love-affair.
Angel. A sweetheart, as a heavenly messenger.
Beau. An escort or lover, as a thing of beauty.
Betrothed. A person engaged to be married.
Captive. One enslaved by beauty, love, passion, or the like.
Cara sponsa [It.]. Dear wife.
Caro sponso [It.]. Dear husband.
Cavalière servente [It]. A gallant.
Cicisbeo [It.]. A professed gallant of a married woman
Cocotte. A mistress; used in a bad sense.
Coquette. A woman who endeavors to attract admiration and advances in love, merely to gratify her vanity.
Darling. One who is tenderly beloved; a little dear.
Duck. A darling.
Dulcinea [Sp.]. A sweetheart; a lady-love.
Enamorata. A lady sweetheart.
Familist. A member of an old sect who held that religion consists in love, not faith.
Favorite, etc. One admired by another. See FAVORITE.
Fiancé [F.]. A betrothed person
Flirt. One who makes love for mere amusement.
Follower. An admirer.
Gallant. A man who pays court and attention to women.
Goddess. A lady-love regarded as divine.
Heart. A sweetheart.
Idol. A person beloved.
Inamorata. A female in love; enamored
Inamorato. A male in love; enamored
Lady-love. A woman who is beloved.
Leman. A sweetheart; a mistress.
Lothario. A character in Rowe's *The Fair Penitent,* represented as a libertine and seducer.
Love. A person beloved.
Lover. A person in love.
Pair of turtle-doves. Two lovers
Paramour. One who is immorally a lover or a mistress.
Suitor. One who seeks a woman's hand in marriage; a wooer.
Swain. A rustic lover.
Sweetheart. One who is particularly loved by or as a lover.
True love. A sweetheart.
Venus. Goddess of love and beauty

Umbrage. Jealousy; resentment at being overshadowed.
Unpopularity. The state or quality of being disliked.

HATE—*Figurative Nouns*

Bad blood. Ill feeling.
Bête noire [F.]. A black beast; an annoyance.
Bitter pill. Anything disagreeable.
Ill blood. Hatred.
Vials of hate. Great hatred.

HATE—*Verbs.*

Abhor. To feel excessive repugnance towards.
Abominate. To hate exceedingly; detest.
Alienate. To estrange; make unfriendly.
Bear a grudge. ⎫
Bear malice. ⎬ To have hatred for. See CHARITABLENESS-MALEV-OLENCE.
Bear spleen. ⎭
Be hateful, etc. To be unfriendly to; be adverse. See *Adjectives*
Conceive an aversion. To form or receive an aversion.
Contemptible. Deserving of scorn.
Despicable. Contemptible, mean.
Despise. To scorn, contemn, disdain.
Detest. To testify against; abhor; abominate.
Disrelish, etc. To feel disgust for. See DESIRE-DISTASTE.
Envenom. To poison; render hateful.
Estrange. To make unfriendly.
Excite hatred. To arouse hatred.
Execrate. To detest completely; curse.
Hate. To dislike and desire to injure.
Hold in abomination.
Horrify, etc. To fill with horror or dread. See PLEASURABLENESS-PAINFULNESS.
Incense. To arouse; make angry against.
Irritate. To annoy; arouse to a slight angry feeling.
Loathe. To feel disgust at; abhor.
Owe a grudge. To hate.
Provoke hatred, etc. See *Nouns*
Recoil at. To withdraw from, as anything repugnant.
Repel. To repulse.
Revolt against. To shrink from.
Rile. To vex; anger.
Scowl. To frown at; look angry. See POLITENESS-IMPOLITENESS.
Set against. To oppose.
Set by the ears. To cause strife between.
Shrink from. To recoil from.
Shudder at. To shake with horror or aversion.
Sow dissension. To cause quarrel or strife.
Stink in the nostrils. To be disgusting or abhorrent.
View with horror.

HATE—*Adjectives.*

Abhorrent. Repugnant; detestable.
Abominable. Detestable; loathsome.
At daggers drawn. At enmity.
Averse from. Repugnant; disliking.
Bitter, etc. Sharp; harsh; stern. See POLITENESS-IMPOLITENESS.
Crossed in love. Thwarted in love.
Disgusting, etc. Sickening; repugnant. See PLEASURABLENESS-PAINFULNESS.
Disliked, etc. Not liked. See DESIRE-DISTASTE.
Forsaken. Abandoned; left alone.
Hateful. Malevolent; abhorrent.
Hating, etc. Loathing; detesting. See *Verbs*
Implacable. Inexorable; unrelenting.
Insulting. Abusive; contemptuous.
Invidious. Hateful; likely to incur hatred or ill will
Irritating. Exasperating; annoying.
Jilted. Discarded after having been encouraged as a lover.
Love-lorn. Forsaken by one's love.
Malicious, etc. Exercising malice; malevolent. See CHARITABLE-NESS-MALEVOLENCE.
Not on speaking terms. Mutually angry. See AMITY-HOSTILITY.
Obnoxious. Hateful; offensive; odious.
Odious. Deserving hate; detestable; disgusting.
Offensive. Causing anger to a certain degree; displeasing.
Provoking. Arousing resentment; irritating.
Rejected. Discarded; cast away from.
Repulsive. Inclined to repel; unattractive.
Set against. Opposed.
Shocking. Horrible; disgusting.
Spiteful. Filled with mean and petty hatred.
Unbeloved. Not loved.
Uncared for. Displeasing.
Undeplored. Not mourned for.

LOVE—HATE—*Continued.*

LOVE—*Verbs*

Adore. To love in the highest degree.
Affect. To love or regard with affection.
Aimer éperdument [F.]. To love to distraction.
Attach. To win the heart of.
Attract. To draw, allure, influence by moral or other qualities
Bear love to. To have love for.
Become enamored, etc. To fall in love. See *Adjectives.*
Be in love with, etc. See *Adjectives.*
Be partial to. To be inclined in favor of.
Be wedded to. To be very much attached to; be married to
Bewitch. To charm; fascinate.
Burn. To be in a state of strong passion or desire.
Captivate. To enthrall the affections.
Care for. To have affection for.
Charm. To fascinate; please very much.
Cherish. To hold dear; care for.
Cherish a love for. To have a love for.
Cling to. To adhere closely to.
Curry favor with. To gain favor by means of flattery.
Desire, etc. To long for eagerly and anxiously. See DESIRE
Dote on. ⎫
Dote upon. ⎬ To be foolishly or excessively fond of.
Enamor. To inflame with love.
Endear. To make more beloved.
Engage the affections. ⎫
Engage the heart. ⎬ To win one's love.
Engage the love. ⎭
Enrapture. To transport with pleasure.
Entertain a love for. To love.
Excite love. To arouse love.
Faire l'aimable [F.]. To do the amiable.
Fall in love with. Become enamored.
Fancy. To be pleased with.
Fascinate. To please very much; charm.
Feast one's eyes on. Look on with pleasure.
Flirt. To play at courtship.
Gain the affections. ⎫
Gain the heart. ⎬ To win the love of.
Gain the love. ⎭
Get into favor. Ingratiate oneself.
Harbor a love for. ⎫ To love.
Have a love for. ⎬
Hold dear. Cherish.
Hug. To embrace closely.
Idolize. To love to excess.
Ingratiate oneself. To bring oneself into favor with.
Insinuate oneself. To obtain favor by means of flattery or stealth
Like. To be pleased with.
Look sweet upon. Make love to.
Lose one's heart. To fall in love.
Love. To regard with affection; be fond of.
Love to distraction. To love excessively.
Make much of. Cherish.
Pay one's court to. To woo; court.
Pet. To fondle; indulge.
Philander. To take liberties with a woman.
Prize. To value; regard highly.
Propitiate. To render favorable.
Regard. To hold in esteem.
Revere. To honor; venerate.
Secure the affections. ⎫
Secure the heart. ⎬ To gain the love of.
Secure the love. ⎭
Seduce. To induce to surrender chastity.
Set one's affections on. To fall in love with.
Set one's cap at. To make love to, try to attract the attention of.
Sympathize with. To have a common feeling with
Take a fancy to. To fancy.
Take an interest in. To be attracted to.
Take the fancy of. To please.
Take to. To like
Turn the head. To infatuate.
Win the affections. ⎫
Win the heart. ⎬ To win one's love.
Win the love. ⎭
Wind round the heart. To fascinate
Worm oneself. To insinuate.

LOVE—*Adjectives.*

Adorable. Lovable; worthy of adoration.
Affectionate. Having great love.

HATE—ADJECTIVES—*Continued.*

Unendeared. Not loved.
Unlamented. Uncared for.
Unloved. Not attached to.
Unmourned. Not cared for.
Unvalued. Not wanted.

HATE—*Phrases.*

Acerrima proximorum odia [L.]. Fiercest is the hatred of those nearest kin. [Tacitus, *History*, iv, 26.]
Odium medicum [L.]. Mutual hatred among physicians.
Odium orthoepicum [L.]. Hatred among orthoepists.

LOVE—ADJECTIVES—*Continued.*

After one's fancy. ⎫
After one's mind. ⎬ Pleasing to one.
After one's own heart. ⎪
After one's taste. ⎭
Amatory. Pertaining to love.
Amiable. Lovable; pleasing.
Amorous. Inclined to love.
Ardent. Passionate; affectionate; eager.
Attached to. Bound to; won over to by moral or other qualities.
Attractive. Pleasing; alluring; having moral qualities that please.
Beloved. Dear to the heart; loved.
Bewitching. Charming; fascinating.
Bitten. Smitten with love.
Captivating. Charming; very pleasing; alluring
Charmed, etc. Fascinated; delighted. See *Verbs.*
Charming, etc. Pleasing; fascinating. See *Verbs.*
Congenial. Allied in nature.
Darling. Very dearly beloved; little dear.
Dear. Much esteemed; beloved.
Dear as the apple of one's eye. ⎫ Very dear.
Dearly beloved. ⎬
Devoted. Given up to; attached to; consecrated to.
Enamored. Deeply in love; captivated.
Enchanting. Charming; pleasing; agreeable.
Engaging. Tending to draw the affection; attractive.
Erotic. Pertaining to love; amatory.
Fascinating. Pleasing; enchanting.
Favorite. Best beloved; most cared for.
Fond of. Tender; affectionate.
In love. Under the influence of love.
In one's good graces, etc. In one's favor. See AMITY.
Interesting. Exciting the emotions or holding the attention.
Like an angel. Lovely.
Little. Small, slight, slender; a term of endearment.
Lovable. Worthy of love.
Loved, etc. Attracted to by some pleasing quality.
Lovely. Possessing qualities that are worthy of love.
Love-sick. Ill with amorous desire.
Loving. Affectionate.
Motherly. Like a mother in manner and action.
Nearest to one's heart. Dearest; most cared for.
Over head and ears in love. Very much in love; infatuated.
Passionate. Moved to strong feeling, as love, desire, or the like.
Pet. Fondled; indulged.
Popular. Well liked; beloved by the people.
Precious. Valuable; dear.
Rapturous. Ravishing; transporting.
Seductive. Tending to lead astray; enticing.
Smitten. Affected with love; enamored.
Struck with. Impressed by.
Sweet. Mild; kind; pleasing.
Sweet upon. In love with.
Sympathetic. Having common feelings or compassion.
Taken with. Pleased with; in love with.
Tender. Gentle; soft.
To one's fancy. ⎫
To one's mind. ⎬ Pleasing.
To one's own heart. ⎪
To one's taste. ⎭
Uxorious. Too much devoted to one's wife.
Wedded to. Much attached to.
Well-beloved. Much or dearly beloved.
Winning. Attracting; charming.

LOVE—Continued.

LOVE—Phrases.

Amantes, amentes [L.]. Lovers, lunatics. [Terence, *Andrea*, I, iii, 13.]

Aut amat aut odit mulier; nihil est tertium [L.]. A woman loves or she hates; no third course exists for her. [Publius Syrus, 6.]

Froides mains, chaudes amours [F.]. Cold hands, warm heart.

Gage d'amour [F.]. Pledge of love.

Ich habe genossen das irdische Glück, ich habe gelebt und geliebet [G.]. I have enjoyed the pleasure of this earth, I have lived and loved. [Schiller, *Wallenstein*, ii, 2.]

Omnia vincit amor [L.]. Love conquers all things. [Virgil, *Eclogues*, x, 69.]

Quem Jupiter vult perdere, dementat prius [L.]. Whom Jupiter wishes to destroy, he first makes mad.

Serus in cælum redeas [L.]. Late return thou to the skies. [Horace, *Odes*, I, ii, 45.]

loved. Cherished. LOVE-HATE.

love'-knot". A knot tied in pledge of love. SIGN.

love'-let"-ter. A letter expressing love for the receiver. BLANDISHMENT.

love'-li-ness. The state of being lovely. PLEASURABLE-NESS-PAINFULNESS.

love'-lorn". Pining for a lover. LOVE-HATE.

love'-ly. Attractive; lovable. BEAUTY-UGLINESS, LOVE-HATE, PLEASURABLENESS-PAINFULNESS, SENSUALITY-SUFFERING.

love'-mak"-ing. Courtship. BLANDISHMENT.

love'-pot". One fond of drink. TEETOTALISM-INTEMPERANCE.

lov'-er. A warm admirer; a devoted friend. DESIRE-DISTASTE, FAVORITE-ANGER, LOVE-HATE, POLITENESS-IMPOLITENESS.

love'-sick". Languishing with love. BLANDISHMENT, LOVE-HATE.

love'-stor"-y. A story of love. BLANDISHMENT, LOVE-HATE.

love'-tale". A tale of love. BLANDISHMENT.

love'-tok"-en. A gift in token of love. BLANDISHMENT, LOVE-HATE, POLITENESS-IMPOLITENESS.

lov'-ing. Affectionate. LOVE-HATE.

lov'-ing-cup". A parting-cup. POLITENESS-IMPOLITENESS, SOCIABILITY-PRIVACY.

lov'-ing-kind"-ness. Tender regard. CHARITABLENESS-MALEVOLENCE.

low. (1) Not high or tall; deep; below usual level; soft; humble; vulgar. COSTLINESS-CHEAPNESS, EXCESS-LACK, GENTILITY-COMMONALTY, HEIGHT-LOWNESS, LOUDNESS-FAINTNESS, MAGNITUDE-SMALLNESS, REPUTATION-DISCREDIT, TASTE-VULGARITY; **at a low ebb**, BETTERMENT-DETERIORATION, ELEVATION-DEPRESSION, MAGNITUDE-SMALLNESS, PROVISION-WASTE, SUPREMACY-SUBORDINACY; **bring low**, ELEVATION-DEPRESSION; **low comedy**, ACTING; **low condition**, GENTILITY-COMMONALTY; **low fellow**, GENTILITY-COMMONALTY; **low life**, GENTILITY-COMMONALTY, TASTE-VULGARITY; **low neighborhood**, CITY-COUNTRY; **low note**, RESONANCE-NONRESONANCE; **low origin**, GENTILITY-COMMONALTY; **low price**, COSTLINESS-CHEAPNESS; **low spirits**, LIGHTHEARTEDNESS-DEJECTION; **low tide**, HEIGHT-LOWNESS; **low tone**, VOCALIZATION-MUTENESS, WHITENESS-BLACKNESS; **low water**, AFFLUENCE-PENURY, DAMPNESS-DRYNESS, EXCESS-LACK, HEIGHT-LOWNESS.

low. (2) To moo. CRY-ULULATION.

low'-born". Of humble birth. GENTILITY-COMMONALTY.

low'-er. (1) To lessen or bring down; to humble. ELEVATION-DEPRESSION, HEIGHT-LOWNESS, INCREASE-DECREASE, SUPREMACY-SUBORDINACY; **lower one's flag**, YIELDING; **lower one's note**, SELFRESPECT-HUMBLENESS; **lower orders**, GENTILITY-COMMONALTY.

low'-er. (2) To look angry or sullen. DIMNESS, FAVORITE-ANGER, FAVORITE-MOROSENESS, LIGHT-DARKNESS, LIGHTHEARTEDNESS-DEJECTION, PROPHECY.

low'-er-ing. (1) Bringing down. ELEVATION-DEPRESSION.

low'-er-ing. (2) Threatening. LIGHTHEARTEDNESS-DEJECTION.

low'-est. Least. SUPREMACY-SUBORDINACY.

low'-lands". Lands low with respect to surrounding country. HEIGHT-LOWNESS.

low'-li-hood. A lowly state. SELFRESPECT-HUMILITY.

low'-ly. Humble. SELFRESPECT-HUMBLENESS.

low'-mind"-ed. Base; vulgar. GENTILITY-COMMONALTY, UPRIGHTNESS-DISHONESTY.

lown. A loon; dolt. GOOD MAN-BAD MAN, SAGE-FOOL.

low'-ness. The quality or state of being low. HEIGHT-LOWNESS, SELFRESPECT-HUMBLENESS, TASTE-VULGARITY.

loy'-al. Constant and faithful in relations implying trust. INSUBORDINATION-OBEDIENCE, OBSERVANCE-NONOBSERVANCE, PATRIOTISM-TREASON, UPRIGHTNESS-DISHONESTY.

loyal en tout [F.] (lwa-yal' an· tu). Loyal in everything. OBSERVANCE-NONOBSERVANCE, UPRIGHTNESS-DISHONESTY.

loy'-al-ty. Devoted allegiance. INSUBORDINATION-OBEDIENCE, PATRIOTISM-TREASON, UPRIGHTNESS-DISHONESTY.

loyauté m'oblige [F.] (lwa-yo-tê' mo-blizh'). Loyalty binds me. DUTY-DERELICTION, UPRIGHTNESS-DISHONESTY.

loz'-enge. A diamond-shaped figure. ANGULARITY.

loz'-enged. Diamond-shaped. **Lozenged window**, ARCHITECTURE.

L. s. d. Abbreviations for pounds, shillings, pence (*libræ, solidi, denarii*). MONEY.

lub'-bard. A lubber; lubberly. ACTIVITY-INDOLENCE, ADEPT-BUNGLER.

lub'-ber. A lout; awkward, ungainly fellow. ACTIVITY-INDOLENCE, ADEPT-BUNGLER, SAGE-FOOL, SCHOLAR-DUNCE.

lub'-ber-ly. Clumsy; clumsily. GREATNESS-LITTLENESS, SKILL-UNSKILFULNESS.

lu'-bri-cate. To lessen friction. DIFFICULTY-FACILITY, FRICTION-LUBRICATION, SMOOTHNESS-ROUGHNESS.

lu'-bri-ca"-ted. Made smooth or slippery. FRICTION-LUBRICATION.

lu"-bri-ca'-tion. The act of lubricating; lubricant. FRICTION-LUBRICATION, SMOOTHNESS-ROUGHNESS.

lu-bric'-i-tate. To make smooth or slippery. FRICTION-LUBRICATION.

lu-bric'-i-ty. Smoothness; slipperiness; unchastity. PULPINESS-OILINESS, PURITY-IMPURITY, SMOOTHNESS-ROUGHNESS.

lu'-bri-cous. Lubric. SMOOTHNESS-ROUGHNESS.

lu'-cent. Luminous. LIGHT-DARKNESS.

lu'-cid. Sane; easily understood; resplendent; translucent. CLEARNESS-OBSCURITY, DIAPHANEITY-OPAQUENESS, LIGHT-DARKNESS, PERSPICUITY-OBSCURITY; **lucid interval**, SANENESS-LUNACY.

lucidus ordo [L.] (lu'-sid-us or'-do). Lucid arrangement. REGULARITY-IRREGULARITY.

Lu'-ci-fer. Satan. ANGEL-SATAN.

lu'-ci-fer. A match. COMBUSTIBILITY.

lu-cif'-er-ous. Giving light. LIGHT-DARKNESS.

lu-cif'-ic. Producing light. LIGHT-DARKNESS.

lu-cid'-i-ty. The quality of being lucid. LIGHT-DARKNESS.

lu-cim'-e-ter. A photometer. OPTICAL INSTRUMENTS.

luck. Chance; good fortune. PURPOSE-LUCK, RATIONALE-LUCK, WELFARE-MISFORTUNE.

luck'-less. Unfortunate. WELFARE-MISFORTUNE.

luck'-y. Fortunate; auspicious. OPPORTUNENESS-UN-SUITABLENESS, SUCCESS-FAILURE, WELFARE-MIS-FORTUNE.

lu'-cra-tive. Highly profitable. GAIN-LOSS.

lu'-cre. Money; profit; greed. AFFLUENCE-PENURY, GAIN-LOSS.

Lu'-cre"-ti-a. A Roman heroine, whose violation and suicide caused the overthrow of the monarchy. PURITY-IMPURITY.

lucri causa [L.] (lu'-crai cau'-sa). For the sake of gain. GAIN-LOSS.

luc-ta'-tion. Struggle for success. STRIFE-PEACE.

lu"-cu-bra'-tion. Close and earnest meditation or study. REFLECTION-VACANCY.

lu'-cu-lent. Brilliant. LIGHT-DARKNESS.

lucus a non lucendo [L.] (lu'-cus ê non lu-sen'-do). A grove (so named) because it is not light; an inconsequence. LIKENESS-UNLIKENESS, NAME-MISNOMER.

lud. Lord. O lud! JUBILATION-LAMENTATION.

ludere cum sacris [L.] (lu'-der-î cum sê'-cris). To sport with things sacred. GODLINESS-UNGODLINESS, USE-MISUSE.

Lud'-dite. One of a band in England who forcibly opposed labor-saving machines. ASSOCIATION, TYRANNY-ANARCHY.

lu-dib'-ri-ous. Ridiculous. ENTERTAINMENT-WEARINESS.

lu'-di-crous. Laughable. SOCIETY-LUDICROUSNESS.

luff. To steer closer to the wind. TRAVELING-NAVIGATION.

lug. To drag; the ear. HEARING-DEAFNESS, PUSH-PULL.

lug'-gage. Baggage. PROPERTY.

lug'-ger. A small vessel. CONVEYANCE-VESSEL.

lu-gu'-bri-ous. Doleful. LIGHTHEARTEDNESS-DEJECTION.

luke'-warm. Moderately warm; not ardent; indifferent. HEAT-COLD, INDIFFERENCE, SENSITIVENESS-APATHY.

lull. To soothe to rest; to compose; to cease. ACTIVITY-INDOLENCE, DISCONTINUANCE-CONTINUANCE, MOVEMENT-REST, SOUND-SILENCE, TURBULENCE-CALMNESS; **lull to sleep,** MOVEMENT-REST.

lull'-a-by. A cradle-song; a berceuse. ACTIVITY-INDOLENCE, ALLEVIATION-AGGRAVATION, MUSIC, POETRY-PROSE, TURBULENCE-CALMNESS.

lum'-bar. Pertaining to the loins. ANATOMY, ANTERIORITY-POSTERIORITY.

lum'-ber. To fill with useless material; to impede; to heap in disorder; to move heavily. OBSTRUCTION-HELP, REGULARITY-IRREGULARITY, STORE, SWIFTNESS-SLOWNESS, USEFULNESS-USELESSNESS.

lum'-ber-ing. Clumsily huge. BEAUTY-UGLINESS, PROPRIETY-IMPROPRIETY.

lum'-ber-room". A chamber for useless articles. CONTENTS-RECEIVER.

lum-bric'-i-form. Like an earthworm. ROUNDNESS.

lu'-mi-na-ry. A source of light; one who enlightens mankind. LUMINARY-SHADE, SAGE-FOOL.

LUMINARY—SHADE.

Aldebaran. A bright star of the first magnitude.

Apollo. The god of the sun; figuratively, the sun.

Aurora. The rising light of the morning.

Aurora borealis. The northern daybreak; a luminous meteoric phenomenon, visible only at night, and supposed to be of electrical origin.

Blazing star. A comet.

Canicula. The Dog Star; the largest and brightest of the fixed stars.

Constellation. A cluster or group of fixed stars.

Dog Star. The brightest of fixed stars.

Étoile du Nord [F.]. The North Star.

Fata morgana [It.]. A mirage by which distant objects appear inverted, displaced, or multiplied.

Firedrake. A fiery meteor.

Firefly. A luminous winged insect.

Flame, etc. A stream of burning vapor or gas. See HEAT.

Fork lightning. Lightning which appears in long narrow streamers with short turns or angles.

Friar's lantern. The *ignis fatuus* or will-o'-the-wisp.

Galaxy. The luminous tract or belt, which is seen at night stretching across the heavens.

Glowworm. A wingless insect which emits light.

Ignis fatuus [L.]. A meteor-like light appearing by night over marshy places.

Jack o' lantern. An *ignis fatuus.*

Light. The source of illumination. Hail, holy light, offspring of heaven first born, or of the Eternal coeternal beam, Bright effluence of bright essence increate. [Milton, *Paradise Lost,* iii, 1.] See LIGHT.

Lightning. A discharge of atmospheric electricity accompanied by a vivid flash of light.

Luminary. Any body that gives light.

Meteor. A transient luminous body seen in the atmosphere.

Northern light. The aurora borealis.

Orb. A sun, planet, or star.

Phœbus. The sun god; the sun.

Phosphorescence. Quality of being luminous without sensible heat.

Phosphorus. The morning star.

Scintilla [L.]. A spark.

Sheet lightning. A diffused glow of electric light flashing out from the clouds, and illuminating their outlines.

Sirius. The Dog Star.

Spark. A small particle of fire or ignited substance.

Star. One of the innumerable luminous bodies seen in the heavens, other than the sun, moon, and comets.

Shade. Comparative obscurity caused by some intervening object cutting the rays of light.

Shadow, etc. Shade within confined limits. See LIGHT-DARKNESS.

Umbrage. Shade.

SHADE—*Nouns of Agency.*

Awning, etc. A cover of canvas to shelter from the sun's rays. See COVER.

Blind. Something used to keep out light.

Cloud. A collection of visible vapor suspended in the upper atmosphere; anything that serves to cast a shadow.

Curtain. A cloth screen intended to darken.

Gathering of clouds. A collection of clouds which causes shade.

Glade. A mantle or mask.

Mist. Anything which dims or darkens, as a cloud of vapor.

Parasol. A small umbrella used for protection against the sun's rays.

Screen. Anything that cuts off the light, and darkens.

Shutter. A cover for a window or other aperture.

Sunshade. A screen to keep off the sun's rays.

Umbrella. A shade, formed of silk or cloth stretched on elastic rods which are fastened to a stick.

Veil. A screen of gauze or other diaphanous material, to hide or protect the face.

SHADE—*Verbs.*

Cast a shadow, etc. To darken. See LIGHT-DARKNESS.

Close a shutter. To pull shut a shutter.

Draw a curtain. To cause a curtain to slide or move so as to obscure.

Put up a shutter. To close up with a shutter.

Veil, etc. To obscure with a veil. See *Nouns.*

SHADE—*Adjectives.*

Shady. Overspread with shade.

Umbrageous. Shady.

LUMINARY—*Continued.*

Summer lightning. Extensive flashes of electric light without thunder, seen at the close of a hot day.

Sun. The luminous orb, the light of which constitutes day, and its absence night.

Will-o'-the-wisp. The *ignis fatuus.*

Zodiacal light. A luminous tract of the sky, lying near the ecliptic.

LUMINARY—*Artificial Lights.*

Argand. A lamp producing a clear, strong light, named after its inventor.

LUMINARY—ARTIFICIAL LIGHTS—*Continued.*

Bougie [F.]. A wax candle.
Brand. A burning piece of wood.
Bull's-eye. A lantern, with a thick glass lens on one side for concentrating the light on any object.
Burner. That part of a lamp, gas-fixture, etc., where the flame is produced.
Candelabrum. A large candlestick, having several branches.
Candle. A slender body of tallow, wax, etc., containing a wick of loosely twisted threads, and used to furnish light.
Candlestick. An instrument for holding a candle.
Chandelier. A candlestick, lamp-stand, or gas-fixture, having several branches.
Dark lantern. A lantern with an opening which may be closed to conceal the light.
Duplex. A double light.
Electric light. A light produced by an electric flash.
Firework. A device for producing a striking display of light
Fizgig. A kind of firework.
Flambeau [F.]. A flaming torch.
Gas. A complex mixture of marsh gas, olefiant gas, and hydrogen, artificially produced by the destructive distillation of coal, etc.
Gaselier. A frame of several gas-burners.
Gaslight. The light produced by burning gas.
Girandole [F.]. A chandelier.

Lamp. A light-producing instrument.
Lantern. Something enclosing a light and protecting it from the wind.
Lanthorn. A lantern.
Lighthouse. A building or tower with a powerful light on top, erected at the entrance of a port to serve as a guide to ships. See SIGN.
Limelight. An intense light produced by the incandescence of lime in burning oxygen and hydrogen gases.
Link. A torch made of tow and pitch.
Luster. A chandelier or candlestick of an ornamental character.
Moderator. A lamp in which fluid pressure, regulated by a piston and spring, serves to supply the wick with oil.
Oil. Any combustible substance, like olive-oil. See PULPINESS-OILINESS.
Pyrotechnics. Fireworks.
Rocket. An artificial firework.
Rushlight. A small feeble light.
Sconce. The circular tube in a candlestick into which the candle is inserted.
Taper. A small wax candle.
Torch. A light formed of some combustible substance, as of resinous wood.
Wick. A loosely twisted braided cord, used in candles and oil lamps

LUMINARY—*Verbs.*

Illuminate, etc. To make light. See LIGHT.

LUMINARY—*Adjectives.*

Phosphorescent. Shining with a faint light.
Phosphoric. Pertaining to phosphorus.

Radiant, etc. Emitting rays of light. See LIGHT.
Self-luminous. Possessing the power to emit light.

lu″-mi-nif′-er-ous. Producing light. LIGHT-DARKNESS.
lu″-mi-nos′-i-ty. The quality of being luminous. LIGHT-DARKNESS.
lu′-mi-nous. Shining; perspicuous. CLEARNESS-OBSCURITY, LIGHT-DARKNESS.
lu′-mi-nous-ness. The quality of being full of light. LIGHT-DARKNESS.
lump. To heap indiscriminately; a shapeless mass; aggregate; a protuberance. CONVEXITY-CONCAVITY, GATHERING-SCATTERING, GREATNESS-SMALLNESS, HEAVINESS-LIGHTNESS, SOLIDITY-RARITY, WHOLE-PART; in the lump, WHOLE-PART; lump of affectation, SOCIETY-AFFECTATION; lump together, COMPOSITION-RESOLUTION, GATHERING-SCATTERING, UNION-DISUNION.
lump′-ish. Like a lump; inert; stupid. ACTIVITY-INDOLENCE, BEAUTY-UGLINESS, GREATNESS-LITTLENESS, HEAVINESS-LIGHTNESS, SOLIDITY-RARITY.
lu′-na-cy. Mental unsoundness. SANENESS-LUNACY.
lu′-nar. Pertaining to the moon. UNIVERSE; lunar caustic, HEATING-COOLING.
lu′-na-tic. Insane; crazy. SANENESS-LUNACY, SANENESS-MANIAC.
lunch. A light meal. NUTRIMENT-EXCRETION.
lunch′-eon. Lunch. NUTRIMENT-EXCRETION.
lune avec les dents, prendre la [F.] (lün a-vec′ lê dan·, pran·dr la). To take the moon by the horns, *i. e.,* to attempt the impossible. MIGHT-IMPOTENCE, POSSIBILITY-IMPOSSIBILITY.
lung. Organ of respiration. ANATOMY.
lunge. To plunge forward; a long thrust with sword or bayonet. ATTACK-DEFENSE, IMPETUS-REACTION.
lungs. Organs for aerial respiration; a loud-voiced fellow. CRY-ULULATION, LOUDNESS-FAINTNESS, RIVER-WIND, VOCALIZATION-MUTENESS.
lu′-ni-form. Crescent-shaped. CURVATION-RECTILINEARITY.
lu′-nu-lar. Having the form of a small crescent. CURVATION-RECTILINEARITY.
lu′-nule. A crescent-shaped part or marking. CURVATION-RECTILINEARITY.
lu-pa′-nar. A brothel. PURITY-IMPURITY.

lupus in fabula [L.] (lu′-pus in fab′-yu-la) The wolf in the story. TRUTHFULNESS-FRAUD.
lurch. A sudden swaying or rolling to one side; an irregular swinging motion; to defeat. ASCENT-DESCENT, PARALLELISM-INCLINATION, SUCCESS-FAILURE, VIBRATION; leave in the lurch, QUEST-ABANDONMENT, TRANSCURSION-SHORTCOMING, TRUTHFULNESS-FRAUD; left in the lurch, SUCCESS-FAILURE.
lure. To entice; to allure. MOTIVE-CAPRICE, TRUTHFULNESS-FRAUD.
lu′-rid. Giving ghastly or dull-red light; gloomy; dismal. DIMNESS, LIGHT-DARKNESS, REDNESS-GREENNESS.
lurk. To lie hidden; to lie unnoticed. ENLIGHTENMENT-SECRECY, MANIFESTATION-LATENCY, VISIBILITY-INVISIBILITY.
lurk′-ing-place″. A hiding-place. EXPOSURE-HIDING-PLACE.
lus′-cious. Rich, sweet, and delicious. PALATABLENESS-UNPALATABLENESS, PLEASURABLENESS-PAINFULNESS, SWEETNESS-ACIDITY.
lush. Fresh and luxuriant; intoxicating drink. ANIMALITY-VEGETABILITY, SOBRIETY-INTEMPERANCE, SWEETNESS-ACIDITY.
lush′-y. Tipsy. TEETOTALISM-INTEMPERANCE.
lusk. Lazy. ACTIVITY-INDOLENCE.
lu′-so-ry. Pertaining to play. ENTERTAINMENT-WEARINESS.
lust. Vehement desire; concupiscence. DESIRE-DISTASTE, PURITY-IMPURITY.
lus′-ter. Refulgence; gloss; renown; a branched candelabrum. LIGHT-DARKNESS, LUMINARY-SHADE, REPUTATION-DISCREDIT.
lust′-ful. Having sensual desire. PURITY-IMPURITY.
lust′-i-hood. State of being lusty. GREATNESS-LITTLENESS, STRENGTH-WEAKNESS.
lust′-i-ly. Strongly; stoutly. LOUDNESS-FAINTNESS, TOIL-RELAXATION; cry out lustily, JUBILATION-LAMENTATION.
lust′-less. Spiritless. MIGHT-IMPOTENCE.
lus-tra′-tion. Act of purification and expiation. ATONEMENT, CLEANNESS-FILTHINESS.
lus′-trous. Shining. LIGHT-DARKNESS.

lus'-trum. A period of five years. PERIOD-PROGRESS.

lust'-y. Able-bodied. GREATNESS-LITTLENESS.

lusus naturæ [L.] (lu'-sus na-tiu'-rî). A monstrosity; a freak of nature. CONVENTIONALITY-UNCONVENTIONALITY.

lute. A musical instrument; a soft adhesive mixture. COHESION-LOOSENESS, CONNECTIVE, MUSICAL INSTRUMENTS.

lu'-te-ous. Of a golden-yellowish color. YELLOWNESS-PURPLE.

Lu'-ther-an. Pertaining to Luther or the Church founded by him. ORTHODOXY-HETERODOXY

lux-a'-tion. Displacement of an organ. UNION-DISUNION.

lux-u'-ri-ance. Vigorous growth; excessive abundance. ENOUGH, FERTILITY-STERILITY.

lux-u'-ri-ant. . Abundant or superabundant in growth. ENOUGH, FERTILITY-STERILITY.

lux-ur'-i-ate. To take inordinate pleasure. **Luxuriate in,** PLEASURE-PAIN, SENSUALITY-SUFFERING.

lux-u'-ri-ous. Pertaining to luxury; supplied with luxuries. MODERATION-VOLUPTUARY, PLEASURABLENESS-PAINFULNESS, SENSUALITY-SUFFERING.

lux-u'-ri-ous-ness. State of being luxurious. MODERATION-SELFINDULGENCE.

lux'-u-ry. Free indulgence in pleasures; voluptuousness; any article that ministers to pleasure; a dainty. EXCESS-LACK, MODERATION-VOLUPTUARY, PLEASURE-PAIN, SENSUALITY-SUFFERING.

ly-can'-thrope. One afflicted with lycanthropy. JOVE-FIEND.

ly-can'-thro-py. A mania in which a person imagines himself to be a wolf. SANENESS-LUNACY.

Ly-ce'-um. The grove in which Aristotle taught; a school; a literary association. SCHOOL.

Lyd-ford law. Better **Lidford law;** punishment without trial. LAW-LAWLESSNESS.

Lyd'-i-an mea'-sure. A kind of soft, slow music of ancient time. MUSIC.

ly'-ing. Prostrate; mendacious; false; untruthfulness. ERECTNESS-FLATNESS, TRUTHFULNESS-FALSEHOOD, UPRIGHTNESS-DISHONESTY.

Ly-king'. The Le-king, the book of rites, the foundation of Chinese manners. REVELATION-PSEUDO-REVELATION.

lymph. A transparent, colorless, alkaline fluid of the body. DIAPHANEITY-OPAQUENESS, LIQUID-GAS, WATER-AIR.

lym-phat'-ic. Pertaining to lymph; absorbent. WATER-AIR.

lynch. To punish by lynch-law. RECOMPENSE-PUNITION; **lynch law,** LAW-LAWLESSNESS, RULE-LICENSE.

lynch'-law''. Punishment without trial. TYRANNY-ANARCHY.

lynx'-eyed''. Keen-sighted. SAGACITY-INCAPACITY, SIGHT-BLINDNESS.

lyre. A stringed musical instrument. MUSICAL INSTRUMENTS, POETRY-PROSE.

lyr'-ic. Musical and emotional. MUSIC; **lyric poetry,** POETRY-PROSE.

lyr'-ic-al. Fitted to be sung to the lyre. POETRY-PROSE.

lyr'-ist. A lyric poet. POETRY-PROSE.

lys'-sa. Hydrophobia. HEALTH-SICKNESS.

M

ma. Mother. PARENTAGE-PROGENY.

Mab. Queen of the fairies. JOVE-FIEND.

mac-ad'-am-ize. To pave with broken stones. SMOOTH-NESS-ROUGHNESS.

Ma''-caire', Ro''-bert'. A criminal. ROBBER.

mac''-a-ro'-ni. A fop. SOCIETY-DANDY.

mac''-a-ron'-ic. Confused; burlesque. ADAGE-NON-SENSE, POETRY-PROSE.

mac''-a-ron'-ics. A jumble of words. LANGUAGE, POETRY-PROSE.

mace. A war-club; a staff of office. SCEPTER, WEAPON.

mace'-bear''-er. An officer. JUDICATURE.

mac'-er-ate. Reduce to a pulp. WATER-AIR.

mac''-er-a'-tion. Softening in a liquid; making lean; mortification. ATONEMENT, AUSTERITY, CEREMONIAL, WATER-AIR.

Mac-heath'. A highwayman. ROBBER.

Ma''-chi-a-vel'-li. Florentine statesman. CRAFT-ARTLESSNESS.

Mach''-i-a-vel'-lian. Crafty. CRAFT-ARTLESSNESS, UPRIGHTNESS-DISHONESTY.

Mach''-i-a-vel'-lism. Political artifice. CRAFT-ARTLESSNESS, TRUTHFULNESS-FALSEHOOD.

mach''-i-co-la'-ted. Defended. ATTACK-DEFENSE.

mach''-i-co-la'-tion. An opening between a wall and parapet; defenses. ARCHITECTURE, ATTACK-DEFENSE, INDENTATION.

mach''-i-na'-tion. The making of a secret plan. CRAFT-ARTLESSNESS, DESIGN; **machinations of the devil,** GOOD-EVIL.

mach'-i-na''-tor. A maker of secret plans. DESIGN.

ma-chine'. A mechanical contrivance. INSTRUMENT; **be a mere machine,** LIBERTY-SUBJECTION.

ma-chin'-er-y. A complex system of appliances. INSTRUMENT.

ma-chin'-ist. A constructor of machines; a shifter of scenes. ACTING, AGENT.

mac'-i-len-cy. Leanness. BREADTH-NARROWNESS.

mac'-i-lent. Lean. BREADTH-NARROWNESS.

mack'-er-el. A pimp; variegated. PURITY-RAKE, VARIEGATION; **mackerel sky,** VARIEGATION, VISCIDITY-FOAM.

mack'-in-tosh. A water-proof garment. DRESS-UNDRESS.

mac''-ro-bi-ot'-ic. Pertaining to long life. LASTINGNESS-TRANSIENTNESS.

mac'-ro-cosm. The great world. UNIVERSE.

mac-rol'-o-gy. Superfluity of words. SIMPLICITY-FLORIDNESS.

Mac-syc'-o-phant, Sir Per'-ti-nax. A worldly man in Macklin's *Man of the World.* FLATTERER-DEFAMER, PRESUMPTION-OBSEQUIOUSNESS.

mac-ta'-tion. The killing of a sacrificial victim. DEVOTION-IDOLATRY.

macte virtute [L.] (mac'-tî vir-tiu'-tî). Proceed in virtue. APPROVAL-DISAPPROVAL.

mac'-u-la. A blotch. EMBELLISHMENT-DISFIGUREMENT.

mac'-u-late. To spot. CLEANNESS-FILTHINESS.

mac''-u-la'-tion. A making spotted; a blemish. EMBELLISHMENT-DISFIGUREMENT, VARIEGATION.

mad. Insane; angry. EXCITATION, SANENESS-LUNACY; **drive one mad,** FAVORITE-ANGER, SANENESS-LUNACY; **go mad,** EXCITABILITY-INEXCITABILITY; **mad after,** DESIRE-DISTASTE; **mad as a March hare,** SANENESS-LUNACY; **mad with rage,** FAVORITE-ANGER.

mad'-am. My lady. MALE-FEMALE.

mad'-brained''. Mentally disordered. SANENESS-LUNACY.

mad'-cap''. Reckless; given to wild follies; a rash person. EXCITABILITY-INEXCITABILITY, RECKLESSNESS-CAUTION, SANENESS-MANIAC, TURBULENCE-CALMNESS, WAG.

mad'-den. Incense. FAVORITE-ANGER, SANENESS-LUNACY.

mad'-dened. Incensed. SANENESS-LUNACY.

mad'-der. A dyeing plant. REDNESS-GREENNESS.

made. Produced. NATURE-ART; **made man,** WELFARE-MISFORTUNE; **made to one's hand,** PREPARATION-NONPREPARATION.

mad''-e-fac'-tion. A making moist. DAMPNESS-DRYNESS.

mad'-man. A lunatic. FAVORITE-ANGER, SANENESS-MANIAC.

mad'-ness. Dementia. SANENESS-LUNACY.

Ma-don'-na. The Virgin Mary. ANGEL-SATAN, GODLINESS-UNGODLINESS.

mad'-ri-gal. A shepherd's song. MUSIC, POETRY-PROSE.

Mael'-strom. A famous whirlpool. REFUGE-PITFALL, REVOLUTION-EVOLUTION, RIVER-WIND.

maestro [It.] (ma-es'-tro). A master in music. MUSIC.

mag''-a-zine'. A warehouse; a periodical. MARK-OBLITERATION, MISSIVE-PUBLICATION, STORE.

Mag'-da-len. A woman, mentioned by Luke. REPENTANCE-OBDURACY.

mage. A magician. DEVOTION-MAGICIAN.

ma-gen'-ta. A color. REDNESS-GREENNESS.

mag'-got. A whim; a worm. BIGOTRY-WHIM, DESIRE-DISTASTE, FANCY, GREATNESS-LITTLENESS; **have a maggot in the brain,** PERSISTENCE-WHIM.

mag'-got-y. Full of maggots; capricious. CLEANNESS-UNCLEANNESS, PERSISTENCE-WHIM; **maggoty-headed,** EXCITABILITY-INEXCITABILITY, SAGACITY-INCAPACITY.

Ma'-gi. The learned caste of the Medes and Persians. ORTHODOXY-HETERODOXY, SAGE-FOOL.

mag'-ic. Sorcery. DEVOTION-MAGIC; **magic lantern,** APPEARANCE-DISAPPEARANCE, ENTERTAINMENT-WEARINESS, OPTICAL INSTRUMENTS.

ma-gi'-cian. Sorcerer. DEVOTION-MAGICIAN.

ma-gilp'. An oil compound used as a vehicle for colors. PULPINESS-ROSIN.

magister ceremoniarum [L.] (ma-jis'-ter ser''-î-mo-ni-ê'-rum). Master of ceremonies. SOLEMNIZATION.

mag''-is-te'-ri-al. Pertaining to a magistrate. PRESUMPTION-OBSEQUIOUSNESS, SELFRESPECT-HUMBLENESS.

mag'-is-ter-y. A precipitate. FRIABILITY.

mag'-is-tra-cy. The office of a magistrate. JUDICATURE, RULE-LICENSE.

mag'-is-trate. An officer. CHIEF-UNDERLING, JUDGE, PRESIDENT-MEMBER.

mag'-is-tra-ture. Government. RULE-LICENSE.

magistri, jurare in verba [L.] (ma-jis'-trai, jiu-rê'-rî in ver'-ba). To swear with the words of a master. DECISION-MISJUDGMENT.

magistri, nullius jurare in verba [L.] (ma-jis'-trai, nul'-li'-us jiu-rê'-rî in ver'-ba). Not to swear in the words of any master. CREDULOUSNESS-SKEPTICISM.

mag'-ma. A crude mixture. MIXTURE-HOMOGENEITY.

Mag'-na Char'-ta. A great English charter. CONTRACT.

magna pars fui quorum [L.] (mag'-na pars fiu'-ai, quo'-rum). Of which I was a great part. AGENT.

mag''-na-nim'-i-ty. Greatness of mind. UNSELFISHNESS-SELFISHNESS.

mag-nan'-i-mous. Generous. UNSELFISHNESS-SELFISHNESS.

mag'-nate. A noble; rich person. GENTILITY-COMMONALTY, LABOR-CAPITAL.

mag'-net. The loadstone; an attractive person. ATTRACTION-REPULSION, CHEMISTRY, DESIRE-DISTASTE.

mag-net'-ic. Pertaining to a magnet. **Magnetic flux,** ELECTRICITY; **magnetic force,** MOTIVE-CAPRICE; **magnetic whirls,** ELECTRICITY.

mag'-net-ism. Power of attraction. ATTRACTION-REPULSION, ELECTRICITY, MIGHT-IMPOTENCE, MOTIVE-CAPRICE; **animal magnetism,** DEVOTION-MAGIC.

mag''-net-i-za'-tion. Act of magnetizing. ELECTRICITY.

mag'-net-ize. To influence. DEVOTION-MAGIC, DOMINANCE-IMPOTENCE, MOTIVE-CAPRICE.

magni nominis umbra [L.] (mag'-nai nom'-i-nis um'-bra). The shadow of a great name. BETTERMENT-DETERIORATION, GENTILITY-COMMONALTY, REPUTATION-DISCREDIT.

mag-nif'-i-cence. Splendor. BEAUTY-UGLINESS, POMP.

mag-nif'-i-cent. Majestic; grand. BEAUTY-UGLINESS, GREATNESS-LITTLENESS, POMP.

mag-nif'-i-co. A Venetian noble. GENTILITY-COMMONALTY.

mag'-ni-fi''-er. That which magnifies. OPTICAL INSTRUMENTS.

magnifique et pas cher [F.] (ma-nyi-fik' ê pa sher). Splendid and not dear. COSTLINESS-CHEAPNESS.

mag'-ni-fy. To make great; to extol. APPROVAL-DISAPPROVAL, DEVOTION-IDOLATRY, ENLARGEMENT-DIMINUTION, GULL-HYPERBOLE, INCREASE-DECREASE, OVERVALUATION-UNDERVALUATION.

mag-nil'-o-quence. Bombastic style. BRAGGING.

mag-nil'-o-quent. Of pompous style; vainglorious. BRAGGING, SIMPLICITY-FLORIDNESS.

mag'-ni-tude. Great size or extent. GREATNESS-LITTLENESS, MAGNITUDE-SMALLNESS, QUANTITY-MEASURE.

MAGNITUDE—SMALLNESS.

Abundance. An overflowing fulness; great plenty.
Best part. The greater part of anything.
Bulk. Magnitude of material substance.
Chief part. The greater part of anything.
Deal. An indefinite quantity, degree, or extent.
Enormity. The quality or state of exceeding a measure or rule.
Essential part. That part which is indispensable.
Fulness. The state of being full.
Greater part. The larger portion.
Greatness. The state of being great. See *Adjectives.*
Immensity. Unlimited or immeasurable extension.
Importance. Quality or state of being important. See CONSEQUENCE.
Infinity. The state of being so great as to have no bounds. See INFINITY.
Intensity. The degree of force.
Magnitude. Extent of dimensions.
Main part. } The greater part of anything.
Major part. }
Mass. The principal part of anything.
Might. Greatness of strength or resources.
Multitude. A great number of persons or things. See MULTITUDE.
Power. Greatness of strength.
Principal part. The greater part of anything.
Quantity. A large portion, bulk, or sum.
Sight. A great number, quantity, or sum.
Size. Comparative greatness. See GREATNESS.
Strength. Greatness of physical power.
Volume. Space occupied, as measured by cubic units.
World. A large quantity.

MAGNITUDE—*Nouns of Measure, etc.*

Bushel. A measure of capacity equal to four pecks.
Cargo. The lading or freight of a ship or other vessel.
Cart-load. As much as will fill a cart.
Flood. A great mass of water; a great mass of anything.
Heap. A large quantity of things not placed in a pile.
Kiloliter. A measure of a thousand liters.
Load. As much as can be carried.
Peck. A measure of capacity containing eight quarts.
Pot. As much as will fill a pot.
Ship-load. As much as a ship can carry.
Spring tide. The high tide which occurs after the new and full moon.
Stock. The amount of anything on hand.
Wagon-load. As much as will fill a wagon.

MAGNITUDE—*Verbs.*

Be great. To be large.
Carry to a great height. To make high.
Enlarge. To make greater.
Know no bounds. To be infinitely great.
Rise to a great height. To become large.
Run high. To cost a great deal.
Soar. To float through the air at a great distance above the earth.
Tower. To rise to a great height.
Transcend. To be greater in degree.

Fewness. Smallness of number. See MULTIPLICITY-PAUCITY.
Finiteness. The state of being limited in quantity, degree, or capacity.
Hardly anything. A scarcely noticeable quantity.
Insignificance. Quality of being small or unimportant. See CONSEQUENCE-INSIGNIFICANCE.
Just enough to swear by. No more than a noticeable quantity.
Littleness. State of being small. See GREATNESS-LITTLENESS.
Meanness. State of being small or of little value.
Mediocrity. A moderate degree or rate.
Moderation. State of being within reasonable limits.
Next to nothing. A quantity hardly noticeable.
Paucity. Smallness of number.
Smallness. State of being of little size.
Tenuity. Slenderness or thinness.

SMALLNESS—*Denotations.*

Ace. A very small quantity or degree.
Animalcule. An animal invisible, or nearly so.
Atom. The smallest particle of matter.
Bit. A small piece of anything.
Cantlet. A piece or fragment.
Capful. As much as a cap will hold.
Cast. A looking for a short time; a glance.
Chip. A fragment or piece broken off.
Chipping. A fragment.
Clipping. A piece separated by clipping.
Corpuscle. A minute particle; especially, a protoplasmic animal cell in the blood
Crumb. A small fragment or piece; especially, a small piece of bread.
Dash. A slight admixture or infusion.
Details. Minute portions.
Dole. A scanty share or allowance.
Dot. Anything small like a speck.
Driblet. A small piece or part.
Drop. The quantity of fluid which falls in one small spherical mass.
Drop in the ocean. A comparatively small portion.
Droplet. A little drop.
Finite quantity. A limited quantity.
Flinders. Small pieces or splinters.
Flitter. A rag; a small piece or fragment.
Fraction. A portion; a fragment. See PLURALITY-FRACTION.
Fragment. A part broken off.
Fritter. A small piece.
Gleam. A small stream of light.
Globule. A small particle of a circular form.
Gobbet. A mouthful.
Grain. A small, hard particle.
Granule. A little grain.
Hair. A very fine filament growing from the skin.
Handful. As much as can be held in the hand.
Idea. A fictitious object or picture created by the imagination.
Inch. A small distance or degree.
Iota. A very small quantity or degree.
Jot. The smallest particle.

MAGNITUDE—SMALLNESS—*Continued.*

MAGNITUDE—*Adjectives*

Above par. Of greater value than the face
Absolute. Great without limitation.
Abundant. Of great frequency in occurrence.
Ample. Of great dimensions.
Arch. Preeminently great.
Arrant. Great in doing evil.
Astonishing. Wonderfully great.
At its height. At the point of greatest importance.
Beyond expression. Too great for words.
Big. Great in size.
Complete. Of entire extent.
Considerable. Worthy of regard as being great
Consummate. Perfectly great
Crass. Coarse.
Decided. Great without uncertainty
Deep. Great in depth.
Desperate. Without hope.
Enormous. Excessive in size.
Essential. Absolutely requisite
Excessive. Too great.
Exorbitant. Too great in price.
Extensive. Of large dimensions.
Extraordinary. Out of the common order.
Extravagant. Beyond bounds or limits.
Extreme. The highest degree of anything
Fabulous. Exceedingly great
Fair. Moderately great
Far gone. Advanced.
Finished. Having reached its largest extent
Flagrant. Notoriously bad.
Full. Complete in measure.
Glaring. Plainly evident.
Goodly. Great in proportion or numbers.
Grave. Of great importance.
Great. Of considerable degree.
Greater. Larger than.
Gross. Very large; coarse
Heavy. Of great weight.
High. Of great height.
Huge. Having great bulk.
Immense. Very great in extent.
Important. Of great consequence.
Incredible. Too greatly improbable to admit of belief.
Indescribable. That cannot be represented in words.
Ineffable. Too good to be represented in words.
Inexpressible. Not to be expressed.
Inordinate. Great beyond the prescribed bounds.
Intense. Very great in degree.
In the zenith. At the culminating point of greatness.
Large. Great in size.
Many. Constituting a great number.
Marked. Distinguished for greatness.
Marvelous. Inspiring wonder.
Mighty. Having great power.
Monstrous. Varying greatly from the natural.
Noble. Distinguished for good qualities.
Noteworthy. Deserving attention.
Of mark. Of great distinction.
Outrageous. Great to excess.
Overgrown. Developed beyond the normal.
Passing. Greater than.
Perfect. Complete in all parts.
Plenary. Complete in all requisites.
Pointed. Direct.
Positive. Inherent in a thing by itself.
Precious. Of great value.
Preposterous Not admitting of the slightest belief
Prodigious. Great beyond all usual limits.
Profound. Of great intellectual depth.
Rank. Strong in a bad sense.
Red-hot. Intense in a degree beyond the usual.
Remarkable. So much out of the usual as to demand attention.
Roaring. Large and noisy.
Sad. Afflicted by grief.
Serious. Of great importance because of attendant danger.
Signal. Large.
Sound. Strong; complete
Stark. Complete.
Starkstaring. Complete; sheer.
Strong. Having great physical power.
Stupendous. So great as to overcome the senses with astonishment.

SMALLNESS—Denotations—*Continued.*

Look. A glance.
Material part. Essential part; an atom.
Material point. Essential point; *minimum sensibile.*
Mere nothing. \
Mere trifle. } A very small portion.
Minim. Anything very minute.
Minimum. The least quantity possible.
Minutiæ. Minute particles.
Mite. Anything very small.
Modicum. A small quantity.
Molecule. The smallest part of a substance which possesses the characteristic properties.
Morsel. A little bite of food.
Mote. A small particle, as of floating dust.
Mouthful. As much as the mouth will hold.
Nutshell. As much as can be contained in a nutshell
Paring. That which is pared off.
Particle. A minute portion of matter.
Patch. A small piece of anything used to repair a breach.
Point. A dot or mark.
Rag. A piece of cloth torn off
Scantling. A little piece.
Scintilla. A spark.
Scrag. Something thin or lean.
Scrap. Something scraped off.
Seed. The small, ripened ovule of plants.
Shade. A minute difference or variation.
Shadow. A small degree.
Shaving. That which is shaved off.
Shive. A thin piece or fragment.
Shiver. One of the small pieces into which a brittle thing is broken.
Shred. A long, narrow piece cut or torn off.
Sip. A small draft taken with the lips.
Slip. A slender piece.
Sliver. A sharp, slender fragment.
Smack. A small quantity; a taste.
Small quantity. A small portion.
Snack. A slight, hasty repast.
Snatch. A small piece or fragment.
Snick. A small cut or mark.
Snip. A bit cut off.
Snippet. A small part or piece.
Sop. A thing of little or no value.
Soupçon [F.]. A suspicion; hence, a very small quantity
Spark. A small particle of fire or ignited substance.
Speck. A very small thing.
Spice. A small quantity or admixture.
Splinter. A thin piece split or rent off lengthwise.
Spoonful. As much as a spoon will hold.
Sprinkling. A small quantity falling in distinct drops or particles.
Sup. A small mouthful.
Tag. Any slight appendage.
Tatter. A part torn and hanging.
The shadow of a shade. The very slightest particle.
Thimbleful. As much as a thimble will hold.
Thought. A small degree or quantity.
Tincture. A slight quality added to anything.
Tinge. A slight degree of color, taste, etc.
Tittle. A minute part.
Touch. A small quantity intermixed.
Trifle. A thing of very little value or importance.
Vanishing point. The point to which all parallel lines in the same plane tend.
Whit. The smallest particle imaginable.

SMALLNESS—*Verbs.*

Be small, etc. See *Adjectives.*
Diminish, etc. To grow smaller. See Increase-Decrease Enlargement-Diminution.
Lie in a nutshell. To be in a small compass.

SMALLNESS—*Adjectives.*

At a low ebb. Small in degree.
Bare. Not more than just sufficient.
Below par. Of smaller value than the face.
Below the mark. Smaller than the average.
Diminutive. Of relatively small size. See Greatness-Littleness.
Evanescent. Small to the point of passing away.
Faint. Slight.
Few. Small in numbers.

MAGNITUDE—SMALLNESS—*Continued.*

MAGNITUDE—Adjectives—*Continued*

Swinging. Free.
Thoroughgoing. Efficient in everything.
Thorough-paced. Trained to perfection, as a race-horse.
Thumping. Heavy; large.
Towering. Rising higher.
Unabated. Not diminished in strength.
Unapproachable. Thoroughly inaccessible.
Unconscionable. Not influenced by mental restraint
Undiminished. Not decreased in size.
Unequivocal. Not admitting of doubt
Unlimited. Having no bounds.
Unmitigated. Not lessened in severity.
Unreduced. Not lessened in size or amount.
Unrestricted. Not limited by the usual bounds.
Unspeakable. That cannot be expressed in words.
Unsuitable. Not fitting.
Unsurpassed. Unexcelled.
Unutterable. Such that it cannot be expressed in words.
Utter. Complete; entire.
Uttermost. That beyond which there is nothing.
Vast. Immeasurably great.
Veriest. In the most eminent degree.
Wholesale. Done on a large scale.
Wide-spread. Extended over a great area
World-wide. Of universal importance.

MAGNITUDE—*Adverbs.*

Absolutely. Without exception.
Abundantly. In a plentiful degree
Acutely. With a keen perception.
A deal. Much.
Amazingly. In a manner momentarily overwhelming the intellect
À outrance [F.]. To the utmost.
Astonishingly. In a manner affecting the emotions powerfully
À toute outrance [F.]. To the uttermost.
Awfully. Excessively.
Beyond all bounds. Without any limit
Beyond compare.
Beyond comparison. } In a manner too high for an estimate relative
Beyond measure. } to anything else.
Bitterly. Painfully.
By wholesale. On a very large scale
Chiefly. For the most part.
Confoundedly. Greatly; in a detestable manner.
Cruelly. Extremely.
Curiously. In a singular manner
Decidedly. Without doubt.
Desperately. Hopelessly.
Deucedly. Excessively.
Devilishly. Maliciously.
Downrightly. Openly; plainly.
Dreadfully. Excessively.
Egregiously. Remarkably.
Emphatically. Forcibly.
Enormously. In a huge degree.
Enough. In a tolerable degree
Entirely. Completely.
Essentially. In an important degree.
Ever so. }
Ever so much. } To a great extent.
Exceedingly. Beyond an ordinary degree
Excessively. Greatly.
Exorbitantly. Enormously.
Exquisitely. In a delicately beautiful manner.
Extravagantly. In a manner running far beyond the natural bounds.
Extremely. Very greatly.
Famously. In a distinguished manner
Far and wide. Universally.
Fearfully. In a fearful manner
For the most part. Especially
Frightfully. Exciting alarm.
Furiously. In a raging manner
Fundamentally. Primarily
Glaringly. In a conspicuous and self-evident manner
Greatly. Extremely; very much
Grievously. Painfully.
Grossly. In a great and coarse degree
Horribly. Dreadfully.
Immeasurably. Immensely.
Immoderately. Unrestrainedly

SMALLNESS—Adjectives—*Continued.*

Half-way. Intermediate,
Homeopathic. Extremely small in quantity.
Inappreciable. Too small to be estimated.
Inconsiderable. Too small to be worthy of notice.
Infinitesimal. Infinitely small.
Light. Small in weight.
Limited. Bounded within small limits.
Little. Below the ordinary size.
Low. Small in height.
Meager. Small in fulness.
Mere. Such and no more.
Middling. Neither small nor large.
Minute. Exceedingly small.
Moderate. Fairly small.
Modest. Not unduly large.
Near ruin. Almost destroyed.
No great shakes. Of little consequence.
Paltry. Of little worth. See CONSEQUENCE-INSIGNIFICANCE.
Scant. Scarcely enough.
Scanty. Small in quantity.
Sheer. Having no modifying conditions.
Simple. Too small for consideration.
Slender. Small in diameter.
Slight. Of small significance.
Small. Having little size.
So-so. Paltry.
Sparing. Scarce.
Stark. Utterly.
Subtle. Nicely discriminating.
Tender. Lacking strength.
Tolerable. Moderately good.
Under par. See BELOW PAR.
Under the mark. See BELOW THE MARK.
Very small. Very much less than the standard.

SMALLNESS—*Adverbs.*

About. Approximately.
After a fashion. To some degree.
A little. Not much.
All but. Not quite.
Almost. Very nearly.
As little as may be. The least possible.
At least.
At most. }
At no hand. } At any rate.
At the least. }
At most. At the furthest.
A wee bit. Just a little.
Barely. By a little.
Be the same more or less. At any rate.
By no manner of means. In no wise at all.
By no means. Certainly not.
Close upon. Hard by.
Comparatively. According to estimate made by comparison.
Ever so little. To a very small extent.
Faintly. In a weak manner.
Hardly. Not quite.
Imperceptibly. So as not to be noticed.
Imperfectly. Not completely.
In a certain degree. To some extent
In a manner. In a sense.
In ever so small a degree. Slightly
In no respect. Not at all.
In no wise. In no manner.
In part. To some degree.
In some degree. Not perfectly.
In some measure. Very slightly.
Insufficiently. In an inadequate manner.
Merely. Barely.
Miserably. Unhappily.
Nearly. Closely approaching.
Near the mark. Nearly up to the standard.
Near upon. At no great distance from.
No more than. To a particular extent, degree, etc.
Not a bit. Not the least.
Not a bit of it. Not at all.
Not a jot. }
Not a shadow } Not the least.
Not at all. }
Not a whit. }

MAGNITUDE—SMALLNESS—*Continued.*

MAGNITUDE—Adverbs—*Continued*

In a great degree. }
In a great measure. } Largely.
In all conscience. Reasonably.
Incalculably. In a degree beyond all calculation
Incredibly. In a manner impossible to be believed.
Indeed. In fact.
Indefinitely. Without a fixed time limit.
Infinitely. Without any limits.
Inordinately. In a manner passing fit limits.
Intensely. To a very great degree.
In the extreme. At the point of greatest distress.
In the main. Mostly.
Kat'exochen [Gr.]. Preeminently.
Lamentably. Causing grief.
Mainly. Principally.
Marvelously. In a manner exciting wonder and surprise.
Mighty. Exceedingly.
Miserably. Causing misery.
Monstrously. Exceedingly.
Most. In the highest degree.
Much. }
Muckle. } In a great degree.
Never so. True at no time.
No end of. In a manner continued indefinitely.
Notably. Markedly.
Not a little. A good deal.
On a large scale. Widely.
Out of all proportion. Unusually.
Painfully. Distressingly.
Particularly. With specific reference.
Peculiarly. In a manner not common to others.
Piteously. Causing pity.
Pointedly. With explicitness.
Powerfully. With great force.
Preeminently. With superiority or distinction above others.
Preposterously. In an eminently absurd manner.
Pretty. Rather.
Pretty well. Satisfactorily.
Prominently. Conspicuously.
Purely. Merely.
Radically. Essentially.
Remarkably. In a manner worthy of notice.
Richly. Strongly.
Sadly. Grievously.
Seriously. Gravely.
Severely. Strictly.
Shockingly. Dreadfully.
Signally. In an eminent manner.
Singularly. In a manner not common to others.
So. In such a manner.
Sorely. Greatly.
Strangely. In an unusual manner.
Strikingly. Forcibly.
Stupendously. In a great and wonderful manner.
Superlatively. In the utmost degree.
Surprisingly. Causing surprise.
Terribly. Causing terror.
To a gigantic extent. Stupendously.

SMALLNESS—Adverbs—*Continued.*

Not in the least. By no means.
Not quite. Not entirely.
No ways. On no account.
No wise. In no manner.
On a small scale. Slightly.
Only. In one manner.
Only just. So much and no more.
On no account. Not at all.
On the brink of. Nearly.
Partially. In part.
Passably. In a fairly good manner.
Peu s'en faut [F.]. Far from it.
Pretty well. In a fair manner.
Pro tanto [L.]. For so much.
Purely. Merely.
Rather. In some degree.
Say. About.
Scarcely. Barely.
Short of. Not up to a standard.
Simply. Without addition.
Slightly. In a small degree.
Some. Not much.
Somewhat. In some degree.
Somewhere about. Nearly.
Tant soit peu [F.]. Never so little.
Thereabouts. Nearly.
Thus far. To a particular extent, degree, etc.
To a certain degree. To some extent.
To a small extent. On a small scale.
Well enough. Sufficiently good.
Well-nigh. Nearly.
Within an ace of. }
Within an inch of. } In a barely sufficient manner.
Within bounds. In a restricted manner.
Wretchedly. In a miserable manner.

MAGNITUDE—Adverbs—*Continued.*

To a great extent. }
To a large extent. } In the main.
Tremendously. In a terrifying manner.
Truly. Really.
Ultra [L.] Excessively.
Uncommonly. Rarely.
Unequivocally. Certainly.
Unusually. Not frequently
Very. To a great extent.
Very much. To a very great degree.
Well. Greatly.
Widely. To a great degree.
With a vengeance. Fearfully.
With a witness. Surely.
Woefully. Dreadfully.
Wonderfully. In a surprising manner.

Magnitude—*Phrase*

A maximis ad minima [L.]. From the greatest to the least

---

magno conatu magnas nugas [L.] (mag'-no co-nē'-tu mag'-nas niu'-gas). Great jokes with a great effort. Consequence-Insignificance, Provision-Waste.
Magnus Apollo [L.] (mag'-nus a-pol'-lo). Great Apollo; one of high authority. Sage-Fool.
mag'-pie. A loquacious person. Talkativeness-Taciturnity.
mags'-man. A street swindler. Robber.
ma''-ha-ra'-ja. A Hindu prince. Chief-Underling.
ma-hog'-a-ny. A kind of wood. Gray-Brown.
Ma-hom'-ed-an. Pertaining to Islam. Orthodoxy-Heterodoxy.
Ma-hom'-et. The founder of Islam. Revelation-Pseudorevelation.
Ma-hom'-et-an-ism. The Moslem religion. Orthodoxy-Heterodoxy.
maid. An unmarried woman; a female servant; a girl. Chief-Underling, Infant-Veteran, Matrimony-

Celibacy; maid of all work, Chief Underling; maid of honor, Friend-Foe.
maid'-en. A maid; initiatory; a beheading-machine. Beginning-End, Infant-Veteran, Recompense-Scourge.
maid'-en-head. Unmarried state. Matrimony-Celibacy.
maid'-en-hood. State of being a maiden. Matrimony-Celibacy.
maid'-en-ly. Like a maiden. Male-Female.
mai'-gre. Pertaining to a fast. Fasting-Gluttony.
mail. Governmental system for conveying and delivering mail matter; armor. Attack-Defense, Messenger; mail coach, Conveyance-Vessel.
maim. To disable. Betterment-Deterioration, Might-Impotence.
main. The ocean; a chief conductor; principal. Aperture-Closure, Consequence-Insignificance,

OCEAN-LAND, WATERCOURSE-AIRPIPE; **in the main,** CONSEQUENCE-INSIGNIFICANCE, MAGNITUDE-SMALL-NESS, SUBJECTIVENESS-OBJECTIVENESS, WHOLE-PART; **look to the main chance,** GENEROSITY-FRU-GALITY, PREVISION, RECKLESSNESS-CAUTION, SKILL-UNSKILFULNESS, UNSELFISHNESS-SELFISHNESS; **main chance,** CONSEQUENCE-INSIGNIFICANCE, GAIN-LOSS, GOOD-EVIL; **main force,** COERCION, STRENGTH-WEAKNESS, TURBULENCE-CALMNESS; **main part,** MAGNITUDE-SMALLNESS, WHOLE-PART; **plow the main,** TRAVELING-NAVIGATION; **with might and main,** TOIL-RELAXATION.

main, coup de [F.] (man', cu de) With main force. ACTION-PASSIVENESS.

main′-land. Principal body of land. OCEAN-LAND.

main′-per-nor. A surety. SECURITY.

main′-sail″. The sail carried on the mainmast. CON-VEYANCE-VESSEL.

main′-spring″. Driving spring of a mechanism; the chief cause. CAUSE-EFFECT.

main′-stay″. A chief support. REFUGE-PITFALL, SAN-GUINENESS-HOPELESSNESS, SUSPENSION-SUPPORT.

mains, chaudes amours, froides [F.] (man', shodz a-mur', frwad). Cold hands, warm heart. LOVE-HATE.

main-tain′. To support; continue; affirm. AGENCY, ASSERTION-DENIAL, CONSERVATION, DISCONTINU-ANCE-CONTINUANCE, MUTATION-PERMANENCE, SUS-PENSION-SUPPORT; **maintain one's course,** DETERMI-NATION-VACILLATION; **maintain one's ground,** AT-TACK-DEFENSE; **maintain the even tenor of one's way,** QUEST-EVASION.

main′-te-nance. Means of support. AFFLUENCE-PENURY.

maintien [F.] (man'-ti-an'). Deportment. CONDUCT.

maison de campagne [F.] (mê-zon′' de can'-pany'). A country-seat. DWELLER-HABITATION.

maison de santé [F.] (mê-zon′' de san'-tê') A hos-pital. REMEDY-BANE.

maitre, coup de [F.] (mêtr, cu de). A master-stroke. GOODNESS-BADNESS, SKILL-UNSKILFULNESS.

maitre, l'œil de [F.] (mêtr, luy de). The eye of a master. CAREFULNESS-CARELESSNESS.

maitre, tel valet, tel [F.] (mêtr, tel va-lê', tel). Like master, like man. DOMINANCE-IMPOTENCE, LIKE-NESS-UNLIKENESS.

majesté, lèse [F.] (ma-zhes-tê', lês) High treason INSUBORDINATION-OBEDIENCE.

ma-jes′-tic. Stately; noble. POMP, REPUTATION-DISCREDIT.

maj′-es-ty. Exalted dignity. CHIEF-UNDERLING, DIVINITY, REPUTATION-DISCREDIT.

ma′-jor. An army officer; greater. CHIEF-UNDER-LING, SUPREMACY-SUBORDINACY; **majordomo,** CHIEF-UNDERLING, MANAGER; **major-general,** CHIEF-UN-DERLING; **major key,** MELODY-DISSONANCE; **major part,** MAGNITUDE-SMALLNESS, WHOLE-PART.

ma-jor′-i-ty. Full legal age; the greater number. MANHOOD, MULTIPLICITY-PAUCITY, SUPREMACY-SUB-ORDINACY.

ma-jus′-cu-læ. Capital letters. LETTER.

make. To attain; to compel; to bring about; to con-stitute; to render; to construct. ARRIVAL-DE-PARTURE, COERCION, COMPLETION-NONCOMPLETION, CONSTITUENT-ALIEN, CONVERSION-REVERSION, CRE-ATION-DESTRUCTION, FORM-FORMLESSNESS, INCLU-SION-OMISSION; **make acquainted with,** EDUCATION-LEARNING, ENLIGHTENMENT-SECRECY; **make after,** QUEST-EVASION; **make a fuss,** ACTIVITY-INDOLENCE, CONSEQUENCE-INSIGNIFICANCE; **make a piece of work,** CONTENTEDNESS-DISCONTENTMENT; **make a present,** GIVING-RECEIVING; **make a push,** ACTIVITY-INDOLENCE; **make a requisition,** ORDER, PETITION-EXPOSTULATION; **make a speech,** SPEECH-INARTICU-LATENESS; **make away with,** CREATION-DESTRUC-TION, KEEPING-RELINQUISHMENT, LIFE-KILLING, USE-DISUSE; **make a wry face,** DESIRE-DISTASTE, PLEASURABLENESS-PAINFULNESS; **make believe,** TRUTHFULNESS-FABRICATION, TRUTHFULNESS-FALSEHOOD, TRUTHFULNESS-FRAUD; **make choice of,** CHOICE-NEUTRALITY; **make fast,** UNION-DISUNION; **make for,** AIM-ABERRATION; **make fun of,** SOCIETY-DERISION, WITTINESS-DULNESS; **make good,** COM-PENSATION, COMPLETION-NONCOMPLETION, EN-TIRETY-DEFICIENCY, ESCAPE, EVIDENCE-COUNTER-EVIDENCE, MUTABILITY-STABILITY, OBSERVANCE-NONOBSERVANCE, PROOF-DISPROOF, RENOVATION-RELAPSE; **make haste,** HURRY-LEISURE; **make hay while the sun shines,** OPPORTUNENESS-UNSUITABLE-NESS; **make interest,** PETITION-EXPOSTULATION; **make its appearance,** VISIBILITY-INVISIBILITY; **make known,** ENLIGHTENMENT-SECRECY; **make light of,** CONSEQUENCE-INSIGNIFICANCE, DIFFICULTY-FACIL-ITY, OVERVALUATION-UNDERVALUATION; **make money,** GAIN-LOSS; **make much of,** AMITY-HOSTIL-ITY, BLANDISHMENT, CONSEQUENCE-INSIGNIFICANCE, GULL-HYPERBOLE; **make no doubt,** FAITH-MISGIV-ING; **make no secret of,** MANIFESTATION-LATENCY; **make no sign,** ENLIGHTENMENT-SECRECY, MANIFES-TATION-LATENCY; **make nothing of,** ASTONISHMENT-EXPECTANCE, CLEARNESS-OBSCURITY, SUCCESS-FAILURE; **make of,** BLANDISHMENT; **make off,** ESCAPE, QUEST-EVASION; **make off with,** THEFT; **make oneself master of,** EDUCATION-LEARNING; **make one's fortune,** WELFARE-MISFORTUNE; **make one's way,** TRANSMISSION, WELFARE-MISFORTUNE; **make out,** CLEARNESS-OBSCURITY, DISCOVERY, DUE-NESS-UNDUENESS, EVIDENCE-COUNTEREVIDENCE, INTERPRETATION-MISINTERPRETATION, KNOWLEDGE-IGNORANCE, PROOF-DISPROOF, SIGHT-BLINDNESS; **make over,** ALIENATION, GIVING-RECEIVING; **make peace,** FIGHTING-CONCILIATION, MEDIATION; **make public,** PUBLICITY; **make ready,** PREPARATION-NON-PREPARATION; **make sure,** CERTAINTY-DOUBT, MUTA-BILITY-STABILITY, PREPARATION-NONPREPARATION; **make terms,** CONTRACT; **make the best of,** YIELDING; **make the land,** ARRIVAL-DEPARTURE; **make things pleasant,** CRAFT-ARTLESSNESS; **make time,** LASTING-NESS-TRANSIENTNESS; **make towards,** AIM-ABERRA-TION; **make use of,** USE-DISUSE; **make way,** AD-VANCE-RETROGRESSION, APERTURE-CLOSURE; **make way for,** COMMUTATION-PERMUTATION, OBSTRUC-TION-HELP, QUEST-EVASION.

ma′-ker. One who makes; the Creator. AGENT; **the Maker,** DIVINITY.

MAKER—DESTROYER

Architect. One who designs or builds something; one who lays the plans and directs the construction of buildings.

Author. One who originates anything; one who composes books, pamphlets, etc.

Founder. One who founds or endows something

Generator. One who generates or produces.

Inventor. One who finds out or makes something not previously existent.

Assassin. A stealthy, treacherous destroyer of life. See LIFE-KILLING. [Arabic, hashish-eater. in the crusades.]

Cankerworm. A caterpillar destructive to trees. See REMEDY-BANE.

Destroyer. One who brings to ruin or kills. See CREATION-DE-STRUCTION.

Executioner. A public official who inflicts capital punishment. See RECOMPENSE-SCOURGE.

Iconoclast. An image destroyer.

MAKER—*Continued.*

Maker. One who makes. See AGENT.
Mover. One who moves or incites to activity.

make'-shift''. A temporary expedient. COMMUTA-TION-PERMUTATION, PRETEXT.
make up. To compensate; to compose. ENTIRETY-DEFICIENCY, INCLUSION-OMISSION; **make up accounts,** ACCOUNTS; **make up a quarrel,** FIGHTING-CONCILIATION; **make up a sum,** OUTLAY-INCOME; **make up for,** COMPENSATION; **make up matters,** ATONEMENT; **make up one's mind,** DECISION-MISJUDGMENT, DETERMINATION-VACILLATION, FAITH-MISGIVING; **make up to,** ADDRESS-RESPONSE, APPROACH-WITHDRAWAL.
make'-weight''. Something used to fill up or increase weight. COMPENSATION, ENTIRETY-DEFICIENCY, EQUALITY-INEQUALITY.
ma'-king of, be the. To be that which contributes to improvement or success. GOODNESS-BADNESS, OBSTRUCTION-HELP, USEFULNESS-USELESSNESS.
mala fides [L.] (mē'-la fai'-diz). Bad faith. UPRIGHTNESS-DISHONESTY.
mal'-a-chite. Native carbonate of copper. REDNESS-GREENNESS.
mal''-a-col'-o-gy. The science of mollusks. ZOOLOGY-BOTANY.
malade imaginaire [F.] (ma-lad' i-ma-zhi-nêr'). Sick in conceit. LIGHTHEARTEDNESS-DEJECTION.

Originator. One who is the producing cause of anything.
Producer. One who produces; one who cultivates for sale.

maladie du pays [F.] (ma-la-di' dü pê-i'). Homesickness. CONTENTEDNESS-REGRET.
mal''-ad-min''-is-tra'-tion. Bad management of affairs. SKILL-UNSKILFULNESS.
maladroit [F.] (ma-la-drwa'). Awkward. SKILL-UNSKILFULNESS.
mal'-a-dy. A disease. HEALTH-SICKNESS.
malaise [F.] (ma-lêz'). Uneasiness. PLEASURE-PAIN, SENSUALITY-SUFFERING.
mal'-a-pert. A saucy person. BRAWLER, PRESUMPTION-OBSEQUIOUSNESS.
Mal'-a-prop, Mrs. A character in Sheridan's *Rivals,* who misapplies words. NAME-MISNOMER.
mal à propos [F.] (mal a pro-po'). Ill-timed. HARMONY-DISCORD, OPPORTUNENESS-UNSUITABLENESS.
ma-la'-ri-a. A diseased condition. HEALTHINESS-UNHEALTHINESS, REMEDY-BANE.
mal'-con''-for-ma'-tion. Ill form. PROPORTION-DEFORMITY.
mal'-con-tent''. A discontented person. ANTAGONIST-ASSISTANT, CONTENTEDNESS-DISCONTENTMENT.
mal du pays [F.] (mal dü pê-i'). Homesickness. CONTENTEDNESS-REGRET.
male. A man; of the sex that begets young. MALE-FEMALE, STRENGTH-WEAKNESS; **male animal,** MALE-FEMALE.

MALE—FEMALE.

Beau [F.]. A ladies' man.
Billy-goat. A male goat.
Blade. A dashing, wild, or reckless fellow.
Boar. The uncastrated male of swine.
Boy. A male child. See INFANCY.
Buck. The male of various animals, as of deer, rabbits, etc.
Bull. The male of various animals, more commonly of domestic cattle.
Bullock. An ox; especially, a beef-ox over four years old.
Capon. A male chicken gelded to increase growth.
Chap. A man or boy of little worth.
Cock. The male of birds, particularly of domestic fowls.
Dog. The male of the dog.
Drake. A male duck.
Elf. A diminutive person; a dwarf.
Entire horse. The uncastrated male of the genus horse.
Fellow. An inferior, worthless, or disreputable man or boy.
Gaffer. An old man; especially, an old countryman.
Gander. A male goose.
Gelding. A castrated horse.
Gentilhomme [F.]. Gentleman.
Gentleman. A well-bred and honorable man.
Gib-cat. A castrated cat.
Goodman. The master of a house or family.
Hart. The male of the red deer.
He. A personal pronoun denoting a male person.
He-goat. A male goat.
Horse. The male of the horse; especially, when castrated.
Husband. A married man. See MATRIMONY.
Male. A person or animal of the male sex.
Man. An adult male of the human kind.
Manhood. The state of being of age. See MANHOOD.
Man-servant. An adult male servant.
Master. A male person who has authority over others.
Mister. A title of address prefixed to the name of a man.
Mr. An abbreviation for Mister.
Ox. An adult castrated male of bovine quadrupeds.
Ram. A male sheep.
Sir. A term of respectful address to men.
Stag. The male of various animals; especially, of the red deer.
Stallion. An uncastrated male horse.
Swain. A rustic gallant.
Tom-cat. The male of the cat.
Tup. A male sheep.
Wight. A person, male or female, generally used in good-humored contempt.
Yeoman. A farmer.

Belle [F.]. A young lady of superior beauty and attractions.
Bitch. The female of the dog and of some other carnivores.
Cow. The female of domestic cattle and of some other animals.
Dame. A woman of high social position.
Doe. The female of the deer, antelope, hare, rabbit, and kangaroo.
Donna [It.]. The title given a lady in Italy.
Dowager. A widow holding dower or jointure.
Ewe. A female sheep.
Fair sex. An expression denoting the female sex.
Female. A person or animal of the female sex.
Feminality. The quality or nature of the female sex.
Gammer. An old woman.
Girl. A female infant or child. See INFANCY.
Goodwife. } The mistress of a house.
Goodwoman. }
Goody. An old woman of an humble class.
Grisette [F.]. A Parisian working girl, especially one of easy virtue.
Gynecæum [Gr.]. That part of a house exclusively set apart for women.
Hen. The female of the domestic fowl.
Hostess. A woman who gives entertainment.
Lady. A refined and well-bred woman.
Lioness. A female lion.
Madam. A title of courtesy addressed to a woman.
Madame [F.]. The original form of Madam.
Mare. The female of the horse.
Matron. A woman of established age and dignity; a married woman.
Matronage. The state of a matron.
Matronhood. The state of being a matron.
Mrs. An abbreviation of the title Mistress.
Muliebrity. The state of being a woman.
Nanny-goat. A female goat.
Nymph. An inferior divinity; a young unmarried woman.
Petticoat. An underskirt worn by women; a woman.
Rani. A Hindu queen or princess.
Roe. The female of any species of deer.
She. A female; a woman.
She-goat. A female goat.
Softersex. An expression denoting the female sex.
Sow. A female hog.
Squaw. An American Indian woman or girl.
The fair. Women.
The sex. Women.
Tigress. A female tiger.
Vixen. A quarrelsome woman.
Weaker vessel. Woman.

MALE—FEMALE—*Continued.*

MALE—*Adjectives.*

Anthropic. Of or pertaining to a man.
He.
Male. } Denoting persons or animals of the male sex.
Masculine.
Manly. Possessing qualities characteristic of a true man
Unmanly. Unbecoming a man; base; cowardly.
Womanish. Characteristic of a woman; chiefly in a disparaging sense.
Virile. Having the characteristics of mature manhood.

FEMALE—*Continued from Column 2*

FEMALE—*Phrase.*

Es de vidrio la mujer [Sp.].   Woman is made of glass.

---

mal, ein, kein mal [G.] (ain mal, kain mal). Just once, nothing counts. FREQUENCY-RARITY, INNOCENCE-GUILT.
mal, si vienes solo, bien vengas [Sp.] (mal, sî vî-en'-es so'-lo, bî-en' ven'-gas). You may come well [you are welcome] misfortune, if you come alone. WELFARE-MISFORTUNE.
mal″-e-dic'-tion. A curse. CHARITABLENESS-CURSE.
mal″-e-fac'-tion. A crime. INNOCENCE-GUILT.
mal″-e-fac'-tor. A criminal. GOOD MAN-BAD MAN.
ma-lef'-ic. Mischief-making. GOODNESS-BADNESS.
ma-lef'-i-cent. Mischievous. CHARITABLENESS-MALEVOLENCE.
ma-lev'-o-lence. Ill will. AMITY-HOSTILITY, CHARITABLENESS-MALEVOLENCE, INNOCENCE-GUILT.
ma-lev'-o-lent. Ill-willed. CHARITABLENESS-MALEVOLENCE, VIRTUE-VICE.
ma-lev'-o-lent-ly. With ill will. CHARITABLENESS-MALEVOLENCE.
mal″-for-ma-tion. Ill formation. PROPORTION-DEFORMITY.
malgré soi [F.] (mal-grê' swa). In spite of himself. READINESS-RELUCTANCE.
mal'-ice. Active malevolence. CHARITABLENESS-MALEVOLENCE, LOVE-HATE; **bear malice,** PARDON-VINDICTIVENESS; **malice prepense,** CHARITABLENESS-MALEVOLENCE.
ma-li'-cious. Spiteful. CHARITABLENESS-MALEVOLENCE, LOVE-HATE.
ma-li'-cious-ness. Spitefulness. CHARITABLENESS-MALEVOLENCE.
ma-lign'. Pernicious; to speak evil of. ADULATION-DISPARAGEMENT, CHARITABLENESS-MALEVOLENCE, GOODNESS-BADNESS.
ma-lig'-nant. Evil in nature. CHARITABLENESS-MALEVOLENCE, GOODNESS-BADNESS.
ma-lig'-ni-ty. Destructive tendency. CHARITABLENESS-MALEVOLENCE, GOODNESS-BADNESS, TURBULENCE-CALMNESS.
ma-lin'-ger. To feign sickness. TRUTHFULNESS-FALSEHOOD.
ma-lin'-ger-ing. Injuring by falsehood. TRUTHFULNESS-FALSEHOOD.
mal'-i-son. A curse. CHARITABLENESS-CURSE.
malis pepercerit, bonis nocet, si quis [L.] (mê'-lis pî-per'-sî-rit, bo'-nis no'-set, sai quis). If any one spares the bad, he injures the good. DUTY-IMMUNITY, HARSHNESS-MILDNESS.
mal'-kin. A mop. CLEANNESS-FILTHINESS.
mall. A public walk; a maul. DWELLER-INHABITANT, IMPETUS-REACTION.
mal″-le-a-bil'-i-ty. Pliancy. HARDNESS-SOFTNESS.
mal'-le-a-ble. Pliant. HARDNESS-SOFTNESS.
mal'-let. A wooden hammer. IMPETUS-REACTION
mal-o'-dor. A bad smell. PERFUME-STENCH

Wench. A damsel or young woman of lowly condition.
Wife. A woman joined to a man in wedlock. See MATRIMONY.
Womanhood. The state of a woman. See MANHOOD.
Womankind. Women collectively

FEMALE—*Adjectives*

Effeminate. Soft, unmanly, or womanish.
Female. Denoting persons or animals of the female sex.
Feminine. Having the qualities of a woman.
Ladylike. Suitable to a well-bred woman; gentle; delicate.
Maidenly. Befitting a maiden; gentle; modest.
Matronly. Advanced in years; elderly.
She. Denoting a female.
Unfeminine. Acting like a man.
Unwomanly. Not suited or becoming to a woman.
Womanly. Having the qualities becoming to a woman.

(Continued on Column 1.)

---

mal-prac'-tise. Improper conduct. INNOCENCE-GUILT.
malt liq'-uor. A drink. NUTRIMENT-EXCRETION.
mal-treat'. To treat ill. CHARITABLENESS-MALEVOLENCE, CONTENTEDNESS-DISCONTENTMENT, GOODNESS-BADNESS.
malum in se [L.] (mê'-lum in sî). A deed wrong in itself. RIGHT-WRONG.
malum prohibitum [L.] (mê'-lum pro-hib'-it-um). An evil prohibited. DUENESS-UNDUENESS.
mal″-ver-sa'-tion. Misconduct. EXTRAVAGANCE-AVARICE, INNOCENCE-GUILT.
mam'-e-lon. A rounded hillock. CONVEXITY-CONCAVITY.
Mam'-e-luke. A cavalryman. BELLIGERENT
mam'-ma. Mother. PARENTAGE-PROGENY.
mam'-mal. An animal. FAUNA-FLORA.
mam'-met. An idol. DELINEATION-CARICATURE.
mam'-mi-form. Shaped like a nipple. CONVEXITY-CONCAVITY.
mam-mil'-la. A nipple. CONVEXITY-CONCAVITY.
Mam'-mon. The god of riches. AFFLUENCE-PENURY.
mam'-moth. Huge. GREATNESS-LITTLENESS.
man. A human being; a husband; an adult; a male servant; courage; to fortify. AGENT, BRAVERY-COWARDICE, CHIEF-UNDERLING, HUMANITY, MALE-FEMALE, MANHOOD, MATRIMONY-CELIBACY, PREPARATION-NONPREPARATION; **make a man of,** BRAVERY-COWARDICE, GOODNESS-BADNESS; **man about town,** CITY-COUNTRY; **man and wife,** MATRIMONY-CELIBACY; **man at arms,** BELLIGERENT; **man in office,** CHIEF-UNDERLING; **man of means,** LABOR-CAPITAL; **man-of-war,** BELLIGERENT, CONVEYANCE-VESSEL; **man-of-war's man,** WAYFARER-SEAFARER; **man on horseback,** TYRANNY-ANARCHY; **man's estate,** MANHOOD; **one's man of business,** CONSIGNEE; **Son of man,** DIVINITY; **to a man,** ASSENT-DISSENT.
man'-a-cle. A handcuff. RELEASE-PRISON, RELEASE-RESTRAINT.
man'-age. To direct. MANAGEMENT, PRESIDENT-MEMBER; **manage to,** SUCCESS-FAILURE.
man'-age-a-ble. Docile. DIFFICULTY-FACILITY.
man'-age-ment. Conduct; intrigue. CONDUCT, SKILL-UNSKILFULNESS.

MANAGEMENT

Administration. Assuming control of public affairs.
Agency. The faculty of exercising power or control.
Charge. Responsibility to oversee something.
Command. See RULE.
Conduct. Guidance; management.
Control. Authority; dominion.
Direction. Guidance.
Director. See MANAGER.
Government. Control; direction

Gubernation. Piloting; steering.
Guidance. Superintendence; leading.
Legislation. Enacting laws to limit the acts of people.
Management. Guide; overseeing.
Managery. The act of managing.
Ministration. Service; ministering.
Oversight. Watchful care.
Pilotage. Direction, as by a pilot.
Regulation. Rules laid down for control of some enterprise or machinery.
Steerage. Act of steering or directing.
Superintendence. Oversight; exercise care over.
Supervision. Oversee; inspection.
Surveillance. Watch; look after.

MANAGEMENT—*Associated Nouns.*

Board of Control. A body of men appointed or elected to manage.
Chair. One who directs the thoughts and proceedings of a deliberative body.
Eye of the master. The skill of a master.
Kingcraft. The governmental policy of kings.
Ministry. A body of officials who carry the policy of a government into execution.
Portfolio. The headship of some department of state; like a cabinet portfolio.
Premiership. Being at the head of a cabinet.
Proctorship. Having the commission to manage or exercise control for another.
Reins. Means of restraining or governing.
Reins of government. Control of the government.
Senatorship. Holding an office in the higher body of Congress.
Statecraft. The art of conducting state affairs.
Statesmanship. Governing the policy of a government by wise counsels.
Stewardship. Being a guardian; a superintendent.

MANAGEMENT—*Nouns of Agency.*

Compass. Instrument to determine direction.
Cynosure. Constellation of the Lesser Bear by which mariners are often directed
Guiding star. A particular star by which sailors direct their course.
Helm. The apparatus by which a ship is steered.
Lodestar. The polestar.
Needle. The pointing instrument of the compass.
Polestar. The star toward which the magnetic needle of the compass points.
Rudder. The apparatus by which a ship is steered.

MANAGEMENT—*Verbs*

Administer. To control; to carry out.
Be at the helm. To direct; to govern.
Be in the chair. To have control.
Conduct. To carry on, to direct.
Control. To guide; to exercise supervision over
Cut out work for. To give a plan to work by
Direct. To lead; to instruct.
Drive. To cause to go in a certain direction.
Govern. To exercise authority over.
Guide. To lead or direct.
Handle the reins. To lead wherever desired.
Have office; have the care of; have the charge of; have the direction of; have the portfolio; have the reins; head; hold office; hold the portfolio; hold the reins; keep in order; lead; lead on; lead the way; legislate for; look after.
Manage. To control; to oversee.
Ministrate. To carry out a religious service.
Occupy the chair. Be in a position to direct.
Order. To give a command; to direct.
Overlook. To superintend; to supervise.
Pilot. To direct the course of, as to pilot a ship
Prescribe. To lay down rules.
Preside. To direct a deliberating body.
Preside at the board. To sit in authority.
Pull the strings.⎫
Pull the wires. ⎬ To try to influence in one's favor
Regulate. To manipulate; to direct.
Rule. See RULE.
See to. To attend to; to exercise vigilance over
Show the way. To direct; to guide.
Steer. To pilot.
Superintend. To exercise control over
Supervise. To oversee.
Tackle. To grasp in order to master.
Take the chair. Assume control of a meeting.

Take the direction. To assume charge of.
Take the helm. To take the pilot's place.
Take the lead. To set a pace for the rest.
Take the reins. To obtain mastery.
Tool. To drive, as a coach.

MANAGEMENT—*Adjectives.*

Directing, etc. See *Verbs.*
Hegemonic. Ruling; guiding.

MANAGEMENT—*Adverbs*

At the head of. In the lead.
At the helm. In control.

man'-a-ger. One who manages. ACTING, MANAGER, PRESIDENT-MEMBER.

MANAGER.

Adviser. See ADVICE.
Ædile. A Roman officer who had charge of public buildings, highways, shows, etc.
Agent. See CONSIGNEE.
Arbiter. See JUDGE.
Bailiff. A deputy sheriff.
Bell-wether. The sheep with the bell on; leader of the flock.
Board. See COUNCIL.
Bureaucrat. One who is at the head of a bureau.
Cabman. One who runs a cab.
Captain. See CHIEF.
Carman. One who conveys goods with a cart or car.
Centerman. The one on whom the others depend for guidance.
Chair. The source of information and direction, as the chair of a deliberative body.
Chairman. The leader of committees.
Charioteer. One who drives a chariot.
Chauffeur. Manager of an automobile.
Clerk of works. One who keeps the records for a company.
Coachman. One who drives a coach.
Comptroller. A city officer who examines public accounts.
Conductor. A leader; a manager.
Corypheus. Leader of a party or cause.
Croupier [F.]. One who presides at a gaming table.
Demagogue. One who artfully sways mobs and the rabble, by his appeals, a political intriguer.
Director. A guide, a manager.
Draco. A famous Athenian lawgiver.
Driver. One who directs a team of horses or oxen
Eparch. Ancient Grecian governor.
Factor. Leader; responsible person.
Factotum. A leader in every kind of work.
Foreman. A boss; a dictator; an overseer.
Fugleman. A drill leader for a company of soldiers.
Functionary. One charged to perform some function.
Governor. A ruler; a controller.
Grand vizier. Chief minister of the Turkish empire
Guide. See ENLIGHTENMENT.
Guiding star. See MANAGEMENT
Headcenter. A director.
Headman. Leader; foreman.
Helmsman. Steersman; guide
Housekeeper. House-mistress, one who oversees the house.
Husband. The head of the family.
Inspector. An overseer; a supervisor.
Intendant. A superintendent of some public business
Jack in office. An insolent fellow in office.
Jehu. A driver; a reckless coachman. [Bible, II *Kings* ix, 20.]
Landreeve. An assistant officer to the steward of a large land estate.
Lawgiver. One who formulates laws.
Lawmaker. One who forms laws
Leader. A guide; a conductor.
Legislator. An enactor of laws.
Linkboy. A man who carries a torch to light passengers.
Lobbyist. A person who tries to influence members of a legislature for the purpose of securing laws according to his own ideas.
Log-roller. A person whose business is to accomplish certain political ends or schemes
Majordomo [L.]. The head man
Manager. Director; supervisor.
Man in office. One who directs public affairs.
Master. See CHIEF
Mayor. See CHIEF
Middleman. A man who rents large tracts of land from proprietors and then rents them in small tracts to peasants.

Minister. One who serves; one of the executive department of a government.

Minos. The famous lawgiver of Crete.

Moderator. One who presides over a deliberative body.

Monitor. An overseer; a guardian.

Muleteer. A mule-driver.

Office-bearer. One who has a specific office or duty to perform

Officer. A public servant; one who sits in authority.

Official. One who holds a public office.

Overlooker. A superintendent.

Overseer. Supervisor.

Person in authority. See CHIEF.

Pilot. One who directs; especially, one who directs the course of a ship.

Politician. One well versed in the science of government.

Postilion. One who guides the first pair of horses hitched to a coach.

Precentor. A leader of a choir.

Premier. The highest official.

President. The head of an organization, corporation, or government.

Prime Minister. See PREMIER.

Principal. Head; chief in control.

Proctor. One who looks after the affairs of another.

Procurator. An agent; a proctor.

Ranger. The keeper of a public park or forest.

Rector. The chief officer of a university; the head of a school.

Red-tapist. One who adheres strictly to official duties.

Reis effendi [Turk.]. Chancellor of the Turkish empire.

Ringleader. The cause of a movement; usually applied in a bad sense.

Secretary. An officer of state whose business is to manage the affairs of a particular department

Secretary of State. The highest cabinet official in the United States Government.

Seneschal. A steward; superintendent of royal domestic ceremonies in the Middle Ages.

Shepherd. The keeper and leader of a flock.

Speaker. One who leads the thoughts of his hearers

State-monger. One who participates in political affairs.

Statesman. One versed in statecraft.

Statist. A statesman.

Steersman. Leader; helmsman

Steersmate. See STEERSMAN.

Steward. A man who manages domestic concerns.

Strategist. One skilled in directing great military movements.

Supercargo. Superintendent of a merchant vessel.

Superintendent. One who has oversight of public or private grounds or works.

Superior. An advanced officer; first in rank.

Supervisor. Overseer; director.

Surveyor. One who acts as superintendent of others.

Taskmaster. One who assigns oppressive tasks.

Teamster. A driver of a team.

Vetturino. One who drives a vettura, a four-wheeled Italian carriage.

Vicar. See REPRESENTATIVE.

Vice-president. One second in authority; successor to the president.

Visitor. A person who makes formal visits of inspection.

Vizier. A high executive officer in Turkey.

Whip. A coach-driver.

Whipper in. One who whips others into line to support certain measures.

Wire-puller. One who gains his power by secret plans.

MANAGER—*Adverb.*

Ex officio [L.]. By virtue of an office.

man'-age-ry. Conduct. MANAGEMENT.

manche après la cognée, jeter le [F.] (man·sh a-prê' la co-nyê', zhe-tê' le). To throw the helve after the hatchet. SANGUINENESS-HOPELESSNESS.

man''-ci-pa'-tion. Slavery. RELEASE-RESTRAINT.

man-da'-mus. An order. ORDER.

man''-da-rin'. A Chinese official. CHIEF-UNDERLING.

man'-date. A command. ORDER.

man'-di-ble. The bone of the lower jaw. NUTRIMENT-EXCRETION.

man'-do-lin. A musical instrument. MUSICAL INSTRUMENTS.

man-drag'-o-ra. An herb. TURBULENCE-CALMNESS.

man'-drel. A shaft. REVOLUTION-EVOLUTION.

man''-du-ca'-tion. Mastication. NUTRIMENT-EXCRETION.

mane. Long hair on a horse's neck. SMOOTHNESS-ROUGHNESS.

man'-eat''-er. An animal that eats human beings. LIFE-KILLING.

manège [F.] (ma-nêzh'). The art of horsemanship. DOMESTICATION-AGRICULTURE, TRAVELING-NAVIGATION.

ma'-nes. Spirits of the dead. LIFE-CORPSE.

manet, alta mente repostum [L.] (mê'-net, al'-ta men'-tî rî-pos'-tum). It abides stored away in the depths of the mind. REMEMBRANCE-FORGETFULNESS.

manet cicatrix [L.] (mê'-net sic'-a-trix). The scar remains. PARDON-VINDICTIVENESS.

ma-neu'-ver. A change of position; a dexterous proceeding. ACTION-PASSIVENESS, CRAFT-ARTLESSNESS.

man'-ful. Brave; sturdy. BRAVERY-COWARDICE, PERSISTENCE-WHIM, STRENGTH-WEAKNESS.

man'-ful-ly. Courageously. DETERMINATION-VACILLATION.

man'-ger. A feeding-trough. CONTENTS-RECEIVER.

manger, cela se laisse [F.] (man-zhê', se-la' se lês). Something fit to eat. PALATABLENESS-UNPALATABLENESS.

manger son blé en herbe [F.] (man-zhê' son· blê an· êrb). To eat one's corn in the blade. EXTRAVAGANCE-AVARICE.

man'-gle. To lacerate; to smooth; a smoothing machine. BETTERMENT-DETERIORATION, SMOOTHNESS-ROUGHNESS, UNION-DISUNION.

man'-gy. Squalid. HEALTH-SICKNESS.

man''-ha''-ter. A misanthrope. HUMANITARIANISM-MISANTHROPY.

man'-hood. Manly quality. BRAVERY-COWARDICE, MANHOOD.

MANHOOD.

Adolescence. The time of growth from childhood to manhood.

Adult. A full-grown individual of either sex.

Adultness. The state of being an adult.

Flower of age. The brightest period of life.

Full age. Mature age.

Majority. The age at which a person may legally manage his own affairs.

Man. An adult male of the human race. See MALE.

Manhood. The state of being of age.

Maturity. The state of having reached full development.

Meridian of life. The culminating point of life.

No chicken. A person by no means young.

Prime of life. The period of full perfection in life.

Pubescence. The state of having arrived at puberty

Ripe age. Fully developed age.

Virility. The state of having the vigor and strength of manhood.

Woman. An adult female of the human race See MALE-FEMALE

MANHOOD—*Verbs.*

Assume the *toga virilis.* } To become legally capable of managing
Attain majority. } one's own affairs.

Come of age. To complete the first twenty-one years of one's life

Come to man's estate. To come to the state of being a man.

Come to years of discretion. To attain to cautious and correct judgment.

Have cut one's eye-teeth. To have had a little experience in the world.

Have sown one's wild oats. To have passed through dissipations in one's youth.

MANHOOD—*Adjectives.*

Adolescent. Growing from childhood to manhood.

Adult. Pertaining to mature life.

Full grown. Having reached the normal size of complete development.

Grown up. Arrived at full growth or stature.

In one's prime. In the period of full perfection in life.

Manly. Worthy of a man.

Marriageable. Of an age suitable to be married.

Matronly. Becoming a mother.

Mature. Having reached full development.

Middle-aged. Between 30 and 50 years of age.

Nubile. Of an age suitable for marriage.

Of age. Having attained majority
Of full age. Mature in age.
Of ripe age. Of a fully developed age.
Out of one's teens. Twenty years or older.
Pubescent. Having arrived at the age of puberty.
Virile. Pertaining to a man in his mature state.
Womanly. Becoming a woman.

ma'-ni-a. Excessive desire; insanity   DESIRE-DIS-TASTE, SANENESS-LUNACY.
ma'-ni-ac. A madman. SANENESS-MANIAC.
ma-ni'-a-cal. Insane. SANENESS-LUNACY.
manibus pedibusque [L.] (man'-i-bus ped-i-bus'-quî) With hands and feet. TOIL-RELAXATION.

Man''-i-che'-ism. A religious philosophy   ANGEL-SATAN.
man'-i-chord. A musical instrument. MUSICAL IN-STRUMENTS.
man'-i-cure. To take care of people's hands and nails. REMEDY-BANE.
ma'-nie. Mania. DESIRE-DISTASTE.
manière [F.] (mɑ-niêr') Manner. SOCIETY-AFFECTA-TION.
man'-i-fest. Evident; clear   MANIFESTATION-LATENCY, VISIBILITY-INVISIBILITY.
man''-i-fes-ta'-tion. Revelation   MANIFESTATION-LA-TENCY.

MANIFESTATION—LATENCY

Bareness. State of being bare.
Demonstration. A proof or reasoning by which anything is made plain to the sight or understanding.
Disclosure. The act or process of making anything plain or clear. See EXPOSURE.
Display. The act of spreading out or bringing to the view or to the mind.
Épanchement [F.]. An outpouring or overflowing by which anything is revealed
Exhibition. Something made plain to the sight.
Exposition. A public show in which things are seen
Expression. The act of declaring or signifying.
Indication. That which serves to mark or point out to the mind or eye. See HEED.
Manifestation. The act of uncovering to the eye or understanding.
Openness. The quality or state of being plain and clear to the sight or mind. See PROBITY; CRAFT-ARTLESSNESS.
Plainness. The quality or state of being clear to the mind or eye. See *Adjectives*.
Plain-speaking. Speaking with plain, clear meaning.
Premonstration. A pointing out or making clear beforehand.
Production. The act or process of bringing forth to view.
Publicity. The state of being open to common knowledge. See PUBLICITY.
Showing. Anything that is presented to the sight or made known. See *Adjectives*.
Showing off. Anything presented to the sight for the purpose of attracting attention.

MANIFESTATION—*Verbs.*

Appear. To come forth into view. See VISIBILITY.
Be manifest. To be clear or plain to the eye or understanding.
Bring forth. Bring into view.
Bring forward. To bring into sight.
Bring into notice. To bring to one's attention.
Bring into view. To bring into range of vision.
Bring out. Bring to the light.
Bring out in strong relief. To bring to view by elevating above the ordinary level.
Bring to light. To make clear or plain by bringing from the darkness.
Bring to the front. To bring into the direct line of sight.
Call into notice. To call attention to.
Demonstrate. To point out; to make clear.
Disclose. To bring to view by uncovering.
Display. To spread out, open, or unfold.
Draw out. Bring from darkness to light.
Elicit. To bring forth, as by some inducement.
Exhibit. To set forth for inspection.
Expose. To disclose the real character or meaning of.
Expose to view. To display openly.
Express. To set forth or clear to the understanding.
Give indication of. To point out something not generally known
Give notice. To inform by any means
Give sign. To point out to the eye.
Give token. To recall or point out to the mind.
Hold up to the mirror. To reveal to oneself.
Hold up to view. To expose to the eye.
Indicate. To point out. See HEED.
Lay before one.
Lay before one's eyes. } To bring into the direct line of sight.
Lay open. To uncover to sight.
Make manifest. To make clear to the eye or mind. See *Adjectives*.
Make no mystery of. To make clear something unknown or unexplained.
Make no secret of. To reveal something known only to a few

Adumbration. A slight shadow or faint resemblance
Anagoge. A spiritual or mystical meaning.
Cabala. A doctrine which teaches that every letter, word, number, and accent of Scripture contains a hidden sense.
Concealment. The act of hiding or withdrawing from sight. See sub CONCEALMENT.
Darkness. That which is hidden or invisible on account of total or partial absence of light.
Hidden meaning. An intention or purpose hidden by the intention stated.
Imperceptibility. That which is hidden from sight or mind
Implication. That which is implied but not expressed.
Inexpression. That which is hidden because it cannot be told in words.
Insinuation. A suggestion by distant allusion.
Invisibility. That which is hidden from the eye.
Latency. State of being hidden or invisible.
Le dessous des cartes [F.]. The secret of an affair.
Mystery. Something unknown or unexplained
Occult mean'ng. A meaning that is not immediately or easily known.
Occultness. State or quality of being hidden from the eye or understanding.
Secret. Something known only to one or a few and kept from others.
Silence. Absence of sound or noise; hidden from the ear. See TACITURNITY
Snake in the grass. A secret or treacherous enemy. See PITFALL.
Something rotten in the state of Denmark. [Shakespeare, *Hamlet*, I, 4.]
Undercurrent. Feeling or opinion in the direction contrary to that which is publicly shown.

LATENCY—*Denotations.*

Allusion. A hint at something hidden.
Delphic oracle. A famous oracle at Delphi which made known the commands or wishes of the gods.
Innuendo. An indirect hint usually derogatory to a person not named. See ENLIGHTENMENT.
More than meets the ear.
More than meets the eye. } A holding back of information.

LATENCY—*Verbs.*

Allude to. To carry the mind or thought to something not plainly known by means of another thing connected with it.
Be latent. To be hidden or invisible. See *Adjectives*.
Escape detection. To remain hidden or unknown.
Escape observation. To remain covered or hidden from sight.
Escape recognition. To be unknown.
Imply. To give a meaning to which is not expressed.
Infer. Produce or bring forward from something not clearly understood.
Involve. Hide from sight or understanding.
Keep back. Withhold from sight or meaning. See SECRECY.
Laugh in one's sleeve. To laugh secretly or so as not to be observed; especially, while showing a grave or serious countenance to the person laughed at.
Leave an inference. Having a meaning beyond that expressed
Lie hid. See SECRECY.
Lurk. To lie hidden in order to make an unexpected attack or to escape notice.
Make no sign. Be hidden "He dies and makes no sign." [Shakespeare, *Henry VI*, II, iii, 2]
Smolder. Exist in a hidden or suppressed state.
Underlie. To be covered
Understand. To learn.
Whisper. To utter in a low and unvocal tone so as not to be generally heard.

MANIFESTATION—LATENCY—*Continued.*

MANIFESTATION—Verbs—*Continued.*

Manifest oneself. To show or make clear one's own actions or intentions

Place before one.
Place before one's eyes. } To bring to view

Proclaim. To make known publicly. See Publicity.

Produce. To bring from the unknown to the known.

Put through one's paces. To reveal the actions or intentions of a person. as of a horse for sale

Rear its head. To show above the ordinary.

Render manifest. To make clear to mind or eye. See *Adjectives.*

Represent. To bring before the mind. as by words or pictures.

Set before one.
Set before one's eyes. } To place in a position to be seen.

Set forth. To place apart from other things.

Show. To cause or permit to be seen.

Show one's colors.
Show one's face. } To make known one's ideas or intentions.

Show up. To hold a person or thing up to view; to expose

Speak for itself. To be clearly seen or known without explanation.

Stand to reason. To be clear and plain.

Stare one in the face. To be so plain that no mistake can be made.

Tell its own tale. To be clear or plain without proof See Clearness.

Tell to one's face. To tell openly

Transpire. To come gradually from secrecy to public notice.

Trot out. To make known.

Unfurl the flag. To make known one's intentions.

Unroll. To spread or open to the light.

Wear one's heart upon his sleeve. To be clear and open in thought and action

MANIFESTATION—*Adjectives.*

Apparent. Clearly seen, or easily understood.

Arrant. Unmitigated.

Autoptical. Seen with one s own eyes.

Bare. Devoid of covering.

Barefaced. Impudent.

Capable of being shown. That may be proved.

Clear. Free from anything that dims or keeps off the light.

Clear as day.
Clear as daylight. } Figurative degrees of clearness
Clear as noonday.

Conspicuous. Clearly visible on account of prominence. See sub Visibility

Defined. Made clear or plain by marking the limits or outlines.

Definite. Known with exactness.

Demonstrative. Showing clearly or plainly.

Disclosed. Brought into view by uncovering. See Exposure.

Distinct. Standing apart, or clearly seen as standing apart from other things

Downright. Without doubt; positive.

Evident. Plain to the mind or senses.

Exoteric. Capable of being readily or fully seen.

Explicit. Expressed plainly.

Express. Set forth or declared with the utmost distinctness

Flagrant. Openly wicked

Frank. Open in manner and disposition.

Free-hearted. Open, unreserved; generous.

Glaring. Open and bold.

Inconcealable. Not able to be hidden from the light.

Intelligible. Capable of being made clear.

In the foreground. Near the eye.

Literal. Exact or plain as to fact or detail.

Manifest. Clear and open.

Manifested. Plain See *Verbs.*

Naked. Exposed to light.

Notable. Clearly seen, conspicuous.

Notorious. Publicly known and the subject of general remark, especially unfavorable See Publicity.

Not to be mistaken. Unmistakable.

Obvious. Easily seen or understood.

Open. Uncovered to the light.

Open as day. Plain and clear as sunlight.

Ostensible. Proper or intended to be shown.

Overt. Open to view.

Palpable. Readily perceived and detected.

Patent. Open to everybody.

Plain. Readily seen or understood

Plain as a pike-staff. Very plain

Plain as the nose on one's face.
Plain as the sun at noonday. } Plain as it can be.
Plain as the way to parish church.

Latency—*Adjectives.*

Allusive. Having reference to something not fully expressed

By implication.
By inference. } Shown or proved to be in connection with.

Concealed. Hidden. See Enlightenment-Secrecy.

Constructive. Not directly expressed, but derived from.

Covert. Covered over.

Crooked. Not straightforward in conduct.

Dark. Without light, or not easily understood.

Delitescent. Lying hid.

Dormant. Not shown.

Impenetrable. Not to be entered by light See Clearness-Obscurity.

Implicit Fairly understood. though not expressed in words.

Implied. Contained or included, though not directly stated. See *Verbs.*

Indirect. Not in direct relation.

Indiscoverable. Not to be brought to light or knowledge.

Inferential. Drawn to light.

In the background. Almost out of view.

Invisible. Not to be seen. See Visibility-Invisibility.

Latent. Hidden.

Lurking. Hiding for an evil purpose. See *Verbs.*

Muffled. Wrapped up so as to conceal; deaden sound.

Not expressed. Not told or shown.

Occult. Hidden from observation or knowledge.

Secret. Unknown to all but a few. See Enlightenment-Secrecy.

Steganographic. Written in characters which are not intelligible except to persons who have the key.

Tacit. Done or made in silence.

Unapparent. Not easily seen.

Unbreathed. Not told.

Underground.
Underhand. } Secretly

Understood. Made clear or plain.

Undeveloped. Covered or folded.

Undisclosed. Kept from view. See Exposure.

Undiscovered. Hidden from knowledge. See Discovery.

Unexplained. Kept from the mind.

Unexplored. Not made known to sight.

Unexposed. Not brought to light.

Unexpressed. Not shown or told.

Uninvented. Not in existence.

Unknown. Hidden from the mind.

Unproclaimed. Not known to the public.

Unpublished. Not generally known.

Unsaid. Known to but one.

Unseen. Hidden from the eye. See sub Vision.

Unsolved. Not clear to the mind.

Unspied. Hidden from the eye.

Unsung. Not celebrated in song or poetry.

Unsuspected. Not regarded as having done an evil act; not brought into light.

Untalked of.
Untold. } See Enlightenment.

Untraced. Not marked out or made known.

Untracked. Not known by following.

Unwritten. Not written.

Latency—*Adverbs.*

Behind one's back.
Behind the scenes. } Secretly.

By a side wind. By indirect means or influence.

In the background. At a distance.

On the tip of one's tongue. To be on the point of telling.

Secretly. Kept separate or hidden from view or knowledge. See Enlightenment-Secrecy.

Sub silentio [L.]. In silence.

Latency—*Phrase.*

Thereby hangs a tale. Suggestion of something more than is told. [Shakespeare, *As You Like It*, ii, 7.]

MANIFESTATION—Adjectives—*Continued.*

Plain-spoken. Spoken with plain, unreserved sincerity. See Artlessness.

Producible. That can be brought to light

Prominent. Easily seen.

Salient. Easily seen because projecting above everything.

Self-evident. Requiring no proof of the truth.

Starkstaring. Showing with undue prominence.

MANIFESTATION—Adjectives—Continued.

Striking. Impressive.
Unconcealable. Not to be hidden from the light.
Undisguised. Not hidden or concealed

Unmistakable. That cannot be taken for something else.
Unreserved. Not withheld in part.
Unshaded. Allowed to come to the full light

MANIFESTATION—Adverbs

Aboveboard. Openly.
At first blush. First view or glance.
Before one's eyes. In plain sight.
Cartes sur table [F.] To deal frankly, openly
Face to face. In plain view
In broad daylight.)
In open daylight. } As plainly and clearly as possible.
In the face of day.)
In market-overt.)
In open court. } Publicly
In the face of heaven.)

In set terms. Spoken plainly and exactly
In the open streets. Publicly.
Manifestly. Openly; plainly
On the face of. In sight.
On the stage. In public.
Openly. Plainly See Adjectives
Prima facie [L.] At first view
To one's face }
Under one's nose. } Openly.
Without reserve. Not withholding a part.

MANIFESTATION—Phrases

Cela saute aux yeux [F.]. That leaps to the eyes; quickly seen or understood.
Cela va sans dire [F.] It goes without saying.
Fari quæ sentiat [L.] To speak what one thinks.
He that runs may read. A phrase denoting something easily understood.
It needs no ghost to tell us. Evident.

Res ipsa loquitur [L.]. The thing speaks for itself; self-explanatory
The meaning lies on the surface. Clear without proof.
Volto sciolto e pensieri stretti [It.]. Countenance open and thoughts closed.
You can see it with half an eye. Plainly

---

man''-i-fes'-ted. Clear. MANIFESTATION-LATENCY.
man''-i-fes'-ted-ly. Clearly. MANIFESTATION-LATENCY
man''-i-fes'-to. A proclamation. PUBLICITY.
man'-i-fold. Numerous; complicated. MULTIPLICITY-PAUCITY, UNIFORMITY-MULTIFORMITY
man'-i-kin. A model of the human body; a dwarf. DELINEATION-CARICATURE, GREATNESS-LITTLENESS.
man'-i-ple. A division of a Roman legion. MULTIPLICITY-PAUCITY.
ma-nip'-u-late. To handle dexterously; to manage. TOUCH, USE-DISUSE.
ma-nip''-u-la'-tion. Management. CONDUCT.
man''-kind'. The whole human race. ETHNOLOGY, HUMANITY
man'-li-hood. Manliness. BRAVERY-COWARDICE.
man'-like. Masculine. STRENGTH-WEAKNESS.
man'-li-ness. Gentlemanly. BRAVERY-COWARDICE.
man'-ly. Having the qualities of a man. BRAVERY-COWARDICE, MALE-FEMALE, MANHOOD, STRENGTH-WEAKNESS.
Mann, der kranke [G.] (man, der kran'-kê) The sick man. MIGHT-IMPOTENCE.
Mann nicht kann meiden, muss Mann willig leiden, was [G.] (vas man niht kan mai'-den, mus man vil'-lih lai'-den) What can't be cured must be endured. VOLITION-OBLIGATION.
man'-na. A kind of food. SWEETNESS-ACIDITY; manna in the wilderness, OBSTRUCTION-HELP, PLEASURABLENESS-PAINFULNESS.
man'-ner. Behavior; kind; style. CONDUCT, DIVISION, STYLE, WAY, by no manner of means, READINESS-RELUCTANCE; in a manner, MAGNITUDE-SMALLNESS; to the manner born, SUBJECTIVENESS-OBJECTIVENESS.
man'-nered. Having a certain way PURITY-CRUDENESS.
man'-ner-ism. Peculiarity of style or manner. CONCEIT-DIFFIDENCE, CONVENTIONALITY-UNCONVENTIONALITY, SOCIETY-AFFECTATION, UNIVERSALITY-PARTICULARITY.
man'-ner-ly. Polite. POLITENESS-IMPOLITENESS.
man'-ners. Politeness; breeding. POLITENESS-IMPOLITENESS, SOCIETY-LUDICROUSNESS.
man'-or. A landed estate. PROPERTY; lord of the manor, HOLDER; manor house, DWELLER-HABITATION.
ma-no'-ri-al. Of a manor. PROPERTY.
manse. A parsonage. FANE.

man'-serv''-ant. A serving-man. CHIEF-UNDERLING, MALE-FEMALE.
man'-sion. A large dwelling. DWELLER-HABITATION.
man'-slaugh''-ter. Killing of man by man. LIFE-KILLING.
man'-sue-tude. Tameness POLITENESS-IMPOLITENESS.
man'-tel-et. A small mantle worn by women; a screen to protect defenders. ATTACK-DEFENSE, DRESS-UNDRESS.
man'-tel-piece''. A shelf above the fireplace. SUSPENSION-SUPPORT.
man'-tel-shelf''. The shelf forming a usual part of a mantel. SUSPENSION-SUPPORT.
man-til'-la. A light cape. DRESS-UNDRESS.
man'-tle. To cover; a loose cloak; a hood for a gas-flame; to flush. DRESS-UNDRESS, EMOTION, ENLARGEMENT-DIMINUTION, EXCITATION, FAVORITE-ANGER, LUMINARY-SHADE, REDNESS-GREENNESS, SCEPTER, VISCIDITY-FOAM.
man'-tlet. A musket-proof roof; a short cloak. ATTACK-DEFENSE, DRESS-UNDRESS.
man-tol'-o-gy. Art of divination. PROPHECY.
man'-tu-a. A woman's loose cloak. DRESS-UNDRESS.
man'-u-al. A handbook; done with the hands. ADVICE, ENLIGHTENMENT-SECRECY, MISSIVE-PUBLICATION, SCHOOL; manual labor, TOIL-RELAXATION.
ma-nu'-bi-al. Taken in war. PLUNDER.
man''-u-fac'-to-ry. A building for manufacturing. WORKSHOP.
man''-u-fac'-ture. The product of manufacturing; to make. CREATION-DESTRUCTION, LABOR-CAPITAL, NATURE-ART.
man''-u-fac'-tured. Not natural. NATURE-ART.
man''-u-fac'-tur-er. One who manufactures. AGENT
manu forti [L.] (mên'-yu for'-tai) With a strong hand. DETERMINATION-VACILLATION, HARSHNESS-MILDNESS, TOIL-RELAXATION.
man''-u-mis'-sion. Act of freeing. RELEASE-RESTRAINT.
man''-u-mit'. Release. RELEASE-RESTRAINT
man'-u-mo''-tor. A hand-carriage for invalids CONVEYANCE-VESSEL
ma-nure'. Dung. CLEANNESS-FILTHINESS, DOMESTICATION-AGRICULTURE, OBSTRUCTION-HELP
man'-u-script. Written by hand. WRITING-PRINTING.
man'-y. A great number, numerous. MULTIPLICITY-

PAUCITY; **for many a day,** LASTINGNESS-TRANSIENT-NESS; **many irons in the fire,** ACTIVITY-INDOLENCE; **many men many minds,** ASSENT-DISSENT; **many times,** FREQUENCY-RARITY, RECURRENCE; **the many,** GENTILITY-COMMONALTY.

man'-y-col"-ored. Having many colors. VARIEGA-TION.

man'-y-si"-ded. Having many sides. LATERALITY-CONTRAPOSITION, UNIFORMITY-MULTIFORMITY.

man'-y-tongued'. Having many tongues. TID-INGS.

map. A chart; to plan. DELINEATION-CARICATURE, ENLIGHTENMENT-SECRECY, POSITION; **map out,** DE-SIGN.

mar. To spoil; to obstruct. BETTERMENT-DETERIORA-TION, OBSTRUCTION-HELP.

Mar'-a-bout. A Mohammedan devotee. FANE.

mar"-a-na'-tha. Word used in anathematizing. CHARI-TABLENESS-CURSE.

ma-ras'-mus. A wasting away. BETTERMENT-DETERI-ORATION, ENLARGEMENT-DIMINUTION, HEALTH-SICK-NESS.

ma-raud'. To pillage. THEFT.

ma-raud'-er. One who pillages. ROBBER.

mar'-ble. A little ball; stone; cold; tablet. HARD-NESS-SOFTNESS, ROUNDNESS, SCULPTURE, SENSI-TIVENESS-APATHY, WRITING-PRINTING.

mar'-bled. Spotted. VARIEGATION.

mar'-ble-heart"-ed. Hard-hearted. CHARITABLE-NESS-MALEVOLENCE.

march. To proceed; a piece of music; a walk. AD-VANCE-RETROGRESSION, EXTENSION-DISTRICT, MU-SIC, TRAVELING-NAVIGATION; **dead march,** LIFE-FUNERAL; **forced march,** HURRY-LEISURE; **march against,** ATTACK-DEFENSE; **march of events,** OCCUR-RENCE-DESTINY; **march off,** ARRIVAL-DEPARTURE; **march of intellect,** BETTERMENT-DETERIORATION, KNOWLEDGE-IGNORANCE; **march of time,** PERIOD-PROGRESS; **march on a point,** AIM-ABERRATION; **march past,** POMP; **on the march,** MOVEMENT-REST; **steal a march,** ACTIVITY-INDOLENCE, CRAFT-ART-LESSNESS, LEADING-FOLLOWING, TRANSCURSION-SHORTCOMING, TRUTHFULNESS-FRAUD.

March, Ides of. The fifteenth of March. VOLITION-OBLIGATION.

march'-es. Regions. BOUNDARY.

mar'-chion-ess. Wife of a marquis. GENTILITY-COM-MONALTY.

march'-man. A man dwelling on a frontier. DWELL-ER-HABITATION.

mar'-cid. Lean. BREADTH-NARROWNESS.

mar'-cor. A wasting away. BREADTH-NARROW-NESS.

mare. A female horse. CONVEYER, MALE-FEMALE;

mare's nest, TRUTHFULNESS-FABRICATION; **mare's tail,** RIVER-WIND, VISCIDITY-FOAM.

ma-ren'-go. Coin. VALUES.

mar-e-schal. A marshal. CHIEF-UNDERLING.

marge. An edge. BORDER.

mar'-gin. Border; difference between cost and selling price; latitude. BORDER, EXCESS-LACK, EXTEN-SION-DISTRICT, LIBERTY-SUBJECTION.

mar'-gin-al. Pertaining to a margin. BORDER.

mar'-gin-ate. To margin. BORDER.

mar'-grave. A German governor. CHIEF-UNDERLING, GENTILITY-COMMONALTY.

mar'-gra-vine. Wife of a margrave. CHIEF-UNDER-LING.

mariage de convenance [F.] (ma-riazh' de con'-ve-nan's'). Marriage of convenience. MATRIMONY-CELIBACY.

ma-rine'. A soldier; naval. BELLIGERENT, CONVEY-ANCE-VESSEL, OCEAN-LAND, WAYFARER-SEAFARER; **marine painter,** ARTIST; **marine painting,** PAINTING; **tell it to the marines,** ADAGE-NONSENSE.

mar'-i-ner. A sailor. TRAVELING-NAVIGATION, WAY-FARER-SEAFARER.

Ma"-ri-ol'-a-try. Worship of Mary. DEVOTION-IDOLATRY.

mar"-i-o-nette'. A puppet. ACTING, DELINEATION-CARICATURE.

mar'-ish. Marshy. SWAMP-ISLAND.

mar'-i-tal. Of marriage. MATRIMONY-CELIBACY.

mar'-i-time. Oceanic; marine. OCEAN-LAND, TRAV-ELING-NAVIGATION.

mark. To observe; distinction; record; degree. CHOICE-NEUTRALITY, CONSEQUENCE-INSIGNIFICANCE, HEED-DISREGARD, MARK-OBLITERATION, MIND-IM-BECILITY, PURPOSE-LUCK, QUANTITY-MEASURE, REPUTATION-DISCREDIT, SIGN, STATION; **beyond the mark,** TRANSCURSION-SHORTCOMING; **leave one's mark,** REPUTATION-DISCREDIT; **man of mark,** GEN-TILITY-COMMONALTY, REPUTATION-DISCREDIT; **mark off,** MARK-OBLITERATION; **mark of recognition,** PO-LITENESS-IMPOLITENESS; **mark out,** CHOICE-NEU-TRALITY; **mark time,** CHRONOLOGY-ANACHRONISM, MOVEMENT-REST; **mark with a red letter,** SOLEMNI-ZATION; **mark with a white stone,** APPROVAL-DISAP-PROVAL, CONSEQUENCE-INSIGNIFICANCE; **near the mark,** REMOTENESS-NEARNESS; **overshoot the mark,** SKILL-UNSKILFULNESS; **put a mark upon,** HEED-DISREGARD; **save the mark,** ASTONISHMENT-EX-PECTANCE; **up to the mark,** DUENESS-UNDUENESS, ENOUGH, GOODNESS-BADNESS, SKILL-UNSKILFUL-NESS; **wide of the mark,** REMOTENESS-NEARNESS, TRUTH-ERROR; **within the mark,** TRANSCURSION-SHORTCOMING.

MARK—OBLITERATION.

Acts of. The record of the doings of.

Affidavit. A sworn statement in writing made before the proper authorities.

Almanac. } A book or table containing a calendar of days, weeks,
Almanack. } and months, and astronomical data.

Annals. A record of events in their chronological order; history.

Archives. Public or state documents which are or may be of historic interest; also, in singular, the place where they are kept.

Biography. The written history of a person's life.

Blue-book. A book of information in regard to affairs of government

Booking. The act of registering in a book.

Calendar. Table or orderly arrangement of the divisions of time.

Cedilla. Mark, indicating the soft sound of "c."

Celebration. A joyful or solemn demonstration.

Certificate. Written evidence as to the qualifications of a person or the truth of a statement.

Chronicle. A record of events arranged chiefly with regard to the order of their occurrence; history. See HISTORY.

Cicatrix [L.]. The mark or scar left after the healing of a wound. See SCAR.

Blot. A spot or stain which covers up something that was written before.

Cancel. The striking out of printed or written matter, usually by drawing lines through.

Cancelation. The act or process of canceling. See CANCEL.

Circumduction. The act or process of nullifying or canceling. See CANCEL.

Deletion. The act of erasing or rendering extinct.

Erasure. The act of erasing. See sub ERASE.

Obliteration. The act of obliterating. See OBLITERATE

Razure. An erasure. See sub ERASURE.

Tabula rasa [L.]. An erased or blank tablet.

OBLITERATION—*Verbs.*

Apply the sponge. To use the sponge in removing written matter, as from a blackboard.

Be effaced, etc See EFFACE.

Blot out. To cover with a stain or blot so as not to be seen or read.

Cancel. To strike out, as an account; usually by drawing lines through.

MARK—OBLITERATION—*Continued.*

Column. A shaft or obelisk.

Commemoration. An observance in honor of some person or event

Compte rendu [F.]. The written report of an agent or official.

Copy. A transcript or reproduction of an original.

Deed. A written instrument for the transfer of property

Deposition. Testimony reduced to writing.

Diary. A register of daily events.

Diptych. A writing on two leaves or folds.

Docket. A list or calendar of business matters.

Document. Written matter usually of a legal nature.

Domesday book. A statistical survey of England made by William the Conqueror.

Dottings. Marks indicating repetition

Duplicate. A written paper which contains the same matter as another and has the same force.

Enrolment. The written record of those belonging

Entry. The record made of any event or action

Ephemeris. A diary.

Footmark.· Footprint. See FOOTPRINT.

Footprint. The impression made by a foot.

Footstep. A footprint. See FOOTPRINT.

Gazette. }
Gazetteer. } A newspaper.

Hansard's debates. The official report of the proceedings of the British Parliament.

Hatchment. The armorial bearings of a deceased person.

History. A systematic account of the events of the past.

Indorsement. That which is written on the back of any paper or document.

Inrolment. See ENROLMENT

Inscription. That which is written on or engraved in.

Jottings. Short notes or memoranda.

Legend. A motto, usually inscribed on a coin, medal, or banner.

Log. The record of a ship's daily progress.

Magazine. A pamphlet published periodically.

Mark. A visible impression made or left upon anything.

Medal. A piece of metal struck with a device, intended to preserve the remembrance of something.

Memento. Anything given to awaken memory.

Memorandum. A brief note.

Memorial. Anything intended to preserve the memory, as a tablet.

Minute. A brief record of, as of a business meeting; usually in the plural.

Monolith. A pillar, monument, or obelisk, of a single stone.

Muniment. Any record or written evidence that can be used to defend a title.

Newspaper. A public print that circulates news.

Notch. A hollow or nick intended to mark.

Note. A brief record; a memorandum.

Obelisk. An upright pillar or monument

Pillar. A monument

Pist. The track of a horseman; a trail.

Proceedings of. See TRANSACTIONS OF.

Procès verbal [F.] An authentic record of an official act or statement.

Record. Any writing or other means of preserving and handing down the knowledge and events of the past.

Recorder. One who records or marks

Register. A formal written record, as of facts or names; a roll.

Registration. An official written record, as of names; an enrolment.

Registry. A written record, as of facts or statements; a registration.

Relic. Some part that is left, the remainder of which has been lost or destroyed; anything preserved in remembrance.

Remains. That which is left after destruction; the ruins. We may have remains at any time, but relics only after the lapse of time.

Return. An official report.

Scar. A mark remaining after the healing of a wound or sore. See CICATRIX.

Scent. The trace of odor left on the ground by an animal in passing over

Scroll. A writing formed into a roll.

Signature A person's name or mark appended to some paper or document.

Slab. A piece of stone intended as a marker.

State paper. An official communication on state affairs, as a president's message.

Statistics. Tabulated facts

Tablet. A flat piece of metal, etc., containing a memorial inscription.

Tabulation. A systematic arrangement of facts in tables.

Testimonial. Written evidence as to one's character or ability; a certificate See CERTIFICATE. A certificate is usually more official than a testimonial.

OBLITERATION—VERBS—*Continued.*

Deface. To render illegible in part, as an inscription.

Draw the pen through. To cancel. See CANCEL.

Efface. To render illegible in any manner by direct action.

Erase. To scratch or rub out.

Expunge. Literally, to pick out with a sharp instrument; to strike out as of no account.

Leave not a rack behind. Literally, to leave not a bit of cloud or flying vapor behind; to leave no trace or vestige. [Shakespeare *Tempest.*]

Leave no trace of. Obliterate.

Obliterate. To render illegible in any manner whatever.

Rase. To erase. See ERASE.

Render illegible. Make unreadable.

Rub off. }
Rub out. } To erase. See sub ERASE.

Scratch out. To remove written matter by scratching, as with a knife.

Sponge out. See APPLY THE SPONGE.

Strike out. To expunge. See EXPUNGE.

Wash out. }
Wipe away. } To erase.
Wipe out. }

OBLITERATION—*Adjectives.*

Intestate. Not disposed of by will.

Leaving no trace. Leaving no mark.

Obliterated, etc. See *Verbs.*

Out of print. No longer on sale, the edition being exhausted.

Printless. Bearing no print or impression.

Unrecorded. Not preserved in writing.

Unregistered. Not entered in the register.

Unwritten. Not put down in writing.

OBLITERATION—*Interjections.*

Dele [L.]. Blot out; destroy.

Out with it.

OBLITERATION—*Phrase.*

Delenda est Carthago [L.]. Carthage must be destroyed. [Cato.]

MARK—*Continued.*

Tilde. A diacritical sign used in writing the Spanish language.

Trace. A visible continued mark left behind which may aid in discovering present conditions or whereabouts.

Track. An impression or footprint; a well-beaten course.

Trail. A route or path through the forest.

Transactions of. Minutes or records of what has been done, as at a meeting of a society.

Trophy. A memento or token of victory.

Vestige. A trace; originally a footprint; any remains of the works of men.

Wake. The track left by a vessel in the water.

MARK—*Associated Nouns.*

Commonplace-book. A book of miscellaneous notes and memoranda.

Day-book. A book in which business transactions are recorded in the order of their occurrence.

Journal. A daily paper; a diary; also, the book in which are entered the accounts from the day-book in condensed form.

Ledger. The final account-book in business transactions containing the debits and credits of each man.

Memorandum-book. A note-book. See sub NOTE-BOOK

Monument. That which stands or remains to preserve the memory.

Note-book. A small book in which are taken down all sorts of observations and memoranda.

Pigeonholes. Small openings in a bookcase or writing-desk for filing papers.

Pocketbook. A note-book. See sub NOTE-BOOK

Portfolio. A portable case for holding writing materials and documents.

MARK—*Collective Nouns*

Adversaria. A collection of miscellaneous notes and remarks.

Cartulary. A collection of legal papers.

Excerpta. A collection of extracts and quotations.

MARK—*Verbs*

Book. To enter in a book; record

Calendar. To register in a calendar.

Chronicle. To arrange in chronological order. See CHRONICLE.

Commemorate. To preserve the memory of by proper observances.

MARK—Verbs—*Continued.*

Commit to writing. To record in writing.

Enroll. To enter in a roll or register.

Enter. To insert in writing.

File. To systematically arrange papers for future reference.

Hand down to posterity. Record.

Inscroll. To write on a scroll.

Insert. To write in, as a name in a register.

Jot down. To note down.

Keep up the memory of. Commemorate.

Make a memorandum of. To take a note of.

Make a minute of. To take a brief note of.

Make an entry of. To make a formal or official record of.

Make a note of. Write down.

Make a return. To make an official report, as of an election.

Mark. To keep record of by means of marks. See Mark.

Mark off. To keep a record of by checking off.

Minute. To make a brief summary of; to place on official record.

Note down. To make a brief note of in writing.

Post. To transfer accounts from the original books of entry to the ledger.

Put down. To write down, as a name.

Put down in black and white. To put down in writing

Put down in writing. Write down.

Put on paper. To record in writing.

Put upon record. To put down in writing; to make record of.

Record. To preserve by committing to writing; to make record of. See Mark.

Reduce to writing. To put verbal matter in the form of writing.

Register. To enter in the register, as one's name.

Report. To give a written account of, or to make an official statement.

Set down. To put in writing.

Set down in black and white. To set down in writing.

Set down in writing. Make a record of.

Sign. To append one's name or its equivalent to any paper or document.

Take a memorandum. Make a note.

Take a minute of. To take a summarized record of.

Take a note of. Set down in writing.

Take down. To take a note of in writing.

Tick off. To check off by making a small mark against.

MARK—*Adverb.*

On record. Written down officially.

marked. Affirmed; great. Assertion-Denial, Magnitude-Smallness; **in a marked degree,** Magnitude-Smallness; **well marked,** Visibility-Invisibility.

mar'-ket. To buy; mart. Buying-Sale, Market; **bring to market,** Buying-Sale; **buy in the cheapest and sell in the dearest market,** Exchange; **in the market,** Buying-Sale, Exchange, Proffer-Refusal; **market-overt,** Manifestation-Latency, Market; **market-place,** Dweller-Habitation, Market; **market price,** Price-Discount; **rig the market,** Exchange.

MARKET.

Bazaar. An Oriental market-place or range of shops.

Booth. A temporary structure at a fair or market.

Bourse. A place where merchants and bankers meet for business at certain hours.

Bureau. An office where business requiring writing is transacted.

Chambers. A hall where a deliberative assembly meets.

Change. A building set apart for mercantile transactions.

Compter. } A table or board on which money is counted and over

Counter. } which business is transacted.

Counting-house. The house or room in which a merchant, trader, or manufacturer keeps his books and transacts business.

Custom-house. The place appointed by the government where duties upon merchandise are collected.

Dépôt [F.] A place of deposit for the storing of goods.

Emporium [L]. A place of trade.

Entrepôt [F]. A distributing commercial center.

Establishment. Any office or place of business with its fixtures.

Exchange. The place where the merchants, brokers, and bankers meet at certain hours to transact business.

Fair. An exhibit and sale of manufactured and agricultural products.

Guildhall. The hall where an association of persons engaged in kindred pursuits meets.

Hall. A trade-building.

Interposit. A depot or station between one commercial city and another.

Market. A meeting of people, at a stated time and place, for the purpose of trade.

Market-overt. An open market.

Market-place. An open square or place in a town where markets or public sales are held.

Mart. A place of public traffic.

Office. A place where a particular kind of business or service is transacted.

Shop. A place for the regular sale of articles at retail.

Stall. A small booth or compartment in a street, market, etc., for the sale of anything.

Staple. Any article that is regularly or constantly produced and sold. See Store.

Store. A place of deposit for goods.

Tattersall's. A market in London for the sale and exchange of horses.

Toll-booth. A place where goods are weighed to ascertain the duties or toll.

Warehouse. A storehouse for goods.

Wareroom. A room in which goods are stored or exhibited for sale.

Wharf. A structure or platform to receive and discharge cargo.

mar'-ket-a-ble. Suitable for sale. Buying-Sale, Exchange.

marks'-man. One who shoots well. Adept-Bungler.

marks'-man-ship. Marksman's skill. Skill-Unskilfulness.

marl. A clay and sand deposit. Ocean-Land.

mar'-ma-lade. A preserve. Sweetness-Acidity.

mar'-mot. An animal. Activity-Indolence.

ma-roon'. A color. Gray-Brown, Redness-Greenness.

mar'-plot''. One who mars a plan. Adept-Bungler, Benefactor-Evildoer, Obstruction-Help.

marque, let'-ters of. A license of reprisal. Theft.

mar-quee'. Outer flap or roof. Cover-Lining.

mar'-quet-ry. Inlaid work. Variegation.

mar'-quis. A title. Gentility-Commonalty.

mar'-quis-ate. The rank of a marquis. Gentility-Commonalty.

mar'-riage. Union of man and woman in wedlock. Matrimony-Celibacy; **ill-assorted marriage,** Matrimony-Celibacy.

mar'-riage-a-ble. Fitted for marriage. Manhood, Matrimony-Celibacy.

mar'-riage-bell''. A bell rung at a marriage. Lightheartedness-Dejection.

mar'-ried. Wedded. Matrimony-Celibacy.

mar'-row. Interior of a bone; essence. Center, Outside-Inside, Subjectiveness-Objectiveness; **chill to the marrow,** Heating-Cooling.

mar'-row-bones'', on one's. Kneeling. Atonement, Petition-Expostulation, Presumption-Obsequiousness, Selfrespect-Humbleness, Yielding.

mar'-row-less. Lacking marrow. Might-Impotence.

mar'-ry. To wed; to fasten end to end; in truth. Assertion-Denial, Composition-Resolution, Matrimony-Celibacy; **marry come up,** Approval-Disapproval, Defiance, Favorite-Anger.

Mars. God of war. Fighting-Conciliation; **Mars orange,** Blueness-Orange.

Mars gravior sub pace latet [L.] (mars grē'-vi-or sub pê'-sî lē'-tet). A more serious war lurks under the peace. Fighting-Conciliation, Strife-Peace, Variance-Accord.

marsh. A swamp. Dampness-Dryness, Swamp-Island.

mar'-shal. To arrange; an officer. Antagonist-As-

SISTANT, CHIEF-UNDERLING, MESSENGER, ORGANIZA-
TION-DISORGANIZATION

Mar'-shal-sea. A prison. RELEASE-PRISON

marsh'-y. Boggy. SWAMP-ISLAND.

mar-su'-pi-al. Having a pouch. CONTENTS-RECEIVER.

mart. A market MARKET.

marte, suo [L.] (mar'-tî, siu'-o). By his own strength
SKILL-UNSKILFULNESS, TOIL-RELAXATION.

mar-tel'-lo tow'-er. A coast defense. ATTACK-DE
FENSE.

mar'-tial. Pertaining to war. FIGHTING-CONCILIA-
TION; **court-martial,** TRIBUNAL; **martial law,** COER-
CION, HARSHNESS-MILDNESS, LAW-LAWLESSNESS,
martial music, MUSIC.

mar''-ti-net'. A strict disciplinarian. HARSHNESS-
MILDNESS.

mar'-tin-gale. A piece of harness. RELEASE-PRISON

Mar'-tin-mas. A festival. CEREMONIAL.

mar'-tyr. A sufferer for faith. AUSTERITY, PLEAS-
URE-PAIN, SENSUALITY-SUFFERING; **martyr to disease,** HEALTH-SICKNESS.

mar'-tyr-dom. Condition of a martyr. AUSTERITY,
LIFE-KILLING, PLEASURE-PAIN, RECOMPENSE-PUNI-
TION, SENSUALITY-SUFFERING, UNSELFISHNESS-SELF-
ISHNESS.

mar'-vel. A wonder; prodigy. ASTONISHMENT-
EXPECTANCE, PHENOMENON; **marvel whether,** HY-
POTHESIS.

mar'-vel-ous. Wonderful; great. ASTONISHMENT-
EXPECTANCE, MAGNITUDE-SMALLNESS; **deal in the
marvelous,** GULL-HYPERBOLE.

mar'-vel-ous-ly. Wonderfully. MAGNITUDE-SMALL-
NESS.

Ma''-sa-ni-el'-lo. Neapolitan insurgent leader. IN-
SUBORDINATION-OBEDIENCE.

mas'-cot. Something that is regarded as bringing
good luck to the possessor. PURPOSE-LUCK.

mas'-cu-line. Strong; male. MALE-FEMALE,
STRENGTH-WEAKNESS; **masculine gender,** NOUN.

mash. Mixture; a semiliquid; to mix. HARDNESS-
SOFTNESS, MIXTURE-HOMOGENEITY, REGULARITY-
IRREGULARITY, VISCIDITY-FOAM.

mask. A cover for the face; pretext. ATTACK-DE-
FENSE, COVER-LINING, DRESS-UNDRESS, ENLIGHTEN-
MENT-SECRECY, EXPOSURE-HIDINGPLACE, LUMINARY-
SHADE, TRUTHFULNESS-FRAUD; **put on the mask,**
TRUTHFULNESS-FALSEHOOD.

ma'-son. A workman. AGENT.

Mas'-o-ra. Jewish writings. REVELATION-PSEUDO-
REVELATION.

masque. Dramatic performance. ACTING.

masqué, bal [F.] (mas-kê', bal) Masquerade. EN-
TERTAINMENT-WEARINESS.

mas''-quer-ade'. A social party; disguise. ENLIGHT-
ENMENT-SECRECY, ENTERTAINMENT-WEARINESS,
TRUTHFULNESS-FALSEHOOD; **masquerade dress,** EX-
POSURE-HIDINGPLACE.

mass. (1) Extent of volume. GATHERING-SCATTER-
ING, GREATNESS-LITTLENESS, HEAVINESS-LIGHT-
NESS, MAGNITUDE-SMALLNESS, QUANTITY-MEASURE,
SOLIDITY-RARITY, WHOLE-PART; **in the mass,**
WHOLE-PART; **mass of society,** GENTILITY-COMMON-
ALTY.

mass. (2) Eucharist. CEREMONIAL, DEVOTION-IDOL-
ATRY; **attend mass,** DEVOTION-IDOLATRY; **mass-book,**
CEREMONIAL.

mas'-sa-cre. To kill. LIFE-KILLING.

mas''-sage'. A scientific remedy by kneading, rubbing,
etc. REMEDY-BANE.

masse, en [F.] (mas, an·). In a body ASSOCIATION.

mass'-es, the. The common people. GENTILITY-
COMMONALTY.

mass'-ive. Huge; massy. GREATNESS-LITTLENESS,
HEAVINESS-LIGHTNESS, SOLIDITY-RARITY.

mass'-y. Ponderous. GREATNESS-LITTLENESS.

mas'-ter. A title; to learn thoroughly; proficient; **to**
overcome; young man. ADEPT-BUNGLER, CHIEF-
UNDERLING, CLEARNESS-OBSCURITY, EDUCATION-
LEARNING, HOLDER, INFANT-VETERAN, INSTRUCTOR-
PUPIL, KNOWLEDGE-IGNORANCE, LIBERTY-SUBJEC-
TION, MALE-FEMALE, MANAGER, PRESIDENT-MEM-
BER, SKILL-UNSKILFULNESS, SUCCESS-FAILURE,
TITLE; **eye of the master,** MANAGEMENT; **hard mas-
ter,** HARSHNESS-MILDNESS; **head master,** PRESIDENT-
MEMBER; **master hand,** ADEPT-BUNGLER; **master-
key,** APERTURE-CLOSURE, INSTRUMENTALITY; **mas-
ter mind,** ADEPT-BUNGLER, SAGE-FOOL; **master of
arts,** SCHOLAR-DUNCE; **master of one's time,** FAITH-
MISGIVING; **master of self,** DETERMINATION-VACIL-
LATION; **master of the position,** SUCCESS-FAILURE;
master of the revels, ENTERTAINMENT-WEARINESS;
master of the rolls, JUDGE, RECORDER; **master of the
situation,** RULE-LICENSE, SUCCESS-FAILURE; **master
one's feelings,** EXCITABILITY-INEXCITABILITY; **master one's passions,** VIRTUE-VICE; **master passion,**
AFFECTIONS; **master spirit of the age,** REPUTATION-
DISCREDIT, SAGE-FOOL.

mas'-ter-dom. Dominion. RULE-LICENSE.

mas'-ter-ful. Arbitrary; skilful. RULE-LICENSE,
SKILL-UNSKILFULNESS.

mas'-ter-mind''. Predominant intellect. SAGE-FOOL.

mas'-ter-piece''. Admirable production. FAULTLESS-
NESS-FAULTINESS, GOODNESS-BADNESS, SKILL-UN-
SKILFULNESS.

mas'-ter-ship. Superiority. SKILL-UNSKILFULNESS.

mas'-ter-stroke''. Masterly achievement. DESIGN,
SUCCESS-FAILURE.

mas'-ter-y. Command. RULE-LICENSE, SKILL-UN-
SKILFULNESS, SUCCESS-FAILURE.

mast-head'. To punish. RECOMPENSE-PUNITION.

mas'-tic. A resin. PULPINESS-ROSIN, VISCIDITY·
FOAM.

mas'-ti-cate. To chew. NUTRIMENT-EXCRETION

mas'-tiff. A breed of dogs. FAUNA-FLORA.

mat. A texture, to be laid on the floor; anything
closely interwoven. CROSSING, SUSPENSION-SUP·
PORT.

mat''-a-dor'. One who slays. LIFE-KILLING.

match. A contest; marriage; similar. COMBUSTIBLE,
EQUALITY-INEQUALITY, HARMONY-DISCORD, IMITA-
TION-ORIGINALITY, LIKENESS-UNLIKENESS, MATRI-
MONY-CELIBACY, STRIFE-PEACE.

match'-less. Peerless. SUPREMACY-SUBORDINACY,
VIRTUE-VICE.

match'-lock''. A kind of musket. WEAPON.

mate. A match; comrade. ANTAGONIST-ASSISTANT,
CHIEF-UNDERLING, EQUALITY-INEQUALITY, FRIEND-
FOE, LIKENESS-UNLIKENESS, MATRIMONY-CELIBACY;
check mate, SUCCESS-FAILURE.

mater, alma [L.] (mê'-ter, al'-ma) Fostering mother.
SCHOOL.

mater familias [L.] (mê'-ter fa-mil'-i-as) Mother of
a family. PARENTAGE-PROGENY.

ma-te'-ri-al. Substance; important. CONSEQUENCE-
INSIGNIFICANCE, MATERIALITY-SPIRITUALITY, MATE-
RIALS; **material for thought,** CONCEPTION-THEME;
material point, MAGNITUDE-SMALLNESS.

ma-te'-ri-al'. Materials collectively. INSTRUMENT.

ma-te'-ri-al-ism. A branch of philosophy. GODLI-
NESS-DISBELIEF, MATERIALITY-SPIRITUALITY, ORTHO-
DOXY-HETERODOXY.

ma-te'-ri-al-ist. A believer in materialism. GODLI-
NESS-DISBELIEF, MATERIALITY-SPIRITUALITY, ORTHO-
DOXY-HETERODOXY.

ma-te''-ri-al-is'-tic. Marked by materialism. MATE-
RIALITY-SPIRITUALITY.

ma-te''-ri-al'-i-ty. State of being material. MATE-
RIALITY-SPIRITUALITY.

MATERIALITY—SPIRITUALITY.

Corporality.
Corporeity. } The state of having a body.
Flesh and blood. Human nature; having a body, as a person.
Materiality.
Materialness. } Being composed of matter.
Physical condition. Having a material body, especially relating to the human body apart from the mind or spirit.
Substantiality The state of having a real or bodily existence.

MATERIALITY—Denotations.

Article. A particular one of various things.
Body. The material organized substance of an animal
Brute matter. Physical, without mental, matter.
Corpus [L.]. Body.
Element. One of the ultimate, undecomposable constituents of any kind of matter.
Frame. Physical constitution.
Hyle. Matter.
Material. The substance or matter of which anything is made.
Materials. etc. Substances entering into the composition of bodies of matter. See MATERIALS.
Matter. That of which the sensible universe and all its bodies are composed.
Object. Something visible or tangible.
Pabulum [L.] Food.
Parenchyma [Gr.]. The soft cellular tissues of plants.
Plenum [L] Space occupied by matter.
Principle. Fundamental substance or energy.
Something. A certain indefinite thing.
Still life. Inanimate objects.
Stocks and stones. Senseless things.
Stuff. The fundamental material of which anything is made up.
Substance. The essential components of anything.
Substratum [L.]. Substance.
Thing. Whatever exists as a separate entity.

MATERIALITY—Scientific Terms.

Experimental philosophy. General laws and principles of matter, based exclusively upon observation and experiment.
Materialism. The doctrine which denies the existence of spiritual substances or agents, and maintains that spiritual phenomena are the result of some peculiar organization of matter
Materialist. One who upholds the doctrine of materialism. See sub MATERIALISM.
Natural philosophy. That branch of physical science which treats of the phenomena and laws of matter and considers those effects only which are unaccompanied by any change of a chemical nature.
Philosophie positive [F.] A system of philosophy originated by M. Auguste Comte, which excludes from philosophy everything but the natural phenomena or properties of knowable things.
Physical science. The science of the causes and connections of natural phenomena.
Physicist. A believer in the theory that the fundamental phenomena of life are to be explained upon purely chemical and physical principles.
Physics. See NATURAL PHILOSOPHY.
Somatics. The science which treats of the general properties of matter.
Somatology. The properties of material substances.

ma-te'-ri-al-ly. Essentially. CONSEQUENCE-INSIG-NIFICANCE.
ma-te'-ri-al-ness. Reality. CONSEQUENCE-INSIG-NIFICANCE.
ma-te'-ri-als. Substances. MATERIALS.

MATERIALS.

Ammunition. Materials of war. See WEAPON.
Baggage. Articles of clothing, etc., carried on a journey. See PROPERTY.
Bandanna. A large red or blue handkerchief.
Bell-metal. An alloy or bronze used for making bells.
Brick. A block of clay tempered with water, sand, etc., and sun-dried or burnt.
Bricks and mortar. Materials for building.
Calico. Cotton cloth used in making clothing.
Celluloid. A substance composed of gun-cotton and camphor, used for making combs, etc.
Cement. A mortar which will harden under water
Clay. Soft earth used in making brick.

Ego [L.]. Self, considered as the seat of consciousness.
I. The spiritual personality.
Immaterialism. The doctrine that spiritual beings exist, or are possible.
Immateriality. The state or quality of being spiritual or without body or substance.
Immaterialness. See IMMATERIALITY.
Incorporeity. The quality of not having a material body or form.
Inextension. Want of length, breadth and thickness; or wanting the property of taking up space.
Me. See EGO.
Myself. See EGO.
Spirit. Life, or living substance, considered independently of bodily existence. See SOUL.
Spiritualism. The doctrine which teaches that all which exists is spirit or soul.
Spiritualist. One who maintains the doctrine of spiritualism
Spirituality. Quality or state of being spiritual
Telepathy. Thought transference.

SPIRITUALITY—Verbs.

Disembody. To divest of body or corporeal existence.
Spiritualize. To convert into, or imbue with a spirit.

SPIRITUALITY—Adjectives.

Asomatous. Without a material body.
Disembodied. Divested of a body.
Extramundane. Beyond the material world.
Immaterial. Not consisting of matter
Immateriate. See IMMATERIAL.
Incorporal.
Incorporeal. } Not having a material body or form.
Personal. Applying to character or conduct.
Pneumatoscopic. Spirit-seeing.
Spiritual. Consisting of spirit; not material. See MIND.
Subjective. Relating to the mind, or intellectual world.
Unearthly. Not of the earth; spiritual.
Unembodied. Existing only in spirit.
Unextended. Being without dimensions.

MATERIALITY—Continued.

MATERIALITY—Adjectives.

Bodily. Having a body or material form.
Corporal.
Corporeal. } Consisting of a material body or substance.
Impersonal. Without the attributes which make up the nature of a person.
Material. Consisting of matter.
Materialistic. Of the nature of materialism. See MATERIALISM
Neuter. Neither matter nor spirit.
Objective. Having the nature of an object.
Palpable. Capable of being touched and felt.
Physical. Cognizable by the senses
Ponderable. Capable of being weighed
Sensible. Capable of being perceived by the senses.
Somatic. Pertaining to the body
Somatoscopic. Physical.
Substantial. Actually existing, real.
Tangible. Perceptible to the touch
Unspiritual. Not of spirit, but matter.

Compo. Composition, as for plastering.
Composition. A mass or body formed by combining two or more substances.
Concrete. A mixture of gravel with cement, used for sidewalks, etc
Contingents. Materials entering into the composition of anything.
Crockery, etc. Vessels formed of baked clay. See HEATING.
Fuel. Materials for fire.
Gingham. A kind of cotton or linen cloth.
Grist. Grain.
Household stuff. Articles of domestic use.
Linoleum. A floor-cloth made by laying hardened linseed oil with cork on a canvas backing.
Material. The substance or matter of which anything is made.
Materials. Substances entering into the composition of anything.
Means, etc. That through which an end is attained. See MEANS.
Metal. An elementary substance entering into the composition of ores.
Munition. War materials.
Nankeen. A species of Chinese cloth.
Ore. The native form of a metal.
Pabulum [L.]. Food. See NUTRIMENT.

Raw material. Material in its natural state.
Reenforcement. That which strengthens or gives assistance.
Relay. A supply of anything for affording relief.
Staple. The principal commodity of traffic in a market.
Stock. A store of goods.
Stone. Rock cut for building purposes.
Stuff. Material which is to be worked up in any process of manufacture
Supplies. That which furnishes aid or need
Taffeta. A fine smooth stuff of silk.
Timber. Wood proper for building purposes.
Wood. The substance of trees used for building purposes.

MATERIALS—*Adjectives.*

Raw. In the natural state. See PREPARATION-NONPREPARATION.
Wooden, etc. Made of wood. See *Nouns.*

ma-te'-ri-a med'-i-ca. Science of medicinal substances. REMEDY-BANE.
ma-ter'-nal. Motherly. CHARITABLENESS-MALEVOLENCE, PARENTAGE-PROGENY; **maternal love,** LOVE-HATE.

ma-ter'-ni-ty. Motherhood. PARENTAGE-PROGENY
math''-e-mat'-ic-al. Rigidly exact. TRUTH-ERROR; **mathematical point,** GREATNESS-LITTLENESS.
math''-e-mat'-ics. Science of quantity. QUANTITY-MEASURE.
ma-the'-sis. Learning in mathematics. QUANTITY-MEASURE.
mat'-in. Belonging to morning. MORNING-EVENING.
mat''-i-née'. An afternoon entertainment. SOCIABILITY-PRIVACY.
mat'-ins. Morning worship. DEVOTION-IDOLATRY.
mat'-rass. A vessel for distilling. CONTENTS-RECEIVER.
mat'-ri-cide. Killing of a mother. LIFE-KILLING.
ma-tric''-u-la'-tion. Act of enrolling. EDUCATION-LEARNING.
mat''-ri-mo'-ni-al. Pertaining to marriage. MATRIMONY-CELIBACY.
mat'-ri-mo-ny. Condition of being married. MATRIMONY-CELIBACY, MIXTURE-HOMOGENEITY.

MATRIMONY—CELIBACY.

Bigamy. The offense of marrying one person when already legally married to another.
Bridal. See sub WEDDING.
Cohabitation. State of living together as if married.
Coverture. The married state.
Deuterogamy.⎫ A second marriage after the death of the first husband or wife.
Digamy. ⎭
Endogamy. Marriage restricted within the tribe
Espousal. See sub SPOUSAL.
Free love. The practise of consorting with the opposite sex, at pleasure, without marriage.
Ill-assorted marriage. A marriage in which the parties are unadapted to one another.
Intermarriage. Marriage between blood-kindred.
Leading to the altar. To marry.
Left-handed marriage. See MORGANATIC MARRIAGE.
Marriage. Legal union of a man and woman as husband and wife.
Marriage state. The condition of a married person.
Matrimony. The act which unites a man and woman as husband and wife.
Mésalliance [F.] A marriage with a person of inferior social position.
Monogamy. Marriage with but one person, husband or wife, at the same time.
Morganatic marriage. A marriage between a man of rank and a woman of inferior position, by which the wife and offspring are debarred the husband's rank and inheritance
Mormonism. Belief in polygamy.
Nuptial benediction. The marriage ceremony.
Nuptials. Marriage rites.
Nuptial tie. The marriage ceremony.
Polyandrism. Having more than one husband at the same time
Polygamy. Having a number of wives or husbands at the same time.
Spousal. Taking to oneself a wife.
Trigamy. Having three husbands or three wives at the same time.
Union. Marriage.
Unlawful marriage. A marriage contracted contrary to or in violation of law.
Vinculum matrimonii [L.] The bond of marriage.
Wedding. The ceremony of a marriage.
Wedlock. The state of being married.

MATRIMONY—*Associated Nouns*

Baron. A husband.
Benedick. A man recently married.
Betrothment. The act of contracting to any one for marriage. See ENGAGEMENT
Bigamist. One guilty of the offense of marrying one person when already legally married to another.
Bride. A woman newly married, or about to be married.
Bridegroom. A man newly married, or about to be married.
Bridesmaid. A female friend who attends on a bride at her wedding.
Bridesman. A male friend who attends a groom at his wedding.
Consort. A wife or husband.
Epithalamium [Gr.] A marriage song.
Feme. A woman
Femecovert. A married woman
Goodman. A husband.

Bachelorhood.⎫ The state of a man who has not been married.
Bachelorship.⎭
Celibacy. The state of an unmarried person; especially that of an unmarried man, or of one bound by vows not to marry.
Maidenhead.⎫ The state of an unmarried woman.
Maidenhood.⎭
Misogamy. Hatred of marriage.
Misogyny. Hatred of women.
Pucelage [F.]. State of being unmarried: applied usually to women.
Single. Unmarried.
Single blessedness. State of being unmarried: usually to men.

CELIBACY—*Denotations.*

Agamist. A person opposed to marriage.
Bachelor. An unmarried man.
Cœlebs. The hero in Hannah More's novel, *Cœlebs in Search of a Wife,* a satire on impossible ideals of womanhood.
Feme sole. An unmarried woman.
Maid. ⎫ An unmarried woman.
Maiden.⎭
Misogamist. A hater of marriage.
Misogynist. A hater of women.
Monogamist. One who has but one husband or wife at the same time.
Old bachelor. An unmarried man.
Old maid. An unmarried woman.
Spinster. An unmarried woman.
Unmarried man. A man without a wife.
Unmarried woman. A woman without a husband.
Virgin. An unmarried woman.

CELIBACY—*Verb.*

Live single. To be unmarrie

CELIBACY—*Adjectives.*

Single. Unmarried.
Spouseless.⎫ Without a wife
Wifeless. ⎭
Unmarried.⎫ Without wife or husband
Unwedded.⎭

MATRIMONY—ASSOCIATED NOUNS—*Continued.*

Goodwife. A wife.
Helpmate. A husband or wife.
Honeymoon. The first month after marriage.
Husband. A man who has a wife.
Hymeneal altar. The marriage altar.
Lady. A wife.
Man. A husband.
Man and wife. A married couple.
Married couple. A man and wife
Married man. A man who has a wife.
Married woman. A woman who has a husband
Match. A suitable marriage partner.
Mate. A husband or wife.

MATRIMONY—Associated Nouns—*Continued*.

Matron.
Matronage.} A married woman.
Matronhood. The state or condition of a married woman.
Neogamist. A person recently married.
Partner. One to whom a person is married.
Spouse. A wife.

Squaw. The wife of an Indian.
Wedded pair. A husband and wife
Wife. A married woman.
Wife of one's bosom. A wife.
Yokemate. A wife or husband.

MATRIMONY—*Figurative Nouns*.

Bed. Used as a symbol of matrimony.
Better half. A wife.
Bluebeard. One married often, as in the well-known story.
Darby and Joan. A lovely, old-fashioned, virtuous couple.
Gray mare. A wife who rules her husband.
Hymen. Marriage.

Old man. Husband.
Old woman. Wife.
Rib. Wife
Temple of Hymen. Marriage.
Torch of Hymen. A bridal torch.
Turk. A cruel husband.

MATRIMONY—*Verbs*.

Affiance. To pledge one's faith to for marriage.
Affy. To promise to marry.
Be asked in church. To publish in church for marriage.
Be married. To be joined in lawful union.
Be spliced. To be married.
Bestow one's hand upon. To give in marriage.
Betroth. To contract to any one for a marriage. See ENGAGEMENT.
Bid the banns. To make an intention to marry publicly known.
Couple. To be joined in marriage. See UNION.
Espouse. To promise in marriage.
Give away.
Give in marriage.} To present the bride to the bridegroom.
Give one's hand to. To bestow in marriage.
Go off. Occur in some specified manner.
Handfast. To betroth by joining hands, in order to cohabitation, before the celebration of marriage.

Intermarry. To marry among.
Join. To unite in marriage.
Lead to the hymeneal altar. To lead to the church altar in order to marry.
Marry. To constitute man and wife according to the laws and customs of a nation.
Pair off. To bring together a man and woman who are adapted to one another.
Publish the banns. To make intention to marry known by reading in a church.
Take for better for worse.
Take to oneself a wife.} To be married.
Tie the nuptial knot. To perform the ceremony which constitutes man and wife.
Wive. To provide with a wife.
Wed. To take for husband or for wife by a formal ceremony

MATRIMONY—*Adjectives*.

Affianced. Pledged to marry.
Betrothed. Promised to marry.
Bridal. Pertaining to a bride or a wedding.
Conjugal. Suitable or appropriate to the marriage state.
Connubial. Pertaining to the marriage state.
Engaged. Bound by promise to marry.
Hymeneal. Relating to marriage.
Levirate. According to the law of the Israelites, by which a woman was married to her dead husband's brother.
Marital. Pertaining to the marriage relation as it affects the husband.

Marriageable. Fitted by age, physical condition, and mental capacity for marriage.
Married. Made man and wife. See *Verbs*.
Matrimonial. Pertaining to marriage or the married state.
Nubile. Of suitable age to marry.
Nuptial. Relating to marriage, especially to the marriage ceremony.
One. Said of a man and woman after union by marriage.
One bone and one flesh. Of a single person by the union of marriage.
Spousal. Pertaining to marriage; generally used in the plural.
Wedded. Joined in lawful union.

MATRIMONY—*Phrases*.

Copula, felices ter et amplius, quos irrupta tenet [L.]. Thrice happy, and more, those whom the marriage-bond unbroken holds.

Mariage de convenance [F.] Marriage of convenience.
The gray mare the better horse. The wife controls her husband

MATRIMONY—DIVORCE.

DIVORCE.

Divorce.
Divorcement.} A legal dissolution of the marriage contract.
Judicial separation. A separation of man and wife which has the effect of making each a single person for all legal purposes, but without ability to contract a new marriage.
Separate maintenance. An allowance made to a wife by a husband under deed of separation.
Separatio a mensa et thoro [L.]. A separation of a married woman from the bed and board of her husband.
Separatio a vinculo matrimonii [L.]. A complete divorce.
Separation. See DIVORCE.

Relict. A widow.
Viduity. Widowhood.
Weeds. An article of dress worn in token of grief.
Widow. A woman who has lost her husband by death.
Widower. A husband who has lost his wife by death.
Widowhood. The state of a widow.

DIVORCE—*Verbs*.

Disespouse. To separate after plighted troth.
Divorce. To free by legal process from the relationship of husband and wife.
Live separate.
Separate.} To live apart.
Put away. To part from one's wife.
Wear the horns. To have the imaginary mark of a cuckold on the forehead.

DIVORCE—*Denotations*.

Cuckold. The husband of an adulteress.
Divorcée. A person who has been divorced.
Dowager. A widow who enjoys a dower from her husband's estate.

---

ma'-trix. That which gives form to anything. COPY-MODEL, WORKSHOP.

ma'-tron. A married woman. MALE-FEMALE, MATRIMONY-CELIBACY.

ma'-tron-age. Condition of being a matron. MALE-FEMALE, MATRIMONY-CELIBACY.

ma'-tron-hood. State of being a matron. MALE-FEMALE, MATRIMONY-CELIBACY.

ma'-tron-ly. Like a matron. INFANCY-AGE, MANHOOD.

ma-tross'. A gunner's assistant. BELLIGERENT.

mat'-ter. Substance; subject; affair; pus. CLEANNESS-FILTHINESS, CONCEPTION-THEME, CONSEQUENCE-INSIGNIFICANCE, MATERIALITY-SPIRITUALITY, MEANING-JARGON, OCCUPATION, SUBSTANCE-NULLITY; **matter in dispute,** INVESTIGATION-ANSWER; **matter in hand,** CONCEPTION-THEME, OCCUPATION; **matter nothing,** CONSEQUENCE-INSIGNIFICANCE; **matter of course,** CERTAINTY-DOUBT, CONVENTIONALITY-UNCONVENTIONALITY, HABIT-DESUETUDE; **matter of**

fact, CERTAINTY-DOUBT, CRAFT-ARTLESSNESS, OC-CURRENCE-DESTINY, TRUTH-ERROR, WITTINESS-DULNESS; **no matter,** CAREFULNESS-CARELESSNESS; **what matter,** CONSEQUENCE-INSIGNIFICANCE; **what's the matter,** INQUISITIVENESS-INDIFFERENCE, INVESTIGATION-ANSWER.

mat'-ting. A coarsely woven floor-covering. CROSSING.

mat'-tock. A tool. SHARPNESS-BLUNTNESS.

mat'-tress. A bed. SUSPENSION-SUPPORT.

mat''-u-ra'-tion. Ripeness. PREPARATION-NONPREPARATION.

ma-ture'. Fully developed; to develop. BETTERMENT-DETERIORATION, CONVERSION-REVERSION, DESIGN, FAULTINESS-FAULTLESSNESS, MANHOOD, NOVELTY-ANTIQUITY, PREPARATION-NONPREPARATION; **mature thought,** REFLECTION-VACANCY.

ma-ture'-ly. Considered. PREDETERMINATION-IMPULSE.

ma-tu'-ri-ty. State of being mature. MANHOOD, NOVELTY-ANTIQUITY, PREPARATION-NONPREPARATION; **bring to maturity,** COMPLETION-NONCOMPLETION.

ma-tu'-ti-nal. Early. MORNING-EVENING.

maud'-lin. Tearful; drunk. ACTIVITY-INDOLENCE, SENSITIVENESS-APATHY, TEETOTALISM-INTEMPERANCE.

mau'-gre. In spite of. COMPENSATION.

mau'-kin. A mop. CLEANNESS-FILTHINESS.

maul. A hammer; to hurt. GOODNESS-BADNESS, IMPETUS-REACTION.

maund. A basket; to mutter. CONTENTS-RECEIVER, SPEECH-INARTICULATENESS.

maun'-der. To talk incoherently. JUBILATION-LAMENTATION, SPEECH-INARTICULATENESS, TERSENESS-PROLIXITY.

mau''-so-le'-um. A tomb. LIFE-FUNERAL.

mauvais gout [F.] (mo-vê' gu) Bad taste. TASTE-VULGARITY.

mauvais quart d'heure [F.] (mo-vê' kar dur). A bad quarter of an hour. PLEASURE-PAIN.

mauvais sujet [F.] (mo-vê' sü-zhe'). A bad subject. GOOD MAN-BAD MAN.

mauvais ton [F.] (mo-vê' ton·). Bad style. TASTE-VULGARITY.

mauvaise honte [F.] (mo-vêz' on·t). Bashfulness. CONCEIT-DIFFIDENCE, SOCIETY-AFFECTATION.

mauvaise plaisanterie [F.] (mo-vêz' plê-zan·t-rî'). Bad jesting. TASTE-VULGARITY.

mauve. A color. YELLOWNESS-PURPLE.

maux, les grandes remèdes, aux grands [F.] (mo, lê gran·d re-med', o gran·). To desperate evils, desperate remedies. REMEDY-BANE.

maw. The stomach. CONTENTS-RECEIVER.

mawk'-ish. Insipid. SAVOR-TASTELESSNESS.

maw'-worm''. A hypocritical character. GODLINESS-UNGODLINESS, GULL-HYPERBOLE.

max'-im. A practical truth. ADAGE-NONSENSE, COUNCIL.

maximis ad minima [L.] (max'-i-mis ad min'-i-ma). From the greatest to the least. ADMISSION-EXCLUSION, MAGNITUDE-SMALLNESS.

max'-i-mum. Supreme; summit. SUPREMACY-SUBORDINACY, TOP-BOTTOM.

may'-be. Perhaps. POSSIBILITY-IMPOSSIBILITY, **as it may be,** RATIONALE-LUCK.

May'-day''. First day of May. COUNTRY, ENTERTAINMENT-WEARINESS.

May'-fly''. A fly that appears in May. LASTINGNESS-TRANSIENTNESS.

may'-hap. Perhaps. POSSIBILITY-IMPOSSIBILITY.

may'-or. The highest city official. CHIEF-UNDERLING, MANAGER, PRESIDENT-MEMBER.

may'-or-al-ty. Office of a mayor. CHIEF-UNDERLING.

May'-pole''. A pole put up for May-day. COUNTRY, HEIGHT-LOWNESS.

May'-queen''. Queen of May-day. EMBELLISHMENT-DISFIGUREMENT.

maz'-ard. The jaw. NUTRIMENT-EXCRETION.

maze. A winding; perplexity. CIRCLE-WINDING, DIFFICULTY-FACILITY, TIDINGS-MYSTERY; **in a maze,** CERTAINTY-DOUBT.

ma'-zed. Perplexed. SANENESS-LUNACY.

ma-zur'-ka. A dance. ENTERTAINMENT-WEARINESS.

me. Personal pronoun. MATERIALITY-SPIRITUALITY.

meâ culpâ [L.] (mî-a cul'-pa). Through my fault. REPENTANCE-OBDURACY.

mead. A liquor; meadow. GULF-PLAIN, SWEETNESS-ACIDITY.

mead'-ow. A tract of low, level land. GULF-PLAIN; **meadow land,** CITY-COUNTRY, DOMESTICATION-AGRICULTURE.

mea'-ger. Scanty; emaciated. BREADTH-NARROWNESS, CONSEQUENCE-INSIGNIFICANCE, ENTIRETY-DEFICIENCY, EXCESS-LACK, FORCE-WEAKNESS, MAGNITUDE-SMALLNESS; **meager diet,** FASTING-GLUTTONY.

meal. Repast; powder. FRIABILITY, NUTRIMENT-EXCRETION.

meal'-y. Farinaceous. FRIABILITY.

meal'-y-mouthed''. Flattering; insincere. ADULATION-DISPARAGEMENT, PRESUMPTION-OBSEQUIOUSNESS, TRUTHFULNESS-FALSEHOOD.

mean. Average; inferior; base; to intend or signify. CONSEQUENCE-INSIGNIFICANCE, EXTRAVAGANCE-AVARICE, GENTILITY-COMMONALTY, GOODNESS-BADNESS, MEANING-JARGON, MEDIUM, MIDCOURSE-CIRCUIT, MIDDLE, PRESUMPTION-OBSEQUIOUSNESS, PURPOSE-LUCK, REPUTATION-DISCREDIT, UNSELFISHNESS-SELFISHNESS, UPRIGHTNESS-DISHONESTY; **golden mean,** MEDIOCRITY, MEDIUM, TURBULENCE-CALMNESS; **mean nothing,** MEANING-JARGON; **mean parentage,** GENTILITY-COMMONALTY; **mean wretch,** GOOD MAN-BAD MAN; **take the mean,** COMPOSITION

me-an'-der. To wind; a winding. AIM-ABERRATION, CIRCLE-WINDING, CIRCUITION, MIDCOURSE-CIRCUIT, RIVER-WIND.

me-an'-der-ing. Diffuse. CIRCLE-WINDING, RIVER-WIND.

me-an'-der-ous. Wandering. RIVER-WIND.

mean'-est ca-pac'-i-ty. Least capacity. SAGACITY-INCAPACITY; **intelligible to the meanest capacity,** CLEARNESS-OBSCURITY.

mean'-ing. Intention. MEANING-JARGON.

MEANING—JARGON

Acceptation. The meaning in which a word or expression is generally received. See INTERPRETATION.

After acceptation. The meaning derived from a word or expression after some thought.

Allusion. A reference to something supposed to be known, but not mentioned. See MANIFESTATION-LATENCY.

Argument. The subject-matter of a discourse, writing, etc.

Bearing. The object toward which the words or expressions used are directed.

Broad meaning. The evident meaning.

Colloquial meaning. The meaning accepted in a particular locality

Absurdity Contrary to reason or sound judgment. See ADAGE-NONSENSE.

A tale told by an idiot. A senseless story. [Shakespeare, *Macbeth*, v, 5.]

Babble. Idle talk.

Balderdash. Unmeaning talk.

Baragonin [F.]. Jargon.

Bavardage [F.]. Babbling.

Bombast. High-sounding words unsuited for the occasion.

Bosh. Empty talk.

Dead letter. That which has lost force or authority.

MEANING—JARGON—*Continued.*

Coloring.   Distinguishing characteristic of one's language.
Drift.   The object not expressly notified, but generally gathered from one s remarks.
Expression.   That which is plainly indicated by language.
Figure of speech.   A mode of expressing abstract ideas by words which suggest pictures or images.
General meaning.   The generally accepted meaning.
Gist.   The substance or pith of a matter.
Honest meaning.   An acceptation plainly intended.
Import.   That which a word or statement is specifically and directly designed to convey.
Literality.
Literal meaning.} Meaning derived from the words.
Matter.   The substance of a speech, etc.
Meaning.   That which is intended to be expressed by words.
Natural meaning.   The most common intention.
Plain meaning.   The intended acceptation.
Primâ facie **meaning.**   Meaning derived from the expression.   See MANIFESTATION
Purport.   That which is suggested to the mind by a continuous speech.
Scope.   That which is purposed to be accomplished by words.
Sense.   The recognized acceptation which is attached to a word or expression.
Significance.   The intention of the terms employed in speaking.
Signification.   The meaning which a sign or character is intended to convey.   See SIGNIFICANCE.
Simple meaning.   The most common meaning.
Spirit.   Real meaning, opposed to the letter or to formal statement.
Subject.   That which is brought under thought or examination.
Subject-matter.   The matter under discussion.
Substantial meaning.   A well-founded meaning.
Suggestion.   Anything introduced indirectly to the thoughts.   See ENLIGHTENMENT.
Sum and substance.   The meaning or force derived from an expression or speech.
Synonym.   One of two or more words which have nearly the same signification.
Tenor.   The general course or character of a speech or continued discourse. *
Text.   Anything chosen as the subject of an argument, composition, etc.
True meaning.   The meaning generally accepted.
Unstrained meaning.   The meaning plainly conveyed by an expression.

MEANING—*Verbs.*

Allude to.   To have reference to a subject not plainly mentioned.
Bear a sense.   To have a particular meaning.
Bespeak.   To indicate by words.
Breathe.   To express.
Convey.   To impart to.
Dec are.   To make known by language.   See ASSERTION.
Drive at   To aim or tend to a point.
Express.   Directly and distinctly stated.
Imply.   To be involved in though not expressed in words
Import.   To carry or include, as meaning or intention.
Indicate.   To direct to a knowledge of.
Involve.   To complicate or make intricate.   See MANIFESTATION-LATENCY.
Mean.   To have in the mind, as a purpose or intention.
Point to.   To direct attention to.
Purport.   To intend to show.
Signify.   To indicate in any way.
Speak of.   To express in words.
Tell of.   To describe.
Touch on.   To refer to.
Understand.   To apprehend the meaning or intention of.   See INTERPRETATION.

MEANING—*Adjectives.*

Allusive.   Having reference to something not fully expressed.
Declaratory.   Making clear or manifest.   See ASSERTION.
Explicit.   Open to the understanding.   See MANIFESTATION.
Expressive.   Vividly representing the meaning intended to be conveyed.
Full of meaning.   Expressing everything that is intended.
Intelligible.   Capable of being understood.   See CLEARNESS.
Literal.   Following the letter or exact words.
Meaning.   Having a particular purpose or intention.   See *Verbs.*
Pithy.   Forceful.
Pregnant with meaning.   Weighty.
Significant.   Expressive.
Significative.   Having a meaning or purpose.

Empty sound.   An expression without meaning.
Fiddle-faddle.   Trifling talk.
Flummery.   Empty compliment.
Fudge.   A made-up story.
Fustian.   Writing in which high-sounding words are used. above the dignity of the subject.
Gibberish.   Without meaning.
Hocus-pocus.   A juggler's talk in pretended incantations; *Hoc est corpus.*
Inanity.   Want of seriousness in talk.
Jabber.   Rapid or incoherent talk.
Jargon.   Confused, unintelligible language.
Mere words.   An expression without meaning.
Moonshine.   Show without reality.
Niaiserie [F.].   Nonsense.
Nonsense.   Words or language which have no meaning, or convey no intelligible ideas.
Nugæ canoræ [L.].   Mere jingling.
Palaver.   Talk intended to deceive.
Platitude.   Staleness of ideas or language.
Rant.   High-sounding language without importance or dignity of thought.
Rigmarole.   A succession of confused or nonsensical statements.
Rodomontade.   Vain boasting.   [Rodomonte, in *Orlando Furioso.*]
Rubbish.   Worthless talk.
Scrabble.   Unmeaning marks or letters.
Sounding brass and a tinkling cymbal.   Figuratively talk without meaning.   [Bible.]
Stuff.   Foolish or irrational language.
Stuff and nonsense.   Foolish and senseless talk.
Trash.   Needless and foolish talk.
Truism.   A proposition needing no proof or argument.
Twaddle.   Silly talk.
Twattle.   Idle talk.
Unmeaningness.   Having no meaning or signification.   See *Adjectives.*
Vagueness.   Unsettled, wandering talk.   See CLEARNESS-OBSCURITY.
Verbiage.   Use of many words without necessity, or with little sense.
Vox et præteræ nil [L.].   Talk and nothing else.
Wish-wash.   Weak, idle talk.

JARGON—*Verbs.*

Be unmeaning.   See *Adjectives.*
Mean nothing.
Quibble.   To evade the point in speaking. by raising unimportant questions.
Scrabble.   To make unmeaning marks or letters.
Twaddle.   To talk in a weak and silly manner.

JARGON—*Adjectives.*

Fiddle-faddle.   Trifling.
Incommunicable.   Incapable of being told or imparted to others.
Inexpressible.   Not capable of utterance in language.
Inexpressive.   Without meaning; inexpressible.   [Browning.]
Insignificant.   Without sense or import.
Meaningless.   Without sense or purpose.
Nonsensical.   Foolish or without sense.
Not expressed.   Implied or left to inference.
Not significant.   Without meaning.   See CLEARNESS.
Quibbling.   Evasive.
Senseless.   Deficient in sense.
Tacit.   Implied but not expressed.   See MANIFESTATION-LATENCY.
Trashy.   Good for nothing.
Trivial.   Trifling.
Trumpery.   Deceptive.
Twaddling.   Silly.
Undefinable.   Not capable of being explained.
Unexpressive.   Without meaning; inexpressible.   [Milton, *Lycidas.*]
Unmeaning.   Having no signification.
Unmeant.   Not intended.
Vacant.   Empty of thought.
Void of sense.   Wanting sense.   See CLEARNESS.
Washy.   Weak, or lacking depth.

MEANING—ADJECTIVES—*Continued.*

Significatory.   See SIGNIFICANT.
Synonymous.   Conveying the same, or nearly the same, idea.
Tantamount.   Equivalent in signification or effect.   See sub EQUALITY

MEANING—*Adverbial Expressions*

That is to say.   See INTERPRETATION.
To that effect.   With that meaning.

mean'-ing-less. Without meaning. MEANING-JARGON.

mean'-ness. Baseness. MAGNITUDE-SMALLNESS, UNSELFISHNESS-SELFISHNESS.

means. Instrument; resources. AFFLUENCE-PENURY, INSTRUMENTALITY, MATERIALS, MEANS, PROPERTY; **by all means,** CONSENT, LEAVE-PROHIBITION, MEANS, READINESS-RELUCTANCE; **by any means,** MEANS; **by no means,** ASSERTION-DENIAL; **means of access,** WAY

MEANS.

Aid. Assistance.

Appliances. The things applied or used as means to an end. See INSTRUMENT.

A shot in the locker. Shot stored away for an emergency.

Capital. Money or stock employed in trade as a means of producing wealth.

Cards to play. Means to success, not yet employed.

Conveniences. Things suited to one's wants.

Expedients. Suitable means to accomplish an end.

Means. That through which or by the help of which an end is attained.

Medium. A secondary agency by or through which a primary agency accomplishes some end.

Provision. That which is brought together or arranged beforehand for the accomplishment of an end. See PROVISION.

Resources. That on which one depends for supply or support.

Sheet anchor. Anything regarded as a sure support in danger.

Stock in trade. A store of goods on hand.

Two strings to one's bow. Extra means.

Ways and means. Suitable means to accomplish an end.

Wherewithal. The necessary means or instrument.

MEANS—*Verbs.*

Find means.
Have means. } See *Nouns.*
Possess means.

MEANS—*Adjectives.*

Instrumental. Serving as a means. See INSTRUMENTALITY.

Mechanical. Operated by the action of forces without a directing intelligence. See INSTRUMENT.

MEANS—*Adverbial Expressions.*

By all means; by any means; by means of; by some means; by the agency of; by the aid of (see OBSTRUCTION); **by what means; herewith; how** (see WAY)· **therewith; through; wherewith; wherewithal; with; with the aid of.**

mean'-time". Interval. DURATION-NEVERNESS.

mean'-while". Interval. DURATION-NEVERNESS.

mea'-sles. A contagious febrile disorder HEALTH-SICKNESS.

meas'-u-ra-ble. Capable of computation. MENSURATION.

meas'-ure. Extent; to judge; time; meter; transaction; moderation. ACTION-PASSIVENESS, ASSIGNMENT, DESIGN, MEASURE, MELODY-DISSONANCE, MENSURATION, POETRY-PROSE, QUANTITY-MEASURE, TURBULENCE-CALMNESS; **angular measure,** ANGULARITY; **full measure,** ENOUGH; **out of measure,** EXCESS-LACK; **without measure,** EXCESS-LACK.

MEASURE.

Measure. The extent, quantity, capacity, volume. or dimensions of anything as ascertained by a certain rule or standard.

MEASURE—*Apothecaries' Fluid Measure.*

Dram. One-eighth of an ounce.
Gallon. A measure of capacity of 231 cubic inches.
Minim. .95 of a grain of water.
Ounce. 455.6 grains.
Pint. 16 ounces.

MEASURE—*Apothecaries' Weight.*

Dram. 60 grains or one-eighth of an ounce.
Grain. One-sixteenth of a pound.
Ounce. 427.5 grains.
Pound. 12 ounces.
Scruple. 20 grains.

MEASURE—*Avoirdupois Weight.*

Dram. One-sixteenth of an ounce.
Grain. The 1-7000 part of a pound.
Hundredweight. 100 pounds.
Ounce. One-sixteenth of a pound.
Pound. 16 ounces.
Quarter. One-fourth of a hundredweight.
Stone. 14 pounds.
Ton. 2000 pounds.

MEASURE—*Cubic Measure.*

Cubic foot. 1728 cubic inches.
Cubic inch. A measure equal to a cube whose edge is one inch.
Cubic yard. A measure equal to a cube whose edge is one yard.
Perch. 25 cubic feet

MEASURE—*Dry Measure.*

Bushel. A measure of capacity of 2150.4 cubic inches.
Peck. One-fourth of a bushel.
Pint. One-half of a quart.
Quart. One thirty-second of a bushel.

MEASURE—*Linear Measure*

Foot. 12 inches.
Furlong. One-eighth of a mile.
Inch. One-twelfth of a foot.
League. 3 statute miles.
Mile. 5280 feet.
Rod. 16½ feet.
Yard. 3 feet.

MEASURE—*Liquid Measure*

Barrel. A measure of 31 gallons.
Cask. 60 gallons.
Gallon. A measure containing 231 cubic inches.
Gill. One-fourth of a pint.
Hogshead. 63 gallons.
Pint. One-half of a quart.
Quart. One-fourth of a gallon.

MEASURE—*Mariners' Measure*

Cable. 100 fathoms.
Fathom. 6 feet.
Foot. 12 inches.
Mile. 5280 feet.
Nautical mile. 2029 yards.
Statute mile. 5280 feet.

MEASURE—*Metric System—Capacity.*

Centiliter. One one-thousandth of a peck.
Decaliter. .284 of a bushel.
Deciliter. One one-hundredth of a peck.
Hectoliter. 2.84 bushels.
Kiloliter. 28.38 bushels.
Liter. .11 of a peck.
Milliliter. .061 cubic inch.

MEASURE—*Metric System—Length.*

Centimeter. .394 inch.
Decameter. 397.7 inches.
Decimeter. 3.94 inches.
Hectometer. 109.36 yards.
Kilometer. .62 of a mile.
Meter. 39.37 inches.
Millimeter. .039 inch.
Myriameter. 6.21 miles.

MEASURE—*Metric System—Surface.*

Are. .02 of an acre.
Centare. 1.19 square yards.
Hectare. 2.47 acres.

MEASURE—*Metric System—Weight.*

Centigram. One-hundredth part of a gram.
Decagram. 154.32 grains.
Decigram. 1.54 grains.
Gram. 15.42 grains.
Hectogram. 3.53 ounces.
Kilogram. 2.2 pounds.
Millier. 19.67 hundredweights.
Milligram. .01 grain.
Myriagram. 22.05 pounds.
Quintal. 220.46 pounds.

MEASURE—*Paper Measure.*

Bale. A large package.
Bundle. Two reams of paper.
Printer's bundle. Two large reams.
Printer's quire. 24 sheets.
Printer's ream. 21½ quires.
Ream. 20 quires.
Roll of parchment.

MEASURE—*Square Measure.*

Acre. 160 square rods.
Square foot. 144 square inches.
Square inch. A measure equal to a surface whose side is one inch.
Square mile. 640 acres.
Square rod. 30¼ square yards.
Square yard. 9 square feet.

MEASURE—*Surveyors' Linear Measure*

Chain. 22 yards.
Link. 7.92 inches.
Mile. 5280 feet.
Rod. 16.5 feet.

MEASURE—*Surveyors' Square Measure.*

Acre. 160 square rods
Square chain. 480 square yards.
Square link. 23.12 square inches
Square rod. 272¼ square feet.
Township. 36 square miles.

MEASURE—*Time Measure.*

Century. 100 years.
Common year. 365 days.
Day. 24 hours.
Hour. 60 minutes.
Leap-year. 366 days.
Minute. One-sixtieth part of an hour.
Second. One-sixtieth part of a minute.
Week. 7 days.

MEASURE—*Troy Weight.*

Grain. 1-5760 part of a pound.
Ounce. 480 grains.
Pennyweight. 24 grains.
Pound. 5760 grains.

MEASURE—*Wood Measure.*

Cord. A measure of wood equal to 128 cubic feet (4 by 4 by 8).
Cord foot. The 128th part of a cord.
Cubic foot. A cube, measuring a foot in length.

meas'-ured. Sufficient; estimated. ENOUGH, MELODY-DISSONANCE, MODERATION-SELFINDULGENCE, TURBULENCE-CALMNESS.
meas'-ure-less. Without measure. INFINITY.
meas'-ure-ment. Computation. MENSURATION.
meas'-ures. Means; acts; extent. **Have no measures with,** VARIANCE-ACCORD; **take measures,** CONDUCT, DESIGN, PREPARATION-NONPREPARATION.
meas'-ur-ing. Computing. MENSURATION.
meat. Animal food. NUTRIMENT-EXCRETION; **broken meat,** USEFULNESS-USELESSNESS.
Mæ-ce'-nas. Roman statesman; patron of letters. FRIEND-FOE, SCHOLAR-DUNCE.
me-chan'-ic. A workman. AGENT, LABOR-CAPITAL.
me-chan'-ic-al. Pertaining to mechanics; automatical. INSTRUMENT, MEANS, VOLITION-OBLIGATION; **mechanical powers,** INSTRUMENT.
mech''-a-ni'-cian. A designer of machinery. AGENT.
mech'-a-nism. Machinery. INSTRUMENT.
medaglia, ha il sus rovescio, ogni [It.] (mê-dal'-ya, ha il sus ro-ves'-cho on'-yî). Every medal has its reverse. ANTERIORITY-POSTERIORITY.
med'-al. An engraved disk given for merit. MARK-OBLITERATION, SCULPTURE, TITLE, TROPHY.
med'-al-ist. A designer of medals. ADEPT-BUNGLER.
me-dal'-lion. A large medal. SCULPTURE.
med'-dle. To interfere officiously. ACTIVITY-INDOLENCE.
med'-dle-some. Intrusive. ACTIVITY-INDOLENCE.
med'-dling. Officious. ACTIVITY-INDOLENCE.
médecin, guéris-toi toi-même [F.] (mêd-san', gê-rî'-

twa' twa''-mem'). Physician, heal thyself. RENOVATION-RELAPSE.
médecin tant pis [F.] (mêd-san·' tan· pî). A doctor so much the worse. LIGHTHEARTEDNESS-DEJECTION.
médecine expectante [F.] (mêd-sîn' ex-pec-tan·t'). A time treatment. EARLINESS-LATENESS, REMEDY-BANE.
Medes and Persians, law of the. MUTATION-PERMANENCE, UNIFORMITY-MULTIFORMITY.
me'-di-al. Mean. MIDDLE.
me'-di-ant. The third above the key-note. MELODY-DISSONANCE.
medias res, in [L.] (mî'-di-as rîz, in). Into the midst of affairs. MIDDLE; **plunge** *in medias res,* INJECTION-EJECTION, SIMPLICITY-FLORIDNESS.
me'-di-ate. Intercede. DIVINITY, INSTRUMENTALITY, MEDIATION, MIDDLE.
me''-di-a'-tion. Intervention; intercession. DIVINITY, INSTRUMENTALITY, MEDIATION, PETITION-EXPOSTULATION.

MEDIATION.

Intercession. The act of mediating between persons, especially in favor of one party.
Interference. The exercise of influence or authority in the concerns of others, for the purpose of modifying an established course of one.
Intermeddling. The act of taking part in the affairs of others without being asked or desired.
Interposition. Taking part with authority in the affairs of others as a prevention of some result that would otherwise occur.
Intervention. Any interference that may affect the affairs of others.
Mediation. Agency between parties, as the equal friend of each, with influence recognized by each.
Mediatization. The act of coming between two parties as the equal friend of each.
Mediatorship. The office or character of a mediator.

MEDIATION—*Denotations.*

Arbitration. The hearing and determining of a cause between parties in controversy, by a person or persons agreed upon by the parties.
Compromise. An arrangement for the settlement of a dispute by mutual concession, involving a partial surrender by both sides. See sub COMPROMISE.
Diplomacy. The art and practise of conducting negotiations between nations.
Diplomatics. The art of deciphering ancient writings, charters, etc.
Flag of truce. A white flag displayed by an enemy, for the purpose of making some communication not hostile. See FIGHTING-CONCILIATION.
Good offices. Voluntary service which one offers to parties in dispute, to effect a settlement.
Negotiation. The mutual intercourse of governments by diplomatic agents, in making treaties, etc.
Parley. An oral conference with an enemy, as with regard to a truce.
Peace-offering. A gift or service offered as satisfaction to an offended person.

MEDIATION—*Nouns of Agent.*

Diplomatist. A person employed or skilled in conducting negotiations. See sub CONSIGNEE.
Go-between. An intermediate agent, usually in a disparaging sense.
Intercessor. One who comes between parties at variance, with a view to reconciliation, by pleading for one party.
Make-peace. A peacemaker.
Mediator. An equal friend of parties in dispute.
Moderator. One who pacifies or restrains.
Negotiator. A person who treats with others in respect to public compacts.
Peacemaker. One who reconciles parties at variance.

MEDIATION—*Verbs.*

Arbitrate. To settle a dispute by parties mutually agreed upon by the disputants.
Intercede. To act between parties by pleading in behalf of one.
Interfere. To take part in the concerns of others, especially to prevent some action.
Interpose. To exercise one's authority in the affairs of others.
Intervene. To interfere in any way to affect the affairs of others.
Magnas componere lites [L.]. To settle great disputes.

Mediate. To interpose between parties, as the equal friend of each.
Mediatize. To cause to act through an agent.
Meet half-way. To agree to a compromise.
Negotiate. To hold intercourse respecting a treaty, league, or convention.
Step in. To take a part in an affair.

MEDIATION—*Adjective.*

Mediatory. Pertaining to mediation or a mediator.

me″-di-a-ti-za′-tion. Reduction from a direct to a mediate relation. MEDIATION.
me′-di-a-tize. Reduce from a direct to a mediate relation. MEDIATION.
me′-di-a″-tor. One who mediates. ANTAGONIST-ASSISTANT.
Me′-di-a″-tor. Saviour. DIVINITY.
me″-di-a-to′-ri-al. Serving to mediate. PRECEDENCE-SUCCESSION.
me′-di-a″-tor-ship. Office of a mediator. MEDIATION.
me′-di-a-to-ry. Pertaining to mediation. MEDIATION.
med′-i-ca, ma-te′-ri-a. The science of medicinal substances. REMEDY-BANE.
med′-i-cal. Relating to medicine. REMEDY-BANE; **medical attendant,** REMEDY-BANE.
med′-i-ca-ment. A healing agency. REMEDY-BANE.
med′-i-cas″-ter. A quack. GULL-DECEIVER.
med′-i-cate. To treat; to tincture. MIXTURE-HOMO-GENEITY, RENOVATION-RELAPSE.
me-dic′-i-nal. Adapted to mitigate bodily diseases. REMEDY-BANE.
med′-i-cine. A curative substance. REMEDY-BANE; **medicine man,** DEVOTION-MAGICIAN.
medicum, odium [L.] (med′-ic-um, o′-di-um). Mutual hatred among physicians. LOVE-HATE.
me-di′-e-ty. The middle part. MIDDLE.
me″-di-e′-val. Belonging to the Middle Ages. NEWNESS-ANTIQUITY.
me″-di-e′-val-ism. Spirit of the Middle Ages. FUTURE-PAST.
me″-di-e′-val-ist. One devoted to the ideas of the Middle Ages. FUTURE-PAST.
mediis rebus, in [L.] (mi′-di-is ri′-bus, in). In the midst of affairs. ACTIVITY-INDOLENCE.
medio tutissimus, in [L.] (mi′-di-o tiu-tis′-im-us, in). Safety in moderation. RECKLESSNESS-CAUTION.
mediocritas, aurea [L.] (mi-di-oc′-ri-tas au′-ri-a). The golden medium. MIDCOURSE-CIRCUIT.
me′-di-o″-cre. Ordinary. FAULTLESSNESS-FAULTINESS.
me″-di-oc′-ri-ty. Middle state; a moderate degree. FAULTLESSNESS-FAULTINESS, MAGNITUDE-SMALLNESS, MEDIOCRITY, MEDIUM.

MEDIOCRITY.

Average circumstances. General or ordinary circumstances.
Golden mean. See MIDCOURSE; TURBULENCE-CALMNESS.
Mediocrity. Ordinary, commonplace ability
Middle classes. Classes that occupy socially an intermediate position.
Moderate circumstances. Limited condition in regard to worldly estate.
Respectability. State of being moderate in excellence.

MEDIOCRITY—*Verbal Expressions.*

Get on fairly; get on peaceably; get on quietly; get on respectably; get on tolerably; go on fairly; go on peaceably; go on quietly; go on respectably; go on tolerably; jog on.

med′-i-tate. To plan in the mind. PURPOSE-LUCK, REFLECTION-VACANCY.
med′-i-ta′-tion. Reflection. REFLECTION-VACANCY
med′-i-ta-tive. Thoughtful. REFLECTION-VACANCY.
med′-i-ter-ra′-ne-an. Enclosed nearly or wholly by land. ENVIRONMENT-INTERPOSITION, MIDDLE.
me′-di-um. Mediocre; atmosphere; a liquid vehicle;

mean; seer. COLOR-ACHROMATISM, DEVOTION-MAGICIAN, ENVIRONMENT-INTERPOSITION, INSTRUMENTALITY, MEDIUM, MIDDLE; **transparent medium,** DIAPHANEITY-OPAQUENESS.

MEDIUM.

Average. The result obtained by dividing the sum by the number of items added.
Balance. The middle, or the part easily thrown on one side or the other.
Compromise. Means of settling by each giving in a little See COMPROMISE.
Generality. The greater part.
Golden mean. Absence of extremes or excess.
Intermedium. Medium.
Mean. The point found according to some law between two extremes.
Mediocrity. Common excellence.
Medium. Agent acting between two things.
Middle. The point half-way between two points.
Neutrality. The state of not acting for or against.

MEDIUM—*Verbal Expressions.*

Pair off; reduce to a mean; split the difference; strike a balance; take the average.

MEDIUM—*Adjectives.*

Average. Ordinary.
Commonplace. Of not much excellence.
Intermediate. Holding a place in the middle.
Mean. Common.
Médiocre [F.]. Of moderate excellence.
Middle. Half-way between two points. See sub MIDDLE.
Middle-class. Intermediate.
Neutral. Not acting for or against anything.

MEDIUM—*Adverbs, etc.*

Communibus annis [L.]. Taking one year with another.
In round numbers; in the long run; on an average; taking all things together; taking it for all in all; taking one with another.

MEDIUM—*Phrase.*

Medium tenuere beati [L.]. The happy hold the middle course.

med′-ley. Jumble; mixture. MIXTURE-HOMOGENEITY, REGULARITY-IRREGULARITY; **chance medley,** RATIONALE-LUCK.
med′-ul-la-ry. Pertaining to marrow or medulla. HARDNESS-SOFTNESS.
meed. Desert; reward. ASSIGNMENT, RECOMPENSE-PUNITION; **meed of praise,** APPROVAL-DISAPPROVAL.
meek. Gentle; humble. EXCITABILITY-INEXCITABILITY, SELFRESPECT-HUMBLENESS.
meek′-ness. Gentleness. SELFRESPECT-HUMBLENESS.
meet. Suitable; to come together. ARRIVAL-DEPARTURE, BRAVERY-COWARDICE, CONCENTRATION-RADIATION, DUENESS-UNDUENESS, DUTY-DERELICTION, GATHERING-SCATTERING, HARMONY-DISCORD, INTERSPACE - CONTACT, OBSERVANCE - NONOBSERVANCE, PROPRIETY-IMPROPRIETY; **make both ends meet,** AFFLUENCE-PENURY, GENEROSITY-FRUGALITY; **meet half-way,** AMITY-HOSTILITY, CHARITABLENESS-MALEVOLENCE, COMPOSITION, FIGHTING-CONCILIATION, MEDIATION, READINESS-RELUCTANCE, VARIANCE-ACCORD; **meet hand to hand,** STRIFE-PEACE, **meet in front,** BRAVERY-COWARDICE; **meet one at every turn,** EXCESS-LACK, PRESENCE-ABSENCE; **meet one's death,** LIFE-DEATH; **meet one's end,** LIFE-DEATH; **meet one's expenses,** GENEROSITY-FRUGALITY; **meet one's wishes,** CONSENT, PLEASURABLENESS-PAINFULNESS; **meet the ear,** HEARING-DEAFNESS; **meet the eye,** VISIBILITY-INVISIBILITY; **meet with,** DISCOVERY, OCCURRENCE-DESTINY, **meet with attention,** HEED-DISREGARD; **unable to make both ends meet,** AFFLUENCE-PENURY, SETTLEMENT-DEFAULT.
meet′-ing. A coming together. ARRIVAL-DEPARTURE, CONCENTRATION-RADIATION, COUNCIL, GATHERING-

SCATTERING, INTERSPACE-CONTACT, VIGOR-INERTIA; hostile meeting, STRIFE-PEACE.

meet'-ing–house". A house for public worship. DWELLER-HABITATION, FANE.

meg'-a-cosm. The great world. UNIVERSE.

Meg-æ'-ra. One of the Greek goddesses of vengeance. TURBULENCE-CALMNESS.

meg'-a-scope. A solar microscope. OPTICAL INSTRUMENTS.

Meg"-a-the'-ri-um. An extinct edentate. NOVELTY-ANTIQUITY.

meglio cader dalle finestre che dal tetto [It.] (mel'-yo ka'-dêr dal'-lê fîn-ês'-trê kê dal tet'-to). It is better to fall from the window than from the roof. HEIGHT-LOWNESS.

me'-grims. Congestion of the brain in a horse. AGITATION, LIGHTHEARTEDNESS-DEJECTION.

Mei-bo'-mi-an. Pertaining to Heinrich Meibom. **Meibomian glands,** ANATOMY.

Mein Herr [G.] (main hêr). Sir. TITLE.

meis'-ter-sing"-er. Poet and musician of Germany. POETRY-PROSE.

me judice [L.] (mî ju'-di-sî). In my opinion. FAITH-MISGIVING.

mel"-an-cho'-li-a. Dejection; insanity. LIGHT-HEARTEDNESS-DEJECTION, SANENESS-LUNACY.

mel"-an-chol'-ic. Low-spirited. LIGHTHEARTEDNESS-DEJECTION, WITTINESS-DULNESS.

mel'-an-chol-y. Gloomy; despondency. CONTENTEDNESS-DISCONTENTMENT, LIGHTHEARTEDNESS-DEJECTION; **away with melancholy,** LIGHTHEARTEDNESS-DEJECTION.

mélange [F.] (mê-lan˙zh'). A mixture. MIXTURE-HOMOGENEITY.

mel'-a-no-scope. An instrument used to distinguish between substances giving red spectral bands. INSTRUMENT.

mel, ibi apes, ibi [L.] (mel, ai'-bai ê'-pîz, ai'-bai). Where the honey is, there are the bees. DESIRE-DISTASTE.

mêlée [F.] (mê-lê'). An affray. REGULARITY-IRREGULARITY, STRIFE-PEACE.

meliora proboque deteriora sequor, video [L.] (mî-li-o'-ra pro-bo'-quî dî-tî'-ri-o'-ra sî'-quor, vid'-î-o). I see the better and approve, the worse I follow. MUTABILITY-STABILITY.

meliora, spero [L.] (mî-li-o'-ra, spî'-ro). I hope for better things. SANGUINENESS-HOPELESSNESS.

me'-lio-rate. To make better. BETTERMENT-DETERIORATION.

me'-lio-ra-tion. Improvement. BETTERMENT-DETERIORATION.

melioribus, da locum [L.] (mî-li-or'-i-bus, da lo'-cum). Give place to your betters. CHIEF-UNDERLING, YIELDING.

melius inquirendum, ad [L.] (mî'-li-us in-qui-ren'-dum, ad). The better for searching. BETTERMENT-DETERIORATION.

mel-lif'-er-ous. Bearing honey. SWEETNESS-ACIDITY.

mel-lif'-lu-ous. Sweetly flowing. MELODY-DISSONANCE, PURITY-CRUDENESS.

mel'-low. Soft; delicate; subdued; tipsy; to become mellow. BETTERMENT-DETERIORATION, COLOR-ACHROMATISM, CONVERSION-REVERSION, HARDNESS-SOFTNESS, INFANCY-AGE, MELODY-DISSONANCE, PREPARATION-NONPREPARATION, TEETOTALISM-INTEMPERANCE.

mel'-low-ness. Ripeness. PREPARATION-NONPREPARATION.

mel'-o'-di-ous. Tuneful. MELODY-DISSONANCE.

mel'-o-dist. A composer of melodies. MUSICIAN

mel"-o-dra'-ma. A musical drama. ACTING.

mel"-o-dra-mat'-ic. Resembling melodrama. ACTING.

mel-o-dy. MELODY-DISSONANCE.

MELODY—DISSONANCE.

Chime. The harmonious sounding together of musical instruments.

Concent. Concord of sounds.

Concord. An agreeable combination of sounds heard at the same time.

Consonance. Pleasing accord and harmony of sounds.

Euphonism. Agreeable and harmonious combination of sounds.

Euphony. An agreeable sound which is pleasing to the ear.

Harmony. The concord resulting from two or more musical strains of different pitch.

Homophony. Sameness of sound.

Melody. The pleasing variety and alternation of sounds, musical and measured, as they succeed each other.

Rhythm. Musical movement; regular recurrence of accent.

Unison. A coincidence of sounds proceeding from different sonorous bodies, but having the same number of vibrations in a given time.

Unisonance. Unison of sounds.

MELODY—*Associated Nouns.*

Acciaccatura [It.]. A grace note.

Appoggiato [It.]. A direction in music that notes are to be so performed that they glide and melt into each other.

Appoggiatura [It.]. A subordinate note preceding an essential tone.

Bar. A vertical line across the staff, which divides the staff into measures.

Brace. A vertical curved line used to connect staves.

Breve. A note equal to two semibreves.

Burden. The verse repeated in a song.

Chords. A combination of tones simultaneously performed.

Chromatic scale. A music scale of thirteen tones.

Clef. A character used in music to determine the position or pitch of the scale.

Composer. An author of a piece of music.

Contrapuntist. One skilled in writing music in parts.

Counterpoint. The writing of music in parts.

Crotchet. A quarter note.

Demisemiquaver. A short note equal in time to one thirty-second of a whole note.

Diapason. The entire compass of tones.

Cacophony. A combination of discordant and inharmonious sounds.

Discord. A combination of musical sounds which strikes the ear harshly on account of the incommensurability of their several vibrations.

Discordance. The state of being discordant.

Dissonance. A combination of discordant sounds.

Harshness, etc. The state of being grating or disagreeable in sound. See CACOPHONY.

DISSONANCE—*Denotations.*

Babel. A confused mixture of sounds, as of voices or languages, as at the building of the tower of Babel.

Caterwauling. The cry of cats.

Cat's concert. Harsh disagreeable noises or cries like the cry of cats.

Dutch concert. A so-called concert in which all the singers sing at the same time different songs.

Marrow-bones and cleavers. Large bones used to make a rhythmical accompaniment by beating.

DISSONANCE—*Verbs.*

Be discordant, etc. To be inharmonious. See *Adjectives.*

Jar, etc. To sound harshly; grate upon the ears. See CACOPHONY.

DISSONANCE—*Adjectives.*

Absonant. Discordant, not consonant.

Cacophonous. Inharmonious.

Discordant. Not in harmony or musical concord.

Dissonant. Inharmonious.

Harsh, etc. Grating on the ear; displeasing See CACOPHONY

Immelodious. Not melodious.

Inharmonious. Out of harmonious accord.

Out of tune. Not in harmony or concord.

Singsong. In a drawling or monotonous manner or tone.

Tuneless. Unmusical.

Unharmonious. Discordant.

Unmelodious. Not pleasing or agreeable to the ear.

Unmusical. Not musical.

Untunable. Not able to be tuned.

MELODY—Associated Nouns—*Continued.*

Diatessaron. An interval of a fourth.

Diatonic scale. A scale consisting of eight sounds with seven intervals.

Dominant. The fifth tone of the scale.

Drone. A monotonous base.

Enharmonic scale. A scale of perfect intonation which recognizes all the notes and intervals that result from the exact tuning of diatonic scales.

Faburden. A counterpoint with a drone bass.

Flat. A character beside a note indicating a semitone lower.

Fourth. The interval of two tones and a semitone.

Fundamental bass. } The root note of a chord.
Fundamental note. }

Gamut. The scale.

Harmonics. Secondary and less distinct tones which accompany any principal tone.

Harmonist. One skilled in the principles of harmony.

High note, etc. An acute or sharp note. See CACOPHONY.

Interval. Difference in pitch between any two tones.

Intonation. The act of sounding the tones of the musical scale.

Key. The fundamental tone of a movement to which its modulations are referred.

Key-note. The first tone of the scale in which a piece is written.

Key scale. The scale in which a piece is written.

Leading note. The seventh note in the ascending scale.

Line. One of the straight horizontal and parallel strokes on and between which the notes are placed.

Low note, etc. A base note. See RESONANCE.

Major key. A key in which one and two, two and three, four and five, five and six, six and seven, make major seconds.

Major mode. The scale as affected by the various positions in it of the intervals.

Major scale. The natural diatonic scale, which has semitones between the third and fourth, and seventh and eighth degrees.

Major tone. The principal tone of a scale.

Measure. The group or grouping of beats, caused by the regular recurrence of accented beats.

Mediant. The third note above the key-note.

Minim. A half note equal in time to two quarters.

Minor key. A key less by a semitone in interval or difference of pitch.

Minor mode. The scale in which the third and sixth are minors.

Minor scale. The scale in which the third and sixth are minors, with a semitone between the seventh and eighth.

Minor tone. A tone lower by a semitone.

Modulation. A change of key.

Musical note. A character in music to indicate the length of a tone

Natural note. A note of the natural scale.

Notes of a scale. The characters used to indicate the tones of a scale.

Octave. The interval between one and eight of the scale.

Part. One of the different melodies of a concerted composition.

Passage. A portion of a musical composition.

Phrase. A short clause or portion of a period.

Piece of music, etc. A musical composition. See MUSIC.

Pitch. The relative acuteness of a tone.

Preparation. The holding over of a note from one chord into the next chord.

Quaver. An eighth note.

Resolution. The passing of a dissonant into its proper consonant chord.

Rest. Silence in music or in one of its parts.

Rime, etc. Correspondence of sound in the terminating words or syllables of two or more verses. See POETRY.

Scale. The graduated series of all the tones from the key-note to its octave.

Second. The interval between any tone and the tone next above it.

Semibreve. A note of half the time of the breve.

Semiquaver. A sixteenth note.

Semitone. Half a tone.

Sharp. A character to indicate that the note before which it is to be placed is to be raised a semitone.

Space. One of the intervals between the lines of the staff.

Staff. The five lines and spaces on which music is written.

Stave. The staff.

Subdominant. The fourth tone above, or fifth below, the tonic.

Submediant. The sixth tone of the scale.

Supertonic. The note next above the key-note.

Suspension. The prolongation of one or more tones of a chord into the chord which follows.

Sustained note. A note held up to a certain pitch.

Syncopation. } The welding into one tone the second half of one beat
Syncope. } with the first half of the beat which follows

Temperament. A system of compromises in the tuning of organs, etc., whereby the tones are mutually modified and in part canceled.

Tetrachord. A scale series of four sounds, of which the first and last constitute a fourth.

Third. The third tone of the scale.

Thorough-bass. The representation of chords by figures placed upon the base.

Timber. The quality of tone distinguishing voices or instruments.

Tonality. The principle of key in music.

Tone. A sound considered as to pitch.

Tonic. The first tone of any scale.

MELODY—*Verbs.*

Accord. To agree in pitch or tone.

Be harmonious, etc. To be agreeable to the ear. See *Adjectives*

Chime. To be in harmony.

Harmonize. To be or put in accord.

Put in tune. To harmonize.

String. To put in tune the strings of a musical instrument.

Symphonize. To put in harmony with.

Transpose. To change from one key to another.

Tune. To harmonize.

MELODY—*Adjectives.*

Assonant. Pertaining to or having a resemblance to sound.

Canorous. Uttering musical sounds.

Chromatic. Pertaining to the scale which proceeds by semitones.

Clear. Easily heard; distinct; entirely musical.

Clear as a bell.

Concentual. Possessing harmony.

Diatonic. Pertaining to the scale of eight tones, the last of which is the octave of the first.

Dulcet. Sweet or pleasing to the ear

Enchanting, etc. Fascinating; very pleasing. See PLEASURABLENESS

Enharmonic. Pertaining to a scale of perfect intonation.

Euphonic. } Pertaining to sounds that are pleasing to the ear.
Euphonical. }

Euphonious. Agreeable or pleasing in sound.

Fine-toned. Excellent or pure in tone.

Full-toned. Clear or distinct in tone.

Harmonical. Pertaining to harmony or music.

Harmonious. Musically concordant.

Homophonous. Having the same pitch.

In concert. In unison.

In concord, etc. See *Nouns.*

In tune. Harmonious.

Isotonic. Having equal tones.

Measured. Regulated; uniform.

Mellifluous. Softly or sweetly flowing.

Mellow. Soft; rich; not harsh.

Melodious. Containing or pertaining to music or melody.

Musical. Pertaining to music.

Rhythmical. Regularly recurring in beats or accents.

Silver-toned. Clear and ringing in tone.

Silvery. Having a clear, tinkling sound.

Soft. Gentle; low; not harsh.

Sweet. Mild; soft; pleasing.

Symphonious. Harmonious in sound; concordant.

Symphonizing. Harmonizing; agreeing with in sound.

Tunable. Possessing the power to be tuned or put in harmony.

Tuneful. Harmonious; melodious.

Unisonant. Being in unison.

MELODY—*Adverbs.*

Harmoniously, etc. In an harmonious manner. See *Adjectives.*

Mel-pom'-e-ne. The muse of tragedy. ACTING.

melt. Liquefy; to become tender. COMPASSION-RUTH-LESSNESS, CONVERSION-REVERSION, HEATING-COOLING, LIQUEFACTION-VOLATILIZATION; **melt away,** AP-

PEARANCE-DISAPPEARANCE, ENTITY-NONENTITY, IN-CREASE-DECREASE, PROVISION-WASTE, SUBSTANCE-NULLITY; **melt in the air**, LOUDNESS-FAINTNESS; **melt into one**, COMPOSITION-RESOLUTION; **melt into tears**, JUBILATION-LAMENTATION; **melt the heart**, COMPASSION-RUTHLESSNESS.

melt'-ing. Mollifying; dissolving. COMPASSION-RUTHLESSNESS, HEATING-COOLING, LIQUEFACTION-VOLATILIZATION.

mem'-ber. A part; councilor. CONSTITUENT-ALIEN, COUNCIL, PRESIDENT-MEMBER, WHOLE-PART.

mem'-brane. A thin structure. LAMINA-FIBER.

même, quand [F.] (mem, kan·). Although. ANTAGONISM-CONCURRENCE.

me-men'-to. A reminder. REMEMBRANCE-FORGETFULNESS.

memento mori [L.] (mî-men'-to mo'-rai). Be mindful of death. LIFE-FUNERAL, LIGHTHEARTEDNESS-DEJECTION.

meminisse juvabit [L.] (mem''-i-nis'-sî ju-vê'-bit). It will help to remember. REMEMBRANCE-FORGETFULNESS.

mem'-oir. A record of something worthy. ACCOUNT, ESSAY.

mem''-o-ra-bil'-i-a. Noteworthy reminiscences. CONSEQUENCE-INSIGNIFICANCE, REMEMBRANCE-FORGETFULNESS.

mem'-o-ra-ble. Remarkable. CONSEQUENCE-INSIGNIFICANCE, REMEMBRANCE-FORGETFULNESS.

mem''-o-ran'-dum. A brief note of things to be remembered. MARK-OBLITERATION, REMEMBRANCE-FORGETFULNESS; **memorandum book**, DIGEST, MARK-OBLITERATION.

memoria, in æterna [L.] (mî-mo'-ri-a, in î-ter'-na). In everlasting remembrance. REMEMBRANCE-FORGETFULNESS.

memoriæ, beatæ [L.] (mî-mo'-ri-î, bî-ê-tî). Of blessed memory. REMEMBRANCE-FORGETFULNESS.

me-mo'-ri-al. A commemoration. MARK-OBLITERATION.

me-mo'-ri-al-ist. One who writes a memorial. RECORDER.

me-mo'-ri-al-ize. To commemorate. REMEMBRANCE-FORGETFULNESS.

me-mo'-ri-als. Records. ACCOUNT.

memoriam, in [L.] (mî-mo'-ri-am, in). In memory. LIFE-FUNERAL, REMEMBRANCE-FORGETFULNESS.

mem'-o-ry. Remembrance; fame. FUTURE-PAST, REMEMBRANCE-FORGETFULNESS, REPUTATION-DISCREDIT; **failing memory**, REMEMBRANCE-FORGETFULNESS; **in the memory of man**, FUTURE-PAST; **memory runneth not to the contrary**, NOVELTY-ANTIQUITY; **short memory**, REMEMBRANCE-FORGETFULNESS.

men'-ace. A threat. CHARITABLENESS-MENACE, WARNING.

men'-ac-ing. Threatening. CHARITABLENESS-MENACE.

me''-nage'. Household management. CONDUCT.

men-ag'-e-rie. A collection of wild animals for exhibit. DOMESTICATION-AGRICULTURE, GATHERING-SCATTERING, STORE.

men-ag'-e-ry. Same as menagerie. STORE.

mend. To restore. BETTERMENT-DETERIORATION; **mend one's manners**, BETTERMENT-DETERIORATION, POLITENESS-IMPOLITENESS.

mendacem memorem esse oportet [L.] (men-dê'-sem mî-mo'-rem es'-sî o-por'-tet). A liar needs to have a good memory. NEED, REMEMBRANCE-FORGETFULNESS.

mendacia linguæ, blandæ [L.] (men-dê'-si-a lin'-gwî, blan'-dî). Falsehoods of a smooth tongue. TRUTHFULNESS-FALSEHOOD.

men-da'-cious. Falsifying. TRUTHFULNESS-FALSEHOOD.

men-dac'-i-ty. Falsehood. TRUTHFULNESS-FALSEHOOD.

men'-di-can-cy. Beggary. AFFLUENCE-PENURY, PETITION-EXPOSTULATION.

men'-di-cant. Begging; a begging friar. AFFLUENCE-PENURY, MINISTRY-LAITY, PETITIONER.

men'-di-cate. To beg. PETITION-DEPRECATION.

mend'-ing. Improving. BETTERMENT-DETERIORATION.

me'-ni-al. Servile; a servant. CHIEF-UNDERLING, GENTILITY-COMMONALTY.

men''-in-gi'-tis. A disease of the brain. HEALTH-SICKNESS.

me-nis'-cus. A lens. OPTICAL INSTRUMENTS.

mensâ et thoro, separatio a [L.] (men'-sa et tho'-ro, sep-a-rê'-shi-o ê). Separation from bed and board. MATRIMONY-DIVORCE.

mens æqua in arduis [L.] (mens î'-qua in ar'-diu-is). A tranquil mind in circumstances of difficulty. EXCITABILITY-INEXCITABILITY, SENSITIVENESS-APATHY.

mens legis [L.] (mens lî'-jis). The spirit of the law. LAW-LAWLESSNESS.

mens sana [L.] (mens sê'-na). A sound mind. SANENESS-LUNACY.

mens sana in corpore sano [L.] (mens sê'-na in cor'-po-rî sê'-no). A sound mind in a sound body. PLEASURE-PAIN.

mens sibi conscia recti [L.] (mens sib'-i cons'-shi-a rec'-tai). A mind conscious of rectitude. INNOCENCE-GUILT, SELFRESPECT-HUMBLENESS.

men'-stru-al. Occurring monthly. PERIODICITY-IRREGULARITY.

men'-stru-um. A solvent. LIQUEFACTION-VOLATILIZATION.

men''-su-ra'-tion. The act of measuring. MENSURATION.

MENSURATION.

Admeasurement. The act or process of ascertaining the dimensions of anything.

Appraisement. The act of estimating the value of anything.

Assessment. The valuation of property for the purposes of taxation.

Assize. Anything fixed or reduced to a certainty in point of weight, measure, etc.

Cadastre [F.]. An official statement of the value of real estate for the purpose of taxation.

Dead reckoning. The method of determining the place of a ship from compass and log without celestial observations.

Estimate. A valuing or rating by the mind, without actually measuring, weighing, or the like.

Estimation. An opinion of the extent or quantity of anything, without using precise data.

Gaging. The act of measuring the contents of anything.

Land surveying. The operation of finding the contour, dimensions, or other particulars of any part of the earth's surface

Measurement. The act of determining the extent, size, capacity, or amount.

Mensuration. The act of computing the dimensions of anything, by a certain rule or standard.

Metage. Measurement, especially of coal.

Reckoning. The calculation of a ship's position, either from astronomical observations, or from compass and log. See NUMBERING

Survey. The determination of the form, extent, position, etc., of a tract of land.

Surveying. See SURVEY.

Valuation. Estimation or measure of worth and value.

MENSURATION—*Nouns of Means or Instrument.*

Armillary sphere. An ancient astronomical sphere on which the positions of the important circles of the celestial sphere were marked.

Astrolabe. An instrument for showing the positions of the stars.

Balance. An apparatus for weighing. See HEAVINESS.

Bathometer. An instrument used in deep-sea soundings.

Callipers. An instrument for measuring the diameter of bodies.

Cardiograph. An instrument for recording the movements of the heart.

Check. A mark for verification; an order for money.

Compass. An instrument for determining directions upon the earth's surface.

Compound arithmetic. The science of compound numbers.

Flood-mark. The mark or line to which the tide rises, from which the height of water is measured.

Foot-rule. A measuring instrument consisting of a graduated bar of wood or metal, marked so as to show feet and fractions.

Gage. } A measure or standard; an instrument to determine dimen-
Gauge. } sions, distance, or capacity.

Geometer. One skilled in geometry.

Graduated scale. A measure or rule marked with lines at regular intervals.

Graduation. The marks on an instrument or vessel to indicate degrees or quantity.

Heliometer. An instrument to measure the diameter of the sun.

Helioscope. An instrument for viewing the sun without injury to the eyes.

High-water mark. That line on the seashore to which the waters ordinarily reach at high water.

Index. A movable finger on a gage, scale, or other graduated instrument.

Landmark. Any mark or fixed object by which the limits of a place are known.

Land surveyor. One who measures land.

Line. A long tape, or ribbon of steel, marked with subdivisions for measuring.

Measure. An instrument by which size or quantity is measured.

Meter. An instrument for measuring and recording the quantity measured.

Nilometer. An instrument for measuring the rise of water in the Nile during its periodical flood.

Odometer. An instrument attached to a wheel to measure the distance traveled.

Pantometer. An instrument for measuring angles and perpendiculars.

Rod. A measure of length containing sixteen and one-half feet.

Rule. A measuring instrument marked so as to show inches and fractions of an inch.

Scale. Succession of ascending steps and degrees.

Standard. That which is established by authority as a rule for the measure of quantity, extent, value, or quality.

Telemeter. An apparatus for determining distance on the earth's surface.

Weights and measures. Tables giving different values of articles.

Yard measure. A measure of length equal to three feet.

Mensuration—*Scientific Terms.*

Altimetry. The art of measuring altitudes or heights.

Altitude and azimuth. The measurements by which the location of a star or celestial object is noted.

Barometer. An instrument for determining the weight or pressure of the atmosphere. See Water.

Coordinates. Lines by means of which the position of any point is defined with respect to certain fixed lines, or planes.

Declination and right ascension. The angular distances by which a heavenly body is located.

Geodesia. See Geodesy.

Geodesy. That branch of applied mathematics which determines the general figure and dimensions of the earth.

Geodetics. See Geodesy.

Geogeny. Study of the shape of the earth.

Geometry. The branch of mathematics which investigates the relations, properties, and measurement of solids, surfaces, lines, and angles.

Goniometer. An instrument for measuring angles, especially angles of crystals.

Hypsometry. That branch of geodesy which measures heights of portions of the earth's surface.

Latitude and longitude. The location of a place on the earth's surface, determined by its distance north or south of the equator, and east or west of a standard meridian.

Metrology. The science of weights and measures.

Nonius. A vernier. See Vernier.

Ordinate and abscissa. Distances of a point from two straight lines intersecting at right angles, by means of which the location of a point is determined.

Orthometry. The art of constructing verses of correct measures, etc.

Polar coordinates. Coordinates made up of a radius vector and its angle of inclination to another line.

Stereometry. The art of measuring the cubical contents of bodies.

Thermometer. An instrument for measuring temperature. See Heat.

Transit. A surveying instrument

Udometer. A rain-gage.

Variometer. An instrument used to determine the variation of magnetic force.

Velo. The velocity of one foot per second.

Vernier. A short scale made to slide along the divisions of a graduated instrument. See Greatness.

Mensuration—*Verbs.*

Apply the compass. See *Nouns.*

Appraise. To measure the value of.

Appreciate. To set a price or value on.

Assess. To measure the rate or amount of tax, etc.

Estimate. To measure the worth of in a general way.

Fathom. To measure by a sounding line.

Form an estimate. To express an opinion of the size or amount without actual measurement.

Gage. To measure the contents or capacity of.

Graduate. To mark with a scale of measurement.

Heave the lead. To take soundings with lead and line.

Heave the log. To ascertain the speed of a vessel by the log.

Measure. To ascertain the extent, quantity, dimensions, or capacity of, by a certain rule or standard.

Mete. To measure.

Pace. To measure by steps or paces.

Plumb. To measure the depth.

Probe. To search to the bottom.

Rate. To set a certain estimate on.

Set a value on. To measure the worth of.

Sound. To measure the depth of by means of a line and plummet.

Span. To measure with the hand.

Step. To measure by steps.

Survey. To determine the form, extent, position, etc

Take an average. See Medium.

Value. To measure the worth of.

Mensuration—*Adjectives*

Geodetical. Determined by the operations of geodesy.

Measurable. Capable of being measured.

Measuring, etc. See *Verbs.*

Metric. Proceeding by measurement.

Metrical. Pertaining to measure.

men'-tal. Pertaining to the mind. Mind-Imbecility; **mental calm,** Excitability-Inexcitability; **mental excitement,** Excitation; **mental pabulum,** Conception-Theme; **mental philosophy,** Mind-Imbecility; **mental reservation,** Enlightenment-Secrecy; **mental suffering,** Pleasure-Pain.

menteur à triple étage [F.] (man·-tur′ a tripl ê-tazh′). A liar in a triple degree. Gull-Deceiver.

men'-tion. Notice. Enlightenment-Secrecy; **above mentioned,** Recurrence; **not worth mentioning,** Consequence-Insignificance.

mentis gratissimus error [L.] (men′-tis gra-tis′-sim-us er′-ror). A most agreeable mental error. Decision-Misjudgment.

men'-tor. A wise teacher and adviser. Advice, Instructor-Pupil.

me-nu'. A bill of fare. Nutriment-Excretion, Record.

Meph-is-toph'-e-les. A familiar spirit. Jove-Fiend.

Meph''-is-to-phe'-li-an. Pertaining to Mephistopheles. Virtue-Vice.

me-phit'-ic. Foul; noxious. Healthiness-Unhealthiness, Perfume-Stench.

me-phi'-tis. A noxious exhalation. Remedy-Bane.

mer à boire, il a le [F.] (mêr a bwar, il a le). He has the sea to drink up (*i. e.*, an impossible job on his hands). Possibility-Impossibility.

me-ra'-cious. Strong. Pungency.

mer'-can-tile. Pertaining to buying and selling. Exchange.

mercatoria, lex [L.] (mer-ca-to′-ri-a, lex). Mercantile law. Law-Lawlessness.

mer'-ca-ture. Traffic. Exchange.

mer'-ce-na-ry. Sordid; a hired soldier. Belligerent, Chief-Underling, Extravagance-Avarice, Price-Discount, Unselfishness-Selfishness.

mer'-chan-dise. Wares. Merchandise.

MERCHANDISE.

Article. A definite one of various things, as an article of merchandise.

Cargo, etc. The goods or merchandise conveyed in a vessel, etc. See CONTENTS.

Commodity. An object of commerce; something bought and sold.

Effects. Movable goods.

Goods. Commodities; wares.

Merchandise. Objects of commerce; things bought and sold in trade.

Produce. The outcome of labor, especially farm labor; hence, agricultural products.

Staple commodity. The chief commodity or the one produced or manufactured in large quantities.

Stock. The goods and merchandise employed in trade or commerce.

Stock in trade, etc. The merchandise kept for sale by a shopkeeper, etc. See STORE.

Ware. Articles of commerce or merchandise.

---

mer'-chant. A dealer. BUYING-SALE, DEALER.

mer'-chant-man. A trading vessel. CONVEYANCE-VESSEL.

mer'-ci-ful. Full of mercy. CHARITABLENESS-MALEVOLENCE, COMPASSION-RUTHLESSNESS.

mer'-ci-less. Without mercy. COMPASSION-RUTHLESSNESS.

mer-cu'-ri-al. Active; fickle. EXCITABILITY-INEXCITABILITY, MOVEMENT-REST, SWIFTNESS-SLOWNESS.

Mercurius, ex quovis ligno non fit [L.] (mer-kiu'-ri-us, ex quo'-vis lig'-no non fit). A Mercury is not to be made out of any chance piece of wood. OPPORTUNENESS-UNSUITABLENESS.

Mer'-cu-ry. The messenger of the gods; a metallic element. CHEMISTRY, MESSENGER, SWIFTNESS-SLOWNESS, WAYFARER-SEAFARER.

mer'-cy. Compassion; levity. CHARITABLENESS-MALEVOLENCE, COMPASSION-RUTHLESSNESS, HARSHNESS-MILDNESS; **cry you mercy,** PETITION-EXPOSTULATION; **for mercy's sake,** PETITION-EXPOSTULATION; **have no mercy,** CHARITABLENESS-MALEVOLENCE, COMPASSION-RUTHLESSNESS; **mercy on us!** ASTONISHMENT-EXPECTANCE; **mercy seat,** TRIBUNAL.

mere. A lake; simple. CONSEQUENCE-INSIGNIFICANCE, LAKE-PLAIN, MAGNITUDE-SMALLNESS; **buy for a mere nothing,** COSTLINESS-CHEAPNESS; **mere nothing,** CONSEQUENCE-INSIGNIFICANCE, MAGNITUDE-SMALLNESS; **mere pretext,** PRETEXT; **mere words,** SIMPLICITY-FLORIDNESS; **mere wreck,** BETTERMENT-DETERIORATION.

mer'-els. A game. ENTERTAINMENT-WEARINESS.

mere'-ly. Only. MAGNITUDE-SMALLNESS.

mer"-e-tri'-cious. False; wanton. PURITY-IMPURITY, TASTE-VULGARITY, TRUTHFULNESS-FRAUD.

mer'-folk. Denizens of the sea. JOVE-FIEND.

merge. Combine; insert. ADMISSION-EXCLUSION, COMPOSITION-RESOLUTION, INJECTION-EJECTION, WATER-AIR; **merge in,** COHESION-LOOSENESS; **merge into,** CONVERSION-REVERSION.

merged. Swallowed up. ENVIRONMENT-INTERPOSITION.

me-rid'-i-an. Noonday; the highest point. EXTENSION-DISTRICT, LIGHT-DARKNESS, MORNING-EVENING, TOP-BOTTOM; **meridian of life,** MANHOOD.

me-rid'-i-o-nal. Highest. TOP-BOTTOM.

mer'-it. Worth. DUENESS-UNDUENESS, GOODNESS-BADNESS, VIRTUE-VICE; **make a merit of,** BRAGGING; **merit notice,** CONSEQUENCE-INSIGNIFICANCE.

mer'-it-ed. Deserve. DUENESS-UNDUENESS.

mer'-it-ing. Deserving. DUENESS-UNDUENESS.

merito, e [L.] (mer'-it-o, î). According to merit. VIRTUE-VICE.

mer"-i-to'-ri-ous. Praiseworthy. APPROVAL-DISAPPROVAL, VIRTUE-VICE.

mer'-maid. A marine creature. CONVENTIONALITY-UNCONVENTIONALITY, JOVE-FIEND.

---

mer'-man. A fabled marine creature, half man, half fish. JOVE-FIEND.

mero motu, ex [L.] (mî'-ro mo'-tiu, ex). Of his own accord. VOLITION-OBLIGATION.

mer'-ri-ment. The state of being merry. ENTERTAINMENT-WEARINESS, LIGHTHEARTEDNESS-DEJECTION.

mer'-ry. Cheerful; drunk. LIGHTHEARTEDNESS-DEJECTION, TEETOTALISM-INTEMPERANCE; **make merry,** ENTERTAINMENT-WEARINESS; **make merry with,** SOCIETY-DERISION, WITTINESS-DULNESS; **merry and wise,** WITTINESS-DULNESS; **wish a merry Christmas,** FELICITATION.

mer'-ry-an"-drew. A clown. WAG.

mer'-ry-go-round. An amusement. ENTERTAINMENT-WEARINESS.

mer'-ry-mak"-ing. A frolic. ENTERTAINMENT-WEARINESS, JUBILATION-LAMENTATION, LIGHTHEARTEDNESS-DEJECTION, SOCIABILITY-PRIVACY.

mer'-ry-thought". The wish-bone. WITTINESS-DULNESS.

mer'-sion. An immersion. WATER-AIR.

meruit ferat, palmam qui [L.] (mer-yu'-it fî'-rat, pal'-mam quai). Let him bear the palm who has won it. REPUTATION-DISCREDIT.

merveille, à [F.] (mer-vêîy', a). Marvelously. SUCCESS-FAILURE.

mes"-al-li"-ance'. A marriage with an inferior. HARMONY-DISCORD, MATRIMONY-CELIBACY.

me-seems'. It seems to me. FAITH-MISGIVING.

mesh. A network. CROSSING, INTERSPACE-CONTACT.

mesh'-es. Trap; difficulty. DIFFICULTY-FACILITY, TRUTHFULNESS-FRAUD; **meshes of sophistry,** RATIOCINATION-CASUISTRY.

mes'-i-al. Median. ANATOMY, MIDDLE.

Mes'-mer. The propounder of the doctrine of mesmerism. DEVOTION-MAGICIAN.

mes'-mer-ism. The art of exercising hypnotic influence. DEVOTION-MAGIC.

mes'-mer-ist. One who mesmerizes. DEVOTION-MAGICIAN.

mes'-mer-ize. Hypnotize. DEVOTION-MAGICIAN.

mesne lord. An intermediate lord. HOLDER.

Mes"-o-zo'-ic. Pertaining to a geological period. **Mesozoic period,** GEOLOGY.

mess. A mixture; portion; meal; disorder. ASSIGNMENT, DIFFICULTY-FACILITY, MIXTURE-HOMOGENEITY, NUTRIMENT-EXCRETION, REGULARITY-IRREGULARITY, SUCCESS-FAILURE; **make a mess,** SKILL-UNSKILFULNESS, SUCCESS-FAILURE.

mes'-sage. A communication. ORDER, TIDINGS-MYSTERY.

Mes"-sa-li'-na. Unchaste wife of the Emperor Claudius. PURITY-RAKE.

mes'-sen-ger. A forerunner; cloud. CHIEF-UNDERLING, CONSIGNEE, MESSENGER, VISCIDITY-FOAM; **messenger balloon,** TRIAL.

MESSENGER

Ambassador, etc. A person of the highest diplomatic rank sent to represent a sovereign or country at a foreign court, etc. See CONSIGNEE.

Apparitor. An attending messenger of an ecclesiastical court.

Bellman. A person who rings a bell and makes announcements in the streets.

Commissionnaire [F.]. A messenger or attendant, in some European cities, who performs miscellaneous services for travelers.

Courier. A special messenger carrying despatches from a distance.

Crier. One who gives public notice by vocal proclamation.

Emissary. One sent on a mission as a secret agent.

Envoy. A person entrusted with a special mission; a diplomatic agent below an ambassador in rank.

Errand-boy. A boy whose business it is to do errands.

Estafet. One of a relay of couriers; a military courier.

Flag-bearer. The one who carries the flag or colors.

Gentleman of the press. A person connected with a newspaper.

Herald. Any bearer of news.

Informer, etc. One who imparts news or informs against others, etc. See ENLIGHTENMENT.

Internuncio. A papal minister to a foreign court, ranking next below a nuncio.

Legate. An envoy or ambassador, especially of the pope.

Marshal. An officer charged with the conduct of ceremonies, preservation of order, points of etiquette, etc.

Messenger. One who carries a message.

Newsboy. A boy who distributes or sells newspapers.

Nuncio. A permanent papal representative at a foreign court.

Own correspondent. One who is a special messenger or correspondent of a publication which calls him its own.

Parlementaire [F.]. A bearer of a flag of truce.

Penny-a-liner. One who furnishes news for a public journal at so much a line.

Post. A messenger carrying letters regularly from place to place.

Pursuivant. A messenger of state.

Reporter. One who bears news or gathers and reports news for the newspapers.

Representative of the press. One who gathers news for a newspaper.

Runner. A messenger.

Scout. A person sent out to gain information concerning the strength or movements of an enemy.

Special correspondent. A representative of the press who is assigned a certain line of news or special cases to report.

Spy. One sent secretly or in disguise within an enemy's lines to gain information and report it to the proper officer.

Trumpeter. One who proclaims or publishes abroad.

MESSENGER—*Denotations.*

Ariel. A spirit of the air or water. [Shakespeare, *Tempest.*]

Iris. The goddess of the rainbow and messenger of the gods.

Mercury. The messenger of the gods.

MESSENGER—*Nouns of Agent.*

Cable. A submarine conductor used for conveying messages.

Carrier-pigeon. A variety of pigeon used to carry letters from a distance to its home.

Dawk. The East-Indian inland mail.

Letter-bag. A bag in which letters are carried.

Mail. The whole governmental system by which letters, parcels, etc., are conveyed and delivered.

Post-office. An office for the reception, transmission, and delivery of the mails.

Telegraph. An apparatus for communicating at a distance.

Wire. An electric telegraph.

Mes-si'ah. The Saviour. DIVINITY.

messieurs les gardes françaises, tirez [F.] (mê-siu' lê gard fran'-sêz', ti-rê'). Gentlemen of the French guard, fire. ORDER.

mess'-mate''. Associate at mess. FRIEND-FOE.

mes'-suage. A large dwelling-house. DWELLER-HABITATION.

met-ab'-o-lism. Processes of cell-creation and destruction. BIOLOGY.

met''-a-cen'-ter. A center. CENTER.

met-ach'-ro-nism. A chronological error. CHRONOLOGY-ANACHRONISM.

me'-tage. Measurement. MENSURATION.

met''-a-gen'-e-sis. Alternation of generations. MUTABILITY-STABILITY.

met''-a-gram'-ma-tism. The act of making anagrams. LETTER.

met'-al. An element. CHEMISTRY, MATERIALS.

met''-a-lep'-sis. A rhetorical figure. TROPE.

met''-al-log'-ra-phy. The science which treats of metallic substances. ORGANIZATION-INORGANIZATION.

met'-al-lur''-gy. Science of metals. ORGANIZATION-INORGANIZATION.

met''-a-mor'-phism. Changes in rocks due to recrystallization. GEOLOGY.

met''-a-mor'-phose. Transmute. MUTATION-PERMANENCE.

met''-a-mor'-pho-sis. A changing of form. BIOLOGY, MUTABILITY-STABILITY.

met'-a-phor. A figure of speech. RHETORIC, TROPE.

met''-a-phor'-ic-al. Figurative. COMPARISON, TROPE; **metaphorical expression,** RHETORIC.

met'-a-phrase. A verbal translation. INTERPRETATION-MISINTERPRETATION.

met'-a-phrast. A literal translator. INTERPRETER.

met''-a-phys'-ic-al. Transcendental. MIND-IMBECILITY.

met''-a-phy-si'-cian. One skilled in metaphysics. MIND-IMBECILITY.

met''-a-phys'-ics. Scientific knowledge of mental phenomena. MIND-IMBECILITY.

met-as'-ta-sis. Change of one thing into another. MUTATION-PERMANENCE, REVERSAL, TRANSFER.

met-ath'-e-sis. A transposition of letters or syllables. CONVERSION-REVERSION, TRANSFER.

mete. To distribute; to measure. ASSIGNMENT, MENSURATION; **mete out,** GIVING-RECEIVING.

met-emp''-sy-cho'-sis. Transmigration of souls. MUTATION-PERMANENCE.

me'-te-or. A bright heavenly body. LUMINARY-SHADE, UNIVERSE.

me''-te-or'-ic. Pertaining to meteors. LIGHT-DARKNESS, TURBULENCE-CALMNESS.

me''-te-or''-o-log'-ic-al. Pertaining to meteorology. WATER-AIR.

me''-te-or-ol'-o-gy. Science of meteors. WATER-AIR.

me'-ter. A measure; rhythmic arrangement of words. MEASURE, MENSURATION, METER, RHETORIC.

me-theg'-lin. A fermented drink. SWEETNESS-ACIDITY.

me-thinks'. It seems to me. FAITH-MISGIVING.

neth'-od. Order; way. CONDUCT, REGULARITY-IRREGULARITY, WAY; **want of method,** REGULARITY-IRREGULARITY.

meth-od'-ic-al. According to method. ORGANIZATION-DISORGANIZATION, REGULARITY-IRREGULARITY.

Meth'-od-ism. The doctrines of the Methodists. ORTHODOXY-HETERODOXY.

Meth'-od-ist. One of a sect. ORTHODOXY-HETERODOXY.

meth'-od-ize. To arrange. ORGANIZATION-DISORGANIZATION.

Me-thu'-se-lah. A Bible character. INFANT-VETERAN; **old as Methuselah,** INFANCY-AGE, NOVELTY-ANTIQUITY; **since the days of Methuselah,** NOVELTY-ANTIQUITY.

mé''-tis. One of mixed blood. CONVENTIONALITY-UNCONVENTIONALITY.

met-on'-y-my. A figure of speech. COMMUTATION, PERMUTATION, RHETORIC, TROPE.

met'-o-pe. Face. ARCHITECTURE.

met''-o-pos'-co-py. The study of physiognomy. ANTERIORITY-POSTERIORITY, APPEARANCE-DISAPPEARANCE, INTERPRETATION-MISINTERPRETATION.

me'-tre. Rhythmic arrangement of words. METER, POETRY-PROSE.

met'-ric. Pertaining to meter. **Metric system,** MEASURE.

met'-ri-cal. Rhythmical; metric. MENSURATION, POETRY-PROSE.

met-rol'-o-gy. Science of weights and measures. MENSURATION.

metron, ariston [Gr.] (met'-ron, ar'-ist-on). The golden mean. MIDCOURSE-CIRCUIT, TURBULENCE-CALMNESS.

me-trop'-o-lis. A chief city. CITY-COUNTRY, DWELLER-HABITATION.

met''-ro-pol'-i-tan. An archbishop. DWELLER-HABITATION, MINISTRY-LAITY.

met'-tle. Ardor; courage. AFFECTIONS, BRAVERY-COWARDICE; **man of mettle,** BRAVERY-COWARDICE; **on one's mettle,** DETERMINATION-VACILLATION; **put on one's mettle,** BRAVERY-COWARDICE, EXCITATION.

met'-tle-some. Brave; ardent; sensitive. BRAVERY-COWARDICE, EXCITABILITY-INEXCITABILITY, SENSITIVENESS-APATHY.

mettre de l'eau dans son vin [F.] (metr de lo dan' son' van'). To put water into wine. STRENGTH-WEAKNESS.

meum et tuum [L.] (mî′-um et tiu′-um). Mine and thine. PROPERTY; **disregard distinction between** *meum et tuum*, THEFT.

mew. To cry; to shed. CRY-ULULATION, DRESS-UNDRESS, JUBILATION-LAMENTATION; **mew up,** RELEASE-RESTRAINT.

mewed up. Shut up. CONFINEMENT.

mewl. To cry like an infant. CRY-ULULATION.

mews. A city stable. DWELLER-HABITATION.

Mez″-zo-fan′-ti. Italian linguist. SCHOLAR-DUNCE.

mezzo-rilievo [It.] (med″-zo-rî-lyê′-vo). Sculpture in half-relief. CONVEXITY-CONCAVITY, SCULPTURE.

mezzo termine [It.] (med′-zo ter′-min-ê). The middle term. COMPOSITION, MIDCOURSE-CIRCUIT, MIDDLE.

mez′-zo-tint. A method of engraving. ENGRAVING.

mi′-asm. Malarial poison. REMEDY-BANE.

mi-ca′-ceous. Consisting of mica. LAMINA-FIBER.

Mich′-ael-mas. Feast of St. Michael. CEREMONIAL.

mick′-le. Large; many. GREATNESS-LITTLENESS, MAGNITUDE-SMALLNESS.

Mi-co′-mi-con. An imaginary kingdom. FANCY.

mi′-cro-cosm. A little world. GREATNESS-LITTLENESS.

mi-crog′-ra-phy. The description of microscopic objects. GREATNESS-LITTLENESS.

mi-crom′-e-ter. An instrument for measuring small dimensions. ASTRONOMY, GREATNESS-LITTLENESS.

mi′-cro-phone. An instrument for intensifying feeble sounds. HEARING-DEAFNESS.

mi′-cro-scope. An instrument for enlarging small objects. GREATNESS-LITTLENESS, OPTICAL INSTRUMENTS.

mi″-cro-scop′-ic. Very minute. GREATNESS-LITTLENESS.

mi′-cro-sco″-pist. One expert in the use of the microscope. OPTICAL INSTRUMENTS.

mi′-cro-sco″-py. Microscopic investigation. OPTICAL INSTRUMENTS.

mid. Middle. ENVIRONMENT-INTERPOSITION, MIDDLE.

Mi′-das. A fabled rich man. AFFLUENCE-PENURY.

mid′-course″. Middle way. MIDCOURSE-CIRCUIT, MIDDLE.

MIDCOURSE—CIRCUIT.

Ariston metron [Gr.]. The middle course is best; the golden mean.

Aurea mediocritas [L.]. The golden mean.

Compromise. A settlement by arbitration, each side conceding something.

Cross-cut. A short cut.

Golden mean. Midway between the two extremes; moderation.

Great-circle sailing. Sailing by the arc of a great circle.

Half-and-half measures. Inadequate or imperfect measures.

Half measures. Weak course of action.

Juste milieu [F.]. The golden mean.

Mean, etc. Midway between the two extremes, etc. See MEDIUM.

Mezzo termine [It.]. The middle part.

Mid-course. The middle course.

Middle, etc. The part equidistant from the extremes, etc. See MIDDLE.

Middle course. The intermediate course, avoiding the extremes; hence, the course of wisdom or mediocrity.

Neutrality. The state of being neutral or on neither side in relation to any contest.

Short cut. An easy way, avoiding the difficulties.

Straight course, etc. A course free from hindrances, etc. See AIM.

Straight path. The unhindered path.

MIDCOURSE—*Verbs.*

Compromise. To settle by mutual concessions.

Go half-way. To concede half the point at issue.

Go straight, etc. Not to deviate from the direct course, etc. See AIM.

Keep in a middle course.

Keep in an even course.

Make a compromise. See *Nouns.*

MIDCOURSE—*Adjectives*

Straight, etc. Having the same direction throughout, etc. See AIM.

MIDCOURSE—*Phrase*

Medium tenuere beati [L.]. The happy hold the middle course.

mid′-day″. Noon. MORNING-EVENING.

mid′-den. A dunghill. CLEANNESS-FILTHINESS.

mid′-dle. Medium; mean. CENTER, MEDIUM, MIDCOURSE-CIRCUIT, MIDDLE; **middle classes,** MEDIOCRITY; **middle constriction,** BREADTH-NARROWNESS; **middle course,** MIDCOURSE-CIRCUIT; **middleman,** CONSIGNEE, MANAGER; **middle term,** COMPOSITION, MIDDLE.

MIDDLE.

Bisection. Separation or cutting into two parts, especially equal parts.

Center, etc. A point equally distant from the extremities or sides; in a circle, a point within equally distant from every point in the circumference. See CENTER.

Equidistance. Equal distance.

Half-distance. Midway.

Interjacence, etc. The state of lying between. See INTERPOSITION.

Ambages. A circuit or winding.

Circuit. The distance around or circumference of any space.

Circumbendibus. A roundabout way.

Détour [F.]. A circuitous route.

Digression. A turning aside from the main subject of discourse or from the right path.

Loop. A fold or doubling of a thread, rope, or the like through which another one may be passed, also a curve in the form of a loop.

Roundabout way.

Winding, etc A turning or a curve. See CIRCUITION.

Zigzag, etc. Something having a series of short turns or angles, etc See AIM-ABERRATION.

CIRCUIT—*Verbs.*

Beat about. To search in various ways.

Beat about the bush.

Go out of one's way.

Go roundabout.

Lead a pretty dance. To make a nice circle in dancing.

Make a *détour*. To take a circuitous journey.

Make two bites of a cherry. To do a thing in a roundabout way or make too much fuss about it.

Meander, etc. To proceed in a winding course, etc. See AIM-ABERRATION.

Perform a circuit. See *Nouns.*

CIRCUIT—*Adjectives.*

Circuitous. Running round in a circuit.

Indirect. Deviating from a straight line or course.

Roundabout. Circuitous.

Zigzag, etc. Having short, sharp turns or angles.

CIRCUIT—*Adverbs, etc.*

By an indirect course.

By a side wind. In an unexpected way.

From pillar to post. From one predicament to another.

In a roundabout way.

Juste milieu, etc. The golden medium. See MIDCOURSE.

Mean, etc. Middle place or point, etc. See MEDIUM.

Mediety. The middle part or state.

Medium. That which lies half-way between.

Mezzo termine [It.] The middle point or term.

Mid-course, etc. The middle course or way. See MIDCOURSE.

Middle. The part or point equally distant from the extremities.

Middle term. In logic the term of the syllogism with which the other two terms are separately compared and by means of which they are brought together in the conclusion.

Midst. The central place or part; the part surrounded by other parts or objects.

Nucleolus. Diminutive of nucleus.

Nucleus. The center about which matter is gathered or aggregated.

MIDDLE—*Denotations.*

Diaphragm. The muscular partition separating the cavity of the chest from that of the abdomen.

Equator. The imaginary great circle on the earth's surface, everywhere equally distant from the two poles.

Half-way house. A place equally distant from the ends of a route.
Midriff. The diaphragm.
Nave. The middle or body of a church.
Navel. A mark or depression in the middle of the abdomen.
Omphalos. The navel.

MIDDLE—*Adjectives*.

Central, etc. In or near the center. See CENTER.
Equatorial. Relating to the equator.
Equidistant. Half-way between.
Intermediate, etc. Coming between or being in the middle place. See ENVIRONMENT-INTERPOSITION.
Mean. Filling a middle place.
Medial. Relating to the middle or mean.
Mediate. Between the two extremes; acting as an intervening agent.
Mediterranean. Closed in or nearly closed in by land.
Mesial. Middle; dividing into two equal parts.
Mid. Occupying the middle part.
Middle. Equidistant from the extremes.
Middlemost. Nearest to the middle.
Midmost. Middlemost or middle.

MIDDLE—*Adverbs*.

Half-way. At the middle point.
In medias res [L.]. In the midst of affairs.
In the middle.
Midships. In the middle of the ship.
Midway. Half-way.

mid'-dle–aged''. Between youth and old age. MANHOOD.
mid'-dle-man. Agent. MANAGER.
mid'-dle-most''. Nearest to the middle. CENTER.
mid'-dling. Of middle rank or quality. FAULTLESSNESS-FAULTINESS, MAGNITUDE-SMALLNESS.
mid'-dy. A midshipman. WAYFARER-SEAFARER.

Mid'-gard''. The earth, the abode of men. UNIVERSE.
midge. A gnat; a dwarf. GREATNESS-LITTLENESS.
mid'-land. The interior of a country. OCEAN-LAND.
mid'-most. Nearest to the middle. MIDDLE.
mid'-night''. Middle of the night; dark. LIGHT-DARKNESS, MORNING-EVENING; **midnight oil,** EDUCATION-LEARNING; **midnight sun,** ASTRONOMY.
mid'-prog''-ress. Moderate progress. ADVANCE-RETROGRESSION.
mid'-riff. The diaphragm. ENVIRONMENT-INTERPOSITION, MIDDLE.
mid'-ship''-man. A naval cadet. WAYFARER-SEAFARER.
mid'-ships''. The midship timbers. MIDDLE.
midst. Middle; in the middle. CENTER, ENVIRONMENT-INTERPOSITION, MIDDLE; **in the midst of,** ACTION-PASSIVENESS, MIXTURE-HOMOGENEITY.
mid'-sum''-mer. Middle of the summer. MORNING-EVENING.
mid'-way''. Half-way. MIDDLE.
mid'-wife''. A woman who assists at childbirth. ANTAGONIST-ASSISTANT, INSTRUMENTALITY, REMEDY-BANE.
mid'-wife''-ry. Assistance at childbirth; obstetrics. CREATION-DESTRUCTION, REMEDY-BANE.
mien. The external appearance. APPEARANCE-DISAPPEARANCE.
miêntras que el sol luziere, recoge tu heno [Sp.] (mî-en'-tras kê el sol lu-thi-ê'-rê, rê-co-hê' tu ê'-no). Make hay while the sun shines. OPPORTUNENESS-UNSUITABLENESS.
miff. Feeling of slight vexation. FAVORITE-ANGER.
might. Ability to do; strength. MAGNITUDE-SMALLNESS, MIGHT-IMPOTENCE, TOIL-RELAXATION, TURBULENCE-CALMNESS.

MIGHT—IMPOTENCE.

Ability. Physical or mental power; power to do.
Ableness. The state of having competent powers; capacity. See *Adjectives*.
Almightiness. All powerfulness.
Ascendency. Governing power.
Attribute. A quality or endowment of a person.
Authority. Rightful power; especially power arising from whatever commands influence or respect. See RULE.
Capability. Power to perform.
Capacity. Power to receive.
Cogency. Power of convincing.
Competency. The state of having sufficient ability.
Control. Regulating or restraining power.
Dint. Force; used in phrase, "by dint of."
Efficacy. Power to produce intended effects.
Efficiency. Power to do works.
Enablement. The state of being able.
Endowment. Any gift; any natural capacity.
Energy. Power to do work. See VIGOR.
Faculty. Any power of the mind.
Force. Power in an individual; power considered as exerting restraint or coercion.
Gift. A natural force; talent.
Influence. Power of impelling or directing. See DOMINANCE.
Might. Power in general; strength.
Omnipotence. All power.
Potency. Innate force; influence.
Potentiality. Inherent capability for doing or achieving.
Power. Ability to do something; ability exerted; strength.
Prepollence. Superior power.
Prepotency. Quality of being very powerful.
Property. Legal right to possess, enjoy and dispose of.
Puissance. Power to do; achieve.
Qualification. Any trait, natural or acquired, that is a power.
Quality. Accomplishment; capacity.
Strength. Muscular force; power in general. See STRENGTH.
Susceptibility. Capability of being affected.
Sway. Power employed in governing.
Validate. Make sound and powerful.
Validity. State of being sound and powerful.
Virtue. Moral excellence or worth; an innate **power; a merit.**

Collapse. A loss of power; the prostration resulting therefrom.
Disability. Lack of ability; incapacity.
Disablement. Deprivation of power to act.
Disqualification. Want of qualification; incompetency.
Emasculation. Deprivation of virile strength.
Exhaustion. State of being exhausted, or deprived of energy.
Failure. The act of failing; proof of inadequacy. See RULE.
Helplessness. Inability to help oneself. See sub *Adjectives*.
Imbecility. Mental impotence.
Impotence. Want of power or energy; weakness.
Impuissance. Want of power.
Inability. Want of adequate powers or capacity.
Inaptitude. Want of that disposition or capacity to adapt **itself** readily to a condition.
Incapability. Natural or legal inability.
Incapacity. Want of power to receive.
Incompetence. Want of adequate power to accomplish.
Indocility. Dulness of intellect; slowness to learn.
Inefficacy. Want of power to produce an intended effect. See USEFULNESS-USELESSNESS.
Inefficiency. No efficiency; habitual want of energy.
Ineptitude. Want of suitableness; want of tact.
Invalidity. Want of force or power, as a legal document.
Palsy. Loss of power of control; impairment of sensation.
Paralysis. Loss of power of moving the muscles.
Prostration. Reduction to extreme weakness.

IMPOTENCE—*Denotations*.

Apoplexy. Loss of power of motion due to pressure on the brain.
Bit of waste paper. A paper without force or authority.
Blank cartridge. A cartridge containing no ball.
Brutum fulmen [L.]. A harmless thunderbolt.
Cripple. One who has lost or never had the use of a limb or limbs.
Dead letter. That which has lost its force or authority.
Dummy. An imitation or copy of something to be used as a substitute.
Flash in the pan. The flashing of the priming in the pan of a flint-lock musket without discharging the piece.
Molly-coddle. An effeminate man.
Muff. A stupid fellow.
Old woman. A name for a clumsy, awkward person.

MIGHT—*Denotations*.

Attraction. The power in nature acting mutually between bodies, tending to draw them together.

Dynamic energy. The action of forces producing or changing motion in bodies.

Elasticity. The property in bodies by which they recover their former figure or dimensions, after the removal of external pressure.

Electricity. A manifestation of energy in nature in light, heat, etc.

Electro-magnetism. The magnetism developed by a current of electricity.

Friction. The resistance a body meets with from the surface on which it moves.

Galvanism. Electricity excited by the mutual action of certain liquids and metals.

Gravity. The tendency of a mass of matter toward the center of attraction.

Magnetism. The manifestation of the force in nature which is seen in a magnet.

Potential energy. Energy due to configuration.

Pressure. A constraining force or impulse of any kind.

Right arm. ⎫
Right hand. ⎬ A symbol of strength.

Suction. The power of drawing, as liquids by exhausting the air.

Vantage ground. A position which gives one an advantage.

Vis inertia [L.]. The power of resistance.

Vis mortua [L.]. Dead power.

Vis viva [L.] Living power.

Voltaic electricity. Electricity as a current produced by chemical decomposition.

Voltaism. That form of electricity developed by the chemical action between metals and different liquids.

MIGHT—*Verbs*.

Arm. To give arms to oneself; to furnish as with arms.

Be in one's power; belong to; be powerful. See *Adjectives*.

Can. To be able.

Compel. To exert force so as to subdue resistance. See COERCION.

Confer power.

Empower. To give power to.

Enable. To confer adequate power upon.

Endow. To give something to.

Endue. To invest as with some gift, etc.

Exercise power. See sub *Nouns*.

Gain power. See *Nouns*.

Give power. Empower; enable.

Indue. To give power to.

Invest. To put on; to assume.

Lie in one's power.

Pertain. To belong to.

Strengthen. See STRENGTH.

MIGHT—*Adjectives*.

Able. Having competent power, skill, or knowledge to do or accomplish; having intellectual powers.

Adequate. Having sufficient power, suitable to the difficulty.

Almighty. All powerful.

Capable. Able to comprehend; having mental ability.

Cogent. Convincing in argument or logic.

Competent. Having requisite qualifications to perform.

Effective. Having power to produce a given effect.

Effectual. Producing an effect.

Efficacious. Producing an intended effect.

Efficient. Producing results; able; competent.

Equal to. Equivalent to.

Forcible. Possessing force; energetic. See VIGOR.

Influential. Having or exerting an influence. See DOMINANCE.

Multipotent. Having manifold powers.

Omnipotent. All powerful.

Plenipotent. Having full power.

Potent. Physically or morally powerful.

Potential. Existing in possibility.

Powerful. Possessing great force, energy, or power.

Productive. Having the power of producing or bringing forth. See FERTILITY.

Puissant. Having power; strong.

Up to. Engaged in; about.

Valid. Based on facts; sound and strong.

MIGHT—*Adverbial Phrases*.

By dint of; by virtue of; powerfully. See *Adjectives*.

IMPOTENCE—DENOTATIONS—*Continued*.

Sideration. A sudden, unexpected stroke.

Softening of the brain. Loss of power due to hemorrhage or inflammation.

Syncope. A fainting.

Tellum imbelle [L.]. An unwarlike weapon.

Vox et præterea nihil [L.]. A voice and nothing else.

IMPOTENCE—*Verbs*.

Becripple. To make a cripple.

Be impotent. See *Adjectives*.

Break the back. ⎫
Break the neck. ⎬ Figurative expressions for to render powerless.

Castrate. To weaken by destroying or removing the genital cells

Clip the wings of. To impair; diminish the strength of.

Collapse. To fall together; fail; succumb.

Cramp. To affect with cramps, or severe pains which draw up the muscles.

Cripple. To injure; weaken.

Deaden. To make dead; diminish greatly the power or vigor of.

Deprive of power. Weaken.

Disable. To make unable; incapacitate.

Disarm. To take away arms; deprive of power to injure.

Disenable. To unfit.

Disqualify. Not to possess the requisite qualities.

Double up. Bring head and feet together, as by blow in the stomach

Draw the teeth of. To disarm.

Drop. Let fall.

Emasculate. To deprive of virile strength; castrate.

End in smoke. See SUCCESS-FAILURE.

Enervate. To make weak and helpless.

Exhaust. To draw off; reduce the strength of.

Faint. To fall into a swoon; lose vigor.

Fall into a swoon. Become insensible.

Garrote. To strangle by the garrote, a Spanish instrument of strangulation.

Geld. To castrate.

Go by the board. To go over the side of the ship: said of the mast.

Hamstring. To cripple by cutting the tendons.

Incapacitate. To render unable; disqualify.

Invalidate. To weaken the effect of; destroy the validity of.

Lame. To make lame.

Maim. To injure the limbs so as to incapacitate from use.

Muzzle. To make fast the mouth to prevent talking or biting.

Not a leg to stand on. To break the legs.

Paralyze. To affect with paralysis; benumb.

Prostrate. To bring down by weakness; deprive of strength.

Put a spoke in one's wheel. To foil one in his plans.

Put *hors de combat*. To disable.

Put out of gear. To deprive of good or fit condition.

Rattan. To deprive of tools used in one's employment by trade-union men.

Render powerless. See *Adjectives*.

Scotch the snake. To wound slightly.

Shatter. To break into pieces; destroy the soundness of.

Silence. To make keep silence; restrain from activity.

Spike the guns. To render the guns useless.

Sprain. To weaken by stretching the cords.

Strangle. To destroy by choking off the wind.

Swoon. To sink into a fainting fit.

Take the wind out of one's sails. To make ineffective.

Throttle. To prevent breathing by pressure.

Tie the hands. To render impotent.

Unfit. To render incompetent; incapacitate.

Unhinge. To take off the hinges; render unsteady.

Unman. To make lose manly qualities.

Unnerve. To deprive of nerves; weaken.

Vouloir prendre la lune avec les dents [F.]. To wish to seize the moon by the teeth.

Vouloir rompre l'anguille au genou [F.]. To wish to break an eel on the knee.

Weaken. See STRENGTH-WEAKNESS.

IMPOTENCE—*Adjectives*.

Armless. Without arms; deprived of defense.

Crippled. Deprived of the use of limbs, having the power of impaired.

Dead beat. Thoroughly defeated or overcome.

Defenseless. Without defense.

Demoralized. Having weakened the morals of.

Disabled. Deprived of or impaired in power.

Disjointed. Unconnected.

Disqualified. Not having the necessary qualities.

MIGHT—IMPOTENCE—*Continued.*

MIGHT—*Phrases.*

À toute force [F.]. With all one's might.
Dos moi pou sto, kai tan gan kinaso [Gr.]. Give me where I may stand, and I will move the earth. [Archimedes.]
Eripuit cælo fulmen, sceptrumque tyrannis [L.]. He [Franklin] snatched from heaven the thunderbolt and the scepter from tyrants.
Fortis cadere, cedere non potest [L.]. The brave man may fall, yield he cannot.
Quid valeant humeri quid ferre recusent [L.]. [Consider] what your shoulders have strength for, what they refuse to bear.

IMPOTENCE—ADJECTIVES—*Continued from Column 2.*

Pregnable. Incapable of resisting an attack.
Rudderless. Having no guide or rudder.
Shattered. Broken in pieces; destroyed as to power.
Sine ictu [L.]. Without a stroke or power.
Sinewless. Without sinews; nerveless; weak.
Unable. Not able.
Unapt. Inapt.
Unarmed. Harmless.
Unendowed. Not gifted by nature.
Unfit. Not fit by nature.
Unfitted. Made unfit.
Unfortified. Not fortified; weak against attacks.
Unfriended. Wanting friends; unsupported.
Unhinged. Off of hinge; unsteady; nervous.
Unnerved. Without nerves; without vigor.
Unqualified. Not having the requisite qualities.
Untenable. Not to be held or maintained.
Vincible. Able to be conquered.
Water-logged. Soaked with water; useless and unmanageable.
Weaponless. Without weapons.
Without a leg to stand upon. Unsupported; powerless.

IMPOTENCE—*Phrase.*

Der kranke Mann [G.]. The sick man.

---

might'-y. Momentous; powerful. GREATNESS-LITTLENESS, MAGNITUDE-SMALLNESS, SELFRESPECT-HUMBLENESS, STRENGTH-WEAKNESS.
mi'-grate. To go from one country to another. TRAVELING-NAVIGATION.
mi-gra'-tion. Change of abode. TRAVELING-NAVIGATION.
mi'-gra-to-ry. Wandering. TRAVELING-NAVIGATION.
mi-ka'-do. The sovereign of Japan. CHIEF-UNDERLING.
milch cow. A cow giving milk. FAUNA-FLORA, FERTILITY-STERILITY, STORE.
mild. Moderate; calm; insipid; warm; courteous. ExCITABILITY-INEXCITABILITY, HARSHNESS-MILDNESS, HEAT-COLD, POLITENESS-IMPOLITENESS, SAVORTASTELESSNESS, TURBULENCE-CALMNESS.
mil'-dew. A decayed condition. CLEANNESS-FILTHINESS, REMEDY-BANE.
mil'-dewed. Spoiled. BETTERMENT-DETERIORATION, CLEANNESS-FILTHINESS.
mild'-ness. Moderation. HARSHNESS-MILDNESS.
mile. A measure of distance. LENGTH-SHORTNESS, MEASURE.
mile'-post". An indicator of distance. SIGN.
mile'-stone". An indicator of distance. SIGN; whistle jigs to a mile-stone, USEFULNESS-USELESSNESS.
milieu, juste [F.] (mi-liu', zhüst). The golden mean. MIDCOURSE-CIRCUIT, TURBULENCE-CALMNESS.
mil'-i-tant. Engaged in conflict. FIGHTING-CONCILIATION.
mil'-i-ta-ry. Martial; warlike. BELLIGERENT, FIGHTING-CONCILIATION; **military power,** RULE-LICENSE; **military time,** EARLINESS-LATENESS; **military train,** BELLIGERENT.
militate against. To have influence against. ANTAGONISM-CONCURRENCE, COOPERATION-OPPOSITION.

IMPOTENCE—ADJECTIVES—*Continued.*

Done up. Exhausted.
Emasculate. Deprived of manly virility.
Exhausted. Drawn off; weakened.
Fatherless. Without a father.
Good for nothing. Absolutely worthless.
Graveled. Embarrassed. See DIFFICULTY.
Harmless. ⎫
Helpless. ⎬ Disabled.
Hors de combat [F.]. ⎭
Imbecile. Having weak mental faculties.
Impotent. Having no power or energy.
Inadequate. Not having sufficient power, ability, etc. See LACK.
Inapt. Unsuitable.
Incapable. Lacking capability or adequate ability.
Incompetent. Not able to fulfil the duties.
Indefensible. Not defensible; not maintainable.
Ineffective. Having no effect.
Ineffectual. Not producing the intended effect. See SUCCESS-FAILURE.
Inefficacious. Not having the requisite power to produce a designed effect. See USEFULNESS-USELESSNESS.
Inefficient. Not producing the required effect; habitually indisposed to activity.
Inept. Unfit; silly; foolish.
Inoperative. Not active or producing an effect.
Laid on one's back. Rendered powerless.
Laid on the shelf. Useless.
Lustless. Lacking vigor.
Marrowless. Without marrow; without vigor.
Nerveless. Without nerves; wanting vigor.
Nugatory. Having no force or meaning.
Null and void. Having no effect.
On one's beam end; out of gear; out of balance, as a ship.
Palsied. Affected with palsy.
Paralytic. Affected or tending to paralysis.
Paralyzed. Deprived of the power of moving or acting.
Pithless. Feeble.
Powerless. Without power; impotent.

(Continued on Column 1.)

---

mi-li'-tia. Citizen soldiers. BELLIGERENT.
milk. A white liquid; to extract milk; moderate. HARSHNESS-MILDNESS, TURBULENCE-CALMNESS, VISCIDITY-FOAM, WHITENESS-BLACKNESS; **flow with milk and honey,** ENOUGH, PLEASURABLENESS-PAINFULNESS, WELFARE-MISFORTUNE; **milk a he-goat into a sieve,** POSSIBILITY-IMPOSSIBILITY; **milk and water,** CONSEQUENCE-INSIGNIFICANCE, FAULTLESSNESS-FAULTINESS, SAVOR-TASTELESSNESS, STRENGTHWEAKNESS, TURBULENCE-CALMNESS; **milk of human kindness,** CHARITABLENESS-MALEVOLENCE; **milk the ram,** USEFULNESS-USELESSNESS.
milk'-i-ness. Mildness. DIAPHANEITY-OPALESCENCE.
milk'-liv"-ered. Cowardly. BRAVERY-COWARDICE.
milk'-maid". Dairymaid. CHIEF-UNDERLING, CITYCOUNTRY.
milk'-man. A milk-pedler. AGENT.
milk'-sop". An effeminate man. BRAVERY-COWARDICE, SAGE-FOOL.
milk'-y. Like milk. DIAPHANEITY-OPALESCENCE, VISCIDITY-FOAM; **milky way,** ASTRONOMY, UNIVERSE.
mill. A machine for grinding; a combat. FRIABILITY, INSTRUMENT, STRIFE-PEACE, WORKSHOP; **like a horse in a mill,** REVOLUTION-EVOLUTION.
mil-len'-ni-um. A thousand years; the thousand years of Christ's kingdom on earth. FANCY, FUTURE-PAST, PERIOD-PROGRESS, SANGUINENESS-HOPELESSNESS.
mil'-ler. One who operates a grist-mill. AGENT.
mil-les'-i-mal. Pertaining to thousandths. FIVEQUINQUESECTION.
mil'let seed. Seed of the millet grass. GREATNESSLITTLENESS.
mil'-liard. A thousand millions. FIVE-QUINQUESECTION.
mil"-lier'. Unit of weight. MEASURE.
mil'-li-gram. Unit of weight. MEASURE.

mil'-li-li''-ter. Unit of liquid measure. MEASURE.

mil'-li-me''-ter. Unit of lineal measure. MEASURE.

mil'-li-ner. One who makes or trims women's hats. DRESS-UNDRESS; **man milliner,** SOCIETY-DANDY.

mil'-li-ner-y. Articles made or sold by milliners. DRESS-UNDRESS, EMBELLISHMENT-DISFIGUREMENT, POMP; **man millinery,** POMP, SOCIETY-AFFECTATION.

mil'-lion. A thousand thousand. FIVE-QUINQUESECTION, GENTILITY-COMMONALTY, HUMANITY, MULTIPLICITY-PAUCITY; **for the million,** CLEARNESS-OBSCURITY, DIFFICULTY-FACILITY.

mil''-lion-aire'. One worth a million or more. AFFLUENCE-PENURY.

mill'-pond''. A pool of water. ERECTNESS-FLATNESS, GULF-PLAIN, STORE.

mill'-stone''. One of two stones used for grinding grain. HEAVINESS-LIGHTNESS.

mime. A mimic; buffoon. ACTING, WAG.

mi'-mer. A mimic. ACTING.

mim'-ic. To imitate. ACTING, DELINEATION-CARICATURE, IMITATION-ORIGINALITY.

mim'-ic-ry. Imitation. IMITATION-ORIGINALITY.

mi-mog'-ra-pher. A composer of mimes. ACTING.

mi-nac'-i-ty. Disposition to threaten. CHARITABLENESS-MENACE.

min'-a-ret. A slender tower. ARCHITECTURE, HEIGHT-LOWNESS.

minauderie [F.] (mi-no-drî'). Airs. SOCIETY-AFFECTATION.

mince. To cut up; to extenuate; affected. JUSTIFICATION-CHARGE, NUTRIMENT-EXCRETION, SOCIETY-AFFECTATION, SPEECH-INARTICULATENESS, SWIFTNESS-SLOWNESS, UNION-DISUNION; **mince the matter,** DESIRE-PARTICULARNESS; **mince the truth,** TRUTHFULNESS-FALSEHOOD; **not mince the matter,** CRAFT-ARTLESSNESS, MANIFESTATION-LATENCY.

mince-'meat'' of, **make.** To utterly destroy. CREATION-DESTRUCTION.

min'-cing. Overnice. SOCIETY-AFFECTATION; **mincing steps,** SWIFTNESS-SLOWNESS.

mind. Intellect; to pay attention; to purpose; to give heed; to remember; to believe. CAREFULNESS-NEGLECT, DESIRE-DISTASTE, DESIRE-PARTICULARNESS, FAITH-MISGIVING, HEED-DISREGARD, MIND-IMBECILITY, PURPOSE-LUCK, READINESS-RELUCTANCE, RECKLESSNESS-CAUTION, REMEMBRANCE-FORGETFULNESS, VOLITION-OBLIGATION, WARNING; **bear in mind,** HEED-DISREGARD, REFLECTION-VACANCY, REMEMBRANCE-FORGETFULNESS; **bit of one's mind,** ENLIGHTENMENT-SECRECY; **food for the mind,** CONCEPTION-THEME; **give the mind to,** HEED-DISREGARD; **have a mind to,** DESIRE-DISTASTE, PURPOSE-LUCK, READINESS-RELUCTANCE; **in the mind,** CONCEPTION-THEME, READINESS-RELUCTANCE, REFLECTION-VACANCY; **make one's mind easy,** EXCITABILITY-INEXCITABILITY; **make up one's mind,** DETERMINATION-VACILLATION, FAITH-MISGIVING; **mind at ease,** PLEASURE-PAIN; **mind one's book,** EDUCATION-LEARNING; **mind one's business,** CAREFULNESS-CARELESSNESS, HEED-DISREGARD, INQUISITIVENESS-INDIFFERENCE; **mind's eye,** FANCY; **mind what one is about,** RECKLESSNESS-CAUTION; **never mind,** CAREFULNESS-CARELESSNESS, CONSEQUENCE-INSIGNIFICANCE; **not mind,** CAREFULNESS-CARELESSNESS; UNCONCERN; **out of mind,** REMEMBRANCE-FORGETFULNESS; **set one's mind upon,** DETERMINATION-VACILLATION; **speak one's mind,** CRAFT-ARTLESSNESS, TRUTHFULNESS-FALSEHOOD; **to one's mind,** LOVE-HATE, PLEASURABLENESS-PAINFULNESS, TASTE-VULGARITY; **willing mind,** READINESS-RELUCTANCE.

MIND—IMBECILITY.

Ability, etc. Physical or mental power. See SKILL.

Association of ideas. The combination or connection of states of mind or their objects with one another, as the result of which one is said to be revived or represented by means of the other.

Capacity. The power of receiving and holding ideas, knowledge.

Cogitative faculties. The faculties of the mind by which we think or meditate.

Conception. The faculty of forming concepts or general notions.

Consciousness. The power of self-knowledge; the inner sense.

Faculties. The natural powers of the mind by which it acts uniformly and with facility in some specific way.

Genius. Exalted intellectual power, marked by an extraordinary faculty for original expression or creation.

Instinct. Unconscious, unreasoning, or involuntary impulse to any mode of action, whether physical or mental, without a distinct apprehension of the end to be accomplished.

Intellect. The faculty of the human soul by which it knows, as distinguished from the sensibility and the will.

Intellection. Exercise of the intellect; hence, thought.

Intellectual faculties. The faculties of the mind.

Intellectuality. Intellectual powers; possession of intellectual force or endowment.

Intelligence. The act or state of knowing; readiness of comprehension.

Intuition. Immediate perception of truth without conscious reasoning.

Judgment. The faculty of judging or of deciding correctly.

Mind. That which thinks, feels, and wills; the entire psychical being of man.

Observation. The act, power, or habit of taking notice.

Parts. Faculties; talents.

Percipience. The faculty or power of perceiving.

Rationality. Reasoning power.

Reason. The entire mental or rational nature of man as distinguished from the intelligence of the brute.

Senses. Rational perceptions accompanied by feeling.

Thinking principle. The original faculty of thinking.

Understanding. The power to understand; the intellectual faculty.

Wisdom, etc. Knowledge, and the capacity to make due use of it. See SAGACITY.

Wit, etc. Mind; intellect; understanding; sense. See SAGACITY.

Wits. Mental faculties or powers of the mind.

Absence of intellect. Imbecility.

Brutality. The condition or quality of being brutal.

Brute force. Compulsory power; violence.

Brute instinct. Unintelligence; brute instinct.

Imbecility. Feebleness, especially of mind.

Incapacity, etc. Lack of intellectual power. See SAGACITY-INCAPACITY.

Want of intellect, etc. See MIND.

IMBECILITY—*Adjective.*

Unendowed with reason. Without the faculty of reason.

MIND—*Continued.*

MIND—*Figurative Nouns.*

Bosom. The breast considered as the seat of the passions.

Brain. The organ of intellect; hence, the understanding.

Brain-pan. The bones which enclose the brain.

Breast. The seat of the affections and passions.

Cerebrum. Brain, especially the upper and anterior part.

Cranium. The skull, especially that part enclosing the brain.

Divina particula auræ [L.]. Divine particle of air.

Ghost. The soul or spirit of a deceased person.

Head. That part of an animal containing the brain and chief sensory organs.

Headpiece. Understanding; mental faculty.

Heart. The seat of the affections or sensibilities.

Heart's core. Inmost character or disposition.

Inner man. The feelings and affections.

Noddle. The head.

Organ of thought. The brain.

Pate. The head of a person.

Penetralia mentis [L.]. The inmost parts of the mind.

Pericranium. The periosteum of the external surface of the cerebrum.

Sconce. A piece of armor for the head; figuratively, the head. brains, sense.

Scull. The skull.

Seat of thought. The brain.

Sensorium. The nervous system, including the cerebrum.
Sensory. See Sensorium.
Skull. The bony framework which encloses the brain; the head or brain.

Soul. The spiritual, rational part of man.
Spirit. The intelligent, immaterial part of man.
Upper story. The head.

Mind—Philosophical Terms.

Craniology. That branch of internal somatology which treats of the characteristics of skulls.
Cranioscopy. Scientific examination of the cranium.
Idealism. The theory that in external perceptions the objects immediately known are ideas and ideas only; quest of the ideal.
Ideality. The state or character of being ideal or imaginary.
Ideology. The science that treats of the evolution of human ideas.
Immateriality, etc. The state or quality of being immaterial, etc See Materiality-Spirituality.
Mental philosophy. The general laws or principles under which all the subordinate phenomena or facts relating to the mind are comprehended.
Metaphysician. One who is versed in metaphysics.
Metaphysics. Philosophy in the wide sense; the principles of philosophy as applied to explain the methods of any particular science.
Moral philosophy. The science which treats of the nature and condition of man as a moral being, of the duties which result from his moral relations, and the reasons on which they are founded.
Philosophy of the mind. Mental philosophy.
Phrenology. A system which teaches that the faculties of the mind are manifested through special organs, or in separate portions of the brain.
Pneumatology. The science of spiritual existence or phenomena of any description.
Psychics. Psychology.
Psychologist, etc. One who is devoted to or versed in psychology.
Psychology. The science of the human soul and its operations.
Spiritualism. The doctrine that there are substances or beings not cognizable by the senses; the intuitional philosophy.
Transcendentalism. That which in religion or philosophy is vague, visionary, or sublimated; any form of transcendental philosophy.

Mind—Verbs.

Appreciate. Perceive or distinguish adequately.
Be aware of. Be conscious or informed of.
Be conscious of. Possess knowledge of; be sensible of.
Fancy, etc. Form a conception of, etc. See Fancy.
Mark. Pay special attention to; heed.
Note. Take notice of, observe.

Notice. Pay attention to; mark; heed.
Realize. Apprehend the meaning or significance of; think of as real.
Ruminate, etc. Meditate upon; muse, etc See Reflection.
Take cognizance of. Take knowledge of; notice.
Take notice of. Observe; note; notice.

Mind—Adjectives.

Cerebral. Pertaining to the cerebrum; mental.
Endowed with reason. Furnished with the faculty of reason.
Ghostly. Relating to the soul.
Immaterial, etc. See Spirituality.
Intellectual. Pertaining to the intellect; possessing intellect or intelligence.
Mental. Pertaining to the mind or the entire rational nature.
Metaphysical. Relating to metaphysics; treating of or devoted to metaphysics; transcendental.

Nooscopic. Observing the reason.
Psychical. Of or pertaining to the mind or soul.
Psychological. Of or pertaining to psychology.
Rational. Pertaining to the reason; having reason; agreeable to reason.
Spiritual. Of or pertaining to spirit; marked by the highest qualities of the human mind.
Subjective. Proceeding from or taking place within the thinking subject.

Mind—Adverb.

In petto [It.]. Within the breast.

Mind—Phrases.

Ens rationis [L.]. A creature of reason.

Locos y niños dicen la verdad [Sp.]. Children and fools speak the truth.

mind'-ed. Willing; disposed. Purpose-Luck, Readiness-Reluctance.
mind'-ful. Heedful; observant. Heed-Disregard, Remembrance-Forgetfulness.
mind'-ful-ness. Observance. Heed-Disregard.
mind'-less. Careless; imbecile; insensible. Heed-Disregard, Remembrance-Forgetfulness, Sagacity-Incapacity, Sensitiveness-Apathy.
mine. A subterranean cavity; a destructive agent; a source of wealth. Aperture-Closure, Attack-Defense, Betterment-Deterioration, Convexity-Concavity, Creation-Destruction, Enough, Store, Truthfulness-Fraud; **dig a mine,** Design, Preparation - Nonpreparation; **mine of wealth,** Affluence-Penury; **spring a mine,** Attack-Defense, Prevision.
mi'-ner. One who mines. Concavity-Convexity; **sapper and miner,** Belligerent.
min'-er-al. An inorganic substance. Organization-Inorganization; **mineral oil,** Pulpiness-Rosin.
min'-er-al-ize. To change from a metal to a mineral. Mineralogy.
min''-er-al-og'-ic-al. Pertaining to mineralogy. Mineralogy.
min''-er-al'-o-gist. Student of mineralogy. Mineralogy.
min''-er-al'-o-gy. Science of minerals. Mineralogy, Organization-Inorganization.

MINERALOGY.

Mineralogy. The science which treats of the description, formation, and classification of minerals.

Mineralogy—Associated Words

Angle. Difference of direction of two or more lines or planes.
Basal pinacoid. Pinacoid cutting the vertical axis of a crystal
Contact-goniometer. Instrument for measuring the angles made by the faces of crystals.
Crystal. Solid mathematical form assumed by homogeneous substances.
Crystallographic axes. The axes of a crystal.
Crystallography. Science of crystals.
Dihexagonal pyramid. Crystal in the form of a pyramid twelve-sided in cross-section.
Diploid. Crystal having 24 trapezoidal faces.
Ditetragonal pyramid. Crystal in the form of an eight-sided pyramid.
Face. One of the plane surfaces of a crystal.
Goniometer. Instrument for measuring angles.
Hemihedrism. State of having half the number of symmetrically arranged planes possible.
Hemimorphism. State of having two ends bounded by dissimilar planes.
Hexagonal system. Crystals having six symmetrical faces.
Hexahedron. Crystal having six faces.
Hexoctahedron. Kind of crystal having 48 similar and equal triangular faces.
Holohedron. Crystal having all the symmetrical faces possible.
Icositetrahedron. Kind of crystal having 24 equal and similar trapeziform faces.

Isometric system. System of crystals having the three axes of equal length.

Mineralogist. One versed in mineralogy.

Monoclinic system. System of crystals having one symmetrical plane.

Octahedron. Crystal having plane faces.

Orthorhombic system. System of crystals having three unlike axes at right angles.

Parameter. The rational multiple of the unit-length of any semi-axis intercepted by a crystal plane determining its position with reference to the fundamental form.

Pinacoid. Form of crystal having two planes cutting one axis while parallel to the other two.

Prism. Form of crystal having three planes making parallel and vertical intersections.

Reflecting goniometer. Instrument for measuring angles by reflected light.

Rhombic dodecahedron. Crystal having 12 rhombic faces.

Symbol. A character or mark indicating the surface of a crystal.

Symmetry. Relative proportion and harmony of the parts of a whole.

Tetartohedrism. State of having but one-fourth the full number of symmetrical faces

Tetragonal prism. Prism of the tetragonal system.

Tetragonal system. System of crystals having four alternately dissimilar planes of symmetry intersecting at angles of 45 degrees and at right angles to a fifth symmetrical plane.

Tetrahexahedron. Crystal having 24 triangular faces.

Triclinic system. System of crystals having full number of faces but no planes of symmetry.

Trisoctahedron. Crystal having 24 faces in eight groups of three each.

Twin crystals. Two similar crystals united so as to be symmetrical with respect to a plane which is not a plane of symmetry for either one.

MINERALOGY—Verbs.

Mineralize. To change from a metallic to a mineral form.

Orientate. To place a crystal so as to show symmetry.

MINERALOGY—Adjectives.

Amorphous. Not crystallized.

Crystalline. In the form of a crystal.

Gyroidal. Pertaining to non-symmetrical forms of crystals in which the planes appear to be twisted in respect to each other.

Heterogeneous. Containing dissimilar elements.

Holohedral. Having all the symmetrical faces possible.

Homogeneous. Having parts of similar form and arrangement.

Interfacial. Formed by two faces of a polyhedron.

Isomorphous. Crystallizing in forms identical with those of some other substance.

Mineralogical. Pertaining to mineralogy.

Orthorhombic. Pertaining to forms of crystals dissimilarly symmetrical in three planes at right angles to each other.

Pentagonal. Having five angles.

Pyramidal. Of the shape of a pyramid.

Rhombohedral. Possessing three common planes of symmetry intersecting at angles of 60 degrees.

Sphenoidal. Pertaining to a crystal of the hemihedral form and included under four equal scalene triangular faces.

Tetragonal. Possessing four alternately dissimilar planes of symmetry intersecting at angles of 45 degrees and cutting a fifth plane at right angles.

Tetrahedral. Possessing four faces which meet at a point.

Trapezohedral. In the form of a trapezohedron.

Minerva, invita [L.] (mi-ner′-va in-vai′-ta). Without genius. DIFFICULTY-FACILITY, READINESS-RELUCTANCE.

Mi-ner′-va press. A London printing-house. ACCOUNT, SIMPLICITY-FLORIDNESS.

min′-gle. To mix. MIXTURE-HOMOGENEITY.

min′-i-a-ture. A small painting. GREATNESS-LITTLENESS, PAINTING; **miniature painter,** ARTIST.

min′-ie ri′-fle. A rifle for using minie balls. WEAPON.

min′-i-kin. Something very small. GREATNESS-LITTLENESS

min′-im. A drop; a half note. MAGNITUDE-SMALLNESS, MEASURE, MELODY-DISSONANCE.

min′-i-mum. The least possible amount or degree. MAGNITUDE-SMALLNESS, SUPREMACY-SUBORDINACY.

min′-ion. A servile favorite. FAVORITE-ANGER.

min″-ion-ette′. A bastard size of type-body. WRITING-PRINTING.

min′-is-ter. An agent; a governmental representative; a pastor; to serve; to supply. AGENT, CEREMONIAL, FANE, GIVING-RECEIVING, INSTRUMENTALITY, MANAGER, MINISTRY-LAITY, OBSTRUCTION-HELP, REMEDY-BANE, REPRESENTATIVE.

min″-is-te′-ri-al. Clerical. CHURCH.

min′-is-ter-ing spir′-it. An angel. ANGEL-SATAN

min′-is-trant. Serving. OBSTRUCTION-HELP.

min′-is-trate. To serve. MANAGEMENT.

min″-is-tra′-tion. Act of performing service. CEREMONIAL, CHURCH, MANAGEMENT.

min′-is-try. Ministers collectively; agency. CHURCH, MANAGEMENT, MINISTRY-LAITY, OBSTRUCTION-HELP.

MINISTRY—LAITY.

Abbé [F.]. The head of an abbey; a title of respect commonly given in France to every one vested with the ecclesiastical dress.

Abbess. A female governess of a nunnery, having the same authority over the nuns that an abbot has over the monks.

Abbot. The superior or head of an abbey.

Abdal. A religious devotee in Persia.

Abuna. Head of the Abyssinian Church.

Acolothist. An acolyte

Acolyte. One who has received the highest of the four minor orders in the Catholic Church, being ordained to carry the wine, water, and lights at the Mass.

Acolyth. See ACOLYTE.

Almoner. One who distributes alms, especially those of a religious house.

Ancient flamen. See FLAMEN.

Archbishop. A head bishop and one who superintends the conduct of the suffragan bishops in his province and exercises episcopal authority in his own diocese.

Archdeacon. In England, an ecclesiastical dignitary, next in rank below a bishop, whom he assists, and by whom he is appointed, though with independent authority.

Augustin. A member of a religious order named after St. Augustine.

Austin Friars. An order of friars established in 1265 by Pope Alexander IV.

Beadle. An inferior parish officer in England, having various duties.

Beadsman. A poor man, supported by a beadhouse, and required to pray for its founder.

Benedictine. One of the order of monks established by St. Benedict of Nursia in the sixth century.

Beneficiary. The holder of a benefice or church living.

Assembly. A company of persons collected together with a common purpose, especially for worship.

Brethren. Fellow men

Catechumen. One who receives rudimentary instruction in the Christian doctrine, preliminary to being received into membership of the church.

Civilian. One whose pursuits are those of civil life; not clerical.

Congregation. An assembly of persons met for worship and religious instruction.

Flock. A Christian congregation or church, considered in relation to their pastor.

Fold. Figuratively, the church or a church.

Laity. The people, as distinguished from the clergy.

Layman. One of the laity.

Parishioner. One connected with a parish.

People. Persons, generally, as distinguished from the clergy; the laity.

Secularist. One who disregards all religious worship and belief, and directs his attention solely to the things of this present life.

Secularization. Conversion from religious to secular possession and uses.

Temporality. [Obs.] The laity.

LAITY—Verb.

Secularize. To convert from spiritual to secular or common uses.

LAITY—Adjectives.

Civil. Pertaining to the city or state.

Laical. Pertaining to the laity.

MINISTRY—LAITY—*Continued.*

Bishop. One ordained to the highest order of the ministry, superior to the priesthood and generally claiming to be a successor of the Apostles.

Blackcoat. A clergyman.

Black friar. A friar of the Dominican order.

Bonhomme. A simple man; an old codger

Bonze. A Buddhist or Fohist priest, monk, or nun.

Brahman. A person of the highest or priestly caste among the Hindus.

Caloyer. A monk of the Greek Church.

Canon. A member of a cathedral chapter; a person who holds a prebend in a cathedral or collegiate church.

Canoness. A woman who holds a canonry in a conventual chapter.

Capitular. A member of a chapter.

Capuchin. A Franciscan monk of the austere branch established in 1526 by Matteo di Baschi, distinguished by wearing the long pointed cowl of St. Francis.

Cardinal. One of the ecclesiastical princes who constitute the pope's council.

Carmelite. A friar of the mendicant order established on Mt. Carmel, in Syria, in the twelfth century.

Carthusian. A member of a very austere religious order, founded at Chartreuse in France by St. Bruno, in 1086.

Cenobite. One of a religious order, dwelling in a convent or religious community.

Chaplain. A clergyman attached to the army or navy, to some public institution, or to a family or a court, for the purpose of performing divine service.

Choir. A band of singers in church service.

Chorister. The leader of the choir in church service.

Churchman. An ecclesiastic or clergyman.

Churchwarden. An officer in an Episcopal church, whose duties vary in different dioceses, but always include the provision of what is necessary for the communion service.

Cistercian. A monk of a branch of the Benedictine order, established by Robert, abbot of Molesme, at Cîteaux, in France, in the year 1098.

Classis. A church court.

Clergy. The body of men, set apart by due ordination, to the service of God, in the Christian Church.

Clergyman. A man, regularly ordained to preach the gospel, and administer its ordinances.

Clericals. The clergy.

Clerk. A clergyman.

Confessor. A priest who hears confessions and administers penance.

Conventual. One living in a convent; a monk or nun.

Corybant. A priest of the goddess Cybele in Phrygia.

Crossed Friars. } A minor order, so named from the crosses they
Crutched Friars. } wore on their garments.

Curate. A clergyman who assists a rector or vicar.

Curé [F.]. A curate or parson.

Deacon. An officer in Christian churches appointed to perform various subordinate duties which vary in different communions.

Deaconess. A female deacon.

Dean. An ecclesiastical dignitary, subordinate to a bishop.

Dervish. A Turkish or Persian monk, especially one professing extreme poverty.

Dignitaries of the church. Those holding ecclesiastical rank above that of parochial priests or clergymen.

Diocesan. A bishop, considered in relation to his diocese.

Divine. A minister of the gospel.

Dominican. One of the order of friars, founded by the Spaniard Dominic de Guzman at Toulouse in 1215.

Druid. One of an order of priests among the ancient Gauls and Britons.

Ebdomarius. Superintendent of divine services in a cathedral.

Ecclesiarch. An officer in the Eastern Church; a kind of chief sexton.

Ecclesiast. Administrator of church affairs.

Ecclesiastic. One officially set apart for the service of the church.

Elder. A church officer of varying rank and function; in the Methodist Episcopal Church, a clergyman ordained to administer all the sacraments.

Eminence. A title of honor applied to a cardinal in the Roman Catholic Church.

Fakir. }
Faquir. } An Oriental religious or begging monk.

Father. A confessor or a priest.

Father in Christ. A title given to a bishop as being divinely appointed.

Field preacher. One who preaches in the open air.

Flamen. A priest devoted to the service of a particular god, from whom he received his name.

Lay. Relating to the laity, as distinct from the clergy

Profane. Not sacred or holy; secular.

Secular. Pertaining to this present world; belonging to the laity.

Temporal. Civil or political, as distinguished from ecclesiastical.

MINISTRY—*Continued*

Fohist. A Buddhist priest.

Franciscan. A monk of the order of St. Francis, an order of mendicant monks founded in 1209 by St. Francis of Assisi.

Friar. A member of a mendicant monastic order

Friars minor. Franciscans.

Gooroo. A spiritual teacher or confessor among the Hindus.

Gray friars. Franciscans.

Hadji. A Mohammedan pilgrim to Mecca; an Armenian or Greek who has visited the sepulcher at Jerusalem.

Hierarch. The chief of a sacred or ecclesiastical order.

Hierophant. The presiding priest who initiates candidates at the Eleusinian mysteries.

High priest. A chief priest; the head of the Jewish priesthood.

Imaum. A Mohammedan minister or priest who performs the regular service of the mosque.

Incumbent. One who is in present possession of a benefice or office.

Jesuit. One of a religious order founded by Ignatius Loyola, and approved in 1540, under the title of the Society of Jesus.

Kaziaskier. A Mohammedan priest of high rank.

Lama. In Tibet, Mongolia, etc., a priest or monk of a belief known as Lamaism, a modified form of Buddhism.

Lay brother. One received into a convent of monks under the three vows, but not in holy orders.

Lecturer. An assistant preacher.

Levite. One of the tribe of Levi; one subordinate to the priests and employed in various duties connected with the tabernacle first, and afterward of the temple.

Lorettine. One of an order of nuns founded in 1812, at Loretto, in Kentucky.

Mendicant. A begging friar.

Metropolitan. An archbishop; a bishop whose see is a metropolis.

Minister. The pastor of a church duly authorized to preach the gospel and administer the sacraments.

Ministry. The clergy, as a body.

Minorites. Franciscan friars.

Missionary. One sent to preach the gospel to the heathen or the poor.

Mollah. A Turkish title of respect for a religious and learned man.

Monk. One who retires from the ordinary temporal affairs of life and devotes himself entirely to religion.

Muezzin. A Mohammedan crier of the hour of prayer.

Mufti. An official expounder of Mohammedan law.

Novice. One who enters a religious house, whether of monks or nuns, as a probationist.

Nun. A woman devoted to religion, and living in a convent, under the vows of poverty, chastity, and obedience.

Observant. An observantine or one of the branch of the Franciscan order who profess to adhere more strictly than the conventuals to the intention of the founder, especially as to poverty.

Padre [It., Pg., Sp.]. Father; a title given to a priest in Italy, Spain, and Spanish America, and in India to all clergymen.

Palmer. A wandering religious votary, especially one who has visited the Holy Lands and carries a palm in token of it.

Papa. A parish priest in the Greek Church.

Parson. A rector or incumbent of a parochial church in full charge; a preacher.

Pastor. A minister in charge of a church and parish.

Patriarch. A dignitary superior to the order of archbishops.

Perpetual curate. Before 1868, a curate having charge of a parish without rector or vicar, but controlled by a layman.

Pilgrim. One who travels far to visit some holy place or shrine as a devotee.

Pontiff. A high priest; the pope.

Pope. The bishop of Rome, the head of the Roman Catholic Church.

Postulant. A candidate.

Preacher. One who discourses in public on religious subjects.

Prebendary. A person who receives a stated income from the revenues of a cathedral or conventual church.

Precentor. A choir leader.

Prelate. A dignitary of the church.

Presbyter. In hierarchical churches, a minister of lower rank than a bishop, but higher than a deacon; a priest; in the Presbyterian Church, a member of a presbytery.

Presbytery. A judicatory consisting of all the ministers within a certain district and one ruling elder from each parish or church, commissioned to represent the church in conjunction with the pastor.

MINISTRY—*Continued.*

Priest. In the Roman Catholic and Greek churches, the lowest order of ecclesiastics empowered to consecrate the Host and perform Mass; in the Protestant Episcopal Church a presbyter.
Priesthood. The collective body of priests.
Primate. An archbishop.
Prior. The superior in a convent of monks, inferior to an abbot
Prioress. The female superior of a nunnery.
Propagandist. One who devotes himself to the spread of a certain system of principles.
Prophet. One inspired by God to declare his purposes.
Rabbi. } A Jewish title of respect for a teacher or doctor of the law
Rabbin. }
Reader. One whose office is to read prayers in church.
Rector. In the Protestant Episcopal Church, a clergyman in charge of a parish.
Religieuse [F] A person under monastic vows; a monk or nun.
Residentiary. An ecclesiast who keeps a certain residue.
Reverence. A priest or other minister.
Reverend. A title of honor applied to a clergyman.
Revivalist. One who promotes revivals of religion.
Rural dean. One having, under the bishop, care of the clergy within certain parishes of the diocese

Sacristan. One who takes general care of the church; a sexton.
Santon. A kind of dervish, regarded by the people as a saint.
Scribe. One skilled in the law and traditions and who read and expounded the law to the people.
Sexton. A sacristan.
Sheik. A Mohammedan ecclesiastic of a high grade
Shepherd. The pastor of a church.
Sidesman. An assistant to the churchwarden.
Sofi. }
Sophi. } One of a certain order of religious men in Persia.
Spiritual director. A minister.
Subdean. The deputy or substitute of a dean.
Suffragan. An assistant bishop.
Suisse [F.]. A porter.
Talapoin. A Buddhist or Fohist monk or priest.
The cloth. The clerical profession.
Trappist. A monk belonging to a branch of the Cistercian order, established in 1660 by Armand de Rancè.
Ulema. A college or corporation in Turkey composed of the hierarchy.
Verger. An attendant on a dignitary, as on a bishop, dean, etc.
Vicar. The incumbent of an appropriated benefice.

MINISTRY—*Verbs.*

Take orders, etc   To enter some grade of the ministry etc.   See sub Church.

MINISTRY—*Adjectives.*

Called to the ministry.
His Eminence. Title applied to a cardinal.
His Grace. Title applied to an archbishop.
His Holiness. Title applied to the pope.
In orders. Belonging to a grade of the ministry.

Ordained. Invested with ministerial or sacerdotal functions.
The Reverend. Worthy of reverence: said of a clergyman.
The Right Reverend. Said of a bishop.
The Very Reverend. Said of a dean.

min'-ne-sing''-er. A lyric poet. Poetry-Prose.
min'-now. A little fish. Greatness-Littleness.
mi'-nor. Inferior; one under legal age. Infant-Veteran, Supremacy-Subordinacy; **minor key,** Melody-Dissonance.
Mi'-nor-ites. Franciscans. Ministry-Laity.
mi-nor'-i-ty. State of being a minor; the smaller number. Infancy-Age; Multiplicity-Paucity, Supremacy-Subordinacy.
Mi'-nos. A king of Crete. Manager.
Min'-o-taur. A fabled monster. Conventionality-Unconventionality.
min'-ster. A church. Fane.
min'-strel. A wandering musician. Musician.
min'-strel-sy. The art of a minstrel. Music.
mint. A place to coin money; to mold; wealth. Affluence-Penury, Copy-Model, Workshop.
min'-u-end. The number from which another is subtracted. Addition-Subtraction.
min'-u-et. A dance. Entertainment-Weariness, Music.
mi'-nus. Less; negative; without positive value. Addition-Subtraction, Credit-Debt, Gain-Loss, Presence - Absence, Settlement - Default, Supremacy-Subordinacy, Transcursion-Shortcoming.
mi-nus'-cule. A small letter. Letter.
min'-ute. The sixtieth part of an hour or degree; a memorandum; an instant. Digest, Eternity-Instantaneity, Mark - Obliteration, Measure, Period-Progress; **to the minute,** Earliness-Lateness.
mi-nute'. Very small; very exact. Greatness-Littleness, Magnitude-Smallness; **minute account,** Account; **minute attention,** Heed-Disregard.
mi-nute'-ness. Quality of being minute. Carefulness-Carelessness.
mi-nu'-ti-æ. Unimportant details. Consequence-Insignificance, Greatness-Littleness, Magnitude-Smallness.
minx. A pert or wanton girl. Brawler, Purity-Rake.
miq'-ue-let. A bandit. Robber.
mir. A Russian local community. Dweller-Habitation.

mirabile dictu [L.] (mi-rab'-i-lĭ dic'-tiu). Wonderful to relate. Astonishment-Expectance.
mirabilis, annus [L.] (mi-rab'-i-lis, an'-nus). Wonderful year. Phenomenon.
mir'-a-cle. A supernatural event. Conventionality-Unconventionality, Phenomenon; **miracle play,** Acting.
mi-rac'-u-lous. Wonderful. Astonishment-Expectance.
mi''-rage'. An optical effect. Sanguineness-Hopelessness, Sight-Dimsightedness, Truthfulness-Fraud.
mire. Soft mud. Cleanness-Filthiness.
mir'-ror. A looking-glass; an exemplar. Faultlessness-Faultiness, Imitation-Originality, Optical Instruments, Reputation-Discredit, Sight-Dimsightedness; **hold the mirror up to nature,** Delineation-Caricature; **hold up the mirror,** Manifestation-Latency; **magic mirror,** Sight-Dimsightedness.
mirth. Jollity. Lightheartedness-Dejection.
mis''-ac-cep-ta'-tion. Understanding in a wrong sense. Anteriority-Posteriority, Interpretation-Misinterpretation.
mis''-ad-ven'-ture. Adversity. Welfare - Misfortune.
mis''-ad-vised'. Ill-advised. Skill - Unskilfulness.
mis'-an-thrope. Hater of mankind. Humanitarianism-Misanthropy.
mis'-an-throp'-ic. Hating mankind. Humanitarianism-Misanthropy.
mis-an'-thro-py. Hatred of mankind. Humanitarianism-Misanthropy.
mis''-ap-ply'. To apply wrongly. Interpretation-Misinterpretation, Skill-Unskilfulness, Use-Misuse.
mis-ap''-pre-hend'. To take in a wrong sense. Interpretation-Misinterpretation, Truth-Error.
mis-ap''-pre-hen'-sion. Mistake. Interpretation-Misinterpretation, Truth-Error.
mis''-ap-pro'-pri-ate. To use for a wrong purpose. Use-Misuse.
mis''-ap-pro''-pri-a'-tion. Misapplication. Use-Misuse

mis″-ar-range′. To place in a wrong order. ORGAN-IZATION-DISORGANIZATION.

mis″-be-come′. Not to become. DUENESS-UNDUE-NESS.

mis-be-com′-ing. Inappropriate. DUENESS-UNDUE-NESS.

mis″-be-got′-ten. Irregularly begotten; despicable. PROPORTION-DEFORMITY, VIRTUE-VICE.

mis″-be-have′. To conduct oneself improperly. DUE-NESS-UNDUENESS, TASTE-VULGARITY, VIRTUE-VICE.

mis″-be-hav′-ior. Improper conduct. INNOCENCE-GUILT, POLITENESS-IMPOLITENESS, TASTE-VULGAR-ITY.

mis″-be-lief′. False belief. FAITH-MISGIVING.

mis″-be-lieve′. Believe wrongly. FAITH-MISGIVING.

mis″-be-liev′-er. An unbeliever. CREDULOUSNESS-SKEPTICISM.

mis-cal′-cu-late. To judge wrongly. DECISION-MIS-JUDGMENT, EXPECTATION-SURPRISE, PREVISION-DIS-APPOINTMENT, TRUTH-ERROR.

mis-cal″-cu-la′-tion. Wrong estimate. DECISION-MISJUDGMENT, EXPECTATION-DISAPPOINTMENT, EX-PECTATION-SURPRISE.

mis-call′. To name improperly. NAME-MISNOMER.

mis-car′-ry. To fail. SUCCESS-FAILURE.

mis″-cel-la′-ne-ous. Promiscuous. MIXTURE-HOMO-GENEITY, UNIVERSALITY-PARTICULARITY.

mis′-cel-la-ny. A medley; a collection of compositions on various subjects. GATHERING-SCATTERING, MIX-TURE-HOMOGENEITY, UNIVERSALITY-PARTICULARITY.

mis-chance′. A mishap; a misfortune. WELFARE-MISFORTUNE.

mis′-chief. Harm. GOOD-EVIL; do mischief, GOOD-NESS-BADNESS; make mischief, GOODNESS-BADNESS.

mis′-chief-ma″-ker. One who makes mischief. BENE-FACTOR-EVILDOER, UPRIGHTNESS-ROGUE.

mis′-chief-ma″-king. Troublesome. GOODNESS-BAD-NESS.

mis′-chie-vous. Harmful. GOODNESS-BADNESS.

mis′-ci-ble. Mixable. MIXTURE-HOMOGENEITY.

mis-cite′. To cite wrongly. TRUTHFULNESS-FALSE-HOOD.

mis-com″-pu-ta′-tion. Wrong reckoning DECISION-MISJUDGMENT, TRUTH-ERROR.

mis″-com-pute′. To compute wrongly. DECISION-MISJUDGMENT, TRUTH-ERROR.

mis″-con-ceive′. To interpret incorrectly; to misjudge. INTERPRETATION - MISINTERPRETATION, TRUTH-ERROR.

mis″-con-cep′-tion. Wrong conception. DECISION-MISJUDGMENT.

mis-con′-duct. Mismanagement; bad behavior. INNO-CENCE-GUILT, SKILL-UNSKILFULNESS.

mis″-con-duct′-ed. Wrongly managed. SKILL-UN-SKILFULNESS.

mis″-con-duct′ one-self. To behave improperly VIR-TUE-VICE.

mis″-con-jec′-ture. A wrong guess. DECISION-MIS-JUDGMENT.

mis″-con-struc′-tion. Erroneous interpretation. IN-TERPRETATION-MISINTERPRETATION, TRUTH-ERROR.

mis-con-strue′. To interpret erroneously. INTERPRE-TATION-MISINTERPRETATION.

mis″-cor-rect′. To fail to correct. EDUCATION-LEARN-ING.

mis-count′. To count wrongly. TRUTH-ERROR.

mis′-cre-ance. Adherence to a false religious faith. FAITH-MISGIVING.

mis″-cre-ant. A vile wretch. GOOD MAN-BAD MAN.

mis″-cre-a′-ted. Formed illegitimately. VIRTUE-VICE.

mis-date′. A wrong date. CHRONOLOGY-ANACHRONISM.

mis-da′-ted. Wrongly dated. CHRONOLOGY-ANACH-RONISM.

mis-deed′. An offense. INNOCENCE-GUILT.

mis″-de-mean′. To behave ill. VIRTUE-VICE.

mis″-de-mean′-ant. One guilty of misdemeanor. GOOD MAN-BAD MAN.

mis″-de-mean′-or. Misbehavior. INNOCENCE-GUILT.

mis″-de-vo′-tion. Mistaken devotion. GODLINESS-UN-GODLINESS.

mis″-di-rect′. To misteach; to give a wrong direction to. EDUCATION-MISTEACHING, SKILL-UNSKILFUL-NESS.

mis″-di-rec′-tion. A missending. SKILL-UNSKILFUL-NESS.

mis-do′. To do badly. VIRTUE-VICE.

mis-do′-ing. A wrong-doing. INNOCENCE-GUILT.

mis-doubt′. Suspicion. FAITH-MISGIVING.

mise en scène [F.] (mîz an· sen). The putting in prep-aration for a theatrical stage. ACTING, APPEAR-ANCE-DISAPPEARANCE, POMP.

mis″-em-ploy′. To employ amiss. USE-MISUSE.

mis″-em-ploy′-ment. Wrong employment. USE-MIS-USE.

mi′-ser. A niggard. EXTRAVAGANCE-AVARICE.

miserabile dictu [L.] (miz-er-ab′-i-lî dic′-tiu). Horrible to relate. JUBILATION-LAMENTATION.

mis″-er-a-ble. Small; grievously unhappy; sordid. PLEASURE-PAIN.

mis′-er-a-bly. Weakly. MAGNITUDE-SMALLNESS.

mis-e-re′-re, sing. To chant mournfully. REPENT-ANCE-OBDURACY.

misericordiam, argumentum ad [L.] (miz-er-i-cor′-di-am, ar-giu-men′-tum ad). Argument to pity. COMPASSION-RUTHLESSNESS.

miseris succurrere disco [L.] (miz′-er-is suc-cur′-rer-î dis′-co). I learn to help the wretched. COMPASSION-RUTHLESSNESS.

mi′-ser-ly. Of the disposition of a miser. EXTRAVA-GANCE-AVARICE.

mis′-er-y. Wretchedness. PLEASURE-PAIN; miseries of human life, PLEASURE-PAIN; put out of one's misery, COMPASSION-RUTHLESSNESS.

mis-es′-ti-mate. To estimate erroneously. DECISION-MISJUDGMENT.

mis-fea′-sance. A trespass; the improper doing of a lawful act. INNOCENCE-GUILT, SKILL-UNSKILFUL-NESS.

mis-for′-tune. A calamity. PLEASURABLENESS-PAIN-FULNESS, WELFARE-MISFORTUNE.

mis-giv′-ing. A feeling of doubt or apprehension. FAITH-MISGIVING, SANGUINENESS-TIMIDITY.

mis-gov′-ern. To govern ill. SKILL-UNSKILFULNESS.

mis-guid′-ance. Evil influence. EDUCATION-MIS-TEACHING.

mis-guide′. To misteach; to guide amiss. EDUCATION-MISTEACHING, TRUTH-ERROR, TRUTHFULNESS-FRAUD.

mis-guid′-ed. Led astray. SKILL-UNSKILFULNESS.

mis-hap′. Evil accident; misfortune. GOOD-EVIL, PLEASURABLENESS-PAINFULNESS, SUCCESS-FAILURE, WELFARE-MISFORTUNE.

Mish′-na. First part of the Talmud. REVELATION-PSEUDOREVELATION.

mis″-in-form′. To give false information to. EDUCA-TION-MISTEACHING, TRUTH-ERROR.

mis-in″-form-a′-tion. Wrong information. EDUCA-TION-MISTEACHING.

mis″-in-formed′. Informed wrongly. KNOWLEDGE-IGNORANCE.

mis″-in-struct′. To instruct amiss. EDUCATION-MIS-TEACHING.

mis″-in-struc′-tion. Wrong teaching. EDUCATION-MISTEACHING.

mis″-in-tel′-li-gence. Misinformation. EDUCATION-MISTEACHING.

mis″-in-ter′-pret. Misunderstand. INTERPRETATION-MISINTERPRETATION.

mis″-in-ter″-pre-ta′-tion. A mistaken interpretation. INTERPRETATION-MISINTERPRETATION.

mis″-in-ter′-pret-ed. Misunderstood. INTERPRETATION-MISINTERPRETATION

mis-join′-der. The uniting of persons or things that should not be united. HARMONY-DISCORD.

mis-joined′. Joined improperly. HARMONY-DISCORD.

mis-join′-ing. Uniting persons or things that should not be united. HARMONY-DISCORD.

mis-judge′. Form an erroneous opinion. DECISION-MISJUDGMENT.

mis-judged′. Judged wrongly. DECISION-MISJUDGMENT.

mis-judg′-ing. Judging wrongly. DECISION-MISJUDGMENT.

mis-judg′-ment. Wrong judgment. CREDULOUSNESS-SKEPTICISM, DECISION-MISJUDGMENT, RATIOCINATION-CASUISTRY.

mis-lay′. To lose; to derange. GAIN-LOSS, ORGANIZATION-DISORGANIZATION.

mis-lead′. To direct wrongly; to lead astray. EDUCATION-MISTEACHING, PATRIOTISM-TREASON, RATIOCINATION-INSTINCT, TRUTH-ERROR, TRUTHFULNESS-FRAUD.

mis-lead′-ing. Leading astray. EDUCATION-MISTEACHING, TRUTH-ERROR.

mis-like′. To dislike. DESIRE-DISTASTE.

mis-man′-age. To manage unskilfully. SKILL-UNSKILFULNESS.

mis-man′-age-ment. Improper management. SKILL-UNSKILFULNESS.

mis-match′. To match unsuitably. HARMONY-DISCORD, VARIATION.

mis-matched′. Not corresponding. HARMONY-DISCORD.

mis-name′. To give a wrong name to. NAME-MISNOMER.

mis-no′-mer. A name wrongly applied. NAME-MISNOMER.

mis-og′-a-mist. A hater of marriage. HUMANITARIANISM-MISANTHROPY, MATRIMONY-CELIBACY.

mis-og′-a-my. Hatred of marriage. MATRIMONY-CELIBACY.

mis-og′-y-nist. Hater of women. MATRIMONY-CELIBACY.

mis-og′-y-ny. Hatred of women. MATRIMONY-CELIBACY.

mis″-per-sua′-sion. A false persuasion. EDUCATION-MISTEACHING.

mis-place′. To derange. ORGANIZATION-DISORGANIZATION.

mis-placed′. Wrongly placed. CONVENTIONALITY-UNCONVENTIONALITY, ESTABLISHMENT-REMOVAL, HARMONY-DISCORD.

mis-place′-ment. Mislocation. ESTABLISHMENT-REMOVAL.

mis-pol′-i-cy. Wrong policy. SKILL-UNSKILFULNESS.

mis-print′. A typographical error. TRUTH-ERROR.

mis-pri′-sion. The concealment of a crime. ENLIGHTENMENT-SECRECY, INNOCENCE-GUILT; **misprision of treason,** INSUBORDINATION-OBEDIENCE, PATRIOTISM-TREASON.

mis-prize′. To slight or undervalue. OVERVALUATION-UNDERVALUATION, REGARD-DISRESPECT.

mis″-pro-nounce′. To pronounce wrongly. SPEECH-INARTICULATENESS.

mis″-pro-por′-tion. Wrong proportion. PROPORTION-DEFORMITY.

mis″-pro-por′-tioned. Ugly; out of due proportion. BEAUTY-UGLINESS, PROPORTION-DEFORMITY.

mis-quote′. To quote wrongly. TRUTHFULNESS-FALSEHOOD.

mis-reck′-on. To miscalculate. DECISION-MISJUDGMENT, TRUTH-ERROR.

mis″-re-la′-tion. Erroneous relation. CONNECTION-INDEPENDENCE.

mis-rel′-ish. To dislike. DESIRE-DISTASTE.

mis″-re-port′. To give a false account of. TRUTH-ERROR, TRUTHFULNESS-FALSEHOOD.

mis-rep″-re-sent′. To represent incorrectly or falsely. EDUCATION-MISTEACHING, INTERPRETATION-MISINTERPRETATION, RATIOCINATION-INSTINCT, TRUTHFULNESS-FALSEHOOD.

mis-rep″-re-sen-ta′-tion. Untrue representation; false account. DELINEATION-CARICATURE, INTERPRETATION-MISINTERPRETATION, TRUTHFULNESS-FABRICATION, TRUTHFULNESS-FALSEHOOD.

mis-rule′. Laxity; disorder. RULE-LICENSE, SKILL-UNSKILFULNESS; **lord of misrule,** ADEPT-BUNGLER.

miss. A girl; to want; to neglect; to fail; mistake; a kept mistress. CAREFULNESS-CARELESSNESS, CLEARNESS-OBSCURITY, DESIRE-DISTASTE, GAIN-LOSS, INFANT-VETERAN, PURITY-RAKE, SUCCESS-FAILURE, TRUTH-ERROR; **miss fire,** SUCCESS-FAILURE; **miss one's aim,** SUCCESS-FAILURE; **miss one's way,** CERTAINTY-DOUBT, SKILL-UNSKILFULNESS; **miss stays,** TRANSCURSION-SHORTCOMING.

missa cantata [L.] (mis′-sɑ cɑn-tɑ′-tɑ). A mass hymn. CEREMONIAL.

mis′-sal. The book containing the mass service. CEREMONIAL.

mis-say′. To say wrongly. SPEECH-INARTICULATENESS, WORD-NEOLOGY.

mis-send′. To send amiss. SKILL-UNSKILFULNESS.

mis-shape′. Deformity. PROPORTION-DEFORMITY.

mis-sha′-pen. Ugly; deformed. BEAUTY-UGLINESS, PROPORTION-DEFORMITY.

mis′-sile. A weapon to be thrown. PUSH-PULL, WEAPON.

miss′-ing. Lost; wanting. APPEARANCE-DISAPPEARANCE, ENTITY-NONENTITY, PRESENCE-ABSENCE.

mis′-sion. A commission; an errand. COMMISSION-ABROGATION, OCCUPATION.

mis′-sion-a-ry. A person sent to teach and preach. INSTRUCTOR-PUPIL, MINISTRY-LAITY.

mis′-sive. A letter. MISSIVE-PUBLICATION.

MISSIVE—PUBLICATION.

Billet. Short communication.
Billet-doux [F.]. Love-letter.
Bulletin. Announcement of news.
Circular A general letter addressed to a number of people.
Correspondence. Communication by letters.
Despatch.}
Dispatch.} A special message
Epistle. A formal letter.
Favor. Commercial term for letter.
Letter. A written communication.
Missive. A letter sent.
Note. A short communication.
Post. Paper measuring 18¾ by 15¼ inches.
Post-card. A card prepared by the government for short messages.
Rescript. The reply of the pope on important questions.

Album. A printed compilation.
Article. A short composition.
Bibliology. Biblical literature; history of books.
Book. Literary composition of considerable length.
Booklet. A small book.
Brochure [F.]. A short sketch.
Circular. A general notice or advertisement.
Codex. An ancient manuscript
Compilation. A book composed of materials gotten from **various** sources.
Cyclopedia. Encyclopedia.
Duodecimo. A book, twelve leaves in a sheet.
Editorial. Article written by the editor of a paper.
Enchiridion. A manual of devotions.
Encyclopedia. A book treating on subjects of knowledge.

MISSIVE—PUBLICATION—*Continued.*

Rescription. A reply.
These presents. Declaration.

MISSIVE—*Verb.*

Correspond. To communicate by sending and receiving letters.

MISSIVE—*Verbal Expressions.*

Correspond with; keep up a correspondence; send a letter to; write to.

MISSIVE—*Adjective.*

Epistolary. Pertaining to letters.

MISSIVE—*Phrase.*

Furor scribendi [L.] Rage for writing.

PUBLICATION—ASSOCIATED NOUNS—*Continued from Column 2.*

Portfolio. A portable case for holding loose papers.
Quire. A collection of 24 sheets of paper.
Ream. A quantity of paper of 480 sheets.
Section. A distinct part or portion of a book or writing.
Sheet. A broad printed piece of paper.
The press. The art or business of printing and publishing; hence, printed publications taken collectively, more especially newspapers.

PUBLICATION—*Nouns of Agent.*

Author. One who composes or writes a book.
Bibliopole. One who sells books.
Bibliopolist. See BIBLIOPOLE.
Book-seller. One who sells books.
Editor. A person who prepares, superintends, revises, and corrects a book, magazine, or newspaper. etc., for publication
Editress. A female editor.
Essayist. A writer of essays.
Gentlemen of the press. Persons connected with newspaper work.
Grub-street writer. A writer of small productions.
Hedge writer. An illiterate or poor writer.
Journalist. One whose business it is to write for a public journal.
Librarian. One who has charge of a library.
Literary hack. A man who does any sort of literary work.
Littérateur [F.] A literary man.
Pen. Style of writing.
Penny-a-liner. One who furnishes matter to public journals for so much a line.
Publisher. One who publishes books, etc.
Reporter. One who gathers news for a newspaper.
Representative of the press. A reporter.
Scribbler. A writer of no reputation.
Sub-editor. An assistant editor.
The scribbling race. Writers of no reputation.
Writer for the press. One who contributes to the public journals.

Ephemeris [Gr.]. Tables of the positions of the stars during **a** period.
Extra. An issue of a paper outside of the regular.
Folio. A book composed of sheets folded once.
Hand-book. A book of useful information on any subject.
Issue. The part of a paper or book given out at one time.
Libretto [It.]. Text of a musical composition.
Livraison [F.]. A single section of a book issued in parts
Magazine. A periodical containing miscellaneous compositions.
Manual. Hand-book.
Number. Issue of a periodical.
Octavo. A book formed by folding a sheet to make eight leaves.
Octo-decimo. A book eighteen of whose leaves form a sheet.
Opuscle. A small or unimportant work.
Pamphlet. A brief essay.
Part. A portion of a book
Periodical. A publication issued at certain intervals.
Publication. A work printed and placed before the public.
Quarto or 4to. A book four of whose leaves make a sheet; a book with pages 7 x 8½, or one 10 x 13 inches in size.
Serial. Periodical.
Tome. A large volume.
Tract. A short religious or moral treatise
Tractate. A short written discussion.
Volume. One of the several parts of a complete work.
Work. } Any written production.
Writing. }

PUBLICATION—*Associated Nouns.*

Bibliography. A history or description of books and manuscripts.
Bibliotheca. A library.
Bill. A paper printed or written to advertise something.
Book-learning, etc. Knowledge derived from books. See KNOWLEDGE.
Broadsheet. A sheet of paper containing one large page, or printed on one side only.
Chapter. A division of a book or treatise.
Clause. A separate portion of a written paragraph.
Editorship. The office or charge of an editor.
Fly-leaf. An unprinted leaf at the beginning or end of a book
Head. A separate part, or topic, of a discourse.
Knowledge of books. Information relative to editions, contents, etc., of books.
Leaf. A folded sheet containing two pages upon its opposite sides.
Leaflet. A little leaf.
Library. A considerable collection of books kept for use and not for merchandise. •
Page. One side of a leaf of a book or manuscript.
Paper. A printed sheet appearing periodically.
Paragraph. A distinct part of a discourse or writing
Passage. A portion of a book.

(*Continued on Column* 1.)

---

mis-spell'. To spell erroneously. INTERPRETATION-MISINTERPRETATION.
mis-spend'. To squander. EXTRAVAGANCE-AVARICE.
mis-state'. To state wrongly. TRUTH-ERROR, TRUTHFULNESS-FALSEHOOD.
mis-state'-ment. An incorrect statement. TRUTH-ERROR, TRUTHFULNESS-FABRICATION, TRUTHFULNESS-FALSEHOOD.
mist. Fog; anything which dims. DIAPHANEITY-OPALESCENCE, LUMINARY-SHADE, VISCIDITY-FOAM; **in a mist,** ENLIGHTENMENT-SECRECY; **mist before the eyes,** SIGHT-DIMSIGHTEDNESS; **mists of error,** TRUTH-ERROR; **seen through a mist,** CLEARNESS-OBSCURITY.
mis-take'. Error; failure; to understand wrongly. INTERPRETATION-MISINTERPRETATION, SKILL-UNSKILFULNESS, SUCCESS - FAILURE, TRUTH - ERROR; **never was a greater mistake,** ASSERTION-DENIAL.
mis"-teach'. Instruct wrongly. RATIOCINATION-CASUISTRY.
mis-teach'-ing. Erroneous instruction. EDUCATION-MISTEACHING.
mis'-ter. A title. MALE-FEMALE.
mis-term'. To miscall. NAME-MISNOMER.
mis-think'. To have erroneous judgment of. DECISION-MISJUDGMENT.

mis-time'. Not to adapt to the time. OPPORTUNENESS-UNSUITABLENESS.
mis-timed'. Inopportune. OPPORTUNENESS-UNSUITABLENESS.
mis'-tral. A northwest wind of the Gulf of Lyons. RIVER-WIND.
mis"-trans-late'. To translate wrongly. INTERPRETATION-MISINTERPRETATION.
mis'-tress. A lady; possessor; master; concubine. CHIEF-UNDERLING, HOLDER, MALE-FEMALE, PURITY-RAKE.
mis-trust'. Want of confidence. FAITH-MISGIVING, SANGUINENESS-TIMIDITY.
mist'-y. Clouded. CLEARNESS-OBSCURITY, DIAPHANEITY-OPAQUENESS, DIMNESS, VISIBILITY-INVISIBILITY.
mis-un"-der-stand'. To understand wrongly. INTERPRETATION-MISINTERPRETATION, TRUTH-ERROR.
mis-un"-der-stand'-ing. A misapprehension; a disagreement. INTERPRETATION-MISINTERPRETATION, TRUTH-ERROR, VARIANCE-ACCORD.
mis-us'-age. Misapplication. GOODNESS - BADNESS USE-MISUSE.
mis-use'. Ill-treatment. PROVISION-WASTE, USE-MISUSE.

mis-used'. Misapplied. Use-Misuse.

mite. A particle; a small coin. Greatness-Little-ness, Magnitude-Smallness, Money.

mi'-ter. The junction of two bodies; a head-dress. Angularity, Union-Disunion, Vestments.

mith'-ri-date. An antidote against poison. Remedy-Bane.

mit'-i-gate. To alleviate; to make mild. Allevia-tion-Aggravation, Betterment-Deterioration, Turbulence-Calmness.

mit''-i-ga'-tion. The act of mitigating. Alleviation-Aggravation, Increase-Decrease, Justification-Charge, Turbulence-Calmness.

mi''-traille'. Shot used in loading cannon. Weapon.

mi''-trail''-leur'. One who operates a mitrailleuse. Weapon.

mi''-trail''-leuse'. Kind of breech-loading gun. Weapon.

mit'-ten. A covering for the hand. Dress-Undress.

mit'-ti-mus. An order. Order.

mix. To mingle. Mixture-Homogeneity, Organ-ization-Disorganization; **mix oneself up with,** Ac-tion-Passiveness, Activity-Indolence, Antago-nism-Concurrence, Organization-Disorganiza-tion.

mixed. Blended. Mixture-Homogeneity.

mix'-en. A dung-heap. Cleanness-Filthiness.

mix'-ture. State of being mixed. Mixture-Homo-geneity; **mere mixture,** Regularity-Irregularity.

MIXTURE--HOMOGENEITY.

Admixtion. } The state or act of mingling or mixing; also, the result
Admixture. } of mixing.

Adulteration. The act of corrupting or debasing by foreign mixture.

Alloyage. The act or process of alloying metals.

Combination, etc. The act or process of joining together persons or things. See Composition.

Commixion. }
Commixtion. } The blending or mixing of ingredients into one com-pound.
Commixture. }

Diffusion. In chemistry, the process of becoming uniformly mixed.

Impregnation. The union or fusion of the male germ cell with the female germ cell to form a new cell with power to develop into a new individual.

Infiltration. The act or process of infiltrating or percolating.

Infusion. The act of infusing or soaking.

Interlarding. Inserting between; diversifying or mingling.

Intermixture. A mass of ingredients mingled.

Interpolation, etc. The act of inserting something spurious. See Environment-Interposition.

Junction, etc. The act of joining or combining. See Union.

Matrimony. The union of a man and woman in wedlock; the married state.

Mixtion. } The act of mixing or mingling or the state of being mixed.
Mixture. }

Seasoning. Qualifying by admixture.

Sophistication. The act of adulterating or making worthless by admixture.

Sprinkling. The act of one who sprinkles or scatters a liquid or the like so that it falls in small particles.

Suffusion. The act of overspreading or covering with a fluid or tincture.

Mixture—Nouns of Means.

Caldron. A large kettle in which things are mixed by boiling.

Dash. A slight adulteration.

Smack. A slight flavor.

Soupçon [F.]. A suspicion; hence, a very small quantity.

Spice. A vegetable substance used to give flavor to food.

Sprinkling. A small scattering quantity.

Tincture. A solution of some principle used in medicine.

Tinge. A faint trace of color imbuing what is otherwise colorless.

Touch. A slight quality or quantity.

Mixture—Nouns of Result.

Alloy. The metal obtained from a mixture of other metals.

All sorts. A mass of many different things.

Amalgam. A mixture of mercury with some other metal or metals.

Ambigu [F.]. A feast consisting of a mixture of dishes.

Cross. The result of a mixing of breeds or stock.

Gallimaufry. A hash consisting of various kinds of meats.

Griff. A mulatto.

Half-and-half. A mixture containing as much of one material as another.

Half-blood. One whose parents are of different races.

Half-caste. One born of mixed European and Asiatic blood.

Hotchpot. A confused mass, as of goods and estates.

Hybrid. The offspring of the union of two different species.

Jumble. A mixture of words. See Regularity-Irregularity.

Magma [L.]. A crude mixture of organic or mineral matter in the state of paste.

Mash. A mass of ingredients blended together.

Medley. A musical composition of detached passages from other compositions.

Mélange [F.]. A medley or mixture.

Mess. A confused or disorderly mixture.

Elimination. The act or process of expelling or discharging.

Homogeneity. The sameness or uniformity of kind or nature.

Purification, etc. The act or process of making pure. See Clean-ness.

Purity. The state of being pure.

Sifting. See Verbs.

Simpleness. State of being simple. See Adjectives.

Homogeneity—Verbs.

Bolt. To sift the bran from the flour; hence, to refine or purify.

Clear. To make free from impurities.

Disentangle, etc. To free from confusion; to clear up, etc. See Disunion.

Eliminate. To expel or to set aside.

Purify, etc. To make pure, etc. See Cleanness.

Render simple. See Adjectives.

Sift. To separate as by a sieve.

Simplify. To make simple.

Winnow. To separate by means of the wind.

Homogeneity—Adjectives.

Clear. Free from mixture or obstruction.

Elementary. With but one constituent element; not compounded.

Exclusive. Tending to exclude or shut out.

Exempt from. Free from.

Free from. Without.

Homogeneous. Having the same nature or similar parts.

Neat. Free from uncleanness or disorder.

Of a piece. Of the same sort or kind.

Pure. Free from mixture or extraneous matter.

Pur et simple [F.]. Pure and simple.

Sheer. Unmingled; being what it seems to be.

Simple. Uncompounded; plain.

Single. Consisting of but one.

Unadulterated. Not adulterated.

Unalloyed. Not reduced in purity by mixture.

Unblended. Not commingled.

Uncombined. Separate.

Uncompounded. Not formed of different ingredients or elements.

Undecomposed. Not dissolved or broken up.

Unfortified. Not strengthened or confirmed.

Uniform. Being the same throughout.

Unmingled. Not blended or mixed.

Unmixed. Separate; distinct.

Unsophisticated. Unadulterated, pure.

Untinged. Unaffected by mixture.

Homogeneity—Adverbs.

Only. Simply.

Simply. See Adjectives.

MIXTURE—Nouns of Result—*Continued.*

Mingled yarn. Tangled skeins of yarn.

Miscellany. A varied collection of literary compositions.

Mongrel. An animal of mixed breed.

Mosaic. A design made by inlaying in patterns small pieces of dif-ferent colored glass, stones, or the like.

Mulatto. A person of half white and half negro blood.

Noah's ark. A mixture of everything.

Octoroon. A person having one-eighth negro and seven-eighths white blood.

Odds and ends. Fragments of different things.

Olio. A varied collection of musical compositions.

MIXTURE—Nouns of Result—*Continued.*

Ollapodrida [Sp.]. A Spanish dish consisting of several kinds of meat and vegetables chopped up together.
Omnium gatherum [L.]. A miscellaneous collection.
Pasticcio [It.]. An olio or medley.
Patchwork. Work made up of heterogeneous materials.
Pewter. An alloy of tin and lead.
Potpourri [F.]. A piece of music, consisting of different airs strung together.
Quadroon. The child of a mulatto and a white person.
Quarteron. A quadroon.

Quinteron. The offspring of an octoroon and a white person.
Salad. A dish of a mixture of green herbs and meat.
Salmagundi. A dish of chopped meat, eggs, onions, etc., with oil, vinegar, and pepper.
Sauce. A dressing for food, composed of several ingredients.
Terceron. A person of one-third white blood.
Tertium quid [L.]. A third something.
Texture. A woven fabric.
Zambo. The child of a mulatto and a negro.

MIXTURE—*Verbs.*

Adulterate. To corrupt by the admixture of a foreign substance.
Alloy. To reduce the purity of by mixture.
Amalgamate. To mix so as to make a uniform compound; to alloy with mercury.
Associate with. To be connected with in any way.
Attemper. To mix in proper proportion.
Be entangled with. To be mixed up in.
Bemingle. To mix or mingle.
Be mixed, etc. To be joined closely together.
Besprinkle. To spread or scatter over.
Blend. To combine intimately.
Brew. To be in a state of preparation or to be mixing.
Combine, etc. To join in a close union, etc. See Composition.
Commingle. To mix together.
Commix. To mingle together.
Compound. To unite into one by a mixture of ingredients.
Cross. To mix the breed.
Dash. To adulterate by throwing something in.
Get among. To go into the company of.
Hash up. To cut up into small bits.
Imbue. To cause to imbibe thoroughly.
Immix. To commingle.
Impregnate with. To infuse with an active principle.
Infect. To affect by communication, especially with something noxious.
Infiltrate. To penetrate a substance gradually by means of pores.

Infuse. To pour in or to steep.
Instil. To infuse gradually.
Interlard, etc. To vary by mixture, etc. See Interposition.
Intermingle. To mix together
Intermix. To mingle together.
Intertwine. To unite by twisting one with the other.
Interweave, etc. To intermingle in texture, etc. See Crossing.
Join, etc. To unite, etc. See Union.
Knead. To work into a mass with the hands.
Medicate. To tincture with anything medicinal.
Mingle. To mix or unite with so as to form one.
Mix. To mingle or blend two or more substances so as to form one.
Mix up with. ⎫
Pound together.⎭ To cause to form one substance.
Season. To mitigate by admixture.
Shuffle, etc. To mix up or confuse, etc. See Organization-Disorganization.
Sophisticate. To corrupt by admixture.
Sprinkle. To scatter on in small particles.
Stir up. To mix thoroughly
Suffuse. To cover over with a color or tincture.
Tincture. To impregnate with something foreign, as an odor or color.
Tinge. To modify, by mixing or by application to the surface
Transfuse. To cause to be imbibed.

MIXTURE—*Adjectives.*

Composite. Made up of separate or distinct parts.
Half-and-half. Composed of equal parts of different substances.
Heterogeneous. Consisting of ingredients of various kinds.
Hybrid. Produced by the mixture of two species.
Implex. Intricate; complex.
Indiscriminate. Lacking discrimination; confused
Linsey-woolsey. Made of linen and wool.

Miscellaneous. Consisting of different kinds or things
Miscible. That may be mixed.
Mixed. See Verbs.
Mongrel. Of mixed breed.
Motley, etc. Made up of different colors or various parts. See Variegation.
Promiscuous. Commingled without order or distinction.

MIXTURE—*Adverbs, etc.*

Amid. ⎫
Amidst.⎭ Among or mingled with.
Among. ⎫
Amongst.⎭ Surrounded by.

In the crowd. In the number or company of.
In the midst of. Surrounded by.
With. In the company of.

---

miz'-zle. Mist-like rain. River-Wind.
mne-mon'-ics. Science of artificial memory. Remembrance-Forgetfulness.
Mne-mos'-y-ne. The goddess of memory. Remembrance-Forgetfulness.
mne''-mo-tech'-nics. Science of artificial memory. Remembrance-Forgetfulness.
moan. To cry or lament. Cry-Ululation, Jubilation-Lamentation.
moat. A ditch on the outside of a fortress wall. Attack-Defense, Enclosure, Groove, Watercourse-Airpipe.
mob. A lawless crowd; the lowest class of people. Approval-Disapproval, Gathering-Scattering, Gentility-Commonalty, Regard-Disrespect; king mob, Gentility-Commonalty; mob cap, Dress-Undress; mob law, Law-Lawlessness, Rule-License.
mo'-bile. Movable; sensitive. Movement-Rest, Mutability-Stability, Sensitiveness-Apathy.
mo-bil'-i-ty, the. The mob. Movement-Rest, Mutability-Stability, Reputation-Discredit, Sensitiveness-Apathy.
mo''-bil-i-za'-tion. An assembling of people. Fighting, Movement-Rest.

mo'-bil-ize. To get ready for active service. Movement-Rest; mobilize troops, Fighting-Conciliation.
mob-oc'-ra-cy. Mob rule. Rule-License.
moc'-ca-sin. A foot-covering. Dress-Undress.
mock. To imitate exactly; to mimic in derision; to deceive by false show. Imitation-Originality, Jubilation-Lamentation, Likeness-Unlikeness, Regard-Disrespect, Society-Derision, Truth-Error, Truthfulness-Fraud; mock danger, Bravery-Cowardice; mock modesty, Society-Affectation.
mock'-ery. Derisive mimicry; a false show; a delusion. Imitation-Originality, Regard-Disrespect, Society-Derision, Substance-Nullity, Truthfulness-Fraud; mockery, delusion, and snare, Ratiocination-Casuistry, Truthfulness-Fraud; solemn mockery, Pomp.
mock'-ing. Imitating. Recurrence.
mock'-ing-bird''. A bird that imitates. Imitation-Originality.
mo'-dal. Denoting a manner. Condition-Situation, Subjectiveness-Objectiveness.

mode. State; method; common fashion; the scale; a verb form used to express action, etc. Condition-Situation, Habit - Desuetude, Melody - Dissonance, Society-Ludicrousness, Way; **imperative mode,** Verb; **indicative mode,** Verb; **infinitive mode,** Verb; **mode of expression,** Style; **participial mode,** Verb; **potential mode,** Verb; **subjunctive mode,** Verb.

mode, à la [F.] (mod, a la). In fashion. Society-Ludicrousness.

mod'-el. A copy; rule; perfection; pattern; an example for imitation. Copy-Model, Delineation-Caricature, Faultlessness-Faultiness, Form-Formlessness, Good Man-Bad Man, Sculpture, Uniformity-Multiformity; **model after,** Imitation-Originality; **model condition,** Uniformity-Multiformity; **new model,** Betterment-Deterioration, Revolution.

mod'-el-er. One who models. Artist.

mod'-er-ate. Within reasonable limits or control; calm; to allay; cheap. Costliness-Cheapness, Enough, Magnitude-Smallness, Moderation-Selfindulgence, President-Member, Swiftness-Slowness, Turbulence-Calmness; **moderate circumstances,** Mediocrity.

mod'-er-ate-ly. In a moderate degree. Faultlessness-Faultiness, Turbulence-Calmness.

mod''-er-at'-ing. Restraining. Turbulence - Calmness.

moderatio, adhibenda est in jocando [L.] (mod-er-ê'-shi-o, ad-hib-en'-da est in jo-can'-do). Moderation is to be observed in joking. Wittiness-Dulness.

mod''-er-a'-tion. State of being moderate; calmness of mind. Excitation, Harshness-Mildness, Magnitude-Smallness, Moderation-Selfindulgence, Turbulence-Calmness.

MODERATION—SELFINDULGENCE—VOLUPTUARY.

Abnegation. Renunciation.
Abstemiousness. The quality of being temperate.
Abstinence. Practise of temperance.
Encratism. Practise of Encratites; abstinence from wine, animal food, and marriage.
Forbearance. Control of temper.
Frugality. A temperate expenditure.
Moderation. The state or quality of being temperate.
Nephalism. Total abstinence from spirituous liquors.
Pythagorism. The doctrine of Pythagoras.
Self-control. Self-restraint. See Determination.
Self-denial. Temperance in one's desires.
Self-restraint. Restraint or control over self.
Sobriety. Habitual temperance.
Stoicism. The maxims of the Stoics wherein they professed temperance and studied indifference to either pleasure or pain.
System of Cornaro. Extreme frugality of diet. [French.]
System of Pythagoras. A Greek system of philosophy founded by Pythagoras.
Teetotalism. The principles of teetotalers. See Nouns.
Temperance. Moderation, particularly in the natural appetites.
Total abstinence. Refraining absolutely from the use of spirituous liquors.
Vegetarianism. The practise of living solely upon vegetables.

Moderation—Nouns of Agent.

Abstainer. One who refrains from the use of liquors; a teetaler.
Gymnosophist. One of a sect of ancient Hindu philosophers who renounced the world and lived in abstinence and contemplation.
Pythagorean. A follower of Pythagoras, the founder of Italian philosophy.
Teetotaler. A total abstainer. See Teetotalism.
Vegetarian. A man who abstains from eating meat.

Moderation—Verbs.

Abstain. To exercise temperance.
Be temperate. See Adjectives.
Deny oneself. To decline to gratify one's appetites.
Forbear. To abstain from.
Know when one has had enough. To know enough to stop drinking before becoming intoxicated.
Refrain. To forbear; abstain.
Spare. To refrain from using.
Take the pledge. To promise to drink no intoxicating liquor.

Moderation—Adjectives.

Abstemious. Eating and drinking temperately.
Abstinent. Totally abstaining, as from intoxicants.
Frugal. Marked by economy.
Measured. See Enough.
Moderate. Keeping within temperate limits.
Pythagorean. Of the philosophy of Pythagoras.
Sober. Even-tempered.
Sparing. Frugal.
Teetotal. Of total abstinence.
Temperate. Observing moderation and self-control, particularly in the case of intoxicants.
Vegetarian. Relating to vegetarianism. See Nouns.
Within compass. Within moderation.

Amativeness. Great propensity to sexual love.
Animalism. The state of animals; actuated only by sensual impulse.
Carnality. Lusts after the flesh; sensuality.
Crapulence. Drunkenness; the illness caused by intemperance.
Debauchery. Intemperance in sensual pleasures.
Dissipation. Intemperate indulgence.
Effeminacy. Indulgence in unmanly pleasures.
Epicureanism. Devotion to luxurious and intemperate habits.
Epicurism. Luxury; sensuality. [Epicurus, Greek philospher.]
Excess. Going out of bounds.
Free living. Unrestrained indulgence of the appetites.
High living. Intemperate living.
Inabstinence. Want of abstinence. See Abstinence.
Indulgence. Freedom to the desires.
Intemperance. Want of moderation; excessive indulgence.
Lap of luxury. Condition fostered by indulgence. [Miss Edgeworth, Moral Tales.]
Lap of pleasure. Condition fostered in pleasure.
Licentiousness. See Adjectives.
Luxuriousness. State or quality of being luxurious.
Luxury. A free indulgence in the gratification of the desires.
Pleasure. Gratification of the desires.
Self-indulgence. Free indulgence of one's desires.
Sensuality. Free indulgence of the carnal desires.
Silkiness. Softness; effeminacy.
Sybaritism. The practise of effeminacy. [Sybaris, an Italian city.]
Too much. Overindulgence in intoxicants and otherwise.
Voluptuousness. See Adjectives.

Selfindulgence—Denotations.

Carousal. An occasion of riotous revelry.
Debauch. An act or season of excessive indulgence of the appetites.
Drinking-bout. A season of drinking or carousing.
Jollification. An act or occasion of festivity.
Orgies. Wild or wanton revelry.
Revelry. Noisy, riotous festivity.
Revels. An occasion of excessive festivity.
Saturnalia. The festival of Saturn, a period of noisy revelry and indulgence.
Wassail. A drinking-bout.

Selfindulgence—Nouns of Agent.

Circean cup. Named after Circe, the Greek sorceress; hence, fascinating but poisonous and evil, as intoxicants.
Hashish. An intoxicating preparation from Indian hemp.

Selfindulgence—Verbs.

Be intemperate. See Adjectives.
Exceed. To go beyond proper bounds.
Give a loose to indulgence. See Nouns.
Indulge. To yield without restraint.
Live hard. } To live intemperately.
Live high. }
Live on the fat of the land. To live luxuriously.
Pamper. To satiate without regard to temperance.
Plunge into dissipation. To rush into intemperance.
Rake. To lead an intemperate, debauched life.
Revel. To feast intemperately.
Run riot. To act without control.
Slake one's appetite. To decrease one's hunger.

MODERATION—SELFINDULGENCE—*Continued.*

MODERATION—*Phrases.*

Appetitus rationi obediant [L.]. Let appetite obey the reason. [Cicero, *Officiis*, 1, 29, 102.]
Trahit sua quemque voluptas [L.]. His own pleasure draws each man. [Virgil, *Eclogues*, 2, 65.]

SELFINDULGENCE—ADJECTIVES—*Continued from Column 2.*

Luxurious. Pertaining to luxury. See *Nouns.*
Nursed in the lap of luxury. Addicted to luxury
Pampered. Indulged intemperately.
Paphian. Pertaining to Paphos, a city sacred to Aphrodite; hence, belonging to Aphrodite or her rites.
Piggish. Acting like a pig; greedy.
Rakish. Dissolute; dissipated.
Self-indulgent. See *Nouns.*
Sensual. Intemperate in the animal nature.
Swinish. Greedy, like swine; gross.
Sybaritical. Luxurious.
Voluptuous. Pertaining to sensual pleasures.
Wild. Intemperate in conduct.

SELFINDULGENCE—VERBS—*Continued.*

Slake one's thirst. To decrease one's thirst.
Sow one's wild oats. To practise youthful excesses.
Swill. To drink intemperately.
Wallow in voluptuousness. See sub *Adjectives.*

SELFINDULGENCE—*Adjectives.*

Bred in the lap of luxury. Reared luxuriously.
Brutish. Of the nature of a brute; gross; carnal.
Crapulous. Ill by intemperance.
Debauched. Given to intemperance.
Dissolute. Given to vice and intemperance.
Epicurean. One given to sensual pleasures.
Fast. Dissipated; intemperate.
Full-fed. Fed to fulness.
Inabstinent. Wanting abstinence. See *Nouns.*
Indulged. Humored to excess.
Intemperate. Given to excessive use of alcoholic drinks.
Licentious. Intemperate in sensual indulgences.

(*Continued on Column 1.*)

MODERATION—VOLUPTUARY.

VOLUPTUARY.

Carpet knight. A knight who has not known the hardships of the field.
Epicure. One devoted to sensual enjoyments.
Epicurean. A believer that happiness is man's chief end, like Epicurus.
Free liver. One who lives in the free enjoyment of sensual pleasures.
Gourmand [F.].
Gourmet [F.]. } A glutton; an epicure.
Hard liver. One who devotes life to the pursuit of sensual pleasures.
Heliogabalus. Emperor of Rome and a notorious debauchée.
Hog. One who has the greediness of a hog for sensual enjoyment.

Libertine. One who leads a life devoted to sensual pleasures without restraint. See PURITY-RAKE.
Man of pleasure. One who indulges freely in sensual pleasures to the exclusion of all else.
Pig. See HOG. [Horace, *Epistles*, I, iv, 15.]
Sardanapalus. A licentious king of Assyria.
Sensualist. One unduly indulgent to his animal appetites.
Swine of Epicurus. A hoggish eater. "The fattest hog in Epicurus' sty." [W. Mason.]
Sybarite. An epicure.
Voluptuary. One addicted to sensual pleasures.
Votary of Epicurus. One who lives for pleasure alone.

mod″-er-a′-to. Moderately. Music.
mod′-er-a″-tor. One who or that which restrains or regulates; the presiding officer of a meeting. LU-MINARY-SHADE, MANAGER, MEDIATOR, PRESIDENT-MEMBER, TURBULENCE-CALMNESS.
mod′-ern. Not ancient. NOVELTY-ANTIQUITY.
mod′-ern-ism. A modern practise. NOVELTY-ANTIQUITY.
mod′-ern-ize. Render modern. NOVELTY-ANTIQUITY.
mod′-est. Unassuming. CONCEIT-DIFFIDENCE, MAGNITUDE-SMALLNESS, PURITY-IMPURITY.
mod′-es-ty. State of being modest; decent propriety. CONCEIT - DIFFIDENCE, OVERVALUATION - UNDERVALUATION, PURITY-IMPURITY, SELFRESPECT-HUMBLENESS; **mock modesty,** SOCIETY-AFFECTATION.
mod′-i-cum. A little. ASSIGNMENT, MAGNITUDE-SMALLNESS.
mod′-i-fi″-a-ble. Changeable. MUTATION-PERMANENCE.
mod″-i-fi-ca′-tion. Variation; qualification. DEVIATION, MODIFICATION, MUTATION-PERMANENCE, VARIATION.

MODIFICATION.

Allowance. Concession.
Coloring. Misrepresentation.
Condition. A necessary state or fact.
Consideration. Regard.
Discount. Lack of credence.
Exception. A taking out.
Exemption. A freeing from.
Extenuating circumstances. Circumstances that modify or diminish the gravity of.
Grains of allowance. Modifying circumstances.
Limitation. Restricting condition.
Modification. Change; variation.
Proviso. A modifying condition.
Qualification. A limiting exception.
Salvo. A saving clause.
Saving clause. A clause that modifies or limits.

MODIFICATION—*Verbs.*

Allow.. To take into account.
Leaven. To imbue.

Limit. To set bounds to.
Modify. To change or alter.
Qualify. To make modifying exceptions.

MODIFICATION—*Verbal Expressions.*

Admit exceptions; give a color to; introduce new conditions; make allowance for; take exception; take into account.

MODIFICATION—*Adjectives.*

Conditional. Subject to conditions.
Contingent. Depending on some uncertain future event. See CERTAINTY-DOUBT.
Exceptional. Implying an exception.
Hypothetical. Assumed for the sake of argument.
Qualifying. Having a modifying condition. See *Verbs.*

MODIFICATION—*Adverbs, etc.*

According as. Just as.
Admitting. Granting that.
After all. All things considered.
Although. Notwithstanding.
At all events. Even though.
But. With the exception of.
Conditionally. With limitations.
Cum grano salis [L.]. With a grain of salt.
Even. So much as.
Exceptis excipiendis [L.]. Exceptions having been made.
For all that. Granting that.
If. Provided that.
If possible. See POSSIBILITY.
On the supposition. If that happens.
Provided. Conditionally.
Provided always. Always excluding that.
Subject to. Limited.
Supposing. Assuming as true.
Though. Granted that.
Unless. If it be not a fact that.
Wind and weather permitting. Subject to conditions.
With grains of allowance. Excepting.
With the understanding. }
With this proviso. } With a certain limitation. See *Nouns.*
Yet. Even.

mod'-i-fy. Change. MODIFICATION, MUTATION-PERMANENCE.

mo-dil'-lion. Bracket. ARCHITECTURE.

mo'-dish. Fashionable. SOCIETY-LUDICROUSNESS.

mod'-u-late. Vary. MUTATION-PERMANENCE.

mod''-u-la'-tion. A change of key. MELODY-DISSONANCE, MUTATION-PERMANENCE.

mod'-ule. A model. COPY-MODEL.

mod'-u-lus. A coefficient. NUMBER.

modus operandi [L.] (mo'-dus op-er-an'-dai). Manner of operation. AGENCY, CONDUCT, WAY.

modus operandi in rebus [L.] (mo'-dus op-er-an'-dai in ri'-bus). Mode of operation in affairs. TURBULENCE-CALMNESS.

Mo'-gul. An important personage. CHIEF-UNDERLING.

Mo-ham'-med-an. A follower of Mohammed. ORTHODOXY-HETERODOXY.

Mo'-hawk. A lawless person. BENEFACTOR-EVILDOER, BRAWLER.

Mo'-hock. A lawless person. BENEFACTOR-EVILDOER.

moi'-der. To bewilder; to confuse. CERTAINTY-DOUBT, HEED-DISREGARD.

moi'-e-ty. A share. DOUBLING-HALVING.

moil. To drudge; to toil. ACTIVITY-INDOLENCE, TOIL-RELAXATION.

moi pou sto kai tan gan kinaso, dos [Gr.] (moy pu sto kai tan gan kin-a'-so, dos). Give me where I may stand and I will move the earth. MIGHT-IMPOTENCE.

moist. Damp. DAMPNESS-DRYNESS.

mois'-ten. Dampen. DAMPNESS-DRYNESS.

moist'-ness. Humidness. DAMPNESS-DRYNESS.

mois'-ture. Sensible wetness. DAMPNESS-DRYNESS, VISCIDITY-FOAM, WATER-AIR.

mokes. The meshes of a net. CROSSING.

mo-las'-ses. A sweet syrup. SWEETNESS-ACIDITY.

mold, molder, moldy, etc. See MOULD, MOULDER, MOULDY, etc.

mole. A breakwater; a spot; a harbor. ATTACK-DEFENSE, CONVEXITY-CONCAVITY, EMBELLISHMENT-DISFIGUREMENT, HEIGHT-LOWNESS, REFUGE-PITFALL.

mo-lec'-u-lar. Consisting of molecules. GREATNESS-LITTLENESS, MAGNITUDE-SMALLNESS.

mol-e-cule. A small particle. CHEMISTRY, GREATNESS-LITTLENESS, MAGNITUDE-SMALLNESS.

mole'-hill''. A little elevation made by a mole; an insignificant obstacle. CONSEQUENCE-INSIGNIFICANCE, GREATNESS-LITTLENESS, HEIGHT-LOWNESS.

mo-lest'. To disturb injuriously. CHARITABLENESS-MALEVOLENCE, PLEASURABLENESS-PAINFULNESS.

mol''-es-ta'-tion. Act of molesting. CHARITABLENESS-MALEVOLENCE, GOODNESS-BADNESS, PLEASURABLENESS-PAINFULNESS.

mol'-lah. A judge; a priest. JUDGE, MINISTRY-LAITY.

mollia tempora [L.] (mol''-li-a tem'-por-a). Favorable opportunities. OPPORTUNENESS-UNSUITABLENESS.

mollia tempora fandi [L.] (mol''-li-a tem'-por-a fan'-dai). Favorable opportunities for speaking. CONVERSATION-MONOLOGUE.

mol''-li-fi-ca'-tion. Mitigation. HARDNESS-SOFTNESS.

mol'-li-fy. To soften; allay. HARDNESS-SOFTNESS, TURBULENCE-CALMNESS.

mol-lus'-cous. Pertaining to Mollusca. FAUNA-FLORA.

mol'-lusk. An invertebrate animal. FAUNA-FLORA.

mol'-ly-cod''-dle. An effeminate man. MIGHT-IMPOTENCE.

Mol'-ly Ma-guire'. One of a lawless secret society. TYRANNY-ANARCHY.

Mo'-loch. A god of the Phenicians; any pernicious influence. JOVE-DEMON, LIFE-KILLING, REVELATION-PSEUDOREVELATION.

mol'-ten. Melted. HEATING-COOLING.

mo'-ment. An instant; consequence. CONSEQUENCE-INSIGNIFICANCE, DURATION-NEVERNESS, ETERNITY-INSTANTANEITY; **for the moment,** LASTINGNESS-TRANSIENTNESS; **lose not a moment,** ACTIVITY-INDOLENCE, HURRY-LEISURE; **not have a moment,** ACTIVITY-INDOLENCE; **on the spur of the moment,** PREDETERMINATION-IMPULSE.

mo'-men-ta-ry. Lasting but a short time. ETERNITY-INSTANTANEITY, LASTINGNESS-TRANSIENTNESS.

mo-men'-tous. Weighty. CONSEQUENCE-INSIGNIFICANCE.

mo-men'-tum. Impetus. IMPETUS-REACTION.

Mo'-mus. God of mockery. JUBILATION-LAMENTATION.

mon'-a-chal. Monkish. CHURCH.

mon'-a-chism. Monasticism. CHURCH.

mon'-a-chy. The monastic manner of life. CHURCH.

mon'-ad. An ultimate atom. GREATNESS-LITTLENESS.

mon'-arch. A sole ruler. CHIEF-UNDERLING.

mon-ar'-chic-al. Pertaining to a monarch. RULE-LICENSE.

mon'-arch-y. Government by a monarch. RULE-LICENSE.

mon'-as-ter-y. A house of religious retirement. FANE.

mon-as'-tic. Pertaining to religious seclusion. CHURCH.

mon'-e-ta-ry. Pecuniary. ACCOUNTS, MONEY; **monetary arithmetic,** ACCOUNTS.

mon'-ey. Wealth; coin. AFFLUENCE-PENURY, MONEY; **bad money,** MONEY; **command of money,** AFFLUENCE-PENURY; **for one's money,** CHOICE-NEUTRALITY; **made of money,** AFFLUENCE-PENURY; **make money,** GAIN-LOSS; **money burning one's pocket,** EXTRAVAGANCE-AVARICE; **money coming in,** OUTLAY-INCOME; **money down,** SETTLEMENT-DEFAULT; **money going out,** OUTLAY-INCOME; **money market,** MONEY; **money matters,** ACCOUNTS; **money paid,** OUTLAY-INCOME; **money's worth,** COSTLINESS-CHEAPNESS, PRICE, USEFULNESS-USELESSNESS; **raise money,** LOAN-BORROWING; **save money,** GENEROSITY-FRUGALITY; **throw away one's money,** EXTRAVAGANCE-AVARICE.

MONEY.

Assets, etc. The property of an insolvent debtor applicable to the payment of his debts. See PROPERTY.

Base coin. Counterfeit coin.

Capital. Accumulated money invested in productive enterprises.

Cash. Money in hand.

Change. Small coins collectively.

Circulating medium. The current money.

Coin. A piece of metal stamped by the authority of the government.

Currency. Money in circulation as a medium of trade.

Doit. A small copper coin used in Holland.

Dollar. The standard monetary unit of the United States, equal to 100 cents.

Earning. Money obtained for labor.

False money. Counterfeit money.

Farthing. The smallest English monetary unit, of the value of one-fourth of a penny.

Funds. A sum of money; resources.

Good sum. A large sum of money.

Groat. A small English silver coin.

Guinea. An English monetary unit equal to 21 shillings.

£. s. d. Abbreviations for pound, shilling, and pence. [*Libra, solidi, denarii.*]

Lac of rupees. The sum of 100,000 rupees, about $50,000.

Louis d'or [F.]. An old gold coin of France.

Mite. A small sum of money.

Money. The common medium of exchange.

Money in hand. Ready money.

Necessary money. Money for personal expenses.

Penny. An English coin equal to one-twelfth of a shilling; a cent.

Petty cash. Money of small denominations.

Piece. A coin.

Pin money. Money for personal expenses for women.

Pocket money. Money for personal expenses.

Pounds, shillings, and pence. English monetary units.

Proceeds, etc. Sum derived from the disposal of goods. See OUTLAY.

Ready money. Money in hand.

Remittance, etc. Money sent for the payment of a debt. See SETTLEMENT.

Rouleau [F.]. A roll of coin.

Round sum. A large sum of money.

Shilling. An English monetary unit equal to about 25 cents.

Small coin. Change.

Sou [F.]. A French coin equal to one cent.

Specie. Coin issued by the government as current money.

Sterling coin. Coin of accepted worth.

Stiver. A small coin used in the Netherlands worth about two cents.

Stock. Money invested in trade.

Supplies. The amount of a commodity available for meeting a demand.

Tael. A Chinese monetary unit.

Treasure. Accumulated riches.

Wampum. Indian money.

Wealth, etc. A great abundance of anything valuable. See AFFLUENCE.

MONEY—*Paper Money, etc.*

Assignat [F.]. A note issued by the French Revolutionary government.

Bank-note. A promissory note issued by a bank as a circulating medium.

Bill. A bank or government note issued as money.

Bill of exchange. A written order from one person to another for the payment of money to a third.

Bond. A written obligation under seal, in which a person binds himself to pay to another a certain sum of money at a specified time.

Check. } An order in writing upon a bank for the payment of money
Cheque.} to some designated person or order.

Coupon. A dated certificate attached, as to a bond, representing interest accrued and payable.

Debenture. An instrument of the nature of a bond, given as an acknowledgment of debt.

Draft. An order drawn by one person on another for the payment of money to a third.

Exchequer bill. An interest-bearing obligation issued by a government for the repayment of money temporarily advanced.

Greenback. A legal tender note of the United States: so called because the back is printed in green.

I O U. A paper having on it these letters, meaning I owe you, followed by a named sum and duly signed.

Money-order. An order for the payment of a specified sum of money.

Note. A signed promise to pay a stated sum of money at a specified time.

Note of hand. A written engagement to pay a certain sum of money at a certain time.

Order. A written instrument directing the payment of money.

Paper money. Paper stamped with the stamp of the government and used as money.

Post-office order. An order from one post-office to another directing the payment of money.

Promissory note. A note or promise to pay a sum of money at a specified time.

Warrant. A written order authorizing the payment of money.

MONEY—*Nouns of Material.*

Bullion. Uncoined gold or silver.

Copper. A metal from which minor coins are made.

Gold. A precious metal of which the highest valued coins are made.

Ingot. A mass of gold or silver prepared for coining.

Nugget. A lump of precious metal found in a free state.

Precious metals. Gold and silver.

Silver. One of the precious metals of which coin is made.

MONEY—*Associated Nouns.*

Accounts. A record or statement of debits and credits. See ACCOUNTS.

Amount. The sum total of quantities.

Balance. The difference between the debit and credit totals of an account.

Balance-sheet. A statement in tabular form to show assets and liabilities.

Coiner. One who coins money.

Credit, etc. The degree of confidence in a person to fulfil financial obligations. See CREDIT.

Drawee. The person upon whom another draws a bill of exchange.

Drawer. One who draws a bill of exchange.

Exchequer. The treasury of a state.

Finance. The management of money and of monetary affairs.

Liability, etc. That sum for which one is responsible. See CREDIT.

Moneyer. A coiner of money.

Money market. The field for the employment or investment of money.

Money matters. Matters in which money is a consideration.

Obligee. The person in whose favor a bond or other obligation is entered into.

Obligor. The person who is bound to perform an obligation.

Payee. A person to whom money has been or is to be paid.

Tester. An officer of a mint who tests bullion and coin.

MONEY—*Figurative Nouns.*

Almighty dollar. Money considered as an irresistible power and an object of devotion. [Washington Irving, *The Creole Village*.]

Argumentum ad crumenam [L.]. An argument to the purse.

Blunt. Ready money.

Breeches pocket. Money.

Chink. Cash.

Coffers. Financial resources.

Dust. Cash or money.

Flash note. A note of doubtful value.

Hard cash. Money.

Kite. A commercial paper of doubtful value.

Mopus. Money.

Needful. Cash.

Plum. A fortune.

Pocket. Money.

Power of money. Resources.

Purse. Money.

Rap. A debased coin; an Irish rapparee.

Rhino. Money.

Salt. Cash.

Sinews of war. Financial resources.

Slip. A counterfeit silver coin.

Tin. Coin.

Ways and means. Financial resources.

Wherewithal. Money.

MONEY—*Scientific Nouns.*

Chrysology. That branch of political economy which relates to the production of wealth.

Numismatics. The science of coins.

MONEY—*Verbs.*

Amount to. To reach an aggregate.

Come to.

Discount, etc. To purchase notes below face value. See PRICE.

Draw. } To issue an order for the payment of money.
Draw upon.}

Indorse, etc. To sign in order to give security. See SECURITY.

Issue. To send forth by official authority.

Mount up to. To rise to.

Touch the pocket. To take one's money.

Utter. To deliver or offer to deliver a counterfeit coin as genuine.

MONEY—*Adjectives.*

Crumenal. Pertaining to a purse.

Economic. Pertaining to money matters or wealth.

Financial. Pertaining to or concerning money matters.

Fiscal. Pertaining to the government treasury.

Monetary. Pertaining to money.

Numismatical. Pertaining to the science of coins.

Pecuniary. Referring to money.

Sterling. Of accepted value; genuine.

Sumptuary. Pertaining to expense.

MONEY—*Phrases.*

Argent comptant [F.]. Ready money.

Barbarus ipse placet dummodo sit dives [L.]. Provided only he is rich, a very barbarian pleases. [Ovid, *Art of Love*, ii, 276.]

Nervos belli pecuniam infinitam [L.]. The sinews of war are unlimited money. [Cicero *Philippics*, 5, 2, 5.]

mon'-ey-bag". A purse. TREASURY.

mon'-ey-box". Box for holding money. TREASURY.

mon'-ey-bro"-ker. A dealer in money. DEALER.

mon'-ey-chan"-ger. One who changes money at a given rate. DEALER, TREASURER.

mon'-eyed. Wealthy. AFFLUENCE-PENURY, MONEY.

mon'-ey-er. A coiner of money. DEALER.

mon'-ey-grub"-bing. Contemptible money-making. GAIN-LOSS.

mon'-ey-less. Impecunious. AFFLUENCE-PENURY.

mon'-ey-ma'-king. Bent upon accumulating wealth GAIN-LOSS.

mon'-ger. A trader. DEALER, UPRIGHTNESS-DISHONESTY.

Mon-go'-li-an. One of the yellow race of men. ETHNOLOGY.

mon'-grel. An incongruous mixture; of mixed breeds; base. CONVENTIONALITY-UNCONVENTIONALITY, FAUNA-FLORA, GOOD MAN-BAD MAN, MIXTURE-HOMOGENEITY.

mon'-ied. Wealthy. AFFLUENCE-PENURY.

mo-nil'-i-form. Like a string of beads. ROUNDNESS.

mo-ni'-tion. Instruction; warning. ENLIGHTENMENT-SECRECY, WARNING.

mon'-i-tive. Monitory. MOTIVE-DEHORTATION.

mon'-i-tor. An adviser; an ironclad; a pupil-teacher; oracle. ADVICE, BELLIGERENT, INSTRUCTOR-PUPIL, MANAGER, SOOTHSAYER, WARNING; **inward monitor,** DUTY-DERELICTION.

mon'-i-to-ry. Admonitory; admonition. MOTIVE-DEHORTATION, PROPHECY, WARNING.

monk. A religious recluse. MINISTRY-LAITY.

mon'-key. An imitative animal; a contrivance; a ridiculous epithet. IMITATION-ORIGINALITY, IMPETUS-REACTION, SOCIETY-LAUGHINGSTOCK; **monkey trick,** ADAGE-NONSENSE, ENTERTAINMENT-WEARINESS; **monkey up,** FAVORITE-ANGER; **play the monkey,** SAGACITY-INCAPACITY.

mon'-key-wrench''. A wrench having a movable jaw for grasping a nut. INSTRUMENT.

monk'-hood. The condition of a monk. AUSTERITY.

monk'-ish. Pertaining to monks. CHURCH.

monk'-ish Lat'-in. Unclassical Latin. WORD-NEOLOGY.

mon'-o-chord. A one-stringed musical instrument. MUSICAL INSTRUMENTS.

mon'-o-chrome. A single colored painting. COLOR-ACHROMATISM, PAINTING.

mon''-o-clin'-ic. Symmetric. MINERALOGY.

mon-oc'-u-lous. One-eyed. SIGHT-DIMSIGHTEDNESS.

mon'-o-drame. A drama acted by one person. ACTING.

mon'-o-dy. A doleful composition; a lyric solo. JUBILATION-LAMENTATION, POETRY-PROSE.

mon-og'-a-mist. One who has but one living spouse. MATRIMONY-CELIBACY.

mon-og'-a-my. Practise of single marriage. MATRIMONY-CELIBACY.

mon'-o-gram. A cipher; letter; diagram. DELINEATION-CARICATURE, LETTER, TIDINGS-MYSTERY.

mon'-o-graph. A description; writing. ACCOUNT, WRITING-PRINTING.

mon'-o-lith. A single stone. MARK-OBLITERATION.

mon''-o-lith'-ic. Peculiar to a monolith. ORTHODOXY-HETERODOXY.

mon'-o-logue. A dramatic soliloquy. ACTING, CONVERSATION-MONOLOGUE.

mon-om'-a-chy. A duel. STRIFE-PEACE.

mon''-o-ma'-ni-a. Insanity confined to one idea or subject. BIGOTRY-APOSTASY, SANENESS-LUNACY.

mon''-o-ma'-ni-ac. One affected by monomania. SANENESS-MANIAC.

mon-om'-e-ter. Having one foot to a verse. RHETORIC.

mon-op'-o-list. One who monopolizes. LABOR-CAPITAL, UNSELFISHNESS-SELFISHNESS.

mon-op'-o-ly. The exclusive right. HOLDING-EXEMPTION, LABOR-CAPITAL, RELEASE-RESTRAINT.

mon'-o-stich. A composition of one verse. TERSENESS-PROLIXITY.

mon'-o-the''-ism. The doctrine that there is but one God. THEOLOGY.

mon''-o-the-is'-tic. Pertaining to monotheism. ORTHODOXY-HETERODOXY.

mon-ot'-o-nous. Without variety; tiresomely uniform. CRASH-DRUMMING, ENTERTAINMENT-WEARINESS, EQUALITY-INEQUALITY, FORCE-WEAKNESS, MUTATION-PERMANENCE, RECURRENCE, UNIFORMITY-DIVERSITY, WITTINESS-DULNESS.

mon-ot'-o-ny. Want of cadence. RECURRENCE.

mon-soon'. A trade-wind. RIVER-WIND.

mon'-ster. A fabulous animal; a very large person or thing; a prodigy; one to be abhorred. BEAUTY-UGLINESS, BENEFACTOR-EVILDOER, CONVENTIONALITY-UNCONVENTIONALITY, GOOD MAN-BAD MAN, GREATNESS-LITTLENESS, PHENOMENON.

mon-stros'-i-ty. Anything unnaturally large or distorted. CONVENTIONALITY-UNCONVENTIONALITY, GREATNESS-LITTLENESS, PROPORTION-DEFORMITY, SOCIETY-LUDICROUSNESS.

mon'-strous. Wonderful; huge; hideous. ASTONISHMENT-EXPECTANCE, BEAUTY-UGLINESS, GREATNESS-LITTLENESS, MAGNITUDE-SMALLNESS, SOCIETY-LUDICROUSNESS, TASTE-VULGARITY.

mon'-strous-ly. Wonderfully. MAGNITUDE-SMALLNESS.

montagne Russe [F.] (mon'-tany' rüs). Russian mountain. ENTERTAINMENT-WEARINESS, PARALLELISM-INCLINATION.

mont de piété [F.] (mon· de piê-tê'). Pawnbroker's shop. LOAN-BORROWING.

Mont-gol'-fi-er. A hot-air balloon. CONVEYANCE-VESSEL.

month. One-twelfth of a year. PERIOD-PROGRESS.

month'-ly. Coming once a month. PERIODICITY-IRREGULARITY; **monthly nurse,** REMEDY-BANE.

mon'-ti-cle. A little hill. HEIGHT-LOWNESS.

mon'-u-ment. A commemorative statue. HEIGHT-LOWNESS, LIFE-FUNERAL, MARK-OBLITERATION.

monumentum œre perennius [L.] (mon-yu-men'-tum î'-rî per-en'-ni-us). A monument more durable than brass. TROPHY.

moo. The lowing of a cow. CRY-ULULATION.

mood. Temper of mind. AFFECTIONS, CONDITION-SITUATION, INCLINATION, MUTATION-PERMANENCE, READINESS-RELUCTANCE, SUBJECTIVENESS-OBJECTIVENESS.

mood'-ish. Out of humor; peevish. FAVORITE-QUARRELSOMENESS.

mood'-ish-ness. Peevishness. FAVORITE-QUARRELSOMENESS, POLITENESS-IMPOLITENESS.

moods and tenses. Manner and time of conceiving and expressing action or being. DEVIATION, VARIATION.

mood'-y. Petulant; sullen; melancholy. EXCITABILITY-INEXCITABILITY, FAVORITE-MOROSENESS, LIGHTHEARTEDNESS-DEJECTION.

moon. A satellite; the time of one revolution of the moon in its orbit. ASTRONOMY, MUTABILITY-STABILITY, UNIVERSE; **bay the moon,** CRY-ULULATION, USEFULNESS-USELESSNESS; **jump over the moon,** SPRING-DIVE; **man in the moon,** FANCY; **moon of green cheese,** CREDULOUSNESS-SKEPTICISM.

moon'-beam''. A ray of moonlight. DIMNESS, LIGHT-DARKNESS.

moon'-calf''. A dolt. SAGE-FOOL.

moon'-eyed''. Having moon-eyes. SIGHT-DIMSIGHTEDNESS.

moon'-shee. A teacher. INSTRUCTOR-PUPIL, SCHOLAR-DUNCE.

moon'-shine''. Moonlight; empty nonsense; unreality; pretense. ADAGE-NONSENSE, DIMNESS, LIKELIHOOD-UNLIKELIHOOD, MEANING-JARGON, PRETEXT, SUBSTANCE-NULLITY, TRUTHFULNESS-FABRICATION.

moon'-struck''. Lunatic; wonder. ASTONISHMENT-EXPECTANCE, SANENESS-LUNACY.

moor. To fasten; a waste tract of land. ESTABLISHMENT-REMOVAL, EXTENSION-INEXTENSION, GULF-PLAIN, HEIGHT-LOWNESS, UNION-DISUNION.

Moore, Old. A fortune-teller. SOOTHSAYER.

moored. Firm. ESTABLISHMENT-REMOVAL, MUTABILITY-STABILITY.

moor'-ings. Condition of a moored ship. CONNECTIVE, ESTABLISHMENT-REMOVAL.

Moor'-ish. Marshy; pertaining to the Moors. SWAMP-ISLAND; **Moorish capital,** ARCHITECTURE.

moor'-land. A moor or marsh. EXTENSION-INEXTENSION, GULF-PLAIN, HEIGHT-LOWNESS.

moor'-y. Marshy. SWAMP-ISLAND.

moot. To investigate; argue. INVESTIGATION-ANSWER, RATIOCINATION-INSTINCT; **moot point,** CONCEPTION-THEME, INVESTIGATION-ANSWER.

moot'-ed. Under discussion. HYPOTHESIS.

mop. An instrument for cleansing. CLEANNESS-FILTHINESS.

mope. To make spiritless. LIGHTHEARTEDNESS-DEJECTION.

mope'-eyed". Short-sighted. SIGHT-DIMSIGHTEDNESS.

mo'-ping. Melancholy LIGHTHEARTEDNESS-DEJECTION.

mo'-pish. Dejected. LIGHTHEARTEDNESS-DEJECTION.

mop'-pet. A little girl. FAVORITE-ANGER.

mop'-sy. An untidy woman. FAVORITE-ANGER, PURITY-RAKE.

mo'-pus. A dreamer; drone; money; sad. ACTIVITY-INDOLENCE, FANCY, LIGHTHEARTEDNESS-DEJECTION, MONEY.

mo'-py. Dejected. LIGHTHEARTEDNESS-DEJECTION.

mora nec requies, nec [L.] (mo'-rɑ nec rî'-qui-îz, nec) Neither delay nor rest. ACTIVITY-INDOLENCE.

mor'-al. Pertaining to conduct in respect to right and wrong, virtue and vice, etc.; a maxim. ADAGE-NONSENSE, DECISION-MISJUDGMENT, DUTY-DERELICTION, RIGHT-WRONG, VIRTUE-VICE; **moral certainty,** CERTAINTY-DOUBT; **moral courage,** DETERMINATION-VACILLATION; **moral education,** EDUCATION-MISTEACHING; **moral obligation,** DUTY-DERELICTION; **moral support,** OBSTRUCTION-HELP; **moral tuition,** EDUCATION-MISTEACHING; **moral turpitude,** UPRIGHTNESS-DISHONESTY **point a moral,** EDUCATION-MISTEACHING.

mo-ral'-i-ty. Moral conduct. DUTY-DERELICTION, VIRTUE-VICE.

mor'-al-ize. To make moral reflections. EDUCATION-MISTEACHING, RATIOCINATION-INSTINCT.

mor'-al phil-os'-o-phy. Science of morals. DUTY-DERELICTION, MIND-IMBECILITY.

mor'-als. Conduct. DUTY-DERELICTION, RIGHT-WRONG, VIRTUE-VICE.

mo-rass'. Marsh. SWAMP-ISLAND.

Mo-ra'-vi-an-ism. The doctrines of the Moravians. ORTHODOXY-HETERODOXY.

mor'-bid. Sickly. HEALTH-SICKNESS.

mor-bid'-i-ty. Morbidness. HEALTH-SICKNESS.

mor-bid-os'-i-ty. Morbidness. HEALTH-SICKNESS.

mor-bif'-er-ous. Producing disease. HEALTHINESS-UNHEALTHINESS.

mor-bif'-ic. Productive of disease HEALTH-SICKNESS, HEALTHINESS-UNHEALTHINESS.

mor-da'-cious. Severe. CHARITABLENESS-MALEVOLENCE.

mor-dac'-i-ty. Biting severity CHARITABLENESS-MALEVOLENCE

mor'-dant. Biting; a substance for fixing dye. COLOR-ACHROMATISM, PUNGENCY, VIGOR-INERTIA.

more. Greater in amount, number, or rank. ADDITION-SUBTRACTION, SUPREMACY-SUBORDINACY; **more last words,** PREDECESSOR-CONTINUATION; **more or less,** MAGNITUDE - SMALLNESS, QUANTITY - MEASURE, TRUTH-ERROR; **more than a match for,** STRENGTH-WEAKNESS, SUPREMACY-SUBORDINACY; **more than enough,** EXCESS-LACK; **more than flesh and blood can bear,** PLEASURABLENESS-PAINFULNESS; **more than meets the eye,** MANIFESTATION-LATENCY **more than one,** PLURALITY-FRACTION.

more, ex [L.] (mo'-rî, ex). According to custom. HABIT-DESUETUDE.

more majorum [L.] (mo-rî mê-jo'-rum). After the manner of our ancestors. CONVENTIONALITY-UNCONVENTIONALITY.

more solito [L.] (mo'-rî sol'-i-to). An unusual custom. CONVENTIONALITY - UNCONVENTIONALITY, HABIT-DESUETUDE.

more suo [L.] (mo'-rî siu'-o) In his own way HABIT-DESUETUDE.

mores, O [L.] (mo'-rîz, o) O customs. APPROVAL-DISAPPROVAL.

more-o'-ver. Besides. ADDITION-SUBTRACTION.

Mo-resque'. Pertaining to the Moors. **Moresque architecture,** ARCHITECTURE.

Morgana, Fata [It.] (mor-gɑ'-nɑ, fɑ'-tɑ) Mirage. FANCY, LUMINARY-SHADE.

mor'-ga-nat'-ic mar'-riage. Marriage of a man of superior rank to a woman of inferior. MATRIMONY-CELIBACY.

morgue [F.] (morg). A deadhouse. LIFE-FUNERAL.

morgue littéraire [F.] (morg li-tê-rêr) Literary style. STYLE.

mori, dulce et decorum est pro patria [L.] (mo'-rɑi, dul'-sî et dî-co'-rum est pro pê'-tri-ɑ). It is sweet and seemly to die for one's fatherland. DUTY-DERELICTION, LIFE-DEATH.

mori, memento [L.] (mo'-rɑi, mî-men'-to) Remember death. LIFE-FUNERAL.

mor'-i-bund. Dying. HEALTH-SICKNESS, LIFE-DEATH.

mo'-ri-ent. Dying. LIFE-DEATH.

mo'-ri-on. A helmet. DRESS-UNDRESS.

Mo-ris'-co. A morris-dancer ENTERTAINMENT-WEARINESS.

mor'-mo [Gr.]. False terror. SANGUINENESS-TIMIDITY

Mor'-mon. One of a religious sect. ORTHODOXY-HETERODOXY.

Mor'-mon-ism. Polygamy, belief of the Mormons MATRIMONY-CELIBACY, ORTHODOXY-HETERODOXY

morn. Early part of the day. MORNING-EVENING.

morn'-ing. Early part of the day. EARLINESS-LATENESS, MORNING-EVENING; **morning dress,** DRESS-UNDRESS; **morning, noon, and night,** FREQUENCY-RARITY, LASTINGNESS - TRANSIENTNESS; **morning star,** ANGEL-SATAN

MORNING—EVENING

Aurora. The rising light of the morning.
Break of day. The first appearance of light in the morning.
Cock-crow. The early morning.
Crepuscule. The twilight between the first dawn and sunrise.
Dawn. The first appearance of light at the break of day
Daybreak. The dawn; the first light.
First blush of the morning. The first appearance of light.
Forenoon. That part of the day which is included between sunrise and midday.
Meridian. Noonday; that period of the day when the sun reaches its highest point.
Midday. The middle of the day.
Midsummer. The middle of the summer
Morn. } That part of the day included between dawn and noon
Morning. }

Afternoon. The period after noon and before sunset.
Autumn. The latter portion of the year; the time of abundance.
Autumnal equinox. The time when the sun crosses the equator going southward.
Bed-time. The time to go to bed.
Close of day. Evening.
Cock-shut. Evening twilight
Curfew. The time of extinguishing lights and retiring to rest
Dead of night. The most quiet time of night
Decline of day. The fall of day
Dewy eve. The time of day when dew falls. [Milton.]
Dusk. The state in the evening between light and darkness
Eleventh hour. The last hour of day
Eve. } That part of the day which precedes darkness.
Evening. }

MORNING—EVENING—*Continued*

Noon. The middle of the day. [L., *nona*, ninth hour.]
Noonday. Midday.
Noontide. The time of noon.
Peep of day. Dawn.
Prime of the morning. Early morning.
Spring. The early portion of the year.
Summer. The middle season of the year.
Sunrise. The appearance of the sun each morning.
Twilight. The period between dawn and sunrise.
Vernal equinox. The time when the sun crosses the equator when proceeding northward.

MORNING—*Adjectives.*

Matin. Pertaining to the morning.
Matutinal. Early; pertaining to the morning.
Vernal. Of or pertaining to spring; early.

MORNING—*Adverbs.*

At sunrise, etc. At dawn. See *Nouns.*
When the morning dawns.
With the lark. " Hark, hark! the lark at heaven's gate sings, and Phœbus 'gins arise." [Shakespeare, *Cymbeline*, II. iii.]

mo-rose'. Sullen; rude. FAVORITE-MOROSENESS, HUMANITARIANISM-MISANTHROPY, POLITENESS-IMPOLITENESS.
mo-ros'-i-ty. Sullenness. FAVORITE-MOROSENESS.
Mor'-pheus. Son of sleep and god of dreams. ACTIVITY-INDOLENCE.
mor'-phew. A scurfy eruption. CLEANNESS-FILTHINESS.
mor''-pho-log''-ic-al. Pertaining to morphology Morphological crystallography, MINERALOGY.
mor-phol'-o-gy. Any science of forms; science of form and structure of animals and plants. BIOLOGY, FORM-FORMLESSNESS, ZOOLOGY-BOTANY.
mor'-ra. A game. ENTERTAINMENT-WEARINESS.
mor'-ris, nine men's. A game. ENTERTAINMENT-WEARINESS.
mor'-ris-chair''. An easy-chair having loose cushions on back and seat. SUSPENSION-SUPPORT.
mor'-ris-dance''. A rustic dance. ENTERTAINMENT-WEARINESS.
mor'-row. First day after the present. FUTURE-PAST.
mors aux dents, prendre le [F.] (morz o dan', pran·dr le). To become headstrong. REPRISAL-RESISTANCE.
mor'-sel. A bit of food; bite. MAGNITUDE-SMALLNESS, NUTRIMENT-EXCRETION, WHOLE-PART.
mors turpi vita potior, honesta [L.] (mors tur'-pai vai'-ta po'-shi-or, ho-nes'-ta). Honorable death is better than base life. LIFE-DEATH, UPRIGHTNESS-DISHONESTY.
mort, guerre à [F.] (mor, gêr a). War to the death FIGHTING-CONCILIATION.
mor'-tal. Subject to death; fatal. ENTERTAINMENT-WEARINESS, HUMANITY, LASTINGNESS-TRANSIENTNESS, LIFE-KILLING; **mortal antipathy**, DESIRE-DISTASTE; **mortal blow**, GOOD-EVIL; **mortal coil**, LIFE-CORPSE; **mortal funk**, SANGUINENESS-TIMIDITY; **mortal remains**, LIFE-CORPSE; **mortal sin**, INNOCENCE-GUILT.
mor-tal'-i-ty. Quality of being mortal. HUMANITY, LASTINGNESS-TRANSIENTNESS, LIFE-DEATH; **bills of mortality**, LIFE-DEATH.
mor'-tar. Cement; pulverizer; cannon. CHEMISTRY, CONNECTIVE, FRIABILITY, WEAPONS.
mortem, post [L.] (mor'-tem, post) After death. LIFE-DEATH, LIFE-FUNERAL
mort'-gage. Sale; credit; to lend; pledge. BUYING-SALE, CREDIT-DEBT, LOAN-BORROWING, SECURITY.
mort''-ga-gee'. The grantee under a mortgage. CREDIT-DEBT, HOLDER.

mort'-ga-gor. One who mortgages property. CREDIT-DEBT, HOLDER.
mor-tif'-er-ous. Fatal. LIFE-KILLING.
mor''-ti-fi-ca'-tion. Austerity; humiliation; gangrene; vexation. AUSTERITY, CONTENTEDNESS-DISCONTENTMENT, HEALTH-SICKNESS, PLEASURABLENESS-PAINFULNESS, PLEASURE-PAIN, SELFRESPECT-HUMBLENESS
mor'-ti-fy. Humiliate. CONTENTEDNESS-DISCONTENTMENT, PLEASURABLENESS-PAINFULNESS.
mor'-ti-fy''-ing. Humiliating. CONTENTEDNESS-DISCONTENTMENT.
mor'-tise. To join; intersect: a cavity in a piece of timber. CROSSING, ENVIRONMENT-INTERPOSITION, UNION-DISUNION.
mort'-main''. Tenure of land. LIBERTY-SUBJECTION; **in mortmain**, KEEPING-RELINQUISHMENT.
mor'-tu-a-ry. Relating .to the burial of the dead. LIFE-DEATH, LIFE-FUNERAL.
mo-sa'-ic. A kind of inlaid work. MIXTURE-HOMOGENEITY, PAINTING, UNIFORMITY-MULTIFORMITY, VARIEGATION.
Mos'-lem. Mohammedan. ORTHODOXY-HETERODOXY.
mosque. A Mohammedan temple. FANE.
moss. A low tufted plant; a bog. SMOOTHNESS-ROUGHNESS, SWAMP-ISLAND, ZOOLOGY-BOTANY.
moss'-grown''. Overgrown with moss. BETTERMENT-DETERIORATION
moss'-troop''-er. A border marauder. BELLIGERENT, TROOPER.
moss-y. Overgrown with moss. FAUNA-FLORA.
most. Greatest amount or number. MAGNITUDE-SMALLNESS; **at most**, MAGNITUDE-SMALLNESS; **for the most part**, HABIT-DESUETUDE, UNIVERSALITY-PARTICULARITY; **make the most of**, BETTERMENT-DETERIORATION, GULL-HYPERBOLE, OVERVALUATION-UNDERVALUATION, SKILL-UNSKILFULNESS, USE-DISUSE; **make the most of one's time**, ACTIVITY-INDOLENCE; **most often**, FREQUENCY-RARITY, HABIT-DESUETUDE; **the most**, SUPREMACY-SUBORDINACY.
mot [F.] (mo). A pithy or witty saying. ADAGE-NONSENSE.
mot à mot [F.] (mot a mo). Word for word. IMITATION-ORIGINALITY.
mot d'énigme [F.] (mo dê-nigm'). The answer to a riddle. INTERPRETATION-MISINTERPRETATION.
mot de passe [F.] (mo de pas) A password. SIGN.
mot d'ordre [F.] (mo dordr) A command. ORDER.
mot du guet [F.] (mo dü ge) A watchword. SIGN.

Eventide. The time of evening.
Fall. The season when leaves fall from the trees; the latter portion of the year.
Fall of day. The close of day.
Fall of the leaf. Autumn; the declining time.
Going down of the sun. Approach of evening.
Midnight. The middle of the night.
Nightfall. The coming of night.
Postmeridian. The afternoon.
Sundown. Evening; the setting of the sun.
Sunset. The daily disappearance of the sun.
Twilight. The period between sunset and darkness.
Winter. The season of cold and short days.
Witching time of night. The time of most witches. [*Hamlet*, III. ii.]

EVENING—*Adjectives.*

Autumnal. Pertaining to autumn.
Nocturnal. Pertaining to the night.
Vespertine. Pertaining to the evening.

MORNING—*Continued.*

MORNING—*Phrase.*

Entre chien et loup [F.]. Between dog and wolf.

mot pour rire [F.] (mo pur rir). A witticism WITTI
NESS-DULNESS.

mote. A match; speck. HEAVINESS-LIGHTNESS,
MAGNITUDE-SMALLNESS; **mote in the eye,** DECISION-
MISJUDGMENT, SIGHT-DIMSIGHTEDNESS.

mo-tet'. A sacred cantata. DEVOTION-IDOLATRY.

moth. An insect that destroys woolen fabrics.
REMEDY-BANE.

moth'-eat''-en. Eaten or damaged by moths. BET-
TERMENT-DETERIORATION, CLEANNESS-FILTHINESS.

moth'-er. Mold; a female parent: native. CLEAN-
NESS-FILTHINESS, PARENTAGE-PROGENY; **mother-
of-pearl,** VARIEGATION; **mother tongue,** LANGUAGE;
mother wit, SAGACITY-INCAPACITY.

moth'-er-hood''. State of being a mother. PARENT-
AGE-PROGENY

moth'-er-land''. The land of one's ancestors.
DWELLER-HABITATION.

moth'-er-ly. Pertaining to a mother. CHARITABLE-
NESS-MALEVOLENCE, LOVE-HATE.

mo'-tion. Movement; design; proposition; topic.
CONCEPTION-THEME, DESIGN, MOVEMENT-REST,
PETITION-EXPOSTULATION, PRESIDENT-MEMBER,
PROFFER-REFUSAL; **make a motion,** HYPOTHESIS,
PROFFER-REFUSAL; **motion downwards,** ASCENT-
DESCENT; **motion from,** APPROACH-WITHDRAWAL,
put in motion, PUSH-PULL; **put oneself in motion,**
ACTION-PASSIVENESS; **set in motion,** USE-DISUSE.

mo'-tion-less. Being at rest. ACTIVITY-INDOLENCE,
MOVEMENT-REST.

mo'-tive. Incentive; moving. MOTIVE-CAPRICE,
absence of motive, MOTIVE-CAPRICE; **motive power,**
MOVEMENT-REST.

MOTIVE—CAPRICE—DEHORTATION.

Advice, etc. Influence toward the acceptance or rejecting of an act or course. See ADVICE.

Advocacy. The act of exerting one's influence in favor of a cause.

Agacerie [F.]. Caressing treatment; enticement.

Allectation. } An allurement.
Allective. }

Allurement. An attracting or tempting influence.

Arrière pensée [F.]. An afterthought.

Attractability. } Susceptibility to attraction
Attractiveness. }

Attraction. An influencing of the mind and affecting favorably.

Bait. Anything which allures or tempts.

Bewitchment. The state of being under the influence of charms.

Blandishment. A soothing or caressing influence.

Bribe. A reward or gift given with a view to pervert the judgment.

Bribery and corruption. The act of influencing the action of another by corrupt inducements.

Cajolery. The act of influencing by flattering or delusive promises.

Call. An influence to do something, as a call to the ministry.

Charm. The power of pleasing.

Consideration. An influence to be taken into account before doing a thing.

Decoy. Anything intended to lead into a snare.

Decoy duck. A duck used to lure wild ducks into a decoy; hence, a person used to lure others into danger.

Dictate. An authoritative command.

Dram. A drink offered as an enticement.

Encouragement. A hopeful or cheering influence.

Enticement. An influence tending to draw toward evil by tempting the desires of a person.

Exhortation. An incitement to do good by means of an earnest appeal.

Fascination. An influence that attracts irresistibly

Fillip. Something serving to arouse or excite.

Forbidden fruit. Any coveted, unlawful pleasure [Bible.]

Goad. Any necessity that urges or stimulates.

Golden apples. Apples in the garden of Hesperus; figuratively, coveted pleasure or desire.

Ground. A reason; primary influence

Honeyed words.

Hortation. An exhortation.

Impressibility. The state of being easily influenced.

Impulse. A sudden mental influence or motive.

Impulsion. A strong, sudden mental impulse.

Incentive. An influence which tends to produce an action.

Incitation. } An impulsion toward a particular action.
Incitement. }

Inducement. An influence that leads toward the doing of an act

Influence. The gradual operation of some unseen cause.

Inspiration. The inbreathing of an influence, usually divine or lofty

Instance. The act of influencing or soliciting.

Instigation. Influence brought to bear to produce an action, usually bad.

Intention, etc. A settled design of the mind toward some aim or end. See PURPOSE.

Keystone. The topmost stone of an arch; figuratively, the object of striving.

Loadstone. A piece of magnetic iron ore possessing polarity like a magnetic needle.

Lure. Anything which tends to influence by means of prospective pleasure.

Absence of motive. Want of reason or cause.

Caprice, etc. A sudden change of mind without reason or cause.

Chance, etc. Absence of law or adequate cause. See PURPOSE.

CAPRICE—*Verbs.*

Have no motive. To be without any reason or cause.

Scruple, etc. To be unwilling; have moral grounds for not doing See READINESS.

CAPRICE—*Adjectives*

Aimless, etc. Without any definite design or intention. See PURPOSE.

Without rime or reason. Without sound or sense.

CAPRICE—*Adverb.*

Out of mere caprice. Capriciously.

MOTIVE—*Continued.*

Magnet. A species of iron ore which has the property of attracting iron.

Magnetic force. Extraordinary personal power to excite the feelings and win the affections.

Magnetism. The power to excite the feelings and gain the affections.

Mainspring. The chief or most powerful motive.

Motive. That influence in the mind which incites it to action.

Persuasibility. The capability of being persuaded or influenced.

Persuasibleness. The quality of being capable to be influenced.

Persuasion. The act of influencing by means of entreaty or reasoning.

Persuasiveness. The power of having influence on other minds

Press. Strong influence brought to bear upon.

Primum mobile [L.]. The first cause of an action.

Principle. The fundamental influence which causes action, an impulse.

Pro and con. For and against.

Prompting. An influence exciting a person to action.

Provocation, etc. An incitation to action. See EXCITATION.

Provocative. That which excites to action.

Reason. The primary motive or cause of a thing

Reason why. The grounds for acting.

Rowel. A spur.

Secret motive. A motive not known from the general actions.

Seducement. The act of influencing so as to draw from duty.

Seduction. The act of enticing to evil.

Softness. The state of being easily influenced.

Solicitation. To ask by entreaty.

Song of the sirens. Anything deceptive or enticing.

Sop. Anything given to propitiate.

Sop for Cerberus. A gift or favor given to pacify an opponent: in allusion to the sop said to have been given to Cerberus on one's entrance to Hades. [Virgil, *Æneid*, VI, 417.]

Spell, etc. The state of being under the influence of magic. See DEVOTION-CHARM.

Springs of action. Cause or motive

Spur. That which goads to action.

Stimulus. Anything which rouses the feelings.

Suasion. The act of persuading.

Susceptibility. The state of being easily influenced.

Tantalization. The act of vexing or provoking, as Tantalus was tantalized in Hades.

MOTIVE—*Continued*

Temptation. The act of influencing for evil.
The why and the wherefore. The reason for a particular course of action.
Trail of a red herring. A clue or series of clues
Voice of the tempter. A temptation.

Whet. That which stimulates.
Whip. An instrument for driving horses.
Witchery. Irresistible influence.
Witching. The act of enchanting.

MOTIVE—*Nouns of Agent*

Circe. A mythological enchantress, who first charmed her victims and then changed them to beasts.
Firebrand. One who inflames factions or causes mischief
Incendiary. One who kindles passion.
Instigator One who incites another to do anything.

Prompter. One who influences to action.
Seducer. }
Seductor. } One who seduces or leads to wrong
Tempter. One who incites to an evil or forbidden action.

MOTIVE—*Verbs.*

Act on principle. To do anything honorably.
Actuate. To incite or impel as by motives.
Act upon. To influence.
Advise, etc. To give counsel to. See ADVICE.
Advocate. To be in favor of, exert one's influence for anything.
Allure. To draw by means of some prospective pleasure.
Animate. To make active, use one's influence in such a manner
Arouse. To stir up; excite
Attract. To draw toward.
Bait the hook. To lure.
Bait with a silver hook. To make very tempting with a bribe.
Beckon. To call toward with a gesture.
Be persuaded, etc. To listen to the advice of another.
Bewitch. To gain power over by means of charms; to please very much.
Bias. To influence in one direction.
Bribe. To offer anything to draw a person from his duty
Bring in its train. To attract.
Bring round. To influence so as to bring to a desired position.
Bring to one's senses. To cause a person to become reasonable.
Cajole, etc. To impose on by flattering. See TRUTHFULNESS-FRAUD.
Call up. To remind
Call upon. To request something of a person.
Captivate. To capture; seize
Carry. To win or succeed.
Carry away. To incite to a state of great feeling or passion.
Charm. To put an influence over by means of some supernatural power some incantation, or rhythmic spell.
Clap on the back. }
Clap on the shoulder. } To give a sign of approval or encouragement.
Coax. To persuade by means of flattery or caresses.
Come over. To change opinions or position.
Come round one. To change one's opinions or position.
Concede, etc To grant; acknowledge as true. See CONSENT.
Conciliate. To settle or pacify
Court. To seek favor.
Dispose. To influence toward some particular purpose.
Drag, etc. To draw along by force See PUSH.
Draw. To attract; have an attractive influence.
Draw on. }
Draw over. } To persuade
Egg on. To urge on; incite
Encourage. To inspire with hope.
Enforce. To compel obedience.
Engage. To attract; please; win over.
Enlist. To gain the favor or interest of.
Entice. To attract or draw towards evil by influencing the desires or hopes
Exercise influence over. }
Exercise influence upon. } To have power with.
Exercise influence with. }
Exhort. To entreat earnestly.
Fascinate. To attract greatly; bewitch; have great influence over
Follow the advice of. To act upon the counsel of the wise.
Follow the bent of. To act according to your nature.
Follow the dictates of. To obey the imperative of conscience.
Force. To necessitate by means of mental power or influence; compel.
Gain over. To win over.
Gild the pill. To make something disagreeable more attractive
Give an impulse to, etc. See *Nouns.*
Goad. To urge on; impel; drive on.
Go round one. To find out one's feelings or the like.
Grease the palm. To corrupt with bribes.
Have influence over. To induce your friends to act.
Have influence upon. To move others to act.

Have influence with. To have a pull with officials.
Hound on. To urge or spur on.
Hurry on. To cause to hasten.
Impel, etc. To drive on, as by force. See IMPETUS
Incite. To move to action.
Incline. To have some tendency toward
Induce. To influence toward an action.
Influence. To act upon by means of moral suasion
Inoculate. To propagate; infest; imbue.
Inspire. To fill with high and noble thoughts.
Inspirit. To enliven; encourage.
Instigate. To incite to an evil action.
Inveigle. To lead astray by means of flattery or deception.
Invite. To allure.
Keep in countenance. To countenance a person by acting like him.
Lash. To drive on as with a whip
Lead. To allure or induce.
Lead by the nose. To lead easily or blindly.
Lure. To entice or attract by the promise of pleasure.
Magnetize. To influence by means of one's personality; hypnotize
Make things pleasant. Give attraction to things
Move. To arouse the feelings or passions.
Obey a call. To comply with a summons.
Operate upon. To have effect upon.
Overcome. To obtain mastery over.
Overpersuade. To influence against one's inclination or opinion.
Pat on the back. } To prove one's sense of your great merit.
Pat on the shoulder. } [Cowper, *On Friendship.*]
Persuade. To succeed in winning over by means of argument or entreaty.
Predispose. To incline beforehand.
Press, etc. To compel by moral force See PETITION.
Prevail upon. }
Prevail with. } To persuade.
Prick. To urge on to action, as by a prick or goad.
Procure. To cause or effect; bring about.
Prompt. To move to action, as another person.
Propel, etc. To force onward. See PUSH
Provoke. To rouse to activity.
Put a sop in the pan. To put a bit of choice food in the pan.
Put up to. To instigate toward an action.
Seduce. To lead astray or toward some wrong action.
Set an example. To determine a precedent.
Set on. To incite; impel.
Set the fashion. To determine what the fashion shall be.
Spirit up. To excite to action; encourage.
Spur. To urge or drive on.
Stimulate, etc. To rouse to greater activity; animate See EXCITATION.
Suborn. To instigate or urge toward an evil act
Sway. To have control over; influence easily, as passions of the people
Talk over. To persuade; convince; win over
Tamper with. To interfere with, fraudulently
Tantalize. To irritate or annoy.
Tempt. To endeavor or attempt to lead toward a wrong action
Throw a sop to. To attempt to pacify.
Turn the head. To turn and face in the opposite direction.
Turn the scales. To settle; determine.
Urge. To impel either by force or argument
Weigh with. To have influence with.
Wheedle. To persuade by means of coaxing or flattering words.
Whip. To urge or drive on.
Win over. To gain over, as to a different position or opinion.
Work upon. To exert influence over.
Yield to temptation. To give in to allurements.

MOTIVE—*Continued*.
MOTIVE—*Adjectives*.

Attractive. Possessing the power to allure or win over; pleasing.
Disposed. Inclined toward.
Fascinating, etc. Charming, enchanting; very pleasing. See PLEASURABLENESS.
Hortative. } Inciting; encouraging.
Hortatory. }
Impulsive. Moved by feeling rather than reflection.
Induced, etc. Influenced as by persuasion to do some act. See *Verbs*.
Inspired by. Stimulated; influenced.
Instinct with. Animated with; imbued with.
Inviting. Pleasing; attractive.

Motive. Having the power to incite to action.
Persuadable, etc. Open to influence or persuasion. See READINESS.
Persuasive. Having the power to persuade or influence.
Protreptical. Hortatory.
Provocative, etc. Having the power to incite or influence. See EXCITATION.
Seductive. Having the power to seduce or lead astray.
Smitten with. Overcome with; very much attracted by.
Spellbound. Influenced or fascinated, as by a magic charm.
Suasive. Persuasive.
Tempting, etc. Attractive; seductive. See *Verbs*

MOTIVE—*Adverbs*.

As. Since; because.
Because. On account of; by reason of.
By reason of. On account of.
For. Because; by reason of.
For all the world.
Forasmuch as. Considering that.
For that reason. Therefore.
For the sake of. On account of affectionate interest felt for a person or thing.

For this reason. Wherefore.
From. Away; forth; hence.
From that motive. From that desire.
From this motive. From this desire.
On account of. For the sake or reason of.
On principle. In accordance with integrity.
On the score of. On account of.
Out of. From that source.
Therefore, etc. For that reason. See RATIONALE.

MOTIVE—*Phrase*.

Fax mentis, incendium 'gloriæ [L.]. A burning desire for glory is a torch to the mind.

MOTIVE—DEHORTATION.

DEHORTATION.

Check. Whatever arrests progress or limits action. See OBSTRUCTION.
Cohibition, etc. Hindrance; restraint. See RELEASE.
Contraindication. The act of doing anything in a manner opposite to what is usual or expected.
Curb. That which restrains or subdues.
Damper. That which checks or discourages.
Dehortation. Advice or counsel against anything.
Deprecation, etc. The act of pleading earnestly against. See PETITION.
Discouragement. The act of depressing the spirits of, or deterring.
Dissuasion. The act of advising or arguing against anything.
Expostulation. The act of reasoning earnestly with a person to convince him of an error in his course.
Reluctance, etc. The act of being unwilling to yield. See READINESS.
Remonstrance. The act of urging reasons against an action or course.
Wet blanket. Anything which dispirits or discourages

DEHORTATION—*Verbs*.

Act as a drag, etc. To restrain. See OBSTRUCTION.
Blunt. To repress, as a desire.
Calm. To soothe; make tranquil.
Chill. To check the enthusiasm of.
Contraindicate. To act contrary to the usual or expected course.
Cool. To lose the heat of excitement or passion.
Cry out against. To oppose.
Damp. To discourage; dishearten.
Decline. To depress; deviate from rectitude.
Dehort. To urge against.
Deter. To restrain by means of some counteracting motive.
Discourage. To depress; dishearten.
Disenchant. To take away a charm, disillusion.

Dishearten. To take away courage or cheer.
Disincline. To excite a slight aversion to.
Dispirit. To discourage; take away the spirit.
Dissuade. To argue or advise against anything.
Expostulate. To earnestly argue with a person in order to deter him from some act.
Hold back. To restrain; hold in check.
Indispose. To render adverse.
Keep back, etc. To hold in restraint. See RELEASE.
Quench. To cause to end or cease.
Quiet. To bring to rest; calm.
Remonstrate. To present and urge reasons in opposition.
Render adverse, etc. To make opposed to. See READINESS
Repel. To drive from.
Shake. To make infirm or unsteady, as a resolution.
Stagger. To cause a person to give way.
Throw cold water on. To discourage; dishearten.
Turn aside, etc. To deviate. See AIM.
Warn. To make aware or give notice of some danger.
Wean from. To estrange, as from former habits.

DEHORTATION—*Adjectives*.

Averse, etc. Turned away or aside in mind. See READINESS.
Dehortatory. Arguing or advising against.
Dissuaded, etc. Advising or attempting to change from some course or action. See *Verbs*.
Dissuading, etc. Arguing against. See *Verbs*.
Dissuasive. Tending to dissuade.
Expostulary. Arguing earnestly to convince a person of an error.
Monitive. } Advising; giving friendly counsel.
Monitory. }
Repugnant, etc. Repulsive to the feelings or taste. See DESIRE.
Uninduced, etc. Not to be influenced. See INFLUENCE.
Unpersuadable, etc. Not to be persuaded; obstinate. See BIGOTRY.

mot'-ley. Variegated in color. MIXTURE-HOMOGENEITY, UNIFORM-MULTIFORM, VARIEGATION; **wearer of the motley,** WAG.
mo'-tor. Machine. ELECTRICITY.
mo'-to-ry. Causing motion. MOVEMENT-REST.
mots, flux de [F.] (mo, flü de). Too much talk. LOQUACITY-TACITURNITY.
mot'-tled. Variegated. VARIEGATION.
mot'-to. Maxim; rule of conduct. ADAGE-NONSENSE, PHRASE, SIGN.
motu, ex mero [L.] (mo'-tiu, ex mi'-ro). Of his own accord. RULE-LICENSE.

motu suo [L.] (mo'-tiu siu'-o). Of his own accord. VOLITION-OBLIGATION.
mou-chard'. A French police spy. ENLIGHTENMENT-SECRECY.
mould. Earthy material; that of which anything is made; a fungous growth; cast; matrix; to fashion; to make the most of. CLEANNESS-FILTHINESS, CONDITION-SITUATION, CONVERSION-REVERSION, COPY-MODEL, DELINEATION-CARICATURE, FORM-FORMLESSNESS, OCEAN-LAND, SCULPTURE, TEXTURE, USE-MISUSE, ZOOLOGY-BOTANY. See MOLD.

mould'-ed. Fashioned. AFFECTIONS; **moulded on,** IMITATION-ORIGINALITY. See MOLDED.

mould'-er. To decay; deteriorate. BETTERMENT-DETERIORATION, CLEANNESS-FILTHINESS. See MOLDER.

mould'-ing. Narrow surface used for decorating. EMBELLISHMENT-DISFIGUREMENT. See MOLDING.

mould'-y. Overgrown with mold. BETTERMENT-DETERIORATION, CLEANNESS-FILTHINESS. See MOLDY.

moulin à paroles [F.] (mu-lan'' a pa-rol'). A chatterbox. TALKATIVENESS-TACITURNITY.

mouline se battre contre des [F.] (mu-lîn' se batr con'tr dê). To fight against the bugbears. USEFULNESS-USELESSNESS.

moult. To shed. DRESS-UNDRESS. See MOLT.

moult'-ing. Shedding the skin or feathers. DRESS-UNDRESS. See MOLTING.

mound. A defense; a hill. ATTACK-DEFENSE, GREATNESS-LITTLENESS, HEIGHT-LOWNESS.

mount. To ascend; hill; display. ASCENT-DESCENT, ELEVATION-DEPRESSION, HEIGHT-LOWNESS, POMP; **mount guard,** CAREFULNESS-CARELESSNESS, SECURITY-INSECURITY; **mount up,** MONEY, PRICE-DISCOUNT.

moun'-tain. A high elevation; something of great magnitude. GREATNESS-LITTLENESS, HEAVINESS-LIGHTNESS, HEIGHT-LOWNESS; **make mountains of molehills,** OVERVALUATION-UNDERVALUATION; **mountain brought forth mouse,** PREVISION-DISAPPOINTMENT; **mountain in labor,** PROVISION-WASTE; **mountain range,** GEOLOGY.

moun''-tain-eer'. One who climbs mountains. WAYFARER-SEAFARER.

moun'-tain-ous. Resembling a mountain. HEIGHT-LOWNESS.

mount'-e-bank. A vendor of quack medicines; a charlatan. ACTING, GULL-DECEIVER, WAG.

mounted rifles. Rifles fixed in a setting. WEAPON.

mourn. To lament; to grieve. JUBILATION-LAMENTATION, LIGHTHEARTEDNESS-DEJECTION, PLEASURE-PAIN.

mourn'-ful. Lamentable; sad; afflicting. JUBILATION-LAMENTATION, LIGHTHEARTEDNESS - DEJECTION, PLEASURABLENESS-PAINFULNESS.

mourn'-ing. Dress manifesting grief. DRESS-UNDRESS, JUBILATION-LAMENTATION **in mourning,** JUBILATION-LAMENTATION, WHITENESS-BLACKNESS.

mouse. A small animal; to prowl about. GREATNESS-LITTLENESS, INVESTIGATION; **mountain brought forth mouse,** EXPECTATION-DISAPPOINTMENT; **not a mouse stirring,** MOVEMENT-REST.

mouse'-col''-ored. Of a grayish color. GRAY-BROWN.

mouse'-hole''. A hole made by a mouse. APERTURE-CLOSURE.

mouse'-trap''. A deceitful device. TRUTHFULNESS-FRAUD.

mousseux [F.] (mu-su'). Foaming. VISCIDITY-FOAM.

mouth. An opening; receptacle; estuary; eat; to enunciate; to drawl. APERTURE-CLOSURE, BEGINNING-END, BORDER, CONTENTS-RECEIVER, ENTRANCE-EXIT, GULF-PLAIN, NUTRIMENT-EXCRETION, SPEECH-INARTICULATENESS, VOCALIZATION-MUTENESS; **deep-mouthed,** CRY - ULULATION, RESONANCE - NONRESONANCE; **down in the mouth,** SELFRESPECT-HUMBLENESS; **make mouths,** REGARD-DISRESPECT; **mouth honor,** ADULATION-DISPARAGEMENT, POMP, TRUTHFULNESS - FALSEHOOD, UPRIGHTNESS - DISHONESTY; **mouth watering,** DESIRE-DISTASTE; **open one's mouth,** SPEECH-INARTICULATENESS; **pass from mouth to mouth,** PUBLICITY; **stop one's mouth,** VOCALIZATION-MUTENESS; **word of mouth,** SPEECH-INARTICULATENESS.

mouth'-ful. As much as the mouth will hold; a small quantity. MAGNITUDE-SMALLNESS, NUTRIMENT-EXCRETION, QUANTITY-MEASURE.

mouth'-piece''. A spokesman. ENLIGHTENMENT-SECRECY, INTERPRETER, MESSENGER, SPEECH-INARTICULATENESS.

mouth'-y. Verbose. SIMPLICITY-FLORIDNESS.

moutonné [F.] (mu-to-nê'). Curled. CONVEXITY-CONCAVITY.

moutons, revenons à nos [F.] (mu-ton'', re-ve-non'' a no). Let us return to our subject. RENOVATION-RELAPSE.

mov'-a-ble. That may be moved. MOVEMENT-REST, TRANSFER.

mov'-a-bles. Personal property. PROPERTY.

move. To change place; incite; begin; propose; a movement. ACTION-PASSIVENESS, BEGINNING-END, ENTERPRISE, EXCITATION, HYPOTHESIS, MOTIVE-CAPRICE, MOVEMENT-REST, PROFFER-REFUSAL; **good move,** DESIGN; **move forward,** ADVANCE-RETROGRESSION; **move from,** APPROACH-WITHDRAWAL; **move heaven and earth,** TOIL-RELAXATION; **move in a groove,** CONVENTIONALITY-UNCONVENTIONALITY; **move off,** APPROACH-WITHDRAWAL, ARRIVAL-DEPARTURE; **move on,** ACTIVITY-INDOLENCE, ADVANCE-RETROGRESSION; **move out of,** ENTRANCE-EXIT; **move quickly,** SWIFTNESS-SLOWNESS; **move slowly,** ACTIVITY-INDOLENCE, HURRY-LEISURE, SWIFTNESS-SLOWNESS; **move to,** POLITENESS-IMPOLITENESS; **on the move,** ARRIVAL-DEPARTURE.

moved with. Influenced by. EMOTION.

move'-less. Motionless. MOVEMENT-REST.

move'-ment. Act of moving; rhythmical procession of a piece. ACTION-PASSIVENESS, ACTIVITY-INDOLENCE, MOVEMENT-REST, MUSIC.

MOVEMENT—REST.

Angular velocity. The rate of revolution around a fixed axis.

Cadence. The act or state of declining or sinking.

Carriage. The act of transporting or conveying.

Course. Motion considered with reference to manner.

Evolution. A prescribed movement of a body of troops, or of a vessel or fleet.

Flow. To glide along smoothly.

Flux. A continuous moving on or passing by.

Footfall. A footstep.

Gait. Manner of walking or stepping.

Going, etc. Movement from place to place. See *Verbs.*

Journey, etc. See TRAVELING.

Kinematics. That branch of mechanics which treats of motion without reference to the forces which produce it.

Laws of motion. Regular modes of the action of force, as of gravitation.

Locomotion. The act of moving from place to place.

Mobility. State of flowing with great ease.

Mobilization. Act of putting into readiness for active service.

Motion. Successive change of place or position.

Motive power. A natural agent used to impart motion.

Calm. } A state of perfect repose.
Dead calm. }

Deadlock. A block or stoppage of business.

Dead stand. } Complete cessation from progress or motion.
Dead stop. }

Fix. A position from which it is difficult to extricate oneself.

Fixity. The state of being fixed.

Full stop. Complete cessation of motion.

Immobility. State of being immovable.

Indisturbance. Calmness or repose.

Lock. A fixed and immovable position.

Lull, etc. A momentary stoppage. See DISCONTINUANCE.

Not a breath stirring. } Perfect quiet or calmness.
Not a mouse stirring. }

Pause. A momentary state of repose.

Peace. A state of quiet or tranquillity.

Quiescence. The state of being at rest.

Quiet. Freedom from motion.

Quietism. The practise of striving after undisturbable tranquillity of mind.

Repose, etc. State of being at rest. See TOIL-RELAXATION.

MOVEMENT—REST—*Continued.*

Movableness. Quality or state of being movable.
Move. The act of moving from one position to another.
Movement. Change of place or posture.
Pace. A single movement from one foot to another in walking
Port. The manner in which a person bears himself.
Progress. A moving or going forward.
Rate. Degree of movement.
Restlessness, etc. State of being unsettled. See MUTABILITY.
Run. Continued movement.
Step. An advance or movement made by one removal of the foot.
Stir. Various movements.
Stream. A continued course.
Stride. The act of passing over with long steps.
Transit, etc. The act of passing from one place to another. See IMPETUS.
Unrest. Want of rest or repose.
Velocity. Quickness of motion.
Voyage. A passage from one place to another by water. See TRAVELING.

MOVEMENT—*Verbs*

Be in motion, etc. To be in a state of successive change of place or position. See *Adjectives.*
Budge. To move; change place or position.
Change one's place. Take a new position.
Change one's quarters. Take a new lodging.
Dodge. To evade by moving quickly to one side.
Drift. To move slowly; float, as in a current.
Flit. To move lightly, as a bird.
Flow. To move smoothly; glide.
Gang. To go.
Glide. To move smoothly and without noise.
Go. To change position by moving from one place to another.
Hie. To move in haste.
Hover about. } To move about or around slowly and lingeringly.
Hover around. }
Impel. To drive forward.
Keep going. Go on.
Keep moving. Move on.
Mobilize. To get into a state of readiness for immediate action.
Move. To change place or position.
Pass. To move in space.
Propel, etc. To cause to move. See PUSH.
Put in motion. Start up.
Render movable. To make movable.
Roll. To move by turning around.
Roll on. To move forward.
Run. To move swiftly on the feet.
Set in motion. Start up.
Shift. To move from place to place.
Shift one's place. Take a new place.
Shift one's quarters. Take new lodgings.
Slide. To move with a gliding, slipping motion.
Stir. To move.
Stream. To move like flowing water.
Sweep along. To carry along with a strong, steady motion.
Walk, etc. To move with steps. See TRAVELING.
Wander, etc. To journey. See AIM.

MOVEMENT—*Adjectives.*

Erratic, etc. Wandering. See AIM.
In motion. Moving; changing position.
Mercurial. Quickly moving or changing, like mercury.
Mobile. Moving; changing.
Motive. Possessing the power to move.
Motory. Having the power to produce motion.
Movable. Possessing the power to move.
Moving, etc. Changing position. See *Verbs.*
Nomadic, etc. Wandering from one place to another. See TRAVELING.
Restless, etc. In a state of motion. See MUTABILITY.
Shifting. Going from place to place.
Transitional. Moving from one place or state to another.
Unquiet. Restless.

MOVEMENT—*Adverbs, etc.*

On the march. }
On the move. }
On the tramp. } Moving from place to place.
On the wing. }
Under way. }

Rest. The act or state of being free from all exertion or motion.
Silence, etc. State of being free from motion or activity. See SOUND-SILENCE.
Sleep, etc. Complete rest or repose. See ACTIVITY-INDOLENCE.
Stagnancy. A standing still.
Stagnation. State of being still.
Stand. State of being inactive or at rest.
Standing still. State of being at rest.
Standstill. A complete pause.
Statue-like repose. Perfect rest.
Stillness, etc. State of being silent or at rest. See *Adjectives.*
Tranquillity. Freedom from disturbing influences.

REST—*Denotations.*

Bivouac. A temporary encampment of soldiers without tents.
Catalepsy. A sudden suspension of consciousness and obstinate muscular rigidity.
Embargo. A prohibition by a government restraining vessels from leaving its ports.
Goal, etc. The objective point or terminus that one is striving to reach. See ARRIVAL.
Haven, etc. A place of anchorage for ships. See REFUGE.
Home, etc. One's fixed place of abode. See DWELLER-HABITATION.
Pillow, etc. A case stuffed with feathers, used as a support when one is reclining or sleeping. See SUSPENSION-SUPPORT.

REST—*Verbs.*

Abide. To remain at rest or continue in a place or condition.
Alight, etc. To come to rest upon. See ARRIVAL
Anchor. To make secure or abiding.
Be at a stand, etc. See *Nouns.*
Becalm. To make quiet or calm.
Be quiescent, etc. To be in a state of rest. See *Adjectives.*
Bring to. To cause a ship to become nearly stationary.
Cast anchor. To throw anchor.
Come to an anchor. Bring to anchor.
Draw up. To set in array.
Dwell, etc. To pause. See PRESENCE.
Go to bed. To retire.
Halt. To stop; stand still.
Heave to. To be almost at a standstill.
Hold. To remain firm or unchanged.
Hold the breath. To remain very still.
Hush. To make quiet.
Keep quiet. To remain still.
Keep within doors. Stay in the house.
Lay an embargo on. To forbid foreign commerce.
Lay to. To come to a stop.
Let alone. To have nothing to do with.
Let well enough alone. To leave untouched what is doing well enough.
Lie still. To remain quiet while lying.
Lie to. To bring a ship to an almost stationary state.
Lull to sleep. To soothe to rest.
Mark time. To go through the movements of walking without advancing.
Not stir a peg. } To stand very still.
Not stir a step. }
Pause. To rest momentarily.
Pull up. To stop.
Quell. To cause to make quiet.
Quieta non movere [L.]. Quiet not to move.
Remain. To continue in one place.
Remain *in situ.* To remain in its natural position.
Repose. To be free from all toil and exertion.
Repose on one's laurels. To be satisfied with one's distinctions and not try for more.
Rest. To cease in activity, to be without motion.
Rest and be thankful. Be quiet and give thanks.
Rest on one's oars. To hold a boat stationary.
Ride at anchor. To float while fastened with an anchor.
Settle, etc. To come to a state of rest. See ESTABLISHMENT.
Stagnate. To become inactive.
Stand. To rest on the feet while in an erect position.
Stand like a post. To stand very still and stiff.
Stand still. Halt.
Stay. To remain in one place.
Stay at home. Remain at home.
Stick. To be attached to.
Stick fast. To be firmly attached to.
Stop, etc. To come to rest or cease from motion. See DISCONTINUANCE.

MOVEMENT—REST—Continued.

Movement—Phrases.

Eppur si muove [It.]. Yet it [the earth] does move. [Galileo.]
Es bildet ein Talent sich in der stille, sich ein Charakter in dem Strom der Welt [G.]. Talent is built up in quiet, character in the stream of the world.

REST—Adjectives—Continued from Column 2.

Still. Silent, without motion.
Still as a mouse.
Still as a post.
Still as a statue.
Still as death.
Stock still. Entirely motionless.
Undisturbed. Without agitation.
Unmoved. Not to be moved; still.
Unruffled. Not discomposed or agitated.
Untraveled. Not passed over.

REST—Adverbs.

At a stand, etc. See *Adjectives*.
At the halt.
Tout court [F.]. Very short.

REST—Interjections.

Avast! A nautical expression meaning halt; halt! hold hard! stay! stop! whoa!

REST—Phrase.

Requiescat in pace [L.]. May he rest in peace; R. I. P.

---

mov'-er. One who causes movement. Maker-Destroyer.
mov'-ing, keep. To cause to stay in motion. Activity-Indolence.
mow. To cut grass; place in a barn where hay or grain is stored. Domestication-Agriculture, Length-Shortness, • Smoothness-Roughness, Store; **mow down,** Creation-Destruction.
mox'-a. A material for cauterizing. Heating-Cooling.
mo-zet'-ta. A cape worn by Roman Catholic Church dignitaries. Vestments.
M. P. Member of Parliament. Council.
Mr. Mister. Male-Female, Title.
Mrs. Mistress. Male-Female.
MS. Manuscript. Writing-Printing.
much. Great in quantity or amount. Magnitude-Smallness; **make much of,** Amity-Hostility, Approval-Disapproval, Blandishment, Consequence-Insignificance, Love-Hate; **much ado,** Difficulty-Facility, Toil-Relaxation; **much ado about nothing,** Consequence-Insignificance, Overvaluation-Undervaluation, Skill-Unskilfulness; **much cry and little wool,** Bragging; **much speaking,** Talkativeness-Taciturnity; **much the same,** Equality-Inequality, Likeness-Unlikeness, Sameness-Contrast; **not say much for,** Approval-Disapproval; **think much of,** Approval-Disapproval, Overvaluation-Undervaluation, Regard-Disrespect.
mu'-cid. Slimy; semiliquid. Cleanness-Filthiness, Viscidity-Foam.
mu'-ci-lage. A gummy substance. Viscidity-Foam.
mu''-ci-lag'-in-ous. Slimy. Viscidity-Foam.
muck. Moist manure. Cleanness-Filthiness; **run amuck,** Attack-Defense, Excitability-Inexcitability, Life-Killing.
muck'-er. A rough, low fellow. Good Man-Bad Man.
muck'-le. Much. Magnitude-Smallness.
muck'-worm''. Miser; low-born. Extravagance-Avarice, Gentility-Commonalty.
mu'-cor. Moldiness. Cleanness-Filthiness.
mu-cos'-i-ty. Mucousness. Viscidity-Foam.

REST—Verbs—Continued.

Stop short. To stop suddenly.
Take breath.

REST—Adjectives.

At anchor. Fastened with an anchor, without motion.
At a stand.
At a standstill.
At rest. Without motion.
Becalmed. Made quiet because of lack of wind, as a ship.
Calm. Motionless; quiet.
Cataleptic. Pertaining to a disease in which consciousness is lost and the muscles become rigid.
Fixed. Made firm or solid; immovable.
Immovable, etc. Fixed; not movable. See Mutability.
Motionless. At perfect rest.
Moveless. Not to be moved.
Quiescent. In a state of repose.
Quiet. In a state of rest or repose.
Restful. At rest; in a state of repose.
Sedentary. Lacking in activity.
Silent, etc. Without sound; still. See Sound.
Sleeping, etc. Pertaining to slumber, rest, or inactivity. See Activity.
Stagnant. At rest, without motion.
Standing still, etc. Motionless. See *Verbs*.
Stationary. At rest, without motion.
Stay-at-home. Pertaining to a person always staying at home.

(Continued on Column 1.)

mu'-cous. Slimy. Viscidity-Foam.
mu'-cro-nate. Ending in a point. Sharpness-Bluntness.
mu'-cro-na''-ted. Pointed. Sharpness-Bluntness
mu'-cu-lent. Slimy. Viscidity-Foam.
mu'-cus. Animal mucilage. Viscidity-Foam.
mud. Moistened earth; mire. Cleanness-Filthiness, Swamp-Island, Viscidity-Foam; **clear as mud,** Clearness-Obscurity; **stick in the mud,** Difficulty-Facility, Success-Failure.
mud'-dle. To confuse; a confused condition; absurd. Adage-Nonsense, Heed-Disregard, Organization-Disorganization, Regularity-Irregularity; **muddle one's brain,** Certainty-Doubt.
mud'-dled. Intoxicated. Teetotalism-Intemperance.
mud'-dle-head''-ed. Stupid. Sagacity-Incapacity.
mud'-dy. Damp; clouded; stupid. Clearness-Obscurity, Color-Achromatism, Dampness-Dryness, Diaphaneity-Opaqueness, Dimness, Sagacity-Incapacity, Swamp-Island, Viscidity-Foam.
mud'-lark''. One who cleans gutters; a street-child. Cleanness-Filthiness, Gentility-Commonalty.
mu-ez'-zin. A public crier. Ministry-Laity.
muff. A bungler; a covering to keep the hands warm; incapable. Adept-Bungler, Dress-Undress, Power-Impotence.
muf'-fle. To wrap; to keep secret; to speak indistinctly; silent. Dress-Undress, Enlightenment-Secrecy, Sound-Silence, Speech-Inarticulateness, Vocalization-Muteness.
muf'-fled. Faint; latent. Loudness-Faintness, Manifestation-Latency; **muffled drums,** Life-Funeral, Resonance-Nonresonance.
muf'-fler. A wrap for the neck. Dress-Undress.
muf'-ti. Citizen's dress; a judge; priest. Dress-Undress, Judge, Ministry-Laity.
mug. Face; cup; pottery. Anteriority-Posteriority, Contents-Receiver, Heating-Cooling.
mug'-gy. Moist; opaque; dim. Dampness-Dryness, Diaphaneity-Opaqueness, Dimness.
mug'-house''. An ale-house. Dweller-Habitation.

mu'-gi-ent. Lowing. CRY-ULULATION.

mujer, es de vidrio la [Sp.] (mu-her', es dê vî'-drî-o, la). Woman is made of glass. MALE-FEMALE.

mu-lat'-to. One having part white and part negro blood. CONVENTIONALITY-UNCONVENTIONALITY, MIXTURE-HOMOGENEITY.

mulct. Fine; to fine. RECOMPENSE-PENALTY, THEFT.

mule. Obstinate; hybrid; beast of burden. BIGOTRY-APOSTASY, CONVENTIONALITY-UNCONVENTIONALITY, CONVEYER.

mu"-le-teer'. A mule-driver. MANAGER.

mu"-li-eb'-ri-ty. Womanhood. MALE-FEMALE.

mulier nihil est tertium, aut amat aut odit [L.] (miu'-li-er nai'-hil est ter'-shi-um, aut ê'-mat aut o'-dit). A woman loves or she hates; no third course exists for her. LOVE-HATE.

mu'-lish. Obstinate. BIGOTRY-APOSTASY.

mull. A promontory; to sweeten. CONVEXITY-CONCAVITY, SWEETNESS-ACIDITY.

mul'-lion. A division-piece in a window. ARCHITECTURE, SUSPENSION-SUPPORT.

mul"-ti-fa'-ri-ous. Having great variety or diversity. CONNECTION-INDEPENDENCE, UNIFORMITY-DIVERSITY, UNIFORMITY-MULTIFORMITY.

mul"-ti-fa'-ri-ous-ness. Great variety. MULTIPLICITY-PAUCITY, RULE-MULTIFORMITY.

mul'-ti-fid. Divided. WHOLE-PART.

mul'-ti-foil. Radiating. ARCHITECTURE.

mul'-ti-fold. Manifold. UNIFORMITY-MULTIFORMITY.

mul'-ti-form. Having many forms. RULE-MULTIFORMITY, UNIFORMITY-DIVERSITY.

mul"-ti-form'-i-ty. Diversity of forms. UNIFORMITY-MULTIFORMITY.

mul"-ti-gen'-er-ous. Having many kinds. UNIFORMITY-MULTIFORMITY.

mul"-ti-lat'-er-al. Having many sides. ANGULARITY, LATERALITY-CONTRAPOSITION, PROPORTION-DEFORMITY.

mul-ti-loc'-u-lar. Many-celled. CONTENTS-RECEIVER.

mul-til'-o-quence. Loquacity. SPEECH-INARTICULATENESS, TALKATIVENESS-TACITURNITY.

mul"-ti-no'-mi-al. Polynomial. MULTIPLICITY-PAUCITY.

mul-tip'-a-rous. Producing many at a birth. FERTILITY-STERILITY.

mul"-ti-par'-tite. Divided into many parts. UNION-DISUNION.

mul'-ti-ple. A quantity containing another an even number of times. MULTIPLICITY-PAUCITY, NUMBER.

mul'-ti-pli-cand". A number multiplied by another. NUMBER.

mul'-ti-pli-ca'-tion. Act of multiplying. FERTILITY-STERILITY, MULTIPLICITY-PAUCITY, NUMBERING, RENEWAL.

mul'-ti-pli-ca"-tor. The multiplying number. NUMBER.

mul"-ti-plic'-i-ty. Condition of being manifold. MULTIPLICITY-PAUCITY.

MULTIPLICITY—PAUCITY.

A quantity. A certain number which can be determined.

Enormous number. }
Greater number. } A number above the usual.

Great number. }
Large number. } A number above the ordinary measure.

Lots. A large number.

Majority. The greater part of any number or quantity: more than half.

Multiple. The resultant obtained by multiplying a quantity by whole numbers.

Multiplication. The process of adding one number to itself as many times as there are units in another number.

Multiplicity. The state of being manifold; a great number.

Multitude. A vast number.

Nonillion. A number represented by a unit with thirty ciphers annexed.

Numbers. An assemblage of units.

Numerality. }
Numerosity. } The state of being in a great number.

Numerousness. The quality of consisting of great numbers.

Profusion, etc. Great abundance. See SUFFICIENCY.

Quadrillion. According to the French system, a unit with fifteen ciphers annexed.

Round number. A full or complete number.

Scores. Twenty taken more than once; a large number.

MULTIPLICITY—*Denotations*.

All the world and his wife. Everybody.

Army. A body of men armed for war.

Array. A body of persons placed in regular arrangement.

Bevy. A collection of persons, especially of ladies.

Brood. The young birds hatched at the same time.

Bushel. A quantity that fills a bushel measure.

Centiped. A venomous insect having a great number of feet.

Cloud. A great crowd or multitude.

Covey. A brood or hatch of birds.

Crowd, etc. A number of persons collected into a close body. See GATHERING.

Draft. A force or detachment of soldiers.

Drove. A collection of cattle driven.

Farrow. A litter of pigs.

Flight. A number of beings or things passing through the air together.

Flock. A company or collection of living creatures.

Fry. A swarm or crowd, especially of little fishes.

Galaxy. A cluster of stars.

Herd. A number of beasts assembled together.

Decimation. The act of destroying a great but indefinite proportion of the people.

Elimination. The act rejecting or casting out a certain number of things as useless.

Fewness, etc. The state of being in a small number; not many. See *Adjectives*.

Infrequency, etc. The state of occurring not often. See FREQUENCY.

Minority. The smaller of two parties or divisions; less than half.

Paucity. Smallness of number.

Rarity. The state of occurring at infrequent intervals.

Reduction. The act of making less.

Sarculation. The act of weeding with a rake.

Small number.

Small quantity.

Weeding, etc. To remove or root out any obnoxious thing. See *Verbs*.

PAUCITY—*Verbs*.

Be few, etc. To be in a small number. See *Adjectives*.

Decimate. To reduce the number of anything greatly.

Diminish the number. To decrease the number.

Eliminate. To sort out and take away the obnoxious parts or persons.

Reduce. To make less in number.

Render few, etc. To make few. See *Adjectives*.

Thin. To make less crowded.

Weed. To root out what is injurious or offensive.

PAUCITY—*Adjectives*.

Few. Not many; small in number.

Few and far between. Widely scattered.

Hardly any. Very few.

Infrequent, etc. At large or distant intervals. See FREQUENCY.

Rare. Occurring at distant intervals.

Rari nantes [L.]. Swimming here and there.

Reduced, etc. Made less. See *Verbs*.

Scant. Scarcely enough.

Scanty. Limited in number.

Scarcely any. Very few; hardly any

Thin. Not crowded.

Thinly scattered.

To be counted on one's fingers. Few in number.

Unrepeated. Not recurring.

PAUCITY—*Adverb*.

Here and there. At intervals.

MULTIPLICITY—Denotations—*Continued.*

Hive. A swarm of bees.
Host. A great number or multitude of anything.
Legion. A great number.
Litter. The young brought forth at one time by a multiparous animal.
Nest. Those who occupy a nest or are associated in the same pursuit.

Peck. As much as will fill a peck measure.
Sea. Anything resembling the sea in vastness.
Shoal. A great multitude assembled.
Sight. A great number, quantity, or sum.
Swarm. A great number or multitude, as of people in motion.

MULTIPLICITY—*Verbs*

Be numerous, etc. To be in great quantities. See *Adjectives*
Come thick upon. To come upon in great numbers.
Creep with. To be covered with.
Crowd. A company of persons more than filling the place they occupy.
Multiply. To increase in numbers.
Outnumber. To exceed in number

People. To fill with persons.
Swarm. To be crowded.
Swarm like bees.
Swarm like locusts.
Swarm with.
Teem with.

MULTIPLICITY—*Adjectives.*

A hundred.
A million. } Expressions meaning in great numbers; numerous.
A myriad.
And heaven knows what not. A great many things beside.
And what not. Much besides.
A thousand.
A thousand and one.
A world of. A great many.
Briarean. Hundred-handed.
Crowded. Having or being filled with great numbers.
Divers. More than one, but not in very great numbers.
Endless, etc. Without limit or end. See INFINITY.
Ever so many. Very many.
Full many. Very many.
Half a dozen. Six.
Half a hundred. Fifty.
In profusion. In great numbers.
Manifold. Numerous.
Many. Composed of or constituting a great number.
Many more.
More than one can tell. In countless numbers.
Multinominal. Having many terms.
Multiple. Consisting of more than one.
Multiplied. Increased by itself.
Multitudinous. Consisting of great numbers.

No end of.
No end to. } Numberless
Not a few. Many
Numberose.
Numerous. } In great numbers.
Numerous as the hairs on the head.
Numerous as the sands on the seashore. } Multitudinous; in great or countless numbers.
Numerous as the stars of the firmament.
Peopled. Filled with inhabitants.
Plenty as blackberries. In great numbers
Populous. Having many inhabitants.
Profuse. Superabundant; in great numbers.
Several. More than one, but not a great number.
Some forty or fifty. An uncertain quantity.
Some ten or a dozen.
Studded. Thickly set, as with gems.
Sundry. A small number; various.
Teeming. Full with or of.
Thick. Dense; containing a great number.
Thick as hail.
Thick as hops. Very numerous.
Thick coming. Coming in great numbers.
Various. Of different kinds; divers.
Very many. A great many

MULTIPLICITY—*Phrases.*

Acervatim [L.]. In heaps.
En foule [F.]. In a crowd.
Their name is "legion." The number of evil spirits. [Bible.]

Vel prece, vel pretio [L.]. Either wit.. prayer or with price; either for love or money.

mul'-ti-pli''-er. The multiplying number. NUMBER.
mul'-ti-ply. Increase. FERTILITY-STERILITY, MULTIPLICITY-PAUCITY, RENEWAL.
mul-tip'-o-tent. Having manifold power MIGHT-IMPOTENCE.
mul'-ti-si''-ded. Many-sided. MULTIPLICITY-PAUCITY, LATERALITY-CONTRAPOSITION.
mul-tis'-o-nous. Emitting much sound. LOUDNESS-FAINTNESS.
mul'-ti-tude. A large number. MAGNITUDE-SMALLNESS, MULTIPLICITY-PAUCITY, PLURALITY-FRACTION; the multitude, GENTILITY-COMMONALTY.
mul''-ti-tu'-di-nous. Manifold. MULTIPLICITY-PAUCITY.
multum in parvo [L.] (mul'-tum in par'-vo) Much in little. DIGEST.
mul'-ture. A grinding of grain. FRIABILITY.
mum. Silent. TALKATIVENESS-TACITURNITY, VOCALIZATION-MUTENESS.
mum'-ble. To chew; mutter. NUTRIMENT-EXCRETION, SPEECH-INARTICULATENESS.
mum'-bo-jum''-bo. A demon; an object of superstitious fear. DEVOTION-CHARM, JOVE-FIEND
mum'-mer. A masked actor. ACTING.
mum'-mer-y. A masked performance; absurdity; parade; imposture. ADAGE-NONSENSE, ENTERTAINMENT-WEARINESS, POMP, TRUTHFULNESS-FRAUD.
mum'-mi-fy. To embalm. LIFE-FUNERAL.
mum'-my. An embalmed corpse. DAMPNESS-DRY-

NESS, LIFE-CORPSE; **beat to a mummy,** RECOMPENSE-PUNITION.
mump. To beg; to mumble. PETITION-EXPOSTULATION, SPEECH-INARTICULATENESS.
mump'-er. A pauper; beggar. AFFLUENCE-PENURY, PETITIONER.
mump'-ish. Sad. LIGHTHEARTEDNESS-DEJECTION.
mumps. Sullenness; dejection. FAVORITE-MOROSENESS, LIGHTHEARTEDNESS-DEJECTION.
munch. To chew. NUTRIMENT-EXCRETION.
Mun'-chau-sen. A noted liar. GULL-HYPERBOLE.
mun'-dane. Pertaining to the world; worldly. GODLINESS-DISBELIEF, UNIVERSE, UNSELFISHNESS-SELFISHNESS.
mun-da'-tion. The act of cleansing. CLEANNESS-FILTHINESS.
mun'-di-fy. Cleanse. CLEANNESS-FILTHINESS.
mun-div'-a-gant. Wandering through the world. TRAVELING-NAVIGATION.
mu'-ner-a-ry. Of the nature of a gift. RECOMPENSE-PUNITION.
mu'-ne-rate. To remunerate. RECOMPENSE-PUNITION.
mu-nic'-i-pal. Pertaining to local self-government. JUDICATURE.
mu-nic''-i-pal'-i-ty. Borough. CITY-COUNTRY.
mu-nif'-i-cence. Generosity GENEROSITY-FRUGALITY.
mu-nif'-i-cent. Generous. GENEROSITY-FRUGALITY.
mu'-ni-ment. Defense; record; security. ATTACK-DEFENSE, MARK-OBLITERATION, SECURITY.

mu'-ral. Resembling a wall. ATTACK-DEFENSE; **mural circle,** ASTRONOMY.

mur'-der. To kill; act of killing. LIFE-KILLING; **murder the King's English,** GRAMMAR-SOLECISM, SPEECH-INARTICULATENESS; **the murder is out,** EXPOSURE-HIDINGPLACE.

mur'-der-er. One who commits murder. GOOD MAN-BAD MAN, LIFE-KILLING.

mur'-der-ous. Brutal. LIFE-KILLING.

mu'-ri-ca"-ted. Full of sharp points SHARPNESS-BLUNTNESS.

murk'-some. Dark. LIGHT-DARKNESS.

murk'-y. Hazy; darkened; gloomy. DIAPHANEITY-OPAQUENESS, LIGHT-DARKNESS, LIGHTHEARTEDNESS-DEJECTION.

mur'-mur. To complain; to sound; to purl. JUBILATION-LAMENTATION, LOUDNESS-FAINTNESS, RIVER-WIND.

mur'-rain. A plague. HEALTH-DISEASE.

Mur'-ray. A guide-book. TRAVELING-NAVIGATION; **Lindley Murray,** SCHOOL.

mur'-rey. Of a mulberry color. WHITENESS-BLACKNESS.

mur'-ri-on. A helmet. DRESS-UNDRESS. [Morion.]

mus, nascitur ridiculus [L.] (mŭs, nas'-si-tŭr ri-dic'-yu-lŭs). A ridiculous mouse was born. CONSEQUENCE-INSIGNIFICANCE, EXPECTATION-DISAPPOINTMENT.

mus'-ca-dine. A fragrant pear. PERFUME-STENCH.

muschio, pietra mossa non, fa [It.] (mŭs'-kî-o, pî-ê'-tra mos'-sa non, fα). A rolling stone gathers no moss. MUTABILITY-STABILITY.

mus'-cle. Muscular strength; flesh. ANATOMY, STRENGTH-WEAKNESS.

mus'-cu-lar. Strong; pertaining to muscle. ANATOMY, STRENGTH-WEAKNESS.

muse. To cogitate. REFLECTION-VACANCY.

Muse. Inspiring power of poetry. POETRY-PROSE; **historic Muse,** ACCOUNT; **unlettered Muse,** PURITY-CRUDENESS.

muse'-ful. Reflective. REFLECTION-VACANCY.

Muses, the. Goddesses presiding over poetry, etc. MUSICIAN.

mu-se'-um. A collection; place where it is kept. GATHERING-SCATTERING, STORE.

mush'-room. A fungus; new; upstart; low-born. FAUNA-FLORA, GENTILITY-COMMONALTY, NOVELTY, ANTIQUITY, WELFARE-MISFORTUNE.

mu'-sic. Melody. MUSIC, NATURE-ART; **music of the spheres,** IRREGULARITY, REGULARITY-IRREGULARITY; **set to music,** MELODY-DISSONANCE.

MUSIC.

Accompaniment. A part performed by instruments accompanying another part performed by voices.

Adagio, etc. Slow movement in a piece of music. See *Adverbs.*

Air. A tune.

Antiphone. The response of one part of a choir to another in a chant

Antiphony. A chant sung alternately by parts of a choir.

Aria. An air or song.

Arietta. A little air.

Ballad. A popular narrative poem adapted for singing.

Balladry. The subject or style of ballads.

Band. A number of musicians who play together upon portable musical instruments.

Bass. The lowest part in a musical composition.

Bravura. An air having several notes to a syllable and requiring great spirit.

Cadence. The close or fall of a strain.

Cadenza. The modulation of the voice in singing.

Canon. A musical composition in which the voices begin in succession and at regular intervals to repeat the same subject.

Cantate. The 98th Psalm used as a canticle.

Canticle. A song, hymn, or passage from the Bible, arranged for chanting in church service.

Canzonet. A song composed of several parts.

Capriccio. A fancifully irregular composition.

Carol. A song of praise or devotion.

Catch. A humorous round so contrived that the singers catch up each other's words.

Cavatina [It.]. An air with little movement.

Chant. } A short and simple melody.
Chaunt. }

Chorale. A sacred tune.

Chorus. A composition of two or more parts, each of which is intended to be sung by two or more voices.

Chronometer. An instrument for beating time in music.

Composer, etc. One who writes or composes music. See MUSICIAN

Composition. A musical production.

Concert. Musical accordance or harmony.

Concerted piece. A composition to be sung by several voices.

Concerto [It.]. A piece of music in which one instrument plays the leading part while others play the accompaniment.

Dance music. A tune by which dancing is regulated.

Descant. A composition in parts.

Dirge, etc. A piece of music of a mournful character. See JUBILATION-LAMENTATION.

Dithyramb. An ancient Greek song to the accompaniment of the flute, in honor of Bacchus.

Ditty. A little poem intended to be sung.

Duet. A composition for two performers, whether vocal or instrumental.

Dump. A melancholy or sad strain of music.

Duo. A composition for two performers.

Fantasia. A fantastic musical composition.

Fugue [F.]. A musical composition in which a theme proposed in one part is repeated and imitated by others which succeed it.

Full score. A score in which all the parts for voices and instruments are given.

Glee. An unaccompanied part song for three or more solo voices.

Head tone. The principal sound as to pitch.

Hymn. An ode or song of praise.

Instrumental music. Music by, or prepared for an instrument.

Lay. A simple lyrical poem.

Lullaby. A song that lulls babes to sleep.

Lydian measures. Soft, pathetic music.

Madrigal. A vocal composition of five or six parts.

March. A piece of music fitted to guide the movement of troops.

Martial music. Music suited for war

Melody, etc. A rhythmical succession of single tones so combined as to form an agreeable musical whole. See MELODY.

Minstrelsy. The singing and playing of a minstrel.

Minuet. The music for a slow, graceful dance.

Movement. The rhythmical progression of a piece.

Music. A succession of sounds so arranged as to be pleasing to the ear and in accordance with the laws of harmony.

Musician, etc. One who performs or is skilled in music.

Notturno [F.]. A sentimental, dreamy musical composition.

Opera. A drama of which music forms an essential part.

Operetta [It.]. A short, light musical drama.

Oratorio. A sacred musical composition consisting of different parts.

Orchestra. The instruments employed by a full band, collectively.

Overture. A musical composition for a full instrumental band, used as an introduction to an opera, etc.

Part song. A song in two or more distinct vocal parts.

Passamezzo [It.]. The music for an Italian dance.

Pastoral. A lyrical composition the subject of which is taken from real life.

Pastorale [It.]. A composition in a soft, rural style.

Pibroch. A wild irregular piece of Scotch music.

Piece of music. A musical composition.

Potpourri [F.]. A medley of different airs.

Psalm. A sacred song.

Psalmody. The art of singing sacred songs.

Quartet. } A composition in four parts, each performed by a single
Quartette. } voice or instrument.

Recitative. A musical composition in which the words are delivered in a declamatory style.

Recitativo [It.]. A musical recitation in which the words are delivered in a manner resembling ordinary declamation.

Rondeau [F.]. A species of lyric poetry.

Rondo [It.]. A lively, cheerful musical composition.

Roulade [F.]. A rapid series of running tones used as an embellishment.

Round. A short vocal piece in which three or four voices follow each other round.

Score. The original draft of a composition with the different parts written on staves one above another.

Second. A subordinate part in a musical composition.

Septet. A musical composition for seven voices or seven musical instruments

Serenade. Music sung or performed in the open air at night

Siren strains. Fascinating charming music.

Slow movement.
Slow music. } A slow progression of a piece of music

Soft music. Music gentle and pleasing to the ear.

Solfeggio [It.]. The system of arranging the scales by the names do, re, mi, fa, sol, la, si.

Solo. A tune or piece played or sung by a single person.

Sonata. A musical composition consisting of several parts.

Song, etc. A poem adapted to vocal music. See POETRY

Stave. The five horizontal parallel bars and the spaces on which music is written.

Strain. A complete musical period or sentence.

Symphony. An instrumental composition for a full orchestra

Technique [F.]. Artistic execution of a musical composition.

Trio. A musical composition sung or played by three persons.

Tune. A rhythmical series of tones for one voice or instrument.

Tweedledum and tweedledee.

Variation. Repetition of a theme or melody with fanciful modifications.

Vocalism. The exercise of the vocal organs.

Vocal music. Music made by the voice

Waltz, etc. A piece of music composed in triple measure for a waltz See ENTERTAINMENT

Music—*Verbs*.

Attune. To adjust so as to make one sound in harmony with another

Compose. To write music.

Perform, etc. To execute; do. See MUSICIAN

Music—*Adjectives*.

Choral. Like or pertaining to a choral.

Harmonious, etc. In musical concord, not discordant. See MELODY

Instrumental. Pertaining to or made by musical instruments.

Lyric. Pertaining to or like the lyre or harp.

Musical. Pertaining to music.

Operatic. Pertaining to or like an opera.

Vocal. Pertaining to music made by the voice.

Wagnerian. Pertaining to Richard Wagner, the German musician

Music—*Adverbs*.

Adagio [It.]. In a slowly moving manner

Affettuoso [It.]. In a soft and tender manner

Alla capella [It]. In an ecclesiastical manner

Allegretto [It]. In a moderately fast manner.

Allegro [It.] In a bright, spirited, and rapid manner

Andante [It.]. In a rather slow manner

Andantino [It] In a manner somewhat faster than andante

Capriccioso [It.]. In a capricious manner

Crescendo [It.]. Increasing in loudness or volume.

Diminuendo [It.] Decreasing in loudness

Larghetto [It.]. Somewhat slowly, but not as slow as largo.

Largo [It.] Slowly.

Legato [It.]. In a closely connected manner

Maestoso [It.]. Majestically.

Moderato [It.]. In a moderately quick manner

Obbligato [It.]. Indispensable, as for a musical composition.

Pizzicato [It.]. With a staccato effect.

Prestissimo [It]. Very fast; with great rapidity

Presto [It.]. Fast; quickly

Rallentando [It.]. Decreasing in time and loudness

Scherzando [It].
Scherzo [It]. } In a playful manner

Spiritoso [It.] In a spirited, lively manner.

Staccato [It.]. In a short, distinct, and disconnected manner

Toccata [It.]. A touch-piece

Veloce [It.]. Rapidly.

Vivace [It.]. In a lively, brisk manner

mu'-sic-al. Pertaining to music. MELODY-DISSONANCE, MUSIC, MUSICIAN; **musical ear,** HEARING-DEAFNESS, MUSICIAN; **musical note,** MELODY-DISSONANCE; **musical voice,** VOCALIZATION-MUTENESS.

mu'-sic-al in-stru'-ments. Instruments for making music. MUSICAL INSTRUMENTS.

MUSICAL INSTRUMENTS

Band. A collection of portable musical instruments.

Musical instruments. Instruments that have the power of producing music.

Orchestra. The instruments employed by a full band

MUSICAL INSTRUMENTS—*Stringed Instruments*

Archlute. A large lute

Bandurria [It.]. A stringed instrument similar to the guitar.

Banjo. A musical instrument with five strings, played with the fingers and hands.

Base-viol. A violin, used for playing bass

Bass. The instrument which plays bass

Bass-viol. See BASE-VIOL.

Bow. An appliance consisting of an elastic rod, with a number of horsehairs stretched from end to end, used in playing on a stringed instrument.

Cithern. A musical instrument resembling the guitar.

Clarichord. A musical instrument in the form of a spinet.

Clavichord. A keyed stringed instrument, now superseded by the pianoforte.

Clavier [F.]. An instrument having a keyboard, especially the square piano

Contra basso [It.] The largest base-viol.

Cremona. A violin made at Cremona, Italy.

Double-bass. The largest and lowest-toned instrument in the viol form.

Dulcimer. A triangular-shaped stringed instrument, played upon by metallic rods.

Eolian harp. A box on which are stretched strings on which the wind produces music.

Fiddle. A stringed instrument played with a bow

Fiddlestick. The bow used in playing a fiddle.

Gittern. An instrument like a guitar.

Guitar. An instrument of six strings, played with the fingers.

Harp. A musical instrument consisting of a triangular frame furnished with strings and played with the fingers.

Harpsichord. A harp-shaped instrument set horizontally on legs, with strings of wire, played by the fingers by means of keys.

Hurdy-gurdy. A stringed musical instrument whose sounds are produced by the friction of a wheel, and regulated by the fingers.

Kit. A small violin

Lute. An instrument similar to a mandolin.

Lyre An instrument like a small harp.

Mandolin. An instrument with metal strings tuned in pairs, and played with a pick.

Manichord. The clavichord

Monochord. An instrument for obtaining the mathematical relations of musical sounds.

Mute. A little utensil on the bridge of a violin or similar instrument to deaden the sound.

Pianino. A small piano.

Piano. A musical instrument consisting of a series of wires of graduated length, struck by hammers moved by keys.

Pianoforte. The piano.

Polychord. A musical instrument of ten strings.

Psaltery. An old Hebrew stringed instrument.

Rebeck. An instrument with cat-gut strings played upon with a bow.

Spinet. A keyed instrument, with one string to each note, sounded by leather or quill plectrums.

Tenor. The instrument that plays tenor.

Theorbo. An instrument like a large lute, but having two heads.

Vielle [F.]. A stringed instrument played with a wheel.

Vina. An East-Indian stringed instrument

Viol.

Viola [It.]. An instrument somewhat larger than a violin.

Viola d'amore [It.]. A violin with a peculiarly soft sourd.

Violoncello [It] A large musical instrument with four strings, giving sounds an octave lower than the tenor violin.

Violin. An instrument with four strings played with a bow

Violone [It]. The double bass.

Virginals. A musical instrument somewhat like a small pianoforte.

Xanorphica. A musical instrument like an harmonichord, and sounded by means of a small bow.

MUSICAL INSTRUMENTS—*Wind Instruments*.

Accordion. A small, portable, keyed instrument whose tones are generated by play of the wind upon free metallic reeds.

Bagpipe. A wind-instrument consisting of a leather wind-bag and three sounding pipes.

Barrel organ. An instrument for producing music by means of a revolving cylinder.

Basset-horn. An instrument blown with a reed.

Bassoon. A wind-instrument similar to the flute.

Bombardon. A deep-toned instrument similar to a bassoon.

Brass band A band of musicians who play upon instruments made of brass.

Bugle. An instrument like the horn.

Bugle-horn. A horn used by buglers.

Cat-call. An instrument that makes a noise like the cry of a cat.
Clarinet. A wind-instrument blown by a single reed.
Clarion. A trumpet whose note is clear and shrill.
Clarionet. See Clarinet.
Concertina. An instrument similar to the accordion.
Cor Anglais [F.]. The English horn.
Cornet. A brass instrument, furnished with valves or pistons, and cupped mouthpiece.
Cornet-à-pistons [F.]. A horn similar to the French horn.
Corno di bassetto [It.]. The basset-horn.
Corno Inglese [It.]. The English horn.
Cornopean. A wind-instrument like a trumpet.
Fagotto [It.]. The bassoon.
Fife. A small shrill pipe used to accompany the drum in military music.
Flageolet. A small wooden pipe having six or more holes and a mouthpiece inserted at one end.
Flute. A musical wind-instrument, consisting of a hollow pipe, with holes along its length.
French horn. A metallic wind instrument, consisting of a long tube twisted into circular folds and gradually expanding.
Hand-organ. A barrel organ operated by a crank.
Harmonicon. A small, flat instrument in which the notes are produced by the vibration of metallic reeds.
Harmoniphon. An old wind-instrument in which the sound was produced by the vibrations of metallic plates.
Harmonium. A musical instrument resembling a small organ.
Hautboy. A wind-instrument similar to a clarinet.
Horn. A wind-instrument, resembling a horn in shape.
Humming-top. A metallic top that produces a low humming noise when spinning.
Oboe. An instrument similar to a clarinet, and sounded by means of a double reed.
Ophicleide. A large brass wind-instrument which produces low, loud sounds.
Organ. A wind-instrument consisting of pipes, which are filled with wind from a bellows, and played upon by means of keys.
Pandean pipes. A primitive wind-instrument, of short graduated pipes.
Piccolo. A small shrill flute.
Pipe. A wind-instrument of music, consisting of a tube or tubes of straw, reed, metal, etc.
Pitch-pipe. A wind-instrument to regulate the pitch of a tune.
Sackbut. An instrument like the trombone.
Saxophone. A brass wind-instrument, shaped like a Dutch pipe and played like a clarinet; a saxhorn.
Seraphina. A wind-instrument whose sounding parts are reeds of brass playing freely through a slot in a plate.
Serpent. A brass wind-instrument of a loud and coarse tone, so called from its form.
Sirene. An instrument in which the sounds are produced by air escaping through holes in a rotating disk.
Sordet. } A contrivance in a musical instrument to deaden vibra-
Sordine. } tions.
Trombone. An instrument of the trumpet kind, consisting of a tube bent twice upon itself, and ending in a bell.
Trumpet. A wind-instrument, consisting of a long tube bent once or twice and ending in a bell.
Union pipes. A variety of bagpipe.
Whistle. An instrument in which air forced through a cavity, or against a thin edge, produces a shrill sound

Musical Instruments—*Vibrating Surfaces.*

Bass drum. The largest kind of drum having two heads, and giving a deep sound.
Bell. A hollow metallic vessel, containing a clapper or tongue, and giving forth a ringing sound when struck.
Bones. Two or four pieces of bone held between the fingers and struck together to make a kind of music.
Castanet. Two small, concave shells of ivory or hard wood, fastened to the thumb and beaten with the middle finger.
Cymbal. A musical instrument of brass shaped like a circular plate, used in pairs to produce a sharp ringing sound.
Drum. An instrument consisting of a hollow cylinder, over each end of which is stretched a piece of skin or vellum, to be beaten with a stick.
Gong. A disk with upturned rim, struck with a metallic knob.
Harmonica. A musical instrument consisting of a series of hemispherical glasses which, by touching the edges with the dampened fingers, give forth the tones.
Kettle-drum. A drum made of thin copper in the form of a hemispherical kettle, with parchment stretched over the mouth of it.
Musical glasses. Glass goblets or bowls so tuned and arranged that when struck they produce musical notes.

Musical stones. Stones which produce musical sounds when struck.
Rattle. An instrument with which a rattling sound is made.
Side drum. A snare drum; a small drum beaten at one end.
Sounding-board. A thin board which propagates the sound in a piano, violin, etc.
Tabor. A small drum used as an accompaniment to a fife.
Taborin. } A small, shallow drum.
Tabourine. }
Tabret. A small drum.
Tambour. } A shallow drum with only one skin, played on with
Tambourine. } the hand.
Tam-tam. } A large flat drum used in India.
Tom-tom. }
Timbrel. A small shallow drum.
Tymbal. A kind of kettle-drum.
Xylophone. An instrument common among the Russians and Poles, consisting of a series of strips of wood or glass graduated in length to the musical scale and struck with two small hammers.
Zambomba. An instrument consisting of a strip of parchment stretched over a jar, and a stick of wood through the parchment.

Musical Instruments—*Vibrating Bars.*

Jew's-harp. An instrument which when placed between the teeth gives by means of a bent metal tongue struck by the finger a sound modulated by the breath.
Musical box. A box or case containing an apparatus moved by clockwork so as to play certain tunes automatically.
Reed. A small piece of cane or wood attached to the mouthpiece of certain instruments, and set in vibration by the breath.
Reed instrument. An instrument in which the wind acts on a set of free reeds.
Triangle. A rod of steel in the form of a triangle open at one end and sounded by being struck with a small metallic rod.
Tuning-fork. A steel instrument consisting of two prongs and a handle, which, being struck, gives a certain tone.

mu'-sic–hall''. Place of amusement. Acting, Entertainment-Weariness.
mu-si'-cian. One skilled in music. Musician.

MUSICIAN.

Accompanist. The performer in music who takes the accompanying part.
Accordionist. One who plays an accordion.
Artiste [F.]. A skilled music performer.
Ballad-monger. A seller or maker of ballads.
Band. A number of musicians who play together upon portable musical instruments.
Bandmaster. One who conducts a band.
Bard, etc. A poet and singer among the Celts.
Cantatrice [It.]. A female professional singer.
Catgut-scraper. A vulgar name for a violinist.
Chanter. A singer; the chief singer of the chantry.
Chantress. A female chanter or singer.
Choir. A band or organized company of singers, especially in church service.
Chorister. A singer in a chorus.
Chorus. A company of singers singing in concert.
Chorus-singer. A member of a chorus.
Composer. An author of a piece of music.
Drummer. One whose office is to beat the drum.
Fiddler. One who plays on a fiddle.
Fifer. One who plays the fife.
Flautist. One who plays the flute.
Harper. } One who plays a harp.
Harpist. }
Instrumentalist. A performer on a musical instrument.
Liedertafel [G.]. A male choir.
Melodist. A composer or singer of melodies.
Minstrel. A singer and harper; a musician.
Musician. A skilled singer or performer on a musical instrument.
Orchestra. A band of instrumental musicians.
Organist. One who plays an organ.
Performer. A musician.
Pianist. One who plays a piano.
Piper. One who plays on a pipe.
Player. One who plays a musical instrument.
Quire. See Choir.
Singer. One who sings.
Songster. One skilled in singing
Songstress. A woman who sings.
Trumpeter. One who sounds a trumpet.
Violinist. One who plays a violin.

Vocalist. A singer or vocal musician.
Waits. Musicians who sing or play at night.
Warbler. One who warbles; a singer.

Musician—*Denotations.*

Apollo. The god of music.
Erato. The Muse who presided over lyric poetry.
Euterpe. The Muse who presided over music.
Nightingale. A bird that sings at night, and is celebrated for the sweetness of its song.
Orpheus. The famous mythic Thracian poet, reputed to have power to entrance beasts and inanimate objects by the music of his lyre.
Philomel. The daughter of Pandion, king of Athens, who was changed into a nightingale; the nightingale.
Siren. A sea-nymph, said to sing with such sweetness that she lured sailors to destruction.
The Muses. The nine goddesses who presided over song and the different kinds of poetry.
Thrush. A small bird noted for the sweetness of its song.
Tuneful choir. }
Tuneful nine. } The Muses.

Musician—*Associated Nouns.*

Execution. The mode of performing on an instrument.
Expression. Manner of playing which gives life and force.
Performance. A musical feat
Solmization. The act of sol-faing.
Touch. The manner of touching or striking the keys of a piano.

Musician—*Verbs.*

Accompany. To play a part of a musical composition.
Arrange. To adapt a musical composition to instruments or voices for which it was not originally written.
Beat the drum. To strike the drum.
Beat time. To measure or regulate time in music by beating with the foot or hand.
Blow the horn. To make music on the horn.
Carol. To praise in a joyful song.
Chant. }
Chaunt. } To sing in the manner of a chant.
Chirp. }
Chirrup. } To make a short sharp sound, such as crickets make.
Compose. To write music.
Execute. To perform a piece of music.
Fiddle. To play on the fiddle or violin.
Grind the organ. To turn the crank which causes an organ to sound.
Have a correct ear. To have an ear which easily distinguishes dis-cords.
Have a musical ear. } To be able to detect differences in musical
Have an ear for music. } sounds.
Hum. To sing with the mouth closed.
Intone. To utter a deep, long sound.
Perform. To play on a musical instrument before an audience.
Pipe. To play on a pipe.
Play. To perform music upon any instrument.
Play a second. To play the accompaniment.
Purl. To make a murmuring sound.
Quaver. To tremble or make the voice vibrate.
Set to music. To arrange to music.
Shake. To vibrate or quaver in music.
Sing. To utter music with the voice.
Sing a second. To sing an accompaniment.
Sol-fa. To pronounce the notes of the gamut.

Sound the horn. To make the horn be heard.
Strike the lyre. To play on the lyre.
Strike up. To begin to play.
Strum. To play an instrument in a coarse, noisy manner.
Sweep the chords. To strike the strings with a long stroke.
Thrum. To play coarsely on an instrument.
Touch the guitar, etc. To play on the guitar. See Musical Instruments.
Trill. To utter with tremulousness or quavering.
Tweedle. To play awkwardly on the violin.
Twitter. To sing with a tremulous and shortly intermitted voice.
Warble. To sing in a thrilling or vibrating voice.
Whistle. To make a sharp, shrill sound by compressing the lips and breathing the air through a small orifice.

Musician—*Adjectives.*

Musical. Pertaining to or having reference to music.
Playing, etc. Performing on musical instruments. See *Verbs.*

Musician—*Adverbs.*

Adagio [It.]. In a slow manner.
Andante [It.], etc. In a moderately slow manner. See Music.

mu'-sing. Deep cogitation. Reflection-Vacancy; **musing on other things,** Heed-Disregard.
musk. A perfume. Perfume-Stench.
mus'-ket. A gun. Weapon; **shoulder a musket,** Fighting-Conciliation.
mus''-ket-eer'. A foot-soldier. Belligerent.
mus''-ket-oon'. A light gun. Belligerent.
mus'-ket-ry. Muskets collectively. Weapon.
mus'-lin. Thin cotton cloth. Diaphaneity-Opalescence.
mus'-nud. A raised seat; council; scepter. Council, Scepter, Suspension-Support.
Mus'-sul-man. Relating to the Moslems. Orthodoxy-Heterodoxy.
must. Be necessary; mold. Cleanness-Filthiness, Coercion; **I must say,** Assertion-Denial; **it must follow,** Proof-Disproof.
mus-tache'. Hair on the upper lip. Smoothness-Roughness.
mus'-tard. A pungent condiment. Condiment, Pungency; **after meat mustard,** Opportuneness-Unsuitableness.
mus'-tard-seed''. A small seed. Greatness-Littleness.
mus'-ter. To collect; roll. Gathering-Scattering, Numbering; **muster courage,** Bravery-Cowardice; **not pass muster,** Faultlessness-Faultiness; **pass muster,** Enough.
mus'-ter-book''. Book containing muster-roll. Record.
mus'-ter-roll''. A list. Record.
must'-y. Stale; having a bad odor. Cleanness-Filthiness, Perfume-Stench.
mu''-ta-bil'-i-ty. State of being unstable. Mutability-Stability.

MUTABILITY—STABILITY.

Agitation. The state of being moved with violence, or with irregular action. See Agitation.
Alternation, etc. Succession of things in time or place. See Vibration.
Changeableness, etc. The quality of being changeable. See *Adjectives.*
Disquiet. Restlessness.
Disquietude. Uneasiness.
Fluctuation. A moving in this and that direction.
Inconstancy. Liability to sudden change.
Inquietude. Disturbed state.
Instability. Want of firmness or stability.
Mobility. The quality or state of being easily moved.
Mutability. The quality of being subject to alteration in form or nature.
Restlessness. State of being continually moving. See *Adjectives.*
Transientness. State of staying for only a short time. See Lastingness-Transientness.
Unrest. Want of rest or repose.

Aplomb [F.]. Self-possession.
Constancy. Firmness of mind; steadiness.
Establishment. Fixed state.
Immobility. The quality of being immovable.
Immutability. The quality of being unchangeable.
Obstinacy. See Bigotry.
Permanence. See Chronology.
Solidity. The state or quality of being sound.
Soundness. The quality or state of being sound.
Stabiliment. The act of making firm.
Stability. Firmness of purpose or character; fixedness.
Stable equilibrium. Fixed and solid position.
Stiffness. Quality or state of being stiff.
Unchangeableness. See *Adjectives.*
Vitality. Capability of living.

Stability—*Denotations.*

Anchylosis. The stiffening of a movable joint.
Ethiopian's skin. The skin of a member of the black race. [Bible.]

MUTABILITY—STABILITY—*Continued.*

Unstable equilibrium. A condition subject to change or overthrow.

Vacillation. A moving one way and the other. See DETERMINATION-VACILLATION.

Versatility. Aptness to change.

Vicissitude. Regular change or succession from one thing to another.

MUTABILITY—*Denotations.*

April showers. Showers occurring very variably during the month of April.

Chameleon. A lizard whose color changes with the color of the objects around it.

Cynthia of the minute.

Fidgets. A nervous restlessness.

Harlequin. A buffoon, dressed in party-colored clothes.

Moon. The celestial orb which revolves round the earth, whose appearance changes from a complete sphere to a crescent.

Proteus. A marine deity who possessed the faculty of readily assuming different shapes.

Quicksilver. A metal, mercury, characterized by its freedom of motion.

Shifting sands. Time, or anything variable.

Weathercock. An instrument to indicate the direction of the wind.

Wheel of fortune. Figuratively, changeable fortune.

MUTABILITY—*Verbs.*

Alternate. To occur by turns; change reciprocally.

Change and change about. To change continually.

Flicker. To waver, as a flame in an air-current.

Flit. To change positions quickly, as a light substance.

Flitter. To flutter.

Flounder. To toss and tumble about.

Fluctuate. To move first in one direction, then in another.

Flutter. To be in agitation or uncertainty.

Have as many phases as the moon. To be changeable.

Oscillate. See VIBRATION.

Oscillate between two extremes. To vary between two opposites.

Ring the changes. To repeat an argument with all possible variations; to produce varied music from chimes.

Scuffle. To struggle confusedly.

Shake. To cause to move with rapid vibrations; to tremble.

Shift. To alter; to vary the direction of.

Shift to and fro. To swing backward and forward; to vary the position of.

Sway to and fro. To incline from side to side.

Totter. To shake as if about to fall.

Tremble. To shake involuntarily, said of persons; totter.

Turn and turn about.

Vacillate. To fluctuate in mind.

Vary. To alter or be altered in any way.

Wamble. To move irregularly backward and forward.

Waver. To move one way, then the other.

MUTABILITY—*Adjectives.*

Afloat. Unfixed; uncontrolled.

Agitating. See AGITATION.

Alterable. Capable of being changed or varied.

Alternating. See *Verbs.*

Capricious. See PERSISTENCE-WHIM.

Changeable. Liable to change.

Changeful. Uncertain.

Changing. See MUTATION.

Chequered. Diversified.

Desultory. Passing from one thing or subject to another without logical connection, as a circus rider leaps from horse to horse.

Erratic. Wandering aimlessly.

Ever-changing.

Fickle. Wavering in opinion or purpose.

Fitful. Irregular; unstable.

Fluctuating. See *Verbs.*

Inconsonant. Inconsistent.

Inconstant. Subject to change.

Irresolute. See DETERMINATION-VACILLATION.

Mobile. Capable of being aroused or excited.

Mutable. Capable of being changed.

Plastic. Creative; easily molded.

Protean. Pertaining to Proteus; changeable

Proteiform. Protean.

Restless. Uneasy; discontented.

Spasmodic. Occurring at intervals.

Touch and go. To touch bottom, as a ship in sailing, with much decrease in speed.

Transient. See LASTINGNESS-TRANSIENTNESS.

Unfixed. Not fixed.

Fixture. That which is attached to something as a permanent appendage.

Foundation. That upon which anything is founded.

Leopard's spots. The spots on the skin of the leopard. [Bible.]

Pillar. A supporting column or structure.

Rock. A mass of stone.

Tower. A firmly built structure.

STABILITY—*Verbs.*

Ascertain. To learn for a certainty; free from doubt or change.

Be firm. See *Adjectives.*

Be stable. See *Adjectives.*

Build one's house on a rock. [Bible.]

Establish. To settle in a firm, fixed manner.

Fasten. See UNION.

Fix. To make firm or definite; to settle down permanently.

Keep firm. To be solid or immovable.

Keep hold. To hang on.

Make good. To maintain; to accomplish.

Make sure. To make firm.

Remain firm. To stand against.

Retain. To keep in possession; to continue to hold.

Set. To make permanent or fixed.

Set on its legs. To place in a solid position.

Settle. To place or become placed in a fixed or lasting condition.

Settle down. To take a fixed position.

Stabilitate. To make stable.

Stablish. To establish.

Stand firm. To be solid.

Stick fast. To be immovable.

Strike root. Take a firm hold.

Take root. To become fixed.

Take up one's abode. See ESTABLISHMENT.

Weather the storm. To remain firm under difficulty or adversity.

STABILITY—*Adjectives.*

Aground. Stranded.

Anchored. Held fast, as by an anchor.

At anchor. When a ship rides by her anchor.

Balanced. Settled and adjusted, as an account.

Confirmed. Strengthened; fixed.

Constant. Not liable to change.

Deep-rooted. Solid.

Durable. Lasting.

Established. See *Verbs.*

Fadeless. Not liable to fade.

Fast. Not loose or unstable.

Firm. Stable in opinion or position.

Firm as a rock. Solid.

Firmly established. See *Verbs.*

Firmly seated. Solid.

Fixed. Immovable.

High and dry. Out of water; stranded.

Immovable. Not movable.

Immutable. Not liable to change.

Imperishable. Not liable to decay.

Incommutable. Not capable of being interchanged.

Incontrovertible. Too clear to admit of dispute.

Indeciduous. Lasting.

Indeclinable. Not altered by terminations.

Indefeasible. Not voidable; not to be defeated.

Indelible. Incapable of being blotted out, lost, or forgotten.

Indestructible. Not liable to be decomposed.

Indissoluble. Perpetually binding.

Indissolvable. Incapable of being dissolved.

Ineradicable. Not capable of being rooted out.

Inextinguishable. Incapable of being destroyed.

Insusceptible. Not capable of being affected.

Insusceptible of change. Unchangeable.

Intransmutable. Incapable of being changed into another substance.

Invariable. Not liable to change.

Inveterate. Firmly established because of long continuance.

Irreducible. Not capable of being reduced.

Irremovable. Incapable of being removed.

Irresoluble. Not capable of being dissolved or released.

Irretrievable. Not capable of recovery or repair.

Irreversible. Not capable of being reversed, repealed, or annulled.

Irrevocable. Not capable of being revoked or recalled.

Moored. Confined or fastened, as by cables or anchors.

Not to be changed.

MUTABILITY—STABILITY—*Continued.*

MUTABILITY—Adjectives—*Continued.*

Unsettled. Not settled.
Unstable. Not steady or firm.
Unstayed. Not sustained; fickle.
Unsteady. Unfixed; variable.
Vagrant. Unsettled; moving with uncertain direction.
Variable. Subject to sudden change.
Versatile. Changeable.
Vibratory. Moving or causing to move to and fro.
Wayward. Full of whims; perverse.

MUTABILITY—*Adverbs.*

Off and on.
See-saw. See VIBRATION.

MUTABILITY—*Phrases.*

Honores mutant mores [L.]. Honors change (men's) manners
Pietra mossa non fa muschis [It.]. "A rolling stone gathers no moss."
Varium et mutabile semper femina [L.]. A thing inconstant and changeable ever is woman. [Virgil, *Æneid,* iv, 569.]

STABILITY—*Continued from Column 2.*

STABILITY—*Phrases.*

Littera scripta manet [L.]. The written word remains.
Video meliora proboque, deteriora sequor [L.]. I see the better and approve, the worse I follow. [Ovid, *Metamorphosis* vii, 20.]

mu′-ta-ble. Changeable. MUTABILITY-STABILITY.

STABILITY—Adjectives—*Continued.*

Obstinate. See BIGOTRY.
On a rock. On a solid foundation.
Perennial. See LASTINGNESS.
Permanent. See MUTATION-PERMANENCE.
Reverseless. Not to be reversed.
Riveted. Firmly fastened; clinched.
Rooted. Firmly fixed.
Settled. Permanently fixed, placed, or adjusted.
Stable. Unwavering; durable.
Steadfast. Firmly established; constant.
Steady. Firm; regular.
Stereotyped. Formed in an unchangeable manner.
Stranded. Driven or run aground.
Stuck fast. Immovable.
Tethered. Confined to certain limits by means of a rope or chain.
Transfixed. Pierced through, as with a dart or spear.
Unalterable. Not to be altered.
Unaltered. Not altered.
Unchangeable. Incapable of being changed.
Undeviating. Regular in rule, principle, or purpose.
Undying. Immortal.
Valid. Forceful.
Vested. Fixed; not dependent on contingencies.

STABILITY—*Interjection.*

Stet [L.]. Let it stand.

(*Continued on Column 1.*)

mu-ta′-tion. The act of changing. MUTATION-PERMA-NENCE.

MUTATION—PERMANENCE.

Alteration. The act of making different; or the state of being made so.
Break. An interruption of continuity.
Change. A passing from one form or condition to another.
Changeableness. Liability to change. See MUTABILITY.
Conversion. See CONVERSION.
Deviation. A departure from the usual course or mode.
Displacement. A putting out of place. See ESTABLISHMENT-REMOVAL.
Innovation. A variation in methods or recognized principles.
Inversion. A reversing of the natural order of things.
Metamorphosis. A change of form.
Modification. A slight variation, or the result of such variation.
Mutation. The act or process of varying the form or qualities.
Permutation. Reciprocal change.
Qualification. The act of limiting or changing.
Revolution. See REVOLUTION.
Transference. The act of conveying from one person or place to another. See TRANSFER.
Transfiguration. A change of form.
Transformation. Conversion into another form.
Transmutation. The change from one form or substance into another.
Turn. Change of direction, course, or tendency.
Variation. Partial change from a former state or nature: the amount of such change.

MUTATION—*Denotations.*

Alterative. A change-producing medicine.
Avatar. The descent of a deity into incarnate man. [Hindu.]
Diversion. That which turns or draws the mind from care or study.
Metempsychosis. The passing of a dead man's soul into the body of some other animal.
Modulation. A change of key in music, or in the pitch of the voice.
Mood. Temporary state of the mind in regard to passions or feeling.
Tergiversation. Fickleness of conduct.
Transanimation. The conveyance of a soul from one body to another.
Transmigration. The act of passing from one country to another; the passing of the soul at death into another mortal body.
Transubstantiation. The changing of the bread and wine of the Mass into the body and blood of Christ.

MUTATION—*Scientific Terms.*

Metagenesis. The production of sexual individuals by non-sexual means.
Metastasis. A sudden and complete change of a disease in its location.

Conservation. The keeping of a thing entire or unchanged.
Conservatism. Opposition to change.
Endurance. Lastingness.
Maintenance. Keeping up.
Obstinacy. See BIGOTRY.
Permanence. The state or quality of being fixed or indefinitely continued.
Persistence. Continuity of policy, condition, or action.
Preservation. The state of being kept from destruction or decay.
Quiescence. See MOVEMENT-REST.
Stability. See MUTABILITY-STABILITY.
Standing. Duration or existence.
Status quo [L.]. The state in which.

PERMANENCE—*Denotations.*

Law of the Medes and Persians. A figurative expression for anything unchangeable. [Bible.]
Standing dish. A dish or article of food always on hand.

PERMANENCE—*Verbs.*

Abide. To continue stable or fixed in some position or condition.
Aby. To suffer; endure.
Bide. To inhabit permanently; remain firm.
Dwell. To have a permanent habitation.
Endure. To remain firm; to continue unyielding.
Hold. To maintain or cause to remain in a fixed position, condition, or relation.
Hold good. To continue in full force and effect.
Hold on. To continue in.
Hold one's footing. To stand firm.
Hold one's ground. To maintain one's position.
Keep one's ground. To stand firm.
Last. To remain unimpaired; to continue indefinitely.
Let alone. To allow to remain without interference.
Let be. Not to molest or interfere with.
Live. To continue in existence.
Maintain. To keep up; to support.
Outlive. To live longer than.
Persist. To continue obstinately in opinion or action.
Remain. To endure in an unchanged form or condition.
Rest. To remain fixed.
Stand. To maintain a fixed position.
Stand fast. To be immovable.
Stand still.
Stay. To continue fixed for an indefinite time.
Subsist. To continue in the present state.

MUTATION—PERMANENCE—*Continued.*

MUTATION—*Verbs.*

Alter. To produce a change in.
Change. To make different; substitute.
Chop. To exchange.
Convert into. See CONVERSION.
Deviate. To depart from the usual course or condition.
Disturb. See ORGANIZATION-DISORGANIZATION.
Diversify. To make various in form or quality
Evert. To overturn.
Give a color to. To modify.
Give a turn to. To change slightly.
Influence. To affect by hidden power, physical or moral.
Innovate. To alter by the introduction of something new
Introduce new blood. To change the breed.
Metamorphose. To change the form of.
Modify. To shape anew; to vary.
Modulate. To vary in tone.
Pass to. To change to.
Qualify. To modify.
Recast. See REVOLUTION.
Resume. To continue after an interruption.
Reverse. See REVERSAL.
Ring the changes. To present facts or arguments in various manners.
Shift. To vary in direction or position.
Shift the scenes. To change location or surroundings.
Shuffle. To change the relative position of; to shift ground.
Shuffle the cards.
Superinduce. To bring in as an addition.
Tack. To change the course of a ship.
Take a turn. To change for better or for worse
Tamper with. To meddle with or alterate unlawfully.
Transfigure. To change the external form or appearance of.
Transform. To make different in substance or shape.
Transmogrify. To change into a different form
Transmute. To make different in nature, shape, or substance.
Transume. To take from one to another.
Turn. To reverse the shape or position of; be changed.
Turn aside. To change from.
Turn over a new leaf. To change from one's bad habits.
Turn the corner. To start changing for the better.
Turn the scale. To change the advantage
Vamp. To patch or repair.
Vary. To make partially different in properties, proportions, or nature.
Veer. To change direction; to turn.
Warp. To bend from the true direction.
Wax and wane. To increase and decrease in size or condition, as the moon
Work a change.

MUTATION—*Adjectives.*

Alterative. Causing change.
Changeable. See MUTABILITY.
Changed. See *Verbs.*
Modifiable. Capable of being diversified by various forms and differences.
Newfangled. Disposed to change frequently.
Transitional. Containing, denoting, or involving change.

PERMANENCE—VERBS—*Continued*

Survive. To exist longer than.
Tarry. To stay in the same place for a time.

PERMANENCE—*Adjectives.*

Conservative. Disposed or tending to maintain existing conditions.
Established. Made firm; well founded.
Intact. Left entire.
Inviolate. Unbroken; unhurt.
Monotonous. Kept up with wearying uniformity.
Permanent. Lasting.
Persistent. Inclined to remain firm.
Persisting. See *Verbs.*
Qualis ab incepto [L.]. The same as from the beginning.
Stable. See MUTABILITY-STABILITY.
Stationary. See MOVEMENT-REST.
Unchanged. Not changed.
Unchequered. Undiversified.
Undestroyed.
Unfailing. Incapable of being exhausted.
Unrenewed. The same as before.
Unrepealed. Not canceled.
Unsuppressed. Not subdued.

PERMANENCE—*Adverbs.*

At a stand. In a fixed state or condition.
At a standstill. At a full stop.
Finally. Lastly.
For good. For evermore.
In statu quo [L.]. In the former state.
Uti possidetis [L.]. The state of present possession.
Without a shadow of turning. With no sign of change.

PERMANENCE—*Phrases.*

Esto perpetua [L.]. Let it be perpetual. [Father Paul, of the state. Blackstone, I, 145.]
J'y suis et j'y reste [F.]. Here I am and here I stay.
Nolumus leges Angliæ mutari [L.]. We do not wish the laws of England to be changed. [The earls and barons of England. Blackstone, I, 19.]

MUTATION—*Continued.*

MUTATION—*Interjection.*

Quantum mutatus [L.]. How changed.

MUTATION—*Phrases.*

"A change came over the spirit of my dream." [Byron, *The Dream.*]
Casaque tourner [F.]. To turn one's coat; to change one's party.
In statu quo ante bellum [L.]. As it was before the war.
Mutatis mutandis [L.]. The necessary changes having been made.
Non sum qualis eram [L.]. I am not what I was. [Horace, *Odes* IV, i, 3.]
Nous avons changé tout cela [F.]. We have changed all that.
Tempora mutantur, et nos mutamur in illis [L.]. The times are changed and we are changed with them.
Vox audita perit, littera scripta manet [L.]. The spoken word perishes, the written word remains.

---

mutatis mutandıs [L.] (miu-tê'-tis miu-tan'-dis). The necessary change being made. COMPUTATION-PERMUTATION, INTERDEPENDENCE, MUTATION-PERMANENCE.

mutato nomine de te fabula narratur [L.] (miu-tê'-to nom'-i-nî dî tî fab'-yu-la nar-rê'-tur). The name being changed, the story is told of you. REPRISAL-RESISTANCE, TROPE.

mute. A *dramatıs persona;* unpronounced; silent; an instrument. ACTING, LETTER, LIFE-FUNERAL, MUSICAL INSTRUMENTS, SOUND-SILENCE, TALKATIVENESS-TACITURNITY, VOCALIZATION-MUTENESS; **deaf mute,** HEARING-DEAFNESS; **render mute,** VOCALIZATION-MUTENESS.

mute'-ness. Dumbness. LOQUACITY-TACITURNITY, SOUND-SILENCE.

mu'-ti-late. To retrench; to maim; to deform. ADDITION-SUBTRACTION, BETTERMENT-DETERIORATION, FORM-FORMLESSNESS.

mu'-ti-la''-ted. Incomplete. ENTIRETY-DEFICIENCY.

mu'-ti-la''-tion. Condition of being mutilated. GOOD-EVIL.

mu''-ti-neer'. To engage in mutiny. INSUBORDINATION-OBEDIENCE, PATRIOTISM-TREASON.

mu''-ti-neer'-ing. Rebelling. INSUBORDINATION-OBEDIENCE.

mu'-ti-nous. Rebellious. INSUBORDINATION-OBEDIENCE, PATRIOTISM-TREASON.

mu'-ti-ny. To rise against authority. INSUBORDINATION-OBEDIENCE, PATRIOTISM-TREASON.

mut'-ter. Faint sound; imperfect speech; to threaten; to grumble. CHARITABLENESS-MENACE, JUBILATION-LAMENTATION, LOUDNESS-FAINTNESS, SPEECH-INARTICULATENESS.

mu'-tu-al. Reciprocally related; correlative. COMPUTATION-PERMUTATION, INTERDEPENDENCE.

mu'-tule. An ornament. ARCHITECTURE.

muz'-zle. The mouth of a thing; to bind; to restrain.

APERTURE-CLOSURE, BORDER, MIGHT-IMPOTENCE, RELEASE-PRISON, RELEASE-RESTRAINT, SOUND-SILENCE, VOCALIZATION-MUTENESS.

muz′-zle–load″-er. A firearm loaded through the muzzle. WEAPON.

muz′-zy. Stupid; tipsy. HEED-DISREGARD, TEETOTALISM-INTEMPERANCE.

my. Personal pronoun. **All my eye,** TRUTHFULNESS-FABRICATION; **my stars!** ASTONISHMENT-EXPECTANCE.

my-col′-o-gy. Science of fungi. ZOOLOGY-BOTANY

myn-heer′. Sir. TITLE.

my-ol′-o-gy. Science of muscular system. TEXTURE.

my′-o-man″-cy. Divination. PROPHECY.

my-o′-pi-a. Defect in vision. SIGHT-DIMSIGHTEDNESS.

my-op′-ic. Near-sighted. SIGHT-DIMSIGHTEDNESS.

myr′-i-ad. Ten thousand; a multitude. FIVE-QUINQUESECTION, MULTIPLICITY-PAUCITY.

myr′-i-a-gram. Unit of weight. MEASURE.

myr′-i-a-me″-ter. Unit of lineal measure. MEASURE.

myr′-mi-don. An unscrupulous follower. BELLIGERENT.

myrrh. A perfume. PERFUME-STENCH.

myr′-tle. A plant sacred to Venus. LOVE-HATE.

my-self′. I; spirit. MATERIALITY-SPIRITUALITY, UNIVERSALITY-PARTICULARITY.

mys-te′-ri-ous. Secret; obscure; mystic. ASTONISHMENT - EXPECTANCE, CLEARNESS - OBSCURITY, ENLIGHTENMENT-SECRECY, VISIBILITY-INVISIBILITY.

mys′-ter-y. A dramatic representation; an enigma; a secret; a trade. ACTING, ENLIGHTENMENT-SECRECY, MANIFESTATION-LATENCY, OCCUPATION, TIDINGS-MYSTERY, VISIBILITY-INVISIBILITY.

mys′-tic. Uncertain; obscure; secret. CERTAINTY-DOUBT, CLEARNESS-OBSCURITY, DEVOTION-MAGIC ENLIGHTENMENT-SECRECY.

mys′-tic-al. Secret. CLEARNESS-OBSCURITY.

mys′-ti-cism. Obscurity. HEAVEN-HELL.

mys″-ti-fi-ca′-tion. Act of mystifying. CLEARNESS-OBSCURITY, ENLIGHTENMENT-SECRECY.

mys′-ti-fy. To confuse; to make obscure; to impose on the credulity of. EDUCATION-MISTEACHING, ENLIGHTENMENT - SECRECY, RATIOCINATION - INSTINCT, TRUTHFULNESS-FRAUD.

myth. A tradition; a fictitious narrative. FANCY, TRUTHFULNESS-FABRICATION.

myth′-ic. Fabulous. FANCY.

myth″-o-log′-ic-al. Fabulous. FANCY.

myth-ol′-o-gy. Science of myths. JOVE-FIEND, ORTHODOXY-HETERODOXY.

N

nab. Catch furtively or suddenly. Taking-Restitution, Truthfulness-Fraud.

na'-bob. Luxurious rich man; viceroy. Affluence-Penury, Order.

na'-cre-ous. Pearly. Variegation.

na'-dir. Lowest possible point. Top-Bottom.

nag. A small horse; a scold. Conveyer, Variance-Accord.

nager entre deux eaux [F.] (nɑ-zhê' ɑn·tr dʉz o). To swim between two streams; to be a trimmer between two parties. Bigotry-Apostasy.

na'-iad. Water-nymph; river-mussel. Jove-Fiend, Ocean-Land.

na'-ik. In British India, a leader or chief. Chief-Underling.

nail. Fix in place; a measure of 2¼ inches; a callosity. Anatomy, Connective, Hardness-Softness, Instrument, Keeping - Relinquishment, Length-Shortness, Suspension-Support, Union-Disunion; **hit the right nail on the head,** Discovery, Skill-Unskilfulness, Success-Failure; **on the nail** Settlement-Default, Time.

nail'-er-y. A place where nails are made. Workshop.

na-ive'. Characterized by unaffected simplicity. Craft-Artlessness.

na''-ive''-te'. Simplicity without art. Craft-Artlessness.

na'-ked. Stripped of clothes; evident. Dress-Undress, Manifestation-Latency; **naked eye,** Sight-Blindness; **naked fact,** Occurrence-Destiny; **naked sword,** Weapon; **naked truth,** Truth-Error.

na'-ked-ness. State of being naked. Nature-Art.

nam''-by-pam'-by. Affectedly pretty; weakly sentimental. Propriety-Impropriety, Society-Affectation.

name. Designation given to anything; nominate; reputation. Commission-Abrogation, Name-Misnomer, Reputation-Discredit, Sign, Word-Neology; **assume a name,** Name-Misnomer; **bad name,** Reputation-Discredit; **call names,** Regard-Disrespect, Uprightness-Dishonesty; **fair name,** Reputation-Discredit; **good name,** Reputation-Discredit; **in the name of,** Dueness-Undueness, Obstruction-Help, Rule-License.

NAME—MISNOMER.

Agnomen. An additional name, or an epithet appended to a name.

Antonomasia. Substitution of a title or epithet for a proper name.

Antonym. A word opposed to another in meaning.

Appellation. Name by which a thing is known descriptively.

Appellative. A common name as distinguished from a proper one.

Baptism. Act of baptizing, calling by the Christian name.

By-name. A nickname; epithet.

By-word. Common expression.

Cant, etc. Phraseology assumed for effect; stock phrases. See Word-Neology.

Cognomen. A name added to a nomen to denote family.

Cognomination. A cognomen or surname.

Compellation. Word of salutation.

Convertible terms, etc. Interchangeable, transformable terms. See Interpretation.

Denomination. Name; specific designation.

Description. A representation in words.

Designation. A distinguishing name or mark.

Empty name. A name destitute of force or meaning.

Empty title. A title or name without weight or value.

Epithet. A word expressive of some real quality in the thing to which it is applied.

Expression. A saying; representation by words.

Handle to one's name. A colloquial title.

Head. } Caption, title, or the like.
Heading. }

Hoosier. Nickname for an inhabitant of Indiana.

Name. That by which a person or thing is called.

Namesake. One who is named after another.

Naming, etc. Act of giving a name. See *Verbs.*

Nomenclature. A list of names, as used in a science or art.

Nomination. Act of mentioning by names.

Noun. Name of anything.

Nuncupation. Act of naming or dedicating.

Onomatopœia. Formation of words by imitation of sounds.

Patronymic. A name derived from an ancestor.

Prænomen. A name added to a family name to denote the individual.

Proper name. A name applied to a particular person, place, or thing.

Style. Title; phrase of appellation.

Surname. A name added to a personal name to make it more specific.

Term. A word or expression used to designate some definite thing.

Title. An inscription to designate the name of a thing.

Alias [L.]. A false or assumed name.

Assumed name. Pretended; fictitious name.

Assumed title. A name or title not generally credited to a person.

By-name. A nickname; epithet.

Lucus a non lucendo [L.]. A far-fetched etymology.

Misnomer. A wrong name; an inapplicable designation.

Nickname. A name sometimes given in derision, sometimes in compliment.

Nom de guerre [F.]. An assumed name on entering the army; a nickname; a traveling name.

Nom de plume [F.]. An assumed literary title.

Pseudonym. A fictitious name; a pen-name.

Pseudonymy. Practise of assuming different names.

Sobriquet [F.]. A fanciful or humorous appellation.

What d'ye call 'em, etc. A colloquialism indicating forgetfulness or contempt for the persons or things referred to. See Neology.

MISNOMER—*Denotation.*

Mrs. Malaprop. A character in Sheridan's *The Rivals,* who uses words inappropriately.

MISNOMER—*Verbs.*

Assume a name. To pretend to possess a name.

Miscall. To give a wrong name to.

Misname. To call by the wrong name.

Misterm. To name erroneously.

Nickname. To call by an opprobrious or complimentary name.

MISNOMER—*Adjectives.*

Anonymous. Bearing no name.

Having no name. Possessing no designation or appellation.

Innominate. Without a specific name.

Misnamed, etc. Wrongly named. See *Verbs.*

Nameless. Having no name; inexpressible.

Pseudonymous. Bearing a false name or signature.

Self-called. Named without outside aid.

Self-christened. Self-named.

Self-styled. Called or styled by oneself.

So-called. Generally styled thus; called as stated.

Soi-disant [F.]. Pretended; would-be; implying false pretense.

Unnamed. Not having received a name.

Without a name. Nameless; possessing no name.

MISNOMER—*Adverb.*

In no sense. By no means; by no process of naming.

NAME—*Continued.*

NAME—*Scientific Nouns*

Orismology.   Science of defining scientific and technical terms.

Technical terms.   Expressions or names in technical sciences.

NAME—*Verbs*

Baptize.   To christen or name.

Be called, etc.   To be appointed or named   See *Verbs*

Bear the name of.   To possess the name of.

Call.   To name; designate.

Characterize.   To mark; especially by stamping or engraving.

Clepe.   To name; call.

Define.   To state precisely the meaning of.

Denominate.   To give a name or epithet to.

Designate.   To mention by a distinctive name.

Distinguish by the name of.   To tell or recognize by the name.

Dub.   To name; entitle

Entitle.   To give a title to; name

Go or be known by the name of.   To be familiarly known by the name of so and so.

Go or pass under the name of.   To be known by.

Label, etc.   To classify or designate.   See MARK.

Name.   To distinguish by giving a particular appellation to

Rejoice in name of.   To take pride in a peculiar appellation

Specify.   To name expressly or particularly

Style.   To give a designation to; call.

Take the name of.   To receive or appropriate a name.

NAME—*Adjectives*

Cognominal.   Pertaining to the surname.

Hight.   Called; named.

Known as.   Recognized; called by name of.

Named, etc.   Nominated; mentioned; spoken of.   See *Verbs.*

Nominal.   Pertaining to a name; existing in name only.

Nuncupative.   Declaratory; existing only in name.

Nuncupatory.   Nuncupative; oral.

Orismological.   Pertaining to orismology

Titular.   Existing in title only, nominal

What one may fairly call.

What one may fitly call.   }   Expressions pertaining to naming,

What one may properly call.   but varying in degree.

What one may well call.

Yclept.   Archaic for called, named.

---

named.   Given a name.   NAME-MISNOMER.

name′-less.   Without reputation; anonymous.   NAME-MISNOMER, REPUTATION-DISCREDIT.

name′-ly.   To wit.   INTERPRETATION-MISINTERPRETATION, UNIVERSALITY-PARTICULARITY.

name′-sake.   Having the same name.   NAME-MISNOMER.

na′-ming.   Giving a name.   NAME-MISNOMER.

Na′-na Sa′-hib.   One of the leaders in the Sepoy mutiny   GOOD MAN-BAD MAN.

nan-keen′.   A Chinese fabric.   MATERIALS.

nan′-ny-goat.   Female goat.   MALE-FEMALE.

nap.   Woolly surface of felt, etc.; short sleep.   ACTIVITY-INDOLENCE, SMOOTHNESS-ROUGHNESS, TEXTURE.

nape.   Back of the neck.   ANTERIORITY-POSTERIORITY.

na′-pha-wa″-ter.   A perfume made by distilling orange-flowers.   PERFUME-STENCH.

naph′-tha.   An inflammable oil distilled from organic bodies.   CHEMISTRY, PULPINESS-OILINESS.

Na′-pier′s bones.   Mathematical contrivance.   NUMBERING.

nap′-kin.   Small cloth.   CLEANNESS-FILTHINESS; **buried in a napkin,** CAREFULNESS-CARELESSNESS; **lay up in a napkin,** USE-DISUSE.

nap′-less.   Without a nap.   DRESS-UNDRESS.

na-po′-le-on.   A form of euchre.   ENTERTAINMENT-WEARINESS.

Na-po′-le-on of fi-nance′.   Financier.   LABOR-CAPITAL.

Napoli, e poi muori, vedi [It.] (na-po′-lî, ê po′-î mu-or′-î, vê′-dî).   See Naples, and die.   BEAUTY-UGLINESS, PLEASURE-PAIN.

nap′-ping.   Unattentive; sleepy.   EXPECTATION-SURPRISE, HEED-DISREGARD, WITTINESS-DULNESS.

nap′-py.   Strong beer or ale.   TEETOTALISM-INTEMPERANCE, VISCIDITY-FOAM.

Nar-cis′-sus.   Mythological being.   BEAUTY-UGLINESS.

nar-cot′-ic.   A drug   HEALTHINESS-UNHEALTHINESS, REMEDY-BANE.

nar-rate′.   To tell; recite.   ACCOUNT.

nar-ra′-tion.   Something related.   ACCOUNT, RHETORIC.

nar′-ra-tive.   An orderly continuous account.   ACCOUNT, RHETORIC.

nar-ra′-tor.   One who relates or narrates.   TIDINGS-MYSTERY

nar′-row.   Contracted.   BREADTH-NARROWNESS, ENLARGEMENT-DIMINUTION; **narrow end of the wedge,** BEGINNING-END; **narrow escape,** ESCAPE;

narrow house, LIFE-FUNERAL, **narrow means,** AFFLUENCE-PENURY, **narrow search,** INVESTIGATION-ANSWER.

nar′-row-ing.   The act of reducing in width.   BREADTH-NARROWNESS.

nar′-row-mind′-ed.   Bigoted; selfish.   DECISION-MISJUDGMENT, UNSELFISHNESS-SELFISHNESS.

nar′-row-ness.   Illiberality.   BREADTH-NARROWNESS.

na′-sal.   Modified or produced by the nose.   SPEECH-INARTICULATENESS.

na′-sal ac′-cent.   Talking through the nose.   SPEECH-INARTICULATENESS.

nas′-cent.   Coming into being.   BEGINNING-END.

nascitur a sociis [L.] (nas′-i-tur ê so′-shi-is).   One is found out from his companions.   CONVENTIONALITY-UNCONVENTIONALITY.

nascitur ridiculus mus [L.] (nas′-i-tur ri-dic′-yu-lus mus).   A ridiculous mouse is born.   EXPECTATION-DISAPPOINTMENT.

naso, omnia suspendens [L.] (nê′-so, om′-ni-a sus-pen′-dens).   Suspending everything from his nose; turning up his nose at everything   [Horace.]   DESIRE-PARTICULARNESS.

nas′-ty.   Filthy; offensive; unsavory.   CLEANNESS-FILTHINESS, PALATABLENESS-UNPALATABLENESS, PLEASURABLENESS-PAINFULNESS; **cheap and nasty,** COSTLINESS-CHEAPNESS.

nata, pro re [L.] (nê′-ta, pro rî).   According to the circumstances.   TERMS.

na′-tal.   Birth; indigenous.   BEGINNING-END, DWELLER-HABITATION.

na-ta′-tion.   Swimming or floating.   TRAVELING-NAVIGATION.

nath′-less.   Nevertheless.   COMPENSATION.

na′-tion.   A race.   HUMANITY; **national guard,** BELLIGERENT.

na″-tion-al′-i-ty.   Patriotism; nation.   HUMANITARIANISM-MISANTHROPY, HUMANITY.

na′-tions, law of.   International law   LAW-LAWLESSNESS.

na′-tive.   Artless; not artificial; inhabitant.   CRAFT-ARTLESSNESS, DWELLER-HABITATION, NATURE-ART; **native accent,** VOCALIZATION-MUTENESS; **native land,** DWELLER-HABITATION; **native soil,** DWELLER-HABITATION; **native tongue,** LANGUAGE.

na-tiv′-i-ty.   Birth.   BEGINNING-END, NATURE-ART; **cast a nativity,** DEVOTION-MAGIC, PROPHECY.

nat′-ty.   Neatly fine.   BEAUTY-UGLINESS.

natura il fece e poi roppe la stampa [It.] (na-tu'-ra îl fê'-chê ê po'-î rop'-pê la stam'-pa). Nature made him, and then broke the mold. Solitude-Company.

natura non fecit saltum [L.] (nê-tiu'-ra non fî'-sit sal'-tum). Nature makes no leap. Regularity-Irregularity.

naturæ, vis medicatrix [L.] (nê-tiu'-rî, vis med-i-kê'-trix). The healing power of nature. Remedy-Bane.

nat'-u-ral. Intrinsic; not sharped or flatted; spontaneous; artless. Craft-Artlessness, Melody-Dissonance, Preparation-Nonpreparation, Purity-Crudeness, Sage-Fool, Subjectiveness-Objectiveness, Truth-Error; **natural condition,** Nature-Art; **natural course of things,** Habit-Desuetude; **natural death,** Completion-Noncompletion, Life-Death; **natural history,** Nature-Art, Organization-Inorganization; **natural law,** Nature-Art; **natural meaning,** Meaning-Jargon; **natural order of things,** Conventionality - Unconventionality; **natural philosophy,** Materiality-Spirituality; **natural religion,** Nature-Art; **natural science,** Nature-Art; **natural state,** Uniformity-Multiform-ity; **natural theology,** Nature-Art, Theology; **natural turn,** Affections.

nat'-u-ral-ism. Adherence to nature. Nature-Art.

nat'-u-ral-ist. Natural scientist. Organization-Inorganization.

nat''-u-ral-i-za'-tion. Conformity; conversion; location. Conventionality-Unconventionality, Conversion-Reversion, Establishment-Removal.

nat'-u-ral-ize. Habituate. Habit-Desuetude.

nat'-u-ral-ized. Inhabitant. Dweller-Habitation.

nat'-u-ral-ly. Spontaneously. Cause-Effect, Nature-Art.

nat'-u-ral-ness. Quality of being natural. Nature-Art.

na'-ture. Existing system of things; inclination; simplicity; affection. Affections, Craft-Artlessness, Inclination, Nature-Art, Subjectiveness-Objectiveness, Truth-Error, Uniformity-Multiformity, Universe; **animated nature,** Organization-Inorganization; **in nature's garb,** Dress-Undress; **organized nature,** Organization-Inorganization; **second nature,** Habit-Desuetude; **state of nature,** Dress-Undress, Preparation-Nonpreparation.

NATURE—ART.

Nature. The condition of the universe in respect to all its phenomena and laws.

Nature—*Associated Nouns.*

Accordance with reality.} Naturalness.
Accordance with truth.}
Character. Fidelity in painting the characteristic features of objects.
Conformity with nature. Agreeableness to nature.
Constitution. The make-up of anything.
Creation. The world of nature.
Essentiality. The essential characteristic of a thing.
Genuineness. Reality.
Ingenuity. Natural cleverness.
Legitimacy. Genuineness.
Nakedness. Natural state.
Natural condition. Naturalness.
Natural history. The study of zoology, botany, etc.
Naturalism. Adherence to nature in all forms of art.
Natural law. Laws governing the phenomena of nature.
Naturalness. State of displaying nothing artificial.
Natural religion. System of beliefs concerning God and duty toward Him derived from the study of nature and not from revelation.
Natural science. The science of material nature.
Natural theology. Theology based on the study of nature and not on revelation.
Nature-deity. A power of nature personified as a deity.
Nature-myth. Myth based on a natural phenomenon.
Nature-worship. The worship of natural objects or phenomena as gods.
Reality. The quality of being real.
Regularity. Quality of having uniformity.
Simplicity. State of being free from elaborateness.
Spontaneity. The quality of proceeding from inherent tendencies.
Unregeneracy. Quality and state of being unregenerate.

Nature—*Adjectives.*

Artless. Honest; frank.
Characteristic. Showing the distinctive qualities or traits of a person or thing.
Consistent with nature. Natural.
Constitutional. Inherent in the structure of the body or mind.
Created. Brought into being; caused to exist.
Essential. Belonging to that which makes a thing what it is.
From nature. Natural.
Genuine. Belonging to the original stock.
Indigenous. Produced, or existing naturally in a country or climate.
Ingenuous. Plain; candid.
Intrinsic. Innate; inward.
Legitimate. Authorized; not false.
Lifelike. Appearing as though possessing life.
Native. Conferred by birth; born in the region in which one lives.
Normal. Conformed to a standard, or nature.
Original. Pertaining to the origin, first in order.
Real. Actually in being or existence.
Regular. According to nature or law.

Art. The practical application of knowledge; study of a branch of learning to be applied; the embodiment of beautiful thoughts in sensuous forms.

Art—*Associated Nouns.*

Architecture. Science and art of constructing buildings.
Arithmetic. Science of numbers and the art of their use in getting results.
Astronomy. Science of the stars.
Copy. An imitation.
Creation of beauty. A beautiful creation.
Embodied beauty. Something showing perfect beauty in every respect.
Fine arts. Arts of beauty: painting, engraving, sculpture, music and poetry.
Geometry. That branch of mathematics which investigates the relations, properties, and measurements of figures.
Grammar. The art of correct use of a language.
Illustration. Representation.
Imitation. Something made to appear like its original.
Liberal arts. Higher branches of learning.
Likeness. That which resembles another thing.
Literature. The written productions of the human mind, embodying power-giving, inspiring, and elevating thought.
Logic. The art of reasoning.
Manufacture. Art of producing goods.
Music. Science and art of the rhythmic combination of tones.
Nativity. Picture representing the birth of Christ.
Painting. Art of representing objects on a surface by means of pigments.
Poetry. The art of expressing beautiful thought, feeling, or action in melodious rhythmical language.
Profession. Occupation requiring some knowledge of the liberal or fine arts.
Representation. Reproduction of an object by art.
Rhetoric. The science and art of discourse.
Science. Systematized knowledge.
Sculpture. The art of reproducing natural objects in solid form.
Skill. Dexterity.

Art—*Adjectives.*

Artificial. Made, or contrived by art; unnatural.
Artistic. Pertaining to art.
Copied. Produced from an original.
Illustrated. Made clear by examples, or figures.
Made. Produced artificially.
Manufactured. Made by hand or machinery.

Nature—*Adjectives—Continued.*

Simple. Open; not obscure; not complex.
Spontaneous. Arising from internal impulse, or natural law.
True. In accordance with the actual condition of things.
Unregenerate. Not changed from a natural to a spiritual state.

NATURE—*Continued.*

NATURE—*Adverbs.*

In course.　In regular succession.
In the course of nature.　By natural means.

Naturally.　According to nature.
Of course.　By consequence.

NATURE—*Phrase.*

"Study nature, not books."

na'-ture–de"-i-ty.　A natural power worshiped as a god.　NATURE-ART.

na'-ture–myth".　Myth about nature.　NATURE-ART.

na'-ture–wor"-ship.　Worship of natural objects.　NATURE-ART.

naught.　Nothing; zero.　PLURALITY-ZERO, SUBSTANCE-NULLITY; bring to naught, SUCCESS-FAILURE; set at naught, ANTAGONISM-CONCURRENCE, OBSERVANCE - NONOBSERVANCE, OVERVALUATION - UNDERVALUATION, REGARD - DISRESPECT, REGARD-SCORN.

naugh'-ty.　Perverse.　VIRTUE-VICE.

nau-ma'-chi-a.　Mock sea-fight.　STRIFE-PEACE.

nau'-se-a.　Disgust; weariness.　DESIRE-DISTASTE, ENTERTAINMENT-WEARINESS.

nau'-se-ate.　Affect with disgust; give pain.　PALATABLENESS-UNPALATABLENESS, PLEASURABLENESS-PAINFULNESS.

nau'-se-a"-ting.　Disgusting; sickening.　PLEASURABLENESS-PAINFULNESS.

nau'-seous.　Disgusting; unpleasant.　DESIRE-DISTASTE, PALATABLENESS-UNPALATABLENESS, PLEASURABLENESS-PAINFULNESS.

nau'-tic-al.　Pertaining to the ocean.　TRAVELING-NAVIGATION; nautical mile, MEASURE.

na'-val.　Relating to the navy.　TRAVELING-NAVIGATION; naval authorities, CHIEF-UNDERLING; naval engagement, STRIFE-PEACE; naval forces, BELLIGERENT.

na'-varch.　An admiral.　CHIEF-UNDERLING.

nave.　Main body of a church; the hub; the navel.　ARCHITECTURE, CENTER, FANE, MIDDLE.

na'-vel.　Central point; depression on the abdomen.　CENTER, MIDDLE.

nav'-i-ga-ble.　Capable of navigation.　TRAVELING-NAVIGATION.

nav"-i-ga'-tion.　State of being navigable.　TRAVELING-NAVIGATION.

nav'-i-ga"-tor.　A sailor.　WAYFARER-SEAFARER.

nav'-vy.　Common laborer; pioneer.　AGENT, PREPARATION-NONPREPARATION.

na'-vy.　Ships; fighters.　BELLIGERENT, CONVEYANCE-VESSEL.

na-wab'.　Moslem ruler.　CHIEF-UNDERLING.

nay.　A denial or refusal.　ASSERTION-DENIAL; nay rather, SAMENESS-CONTRAST.

Naz"-a-rene'.　Disparaging name given to Christ and early Christians.　GODLINESS-DISBELIEF.

N. B.　*Nota bene* (note well).　HEED-DISREGARD.

N. by E.　North by east.　AIM-ABERRATION.

N. E.　Northeast.　AIM-ABERRATION.

N. E. by N.　Northeast by north.　AIM-ABERRATION.

ne plus ultra [L.] (nî plus ul'-tra).　No more beyond; nothing superior to it.　BOUNDARY, COMPLETION-NONCOMPLETION, ENTIRETY - DEFICIENCY, FAULTLESSNESS - FAULTINESS, REMOTENESS - NEARNESS, SUPREMACY-SUBORDINACY, TOP-BOTTOM.

neaf.　The fist or hand.　KEEPING-RELINQUISHMENT.

neap.　Low; ebb.　ENLARGEMENT-DIMINUTION, HEIGHT-LOWNESS.

neap tide.　Low tide.　HEIGHT-LOWNESS.

near.　Like; not distant in time or place; to approach; miserly.　APPROACH-WITHDRAWAL, EARLINESS-LATENESS, EXTRAVAGANCE-AVARICE, FUTURE-PAST, LIKENESS-UNLIKENESS, OCCURRENCE-DESTINY, REMOTENESS-NEARNESS; bring near, LIKENESS-UNLIKENESS; come near, APPROACH - WITHDRAWAL; draw near, REMOTENESS-NEARNESS; near at hand, EARLINESS-LATENESS; near one's end, LIFE-DEATH; near relation, RELATIONSHIP; near run, MAGNITUDE-SMALLNESS; near side, RIGHT-LEFT; near sight, SIGHT - DIMSIGHTEDNESS; near - sightedness, SIGHT-DIMSIGHTEDNESS; near the mark, MAGNITUDE-SMALLNESS; near the truth, DISCOVERY; near upon, MAGNITUDE-SMALLNESS; sail near the wind, RECKLESSNESS-CAUTION, SKILL-UNSKILFULNESS.

near'-ly.　Within a little.　MAGNITUDE-SMALLNESS; nearly all, WHOLE-PART; nearly allied, RELATIONSHIP; nearly related, RELATIONSHIP.

near'-ness.　Closeness.　REMOTENESS-NEARNESS.

neat.　Clean; orderly; spruce; trim.　BEAUTY-UGLINESS, CLEANNESS-FILTHINESS, MIXTURE-HOMOGENEITY, PURITY-CRUDENESS, REGULARITY-IRREGULARITY, SIMPLICITY-FLORIDNESS TERSENESS-PROLIXITY; neat's-foot oil, PULPINESS-OIL.

neat'-hand"-ed.　Deft.　SKILL-UNSKILFULNESS.

neat'-herd".　A cow-keeper.　DOMESTICATION-AGRICULTURE.

neb.　The beak or bill.　CONVEXITY-CONCAVITY.

neb'-u-la.　Star-cluster; mist.　ASTRONOMY, UNIVERSE, VISCIDITY-FOAM.

neb"-u-los'-i-ty.　Cloudiness; nebulousness.　DIMNESS, VISCIDITY-FOAM.

neb'-u-lous.　Misty; obscure.　CLEARNESS-OBSCURITY, VISCIDITY-FOAM.

nec"-es-sa'-ri-an.　Pertaining to necessarianism.　VOLITION-OBLIGATION.

nec'-es-sa-ries.　Essential requisites.　NEED.

nec'-es-sa"-ri-ly.　By inevitable consequence.　CAUSE-EFFECT.

nec'-es-sa-ry.　Needful.　VOLITION-OBLIGATION.

ne-ces"-si-ta'-ri-an.　One who believes in fatalism.　VOLITION-OBLIGATION.

necessitas non habet legem [L.] (nî-ses'-si-tas non hê'-bet lî'-jem).　Necessity has no law.　NEED.

necessitate rei, ex [L.] (nî-ses-si-tê'-tî rî'-ai, ex).　From the necessity of the thing.　ACTION-PASSIVENESS.

ne-ces'-si-tate.　Make necessary.　NEED.

ne-ces"-si-ta'-tion.　Compulsion.　VOLITION-OBLIGATION.

ne-ces'-si-tous.　Extremely needy.　AFFLUENCE-PENURY.

ne-ces'-si-ty.　Fate; an essential requisite; poverty.　AFFLUENCE-PENURY, COERCION, NEED, VOLITION-OBLIGATION; make a virtue of necessity, SKILL-UNSKILFULNESS.

neck.　Long slender part of anything; part between the shoulders and the head.　ANATOMY, BREADTH-NARROWNESS, ENLARGEMENT-DIMINUTION; break one's neck, LIFE-DEATH; neck and crop, ADMISSION-EXPULSION, ENTIRETY-DEFICIENCY; neck and neck, EQUALITY-INEQUALITY; neck of land, OCEAN-LAND; neck or nothing, DETERMINATION-VACILLATION, RECKLESSNESS-CAUTION.

neck'-cloth".　A cravat.　DRESS-UNDRESS.

neck'-er-chief.　A kerchief for the neck.　DRESS-UNDRESS.

neck'-er-cloth.　A cloth for the neck.　DRESS-UNDRESS.

neck'-lace. Ornament; encircling molding. CIRCLE-WINDING, EMBELLISHMENT-DISFIGUREMENT.

necks. Water sprites. JOVE-FIEND.

nec-rol'-o-gy. A register of deaths. ACCOUNT, LIFE-DEATH.

nec'-ro-man''-cer. A magician. DEVOTION-MAGICIAN.

nec'-ro-man''-cy. Black art. DEVOTION-MAGIC.

nec-rop'-o-lis. A city of the dead. LIFE-FUNERAL.

nec'-rop-sy. Autopsy. LIFE-FUNERAL.

nec'-ro-scop'-ic. Pertaining to necropsy. LIFE-FUNERAL.

nec-ro'-sis. Mortification. HEALTH-SICKNESS.

nec'-tar. Sweet and delicious drink of the gods. PALATABLENESS - UNPALATABLENESS, SWEETNESS-ACIDITY.

nec-ta'-ri-ous. Like nectar. SWEETNESS-ACIDITY.

nec tecum possum vivere, nec sine te [L.] (nec tî'-cum pos'-sum viv'-er-î, nec sai'-nî tî). Neither with thee can I live, nor without thee. NEED.

need. Necessity; want; poverty; desire. AFFLUENCE - PENURY, DESIRE - DISTASTE, EXCESS - LACK, NEED; **friend in need,** ANTAGONIST-ASSISTANT; **in one's utmost need,** WELFARE-MISFORTUNE.

NEED.

Call for. A need.
Case of life or death. An extremely urgent necessity.
Case of need. Pressing occasion for something.
Demand for. Manifested want.
Desideratum. That which is desired.
Essentiality. The condition of being essential. See *Adjectives.*
Exigency. The condition of demanding immediate aid or assistance.
Indispensability. The condition of being indispensable. See *Adjectives.*
Matter of necessity. Something indispensable.
Necessaries. Those things which must be had unconditionally.
Necessaries of life. Those things which must be had to sustain life.
Necessities. Those things which must be had to satisfy certain wants or habits, but not so essential to the entire well-being as the necessaries.
Necessity. The condition which demands that certain things must be had.
Need. The condition of something being necessary or very desirable: used chiefly of concrete things.
Needfulness. Necessity for supply or relief.
Pinch. A case of need or emergency.
Requirement. That which is insisted upon as a necessary condition.
Requisite. Something which the very nature of things makes necessary
Run on. Continued and pressing demands, especially for payment of obligations; as, a run on a bank.
Sine qua non [L.]. An indispensable condition.
Stress. Great need; distress.
Urgency. The condition of being urgent. See *Adjectives.*
Want. The condition of being without that which contributes to our comfort or satisfies our desires.
Wants. Those things which contribute to our comfort or satisfy our desires.

NEED—*Verbs.*

Be necessary, etc. Impossible to be dispensed with.
Call for. To demand.
Create a necessity for. To make essential.
Desiderate. To feel a desire or need for.
Desire. To wish or long for.
Have occasion for. To have need or requirement.
Lack. To be deficient.
Make a requisite. To make necessary or needful.
Necessitate. To render necessary.
Need. To be in a condition of need. See *Nouns.*
Not able to do without. To have a great need for.
Not able to dispense with. To be necessary.
Prerequire. To require beforehand.
Put in requisition. To make an authoritative demand for.
Render necessary. To make necessary.
Require. To authoritatively make a necessary condition.
Stand in need of. To be in need of.

NEED—*Adjectives.*

Absorbing. Fully occupying; requiring one's whole time or attention.

Called for. Needed; required.
Crying. Calling for.
Destitute. Entirely bereft or lacking.
Essential. Of the very basis or essence, and without which a thing cannot exist.
Exigent. Demanding immediate aid or action.
Imperative. Absolutely required or necessary.
In demand. Necessary.
Indispensable. Not capable of being omitted; not so strong as essential.
In request. Sought after.
Instant. Pressing; urgent.
In want of. Needing or desiring.
Necessary. Of such a nature that it cannot be given up.
Needful. Necessary to the purpose.
Prerequisite. Necessary beforehand.
Pressing. Urgent.
Required. Made a necessary condition.
Requisite. Necessary from the nature of things.
Urgent. Of pressing need.

NEED—*Adverbs.*

Ex necessitate rei [L.]. From the necessity of the case.
Of necessity. Impossible to be otherwise.

NEED—*Phrases.*

It cannot be dispensed with.
It cannot be spared.
Mendacem memorem esse oportet [L.]. A liar needs to have a good memory. [Quintilian, 4, 2, 91.]
Necessitas non habet legem [L.]. Necessity has no law.
Nec tecum possum vivere, nec sine te [L.]. Neither with thee can I live, nor without thee. [Martial, XII, xlvii, 2.]
There's no time to lose.

need'-ful. Necessary; requisite. MONEY, NEED, VOLITION-OBLIGATION; **do the needful,** SETTLEMENT-DEFAULT.

need'-ful-ness. The state of being needful. NEED.

need'-i-ness. The state of being needy. AFFLUENCE-PENURY.

nee'-dle. Perforator; compass. MANAGEMENT, PERFORATOR-STOPPER, SHARPNESS-BLUNTNESS; **as the needle to the pole,** OBSERVANCE-NONOBSERVANCE, TRUTHFULNESS-FALSEHOOD, UPRIGHTNESS-DISHONESTY.

nee'-dle-gun''. Small gun. WEAPON.

nee'-dle-point''-ed. Sharp at the point. SHARPNESS-BLUNTNESS.

nee'-dle-shaped''. Shaped like a needle. SHARPNESS-BLUNTNESS.

need'-less. Useless. EXCESS-LACK.

nee'-dle-wit'-ted. Keen. SAGACITY-INCAPACITY.

nee'-dle-wom''-an. A seamstress. AGENT.

need'-y. Being in need. AFFLUENCE-PENURY.

ne'-er'-a-one''. Not a one. SUBSTANCE-NULLITY.

ne'-er'-do-well''. Good for nothing. GOOD MAN-BAD MAN.

ne-fa'-ri-ous. Heinous. VIRTUE-VICE.

ne-ga'-tion. Denial in general. ASSERTION-DENIAL.

neg'-a-tive. Inexisting; denial; minus quantity; prototype; confutation. ASSERTION-DENIAL, ENGRAVING, ENTITY-NONENTITY, NUMBER, PROFFER-REFUSAL, PROOF-DISPROOF, SAMENESS-CONTRAST; **prove a negative,** EVIDENCE-COUNTEREVIDENCE.

neg'-a-tive-ly. In a negative manner. ASSERTION-DENIAL, ENTITY-NONENTITY.

neg'-a-tive-ness. The state of being negative. ENTITY-NONENTITY.

neg'-a-to-ry. Signifying negation. ASSERTION-DENIAL.

neg-lect'. Carelessness; disregard; negligence. ACTION-PASSIVENESS, CAREFULNESS-CARELESSNESS, COMPLETION-NONCOMPLETION, DUTY-DERELICTION, ENTIRETY - DEFICIENCY, HURRY - LEISURE, INCLUSION-OMISSION, OBSERVANCE-NONOBSERVANCE, REGARD-DISRESPECT, USE-DISUSE; **neglect of time,** CHRONOLOGY-ANACHRONISM.

neg-lect'-ed. Disregarded. CAREFULNESS-CARELESS-NESS.

neg-lect'-ful. Careless. CAREFULNESS-CARELESSNESS, OVERVALUATION-UNDERVALUATION.

neg''-li-gee'. Careless attire. DRESS-UNDRESS.

neg'-li-gence. Disregard for appearances. CAREFULNESS-CARELESSNESS.

neg'-li-gent. Act of omitting what ought to be done. CAREFULNESS-CARELESSNESS.

neg'-li-gent-ly. Carelessly. CAREFULNESS - CARELESSNESS.

ne-go'-ti-ate. Mediate; bargain; transfer; traffic. ALIENATION, CONTRACT, EXCHANGE, MEDIATION.

ne-go''-ti-a'-tion. Act of transacting business. CONTRACT, EXCHANGE, MEDIATION.

ne-go'-ti-a''-tor. Mediator; agent. CONSIGNEE, CONTRACT, MEDIATION.

ne'-gro. Black man; slave. CHIEF-UNDERLING, ETHNOLOGY, WHITENESS-BLACKNESS.

ne'-gus. A drink. NUTRIMENT-EXCRETION.

neif. The fist or hand. KEEPING-RELINQUISHMENT.

neigh. Whinny; boast. BRAGGING, CRY-ULULATION.

neigh'-bor. One who is near; a friend. FRIEND-FOE, REMOTENESS-NEARNESS.

neigh'-bor-hood. Vicinity. REMOTENESS-NEARNESS.

neigh'-bor-ing. Adjoining. REMOTENESS-NEARNESS.

neigh'-bor-ly. Friendly; sociable; courteous; helpful. AMITY-HOSTILITY, OBSTRUCTION-HELP, POLITENESS-IMPOLITENESS, SOCIABILITY-PRIVACY.

nei'-ther. Not either. CHOICE-REJECTION; **neither here nor there,** CONNECTION-INDEPENDENCE, PRESENCE-ABSENCE; **neither more nor less,** EQUALITY-INEQUALITY, TRUTH-ERROR; **neither one thing nor another,** CONVENTIONALITY-UNCONVENTIONALITY.

nem. con. [L.] (nem. con.) Unanimously. ASSENT-DISSENT.

Nem'-e-sis. Goddess of chastisement and vengeance; retributive justice. EXCULPATION-PUNITION, PARDON-VINDICTIVENESS, RIGHT-WRONG.

nemine contradicente [L.] (nem'-i-nî con-tra-di-sen'-tî). Unanimously. ASSENT-DISSENT.

nemo me impune lacessit [L.] (nî'-mo mî im-piu'-nî la-ses'-sit). No one attacks me with impunity. DEFIANCE.

ne'-ni-a. An elegy. JUBILATION-LAMENTATION.

ne-og'-a-mist. A newly married person. MATRIMONY-CELIBACY.

ne''-o-log'-ic. Pertaining to the coinage or usage of new words or new meanings of words. WORD-NEOLOGY.

ne''-o-log'-ic-al. Pertaining to neology. WORD-NEOLOGY.

ne-ol'-o-gism. A new word or phrase. WORD-NEOLOGY.

ne-ol'-o-gist. A coiner of new words or meanings of words. WORD-NEOLOGY.

ne-ol'-o-gy. Coining or using of new words. WORD-NEOLOGY.

ne'-o-phyte. A novice. INSTRUCTOR-PUPIL.

Ne''-o-pla'-to-nism. An old system of philosophy. ORTHODOXY-HETERODOXY.

ne''-o-ter'-ic. New; modern. NOVELTY-ANTIQUITY.

ne-pen'-the. A drug said to banish pain and sorrow. LIGHTHEARTEDNESS-DEJECTION, REMEDY-BANE.

neph'-a-lism. The practise of total abstinence from intoxicating liquors. AUSTERITY, MODERATION-SELF-INDULGENCE.

neph''-el-og'-no-sy. The science of clouds. VISCIDITY-FOAM.

neph'-ew. Son of a sister or brother. RELATIONSHIP.

nep'-o-tism. Favoritism extended towards relatives. RELATIONSHIP, RIGHT-WRONG, TYRANNY-ANARCHY, UNSELFISHNESS - SELFISHNESS, UPRIGHTNESS - DISHONESTY.

nep'-o-tist. One who practises nepotism. UNSELFISHNESS-SELFISHNESS.

Nep'-tune. Mythological god of the sea; a planet. ASTRONOMY, OCEAN-LAND.

Ne'-re-id. One of the sea-nymphs. JOVE-FIEND, OCEAN-LAND.

nerve. Strength; intrepidity; part of the nervous system. ANATOMY, BRAVERY-COWARDICE, STRENGTH-WEAKNESS.

nerve'-less. Having no strength. MIGHT-IMPOTENCE.

nervos belli pecuniam infinitam [L.] (ner'-vos bel'-lai pî-kiu'-ni-am in-fi-nai'-tam). The sinews of war are unlimited money. WEAPON, MONEY.

nerv'-ous. Weak; timid; modest; style. CONCEIT-DIFFIDENCE, FORCE - WEAKNESS, SANGUINENESS-TIMIDITY, STRENGTH-WEAKNESS.

nerv'-ous-ness. The state of being nervous. SANGUINENESS-TIMIDITY.

nes'-cience. Ignorance. KNOWLEDGE-IGNORANCE.

nest. Series; retreat; cradle. CAUSE-EFFECT, DWELLER-HABITATION, MULTIPLICITY-PAUCITY; **nest of boxes,** LAMINA-FIBER.

nest'-egg'. An egg to attract a fowl when about to lay an egg. STORE.

nes'-tle. Fondle; snuggle. BLANDISHMENT, PRESENCE-ABSENCE, SECURITY-INSECURITY.

nes'-tling. Recently hatched. INFANT-VETERAN.

Nes'-tor. One of the Greek chiefs before Troy; an adviser. ADVICE, INFANT-VETERAN, SAGE-FOOL.

Nes-to'-ri-an. One of a sect of Christians, part of which still exists in Persia and Turkey. ORTHODOXY-HETERODOXY.

net. Snare; cover; gain; openly-woven fabric. CONTENTS-RECEIVER, CRAFT-ARTLESSNESS, CROSSING, DIFFICULTY-FACILITY, GAIN-LOSS, INCREMENT-REMNANT, ENCLOSURE, TRUTHFULNESS-FRAUD; **net profit,** GAIN-LOSS, OUTLAY-INCOME.

neth'-er. Lower. HEIGHT-LOWNESS.

neth'-er–most''. Lowest. HEIGHT - LOWNESS, TOP-BOTTOM.

net'-ting. Fabric of open-work. CROSSING.

net'-tle. An herb with stinging hairs; provoke. FAVORITE - ANGER, PLEASURABLENESS - PAINFULNESS, REMEDY-BANE.

net'-work. A system of cross-lines. CROSSING, REGULARITY-IRREGULARITY.

neur-al'-gi-a. Acute pain in the nerves. HEALTH-SICKNESS, PLEASURABLENESS-PAINFULNESS.

neu-rol'-o-gy. Science of the nervous system. TEXTURE.

neu-rot'-ic. Disease seated in the nerves. REMEDY-BANE.

neu'-ter. Taking neither side; sexless. CHOICE-NEUTRALITY, MATERIALITY-SPIRITUALITY; **neuter gender,** NOUN; **neuter verb,** VERB; **remain neuter,** DETERMINATION-VACILLATION; **stand neuter,** UNCONCERN.

neu'-tral. Mean; no choice; avoidance. CHOICE-NEUTRALITY, MEDIUM, QUEST-EVASION; **neutral tint,** COLOR-ACHROMATISM, GRAY-BROWN.

neu-tral'-i-ty. Mid-course; peace; insensibility; indifference. CHOICE-NEUTRALITY, MEDIUM, MIDCOURSE-CIRCUIT, QUEST-EVASION, SENSITIVENESS-APATHY, STRIFE-PEACE, UNCONCERN.

neu''-tral-i-za'-tion. The state of being neutralized. COMPENSATION, COOPERATION-OPPOSITION.

neu'-tral-ize. Counteract; compensate. COMPENSATION, COOPERATION-OPPOSITION.

ne''-vee'. Upper part of a glacier. HEAT-COLD.

nev'-er. Not at any time. DURATION-NEVERNESS; **it will never do,** APPROVAL-DISAPPROVAL, CONTENTEDNESS-DISCONTENTMENT, LEAVE-PROHIBITION, PROPRIETY-IMPROPRIETY; **never a one,** SUBSTANCE-NULLITY; **never-dying,** ETERNITY-INSTANTANEITY; **never-ending,** ETERNITY - INSTANTANEITY; **never-fading,**

Eternity-Instantaneity, Reputation-Discredit; **never forget,** Thankfulness-Thanklessness; **never hear the last of,** Entertainment-Weariness, Recurrence; **never indebted,** Settlement-Default; **never mind,** Carefulness-Carelessness, Consequence-Insignificance, Regard-Scorn, Sensitiveness-Apathy, Unconcern; **never-more,** Duration-Neverness; **never otherwise,** Uniformity-Diversity; **never say die,** Lightheartedness-Dejection, Persistence-Whim, Sanguineness-Hopelessness; **never so,** Magnitude-Smallness; **never tell me,** Assent-Dissent; **never thought of,** Purpose-Luck; **never tired,** Activity-Indolence; **never-tiring,** Persistence-Whim; **never to be forgotten,** Consequence-Insignificance; **never to return,** Future-Past.

nev'-er-ness. Having the quality of being beyond time or occurrence. Duration-Neverness.

nev"-er-the-less'. None the less. Compensation.

new. Novel; different; unfamiliar. Habit-Desuetude, Likeness-Unlikeness, Novelty-Antiquity; **give new life to,** Excitation, Obstruction-Help; **new birth,** Renovation-Relapse; **new blood,** Betterment-Deterioration, Excitation, Mutation-Permanence; **new brooms,** Activity-Indolence, Habit-Desuetude; **new-comer,** Constituent-Alien, Dweller-Habitation; **new conditions,** Modification; **new departure,** Beginning-End; **new edition,** Betterment-Deterioration, Recurrence, Renewal; **new ideas,** Education-Misteaching; **put on the new man,** Repentance-Obduracy; **turn over a new leaf,** Betterment-Deterioration, Mutation-Permanence, Repentance-Obduracy; **view in a new light,** Betterment-Deterioration.

ne-waub'. A deputy ruler in India. Chief-Underling.

new'-born". Lately born; infant. Infant-Veteran, Novelty-Antiquity.

New'-cas"-tle, car'-ry coals to. Throw away one's labor. Excess-Lack.

new"-fan'-gled. Novel; change; neology. Conventionality-Unconventionality, Mutation-Permanence, Novelty-Antiquity, Society-Ludicrousness, Taste-Vulgarity, Word-Neology.

new"-fash'-ioned. Lately come into fashion. Novelty-Antiquity.

new"-fledged'. Lately feathered. Infant-Veteran, Novelty-Antiquity.

New'-found-land dog. One of a breed of large dogs. Fauna-Flora.

New'-gate. Imprison. Release-Prison.

new'-gilt. Recently ornamented. Embellishment-Disfigurement.

new'-ly. Recently. Novelty-Antiquity.

new"-mod'-el. Revolutionize; improve; make anew. Betterment-Deterioration, Conversion-Reversion, Revolution.

new'-ness. Novelty. Novelty-Antiquity.

news. Anything new. Enlightenment-Secrecy, Tidings-Mystery.

news'-boy". A boy who sells or delivers papers. Messenger.

news'-mon"-ger. A gossip; one curious to know. Enlightenment-Secrecy, Inquisitiveness-Indifference, Tidings-Mystery.

new'-span"-gled. Newly adorned. Stream.

news'-pa"-per. A periodical. Mark-Obliteration, Publicity; **newspaper correspondent,** Consignee.

New'-year's day. The first day of the year. Determination-Vacillation, Periodicity-Irregularity.

next. Following; near; future; later. Antecedence-Sequence, Future-Past, Precedence-Succession, Remoteness-Nearness; **next friend,** Representative; **next of kin,** Relationship; **next to nothing,** Magnitude-Smallness; **next world,** Occurrence-Destiny.

Ni-ag'-a-ra. An American cataract. River-Wind.

niaiserie [F.] (ni-êz-rî') Foolery; nonsense. Meaning-Jargon.

ni'-as. A simpleton. Sage-Fool.

nib. Cut; point or extremity of anything. Beginning-End, Sharpness-Bluntness, Top-Bottom, Union-Disunion.

nib'-ble. Eat little bits of. Nutriment-Excretion; **nibble at,** Approval-Disapproval; **nibble at the bait,** Indentation, Readiness-Reluctance.

nice. Savory; fastidious; discerning; honorable. Desire-Particularness, Differentiation-Indiscrimination, Goodness-Badness, Palatableness-Unpalatableness, Pleasurableness-Painfulness, Truth-Error, Uprightness-Dishonesty; **nice distinction,** Variation; **nice ear,** Hearing-Deafness; **nice hand,** Adept-Bungler; **nice perception,** Differentiation-Indiscrimination; **nice point,** Difficulty-Facility.

nice'-ly. Completely. Entirety-Deficiency, Taste-Vulgarity.

Ni'-cene" Creed. The Trinitarian creed adopted at Nice, A. D. 325. Orthodoxy-Heterodoxy.

ni'-ce-ty. A minute distinction. Differentiation-Indiscrimination, Uprightness-Dishonesty.

niche. Recess; receptacle; angle. Angularity, Architecture, Contents-Receiver, Extension-Place; **niche in the temple of fame,** Reputation-Discredit.

nicher, se [F.] (ni-shê', se). To make one's nest. Establishment-Removal.

nicht wahr? [G.] (niʜt var). Not true? Is it not so? Investigation-Answer.

nick. Notch; deceive; mark. Indentation, Sign, Truthfulness-Fraud; **nick it,** Success-Failure; **nick of time,** Opportuneness-Unsuitableness.

Nick, Old. The devil. Angel-Satan.

nick'-el. An element; a coin. Chemistry, Values.

nick'-nack". A small article. Consequence-Insignificance.

nick'-name". A by-name. Name-Misnomer.

nic'-o-tine. Pungent; poison. Pungency, Remedy-Bane.

nic'-ti-tate. Wink. Sight-Dimsightedness.

nic"-ti-ta'-tion. The act of winking. Sight-Dimsightedness.

nidg'-et. A simpleton. Bravery-Cowardice.

nid"-i-fi-ca'-tion. Act of building a nest. Dweller-Habitation.

ni'-dor. Odor, as of cooked food. Odor-Inodorousness.

ni'-dor-ous. Emitting an odor, as of cooked meat. Perfume-Stench.

ni'-dus. A center of infection; nest. Cause-Effect, Dweller-Habitation.

niece. Daughter of a brother or sister. Relationship.

niente, tanto buon che val [It.] (ni-en'-tê, tan'-to bu'-on ke val). So good as to be worth nothing. Consequence-Insignificance, Usefulness-Uselessness.

nig'-gard. A miser. Extravagance-Avarice.

nig'-gard-ly. Meanly avaricious. Consequence-Insignificance, Extravagance-Avarice.

nig'-ger. A negro. Whiteness-Blackness.

nig'-gle. Befool. Regard-Disrespect.

nig'-gling. Trifling. Consequence-Insignificance.

nigh. Near. Remoteness-Nearness.

night. Period during which the sun is below the horizon. Light-Darkness; **labor day and night,** Toil-Relaxation; **night and day,** Frequency

RARITY; **orb of night,** UNIVERSE; **time of night,** TURBULENCE-CALMNESS.

night'–cap". Cap for wearing during sleep. DRESS-UNDRESS.

night'–fall". Evening: MORNING-EVENING.

night'–in-gale. A small bird. MUSICIAN.

night'–gown". A loose gown worn in bed. DRESS-UNDRESS.

night'–mare". An oppressive condition in sleep; any oppressive influence. FANCY, OBSTRUCTION-HELP, PLEASURE-PAIN, SANGUINENESS-TIMIDITY, SENSUALITY-SUFFERING.

night'–shade". A plant of the genus Solanum. REMEDY-BANE.

night'–shirt". A nightgown for men. DRESS-UNDRESS.

nig-res'–cent. Growing black. WHITENESS-BLACKNESS.

nig"-ri-fi-ca'-tion. Process of making black. WHITENESS-BLACKNESS.

nihil ad rem [L.] (nai'-hil ad rem). Nothing to the point. CONNECTION-INDEPENDENCE.

nihil tetigit quod non ornavit [L.] (nai'-hil tet'-i-jit quod non or-nê'-vit). He touched nothing without embellishing it. TASTE-VULGARITY.

ni'–hil-ism. The doctrine that nothing either exists or can be known; anarchy. GODLINESS-DISBELIEF, TYRANNY-ANARCHY, RULE-LICENSE, VIRTUE-VICE.

ni'–hil-ist. Advocate of nihilism. GODLINESS-DISBELIEF, GOOD MAN-BAD MAN, TYRANNY-ANARCHY, UPRIGHTNESS-ROGUE.

ni-hil'–i-ty. Nothingness. ENTITY-NONENTITY, SUBSTANCE-NULLITY.

nihilo, ex . . . nihil fit [L.] (ex nai'-hil-o nai'-hil fit). Out of nothing, nothing is made. CREATION-DESTRUCTION.

nil [L.] (nil). Nothing. ENTITY-NONENTITY, SUBSTANCE-NULLITY.

nil admirari [L.] (nil ad-mi-rê'-rai). To wonder at nothing. APPROVAL-DISAPPROVAL, ASTONISHMENT-EXPECTANCE, SENSITIVENESS-APATHY.

nil conscire sibi nulla pallescere culpa [L.] (nil consai'-rî sib'-i nul'-la pal-les'-ser-î cul'-pa). To be conscious of and to grow pale at no fault. INNOCENCE-GUILT.

nil desperandum [L.] (nil des-per-an'-dum). Never despair. SANGUINENESS-HOPELESSNESS.

nill. Will not. PROFFER-REFUSAL, READINESS-RELUCTANCE.

ni-lom'–e-ter. A river-gage. MENSURATION.

nim. Steal. THEFT.

nim'–ble. Agile. ACTIVITY-INDOLENCE, SWIFTNESS-SLOWNESS.

nim'–ble-foot"-ed. Speedy. SWIFTNESS-SLOWNESS.

nim'–ble-ness. Agility. ACTIVITY-INDOLENCE.

nim'–ble-wit"-ted. Quick-witted. SAGACITY-INCAPACITY, WITTINESS-DULNESS.

nim'–bus. A dark heavy rain-bearing cloud; a halo of light and glory. LIGHT-DARKNESS, REPUTATION-DISCREDIT, VISCIDITY-FOAM.

ni-mi'–e-ty. Excess. EXCESS-LACK.

nimis, ne quid [L.] (nai'-mis, nî quid). Not anything too much. GENEROSITY-FRUGALITY.

nimium ne crede colori [L.] (nim'-i-um nî crî'-dî co-lo'-rai). Trust not too much to looks. FAITH-MISGIVING.

n'importe [F.] (nan'-port'). It matters not. CONSEQUENCE-INSIGNIFICANCE.

Nim'–rod. A mighty hunter. LIFE-KILLING, QUEST-EVASION.

nin'–com-poop. Simpleton. SAGE-FOOL.

nine. Eight and one. FIVE-QUINQUESECTION; **nine days' wonder,** ASTONISHMENT-EXPECTANCE, CONSE-QUENCE-INSIGNIFICANCE, LASTINGNESS-TRANSIENTNESS; **nine lives,** LIFE-DEATH; **nine men's morris,** ENTERTAINMENT-WEARINESS; **nine points of the law,** HOLDING-EXEMPTION; **tuneful nine,** MUSICIAN, POETRY-PROSE.

nine'–fold". Nine times as many. FIVE-QUINQUESECTION.

nine'–pins. A game. ENTERTAINMENT-WEARINESS.

nine'–teenth". Ninth in order after the tenth. **Nineteenth century,** TIME.

nine'–ty. Nine times ten. FIVE-QUINQUESECTION.

nin'–ny. A foolish person. SAGE-FOOL.

nin'–ny–ham"-mer. A simpleton. SAGE-FOOL.

ninth. Next succeeding the eighth. FIVE-QUINQUESECTION.

Ni'–o-be. Daughter of Tantalus; wife of Amphion of Thebes. JUBILATION-LAMENTATION; **like Niobe all tears,** JUBILATION-LAMENTATION.

nip. Cut; bite. CREATION-DESTRUCTION, HEATING-COOLING, LENGTH-SHORTNESS, NUTRIMENT-EXCRETION, PUNGENCY, UNION-DISUNION; **nip in the bud,** LIFE-KILLING, OBSTRUCTION-HELP; **nip up,** TAKING-RESTITUTION.

nip'–per-kin. A small cup. CONTENTS-RECEIVER.

nip'–pers. Tools for nipping. KEEPING-RELINQUISHMENT.

nip'–ping. Biting cold. HEAT-COLD.

nip'–ple. The cone-shaped process of the breast. CONVEXITY-CONCAVITY.

Nir-va'–na. Annihilation. HEAVEN-HELL.

nis. A water-sprite. JOVE-FIEND.

nisi prius [L.] (nai'-sai prai'-us). Not before: a term applied to terms of court. EXCESS-LACK, LITIGATION.

Ni'–sus and Eu-ry'–a-lus. Two bosom friends. [Virgil, Æneid.] FRIEND-FOE.

nisus formativus [L.] (nai'-sus for-mê-tai'-vus). Creative energy. CREATION-DESTRUCTION.

ni'–ten-cy. Brightness. LIGHT-DARKNESS.

ni'–ter. Saltpeter. PUNGENCY.

nit'–id. Bright. LIGHT-DARKNESS.

nitor in adversum [L.] (nai'-tor in ad-ver'-sum). I strive against opposition. ANTAGONISM-CONCURRENCE.

ni'–tric. Pertaining to niter. **Nitric acid,** CHEMISTRY.

ni'–trous. Containing niter. **Nitrous oxid,** FEELING-INSENSIBILITY.

niv'–e-ous. Snowy. HEAT-COLD, WHITENESS-BLACKNESS.

nix'–e. A water-sprite. JOVE-FIEND.

nix'–ie. A mischievous water-spirit. JOVE-FIEND.

ni-zam'. Native sovereign of Hyderabad. CHIEF-UNDERLING.

niz'–ey. A simpleton. SAGE-FOOL.

no. Not so. ASSENT-DISSENT, ASSERTION-DENIAL, CHOICE-REJECTION, PROFFER-REFUSAL, READINESS-RELUCTANCE; **and no mistake,** CERTAINTY-DOUBT; **at no great distance,** REMOTENESS-NEARNESS; **at no hand,** MAGNITUDE-SMALLNESS; **at no time,** DURATION-NEVERNESS; **give no quarter,** LIFE-KILLING; **have no business there,** CONVENTIONALITY-UNCONVENTIONALITY; **have no end,** ETERNITY-INSTANTANEITY; **have no notion of,** ASSENT-DISSENT; **in no degree,** MAGNITUDE-SMALLNESS; **make no scruple of,** READINESS-RELUCTANCE; **no chance,** LIKELIHOOD-UNLIKELIHOOD; **no chicken,** INFANCY-AGE, MANHOOD; **no choice,** CHOICE-NEUTRALITY, VOLITION-OBLIGATION; **no conjurer,** ADEPT-BUNGLER, SAGE-FOOL; **no consequence,** CONSEQUENCE-INSIGNIFICANCE; **no doubt,** ASSENT-DISSENT, CERTAINTY-DOUBT; **no end of,** LENGTH-SHORTNESS, MAGNITUDE-SMALLNESS, MULTIPLICITY-PAUCITY; **no go,** SUCCESS-FAILURE, TRANSCURSION-SHORTCOMING; **no great shakes,** CONSEQUENCE-INSIGNIFICANCE, FAULTLESSNESS-FAULTI-

NESS, MAGNITUDE-SMALLNESS; **no less,** ENOUGH; **no longer,** FUTURE-PAST; **no love lost between them,** LOVE-HATE; **no matter,** CAREFULNESS-CARELESSNESS, CONSEQUENCE-INSIGNIFICANCE; **no more,** ENTITY-NONENTITY, FUTURE-PAST, LIFE-DEATH; **no more than,** MAGNITUDE-SMALLNESS; **no object,** CONSEQUENCE-INSIGNIFICANCE; **no one,** SUBSTANCE-NULLITY; **no one knows who,** GENTILITY-COMMONALTY; **no other,** SAMENESS-CONTRAST, SOLITUDE-COMPANY; **no scholar,** SCHOLAR-DUNCE; **no sooner said than done,** ACTIVITY-INDOLENCE, EARLINESS-LATENESS, ETERNITY-INSTANTANEITY, HURRY-LEISURE; **no stranger to,** KNOWLEDGE-IGNORANCE; **no such thing,** ASSERTION-DENIAL, ENTITY-NONENTITY, LIKENESS-UNLIKENESS, SAMENESS-CONTRAST, SUBSTANCE-NULLITY; **no surrender,** ATTACK-DEFENSE, BIGOTRY-APOSTASY; **no thank you,** PROFFER-REFUSAL; **no wonder,** ASTONISHMENT-EXPECTANCE; **on no account,** LEAVE-PROHIBITION, PROFFER-REFUSAL; **to no purpose,** SUCCESS-FAILURE, TRANSCURSION-SHORTCOMING, USEFULNESS-USELESSNESS; **unable to say no,** DETERMINATION-VACILLATION; **with no interval,** INTERSPACE-CONTACT.

No'-ah's ark. The ark in which Noah and his family were saved at the time of the flood. GATHERING-SCATTERING, MIXTURE-HOMOGENEITY.

nob. The head. TOP-BOTTOM.

no-bil'-i-tate. Make noble. INCREASE-DECREASE, REPUTATION-DISCREDIT.

no-bil'-i-ty. Those ranking by title above the common people. GENTILITY-COMMONALTY.

no'-ble. Excellent; worthy. CONSEQUENCE-INSIGNIFICANCE, GENTILITY-COMMONALTY, MAGNITUDE-SMALLNESS, REPUTATION-DISCREDIT, UNSELFISHNESS-SELFISHNESS, VIRTUE-VICE.

no'-ble-man. One of the nobility. GENTILITY-COMMONALTY.

no'-ble-mind''-ed. Magnanimous. UNSELFISHNESS-SELFISHNESS.

no'-ble-ness. Elevation of mind. VIRTUE-VICE.

no-blesse'. The body of the nobility. GENTILITY-COMMONALTY.

no'-bod''-y. No one. GENTILITY-COMMONALTY, PLURALITY-ZERO, PRESENCE-ABSENCE, SUBSTANCE-NULLITY; **nobody knows,** KNOWLEDGE-IGNORANCE; **nobody knows where,** REMOTENESS-NEARNESS; **nobody on earth,** PRESENCE-ABSENCE; **nobody present,** PRESENCE-ABSENCE; **nobody would think,** EXPECTATION-SURPRISE.

noct-am''-bu-la'-tion. Walking in one's sleep. TRAVELING-NAVIGATION.

noc-tiv'-a-gant. Wandering about in the night. LIGHT-DARKNESS, TRAVELING-NAVIGATION.

noc''-ti-va-ga'-tion. The act of wandering around in the night. LIGHT-DARKNESS.

noc'-to-graph. A writing-frame used by the blind. SIGHT-BLINDNESS.

noc-tur'-nal. Occurring or performed at night. LIGHT-DARKNESS, MORNING-EVENING, WHITENESS-BLACKNESS.

noc'-u-ous. Venomous; causing harm. GOODNESS-BADNESS.

nod. Motion of the head indicative of assent, sleepiness, command, etc. ACTIVITY-INDOLENCE, ASSENT-DISSENT, ORDER, POLITENESS-IMPOLITENESS, SIGN, VIBRATION; **nod of approbation,** APPROVAL-DISAPPROVAL; **nod of assent,** ASSENT-DISSENT.

nod'-ding. Inclining the head forward. ACTIVITY-INDOLENCE.

nod'-ding to its fall. About to tumble down. ASCENT-DESCENT, BETTERMENT-DETERIORATION, CREATION-DESTRUCTION.

nod'-dle. The head. MIND-IMBECILITY, TOP-BOTTOM.

nod'-dy. A dunce. SAGE-FOOL.

node. Swelling. CONVEXITY-CONCAVITY.

no-dos'-i-ty. Knottiness. CONVEXITY-CONCAVITY, SMOOTHNESS-ROUGHNESS.

nods and becks and wreath''-ed smiles. Expression of approval. POLITENESS-IMPOLITENESS.

nod'-u-lar. Having nodules. CONVEXITY-CONCAVITY.

nod'-ule. A little knot or lump. CONVEXITY-CONCAVITY.

nodus, dignus vindice [L.] (no'-dus, dig'-nus vin'-di-si). A knot worthy to be untied. DIFFICULTY-FACILITY, PHENOMENON.

noëmata [Gr.] (no-ê'-ma-ta). Thoughts. CONCEPTION-THEME.

nog'-gin. A mug. CONTENTS-RECEIVER.

noise. Loud, disagreeable sound. LOUDNESS-FAINTNESS, SOUND-SILENCE; **loud noise,** LOUDNESS-FAINTNESS; **make a noise in the world,** REPUTATION-DISCREDIT; **noise abroad,** PUBLICITY.

noise'-less. Silent. SOUND-SILENCE.

noi'-some. Very offensive; disgusting. GOODNESS-BADNESS, HEALTHINESS-UNHEALTHINESS, PERFUME-STENCH.

nois'-y. Making a loud noise. LOUDNESS-FAINTNESS.

nolens volens [L.] (no'-lens vo'-lens). Whether he will or not. COERCION, READINESS-RELUCTANCE, VOLITION-OBLIGATION.

noli me tangere [L.] (no'-lai mî tan'-jer-î). Do not touch me. DEFIANCE, DESIRE-PARTICULARNESS, EXCITABILITY-INEXCITABILITY, SOCIABILITY-PRIVACY.

no-li'-tion. Unwillingness. READINESS-RELUCTANCE.

nol-le'-i-ty. Unwillingness. READINESS-RELUCTANCE.

nolumus leges Angliæ mutari [L.] (nol'-yu-mus lî'-jîz an'-gli-î miu-tê'-rai). We do not wish the laws of England to be changed. CONSERVATION, DISCONTINUANCE-CONTINUANCE, MUTATION-PERMANENCE.

nom de guerre [F.] (non· de ger). War name. NAME-MISNOMER.

nom de plume [F.] (non· de plüm). An assumed or literary title. NAME-MISNOMER.

no'-mad. Rover. WAYFARER-SEAFARER.

no-mad'-ic. Wandering. MOVEMENT-REST, TRAVELING-NAVIGATION.

nom'-ad-ism. Nomadic tendency. TRAVELING-NAVIGATION.

nom'-ad-ize. To lead the life of a nomad. TRAVELING-NAVIGATION.

no'-man-cy. Divination by means of the letters in one's name. PROPHECY.

no'-men-cla''-ture. Glossary. NAME-MISNOMER.

nom'-i-nal. Existing in name only. NAME-MISNOMER, SUBSTANCE-NULLITY, WORD-NEOLOGY; **nominal price,** COSTLINESS-CHEAPNESS.

nom'-i-nate. To designate, as a candidate for an office. COMMISSION-ABROGATION.

nom''-i-na'-tion. Act of naming a man for office. COMMISSION-ABROGATION, NAME-MISNOMER.

nom'-i-na-tive. The case of the subject of a finite verb. NOUN.

nom''-i-nee'. Receiver of a nomination. CONSIGNEE.

nominis umbra [L.] (nom'-i-nis um'-bra). Shadow of a name. SUBSTANCE-NULLITY.

no-mol'-o-gy. Science of law and lawmaking. LAW-LAWLESSNESS.

non compos mentis [L.] (non com'-pos men'-tis) Not sound in mind. SANENESS-LUNACY.

non constat [L.] (non con'-stat). It does not appear RATIOCINATION-INSTINCT.

non deficit alter [L.] (non def'-i-sit al'-ter). Nothing is wanting. PLURALITY-FRACTION.

non inventus [L.] (non est in-ven'-tus) He has not been found. PRESENCE-ABSENCE.

non hæc in fœdera [L.] (non hec in fed'-er-a). Not into these alliances. ASSERTION-DENIAL, CHOICE-REJECTION.

non nobis, Domine [L.] (non no'-bis, dom'-in-î). Not to us, Lord. DEVOTION-IDOLATRY.

non nobis solum [L.] (non no'-bis so'-lum). Not for ourselves alone. UNSELFISHNESS-SELFISHNESS.

non nostrum tantas componere lites [L.] (non nos'-trum tan'-tas com-pon'-er-î lai'-tîz). It is not our duty to settle such grave disputes. POSSIBILITY-IMPOSSIBILITY, VARIANCE-ACCORD.

non obstante [L.] (non ob-stan'-tî). Notwithstanding. OBSTRUCTION-HELP.

non possumus [L.] (non pos'-su-mus). We are not able. BIGOTRY-APOSTASY, POSSIBILITY-IMPOSSIBILITY, PROFFER-REFUSAL.

non scripta, lex [L.] (non scrip'-ta, lex). The unwritten law. LAW-LAWLESSNESS.

non semper erit æstas [L.] (non sem'-per î'-rit es'-tas). It will not always be summer. LASTINGNESS-TRANSIENTNESS.

non sequitur [L.] (non seq'-wi-tur). It does not follow. RATIOCINATION-INSTINCT.

non sum qualis eram [L.] (non sum quê'-lis î'-ram). I am not what I was. MUTATION-PERMANENCE, STRENGTH-WEAKNESS.

non''-ad-di'-tion. Lack of addition. ADDITION-SUBTRACTION.

non''-ad-mis'-sion. Lack of admission. INCLUSION-OMISSION.

non'-age. The period of minority. INFANCY-AGE.

non''-a-ge-na'-ri-an. A person between the ages of ninety and a hundred. INFANT-VETERAN.

non''-ap-par'-ent. Not apparent. VISIBILITY-INVISIBILITY.

non''-ap-pear'-ance. Lack of appearance. VISIBILITY-INVISIBILITY.

non''-as-sem'-blage. Lack of assemblage. GATHERING-SCATTERING.

non''-at-tend'-ance. Lack of attendance. PRESENCE-ABSENCE.

nonce. Present time. TIME; **for the nonce,** OPPORTUNENESS-UNSUITABLENESS, TIME.

non''-cha-lance'. Indifference. CAREFULNESS-CARELESSNESS, DESIRE-DISTASTE, SENSITIVENESS-APATHY.

non''-cha-lant'. Indifferent. SENSITIVENESS-APATHY.

non''-co-he'-sive. Lacking cohesion. COHESION-LOOSENESS.

non''-co-in'-ci-dence. Lack of coincidence. SAMENESS-CONTRAST.

non'-com-mis''-sioned of'-fi-cer. An officer appointed by a regimental commander. CHIEF-UNDERLING.

non''-com-ple'-tion. Lack of completion. CAREFULNESS-CARELESSNESS, COMPLETION-NONCOMPLETION, ENTIRETY-DEFICIENCY.

non''-com-pli'-ance. Lack of compliance. ASSENT-DISSENT, INSUBORDINATION-OBEDIENCE, PROFFER-REFUSAL, TRANSCURSION-SHORTCOMING.

non''-con-form'-ist. A dissenter. CONVENTIONALITY-UNCONVENTIONALITY, ORTHODOXY-HETERODOXY.

non''-con-form'-i-ty. Refusal to conform. ASSENT-DISSENT, CONVENTIONALITY-UNCONVENTIONALITY.

non''-con-tent'. A member of the British House of Lords who votes in the negative. ASSENT-DISSENT.

non'-de-script. A person difficult to describe; indescribable. CONVENTIONALITY-UNCONVENTIONALITY.

none. Not one. PLURALITY-ZERO; **none else,** SOLITUDE-COMPANY; **none in the world,** SUBSTANCE-NULLITY; **none such,** CONVENTIONALITY-UNCONVENTIONALITY, GOODNESS-BADNESS, SUPREMACY-SUBORDINACY; **none the worse,** RENOVATION-RELAPSE; **none to spare,** EXCESS-LACK.

non''-en-dur'-ance. Lack of endurance. EXCITABILITY-INEXCITABILITY.

non-en'-ti-ty. Nothingness. CONSEQUENCE-INSIG-

NIFICANCE, ENTITY-NONENTITY, SUBSTANCE-NULLITY.

non''-es-sen'-tial. Not essential. CONSEQUENCE-INSIGNIFICANCE, SUBJECTIVENESS-OBJECTIVENESS.

non''-ex-ist'-ence. Absence of existence. ENTITY-NONENTITY.

non''-ex-ist'-ent. Not existing. ENTITY-NONENTITY.

non''-ex-pect'-ant. Not having an expectation. EXPECTATION-SURPRISE.

non''-ex-pec-ta'-tion. Lack of expectance. EXPECTATION-SURPRISE.

non''-ex-ten'-sion. Lack of extension. EXTENSION-INEXTENSION.

non''-ful-fil'-ment. Lack of fulfilment. COMPLETION-NONCOMPLETION, SUCCESS-FAILURE; **non-fulfilment of one's hopes,** EXPECTATION-DISAPPOINTMENT.

no-nil'-lion. The tenth power of a thousand. MULTIPLICITY-PAUCITY.

non–im''-i-ta'-tion. Lack of imitation. IMITATION-ORIGINALITY.

non–in''-ter-fer'-ence. Lack of interference. ACTION-PASSIVENESS, LIBERTY-SUBJECTION.

no'-ni-us. A small movable auxiliary scale. MENSURATION.

non-ju'-ring. Not swearing assent. ASSENT-DISSENT.

non-ju'-ror. A clergyman in English orders who refused to take the oath of allegiance, after the Revolution of 1688, to William and Mary. ASSENT-DISSENT, ORTHODOXY-HETERODOXY.

non''-nat'-u-rals. Things not constituting the being or nature of man, but necessary to his existence. HEALTHINESS-UNHEALTHINESS.

non'-ny. A ninny. SAGE-FOOL.

non''-ob-serv'-ance. Lack of observance. CONSEQUENCE-INSIGNIFICANCE, DUTY-DERELICTION, HEEDDISREGARD, INSUBORDINATION-OBEDIENCE, OBSERVANCE-NONOBSERVANCE.

non''-ob-serv'-ant. Inattentive. HABIT-DESUETUDE.

non''-pa-reil'. One who or that which is of unequaled excellence. GOODNESS-BADNESS.

non''-pay'-ment. Lack of payment. SETTLEMENT-DEFAULT.

non''-per-form'-ance. Failure to perform. COMPLETION-NONCOMPLETION, DUTY-DERELICTION.

non'-plus. Perplexity. DIFFICULTY-FACILITY, SUCCESS-FAILURE.

non–prep''-a-ra'-tion. Lack of preparation. PREPARATION-NONPREPARATION.

non''-prev'-a-lence. Lack of prevalence. HABIT-DESUETUDE.

non''-res'-i-dence. The state or condition of not being resident in a given place. PRESENCE-ABSENCE.

non''-res'-i-dent. Not residing in a particular place. PRESENCE-ABSENCE.

non''-re-sist'-ance. Absence of opposition. INSUBORDINATION-OBEDIENCE, YIELDING.

non''-re-sist'-ing. Making no resistance. YIELDING.

non''-res'-o-nance. Lack of the quality of resonance. RESONANCE-NONRESONANCE.

non'-sense. Absurdity; trifles. ADAGE-NONSENSE, CONSEQUENCE-INSIGNIFICANCE, MEANING-JARGON; **talk nonsense,** SAGACITY-INCAPACITY, TALKATIVENESS-TACITURNITY.

non-sen'-sic-al. Absurd; trifling. ADAGE-NONSENSE, MEANING-JARGON, RATIOCINATION-INSTINCT, SAGACITY-INCAPACITY.

non''-sub-sist'-ence. Lack of subsistence. ENTITY-NONENTITY.

non''-suc-cess'. Failure. SUCCESS-FAILURE.

non'-such. An unexampled thing. CONVENTIONALITY-UNCONVENTIONALITY, GOODNESS-BADNESS, SUPREMACY-SUBORDINACY.

non'-suit''. Abandonment of a suit by the plaintiff. EXCULPATION-CONVICTION, SUCCESS-FAILURE.

non'-suit"-ed. Dropped. EXCULPATION-CONVICTION, SUCCESS-FAILURE.

nonum prematur in annum [L.] (no'-num pri-mê'-tur in an'-num). Let it be kept for nine years. EARLINESS-LATENESS.

non-u"-ni-form'-i-ty. Variableness. UNIFORMITY-DIVERSITY.

non'-un"-ion. Not belonging to a trades-union. CONVENTIONALITY-UNCONVENTIONALITY.

noo'-dle. A blockhead. SAGE-FOOL.

nook. A narrow and retired place. ANGULARITY, CONTENTS-RECEIVER, EXTENSION-PLACE

noon. Midday. MORNING-EVENING.

noon'-day. Noon. LIGHT-DARKNESS; **clear as noonday,** CLEARNESS-OBSCURITY, MANIFESTATION-LATENCY; **bright as noonday,** LIGHT-DARKNESS.

noon'-tide". The time of midday. LIGHT-DARKNESS, MORNING-EVENING.

no"-o-scop'-ic. Metaphysical. MIND-IMBECILITY.

noose. Slip-knot. CIRCLE-WINDING, CONNECTIVE, RECOMPENSE-SCOURGE, TRUTHFULNESS-FRAUD.

N or M. General symbol for the name of any person. UNIVERSALITY-PARTICULARITY.

norma loquendi [L.] (nor'-ma lo-quen'-dai). Standard of speaking. GRAMMAR-SOLECISM.

nor'-mal. Regular; perpendicular. CONVENTIONALITY-UNCONVENTIONALITY, ERECTNESS-FLATNESS, NATURE-ART, SUBJECTIVENESS-OBJECTIVENESS; **normal condition,** UNIFORMITY-MULTIFORMITY.

normand, répondre en [F.] (nor-man", rê-pon·dr' an'). To give an evasive answer. TRUTHFULNESS-FALSEHOOD.

north. One of the four cardinal points of the compass. AIM-ABERRATION; **north and south,** LATERALITY-CONTRAPOSITION.

north'-er-ly. Toward the north. CONVEYANCE-VESSEL.

north'-ern. Situated toward the north. CONVEYANCE-VESSEL, LATERALITY-CONTRAPOSITION; **northern light,** YELLOWNESS-PURPLE; **northern star,** UPRIGHTNESS-DISHONESTY.

North"-west' Pas'-sage. A passage from the Atlantic to the Pacific along the northern coasts of America. CIRCUITION.

nosce te [L.] (nos'-sî tî). Know thyself. SAGACITY-INCAPACITY.

nosce tempus [L.] (nos'-sî tem'-pus). Know thy time. OPPORTUNENESS-UNSUITABLENESS.

noscitur à sociis [L.] (nos'-si-tur ê so'-shi-is). He is known by his companions. CONVENTIONALITY-UNCONVENTIONALITY.

nose. The part of the face which contains the nostrils and the organ of smell. ANATOMY, CONVEXITY-CONCAVITY, ODOR-INODOROUSNESS; **lead by the nose,** JUSTIFICATION-CHARGE, LIBERTY-SUBJECTION, MOTIVE-CAPRICE; **led by the nose,** LIBERTY-SUBJECTION; **not see beyond one's nose,** DECISION-MISJUDGMENT, SAGACITY-INCAPACITY, SKILL-UNSKILFULNESS; **put one's nose out of joint,** REPUTATION-DISCREDIT, SUCCESS-FAILURE; **speak through the nose,** SPEECH-INARTICULATENESS; **thrust one's nose in,** ACTIVITY-INDOLENCE, ENVIRONMENT-INTERPOSITION; **under one's nose,** DEFIANCE, MANIFESTATION-LATENCY, PRESENCE-ABSENCE, REMOTENESS-NEARNESS.

nose'-gay. A bunch of fragrant flowers. EMBELLISHMENT-DISFIGUREMENT, PERFUME-STENCH.

nos-ol'-o-gy. Systematic classification of diseases. HEALTH-SICKNESS.

nos-tal'-gi-a. Homesickness. CONTENTEDNESS-REGRET.

nos'-tril. One of the anterior openings of the nose. WATERCOURSE-AIRPIPE; **breath of one's nostrils,** INVESTIGATION-ANSWER, LIFE-DEATH; **stink in the nostrils,** PERFUME-STENCH.

nos'-trum. Scheme; quack medicine. DESIGN, REMEDY-BANE.

not. In no manner. ASSERTION-DENIAL; **it will not do,** RIGHT-WRONG; **not a bit,** ASSERTION-DENIAL, MAGNITUDE-SMALLNESS; **not act,** ACTION-PASSIVENESS; **not a few,** MULTIPLICITY-PAUCITY; **not a leg to stand on,** MIGHT-IMPOTENCE; **not a little,** MAGNITUDE-SMALLNESS; **not allowed,** LAW-LAWLESSNESS; **not amiss,** BEAUTY-UGLINESS, FAULTLESSNESS-FAULTINESS, GOOD-EVIL; **not any,** PLURALITY-ZERO; **not a particle,** SUBSTANCE-NULLITY; **not a pin to choose,** EQUALITY-INEQUALITY; **not a soul,** PLURALITY-ZERO; **not at all,** ASSERTION-DENIAL, MAGNITUDE-SMALLNESS; **not a whit,** MAGNITUDE-SMALLNESS; **not bad,** FAULTLESSNESS-FAULTINESS; **not bargain for,** EXPECTATION-SURPRISE; **not come up to,** EQUALITY-INEQUALITY, SUPREMACY-SUBORDINACY; **not expect,** EXPECTATION-SURPRISE; **not fail,** UPRIGHTNESS-DISHONESTY; **not far from,** REMOTENESS-NEARNESS; **not fit to be seen,** BEAUTY-UGLINESS; **not following,** RATIOCINATION-INSTINCT; **not for the world,** ASSENT-DISSENT, PROFFER-REFUSAL, READINESS-RELUCTANCE; **not grant,** PROFFER-REFUSAL; **not guilty,** INNOCENCE-GUILT; **not hardened,** REPENTANCE-OBDURACY; **not having,** HOLDING-EXEMPTION, PRESENCE-ABSENCE; **not hear of,** PROFFER-REFUSAL; **not identical,** SYNONYM-ANTONYM; **not included,** INCLUSION-EXCLUSION; **not know what to make of,** CERTAINTY-DOUBT, CLEARNESS-OBSCURITY; **not matter,** CONSEQUENCE-INSIGNIFICANCE; **not mind,** REGARD-SCORN, SENSITIVENESS-APATHY; **not often,** FREQUENCY-RARITY; **not of the earth,** GODLINESS-UNGODLINESS; **not one,** PLURALITY-ZERO; **not on speaking terms,** AMITY-HOSTILITY; **not particular,** CONTENTEDNESS-DISCONTENTMENT; **not pay,** SETTLEMENT-DEFAULT; **not quite,** MAGNITUDE-SMALLNESS; **not reach,** TRANSCURSION-SHORTCOMING; **not right,** SANENESS-LUNACY; **not sorry,** PLEASURE-PAIN; **not submit,** REPRISAL-RESISTANCE; **not the thing,** DUENESS-UNDUENESS, LOVE-HATE; **not to be borne,** PLEASURABLENESS-PAINFULNESS; **not to be despised,** CONSEQUENCE-INSIGNIFICANCE; **not to be had,** COSTLINESS-CHEAPNESS, EXCESS-LACK, POSSIBILITY-IMPOSSIBILITY; **not to be put down,** DETERMINATION-VACILLATION; **not to be thought of,** APPROVAL-DISAPPROVAL, DUENESS-UNDUENESS, LEAVE-PROHIBITION, POSSIBILITY-IMPOSSIBILITY, PROFFER-REFUSAL, REFLECTION-VACANCY, SANGUINENESS-HOPELESSNESS; **not to mention,** ADDITION-SUBTRACTION; **not trouble oneself about,** CAREFULNESS-CARELESSNESS; **not understand,** CLEARNESS-OBSCURITY; **not vote,** CHOICE-NEUTRALITY; **not within previous experience,** FREQUENCY-RARITY; **not wonder,** ASTONISHMENT-EXPECTANCE; **not worth,** CONSEQUENCE-INSIGNIFICANCE, USEFULNESS-USELESSNESS; **what is not,** TRUTHFULNESS-FABRICATION; **what ought not,** RIGHT-WRONG.

nota bene [L.] (no'-ta bî'-nî). Give good heed. HEED-DISREGARD.

notabilia [L.] (no-ta-bil'-i-a). Notable things. CONSEQUENCE-INSIGNIFICANCE.

no"-ta-bil'-i-ties. Persons of distinction. GENTILITY-COMMONALTY.

no"-ta-bil'-i-ty. A person of distinction. CONSEQUENCE-INSIGNIFICANCE, REPUTATION-DISCREDIT.

no'-ta-ble. Remarkable; distinguished; readily seen. ACTIVITY-INDOLENCE, CONSEQUENCE-INSIGNIFICANCE, MANIFESTATION-LATENCY, REPUTATION-DISCREDIT.

no'-ta-bles. Those worthy of note. GENTILITY-COMMONALTY.

no'-ta-bly. In a notable degree. MAGNITUDE-SMALLNESS.

no'-ta-ry. An officer empowered by law to note protests, administer oaths, etc. RECORDER, ADVOCATE; **notary public,** ADVOCATE.

no-ta'-tion. Convenient system of signs, figures, or abbreviations used in any science. NUMBERING.

notch. Hollow cut in anything. ANGULARITY, INDENTATION, MARK-OBLITERATION, SIGN.

notched. Indented. INDENTATION.

note. Remark; sign; explanation; epistle; fame; a musical character; a mark used to call attention to something; take cognizance. DIGEST, HEED-DISREGARD, INTERPRETATION-MISINTERPRETATION, MARK-OBLITERATION, MELODY-DISSONANCE, MIND-IMBECILITY, MISSIVE-PUBLICATION, MONEY, REPUTATION-DISCREDIT, SIGN, WRITING-PRINTING; **change one's note,** BIGOTRY-APOSTASY; **make a note of,** MARK-OBLITERATION, REMEMBRANCE-FORGETFULNESS; **note of admiration,** ASTONISHMENT-EXPECTANCE; **note of alarm,** ALARM; **note of preparation,** PREPARATION-NONPREPARATION; **of note,** CONSEQUENCE-INSIGNIFICANCE, REPUTATION-DISCREDIT; **take note of,** HEED-DISREGARD.

note'-book". A book in which to enter notes. DIGEST, MARK-OBLITERATION.

no'-ted. Famous. KNOWLEDGE-IGNORANCE, REPUTATION-DISCREDIT.

note'-wor"-thy. Remarkable. CONVENTIONALITY-UNCONVENTIONALITY, MAGNITUDE-SMALLNESS.

noth'-ing. No thing; not anything important. CONSEQUENCE-INSIGNIFICANCE, PLURALITY-ZERO, SUBSTANCE-NULLITY; **come to nothing,** FERTILITY-STERILITY, SUCCESS-FAILURE, TRANSCURSION-SHORTCOMING; **do nothing,** ACTION-PASSIVENESS; **for nothing,** COSTLINESS-CHEAPNESS; **go for nothing,** CONSEQUENCE-INSIGNIFICANCE; **good for nothing,** USEFULNESS-USELESSNESS; **have nothing to do with,** CONNECTION-INDEPENDENCE; **make nothing of,** ASTONISHMENT-EXPECTANCE, OVERVALUATION-UNDERVALUATION, SUCCESS-FAILURE; **nothing at all,** SUBSTANCE-NULLITY; **nothing comes amiss,** CONTENTEDNESS-DISCONTENTMENT; **nothing in it,** SUBSTANCE-NULLITY; **nothing loth,** READINESS-RELUCTANCE; **nothing more to be said,** PROOF-DISPROOF; **nothing of the kind,** ASSERTION-DENIAL, LIKENESS-UNLIKENESS; **nothing on,** DRESS-UNDRESS; **nothing on earth,** SUBSTANCE-NULLITY; **nothing to do,** ACTION-PASSIVENESS; **nothing to do with,** PROFFER-REFUSAL; **nothing to go upon,** POSSIBILITY-IMPOSSIBILITY; **nothing to signify,** CONSEQUENCE-INSIGNIFICANCE; **nothing whatever,** SUBSTANCE-NULLITY; **take nothing by,** SUCCESS-FAILURE; **think nothing of,** REGARD-SCORN; **worse than nothing,** SETTLEMENT-DEFAULT.

noth'-ing-ness. Worthlessness. CONSEQUENCE-INSIGNIFICANCE.

no'-tice. Observe; intelligence; warning. ADEPT-BUNGLER, DECISION-MISJUDGMENT, ENLIGHTENMENT-SECRECY, HEED-DISREGARD, MIND-IMBECILITY, PUBLICITY, WARNING; **bring into notice,** MANIFESTATION-LATENCY; **deserve notice,** CONSEQUENCE-INSIGNIFICANCE; **give notice,** ENLIGHTENMENT-SECRECY, MANIFESTATION-LATENCY, SIGN; **notice is hereby given,** PUBLICITY; **notice to quit,** KEEPING-RELINQUISHMENT; **short notice,** SIGN; **take no notice of,** CAREFULNESS-CARELESSNESS; **take notice of,** MIND-IMBECILITY, PUBLICITY; **this is to give notice,** HEED-DISREGARD; **worthy of notice,** CONSEQUENCE-INSIGNIFICANCE.

no"-ti-fi-ca'-tion. Notice given in writing or by signs. ENLIGHTENMENT-SECRECY, SIGN.

no'-tion. Idea. CONCEPTION-THEME.

no'-tion-al. Ideal. FANCY.

no"-to-ri'-e-ty. State of being too well known or unfavorably known. PUBLICITY, REPUTATION-DISCREDIT.

no-to'-ri-ous. Famous; infamous. KNOWLEDGE-IGNORANCE, MANIFESTATION-LATENCY, PUBLICITY, REPUTATION-DISCREDIT.

Notre Dame [F.] (notr dam). Our Lady; the Blessed Virgin. DIVINITY, INNOCENCE-GUILT, PIETY-IMPIETY, PURITY-IMPURITY.

notturno [It.] (not-tur'-no). A nocturne. MUSIC.

not"-with-stand'-ing. Despite. COMPENSATION.

nought. Zero. ZERO.

noun. A name of an object of thought. NOUN; **abstract noun,** NOUN; **collective noun,** NOUN; **common noun,** NOUN; **compound noun,** NOUN; **concrete noun,** NOUN; **derivative noun,** NOUN; **diminutive noun,** NOUN; **material noun,** NOUN; **participial noun,** NOUN; **primary noun,** NOUN; **proper noun,** NOUN; **simple noun,** NOUN.

NOUN.

Noun. Name of an object of thought.
Substantive. A noun; a word or phrase used as a noun.

NOUN—*Kinds.*

Abstract noun. Name of a quality, action, or condition.
Collective noun. Noun which denotes plurality without a plural termination.
Common noun. Name of a class, or of each one of a class.
Compound noun. Noun composed of two or more other words in composition.
Concrete noun. Name of a substance or material object; or of a quality, action, or condition inherent in that substance.
Derivative noun. Noun derived from another word by means of some affix.
Diminutive noun. Noun which expresses diminutive size.
Material noun. Name of a material.
Participial noun. A participle used as a noun.
Primary noun. Noun not formed by derivation.
Proper noun. An individual name.
Simple noun. Noun not formed by composition.

NOUN—*Associated Words.*

Case. The relation of a noun to other words.
　Ablative. Case denoting usually the relation indicated in English by with, from, by, in, etc.
　Accusative. Case equivalent to the English objective.
　Dative. Case of the indirect object.
　Genitive. Case denoting the relation indicated in English by the possessive, or the preposition *of.*
　Nominative. The case in English of the subject of a finite verb, the predicate noun after a nominative, the person or thing addressed, the subject of a participle, and the independent noun.
　Objective. The case of the object of a verb, the predicate noun after an object, the subject of an infinitive and after a preposition.
　Possessive. The case indicating the possessor.
　Vocative. Case in several languages of address.
Gender. A grammatical distinction expressing the natural distinction of sex.
　Feminine gender. Gender of the names of females.
　Masculine gender. Gender of the names of males.
　Neuter gender. Gender of the names of things without sex.
Number. Grammatical distinction between one or more than one.
　Dual number. Number expressing two.
　Plural number. Number denoting more than one.
　Singular number. Number denoting but one.
Person. Grammatical distinction to express the relation of a noun to the speaker.
　First person. The speaker.
　Second person. The person spoken to.
　Third person. The person or thing spoken of

nour'-ish. To feed. OBSTRUCTION-HELP.

nour'-ish-ment. Food. LIFE-DEATH, NUTRIMENT-EXCRETION, OBSTRUCTION-HELP.

nous. Mind. MIND-IMBECILITY.

nous avons changé tout cela [F.] (nuz a-von·' shan·-zhě' tu se-la'). We have changed all that. MUTATION-PERMANENCE.

nou'-sel. To ensnare. TRUTHFULNESS-FRAUD.

nou'-sle. Ensnare. TRUTHFULNESS-FRAUD.

Nova Zembla. Two Russian islands in the Arctic Ocean. HEAT-COLD.

No-va'-tian. One of a sect of Cathari founded by Novatianus. ORTHODOXY-HETERODOXY

no-va′-tion. A making new. CHOICE-NEUTRALITY.
nov′-el. A fictitious tale; new. ACCOUNT, KNOWL-EDGE-IGNORANCE, LIKENESS-UNLIKENESS; NOV-ELTY-ANTIQUITY.
nov′-el-ist. A writer of novels. ACCOUNT.

novello, di . . . tutto par bello [It.] (dî no-vel′-lo tut′-to par bel′-lo). Everything new is fair to view. BEAUTY-UGLINESS, NOVELTY-ANTIQUITY.
nov′-el-ty. Strangeness. LIKENESS-UNLIKENESS, NOV-ELTY-ANTIQUITY.

NOVELTY—ANTIQUITY.

Gloss of novelty. Attractiveness caused by newness or unfamiliarity.
Immaturity. Unripeness; incompleteness.
Innovation. Something new in customs, rites, etc.
Newness. State or quality of being new; recentness.
Novelty. A new or strange thing.
Recency. Lateness in time; freshness.
Renovation, etc. Making new after decay; renewal. See RENOVA-TION.
Youth, etc. That part of life between childhood and manhood. See INFANCY.

NOVELTY—*Denotations.*

Latest fashion. The prevailing mode or style, especially of dress.
Modernism. A modern usage or mode of expression.
Mushroom. One who rises suddenly from a low condition in life.
Parvenu [F.]. A man newly risen into notice.

NOVELTY—*Verbs.*

Modernize. To render modern.
Renew, etc. To make or begin over again. See RENOVATION.

NOVELTY—*Adjectives.*

Brand-new. Bright and fresh.
Evergreen. Retaining greenness; always fresh.
Fresh. Newly prepared or produced.
Fresh as a daisy. Bright and cheerful.
Fresh as a rose. Ruddy and beautiful.
Fresh as paint. Recently grown, made, etc.
Green. Immature; unripe.
Immature. Undeveloped; imperfect.
Just out. Appearing at this moment.
Late. Recent; coming after a suitable time.
Modern. Pertaining to the present.
Neoteric. New; recent origin.
New. Lately come into existence.
New-born. Lately born.
New-fangled. New-made or new-fashioned.
New-fashioned. Made in new style.
New-fledged. Lately feathered.
Novel. Unusual; strange.
Of yesterday. Recent.
Raw. Newly done; fresh.
Recent. Pertaining to time not long past.
Renovated. Made new and vigorous.
Spick and span. Bright; quite new.
Unbeaten. Not trodden down; new.
Unhandled. Not previously used.
Untried. Not yet experienced.
Untrodden. Unfrequented; not marked by feet.
Vernal. Belonging to the spring.
Virgin. Pertaining to a virgin; first.
Young, etc. Not long born. See INFANCY

NOVELTY—*Adverbs.*

Afresh. As a new act; over again
Anew. Once more; again.
Just now. The present moment; immediately.
Lately. Not long ago.
Latterly. In time not long past.
Newly, etc. Lately; recently. See *Adjectives.*
Of late. In times past; near the present.
Only yesterday. Long past time conceived of as quite recent.
The other day. Indefinite past time.

NOVELTY—*Phrases*

Di novello tutto par bello [It.]. Everything new is fair to view.
Nullum est jam dictum quod non dictum est prius [L.]. Nothing is said nowadays that has not been said before.
Tempi passati [L.]. Times gone by.
Una scopa nova spazza bene [It.]. A new broom sweeps clean.

Age. A period of time; state of being old.
Antiquity. Times long past.
Oldness. State of being advanced in years. See *Adjectives.*

ANTIQUITY—*Nouns of Result.*

Decay. Gradual decline; deterioration.
Decline. Tendency to a worse state; a falling off.
Maturity. Ripeness; state of perfection.
Senility, etc. Old age; dotage. See INFANCY-AGE.

ANTIQUITY—*Denotations.*

Archaism. An ancient, or old-fashioned, word, expression, or idiom.
Cobwebs of antiquity. The marks and results of old age.
Common law. The law which receives its binding force from im-memorial usage.
Custom. Long-established practise.
Immemorial usage. A custom or practise antedating history.
Megatherium. An extinct gigantic mammal.
Prescription. Custom continued until it has the force of law.
Relic of the past. Anything preserved in remembrance of past years.
Sanskrit. The ancient Hindu language.
Thing of the past. Anything out of date.
Tradition. Knowledge or belief transmitted from ancestors to pos-terity

ANTIQUITY—*Nouns of Degree.*

Eldership. Office of an elder in a church; state of being older.
Primogeniture. State of being the first-born child of the same par-ents.
Seniority. Priority of birth or office.

ANTIQUITY—*Verbs.*

Age. To grow old.
Become old. To begin to take on the characteristics of age. See *Adjectives.*
Be old, etc. To be advanced in years. See *Adjectives*
Fade. To decay or wither.
Have had. To be past.
Have seen its day. To have passed into a state of decay or deteriora-tion.

ANTIQUITY—*Adjectives.*

Aboriginal, etc. Native to the soil; first; primitive. See BEGIN-NING.
After age. Succeeding time.
Ancestral black-letter. Printed in the old English or Gothic letter.
Ancient. Of great age.
Antediluvian. Pertaining to times before the flood.
Antemundane. Before the creation of the world.
Antiquated. Grown old; old-fashioned.
Antique. Old; ancient.
Archaic. Obsolete.
Behind the age. Not up with the thought or methods of the day.
Classic. Pertaining to ancient literature or art of the highest type.
Crumbling, etc. Falling to pieces through age. See BETTERMENT-DETERIORATION.
Customary. Usual; habitual.
Diluvian. Pertaining to the deluge.
Elder. Senior; older.
Eldest. Most advanced in age.
Exploded. Rejected; condemned.
First-born. First brought forth; preeminent.
Fossil. Dug out of the earth; that which is antiquated.
Gone by. Omitted.
Gone out. Died away.
Immemorial. Beyond memory; long ago.
Inveterate. Deep-rooted; obstinate from long continuance.
Medieval. Belonging to the middle ages.
Obsolete. Gone out of use; out of date.
Of long standing. In existence for a long time.
Of other times. Old-fashioned.
Of the old school. Belonging to an earlier time.
Old. Aged; far advanced in years.

ANTIQUITY—Adjectives—*Continued.*

Old as Adam.
Old as history.
Old as Methuselah. } Expressions employed to denote time long past.
Old as the hills.
Old-fashioned. Antiquated; having characteristics of former times.
Out of date. Behind the times; out of use.
Out of fashion. Not in vogue.
Palæocrystic. Ice-covered regions of the Arctic and Antarctic Oceans.
Palæozoic. Pertaining to the lowest geological strata in which forms of life appear.
Passé [F.]. Past; out of use.
Patriarchal. Pertaining to the ruler of a family.
Preadamite. Existing before Adam.
Preglacial. Prior to the glacial period.
Prehistoric. Relating to a period antecedent to written history.
Prerafaelite. Pertaining to a style of art which preceded Rafael.
Prescriptive. Acquired by immemorial use.
Prime. First in time or order; beginning.

Primeval. Original; belonging to the first ages.
Primigenous. First formed; original.
Primitive. Belonging to early times; ancient.
Primordial. Existing from the beginning.
Primordinate. Of earliest origin.
Rococo. Having a tendency to be bizarre in art and literature: fantastic.
Rooted. Deep; radical.
Run out. Ended; consumed; spent.
Second-hand. That which has been used before.
Senile, etc. Affected by old age. See INFANCY-AGE.
Stale. Having lost freshness.
Time-honored. Honored from former times.
Time-worn. Impaired by time; weather-beaten.
Traditional. Transmitted by word of mouth only.
Venerable. Rendered sacred by age.
Whereof the memory of man runneth not to the contrary. Immemorial.

ANTIQUITY—*Adverbs.*

Since the days of Methuselah.
Since the world was made. } Expressions which denote time long past.
Since the year one.

---

nov'-ice. A beginner in any business or occupation; one who enters a religious order on probation. ADEPT - BUNGLER, INSTRUCTOR - PUPIL, MINISTRY-LAITY, SCHOLAR-DUNCE.

no-vi'-ti-ate. State or time of being a novice. EDUCATION-LEARNING, PREPARATION-NONPREPARATION.

novus homo [L.] (no'-vus ho'-mo). A stranger; an upstart. CONSTITUENT - ALIEN, GENTILITY - COMMONALTY.

now. At the present time. TIME; **now and then,** FREQUENCY-RARITY; **now or never,** OPPORTUNENESS-UNSUITABLENESS.

now'-a-days''. In the present time. TIME.

no'-ways''. In no way or manner. MAGNITUDE-SMALLNESS.

no'-where''. In no place. PRESENCE-ABSENCE.

no'-wise''. In no manner or degree. ASSERTION-DENIAL, MAGNITUDE-SMALLNESS.

nox'-ious. Tending to cause injury, especially to health or morals. GOODNESS-BADNESS, HEALTHINESS-UNHEALTHINESS.

no''-yade'. Act of drowning. EXCULPATION-PUNITION, LIFE-KILLING.

noyerait dans une goutte d'eau, il se [F.] (noy-er-ê' dan·z ün gut do, il se). He will drown himself in a drop of water. SKILL-UNSKILFULNESS.

noz'-zle. A projecting spout or pipe for discharging water. APERTURE-CLOSURE, CONVEXITY-CONCAVITY, WATERCOURSE-AIRPIPE.

nu''-ance'. Shade of difference in color. DIFFERENTIATION-INDISCRIMINATION, VARIATION.

nubes, occurrent [L.] (niu'-biz, oc-cur'-rent). Clouds will intervene. OBSTRUCTION-HELP.

nubibus, in [L.] (niu'-bi-bus, in). In the clouds; imaginary. ENTITY-NONENTITY, FANCY.

nu-bif'-er-ous. Cloud-bearing. DIAPHANEITY-OPAQUENESS.

nu'-bile. Marriageable. MANHOOD, MATRIMONY-CELIBACY.

nu-cle'-o-lus. A little nucleus. CENTER, MIDDLE.

nu'-cle-us. A center of growth; a kernel. CAUSE-EFFECT, CENTER, CONSEQUENCE-INSIGNIFICANCE, MIDDLE.

nu-da'-tion. The act of making nude. DRESS-UNDRESS.

nuda veritas [L.] (niu'-da ver'-i-tas). The naked truth. TRUTH-ERROR.

nude. Destitute of covering. DRESS-UNDRESS.

nudge. To touch or push gently as a warning. SIGN.

nu'-di-ty. State of being nude. DRESS-UNDRESS.

nu-gac'-i-ty. Trifling talk or behavior. SAGACITY-INCAPACITY, USEFULNESS-USELESSNESS.

nugæ canoræ [L.] (niu'-jî ca-no'-rî). Silly verses. MEANING-JARGON, WITTINESS-DULNESS.

nugas, magno conatu magnas [L.] (niu'-gas, mag'-no co-nê'-tiu mag'-nas). Much nonsense at great effort. CONSEQUENCE-INSIGNIFICANCE.

nu'-ga-to-ry. Having no power or force. MIGHT-IMPOTENCE.

nug'-get. A mass, especially of precious metal. GREATNESS-LITTLENESS, MONEY.

nui'-sance. That which causes trouble or annoyance. GOOD-EVIL, PLEASURABLENESS-PAINFULNESS.

null. Of no legal effect or force. SUBSTANCE-NULLITY; **declare null and void,** COMMISSION-ABROGATION, OBSERVANCE-NONOBSERVANCE; **null and void,** FERTILITY-STERILITY, LAW-LAWLESSNESS, MIGHT-IMPOTENCE.

nulla dies sine linea [L.] (nul'-la dai'-îz sai'-nî lin'-î-a). Not a day without a line. ACTIVITY-INDOLENCE.

nulla pallescere culpa, nil conscire sibi [L.] (nul'-la pal-les'-ser-î cul'-pa, nil con-sai'-rî sib'-i). To be conscious of no fault pales at no charge. INNOCENCE-GUILT.

nulli secundus [L.] (nul'-lai sî-cun'-dus). Second to none. SUPREMACY-SUBORDINACY.

nul''-li-bi'-e-ty. State of being nowhere. PRESENCE-ABSENCE.

nul''-li-fi-ca'-tion. The act of nullifying. COMMISSION-ABROGATION, OBSERVANCE-NONOBSERVANCE.

nul'-li-fy. To deprive of force or effect. COMMISSION-ABROGATION, COMPENSATION, CREATION-DESTRUCTION, ENTITY - NONENTITY, OBSERVANCE - NONOBSERVANCE, SETTLEMENT-DEFAULT.

nul'-li-ty. State or quality of being void or not existing. ENTITY-NONENTITY, SUBSTANCE-NULLITY.

nullius jurare in verba magistri [L.] (nul-lai'-us ju-rê'-rî in ver'-ba ma-jis'-trai). To testify to nothing in words of a master. CREDULOUSNESS-SKEPTICISM.

nullus in singulis, aliquis in omnibus [L.] (nul'-lus in sin'-giu-lis, al'-i-quis in om'-ni-bus). Dabbler in all things, good for nothing in each particular thing. ADEPT-BUNGLER.

numb. Destitute of sensation. FEELING-INSENSIBILITY, SENSITIVENESS-APATHY, TINGLING-NUMBNESS.

numbed. Deprived of the power of sensation. SENSITIVENESS-APATHY.

num'-ber. To count; a numeral; many; one of a series of periodicals; a grammatical distinction. MISSIVE-PUBLICATION, NOUN, NUMBER, NUMBERING, PLURALITY-FRACTION, VERB; **dual number,** NOUN; **mixed number,** NUMBER; **number among,**

ADMISSION-EXCLUSION; **number of times**, RECURRENCE; **plural number**, NOUN; **singular number**, NOUN; **take care of number one**, UNSELFISHNESS-SELFISHNESS.

NUMBER.

Aliquot part. A part which is contained exactly in a number.
Antilogarithm. The number corresponding to any logarithm.
Arithmetical progression. A progression in which the terms increase or decrease by equal differences.
Cipher. The character o.
Circulating decimal. A decimal fraction repeating a set of figures without end.
Coefficient. A number or letter put before an algebraic expression which is to be multiplied by that number.
Combination. A joining together to form a whole.
Common measure. Any quantity regarded as a standard of comparison with other quantities.
Complement. Full number or allowance.
Counter. A piece of wood, ivory, etc., used in counting; a coin.
Decimal. A tenth; a fraction in decimal notation.
Denominator. That which is used as a unit or divisor.
Difference. Result obtained by subtracting one number from another.
Differential. An infinitesimal difference between two values of a quantity.
Digit. Any one of the ten Arabic numerals.
Dividend. A quantity divided into equal parts.
Divisor. That by which a number or quantity is divided.
Election. Choice in general.
Exponent. A symbol indicating a power.
Factor. One of two or more quantities that, when multiplied together, produce a given quantity.
Figure. A character representing a number.
Figurative numbers. Such numbers as do or may represent some geometrical figure, in relation to which they are always considered, as triangular, pyramidal, etc., numbers.
Fluent. A variable quantity in fluxions which is continually increasing or decreasing, whether it be line, surface, etc.; an integral.
Fluxion. The rate of flow or variation of a changing quantity.
Formula. A rule or principle expressed in algebraic symbols.
Fraction. A quantity less than a unit
Function. A quantity whose value is dependent on the value of some other quantity.
Geometrical progression. A progression in which the terms increase or decrease by equal ratios.
Harmonical progression. One in which the terms are the reciprocals of quantities in arithmetical progression.
Index. The indicator of the power of a quantity.
Integer. A whole number in contradistinction to a fraction.
Integral A mathematical function of variables that remains constant.
Logarithm. The exponent of the power to which a fixed number, called the base, must be raised in order to produce a given number.
Mixed number. A whole number and a fraction taken together.
Modulus. A number, coefficient, or quantity that measures a force, function, or effect.
Multiple. A resultant of multiplying a quantity by whole numbers.
Multiplicand. A number multiplied, or to be multiplied, by another
Multiplicator. The number by which another number is multiplied.
Multiplier. The multiplying number.
Number. One of a series of symbols used in arranging or classifying quantities.
Numeral. A symbol or character used to express a number.
Numerator. In a vulgar fraction, the term that denotes how many of the parts of a unit are taken.
Percentage. Rate per hundred, or proportion in a hundred parts.
Permutation. Arrangement of a number of elements or things with reference to their order of sequence.
Polygonal numbers. See PYRAMIDAL NUMBERS.
Power. A number multiplied by itself any number of times.
Prime number. Any number divisible only by itself or unity.
Product. The result obtained by multiplication.
Progression. A series of numbers or quantities each of which is derived from the preceding by a constant law.
Proportion. An equality or identity between ratios.
Pyramidal numbers. Certain series of figurate numbers expressing the number of balls or points that may be arranged in the form of pyramids.
Quotient. The result obtained by division.
Ratio. The relation between two numbers or two magnitudes of the same kind.
Reciprocal. The quotient obtained by dividing unity by a number.

Repetend. That part of a circulating decimal which is repeated indefinitely.
Root. A quantity that, taken a specified number of times as a factor, will give another quantity called its power.
Round number. A number that ends in a cipher, or that is divisible by ten.
Series. An orderly arrangement of one thing after another.
Submultiple. A number or quantity of which another is a multiple.
Subtrahend. That which is to be subtracted.
Sum. The result obtained by addition.
Symbol. A sign or mark by which one knows or infers a thing.
Variation One of the different arrangements which can be made of any number of quantities, taking a certain number of them together.

NUMBER—*Adjectives*.

Aliquot. Contained in another number without remainder.
Complementary. Supplying a deficiency.
Decimal. Founded on the number 10.
Differential. Pertaining to differentials.
Divisible. Admitting of division without remainder.
Exponential. Of or pertaining to exponents.
Figurate. According to number
Fluxional. Pertaining to fluxions
Fractional. Pertaining to fractions.
Imaginary. An algebraic expression having no assignable numerical interpretation.
Impossible. Pertaining to an imaginary quantity.
Incommensurable. Having no standard of comparison.
Integral. Pertaining to an integer.
Irrational. Not equal to the quotient of any two entire quantities
Logarithmic. Consisting of logarithms.
Logometric. Denoting a scale to ascertain chemical equivalents.
Negative. Less than zero.
Numeral. Relating to number.
Positive. Greater than zero.
Prime. Condition of being divisible by no whole number except itself and unity.
Proportional. Pertaining to proportion.
Radical. Pertaining to the root of a number.
Rational. Expressible as the ratio of two whole numbers.
Real. Not imaginary.
Reciprocal. Used to denote different kinds of mutual relation.
Surd. Irrational.

num″-ber-al′-i-ty. State of being numerous. MULTIPLICITY-PAUCITY.
num′-bered. Counted. **Days numbered**, LIFE-DEATH, LIFE-KILLING, SANGUINENESS-HOPELESSNESS, VOLITION-OBLIGATION; **numbered with the dead**, LIFE-DEATH.
num′-ber-ing. Counting. NUMBERING.

NUMBERING.

Algorithm. The Arabic or decimal system of numeration.
Calculation. The result of an arithmetical operation.
Computation. The act of estimating numerically.
Dactylonomy. The art of counting by the fingers.
Enumeration. Detailed mention of things in succession.
Measurement. The act or result of measuring.
Numbering. The act of counting.
Numeration. The art of reading or naming numbers.
Pagination. The process of paging a book.
Recension. A critical revision.
Reckoning. The act of calculating, counting, or computing.
Rhabdology. The art of computing by means of Napier's rods.
Statistics. Systematized numerical facts collectively.
Summation. The operation of obtaining a sum.
Supputation. Reckoning; account.
Tale. A counting or enumeration.

NUMBERING—*Denotations*.

Algebra. That branch of mathematics which treats of the relations and properties of quantity by means of letters and other symbols.
Analysis. The resolving of problems by reducing the conditions that are in them to equations.
Arithmetic. The art of computation by figures.
Calculus. A process of mathematical reasoning by the use of symbols.
Calculus of differences. A branch of mathematics in which the laws of dependence which bind the variable quantities are themselves subject to change.

Differential calculus. A method of investigating mathematical questions by using the ratio of certain indefinitely small quantities.

Fluxions. The method of analysis based on the conception of all magnitudes as generated by motion.

Infinitesimal calculus. Differential and integral calculus in which the increments given to variables are regarded as infinitesimal.

Integral calculus. A method of investigating mathematical questions by finding expressions from the differentials of that expression.

Numbering—*Nouns of Statistics*.

Account. A record of business transactions.

Capitation. Individual assessment.

Census. Authoritative enumeration of the inhabitants of a country.

Dead-reckoning. Computation of a vessel's situation at sea without astronomical observations.

Muster. The roll of troops on parade.

Poll. The list or enumeration of persons.

Recapitulation. A summary of the principal points in a discourse or essay; a summing up.

Roll-call. The act of calling over a list of names of persons.

Numbering—*Nouns of Operation*.

Addition. The act of adding; an increase.

Approximation. A continual approach nearer and nearer to a result.

Differentiation. The act of differentiating.

Division. Ratio of one quantity to another.

Equations. Propositions asserting the equality of two quantities.

Evolution. Extraction of roots.

Extraction of roots. The operation of finding the roots of given numbers or quantities.

Factoring. The act of resolving into factors.

Integration. Bringing together parts into a whole.

Interpolation. The process of deriving intermediate values of a quantity from a series of given values.

Involution. Raising of a number or quantity to any given power.

Multiplication. The act or process of increasing in number.

Notation. The art of recording by figures or other marks

Practise. A rule in arithmetic.

Reduction. Changing from one denomination to another without altering the value.

Rule of three. A rule for finding any term of a proportion, the three others being given.

Subtraction. The operation of finding the difference of two quantities.

Numbering—*Nouns of Instrument*.

Abacist. A calculator.

Abacus. A reckoning table with sliding balls

Arithmetician. One skilled in arithmetic.

Calculating machine. A device to aid computation.

Calculator. A calculating machine; a set of tables for ready reckoning.

Difference machine. A machine for calculating mathematical tables.

Logometer. A scale for measuring chemical equivalents.

Napier's bones. A contrivance for facilitating calculations in multiplication or division.

Sliding-rule. A rule used by draftsmen in rapid calculations.

Swan-pan. A Chinese form of abacus.

Tallies. Sticks on which notches are cut for the purpose of keeping and checking accounts.

Numbering—*Verbs*.

Add. To find the sum of.

Affix numbers to. To add numbers to the end.

Amount to. To be equivalent.

Audit. To examine and adjust, as accounts.

Balance. To regulate and adjust.

Calculate. To compute mathematically.

Call over. To go over by reading aloud name by name.

Cast up. To compute; to reckon.

Check. To verify; to make secure by means of a mark.

Cipher. To calculate arithmetically.

Come to. To amount to.

Compute. To sum up or reckon.

Count. To name one by one; to number.

Demonstrate. To point out.

Divide. To separate into pieces.

Enumerate. To name one by one.

Extract roots. To ascertain the root of a quantity.

Multiply. To grow in number.

Muster. To collect; to assemble, as for military review.

Number. To reckon, as one of a collection.

Overhaul. To re-examine, as accounts.

Page. To number in pages.

Poll. To enroll for taxation and the like.

Prove. To ascertain by trial.

Recapitulate. To sum up.

Recite. To tell over in detail.

Run over. To go over hastily.

Score. To keep account of.

Subtract. To withdraw from the rest.

Sum. To add into one whole.

Sum up. To ascertain the totality of.

Suppute. To reckon; to compute.

Take an account of. To take note of.

Take stock. To make an inventory of goods.

Tell. To count one at a time.

Tell off. To count, as a number of men, for a particular duty.

Numbering—*Adjectives*.

Algebraic. Pertaining to algebra.

Analytic. Resolving into first principles.

Arithmetical. Pertaining to arithmetic.

Calculable. That may be calculated.

Commensurable. Having a common measure.

Commensurate. Proportional

Computable. That can be computed.

Factorial. A name given to factors of a continued product.

Incommensurable. Having no common measure.

Incommensurate. Not admitting of a common measure.

Numerable. That may be numbered.

Numeral. Pertaining to number.

Numerical. Consisting in number.

Statistical. Pertaining to statistics.

Tabular. Computed by the use of tables.

num'-ber-less. Very numerous. Infinity.

num″-ber-os'-i-ty. State of being numerous. Multiplicity-Paucity.

num'-ber-ous-ness. State of being numerous. Multiplicity-Paucity.

num'-bers. Many; verse. Multiplicity-Paucity, Poetry-Prose.

numb'-ness. State of being without feeling. Sensitiveness-Apathy, Tingling-Numbness.

nu'-mer-a-ble. That may be counted. Numbering.

nu'-mer-al. Pertaining to a number. Number, Numbering.

nu″-mer-a'-tion. Act of reading or naming numbers. Numbering.

nu'-mer-a″-tor. Term of a fraction. Number.

nu-mer'-i-cal. Expressed in numbers. Numbering.

nu″-mer-ose'. Multiplicity - Paucity, Purity-Crudeness.

nu″-mer-os'-i-ty. Harmony. Purity-Crudeness.

nu'-mer-ous. Consisting of a great number of units. Multiplicity-Paucity.

nu″-mis-mat'-ic-al. Pertaining to coins or medals. Money.

nu″-mis-mat'-ics. Science of coins and medals. Money.

numps. A blockhead. Sage-Fool.

num'-skull. A dunce. Sage-Fool.

nun. A woman devoted to religious life. Ministry-Laity.

nunc aut nunquam [L.] (nunc aut nun'-quam). Now or never. Opportuneness-Unsuitableness.

Nunc Dimittis [L.] (nunc di-mit'-tis). Now dismiss. Devotion-Idolatry. [*Luke* ii, 26.]

nun'-ci-o. An ambassador. Consignee, Messenger.

nun″-cu-pa'-tion. A public declaration. Name-Misnomer.

nun-cu'-pa-tive. Oral. Name-Misnomer.

nun-cu'-pa-to-ry. Orally. Enlightenment-Secrecy, Name-Misnomer.

nun″-di-na'-tion. Buying and selling at fairs. Exchange.

nun'-ner-y. A convent for nuns. Fane.

nup'-tial. Pertaining to marriage. Matrimony-Celibacy.

nup'-tials. Marriage. Matrimony-Celibacy.

nurse. To attend and take care of; one who nurses. CHIEF - UNDERLING, CONSERVATION, GUARD - PRISONER, OBSTRUCTION-HELP, REMEDY-BANE; **nurse-maid,** CHIEF-UNDERLING; **put to nurse,** EDUCATION-MISTEACHING.

nurs'-er-y. A room for children; a place where trees and plants are raised; place where anything is fostered. CAUSE-EFFECT, CONTENTS-RECEIVER, DOMESTICATION-AGRICULTURE, INFANCY-AGE, SCHOOL, WORKSHOP; **nursery - maid,** CHIEF - UNDERLING; **nursery rhymes,** POETRY-PROSE; **nursery tale,** ACCOUNT, FANCY.

nurs'-ling. An infant. INFANT-VETERAN.

nur'-ture. Feeding; education. EDUCATION-MIS-TEACHING, NUTRIMENT-EXCRETION, OBSTRUCTION-HELP, PREPARATION-NONPREPARATION; **nurture a belief,** FAITH-MISGIVING; **nurture an idea,** MIND-IMBECILITY.

nut. A fruit consisting of a kernel enclosed in a hard shell; a puzzle. **Nut oil,** PULPINESS-OIL; **nut to crack,** DIFFICULTY-FACILITY, TIDINGS-MYSTERY.

nu-ta'-tion. A revolving movement. VIBRATION.

nut'-brown''. Brown color. GRAY-BROWN.

nut'-meg-gra''-ter. A device for grating nutmegs. FRIABILITY.

nu'-tri-ment. That which nourishes. NUTRIMENT-EXCRETION.

NUTRIMENT—EXCRETION.

Aliment. Substance necessary to the natural growth of an organism.
Ambrosia. The immortality-giving food of the gods.
Artichoke. A thistle-like plant whose tubers are edible.
Beef. The flesh of cattle.
Beefsteak. A slice of beef suitable for broiling.
Beet. An edible root.
Belly timber. Figuratively, food.
Bisque. Biscuit
Blackberry. A small edible berry.
Blanc mange. Cornstarch, etc., boiled in milk for desserts
Bloater. A selected herring slightly cured.
Board. Food which is served at the table.
Bread. A principal article of food made of flour or meal of grain.
Bread and cheese. Common expression for food.
Breadfruit. A fruit of a tropical tree.
Breadstuff. Materials for bread.
Broth. A thin soup.
Cates. Delicate or luxurious food.
Cerealia [L.]. The cereals.
Chowder. Fish boiled with pork, vegetables, etc
Chyle. Partially digested food.
Clam. A shell-fish.
Comestibles. Something fit for the table.
Commissariat. Food-supply. See PROVISION.
Commons. Rations.
Condiment. Spice used to season food.
Consommé [F.]. A strong meat soup.
Contents of the larder. Provisions.
Cornstarch. Starch made from corn.
Creature comforts. Things that refresh the body.
Dainty. A rare and costly food.
Delicacy. Food suited to a fine taste.
Diet. Properly prescribed food.
Dietary. A system of diet.
Eatables. Food prepared for eating.
Eatage. Pasturage.
Edibles. Food fit for eating.
Entrée [F.]. A side-dish.
Entremets [F.]. A side-dish.
Fare. Daily food.
Feed. Food for domestic animals.
Flesh-pots. Food.
Fodder. Food for domestic animals.
Food. Whatever is taken to maintain life.
Forage. Food for horses or cattle.
Fricassee. A dish of rabbit, chicken, or other meat cut into small pieces and stewed or fried.
Good cheer. Provisions for a feast.
Good living. Good food.
Grub. Food.
Hash. Chopped meat stewed or fried.
Hoe-cake. A cake of Indian meal.
Hors d'œuvre [F.]. A side-dish.
Ice-cream. Frozen cream flavored.
Ingesta. Food.
Joint. One of the pieces into which a carcass is cut by a butcher.
Keep. Means of subsistence.
Kickshaws. An unsubstantial dish of food.
Lettuce. A salad.
Meat. The flesh of animals used as food.
Mince. Meat chopped very fine.
Nourishment. That which sustains life.
Nurture. That which nourishes.
Nutriment. Food.
Oatcake. A cake made from oats.

Bleeding. Emission of blood.
Catarrh. Discharge from an inflammation of the membranes of the air-passages.
Dejection. Matter voided.
Diaphoresis. Perspiration.
Diarrhea. Frequent and profuse discharge from the intestines.
Discharge. That which is emitted or discharged.
Effusion That which is poured out.
Egesta [L.]. Matter secreted and thrown off.
Ejecta [L.]. Matter thrown out.
Emanation. A constantly and necessarily flowing efflux.
Evacuation. That which is evacuated; particularly from the bowels.
Excrement. Matter secreted and ejected.
Excreta [L.]. The excrements.
Excretion. Excrement.
Exhalation. That which is discharged in the form of vapor.
Extravasation. Matter escaped from its proper vessel.
Extrusion. Something forced or pressed out.
Exudation. Matter discharged through pores or incisions.
Exuviæ [L]. Part of animals cast off.
Fæces [L.]. Excrement.
Hemorrhage. A discharge of blood.
Lava. Molten matter discharged from a volcano.
Outpouring. A great effusion.
Perspiration. Matter given off through the pores of the skin.
Ptyalism. Excessive secretion of saliva.
Rheum. A discharge from the eyes or nose.
Saliva. The secretion from the salivary glands.
Salivation. An excessive secretion of saliva.
Secretion. Matter collected for use or excretion.
Sewage. Refuse matter carried off by a sewer.
Spittle. Saliva.
Sputa. Matter spit out, especially during disease.
Subation. Discharge.
Sweat. Perspiration.

EXCRETION—*Verbs.*

Emanate. To come off in form of vapor.
Excrete. To secrete and throw off.

NUTRIMENT—*Continued.*

Oatmeal. A food made from oats.
Omelet. A dish of eggs and milk, stirred together and fried.
Oyster. A shell-fish much used as food.
Pabulum. Food.
Pastry. Food made with crust of shortened dough.
Pasturage. } Grass which horses and cattle graze upon.
Pasture. }
Pasty. A pie, usually of meat.
Pie. Prepared food baked between two layers of pastry.
Pièce de résistance [F.]. The most substantial dish of a dinner.
Potage. Pottage.
Pottage. A stew of meat and vegetables.
Prey. Any animal seized by another for food.
Prog. Victuals of any kind.
Provender. Food provided for cattle.
Provisions. Supply of food.
Prunelle. A small prune.
Pudding. A dish consisting of a mixture of fruit, milk, eggs, etc.
Purée [F.]. A thick soup.
Ragout. A dish made of meat and vegetables, cut fine, stewed, and highly seasoned.
Raisin. A dried grape.

NUTRIMENT—*Continued.*

Ration. A fixed allowance of food.
Ravin. Prey.
Rusk. A sweet biscuit.
Réchauffé [F.]. Food warmed over.
Relêve [F.]. A delicacy, as olives or radishes.
Remove. A dish or course at dinner.
Roast and boiled. Meats.
Sirloin. The upper part of a loin of beef.
Soup. Liquid food made by boiling meat or vegetables in water.
Spoonmeat. Food to be taken with a spoon.
Staff of life. Bread.
Steak. A slice of meat for frying.
Stew. A preparation of meat with vegetables cooked by stewing.
Subsistence. That upon which one feeds.
Succotash. Corn and beans cooked together.
Sustenance. That which supports life.

Sustentation. The support of life.
Sweets, etc. Sweet accompaniments of a meal.
Taffy. A sugar candy.
Tapioca. The dried starch obtained from the roots of the cassava.
Tomato. The fruit of a plant of the Nightshade family, used as food.
Vanilla. An oil extracted from the berries of the vanilla plant, used as a flavor.
Veal. The flesh of a calf.
Vermicelli. The flour of a hard and small-grained wheat.
Viands. Articles of food.
Victuals. Food for human beings as prepared for eating.
Vol-au-vent [F.]. A meat pie.
Waffle. A soft cake cooked in a waffle-iron.
Walnut. The fruit of the walnut-tree.
Yolk. The yellow part of an egg.

NUTRIMENT—*Beverages.*

Ale. A beverage made from a fermented infusion of malt.
Beer. An alcoholic beverage produced from various substances containing starch.
Beverage. A refreshing drink.
Bishop. A hot drink made from mulled wine, sugar, oranges, etc.
Broth. A fluid food.
Chocolate. A beverage made from a cake of cacao-seeds.
Cider. The expressed juice of apples used as a beverage.
Claret. A red table-wine.
Cocktail. An iced drink of spirits mixed with bitters, sugar, etc.
Coffee. A beverage made from the coffee-berry after it is roasted and ground.
Cup. A beverage made with wine, generally iced, and with flavoring herbs.
Draft. The amount drunk at one time.
Dram. A drink of spirits.
Drench. A drink.
Drink. Any liquid beverage.
Flip. A hot drink, chiefly of ale spiced and sugared.
Gin, etc. An alcoholic liquor distilled from various grains and flavored with juniper-berries. See TEETOTALISM-INTEMPERANCE.
Grog. An unsweetened mixture of spirits and water.
Gulp. A swallow.
Heavy wet. Malt liquor, as making the drinker stupid.

Hyson. A grade of green tea.
Ice-water. Water chilled by ice.
Liqueur [F.]. An alcoholic cordial sweetened and flavored with aromatic substances.
Liquor. Any intoxicating liquid.
Lisbon. A sweet wine.
Malt liquor. Any alcoholic beverage brewed from malt.
Negus. A drink made of wine, water, and lemon-juice, sweetened.
Nip. A dram of strong drink.
Potion. A draft.
Punch. An alcoholic beverage composed of wine or spirits, sweetened, and flavored with lemon or orange.
Sip. A mere taste.
Sir John Barleycorn. A personification of malt or intoxicating liquors.
Spirits. A strong distilled liquor, especially alcohol.
Stingo. Strong beer or ale.
Sup. A taste of liquid.
Swill. Liquor drunk regularly.
Tea. A beverage made from the leaves of the tea-plant; the cup that cheers but not inebriates. [Cowper.]
Toddy. A beverage of spirits, hot water, and sugar.
Wassail. The liquor prepared for a drinking-bout.
Wine. The fermented juice of the grape.

NUTRIMENT—*Nouns of Action.*

Deglutition. The act of swallowing.
Drinking, etc. The act of swallowing fluids. See *Verbs.*
Eating. The act of taking food. See *Verbs.*
Epulation. A feasting.
Gluttony, etc. The act of eating to excess. See FASTING-GLUTTONY
Gulp. A swallowing.

Hippophagy. The act of eating horse-flesh.
Ichthyophagy. The practise of feeding on fish.
Libation. The act of pouring out wine.
Manducation. } The act of chewing.
Mastication. }
Rumination. The act of chewing the cud.

NUTRIMENT—*Associated Nouns.*

Bait. A light meal for man or beast.
Banquet. A sumptuous feast.
Bever. A small lunch between meals.
Bill of fare. A list of articles or dishes provided for a meal.
Blowout. A jovial feast.
Bolus. A mouthful.
Breakfast. The first meal of the day.
Carousal, etc. A feast. See ENTERTAINMENT.
Collation. A lunch or light repast.
Course. A portion of a meal served at one time.
Cuisine. The cooking department.
Déjeûner [F.]. Breakfast.
Déjeûner à la fourchette [F.]. A meat breakfast.
Dessert. The last course of a dinner.
Dinner. The principal meal of the day, eaten about midday.
Dish. A particular kind of food.
Drunkenness, etc. Excessive indulgence in alcoholic liquors. See TEETOTALISM-INTEMPERANCE.
Eater. One who eats.
Eating-house. A house where cooked provisions are sold, to be eaten on the premises
Feast. A festive or joyous meal.
Feed. A meal.
Festal board. A meal prepared for a festival.
Gobbet. A mouthful.
Hearty meal. An enjoyable meal.
Junket. A feast.
Lunch. A light meal between breakfast and dinner.

Luncheon. A light repast.
Meal. A repast.
Menu. A bill of fare.
Mess. A quantity of food set on a table at one time.
Morsel. A little bite of food.
Mouthful. As much as is usually put into the mouth at one time.
Ordinary. A dining-room or eating-house where a meal is prepared for all comers, at a fixed price for a meal, in distinction from one where each dish is separately charged.
Picnic. An entertainment at which each person contributes some dish to a common table.
Plate. A small, shallow, and usually circular vessel from which food is eaten at table.
Pot-luck. Whatever may chance to be provided for a meal.
Refection. A lunch.
Refreshment. An article of food or drink.
Regale. A banquet.
Regalement. An entertainment or festival.
Repast. A meal.
Sippet. A small sop.
Snack. A slight, hasty repast.
Sop. Anything dipped and softened in any liquid.
Spread. A feast.
Supper. A meal taken at the close of a day.
Table. Figuratively, the food spread upon a table.
Table d'hôte [F.]. A common table for guests at a hotel.
Tiffin. A lunch.
Whet. An appetizer.

NUTRIMENT—*Continued.*

NUTRIMENT—*Verbs.*

Banquet.
Batten. } To treat to a feast.
Batten upon. To grow fat upon rich food.
Bite. To seize or cut with the teeth.
Bolt. To swallow hurriedly or without chewing.
Break bread. To dine.
Breakfast. To take the first meal of the day.
Break one's fast. To take food.
Browse. To feed upon leaves, twigs, and grass.
Carouse. To drink deeply and in a boisterous manner.
Champ. To bite upon impatiently.
Chew. To cut or grind with the teeth.
Crack a bottle. To join in a drink.
Cranch. See CRUNCH.
Craunch. See CRUNCH.
Crop. To eat the ends off of grass and plants.
Crunch. To crush audibly in the mouth.
Despatch. To dispose of speedily.
Devour. To eat up greedily, as a beast of prey.
Dine. To eat the chief meal of the day.
Discuss. To test by eating or drinking.
Dispatch. See DESPATCH.
Do justice to. Eat much of with relish.
Drain the cup. To drink all that is in the cup.
Drink in. To drink.
Drink one's fill. To drink until one is satisfied.
Drink up. To drink all that a cup contains.
Eat. To chew and swallow food.
Eat heartily. Eat a cheerful meal.
Empty one's glass. To drink all that a glass contains.
Fall to. To begin to eat hastily.
Fare. To live as regards food and drink.
Fatten on. To grow fat from feeding on something.
Feast on. To dine on rich provisions.
Feed. To give food to.
Feed on. To live on.
Get down. To eat or drink.
Gnaw. To bite off little by little.

Gormandize. To greedily eat very much.
Graze. To feed on grass.
Gulp.
Gulp down. } To swallow eagerly and in large mouthfuls.
Lap. To take up liquid with the tongue.
Lick. To take food into the mouth in bits by drawing the tongue over it.
Live on. To eat sufficient of to maintain life.
Lunch. To take light food between meals.
Masticate. To prepare food in the mouth for swallowing.
Mumble. To chew gently; to eat with a muttering sound.
Munch. To masticate noisily.
Nibble. To bite off and eat little bits.
Peck. To pick up with the beak.
Pick. To eat slowly and daintily.
Play a good knife and fork. To be a good eater
Purvey. To furnish supplies.
Quaff. To drink copiously or with relish.
Quass. To quaff; drink.
Regale. To entertain in a regal manner.
Royne. To gnaw.
Sip. To take with the lips in small drafts.
Snap. To close the mouth suddenly.
Suck.
Suck up. } To draw into the mouth with the lips.
Sup. To eat the evening meal.
Swallow. To receive through the gullet into the stomach.
Swig. To take deep drafts.
Swill. To drink greedily and to excess.
Take. To eat.
Take down. To eat.
Take tea. To eat supper.
Tipple. To drink strong drink frequently.
Toss off. To drink at one draft.
Toss one's glass. To toss off a glassful.
Tuck in. To eat.
Wash down. To follow the meal with wine.
Wet one's whistle. To take a drink.

NUTRIMENT—*Adjectives.*

Alimentary. Pertaining to aliment.
Bibulous. Fond of drinking.
Carnivorous. Eating or living on flesh.
Cereal. Pertaining to edible grains.
Cibarious. Pertaining to food.
Comestible. Suitable to be eaten.
Culinary. Pertaining to cooking.
Dietetic. Relating to diet.
Eatable. In a condition suitable for eating.
Edible. Fit to be used as food.
Esculent. Edible.

Graminivorous. Feeding upon grass.
Granivorous. Feeding upon grain.
Herbivorous. Subsisting on herbs.
Ichthyophagus. Subsisting on fish.
Nutritious.
Nutritive. } Nourishing.
Omnivorous. Living upon food of all kinds.
Phytivorous. Herbivorous.
Potable.
Potulent. } Fit for drinking.
Succulent. Pertaining to thick, fleshy, juicy plants.

nu-tri′-tion. Process by which growth is promoted and waste repaired in the body. BIOLOGY, OBSTRUCTION-HELP.

nu-tri′-tious. Nourishing. HEALTHINESS-UNHEALTHINESS, NUTRIMENT-EXCRETION, REMEDY-BANE.

nu′-tri-tive. Having nutritious properties. NUTRIMENT-EXCRETION, REMEDY-BANE.

nuts. Something that gives particular pleasure. GOOD-EVIL, PLEASURABLENESS-PAINFULNESS.

nut′-shell. The shell of a nut; a small space. MAGNITUDE-SMALLNESS; **lie in a nutshell,** DIGEST, GREATNESS-LITTLENESS.

nux″ vom′-i-ca. The seed of a plant containing strychnin and brucin. REMEDY-BANE.

nuz′-zle. To fondle. BLANDISHMENT.

nych-the′-me-ron. The whole day of 24 hours. PERIODICITY-IRREGULARITY.

nyc′-ta-lo″-py. Day blindness. SIGHT-DIMSIGHTEDNESS.

nymph. A mythological female divinity, inhabiting a grove or spring. JOVE-FIEND, MALE-FEMALE; **sea-nymph,** OCEAN-LAND.

nys-tag′-mus. A spasmodic movement of the eyes. SIGHT-DIMSIGHTEDNESS.

O

O! An exclamation. ASTONISHMENT-EXPECTANCE; **O for,** DESIRE-DISTASTE.

oaf. An imbecile. SAGE-FOOL.

oak. A tree. STRENGTH - WEAKNESS; **heart of oak,** BRAVERY - COWARDICE, HARDNESS - SOFTNESS, STRENGTH-WEAKNESS.

oak'-um. Hemp-fiber. LAMINA-FIBER.

oar. A paddle. INSTRUMENT, TRAVELING-NAVIGA-TION, WAYFARER-SEAFARER; **lie upon one's oars,** ACTION-PASSIVENESS; **ply the oar,** TOIL-RELAXATION, TRAVELING-NAVIGATION; **pull an oar,** ACTION-PAS-SIVENESS; **put in an oar,** ACTIVITY-INDOLENCE, EN-VIRONMENT-INTERPOSITION; **rest on one's oars,** DIS-CONTINUANCE - CONTINUANCE, MOVEMENT - REST, TOIL-RELAXATION.

oars'-man. A rower. WAYFARER-SEAFARER.

o'-a-sis. Fertile place in a desert. CONVENTIONALITY-UNCONVENTIONALITY, OCEAN - LAND, UNION - DIS-UNION.

oat. A cereal grass and its edible grain. DOMESTICA-TION-AGRICULTURE.

oat'-cake". A cake made of oatmeal. NUTRIMENT-EXCRETION.

oath. A solemn affirmation; a curse. ASSERTION-DENIAL, CHARITABLENESS-CURSE, ENGAGEMENT-RE-LEASE; **rap out oaths,** PRESUMPTION-OBSEQUIOUS-NESS; **upon oath,** ASSERTION-DENIAL, ENGAGE-MENT-RELEASE.

oat'-meal". The meal of oats. NUTRIMENT-EXCRE-TION.

ob"-bli-ga'-to. A necessary accessory; a secondary accompaniment. MUSIC, SOLITUDE-COMPANY.

ob'-duc-tion. A drawing over. COVER-LINING.

ob'-dur-ate. Inexorable; unyielding; impenitent. BIGOTRY - APOSTASY, HARSHNESS - MILDNESS, RE-PENTANCE-OBDURACY, VIRTUE-VICE.

o-be'-di-ence. Submissiveness. INSUBORDINATION-OBEDIENCE, LIBERTY - SUBJECTION, OBSERVANCE-NONOBSERVANCE, YIELDING.

o-be'-di-ent. Submissive. INSUBORDINATION-OBEDI-ENCE.

o-be'-di-ent-ly. Submissively. INSUBORDINATION-OBEDIENCE.

o-bei'-sance. A bow. ELEVATION-DEPRESSION, PO-LITENESS - IMPOLITENESS, REGARD - DISRESPECT, YIELDING.

ob'-el-isk. A four-sided pillar. HEIGHT-LOWNESS, MARK-OBLITERATION.

Ob'-er-on. The king of the fairies. JOVE-FIEND.

o-bese'. Fat. ENLARGEMENT-DIMINUTION, EXCESS-LACK.

o-bes'-i-ty. Corpulence. GREATNESS-LITTLENESS, EN-LARGEMENT-DIMINUTION.

o-bey'. To comply with; to be subject to. INSUBOR-DINATION-OBEDIENCE, LIBERTY-SUBJECTION, YIELD-ING; **obey a call,** MOTIVE-CAPRICE; **obey the helm,** DIFFICULTY-FACILITY; **obey rules,** CONVENTIONALITY-UNCONVENTIONALITY.

ob-fus'-cate. To muddle. DIAPHANEITY-OPAQUE-NESS, LIGHT-DARKNESS; **obfuscated,** DIAPHANEITY-OPAQUENESS, TEETOTALISM-INTEMPERANCE.

o'-bit. The death of a person. LIFE-DEATH, LIFE-FUNERAL.

obit, post [L.] (o'-bit, post). After death. LIFE-DEATH, LIFE-FUNERAL.

obiter dictum [L.] (ob'-i-ter dic'-tum). An irrelevant remark. CONNECTION - INDEPENDENCE, ENVIRON-MENT-INTERPOSITION, OPPORTUNENESS-UNSUITABLE-NESS.

o-bit'-u-a-ry. A death-notice. ACCOUNT, LIFE-DEATH.

ob-ject'. To disapprove. **Object to,** APPROVAL-DIS-APPROVAL, DESIRE-DISTASTE.

ob'-ject. A thing; aim; something ugly. BEAUTY-UGLINESS, MATERIALITY-SPIRITUALITY, PURPOSE-LUCK, SUBSTANCE-NULLITY; **be an object,** CONSE-QUENCE-INSIGNIFICANCE.

ob-jec'-tion. An adverse argument. APPROVAL-DIS-APPROVAL, OBSTRUCTION-HELP; **no objection,** CON-SENT.

ob-jec'-tion-a-ble. Open to objection. PROPRIETY-IMPROPRIETY, RIGHT-WRONG.

ob-jec'-tive. External; material. MATERIALITY-SPIRITUALITY, SUBJECTIVENESS-OBJECTIVENESS.

ob-jec'-tive-ness. Externality. SUBJECTIVENESS-OB-JECTIVENESS.

ob-jur'-gate. To scold. APPROVAL-DISAPPROVAL.

ob-jur-ga'-tion. Rebuke. APPROVAL-DISAPPROVAL.

ob-jur'-ga-to-ry. Rebukingly. APPROVAL-DISAP-PROVAL.

ob-late'. Flattened at the poles. LENGTH-SHORTNESS, ROUNDNESS.

ob-la'-tion. Anything offered in worship. DEVOTION-IDOLATRY, GIVING-RECEIVING.

ob"-lec-ta'-tion. A delight. PLEASURE-PAIN.

ob"-li-ga'-tion. A binding promise; a duty; a require-ment. CREDIT-DEBT, ENGAGEMENT - RELEASE, TERMS, THANKFULNESS-THANKLESSNESS, VOLITION-OBLIGATION; **confer an obligation,** GOODNESS-BAD-NESS; **feeling of obligation,** THANKFULNESS-THANK-LESSNESS; **under an obligation,** DUTY-DERELICTION, THANKFULNESS-THANKLESSNESS.

ob-li-ga'-to. Necessary. SOLITUDE-COMPANY.

ob'-li-ga-to"-ry. Binding. COMPOSITION, DUTY-DERE-LICTION.

o-blige'. To compel; to accommodate. DUTY-DERE-LICTION, OBSTRUCTION-HELP, OCCASION.

obligé, bien [F.] (o-bli-zhê', bi-an·'). Greatly obliged. PROFFER-REFUSAL.

ob-liged'. Grateful; bound: DUTY - DERELICTION, THANKFULNESS-THANKLESSNESS.

ob"-li-gee'. One obliged. MONEY.

ob-li'-ging. Helpful. CHARITABLENESS-MALEVO-LENCE, OBSTRUCTION-HELP, POLITENESS-IMPOLITE-NESS.

ob"-li-gor'. A debtor. MONEY.

ob"-li-qua'-tion. Deviation. AIM-ABERRATION.

ob-lique'. Slanting. ANGULARITY, CURVATION-REC-TILINEARITY, PARALLELISM-INCLINATION.

ob-lique'-ly. Slantingly. AIM-ABERRATION, PARAL-LELISM-INCLINATION.

ob-liq'-ui-ty. Inclination; wickedness. ANGULARITY, PARALLELISM-INCLINATION, VIRTUE-VICE; **obliquity of judgment,** DECISION-MISJUDGMENT.

ob-lit'-er-ate. To erase. MARK-OBLITERATION.

ob-lit'-er-a-ted. Erased. MARK-OBLITERATION.

ob-lit"-er-a'-tion. A blotting out. MARK-OBLITERA-TION; **obliteration of the past,** REMEMBRANCE-FOR-GETFULNESS.

ob-liv'-i-on. Utter forgetfulness. PARDON-VINDICTIVE-NESS, REMEMBRANCE-FORGETFULNESS; **oblivion of**

benefits, Thankfulness-Thanklessness; **oblivion of time,** Chronology-Anachronism; **redeem from oblivion,** Remembrance-Forgetfulness.

ob-liv'-i-ous. Forgetful. Remembrance-Forgetfulness.

ob'-long. Longer than broad. Length-Shortness; **oblong spheroid,** Roundness.

ob'-lo-quy. Infamy; defamation. Adulation-Disparagement, Approval-Disapproval, Reputation-Discredit.

ob''-mu-tes'-cence. Muteness. Talkativeness-Taciturnity, Vocalization-Muteness.

ob-nox'-ious. Odious. Contentedness-Discontentment, Goodness-Badness, Love-Hate; **obnoxious to,** Contingency.

ob-nu'-bil-a''-ted. Beclouded. Dimness.

o'-bo-e. A wind-instrument. Musical Instruments.

obra de comun, obra de ningun [Sp.] (o'-bra dê co-mun', o'-bra dê nin-gun'). Everybody's business is nobody's business. Occupation, Organization-Disorganization.

ob-rep'-tion. Stealthiness. Enlightenment-Secrecy.

ob''-rep-ti'-tious. Fraudulent. Enlightenment-Secrecy.

ob-scene'. Indecent. Purity-Impurity.

ob-scen'-i-ty. Lewdness. Purity-Impurity.

ob''-scu-ra'-tion. Hiding. Light-Darkness.

ob-scure'. Dusky; humble; abstruse. Ambiguity, Dimness, Gentility-Commonalty, Light-Darkness, Perspicuity - Obscurity, Reputation - Discredit, Visibility-Invisibility, Whiteness-Blackness.

ob-scu'-ri-ty. Lack of distinctness. Certainty-Doubt, Clearness - Obscurity, Gentility - Commonalty, Light-Darkness, Perspicuity-Obscurity.

obscurum per obscurius [L.] (ob-sciu'-rum per ob-sciu'-ri-us). Making more obscure by explanation. Clearness-Obscurity.

ob''-se-cra'-tion. A supplication. Petition-Expostulation.

ob'-se-quies. Funeral rites. Life-Funeral.

ob-se'-qui-ous. Servile. Politeness-Impoliteness, Presumption - Obsequiousness, Regard - Disrespect.

ob-se'-qui-ous-ness. Servility. Insubordination-Obedience, Politeness-Impoliteness, Presumption-Obsequiousness, Regard-Disrespect.

ob-serv'-ance. A custom; a ceremony. Ceremonial, Conduct, Conventionality-Unconventionality, Duty-Dereliction, Habit-Desuetude, Heed-Disregard, Insubordination-Obedience, Observance-Nonobservance.

OBSERVANCE—NONOBSERVANCE.

Acknowledgment. Admittance as genuine; recognition.
Acquittal. Discharge or performance, as of duty or obligation.
Acquittance. See Acquittal.
Adhesion. Firmness in opinion.
Compliance. The act of submitting; observance.
Discharge. The performance of a duty.
Exact observance, etc. Strict or accurate performance; rule of practise.
Fidelity, etc. Strict adherence to duty or obligation. See Uprightness.
Fulfilment. Performance; accomplishment.
Obedience, etc. Submission to duty; observance of a law or custom. See Insubordination-Obedience.
Observance. The act of complying with a custom; compliance.
Performance. The act of carrying out anything; completion.
Satisfaction. The extinguishment of a claim or obligation.

Observance—Verbs.

Abide by. To submit to; accept.
Acknowledge. To recognize as imposing responsibility.
Acquit oneself of an obligation. To be freed from a duty.
Act up to. To perform; to.
Be faithful to. To be true to.
Carry into execution. }
Carry out. } To do.
Cling to. To adhere to.
Comply with. To be in conformity with; obey.
Discharge. To do one's duty; perform.
Discharge an obligation. To do one's duty.
Do one's office. To act in compliance with one's duty.
Execute. To accomplish; bring to an end.
Fulfil. To bring about; bring to pass.
Fulfil an obligation. To satisfy a claim upon one's services.
Keep. To observe; to act in compliance with.
Keep faith with. }
Keep one's promise. } To do as one has promised.
Keep one's word. }
Make good. To make amends; compensate.
Make good one's promise. } To do what one has promised to do.
Make good one's word. }
Meet. To satisfy; observe one's responsibilities.
Observe. To heed; follow out; comply with.
Perform. To execute; accomplish.
Perform an obligation. To do one's duty.
Redeem one's pledge. To keep one's promise.
Respect. To treat in accordance with custom.
Satisfy. To supply fully.
Stand to one's engagement. To keep one's engagement

Observance—Adjectives.

As good as one's word. Truthful; true to one's promise.
Faithful. Trustworthy in the observance of promises.

Bad faith, etc. Non-fulfilment of a promise. See Uprightness-Dishonesty.
Disobedience, etc. Lack of submission to duty. See Insubordination.
Evasion. The act of avoiding.
Failure. Neglect; non-observance.
Forfeiture. The act of losing anything on account of omission.
Informality. The state of being not formal.
Infraction. A violation as of a rule.
Infringement. Disregard of a law or rule.
Inobservance. The act of not complying with a law or custom.
Laches. Neglect of law.
Lawlessness. Neglect of obedience to law.
Laxity. Looseness; inexactness.
Neglect. Want of attention; carelessness.
Non-observance, etc. The state of not paying attention. See Observance.
Nullification. The act of depriving of legal force.
Omission. Failure to do a thing.
Protest. Objection.
Repudiation. The act of refusing to pay a claim or debt; the disavowing of a custom.
Retraction. The act of drawing back.
Transgression. The breaking of a law or custom.
Violation. A transgression.

Nonobservance—Verbs.

Be off. Depart from.
Break. To violate.
Cancel, etc. To render null and void. See Mark-Obliteration.
Close one's eyes to. To be not attentive.
Declare null and void. To make known as invalid.
Discard. To reject; turn away as not wanted.
Do violence to. To transgress; to break through.
Drive a coach and six through. To violate.
Elude. To evade; avoid.
Evade. To avoid by artifice.
Fail. To disappoint.
Fling to the winds. To consider of no account.
Forfeit. To lose on account of some fault.
Give the go-by to. To pay no heed to.
Go back from. To repudiate.
Go from one's word. To break one's word.
Ignore. To pay no attention to.
Infringe. To disregard any law or custom.
Neglect. To pay no heed; disregard.
Nullify. To render void.
Omit. To neglect to do.
Palter. To act in a trifling manner.
Protest. To object to.

OBSERVANCE—NONOBSERVANCE—*Continued.*

OBSERVANCE—Adjectives—*Continued.*

Honorable, etc.　In accordance with the principles of honor.　See UPRIGHTNESS.
Literal, etc.　Exact as to details.　See TRUTH.
Loyal.　Constant; faithful.
Observant.　Watchful; paying close attention to one's duty.
Punctilious.　Exact in regard to the forms and usages of society.
Punctual.　Observant in regard to an appointed time.
True.　In conformity with fact; not false.
True as the dial of the sun.　Exact as the sun-dial.
True as the needle to the pole.　As true as the magnetic needle is to the pole.

OBSERVANCE—*Adverbs.*

Faithfully, etc.　In a true manner.　See *Adjectives.*

OBSERVANCE—*Phrases.*

Gardez la foi [F.].　Keep the faith.
Ignoscito sæpe alteri, numquam tibi [L.].　Pardon another often, never thyself.
Loyal in tout [F.].　Loyal in everything.
Tempori parendum [L.].　One must yield to the times.

NONOBSERVANCE—Verbs—*Continued.*

Repudiate.　To refuse to acknowledge.
Retract.　To recall or take back.
Set aside.　To put aside.
Set at naught.　To regard as valueless.
Shut one's eyes to.　To pay no attention to.
Strain a point. }
Stretch a point. } To exaggerate.
Trample under foot.　To utterly disregard.
Transgress.　To violate a command or law.
Violate.　To set at naught.

NONOBSERVANCE—*Adjectives.*

Elusive.　Having the tendency to slip away.
Evasive.　Having the tendency to elude.
Lawless.　Without law.
Transgressive.　Faulty; liable to transgress.
Unfulfilled, etc.　In a manner that is not fulfilled.　See OBSERVANCE.
Violating, etc.　Apt to violate.　See *Verbs.*

Ob-serv'-ant.　A friar of the strictest Franciscan order.　MINISTRY-LAITY.
ob-serv'-ant.　Watchful.　HEED-DISREGARD, OBSERVANCE-NONOBSERVANCE.
ob''-ser-va'-tion.　Close attention; a remark.　ASSERTION-DENIAL, CONCEPTION-THEME, HEED-DISREGARD, MIND-IMBECILITY.
ob-serv'-a-to-ry.　A building fitted for observing the sky.　UNIVERSE.
ob-serve'.　To remark; to heed; to notice.　ASSERTION-DENIAL, CONVENTIONALITY-UNCONVENTIONALITY, DUTY-DERELICTION, HEED-DISREGARD, OBSERVANCE-NONOBSERVANCE; **observe a duty,** DUTY-DERELICTION; **observe rules,** CONVENTIONALITY-UNCONVENTIONALITY.
ob-serv'-er.　A spectator.　ONLOOKER.
ob-serv'-ing.　Watchful.　HEED-DISREGARD.
ob-ses'-sion.　A siege.　ATTACK-DEFENSE.
ob-sid'-i-an.　Volcanic rock.　GEOLOGY.
ob-sid'-i-o-nal.　Pertaining to a siege.　ATTACK-DEFENSE.
ob'-so-lete.　Out of use.　FUTURE-PAST, NOVELTY-ANTIQUITY, TASTE-VULGARITY, USEFULNESS-USELESSNESS, WORD-NEOLOGY.

ob'-sta-cle.　A hindrance.　OBSTRUCTION-HELP.
obstant, Fata [L.] (ob'-stant, fê'-ta).　The Fates oppose.　VOLITION-OBLIGATION.
ob''-stet-ri'-cian.　An accoucheur.　INSTRUMENTALITY.
ob-stet'-rics.　Midwifery.　CREATION-DESTRUCTION, REMEDY-BANE.
ob'-sti-na-cy.　Stubbornness.　ACTIVITY-INDOLENCE, BIGOTRY-APOSTASY, DECISION-MISJUDGMENT, DETERMINATION-VACILLATION, FAVORITE-QUARRELSOMENESS, MUTABILITY-STABILITY, MUTATION-PERMANENCE, TURBULENCE-CALMNESS.
ob'-sti-nate.　Stubborn.　BIGOTRY-APOSTASY, DETERMINATION-VACILLATION, MUTABILITY-STABILITY.
ob'-sti-nate-ly.　Stubbornly.　BIGOTRY-APOSTASY.
ob'-sti-nate-ness.　Stubbornness.　BIGOTRY-APOSTASY.
ob''-sti-pa'-tion.　Constipation.　APERTURE-CLOSURE.
ob-strep'-er-ous.　Clamorous.　LOUDNESS-FAINTNESS, TURBULENCE-CALMNESS.
ob-struct'.　To block up; to hinder.　APERTURE-CLOSURE, OBSTRUCTION-HELP, RIVER-WIND; **obstruct the passage of light,** DIAPHANEITY-OPAQUENESS.
ob-struc'-tion.　An obstacle.　APERTURE-CLOSURE, DIFFICULTY-FACILITY, OBSTRUCTION-HELP.

OBSTRUCTION—HELP.

Bafflement.　A foiling.
Check.　A sudden or continued restraint or obstruction.
Coercion.　Restraint of freedom.
Counterpoise.　A force or power equal to and acting in opposition to another.
Difficulty, etc.　The state of being hard to accomplish; obstruction.　See DIFFICULTY.
Discountenance.　Disapprobation.
Discouragement.　That which tends to deter from anything.
Embarrassment.　The state of being in confusion or perplexity in regard to one's actions, manners, and the like.
Encumbrance.　Anything which impedes, checks, or hinders.
Hindrance.　Anything that stops or obstructs
Impediment.　That which hinders or obstructs.
Impedimenta.　Things which obstruct or hinder, especially the baggage of an army.
Impedition.　The act of hindering.
Incumbrance.　Anything that impedes or makes difficult an action or motion.
Inhibition, etc.　The act of restraining or the state of being restrained.　See LEAVE-PROHIBITION.
Interception.　The act of obstructing the progress of anything.
Interclusion.　The act of intercepting.
Interference.　The act of working in opposition or interposing; the state of interfering.
Interposition.　The act of placing or coming in between; the state of being in between.
Interruption.　Obstruction caused by breaking in upon any progress, motion, or the like

Accommodation.　That which supplies a want.
Adjunct.　Something joined to or connected with another thing.
Advance.　An assistance beforehand; an offer.
Advocacy.　The act of pleading for or supporting.
Aid.　That which helps or assists.
Aidance.　The act of aiding.
Alimentation.　Provision for support.
Ally, etc.　A person or thing connected with another in some relation of helpfulness.　See ANTAGONIST-ASSISTANT.
Assistance.　Aid; help; support.
Championship.　The state of contending in another's behalf.
Coadjuvancy, etc.　Assistance; cooperation.　See ANTAGONISM-CONCURRENCE.
Contingents.　Quotas of troops.
Countenance.　Aid; assistance; support.
Deus ex machina [L.].　A god let down by a machine; a mechanical stage device.
Favor.　Support; encouragement.
Food, etc.　That which is eaten or drunk for the support of life.　See NUTRIMENT.
Furtherance.　The act of assisting or promoting.
Help.　Very urgent need of aid; assistance.
Help at a dead lift.　Help without the aid of mechanical apparatus.
Interest.　Especial attention to some object.
Lift.　The act of lifting or raising.
Manna in the wilderness.　Figuratively, divine food.
Means, etc.　The medium through which anything is done.　See MEANS
Ministration.　The act of performing service.

OBSTRUCTION—HELP—*Continued.*

Objection. Anything presented in obstruction to.
Obstacle. Anything which impedes, obstructs, or hinders.
Obstruction. Anything which impedes or hinders.
Obtrusion. The act of thrusting upon others by force or contrary to their wishes.
Oppilation. The act of filling with obstructions.
Preclusion. The act of shutting out by previous obstacles.
Prevention. The act of hindering or obstruction of access.
Preventive. Anything which intercepts or obstructs approach.
Restraint, etc. That which hinders or obstructs. See RELEASE-RESTRAINT.
Restriction. Anything that holds in check or within confinement.
Retardation. The act of hindering or obstructing.
Retardment. The act of retarding.
Stoppage. The act of arresting motion.
Stricture. A hindrance or compression.

OBSTRUCTION—*Nouns of Means and Instrument.*

Bar. A piece of wood or metal forming a barrier or obstruction to a passageway.
Barricade, etc. A barrier hastily built of objects nearest at hand. See ATTACK-DEFENSE.
Barrier. Something that bars, keeps out, or obstructs progress.
Block. Anything that stops effectually the progress or operation of.
Blockade, etc. Any hindrance or obstruction to action or progress. See APERTURE-CLOSURE.
Boom. A strong cable or line of spars, bound together, stretched across a river or harbor to prevent navigation.
Breakwater. A wall or structure for protecting a harbor from the force of waves.
Buffer. Anything that lessens the shock of an opposing force.
Bulkhead. A partition in a ship to render apartments water-tight.
Burden. A heavy or taxing load.
Burrock. A small weir.
Chainweight. A weight or obstruction attached to something by a chain.
Clog. Anything attached so as to impede motion or action.
Contretemps [F.]. A chance accident which throws everything into confusion.
Dam. A barrier to confine the flow of a stream.
Damper. That which damps or checks.
Dead wall. A wall without break or variation.
Dead weight. A burden borne without aid.
Drag weight. A weight to check motion.
Drawback. Anything that hinders progress.
Ephialtes. The nightmare.
Estoppel. An act or admission that cannot legally be denied.
Fardel. A bundle or burden.
Gate. A movable barrier closing a passage.
Head-wind. A wind blowing in opposition to.
Hinderer. One who interferes with or hinders.
Hitch. An obstruction which causes a sudden stoppage.
Holdback. That which keeps back; a check.
Ill-wind. A wind that is unfavorable to progress.
Incubus. The form in which the nightmare appears.
Insuperable obstacle. An obstruction that cannot be overcome.
Interloper. One who interferes officiously
Killjoy. One who spoils pleasure.
Knag. A knot in wood.
Knot. An intertwining of the parts of one or more ropes or cords, for the purpose of fastening them together.
Let. Anything that obstructs or hinders.
Lion in the path. Figuratively, an impassable obstacle.
Load. Anything that is borne with difficulty.
Lumber. A superfluous weight or bulk.
Marplot. One who mars or spoils a plot by officious interference.
Millstone round one's neck. An insurmountable obstacle.
Nightmare. An oppressive condition in sleep, giving the sense of a difficulty or danger from which one cannot escape.
Old man of the sea. An oppressive burden; from the story of Sindbad, *Arabian Nights.*
Onus. A burden or responsibility
Opponent. One who opposes another. See ANTAGONIST
Pack. A bundle or package.
Portcullis. Iron-pointed timbers hung over the gateway of a fortified place and let down to obstruct the passage.
Prophylactic. A medicine that prevents disease from spreading.
Remora. An impediment.
Screw loose. Anything that prevents freedom of motion or regular movement.
Shoe. A drag placed under a wheel to obstruct its rotation.

Ministry. The act of giving needful things.
Nourishment. }
Nutrition. } That which sustains or promotes growth.
Opitulation. The act of helping or assisting.
Parbuckle. A sling made by passing both ends of a rope through its bight, used in moving heavy objects.
Patronage. Especial favor or assistance.
Promotion. The act of contributing to the growth or enlargement of anything.
Recruits. A new supply of something necessary or useful.
Reinforcements. Additional troops sent to strengthen a position.
Relief. A person or persons taking the place of another in some duty.
Rescue. Deliverance, as from danger.
Subministration. The act of supplying or furnishing.
Subvention. The act of coming to relief or assistance.
Succor. Relief; assistance.
Succors. Auxiliary troops.
Supernatural aid. Divine aid.
Supplies. Accumulated stores reserved for distribution.
Support, etc. That which helps, upholds, or assists. See SUSPENSION-SUPPORT.
Sustentation. Support.

HELP—*Verbs.*

Abet. To encourage by aid; chiefly in a bad sense.
Accommodate. To furnish with something desired or needed.
Administer to. To supply with; contribute to.
Adopt the cause of. To take up the cause of.
Advance. To assist by giving aid.
Advocate. To be or plead in favor of.
Afford aid. See *Nouns.*
Aid. To assist another's exertions; help.
Assist. To give support, help, or succor.
Attend. To minister; serve.
Back. To support; strengthen by aid.
Back up. To uphold by the aid of money or influence.
Bear a hand. }
Bear a helping hand. } To give aid to.
Bear through. To pass through by force.
Beat up for recruits. To look for aid for a cause.
Befriend. To aid; countenance; benefit.
Benefit, etc. To do good to; help; assist. See GOODNESS.
Be of use to. To give help to.
Be the making of. To influence one's behavior or position.
Bolster. To support; hold up; maintain.
Bring aid. To help.
Cheer. To encourage.
Cherish. To hold dear; encourage.
Come to the aid of, etc. See *Nouns.*
Conduce, etc. To promote; further. See INCLINATION.
Consult the wishes of. To do as one wishes one to do.
Contribute. To give aid to; assist.
Countenance. To favor; approve; aid; support.
Cradle. To nurse in infancy.
Cultivate. To foster; cherish; turn special attention upon.
Do service to. To help.
Dry-nurse. To attend; bring up and feed without the breast.
Encourage. To give courage to; embolden; countenance.
Enlist under the banners of. To exert one's power or influence in a cause.
Entertain. To maintain; support.
Espouse the cause of. To adopt the cause of.
Expedite. To relieve of burdens; hasten.
Fan the flame. }
Feed the flame. } To stir up or influence.
Favor. To support; aid; have the disposition to aid.
Foment. To cherish; abet.
Forward. To hasten; advance; promote.
Foster. To encourage; promote.
Furnish aid. To give help to.
Further. To help forward; promote; assist.
Give a hand. }
Give a helping hand. }
Give aid. }
Give a lift to. } To help.
Give an impulse to. }
Give a shove to. }
Give moral support to. To give assent to without giving material assistance.
Give new life to. To aid or encourage.
Give one a lift. To assist a person.
Give one a turn. To assist.
Hasten. To hurry; push on.

OBSTRUCTION—HELP—*Continued.*

OBSTRUCTION—Nouns of Means and Instrument—*Continued.***

Skid. A chain used to fasten a wheel to prevent its rotation when going down a hill.

Snag. A hidden obstacle or impediment.

Snag and sawyers. Fallen trees that rest at the root-end on the bottom of a stream, and continually rise and fall under the action of the current.

Spoke. A stick or bar for insertion in a wheel to prevent its turning.

Stay. A rod or bar for holding something in position.

Stile. A step or steps on each side of a wall to aid in surmounting it.

Stop. An obstruction or obstacle.

Stopper. One who or that which stops up or closes.

Stumbling-block. } Any obstruction or hindrance causing one to
Stumbling-stone. } stumble.

Tether, etc. Something used to check or confine. See Release-Prison.

Trammel. That which limits freedom or activity.

Turnpike. A gate set across a road to stop travelers until toll is paid.

Turnstile. A wooden frame or gate at the entrance of a building or passage.

Wall. A structure of stone or brick for defense or security.

Weir. An artificial obstruction placed in a stream to raise the water.

Wet blanket. A discouragement or damper.

OBSTRUCTION—*Verbs.*

Act as a drag. To hinder.

Antevert. To prevent.

Avert. To cause to turn off.

Baffle. To frustrate or defeat.

Balk. To frustrate or baffle.

Bar. To hinder; obstruct; prevent.

Barricade. To fortify in order to check the advance of an enemy.

Be in the way of. To obstruct the passage.

Belay. To obstruct or block up.

Block. To obstruct.

Block the way. }
Block up. } To prevent passage.

Bolt. To close by means of bolts.

Break in upon. To rush upon.

Check. To restrain.

Choke. To obstruct by filling up a passage.

Circumvent. To deceive; delude.

Clip the wings of. To cut the feathers of birds to prevent their flight.

Clog. To obstruct a passage so as to hinder motion.

Clog the wheel. To check the motion of.

Contravene. To oppose.

Counteract. To work in opposition to.

Countercheck. To stop or check by some obstacle.

Cramp. To confine; impede; check.

Cripple, etc. To deprive of activity or use. See Betterment-Deterioration.

Cross the path of. To obstruct.

Cumber. To hinder by a weight or burden.

Cut off. To obstruct approach to.

Cut the ground from under one. To take away all support.

Damp. To dishearten.

Dam up, etc. To obstruct the flow of. See Aperture-Closure.

Debar. To exclude or shut out.

Defeat, etc. To overcome; render null and void. See Success.

Discommode. To trouble; inconvenience.

Discompose. To interfere with; annoy.

Disconcert. To frustrate; annoy.

Discountenance. To refuse to support.

Dishearten, etc. To discourage; depress. See Motive-Dehortation.

Draw off. To withdraw.

Drive into a corner. To drive into a position which necessitates surrender.

Embarrass. To put into a difficult position.

Encumber. To weigh down; obstruct.

Estop. To impede the progress of, as in law.

Fall foul of. To make an attack upon.

Foil. To frustrate.

Foreclose. To stop; exclude; prevent.

Forefend. To hinder; prevent the approach of.

Frustrate. To baffle; disappoint; succeed in obstructing.

Hamper. To hinder.

Hang like a millstone round one's neck. To impede; trouble; annoy.

Hedge in. }
Hedge round. } To surround. or place in a difficult position.

Hinder. To keep from action, motion, etc.

HELP—Verbs—*Continued.***

Help. To furnish with means of assistance when in distress; aid; assist.

Help a lame dog over a stile. To give assistance when in need or **a** difficulty.

Hold a hand. }
Hold a helping hand. } To aid. ·

Hold up. To support; sustain.

Humor. To help or assist by favoring treatment.

Keep in countenance. To preserve in an assured condition.

Lend a hand. }
Lend a helping hand. } To help.

Lend one's aid. To give one's assistance.

Lend one's countenance to. To give one's assent to.

Lend oneself to. To give oneself in support to.

Lend wings to. To hasten.

Make interest for. To work to the advantage of another.

Manure. To fertilize or enrich.

Minister to. To supply with needs.

Nourish. To sustain; supply with necessaries for subsistence.

Nurse. To nourish; cherish; care for.

Nurture. To train with a fostering care.

Oblige. To accommodate.

Pander to. To minister to the evil designs or lusts of another.

Patronize. To support; maintain: often in an unfavorable sense.

Pay the piper. To satisfy any demand, usually unwillingly. ·

Press into service. To compel to serve.

Promote. To advance; further.

Prop. To support; prevent from falling.

Pull through. To help through a difficulty.

Push forward. }
Put forward. } To assist.

Put out to nurse. To bring up or foster.

Quicken. To hasten; incite.

Recruit. To supply deficiency or lack.

Reinforce. To strengthen with new forces, aid, or assistance.

Relieve. To free from any burden, trouble, or the like.

Render a service, etc. To give assistance. See Usefulness.

Rescue. To deliver from danger, trouble, or the like.

Second. To assist; encourage.

Serve. To assist as an inferior.

Set agoing. To start moving.

Set forward. To urge on.

Set on one's legs. To give aid to.

Set up. To erect; establish.

Shine upon. To favor; encourage.

Side with, etc. To embrace the opinions of another. See Antagonism-Concurrence.

Smile upon. To express approval of.

Smooth the bed of death. To help in the last extremity

Speed. To hasten.

Squire. To wait upon, as a squire.

Stand by. To defend; support; not to desert.

Stick up. Not to forsake.

Stick up for. To defend.

Stretch out a hand. }
Stretch out a helping hand. } To give aid to.

Subminister to. To supply.

Subscribe to. To assent; agree.

Subserve, etc. To assist forward; promote. See Instrumentality.

Succor. To relieve; assist; help.

Suckle. To nurse at the breast.

Supply aid to. See Nouns.

Support. To uphold; aid; furnish what is necessary for life.

Sustain. To maintain; support; nourish.

Take by the hand. To assist; help.

Take care of, etc. See Carefulness.

Take in hand. To lend one's assistance to.

Take in tow. To assist in promoting.

Take up the cause of. To aid another in a cause.

Take up the cudgels for. To support.

Tend. To be directed to some end.

Tender to. To offer to.

Uphold. To support; assist.

Wait on. To serve.

Work for. To perform service for.

HELP—*Adjectives.*

Accessory. Aiding in producing some effect.

Adjuvant. Helping; assisting.

Aiding, etc Assisting, helping.

Amicable. Friendly.

OBSTRUCTION—HELP—*Continued*

OBSTRUCTION—Verbs—*Continued.*

Hustle. To handle roughly; eject forcibly.
Impede. To stop in progress.
Impedite. To impede.
Incommode. To inconvenience.
Incumber. To burden, as with a load.
Inhibit, etc. To check; hinder; hold in restraint. See Leave-Prohibition.
Intercept. To stop on the passage; obstruct the progress of.
Interclude. To shut out; intercept
Interfere. To enter into the affairs of another.
Intermeddle, etc. To interfere officiously See Activity.
Interpose. To thrust in; intrude as an objection.
Interrupt. To stop or check the progress of.
Keep off. To restrain.
Lay a wet blanket on. To dampen; discourage.
Let. To retard or hinder by obstacles.
Load with. To weigh down with
Lock. To close or fasten with lock and key.
Lock the wheel. To prevent the wheel from rotating.
Lumber. To put in a disorderly heap.
Mar. To spoil.
Nip in the bud. To destroy in the beginning.
Obstruct. To hinder, with the idea of prevention.
Obviate. To make clear of; prevent by interception.
Oppose, etc. To resist; hinder; obstruct. See Antagonism.
Overlay. To oppress by laying on too great weight
Overload. To put too great weight on.
Override. To annul or set aside.
Preclude. To shut out by an anticipated action.
Prevent. To hinder; obstruct entirely.
Put an extinguisher on. To put out.
Put a spoke in the wheel. To fasten a wheel with a contrivance so as to cause it to slide.
Put a stop to. To prevent activity.
Put on the brake, etc. To impede or obstruct by means of a brake. See *Nouns.*
Put to inconvenience. To hinder.
Restrict. To restrain.
Retard. To delay; hinder.
Run foul of. To rush upon with haste.
Saddle with. To load down; encumber.
Scotch the wheel. To prevent a wheel from rotating.
Shackle, etc. To bind or confine, so as to obstruct. See Release-Restraint.
Slacken. To check; repress.
Snub. To rebuke or check with a short biting remark
Spike guns, etc. To render guns useless by driving a spike or nail into the touch-hole. See Usefulness-Uselessness.
Spoil. To render useless.
Spoil sport. To place obstacles in the way of players.
Stand in the way of. To obstruct a person's passage.
Stave off. To push off.
Stay. To hinder; restrain.
Stop. To hinder or obstruct officiously.
Stop the way. To prevent passage.
Take the wind out of one's sails. To check one's progress.
Throw a wet blanket on. To discourage; dampen.
Throw cold water on. To check the enthusiasm of.
Thwart. To oppose successfully; frustrate.
Tie one's hands. To make a person helpless.
Trammel. To shackle; hamper.
Traverse. To obstruct; thwart.
Turn aside. To compel one by obstruction to turn from a path.
Undermine. To ruin in an underhand or treacherous manner.
Ward off. To keep off.

OBSTRUCTION—*Adjectives.*

Alone. Apart from others.
Burdensome. Oppressive; heavy to be borne.

---

ob-struct'-ive. Tending to obstruct. Antagonist-Assistant, Obstruction-Help.
ob'-stru-ent. Causing obstruction. Obstruction-Help.
ob-stu''-pe-fac'-tion. Stupefaction. Sensitiveness-Apathy.
obstupui steteruntque comæ et vox faucibus hæsit [L.] (ob-stiu'-piu-ɑi stet-er-unt'-quî co'-mî et vox fau'-si bus hî'-sit). I was astounded and my hair stood on end. Sanguineness-Timidity

HELP—Adjectives—*Continued*

Ancillary. Subordinate; helping.
At one's beck. Close at hand.
Auxiliary. Helping; assisting
Coadjuvant, etc. Assisting; aiding. See Antagonism-Concurrence.
Favorable. Inclined towards; friendly.
Friendly Kindly disposed towards.
Helpful. Giving help.
Ministrant. Attendant; serving, as a minister.
Neighborly. Living close by; friendly.
Obliging, etc. Having the disposition to do favors; eager to help. See Charitableness.
Propitious. Fortunate; lucky; favorable.
Subservient. Serving; subordinate.
Subsidiary. Serving to help; assistant.
Well-disposed. Favorable.

HELP—*Adverbs, etc.*

By the aid of, etc. With the assistance of. See *Nouns.*
For the sake of. For the advantage of.
In aid of.
In behalf of.
In favor of. } To one's interest, advantage, or defense.
In furtherance of.
In the name of.
In the service of.
Non obstante [L.]. Notwithstanding.
On account of. To one's favor.
On behalf of. For the sake of.
On the part of. To one's aid.
With the aid of, etc. See *Nouns.*

HELP—*Interjections*

Help! save us! to the rescue!

OBSTRUCTION—Adjectives—*Continued.*

Cumbersome. Hindering; burdensome; heavy.
Cumbrous. Serving to hinder or obstruct.
Deserted, etc. Forsaken; left alone. See Quest-Abandonment.
Hard-pressed. In a difficult position.
Heavy-laden. Weighed down heavily.
Hindered, etc. Opposed; obstructed. See Verbs.
Hindering, etc. Opposing. See Verbs.
Impedient. Hindering.
Impeditive. Obstructive; causing hindrance.
Incommodious. Inconvenient.
Intercipient. Stopping, intercepting.
In the way of. Obstructing.
Obstructive. Hindering; tending to obstruct.
Obstruent. Obstructing; blocking up.
Obtrusive. Inclined to intrude uninvited.
Onerous. Burdensome; oppressive.
Prophylactic, etc. Defending from disease. See Remedy.
Single-handed. Alone; without assistance.
Unassisted, etc. Without help or assistance. See Obstruction-Help.
Unfavorable. Not favorable.
Water-logged. Rendered heavy and clumsy, like a log.
Wind-bound. Prevented from sailing by an opposing wind.

OBSTRUCTION—*Phrase*

Occurent nubes [L.]. Clouds will intervene.

---

ob-tain'. To get; to be prevalent. Entity-Nonentity, Gain-Loss; **obtain under false pretenses,** Theft.
ob-tain'-a-ble. Procurable. Possibility-Impossibility.
ob-tain'-ment. Acquirement. Gain-Loss.
ob-ten''-e-bra'-tion. A darkening. Light-Darkness.
ob''-tes-ta'-tion. Entreaty. Advice, Petition-Expostulation.

ob″-trec-ta′-tion. Slander. ADULATION-DISPARAGEMENT.

ob-trude′. To thrust into. ACTIVITY-INDOLENCE, INJECTION-EJECTION.

ob-trun′-cate. To lop. LENGTH-SHORTNESS.

ob-tru′-sion. An obtruding. ENVIRONMENT-INTERPOSITION, OBSTRUCTION-HELP.

ob-tru′-sive. Tending to obtrude. ENVIRONMENT-INTERPOSITION, OBSTRUCTION-HELP, POLITENESS-IMPOLITENESS, TASTE-VULGARITY.

ob-tund′. To blunt. FEELING-INSENSIBILITY, SHARPNESS-BLUNTNESS, TURBULENCE-CALMNESS.

ob-tuse′. Dull. FEELING-INSENSIBILITY, SAGACITY-INCAPACITY, SENSITIVENESS-APATHY, SHARPNESS-BLUNTNESS; **obtuse angle,** ANGULARITY.

ob-tuse′-ness. Bluntness. FEELING-INSENSIBILITY.

ob-um′-brate. Overhung. LIGHT-DARKNESS.

ob′-verse. The face of a coin. ANTERIORITY-POSTERIORITY.

ob′-vi-ate. To prevent by interception. OBSTRUCTION-HELP.

ob′-vi-ous. Manifest. CLEARNESS-OBSCURITY, MANIFESTATION-LATENCY, VISIBILITY-INVISIBILITY.

occasio calva post est, fronte capillato [L.] (oc-kê′-shi-o cal′-va post est, fron′-tî cap-il-lê′-to). Opportunity, though she has hair in front, is bald behind. ACTION-PASSIVENESS, SUCCESS-FAILURE.

occasio facit furem [L.] (oc-kê′-shi-o fê′-sit fiu′-rem). Opportunity makes the thief. OPPORTUNENESS-UNSUITABLENESS.

oc-ca′-sion. A juncture; an opportunity. CAUSE-EFFECT, CONDITION-SITUATION, OPPORTUNENESS-UNSUITABLENESS; **benefit the occasion,** PROPRIETY-IMPROPRIETY; **have the occasion for,** NEED; **on the present occasion,** TIME; **on the spur of the occasion,** PREDETERMINATION-IMPULSE.

oc-ca′-sion-al. Occurring sometimes. CERTAINTY-DOUBT.

oc-ca′-sion-al-ly. Sometimes. FREQUENCY-RARITY.

oc-ca′-sion-er. Cause. CAUSE-EFFECT.

Oc″-ci-den′-tal. Western. LATERALITY-CONTRAPOSITION.

oc′-ci-put. The hindhead. ANTERIORITY-POSTERIORITY

oc-ci′-sion. A killing. LIFE-KILLING.

oc-clude′. To close. APERTURE-CLOSURE.

oc-clu′-sion. A stopping up. APERTURE-CLOSURE.

oc-cult′. Concealed. CLEARNESS-OBSCURITY, ENLIGHTENMENT-SECRECY, MANIFESTATION-LATENCY; **occult art,** DEVOTION-MAGIC.

oc″-cul-ta′-tion. Concealment. APPEARANCE-DISAPPEARANCE, ASTRONOMY, ENLIGHTENMENT-SECRECY.

oc-cult′-ness. Concealment. MANIFESTATION-LATENCY.

oc′-cu-pan-cy. Holding in possession. HOLDING-EXEMPTION, PRESENCE-ABSENCE.

oc′-cu-pant. One who occupies. DWELLER-HABITATION, HOLDER.

oc″-cu-pa′-tion. Business. OCCUPATION, PRESENCE-ABSENCE; **in the occupation of,** DWELLER-HABITATION; **occupation road,** WAY.

OCCUPATION.

Affair. Something done or to be done.

Agendum [L.]. A thing to be done.

Art. The use of means for the accomplishment of some desired end; a system of rules or accepted methods for accomplishing some practical end.

Avocation. An occupation which calls one away from one's regular employment.

Beat. A circuit or district regularly gone over in the line of duty.

Berth. Employment or office.

Business. That which occupies one's time and attention.

Calling. An employment to which one is called by a special fitness or sense of duty.

Capacity. Specific profession or occupation.

Care. Protection or oversight.

Career. The conduct in some calling in life.

Case. Special facts or conditions involved in a suit at law.

Charge. Care or custody of any person or thing.

Chargeship. Office of a *charge d'affairs*.

Cloth. The distinguishing dress of any profession, especially of the clergy; hence, the clerical office.

Commission. The duty or office entrusted to the care of any person or persons.

Concern. That which relates to one.

Craft. An occupation necessitating technical skill or manual dexterity.

Cue. A part to be performed.

Department. A division or subdivision of business or official duty.

Duty, etc. Any service or business which is assigned. See DESIGN.

Employ. That which engages one.

Employment. That which engages one's time or attention; occupation.

Engagement. An engrossing or absorbing occupation.

Errand. Special business given into the hands of a messenger.

Exercise. The performance of an office or religious duty.

Faculty. The ability to do or perform.

Field. Favorable opportunity for action or achievement.

Function. A course of action pertaining peculiarly to any public office.

Handicraft. An occupation requiring manual skill.

Incumbency. Full possession and exercise of an office or benefice.

Industrial arts. Arts relating to the processes or products of manufacture or commercial production.

Industry. A single department of productive activity.

Irons in the fire. Different duties or objects of attention.

Job. A situation; an engagement to work.

Line. A department or branch of mercantile business.

Living. The benefice of a clergyman.

Lookout. An object of forethought or care.

Matter. That with which one is concerned; affair.

Matter in hand. Business engaging one at the present time.

Mission. The service with which an agent or messenger is charged.

Mystery. The business with which one is accustomed to be occupied.

Occupation. The chief business of one's life.

Office. A position of authority and trust.

Orb. Sphere of action.

Part. That which falls to one; duty; office.

Place. A position occupied by one.

Post. A position or office.

Press of business, etc. Rush of business. See ACTIVITY.

Profession. The occupation, if not agricultural, mechanical, or the like, which one follows.

Province. The proper business or office of a person or order.

Pursuit, etc. Continued business or employment. See QUEST.

Race. Course of life; career.

Rôle [F.]. A part or function played by any one.

Round. A series of duties or tasks to be performed in regular order, and then repeated.

Routine. A regular or habitual course of action.

Service, etc. Duty performed or required. See LIBERTY-SUBJECTION.

Situation. Steady employment or position.

Sphere. Range of action; employment.

Task. Duty assigned; undertaking.

Thing to do. Work.

Trade, etc. The business of exchanging commodities. See EXCHANGE.

Undertaking. Any business or project engaged in by a person.

Vocation. Destined employment or calling.

Walk. Course of action.

Walk of life. Vocation.

What one is about. }
What one is doing. } Occupation.

Work, etc. Employment; physical labor. See ACTION.

OCCUPATION—*Verbs.*

Act. To exert power or perform an office or duty.

Act one's part. To fulfil one's duties

Attend to business. }
Attend to one's work. } To be engaged in one's employment.

Be about. To attend to one's business.

Bear the burden. To sustain business responsibilities.

Be at work on. To be busy with.

Be doing. To work.

Be employed in. }
Be engaged in. } To be engaged in a particular task.

Be in the hands of. To have work to do.

Be occupied with. To be busy.

Be on the anvil. To be in the formative state, but not matured.
Be on the stocks. To be well on the way in the process of making.
Betake oneself to. To engage in.
Carry on a trade. }
Carry on business. } To be engaged in a particular work. See *Nouns*.
Concern oneself with. To be engaged in.
Discharge the duties of. }
Discharge the functions of. } To do a particular line of work.
Discharge the office of. }
Do a trade. }
Do business. } To be occupied with one's work. See *Nouns*.
Do duty. To work.
Drive a trade. To be engaged in a particular line of work.
Employ oneself in. }
Employ oneself upon. } To work upon.
Employ one's time in. }
Enter a profession. To take up the work of one's life. See *Nouns*.
Fill an office. To perform the duties pertaining to the office.
Fill a place. }
Fill a situation. } To be assigned to a duty.
Have in hand. To be occupied with.
Have one's hands full, etc. To be pressed with business. See ACTIVITY.
Have one's hands in. To be accustomed to a particular business.
Have on one's hands. To have in one's care.
Have on one's shoulders. To bear the responsibility of.
Have to do with, etc. To be concerned with. See ACTION.
Hold an office. }
Hold a place. } To do a particular work. See *Nouns*.
Hold a portfolio. To perform the functions of a minister of state or member of the cabinet.
Hold a situation. See *Nouns*.
Keep a shop. To be in business on a small scale.
Labor in one's vocation. To be engaged in one's life-work. See *Nouns*.
Make it one's business. To devote one's time to. See *Nouns*.
Occupy oneself with. To be busy with.
Officiate. To conduct the business of an office or public trust.
Pass one's time in. To work upon.
Pass through one's hands. To transact business.
Perform the duties of. }
Perform the functions of. } To do the work connected with a particular place.
Perform the office of. }
Play one's part. To perform the duty assigned to one.
Ply one's task. To diligently perform one's duty or office.
Ply one's trade. To work diligently at one's trade or occupation.
Pursue the even tenor of one's way. To preserve the golden mean in all the affairs of life.
Serve. To work in behalf of.
Spend one's time in. To engage in work.

Transact a trade. To carry on or perform a trade.
Transact business. To do business.
Turn one's hand to. To engage in or apply oneself to.
Undertake, etc. To set about or take in hand. See ENTERPRISE.

Occupation—*Adjectives.*

Acting. Doing duty in place of another.
Afoot. In active operation.
Business-like. According to right business methods.
Busy, etc. Occupied with work or serious affairs, etc. See ACTIVITY.
Functional. Pertaining to a duty or function.
Going on. Doing or proceeding.
Industrial. Of or pertaining to occupations.
In hand. In the course of transaction.
In one's hands. In one's possession or at one's risk.
Official. Relating to an office or public trust.
On foot. In operation.
On hand. In immediate possession.
On one's hands. In one's care.
On the anvil. In a formative or immature state or condition.
Professional. Relating to a profession or calling.
Work-a-day. Week-day or work-day.

Occupation—*Adverbs, etc.*

All in one day's work.
In the course of business.
Professionally. Relations to one's business or profession. See *Adjectives*.

oc'-cu-pied. Employed. ACTIVITY-INDOLENCE; **occupied by,** DWELLER-HABITATION; **occupied with,** HEED-DISREGARD, OCCUPATION.
oc'-cu-pi"-er. A tenant. DWELLER-HABITATION, HOLDER.
oc'-cu-py. To employ; to hold. HOLDING-EXEMPTION, PRESENCE-ABSENCE; **occupy a post,** RULE-LICENSE; **occupy oneself with,** HEED-DISREGARD, OCCUPATION; **occupy the chair,** MANAGEMENT; **occupy the mind,** HEED-DISREGARD, REFLECTION-VACANCY; **occupy time,** DURATION-NEVERNESS.
oc'-cu-py"-ing. Holding. PRESENCE-ABSENCE.
oc-cur'. To happen. ENTITY-NONENTITY, OCCURRENCE-DESTINY; **occur in a place,** PRESENCE-ABSENCE; **occur to the mind,** REFLECTION-VACANCY.
oc-cur'-rence. A happening. OCCURRENCE-DESTINY; **of daily occurrence,** HABIT-DESUETUDE.

OCCURRENCE—DESTINY.

Accident. Anything that happens unexpectedly or undesignedly.
Advent. A coming event.
Adventure. An exciting experience coming unexpectedly.
Affair. That which is done or is to be done.
Affairs. Business of any kind.
Affairs in general. Usual proceedings or actions.
Business. That which engages the time, labor, or attention of any one.
Casualty. A fatal chance or occurrence.
Chapter of accidents. Chance. See RATIONALE-LUCK.
Circumstance. That which in some way affects a fact or event.
Concern. That which affects the welfare or happiness.
Consequence. A result.
Contingency. Possibility of happening.
Course of events. }
Course of things. } A series of happenings.
Crisis. A decisive point.
Current of events. A series of connected events.
Current of things. The progress of affairs.
Doings. Anything done.
Emergency. An unexpected turn in circumstances.
Event. That which happens.
Eventuality. A possible or a consequential event.
Fact. An effect produced or achieved.
Incident. A minor occurrence.
Life. A certain way or manner of living with respect to conditions, circumstances, etc.
March of events. }
March of things. } The course or onward movement of affairs.
Matter of fact. An actual occurrence.
Naked fact. A fact without addition or exaggeration.

After life. Existence after death.
Destiny. The end toward which anything is going.
Everlasting death. The lot of the wicked after death.
Everlasting life. The condition of the sanctified after death.
Future existence. }
Future state. } The condition or state of mortals after death.
Futurity. The state of being in time to come.
Next world. The world after death.
Postexistence. That part of life which has been lived.
Prospect. Foresight. See EXPECTATION.
World to come. The existence after the existence of this world.

DESTINY—*Verbs.*

Approach. To come near.
Await. To be reserved for.
Come on. To be about to occur.
Doom. To preordain to an evil lot.
Foreordain. To determine beforehand.
Impend. To hang over; be nearly upon.
Loom. To rise gradually into view.
Predestine. }
Preordain. } To appoint beforehand.
Threaten. To express intentions to do something disagreeable.

DESTINY—*Verbal Expressions.*

Hang over; have in store for; lie over; stare one in the face.

DESTINY—*Adjectives.*

About to be. }
About to happen. } Coming to pass almost immediately.
At hand. }

OCCURRENCE—DESTINY—*Continued.*

Occurrence. An incident or event.
Order of the day. The special business appointed for a specified day.
Particular. An individual fact or circumstance.
Pass. The state of things.
Passage. Change from one state to another.
Phenomenon. An unusual happening.
Proceeding. A measure or step taken in the course of business.
Run of events. ⎱
Run of things. ⎰ The course of procedure.
Situation. Position as regards the condition and circumstances. See CONDITION-SITUATION.
State of affairs. The circumstances or condition of things.
Stream of events. ⎱
Stream of things. ⎰ The onward movement of affairs.
The times. The period at which any definite event occurred.
The world. The sum of human affairs and interests.
Things. Transactions or occurrences.
Things in general. The sum of passing events.
Tide of events. ⎱ ⎰The progress of affairs, " which taken at the flood
Tide of things. ⎰ ⎱ leads on to fortune." [Shakespeare, *Julius Cæsar*, V, iii.]
Transaction. That which is done.
Ups and downs of life. Alternate states of conditions or circumstances in life.

OCCURRENCE—*Verbs.*

Arise. To come into existence.
Arrive. To come.
Bechance. To happen by chance.
Befall. To come by accident.
Betide. To come upon; to happen.
Come. To be brought about.
Effect. To bring about.
Encounter. To meet.
Endure. To undergo. See FEELING.
Ensue. To follow.
Eventuate. Come to pass, to result.
Experience. To undergo.
Fall. To befall; take place.
Find. To come upon accidentally.
Happen. To take place.
Hold. To occupy the time.
Issue. To end or terminate; result.
Occur. To happen.
Pass. To happen.
Prove. To come to pass.
Run. To occur or be found.
Start. To begin.
Supervene. To happen in addition; happen.
Undergo. To pass through.

OCCURRENCE—*Verbal Expressions.*

Become of; be one's chance; be one's fortune; be one's lot; be on foot; cast up; come about; come forth; come into existence; come off; come on; come round; come to pass; crop up; draw on; fall in; fall out; fall to the lot of; go through; meet with; pass off; pass through; present itself; spring up; take effect; take its course; take place; turn out; turn up.

OCCURRENCE—*Adjectives.*

Afloat. In circulation.
At issue. Undecided.
Bustling. Characterized by confused activity
Current. In circulation.
Doing. Taking place.
Eventful. Rich in events or incidents.
Full of incident. Full of events.
Going on. Happening.

oc-cur'-sion. A meeting. IMPETUS-REACTION.

DESTINY—ADJECTIVES—*Continued.*

Brewing. In preparation.
Close at hand. About to happen in a very short time.
Coming. Going to be present at some future time.
Destined. Determined for the future.
Forthcoming. About to appear.
Going to happen. About to take place.
Hanging over one's head. Almost ready to happen.
Imminent. Likely to befall very soon.
Impending. Almost sure to happen at some uncertain time.
In embryo. In its earliest stage.
In prospect. Contemplated. See EXPECTATION.
In reserve. Retained for future use.
Instant. About to occur at once.
In store. Ready or prepared for future use.
In the wind. Astir.
In the womb of futurity. ⎱
In the womb of time. ⎰ Getting ready to appear at a future time.
Looming in the distance. ⎱
Looming in the future. ⎰ Giving remote indications of happening.
Looming in the horizon. ⎰
Near. ⎱
Near at hand. ⎰ Not far off in time.
On the cards. Likely to happen.
Overhanging. Imminent.
Pregnant. About to appear. See CREATION.
Preparing. Getting ready to happen.
To come. Future.
That is to be. ⎱
That will be. ⎰ Thought of as being in the future.
Unborn. Having not yet occurred.

DESTINY—*Adverbs, etc.*

All in good time. At the proper time.
As chance would have it. Accidentally.
Eventually. Finally. See OCCURRENCE.
In the long run. As the average of a long series of events.
In time. After the lapse of time.
Whatever may happen. Regardless of events. See CERTAINTY.

———

OCCURRENCE—ADJECTIVES—*Continued.*

Happening. Taking place.
Incidental. Occurring as minor to something else.
In question. Under examination.
In the wind. Rumored; impending.
On foot. Astir, begun.
On the tapis. Under consideration.

OCCURRENCE—*Adverbs, etc.*

As it may happen. Depending on chance.
As it may turn out. Depending on the result.
As the cat jumps. Depending on the turn of affairs.
As the tree falls. By chance.
As the world goes. Conforming to the present conditions.
As the world wags. In a time-serving manner.
As things go. ⎱
As times go. ⎰ Considering the conditions of the times.
Eventually. Finally.
In case. If it happen that.
In the course of things. During the progress of events.
In the event of. In case.
In the natural course of things. ⎱
In the ordinary course of things. ⎰ If nothing unusual happens.
The plot thickens. The conspiracy becomes more fully developed.

o'-cean. The sea. OCEAN-LAND; **plow the ocean,** WAYFARER-SEAFARER.

OCEAN—LAND.

Billows. Great waves or swells on the ocean; the ocean itself.
Brine. The sea water; the ocean.
Deep. The sea; ocean.
Great waters. The ocean.
High seas. The waters of the ocean beyond those assigned to the nations.
Main. The ocean
Ocean. A great tract of salt water
Offing. That portion of the sea at such a distance from the shore as to have deep water.

Acres. The extent of measured land
Alluvion. Earthy matter deposited by floods.
Alluvium. Deposits of earthy matter where the flow of water is checked.
Bank. The rising ground bordering a lake, river, or sea.
Beach. The shore of the sea, or of a lake, washed by the waves
Clay. Soft earth.
Clod. ⎱
Clot. ⎰ A lumpy clayey mass of earth.
Coast. The seashore, or land near it.

OCEAN—LAND—*Continued.*

Salt water. The briny water of the ocean; the ocean itself.

Sea. The body of salt water covering the larger part of the earth's surface; the ocean.

Tide, etc. The alternate rising and falling of the waters of the ocean. See RIVER.

Vasty deep. The ocean.

Waters. A body of waters such as the sea.

Watery waste. The ocean.

Waves. The sea; waters in general.

OCEAN—*Scientific Nouns.*

Hydrographer. One who makes charts pertaining to navigation.

Hydrography. The science of making charts pertaining to navigation

OCEAN—*Figurative Nouns.*

Dolphin. A large fish, emblematic of the ocean.

Naiad. A water-nymph presiding over rivers and brooks.

Neptune. The god of the seas.

Nereid. A sea-nymph one of the daughters of Nereus and Doris.

Sea-nymph. A female divinity of the sea.

Siren. A sea-nymph, half woman, half bird, drawing travelers to them by their sweet singing to destroy them.

Thetis. A sea-nymph.

Trident. The three-pronged fork, the emblem of Neptune.

Triton. A sea-god, the son of Neptune.

OCEAN—*Adjectives.*

Cotidal. Simultaneity in tides.

Hydrographic. Relating to maritime maps or charts.

Marine. Pertaining to the ocean.

Maritime. Pertaining to the sea; marine.

Oceanic. Like to or pertaining to the ocean.

Pelagian. }
Pelagic. } Pertaining to the deep sea.

Sea-going. Pertaining to a vessel going out on the ocean or deep sea.

OCEAN—*Adverbs, etc.*

Afloat. In a floating state.

At sea. Upon the ocean.

On sea. Upon the sea.

LAND—ADJECTIVES—*Continued from Column 2.*

Landed. Having or owning land.

Littoral. Pertaining to the shore.

Midland. Pertaining to the interior country.

Predial. Consisting of land.

Riparian. Pertaining to the river-bank.

Terrene, etc. Pertaining to the earth. See UNIVERSE.

Territorial. Pertaining to a territory.

LAND—*Adverbs, etc.*

Ashore. }
On land. } Upon the shore.
On shore. }

Continent. One of the grand divisions of land on the globe.

Crag. A steep, rugged rock.

Delta. An alluvial deposit at the mouth of a river.

Derelict. Land gained by the withdrawing of the sea.

Dry land. The land not covered by water.

Earth. The solid portion of the globe.

Glebe. A tract of church land.

Ground. The firm, solid portion of the earth.

Highland, etc. Elevated or mountainous land. See HEIGHT.

Innings. Land recovered from the sea.

Iron-bound shore. The rugged, broken land along the sea.

Isthmus. A narrow neck of land joining two larger bodies of land.

Land. That portion of the earth not covered by water.

Landsman. One who lives on the land.

Lea. Meadow land.

Loam. An earthy mixture of clay and sand.

Loom of the land. The rise of the land above the surrounding country.

Mainland. The continent.

Marl. A peculiar earth used for fertilizing.

Mold. Earthy material.

Neck of land. A long narrow tract of land projecting from a main body.

Oasis. A fertile spot of land in a desert.

Peninsula. A portion of land projecting into the water.

Promontory. A high cape. See CONVEXITY.

Real estate. Property in houses and lands. See PROPERTY.

Rock. A large mass of stony material.

Scar. A bare detached rock.

Sea-bank. The seashore.

Sea-beach. A beach lying along the sea.

Sea-board. The land bordering on the sea.

Sea-coast. The shore of the land adjacent to the sea.

Sea-side. The land bordering on the sea.

Shore. The land bordering along the ocean.

Soil. The upper stratum of the earth.

Strand. The beach of the sea.

Sub-soil. The bed of earth which lies immediately beneath the surface soil.

Terra firma [L.]. The solid land.

Tongue of land. A long, narrow neck of land projecting into the water.

LAND—*Verbs.*

Come ashore. }
Go ashore. } To come to land.

Come to land. To go on land.

Land. To go on firm ground from the sea.

Set foot on dry land. }
Set foot on the soil. } To land.

LAND—*Adjectives.*

Alluvial. Pertaining to earthy matter deposited by rivers.

Continental. Pertaining to the continent.

Earthy. Like earth; pertaining to the earth.

(Continued on Column 1.)

---

o″-ce-an′-ic. Pertaining to the ocean. OCEAN-LAND.

O-ce′-a-nus. God of the waters. JOVE-FIEND.

o′-cher. A brownish-yellow pigment. BLUENESS-ORANGE, GRAY-BROWN; **yellow ocher,** YELLOWNESS-PURPLE.

o′-cher-ous. Like ocher. BLUENESS-ORANGE.

och-loc′-ra-cy. Mob rule. RULE-LICENSE.

o′-clock′. By the clock. CHRONOLOGY-ANACHRONISM; **know what's o'clock,** SKILL-UNSKILFULNESS.

oc′-ta-gon. A figure. ANGULARITY.

oc′-ta-he″-dron. An eight-sided solid. ANGULARITY, MINERALOGY.

oc′-tant. An eighth part of a circle. ANGULARITY, WHOLE-PART.

Oc′-ta-teuch. The first eight books of the Bible. REVELATION-PSEUDOREVELATION.

oc′-tave. An interval of seven degrees. MELODY-DISSONANCE.

oc-ta′-vo. Folded into eight leaves. MISSIVE-PUBLICATION.

Oc-to′-ber. The tenth month of the year; earlier, the eighth. PERIODICITY-IRREGULARITY.

oc″-to-dec′-i-mo. Folded into eighteen leaves. MISSIVE-PUBLICATION.

oc′-to-fid. Cleft into eight divisions. FIVE-QUINQUESECTION.

oc′-to-ge-na″-ri-an. A person eighty years old. INFANT-VETERAN.

oc″-to-roon′. An eighth-blooded person. MIXTURE-HOMOGENEITY.

oc″-troi. A tax. PRICE-DISCOUNT.

oc′-tu-ple. Having eight parts. FIVE-QUINQUESECTION.

oc′-u-lar. Pertaining to the eyes. SIGHT-BLINDNESS; **ocular demonstration,** SIGHT-BLINDNESS, VISIBILITY-INVISIBILITY; **ocular inspection,** SIGHT-BLINDNESS.

oculis subjecta fidelibus [L.] (oc′-yu-lis sub-jec′-ta fid-el′-i-bus). Under one's faithful eyes. VISIBILITY-INVISIBILITY.

oc′-u-list. An eye-doctor. REMEDY-BANE.

o′-da-lisk. A female slave. CHIEF-UNDERLING.

odd. Not even; remaining; peculiar; ridiculous; single. CONVENTIONALITY-UNCONVENTIONALITY, IN-

CREMENT-REMNANT, NUMBERING, SANENESS-LUN-
ACY, SOCIETY-LUDICROUSNESS, TASTE-VULGARITY;
odd fish, SOCIETY-LAUGHINGSTOCK.

odd'-i-ty. Singularity. CONVENTIONALITY-UNCON-
VENTIONALITY, SANENESS-LUNACY, SOCIETY-LAUGH-
INGSTOCK, SOCIETY-LUDICROUSNESS.

odd'-ments. Things incidental to. WHOLE-PART.

odds. Advantage; chances; variance. EQUALITY-
INEQUALITY, RATIONALE-LUCK, VARIANCE-ACCORD;
at odds, HARMONY-DISCORD, VARIANCE-ACCORD;
long odds, DIFFICULTY-FACILITY; **odds against one,**
SECURITY-INSECURITY; **odds and ends,** INCREMENT-
DECREMENT, MIXTURE-HOMOGENEITY, USEFULNESS-
USELESSNESS, WHOLE-PART; **the odds are,** LIKELI-
HOOD-UNLIKELIHOOD; **what's the odds,** CONSE-
QUENCE-INSIGNIFICANCE.

ode. A brief poem. POETRY-PROSE.

o-de'-on. A Grecian trial theater. DWELLER-HABITA-
TION.

odeur, en mauvaise [F.] (o-dur', an· mo-vêz'). In bad
odor. APPROVAL-DISAPPROVAL.

od force. A hypothetical force. DEVOTION-MAGIC.

odi profanum vulgus [L.] (o'-dai pro-fê'-num vul'-gus).
I hate the vulgar crowd. SELFRESPECT-HUMBLE-
NESS.

O'-din. The chief of the gods. JOVE-FIEND.

o'-di-ous. Hateful. BEAUTY-UGLINESS, LOVE-HATE,
PLEASURABLENESS-PAINFULNESS.

o'-di-um. Disgrace. APPROVAL-DISAPPROVAL, LOVE-
HATE, REPUTATION-DISCREDIT.

odium theologicum [L.] (o'-di-um thî-o-loj'-i-cum).
The enmity of theologians. CHURCH, DECISION-
MISJUDGMENT, GODLINESS-UNGODLINESS.

o-dom'-e-ter. An implement for measuring distance
traveled. MENSURATION.

o-don'-toid. Tooth-like. CONVEXITY-CONCAVITY,
SHARPNESS-BLUNTNESS.

o'-dor. Smell. ODOR-INODOROUSNESS; **in bad odor,**
APPROVAL-DISAPPROVAL; **odor of sanctity,** GODLI-
NESS-UNGODLINESS.

ODOR—INODOROUSNESS.

Catnip. Mint having a strong odor pleasing to cats.
Effluvium. A disagreeable odor, an invisible emanation from putre-
fying matter.
Emanation. A flowing forth from a source, as an evil odor.
Essence. Perfume; scent; odor.
Exhalation. The breathing out of a vapor or effluvium.
Fume. An odorous vapor.
Nidor. The odor of cooked or cooking food.
Odor. That quality of a substance which renders it perceptible to
the sense of smell.
Odorament. A strong scent.
Redolence. A pleasing odor or scent.
Scent. That property of a body which affects the sense of smell.
Smell. That which is perceived by the olfactory organs.

ODOR—*Nouns of Agent.*

Act of smelling, etc. The act of perceiving an odor. See *Verbs.*
Scent. The odor left by an animal by which it can be tracked.
Sense of smell. The power to perceive an odor.
Trail. The scent left by an animal by which it may be pursued.

ODOR—*Verbs.*

Exhale. To breathe out.
Give out a smell, etc. To emanate an odor. See *Nouns.*
Have an odor, etc. To have the power to become perceptible to the
sense of smell. See *Nouns.*
Inhale. To draw in an odor, scent, or the like.
Nose. }
Scent. } To perceive by the sense of smell.
Smell. }
Smell of. } To give forth a certain odor.
Smell strong of. }
Sniff. To attempt to smell by short rapid inhalations.

Absence of smell. Lack of the power to become perceptible to the
sense of smell.
Inodorousness. Want of odor or smell.
Want of smell. Absence of smell.

INODOROUSNESS—*Verbs.*

Be inodorous, etc. Not to smell. See *Adjectives.*
Deodorize. To make inodorous.
Not smell. To be inodorous.

INODOROUSNESS—*Adjectives.*

Deodorized. } Made inodorous.
Deodorizing. }
Inodorate. } Without smell or odor.
Inodorous. }
Scentless. Without scent.
Wanting smell. } Not to be perceived by the sense of smell. See
Without smell. } ODOR.

ODOR—*Verbs—Continued*

Snuff. To inhale the air through the nose as dogs and other animals;
sniff.
Snuff up. To draw up into the nose.

ODOR—*Adjectives.*

Graveolent. Having a strong scent or odor.
Nidorous. Resembling the odor of roast meat or decaying animal
matter.
Odoriferous. Diffusing an odor.
Odorous. Having an odor.
Olfactory. Pertaining to the sense of smell.
Pungent. Sharp or stinging to the sense.
Quick-scented. Acute of smell.
Redolent. Odorous, full of a pleasing smell.
Smelling. Odorous.
Strong-scented. Having a very perceptible odor.

o'-dor-a-ment. A perfume. ODOR-INODOROUSNESS.

o''-dor-if'-er-ous. Fragrant. ODOR-INODOROUSNESS.

o'-dor-ous. Fragrant. ODOR-INODOROUSNESS.

o-dyl'-lic force. A hypothetical force. DEVOTION-
MAGIC.

od-zoo'-kens. An exclamation of surprise. ASTONISH-
MENT-EXPECTANCE.

œc''-u-men'-i-cal. Universal. UNIVERSALITY-PAR-
TICULARITY.

œ-dem'-a-tous. Dropsical. ENLARGEMENT-DIMINU-
TION, HARDNESS-SOFTNESS.

Œd'-i-pus. The solver of the Sphinx's riddle. IN-
TERPRETER, INVESTIGATION-ANSWER.

Œdipus, Davus sum, non [L.] (ed'-i-pus, dê'-vus sum,
non). I am Davus, not Œdipus. CRAFT-ARTLESS-
NESS, WITTINESS-DULNESS.

œil de maitre [F.] (uy de mêtr). The eye of a master.
CAREFULNESS-CARELESSNESS.

œ''-ti-ol'-o-gy. The science of the causes of disease.
HEALTH-SICKNESS.

of. Belonging to; out from. **Of all things,** SUPREM-
ACY-SUBORDINACY; **of a piece,** HARMONY-DISCORD,
LIKENESS-UNLIKENESS, UNIFORMITY-DIVERSITY; **of
course,** CONVENTIONALITY-UNCONVENTIONALITY,
NATURE-ART, RATIONALE-LUCK, VOLITION-OBLIGA-
TION; **of late,** NOVELTY-ANTIQUITY; **of no effect,**
FERTILITY-STERILITY; **of old,** NOVELTY-ANTIQUITY;
of one mind, HARMONY-DISCORD; **of similar mean-
ing,** SYNONYM-ANTONYM; **of the same meaning,**
SYNONYM-ANTONYM; **of yore,** FUTURE-PAST.

off. Away. REMOTENESS-NEARNESS; **be off,** QUEST-
EVASION; **keep off,** QUEST-EVASION, REMOTENESS-

NEARNESS; **make off with,** THEFT; **move off,** AP-PROACH-WITHDRAWAL; **off and on,** DETERMINATION-VACILLATION, MUTABILITY-STABILITY, PERIODICITY-IRREGULARITY; **off one's balance,** DETERMINATION-VACILLATION; **off one's guard,** EXPECTATION-SUR-PRISE; **off one's hands,** GAIN-LOSS; **off one's legs,** PUSH-PULL, SPRING-DIVE; **off one's mind,** REFLEC-TION-VACANCY; **off side,** RIGHT-LEFT; **off with you,** ADMISSION-EXPULSION; **sheer off,** APPROACH-WITH-DRAWAL; **stand off,** APPROACH-WITHDRAWAL; **start off,** ARRIVAL-DEPARTURE; **take off one's hands,** GIVING-RECEIVING; **throw off one's center,** REPUTA-TION-DISCREDIT; **throw off the scent,** CERTAINTY-DOUBT, QUEST-EVASION.

of'-fal. Refuse. CLEANNESS-FILTHINESS.

off'-cut". A surplus margin cut from paper. UNION-DISUNION, WRITING-PRINTING.

of-fend'. To displease; to sin. PLEASURABLENESS-PAINFULNESS, VIRTUE-VICE; **offend against the law,** LAW-LAWLESSNESS.

of-fend'-ed. Displeased. FAVORITE-ANGER.

of-fend'-ing Ad'am. VIRTUE-VICE.

of-fense'. An offending; a sin; resentment. ATTACK-DEFENSE, FAVORITE-ANGER, INNOCENCE-GUILT.

of-fen'-sive. Disagreeable; injurious; serving for attack. ATTACK-DEFENSE, CLEANNESS-FILTHINESS, DESIRE-DISTASTE, PALATABLENESS-UNPALATABLE-NESS, PERFUME-STENCH; **offensive and defensive alliance,** ASSOCIATION; **offensive to ears polite,** PURITY-CRUDENESS.

of'-fer. To tender a proposal. BUYING-SALE, GIVING-RECEIVING, PROFFER-REFUSAL; **offer a choice,** CHOICE-NEUTRALITY; **offer for sale,** BUYING-SALE; **offer oneself,** PROFFER-REFUSAL; **offer sacrifice,** DE-VOTION-IDOLATRY; **offer the alternative,** CHOICE-NEUTRALITY; **offer up prayers,** DEVOTION-IDOLA-TRY.

of'-fer-ing. A donation; a sacrifice. GIVING-RE-CEIVING, PETITION-EXPOSTULATION, PROFFER-RE-FUSAL; **burnt offering,** DEVOTION-IDOLATRY; **sin offering,** ATONEMENT.

of'-fer-to"-ry. A part of the mass; a contribution. CEREMONIAL, DEVOTION-IDOLATRY, GIVING-RECEIV-ING.

off'-hand". Without preparation. CAREFULNESS-CARELESSNESS, EARLINESS-LATENESS, HEED-DIS-REGARD, PREDETERMINATION-IMPULSE.

of'-fice. A function; a business; a room for business; a devotional service. AGENCY, CONTENTS-RECEIVER, DEVOTION-IDOLATRY, MARKET, OCCUPATION; **do an ill office,** CHARITABLENESS-MALEVOLENCE, RULE-LICENSE; **do one's office,** OBSERVANCE-NONOB-SERVANCE; **good offices,** CHARITABLENESS-MALEVO-LENCE; **hold office,** MANAGEMENT; **kind offices,** CHARITABLENESS-MALEVOLENCE, MEDIATION; **man in office,** CHIEF-UNDERLING, MANAGER.

of'-fice-bear"-er. An officer. MANAGER.

of'-fi-cer. A director. BELLIGERENT, CHIEF-UNDER-LING, JUDICATURE, MANAGER.

of'-fi-ces. Outhouses. CONTENTS-RECEIVER.

of-fi'-cial. Pertaining to an office; authoritative; a public officer. CERTAINTY-DOUBT, CHIEF-UNDER-LING, MANAGER, OCCUPATION, RULE-LICENSE.

of-fi'-cial-ism. Official stringency. HARSHNESS-MILD-NESS.

of-fi'-ci ate. To conduct. ACTION-PASSIVENESS, CER-EMONIAL, CONDUCT, OCCUPATION.

officina gentium [L.] (of-fi-sai'-na jen'-shi-um). Work-shop of nations. WORKSHOP.

officio, ex [L.] (of-fish'-i-o, ex). By virtue of office. DUENESS-UNDUENESS, MANAGER, RULE-LICENSE, TRUTH-ERROR.

of-fi'-cious. Intermeddling. ACTIVITY-INDOLENCE.

of-fi'-cious-ness. Meddling. ACTIVITY-INDOLENCE.

off'-ing. Sea far from the eye. OCEAN-LAND, RE-MOTENESS-NEARNESS.

off'-scour"-ings. Refuse. CLEANNESS-FILTHINESS, USEFULNESS-USELESSNESS.

off'-scum. Scum. CLEANNESS-FILTHINESS.

off'-set". A sum balancing another; a small branch. COMPENSATION, PARENTAGE-PROGENY.

off'-shoot". Something branching off. INCREMENT-REMNANT, PARENTAGE-PROGENY, RATIONALE-LUCK, WHOLE-PART.

off'-spring". Issue. CAUSE-EFFECT, PARENTAGE-PROGENY.

of-fus'-cate. To darken. DIAPHANEITY-OPAQUENESS, FUTURE-PAST, LIGHT-DARKNESS.

of"-fus-ca'-tion. Darkness. LIGHT-DARKNESS.

oft. Frequently. FREQUENCY-RARITY, RECURRENCE.

oft'-en. Many a time. FREQUENCY-RARITY, RECUR-RENCE; **most often,** HABIT-DESUETUDE.

oft'-ness. Frequency. FREQUENCY-RARITY.

oft'-times. Often. FREQUENCY-RARITY.

og'-ham. Ancient Irish writing. WRITING-PRINTING.

o'-gle. To look at amorously. BLANDISHMENT, DESIRE-DISTASTE, POLITENESS-IMPOLITENESS, SIGHT-BLIND-NESS.

o'-gre. A monster. ANGEL-SATAN, HUMANITARIAN-ISM-MISANTHROPY, SANGUINENESS-TIMIDITY.

o'-gress. A female ogre. JOVE-FIEND.

oh. An exclamation. APPROVAL-DISAPPROVAL.

Ohm. A noted electrician. **Ohm's law,** ELECTRICITY.

oil. To lubricate. FRICTION-LUBRICATION, PULPINESS-OIL, PULPINESS-OILINESS; **pour oil on,** ALLEVIATION-AGGRAVATION; **pour oil on the troubled waters,** TUR-BULENCE-CALMNESS.

oil'-col-or. Paint. PAINTING.

oil'-ing. Greasing. FRICTION-LUBRICATION.

oil'-paint. Oil-color. PAINTING.

oil"-paint'-ing. A painting in oils. PAINTING.

oils. Paints. PAINTING.

oil'-y. Greasy; unctuous. ADULATION-DISPARAGE-MENT, POLITENESS-IMPOLITENESS, PRESUMPTION-OB-SEQUIOUSNESS, PULPINESS-OILINESS, SMOOTHNESS-ROUGHNESS, TURBULENCE-CALMNESS.

oi"-no-ma'-ni-a. Desire for drink. TEETOTALISM-IN-TEMPERANCE.

oint'-ment. An unguent. PULPINESS-OIL, REMEDY-BANE.

old. Aged. NOVELTY-ANTIQUITY; **die of old age,** COM-PLETION-NONCOMPLETION; **of old,** FUTURE-PAST; **old Adam,** VIRTUE-VICE; **old age,** INFANCY-AGE; **old bachelor,** MATRIMONY-CELIBACY; **old clothes,** DRESS-UNDRESS; **old fogy,** SAGE-FOOL, SOCIETY-LAUGH-INGSTOCK; **old homestead,** CITY-COUNTRY; **old joke,** WITTINESS-DULNESS; **old maid,** ENTERTAINMENT-WEARINESS, MATRIMONY-CELIBACY; **old man,** IN-FANT-VETERAN, MATRIMONY-CELIBACY; **old man of the sea,** OBSTRUCTION-HELP; **old oaken bucket,** CITY-COUNTRY; **old school,** BIGOTRY-APOSTASY, HABIT-DESUETUDE, NOVELTY-ANTIQUITY; **old song,** CONSE-QUENCE-INSIGNIFICANCE, COSTLINESS-CHEAPESS, RECURRENCE; **old stager,** ADEPT-BUNGLER, INFANT-VETERAN; **old story,** LOVE-HATE, RECURRENCE, TIDINGS-MYSTERY; **old times,** FUTURE-PAST; **old woman,** MATRIMONY-CELIBACY, SAGE-FOOL; **one's old way,** HABIT-DESUETUDE; **pay off old scores,** AT-TACK-DEFENSE.

Oldbuck. An antiquarian. FUTURE-PAST.

old'-er. More old. INFANCY-AGE.

old'-est. Most advanced in years. INFANCY-AGE.

old'-est in-hab'-it-ant. The earliest settler. **Not in the memory of the oldest inhabitant,** FREQUENCY-RARITY.

old"-fash'-ioned. Antiquated. NOVELTY-ANTIQUITY.

old'-ness. Antiquity. NOVELTY-ANTIQUITY.

o"-le-a-gine'. An oily substance. PULPINESS-OIL

o''-le-o-mar'-ga-rine. Artificial butter. PULPINESS-OILINESS.

oleum addere camino [L.] (o'-li-um ad'-der-î cam-ai'-no). To add oil to the fire. INCREASE-DECREASE, TURBULENCE-CALMNESS.

ol-fac'-to-ry. Pertaining to smelling. ODOR-INODOROUSNESS.

ol'-id. Stinking. PERFUME-STENCH.

ol'-id-ous. Rancid. PERFUME-STENCH.

ol'-i-garch. A ruler. CHIEF-UNDERLING.

ol''-i-gar'-chic. Pertaining to an oligarchy. RULE-LICENSE.

ol'-i-gar''-chy. The rule of a few. RULE-LICENSE.

o'-li-o. A medley. MIXTURE-HOMOGENEITY.

ol'-ive-branch''. An emblem of peace; a youngster. FIGHTING-CONCILIATION, INFANT-VETERAN, PARENTAGE-PROGENY.

ol'-ive-green''. Dark green. REDNESS-GREENNESS.

ol'-la po-dri'-da. A mixture. MIXTURE-HOMOGENEITY.

O-lym'-pus. The home of the gods. HEAVEN-HELL.

om'-ber. A game of cards. ENTERTAINMENT-WEARINESS.

ombres chinoises [F.] (on·br shi-nwaz'). Chinese shadows. APPEARANCE-DISAPPEARANCE.

o-me'-ga. The last. BEGINNING-END.

om'-e-let. A dish of eggs. NUTRIMENT-EXCRETION.

o'-men. A portent. PORTENT.

om'-i-nate. To presage. PROPHECY.

om'-i-nous. Portentous. PROPHECY, SECURITY-INSECURITY.

om'-i-nous-ness. Inauspiciousness. PROPHECY.

o-mis'-sion. A leaving out; failure to do. CAREFULNESS-CARELESSNESS, CONSTITUENT-ALIEN, ENTIRETY-DEFICIENCY, INNOCENCE-GUILT, OBSERVANCE-NONOBSERVANCE, SUCCESS-FAILURE.

o-mit'. Leave out. CAREFULNESS-CARELESSNESS, INCLUSION-OMISSION, OBSERVANCE-NONOBSERVANCE.

o-mit'-ted. Left out. ENTITY-NONENTITY, PRESENCE-ABSENCE.

omne, nec scire fas est [L.] (om'-ne, nec sai'-rî fas est). To know all things is not permitted. KNOWLEDGE-IGNORANCE.

omne tulit punctum [L.] (om'-ne tiu'-lit punc'-tum). He has gained every point. SUCCESS-FAILURE.

om'-ni-bus. A public conveyance. CONVEYANCE-VESSEL.

om''-ni-fa''-ri-ous. Of all kinds. UNIFORMITY-MULTIFORMITY.

om-nif'-ic. All-creating. FERTILITY-STERILITY.

om'-ni-form. Having all forms. UNIFORMITY-MULTIFORMITY.

om-ni-form'-i-ty. Quality of having every shape. UNIFORMITY-MULTIFORMITY.

om-nig'-en-ous. Consisting of all kinds. UNIFORMITY-MULTIFORMITY.

om-nip'-o-tence. Unlimited power; God. DIVINITY, MIGHT-IMPOTENCE.

om-nip'-o-tent. All powerful. MIGHT-IMPOTENCE.

om''-ni-pres'-ence. Universal presence. DIVINITY, PRESENCE-ABSENCE.

om''-ni-pres'-ent. Universally present. PRESENCE-ABSENCE.

om-nis'-cience. Infinite knowledge. DIVINITY, KNOWLEDGE-IGNORANCE.

om-nis'-cient. All-knowing. KNOWLEDGE-IGNORANCE.

om''-ni-um-gath''-er-um. A medley. GATHERING-SCATTERING, MIXTURE-HOMOGENEITY, REGULARITY-IRREGULARITY.

om-niv'-o-rous. All-devouring. DESIRE-DISTASTE, FASTING-GLUTTONY, NUTRIMENT-EXCRETION.

om'-phal-os. The navel. MIDDLE.

on. Forward. ADVANCE-RETROGRESSION; on a bed of roses, SENSUALITY-SUFFERING; on account of, RATIONALE-LUCK; on a large scale, MAGNITUDE-SMALL-

NESS; on all accounts, ENTIRETY-DEFICIENCY; on all fours, HARMONY-DISCORD, SAMENESS-CONTRAST; on an average, MEDIUM; on a par, EQUALITY-INEQUALITY; on foot, ACTIVITY-INDOLENCE, AGENCY, DURATION-NEVERNESS, OCCURRENCE-DESTINY, PREPARATION-NONPREPARATION, TRAVELING-NAVIGATION; on no occasion, DURATION-NEVERNESS; on no account, MAGNITUDE-SMALLNESS; on one's head, REVERSAL; on that account, RATIONALE-LUCK; on the brink of, MAGNITUDE-SMALLNESS; on the cards, OCCURRENCE-DESTINY; on the increase, INCREASE-DECREASE; on the move, MOVEMENT-REST; on the nail, TIME; on the other hand, COMPENSATION; on the part of, CONNECTION-INDEPENDENCE; on the point of, LASTINGNESS-TRANSIENTNESS; on the present occasion, TIME; on the whole, WHOLE-PART.

once. In the past; one time. FREQUENCY-RARITY, FUTURE-PAST; at once, EARLINESS-LATENESS, ETERNITY-INSTANTANEITY; once for all, BEGINNING-END, CHOICE-NEUTRALITY, DETERMINATION-VACILLATION, ENLIGHTENMENT-SECRECY, FREQUENCY-RARITY; once in a blue moon, FREQUENCY-RARITY; once in a way, FREQUENCY-RARITY; once more, DOUBLING-HALVING, RECURRENCE; once upon a time, DURATION-NEVERNESS, FUTURE-PAST, TIME.

on'-dine. A water-nymph. JOVE-FIEND.

on dit [F.] (on· di). One says. CONVERSATION-MONOLOGUE, TIDINGS-MYSTERY.

one. Unit; same; single. HUMANITY, MATRIMONY-CELIBACY, SAMENESS-CONTRAST, SOLITUDE-COMPANY, WHOLE-PART; all one to, SENSITIVENESS-APATHY; as one man, ANTAGONISM-CONCURRENCE, ASSENT-DISSENT; at one with, COOPERATION-OPPOSITION, EQUALITY-INEQUALITY, VARIANCE-ACCORD; both the one and the other, DUALITY; from one to another, ALIENATION; make one of, PRESENCE-ABSENCE; neither one nor the other, CHOICE-NEUTRALITY; one and a half, SOLITUDE-COMPANY; one bone and one flesh, MATRIMONY-CELIBACY; one by one, SOLITUDE-COMPANY, UNION-DISUNION, UNIVERSALITY-PARTICULARITY; one fell swoop, ETERNITY-INSTANTANEITY, TURBULENCE-CALMNESS; one fine morning, DURATION-NEVERNESS, TIME; one idea, DECISION-MISJUDGMENT; one in a way, CONVENTIONALITY-UNCONVENTIONALITY; one in ten thousand, GOOD MAN-BAD MAN, GOODNESS-BADNESS; one jump, ETERNITY-INSTANTANEITY; one leg in the grave, STRENGTH-WEAKNESS; one of these days, FUTURE-PAST, TIME; one or two, PLURALITY-FRACTION; one thing with another, RATIOCINATION-INSTINCT; one way or another, IMITATION-ORIGINALITY; on one side, LATERALITY-CONTRAPOSITION, PARALLELISM-INCLINATION; with one voice, ASSENT-DISSENT.

one''-eyed'. Having one eye. SIGHT-DIMSIGHTEDNESS.

o-nei'-ro-crit''-ic. An interpreter of dreams. INTERPRETER.

o-nei'-ro-man''-cy. Divination by dreams. PROPHECY.

one'-ness. Unity. SOLITUDE-COMPANY.

on'-er-ous. Burdensome. DIFFICULTY-FACILITY, GOODNESS-BADNESS, OBSTRUCTION-HELP, PLEASURABLENESS-PAINFULNESS.

one''-self'. One's self. SAMENESS-CONTRAST; be oneself again, RENOVATION-RELAPSE; have all to oneself, HOLDING-EXEMPTION; kill oneself, LIFE-KILLING; take merit to oneself, BRAGGING; take upon oneself, DETERMINATION-VACILLATION, ENTERPRISE, VOLITION-OBLIGATION; talk to oneself, CONVERSATION-MONOLOGUE; true to oneself, PERSISTENCE-WHIM.

one'-si''-ded. Partial. DECISION-MISJUDGMENT, RIGHT-WRONG, UPRIGHTNESS-DISHONESTY.

on'-go''-ing. Progress. ADVANCE-RETROGRESSION.

on'-ion. A culinary plant. CONDIMENT.
on'-look''-er. A spectator ONLOOKER.

ONLOOKER.

Beholder.   One who looks upon with attention and interest.
Bystander.   A chance onlooker.
Eye-witness.   One who has seen the occurrence with his own eyes.
Looker-on.   One who looks on without interest or taking part.
Observer.   One who looks on with careful attention.
Onlooker.   One who stands by and looks on passively
Passer-by.   One who looks on while passing.
Sentinel, etc.   A soldier on guard to look out for danger. See WARN-ING.
Sight-seer.   One who spends his time looking at objects of interest
Spectator.   One present and looking on at some happening.
Spy.   One who looks on secretly.
Witness.   One who sees by being personally present.

ONLOOKER—Verbs.

Behold, etc.   To look on with careful attention. See SIGHT.
Look on, etc.   To regard without personal interest. See PRESENCE.
Witness.   To see by being personally present.

on'-ly. Solitary; merely. FAULTLESSNESS-FAULTI-NESS, GREATNESS-SMALLNESS, MIXTURE-HOMOGE-NEITY, SOLITUDE-COMPANY; only think, ASTONISH-MENT-EXPECTANCE; only yesterday, NOVELTY-AN-TIQUITY.

on'-o-man''-cy. Divination by names. PROPHECY.

on''-o-mat''-o-pœ'-ia. Imitation of natural sounds. LANGUAGE, NAME-MISNOMER.

on'-set''. An attack. ATTACK-DEFENSE, BEGINNING-END.

on'-slaught''. An assault. ATTACK-DEFENSE.

on-tog'-e-ny. Germ-history. BIOLOGY.

on-tol'-o-gy. The science of real being. ENTITY-NON-ENTITY.

onus [L.] (o'-nus). A burden; duty. DUTY-DERELIC-TION, OBSTRUCTION-HELP.

onus probandi [L.] (o'-nus pro-ban'-dai). The burden of proof. CERTAINTY-DOUBT, FAITH-MISGIVING.

on'-ward. Forward. ADVANCE-RETROGRESSION.

on'-y-cho-man''-cy. Divination by nails. PROPHECY.

o'-nyx. A kind of quartz. EMBELLISHMENT-DISFIG-UREMENT.

o''-o-gen'-e-sis. Development of the ovum. BIOLOGY.

ooze. To leak out. ADMISSION-EXPULSION, EN-TRANCE-EXIT, RIVER-WIND, VISCIDITY-FOAM; ooze out, EXPOSURE-HIDINGPLACE.

oo'-zing. Dropping. ENTRANCE-EXIT.

o-pac'-i-ty. Obscurity. DIAPHANEITY-OPAQUENESS.

o-pa'-cous. Opaque. DIAPHANEITY-OPAQUENESS.

o'-pal. A variegated mineral. EMBELLISHMENT-DIS-FIGUREMENT, VARIEGATION.

o'-pal-es'-cence. Semi-transparency. DIAPHANEITY-OPALESCENCE.

o''-pal-es'-cent. Iridescent. DIAPHANEITY-OPAQUE-NESS, VARIEGATION.

o' pal-ine. Opalescent. DIAPHANEITY-OPALESCENCE, VARIEGATION.

o-paque'. Not transparent. DIAPHANEITY-OPAQUE-NESS.

o-paque'-ness. Imperviousness to light. DIAPHANE-ITY-OPAQUENESS.

o'-pen. Not closed or hidden; frank. APERTURE-CLOSURE, BEGINNING-END, CRAFT-ARTLESSNESS, EN-LARGEMENT-DIMINUTION, EXPOSURE-HIDINGPLACE, MANIFESTATION-LATENCY, PUBLICITY, TRUTHFUL-NESS-FALSEHOOD; in open court, MANIFESTATION-LATENCY, PUBLICITY; lay oneself open to, CONTIN-GENCY, SECURITY-INSECURITY; lay open, DRESS-UN-DRESS; leave the matter open, SUBSTANCE-NULLITY; open a case, RATIOCINATION-INSTINCT; open a dis-cussion, RATIOCINATION-INSTINCT; open air, OUT-SIDE-INSIDE, WATER-AIR; open and above board, UP-RIGHTNESS-DISHONESTY; open arms, ●AMITY-HOS-TILITY, FIGHTING-CONCILIATION, POLITENESS-IMPO-LITENESS, READINESS-RELUCTANCE, SOCIABILITY-PRIVACY; open country, GULF-PLAIN; open enemy, FRIEND-FOE; open eyes, ASTONISHMENT-EXPEC-TANCE, DISCOVERY, EDUCATION-MISTEACHING, EX-PECTATION - SURPRISE, EXPOSURE - HIDINGPLACE, HEED-DISREGARD, MANIFESTATION-LATENCY, PRE-DETERMINATION-IMPULSE, SIGHT-BLINDNESS; open fire, ATTACK-DEFENSE, BEGINNING-END; open house, SOCIABILITY-PRIVACY; open into, CONVERSION-RE-VERSION, RIVER-WIND; open one's mind, EXPOSURE-HIDINGPLACE; open one's purse-strings, OUTLAY-IN-COME; open order, ENLARGEMENT-DIMINUTION; open question, CERTAINTY-DOUBT, INVESTIGATION-AN-SWER; open rupture, VARIANCE-ACCORD; open-sesame, APERTURE-CLOSURE, DEVOTION-CHARM, INSTRUMEN-TALITY, SIGN; open space, EXTENSION-DISTRICT; open the ball, BEGINNING-END, PRECEDENCE-SUCCESSION; open the door to, BEGINNING-END, CAUSE-EFFECT, DIFFICULTY-FACILITY, ENTRANCE-EXIT, LEAVE-PRO-HIBITION, PREPARATION-NONPREPARATION; open the lips, EXPOSURE-HIDINGPLACE; open the lock, DIS-COVERY; open the sluices, ADMISSION-EXPULSION; open the trenches, ATTACK-DEFENSE; open to, CON-TINGENCY, DIFFICULTY-FACILITY, SECURITY-INSE-CURITY; open to discussion, RATIOCINATION-IN-STINCT; open to suspicion, FAITH-MISGIVING; open to the view, VISIBILITY-INVISIBILITY; open up, BEGIN-NING-END, EXPOSURE-HIDINGPLACE; open war, AM-ITY-HOSTILITY, FIGHTING-CONCILIATION; throw open, ADMISSION-EXPULSION; with open doors, PUBLICITY.

o'-pen-er. Porter; key. APERTURE-CLOSURE.

o'-pen-eyed''. Vigilant. EXPECTATION-SURPRISE, HEED-DISREGARD.

o'-pen-ing. A vacant space; a beginning; an oppor-tunity. APERTURE-CLOSURE, BEGINNING-END, EX-TENSION-DISTRICT, INTERSPACE-CONTACT, OPPOR-TUNENESS-UNSUITABLENESS, RATIOCINATION-IN-STINCT.

o'-pen-hand''-ed. Generous. GENEROSITY-FRUGALITY.

o'-pen-heart''-ed. Candid. CRAFT-ARTLESSNESS, GEN-EROSITY-FRUGALITY, TRUTHFULNESS-FALSEHOOD, UPRIGHTNESS-DISHONESTY.

o'-pen-ly. Without concealment. MANIFESTATION-LATENCY.

o'-pen-mouthed''. Loquacious; showing expectation or wonder. ASTONISHMENT-EXPECTANCE, CRY-ULULA-TION, DESIRE-DISTASTE, EXPECTATION-SURPRISE, TALKATIVENESS-TACITURNITY.

o'-pen-ness. Candor. MANIFESTATION-LATENCY.

op'-e-ra. A musical drama. ACTING, MUSIC, POETRY-PROSE; opera-glass, OPTICAL INSTRUMENTS; opera-house, ACTING.

opéra bouffe [F.] (o-pê-ra' buf). A comic opera. ACTING.

operæ pretium est [L.] (op'-er-î prí'-shi-um est). It is worth while. PROPRIETY-IMPROPRIETY.

operandi, modus [L.] (op-er-an'-dai, mo'-dus). A mode of operation. AGENCY, CONDUCT, WAY.

op'-er-ate. To act; to work. ACTION-PASSIVENESS, AGENCY, CAUSE-EFFECT, CREATION-DESTRUCTION; operate upon, MOTIVE-CAPRICE.

op''-e-rat'-ic. Pertaining to operas. ACTING, MUSIC.

op''-er-a'-tion. A mode of action. ACTION-PASSIVE-NESS, AGENCY, CAUSE-EFFECT, CREATION-DESTRUC-TION, REMEDY-BANE; in operation, ACTION-PASSIVE-NESS, AGENCY; put in operation, USE-DISUSE; surgi-cal operation, REMEDY-BANE.

op'-er-a-tive. Exerting power; a worker in a factory. AGENCY, AGENT, LABOR-CAPITAL.

op'-er-a''-tor. A skilled worker. AGENT, REMEDY-BANE, LABOR-CAPITAL.

o-per′-cu-la″-ted. Fitted with a cover. APERTURE-CLOSURE.

o-per′-cu-lum. A cover. COVER-LINING.

op″-e-ret′-ta. A short opera. MUSIC.

op′-er-ose″. Laborious. DIFFICULTY-FACILITY, TOIL-RELAXATION.

op′-er-ose″-ness. Laboriousness. TOIL-RELAXATION.

oph′-i-cleide. A brass wind-instrument. MUSICAL INSTRUMENTS.

oph″-i-ol′-o-gy. The science of serpents. ZOOLOGY-BOTANY.

oph′-i-o-man-cy. Divination by serpents. PROPHECY.

oph-thal′-mi-a. Inflammation of the eye. SIGHT-DIMSIGHTEDNESS.

oph-thal′-mic. Pertaining to the eye. SIGHT-BLINDNESS.

o′-pi-ate. A narcotic. TURBULENCE-CALMNESS.

o-pine′. To think. FAITH-MISGIVING.

o-pin′-i-a-tive. Bigoted. DECISION-MISJUDGMENT.

o-pin′-i-a-tive-ness. Bigotry. BIGOTRY-APOSTASY.

o-pin′-i-a″-tor. A bigot. BIGOTRY-APOSTASY.

opiniâtre [F.] (o-pi-ni-ɑtr′). Headstrong. DECISION-MISJUDGMENT.

o-pin′-i-a-try. The disposition to give opinions and cling to them. BIGOTRY-APOSTASY.

o-pin′-ion. A judgment. DECISION-MISJUDGMENT, FAITH-MISGIVING; **give an opinion,** DECISION-MISJUDGMENT; **have too high an opinion of oneself,** CONCEIT-DIFFIDENCE, OVERVALUATION-UNDERVALUA-TION; **popular opinion,** ASSENT-DISSENT; **system of opinions,** FAITH-MISGIVING; **wedded to an opinion,** BIGOTRY-APOSTASY.

o-pin′-ion-ate. Stiff in opinion. BIGOTRY-APOSTASY, DECISION-MISJUDGMENT.

o-pin′-ion-a″-ted. Headstrong. DECISION-MISJUDGMENT; **self-opinionated,** CONCEIT-DIFFIDENCE.

o-pin′-ion-a-tist. A bigot. BIGOTRY-APOSTASY.

o-pin′-ioned. Bigoted. DECISION-MISJUDGMENT.

o-pin′-ion-ist. One fond of his own opinions. BIGOTRY-APOSTASY, CERTAINTY-DOUBT.

o-pit′-u-la″-tion. Help. OBSTRUCTION-HELP.

o′-pi-um. A sedative drug. FEELING-INSENSIBILITY, TURBULENCE-CALMNESS.

o′-pi-um—eat″-er. A consumer of opium. ACTIVITY-INDOLENCE.

o-pos′-sum. An animal which plays off dead when caught or seen. GULL-DECEIVER.

op′-pi-dan. A townsman. CITY-COUNTRY, DWELLER-HABITATION.

op″-pi-la′-tion. A blocking up. OBSTRUCTION-HELP.

op-po′-nent. Antagonist. ANTAGONIST-ASSISTANT, FRIEND-FOE, OBSTRUCTION-HELP.

op′-por-tune′. Timely. OPPORTUNENESS-UNSUITABLENESS, PROPRIETY-IMPROPRIETY.

op″-por-tune′-ly. Timely. OPPORTUNENESS-UNSUITABLENESS.

op″-por-tune′-ness. Timeliness. OPPORTUNENESS-UNSUITABLENESS.

OPPORTUNENESS—UNSUITABLENESS.

Conjuncture. A combination of events or circumstances.

Crisis. The point of time when it is to be decided whether a course of action must go on or be modified.

Favorable opportunity. } A suitable combination of conditions for the
Fine opportunity. } success of an action, etc.

Given time. A time fixed for the performance of an act, duty, etc.

High time. Full time for the occasion.

Juncture. A point of time critical or important by a concurrence of circumstances.

Mollia tempora [L.] Favorable occasion.

Nick of time. The exact point or critical moment.

Occasion. A convenient or timely chance.

Opening. An opportunity.

Opportuneness, etc. Favorableness of opportunity See *Adjectives.*

Opportunity. A time or place favorable for executing a purpose.

Proper season. } A time suitable in all respects.
Proper time. }

Room. Fit occasion.

Suitable season. } A time favorable to the success of an action.
Suitable time. }

Tempestivity. Seasonableness.

Turn. Occasion or convenience.

Turning-point. The point upon which a question turns and which decides a case.

Well-timed opportunity. A favorable or suitable opportunity.

OPPORTUNENESS—*Figurative Nouns.*

Clear stage. An uninterrupted sphere of activity.

Fair field. A fair or equal chance.

Golden opportunity. An opportunity very likely to bring success.

Fata Morgana [It.]. A mirage by which distant objects appear multiplied.

OPPORTUNENESS—*Verbs.*

Battre le fer l'enclume [F.]. To strike the iron on the anvil.

Give an occasion. } To give a favorable chance to See GIVING.
Give an opportunity. }

Improve the occasion. To make good use of an occasion.

Make hay while the sun shines. To seize the opportunity.

Prendre la balle au bond [F.]. To seize the ball on the bound.

Seize the occasion. } To act at a favorable time.
Seize the opportunity. }

Strike the iron while it is hot. To seize an opportunity while there is time.

Suit the occasion, etc. To make expedient. See PROPRIETY.

Take time by the forelock. To seize an opportunity while there is time, before it turns its bald head to you.

Use an occasion. } See USE.
Use an opportunity. }

Anachronism, etc. An error in chronology. See CHRONOLOGY.

Contretemps [F.]. An unexpected accident.

Evil hour. A time of misfortune.

Improper time. An unfavorable occasion.

Intempestivity. Untimeliness.

Intrusion. Encroachment upon one's time.

Unreasonableness, etc. Out of proper time. See *Adjectives*

Unsuitable time. An unfavorable chance.

UNSUITABLENESS—*Verbal Expressions.*

Allow the occasion to escape; allow the occasion to go by; allow the occasion to lapse; allow the occasion to pass by; allow the occasion to slip by; allow the opportunity to escape; allow the opportunity to go by; allow the opportunity to lapse; allow the opportunity to pass by; allow the opportunity to slip by; be busy; be ill-timed; be occupied, etc. (see, *Adjectives*); **break in upon; come amiss; have other fish to fry; intrude; let slip through the fingers; lock the stable door when the steed is stolen; lose an opportunity; mistime; neglect an opportunity; suffer the occasion to escape; suffer the occasion to go by; suffer the occasion to lapse; suffer the occasion to pass by; suffer the occasion to slip by; suffer the opportunity to escape; suffer the opportunity to go by; suffer the opportunity to lapse; suffer the opportunity to pass by; suffer the opportunity to slip by; throw away an opportunity; waste an opportunity; waste time,** etc. (see *Adjectives*).

UNSUITABLENESS—*Adjectives.*

Ill-timed. Poorly timed.

Inauspicious. Unfortunate.

Inexpedient, etc. Not expedient. See PROPRIETY.

Inopportune. Unfavorable

Intrusive. Coming without invitation.

Mal à propos [F.]. Unsuitable.

Mistimed. Poorly timed or judged.

Out of date. } At an unfavorable time.
Out of season. }

Premature, etc. Done before time, untimely. See EARLINESS.

Timeless. Done at an improper time.

Too late for. } At the wrong time
Too soon for. }

Unfavorable. Not propitious.

Unfortunate. Having ill fortune

Unlucky. Unfortunate.

Unpropitious. Not advantageous; unfavorable.

Unpunctual, etc. Not on time. See EARLINESS.

Unseasonable. Not in proper season.

Unsuited, etc. Unfitted. See HARMONY.

Untimely. Unpropitious; ill-timed.

Untoward. Unfavorable; annoying.

OPPORTUNENESS—UNSUITABLENESS—*Continued.*

OPPORTUNENESS—*Adjectives.*

Auspicious. Favorable; fortunate.
Critical. Momentous; perilous.
Favorable. Advantageous; propitious.
Fortunate. Happy; lucky.
Happy. Fortunate; lucky; opportune.
Lucky. Auspicious; fortunate.
Obiter dicta [L.]. Spoken casually.
Opportune. Timely; fortunate; lucky.
Propitious. Auspicious; favorable.
Providential. Brought about by the providence of God.
Seasonable. Timely; done at the proper time.
Suitable, etc. Fitting; appropriate. See HARMONY.
Timeful. Seasonable; timely.
Timely. Opportune; seasonable.
Well-timed. Done or said opportunely.

OPPORTUNENESS—*Adverbs, etc.*

All in good time. Timely.
À propos [F.]. Opportunely.
At the eleventh hour. At the last moment; just in time
By the by. By the way; incidentally.
By the way. Incidentally.
By way of parenthesis. Incidentally.
En passant [F.]. In passing.
Ex tempore [F.]. Without preparation.
For the nonce. For the present time.
In due course.⎫
In due season.⎬Opportunely.
In due time.⎭
In the fulness of time.⎫
In the nick of time.⎬ At the proper moment.
Just in time. At the last moment.
Now or never. At the most favorable time.
On the spot, etc. At once. See EARLINESS.
On the spur of the moment.⎫
On the spur of the occasion.⎬Hurriedly.
Opportunely, etc. In an opportune or favorable manner. See *Adjectives.*

UNSUITABLENESS—*Adverbs, etc.*

A day after the fair. Too late.
As ill luck would have it. Inopportunely; unfortunately.
In an evil hour. In an unfortunate moment.
Inopportunely, etc. In an unfortunate manner. See *Adjectives.*
The time having gone by. Too late; not seized in time.

UNSUITABLENESS—*Phrases.*

After death the doctor. To pay attention after it is too late.
After meat mustard. Out of season.

OPPORTUNENESS—ADVERBS, ETC.—*Continued.*

Parenthetically. In an episodical or explanatory manner.
Par parenthèse [F.]. By parenthesis.
Pro hac vice [L.]. On this occasion.
Proper course.⎫
Proper season.⎬Timely.
Proper time.⎭
Pro re nata [L.]. Special; for special business.
While speaking of.⎫
While speaking on the subject.⎬ In a moment.

OPPORTUNENESS—*Phrases.*

Bien perdu, bien connu [F.] Blessing flown is a blessing known.
Carpe diem [L.]. Seize the day.
È sempre l'ora [It.]. It is always time.
Ex quovis ligno non fit Mercurius [L.]. A Mercury is not made of any chance piece of wood.
Nosce tempus [L.]. Know thy opportunity.
Nunc aut nunquam [L.]. Now or never.
Occasionem cognosce [L.]. Seize the occasion.
One's hour is come. The time to act.
Recoge tu heno mientras que el sol luziere [Sp.]. "Make hay while the sun shines."
That reminds me.

---

op″-por-tu′-ni-ty. Favorable occasion. OPPORTUNENESS-UNSUITABLENESS; **lose an opportunity,** OPPORTUNENESS-UNSUITABLENESS.

op-pose′. To resist. ANTAGONISM-CONCURRENCE, CO-OPERATION-OPPOSITION, EVIDENCE-COUNTEREVIDENCE, READINESS-RELUCTANCE, REPRISAL-RESISTANCE, SAMENESS-CONTRAST.

op-posed′. Opposite; unfavorable. ANTAGONISM-CONCURRENCE, SAMENESS-CONTRAST.

op-pos′-ing. Opposite; resisting. ANTAGONISM-CONCURRENCE, SAMENESS-CONTRAST.

op′-po-site. Contrary. HARMONY-DISCORD, REVERSAL, SAMENESS-CONTRAST, STRIFE-PEACE; **opposite scale,** COMPENSATION; **opposite side,** LATERALITY-CONTRAPOSITION.

op′-po-site-ness. Contrariety. SAMENESS-CONTRAST.

op″-po-si′-tion. Resistance. ANTAGONISM-CONCURRENCE, COOPERATION-OPPOSITION, INTERSPACE-CONTACT, LATERALITY-CONTRAPOSITION, REPRISAL-RESISTANCE, SAMENESS-CONTRAST, STRIFE-PEACE; **the opposition,** ANTAGONIST-ASSISTANT.

op″-po-si′-tion-ist. An opponent of the party in power. ANTAGONIST-ASSISTANT.

op-press′. To weigh down. CHARITABLENESS-MALEVOLENCE, GOODNESS-BADNESS, HARSHNESS-MILDNESS; **oppressed with melancholy,** LIGHTHEARTEDNESS-DEJECTION.

op-pres′-sion. Languor; tyranny. LIBERTY-SUBJECTION, TYRANNY-ANARCHY, WELFARE-MISFORTUNE.

op-press′-ive. Tyrannical; depressing. HARSHNESS-MILDNESS, HEAT-COLD, LIBERTY-SUBJECTION, PLEASURABLENESS-PAINFULNESS.

op-press′-or. A tyrant. BENEFACTOR-EVILDOER, HARSHNESS-MILDNESS, TYRANNY-ANARCHY.

op-pro′-bri-ous. Contumelious. REPUTATION-DISCREDIT.

op-pro′-bri-um. Contumely. REPUTATION-DISCREDIT.

op-pugn′. To oppose. ANTAGONISM-CONCURRENCE.

op-pug′-nan-cy. Opposition. ANTAGONISM-CONCURRENCE.

op-pug′-na-tion. Opposition. ANTAGONISM-CONCURRENCE, REPRISAL-RESISTANCE.

op′-ta-tive. Discretionary. DESIRE-DISTASTE.

op′-tic. Pertaining to the eye. SIGHT-BLINDNESS; **optic nerve,** ANATOMY.

op′-tic-al. Pertaining to optics. SIGHT-BLINDNESS.

op′-tic-al in′-stru-ments. Instruments to aid vision. OPTICAL INSTRUMENTS.

OPTICAL INSTRUMENTS.

Actinometer. An instrument for measuring the chemical effects of the sun's rays.
Barnacles. Spectacles.
Binocular. A telescope, microscope, etc., adapted to the use of both eyes.
Camera lucida. An instrument by which an apparent image is cast on a paper and the same may be outlined.
Camera obscura. An optical apparatus by which images are cast upon a surface in a darkened box.
Cheval-glass. A swinging mirror in which the full length of the figure can be imaged.
Chromatrope. An instrument by which a kaleidoscopic effect is produced.
Eriometer. An instrument for measuring minute particles by the diffraction of light produced.
Eye-glasses. Spectacles without bows.
Eyepiece. Part of a telescope or microscope.
Field-glass. A small portable telescope; a spy-glass.
Glass. A mirror.
Glasses. Spectacles or eye-glasses.
Goggles. Spectacles with tubes and glasses worn to protect the eyes; spectacles.
Graphoscope. Single magnifying lens.
Kaleidoscope. An optical instrument by which objects viewed through it appear repeated in symmetrical patterns.
Lens. A piece of glass having surfaces of different curvatures used to make rays of light converge or diverge.

Looking-glass. A mirror.

Lorgnette. A pair of eye-glasses carried on a long handle.

Lucimeter. An instrument for measuring the evaporating power of the sun.

Magic lantern. A device for throwing on a screen an enlarged picture of an object. See APPEARANCE.

Magnifier. Any instrument that increases the apparent size of an object.

Megascope. A solar microscope for throwing enlarged images on a screen.

Meniscus. A lens convex on one side and concave on the other.

Microscope. An instrument for increasing the size of a minute object so as to be visible to the eye.

Microscopy. The art or practise of using a microscope.

Mirror. An object having a reflecting surface, made of an amalgam of tin, or silver with mercury, or of polished metal.

Opera-glass. A binocular telescope magnifying a given field without inversion.

Optical instruments. Instruments fitted to aid sight.

Periscopic lens. A microscopic lens having two plano-convex lenses.

Photometer. An instrument for measuring the intensity of light.

Pier-glass. A high and narrow mirror to be put between windows.

Pince-nez [F.]. Eye-glasses held in place by a spring pressing both sides of the nose.

Polariscope. An instrument used for polarizing light and analyzing its properties.

Polemoscope. An opera-glass or field-glass having an oblique mirror for seeing objects not directly before the eye.

Polyscope. A glass making an object appear many times.

Prism. A transparent body with parallel, triangular bases and rectangular faces, used to disperse a ray of light.

Pseudoscope. An instrument which shows objects with their proper relief reversed.

Radiometer. An instrument used for measuring the mechanical energy of radiant heat.

Reflector. Anything having a polished surface and reflecting heat, light, sound, etc.; a telescope.

Spectacles. Two lenses worn before the eyes to protect, assist, or conceal a defect of the eye.

Spectroscope. An instrument for examining the spectra of volatile substances so as to determine their properties.

Speculum. A mirror; a reflector of polished metal used in reflecting telescopes.

Spy-glass. A small terrestrial telescope.

Stereoscope. An instrument used to give to pictures a solid appearance. It is done by superimposing one picture upon the other, each eye seeing a picture.

Teinoscope. An optical instrument which makes objects appear stretched out.

Telescope. An optical instrument used to look at objects at a great distance, especially heavenly bodies.

Thaumatrope. An optical instrument demonstrating the persistence of an impression upon the retina after the luminous body is removed.

OPTICAL INSTRUMENTS—*Noun of Agency.*

Microscopist. One skilled in using the microscope.

op′-tics. The science of light and vision. LIGHT-DARKNESS, SIGHT-BLINDNESS.

op′-ti-ma-cy. The nobility. GENTILITY-COMMONALTY.

op″-ti-ma′-tes. The aristocrats of Rome. GENTILITY-COMMONALTY.

optime [L.] (op′-tim-î) Very well. APPROVAL-DISAPPROVAL.

op′-ti-mism. Sanguineness. LIGHTHEARTEDNESS-DEJECTION, OVERVALUATION - UNDERVALUATION, SANGUINENESS-HOPELESSNESS.

op′-ti-mist. A sanguine person. CERTAINTY-DOUBT, FLATTERER-DEFAMER, OVERVALUATION-UNDERVALUATION, SANGUINENESS-HOPELESSNESS.

op′-tion. Choice. CHOICE-NEUTRALITY, VOLITION-OBLIGATION.

op′-tion-al. Elective. VOLITION-OBLIGATION.

op′-tion-al-ly. At will. CHOICE-ABSENCE OF CHOICE.

op′-u-lence. Wealth. AFFLUENCE-PENURY.

op′-u-lent. Wealthy. AFFLUENCE-PENURY.

opus, materiam superabat [L.] (o′-pus, mê-tî′-ri-am su-per-ê′-bat). The workmanship surpasses the material. CREATION-DESTRUCTION, SKILL-UNSKILFULNESS.

o-pus′-cule. An unimportant work. MISSIVE-PUBLICATION.

or. Either. CHOICE-NEUTRALITY.

or. Gold. BLUENESS-ORANGE, YELLOWNESS-PURPLE.

or, drap d' [F.] (or, dra d'). Cloth of gold. EMBELLISHMENT-DISFIGUREMENT.

ora et labora [L.] (o′-ra et lab-o′-ra). Worship and work. DEVOTION-IDOLATRY, TOIL-RELAXATION.

ora e sempre [It.] (o′-rî ê sem′-prê). Now and always. ETERNITY-INSTANTANEITY.

or′-a-cle. A sage. INTERPRETER, SAGE-FOOL, SOOTHSAYER; **Sir Oracle,** BRAWLER, CERTAINTY-DOUBT, CONCEIT-DIFFIDENCE, INVESTIGATION-ANSWER.

o-rac′-u-lar. Wise in predicting; ambiguous. CERTAINTY-DOUBT, PROPHECY, SAGACITY-INCAPACITY.

o′-ral. Spoken. SPEECH-INARTICULATENESS, VOCALIZATION-MUTENESS; **oral communication,** CONVERSATION-MONOLOGUE, SPEECH-INARTICULATENESS; **oral evidence,** EVIDENCE-COUNTEREVIDENCE.

o′-ral-ly. By word of mouth. SPEECH-INARTICULATENESS.

or′-ange. A roundish fruit; reddish-yellow. BLUENESS-ORANGE, ROUNDNESS.

or′-ange-ry. An orange-grove. DOMESTICATION-AGRICULTURE.

orasse, est bene studuisse, bene [L.] (o-ras′-sî, est bî′-nî stiu-diu-is′-sî, bî-nî). To have prayed well is to have studied well. DEVOTION-IDOLATRY.

o-ra′-tion. A public speech. RHETORIC, SPEECH-INARTICULATENESS; **funeral oration,** LIFE-FUNERAL.

or′-a-tor. A public speaker. SPEECH-INARTICULATENESS.

or″-a-tor′-ic-al. Eloquent. SPEECH-INARTICULATENESS.

or″-a-to′-ri-o. A sacred composition. MUSIC.

or′-a-to-ry. Eloquence; a private chapel. FANE, SPEECH-INARTICULATENESS.

or′-a-tress. A female orator. SPEECH-INARTICULATENESS.

or′-a-trix. A female orator. SPEECH-INARTICULATENESS.

orb. Anything circular. CIRCLE-WINDING, EXTENSION - DISTRICT, LUMINARY - SHADE, OCCUPATION, SIGHT-BLINDNESS; **orb of day,** LUMINARY-SHADE, UNIVERSE; **orb of night,** UNIVERSE.

or-bic′-u-lar. Well-rounded. CIRCLE-WINDING.

or′-bit. The path of a heavenly body. ASTRONOMY, CIRCLE-WINDING, UNIVERSE, WAY.

or′-chard. An assemblage of fruit trees. CITY-COUNTRY, DOMESTICATION-AGRICULTURE.

or′-ches-tra. A band of musicians; a part of a theater. ACTING, MUSIC, MUSICAL INSTRUMENTS, MUSICIAN.

or-dain′. To enact; to appoint. CHURCH, COMMISSION-ABROGATION, DIVINITY, DUENESS-UNDUENESS, LAW-LAWLESSNESS, ORDER.

or-dained′. Appointed; determined. DUENESS-UNDUENESS, MINISTRY-LAITY.

or′-de-al. Severe trial. DEVOTION-MAGIC, PLEASURE-PAIN, TRIAL; **ordeal of battle,** FIGHTING-CONCILIATION.

or′-der. Regular arrangement; rule; written direction to pay money; rank; class; to direct; to command. DIVISION, GENTILITY-COMMONALTY, LAW-LAWLESSNESS, MANAGEMENT, MONEY, ORDER, PRECEPT, PRESIDENT-MEMBER, REGULARITY-IRREGULARITY, REPUTATION-DISCREDIT, SOLITUDE-COMPANY; **at one's order,** INSUBORDINATION-OBEDIENCE; **call to order,** APPROVAL-DISAPPROVAL, ORDER; **in order,** PURPOSE - LUCK, REGULARITY - IRREGULARITY; **in working order,** PREPARATION-NONPREPARATION; **keep in order,** MANAGEMENT; **money order,** MONEY; **occur in regular order,** PERIODICITY-IRREGULARITY; **order of the day,** CONVENTIONALITY-UNCONVENTIONALITY, HABIT-DESUETUDE, OCCURRENCE-DESTINY,

ORDER, STORE, out of order, CONVENTIONALITY-UN-CONVENTIONALITY, FAULTLESSNESS-FAULTINESS, REGULARITY-IRREGULARITY; **pass to the order of the day**, QUEST-ABANDONMENT, DESIGN; **put in order**, ORGANIZATION-DISORGANIZATION, PREPARATION-NONPREPARATION, RENOVATION-RELAPSE; **set in order**, ORGANIZATION-DISORGANIZATION, PREPARATION-NONPREPARATION; **set one's house in order**, PREPARATION-NONPREPARATION; **standing order**, HABIT-DESUETUDE.

ORDER.

Act. A decree; an edict
Appointment. A decree or direction.
Beat of drum. A command sounded on a drum.
Beck. A motion with the head or hand.
Behest. A mandate.
Bidding. Request.
Brevet. A warrant from a government, granting title, privilege, or dignity.
Bugle-call. An order sounded by the bugle.
Bull. A papal decree.
Call. Order
Caveat [L.] Caution; warning.
Charge. Injunction.
Citation. An official notice to appear for a hearing.
Claim. A demand on the ground of right.
Command. An authoritative order requiring obedience
Decree. An order of an absolute sovereign.
Decretal. A letter from the Pope determining some point in ecclesiastical law.
Demand. Asking with authority.
Dictate. A statement delivered with authority.
Dictation. The act of dictating.
Dictum. An authoritative statement.
Direction. Government; supervision.
Dispatch. An order sent with a messenger.
Dispensation. The act of enjoining something to another
Edict. A command by public authority.
Enactment. A law passed by a legislative body. See LAW
Exaction. The act of demanding with authority.
Fiat. An effectual decree.
Firman. An order given to a traveler by an Oriental monarch, assuring protection.
Fixture. An appointment, in reference to English sports.
Hattisheriff. An irrevocable Turkish decree countersigned by the Sultan.
Hest. Precept.
Imposition. Something charged.
Instructions. Orders; commands.
Interpellation. A question raised as to action taken.
Mandamus. A writ issued by a superior court to an inferior court for the heeding of some special duty
Mandate. Order, command.
Message. A written order or request.
Mittimus. A warrant granted by a justice for committing to prison a person charged with crime.
Mot d'ordre [F]. Word of command.
Nisi prius [L]. Unless before: a phrase applied to terms of court.
Nod. A motion with the head.
Order. A command, a mandate.
Order of the day. Program to be carried out.
Ordinance. A rule of action.
Ordination The act of appointing.
Passport A document given by a competent state officer to travelers for freedom from molestation on land and sea.
Placit. A determination; a dictum.
Plebiscite. A vote by universal male suffrage.
Precept. Order; command.
Prescript. Direction; model prescribed.
Prescription. The act of dictating.
Reclamation. Remonstrance.
Request. An expression of one's desire to another person that he should do or give something. See PETITION
Requirement. An exaction.
Requisition. A demand.
Revendication. A claim for the restoration of.
Senatus consultum [L]. The decree of the Senate
Subpœna. To compel to appear as a witness.
Summons. The order of a superior
Tattoo. A beat of drum, or sound of trumpet, at night, giving notice to retreat, or to repair to quarters.

Trumpet-call. An order sounded by trumpet.
Ukase. An order issued by the Czar of Russia.
Ultimatum. A final statement of terms or conditions. See TERMS.
Warrant. A commission giving authority or justifying the doing of anything.
Word. An order or command.
Word of command. An order.
Writ. A sealed instrument given by the proper authority commissioning the person to whom it is given to perform or not to perform some function.

ORDER—*Verbs*.

Appoint. To ordain; to prescribe.
Assume the command. To have authority over See RULE.
Beckon. To make a significant sign.
Be ordered. To be commanded to do. See *Nouns*
Bid. To order; command.
Call for. To request to come forth.
Call to order. To bring to silence.
Call upon. To address a request to.
Charge. To instruct; to request.
Cite. To summon before a court authoritatively.
Claim. To demand a right.
Command. To order; to request.
Decree To appoint by law.
Demand. To ask for by right or authority. See *Nouns*.
Dictate. To command with authority.
Direct. To point out; to instruct.
Enact. To pass as a law.
Enjoin. To commission.
Exact. To require by force.
Give orders. To direct to do.
Give the law. To command to do or not to do.
Give the signal. To notify by signs
Give the word. ⎫
Give the word of command. ⎭ To order.
Impose. To require of.
Impose a task. To give work to.
Insist on. To make repeated demand or request. See COERCION.
Instruct. To teach.
Issue a command. ⎫
Issue a decree. ⎬ To command.
Issue an order. ⎪
Issue a requisition. ⎭
Lay claim to. To claim as one's own.
Lay down the law. To direct in a particular line of action.
Make a decree. ⎫
Make an order. ⎬ To order
Make a requisition. ⎭
Mark out. To give instructions.
Ordain. To establish by decree or law
Order. To command.
Prescribe. To set down as a decree.
Prescribe a task. To command to do a work.
Promulgate a decree. ⎫
Promulgate an order. ⎬ To command.
Promulgate a requisition. ⎭
Put in requisition. To demand.
Receive an order. To be commanded.
Reclaim. To claim again.
Remand. To send back.
Require. Make demands of.
Require at the hands of. To demand from.
Revendicate. To demand restoration of.
Send for. To call to appear
Set a task. Impose a task.
Set to work. To assign duty to
Subpœna. To summon to appear as a witness.
Summon. To command to appear at a specific time and place.
Task. To assign some labor or duty.
Tax. To burden.

ORDER—*Adjectives*.

Authoritative. By power or authority See RULE.
Commanding. Ordering. See *Verbs*
Decretal. Pertaining to a decree.
Decretive. Determining.
Decretory. Established by a decree.

ORDER—*Adverbs, etc.*

At beat of drum. At a given signal
By a dash of the pen. ⎫
By a stroke of the pen. ⎭ By decree or order.
By order. According to command

In a commanding tone.   Authoritatively
On the first summons.   Immediately.

ORDER—*Phrases.*

Boutez en avant [F.].   Push forward.
Le roi le veut [F.]   The king wishes it.
Messieurs les gardes françaises, tirez [F.].   Gentlemen of the French Guard, fire.   [English command to the French at the battle of Fontenoy.]
Sic volo, sic jubeo [L.].   As I wish, thus I command.
The decree is gone forth.

or'-der-less.   Without arrangement.   REGULARITY-IRREGULARITY.
or'-der-li-ness.   Regularity.   REGULARITY-IRREGU-LARITY.
or'-der-ly.   Regular; a subordinate.   CHIEF-UNDER-LING, CONVENTIONALITY-UNCONVENTIONALITY, OR-GANIZATION - DISORGANIZATION, PRECEDENCE-SUC-CESSION, REGULARITY-IRREGULARITY, UNIFORMITY-MULTIFORMITY.
or'-ders, ho'-ly.   The ministry.   CHURCH; **in orders,** MINISTRY-LAITY.
or'-di-nal.   A collection of rubrics.   CEREMONIAL.
or'-di-nance.   A law; a rite.   CEREMONIAL, LAW-LAW-LESSNESS, ORDER.
or'-di-na-ry.   Usual; common; a *table d'hôte.*   ASTON-ISHMENT-EXPECTANCE, BEAUTY-UGLINESS, CONSE-QUENCE-INSIGNIFICANCE, CONVENTIONALITY-UNCON-VENTIONALITY, EMBELLISHMENT-SIMPLICITY, FAULT-LESSNESS-FAULTINESS, HABIT-DESUETUDE, NUTRI-MENT-EXCRETION; **in ordinary,** STORE; **lay up in ordinary,** USE-DISUSE; **lie in ordinary,** ACTION-PAS-SIVENESS; **ordinary condition,** UNIFORMITY-MULTI-FORMITY; **ordinary course of things,** HABIT-DESUE-TUDE.
or'-di-nate.   A mathematical term.   DIFFERENTIA-TION-INDISCRIMINATION.
or''-di-na'-tion.   The rite of ordaining; appointment; disposition.   CEREMONIAL, CHURCH, COMMISSION-ABROGATION, ORDER.
ord'-nance.   Weapons.   WEAPON.
or'-don-nance.   A law.   LAW-LAWLESSNESS.
or'-dure.   Excrement.   CLEANNESS-FILTHINESS.
ore.   Metal.   MATERIALS.
ore rotundo [L.] (o'-rî ro-tun'-do).   With full utterance.
or'-gan.   A wind-instrument; an instrument.   IN-STRUMENT, MUSICAL INSTRUMENTS, VOCALIZATION-MUTENESS.
or-gan'-ic.   Structural; protoplastic.   CONDITION-SITUATION, ORGANIZATION-INORGANIZATION, TEX-TURE; **organic change,** REVOLUTION; **organic chem-istry,** ORGANIZATION-INORGANIZATION; **organic re-mains,** LIFE-CORPSE, ORGANIZATION-INORGANIZA-TION.
or'-gan-ism.   A living being.   TEXTURE.
or'-gan-ist.   An organ-player.
or''-gan-i-za'-tion.   Constitution in parts; that which is organized.   CREATION-DESTRUCTION, DESIGN, ORGANIZATION - DISORGANIZATION, ORGANIZATION-INORGANIZATION, TEXTURE.

ORGANIZATION—DISORGANIZATION.

Allocation.   A placing or arrangement.
Allotment.   Distribution in parts or parcels; assignment.
Analysis.   Separation of a whole into its parts.
Apportionment.   Assignment of definite portions.
Arrangement.   Methodical disposition of parts in due order.
Assortment.   Act of separating into classes.
Classification.   Distribution into groups or sets
Collocation.   Stationing of things in due place.
Digestion.   Conversion of things for assimilation or mental reception.
Disposal.   A putting in order.
Disposition.   The act of ordering or regulating.
Distribution.   Classification into an orderly way.
Division   Separation into parts.
Graduation.   Arrangement by successive steps.
Organization.   Constitution in parts having a special relation
Plan.   Method or scheme of action.   See DESIGN.
Preparation.   Making ready for a special purpose.   See PREPARA-TION.
Sorting.   Reducing to order; separation into classes.
Syntaxis.   Connected system.
Taxis.   A medical operation; manipulation with the finger.
Taxonomy.   The science that deals with classifications.

ORGANIZATION—*Results of Classification.*

Architecture.   Art of building according to a well-developed plan.
Digest.   An arrangement of materials into a summary.
Organism.   An arrangement of parts whose functions are essential to life and mutually dependent.
Register.   A written record of acts kept for reference.
Synopsis.   Concise classification into heads.
Syntagma.   An orderly arrangement or collection of writings, music, etc.
Table.   A set of related signs arranged in concise form.

ORGANIZATION—*Nouns of Instrument.*

Riddle.   A sieve of coarse meshes.
Screen.   A long, coarse sieve used for heavy matter.
Sieve.   An instrument to separate coarse from fine material.

ORGANIZATION—*Verbs.*

Allot.   To give out by lot.
Arrange.   To put together in order.
Assign places to.   To indicate the proper place.
Assign the parts.   To mark the share, or portion.
Assort.   To divide off into classes.
Bring into order.   To render or produce order or system.

Corrugation.   Derangement of the face into wrinkles.   See PLICA-TURE.
Deorganization.   Destruction of character as an organ.
Derangement.   Disturbing of arrangement.   See *Verbs.*
Discomposition.   Discomposure, derangement.
Dislocation.   Displacement from regular order.
Disorder.   Lack of order, or arrangement.   See REGULARITY-IRREGULARITY.
Disorganization.   State of being thrown into confusion; destruction of order or system.
Disturbance.   The act of disordering.
Evection.   Largest derangement of the moon in its orbit.
Interruption.   Breaking in upon an orderly course.
Inversion.   Change in natural order.   See REVERSAL.
Perturbation.   Disarrangement in the composure of the mind.
Shuffling.   Mixing up; confusing.   See *Verbs.*

DISORGANIZATION—*Verbs.*

Bedevil.   To muddle; throw into disorder, as if by the devil.
Break in upon. }
Break the ranks. } To approach violently; throw into confusion.
Bring into disorder.   To break the regular order.
Complicate.   To entangle; confuse.
Confound.   To cast into confusion and astonishment.
Confuse.   To mix up so as to be undistinguishable.
Convulse.   To draw together; shake up, as by violent action or emotion.
Decompose.   To separate into elements; decay.
Deorganize.   To deprive of its organic character
Derange.   To put into disorder; disturb.
Disarrange.   To throw out of place; derange
Disconcert.   To destroy the harmony of confuse.
Dishevel.   To throw the hair into disorder.
Dislocate.   To put off from its due place; misplace
Disorder.   To put out of order or arrangement.
Disorganize.   To break up a regular system into confusion
Displace.   Put out of its position; change the place of.
Disturb.   To overthrow the composure of; disorder.
Embrangle.   To complicate; entangle.
Embroil.   To involve in confusion or discord.
Entangle.   To become twisted into a tangle; to perplex.
Fumble.   To put in a confusion; mix up; handle clumsily.
Huddle.   To collect in a mass.
Hustle.   To jostle along in disorder.
Imbrangle.   To entangle; involve in complication
Involve.   To roll into difficulty; entangle.

ORGANIZATION—DISORGANIZATION—*Continued.*

ORGANIZATION—VERBS—*Continued.*

Card. To comb out wool.
Cast the parts. To fix or distribute the parts.
Catalogue. To make an enumeration of in regular order; to make a methodical list of.
Class. To put in groups.
Classify. To put in classes.
Collocate. To put in place; to station.
Coordinate. To put alongside in the same order.
Deal. To divide; to distribute.
Digest. To systematize; to classify.
Disembroil. To free from perplexity.
Disentangle. To set free; to separate from difficulties.
Dispose. To arrange in order.
Dispose of. To put definitely in its place.
Distribute. To give among many; to deal out.
Divide. To separate into parts.
File. To put on a file; to arrange for reference.
Fix. To fasten; arrange.
Form. To put in a particular form· to arrange.
Graduate. To arrange in degrees.
Group. To form in a group.
Index. To provide with a guide, or a pointer.
Introduce order into. To bring order into in place of disorder.
Marshal. To gather and assemble in order.
Methodize. To give method to; to regulate.
Organize. To arrange the several parts that they may cooperate together.
Pack. To arrange in order for transportation.
Parcel out. To divide out in small parts.
Place. To put in a special spot; to order.
Place in order. To put in its proper place.
Put in array. ⎫
Put in order. ⎪
Put in shape. ⎬ To arrange in regular order.
Put in trim. ⎪
Put to rights. ⎭
Rally. To collect and give order to.
Range. To set in a row; arrange.
Rank. To arrange in a particular class or division.
Ravel. To be disengaged, as tangled fibers.
Reduce to order. To bring into an orderly condition.
Register. To enter in a book; to schedule. See MARK
Regulate. To put together in order according to rule.
Riddle. To sift; to separate good from worthless.
Set in array. ⎫
Set in order. ⎬ To arrange in some regular order.
Set in trim. ⎭
Set out. ⎫
Set to rights. ⎬ To arrange.
Settle. To put down firmly; adjust.
Sift. To use a sieve; to separate.
Size. To arrange according to size.

DISORGANIZATION—VERBS—*Continued.*

Jumble. To throw together in confusion.
Litter. To scatter, as hay or straw.
Misarrange. To wrongly arrange.
Mislay. To lay in a wrong place.
Misplace. To wrongly place.
Mix. To unite substances in a mass; mingle. See MIXTURE.
Muddle. To confuse the brain.
Perplex. To fold up in difficulties and complications.
Perturb. To disturb the mind; vex; annoy.
Put into disorder. To confuse.
Put out of joint. To put out of working order.
Ravel. To bring into confusion; entangle.
Riot. To act in a riotous manner; raise a disturbance.
Ruffle. To agitate.
Rumple. To make ridges or crumples. See PLICATURE.
Scatter. To throw broadcast; disperse.
Shuffle. To move awkwardly; mix up in confusion
Tangle. To twist up so as difficult to unravel.
Throw into disorder. To confuse. See REGULARITY-IRREGULARITY.
Throw out of gear. To put out of working order.
Toss. To agitate.
Towzle. To disorder or make shaggy.
Trouble. Put in commotion of any kind; agitate.
Tumble. To turn over and over; throw in confusion.
Turn topsy-turvy. To turn things upside down.
Unhinge. To take off of hinge; unbalance.
Unsettle. To destroy the firmness of.

DISORGANIZATION—*Adjectives.*

Deranged. Unbalanced; disordered. See *Adjectives.*
Syncretic. ⎫
Syncretical. ⎬ Uniting different systems of philosophy or religion.

ORGANIZATION—VERBS—*Continued.*

Sort. To separate into kinds, or classes.
String together. To put on a string in orderly succession.
Systematize. To reduce to orderly arrangement.
Tabulate. To arrange in a list
Thread. To pierce through, as a narrow and difficult way.
Unravel. To separate tangled parts.

ORGANIZATION—*Adjectives.*

Arranged. Put together in order. See *Verbs.*
Cut and dried. Arranged beforehand, like hay or firewood.
Embattled. Arranged in order for battle.
In battle array. Drawn up in lines of battle.
Methodical. Having arrangement and regularity.
Orderly. Having order, systematic.
Regular. Going according to rule.
Systematic. Acting according to a comprehensive plan.

ORGANIZATION—INORGANIZATION.

Albumen. A nitrogenous substance, the chief constituent of the white of eggs.
Animated nature. The world of existing or living creatures.
Fossils. Petrified remains of prehistoric organic bodies.
Living beings. The living existences, as distinguished from lifeless existences.
Living nature. The world of living creatures.
Organic remains. That which is left of living creatures after death.
Organism. An organized living being.
Organization. The state of being in systematic connection and cooperation.
Organized nature. ⎫ The creation as following a system of arrange-
Organized world. ⎬ ments and laws.
Protein. Alkali albumen, originally considered to be the basis of all albuminous substances.
Protoplasm. A soft, viscid, organic compound constituting the greater part of an animal or vegetable cell.
Structure, etc. The organic combination and arrangement of the parts of a body or object. See TEXTURE.

ORGANIZATION—*Scientific Nouns.*

Anatomy. The science which treats of the structure of organisms. See ANATOMY
Biology. The science of life. See BIOLOGY.
Botany. The science which treats of plants. See BOTANY.
Chemistry. The science which treats of matter as composed of atoms.

Brute matter. The world of irrational and unthinking beings.
Inanimate matter. The world of lifeless or inactive substances
Inorganic matter. Substance devoid of organized structure, or the organs necessary to life.
Inorganization. The state of being devoid of physical structure.
Mineral kingdom. ⎧ That grand division of nature which embraces all
Mineral world. ⎨ inorganic objects, as distinguished from plants
      ⎩ or animals.
Unorganized matter. Matter devoid of the organs necessary to life.

INORGANIZATION—*Scientific Nouns.*

Geology. The science which treats of the structure of the earth. See GEOLOGY.
Geognosy. That branch of geology which treats of the materials of the earth's structure.
Geoscopy. Knowledge of the earth obtained by investigation.
Lithology. That branch of geology which treats of rocks and their microscopic character.
Metallography. The science which treats of metals.
Metallurgy. The science of extracting metals from ores.
Mineralogy. The science which treats of minerals.
Oryctography. That branch of natural history in which fossils are described.
Oryctology. The science which treats of fossil organisms.

ORGANIZATION—INORGANIZATION—*Continued.*

ORGANIZATION—Scientific Nouns—*Continued*

→**Natural history.** That branch of history which treats of nature as separated from man
Naturalist One who studies nature
Organic chemistry. Chemistry which treats of the substances which form the structure of organized beings
Physiology. The science which treats of the functions of the organs of the body
Zoology. The science of animal life

ORGANIZATION—*Adjectives*

Organic. Pertaining to or composed of animal or vegetable structures
Organized. Brought into systematic connection.

or'-gan-ize. To arrange in parts. CREATION-DESTRUCTION, DESIGN, ORGANIZATION-DISORGANIZATION; **organized hypocrisy,** TRUTHFULNESS-FALSEHOOD.
or'-gan-ized. Arranged. ORGANIZATION-INORGANIZATION.
or''-gan-ol'-o-gy. The science of the organs of the body. TEXTURE.
or'-gasm. Immoderate excitement. TURBULENCE-CALMNESS.
or'-gies. Wanton revelry. MODERATION - SELFINDULGENCE.
o'-ri-el. A window. ANGULARITY, ARCHITECTURE, CONTENTS-RECEIVER, FANE.
O'-ri-ent. The East. LATERALITY-CONTRAPOSITION, LIGHT-DARKNESS.
O''-ri-en'-tal. Eastern. LATERALITY - CONTRAPOSITION; **Oriental topaz,** EMBELLISHMENT - DISFIGUREMENT.
o''-ri-en'-tate. To show symmetry. MINERALOGY.
o''-ri-en-ta'-tion. A principle in architecture. LATERALITY-CONTRAPOSITION.
or'-i-fice. An aperture. APERTURE-CLOSURE, BEGINNING-END.
or'-i-flamme. An ensign. SIGN.
Or'-i-gen-ism. The doctrines of Origen. ORTHODOXY-HETERODOXY.
or'-i-gin. Commencement. BEGINNING-END, CAUSE-EFFECT; **derive its origin,** CAUSE-EFFECT.
o-rig'-i-nal. First in order; not imitated; exceptional; inventive; singular. CAUSE-EFFECT, CONVENTIONALITY-UNCONVENTIONALITY, COPY-MODEL, FANCY, IMITATION - ORIGINALITY, LIKENESS - UNLIKENESS, NATURE-ART, SOCIETY-LAUGHINGSTOCK, UNIVERSALITY-PARTICULARITY, VOLITION-OBLIGATION; **return to original state,** RENOVATION-RELAPSE.
o-rig''-i-nal'-i-ty. Inventiveness. CONVENTIONALITY-UNCONVENTIONALITY, FANCY, IMITATION-ORIGINALITY, LIKENESS-UNLIKENESS, VOLITION-OBLIGATION, **want of originality,** WITTINESS-DULNESS.
o-rig'-i-nate. To spring from; to create. BEGINNING-END, CAUSE-EFFECT, FANCY, VOLITION-OBLIGATION; **originate in,** CAUSE-EFFECT.
o-rig''-i-na'-tion. Beginning. CAUSE-EFFECT.
o-rig''-i-na''-tor. Inventor. MAKER-DESTROYER.
O-ri'-on's belt. A constellation. UNIVERSE.

INORGANIZATION—*Continued.*

INORGANIZATION—*Verb*

Turn to dust. To change into inorganic matter

INORGANIZATION—*Adjectives*

Azoic. Inorganic, without life
Inanimate. Without life
Inorganic. Devoid of systematic physical structure.
Mineral Inorganic, pertaining to or like a mineral.

or''-is-mo-log'-ic-al. Pertaining to orismology. NAME-MISNOMER.
or''-is-mol'-o-gy. The science of defining. NAME-MISNOMER, WORD-NEOLOGY.
or'-i-son. A prayer. DEVOTION-IDOLATRY, PETITION-EXPOSTULATION.
Or'-muzd. The spirit of good. JOVE-FIEND.
or'-na-ment. An adornment. EMBELLISHMENT-DISFIGUREMENT, EMBELLISHMENT-SIMPLICITY, REPUTATION-DISCREDIT, RHETORIC, SIMPLICITY-FLORIDNESS, **ornamental art,** EMBELLISHMENT-DISFIGUREMENT, PAINTING; **ornamental garden,** OCEAN-LAND.
or''-na-men-ta'-tion. Decoration. EMBELLISHMENT-DISFIGUREMENT.
or'-na-ment-ed. Decorated. EMBELLISHMENT-DISFIGUREMENT, SIMPLICITY-FLORIDNESS.
or-nate'. Greatly ornamented. EMBELLISHMENT-DISFIGUREMENT, SIMPLICITY-FLORIDNESS.
or-nate'-ness. Beauty. EMBELLISHMENT-DISFIGUREMENT.
or'-na-ture. Decoration. EMBELLISHMENT-DISFIGUREMENT.
ornavit, nihil tetigit quod non [L.] (or-nê'-vit, naï'hil tet'-i-jit quod non). He touched nothing without embellishing it. TASTE-VULGARITY
or-nis'-co-py. Divination by birds. PROPHECY.
or''-nith-ol'-o-gy. The science of birds. ZOOLOGY-BOTANY.
or'-nith-o-man'-cy. Augury. PROPHECY.
oro todo le que reluce, no es [Sp.] (o'-ro to'-do lê kê rê-luth'-ê, no es). All is not gold that glitters. CREDULOUSNESS-SKEPTICISM, TRUTHFULNESS-FRAUD.
or'-phan. A child deprived of its parents by death. INFANT-VETERAN.
Or'-pheus. A great musician. MUSICIAN.
or'-pi-ment. A yellow pigment. YELLOWNESS-PURPLE.
or'-re-ry. An astronomical apparatus. ASTRONOMY, UNIVERSE.
or'-tho-dox. Holding the correct or generally accepted doctrine. CONVENTIONALITY-UNCONVENTIONALITY, ORTHODOXY-HETERODOXY, TRUTH-ERROR; **orthodox dissenter,** ORTHODOXY-HETERODOXY.
or'-tho-dox''-y. The correct belief. ORTHODOXY-HETERODOXY.

ORTHODOXY—HETERODOXY.

Hyperorthodoxy. Excessive orthodoxy
Orthodoxy Correctness and soundness in religious doctrine
Soundness. Correct views in regard to creed.
Strictness. Close conformity to doctrine or creed.
True faith. The correct belief.
Truth, etc. Correct accordance with divine law See TRUTH

ORTHODOXY—*Denotations*

Anglicanism. The principles of the established Church of England.
Apostles' Creed. The most widely accepted confession of faith in Christendom.

Apostasy. A total falling from one's religion or creed.
Error, etc. A mistake, something false See TRUTH-ERROR.
False doctrine. Incorrect doctrine.
Heresy. A view of religious matters at variance from accepted doctrines
Heterodoxy. The state of being at variance from any established religious doctrine
Schism. A division of a Church into factions.
Schismaticalness. The state of being separated from the established Church because of a variance in doctrine.
Schismaticism. A schism.

ORTHODOXY—HETERODOXY—*Continued*

ORTHODOXY—Denotations—*Continued.*

Apostolic Church. The Church universal holding the apostolic faith.

Athanasian Creed. The confession of faith said to have been written by Athanasius.

Baptist. A denomination of Christians who deny the validity of infant baptism, and insist that infant baptism should be by immersion.

Body of Christ. The collective body of Christians.

Broad Church. A portion of the Church of England.

Calvinism. The theological doctrine of John Calvin.

Calvinist. A believer in Calvinism.

Canonist, etc. A person well-versed in Church or canon law. See THEOLOGY.

Canons. Those books of the Bible recognized as inspired. See FAITH.

Catechism. A short outline of the rudiments of a religious creed.

Catholic. A person who accepts the creeds which are received in common by all parts of the orthodox Christian Church.

Catholic Church. The universal Church.

Catholicism. The practises and doctrines of the universal Church.

Catholicity. Conformity to the system of doctrine held by all parts of the orthodox Christian Church

Christendom. That part of the world where Christianity prevails.

Christian. A believer in Christ.

Christian community. A body of Christians.

Christianism. Christianity

Christianity. Christian doctrines and beliefs.

Christian Science. A cult organized by Mary Eddy for curing disease by prayer.

Church. The body of Christian believers.

Church of Christ. The Christian Church.

Church of Rome. The Roman Catholic Church.

Collective body of Christians. The body of Christian believers.

Congregationalist. One who belongs to the Congregational Church.

Disciples of Christ. A Christian denomination which rejects human creeds and sectarian names

Dowieite. A follower of Alexander Dowie a healer by prayer.

Episcopalian. One who belongs to an Episcopal Church, or adheres to the episcopal form of Church government.

Erastian. One of the followers of Thomas Erastus, who held that the holy communion was open to all.

Established Church. A Church supported by the civil power, the Church of England.

Followers of Christ. The body of Christians.

Free Church. An ecclesiastical body that separated from the Church of Scotland.

Greek Church. The Greek Catholic Church.

High Church. An ecclesiastical body in the Church of England and the Protestant Episcopal Church, who emphasize the doctrine of apostolic succession, etc.

Huguenot. A French Protestant.

Iconoclasm. The destruction of images of worship

Independent. One who believes that an organized Christian Church is independent of all ecclesiastical authority.

Irvingite. A body of Christians highly ritualistic in worship, who look for a speedy coming of Christ. [Rev. Edward Irving, 1830.]

Latter-day Saint. A member of the Mormon Church.

Low Church. An ecclesiastical body in the Church of England and the Protestant Episcopal Church, which rejects the tenets of the High Church school.

Lutheran. One who adheres to the doctrines of Luther or the Lutheran Church.

Members of Christ. Christian believers.

Methodism. The doctrines of a sect of Christians, which teach a methodical strictness in all religious duties.

Methodist. A believer in Methodism

Moravianism. The religious system of the Moravians, a branch of the Hussites.

Mormon. A follower of Joseph Smith, who believes in polygamy and Church control over civil matters.

Nicene Creed. The Trinitarian creed adopted at Nice, Asia Minor.

Orthodox dissenter. One who separates from the worship and service of an established Church

Papacy. The Roman Catholic religion.

Papism. Religion of the Roman Catholic Church: an offensive term.

Papistry. The doctrines and ceremonies of the Church of Rome.

Presbyterian. A member of the Presbyterian Church.

Protestant. A Christian who does not belong to the Roman Catholic or Greek Church.

Protestantism. The principles or religion of the Protestants.

Puritan. English Protestants and their followers who advocated simpler forms of faith and worship than those established by law.

Puritanism. The teachings of the Puritans.

HETERODOXY—*Denotations.*

Abdal. A Mohammedan worshiper.

Albigenses. A sect of reformers.

Anabaptism. The doctrine of a mystical German sect very radical in its opinions.

Anabaptist. A believer in Anabaptism.

Antichrist. An opponent of Christ.

Antinomianism. A doctrine that faith frees a Christian from moral law.

Arianism. The doctrines of Arius, who held Christ to be inferior to God the Father, in nature and dignity.

Atheism. Disbelief or denial of the existence of a God. See GODLINESS-DISBELIEF.

Backsliding. A falling back into sin or error.

Bibliolatry. Excessive worship of the letter of the Bible.

Bigot. A person who regards his own faith and views in matters of religion as unquestionably right.

Bigotry. Unreasoning attachment to one's own belief and opinions. See BIGOTRY.

Brahman.}
Brahmin.} A person of the highest priestly class among the Hindus.

Brahminism. The religion or system of doctrines taught by Brahma.

Brownian. A member of an independent Church.

Bryanite. A Bible Christian.

Buddhism. The religion taught by the Hindu sage, Buddha.

Buddhist. One who accepts the teachings of Buddha.

Deism. A belief in God, but a denial of supernatural revelation.

Deist. One who believes in the existence of a God, but denies revealed religion.

Dissent, etc. Separation from an established Church See ASSENT-DISSENT.

Dissenter. One who separates from the service and worship of an established Church.

Ditheism. The belief that there are two equal gods.

Dualism. The doctrine that a distinct divine and human personality exists in Christ.

Ebionite. One of a sect of heretics in the first centuries of the Church, whose doctrine was a mixture of Judaism and Christianity.

Emanatist. One who maintains that all things are produced by an evolution from a Divine Being.

Erastianism. The doctrine that the state has supreme control in Church matters.

Essene. One of a sect of Jews remarkable for their strictness and abstinence.

Ethicism. The belief that ethics should govern all human conduct.

Eusebian. A believer in Arianism.

Familist. A religious sect who held that religion consists wholly in love.

Fanatic. One who indulges wild and extravagant notions of religion.

Fanaticism. Wild and extravagant notions on religion.

Fire-worshiper. One who worships fire.

Gentile. A worshiper of false gods.

Gentilism. The state of being a Gentile.

Gentoo. A Hindu.

Giaour. The Moslem name for a person who does not believe in their religion.

Glassite. A member of a small Christian sect holding communion weekly.

Gnostic. A believer in Gnosticism.

Gnosticism. A semi-pagan, semi-Christian system of religion, existing until the sixth century.

Gymnosophist. One of a sect of philosophers in India, who denied themselves the use of flesh, bodily pleasures, and employed themselves in the contemplation of nature.

Heathen. One who worships idols.

Heathendom. That part of the world where heathenism prevails.

Heathenism. The religious system or rites of a heathen nation.

Hebrew. A descendant of Abraham.

Heretic. One who believes some doctrine contrary to the established faith.

Hinduism. The religious doctrines and rites of the Hindus.

Hylotheism. The doctrine that God and the natural universe are identical.

Iconoclast. An image-breaker.

Idolater, etc. A worshiper of idols. See DEVOTION-IDOLATRY.

Idolatry. The worship of anything which is not God.

Islamism. The faith or religious system of the Mohammedans.

Jansenism. A system in the Roman Catholic Church holding the doctrines of irresistible grace and total depravity.

Jew. A descendant of Abraham.

Jovianist. A believer in the doctrines of Jovinian, who denied the virginity of Mary

ORTHODOXY—HETERODOXY—*Continued.*

ORTHODOXY—Denotations—*Continued.*

Quakerism. The doctrines of the Quakers.

Religious sects. Religious societies having distinguishing doctrines or forms of worship.

Religious truth. The doctrine as upheld by a particular denomination.

Roman Catholic. A member of the Church of Rome.

Romanism. The principles of the Church of Rome.

Romanist. One who adheres to the tenets of the Church of Rome.

Sandemanian. A follower of Robert Sandeman, a Scotch sectary of the eighteenth century.

Sublapsarian. One of a class of Calvinists who consider the election of grace is made from men considered as fallen.

Supralapsarian. A class of Calvinists who regard the election as made from men considered without reference to the fall.

Swedenborgian. A follower of Emanuel Swedenborg.

Temple of the Holy Ghost. The Christian believer.

Textuary. One who adheres closely to the text.

The Church. The body of Christian believers.

The Faith once delivered to the saints. The apostolic faith.

Thirty-nine Articles. The thirty-nine doctrines formulated by a convocation of the Church of England.

True believer. An orthodox Christian.

Universal Church. The Christian Church.

Wesleyan. A follower of John Wesley.

Zion. The Christian Church.

ORTHODOXY—*Adjectives.*

Catholic. Not heretical; in accordance with the adopted faith.

Christian. Of or pertaining to Christ or His doctrine.

Divine. Pertaining to or of God.

Evangelical. Pertaining to the fundamental Protestant doctrines.

Faithful. Full of faith; strong in his convictions.

Monotheistic. Believing in one God.

Orthodox. Sound or correct in religious doctrine.

Protestant. Opposed to the Roman Catholic Church.

Reformed. Corrected or amended in religious doctrine.

Romish. Belonging to the Roman Church.

Schismless. Without division in a Church.

Scriptural. According to Scripture.

Sound. Correct in creed.

Strict. Observing exactly.

True, etc. Correct. See Truth.

HETERODOXY—Denotations—*Continued from Column 2.*

Skeptic, etc. A person who doubts the existence and perfections of God. See Godliness-Disbelief.

Sofi. A member of a sect of Persian mystics, who believe in a form of pantheism.

Soofeeism. A refined mysticism among a sect of Mohammedans.

Superstition, etc. Irrational worship of the Supreme Being. See Credulousness.

Syncretism. A 17th century movement to unite all Protestant Churches.

Synergism. The doctrine of the cooperation of the soul with divine grace in its salvation

Theism. Belief in the existence of a God.

Theist. One who believes in God.

Tractarian. One of the writers of the Oxford Tracts on the sacramental system and the authority of the Church of England.

Tractarianism. The principles of the Tractarians.

Tritheism. The doctrine that the Father, Son, and Holy Ghost are three distinct Gods.

Turkism. The Turkish religion.

Ubiquitarian. One of a group of Lutheran divines who believed that the body of Christ was everywhere, especially in the eucharist.

Ultramontane. One who maintains extreme views favoring the pope's supremacy

Ultramontanism. The principles of those within the Roman Catholic Church who maintain extreme views favoring the pope's supremacy.

Unitarian. One who believes that God exists only in one person.

Wahabi. One of a Mohammedan sect.

HETERODOXY—*Adjectives.*

Antichristian. Opposed to Christianity.

Antiscriptural. Opposed to Scripture.

Apocryphal. Pertaining to the fourteen books contained in the Vulgate version, but held uncanonical by Protestant Churches.

Bigoted, etc. Stubbornly attached to a creed. See Bigotry.

Boodhist. Relating to Buddhism.

Brahminical. Relating to Brahminism.

Dissenting. }
Dissident } Not agreeing with; differing from.

HETERODOXY—Denotations—*Continued.*

Judaism. The religious doctrines and rites of the Jews.

Labadist. A believer in mysticism, and the obligation of community of property among Christians.

Lamaism. A modified form of Buddhism.

Latitudinarian. One indifferent to a strict application of any standard of belief.

Latitudinarianism. Indifference to any fixed standard of belief.

Magi. A member of an ancient Persian priesthood.

Materialism. The doctrine of a materialist.

Materialist. One who denies the existence of spiritual substances or agents.

Moslem. }
Mussulman. } An orthodox Mohammedan.

Mythology. The collective myths which describe the gods of a heathen people.

Neoplatonism. A pantheistic school of philosophy. See Neoplatonism.

Nestorian. An adherent of Nestorius, who maintained that the divine and human natures were not merged into one in Christ.

Non-conformist. One who does not conform to an established Church

Non-conformity. Refusal to unite with an established Church.

Nonjuror. A Jacobite.

Novatians. One of the sect of Novatians who held that the lapsed might not be received into communion, and that second marriages were unlawful.

Origenism. The doctrine of Origen, that all created beings, including Satan, will be saved.

Osmanly. A Turk.

Pagan. One who worships false gods.

Paganism. The practise of worshiping false gods.

Painim. A pagan; an infidel.

Pantheist. One who believes that the universe, taken as a whole, is God.

Parsee. One who adheres to the old Persian religion.

Paynim. A pagan.

Polytheism. Belief in many gods.

Polytheist. One who believes in many gods.

Positivism. A philosophical system holding that man can know nothing but the phenomena of things.

Positivist. A believer in positivism, a system of philosophy which deals only with positives.

Precisianism. The practise of one ceremoniously exact in the observance of religious rules.

Puseyism. The system of doctrines propounded by Dr. Pusey and other English clergymen.

Quietism. The doctrine that spiritual exaltation is attained only by fixing the soul on religious contemplation.

Rabbist. One among the Jews who adhered to the Talmud and the traditions of the rabbins.

Recusancy. Non-conformity.

Recusant. A non-conformist.

Ritualism. Adherence to a prescribed form of religious worship.

Ritualist. One who advocates ritualism.

Rosicrucian. One of a school of philosophy, claiming to be deeply versed in the secrets of nature.

Sabbatarianism. The doctrine which teaches the observance of the seventh day of the week as holy.

Sabellianism. The doctrine that there is only one person in the Godhead.

Sabian. One of a small Oriental sect whose doctrines were a mixture of Christianity, Judaism, Mohammedanism, and heathenism.

Sabianism. That species of idolatry which consists in worshiping the sun, moon, and stars.

Sacramentarian. One opposing Luther's doctrine of the eucharist.

Sadducee. One of a sect among the ancient Jews who denied the resurrection, a future state, and the existence of angels.

Sandemanian. One of the sect of Glassites.

Scarlet Woman. A personification of pagan or papal Rome. [*Revelation* xvii, 4, 5.]

Schismatic. One who creates or takes part in schism.

Seceder. One who withdraws from an established Church.

Sectarian. A member or adherent of a special denomination.

Sectarianism. }
Sectarism. } Excessive denominational zeal.

Sectarist. A sectary

Sectary. A dissenter.

Secularism. The practise of rejecting every form of religious faith, and accepting only the facts and influences of the present life.

Separatist. One who withdraws from an established Church.

(*Continued on Column* 1.)

HETERODOXY—Adjectives—*Continued.*

Ethnic. } **Ethnical.** } Pagan; pertaining to nations neither Christian nor Jew.
Fanatical. Moved with excessive and intemperate zeal.
Gentile. Pertaining to a person that is not a Jew.
Heathen. Irreligious; a dweller on the heath.
Heathenish. Like a heathen.
Heretical. At variance with accepted religious views.
Heterodox. Differing from accepted doctrines or religious opinions.
Iconoclastic. Pertaining to iconoclasm or image-breaking.
Idolatrous, etc. Pertaining to the worship of heathen gods. See Devotion-Idolatry.
Judaical. Relating to the Jews.
Judaism, etc. Pertaining to the Jewish religion. See *Nouns.*
Mohammedan. Relating to the Mohammedan religion.
Pagan. Heathen, not Christian, pertaining to the worship of heathen gods; a dweller in a village.

Painim. Pagan.
Pantheistic. Pertaining to the belief that the universe and God are identical.
Polytheism. Pertaining to the belief in many gods.
Recusant. Refusing to conform to accepted doctrines.
Schismatic. Pertaining to a schism or a division in a Church.
Sectarian. Excessively devoted to a sect.
Secular, etc. Pertaining to the present life. See Ministry.
Superstitious, etc. Pertaining to credulous belief in the supernatural. See Credulousness.
Uncanonical. Not according to canon.
Unchristian. Not Christian.
Unorthodox. Not firm and sound in doctrine.
Unscriptural. Not in accordance with Scripture.
Visionary, etc. Pertaining to dreams or apparitions. See Fancy.

or'-tho-ep"-y. Pronunciation. Vocalization-Muteness.
or-thog'-o-nal. Rectangular. Erectness-Flatness.
or-thog'-ra-phy. Spelling. Letter.
or-thol'-o-gy. Naming. Truth-Error.
or-thom'-e-try. Versification. Mensuration, Poetry-Prose.
or"-tho-pe'-di-a. Surgery. Remedy-Bane.
or'-tho-prax"-y. Right-doing. Remedy-Bane.
or"-tho-rhom'-bic. Pertaining to crystal-forms. Mineralogy.
orts. Leavings. Increment-Remnant, Usefulness-Uselessness.
or-yc-tog'-ra-phy. Description of fossils. Organization-Inorganization.
or"-yc-tol'-o-gy. Science of fossils. Organization-Inorganization, Zoology-Botany.
os, aux absents, les [F.] (oz, oz ab-san't', lez). The bones for the absent ones. [Let them take what they can get.]
os'-cil-late. To waver. Mutability-Stability, Vibration.
os'-cil-la-ting. Wavering. Vibration.
os"-cil-la'-tion. Swinging. Periodicity-Irregularity, Vibration; center of oscillation, Center.
os'-cil-la-to"-ry. Swinging. Vibration.
os'-ci-tan-cy. Dulness; yawning. Activity-Indolence, Aperture-Closure.
os'-ci-tant. Yawning. Aperture-Closure.
os"-ci-ta'-tion. Yawning lazily. Activity-Indolence.
os'-cu-late. To kiss. Interspace-Contact.
os"-cu-la'-tion. Kissing. Blandishment, Interspace-Contact.
os'-cu-la-to"-ry. Pertaining to kissing. Interspace-Contact.
O-si'-ris. Egyptian god. Jove-Fiend.
Os-man'-li. Turkish official. Orthodoxy-Heterodoxy.
Os'-sa on Pe'-li-on. Mountain piled on mountain. Gathering-Scattering, Heaviness-Lightness.
os'-se-ous. Bony. Hardness-Softness.
os-sif'-ic. Bone-forming. Hardness-Softness.
os"-si-fi-ca'-tion. Formation of bones. Hardness-Softness.
os'-si-fy. To change to bone. Hardness-Softness.
os'-su-a-ry. Grave-mound. Life-Funeral.
os-ten'-si-ble. Seeming. Appearance-Disappearance, Likelihood-Unlikelihood, Manifestation-Latency, Pretext.
os-ten'-si-bly. Seemingly. Appearance-Disappearance, Pretext.
os"-ten-ta'-tion. Show. Conceit-Diffidence, Pomp.
os"-ten-ta'-tious. Showy. Conceit-Diffidence, Pomp.
os"-te-ol'-o-gy. Science of the bones. Texture.
os'-ti-a-ry. Estuary. Aperture-Closure, Gulf-Plain.

os'-tra-cism. Exclusion. Approval-Disapproval, Exculpation-Punition, Sociability-Privacy.
os'-tra-cize. To banish. Approval-Disapproval, Recompense-Punition, Sociability-Privacy.
os'-trich. Large bird. Stomach of an ostrich, Fasting-Gluttony.
O-thel'-lo. A Moor in Shakespeare's *Othello.* Othello's occupation's gone, Commission-Retirement.
oth'-er. Not oneself. Variation; do unto others as we would men should do unto us, Unselfishness-Selfishness; enter into the feelings of others, Charitableness-Malevolence; every other, Periodicity-Irregularity; in other words, Interpretation-Misinterpretation; just the other way, Sameness-Contrast; other extreme, Sameness-Contrast; other side of the shield, Evidence-Counterevidence; other things to do, Activity-Indolence; other time, Time; put oneself in the place of others, Unselfishness-Selfishness; the other day, Novelty-Antiquity.
oth'-er-wise". Different. Likeness-Unlikeness.
otia fecit, Deus nobis hæc [L.] (o'-shi-a fï'-sit, dï'-us no'-bis hec). God has given us this ease. Entertainment-Weariness.
otium cum dignitate [L.] (o'-shi-um cum dig'-ni-tê'-tî). Rest with honor. Hurry-Leisure.
ot'-ter-hound". A dog. Fauna-Flora.
ot'-to-man. Seat. Suspension-Support.
ou"-bli-ette'. Dungeon. Exposure-Hidingplace, Release-Prison.
oufe. Elf. Jove-Fiend.
ough. Fie, for shame. Reputation-Discredit.
ought. Owes. Ought to be, Right-Wrong; ought to be done, Duty-Dereliction.
oui-dire [F.] (uî-dîr'). Hearsay. Tidings.
ounce. Small weight. Heaviness-Lightness, Measure.
our-selves'. A first person reflexive pronoun. Humanity.
oust. To eject. Admission-Expulsion, Commission-Abrogation, Taking-Restitution.
out. Outside; in error. Outside-Inside, Truth-Error; come out, Exposure-Hidingplace, Visibility-Invisibility; go out, Entrance-Exit, Heating-Cooling; out and out, Entirety-Deficiency; out at elbows, Affluence-Penury, Reputation-Discredit; out at heels, Affluence-Penury; out in one's reckoning, Truth-Error; out of, Excess-Lack, Motive-Caprice; out upon it, Approval-Disapproval, Charitableness-Curse; out with it, Charitableness-Curse, Exposure-Hidingplace, Mark-Obliteration.
out-bal'-ance. To weigh down. Compensation, Supremacy-Subordinacy.
out-bid'. To bid more than. Exchange.
out-brave'. To be braver than. Presumption-Obsequiousness.

out-bra'-zen. To be bolder than. PRESUMPTION-OB-SEQUIOUSNESS.

out'-break''. Beginning; excitement; riot. ATTACK-DEFENSE, BEGINNING-END, ENTRANCE-EXIT, EXCITABILITY-INEXCITABILITY, INSUBORDINATION-OBEDIENCE, TURBULENCE-CALMNESS, VARIANCE-ACCORD.

out'-burst''. Riot; excitement. ENTRANCE-EXIT, EXCITABILITY-INEXCITABILITY, TURBULENCE-CALMNESS.

out'-cast''. Exile. CONVENTIONALITY-UNCONVENTIONALITY, GOOD MAN-BAD MAN, SOCIABILITY-PRIVACY.

out'-come''. Result. ENTRANCE-EXIT, GAIN-LOSS.

out'-crop''. Exposed rock. GEOLOGY.

out'-cry''. Loud cry. APPROVAL-DISAPPROVAL, CRY-ULULATION, JUBILATION-LAMENTATION.

out-do'. Exceed. ACTIVITY-INDOLENCE, SUBORDINACY, SUCCESS-FAILURE, SUPREMACY-SUBORDINATION, TRANSCURSION-SHORTCOMING.

out'-door''. Outside. OUTSIDE-INSIDE.

out'-er. Without. OUTSIDE-INSIDE.

out'-er-most''. Farthest out. OUTSIDE-INSIDE.

out-face'. To defy. PRESUMPTION-OBSEQUIOUSNESS.

out'-fit. Garments; equipment. DRESS-UNDRESS, PREPARATION-NONPREPARATION.

out-flank'. To pass around; to defeat. LATERALITY-CONTRAPOSITION, SUCCESS-FAILURE.

out'-gate''. Outlet. ENTRANCE-EXIT.

out-gen'-er-al. Surpass in maneuver. SUCCESS-FAILURE.

out''-go'. To go faster than. TRANSCURSION-SHORTCOMING.

out'-go''-ing. Leaving. ENTRANCE-EXIT.

out'-go''-ings. Expenses. OUTLAY-INCOME.

out-grow'. To grow faster than. ENLARGEMENT-DIMINUTION.

out'-growth''. Excrescence. CAUSE-EFFECT.

out''-Her'-od. To outdo in cruelty. SUPREMACY-SUBORDINACY, TURBULENCE-CALMNESS.

out'-house''. Small building. CONTENTS-RECEIVER.

out'-ing. Excursion. TRAVELING-NAVIGATION.

out''-jump'. To excel in jumping. REPUTATION-DISCREDIT, TRANSCURSION-SHORTCOMING.

out-land'-ish. Uncouth; foreign. CONNECTION-INDEPENDENCE, CONVENTIONALITY-UNCONVENTIONALITY, SOCIETY-LUDICROUSNESS, TASTE-VULGARITY.

out-last'. To endure longer than. LASTINGNESS-TRANSIENTNESS.

out'-law''. A freebooter. CONVENTIONALITY-UNCONVENTIONALITY, GOOD MAN-BAD MAN, SOCIABILITY-PRIVACY.

out'-law''-ry. The state of being proscribed. LAW-LAWLESSNESS.

out'-lay''. Expense. OUTLAY-INCOME.

OUTLAY—INCOME.

Bribe. A price, reward, or gift promised with a view to pervert the judgment or corrupt the conduct of a person. See RECOMPENSE.

Circulation. Circulating coin.

Contingent. Monthly allowance to an army captain to defray incidental charges.

Deposit. Money lodged with a bank subject to order.

Disbursement. That which is paid out.

Donation. That which is given as a present. See GIVING.

Earnest. Money deposited as evidence of good faith.

Expenditure. } That which is expended or paid out.
Expenses. }

Fee. Compensation for services rendered.

Footing. A sum paid on entering a position or profession to treat one's companions.

Garnish. A fee paid by a new prisoner.

Handsel. Earnest money.

Instalment. A sum of money which is divided into portions payable at different times.

Investment. The amount of money paid in the purchase of some species of property.

Money going out. Expenditure.

Outgoings. The amount of money which goes out.

Outlay. That which is expended.

Pay in advance. Money given before its equivalent is received

Payment. That which is given in discharge of a debt.

Prime cost. The first or lowest cost. See PRICE.

Purchase. That which is obtained for a price in money. See BUYING.

Quota. A proportional part or share.

Run upon a bank. A sudden withdrawal of money from a bank by many depositors.

Subsidy. A grant to assist in the establishment or support of an enterprise

Tribute. A stated sum of money paid by one ruler or nation to another, either as an acknowledgment of submission, or as the price of peace and protection.

OUTLAY—Verbs.

Bleed. To get money from by artifice.

Disburse. To give out from the treasury

Expend. To spend in large amounts.

Fee. To pay a fee to. See RECOMPENSE.

Invest. To lay out capital so as to get gain from it.

Pay. To give value in return.

Spend. To give out money for anything.

Subscribe. To promise to pay for the benefit of some common interest.

Subsidize. To pay a regular allowance in furtherance of some project.

OUTLAY—Verbal Expressions

Fork out; get through; lay out; loose the purse-strings; make up a sum; open the purse-strings; pay one's way; run through; shell out; sink money; untie the purse-strings.

Alimony. Money allowed a divorced woman from her former husband's estate.

Annuity. An annual allowance.

Bonus. An extra allowance depending on conditions.

Earnings. That which a person earns See GAIN.

Emolument. Compensation connected with an office or position. See RECOMPENSE.

Gross receipts. Total receipts, before they are diminished by any reduction, as for expenses.

Income. }
Incomings. } Amount of salary, wages, etc., per month or year.
Innings. }

Jointure. Settlement of lands, instead of a dower, on a woman upon marriage. See PROPERTY.

Money coming in. Income.

Net profit. The sum left after all expenses are paid.

Pension. Regular allowance made to one for services rendered.

Pittance. A very small allowance.

Premium. Prize given for excellence.

Proceeds. Amount gotten in any business transaction.

Rack rent. Excessive rent, nearly equal to the annual value of the property rented.

Receipt. That which is received.

Rent. Sum paid at stated periods for use of property.

Rentage. }
Rental. } The whole sum paid for use of property.

Rent roll. An account of rents or income.

Return. Profit.

Revenue. Income.

Sweepstakes. Stakes so arranged in betting that one person wins all.

Tontine. An annuity granted to several so that at the death of one his share goes to the others.

Value received. Consideration given for anything.

INCOME—Verbs.

Accrue. To increase, as profit. See GIVING-RECEIVING.

Acquire. To gain gradually. See GAIN.

Afford. To be able to bear the expense.

Bring in. To gain by exertion or effort.

Derive from. }
Draw from. } To obtain an income from.

Pay. To give value in return.

Receive. To get. See sub RECEIVING.

Return. To repay.

Take. To get possession of property.

Take money. To receive money in exchange.

Yield. To produce.

INCOME—Adjectives.

Profitable. Bringing in gain. See GAIN.

Received. Gotten from any source.

Receiving. Coming in. See Verbs.

OUTLAY—*Continued.*

OUTLAY—*Adjectives.*

Expended. Paid out. See sub *Verb.*
Expending. Being paid out.

Sumptuary. Relating to expenses.

OUTLAY—*Phrase.*

Vectigalia nervos esse reipublicæ [L.]. Revenues are the sinews of the commonwealth. [Cicero, *Manilian Law,* 7.]

out″-leap′. To excel in leaping. TRANSCURSION-SHORTCOMING.

out′-let″. Vent. APERTURE-CLOSURE, ENTRANCE-EXIT.

out′-li″-er. One whose residence is not in the same place where his business is situated. UNION-DISUNION, REMOTENESS-NEARNESS.

out′-line″. Features; plan. APPEARANCE-DISAPPEARANCE, DELINEATION-CARICATURE, DESIGN, OUTLINE, PAINTING.

OUTLINE.

Ambit. A circumference.
Circlet, etc. A small circumference. See CIRCLE.
Circuit. A circumference.
Circumference. The line which bounds a circle.
Contour. The outline of a figure or body.
Outline. The bordering line.
Perimeter. The bounding line of any figure of two or more dimensions.
Periphery. A circumference.
Profile. An outline.
Silhouette. A representation of the outlines of a figure filled in with black.
Tournure [F.]. Outline.

OUTLINE—*Denotations.*

Baldric. A belt worn over one shoulder and across the breast.
Band. A fillet, strap, or any narrow ligament with which a thing is encircled.
Belt. That which engirdles a person or thing.
Cingle. A band which encircles the body.
Clasp. A throwing of the arms around.
Cordon. An extended line of soldiers surrounding a place.
Girdle. That which girds, encircles, or encloses.
Girt. }
Girth. } A band or strap which encircles the body.
Lines. Long narrow marks forming the outlines of a figure.
Zodiac. An imaginary belt encircling the heavens.
Zone. An imaginary band surrounding the earth.

out′-lines″. Borders; framework of a book. BEGINNING-END, DIGEST.

out′-live′. To survive. MUTATION-PERMANENCE.

out′-look″. View; to outstare. APPEARANCE-DISAPPEARANCE, PRESUMPTION-OBSEQUIOUSNESS.

out′-ly″-ing. Outside. INCREMENT-REMNANT, OUTSIDE-INSIDE.

out″-ma-neu′-ver. To excel in maneuvering. SUCCESS-FAILURE, TRUTHFULNESS-FRAUD.

out-march′. Excel in marching. SWIFTNESS-SLOWNESS.

out-num′-ber. To exceed in number. MULTIPLICITY-PAUCITY.

out of. Lacking. EXCESS-LACK, MOTIVE-CAPRICE; get out of the way, QUEST-EVASION; get well out of, ESCAPE; go out of one's way, MIDCOURSE-CIRCUIT; out of all proportion, MAGNITUDE-SMALLNESS; out of breath, WEARINESS-REFRESHMENT; out of cash, AFFLUENCE-PENURY; out of character, HARMONY-DISCORD; out of conceit with, DESIRE-DISTASTE; out of countenance, REPUTATION-DISCREDIT, SELFRESPECT-HUMBLENESS; out of danger, SECURITY-INSECURITY; out of date, CHRONOLOGY-ANACHRONISM, NOVELTY-ANTIQUITY, OPPORTUNENESS-UNSUITABLENESS; out of doors, OUTSIDE-INSIDE; out of employ, ACTION-PASSIVENESS; out of favor, DESIRE-DISTASTE; out of focus, VISIBILITY-INVISIBILITY; out of gear, MIGHT-IMPOTENCE, PREPARATION-NONPREPARATION, REGU-LARITY-IRREGULARITY; out of hand, COMPLETION-NONCOMPLETION, EARLINESS-LATENESS; out of harness, LIBERTY-SUBJECTION, RELEASE-RESTRAINT; out of health, HEALTH-SICKNESS; out of hearing, HEARING-DEAFNESS, REMOTENESS-NEARNESS; out of humor, CONTENTEDNESS-DISCONTENTMENT, LIGHTHEARTEDNESS-DEJECTION, PLEASURE-PAIN; out of joint, GOOD-EVIL, HARMONY-DISCORD, MIGHT-IMPOTENCE, REGULARITY-IRREGULARITY; out of luck, WELFARE-MISFORTUNE; out of one's depth, DEEPNESS-SHALLOWNESS, DIFFICULTY-FACILITY, RECKLESSNESS-CAUTION, TRANSCURSION-SHORTCOMING; out of one's mind, SANENESS-LUNACY; out of one's power, POSSIBILITY-IMPOSSIBILITY; out of one's reckoning, CERTAINTY-DOUBT, EXPECTATION-DISAPPOINTMENT, EXPECTATION-SURPRISE, TRUTH-ERROR; out of one's teens, MANHOOD; out of one's wits, EXCITATION, SANENESS-LUNACY; out of order, CONVENTIONALITY-UNCONVENTIONALITY, FAULTLESSNESS-FAULTINESS, PREPARATION-NONPREPARATION, REGULARITY-IRREGULARITY; out of patience, EXCITABILITY-INEXCITABILITY; out of place, CONVENTIONALITY-UNCONVENTIONALITY, ESTABLISHMENT-REMOVAL, PROPRIETY-IMPROPRIETY, REGULARITY-IRREGULARITY; out of pocket, AFFLUENCE-PENURY, CREDIT-DEBT, GAIN-LOSS; out of print, MARK-OBLITERATION; out of reach, POSSIBILITY-IMPOSSIBILITY, REMOTENESS-NEARNESS; out of repair, BETTERMENT-DETERIORATION; out of repute, REPUTATION-DISCREDIT; out of season, HARMONY-DISCORD, OPPORTUNENESS-UNSUITABLENESS; out of shape, PREPARATION-NONPREPARATION; out of sorts, HEALTH-SICKNESS, LIGHTHEARTEDNESS-DEJECTION, REGULARITY-IRREGULARITY; out of spirits, LIGHTHEARTEDNESS-DEJECTION; out of the common, CONVENTIONALITY-UNCONVENTIONALITY; out of the perpendicular, PARALLELISM-INCLINATION; out of the question, ASSENT-DISSENT, CHOICE-NEUTRALITY, DUENESS-UNDUENESS, POSSIBILITY-IMPOSSIBILITY, PROFFER-REFUSAL, SANGUINENESS-HOPELESSNESS; out of the sphere of, REMOTENESS-NEARNESS; out of the way, CONNECTION-INDEPENDENCE, CONVENTIONALITY-UNCONVENTIONALITY PRESENCE-ABSENCE, REMOTENESS-NEARNESS, SOCIABILITY-PRIVACY, SOCIETY-LUDICROUSNESS; out of the world, LIFE-DEATH, SOCIABILITY-PRIVACY; out of tune, BETTERMENT-DETERIORATION, FAULTLESSNESS-FAULTINESS, MELODY-DISSONANCE, VARIANCE-ACCORD; out of work, ACTION-PASSIVENESS; put out of sight, ENLIGHTENMENT-SECRECY, VISIBILITY-INVISIBILITY; turn out of doors, ADMISSION-EXPULSION.

out′-post″. Advanced station. ANTERIORITY-POSTERIORITY, ENVIRONMENT-INTERPOSITION, REMOTENESS-NEARNESS.

out-pour′. An outflow. ENTRANCE-EXIT.

out′-pour″-ing. Effusion. ENLIGHTENMENT-SECRECY, ENOUGH, ENTRANCE-EXIT, NUTRIMENT-EXCRETION.

out′-put″. Production. ENTRANCE-EXIT, GAIN-LOSS.

out′-rage. Violence; badness; guilt. BETTERMENT-DETERIORATION, CHARITABLENESS-MALEVOLENCE, GOOD-EVIL, GOODNESS-BADNESS, INNOCENCE-GUILT, REGARD-DISRESPECT, TURBULENCE-CALMNESS.

out″-ra′-geous. Atrocious. MAGNITUDE-SMALLNESS, REPUTATION-DISCREDIT, TURBULENCE-CALMNESS.

outrance, à [F.] (u-tran′s′, a). To the uttermost. ENTIRETY-DEFICIENCY, MAGNITUDE-SMALLNESS, TURBULENCE-CALMNESS.

outrance, à toute [F.] (u-tran's', a tut). To the uttermost. TURBULENCE-CALMNESS.

outrance, guerre à [F.] (u-tran's', gêr a). War to the death. FIGHTING-CONCILIATION.

out'-rank''. To be of a higher rank. SUPREMACY-SUBORDINACY.

outré [F.] (u-trê'). Excessive; strained. CONVENTIONALITY-UNCONVENTIONALITY, GULL-HYPERBOLE, SOCIETY-LUDICROUSNESS.

outre-mer [F.] (utr''-mer'). Beyond the sea. REMOTENESS-NEARNESS.

out-reach'. To cheat. TRUTHFULNESS-FRAUD.

out-reck'-on. To exceed in reckoning. OVERVALUATION-UNDERVALUATION.

out'-ride''. To ride faster than. TRANSCURSION-SHORTCOMING.

out'-ri''-der. Servant riding on ahead. PREDECESSOR-CONTINUATION.

out'-rig''-ger. Support. CONVEYANCE-VESSEL, SUSPENSION-SUPPORT.

out'-right''. Utterly. ENTIRETY-DEFICIENCY.

out-ri'-val. To defeat. REPUTATION-DISCREDIT, SUPREMACY-SUBORDINACY, TRANSCURSION-SHORTCOMING.

out'-room''. An outer room. CONTENTS-RECEIVER.

out-run'. To excel in running. TRANSCURSION-SHORTCOMING; **outrun the constable,** CREDIT-DEBT, EXTRAVAGANCE-AVARICE.

out'-scour''-ings. That which is washed out. CLEANNESS-FILTHINESS.

out'-set''. Beginning; start. ARRIVAL-DEPARTURE, BEGINNING-END.

out-shine'. To shine brighter than. REPUTATION-DISCREDIT.

out-side'. Outer part of anything. APPEARANCE-DISAPPEARANCE, OUTSIDE-INSIDE; **clean the outside of the platter,** POMP; **mere outside,** TRUTHFULNESS-FALSEHOOD; **outside car,** CONVEYANCE-VESSEL.

OUTSIDE—INSIDE.

Circumjacence. Condition of lying on every side.
Excentricity. State of being without the center.
Exterior. The outside.
Exteriority. The outside.
Face. Principal part of the outside.
Outside. Part of anything exposed to view.
Superficies.} Covering or external view of anything.
Surface.}

OUTSIDE—*Denotations.*

Disc.} Anything nearly flat and circular.
Disk.}
Facet. One of the faces cut on a diamond.
Skin. The outside of the body. See COVER.
Superstratum. One layer placed above another.

OUTSIDE—*Verbal Expressions.*

Be exterior (see *Adjectives*); **lie around** (see ENVIRONMENT); **place exteriorly; place outside; place outwardly; put out; turn out.**

OUTSIDE—*Adjectives.*

Ab extra [L.]. From without.
À la belle etoile [F.]. In the open air.
Al fresco [It.]. To the open air.
Discoid. Resembling a disk.
Excentric. Away from the center.
Exterior. Helping to form the outside.
External. Closely connected with the outside.
Extramural. Outside the walls.
Extra muros [L.]. Without the walls.
Extraregarding. Looking at what is beyond us.
Extrinsic. Unnatural: foreign.
Frontal. Situated in the front.
In the open air. Outside.
Outdoor. In the open air.
Outer. Farther out.
Outermost. Farthest out.
Outlying. Adjacent to.
Out of doors. Outside.
Outside. Pertaining to the outside.
Outstanding. Located on the outside.
Outward. Directed toward the outside.
Round about. Surrounding.
Skin deep. Not going in far.
Sub dio [L.].}
Sub Jove [L.].} Under the open sky
Superficial. Lying on the surface.

OUTSIDE—*Adverbs.*

Externally. On the outside.
Out. Not in.
Outwards. Toward the outside.
Over. Beyond
Without. On the outside.

Inside. The part beneath the surface.
Interior. The inside of something large or magnificent.
Interiority. The state or condition of being inside.

INSIDE—*Denotations.*

Backbone. The column of bones in the back which gives firmness to the frame. See CENTER.
Belly. That part of the human body which contains the intestines.
Bosom. The breast of a human being.
Bowels. The entrails of a man.
Breast. The fore part of the body between the neck and belly.
Cave. A hollow place in the earth.
Chitterlings. The small intestines of the swine.
Contents. The thing or things held by a receptacle. See CONTENTS.
Entrails. The internal parts of animal bodies.
Guts. The entrails of an animal.
Heart. The part nearest the middle or center; the organ which keeps the blood in circulation.
Innermost recesses. The parts most remote from the outward parts. See CONVEXITY-CONCAVITY.
Interspace. The intervening space.
Intestines. The entrails.
Lap. The position formed by the knees and thighs when one sits down.
Marrow. The tissue which fills the cavities of bones.
Penetralia [L.]. The innermost parts of a thing.
Pith. The soft spongy substance in the center of the stems of many plants.
Recesses. Places of retirement, retreat, or secrecy.
Subsoil. The bed of earth which lies immediately beneath the surface soil.
Substance. That which underlies all outward manifestations.
Substratum. A layer of earth lying under another.
Viscera. The organs contained in the abdomen.
Vitals. One of the necessary organs of life.
Womb. The place where anything is generated or produced.

INSIDE—*Verbs.*

Enclose. To shut up in something. See CONFINEMENT.
Imbed. To fix solidly in See INJECTION.
Intern. To confine.

INSIDE—*Verbal Expressions.*

Be inside (see *Adjectives*); **be within** (see *Adverbs*); **keep within, place within.**

INSIDE—*Adjectives.*

Deep-seated. Permanent, intense.
Domestic. Not pertaining to outsiders.
Enclosed. Limited. See *Verbs*
Endemic. Prevalent among a certain people.
Home. Arising from or pertaining to the home.
Indoor. Inside.
Inland. At a distance from the coast.
Inmost. Farthest in.
Inner. Farther in.
Innermost. Inmost.
Inside. Within.

INSIDE—Adjectives—*Continued.*

Interior. Inside
Internal. On the inside
Interstitial. Situated within the tissues of an organ
Intestinal. Pertaining to the intestines
Intestine. Domestic.
Intramural. Situated within the walls of a city

Intraregarding. Looking within oneself.
Inward. Directed toward the inside.
Inwrought. Worked in. See Subjectiveness.
Subcutaneous. Situated just beneath the skin.
Vernacular. Belonging to one's native country.

INSIDE—*Adverbs, etc*

Ab intra [L.]. From within
At home. In seclusion.
Herein. In this matter or place.
In. Not outside.
Indoors. Not in the open air
Inly. Inwards.
Internally. On the inside.

In the bosom of one's family. Retired.
Inwards. Towards the inside.
Therein. In that place.
Wherein. In which.
Within. Inside.
Withindoors.}
Withinside.} Not in the open air.

out'-skirts''. Border. Environment-Interposition, Remoteness-Nearness.
out-speak'. To speak out. Speech-Inarticulateness.
out'-spok''-en. Frank. Craft-Artlessness, Speech-Inarticulateness, Truthfulness-Falsehood; **be outspoken,** Approval-Disapproval.
out-spread'. To spread out. Breadth-Narrowness.
out-stand'-ing. Outside; due. Credit-Debt, Increment-Remnant, Outside-Inside; **outstanding debt,** Credit-Debt.
out-stare'. Browbeat. Presumption-Obsequiousness.
out-step'. To step faster than. Transcursion-Shortcoming.
out-stretched'. Stretched out. Breadth-Narrowness, Length-Shortness; **with outstretched arms,** Politeness-Impoliteness.
out-strip'. Excel. Leading-Following, Supremacy-Subordinacy, Swiftness-Slowness, Transcursion-Shortcoming.

out-talk'. To talk more than. Talkativeness-Taciturnity.
out-vie'. To excel. Reputation-Discredit, Strife-Peace.
out-vote'. To cast more votes than. Success-Failure.
out'-ward. Outside. Outside-Inside, Subjectiveness-Objectiveness; **outward bound,** Arrival-Departure.
out'-wards. Outside. Outside-Inside.
out-weigh'. To be heavier than. Dominance-Impotence, Supremacy-Subordinacy.
out-wit'. Overreach. Success-Failure, Truthfulness-Fraud.
out'-work''. Defense. Attack-Defense.
o'-val. Elliptical. Circle-Winding.
o'-va-ry. Part of a flower. Biology.
o'-vate. Egg-shaped. Circle-Winding.
o-va'-tion. Reception. Solemnization.
ov'-en. Stove. Oven-Refrigerator; **like an oven,** Heat-Cold.

OVEN—REFRIGERATOR.

Alembic. An apparatus formerly used in distillation.
Athanor. A furnace used by the alchemists.
Bake-house. Bakery
Bakery. A place of baking.
Boiler. A large utensil in which food etc , is cooked.
Brasier. An open pan for holding live coals
Caboose. Cooking room on board ship.
Caldron. A large boiler
Chafing-dish. Pan with coal-basin attached.
Conservatory. A room properly heated for preserving tender plants.
Crucible. A pot for melting metals or minerals.
Fiery furnace. A place of intense heat
Fireplace. A recess to put a fire in.
Focus. Burning point of light passed through a sun-glass.
Forge. An open fireplace with forced draft
Franklin stove. A kind of stove introduced by Benjamin Franklin.
Furnace. An enclosed fireplace for producing a high degree of heat.
Grate. A frame of iron bars for holding burning fuel
Hearth. Floor of a fireplace
Heater. An apparatus for heating, as a coil of steam-pipes
Hothouse. A glazed building for rearing tender plants
Hypocaust. A furnace, the heat of which was led to rooms above.
Kettle. A metallic vessel for stewing.
Kiln. A furnace for baking brick, etc
Kitchener. A cook-stove.
Laundry. An establishment for washing and ironing clothes.
Limekiln. A kiln in which limestone is reduced to lime
Oven. A chamber in which substances are artificially heated.
Pot. A circular vessel, deeper than broad, used for boiling meat and vegetables.
Range. A large, improved cook-stove.
Retort. A bulb with a beak, for distilling
Reverbatory. A furnace with a vaulted ceiling that deflects the heat toward the hearth.
Russian bath. A vapor bath, or long exposure of the body to steam.
Seething caldron. A caldron filled with a boiling liquid.
Still. An apparatus for vaporizing liquids.
Stove. An apparatus in which fuel is burned for heating or cooking.
Sudatory. A hot-air bath.
Turkish bath. A bath in which a profuse perspiration is produced by hot air

Cooler. A vessel for cooling liquids.
Damper. An attachment to a stove for regulating heat.
Freezing mixture. One that causes freezing.
Frigidarium. Cooling room of Roman *thermæ.*
Ice-bag. A bag of rubber or the like for holding chopped ice.
Ice-house. A building padded with sawdust for storing ice
Ice-pail. A vessel partly filled with ice for cooling bottles of wine.
Refrigerator. A chamber for cooling substances.
Refrigeratory. Chamber in an ice-plant where the ice is formed.
Wine-cooler. An arrangement for cooling wine.

———

OVEN—*Continued.*

Urn. A cylindrical vessel, with a fire-pan or spirit-lamp in the bottom.
Vapor bath. The application of vapor to the body in a close place.
Volcano. A mountain from which heated matter is ejected.
Warm bath. A bath in warm water, vapor, etc.
Warming-pan. A metal vessel for holding hot coals for warming a bed.
Wash-house. A laundry

Oven—*Associated Nouns.*

Andiron. A utensil for supporting wood in a fireplace.
Back-log. A large stick of wood, forming the back of a fire on the hearth
Fire-dog. A support for wood in a fireplace.
Fire-irons. Utensils for the fireplace, as tongs, poker, and shovel
Frying-pan. An iron pan with a long handle used for frying food.
Gridiron. A grated iron utensil for broiling flesh and fish over coals.
Hob. An iron shelf at the side of a fireplace where things are put to keep warm.
Poker. A metal bar used in stirring the fire.
Salamander. A large poker; a culinary utensil.
Shovel. An iron or tin implement used about a fireplace.
Stew-pan. A pan used for stewing.
Tongs. An instrument of two long arms for handling hot coals.
Trivet. A stand to hold a kettle near the fire.
Tuyere. A nozzle or fixture through which the blast is delivered to the interior of a blast furnace.

o'-ver. Remaining; past; above; too much. Beginning-End, Excess-Lack, Future-Past, Height-Lowness, Increment-Remnant, Outside-Inside, Supremacy-Subordinacy; **all over,** Completion-Noncompletion; **all over with,** Creation-Destruction, Life-Death, Success-Failure, Welfare-Misfortune; **danger over,** Security-Insecurity; **fight one's battles over again,** Account; **get over,** Renovation-Relapse; **make over,** Giving-Receiving; **over again,** Recurrence; **over against,** Laterality-Contraposition; **over and above,** Addition-Subtraction, Excess-Lack, Increment-Remnant, Supremacy-Subordinacy; **over head and ears,** Deepness-Shallowness, Emotions, Entirety-Deficiency, Height-Lowness; **over the border,** Remoteness-Nearness; **over the hills and far away,** Remoteness-Nearness; **over the mark,** Supremacy-Subordinacy;**·over the way,** Laterality-Contraposition; **set over,** Commission-Abrogation; **turn over,** Reversal.

o''-ver-a-bound'. To be too plenteous. Excess-Lack.

o''-ver-act'. To overdo. Activity-Indolence, Society-Affectation.

o''-ver-act'-ed. Affected. Society-Affectation.

o'-ver-all. Trousers. Dress-Undress.

o'-ver-anx-i''-e-ty. To much anxiety. Desire-Distaste.

o''-ver-arch'. To arch over. Cover-Lining.

o''-ver-awe'. To awe greatly. Duty-Dereliction, Rule-License, Sanguineness-Timidity.

o''-ver-bal'-ance. To weigh down. Compensation, Supremacy-Subordinacy.

o''-ver-bal'-anced. Overweighted. Equality-Inequality.

o''-ver-bear'. To oppress. Dominance-Impotence.

o''-ver-bear'-ance. Arrogance. Presumption-Obsequiousness.

o''-ver-bear'-ing. Domineering. Presumption-Obsequiousness.

o'-ver-board''. Over the side of a boat. **Throw overboard,** Admission-Expulsion, Choice-Rejection, Commission-Abrogation, Keeping-Relinquishment, Use-Disuse.

o''-ver-borne'. Overpowered. Liberty-Subjection, Success-Failure

o''-ver-bur'-den. To load too heavily. Excess-Lack, Goodness-Badness, Weariness-Refreshment.

o''-ver-cast'. To cover. Dimness, Light-Darkness, Viscidity-Foam.

o''-ver-cau'-tious. Too cautious. Recklessness-Caution.

o''-ver-charge'. To strain. Costliness-Cheapness, Excess-Lack, Gull-Hyperbole, Simplicity-Floridness.

o'-ver-coat''. Garment. Dress-Undress

o''-ver-col'-or. To exaggerate. Gull-Hyperbole.

o''-ver-come'. To conquer; to persuade. Lightheartedness-Dejection, Motive-Caprice, Reputation-Discredit, Success-Failure, Teetotalism-Intemperance; **overcome an obstacle,** Success-Failure.

o''-ver-con'-fi-dence. Sanguineness Recklessness-Caution.

o''-ver-con'-fi-dent. Too confident Credulousness-Skepticism, Recklessness-Caution

o''-ver-cred'-u-lous. Too credulous. Credulousness-Skepticism.

o''-ver-cu'-ri-ous. Too curious. Inquisitiveness-Indifference

o''-ver-date'. Postdate. Chronology-Anachronism

o''-ver-dis-ten'-tion. Strain. Enlargement-Diminution.

o''-ver-do'. To do excessively. Activity-Indolence, Excess-Lack, Society-Affectation

o''-ver-done'. Affected. Society-Affectation.

o'-ver-dose''. Large dose. Excess-Lack.

o''-ver-draw'. Exaggerate; to draw more than **one is** credited with. Delineation-Caricature, Extravagance-Avarice, Gull-Hyperbole.

o''-ver-due'. Not on time. Chronology-Anachronism.

o''-ver-ea'-ger. Too eager. Desire-Distaste.

o''-ver-eat'. To gormandize. Fasting-Gluttony.

o''-ver-es'-ti-mate. Value too highly. Decision-Misjudgment, Gull-Hyperbole, Overvaluation-Undervaluation.

o''-ver-es'-ti-ma-ted. Valued too highly. Adulation-Disparagement, Overvaluation - Undervaluation.

o''-ver-es''-ti-ma''-tion. Excessive estimation. Alleviation-Aggravation, Overvaluation-Undervaluation.

o''-ver-fa-tigued'. Too tired. Weariness-Refreshment.

o''-ver-fed'. Fed too much. Fasting-Gluttony.

o''-ver-feed'. To feed excessively. Excess-Lack.

o''-ver-flow'. To flow over. Excess-Lack, River-Wind; **overflow with gratitude,** Thankfulness-Thanklessness.

o''-ver-flow'-ing. Superfluous. Excess-Lack.

o''-ver-fond''. Fond to excess. Excess-Lack.

o''-ver-go'. To go a distance. Transcursion-Shortcoming.

o''-ver-gorge'. To gormandize. Fasting-Gluttony.

o''-ver-gorged'. Satisfied to disgust. Desire-Repletion, Fasting-Gluttony.

o''-ver-grown'. Large. Enlargement-Diminution, Greatness-Littleness, Magnitude-Smallness.

o'-ver-growth''. Excessive growth Enlargement-Diminution.

o''-ver-hang'. To hang over. Height-Lowness.

o''-ver-hang'-ing. Impending. Height-Lowness, Occurrence-Destiny.

o''-ver-ha'-sty. Too hasty. Favorite-Quarrelsomeness.

o''-ver-haul'. Examine, reprove. Approval-Disapproval, Heed-Disregard, Investigation-Answer, Numbering

o''-ver-head'. Above. Height-Lowness.

o''-ver-hear'. To hear accidentally. Enlightenment-Secrecy, Hearing-Deafness.

o''-ver-joyed'. Very glad. Pleasure-Pain.

o''-ver-jump'. To jump beyond. Transcursion-Shortcoming.

o''-ver-lap'. To lap over. Dress-Undress, Transcursion-Shortcoming.

o''-ver-lay'. To cover; to obscure. Activity-Indolence, Cover-Lining, Excess-Lack, Gull-Hyperbole; **overlay with ornament,** Simplicity-Floridness.

o''-ver-leap'. To leap beyond Geology, Transcursion-Shortcoming.

o''-ver-lib'-er-al. Too liberal. Extravagance-Avarice.

o''-ver-lie'. To lie upon. Cover-Lining.

o''-ver-load'. To burden too much. Excess-Lack, Obstruction-Help

o''-ver-look'. To slight, to manage; to forgive. Carefulness-Carelessness, Heed-Disregard, Management, Pardon-Vindictiveness, Regard-Disrespect.

o''-ver-looked'. Not noticed Consequence-Insignificance; **not to be overlooked,** Consequence-Insignificance.

o''-ver-look'-er. Superintendent. Manager.

o'-ver-ly'-ing. Lying above. Height-Lowness.

o''-ver-mas'-ter. To conquer. Success-Failure.

o''-ver-match'. To defeat or excel. Equality-Inequality, Strength-Weakness, Success-Failure, Supremacy-Subordinacy.

o″-ver-meas′-ure. To estimate too high. EXCESS-LACK.

o″-ver-mod′-est. Diffident. CONCEIT-DIFFIDENCE.

o″-ver-much′. Too much. EXCESS-LACK.

o″-ver-night′. During the night. FUTURE-PAST.

o″-ver-of-fi′-cious. Too officious. ACTIVITY-INDOLENCE.

o″-ver-paid′. Getting too much pay. GENEROSITY-FRUGALITY.

o″-ver-pass′. To pass by; to overlook. SUPREMACY-SUBORDINACY, TRANSCURSION-SHORTCOMING.

o″-ver-per-suade′. To win over. MOTIVE-CAPRICE.

o′-ver-plus. Surplus. EXCESS-LACK, INCREMENT-REMNANT.

o″-ver-poise′. To outweigh. COOPERATION-OPPOSITION.

o″-ver-pow′-er. To subdue. EXCITATION, SUCCESS-FAILURE.

o″-ver-pow′-er-ing. Conquering. EXCITATION, STRENGTH-WEAKNESS.

o″-ver-praise′. To flatter. ADULATION-DISPARAGEMENT, GULL-HYPERBOLE, OVERVALUATION-UNDERVALUATION.

o″-ver-prize′. To exceed in value. OVERVALUATION-UNDERVALUATION.

o″-ver-rate′. To rate too high. OVERVALUATION-UNDERVALUATION.

o″-ver-reach′. To go beyond; to cheat. CRAFT-ARTLESSNESS, SUCCESS-FAILURE, TRANSCURSION-SHORTCOMING, TRUTHFULNESS-FRAUD.

o″-ver-reck′-on. Estimate excessively. OVERVALUATION-UNDERVALUATION.

o′-ver-re-fined″. Subtle. RATIOCINATION-INSTINCT.

o′-ver-re-fine′-ment. Too much refinement. RATIOCINATION-INSTINCT.

o″-ver-re-lig′-ious. Too enthusiastic in religion. AUSTERITY.

o″-ver-ride′. To overcome; to annul; to pass. COMMISSION-ABROGATION, DOMINANCE-IMPOTENCE, HARSHNESS-MILDNESS, OBSTRUCTION-HELP, RULE-LICENSE, SUCCESS-FAILURE, SUPREMACY-SUBORDINACY, TRANSCURSION-SHORTCOMING.

o″-ver-right′-eous. Too righteous. GODLINESS-UNGODLINESS.

o″-ver-rule′. To control; to set aside. COMMISSION-ABROGATION, RULE-LICENSE.

o″-ver-rul′-ing. Controlling. CONSEQUENCE-INSIGNIFICANCE, RULE-LICENSE.

o″-ver-run′. To spread; to pillage; to go beyond. BETTERMENT-DETERIORATION, ENLARGEMENT-DIMINUTION, EXCESS-LACK, PRESENCE-ABSENCE.

o″-ver-scru′-pu-lous. Too scrupulous. UPRIGHTNESS-DISHONESTY.

o″-ver-se′-er. Superintendent. MANAGER.

o″-ver-sen′-si-tive. Too sensitive. OVERVALUATION-UNDERVALUATION, SENSITIVENESS-APATHY.

o″-ver-set′. To upset; to fall. ELEVATION-DEPRESSION, REVERSAL, SUCCESS-FAILURE.

o″-ver-shad′-ow. To cast a shadow over. LIGHT-DARKNESS, REPUTATION-DISCREDIT.

o″-ver-shoot′ the mark. To shoot too high; to overdo. ACTIVITY-INDOLENCE, EXCESS-LACK, GULL-HYPERBOLE, SKILL-UNSKILFULNESS, TRANSCURSION-SHORTCOMING.

o′-ver-sight″. Management; error. HEED-DISREGARD, MANAGEMENT, SUCCESS-FAILURE, TRUTH-ERROR.

o″-ver-skip′. To go beyond. TRANSCURSION-SHORTCOMING.

o″-ver-sleep′. To sleep too long. ACTIVITY-INDOLENCE.

o″-ver-spent′. Tired out. WEARINESS-REFRESHMENT.

o″-ver-spread′. To spread over. BOUNDARY, GATHERING-SCATTERING, PRESENCE-ABSENCE.

o″-ver-state′. To exaggerate. GULL-HYPERBOLE.

o″-ver-step′. To step beyond. TRANSCURSION-SHORTCOMING.

o″-ver-stock′. To supply too much. EXCESS-LACK.

o″-ver-strain′. To strain too much. OVERVALUATION-UNDERVALUATION, WEARINESS-REFRESHMENT.

o″-ver-sup-ply′. Overabundance. EXCESS-LACK.

o′-vert″. Open. MANIFESTATION-LATENCY; **overt act,** ACTION-PASSIVENESS.

o″-ver-take′. To come up to. ARRIVAL-DEPARTURE.

o″-ver-tak′-en. Intoxicated. TEETOTALISM-INTEMPERANCE.

o″-ver-task′. To burden too heavily. USE-MISUSE, WEARINESS-REFRESHMENT.

o″-ver-tax′. To burden too much. USE-MISUSE, WEARINESS-REFRESHMENT.

o′-ver-throw″. To destroy; to defeat. CREATION-DESTRUCTION, ELEVATION-DEPRESSION, PROOF-DISPROOF, SUCCESS-FAILURE.

o″-ver-thwart′. To oppose. ANTAGONISM-CONCURRENCE.

o″-ver-tired′. Very tired. WEARINESS-REFRESHMENT.

o″-ver-top′. To tower over. HEIGHT-LOWNESS, SUPREMACY-SUBORDINACY, TOP-BOTTOM.

o′-ver-ture. Prelude; offer. MUSIC, PETITION-EXPOSTULATION, PREDECESSOR-CONTINUATION, PROFFER-REFUSAL.

o″-ver-turn′. To destroy; to refute. CREATION-DESTRUCTION, ELEVATION-DEPRESSION, PROOF-DISPROOF, REVERSAL.

o″-ver-val″-u-a′-tion. Estimating too highly. OVERVALUATION-UNDERVALUATION.

OVERVALUATION—UNDERVALUATION.

Exaggeration, etc. The act of describing a thing with extravagant and untruthful additions. See GULL-HYPERBOLE.

Fine talking. Boasting.

Optimism. The doctrine that this is the best of all possible worlds

Optimist. One who believes in optimism.

Overestimation. Rating at more than full value

Pessimism. The doctrine that the world is the worst possible world.

Pessimist. One who believes in pessimism.

Vanity, etc. Overestimation of oneself. See CONCEIT.

OVERVALUATION—*Figurative Expressions.*

Much ado about nothing. A great deal of trouble about nothing. [Shakespeare.]

Much cry and little wool. Great promises and small results; shearing swine.

Storm in a teacup. A great annoyance about a little matter.

OVERVALUATION—*Verbs.*

Attach too much importance to. To overvalue.

Catch at straws. To put too much confidence in.

Depreciation, etc. The act of losing in value. See ADULATION-DISPARAGEMENT.

Modesty, etc. The state of undervaluing one's qualities. See CONCEIT-DIFFIDENCE.

Pessimism. The tendency to consider all things as bad; the belief that this is the worst of all possible worlds.

Pessimist. A believer in pessimism.

Underestimation. Regarding anything at a lower value than it really has.

Undervaluing, etc. Holding below value. See *Verbs*

UNDERVALUATION—*Verbs.*

Depreciate. To lessen the worth of.

Disparage, etc. To undervalue. See ADULATION

Disprize. To hold in low esteem.

Make light of.
Make little of.
Make no account of. } To belittle or regard as worthless.
Make nothing of.

Misprize. To hold in wrong esteem.

OVERVALUATION—UNDERVALUATION—*Continued.*

OVERVALUATION—Verbs—*Continued*

Estimate too highly. To have too high an opinion of.
Exaggerate, etc To describe with additions See Gull-Hyperbole.
Extol. To magnify, to lift up
Extol to the skies. To praise very highly; to raise very high.
Have too high an opinion of oneself, etc. To be vain See Conceit
Magnify. To increase the size of.
Make mountains of mole-hills. To exaggerate, magnify.
Make much of ⎫
Make too much of. ⎭ To exaggerate
Make the best of. ⎫
Make the most of. ⎭ To look favorably upon
Make the worst of. To belittle.
Make two bites of a cherry. To exaggerate or hold of undue importance.
Outreckon. To estimate too highly
Overestimate To rate too highly.
Overpraise. To commend too much.
Overprize. To esteem too highly.
Overrate. ⎫
Overreckon. ⎭ To value too highly
Overstrain. To exert too much.
Overvalue. ⎫
Overweigh. ⎭ To estimate too highly
Set too high a value upon. To overvalue.
Strain. To stretch; exaggerate.
Think much of. ⎫
Think too much of. ⎭ To exaggerate.

OVERVALUATION—*Adjectives*

Overestimated, etc Rated too highly. See *Verbs*.
Oversensitive, etc. Too easily affected See Sensitiveness

UNDERVALUATION—Verbs—*Continued.*

Neglect, etc. To fail to treat with due consideration See Carefulness-Neglect
Not to do justice to. Not to regard at true value.
Ridicule, etc To deride. See Society-Derision
Set at naught. To hold as nothing.
Set no store by. To regard as of little importance
Shake off as dew-drops from a lion's mane. To consider of no account.
Slight, etc To neglect wilfully· disregard. See Regard-Scorn
Slur over. To pass over lightly
Think nothing of To belittle.
Underestimate. To value too lowly
Underrate. To estimate too lowly.
Underreckon To count of too little value
Undervalue. To rate too lowly.

UNDERVALUATION—*Adjectives.*

Depreciated. Lowered in worth.
Depreciating, etc. Losing in value. See *Verbs*.
Unprized. Without prize.
Unvalued. Without value· having no value.

OVERVALUATION—*Continued.*

OVERVALUATION—*Phrases*

All his geese are swans. Boasting, in an exaggerative manner
Parturiunt montes [L.] The mountains are in labor (mice will be born)

---

o″-ver-val′-ue. To value too much. Overvaluation-Undervaluation.
o″-ver-ween′-ing. Arrogant. Conceit-Diffidence, Excess-Lack, Presumption-Obsequiousness, Recklessness-Caution, Selfrespect-Humbleness.
o″-ver-weigh′. To exceed in weight. Dominance-Impotence, Overvaluation-Undervaluation, Supremacy-Subordinacy.
o″-ver-whelm′. To ruin; to overcome. Creation-Destruction, Excess-Lack, Excitation.
o″-ver-whelmed′. Defeated. Liberty-Subjection, Success-Failure.
o″-ver-whelm′-ing. Powerful; sublime. Astonishment-Expectance, Excitation, Strength-Weakness.
o″-ver-wise′. Too wise. Conceit-Diffidence.
o″-ver-work′. To work too much. Use-Misuse, Weariness-Refreshment.
o″-ver-wrought′. Overdone, excited. Excitation, Gull-Hyperbole, Society-Affectation.
o″-ver-zeal′-ous. Too zealous. Excitability-Inexcitability.
o′-vi-form. Egg-shaped; elliptical. Roundness
ovo, in [L.] (o′-vo, in). In the egg. Cause-Effect
o′-void. Egg-shaped. Roundness
o′-vule. Seed. Circle-Winding.
o′-vum. Part of an ovary. Biology
owe. To be in debt. Credit-Debt; owe to oneself, Duty-Dereliction.
ow′-ing. In debt. Credit-Debt, owing to, Cause-Effect, Rationale-Luck.
owl. Figurative name for a wise man. Sage-Fool, owl's light, Dimness; screech-owl, Cry-Ululation.
own. Possess; acknowledge. Assent-Dissent, Exposure-Hidingplace, Holding-Exemption, Property; act on one's own responsibility, Rule-License; after one's own heart, Love-Hate; at one's own risk, Duty-Dereliction; come by one's own, Gain-Loss; condemned out of one's own mouth,

Proof-Disproof; consult one's pleasure, Unselfishness-Selfishness; have one's own way, Difficulty-Facility, Liberty-Subjection, Rule-License, Success-Failure, Volition-Obligation; hold one's own, Attack-Defense, Rule-License; know one's own mind, Persistence-Whim; look after one's own interest, Unselfishness-Selfishness; look with one's own eyes, Carefulness-Carelessness; not know one's own mind, Determination-Vacillation; not know one's own interest, Skill-Unskilfulness; of one's own accord, Readiness-Reluctance, Volition-Obligation; out of one's own head, Volition-Obligation; own flesh and blood, Relationship; own oneself in the wrong, Repentance-Obduracy; own to the soft impeachment, Exposure-Hidingplace; pay in one's own coin, Reprisal-Resistance; stand in one's own light, Skill-Unskilfulness; take the law into one's own hands, Fighting-Conciliation, Law-Lawlessness, Volition-Obligation; throw a stone in one's own garden, Reprisal-Resistance, Skill-Unskilfulness; will of one's own, Determination-Vacillation
own′-er. Possessor. Holder; without an owner, Holding-Exemption.
own′-er-ship. The state of being owner Holding-Exemption, Property.
ox. Animal. Fauna-Flora, Male-Female; hot enough to roast an ox, Heat-Cold.
ox′-goad″. A pointed stick to drive oxen. Weapon
ox′-id. Compound of oxygen. Chemistry.
ox″-i-da′-tion. The process of becoming oxidized. Betterment-Deterioration, Biology.
o′-yer. Trial. Court of oyer and terminer, Tribunal.
o′-yes″ Hear. Hearing-Deafness, Heed-Disregard, Publicity.
oys′-ter. An edible bivalve found in salt water. Nutriment-Excretion
o′-zone. Kind of gas. Chemistry.

P

P. The sixteenth letter of the alphabet. **Mind one's P's and Q's,** CAREFULNESS-CARELESSNESS, DUTY-DERELICTION, POLITENESS-IMPOLITENESS; **P-coat,** DRESS-UNDRESS..

pab′-u-lum. Food. MATERIALITY-SPIRITUALITY, MATERIALS, NUTRIMENT-EXCRETION; **mental pabulum,** CONCEPTION-THEME.

pace. A step; a particular gait. MENSURATION, MOVEMENT-REST, TRAVELING-NAVIGATION; **keep pace with,** COOPERATION-OPPOSITION, SWIFTNESS-SLOWNESS; **pace up and down,** TRAVELING-NAVIGATION; **put through one's paces,** MANIFESTATION-LATENCY; **show one's paces,** POMP.

pacem para bellum, si vis [L.] (pê′-sem pê′-ra bel′-lum, sai vis). If you wish peace, prepare for war. FIGHTING-CONCILIATION, PREPARATION-NONPREPARATION.

pach″-y-der′-ma-tous. Thick-skinned; pertaining to a former order of hoofed mammals. FEELING-INSENSIBILITY, SENSITIVENESS-APATHY.

pa-cif′-ic. Calm. STRIFE-PEACE, TURBULENCE-CALMNESS.

pa-cif″-i-ca″-tion. Act of making peace. FIGHTING-CONCILIATION, TURBULENCE-CALMNESS.

pac′-i-fi-ca″-tor. A peacemaker. STRIFE-PEACE.

pac′-i-fied. Calmed. FIGHTING-CONCILIATION, VARIANCE-ACCORD.

pac′-i-fy. To calm. FIGHTING-CONCILIATION, TURBULENCE-CALMNESS.

pack. A bundle; a crowd; to make full. ENLARGEMENT-DIMINUTION, GATHERING-SCATTERING, OBSTRUCTION-HELP, ORGANIZATION-DISORGANIZATION, PREPARATION-NONPREPARATION, PRESENCE-ABSENCE; **pack off,** ADMISSION-EXPULSION, ARRIVAL-DEPARTURE; **pack of nonsense,** CONSEQUENCE-INSIGNIFICANCE, **pack up,** CONFINEMENT; **send packing,** ADMISSION-EXPULSION.

pack′-age. A bundle. ESTABLISHMENT-REMOVAL, GATHERING-SCATTERING.

pack′-et. A small package; a vessel. CONVEYANCE-VESSEL, GATHERING-SCATTERING.

pack′-horse. A horse which carries heavy bundles. CONVEYER.

pack′-ing. Arranging closely. ESTABLISHMENT-REMOVAL.

pack′-sad-dle. A saddle for a pack-horse SUSPENSION-SUPPORT.

pack′-thread″. Thread used for sewing packages. LAMINA-FIBER.

pact. An agreement. CONTRACT.

Pac-to′-lus. A river in ancient Lydia famous for its golden sands. AFFLUENCE-PENURY.

pad. To stuff; a road-horse. CONVEYER, COVER-LINING, ENLARGEMENT-DIMINUTION.

pad′-ding. Material for stuffing. COVER-LINING, HARDNESS-SOFTNESS, PERFORATOR-STOPPER.

pad′-dle. To beat the water with oars; an oar. INSTRUMENT, TRAVELING-NAVIGATION; **paddle one's own canoe,** CONDUCT, LIBERTY-SUBJECTION; **paddle steamer,** CONVEYANCE-VESSEL.

pa″-di-shah′. Chief ruler; a title of the Sultan of Turkey. CHIEF-UNDERLING.

pad′-lock. A lock for a staple. CONNECTIVE, RELEASE-PRISON; **put a padlock on one's lips,** TALKATIVENESS-TACITURNITY.

pa′-dre. Father. MINISTRY-LAITY.

pa-dro′-ne. A patron. CHIEF-UNDERLING.

pæ′-an. Song of triumph. APPROVAL-DISAPPROVAL, DEVOTION-IDOLATRY, JUBILATION-LAMENTATION, SOLEMNIZATION, THANKFULNESS-THANKLESSNESS.

pa′-gan. A heathen. ORTHODOXY-HETERODOXY.

pa′-gan-ism. Worship of false gods. ORTHODOXY-HETERODOXY.

pag′-eant. A pompous show. APPEARANCE-DISAPPEARANCE, POMP.

pag′-eant-ry. Display. APPEARANCE-DISAPPEARANCE, POMP.

pag″-i-na′-tion. The act of paging, as a book. PREDECESSOR-CONTINUATION.

pa-go′-da. An Eastern temple. FANE.

pah. A kind of entrenchment. ATTACK-DEFENSE.

paid. Recompensed. SETTLEMENT-DEFAULT.

pail. A vessel for water, etc. CONTENTS-RECEIVER.

paillard [F.] (pai-yar′). A lewd person. PURITY-RAKE.

pail″-lasse′. A mattress of cheap material. SUSPENSION-SUPPORT.

pain. Distress; punishment. GOODNESS-BADNESS, PLEASURABLENESS-PAINFULNESS, PLEASURE-PAIN, RECOMPENSE-PENALTY, SENSUALITY-SUFFERING.

pained. Distressed. PLEASURE-PAIN, SENSUALITY-SUFFERING.

pain′-ful. Giving pain. PLEASURABLENESS-PAINFULNESS, SENSUALITY-SUFFERING.

pain′-ful-ly. With suffering. MAGNITUDE-SMALLNESS, PLEASURABLENESS-PAINFULNESS.

pain′-ful-ness. Suffering of body or mind. GOOD-EVIL; GOODNESS-BADNESS, PLEASURABLENESS-PAINFULNESS, REMEDY-BANE.

pai′-nim. Pagan. ORTHODOXY-HETERODOXY.

pain′-less. Free from pain. PLEASURE-PAIN.

pains. Carefulness. TOIL-RELAXATION; **get for one's pains,** RECOMPENSE-PUNITION; **pains and penalties,** RECOMPENSE-PENALTY; **take pains,** ACTIVITY-INDOLENCE, TOIL-RELAXATION.

pains′-ta″-ker. A careful person. CAREFULNESS-CARELESSNESS.

pains′-ta″-king. Taking pains; diligent work. ACTIVITY-INDOLENCE, TOIL-RELAXATION.

paint. A pigment; to portray. COLOR-ACHROMATISM, COVER-LINING, DELINEATION-CARICATURE, EMBELLISHMENT-DISFIGUREMENT, PAINTING, TRUTHFULNESS-FRAUD; **paint the lily,** EXCESS-LACK.

paint′-ed. Portrayed. PAINTING.

paint′-er. A rope at the bow of a boat; one who paints. ARTIST, CONNECTIVE.

paint′-ing. The act of laying on paints with a brush; a picture. DELINEATION-CARICATURE, NATURE-ART, PAINTING.

PAINTING.

Cabinet pictures. Small and highly finished pictures suitable to a small room and for close inspection.

Calotype. A picture obtained from paper rendered sensitive by iodid of silver.

Canvas. A picture made on canvas.

Cartoon. A picture of caricature.

Chiaroscuro. The art of mingling dark and light colors in a pleasing effect. See LIGHT.

Composition. Anything put together of artistic effects.

Daguerreotype. An early photograph made according to the plan of Daguerre, the inventor.

Depicting. A picturing with words or colors.

Design. An artistic representation.

Diorama. A painting or paintings so arranged as to be seen in rapid succession by the spectators.

Draft. } A plan drawn to a scale.
Draught. }

Drawing. Any picture or representation of an object by crayon, pencil, or otherwise. See *Verbs*.

Easel-picture. A picture suited in size and subject to an easel.

Enamel. A painting finished in enamel.

Encaustic painting. A painting in which the colors are fixed by burning.

Flower painting. A painting of flowers

Fresco. A picture depicted on a wall.

Full-length. A portrait of the entire person.

Genre [F.]. Style

Gouache [F.]. A painting made by opaque colors mixed in water and gum.

Grisaille [F.]. A style of painting in grayish tints in imitation of bas-reliefs.

Half-length. A portrait showing the upper half of the body

Head. A portrait of the head.

Heliograph. A photograph taken by sunlight.

Heliography. Art of taking pictures by sunlight.

Heliotype. A picture made by heliotypy or the process of transferring a picture from negatives to the printed plate.

High art. Artistic skill.

Historical painting. A painting of historical scenes.

Kit-kat. A picture about 28x36 inches, so called because the members of the Kit-Kat Club had their portraits painted of that size.

Landscape. A picture of natural scenery.

Landscape painting. Painting confined to natural scenery

Marine painting. Painting of sea views.

Miniature. } A painting of small size and careful workman-
Miniature painting. } ship, or the act of painting such.

Monochrome. Painting in different shades of the same color.

Mosaic. A surface inlaid with bits of stone, glass, etc., arranged in an artistic manner.

Oil-painting. A painting done in oils.

Ornamental art. Painting. See EMBELLISHMENT.

Outline. A sketch of an object bringing out its principal lines.

Painting. The art of depicting; the thing depicted.

Panorama. A series of pictures passing continuously before the spectators; a widely extended view in all directions.

Pencil drawing. A drawing executed with a pencil.

Perspective. The art of delineating cubical objects on a surface so that they shall appear as real objects.

Photograph. A picture due to the action of light on a sensitized film.

Photography. The process of forming an image by the chemical action of light.

Picture. Representation of an object, as by painting.

Piece. Anything finished in itself, as music, sculpture, etc.

Polychrome. A picture in several colors.

Portrait. Representation of an individual by any process. See DELINEATION.

Portrait painting A painting or picture of a person.

Portraiture. A representation of an object, as by drawing, painting.

Priming. The first ground.

Profile. A drawing in which the outlines are shown

Prospect. A distant view spread out to the eye.

Scene. A stretch of country seen at a distance.

Scene painting. A painting of some scene, or the art of painting such.

Scenography. The art of representing an object in perspective.

School. The body of disciples of a teacher or system.

Sciagraphy. The art of painting shadows properly.

Sea view. A scene of the sea.

Shade. The dark part of a picture.

Silhouette [F.]. A very simple, profile drawing.

Sketch. An incomplete drawing.

Still life. A dead, inanimate representation.

Study. A first sketch from nature or the living model.

Style. Mode of presentation or execution.

Sun painting. Depiction by the action of sunlight.

Tableau. A representation of a scene by motionless persons.

Talbotype. A picture obtained from sensitive paper.

Tapestry. A textile fabric with elaborate designs inwoven.

The grand art. } Artistic art
The grand style. }

Treatment. The act of treating of anything.

View. That which is seen.

Water-color drawing. A drawing or sketch in water-colors.

Whole-length. A picture which shows the whole person.

PAINTING—*Associated Nouns*

Blacklead. Plumbago.

Body-color. A color possessing body or substance in a great degree.

Brush. A painting instrument made of hair, bristles, etc., attached to a handle.

Chalk. A piece of soft limestone used to make marks.

Charcoal. A drawing pencil made of charcoal-dust.

Crayons. A cylindrical piece of prepared chalk of various colors used in lithography.

Distemper. A pigment mixed with a vehicle, as yolk of eggs or glue.

Easel. A small frame for supporting pictures.

Gouache [F.]. A method of painting with colors mixed in water and gum.

Oil color. A painting color made of a pigment mixed in oil.

Oil paint. A painting whose colors are oil colors; paint made by the addition of oil.

Oils. A liquid insoluble in water, much used in painting.

Paint. A coloring substance of any kind, dry or liquid. See COLOR.

Palette. } A small, oval, paint-holding board used by artists
Pallet. }

Pastel. A paste of varied colors used like a crayon.

Pencil. A small piece of lead covered with wood, and used in drawing, sketching, etc.

Stump. A short roll of paper used in shading and toning crayon sketches.

Tempera [It.]. An Italian method of painting in distemper.

Varnish. A resinous matter spread over smooth surfaces to give a glossy appearance. See PULPINESS-ROSIN.

Vergette [F.]. A palette.

Water-color. A coloring pigment mixed in water.

Water-glass. Glass made liquid by boiling in an alkali.

PAINTING—*Nouns of Place.*

Atelier [F.]. Workshop of an artist.

Picture gallery. A place where pictures are kept for exhibition.

Studio. An artist's study or workshop.

PAINTING—*Verbs.*

Chalk out. To outline in the rough.

Color. To give colors to; paint.

Dash off. To sketch rapidly.

Dead color. To deprive of its glossiness.

Depict. To delineate; portray.

Design. To draw something with an end in view

Draw. To make a diagram of, as with a pencil.

Draw in pencil. See *Nouns*.

Hatch. To mark with hatchings or to fill with cross lines for purposes of shading.

Limn. To draw or decorate.

Paint. To represent in colors.

Paint in oils. See *Nouns*.

Pencil. To draw as with a pencil.

Scratch. To draw clumsily.

Shade. To cause to blend by gradations

Sketch. To draw rapidly an outline of an object.

Square up. To put on the last touches.

Stencil. To make or decorate as with a stencil.

Stipple. To sketch with dots instead of lines.

Varnish. To cover with varnish; make glossy.

Wash. To spread India ink over surface of.

PAINTING—*Adjectives.*

Graphic. Pertaining to writing or drawing.

Oil. Covering with oil. See *Nouns*.

Painting. Drawing in colors. See *Verbs*.

Pencil. Made with a pencil.

Pictorial. Of or characteristic of a picture.

Picturesque. Having the beauty of a picture.

PAINTING—*Adverb*

In pencil. See *Nouns*.

PAINTING—*Phrases*

Delineavit [L.]. He painted it.

Fecit [L.]. He made it.

Mutum est pictura poema [L.] A picture is a mute poem

pair. Two of anything. DUALITY, LIKENESS-UNLIKENESS; **pair off**, MATRIMONY-CELIBACY, MEDIUM

pair'-oar. A boat. CONVEYANCE-VESSEL.

pairs. A game of cards. ENTERTAINMENT-WEARINESS.

Paix'-han. A French general. **Paixhan gun**, WEAPON.

pájaro en mano que buitre volando, más vale [Sp.] (pa'-har-o en ma'-no kê bu-i'-trê vo-lan'-do, mas val'-ê). A sparrow on the hand is better than a vulture on the wing. CERTAINTY-DOUBT.

pal. A chum. ANTAGONIST-ASSISTANT, FRIEND-FOE.

pal'-ace. A grand house DUALITY, **bishop's palace,** FANE.

pal'-a-din. A paragon of knighthood ATTACK-DEFENSE, BELLIGERENT.

pa''-læ-o-crys'-tic. Pertaining to ice that exists from year to year. NOVELTY-ANTIQUITY.

pa''-læ-ol'-o-gy. The study of antiquity FUTURE-PAST, LANGUAGE, WORD-NEOLOGY.

pa-læs'-tra. A wrestling-court. LISTS, SCHOOL.

pa-læ''-ti-ol'-o-gy. Oratory as taught in the Greek gymnasium. FUTURE-PAST

palais de vérité [F.] (pɑ-lê' de vê-ri-tê'). The palace of truth. CRAFT-ARTLESSNESS.

pal''-an-quin'. Oriental carriage borne on men's shoulders. CONVEYANCE-VESSEL.

pal'-a-ta-ble. Agreeable to the taste. PALATABLENESS-UNPALATABLENESS, PLEASURABLENESS-PAINFULNESS, SAVOR-TASTELESSNESS, SENSUALITY-SUFFERING.

pal'-a-ta-ble-ness. The quality of being palatable. PALATABLENESS-UNPALATABLENESS.

PALATABLENESS—UNPALATABLENESS.

Relish. The sensation of pleasant taste.
Savoriness. The quality of being pleasant to the taste or smell.
Zest. An agreeable flavor, especially that added to give piquancy

PALATABLENESS—Denotations.

Ambrosia. The immortality-giving food of the gods, sometimes supposed to be used as an unguent.
Bonne bouche [F.]. A delicate morsel.
Dainty. A luscious morsel.
Delicacy. A luxury or dainty.
Game. The flesh of wild animals prepared for food.
Nectar. The drink of the gods.
Tit-bit. A morsel of choice food.
Turtle. The flesh of the turtle prepared for food.
Venison. The flesh of deer prepared for food.

PALATABLENESS—Verbs

Be savory, etc. See *Adjectives*.
Flatter the palate. To have a very agreeable taste.
Like. To enjoy the taste of.
Relish. To like the taste of.
Render palatable. To make pleasing to the taste See *Adjectives*
Smack the lips. To take pleasure in eating.
Tickle the appetite. To have a very agreeable taste
Tickle the palate. To be agreeable to the taste.

PALATABLENESS—Adjectives.

Ambrosial. Divinely flavored.
Appetizing. Tending to increase or please the appetite.
Dainty. Having a refined, delicate taste.
Delectable. Capable of being greatly enjoyed.
Delicate. Refinedly pleasing to the taste.
Delicious. Extremely delightful to the sense of taste.
Exquisite. Characterized by a very delicate flavor.
Good. Having a pleasant savor
Gustful. Having a good taste.
Lickerish. Tempting the appetite.
Luscious. Exceedingly delightful to the sense of taste.
Nice. Having a pure, refined taste.
Palatable. Capable of being eaten with a relish.
Rich. Having many qualities that are pleasant to the taste.
Savory. Having a pleasing flavor.
Tasty. Having a fine taste.
To one's taste. Agreeable to one's taste
Toothful. } Eaten with enjoyment.
Toothsome. }
Well-tasted. With a good taste.

PALATABLENESS—Phrases.

Cela se laisse manger [F.]. This is fit to eat.
Per amusare la bocca [It.] To please the palate.

Acerbity. Sourness combined with bitterness.
Acrimony. Extreme bitterness of taste.
Acritude. The quality of being sharp or biting to the taste.
Amaritude. Bitterness.
Austerity. Sourness of taste.
Gall and wormwood. Intense bitterness.
Roughness. Astringency or harshness to the taste. See SWEETNESS-ACIDITY.
Sickener. Anything that tends to sicken or nauseate.
Unsavoriness. The quality of having no flavor; tasteless.

UNPALATABLENESS—Denotations.

Aloes. An intensely bitter resinous substance.
Asafetida. The dried juice of certain plants, having an exceedingly offensive odor and bitter taste.
Quassia. The bitter wood of the bitter ash.
Rue. A very bitter, acrid plant.

UNPALATABLENESS—Verbs.

Be unpalatable. Unpleasant to the taste. See *Adjectives*.
Disgust. To offend the sense of taste.
Nauseate. To cause nausea or disgust.
Pall. To be insipid and tasteless.
Sicken. To cause to be sick.
Turn the stomach. Cause stomach sickness.

UNPALATABLENESS—Adjectives.

Acrid. Having a biting, burning taste
Acrimonious. Very bitter.
Bitter. Having a biting, unpleasant taste, as of gall or aloes.
Bitter as gall. Bitter, like gall.
Ill-flavored. Not having a good taste.
Loath. Filled with disgust or aversion.
Loathfulsome. Causing an intense feeling of dislike.
Nasty. Disgusting to the sense of taste.
Nauseous. Causing sickness of the stomach.
Offensive. Extremely unpleasant.
Repulsive. Causing extreme dislike for.
Rough. Causing a puckering feeling in the mouth.
Sickening. See *Verbs*.
Unpalatable. Unpleasant to the taste.
Unpleasant. Disliked. See PLEASURABLENESS-PAINFULNESS.
Unsavory. Without taste.
Unsweet. Bitter or sour.

pal'-ate. The seat of taste. SAVOR-TASTELESSNESS; **tickle the palate,** PALATABLENESS-UNPALATABLENESS, PLEASURABLENESS-PAINFULNESS, SAVOR-TASTELESSNESS.

pa-la'-tial. Grand; pertaining to a palace. DWELLER-HABITATION, POMP.

pa-lat'-i-nate. A political division ruled over by a prince. RULE-LICENSE.

pal'-a-tine–court. A high judicial function. TRIBUNAL.

pa-la'-ver. Idle talk. CONVERSATION-MONOLOGUE, COUNCIL, MEANING-JARGON, SPEECH-INARTICULATENESS, TALKATIVENESS-TACITURNITY.

pale. A picket; wan. BOUNDARY, COLOR-ACHROMATISM, DIMNESS, ENCLOSURE, EXTENSION-DISTRICT, SANGUINENESS-TIMIDITY, **pale its ineffectual fire,** DIMNESS, REPUTATION-DISCREDIT; **pale of the church,** CHURCH; **turn pale,** COLOR-ACHROMATISM, EMOTION, SANGUINENESS-TIMIDITY.

pale'-faced. Having a pale face. COLOR-ACHROMATISM.

pale'-ness. A pale color. COLOR-ACHROMATISM, DIMNESS.

pa''-le-og'-ra-phy. Ancient writings. FUTURE-PAST, LANGUAGE.

pa''-le-ol'-o-gy. The study of antiquity. FUTURE-PAST, LANGUAGE, WORD-NEOLOGY.

pa''-le-on-tol'-o-gy. The branch of biology that treats of the ancient life of the globe. FUTURE-PAST, GEOLOGY, ZOOLOGY-BOTANY.

pa″-le-o-zo′-ic. Pertaining to the lowest geological age. NOVELTY-ANTIQUITY; **paleozoic period,** GEOLOGY.

pa-les′-tric. Pertaining to wrestling. STRIFE-PEACE, TOIL-RELAXATION.

pa-les′-tric-al. Pertaining to wrestling. STRIFE-PEACE.

pal′-e-tot. A loose overcoat. DRESS-UNDRESS.

pal′-ette. A small oval board on which a painter mixes his colors. PAINTING.

pal′-frey. A saddle-horse, especially for ladies. CONVEYER.

pal′-imp-sest. A parchment written upon twice. COMMUTATION-PERMUTATION.

pal′-in-drome. A word or words that read the same forward or backward. REVERSAL, WORD-NEOLOGY.

pa′-ling. A picket; an enclosure. ATTACK-DEFENSE, ENCLOSURE, RELEASE-PRISON.

pal″-in-ge-ne′-si-a. Regeneration. RENEWAL.

pal″-in-gen′-e-sis. A new birth into a higher life. RENOVATION-RELAPSE.

pal′-i-node. A metrical recantation. BIGOTRY-APOSTASY.

pal′-i-no″-dy. Retracting. BIGOTRY-APOSTASY.

pal″-i-sade′. A fortification of stakes. ATTACK-DEFENSE, RELEASE-PRISON.

pall. A cloak; a covering for the dead; distasteful. DESIRE-DISTASTE, DESIRE-REPLETION, DRESS-UNDRESS, ENTERTAINMENT-WEARINESS, FEELING-INSENSIBILITY, LIFE-FUNERAL, PALATABLENESS-UNPALATABLENESS, SCEPTER, VESTMENTS.

pal-la′-di-um. A safeguard. SECURITY-INSECURITY.

pal′-let. A small bed. SUSPENSION-SUPPORT

pal′-li-a-ment. A robe. DRESS-UNDRESS.

pal′-li-ate. Extenuate; abate. ALLEVIATION-AGGRAVATION, BETTERMENT-DETERIORATION, JUSTIFICATION-CHARGE, REMEDY-BANE, TURBULENCE-CALMNESS.

pal″-li-a′-tion. Alleviation. ALLEVIATION-AGGRAVATION, JUSTIFICATION-CHARGE.

pal′-li-a-tive. Relieving. ALLEVIATION-AGGRAVATION, REMEDY-BANE.

pal′-lid. Wan. COLOR-ACHROMATISM.

pal-lid′-i-ty. Paleness. COLOR-ACHROMATISM.

pal′-li-um. A mantle worn by the clergy. VESTMENTS.

pall″-mall′. A game. ENTERTAINMENT-WEARINESS.

pal-lo′-ne. A game resembling tennis. ENTERTAINMENT-WEARINESS.

pal′-lor. Paleness. COLOR-ACHROMATISM.

palm. To steal; a trophy. LENGTH-SHORTNESS, THEFT, TITLE, TROPHY; **bear the palm,** REPUTATION-DISCREDIT; **grease the palm,** GIVING-RECEIVING, MOTIVE-CAPRICE, SETTLEMENT-DEFAULT; **itching palm,** DESIRE-DISTASTE, EXTRAVAGANCE-AVARICE; **palm off,** TRUTHFULNESS-FRAUD; **palm upon,** TRUTHFULNESS-FRAUD; **win the palm,** SUCCESS-FAILURE.

pal′-ma-ted. Resembling the hand. INDENTATION.

palm′-er. A wandering religious votary. MINISTRY-LAITY, WAYFARER-SEAFARER.

pal′-mis-try. The pretended art of reading one's future by the marks in the palm of the hand. PROPHECY.

palm′-y. Flourishing. LIGHTHEARTEDNESS-DEJECTION, PLEASURABLENESS-PAINFULNESS, WELFARE-MISFORTUNE; **palmy days,** PLEASURE-PAIN, WELFARE-MISFORTUNE.

pal″-pa-bil′-i-ty. Perceptibility by touch. TOUCH.

pal′-pa-ble. Obvious; perceptible by touch. MANIFESTATION-LATENCY, MATERIALITY-SPIRITUALITY, TOUCH, VISIBILITY-INVISIBILITY; **palpable obscure,** LIGHT-DARKNESS.

pal-pa′-tion. A digital exploration. TOUCH.

pal′-pi-tate. To beat quickly. AGITATION, EMOTION, SANGUINENESS-TIMIDITY.

pal″-pi-ta′-tion. Rapid pulsation. AGITATION, EMOTION, SANGUINENESS-TIMIDITY.

pal′-sied. Paralytic. FEELING-INSENSIBILITY, HEALTH-SICKNESS, MIGHT-IMPOTENCE, STRENGTH-WEAKNESS.

pal′-sy. Paralysis. FEELING-INSENSIBILITY, HEALTH-SICKNESS, MIGHT-IMPOTENCE, SENSITIVENESS-APATHY.

pal′-sy–strick″-en. Paralyzed. SENSITIVENESS-APATHY.

pal′-ter. Trifle. DETERMINATION-VACILLATION, OBSERVANCE-NONOBSERVANCE, TRUTHFULNESS-FALSEHOOD.

pal′-tri-ness. Trifling. CONSEQUENCE-INSIGNIFICANCE.

pal′-try. Mean; worthless. CONSEQUENCE-INSIGNIFICANCE, MAGNITUDE-SMALLNESS, UPRIGHTNESS-DISHONESTY.

pal′-u-dal. Fenny. SWAMP-ISLAND.

pam′-pas. The great plains of South America. GULF-PLAIN.

pam′-per. To glut. FASTING-GLUTTONY, MODERATION-SELFINDULGENCE.

pam′-pered. Indulged. FASTING-GLUTTONY, MODERATION-SELFINDULGENCE.

pam′-phlet. A small book. MISSIVE-PUBLICATION

pam″-phlet-eer′. A scribbler. ESSAY.

pan. A shallow, open dish. CONTENTS-RECEIVER.

pan″-a-ce′-a. A cure-all. REMEDY-BANE.

pa″-nache′. A plume. EMBELLISHMENT-DISFIGUREMENT, SMOOTHNESS-ROUGHNESS.

Pan″-A-mer′-i-can. Including the whole of America. UNIVERSALITY-PARTICULARITY.

pan′-cre-as. Gland of the body. ANATOMY.

pan″-cre-at′-ic. Pertaining to the pancreas. ANATOMY

pan′-dar. A procurer. PURITY-RAKE.

Pan-de′-an. Pertaining to Pan. **Pandean pipes,** MUSICAL INSTRUMENTS.

pan′-dect. A treatise. DIGEST, ESSAY, KNOWLEDGE-IGNORANCE, LAW-LAWLESSNESS.

pan″-de-mo′-ni-um. The abode of all demons. HEAVEN-HELL; **inhabitants of pandemonium,** ANGEL-SATAN.

pan′-der. To minister to the evil designs of others. PURITY-RAKE; **pander to,** ADULATION-DISPARAGEMENT, INSTRUMENTALITY, OBSTRUCTION-HELP.

pan″-dic-u-la′-tion. The act of stretching the body and limbs; yawning. ACTIVITY-INDOLENCE, APERTURE-CLOSURE, ENLARGEMENT-DIMINUTION.

pan′-door. An inhuman soldier. BELLIGERENT.

Pan-do′-ra. A beautiful woman in classical mythology. **Bottom of Pandora's box,** SANGUINENESS-HOPELESSNESS; **Pandora's box,** GOOD-EVIL.

paned. Having panels of a different color from the rest of the fabric. VARIEGATION.

pan″-e-gyr′-ic. Eulogy. APPROVAL-DISAPPROVAL, RHETORIC.

pan″-e-gyr′-ic-al. A eulogy. APPROVAL-DISAPPROVAL.

pan′-e-gy-rize. To pronounce a panegyric on. APPROVAL-DISAPPROVAL.

pan′-el. Square of wainscot; jury-roll. ENVIRONMENT-INTERPOSITION, JUSTIFICATION-CHARGE, RECORD; **sliding panel,** TRUTHFULNESS-FRAUD.

pan′-el-ing. Work in panels. EMBELLISHMENT-DISFIGUREMENT.

pang. A pain. PLEASURE-PAIN, SENSUALITY-SUFFERING.

Pan′-gloss. A character in Voltaire's *Candide.* SCHOLAR-DUNCE.

pan″-har-mon′-ic. Embracing all harmony. UNIVERSALITY-PARTICULARITY.

pan′-ic. Sudden fright. SANGUINENESS-TIMIDITY.

pan′-ic–strick″-en. Stricken with panic. SANGUINENESS-TIMIDITY.

pan'-ic–struck''. Struck with panic SANGUINENESS-TIMIDITY.

pan'-ier. Bustle for a woman's dress. DRESS-UNDRESS.

pan'-nel. A rustic saddle. ERECTNESS-FLATNESS, SUSPENSION-SUPPORT.

pan'-nier. A wicker basket. CONTENTS-RECEIVER.

pan'-o-plied. Arranged in complete armor. ATTACK-DEFENSE, SECURITY-INSECURITY.

pan'-o-ply. Armament. ATTACK-DEFENSE, WEAPON

pan-op'-ti-con. A prison. RELEASE-PRISON.

pan-o-ra'-ma. Complete view. APPEARANCE-DISAPPEARANCE, PAINTING.

pan-o-ram'-ic. Like a panorama VISIBILITY-INVISIBILITY.

Pan''-slav'-ic. Pertaining to all the peoples of Slavic blood UNIVERSALITY-PARTICULARITY.

pan'-so-phy. A scheme of universal knowledge KNOWLEDGE-IGNORANCE.

pant. To breathe quickly. EMOTION, HEAT-COLD, WEARINESS-REFRESHMENT; **pant for,** DESIRE-DISTASTE.

pan''-ta-loon'. A buffoon. ACTING, INFANT-VETERAN, WAG.

pan''-ta-loons'. Trousers. DRESS-UNDRESS.

pan'-the-ism. The doctrine that the universe is God. ORTHODOXY-HETERODOXY.

pan'-the-ist. A believer in pantheism. ORTHODOXY-HETERODOXY.

pan''-the-is'-tic. Relating to pantheism ORTHODOXY-HETERODOXY.

Pan'-the-on. A circular temple at Rome. FANE, JOVE-FIEND.

pan'-ther. A leopard. BRAVERY-COWARDICE.

pan'-tile. A peculiar tile. COVER-LINING, WATERCOURSE-AIRPIPE.

pant'-ing. Quick breathing. EMOTION.

pan''-ti-soc'-ra-cy. Equal rank and authority for all. GENTILITY-COMMONALTY, RULE-LICENSE.

pan-tol'-o-gist. An expert in pantology. ADEPT-BUNGLER, SCHOLAR-DUNCE.

pan-tol'-o-gy. A system involving all departments of human knowledge. KNOWLEDGE-IGNORANCE.

pan-tom'-e-ter. An instrument for measuring angles and determining perpendiculars. MENSURATION.

pan'-to-mime. A series of actions used to express ideas. ACTING, LANGUAGE, SIGN.

pan''-to-mim'-ic. A series of actions used to express ideas. SIGN.

pan'-to-mim''-ist. One who employs pantomime. ACTING, SOCIETY-LAUGHINGSTOCK.

pan'-try. Closet for provisions. CONTENTS-RECEIVER.

pan'-ur-gy. Universal skilfulness. SKILL-UNSKILFULNESS.

pap. A teat; soft food for infants. CONVEXITY-CONCAVITY, PULPINESS-OILINESS.

pa-pa'. Father. PARENTAGE-PROGENY.

Pa-pa'. The pope. MINISTRY-LAITY.

pa'-pa-cy. Office of the pope. ORTHODOXY-HETERODOXY.

pa'-pal. Belonging to the pope. CHURCH.

pa'-per. A substance for writing or printing on; written promises to pay. COVER-LINING, MISSIVE-PUBLICATION, SECURITY, WHITENESS - BLACKNESS, WRITING - PRINTING; **paper credit,** CREDIT - DEBT; **paper money,** MONEY; **paper pellet,** CONSEQUENCE-INSIGNIFICANCE; **paper war,** RATIOCINATION-INSTINCT, STRIFE-PEACE.

pap-es'-cent. Containing pap. PULPINESS-OILINESS.

Pa'-phi-an. A prostitute. MODERATION-SELFINDULGENCE, PURITY-IMPURITY.

pa-pil'-la. The nipple of the mammary glands. CONVEXITY-CONCAVITY.

pa'-pism. Papacy. ORTHODOXY-HETERODOXY.

pa'-pist-ry. The religion of the papists. ORTHODOXY-HETERODOXY.

pap-oose'. A North-American Indian infant. INFANT-VETERAN.

pap'-pous. Having a pappus or down SMOOTHNESS-ROUGHNESS.

pap'-u-la. A pimple. CONVEXITY-CONCAVITY.

pap'-u-lose. Full of papulæ. CONVEXITY-CONCAVITY.

pap'-u-lous. Full of papulæ CONVEXITY-CONCAVITY.

pa-py'-rus. The writing-paper of the ancient Egyptians WRITING-PRINTING

par. State of equality. EQUALITY-INEQUALITY; **above par,** GOODNESS-BADNESS; **below par,** FAULTLESSNESS-FAULTINESS, GOODNESS-BADNESS, HEIGHTLOWNESS

par excellence [F.] (par ec''-se-lan·s'). Preeminently. CONSEQUENCE-INSIGNIFICANCE, SUPREMACY-SUBORDINACY.

par le roi, de [F.] (par le rwa, de) In the king's name. RULE-LICENSE.

par nobile fratrum [L.] (par nob'-i-lî frê'-trum). A noble pair of brothers. FRIEND-FOE, LIKENESS-UNLIKENESS.

par parenthèse [F.] (par pa-ran·-tez'). Parenthetically. OPPORTUNENESS-UNSUITABLENESS.

par pari refero [L.] (par pê-rai ref'-er-o). I return like for like. REPRISAL-RESISTANCE.

par'-a-ble. A moral fable. ACCOUNT, EDUCATION-MISTEACHING, TROPE.

pa-rab'-o-la. One of the conic sections. CURVATION-RECTILINEARITY.

par'-a-bol-ic. Expressed by parable. TROPE.

par''-a-cen-te'-sis. The operation of drawing off fluid, as in dropsy. ADMISSION-EXPULSION.

par-ach'-ro-nism. A chronological error by which a date is placed too late. CHRONOLOGY-ANACHRONISM.

par'-a-chute. An apparatus for descending from a balloon. CONVEYANCE-VESSEL, REFUGE-PITFALL.

Par'-a-clete. The Comforter. DIVINITY.

pa-rade'. A showy exhibition. DWELLER-HABITATION, POMP.

par'-a-digm. A model. COPY-MODEL.

par'-a-dise. Heaven; place of bliss. HEAVEN-HELL, PLEASURE-PAIN; **fool's paradise,** SANGUINENESS-TIMIDITY; **in paradise,** PLEASURE-PAIN.

par''-a-di-si'-a-cal. Blissful. HEAVEN-HELL

par'-a-dox. A tenet seemingly absurd, yet true. ADAGE-NONSENSE, CLEARNESS-OBSCURITY, DIFFICULTY-FACILITY, TIDINGS-MYSTERY.

par-a-dox'-ic-al. Having the nature of a paradox. CERTAINTY-DOUBT, CLEARNESS-OBSCURITY.

par'-af-fin. A waxy substance obtained from tar PULPINESS-ROSIN.

par''-a-gen'-e-sis. Branch of chemical geology. GEOLOGY.

par''-a-go'-ge. Rhetorical figure. RHETORIC.

par'-a-gon. A model of perfection. FAULTLESSNESS-FAULTINESS, GOOD MAN-BAD MAN, REPUTATION-DISCREDIT.

par'-a-gram. A pun. AMBIGUITY, WORD-NEOLOGY.

par'-a-graph. A part of a discourse; a mark. MISSIVE-PUBLICATION, PHRASE, RHETORIC, WHOLE-PART.

par''-a-leip'-sis. A feigned omission. CAREFULNESS-CARELESSNESS.

par'-al-lax. Such difference of position of a heavenly body as would appear if viewed from two points. ASTRONOMY, REMOTENESS-NEARNESS.

par'-al-lel. Extending in the same direction but never meeting. COMPARISON, IMITATION-ORIGINALITY, LIKENESS-UNLIKENESS, PARALLELISM-INCLINATION,

PROPORTION-DEFORMITY; **draw a parallel,** COMPARISON; **none but himself can be his parallel,** REPUTATION-DISCREDIT; **run parallel,** COOPERATION-OPPOSITION.

par'-al-lel-ism. State of being parallel. HARMONY-DISCORD, LIKENESS-UNLIKENESS, PARALLELISM-INCLINATION, PROPORTION-DEFORMITY, VARIANCE-ACCORD.

PARALLELISM—INCLINATION.

Coextension. The act or state of being equal or of having the same limits.
Parallelism. State of being parallel; resemblance.

PARALLELISM—*Adjectives.*

Coextensive. Extending equally; having same limits.
Parallel. Running side by side in same direction; similar.

PARALLELISM—*Adverb*

Alongside. Lying by the side of. See LATERALITY

INCLINATION—VERBS—*Continued from Column 2*

Render oblique. To move away from the perpendicular.
Sag. To bend down in the middle; lean from its own weight.
Seel. To lean to the side; careen, heel
Shelve. To tilt; slope by degrees.
Sidle. To move with the side in the front
Slant. To turn from a direct line.
Slope. To incline from a given line.
Slouch. To walk leaning forward and in an awkward manner.
Stoop. To incline forward with old age or from disease
Swag. To have a swaying motion
Sway. To move from side to side.
Tilt. To push forward; incline from an upright position

INCLINATION—*Adjectives.*

Abrupt. Broken off suddenly; steep; broken.
Acclivous. Sloping upward.
Ajee. Turned to one side, awry
Anticlinal. Inclining in two directions
Antiparallel. Parallel, but in different directions.
Ascending. Moving upward.
Askew. In an inclining manner; awry
Aslant. In a slanting position.
Athwart. In a transverse manner; across
Awry. To one side; atwist
Bevel. Sloping off, oblique
Breakneck. Endangering the neck or life of one.
Clinal. Inclining.
Crooked. Bent; not straight, as in conduct.
Curved. Having no angles or corners See CURVATION
Declining Bending downward.
Declivous. Opposed to acclivous.
Descending. Moving downward and in a sloping manner.
Devex. Bending downward
Diagonal. Drawn obliquely; passing from corner to opposite corner
Downbill. Sloping down
Falling. Going from higher to lower spot, descending.
Inclined. Leaning forward biased
Indirect. Not direct, crooked, oblique.
Knock-kneed. Having the knees sagging together See PROPORTION-DEFORMITY
Oblique. Leaning from the vertical indirect
Out of the perpendicular. Oblique
Plagiedral. Having an oblique spiral arrangement of planes.
Precipitous Sloping greatly, steep.
Recumbent. Lying back; leaning.
Rising. Moving upward; ascending
Skew. Shaped in an oblique manner
Slant. Inclined from a straight line, sloping.
Sloping. Inclined to the horizontal See *Verbs*
Steep. Greatly sloping; precipitous
Tilted. Pushed forward; raised as to one end out of the horizontal. See *Verbs*
Transversal. Running crosswise
Transverse. Lying in an athwart position
Uphill. Moving up; ascending.
Wry. Twisted to one side; distorted

INCLINATION—*Adverbs, etc.*

All on one side. Leaning very much.
Askance.⎫ Obliquely
Askant. ⎭
Askew. In a twisted manner
At an angle. Sloping.

Acclivity. A sloping; an inclining.
Ascent. A gradual rising.
Bend. The act of crooking; a crook; a turning from the straight line. See CURVATION.
Bevel. An inclination of two surfaces to each other.
Bias. A bending from the straight line, prejudice.
Cant. An inclination from a horizontal line
Crookedness. State of being crooked or bent See *Adjectives.*
Declivity. A downward decline; a sloping downward.
Devexity. A sloping downward, a declivity.
Dip. Inclination or slope
Distortion. The act of twisting aside. See PROPORTION-DEFORMITY
Downhill. A slope
Easy ascent. A slight inclination.
Easy descent. A gradual slope.
Gentle slope. A slight incline.
Gradient. A grade.
Inclination. Deflection from a given direction, mental divergence; bias.
Leaning. State of being inclined from a vertical position. See *Verbs*
List. Inclination to one side; a careening.
Lurch. A sudden deviation from its true course
Obliquity. Deviation from the horizontal or vertical; mental crookedness
Rapid slope. A steep incline.
Rise. A gradual ascent
Slant. A leaning obliquely.
Slope. Any surface inclining to the plane of the horizon.
Slopeness. The state of being a slope
Steepness. Great inclination to the horizon See *Adjectives*
Swag. A swaying motion
Tilt. An inclination from the perpendicular
Twist. A turning, state of being twisted
Zigzag. A series of short sharp turns from one side to another

INCLINATION—*Scientific Nouns*

Angle. An opening between two lines that meet, or will meet if prolonged
Clinometer. An instrument for measuring angular inclination.
Cosine. A function of trigonometry; in a right triangle it is the adjacent side divided by hypotenuse.
Cotangent. A trigonometrical function
Hypotenuse. The side of a right-angled triangle opposite to the right angle.
Sine. A trigonometrical function

INCLINATION—*Denotations.*

Bank. The slope of a hillside
Cliff. A steep slope.
Diagonal. A straight line or plane passing from one angle or corner to an angle or corner not adjacent to it.
Escarpment. A steep slope.
Facilis descensus Averni [L.] The easy descent to Avernus.
Hill. A natural elevation of earth.
Montagne Russe [F.] Russian mountain, suitable for coasting.
Precipice. A high and very steep cliff See ERECTNESS
Scarp. A steep slope.
Shelving beach. A ledge that forms shelves.
Tower of Pisa. A tower at Pisa, Italy, that leans out of the perpendicular

INCLINATION—*Verbs*

Bend. To make crooked; deflect
Be oblique. See *Adjectives.*
Bias. To swerve in rolling.
Cant. To incline forward; tilt.
Careen. To incline to one side: said of a ship.
Crook. To make crooked; bend.
Decline. To bend downward or aside.
Descend. To climb down; go from higher to lower.
Distort. To twist awry; turn aside from true meaning See PROPORTION-DEFORMITY.
Heel. To incline to one side.
Incline. To cause to lean from the erect position; bend.
Lean. To move out of erect posture; incline forward or backward.

(Continued on Column 1.)

INCLINATION—Adverbs—*Continued.*

By a side wind. Obliquely.
Edgewise. In the direction of the edge.
Obliquely. Slantingly. See *Adjectives.*
On one side. Leaning.

Sidelong. Along the side.
Sideways. In the direction of the side.
Slantwise.}
Slopewise.} Obliquely.

---

par″-al-lel′-o-gram. A quadrilateral whose opposite sides are parallel. ANGULARITY.

par″-al-lel-o-pi′-ped. A regular solid bounded by six parallelograms, the opposite ones parallel and equal. ANGULARITY.

par-al′-o-gism. Any act of false reasoning. RATIOCI-NATION-INSTINCT.

par-al′-o-gy. False reasoning. RATIOCINATION-IN-STINCT.

par-al′-y-sis. Loss of voluntary motion. FEELING-INSENSIBILITY, HEALTH-SICKNESS, MIGHT-IMPO-TENCE, SENSITIVENESS-APATHY.

par″-a-lyt′-ic. Affected with paralysis. FEELING-IN-SENSIBILITY, HEALTH-SICKNESS, MIGHT-IMPOTENCE.

par′-a-lyze. To affect with paralysis. FEELING-IN-SENSIBILITY, MIGHT-IMPOTENCE, SENSITIVENESS-APATHY.

par′-a-lyzed. Affected with paralysis. MIGHT-IMPO-TENCE.

par-am′-e-ter. Term used in study of crystals. MIN-ERALOGY.

par′-a-mount. Chief. CONSEQUENCE-INSIGNIFI-CANCE, RULE-LICENSE, SUPREMACY-SUBORDINACY; **lord paramount,** CHIEF-UNDERLING, HOLDER; **paramount estate,** PROPERTY.

par′-a-mour. A lover in a bad sense. LOVE-HATE.

par′-a-no-ma′-si-a. See PARONOMASIA.

par′-a-pet. Breastwork. ATTACK-DEFENSE.

par′-aph. To sign the initials. SIGN.

par″-a-pher-na′-li-a. Ornaments. INSTRUMENT, PROPERTY.

par′-a-phrase. A loose or free translation. COPY-MODEL, IMITATION-ORIGINALITY, MARK-OBLITERA-TION, PHRASE.

par′-a-phrast. One who paraphrases. INTERPRETER.

par′-a-phras″-tic. Like a paraphrase. IMITATION-ORIGINALITY, INTERPRETATION-MISINTERPRETATION.

par′-a-site. A hanger-on. CHIEF-UNDERLING, FLAT-TERER-DEFAMER, PRESUMPTION-OBSEQUIOUSNESS.

par″-a-sit′-ic. Living on another. LIBERTY-SUBJEC-TION, PRESUMPTION-OBSEQUIOUSNESS, TAKING-RES-TITUTION.

par″-a-sit′-ic-al. Living on another. LIBERTY-SUB-JECTION, PRESUMPTION-OBSEQUIOUSNESS.

par′-a-sol. A small umbrella. COVER-LINING, LUMI-NARY-SHADE.

par″-a-tax′-is. The arrangement of clauses without connectives. GRAMMAR-SOLECISM.

par-ath′-e-sis. Apposition, as of nouns. GRAMMAR-SOLECISM.

paratus, in utrumque [L.] (pa-rê′-tus, in yu-trum′-que). Prepared for either alternative. DETERMINATION-VACILLATION, PREPARATION-NONPREPARATION.

paratus, semper [L.] (pa-rê′-tus, sem′-per). Always prepared. PREPARATION-NONPREPARATION.

parbleu [F.] (par′-blu). A polite French oath. CHARI-TABLENESS-CURSE, TASTE-VULGARITY.

par′-boil″. To boil partially. HEATING-COOLING.

par′-buck″-le. An apparatus for rolling barrels or heavy objects up or down an incline. OBSTRUCTION-HELP.

Par′-cæ. The Latin name of the Fates. VOLITION-OBLIGATION.

par′-cel. A bundle. GATHERING-SCATTERING, WHOLE-PART; **parcel out,** ASSIGNMENT, ORGANIZATION-DIS-ORGANIZATION; **part and parcel,** CONSTITUENT-ALIEN.

par′-cels. Collections of anything. PROPERTY.

parcere subjectis [L.] (par′-ser-î sub-jec′-tis). To spare the conquered. COMPASSION-RUTHLESSNESS, HARSH-NESS-MILDNESS.

parch. To scorch; extremely dry. DAMPNESS-DRY-NESS, HEAT-COLD, HEATING-COOLING.

parched. Scorched. **Parched with thirst,** DESIRE-DIS-TASTE.

parch′-ment. Skin prepared for writing on. SECURITY, WRITING-PRINTING.

par′-ci-ty. Frugality. EXTRAVAGANCE-AVARICE.

par′-don. Forgiveness. EXCULPATION-CONVICTION, PARDON-VINDICTIVENESS; **beg pardon,** ATONEMENT; **pardon me,** ASSENT-DISSENT.

PARDON—VINDICTIVENESS—JEALOUSY—ENVY.

Absolution. Remission of sin by authority of the priestly office.

Act of indemnity. An act or law passed in order to relieve persons, especially in an official station, from some penalty to which they are liable in consequence of acting illegally.

Amantium iræ [L.]. Lovers' quarrels.

Amnesty. Pardon by the chief executive to a whole class of offenders against the state.

Bill of indemnity. See ACT OF INDEMNITY.

Conciliation. Gaining the good will of.

Condonation. Forgiveness by one of a married couple to the other for breach of married duty.

Covenant of indemnity.} A legal agreement granting release of an
Deed of indemnity.} obligation.

Exculpation. The act of freeing from blame.

Excuse. Overlooking small faults.

Exoneration. A freeing or freedom from a charge, accusation, etc.

Forgiveness. Foregoing of punishment, and extinguishment of resentment.

Grace. Divine favor toward man.

Indemnity. That which is paid for a loss.

Indulgence. Forbearance of restraint or control.

Locus pœnitentiæ [L.]. Place for repentance.

Longanimity. Disposition to bear injuries patiently.

Oblivion. Public remission and pardon of offenses.

Pardon. Removal of penalty of one found guilty.

Placability. Willingness to be appeased.

Propitiation. Act of appeasing and rendering favorable.

Avengeance.}
Avengement.} Retributive punishment.

Blood for blood. Revenge.

Day of reckoning. Time for judgment.

Implacability. Quality of being unappeasable.

Malevolence. See CHARITABLENESS-MALEVOLENCE.

Rancor. Bitter, deep-rooted enmity.

Retaliation. Giving back like for like.

Revenge. Punishment inflicted in a malignant spirit.

Ruthlessness. Want of compassion

Sweet revenge. Revenge regarded as satisfying an angry passion.

Vendetta [It.]. A blood-feud.

Vengeance. Passionate and unsparing revenge.

Vindictiveness. Quality of having a revengeful spirit.

VINDICTIVENESS—*Nouns of Agent.*

Avenger. One who exacts satisfaction for

Eumenides. The Furies, the avengers of wrong in classic mythology.

Nemesis. A divinity of chastisement and vengeance in Greek myth-ology

Vindicator. One who inflicts punishment for wrong done.

VINDICTIVENESS—*Verbs.*

Avenge. To revenge passionately and without mercy.

Bear malice. To have malicious feelings.

Breathing revenge.}
Breathing vengeance.} To be full of revenge.

PARDON—VINDICTIVENESS—*Continued.*

Quittance. Release from debt or obligation.
Reconciliation. Making those friends again who are enemies.
Release. Discharge from responsibility or claim.
Remission. Act of not exacting the penalty; forgiveness.
Reprieve. Temporary withdrawal of sentence.

PARDON—*Verbs.*

Absolve. To set free or release, as from sins.
Acquit. To declare innocent.
Allow for. To excuse on account of.
Ask pardon. To beseech.
Bear with. To endure patiently.
Beg pardon. To ask forgiveness.
Conciliate. To gain the good will of.
Condone. To overlook.
Excuse. To overlook small faults.
Forget an injury. To forgive.
Forgive. To forego punishment and hold no resentment.
Forgive and forget. To pardon absolutely.
Give absolution. To forgive the sins or offenses of
Implore pardon. To ask forgiveness.
Let bygones be bygones. To forgive.
Let off. To pardon.
Let one down easily. To inflict light punishment.
Let the wound heal. To forgive.
Make allowances for. To excuse on account of.
Make up a quarrel. To be friends again
Not be too hard upon. To inflict light punishment.
Overlook. To purposely disregard.
Pardon. To remove penalty from one found guilty.
Passover. To cease to cherish displeasure.
Placate. To appease the wrath of.
Pocket the affront. Not to resent it.
Propitiate. To appease and render favorable.
Remit. To refrain from exacting or enforcing.
Reprieve. To withdraw sentence temporarily.
Shake hands. To be friends again.
Think no more of. To forgive and forget.
Wink at. To overlook.

PARDON—*Adjectives.*

Conciliated. Freed from resentment. See *Verbs.*
Conciliatory. Tending to make peace; pacific.
Forgiving. Prone to forgive.
Placable. Capable of being appeased.
Unavenged.
Unresented. } Permitted to pass by without seeking satisfaction for.
Unrevenged.

VINDICTIVENESS—Verbs—*Continued.*

Harbor revenge.
Harbor vindictive feeling. } To have a revengeful spirit.
Have accounts to settle.
Have a crow to pluck. } To have a grievance against some one.
Have a rod in pickle.
Have one's revenge. To take revenge.
Keep the wound green. To be unforgiving.
Rankle. To produce irritation.
Rankle in the breast. To have a bitter feeling against one.
Revenge. To inflict punishment in a malignant spirit.
Take revenge.
Wreak one's anger. } To inflict injury or pain maliciously in return for injury done.
Wreak one's vengeance.

VINDICTIVENESS—*Adjectives.*

Æternum servans sub pectore vulnus [L.]. A wound ever rankling in the breast.
Avenging. Disposed to avenge.
Immitigable. Not to be mitigated.
Implacable. Not to be appeased.
Inexorable. Not to be moved by entreaty.
Manet alta mente repostum [L.]. It remains deeply fixed in the mind.
Manet cicatrix [L.]. The scar remains.
Pitiless. Hard-hearted; cruel.
Rancorous. Bitter vindictive enmity.
Rankling. Irritating.
Remorseless. Without mercy.
Revengeful. Vindictive in mind.
Rigorous. Severe and exacting.
Ruthless. Cruel.
Stony-hearted. Pitiless or implacable.
Unforgiving. Not disposed to forgive
Unrelenting. Inexorable.
Vengeful.
Vindictive. } Disposed to take revenge.

VINDICTIVENESS—*Phrase.*

Dies iræ, dies illa [L.]. Judgment day.

PARDON—*Continued.*

PARDON—*Phrases.*

Comprendre c'est tout pardonner, tout [F.]. To understand all is to pardon all.
Cry you mercy.
Ignoscito sæpe alteri, nunquam tibi [L.]. Pardon another often, thyself never.
Veniam petimus damusque vicissim [L.]. Pardon we seek and give in turn. [Horace, *To Pisa,* XI.]

PARDON—JEALOUSY.

JEALOUSY.

Green-eyed monster. A figurative expression for jealousy.
Jaundiced eye. Disposition to be jealous.
Jealousness.
Jealousy. } Earnest and anxious suspicion.
Juno. The consort of Jupiter: very jealous goddess.
Yellows. Jealousy; a jealous frame of mind.

JEALOUSY—*Verbs.*

Be jealous. Disposed to suspect rivalry in matters of interest and affection.

View with a jealous eye.
View with jealousy. } To have a feeling of jealousy for.

JEALOUSY—*Adjectives.*

Horn-mad. Mad from being made a cuckold.
Jaundiced. Affected with jealousy.
Jealous. Filled with jealousy.
Jealous as a Barbary pigeon. Very jealous.
Yellow-eyed. Disposed to be jealous.

PARDON—ENVY.

ENVY.

Enviousness. See *Adjectives.*
Envy. Ill will toward another on account of his superior excellence, possessions, etc.
Jalousie de metier [F.]. Professional jealousy.
Rivalry. Striving to obtain the same object another is pursuing.

ENVY—*Verbs.*

Burst with envy. To be passionate with envy.
Covet. To desire eagerly; desire unlawfully.

Envy. To have ill will toward another on account of his superior excellence.

ENVY—*Adjectives.*

Alieni appetens [L.]. Coveting others' goods.
Covetous. Eagerly desirous; unlawfully desirous.
Envious. Displaying envy.
Invidious. Provoking envy or ill will.

ENVY—*Phrase.*

Cæca invidia est [L.] Envy is blind.

---

par'-don-a-ble. Excusable. JUSTIFICATION-CHARGE.
pare. To cut off; to remove the outside of anything. ADDITION-SUBTRACTION, DRESS-UNDRESS, ENLARGE-MENT-DIMINUTION, LAMINA-FIBER; **pare down,** LENGTH-SHORTNESS.
par''-e-gor'-ic. A medicine. REMEDY-BANE.

par-en'-chy-ma. The soft cellular substance of the glands. MATERIALITY-SPIRITUALITY, TEXTURE.

par'-ent. A father or mother. PARENTAGE-PROGENY.

par'-ent-age. Birth. PARENTAGE-PROGENY, RELATIONSHIP.

PARENTAGE—PROGENY.

Abba. Father.
Ancestor. One from whom a person is descended.
Ancestry. A series of ancestors.
Birth. Lineage; descent.
Clan. A collection of families regarded as having the same common ancestor.
Consanguinity. Relation by blood.
Dad. Father.
Dam. A female parent.
Descent. Procedure by generation.
Extraction. Derivation from a stock or family.
Family. Those who descend from one common progenitor.
Father. A male parent.
Forefather. One who precedes another in the line of genealogy.
Genealogy. Regular descent of a person or family from a progenitor.
Genitor. One who begets.
Godfather. A man who becomes sponsor for a child at baptism and makes himself a surety for its Christian training and instruction.
Godmother. A woman who becomes sponsor for a child at baptism.
Grandsire. A grandfather; any ancestor.
House. A family of ancestors, descendants, and kindred.
Line. A series or succession of ancestors.
Lineage. Descent in a line from a common progenitor.
Ma. Mother.
Mama. Mother.
Materfamilias [L.]. Mother of a family.
Maternity. The state of being a mother.
Mother. A female parent.
Motherhood. State of being a mother.
Papa. Father.
Parent. One who brings forth offspring.
Parentage. Relation of father and child.
Paterfamilias [L.]. Father of the family.
Paternity. State of being a parent.
Patriarch. One who governs his family and descendants by paternal right.
Pedigree. A line of ancestors.
Procreator. One who begets.
Progenitor. An ancestor in the direct line.
Race. The descendants of a common ancestor.
Sept. A clan.
Sire. A male parent.
Stem. A race or generation of progenitors.
Stirps. Stock; race
Stock. The race or line of a family.
Tree. Representation of ancestry in the form of a tree.
Tribe. A series of generations descending from the same progenitor.
Trunk. Figuratively, the direct line of ancestry.

PARENTAGE—*Adjectives.*

Ancestral. Pertaining to an ancestor.
Family. Of or belonging to a family.
Linear. Descendant in a direct line.
Maternal. Pertaining to the mother.
Parental. Characteristic of a father or parents.
Paternal. Pertaining to a father.
Patriarchal. Pertaining to the head of a family.

pa-ren'-tal. Pertaining to a parent. PARENTAGE-PROGENY.

pa-ren'-the-sis. Something inserted for explanation. ATTRACTION - REPULSION, CONTINUITY - INTERRUPTION, INTERSPACE-CONTACT, REVERSAL; **by way of parenthesis,** OPPORTUNENESS-UNSUITABLENESS.

par''-en-thet'-ic-al. Expressed in a parenthesis. CONNECTION-INDEPENDENCE, ENVIRONMENT-INTERPOSITION.

par''-en-thet'-ic-al-ly. Thrown in. CONNECTION-INDEPENDENCE, ENVIRONMENT-INTERPOSITION, OPPORTUNENESS-UNSUITABLENESS.

pari passu [L.] (pê'-rai pas'-su). Together. COEXISTENCE, EQUALITY-INEQUALITY.

Pa'-ri-ah. One of the primitive people of southern India; an outcast. GENTILITY-COMMONALTY, SOCIABILITY-PRIVACY.

Bantling. A young, small child.
Breed. Descendants of one strain; a race.
Brood. All the young chickens hatched at one time.
Child. One of a progeny.
Daughter. A female descendant.
Descendant. One who descends lineally.
Family. A group of persons united by ties of blood.
Farrow. A litter of pigs.
Filiation. The relationship between parent and child
Fils [F.]. Son.
Godchild. Child for whom one has become sponsor at its baptism.
Grandchildren. The children of children.
Heir apparent. One whose right to an estate is indefeasible if he survives the ancestor.
Heiress. A female heir.
Heir presumptive. One who, if the ancestor should die immediately, would be his heir, but whose right to the inheritance may be defeated by the birth of a nearer relative.
Heirs. Persons who succeed to a deceased person's property.
Issue. That which is produced or given out.
Line. A series of persons in direct descent.
Lineage. A line of descendants.
Litter. A number of young brought forth at once
Offset. A branch of a family
Offshoot. An issue of a family.
Offspring. That which is produced.
Posterity. The descendants of a progenitor.
Primogeniture. Being the first born of parents.
Progeny. The offspring, the descendants of human beings.
Ramification. A small branch or offshoot.
Rising generation. A young generation.
Scion. A descendant.
Seed. That which is produced; an offspring.
Son. A male child.
Sonship. State of being a son.
Spat. A spawn of shell-fish.
Spawn. The offspring of fishes; derisively the offspring of any animal.
Straight descent. Descendants direct from an ancestor.

PROGENY—*Figurative Nouns.*

Branch. A division of a race or family.
Chip of the old block. A child who resembles either of his parents.
Olive branch. Figuratively, a child
Shoot. An offspring from a family tree.
Sprit. }
Sprout. } A descendant.

PROGENY—*Adjective.*

Filial. Of or pertaining to a son or daughter.

PARENTAGE—*Continued.*

PARENTAGE—*Phrases.*

Avi numerantur avorum [L.]. Ancestors of ancestors are counted to me.

Hombre bueno no le busquen abolengo [Sp.]. No one explores a good man's pedigree

pa'-ri-an. White statuary-marble. SCULPTURE.

pa-ri'-e-tal. Pertaining to a wall. ANATOMY, LATERALITY-CONTRAPOSITION.

pa-ri'-e-tes. The walls of any cavity in the body. COVER-LINING, LATERALITY-CONTRAPOSITION.

par'-ing. Cutting off. MAGNITUDE-SMALLNESS.

par'-ing-knife''. A knife for paring fruit. SHARPNESS-BLUNTNESS.

par'-ish. District under one pastor. DWELLER-HABITATION, EXTENSION-DISTRICT; **bring to the parish,** AFFLUENCE-PENURY; **come upon the parish,** AFFLUENCE-PENURY.

pa-rish'-ion-er. One connected with a parish. MINISTRY-LAITY.

parisienne, à la [F.] (pa-ri''-zi-en', a la). In the Parisian style. SOCIETY-LUDICROUSNESS.

par'-i-tor. An apparitor. JUDICATURE.

par'-i-ty. Equality. EQUALITY-INEQUALITY.

park. A pleasure-ground; a train of cannon. CITY-COUNTRY, DOMESTICATION-AGRICULTURE, DWELLER-HABITATION, ENTERTAINMENT-WEARINESS, FAUNA-FLORA, GULF-PLAIN, WEAPON; **park paling,** ENCLOSURE.

par'-lance. Talk. SPEECH-INARTICULATENESS; **in common parlance,** SIMPLICITY-FLORIDNESS.

parlementaire [F.] (par-le-man'-têr'). Parliamentary. FIGHTING-CONCILIATION, MESSENGER.

parler à tort et à travers [F.] (par-lê' a tor ê a tra-vêr'). To speak gibberish. ADAGE-NONSENSE, RATIOCINATION-INSTINCT.

parler, façon de [F.] (par-lê', fa-son·' de). Manner of speaking. TROPE.

par'-ley. Conference. CONVERSATION-MONOLOGUE, MEDIATION.

par'-lia-ment. The legislature of Great Britain. COUNCIL.

par-lia-men'-ta-ry. Pertaining to parliament. **Parliamentary securities,** TREASURY.

par'-lor. A reception-room. CONTENTS-RECEIVER.

par'-lor-maid. A servant. CHIEF-UNDERLING.

par'-lous. Perilous. SECURITY-INSECURITY.

Par-nas'-sus. A mountain in Greece sacred to the Muses. POETRY-PROSE.

pa-ro'-chi-al. Belonging to a parish. EXTENSION-DISTRICT.

par'-o-dy. A travesty. COPY-MODEL, IMITATION-ORIGINALITY, INTERPRETATION-MISINTERPRETATION, SOCIETY-DERISION.

pa-role'. Word of honor. ENGAGEMENT-RELEASE, SECURITY, SPEECH-INARTICULATENESS; **on parole,** ENGAGEMENT-RELEASE, GUARD-PRISONER, RELEASE-RESTRAINT.

parole d'honneur [F.] (pa-rol' do-nur'). Word of honor. UPRIGHTNESS-DISHONESTY.

Pa-rol'-les. A character in Shakespeare's *All's Well that Ends Well.* BRAWLER.

par'-o-no-ma'-si-a. A play upon words. RHETORIC, SIMPLICITY-FLORIDNESS, WORD-NEOLOGY.

par'-ox-ysm. A convulsion. EXCITABILITY-INEXCITABILITY, FAVORITE-ANGER, TURBULENCE-CALMNESS.

par'-quet-ry. Wooden mosaic. VARIEGATION.

Parr, Old. Thomas Parr, a reputed centenarian. INFANT-VETERAN.

par'-ri-cide. One who murders father or mother. LIFE-KILLING.

par'-rot. A tropical bird; imitate. IMITATION-ORIGINALITY, TALKATIVENESS-TACITURNITY; **repeat as a parrot,** REMEMBRANCE-FORGETFULNESS.

Par'-rott. An American inventor. **Parrott gun,** WEAPON.

par'-ry. Avoid. ATTACK-DEFENSE, PROOF-DISPROOF, QUEST-EVASION.

pars magna fui, quorum [L.] (pars mag'-na fiu'-ai, quo'-rum). Of which things I was a great part. AGENT.

parse. To analyze grammatically. GRAMMAR-SOLECISM, INVESTIGATION-ANSWER.

Par'-see. A Zoroastrian. ORTHODOXY-HETERODOXY.

par''-si-mo'-ni-ous. Penurious. EXTRAVAGANCE-AVARICE, GENEROSITY-FRUGALITY.

par''-si-mo'-ni-ous-ness. Penuriousness. EXTRAVAGANCE-AVARICE.

par'-si-mo-ny. Excessive economy. EXTRAVAGANCE-AVARICE, GENEROSITY-FRUGALITY.

par'-son. Clergyman. MINISTRY-LAITY.

par'-son-age. House belonging to a parish. FANE.

part. To divide; a rôle; a duty. ACTING, CONCENTRATION-RADIATION, DUTY-IMMUNITY, MELODY-DISSONANCE, MISSIVE-PUBLICATION, OCCUPATION, PLURALITY-FRACTION, UNION-DISUNION, WHOLE-PART; **act a part,** ACTION-PASSIVENESS, SOCIETY-AFFECTATION, USEFULNESS-USELESSNESS; **bear part in,** ANTAGONISM-CONCURRENCE; **component part,** CONSTITU-ENT-ALIEN, WHOLE-PART; **for my part,** UNIVERSALITY-PARTICULARITY; **fractional part,** PLURALITY-FRACTION; **in part,** MAGNITUDE-SMALLNESS, WHOLE-PART; **on the part of,** CONNECTION-INDEPENDENCE, OBSTRUCTION-HELP; **part and parcel,** CONSTITUENT-ALIEN; **part by part,** WHOLE-PART; **part company,** QUEST-EVASION, UNION-DISUNION, VARIANCE-ACCORD; **part of speech,** GRAMMAR-SOLECISM, WORD-NEOLOGY; **part song,** MUSIC; **part with,** GIVING-RECEIVING, KEEPING-RELINQUISHMENT; **play a part in,** DOMINANCE-IMPOTENCE; **principal part,** CONSEQUENCE-INSIGNIFICANCE, MAGNITUDE-SMALLNESS; **take an active part,** ACTIVITY-INDOLENCE; **take a part in,** ACTION-PASSIVENESS; **take no part in,** QUEST-EVASION; **take part with,** ANTAGONISM-CONCURRENCE; **take the part of,** ANTAGONISM-CONCURRENCE.

parta male dilabuntur, male [L.] (par'-ta mê'-lî dil-a-bun'-tur, mê'-lî). Gains ill-gotten are ill made away with. UPRIGHTNESS-DISHONESTY.

par-take'. To have a part. PARTICIPATION; **partake of the sacrament,** CEREMONIAL.

par-ta'-king. Participating. PARTICIPATION.

parte, ex [L.] (par'-tî, ex). Of one side only. DECISION-MISJUDGMENT.

par''-terre'. A flower-garden with beds arranged in a pattern. DOMESTICATION-AGRICULTURE, ERECTNESS-FLATNESS.

Parthis mendacior [L.] (par'-this men-dê'-shi-or). More deceptive than the Parthians. TRUTHFULNESS-FALSEHOOD.

parti pris [F.] (par-ti' prî). Prejudgment. PREDETERMINATION-IMPULSE.

par'-tial. Biased; not general. DECISION-MISJUDGMENT, EQUALITY-INEQUALITY, RIGHT-WRONG, UNIVERSALITY-PARTICULARITY; **partial shadow,** DIMNESS.

par''-ti-al'-i-ty. Quality of being partial. DECISION-MISJUDGMENT, DESIRE-DISTASTE, EQUALITY-INEQUALITY, LOVE-HATE, RIGHT-WRONG, SUPREMACY-SUBORDINACY.

par'-tial-ly. In part; with undue bias. MAGNITUDE-SMALLNESS, WHOLE-PART.

particeps criminis [L.] (par'-ti-seps crim'-i-nis). A sharer in a crime. AGENT, ANTAGONIST-ASSISTANT.

par-tic'-i-pate. To partake. ANTAGONISM-CONCURRENCE, PARTICIPATION; **participate in,** ACTION-PASSIVENESS.

par-tic''-i-pa'-tion. A sharing with others. ANTAGONISM-CONCURRENCE, PARTICIPATION.

PARTICIPATION.

Coheirship. State of being one of many entitled to an inheritance.
Common stock. Anything held in common.
Communion. Act of sharing.
Communism. Common possession of property.
Community of goods. Equal participation or share in all property.
Community of possession. Holding in common.
Cooperation. Participation in the same work.
Coparcenary. Equal sharing of an estate.
Coparceny. A share of an inheritance.
Copartnership. A sharing in business.
Coportion. A portion in common with others
Cotenancy. Joint tenancy.
Gavelkind. A tenure by which land descended from a father to all his sons in equal portions.
Hotchpot. A blending of property for equality of division.
Joint stock. Shares held in common with others.
Joint tenancy. Tenure in land by unity of possession, time, interest, and title, so that it goes to the survivor.
Participation. A sharing in common with others.
Partnership. State of a partner; joint possession.
Picnic. A pleasure party in which each person contributes something to a common table.
Possession in common. Community of goods.
Snacks. A share.
Socialism. A system of social reform which contemplates an equitable distribution of property and labor.
Tenancy in common. A tenant's interest in common with others.

PARTICIPATION—*Nouns of Agency.*

Coheir. An heir with others.
Communist. One who practises and teaches the doctrine of the community of goods.
Coparcener. One who has an equal share in an estate of inheritance.
Copartner. One in common with another or others in any enterprise.
Cotenant. A tenant in common with others.
Joint tenant. One who holds an estate in joint tenancy, with right of survivorship.
Participator. One who has a share in.
Partner. One who take a share in an enterprise of any kind.
Shareholder. One who has a share or shares in a company.
Sharer. One who participates.
Socialist. One who advocates socialism.
Tenants in common. Those holding real or personal property in common.

PARTICIPATION—*Verbs.*

Be seized as a joint tenant. To have possession as a joint tenant.
Be seized in common. To hold in common.
Come in for a share. To join in a division.
Go halves.
Go shares. } To hold with others.
Go snacks.
Have a hand in. To own partly. See ANTAGONISM-CONCURRENCE.
Have as joint tenant. To hold in common with others, with survivorship.
Have in common.
Join in. } To share with another.
Partake. To receive a share of.
Participate. To have a share in.
Possess as joint tenants. To be a part holder. See *Nouns*.
Possess in common. To hold in common with others.
Share. To hold partly.
Share and share alike. To divide equally throughout.
Share in. To secure part of a distribution.

PARTICIPATION—*Adjectives.*

Communistic. Pertaining to communism.
Partaking. See *Verbs*.

PARTICIPATION—*Adverb.*

Share and share alike. Equally divided.

par-tic′-i-pa″-tor. One who shares. ACTION-PASSIVE-NESS, PARTICIPATION.
par′-ti-cle. An atom; one of the minor uninflected parts of speech. FRIABILITY, MAGNITUDE-SMALLNESS, PARTICLE.

PARTICLE.

Particle. One of the minor uninflected parts of speech.

PARTICLE—*Kinds.*

Adverb. Word used to modify a verb, adjective, or other adverb. Some are compared (see *Adjectives*), and these are not truly particles. They denote time, place, number, degree. manner, etc.
Conjunction. Word used to connect sentences, clauses, and like parts of sentences.
Absolute adversative. A conjunction used where there is a simple opposition of the same attribute to different subjects, or of different attributes in the same subjects, or of different attributes in different subjects.
Adequate adversative. A conjunction used of events and their causes or consequences, and indicating a sufficient condition for the conclusion.
Adversative. A conjunction indicating a contrast.
Causal. A conjunction indicating a cause or reason, or effect or inference.
Collective. A conjunction subjoining effects to causes.
Comparative adversative. · A conjunction that marks the equality or excess of the same attribute in different subjects.
Connective. A conjunction that connects the meaning of sentences.
Continuative. A conjunction that consolidates sentences into one continuous whole.
Copulative. A conjunction which only couples sentences.
Disjunctive. A conjunction which does not connect the meaning of sentences.
Inadequate adversative A conjunction indicating an insufficient condition for the conclusion.
Positive. A conjunction used to imply necessary connection and existence.

Simple disjunctive. A conjunction that disjoins and opposes indefinitely
Suppositive. A conjunction used to imply necessary connection, but not to assert existence.
Inseparable prefix. Prefix never used as a separate word.
Interjection. A word used to express emotion.
Preposition. A word used to connect words, and indicate their relations.

par-tic′-u-lar. Specific; a detail. CAREFULNESS-CARE-LESSNESS, DESIRE-DISTASTE, HEED-DISREGARD, OCCURRENCE-DESTINY, PERSISTENCE-WHIM, TASTE-VULGARITY, TRUTH-ERROR, UNIVERSALITY-PARTICULARITY, WHOLE-PART; **in particular,** UNIVERSALITY-PARTICULARITY; **particular account,** ACCOUNT; **particular estate,** PROPERTY.
par-tic″-u-lar′-i-ty. A nicety in taste. HEED-DISRE-GARD, UNIVERSALITY-PARTICULARITY.
par-tic′-u-lar-ize. To mention in particular. ACCOUNT, UNIVERSALITY-PARTICULARITY.
par-tic′-u-lar-ly. Especially. MAGNITUDE-SMALLNESS, SUPREMACY-SUBORDINACY.
par-tic′-u-lars. Important facts. ACCOUNT, UNIVERSALITY-PARTICULARITY.
partie carrée [F.] (par-tî′ ca-rê′). Party made up of two men and two women. SOCIABILITY-PRIVACY.
part′-ing. A separation. UNION-DISUNION.
par-ti′-tion. A dividing. ASSIGNMENT, ENVIRONMENT-INTERPOSITION, WHOLE-PART.
par′-ti-zan. A follower. ANTAGONIST-ASSISTANT, FRIEND-FOE, PATRIOTISM-TREASON, WEAPON.
par′-ti-zan-ship. Adherence to a party. ANTAGONISM-CONCURRENCE, DECISION-MISJUDGMENT.
part′-let. A hen. FAUNA-FLORA.
part′-ly. In some degree. WHOLE-PART.
part′-ner. Associate in business; companion. ANTAGONIST-ASSISTANT, FRIEND-FOE, MATRIMONY-CELIBACY, PARTICIPATION, SOLITUDE-COMPANY; **sleeping partner,** ACTIVITY-INDOLENCE.
part′-ner-ship. Union in business. ASSOCIATION, CO-OPERATION-OPPOSITION, SOLITUDE-COMPANY; **join partnership with,** ANTAGONISM-CONCURRENCE.
parts. Wisdom; skill; faculties. MIND-IMBECILITY, SAGACITY-INCAPACITY, SKILL-UNSKILFULNESS.
par-tu′-ri-ent. Bringing forth young. CREATION-DE-STRUCTION, FERTILITY-STERILITY.
par″-tu-ri′-tion. The act of bringing forth young. CREATION-DESTRUCTION.
parturiunt montes [L.] (par-tiu′-ri-unt mon′-tîz). The mountains are in labor. EXPECTATION-DISAPPOINTMENT, OVERVALUATION-UNDERVALUATION, SUCCESS-FAILURE.
par′-ty. Body of persons; faction; one of two litigants. ASSOCIATION, ENTERTAINMENT-WEARINESS, GATHERING-SCATTERING, HUMANITY, SOCIABILITY-PRIVACY, UNIVERSALITY-PARTICULARITY; **party spirit,** ANTAGONISM-CONCURRENCE, DECISION-MISJUDGMENT, RIGHT-WRONG; **party to,** ACTION-PASSIVENESS, AGENT, ANTAGONISM-CONCURRENCE; **party to a suit,** LITIGATION; **party wall,** ENVIRONMENT-INTERPOSITION.
par′-ty-col″-ored. Having various colors. VARIEGATION.
pa-rure′. Decoration. EMBELLISHMENT - DISFIGUREMENT.
parva componere magnis [L.] (par′-va com-pon′-er-î mag′-nis). To compare small things with great. COMPARISON.
par′-ve-nu″. An upstart. GENTILITY-COMMONALTY, NOVELTY-ANTIQUITY, TASTE-VULGARITY, WELFARE-MISFORTUNE.
par-vi-tude. Smallness. GREATNESS-LITTLENESS.
par′-vi-ty. Smallness. GREATNESS-LITTLENESS.
parvum parvo magnus acervus erit, adde [L.] (par′-vum par′-vo mag′-nus a-ser′-vus î′-rit, ad′-dî). Add little

to little, a great heap will be. ADDITION-SUBTRACTION, GENEROSITY-FRUGALITY, STORE.

pas. Precedence. LEADING-FOLLOWING, PRECEDENCE-SUCCESSION, REPUTATION-DISCREDIT, STATION.

pas, le [F.] (pa, le). The precedence. LEADING-FOLLOWING.

pas le sou, qui n'a [F.] (pa le su, kî na). He who is not worth a cent. AFFLUENCE-PENURY.

pas si bête [F.] (pa sî bêt). Not such a fool. SAGACITY-INCAPACITY.

pas'-chal. Pertaining to the Passover. CEREMONIAL, PERIODICITY-IRREGULARITY.

pa-sha'. An Ottoman ruler. CHIEF-UNDERLING, TYRANNY-ANARCHY.

pa-shaw'. A Turkish governor. CHIEF-UNDERLING.

pa-shaw'-lick. The province of a pashaw. RULE-LICENSE.

pasigraphie [F.] (pa-sî-gra-fî'). A universal writing. LANGUAGE.

pa-sig'-ra-phy. An international system of written signs. WRITING-PRINTING.

pas-quin-ade'. Lampoon. ADULATION - DISPARAGEMENT.

pass. Go beyond; endure; adopt; overlook. APPEARANCE-DISAPPEARANCE, ATTACK-DEFENSE, BREADTH-NARROWNESS, CONDITION-SITUATION, DIFFICULTY-FACILITY, FUTURE-PAST, INTERSPACE-CONTACT, LEAVE-PROHIBITION, MOVEMENT-REST, MULTIPLICITY-PAUCITY, OCCURRENCE-DESTINY, PASSAGE, PERIOD-PROGRESS, SUPREMACY-SUBORDINACY, TRANSFER, TRANSMISSION, WAY; **barely pass,** FAULTLESSNESS - FAULTINESS; **barely pass muster,** FAULTLESSNESS-FAULTINESS; **let it pass,** CAREFULNESS-CARELESSNESS; **make a pass at,** ATTACK-DEFENSE; **pass a law,** LAW - LAWLESSNESS; **pass an examination,** GOODNESS-BADNESS, REPUTATION-DISCREDIT; **pass and repass,** TRANSMISSION; **pass an opinion,** DECISION-MISJUDGMENT; **pass as,** ALIENATION, GIVING-RECEIVING; **pass away,** BEGINNING-END, DISCONTINUANCE-CONTINUANCE, ENTITY-NONENTITY, FUTURE - PAST, LASTINGNESS - TRANSIENTNESS, LIFE-DEATH; **pass by,** CAREFULNESS-CARELESSNESS, FUTURE-PAST, HEED-DISREGARD, PERIOD-PROGRESS, REGARD-DISRESPECT, REGARD-SCORN; **pass comprehension,** CLEARNESS-OBSCURITY; **pass current,** FAITH-MISGIVING, PUBLICITY; **pass in review,** HEED-DISREGARD; **pass in the mind,** CONCEPTION-THEME, REFLECTION-VACANCY; **pass into,** CONVERSION-REVERSION; **pass into one's hands,** GIVING-RECEIVING; **pass judgment,** DECISION-MISJUDGMENT; **pass muster,** APPROVAL - DISAPPROVAL, CONVENTIONALITY - UNCONVENTIONALITY, ENOUGH, GOODNESS-BADNESS; **pass off,** ENTRANCE-EXIT, FUTURE-PAST, OCCURRENCE-DESTINY; **pass off for,** TRUTHFULNESS-FALSEHOOD; **pass on,** ADVANCE-RETROGRESSION; **pass one's time in,** OCCUPATION; **pass one's word,** ENGAGEMENT-RELEASE; **pass out of,** ENTRANCE-EXIT; **pass over,** CAREFULNESS-CARELESSNESS, DUTY-IMMUNITY, GIVING-RECEIVING, INCLUSION-OMISSION, PARDON-VINDICTIVENESS, TRANSMISSION; **pass over to,** ANTAGONISM-CONCURRENCE; **pass sentence on,** EXCULPATION-CONVICTION; **pass the eyes over,** HEED-DISREGARD; **pass the fingers over,** TOUCH; **pass the Rubicon,** BEGINNING-END, CHOICE - NEUTRALITY; **pass through,** OCCURRENCE-DESTINY, TRANSMISSION; **pass through one's hands,** OCCUPATION; **pass time,** DURATION-NEVERNESS, ENTITY-NONENTITY; **pass to,** CONVERSION-REVERSION, MUTATION-PERMANENCE; **pass to the order of the day,** QUEST-ABANDONMENT; **pretty pass,** DIFFICULTY-FACILITY.

pass'-a-ble. Capable of being passed. BEAUTY-UGLINESS, CONSEQUENCE-INSIGNIFICANCE, FAULTLESSNESS-FAULTINESS, MAGNITUDE-SMALLNESS.

pass'-a-bly. Fairly well. MAGNITUDE-SMALLNESS.

passade [F.] (pas-sad'). In fencing, a motion forward and thrust. ATTACK-DEFENSE.

pas'-sage. Act of passing; a hall or way; incident; portion of a book. ACTION-PASSIVENESS, APERTURE-CLOSURE, CONTENTS-RECEIVER, CONVERSION-REVERSION, DWELLER-HABITATION, MELODY-DISSONANCE, MISSIVE-PUBLICATION, OCCURRENCE-DESTINY, TRANSFER, TRANSMISSION, TRAVELING-NAVIGATION, WAY, WHOLE-PART; **cut a passage,** APERTURE-CLOSURE; **force a passage,** PASSAGE; **passage of arms,** STRIFE-PEACE.

passage d'armes [F.] (pa-sazh' darm). Passage of arms. STRIFE-PEACE.

pas''-sa-mez'-zo. Music for a quick dance played in common time. MUSIC.

passant, en [F.] (pa-san'', an·). In passing. PURPOSE-LUCK, TRANSFER, TRANSMISSION.

pass'-book''. A book in which merchants enter account of things sold on credit. ACCOUNTS.

passé [F.] (pa-sê'). Over; gone. BETTERMENT-DETERIORATION, INFANCY-AGE, NOVELTY-ANTIQUITY.

passe, mot de [F.] (pas, mo de). A password. SIGN.

passed. Already gone. **Passed away,** FUTURE-PAST.

pas'-sen-ger. A traveler. WAYFARER-SEAFARER; **passenger train,** CONVEYANCE-VESSEL.

passe-parole [F.] (pas''-pa-rol'). Password. SIGN.

passe-partout [F.] (pas''-par-tu'). A light picture-frame; a master-key. APERTURE-CLOSURE, INSTRUMENTALITY.

pass'-er-by'. One who passes. ONLOOKER.

passer le temps, pour [F.] (pa-sê' le tan·, pur). To pass away the time. ACTION-PASSIVENESS.

passe-temps [F.] (pas''-tan·'). Pastime. ENTERTAINMENT-WEARINESS.

pas'-sim. Here and there. EXTENSION-PLACE, GATHERING-SCATTERING, POSITION.

pass'-ing. Going by; cursory. LASTINGNESS-TRANSIENTNESS, MAGNITUDE-SMALLNESS, TRANSMISSION; **passing bell,** LIFE-FUNERAL; **passing strange,** ASTONISHMENT-EXPECTANCE; **passing word,** ENLIGHTENMENT-SECRECY.

pas'-sion. A suffering; anger; great desire. AFFECTIONS, DESIRE-DISTASTE, EMOTION, EXCITABILITY-INEXCITABILITY, EXCITATION, FAVORITE - ANGER, LOVE-HATE, PLEASURE-PAIN, VIOLENCE-CALMNESS; **ruling passion,** BIGOTRY-APOSTASY.

pas'-sion-ate. Easily moved to anger or strong feeling. EMOTION, EXCITABILITY-INEXCITABILITY, FAVORITE-QUARRELSOMENESS, LOVE-HATE.

pas'-sion-less. Without passion. SENSITIVENESS-APATHY.

Pas'-sion week'. The week beginning with the fifth Sunday in Lent. CEREMONIAL.

pas'-sive. Inert; patient; receiving influences. ACTION-PASSIVENESS, EXCITABILITY-INEXCITABILITY, INSUBORDINATION-OBEDIENCE, VIGOR-INERTIA.

pass'-ive-ness. Inactivity. ACTION-PASSIVENESS, EXCITABILITY-INEXCITABILITY, INSUBORDINATION-OBEDIENCE.

pass'-key''. A night-key. INSTRUMENTALITY.

Pass'-o''-ver. The feast of unleavened bread. CEREMONIAL.

pass'-port. An official warrant of protection. INSTRUMENTALITY, LEAVE-PROHIBITION, ORDER.

pass'-word''. A watchword. FIGHTING-CONCILIATION, INVESTIGATION-ANSWER, SIGN.

past. Gone by; spent. FUTURE-PAST; **danger past,** SECURITY - INSECURITY; **insensibility to the past,** REMEMBRANCE-FORGETFULNESS; **obliteration of the past,** REMEMBRANCE-FORGETFULNESS; **past bearing,** PLEASURABLENESS-PAINFULNESS; **past comprehension,** CLEARNESS-OBSCURITY; **past cure,** BETTERMENT - DETERIORATION, SANGUINENESS - HOPELESSNESS; **past dispute,** CERTAINTY - DOUBT; **past one's**

prime, Infancy-Age; **past praying for,** Virtue-Vice; **past recollection,** Remembrance-Forgetfulness; **past work,** Betterment-Deterioration, Usefulness-Uselessness; **thing of the past,** Novelty-Antiquity.

paste. An adhesive mixture. Cohesion-Looseness, Connective, Embellishment-Disfigurement, Pulpiness-Oiliness, Truthfulness-Fraud; **scissors and paste,** Choice-Neutrality.

paste'-board''. A paper board. Pulpiness-Oiliness.

pas'-tel''. A picture drawn with colored crayons. Painting.

pasticcio [It.] (pas''-tît'-chi-o). A work made of fragments. Mixture-Homogeneity.

pas'-til. A compound for fumigating hospitals. Perfume-Stench.

pas'-time''. Diversion. Entertainment-Weariness.

pas'-tor. A minister. Ministry-Laity, Instructor-Pupil.

pas'-tor-al. A poem of shepherd life; pertaining to the care of the soul. Ceremonial, Church, City-Country, Domestication-Agriculture, Music, Poetry.

pas''-to-ra'-le. In music, a composition in rural style. Music.

pa'-stry. Pies, tarts, etc. Nutriment-Excretion, Sweetness-Acidity.

pas'-tur-age. Grass on which cattle feed. Fauna-Flora, Gulf-Plain.

pas'-ture. Ground for grazing. Fauna-Flora, Country, Nutriment-Excretion.

pa'-sty. Like paste; a pie. Nutriment-Excretion, Viscidity-Foam.

pat. Tap; fitting. Harmony-Discord, Impetus-Reaction; **pat on the back,** Alleviation-Aggravation, Approval-Disapproval, Blandishment, Bravery-Cowardice, Motive-Caprice; **pat on the cheek,** Blandishment; **pat on the head,** Blandishment.

Pat''-a-go'-ni-an. An inhabitant of Patagonia who is noted for his tallness. Height-Lowness.

patch. Mend; a blemish. Embellishment-Disfigurement, Extension-District, Magnitude-Smallness; **patch up,** Composition, Renovation-Relapse.

patch'-work''. A fabric made of patches. Continuity-Interruption, Mixture-Homogeneity, Variegation.

pate. The top of the head. Mind-Imbecility, Top-Bottom.

pat''-e-fac'-tion. The act of opening. Aperture-Closure.

pa-tel'-la. Kneecap; a cup-like part. Anatomy, Contents-Receiver.

pat'-ent. Manifest; to secure a patent. Aperture-Closure, Leave-Prohibition, Manifestation-Latency, Property.

pat'-e-ra. A shallow vessel used by the Romans in libation. Architecture, Ceremonial, Contents-Receiver.

pa''-ter-fa-mil'-i-as. The father of the family. Parentage-Progeny.

pa-ter'-nal. Fatherly. Charitableness-Malevolence, Parentage-Progeny; **paternal domicile,** Dweller-Habitation.

pa-ter'-nal-ism. The practise of government by or after the manner of a father. Rule-License.

pa-ter'-ni-ty. The condition of being a father. Parentage-Progeny.

pa''-ter-nos'-ter. The beginning of the Lord's Prayer. Devotion-Idolatry.

pater patriæ [L.] (pê'-ter pê'-tri-î). Father of his country. Benefactor-Evildoer.

path. A walk. Aim-Aberration, Aperture-Closure, Conduct, Entrance-Exit, Escape, Passage, Way; **cross the path,** Obstruction-Help; **secret path,** Exposure-Hidingplace.

pa-thet'-ic. Affecting the passions. Pleasurableness-Painfulness.

path'-less. Having no path. Aperture-Closure, Difficulty-Facility, Extension-District.

pa-thog''-no-mon'-ic. Pertaining to symptoms that are characteristic of a disease. Sign.

pa-thol'-o-gy. Science of diseases. Health-Sickness.

pa'-thos. That which excites feeling. Emotion.

path-o-scop'-ic. Pertaining to disease. Affections.

path'-way''. Path. Way.

pa'-tience. Perseverance. Entertainment-Weariness, Excitability-Inexcitability, Persistence-Whim.

pa'-tient. A sick person. Health-Sickness.

pa''-tois'. An illiterate dialect. Word-Neology.

patria, omne solum forti [L.] (pê'-tri-a, om'-nî so'-lum for'-tai). Every soil is fatherland to the brave man. Bravery-Cowardice.

patriæ, amor [L.] (pê'-tri-î, ê'-mor). Love of fatherland. Humanitarianism-Misanthropy.

pa'-tri-arch. An aged man; chief. Infant-Veteran, Ministry-Laity, Parentage-Progeny.

pa''-tri-ar'-chal. Pertaining to a patriarch. Infancy-Age, Novelty-Antiquity, Parentage-Progeny.

pa-tri'-cian. One of the upper classes. Gentility-Commonalty.

pat'-ri-mo-ny. An inheritance from an ancestor. Property.

pa'-tri-ot. One who loves his country. Humanitarianism-Misanthropy, Patriotism-Treason.

pa''-tri-ot'-ic. Full of patriotism. Humanitarianism-Misanthropy, Patriotism-Treason.

pa'-tri-ot-ism. Devotion to one's country. Humanitarianism-Misanthropy, Patriotism-Treason.

PATRIOTISM—TREASON.

Amor patriæ [L.]. Love of one's fatherland.
Chauvinism. Excessive patriotism.
Chivalry. Knightly reverence for one's country and women
Fidelity. Faithfulness in executing a public trust.
Honor. A high and patriotic system of conduct.
Jingoism. Fanatic and aggressive patriotism.
Loyalty. Unswerving devotion to one's country.
Patriotism. Love of one's country and the desire to protect it.

Patriotism—*Nouns of Agent.*

Adherer. One who is attached or devoted to.
Bigot. One obstinately devoted to a cause.
Champion. One who acts or speaks in behalf of a person or cause.
Defender. One who supports or protects.
Devotee. One who is wholly devoted to.
Fanatic. A person affected by excessive enthusiasm for a cause.
Father of his country. A title applied to George Washington.

Betrayal. Act of dealing treacherously toward one's own country.
Faithlessness. State of lacking loyalty.
Misprision of treason. The concealing of a knowledge of treason without aiding the traitors.
Mutiny. Rebellion against legal authority as represented in a commander.
Perjury. The act of swearing to a lie.
Sedition. The act of stirring up an insurrection.
Treason. The act of plotting to aid the enemies of one's country.

Treason—*Nouns of Agent.*

Apostate. One who forsakes the principles or cause to which he belongs.
Backslider. One who deserts a cause which he formerly maintained.
Benedict Arnold. An American traitor in the Revolutionary War.
Betrayer. One who betrays a cause.
Deserter. One who forsakes a party or cause.

PATRIOTISM—TREASON—*Continued.*

PATRIOTISM—Nouns of Agent—*Continued.*

First in war, first in peace, and first in the hearts of his countrymen. Said of George Washington.

Partizan. An adherent to a cause.

Patriot. A lover of his country.

PATRIOTISM—*Associated Nouns.*

America. The national hymn of the United States.

American Eagle. The emblem of the United States of America.

Badge of the Grand Army of the Republic. The badge of the survivors of the armies of the United States engaged in the Civil War.

Badge of the Order of St. Andrew. The badge of a Scotch patriotic society.

Badge of the Order of St. Patrick. The badge of an Irish patriotic society.

Badge of the Order of the Golden Fleece. The badge of an order of European knighthood.

Badge of the Order of the Thistle. The emblem of a Scotch patriotic society.

Battle Hymn of the Republic. A national hymn of the United States.

Black Eagle. A Prussian medal given for valor in battle.

British Lion. An emblem of the British Empire.

Brother Jonathan. A sportive name for the people of the United States, like John Bull for the people of England. It has been connected with Gov. Jonathan Trumbull of Connecticut, a scriptural Brother Jonathan of General Washington.

Die Wacht am Rhein [G.]. A national song of Germany.

Dixie. The national song of the Southern Confederacy.

Fleur-de-lis [F.]. The national flower of royal France.

G. A. R. Grand Army of the Republic.

God Save the King. The national hymn of Great Britain.

Iron Cross. A decoration of a Prussian order of military merit.

La Marseillaise [F.]. The French national hymn.

Lilies of France. The emblem of monarchical France.

Rose. The national flower of England.

Russian Bear. The emblem of the Russian Empire.

Santiago [Sp.]. Saint James: a Spanish battle-cry.

Shamrock. The national flower of Ireland.

Star-Spangled Banner. The national song of the United States.

St. Andrew. The Scottish patron saint.

St. David. The patron saint of Wales.

St. George. The patron saint of England.

St. Patrick. The patron saint of Ireland.

Tricolor. The standard of the French Republic.

Union Jack. A flag. containing only the union, without the fly, hoisted on a jackstaff.

Wearing of the Green. An Irish national song

Yankee Doodle. An American national song.

PATRIOTISM—*Verbs.*

Champion. To contend for.

Cherish. To care for kindly.

TREASON—Nouns of Agent—*Continued.*

Heretic. One who believes some wrong doctrine or adheres to a wrong cause.

Judas. A traitor; the betrayer of Christ.

Mutineer. One who causes a mutiny.

Rebel. One who attempts to overthrow legal authority.

Recreant. One who yields in combat, and begs for mercy.

Renegade. A deserter.

Turncoat. One who forsakes his party or principles.

TREASON—*Verbs.*

Be false to. To betray.

Betray. To deliver over by fraud.

Corrupt. To debase.

Disclose the secrets of. To betray.

Dishonor. To bring reproach upon.

Ensnare. To lead into evil.

Give over to the foe. To betray.

Inveigle. To lead astray.

Lead astray. To lead to wrong.

Mislead. To direct wrongly.

Prove recreant to. To desert.

Rebel. To resist the laws of the land by force.

Violate the confidence of. To betray.

TREASON—*Adjectives.*

Apostate. Guilty of desertion from one's party.

False. Marked by bad faith.

Mutinous. Engaged in mutiny.

Seditious. Stirring up insurrection.

Treacherous. Practising treachery.

PATRIOTISM—Verbs—*Continued.*

Defend. To guard against attack.

Foster. To give aid and protection to.

Lay down one's life for one's country. ⎱
Lay one's life on the altar of one's country. ⎰ To die for one's country.

Secure from danger. To rescue.

PATRIOTISM—*Adjectives.*

Chauvinistic. Excessively patriotic.

Chivalric. Devoted to one's country.

Fanatical. Controlled by intemperate zeal.

Loyal. Constant in one's affection to one's country

Patriotic. Loving one's fatherland.

PATRIOTISM—*Phrase.*

Dulce et decorum est pro patria mori [L.]. It is sweet and beautiful to die for one's country. [Horace, *Odes*, III, ii, 13.]

---

pa-trol'. A guard at camp. SECURITY-INSECURITY, TRAVELING-NAVIGATION.

pa'-tron. One who protects. ANTAGONIST-ASSISTANT, BUYING-SALE, FRIEND-FOE.

pat'-ron-age. Special support. DOMINANCE-IMPOTENCE, OBSTRUCTION-HELP, RULE-LICENSE.

pat'-ron-ize. Support. OBSTRUCTION-HELP.

pat''-ro-nym'-ic. Formed after one's father's name. NAME-MISNOMER.

pat'-ten. A clog. DRESS-UNDRESS.

pat'-ter. To strike as drops of rain; mumble. CRASH-DRUMMING, IMPETUS-REACTION, TALKATIVENESS-TACITURNITY.

pat'-ter-er. One who mumbles. SPEECH-INARTICULATENESS.

pat'-tern. A model. CONVENTIONALITY-UNCONVENTIONALITY, COPY-MODEL, EMBELLISHMENT-DISFIGUREMENT, FAULTLESSNESS-FAULTINESS, SIGN.

pattes de mouche [F.] (pat de mush). Scribbling. WRITING-PRINTING.

pattes de velours, faire [F.] (pat de ve-lur', fêr). To be all smirks and smiles. TRUTHFULNESS-FALSEHOOD, TRUTHFULNESS-FRAUD.

pat'-u-lous. Spreading. ENLARGEMENT-DIMINUTION.

pau-cil'-o-quy. The utterance of few words. TALKATIVENESS-TACITURNITY.

pau'-ci-ty. Fewness. EXCESS-LACK, MAGNITUDE-SMALLNESS, MULTIPLICITY-PAUCITY.

Paul Jones. A Scottish-American naval adventurer. ROBBER.

Paul Pry. A newsmonger. CONVERSATION-MONOLOGUE, INQUISITIVENESS-INDIFFERENCE.

paulo post futurum [L.] (pau'-lo post fiu-tiu'-rum). One of these days. FUTURE-PAST.

paunch. To disembowel. CONTENTS-RECEIVER.

pau'-per. A poor person. AFFLUENCE-PENURY.

pause. To stop; to wait. ACTION-PASSIVENESS, CONTINUITY-INTERRUPTION, DETERMINATION-VACILLATION, DISCONTINUANCE-CONTINUANCE, FAILURE-UNBELIEF, MISGIVING, MOVEMENT-REST, TOIL-RELAXATION.

pauvre diable [F.] (povr di-abl'). Poor devil. AFFLUENCE-PENURY.

pave. To lay with stone or brick. COVER-LINING; **pave the way,** DIFFICULTY-FACILITY.

pavé [F.] (pa-vê'). Pavement. **On the** *pavé*, PURITY-IMPURITY.

pave'-ment. A paved foot-path. CITY, COVER-LINING, TOP-BOTTOM, WAY.

pa-vil'-ion. A canopy. ARCHITECTURE, DWELLER-HABITATION.

pa'-ving. The laying of pavement. TOP-BOTTOM.

pa'-vi-or. A paver. PREPARATION - NONPREPARATION.

paw. Foot of a beast; to scrape. KEEPING-RELINQUISHMENT, TOUCH.

paw'-ky. Shrewd. CRAFT-ARTLESSNESS.

pawn. A pledge deposit. LOAN-BORROWING, SECURITY.

pawn'-bro''-ker. One who lends money on pledge. LOAN-BORROWING.

pawn'-shop''. A shop where property can be pawned. LOAN-BORROWING.

pax [L.] (pax) Peace. CEREMONIAL, SOUND-SILENCE.

pax in bello [L.] (pax in bel'-lo) Peace in war FIGHTING-CONCILIATION.

pax vobiscum [L.] (pax vo-bis'-cum). Peace be with you. POLITENESS-IMPOLITENESS.

pay. To compensate; return; profit. BUYING-SALE, COVER-LINING, GAIN-LOSS, GIVING-RECEIVING, OUTLAY-INCOME, RECOMPENSE-PUNITION, SETTLEMENT-DEFAULT; **in one's pay,** BUYING-SALE, CHIEF-UNDERLING; **pay attention to,** CAREFULNESS-CARELESSNESS, HEED-DISREGARD; **pay a visit,** POLITENESS-IMPOLITENESS, SOCIABILITY-PRIVACY; **pay back,** REPRISAL-RESISTANCE; **pay down,** SETTLEMENT-DEFAULT; **pay dues,** DUENESS-UNDUENESS; **pay homage,** DEVOTION-IDOLATRY, REGARD-DISRESPECT, YIELDING; **pay in advance,** OUTLAY-INCOME; **pay in full,** SETTLEMENT-DEFAULT; **pay in one's own coin,** REPRISAL-RESISTANCE; **pay no attention, etc., to,** HEED-DISREGARD; **pay off,** REPRISAL-RESISTANCE; **pay old debts,** SETTLEMENT-DEFAULT; **pay one's respects,** POLITENESS-IMPOLITENESS; **pay one's way,** GENEROSITY-FRUGALITY, SETTLEMENT-DEFAULT; **pay out,** RECOMPENSE-PUNITION; **pay regard to,** REPUTATION-DISCREDIT; **pay the debt of nature,** LIFE-DEATH; **pay the penalty,** ATONEMENT; **pay the piper,** OBSTRUCTION-HELP; **pay through the nose,** COSTLINESS-CHEAPNESS, EXTRAVAGANCE-AVARICE; **pay too much,** COSTLINESS-CHEAPNESS.

pay-ee'. A person to whom money has been or is to be paid. MONEY.

pay'-er. One who pays. SETTLEMENT-DEFAULT.

pay'-mas''-ter. One who pays employees. TREASURER.

pay'-ment. The act of paying. OUTLAY-INCOME, RECOMPENSE-PUNITION, SETTLEMENT-DEFAULT.

pay'-nim. Pagan. ORTHODOXY-HETERODOXY.

pays, mal du [F.] (pê-î', mal dû). Homesickness. CONTENTEDNESS-REGRET.

pea. A climbing herb. ROUNDNESS.

peace. Quietness; freedom from war. AMITY-HOSTILITY, MOVEMENT-REST, SOUND-SILENCE, STRIFE-PEACE, VARIANCE-ACCORD; **at peace,** VARIANCE-ACCORD; **commission of the peace,** JUDICATURE; **justice of the peace,** JUDGE; **keep the peace,** TURBULENCE-CALMNESS, VARIANCE-ACCORD; **make peace,** FIGHTING-CONCILIATION, STRIFE-PEACE; **make peace with,** CONTENTEDNESS-DISCONTENTMENT; **Prince of peace,** DIVINITY; **speak peace,** CONTENTEDNESS-DISCONTENTMENT.

peace'-a-ble. Inclined to peace. STRIFE-PEACE, TURBULENCE-CALMNESS.

peace'-a-bly. Quietly. **Get on peaceably,** MEDIOCRITY, STRIFE-PEACE.

peace'-ful. Undisturbed. EXCITABILITY-INEXCITABILITY, TURBULENCE-CALMNESS.

peace'-ma''-ker. One who quiets strife. CONTENTEDNESS-DISCONTENTMENT, MEDIATION, VARIANCE-ACCORD.

peace'-of''-fer-ing. An offering of thanks for peace. ATONEMENT, FIGHTING-CONCILIATION, GIVING-RECEIVING, MEDIATION.

peach. To tell on an accomplice. EXPOSURE-HIDING-PLACE.

peach'-col''-ored. Bright-reddish. REDNESS-GREENNESS.

pea'-cock''. A beautiful fowl. BEAUTY-UGLINESS, CONCEIT-DIFFIDENCE, POMP, SELFRESPECT-HUMBLENESS, VARIEGATION; **jackdaw in peacock's feathers,** ADEPT-BUNGLER.

pea'-green''. A shade of green. REDNESS-GREENNESS.

pea'-jack''-et. A coat worn by seamen in rough weather. DRESS-UNDRESS.

peak. Summit. HEALTH-SICKNESS, HEIGHT-LOWNESS, SHARPNESS-BLUNTNESS, TOP-BOTTOM.

peak'-ed. Pointed. SHARPNESS-BLUNTNESS.

peal. A loud, long sound. CRASH-DRUMMING, LOUDNESS-FAINTNESS; **peal of bells,** CRASH-DRUMMING; **peal of laughter,** JUBILATION-LAMENTATION.

pearl. A white substance found in the oyster; to adorn with pearls. EMBELLISHMENT-DISFIGUREMENT, GOODNESS-BADNESS, REPUTATION-DISCREDIT, **cast pearls before swine,** PROVISION-WASTE, USEFULNESS-USELESSNESS; **mother-of-pearl,** VARIEGATION.

pearl'-i-ness. The quality of being pearly. DIAPHANEITY-OPALESCENCE.

pearl'-y. Like pearl. COLOR-ACHROMATISM, DIAPHANEITY-OPALESCENCE, GRAY-BROWN, VARIEGATION, WHITENESS-BLACKNESS.

pear'-shape. Shaped like a pear. ROUNDNESS.

peas'-ant. A farm-hand. GENTILITY-COMMONALTY.

peat. A fuel. COMBUSTIBLE.

peb'-ble. A small, roundish stone. GREATNESS-LITTLENESS, HARDNESS-SOFTNESS.

pec''-ca-bil'-i-ty. Sinning. VIRTUE-VICE.

pec''-ca-ble. Capable of sinning. INNOCENCE-GUILT.

pec''-ca-dil'-lo. A slight sin. INNOCENCE-GUILT.

pec''-can-cy. The quality of being peccant or sinful. FAULTLESSNESS-FAULTINESS, GOODNESS-BADNESS.

pec'-cant. Being a sinner; diseased. CLEANNESS-FILTHINESS, FAULTLESSNESS-FAULTINESS, GOODNESS-BADNESS, HEALTH-SICKNESS; **peccant humor,** CLEANNESS-FILTHINESS, HEALTH-SICKNESS.

peccare in bello non licet, bis [L.] (pec-kê'-rî in bel'-lo non lai'-set, bis). To blunder twice in war is not permitted. ADEPT-BUNGLER, FIGHTING-CONCILIATION.

peccavi [L.] (pec-kê'-vai). I have sinned. REPENTANCE-OBDURACY.

peck. The fourth of a bushel; a sharp, quick blow MAGNITUDE-SMALLNESS, MEASURE, MULTIPLICITY-PAUCITY, NUTRIMENT-EXCRETION; **peck at,** APPROVAL-DISAPPROVAL; **peck of trouble,** DIFFICULTY-FACILITY, PLEASURE-PAIN, WELFARE-MISFORTUNE.

peck'-ish. Inclined to eat. DESIRE-DISTASTE.

Peck'-sniff. A hypocrite in Dickens's *Martin Chuzzlewit.* GULL-DECEIVER.

pec'-tin-at-ed. Resembling the teeth of a comb. SHARPNESS-BLUNTNESS.

pec'-u-late. To steal. THEFT.

pec'-u-la'-tion. Stealing. THEFT.

pec'-u-la''-tor. A thief. ROBBER.

pe-cu'-liar. Especial. CONVENTIONALITY-UNCONVENTIONALITY, UNIVERSALITY-PARTICULARITY.

pe-cu''-li-ar'-i-ties. Characteristics. SUBJECTIVENESS-OBJECTIVENESS.

pe-cu''-li-ar'-i-ty. Characteristic. CONVENTIONALITY-UNCONVENTIONALITY, UNIVERSALITY-PARTICULARITY.

pe-cu'-liar-ly. Especially. MAGNITUDE-SMALLNESS, SUPREMACY-SUBORDINACY.

pe-cu'-ni-a-ry. Monetary. MONEY.

pe-cu'-ni-ous. Rich. AFFLUENCE-PENURY.

ped'-a-gogue. A schoolmaster. INSTRUCTOR-PUPIL, SCHOLAR-DUNCE, SOCIETY-AFFECTATION.

ped'-al. The foot-keys of an organ; pertaining to **the** foot ANATOMY, INSTRUMENT

ped'-ant. One who makes a vain show of his learning. SCHOLAR-DUNCE, SOCIETY-AFFECTATION.

pe-dan'-tic. Ostentatious of learning. KNOWLEDGE-IGNORANCE, SIMPLICITY-FLORIDNESS, SOCIETY-AFFECTATION.

ped'-ant-ry. A boastful display of knowledge. DECISION-MISJUDGMENT, KNOWLEDGE-IGNORANCE, SOCIETY-AFFECTATION.

ped'-dle. To travel and retail goods. ACTIVITY-INDOLENCE.

ped'-dling. Selling from house to house. CONSEQUENCE-INSIGNIFICANCE, EXTRAVAGANCE-AVARICE.

ped''-e-re'-ro. A swivel-gun. WEAPON.

ped'-es-tal. The base of a column, etc. ARCHITECTURE, SUSPENSION-SUPPORT; **place on a pedestal,** ELEVATION-DEPRESSION.

pe-des'-tri-an. One who walks. WAYFARER-SEAFARER.

ped'-i-cel. A footstalk by which a leaf is fixed to a tree. SUSPENSION-SUPPORT.

ped'-i-gree. Lineage. CONTINUITY-INTERRUPTION, PARENTAGE-PROGENY, RATIONALE-LUCK.

ped'-i-ment. An ornamental top for the front of a building. ARCHITECTURE, SUSPENSION-SUPPORT, TOP-BOTTOM.

pedir peras al olmo [Sp.] (pê-dir' pê'-ras al ol'-mo). To look for pears on the elm. LIKELIHOOD-UNLIKELIHOOD.

ped'-ler. A merchant who sells from house to house. DEALER; **pedler's French,** WORD-NEOLOGY.

ped-om'-e-ter. A distance gage. LENGTH-SHORTNESS.

ped-un'-cle. The stem of a flower and fruit of a plant. SUSPENSION-SUPPORT.

ped-un'-cu-late. Borne on a peduncle. SUSPENSION-SUPPORT.

peel. Rind; take off rind. COVER-LINING, DRESS-UNDRESS, LAMINA-FIBER; **peel off,** UNION-DISUNION.

peel'-house''. A fortress. ATTACK-DEFENSE.

peep. Sly look. SIGHT-BLINDNESS; **peep behind the curtain,** INVESTIGATION-ANSWER; **peep of day,** MORNING-EVENING; **peep into the future,** PREVISION; **peep out,** EXPOSURE-HIDINGPLACE, VISIBILITY-INVISIBILITY.

peep'-hole''. A hole through which one may look undiscovered. APERTURE-CLOSURE.

peep'-show''. A small show viewed through a magnifying glass. APPEARANCE-DISAPPEARANCE, ENTERTAINMENT-WEARINESS.

peer. Equal; to peep. EQUALITY-INEQUALITY, GENTILITY-COMMONALTY, INVESTIGATION-ANSWER, SIGHT-BLINDNESS; **peer out,** VISIBILITY-INVISIBILITY.

peer'-age. The nobility. GENTILITY-COMMONALTY.

peer'-less. Of unequaled excellence. REPUTATION-DISCREDIT, SUPREMACY-SUBORDINACY, VIRTUE-VICE.

pee'-vish. Fretful. FAVORITE-QUARRELSOMENESS, POLITENESS-IMPOLITENESS.

peg. Wooden nail or pin; a degree. CONVEXITY-CONCAVITY, INSTRUMENT, STATION, SUSPENSION-SUPPORT; **come down a peg,** ASCENT-DESCENT; **let down a peg,** ELEVATION-DEPRESSION; **not stir a peg,** ACTION-PASSIVENESS, MOVEMENT-REST; **peg away,** ACTIVITY-INDOLENCE; **peg on,** TRAVELING-NAVIGATION; **peg to hang on,** PRETEXT.

Peg'-a-sus. The winged horse of the Muses. CONVEYER.

peg'-o-man''-cy. Divination by fountains. PROPHECY.

pegs. The legs. TRAVELING-NAVIGATION.

peindre, fait à [F.] (pan·dr, fêt a). Well-made. BEAUTY-UGLINESS.

peine forte et dure [F.] (pên fort ê dür). Strong and severe punishment. RECOMPENSE-PENALTY.

pel-a'-gi-an. A deep-sea animal. OCEAN-LAND.

pel-ag'-ic. Pertaining to the inhabitants of the ocean. OCEAN-LAND.

pel'-er-ine. A cape worn by women. DRESS-UNDRESS.

pelf. Money; wealth. AFFLUENCE-PENURY, GAIN-LOSS, PROPERTY.

pel'-i-can. A fish-eating bird. PROVISION-WASTE.

pe-lisse'. A long cloak. DRESS-UNDRESS.

pel'-let. A small round ball. ROUNDNESS; **paper pellet,** CONSEQUENCE-INSIGNIFICANCE.

pel'-li-cle. A thin layer. COVER-LINING, LAMINA-FIBER.

pell''-mell'. In utter confusion. REGULARITY-IRREGULARITY.

pel-lu'-cid. Clear. DIAPHANEITY-OPAQUENESS.

pel-lu-cid'-i-ty. Translucency. DIAPHANEITY-OPAQUENESS.

pelote [F.] (plot). A ball. ROUNDNESS.

pelt. Skin of a beast with hair on; to throw. ATTACK-DEFENSE, COVER-LINING, DRESS-UNDRESS, IMPETUS-REACTION, RECOMPENSE-PUNITION.

pelt'-ry. Skins. COVER-LINING.

pen. Instrument for writing; enclosure for beasts. DWELLER-HABITATION, ENCLOSURE, MISSIVE-PUBLICATION, RELEASE-PRISON, RELEASE-RESTRAINT, WRITING-PRINTING; **draw the pen through,** MARK-OBLITERATION; **pen and ink,** WRITING-PRINTING; **pen in hand,** WRITING-PRINTING; **ready pen,** STYLE; **slip of the pen,** GRAMMAR-SOLECISM, TRUTH-ERROR; **stroke of the pen,** ORDER, RULE-LICENSE, WRITING-PRINTING.

pe'-nal. Incurring punishment. RECOMPENSE-PUNITION; **penal servitude,** RECOMPENSE-PUNITION; **penal settlement,** RELEASE-PRISON.

pen'-al-ty. Judicial punishment. RECOMPENSE-PENALTY, RECOMPENSE-PUNITION.

pen'-ance. Suffering for sin. ATONEMENT, AUSTERITY, CEREMONIAL, RECOMPENSE-PENALTY, REPENTANCE-OBDURACY.

Pen-a'-tes. The old Latin household gods. **Lares and Penates,** DEVOTION-IDOLATRY, DWELLER-HABITATION.

pen''-chant'. A strong inclination. DESIRE-DISTASTE, LOVE-HATE, READINESS-RELUCTANCE.

pen'-cil. An instrument for writing; a brush. GATHERING-SCATTERING, LIGHT-DARKNESS, PAINTING, WRITING-PRINTING.

pen'-cil-draw'-ing. A drawing made with a pencil. PAINTING.

pen'-craft. Penmanship. WRITING-PRINTING.

pend'-ant. A jewel; a flag; projection. ARCHITECTURE, LIKENESS-UNLIKENESS, SIGN.

pend'-en-cy. Suspense; hanging. DURATION-NEVERNESS, SUSPENSION-SUPPORT.

pend'-ent. Hanging. SUSPENSION-SUPPORT.

pendente lite [L.] (pen-den'-tî lai'-tî). Pending suit. CERTAINTY-DOUBT, DURATION-NEVERNESS, LITIGATION.

pend'-ing. Awaiting. DURATION-NEVERNESS.

pend'-u-lous. Hanging. SUSPENSION-SUPPORT, VIBRATION.

pend'-u-lum. A body suspended and vibrating. CHRONOLOGY-ANACHRONISM, SUSPENSION-SUPPORT; **motion of a pendulum,** VIBRATION.

Pe-nel'-o-pe. A character in Greek legend. **Work of Penelope,** COMPLETION-NONCOMPLETION, USEFULNESS-USELESSNESS.

pen''-e-tra''-ble. That may be penetrated. ENTRANCE-EXIT.

pen''-e-tra'-li-a. The interior parts of anything. OUTSIDE-INSIDE.

penetralia mentis [L.] (pen''-e-trê'-li-a men'-tis). The inner parts of the mind. AFFECTIONS, MIND-IMBECILITY.

pen'-e-trate. To enter. ENTRANCE-EXIT, EXCITATION, SAGACITY-INCAPACITY, TRANSMISSION; **penetrate the soul,** EXCITATION.

pen'-e-tra''-ted with. Thoroughly moved by; full of. AFFECTIONS, EMOTION, FAITH-MISGIVING.

pen'-e-tra''-ting. Acute; discerning. EMOTION, SAGACITY - INCAPACITY; **penetrating glance,** SIGHT-BLINDNESS.

pen''-e-tra'-tion. Acuteness. APERTURE-CLOSURE, ENTRANCE-EXIT, INJECTION-EJECTION, SAGACITY-INCAPACITY.

pen'-fold. A temporary pen for straying cattle that are doing damage. ENCLOSURE.

pen-in'-su-la. Land nearly surrounded by water.

pen'-i-tence. Contrition. REPENTANCE-OBDURACY, SOLEMNIZATION.

pen'-i-tent. Sorry. REPENTANCE-OBDURACY.

pen''-i-ten'-tial. Pertaining to penitence. REPENTANCE-OBDURACY.

pen''-i-ten'-tia-ry. A house of correction. RELEASE-PRISON, REPENTANCE-OBDURACY.

pen'-knife''. A small pocket-knife. SHARPNESS-BLUNTNESS.

pen'-man. One who writes a good hand. WRITING-PRINTING; **inspired penman,** REVELATION-PSEUDOREVELATION.

pen'-man-ship. Handwriting. WRITING-PRINTING.

pen'-nant. A small flag. SIGN

pen'-ni-less. Poverty-stricken. AFFLUENCE-PENURY.

pen'-non. A small flag. SIGN.

pen'-ny. One-twelfth of a shilling. MONEY; **cost a pretty penny,** COSTLINESS-CHEAPNESS; **in for a penny in for a pound,** ENGAGEMENT-RELEASE; **no penny no paternoster,** PRICE-DISCOUNT; **not have a penny,** AFFLUENCE-PENURY; **penny trumpet,** CACOPHONY; **turn a penny,** GAIN-LOSS

pen'-ny-a-lin'-er. A term of contempt for those who write at a penny a line. MESSENGER, MISSIVE-PUBLICATION.

pen'-ny-a-lin'-ing. Writing at a penny a line. TERSENESS-PROLIXITY.

pen''-ny-an'-te. A game of poker in which the ante is limited to one cent. ENTERTAINMENT-WEARINESS.

pen''-ny-weight''. The twentieth part of the troy ounce HEAVINESS-LIGHTNESS.

pen'-ny-wise''. Economical in small matters. EXTRAVAGANCE-AVARICE; **penny-wise and pound-foolish,** EXTRAVAGANCE-AVARICE, PERSISTENCE-WHIM, PROVISION-WASTE.

pen'-ny-worth''. A penny's worth. PRICE-DISCOUNT.

pe-nol'-o-gist. A student of penology. SCIENTIST.

pe-nol'-o-gy. The science that treats of the punishment and prevention of crime and of the management of prisons. RECOMPENSE-PUNITION.

pensée, arrière [F.] (pɑn-sê', ɑ-riar'). A mental reservation. ENLIGHTENMENT-SECRECY, PURPOSE-LUCK.

penseroso [It.] (pên-ser-o'-so). Sadness. LIGHTHEARTEDNESS-DEJECTION.

pen'-sile. Hanging loosely. SUSPENSION-SUPPORT.

pen'-sion. A yearly allowance by government OUTLAY-INCOME.

pen'-sion-a-ry. Living by means of a pension. CHIEF-UNDERLING, GIVING-RECEIVING.

pen'-sion-er. One who receives a pension. CHIEF-UNDERLING, GIVING-RECEIVING.

pen'-sive. Thoughtful; sad. LIGHTHEARTEDNESS-DEJECTION, MIND-IMBECILITY.

pen'-stock''. A conduit from a mill-race to a water-wheel gate. WATERCOURSE-AIRPIPE.

pen'-ta-gon. A figure having five sides and five angles ANGULARITY.

pen-tag'-o-nal. Like a pentagon. MINERALOGY.

pen''-ta-he'-dron. A solid bounded by five plane faces. ANGULARITY.

pen-tam'-e-ter. A poetic verse of five metrical feet. POETRY-PROSE, RHETORIC.

pen'-ta-style. Portico. ARCHITECTURE.

Pen'-ta-teuch. The five first books of the Old Testament. REVELATION-PSEUDOREVELATION.

Pen'-te-cost. A Jewish festival occurring fifty days after the Passover. CEREMONIAL.

Pen''-the-si-le'-an. Like Penthesilea, who was queen of the Amazons. BRAVERY-COWARDICE.

pent'-house. A lean-to. CONTENTS-RECEIVER.

pen'-tile. A tile for covering the sloping part of a roof COVER-LINING.

pent'-roof''. Roof having one inclination ARCHITECTURE

pent up. Fast; enclosed. RELEASE-RESTRAINT; **pent up in one's memory,** REMEMBRANCE-FORGETFULNESS

pe-nul'-ti-mate. Being the last but one MIDDLE.

pe-num'-bra. A margin of a shadow. LIGHT-DARKNESS.

pe-nu'-ri-ous. Niggardly. EXTRAVAGANCE-AVARICE.

pen'-u-ry. Poverty. AFFLUENCE-PENURY

pe'-on. A foot-soldier. BELLIGERENT.

peo'-ple. Number of persons; nation DWELLER-HABITATION, GENTILITY-COMMONALTY, HUMANITY, MINISTRY-LAITY, MULTIPLICITY-PAUCITY, PRESENCE-ABSENCE.

peo'-pled. Inhabited. MULTIPLICITY-PAUCITY, PRESENCE-ABSENCE.

pe-pas'-tic. A medicine for wounds. REMEDY-BANE

pep'-per. A plant and its seed. ATTACK-DEFENSE, CONDIMENT, PUNGENCY; **hot as pepper,** HEAT-COLD; **pepper-and-salt,** GRAY-BROWN, VARIEGATION.

pep'-per-corn. An insignificant quantity. CONSEQUENCE-INSIGNIFICANCE; **peppercorn rent,** COSTLINESS-CHEAPNESS.

pep'-per-y. Like pepper. FAVORITE-MOROSENESS, PUNGENCY.

pep'-tic. Promotive of digestion. REMEDY-BANE.

per contra [L.] (per con'-trɑ). Contrariwise. ANTAGONISM-CONCURRENCE, EVIDENCE-COUNTEREVIDENCE, SAMENESS-CONTRAST.

per saltum [L.] (per sal'-tum). By a jump. CONTINUITY-INTERRUPTION, ETERNITY-INSTANTANEITY.

per se [L.] (per si). By itself considered. SOLITUDE-COMPANY.

per''-ad-ven'-ture. Perhaps. POSSIBILITY-IMPOSSIBILITY.

per'-a-grate. To wander over. TRAVELING-NAVIGATION.

per-am'-bu-late. To walk around. TRAVELING-NAVIGATION

per-am''-bu-la'-tion. Walking through or over, especially for the purpose of surveying. TRAVELING-NAVIGATION.

per-am'-bu-la''-tor. One who walks about. CONVEYANCE-VESSEL, LENGTH-SHORTNESS.

per-ceiv'-a-ble. Able to be perceived. PERCEIVE.

per-ceive'. To feel; to discern. FEELING-INSENSIBILITY, KNOWLEDGE-IGNORANCE, SIGHT-BLINDNESS.

per-cent'-age. Allowance on a hundred. NUMBER, PRICE-DISCOUNT.

per-cep''-ti-bil'-i-ty. Cognizability VISIBILITY-INVISIBILITY.

per-cep'-ti-ble. That can be seen. VISIBILITY-INVISIBILITY.

per-cep'-tion. The power or act of perceiving. CONCEPTION-THEME, KNOWLEDGE-IGNORANCE.

per-cep'-tive. Able to perceive. FEELING-INSENSIBILITY.

per''-cep-tiv'-i-ty. Power of perception. FEELING-INSENSIBILITY.

perch. A roost; rod. DWELLER-HABITATION, ESTABLISHMENT-REMOVAL, HEIGHT-LOWNESS, MEASURE, PRESENCE-ABSENCE, SUSPENSION-SUPPORT; **perch up,** ELEVATION-DEPRESSION.

per-chance'. Perhaps. POSSIBILITY-IMPOSSIBILITY, RATIONALE-LUCK.

per-cip'-i-ence. Perception. MIND-IMBECILITY.

per′-co-late. Filter. ENTRANCE-EXIT, RIVER-WIND.
per″-co-la′-tion. Filtration. ENTRANCE-EXIT.
per-cus′-sion. A stroke. IMPETUS-REACTION; **center of percussion,** CENTER.
per-cus′-so-ry. Running over slightly or in haste. HEED-DISREGARD.
per-di′-tion. Ruin. CREATION-DESTRUCTION, GAIN-LOSS, SUCCESS-FAILURE.
perdre son Latin [F.] (perdr son· la-tan′). To lose his Latin. DIFFICULTY-FACILITY.
perdrix, toujours [F.] (per-dri′, tu-zhur′). Always partridge. ENTERTAINMENT-WEARINESS.
perdu, enfant [F.] (per-dü′, an·-fan′). A lost child. RECKLESSNESS-CAUTION, SANGUINENESS-HOPELESSNESS.
perdu, un bien fait n′est jamais [F.] (per-dü′, un· bi-an·′ fê nê zha-mê′). A kind act is never lost. HUMANITARIANISM-MISANTHROPY.
per′-dy. In truth. ASSERTION-DENIAL.
per′-e-gri-nate. To travel from place to place. TRAVELING-NAVIGATION.
per″-e-gri-na′-tion, Traveling. TRAVELING-NAVIGATION.
per″-e-gri-na′-tor. A traveler. WAYFARER-SEAFARER.
per′-emp-to″-ry. Positively. ASSERTION-DENIAL, COERCION, DETERMINATION-VACILLATION, DUTY-DERELICTION, HARSHNESS-MILDNESS, RULE-LICENSE; **peremptory refusal,** PROFFER-REFUSAL.
per-en′-ni-al. Durable. CONTINUITY-INTERRUPTION, FAUNA-FLORA, LASTINGNESS-TRANSIENTNESS, MUTABILITY-STABILITY.
perennius, œre [L.] (per-en′-ni-us, i′-rî). More enduring than bronze. REPUTATION-DISCREDIT.

per′-er-ra′-tion. A wandering. TRAVELING-NAVIGATION.
père tel fils, tel [F.] (pêr tel fis, tel). Like father, like son. LIKENESS-UNLIKENESS.
per′-fect. Complete; finished. COMPLETION-NONCOMPLETION, ENTIRETY-DEFICIENCY, FAULTLESSNESS-FAULTINESS, MAGNITUDE-SMALLNESS.
per-fec′-tion. State of being perfect. ENTIRETY-DEFICIENCY, FAULTLESSNESS-FAULTINESS, GOODNESS-BADNESS; **bring to perfection,** COMPLETION-NONCOMPLETION, FAULTLESSNESS-FAULTINESS.
per′-fect-ly. In a perfect manner. FAULTLESSNESS-FAULTINESS.
per′-fect-ness. Supreme excellence. FAULTLESSNESS-FAULTINESS.
perfervidum ingenium [L.] (per-fer′-vid-um in-ji′-ni-um). One of superheated mettle. ACTIVITY-INDOLENCE.
per-fid′-i-ous. Treacherous. TRUTHFULNESS-FALSEHOOD, UPRIGHTNESS-DISHONESTY.
per-fid′-i-ous-ness. Treachery. UPRIGHTNESS-DISHONESTY.
per′-fi-dy. Violation of faith. TRUTHFULNESS-FALSEHOOD, UPRIGHTNESS-DISHONESTY.
per′-flate. To blow through. RIVER-WIND.
per-fla′-tion. A blowing through. RIVER-WIND.
per′-fo-rate. To bore or pierce through. APERTURE-CLOSURE, TRANSMISSION.
per′-fo-ra″-ted. Bored through. APERTURE-CLOSURE.
per″-fo-ra′-tion. A boring through. APERTURE-CLOSURE, GROOVE.
per″-fo-ra″-tor. One who or that which pierces. PERFORATOR-STOPPER.

PERFORATOR—STOPPER.

Auger. A carpenter's tool for boring holes.
Awl. A pointed instrument for piercing small holes.
Bodkin. A steel, bone, or ivory implement with a sharp point, used in needlework for piercing holes.
Borer. An instrument for boring.
Bradawl. A straight awl with chisel edge, used to make holes for brads.
Corkscrew. An instrument for drawing corks.
Dibble. A pointed wooden instrument for making holes in the ground to plant seed.
Drill. An instrument with an edged or pointed end for making holes.
Gimlet. A tool for boring small holes.
Gouge. A round hollow chisel for cutting grooves in wood or stone.
Lancet. A small, sharp, two-edged knife used by surgeons.
Needle. A small, sharply pointed steel instrument used for sewing.
Perforator. That which is used for making holes.
Piercer. Something used to penetrate or puncture.
Probe. A small slender rod for examining wounds.
Punch. An iron or steel tool for piercing holes by stamping out a piece.
Puncheon. A figured punch used by goldsmiths.
Rimer. An instrument used in making the rounds of a ladder.
Scoop. A spoon-shaped surgical instrument used in extracting foreign substances.
Spear. A long, sharp-pointed fighting weapon. See WEAPON.
Spikebit. A long slender instrument for boring.
Stiletto. A pointed instrument for making eyelet holes; a dagger.
Stylet. A stiletto.
Terrier. An auger.
Trepan. A crown saw for perforating the skull, turned, when used, like an auger.
Trocar. A stylet with a triangular point, used in exploring tissues, or for inserting drainage tubes.
Warder. A staff.
Wimble. A gimlet.

———

STOPPER—NOUNS OF AGENT—*Continued from Column 2.*

Porter. A man in charge of a door or gate.
Warder. The turnkey of a prison.

Bung. The large stopper of a cask.
Cork. A stopper for a bottle or cask.
Cover. Anything laid or spread over something else.
Dossil. A plug or spigot.
Padding. Material with which anything is padded or stuffed.
Piston. The plunger in a pump or steam-engine.
Pledget. A little plug.
Plug. A piece of wood or other substance used to stop a hole.
Ram. The plunger of an hydraulic press.
Rammer. A rod for forcing down the charge of a gun.
Ramrod. The rod used for driving home the charge of a gun.
Side-valve. A valve which opens and closes a passageway by sliding over a post.
Spigot. A peg to stop the vent-hole of a cask.
Spike. An iron rod driven into the vent of a gun.
Spill. A peg or pin for plugging a hole.
Stop-cock. An instrument used to regulate the supply of water, gas, etc., flowing through pipes.
Stop-gap. That which closes up a gap; an expedient
Stopper. That which fills a hole or vent in a vessel.
Stopping. Material for filling a cavity.
Stopple. That which closes the mouth of a vessel.
Stuffing. That which is used in filling anything.
Tap. A plug for stopping the hole in a cask.
Tompion. A stopper of a gun or cannon.
Tourniquet. A surgical instrument for stopping hemorrhages.
Valve. A lid or cover or plug, used to close an aperture.
Vent-peg. A peg for filling the vent of a barrel.
Wadding. Material used for wads

STOPPER—*Nouns of Agent.*

Beadle. An inferior parish officer in England who punishes offenders, etc.
Cerberus. In mythology, the three-headed monster that guarded the entrance into the infernal regions.
Doorkeeper. One who guards the door.
Janitor. A doorkeeper.

(*Continued on Column 1.*)

per-force′. By force. COERCION, READINESS-RELUCTANCE, VOLITION-OBLIGATION.

per-form′. To do; to complete. ACTING, ACTION-PASSIVENESS, AGENCY, COMPLETION-NONCOMPLETION,

Creation-Destruction, Music, Musician, Observance-Nonobservance; **perform a circuit**, Midcourse-Circuit; **perform a duty**, Duty-Dereliction; **perform a function**, Usefulness-Uselessness; **perform a funeral**, Life-Funeral; **perform an obligation**, Observance-Nonobservance; **perform a part**, Acting, Action-Passiveness; **perform a service**, Ceremonial; **perform the duties of**, Occupation.

per-form′-a-ble. Capable of being done. Possibility-Impossibility.

per-form′-ance. The act of performing. Acting, Action-Passiveness, Agency, Completion-Noncompletion, Creation-Destruction, Music, Musician, Observance-Nonobservance.

per-form′-er. One who performs. Acting, Agent, Musician, Society-Affectation.

per-fu′-ma-to-ry. Yielding perfume. Perfume-Stench.

per-fume′. A sweet scent. Perfume-Stench.

PERFUME—STENCH.

Aroma. A delicate, spicy odor.
Aromatic perfumes. Those from aromatic plants
Attar. A fragrant essential oil.
Balm. Any fragrant ointment
Bay rum. An aromatic liquid from bay leaves
Bergamot. A perfume from the fruit of the bergamot tree.
Bouquet. A perfume
Civet. A musky perfume from the civet
Eau de Cologne [F] Cologne water
Fragrance. Sweet perfume
Frankincense. A rosin used as an incense
Incense. The perfume and odor from spices and gums used in celebrating religious rites.
Musk. A perfume from the navel of the musk deer
Myrrh. A gum rosin of an aromatic odor.
Napha-water. Perfume distilled from orange-flowers
Nosegay. A bunch of odorous flowers
Pastil. }
Pastille. } A perfumery for scenting the air of a room
Perfume. A pleasant odor, especially from flowers.
Perfumery. Perfumes in general.
Perfumes of Arabia. Perfumes coming from Arabia. [Shakespeare, *Macbeth*.]
Potpourri [F.] A packet of flowers, leaves, etc., to scent a room.
Pulvil. Powdery perfume.
Redolence. Quality of diffusing fragrance
Sachet. A scent-bag.
Sassafras. An American tree, the bark of which has a strong aromatic odor.
Scent. The effluvium left by animals in their movements.
Scent-bag. A small pouch for carrying perfumes
Smelling-bottle. A bottle for carrying smelling-salts, or the like
Sweet smell. A pleasing odor.
Thurification. Act of burning
Vinaigrette [F] A small perforated box for holding smelling-salts, etc.

PERFUME—*Verbs.*

Be fragrant. To please the sense of smell. See *Adjectives.*
Embalm. To imbue with fragrance
Have a perfume. To have a pleasing odor See *Nouns.*
Perfume. To render odorous
Scent. To cause to be fragrant.
Smell sweet. To emit a sweet odor

PERFUME—*Adjectives*

Ambrosial. Divinely fragrant
Aromatic. Having a spicy odor.
Balmy. Fragrant like aromatic balm
Fragrant. Having a sweet perfume
Fragrant as a rose.
Muscadine. Having the fragrance of the Southern fox-grape.
Perfumatory. Yielding a pleasant odor.
Perfumed. Sweet-scented. See *Verbs.*
Redolent. Diffusing a pervasive odor; fragrant.
Scented. Smelling. See *Verbs*
Spicy. Having a pungent odor
Sweet-scented. }
Sweet-smelling. } Pleasing to the smell
Thuriferous. Producing or bearing frankincense

Bad odor. A bad smell, usually artificial
Bad smell. That which gives an unpleasant sensation to the olfactory nerves
Empyreuma. The smell of animal or vegetable matter burned in a closed vessel.
Fetor. An offensive disgusting odor
Foulness. The quality of being filthy and offensive
Mustiness. Bad smell resulting from mold or age.
Rancidity. Smell of fats and oils in bad condition.
Stench. }
Stink. } An offensive disgusting odor.
Strong odor. }
Strong smell. } A disagreeable or offensive smell

STENCH—*Denotations.*

Asafetida. The fetid gum resin of a plant
Fungus. Organisms or plants of the family mold mildew, etc.
Garlic. A plant having a very strong, pungent smell
Polecat. An animal whose scent-glands secrete a substance of an exceedingly disagreeable odor
Skunk. An animal whose scent-glands secrete an extremely fetid liquid
Stinkpot. An earthen jar charged with powder, grenades and materials of an offensive smell.
Stoat. The ermine or brown weasels whose scent is disagreeable.

STENCH—*Verbs*

Have a bad smell, etc To be disagreeable to the sense of smell See *Nouns*
Smell To have an odor or scent.
Smell offensively. }
Smell strong. }
Stink. } To be disagreeable to the sense of smell
Stink in the nostrils. }
Stink like a polecat. }

STENCH—*Adjectives*

Bad. Unpleasant
Empyreumatic. Pertaining to empyreuma. See *Nouns.*
Fetid. Having a strong, offensive smell.
Frowzy. Having a musty smell
Fulsome. Disgusting by its grossness.
Fusty. Musty, moldy.
High. Tainted: said of meat.
Mephitic. Pertaining to noxious exhalations.
Musty. Having the smell of mold or old age.
Nidorous. Smelling like cooked meat
Noisome. Very disagreeable to sense of smell
Offensive. Causing disgust.
Olid. }
Olidous. } Of a strong, disagreeable smell
Putrid. Produced by putrefaction.
Rancid. Like fats or oils in bad condition.
Rank. Strong and disagreeable.
Reasty. Rancid: as of bacon.
Smelling. Being disagreeable to the sense of smell.
Stinking. Annoying with an offensive smell.
Strong. }
Strong smelling. } Disagreeable.
Suffocating. So strong as to make breathing difficult.
Tainted. Smelling as if slightly decayed.

per-fumed′. Rendered odorous. Perfume-Stench.
per-fu′-mer. One who deals in perfumes. Perfume-Stench.
per-func′-to-ry. Done to get rid of the duty. Carefulness-Carelessness, Entirety-Deficiency, Excess-Lack, Transcursion-Shortcoming.
per-haps′. Possibly. Hypothesis, Possibility-Im-

POSSIBILITY.
pe′-ri. A fairy. Beauty-Ugliness, Jove-Fiend.
per′-i-apt. An amulet. Devotion-Charm.
per′′-i-cra′-ni-um. The region round the cranium. Mind-Imbecility.
pe-ric′-u-lous. Dangerous. Security-Insecurity.
periculum concordiam parit, commune [L.] (per-ic-

yu'-lum con-cor'-di-am pê-rit, com-miu'-nî). Common danger produces concord. STRIFE-PEACE, VARIANCE-ACCORD.

per'-i-dot. Chrysolite. EMBELLISHMENT-DISFIGUREMENT.

per'-i-gee. Point of the moon's orbit nearest the earth. ASTRONOMY.

per''-i-he'-li-on. The point in a planet's orbit nearest the sun. REMOTENESS-NEARNESS.

per'-il. Danger. SECURITY-INSECURITY; **at your peril,** CHARITABLENESS-MENACE; **take heed at one's peril,** WARNING

per-i-lep'-sis. Comprehension. RATIOCINATION-INSTINCT.

per'-il-ous. Hazardous. SANGUINENESS-TIMIDITY, SECURITY-INSECURITY.

per-im'-e-ter. The outer boundary of a figure. OUTLINE.

pe'-ri-od. A point; a portion of time. BEGINNING-END, DISCONTINUANCE-CONTINUANCE, DURATION-NEVERNESS, PERIODICITY-IRREGULARITY, PERIOD-PROGRESS, STATION; **at fixed periods,** PERIODICITY-IRREGULARITY; **well-rounded periods,** PURITY-CRUDENESS, SIMPLICITY-FLORIDNESS.

PERIOD—PROGRESS.

Age. A particular period of time.
Annus magnus [L.] The great year.
Century. A hundred years.
Day. The period of one complete revolution of the earth on its axis.
Decade. A space of ten years.
Decennium. A period of ten years.
Generation. The ordinary period of time at which one rank follows another or father is succeeded by child, usually a third of a century.
Hour. The twenty-fourth part of a day.
Lifetime. The duration of life
Lustrum [L.] A period of five years.
Millennium. A thousand years.
Minute. The sixtieth part of an hour
Month. The twelfth part of a year
Period. A stated length of time.
Quarter. A fourth part of the moon's period.
Quinquennium. A period of five years.
Second. The sixtieth part of a minute.
Week. A period of seven days
Year. The time of one revolution of the earth around the sun.

PERIOD—*Adjectives.*

Annual, etc. Coming once a year. etc. See PERIODICITY.
Horary. Happening once an hour.
Hourly. Occurring hour by hour.

PROGRESS—*Continued from Column 2.*

PROGRESS—*Adverbs, etc.*

In course. In regular succession.
In due season. At the proper time.
In due time. At the proper moment.
In process. Begun, but not completed.
In the fulness of time. When all things are prepared.
In time. In good season.

PROGRESS—*Phrases.*

Fugaces labuntur anni [L.]. The fleeting years slip away. [Horace, *Odes,* II, xiv, 2.]
Labitur et labetur [L.]. It glides along and will continue to glide. [Horace, *Epistles,* I, ii, 43]
"**To-morrow and to-morrow creeps in this petty pace from day to day.**" [Shakespeare, *Macbeth,* V, iii]
Truditur dies die [L.]. One day is pressed onward by another [Horace, *Odes,* II, xviii, 15]

Aorist. A past tense in Greek, so named from its use as the indefinite or general tense
Course of time. } The passage of time.
Current of time. }
Duration, etc. Continuance in time, etc. See DURATION.
Flight of time.
Flow of time.
Flux of time.
Lapse of time. } The passing away of time.
March of time.
Process of time.
Progress of time.
Step of time.
Stream of time.
Succession of time. } The changing from day to day.
Tide of time.
Tract of time.

PROGRESS—*Verbs.*

Advance. To move forward.
Be past, etc. To have happened. See FUTURE-PAST.
Elapse. To slip away.
Expire. To come to an end.
Flit. To pass rapidly.
Flow. To glide along smoothly.
Fly. To pass swiftly.
Glide. To move gently and smoothly.
Go. To pass away.
Lapse. To pass slowly or by degrees.
Out. To come or go out.
Pass. To go by; be spent.
Pass by. To elapse.
Press on. To advance strenuously.
Proceed. To go on.
Roll on. To pass by.
Run. To proceed; pass.
Run its course. To pass away.
Slide. To move smoothly onward.
Slip. To pass along unobservedly.
Wear on. To pass tediously.

PROGRESS—*Adjectives.*

Aoristic. Indefinite.
Elapsing. Passing away. See *Verbs.*
Progressive. Moving forward.

(*Continued on Column* 1.)

pe''-ri-od'-ic. Having regular recurrence. PERIODICITY-IRREGULARITY; **periodic law,** CHEMISTRY; **periodic sentence,** RHETORIC.

pe''-ri-od'-ic-al. Regularly recurring; a book which appears at set intervals. MISSIVE-PUBLICATION.

PERIODICITY-IRREGULARITY.
pe''-ri-od'-ic-al-ly. Regularly. PERIODICITY-IRREGULARITY.

pe''-ri-o-dic'-i-ty. Regularly recurrent. PERIODICITY-IRREGULARITY.

PERIODICITY—IRREGULARITY

Alternateness. The quality of following by turns
Alternation. The act of doing in turns.
Alternativeness. The quality of offering a choice between two.
Alternity. Succession by turns.
Anniversary. The annual return of the day on which any notable event took place.
Beat. A recurring stroke or throb.
Bout. As much as can be performed at one turn.
Cycle. The revolution of a certain period of time, marked by the recurrence of something peculiar.

Fitfulness. The state of being marked by sudden impulses or starts.
Irregularity. The state or quality of departing from the usual or proper form or order
Uncertainty. The quality of being not sure or doubtful.
Unpunctuality. State of being not observant and exact as to appointed time.

IRREGULARITY—*Adjectives.*

Capricious. Apt to change suddenly, as a goat ([L.] *Capra*) moves.
Desultory. Jumping from one thing or subject to another, as a circus rider from horse to horse.

PERIODICITY—IRREGULARITY—*Continued.*

Intermittence. State of being periodic or recurrent

Oscillation, etc. The act of varying between fixed limits, etc. See VIBRATION

Periodicity The state of being regularly recurrent.

Pulsation A beat or throb of a series

Pulse A measured beat

Punctuality Scrupulous exactness as to time.

Regularity The quality of returning at stated intervals

Revolution The period measured by the regular return of a revolving body

Rhythm. The dividing into short periods by a regular succession of motions, etc

Rotation. A succession in a series

Round. A succession or periodical revolution

Steadiness, The quality of being regular or steady

Turn, A revolution.

PERIODICITY—*Denotations*

Ash Wednesday. The first day of Lent [Funereal ashes.]

Bicentennial. The two hundredth year or anniversary

Birthday The anniversary of one's birth.

Centenary The celebration of an event occurring a hundred years before

Christmas. The 25th day of December the anniversary of the birth of Christ.

Days of the week. The days from one Sunday to the next

Easter. The anniversary of the resurrection of Christ, originally a festival of Easter, goddess of spring

Fast. A period of abstinence from food.

Feast. A joyous anniversary

February. The second month of the year; earlier the last month [Februa, purification.]

Hallowe'en The evening preceding All Saints' Day.

January. The first month of the year, named from Janus, a Roman god of openings

Jubilee. The fiftieth anniversary of an event

Leap-year. Every fourth year, which leaps over a day more than the common year.

Monday. The second day of the week. [L.] *La lunæ dies,* moon s day.

Months of the year. Twelve calendar or thirteen lunar months constitute a year.

New year's day. The first day of the year.

Nycthemeron. The space of twenty-four hours [Gr night and day.]

October. The tenth month of the year, originally the eighth month

Period. A stated and recurring interval of time

Rota. An ecclesiastical court of Rome that held annual sessions

Routine. A round of business or pleasure daily pursued.

Stated time. A fixed time for the performance of an act.

Sunday. The first day of the week *Dies solis,* day of the sun.

Wednesday. The fourth day of the week Woden's day, *Jovis dies.*

Year-book A book published yearly

Yule. Christmas Originally a heathen festival of Yule.

Yule-tide. Christmas time

PERIODICITY—*Verbs*

Alternate. To cause to succeed by turns.

Beat. To strike repeatedly

Come again. ⎫

Come in its turn. ⎪ To recur or happen in regular order.

Come round. ⎬

Come round again. ⎭

Intermit. To cease at intervals.

Pulsate. To throb or beat.

Recur in regular order. ⎫ To come at fixed times.

Recur in regular succession. ⎭

Return. To come again.

Revolve. To cause to move in a circle

PERIODICITY—*Adjectives.*

Alternate. Following each other in succession of time.

Annual. Coming once a year.

Biennial. Taking place once in two years.

Fitful. Marked by fits: irregularly variable.

Flickering. Wavering unsteadily

Irregular. Not according to usual forms or rules

Rambling. Wandering, discursive.

Rhapsodical. Unconnected, confused.

Spasmodic. Convulsive, intermittent.

Uncertain. Inconstant variable

Unpunctual. Not done at the exact time.

IRREGULARITY—*Adverbs, etc*

By fits and starts, etc. Irregularly See CONTINUITY-INTERRUPTION.

Irregularity. Not happening at fixed times. See *Adjectives*

PERIODICITY—ADJECTIVES—*Continued*

Biweekly Happening once every two weeks.

Centennial. Coming once in a hundred years.

Cyclical. Moving in cycles.

Daily. Occurring once a day

Diurnal. Recurring each day

Every other. Alternate.

Fortnightly. Occurring once every two weeks.

Hebdomadary. ⎫

Hebdomadal. ⎬ Happening every seven days

Hebdomad. ⎭

Hourly Occurring once an hour

Intermittent. Beginning and ceasing at intervals.

Lenten. Relating to the fast called Lent.

Menstrual. Monthly.

Monthly. Done once a month, or performed in a month.

Paschal. Relating to the Paschal feast or Easter

Periodic. ⎫ Happening at stated intervals

Periodical. ⎭

Punctual. Performed at the exact time.

Quadrennial. Occurring once in four years.

Quotidian. Coming daily

Recurrent. Returning from time to time.

Recurring. Following in succession. See *Verbs.*

Regular. Pursued with uniformity.

Regular as clockwork. Very steady.

Remittent. Having remissions.

Rhythmical. Pertaining to rhythm

Secular. Relating to an age.

Serial. Appearing in successive parts.

Steady. Regular, constant.

Tertian. Occurring every third day.

Triennial. Coming every three years.

Weekly. Once a week.

Yearly. Once a year

PERIODICITY—*Adverbs, etc.*

Alternately. Succeeding by turns.

At established periods. ⎫

At fixed periods. ⎪

At regular intervals. ⎬ Regularly

At stated times. ⎭

By turns. Alternately.

Day by day. Daily

De die in diem [L.]. From day to day

Every other day.

From day to day.

In rotation.

In turn.

Off and on.

Periodically. See *Adjectives*

Punctually. See *Adjectives*

Ride and tie. In turn with another in labor and rest

Round and round.

---

per″-i-pa-tet′-ic. Walking about. TRAVELING-NAVIGATION, WAYFARER-SEAFARER.

per-iph′-er-y. The outer surface. OUTLINE.

per′-i-phrase. To express in a roundabout manner. PHRASE, TERSENESS-PROLIXITY.

per-iph′-ra-sis. Circumlocution. TERSENESS-PROLIXITY.

per″-i-phras′-tic. Employing indirect words. TERSENESS-PROLIXITY.

per′-i-plus. Circumnavigation. TRAVELING-NAVIGATION.

per′-i-scope. A general view. SIGHT-BLINDNESS.

per″-i-scop′-ic. Viewing on all sides; VISIBILITY-INVISIBILITY; periscopic lens, OPTICAL INSTRUMENTS.

per′-ish. To die; to go to ruin. BETTERMENT-DETERIORATION, CREATION-DESTRUCTION, LIFE-DEATH, SUBSTANCE-NULLITY; **perish with cold,** HEAT-COLD; **perish with hunger,** FASTING-GLUTTONY.

per'-ish-a-ble. Liable to perish. LASTINGNESS-TRANSIENTNESS.

per'-ished. Decayed; passed out of existence. ENTITY-NONENTITY.

per'-ish-ing. Passing out of existence. CREATION-DESTRUCTION.

per''-is-sol'-o-gy. Superfluity of words. TERSENESS-PROLIXITY.

per''-i-stal'-tic. Applied to the motion of the intestines. CIRCLE-WINDING.

per'-i-style. System of columns. ARCHITECTURE.

per'-i-wig. A small wig; a peruke. DRESS-UNDRESS.

per'-jured. Having sworn falsely. UPRIGHTNESS-DISHONESTY.

per'-jur-er. One who bears false witness. GULL-DECEIVER.

per'-ju-ry. Solemn assertion of a falsity. PATRIOTISM-TREASON, TRUTHFULNESS-FALSEHOOD.

perk. To make trim. DRESS-UNDRESS; **perk up,** ELEVATION - DEPRESSION, LIGHTHEARTEDNESS - DEJECTION, WEARINESS-REFRESHMENT.

perked'-up. Proud. SELFRESPECT-HUMBLENESS.

per''-lus-tra'-tion. The act of viewing all over. SIGHT-BLINDNESS.

per'-ma-nence. Fixedness. LASTINGNESS-TRANSIENTNESS, MUTABILITY-STABILITY, MUTATION-PERMANENCE, PERSISTENCE-WHIM, VIGOR-INERTIA.

per'-ma-nent. Fixed. DURATION-NEVERNESS, HABIT-DESUETUDE, LASTINGNESS-TRANSIENTNESS, MUTABILITY-STABILITY, MUTATION-PERMANENCE.

per'-me-a-ble. That may be passed through. APERTURE-CLOSURE.

per'-me-ate. To pass through; to fill. ENVIRONMENT-INTERPOSITION, PRESENCE-ABSENCE, TRANSMISSION.

per'-me-a-tion. Diffusing. ESTABLISHMENT-REMOVAL, TRANSMISSION.

Per'-mi-an. Relating to a certain group of strata. **Permian period,** GEOLOGY.

per-mis'-si-ble. That may be allowed. LEAVE-PROHIBITION.

per-mis'-sion. Consent. DIFFICULTY-FACILITY, LEAVE-PROHIBITION, RULE-LICENSE.

permission, avec [F.] (per-mi-si-on·', a-vec'). With permission. LEAVE-PROHIBITION.

per-mis'-sive. Granting. LEAVE-PROHIBITION.

per-mit'. Allow. ASSENT-DISSENT, CONSENT, DIFFICULTY-FACILITY, LEAVE-PROHIBITION.

per-mit'-ted. Allowed. LEAVE-PROHIBITION.

per-mit'-ting. Allowing. LEAVE-PROHIBITION; **weather, etc., permitting,** MODIFICATION, POSSIBILITY-IMPOSSIBILITY.

per-mu-ta'-tion. The arrangement of things in every possible order. COMMUTATION-PERMUTATION, MUTATION-PERMANENCE, NUMBER.

per-ni'-cious. Deadly. GOODNESS-BADNESS.

per-nic'-i-ty. Swiftness. SWIFTNESS-SLOWNESS.

per'-o-rate. To harangue. TERSENESS-PROLIXITY.

per''-o-ra'-tion. The conclusion of an oration. BEGINNING-END, PREDECESSOR-CONTINUATION, SPEECH-INARTICULATENESS.

per'-pend. Consider carefully. MIND-IMBECILITY.

per''-pen-dic'-u-lar. Exactly upright. ERECTNESS-FLATNESS.

per''-pen-dic''-u-lar'-i-ty. Erectness. ERECTNESS-FLATNESS.

per-pen'-sion. Pondering. HEED-DISREGARD.

per'-pe-trate. To commit. ACTION-PASSIVENESS; **perpetrate a pun,** etc., WITTINESS-DULNESS.

per''-pe-tra'-tion. Performance. ACTION-PASSIVENESS.

per'-pe-tra''-tor. One who perpetrates a crime. AGENT.

perpetua, esto [L.] (per-pet'-yu-a, es'-to). Let it endure forever. APPROVAL-DISAPPROBATION, MUTATION-PERMANENCE, REGARD-DISRESPECT.

per-pet'-u-al. Incessant. ETERNITY-INSTANTANEITY, FREQUENCY-RARITY, INFINITY, LASTINGNESS-TRANSIENTNESS; **perpetual curate,** MINISTRY-LAITY.

per'-pet-u-al-ly. Continually. ETERNITY-INSTANTANEITY, FREQUENCY-RARITY.

per-pet'-u-ate. Make perpetual. DISCONTINUANCE-CONTINUANCE, ETERNITY-INSTANTANEITY, MUTABILITY-STABILITY.

per-pet''-u-a'-tion. Continuance. ETERNITY-INSTANTANEITY.

per''-pe-tu'-i-ty. The quality of being perpetual. ETERNITY-INSTANTANEITY, INFINITY, LASTINGNESS-TRANSIENTNESS.

per-plex'. Puzzle. CERTAINTY-DOUBT, CLEARNESS-OBSCURITY, HEED-DISREGARD, ORGANIZATION-DISORGANIZATION, PLEASURABLENESS-PAINFULNESS.

per-plexed'. Puzzled. CIRCLE-WINDING, CLEARNESS-OBSCURITY, REGULARITY-IRREGULARITY.

per-plex'-ing. Puzzling. CERTAINTY-DOUBT, DIFFICULTY-FACILITY.

per-plex'-i-ty. Embarrassment. CERTAINTY-DOUBT, CLEARNESS-OBSCURITY, DIFFICULTY-FACILITY, REGULARITY-IRREGULARITY.

per'-qui-site. An allowance. RECOMPENSE-PUNITION.

per''-qui-si'-tion. A thorough search. INVESTIGATION-ANSWER.

per''-scru-ta'-tion. A thorough searching. INVESTIGATION-ANSWER.

per'-se-cute. To harass. CHARITABLENESS-MALEVOLENCE, GOODNESS-BADNESS, PLEASURABLENESS-MALEVOLENCE.

per''-se-cu'-tion. Oppression. CHARITABLENESS-MALEVOLENCE.

per''-se-ver'-ance. Persisting in what is undertaken. ACTIVITY-INDOLENCE, BIGOTRY-APOSTASY, DETERMINATION-VACILLATION, DISCONTINUANCE-CONTINUANCE, PERSISTENCE-WHIM.

per''-se-vere'. To persist. PERSISTENCE-WHIM.

per''-se-ver'-ing. Persistent. PERSISTENCE-WHIM.

Per-si'-des. Children of Perseus. SUSPENSION-SUPPORT.

per''-si''-flage'. Banter. SOCIETY-DERISION.

per-sist'. Endure. DETERMINATION-VACILLATION, DISCONTINUANCE - CONTINUANCE, MUTATION - PERMANENCE, PERSISTENCE-WHIM, RECURRENCE.

per-sist'-ence. Perseverance. ACTIVITY-INDOLENCE, DISCONTINUANCE-CONTINUANCE, LASTINGNESS-TRANSIENTNESS, MUTATION-PERMANENCE, PERSISTENCE-WHIM.

PERSISTENCE—WHIM.

Backbone. Firmness; stability of purpose.

Bottom Power of endurance

Bulldog courage. Stubborn or persevering courage

Constancy Firmness of mind; unshaken determination.

Continuance. A remaining in a particular state. See CONTINUANCE

Firmness, etc The quality of being firm, etc. See MUTABILITY-STABILITY

Game. Unyielding spirit.

Boutade [F.]. An outbreak, a whim

Capriccio [It.]. A caprice or fancy.

Caprice. An abrupt change of opinion, feeling, or action without sufficient motive.

Capriciousness. Sudden or groundless changes of mind. See *Adjectives.*

Crotchet. A whimsical notion.

Escapade [F.]. An act disregarding the rules of propriety or common sense.

Indefatigability. The state of being unflagging.
Indefatigableness. Persistency.
Iteration. Repetition.
Patience. The exercise of sustained endurance and perseverance.
Permanence, etc. Continuance in one state without change, etc. See MUTATION-PERMANENCE.
Perseverance. Continued pursuit or progress.
Persistence. The state of being determined.
Pertinaciousness. The state of being pertinacious or constant.
Pertinacity. Great firmness in holding to a thing or aim.
Plodding. Laborious diligence.
Pluck. Indomitable resolution.
Sedulity. Constant application.
Singleness of purpose. Sincerity of purpose or persistence in one line.
Stamina. Power of endurance.
Steadiness. The quality of being steadfast.
Tenacity of purpose. Persistence in one's aim or plan.

PERSISTENCE—*Verbs.*

Adhere to. To hold fast to
Bear up. To be firm.
Be in at the death. In hunting, to arrive before the dogs have killed the fox.
Cling. To hold on firmly.
Cling to. To stick at.
Continue. To persevere in any course, etc. See CONTINUANCE.
Die in harness. To continue steadfast to the end.
Die in the last ditch. To die rather than give up.
Follow up. To pursue diligently.
Hold on. To continue.
Hold out. To endure.
Hold up. To support oneself.
Keep on. To persist.
Keep to one's course. }
Keep to one's ground } To remain firm.
Keep up. To continue on.
Maintain one's course. }
Maintain one's ground. } To persist.
Persevere. To continue in one course despite discouragements in order to attain an end.
Persist. To continue from a determination not to give up.
Plod. To toil or study laboriously and patiently.
Stick to. To persevere in holding to.
Stick to one's text. To continue in the same course or manner.
Stick to work, etc. To continue labor. See TOIL.

PERSISTENCE—*Adjectives.*

Constant. Unchangeably fixed; continuous.
Game to the last. Unyielding to the end.
Indefatigable. Unremitting in labor or effort.
Indomitable. That cannot be subdued.
Industrious. Assiduously occupied in some work or pursuit, etc. See ACTIVITY.
Never tiring. Always at work.
Persevering. Continuing. See *Verbs.*
Persistent. Tenacious of purpose.
Persisting. Continuing in doing. See *Verbs.*
Pertinacious. Stubbornly persistent.
Plodding. Working laboriously. See *Verbs.*
Solid. Firm
Staunch. Constant and zealous.
Steadfast. Firm in devotion to duty.
Steady. Constant in purpose.
Steady as time. Constant.
Strenuous, etc. Eagerly pressing; zealous, etc. See TOIL.
Sturdy. Resolute in a good sense; having an unyielding quality.
True to oneself. Unchangeable in purpose.
Unchangeable, etc. Not subject to change, etc. See MUTABILITY-STABILITY.
Unconquerable Indomitable, etc. See STRENGTH.
Undeviating. Not deviating or turning aside from its course.
Undrooping. Not to be dispirited or depressed.
Unfaltering. Not hesitating or trembling.
Unflagging. Not languishing or drooping.
Unflinching. Not failing in persevering or doing.
Unintermitting. Not being interrupted.
Unremitting. Incessant.
Unsleeping. Vigilant
Unswerving. Not departing from a rule of duty.
Untiring. Never becoming weary or fatigued.
Unwavering. Fixed in opinion.
Unwearied. Persistent; indefatigable.

Fad. A freak or whim.
Fancy. A liking or fondness, formed by caprice rather than reason.
Fit. A passing whim.
Flimflam. A freak or trick.
Freak. A sudden, causeless change of mind.
Humor. A funny turn of thought.
Maggot. An odd fancy.
Prank. A mischievous trick.
Quirk. A smart retort or artful turn for evasion.
Vagary. A wandering of the thoughts; a fanciful freak.
Whim. A sudden turn or deviation of the mind from its natural course.
Whimsy. A fanciful conceit or capricious notion.
Whimwham. A whim or whimsy.
Wild-goose chase. The pursuit of something unattainable.

WHIM—*Verbs.*

Be capricious. To be subject to unexpected changes of mind. See *Adjectives.*
Blow hot and cold. To favor a thing at one time and treat it coldly at another.
Have a maggot in the brain. To have a whim or fancy; be capricious.
Play fantastic tricks. To be changeable of purpose.
Play fast and loose. To behave or deal with others whimsically.
Strain at a gnat and swallow a camel. To scruple at doing some small thing and then do something very much worse; hence, to act contrary to reason. [Bible.]
Take it into one's head. To have a sudden notion.

WHIM—*Adjectives.*

Arbitrary. Done according to one's own will or caprice.
Capricious. Characterized by caprice.
Captious. Given to finding fault.
Contrary. Given to opposition.
Crotchety. Subject to whims or caprices.
Eccentric. Deviating from the usual course; odd.
Erratic. Departing from the common course in conduct or opinion.
Fanciful. Guided by fancy rather than reason or experience.
Fantastical. Whimsical or capricious.
Fickle, etc. Having a very changeable mind, etc. See DETERMINATION-VACILLATION.
Fitful. Characterized by fits or variableness.
Freakish. Given to sudden changes of mind.
Frivolous. Marked by trifling.
Full of whims. Changeable. See *Nouns.*
Giddy. Unstable, fickle; heedless.
Humorsome. Whimsical or moody.
Hysterical. Affected with hysteria, a nervous affection occurring in women.
Inconsistent. Not uniform in opinion or action.
Maggoty. Full of caprices or whims.
Particular. Concerned with details; fastidious.
Penny-wise and pound-foolish. Saving small sums while losing larger ones.
Skittish. Changeable; humorsome.
Sleeveless. Lacking a pretext; unreasonable.
Unconformable. Not consistent.
Volatile. Changeable; fickle.
Wanton. Straying from moral rectitude.
Wayward. Disobedient; perverse.
Whimsical. Full of whims.

WHIM—*Adverbs,* etc.

By fits and starts. Irregularly.
Without rhyme or reason. Without sound or sense.

WHIM—*Phrases.*

Nil fuit unquam sic impar sibi [L.]. Nothing was ever so inconsistent in itself.
The deuce is in him.
Tourner casaque [F.]. To turn one's coat.

PERSISTENCE—*Continued.*

PERSISTENCE—*Adverbs,* etc.

At any price. Bound to be done.
Per fas et nefas [L.]. Through right and wrong.
Sink or swim. Regardless of consequences.
Through evil report and good report. }
Through fire and water. } Through the greatest difficulties.
Through thick and thin. }
Vogue la galère [F.]. Forward, come what may.
Without fail. Certain.

PERSISTENCE—*Continued.*

PERSISTENCE—*Phrases*

Aut vincere aut mori [L.]. Either conquer or die.
La garde meurt et ne se rend pas [F.]. The guard dies, it does not surrender
Never say die. Indomitable.

Tout vient à temps pour qui sait attendre [L.]. Everything comes seasonably to him who knows how to wait.
Vestigia nulla retrorsum [L.]. No footsteps backward.

per-sist'-ent. Determined. LASTINGNESS-TRANSIENT-NESS, MUTATION-PERMANENCE, PERSISTENCE-WHIM.
per-sist'-ing. Firmly adhering. PERSISTENCE-WHIM.
per'-son. A human being; a form of the verb. MALE-FEMALE, SUBSTANCE-NULLITY, VERB; **without distinction of persons,** RIGHT-WRONG.
per'-son-a-ble. Attractive in person. BEAUTY-UGLINESS.
personæ, dramatis [L.] (per-so'-nî, dram'-ɑ-tis). Characters represented in drama. ACTING, AGENT.
per'-son-age. A person; a distinction. HUMANITY.
per'-son-al. Belonging to a person. HUMANITY, MALE-FEMALE, MATERIALITY-SPIRITUALITY, SUBSTANCE-NULLITY, UNIVERSALITY-PARTICULARITY; **personal estate,** PROPERTY; **personal government,** TYRANNY-ANARCHY; **personal narrative,** ACCOUNT; **personal property,** PROPERTY; **personal security,** SECURITY.
per''-son-al'-i-ty. That which characterizes a person. ADULATION - DISPARAGEMENT, APPROVAL - DISAPPROVAL, HUMANITY, MALE-FEMALE, MATERIALITY-SPIRITUALITY, POLITENESS-IMPOLITENESS, REGARD-

DISRESPECT, SUBSTANCE-NULLITY, UNIVERSALITY-PARTICULARITY.
per'-son-al-ty. Personal property. PROPERTY.
per'-son-ate. Represent. DELINEATION-CARICATURE, IMITATION-ORIGINALITY.
per''-son-a'-tion. Assuming a character. ACTING, DELINEATION-CARICATURE, IMITATION-ORIGINALITY.
per-son''-i-fi-ca'-tion. Typical representation. DELINEATION-CARICATURE, RHETORIC.
per-son'-i-fy. To ascribe to a thing the qualities of a person. DELINEATION-CARICATURE, TROPE.
per-spec'-tive. Relating to vision. APPEARANCE-DISAPPEARANCE, EXPECTATION-SURPRISE, PAINTING; **in perspective,** LENGTH-SHORTNESS.
per''-spi-ca'-cious. Quick-eyed. SAGACITY-INCAPACITY.
per''-spi-cac'-i-ty. Mental penetration. SAGACITY-INCAPACITY, SIGHT-BLINDNESS.
per'-spi-ca-cy. Penetration. SAGACITY-INCAPACITY.
per''-spi-cu'-i-ty. Clearness of expression and style. CLEARNESS - OBSCURITY, PERSPICUITY - OBSCURITY, RHETORIC.

PERSPICUITY—OBSCURITY

Definiteness. The state of being definite; precision.
Exactness, etc. Carefulness in method and conformity to truth, etc. See TRUTH.
Perspicuity, etc. Clearness in the expression of thought, etc. See CLEARNESS.
Plain speaking, etc. See MANIFESTATION.

PERSPICUITY—*Denotation.*

Definition. An explanation of the meaning of a word or term.

PERSPICUITY—*Adjectives.*

Exact, etc. Scrupulously careful to conform to a rule or standard, etc. See TRUTH.
Explicit, etc. Set forth in the plainest language, so that it cannot be misunderstood, etc. See MANIFESTATION.
Lucid, etc. Clear; easily understood, etc. See CLEARNESS.

Ambiguity, etc. Uncertainty as to meaning, etc. See AMBIGUITY
Hard words. Words difficult to understand
Inexactness. Lack of exactness
Involution. The state of being involved or complicated.
Obscurity, etc. The quality of being obscure or unintelligible, etc. See PERSPICUITY-OBSCURITY.
Vagueness, etc. The state of being vague or indefinite, etc. See CERTAINTY-DOUBT.
What d'ye call 'em See WORD-NEOLOGY

OBSCURITY—*Adjectives.*

Confused. Rendered indistinct or obscure.
Crabbed. Obscure; perplexing.
Involved. Made intricate or complicated.
Obscure. Not easily understood.

per-spic'-u-ous. Lucid. CLEARNESS-OBSCURITY.
per-spi-ra'-tion. Sweat. ENTRANCE-EXIT, NUTRIMENT-EXCRETION; **in a perspiration,** HEAT-COLD.
per-spire'. To sweat. ADMISSION-EXPULSION, ANATOMY, DAMPNESS-DRYNESS, ENTRANCE-EXIT.
per-stringe'. To touch. HEED-DISREGARD.
per-sua'-da-ble. That may be persuaded. READINESS-RELUCTANCE.
per-suade'. To induce by argument or entreaty. FAITH-MISGIVING, MOTIVE-CAPRICE.
per-sua''-si-bil'-i-ty. Capable of being persuaded. MOTIVE-CAPRICE, READINESS-RELUCTANCE.
per-sua'-si-ble. Persuasive. READINESS-RELUCTANCE.
per-sua'-si-ble-ness. The quality of being persuasible. MOTIVE-CAPRICE, READINESS-RELUCTANCE.
per-sua'-sion. A persuading; a motive. EDUCATION-MISTEACHING, FAITH-MISGIVING, MOTIVE-CAPRICE; **religious persuasion,** THEOLOGY.
per-sua'-sive. Tending to persuade. MOTIVE-CAPRICE; **persuasive reasoning,** RATIOCINATION-INSTINCT.
per-sua'-sive-ness. Eloquence. MOTIVE-CAPRICE.
pert. Smart; saucy. CONCEIT-DIFFIDENCE, POLITENESS-IMPOLITENESS, PRESUMPTION-OBSEQUIOUSNESS.
per-tain' to. Relate to. ADMISSION-EXCLUSION, CONNECTION-INDEPENDENCE, DUTY-DERELICTION, HOLDING-EXEMPTION, MIGHT-IMPOTENCE, PROPERTY.

perte de vue, à [F.] (pert de vü, ɑ). Beyond one's view. REMOTENESS-NEARNESS, VISIBILITY-INVISIBILITY.
per''-ti-na'-cious. Persistent. PERSISTENCE-WHIM.
per''-ti-na'-cious-ness. Persistency. PERSISTENCE-WHIM.
per-ti-nac'-i-ty. Obstinacy in adherence. PERSISTENCE-WHIM.
per'-ti-na-cy. Unyielding tenacity. PERSISTENCE-WHIM.
per'-ti-nence. Fitness. HARMONY-DISCORD
per'-ti-nen-cy. Fitness. HARMONY-DISCORD.
per'-ti-nent. Appropriate to the case. CONNECTION-INDEPENDENCE, HARMONY-DISCORD.
per'-ti-nent-ly. In a fit manner. CONNECTION-INDEPENDENCE, HARMONY-DISCORD.
per-tin'-gent. Touching. INTERSPACE-CONTACT.
pert'-ness. Sauciness. PRESUMPTION-OBSEQUIOUSNESS.
per-turb'. To agitate. EXCITATION, ORGANIZATION-INORGANIZATION.
per''-tur-ba'-tion. The act of disturbing. AGITATION, ASTRONOMY, EMOTION, EXCITABILITY - INEXCITABILITY, EXCITATION, ORGANIZATION-DISORGANIZATION, SANGUINENESS-TIMIDITY, VIGOR-INERTIA.
per-tu'-sion. The act of piercing. APERTURE-CLOSURE.
per-uke'. A wig. DRESS-UNDRESS.

pe-ru'-sal. A careful reading. EDUCATION-LEARNING.

pe-ruse'. To read with attention. EDUCATION-LEARNING.

per-vade'. To be in all parts. DOMINANCE-IMPOTENCE, PRESENCE-ABSENCE; **pervade the soul,** EXCITATION.

per-va'-ding. Permeating. EMOTION; **pervading spirit,** AFFECTIONS.

per-va'-sion. Permeation. PRESENCE-ABSENCE.

per-verse'. Obstinate in wrong. BIGOTRY-APOSTASY, DIFFICULTY-FACILITY, FAVORITE-MOROSENESS, POLITENESS-IMPOLITENESS.

per-ver'-sion. A diverting from the proper use. BETTERMENT-DETERIORATION, EDUCATION-MISTEACHING, GODLINESS-UNGODLINESS, INTERPRETATION-MISINTERPRETATION, RATIOCINATION-CASUISTRY, TRUTHFULNESS-FABRICATION.

per-ver'-si-ty. Perverseness. FAVORITE-MOROSENESS, POLITENESS-IMPOLITENESS.

per'-vert. To corrupt. BETTERMENT-DETERIORATION, BIGOTRY-APOSTASY, CONVERSION, EDUCATION-MISTEACHING, GODLINESS-UNGODLINESS, INTERPRETATION-MISINTERPRETATION, RATIOCINATION-INSTINCT, TRUTHFULNESS-FABRICATION.

per-vert'-ed. Corrupted ORTHODOXY-HETERODOXY, TRUTH-ERROR.

per-ves''-ti-ga'-tion. Thorough investigation. INVESTIGATION-ANSWER.

per''-vi-ca'-cious. Obstinate. BIGOTRY-APOSTASY.

per''-vi-cac'-i-ty. Stubbornness. BIGOTRY-APOSTASY.

per''-vi-ca-cy. Stubbornness. BIGOTRY-APOSTASY.

pervigilium [L.] (per-vi-jil'-i-um). A watching all night. ACTIVITY-INDOLENCE.

per'-vi-ous. That may be penetrated. APERTURE-CLOSURE.

pe-se'-ta. Coin. VALUES.

pes'-si-mism. Complaining that everything is for the worst. LIGHTHEARTEDNESS-DEJECTION, OVERVALUATION-UNDERVALUATION, SANGUINENESS-HOPELESSNESS.

pes'-si-mist. One who always looks for the worst. BRAVERY-COWARDICE.

pes'-so-man''-cy. Divination with pebbles. PROPHECY.

pessoribus orti [L.] (pes-sor'-i-bus or'-tai). A nobody. GENTILITY-COMMONALTY.

pest. Plague. PLEASURABLENESS-PAINFULNESS, REMEDY-BANE.

pes'-ter. Tease. PLEASURABLENESS-PAINFULNESS.

pes'-ter-ing. Annoying. PLEASURABLENESS-PAINFULNESS.

pest'-house''. A house for persons having contagious diseases. REMEDY-BANE.

pes-tif'-er-ous. Carrying pestilence. HEALTHINESS-UNHEALTHINESS.

pes'-ti-lence. A plague. GOODNESS-BADNESS, HEALTH-SICKNESS.

pes'-ti-lent. Pernicious; harboring disease. HEALTHINESS-UNHEALTHINESS.

pes''-ti-len'-tial. Breeding pestilence. HEALTHINESS-UNHEALTHINESS.

pes'-tle. An instrument for pounding things in a mortar. **Pestle and mortar,** FRIABILITY.

pet. A tame, fondled animal. ADULATION-DISPARAGEMENT, BLANDISHMENT, FAVORITE-ANGER.

pe-tard'. A device for blowing up works. WEAPON; **hoist on one's own petard,** REPRISAL-RESISTANCE, SUCCESS-FAILURE.

Pe'-ter. One of the twelve Apostles. **Borrow of Peter to pay Paul,** LOAN-BORROWING; **rob Peter to pay Paul,** RIGHT-WRONG, THEFT.

petit maitre [F.] (pe-ti' mêtr). A fop. SOCIETY-AFFECTATION, SOCIETY-DANDY.

petite dame [F.] (pe-tît' dam). A prostitute. PURITY-RAKE.

petitio principii [L.] (pe-tish'-i-o prin-sip'-i-ai). A begging of the question. RATIOCINATION-CASUISTRY.

pe-ti'-tion. A request. DEVOTION-IDOLATRY, PETITION-EXPOSTULATION.

PETITION EXPOSTULATION.

Address. A formal communication, usually of some length.

Apostrophe. An address to an absent person or thing.

Appeal. An urgent request for help.

Application. A formal request, as for a position.

Asking. The act of asking. See *Verbs.*

Begging. The act of asking for alms.

Begging-letter. A letter sent around making request for gifts of money, etc.

Canvass. The act of going around soliciting votes and the like.

Claim. To demand as being due one by right.

Entreaty. A very earnest request, more personal than an appeal.

Imploration. The act of seeking with tears.

Importunity. The act of seeking urgently and persistently.

Imprecation. The act of praying that evil may befall.

Incantation. The saying or singing of magical words as a means of enchantment.

Instance. The act of seeking by suggestion.

Interpellation. A formal demand for an official statement in matters of government.

Invitation. A courteous solicitation to come.

Invocation. The act of calling upon earnestly and solemnly for aid or protection.

Mendicancy. The condition of being mendicant. See *Adjectives.*

Motion. A formal proposal or suggestion, usually one made in a deliberative assembly.

Obsecration. An oratorical appeal for divine or human aid.

Obtestation. Earnest entreaty.

Orison. An earnest prayer; used chiefly in poetry.

Overture. The act of seeking something by making certain preliminary proposals.

Petition. A formal request, usually made to persons in authority and for ordinary wants.

Postulation. Supplication.

Prayer. A request; usually one made to the Supreme Being.

Request. The act of asking for something in a courteous and formal manner.

Deprecation. Prayer or petition for the averting of some threatening evil.

Expostulation. Pleading or entreating with another against some proposed action or course of conduct.

Intercession. Prayer or entreaty in behalf of another.

Mediation. The act of seeking to reconcile those who are at variance.

EXPOSTULATION—*Verbs.*

Deprecate. To pray or entreat against some threatening evil.

Enter a protest. To make a formal and written protest or objection against.

Expostulate. To argue with. See *Nouns.*

Intercede for. To make entreaty in behalf of another.

Protest. To make positive and usually formal objection to.

EXPOSTULATION—*Adjectives.*

Deprecated, etc. See *Verbs.*

Deprecatory. Serving or tending to avert evil.

Expostulatory. Containing or expressing expostulation.

Intercessory. Containing or expressing intercession.

Mediatorial. Serving to mediate.

Protested. Objected to.

Unasked. Without asking for.

Unbesought. Unasked.

Unsought. Unasked for

EXPOSTULATION—*Interjections.*

Cry you mercy! far be it from! forbid it heaven! God forbid! hands off! heaven forbid! heaven forefend! *longe absit* [L.]. Far be it.

PETITION—*Continued.*

Requisition. An authoritative demand.

Rogation. A formal request; used chiefly of governmental bodies.

PETITION—*Continued.*

Round robin.   A petition with signatures written in a circle.
Solicitation.   An earnest and persistent request.

Suit.   The act of suing.   See *Verbs*.
Supplication.   A prayer of the greatest earnestness and intensity.

PETITION—*Verbs.*

Address a petition.   To make a formal written supplication
Address a prayer.   To entreat.
Address a request.   To ask from
Adjure.   To entreat most earnestly.
Appeal to.   To make an earnest supplication to.
Apply to.   To make formal request of.
Ask.   To express a wish for something to another.
Beg.   To ask with importunity.
Beg a boon.   To beg a favor or gift.
Beg from door to door.   To be reduced to the lowest extremity.
Beg hard.   To beg persistently.
Beg leave.   To ask permission.
Beg one's bread.   To be in the condition of a beggar.
Beseech.   To entreat humbly but with great earnestness.
Beset.   To seek or urge upon in such a manner as to embarrass.
Besiege.   To seek to capture by laying siege to.
Bespeak.   To ask for in advance.
Bid for.   To ask for.
Cadge.   To get by begging.
Call for.   To require.
Call to.   To summon to the discharge of some particular duty
Call upon.   To entreat or beseech.
Canvass.   To go around seeking votes and the like
Claim.   To demand as belonging by right.
Clamor for.   To make demand for noisily and persistently
Come down on one's marrow-bones.   To beg, kneeling.
Conjure.   To entreat earnestly.
Court.   To seek the favor of.
Crave.   To ask for humbly but persistently
Cry aloud.   To ask for with a loud voice.
Cry for help.   To be in great distress
Cry to.   To ask help.
Dance attendance on.   To seek the favor of by continual service.
Dun.   To demand or repeatedly demand payment.
Entreat.   To make an earnest request.
Evoke.   To call or summon forth.
Fall on one's knees.   To entreat or pray to
Go a-begging.   To solicit in charity.
Impetrate.   To gain by entreaty
Implore.   To seek with weeping.
Importune.   To ask for persistently.

Imprecate.   To pray that evil may befall
Invite.   To ask to come.
Invoke.   To call upon earnestly and solemnly for aid or protection.
Kneel to.   To entreat.
Knock at the door.   To make a request upon.
Make a petition.   To solicit.
Make application.   To apply.
Make a prayer.   To ask humbly.
Make a request.   To express one's desire.
Make a requisition.   To demand.
Make bold to ask.   To make an appeal to
Make interest.   To seek favor
Mendicate.   To beg.
Mump.   To play the beggar.
Obtest.   To address with earnest entreaty
Offer up prayers.   To beseech God.
Petition.   To formally ask or request.
Plead.   To seek to gain by argument or persuasion.
Ply.   To request or ask importunately.
Pop the question.   To propose marriage.
Pray.   To petition devoutly or earnestly.
Prefer a petition.   To formally present a petition.
Prefer a prayer.   To make a formal prayer.
Prefer a request.   To make a formal request.
Press.   To seek or urge upon persistently.
Publish the banns.   To give public notice of a marriage.
Put to.   To press hard upon; urge.
Put up a petition.
Put up a prayer. } To offer a petition.
Put up a request.
Request.   To ask in a courteous manner.   See *Nouns*.
Seek.   To endeavor to get what is desired by any means whatever.
Send the hat round.   To collect.
Solicit.   To ask for earnestly and persistently.
Sue.   To endeavor to persuade by entreaty; to follow up.
Supplicate.   To pray with the greatest fervency, kneeling.
Tax.   To make demands upon.
Throw oneself at the feet of.   To take an attitude of supplication.
Trouble one for.   To ask for.
Urge.   To entreat or importune.
Whistle for.   To call or summon by whistling.

PETITION—*Adjectives*

Cap in hand.   Submissive or servile.
Clamorous.   Making or made with any loud, repeated outcry
Importunate.   Persistent in entreaty
Mendicant.   Reduced to beggary.
On one's bended knees.
On one's knees. } In an attitude of supplication.
On one's marrow-bones.

Precatory.   Given to entreaty.
Requesting, etc.   Asking with authority   See *Verbs*
Suppliant.
Supplicant. } Asking or entreating fervently.
Supplicatory.   Expressing supplication.
Urgent.   Eagerly importunate or insistent.

PETITION—*Adverbs, etc*

Be good enough.
Be so good as. } Be kind
Do.   An expression of entreaty
Have the goodness.
If you please. } Forms of polite request or entreaty
I pray thee.

Please.
Pray. } Forms of polite request or entreaty.
Prithee.   I pray thee.
Vouchsafe.   Graciously bestow.
Will you.   A form of request

PETITION—*Phrases*

Dieu vous garde [F.]   God guard you
Dirige nos, Domine [L.].   Lord direct us.
For God's sake.

For goodness' sake.
For heaven's sake.
For mercy's sake.

pe-ti'-tion-er.   One who asks.   PETITIONER.

PETITIONER

Applicant.   One who applies for anything.
Aspirant.   One who eagerly seeks something.
Beggar.   One who begs or depends on others for support.
Bidder.   One who offers a price for something.
Cadger.   Itinerant huckster.
Candidate.   One who puts himself forward or is put forward as an aspirant for an office or honor.
Canvasser.   One who canvasses or solicits by traversing a district
Claimant.   One who claims something as a right.

Competitor.   A person who seeks or claims something that is sought or claimed by another.
Mendicant.   A beggar or a begging friar
Mumper.   A beggar.
Petitioner.   One who petitions or solicits; one who presents a petition
Place-hunter.   A persistent aspirant for public office
Postulant.   One who demands; a candidate.
Pot-hunter.   A sportsman who shoots anything he comes across without regard to the rules of the sport, being anxious only to fill his bag.
Prizer.   One who contests for a prize.
Solicitor.   One who entreats or asks earnestly, especially for another
Suitor.   One who sues; a wooer; a petitioner.

Suppliant. One who humbly entreats.
Supplicant. A petitioner who earnestly entreats or asks
Sturdy beggar. A strong, lusty fellow who gains his living by begging.
Touter. One who loiters about places frequented by tourists, to render services or to secure their patronage for a particular inn.

pet'-rel. A sea-bird. WARNING.
pet''-ri-fac'-tion. Fossilization. SOLIDITY-RARITY.
pet'-ri-fy. To convert into stone. ASTONISHMENT-EXPECTANCE, EXCITATION, HARDNESS-SOFTNESS, HEATING-COOLING, SANGUINENESS-TIMIDITY, SOLIDITY-RARITY.
pe-tro'-le-um. A liquid mineral pitch. PULPINESS-ROSIN.
pétroleur [F.] (pê''-tro-lur'). Incendiary using petroleum. TYRANNY-ANARCHY.
pétroleuse [F.] (pê-tro-luz'). One who uses petroleum for incendiary purposes. HEATING-COOLING.
pet-rol'-o-gy. Science of rocks. GEOLOGY.
pet'-ro-nel. A firearm. WEAPON.
pet'-ti-coat. A woman's undergarment. DRESS-UNDRESS, MALE-FEMALE; **petticoat government,** RULE-LICENSE, SKILL-UNSKILFULNESS.
pet'-ti-fog''-ger. An inferior lawyer. ADVOCATE.
pet'-ti-fog''-ging. Paltry; mean. RATIOCINATION-CASUISTRY, UPRIGHTNESS-DISHONESTY, VARIANCE-ACCORD.
pet'-tish. Peevish. FAVORITE-QUARRELSOMENESS.
petto, in [It.] (pet'-to, in). Within the breast. CONCEPTION-THEME, ENLIGHTENMENT-SECRECY, MIND-IMBECILITY, PURPOSE-LUCK.
pet'-ty. Of little worth. CONSEQUENCE-INSIGNIFICANCE, GREATNESS-LITTLENESS; **petty cash,** MONEY; **petty larceny,** THEFT; **petty sessions,** TRIBUNAL; **petty treason,** INSUBORDINATION-OBEDIENCE.
pet'-u-lance. Peevishness. FAVORITE-QUARRELSOMENESS, PRESUMPTION-OBSEQUIOUSNESS.
pet'-u-lant. Fretful. FAVORITE-QUARRELSOMENESS, FORCE-WEAKNESS.
peu de chose [F.] (pu de shoz). A trifle. CONSEQUENCE-INSIGNIFICANCE.
peu s'en faut [F.] (pu san· fo). MAGNITUDE-SMALLNESS.
peut, celui qui veut celui la [F.] (pu, se-lwî ki vu se-lwî' la). Who has the will, he has the skill. DETERMINATION - VACILLATION, SKILL - UNSKILFULNESS.
pew. An enclosed seat in a church. CONTENTS-RECEIVER, FANE.
pew'-ter. An alloy consisting of tin and lead, but sometimes containing antimony, bismuth, and copper. MIXTURE-HOMOGENEITY.
pfennig [G.] (fen'-ig). Coin. VALUES.
pha'-e-ton. A carriage. CONVEYANCE-VESSEL.
pha-lan'-ges. Bones of fingers and toes. ANATOMY.
pha'-lanx. A compact body of soldiers. ASSOCIATION, BELLIGERENT.
phan'-tasm. A specter. APPEARANCE-DISAPPEARANCE, FANCY, SIGHT-DIMSIGHTEDNESS.
phan-tas'-ma. A day-dream. SIGHT-DIMSIGHTEDNESS.
phan-tas''-ma-go'-ri-a. An optical effect produced by a magic lantern. APPEARANCE-DISAPPEARANCE.
phan'-ta-sy. Fancy. CONCEPTION-THEME, FANCY.
phan'-tom. An apparition. APPEARANCE-DISAPPEARANCE, FANCY, SIGHT-DIMSIGHTEDNESS, SUBSTANCE-NULLITY.
Pha'-raoh. King of Egypt. TYRANNY-ANARCHY.
phar''-i-sa'-ic-al. Like the Pharisees. GODLINESS-UNGODLINESS, TRUTHFULNESS-FRAUD.
phar'-i-sa''-ism. Hypocrisy. GODLINESS-UNGODLINESS, TRUTHFULNESS-FALSEHOOD.
Phar'-i-see. A Jew strict in the externals of religion. GODLINESS-UNGODLINESS, GULL-DECEIVER.
phar''-ma-ceu'-tics. Pharmacy. REMEDY-BANE.

phar''-ma-col'-o-gy. The science of medicines. REMEDY-BANE.
phar''-ma-cop'-o-list. A druggist. REMEDY-BANE.
phar'-ma-cy. The art of compounding medicines. REMEDY-BANE.
Pha'-ros. An old lighthouse on the island of Pharos; a lighthouse. SIGN.
phase. Aspect. APPEARANCE-DISAPPEARANCE, ASTRONOMY, CONDITION-SITUATION, CONVERSION-REVERSION, FORM-FORMLESSNESS; **assume a new phase,** CONVERSION-REVERSION; **have many phases,** MUTABILITY-STABILITY; **view in all its phases,** INVESTIGATION-ANSWER.
pha'-sis. Aspect. APPEARANCE-DISAPPEARANCE.
phas'-ma. A phantom. SIGHT-DIMSIGHTEDNESS.
phe-nom'-en-on. An appearance. APPEARANCE-DISAPPEARANCE, OCCURRENCE-DESTINY, PHENOMENON.

PHENOMENON.

Curiosity. Any object that arouses inquiry and fastens attention.
Gazing-stock. Anything gazed at with curiosity or contempt.
Marvel. Anything exciting wonder.
Miracle. Anything wonderful or amazing; a supernatural event or happening.
Phenomenon. That which strikes one as strange, unusual, or unaccountable.
Portent. A momentous event. See PORTENT.
Prodigy. Something unusual or extraordinary causing wonder or surprise.
Sight. Something strange and worthy of notice.
Sign. A remarkable event, considered by the ancients as indicating the will of some deity.
Spectacle. A grand display.
Wonder. An unaccountable thing.
Wonderment. A wonderful thing.

PHENOMENON—*Denotations.*

Annus mirabilis [L.]. The wonderful year.
Bursting of a bomb. ⎱ Something resembling an explosion of a bomb
Bursting of a shell. ⎰ in suddenness and effectiveness.
Coup de théâtre [F.]. A theatrical effect.
Dignus vindice nodus [L.]. A knot worthy to be untied.
Jeu de théâtre [F.]. A stage trick.
Lion. An object of interest and curiosity, especially a person who is so regarded.
Monster. Something of unnatural size, shape, or quality. See CONVENTIONALITY-UNCONVENTIONALITY.
Peal of thunder. A loud and sudden crash, as of thunder.
Saint Elmo's fire. A luminous flame-like appearance, sometimes seen in dark, tempestuous nights, at some prominent point on a ship.
Thunderbolt. Something resembling lightning in suddenness and effectiveness.
Thunderclap. A sharp burst of thunder.
Volcanic eruption. A violent throwing out of flames, lava, etc., from a volcano.
What no words can paint. An object, effect, or feeling that cannot be described.
Wonders of the world. Things of uncommon interest, usually said to be seven.
Xiphopagus. A double monster.

PHENOMENON—*Phrase*

Natura il fece, e poi roppe la stampa [It.]. Nature made him, and then broke the mold.

phi'-al. A glass bottle. CONTENTS-RECEIVER.
Phid'-i-as. A famous Greek sculptor. ARTIST.
phi-lan'-der. Make love. BLANDISHMENT.
phil''-an-throp'-ic. Benevolent. CHARITABLENESS-MALEVOLENCE.
phi-lan'-thro-pist. A benevolent man. HUMANITARIANISM-MISANTHROPY.
phi-lan'-thro-py. The love of mankind. CHARITABLENESS - MALEVOLENCE, HUMANITARIANISM - MISANTHROPY.
phil'-i-beg. A kilt. DRESS-UNDRESS.
Philip drunk to Philip sober. **Appeal from Philip drunk to Philip sober,** BETTERMENT-DETERIORATION.

phi-lip′-pic. Any invective speech. APPROVAL-DIS-APPROVAL.

Phi-lis′-tine. Sordid. GENTILITY-COMMONALTY, KNOWLEDGE-IGNORANCE.

phi-lol′-o-gist. An expert in linguistics. SCHOLAR-DUNCE.

phi-lol′-o-gy. The study of languages in connection with history and literature. GRAMMAR-SOLECISM, LANGUAGE.

phil′-o-math. A scholar. SCHOLAR-DUNCE.

phil′-o-mel. The nightingale. MUSICIAN.

phi-los′-o-pher. A student of philosophy. SCHOLAR-DUNCE; **philosopher's stone,** FAULTLESSNESS-FAULT-INESS, REMEDY-BANE.

phil′′-o-soph′-ic. Rational. EXCITABILITY-INEXCIT-ABILITY.

phil′′-o-soph′-ic-al. According to philosophy. EX-CITABILITY-INEXCITABILITY, REFLECTION-VACANCY.

phi-los′-o-phy. Principles of science. EXCITABILITY-INEXCITABILITY, KNOWLEDGE-IGNORANCE; **moral philosophy,** MIND-IMBECILITY; **philosophy of the mind,** MIND-IMBECILITY.

phil′-ter. A love-potion. DEVOTION-CHARM.

phiz. Face. ANTERIORITY-POSTERIORITY, APPEAR-ANCE-DISAPPEARANCE.

phle-bot′-o-my. Bloodletting. ADMISSION-EXPUL-SION, REMEDY-BANE.

phlegm. The thick viscid matter discharged by coughing. SENSITIVENESS-APATHY, VISCIDITY-FOAM.

phleg-mat′-ic. Abounding with phlegm. SENSITIVE-NESS-APATHY, UNCONCERN.

phlo-gis′-tic. Pertaining to phlogiston. HEAT-COLD.

pho. An interjection. ADAGE-NONSENSE.

Phœ′-bus. The sun-god. LUMINARY-SHADE, UNI-VERSE.

phœ′-nix. A fabulous bird. CONVENTIONALITY-UN-CONVENTIONALITY, FAULTLESSNESS-FAULTINESS, RE-NEWAL, RENOVATION-RELAPSE.

phonanta sunetoisi [Gr.] (fo-nan′-ta syn-e′-toi-si). A word to the wise. CLEARNESS-OBSCURITY.

pho-net′-ic. Relating to the representation of sounds by letters. EXPECTATION-SURPRISE, SOUND-SI-LENCE, SPEECH-INARTICULATENESS; **phonetic spell-ing,** LETTER.

phon′-ics. The science of sounds. SOUND-SILENCE.

pho′-no-graph. An instrument which records sounds and reproduces them. HEARING-DEAFNESS.

pho-nog′-ra-phy. A representation of sounds. LET-TER, SOUND-SILENCE, WRITING-PRINTING.

pho-nol′-o-gy. Science of vocal sounds SOUND-SILENCE, VOCALIZATION-MUTENESS.

phos′′-phor-es′-cence. A faint light without heat LIGHT-DARKNESS, LUMINARY-SHADE.

phos′′-phor-es′-cent. Luminous without heat LIGHT-DARKNESS, LUMINARY-SHADE.

phos-phor′-ic. Phosphorescent. LUMINARY-SHADE.

phos′-phor-us. A combustible substance exhibiting a faint light in the dark. LUMINARY-SHADE.

pho′′-to-gen′-ic. Photographic. LIGHT-DARKNESS.

pho′-to-graph. A likeness. DELINEATION-CARICA-TURE, LIKENESS-UNLIKENESS, PAINTING.

pho-tog′-ra-phy. The art of producing pictures. LIGHT-DARKNESS, PAINTING, TRUTHFULNESS-FALSE-HOOD.

pho′′-to-gra-vure′ A process in engraving. EN-GRAVING.

pho′′-to-lith′-o-graph. To produce a printing-surface on stone. ENGRAVING.

pho′′-to-lith-og′-ra-phy. The art of photolithograph-ing. ENGRAVING.

pho-tol′-o-gy. The science of light LIGHT-DARK-NESS.

pho-tom′-e-ter. An instrument for measuring the in-tensity of light. LIGHT-DARKNESS, OPTICAL IN-STRUMENTS.

pho-tom′-e-try. Science of measuring the intensity of light. LIGHT-DARKNESS.

pho′-to-sphere. The visible shining surface of a planet. UNIVERSE.

phrase. A brief expression. MELODY-DISSONANCE, PHRASE, RHETORIC, TROPE, WORD-NEOLOGY

PHRASE.

Expression. A form of words conveying an idea or sentiment; mode of speech.

Figure of speech. A mode of expressing abstract ideas by words which suggest pictures or images from the physical world. See TROPE.

Idiom. The structural form peculiar to any language, especially if it be an irregularity.

Idiotism. The mode of expression of a particular language or person.

Motto. A short, suggestive expression of a guiding principle. See ADAGE.

Paragraph. A distinct part of a discourse or writing.

Paraphrase, etc. A setting forth the signification of a text in other and ampler terms.

Periphrase, etc. A roundabout or indirect way of speaking.

Phrase. A mode or form of expression.

Phraseology, etc. Style of expression or peculiarity of diction, etc. See STYLE.

Sentence. A combination of words which expresses a thought.

Set phrase. A regular or formal mode of expression.

Turn of expression. Form of expression.

PHRASE—*Verbs.*

Arrange in words. } **Clothe in words.** } To give expression to one's thoughts.

Couch in terms. To express in words.

Express. To utter; denote; designate

Express by words. **Find words to express.** } **Give expression to.** } To express what one has in mind. **Give words to.** }

Phrase. To express in proper words.

Put into words. To speak.

Speak by the card. To speak correctly or from definite information.

Word. } **Word it.** } To express in words.

PHRASE—*Adjectives.*

Expressed. Uttered in words. See *Verbs.*

Idiomatic. Conforming to idiom.

PHRASE—*Adverbs, etc*

In good set terms. Accurately expressed.

In round terms. Plainly.

In set phrases. In formal language.

In set terms. Formally

phrase′-mon-ger. A wordy speaker or writer. SIM-PLICITY-FLORIDNESS.

phra′′-se-ol′-o-gy. Mode of speech. LANGUAGE, PHRASE, RHETORIC, STYLE.

phren-et′-ic. Pertaining to phrenitis SANENESS-LUNACY.

phren-i′-tis. Brain fever. SANENESS-LUNACY.

phre-nol′-o-gy. Science of the mind. MIND-IMBE-CILITY.

phren′′-o-typ′-ics. Science of memory REMEM-BRANCE-FORGETFULNESS.

phren′-sy. Violent excitement; frenzy. EXCITABIL-ITY-INEXCITABILITY, FANCY, SANENESS-LUNACY.

phren′-sied. Frenzied; mad. SANENESS-LUNACY.

Phry′-ne. A celebrated Athenian hetæra. PURITY-RAKE.

phthi′′-so-zo′-ics. The art of destroying hurtful ani-mals DOMESTICATION-AGRICULTURE, LIFE-KILL-ING.

phy-lac′-ter-ic. Charm-like. ADAGE-NONSENSE, DEVOTION-MAGIC.

phy-lac′-ter-y. A charm to protect from danger. ADAGE-NONSENSE, DEVOTION-CHARM.

phy-log'-e-ny. History of evolution. BIOLOGY.

phys'-ic. Art of healing. REMEDY-BANE, RENOVATION-RELAPSE.

phys'-ic-al. Pertaining to nature. MATERIALITY-SPIRITUALITY; **physical crystallography,** MINERALOGY; **physical education,** EDUCATION-MISTEACHING, MATERIALITY-SPIRITUALITY; **physical force,** COERCION, STRENGTH-WEAKNESS; **physical pain,** SENSUALITY-SUFFERING; **physical pleasure,** SENSUALITY-SUFFERING; **physical science,** MATERIALITY-SPIRITUALITY; **physical sensibility,** FEELING-INSENSIBILITY, SENSITIVENESS-APATHY.

phy-si'-cian. Doctor. ADVICE, REMEDY-BANE.

phys'-i-cist. A specialist in physics. MATERIALITY-SPIRITUALITY.

phys'-ics. The science of nature. MATERIALITY-SPIRITUALITY.

phys''-i-og'-no-my. The art of discerning the character of the mind from the face. ANTERIORITY-POSTERIORITY, APPEARANCE-DISAPPEARANCE, INTERPRETATION-MISINTERPRETATION.

phys''-i-o-graph'-ic-al. Descriptive of nature. **Physiographical geography,** GEOLOGY.

phys''-i-o-log'-ic-al. Pertaining to physiology. **Physiological chemistry,** CHEMISTRY.

phys''-i-ol'-o-gy. The science of living beings. BIOLOGY, LIFE-DEATH, ORGANIZATION-INORGANIZATION; **vegetable physiology,** ZOOLOGY-BOTANY.

phy-sique'. The physical structure of a person. ANIMALITY-VEGETABILITY, STRENGTH-WEAKNESS.

phy-tiv'-o-rous. Feeding on plants or herbage. NUTRIMENT-EXCRETION.

phy-tog'-ra-phy. Descriptive botany. ZOOLOGY-BOTANY.

phy-tol'-o-gy. Botany. ZOOLOGY-BOTANY.

phy-tot'-o-my. Vegetable anatomy. ZOOLOGY-BOTANY.

pi. To mix up type. WRITING-PRINTING.

piacere, al [It.] (pî-a-chê'-rê al). As you please. VOLITION-OBLIGATION.

pi-ac'-u-lar. Expiatory. ATONEMENT.

pi-ac'-u-lous. Criminal. ATONEMENT.

pi''-a-ni'-no. A small piano. MUSICAL INSTRUMENTS.

pi''-a-nis'-si-mo. Very soft. LOUDNESS-FAINTNESS, MUSIC.

pi-an'-ist. A piano player. MUSICIAN.

pia'-no. Soft; gentle. LOUDNESS-SOFTNESS, MUSICAL INSTRUMENTS, SWIFTNESS-SLOWNESS, TURBULENCE-CALMNESS.

pi-an''-o-for'-te. A keyed musical instrument. MUSICAL INSTRUMENTS.

pi-az'-za. A covered walk. DWELLER-HABITATION.

pi'-broch. Wild music. FIGHTING-CONCILIATION, MUSIC.

pi'-ca. A size of type. WRITING-PRINTING.

picaresco, gusto [Sp.] (pî-car-ês'-co, gus'-to). A roguish taste. VIRTUE-VICE.

pic''-a-roon'. Rogue. ROBBER.

pic'-co-lo. A small flute. MUSICAL INSTRUMENTS.

pick. Select; a picking tool. CHOICE-NEUTRALITY, CLEANNESS-FILTHINESS, GAIN-LOSS, GOODNESS-BADNESS, NUTRIMENT-EXCRETION, SHARPNESS-BLUNTNESS; **pick a quarrel,** VARIANCE-ACCORD; **pick holes,** ADULATION-DISPARAGEMENT, APPROVAL-DISAPPROVAL; **pick one's steps,** CAREFULNESS-CARELESSNESS; **pick one's way,** CHOICE-NEUTRALITY, TRAVELING-NAVIGATION, VENTURE; **pick out,** CHOICE-NEUTRALITY, INJECTION-EJECTION; **pick the brains of,** TRIAL-ANSWER; **pick the lock,** DISCOVERY; **pick to pieces,** APPROVAL-DISAPPROVAL, CREATION-DESTRUCTION, UNION-DISUNION; **pick up,** BETTERMENT-DETERIORATION, CHOICE-NEUTRALITY, EDUCATION-LEARNING, GAIN-LOSS.

pick'-a-nin''-ny. A little child, especially a negro. INFANT-VETERAN.

pick'-ax''. A picking tool. SHARPNESS-BLUNTNESS.

picked. Chosen. GOODNESS-BADNESS; **picked men,** ADEPT-BUNGLER.

pick-eer'. To maraud. THEFT.

pick-eer'-er. One who pickeers. ROBBER.

pick''-el-haube'. A helmet. ATTACK-DEFENSE, DRESS-UNDRESS.

pick'-et. A camp guard; a short stake. ATTACK-DEFENSE, BELLIGERENT, CONFINEMENT, ESTABLISHMENT-REMOVAL, RECOMPENSE-PUNITION, RELEASE-PRISON, RELEASE-RESTRAINT, UNION-DISUNION, WARNING.

pick'-et-ing. Placing on guard; a mode of torture. RECOMPENSE-PUNITION.

pick'-ings. Booty. GAIN-LOSS, PLUNDER.

pick'-le. To preserve in the brine of vinegar; a scrape; a grain of corn. CONDIMENT, CONDITION-SITUATION, CONSERVATION, DIFFICULTY-FACILITY, PUNGENCY, WATER-AIR; **have a rod in pickle,** PREPARATION-NONPREPARATION; **in a fine pickle,** DIFFICULTY-FACILITY.

pick'-le-her''-ring. Pickled herring; a buffoon. WAG.

pick'-pock''-et. One who steals from pockets. ROBBER; **abuse like a pickpocket,** APPROVAL-DISAPPROVAL.

pick'-purse. One who steals from purses. ROBBER.

pick'-thank''. A flatterer. ACTIVITY-INDOLENCE, PRESUMPTION-OBSEQUIOUSNESS.

pic'-nic. An outdoor pleasure-party. ADMISSION-EXPULSION, ENTERTAINMENT-WEARINESS, PARTICIPATION.

pic-quet'. A game of cards. ENTERTAINMENT-WEARINESS.

pic-to'-ri-al. Pertaining to pictures. BEAUTY-UGLINESS, PAINTING; **pictorial language,** RHETORIC.

pictura pascit inana animum [L.] (pic-tiu'-ra pas'-sit in-ê-na an'-i-mum). He feeds his mind with an empty picture. REFLECTION-VACANCY.

pictura poema mutum est [L.] (pic-tiu'-ra po-î'-ma miu'-tum est). A picture is a mute poem. PAINTING, POETRY-PROSE.

pic'-ture. A resemblance. ACCOUNT, APPEARANCE-DISAPPEARANCE, DELINEATION-CARICATURE, PAINTING; **picture to oneself,** FANCY; **the picture of,** LIKENESS-UNLIKENESS.

pic'-ture-gal'-ler-y. A place for collecting pictures. PAINTING.

pic''-tur-esque'. Beautiful to the eye. BEAUTY-UGLINESS, PAINTING.

pid'-dle. Dawdle. ACTIVITY-INDOLENCE.

pid'-dling. Dawdling. CONSEQUENCE-INSIGNIFICANCE.

pie. A food. NUTRIMENT-EXCRETION, SWEETNESS-ACIDITY, WRITING-PRINTING.

pie'-bald''. Of various colors. VARIEGATION.

piece. A bit; a selection; a coin. ACTING, MONEY, PAINTING, PURITY-RAKE, WEAPON, WHOLE-PART; **fall to pieces,** CREATION-DESTRUCTION, TOUGHNESS-BRITTLENESS; **give a piece of advice,** ADVICE; **in pieces,** FRIABILITY; **make a piece of work about,** CONSEQUENCE-INSIGNIFICANCE; **of a piece,** HARMONY-DISCORD, LIKENESS-UNLIKENESS, MIXTURE-HOMOGENEITY, UNIFORMITY-DIVERSITY; **piece of good fortune,** GOOD-EVIL; **piece of music,** MELODY-DISSONANCE, MUSIC; **piece of news,** TIDINGS-MYSTERY; **piece of work,** VARIANCE-ACCORD; **piece out,** ENTIRETY-DEFICIENCY; **piece together,** UNION-DISUNION; **pull to pieces,** CREATION-DESTRUCTION.

pièce de résistance [F.] (piês de rê-zis-tan·s'). A solid joint of meat. NUTRIMENT-EXCRETION.

pièce justificative [F.] (piês zhüs-ti-fi-ca-tîv'). Proof and illustration. EVIDENCE-COUNTEREVIDENCE.

piece'-meal''. Piece by piece. WHOLE-PART.

pied. Variegated. VARIEGATION.

pied de la lettre, au [F.] (piè de la letr, o). Literally. TRUTH-ERROR.

pie-poudre, court of. An ancient court of England. TRIBUNAL.

pier. A wharf; a support for an arch. REFUGE-PIT-FALL.

pierce. To perforate; wound. APERTURE-CLOSURE, BETTERMENT-DETERIORATION, EXCITATION, GOODNESS-BADNESS, HEATING-COOLING, PLEASURABLENESS-PAINFULNESS, SENSUALITY-SUFFERING; **pierce the head,** CACOPHONY; **pierce the heart,** PLEASURABLENESS-PAINFULNESS.

pier'-cer. One who or that which pierces. PERFORATOR-STOPPER.

pier'-cing. Cutting; shrill. APERTURE-CLOSURE, CACOPHONY, EMOTION, HEAT-COLD, LOUDNESS-FAINTNESS, SAGACITY-INCAPACITY; **piercing eye,** SIGHT-BLINDNESS; **piercing pain,** SENSUALITY-SUFFERING.

pier'-glass". A large high mirror between two openings in a wall. OPTICAL INSTRUMENTS.

Pi-e'-ri-an Spring. Spring of the Muses. POETRY-PROSE.

pierre fendr, a [F.] (pièr fan·dr, a). A heavy frost. HEAT-COLD.

pietas [L.] (pai'-et-as). Godliness. CEREMONIAL.

piété, mont de [F.] (pi-ê-tê', mon· de). Pawnbroker. LOAN-BORROWING.

pi'-et-ism. Strict devotion. GODLINESS-UNGODLINESS.

pi'-et-ist. One who makes a display of religious feeling. GODLINESS-UNGODLINESS.

pi"-et-is'-tic. Characterized by religious emotionalism. GODLINESS-UNGODLINESS.

pi"-et-is'-tic-al. Characterized by religious emotionalism. GODLINESS-UNGODLINESS.

pi'-et-y. Veneration of God. GODLINESS-UNGODLINESS.

pig. A hog. FAUNA-FLORA, MODERATION-SELFINDULGENCE; **pig in a poke,** CERTAINTY-DOUBT, PURPOSE-LUCK, RECKLESSNESS-CAUTION; **pig together,** GATHERING-SCATTERING.

pig'-eon. A dove; one who is easily swindled. GULL-DECEIVER, THEFT.

pigeon, gorge de [F.] (pi-zhon·', gorzh de). Dove-color. VARIEGATION.

pig'-eon—Eng'-lish. A dialect of English used in China. WORD-NEOLOGY.

pig'-eon—heart'-ed. Timid. BRAVERY-COWARDICE.

pig'-eon—hole". A small box-like hole. APERTURE-CLOSURE, CONTENTS-RECEIVER.

pig'-eon-holes". Small box-like holes. MARK-OBLITERATION.

pig'-gin. A long-handled dipper. CONTENTS-RECEIVER.

pig'-gish. Greedy. MODERATION-SELFINDULGENCE.

pig'-head"-ed. Obstinate. BIGOTRY-APOSTASY, SAGACITY-INCAPACITY.

pig'-ment. Any coloring material. COLOR-ACHROMATISM.

pig'-my. A dwarf. GREATNESS-LITTLENESS.

pig"-no-ra'-tion. The act of pawning. SECURITY.

pig'-stick"-ing. Boar-hunting. LIFE-KILLING.

pig'-sty. A pigpen. CLEANNESS-FILTHINESS.

pig'-tail. Chinaman's cue. SUSPENSION-SUPPORT.

pig'-wid"-geon. A cant word for anything petty. GREATNESS-SMALLNESS, JOVE-FIEND.

pike. A lance. HEIGHT-LOWNESS, SHARPNESS-BLUNTNESS, WEAPON.

pike'-man. A soldier armed with a pike. BELLIGERENT.

pike'-staff. The staff of a pike. HEIGHT-LOWNESS, MANIFESTATION-LATENCY.

pi-las'-ter. A square column. CONVEXITY-CONCAVITY, EMBELLISHMENT-DISFIGUREMENT, SUSPENSION-SUPPORT.

pile. A heap; a large building. ARCHITECTURE, CREATION-DESTRUCTION, GATHERING-SCATTERING, SMOOTHNESS-ROUGHNESS, **funeral pile,** LIFE-FUNERAL; **pile up,** EXCESS-LACK, GULL-HYPERBOLE.

pile'-dri"-ving—en"-gine. An apparatus for driving down piles. IMPETUS-REACTION.

pil'-fer. Steal. THEFT.

pil'-fer-er. One who steals. ROBBER.

pil-gar'-lic. A sneaking fellow. SOCIABILITY-PRIVACY.

pil'-grim. A traveler. MINISTRY-LAITY, WAYFARER-SEAFARER.

pil'-grim-age. A journey to some sacred place. ENTERPRISE, TRAVELING-NAVIGATION.

pill. A medicine in the form of a sphere. REMEDY-BANE, ROUNDNESS; **bitter pill,** PLEASURABLENESS-PAINFULNESS, WELFARE-MISFORTUNE.

pil'-lage. Plunder. BETTERMENT-DETERIORATION, THEFT.

pil'-la-ger. Plunderer. ROBBER.

pil'-lar. A support; a monument. HEIGHT-LOWNESS, MARK-OBLITERATION, MUTABILITY-STABILITY, SUSPENSION-SUPPORT, WRITING-PRINTING; **from post to pillar,** AGITATION, MIDCOURSE-CIRCUIT, REMEMBRANCE-FORGETFULNESS; **pillar of the state,** REPUTATION-DISCREDIT; **pillars of Hercules,** SIGN.

pil'-lion. A pad for a second person on a horse. SUSPENSION-SUPPORT.

pil'-lo-ry. A frame to confine criminals by neck and head. RECOMPENSE-SCOURGE.

pil'-low. A cushion for the head. FEELING-INSENSIBILITY, HARDNESS-SOFTNESS, MOVEMENT-REST, SUSPENSION-SUPPORT; **consult one's pillow,** EARLINESS-LATENESS, REFLECTION-VACANCY.

pi'-lot. One who steers a ship. ENLIGHTENMENT-SECRECY, MANAGEMENT, MANAGER, WAYFARER-SEAFARER.

pi'-lot-age. Guidance. MANAGEMENT.

pi'-lot bal-loon'. A guide balloon. CONVEYANCE-VESSEL, TRIAL.

pi'-lot—boat. A boat to receive and carry pilots as they leave vessels. CONVEYANCE-VESSEL.

pi'-lose. Hairy. SMOOTHNESS-ROUGHNESS.

pimp. A pander. PURITY-RAKE.

pim'-ple. A small pointed elevation on the skin. CONVEXITY-CONCAVITY, EMBELLISHMENT-DISFIGUREMENT, HEALTH-SICKNESS.

pin. A short stiff piece of wire with a point. CONNECTIVE, CONSEQUENCE-INSIGNIFICANCE, ESTABLISHMENT-REMOVAL, REVOLUTION-EVOLUTION, SHARPNESS-BLUNTNESS, UNION-DISUNION; **might hear a pin drop,** SOUND-SILENCE; **not a pin to choose,** CHOICE-NEUTRALITY, EQUALITY-INEQUALITY; **pin down,** COERCION, RELEASE-RESTRAINT; **pin oneself upon,** CHIEF-UNDERLING, PRESUMPTION-OBSEQUIOUSNESS; **pin one's faith upon,** FAITH-MISGIVING, SANGUINENESS-HOPELESSNESS; **point of a pin,** GREATNESS-LITTLENESS.

pin'-a-coid". Kind of crystal. MINERALOGY.

pin'-a-fore". A little apron. DRESS-UNDRESS.

pince'-nez". A kind of eye-glasses. OPTICAL INSTRUMENTS.

pin'-cers. A grasping instrument. KEEPING-RELINQUISHMENT.

pinch. To squeeze; in need. CONDITION-SITUATION, DIFFICULTY-FACILITY, ENLARGEMENT-DIMINUTION, EXTRAVAGANCE-AVARICE, HEATING-COOLING, NEED, PLEASURABLENESS-PAINFULNESS, SENSUALITY-SUFFERING; **at a pinch,** DIFFICULTY-FACILITY; **jack at a pinch,** ANTAGONIST-ASSISTANT; **pinch of snuff,** CONSEQUENCE-INSIGNIFICANCE; **where the shoe pinches,** ANTAGONISM-CONCURRENCE, GOODNESS-BADNESS, OBSTRUCTION-HELP, PLEASURABLENESS-PAINFULNESS.

pinch'-beck. An alloy of copper and zinc. EMBELLISHMENT-DISFIGUREMENT, TRUTHFULNESS-FRAUD.

pinched. In hard circumstances. Affluence-Penury, Condition-Situation, Difficulty-Facility, Enlargement-Diminution, Extravagance-Avarice, Heating-Cooling, Need, Obstruction-Help, Pleasurableness-Painfulness, Sensuality-Suffering; **pinched with hunger,** Desire-Distaste.

pinch'-ing. Nipping. Extravagance-Avarice, Heat-Cold.

Pin-dar'-ic. Pertaining to Pindar. Poetry.

pine. To waste away. Health-Sickness, Lightheartedness-Dejection, Pleasure-Pain; **pine away,** Lightheartedness-Dejection; **pine for,** Desire-Distaste.

pin'-er-y. A pine forest. Domestication-Agriculture.

pi-ne'-tum. A forest of pines. Domestication-Agriculture.

pin'-guid. Fat. Pulpiness-Oiliness.

ping-pong. Table tennis. Tennis.

pin'-hole. A place where a pin is fixed. Aperture-Closure.

pin'-ion. A quill; a small toothed wheel. Instrument, Release-Prison, Release-Restraint, Traveling-Navigation, Union-Disunion.

pink. A reddish color; pierce; perfection. Aperture-Closure, Faultlessness-Faultiness, Impetus-Reaction, Redness-Greenness, Reputation-Discredit; **pink of,** Beauty-Ugliness; **pink of fashion,** Society-Ludicrousness; **pink of perfection,** Faultlessness-Faultiness; **pink of politeness,** Politeness-Impoliteness.

pin'-mon''-ey. Spending- or pocket-money. Money.

pin'-nace. A boat. Conveyance-Vessel.

pin'-na-cle. A turret. Architecture, Top-Bottom.

pins. Legs. Traveling-Navigation; **pins and needles,** Pleasure-Pain, Sensuality-Suffering, Tingling-Numbness.

pint. Unit of measure. Measure.

Pin'-to, Fer-na'-o Men'-dez. Portuguese adventurer. Gull-Deceiver.

pi-o-neer'. One who goes before to clear the way. Anteriority-Posteriority, Instructor-Pupil, Predecessor-Continuation, Preparation-Nonpreparation.

pi'-ous. Devout. Godliness-Ungodliness; **pious fraud,** Godliness-Ungodliness, Truthfulness-Fabrication.

pipe. A tube; a sound; a cry. Cacophony, Cry-Ululation, Jubilation-Lamentation, Musical Instruments, Musician, Way; **no pipe, no dance,** Price-Discount; **pipe of peace,** Strife-Peace; **pipe one's eye,** Jubilation-Lamentation.

pipe'-clay''. A white clay used for pottery. Habit-Desuetude, Harshness-Mildness.

pi'-per. One who plays a pipe. Musician; **drunk as a piper,** Teetotalism-Intemperance; **pay the piper,** Obstruction-Help, Settlement-Default.

pi'-ping. Playing the pipe; smoking. **Piping hot,** Heat-Cold; **piping time,** Strife-Peace, Welfare-Misfortune.

pip'-kin. A small earthen jar. Contents-Receiver.

pi'-quan-cy. Sharpness; cleverness. Excitation, Force-Weakness, Pungency.

pi'-quant. Sharp. Emotion, Force-Weakness, Pungency.

pi'-quante. Sharp. **Piquante sauce,** Condiment, Pleasurableness-Painfulness.

pique. To offend; to stimulate. Excitation, Favorite-Anger, Love-Hate, Pleasurableness-Painfulness; **pique oneself,** Conceit-Diffidence, Self-respect-Humbleness.

pi-queer'-er. One who marauds; a pickeerer. Robber.

pi''-quet'. Picket. Attack-Defense, Belligerent.

pi'-ra-cy. Robbery on the sea. Theft.

pi'-rate. A sea-robber. Robber, Theft.

pi-rat'-ic-al. Pertaining to pirates. Theft.

pir''-ou-ette'. A wheeling about on the toes when dancing. Reversal, Revolution-Evolution; **turn a pirouette,** Persistence-Whim.

Pi'-sa. The capital of the province of Pisa, Italy. **Tower of Pisa,** Parallelism-Inclination.

pis-aller [F.] (piz''-a-lê'). The last shift. Commutation-Permutation, Volition-Obligation.

pis''-ca-to'-ri-al. Pertaining to fishes. Fauna-Flora, Life-Killing.

pis'-ca-to-ry. Pertaining to fishes. Fauna-Flora, Life-Killing.

piscem natare docere [L.] (pis'-sem nat-ê'-rî do-sî'-rî). To teach a fish to swim. Education-Misteaching, Excess-Lack.

Pis'-ces. Sign of the zodiac. Astronomy.

pis'-ci-cul''-ture. The hatching of fish as an industrial art. Domestication-Agriculture.

pish. An exclamation of contempt. Adage-Nonsense, Consequence-Insignificance, Excitability-Inexcitability, Favorite-Quarrelsomeness.

piste. The track a horseman makes upon the ground he goes over. Mark-Obliteration.

pis'-tol. A hand gun. Weapon.

pis'-to-let. A small pistol. Weapon.

pis'-tol-shot''. The distance a pistol shoots. Remoteness-Nearness.

pis'-ton. A short cylinder fitted to a hollow one within which it moves. Perforator-Stopper.

pit. A deep hole; the main floor of a theater. Acting, Aperture-Closure, Convexity-Concavity, Deepness-Shallowness, Life-Funeral; **bottomless pit,** Heaven-Hell; **pit of Acheron,** Heaven-Hell; **pit against,** Antagonism-Concurrence, Variance-Accord; **pit against one another,** Comparison.

pit'-a-pat''. Flutteringly. Agitation, Crash-Drumming, Emotion, Excitability-Inexcitability.

pitch. A substance which exudes from the pine; to throw; slant. Ascent-Descent, Elevation-Depression, Establishment-Removal, Height-Lowness, Melody-Dissonance, Pulpiness-Rosin, Push-Pull, Quantity-Measure, Station, Top-Bottom, Vibration, Whiteness-Blackness; **pitch and toss,** Purpose-Luck; **pitch dark,** Light-Darkness; **pitch into,** Attack-Defense, Recompense-Punition, Strife-Peace; **pitch of one's breath,** Cry-Ululation; **pitch one's tent,** Arrival-Departure; **pitch overboard,** Keeping-Relinquishment; **pitch upon,** Arrival-Departure, Choice-Neutrality, Discovery, Gain-Loss.

pitched' bat''-tle. A general battle. Strife-Peace.

pitch'-er. A vessel with a spout for pouring out liquids. Contents-Receiver.

pitch'-fork''. A farm utensil. Conveyance-Vessel, Push-Pull; **rain pitchforks,** River-Wind.

pitch'-pipe''. An instrument to give the key-note. Musical Instruments.

pitch'-y. Pitch-like. Light-Darkness, Pulpiness-Rosin, Whiteness-Blackness.

pit'-e-ous. That may excite pity. Pleasurableness-Painfulness.

pit'-e-ous-ly. Mournfully. Magnitude-Smallness.

pit'-fall''. A pit used as a trap. Exposure-Hiding-place, Refuge-Pitfall, Truthfulness-Fraud.

pith. Vital part; substance. Center, Consequence-Insignificance, Meaning-Jargon, Outside-Inside, Strength-Weakness, Subjectiveness-Objectiveness.

pith'-i-ness. Concentrated force. Strength-Weakness.

pith'-less. Without pith. Might-Impotence.

pith′-y. Full of pith; concise. FORCE-WEAKNESS, MEANING-JARGON, TERSENESS-PROLIXITY.

pit′-i-a-ble. Deserving pity. GOODNESS-BADNESS, PLEASURABLENESS-PAINFULNESS, REGARD-SCORN.

pit′-ied. Had sympathy expressed for. PLEASURE-PAIN.

pit′-i-ful. Compassionate. COMPASSION-RUTHLESSNESS, CONSEQUENCE - INSIGNIFICANCE, GOODNESS-BADNESS, REGARD-SCORN, REPUTATION-DISCREDIT.

pit′-i-less. Without pity. COMPASSION - RUTHLESSNESS, PARDON-VINDICTIVENESS.

pit′-i-less-ness. Hardheartedness. COMPASSION-RUTHLESSNESS.

pit′-tance. Any meager allowance. ASSIGNMENT, EXCESS-LACK, OUTLAY-INCOME.

pit′-ted. Marked with little pits, as in smallpox. EMBELLISHMENT-DISFIGUREMENT.

pit′-u-ite. Mucus. VISCIDITY-FOAM.

pit′-u-i-tous. Full of mucus. VISCIDITY-FOAM.

pit′-y. Compassion. COMPASSION-RUTHLESSNESS; **express pity,** CONDOLENCE; **for pity's sake,** COMPASSION-RUTHLESSNESS; **what a pity,** CONTENTEDNESS-REGRET, JUBILATION-LAMENTATION.

pit′-y-ing. Compassionating. COMPASSION-RUTHLESSNESS.

piv′-ot. A pin on which anything turns. CAUSE-EFFECT, REVOLUTION-EVOLUTION, SUSPENSION-SUPPORT, UNION-DISUNION.

pix. A box. CEREMONIAL, CONTENTS-RECEIVER, TRIAL.

pix′-y. An elf. JOVE-FIEND.

piz″-zi-ca′-to. A direction to violinists to pluck the strings with the fingers. MUSIC.

pla″-ca-bil′-i-ty. Complaisance. PARDON-VINDICTIVENESS.

pla′-ca-ble. Willing to forgive. PARDON-VINDICTIVENESS.

plac′-ard. A window-bill. PUBLICITY.

pla′-cate. Pacify. FIGHTING-CONCILIATION, PARDON-VINDICTIVENESS.

place. Situation; rank; room. CONDITION-SITUATION, DWELLER-HABITATION, ESTABLISHMENT-REMOVAL, EXTENSION-PLACE, OCCUPATION, ORGANIZATION-DISORGANIZATION, POSITION, REGULARITY-IRREGULARITY, REPUTATION - DISCREDIT, STATION; **burial-place,** LIFE-FUNERAL; **give place to,** QUEST-EVASION; **have place,** ENTITY-NONENTITY; **in place,** POSITION; **in place of,** COMMUTATION-PERMUTATION; **make a place for,** ESTABLISHMENT-REMOVAL; **out of place,** CONVENTIONALITY-UNCONVENTIONALITY, ESTABLISHMENT-REMOVAL, HARMONY-DISCORD, PROPRIETY-IMPROPRIETY; **place in order,** ORGANIZATION-DISORGANIZATION; **place itself,** REGULARITY-IRREGULARITY; **place to one's credit,** CREDIT-DEBT; **place under,** ADMISSION-EXCLUSION, **place upon record,** MARK-OBLITERATION.

placebit, decies repetita [L.] (pla-si′-bit, di′-si-iz rep″-e-tai′-ta). Though ten times repeated it will please. PLEASURABLENESS-PAINFULNESS.

placebo [L.] (pla-si′-bo). Please. ADULATION-DISPARAGEMENT.

place′-hunt″-er. One who seeks a situation. PETITIONER.

place′-man. One who holds a place. CONSIGNEE.

plac′-id. Quiet. EXCITABILITY-INEXCITABILITY.

plac′-it. A decree. ORDER.

pla′-gi-a-rism. Literary theft. IMITATION-ORIGINALITY, LOAN-BORROWING, THEFT.

pla′-gi-a-rist. A literary thief. ROBBER.

pla′-gi-a-rize. To appropriate literary work as one's own production. REPRISAL-RESISTANCE.

pla′-gi-a-ry. Practising plagiarism. REPRISAL-RESISTANCE..

Pla′-gia-ry, Sir Fretful. A character in *The Critic,* by Sheridan. FAVORITE-QUARRELSOMENESS.

pla″-gi-he′-dral. Having an oblique spiral arrangement of planes. PARALLELISM-INCLINATION.

plague. A contagious disease. HEALTH-SICKNESS, PLEASURABLENESS-PAINFULNESS; PLEASURE-PAIN, **a plague upon,** CHARITABLENESS-CURSE.

plague′-spot. A mark of the plague. GOODNESS-BADNESS, HEALTHINESS-UNHEALTHINESS.

pla′-guing. Annoying. PLEASURABLENESS-PAINFULNESS.

pla′-guy. Troublesome. DIFFICULTY-FACILITY, PLEASURABLENESS-PAINFULNESS.

plaid. An outer garment. DRESS-UNDRESS, VARIEGATION.

plaidoyer [F.] (plê-dwa-yê′) Counsel's speech. RATIOCINATION-INSTINCT.

plain. Manifest; simple; flat. BEAUTY-UGLINESS, CLEARNESS-OBSCURITY, CRAFT-ARTLESSNESS, EMBELLISHMENT - DISFIGUREMENT, ERECTNESS-FLATNESS, GULF-PLAIN, MANIFESTATION-LATENCY, SIMPLICITY-FLORIDNESS, VISIBILITY-INVISIBILITY; **plain English,** SIMPLICITY-FLORIDNESS; **plain dealing,** TRUTHFULNESS-FALSEHOOD; **plain interpretation,** AMBIGUITY; **plain question,** INVESTIGATION-ANSWER; **plain sailing,** DIFFICULTY-FACILITY; **plain sense,** SAGACITY-INCAPACITY; **plain speaking,** CLEARNESS-OBSCURITY, CRAFT-ARTLESSNESS, MANIFESTATION-LATENCY; **plain terms,** AMBIGUITY, CLEARNESS-OBSCURITY, SIMPLICITY-FLORIDNESS; **plain truth,** TRUTH-ERROR; **plain words,** CRAFT-ARTLESSNESS, TRUTHFULNESS-FALSEHOOD.

plain′-ly. Clearly. **Tell one plainly,** ENLIGHTENMENT-SECRECY.

plain′-ness. Without ornament. EMBELLISHMENT-SIMPLICITY, MANIFESTATION-LATENCY, SIMPLICITY-FLORIDNESS.

plain′-song. The Gregorian chant. DEVOTION-IDOLATRY.

plain′-spo″-ken. Speaking with sincerity. CRAFT-ARTLESSNESS, MANIFESTATION-LATENCY.

plaint. A cry of distress. CRY-ULULATION, JUBILATION-LAMENTATION.

plaint′-ful. Expressing sorrow. JUBILATION-LAMENTATION.

plain′-tiff. He who commences a lawsuit. DUENESS-UNDUENESS, JUSTIFICATION-CHARGE.

plain′-tive. Mournful. JUBILATION-LAMENTATION.

plain′-tive-ness. Expression of subdued sadness. JUBILATION-LAMENTATION.

plai″-sance′. A pleasure ground; part of a park. DWELLER - HABITATION, ENTERTAINMENT - WEARINESS.

plaisanterie [F.] (plê-zant-ri′) Jest. WITTINESS-DULNESS.

plaisir, avec [F.] (plê-zir′, a-vec′). With pleasure. ASSENT-DISSENT, READINESS-RELUCTANCE.

plaisir de vous revoir, au [F.] (plê-zir′ de vu re-vwar′, o). Till I have the pleasure of seeing you again. ARRIVAL-DEPARTURE.

plais′-ter. Plaster. COVER-LINING.

plait. A fold. CROSSING, PLICATURE.

plan. Scheme. CONDUCT, DELINEATION-CARICATURE, DESIGN, ENLIGHTENMENT - SECRECY, TRAVELING-NAVIGATION.

plane. A level surface. ASCENT-DESCENT, CONVEXITY-CONCAVITY, ERECTNESS-FLATNESS, SMOOTHNESS-ROUGHNESS; **inclined plane,** INSTRUMENT.

plan′-et. A celestial body revolving about the sun. ASTRONOMY, UNIVERSE, VOLITION-OBLIGATION.

plan′-et-a-ry. Pertaining to the planets. ASTRONOMY.

plan′-et-oid. A minor planet. UNIVERSE.

plan′-et-struck″. Affected by the influence of planets. ASTONISHMENT - EXPECTANCE, WELFARE - MISFORTUNE.

plank. A thick board. LAMINA-FIBER, REFUGE-PITFALL, WAY.

planned. Designed. DESIGN.

plan'-ning. Designing. DESIGN.

plant. An herb; to set in the earth. DOMESTICATION-AGRICULTURE, ESTABLISHMENT-REMOVAL, FAUNA-FLORA, INJECTION-EJECTION, INSTRUMENT, PROPERTY, TRUTHFULNESS-FRAUD; **plant a battery,** ATTACK-DEFENSE; **plant a dagger in the breast,** PLEASURABLENESS-PAINFULNESS; **plant a thorn in the side,** PLEASURABLENESS-PAINFULNESS; **plant oneself,** ESTABLISHMENT-REMOVAL.

plan-ta'-tion. Any place that is planted; a colony. DOMESTICATION-AGRICULTURE, ESTABLISHMENT-REMOVAL, PROPERTY.

planter ses choux, aller [F.] (plan'-tê' sê shu, a-lê'). To go and live [plant cabbages] in the country. SOCIABILITY-PRIVACY.

plant'-ing. To set in the ground. INJECTION-EJECTION.

plash. A puddle of water; to play in water. GULF-PLAIN, RESONANCE-NONRESONANCE, RIVER-WIND.

plash'-y. Muddy. SWAMP-ISLAND.

plasm. A mold. COPY-MODEL.

plas'-ma. A quartz used for engraved ornaments. EMBELLISHMENT-DISFIGUREMENT.

plas'-mic. Pertaining to plasma. FORM-FORMLESSNESS.

plas'-ter. A composition of lime, sand, and water. CONNECTIVE, COVER-LINING, REMEDY-BANE; **plaster up,** RENOVATION-RELAPSE.

plas'-tic. Giving form. FORM-FORMLESSNESS, HARDNESS-SOFTNESS, MUTABILITY-STABILITY.

plas-tic'-i-ty. Capacity of being molded. HARDNESS-SOFTNESS.

plat. To interweave. CROSSING, GULF-PLAIN.

plate. A dish; a covering of metal. CONTENTS-RECEIVER, COVER-LINING, ENGRAVING, LAMINA-FIBER, LEVELNESS, NUTRIMENT-EXCRETION; **plate-engraving,** ENGRAVING; **plate-printing,** ENGRAVING, WRITING-PRINTING.

pla-teau'. A table-land. ERECTNESS-FLATNESS, GULF-PLAIN.

plat'-form. A raised floor; a scheme. ADDRESS-RESPONSE, DESIGN, ERECTNESS-FLATNESS, LISTS, SCHOOL, SUSPENSION-SUPPORT; **platform orator,** SPEECH-INARTICULATENESS.

plat'-i-num. An element. CHEMISTRY.

plat'-i-tude. An empty remark. MEANING-JARGON, WITTINESS-DULNESS.

Pla-ton'-ic. Relating to Plato; pure. EXCITABILITY-INEXCITABILITY, PURITY-IMPURITY, REFLECTION-VACANCY; **Platonic bodies,** ANGULARITY.

Pla'-to-nism. The philosophy of Plato. REFLECTION-VACANCY.

pla-toon'. A small body of soldiers. BELLIGERENT; **platoon fire,** ATTACK-DEFENSE.

plat'-ter. An oblong dish. CONTENTS-RECEIVER, LAMINA-FIBER, LEVELNESS; **clean the outside of the platter,** POMP, TRUTHFULNESS-FALSEHOOD.

plau'-dit. Praise bestowed. APPROVAL-DISAPPROVAL.

plau''-si-bil'-i-ty. Apparent correctness. LIKELIHOOD-UNLIKELIHOOD.

plau'-si-ble. Apparently right. ADULATION-DISPARAGEMENT, APPROVAL-DISAPPROVAL, JUSTIFICATION-CHARGE, LIKELIHOOD-UNLIKELIHOOD, RATIOCINATION-INSTINCT, TRUTHFULNESS-FALSEHOOD.

play. To sport; to gamble; to act the part of. ACTING, ACTION-PASSIVENESS, AGENCY, DELINEATION-CARICATURE, DOMINANCE-IMPOTENCE, ENTERTAINMENT-WEARINESS, EXTENSION-DISTRICT, LIBERTY-SUBJECTION, MUSICIAN, USE-DISUSE, VIBRATION; **at play,** ENTERTAINMENT-WEARINESS; **bring into play,** AGENCY, USE-DISUSE; **full of play,** LIGHTHEARTEDNESS-DEJECTION; **full play,** DOMINANCE-IMPOTENCE; **give play to the imagination,** FANCY; **have free play,** AGENCY; **in play,** AGENCY, WITTINESS-DULNESS; **play a deep game,** CRAFT-ARTLESSNESS; **play a game,** CONDUCT, ENTERTAINMENT-WEARINESS, QUEST-EVASION; **play a part,** ACTION-PASSIVENESS, ACTING, TRUTHFULNESS-FALSEHOOD; **play at cross purposes,** AMBIGUITY, ANTAGONISM-CONCURRENCE, CLEARNESS-OBSCURITY, REGULARITY-IRREGULARITY, TRUTH-ERROR; **play fast and loose,** BIGOTRY-APOSTASY, DETERMINATION-VACILLATION, PERSISTENCE-WHIM, TRUTHFULNESS-FALSEHOOD; **play first fiddle,** CONSEQUENCE-INSIGNIFICANCE, REPUTATION-DISCREDIT, SUPREMACY-SUBORDINACY; **play for,** PURPOSE-LUCK; **play havoc,** BETTERMENT-DETERIORATION; **play hide and seek,** ENLIGHTENMENT-SECRECY, QUEST-EVASION; **play into the hands of,** ANTAGONISM-CONCURRENCE; **play of colors,** VARIEGATION; **play off,** TRUTHFULNESS-FRAUD; **play one a trick,** EXPECTATION-DISAPPOINTMENT, TRUTHFULNESS-FRAUD; **play one false,** EXPECTATION-DISAPPOINTMENT, TRUTHFULNESS-FALSEHOOD, TRUTHFULNESS-FRAUD; **play one's best card,** SKILL-UNSKILFULNESS, TOIL-RELAXATION; **play one's part,** CONDUCT, OCCUPATION; **play on the feelings,** EXCITATION; **play second fiddle,** INSUBORDINATION-OBEDIENCE, LIBERTY-SUBJECTION, SUPREMACY-SUBORDINACY; **play the deuce,** EXCITABILITY-INEXCITABILITY; **play the devil with,** CHARITABLENESS-MALEVOLENCE; **play the fool,** ENTERTAINMENT-WEARINESS, SAGACITY-INCAPACITY, SKILL-UNSKILFULNESS, SOCIETY-LUDICROUSNESS; **play the monkey,** SAGACITY-INCAPACITY; **play tricks with,** CRAFT-ARTLESSNESS, SKILL-UNSKILFULNESS; **play truant,** QUEST-EVASION; **play upon,** SOCIETY-DERISION, TRUTHFULNESS-FRAUD; **play upon words,** AMBIGUITY, WITTINESS-DULNESS, WORD-NEOLOGY; **play with,** CAREFULNESS-CARELESSNESS.

play'-day''. A holiday. ENTERTAINMENT-WEARINESS.

played'-out''. Exhausted; completed. BEGINNING-END, COMPLETION-NONCOMPLETION, SUCCESS-FAILURE, WEARINESS-REFRESHMENT.

play'-er. A musician; an actor. ACTING, MUSICIAN.

play'-fel''-low. An associate in games, etc. FRIEND-FOE.

play'-ful. Frolicsome. ENTERTAINMENT-WEARINESS, LIGHTHEARTEDNESS-DEJECTION, WITTINESS-DULNESS; **playful imagination,** FANCY.

play'-ground''. A piece of ground used for recreation. ENTERTAINMENT-WEARINESS, LISTS.

play'-house''. A theater. ACTING.

play'-mate''. A playfellow. FRIEND-FOE.

play'-some''. Playful. LIGHTHEARTEDNESS-DEJECTION.

play'-thing''. A toy. CONSEQUENCE-INSIGNIFICANCE, ENTERTAINMENT-WEARINESS; **make a plaything of,** LIBERTY-SUBJECTION.

play'-wright''. A maker of plays. ACTING.

pla'-za. Market-place. CITY.

plea. What is advanced in support of a cause. EVIDENCE-COUNTEREVIDENCE, JUSTIFICATION-CHARGE, LITIGATION, PRETEXT.

plead. To argue. EVIDENCE-COUNTEREVIDENCE, PETITION-EXPOSTULATION, PRETEXT, TRIBUNAL; **plead guilty,** REPENTANCE-OBDURACY; **plead one's cause,** JUSTIFICATION-CHARGE.

plead'-er. A lawyer. ADVOCATE.

plead'-ing. The act of advocating. **Special pleading,** RATIOCINATION-INSTINCT.

plead'-ings. The pleas of the plaintiff and defendant. LITIGATION.

pleas'-ant. Gratifying. CONNECTION-INDEPENDENCE, ENTERTAINMENT-WEARINESS, PLEASURABLENESS-PAINFULNESS, WITTINESS-DULNESS; **make things pleasant,** ADULATION-DISPARAGEMENT, MOTIVE-

CAPRICE, PLEASURABLENESS-PAINFULNESS, TRUTH-FULNESS-FRAUD.

pleas'-ant-ness.   Cheerfulness.   PLEASURABLENESS-PAINFULNESS.

pleas'-ant-ry.   Sprightly talk.   ENTERTAINMENT-WEARINESS, PETITION-EXPOSTULATION, WITTINESS-DULNESS.

please.   To give pleasure.   ENTERTAINMENT-WEARINESS; **as you please,** CONSENT, INSUBORDINATION-OBEDIENCE; **do what one pleases,** LIBERTY-SUBJECTION; **if you please,** CONSENT, INSUBORDINATION-OBEDIENCE, PETITION-EXPOSTULATION; **please oneself,** UNSELFISHNESS-SELFISHNESS.

pleas'-ing.   Giving pleasure.   ENTERTAINMENT-WEARINESS, LIGHTHEARTEDNESS-DEJECTION, PLEASURABLENESS-PAINFULNESS, PLEASURE-PAIN.

pleas'-ur-a-ble-ness.   The quality of being able to give pleasure.   PLEASURABLENESS-PAINFULNESS.

PLEASURABLENESS—PAINFULNESS.

Agreeableness.   The quality of being agreeable or pleasant.

Amenity.   The state of being pleasant or agreeable.

Amiability.   Sweetness of disposition.

Amusement, etc.   Pleasurable excitement, etc.   See ENTERTAINMENT.

Attractability.   The quality of being alluring or inviting.

Attraction, etc.   The power of alluring or engaging, etc.   See MOTIVE.

Attractiveness.   The quality of being attractive or pleasing.

Bittersweet.   A plant whose taste is at first bitter then sweet.

Bright side.   Anything that gives cheerfulness and joy.

Charm.   Any alluring quality, especially of song.

Dainty.   That which is delicious and delicate.

Delectability.   The quality of giving delight or being charming.

Enchantment.   That which has power to fascinate or highly delight.

Fair weather.   Figuratively. a season of pleasure.

Fascination.   Irresistible influence or charm.

Goodness, etc.   The state of being good, general excellence, etc.   See GOODNESS.

Hedonism.   The theory that finds the explanation of duty in its tendency to give pleasure.

Hedonist.   A believer in Hedonism.

Invitingness.   The quality of being attractive or inviting.

Jocundity.   The quality of being jocund, cheerful, or sportive.

Land flowing with milk and honey.   Figuratively, a land of great fertility.   [Bible.]

Loveliness, etc.   The quality of being lovely or charming, etc.   See BEAUTY.

Manna in the wilderness.   An unexpected satisfaction.   [Bible.]

Nuts.   Something that gives particular pleasure.

Pleasantness.   The state of being pleasant or agreeable.

Pleasurableness.   The quality of being capable of giving pleasure or delight.

Pleasure-giving.

Regale.   A banquet.

Sauce piquante [F.].   Appetizing foods.

Seduction.   Enticement to evil.

Sunny side.   The bright or cheery aspect of affairs.

Sweets.   Things sweet or pleasant to the taste.

Tidbits. }
Titbits. }   A bit or morsel, as of choice food.

Treat.   That which affords entertainment.

Winning ways.   A pleasing disposition.

Witchery.   Irresistible influence; fascination.

PLEASURABLENESS—*Verbs.*

Afford pleasure.   To delight.   See PLEASURE.

Allure, etc.   To attempt to draw to as by a charm or some prospect of pleasure or advantage. etc.   See MOTIVE.

Amuse, etc.   To entertain pleasantly. etc.   See ENTERTAINMENT.

Attract.   To draw by a moral or emotional influence.

Beautify.   To make beautiful.

Bewitch.   To so please as to take away the power of resistance.

Bless.   To make happy.

Captivate.   To gain ascendency over by some art or attraction.

Cause pleasure.   To gratify.   See PLEASURE.

Charm.   To attract irresistibly.

Create pleasure.   To excite agreeable sensations.   See PLEASURE.

Delight.   To give great pleasure to.

Do one's heart good.   To be a joy to.

Enchant.   To charm by sorcery; fill with delight.

Enliven.   To make lively or cheerful.

Enrapture.   To transport with pleasure or delight.

Enravish.   To throw into a state of ecstasy; delight beyond measure.

Entrance.   To ravish with delight.

Fascinate.   To allure irresistibly.

Flatter.   To attempt to gratify the vanity of.

Gild and frill.   To render agreeable in appearance.

Give pleasure.   To be agreeable to.   See PLEASURE.

Gladden, etc.   To make glad or joyful, etc.   See LIGHTHEARTEDNESS.

Gladden the heart.   To make happy.

Affliction.   The cause of continued pain of body or mind.

Affront, etc.   A designed mark of disrespect, etc.   See REGARD-DISRESPECT.

Annoyance.   The act of annoying; vexation.

Care, etc.   An oppressive sense of responsibility, etc.   See PLEASURE-PAIN.

Curse.   The cause of great harm or misfortune.

Désagrément [F.].   Disagreeableness.

Grievance.   A cause of uneasiness or annoyance.

Infestation.   The act of annoying by presence and numbers; molestation.

Infliction.   The act of causing another to suffer.

Malignity, etc.   Disposition to do evil, etc.   See CHARITABLENESS-MALEVOLENCE.

Misfortune, etc.   Bad luck; an evil accident, etc.   See WELFARE-MISFORTUNE.

Mishap.   An unfortunate accident.

Molestation.   The act of disturbing.

Mortification.   The act of humiliating.

Nul bien sans peine [F.].   No good without pain.

Painfulness.   Suffering of body or mind.

Provocation.   The act of causing anger or resentment.

Trial.   That which afflicts or harasses.

Trouble.   That which annoys or afflicts; uneasiness.

Vexation.   The act of disquieting irritation.

PAINFULNESS—*Denotations.*

Bitter draft. }
Bitter pill. }   Anything causing pain or distress to the mind.

Blow.   Something that produces mental or physical suffering.

Bore.   A person or thing that wearies.

Bother.   One who, or that which causes annoyance or perplexity.

Burden.   That which is wearisome or oppressive.

Cancer.   A malignant growth attended with great pain and ulceration.

Canker.   A spreading gangrenous ulcer.   See REMEDY-BANE.

Cankerworm of care.   Care or trouble which causes a breaking down of health.

Carking care.   Distressing or worrying duties or troubles.

Dagger, etc.   A short weapon used for stabbing.   See WEAPON.

Esclandre [F].   A scandal or exposure.

Gall and wormwood.   Anything extremely bitter, or that causes pain.

Head and front of one's offending.   The chief object or act of offense.   [Shakespeare, *Othello,* I, ii.]

Heavy news.   Distressing news.

Hornet's nest.   A source of irritation and trouble.

Hot water.   Figuratively, an uncomfortable position.

Load.   Care or trouble.

Neuralgia.   A disease, the chief symptom of which is a very acute pain which follows the course of a nervous branch.

Nuisance.   That which annoys or gives trouble and vexation.

Pest.   One who or that which is troublesome or destructive.

Plague.   That which smites, wounds, or troubles.

Pother.   Annoyance.

Rub.   Something grating to the feelings.   [Shakespeare, *Hamlet,* III. i.]

Scorpion.   A painful scourge.   See BENEFACTOR-EVILDOER.

Scourge.   A means of inflicting punishment or suffering.   See RECOMPENSE-SCOURGE.

Sea of troubles.   A mass of troubles resembling the sea in vastness.   [Shakespeare, *Hamlet,* III. i.]

Sickener.   That which renders sick.

Skeleton in the closet.   A distressing family secret.

Sore object.   A disagreeable sight.

Sorry sight.   A sight that causes pity.

Source of annoyance. }
Source of irritation. }   Anything that causes bother or trouble.

Sting.   Anything that causes acute bodily or mental pain.

Stroke.   Any affliction or calamity.

PLEASURABLENESS—PAINFULNESS—*Continued.*

PLEASURABLENESS—Verbs—*Continued.*

Gratify. To give pleasure to; satisfy.
Gratify desire, etc. To please. See DESIRE.
Hit one's fancy. To be agreeable to.
Humor. To indulge the fancies, moods, and caprices of.
Indulge. To yield to the desire of.
Interest. To arouse emotion or passion in behalf of a person or thing.
Make things pleasant. To please.
Meet one's wishes. To be pleasing to.
Offer pleasure. To satisfy. See PLEASURE.
Please. To excite agreeable emotions or sensations in.
Popularize. To make acceptable to the common people.
Present pleasure. }
Procure pleasure. } To excite agreeable emotions in. See PLEASURE.
Produce pleasure. }
Quench. To make an end of or satisfy emotions or sensations.
Ravish. To carry away with joy or delight.
Refresh. To make as if new.
Regale. To entertain sumptuously.
Rejoice the heart. To make one glad.
Satiate. To satisfy fully the desire of
Satisfy. To supply to the full; make content.
Slake. To render inoperative by satisfying, assuage.
Stimulate, etc. To excite to activity, etc. See EXCITATION.
Sweeten. To make pleasing to the mind or feelings.
Take. To gain reception; please.
Tickle. To please or gratify.
Tickle one's fancy. To delight one.
Tickle the palate, etc. To be agreeable to the taste. See PALATA-
BLENESS.
To take one's fancy. To be pleasing to.
Transport. To ravish with pleasure.
Treat. To furnish gratuitous entertainment.
Warm the cockles of the heart. To warm the inner chambers of the
heart; delight. [Scott, Southey, Darwin]
Win the heart. To secure the affections of.
Yield pleasure. To excite agreeable sensations. See PLEASURE.

PLEASURABLENESS—*Adjectives.*

Acceptable. Worthy of being accepted with pleasure.
Agreeable. Pleasing to the mind or senses.
Alluring. Attractive. See *Verbs.*
Appetizing, etc. Exciting any physical craving or desire. See Ex-
CITATION.
Attractive, etc. Drawing by moral influence or pleasing emotion, etc.
See MOTIVE.
Beatic. }
Beatific. } Having power to impart blissful enjoyment.
Bewitching. }
Captivating. } Charming. See *Verbs.*
Causing pleasure. Delighting. See *Verbs.*
Charming. Attractive. See *Verbs.*
Cheering, etc. Comforting, etc. See LIGHTHEARTEDNESS.
Comfortable. Giving comfort or consolation.
Cordial. Sincere; affectionate; giving strength or spirits.
Dainty. Delicate; elegant in manner or breeding.
Delectable. Very pleasing. [Bunyan, *Pilgrim's Progress.*]
Delicate. Pleasing to the senses.
Delicious. Affording great pleasure; charming.
Delightful. Highly pleasing.
Dulcet. Sweet to the ear. [Shakespeare, *Midsummer Night's Dream*
II, ii]
Ecstatic. Immeasurably delightful.
Elysian, etc. Relating to the abode of the blessed after death; pleas-
ing in the highest degree, etc. See HEAVEN.
Empyrean. Pertaining to the highest and purest region of heaven.
Enchanting. Charming. See *Verbs.*
Engaging. Attractive.
Enravishing. Delighting. See *Verbs.*
Enticing. Having power to entice or allure.
Entrancing. Charming. See *Verbs*
Exquisite. Of surpassing quality, delightfully excellent.
Fascinating. Having an irresistible power over. See *Verbs.*
Favorite. Regarded with particular affection or preference.
Felicitous. Delightful, prosperous.
Genial. Sympathetically cheerful and happy.
Glad. Moderately joyful.
Gladsome. Pleasing; cheerful.
Grateful. Willing to acknowledge favors, affording pleasure.
Gratifying. Satisfying a desire. See *Verbs*
Halcyon. Calm; peaceful (the sea being still while the bird broods).
Heartfelt. Sincere; hearty.

PAINFULNESS—Denotations—*Continued.*

Thorn. That which pricks or annoys.
Thorn in one's side. }
Thorn in the flesh. } A source of continual annoyance or trouble.
Ulcer. Anything that festers and corrupts like an open sore.
Waters of bitterness. Anything causing pain or distress to the mind.
Where the shoe pinches. A cause of annoyance or trouble.
Wound. An injury or hurt to the feeling, faculty, or reputation.

PAINFULNESS—*Verbs.*

Add a nail to one's coffin. To do something injurious to one's health
Afflict. To trouble grievously.
Affront. To insult to the face.
Aggrieve. To give pain or sorrow to.
Agonize. To suffer extreme anguish, as a wrestler in the games
Annoy. To irritate by repeated acts; vex.
Appal. To depress or overcome with fear or sudden horror.
Assail. To attack in a hostile manner.
Badger. To worry or irritate persistently.
Bait. To harass or torment for sport.
Barb the dart. To make more cutting or severe.
Beset. To set upon on all sides; perplex.
Bite. To cause sharp pain to.
Bore. To harass or weary by importunity or iteration.
Bother. To annoy or perplex.
Break on the wheel. To execute or torture.
Break the heart. To crush with grief.
Bring one's gray hairs with sorrow to the grave. To cause great sor-
row to.
Bring pain. To cause suffering to. See PLEASURE-PAIN.
Cause pain, etc. To grieve. See PLEASURE-PAIN.
Chafe. To excite anger in; irritate.
Convulse. To agitate greatly.
Corrode. To eat away by degrees; prey upon.
Create pain, etc. To cause to suffer. See PLEASURE-PAIN.
Cross. To crash or interfere with.
Cruciate. To torment.
Crucify. To put to death by nailing the hands and feet to a cross.
Cut. To pierce or lacerate.
Cut to the heart. To deeply wound the sensibilities of.
Cut to the quick. To cause mental suffering.
Cut up. To injure or wound.
Discompose. To put into disorder; agitate.
Disenchant. To free from enchantment.
Disgust. To excite aversion in.
Displease. To offend or be disagreeable to.
Disquiet. To disturb the peace or tranquillity of.
Distress. To afflict with pain or calamity.
Disturb. To agitate the mind of, throw into confusion.
Draw tears from the eyes. To give cause for weeping.
Enchafe. To chafe or heat.
Enrage. To excite to anger; make furious.
Fash. To tease or vex.
Freeze the blood. To frighten
Fret. To irritate or vex.
Gall. To break the skin by rubbing; vex.
Give offense, etc To cause one to be angry. See FAVORITE-ANGER.
Give pain, etc. To cause one sorrow or suffering. See PLEASURE-
PAIN
Gnaw. To corrode or fret away.
Go against the grain. To oppose.
Go against the stomach. To sicken.
Grate on the ear. To be harsh-sounding.
Grate upon the feelings. To be disagreeable.
Grieve. To cause grief to; wound the feelings.
Gripe, etc. To pinch or distress, etc. See SENSUALITY-SUFFERING.
Harass. To tire or weary by importunity or fretting
Harrow. To break, as with a harrow; vex.
Harry. To agitate or worry.
Haunt the memory. To be unable to forget.
Horrify. To strike with extreme dread or terror mixed with detesta-
tion
Hurt. To injure or wound the feelings of.
Hurt the feelings of. To displease.
Importune. To press again and again with the same request: tease.
Incommode. To cause inconvenience to; disturb
Induce pain, etc To hurt. See PLEASURE-PAIN.
Infest. To trouble greatly by presence and numbers.
Inflict pain, etc. To injure. See PLEASURE-PAIN.
Irk. To weary or annoy; used impersonally.
Irritate. To cause to become angry or displeased; provoke.
Jar upon the feelings. To displease.

PLEASURABLENESS—PAINFULNESS— *Continued.*

PLEASURABLENESS—Adjectives—*Continued.*

Inviting. Alluring; tempting.
Killing. Captivating; irresistible.
Leef.
Lief. } Pleasing; agreeable.
Lovely, etc. Charming; amiable, etc. See BEAUTY.
Luscious, etc. Delicious; sweet, etc. See SWEETNESS.
Luxurious. Pertaining to luxury.
Nice. Delicate; dainty.
Palatable, etc. Agreeable to the taste; acceptable, etc. See PALATA-
   BLENESS.
Palmy. Prosperous; flourishing.
Pleasant. Agreeable to the mind or senses.
Pleasing. Giving pleasure. See *Verbs.*
Pleasurable. Capable of giving pleasure.
Pleasure-giving. Pleasing.
Prepossessing. Attracting confidence, esteem, or love.
Rapturous. Ecstatic; transporting.
Ravishing. Transporting.
Refreshing. Reviving.
Satisfactory, etc. Giving satisfaction, etc. See GOODNESS.
Saturnian. Distinguished for peacefulness, as the reign of Saturn.
Seducing. Enticing from the right. See *Verbs.*
Seductive. Tending to lead astray.
Sensual, etc. Given to the pleasures of sense and appetite, etc. See
   SENSUALITY.
Seraphic. Sublime; angelic.
Sweet. Pleasing to the senses or mind; amiable; winning.
Taking. Attracting. See *Verbs.*
Thrilling. Producing a tingling or exquisite sensation.
To one's liking.
To one's mind. } Pleasing.
To one's taste.
Voluptuous. Ministering to sensual gratification or given to the en-
   joyments of luxury and pleasure.
Welcome. Received gladly; grateful.
Welcome as the roses in May. Delightful.
Welcomed. Received or saluted with kindness.
Winning. Suited to gain favor.
Winsome. Causing pleasure; gladsome.

PLEASURABLENESS—*Phrases.*

Chose qui plait est à demi vendue [F.]. A thing that pleases is half
   sold.
Decies repetita placebit [L.]. Though repeated ten times, it will
   please.

PAINFULNESS—Verbs—*Continued from Column 2.*

Wound the feelings. To hurt or distress.
Wound to the quick. To cause mental suffering.
Wring. To twist; afflict.
Wring the heart. To cause intense pain or anguish to.

PAINFULNESS—*Adjectives.*

Abhorrent. Detesting; repugnant to.
Acute. Sharp; keen; intense.
Affecting. Moving the emotions; pathetic.
Afflicting. Causing suffering. See *Verbs.*
Afflictive. Causing pain or grief; distressing.
Aggravating. Making more heinous; provoking.
Agonizing. Causing intense pain. See *Verbs.*
Annoying. Disturbing. See *Verbs.*
Appalling. Making pale with fear. See *Verbs.*
Awkward. Embarrassing.
Biting. Causing intense mental or physical suffering. See *Verbs.*
Bitter. Having an acrid, biting taste; distressing; painful.
Bothering. Causing trouble. See *Verbs.*
Burdensome. Grievous to be borne.
Calamitous. Producing distress or misery; unhappy.
Carking. Distressing; corroding.
Causing pain. Hurtful. See PLEASURE-PAIN.
Caustic. Burning; severe; sharp.
Cheerless. Without joy or comfort.
Comfortless. Wanting comfort; in distress.
Consuming. Destroying; wasting.
Corroding. Gnawing; wasting away. See *Verbs.*
Cruel. Having pleasure in giving pain to others; bloody.
Crushing. That crushes or oppresses grievously.
Cumbersome. Burdensome; vexatious.
Cumbrous. Making action difficult
Cutting. Paining. See *Verbs.*

PAINFULNESS—Verbs—*Continued.*

Lacerate the heart. To afflict.
Lancinate. To tear or pierce.
Make one shudder. To frighten
Make one sick. To be very disagreeable to.
Make the blood curdle. } To have a sensation as of the freezing of
Make the blood run cold. } the blood, caused by fright, pain, etc.
Make the flesh creep. To cause a sensation as of insects creeping
   over the skin.
Make the hair stand on end. To frighten.
Make the heart bleed. To cause intense pain or sorrow to.
Make unhappy, etc. To cause sorrow or grief. See PLEASURE-PAIN.
Maltreat. To treat badly or abuse.
Molest. To annoy by trespass or interference.
Mortify. To affect with vexation or humiliation.
Nauseate. To affect with a feeling of nausea; loathe.
Nettle. To excite irritation or uneasiness in; provoke.
Occasion pain, etc. To cause mental or physical suffering. See
   PLEASURE-PAIN.
Offend. To make angry or affront.
Pain. To render uneasy in body or mind; torment; distress.
Perplex. To distress with doubt or anxiety; puzzle.
Persecute. To harass with importunity; beset with cruelty.
Pester. To harass with little vexations or annoyances.
Pierce. To affect deeply.
Pierce the heart. To cause pain to.
Pinch. To press or squeeze so as to cause pain; distress.
Pique. To excite irritation in; nettle.
Plague. To infest with disease or calamity; vex.
Plant a dagger in the breast. } To cause intense pain or sorrow to.
Plant a thorn in one's side. } To cause intense pain or sorrow to.
Plunge into sorrow. To cause pain or suffering to.
Pother. To perplex or worry.
Prey on the heart. }
Prey on the mind. } To have trouble which causes a wasting or
Prey on the spirits. } pining away.
Prick. To affect with sharp pain.
Produce pain, etc. To hurt. See PLEASURE-PAIN.
Provoke. To call forth into action; make angry.
Put to the question. To subject to a test.
Put to the rack. To subject to punishment; torture.
Rack. To torment; oppress by extortion.
Rankle. To fester; cause a sore.
Rend the heart. }
Rend the heart-strings. } To break one's heart.
Repel. To repulse; drive or keep away.
Revolt. To do violence to.
Rile. To stir up or make angry.
Ruffle. To disturb or agitate.
Sadden. To make grave or sorrowful; become sad.
Scarify. To scratch or cut the skin of.
Set the teeth on edge. To cause a grinding of the teeth, as by anger
   or pain.
Shock. To meet with hostile violence; strike with horror or disgust.
Sicken. To make sick; disgust.
Smite, etc. To strike or afflict, etc. See RECOMPENSE-PUNITION.
Snap at. To utter harsh, angry words to.
Sour the temper. To make the temper disagreeable.
Stick in one's gizzard. To harbor resentment.
Stick in one's throat. To be overcome by fear, etc., as to be unable
   to speak.
Sting. To pain sharply.
Sting to the quick. To cause intense mental pain to.
Stink in the nostrils. To be a constant source of irritation or trouble.
Tear the heart-strings. To break one's heart.
Tease. To give slight or playful annoyance.
Tire. To become weary or fatigued.
Torment. To subject to extreme pain or anguish.
Torture. To cause to suffer keenly.
Trouble. To put into confusion; distress.
Try the patience. To torment.
Turn the stomach. To sicken.
Tweak the nose. To pinch the nose and pull it with a sudden jerk
   and twist.
Vex. To make angry or to annoy by petty provocations; irritate.
Weigh on the heart. }
Weigh on the mind. } To be unable to get rid of a source of pain or
Weigh on the spirits. } trouble.
Wherret. To trouble or tease.
Worry. To attack repeatedly; beset with importunity.
Wound. To hurt so as to draw blood; hurt the feelings of.

(Continued on Column 1.)

PAINFULNESS—Adjectives—*Continued.*

Deplorable. Worthy of being lamented; causing grief.
Depressing. Casting a gloom upon.
Depressive. Tending to cast down.
Desolating. Making desolate; ruining.
Dire. Evil in a degree; very calamitous.
Disagreeable. Not agreeable; unpleasant.
Disastrous. Attended with suffering or disaster.
Disgusting. Sickening. See *Verbs.*
Disheartening. Depriving of courage and hope.
Dismal. Gloomy; depressing to the feelings.
Displeasing. Disagreeable to. See *Verbs.*
Distasteful. Unpleasant to the taste; offensive to the feelings.
Distressing. Causing pain or trouble. See *Verbs.*
Dolorific. Causing grief.
Dolorous. Full of grief; sorrowful.
Dreadful. Inspiring dread or great fear.
Dreary. Arousing cheerless sensations or associations.
Enough to drive one mad.
Enough to make a parson swear. } To be a cause of irritation or anger.
Enough to provoke a saint.
Envenomed. Tainted with bitterness or hatred.
Excruciating. Inflicting agonizing pain upon.
Execrable. Very hateful, abominable.
Fearful. Inspiring fear or awe.
Frightful. Exciting alarm or terror.
Fulsome. Disgusting by excess or grossness.
Galling. Causing pain or bitterness. See *Verbs.*
Grating. Making a harsh sound.
Grave. Weighty; solemn
Grievous. Causing grief; afflictive.
Grim. Having a fear-inspiring aspect.
Grinding. Oppressing by severe exactions.
Harassing. Troubling continually. See *Verbs.*
Hard. Not easy; cruel.
Harrowing. Inflicting pain. See *Verbs.*
Harsh. Repulsive to the sensibilities.
Hateful. Exciting great dislike or disgust.
Heart-breaking.
Heart-corroding.
Heart-rending. } Causing overpowering sorrow.
Heart-sickening.
Heart-wounding.
Hideous, etc. Exciting terror, etc. See EMBELLISHMENT-DISFIGUREMENT.
Horrible. Exciting horror or fear.
Horrid. Suited to excite horror.
Horrific. Causing horror.
Horrifying. Frightening. See *Verbs.*
Hurtful, etc. Causing loss or injury, etc. See GOODNESS-BADNESS.
Hurting. Causing pain or suffering. See *Verbs.*
Importunate. Overpressing in demand.
Insufferable. Offensive beyond endurance.
Insupportable. That cannot be borne or endured.
Intolerable. That cannot be tolerated.
Invidious. Likely to produce ill will.
Irksome. Causing uneasiness by long continuance.
Irritating. Causing trouble. See *Verbs.*
Joyless. Without joy; not causing joy.
Lamentable. Sorrowful; suited to awaken lament.
Loathful. Hating; disgusting.
Loathsome. Exciting loathing or disgust.
Melancholy. Depression of spirits, as by black bile.
More than flesh and blood can bear. Overcoming by pain or sorrow
Mortifying. Disheartening; death-making. See *Verbs.*
Mournful. Full of sorrow; saddening.
Nasty. Disgusting; offensive.

Nauseating. Sickening. See *Verbs.*
Nauseous. Causing nausea or seasickness; loathsome.
Not to be borne.
Not to be endured. } Unbearable.
Obnoxious. Exposed to censure; blameworthy.
Odious. Provoking hatred or disgust.
Offensive. Causing pain or unpleasant sensations.
Onerous. Oppressive
Oppressive. Unjustly severe or harsh.
Painful. Full of pain; causing pain or distress.
Past bearing. Painful or irritating, as to be unbearable.
Pathetic. Moving to pity or grief.
Pestering. Paining by continuous annoyance. See *Verbs.*
Piteous. Miserable; fitted to excite pity
Pitiable. Worthy of pity.
Plaguing. Worrying. See *Verbs.*
Plaguy. Troublesome; tormenting.
Provoking. Teasing. See *Verbs.*
Racking. Unfeeling. See *Verbs.*
Rending. Tearing asunder; bursting.
Repellent. Able or tending to repel.
Repulsive. Serving to repulse.
Revolting. Causing gross offense to. See *Verbs.*
Rueful. Mournful; sorrowful.
Ruinous. Causing ruin; pernicious.
Sad. Affected with grief; calamitous.
Searching. Penetrating; trying.
Severe. Sharp; distressing.
Sharp. Keen; biting; violent.
Shocking. Causing to recoil with horror or disgust. See *Verbs.*
Sickening. Making sick. See *Verbs.*
Sore. Painful; sensitive; distressing.
Stinging. Inflicting sharp pain. See *Verbs.*
Teasing. Annoying. See *Verbs.*
Terrific. Causing terror or great fear.
Thankless. Ungrateful.
Thrilling. Penetrating; feeling a tingling sensation through the body.
Tiresome. Tending to tire; tedious.
Tormenting. Troublesome. See *Verbs.*
Touching. Affecting; pathetic.
Tragical. Expressive of the loss of life or of sorrow.
Tremendous. Suited to excite terror or fear; terrible.
Troublesome. Causing trouble or anxiety.
Unacceptable. Not acceptable.
Unaccommodating. Not disposed to please.
Unbearable. That cannot be endured.
Uncomfortable. Unpleasant.
Undesirable.
Undesired. } Disagreeable.
Unendurable. Not to be borne.
Uninviting. Not wished for
Unlucky. Unhappy.
Unpalatable. Not pleasant to the taste.
Unpleasant.
Unpleasing. } Not pleasant.
Unpopular. Not pleasing to the people.
Unsatisfactory. Unable to cause a feeling of satisfaction.
Untoward. Perverse; troublesome.
Unwelcome. Not desired.
Vexatious. Causing annoyance or trouble.
Vile, etc. Mean; morally impure, etc. See GOODNESS-BADNESS.
Wearisome. Making weary or tired.
Withering. Causing to languish or pass away.
Woful. Causing calamity or distress.
Worrying. Causing mental pain to. See *Verbs.*

PAINFULNESS—*Adverbs, etc.*

Deuced. Devilishly; confoundedly.
Painfully. Hurtful. See *Adjectives.*

With pain, etc. Injuriously See PLEASURE-PAIN.

PAINFULNESS—*Interjection.*

Hinc illæ lachrymæ [L.]. Hence these tears.

PAINFULNESS—*Phrases.*

Surgit amari aliquid [L.] Something bitter rises.
The iron entering into the soul. A cause of mental suffering.

The place being too hot to hold one. In an uncomfortable or disagreeable position.

pleas'-ure. Delight. ENTERTAINMENT-WEARINESS, MODERATION-SELFINDULGENCE, PLEASURE - PAIN, READINESS - RELUCTANCE, SENSUALITY - SUFFERING,

VOLITION-OBLIGATION; **at pleasure,** VOLITION-OBLIGATION; **at one's pleasure,** CHOICE-NEUTRALITY, RULE-LICENSE; **during pleasure,** CONTINGENT-DURA-

TION; **give pleasure,** Pleasurableness-Painful-ness, Sensuality-Suffering; **man of pleasure,** Moderation-Voluptuary; **take one's pleasure,**

Entertainment-Weariness; **will and pleasure,** Volition-Obligation; **with pleasure,** Readiness-Reluctance, Way.

PLEASURE—PAIN.

Beatitude. Consummate bliss.
Bliss. Heavenly joy.
Cheer. Mirth; cheerfulness.
Cheerfulness. A state of moderate joy.
Comfort. Positive enjoyment of a strength-giving kind.
Complacency. Quiet contentment.
Delectation. Great pleasure.
Delight. Extreme pleasure.
Ease. Tranquillity; comfort.
Ecstasy. Extreme delight; rapture.
Enchantment. An overpowering or irresistible influence which fascinates or delights.
Enjoyment. Pleasure or satisfaction.
Felicity. Intense happiness.
Fruition. The pleasure or satisfaction derived from possession or use.
Gladness. The state of being glad; cheerfulness.
Glee. Joy; gaiety.
Good, etc. Welfare; prosperity, etc. See Good.
Gratification. Satisfaction; delight.
Gusto, etc. Keen enjoyment, etc. See Sensuality.
Happiness. The state of mind resulting from the enjoyment of good.
Joy. Exhilaration of spirit.
Mind at ease. A condition of satisfaction and pleasure.
Oblectation. The state of being greatly delighted.
Pleasure. The gratification of the mind.
Rapture. Extreme pleasure or joy; ecstasy.
Ravishment. Transport of joy.
Sans souci [F.]. Without care.
Satisfaction. Complacency of mind resulting from compliance with its desires.
Snugness. The state of being cozy.
Summum bonum [L.]. The highest good.
Transport. Great emotion; rapture.
Unalloyed happiness. Pure and unlimited happiness.
Well-being. Happiness; prosperity.
Zest. Agreeable excitement of mind accompanying mental exercise.

Pleasure—Nouns of Cause.

Amusement, etc. That which amuses; a diversion, etc. See Entertainment.
Beatification. The act of making happy.
Cushion, etc. A soft pillow, also a riotous kind of dance, formerly common at weddings, etc. See Suspension-Support.
Luxury, etc. Something rare or costly which gives pleasure, etc. See Sensuality.
Refreshment. That which refreshes or reanimates.
Relish. The power of pleasing.
Sunshine. A cheering influence.
Treat. An entertainment given as an expression of regard.

Pleasure—Nouns of Time.

Golden age. The fabulous age of primeval simplicity and purity of manners.
Golden time. Time of greatest enjoyment or opportunity.
Halcyon days. Happy days of rest in strenuous life.
Honeymoon. The first month after marriage.
Palmy days. Prosperous or flourishing days.
Saturnalia regna [L.]. A Roman festival during which unrestrained license and merriment reigned.

Pleasure—Nouns of Place.

Agapemone. A religious community of men and women, organized, in 1846, at Charlynch, England.
Arcadia. A district of Greece, noted for the contentment and happiness of its people; hence, figuratively, any region of pleasure and quiet happiness.
Elysium, etc. The seat of future happiness, etc. See Heaven.
Happy valley. In Johnson's *Rasselas*, a valley of delights, situated in Abyssinia.
Paradise. The abode of sanctified souls after death; hence, any region of delight.
Seventh heaven.⎫ A sublime or exalted condition referred to by the
Third heaven. ⎭ Apostle Paul.

Pleasure—Verbs.

Bask in the sunshine. To be under warming or cheering influences.
Be in clover, etc. To be in pleasant circumstances, etc. See Sensuality.

Ache. A dull, protracted pain.
Aching heart. A condition of continued pain.
Affliction. Sore distress of mind; flogging.
Agony. Intense suffering of mind.
Anguish. Excessive grief or mental pain.
Annoyance. The state of being annoyed or irritated.
Anxiety. Distress of mind about something in the future.
Bitterness. Deep distress or vexation of mind.
Bleeding heart. A condition of great grief or suffering.
Bother. Petty trouble.
Botheration. The state of being annoyed.
Broken heart. Crushed or depressed spirit.
Care. Trouble caused by onerous duties.
Cark. Solicitude; worry.
Chagrin. A keen sense of mortification.
Concern. Solicitude or anxiety for any person or thing.
Dejection, etc. Mental depression, etc. See Lightheartedness-Dejection.
Depth of misery. A condition of greatest misery.
Desolation. Sadness; gloominess.
Despair, etc. Utter hopelessness, etc. See Sanguineness-Hopelessness.
Discomfort. Lack of comfort; mental unrest.
Discomposure. Mental agitation.
Discontent, etc. Uneasiness of mind, etc. See Contentedness-Discontentment.
Displeasure. Irritation of mind; dissatisfaction.
Disquiet. An unsettled condition of mind; restlessness.
Dissatisfaction. Discontent.
Distress. Extreme pain or anguish of mind.
Dole. Sorrow or grief.
Dolor. Pain or distress.
Ephialtes. The nightmare.
Extremity. The highest degree of pain or suffering.
Fiery ordeal. A painful experience.
Fret. Irritation of temper.
Gnawing grief. A continual cause of mental suffering.
Grief. Sorrow for some definite cause, usually in the past.
Heartache. Sorrow or anguish of mind.
Heavy affliction.⎫ A state of pain, distress, or grief.
Heavy heart. ⎭
Hell upon earth. A continuous state of mental torment.
Ills that flesh is heir to. Whatever annoys or impairs happiness. [Shakespeare, *Hamlet*, III, i.]
Incubus. The nightmare.
Infelicity. Unhappiness; misery.
Infliction. Mental punishment or disgrace.
Inquietude. Disturbed state of mind.
Irritation. Excitement of passion or anger.
Malaise [F.]. Uneasiness.
Mauvais quart d'heure [F.]. A bad quarter of an hour.
Mental suffering.
Miseries of human life. Pain of body or mind.
Misery. Excessive pain of mind; wretchedness.
Mortification. Depression caused by disappointment.
Nightmare. A condition in sleep characterized by extreme uneasiness or discomfort.
Ordeal. A painful experience.
Pain. Distressing or afflicting emotion.
Pang. A fit of extreme pain or anguish.
Passion. Violent agitation of mind in anger.
Peck of trouble. A great deal of trouble.
Prostration. Great depression.
Purgatory. A state or place of purification after death. See Heaven-Hell.
Sea of troubles. Troubles resembling the sea in vastness. [Shakespeare, *Hamlet*, III, i.]
Shock. A sudden agitation of the mind or feelings.
Smart, etc. Lively pain; pungent grief, etc. See Sensuality-Suffering.
Solicitude. Mental unrest on account of fear of evil or desire of good.
Sorrow. Mental pain caused by some loss or disappointment.
Stew. A state of worry.
Sufferance. The state of suffering.
Suffering. See *Verbs*.
Taking. Distress of mind.
Torment. Extreme pain or anguish.

PLEASURE—PAIN—*Continued.*

PLEASURE—Verbs—*Continued.*

Be in elysium, etc.   To be in a delightful place, etc.   See Heaven.
Be pleased, etc.   To have agreeable sensations.   See Pleasurableness.
Be pleased with, etc.   To derive pleasure from.   See Pleasurableness.
Breathe freely.   To be comfortable.
Delight in.   To take great pleasure in.
Derive pleasure from.   To be satisfied with.
Enjoy.   To possess and use with satisfaction.
Enjoy oneself.   To derive pleasure from.
Enter into the spirit of.   To approve and gain pleasure from.
Experience pleasure.   To have agreeable emotions.   See *Nouns.*
Fall into raptures.   To be very much delighted.   See *Nouns.*
Feel at home.   To be free from care.
Feel pleasure.   To be pleased with.
Gloat over, etc.   To exhibit evil pleasure over, etc.   See Sensuality.
Go into raptures.   To be carried away by pleasure.   See *Nouns.*
Have a liking for.   To be pleased with.
Hug oneself.   To congratulate oneself.
Indulge in.   To give oneself up to.
Joy.   To rejoice or delight.
Like.   To be pleased with.
Love, etc.   To regard with affection, etc.   See Love.
Luxuriate in.   To indulge in with unrestrained delight.
Receive pleasure from.   To enjoy oneself.
Rejoice in.   To feel joy in.
Relish.   To eat with pleasure; enjoy.
Solace oneself with.   To derive comfort from.
Take a fancy to.   To like.
Take in good part.   To make the best of.
Take pleasure in.   To be delighted with.
Take to.   To be fond of.
Tread on enchanted ground.   To be in a state of high delight.
Treat oneself to.   To enjoy.

PLEASURE—*Adjectives.*

At ease.   Without care.
Beatic.   Happy.
Beatified.   Made happy.
Blessed. } Enjoying happiness.
Blest. }
Blissful.   Full of joy and felicity.
Captivated.   Charmed or fascinated.
Cloudless.   Clear; bright.
Comfortable, etc.   Contented; cheering, etc.   See Sensuality.
Content, etc.   Limited in desires to what one possesses, etc.   See Contentedness.
Ecstatic.   Delightful beyond measure.
Enchanted.   Under the power of enchantment.
Enjoying.   Deriving pleasure from.   See *Verbs.*
Enraptured.   Transported with pleasure.
Enravished.   Delighted beyond measure.
Entranced.   Ravished with delight.
Fascinated.   Operated on by an irresistible charm.
Glad.   Happy; pleased.
Gladsome.   Pleased; causing joy.
Happy.   Enjoying good of any kind.
Happy as a king. } Degrees of enjoyment.
Happy as the day is long. }
In a blissful state.   Happy.
In a transport of delight.   Delighted.
In ecstasies. } In a state or condition of overcoming pleasure.   See *Nouns.*
In paradise. }
In raptures.   In a state of agreeable excitement.
Joyful, etc.   Full of joy, etc.   See Lightheartedness.
Not sorry.   Glad.
Overjoyed.   Extremely gratified.
Painless.   Without pain.
Pleased, etc.   Enjoying.   See Pleasurableness.
Pleased as Punch.   Very much pleased.
Pleasing, etc.   Deriving pleasure from.   See Pleasurableness.
Raptured.   Enraptured.
Ravished.   Delighted to ecstasy.
Sans souci [F.].   Without care.
Ter quaterque beatus [L.].   Thrice and four times happy.
Thrice happy.   Very happy.
Transported.   Carried away with pleasure.
Unalloyed.   Not mixed with misfortune.
With a joyful face.   Delighted.
Without alloy.   With unrestrained pleasure.
With sparkling eyes.   Happy.

Torture.   Anguish of mind.
Trial.   That which tries or afflicts.
Tribulation.   Severe affliction; thrashing.
Trouble.   That which causes disturbance or affliction.
Uneasiness.   The state of being uneasy or restless.
Unhappiness.   The state of being unhappy or sorrowful.
Unkindest cut of all.   The most unjust or cruel blow or treatment.   [Shakespeare, *Cæsar*, III, ii.]
Vexation.   The state of being vexed; agitation.
Vexation of spirit.   A cause of trouble or disquiet.
Weariness.   The state of being weary or exhausted of strength.
Wo.   Overwhelming sorrow.
Worry.   A state of undue anxiety or care.
Wretchedness.   Extreme misery.

PAIN—*Nouns of Cause*

Blow.   A sudden calamity.
Bore.   A tiresome person or thing.
Burden.   That which is grievous or oppressive.
Esclandre [F.].   A scandal or exposure.
Load.   That which burdens or oppresses.
Plague.   That which smites or troubles; a calamity.
Visitation.   A retributive calamity.

PAIN—*Figurative Expressions.*

Iron age.   A degenerate or unjust period.
Reign of Terror.   The period in the French Revolution from May, 1793, to August, 1794, in which thousands were guillotined; hence, any period of great distress.
Slough of despond, etc.   A fit of mental depression or distress, etc.   See Welfare-Misfortune.   [Bunyan, *Pilgrim's Progress.*]

PAIN—*Associated Nouns.*

Martyr.   One who suffers death for his religion; a witness.
Object of compassion.   A person or thing to be pitied.
Prey.   One given up as a victim.
Shorn lamb.   A person overcome by suffering or sorrow.   "God tempers the wind to the shorn lamb."   [Sterne.]
Sufferer.   One who has a painful experience.
Victim.   One who is injured, killed, or sacrificed.
Wretch.   A miserable person or one sunken in vice.

PAIN—*Verbs.*

Ache, etc.   To be in continued pain, etc.   See Sensuality-Suffering.
Ail.   To affect with pain; trouble.
Bear pain.   To endure.   See *Nouns.*
Be in a taking.   To be suddenly seized with pain.
Be on pins and needles.   To be in an uncomfortable state.
Be the victim of.   To be pained or injured by.   See *Nouns.*
Bleed.   To feel deep sympathy or grief.
Break one's heart.   To cause one grief or sorrow.
Chafe.   To be vexed or irritated.
Come to grief.   To fail or be disappointed.
Despair, etc.   To give up all hope, etc.   See Sanguineness-Hopelessness.
Drain the cup of misery to the dregs.   To undergo the greatest distress or vexation.
Droop.   To despond or languish.
Endure pain. } To suffer.
Experience pain. }
Fall on evil days, etc.   To be in a season of distress.   See Welfare-Misfortune.
Feel pain.   To suffer.
Fret.   To be vexed or agitated.
Fret and fume.   To be irritated.
Give way.   To yield to pressure.
Go hard with.   To meet with troubles.
Grieve.   To cause to suffer; mourn.
Have a bad time of it.   To be in trouble.
Labor under afflictions.   To be in pain or suffering.
Languish.   To become languid; to pine away.
Mourn, etc.   To be sorrowful or in a state of grief, etc.   See Jubilation-Lamentation.
Pine.   To waste away under anxiety of mind.
Quaff the bitter cup.   To be subject to misery or vexation.
Repine.   To feel inward distress that preys on the spirits.
Sink.   To cause to decline.
Sit on thorns.   To be in a most uncomfortable position.
Smart.   To feel a pricking pain of mind.
Suffer.   To endure or undergo with pain.
Suffer pain.   To be in mental or physical trouble.

PLEASURE—PAIN—*Continued.*

PLEASURE—*Adverbs, etc.*

Happily. With happiness. See *Adjectives.*
With glee. Joyfully. See *Nouns.*
With pleasure. Obligingly. See READINESS.

PLEASURE—*Phrases.*

Empta dolore docet experientia [L.]. Experience bought with pain teaches.
Est quædam flere voluptas [L.]. There is in weeping a certain pleasure. [Ovid, *Tristia*, IV, iii, 37.]
Mens sana in corpore sano [L.]. A sound mind in a sound body. [Juvenal, 10, 356.]
Nessun maggior dolore che ricordarsi del tempo felice nella miseria [It.]. There is no greater sorrow than to recall happiness in misery. [Dante, *Inferno*, V, 121.]
One's heart leaping with joy.
Vedi Napoli, e poi muori [It.]. See Naples, and die.
Voluptas quædam fleri est [L.]. There is in weeping a certain pleasure.

PAIN—ADJECTIVES—*Continued from Column 2.*

Miserable. Extremely unhappy.
On the rack. Suffering torture.
Out of humor, etc. See FAVORITE-MOROSENESS.
Pained. Suffering. See *Verbs.*
Plunged in grief. Sorrowing.
Poor. Deserving of pity or sympathy.
Sore, etc. Easily grieved or vexed, etc. See SENSUALITY-SUFFERING.
Sorrowful. Full of sorrow; distressed.
Sorrowing. Feeling pain or grief on account of evil experienced.
Sorry. Feeling regret.
Steeped to the lips in misery. In a state of utter hopelessness or misery. [Longfellow, *Goblet of Life.*]
Stranded. Left helpless or perplexed.
Stricken. Afflicted; smitten.
Suffering. In pain. See *Verbs.*
To be pitied. Poor and suffering.
Uncomfortable. Uneasy; gloomy.
Undone. Ruined.
Uneasy. Disturbed by pain or anxiety.
Unfortunate, etc. Not fortunate; unhappy, etc. See WELFARE-MISFORTUNE.
Unhappy. Sorrowful.
Victimized. Made a victim of; duped.
Weary, etc. Exhausted in patience; tired, etc. See ENTERTAINMENT-WEARINESS.
Wobegone. Steeped in grief or sorrow.
Worried. Harassed with care and anxiety, annoyed.
Wretched. Sunk in affliction and distress.

PAIN—*Phrases.*

Haret lateri lethalis arundo [L.]. The deadly arrow sticks in his side. [Virgil, *Æneid*, IV, 73.]
One's heart bleeding.
The iron entered into our soul. [Psalter, 105, 18.]

PAIN—VERBS—*Continued.*

Sup full of horrors. To be subject to continual dangers or miseries. [Shakespeare, *Macbeth*, V, iii.]
Take on. To assume; take on oneself.
Take to heart. To grieve over.
Undergo pain. To suffer.
Weigh upon the heart. To cause grief.
Wince. To shrink, as from pain.
Worry oneself. To allow oneself to be troubled or vexed.
Yearn. To be made uneasy with longing.

PAIN—*Adjectives.*

Accursed. Doomed to misery or destruction.
Aching. Painful. See *Verbs.*
Afflicted. Troubled grievously.
A prey to. } Stricken by.
A prey to grief.
Between hawk and buzzard. In great anxiety.
Broken-hearted. Having the spirits broken by grief or despair.
Careworn. Burdened with care.
Chagrined. Vexed or annoyed.
Cheerless, etc. Without joy and gladness, etc. See LIGHTHEARTEDNESS-DEJECTION.
Concerned. Anxious or solicitous for any person or thing.
Crushed. Grievously oppressed.
Cut up. Injured or wounded.
Devoted. Doomed to evil.
Discontented, etc. Uneasy in mind, etc. See CONTENTEDNESS-DISCONTENTMENT.
Displeased, etc. Not pleased; offended; vexed, etc. See PLEASURABLENESS-PAINFULNESS.
Disturbed. Agitated in mind.
Doomed. Destined to calamity or ruin.
Full of pain. Causing pain or trouble.
Griped. Distressed.
Heart-broken. Deeply grieved.
Heart-scalled. Greatly distressed.
Heart-stricken. Dismayed.
Heavy-laden. Weighed down with care or grief.
Horrified. Stricken with horror.
Horror-stricken. Struck with an excessive degree of fear with a shuddering.
Ill at ease. Uneasy; anxious.
Ill-used. Badly treated.
In a state of pain. Painful.
In a taking. In a fit of sickness, etc. See *Nouns.*
In a way. Perplexed; discomfited.
In despair, etc. Hopeless. See SANGUINENESS-HOPELESSNESS.
Infelicitous. Unhappy or unfortunate.
In grief. Weeping.
In limbo. In confinement or imprisoned.
In pain. Suffering.
In tears, etc. Very sorrowful, etc. See JUBILATION-LAMENTATION.
Lost. Perplexed, bewildered.

(Continued on Column 1.)

---

pleas'-ure–giv'-ing. Full of enjoyment. PLEASURABLENESS-PAINFULNESS.
pleas'-ure–ground". A playground. DWELLER-HABITATION, ENTERTAINMENT-WEARINESS.
ple-be'-ian. One of the common people. GENTILITY-COMMONALTY.
pleb'-i-scite. A popular vote. CHOICE-NEUTRALITY, DECISION-MISJUDGMENT, LAW-LAWLESSNESS, ORDER.
pleb"-i-sci'-tum. A law enacted by public vote. CHOICE-NEUTRALITY.
plectuntur Achivi, delirant reges [L.] (plec-tun'-tur a-kai'-vai, de-lai'-rant rî-jîz). The kings rage, the people suffer. HARSHNESS-MILDNESS.
pledge. Promise; security. ENGAGEMENT-RELEASE, LOAN-BORROWING, POLITENESS-IMPOLITENESS, SECURITY, SOLEMNIZATION; **hold in pledge,** SECURITY; **pledge oneself,** ENGAGEMENT-RELEASE; **pledge one's word,** ENGAGEMENT-RELEASE; **take the pledge,** MODERATION-SELFINDULGENCE, SECURITY, TEETOTALISM-INTEMPERANCE.

pledg'-et. A small plug; a wad of lint. PERFORATOR-STOPPER, REMEDY-BANE.
Plei'-a-des. A group of stars in Taurus. GATHERING-SCATTERING, UNIVERSE.
ple'-na-ry. Entire. ENTIRETY-DEFICIENCY, MAGNITUDE-SMALLNESS.
ple-nip'-o-tent. Possessing full power. MIGHT-IMPOTENCE.
plen"-i-po-ten'-ti-a-ry. One having full power. CONSIGNEE-REPRESENTATION.
plen'-i-tude. Fulness. ENOUGH, EXCESS-LACK; **in the plenitude of power,** STRENGTH-WEAKNESS.
plen'-te-ous. Abundant. ENOUGH.
plen'-ti-ful. Ample. ENOUGH.
plen'-ty. Abundance. ENOUGH, MULTIPLICITY-PAUCITY; **plenty to do,** ACTIVITY-INDOLENCE.
ple'-num. That state in which every part of space is supposed to be full of matter. MATERIALITY-SPIRITUALITY, SUBSTANCE-NULLITY.
ple'-o-nasm. Redundancy of words. EXCESS-LACK, RHETORIC, TERSENESS-PROLIXITY.

ple″-o-nas′-tic. Redundant. TERSENESS-PROLIXITY.

ple-roph′-o-ry. Fulness; full persuasion. FAITH-MIS-GIVING.

pleth′-o-ra. Fulness of blood. EXCESS-LACK.

ple-thor′-ic. Affected with plethora. EXCESS-LACK.

plex′-us. A complication of parts. CROSSING.

pli″-a-bil′-i-ty. Flexibility. HARDNESS-SOFTNESS, READINESS-RELUCTANCE.

pli′-a-ble. Flexible. HARDNESS-SOFTNESS.

pli′-a-ble-ness. Flexibility. HARDNESS-SOFTNESS.

pli′-an-cy. Flexibility. DETERMINATION-VACILLATION, HARDNESS-SOFTNESS.

pli′-ant. Easily bent. DETERMINATION-VACILLATION, DIFFICULTY-FACILITY, HARDNESS-SOFTNESS, PRESUMPTION-OBSEQUIOUSNESS.

pli′-cate. Plaited. PLICATURE.

pli-ca′-tion. Folding. GEOLOGY.

plic′-a-ture. A fold. PLICATURE.

PLICATURE.

Corrugation. An alternation of ridges and grooves.
Crankle.
Crinkle. } A short turn, as in a string.
Crease. The mark made by a fold.
Crumple. An irregular fold.
Doubling.
Duplicature. } Fold.
Elbow. A sudden bend or turn. [*Ell*, arm.]
Flection. A turned or curved part.
Flexure. A bend, as in a bone.
Fold. A part doubled over.
Joint. Place where two or more things unite, often by a fold.
Plication.
Plicature. } A fold.
Rimple. Wrinkle.
Rivel. Crease.
Ruck. A crease or ridge, as in cloth or paper. [Prov Eng.]
Rumple. An irregular wrinkle.
Wrinkle. A slight ridge, made as by contraction.

PLICATURE—*Denotations.*

Crow's feet. The wrinkles that appear under and around the outer corners of the eyes.
Dog's ears. The corners of the leaves of a book turned down.
Flounce. An ornamental appendage to the skirt of a woman's dress.
Frounce. A wrinkle, plait, or curl.
Gather. A plait or fold in cloth made by drawing a thread through it.
Lapel. That part of a garment which is turned back, as the lap or fold of the front of a coat.
Plait. A doubling, as of cloth.
Ply. A fold or plait.
Pucker. A fold or wrinkle.
Ruffle. A strip of lace, etc., plaited or gathered and used as a trimming.
Tuck. A horizontal sewed fold, such as is made in a garment, to shorten it.

PLICATURE—*Verbs.*

Cocker. To coddle.
Cockle up. To pucker.
Corrugate. To contract into alternate ridges and furrows.
Crankle. To fill with short turns.
Crease. To mark by making folds.
Crimple. To contract with wrinkles.
Crinkle. To bend or fold.
Crumple. To crush with irregular folds.
Curl. To form into coils, curves, or ripples.
Double. To fold.
Flounce. To furnish with flounces.
Fold. To turn back upon itself.
Frizzle. To cause to crinkle or curl up.
Frounce. To form wrinkles in the forehead.
Gather. To pucker.
Hem. To fold and sew down the edge.
Plait. To fold in strips.
Plicate. To fold in plaits like a fan.
Pucker. To gather in small folds.
Rimple. To rumple.
Rivel. To crease.
Ruck. To ridge.
Ruffle. To rumple; furnish with ruffles.

Rumple. To crush with irregular folds.
Tuck. To fold under.
Turn double.
Turn down. } To make a fold in.
Turn under.
Twill. To weave in such a manner as to produce a diagonal appearance upon surface.
Wrinkle. To fill with ridges and grooves.

PLICATURE—*Adjectives*

Folded. See *Verbs.*
Retrorse. Turned, bent, or directed backward.

pli′-ers. A kind of pincers. INJECTION-EJECTION, KEEPING-RELINQUISHMENT.

plight. To pledge. CONDITION-SITUATION, ENGAGEMENT-RELEASE, SECURITY; **evil plight,** WELFARE-MISFORTUNE; **plight one's faith,** BLANDISHMENT; **plight one's troth,** BLANDISHMENT, ENGAGEMENT-RELEASE.

plight′-ed love. Engagement. BLANDISHMENT, LOVE-HATE.

plinth. The square block at the base of a column. SUSPENSION-SUPPORT, TOP-BOTTOM.

plod. To drudge. ACTIVITY-INDOLENCE, PERSISTENCE-WHIM, SWIFTNESS-SLOWNESS, TRAVELING-NAVIGATION.

plod′-ding. Slow motion or study. ACTIVITY-INDOLENCE, PERSISTENCE-WHIM, WITTINESS-DULNESS.

plough. A plow; an instrument to break the soil. DOMESTICATION-AGRICULTURE, GROOVE; **plough in,** ENVIRONMENT-INTERPOSITION; **plough one's way,** TRAVELING-NAVIGATION; **plough the ground,** PREPARATION-NONPREPARATION; **plough the waves,** TRAVELING-NAVIGATION.

plough′-boy. A boy who guides a plow; a rustic. GENTILITY-COMMONALTY.

plough′-share. The blade of a plow. SHARPNESS-BLUNTNESS.

plot. A scheme; a portion of ground. CRAFT-ARTLESSNESS, DESIGN, ENLIGHTENMENT-SECRECY, EXTENSION-DISTRICT, GULF-PLAIN; **the plot thickens,** ACTIVITY-INDOLENCE, GATHERING-SCATTERING, OCCURRENCE-DESTINY.

plow. A better spelling of **plough.**

pluck. Determination; take. BRAVERY-COWARDICE, CHOICE-REJECTION, DETERMINATION-VACILLATION, PERSISTENCE-WHIM, TAKING-RESTITUTION, THEFT, TRUTHFULNESS-FRAUD; **pluck a crow with,** APPROVAL-DISAPPROVAL; **pluck out,** INJECTION-EJECTION; **pluck up courage,** BRAVERY-COWARDICE.

pluck′-y. Full of spirit. BRAVERY-COWARDICE.

plug. A stopper. APERTURE-CLOSURE, PERFORATOR-STOPPER.

plum. A fruit; a handsome fortune. FIVE-QUINQUE-SECTION, MONEY, SWEETNESS-ACIDITY.

plu′-mage. Feathers of a bird. SMOOTHNESS-ROUGHNESS.

plum′-col″-ored. The color of a plum. YELLOWNESS-PURPLE.

plumb. A leaden weight on a line. APERTURE-CLOSURE, MENSURATION.

plumb′-line″. A perpendicular line. ERECTNESS-FLATNESS.

plume. A feather used as an ornament. EMBELLISHMENT-DISFIGUREMENT, SMOOTHNESS-ROUGHNESS; **borrowed plumes,** LOAN-BORROWING; **plume oneself,** SELFRESPECT-HUMBLENESS.

plume, coup de [F.] (plŭm, cu de). A literary attack. WRITING-PRINTING.

plume, nom de [F.] (plŭm, non′ de). An assumed title. NAME-MISNOMER.

plu-mig′-er-ous. Feathered. SMOOTHNESS-ROUGHNESS.

plum'-met. A piece of lead for sounding. Deepness-Shallowness, Erectness-Flatness.

plu'-mose. Bearing feathers. Smoothness-Roughness.

plu-mos'-i-ty. The state of being plumose. Smoothness-Roughness.

plump. Fat; to fall suddenly. Eternity-Instantaneity, Expectation-Surprise, Greatness-Littleness, Spring-Plunge; **plump down,** Ascent-Descent; **plump upon,** Arrival-Departure.

plump'-er. One who plumps himself; a vote given to one candidate only when two or more are to be elected. Choice-Neutrality, Enlargement-Diminution.

plun'-der. Pillage; booty. Plunder, Theft.

PLUNDER.

Blackmail. Extortion of money by threats or accusation.
Booty. Something taken by violence or robbery, especially in war.
Loot. Plunder taken from a sacked city by the conquering army.
Pickings. That which is obtained from petty thefts.
Plunder. Something obtained by plundering or by open force from an enemy.
Prey. Anything obtained by violence.
Prize. Something taken by superior force.
Ravin. Spoliation; prey.
Spolia opima [L.]. The richest plunder.
Spoil. Anything taken from another by violence.
Stolen goods. Articles in one's possession to which one has no right.
Swag. The plunder of a burglar or thief.

PLUNDER—*Adjective.*

Manubial. Belonging to booty; obtained in war.

plunge. Dive; to rush. Deepness-Shallowness, Hurry-Leisure, Injection-Ejection, Revolution, Spring-Dive, Water-Air; **plunge headlong,** Hurry-Leisure; **plunge in** *medias res*, Determination-Vacillation, Injection-Ejection, Simplicity-Floridness; **plunge into,** Enterprise; **plunge into difficulties,** Difficulty-Facility; **plunge into dissipation,** Moderation-Selfindulgence; **plunge into sorrow,** Pleasurableness-Painfulness.

plunged. Cast. **Plunged in debt,** Credit-Debt; **plunged in grief,** Pleasure-Pain.

plu'-ral. More than one. Plurality-Fraction.

plu-ral'-i-ty. A greater number. Plurality-Fraction.

PLURALITY—FRACTION.

A certain number. A fixed amount or quantity.
A few A small or limited number.
A number. A collection of many individuals.
Multitude, etc. A great number of persons or things taken collectively, etc. See Multiplicity.
One or two. A small indefinite number.
Plurality. A number consisting of more than one of the same kind.
Several. Persons or things, more than two, but not very many.
Two or three. A small indefinite number.

PLURALITY—*Adjectives.*

Certain. Fixed or stated; regular.
More than one. Many.
Not alone, etc. Being with others. See Solitude.
Plural. Containing more than one.

Fraction. A portion or a fragment.
Fractional part. One of the parts into which anything may be divided.
Part, etc. One of the portions into which anything is divided, or regarded as divided, etc. See Whole-Part.

PLURALITY—Adjectives—*Continued.*

Some. Considerable in number.
Upwards of. More than; above.

PLURALITY—*Adverb.*

Et cetera [L.]. Etc.; and the rest.

PLURALITY—*Phrase.*

Non deficit alter [L.]. The second is not wanting.

PLURALITY—ZERO.

ZERO.

Absence, etc. The state of being withdrawn or absent; want, etc. See Presence-Absence.
A me qui vive [F.]. A living soul.
Cipher. A character which expresses nothing.
Naught. Nothing.
Nobody. Not a single person.
None. Not one.
Not a soul. Not a person.
Nothing. Not anything.
Nought. Nothing.
Unsubstantiality, etc. The state of containing no matter or substance, etc. See Substance-Nullity.
Zero. Nothing; naught.

ZERO—*Adjectives.*

Not any.⎫
Not one.⎭ None.

plus. Increased by. Addition-Subtraction.

plush. Shaggy cloth. Smoothness-Roughness.

Plu'-to. The god of the lower world. Heaven-Hell; **realms of Pluto,** Heaven-Hell.

plu-toc'-ra-cy. A wealthy class in a political community who control the doings of the government. Affluence-Penury, Labor-Capital.

Plu-ton'-ic. Pertaining to Pluto. Heat-Cold.

Plu'-tus. The god of wealth. Affluence-Penury.

plu'-vi-al. Rainy. River-Wind.

ply. To work at closely; a fold. Petition-Expostulation, Plicature, Toil-Relaxation, Use-Disuse; **ply a trade,** Exchange; **ply one's task,** Action-Passiveness, Occupation; **ply one's trade,** Occupation.

P. M. Postmeridian; past midday. Morning-Evening.

pneu-mat'-ics. The science which treats of the mechanical properties of the air. Liquid-Gas.

pneu''-ma-tol'-o-gy. The science of spiritual existence. Mind-Imbecility.

pneu''-ma-to-scop'-ic. Spiritual. Materiality-Spirituality.

poach. To steal game. Law-Lawlessness, Theft.

poach'-er. One who steals game. Robber.

poach'-y. Easily trodden into holes by cattle. Swamp-Island.

pobreza no hay verguenza, à [Sp.] (po-breth'-a no a'-î ver-gu-en'-tha). Poverty has no shame. Affluence-Penury, Selfrespect-Humbleness.

pock. A pustule on the skin in smallpox. Convexity-Concavity.

pock'-et. A small bag; to take. Contents-Receiver, Establishment-Removal, Excitability-Inexcitability, Giving-Receiving, Greatness-Littleness, Money, Treasury; **button up one's pocket,** Settlement-Default; **out of pocket,** Credit-Debt, Gain-Loss; **pocket the affront,** Pardon-Vindictiveness, Yielding; **touch the pocket,** Money.

pock'-et-book. A purse; a note-book. Mark-Obliteration.

pock′-et–hand′-ker-chief. A cloth used for the nose. DRESS-UNDRESS.

pock′-et–mon′-ey. Spending-money. MONEY.

pock′-et–pis′-tol. A liquor-flask. CONTENTS-RECEIVER.

pococurante [It.] (po′′-co-cu-ran-tê′). Easy-going. DESIRE-DISTASTE, SENSITIVENESS-APATHY.

pocula, inter [L.] (poc′-yu-la, in′-ter). At one's cups. TEETOTALISM-INTEMPERANCE.

pod. A seed-case. CONTENTS-RECEIVER, COVER-LINING.

podestà [It.] (po′′-des-ta′). A legal officer. JUDGE.

po′-em. A composition in verse. POETRY-PROSE.

pœnitentiæ, locus [L.] (pen-i-ten′-shi-î, lo′-cus). Place for repentance. COMPASSION-RUTHLESSNESS, JUSTI-FICATION-CHARGE, PARDON-VINDICTIVENESS, REPENTANCE-OBDURACY.

po′-e-sy. Poetry. POETRY-PROSE.

po′-et. One who writes poetry. POETRY-PROSE.

po′-et-as′′-ter. A mere rimer. POETRY-PROSE, SOCIETY-AFFECTATION.

po-et′-ic. Suitable for poetry. FORCE-WEAKNESS, POETRY-PROSE.

po-et′-ic-al. Pertaining to poetry. POETRY-PROSE.

po′-et-ics. The art of poetry. POETRY-PROSE.

po′-et-ize′′. To make poetic. POETRY-PROSE.

po′-et-ry. The work of poets. NATURE-ART, POETRY-PROSE, RHETORIC.

POETRY—PROSE.

Alexandrine. An iambic hexameter verse, used in early French poems upon Alexander the Great.

Anacreontic. An erotic, amatory poem in the manner of the Greek poet Anacreon.

Anthology. A collection of beautiful passages [flowers] from authors.

Antistrophe. The lines of an ode alternating with the strophe

Ballad. Any popular poem, narrative in content and generally lyric in form.

Bucolic. A pastoral poem.

Canto. A part of a long poem.

Canzonet. A short, airy song.

Cento. A patchwork poem.

Couplet. Two lines of verse in immediate sequence and riming together.

Disjecti membra poetæ [L.] Members of a disjointed poet. [Horace, *Satires,* I iv, 62.]

Distich. Two lines making complete sense.

Dithyramb. A wild, irregular poem.

Doggerel. A trivial, clumsy verse.

Dramatic poetry. That kind of poetry of which scenic representation is possible.

Drinking song. A musical, poetical composition adapted to the occasion of drinking.

Eclogue. A short, pastoral poem.

Elegiac poetry. } Poetry expressing sorrow or lamentation. See
Elegiac verse. } *Adjectives.*

Elegiacs. Sad, plaintive poetry.

Elegy. A lyric poem lamenting the dead, or on a sorrowful theme.

Epic. An heroic poem.

Epic poetry. Heroic verse.

Epode. A lyric poem in which a longer verse is followed by a shorter

Epopee. }
Epopœia. } An epic poem or poetry.

Hudibrastic verse. Satirical poetry, like the *Hudibras* of Butler.

Iambus. A verse whose predominating foot is the iambus.

Idyl. A narrative poem of romance or fancy.

Lay. A song or ballad in simple style.

Leonine verse. A medieval rimed Latin verse.

Licentia vatum [L.] Poetic license.

Love song. A song expressive of love.

Lullaby. A song to please a child.

Lyric. A lyric poem.

Lyric poetry. The kind of poetry that expresses the individual emotions of the writer.

Macaronics. } A mixed, jumbled poem, so as to make a burlesque
Macaronic verse. } composition.

Madrigal. A short song, amatory or pastoral, and iambic in meter.

Making verses. The art of writing poetry.

Monody. A mourning poem sung by one person in which he laments.

Music. A rhythmical succession of tones. See MUSIC.

Nursery rimes. Short songs used in the nursery.

Ode. A form of lyric poetry used for the expression of sentiment or imaginative thought.

Opera. Musical dramatic poetry accompanied by choruses, scenery, acting, etc.

Orthometry. The art of writing poetry correctly.

Pastoral. A poem relating to rural scenes and customs.

Poem. A composition in verse characterized by poetic thought and beauty

Poesy. Poetry.

Poetics. The art or principles of poetry.

Poetry. Imaginative metrical composition.

Posy. A brief, poetical sentiment.

Prose run mad. Poetry.

Prosody. That part of grammar that treats of versification.

Prosaism. A prosaic style or expression.

Prose. Ordinary speech, opposed to poetry, without metrical structure.

Weldliteratur [G.]. World-literature.

PROSE—*Nouns of Agency.*

Prosaist. A writer of prose.

Proser. A dull tedious writer.

Prose writer. One who writes prose.

PROSE—*Verbs.*

Prose. To compose in prose, to speak in prose.

Write in prose. } To write without regard to rhythm, etc.
Write prose. }

PROSE—*Adjectives.*

In prose. Without regard to rhythm, etc.

Not in verse. In prose.

Prosaic. Pertaining to prose; unimaginative.

Prosy. Having the nature of prose, dull, commonplace.

Rimeless. Without rimes.

Unpoetical. Not having the characteristics of poetry.

Unrimed. Not rimed.

POETRY—*Continued.*

Quatrain. A stanza of four lines.

Riming. The art of making rimes.

Rondeau. A poem of prescribed form, having repetitions recurring according to a fixed law.

Roundelay. See RONDEAU

Rondo. A lively poem in which the first strain follows every other strain.

Runes. An obscure or mystic poem or verse.

Sea song. A song used on the sea.

Song. Poetry, a poetical composition adapted to singing.

Sonnet. A poem of fourteen lines, originally composed of an octave and a sextet

Stanza. A group of rimed lines, usually four or more, into which poems are frequently divided.

Strain. A distinctive portion of a poem.

Strophe. In ancient poetry, the first of two corresponding stanzas.

Triplet. A group of three lines riming together.

Verse. Metrical composition as distinguished from prose.

Versification. The art of writing poetry.

War song. A song pertaining to war; a song full of incitement to ardor.

POETRY—*Associated Nouns.*

Accentuation. The application of the accent. See VOCALIZATION.

Alliteration Rhythmical repetition of letters at the beginning of accented syllables.

Anacrusis. A prefix of one or two unaccented syllables to a verse properly beginning with an accented syllable.

Anapest. A metrical foot consisting of two unaccented syllables and one accented syllable.

Antispast. A foot of four syllables, the first and fourth unaccented, and the second and third accented.

Assonance. A species of rime.

Calliope. The Muse that presides over heroic poetry.

Choriambus. A foot of four syllables, of which the first and last are long, and the second and third short.

Dactyl. A poetical foot of one long followed by two short syllables.

Elegiac meter. The meter used in writing poems of lamentation.

Foot. A combination constituting a metrical element of a verse

Helicon. A mountain in Greece, the abode of Apollo and the Muses

POETRY—Associated Nouns—*Continued*.

Hexameter. A verse of six feet, the first four of which may be either dactyls or spondees, the fifth must be a dactyl, and the sixth a spondee.

Ictus. The stress of voice upon an accented syllable of a word.

Line. A verse, or the words which form a certain number of feet.

Measure. The manner of combining the long and short syllables of a verse.

Meter. Rhythmical arrangement of words or syllables into verses.

Muse. One of the nine goddesses who presided over song and the different kinds of poetry.

Numbers. Poetic measure, as divisions of time or number of syllables.

Parnassus. A mountain in Greece, sacred to Apollo and the Muses.

Pentameter. A verse of five feet.

Pierian Spring. The spring of the Muses.

Pierides. The Muses.

Rhyme. Correspondence of sound in the terminating words or syllables of two verses; end rime.

Rhythm. Movement in musical time, with periodic recurrence of accent.

Rime. Rhythmical repetition of letters in poetry, as alliteration, assonance, rhyme. etc.

Spondee. A poetic foot of two long syllables.

Trochee. A foot of two syllables, the first long and the second short.

Tuneful Nine. The Muses.

POETRY—*Nouns of Agency*.

Bard. Any poet; but in ancient times one who sang of heroic deeds of men.

Genus irritabile vatum [L.]. Irritable race of poets.

Idylist. An idyllic poet.

Improvisatore. One who devises on the spur of the moment.

Laureate. The poet officially crowned with the title of laureate.

Lyrist. A lyric poet.

Meistersinger. One of the poets and musicians who succeeded the minnesingers.

Minnesinger. A lyric poet of mediæval Germany.

Poet. One who makes verses or composes poetry.

Poetaster. One who dabbles in poetry.

Poet laureate. Laureate; a title conferred by the king.

Rimer.
Rimester. } One who makes rimes, or bad poetry; a rhymer, etc.
Rimist.

Runer. An early Gothic bard.

Scald. One of the ancient Scandinavian minstrels.

Sonneteer. A writer of sonnets.

Troubadour. A lyric poet that lived in medieval France and Spain.

Trouvére. One of a class of epic poets who flourished in France during the 11th, 12th, 13th, and 14th centuries.

Versifier. One who makes verses

POETRY—*Verbs*.

Make verses. To write poetry.

Poetize. To turn into poetry; make poetry.

Rime. To put into rime.

Scan. To separate a verse into feet; indicate such separation in reading.

Sing. To celebrate in song; compose poetry.

Versify. To make verses, or turn into poetry.

POETRY—*Adjectives*.

Acatalectic. Said of a verse having the required number of feet.

Alcaic. Of or like the poetry of Alcæus, having the meter of Alcæus.

Anapestic. Having for its principal foot an anapest.

Catalectic. Incomplete, having one or two syllables lacking to make a complete verse.

Dithyrambic. Wild and irregular. See *Nouns*.

Elegiac. Pertaining to or having the characteristics of an elegy.

Epic. Having the characteristics of an epic poem.

Iambic. Having its principal foot an iambus.

Idyllic. Having the qualities of a pastoral poem.

Ionic. Pertaining to Ionia, or its poetry or literature.

Lyric.
Lyrical. } Pertaining to lyric poetry.

Metrical. Put in poetical measure; relating to meter.

Pindaric. Relating to Pindar, a Greek lyric poet.

Poetic.
Poetical. } Relating or pertaining to poetry.

Sapphic. Relating to Sappho, a writer of amatory poems and lyrics.

Trochaic. Having principal foot a trochee.

Tuneful. Harmonious; musical; poetical.

POETRY—*Phrases*.

Dichtung und wahrheit [G.]. Poetry and truth.

Furor poeticus [L]. Poetic rage.

Licentia vatum [L.]. Poetic license.

Mutum est pictura poema [L.]. A picture is a mute poem.

Volk der dichter und denker [G.]. Nation of poets and thinkers.

poign'-an-cy. Severity. AFFECTIONS, PUNGENCY, VIGOR-INERTIA.

poign'-ant. Cutting. EMOTION, VIGOR-INERTIA.

point. The sharp end of anything; a speck; topic; place. BEGINNING-END, CONCEPTION-THEME, CONDITION-SITUATION, EXTENSION-INEXTENSION, EXTENSION-PLACE, FORCE-WEAKNESS, GREATNESS-LITTLENESS, MAGNITUDE-SMALLNESS, PURPOSE-LUCK, QUANTITY-MEASURE, SHARPNESS-BLUNTNESS, SIGN, STATION, UPRIGHTNESS-DISHONESTY, VIGOR-INERTIA, WITTINESS-DULNESS; **at the point of,** REMOTENESS-NEARNESS; **at the point of the bayonet,** FIGHTING-CONCILIATION, TURBULENCE-CALMNESS; **at the point of the sword,** COERCION, HARSHNESS-MILDNESS, TURBULENCE-CALMNESS; **come to the point,** HEED-DISREGARD, RATIOCINATION-INSTINCT, SIMPLICITY-FLORIDNESS, TERSENESS-PROLIXITY, UNIVERSALITY-PARTICULARITY; **culminating point,** TOP-BOTTOM; **disputed point,** VARIANCE-ACCORD; **from all points,** EXTENSION-DISTRICT; **full of points,** FORCE-WEAKNESS; **go straight to the point,** AIM-ABERRATION; **in point,** CONNECTION-INDEPENDENCE, CONVENTIONALITY-UNCONVENTIONALITY, HARMONY-DISCORD; **in point of fact,** ENTITY-NONENTITY; **knotty point,** DIFFICULTY-FACILITY, EXCESS-LACK; **make a point of,** COERCION, DETERMINATION-VACILLATION, DUENESS-UNDUENESS, STRIFE-PEACE, TERMS, UPRIGHTNESS-DISHONESTY; **on the point of,** FUTURE-PAST, LASTINGNESS-TRANSIENTNESS; **point a moral,** EDUCATION-MISTEACHING; **point an antithesis,** PURITY-CRUDENESS; **point at,** AIM-ABERRATION, APPROVAL-DISAPPROVAL, HEED-DISREGARD, POLITENESS-IMPOLITENESS, PURPOSE-LUCK, REGARD-DISRESPECT; **point in dispute,** INVESTIGATION-ANSWER; **point of attack,** ATTACK-DEFENSE; **point of convergence,** GATHERINGPLACE; **point of death,** LIFE-DEATH; **point of etiquette,** SOCIETY-LUDICROUSNESS; **point of honor,** UPRIGHTNESS-DISHONESTY; **point of land,** CONVEXITY-CONCAVITY; **point of order,** PRESIDENT-MEMBER; **point of the compass,** AIM-ABERRATION; **point of view,** APPEARANCE-DISAPPEARANCE, CONCEPTION-THEME, SIGHT-BLINDNESS; **point out,** ENLIGHTENMENT-SECRECY, HEED-DISREGARD, RATIONALE-LUCK; **point the finger of scorn,** REGARD-SCORN; **point to,** AIM-ABERRATION, HEED-DISREGARD, LIKELIHOOD-UNLIKELIHOOD, MEANING-JARGON, PROPHECY, RATIONALE-LUCK; **to the point,** TERSENESS-PROLIXTIY. *point d'appui* [F.] (pwan· da-pwî'). Point of support. SUSPENSION-SUPPORT.

point″-blank′. Direct; plain. Aim-Aberration, Proffer-Refusal, Simplicity-Floridness.

point′-cham-pain′. Line of dishonor in heraldry. Reputation-Discredit.

point′-ed. Having a point. Assertion-Denial, Force-Weakness, Magnitude-Smallness, Sharpness-Bluntness, Sign.

point′-ed-ly. In a pointed manner. Purpose-Luck.

point′-er. A dog; an indicator. Fauna-Flora, Sign.

point′-less. Without a point. Wittiness-Dulness.

poise. To balance. Equality-Inequality, Heaviness-Lightness.

poi′-son. Anything noxious to life or health. Betterment-Deterioration, Remedy-Bane.

poi′-soned. Infected with poison. Commend the poison chalice, Goodness-Badness, Truthfulness-Falsehood.

poi′-son-ing. The state of being poisoned. Betterment-Deterioration.

poi′-son-ous. Deadly. Healthiness-Unhealthiness, Remedy-Bane.

poke. A pocket. Contents-Receiver; **pig in a poke,** Certainty-Doubt, Purpose-Luck, Recklessness-Caution; **poke at,** Attack-Defense, Impetus-Reaction; **poke fun at,** Society-Derision; **poke one's nose in,** Activity-Indolence; **poke out,** Convexity-Concavity; **poke the fire,** Heating-Cooling.

po′-ker. An iron rod for poking a fire. Oven-Refrigerator.

po-lac′-ca. A vessel. Conveyance-Vessel.

po-la′-cre. A vessel. Conveyance-Vessel.

po′-lar. Pertaining to the poles. Top-Bottom; **polar coordinates,** Mensuration.

po-lar′-i-scope. An optical instrument. Optical Instruments.

po-lar′-i-ty. The quality of having opposite poles. Co-operation-Opposition, Duality, Laterality-Contraposition.

po″-lar-i-za′-tion. Act of polarizing. Electricity.

pole. A rod; either of the extremities of an axis of a sphere; point of greatest electrification. Center, Height-Lowness, Electricity, Length-Shortness, Revolution-Evolution, Top-Bottom; **from pole to pole,** Extension-District, Remoteness-Nearness; **greasy pole,** Entertainment-Weariness; **opposite poles,** Laterality-Contraposition.

pole′-ax″. An ancient battle-ax. Weapon.

pole′-cat″. An animal allied to the weasel. Perfume-Stench.

po-lem′-ic. Disputatious. Belligerent, Ratiocination-Instinct, Strife-Peace, Variance-Accord.

po-lem′-ic-al. Disputatious. Ratiocination-Instinct.

po-lem′-ics. The art of controversy. Ratiocination-Instinct, Strife-Peace, Variance-Accord.

po-lem′-o-scope. An opera-glass with a mirror for seeing objects not directly ahead. Optical Instruments.

pole′-star. The largest star near the north pole of the heavens. Management, Sign.

po-lice′. A body of civil officers. Judicature; **police court,** Tribunal; **police department,** City-Country; **police magistrate,** Judge.

po-lice′-man. A member of the police. Judicature, Security-Insecurity.

pol′-i-cy. Plan. Conduct, Design.

pol′-ish. To make smooth; refined in manners. Beauty-Ugliness, Betterment-Deterioration, Embellishment-Disfigurement, Friction-Lubrication, Politeness-Impoliteness, Smoothness-Roughness, Taste-Vulgarity; **polish off,** Completion-Noncompletion.

Po″-lish-bank′. A game. Entertainment-Weariness.

pol′-ished. Made smooth and glossy. City-Country, Politeness-Impoliteness, Purity-Crudeness, Society-Ludicrousness.

polisson [F.] (po-li-son′). Scamp. Good Man-Bad Man.

po-lite′. Refined in manner. Politeness-Impoliteness; **polite literature,** Language; **polite society,** Society-Ludicrousness; **offensive to ear polite,** Purity-Crudeness.

po-lite′-ness. Courtesy. Politeness-Impoliteness.

POLITENESS—IMPOLITENESS.

Affability. Ease and courtesy of manner.
Amability. Lovableness.
Amenity. Agreeableness in any respect.
Amiability. Quality of heart which attracts love.
Bienséance [F.]. Civility.
Breeding. Presence of polish and agreeableness.
Civility. Observance of slight external courtesies.
Civilization. The condition of a people with regard to their progress in the sciences, arts, government, etc.
Comity. Courtesy between equals.
Complacency. The state of being satisfied with one's state or surroundings.
Complaisance. Desire to please.
Condescension, etc. The act of stooping to the condition of inferiors, etc. See Selfrespect-Humbleness.
Courtesy. Graceful respectfulness.
Duty. The course of conduct that one is morally bound to follow.
Easy temper. Calmness or composure of mind.
Gallantry. Attention shown a weaker person, especially a woman.
Gentility. The air of one well-born.
Good behavior. External grace of deportment.
Good breeding. Good manners.
Good humor. Pleasing frame of mind.
Good manners. The effect of training on character and behavior.
Good temper. Composure of mind.
Manners. Conduct in social intercourse.
Mansuetude. Mildness.
Obsequiousness. Slavish submission. See Presumption-Obsequiousness.
Pink of courtesy. } Highest degree of courtesy and politeness.
Pink of politeness. }
Polish. Absence of anything making one offensive in social intercourse.

Acerbity. Want of natural mildness or sweetness.
Acrimony. Sourness shown habitually in small things.
Asperity. Spontaneous but well-meant roughness of manner or severity of speech.
Austerity. Serious disposition.
Bad manners. Impolite behavior.
Barbarism. Rudeness of conduct.
Barbarity. Brutal conduct.
Blackguardism. The conduct of a mean, low fellow.
Brusquerie [F.]. Bluntness.
Brutality. Coarseness of conduct.
Captiousness, etc. Readiness to be offended, etc. See Favorite-Quarrelsomeness.
Churlishness. The quality of being rude or ill-bred.
Conduct unbecoming a gentleman. Rudeness.
Cynicism. Contempt for the opinions of others.
Discourtesy. Lack of graceful respect.
Displacency. Envious displeasure.
Disrespect, etc. Lack of respect, etc. See Regard-Disrespect.
Grossièreté [F.]. Coarseness.
Ill-breeding. Poor bringing up or training.
Illiberality. Lack of breadth and variety of culture.
Ill-manners. Ill-behavior.
Impudence. A jaunty disrespect.
Incivility. Neglect of civility.
Insuavity. Absence of a winning sweetness.
Inurbanity. Lack of agreeableness of manner.
Misbehavior. Improper behavior.
Moodishness. Capriciousness of mood.
Moroseness, etc. Harshness of feeling toward inferiors, etc. See Favorite-Moroseness.
Perversity. Disposition to do the opposite of what is required.
Procacity. Impudence.

POLITENESS—IMPOLITENESS—*Continued.*

Politeness. Conventional expression of proper respect.
Presence. Appearance.
Prévenance [F.]. Kind attention.
Respect. Conduct showing deference.
Suavity. Sweetness of disposition.
Urbanity. Agreeableness of manners.

POLITENESS—*Associated Nouns.*

Abord [F.]. Manner of accosting.
Accolade [F.]. The salutation given to one on whom knighthood has been conferred.
Accueil [F.]. Reception; welcome.
Best love. Devoted affection.
Bow. A salutation made by an inclination of the body or head forward.
Bowing and scraping. Gaining acquaintance by rude or unusual ways.
Buss. A kiss.
Capping. Doffing the cap in salutation.
Ceremonial. The observance of conventional forms in social intercourse.
Compliment. A formal expression of admiration or commendation.
Condolence. Expression of sympathy.
Curtsy. A downward movement of the body by bending the knees.
Devoir [F.]. Respectful notice due to another.
Embrace. A clasping in the arms.
Fair words. Flattering speech.
Genuflexion. A bending of the knee in worship. See DEVOTION.
Greeting. Salutation on meeting, or by message or letter
Grip of the hand. A clasping of the hands in greeting.
Honeyed phrases. Endearing or flattering talk.
Hug. A close embrace.
Introduction. The act of making acquainted.
Kind regards.
Kind remembrances. } Courteous greeting or message.
Kiss. A salute or caress with the lips.
Kneeling. A falling on the knees.
Kotow. A Chinese obeisance made by touching the ground with the forehead.
Love. Devoted affection or attachment to.
Love token. A gift in token of love. See BLANDISHMENT.
Mark of recognition. Friendly notice, salutation, or attention.
Nod. A forward and downward motion of the head, as a sign of recognition.
Nods and becks and wreathed smiles. Actions to attract attention for mere amusement or pleasure.
Obeisance, etc. An act of courtesy or reverence made by the inclination of the body or the bending of the knee. See REGARD.
Pledge. A token of good-will or friendship.
Presentation. The act of making personally acquainted.
Reception. The act of receiving or welcoming others.
Recognition. Friendly notice, salutation, or attention.
Regards. Courteous greeting.
Remembrance. A token or gift reminding of gratitude, friendship, or love.
Respects. Expression of consideration, esteem, or compliment.
Salaam. A bow with the hand upon the forehead.
Salutation. A form of greeting or welcoming.
Salute. A display of honors out of respect.
Scrape. A scraping or drawing back of the foot in bowing.
Shaking hands. Grasping hands mutually as a salute at meeting or parting. See *Verbs.*
Soft tongue.
Soft words. } Flattery.
Squeeze. A close clasp.
Sweet words. Flattering speech.
Valediction. A bidding farewell. See ARRIVAL-DEPARTURE.
Vin d'honneur [F.]. Wine offered to distinguished guests.
Welcome. A hearty greeting given.

POLITENESS—*Verbs.*

Bow. To bend the body, knee, or head in token of respect.
Cap. To salute by removing the cap.
Cheer. To applaud with cheers.
Civilize. To instruct in the ways of civilization.
Conciliate. To obtain the friendship of.
Courtesy. To bend the knee in token of obedience or respect.
Embrace, etc. To grasp in the arms, etc. See BLANDISHMENT.
Greet. To address or make some sign of recognition upon meeting.
Hail. To call to.
Humanize. To make more humane.
Kiss. To greet with the lips.

Rusticity. Want of refinement or culture.
Spinosity. Crabbedness; thorniness.
Sternness. Severity of manner.
Tartness. Slight asperity; pungent readiness of mind.
Uncourteousness, etc. Lack of courtesy, etc. See *Adjectives.*
Ungainly manners. Impoliteness.
Virulence. Extreme bitterness of disposition.
Vulgarity, etc. Depravity of taste and manners. See TASTE-VULGARITY.

IMPOLITENESS—*Associated Nouns*

Bear. An ill-mannered or morose person.
Beast. A brutal or rude person.
Blackguard. A low, coarse, abusive fellow.
Black looks. Frowns, or mark of displeasure.
Bruin. An ill-mannered person; a bear.
Brute. A brutal, coarse person.
Contumely. Haughty or contemptuous language.
Cross-patch. A cross person.
Frown. A knitting of the brow, as in dislike or anger.
Frump. An old, ill-tempered woman.
Personality. A disparaging or derogatory remark.
Rebuff. A sudden repulse or curt denial.
Sauce-box, etc. A very saucy or pert person. See BRAWLER.
Scowl. A lowering of the brows, as in anger or strong disapproval.
Unlicked cub. An ill-mannered person.
Unparliamentary language. Language contrary to the rules that govern the proceedings of deliberative bodies.

IMPOLITENESS—*Verbs*

Brutalify.
Brutalize. } To treat brutally.
Cut. Not to recognize another purposely.
Frown. To contract the brow in displeasure.
Glower. To stare frowningly.
Growl. To talk in an angry, surly manner.
Insult, etc. To talk offensively, etc. See REGARD-DISRESPECT.
Ogle. To look at in a coquettish manner.
Pout. To hang or stick out the lips in anger.
Scowl. To frown.
Snap. To talk in a quick sharp manner.
Snarl. To talk crossly.

IMPOLITENESS—*Verbal Expressions.*

Be rude, etc. (see *Adjectives*); give the cold shoulder to; keep at a distance; keep at arm's length; look black upon; look cold upon; look cool upon; lose one's temper, etc. (see FAVORITE-ANGER); make bold with; make free with; point at; put to the blush; render rude, etc. (see *Adjectives*); send away with a flea in the ear; show the door to; stare out of countenance; take a liberty; take a name in vain; treat with discourtesy; turn one's back upon; turn on one's heel; turn the cold shoulder to.

IMPOLITENESS—*Adjectives.*

Abusive. Uttering harsh language against a person.
Acrimonious. Exhibiting bitterness in speaking.
Austere. Very serious.
Bearish. Snarling and gruff in conduct.
Biting. Indiscriminately censorious and unfeeling.
Bitter. Marked by sharpness or severity.
Blackguard. Characteristic of a blackguard.
Bluff. Somewhat rude or abrupt, but kindly.
Blunt. Abrupt in manner.
Boorish. Awkward and rude from want of training.
Brusque [F.]. Blunt; coarse.
Brutal. Treating others with brutality.
Caustic. Marked by a sharp and penetrating spite.
Cavalier. Easy; gay.
Churlish. Wanting in kindness and courtesy.
Contumelious. Full of unmerited disrespect and insolence.
Cool. Not allowing much intimacy.
Crabbed. Morose.
Dedecorous. Unbecoming.
Discourteous. Uncourteous.
Forward. Immodest.
Foul-mouthed.
Foul-spoken. } Using indecent language habitually.
Grim. Surly.
Gruff. Stern.
Harsh. Sour and unpleasant.
Ill-behaved.
Ill-bred.
Ill-conditioned. } Impolite; rude.
Ill-mannered.

POLITENESS—IMPOLITENESS—*Continued.*

POLITENESS—Verbs—*Continued.*

Kneel.   To fall on the knees.
Pledge.   To drink with in friendship.
Polish.   To deprive of that which makes one offensive in social intercourse.
Receive.   To entertain.
Salute.   To greet with some sign, as raising the hand to the head.
Scrape.   To get in an unusual way.
Serenade.   To entertain with a serenade.
Uncover.   To remove the hat in respect.
Usher.   To introduce.
Visit.   To make a friendly call on.
Welcome.   Receive gladly.

POLITENESS—*Verbal Expressions.*

Be all things to all men; be courteous (see *Adjectives*); behave oneself; bend the knee; bid Godspeed; bid welcome; bob a courtesy; bob a curtsy; bow the knee; dance attendance, etc. (see PRESUMPTION-OBSEQUIOUSNESS); doff the cap; do homage to, etc., (see REGARD), do the amiable; do the honors; drink to; give one's duty; hob and nob; hold out the hand; kiss the hands; look as if butter would not melt in one's mouth; make a leg; make one's bow; make the amiable; make way for; mend one's manners; mind one's P's and Q's; move to; nod to; pay attention to; pay a visit, etc. (see SOCIABILITY); pay one's respects; present arms; present oneself; press the hand; prostrate oneself, etc. (see DEVOTION). render polite, etc. (see *Adjectives*); send one's duty; shake hands; show courtesy; smile upon; speak one fair; speed the parting guest; squeeze the hand; take in good part; take off the hat; touch the hat; wait upon; welcome with open arms.

POLITENESS—*Adjectives.*

Affable.   Courteous in intercourse.
Bland.   Having a pleasantness of talk or manners.
Civil.   Observing slight courtesies.
Civilized.   Advanced in civilization.
Complacent. }
Complaisant. }   Agreeable; courteous.
Conciliatory.   Tending to gain the good-will of another.
Cordial.   Hearty.
Courteous.   Gracefully respectful.
Cultivated.   Refined.
Fair-spoken.   Having grace of speech.
Familiar.   Closely acquainted.
Fine-spoken.   Speaking politely.
Gallant.   Very attentive to women.
Gentle.   Quiet and refined in manners.
Gentlemanlike.   Becoming a gentleman.
Good-humored.   Of a friendly and easy disposition.
Good-mannered.   Well-bred.
Gracious.   Disposed to do good to those who have deserved ill.
Honey-mouthed. }
Honey-tongued. }   Sweet or persuasive of speech.
Ingratiating.   Making oneself acceptable by his pleasing manners.
Mannerly.   Showing good manners.
Mild.   Having the qualities of harshness and severity subdued.
Neighborly.   Social.
Obliging.   Disposed to do services for others.
Obsequious, etc.   Striving to gain another's favor by consulting his pleasure and making personal sacrifice, etc.   See PRESUMPTION-OBSEQUIOUSNESS.
Oily.   Deceitfully complaisant.
Polished.   Having all roughness of manner and speech removed.
Polite.   Showing proper respect according to the rules of society.
Refined, etc.   Freed from everything coarse, low, vulgar, or inelegant, etc.   See TASTE.
Soft-spoken.   Having a soft or gentle voice.
Urbane.   Agreeable in manners.
Well-behaved. }
Well-bred. }
Well brought up. }   Polite and gentlemanly.
Well-mannered. }
Winning.   Attractive.

POLITENESS—*Adverbs, etc.*

A bras ouverts [F.].   With open arms.
Courteously, etc.   Politely.   See *Adjectives.*
In good humor.   In a good frame of mind.
Suaviter in modo [L.].   Gentle in manner.

IMPOLITENESS—Adjectives—*Continued.*

Impolite.   Not polite.
Imprudent.   Lacking prudence.
Inaffable.   Not easy of approach.
Obtrusive.   Inclined to make one's company unwelcome.
Peevish, etc.   Unreasonably cross or querulous, etc.   See FAVORITE-MOROSENFSS.
Pert.   Regardless of the respect due superiors.
Perverse.   Inclined to do the opposite of what is required.
Precocious.   Forwardness.
Repulsive.   Forbidding.
Rough.   Lacking in politeness.
Rude.   Very rough, so as to be offensive.
Rugged.   Crabbed.
Sarcastic.   Unjustifiably bitter, and personal.
Saucy.   Marked by sharp impertinence.
Sharp.   Cutting in speech.
Short.   Petulant.
Snarling, etc.   Talking in a surly, growling manner, etc.   See *Verbs.*
Sour.   Unpleasant in countenance.
Stern.   Stiff or unsympathetic in manner or conduct.
Sullen, etc.   Discontented and morose, etc.   See FAVORITE-MOROSE-NESS.
Surly.   Quarrelsome; cross.
Surly as a bear.   Very surly.
Tart.   Slightly pungent.
Trenchant.   Cutting.
Unaccommodating.   Not disposed to please.
Unbred.   Not trained.
Unceremonious.   Not according to rite or ceremony.
Uncivil.   Impolite.
Uncivilized.   Rude and barbarous.
Uncomplaisant.   Disagreeable.
Uncourteous. }
Uncourtly. }   Impolite.
Ungainly.   Not attractive.
Ungallant.   Impolite.
Ungenteel.   Ill-bred.
Ungentle.   Ill-mannered.
Ungentlemanlike.   Impolite.
Ungentlemanly.   Impolite.
Ungracious.   Unkind.
Unladylike.   Not like a lady.
Unmannered. }
Unmannerly. }   Without training or manners.
Unneighborly.   Not social.
Unpolished.   Rude.
Unpolite.   Discourteous.
Venomous.   Malignant.
Virulent.   Moved by a desire to injure.
Vulgar, etc.   Indicating a low state of taste and manners, etc.   See TASTE-VULGARITY.

IMPOLITENESS—*Adverbs.*

Discourteously, etc.   With lack of courtesy, etc.   See *Adjectives.*
With a bad grace.   Unwillingly.
With discourtesy, etc.   Impolitely, etc.   See *Nouns.*

POLITENESS—Adverbs, etc.—*Continued.*

With a good grace.   Cheerfully.
With open arms. }
With outstretched arms. }   Gladly or joyously.

POLITENESS—*Interjections.*

Aller vostra salute [It.].   To your health.
All hail!
Ave [L.].   Hail.
Bon jour [F.].   Good morning.
Bon soir [F.].   Good evening.
Godspeed!
Good day!
Good morning!
Good morrow!
Hail!
May your shadow never be less.
Pax vobiscum [L.].   Peace be with you.
Serus in cælum redeas [L.].   Late return thou to the skies;
Welcome!
Well met!

pol'-i-tic. Crafty; sagacious. CRAFT-ARTLESSNESS, RECKLESSNESS - CAUTION, SAGACITY - INCAPACITY; **body politic,** HUMANITY, RULE-LICENSE.

po-lit'-ic-al e-con'-o-my. Economics. CONDUCT.

pol-i-ti'-cian. One versed in politics. ADEPT-BUNGLER, MANAGER.

pol'-i-tics. The science of government. CRAFT-ARTLESSNESS.

pol'-i-ty. Civil constitution. CONDUCT, DUTY-DERELICTION.

pol'-ka. A dance. ENTERTAINMENT-WEARINESS.

poll. Count; vote; a parrot. CHOICE-NEUTRALITY, NUMBERING, TALKATIVENESS-TACITURNITY.

pol'-lard. A tree shorn of its top GREATNESS-LITTLENESS, LENGTH-SHORTNESS.

polloi, oi [Gr.] (pol-loi', hoi). The mass. GENTILITY-COMMONALTY.

poll'-par''-rot. A parrot. TALKATIVENESS-TACITURNITY.

pol-lute'. Corrupt. BETTERMENT-DETERIORATION, CLEANNESS-FILTHINESS.

pol-lu'-tion. Corruption. BETTERMENT-DETERIORATION, HEALTH-SICKNESS, REPUTATION-DISCREDIT, VIRTUE-VICE.

po'-lo. A game. ENTERTAINMENT-WEARINESS.

pol-troon'. A mean coward. BRAVERY-COWARDICE.

pol'-y-an'-drism. The civil condition of having more than one husband. MATRIMONY-CELIBACY.

pol'-y-chord. A musical instrument. MUSICAL INSTRUMENTS.

pol''-y-chro-mat'-ic. Containing more than one atom of chromium. COLOR-ACHROMATISM, VARIEGATION.

pol'-y-chrome. A picture in several colors. PAINTING, VARIEGATION.

po-lyg'-a-my. The condition of having more than one wife or husband. MATRIMONY-CELIBACY.

pol''-y-gas'-tric. Having several bellies. CONTENTS-RECEIVER.

pol'-y-glot. Expressed in many languages. INTERPRETATION-MISINTERPRETATION, LANGUAGE.

pol'-y-gon. A figure having many sides and many angles. ANGULARITY, DWELLER-HABITATION.

po-lyg'-ra-phy. The use of a polygraph. WRITING-PRINTING.

po-lyl'-o-gy. Talkativeness. TERSENESS-PROLIXITY.

po-lyl'-o-gist. A chatterbox. VOCALIZATION-MUTENESS.

pol''-y-mor'-phism. The quality of presenting many forms. BIOLOGY.

po-lyph'-o-nism. Polyphony VOCALIZATION-MUTENESS.

pol'-y-pus. A tumor. CONVEXITY-CONCAVITY.

pol'-y-scope. A multiplying glass. OPTICAL INSTRUMENTS.

pol''-y-syl'-la-ble. A word of several syllables. LETTER.

pol'-y-the''-ism. The doctrine of a plurality of wives ORTHODOXY-HETERODOXY.

pol'-y-the''-ist. A believer in many gods. ORTHODOXY-HETERODOXY.

pol''-y-the-is'-tic. Believing in many gods. ORTHODOXY-HETERODOXY.

pom'-mel. A knob. RECOMPENSE-PUNITION, ROUNDNESS, SUSPENSION-SUPPORT.

Po-mo'-na. The goddess of fruit-trees. ZOOLOGY-BOTANY.

pomp. Ostentation. POMP.

POMP.

Array. Imposing arrangement.
Ceremonial. A system of rules and ceremonies.
Ceremony. Formal method of performing acts of civility.
Chic. Style or good form.
Claptrap. A device or trick to gain applause.

Dash. A vain show.
Demonstration. A show.
Display. Exhibition for effect.
Dress. That which is used as covering or ornament of the body.
Étalage [F.] Laying out for show
Flourish. Something done by way of ostentation.
Flying colors. Flags waving in the air hence, anything showy.
Foppery. Affectation of show
Form. } Show without substance.
Formality. }
Frippery. Second-hand finery or ornament.
Fuss. Unnecessary ado about trifles.
Gala. Pomp or show.
Glitter. Brilliant and showy luster.
Grand doings. Acts done for show.
Insubstantial pageant. A show or display.
Magnificence. Grandeur or splendor.
March past. A parade, with strutting.
Mouth honor. Insincere civility.
Mummery. Farcical show.
Pageant. A theatrical exhibition or show
Pageantry. Splendor.
Parade. Pompous show.
Pomp. Show of magnificence.
Pomposity. The quality or state of being pompous.
Pretense. False, deceptive show.
Pretensions. A holding out the appearance of a certain character.
Procession. A ceremonious train.
Promenade. A walk for pleasure or display.
Punctilio. } Particularity or exactness in forms.
Punctiliousness. }
Puncto. A nice point of form or ceremony.
Review. An inspection.
Ritual. The code of ceremonies observed by an organization.
Set out. A display.
Show. Proud or ostentatious display
Showing off. Parade or pomp.
Solemnity. Affected gravity or seriousness.
Solemn mockery. A counterfeit appearance.
Spectacle. Something exhibited to view
Splash. A show of ornament.
Splendor. Magnificence or parade.
Stage effect. A theatrical entertainment.
Starchedness. Stiffness in manners; formality.
State. Appearance of grandeur.
Stateliness. The quality of being grand.
Strut. A pompous step or walk.
Tomfoolery. Trifling.
Turnout. That which is prominently exhibited.

POMP—*Denotations*

Attitudinarian. A posture maker.
Ball dress. Apparel for social entertainments
Coup de théâtre [F.] Theatrical effect.
Coup d'œil [F.] A glance.
Court dress. Apparel worn at court.
Equipage. A showy turnout.
Etiquette. The forms to be observed in social or official life
Evening dress. Apparel worn at evening social functions.
Fancy dress. Showy apparel.
Fête. A festival.
Field day. A day of unusual display.
Flourish of trumpets. A noise to attract attention.
Fop, etc. One whose ambition is to gain admiration by showy dress. See SOCIETY-DANDY.
Full dress. Dress worn on occasions of ceremony
Man millinery. Articles of a man's dress.
Millinery. Articles, as head-dresses, hats, etc.
Mise en scène [F.] Getting up of a dramatic piece.
Stage trick. A contrivance used in a theatrical entertainment.
Tailoring. The work of a tailor
Tour de force [F.] A show of force.

POMP—*Verbs.*

Attract attention. To be looked upon on account of some unusual appearance.
Be ostentatious, etc. To show off. See *Adjectives.*
Blazon forth. To make widely known.
Brandish. To wave or shake triumphantly or conspicuously.
Clean the outside of the platter, etc. To misrepresent or disguise. See DELINEATION.
Come forward. To come into public view.
Cry up, etc. To make known. See APPROVAL.

Cut a dash.
Cut a figure. } To make a striking display.
Cut a splash.
Dangle. To hang loosely suspended.
Dangle before the eyes. To show off.
Display. To exhibit; expose to view
Emblazon. To display; extol.
Exhibit. To bring into public view; display.
Figure. To take a prominent part.
Flaunt. To display with ostentation.
Glitter. To shine; sparkle: gleam.
Hang out. To show off.
Have framed and glazed. To arrange or place as to show off well.
Hold up. To bring into notice.
Make a dash.
Make a display.
Make a figure.
Make a glitter. } To make a striking display
Make a show.
Make a splash.
March past. To attract attention.
Mount. To fasten to anything for exhibition.
Parade. To make an ostentatious display or show.
Prink. To dress for show or display.
Put a good face upon. To make anything seem pleasant or agreeable.
Put a smiling face upon. To show off agreeably.
Put forward. To bring to notice.
Put oneself forward. To draw attention to oneself.
Set off. To exhibit.
Show off. To display ostentatiously.
Sport. To display with ostentation.
Star it. To be conspicuous.
Trot out. To bring into notice.

POMP—*Adjectives.*

Ceremonial.
Ceremonious. } In accordance with form.
Dashing. Boastingly showy.
Dramatic. Theatrical; showy.
Endimanche [F.] In Sunday clothes.
En grande tenue [F.] In full dress.
Flaming. Brilliant; shining.
Flashing. Cheaply pretentious and showy.
Flaunting. Make an ostentatious display; showy.
Formal. According to a prescribed form.
Garish. Extravagantly showy or flashing.
Gaudy. Of brilliant colors; garish.
Gaudy as a butterfly.
Gaudy as a peacock. } Showy.
Gaudy as a tulip.
Gay, etc. Brilliant; showy. See EMBELLISHMENT.
Glittering. Shining; sparkling.
Grand. Magnificent; wonderful.
High sounding. Ostentatious; boasting.
In best bib and tucker. In best clothes.
In Sunday clothes. In best clothes.
Janty.
Jaunty. } In a careless or self-satisfied manner.
Magnificent. Exhibiting great splendor.
Majestic. Imposing and attractive.
Ostentatious. Exhibiting a vain or boastful display.
Palatial. Like a palace; grand.
Pompous. Displaying great power or wealth.
Pretentious. Marked by affectation or conceit.
Punctilious. Exact in forms of etiquette.
Ritual. According to form or ritual.
Showy. Making a great display.
Solemn. Stiff.
Spectacular. Pertaining to a grand scenic display.
Splendid. Fine; excellent
Starched. Formal.
Stately. Grand; imposing.
Stiff. Formal.
Sumptuous. Involving great expenditure.
Theatrical. Artificial; pompous.
Turgid, etc. Full of bombast. See SIMPLICITY-FLORIDNESS.

POMP—*Adverbs, etc.*

Ad captandum vulgus [L.] To catch the common crowd.
With beat of drums.
With flourish of trumpet. } With noise and show.
With flying colors.

POMP—*Phrase.*

Honores mutant mores [L.] Honors change men's manners.

pom-pos'-i-ty. The state of being pompous. POMP.
pom'-pous. Pretentious. POMP, SIMPLICITY-FLORIDNESS.
pon'-cho. A garment worn by Spanish-Americans. DRESS-UNDRESS.
pond. A small body of water. GULF-PLAIN, STORE; **fish-pond,** DOMESTICATION-AGRICULTURE, GULF-PLAIN.
pon'-der. Consider thoughtfully. HEAVINESS-LIGHTNESS, REFLECTION-VACANCY.
pon'-der-a-ble. Capable of being weighed. HEAVINESS-LIGHTNESS, MATERIALITY-SPIRITUALITY.
pon'-der-ance. Weight. EQUALITY-INEQUALITY.
pon''-der-a'-tion. The act of weighing. DECISION-MISJUDGMENT, HEAVINESS-LIGHTNESS.
pondus fumo, dare [L.] (pon'-dus fiu'-mo, dê'-rî). To give weight to smoke. DECISION-MISJUDGMENT.
pon'-iard. A small dagger. WEAPON.
pons asinorum [L.] (pons as-in-o'-rum). The asses' bridge. CLEARNESS-OBSCURITY, DIFFICULTY-FACILITY.
pontem et fontem, misericordia Domini, inter [L.] (pon'-tem et fon'-tem, mis''-er-i-cor'-di-a dom'-i-nai, in'-ter). 'Twixt bridge and wave the Lord may save. POSSIBILITY-IMPOSSIBILITY.
pon'-tiff. A high priest. MINISTRY-LAITY.
pon-tif'-ic-al. Papal. CHURCH.
pon-tif'-ic-als. The dress of a pontiff. VESTMENTS.
pon-tif'-i-cate. The office of a pontiff. CHURCH.
pon-toon'. A boat; a bridge. CONVEYANCE-VESSEL, WAY.
po'-ny. A small horse. CONVEYER.
poo'-dle. A dog. FAUNA-FLORA.
pooh'-pooh''. Speak sneeringly. CONSEQUENCE-INSIGNIFICANCE, REGARD-SCORN.
pool. A small lake; billiards. ENTERTAINMENT-WEARINESS, GAIN-LOSS, GULF-PLAIN.
poop. The stern of a vessel. ANTERIORITY-POSTERIORITY.
poor. Destitute; lean; weak. AFFLUENCE-PENURY, CONSEQUENCE-INSIGNIFICANCE, EXCESS-LACK, FORCE-WEAKNESS, PLEASURE-PAIN, RATIOCINATION-CASUISTRY, STRENGTH-WEAKNESS, WELFARE-MISFORTUNE; **cut a poor figure,** BEAUTY-UGLINESS; **poor hand,** ADEPT-BUNGLER; **poor head,** SAGACITY-INCAPACITY; **poor in spirit,** CONCEIT-DIFFIDENCE; **poor man,** AFFLUENCE-PENURY; **poor thing,** COMPASSION-RUTHLESSNESS.
poor'-ly. In bad health. HEALTH-SICKNESS; **poorly off,** AFFLUENCE-PENURY.
poor'-ness. Poverty. EXCESS-LACK.
poor'-spir''-it-ed. Mean. BRAVERY-COWARDICE.
pop. A quick noise. CRASH-DRUMMING, EXPECTATION-SURPRISE; **pop a question,** INVESTIGATION-ANSWER; **pop at,** ATTACK-DEFENSE; **pop in,** ENTRANCE-EXIT, INJECTION-EJECTION; **pop off,** LIFE-DEATH; **pop the question,** BLANDISHMENT, PETITION-EXPOSTULATION; **pop upon,** ARRIVAL-DEPARTURE, DISCOVERY.
pope. The Bishop of Rome. CERTAINTY-DOUBT, MINISTRY-LAITY.
pope'-dom. The dominion of the pope. CHURCH.
Pope Joan. A game. ENTERTAINMENT-WEARINESS.
po'-per-y. The Roman Catholic religion. ORTHODOXY-HETERODOXY
pop'-gun''. A toy gun. CONSEQUENCE-INSIGNIFICANCE.
pop'-in-jay. A coxcomb. SOCIETY-DANDY.
pop'-lar. A tree. **Tall as a poplar,** HEIGHT-LOWNESS.
pop'-py. A soporific plant. TURBULENCE-CALMNESS.
pop'-py-head''. Carved finial. ARCHITECTURE.
pop'-u-lace. The masses. GENTILITY-COMMONALTY.

pop'-u-lar. Pleasing; approved. APPROVAL-DISPAR-AGEMENT, LOVE - HATE, REPUTATION - DISCREDIT; **popular opinion,** ASSENT-DISSENT.

popularis, aura [L.] (pop-yu-lê'-ris, au'-ra). The gale of popular favor. REPUTATION-DISCREDIT.

pop''-u-lar'-i-ty. Public favor. APPROVAL - DISAP-PROVAL.

pop'-u-lar-ize. Make popular. CLEARNESS-OBSCURITY, DIFFICULTY-FACILITY, PLEASURABLENESS-PAINFUL-NESS.

pop'-u-lar-ized. Made popular CLEARNESS-OB-SCURITY.

pop''-u-la'-tion. The whole people of a country. DWELLER-HABITATION, HUMANITY.

populi, fæx [L.] (pop'-yu-lai, fex). The scum of society. GENTILITY-COMMONALTY.

populi, regnant [L.] (pop'-yu-lai, reg'-nant). The people rule. LIBERTY-SUBJECTION, RULE-LICENSE.

populi, vox [L.] (pop'-yu-lai, vox). Public senti-ment. CHOICE-NEUTRALITY, PUBLICITY, RULE-LICENSE.

pop'-u-lous. Densely populated. GATHERING-SCAT-TERING, MULTIPLICITY - PAUCITY, PRESENCE - AB-SENCE.

pop'-u-lous-ness. The state of being populous. GATH-ERING-SCATTERING.

por'-ce-lain. The finest kind of earthenware. HEAT-ING-COOLING, SCULPTURE.

porch. A portico. APERTURE-CLOSURE, ARCHITEC-TURE, BEGINNING-END, BORDER, CONTENTS-RE-CEIVER.

por'-cu-pine. An animal covered with spines. FA-VORITE-QUARRELSOMENESS, SHARPNESS-BLUNTNESS.

pore. A small passage in the skin. APERTURE-CLO-SURE, WATERCOURSE-AIRPIPE; **pore over,** EDUCA-TION-LEARNING, HEED-DISREGARD, SIGHT-BLIND-NESS.

po'-rism. A corollary. DECISION-MISJUDGMENT, IN-VESTIGATION-ANSWER.

por' -no-graph'-ic. Licentious. PURITY-IMPURITY.

po-ros'-i-ty. The state of having pores. APERTURE-CLOSURE.

po'-rous. Having pores. APERTURE-CLOSURE, CON-VEXITY-CONCAVITY.

po'-rous-ness. The state of being porous. APERTURE-CLOSURE.

por'-poise. A large fish. GREATNESS-LITTLENESS.

por'-rin-ger. A small dish. CONTENTS-RECEIVER.

port. Carriage; a harbor. APPEARANCE-DISAPPEAR-ANCE, ARRIVAL-DEPARTURE, DWELLER-HABITATION, MOVEMENT-REST, REFUGE-PITFALL, RIGHT-LEFT; **port admiral,** CHIEF-UNDERLING; **port fire,** COMBUS-TIBLE; **port wine,** TEETOTALISM-INTEMPERANCE.

port'-a-ble. Light; that may be carried. GREAT-NESS-LITTLENESS, HEAVINESS-LIGHTNESS, TRANS-FER.

port'-age. The act of transporting. TRANSFER.

por'-tal. Entrance. APERTURE-CLOSURE, BEGINNING-END, BORDER.

por'-ta-tive. Portable. GREATNESS - LITTLENESS, TRANSFER.

port-cul'-lis. A framework of crossed timber for obstructing a passage. ATTACK - DEFENSE, OB-STRUCTION-HELP.

porte-monnaie [F.] (port''-mo-nê') A pocket-book or purse. TREASURY.

por-tend' To foretoken. PROPHECY.

por-tent'. An omen of ill. PHENOMENON, PORTENT

PORTENT

Augury. A portent; an omen.
Auspice. A favorable omen.
Bird of ill omen. A bird regarded as a sign of bad luck.

Gathering clouds. Evil omens.
Harbinger, etc. A foretelling of something that is going to happen. See PREDECESSOR.
Omen. A sign foretelling something that is going to happen
Portent. Any phenomenon that indicates the happening of some momentous future event.
Prefiguration. A foreshadowing; a sign anticipating some future event.
Presage. A presentiment; a prophetic indication.
Prognostic. A sign or indication of some future event.
Sign. A remarkable event, considered by the ancients as indicating the will of some deity. See SIGN.
Signs of the times. An event considered as indicating the divine will.
Warning. Caution against danger. See WARNING.
Yule candle. A large candle used to light the festivities of Christmas eve. It was an evil omen for the candle to burn out before the eve-ning was at an end.

PORTENT—*Adjective.*

Ill-boding. Promising ill.

PORTENT—*Phrase.*

Auspicium melioris ævi [L.]. Augury of a happier time.

por-tent'-ous. Ominous. PROPHECY, SANGUINENESS-TIMIDITY.

por'-ter. A janitor. CONVEYER, PERFORATOR-STOP-PER.

por'-ter-age. The work of a porter. TRANSFER.

port-fo'-li-o. A portable case for papers. CONTENTS-RECEIVER, MANAGEMENT, MARK - OBLITERATION, MISSIVE-PUBLICATION, SCEPTER, STORE.

port'-hole. A gun-hole. APERTURE-CLOSURE.

por'-ti-co. A piazza. ARCHITECTURE, BEGINNING-END, CONTENTS-RECEIVER.

por'-tion. A share. ASSIGNMENT, WHOLE-PART; **por-tion out,** WHOLE-PART.

port'-ly. Large. GREATNESS-LITTLENESS.

port-man'-teau. A bag to carry clothes in. CON-TENTS-RECEIVER.

por'-trait. A likeness. COPY-MODEL, DELINEATION-CARICATURE, PAINTING.

por'-trait-paint'-er. One who makes portraits. ARTIST.

por'-trait-paint'-ing. To paint portraits. PAINTING.

por'-trai-ture. The drawing of portraits. DELINEA-TION-CARICATURE, PAINTING.

por-tray'. To paint the likeness of. ACCOUNT, DE-LINEATION-CARICATURE.

port'-reeve''. A port-warden. CHIEF - UNDERLING, JUDICATURE.

po-sa'-da. An inn. DWELLER-HABITATION.

pose. Position; puzzle. CERTAINTY-DOUBT, DIF-FICULTY-FACILITY, FORM-FORMLESSNESS, POSITION, SOCIETY-AFFECTATION; **pose as,** DELINEATION-CA-RICATURE.

po'-ser. A puzzling question. DIFFICULTY-FACILITY.

pos'-it-ed. Placed. ESTABLISHMENT-REMOVAL.

po-si'-tion. Situation; office: ASSERTION-DENIAL, CONDITION-SITUATION, HYPOTHESIS, POSITION, REP-UTATION-DISCREDIT, STATION; **position in society,** REPUTATION-DISCREDIT.

POSITION.

Aspect. Position as regards view or outlook.
Attitude. Position, as of the body, expressive of some feeling.
Bearings, etc. Situation of an object in relation to another object or other points or places. See AIM.
Footing. A place to put the foot.
Latitude and longitude. Position expressed in degrees of latitude and longitude.
Locality. A definite spot or region, especially a geographical position.
Place. A particular point or portion of space.
Pose. Position of the body with reference to artistic effect.
Position. Arrangement of the body or parts of the body.
Post. Fixed or assigned place or station.
Posture. Disposition of parts of a body, assumed or natural.
Seat. A place to sit in or of abode.
Site. Position with special reference to surroundings.

Situation. Location in respect to something else.
Spot, etc. A particular place of small extent. See EXTENSION-PLACE.
Stage. A large scene of action.
Standing. A place to stand in; relative position, as in social or other relations.
Standpoint. Position from which something is viewed or regarded.
Station. An assigned place.
Status. Condition with reference to some special circumstances.
Venue. Place where a crime is committed or from which a jury must be summoned.
Whereabouts. Place in or near which a person is.

POSITION—Denotation.

Map. A representation of some portion of the surface of the earth.

POSITION—Scientific Nouns.

Chorography. The mapping out of regions or districts.
Geography. The science that treats of the surface of the earth.
Topography. Representation of physical features of a region on a map in detail.

POSITION—Verbs.

Be situate. } To have a particular position. See *Adjectives.*
Be situated. }
Have its seat in. To be located in a particular place.
Lie. Have a location or fixed position.

POSITION—Adjectives.

Local. Pertaining to or existing in a locality.
Situate. Having a fixed or relative position.
Situated. Given a specific position.
Topical. Belonging to a place; local.
Topographical. Pertaining to topography or, in general, relative position.

POSITION—Adverbs, etc.

Amidst such and such *entourage.* Having particular boundaries.
Amidst such and such environs. Having such boundaries.
Amidst such and such surroundings. Located.
Here. In or at this particular place.
Hereabouts. Somewhere near here.
Here and there. Scattered.
In loco [L.]. In the place.
In place. Situated.
In situ [L.]. In its original or proper situation.
In such and such *entourage.* }
In such and such environs. } Located in that particular place.
In such and such surroundings. }
Passim [L.]. Everywhere; throughout.
There. In that place.
Thereabout. Somewhere near that place.
Whereabouts. Near what place.

pos′-i-tive. Certain; absolute; a degree of comparison. ASSERTION-DENIAL, BIGOTRY-APOSTASY, CERTAINTY-DOUBT, CLEARNESS-OBSCURITY, CONVENTIONALITY-UNCONVENTIONALITY, DECISION-MISJUDGMENT, ENTITY - NONENTITY, FAITH - MISGIVING, HARSHNESS-MILDNESS, MAGNITUDE-SMALLNESS, NUMBER, PARTICLE; **philosophie positive,** MATERIALITY-SPIRITUALITY; **positive color,** COLOR-ACHROMATISM; **positive degree,** MAGNITUDE-SMALLNESS; **positive fact,** CERTAINTY-DOUBT.
pos′-i-tive-ness. Certainty. CERTAINTY-DOUBT, ENTITY-NONENTITY.
pos′-i-tiv-ism. A philosophy of positives. GODLINESS-DISBELIEF, ORTHODOXY-HETERODOXY.
pos′-i-tiv-ist. Comtist. GODLINESS-DISBELIEF, ORTHODOXY-HETERODOXY.
pos′-net. A little basin. CONTENTS-RECEIVER.
po-sol′-o-gy. The science of doses. REMEDY-BANE.
pos′-se. A force of men. ASSOCIATION, GATHERING-SCATTERING, POSITION; *posse comitatus,* BELLIGERENT, GATHERING-SCATTERING, JUDICATURE, RULE-LICENSE.
posse, in [L.] (pos′-sî, in). Possible. POSSIBILITY-IMPOSSIBILITY.
pos-sess′. Own. HOLDING-EXEMPTION, PROPERTY; **possess a state,** CONDITION-SITUATION; **possess knowledge,** KNOWLEDGE-IGNORANCE; **possess ·oneself of,** TAKING-RESTITUTION; **possess the mind,** FAITH-MISGIVING; **possess the soul,** EXCITATION.
pos-sessed′. Crazy. SANENESS-LUNACY.
pos-sessed′ with a dev′-il. Wicked. SANENESS-LUNACY.
pos-ses′-sion. Ownership. HOLDING - EXEMPTION, PROPERTY; **come into possession,** ALIENATION, GAIN-LOSS; **in one's possession,** HOLDING-EXEMPTION; **person in possession,** HOLDER; **put one in possession of,** ENLIGHTENMENT-SECRECY; **remain in possession of the field,** SUCCESS-FAILURE.
pos-sess′-or. The person who holds or occupies. HOLDER.
pos″-si-bil′-i-ty. The state of being possible. CONTINGENCY, POSSIBILITY-IMPOSSIBILITY, PROPERTY, RATIONALE-LUCK; **possibility upon a possibility,** CERTAINTY-DOUBT.

POSSIBILITY—IMPOSSIBILITY.

Chance. An event resulting from no assignable cause. See PURPOSE-LUCK.
Compatibility. State of being congruous. See HARMONY.
Contingency. A possibility of an event happening.
Feasibility. State of being feasible or capable of being done or performed.
Possibility. State of being possible, or able to happen.
Potentiality. Possibility; capability.
Practicability. } State of being feasible or practicable. See *Adjectives.*
Practicableness. } *tives.*
What is possible. } Things that may happen, or may be done.
What may be possible. }

POSSIBILITY—Verbs

Admit of. To be possible of; allow
Bear. To endure; allow.
Be possible. Capable of being done. See *Adjectives.*
Put in the way of. To place in such a condition as it may be done.
Render possible. To make capable of being done. See *Adjectives.*
Stand a chance. To have a possibility

POSSIBILITY—Adjectives.

Accessible. Capable of being reached or attained.
Achievable. Capable of being done.
Attainable. That which can be attained, or acquired.
Compatible. Able to exist together See HARMONY.
Conceivable. Able to be conceived; apprehensible.
Contingent. Possible to happen. See CERTAINTY-DOUBT.
Credible. Possible to be believed.
Feasible. Able to be executed or done.

Hopelessness. State of being destitute of hope. See SANGUINENESS-HOPELESSNESS.
Impossibility. State of being unable to do or perform. See *Adjectives.*
What can never be. } Impossibility of occurring.
What cannot be. }

IMPOSSIBILITY—Denotation.

Sour grapes. Things which persons, like the fox in the fable, affect to despise because they cannot obtain them.

IMPOSSIBILITY—Verbs.

Attempt impossibilities. To attempt what cannot be done.
Be impossible. To be incapable of being done. See *Adjectives.*
Be in two places at once. }
Build castles in the air. }
Catch a weasel asleep. } To attempt impossibilities.
Extract sunbeams from cucumbers. }
Have no chance whatever. } To be impossible.
Have nothing to go upon. }
Make a silk purse out of a sow's ear. }
Make bricks without straw. } To attempt the impossible.
Milk a he goat into a sieve. }
Prendre la lune avec les dents [F.]. To seize the moon by the teeth.
Rompre l'anguille au genou [F.]. To break the eel on the knee.
Set the Thames on fire. }
Skin a flint. }
Square the circle. } To do or attempt the impossible.
Wash a blackamoor white. }
Weave a rope of sand. }

POSSIBILITY—IMPOSSIBILITY—*Continued.*

POSSIBILITY—Adjectives—*Continued.*

In posse [L]. In possibility.
Obtainable. Possible of being attained or acquired.
On the cards. Likely to happen.
On the dice. Possible to happen.
Performable. Able to be accomplished.
Possible. Able to happen or not.
Practicable. Able to be practised; feasible.
Superab'e. Able to be overcome.
Surmountable. Rising above; able to conquer.
Within reach. Capable of being attained or done.
Within the bounds of possibility. Liable to happen.

POSSIBILITY—Adverbs, *etc.*

By possibility. By a chance.
Deo volente [L.]. God willing
D. V. [L]. *Deo volente:* God willing.
God willing. Possible if God wills it.
Haply. Perhaps.
If possible. If capable of being done
Maybe. } Perhaps.
Mayhap. }
Peradventure. Perhaps it may be.
Perchance. By chance.
Perhaps. It may be.
Possibly. By a chance.
Wind and weather permitting: If conditions are favorable.

POSSIBILITY—Phrase

Misericordia Domini inter pontem et fontem [L]. 'Twixt bridge and wave the Lord may save.

IMPOSSIBILITY—Adjectives—*Continued from Column 2*

Unsurmountable. Not to be passed or overcome
Visionary. Dreamy; impracticable.

IMPOSSIBILITY—Phrases.

Chercher une aigille dans une botte de foin [F.]. To look for a needle in a haystack.
Il a le mer à boire [F.]. He has the sea to drink.
Non nostrum tantas componere lites [L]. It is not our duty to settle such grave disputes. [Virgil, *Ecloques,* 3 108]
Non possumus [L.]. We are not able.
The grapes are sour.
Ultra crepidam [L.]. Beyond the sole or lasts.

IMPOSSIBILITY—Adjectives.

Absurd. Contrary to reason; opposed to common-sense.
Beyond control. }
Beyond one's depth. }
Beyond one's grasp. }
Beyond one's power. }
Beyond one's reach. } Impossible to be done.
Beyond the bounds of possibility. }
Beyond the bounds of reason. }
Contrary to reason. }
Desperate. Heedless or careless of safety.
From which reason recoils. Unreasonable
Impassible. Not affected by feeling.
Impervious. Not permitting entrance or passage through
Impossible. Not capable of happening.
Impracticable. Not practicable.
Inaccessible. Not easy of being reached.
Incompatible. Not congruous; not existing together. See HARMONY-DISCORD.
Inconceivable. Not conceivable; not imaginable. See LIKELIHOOD-UNLIKELIHOOD.
Incredible. Not believable. See FAITH-MISGIVING.
Inextricable. Not capable of being freed from difficulties.
Infeasible. Not practicable.
Inimaginable. Unimaginable.
Innavigable. Not capable of being sailed.
Insuperable. Not surmountable.
Insurmountable. Not to be overcome or conquered.
Not possible. Not to be done.
Not to be had. }
Not to be thought of. }
Out of one's depth. }
Out of one's grasp. } Impossible to be accomplished.
Out of one's power. }
Out of reach. }
Out of the question. }
Prodigious. Enormous; unusual. See ASTONISHMENT
Too much for. Beyond one's power.
Unachievable. Not to be accomplished.
Unattainable. Not to be acquired.
Uncomeatable. Not to be reached.
Unfeasible. Not to be done.
Unimaginable. Not imaginable.
Unobtainable. Not to be secured.
Unreasonable. Against reason. See RATIOCINATION-INSTINCT.

(*Continued on Column* 1.)

---

pos'-si-ble. That may be. CONTINGENCY, POSSIBILITY-IMPOSSIBILITY, PURPOSE-LUCK, RATIONALE-LUCK.
pos'-si-bly. Perhaps. POSSIBILITY-IMPOSSIBILITY.
possidetis, uti [L.] (pos-si-dĭ'-tis, yu'-tai). As you possess. HOLDING-EXEMPTION, KEEPING-RELINQUISHMENT.
post. Location; support; despatch. ACCOUNT, CONNECTIVE, ESTABLISHMENT-REMOVAL, MARK-OBLITERATION, MESSENGER, MISSIVE-PUBLICATION, OCCUPATION, POSITION, PUBLICITY, RECOMPENSE-PUNITION, REPUTATION-DISCREDIT, SIGN, SUSPENSION-SUPPORT, SWIFTNESS-SLOWNESS; **at one's post,** DUTY-DERELICTION, PREPARATION - NONPREPARATION; **driven from post to pillar,** DIFFICULTY-FACILITY; **signpost,** SIGN; **stand like a post,** MOVEMENT-REST.
post hoc, ergo propter hoc [L.] (post hoc, er'-go prop'-ter hoc). After this, therefore on account of this. RATIOCINATION-INSTINCT.
post'-boy". A courier. WAYFARER-SEAFARER.
post'-card". A card used for mail correspondence. MISSIVE-PUBLICATION.
post'-chaise". A carriage. CONVEYANCE-VESSEL.
post'-date". A date put to a paper later than when it was made. CHRONOLOGY-ANACHRONISM.
post"-di-lu'-vi-al. Happening after the flood in Noah's day. ANTECEDENCE-SEQUENCE, PRECEDENCE-SUCCESSION.
post"-di-lu'-vi-an. One living after the deluge. ANTECEDENCE-SEQUENCE.

post'-er. A bill-poster. PUBLICITY.
pos-te'-ri-or. Later in time or order. ANTECEDENCE-SEQUENCE, ANTERIORITY - POSTERIORITY, PRECEDENCE-SUCCESSION.
pos-te"-ri-or'-i-ty. The state of being later. ANTECEDENCE-SEQUENCE, ANTERIORITY-POSTERIORITY.
pos-ter'-i-ty. Descendants. FUTURE-PAST, PARENTAGE-PROGENY; **hand down to posterity,** MARK-OBLITERATION, REPUTATION-DISCREDIT.
pos'-tern. A back gate. ANTERIORITY-POSTERIORITY, APERTURE-CLOSURE, BEGINNING-END.
post"-ex-ist'-ence. Subsequent existence. OCCURRENCE-DESTINY.
post"-haste'. With speed. HURRY-LEISURE, RECKLESSNESS-CAUTION, SWIFTNESS-SLOWNESS.
post"-horse'. A horse for rapid travel from one station to another. CONVEYER.
pos'-thu-mous. Being after one's death. ANTECEDENCE - SEQUENCE, EARLINESS - LATENESS; **posthumous fame,** REPUTATION-DISCREDIT.
pos-til'-ion. One who rides a coach-horse. MANAGER, WAYFARER-SEAFARER.
post"-li-min'-i-ous. Done subsequently. ANTECEDENCE-SEQUENCE, EARLINESS-LATENESS.
post"-me-rid'-i-an. Pertaining to the afternoon. MORNING-EVENING.
post"-mor'-tem. Expert examination of a body after death. LIFE-DEATH, LIFE-FUNERAL.
post'-nate". Subsequent. ANTECEDENCE-SEQUENCE.

post″–o′-bit. A kind of bond. Life - Death, Life-Funeral.

post′–of″-fice. A place where mail is received and delivered. Messenger; **post-office order,** Money.

post-pone′. Delay. Earliness-Lateness.

post-pone′-ment. A deferring. Earliness-Lateness.

post′-script. A part added to a writing. Predecessor-Continuation.

pos′-tu-lant. A petitioner. Ministry-Laity, Petition-Expostulation, Petitioner.

pos′-tu-late. Assume without proof. Hypothesis, Ratiocination-Instinct.

pos′-tu-la′-tion. Assumption; request. Hypothesis, Petition-Expostulation.

pos′-tu-la-to″-ry. Assuming without proof. Hypothesis.

pos′-ture. Attitude. Condition-Situation, Form-Formlessness, Position.

pos′-ture-mas′-ter. Actor. Acting, Wag.

po′-sy. A motto; a nosegay. Embellishment-Disfigurement, Poetry-Prose, Sign.

pot. An earthen vessel. Conservation, Contents-Receiver, Heating-Cooling, Magnitude-Smallness, Oven-Refrigerator; **death in the pot,** Healthiness-Unhealthiness, Refuge-Pitfall; **go to pot,** Creation-Destruction, Success-Failure; **keep the pot boiling,** Activity-Indolence, Discontinuance-Continuance, Excitation; **make the pot boil,** Gain-Loss.

pot au lait, le [F.] (pot o lê, le). The pot of milk. Fancy, Sanguineness-Hopelessness.

po′-ta-ble. Suitable for drinking. Nutriment-Excretion; **potable water,** Chemistry.

pot′-age. Pottage: obsolete except as a French word. Nutriment-Excretion.

pot′-a-ger. A metal vessel.. Contents-Receiver.

po-ta′-tion. A beverage. Nutriment-Excretion, Teetotalism-Intemperance.

pot′–bel″-lied. Corpulent. Enlargement-Diminution.

pot′–com-pan″-ion. A boon companion. Friend-Foe.

po′-ten-cy. Relative power. Might-Impotence.

po′-tent. Powerful. Might-Impotence, Possibility-Impossibility, Strength-Weakness.

po′-ten-tate. Ruler. Chief-Underling.

po-ten′-tial. Having power. Entity-Nonentity.

po-ten″-ti-al′-i-ty. Inherent. capacity for development. Might-Impotence, Possibility-Impossibility.

poth′-er. To harass or perplex. Emotion, Excitability-Inexcitability, Pleasurableness-Painfulness, Regularity-Irregularity.

pot′–herbs″. Culinary plants. Condiment.

pot′–hooks″. Written characters made like pot-hooks. **Pot-hooks and hangers,** Writing-Printing.

pot′–house″. An ale-house. Dweller-Habitation.

pot′–hun″-ter. One who shoots any kind of game regardless of the laws; a place hunter. Petitioner.

po′-tion. A draft. Nutriment-Excretion, Remedy-Bane.

pot′–luck″. Whatever may chance to be in the pot. Nutriment-Excretion, Purpose-Luck.

Po-to-si′. The southwestern part of Bolivia, noted for its richness in metals. Affluence-Penury.

pot″–pour″-ri′. A mixture. Mixture-Homogeneity, Music, Perfume-Stench.

pot′-tage. A thick broth of meat and vegetables. Nutriment-Excretion.

pot′-ter. To idle. Activity-Indolence.

pot′-ter-ing. To work without spirit. Activity-Indolence.

pot′-ter-y. The wares of a potter. Heating-Cooling, Sculpture.

pot′-tle. A pot. Contents-Receiver.

pot′-u-lent. Fit to drink; drunk. Nutriment-Excretion, Teetotalism-Intemper.′nce.

pot′–val″-iant. Having courage by drink. Teetotalism-Intemperance.

pot′–wal″-lop-er. In England, a voter under peculiar restriction before the Reform Law of 1832. Gentility-Commonalty.

pouch. A small bag. Contents-Receiver.

poudre aux yeux, jeter de la [F.] (pudr oz yu, zhe-tê′ de la). To throw dust into the eyes of a person. Sight-Blindness.

puodre, qui n'a pas inventé la [F.] (pudr, ki na pa an·van-tê′ la). He did not invent gunpowder. Adept-Bungler, Sage-Fool.

poul′-tice. A soothing application for sores. Alleviation-Aggravation, Pulpiness-Oiliness, Remedy-Bane.

poul′-try. Domestic fowls. Fauna-Flora.

pounce′ up-on′. Jump upon. Attack-Defense, Expectation-Surprise, Taking-Restitution.

pound. A weight of 16 ounces avoirdupois, or 12 troy; coin. Enclosure, Friability, Heaviness-Lightness, Measure, Release-Prison, Value; **pound together,** Mixture-Homogeneity.

pound′-age. Charge made for shutting up stray cattle in a pound. Price-Discount.

pounds, shillings and pence. English money. Money.

pour. To throw out in a continuous stream. Enough, Entrance-Exit, River-Wind; **it never rains but it pours,** Excess-Lack; **pour a broadside into,** Attack-Defense; **pour forth,** Admission-Expulsion, Speech-Inarticulateness, Talkativeness-Taciturnity; **pour forth like water,** Extravagance-Avarice; **pour in,** Concentration-Radiation, Enough, Entrance-Exit; **pour on,** Giving-Receiving; **pour out,** Admission-Expulsion, Entrance-Exit, River-Wind; **pour out blood like water,** Life-Killing; **pour water into a sieve,** Extravagance-Avarice, Provision-Waste; **pour with rain,** River-Wind.

pourboire [F.] (pur″-bwar′). Drink-money. Giving-Receiving.

pourparler [F.] (pur″-par″-lê′). A consultation preliminary to a treaty. Advice, Conversation-Monologue, Council.

pou sto [Gr.] (pu sto). Where I may stand. Suspension-Support.

pout. A sullen look. Convexity-Concavity, Favorite-Anger, Favorite-Moroseness, Lightheartedness-Dejection, Politeness-Impoliteness.

pov′-er-ty. Want. Affluence-Penury, Consequence-Insignificance, Excess-Lack; **poverty of intellect,** Sagacity-Incapacity.

pow′-der. A fine dust; composition for firing guns. Completion-Noncompletion, Embellishment-Disfigurement, Friability, Greatness-Littleness; **food for powder,** Belligerent; **gunpowder,** Weapon; **keep one's powder dry,** Preparation-Nonpreparation; **not worth powder,** Usefulness-Uselessness; **powder and shot,** Weapon; **smell powder,** Fighting-Conciliation; **waste powder,** Provision-Waste.

pow′-dered. Reduced to a powder. Variegation.

pow′-der-ing. To cover the body with powder. Embellishment-Disfigurement.

pow′-er. Strength; authority. Force-Weakness, Loudness - Faintness, Magnitude - Smallness, Might - Impotence, Number, Rule - License, Strength-Weakness; **do all in one's power,** Toil-Relaxation; **give power,** Leave-Prohibition; **in the power of,** Liberty-Subjection, Rule-License; **literary power,** Style; **power of attorney,** Commission-Abrogation; **power of money,** Money.

pow′-er-ful. Strong. FORCE-WEAKNESS, LOUDNESS-FAINTNESS, MAGNITUDE-SMALLNESS, STRENGTH-WEAKNESS; **powerful voice,** VOCALIZATION-MUTENESS.

pow′-er-less. Weak. DOMINANCE-IMPOTENCE, FORCE-WEAKNESS, MIGHT-IMPOTENCE, PREPARATION-NONPREPARATION, STRENGTH-WEAKNESS.

pow′-ers that be. Living powers. CHIEF-UNDERLING.

pox. An eruptive disease. HEALTH-SICKNESS.

praam. A flat-bottomed barge. CONVEYANCE-VESSEL.

prac′-ti-ca-ble. That may be done. POSSIBILITY-IMPOSSIBILITY.

prac′-ti-cal. Useful; capable of being turned out. AGENCY, CONDUCT; **practical chemistry,** CHEMISTRY; **practical joke,** REGARD-DISRESPECT, SOCIETY-DERISION, TRUTHFULNESS-FRAUD; **practical knowledge,** KNOWLEDGE-IGNORANCE, SKILL-UNSKILFULNESS.

prac′-ti-cal-ly. In a practical manner. SUBJECTIVENESS-OBJECTIVENESS.

prac′-tice. Training; conduct. CONDUCT, EDUCATION-MISTEACHING, GULL-DECEIVER, HABIT-DESUETUDE, NUMBERING; **in practice,** PREPARATION-NONPREPARATION, SKILL-UNSKILFULNESS; **out of practice,** SKILL-UNSKILFULNESS; **put in practice,** ACTION-PASSIVENESS, COMPLETION-NONCOMPLETION, CONDUCT, USE-DISUSE.

prac′-tise. Train; act. ACTION-PASSIVENESS, EDUCATION-MISTEACHING, USE-DISUSE; **practise at the bar,** ADVOCATE; **practise on one's credulity,** TRUTHFULNESS-FRAUD; **practise upon,** TRIAL, TRUTHFULNESS-FRAUD.

prac′-tised. Skilled. PREPARATION-NONPREPARATION, SKILL-UNSKILFULNESS; **practised eye,** ADEPT-BUNGLER; **practised hand,** ADEPT-BUNGLER.

prac-ti′-tion-er. One engaged in a profession. AGENT, REMEDY-BANE.

præ-cog′-ni-ta. Things previously known. EVIDENCE-COUNTEREVIDENCE.

præ-no′-men. The first name. NAME-MISNOMER.

præ′-tor. A civil governor among the ancient Romans. JUDGE.

prag-mat′-ic sanc′-tion. A solemn decree issued by the head of a state on weighty matters. CONTRACT.

prag-mat′-ic-al. Self-important. CONCEIT-DIFFIDENCE, SOCIETY-AFFECTATION.

pra′-hu. A vessel. CONVEYANCE-VESSEL.

prai′-rie. An open plain. FAUNA-FLORA, GULF-PLAIN.

praise. Commendation. APPROVAL-DISAPPROVAL, DEVOTION-IDOLATRY, THANKFULNESS-THANKLESSNESS.

praised. Approved of. APPROVAL-DISAPPROVAL.

praise′-wor″-thy. Deserving of praise. APPROVAL-DISAPPROVAL, GOODNESS-BADNESS, VIRTUE-VICE.

prance. To spring about. AGITATION, TRAVELING-NAVIGATION.

prank. A trick; to adorn. DETERMINATION-VACILLATION, EMBELLISHMENT-DISFIGUREMENT, ENTERTAINMENT-WEARINESS.

prate. Idle talk. CONVERSATION-MONOLOGUE, TALKATIVENESS-TACITURNITY.

prat′-tle. Childish talk. SPEECH-INARTICULATENESS, TALKATIVENESS-TACITURNITY.

prav′-i-ty. Depravity. VIRTUE-VICE.

prax′-is. An example for exercise. ACTION-PASSIVENESS, GRAMMAR-SOLECISM.

Prax-it′-e-les. A celebrated Greek sculptor. ARTIST.

pray. To supplicate. DEVOTION-IDOLATRY, PETITION-EXPOSTULATION.

prayer. A petition. DEVOTION-IDOLATRY, PETITION-EXPOSTULATION; **house of prayer,** FANE.

prayer′-book″. Book of worship. CEREMONIAL.

prayer′-ful. Devout. DEVOTION-IDOLATRY.

preach. To discourse on a religious subject. CEREMONIAL, EDUCATION-MISTEACHING; **preach to the winds,** USEFULNESS-USELESSNESS; **preach to the wise,** EDUCATION-MISTEACHING.

preach′-er. A minister. INSTRUCTOR-PUPIL, MINISTRY-LAITY.

preach′-ing. Public religious speaking. CEREMONIAL.

preach′-ment. A sermon. EDUCATION-MISTEACHING.

pre-ad′-am-ite. Existing before Adam. INFANT-VETERAN, NOVELTY-ANTIQUITY.

pre-am″-ble. An introductory writing. PREDECESSOR-CONTINUATION.

pre-ap″-pre-hen′-sion. An opinion formed before examination. DECISION-MISJUDGMENT.

preb′-end. A stipend in a cathedral church. CHURCH.

preb′-en-da-ry. One who receives a stipend. MINISTRY-LAITY.

preb′-en-da-ry-ship″. The office of a prebendary. CHURCH.

pre-ca′-ri-ous. Uncertain; dangerous. CERTAINTY-DOUBT, LASTINGNESS-TRANSIENTNESS, SECURITY-INSECURITY.

pre-ca′-ri-ous-ness. Insecurity. SECURITY-INSECURITY.

prec′-a-to-ry. Suppliant. PETITION-EXPOSTULATION.

pre-cau′-tion. Previous care. CAREFULNESS-CARELESSNESS, DESIGN, PREPARATION-NONPREPARATION, SECURITY-INSECURITY.

pre-cede′. To go before. ANTECEDENCE-SEQUENCE, LEADING-FOLLOWING, PRECEDENCE-SUCCESSION, SUPREMACY-SUBORDINACY.

pre-ce′-dence. Priority in time; superior rank or influence. ANTECEDENCE-SEQUENCE, LEADING-FOLLOWING, PRECEDENCE-SUCCESSION, REPUTATION-DISCREDIT.

PRECEDENCE—SUCCESSION.

Antecedence. A going before.

Antecedency. The state of going before; priority.

Anteposition. A placing before.

Anteriority. State of being anterior, or of being prior in time or place. See ANTERIORITY.

Coming before. Arrival sooner than. See *Verbs*.

Importance. State of being important; consequence.

Le pas [F.]. The pass; the step; the precedence.

Precedence. The act of going before in order of time.

Precession. A moving before. See LEADING.

Precursor. A forerunner.

Priority. State of preceding in time, rank, etc. See ANTECEDENCE.

Superiority. State of being superior, or higher in rank, position, authority, etc. See SUPREMACY.

The lead. The being at the head; preceding.

Coming after. A following.

Consecution. Condition of being consecutive or following each other in regular order.

Continuation. Unbroken succession; carrying on without a break.

Going after. A following in the rear. See LEADING-FOLLOWING.

Order of succession. Regularity in following.

Posteriority. State or condition of being posterior, or of coming after one another in order. See ANTECEDENCE-SEQUENCE.

Secondariness. State of being secondary, or of following in order.

Sequence. The condition of following; succession.

Subordinacy. State of being subordinate, or of being placed in a lower rank. See SUPREMACY-SUBORDINACY.

Succession. A following in regular order.

Successiveness. The quality of being successive or following in an uninterrupted order.

PRECEDENCE—SUCCESSION—*Continued.*

PRECEDENCE—*Verbs.*

Come before. ⎫
Come first. ⎬ To go before in order of time.
Have precedence. ⎮
Have the pas. ⎭
Have the start. To start earlier than. See LEADING.
Head. To be before.
Introduce. To bring into presence of and acquaint with
Lead. To move in front of; be chief or a superior.
Lead in the dance. ⎫
Lead in the way. ⎬ To begin or be the first.
Open the ball. ⎭
Place before. To be at the head.
Precede. To go before; outrank.
Preface. To introduce by preliminary remarks.
Prefix. To put or fix on before.
Prelude. To introduce with a prelude, or something that opens or foretells what is coming.
Premise. To set forth beforehand a proposition that is assumed true.
Set the fashion. To be the first to use. See DOMINANCE.
Take precedence. To assume first place in importance.
Take the lead. To surpass; be superior; be in advance.
Usher in. To precede as an usher, one who conducts another to a seat.

PRECEDENCE—*Adjectives.*

Above mentioned. ⎫
Aforesaid. ⎬ Said or mentioned before.
Antecedent. Prior in time, rank, etc.
Anterior. Toward the front.
Before. ⎫
Before mentioned. ⎬ Toward the beginning.
Foregoing. ⎫
Former. ⎬ Going before.
Introductory. Leading up to something more important.
Precedent. Going before; prior.
Preceding. Going before. See *Verbs.*
Precursive. ⎫
Precursory. ⎬ Going before as a forerunner.
Prefatory. Pertaining to a preface; introductory.
Preliminary. Going before something else; antecedent.
Prelusive. ⎫
Prelusory. ⎬ Characteristic of a prelude; telling beforehand.
Preparatory. Having to do with preparation; preliminary.
Prevenient. Going before; preventing.
Prior. Preceding in time, rank, etc.; previous. See ANTECEDENCE.

SUCCESSION—*Verbs.*

Alternate. To succeed by turns; follow by turns.
Append. To add something subordinate.
Come after. ⎫
Come next. ⎬ To follow.
Come on. ⎭
Ensue. To follow, as a natural consequence.
Follow. To come after or go after in same way and direction.
Place after. To place toward the rear.
Step into the shoes of. To succeed.
Succeed. To follow in regular order.
Suffix. To add as a suffix or something subordinate.

SUCCESSION—*Adjectives.*

Consecutive. Following in regular order; resulting as a consequence. See CONTINUITY.
Consequent. Following as a natural result.
Latter. Coming or happening after something else.
Next. Following directly after.
Posterior. Toward the rear. See ANTECEDENCE-SEQUENCE.
Proximate. Lying next to; nearest.
Sequacious. Inclined to follow; logically following in a series.
Sequent. Following; succeeding.
Subsequent. Coming or being after something else.
Succeeding. Following in regular order.

SUCCESSION—*Adverbs.*

After. Later in time.
Behind. Toward the rear. See ANTERIORITY-POSTERIORITY.
Subsequently. Coming after in time.

SUCCESSION—*Phrase.*

Et sequentia [L.]. And the things following.

PRECEDENCE—ADJECTIVES—*Continued*

Proemial. Of or pertaining to a proem or an introductory statement.
Said. As a legal term meaning aforesaid.

PRECEDENCE—*Adverbs.*

Before. ⎫
In advance. ⎬ Toward the front. See LEADING.

PRECEDENCE—*Phrases.*

Prior tempore, prior jure [L.]. First in time, first in right.
Seniores priores [L.]. Elders first.

---

prec'-e-dent. Something done or said that serves as an example. COPY-MODEL, HABIT-DESUETUDE, LITIGATION, PRECEDENCE-SUCCESSION, UNIFORMITY-MULTIFORMITY; follow precedents, CONVENTIONALITY-UNCONVENTIONALITY.

pre-ce'-ding. Going before. ANTECEDENCE-SEQUENCE.

pre-cen'-tor. Music-leader in a church. MANAGER, MINISTRY-LAITY.

pre'-cept. An order. LEAVE-PROHIBITION, ORDER, PRECEPT.

PRECEPT.

Act. A public determination of action; an edict, or law.
Canon. A law or rule of conduct.
Charge. An injunction; an instruction.
Code. A compilation of laws by public authority
Corpus juris [L.]. The body of the law.
Direction. The act of directing and the result of directing; a command.
Form. Established way of proceeding.
Golden rule. A rule of conduct, commanding to do as you would be done by. [Bible.]
Formula. An exact rule to be followed with care.
Formulary. A book of precedents.
Instruction. Commands; charges.
Law. A rule of conduct.
Lex scripta [L.]. The written law; statute law.
Maxim. A brief statement of a practical truth. See ADAGE.
Order. That which is ordered; a regulation; a command. See ORDER.
Precept. Any rule of conduct, especially moral conduct.
Prescript. A direction.
Prescription. That which is prescribed; a physician's formula.

Receipt. ⎫
Recipe. ⎬ A formulaic direction for making something.
Regulation. A rule for governing certain actions.
Rubric. A direction in a prayer-book; any rule of conduct.
Rule. Regular course in any procedure; an enactment.
Stage directions. Rules for the guidance of players.
Statute. A legislative enactment sanctioned according to full forms of law.
Technicality. That which is peculiar to a trade, profession, etc.

pre-cep'-tor. A teacher. INSTRUCTOR-PUPIL.

pre-ces'-sion. A going before. ASTRONOMY, LEADING-FOLLOWING, PRECEDENCE-SUCCESSION.

prece, vel pretio, vel [L.] (prī'-sî, vel prī'-shi-o, vel). Either with prayer or with price; either for love or money. COSTLINESS-CHEAPNESS, MULTIPLICITY-PAUCITY.

précieuse ridicule [F.] (prê-si-uz' ri-di-cūl'). Romantic ladies. SOCIETY-AFFECTATION.

pre'-cinct. Environs; boundary. BOUNDARY, CITY-COUNTRY, ENVIRONMENT-INTERPOSITION, EXTENSION-DISTRICT, EXTENSION-PLACE.

pre'-cious. Of great value or price. COSTLINESS-CHEAPNESS, GOODNESS-BADNESS, LOVE-HATE, MAGNITUDE-SMALLNESS; precious metals, MONEY; precious stone, EMBELLISHMENT-DISFIGUREMENT, GOODNESS-BADNESS.

prec'-i-pice. A steep descent of land or rock. ERECTNESS-FLATNESS, PARALLELISM-INCLINATION, REFUGE-PITFALL; on the verge of a precipice, SECURITY-INSECURITY.

pre-cip'-i-tan-cy. Headlong hurry; rashness. HURRY-LEISURE, RECKLESSNESS-CAUTION.

pre-cip'-i-tate. To throw headlong; hurry; rash. CLEANNESS-FILTHINESS, EARLINESS-LATENESS, ELEVATION-DEPRESSION, HURRY-LEISURE, RECKLESSNESS-CAUTION; **precipitate oneself,** ASCENT-DESCENT.

pre-cip'-i-tate-ly. Rashly. HURRY-INDOLENCE.

pre-cip"-i-ta'-tion. Hurry. EARLINESS-LATENESS.

pre-cip'-i-tous. Very steep. PARALLELISM-INCLINATION.

pre-cip'-i-tous-ness. Hastiness. HURRY-LEISURE.

pre"-cis'. A summary. DIGEST.

pre-cise'. Exact. TRUTH-ERROR.

pre-cise'-ly. Exactly. ASSENT-DISSENT.

pre-cise'-ness. Exactness. TRUTH-ERROR.

pre-ci'-sian. A formalist. GODLINESS-UNGODLINESS.

pre-ci'-sian-ism. The art of being precise. GODLINESS-UNGODLINESS, ORTHODOXY-HETERODOXY, SOCIETY-AFFECTATION.

pre-ci'-sion. Accuracy. PURITY-CRUDENESS.

pre-clude'. Prevent. OBSTRUCTION-HELP.

pre-co'-cious. Immature; rude. EARLINESS-LATENESS, POLITENESS-IMPOLITENESS, PREPARATION-NONPREPARATION, PRESUMPTION-OBSEQUIOUSNESS.

pre"-cog-ni'-tion. Previous knowledge. KNOWLEDGE-IGNORANCE, PREVISION.

pre"-con-ceived'. Conceived beforehand. DECISION-MISJUDGMENT.

pre"-con-cep'-tion. Previous thought. DECISION-MISJUDGMENT.

pre"-con-cert'. To plan beforehand. DESIGN, PREDETERMINATION-IMPULSE.

pre"-con-cer'-ta-tion. Previous preparation. PREPARATION-NONPREPARATION.

pre-cur'-sive. Anticipative. PRECEDENCE-SUCCESSION.

pre-cur'-sor. A forerunner. ANTECEDENCE-SEQUENCE, LEADING-FOLLOWING, PRECEDENCE-SUCCESSION, PREDECESSOR-CONTINUATION.

pre-cur'-so-ry. Going before. PREDECESSOR-CONTINUATION.

pre-da'-ceous. Living by prey. TAKING-RESTITUTION, THEFT.

pre'-dal. Given to plundering, taking to plundering. TAKING-RESTITUTION, THEFT.

pred-a-to'-ri-al. Pillaging. TAKING-RESTITUTION, THEFT.

pred'-a-to-ry. Plundering. TAKING-RESTITUTION, THEFT.

pred-e-ces'-sor. One who has gone before. PREDECESSOR-CONTINUATION.

PREDECESSOR—CONTINUATION.

Avant-coureur [F.]. A forerunner.

Bell-wether. The sheep having a bell and leading the others.

Forerunner. One who goes before; an announcer.

Harbinger. One who or that which announces something.

Herald. One whose business was to bear challenges, etc.; one who announces.

Leader. One who guides; that which goes first.

Outrider. A servant who goes in advance of a carriage.

Pioneer. One who goes first into a country for exploration or settlement.

Precursor. One who or that which goes before and warns of the approach.

Predecessor. One who has preceded another.

Prodrome. A forerunner.

Prodromus. A prodrome.

Vancourier. One sent in advance of an army.

PREDECESSOR—*Denotations.*

Antecedent. That which goes before in time.

Avant propos [F.]. Introduction.

Dawn. Show of approaching sunrise.

Exordium. The introductory part of a discourse.

Frontispiece. An ornamental figure fronting the first page of a book.

Groundwork. That which forms the foundation or support of anything.

Heading. That which stands at the head.

Introduction. That part of a book or discourse which introduces or leads the way to the main subject.

Omen. An occurrence supposed to show the character of some future event.

Overture. A musical composition, designed as an introduction to an opera, etc.

Preamble. The introductory part of a statute, which states the reasons and intent of the law.

Precedent. Something done that may serve as an example to authorize a subsequent act of the same kind.

Preface. An introduction to a book.

Prefigurement. The act of showing or announcing by antecedent types and similitudes.

Prefix. One or more letters or syllables joined to the beginning of a word to modify its signification.

Prelude. An introductory performance.

Premises. Something stated or assumed as the basis of further argument.

Preparation. The act of fitting beforehand for a particular purpose

Proem. } A preface or introduction.
Proemium. }

Prolegomena. A preliminary remark or observation.

Prolepsis. A figure by which objections are anticipated or prevented.

Prologue. The preface or introduction to a poem, discourse, or play.

Prolusion. A trial before the principal performance.

Protasis. The introductory or subordinate member of a sentence.

Symphony. A musical prelude.

Appendage. An addition not essential.

Continuation. A carrying on without a break.

Postscript. An addition or continuation of a letter.

Sequel. That which follows and concludes.

Sequela. That which follows in condition after a disease.

Successor. One who takes the place which another has left.

CONTINUATION—*Denotations.*

Aftercourse. Something happening after an affair is supposed to have ended.

Aftergame. A subsequent scheme or expedient.

Afterpart. A part or portion attached to the rear.

Afterpiece. A piece performed after a play

Afterthought. Reflection after an act.

Appendix. Any literary matter added to a book, but not essential to its completeness.

Arrière pensée [F.]. An afterthought.

Codicil. A clause added to a will.

Colophon. An inscription containing the place and date of publication, printer's name, etc., formerly placed on the last page of a book.

Epilogue. A speech or short poem recited after a play.

Heel-piece. A piece of armor to protect the heels.

More last words. Words spoken after a discourse is supposed to have ended.

Peroration. The concluding part of an oration.

Queue. A tail-like appendage of hair.

Rear. The back or hindmost part.

Retinue. A body of retainers who follow a distinguished person.

Second thought. Reflection after an act.

Suffix. A letter, letters, syllable, or syllables added to the end of a word to modify the meaning.

Suite. A company of attendants.

Tag. A direction card or label.

Tail. The terminal posterior appendage of an animal.

Tail-piece. A piece at the end.

Trail. A track left by man or beast.

Train. A number of followers, or body of attendants.

PREDECESSOR—*Continued.*

PREDECESSOR—*Adjectives.*

Inaugural. Pertaining to or done at an inauguration.

Introductory. Used as an introduction, preliminary.

Precedent. Preceding. See ANTECEDENCE.

Precursory. Preceding and giving warning.

Prefatory. Of or pertaining to a preface.

Preliminary. Introductory.

Preludious. Pertaining to a prelude.

Prelusive. } Characteristic of a prelude.
Prelusory. }

Prodromous Precursory

Proemial. Pertaining to a proem.

pre'-de-lib''-er-a-''tion. Previous deliberation. PREDE-TERMINATION-IMPULSE, PREVISION.

pre-des''-ig-na'-tion. A word used at the beginning of a proposition to indicate its quantity. RATIOCINATION-INSTINCT.

pre'-de-sign'-ed. To design beforehand. PREDETERMINATION-IMPULSE.

pre-des'-ti-nate. To foreordain. DIVINITY.

pre-des''-ti-na'-tion. The unchangeable purpose of God. DIVINITY, VOLITION-OBLIGATION.

pre-des'-tine. To order beforehand. OCCURRENCE-DESTINY, VOLITION-OBLIGATION.

pre'-de-ter''-mi-na-tion. Previous determination. PREDETERMINATION-IMPULSE, VOLITION-OBLIGATION.

PREDETERMINATION—IMPULSE.

Foregone conclusion. A conclusion decided beforehand.
Intention. A settled purpose of the mind. See PURPOSE.
Parti pris [F.]. Well-settled determination.
Predeliberation. Deliberation beforehand.
Predetermination. A purpose formed beforehand.
Premeditation. A thinking over beforehand.
Project. Something that is designed or thrown out for consideration. See PLAN.
Propendency. Careful deliberation.
Resolution. Fixed determination.

PREDETERMINATION—*Verbs.*

Preconcert. To arrange beforehand.
Predetermine. To settle definitely beforehand.
Premeditate. To consider well in the mind.
Preresolve. To determine fixedly beforehand.
Resolve beforehand. To make up one's mind in advance.

PREDETERMINATION—*Adjectives.*

Advised. Done with a purpose; counseled.
Aforethought. Premeditated.
Calculated. Ascertained or determined by a process of thought.
Cunning. Having craft or forethought.
Designed. Specifically purposed or intended.
Intended. Settled as to the mind upon a purpose, designed. See PURPOSE.
Maturely considered. Well and carefully considered.
Predesigned. Designed beforehand.
Premeditated. Thought over well beforehand. See *Verbs.*
Prepense. Considered beforehand.
Studied. Closely examined; premeditated.
Well-devised. ⎫
Well-laid. ⎬ Determined after careful consideration.
Well-weighed. ⎭

PREDETERMINATION—*Adverbs, etc.*

Advisedly. Purposely. See *Adjectives.*
All things considered. After careful consideration.
Deliberately. With one's mind made up.
In cold blood. Deliberately, and without sudden passion.
Intentionally. Of purpose. See PURPOSE.
With eyes open. Knowingly.
With premeditation. After thinking and consideration.

IMPULSE—Adverbs—*Continued from Column 2.*

On the spur of the moment. ⎫ Without previous thought or prepa-
On the spur of the occasion. ⎭ ration.

Creature of impulse. A being governed by passion.
Flash. A sudden burst of light; a short momentary state.
Impromptu. Anything done without preparation.
Improvisation. Anything devised on the spur of the moment.
Improvisatore. One who composes and sings extemporaneously.
Impulse. The act of impelling; any mental activity sudden and momentary.
Inspiration. An influence which stimulates to activity, especially lofty and noble activity.
Spurt. A sudden gushing as of liquid; a sudden outbreak.
Sudden thought. That which occurs to one in a moment.

IMPULSE—*Verbs.*

Extemporize. To speak without premeditation or preparation.
Flash on the mind. To come to the mind with suddenness or without effort.
Improvise. To contrive on the spur of the moment.
Say what comes uppermost. To speak without premeditation.

IMPULSE—*Adjectives.*

Extemporaneous. Spoken without preparation.
Improvisate. Unpremeditated.
Improvisatory. Pertaining to improvisation.
Improvisé [F.]. Improvised.
Improvised. Devised on the spur of the moment.
Impulsive. Having the power to move with an impulse; actuated by impulse and not thought.
Indeliberate. Done without thought or reflection.
Instinctive. Acting without the assistance or direction of instruction or experience; spontaneous. See VOLITION-OBLIGATION.
Natural. Not acquired; given by nature.
Spontaneous. Done without special determination of the will. See VOLITION.
Unguarded. Done or said with carelessness.
Unguided. Without guides or restraints.
Unmeditated. Not thought over.
Unpremeditated. Not thought over beforehand.
Unprompted. Not excited to activity or exertion; not assisted by another in the action.

IMPULSE—*Adverbs, etc.*

A l'improviste [F.]. Unexpectedly.
Extemporaneously. ⎫ Without previous study or meditation.
Extempore. ⎭
Impromptu. Offhand.
Improviso. ⎫ Not prepared beforehand.
Offhand. ⎭

(*Continued on Column 1.*)

---

pre''-de-ter'-mine. To decide beforehand. CHOICE-NEUTRALITY, DESIGN.

pre'-di-al. Consisting of land. DOMESTICATION-AGRICULTURE, OCEAN-LAND, PROPERTY.

pre-dic'-a-ment. State; particular condition. CONDITION-SITUATION, DIVISION.

pred'-i-cate. What is affirmed or denied. ASSERTION-DENIAL, CEREMONIAL.

pred''-i-ca'-tion. An assertion; preaching. ASSERTION-DENIAL, CEREMONIAL.

pred'-i-ca-to-ry. Affirmative. ASSERTION-DENIAL.

pre-dict'. To foretell. PREVISION, PROPHECY.

pre-dic'-tion. A prophecy. PROPHECY.

pre-dict'-ive. Foreboding. PROPHECY.

pre''-di-lec'-tion. Preference. AFFECTIONS, DECISION-MISJUDGMENT, DESIRE-DISTASTE.

pre''-dis-pose'. To adapt previously. MOTIVE-CAPRICE, PREPARATION-NONPREPARATION.

pre''-dis-posed'. Adapted previously. AFFECTIONS, PREPARATION-NONPREPARATION, READINESS-RELUCTANCE.

pre-dis''-po-si'-tion. Previous propensity.

pre-dom'-i-nance. ⎫ Prevalence. DOMINANCE-IMPO-
pre-dom'-i-nan-cy. ⎭ TENCE.

pre-dom'-i-nant. Prevalent. DOMINANCE-IMPOTENCE, RULE-LICENSE.

pre-dom'-i-nate. To be superior. DOMINANCE-IMPOTENCE, SUPREMACY-SUBORDINACY.

pre-em'-i-nence. Superiority. SUPREMACY-SUBORDINACY.

pre-em'-i-nent-ly. Supremely. MAGNITUDE-SMALLNESS, SUPREMACY-SUBORDINACY.

pre-em'-i-nent. Surpassing others. REPUTATION-DISCREDIT, SUPREMACY-SUBORDINACY.

pre-emp'-tion. Act of buying before others. BUYING-SALE.

pre''-en-gage'. To engage by previous contract. EARLINESS-LATENESS.

pre''-en-gage'-ment. Engagement by previous contract. ENGAGEMENT-RELEASE.

pre''-es-tab'-lish. To establish beforehand. DESIGN.

pre″-ex-am′-ine. To examine beforehand. Investigation-Answer.

pre″-ex-ist′. To exist previously. Antecedence-Sequence.

pref′-ace. An introductory speech or writing. Precedence-Succession, Predecessor-Continuation.

pre′-fect. A governor. Chief-Underling, Liberty-
Subjection, President-Member.

pre′-fec-ture. The office of a prefect. Rule-License.

pre-fer′. To esteem above others. Choice-Neutrality, Church, Desire-Distaste; **prefer a claim,** Litigation; **prefer a petition,** Petition-Expostulation.

pref′-er-ence. Predilection. Choice-Neutrality.

pref″-er-en′-tial. Possessing preference. Choice-Neutrality.

pre-fer′-ment. Advancement. Betterment-Deterioration, Church.

pre-fig′-ure. Foreshow. Prophecy.

pre-fig′-ure-ment. Antecedent representation. Sign.

pre-fix′. To place before. Precedence-Succession,
Predecessor-Continuation.

pre-gla′-cial. Prior to the glacial period. Novelty-
Antiquity.

preg′-na-ble. Capable of being taken. Might-Impotence.

preg′-nan-cy. Gestation. Fertility-Sterility.

preg′-nant. Fertile. Consequence-Insignificance,
Creation-Destruction, Fertility-Sterility, Occurrence-Destiny, Prophecy, Terseness-Prolixity; **pregnant with meaning,** Meaning-Jargon.

pre-hen′-sion. The act of grasping. Taking-Restitution.

pre″-his-tor′-ic. Pertaining to the ages before written
history. Novelty-Antiquity.

pre″-in-struct′. To instruct beforehand. Education-
Misteaching.

pre-judge′. To decide beforehand. Decision-Misjudgment.

pre-ju′-di-cate. To prejudge. Decision-Misjudgment.

prej′-u-dice. Bias; injury. Betterment-Deterioration, Decision-Misjudgment, Good-Evil.

prej′-u-diced. Showing prejudice. Decision-Misjudgment.

prej″-u-di′-cial. Detrimental. Goodness-Badness.

prel′-a-cy. The system of government by prelates.
Church.

prel′-ate. A bishop. Ministry-Laity.

pre-lat′-i-cal. Pertaining to a prelate. Church.

pre-la′-tion. Preference. Choice-Neutrality.

pre-lec′-tion. A public lecture. Education-Misteaching.

pre-lec′-tor. A lecturer in a university. Instructor-
Pupil.

pre-lim′-i-na-ries. Those things that precede. **Preliminaries of peace,** Fighting-Conciliation; **settle
preliminaries,** Preparation-Nonpreparation.

pre-lim′-i-na-ry. That precedes. Precedence-Succession, Predecessor-Continuation.

pre′-lude. An overture. Precedence-Succession,
Predecessor-Continuation, Preparation-Nonpreparation.

pre-lu′-sive. Presaging. Precedence-Succession,
Predecessor-Continuation.

pre-lu′-so-ry. Presaging. Precedence-Succession,
Predecessor-Continuation.

pre″-ma-ture′. Ripe too soon; too hasty. Earliness-Lateness, Preparation-Nonpreparation.

pre-med′-i-tate. To meditate beforehand. Predetermination-Impulse, Purpose-Luck.

pre-med′-i-ta″-ted. Deliberated upon beforehand.
Predetermination-Impulse.

pre-med″-i-ta′-tion. Forethought. Predetermination-Impulse.

prem′-i-ces. First-fruits. Cause-Effect.

pre′-mi-er. First minister of state. Manager, Representation.

premier pas [F.] (pre-miê′ pa). The first step. Beginning-End.

pre′-mi-er-ship. The office of a premier. Management.

pre-mise′. Prefix; announce. Precedence-Succession, Prophecy.

prem′-i-ses. Suppositions. Antecedence-Sequence,
Evidence-Counterevidence, Extension-Place,
Predecessor-Continuation, Ratiocination-In-
stinct.

pre′-mi-um. Reward. Outlay-Income, Recompense-Punition; **at a premium,** Costliness-Cheapness.

pre-mon′-ish. Forewarn. Warning.

pre-mon′-ish-ment. Previous warning. Warning.

pre″-mo-ni′-tion. Forewarning. Prophecy, Warning.

pre-mon′-i-to-ry. Giving previous admonition. Prophecy, Warning.

pre″-mon-stra′-tion. Foreshowing. Appearance-Disappearance, Manifestation-Latency, Prophecy.

pre″-mu-ni′-re. The offense of introducing foreign
authority into England. Insubordination-Obedience, Recompense-Punition.

prendre la balle au bond [F.] (pran·dr la bal o bon·).
To take the ball at the rebound. Opportuneness-
Unsuitableness.

pre-no′-tion. A preconception. Decision-Misjudgment, Prevision.

pren-sa′-tion. The act of seizing with violence. Taking-Restitution.

pren′-tice. An apprentice. Instructor-Pupil.

pren′-tice-ship. Serving as an apprentice. Education-Learning.

pre-oc′-cu-pan-cy. Previous possession. Holding-
Exemption.

pre-oc″-cu-pa′-tion. The act of taking possession of
beforehand. Heed-Disregard.

pre-op′-tion. Right of first choice. Choice-Neutrality.

pre″-or-dain′. To ordain beforehand. Occurrence-
Destiny, Volition-Obligation.

prep″-a-ra′-tion. The state of being ready. Education-Misteaching, Melody-Dissonance, Organization-Disorganization, Predecessor-Continuation, Preparation-Nonpreparation; **in course
of preparation,** Design.

PREPARATION—NONPREPARATION.

Adjustment. Act of making fit; of suiting to the thing. See Harmony.

Anticipation. The act of looking forward to and preparing for. See
Prevision.

Arrangement. The act or result of arranging; preparation.

Array. Regular arrangement, as for battle.

Brewing. The process of making malt liquors.

Clearance. The act of clearing; of freeing from encumbrances.

Concoction. The act of preparing by mixing together.

Cooking. The process of preparing food for the table.

Abortion. An arrestment of development; a miscarriage.

Absence of preparation. Neglect or want of training.

Crudity. The state of being crude or of being unprepared.

Disqualification. State of being disqualified; of being unfit for a
position.

Immaturity. Want of development.

Improvidence. Want of foresight or economy.

Improvisation. Art of speaking extemporarily; extemporaneously.
See Predetermination-Impulse.

Inconcoction. Unripeness; immaturity.

PREPARATION—NONPREPARATION—*Continued.*

Cultivation. Working of ground for the purpose of raising crops.
Digestion. The preparation of the food for assimilation.
Elaboration. Developing into careful work; working up into something better.
Equipment. The act of equipping; the state of preparing for any special purpose.
Evolution. The act of evolving; of developing into a higher state.
Forecast. A foresight of conditions and preparation for them. See ENTERPRISE.
Gestation. The act of bearing in the womb.
Hatching. The act of producing young.
Incubation. Hatching by any means.
Inurement. Act of hardening up for difficulty. See HABIT.
Maturation. The process of ripening or coming to maturity.
Maturity. Full development of body or mind.
Mellowness. Quality of being ripe, or fully developed.
Plowing. The process of preparing the ground for tilling.
Precaution. Careful forethought or preparation for any emergency.
Preconcertation. The act of determining upon by previous agreement.
Predisposition. The act of previously arranging.
Preparation. The act of preparing; readiness; preliminary work.
Preparedness. State of being prepared.
Providence. Exercise of care as to the future.
Providing. Making or procuring for future use. See *Verbs.*
Provision. A making ready for the future; measures taken beforehand.
Readiness. State of being ready; preparedness.
Rehearsal. A preparatory recital or performance.
Ripeness. Fully developed.
Ripening. The act of becoming ripe. See *Verbs.*
Semination. The act of sowing or spreading.
Sitting. A brooding on eggs, so as to hatch them.
Sowing. The process of scattering seed.
Tilling. The process of putting in order for raising crops.
Training. Systematic instruction or preparation for an end. See EDUCATION.
Tuning. Putting in tune; adjusting to a purpose.

PREPARATION—*Denotations.*

Accouterment. Equipment or trappings of a soldier.
Armament. The equipment of a vessel or fortification.
Cookery. The art or practise of cooking.
Cradle. A rocking bed for an infant.
Culinary art. The art of cooking.
Échafaudage [F.]. Scaffolding.
First stone. Preparatory work.
Foundation. A structure upon which anything is erected.
Groundwork. That which furnishes a foundation or support for anything.
Novitiate. A period of probation.
Outfit. A fitting out or equipment.
Scaffold.   } A platform built against the side of a building for the
Scaffolding. } support of workmen. See SUSPENSION-SUPPORT.
Stepping-stone. Anything by which one rises or advances.
Un impromptu fait à loisir [F.]. A premeditated impromptu.

PREPARATION—*Nouns of Agent.*

Avant coureur [F.]. A forerunner.
Avant courier [F.]. A harbinger.
Navvy. One employed in building canals, etc.
Pavior. One who paves.
Pioneer. One who enters and opens up a country.
Preparer. One who makes preparation.
Sappers and miners. Those who are employed in digging ditches and rearing fortifications.
Trainer. One who prepares others for any contest, especially a physical contest.
Warming-pan. A large pan into which live coals are put, for warming beds.

PREPARATION—*Verbs.*

Accouter. To equip.
Adjust. To make fit. See EQUALITY.
Anneal. To heat glass or metals in order to remove brittleness or fix colors.
Anticipate. To look forward to and prepare for. See PREVISION.
Arm. To prepare for conflict.
Array. To draw up in battle order.
Attune. To harmonize.
Betrim. To set in good order.
Breed. To cause to produce; to train.
Brew. To make malt liquors.

Inculture. Want of preparation or culture.
Non-preparation. Neglect or want of preparation.
Rawness. Quality or state of being raw. See *Adjectives.*
Want of preparation. Neglect or want of training.

NONPREPARATION—*Denotations.*

Germ. The earliest stage of an organism.
Nature. The existing universe.
Neglect. Omission to do something that should be done. See CAREFULNESS-NEGLECT.
Raw material. Material in a natural state. See MATERIALS.
Rough copy. An unfinished or approximate copy. See DESIGN.
State of nature. Rude and unworked condition.
Unweeded garden. A place unprepared for cultivation. [Shakespeare, *Hamlet,* I, ii, 135.]
Virgin soil. Uncultivated soil.

NONPREPARATION—*Verbs.*

Be unprepared. Not ready. See *Adjectives.*
Dismantle. To deprive of equipments, etc. See USEFULNESS-USELESSNESS.
Extemporize. To make an unprepared speech.
Improvise. To do or speak offhand.
Lack preparation. To be without training.
Lie fallow. To be uncultivated.
Live from hand to mouth. To live without regard to the future.
S'embarquer sans biscuits [F.]. To go on board a ship without biscuits.
Undress. To divest of covering. See DRESS-UNDRESS.
Want preparation. To lack training.

NONPREPARATION—*Adjectives.*

Abortive. Wanting full development.
Caught napping. Unprepared. See EXPECTATION-SURPRISE.
Coarse. Composed of rough parts; unrefined.
Crude. Not having reached full development.
Dismantled. Stripped of equipment. See *Verbs.*
Disqualified. Not having the necessary qualifications.
Embryonic. Pertaining to the embryo; undeveloped.
En deshabille [F.]. In undress.
Fallow. Uncultivated.
Green. Unripe; immature.
Happy-go-lucky. Improvident; confiding in luck.
Ill-digested. Badly digested.
Immature. Not full grown.
Improvident. Not preparing for the future; reckless.
In a state of nature. Not prepared by artificial means.
Incomplete. Not fully developed. See ENTIRETY-DEFICIENCY.
Indigested. Not digested; crude.
In dishabille. In undress.
In the rough. Unworked.
Natural. Not artificial.
Out of gear. } Not suited for working.
Out of order. }
Precocious. Premature development.
Premature. Ripening or happening before the proper or normal time.
Raw. Not prepared by cooking; unprepared.
Rough. Lacking finish or completeness.
Rough cast. Cast without attention to detail.
Rough hewn. Roughly shapen.
Rudimental. As yet undeveloped.
Shiftless. Incapable of providing for oneself; thriftless.
Thoughtless. Without thought; manifesting no preparation.
Unarranged. Not placed in order.
Unbegun. Not started.
Unblown. Not blown.
Unboiled. Not boiled.
Uncultivated. Unprepared for planting.
Unconcocted. Unmixed.
Uncooked. Not prepared for eating.
Undigested. Not properly acted upon by the digestive organs.
Undressed. Not covered; not trimmed.
Undrilled. Not trained.
Uneducated. Without bringing up; without education.
Unequipped. Not fitted with equipment.
Unexercised. Not trained.
Unfashioned. Not shaped.
Unfitted. Not adjusted to.
Unfledged. Not provided with feathers.
Unformed. Without shape.
Unfurnished. Without furniture.

PREPARATION—NONPREPARATION—*Continued.*

PREPARATION—Verbs—*Continued.*

Cook. To prepare food for eating.
Dress. To put in order; to adorn.
Elaborate. To produce by carefulness and labor.
Equip. To fit for service.
Fettle. To put in order.
Fledge. To provide with feathers.
Forearm. To prepare beforehand.
Forecast. To calculate beforehand. See DESIGN.
Furnish. To supply with what is necessary.
Garnish. To decorate.
Hatch. To produce young from eggs.
Infumate. To cure by drying in smoke.
Inure. To harden. See HABIT.
Mature. To ripen.
Mellow. To bring to perfection.
Nurture. To nurse or train. See OBSTRUCTION-HELP.
Pack. To arrange in order.
Predispose. To arrange beforehand.
Prime. To put in a state of readiness.
Provide. To supply with necessaries.
Refurbish. To polish.
Rehearse. To repeat for experiment or preparation.
Rig. To furnish with what is needed for the occasion.
Ripen. To make ripe.
Rough-hew. To shape roughly. [Shakespeare, *Hamlet*, V, ii.]
Season. To render suitable for use.
Set. To place in order.
Temper. To bring to proper condition by heating.
Train. To cause to exercise. See EDUCATION.

PREPARATION—*Verbal Expressions.*

Beat up for recruits; be prepared; be ready (see *Adjectives*); block out; bring into maturity; brush up; buckle on one's armor; clear decks; clear for action; close one's ranks; cultivate the soil; cut out work; dig a mine; dig the foundation; dress the ground; dress up; erect the scaffolding; feather one's nest; fit out; fit up; fix the basis; fix the foundation; fix the groundwork; furbish up; get into harness; get ready; get the steam up; get up; guard against; hammer out; have a rod in pickle; hold oneself in readiness; keep one's powder dry; keep on foot; lay a train; lay in provisions; lay oneself out for; lay the basis; lay the foundation; lay the groundwork; lay the first stone (see FORM); lie in wait for (see EXPECTATION); lick into shape (see FORM); make all snug; make investments; make preparation; make provisions for; make ready; make sure; make sure against; *obstare principiis* [L.], to withstand the first beginnings; open the door to (see DIFFICULTY-FACILITY); plow the ground; prepare for; prepare for the evil day; prepare oneself; prepare the ground; prime and load; provide against; provide against a rainy day; put a groove in; put in gear; put in harness; put in order (see BEGINNING); put in train; put in tune; put in working order; put the horses to; *reculer pour mieux sauter* [F.], to look before one leaps; screw up; serve an apprenticeship (see EDUCATION-LEARNING); set in order; set one's house in order; settle preliminaries; sharpen one's tools; shoulder arms; shuffle the cards; sound the note of preparation; sow the seed; take measures; take precaution; take steps; till the soil; trim one's sails; vamp up; *veniente occurrere morbo* [L.], to meet the coming sickness; whet the knife; whet the sword; wind up.

PREPARATION—*Adjectives.*

Afloat. In a floating condition; moving.
Afoot. Able to walk.
Armed at all points. Fully prepared.
Armed *cap à pie*.
Armed to the teeth. } Armed from head to foot.
At harness. Prepared for action.
At one's post. Ready.
Booted and spurred. Ready for riding.
Brewing. Making of ale or beer.
Brooding. Sitting on eggs to hatch them.
Cut and dried. Prepared beforehand.
Elaborate. Highly and thoroughly finished.
Forthcoming. Ready to appear.
Handy. Ready at hand.
Hatching. Producing.
Highly wrought. Well finished.
In agitation. Excited.
In arms. Prepared for war.
In battle array. Ready for battle.
In best bib and tucker. In best attire.
Inchoate. In an imperfect state.

NONPREPARATION—Adjectives—*Continued.*

Unguarded. Open; not protected.
Unhatched. Not yet produced; not having chipped the shell.
Unhewn. Not cut.
Unlabored. Not worked upon.
Unleavened. Without leaven.
Unlicked. Not licked into shape.
Unmellowed. Unripe.
Unnurtured. Not nourished up.
Unorganized. Not arranged in order.
Unpolished. Rough.
Unpremeditated. Thoughtless. See PREDETERMINATION IMPULSE.
Unprepared. Not ready. See PREPARATION.
Unprovided. Without supplies.
Unqualified. Not fitted for.
Unready. Not prepared.
Unripe. Green.
Unseasoned. Not suited to.
Unsown. Without seed.
Untaught. Ignorant; unlearned.
Untilled. Not prepared for planting.
Untrained. Lacking exercise.
Untrimmed. Without ornament; unpruned; shaggy.
Untutored. Untaught.
Unwrought. Not worked.
Without preparation. Not ready. See PREPARATION.

NONPREPARATION—*Adverb.*

Extempore. Without preparation. See PREDETERMINATION-IMPULSE.

PREPARATION—*Adjectives—Continued.*

In course of preparation. Unfinished.
In embryo. In progress of growth.
In full feather. Fully developed.
In gear. In working order.
In hand. In progress.
In harness. At work.
In practise.
In preparation. } Training.
In readiness. Prepared.
In reserve. Prepared for action.
In saddle. Ready for riding.
In store for. Ready for use.
In training. Exercising.
In utrumque paratus [L.]. Prepared on all sides.
In war-paint. Ready for fighting.
In working gear. Ready for work.
In working order. Prepared for work.
Labored. Earnestly engaged in some labor, thoroughly prepared.
Made to one's hand. Ready for use.
Mature. Completely developed.
Mellow. Ripened.
On foot. In progress.
On the alert. Watchful. See CAREFULNESS.
On the anvil.
On the stocks. } In course of construction or discussion.
On the table.
Practised. Trained. See SKILL.
Precautionary. Having prudent forethought.
Preliminary. Preparatory; antecedent.
Preparative.
Preparatory. } Serving to make ready.
Prepared. Ready. See PRECEDENCE.
Preparing. Making ready.
Provident. Exercising foresight.
Provisional. Provided for a present service.
Ready. Prepared for use or action.
Ready-made. Fit to be used.
Ready to one's hand. Ready for use.
Ripe. Grown to maturity.
Semper paratus [L.]. Always prepared.
Smelling of the lamp. Laboriously prepared, like the orations of Demosthenes.
Snug. Fitting tight but comfortable.
Sword in hand. Prepared for battle.
Under consideration.
Under revision. } In mental preparation.
Up in arms. Ready to fight.
Worked up. Excited.

PREPARATION—*Continued.*

PREPARATION—*Adverbs, etc.*

Against. In opposition to.	**In anticipation of.** With confident expectation.
For. In favor of.	**In preparation of.** Making ready.

PREPARATION—*Phrases.*

A bove majort discit arare minor [L.]. From the older ox the younger learns to plow.

Si vis pacem, para bellum [L.]. If you wish peace, prepare for war.

pre-par′-a-to-ry. Preceding. PRECEDENCE-SUCCESSION.

pre-pare′. To make ready. DESIGN, EDUCATION-MISTEACHING.

pre-par′-er. One who prepares. PREPARATION-NONPREPARATION.

pre-pared′. Ready. PREPARATION-NONPREPARATION, SKILL-UNSKILFULNESS.

pre-par′-ing. Making ready. OCCURRENCE-DESTINY, PREPARATION-NONPREPARATION.

pre-pense′. Predetermination. PREDETERMINATION-IMPULSE, PURPOSE-LUCK, VOLITION-OBLIGATION; malice prepense, CHARITABLENESS-MALEVOLENCE.

pre-pol′-lence. Superior in power. MIGHT-IMPOTENCE.

prepon, to [Gr.] (prep′-on, to). The fit; the becoming. DUTY-DERELICTION, TASTE-VULGARITY.

pre-pon′-der-ance. Superiority. DOMINANCE-IMPOTENCE, RULE-LICENSE, SUPREMACY-SUBORDINACY.

prep″-o-si′-tion. The part of speech that denotes the relation of an object to an action or thing. PARTICLE.

pre″-pos-sess′. To preoccupy. DECISION-MISJUDGMENT.

pre″-pos-sessed′. Biased. BIGOTRY-APOSTASY.

pre″-pos-sess′-ing. Attractive. PLEASURABLENESS-PAINFULNESS.

pre″-pos-ses′-sion. Bias; preoccupation. DECISION-MISJUDGMENT, HOLDING-EXEMPTION.

pre-pos′-ter-ous. Absurd. ADAGE-NONSENSE, DUENESS-UNDUENESS, GULL-HYPERBOLE, MAGNITUDE-SMALLNESS, SOCIETY-LUDICROUSNESS.

pre-po′-ten-cy. Predominance. MIGHT-IMPOTENCE.

Pre′-raf″-fa-el-ite. Before the methods of Raffael. FUTURE-PAST, NOVELTY-ANTIQUITY.

Pre-raf′-fa-el-i″-tism. A style of art. FUTURE-PAST.

pre″-re-quire′. To require beforehand. NEED.

pre-req′-ui-site. A necessary condition. NEED.

pre″-re-solve′. To resolve beforehand. PREDETERMINATION-IMPULSE.

pre-rog′-a-tive. Peculiar privilege. DUENESS-UNDUENESS, RULE-LICENSE.

pre-sage′. To foreshow. PORTENT, PROPHECY.

pres-by-o′-pi-a. A defect of vision in old age. SIGHT-DIMSIGHTEDNESS.

pres″-by-op′-ic. Dimsighted from age. SIGHT-DIMSIGHTEDNESS.

pres′-by-ter. A priest; an elder. MINISTRY-LAITY.

Pres′-by-te′-ri-an. A Church denomination. ORTHODOXY-HETERODOXY.

pres′-by-ter″-y. A body of pastors and ruling elders. CHURCH, MINISTRY-LAITY.

pre′-science. Foreknowledge. PREVISION.

pre′-scient. Foreknowing. PREVISION.

pre′-scious. Foreknowing. PROPHECY.

pre-scribe′. Direct. ADVICE, DUENESS-UNDUENESS, DUTY-DERELICTION, MANAGER, ORDER.

pre-scribed′. Directed. DUENESS-UNDUENESS.

pre′-script. A direction. ORDER, PRECEPT.

pre-scrip′-tion. A medical direction of remedies. HABIT-DESUETUDE, NOVELTY-ANTIQUITY, ORDER, PRECEPT, REMEDY-BANE.

pre-scrip′-tive. Arising from prescription. DUENESS-UNDUENESS, HABIT-DESUETUDE, NOVELTY-ANTIQUITY.

pres′-ence. Being present. APPEARANCE-DISAPPEARANCE, POLITENESS-IMPOLITENESS, PRESENCE-ABSENCE; in the presence of, REMOTENESS-NEARNESS; presence of God, HEAVEN-HELL; presence of mind, EXCITABILITY-INEXCITABILITY, RECKLESSNESS-CAUTION; real presence, CEREMONIAL; saving one's presence, REGARD-DISRESPECT.

PRESENCE—ABSENCE.

Attendance. The act of being present, or of watching over.

Diffusion. The act of spreading abroad; state of being present everywhere. See GATHERING-SCATTERING.

Occupancy. The state of being in possession of, or of being present.

Occupation. That which requires one's presence and takes one's attention.

Omnipresence. Everywhere present at the same time.

Permeation. The act or state of permeating, or of spreading through.

Pervasion. The act or state of spreading through every part.

Presence. The state of being present; the opposite of absence the state of being near.

Ubiety. The state of being in a place.

Ubiquitariness. State of being everywhere.

Ubiquity. Existence in all places at the same time.

Whereness. The quality of having a place.

PRESENCE—*Denotation.*

Bystander. One who stands by or is passively present. See ONLOOKER.

PRESENCE—*Verbs.*

Abide. To stay in a place; continue.

Assister [F.]. To attend.

Attend. To be present; accompany.

Be diffused through. ⎫
Be disseminated through. ⎬ To be spread in all its parts.

Be present. Being in a place referred to. See *Adjectives.*

Dwell. To continue for a long time in a place.

Exist in space. To have actual existence.

Absence. The state of being absent; the being away.

Absenteeism. The practise of being absent from one's accustomed place.

Emptiness. A being empty; lack or absence of something. See *Adjectives.*

Exemption. Freedom from penalties, etc.

Inexistence. Absence of existence. See ENTITY-NONENTITY.

Non-attendance. Want of attendance.

Non-residence. The state of being a non-resident.

Vacancy. Condition of being void or unoccupied.

Vacuity The state of being a vacuum.

ABSENCE—*Denotations.*

Absentee. One who is absent.

Âme qui vive [F.]. Not a living soul.

Alibi. A form of defense by which the accused undertakes to show that he was elsewhere when the crime was committed.

Hiatus. A break or vacancy, as in a manuscript or connected series.

Nobody. ⎫
Nobody on earth. ⎬ No person.

Nobody present. Absence of people.

Not a soul. Not a person.

Tabula rasa [L.]. An erased tablet.

Truant. One who absents himself from the place of duty.

Vacuum. ⎫
Void. ⎬ A space entirely devoid of matter.

ABSENCE—*Verbs.*

Absent oneself. To keep away from.

Be absent. Being away. See *Adjectives.*

PRESENCE—ABSENCE—*Continued.*

PRESENCE—VERBS—*Continued.*

Fall in the way. To meet with; be present along with.
Fill. To occupy entirely.
Find oneself. To be.
Frequent. To be present often.
Haunt. To visit frequently; be present much in the mind.
Inhabit. To live or dwell in a place.
Lie. To continue in a place; be situated.
Line. To mark the situation of.
Lodge. To live temporarily in a place.
Look on. To be a spectator; be present.
Make one at.}
Make one of.} To be one of a number or company.
Meet one at every turn. To be present everywhere.
Nestle. To place in a nest; fondle.
Occupy. To employ one's attention; have possession of.
Occur in a place. To be in a particular place.
Overspread. To spread over; scatter over.
Overrun. To run over; be present in all places.
People. To give inhabitants to.
Perch. To put on an elevated support.
Permeate. To spread all through.
Pervade. To go through in all directions.
Present oneself. To come into the presence of a person.
Remain. To continue in one place.
Reside. To be in one place for a considerable time
Resort to. To visit; frequent.
Revisit. To visit again.
Roost. To sit upon, as a roost.
Run through. To be in a place for a very short time.
Show one's face. To be present.
Sojourn. To stay for a period in one place.
Stand. To be fixed in a certain place.
Stay. To continue to be in a specified place.
Take up one's abode. To make one's permanent home. See ESTABLISHMENT.
Tenant. To hold as a tenant.

PRESENCE—*Adjectives.*

Domiciled. Provided with a home.
Full of people. Well populated.
Inhabiting. Dwelling. See *Verbs.*
Inhabited. Occupied by people.
Moored. Fastened. See ESTABLISHMENT.
Occupying. Holding.
Omnipresent. Present in all places at the same **time.**
Peopled. Having people.
Populous Full of people.
Present. Being in a place referred to.
Resiant. Resident.
Resident. Having an abode.
Residentiary. Having a residence.
Ubiquitary.}
Ubiquitous.} Ubiquitous; everywhere present.

PRESENCE—*Adverbs, etc.*

Abroad. Far and wide
Afield. In or to the field.
At home. At one's own abode.
Before. Face to face with.
Everywhere. In all places.
Here. In this place.
Here, there, and everywhere. Everywhere. See EXTENSION.
In presence of. Face to face.

ABSENCE—VERBS—*Continued.*

Go away. To depart from. See ARRIVAL-DEPARTURE.
Keep away. Remain absent.
Keep out of the way.
Make oneself scarce. To run away
Play truant. Play the runaway.
Stay away. Keep at a distance.
Vacate. To make vacant; leave.
Withdraw. To draw back; retire.

ABSENCE—*Adjectives.*

Absent.}
Away.} Not present to.
Desert. Uninhabited.
Deserted. Left; abandoned.
Devoid. Not in possession of.
Empty. Without contents; not filled.
Exempt from. Free from; released as from an obligation or duty.
Gone from home. Away from one's usual place.
Inexistent. Having no existence. See ENTITY-NONENTITY
Lost. Gone from the presence or possession of.
Missing. Absent from proper place; lost.
Omitted. Left out; not included.
Non-resident. Not residing in.
Not having. Without.
Not present. Absent.
Nowhere to be found. Lost.
Tenantless. Without a tenant; unoccupied.
Unhabitable.}
Uninhabitable.} Not suitable for abode
Uninhabited. Without dwellers.
Unoccupied.}
Untenanted.} Not taken up or occupied.
Vacant.}
Vacuous.} Empty.
Void. Devoid of matter.
Wanting. Without.

ABSENCE—*Adverbs, etc.*

Behind one's back. Secretly; out of sight.
Elsewhere. In another place.
In default of. Owing to lack of.
Minus. Wanting.
Neither here nor there.}
Nowhere.} In no place
Sans [F.]. Without.
Without. Wanting.

ABSENCE—*Phrases*

Aux absents les os [F.]. The bones for the absent ones.
Briller par son absence [F.]. To be conspicuous by one's absence.
Non est inventus [L.]. He has not been found.
The bird has flown.

PRESENCE—ADVERBS—*Continued.*

In propria persona [L.]. In person.
In the face of. Before.
On board. On a vessel.
On the spot. In a particular place.
There. In that place.
Under the eyes of.}
Under the nose of.} In the presence of.
Where. In what place.

---

pres′-ence–cham″-ber. The room in which a high dignitary or ruler receives assemblies. CONTENTS-RECEIVER.
pres′-ent. Taking place or existing at the time of the thought; being in view PRESENCE-ABSENCE, TIME; **at present,** TIME; **present time,** ETERNITY-INSTANTANEITY, TIME; **present to the mind,** HEED-DISREGARD, REMEMBRANCE-FORGETFULNESS; **these presents,** MISSIVE-PUBLICATION, WRITING-PRINTING.
pre-sent′. Bestow; point or aim; offer as a candidate. CHURCH, GIVING-RECEIVING, PROFFER-REFUSAL; **present a bold front,** BRAVERY-COWARDICE; **present a front,** REPRISAL-RESISTANCE; **present arms,** POLITENESS-IMPOLITENESS, REGARD-DISRESPECT; **present itself,** OCCURRENCE-DESTINY, REFLECTION-VACANCY, VISIBILITY-INVISIBILITY; **present oneself,** POLITENESS-IMPOLITENESS, PRESENCE-ABSENCE, PROFFER-REFUSAL; **present to the view,** APPEARANCE-DISAPPEARANCE.
pre-sent′-a-ble. In suitable condition. SOCIETY-LUDICROUSNESS.
pres″-en-ta′-tion. Act of bestowing; introduction. CHURCH, GIVING-RECEIVING, POLITENESS-IMPOLITENESS, PROFFER-REFUSAL, SOLEMNIZATION.
pre-sen′-ti-ment. Foreboding; prophetic apprehension of something future. DECISION-MISJUDGMENT, ENLIGHTENMENT-SECRECY, PREVISION, RATIOCINATION-INSTINCT.
pres′-ent-ly. After a little time. EARLINESS-LATENESS.

pre-sent'-ment. Report made by a grand jury. EN-LIGHTENMENT-SECRECY, GIVING-RECEIVING, LITIGA-TION.

pres"-er-va'-tion. Conservation. CONSERVATION, DIVINITY, MUTATION - PERMANENCE, SECURITY - IN-SECURITY.

pre-serv'-a-tive. Tending to preserve. CONSERVA-TION, SECURITY-INSECURITY.

pre-serv'-a-to-ry. A means of preserving. CONSERVA-TION.

pre-serve'. Save from decay; cooked fruit. STORE, SWEETNESS-ACIDITY.

pre-served'. Kept intact. CONSERVATION.

pre-serv'-er. One who or that which preserves. DEITY, PREPARATION - NONPREPARATION, SECURITY - INSE-CURITY.

pre-serv'-ing. Saving. CONSERVATION.

pre-show'. Show beforehand. PROPHECY.

pre-side'. Act as head. PRESIDENT-MEMBER; **preside at the board,** MANAGEMENT; **preside over,** RULE-LI-CENSE.

pres'-i-den-cy. Office of president. RULE-LICENSE.

pres'-i-dent. One chosen by election to preside over an organized body. CHIEF-UNDERLING, MANAGER, PRES-IDENT-MEMBER; **president pro tem.,** PRESIDENT-MEM-BER.

PRESIDENT—MEMBER.

Archon. The chief magistrate in ancient Athens.
Burgess. Magistrate of a borough.
Burgomaster. Chief magistrate of a municipal town in Holland.
Chair. The office of a magistrate, or presiding officer.
Chairman. Presiding officer of any organized body.
Chancellor. The presiding officer of a chancery court.
Chief. The head or leader of any body of men.
Chief justice. The presiding judge of a court.
Consul. One of the two chief magistrates of the Roman republic.
Governor. A chief ruler or magistrate.
Grand master. The presiding officer of an organized body.
Headmaster. The presiding officer of a school.
Judge. Presiding officer of a court.
Magistrate. A person clothed with directing power.
Manager. A director or conductor of persons or business.
Master. The director of a number of persons.
Mayor. Chief officer of a city.
Moderator. An officer who presides over an assembly.
Prefect. A superintendent of a department of police.
President. A presiding officer, as of a legislative body.
President pro tem. Presiding officer in the absence of the president.
Principal. A leader or head who has controlling influence.
Provost. A person who is appointed to superintend or preside over something.
Regent. One of a governing board.
Sachem. A chief of a tribe of American Indians.
Sagamore. A sachem.
Speaker. One who presides over, or speaks for a deliberative assembly.
Superintendent. One who has the charge or direction of affairs.
Teacher. One who has charge of a school.
Temporary chairman. One who acts or presides in the absence of a chairman.
Tribune. An officer who presided over the meetings of the Roman plebeians.
Vice-president. An officer who presides during the president's absence.

PRESIDENT—Verbs.

Act as president. To preside over an organized body.
Adjourn. To put off to another day.
Call to order. To request to come to order.
Control. To keep order.
Direct. To guide the business of an assembly.
Govern. To direct or control the actions of an organized body.
Have the chair. To be the presiding officer.
Manage. To have the direction of.
Moderate. To preside over or regulate.
Preside. To occupy the place of president, chairman, or moderator.
Rule. To control the will and actions of.
Take the chair. To become the presiding officer.

Alderman. One of a board of municipal officers.
Assemblyman. A member of an assembly.
Club. An association of persons for the pursuit of some common object.
Committee. One or more persons of an organized body, to whom any matter of business is referred.
Committee of the whole. A committee embracing all the members of a deliberative assembly.
Commoner. A member of the House of Commons.
Congressman. A member of the Congress of the United States especially of the House of Representatives.
Constituent. A person who is a member of a body of organized men, and is represented by a public officer.
Councilman. A member of a council.
Delegate. One sent to a legislative body to represent others.
Deliberative assembly. An assembly that meets for the transaction of business, especially legislative affairs.
Deputy. One empowered to act for another in the business of an assembly.
Member. One of the persons composing a society or assembly.
Proxy. A person who is deputed to act or vote for another.
Representative. A member of the branch of the United States Congress directly representing the people.
Seat. The privilege of the members of an assembly.
Senator. A member of the branch of the United States Congress elected by the legislatures of the States.
Standing committee. In legislative bodies, a committee appointed for the consideration of all subjects of a particular class.
Subcommittee. A part or division of a committee.
Subordinate. A member.

MEMBER—Associated Nouns.

Amendment. A change made in a law, bill, or motion.
Commitment. The referring of a bill to a committee.
Debate. Argument for and against.
Division. A voting of a legislative body.
Motion. A formal proposition made in a deliberative body.
Order. Rule of business.
Point of order. A question of procedure under parliamentary rules.
Privileged question. A question affecting the rights of a legislative body, or the rights or conduct of its individual members.
Quorum. Such a number of persons in a deliberative body as is necessary to transact business.
Reconsideration. The restoration of a matter on which a vote has been taken to parliamentary action.
Resolution. A statement, or formal expression proposed to a deliberating body.
Secret session. A session of a deliberating body whose proceedings are secret.
Vote. A formal expression of will or opinion in regard to a question submitted.

press. Plead pertinaciously; compel; dense throng; a machine for printing ; the newspapers of a country. COERCION, CONNECTIVE, CONTENTS-RECEIVER, GATH-ERING-SCATTERING, HEAVINESS-LIGHTNESS, MISSIVE-PUBLICATION, MOTIVE-CAPRICE, PETITION-EXPOSTU-LATION, PROFFER-REFUSAL, PUBLICITY, WRITING-PRINTING; **go to press,** WRITING-PRINTING; **press in,** INJECTION-EJECTION; **press into the service,** OB-STRUCTION-HELP, USE-DISUSE; **press of business,** AC-TIVITY-INDOLENCE, OCCUPATION; **press on,** ADVANCE-RETROGRESSION, HURRY-LEISURE, PERIOD-PROG-RESS, QUEST-EVASION; **press one hard,** ATTACK-DE-FENSE; **under press of,** COERCION; **writer for the press,** MISSIVE-PUBLICATION, WRITING-PRINTING.

pressed. Constrained; placed in an exigency. **Hard pressed,** DIFFICULTY-FACILITY, HURRY-LEISURE, OB-STRUCTION-HELP; **pressed for time,** HURRY-LEI-SURE.

press'-gang". An impress-gang. JUDICATURE

press'-ing. Urgent. CONSEQUENCE-INSIGNIFICANCE, NEED.

pres'-sure. Urgency; stress. CONSEQUENCE-INSIGNIFI-CANCE, DOMINANCE-IMPOTENCE, HEAVINESS-LIGHT-NESS, MIGHT-IMPOTENCE, WELFARE-MISFORTUNE;

center of pressure, CENTER; **high pressure,** EXCITATION, VIGOR-INERTIA.

Pres′ter John. A fabulous Christian monarch. FANCY.

pres″-ti-dig″-i-ta′-tion. The practise of sleight of hand. TRUTHFULNESS-FRAUD.

pres″-ti-dig″-i-ta″-tor. Juggler. GULL-DECEIVER.

pres′-tige. Authority based on past achievements, ascendancy based on recognition of power. DECISION-MISJUDGMENT, DESIRE-DISTASTE, REPUTATION-DISCREDIT, RULE-LICENSE.

pres-tig″-i-a′-tion. Legerdemain. TRUTHFULNESS-FRAUD.

pres-tig′-i-a-to-ry. Delusive. TRUTHFULNESS-FRAUD.

pres-tig′-i-ous. Deceptive. TRUTHFULNESS-FRAUD.

prestissimo [It.] (pres-tis′-si-mo). In very quick time. MUSIC.

pres′-to. In quick time. ETERNITY-INSTANTANEITY, MUSIC.

pre-stric′-tion. Defect of sight. SIGHT-BLINDNESS.

pre-su′-ma-ble. Fair to suppose. LIKELIHOOD-UNLIKELIHOOD.

pre-sume′. Suppose; take as likely; behave arrogantly. DECISION-MISJUDGMENT, FAITH-MISGIVING, HYPOTHESIS, SANGUINENESS-HOPELESSNESS, SECURITY-INSECURITY, SELFRESPECT-HUMBLENESS.

pre-sump′-tion. Blind confidence; judgment on probable grounds; an argument carrying weight; effrontery. DECISION-MISJUDGMENT, DUENESS-UNDUENESS, FAITH-MISGIVING, HYPOTHESIS, LIKELIHOOD-UNLIKELIHOOD, OVERVALUATION-UNDERVALUATION, PRESUMPTION - OBSEQUIOUSNESS, RECKLESSNESS-CAUTION, SANGUINENESS-HOPELESSNESS, SELFRESPECT-HUMBLENESS.

PRESUMPTION—OBSEQUIOUSNESS.

Airs. An affected manner.

Arrogance. The state of being unduly proud and haughty.

Assumption. The state of taking too much upon oneself.

Assumption of infallibility. The act of assuming the pretense of being able to make no mistakes.

Assurance. Entire confidence in oneself.

Audacity. Boldness.

Bluster. Insolent and noisy talk.

Bounce. An insolent lie.

Brass. Insolent assurance.

Dicacity. Pertness.

Domineering, etc. The quality of ordering others about in an insolent manner. See *Verbs*.

Effrontery. Shameless insolence.

Face. Undue assurance.

Face of brass. Unblushing and insolent assurance.

Flippancy. Insolent frivolity.

Front. Bold or brazen assurance.

Hardened front. Insolent and callous assurance.

Hardihood. Audacious boldness.

Haughtiness, etc. Disdainful and overbearing pride. See *Adjectives*.

Impertinence. The state of being insolently presumptuous.

Impudence. The state of being insolently bold.

Insolence. The state of being haughty and contemptuous towards others.

Overbearance. The state of being arrogant and domineering.

Pertness. Vivid, keen, but undignified sprightliness.

Petulance. Capricious insolence.

Presumption. Insolent self-assertion.

Procacity. Shameless boldness.

Sauciness, etc. Impertinent boldness. See *Adjectives*.

Shamelessness, etc. The state of being insensible to disgrace. See *Adjectives*.

Swagger. An insolent carriage.

Swaggering, etc. Insolent conduct in public. See *Verbs*.

Terrorism. The act of overwhelming with fear.

Tyranny. Absolute power administered in an insolent and unjust manner. See HARSHNESS.

Usurpation. The act of assuming in an insolent and arrogant manner.

PRESUMPTION—*Denotations.*

Saucebox, etc. A saucy person. See BRAWLER.

Tag-tail. A hanger-on.

PRESUMPTION—*Verbs.*

Act the grand seigneur. To act in an imperious and overbearing manner.

Arrogate. To claim proudly and without reason.

Assume. To take upon oneself.

Assume a lofty bearing. To act in a supercilious manner.

Beard. To defy in an insolent manner; to take by the beard.

Bear down. To treat tyrannically.

Beat down. To suppress in a high-handed and overweening manner.

Be insolent, etc. To be saucy or impertinent. See *Adjectives*.

Bluster. To talk boisterously.

Brazen out. To act in a shameless manner.

Browbeat. To intimidate by blustering.

Bully. To intimidate by insolence and overbearing.

Carry with a high hand. To act overbearingly.

Abasement. The act of bringing low.

Fawning, etc. The act of seeking favor by cringing. See *Verbs*.

Flunkyism. Servile imitation.

Genuflection, etc. The act of bending the knee, especially in worship. See DEVOTION.

Humility, etc. The quality of being modest in regard to one's own worth. See SELFRESPECT-HUMBLENESS.

Obsequiousness, etc. The state of being meanly condescending. See *Adjectives*.

Prosternation. The state of being cast down.

Prostration. The act of bowing in humility.

Servility. The state of abject submission.

Slavery, etc. Entire subjection to another person's will. See LIBERTY-SUBJECTION.

Subserviency. The state of serving in a subordinate position.

Sycophancy, etc. Servile flattery. See ADULATION.

Time-serving. Obsequious compliance with the ruling powers.

Tuft-hunting. Courting persons of wealth or influence in a servile manner.

OBSEQUIOUSNESS—*Denotations.*

Âme damnée [F.]. One who does another's dirty work.

Carpet knight. A stay-at-home soldier.

Cavalier servant [F.]. A gallant acting the slave to his mistress.

Courtier. One who seeks to gain favors by flattery.

Doer of the dirty work. One who does low, base work for another.

Flatterer, etc. One who flatters, with the hope of gaining favor. See ADULATION.

Flunky. A servile imitator or flatterer.

Fortune-hunter. One who seeks to marry a fortune.

Græculus esuriens [L.]. The hungry Greekling.

Hanger-on. One who attaches himself to a person or place without being engaged.

Lap-dog. A person seeking to be fondled like a lap-dog.

Led-captain. A person under the influence or control of another.

Lick-spittle. A cringing or fawning person.

Parasite. An obsequious flatterer who lives lazily at another's expense.

Pick-thank. One who seeks the favor of others by officious attentions.

Reptile. A groveling, abject person.

Sir Pertinax Macsycophant. A pertinacious old sycophant, in Macklin's *Man of the World*.

Slave. A person in subjection to another, like the Slavs to the Germans.

Smell-feast. A person who looks for and frequents good tables.

Snob. A person who vulgarly affects gentility.

Spaniel. One who follows a person like a dog.

Sycophant. A cringing, servile flatterer.

Time-server. One who serves or adapts himself to the time in which he lives.

Toad. Figuratively, any person regarded as an object of scorn.

Toad-eater. A fawning parasite.

Toady. A fawning, servile person.

Tuft-hunter. One who courts persons of wealth or influence in a servile manner.

Vicar of Bray. A vicar of the village of Bray, England, who repeatedly changed his religion with the changes of government; hence, a political and religious trimmer.

OBSEQUIOUSNESS—*Verbs.*

Avaler les couleuvres [F.]. To put up with mortifications.

Bend the knee. To show humble submission.

PRESUMPTION—OBSEQUIOUSNESS—*Continued.*

PRESUMPTION—Verbs—*Continued.*

Dictate. To order in an imperious manner.
Domineer. To rule insolently.
Dragoon. To intimidate in an insolent manner.
Exact. To force to pay.
Fly in the face of. To defy boldly.
Give an inch and take an ell. To assume a great deal for oneself.
Give oneself airs. To act in an affected and arrogant manner
Hector. To domineer over in a bullying manner, like Hector in the Early English, rather than in Homer.
Huff. To offend.
Intimidate. To inspire with fear.
Kick up a dust. To talk in a boisterous and bullying manner.
Lay down the law. To dictate.
Look big. To assume an arrogant appearance.
Lord it over. To domineer.
Make bold.
Make free. } To take the liberty.
Mount the high horse. To act in an imperious manner.
Outbrave. To surpass in overbearing.
Outbrazen. To overcome with impudence.
Outface. To put out of countenance with bold looks.
Outlook. To browbeat.
Outstare. To overcome with effrontery in looking.
Presume. To act with assurance beyond all proper limits.
Put on big looks. To look affected.
Put to the blush. To act so as to make others blush.
Rap out oaths. To be profane in an insolent manner.
Regarder de haut en bas [F.]. To regard contemptuously.
Ride roughshod over. To pursue a selfish course regardless of consequences to others.
Ride the high horse. To act imperiously.
Roister. To act in a blustering manner.
Snap one's fingers. To treat with contempt.
Snub. To slight in a contemptuous manner.
Swagger. To conduct oneself in a boisterous manner.
Swear, etc. To express oneself in profane and insolent manner. See ASSERTION.
Swell. To expand with pride or wrath.
Take a liberty. To neglect the laws of courtesy.
Talk big. To bluster.
Teach one's grandmother to suck eggs. To show presumption towards people of more experience.
Tempt Providence. To act with great hardihood.
Toss the head. To express contempt.
Traiter de haut en bas [F.]. To treat with contempt.
Trample down. To treat with contempt and pride.
Trample under foot. To treat with scorn, pride, and contempt.
Tread down.
Tread under foot. } To despise.
Vapor. To talk arrogantly and with little meaning.
Want snuffing. To be so arrogant as to need to be put down.

PRESUMPTION—*Adjectives.*

Arbitrary. Having no control to limit one's own selfish desire.
Arrogant. Claiming for oneself proudly and without reason.
Assuming. Taking upon oneself without due cause.
Audacious. Displaying defiant boldness.
Aweless. Lacking reverential fear.
Barefaced. Shameless.
Bluff. Rough but kind in speech.
Blustering. Talking boisterously.
Boldfaced. Impudent.
Brazen. Of hardened impudence.
Brazen-faced. Excessively bold.
Bumptious. Self-conceited.
Cavalier. Slighting.
Contumelious. Expressing scornful insolence.
Dead to shame. Having lost all sense of shame from long association with evil.
Devil-may-care. Reckless.
Dictatorial. Given to speaking in an overbearing manner.
Domineering. Ruling insolently.
Fire-eating. Always desirous to fight.
Flippant. Frivolously insolent.
Forward. Too eager to display oneself.
Free and easy. Acting under no restraint.
"Full of sound and fury." Ferocious and boastful. " Told by an idiot, signifying nothing." [Shakespeare, *Macbeth*, V, v.]
Haughty. Disdainful and overbearingly proud.
Hectoring. Domineering over, as a bully. See *Verbs.*
High and mighty. Great and powerful in one's own opinion.

OBSEQUIOUSNESS—Verbs—*Continued.*

Bow. To bend the body as a mark of reverence.
Cower. To shrink from fear.
Crawl. To act in a servile manner.
Cringe. To bow with base humility.
Crouch. To act in a slavish manner.
Dance attendance on. To be obsequiously helpful.
Do the dirty work of. To do one's low, disagreeable work.
Fall on one's knees. To make a request in a servile manner.
Fatten on. To be a parasite of.
Fawn. To seek favor by cringing.
Feed on. To be a parasite of.
Fetch and carry. To do as another commands.
Go with the stream. To follow the majority.
Grovel. To act in an abject and mean manner.
Hang on the sleeve of. To fawn on continually.
Hold with the hare and hounds. To take the most popular course of action.
Keep time to. To curry favor by being helpful.
Kiss the hem of one's garment. To show the deepest humility and respect for a person.
Kneel. To bend the knee as a sign of humility.
Lick the feet of. To curry favor by extreme servility.
Pay court to. To try to gain the favor of by flattery.
Pin oneself upon. To pay close attention to a person in order to win favor.
Prostrate oneself. To lie down upon the ground in humility.
Sneak. To act with servility.
Stoop. To submit in a servile manner.
Truckle to. To yield in an obsequious manner.
Worship, etc. To honor with extreme submission. See DEVOTION.
Worship the rising sun. To bestow one's attentions upon a person beginning to succeed.

OBSEQUIOUSNESS—*Adjectives.*

Abject. In a servile condition.
Base. Low and untrustworthy in conduct towards others.
Beggarly. Miserably mean.
Cringing. Acting with base humility.
Crouching. See *Verbs.*
Down on one's marrow-bones. In an abject condition.
Fawning. Seeking favor by cringing.
Groveling. Acting in an abject and mean condition.
Mealy-mouthed. Speaking in a deferential and insincere manner.
Mean. Of an ignoble and hateful disposition.
Obsequious. Meanly condescending.
Oily. Deceitfully polite in speech and manners.
Parasitical. Gaining a living by fawning upon a person.
Pliant. Easily influenced.
Prostrate. Showing extreme humility.
Servile. Wanting independence.
Slavish. Like a slave.
Sneaking. Acting with servility.
Sniveling. Affecting tender emotions in a hypocritical manner.
Soapy. Flattering.
Supple. Compliant to the humors of others.
Supple as a glove. Glove fitting.
Sycophantic. Fawning and cringing.

OBSEQUIOUSNESS—*Adverbs.*

Cap in hand.
Hat in hand. } In a fawning manner.

PRESUMPTION—Adjectives—*Continued.*

High-flown. Excessively proud.
High-handed. Using violence to oppress.
Imperious. Commanding in an insolent manner.
Impertinent. Insolently presumptuous.
Impudent. Insolently bold.
Insolent. Haughty and contemptuous towards others.
Intolerant. Not enduring a difference of opinion.
Janty.
Jaunty. } Marked by an affected ease of manners.
Lost to shame. Having no sense of shame.
Magisterial. Showing authority in an overbearing manner.
Malapert. Bold and insolent.
Overbearing. Arrogant and domineering.
Overweening. Marked by presumptuous pride.
Pert. Insolently forward, malapert, sprightly.
Precocious. Too forward in displaying one's accomplishments.
Presumptuous. Insolently self-asserting.

PRESUMPTION—Adjectives—Continued.

Roistering.   Acting in a blustering manner.
Rollicking.   Acting in a careless, swaggering manner.
Saucy.   Impertinently bold, so as to give a sauce to his good wit.
Shameless.   Insensible to shame.
Supercilious.   Disdainful because of haughty pride; raising the eyebrows.
Swaggering.   Acting insolently in public.

Thrasonic.   Marked by insolent boasting, like Thraso, a braggart soldier in Terence's *Eunuch.*
Unabashed.   Not confused by shame.
Unblushing.   Having an insolent countenance.
Vaporing.   Boasting vainly.
Would be.   Pretending to be what one is not.

PRESUMPTION—Adverbs, etc.

Ex cathedra [L.].   With high authority.

With a high hand.   In an arbitrary and overweening manner.

PRESUMPTION—Phrases.

Homme de cour [F.].   Courtier.
One's bark being worse than one's bite.   Making idle threats.

Quid times? Cæsarem vehis [L.].   What do you fear? You carry Cæsar. To the sailors. [Plutarch, *Cæsar.* VII.]
Zapatero a tu zapato [Sp].   Shoemaker, mind thy shoe.

pre-sump'-tive.   Probable.   DUENESS-UNDUENESS, HYPOTHESIS, LIKELIHOOD-UNLIKELIHOOD; **heir presumptive,** HOLDER, PARENTAGE-PROGENY; **presumptive evidence,** EVIDENCE-COUNTEREVIDENCE, LIKELIHOOD-UNLIKELIHOOD.

pre-sump'-tu-ous.   Insolent.   PRESUMPTION-OBSEQUIOUSNESS.

pre"-sup-pose'.   Imply as a necessary condition.   DECISION-MISJUDGMENT, HYPOTHESIS.

pre"-sur-mise'.   Surmise previously formed.   HYPOTHESIS, PREVISION.

pre-tend'.   Simulate; allege untruly.   ASSERTION-DENIAL, TRUTHFULNESS-FALSEHOOD.

pre-tend'-ed.   Simulated.   TRUTHFULNESS-FRAUD.

pre-tend'-er.   Hypocrite; one who puts forth a false claim.   BRAGGING, DUENESS-UNDUENESS, GULL-DECEIVER.

pre-tend'-ing.   Simulating.   TRUTHFULNESS-FALSEHOOD.

pre-tense'.   Excuse; affectation; act of simulation.   BRAGGING, POMP, PRETEXT, TRUTHFULNESS-FABRICATION, TRUTHFULNESS-FALSEHOOD.

pre-ten'-sion.   Claim as to right, dignity, possession; affectation.   AFFECTATION, DUENESS-UNDUENESS, SIMPLICITY-FLORIDNESS, SOCIETY-AFFECTATION.

pre-ten'-sions.   Claims.   BRAGGING, CONCEIT-DIFFIDENCE, POMP.

pre-ten'-tious.   Affected; ostentatious.   BRAGGING, CONCEIT-DIFFIDENCE, DUENESS-UNDUENESS, SENSITIVENESS-APATHY, SOCIETY-AFFECTATION.

pret"-er-i'-tion.   Act of passing over.   FUTURE-PAST.

pre"-ter-lapsed'.   Past and gone.   FUTURE-PAST.

pre"-ter-mit'.   Neglect the doing of.   CAREFULNESS-CARELESSNESS.

pre"-ter-nat'-u-ral.   Extraordinary.   CONVENTIONALITY-UNCONVENTIONALITY.

pre"-ter-per'-fect.   Preterit.   FUTURE-PAST.

pre"-ter-plu'-per"-fect.   Past pluperfect.   FUTURE-PAST.

pre'-text   Excuse.   PRETEXT, TRUTHFULNESS-FABRICATION.

PRETEXT.

Advocation.   The act of pleading; a plea.
Allegation.   A formal averment or affirmation.
Blind.   Something intended to conceal an ulterior purpose.
Cheval de bataille [F.].   A war-horse; a main reliance.
Color.   In law, an apparent right.
Come-off.   An evasion or excuse.
Cue.   A hint or suggestion.
Dust thrown in the eyes.   Anything intended to conceal the true actions or intentions.
Excuse, etc.   A plea offered in extenuation of a fault, etc.   See JUSTIFICATION.
False plea.   A plea intended to deceive.
Gloss.   A false explanation.
Guise.   External appearance.
Handle.   The instrument or occasion for effecting a purpose.
How to creep out of.   Any means of escape.

Lame apology.   An apology not strong or efficient.
Lame excuse.   An insufficient excuse.
Locus standi [L.].   Standing place.   [Gr. *pou sto.*]
Loophole.   A means of escape.
Makeshift.   A temporary contrivance in an emergency.
Mere pretext.   An excuse.
Moonshine.   Empty nonsense.
Ostensible ground.
Ostensible motive. } The apparent ground or reason for an action.
Ostensible reason.
Peg to hang on.   A reason or excuse for an action.
Plea.   Something alleged in defense or justification.
Pretense.   That which is pretended as a motive or excuse.   See TRUTHFULNESS-FABRICATION.
Pretext.   An apparent reason assigned as a cover for the real reason or motive.
Put off.   An evasion or excuse.
Room.   Warrantable occasion.
Salvo.   A saving clause.
Shallow pretext.   A poor excuse.
Shift.   A dodge or trick.
Soft-sawder.   Flattery.   See ADULATION.
Sour grapes.   That which a person, like the fox in the fable, affects to despise because it is beyond his attainment.
Special pleading.   A plea, which, while admitting the plaintiff's allegations, avoids them by setting up new matter.
Stalking-horse.   A horse behind which a hunter conceals himself while stalking game; hence, anything serving to conceal the real intention.
Starting-hole.   Means of evasion.
Tub to a whale.   A trivial concession.
White lie.   A false statement made without intention of malice.

PRETEXT—Verbs.

Allege.   To urge as a plea or excuse.
Excuse, etc.   To justify by extenuating a fault, etc.   See JUSTIFICATION.
Furnish a handle.   To give an occasion or means.
Lend a color to.   To have the appearance of being true.   See *Nouns.*
Make a handle of.   To use to one's advantage.   See *Nouns.*
Make a pretext.   To give an excuse.   See *Nouns.*
Make capital out of.   To make a big thing out of something trivial.
Plead.   To adduce in proof or vindication.
Pretend, etc.   To hold out falsely, etc.   See TRUTHFULNESS-FALSEHOOD.
Shelter oneself under the plea of.   To give excuse for.
Take one's stand upon.   To rely upon.
Use as a plea.   To attempt to justify oneself by   See *Nouns.*

PRETEXT—Adjectives

Alleged.   Asserted to be true.   See *Verbs*
Apologetic.   Said or written in defense of.
Ostensible, etc.   Avowed; apparent, etc.   See MANIFESTATION.
Pretended, etc.   Making a false appearance, etc.   See TRUTHFULNESS-FRAUD.

PRETEXT—Adverbs, etc.

Ostensibly.   Seemingly.   See *Adjectives.*
Under color of.   Under the appearance of.   See *Nouns.*
Under the plea of.
Under the pretense of. } With that excuse.

pret'-ty.   Tolerable; beautiful.   BEAUTY-UGLINESS, FAULTLESSNESS-FAULTINESS, MAGNITUDE-SMALLNESS; **pretty fellow,** SAGE-FOOL; **pretty good,** FAULT-

LESSNESS-FAULTINESS; **pretty kettle of fish,** DIFFI-CULTY-FACILITY, REGULARITY-IRREGULARITY; **pretty pass,** etc., DIFFICULTY-FACILITY; **pretty well,** CONSE-QUENCE - INSIGNIFICANCE, FAULTLESSNESS - FAULTI-NESS, MAGNITUDE-SMALLNESS.

preux chevalier [F.] (prʋ she-va-liê'). A brave knight. UPRIGHTNESS-DISHONESTY.

pre-vail'. Triumph; be predominant. DOMINANCE-IMPOTENCE, ENTITY-NONENTITY, HABIT-DESUETUDE, SUCCESS-FAILURE, SUPREMACY-SUBORDINACY, UNI-VERSALITY-PARTICULARITY; **prevail upon,** MOTIVE-CAPRICE.

pre-vail'-ing. Widely extended. DOMINANCE-IMPO-TENCE, UNIVERSALITY-PARTICULARITY; **prevailing taste,** SOCIETY-LUDICROUSNESS.

prev'-a-lence. Common occurrence; dominance. DOMINANCE-IMPOTENCE, ENTITY-NONENTITY, HABIT-DESUETUDE, SUCCESS-FAILURE, SUPREMACY-SUBOR-DINACY, UNIVERSALITY-PARTICULARITY.

prev'-a-lent. Predominant. DOMINANCE-IMPOTENCE, UNIVERSALITY-PARTICULARITY.

pre-var'-i-cate. Quibble. HABIT-DESUETUDE, TRUTH-FULNESS-FALSEHOOD.

pre-var''-i-ca'-tion. A lie. TRUTHFULNESS-FALSEHOOD.

prévenance [F]. (prêv-nans'). Kindness. POLITENESS-IMPOLITENESS.

pre-ve'-nient. Preceding. EARLINESS-LATENESS, PRE-CEDENCE-SUCCESSION.

pre-vent'. To stop. OBSTRUCTION-HELP.

pre-ven'-tion. Obstruction; prejudice. DECISION-MIS-JUDGMENT, OBSTRUCTION-HELP; **prevention of waste,** GENEROSITY-FRUGALITY.

pre-ven'-tive. An obstacle. OBSTRUCTION-HELP.

pre'-vi-ous. Antecedent. ANTECEDENCE-SEQUENCE; **move the previous question,** QUEST-ABANDONMENT; **not within previous experience,** FREQUENCY-RARITY.

pre'-vi-ous-ly. Beforehand. ANTECEDENCE-SEQUENCE.

pre-vi'-sion. Foresight. PREVISION.

PREVISION.

Anticipation. Taking into the mind as a conception of the future.
Forecast. A calculation regarding the future.
Foregone conclusion. Only possible outcome.
Foreknowledge. Knowledge of an event before it happens.
Foresight. Ability to provide for contingencies.
Foretaste. Enjoyment by anticipation.
Forethought. Provident care.
Longsightedness. Ability to see far ahead.
Precognition. Previous knowledge.
Predeliberation. Deliberation beforehand.
Prenotion. Notion without slightest basis of fact.
Prescience. Foreknowledge.
Presentiment. Prophetic apprehension of something future.
Presurmise. Surmise with but slight basis of fact.
Prevision. Prophetic discernment.
Prognosis. Prediction as to future course of a disease.
Prospect. What the future seems to have in store.
Prospectus. Paper containing information of a proposed work.
Prospicience. Habit of looking forward.
Providence. Foresight and care for the future.
Prudence. Exercise of caution and provision.
Sagacity. Power of ready, accurate, and far-reaching inference from observed facts.
Second sight. Superstitious power of seeing future events.

PREVISION—*Verbs.*

Anticipate. To take into the mind as a conception of the future.
Avise le fin [F.]. Weigh well the end.
Be beforehand. Be previous in time.
Expect. To await with confidence.
Forecast. To calculate regarding the future.
Forejudge. To judge before hearing the facts and arguments.
Foreknow. To know beforehand.
Foresee. To know the future from present indications.
Forewarn. To warn beforehand.
Have an eye to the future. } To be watchful and provident.
Have an eye to the main chance. }
Keep a sharp lookout. To look ahead carefully.
Look. }
Look ahead. }
Look beyond. } To exercise foresight.
Look forward to. }
Look into the future. }
Peep into the future. To foresee.
Predict. To tell beforehand.
Presurmise. To hold an opinion from the most fanciful grounds.
Pry into the future. To use prophetic vision.
Respicere finem [L.]. To regard the end.
Scent from afar. To foresee.
See how the cat jumps. To watch how events turn.
See how the land lies. To learn the state of affairs.
See how the wind blows. To watch the tendencies of a movement.
See one's way. To foresee a course of action.

PREVISION—*Adjectives.*

Farseeing. }
Farsighted. } Having foresight.
Foreseeing. }
Prescient. Foreknowing.
Prospective. Looking to the future.
Provident. Exercising foresight.
Sagacious. Able to discern and distinguish with wise perception.
Weather-wise. Experienced in making predictions as to coming weather.

PREVISION—*Adverbs, etc.*

Against the time when.

PREVISION—*Phrases.*

Cernit omnia Deus vindex [L.]. The avenging divinity sees all.
Mihi cura futuri [L.]. My care is for the future.

pre-warn'. Forewarn. WARNING.

prey. Booty; victim. NUTRIMENT-EXCRETION, PLEAS-URE-PAIN, PLUNDER, PURPOSE-LUCK; **fall a prey to,** GOOD MAN-BAD MAN, SUCCESS-FAILURE; **prey on the mind,** CONTENTEDNESS-REGRET, EXCITATION, LIGHT-HEARTEDNESS-DEJECTION, PLEASURABLENESS-PAIN-FULNESS, SANGUINENESS-TIMIDITY; **prey on the spirits,** LIGHTHEARTEDNESS-DEJECTION; **prey to grief,** PLEASURE-PAIN; **prey to melancholy,** LIGHTHEARTED-NESS-DEJECTION.

price. Valuation. COMMUTATION-PERMUTATION, GOOD-NESS-BADNESS, PRICE-DISCOUNT; **at any price,** PER-SISTENCE-WHIM, READINESS-RELUCTANCE; **beyond price,** COSTLINESS-CHEAPNESS; **cheap at the price,** COSTLINESS-CHEAPNESS; **have one's price,** PRICE-DIS-COUNT; **of great price,** COSTLINESS-CHEAPNESS, GOOD-NESS-BADNESS.

PRICE—DISCOUNT.

Amount. The sum total.
Appraisement. An official valuation.
Assessment. A valuation of property for taxation; the amount so valued.
Benevolence. In English history, a compulsory tax illegally exacted under the guise of a gift.
Bill. A statement of an account or of money due. See ACCOUNTS.
Brokerage. A broker's charges for services.
Cess. A tax.
Charge. The price demanded for a commodity.

Abatement. A reduction from the original amount or demand.
Agio. A discount from bank-notes over current coin; money paid for changing one kind of money into another.
Allowance. A deduction; deviation from the price.
Backwardation. A premium paid by a seller to a [buyer for the privilege of holding back the delivery of his goods.
Contango. Premium paid by buyer to seller for the privilege of with-holding payment for a certain time.
Depreciation. A falling in value or price.
Discount. Amount deducted from a debt, etc.

PRICE—DISCOUNT—*Continued.*

Cost. The amount paid.
Custom. A duty established by law.
Damages. Compensation for injury done.
Demand. That which is demanded; a requirement.
Dues. That which is owed.
Duty. Tax or custom assessed by the government.
Exactments. That which is required of right.
Excise. A duty on goods.
Expense. That which is expended or paid out.
Fare. Money paid for carrying passengers.
Figure. Amount; price.
Freightage. Amount paid for carrying freight.
Gabel. Rent; service; tax.
Gabelle. A tax on salt.
Gavel. Tribute.
Groundage. Charge made for the space occupied by a ship in port.
Hire. Compensation paid for labor or for use of another's property.
Impost. A tax or duty.
Levy. That which is taken by a levy.
Market price. Its price in an open market.
Money's worth. Value received for the money one gives.
Octroi. A tax levied on goods brought within the walls of a city.
Pennyworth. As much as is sold for a penny.
Price. Any equivalent given in exchange; value.
Price-current. A statement of the price of stocks, merchandise. etc., or the price itself.
Prime cost. The very first cost.
Quotation. Price-current.
Ransom. Compensation paid to a captor for release of a prisoner.
Rate. Established portion or valuation.
Salvage. Compensation allowed for saving a vessel.
Sess. A tax.
Shot. A reckoning or charge.
Tailage. To tax or make a levy upon.
Tallage. Tax paid by knights, barons, etc., toward public expenses.
Tariff. A duty; money paid for exportation or importation of merchandise.
Tax. Money levied for public services.
Taxation. A levy by the government on persons, business, and property under its direction.
Tenths. A tax of one-tenth.
Tithe. A tax of one-tenth for support of the clergy.
Toll. A fixed charge paid for some privilege; a miller's compensation for grinding grain.
Valuation. Calculated worth.
Value. Power in exchange.
Wages. Compensation paid to hired labor. See RECOMPENSE.
Wharfage. Consideration paid for use of wharf.
What it will fetch. The selling price of an article.
Worth. That which makes it desirable; value.

PRICE—*Verbs.*

Afford. To be able to expend.
Amount to. To result in the aggregate.
Appraise. To make an official valuation.
Ask. To demand; claim.
Assess. To fix the amount of tax to be paid.
Bear a price. To be worth a certain amount.
Bring in. To fetch so much; have exchange value.
Charge. To put on a price and demand it.
Come to. To amount to.
Cost. To require to be given in exchange.
Demand. To require; ask for.

Drawback. A rebate.
Percentage. The allowance, or duty, on a hundred.
Poundage. A subsidy to the crown on the pounds of merchandise.
Qualification. A limitation; an abatement.
Rebate. Any deduction from the aggregate sum.
Rebatement. The act of rebating.
Reduction. Diminishing in value, price, size, etc.
Salvage. Amount paid for saving a vessel or its cargo.
Set-off. An equivalent compens tion; a rebate.
Tare and tret. Allowance to purchasers of waste in merchandise.

DISCOUNT—*Verbs.*

Abate. To lessen in number; decrease.
Allow. To make an abatement or deduction.
Bate. To strike off; abate.
Discount. To deduct; make an abatement of.
Give. To hand over to another.
Make allowance. To deduct.
Rebate. To make an allowance.
Reduce. To lessen in the amount.
Take off. To reduce in price.
Tax. To fix the amount that is to be paid.

DISCOUNT—*Adjective.*

Discounting. Deducting from the sum owing or to be paid See *Verbs.*

DISCOUNT—*Adverbs, etc.*

At a discount. At a reduction.
Below par. Below nominal value.

PRICE—VERBS—*Continued.*

Distrain. To take or seize in security for debt.
Exact. To force the payment of; require with authority.
Fetch. To bring, as a price.
Fix a price. To determine the value of.
Have one's price.⎱ To be the sum total of.
Mount up to.⎰
Price To set a price upon; ask the price of.
Require. To demand as a condition to possession.
Run up. To amount to.
Run up a bill. To buy on credit. See CREDIT-DEBT.
Sell for. To bring a certain price
Set a price. To determine worth or value.
Stand one in. To bring in.
Yield. To give in return for labor applied.

PRICE—*Adjectives.*

Ad valorem [L.]. A duty charged upon goods according to value at a certain percentum.
Mercenary. Serving for pay.
Priced. Having the price fixed. See *Verbs.*
To the tune of. At that price.
Venal. Capable of being bought; purchasable.

PRICE—*Phrases.*

À bon marche [F.]. At a good bargain.
No longer pipe, no longer dance.
No penny, no paternoster.
No song, no supper.
One may have it for.
Point d'argent, point de Suisse [F.]. No silver, no Swiss

---

priced. Having a price. PRICE-DISCOUNT.
price′-cur″-rent. Statement of the ruling price of stocks, merchandise, or other property. PRICE-DISCOUNT.
price′-less. Invaluable. COSTLINESS - CHEAPNESS, GOODNESS-BADNESS, USEFULNESS-USELESSNESS.
prick. Pierce slightly; mental sting. APERTURE-CLOSURE, MOTIVE-CAPRICE, PLEASURABLENESS-PAINFULNESS, SENSUALITY-SUFFERING, SHARPNESS-BLUNTNESS, TINGLING-NUMBNESS; **kick against the pricks,** REPRISAL-RESISTANCE, USEFULNESS-USELESSNESS; **prick up one's ears,** EXPECTATION-SURPRISE, HEARING-DEAFNESS, HEED-DISREGARD, INQUISITIVENESS-INDIFFERENCE.
prick′-le. Puncture slightly; give a tingling sensation

to. SHARPNESS-BLUNTNESS, TINGLING-NUMBNESS.
prick′-ly. Stinging. SHARPNESS-BLUNTNESS, SMOOTHNESS-ROUGHNESS.
pride. Unreasonable conceit; ornament. CONCEIT-DIFFIDENCE, EMBELLISHMENT - DISFIGUREMENT, SELFRESPECT-HUMBLENESS; **take a pride in,** SELFRESPECT-HUMBLENESS.
priest. One consecrated to the service of a divinity. MINISTRY-LAITY.
priest′-craft″. Policy of a priesthood. CHURCH.
priest′-hood. The priestly office or character. CHURCH, MINISTRY-LAITY.
priest′-ly. Sacerdotal. CHURCH.
Priest′-ly. Noted chemist. **Priestly's apparatus,** CHEMISTRY.

priest'-rid"-den. Completely dominated by priests. CHURCH, GODLINESS-UNGODLINESS.

prig. Pedant; steal. BRAWLER, SOCIETY-AFFECTATION, SOCIETY-DANDY, STEALING.

prig'-gish. Conceited; affected. CONCEIT-DIFFIDENCE, SOCIETY-AFFECTATION.

prig'-gish-ness. Conceit. CONCEIT-DIFFIDENCE.

prig'-gism. Pedantry. CONCEIT-DIFFIDENCE.

prim. Stiffly proper. SELFRESPECT-HUMBLENESS, SOCIETY-AFFECTATION.

prima donna [It.] (prī'-ma don'-a). A leading female singer. ACTING, ADEPT-BUNGLER, CONSEQUENCE-INSIGNIFICANCE.

pri'-ma-cy. State of being first in rank. CHURCH, REPUTATION-DISCREDIT.

prima facie [L.] (prai'-ma fê'-shi-î). At first view. APPEARANCE-DISAPPEARANCE, LIKELIHOOD-UNLIKELIHOOD, MANIFESTATION-LATENCY, MEANING-JARGON, SIGHT-BLINDNESS.

pri'-ma-ry. Original. CAUSE-EFFECT, CONSEQUENCE-INSIGNIFICANCE; **primary color,** COLOR-ACHROMATISM; **primary education,** EDUCATION-MISTEACHING; **primary school,** SCHOOL.

pri'-mate. One exercising special jurisdiction over the bishops in a province. MINISTRY-LAITY.

pri'-mates. Persons highest in rank. GENTILITY-COMMONALTY.

prime. First in rank, dignity, or importance. CONSEQUENCE-INSIGNIFICANCE, EARLINESS-LATENESS, EDUCATION-MISTEACHING, GOODNESS-BADNESS, MORNING-EVENING, NOVELTY-ANTIQUITY, NUMBER, PREPARATION-NONPREPARATION; **in one's prime,** MANHOOD; **prime and load,** PREPARATION-NONPREPARATION; **prime cost,** COSTLINESS-CHEAPNESS, OUTLAY-INCOME, PRICE-DISCOUNT; **prime minister,** MANAGER; **prime mover,** CAUSE-EFFECT; **prime number,** NUMBER; **prime of life,** INFANCY-AGE, MANHOOD; **prime of the morning,** MORNING-EVENING; **prime vertical,** ASTRONOMY.

primed. Exhilarated by drink; skilled. SKILL-UNSKILFULNESS, TEETOTALISM-INTEMPERANCE.

prim'-er. An elementary reading-book. SCHOOL.

pri-me'-val. Belonging to the first ages. NOVELTY-ANTIQUITY.

pri-mig'-e-nous. First-formed. BEGINNING-END, NOVELTY-ANTIQUITY.

pri'-ming. A combustible used to ignite a charge of powder; the first layer of color. PAINTING, WEAPON.

prim'-i-tive. Earliest. CAUSE-EFFECT, NOVELTY-ANTIQUITY; **primitive color,** COLOR-ACHROMATISM.

pri"-mo-ge'-ni-al. Primal. BEGINNING-END.

pri"-mo-gen'-i-ture. Seniority by birth. INFANCY-AGE, NOVELTY-ANTIQUITY, PARENTAGE-PROGENY.

pri-mor'-di-al. First in order. CAUSE-EFFECT, NOVELTY-ANTIQUITY.

pri-mor'-di-ate. Original. NOVELTY-ANTIQUITY.

prim'-rose-col"-ored. Of the color of the primrose. YELLOWNESS-PURPLE.

primum mobile [L.] (prai'-mum mob'-i-lî). Any original source of motion, power, or action. CAUSE-EFFECT, MOTIVE-CAPRICE.

primus inter pares [L.] (prai'-mus in'-ter pê-rîz). First among his peers. SUPREMACY-SUBORDINACY.

prince. A male monarch; a leader. CHIEF-UNDERLING, FAULTLESSNESS-FAULTINESS, GENTILITY-COMMONALTY; **prince of darkness,** ANGEL-SATAN.

prince'-kin. A little or low prince. CHIEF-UNDERLING.

prince'-ly. Like a prince. GENEROSITY-FRUGALITY, GENTILITY-COMMONALTY, REPUTATION-DISCREDIT, RULE-LICENSE, UNSELFISHNESS-SELFISHNESS.

prin'-cess. One of the female members of a royal family. CHIEF-UNDERLING, GENTILITY-COMMONALTY.

prin'-ci-pal. First in importance; director. CONSEQUENCE-INSIGNIFICANCE, MANAGER, PRESIDENT-MEMBER; **principal part,** MAGNITUDE-SMALLNESS, WHOLE-PART.

prin"-ci-pal'-i-ty. Territory of a reigning prince. EXTENSION-INEXTENSION, PROPERTY.

prin-cip'-i-a. First principles. ADAGE-NONSENSE.

principiis obstare [L.] (prin-sip'-i-is ob-stê'-rî). Resist the first beginnings. PREPARATION-NONPREPARATION.

principio, la mitad es hecha, buen [Sp.] (prin-thi'-pî-o, la mî-tad' es ê-tcha', bu-en'). Well begun is half done. TOIL-RELAXATION.

prin'-ci-ple. Source; general truth; settled law; motive. ADAGE-NONSENSE, CAUSE-EFFECT, FAITH-MISGIVING, MATERIALITY-SPIRITUALITY, MOTIVE-CAPRICE, RATIOCINATION-INSTINCT, SUBJECTIVENESS-OBJECTIVENESS, UNIFORMITY-MULTIFORMITY, UPRIGHTNESS-DISHONESTY; **on principle,** MOTIVE-CAPRICE; **want of principle,** VIRTUE-VICE.

prink. Arrange with nicety. EMBELLISHMENT-DISFIGUREMENT, POMP.

print. Impression from type; a printed picture design. ENGRAVING, SIGN, WRITING-PRINTING; **out of print,** MARK-OBLITERATION.

print'-ed. Impressed. WRITING-PRINTING.

print'-er. One engaged in printing. WRITING-PRINTING; **printer's bundle,** MEASURE; **printer's quire,** MEASURE; **printer's ream,** MEASURE.

print'-ing. Art of making and issuing matter for reading, by means of type and the printing-press. WRITING-PRINTING.

pri'-or. Preceding in time, order, or importance; a monastic officer. ANTECEDENCE-SEQUENCE, FUTURE-PAST, MINISTRY-LAITY, PRECEDENCE-SUCCESSION.

pri'-or-ess. A nun. CHURCH.

pri'-ori reas'-on-ing, a. Presumptive reasoning. RATIOCINATION-INSTINCT.

pri-or'-i-ty. Antecedence. ADVANCE-RETROGRESSION, ANTECEDENCE-SEQUENCE, PRECEDENCE-SUCCESSION.

prior tempore, prior jure [L.] (prai'-or tem'-po-rî, prai'-or ju'-rî). First in time, first in right; "first come, first served." ANTECEDENCE-SEQUENCE, PRECEDENCE-SUCCESSION.

pri'-or-y. A monastic house presided over by a prior. FANE.

Pris'-cian's head, break. Make a bad blunder in grammar. GRAMMAR-SOLECISM.

prism. A solid whose bases are any similar, equal, and parallel plane figures, and whose lateral faces are parallelograms. ANGULARITY, COLOR-ACHROMATISM, MINERALOGY, OPTICAL INSTRUMENTS; **see through a prism,** SIGHT-DIMSIGHTEDNESS.

pris-mat'-ic. Resembling the spectrum. COLOR-ACHROMATISM, VARIEGATION.

pris'-on. A place of confinement. ENCLOSURE, RELEASE-PRISON, SECURITY-INSECURITY; **cast into prison,** RELEASE-RESTRAINT; **in prison,** GUARD-PRISONER.

pris'-on-er. One held in custody. GUARD-PRISONER, JUSTIFICATION-CHARGE, RELEASE-RESTRAINT; **take prisoner,** RELEASE-RESTRAINT, TAKING-RESTITUTION.

pris'-on-house, se'-crets of the. EXPOSURE - HIDING-PLACE, TIDINGS-MYSTERY.

pris'-tine. Primitive. FUTURE-PAST.

prith'-ee. I pray thee. PETITION-EXPOSTULATION.

prit'-tle-prat"-tle. Idle talk. CONVERSATION-MONOLOGUE.

pri'-va-cy. A secluded state. ENLIGHTENMENT-SECRECY, SOCIABILITY-PRIVACY.

pri'-vate. Retired. BELLIGERENT, ENLIGHTENMENT-SECRECY, SOCIABILITY-PRIVACY, UNIVERSALITY-PARTICULARITY; **in private,** ENLIGHTENMENT-SECRECY; **keep private,** CONCEIT-DIFFIDENCE; **private road,** WAY; **private soldier,** BELLIGERENT; **talk to in**

private, ADDRESS-RESPONSE, CONVERSATION-MONO-LOGUE; **to gain some private ends,** UNSELFISHNESS-SELFISHNESS.

pri″-va-teer′. One who engages in privateering. BELLIGERENT, ROBBER.

pri″-va-teer′-ing. Act of committing hostilities in a privateer. THEFT.

pri′-vate-ly. In a private or secret manner. CONCEIT-DIFFIDENCE.

pri-va′-tion. Want of the common comforts of life; deprivation. AFFLUENCE-PENURY, GAIN-LOSS.

priv′-a-tive. Depriving. TAKING-RESTITUTION.

priv′-i-lege. Peculiar benefit, favor, or advantage. DUENESS-UNDUENESS, LEAVE-PROHIBITION.

priv′-i-leged. Favored. DUENESS-UNDUENESS; **privileged question,** PRESIDENT-MEMBER.

priv′-i-ty. Private knowledge. KNOWLEDGE-IGNORANCE.

priv′-y. Privately knowing; latrines. CLEANNESS-FILTHINESS, ENLIGHTENMENT-SECRECY; **privy cabinet,** COUNCIL; **privy council,** COUNCIL; **privy to,** KNOWLEDGE-IGNORANCE.

prize. Reward for excellence or success; place value on. APPROVAL-DISAPPROVAL, GAIN-LOSS, GOOD-EVIL, LOVE-HATE, PLUNDER, SUCCESS-FAILURE, TRIBUNAL, TROPHY; **win the prize,** SUCCESS-FAILURE.

pri′-zer. A competitor. PETITIONER.

prize′-fight″-er. Pugilist. BELLIGERENT.

prize′-fight″-ing. The sport of engaging in prize-fights. STRIFE-PEACE.

prize′-man. A prize-winner. ADEPT-BUNGLER.

pro. and con. For and against. MOTIVE-CAPRICE, RATIOCINATION-INSTINCT.

pro forma [L.] (pro for′-ma). For the sake of form. CONVENTIONALITY-UNCONVENTIONALITY.

pro hac vice [L.] (pro hac vai′-si). For this turn. FREQUENCY-RARITY, OPPORTUNENESS-UNSUITABLENESS, TIME, UNIVERSALITY-PARTICULARITY.

pro re nata [L.] (pro rî nê′-ta). For a special emergency. CONDITION-SITUATION, CONNECTION-INDEPENDENCE, OPPORTUNENESS-UNSUITABLENESS, TERMS, UNIVERSALITY-PARTICULARITY.

pro tanto [L.] (pro tan′-to). For so much. MAGNITUDE-SMALLNESS, QUANTITY-MEASURE.

pro tempore [L.] (pro tem′-por-î). For the time being. LASTINGNESS-TRANSIENTNESS.

pro′-a. A swift Malaysian vessel. CONVEYANCE-VESSEL.

prob″-a-bil′-i-ty. Likelihood. LIKELIHOOD-UNLIKELIHOOD, RATIONALE-LUCK.

prob′-a-ble. Likely. FAITH-UNBELIEF, SANGUINE-NESS-HOPELESSNESS.

prob′-a-bly. In all likelihood. LIKELIHOOD-UNLIKELIHOOD.

pro′-bate. Formal, official, legal proof. SECURITY.

pro′-bate, court of. A court having jurisdiction of the proof of wills, etc. TRIBUNAL.

pro-ba′-tion. Trial. PROOF-DISPROOF, TRIAL, VENTURE.

pro-ba′-tion-a-ry. Serving for trial. TRIAL, VENTURE.

pro-ba′-tion-er. One who is on trial. INSTRUCTOR-PUPIL.

pro′-ba-tive. Proving. PROOF-DISPROOF.

pro′-ba-to-ry. Serving for proof. TRIAL.

probatum, est [L.] (pro-bê′-tum, est). It is proved. APPROVAL-DISAPPROVAL, PROOF-DISPROOF.

probe. Search through and through; a smooth, slender rod, used for exploring cavities. DEEPNESS-SHALLOWNESS, INVESTIGATION-ANSWER, MENSURATION, PERFORATOR-STOPPER.

probitas laudatur, et alget [L.] (prob′-it-as lau-dê′-tur, et al′-jet). Integrity is praised, and freezes. UPRIGHTNESS-DISHONESTY.

prob′-i-ty. Integrity. TRUTHFULNESS-FALSEHOOD, UPRIGHTNESS-DISHONESTY.

prob′-lem. A question for solution. CONCEPTION-THEME, INVESTIGATION-ANSWER, TIDINGS-MYSTERY.

prob″-lem-at′-ic-al. Constituting or involving an unsettled problem. CERTAINTY-DOUBT.

pro-bos′-cis. A prolonged, flexible snout. CONVEXITY-CONCAVITY.

pro-cac′-i-ty. Impudence. FAVORITE-QUARRELSOME-NESS, POLITENESS-IMPOLITENESS, PRESUMPTION-OBSEQUIOUSNESS.

pro-ce′-dure. Manner of proceeding. ACTION-PASSIVENESS, CONDUCT, WAY.

pro-ceed′. Go on or forward. ADVANCE-RETROGRESSION, PERIOD-PROGRESS; **proceed from,** CAUSE-EFFECT; **proceed with,** CONDUCT.

pro-ceed′-ing. Act or course of action. ACTION-PASSIVENESS, COMPLETION-NONCOMPLETION, ENTIRETY-DEFICIENCY, OCCURRENCE-DESTINY; **course of proceeding,** CONDUCT.

pro-ceed′-ings of. Records of. MARK-OBLITERATION.

pro′-ceeds. Material results of an action or course. GAIN-LOSS, MONEY, OUTLAY-INCOME.

pro-cer′-i-ty. Tallness. HEIGHT-LOWNESS.

proc′-ess. A systematic series of actions; an accessory outgrowth. CONDUCT, CONVEXITY-CONCAVITY; **in process of time,** ANTECEDENCE-SEQUENCE; **legal process,** LAW-LAWLESSNESS; **process of time,** PERIOD-PROGRESS.

pro-ces′-sion. Act of proceeding; an array. CONTINUITY-INTERRUPTION, POMP, TRAVELING-NAVIGATION.

pro-ces′-sion-al. Hymn sung during a religious procession. CEREMONIAL.

procès verbal [F.] (pro″-sê′ ver″-bal′). Detailed statement relating to the commission of a crime. LITIGATION, MARK-OBLITERATION.

pro′-chro-nism. Antedating. CHRONOLOGY-ANACHRONISM.

pro-claim′. Publish with authority. PUBLICITY.

proc″-la-ma′-tion. A formal declaration. PUBLICITY.

pro-cliv′-i-ty. Propensity. AFFECTIONS, INCLINATION.

pro-con′-sul. A Roman official. REPRESENTATIVE.

pro-con′-sul-ship. Office of a proconsul. RULE-LICENSE.

pro-cras′-ti-nate. To put off. EARLINESS-LATENESS.

pro-cras′-ti-na′-tion. Dilatoriness. ACTIVITY-INDOLENCE, EARLINESS-LATENESS.

pro′-cre-ant. Productive. FERTILITY-STERILITY.

pro′-cre-ate. Produce by generating. CREATION-DESTRUCTION, FERTILITY-STERILITY.

pro″-cre-a′-tion. Generation. CREATION-DESTRUCTION, FERTILITY-STERILITY.

pro′-cre-a″-tive. Tending to generate. FERTILITY-STERILITY.

pro′-cre-a″-tor. One who begets. PARENTAGE-PROGENY.

pro-crus′-te-an. Ruthlessly forcing into conformity. CONVENTIONALITY-UNCONVENTIONALITY; **procrustean law,** UNIFORMITY-MULTIFORMITY.

Pro-crus′-tes. A legendary Greek robber. **Stretch on the bed of Procrustes,** EQUALITY-INEQUALITY.

proc′-tor. An agent acting for another; attorney. ADVOCATE, CONSIGNEE, MANAGER.

proc′-tor-ship. Office of a proctor. MANAGEMENT.

pro-cum′-bent. Lying flat on the ground. ERECT-NESS-FLATNESS.

proc″-u-ra′-tion. The act of procuring. COMMISSION-ABROGATION, GAIN-LOSS.

proc′-u-ra″-tor. One authorized to manage the affairs of another. MANAGER.

pro-cure′. Obtain. BUYING-SALE, CAUSE-EFFECT, GAIN-LOSS, MOTIVE-CAPRICE.

pro-cure′-ment. Obtainment. GAIN-LOSS.

pro-cur'-ess. Bawd. PURITY-RAKE.

prod. Goad. IMPETUS-REACTION.

prod'-i-gal. Wasteful. EXCESS-LACK, EXTRAVAGANCE-AVARICE, GOOD MAN-BAD MAN.

prod''-i-gal'-i-ty. Wastefulness. EXTRAVAGANCE-AVARICE, PROVISION-WASTE.

prod'-i-gence. Waste. EXTRAVAGANCE-AVARICE.

pro-dig'-ious. Immense. ASTONISHMENT-EXPECTANCE, MAGNITUDE-SMALLNESS.

prod'-i-gy. A person or thing of very remarkable gifts. CONVENTIONALITY-UNCONVENTIONALITY, PHENOMENON, POSSIBILITY-IMPOSSIBILITY; **prodigy of learning,** ADEPT-BUNGLER.

pro-di'-tion. Betrayal. UPRIGHTNESS-DISHONESTY.

pro'-drome. Forerunner. PREDECESSOR-CONTINUATION.

prodromos [Gr.] (prod'-ro-mos). Forerunner. PREDECESSOR-CONTINUATION.

prod'-ro-mous. Precursory. PREDECESSOR-CONTINUATION.

pro-duce'. Bring forth; lead to. CAUSE-EFFECT, CREATION-DESTRUCTION, FERTILITY-STERILITY, LENGTH-SHORTNESS, MANIFESTATION-LATENCY; **produce itself,** VISIBILITY-INVISIBILITY.

prod'-uce. That which is produced. GAIN-LOSS, LABOR-CAPITAL, MERCHANDISE.

pro-duced'. Brought forth. CREATION-DESTRUCTION.

pro-du'-cer. One who produces. LABOR-CAPITAL, MAKER-DESTROYER.

pro-du'-ci-ble. That may be brought forward. MANIFESTATION-LATENCY.

prŏ-du'-cing. Bringing forth. FERTILITY-STERILITY.

prod'-uct. Anything produced; result of multiplication. CAUSE-EFFECT, GAIN-LOSS, NUMBER.

pro-duc'-tion. Act of producing, or what is produced. CAUSE-EFFECT, CREATION-DESTRUCTION, GAIN-LOSS, LENGTH-SHORTNESS, MANIFESTATION-LATENCY, MERCHANDISE.

pro-duc'-tive. Able to produce. MIGHT-IMPOTENCE.

pro-duc'-tive-ness. Fertility. FERTILITY-STERILITY.

pro'-em. An introductory statement. PREDECESSOR-CONTINUATION.

pro-em'-i-al. Introductory. BEGINNING-END, PRECEDENCE-SUCCESSION, PREDECESSOR-CONTINUATION.

præmium [L.] (pri'-mi-um). A preface. PREDECESSOR-CONTINUATION.

prof''-a-na'-tion. Desecration. GODLINESS-UNGODLINESS.

pro-fane'. Desecrate; blasphemous; secular. GODLINESS-UNGODLINESS, MINISTRY-LAITY, USE-DISUSE; **profane swearing,** CHARITABLENESS-CURSE.

pro-fan'-i-ty. Irreverence. GODLINESS-UNGODLINESS, USE-DISUSE.

profanum vulgus [L.] (pro-fê'-num vul'-gus). The profane herd. GENTILITY-COMMONALTY.

pro-fes'-sion. Occupation; declaration of faith; pretense. ASSERTION-DENIAL, ENGAGEMENT-RELEASE, NATURE-ART, OCCUPATION, TRUTHFULNESS-FABRICATION; **enter a profession,** OCCUPATION; **profession of faith,** FAITH-MISGIVING, ORTHODOXY-HETERODOXY.

pro-fes'-sion-al. Pertaining to a profession. OCCUPATION.

pro-fes'-sion-al-ly. In a professional manner. OCCUPATION.

pro-fess'-or. Public teacher. INSTRUCTOR-PUPIL, SCHOLAR-DUNCE.

prof''-es-so'-ri-al. Pedagogic. INSTRUCTOR-PUPIL.

pro-fess'-or-ship. Office of a professor. INSTRUCTOR-PUPIL, SCHOOL.

prof'-fer. Act of proffering. PROFFER-REFUSAL.

PROFFER—REFUSAL.

Bid. A verbal offer.

Candidature. The state of being a candidate.

Invitation. An asking to come to some place or to do some act.

Motion. A setting forth for consideration of a plan or course of action.

Offer. The act of tendering something for refusal or acceptance.

Offering. The act of making an offer. See GIVING.

Overture. The opening of negotiations, usually to bring about a reconciliation.

Presentation. The act of presenting for approval, acceptance, etc.

Proffer. The act of offering anything.

Proposal. The offer of something for acceptance and action.

Proposition. An offer of terms for consideration.

Tender. An offer meant to be accepted.

PROFFER—*Verbs.*

Be a candidate. To offer oneself for an office.

Be at one's service. To offer to do something for another.

Bid. To make an offer.

Bid for. To make an offer for something.

Bribe, etc. To offer anything in order to corrupt. See GIVING.

Come forward. To come out and offer oneself, as for an office.

Go a begging. To offer oneself without being accepted.

Hawk about. To sell or offer for sale publicly.

Hold out. To offer oneself.

Invite. To draw by some offer to the inclinations.

Lay at one's feet. To offer anything, often in a servile manner.

Make advances. To make the first efforts, as towards a reconciliation.

Make a motion. To make a formal proposal for an action in a parliamentary body.

Move. To make a motion.

Offer. To tender anything for acceptance or refusal.

Offer for sale, etc. To put upon the market. See BUYING-SALE.

Offer oneself. To express a wish to aid.

Place in one's way. To offer in a conspicuous manner.

Present. To offer openly.

Present oneself. To make an offer of one's services.

Press, etc. To offer anything persistently and eagerly. See PETITION.

Proffer. To offer for acceptance.

Propose. To offer a question for discussion or consideration.

Abnegation. An abjuration; denial.

Declension. The act of declining.

Declining. Rejection; non-acceptance. See *Verbs.*

Denial. A refusal to admit or acknowledge anything.

Disclaimer. A denial; a disavowal.

Discountenance. Disapproval or disfavor.

Dissent. Refusal to assent, approve, or agree. See ASSENT-DISSENT.

Flat refusal. A positive refusal.

Incompliance. The act of refusing to acquiesce.

Non-compliance. Incompliance.

Peremptory refusal. A decisive refusal.

Pointblank refusal. A plain, direct refusal.

Protest. A solemn or formal objection.

Rebuff. A peremptory or unexpected rejection.

Recusancy. The state of persistently refusing to comply with authority.

Refusal. The act of declining to do a thing.

Rejection. Refusal to acknowledge.

Repulse. The act of refusing to have anything to do with; refusal.

Revocation. Repeal; reversal. See COMMISSION.

REFUSAL—*Verbs.*

Be deaf to. To pay no attention to; refuse.

Begrudge. To envy another of his possessions.

Be slow to. To agree to unwillingly.

Cast behind one. To reject.

Close the hand. } To refuse to give monetary help to.
Close the purse. }

Cross. To obstruct; contradict.

Decline. To refuse to accept.

Deny. To refuse to acknowledge as true.

Deny oneself. To refuse oneself something; **refuse to acknowledge oneself.**

Discard. To reject as undesirable.

Disclaim. To disavow; refuse to acknowledge.

Discountenance. To disapprove of.

Dissent, etc. To disagree with. See ASSENT-DISSENT.

Forswear. To reject utterly.

Grudge. To envy a person.

Hang fire. To hesitate; hang in suspense.

PROFFER—REFUSAL—*Continued.*

PROFFER—Verbs—*Continued.*

Put forward. To offer or bring to notice.
Seek. To try to secure.
Stand for. To offer oneself, as for an office.
Start. To begin, make the first offers towards anything.
Tender. To offer; proffer.
Volunteer. To offer oneself willingly to do something.

PROFFER—*Adjectives.*

Disengaged. Not occupied; hence, in a state to be offered.
For sale. Offered to be sold.
In the market. In a state to be offered.
Offered, etc. } Bringing before one for acceptance or refusal. See
Offering, etc. } *Verbs.*
On hire. In a position to be hired.
To let. For rent or hire.

REFUSAL—Adjectives—*Continued from Column 2.*

Not willing to hear of. Not willing to pay any attention to.
Out of the question. Not worthy of consideration; impossible.
Recusant. Persistently refusing to conform to authority.
Refusing, etc. Not wishing to yield. See *Verbs.*
Restiff. } Difficult to restrain.
Restive. }
Uncomplying. Not yielding.
Unconsenting. Not agreeing with.
Ungranted. Not given.

REFUSAL—Adverbs, *etc.*

No, etc. The negative reply. See Assertion-Affirmation.
Not for the world. On no account.
No, thank you. A polite form of refusal.
On no account. By no means.

REFUSAL—*Phrases.*

Bien obligé [F.]. Much obliged.
Non possumus [L.]. No, we cannot.
Your humble servant. Pardon me.

REFUSAL—Verbs—*Continued.*

Have nothing to do with. To refuse to associate with.
Negative. To deny the truth of.
Nill. To refuse.
Not be at home to. To refuse to see any one.
Not grant, etc. To refuse anything. See Consent.
Not hear of. To reject altogether.
Not yield an inch, etc. To refuse to move. See Bigotry.
Protest. To assert a thing earnestly; refuse to acknowledge a thing.
Rebuff. To repel suddenly or rudely.
Refuse. To decline to do a thing or to yield.
Refuse one's assent. To refuse to agree with
Reject. To refuse to receive.
Repel. To check; drive back.
Repulse. To beat or drive back; reject.
Rescind, etc. To make void; abrogate. See Commission.
Resist. To oppose, strive against, or obstruct.
Send away with a flea in the ear. To send away with an unexpected and annoying reply.
Send back. }
Send to the right-about. } To send away with a refusal.
Set aside. To refuse to consider.
Set one's face against. To oppose anything, refuse to consider it fairly.
Shake the head. To refuse by shaking the head.
Shut the door in one's face. } To refuse admittance.
Slam the door in one's face. }
Stand aloof. To stand aside.
Turn a deaf ear to. To refuse to pay any attention to.
Turn one's back upon. To refuse to have anything to do with a person or thing.
Wash one's hands of. To absolve oneself from any guilt.
Withhold one's assent. To refuse to agree.

REFUSAL—*Adjectives.*

Deaf to. Not to pay any attention to.
Impossible. That which cannot come to pass.
Not to be thought of. Not to be considered; refused.

(*Continued on Column* 1.)

---

pro-fi'-cien-cy. Skill. Knowledge-Ignorance, Skill-Unskilfulness, Success-Failure.
pro-fi'-cient. Expert. Adept-Bungler, Knowledge-Ignorance, Skill-Unskilfulness.
pro-fic'-u-ous. Profitable. Usefulness-Uselessness.
pro'-file. An outline; a drawing in outline. Appearance-Disappearance, Laterality-Contraposition, Outline, Painting.
prof'-it. Benefit; return. Gain-Loss, Good-Evil, Goodness-Badness, Usefulness-Uselessness; **profit by,** Goodness-Badness, Success-Failure, Use-Disuse.
prof'-it-a-ble. Yielding profit; useful. Fertility-Sterility, Gain-Loss, Goodness-Badness, Usefulness-Uselessness.
prof'-it-less. Yielding no profit. Usefulness-Uselessness.
prof'-li-ga-cy. Shameless viciousness. Virtue-Vice.
prof'-li-gate. Depraved. Virtue-Vice.
prof'-lu-ence. A flowing forth. River-Wind.
prof' lu-ent. Flowing forth. Advance-Retrogression, River-Wind.
pro-found'. Deep; sagacious. Craft-Artlessness, Deepness-Shallowness, Emotion, Knowledge-Ignorance, Magnitude-Smallness, Sagacity-Incapacity; **profound attention,** Heed-Disregard; **profound knowledge,** Knowledge-Ignorance; **profound secret,** Tidings-Mystery.
profundis, de [L.] (pro-fun'-dis, dī). Out of the depths. Jubilation-Lamentation, Repentance-Obduracy.
pro-fun'-di-ty. Depth. Craft-Artlessness, Deepness-Shallowness, Emotion, Knowledge-Ignorance, Magnitude-Smallness, Sagacity-Incapacity.

pro-fuse'. Copious. Excess-Lack, Extravagance-Avarice, Multiplicity-Paucity, Terseness-Prolixity.
pro-fuse'-ness. Abundance. Excess-Lack.
pro-fu'-sion. Exuberant plenty. Enough, Excess-Lack, Extravagance-Avarice, Multiplicity-Paucity.
prog. Go about begging. Nutriment-Excretion.
pro-gen'-er-ate. Procreate. Creation-Destruction.
pro-gen''-er-a-tion. Procreation. Parentage-Progeny.
pro-gen'-i-tor. An ancestor in the direct line. Parentage-Progeny.
prog'-e-ny. Offspring. Parentage-Progeny.
prog-no'-sis. Prediction of the future course of disease. Prevision, Prophecy.
prog-nos'-tic. Omen. Portent.
prog-nos'-ti-cate. Foretell by means of tokens. Prophecy.
pro'-gram. Plan of proceedings. Design, Prophecy, Record.
pro-gress'. Make to advance. Advance-Retrogression.
prog'-ress. Advance. Advance-Retrogression, Conversion-Reversion, Movement-Rest; **in mid progress,** Transfer; **in progress,** Advance-Retrogression, Completion-Noncompletion, Entirety-Deficiency; **make progress,** Activity-Indolence, Advance-Retrogression, Success-Failure; **progress of science,** Knowledge-Ignorance; **progress of time,** Period-Progress.
pro-gres'-sion. Advancement; a series of numbers. Advance-Retrogression, Continuity-Interruption, Number, Regularity-Irregularity.
pro-gress'-ive. Advancing; bettering. Advance-Retrogression, Betterment-Deterioration, Con-

TINUITY - INTERRUPTION, PERIOD - PROGRESS; **progressive form**, VERB.

pro-hib'-it. To forbid. LEAVE-PROHIBITION.

pro-hib'-it-ed. Forbidden. LAW-LAWLESSNESS, LEAVE-PROHIBITION, RELEASE-RESTRAINT.

pro''-hi-bi'-tion. An order forbidding something. ASSERTION - DENIAL, LEAVE - PROHIBITION, RELEASE-RESTRAINT.

pro-hib'-it-ive. Tending to prohibit. LEAVE-PROHIBITION.

pro-hib'-it-or-y. That which prohibits. LEAVE-PROHIBITION.

pro''-hi-bi'-tion-ist. One who favors the prohibition by law of the manufacture and sale of alcoholic liquors. TEETOTALISM-INTEMPERANCE.

pro-ject'. Shoot or throw forth; devise. CONVEXITY-CONCAVITY, DESIGN, PURPOSE-LUCK, PUSH-PULL.

proj'-ect. Scheme. DESIGN, PURPOSE-LUCK.

pro-ject'-ile. Missile. PUSH-PULL, WEAPON.

pro-jec'-tion. A jutting out; a plan. CONVEXITY-CONCAVITY, DELINEATION-CARICATURE.

pro-ject'-or. One who devises schemes. DESIGN.

pro'-late. Drawling. VOCALIZATION-MUTENESS.

pro-la'-tion. Pronunciation. SPEECH-INARTICULATENESS, VOCALIZATION-MUTENESS.

prole, sine [L.] (pro'-lĭ, sai'-nĭ). Without offspring. FERTILITY-STERILITY.

pro''-leg-om'-en-a. Introductory remarks. PREDECESSOR-CONTINUATION.

pro-lep'-sis. Anticipation; assigning to an event a date earlier than the true one. CHRONOLOGY-ANACHRONISM, PREDECESSOR-CONTINUATION.

pro''-le-taire'. A person of the lowest class. GENTILITY-COMMONALTY.

prol''-e-ta'-ri-an. A person of the lowest class. GENTILITY-COMMONALTY.

prol''-e-ta'-ri-at. The indigent classes. GENTILITY-COMMONALTY, LABOR-CAPITAL.

pro-lif'-ic. Fruitful. CREATION-DESTRUCTION, FERTILITY-STERILITY, USEFULNESS-USELESSNESS.

pro'-lix. Verbose. TERSENESS-PROLIXITY.

pro-lix'-i-ty. Verbosity. TERSENESS-PROLIXITY.

pro-loc'-u-tor. Advocate. INSTRUCTOR-LEARNER, SPEECH-INARTICULATENESS.

pro'-logue. A prefatory statement. ACTING, PREDECESSOR-CONTINUATION.

pro-long'. Lengthen. EARLINESS-LATENESS, LASTINGNESS-TRANSIENTNESS, LENGTH-SHORTNESS.

pro-longed'. Lengthened. LASTINGNESS-TRANSIENTNESS.

pro-lu'-sion. Preliminary step or proceeding. PREDECESSOR-CONTINUATION.

prom''-en-ade'. Walk for amusement or exercise. CITY-COUNTRY, POMP, TRAVELING-NAVIGATION.

Pro-me'-the-an. Like Prometheus. LIFE-DEATH.

Pro-me'-the-us. The founder of civilization. LIFE-DEATH.

prom'-i-nence. Eminence. ELEVATION-DEPRESSION, HEIGHT-LOWNESS.

prom'-i-nent. Jutting out; eminent. CONSEQUENCE-INSIGNIFICANCE, CONVEXITY-CONCAVITY, HEIGHT-LOWNESS, MANIFESTATION-LATENCY, REPUTATION-DISCREDIT.

prom'-i-nent-ly. Eminently. MAGNITUDE-SMALLNESS, SUPREMACY-SUBORDINACY.

pro-mis'-cu-ous. Confusedly mingled; accidental. MIXTURE-HOMOGENEITY, PURPOSE-LUCK, REGULARITY-IRREGULARITY.

prom'-ise. Engage to do or not to do for another; assure. CONSENT, ENGAGEMENT-RELEASE, PROPHECY, SANGUINENESS-HOPELESSNESS; **keep one's promise,** UPRIGHTNESS-DISHONESTY; **keep promise to ear and break to hope,** TRUTHFULNESS-FRAUD; **promise one-** self, EXPECTATION-SURPRISE, SANGUINENESS-HOPELESSNESS.

prom'-is-ing. Giving good hopes for the future. SANGUINENESS-HOPELESSNESS.

prom'-is-so''-ry. Containing a promise. ENGAGEMENT-RELEASE; **promissory note,** MONEY, SECURITY.

prom'-on-to''-ry. A headland. CONVEXITY-CONCAVITY, HEIGHT-LOWNESS, OCEAN-LAND.

pro-mote'. Further. BETTERMENT-DETERIORATION, INCLINATION, OBSTRUCTION-HELP.

pro-mo'-ter. Forwarder. DESIGN.

pro-mo'-tion. Advancement. BETTERMENT-DETERIORATION, OBSTRUCTION-HELP.

prompt. Suggest; early; induce. ACTIVITY-INDOLENCE, ADVICE, EARLINESS-LATENESS, ENLIGHTENMENT-SECRECY, MOTIVE-CAPRICE, REMEMBRANCE-FORGETFULNESS; **prompt memory,** REMEMBRANCE-FORGETFULNESS.

prompt'-book''. A book intended for a stage-prompter. REMEMBRANCE-FORGETFULNESS.

prompt'-er. One who prompts. ACTING, ADVICE, MOTIVE-CAPRICE.

prompt'-ing. Inciting; suggesting. MOTIVE-CAPRICE, REMEMBRANCE-FORGETFULNESS.

prompt'-i-tude. The quality of being prompt. ACTIVITY-INDOLENCE, EARLINESS-LATENESS.

prompt'-u-a-ry. Storehouse. STORE.

pro-mul'-gate. Proclaim. PUBLICITY; **promulgate a decree,** ORDER.

pro-mul'-ga''-tion. Proclaiming. PUBLICITY.

pro'-na-tion and su'-pi-na''-tion. Act of turning the palm of the hand upward and downward. REVERSAL.

prone. Prostrate. AFFECTIONS, ERECTNESS-FLATNESS.

prone'-ness. Propensity. AFFECTIONS, ERECTNESS-FLATNESS, INCLINATION.

prôner [F.] (pro-nê'). Cry up. APPROVAL - DISAPPROVAL, POMP.

prôneur [F.] (pro-nur'). Lecturer. FLATTERER-DEFAMER.

prong. A tine of a fork. DOUBLING-HALVING.

pro'-noun. A word which can be used instead of a noun. PRONOUN; **adjective pronoun,** PRONOUN; **adverbial pronoun,** PRONOUN; **demonstrative pronoun,** PRONOUN; **distributive pronoun,** PRONOUN; **emphatic pronoun,** PRONOUN; **indefinite pronoun,** PRONOUN; **interrogative pronoun,** PRONOUN; **personal pronoun,** PRONOUN; **possessive pronoun,** PRONOUN; **reciprocal pronoun,** PRONOUN; **reflexive pronoun,** PRONOUN; **relative pronoun,** PRONOUN.

PRONOUN.

Pronoun. Word which can be used instead of a noun.

PRONOUN—*Kinds.*

Adjective pronoun. One that can be used either as an adjective or pronoun. They include the demonstratives, indefinites, distributives, and reciprocals.

Adverbial pronoun. One that can be used either as an adverb or pronoun, as where, whither, etc.

Demonstrative pronoun. One that points out specifically.

Distributive pronoun. One that points out objects to be taken singly.

Emphatic pronoun. One that denotes emphasis.

Indefinite pronoun. One that defines generally.

Interrogative pronoun. One used in asking questions.

Personal pronoun. One that shows by its form its person.

Possessive pronoun. One denoting possession.

Reciprocal pronoun. One indicating a mutual relation.

Reflexive pronoun. One used after a transitive verb to denote the same person or thing as the subject.

Relative pronoun. One that acts both as a pronoun and a conjunction.

pro-nounce'. To utter; declare; speak. ASSERTION-DENIAL, DECISION-MISJUDGMENT, SPEECH-INARTICULATENESS, VOCALIZATION-MUTENESS.

pro-nun''-ci-a'-tion. Act of pronouncing words or syllables. VOCALIZATION-MUTENESS.

pro-nun'-ci-a-tive. Asserting with confidence. ASSERTION-DENIAL.

proof. Establishment of a fact by evidence; a printed trial-sheet. DESIGN, FEELING-INSENSIBILITY, HARDNESS-SOFTNESS, PROOF-DISPROOF, SIGN, TRIAL, WRITING-PRINTING; **ocular proof,** VISIBILITY-INVISIBILITY; **proof against,** ATTACK-DEFENSE, DETERMINATION-VACILLATION, REPRISAL-RESISTANCE, SECURITY-INSECURITY, SENSITIVENESS-APATHY, STRENGTH-WEAKNESS.

PROOF—DISPROOF.

Apodixis. Absolute demonstration.
Argument. A reason offered for or against an opinion. See RATIOCINATION.
Comprobation. Proof; common assent to an explanation.
Conclusiveness. The quality of being decisive.
Demonstration. Proof by such evidence of facts as precludes reasonable doubt.
Experimentum crucis [L.]. A severe trial. See TRIAL.
Logic of facts. Natural and inevitable conclusion from any set of circumstances. See EVIDENCE.
Probation. The time of testing.
Proof. Any effort to establish the truth or falsity of something.

PROOF—Verbs.

Demonstrate. To prove; show clearly by giving true evidence.
Draw a conclusion. To come to an opinion or decision about. See DECISION.
Establish. To set on indisputable ground.
Evince. To show plainly and with certainty. See EVIDENCE.
Follow. To accept the conclusions or opinions of some one else.
Follow of course. To follow as a natural consequence.
Have the best of an argument. To prove one's contention.
Hold good. To be able to stand thorough investigation.
Hold water. To hold the bottom or foundation of an argument solid.
Make good. To be able to prove by evidence what one asserts.
Make out. To draw a conclusion from the facts.
Make out a case. To start a case based on the claims of the client.
Prove. To establish, show clearly by logical steps of reasoning.
Prove one's point. To establish one's claim.
Reduce to demonstration. To bring into subjection of reason and judgment ; to put into the form of a logical demonstration.
Set the question at rest. To free from further discussion
Settle the question To decide the question.
Show. To demonstrate. prove
Stand to reason. To submit to the passing of logical judgments.
Verify. To prove to be true. See EVIDENCE.

PROOF—Adjectives.

Apodictic. } Showing by argument.
Apodictical. }
Categorical. Absolute.
Consectary. Following necessarily.
Consequential. Following or resulting.
Crucial. Determining absolutely the falsity of a view.
Decisive. Putting an end to uncertainty.
Deducible. Capable of being derived or inferred.
Demonstrated. Proved. See *Verbs.*
Demonstrating. Proving. See *Verbs.*
Demonstrable. Able to be demonstrated.

PROOF—Adjectives.

Demonstrative. Convincing; showing clearly.
Evident. Manifest or plain. See CERTAINTY.
Following. To come after in logical order.
Inferential. That which can be deducible from what is known.
Irrefragable. Not to be overthrown or refuted.
Irrefutable. Unanswerable, indisputable.
Irresistible. Not to be opposed with success.
Probative. Serving for investigation, trial, or probation.
Proved. That which has been demonstrated.
Unanswerable. Not able to be answered or replied to.
Unanswered. Not to be refuted.
Unconfuted. Not confuted, not proved false.
Unrefuted. Unopposed, unassailed.

PROOF—Adverbs, etc.

As a matter of course. It goes without saying.
Consequently. For that reason.
In consequence. As a result.
Of course. Surely; truly.

PROOF—Phrases.

Exitus acta probat [L.]. The event approves the act.
It must follow.
Probatum est [L.]. It has been proved.

Answer. A reply, a refutation.
Clincher. A decisive argument; that which binds the other statements.
Complete answer. Full reply.
Confutation. The act of disproving something.
Conviction. The act of believing something firmly.
Disproof. Refutation, denial.
Exposition. Bringing to view.
Exposure. Laying open an argument.
Invalidation. Making a thing null and void.
Knock-down argument. One that prostrates everything before it.
Redargution. The act of arguing in return, reply.
Reductio ad absurdum [L.∥]. A reducing to an absurdity.
Refutation. Answer, reply to charges.
Retort. A keen or sharp rejoinder.
Tu quoque argument. A *thou-too* argument.

DISPROOF—Verbs.

Be confuted. To prove invalid.
Clinch an argument. To make it impossible to be overthrown.
Clinch a question. To decide; settle.
Confute. To show the falsity of.
Cut the ground from under one's feet. To put limits to an opponent's arguments.
Defeat. To conquer; overcome.
Demolish. To bring to naught, overthrow.
Disprove. To show the fallacy.
Explode. To shatter; riddle to pieces.
Expose. To show the weakness or falsity.
Fail. To miss the mark; prove defective.
Give one a set down. To check; repulse.
Have. To own, possess.
Have on the hip. To have the advantage over, as in wrestling.
Invalidate. To render null or void.
Negative. To deny; gainsay.
Not leave a leg to stand on. To defeat in an argument.
Overthrow. To upset; defeat.
Overturn. To destroy, cause to fall.
Parry. To ward off, check.
Put to silence. To shut up; cause to keep quiet.
Rebut. To beat back; repel.
Redargue. To overcome by argument or proof. See *Nouns.*
Reduce to silence. To quiet.
Refute. To dispute, disprove.
Scatter to the winds. To shatter, rout.
Show one's weak point. To expose the fallacy, the inconsistency of an argument.
Show the fallacy of. To prove the premises false or insufficient.
Shut up. To quiet; silence.
Silence. To overwhelm; shut up.
Stop the mouth. To put to silence; quiet.

DISPROOF—Adjectives.

Capable of refutation. Able to be refuted, or to be replied to.
Condemned on one's showing. Proved guilty by one's own admission.
Condemned out of one's mouth. Condemned by one's own evidence.
Confutable. Capable of being shown false.
Confuted. Replied to; answered.
Confuting. Opposing in argument.
Reconfutable. Able to be overcome in argument.

DISPROOF—Phrases.

Cadit quæstio [L.]. The question fails; there is no further question.
It does not hold water. Unsound, can't be depended on.
Suo sibi gladio hunc jugula [L.]. Fight him with his own weapons.
The argument falls to the ground.

PROOF—PHRASES—Continued.

Q. E. D. That which was to be demonstrated; *quod erat demonstrandum.*
There is nothing more to be said.

prop. Support. CONNECTIVE, OBSTRUCTION-HELP, SUSPENSION-SUPPORT.

pro''-pæ-deu'-tics. Preliminary knowledge. EDUCATION-MISTEACHING.

prop'-a-ga-ble. Capable of being spread. FERTILITY-STERILITY.

prop''-a-gan'-da. An institution for propagating a doctrine or system. EDUCATION - MISTEACHING, FAITH-MISGIVING, SCHOOL.

prop''-a-gan'-dism. Art or system of propagating tenets or principles. EDUCATION-MISTEACHING.

prop''-a-gan'-dist. One who zealously propagates any doctrine. INSTRUCTOR-PUPIL, MINISTRY-LAITY.

prop'-a-gate. Beget; promulgate. CREATION-DESTRUCTION, PUBLICITY.

prop''-a-ga'-tion. Diffusion. FERTILITY-STERILITY.

pro-pel'. Drive forward. MOTIVE-CAPRICE, MOVEMENT-REST, PUSH-PULL.

pro-pelled'. Urged forward. PUSH-PULL.

pro-pel'-ling. Urging forward. PUSH-PULL.

pro-pend'. Incline towards. READINESS-RELUCTANCE.

pro-pend'-en-cy. Propensity. AFFECTIONS, PREDETERMINATION-IMPULSE.

pro-pense'. Having a propensity. READINESS-RELUCTANCE.

pro-pen'-sion. A mental tendency. AFFECTIONS.

pro-pen'-si-ty. Proclivity. AFFECTIONS, DESIRE-DISTASTE, INCLINATION.

pro-pen'-sed-ness. Proclivity. AFFECTIONS.

prop'-er. Specially suited; of becoming appearance. BEAUTY-UGLINESS, DUENESS-UNDUENESS, PROPRIETY-IMPROPRIETY, UNIVERSALITY - PARTICULARITY; **in its proper place,** REGULARITY-IRREGULARITY; **proper name,** NAME-MISNOMER; **proper time,** OPPORTUNENESS-UNSUITABLENESS; **show a proper spirit,** UPRIGHTNESS-DISHONESTY; **the proper thing,** DUTY-DERELICTION.

prop'-er-ties, the-at'-ri-cal. Stage requisites. ACTING, DRESS-UNDRESS.

prop'-er-ty. Anything that may be owned. AFFLUENCE-PENURY, MIGHT-IMPOTENCE, PROPERTY.

PROPERTY.

Absolute interest. Ownership without limitation or condition.

Acquest. Property acquired otherwise than by inheritance.

Acres. Land.

Alimony. An allowance made to a wife out of her husband's estate, upon her divorce or legal separation from him.

Allodium. Land which is the absolute property of the owner. See LIBERTY.

Appanage. The portion of land assigned by a sovereign prince for the support of his younger sons.

Appurtenances. Things annexed to other things more worthy.

Assets. Property of a deceased person or debtor, subject by law to the payment of his debts.

Bag and baggage. All that belongs to one.

Baggage. The articles which a traveler carries with him on a journey.

Barony. The domain of a baron.

Belongings. Goods or effects.

Beneficial interest. The right of receiving, or entitled to have the advantage, use, or benefit.

Benefit. Whatever promotes prosperity, or adds value to property.

Cargo. The freight of a ship.

Chattels. An item of movable or immovable property except the freehold.

Chattels real. The rights in land that are less than a freehold, as leases, mortgages, etc.

Chose in action. A right to personal property not in possession but obtainable by action.

Circumstances. State of property.

Claim. A title to any debt, privilege or other thing in possession of another.

Contingent interest. A right in anything dependent upon something that may or may not occur.

Copyhold. A tenure of estate by copy of court-roll.

Copyright. The right of an author to print and publish his works, exclusive of all other persons.

Corporeal hereditaments. Inherited property which may be seen and handled; land.

Credit. Trust given or received. See CREDIT.

Debt. That which is due from one person to another. See CREDIT-DEBT.

Demand. The right or title in virtue of which anything may be claimed.

Demesne. A lord's chief manor place, with the lands belonging thereto.

Dependency. A territory subject to a kingdom or state.

Domain. The territory over which dominion or authority is exerted.

Dower. The property with which a woman is endowed.

Dowry. That part of the real estate of a man which a widow enjoys during her life.

Easement. A liberty, privilege, or advantage, which one proprietor has in the estate of another proprietor, distinct from the ownership of the soil.

Effects. Goods; personal estate.

Empire. The dominion of an emperor.

Equipage. Furniture or outfit. See INSTRUMENT.

Equitable estate. An estate that can be sustained or made available in a court of equity.

Equitable interest. A right in anything that may be made effective in a court of equity.

Estates. Property which a person possesses.

Estates and effects. Real and personal property.

Estates for life. Interest or ownership in real estate for life.

Estates for years. Ownership of property for a term of years.

Estates in fee. Land held in consideration of some service rendered to the lord.

Estates in tail. An estate limited to particular heirs.

Estates in tail female. Estates of inheritance limited to female heirs.

Estates in tail general. Estates of inheritance not limited to particular heirs.

Estates in tail male. Estates of inheritance limited to male heirs.

Estates par auter vie. Right or ownership of property during the life of another person.

Estates tail. Estates limited to certain heirs.

Expectancy. An estate, the possession of which a person is entitled to have at some future time.

Farm. The land held under lease and by payment of rent.

Fee simple. Ownership without conditions or limits.

Fee tail. An estate of inheritance limited to particular heirs.

Feoff. A fief.

Feud. A fief.

Fief. An estate held of a superior on condition of military service.

Fixtures. Anything of an accessory character annexed to houses and lands.

Freehold. An estate in real property, of inheritance, or for life.

Goods. Personal property.

Ground. A portion of territory. See OCEAN-LAND.

Hacienda [Sp.]. A productive landed estate.

Heirloom. Any furniture, or personal chattel, which, by law, descends to the heir along with the inheritance.

Hereditaments. Any species of property that may be inherited.

Heritage. That which is inherited.

Holding. A farm or other estate held of another.

Honor. A lordship held of the king.

Impedimenta. Baggage.

Income. The gain which proceeds from labor, business, property, or capital. See OUTLAY-INCOME.

Incorporeal hereditaments. Inheritable property that is incapable of actual visible seizin or possession.

Inheritance. That which may be inherited.

Interest. Participation in advantage or profit.

Jointure. An estate settled on a wife, which she is to enjoy after her husband's decease, for her own life at least, in satisfaction of dower.

Kingdom. The territory governed by a king.

Lading. That which constitutes a load or cargo.

Land. } Any portion of the earth's surface considered as belonging to
Lands. } an individual, etc.

Landed estate. An estate in lands.

Landed property. Ownership of land.

Lease. Tenure of lands for a specified time for rent or compensation.

Leasehold. A tenure by lease.

Legacy. A gift of property by will. See GIVING-RECEIVING.

Legal estate. An estate held in accordance with the rules of law.

Limitation. A settling of an estate or property by specific rules.

Luggage. Baggage.

Manor. The land belonging to a lord or nobleman, as his residence.

Means. Property, revenue, or the like.

Meum et tuum [L.]. Mine and thine.

Money. The medium of exchange. See Money.

Movables. Personal property.

Ownership. The right to own.

Paramount estate. A right in an estate superior to all other claims.

Paraphernalia. Something reserved to a wife, over and above her dower.

Parcels. A part or portion, as of land.

Particular estate. An estate claimed from some particular charge or claim growing out of the estate.

Patent. A writing securing to an inventor the exclusive right in his invention.

Patrimony. A right or estate inherited from one's father.

Pelf. Money; riches.

Personal effects. ⎫

Personal estates. ⎬ Movables; chattels.

Personal property. ⎭

Personalty. Personal property.

Plant. The whole machinery and apparatus employed in carrying on a trade.

Plantation. Land under cultivation.

Possession. The having, holding, or detention of property in one's power.

Possibility. A contingent interest in property.

Principality. The domain of a prince.

Property. Anything that a man may legally possess and hold.

Proprietorship. Ownership.

Rattletraps. A machine or vehicle.

Real estate. Lands, tenements, and hereditaments.

Realm. A royal domain.

Real property. ⎫ Real estate.

Realty. ⎭

Remainder. An estate in expectancy which becomes an estate in possession upon the determination of a particular prior estate.

Rent-roll. A rental.

Resources. Funds; money.

Reversion. The returning of an estate to the grantor or his heirs.

Right. That which one has a legal claim to.

Right of common. The right of feeding beasts on land belonging to the community.

Right of user. The right to the benefit and profit of lands.

Seigniority. The dominion of a lord.

Seizin. Possession of an estate or freehold.

Settlement. A disposition of property for the benefit of some person.

Stake. That which is laid down as a wager.

State. The territory of a body politic.

Stock. ⎫

Stock in trade. ⎭ Money or capital which is employed in trade.

Strict settlement. A settlement of an estate to particular persons.

Suum cuique [L.]. Each one his own.

Tenements. Any species of permanent property.

Tenure. The right of holding, as property.

Term. The limitation of an estate.

Territory. A large extent or tract of land.

Things. Clothes; furniture, etc.

Title. That which is the foundation of ownership of property.

Toft. A place where a messuage has once stood.

Traps. Equipments.

Trust. Deliverance of property upon promise of future payment.

Use. The benefit or profit of lands and tenements.

Vested interest. A right in anything which does not depend on a contingency.

Wealth. Large possessions. See Affluence.

What one is worth. Extent of one's wealth.

What one will cut up for. Value of one s possessions.

Zemindary. The land possessed by a zemindar, or an Indian lord.

PROPERTY—Verbs.

Appertain to. To belong to by any means.

Belong to. To be one's property.

Be one's property. To own. See Nouns.

Be the possessor of. To have in one's power. See Holder.

Come in for. To fall heir to.

Have for one's own. ⎫ To hold legally.

Have for one's very own. ⎭

Inherit. To receive by descent from an ancestor.

Own. To have legal title to.

Pertain to. To belong to.

Possess. To have ownership; have the right of property in actual exercise. See Holding.

Savor of the realty. To manifest the characteristics of a realty.

PROPERTY—Adjectives

Allodial. Pertaining to the absolute ownership of land in distinction from feudal lands.

Copyhold. Pertaining to tenure of land held by copy of court-roll.

Feodal. Same as feudal.

Feudal. Relating to a fee or feud.

Freehold. Held by a full legal tenure.

Landed. Consisting of real estate or land.

Manorial. Pertaining to a manor.

One's own. Belonging to one.

Predial. Consisting of lands, belonging to real estate.

PROPERTY—Adverbs, etc.

To one and his executors, administrators, and assigns.

To one and his heirs and assigns.

To one and his heirs forever.

To one and the heirs of his body.

To one's account. ⎫

To one's credit. ⎬ To one's credit or advantage.

To the good. ⎭

prop'-er-ty-man''. A person who has charge of portable articles used in plays. Acting.

proph'-e-cy. A prediction. Prophecy.

PROPHECY.

Abodement. ⎫

Aboding. ⎭ An omen or foreboding.

Announcement. A publishing of something that is to come.

Ariolation. A soothsaying.

Auguration. The practise of augury.

Augury. Foretelling events by flights of birds, etc.

Auspices. Favoring omens, or influence

Bodement. A prediction.

Divination. The act of divining; foreseeing future events

Foreboding. Anticipation or expectation of evil.

Forecast. A previous determination of an event.

Fortune-telling. The act of forecasting the future events in the life of others.

Hariolation. Soothsaying.

Horoscope. The representation of the heavens at time of birth by which astrologers essay to foretell the events of the life.

Nativity. Representation of the positions of the heavenly bodies at birth, used as a means to determine future events.

Necromancy. Art of foretelling future events by communication with the dead. See Devotion-Magic.

Omen. A prophetic indication of the future. See Portent.

Omination. A foreboding.

Ominousness. State of being ominous or foreboding evil.

Ornithomancy. Divination by the flight of birds.

Prediction. Act of making known beforehand; a prophecy.

Prefiguration. The act of announcing by antecedent signs.

Prefigurement. Act of prefiguring; prefiguration.

Premonition. A warning of something to come. See Warning.

Premonstration. A foreshadowing.

Prognosis. Any prediction, especially in respect to the future course and end of a disease.

Prognostication. The act of foretelling; that which predicts.

Program. A plan announcing a course of proceedings. See Design.

Prophecy. The foretelling of future events through divine help.

Sooth. Augury; truth.

Soothsaying. The foretelling of events; truth-telling.

Vaticination. Prophecy.

PROPHECY—Denotations.

Prototype. A general design to which subsequent forms are traced.

Type. An example, model, or pattern.

PROPHECY—Noun of Place.

Adytum. The inner shrine where oracles are delivered.

PROPHECY—Scientific Nouns.

Astrology. The science or art of judging future events by the stars.

Horoscopy. The art of casting horoscopes.

Judicial astrology. The doctrine of the influence of the stars upon events.

Mantology. The art of divination.

PROPHECY—Forms of Divination.

Aeromancy. Divination by atmospheric appearances.

Alectoromancy. ⎫ Divination by the order in which a cock picks up

Alectryomancy. ⎭ grain covering letters traced in the ground.

Aleuromancy. ⎫

Alphitomancy. ⎭ Divination by meal.

Anthropomancy. Divination by the entrails of a human sacrifice.

Anthroposcopy. Divination by the features.

Arithmancy.   Divination by numbers.
Aruspicy.   Haruspicy.
Austromancy.   Divination by winds.
Axinomancy.   Divination by a balanced hatchet.
Belomancy.   Divination by arrows.
Bibliomancy.   Divination by the Bible.
Bletonism.   The gift of being able to find subterranean springs by sensation.
Botanomancy.   Divination by herbs.
Capnomancy.   Divination by the rising of smoke.
Catopromancy.   Divination by mirrors.
Ceromancy.   Divination by dropping melted wax into water.
Chaomancy.   Aeromancy.
Chiromancy.   Divination by the hand.
Cleromancy.   Divination by dice.
Coscinomancy.   Divination by a balanced sieve.
Cristallomantia.   Divination by spirits seen in a magic lens.
Crithomancy.   Divination by dough of cakes.
Dactyliomancy.   Divination by a finger-ring.
Gastromancy.   Divination by ventriloquism.
Geloscopy.   Divination by the laugh.
Genethliacs.   Divination by the stars at birth.
Geomancy.   Divination by dots made at random on paper.
Gyromancy.   Divination by walking in a circle.
Halomancy.   Divination by salt.
Haruspicy. }
Hieromancy. } Divination by the appearance of the entrails of sacrifices.
Hieroscopy. }
Hydromancy.   Divination by water.
Ichthyomancy.   Divination by the entrails of fishes.
Lithomancy.   Divination by precious stones.
Meteoromancy.   Divination by meteors.
Myomancy.   Divination by mice.
Nomancy.   Divination by the letters forming the name of the person.
Oneiromancy.   Divination by dreams.
Onomancy.   Nomancy.
Onychomancy.   Divination by nails reflecting the sun's rays.
Ophiomancy.   Divination by fishes.
Orniscopy. }
Ornithomancy. } Divination by birds.
Palmistry.   See CHIROMANCY.
Pegomancy.   Divination by fountains.
Pessomancy.   Divination by pebbles.
Psephomancy.   Divination by pebbles drawn from a heap.
Psychomancy.   Divination by ghosts.
Pyromancy.   Divination by sacrificial fire.
Rhabdomancy.   Divination by a wand.
Sciomancy.   Divination by departed spirits.
Sideromancy.   Divination by red-hot iron.
Sortilege.   Divination by drawing lots.
Stichomancy.   Divination by passages in books.
Tephramancy.   Divination by writings in ashes.
Theomancy.   Divination by oracles.

PROPHECY—Verbs.

Abode.   To foreshadow.
Advise.   To announce; give counsel.
Announce.   To declare what is to come.
Augur.   To predict by signs and omens, as the flight of birds.
Augurate.   To take auguries.
Be the precursor.   To be the forerunner or announcer.   See PREDECESSOR.
Betoken.   To give a promise or sign of.
Bid fair.   To give promise of.
Bode.   To have a sign of; presage.
Cast a horoscope. }
Cast a nativity. } To calculate a horoscope or nativity.
Divine.   To foresee; presage.
Excite expectation. }
Excite hope. } To show a good omen.
Forebode.   To presage; have a premonition of.
Foretell.   To declare beforehand.
Foretoken.   To betoken.
Forewarn.   To admonish beforehand.   See WARNING.
Herald.   To announce as a herald.
Hold out expectation. }
Hold out hope. } To have a favorable omen or prospect.
Lead one to expect. }
Lower.   To be threatening.
Ominate.   To foreshadow; presage.
Point to.   To indicate.
Predict.   To make an event known before it happens.
Prefigure.   To show by antecedent signs.
Premise.   To make an antecedent statement.

Presage.   To indicate by a present fact what is to follow.
Preshadow.   To foreshadow.
Preshow.   To foreshow.
Prognosticate.   To prophesy from present events.
Promise.   To give assurance of; engage to do something in the future.
Prophesy.   To speak in the place of God; foretell.
Protypify.   To foreshow by an image or type.
Raise expectation. }
Raise hope. } To show signs of good omen.
Shadow forth.   To signify beforehand.
Signify.   To make known by any process.
Soothsay.   To foretell.
Tell fortunes.   To foretell the acts or course of one's life.
Typify.   To represent by a type; signify.
Usher in.   To announce or introduce as by an usher.
Vaticinate.   To foretell.

PROPHECY—Adjectives.

Augurial.   Pertaining to auguries.
Augurous.   Full of augury.
Auspicial.   Of or pertaining to auspices.
Auspicious.   Promising success from certain signs.
Big with the fate of.   Showing many signs.
Extispicious.   Relating to the inspection of entrails.
Fatidical.   Having power to foretell future events.
Monitory.   Conveying warnings.
Ominous.   Full of omens.
Oracular.   Pertaining to oracles; prophetic.
Portentous.   Full of portents or strange happenings.
Predicting.   Foretelling.   See *Verbs*.
Predictive.   Foretelling; foreboding.
Pregnant.   Full of consequence, implying more than is expressed.
Premonitory.   Containing premonitions.
Prescious.   Foreknowing.
Prophetic.   Pertaining to prophecy.
Sibylline.   Pertaining to the Sibyl; prophetic.
Significant of.   Expressive of something beyond the external mark or sign.
Vaticinal.   Prophetic.
Weather-wise.   Skillful in predicting the state of the weather.

PROPHECY—Phrases.

"**Coming events cast their shadows before.**"   [Campbell *Lochiel*.]
Dicamus bona verba [L.].   Let us speak words of good omen.

proph'-e-sy.   To predict.   PROPHECY.
proph'-et.   One who speaks as the inspired representative of a divine being.   MINISTRY-LAITY, SOOTHSAYER; false prophets, REVELATION-PSEUDOREVELATION; **in the name of the Prophet—figs!**   ADAGE-NONSENSE.
pro-phet'-ic.   Predictive.   PROPHECY, REVELATION-PSEUDOREVELATION.
Prophets, the.   The Old Testament books written by the prophets.   REVELATION-PSEUDOREVELATION.
pro''-phy-lac''-tic.   Preventive.   CONSERVATION, HEALTHINESS-UNHEALTHINESS, OBSTRUCTION-HELP, REMEDY-BANE.
pro''-phy-lax'-is.   Preservative treatment for disease.   CONSERVATION.
pro-pin'-qui-ty.   Local nearness.   REMOTENESS-NEARNESS.
pro-pi'-ti-ate.   Appease; conciliate.   ATONEMENT, COMPASSION-RUTHLESSNESS, CONTENTEDNESS-DISCONTENTMENT, DEVOTION-IDOLATRY, DIVINITY, EXCITABILITY-INEXCITABILITY, FIGHTING-CONCILIATION, LOVE-HATE, PARDON-VINDICTIVENESS.
pro-pi''-ti-a'-tion.   Reconciliation.   ATONEMENT, DIVINITY.
pro-pi'-ti-a-to''-ry.   Conciliatory.   ATONEMENT.
pro-pi'-tious.   Gracious; favorable.   GOODNESS-BADNESS, OBSTRUCTION-HELP, OPPORTUNENESS-UNSUITABLENESS, PARDON-VINDICTIVENESS, SANGUINENESS-HOPELESSNESS, WELFARE-MISFORTUNE.
pro'-plasm.   A matrix or mold.   COPY-MODEL.
pro-por'-tion.   Share; comparative relation; equality of ratios.   ASSIGNMENT, CONNECTION-INDEPENDENCE, NUMBER, PROPORTION-DEFORMITY.

PROPORTION—DEFORMITY.

Arborescence. Having the quality of branching like a tree.
Beauty. The perfection of form or shaping. See BEAUTY.
Bilateral symmetry. Symmetry of bilateral bodies or figures.
Branching. Division into parts or branches.
Centrality. State of being central.
Eurythmy. Harmony and just proportion.
Finish. That which completes or perfects.
Multilateral symmetry. Symmetry of many-sided figures or bodies.
Parallelism. Essential likeness.
Proportion. The relation or adaptation of one portion to another.
Ramification. Process of branching.
Shapeliness. Quality of being well proportioned in form.
Symmetry. Quality of having the parts or elements balanced; relative proportion.
Trilateral symmetry. Symmetry of bodies having three sides.
Uniformity. Quality of being the same at all times, etc.

PROPORTION—*Adjectives.*

Arborescent. Resembling a tree.
Arboriform. Having the form of a tree.
Balanced. Well proportioned; applied to the mind.
Beautiful. Perfect in form or shaping. See BEAUTY.
Branching. Having branches or parts.
Chaste. Pure from unlawful sexual intercourse, or from obscenity.
Classic. Pertaining to or like the productions of ancient Greece and Rome.
Coextensive. Having equal extent.
Dendriform. Having the appearance of a tree.
Dendroid. Resembling a tree or shrub.
Equal. Of just proportion and relation. See EQUALITY.
Finished. Completed; perfected.
Parallel. Essentially alike.
Ramose. }
Ramous. } Full of branches.
Regular. Conforming to the usual rule.
Severe. Exactly conforming to a standard.
Shapely. Well proportioned in form.
Symmetrical. Having the parts balanced; relatively proportioned.
Uniform. The same throughout.
Well-set. Having good symmetry of parts.
Well-shaped. Having good form or proportion.

———

DEFORMITY—ADJECTIVES—*Continued from Column 2.*

Misshapen. Badly shapen.
Not straight. Crooked.
Not true. Not precisely right or accurately adjusted.
On one side. Obliquely set.
Out of shape. Deformed.
Round-shouldered. Having an unnatural turn of the shoulders.
Scalene. Having no two sides equal: said of triangles.
Snub-nosed. Having a short and slightly turned-up nose.
Splay-footed. Having the foot turned outward.
Stumpy. Short and thick.
Taliped. Club-footed.
Unsymmetric. Misshapen.
Wry. Bent to one side; distorted.

DEFORMITY—*Adverb.*

All manner of ways. Without order or regularity.

Anamorphosis. A distorted representation, so made that when viewed from a certain point it appears regular.
Contortion. Partial displacement of a limb by twisting.
Crookedness. The quality of having angles and curves in it.
Deformity. Lack of beauty, harmony, or symmetry.
Detortion. }
Distortion. } A twisting or forcing out of shape.
Harelip. A lip having a fissure like that of a hare.
Grimace. A distortion of the features.
Malconformation. An irregularity in the general structure.
Malformation. An irregularity in the formation or correlation of parts.
Misproportion. Lack of due proportion.
Monstrosity. Anything greatly unnatural in form or size.
Teratology. Science of vegetable or animal monstrosities.
Twist. A distortion resembling the curves in a rope.
Ugliness. Offensiveness of aspect.
Want of symmetry. Lack of perfect form.

DEFORMITY—*Verbs.*

Contort. To displace partially by twisting; writhe unnaturally.
Deform. To mar or distort the form.
Distort. To twist or force out of shape; strain the meaning.
Make faces. To distort the features.
Misshape. To shape ill.
Twist. To turn as if making a rope.
Warp. To turn out of shape by contraction, heat, etc.
Wrest. To pull or force away by violent twisting.
Writhe. To twist the body, face, etc., as in pain or agony.

DEFORMITY—*Adjectives.*

Askew. Obliquely.
Awry. Turned to one side.
Bandy. }
Bandy-legged. } Crooked outward at the knees.
Bloated. Morbidly enlarged.
Bow-kneed. }
Bow-legged. } Having the legs bent in an outward curve.
Bunchbacked. Having a bunch on the back; crooked-backed.
Club-footed. Having a congenital distortion of the feet.
Crooked. Considerably bent.
Crooked as a rainbow. Having a long curve or bend.
Crooked-backed. Stooped.
Crump. Crooked.
Curtailed of one's fair proportions. Deformed.
Deformed. Marred or distorted in form.
Distorted, etc. Twisted out of shape. See *Verbs.*
Gaunt. Lean, as with fasting or suffering.
Grotesque. Ludicrously misshapen.
Humpbacked. }
Hunchbacked. } Crooked-backed.
Ill-made. Not well made.
Ill-proportioned. Not well proportioned.
Irregular. Not consistent throughout; not according to the usual rule.
Knock-kneed. Having the legs bent inward at the knees.
Misbegotten. Irregularly or unlawfully begotten.
Misproportioned. Badly proportioned.

(*Continued on Column 1.*)

———

pro-por'-tion-a-ble. Duly proportioned. NUMBER.
pro-por'-tion-al. Duly proportioned. NUMBER.
pro-por'-tion-ate. Being in proportion. HARMONY-DISCORD.
pro-por'-tions. Relative magnitudes. EXTENSION-DISTRICT, GREATNESS-LITTLENESS.
pro-po'-sal. Offer. DESIGN, PROFFER-REFUSAL, PURPOSE-LUCK.
pro-pose'. Offer for consideration; purpose; offer oneself in marriage. ASSERTION-DENIAL, BLANDISHMENT, HYPOTHESIS, PROFFER-REFUSAL, PURPOSE-LUCK; propose a question, INVESTIGATION-ANSWER.
pro-posed'. Purposed. INVESTIGATION-ANSWER.
prop''-o-si'-tion. Thing proposed; statement of a truth to be demonstrated. CONCEPTION-THEME,

DESIGN, HYPOTHESIS, PROFFER-REFUSAL, RATIOCINATION-INSTINCT.
pro-pound'. Offer for consideration. ASSERTION-DENIAL, HYPOTHESIS; propound a question, INVESTIGATION-ANSWER.
propriâ personâ, in [L.] (pro'-pri-a per-so'-na, in). In one's own person. PRESENCE-ABSENCE, UNIVERSALITY-PARTICULARITY.
pro-pri'-et-a-ry. Owner. HOLDER.
pro-pri'-et-or. One having a legal right to anything. HOLDER.
pro-pri'-et-or-ship. Ownership. PROPERTY.
pro-pri'-et-y. Fitness; suitableness. DUTY-DERELICTION, HARMONY-DISCORD, PROPRIETY-IMPROPRIETY, RIGHT-WRONG, SOCIETY-LUDICROUSNESS.

PROPRIETY—IMPROPRIETY.

Desirability.
Desirableness.} The state or quality of being pleasing or agreeable.
Expedience.
Expediency.} The quality of being personally advantageous.
Fitness. Appropriateness in every way. See HARMONY
High time. The extreme limit of time.
Propriety. Conformity to custom.
Utility. The ability to be useful.

PROPRIETY—Verbs.

Befit. To be becoming to.
Conform. To measure up to a certain standard.
Suit. To agree to our ideas of things.

PROPRIETY—Verbal Expressions.

Be expedient; befit the occasion; befit the season; befit the time; suit the occasion; suit the season; suit the time.

PROPRIETY—Adjectives.

Acceptable. Worthy of being accepted.
Advisable. Agreeing with good sense.
Applicable. Suitable for use. See USEFULNESS
Becoming.
Befitting.} Suitable to the person, occasion, etc.
Convenient. Requiring the loss of no time, effort, etc.
Desirable. To be wished for.
Due. Rightly claimed.
Eligible. Worthy of being chosen.
Expedient. Personally advantageous.
Fit.
Fitting.} Right and proper.
In loco [L.] In place.
Meet. Fit.
Opportune. Coming at the proper time. See OPPORTUNENESS.
Proper. Conforming to usage.
Seemly. To be in taste.
Suitable. Agreeable to our notions. See HARMONY.
Worth while. Advantageous.

PROPRIETY—Adverbs, etc.

Conveniently. In a convenient manner.
In the right place. Suitably.

PROPRIETY—Phrase.

Operæ pretium est [L.]. It pays, or is worth while.

IMPROPRIETY—ADJECTIVES—Continued from Column 2

Unsubservient. Not servile. See USEFULNESS-USELESSNESS.
Unwieldy. Ponderous.

IMPROPRIETY—Phrase.

It will never do.

Discommodity. The state of not being handy or suitable.
Impropriety. Non-conformity to present usage.
Inexpedience.
Inexpediency.} The condition of not being advantageous.
Inutility. Inability to be made use of.
Undesirability.
Undesirableness.} Want of the quality of desirableness. See *Adjectives.*
Unfitness. Lack of fitness. See HARMONY-DISCORD.

IMPROPRIETY—Verbs.

Embarrass. To confuse.
Be inexpedient. To be useless. See *Adjectives.*
Come amiss. To be useless or inconvenient.
Pay too dear for one's whistle. To pay more than something is worth, as Franklin did for his whistle.
Put to inconvenience. To cause trouble to.

IMPROPRIETY—Adjectives.

Awkward. Ungainly in movement.
Clumsy. Lack of gracefulness in appearance.
Cumbersome.
Cumbrous.} Burdensome.
Disadvantageous. Not benefiting.
Discommodious. Incommodious.
Hulky. Clumsy.
Ill-advised. Not based on good judgment.
Ill-contrived. Not well contrived.
Impedient. Hindering.
Improper. Not proper.
Inadmissible. Not to be admitted.
Inadvisable. Not advisable.
Inappropriate. Not suitable to the time, etc.
Inapt. Not suited by nature.
Incommodious. Not convenient.
Inconvenient. Causing annoyance.
Ineligible. Not qualified.
Inexpedient. Not expedient.
Inopportune. Happening at the wrong time.
In the wrong place. M sfitting.
Lumbering. Moving as if heavily burdened.
Mal entendu [F.] Ill-advised.
Objectionable. Worthy of disapproval.
Out of place. Unsuitable.
Unadvisable. Not advisable.
Undesirable. Not to be wished for.
Unfit. Not right or proper. See HARMONY-DISCORD.
Unmanageable. Not easily directed. See DIFFICULTY.
Unnecessary. Not necessary See EXCESS.
Unprofitable. Not producing gain.
Unsatisfactory. Not satisfactory.
Unseemly. Not in good taste.

(Continued on Column 1.)

---

proprio motu [L.] (pro'-pri-o mo'-tu). By its own motion. VOLITION-OBLIGATION.
propter hoc [L.] (prop'-ter hoc). On account of this. RATIONALE-LUCK.
pro-pugn'. To vindicate; defend. ATTACK-DEFENSE, JUSTIFICATION-CHARGE.
pro''-pug-na'-tion. Defense. ATTACK-DEFENSE.
pro-pugn'-er. Defender. ATTACK-DEFENSE.
pro-pul'-sion. Driving. PUSH-PULL.
pro-pul'-sive. Driving on. PUSH-PULL.
prop'-y-lon. A monumental gateway. BEGINNING-END.
prore. A prow. ANTERIORITY-POSTERIORITY.
pro''-ro-ga'-tion. Adjournment. SUPREMACY-SUBORDINACY.
pro-rogue'. To postpone. EARLINESS-LATENESS.
pro-rup'-tion. A bursting out. ENTRANCE-EXIT.
pro-sa'-ic. Commonplace. FORCE-WEAKNESS, POETRY-PROSE, RHETORIC, SAGACITY-INCAPACITY, WITTINESS-DULNESS.
pro-sa'-ism. A prosaic manner. POETRY-PROSE.
pro-sce'-ni-um. Part of a theater. ACTING, ANTERIORITY-POSTERIORITY.
pro-scribe'. To ostracize. CHARITABLENESS-CURSE, EXCULPATION-CONVICTION, LEAVE-PROHIBITION, SOCIABILITY-PRIVACY,

pro-scrip'-tion. Denunciation. CHARITABLENESS-CURSE, EXCULPATION-CONVICTION, LEAVE-PROHIBITION, SOCIABILITY-PRIVACY.
prose. Not poetry; tedious. POETRY-PROSE, TALKATIVENESS-TACITURNITY, TERSENESS-PROLIXITY; **prose run mad,** POETRY-PROSE, RHETORIC, SIMPLICITY-FLORIDNESS; **prose-writer,** POETRY-PROSE, WITTINESS-DULNESS.
pros'-e-cute. To carry on; to carry on a judicial proceeding. ACTION-PASSIVENESS, JUSTIFICATION-CHARGE, LITIGATION, QUEST-EVASION; **prosecute an inquiry,** INVESTIGATION-ANSWER.
pros''-e-cu'-tion. Accusation. LITIGATION.
pros'-e-cu''-tor. One who prosecutes. JUSTIFICATION-CHARGE.
pros'-e-lyte. One won over to a different religion. INSTRUCTOR-PUPIL, PERSISTENCY-APOSTASY.
pros'-e-ly''-tism. The state of a convert to a religion. EDUCATION-MISTEACHING.
pro'-ser. A dull writer or talker. ENTERTAINMENT-WEARINESS, POETRY-PROSE, TALKATIVENESS-TACITURNITY.
pro'-sing. Tedious. FORCE-WEAKNESS, TERSENESS-PROLIXITY, WITTINESS-DULNESS.

pros′-o-dy. The science of poetical forms. POETRY-PROSE.

pros″-o-po-pe′-ia. Personification. RHETORIC, TROPE.

pros′-pect. To look over; an outlook; promise. APPEARANCE-DISAPPEARANCE, EXPECTATION-SURPRISE, FUTURE-PAST, LIKELIHOOD-UNLIKELIHOOD, OCCURRENCE-DESTINY, PAINTING, PREVISION; **good prospect,** SANGUINENESS-HOPELESSNESS; **in prospect,** OCCURRENCE-DESTINY, PURPOSE-LUCK.

pro-spec′-tion. Foresight. EXPECTATION-SURPRISE.

pro-spec′-tive. Anticipated. EXPECTATION-SURPRISE.

pro-spec′-tive-ly. Anticipated. FUTURE-PAST.

pro-spec′-tus. An outline of a plan. DESIGN, DIGEST, PREVISION, RECORD.

pros′-per. To succeed. SUCCESS-FAILURE, WELFARE-MISFORTUNE.

prosperita è non aver necessità, vera [It.] (pros-pêr′-i-ta ê non av′-êr nê-ches′-si-ta, vê′-ra). True wealth is to have no want. AFFLUENCE-POVERTY.

pros-per′-i-ty. Successful progress. WELFARE-MISFORTUNE.

pros′-per-ous. Successful. WELFARE-MISFORTUNE.

pros′-per-ous-ly. Successfully. WELFARE-MISFORTUNE.

pro-spi′-cience. The habit of looking forward. PREVISION.

pros″-ter-na′-tion. Prostration; dejection. LIGHTHEARTEDNESS-DEJECTION, PRESUMPTION-OBSEQUIOUSNESS.

pros′-the-sis. Rhetorical figure. RHETORIC.

pros′-ti-tute. To apply to base purposes; a harlot. BETTERMENT-DETERIORATION, PURITY-IMPURITY, PURITY-RAKE, USE-MISUSE.

pros″-ti-tu′-tion. Misuse. BETTERMENT-DETERIORATION, USE-MISUSE.

pros′-trate. To lie flat. CREATION-DESTRUCTION, ELEVATION-DEPRESSION, ERECTNESS-FLATNESS, HEALTH-SICKNESS, HEIGHT-LOWNESS, LIGHTHEARTEDNESS-DEJECTION, MIGHT-IMPOTENCE, PRESUMPTION-OBSEQUIOUSNESS; **fall prostrate,** ASCENT-DESCENT; **prostrate oneself,** DEVOTION-IDOLATRY, PRESUMPTION-OBSEQUIOUSNESS, REGARD-DISRESPECT.

pros-tra′-tion. The state of being prostrate. CREATION-DESTRUCTION, DEVOTION-IDOLATRY, ELEVATION-DEPRESSION, ERECTNESS-FLATNESS, GODLINESS-UNGODLINESS, HEALTH-SICKNESS, HEIGHT-LOWNESS, LIGHTHEARTEDNESS-DEJECTION, MIGHT-IMPOTENCE, PLEASURE-PAIN, PRESUMPTION-OBSEQUIOUSNESS, REGARD-DISRESPECT, TASTE-VULGARITY, WEARINESS-REFRESHMENT, YIELDING.

pro′-sy. Tiresome. ENTERTAINMENT-WEARINESS, FORCE-WEAKNESS, POETRY-PROSE, WITTINESS-DULNESS.

pro-syl′-lo-gism. Part of a combined syllogism. RATIOCINATION-INSTINCT.

prot-ag′-o-nist. The chief actor in a Greek drama. ACTING, ADEPT-BUNGLER.

pro tanto [L.] (pro tan′-to). To that extent. QUANTITY-MEASURE.

prot′-a-sis. A conditional clause; the introduction to a Greek drama. ADAGE-NONSENSE, PREDECESSOR-CONTINUATION.

pro′-te-an. Changeable. MUTABILITY-STABILITY.

pro-tect′. To keep from harm. CAREFULNESS-CARELESSNESS, SECURITY-INSECURITY.

pro-tect′-ed. Guarded. SECURITY-INSECURITY.

pro-tect′-ing. Guarding. SECURITY-INSECURITY.

pro-tec′-tion. Shelter. ATTACK-DEFENSE, DOMINANCE-IMPOTENCE, RELEASE-RESTRAINT, SECURITY-INSECURITY.

pro-tect′-or. One who protects. ATTACK-DEFENSE, CHIEF-UNDERLING, GUARD-PRISONER, SECURITY-INSECURITY.

pro-tect′-or-ate. A relation of a powerful nation over a weaker one under its control. RULE-LICENSE.

pro″-té″-gé′. One cared for by another. CHIEF-UNDERLING, FRIEND-FOE.

pro′-te-i-form″. Protean. MUTABILITY-STABILITY.

pro′-te-in. Compounds of proteids. ORGANIZATION-INORGANIZATION, VISCIDITY-FOAM.

pro-ter′-vi-ty. Peevishness. FAVORITE-QUARRELSOMENESS.

pro-test′. To deny. ASSENT-DISSENT, ASSERTION-DENIAL, OBSERVANCE-NONOBSERVANCE, PETITION-EXPOSTULATION, PROFFER-REFUSAL, SETTLEMENT-DEFAULT; **protest against,** ANTAGONISM-CONCURRENCE, APPROVAL-DISAPPROVAL.

pro′-test. The act of protesting. **Counter-protest,** EVIDENCE-COUNTEREVIDENCE; **enter a protest,** PETITION-EXPOSTULATION; **under protest,** ASSENT-DISSENT, COERCION, READINESS-RELUCTANCE.

prot′-es-tant. One supporting a protest. ASSENT-DISSENT.

Prot′-es-tant. Opposed to Roman Catholicism. ORTHODOXY-HETERODOXY.

Prot′-es-tant-ism. State of being a Protestant. ASSENT-DISSENT, ORTHODOXY-HETERODOXY.

prot″-es-ta′-tion. Dissent. ASSERTION-DENIAL.

pro-test′-ed. Denied. **Protested bills,** PETITION-EXPOSTULATION, SETTLEMENT-DEFAULT.

Pro′-te-us. A marine deity who could assume any shape. MUTABILITY-STABILITY.

proth′-es-is. A credence-table. FANE.

pro-thon′-o-ta-ry. A notary. RECORDER.

pro′-to-col. An informal treaty. CONTRACT-DESIGN.

pro′-to-plasm. The principal portion of an animal cell. BIOLOGY, COPY-MODEL, FERTILITY-STERILITY, ORGANIZATION-INORGANIZATION.

pro′-to-plast. The original. COPY-MODEL.

pro′-to-type. A primitive form. COPY-MODEL, PROPHECY.

pro-tract′. To prolong. EARLINESS-LATENESS, LENGTH-SLOWNESS, PLURALITY-FRACTION, TERSENESS-PROLIXITY.

pro-tract′-ed. Prolonged. LASTINGNESS-TRANSIENTNESS, TERSENESS-PROLIXITY.

pro-trac′-tion. A lengthening out. EARLINESS-LATENESS, LENGTH-SHORTNESS.

pro-trep′-tic-al. Hortatory. MOTIVE-CAPRICE.

pro-trude′. To thrust out. CONVEXITY-CONCAVITY.

pro-tru′-sion. A bulging out. CONVEXITY-CONCAVITY.

pro-tu′-ber-ance. Prominence. CONVEXITY-CONCAVITY.

pro-tu′-ber-ant. Bulging out. CONVEXITY-CONCAVITY.

pro-typ′-i-fy. To foreshadow. PROPHECY.

proud. Arrogant; high-mettled. REPUTATION-DISCREDIT, SELFRESPECT-HUMBLENESS; **proud flesh,** CONVEXITY-CONCAVITY.

prove. Demonstrate. EMOTION, NUMBERING, OCCURRENCE-DESTINY, PROOF-DISPROOF, TRIAL; **prove one's case,** JUSTIFICATION-CHARGE; **prove recreant,** PATRIOTISM-TREASON; **prove true,** TRUTH-ERROR.

proved′. Demonstrated. PROOF-DISPROOF.

prov′-en-der. Food for cattle; provisions. NUTRIMENT-EXCRETION, PROVISION-WASTE.

prov′-erb. An adage. ADAGE-NONSENSE.

proverbe [F.] (pro-verb′). A kind of comedy. ACTING.

pro-ver′-bi-al. Well-known. ADAGE-NONSENSE, KNOWLEDGE-IGNORANCE.

pro-vide′. To furnish. PROVISION-WASTE; **provide against,** PREPARATION-NONPREPARATION; **provide against a rainy day,** GENEROSITY-FRUGALITY, PROVISION-WASTE.

pro-vi′-ded. On condition; furnished. CONDITION-SITUATION, HYPOTHESIS, MODIFICATION, PREPARATION-NONPREPARATION; **provided for,** AFFLUENCE-PENURY; **well-provided,** ENOUGH.

prov'-i-dence. Foresight; God's care. DIVINITY, PREPARATION-NONPREPARATION, PREVISION.

Prov'-i-dence. God. DIVINITY; **waiter on Providence,** ACTIVITY-INDOLENCE, CONTENTEDNESS-DISCONTENT-MENT.

prov'-i-dent. Exercising foresight. CAPACITY-INCAPACITY, CAREFULNESS-CARELESSNESS, PREPARATION-NONPREPARATION.

prov''-i-den'-tial. Resulting from God's providence. OPPORTUNENESS-UNSUITABLENESS, WELFARE-MISFORTUNE,

prov'-ince. A subjected country; a department. DIVI-SION, DWELLER-HABITATION, EXTENSION-DISTRICT, OCCUPATION.

pro-vin'-cial. Pertaining to a province. DIVISION, DWELLER-HABITATION, EXTENSION-DISTRICT, OCCUPATION, TASTE-VULGARITY.

pro-vin'-cial-ism. A provincial speech. RHETORIC, WORD-NEOLOGY.

pro-vi'-sion. A stipulation; victuals; preparation. AFFLUENCE-PENURY, MEANS, NUTRIMENT-EXCRETION, PREPARATION-NONPREPARATION, PROVISION-WASTE.

PROVISION—WASTE.

Commissariat. Food supplied to an army through the regular department.

Grist. Grain to be ground: a supply.

Grist to the mill. A supply.

Provender. Food for cattle; sometimes food in general. See NUTRIMENT.

Providing. That which is furnished for future use. See *Verbs.*

Provisions. A supply of food of any kind.

Purveyance. Anything provided; food; provisions.

Reenforcement. An additional supply of forces for an army.

Resources. Means or property that are available. See MEANS.

Subvention. The act of aiding; a supporting; a governmental aid. See OBSTRUCTION-HELP.

Supply. Food and the like necessary to the maintenance of an army, etc.

Viaticum [L.]. An allowance for traveling expenses.

PROVISION—*Nouns of Agent.*

Batman. A servant who looks after a packhorse in war.

Caterer. One who furnishes food for an entertainment.

Cateress. A woman purveyor.

Commissary. A military officer in charge of subsistence.

Comprador [It.]. Caterer.

Feeder. One who furnishes food.

Grocer. One who sells provisions.

Jackal. One who serves another's purpose: from the supposition that the jackal finds prey for the lion.

Pelican. A large bird, fabled to feed its young with blood from its breast.

Purveyor. One who furnishes food.

Quartermaster. An officer of army or government charged with issuing clothing, food, supplies, etc.

Restaurateur [F.]. A keeper of an eating-house.

Sutler. A small trader, following an army, who sells eatables to the soldiers. See DEALER.

Victualler. One who supplies victuals.

PROVISION—*Verbs.*

Arm. To furnish with what is necessary to an increase of one's efficiency, as food or weapons.

Beat up for. To stir about and try to get.

Cater. To furnish food for an entertainment.

Feed. To give food to; take food.

Fill. To supply to sufficiency.

Fill up. To provide.

Find. To furnish or provide.

Find one in. To see that one has what he needs.

Forage. To overrun a country in quest of food for men or horses.

Furnish. To give a supply; supply with anything needful.

Have in reserve.
Have in store. } To keep back in the present for use in the future.
Have to fall back upon.

Keep.
Keep by one. } To have in one's use, for one's benefit or pleasure.
Keep on foot.

Lay in. To collect and store.

Lay in a stock.
Lay in a store. } To gather a reserve supply that may be
Make due provisions for. } drawn on at will.

Make good. To supply, as a defect.

Make provision for. To collect for future use.

Provide. To put in a state of preparation; furnish supplies.

Provide against a rainy day. To take heed to the future.

Provision. To furnish with food.

Purvey. To provide; furnish, as supplies.

Recruit. To restore or repair what is lacking or deficient; collect men anew.

Consumption. A gradual destruction, or using up.

Dispersion. A vanishing away; a scattering in many directions. See GATHERING-SCATTERING.

Ebb. Decrease; decline.

Exhaustion. Deprivation of strength or energy.

Expenditure. Act of expending; a paying out; a diminishing, as of money.

Leakage. Waste, as by leaking. See ENTRANCE-EXIT.

Loss. The state of being lost, or of having suffered destruction. See GAIN-LOSS.

Misuse. The act of using wrongfully or foolishly. See USE-MISUSE.

Mountain in labor. Wasted or unnecessary toil (a mouse is brought forth).

Prodigality. Excessive waste. See EXTRAVAGANCE.

Rubbish. Waste, refuse, or rejected matter. See USEFULNESS-USELESSNESS.

Waste. Act of squandering; an incessant diminishing of strength, energy, etc.

Wasting. A gradual destruction. See *Verbs.*

Wear and tear. Loss by service, exposure, or injury incident to the ordinary use of a thing.

WASTE—*Verbs.*

Break a butterfly on a wheel. To exert unnecessary effort; waste one's toil.

Burn the candle at both ends. To be wasteful.

Cast away. To throw away; waste.

Cast one's bread upon the waters. To throw away in the present so as to gather in the future.

Cast one's pearls before swine. To do a foolish, wasteful act.

Consume. To waste away gradually.

Cut blocks with a razor. To waste one's energy or resources.

Disperse. To scatter in all directions, waste. See GATHERING-SCATTERING.

Drain. To exhaust gradually; diminish the amount of.

Dry up. To cease to flow.

Ebb. To flow back; decline.

Employ a steam-engine to crack a nut. To do unnecessary work.

Empty. To remove the contents of; exhaust.

Exhaust. To draw off; diminish the strength, supply, etc., of.

Expend. To use up.

Fling away. To discard.

Fritter away. To waste away in a trifling matter.

Impoverish. To make poor.

Labor in vain. To do work which is fruitless. See USEFULNESS-USELESSNESS.

Leak. To pass gradually away. See ENTRANCE-EXIT.

Melt away. To disappear; be dissipated.

Pour water into a sieve. To do useless work.

Run dry. To cease to flow.

Run to waste. To accomplish no useful end.

Spend. To consume; lose force or energy.

Spill. To pour out; scatter and be wasted.

Squander. To spend foolishly and wastefully. See EXTRAVAGANCE.

Swallow up. To cause to disappear.

Throw away.

Use. To employ for a purpose.

Waste. To squander foolishly; make lose strength, etc.

"Waste its sweetness on the desert air." To bloom or flourish without being seen. [Gray's *Elegy.*]

Waste powder and shot. To shoot uselessly.

WASTE—*Adjectives.*

At a low ebb. Wasting away.

Penny-wise and pound-foolish. Economical in small things, extravagant in large things.

PROVISION—WASTE—*Continued.*

PROVISION—VERBS—*Continued.*

Replenish. To fill again after depletion.
Stock. To furnish with stock; lay by, as supplies.
Stock with. To supply.
Store. To collect and put in a place of safe-keeping for future use. See STORE.
Suppeditate. To supply.
Supply. To furnish with what is necessary.
Victual. To furnish with victuals.

WASTE—ADJECTIVES—*Continued.*

Wasted. Passed away. See *Verbs.*
Wasteful. Inclined to waste; causing waste and loss.

WASTE—*Phrases.*

Le jeu ne vaut pas la chandelle [F.]. The game is not worth the candle.
Magno conatu magnas nugas [L.]. Great trifles from a great effort.

pro-vi′-sion-al. Temporary. CONDITION - SITUATION, LASTINGNESS - TRANSIENTNESS, PREPARATION - NON-PREPARATION.
pro-vi′-sions. Conditions. TERMS.
pro-vi′-so. A conditional stipulation. MODIFICATION, TERMS.
pro-vi′-so-ry. Conditional; provisional. LASTINGNESS-TRANSIENTNESS.
prov″-o-ca′-tion. A cause of anger; incitement to action. EXCITATION, FAVORITE-ANGER, MOTIVE-CAPRICE, PLEASURABLENESS-PAINFULNESS.
pro-vo′-ca-tive. Serving to provoke. EXCITATION, MOTIVE-CAPRICE.
pro-voke′. Irritate; incite. CAUSE-EFFECT, EXCITATION, FAVORITE-ANGER, MOTIVE-CAPRICE, PLEASURABLENESS-PAINFULNESS; **provoke desire,** DESIRE-DISTASTE; **provoke hatred,** LOVE-HATE.
pro-vo′-king. Irritating. LOVE-HATE, PLEASURABLE-NESS-PAINFULNESS.
provoquant [F.] (pro-vo-kɑn′). Incensing. EXCITATION.
prov′-ost. A person having charge over others. CHIEF-UNDERLING, PRESIDENT - MEMBER, REPRESENTATIVE.
prow. The fore part of a vessel. ANTERIORITY-POSTERIORITY.
prow′-ess. Daring valor. BRAVERY-COWARDICE.
prowl. To go about stealthily. ENLIGHTENMENT-SECRECY, TRAVELING-NAVIGATION; **prowl after,** QUEST-EVASION.
prox′-i-mate. Next; near. PRECEDENCE-SUCCESSION, REMOTENESS-NEARNESS; **proximate cause,** CAUSE-EFFECT.
prox-im′-i-ty. Nearness. INTERSPACE-CONTACT, REMOTENESS-NEARNESS.
prox′-i-mo. Next month. FUTURE-PAST.
proximus ardet [L.] (prox′-im-ʊs ɑr′-det). The next burns. REFUGE-PITFALL.
prox′-y. One representing another. PRESIDENT-MEMBER, REPRESENTATIVE, SECURITY-INSECURITY.
prude. A person affecting modesty. PURITY-IMPURITY, SOCIETY-AFFECTATION.
pru′-dence. Caution. CAREFULNESS-CARELESSNESS, RECKLESSNESS-CAUTION.
pru′-dent. Judicious. CAREFULNESS-CARELESSNESS, RECKLESSNESS-CAUTION, SAGACITY-INCAPACITY.
pru′-der-y. Assumed coyness. DESIRE-PARTICULAR-NESS, SOCIETY-AFFECTATION.
pru′-dish. Acting like a prude. SOCIETY-AFFECTATION.
prune. To trim; to cut off. ADDITION-SUBTRACTION, BETTERMENT-DETERIORATION, LENGTH-SHORTNESS.
pru-nel′-la. A cloth for the uppers of shoes. **Leather or prunella,** CONSEQUENCE-INSIGNIFICANCE.
pru-nelle′. A small acid French prune. NUTRIMENT-EXCRETION.
pru′-ri-ence. Lascivious craving. DESIRE-DISTASTE.
pru′-ri-en-cy. Inclination to lascivious thoughts. PURITY-IMPURITY.
pru′-ri-ent. Craving. PURITY-IMPURITY.
Prus′-sian. Pertaining to Prussia. **Prussian blue,** BLUENESS-ORANGE.

prus′-sic. Derived from Prussian blue. **Prussic acid,** REMEDY-BANE.
pry. To scrutinize. INQUISITIVENESS-INDIFFERENCE, INVESTIGATION-ANSWER, SIGHT-BLINDNESS; **pry into the future,** PREVISION.
pry′-ing. Scrutinizing. INQUISITIVENESS-INDIFFERENCE, INVESTIGATION-ANSWER.
pryt″-a-ne′-um. A public building in a Greek city. APPROVAL-DISAPPROVAL.
psalm. A hymn of praise. DEVOTION-IDOLATRY, MUSIC.
psalm′-book″. A psalter. CEREMONIAL.
psal′-mo-dy. Psalm-singing. MUSIC.
Psal′-ter. The Book of Psalms. CEREMONIAL, DEVOTION-IDOLATRY.
psal′-ter-y. A musical instrument. MUSICAL INSTRUMENTS.
pse′-pho-man″-cy. Divination with pebbles. PROPHECY.
pseu′-do. Pretended. LIKENESS-UNLIKENESS, TRUTHFULNESS-FRAUD.
pseu″-do-blep′-sis. False sight. SIGHT-DIMSIGHTEDNESS.
pseu-dol′-o-gy. Falsehood of speech. WORD-NEOLOGY.
pseu′-do-nym. A fictitious name. NAME-MISNOMER, WORD-NEOLOGY.
pseu″-do-rev″-e-la′-tion. A false revelation. REVELATION-PSEUDOREVELATION.
pseu′-do-scope. An instrument which shows objects reversed. OPTICAL INSTRUMENTS.
pshaw. An exclamation of dissatisfaction. CONSEQUENCE - INSIGNIFICANCE, EXCITABILITY - INEXCITABILITY.
psy′-chic-al. Pertaining to the soul. MIND-IMBECILITY.
psy′-chics. Pertaining to the mind. MIND-IMBECILITY.
psy″-cho-log′-i-cal. Pertaining to psychology. MIND-IMBECILITY.
psy-chol′-o-gist. Mental philosopher. MIND-IMBECILITY.
psy-chol′-o-gy. The science of the soul. MIND-IMBECILITY.
psy′-cho-man″-cy. Necromancy. PROPHECY.
ptis′-an. A medicine. REMEDY-BANE.
pty′-a-lism. Salivation. NUTRIMENT-EXCRETION.
pu′-ber-ty. The age at which one is capable of generation. INFANCY-AGE.
pu-bes′-cence. Quality of being pubescent. MANHOOD.
pu-bes′-cent. Arrived at the age of puberty. MANHOOD.
pu′-bis. A bone. ANATOMY.
pub′-lic. People at large. HUMANITY, PUBLICITY; **general public,** HUMANITY; **go to the public house,** TEETOTALISM-INTEMPERANCE; **make public,** EXPOSURE-HIDINGPLACE, PUBLICITY; **public enemy,** FRIEND-FOE; **public house,** DWELLER-HABITATION; **public opinion,** ASSENT-DISSENT; **public park,** CITY-COUNTRY; **public press,** PUBLICITY; **public spirit,** HUMANITARIANISM-MISANTHROPY.
pub″-li-ca′-tion. That which is published. CREATION-DESTRUCTION, MISSIVE-PUBLICATION, PUBLICITY.
pub′-li-cist. A writer on international law. ADVOCATE.

pub-lic'-i-ty.   Notoriety.   MANIFESTATION-LATENCY,
PUBLICITY.

PUBLICITY.

Bruit.   Report or rumor noised abroad.
Circulation.   Diffusion; the act of scattering or spreading abroad.
Cry.   Genera report or rumor.
Currency.   The state of being current; general esteem or standing.
Edition.   Total number of copies of a book, newspaper, etc., issued at one time.
Flagrancy.   Notoriousness; heinousness.
Hue and cry.   A great stir and clamor about any matter.
Indication.   The act of showing or pointing out.
Notoriety.   The character of being notorious; common knowledge or talk.
Proclamation.   The act of proclaiming or publishing.
Promulgation.   The act of announcing to the public.
Propagation.   A spreading from person to person.
Public announcement, etc.   Announcement to the people.   See EN-LIGHTENMENT.
Publication.   The act of offering to public notice.
Publicity.   The state of being public or open to common knowledge; notoriety.
Report.   Common talk, or rumor.   See TIDINGS.
Vox populi [L.].   The voice of the people.

PUBLICITY—*Nouns of Means.*

Advertisement.   ˙A public notice, as in a newspaper.
Affiche [F.]   A placard or bill.
Bill.   Something conta ning a public notice or advertisement.
Broadside.   A large sheet of paper, printed on one side.
Circular.   A circular letter or announcement, usually a printed advertisement, for special or general circulation.
Circular letter.   A letter addressed to a circle, or to a number of persons having a common interest.
Gazette.   A newspaper, or printed account of current events.
Imprint.   A mark or character made by printing, stamping, or pressing; a publisher's or printer's name, etc., printed in a book or other publication.
Journal.   A periodical making public daily current events.
Manifesto.   A public, official, and authoritative declaration or proc lamation.
Newspaper.   A publication issued for general circulation at frequent and regular intervals.
Notice, etc.   An announcement, often accompanied by comments or remarks, etc.   See ENLIGHTENMENT.
Placard.   A printed or written paper publicly displayed, as a proclamation or advertisement.
Poster.   An advertising sheet posted on a wall, paling, or the like.
Public press.   Publications for the public or the people.
Publisher, etc.   One who makes a business of publishing books or periodicals, etc.   See *Verbs.*
Telegraphy.   The art or process of conveying intelligence by telegraph.
The Press.   The publications of a country.

PUBLICITY—*Verbs.*

Advertise.   To make public by advertisement.
Afficher [F.]   To stick up; post.
Blazon.   To proclaim; make widely known.
Broach.   To introduce for the first time; make public.
Circulate.   To spread abroad; disseminate.
Diffuse.   To spread abroad freely; circulate.
Disseminate.   To sow broadcast; scatter.
Edit.   To oversee the preparation of for publication.
Emit.   To send forth authoritatively.
Evulgate.   To publish abroad.
Herald.   To announce by a herald; proclaim.
Issue.   To send forth officially; put into circulation.
Placard.   To announce by placards; post placards.
Post.   To bring to the public notice by putting up placards or posters.
Proclaim.   To promulgate; announce aloud.
Promulgate.   To announce officially and formally; publish.
Propagate.   To spread abroad; disseminate.
Publish.   To make known or announce publicly; proclaim.
Rumor.   To circulate as a rumor; report abroad
Spread.   To distribute about; make widely known; diffuse.
Utter.   In law, to publish; to give forth with audible sound

PUBLICITY—*Verbal Expressions.*

Acquire currency; announce with beat of drum; announce with flourish of trumpets; bandy about; become public, etc. (see *Adjectives*); be public, etc. (see *Adjectives*); be published; blaze about; blaze abroad; blow about; bring before the public; bruit about; buzz

about; come out; drag before the public; drag into the open day; find vent; fly about; get about; get abroad; get afloat; get out; get wind; give forth; give out; give tongue; give to the world; go about; go forth; go the round of the newspapers; go the rounds; go through the length and breadth of the land; hawk about; lay before the public; make known, etc. (see ENLIGHTENMENT); make public; noise abroad; pass current; pass from mouth to mouth; post up; proclaim at Charing Cross, to proclaim publicly and officially, Charing Cross being one of the principal streets of London; proclaim from the housetops; publish in the Gazette; put about; put forth; put forward; raise a cry; raise a hue and cry; raise a report; run like wildfire; see the light; send forth; send round the crier; set news afloat; sound a trumpet; speak of; spread abroad; spread like wildfire; take air; talk of; thunder forth; trumpet forth; *virum volitare per ora* [L.], to fly through the mouths of men; whisper about.

PUBLICITY—*Adjectives.*

Arrant.   Notoriously bad.
Current, etc.   Circulating etc.   See TIDINGS.
Encyclical.   Intended for general circulation.
Exoteric.   External; public.
Flagrant.   Notorious; heinous.
In circulation.   Circulating.
Notorious.   Publicly known, especially unfavorably known to the general public.
Open, etc.   Not private; public, etc.   See MANIFESTATION.
Promulgatory.   Spreading from person to person.
Public.   Open to all; well-known.
Published, etc.   Made public; promulgated, etc.   See *Verbs.*
Trumpet-tongued.   Having a powerful, far-reaching voice or speech.

PUBLICITY—*Adverbs, etc.*

In open court.   In a court opened to the public.
Publicly, etc.   In a public manner, etc.   See *Adjectives.*
With open doors.   Not secretly; publicly.

PUBLICITY—*Interjections.*

Notice!   Take notice.
O yes!
Oyez!   [Anglo-F.].   Hear.   A term used by criers of courts to secure silence before making a proclamation.

PUBLICITY—*Phrases.*

Nomina stultorum parietibus hærent [L.].   Fools' names are stuck on house walls.
Notice is hereby given.
Semel emissum volat irrevocabile verbum [L.].   Once sent forth the word flies irrevocable.
These are to give notice.
This is to give notice.

pub'-lic-ly.   In a public manner.   **Publicly rumored,** TIDINGS-MYSTERY.
publico, pro bono [L.] (pub'-lic-o, pro bo'-no).   For the public good.   HUMANITARIANISM-MISANTHROPY, USEFULNESS-USELESSNESS.
pub'-lish.   To make public.   PUBLICITY; **publish the banns,** ENLIGHTENMENT-SECRECY, PETITION-EXPOSTULATION, WRITING-PRINTING.
pub'-lish-er.   One who publishes.   MISSIVE-PUBLICATION, PUBLICITY.
puce.   Of a brownish-purple color.   YELLOWNESS-PURPLE.
pu'-cel-age.   Virginity.   INFANCY-AGE, MATRIMONY-CELIBACY, PURITY-IMPURITY.
Puck.   An elf.   JOVE-FIEND; **play Puck,** ACTING.
puck'-er.   To contract; agitation.   FAVORITE-ANGER, PLICATION; **in a pucker,** EXCITATION, FAVORITE-ANGER.
pud'-der.   A tumult.   ACTIVITY-INDOLENCE, REGULARITY-IRREGULARITY.
pud'-ding.   A species of food.   HARDNESS-SOFTNESS, NUTRIMENT-EXCRETION, PULPINESS-OILINESS, SWEETNESS-ACIDITY; **in pudding time,** EARLINESS-LATENESS.
Pud'-ding, Jack.   A clown.   ACTING, BRAGGING.
pud'-dle.   A muddy plash.   GULF-PLAIN.
pud'-dler.   One who puddles.   ACTIVITY-INDOLENCE.
pud'-dock.   A small enclosure adjoining a stable; a paddock.   ENCLOSURE.

pu-dic'-i-ty. Chastity. Purity-Impurity.

pudor, proh [L.] (piu'-dor, pro). O for shame! Reputation-Discredit.

pu'-er-ile. Juvenile. Consequence-Insignificance, Force-Weakness, Infant-Veteran, Sagacity-Incapacity.

pu-er'-per-al. Pertaining to childbirth. Creation-Destruction.

puff. To blow; to distend. Adulation-Disparagement, Approval-Disapproval, Bragging, Enlargement-Diminution, Gull-Hyperbole, River-Wind, Sweetness-Acidity, Weariness-Refreshment; **puff of smoke,** Friability; **puff up,** Conceit-Diffidence.

puffed. Distended. **Puffed up,** Conceit-Diffidence, Selfrespect-Humbleness.

puff'-er. One who praises extravagantly. Flatterer-Defamer.

puff'-er-y. The practise of puffing. Bragging, Gull-Hyperbole.

puff'-y. Bloated. Enlargement-Diminution, Greatness-Littleness.

pug. Snub; a kind of dog. Fauna-Flora, Length-Shortness.

pugh. An exclamation of contempt. Consequence-Insignificance.

pu'-gil-ism. The art of boxing. Strife-Peace.

pu'-gil-ist. A prize-fighter. Belligerent.

pu-gil-is'-tic. Pertaining to prize-fighting. Strife-Peace.

pug-na'-cious. Quarrelsome. Bravery-Cowardice, Humanitarianism-Misanthropy, Strife-Peace.

pug-nac'-i-ty. Quarrelsomeness. Favorite-Quarrelsomeness, Strife-Peace.

puis'-ne. Younger; inferior. Antecedence-Sequence, Infancy-Age.

pu'-is-sance. Prowess. Might-Impotence.

pu'-is-sant. Prowess. Might-Impotence, Strength-Weakness.

puke. To vomit. Admission-Expulsion.

pul'-chri-tude. Beauty. Beauty-Ugliness.

pule. To cry plaintively. Cry-Ululation, Jubilation-Lamentation.

pull. To draw; to row. Push-Pull, Traveling-Navigation, Writing-Printing; **a long and a strong pull,** Antagonism-Concurrence, Toil-Relaxation; **pull about one's ears,** Elevation-Depression; **pull an oar,** Action-Passiveness; **pull by the sleeve,** Remembrance-Forgetfulness; **pull different ways,** Variance-Accord; **pull down,** Creation-Destruction, Elevation-Depression; **pull in,** Release-Restraint; **pull out,** Injection-Ejection; **pull the check-string,** Discontinuance-Continuance; **pull the wires,** Management; **pull through,** Obstruction-Help, Renovation-Relapse; **pull together,** Antagonism-Concurrence, Cooperation-Opposition; **pull to pieces,** Adulation-Disparagement, Approval-Disapproval, Creation-Destruction, Union-Disunion; **pull towards,** Attraction-Repulsion, Variance-Concord; **pull up,** Approval-Disapproval, Discontinuance-Continuance, Injection-Ejection, Justification-Charge, Litigation, Movement-Rest; **pull upon the purse,** Costliness-Cheapness; **strong pull,** Toil-Relaxation.

pulled. Drawn. **Pulled down,** Strength-Weakness, Weariness-Refreshment.

pul'-let. A young hen. Infant-Veteran.

pul'-ley. An elementary mechanical power. Instrument.

Pull'-man. A car-builder. **Pullman car,** Conveyance-Vessel.

pul'-lu-late. To germinate. Creation-Destruction, Enlargement-Diminution.

pul'-mo-na-ry. Pertaining to the lungs. Anatomy, River-Wind.

pul-mon'-ic. Pertaining to the lungs. River-Wind.

pulp. A moist, soft mass of matter, usually organic. Pulpiness-Oiliness.

pulp'-i-ness. The state of being pulpy. Pulpiness-Oiliness.

PULPINESS—OILINESS.

Curd. The coagulated portion of milk of which cheese is made.

Dough. A soft mass of moistened flour or meal, mixed for cooking into bread, etc.

Grume. A viscid, semifluid mass.

Jam. A pulpy, sweet conserve of fruit.

Oleomargarine. A substitute for butter.

Pap. Any soft, pulpy food for babes.

Paste. A pulpy, adhesive compound, of which the basis is usually flour and water.

Pasteboard. Paper pulp compressed into a sheet.

Poultice. A mollifying remedy in a moist mealy form, applied to sores.

Pudding. A dish of soft food, often sweetened and flavored, as for dessert.

Pulp. A moist, soft, slightly cohering mass of matter, usually organic.

Pulpiness, etc. The state of being pulpy, etc. See *Adjectives.*

Rob. The inspissated juice of ripe fruit; rhob.

PULPINESS—*Adjectives.*

Grumous. Resembling grume; thick; clotted.

Papescent. Containing or having the qualities of pap.

Pulpy, etc. Like pulp; soft; succulent. See *Nouns.*

Pultaceous. Macerated; softened; nearly fluid.

OILINESS—Adjectives—*Continued from Column 2.*

Soapy. Resembling, containing, or consisting of soap; smeared with soap.

Unctuous. Like a salve; greasy; soapy to the touch.

Waxy. Like wax; plastic; yielding.

Anointment. The act of anointing, or the state of being anointed; also an ointment.

Lubrication, etc. The act of supplying an oily substance, as bearings, to lessen friction, etc. See Friction-Lubrication.

Lubricity. The state of being slippery and oily.

Naphtha. Mixture of volatile, liquid, inflammable hydrocarbons.

Ointment, etc. A fatty, semisolid preparation, with which some medicine has been incorporated: used as a remedy of burns, sores, etc. See Pulpiness-Oil.

Unctuosity. The state or quality of being greasy or soapy.

Unctuousness, etc. The quality of being oily or greasy, etc. See *Adjectives.*

OILINESS—*Verbs.*

Oil, etc. Smear, rub, soak, or treat with oil, etc. See Friction-Lubrication.

OILINESS—*Adjectives.*

Adipose. Fatty.

Butyraceous. Having the qualities of butter.

Fat. Oily; greasy.

Fatty. Consisting of, containing, or having the qualities of fat; **fat.**

Greasy. Smeared with grease; like grease or oil.

Lardaceous. Like lard; fatty.

Oily. Pertaining to or containing oil; greasy.

Oleaginous. Pertaining to oil; oily.

Pinguid. Fat; unctuous; greasy.

Saponaceous. Having the nature or quality of soap.

Sebaceous. Fatty; oily; containing, secreting, or consisting of fat matter.

Slippery. Smooth so as to be hard to hold.

(Continued on Column 1.)

PULPINESS—OIL.

OIL.

Adipocere. A fatty oil formed by the decomposition of animal matter with the presence of moisture and the absence of air.
Animal-oil. Oil derived from the bones of animals.
Blubber. A layer of oil-yielding fat beneath the skin of some marine animals.
Butter. The fatty constituent of milk.
Cerement. A waxed cloth.
Colza-oil. Oil derived from the summer rape or coleseed.
Cream. The thick oily substance that gathers on the surface of milk.
Crystal-oil. A clear oil.
Dripping. The fat which runs from meat when roasting.
Elain. Olein.
Exunge. Ointment.
Fat. A white, greasy, easily melted compound forming a part of animal tissue.
Glycerin. A sweet, liquid, oily compound formed by the decomposition of natural fats with alkalis.
Grease. The fat of animals.
Lard. The semisolid oil of hog's fat.
Liniment. A liquid, oily preparation for rubbing on the skin in case of bruises, etc.
Linseed-oil. The oil expressed from flaxseed.
Mineral-oil. Petroleum.
Neat's-foot oil. The oil expressed from the feet of cattle.

Nut-oil. Oil derived from various nuts.
Oil. A neutral substance of animal or vegetable origin insoluble in water.
Ointment. A fatty preparation mixed with some medicinal substance.
Oleagin. Olein.
Olein. A colorless, oily, liquid compound, the chief constituent of fatty oils.
Olive-oil. Oil expressed from the fruit of the olive.
Paraffin. A colorless, waxy substance derived from methane.
Petroleum. An inflammable oily liquid which exudes from the earth.
Rock-oil. Petroleum.
Salad-oil. Oil used for dressing salad.
Soap. Any compound formed by the union of a fatty acid with a base, usually hardened by pressure.
Soft soap. Any compound formed by the union of a fatty acid with a base.
Spermaceti. Oil derived from the sperm-whale.
Stearin. A white compound contained in animal fats.
Suet. The fatty tissues in the region of the loins of various animals.
Tallow. A substance composed of hard and less fusible fats.
Train-oil. The oil from the blubber of whales.
Unguent. An oil used as an ointment.
Vegetable-oil. Oil derived from various vegetables.
Wax. A fatty solid substance secreted by bees.

PULPINESS—ROSIN.

ROSIN.

Amber. A fossilized vegetable resin, yellowish in color and translucent.
Ambergris. A waxy concretion from the sperm-whale.
Asphalt. Mineral pitch or compound native bitumen.
Asphalte. ⎫
Asphaltum. ⎬ Asphalt.
Bitumen. Any native mixture of hydocarbons; mineral pitch.
Camphor. Gumlike, fragrant compound.
Copal. A transparent resin used in varnishes
Gum. Properly, only vegetable secretions that are soluble in water.
Japan. A varnish made of shellac or other resin.
Lac. A resinous exudation from an insect.
Lacquer. A varnish made from shellac
Magilp. A mixture used as a vehicle for colors
Mastic. A resinous exudation used as an aromatic in varnishes, etc.
Pitch. The resinous exudation of pines.

Resin. Any vegetable exudation, soluble in alcohol, but not in water.
Rosin. The amber-colored substance left after the distilling of oil of turpentine.
Sealing-wax. A mixture of resinous materials and pigments.
Tar. A dark-colored viscid liquid obtained by the distillation of organic bodies and bituminous minerals.
Varnish. A resinous solution used in painting.

ROSIN—*Verb.*

Varnish. To cover with varnish.

ROSIN—*Adjectives.*

Bituminous. Of the nature of bitumen; containing much volatile hydrocarbon.
Pitchy. Sticky.
Resinous. Of the nature of resin.
Tarry. Like tar; covered with tar.

---

pul'-pit. An elevated desk for a preacher. FANE, SCHOOL.
pulp'-y. Soft. PULPINESS-OILINESS.
pul'-sate. To throb. AGITATION, PERIODICITY-IRREGULARITY, VIBRATION.
pul'-sa-tion. Throbbing. EMOTION, VIBRATION.
pulse. The beating of the heart; peas, beans, etc. FAUNA-FLORA, PERIODICITY-IRREGULARITY, VIBRATION; **feel the pulse,** INVESTIGATION-ANSWER, TRIAL.
pul'-sion. Driving forward. IMPETUS-REACTION.
pul-ta'-ceous. Softened. PULPINESS-OILINESS.
pul'-ver-i''-za-ble. Capable of being reduced to powder. FRIABILITY.
pul''-ver-i-za'-tion. Act of reducing to fine powder. FRIABILITY.
pul'-ver-ize. Reduce to powder. FRIABILITY.
pul-ver'-u-lence. Dustiness. FRIABILITY.
pul-ver'-u-lent. Powdery. FRIABILITY.
pul'-vil. A sweet-scented powder. PERFUME-STENCH.
pum'-mel. Beat; a knob. RECOMPENSE-PUNITION, ROUNDNESS, SUSPENSION-SUPPORT.
pump. An engine for raising water; to draw out. DRESS-UNDRESS, INVESTIGATION-ANSWER, RIVER-WIND.
pump'-room. A room in which a pump is worked. DWELLER-HABITATION, REMEDY-BANE.
pun. A play upon words. ADAGE-NONSENSE, AMBIGUITY, RHETORIC, UNIFORMITY-DIVERSITY, WITTINESS-DULNESS.

punch. A blow; a beverage. ACTING, APERTURE-CLOSURE, CONVEYER, COPY-MODEL, ENGRAVING, IMPETUS-REACTION, NUTRIMENT-EXCRETION, PERFORATOR-STOPPER, TEETOTALISM-INTEMPERANCE.
Punch. A clown. WAG; **Punch and Judy,** ACTING.
punch'-bowl. A bowl for punch. CONTENTS-RECEIVER, SHARPNESS-BLUNTNESS, TEETOTALISM-INTEMPERANCE.
pun'-cheon. A tool; a cask. CONTENTS-RECEIVER, PERFORATOR-STOPPER.
Pun''-chi-nel'-lo. A character in an Italian burlesque. ACTING.
punc'-ta-ted. Pointed; covered with small points. VARIEGATION.
punc-til'-io. A nice point. POMP, SOCIETY-LUDICROUSNESS, UPRIGHTNESS-DISHONESTY.
punc-til'-ious. Very exact. OBSERVANCE-NONOBSERVANCE, POMP, UPRIGHTNESS-DISHONESTY.
punc-til'-ious-ness. Precise etiquette. POMP.
punc'-to. A nice point of form. POMP.
punc'-tu-al. Exact; strict. EARLINESS-LATENESS, OBSERVANCE-NONOBSERVANCE, PERIODICITY-IRREGULARITY, TRUTH-ERROR, UPRIGHTNESS-DISHONESTY.
punc''-tu-al'-i-ty. Promptness. ACTIVITY-INDOLENCE, EARLINESS-LATENESS, PERIODICITY-IRREGULARITY, TRUTH-ERROR, UPRIGHTNESS-DISHONESTY.
punc'-tu-al-ly. Promptly. EARLINESS-LATENESS, PERIODICITY-IRREGULARITY.

punc'-tu-ate. To mark with points. GRAMMAR-SOLE-
CISM.
punc'-tu-a-tion. The art of dividing sentences by
points. GRAMMAR-SOLECISM.
punc'-ture. A small hole. APERTURE-CLOSURE.
pun'-dit. A learned man. ADVOCATE, SCHOLAR-
DUNCE.
pun'-gen-cy. Sharpness. PUNGENCY, VIGOR-INERTIA.

PUNGENCY

Acrimony. Harsh or biting sharpness, as of juices.
Haut goût [F.]. High taste.
Piquancy. The quality or state of being piquant.
Poignancy. The quality or state of being poignant.
Pungency. Keenness; sharpness; piquancy.
Race. Peculiar flavor, taste, or strength.
Roughness, etc. Astringency or harshness to the taste, etc. See
ACIDITY.
Sharpness, etc. Pungency; sourness, etc. See *Adjectives*.
Strong taste. Flavor affecting the taste forcibly.
Twang. Disagreeable flavor left in the mouth.
Unsavoriness, etc. The condition or quality of being unsavory, etc.
See PALATABLENESS-UNPALATABLENESS.

PUNGENCY—*Denotations*.

Brine. Water saturated with salt.
Cavendish. A brand of American tobacco prepared by mixing with
molasses.
Caviare. The roes of the sturgeon.
Cayenne. Red pepper.
Cigar. A roll of tobacco-leaves for smoking.
Cigarette. A little cigar made of finely cut tobacco wrapped in
paper.
Cordial. A sweet and aromatic alcoholic liquor.
Dram. A drink of spirits.
Fragrant weed. Tobacco.
Indian weed. A famous quack vegetable medicine.
'Mustard. The seed of the mustard-plant, crushed and used as a
condiment.
Nicotin. A poisonous alkaloid contained in the leaves of tobacco.
Nip. A small dram of strong drink.
Niter. Saline potassium nitrate.
Quid. A small portion of tobacco for chewing.
Rappee. A strong-flavored snuff.
Saltpeter. Niter.
Seasoning, etc. Something added to food to give it relish. See CON-
DIMENT.
Segar. Cigar.
Snuff. Tobacco, fermented, dried, and pulverized, inhaled into the
nostrils.
Tobacco. The leaves of the tobacco-plant prepared for smoking,
chewing, etc.
Weed. Tobacco.

PUNGENCY—*Verbs*.

Be pungent, etc. Be sharp, keen, racy, etc. See *Adjectives*.
Bite the tongue. Cause sharp pain or smarting in the mouth.
Brine. Sprinkle with salt or brine.
Chew. Chew tobacco.
Devil. Grill with Cayenne pepper; season highly, as with pepper.
Pepper. Sprinkle with pepper.
Pickle. Preserve or season with pickle.
Render pungent, etc. Make sharp or racy, etc. See *Adjectives*.
Salt. Sprinkle, supply, or season with salt
Season. Fit for taste; render palatable.
Smoke. Inhale and exhale the smoke of, as tobacco.
Spice. Season with spice.
Take snuff. Snuff pulverized tobacco.

PUNGENCY—*Adjectives*.

Acrid. Pungent; bitter.
Acrimonious. Full of bitterness; sharp.
Biting. Keen; pungent; nipping.
Bitter. Having a peculiar acrid taste.
Brackish. Somewhat saline.
Briny. Impregnated with salt.
Escharotic. Serving or tending to form an eschar; caustic.
Full-flavored. Abundantly or highly flavored.
Gamy. Having the flavor of game; high-flavored.
High-flavored. Richly or spicily flavored.
High-seasoned. Enriched with spice and condiments.
High-tasted. Having a strong relish; piquant.
Hot. Acrid; biting; pungent.
Hot as pepper.

Meracious. Without mixture or adulteration; strong; racy.
Mordant. Biting; caustic.
Peppery. Like pepper; hot; pungent.
Piquant [F.]. Stinging; sharp; pungent.
Pungent. Causing a sharp sensation, as of the taste, smell, or
feelings.
Racy. Having a strong flavor indicating origin; rich; peculiar and
piquant.
Rough, etc. Harsh to the taste, etc. See ACIDITY
Saline. Constituting or consisting of salt; salty.
Salt. Saline; briny.
Salt as a herring. ⎫
Salt as brine. ⎬ Figurative degrees of saltness.
Salt as Lot's wife. [Bible.] ⎭
Seasoned, etc. Fitted for taste, etc. See *Verbs*.
Sharp. Having a stinging pungent taste.
Spicy. Containing, flavored, or fragrant with spices.
Stinging. Pungent; biting.
Strong. Making a keen impression upon the senses; pungent.
Unsavory, etc. Having a disagreeable taste or odor, etc. See
PALATABLENESS-UNPALATABLENESS.
Vellicating. Causing to twitch or contract convulsively.

pun'-gent. Sharp; acrid. EMOTION, FORCE-WEAK-
NESS, ODOR-INODOROUSNESS, PUNGENCY.
Punica fides [L.] (piu'-ni-ca fai'-dîz). Punic faith.
UPRIGHTNESS-DISHONESTY.
pun'-ish. To chastise. RECOMPENSE-PUNITION.
pun'-ish-ing. Chastising. RECOMPENSE-PUNITION.
pun'-ish-ment. A penalty. RECOMPENSE-PUNITION.
pu-ni'-tion. Punishment. RECOMPENSE-PUNITION.
pu'-ni-tive. Punishing. RECOMPENSE-PUNITION.
pu'-ni-to-ry. Punishing. RECOMPENSE-PUNITION.
punk. A prostitute. PURITY-RAKE.
pun'-kah. A fan. RIVER-WIND.
pun'-ning. Playing on words. WITTINESS-DULNESS.
pun'-ster. One who puns. WAG.
punt. A flat-bottomed boat. CONVEYANCE-VESSEL,
TRAVELING-NAVIGATION.
pu'-ny. Little and weak. GREATNESS-LITTLENESS.
pup. The young of various animals. CREATION-DE-
STRUCTION, FAUNA-FLORA, INFANT-VETERAN.
pu'-pil. A scholar; a part of the eye. ANATOMY, IN-
STRUCTOR-PUPIL, SIGHT-BLINDNESS.
pu'-pil-age. The state of a scholar. EDUCATION-
LEARNING, INFANCY-AGE, INSTRUCTOR-PUPIL.
pu''-pi-lar'-i-ty. Minority. EDUCATION-LEARNING.
pupillari, in statu [L.] (piu-pil-lê'-rai, in stê'-tiu). In
state of pupilage. EDUCATION-LEARNING, IN-
STRUCTOR-PUPIL.
pup'-pet. A small doll; a tool. ANTAGONIST-ASSIST-
ANT, CHIEF-UNDERLING, DELINEATION-CARICATURE,
GREATNESS-LITTLENESS, GULL-DECEIVER; **be the
puppet of,** LIBERTY-SUBJECTION; **make a puppet of,**
RULE-LICENSE.
pup'-pet–show''. A mock drama performed by puppets. ACTING, ENTERTAINMENT-WEARINESS.
pup'-py. A young dog; a silly fop. BRAGGING,
BRAWLER, FAUNA-FLORA, SOCIETY-DANDY.
pup'-py-ism. Meanness. SOCIETY-AFFECTATION.
pur et simple [F.] (pür ê san'pl). Pure and simple.
MIXTURE-HOMOGENEITY.
pur sang [F.] (pür san·). Pure blood. GENTILITY-
COMMONALTY.
Pu-ra'-na. One of a class of sacred Hindu poetical
works. REVELATION-PSEUDOREVELATION.
pur'-blind. Near-sighted. DECISION-MISJUDGMENT,
SIGHT-DIMSIGHTEDNESS.
pur'-blind-ness. Near-sightedness. SIGHT-DIMSIGHTED-
NESS.
pur'-chase. Buy; a support. BUYING-SALE, DOMI-
NANCE-IMPOTENCE, GAIN-LOSS, SETTLEMENT-DE-
FAULT, SUSPENSION-SUPPORT.
pur'-chased. Bought. BUYING-SALE.
pur'-chase–mon'-ey. The money paid for anything.
COMMUTATION-PERMUTATION

pur'-chas-er. One who buys. Buying-Sale.

pur'-cha-sing. Buying. Buying-Sale.

pure. Simple; clean; innocent; chaste. Cleanness-Filthiness, Craft-Artlessness, Devotion-Idolatry, Godliness-Ungodliness, Innocence-Guilt, Mixture-Homogeneity, Purity-Crudeness, Purity-Impurity, Simplicity-Floridness, Taste-Vulgarity, Truth-Error, Truthfulness-Falsehood, Uprightness-Dishonesty, Virtue-Vice; **pure accent,** Vocalization-Muteness; **pure color,** Color-Achromatism.

pu''-ree'. A thick soup. Nutriment-Excretion.

pure'-ly. In a pure manner; merely. Magnitude-Smallness.

pur-ga'-tion. A purifying. Atonement, Cleanness-Filthiness.

pur'-ga-tive. A purifier. Cleanness-Filthiness.

pur'-ga-to-ry. A place for purifying souls. Atonement, Heaven-Hell, Pleasure-Pain.

purge. Cleanse. Admission-Expulsion, Atonement, Cleanness-Filthiness.

pu''-ri-fi-ca'-tion. Cleansing; refinement. Betterment-Deterioration, Cleanness-Filthiness, Mixture-Homogeneity.

pu'-ri-fi''-er. Something that refines. Cleanness-Filthiness.

pu'-ri-fy. To cleanse. Betterment-Deterioration, Cleanness-Filthiness.

pur'-ism. Extreme strictness. Society-Affectation.

puris naturalibus, in [L.] (piu'-ris na-tiu-ral'-i-bus, in). Naked. Dress-Undress.

pur'-ist. One overnice in the choice of words. Godliness-Ungodliness, Purity-Crudeness, Society-Affectation.

Pu'-ri-tan. A dissenter in the reign of Elizabeth. Austerity, Orthodoxy-Heterodoxy.

pu'-ri-tan. Overscrupulous. Godliness-Ungodliness.

pu''-ri-tan'-ic-al. Strict. Austerity, Society-Affectation.

Pu'-ri-tan-ism. Practises of the Puritans; austerity. Austerity, Orthodoxy-Heterodoxy.

pu'-ri-ty. Cleanness. Mixture-Homogeneity, Purity-Crudeness, Purity-Impurity.

PURITY—CRUDENESS.

Antithesis. Placing in contrast for effect. See Embellishment.

Concinnity. Harmony.

Ease. Freedom from strain.

Elegance. Beauty arising from materials being nicely chosen and harmoniously disposed.

Euphony. Agreeableness of sounds.

Flowing periods. Expressions that move along as with the soft movement of a stream.

Grace. } Agreeableness of form or motion resulting from
Gracefulness. } nature aided by art.

Numerosity. Harmonious flow.

Purist. One who is overparticular as to purity of literary style.

Purity. Freedom from blemish.

Readiness. Quick adaptability to needs.

The right word in the right place. Exactness of speech.

Well-rounded periods. } Accurate and gliding sentences.
Well-turned periods. }

Purity—*Verbs.*

Point an antithesis. To put in contrast.

Round a period. To close a sentence.

Purity—*Adjectives.*

Academical. Classical.

Artistic. Embodying the principles of art.

Attic. Of the best quality.

Chaste. Free from defect.

Ciceronian. Polished, fluent, and copious.

Classical. Conforming to the highest standards in art.

Correct. Faultless.

Easy. Not strained.

Elegant. Having parts well-proportioned.

Euphemistic. Substituting a less offensive term for a more disagreeable one.

Euphonious. Sounding well to the ear.

Felicitous. Enjoying deep and continued happiness.

Flowing. } Proceeding without hesitation.
Fluent. }

Graceful. Possessing grace.

Happy. Marked by pointedness.

Mellifluous. Flowing smoothly.

Natural. Reflecting nature.

Neat. Marked by good order.

Neatly expressed. } Cleverly expressed.
Neatly put. }

Numerose. Melodious.

Polished. Freed from coarseness.

Pure. Freed from any foreign elements.

Readable. Attractive for reading.

Rhythmical. Having a regular recurrence of accent, etc.

Saxon. Strong and vigorous in the use of language.

Tripping. To move lightly and rhythmically.

Unaffected. Not assuming anything unnatural.

Barbarism. Violation of the law of purity in rhetoric.

Cacophony. Harsh sound of words.

Euphemism. The use of pleasantly sounding words to tell a disagreeable fact; fair words for ugly things.

Fustian. Bombastic language. See sub Ornament.

Inelegance. The lack of elegance.

Mannerism. Monotony of style. See Society-Affectation.

Slang. Jargon not accepted in the standard language. See Word-Neology.

Solecism. Violation of the laws of grammar.

Stiffness. Lack of elasticity or variation. See sub *Adjectives.*

Unlettered muse. An uneducated writer. "Their name, their years, spelt by the unlettered Muse, the place of fame and elegy supply." [Gray, *Elegy in a Country Churchyard.*]

Words that break the jaw. } Words not easily pronounced.
Words that dislocate the jaw. }

Crudeness—*Verb.*

Be inelegant. Crude and imperfect. See *Adjectives.*

Crudeness—*Adjectives.*

Abrupt. Breaking off suddenly.

Affected. Having assumed something not one's own.

Artificial. Not natural.

Barbarous. Violating the rule of purity in rhetoric.

Cramped. Limited.

Crude. Not skilfully finished.

Dry. Not interesting.

Euphemistic. Describing an unpleasant fact by a softened expression.

Forced. Not flowing easily.

Formal. Marked by the observance of form or style.

Graceless. Lacking grace.

Grotesque. Ridiculously odd.

Guindé [F.]. Bombastic; stiff.

Halting. Hesitating.

Harsh. Unpleasant to the ear.

Inelegant. Not elegant.

Labored. Not proceeding easily.

Mannered. Practising bad manners.

Offensive to polite ears. Inelegant or offensive of speech.

Ponderous. Lacking in animation; weighty.

Rude. Unskilled in make, or action.

Stiff. Not elastic.

Turgid. Bombastic. See sub Ornament.

Uncouth. Not gracefully developed.

Ungraceful. Not graceful.

PURITY—*Adjectives—Continued.*

Unlabored. Easily executed.

Well put. Strongly expressed.

PURITY—IMPURITY.

Chastity. Freedom from unlawful sexual intercourse or indulgence.
Continence. Self-restraint, especially with respect to the sexual passion.
Decency. Freedom from immodesty or obscenity
Decorum. Propriety, as in manner, conduct, etc.
Delicacy. The quality or state of being pure or chaste.
Honesty. The quality or state of being honest; especially of women, chastity.
Modesty. The state, quality, or character of being modest; decent reserve and propriety.
Pucelage [F.]. Virginity.
Pudicity. Modesty; chastity.
Purity. Freedom from guilt or the defilement of sin; innocence, chastity.
Shame. A painful sensation excited by a consciousness of guilt or impropriety.
Virginity. Undefiled purity or chastity; maidenhood.
Virtue. Moral excellence, purity of soul; specifically, chastity.

PURITY—Denotations.

Diana. A virgin goddess who presided over virtue, chastity, and marriage.
Hippolytus. Son of Theseus, who resisted the advances of his stepmother, Phædra.
Joseph. Son of Jacob; when he was in Egypt, Potiphar's wife tried to seduce him but was repulsed.
Lucretia. Wife of Tarquinius Collatinus· her rape by Sextus Tarquinius led to the overthrow of the Tarquins and the establishment of the republic.
Prude. A woman of affected modesty, reserve, or coyness.
Vestal. One of the virgin priestesses of Vesta, on whose purity the safety of Rome depended; a woman of pure character.
Virgin. A woman who has had no carnal knowledge of man.

PURITY—Adjectives.

Chaste. Pure undefiled.
Continent. Exercising restraint as to indulgence of passions.
Decent. Fit; proper; seemly.
Decorous. Becoming; proper; seemly
Delicate. Pure; chaste.
Honest. Chaste; virtuous.
Modest. Characterized by reserve, propriety, or purity.
Platonic Purely spiritual, or devoid of sensual feeling.
Pure. Free from moral defilement; innocent.
Undefiled. Not corrupted as to chastity; unviolated.
Virtuous. Having moral excellence; chaste; pure.

PURITY—Phrase.

Notre Dame [F.]. Our Lady; the Blessed Virgin.

IMPURITY—Verbs—Continued from Column 2

Commit adultery, etc. To have illicit sexual intercourse with. See *Adjectives.*
Debauch. To make or become corrupt in morals; make vicious, dishonest, or unchaste.
Defile. To make filthy or impure; befoul.
Deflower. To despoil of purity or virginity.
Intrigue. To engage in clandestine love affairs.
Prostitute. To offer for lewd purposes, as a woman.
Seduce. To entice to surrender chastity.
Violate. To commit rape upon; ravish.

IMPURITY—Adjectives.

Adulterous. Given to adultery; illicit.
Bawdy. Obscene; filthy; unchaste.
Bestial. Brutish; sensual; depraved.
Broad. Loose; indelicate; bold.
Carnal. Sensual.
Carnal-minded. Fleshly· lustful; sensual.
Coarse. Not refined or modest; low; vulgar.
Concupiscent. Lustful, carnal; sensual.
Debauched. Corrupted in morals; made unchaste.
Dissipated. Pursuing pleasure to excess.
Dissolute. Abandoned; lewd; profligate.
Equivocal. Ascribable either to good or bad motives, questionable.
Erotic. Amorous; amatory.
Frail. Deficient in moral strength liable to be led away.
Free. Unduly familiar; indelicate, immodest.
Fulsome. Coarse; indelicate.
Gallant. Polite and attentive to ladies.
Gay. Loving pleasure; wanton.

Abuse. A corrupt, immoral, or vicious practise or act; violation; rape.
Adultery. Sexual intercourse of two persons, either of whom is married to a third person.
Advoutry. Adultery.
Amour [F.]. Illicit love affair
Amourette [F.]. Intrigue.
Bawdry. Unchastity; obscene language.
Carnality. Fleshly lust, or the indulgence of lust.
Concubinage. The state of being a concubine or of having concubines.
Concupiscence. Undue lustful appetite or passion; illicit sexual desire.
Crim. con. Criminal conversation.
Cuckoldom. The state of being the husband of an adulteress.
Debauchery. Seduction from virtue; excessive indulgence of the appetites; sensuality.
Defilement. Pollution; foulness.
Defloration. The act of depriving of virginity.
Dissipation. Profuseness in vicious indulgence, as late hours, riotous living, etc.
Double entendre [F.]. Double meaning, one meaning being indelicate.
Equivoque [F.]. Equivocation.
Faux pas [F.]. A false step; a mistake.
Flesh. The carnal and sinful nature of man.
Fornication. Illicit sexual intercourse of unmarried persons.
Free-love. The practise of consorting with the opposite sex, at pleasure without marriage.
Gallantry. Excessive attention paid to women.
Grossness, etc. Shamefulness, etc. See *Adjectives.*
Harlotry. The trade of a harlot; habitual lewdness.
Immodesty Want of modesty, delicacy, or decent reserve.
Impudicity. Immodesty.
Impurity. The condition or quality of being impure in any sense; defilement; foulness; foul matter, language, action, etc.
Incest. Sexual intercourse between persons too nearly related for legal marriage.
Incontinence. Failure to restrain the passions; indulgence of lust.
Indecency. Want of decency, modesty, or good manners; obscenity; an indecent word or act.
Indelicacy. Want of a nice sense of, or regard for, purity, propriety, or of refinement.
Intrigue. A secret and illicit love affair between two persons of different sexes.
Lasciviency. Lasciviousness; wantonness.
Lechery. Free or scandalous indulgence in lust.
Liaison [F.]. Intrigue.
Libertinage [F.]. Libertinism; lewdness.
Libertinism. Unrestrained indulgence in licentious practises.
Lubricity. Lewdness.
Lust. Unlawful or inordinate desire for carnal pleasure.
Obscenity. Obscene character or quality; lewdness; lewd actions.
Pruriency. The quality or state of being inclined to lascivious thoughts and desires.
Rape. Sexual connection with a woman without her consent.
Ribaldry. Low, vulgar language; indecency; obscenity; lewdness.
Salacity. Strong propensity to venery; lust.
Seduction. Enticement to do wrong; enticing a woman to consent to unlawful sexual intercourse.
Smut. Obscene language; ribaldry
Social evil. Prostitution.
Stupration. Violation of chastity by force.
Uncleanness, etc. Moral impurity, etc. See CLEANNESS-FILTHINESS.
Venery. Sexual indulgence, especially when excessive.
Violation. Ravishment; rape, outrage.
Wenching. Act of frequenting houses of ill fame.
Whoredom. The practise of unlawful sexual intercourse; fornication.

IMPURITY—Associated Nouns.

Bagnio. A brothel.
Bawdy-house.
Bordel. } A house devoted to prostitution.
Brothel.
Harem. The apartments of the wives and concubines of a Mohammedan.
House of ill fame. A brothel.
Seraglio. A harem.
Stew. A brothel.
Supanar [L.]. A house of ill fame.

IMPURITY—Verbs.

Abuse. To violate; ravish.
Be impure, etc. To be defiled by sin. See *Adjectives.*

(Continued on Column 1.)

IMPURITY—Adjectives—*Continued.*

Gross. Coarse in meaning.
Immodest. Wanting in modesty; impure; sensual.
Impure. Foul; defiled by sin; unchaste.
Incestuous. Guilty of incest; of the nature of incest.
Incontinent. Exercising no restraint over the passions.
Indecent. Immodest, gross; obscene.
Indecorous. Contrary to recognized rules of good breeding; unseemly; rude.
Indelicate. Coarse; immodest.
Lascivious. Having, denoting, or tending to produce wanton desires; lustful.
Lecherous. Given to or characterized by lewdness or lust.
Lewd. Characterized by lust; libidinous.
Libidinous. Characterized by lewdness.
Licentious. Wanton; lascivious; lewd.
Lickerish. Tempting or tempted by appetite; lustful.
Light. Characterized by moral laxity.
Loose. Dissolute; lewd.
Lustful. Having carnal or sensual desire.
Meretricious. Vulgar and tawdry; pertaining to a harlot; wanton.
No better than she should be. Unchaste.
Not to be mentioned to ears polite. Indecent; indecorous.
Obscene. Offensive to chastity, decency, or modesty.

Of easy virtue. Easily seduced.
Of loose character. Lewd; dissolute.
On the loose. Obtaining one's living by prostitution.
On the pavé [F.]. On the pavement; being a prostitute.
On the streets. } Being a prostitute.
On the town. }
Paphian. A native of Paphos; a prostitute, as a votary of Venus.
Pornographic. Pertaining to licentious painting or literature; lascivious.
Prurient. Inclined to lascivious thoughts and desires.
Rakish. Dissolute; profligate.
Rampant. Unbridled; unrestrained.
Ribald. Indulging in or manifesting coarse indecency.
Riggish. Like a rig or wanton.
Ruttish. Inclined to rut; lustful.
Salacious. Lustful; lecherous.
Shameless. Wanting modesty; indecent.
Smutty. Obscene; not modest or pure.
Unchaste. Not continent; lewd.
Unclean, etc. Foul; dirty; filthy; morally impure, etc. See CLEAN-NESS-FILTHINESS.
Voluptuous. Exciting sensual desires; sensual.
Wanton. Loose; dissolute; lustful.

PURITY—RAKE.

RAKE.

Adulterer. A man who commits adultery.
Adulteress. A woman who commits adultery.
Advoutress. An adulteress.
Aspasia. The mistress of Pericles of Athens.
Baggage. A disreputable woman.
Bawd. The keeper of a brothel.
Bitch. A wench or lewd woman.
Bluebeard. A cruel or tyrannical husband, a hero of medieval romance.
Bona roba [It.]. A courtezan.
Chartered libertine. A privileged loose liver.
Chère amie [F.]. A mistress.
Cocotte [F.]. A professionally lewd woman.
Conciliatrix [L.]. A woman who secures girls for immoral purposes.
Concubine. A kept mistress.
Courtezan. A woman who prostitutes herself for gain.
Cyprian. A lewd woman.
Debauchee. A sensual or dissipated person.
Delilah. The mistress of Samson.
Demi-monde. A class of persons of equivocal reputation.
Demirep. A woman of questionable chastity.
Don Juan. An aristocratic libertine hero of Molière, Gluck, Mozart, Byron and others.
Doxy. A mistress.
Drab. A prostitute.
Fast man. A man of loose morals.
Fille de joie [F.]. A woman of licentious pleasure.
Fornicator. A man who commits fornication.
Fornicatress. A woman who commits fornication.
Frail sisterhood. Women of easy virtue.
Gallant. A man who pays court to women: used sometimes in a bad sense.
Gay Lothario. A licentious character in Rowe's play, *The Fair Penitent.*
Goat. A lecher.
Grisette. A French working girl of easy virtue.
Harlot. A woman who prostitutes her body for hire.
Harridan. A vixenish hag.
Hussy. A pert or forward girl.
Intrigant [F.]. A man given to intrigue.
Jade. A vicious woman.
Jezebel. The wife of Ahab, king of Israel, notorious for profligacy.
Lais. A notorious Grecian courtezan.
Lecher. An habitually lewd man.
Libertine. One who leads a dissolute and licentious life.
Loose fish. People of easy virtue.

Lorette [F.]. The select class of prostitutes in Paris.
Mackerel. Bawd.
Messalina. The dissolute and licentious wife of the Emperor Claudius.
Minx. A forward girl.
Miss. A mistress.
Mistress. A woman who unlawfully fills the place of a wife.
Mopsy. A slovenly, untidy woman.
Paillard [F.]. A rake.
Pandar. } A man who obtains for others the means for gratifying
Pander. } lust. [Homer, Shakespeare, *Troilus and Cressida.*]
Petite dame [F.]. A mistress.
Phryne. A celebrated Athenian courtezan.
Piece. A low, bold person.
Pimp. A pander.
Procuress. A woman who procures girls for immoral purposes.
Prostitute. A woman who practises lewdness for hire.
Punk. A prostitute.
Quean. A low, worthless woman.
Rake. A disorderly, loose person given to lewdness.
Rake-hell. An utterly abandoned wretch.
Rig. A strumpet.
Rip. A dissipated or depraved person.
Satyr. A very lascivious person.
Seducer. One who persuades a woman to surrender her chastity.
Skit. A frivolous girl.
Slut. A wench.
Street-walker. A prostitute who solicits in the streets.
Strumpet. A prostitute.
Thais. The mistress of Alexander the Great.
Trollop. A prostitute.
Trull. A common prostitute.
Unfortunate. }
Unfortunate female. } A woman who prostitutes herself for hire.
Unfortunate woman. }
Voluptuary, etc. One addicted to sensual and lustful pleasures. See MODERATION-VOLUPTUARY.
Wench. A woman of ill fame.
Whore. A woman who practises sexual intercourse for hire.
Whoremonger. A man who has intercourse with whores.
Wittol. A man who knows his wife's infidelity and tamely submits to it.
Woman. A woman of doubtful reputation.
Woman of easy virtue, etc. A woman of ill fame. See PURITY-IMPURITY.
Woman of the town. A street-walker.

purl. To flow with a gentle noise. LOUDNESS-FAINTNESS, MUSICIAN, RIVER-WIND.
pur'-lieus. Environs. ENVIRONMENT-INTERPOSITION, REMOTENESS-NEARNESS.
pur-loin'. To steal. THEFT.
pur'-ple. Red tinged with blue. REDNESS-GREENNESS, SCEPTER, YELLOWNESS-PURPLE; **purple and fine linen,** SENSUALITY-SUFFERING.

pur'-port. Intent. MEANING-JARGON.
pur'-pose. Aim. PURPOSE-LUCK; **infirm of purpose,** DETERMINATION-VACILLATION; **on purpose,** PURPOSE-LUCK; **serve a purpose,** USEFULNESS-USELESSNESS; **tenacity of purpose,** PERSISTENCE-WHIM; **to little or no purpose,** SUCCESS-FAILURE, USEFULNESS-USELESSNESS; **to some purpose,** SUCCESS-FAILURE.

PURPOSE—LUCK.

Aim. That which is intended.
Ambition. An eager desire or steadfast purpose to achieve something.
Animus. The animating thought or purpose.
Arrière pensée [F.]. An afterthought.
Bull's-eye. The central division of a target aimed at.
Butt. A subject aimed at in criticism.
Contemplation. The act of keeping the eye or mind upon some object or subject.
Cui bono [L.]. To what end: for whose good.
Decision. The definite determination of a contest or question.
Design. A fixed purpose or intention.
Destination. The point to which one directs his course.
Determination. The formation of a fixed purpose.
Drift, etc. The end toward which anything moves. See MEANING.
End. The purpose in view.
Final cause. The designed or intended result.
Game. A plan or scheme pursued.
Goal. The point toward which effort or movement is directed.
Intent.
In ention. } That which is designed or purposed.
Intentionality.
Look out. The act of observing or watching.
Mark. An object serving to guide or direct.
Mind. Disposition or mental tendency.
Motive. That which incites to action.
Object. That on which one sets his mind as an end to be realized.
Point. That to which effort is directed.
Predetermination. The act of disposing or ordering before the event. See PREDETERMINATION.
Prey. That upon which one exerts his power or influence.
Project. Something projected or mapped out in the mind.
Proposal. An offer proposing something to be accepted or adopted.
Purpose. The idea or ideal kept before the mind as an end of effort or action.
Purview. The extent or scope of anything.
Quarry. Anything hunted or eagerly pursued.
Quintain. An object or person set up to be tilted at.
Quo animo [L.]. With what mind or intention.
Raison d'être [F.]. The reason for existence.
Resolution. The purpose or course resolved upon. See PERSISTENCE.
Resolve.
Set purpose. } Fixed purpose.
Settled purpose. Firm intention.
Study. The application of thought to a subject.
Target. Figuratively, that which is made an object of attack or center of intention.
Tendency. The state of tending toward some purpose, end, or result. See INCLINATION.
The be-all and the end-all. That toward which all effort is directed. [Shakespeare. *Macbeth*, 1, 7.]
Ultimatum. The last or only condition.
Undertaking. Any work or project which a person engages in or attempts to perform.
View. Range or scope of thought.
Wish. Strong and persistent desire or longing.

PURPOSE—*Scientific Noun.*

Teleology. The study of final causes.

PURPOSE—*Verbs.*

Calculate. To adjust for a purpose.
Compass. To purpose; intend.
Contemplate. To consider or have in view; look forward to.
Design. To intend or purpose.
Desire. To long for; express a wish for. See DESIRE.
Destinate.
Destine. } To determine the future condition or application of.
Intend. To set the mind upon to accomplish; purpose to convey as a meaning.
Mean. To intend as a matter of present effect or expression; purpose.
Meditate. To plan in the mind.
Premeditate. To revolve in the mind or meditate upon beforehand. See PREDETERMINATION.
Project. To sketch out or purpose in the mind. See DESIGN.
Propose. To formulate, as a purpose.
Purpose. To have or place before oneself, as an aim or intent.
Pursue. To follow with a purpose. See QUEST.

PURPOSE—*Verbal Expressions.*

Aim at; aspire after; aspire at; be after; be at; bid for; dream of: drive at; endeavor after; harbor a design; have a mind to (see

Chance, etc. That which happens in virtue of laws of whose operations we are more or less ignorant. See RATIONALE-LUCK.
Fate, etc. Predetermined and inevitable necessity. See VOLITION-OBLIGATION.
Good luck, etc. A degree of luck. See GOOD.
Hazard. Exposure to the chance of loss or injury.
Lot. That which falls to any one as his fortune.
Luck. A casual event, good or ill, affecting any one.

LUCK—*Denotations.*

Bet. The act of betting.
Betting. The risking of a certain thing or sum against another thing or sum on the issue of an uncertain event.
Blind bargain. A bargain made without intelligent direction or control.
Chuck-farthing. A game in which coins are pitched.
Cross and pile. The game called heads or tails.
Cup-tossing. A game of chance.
Drawing lots. Determination of anything by chance.
Faro. A gambling game in which all the players play against the dealer.
Faro-bank. The venture of the owner of a faro-table.
Fluke. Any unexpected advantage.
Game of chance. A game in which the result is uncertain.
Heads or tails. A phrase used when tossing a coin to decide a proposition.
Leap in the dark.
Mere shot. } An effort without purpose or intention.
Pig in poke, etc. A blind bargain. See CERTAINTY-DOUBT.
Pitch-and-toss. A game in which pennies are pitched at a mark, the player coming nearest being allowed to toss all the pennies in the air and retain those that come down with the heads up.
Pot-luck. Whatever may chance to be in the pot to eat.
Random shot. A shot without aim.
Rouge et noir [F.]. A game of cards in which stakes are deposited upon red or black compartments of a table.
Roulette. A gambling game.
Sortes [L.]. Lots
Sortes Virgilianæ [L.] A kind of divination in which a passage of Virgil was drawn at random to indicate future events.
Sortilegy. Divination by drawing lots.
Sortition. Selection by lot.
Speculation. A more or less risky investment of money.
Stake. Something wagered or risked on a competition.
The turf. The race-course.
Venture. An undertaking attended with risk.
Wager. An agreement between two or more persons that a certain sum of money or other thing shall be paid to one of them on the happening or not happening of an event.

LUCK—*Nouns of Instrument.*

Dice-box. The box from which dice are thrown in gaming.
Mascot. Something regarded as bringing good luck to the possessor.

LUCK—*Nouns of Place.*

Betting-house. A place where betting is done.
Betting-ring. The betting arena on a race-course.
Gambling-house.
Gaming-house. } Any place for playing games for stakes or wagers.
Hell. A gambling-house.

LUCK—*Nouns of Agent.*

Adventurer. One who risks a thing on chance; an unprincipled schemer.
Dicer. A dice player.
Gambler. One who gambles.
Gamester. One who is viciously addicted to play for money.

LUCK—*Verbs.*

Bet. To stake or pledge on an uncertain issue.
Buy a pig in a poke. To purchase blindly, as a pig in a bag.
Cast lots. To throw dice or similar objects for the purpose of determining a question.
Chance, etc. To occur without design. See RATIONALE-LUCK.
Chance it. To venture upon.
Draw lots. To determine a question by drawing one thing from another whose marks are concealed from the drawer.
Encounter chance.
Encounter the risk. } To take a risk.
Gamble. To play a game for a stake.
Game. To lose or wager at play.
Hazard. To venture to take the risk involved in.
Incur chance. To risk.

PURPOSE—LUCK—*Continued.*

PURPOSE—Verbal Expressions—*Continued.*

Readiness); have an eye to; have in contemplation; have in one's eye; have *in petto* to have in the breast, hence in secrecy; have in view; have to; labor at; labor for; level at; point at; propose to oneself; set before oneself; study to; take aim; take into one's head; take upon oneself (see Enterprise); talk of; think of.

Purpose—*Adjectives.*

Advised. Done with intention and forethought.
At stake. In danger; pledged.
Bent upon. With fixed purpose.
Bound for. Having a definite intention or direction.
Determinate. Determined or resolved upon.
Express. Intended for a particular purpose.
In petto [It.] In the breast; in secrecy.
In prospect. In anticipation.
Intended. }
Intending. } Purposed to be done. See *Verbs.*
Intentional. With forethought. See *Nouns.*
In the breast of. In secrecy.
In view. In anticipated foresight.
Minded. Disposed; inclined.
On the anvil. Under discussion.
On the *tapis.* On the table; hence, under consideration.
Prepense, etc. Considered beforehand. See Predetermination.
Teleological. Of or pertaining to teleology, the doctrine of design.

Purpose—*Adverbs*

Advisedly. With forethought and advice.
Deliberately. With careful consideration. See Predetermina-
tion.
Designedly Purposely.
For. In view of.
Intentionally. With forethought. See *Adjectives.*
Knowingly. In a knowing manner.
Pointedly. In a pointed or direct manner.
Purposely. According to purpose or design.
Studiously. Earnestly.
Wittingly. With knowledge and by design.

Purpose—*Adverbial Phrases.*

Advised by; by design; for the purpose of; in cold blood; in contemplation of; in order that; in order to; in pursuance of; on account of; on purpose; pursuant to; *quo animo* [L.], in what mind; to all intents and purposes; to the end that; with an eye to; with a view of; with intent; with one's eyes open; with the intent that; with the view of.

LUCK—Adverbs, etc.—*Continued from Column 2.*

Casually, etc. Without being expected or foreseen. See Rationale-
Luck
En passant [F.]. By the way.
Incidentally. Without design.
Unintentionally, etc. Without design. See *Adjectives.*
Unwittingly. Without knowledge.

Luck—*Phrases.*

Dertro tempore [L.]. At a lucky moment.
Acierta errando [Sp.]. He blunders into the right.

pur'-pose-less. Without purpose. Purpose-Luck.
pur'-pose-ly. Intentionally. Purpose-Luck, Volition-Obligation.
pur'-pure. Purple. Yellowness-Purple.
purr. To murmur as a cat Cry-Ululation
purse. A money bag. Money, Treasury; **long purse,**
Affluence-Penury; **purse up,** Enlargement-
Diminution; **put into one's purse,** Giving-Receiving.
purse'-bear''-er. One who takes charge of the money.
Treasurer.
purse'-proud''. Proud of money. Selfrespect-Humbleness.
purs'-er. A paymaster of a ship. Treasurer.
purse'-strings''. Fastening of a purse. Treasury;
draw the purse-strings, Settlement-Default; **open
the purse-strings,** Outlay-Income.

LUCK—Verbs—*Continued.*

Incur the risk. To take the consequences
Lay. To deposit as a wager; risk.
Lay a wager. }
Leave to chance. } To risk a sum of money or other thing on the hap-
Make a bet. } pening or not happening of an uncertain event.
Play at chuck-farthing. To play the game in which a farthing is pitched into a hole.
Play for. To gamble for.
Put into a lottery. To risk in an affair of chance.
Raffle. To dispose of by drawing lots.
Risk. To expose to a chance of injury or loss.
Run chance. }
Run the risk. } To take the risk involved in.
Set on a cast. To entrust to chance.
Shuffle the cards. To gamble.
Speculate. To make a venturesome transaction.
Stake. To wager; hazard.
Stand a chance, etc. To have a good opportunity of occurring. See Possibility.
Stand the hazard of the die. To venture something on the throw of dice.
Take one's chance. To risk.
Tempt fortune. To try one's luck.
Toss up. To leave to chance.
Trust to chance. To venture.
Trust to the chapter of accidents. To trust to chance.
Venture. To run the risk of.
Wager. To stake on an uncertain event.

Luck—*Adjectives.*

Accidental. Happening by chance.
Aimless. Without aim
Causeless. Self-originating; uncreated.
Designless. Happening without intention.
Driftless. Having no drift or direction; purposeless.
Fortuitous, etc. Happening by chance. See Rationale-Luck.
Indiscriminate. Confused; promiscuous.
Never thought of. Seemingly impossible.
Not meant. Contrary to intention.
Possible, etc. Barely able to be, or to come to pass. See Possi-
bility.
Promiscuous. Confused; mingled indiscriminately.
Purposeless. Having no purpose or result.
Random. Done at hazard: left to chance.
Undesigned. Not intended.
Undirected. Not guided.
Unintended. Not designed.
Unintentional. Happening by chance.
Unpremeditated, etc. Not done by design. See Predetermina-
tion-Impulse.
Unpurposed. Not intentional.
Without purpose. Aimless.

Luck—*Adverbs, etc.*

As it may happen. By chance.
At a venture. Without seeing the end or mark.
At haphazard. Without foreseeing the issue.
At random. By chance; at hazard.
By the way. By chance.

(Continued on Column 1.)

pur-su'-ant to. In accordance with. Purpose-Luck.
pur-sue'. Follow; chase. Approach-Withdrawal,
Discontinuance-Continuance, Leading-Following, Purpose-Luck, Quest-Evasion; **pursue a
course,** Action-Passiveness; **pursue an inquiry,** Investigation-Answer; **pursue the tenor of one's
way,** Conceit-Diffidence, Occupation.
pur-su'-er. One who chases. Approach-Withdrawal,
Quest-Evasion
pur-suit'. Chase. Occupation-Abandonment, Quest-
Evasion.
pur'-sui-vant. A royal messenger. Messenger.
pur'-sy. Short-breathed. Enlargement-Diminution.
pu'-ru-lent. Consisting of pus. Cleanness-Filthiness.
pur-vey'. To provide. Nutriment-Excretion, Provision-Waste.

pur-vey'-ance. Supplying. PROVISION-WASTE, SUBSTI-TUTE.

pur-vey'-or. A commissary. PROVISION-WASTE.

pur'-view. Scope. PURPOSE-LUCK.

pus. The matter of an ulcer. CLEANNESS-FILTHINESS

Pu'-sey-ism. A kind of ritualism. ORTHODOXY-HETERODOXY.

Pu'-sey-ite. One who holds the principles of Puseyism. ORTHODOXY-HETERODOXY.

push. Impel; activity. ACTIVITY-INDOLENCE, AD-VANCE-RETROGRESSION, CONDITION-SITUATION, IMPETUS-REACTION, PUSH-PULL, VENTURE; **come to the push,** DIFFICULTY-FACILITY; **push aside,** ADMISSION-EXPULSION, CAREFULNESS-CARELESSNESS, REGARD-DISRESPECT; **push forward,** ACTIVITY-INDOLENCE, ADVANCE-RETROGRESSION, HURRY-LEISURE, OBSTRUCTION-HELP; **push from,** ATTRACTION-REPULSION; **push on,** HURRY-LEISURE; **push out,** HEIGHT-LOWNESS; **push to the last,** EARLINESS-LATENESS.

PUSH—PULL.

Discharge. The act of discharging or of sending forth, or pushing forth.

Ejaculation. A throwing out suddenly, as of the voice.

Ejection. The act of ejecting, or of driving out with force; an expulsion. See ADMISSION-EXPULSION.

Fling. The act of casting out; a kick.

Projection. The act of projecting, or of shooting forth.

Propulsion. The act of propelling; an impulse given.

Push. A propelling; a repulsion. See IMPETUS.

Shot. A stroke or hit, as if delivered by a propelling force.

Shy. A throwing with a sidelong motion or at random.

Throw. An act of throwing or hurling.

Toss. An upward throwing from the hand.

Vis a tergo [L.⟧. A force from behind.

PUSH—Denotations.

Archery. The art of shooting with the bow.

Arrow. A missile weapon to be shot from a bow.

Ball. A round body used in various games; the projectile from a gun.

Ballistics. The science that deals with the impact, path, and velocity of projectiles.

Brickbat. A piece of a brick used as a missile.

Discus. The quoit of the ancients.

Gun. A metal tube for firing projectiles. See WEAPON.

Missile. An object thrown, or intended to be thrown.

Projectile. A missile for discharge from a large gun or cannon.

Quoit. A circular piece of iron with a round hole in the center, to be thrown at iron pins or stakes.

Shot. A projectile from a gun.

PUSH—Nouns of Agent.

Archer. One who uses bow and arrow.

Bowman. One who uses a bow.

Crack shot.⎫
Good shot.⎭ A man expert in shooting.

Marksman. One skilled in shooting at a mark.

Rifleman. One who uses a rifle.

Sharpshooter. One skilled with the rifle. See BELLIGERENT.

Shooter.⎫
Shot.⎭ A marksman.

Toxophilite. One skilled in archery.

PUSH—Verbs.

Bolt. To expel with force.

Boost. To shove up from behind.

Carry off one's legs. To push off one's support.

Cast. To throw off; drive with force.

Chuck. To throw at a short distance.

Dart. To throw suddenly; shoot out.

Dash. To throw violently; break into pieces by throwing.

Discharge. To send forth; make pass out, as a charge in a gun.

Drive. To push in front of oneself; urge forward.

Ejaculate. To throw out suddenly, as the voice; exclaim.

Expel. To drive out with violence. See ADMISSION-EXPULSION.

Fillip. To strike by a fillip; impel by some inciting force.

Fire off. To discharge, as a gun.

Fling. To throw with suddenness; send forth freely.

Flirt. To wave lightly; toss about playfully or lightly.

Fulminate. To thunder; issue decrees with menaces or censures.

Give an impulse to.⎫
Give a start to.⎭ To push forward.

Heave. To throw with strong effort.

Hurl. To throw with violence and force.

Impel. To drive forward. See IMPETUS.

Jaculate. To throw or cast.

Jerk. To throw with a jerk; emit with a short, sharp, sudden motion.

Draft. The act of drawing; a haul.

Drawing. The act of drawing, or of causing to move by a pull. See Verbs.

Haul. A pulling with force.

Haulage. The act of hauling or dragging.

Pull. The act of drawing with force.

Rake. An instrument for pulling together, as a hay-rake; a pull.

Towage. The act of towing.

Traction. The act of drawing by some power.

PULL—Verbs.

Drag. To pull what is not fitted to pull, or what resists pulling.

Draw. To cause to move with oneself or in the same direction.

Haul. To draw a heavy object slowly.

Jerk. To pull in a jerking manner.

Lug. To pull with great labor.

Pull. To exert a drawing force of any kind.

Rake. To gather or pull together with a rope.

Swig. To tighten a rope.

Take in tow. To pull with a tow-line.

Touse. To pull to pieces.

Tow. To drag behind, as a boat.

Trail. To drag lightly, as a garment.

Train. To bring into a particular course.

Tug. To pull with a continuous effort.

Twitch. To pull sharply.

Wrench. To pull violently from its proper place or meaning.

Yank. To pull.

PULL—Adjectives

Drawing. Moving forward. See Verbs.

Tractile. Capable of being drawn out.

PULL—Phrase.

"A long pull, a strong pull, and a pull all together."

PUSH—Verbs—Continued.

Lance. To thrust with a lance or as with a lance.

Launch. To push, as a boat in the water; send forth.

Let fly.⎫
Let off.⎭ To discharge.

Pitch. To send forth from the hand.

Pitchfork. To handle with a pitchfork.

Project. To send forth; shoot out.

Propel. To drive forward.

Put in motion. To start.

Put to flight. To drive away; scatter.

Send. To drive by force; throw.

Send forth.⎫
Send off.⎭ To move.

Set agoing.⎫
Set in motion.⎭ To start.

Shoot. To make to go out with force: said of a weapon: cause to pass out.

Shy. To fling carelessly.

Sling. To fling as with a sling; cast forth suddenly.

Start. To set in motion.

Throw. To cast forth to a distance; spread carelessly.

Tilt. To thrust, as with a lance.

Toss. To throw about; throw lightly with the hand.

Trundle. To roll along on small wheels. See REVOLUTION.

PUSH—Adjectives.

Projectile. Impelling forward.

Propelled.⎫
Propelling.⎭ Driven forward. See Verbs.

Propulsive. Having the power to propel.

push'-ing. Urging; active. ACTIVITY-INDOLENCE, HURRY-LEISURE.

pu''-sil-la-nim'-i-ty. Cowardice. BRAVERY-COWARDICE.

puss. A cat. FAUNA-FLORA; **play puss in the corner,** COMMUTATION-PERMUTATION.

pus'-sy. A cat. FAUNA-FLORA.

pus'-tule. A pimple. CONVEXITY-CONCAVITY, EMBELLISHMENT-DISFIGUREMENT.

put. Place; a game of cards; a fool. ENTERTAINMENT-WEARINESS, ESTABLISHMENT-REMOVAL, GENTILITY-COMMONALTY, SAGE-FOOL; **neatly put,** PURITY-CRUDENESS; **put about,** ADVANCE-RETROGRESSION, CIRCUITION, PUBLICITY; **put a case,** CONVENTIONALITY-UNCONVENTIONALITY, HYPOTHESIS; **put a construction on,** INTERPRETATION-MISINTERPRETATION; **put a mark upon,** HEED-DISREGARD; **put an end to,** BEGINNING-END, CREATION-DESTRUCTION, DISCONTINUANCE-CONTINUANCE, LIFE-KILLING; **put a question,** INVESTIGATION, ANSWER; **put aside,** CAREFULNESS-CARELESSNESS, HEED-DISREGARD, INCLUSION-OMISSION, KEEPING-RELINQUISHMENT, USE-DISUSE; **put away,** KEEPING-RELINQUISHMENT, MATRIMONY-DIVORCE; **put away thought,** REFLECTION-VACANCY; **put back,** ADVANCE-RETROGRESSION, BETTERMENT-DETERIORATION, ESTABLISHMENT-REMOVAL, RENOVATION-RELAPSE; **put before,** ENLIGHTENMENT-SECRECY; **put by,** STORE; **put down,** COERCION, CREATION-DESTRUCTION, MARK-OBLITERATION, REPUTATION-DISCREDIT, SETTLEMENT-DEFAULT, SUCCESS-FAILURE; **put forth,** ASSERTION-DENIAL, ENLARGEMENT-DIMINUTION, HYPOTHESIS, PROFFER-REFUSAL, PUBLICITY; **put forward,** ASSERTION-DENIAL, HYPOTHESIS, OBSTRUCTION-HELP, POMP, PUBLICITY; **put in commission,** COMMISSION-ABROGATION; **put in force,** COERCION, COMPLETION-NONCOMPLETION; **put off,** ARRIVAL-DEPARTURE, DRESS-UNDRESS, EARLINESS-LATENESS, PRETEXT; **put on,** DRESS-UNDRESS, HURRY-LEISURE, SOCIETY-AFFECTATION, SWIFTNESS-SLOWNESS, TRUTHFULNESS-FALSEHOOD; **put on paper,** MARK-OBLITERATION; **put one's hand to,** ENTERPRISE; **put one's nose out of joint,** REPUTATION, DISCREDIT, SUPREMACY-SUBORDINACY; **put one's trust in,** FAITH-MISGIVING; **put right,** VOLITION-OBLIGATION; **put the horses to,** PREPARATION-NONPREPARATION; **put the saddle on the right horse,** RATIONALE-LUCK; **put the seal to,** COMPLETION-NONCOMPLETION, CONTRACT; **put to convenience,** PROPRIETY-IMPROPRIETY; **put together,** COMPOSITION-RESOLUTION, CREATION-DESTRUCTION, UNION-DISUNION; **put upon,** GOODNESS-BADNESS, TRUTHFULNESS-FRAUD.

put in. To place in. ARRIVAL-DEPARTURE, INJECTION-EJECTION; **put in a word,** CONVERSATION-MONOLOGUE, SPEECH-INARTICULATENESS; **put in an affidavit,** ASSERTION-DENIAL; **put in hand,** ENTERPRISE; **put in mind,** REMEMBRANCE-FORGETFULNESS; **put in motion,** MOVEMENT-REST; **put in one's head,** HYPOTHESIS; **put in one's pocket,** GIVING-RECEIVING; **put in order,** ORGANIZATION-DISORGANIZATION; **put in practise,** CONDUCT; **put in remembrance,** REMEMBRANCE-FORGETFULNESS; **put in shape,** ORGANIZATION-DISORGANIZATION; **put in the place of,** COMMUTATION-PERMUTATION; **put in the way of,** POSSIBILITY-IMPOSSIBILITY; **put in trim,** ORGANIZATION-DISORGANIZATION, PREPARATION-NONPREPARATION.

put out. Place out. CERTAINTY-DOUBT, CONTENTEDNESS-DISCONTENTMENT, CREATION-DESTRUCTION, DIFFICULTY-FACILITY, HEATING-COOLING, HEED-DISREGARD, LIGHT-DARKNESS, OUTSIDE-INSIDE; **oneself put out of court,** RATIOCINATION-INSTINCT, SKILL-UNSKILFULNESS; **put out of countenance,** REPUTATION-DISCREDIT; **put out of gear,** MIGHT-IMPOTENCE; **put out of joint,** ORGANIZATION-DISORGANIZATION; **put out of one's head,** HEED-DISREGARD;

put out of one's misery, COMPASSION-RUTHLESSNESS; **put out of order,** REGULARITY-IRREGULARITY; **put out to nurse,** OBSTRUCTION-HELP.

put to. Given; hardly pressed. PETITION-EXPOSTULATION, RATIONALE-LUCK; **put to death,** LIFE-KILLING; **put to it,** DIFFICULTY-FACILITY; **put to one's oath,** ENGAGEMENT-RELEASE; **put to press,** WRITING-PRINTING; **put to rights,** ORGANIZATION-DISORGANIZATION; **put to sea,** ARRIVAL-DEPARTURE; **put to shame,** REPUTATION-DISCREDIT; **put to silence,** VOCALIZATION-MUTENESS; **put to task,** USE-DISUSE; **put to the blush,** SELFRESPECT-HUMBLENESS; **put to the door,** APERTURE-CLOSURE; **put to the proof,** TRIAL; **put to the question,** PLEASURABLENESS-PAINFULNESS; **put to the rack,** PLEASURABLENESS-PAINFULNESS; **put to the sword,** LIFE-KILLING; **put to the vote,** CHOICE-NEUTRALITY; **put to use,** USE-DISUSE.

put up. Placed; endure. ESTABLISHMENT-REMOVAL, GATHERING-SCATTERING, STORE; **put up a petition,** DEVOTION-IDOLATRY, PETITION-EXPOSTULATION; **put up a prayer,** DEVOTION-IDOLATRY, PETITION-EXPOSTULATION; **put up a shutter,** LUMINARY-SHADE; **put up for,** DESIRE-DISTASTE; **put up for sale,** BUYING-SALE; **put up the sword,** FIGHTING-CONCILIATION; **put up to,** MOTIVE-CAPRICE; **put up to auction,** BUYING-SALE; **put up with,** COMMUTATION-PERMUTATION, EXCITABILITY-INEXCITABILITY.

pu'-ta-tive. Supposed. FAITH-MISGIVING, HYPOTHESIS, RATIONALE-LUCK.

pu''-tid. Worthless. CONSEQUENCE-INSIGNIFICANCE.

pu''-tre-fac-tion. Decomposition. BIOLOGY, CLEANNESS-FILTHINESS.

pu'-tre-fied. Rotted. CLEANNESS-FILTHINESS.

pu'-tre-fy. Rot. CLEANNESS-FILTHINESS.

pu-tres'-cence. Rottenness. CLEANNESS-FILTHINESS.

pu-tres'-cent. Becoming putrid. CLEANNESS-FILTHINESS.

pu'-trid. Corrupt. CLEANNESS-FILTHINESS, PERFUME-STENCH.

put'-ty. A paste of whiting and linseed-oil. CONNECTIVE.

puz'-zle. To perplex. CERTAINTY-DOUBT, DIFFICULTY-FACILITY, ENLIGHTENMENT-SECRECY, TIDINGS-MYSTERY.

puz'-zled. Perplexed. CERTAINTY-DOUBT, DIFFICULTY-FACILITY.

puz'-zle-head'-ed. Full of confused notions. SAGACITY-INCAPACITY.

puz'-zling. Perplexing. CLEARNESS-OBSCURITY.

Pyl'-a-des and O-res'-tes. Characters in Greek legend. FRIEND-FOE.

pyr'-a-mid. A solid, having a rectilinear base, and its sides triangles having a common vertex. ANGULARITY, GATHERING-SCATTERING, SHARPNESS-BLUNTNESS.

py-ram'-i-dal. Having the form of a pyramid. ANGULARITY, MINERALOGY, SHARPNESS-BLUNTNESS.

pyr'-a-mids. A game of pool in which the balls are placed in a triangle. ENTERTAINMENT-WEARINESS.

pyre. A funeral pile. LIFE-FUNERAL.

pyr-he''-li-om'-e-ter. Scientific instrument. ASTRONOMY.

pyr'-i-form. Pear-shaped. ROUNDNESS.

py''-ro-clas'-tic. Formed from a kind of lava. GEOLOGY.

py-rol'-o-gy. Blowpipe analysis. ADVANCE-RETROGRESSION.

py'-ro-man''-cy. Divination by fire. PROPHECY.

py-rom'-e-ter. A high-temperature thermometer. THERMOMETER.

py''-ro-tech'-nics. The art of making fireworks. LUMINARY-SHADE.

py''-ro-tech'-ny. The use of fire and the cautery in art and surgery. HEAT-COLD.

pyr'-rho-nism. Skepticism. CREDULOUSNESS-SKEPTI-CISM, GODLINESS-DISBELIEF.

Pyr'-rho-nist. Disciple of Pyrrho; an absolute skeptic. FAITH-MISGIVING, GODLINESS-DISBELIEF.

Py-thag''-o-re'-an. Pertaining to Pythagoras. MODERATION-SELFINDULGENCE.

Pyth'-i-a. Delphi. SOOTHSAYER.

py'-thon. A soothsayer.

pyth'-o-ness. SOOTHSAYER.

pyx. A vessel; a box for coins. CEREMONIAL, CONTENTS-RECEIVER, FANE.

Q

Q. C. Queen's Counsel. ADVOCATE.

Q. E. D. *Quod erat demonstrandum* [L.]. Which was to be proved. PROOF-DISPROOF.

quab. An unfledged bird. INFANT-VETERAN.

quack. A croaking sound; a medical impostor. CRY-ULULATION, GULL-DECEIVER.

quack'-er-y. Fraudulent practise. SKILL-UNSKILFULNESS, SOCIETY-AFFECTATION, TRUTHFULNESS-FALSEHOOD.

quack'-salv''-er. A medical impostor. GULL-DECEIVER.

quad. A quadrangle. DWELLER-HABITATION.

quad''-ra-ges'-i-ma. Lent. FASTING-GLUTTONY.

quad'-ran''-gle. A four-sided plane figure; a four-sided court. ANGULARITY, DWELLER-HABITATION.

quad-ran'-gu-lar. Having four angles. ANGULARITY.

quad'-rant. A right angle; the quarter of a circle. ANGULARITY, CIRCLE-WINDING.

quad'-rate with. To agree with. HARMONY-DISCORD.

quad-rat'-ic. Pertaining to a square. QUATERNITY.

quad'-ra-ture. A squaring. ANGULARITY, QUATERNITY.

quad-ren'-ni-al. Occurring once in four years. PERIODICITY-IRREGULARITY.

quad'-ri-ble. That may be squared. QUATERNITY.

quad''-ri-fa'-ri-ous. Arranged in four rows. QUADRUPLICATION-QUADRISECTION.

quad'-ri-fid. Split into four parts. QUADRUPLICATION-QUADRISECTION.

quad''-ri-gem'-i-nal. Fourfold. QUADRUPLICATION-QUADRISECTION.

quad''-ri-lat'-er-al. Having four sides and four angles. ANGULARITY, LATERALITY-CONTRAPOSITION.

qua-drille'. A square dance. ENTERTAINMENT-WEARINESS.

quad-ril'-lion. A unit with fifteen ciphers annexed. MULTIPLICITY-PAUCITY.

quad''-ri-par'-tite. Consisting of four parts. QUADRUPLICATION-QUADRISECTION.

quad''-ri-par-ti'-tion. A division into four parts. QUADRUPLICATION-QUADRISECTION.

quad'-ri-reme. A galley with four banks of oars. CONVEYANCE-VESSEL.

quad''-ri-sec'-tion. A subdivision into four parts. QUADRUPLICATION-QUADRISECTION.

quad''-ri-si'-ded. Four-sided. LATERALITY-CONTRAPOSITION.

quad-roon'. A quarter-blooded person. MIXTURE-HOMOGENEITY.

quad'-ru-ped. A four-footed animal. FAUNA-FLORA.

quad'-ru-ple. Fourfold. QUADRUPLICATION-QUINQUESECTION.

quad-ru''-pli-cate. Four times as much. QUADRUPLICATION-QUINQUESECTION.

quad'-ru''-pli-ca'-tion. The act of making fourfold. QUATERNITY.

QUADRUPLICATION—QUADRISECTION.

Quadruplication. The making four times as much.

QUADRUPLICATION—*Verbs.*

Biquadrate. To square the square of a number.

Multiply by four. To increase fourfold.

Quadruplicate. To double twice.

QUADRUPLICATION—*Adjectives.*

Fourfold. Taken four times.

Fourth. Next after the third.

Quadrible. Capable of being squared.

Quadrifarious. Arranged in four rows or ranks.

Quadrigeminal. Having four similar parts.

Quadruple. Of four parts; made four times as great.

Quadruplicate. Twice double.

QUADRUPLICATION—*Adverbs, etc.*

Fourthly. In the fourth place.

Four times. Increased fourfold.

In the fourth place. The position after the third.

Farthing. The fourth part of a penny.

Fourth. One of the four equal parts of anything.

Quadripartition. Division by or into four parts.

Quadrisection. Subdivision into four parts.

Quart. The fourth part of a gallon.

Quarter. A fourth; one-fourth of a dollar.

Quartering, etc. The act of dividing into four parts. See *Verbs.*

Quartern. A quarter, especially of a pint, or peck.

QUADRISECTION—*Verbs.*

Divide into four parts.

Quarter. To divide into four equal parts.

QUADRISECTION—*Adjectives.*

Quadrifid. Deeply cleft into four parts.

Quadripartite. Composed of four parts.

Quartered, etc. Divided into four parts. See *Verbs.*

quære [L.] (quï'-rï). Investigate. INVESTIGATION-ANSWER.

quaff. To drink deeply. NUTRIMENT-EXCRETION; **quaff the bitter cup,** PLEASURE-PAIN.

quag'-gy. Soft and muddy. SWAMP-ISLAND.

quag'-mire''. Soft and muddy ground. CLEANNESS-FILTHINESS, SWAMP-ISLAND.

quail. To lose heart. BRAVERY-COWARDICE, SANGUINENESS-TIMIDITY.

quaint. Pleasingly odd. BEAUTY-UGLINESS, CONVENTIONALITY-UNCONVENTIONALITY, SOCIETY-LUDICROUSNESS, TERSENESS-PROLIXITY.

quake. To tremble rapidly. AGITATION, HEAT-COLD, SANGUINENESS-TIMIDITY, VIBRATION.

Qua'-ker-ish. Like a Quaker. SOCIETY-AFFECTATION.

Qua'-ker-ism. The practise of the Friends. EXCITABILITY-INEXCITABILITY, ORTHODOXY-HETERODOXY.

qual''-i-fi-ca'-tion. That which qualifies. ASSERTION-DENIAL, MIGHT-IMPOTENCE, MODIFICATION, MUTATION-PERMANENCE, PRICE-DISCOUNT, SKILL-UNSKILFULNESS, TEACHING-MISTEACHING.

qual'-i-fied. Fitted; adapted. CONVENTIONALITY-UNCONVENTIONALITY.

qual'-i-fy. To fit for a particular position; to modify. ASSERTION-DENIAL, MIGHT-IMPOTENCE, MODIFICATION, MUTATION-PERMANENCE, PRICE-DISCOUNT, SKILL-UNSKILFULNESS, TEACHING-MISTEACHING.

qual'-i-fy''-ing. Rendering competent. MODIFICA-TION.

qualis ab incepto [L.] (quê'-lis ab in-sep'-to). The same as at the beginning. MUTATION-PERMANENCE.

qual'-i-ties. Distinguishing characteristics. AFFECTIONS.

qual'-i-ty. Essential property; social rank. GENTILITY-COMMONALTY, INCLINATION, POWER - IMPOTENCE, SUBJECTIVENESS-OBJECTIVENESS.

qualm. Conscientious scruple. BELIEF-MISGIVING, READINESS-RELUCTANCE, SANGUINENESS-TIMIDITY; **qualms of conscience,** READINESS-RELUCTANCE, REPENTANCE-OBDURACY.

quamdiu se bene gesserit [L.] (quam''-dai'-yu sî bî'-nî jes'-ser-it). During good behavior. CONTINGENT, DURATION, DUTY-DERELICTION.

quan'-da-ry. A perplexing situation. DIFFICULTY-FACILITY.

quand même [F.] (kan· mem). Even though. COMPENSATION, ANTAGONISM-CONCURRENCE.

quan'-ti-ta-tive. Having to do with quantities only. QUANTITY-MEASURE.

quan'-ti-ty. Comparative amount or number; a considerable amount or number. GATHERING-SCATTERING, MAGNITUDE-SMALLNESS, MULTIPLICITY-PAUCITY, QUANTITY-MEASURE.

QUANTITY—MEASURE.

Amount. Quantities taken as a whole, or as measured.
Amplitude. The amount of extension.
Batch. Quantities taken in a lump.
Capful, etc. A quantity equivalent to capacity of a cap.
Dose. A quantity of medicine taken at one time.
Handful. As much as a hand will hold.
Hay-mow. Mass of hay stored away in a barn.
Lot. A considerable amount.
Magnitude. Amount of measurable extent or volume.
Mass. A collection of substances making one quantity.
Measure. The amount of extent or volume referred to some standard.
Mouthful. As much as is usually taken into the mouth.
Quantity. The property of an object which admits being measured.
Quantum [L.]. Anything having quantity; the property of quantity.
Size. Relative magnitude. See GREATNESS.
Spoonful. As much as a spoon will hold.
Stock. A reserved quantity or quantities from which different amounts are taken.
Strength. The degree in which anything possesses its distinctive properties.
Substance. That of which anything is composed.

QUANTITY—Scientific Nouns.

Mathematics. The science of quantity.
Mathesis. A knowledge of mathematics.

QUANTITY—Adjectives.

Any. To an indefinite extent or degree.
More or less. About.
Quantitative. Relating to differences of quantity.
Some. Of indeterminate quantity.

QUANTITY—Adverb.

To the tune of. To the amount of.

QUANTITY—Phrase.

Digrado in grado [It.]. By degrees.

MEASURE—Adverbs—Continued from Column 2.

Howsoever. To what degree soever; in what manner soever.
Inasmuch. In like degree.
Inch by inch. Little by little.
In some degree. } Indefinitely.
In some measure. }
Little by little. Gradually.
Pro tanto [L.]. To that extent.
Step by step. Slowly.
To some extent. Considerably.

Amount. A quantity or quantities viewed as a whole.
Amplitude. Amount of extent.
Caliber. Degree of capacity.
Compass. Range within certain limits.
Degree. Relative proportion or amount.
Extent. Degree to which anything is extended.
Gradation. Arrangement according to size.
Grade. Relative position in some fixed order.
Height. Amount of extent upward.
Intensity. Degree of force or influence.
Mark. The proper or usual standard.
Measure. Amount of extent referred to some standard.
Pitch. Degree of elevation or depression.
Point. One of a series of graded positions.
Range. Amount of affected area or extent; the extent of a series.
Rank. Degree of worth; high position.
Rate. Comparative measure or valuation.
Ratio. Relation of number, degree, etc.
Reach. The limit of the extent of the effect or influence of anything.
Scope. Range of or capacity for achievement.
Shade. A very slight degree.
Sort. Degree of quality or value.
Sphere. Range of operations, influence, or knowledge.
Stage, etc. A marked point in the development or progression of anything. See STATION.
Standard. A measure used as the unit of value, etc.; a type or model.
Standing. Relative position in the estimation of others.
Station. Place in society or business; especially, high rank.
Stint. A fixed amount, as of work, for a given time.
Strength, etc. Degree of effect on other bodies; ability to act. See MAGNITUDE.
Tenor. The general drift, character, or course of anything.
Vedro. A Russian liquid measure.
Way. Sphere of observation.

MEASURE—Adjectives.

Comparative. Thought of as greater or less than something else.
Gradual. Proceeding or marked by degrees.
Shading off. Differing by a slight degree.
Within the bounds, etc. See BOUNDARY.

MEASURE—Adverbs.

Bit by bit. A little at a time.
By degrees. Gradually.
By inches. An inch at a time.
By little and little. Smaller by degrees.
By slow degrees. Very slowly.
Drop by drop. Gradually.
Gradually. In a gradual manner, slowly.
However. In whatever manner.

(Continued on Column 1.)

---

quantum [L.] (quan'-tum). A certain amount. ASSIGNMENT, QUANTITY-MEASURE.

quantum mutatus [L.] (quan'-tum miu-tê'-tus). A variable quantity. MUTATION-PERMANENCE.

quantum sufficit [L.] (quan'-tum suf'-fi-sit). As much as is sufficient. ENOUGH.

quaquaversum [L.] (quê'-qua-ver'-sum). To all sides. AIM-ABERRATION.

quar''-an-tine'. Enforced isolation. SECURITY-INSECURITY.

quar'-rel. A contention. VARIANCE-ACCORD; **quarrel with one's bread and butter,** CONTENTEDNESS-DISCONTENTMENT, SKILL-UNSKILFULNESS, VARIANCE-ACCORD.

quar'-rel-some. Contentious. FAVORITE-QUARRELSOMENESS.

quar'-ry. A stone mine; anything pursued. PURPOSE-LUCK, STORE.

quar'-ry-man. A man engaged in quarrying stone. AGENT.

quart. A fourth of a gallon. Measure, Quadrupli-cation-Quadrisection.

quar'-ter. A fourth; a locality; a lodging-place; direction; mercy shown an enemy. Aim-Aberra-tion, Compassion-Ruthlessness, Dweller-Hab-itation, Establishment-Removal, Extension-District, Harshness-Mildness, Laterality-Con-traposition, Measure, Period-Progress, Quad-ruplication-Quadrisection, Quaternity; **give no quarter,** Compassion-Ruthlessness, Life-Kill-ing; **give quarter,** Compassion - Ruthlessness, Harshness-Mildness; **quarter of a hundred,** Five-Quinquesection; **quarter upon,** Establishment-Removal.

quar'-ter-deck. The highest deck. Top-Bottom.

quar'-tered. Divided into four parts. Quadruplica-tion-Quadrisection.

quar'-ter-ing. A dividing into four parts. Quadru-plication-Quadrisection.

quar'-ter-mas''-ter. A military officer attending to provisions. Provision-Waste.

quar'-tern. A fourth part. Quadruplication-Quin-quesection.

quar'-ter-on. A fourth part. Mixture-Homogeneity.

quar'-ters. A lodging-place. Dweller-Habitation; **high quarters,** Gentility - Commonalty; **take up one's quarters,** Establishment-Removal.

quar'-ter-ses''-sions. A court held quarterly. Tribu-nal.

quar'-ter-staff''. A long, stout staff. Strife-Peace, Weapon.

quar'-tet. Four things or persons in harmony. Qua-ternity.

quar'-tile. Quadrate. Quaternity.

quar'-to. One-fourth the size of a sheet. Missive-Publication.

quartz. Rock crystal. Hardness-Softness.

quash. To suppress utterly. Commission-Abroga-tion, Creation-Destruction.

qua'-si. Appearing as if. Hypothesis, Likeness-Unlikeness.

quas'-si-a. A bitter tonic. Palatableness-Unpal-atableness.

quass. A thin, sour beer. Nutriment-Excretion.

qua-ter'-nal. Fourfold. Quaternity.

qua-ter'-na-ry. Group of four things; geologic period. Quaternity; **quaternary period,** Geology.

qua-ter'-ni-on. Set of four. Quaternity.

qua-ter'-ni-ty. The union of four in one. Quaternity.

QUATERNITY.

Four. A cardinal number equal to twice two.
Quadrature. The area of square equivalent to a given area, a square or the act of squaring.
Quarter. The fourth part of anything.
Quartet. A combination of four players or singers.
Quaternion. A system or combination of four persons or things.
Quaternity. The union of four in one; state of being composed of four parts.
Tetrad. A combination of four.
Square. A figure of four equal sides and four right angles.

QUATERNITY—*Verbs.*

Reduce to a square.
Square. To make into the form of a square; to multiply by itself.

QUATERNITY—*Adjectives.*

Four. Composed of one more than three.
Quadratic. Like a square.
Quartile. Having four equal sides.
Quaternal. Fourfold.
Quaternary. Consisting of four or occupying fourth place.
Tetractic. Having four rays.

quat'-rain. A stanza of four lines. Poetry-Prose.

quatre èpingles, tiré à [F.] (kɑtr ê-pɑn·gl', tir-ê' ɑ). Precise to a pin's point. Society-Affectation.

qua'-ver. Tremulous motion. Agitation, Crash-Drumming, Melody-Dissonance, Musician, San-guineness-Timidity.

quay. A wharf. Dweller-Habitation, Refuge-Pitfall.

quean. A low woman. Purity-Rake.

quea'-si-ness. Nausea. Desire-Distaste.

quea'-sy. Squeamish. Desire-Particularness.

queen. A female sovereign. Chief-Underling.

queen'-craft''. Craft in policy on the part of a queen. Rule-License.

queen'-hood. The state or personality of a queen. Chief-Underling, Gentility-Commonalty.

queen'-li-ness. Stateliness. Gentility-Commonalty, Reputation-Discredit.

queen'-post''. Supporting post. Architecture.

Queen's Bench. A high English court. Release-Prison, Tribunal.

Queen's Coun'-sel. A barrister who pleads for the crown. Advocate.

Queen's Eng'-lish. Pure English. Language; **murder the queen's English,** Grammar-Solecism, Speech-Inarticulateness.

Queen's ev'-i-dence. State's evidence. Exposure-Hidingplace.

Queen's high'-way. A public road. Way.

queer. Peculiar. Conventionality-Unconven-tionality, Society-Ludicrousness; **queer fish,** Society-Laughingstock.

quell. To put down. Creation-Destruction, Movement-Rest, Success-Failure, Turbulence-Calmness.

quench. To put out. Creation-Destruction, De-sire-Repletion, Heating-Cooling, Motive-De-hortation, Pleasurableness-Painfulness.

quench'-less. Not to be quenched. Desire-Dis-taste.

quer''-i-mo'-ni-ous. Fretful. Lightheartedness-Dejection.

que'-rist. An inquirer. Investigation-Answer.

quern. A hand-mill. Friability.

quer'-u-lous. Complaining. Desire-Particular-ness, Favorite-Quarrelsomeness, Lightheart-edness-Dejection.

quer'-u-lous-ness. The state of being faultfinding. Contentedness-Discontentment.

que'-ry. A question. Investigation-Answer.

que-sal'. A Central-American bird, noted for its beauty. Beauty-Ugliness.

quest. A search. Investigation-Answer, Quest-Evasion.

QUEST—EVASION.

Adventure, etc. Hazardous undertaking or enterprise; a com-mercial venture. See Venture.
Business, etc. A pursuit or occupation that employs or requires energy, time, and thought. See Occupation.
Enterprise, etc. Any projected task or work to which one applies himself. See Enterprise.
Game. A contest for recreation or amusement, to be won by chance, skill, or endurance, athletic contests.

Abstention. A refraining or abstaining.
Abstinence. Act, practise, or state of abstaining; especially, a total abstaining from the use of intoxicating drinks.
Avoidance. Act of avoiding or shunning.
Avolation. Act of flying away; flight; evaporation.
Departure, etc. Act of departing; a going away; deviation; death. See Arrival-Departure.
Elusion. Act of escaping by dexterity or strategy.

Hobby. A subject or pursuit in which a person takes extravagant or persistent interest.

Hue and cry. A loud outcry with which felons were anciently pursued, and which all who heard it were obliged to take up, joining in the pursuit till the malefactor was taken; in later usage, a written proclamation issued on the escape of a felon from prison, requiring all persons to aid in retaking him.

Prosecution. The act or process of pursuing with a view to attain, accomplish, or execute; in law, the act or process of carrying on a judicial proceeding against.

Pursuance. A following after or following out.

Pursuing, etc. Persistent following with the purpose of seizing or securing, etc. See *Verbs*.

Pursuit. Act of pursuing; earnest endeavor to attain or gain; continued employment.

Quest. Act of seeking; looking for something; search.

Scramble. Act of seeking something hurriedly and eagerly.

Quest—*Denotations*.

Angling. The action or art of fishing with a rod.

Battue [F.]. Act of beating the woods for game.

Chase. The practise of hunting game.

Coursing. The sport of chasing the hare or other game with greyhounds.

Fishing. The art or sport of catching fish.

Fox-chase. A fox-hunt.

Hawking. The sport of hunting small game with falcons or hawks.

Hunt.
Hunting. } The act of pursuing game.

Race. A competitive trial of speed.

Shooting. The killing of game with firearms.

Sport. Outdoor game or amusement.

Sporting. Act of engaging in field-sports.

Steeple-chase. A race on horseback across country, in which fences, ditches, etc., are to be leaped.

Venation.
Venery. } The art or practise of hunting game.

Quest—*Nouns of Agent*.

Falconer. One who follows the sport of fowling with hawks.

Hound, etc. A dog which hunts game by scent. See FAUNA.

Hunter. One who or that which hunts.

Huntsman. One who practises hunting.

Nimrod. Son of Cush, grandson of Ham, famous for his exploits as a hunter.

Pursuer. One who pursues.

Sportsman. One who practises field-sports.

Quest—*Verbs*.

Chase. Follow with intent to catch, seize, obtain, etc.

Course. Pursue with greyhounds, as hares.

Court, etc. Seek the favor of; seek to obtain by assiduous attentions, etc. See PETITION.

Dog. Follow as a dog, or with a dog; follow persistently.

Endeavor, etc. Undertake and strive for; exert oneself to accomplish an object. See VENTURE.

Follow. Pursue; strive to attain.

Hound. Hunt with or as with hounds; set on the chase; trail.

Hunt. Pursue, as game, for the purpose of killing or catching; search diligently for.

Prosecute. Pursue or follow up with a view to attain, accomplish, or execute; in law, to carry on a judicial proceeding against.

Pursue. Follow persistently with the purpose of seizing or securing; chase; hunt; seek.

Seek, etc. Go in search or quest of; strive for. See INVESTIGATION.

Still-hunt. To hunt quietly.

Quest—*Verbal Expressions*.

Aim at, etc. (see PURPOSE); be after; bend one's course; bend one's steps; carry on, etc. (see ACTION); direct one's course; direct one's steps; elbow one's way; engage in, etc. (see ENTERPRISE); fight one's way; fish for, etc. (see TRIAL); follow on the heels of, etc. (see LEADING-FOLLOWING); follow the trail, etc. (see INVESTIGATION), follow up; give chase; go in for; hold a course; hunt after; make after; make a jump at; make a leap at; make a snatch at; play a game; press on, etc. (see HURRY); prowl after; ride full tilt at; ride one's hobby; run after; run a race, etc. (see SWIFTNESS), run down; run full tilt at; rush headlong, etc. (see TURBULENCE), rush upon; set about, etc. (see BEGINNING); shape one's course; shape one's steps; start game; take a course; take to; take up; tread a path; tread on the heels of, etc. (see LEADING-FOLLOWING).

Escape, etc. Flight in which one succeeds in getting away from custody, pursuit, or annoyance. See ESCAPE.

Evasion. Act, means, or result of evading or avoiding, as by artifice or sophistry.

Flight. Act of fleeing or escaping; a running away; in law, the evading of justice by going away.

Forbearance. A refraining from retaliation or retribution.

Inaction, etc. Evasion of labor; idleness. See ACTION-PASSIVENESS.

Neutrality. The condition of being unengaged in contests between others.

Recoil, etc. A shrinking back; a rebound. See IMPETUS-REACTION.

Refraining, etc. Not following. See *Verbs*.

Rejection, etc. Act of refusing to accept or receive. See CHOICE-NEUTRALITY.

Retreat, etc. Act of withdrawing from a position, as of an army before an enemy. See APPROACH-WITHDRAWAL.

Seclusion, etc. Act of removing and keeping apart, as from company; solitude; retirement. See SOCIABILITY-PRIVACY.

Evasion—*Nouns of Agent*.

Fugitive. One who or that which flees, as from pursuit, restraint, or duty; a runaway or deserter.

Refugee. One who flees to a refuge.

Runagate. One who deserts a cause.

Runaway. One who or that which runs away, as a deserter or runaway horse.

Shirker, etc. One who shirks or evades duty. See *Verbs*.

Truant. One who absents himself from a place of duty; especially, a child who stays away from school without leave.

Evasion—*Verbs*.

Abandon, etc. Forsake or renounce utterly. See QUEST-ABANDONMENT.

Abscond. Depart suddenly and secretly.

Absquatulate. Take oneself off; decamp.

Abstain. Keep oneself back; refrain.

Avoid. Keep away from; shun; evade.

Blench. Draw back from lack of courage or resolution.

Blink. Shut out of sight; purposely evade.

Bolt. Dash off unexpectedly; break away from restraint.

Decamp. Break camp; march away; run away.

Desert. Depart from or leave, as a person having legal or moral claims upon one; forsake.

Dodge. Avoid by suddenly turning aside.

Elope. Run away from home with a lover or paramour.

Elude. Evade the search, pursuit, or inquiry of.

Escape, etc. Slip out or away from, etc. See ESCAPE.

Eschew. Shun, as something unworthy.

Evade. Avoid by artifice; elude or baffle.

Flee. Run away from; avoid; shun.

Flinch. Waver because of danger; shrink back.

Flit. Fly or move rapidly from place to place.

Fly. Flee from; shun; flee.

Levant. Run away from one's debts.

Parry. Ward off; evade; avoid.

Recoil. Start back as in dismay or loathing; shrink. See IMPETUS-REACTION.

Refrain. Abstain from action; hold within bounds.

Reject, etc. Refuse to accept; repel; discard. See CHOICE-NEUTRALITY.

Retire, etc. Go into privacy or seclusion; withdraw oneself, as for rest. See APPROACH-WITHDRAWAL.

Run. Hasten; speed; flee.

Shirk. Avoid the doing or right doing of; neglect purposely.

Shrink. Draw back; withdraw; recoil, as in horror.

Shun. Keep clear of; avoid.

Shy. Start suddenly aside: said of a horse.

Skedaddle. Flee in haste; scamper.

Spare. Refrain from using.

Evasion—*Verbal Expressions*.

Beat a retreat; be off; be off like a shot; break away; break away from; burst away; burst away from; cut and run; cut one's stick; deny oneself; draw back; fight shy of; flee from; fly from; get out of the way; give leg-bail; give one the go-by; give place to; go away, etc. (see sub DEPARTURE); hang back; have no hand in; have nothing to do with; hold aloof; hold back; hold off; keep aloof; keep at a respectful distance; keep clear of; keep from; keep off; keep one's distance; keep out of the way; lead one a dance; lead one a pretty dance; let alone; maintain the even tenor of one's way; make off; make oneself scarce; make way

QUEST—EVASION—*Continued.*

QUEST—*Adjectives.*

In full cry. In eager chase: said of hounds that have caught the scent, and give tongue together.
In hot pursuit. Pursuing eagerly.
In pursuit. Pursuing.
In quest of. Searching; seeking.
On the scent. On the track of discovery.
Pursuing, etc. Persistently following with the purpose of seizing or securing, etc. See *Verbs.*

QUEST—*Adverbs, etc.*

After. In the rear; behind.
In pursuance of, etc. In accordance with: in prosecution or fulfilment of.

QUEST—*Interjections.*

So-ho! A sportsman's halloo.
Tally-ho! The huntsman's cry to urge on or incite his hounds.
Yoicks! A cry of encouragement to foxhounds.

EVASION—*Continued from Column 2.*

EVASION—*Interjections.*

Devil take the hindmost!
Forbear!
Hands off!
Keep off!
Sauve qui peut [F.]. Save himself who can.

EVASION—VERBAL EXPRESSIONS—*Continued*

for; not attempt; not do, etc. (see ACTION-PASSIVENESS); **part company;** play at hide and seek; play truant; run away; **run away from;** run for one's life; scamper off; set one's face against; sheer off; show a light pair of heels; shuffle off; slink away; slink away from; slip away; slip away from; slip cable; sneak off; sneak out of; stand aloof; stand off; steal away; steal away from; steer clear of; take flight; take French leave; take no part in; take to flight; take to one's heels; tear oneself away; tear oneself away from; throw off the scent; turn away from; turn one's back; turn on one's heel; turn tail; walk one's chalks.

EVASION—*Adjectives.*

Avoiding, etc. Tending to flee from. See *Verbs*
Elusive. Tending to slip away or escape.
Evasive. Tending or seeking to evade; escaping ready apprehension
Fugitive. Escaping or escaped; runaway.
Neutral. Refraining from interference in a contest of any kind.
Runaway. Escaping or escaped from restraint or control.
Shy. Easily frightened or startled.
Shy of, etc. Avoiding a person or thing through caution or timidity. See READINESS-RELUCTANCE.
Unattempted. Not attempted or tried.
Unsought. Not searched for.
Wild. Unrestrained.

EVASION—*Adverbs, etc.*

In order to avoid. For the purpose of avoiding.
Lest. In order that not.

(*Continued on Column* 1.)

QUEST—ABANDONMENT.

ABANDONMENT.

Abandonment. Act of abandoning, or the state of being abandoned; total desertion.
Abrogation. Act of annulling by an authoritative act; repeal by authority.
Cave of Adullam. Cave to which David withdrew from Gath
Cession, etc. A yielding, or surrender, as of property or rights, to another person. See KEEPING-RELINQUISHMENT.
Defection. Act of abandoning a person or cause to which one is bound by allegiance or duty, or to which one has attached himself; desertion.
Desertion. Abandonment of a service, a cause, a party, a friend, or any post of duty.
Desuetude, etc. Discontinuance of practise, custom, or fashion. See HABIT-DESUETUDE.
Discontinuance, etc. Breaking of; want of continuity; cessation; interruption. See CONTINUANCE-DISCONTINUANCE.
Relinquishment. Act of withdrawing from, leaving behind, or abandoning.
Renunciation, etc. Act of rejecting or declining formally. See BIGOTRY-APOSTASY.
Resignation, etc. Act of resigning or giving up, as a claim, office See COMMISSION-RETIREMENT.
Secession. Separation from fellowship or association with others; in United States history, the withdrawal of a state from the national Union.
Withdrawal. Act of withdrawing; retreat.

ABANDONMENT—*Verbal Expressions.*

Abandon. Forsake or renounce utterly.
Desert. Depart from or leave, as a place where one is expected to remain; forsake.
Desist. Cease from action; forbear.

Discard, etc. Turn off as useless; reject, etc. See KEEPING-RELINQUISHMENT.
Drop. Have done with; give up abruptly.
Forego. Give up; relinquish.
Forsake. Leave or withdraw from; abandon.
Leave. Depart from; quit; let alone.
Quit. Let go; forsake; abandon.
Relinquish. Recede or withdraw from; abandon.
Renounce, etc. Refuse to acknowledge longer; abandon the use or pursuit of. See BIGOTRY-APOSTASY.
Stop, etc. Come to an end; discontinue. See CONTINUANCE-DISCONTINUANCE.
Vacate, etc. Surrender possession of by removal; quit. See COMMISSION-RETIREMENT.

ABANDONMENT—*Verbs.*

Back out of; bid a long farewell; break off; depart from; drop all idea of; give over; give up; give up the argument; give up the point; have done with; hold one's hand; leave in the lurch; leave off, desist; move the previous question; pass to the order of the day; quit one's hold; secede from; shut up shop; stay one's hand; take leave of; throw up the cards; throw up the game; wash one's hands of; withdraw from.

ABANDONMENT—*Adjectives.*

Relinquished, etc. Given up. See *Verbs.*
Relinquishing, etc. Surrendering. See *Verbs.*
Unpursued. Not pursued or followed.

ABANDONMENT—*Interjections.*

Aufgeschoben ist nicht aufgehoben [G.]. Put off is not given up
Avast, etc. Cease; stop. See CONTINUANCE-DISCONTINUANCE.
Entbehre gern was du nicht hast [G.]. Willingly renounce what you do not possess.

---

ques'-tion. Something asked. FAITH-MISGIVING, GODLINESS-DISBELIEF, INVESTIGATION-ANSWER; **in question,** CONCEPTION-THEME, INVESTIGATION-ANSWER, OCCURRENCE-DESTINY, SECURITY-INSECURITY; **out of the question,** SANGUINENESS-HOPELESSNESS; **pop the question,** BLANDISHMENT; **put to the question,** INVESTIGATION-ANSWER, PLEASURABLENESS-PAINFULNESS; **question at issue,** INVESTIGATION-ANSWER, VARIANCE-ACCORD.
ques'-tion-a-ble. Open to question. CERTAINTY-DOUBT, FAITH-MISGIVING, REPUTATION-DISCREDIT.

ques'-tion-ing. Interrogating. INVESTIGATION-ANSWER.
ques'-tion-ist. An inquirer. INSTRUCTOR-PUPIL.
ques'-tion-less. Certain. CERTAINTY-DOUBT.
ques'-tor. A public treasurer. TREASURER.
queue. A tail-piece. PREDECESSOR-CONTINUATION.
quib. A gibe. SOCIETY-DERISION.
quib'-ble. An evasion. AMBIGUITY, MEANING-JARGON, RATIOCINATION-INSTINCT, TRUTHFULNESS-FALSEHOOD, WITTINESS-DULNESS; **verbal quibble,** ADAGE-NONSENSE, WITTINESS-DULNESS.

quib′-bling. The act of shuffling in argument. ADAGE-NONSENSE, MEANING-JARGON.

quick. Alive; swift. ACTIVITY-INDOLENCE, EMOTION, FAVORITE-QUARRELSOMENESS, LASTINGNESS-TRANSIENTNESS, LIFE-DEATH, SAGACITY-INCAPACITY, SKILL-UNSKILFULNESS, SWIFTNESS-SLOWNESS; **cut to the quick,** EXCITATION, PLEASURABLENESS-PAINFULNESS; **probe to the quick,** INVESTIGATION-ANSWER; **sting to the quick,** FAVORITE-ANGER, PLEASURABLENESS-PAINFULNESS; **to the quick,** FEELING - INSENSIBILITY, SENSITIVENESS-APATHY; **touch to the quick,** EXCITATION, SENSITIVENESS-APATHY; **quick ear,** HEARING - DEAFNESS; **quick eye,** SIGHT-BLINDNESS; **quick succession,** FREQUENCY-RARITY; **quick as thought,** ETERNITY-INSTANTANEITY.

quick′-en. To make alive; to accelerate. AGENCY, EXCITATION, HURRY - LEISURE, LIFE - DEATH, OBSTRUCTION-HELP, TURBULENCE-CALMNESS.

quick′-en-ing pow′-er. Animating power. AGENCY.

quick′-eyed″. Having a keen sight. SAGACITY-INCAPACITY.

quick′-ly. Rapidly. EARLINESS-LATENESS.

quick′-sand″. Yielding sand. DIFFICULTY-FACILITY, REFUGE-PITFALL.

quick′-scen″-ted. Having a keen sense of smell. ODOR-INODOROUSNESS.

quick′-set″ hedge. A hedge of living shrubs. ENCLOSURE.

quick′-sight″-ed. Having a keen sight. SAGACITY-INCAPACITY.

quick′-sil″-ver. Mercury. MUTABILITY-STABILITY, SWIFTNESS-SLOWNESS, VIGOR-INERTIA.

quick′-wit″-ted. Keen. SAGACITY-INCAPACITY, WITTINESS-DULNESS.

quid. A chew of tobacco. PUNGENCY.

quid pro quo [L.] (quid pro quo). An equivalent. COMMUTATION-PERMUTATION, COMPENSATION, EXCHANGE, RECOMPENSE-PUNITION, REPRISAL-RESISTANCE.

quid valeant humeri, quid ferre recusant [L.] (quid val′-e-ant hiu′-mer-ai, quid fer′-rî rî-kiu′-sant). What the shoulders can, that they refuse to bear. MIGHT-IMPOTENCE.

quid′-di-ty. Essence. RATIOCINATION-INSTINCT, SUBJECTIVENESS-OBJECTIVENESS, WITTINESS-DULNESS.

quid′-nunc. An inquisitive person. INQUISITIVENESS-INDIFFERENCE.

qui-es′-cence. Inaction. MOVEMENT-REST, MUTATION-PERMANENCE.

qui-es′-cent. Being in a state of inaction. MOVEMENT-REST.

qui′-et. Still. EXCITABILITY-INEXCITABILITY, HURRY-LEISURE, MOTIVE-DEHORTATION, MOVEMENT-REST, TURBULENCE-CALMNESS; **keep quiet,** ACTION - PASSIVENESS; **quiet life,** STRIFE-PEACE.

quieta non movere [L.] (qui-î′-ta non mo-vî′-rî). Things that are at rest not to move. ACTION-PASSIVENESS, DISCONTINUANCE-CONTINUANCE, MOVEMENT-REST.

qui′-et-ism. Mystic meditation. GODLINESS-DISBELIEF, MOVEMENT - REST, ORTHODOXY - HETERODOXY, SENSITIVENESS-APATHY.

qui′-et-ly. In a quiet manner. CONCEIT-DIFFIDENCE; **get on quietly,** MEDIOCRITY.

qui′-e-tude. Repose. EXCITABILITY-INEXCITABILITY.

qui-e′-tus. The act of quieting. EXCULPATION-CONVICTION, LIFE-DEATH, LIFE-KILLING, SUCCESS-FAILURE; **give a quietus,** LIFE-KILLING; **receive its quietus,** COMMISSION-ABROGATION.

quill. A feather. WRITING-PRINTING.

quill′-dri″-ver. A writer. WRITING-PRINTING.

quill′-driv″-ing. Writing. WRITING-PRINTING.

quills. Sharp spines. SMOOTHNESS-ROUGHNESS; **quills upon the fretful porcupine,** SMOOTHNESS-ROUGHNESS.

quilt. A bedcover. COVER-LINING, VARIEGATION.

qui′-na-ry. Consisting of five parts. FIVE-QUINQUESECTION.

quin′-cunx. An arrangement of five things. DWELLER-HABITATION, FIVE-QUINQUESECTION.

quin″-quar-tic′-u-lar. Consisting of five articles. FIVE-QUINQUESECTION.

quin′-que-fid. Five-cleft. FIVE-QUINQUESECTION.

quin-quen-ni′-um. A period of five years. PERIOD-PROGRESS.

quin″-que-par′-tite. Five-parted. FIVE-QUINQUESECTION.

quin″-que-sec′-tion. A subdivision into five parts. FIVE-QUINQUESECTION.

quint. A fifth. FIVE-QUINQUESECTION.

quin′-tain. A tilting game. ENTERTAINMENT-WEARINESS, PURPOSE-LUCK.

quin′-tal. A hundredweight. HEAVINESS-LIGHTNESS.

quin′-tes-sence. The most essential part. SUBJECTIVENESS-OBJECTIVENESS.

quin′-troon. The offspring of an octoroon and a white person. MIXTURE-HOMOGENEITY.

quin′-tu-ple. Consisting of five. FIVE-QUINQUESECTION.

quinze. A game of cards. ENTERTAINMENT-WEARINESS.

quip. A taunt. ENTERTAINMENT-WEARINESS, REGARD-DISRESPECT, SOCIETY-DERISION, WITTINESS-DULNESS; **"quips and cranks and wanton wiles"** [Milton, *L'Allegro*]. ENTERTAINMENT-WEARINESS.

qui pro quo [L.] (quai pro quo). Who for whom. TRUTH-ERROR, WITTINESS-DULNESS.

quire. A band of singers; a chancel; twenty-four sheets of paper. FANE, MISSIVE-PUBLICATION, MUSICIAN.

quirk. A quibble. BIGOTRY-APOSTASY, DECISION-MISJUDGMENT, ENTERTAINMENT-WEARINESS, RATIOCINATION-INSTINCT, WITTINESS-DULNESS.

quis custodiet istos custodes [L.] (quis cus-to′-di-et is′-tos cus-to′-dîz). Who shall keep the keepers themselves. CAREFULNESS-CARELESSNESS.

quit. To cease; to repay; to free. ARRIVAL-DEPARTURE, QUEST-ABANDONMENT, SETTLEMENT-DEFAULT; **quitclaim,** DUTY - IMMUNITY; **quit one's hold,** KEEPING-RELINQUISHMENT; **quit of,** GAIN-LOSS, KEEPING-RELINQUISHMENT; **quit scores,** SETTLEMENT-DEFAULT.

qui tam. An action at law. LITIGATION.

quite. Entirely. ENTIRETY - DEFICIENCY; **quite another thing,** CONNECTION-INDEPENDENCE, LIKENESS-UNLIKENESS; **quite the reverse,** SAMENESS-CONTRAST; **quite the thing,** HARMONY-DISCORD.

quits. Release from demands. ATONEMENT, EQUALITY-INEQUALITY; **be quits with,** REPRISAL-RESISTANCE, SETTLEMENT-DEFAULT.

quit′-tance. Release; recompense. ATONEMENT, PARDON - VINDICTIVENESS, RECOMPENSE - PUNITION, SECURITY, SETTLEMENT-DEFAULT.

quiv′-er. An arrow-case; a shaking. AGITATION, CONTENTS-RECEIVER, EMOTION, HEAT-COLD, SANGUINENESS-TIMIDITY, STORE, VIBRATION; **in a quiver,** EMOTION, EXCITATION; **quiver with rage,** FAVORITE-ANGER.

quiv′-er-ing. Trembling. SANGUINENESS-TIMIDITY.

qui vive [F.] (kî vîv). Who goes there. CAREFULNESS-CARELESSNESS; **on the** *qui vive,* CAREFULNESS-CARELESSNESS, EXCITATION.

Quix′-ote, Don. A mad knight. RECKLESSNESS-CAUTION, SANENESS-MANIAC.

Quix-ot′-ic. Ridiculously chivalrous. FANCY, RECKLESSNESS-CAUTION.

quix′-ot-ism. Ridiculous chivalry. EXCITABILITY-INEXCITABILITY, RECKLESSNESS-CAUTION.

quix′-ot-ry. Quixotic practises. EXCITABILITY-INEXCITABILITY.

quiz. To banter. SOCIETY-DERISION, SOCIETY-LAUGHINGSTOCK.

quiz′-zi-cal. Queer. SOCIETY - DERISION, SOCIETY-LUDICROUSNESS.

quiz′-zing. Examining; questioning. SOCIETY-DERISION.

quo animo [L.] (quo an′-i-mo). With what intention. PURPOSE-LUCK.

quoad minus [L.] (quo′-ad mai′-nus). So much the less. COMPENSATION.

quod. A prison. RELEASE-PRISON; **in quod,** GUARD-PRISONER.

quod′-lib-et. A debatable point. INVESTIGATION-ANSWER, RATIOCINATION - INSTINCT, WITTINESS-DULNESS.

quoin. Corner-stone. ARCHITECTURE.

quoits. A pitching game. ENTERTAINMENT-WEARINESS.

quon′-dam. Former. FUTURE-PAST.

quo′-rum. Enough members of an association to act for the whole. COUNCIL, PRESIDENT-MEMBER.

quot homines, tot sententiæ [L.] (quot hom-i′-nîz, tot sen-ten′-shi-i). Many men, many minds. ASSENT-DISSENT, VARIANCE-ACCORD.

quo′-ta. Share. ASSIGNMENT, OUTLAY-INCOME; **furnish its quota,** GIVING-RECEIVING.

quo-ta′-tion. A passage; a price-current. CONVENTIONALITY-UNCONVENTIONALITY, IMITATION-ORIGINALITY, PRICE-DISCOUNT.

quote. To cite. CONVENTIONALITY-UNCONVENTIONALITY, EVIDENCE-COUNTEREVIDENCE.

quoth. Said. SPEECH-INARTICULATENESS.

quo-tid′-i-an. Daily. PERIODICITY-IRREGULARITY.

quo′-tient. The result obtained by division. NUMBER.

R

rab′-bet. Joint. CONNECTIVE.

rab′-bi.
rab′-bin. } Jewish teacher. MINISTRY-LAITY.

rab′-bin-ist. One of a sect of the Jews. ORTHODOXY-HETERODOXY.

rab′-bit. Small wild animal. FERTILITY-STERILITY.

rab′-ble. Mob. GATHERING-SCATTERING, GENTILITY-COMMONALTY.

rab′-id. Fanatic; furious. DESIRE-DISTASTE, EMOTION, EXCITABILITY-INEXCITABILITY, FAVORITE-ANGER, SANENESS-LUNACY.

ra′-bi-es. Hydrophobia. SANENESS-LUNACY.

raccroc [F.] (ra-kro′). Good luck. RATIONALE-LUCK.

race. Nation; career; speed-trial; channel. ANTAGONISM-CONCURRENCE, CONDUCT, CONTINUITY-INTERRUPTION, DIVERSION, ETHNOLOGY, OCCUPATION, PARENTAGE-PROGENY, PUNGENCY, QUEST-EVASION, RELATIONSHIP, RIVER-WIND, STRIFE-PEACE, SWIFTNESS-SLOWNESS, WATERCOURSE-AIRPIPE; **one's race is run,** LIFE-DEATH; **run a race,** QUEST-EVASION, STRIFE-PEACE; **run in a race,** ACTION-PASSIVENESS; **run one's race,** COMPLETION-NONCOMPLETION.

race′-course″. Race-track. LISTS.

race′-horse″. Horse trained for racing. CONVEYER, SWIFTNESS-SLOWNESS.

ra′-cer. A race-horse. CONVEYER.

ra′-ci-ness. Spirit. FORCE-WEAKNESS.

rack. Framework; pain; instrument of torture. CLEANNESS-FILTHINESS, CONTENTS-RECEIVER, PLEASURABLENESS-PAINFULNESS, RECOMPENSE-PUNITION, RECOMPENSE-SCOURGE, SENSUALITY-SUFFERING, SUSPENSION-SUPPORT, VISCIDITY-FOAM; **go to rack and ruin,** WELFARE-MISFORTUNE; **on the rack,** PLEASURE-PAIN; **rack one's brains,** FANCY, REFLECTION-VACANCY; **rack-rent,** OUTLAY-INCOME.

rack′-et. Noise. AGITATION, CRASH-DRUMMING, LOUDNESS-FAINTNESS, VARIANCE-ACCORD.

rack′-et-court″. Tennis-court. ENTERTAINMENT-WEARINESS.

rack′-et-ing. Reveling. ACTIVITY-INDOLENCE, ENTERTAINMENT-WEARINESS.

rack′-ets. Game like tennis. ENTERTAINMENT-WEARINESS.

rack′-et-y. Noisy. LOUDNESS-FAINTNESS.

rack′-ing. Torture. PLEASURABLENESS-PAINFULNESS.

ra′-cy. Spicy. EMOTION, FORCE-WEAKNESS, PUNGENCY, VIGOR-INERTIA.

rad′-dle. To weave. CROSSING.

rad′-dled. Done to excess. TEETOTALISM-INTEMPERANCE.

ra′-di-al. Pertaining to the radius. ANATOMY.

ra′-di-ance. Brightness. BEAUTY-UGLINESS, LIGHT-DARKNESS.

ra′-di-ant. Shining. CONCENTRATION-RADIATION, LIGHT-DARKNESS, REPUTATION-DISCREDIT.

ra′-di-ate. To emit rays. CONCENTRATION-RADIATION, LIGHT-DARKNESS.

ra″-di-a′-tion. Emission of rays. CONCENTRATION-RADIATION, LIGHT-DARKNESS.

rad′-i-cal. Extreme; fundamental. BETTERMENT-DETERIORATION, CAUSE-EFFECT, CONSEQUENCE-INSIGNIFICANCE, ENTIRETY-DEFICIENCY, NUMBER, SUBJECTIVENESS-OBJECTIVENESS; **radical change,** REVOLUTION; **radical cure,** REMEDY-BANE; **radical reform,** BETTERMENT-DETERIORATION.

rad′-i-cal-ly. In a radical manner. MAGNITUDE-SMALLNESS.

rad″-i-ca′-tion. Process of taking root. HABIT-DESUETUDE.

ra′-di-o-graph. Photograph produced by Roentgen rays penetrating opaque substances. SCIAGRAPH.

ra″-di-om′-e-ter. Kind of scientific apparatus. OPTICAL INSTRUMENTS.

ra′-di-us. Semidiameter; bone. ANATOMY, BREADTH-NARROWNESS, LENGTH-SHORTNESS.

ra′-dix. Root. CAUSE-EFFECT.

radoter [F.] (ra-do-tê′). To dote. SAGACITY-INCAPACITY.

radoteur [F.] (ra-do-tur′). Dotard. SAGACITY-INCAPACITY.

raff. Rabble; refuse. GENTILITY-COMMONALTY, PREPARATION-NONPREPARATION.

raff′-ish. Worthless. GENTILITY-COMMONALTY.

raf′-fle. A game of chance. PURPOSE-LUCK.

raft. Float. CONVEYANCE-VESSEL.

raft′-er. Support for a roof. SUSPENSION-SUPPORT.

rag. Piece of cloth. MAGNITUDE-SMALLNESS.

rag′-a-muf″-fin. Vagabond. GENTILITY-COMMONALTY.

rage. Wrath; ardor; fad. DESIRE-DISTASTE, DOMINANCE-IMPOTENCE, EXCITABILITY-INEXCITABILITY, EXCITATION, SOCIETY-LUDICROUSNESS, TURBULENCE-CALMNESS; **the battle rages,** FIGHTING-CONCILIATION.

rage′-ful. Furious. FAVORITE-ANGER.

rag′-ged. Torn. DRESS-UNDRESS.

ra′-ging. Very angry. EXCITABILITY-INEXCITABILITY, EXCITATION, FAVORITE-ANGER, TURBULENCE-CALMNESS.

rag′-man. A man who buys or picks up rags. AGENT.

ragout [F.] (ra-gu′). A highly seasoned dish. NUTRIMENT-EXCRETION.

rags. Torn clothing. DRESS-UNDRESS, USEFULNESS-USELESSNESS; **do to rags,** HEATING-COOLING; **tear to rags,** CREATION-DESTRUCTION; **worn to rags,** BETTERMENT-DETERIORATION.

raid. Foray. ATTACK-DEFENSE.

rail. A protecting bar; to rage. ENCLOSURE, RELEASE-PRISON; **rail at,** APPROVAL-DISAPPROVAL; **rail in,** CONFINEMENT, RELEASE-RESTRAINT.

rail′-ing. Rail. ENCLOSURE.

raillerie [F.] (rai-ye-rî′). Jest.

raillerie, ne pas entendre [F.] (rai-ye-rî, ne paz an′-tan·dr′). Not to take a joke well. FAVORITE-ANGER.

rail′-ler-y. Banter. SOCIETY-DERISION.

rail′-road″.
rail′-way″. } Parallel lines of iron or steel for cars to run upon. WAY.

rai′-ment. Clothing. DRESS-UNDRESS.

rain. Condensed vapor. ENOUGH, RIVER-WIND; **it never rains but it pours,** EXCESS-LACK.

rain′-bow″. Arch of the spectrum colors. VARIEGATION.

rain′-fall″. A shower. RIVER-WIND.

rain′-less. Lacking rain. DAMPNESS-DRYNESS.

rain′-proof″. Proof against the entrance of rain. ATTACK-DEFENSE.

rain′-y. Pertaining to rain. RIVER-WIND; **rainy day,** WELFARE-MISFORTUNE; **provide against a rainy day,** GENEROSITY-FRUGALITY, PREPARATION-NONPREPARATION.

raise. To lift; to grow; to arouse. CONVEXITY-CONCAVITY, CREATION-DESTRUCTION, ELEVATION-DEPRESSION, EXCITATION, INCREASE-DECREASE; **raise a**

cry, Publicity, Sign; **raise a dust**, Activity-Indolence; **raise a hue and cry against**, Approval-Disapproval; **raise alarm**, Alarm, Sanguineness-Timidity; **raise a laugh**, Entertainment-Weariness; **raise anger**, Favorite-Anger; **raise an uproar**, Tyranny-Anarchy; **raise a question**, Faith-Misgiving, Investigation-Answer; **raise a report**, Publicity; **raise a siege**, Fighting-Conciliation; **raise a storm**, Turbulence-Calmness; **raise expectations**, Sanguineness-Hopelessness; **raise funds**, Gain-Loss; **raise hope**, Prophecy; **raise money**, Gain-Loss, Loan-Borrowing; **raise one's head**, Betterment-Deterioration, Reputation - Discredit, Weariness-Refreshment, Welfare - Misfortune; **raise one's voice**, Assertion-Denial, Speech-Inarticulateness; **raise one's voice against**, Approval-Disapproval, Assent - Dissent; **raise spirits from the dead**, Devotion-Magic; **raise the finger**, Sign; **raise the mask**, Loan-Borrowing; **raise the red flag**, Tyranny-Anarchy; **raise the spirits**, Lightheartedness-Dejection; **raise the wind**, Gain-Loss, Loan-Borrowing; **raise troops**, Fighting-Conciliation; **raise up vertical**, Erectness-Flatness, Excitation.

raised. Projecting. Convexity-Concavity.
rai'-sin. A dried grape. Nutriment-Excretion.
raison d'etre [F.] (rê-zon′ dêtr). The reason for being. Purpose-Luck.
raison de plus [F.] (rê-zon′ de plü). All the more reason. Evidence-Counterevidence.
ra'-jah. Hindu prince. Chief-Underling.
raj′-poot′. A Hindu of the warrior caste.
rake. Garden tool; libertine. Atonement, Domestication-Agriculture, Good Man-Bad Man, Moderation - Selfindulgence, Purity - Rake, Push-Pull; **rake out**, Injection-Ejection; **rake up**, Excitation, Gathering-Scattering, Injection-Ejection, Remembrance-Forgetfulness; **rake up evidence**, Evidence-Counterevidence.
rake'-hell''. Utterly abandoned wretch. Good Man-Bad Man, Purity-Rake.
ra''-king–fire′. Firing passing lengthwise of the vessel. Attack-Defense.
ra'-kish. Dissolute. Health-Sickness, Renovation-Relapse.
rallentando [It.] (ral′′-len-tan′-do) Gradually slower. Music.
ral′-ly. Meeting; to encourage. Betterment-Deterioration, Bravery-Cowardice, Organization-Disorganization, Renovation-Relapse, Society-Derision; **rally round**, Antagonism-Concurrence, Regularity-Irregularity.
ral′-ly-ing. Arousing. **Rallying cry**, Bravery-Cowardice, Sign; **rallying point**, Gatheringplace.
ram. Male sheep; war-vessel; thrust. Belligerent, Fauna-Flora, Impetus-Reaction, Male-Female, Perforator-Stopper; **milk the ram**, Usefulness-Uselessness; **ram down**, Aperture-Closure, Solidity-Rarity; **ram in**, Injection-Ejection.
ram′′-a-dan′. Annual Mohammedan fast Ceremonial, Fasting-Gluttony.
ram′-age. Wild. Fauna-Flora.
ram′′-a-zan′. Ramadan. *q. v.*
ram′-ble. To roam. Aim-Aberration, Sagacity-Incapacity, Saneness-Lunacy, Terseness-Prolixity, Traveling-Navigation.
ram′-bler. One who roams. Wayfarer-Seafarer.
ram′-bling. Wandering; irregular; weak. Aim-Aberration, Force-Weakness, Saneness-Lunacy, Terseness-Prolixity, Traveling-Navigation.
ram′′-i-fi-ca′-tion. The act of spreading out. Concentration-Radiation, Doubling-Halving, Lamina-Fiber, Parentage-Progeny, Proportion-Deformity, Whole-Part.

ram′-i-fy. To divide. Concentration - Radiation, Doubling-Halving.
ram′-mer. That which rams. Impetus-Reaction, Perforator-Stopper.
ra′-mose. } Branching. Proportion-Deformity.
ra′-mous. }
ramp. To spring; to grow luxuriantly. Ascent-Descent, Spring-Dive.
ram′-page. Noisiness. Turbulence-Calmness.
ram′-rod′′. Stick used in loading guns. Perforator-Stopper.
ram′-shack′′-le. Shaky. Security-Insecurity.
ran′-cid. Rank. Cleanness-Filthiness, Perfume-Stench.
ran-cid′-i-ty. Stench. Perfume-Stench.
ran′-cor. Malice. Charitableness-Malevolence, Pardon-Vindictiveness.
ran′-cor-ous. Vindictive. Charitableness-Malevolence, Pardon-Vindictiveness.
ran′-dan. Kind of boat. Conveyance-Vessel.
ran′-dom. Casual. Certainty-Doubt, Conveyance-Vessel, Purpose-Luck, Rationale-Luck; **talk at random**, Gull - Hyperbole, Ratiocination - Instinct, Talkativeness-Taciturnity.
range. Stove; extent; to station. Aim-Aberration, Continuity-Interruption, Diversion, Extension-District, Liberty-Subjection, Organization-Disorganization, Oven - Refrigerator, Quantity-Measure, Remoteness-Nearness, Station, Traveling-Navigation; **long range**, Remoteness-Nearness; **range itself**, Regularity - Irregularity; **range under**, Admission-Expulsion; **range with**, Admission - Expulsion; **within range**, Contingency.
ran′-ger. One who ranges. Guard-Prisoner, Manager, Robber.
ra′-ni. Hindu queen. Chief-Underling, Male-Female.
rank. Degree; flourishing; smelling bad. Animality-Vegetability, Belligerent, Continuity-Interruption, Decision-Misjudgment, Goodness-Badness, Magnitude-Smallness, Organization-Disorganization, Perfume-Stench, Quantity-Measure, Regularity-Irregularity, Reputation-Discredit, Station; **man of rank**, Gentility-Commonalty, Reputation-Discredit; **person of rank**, Gentility-Commonalty; **rank and file**, Belligerent, Continuity - Interruption, Gentility - Commonalty.
ran′-kle. To irritate. Betterment-Deterioration, Cleanness-Filthiness, Favorite-Anger, Pardon-Revenge, Pleasurableness-Painfulness, Remembrance-Forgetfulness.
ranks. Common soldiers. **Fill up the ranks**, Renovation-Relapse; **risen from the ranks**, Gentility-Commonalty.
ran′-sack. To search. Investigation - Answer, Theft; **ransack one's brains**, Fancy, Reflection-Vacancy
ran′-som. Redemption. Atonement, Price-Discount, Rescue.
rant. Rave. Acting, Excitability-Inexcitability, Gull-Hyperbole, Meaning-Jargon, Simplicity-Floridness, Speech-Inarticulateness, Terseness-Prolixity.
rant′-er. One who raves. Godliness-Ungodliness, Talkativeness-Taciturnity.
rant′-i-pole. Noisy speaker. Heed-Disregard.
rap. Knock; coin of little value. Consequence-Insignificance, Crash-Drumming, Impetus-Reaction, Money; **not worth a rap**, Affluence-Penury; **rap on the knuckles**, Approval-Disapproval, Favorite-Anger, Recompense-Punition; **rap out**, Assertion-Denial, Speech-Inarticulateness, Vocalization-

Muteness; **rap out oaths,** Charitableness, Curse, Presumption-Obsequiousness.

ra-pa'-cious. Greedy; plundering. Desire-Distaste, Extravagance-Avarice, Taking-Restitution.

ra-pac'-i-ty. Desire to grasp. Desire-Distaste, Taking-Restitution, Theft.

rape. Snatching; carnal knowledge. Purity-Impurity, Theft.

rap'-id. Speedy. Swiftness-Slowness; **rapid slope,** Parallelism-Inclination; **rapid strides, rapid succession,** Frequency-Rarity.

ra-pid'-i-ty. Swiftness. Swiftness-Slowness.

rap'-ids. Swift water. River-Wind.

ra'-pi-er. Kind of sword. Weapon.

rap'-ine. Plunder. Theft.

rap''-pa-ree'. Vagabond. Robber.

rap-pee'. A snuff. Pungency.

rap-pel'. Drum-roll. Crash-Drumming, Fighting-Conciliation.

rap'-ping. Knocking. **Rapping spirit,** Devotion-Magic.

rapports, sous tous les [F.] (ra-port', sü tu lê) In every respect. Truth-Error.

rapprochement [F.] (ra-prosh-man·'). Junction. Amity-Hostility, Variance-Accord.

rap-scal'-lion. Vagabond. Good Man-Bad Man.

rapt. Enraptured. Emotion, Heed-Disregard.

rap-to'-ri-al. Pertaining to a kind of bird. Taking-Restitution, Theft.

rap'-ture. Ecstasy. Love-Hate, Pleasure-Pain.

rap'-tured. Joyous. Pleasure-Pain.

rap'-tur-ous. Transporting. Emotion, Love-Hate, Pleasurableness-Painfulness.

rara avis [L.] (rê'-ra ê'-vis). A rare bird. Conventionality-Unconventionality, Goodness-Badness, Reputation-Discredit.

rare. Scarce. Consequence-Insignificance, Conventionality-Unconventionality, Frequency-Rarity, Goodness-Badness, Likelihood-Unlikelihood, Multiplicity-Paucity, Solidity-Rarity.

rar'-ee-show''. Peep-show. Appearance-Disappearance, Entertainment-Weariness.

rar''-e-fac'-tion. Process of making rare. Enlargement-Diminution, Solidity-Rarity.

rar'-e-fied. Expanded. Solidity-Rarity.

rar'-e-fy. To make rare. Enlargement-Diminution, Solidity-Rarity.

rare'-ly. Seldom. Frequency-Rarity.

rare'-ness. Infrequency. Frequency-Rarity.

rari nantes [L.] (rê'-rai nan'-tîz). Rare ducks. Multiplicity-Paucity.

rar'-i-ty. Scarceness. Conventionality-Unconventionality, Frequency-Rarity, Multiplicity-Paucity, Solidity-Rarity.

rasa, tabula [L.] (rê'-sa, tab'-yu-la). An erased tablet. Mark-Obliteration.

ras'-cal. Knave. Good Man-Bad Man, Uprightness-Rogue.

ras-cal'-i-ty. Trickishness. Uprightness-Dishonesty.

ras-cal'-lion. A rascal. Good Man-Bad Man.

ras'-cal-ly. Knavish. Uprightness-Dishonesty.

rase. To destroy. Mark-Obliteration.

rash. Disease; reckless. Health-Sickness, Recklessness-Caution, Sagacity-Incapacity.

rash'-er. Slice of meat. Lamina-Fiber.

rash'-ling. A rash person. Recklessness-Caution.

rash'-ness. Recklessness. Bravery-Cowardice, Recklessness-Caution.

rasp. Instrument for scraping. Friability, Friction-Lubrication.

rasp'-er. That which rasps; high fence. Difficulty-Facility.

ra'-sure. Erasure. Mark-Obliteration.

rat. Formerly a union man, but now generally applied to printers who do not belong to the union; a small rodent. Bigotry-Apostasy; **smell a rat,** Discovery, Faith-Misgiving.

ra-tan'. Rattan. Recompense-Scourge.

ratch'-et. Piece of mechanism. Sharpness-Bluntness.

rate. Amount. Approval-Disapproval, Decision-Misjudgment, Mensuration, Movement-Rest, Price-Discount, Quantity-Measure; **at a great rate,** Swiftness-Slowness.

rath. Early; fort. Attack-Defense, Earliness-Lateness.

rath'-er. Somewhat. Choice-Rejection, Consequence-Insignificance, Faultlessness-Faultiness, Magnitude-Smallness; **had rather,** Choice-Neutrality; **had rather not,** Desire-Distaste; **have good,** Faultlessness-Faultiness.

rat''-i-fi-ca'-tion. Confirmation. Assent-Dissent, Consent, Contract, Evidence-Counterevidence.

rat'-i-fy. To approve; make binding. Assent-Dissent, Contract, Evidence-Counterevidence.

ra'-ting. A scolding. Approval-Disapproval.

ra'-tio. Rate. Assignment, Connection-Independence, Number, Quantity-Measure.

ra''-ti-oc''-i-na'-tion. Reason. Ratiocination-Instinct.

RATIOCINATION—INSTINCT.

Argumentation. The process of inferring propositions and drawing conclusions, not known or admitted as true, from principles or facts, admitted or proved to be true.

Art of reasoning. The application of the laws of reasoning.

Debate. Argumentation for and against.

Deduction. The applying of some general law or principle to an individual case.

Generalization. The deriving of general principles or laws from individual cases.

Induction. The forming of general principles or notions from particular instances.

Inference. The process of deriving conclusions from previous arguments or evidence.

Predesignation. Act of designating in advance.

Ratiocination. The process of drawing conclusions from the premise stated.

Reasoning. The process of arriving at conclusions by a systematic comparison of facts.

Wrangling. Angry and noisy dispute.

Ratiocination—*Nouns of Agency*

Arguer. One who argues. See *Verbs.*

Casuist. One who works out the niceties of moral questions.

Association. A relation or connection of ideas not due to the reasoning powers.

Instinct. Discernment of what is fitting or necessary without reasoning.

Intuition. An immediate grasping of truth or knowledge prior to all teaching or reasoning.

Presentiment. A prophetic insight into the future; a foreboding.

Instinct—*Denotations.*

Ignotum per ignotius [L.]. Unknown by a thing still more unknown; confusing explanation.

Misjudgment. Mistaken conclusion arrived at without reasoning.

Nonsense. That which has no sense or reason in it.

Post hoc, ergo propter hoc [L.]. After this, therefore because of this.

Rule of thumb. Any primitive method, more practical than scientific.

Instinct—*Scientific Nouns.*

Bad case. A case in which there is lack of reasoning, or in which the reasoning is faulty.

Ignoratia elenchi [L.]. Lack of reasoning power to discern the real point at issue.

Non sequitur [L.]. It does not follow; a conclusion unwarranted by sound reasoning.

RATIOCINATION—INSTINCT—*Continued.*

RATIOCINATION—Nouns of Agency—*Continued.*

Controversialist. One given to controversy. See *Nouns of Manner.*
Controvertist. Controversialist
Debater. One given to debate
Dialectician. One who reasons skilfully
Disputant. A party in a dispute
Logician. An expert in reasoning.
Plaidoyer [F] A defense, a speech at the bar.
Polemic. One who undertakes to defend a theory or doctrine.
Rationalist. A believer in rationalism· that the reason is the source of all knowledge.
Reasoner. One much given to reasoning.
Scientist. A scientific investigator
Wrangler. A debater who is easily angered, the highest grader in mathematics in the University of Cambridge, England.

RATIOCINATION—*Nouns of Manner.*

Analysis. The logical separation of a compound into its original parts.
Argument. A formal process of reasoning.
Case. A cause of dispute or reasoning.
Cogent reasoning. Convincing reasoning.
Comment. Informal discussion of any matter.
Comprehensive argument. An argument that covers all points in dispute.
Conclusive reasoning. Reasoning which leaves no doubt as to the conclusions drawn
Consectary reasoning. Reasoning which necessarily follows from the premises stated.
Contention. Maintaining by argument.
Controversy. A prolonged discussion. usually in writing.
Correct reasoning. Reasoning which logically follows step by step.
Dialectics. That branch of logic which teaches the rules and modes of reasoning
Disceptation. Controversy
Discussion. The process of giving the reasons on both sides of a question
Disputation. The arguing of any question, usually more heated than discussion.
Force of argument. Power of the argument to convince.
Forcible reasoning. Reasoning that compels belief.
Good case. One in which the line of reasoning is complete.
Inquiry. Investigation
Just reasoning. Correct reasoning.
Logic. The science of correct thinking.
Logical reasoning. Consistent reasoning
Logical sequence. Reasoning which follows in a logical order.
Logomachy. A dispute over mere words.
Paper war. A controversy in writing
Persuasatory reasoning.
Persuasive reasoning. } Reasoning which compels belief.
Polemics. The art or practise of carrying on disputations.
Process of reasoning. The whole course or line of reasoning.
Rationalism. The system which makes rational power the basis of truth
Sound reasoning. Correct reasoning.
Strong argument. An argument that convinces.
Strong point. That part of the argument which has the most telling effect
Subtle reasoning. Reasoning with great nicety.
Synthesis. The combining of separate elements into one whole.
Valid reasoning. Correct reasoning.
Ventilation. Free public discussion of any question.
Wrangle. A contentious discussion.

RATIOCINATION—*Scientific Nouns.*

A priori reasoning. Reasoning from antecedent cause to consequent effect.
Arguments. Connected series of statements or reasons intended to establish a position.
Argumentum ad hominem [L.]. An argument against the practises of an opponent and not against the principles which he advocates.
Datum. The premise or starting-point of an argument.
Dilemma. An argument which presents two or more alternatives.
Empirema. Proposition based on experience.
Enthymeme. An argument in which one of the premises is suppressed.
Epagoge. Inductive reasoning.
Horns of a dilemma. The two or more alternatives of a dilemma.
Judgment. The comparison of the two terms of a syllogism and their union or disunion affirmed.
Lemma. A proposition assumed to be true.

INSTINCT—*Figurative Expressions.*

At the end of one's tether. Without an answer.
Au bout de son Latin [F.]. At the end of his Latin; at his wit's end.
Lame and impotent argument. A weak argument.

INSTINCT—*Verbs.*

Hazard a proposition. Take chances on a proposition without basing it on sufficient reason.
Judge by intuition. To judge without reasoning. See *Nouns.*
Judge intuitively. Judge by intuition.
Misjudge. To err in judgment.
Not have a leg to stand on. To be entirely unsupported by reason.
Parler à tort et à travers [F] To speak at random, right and left.
Reason falsely. } To make mistakes in reasoning.
Reason ill. }
Talk at random. To talk in a haphazard manner.
Travel out of the record. To wander from the point at issue.

INSTINCT—*Adjectives.*

Absonant. Not concordant; inconsistent.
Absonous. Absonant.
Anterior to reason. Arrived at without the use of the reasoning powers.
Feeble. Weak: as, a feeble argument.
Flimsy. Of little strength or force.
Foolish. Void of reason.
Frivolous. Insufficient; lacking weight.
Gratuitous. Without sufficient warrant.
Groundless. With no basis of reason.
Hazarded. Taken chances on
Illogical. Without sound reasoning.
Impulsive. Acting without due thought.
Inconclusive. Not warranting a conclusion.
Inconsequent. Not following according to the laws of reason.
Inconsequential Inconsequent.
Inconsistent. Not agreeing with the rules of logic.
Incorrect. Not following the laws of reasoning.
Independent of reason. Intuitive.
Instinctive. Discerned by instinct See *Nouns.*
Intuitive. Known by intuition. See *Nouns.*
Invalid Not sound
Irrational. Not according to reason.
Irrelevant. Not pertaining to the subject.
Loose. Not connected.
Nonsensical. Void of reason.
Not following. Inconsequent.
Poor. Weak.
Unconnected. Not logically related.
Unproved. Not supported by reason.
Unreasonable. Contrary to or exceeding reason.
Unscientific. Not according to the principles of science.
Unsound. Not based on sound reasoning.
Untenable. Not to be defended by good reasons.
Unwarranted. Lacking evidence or authority.
Vague. Unauthorized.
Weak. Lacking force.

INSTINCT—*Adverbs.*

By intuition. Without reasoning. See *Nouns.*
Illogically. Not according to the rules of logic.
Intuitively. By intuition.

INSTINCT—*Phrases.*

A mockery, a delusion, and a snare.
Non constat [L.]. It does not appear.
That goes for nothing.

RATIOCINATION—Scientific Nouns—*Continued.*

Opening. The beginning of an argument or suit.
Perilepsis. Comprehension.
Postulate. A self-evident truth.
Premise. A proposition laid down as a basis for argument.
Principle. A fundamental truth; a ground of action.
Proposition. A judgment expressed in words. See DECISION.
Pros and *cons* [L.]. Arguments for and against.
Prosyllogism. A syllogism which is used to prove the premise of another.
Reasons. That which is given as supporting an argument.
Reductio ad absurdum [L.]. Proving a proposition by showing the absurdity of its contrary

RATIOCINATION—Scientific Nouns—*Continued.*

Sorites. A series of syllogisms abridged.
Starting-point. The beginning of an argument or case.

Syllogism. The regular logical form of argument.
Terms. The three parts of a syllogism.

RATIOCINATION—*Figurative Expressions.*

Chain of reasoning.
Train of reasoning. } Connected steps or points of reasoning.

RATIOCINATION—*Verbs.*

Agitate a question. To excite interest in or draw attention to.
Argue. To advance reasons for or against.
Bandy arguments. To give and receive arguments.
Bandy words. To exchange words; retort in words.
Be at issue. To be in dispute.
Canvass. To discuss and sift; to carefully examine.
Carry on an argument. To maintain an argument.
Chop logic. To wrangle, as if in formal logic.
Come to the point. To stick to the argument.
Comment upon. To discuss in an informal manner.
Consider. To ponder in the mind.
Contend. To enter into argument.
Controvert. To oppose by argument.
Debate. To formally argue a question.
Deny. To declare untrue.
Discuss. To enter into discussion. See *Nouns of Manner.*
Dispute. To enter into disputation. See *Nouns of Manner.*
Examine. To carefully sift; to weigh.
Hold on an argument. To continue the line of reasoning.
Infer. To draw conclusions.

Insist. To urge an argument with earnestness.
Join issue. To take opposite sides of an argument.
Lay stress upon. To make emphatic.
Moot. To argue or debate.
Moralize. To discuss questions with regard to the moral lessons to be drawn.
Open a case. To begin a suit.
Open a discussion. To begin an argument.
Reason. To exercise the power of reasoning. See *Nouns.*
Stir a question. To agitate a question.
Take one's stand upon. To place entire dependence upon, as an argument.
Take up a case. Take up a suit in court.
Take up a side. To support one point of view in an argument.
Torture an argument. To pervert or twist an argument to suit one's purpose.
Try conclusions with. To contend with for superiority.
Ventilate. To open to public discussion.
Wrangle. To enter into a wrangle. See Wrangle.

RATIOCINATION—*Adjectives.*

Argumentative. Characterized by arguments; given to arguing.
Aristotelian. Like the reasoning of Aristotle.
Controversial. Given to controversy.
Controvertible. Capable of being disputed.
Debatable. Capable of being debated.
Dialectic. Logical.
Discursive. Exhibiting the power of connected thought.
Discursory. Discursive.

Disputatious. Eager to enter into disputes.
Logical. Following the laws of reasoning.
Polemical. Given to polemics.
Rationalistic. Relying on reason alone.
Reasoning. Endowed with the power of reasoning.
Relevant. Suited to the purpose.
Synthetic. Constructing wholes from particulars.

RATIOCINATION—*Adverbs, etc.*

Accordingly. In a fitting or conformable manner.
A fortiori [L.]. Much more so.
After all. All things considered.
Au bout du compte [F.]. When all is done.
Because. For that reason.
Consequently. It naturally follows.
Considering. All things taken into account.
Ergo [L.]. Therefore.
Ex concesso [L.]. From what has been conceded.
Finally. In conclusion.
For. Owing to the fact that.
Forasmuch. Considering that.
For that reason.
For this reason. } Wherefore.
For which reason.
Hence. From this cause; therefore.
Inasmuch. Considering that.

In conclusion. Finally.
In consideration of. Considering these things are so.
In fine. In conclusion.
On the whole. All things considered.
Seeing that. Considering that.
Since. Following upon the fact.
Sith. Since.
So. For this cause or reason.
Take one thing with another. All things considered.
Then. As a consequence.
Thence. Following all that has gone before.
Therefore. For this or that reason.
Thus. On these grounds; in this case.
Whence. For which reason.
Whereas. Since the circumstances or facts are such.
Wherefore. For which reason.

RATIOCINATION—*Phrase.*

Ab actu ad posse valet consecutio [L.]. From what has been to what may be, the inference holds.

RATIOCINATION—CASUISTRY.

CASUISTRY.

Casuistry. False reasoning or teaching in regard to duties, obligations, and morals.
Chicane. Trickery; artifice.
Chicanery. Use of trickery or artifice.
Equivocation. The use of a word of doubtful meaning with a purpose to mislead.
Evasion. Avoiding the question in dispute.
False reasoning.
False teaching. } Sophistry.
Inconsistency. Logical disagreement.
Jesuitry. Subtle argument.
Misjudgment. Wrong or mistaken judgment.
Mystification. Act of artfully perplexing the mind of an opponent.
Paralogy. Mistaken reasoning; sometimes false reasoning.
Perversion. Twisting of an argument to suit one's purpose.
Sophistry. A pretense of sound reasoning intended to deceive.
Speciousness. Having the appearance of sound reasoning.
Vicious reasoning. Reasoning which is defective in logical soundness.

CASUISTRY—*Nouns of Agent.*

Pettifogger. A lawyer who resorts to cunning and artifice.
Quibbler. One who resorts to petty and trivial distinctions.
Special pleader. One who engages in special pleading. See sub Special pleading.

CASUISTRY—*Nouns of Manner.*

Antilogy. Inconsistency; self-contradiction.
Claptrap. A trick or device designed to win applause.
Overrefinement. Making too nice distinctions.
Quibble. A shuffling evasion of a point or question.
Quirk. An artful turn or evasion in an argument.
Subterfuge. Evading the force of an argument by some artifice or strategy.

CASUISTRY—*Nouns of Means.*

Elench. A false refutation.
Fallacy. Any unsound or delusive mode of reasoning.
Paralogism. A mistake or falsity in reasoning.
Solecism. Monstrosity of statement.
Sophism. A false argument used with the purpose of deceiving.

RATIOCINATION—CASUISTRY—*Continued.*

CASUISTRY—*Nouns of Result.*

Mere words. Words without meaning.
Nonsense. That which is without sense.
Quiddity. A trifling subtlety.
Quillet. A subtlety.
Quodlibet. A nice point; a subtlety.
Subtlety. An overnice distinction.
Weak point. A statement that does not convince.

CASUISTRY—*Scientific Nouns.*

Elenchus. A method of unsound reasoning; a sophism.
Petitio principii · [L.]. Begging the question; assuming in the premise what is to be proved in the conclusion.
Special pleading. In law, avoiding the allegations of the plaintiff by introducing new matter.

CASUISTRY—*Figurative Nouns.*

Cobwebs of sophistry. Fine-spun fallacious reasoning.
Flaw in an argument. A weak point in an argument.
Hair-splitting. The making of overnice or trivial distinctions.
Meshes of sophistry. Cobwebs of sophistry.

CASUISTRY—*Verbs.*

Beat about the bush. To approach a subject in a roundabout way.
Beg the question. To avoid the point at issue.
Cavil. To pick flaws without good reason.
Cut blocks with a razor. To do useless talking.
Elude. To evade.
Equivocate. To use a word of doubtful meaning with the purpose of deceiving.
Evade. To avoid the force of an argument by artifice or cunning.
Gloss over. To give a specious appearance.
Mislead. To deceive.
Misrepresent. To pervert; to give a false impression.
Mystify. To cause mystification.
Pervert. To wilfully twist or misinterpret the meaning.

Play fast and loose. To say one thing and do another.
Prove that black is white and white is black. To pervert the truth by sophistry.
Put oneself out of court. To be dismissed or dropped from the cause, usually for some default or defect in the case.
Quibble. To make overnice distinctions or to evade the question in an argument.
Reason in a circle. To engage in an inconclusive form of argument in which two or more unproved statements are used to prove each other.
Refine. To make overnice distinctions.
Split hairs. To insist upon oversubtle or trivial distinctions.
Subtilize. To spin into niceties.
Varnish. To hide a fault or error by fair words.

CASUISTRY—*Adjectives.*

Ad captandum vulgus [L.]. To catch the crowd; pleasing.
Deceptive. Misleading.
Evasive. Avoiding by artifice or sophistry.
Fallacious. Involving fallacies.
Fallible. Liable to be incorrect or false, as an argument.
False. Contrary to truth; sometimes designedly intended to deceive.
Fine-spun. Worked out with too much subtlety.
Illusive. Deceiving.
Illusory. Illusive.
Jesuitical. Given to subtle sophistries.
Overrefined. Too subtle.
Pettifogging. Characteristic of a pettifogger.
Plausible. Seeming to be true.
Quibbling. Given to quibbles.
Sophistical. Characterized by or given to sophistry.
Specious. Having only the appearance of truth.

CASUISTRY—*Phrase.*

A mockery, a delusion, and a snare.

---

ra′-tion. Allowance of food. ASSIGNMENT, NUTRIMENT-EXCRETION.
ra′-tion-al. Reasonable; not radical. MIND-IMBECILITY, NUMBER, SAGACITY-INCAPACITY, SANENESS-LUNACY.
ra″-tio-na′-le. Logical basis. CAUSE-EFFECT, INTERPRETATION-MISINTERPRETATION, INVESTIGATION-ANSWER, PURPOSE-LUCK.

RATIONALE—LUCK.

Accounting for. An assignment of a reason for. See *Verbs.*
Affiliation. Close association or relationship.
Ascription. The act of ascribing or referring an effect to a cause.
Attribution. The act of referring, as to a cause.
Derivation from. Deduction of a fact or principle from a fixed law or standard.
Explanation. Meaning assigned to anything; a definition. See INTERPRETATION.
Filiations. Connections.
Imputation. The act of imputing, or of referring to a cause.
Pedigree. A table of descent and relationship. See PARENTAGE.
Rationale. Reasonable exposition of the principles of some reason.
Reason why. That which accounts for anything. See CAUSE.
Reference to. Allusion to.
Theory. An inferential explanation of phenomena.

RATIONALE—*Scientific Nouns.*

Etiology. Science of cause.
Paletiology. A causative explanation of the past conditions of the earth.

RATIONALE—*Verbs.*

Account for. To give reasons for.
Ascribe to. To assign reasons for.
Assign as a cause. To designate as a cause.
Attribute to. To ascribe to as appropriate.
Bring home to. To bring to the source or cause.
Charge on. To ascribe, as a crime.
Derive from. To draw from.
Father upon. To ascribe anything to one, as if to a father.
Ground on. To base on a given principle.
Impute to. To ascribe to.
Invest with. To put on, as clothing.
Lay at the door of. To put down as belonging to one.
Lay to. To charge with.
Point out the reason. To give a reason for See CAUSE.
Point to. To indicate as the cause.

Accident. A sudden and undesigned event.
Adventure. That which happens undesignedly.
Assurance. That which inspires confidence in what was before doubtful.
Book-making. The art of professional betting.
Casualty. An accidental but unimportant event.
Chance. That which happens without any known cause.
Chance-medley. The killing of another in self-defense upon an unexpected attack.
Chapter of accidents. A series of accidents.
Contingence. The possibility of an event happening or not.
Contingency. Contingence.
Equal chance. Equal probability of occurring or not occurring.
Fate. A predetermined event. See VOLITION-OBLIGATION.
Fortune. That which happens to a man; luck.
Gaming. Playing games for stakes. See PURPOSE-LUCK.
Hap. A casual occurrence.
Haphazard. Extra risk or chance.
Hazard. Uncertainty as to whether an event will turn out good or bad.
Hazard of the die. A risking of stakes upon a throw of dice.
Heads or tails. This side or the other of a coin.
Hit. A stroke of luck.
Indetermination. Want of resolution or decision.
Long odds. Little chance of occurring.
Lottery. Distribution of prizes by lots or chance.
Luck. Anything that happens to a person.
Odds. The superiority of chances.
Possibility. State of being possible; that a thing may happen or not.
Probability. More likelihood of happening than of not happening.
Raccroc [F.]. A chance.
Random. Want of purpose.
Run of luck. A series of fortunate events.
Sortes [L.]. A lot.
Sortes Virgilianæ [L.]. A form of divination in which the first passage that the eye drops on in opening at random Virgil's poems is used to direct the course of the individual in a difficulty.

RATIONALE—LUCK—*Continued.*

RATIONALE—Verbs—*Continued.*

Put the saddle on the right horse. To fit on the right place; ascribe aright.
Put to. To charge with.
Refer to. To allude to.
Set down to. To ascribe to.
Tell how it comes. To state the reason for.
Theorize. To have a theory; have opinions in theory.
Trace to. To follow up to; ascribe.

RATIONALE—*Adjectives.*

Attributable. Able to be attributed. See *Verbs.*
Attributed. Ascribed. See sub *Verbs.*
Derivable from. Known by inference from.
Due to. Deserving of; meriting.
Owing to. In consequence of.
Putative. Reputed; supposed.
Referable. }
Referrible. } Capable of being ascribed.

RATIONALE—*Adverbs, etc.*

Because. For this reason.
From that cause. }
From this cause. } Owing to this.
For. Because.
For as much as. Since.
Hence. Therefore.
How comes it. }
How does it happen. }
How happens it. } What is the cause or reason?
How is it. }
In some such way. }
In some way. } From a certain cause or reason.
On account of. }
On that account. } Owing to.
Owing to. Because.
Propter hoc [L.]. On account of.
Since. Following upon the fact that.
Somehow. }
Somehow or other. } For some indefinite cause or reason.
Thanks to. Owing to.
Thence. From the fact.
Therefore. For this reason.
Whence. From the fact.
Wherefore. From this cause.
Why. For what cause?

RATIONALE—*Phrases.*

Fortes fortuna adjuvat [L.]. Fortune favors the brave.
Fortuna favet fatuis [L.]. Fortune favors fools.

ra′-tion-al-ism. Reliance upon reason. Godliness-Disbelief, Ratiocination-Instinct.
ra′-tion-al-ist. A believer in rationalism. Ratiocination-Instinct.
ra″-tion-al-is′-tic. Reasonable. Certainty-Doubt.
ra″-tion-al′-i-ty. Reasonableness. Mind-Imbecility, Sagacity-Incapacity, Saneness-Lunacy.
rat′-lings. The rope rungs of a ship's ladders. Ascent-Descent, Conveyance-Vessel, Suspension-Support.
rat-tan′. A switch. Might-Impotence, Recompense-Scourge.
rat′-ten. To persecute. Might-Impotence.
rat′-tle. Noise. Crash-Drumming, Musical Instruments, Talkativeness-Taciturnity; **death-rattle,** Life-Death; **rattle on,** Talkativeness-Taciturnity.
rat′-tle-snake″. Kind of venomous snake. Benefactor-Evildoer.
rat′-tle-traps″. Rickety objects. Property.
rat′-tling. Lively. Lightheartedness-Dejection; **rattling pace,** Swiftness-Slowness.
rau′-ci-ty. Hoarseness. Loudness-Faintness, Vocalization-Muteness.
rau′-cous. Hoarse. Vocalization-Muteness.
rav′-age. To pillage. Betterment-Deterioration, Creation-Destruction; **ravages of time,** Betterment-Deterioration, Duration-Neverness.

Speculation. A more or less risky investment of money.
Throw of the dice. A hazard or venture.
Toss up. A venture.
Turn of the cards. }
Turn of the table. } A chance in luck.
Wheel of fortune. Chance or fortune.

Luck—*Scientific Nouns.*

Theory of chances. } { A theory in which are set forth the relations
Theory of probabilities. } { of events to each other, their chances or probabilities of happening.

Luck—*Verbs.*

Be one's fate. To be one's appointed lot. See Volition-Obligation.
Chance. To happen without cause.
Fall to one's lot. To happen without any intent of the person.
Hap. To happen.
Light upon. To come upon by chance.
Stumble on. To happen without design.
Take one's chance. To hazard it. See Purpose-Luck.
Turn up. To come up; come to pass.

Luck—*Adjectives.*

Accidental. Not designed or planned.
Adventitious. Not essential; casual.
Casual. Occurring by chance.
Causeless. Happening without cause.
Contingent. Likely to occur.
Fortuitous. Happening without any known cause.
Incidental. Coming without regularity.
Indeterminate. Not determined or precise.
Possible. Capable of happening or not. See Possibility.
Uncaused. Having no cause or reason.
Undetermined. Not settled or established.
Unintentional. Happening without design.

Luck—*Adverbial Expressions.*

As bad would have it; as good would have it; as ill-luck would have it; as it may be; as it may chance; as it may happen; as it may turn up; as the case may be; by accident; by chance; casually; for aught one knows.

RATIONALE—Phrases—*Continued.*

Hinc illæ lachrymæ [L.]. Hence these tears.
That is why.

rave. To rage. Excitability-Inexcitability, Excitation, Saneness-Lunacy; **rave against,** Approval-Disapproval.
rav′-el. To unknit. Crossing, Difficulty-Facility, Organization-Disorganization.
rav′-eled. Unknit. Circle-Winding, Regularity-Irregularity.
rave′-lin. Kind of fort. Attack-Defense.
rav′-el-ing. A tangle. Regularity-Irregularity.
rav′-elled. See Raveled.
ra′-ven. Kind of bird; black; prey upon. Fasting-Gluttony, Vocalization-Muteness, Whiteness-Blackness; **raven for,** Desire-Distaste.
rav′-en-ing. Preying upon. Desire-Distaste, Turbulence-Calmness.
rav′-en-ous. Voracious. Desire-Distaste, Taking-Restitution.
rav′-en-ous-ness. Greediness. Desire-Distaste.
ra′-ver. One who raves. Saneness-Maniac.
rav′-in. Ravage. Nutriment-Excretion, Plunder.
ra-vine′. Gully. Breadth-Narrowness, Groove, Interspace-Contact.
ra′-ving. Furious. Emotion, Excitability-Inexcitability, Excitation, Saneness-Lunacy.
rav′-ish. To violate; to enrapture. Pleasurableness-Painfulness, Taking-Restitution.
rav′-ished. Pleased. Pleasure-Pain.

rav′-ish-ing. Rapturous. PLEASURABLENESS - PAIN-FULNESS.

rav′-ish-ment. Delight. EXCITATION, PLEASURE-PAIN.

raw. Not cooked; inexperienced; sensitive. COLOR-ACHROMATISM, HEAT-COLD, MATERIALS, NOVELTY-ANTIQUITY, PREPARATION-NONPREPARATION, SENSUALITY-SUFFERING, SKILL-UNSKILFULNESS; **raw head and bloody bones,** SANGUINENESS-TIMIDITY; **raw levies,** BELLIGERENT; **raw material,** MATERIALS, PREPARATION-NONPREPARATION.

raw′-boned″. Bony. BREADTH-NARROWNESS.

raw′-ness. Crudeness. PREPARATION - NONPREPARATION.

ray. Line of light. LIGHT-DARKNESS; **ray of comfort,** CONTENTEDNESS-DISCONTENTMENT.

raze. To destroy. CREATION-DESTRUCTION; **raze to the ground,** ELEVATION-DEPRESSION.

ra′-zor. Cutting instrument. SHARPNESS-BLUNTNESS; **cut blocks with a razor,** PROVISION-WASTE, SKILL-UNSKILFULNESS, USE-MISUSE; **keen as a razor,** EMOTION, SHARPNESS-BLUNTNESS.

raz′-zi-a. Foray. ATTACK-DEFENSE, CREATION-DESTRUCTION, THEFT.

re″-ab-sorb′. Absorb again. ADMISSION-EXPULSION.

reach. To attain to; to get; expanse. ARRIVAL-DEPARTURE, COMPLETION-NONCOMPLETION, EQUALITY-INEQUALITY, MEDIOCRITY, QUANTITY-MEASURE, REMOTENESS-NEARNESS, RIVER-WIND, TAKING-RESTITUTION, TRANSFER, TRUTHFULNESS-FRAUD; **reach of** thought, SAGACITY-INCAPACITY; **reach the ear,** LIGHTENMENT-SECRECY, HEARING-DEAFNESS; **reach to,** LENGTH-SHORTNESS, REMOTENESS-NEARNESS; **within reach,** DIFFICULTY-FACILITY, POSSIBILITY-IMPOSSIBILITY, REMOTENESS-NEARNESS.

re-act′. To recoil; act opposite. COOPERATION-OPPOSITION, IMPETUS-REACTION.

re-ac′-tion. Backward movement. COMPENSATION, COOPERATION - OPPOSITION, IMPETUS - REACTION, RENOVATION-RELAPSE, REPRISAL-RESISTANCE.

re-ac′-tion-a-ry. Pertaining to a reaction. ADVANCE-RETROGRESSION, BIGOTRY-APOSTASY, CONVERSION-REVERSION, COOPERATION-OPPOSITION, IMPETUS-REACTION.

re-ac′-tion-ist. Conservative. ANTAGONIST-ASSISTANT, IMPETUS-REACTION.

read. To interpret; to study. EDUCATION-LEARNING, INTERPRETATION-MISINTERPRETATION; **read a lecture,** APPROVAL - DISAPPROVAL, EDUCATION - MISTEACHING; **well read,** KNOWLEDGE-IGNORANCE.

read′-a-ble. Easy to read. PURITY-CRUDENESS.

read′-er. One who reads; book. INSTRUCTOR-PUPIL, MINISTRY-LAITY, WRITING-PRINTING.

read′-er-ship. The office of reader. SCHOOL.

read′-i-ly. Promptly. DIFFICULTY-FACILITY.

read′-i-ness. State of being prepared. PREPARATION-NONPREPARATION, PURITY-CRUDENESS, READINESS-RELUCTANCE, REMEMBRANCE - FORGETFULNESS, SKILL-UNSKILFULNESS.

READINESS—RELUCTANCE.

Alacrity. A cheerful readiness or promptitude to do some act.

Animus [L.]. Spirit; temper; especially, hostile spirit or angry temper.

Aptitude, etc. Readiness in learning; a natural or acquired disposition. See SKILL.

Assent. The giving of consent, approval, or sanction. See ASSENT.

Bent, etc. Disposition toward something; inclination. See AFFECTIONS.

Compliance. A yielding to or acting in accordance with a wish.

Cordiality. Hearty warmth of heart; genial sincerity.

Disposition. Temper or natural constitution of the mind.

Docibleness. Teachableness; aptness to be taught.

Docility. Readiness to learn; tractableness.

Eagerness, etc. Ardor of inclination; ardent desire for anything. See DESIRE.

Earnestness. Zeal in the pursuit of anything; intenseness of desire.

Forwardness. The quality of being ready and prompt.

Frame of mind. Temper; inclination; disposition.

Geniality. Sympathetic cheerfulness or cordiality.

Good-will. A desire for the prosperity and well-being of others.

Heart. Disposition of mind; courage; spirit.

Humor. Turn of mind; disposition, or rather peculiarity of disposition, often temporary.

Inclination. Bias of mind or will, propensity.

Labor of love. A work done with willingness and pleasure. See VOLITION.

Leaning. Tendency of the mind; bias.

Mood. A temporary state of the mind; disposition.

Penchant, etc. [F]. Strong inclination; decided taste; liking. See DESIRE.

Persuasibility. Capability of being influenced by argument, advice, or entreaty.

Persuasibleness. The quality of being persuasive.

Pliability, etc. The quality of yielding to moral force or influence. See HARDNESS-SOFTNESS.

Readiness. Freedom from reluctance; promptitude; being in a state of preparation.

Vein. Tendency or turn of the mind; particular mood for the time being.

Voluntariness, etc. The state of being produced by the free will or choice.

Volunteer. One who enters into any service of his own free will.

Volunteering. Act of undertaking of his own free will.

Willingness. Readiness of the mind to do or to refrain from doing.

Willing mind. A mind ready to do.

Aversation. A turning from with disgust or dislike; aversion.

Averseness, etc. Repugnance or opposition of mind; unwillingness. See DESIRE-DISTASTE.

Backwardness, etc. Dilatoriness or dulness in action; tardiness. See *Adjectives.*

Demure. Suspension of decision or action.

Disinclination. Want of inclination; slight dislike or aversion.

Dissent. Refusal of assent or agreement. See ASSENT-DISSENT.

Fastidiousness, etc. State of being hard to please; squeamishness of mind. See DESIRE-PARTICULARNESS.

Hesitation, etc. Suspension of opinion or action. See DETERMINATION-VACILLATION.

Indifference, etc. Absence of interest as to what is presented to the mind; unconcernedness. See UNCONCERN.

Indisposedness. } State of being indisposed; disinclination; aversion
Indisposition. }

Indocility, etc. State of being indocile; unteachableness. See BIGOTRY.

Nolition. Opposed to volition—the power of willing.

Nolleity. Unwillingness; nolition.

Qualm. } Moral scruple.
Qualms of conscience. }

Recoil. A shrinking from.

Refusal. Denial of what is asked. See PROFFER-REFUSAL.

Reluctance. State of striving against doing something; state of acting with repugnance.

Renitence. Moral resistance.

Scruple. Hesitation proceeding from motives of conscience.

Scrupulosity. } Caution or tenderness arising from fear of doing
Scrupulousness. } wrong or offending.

Shrinking. A drawing back from.

Slowness, etc. Want of readiness or promptness. See SWIFTNESS-SLOWNESS.

Unwillingness, etc. Want of inclination; slight dislike or aversion. See *Adjectives.*

Want of alacrity. A conspicuous absence of cheerful readiness.

Want of readiness. Lack of promptness or willingness.

RELUCTANCE—*Verbs.*

Avoid, etc. To keep at a distance from; shun. See QUEST-EVASION.

Begrudge. To give with reluctance; feel discontent.

Be unwilling, etc. To be disinclined; be reluctant. See *Adjectives.*

Demur. To linger; doubt of or hesitate about.

Dislike, etc. To regard with displeasure or aversion; disapprove. See DESIRE-DISTASTE.

Dissent, etc. To differ in opinion; disagree. See ASSENT-DISSENT.

READINESS—RELUCTANCE.

READINESS—*Verbs.*

Be willing, etc. To be ready; be inclined to do anything. See *Adjectives*.

Catch at. To be eager to get or to use.

Cling to. To apply firmly and closely.

Comply with, etc. To consent; acquiesce; agree. See CONSENT.

Desire, etc. To wish or long for; request; petition. See DESIRE.

Give a willing ear. To give attention to; listen.

Gorge the hook. To swallow with greediness; glut; satiate.

Had as lief. Would gladly; would willingly.

Have a great mind to. ⎫
Have a mind to. ⎬ To be inclined to; disposed to.
Have half a mind to. ⎭

Have no scruple of. To experience no doubt or hesitancy about doing a thing.

Hold to. To cling or cleave to; adhere.

Incline. To be disposed; have a propensity.

Jump at. To accept suddenly or eagerly.

Lean to. To incline in opinion or desire; conform in conduct.

Lend a willing ear. To give earnest attention.

Lend a willing hand. To give assistance; help.

Make no bones of. To make no scruple of; not to hesitate.

Make no scruple of. Not to hesitate from conscientious motives; not to question.

Meet half-way. To yield half the difference in order to effect a compromise.

Mind. To regard with attention; consider.

Nibble at the bait. To bite gently; make a petty attack.

Propend. To lean toward a thing; be favorably disposed.

See fit. To be inclined.

See good. To consider expedient.

See proper. To consider proper or appropriate.

Set abroach. To set running, as liquor.

Swallow the bait. To receive implicitly; accept without examination.

Think fit. To deem suitable.

Think good. To approve.

Think proper. To consider advisable or becoming.

Turn a willing ear. To be open to conviction; be ready to listen to.

Volunteer. To offer voluntarily, without solicitation or compulsion.

READINESS—*Adjectives.*

Bent upon, etc. Strongly inclined toward something. See DESIRE.

Content, etc. Not disposed to grumble; satisfied; contented. See ASSENT.

Cordial. Proceeding from the heart; sincere; affectionate.

Disposed. Inclined; minded.

Docile. Disposed to be taught; easily managed.

Eager. Ardently desirous; impetuous; vehement.

Earnest. Done with a will; zealous with sincerity.

Easily persuaded. Readily convinced; easily prevailed upon.

Easy-going. Mild-tempered; ease-loving.

Facile. Ready; quick; expert.

Fain. Well-pleased; glad; eager.

Favorable. Tending to promote or facilitate; friendly.

Favorably disposed. ⎫
Favorably inclined. ⎬ Favorable to.
Favorably minded. ⎭

Forward. Ready; prompt; presumptuous.

Genial. Cheering; enlivening.

Gracious. Disposed to show kindness or favor; merciful.

Gratuitous. Free; taken without ground or proof.

Hearty. Willing; energetic; warm; cordial.

Inclined. Having a tendency toward, or away from, a thing; disposed.

In the humor. In a pleased state of mind.

In the mind. In good spirits.

In the mood. In a pleasant frame of mind.

In the vein. In a favorable disposition.

Minded. Disposed; inclined.

Nothing loth. Willing; not reluctant; not backward.

Persuadable. That may be convinced.

Persuasible. Persuadable; that may be influenced by reasons offered.

Predisposed. Inclined beforehand; adapted previously.

Propense. Leaning forward, in a moral sense; prone.

Ready. Prepared; willing; not reluctant.

Spontaneous. Done without compulsion; voluntary.

Suasible. Easily persuaded.

Tractable, etc. Capable of being easily managed; docile. See HARDNESS-SOFTNESS.

RELUCTANCE—*Verbs*—*Continued.*

Grudge. To give or take unwillingly; complain.

Hang fire. To hesitate; hold back, as if in suspense

Hesitate, etc. To stop or pause respecting decision or action; doubt. See DETERMINATION-VACILLATION.

Nill. To be unwilling; refuse.

Not be able to find it in one's heart. Not to be willing or disposed.

Not have the stomach to. To be unwilling to brook or resent.

Oppose, etc. To resist or antagonize; strive against. See ANTAGONISM.

Recoil. To draw back; shrink; withdraw oneself.

Refuse, etc. To decline to do or grant; not to comply. See PROFFER-REFUSAL.

Run rusty. To become stubborn or rebellious.

Scruple. To be reluctant on account of considerations of conscience; hesitate at.

Shrink. To withdraw or retire; decline action.

Stick at. To scruple; hesitate.

Stickle. To contend; wrangle; take part with one side or other.

Swerve. To wander; stray; deviate, as from duty.

RELUCTANCE—*Adjectives.*

Adverse, etc. Acting against or in a contrary direction; opposed. See ANTAGONISM.

Averse. Having a repugnance or opposition of mind; disinclined.

Backward. Unwilling; hesitating; slow.

Demurring, etc. Suspending judgment on account of a doubt or difficulty. See *Verbs*.

Disinclined. Unwilling; unfavorable.

Indifferent, etc. Having no inclination or interest; apathetic. See UNCONCERN.

Indisposed. Rendered averse or unfavorable; disinclined.

Involuntary, etc. Not proceeding from choice; done unwillingly. See VOLITION-OBLIGATION.

Laggard. Slow; sluggish; backward.

Loth. Filled with disgust or aversion; unwilling.

Not content. Disposed to repine or grumble; dissatisfied.

Not in the vein. Indisposed; not in good humor.

Reluctant. Striving against; disinclined; unwilling.

Remiss. Not attending to duty or engagements; slow; dilatory.

Repugnant, etc. Characterized by opposition; distasteful to a high degree. See DESIRE-DISTASTE.

Restive. ⎫
Restiff. ⎬ Unwilling to stir; impatient under restraint; stubborn.

Scrupulous. Hesitating to determine or to act, from a fear of offending.

Shy of. Disinclined to familiar approach; cautious.

Slack. Not earnest or eager; backward; remiss.

Slow to. Not precipitate or hasty; deliberate; forbearing.

Squeamish, etc. Overnice; easily disgusted. See DESIRE-PARTICULARNESS.

Unconsenting, etc. Not concurring; disagreeing; refusing. See PROFFER-REFUSAL.

Unwilling. Not willing; disinclined; reluctant.

RELUCTANCE—*Adverbs, etc.*

À contra cœur [F.]. Against the grain; reluctantly.

Against one's will. Grudgingly.

Against one's wishes. Contrary to one's plans or desires.

Against the grain. Reluctantly.

Far be it from me. Very unwillingly.

Grudgingly. With reluctance or discontent.

In spite of oneself. In defiance of opposition.

In spite of one's self. In opposition to every effort.

Invita Minerva [L.]. Against the will of Minerva; against one's inclination; inspiration failing.

Longe absit [L.]. Far be it.

Malgré soi [F.]. In spite of oneself.

No, etc. A word of denial or refusal. See ASSERTION-DENIAL.

Nolens volens, etc. [L.] Whether he will or not. See VOLITION-OBLIGATION.

Not for the world. Not for any consideration.

Perforce, etc. By force; of necessity; at any rate. See COERCION.

Sore against one's will. ⎫
Sore against one's wishes. ⎬ Very reluctantly or grudgingly.
Sore against the grain. ⎭

Under protest. Without agreement.

Unwillingly, etc. In an unwilling or disinclined or reluctant manner. See *Adjectives*.

With a bad grace. In a forced or reluctant manner.

With an ill grace. In a perfunctory manner; ungraciously.

With a heavy heart. In a depressed manner; reluctantly.

READINESS—Adjectives—Continued.

Unasked, etc. Unsolicited; not sought by entreaty. See PETITION.	**Voluntary.** Acting from choice; done without compulsion.
Unforced, etc. Not constrained; not impelled. See LIBERTY.	**Willing.** Inclined to anything; ready; consenting.

READINESS—Adverbs, etc.

À *la bonne heure* [F.]. With all my heart; at the right time.
As lief. As soon as not.
Avec plaisir [F.]. With pleasure.
By all manner of means. } Certainly; without fail.
By all means.
Con amore [It.]. With love; earnestly.
De bonne volonté [F.]. Willingly.
Ex animo [L.]. Heartily; sincerely.
Fain. With joy; gladly.
Freely. Without compulsion.
Graciously. Mercifully; favorably.
Heart and soul. With utmost earnestness.
Heart in hand. Warm and affectionate greeting.

Nothing loth. Satisfied.
Of one's own accord. Willingly; voluntarily.
To one's heart's content. As long as one desires.
Willingly, etc. In a willing manner; cheerfully. See *Adjectives*.
With all one's heart. Very earnestly; devotedly.
With good grace. Readily.
With good will. Willingly.
With open arms. In a very hospitable manner; affectionately.
Without reluctance. With free will; willingly.
With pleasure. Gladly.
With right good will. Contentedly.
Yes. An expression of affirmation or consent. See ASSENT.

read'-ing. Recital; study; interpretation. EDUCATION-LEARNING, INTERPRETATION-MISINTERPRETATION, KNOWLEDGE-IGNORANCE, UNIVERSALITY-PARTICULARITY; **reading in,** CHURCH.

read'-ing-desk". Place for resting a book while reading. FANE, SCHOOL.

re"-ad-just'. To settle again. EQUALITY-INEQUALITY, HARMONY-DISCORD.

re"-ad-just'-ment. .The act of readjusting. EQUALITY-INEQUALITY.

re'-ad-mit'. To admit again. ADMISSION-EXPULSION.

read'-y. Prompt; prepared; skilful. ACTIVITY-INDOLENCE, EXPECTATION-SURPRISE, MONEY, PREPARATION - NONPREPARATION, READINESS - RELUCTANCE, SKILL-UNSKILFULNESS, USEFULNESS-USELESSNESS; **get ready,** PREPARATION-NONPREPARATION; **make ready,** PREPARATION-NONPREPARATION; **ready made,** PREPARATION-NONPREPARATION; **ready memory,** REMEMBRANCE-FORGETFULNESS; **ready money,** MONEY, SETTLEMENT-DEFAULT; **ready pen,** STYLE; **ready to burst forth,** EXCITABILITY-INEXCITABILITY; **ready to sink,** EXCITATION; **ready wit,** WITTINESS-DULNESS.

re"-af-firm'. To assert again. ASSERTION-DENIAL.

re-a'-gent. That which reacts. TRIAL.

re'-al. Actual. ENTITY - NONENTITY, NATURE - ART, NUMBER, TRUTH-ERROR; **real estate,** OCEAN-LAND, PROPERTY; **real property,** PROPERTY; **real security,** SECURITY.

re'-al-ism. A doctrine of philosophy. TRUTH-ERROR.

re"-al-is'-tic. True to fact. TRUTH-ERROR.

re-al'-i-ty. Actual fact or existence. ENTITY-NONENTITY, NATURE-ART, TRUTH-ERROR.

re'-al-ize. To perceive; to make real; to obtain. BUYING-SALE, COMPLETION-NONCOMPLETION, DISCOVERY, FAITH-MISGIVING, FANCY, GAIN-LOSS, KNOWLEDGE-IGNORANCE, MIND-IMBECILITY, UNIVERSALITY-PARTICULARITY.

re'-al-ly. Actually. ASTONISHMENT-EXPECTANCE.

realm. Region; empire. EXTENSION-DISTRICT, HUMANITY, PROPERTY, RULE-LICENSE.

re'-al-ty. Real estate. PROPERTY.

ream. 480 sheets of paper. MEASURE, MISSIVE-PUBLICATION.

ream'-er. Tool for making holes. PERFORATOR-STOPPER.

re-an'-i-mate. Revive. LIFE-DEATH, RENEWAL, RENOVATION-RELAPSE.

re-an"-i-ma'-tion. Revival. RENEWAL, RENOVATION-RELAPSE.

reap. To harvest; to get as the result of something. DOMESTICATION-AGRICULTURE, LENGTH-SHORTNESS, TAKING-RESTITUTION; **reap and carry,** GAIN-LOSS; **reap the benefit of,** BETTERMENT-DETERIORATION, SUCCESS-FAILURE, USEFULNESS-USELESSNESS; **reap the fruits,** GAIN-LOSS, RECOMPENSE-PUNITION, SUCCESS-FAILURE; **reap the whirlwind,** CAUSE-EFFECT,

SUCCESS-FAILURE; **reap where one has not sown,** RIGHT-WRONG.

re"-ap-pear'. To appear again. RECURRENCE, RENOVATION-RELAPSE, VISIBILITY-INVISIBILITY.

re"-ap-pear'-ance. A second appearance. RECURRENCE, RENEWAL.

re"-ap-pear'-ing. Appearing again. RENEWAL.

rear. To construct; to bring up. ANTERIORITY-POSTERIORITY, BEGINNING-END, CREATION-DESTRUCTION, EDUCATION - MISTEACHING, ELEVATION - DEPRESSION, ERECTNESS-FLATNESS, PREDECESSOR-CONTINUATION; **in the rear,** ANTERIORITY-POSTERIORITY, LEADING-FOLLOWING; **rear its head,** MANIFESTATION-LATENCY; **rear one's head,** SELFRESPECT-HUMBLENESS; **rear rank,** ANTERIORITY-POSTERIORITY.

rear'-ad"-mi-ral. Navy officer. CHIEF-UNDERLING.

rear'-ward. Coming last. ANTERIORITY-POSTERIORITY.

rea'-son. Cause; proof; mind. CAUSE-EFFECT, MIND-IMBECILITY, MOTIVE-CAPRICE, RATIOCINATION-INSTINCT, SAGACITY-INCAPACITY; **by reason of,** MOTIVE-CAPRICE; **feast of reason,** CONVERSATION-MONOLOGUE; **in reason,** RIGHT - WRONG, TURBULENCE-CALMNESS; **listen to reason,** SAGACITY-INCAPACITY; **reason in a circle,** RATIOCINATION-INSTINCT; **reason why,** CAUSE-EFFECT, MOTIVE-CAPRICE, RATIONALE-LUCK; **stand to reason,** CERTAINTY-DOUBT, MANIFESTATION-LATENCY, PROOF-DISPROOF; **what's the reason,** INVESTIGATION-ANSWER; **without rime or reason,** MOTIVE-CAPRICE.

rea'-son-a-ble. Sensible; cheap. COSTLINESS-CHEAPNESS, LIKELIHOOD-UNLIKELIHOOD, RIGHT-WRONG, SAGACITY-INCAPACITY, SANENESS-LUNACY, TURBULENCE-CALMNESS; **reasonable prospect,** LIKELIHOOD-UNLIKELIHOOD.

rea'-son-a-ble-ness. Rationality. SAGACITY-INCAPACITY.

rea'-son-er. One who reasons. RATIOCINATION-INSTINCT.

rea'-son-ing. Argument. RATIOCINATION-INSTINCT.

rea'-son-less. Without reason. SAGACITY-INCAPACITY, SANENESS-LUNACY.

rea'-sons. Motives. SAGACITY-INCAPACITY.

re"-as-sem'-ble. To meet again. GATHERING-SCATTERING.

re"-as-sert'. To assert again. ASSERTION-DENIAL.

re"-as-sur'-ance. Renewed assurance. SANGUINENESS-HOPELESSNESS.

re"-as-sure'. Encourage. BRAVERY-COWARDICE, SANGUINENESS-HOPELESSNESS.

re"-as-sured'. With renewed courage. BRAVERY-COWARDICE.

re"-as-sur'-ing. Encouraging. SANGUINENESS-HOPELESSNESS.

reast'-y. Rancid. CLEANNESS-FILTHINESS, PERFUME-STENCH.

reave. Rob. TAKING-RESTITUTION.

re-bate'. Allow a reduction. PRICE-DISCOUNT, TURBULENCE-CALMNESS.

re-bate'-ment. Discount. PRICE-DISCOUNT.

re'-bec. Violin. MUSICAL INSTRUMENTS.

re-bel'. Disobey. INSUBORDINATION-OBEDIENCE, PATRIOTISM-TREASON.

reb'-el. One who disobeys. INSUBORDINATION-OBEDIENCE, PATRIOTISM-TREASON.

re-bel'-lion. Insurrection. INSUBORDINATION-OBEDIENCE.

re-bel'-low. To echo loudly. CRY-ULULATION.

re''-bo-a'-tion. Reverberating sound. CRY-ULULATION.

re-bound'. Bounding back. ADVANCE-RETROGRESSION, IMPETUS-REACTION.

rebours, à [F.] (re-bur', a). On the rebound. ADVANCE-RETROGRESSION, CONVERSION-REVERSION, DIFFICULTY-FACILITY.

re-buff'. To reject. APPROVAL-DISAPPROVAL, IMPETUS-REACTION, POLITENESS-IMPOLITENESS, PROFFER-REFUSAL, REPRISAL-RESISTANCE, SUCCESS-FAILURE.

re-build'. Build anew. RENOVATION-RELAPSE.

re-buke'. To reprove. APPROVAL-DISAPPROVAL.

re'-bus. Puzzle. TIDINGS-MYSTERY.

rebus, in mediis [L.] (ri'-bus, in mi'-di-is). In the midst of affairs. ACTIVITY-INDOLENCE.

re-but'. To refute. ASSERTION-DENIAL, EVIDENCE-COUNTEREVIDENCE, INVESTIGATION-ANSWER, PROOF-DISPROOF.

re-but'-ter. One who rebuts. INVESTIGATION-ANSWER, LITIGATION.

re-cal'-ci-trant. Rebellious. IMPETUS-REACTION, INSUBORDINATION-OBEDIENCE, REPRISAL-RESISTANCE.

re-cal'-ci-trate. To rebel. IMPETUS-REACTION, REPRISAL-RESISTANCE.

re-cal''-ci-tra'-tion. Opposition. IMPETUS-REACTION, REPRISAL-RESISTANCE.

re-call'. To recollect; to call back. BIGOTRY-APOSTASY, COMMISSION-ABROGATION, REMEMBRANCE-FORGETFULNESS; **recall to life,** RENOVATION-RELAPSE.

re-cant'. To retract. ASSENT-DISSENT, ASSERTION-DENIAL, BIGOTRY-APOSTASY, COMMISSION-ABROGATION, REPENTANCE-OBDURACY.

re''-can-ta'-tion. Retraction. ASSENT-DISSENT, BIGOTRY-APOSTASY, COMMISSION-ABROGATION, REPENTANCE-OBDURACY.

re''-ca-pit''-u-late. To sum up. ACCOUNT, DIGEST, NUMBERING, RECURRENCE.

re''-ca-pit''-u-la'-tion. A summing up. DIGEST, NUMBERING, RECURRENCE.

re-cap'-per. A tool for fixing percussion-caps in cartridges. INSTRUMENT.

re-cast'. To form anew. DESIGN, MUTATION-PERMANENCE, REVOLUTION.

re-cede'. To move back. ADVANCE-RETROGRESSION, APPROACH-WITHDRAWAL; **recede into the shade,** REPUTATION-DISCREDIT.

re-ce'-ding. To withdraw. ADVANCE-RETROGRESSION, APPROACH-WITHDRAWAL.

re-ceipt'. Recipe; acknowledgment of having received something. DESIGN, OUTLAY-INCOME, PRECEPT, REMEDY-BANE, SECURITY, SETTLEMENT-DEFAULT; **receipt in full,** SETTLEMENT-DEFAULT.

re-ceive'. To get; to admit; to welcome. ADMISSION-EXCLUSION, ADMISSION-EXPULSION, ASSENT-DISSENT, FAITH-MISGIVING, GAIN-LOSS, GIVING-RECEIVING, OUTLAY-INCOME, POLITENESS-IMPOLITENESS, SOCIABILITY-PRIVACY, TAKING-RESTITUTION; **receive Christ,** GODLINESS-UNGODLINESS.

re-ceived'. Accepted. GIVING-RECEIVING, HABIT-DESUETUDE, KNOWLEDGE-IGNORANCE, OUTLAY-INCOME; **received maxim,** ADAGE-NONSENSE.

re-ceiv'-er. Receptacle; one who receives. CONTENTS-RECEIVER, TREASURER; **receiver of stolen goods,** ROBBER, TAKING-RESTITUTION.

re-ceiv'-ing. Accepting. GIVING-RECEIVING, OUTLAY-INCOME.

re'-cen-cy. Newness. NOVELTY-ANTIQUITY.

re-cen'-sion. Critical revision. NUMBERING.

re'-cent. Modern. FUTURE-PAST, NOVELTY-ANTIQUITY.

re-cep'-ta-cle. Receiving vessel. CONTENTS-RECEIVER.

re-cep'-tion. Admission; welcome. ACCOUNT, ADMISSION-EXCLUSION, ADMISSION-EXPULSION, ARRIVAL-DEPARTURE, CONVERSATION-MONOLOGUE, GIVING-RECEIVING, SOCIABILITY-PRIVACY, TAKING-RESTITUTION; **warm reception,** SOCIABILITY-PRIVACY.

re-cep'-tion-room''. Room for callers. CONTENTS-RECEIVER.

re-cess'. Alcove; vacation. ADVANCE-RETROGRESSION, ANGULARITY, CONTENTS-RECEIVER, EXPOSURE-HIDINGPLACE, SOCIABILITY-PRIVACY, TOIL-RELAXATION.

re-cess'-es. Niches. OUTSIDE-INSIDE; **secret recesses of one's heart,** AFFECTIONS.

re-ces'-sion. Withdrawal. ADVANCE-RETROGRESSION, APPROACH-WITHDRAWAL, BETTERMENT-DETERIORATION.

réchauffé [F.] (rê''-sho-fê'). A literary rehash. COPY-MODEL, HEATING-COOLING, NUTRIMENT-EXCRETION, RECURRENCE, RENOVATION-RELAPSE.

recherché [F.] (re-sher''-shê'). Sought for. GOODNESS-BADNESS, SOCIETY-LUDICROUSNESS.

re-cid'-i-vate. To backslide. RENOVATION-RELAPSE.

re-cid''-i-va'-tion. Backsliding. ADVANCE-RETROGRESSION, RENOVATION-RELAPSE.

re-cid'-i-vous. Liable to backslide. ADVANCE-RETROGRESSION.

rec'-i-pe. Formula. PRECEPT, REMEDY-BANE.

re-cip'-i-ent. One who receives. CONTENTS-RECEIVER, GIVING-RECEIVING.

re-cip'-ro-cal. Mutual. COMMUTATION-PERMUTATION, INTERDEPENDENCE, NUMBER.

re-cip'-ro-cal-ly. Mutually. INTERDEPENDENCE.

re-cip'-ro-cal-ness. Mutuality. INTERDEPENDENCE.

re-cip'-ro-cate. Interchange. COMMUTATION-PERMUTATION, DWELLER-HABITATION, INTERSPACE, REPRISAL-RESISTANCE, VARIANCE-ACCORD.

re-cip''-ro-ca'-tion. Mutual interchange. INTERDEPENDENCE, MUTABILITY-STABILITY, REPRISAL-RESISTANCE.

rec''-i-proc'-i-ty. Mutual interchange. INTERDEPENDENCE.

re-ci'-sion. Act of cutting off. ADDITION-SUBTRACTION.

re-cit'-al. Spirited description. ACCOUNT.

rec''-i-ta'-tion. A rehearsal. SPEECH-INARTICULATENESS.

rec''-i-ta-tive'. Speech uttered in musical tones. MUSIC.

recitativo [It.] (rê''-chî-ta-tî'-vo). Recitative. MUSIC.

re-cite'. To tell. ACCOUNT, NUMBERING, SPEECH-INARTICULATENESS.

reck. To heed. CAREFULNESS-CARELESSNESS.

reck'-less. Heedless. CAREFULNESS-CARELESSNESS, RECKLESSNESS-CAUTION.

reck'-less-ness. Rashness. RECKLESSNESS-CAUTION, UNCONCERN.

RECKLESSNESS—CAUTION.

Audacity. The condition of being unrestrained by law or decency; boldness or daring.

Calculation. A careful estimation of probable results.

Cautel. A precautionary measure or proceeding.

RECKLESSNESS—CAUTION—*Continued.*

Blind bargain. A bargain on which chances are taken.

Carelessness. The state or quality of being neglectful of either danger or duty.

Daring. Heroic courage carried to the extreme.

Desperation. Blind and rash fury.

Fire-eating. Restlessness; daring.

Foolhardihood.} The quality of being bold without consideration or

Foolhardiness.} judgment.

Fool's paradise. A place of happiness founded on vain hopes.

Gambling. Risking of money on the chance of an event occurring.

Gaming. Gambling.

Hastiness. Rash eagerness.

Heedlessness. Carelessness; thoughtlessness.

Impetuosity. Rashness.

Imprudence. Lack of prudence or discretion.

Incautiousness. Want of caution.

Indiscretion. The state or quality of lacking wise judgment.

Knight-errantry. Chivalry.

Levity. Want of earnestness.

Overconfidence. Belief, usually in oneself, beyond the warrant of reason; too great reliance or trust.

Precipitancy. Inconsiderate haste.

Precipitation. Headlong or rash haste or hurry.

Presumption. Extreme confidence or self-assertion; too great confidence in the uncertain.

Quixotism. Chivalry gone mad, like Don Quixote [Cervantes], who fights wind-mills, thinking them to be giant oppressors of the people.

Rashness. Inconsiderate promptness; too great readiness to decide or act.

Temerity. An unreasonable contempt of danger.

Thoughtlessness. Lack of care and consideration.

Want of caution. Want of careful consideration.

RECKLESSNESS—*Nouns of Agent.*

Adventurer. One who seeks his fortune in new or hazardous enterprises.

Bravo [It.]. A daring villain.

Bully. A noisy fellow who is more insolent than courageous.

Daredevil. A reckless fellow.

Desperado [Sp.]. A reckless, furious man.

Don Quixote. The hero of Cervantes' *Don Quixote*, written to ridicule knight-errantry.

Enfant perdu [F.]. The lost child of an army; the forlorn hope.

Fire-eater. An excitable person always ready to fight.

Gambler. One who engages in games of chance.

Gamester. One accustomed to play for a stake.

Hector. A blustering, insolent fellow in English plays, different from the Hector of the *Iliad*.

Hotspur. A fiery-tempered man. [Shakespeare, *Henry IV.*]

Icarus. A mythic person who attempted to fly; a reckless person.

Knight errant. A wandering knight of the Middle Ages, who rode in search of adventures.

Madcap. One given to wild follies.

Rashling. A rash person.

Scapegrace. A reckless, unprincipled person.

RECKLESSNESS—*Verbs.*

Be rash, etc. To hurry into action without caution. See *Adjectives.*

Buy a pig in a poke. To buy something concealed, as a pig in a bag, until the price is paid.

Carry too much sail. To be reckless or incautious.

Catch at straws. To depend upon a slight chance or hope.

Count one's chickens before they are hatched. To base one's hopes or plans upon something that has not yet happened and may not happen.

Dormer tête baissée [F.] To go with head down, to rush headlong into anything.

Go on a forlorn hope. To be led by a very slight hope of success.

Go out of one's depth. To attempt what is beyond one's power.

Kick against the pricks. To oppose that which cannot be overcome.

Knock one's head against the wall. To be unskilful or stupid.

Lean on a broken reed. To have no basis for one's plans or actions.

Play at a desperate game. To attempt to overcome what is hopelessly against one.

Play with edged tools. To use means with which one is unfamiliar.

Play with fire. To use means of which one knows not the power.

Reckon without one's host. To neglect important facts in reaching a conclusion, as in reckoning up your bill at a hotel.

Ride at single anchor. To stake everything on a single hope or event.

Run into danger. To be careless or reckless.

Rush on destruction. To rush into danger.

Caution. Great care exercised in the midst of dangers.

Cautiousness. The quality of exercising caution.

Circumspection. Great care and consideration.

Coolness. The state or quality of being cool. See *Adjectives.*

Deliberation. Slow and careful consideration in regard to any action or measure.

Discretion. Careful and correct judgment in regard to any action.

Foresight. The capacity or power of foreseeing.

Heed. Careful attention.

Presence of mind. A cool and self-possessed state of mind.

Prudence. The quality of being prudent. See *Adjectives.*

Self-command. The state or quality of having all the feelings and powers at perfect command.

Self-possession. The quality of being self-possessed. See *Adjectives.*

Vigilance. Alertness in guarding against danger.

Warning. Caution against danger and error.

Worldly wisdom. Prudence; a careful knowledge of the practical affairs of life.

CAUTION—*Denotations.*

Cunctator. A name given to Quintus Fabius Maximus because he practised the policy of delay against Hannibal.

Delayer. Another name given to Quintus Fabius Maximus because of his dilatory tactics.

Fabian policy. The delaying policy of Fabius.

Sang froid [F.]. Cool blood; presence of mind.

Well-regulated mind. A mind carefully balanced; not easily excited.

CAUTION—*Verbs.*

Be cautious, etc. To act with caution. See CAUTION.

Be early. Be prepared for whatever may come

Be on one's guard. To be vigilant.

Be on the safe side. To be secure from risk or danger.

Bespeak. To make preparation against the future.

Bridle one's tongue. To speak or assert oneself with caution.

Caution. To advise against the future.

Count the cost. To have regard to consequences.

Cut one's coat according to one's cloth. To regulate one's action by one's circumstances.

Feel one's ground. To make careful preparation before proceeding with any measure.

Feel one's way. To advance with cautious steps.

Foresee. To know results beforehand.

Gardez [F.]. Take care.

Gardez bien [F.]. Take good care.

Have a care. Be careful.

Husband one's resources. To make ready for some future emergency.

Keep at a respectful distance. To keep in a place of safety.

Keep on the safe side. To avoid risks and chances.

Keep out of harm's way. To avoid danger.

Keep out of troubled waters. To keep out of danger.

Keep watch. Be vigilant.

Let well, or well enough, alone. To refrain from trying to do better what is already good enough.

Look before one leaps. To take proper regard for the consequences before any act or assertion.

Look on the main chance. To work in the direction which seems most probable to yield success.

Make assurance doubly sure. To secure oneself against all risks.

Mind. To regard with care and concern.

Mind what one is about. To act with care and consideration.

Prepare. Make ready for the future.

Reculer pour mieux sauter [F.]. To go back for a better leap.

See how the land lies. To examine beforehand.

Stand aloof. To decline to do until better acquainted with.

Take care.}

Take good care.} To be careful.

Take heed.}

Think twice. To consider one's course of action.

Wait to see the cat jump. To await the turn of events before acting.

CAUTION—*Adjectives.*

Careful. Acting with care.

Cautelous. Wary; crafty.

Cautious. Acting with caution. See *Nouns.*

Cavendo tutus [L.]. Safe by taking heed.

Chary. Reluctant or cautious, as in giving a pledge.

Circumspect. Acting with circumspection. See *Nouns.*

Cool. Not excited.

Discreet. Having good judgment; prudent.

Guarded. Acting with care and caution.

Heedful. Giving heed. See *Nouns.*

In medio tutissimus [L.]. Safety lies in the middle course.

RECKLESSNESS—CAUTION—*Continued.*

RECKLESSNESS—Verbs—*Continued.*

Sail too near the wind. To sail windward at a comparatively small angle with the wind; hence, to come near the limit, as of a danger-line.

Stick at nothing. To hesitate or scruple at nothing.

Take a leap in the dark. To be reckless. "I am just going to leap into the dark." [Rabelais at death.]

Tempt Providence. To attempt an impossible feat.

Trust to a broken reed. To depend upon useless expedients.

RECKLESSNESS—*Adjectives.*

Adventurous. Delighting in adventures or risks.

Breakneck. Extremely hazardous.

Careless. Neglectful of danger or duty.

Cavalier. Of or pertaining to the Cavaliers under Charles II.; high-spirited; gallant; horseman.

Desperate. Rendered reckless or heroic by extremity of circumstances.

Devil-may-care. Careless; reckless.

Fire-eating. Having the spirit of a fire-eater.

Foolhardy. Unreasonably daring or bold.

Free-and-easy. Showing little regard for customs or conventionalities.

Giddy. Marked by foolish recklessness; frivolous.

Harebrained. Wild and foolish like the hare.

Headlong. Acting with haste and rashness.

Headstrong. Stubbornly self-willed.

Heedless. Without care or attention.

Heels over head. In a tumbled or overturned condition.

Hot-blooded. Quick-tempered; irritable.

Hot-brained. Violent; rash.

Hot-headed. Easily angered.

Icarian. Like Icarus; reckless. He flew over the sea and fell in.

Improvident. Prodigal; lacking in foresight.

Imprudent. Unadvised; wanting in a due regard for consequences.

Impulsive. Easily aroused; acting on the spur of the moment.

Incautious. Acting without caution. See *Nouns.*

Indiscreet. Injudicious; lacking good judgment.

Jaunty. Sprightly; putting on airs of careless ease.

Madcap. Full of wild follies.

Off one's guard. Unprepared; not on the watch.

Overconfident. Too self-reliant.

Overweening. Extremely self-confident; arrogant.

Precipitate. Overhasty; acting with too great eagerness.

Quixotic. Acting like Don Quixote. See *Nouns.*

Rash. Characteristic of one who acts with too great haste and too little regard for consequences.

Reckless. Entirely disregarding consequences.

Temerarious. Acting with temerity.

Uncalculating. Without properly estimating what the chances are or the consequences will be.

Venturesome. Inclined to take risks.

Venturous. Daring; bold.

Wanton. Extravagant; lacking reason and consideration.

Wild. Profligate; highly excited, as with passion.

Without ballast. Without any steadying influence; inconstant.

CAUTION—Adjectives—*Continued.*

On one's guard. Prepared; ready.

Overcautious. Acting with too great care and consideration.

Politic. Crafty; acting with prudence rather than principle.

Prudent. Careful for the future; possessed of foresight.

Shy of. Wary; backward.

Skilful. With careful and well-trained powers.

Steady. Cool; not impulsive.

Stealthy. Acting with wariness and great secrecy.

Sure-footed. To be depended upon; not given to making mistakes.

Unadventurous. Not wont to take risks or ventures.

Unenterprising. Lacking boldness and energy.

Wary. Always guarding against deceptions and dangers, even to timidity.

Watchful. Full of care and vigilance.

CAUTION—*Adverbs.*

Cautiously, etc. Acting with great care and guardedness. See *Adjectives.*

Edgingly. Cautiously.

CAUTION—*Interjection.*

Have a care!

CAUTION—*Phrases.*

Ante victoriam ne canas triumphum [L.] Do not chant your triumph before you conquer.

Festina lente [L.]. Hasten slowly. [Augustus Cæsar's saying.]

Il rit bien qui rit le dernier [F.]. He laughs best who laughs last.

Le silence du peuple est la leçon des rois [F.]. The silence of the people is the lesson of kings.

Na pas reveiller le chat qui dort [F.]. One must not arouse the sleeping cat.

Ni bebas aqua que no veas [Sp.]. Look at the water before you drink.

Noli irritare leones [L.]. Avoid irritating the lions.

Timeo Danaos [L.]. I fear the Greeks. [Virgil, *Æneid*, ii, 49.]

RECKLESSNESS—*Continued.*

RECKLESSNESS—*Adverbs, etc.*

A corps perdu [F.]. Headlong; at breakneck speed.

Hand over head. Negligently; rashly; without seeing what one does.

Happen what may. Taking the chances.

Head foremost. Precipitately, as in diving.

Post haste. With the speed of the post; rapidly.

Tête baissée [F.]. With head down; headlong.

RECKLESSNESS—*Phrases.*

Neck or nothing. With the risk of everything.

The devil being in one. Possessed of some spirit, as it were of the devil, which urges one on headlong into some hasty action or danger.

Too many eggs in one basket.

---

reck'-on. To count. NUMBERING; **reckon among,** ADMISSION-EXCLUSION; **reckon one's chickens before they are hatched,** SANGUINENESS-HOPELESSNESS; **reckon upon,** FAITH-MISGIVING; **reckon with,** SETTLEMENT-DEFAULT; **reckon without one's host,** BRAVERY-COWARDICE, RECKLESSNESS-CAUTION, SKILL-UNSKILFULNESS, SUCCESS-FAILURE, TRUTH-ERROR.

reck'-on-ing. Account. ACCOUNTS, EXPECTATION-SURPRISE, MENSURATION, NUMBERING, RECOMPENSE-PUNITION; **day of reckoning,** PARDON-VINDICTIVENESS.

re-claim'. To claim back. ATONEMENT, DUENESS-UNDUENESS, ORDER, RENOVATION-RELAPSE, REPENTANCE-OBDURACY.

re-claimed'. Reformed. REPENTANCE-OBDURACY

rec"-la-ma'-tion. A reclaiming. ATONEMENT, ORDER, RENOVATION-RELAPSE.

rec"-li-na'tion. Recumbency. ERECTNESS-FLATNESS.

re-cline'. To lean; to repose. ELEVATION-DEPRESSION, ERECTNESS-FLATNESS, TOIL-RELAXATION; **recline on,** SUSPENSION-SUPPORT.

re-cluse'. Hermit. SOCIABILITY-PRIVACY.

re-clu'-sion. Seclusion. SOCIABILITY-PRIVACY.

rec"-og-ni'-tion. Notice; acknowledgment. ASSENT-DISSENT, KNOWLEDGE-IGNORANCE, POLITENESS-IMPOLITENESS, REMEMBRANCE-FORGETFULNESS, THANKFULNESS-THANKLESSNESS; **means of recognition,** SIGN.

rec'-og-ni"-za-ble. Easily recognized. CLEARNESS-OBSCURITY, VISIBILITY-INVISIBILITY.

re-cog'-ni-zance. Avowal. SECURITY.

rec'-og-nize. To notice; to acknowledge. ASSENT-DISSENT, DISCOVERY, HEED-DISREGARD, KNOWLEDGE-IGNORANCE, LEAVE-PROHIBITION, REMEMBRANCE-FORGETFULNESS, SIGHT-BLINDNESS.

rec'-og-nized. Admitted. DOMINANCE-IMPOTENCE, HABIT-DESUETUDE, KNOWLEDGE-IGNORANCE; **recognized maxim,** ADAGE-NONSENSE.

re-coil'. Whirl backward. APPROACH-WITHDRAWAL, CONVERSION-REVERSION, COOPERATION-OPPOSITION, IMPETUS-REACTION, QUEST-EVASION, READINESS-RELUCTANCE; **from which reason recoils,** POSSIBIL-

ITY-IMPOSSIBILITY; **recoil at,** LOVE-HATE; **recoil from,** DESIRE-DISTASTE.

re-coil'-ing. Reaction. IMPETUS-REACTION.

rec''-ol-lect'. To remember. REMEMBRANCE-FORGETFULNESS.

rec''-ol-lec'-tion. Memory. REMEMBRANCE-FORGETFULNESS.

re''-com-mence'. To commence again. BEGINNING-END.

rec''-om-mend'. To give a favorable report of. ADVICE, APPROVAL-DISAPPROVAL; **recommend itself,** APPROVAL-DISAPPROVAL.

rec''-om-men-da'-tion. Favorable representation. ADVICE.

rec''-om-mend'-a-tory. Favorable. ADVICE.

rec'-om-pense. Reward. RECOMPENSE - PUNITION, RIGHT-WRONG.

RECOMPENSE—PUNITION.

Acknowledgment. The act of acknowledging; avowal; recognition.

Allowance. A portion or amount granted for some purpose.

Amends. Reparation; satisfaction; compensation.

Atonement. Any satisfaction, amends, reparation, or expiation made for wrong or injury.

Batta. Extra pay, especially to an English officer in India.

Blackmail. Reward extorted by threats or intimidation.

Bribe. A gift, or advantage given to influence one's conduct.

Carcelage. Prison fees.

Compensation. Whatever makes good for loss or lack.

Consideration. Allowance made for anything; regard.

Crown. A reward for meritorious service. See GIVING.

Douceur [F.]. A gift for service done or to be done.

Emolument. The remuneration connected with any office, occupation, or service.

Fee. A payment for services done or to be done.

Guerdon. A reward or recompense.

Hire. The compensation of labor and services.

Honorarium. A reward to a professional man.

Hush-money. A bribe to secure silence.

Indemnification.⎫ That which is paid or given as compensation or re-
Indemnity. ⎭ imbursement for a loss.

Meed. That which is awarded on account of desert.

Pay. Money paid for service.

Payment. That which is given as a recompense.

Perquisite. Any privilege or benefit claimed as due.

Premium. Something offered as a recompense in recognition of an excellent performance or production.

Quid pro quo [L.]. One thing for another; an equivalent.

Quittance. Recompense; return.

Reckoning. An adjustment of reward or penalty on the basis of merit.

Recompense. An equivalent received or returned for anything given, done, or suffered.

Redress. Satisfaction made; reparation.

Reguerdon. A reward.

Remuneration. Compensation; recompense made.

Reparation. Satisfaction; indemnity.

Requital. Adequate recompense for good or evil.

Retribution. That which is done or given in requital.

Return. Restitution; requital.

Reward. That which is given in return for good or evil done or received.

Salary. A periodical allowance made to a person for his services.

Salvage. The compensation allowed for saving, or helping a vessel in distress.

Scot. Money given or paid as a contribution.

Shot. A share of a reckoning or charge.

Smart money Money paid for a release from an engagement or from a painful situation.

Solatum [L.]. Compensation; solace.

Sop. Anything given to pacify.

Stipend. A definite amount paid at stated periods for services.

Vail. Money given to servants as a gratuity. See GIVING.

Wages. The remuneration of hired labor.

RECOMPENSE—Verbs.

Acknowledge. To give recognition to.

Atone. To make recompense for.

Compensate. To make amends or recompense.

Fee. To reward for services; to recompense.

Get for one's pains. To receive recompense for trouble.

Indemnify. To make compensation or recompense for.

Make amends. To render recompense.

Munerate. To remunerate.

Pay one's footing. To pay one's bill. See SETTLEMENT.

Reap the fruits of. To receive recompense for.

Recompense. To render an equivalent to for service or loss; to compensate.

Remunerate. To reward for service done.

Repay. To pay back.

Requite. In a good sense, to recompense.

Argumentum baculinum [L.]. Club law.

Auto da fé [Port.]. An act of faith; the name given in Spain and Portugal to the burning of the Jews and heretics.

Banishment. Expulsion from one's country.

Bastinado. An Oriental punishment, by beating with a stick on the soles of the feet.

Beating. Punishment by blows.

Blow. A sudden or violent stroke administered. See IMPETUS.

Box on the ear. A slap on the ear.

Buffet. A blow with the hand.

Capital punishment. Punishment inflicting death.

Castigation. Corrective punishment.

Chastening. Act of disciplining by pain.

Chastisement. Pain inflicted for punishment and correction.

Correction. The act of reproving or punishing.

Coup de grâce [F.]. A death-blow.

Crucifixion. The act of putting to death by nailing on a cross.

Cuff. A slap.

Decapitation. The act of putting to death by beheading.

Decollation. The act of beheading.

Discipline. Punishment inflicted by way of correction and training.

Douse. A blow.

Dragonade [F.]. The persecution of the French Protestants under Louis XIV.

Estrapade [F.]. Strappado.

Execution. The infliction of capital punishment in accordance with a decree of a court.

Exile. Banishment from one's home or native land.

Expulsion. The act of expelling.

Flagellation. A whipping.

Fustigation. Punishment by beating with a stick or club.

Gantlet. A military punishment, wherein the offender was made to run between two lines of soldiers who struck him as he passed.

Garrote. A Spanish mode of execution by strangulation

Garotto [Sp.]. Hanging.

Hanging. Death on the gallows. See *Verbs.*

Happy despatch. A quick death.

Hara-kiri [Jap.]. Suicide by slashing the stomach, commanded by the Japanese government in the case of disgraced officials.

Hard labor. Punishment by which the offender is compelled to labor during imprisonment.

Impalement. Putting to death by thrusting through with or fixing upon a pale.

Imprisonment. Restraint of liberty. See RELEASE-RESTRAINT.

Infliction. That which is inflicted, as pain or punishment.

Involuntary exile. Banishment.

Judgment. The sentence of a court in a civil or criminal proceeding wherein the punishment is decreed.

Kick. A blow with the foot.

Martyrdom. Submission to death or persecution for the sake of faith or principle.

Nemesis. The Greek divinity of chastisement and punishment.

Noyade [F.]. Execution by drowning; practised on political prisoners during the Reign of Terror.

Ostracism. Banishment by a popular vote with oyster shells.

Penal servitude. Servitude as a punishment for crime.

Penalty. The consequences, as punishment and suffering, which follow transgression. See RECOMPENSE-PENALTY.

Penology. The science which treats of the punishment and prevention of crime.

Picket. ⎫ Punishment by compelling to stand with one foot on a
Picketing. ⎭ pointed stake.

Pummel. A beating, as with the pommel of a sword.

Punishment. Pain or any other penalty inflicted on a person as a consequence of wrong-doing.

Punition. Punishment.

Rack. Torture or punishment, as by the rack.

Rap on the knuckles. A blow with a stick on the knuckles.

Requital. Retribution; punishment. See RECOMPENSE.

Slap. ⎫
Slap in the face. ⎭ A blow with the open hand.

RECOMPENSE—PUNITION—*Continued.*

RECOMPENSE—Verbs—*Continued.*

Reward. To give in return, whether good or evil.
Satisfy. To give what is due to; to make full recompense.

RECOMPENSE—*Adjectives.*

Compensatory. Making amends.
Munerary. Having the nature of a gift.
Remunerative. Affording remuneration. See *Nouns.*
Remuneratory. Rewarding.
Reparatory. Tending to repair.
Retributive. Involving retribution or recompense.

RECOMPENSE—*Phrases.*

Fideli certa merces [L.]. To the faithful one sure reward.
Honor virtutis præmium [L.]. Honor is the reward of virtue. [Cicero, *Brutus*, 81.]
Tibi seris, tibi metis [L.]. For yourself you sow, for yourself you reap.

PUNITION—Verbs—*Continued from Column 2.*

Give a lesson to. To teach by punishment.
Give it one. To give a beating.
Give the stick. To beat with a stick.
Guillotine. To behead with the guillotine.
Hang. To execute on the gallows.
Hang, draw, and quarter. To hang, disembowel, and cut in quarters: a former mode of punishment in Great Britain.
Have a rod in pickle for. To be ready to give a beating to.
Horse-whip. To beat with a horse-whip.
Impale. To empale.
Inflict punishment. To chastise; to administer correction.
Keelhaul. To haul a man through the water under a vessel's keel; a punishment formerly in various navies.
Lace. To mark with stripes or wales; lash.
Lace one's jacket. To punish by lashing.
Lapidate. To punish or execute by stoning.
Larrup. To beat; thrash.
Lash. To punish with the lash.
Lay about one. To deal blows on all sides.
Lay on. To inflict, as punishment.
Leather. To flog or beat with or as with a leather thong.
Lick. To whip in a fight.
Lynch. To punish for imputed crime by lynch-law, usually by death.
Make an example of. To make an illustration of punishment to serve as a warning.
Make short work of. To put an end to at once.
Masthead. To send to the head or top of a mast to remain for a time as a punishment.
Ostracize. To exile by ostracism; to banish by popular vote.
Pay.
Pay out. } To retort or revenge upon; to requite; punish.
Pelt. To strike with missiles.
Picket. To punish by torturing with pickets. See *Nouns.*
Pitch into. To attack; to assault.
Post. To hold up to public blame.
Pummel. To beat soundly.
Punish. To afflict with pain, loss, or suffering for a crime or fault.
Put on. To attach the blame to.
Put onto the rack. To torture by putting on the rack.
Rib-roast. To beat soundly; cudgel.
Rub down with an oaken towel. To beat with an oaken stick.
Rusticate. To punish a student by compelling him to leave the institution for a while and go into the country.
Scourge. To beat with a scourge or whip.
Serve one right. To treat or cause to befall one according to his deserts.
Serve out. To distribute one's deserts.
Shoot. To discharge a missile.
Slap. To strike with the open hand or something broad.
Slap the face. To strike the face with the open hand.
Smack. To make a sharp noise by striking; as with the lips.
Smite. To destroy the life of by beating.
Spank. To strike, as the breech, with the open hand.
Stone. To pelt, beat, or kill with stones.
Strap. To beat with a strap.
Strike. To hit; to give blows. See IMPETUS.
Strike off the roll. To erase or cancel one's name from membership as punishment for some act of omission or commission.
Suffer. To endure pain.
Suffer for.
Suffer punishment for. } To undergo punishment for the sake of.

Strappado. A former military punishment in which the offender was drawn up at the end of a rope and allowed to fall suddenly till he was stopped with a jerk near the ground.
Stripe. A blow with a whip.
Torture. Infliction of extreme physical pain.
Transportation. The sending away of a convict to a remote place as a means of punishment.
Wipe. A sweeping blow.

PUNITION—*Nouns of Instrument.*

Galleys. Vessels propelled by oars manned by convicts. See RECOMPENSE-SCOURGE.
Lash. The thong of a whip.
Scaffold. A stage for the execution of a criminal. See RECOMPENSE-SCOURGE.

PUNITION—*Verbs.*

Administer correction. To punish as a means of discipline. See *Nouns.*
Administer the lash. To whip. See *Nouns.*
Bang. To punish by beating.
Banish. To punish by exile.
Baste. To beat with a stick.
Bastinado [Sp.]. To beat with a stick on the soles of the feet. See *Nouns.*
Beat. To punish by blows.
Beat black and blue. To cause bruises by beating.
Beat to a jelly. To crush by beating into a shapeless mass.
Beat to a mummy. To beat soundly or until senseless.
Be flogged. To be beaten with a whip or the like.
Be hanged. To be executed on the gallows.
Behead. To execute by cutting off the head of.
Belabor. To beat soundly.
Be rightly served. To be justly punished.
Birch. To whip with a birch stick.
Bowstring. To strangle with the bowstring.
Box the ears. To cuff or buffet over the ears.
Break on the wheel. To punish by tying to a wheel and breaking the limbs with a bar.
Bring to the block. To cause to be beheaded.
Bring to the gallows. To cause to be hanged.
Buffet. To beat about with repeated blows.
Burn. To execute by fire.
Cane. To strike or beat with a cane.
Castigate. To punish with or as with the rod.
Chastise. } To discipline by physical pain; subject to punitive meas-
Chastisen. } ures.
Cob. To beat or knock on the buttocks, as with the knee or with a board or strap.
Comb. To rake as with a comb.
Come to the gallows. To come to execution by hanging.
Correct. To punish in order to moral amendment, or to the removal of a fault.
Crucify. To put to death by fastening to a cross.
Cuff. To strike in any way; to buffet.
Dance upon nothing. Figurative, for to be hanged.
Deal a blow to. To strike at.
Deal retributive justice. To deal deserved punishment.
Decapitate. To behead.
Decimate. To kill one out of every ten persons.
Decollate. To behead.
Die in one's shoes. To die a violent death.
Disbar. To deprive of the right to appear at court as attorney.
Disbench. To deprive of the privilege of a bencher.
Dismiss. To put out of office or service by an act of authority.
Do for. To kill, or to injure fatally.
Dress. To punish or defeat thoroughly.
Drub. To beat, usually with a stick.
Drum out. To expel, as from a camp or regiment, usually to the accompaniment of a drum-beat.
Dust one's jacket. To smite; beat.
Empale. To punish by thrusting a pale or sharp stick through.
Execute. To put to death, especially in accordance with legal sentence.
Exile. To punish by banishment from one's home or native land.
Expel. To punish by ejection or driving out.
Flagellate. To beat with a rod; whip.
Flay. To strip off the skin from.
Flog. To punish by striking with a whip or the like.
Fustigate. To beat with a stick.
Gibbet. To hang and expose on a gibbet; to execute by hanging.
Give a black eye. To hit and bruise the eye.
Give a dressing. To beat soundly.

(Continued on Column 1.)

PUNITION—Verbs—*Continued.*

Swinge. To beat soundly; to whip; to chastise.
Switch. To strike with a small flexible rod; to whip.
Tar and feather. To smear with tar and cover with feathers as a degrading punishment.
Thrash. }
Thresh. } To beat soundly; drub.
Thump. To strike or beat with something heavy.
Thwack. To bang; thump.
Torture. To punish by inflicting pain and agony.
Towel. To beat with a stick.
Transport. To punish by carrying into banishment.

Trim. To rebuke; beat.
Trounce. To punish or beat severely.
Tund. To thump; to hammer.
Turn off. To dismiss contemptuously.
Unfrock. To deprive of priestly privileges.
Visit upon. To inflict.
Warm. To furnish heat by beating; beat.
Whallup. To flog; to whip.
Whip. To punish with a whip, scourge, or rod.
Whop. To beat or strike.
Wipe. To hit or beat.

PUNITION—*Adjectives.*

Castigatory. Punitive in order to amendment.
Inflictive. Causing the infliction of punishment.
Penal. Of or pertaining to punishment, penalties, or to crimes and offenses.

Punished. }
Punishing. } Having punishment inflicted.   See *Verbs.*
Punitive. }
Punitory. } Tending to punishment.

PUNITION—*Interjection.*

À la lanterne [F.]. To the lamp, to hang: a cry of the mob in Paris.

PUNITION—*Phrases.*

Culpam pœna premit comes [L.]. Punishment presses close upon crime. [Horace, *Odes*, iv, v, 24.]

Gravis ira regum est semper [L.]. Heavy is ever the ire of kings. [Seneca, *Medea*, 494.]

RECOMPENSE—PENALTY

PENALTY.

Amercement. A pecuniary penalty inflicted on an offender at the discretion of the court.
Confiscation. Forfeiting of private property to the public use for the wrong-doing of the owner.
Damages. Money recoverable as amends for a wrong and injury sustained.
Deodand. Any personal chattels that had been immediately instrumental in causing the death of a person, and were therefore forfeited to the crown for pious uses.
Escheat. Forfeiture of property for any default.
Fine. Money paid as a penalty for an offense against the criminal law
Forfeit. A thing lost to its owner by way of penalty.
Forfeiture. A penalty for misconduct, crime, or breach of duty.
Mulct. A fine or similar penalty.
Pain. Punishment suffered or denounced.
Peine forte et dure [L.]. Strong and severe punishment.
Penalty. Punishment for crime or offense.
Penance. Pain: punishment. See ATONEMENT.
Premunire [L.]. The penalty ascribed for the offense of introducing foreign authority into England.

Punition. Punishment.
Retribution. Condign punishment for evil or wrong. See RECOMPENSE-PUNITION.
Sequestration. The setting aside of property pending a lawsuit.
Wergild. A fine, the payment for a man killed.

PENALTY—*Verbs.*

Amerce. To punish by a pecuniary penalty.
Confiscate. To seize as forfeited to the public treasury.
Escheat. To take possession of as lapsed or forfeited.
Estreat. To levy an amercement under estreat of record.
Fine. To lay a pecuniary penalty upon because of some breach of the laws or other offense.
Forfeit. To lose title to as a penalty.
Mulct. To sentence to a pecuniary penalty or forfeiture as a punishment.
Sconce. To fine; mulct; used especially for light fines inflicted for irregularities in the universities of England.
Sequester. } To seize, especially for the use or disposal of the government; confiscate.
Sequestrate. }

RECOMPENSE—SCOURGE.

SCOURGE.

Ax. The instrument used for beheading.
Birch. }
Birch-rod. } A bunch of twigs for whipping.
Block. The wooden billet on which condemned prisoners are beheaded.
Boot. A medieval instrument of torture in which the foot and leg were crushed.
Bowstring. A string for strangling criminals.
Brank. A metal frame enclosing the head with a gag for the tongue.
Cane. A rod for punishment.
Cat. A cat-o'-nine-tails.
Cat-o'-nine-tails. An instrument of punishment by flogging, consisting of nine pieces of cord, each with three knots, attached to a thick rope handle.
Cowhide. A heavy flexible leather whip.
Crank. A paddle-like wheel made to be turned by hand in a box filled with gravel: used for punishment.
Cross. An ancient instrument of torture on which criminals were fastened and exposed until they died of exhaustion.
Cucking-stool. A chair in which persons were tied and exposed to derision as a punishment.
Drop. The platform of a gallows, the fall of which allows the condemned murderer to drop.
Ducking-stool. A stool in which common scolds were formerly tied and ducked in water.
Ferule. A flat stick or rod used for punishing.
Galley. A vessel propelled by oars which were usually manned by convicts.

Gallows. A framework of one or two posts with a cross-beam, used for the execution of a criminal by hanging.
Gaol. A jail.
Gibbet. A gallows.
Guillotine. A machine for beheading criminals.
Halter. A hangman's rope.
House of correction. A prison. See RELEASE-PRISON.
Iron heel. Any instrument of punishment.
Knout. A whip of leather thongs, usually twisted with wire.
Lash. A whip.
Maiden. A kind of beheading machine used in Scotland in the 16th and 17th centuries.
Noose. A loop with a running knot used for hanging criminals.
Pillory. A wooden framework in which an offender is fastened between boards by the neck and wrists.
Rack. An instrument of torture, for stretching or dislocating the joints of offenders.
Ratan. }
Rattan. } A switch.
Rod. A switch or instrument of punishment.
Rod in pickle. See RECOMPENSE-PUNITION.
Rope. The cord used for hanging murderers.
Rope's end. The noose.
Scaffold. A gallows.
Scourge. An instrument of punishment.
Stake. A post to which a person is bound to be burned alive.
Stick. A rod or whip.

RECOMPENSE—SCOURGE—*Continued.*

Stocks. An apparatus formerly used for punishing petty offenders, consisting of a frame of heavy timbers with holes for the confinement of the limbs.

Strap. A strip of leather used in flogging.

Switch. A whip.

Thong. A long narrow strip of leather used for a lash.

Thumb-screw. An instrument of torture for compressing the thumb by means of a screw.

Treadmill. A mechanism operated by the stepping or walking motion of one or more persons, used as a hard labor punishment.

Tree. A gibbet or cross.

Triangle. A triangle made of three halberds on which offenders were whipped.

Truncheon. A club or staff.

Wheel. An instrument of torture.

Whip. An instrument for administering punishment.

Whipping-post. A post to which those sentenced to flogging were fastened.

Wooden-horse. A block or frame on which soldiers are mounted as a punishment.

SCOURGE—*Nouns of Agent.*

Executioner. One who puts to death in accordance with the sentence of a court.

Gaoler. A jailer.

Hangman. A public executioner who hangs criminals convicted of capital crimes.

Headsman. A public executioner who beheads criminals convicted of capital crimes.

Jack Ketch. A public executioner or hangman.

Jailer. The officer in charge of a jail.

---

rec′-on-ci″-la-ble. Capable of being reconciled. HARMONY-DISCORD.

rec′-on-cile. To restore friendship. CONTENTEDNESS-DISCONTENTMENT, FIGHTING-CONCILIATION, HARMONY-DISCORD; **reconcile oneself,** EXCITABILITY-INEXCITABILITY.

rec′-on-cile″-ment. Reconciliation. FIGHTING-CONCILIATION, HARMONY-DISCORD.

rec″-on-cil″-i-a′-tion. Renewed harmony. CONTENTEDNESS-DISCONTENTMENT, FIGHTING-CONCILIATION, HARMONY-DISCORD, PARDON-VINDICTIVENESS.

rec′-on-dite″. Obscure. CLEARNESS-OBSCURITY, ENLIGHTENMENT-SECRECY.

re-con′-nais-sance. Survey. INVESTIGATION-ANSWER, SIGHT-BLINDNESS.

rec″-on-noi′-ter. To survey. INVESTIGATION-ANSWER, SIGHT-BLINDNESS.

rec″-on-noi′-ter-ing. Surveying. INVESTIGATION-ANSWER.

re″-con-sid′-er. To consider again. REFLECTION-VACANCY.

re″-con-sid″-er-a′-tion. A thinking over again. PRESIDENT-MEMBER, REFLECTION-VACANCY; **on reconsideration,** BETTERMENT-DETERIORATION.

re-con′-sti-tute. To reform. RENOVATION-RELAPSE.

re″-con-struct′. To build over. RENOVATION-RELAPSE.

re″-con-struc′-tion. Reestablishment. RENOVATION-RELAPSE.

re″-con-ver′-sion. A second conversion. RENOVATION-RELAPSE.

re″-con-vert′. To change again. RENOVATION-RELAPSE.

rec′-ord. Account. EVIDENCE-COUNTEREVIDENCE, MARK-OBLITERATION, SECURITY, SIGN; **court of record,** TRIBUNAL.

RECORD.

Account. A statement of business dealings.

Bead-roll. A list or catalogue.

Bill. A statement of particulars.

Bill of costs. An account of the costs in legal proceedings.

Bill of fare. A list of articles or dishes provided for a meal.

Bill of lading. A written acknowledgment by a carrier of the receipt of goods for transportation.

Blue Book. A pamphlet containing reports of government officials.

Book. A bound collection of printed or written matter.

Cadaster. An official statement of real estate for fixing taxes.

Calendar. A schedule or list of things or events.

Carte [F.]. A list or record.

Cartulary. A register of charters.

Catalogue. A list or enumeration of names, titles, persons, or things.

Catalogue raisonné [F.]. A catalogue according to subjects.

Census. An official numbering of the people of a country.

Check-roll. A list by which something may be checked or verified.

Chequer-roll. A check-roll.

Contents. A list of the subjects treated of in a book.

Diptych. A double catalogue.

Directory. An alphabetical list of the names and addresses of the inhabitants of a district.

Domesday Book. A book containing the record of the statistical survey of England made by William the Conqueror.

File. A collection of papers or documents arranged systematically.

Gazetteer. A dictionary of geographical names.

Index. An alphabetical list of matters discussed in a book.

Inventory. A detailed account of property, merchandise, etc.

Ledger. The principal book of accounts of a business establishment in which all the transactions of each day are entered.

List. A roll or catalogue.

Menu. A bill of fare.

Muster-book. A book containing a muster-roll.

Muster-roll. A return of all troops accounted for at muster-day.

Panel. The official list of persons summoned for jury duty.

Program. A list of exercises making up an entertainment, etc.

Prospectus. An outline or plan of something proposed.

Register. An official written record or account. See MARK.

Returns. A formal report of facts.

Roll. A list or register.

Roster. A list of officers and men enrolled for duty.

Schedule. An inventory or list.

Score. An account kept by notches.

Statistics. A systematized collection of facts.

Syllabus. A concise statement.

Synopsis. A brief outline.

Table. A tabular statement.

Tableau [F.]. Table; tabular statement.

Tally. Account kept by notches.

Terrier. A land-survey setting forth the number of acres, tenants, etc., in a given district.

RECORD—*Adjective.*

Cadastral. Pertaining to an official register of lands.

---

re-cord′-er. One who records. JUDGE, MARK-OBLITERATION, RECORDER.

RECORDER.

Amanuensis. One who writes down what another dictates, or copies what another has written.

Annalist. One who writes annals.

Antiquary. One who studies the past through relics, etc.

Biographer. One who writes of the life and character of particular persons.

Bookkeeper. One who keeps a systematic account of business transactions.

Chronicler. One who records events in the order of their occurrence; in general, any historian.

Clerk. One who keeps the records; a secretary.

Custos rotulorum [L.]. The principal justice of the peace of an English county, who has charge of the records of the sessions.

Historian. One who writes history.

Historiographer. A writer of history; especially, an official historian.

Journalist. One engaged in journalistic or newspaper work.

Master of the rolls. An official who keeps the record of the English courts

Memorialist. One who writes or signs anything intended to preserve the memory of a person or event.

Notary public. A public officer who is authorized to attest deeds and other commercial papers.

Prothonotary. A chief clerk of the court.

Recorder. A public officer charged with the making and keeping of public records.

Register. A registrar.

Registrar. One authorized to make and preserve the records.

Registrary. A registrar.

Remembrancer. One who or that which preserves or stirs up the memory.

Scribe. A custodian and writer of the official records of the Jewish people; a clerk.

Secretary. One who keeps the records and has charge of the official correspondence of an individual or body; a clerk.

re-count'. To relate. ACCOUNT.

re-coup'. Indemnify. TAKING-RESTITUTION.

re-course'. Resort. USE-DISUSE.

re-cov'-er. To regain; get well. BETTERMENT-DETERIORATION, GAIN-LOSS, HEALTH-SICKNESS, RENOVATION-RELAPSE, TAKING-RESTITUTION.

re-cov'-er-y. Restoration. BETTERMENT-DETERIORATION, GAIN-LOSS, RENOVATION-RELAPSE; TAKING-RESTITUTION; **recovery of strength,** WEARINESS-REFRESHMENT.

rec'-re-ant. Apostate. BRAVERY-COWARDICE, GOOD-MAN-BAD MAN, PATRIOTISM-TREASON, UPRIGHTNESS-DISHONESTY, UPRIGHTNESS-ROGUE, VIRTUE-VICE.

rec'-re-ate. To refresh. ENTERTAINMENT-WEARINESS.

rec'-re-a-tive. Tending to refresh. ENTERTAINMENT-WEARINESS.

rec'-re-ment. Waste. CLEANNESS-FILTHINESS.

re-crim'-i-nate. To counter-accuse. APPROVAL-DISAPPROVAL.

re-crim''-i-na'-tion. Countercharge. JUSTIFICATION-CHARGE, REPENTANCE-OBDURACY, REPRISAL-RESISTANCE.

re''-cru-des'-cence. The state of being raw. RENOVATION-RELAPSE.

re-cruit'. A new soldier or member; to build up. ANTAGONIST-ASSISTANT, BELLIGERENT, BETTERMENT-DETERIORATION, HEALTH-SICKNESS, INSTRUCTOR-PUPIL, OBSTRUCTION-HELP, PROVISION-WASTE, RENOVATION-RELAPSE, STRENGTH-WEAKNESS, WEARINESS-REFRESHMENT; **beat up for recruits,** OBSTRUCTION-HELP, PREPARATION-NONPREPARATION.

re-cruit'-ing. Replenishing. RENOVATION-RELAPSE.

re-cruits'. Reenforcements. OBSTRUCTION-HELP.

rect'-an''-gle. Right-angled parallelogram. ANGULARITY.

rect-an'-gu-lar. Having a right angle. ANGULARITY, ERECTNESS-FLATNESS.

rec''-ti-fi-ca'-tion. Correction. RENOVATION-RELAPSE.

rec'-ti-fy. Correct. BETTERMENT-DETERIORATION, CURVATION-RECTILINEARITY, RENOVATION-RELAPSE.

rec''-ti-lin'-e-al. Straight. CURVATION-RECTILINEARITY.

rec''-ti-lin'-e-ar. Straight. CURVATION-RECTILINEARITY.

rec''-ti-lin''-e-ar'-i-ty. State of consisting of straight lines. CURVATION-RECTILINEARITY.

rec'-ti-tude. Uprightness. UPRIGHTNESS-DISHONESTY, VIRTUE-VICE.

rec'-tor. Manager; pastor. MANAGER, MINISTRY-LAITY.

rec'-tor-ship. Office of a rector. CHURCH.

rec'-to-ry. Rector's house. FANE.

rec'-trix. A rectoress; one of the quills of a bird's tail. CHIEF-UNDERLING, ZOOLOGY-BOTANY.

rectus in curia [L.] (rec'-tus in ciu'-ri-a). Of good standing in court. INNOCENCE-GUILT.

reculade [F.] (re-cü-lad'). A falling back. ADVANCE-RETROGRESSION.

reculer pour mieux sauter [F.] (re-cü-lê' pur miu so-tê').

To go back so as to be able to leap better. CRAFT-ARTLESSNESS, PREPARATION-NONPREPARATION, RECKLESSNESS-CAUTION.

reculons, à [F.] (re-cü-lon·', a). Backwards. ADVANCE-RETROGRESSION.

re-cum'-ben-cy. Reclining. ERECTNESS-FLATNESS.

re-cum'-bent. Leaning. ERECTNESS-FLATNESS, PARALLELISM-INCLINATION.

re-cu''-per-a'-tion. The process of gaining strength. TAKING-RESTITUTION.

re-cu'-per-a-tive. Tending to recovery. RENOVATION-RELAPSE, TAKING-RESTITUTION, WEARINESS-REFRESHMENT.

re-cur'. To be repeated. FREQUENCY-RARITY, PERIODICITY-IRREGULARITY, RECURRENCE; **recur to,** USE-DISUSE; **recur to the mind,** REMEMBRANCE-FORGETFULNESS.

re-cure'. To recover. RENOVATION-RELAPSE.

re-cur'-rence. A second happening. CONTINUITY-INTERRUPTION, PERIODICITY-IRREGULARITY, RECURRENCE, REMEMBRANCE-FORGETFULNESS, RENOVATION-RELAPSE.

RECURRENCE.

Battology. A needless repetition of words in speaking or writing.

Harping. A continual dwelling on one subject.

Iteration. Saying or doing the same thing over again.

Monotony. The state of being monotonous. See *Adjectives*.

Periodicity. The condition of recurring at regular intervals.

Reappearance. The act of coming into view again.

Recurrence. The state of occurring or happening again or at stated intervals.

Reiteration. Saying or doing a thing over and over again in an emphatic and exact manner.

Renewal. The act or process of making or beginning over again.

Repetend. Something repeated.

Repetition. The act of doing or saying over again.

Reproduction. The act or power of bringing forward anew.

Reverberation. A beating or sounding back.

Rhythm. Movement characterized by a harmonious succession of sounds, beats, etc.

Rifacimento [It.]. A re-making.

Run. Continued repetition: said of a play.

Succession. The act of following in regular order.

Tautology. The unnecessary repetition of a word or idea.

Tautophony. Repetition of the same sound.

RECURRENCE—*Denotations*.

Burden of a song. That part of a song that is repeated.

Chimes. A set of bells so arranged and tuned as to produce melodies when struck successively.

Drumming. The noise made by beating a drum.

Echo. A sound returned to its source by an opposing surface.

New edition. A reproduction of a book or literary work.

Old song. }
Old story. } A story often repeated.

Réchauffé [F.]. Food warmed over; a literary rehash.

Refrain. A phrase or strain repeated at intervals in a poem or song.

Rehearsal. A preparatory recital or performance for practise.

Ritornello [It.]. A refrain.

Second edition. A republication of a book.

Twice-told tale. A story oft repeated.

RECURRENCE—*Verbs*.

Battologize. To repeat or multiply words unnecessarily in speaking or writing.

Begin again.

Conjugate in all its moods, tenses, and inflections. To repeat a word very often.

Din in the ear. To say over and over again.

Do over again. To repeat.

Drum. To force on the attention by constant repetition.

Drum in the ear. To repeat continually.

Echo. To repeat or reflect a sound.

Go over the same ground. To repeat.

Go the same round. To do over.

Hammer. To strike repeated blows, literally or figuratively.

Harp on the same string. To talk continually on the same subject.

Harp upon. To dwell on or refer to until it becomes tedious.

Iterate. To repeat.

Never hear the last of. To hear at all times.
Reappear. To appear again.
Recapitulate. To repeat or sum up the main points, as in a debate.
Recur. To happen again at certain intervals.
Redouble. To increase greatly by repeated additions.
Reecho. To echo again.
Rehearse. To go over in preparation.
Reiterate. To say or do again and again.
Renew. To begin over again.
Repeat. To say or do over again in any manner whatever.
Reproduce. To bring forth anew.
Resume. To begin again after a cessation.
Return. To come back again.
Return to. To begin again.
Revert. To turn or come back to.
Reword. To repeat in other words.
Ring the changes on. To repeat the same thought in a great variety of ways.
Say over again. To repeat.

RECURRENCE—*Adjectives.*

Above-mentioned. Spoken of before.
Afore-named. Named before.
Aforesaid. Mentioned before.
Another. Repeated.
Chiming. Repeating in harmony.
Ever-recurring. Coming to view repeatedly.
Frequent. Happening often.
Habitual. Recurring constantly.
Harping. Always talking about. "Still harping on my daughter." [Shakespeare, *Hamlet*, II, ii.]
Incessant. Without ceasing.
Iterative. Repeating.
Mocking. Repeating in a jesting or derisive manner.
Monotonous. Tiring by repetition.
Recurrent. Occurring again and again. See *Verbs.*
Recurring. Repeating. See *Verbs.*
Repeated, etc. Done or said over again. See *Verbs.*
Repetitional. Said over again. See *Nouns.*
Repetitionary. Repetitional. See *Nouns.*
Retold. Repeated or told again.
Said. Aforesaid; above-mentioned.
Thick-coming. Coming rapidly or repeatedly.

RECURRENCE—*Adverbs, etc.*

Afresh. Again after a rest.
Again. Once more.
Again and again. Repeatedly.
Anew. Again after a cessation.
A number of times. Frequently.
Bis. Twice.
Da capo [It.]. From the beginning.
Day by day. Daily.
De novo [L.]. Anew.
Ding-dong. With monotonous repetition.
Ditto. In the same manner.
Encore. Once more.
Frequently. Occurring often. See *Adjectives.*
Full many a time. ⎫
Many a time. ⎬ Often.
Many times. ⎪
Many times over. ⎭
Often. Many times.
Once more. ⎫ Repeatedly.
Over again. ⎭
Over and over. Again and again.
Over and over again. Very often.
Several times. More than once.
Time after time. Repeatedly.
Year after year. Successively.

RECURRENCE—*Phrases.*

Cut and come again. To help yourself and take more when wanted.
Ecce iterum Crispinus [L.]. Here he comes again.
Nullum est jam dictum quod non dictum sit prius [L.]. Nothing is said nowadays that has not been said before. [Terence, *Eunuch Prol.*, 41.]
To-morrow and to-morrow. Again and again.
Toujours perdrix [F.]. Always partridge; too much of a good thing.

re-cur'-ring. Happening again. PERIODICITY-IRREGULARITY, RECURRENCE.
re-cur'-sion. Return. ARRIVAL-DEPARTURE.
re''-cur-va'-tion. The act of curving back. CURVATION-RECTILINEARITY.
re-curve'. To bend back. CURVATION-RECTILINEARITY.
re-curved'. Curved back. CURVATION-RECTILINEARITY.
re-curv'-i-ty. The act of recurving. CURVATION-RECTILINEARITY.
re-curv'-ous. Bent back. CURVATION-RECTILINEARITY.
rec'-u-sance. Persistent disobedience. REPENTANCE-OBDURACY.
rec'-u-san-cy. Recusance. ASSENT-DISSENT. ASSERTION-DENIAL, ORTHODOXY-HETERODOXY, PROFFER-REFUSAL.
rec'-u-sant. Non-conformist. ASSENT-DISSENT, ASSERTION-DENIAL, INSUBORDINATION-OBEDIENCE, ORTHODOXY-HETERODOXY, PROFFER-REFUSAL, REPENTANCE-OBDURACY.
rec''-u-sa'-tion. Refusal. ASSERTION-DENIAL.
red. A kind of color. REDNESS-GREENNESS; **red and yellow**, BLUENESS-ORANGE; **Red Book**, RECORD; **red-coat**, BELLIGERENT; **red cross**, REMEDY-BANE; **red flag**, ALARM; **red hot**, EMOTION, EXCITATION, HEAT-COLD, MAGNITUDE-SMALLNESS, TURBULENCE-CALMNESS; **red lead**, REDNESS-GREENNESS; **red letter**, SIGN, SOLEMNIZATION; **red-letter day**, CONSEQUENCE-INSIGNIFICANCE, ENTERTAINMENT-WEARINESS, SOLEMNIZATION, TOIL-RELAXATION; **red light**, ALARM; **red republican**, INSUBORDINATION-OBEDIENCE; **red tape**, HABIT-DESUETUDE; **red-tapist**, MANAGER; **turn red**, EMOTION.
re-dan'. Rampart. ATTACK-DEFENSE.
red-ar'-gue. To disprove. PROOF-DISPROOF.
red''-ar-gu'-tion. Disproof. PROOF-DISPROOF.
red'-den. To make red. FAVORITE-ANGER, REDNESS-GREENNESS, SELFRESPECT-HUMBLENESS.
red'-dened. Made red. REDNESS-GREENNESS.
red'-dish. Slightly red. REDNESS-GREENNESS.
red-di'-tion. Surrender. INTERPRETATION-MISINTERPRETATION, TAKING-RESTITUTION.
red'-dle. Redness. REDNESS-GREENNESS.
re-deem'. To regain; to make good. ATONEMENT, COMMUTATION-PERMUTATION, COMPENSATION, DIVINITY, GAIN-LOSS, RENOVATION-RELAPSE, RESCUE, SETTLEMENT-DEFAULT, TAKING-RESTITUTION; **redeem from**, REMEMBRANCE-FORGETFULNESS; **redeem one's pledge**, BELLIGERENT, DUTY-DERELICTION, UPRIGHTNESS-DISHONESTY, VIRTUE-VICE.
re-deem'-a-ble. Capable of being redeemed. RESCUE.
re-deem'-a-ble-ness. The quality of being redeemable. RESCUE.
Re-deem'-er. Christ. DIVINITY.
re-demp'-tion. The act of redeeming. ATONEMENT, DIVINITY, DUTY-DERELICTION, RELEASE-RESTRAINT, RENOVATION-RELAPSE, RESCUE.
red'-hand''-ed. Having committed murder. ACTION-PASSIVENESS, INNOCENCE-GUILT, LIFE-KILLING.
red-in'-te-grate. Renew. RENOVATION-RELAPSE.
redintegratio amoris [L.] (red-in''-tĭ-grē'-shi-o a-mo'-ris). Renewal of love. BIGOTRY-APOSTASY.
red-in''-te-gra'-tion. Renewal. RENOVATION-RELAPSE.
red''-i-vi'-vus. Renewed. RENOVATION-RELAPSE.
red'-ness. The state of being red. REDNESS-GREENNESS.

REDNESS—GREENNESS.

Blush. A slight reddening of the face or cheeks, as in shame or confusion. "Celestial rosy red, love's proper hue." [Milton, *Paradise Lost*, viii, 618.]

Aquamarine. A bluish-green color; also a variety of beryl.
Green. The color of the spectrum between blue and yellow; the color of growing grass.

REDNESS—GREENNESS—*Continued.*

Carbuncle. The red tincture of a nobleman's escutcheon.
Color. A ruddiness of complexion indicating good health.
Erubescence. The act of becoming red or blushing.
Gules. The red tincture on seals, etc., indicated by parallel vertical lines; hence, used poetically for redness.
Red. The color of the spectrum produced by waves of light of the longest vibration; the color of human blood.
Redness. The quality of being red.
Rubescence. The quality or condition of growing or turning red.
Rubicundity. A condition of slight redness.
Rubification. A making red.
Warmth. The condition of predominating in red or yellow tones.

REDNESS—*Denotations.*

Cedar. A tree whose wood is of a red color.
Human blood. The red liquid which circulates in the blood-vessels of the body.
Red ink. Ink of a red color.

REDNESS—*Nouns of Degree.*

Carmine. A rich red color bordering on purple.
Carnation. The color of human flesh, ranging from pink to deep crimson.
Couleur de rose [F.]. The color of the rose; a deep purplish-pink.
Crimson. A red color having a tinge of blue; in general, deep-red.
Damask. Deep-pink or rose-color; the color of the damask rose.
Flesh-color. The color of human flesh; carnation.
Flesh-tint. Flesh-color.
Fresh-color. A bright, healthy color.
High-color. A strong, deep, or glaring color.
Iron-mold. The color or stain which iron-rust leaves on cloth.
Maroon. A dull-red color, bordering on brownish red.
Pink. A very light-red color; the color of the garden pink.
Purple. A color formed by mixing the primary colors, red and blue, and varying between violet and crimson.
Rose. Rose-red; the color of the rose.
Rose du Barry [F.]. A pink or light-crimson color in porcelain decoration, named from Madame Du Barry, mistress of Louis XV.
Ruby. A rich red color like that of the ruby, slightly bordering on crimson.
Rust. The brownish-red color which iron takes on when exposed to moisture.
Scarlet. A brilliant-red color with a slight tinge of orange or yellow.
Vermilion. A bright-red color.

REDNESS—*Nouns of Source.*

Annatto. A yellowish-red dye obtained from the annatto-tree of Central America.
Cinnabar. Red sulfid of mercury, used as a pigment, giving the color of vermilion.
Cochineal. A dyestuff obtained from the cochineal-insect, giving a brilliant scarlet color.
Fuchsin. A coal-tar dyestuff, dark-red in solution.
Indian red. A purplish-red earth or pigment.
Lake. A pigment made by combining some animal or vegetable matter with a metallic oxid.
Light-red. An orange-red ocher.
Madder. A plant, the root of which is much used in dyeing and as a pigment, giving a red color.
Magenta. A coal-tar dyestuff.
Reddle. A variety of red iron-ore used as a pigment; red ocher.
Red lead. A vivid-red lead oxid, used chiefly as a pigment.
Venetian red. A mixture of ferric oxid and lime, used chiefly as a pigment.

REDNESS—*Verbs.*

Become red, etc. To take on a red color. See *Adjectives.*
Be red, etc. To be of a red color. See *Adjectives.*
Blush. To turn red, especially in the face, as in confusion or shame.
Color up. To turn red in the face; blush.
Flush. To turn red suddenly, as the face in anger.
Incarnadine. To dye red or flesh-colored. " This my [bloody] hand will rather the multitudinous seas incarnadine." [Shakespeare, *Macbeth*, II, ii.]
Mantle. To become overspread with color, usually red; blush.
Redden. To grow red; blush.
Render red. To color or make red.
Rouge. To heighten or imitate the natural color of the skin by applying any cosmetic or coloring.
Rubify. To make red.
Rubricate. To mark red for the purpose of distinguishing or calling attention to, as parts of a book.
Ruddle. To color coarsely red, as to mark sheep with ruddle.

Greenness. The condition of having a green color.
Sea-green. The color of the ocean.
Verdure. The fresh greenness of growing vegetation.
Viridescence. The condition of being slightly green.
Viridity. The condition of having a fresh green color; verdant.

GREENNESS—*Denotations.*

Absinthe. A volatile, green, intoxicating liquor.
Beryl. A vitreous green aluminum silicate.
Emerald. A bright-green variety of beryl.
Grass. The green plants on which cattle feed.
Malachite. A green mineral.
Verd-antique. A mottled green serpentine marble.
Vert. The tincture green in heraldry.

GREENNESS—*Nouns of Source.*

Blue and yellow. The combination which produces green.
Terre verte [F.]. Green earth.
Verdigris. A green pigment obtained by the action of acetic acid on copper.
Verditer. A light-blue pigment which, when boiled, becomes a green pigment.

GREENNESS—*Adjectives.*

Apple-green. Of the color of an apple.
Bottle-green. Of the color of green glass bottles.
Emerald-green. Of the color of an emerald.
Glaucous. Sea-green.
Grass-green. }
Green as grass. } Of the color of grass.
Green. Having the color of growing grass.
Greenish. Slightly green.
Olive. }
Olive-green. } Of the color of the olive.
Pea-green. Of the color of green pea-pods.
Sea-green. Of the color of sea-water.
Verdant. Green with vegetation.
Virent. Verdant; green.
Virescent. Greenish; growing green.

REDNESS—*Continued.*

REDNESS—*Adjectives.*

Blood-red. Colored with or like blood.
Blowzed. Having a coarsely red or flushed face.
Blowzy. Blowzed.
Blushing, etc. Becoming red. See *Verbs.*
Brick-colored. Of the color of bricks; brownish-red.
Brickdust-colored. Brick-colored.
Buff. A light yellow verging toward pink, gray, or brown.
Burnt. Having the color of that which has been burnt; brownish-red.
Carroty. Like a carrot in color; reddish-yellow.
Cherry-colored. Of the color of a cherry.
Claret. Having the color of claret; deep purplish-red.
Erubescent. Tending to grow red; blushing.
Flame-colored. Of the color of a flame.
Flesh-colored. Having the color of human flesh; carnation.
Florid. Flushed with red.
Foxy. Of the color of a fox; reddish-brown.
Hot. Fiery red.
Incarnadin. Flesh-colored.
Lateritious. Of the color of red brick.
Lurid. Giving a ghastly dull-red light.
Murrey. Of a dark reddish-brown or mulberry color.
Peach-colored. Having the bright reddish tint of the peach.
Red. Having the color of arterial human blood
Red as a lobster. }
Red as a turkey-cock. }
Red as blood. } Figurative degrees of redness.
Red as fire. }
Red as scarlet. }
Reddened, etc. Made red. See *Verbs.*
Reddish. Slightly red.
Roseate. Tinged with rose-color or red.
Rose-colored. Of the color of a rose.
Rosy. Of the color of the rose; rose-red.
Rubicund. Having a reddened face; flushed.
Rubiform. Red in color.
Ruby-colored. Of the color of the ruby.
Ruddy. Tinged with red.
Rufous. Brownish-red; rust-colored.

REDNESS—Adjectives—*Continued.*

Russet. Of a reddish-brown color.
Salmon-colored. Of a reddish-yellow or orange color
Sanguine. Having the color of blood; red.

Sorrel. Of a reddish- or yellowish-brown color.
Stammel. Having the color of stammel; of an inferior red color.
Warm. Having predominating tones of red or yellow.

red'-o-lence. Fragrance. Odor-Inodorousness, Perfume-Stench.

red'-o-lent. Odorous. Odor-Inodorousness.

re-doub'-le. To increase. Doubling-Halving, Increase-Decrease, Recurrence; **redouble one's efforts**, Toil-Relaxation.

re-dound'. To contribute. Inclination; **redound to one's honor**, Approval-Disapproval, Reputation-Discredit, Uprightness-Dishonesty.

re-dout'. To fortify. Attack-Defense.

re-dout'-a-ble. Formidable. Action-Passiveness.

red'-ow-a. A round dance. Entertainment-Weariness.

re-dress'. Remedy; compensation. Recompense-Punition, Remedy-Bane, Renovation-Relapse.

red''-ta'-pist. One who is very formal. Manager.

re-duce'. To subdue; to lessen; to lower. Affluence-Penury, Elevation-Depression, Enlargement-Diminution, Increase-Decrease, Length-Shortness, Multiplicity - Paucity, Price-Discount, Strength-Weakness, Success-Failure; **reduce in strength**, Strength-Weakness; **reduce the speed**, Swiftness-Slowness; **reduce to**, Conversion-Reversion; **reduce to a mean**, Medium; **reduce to ashes**, Heating-Cooling; **reduce to demonstration**, Proof-Disproof; **reduce to order**, Organization-Disorganization; **reduce to poverty**, Affluence-Penury; **reduce to powder**, Friability; **reduce to subjection**, Liberty-Subjection; **reduce to writing**, Mark-Obliteration.

re-duced'. Made fewer; lowered. Affluence-Penury, Multiplicity-Paucity, Supremacy - Subordinacy; **reduced to a skeleton**, Betterment-Deterioration; **reduced to straits**, Difficulty-Facility; **reduced to the last extremity**, Security-Insecurity.

reductio ad absurdum [L.] (rĭ-dŭc'-shi-o ad ab-sur'-dum). A reducing a position to an absurdity. Proof-Disproof, Ratiocination-Instinct.

re-duc'-tion. Act of reducing. Conversion-Reversion, Elevation-Depression, Enlargement-Diminution, Increase-Decrease, Length-Shortness, Multiplicity - Paucity, Numbering, Sameness-Contrast; **at a reduction**, Costliness-Cheapness; **reduction of temperature**, Heating-Cooling.

re-dun'-dance. Surplus. Excess - Lack, Terseness-Prolixity, Transcursion-Shortcoming.

re-dun'-dant. Excessive. Excess-Lack.

re-du'-pli-cate. To repeat. Doubling-Halving.

re-du''-pli-ca'-tion. A repetition. Doubling-Halving, Imitation-Originality.

re-ech'-o. To echo back. Imitation-Originality, Recurrence, Resonance-Nonresonance.

reech'-y. Smoky. Cleanness-Filthiness.

reed. Arrow; kind of grass. Musical Instruments, Strength-Weakness, Weapon; **lean on a broken reed**, Recklessness-Caution; **reed instrument**, Musical Instruments; **trust to a broken reed**, Skill-Unskilfulness.

reef. Ridge of rocks; to reduce. Refuge-Pitfall, Swamp-Island, Swiftness-Slowness; **double reef topsails**, Security-Insecurity.

reefs. Dangerous rocks. Refuge-Pitfall.

reek. Steam; smoke. Cleanness-Filthiness, Heat-Cold, Liquefaction-Volatilization, Liquid-Gas, Water-Air.

reek'-ing. Emitting steam or smoke. Cleanness-Filthiness, Dampness - Dryness, Heat - Cold, Liquefaction-Volatilization.

reek'-y. Smoky. Cleanness-Filthiness.

reel. Bobbin; dance; to stagger. Agitation, Entertainment-Weariness, Vibration; **off the reel**, Talkativeness-Taciturnity; **reel back**, Yielding.

re''-em-bod'-y. To embody again. Composition-Resolution, Union-Disunion.

re''-en-force'. To strengthen. Addition-Subtraction, Obstruction-Help, Renovation-Relapse, Strength-Weakness.

re''-en-force'-ment. Help. Addition-Subtraction, Increment-Remnant, Materials, Obstruction-Help, Provision-Waste.

re''-en-force'-ments. Fresh troops. Obstruction-Help.

re'-en-ter. To enter again. Curvation-Rectilinearity.

re-en'-ter-ing. Reentrant. **Reentering angle**, Angularity.

re''-es-tab'-lish. To establish again. Renovation-Relapse.

re''-es-tab'-lish-ment. A restoration. Renovation-Relapse.

re''-es-tate'. To reinstate. Renovation-Relapse.

re-fash'-ion. To form again. Renewal.

re-fect'. To restore. Strength-Weakness.

re-fec'-tion. Food. Nutriment-Excretion, Weariness-Refreshment.

re-fec'-to-ry. Eating-room. Contents-Receiver.

re-fer. To relate; to assign; seek advice. Admission-Exclusion, Advice, Connection-Independence, Evidence-Counterevidence, Rationale-Luck.

ref'-er-a-ble. Assignable. Connection - Independence, Rationale-Luck.

ref'-er-ee'. Umpire. Decision-Misjudgment, Judge.

ref'-er-ence. Act of referring. Advice, Connection-Independence, Evidence-Counterevidence, Rationale-Luck.

ref''-er-en'-da-ry. Referee. Judge.

ref''-er-en'-dum. Proposition for consideration. **Leave referendum**, Persistence-Whim.

referendum, ad [L.] (ref''-er-en'-dum, ad). For consideration. Investigation-Answer.

re-fer'-ment. Reference. Advice.

re-fer'-ri-ble. Referable. Connection-Independence, Ratiocination-Instinct, Rationale-Luck.

re-fine'. To purify. Cleanness-Filthiness; **refine upon**, Betterment-Deterioration.

re-fined'. Cultured. Beauty-Ugliness, Politeness-Impoliteness, Society-Ludicrousness, Taste-Vulgarity; **refined taste**, Taste-Vulgarity.

re-fine'-ment. Culture. Beauty-Ugliness, Betterment-Deterioration, Differentiation-Indiscrimination, Sagacity-Incapacity, Strength-Weakness, Taste-Vulgarity; **overrefinement**, Ratiocination-Instinct.

re-fit'. To repair. Renovation-Relapse.

re-flect'. To think; to mirror. Imitation-Originality, Reflection-Vacancy; **reflect dishonor**, Reputation-Discredit; **reflect light**, Light-Darkness; **reflect upon**, Approval-Disapproval.

re-flect'-ing. Careful. Sagacity-Incapacity; **reflecting goniometer**, Mineralogy.

re-flec'-tion. Thought; blame; image. Adage-Nonsense, Advance-Retrogression, Approval-Disapproval, Conception-Theme, Heed-Disregard, Light-Darkness, Reflection-Vacancy.

REFLECTION—VACANCY.

Abstraction. The act of separating mentally the qualities or properties of an object.

Abstract thought. A thought general and abstruse; hence, difficult.

Afterthought. Consideration after an act.

Application. Intenseness of thought. See HEED.

Association of thought. Mental grouping of ideas.

Brain-work. Mental exercise.

Brown study. A state of absent-mindedness, as in deep thought. See HEED-DISREGARD.

Cerebration. Exertion of the brain in thought.

Close study. Attentive application to mental work.

Cogitation. The act or process of thinking about.

Consideration. Thoughtful feeling or treatment.

Contemplation. The act of considering thoughtfully.

Current of ideas.
Current of thought. } A series of successive thoughts.

Deep reflection. Intense thought.

Deliberation. Careful and considerate thought.

Depth of thought. Profoundness of contemplation.

Examination. Careful inquiry or inspection. See INVESTIGATION.

Excogitation. Attentive thought.

Exercise of the intellect.
Exercitation of the intellect. } Exertion of the mind.

Flow of thought. A gentle procedure of reasoning, uninterrupted and copious.

Head-work. Mental labor.

Inmost thoughts. Thoughts hidden farthest from public view.

Invention. The faculty or power of inventing. See FANCY.

Lucubration. Intense and earnest thought.

Mature thought. Well-developed thought.

Meditation. The act of thinking carefully.

Musing. The act of thinking deeply.

Platonism. The philosophy of Plato.

Pondering. Deliberative thought.

Reconsideration. To think over again.

Reflection. The act of turning back the thoughts; pondering.

Retrospection. The act of looking back on things. See FANCY.

Reverie. An idle train of thought.

Second thoughts. Reflection after an action.

Self-communing. Consideration of one's own thoughts.

Self-consultation. Deliberation with oneself.

Self-counsel. To advise oneself.

Speculation. Thinking proceeding from intuitive principles.

Study. Learning by mental application.

Succession of thought. A consecutive following of thought.

Thought. The act, process, or power of thinking.

Thoughtfulness. Attentiveness. See *Adjectives.*

Thoughts. What are produced by thinking.

Train of thought. A connected line of thought.

Workings of the mind. Mental labors.

REFLECTION—*Verbs.*

Advise with one's pillow. To deliberate alone after retiring.

Animadvert. To criticize or censure.

Apply the mind. To pay attention. See HEED.

Appreciate. To estimate duly.

Bear in mind. Retain in thought.

Beat one's brains. To think searchingly.

Bend the mind. To apply the mind to. See HEED.

Bestow consideration upon. To give careful thought to.

Bestow thought. To give attention.

Bethink oneself. To bring to one's consideration.

Be uppermost in the mind. To hold the first place in the thoughts.

Brood over. To think long and anxiously upon.

Cherish an idea. To think. See CONCEPTION.

Chew the cud upon. Figurative for to meditate deeply upon.

Cogitate. To think over.

Collect one's thoughts. To gain command over one's dispersed thoughts.

Come into one's head. To enter the mind.

Come uppermost. To take the first place in the mind.

Commune with oneself. To think in solitude.

Con over. To study carefully.

Consider. To fix the mind on.

Contemplate. To think studiously.

Crack one's brains. To think very earnestly.

Cross the mind. To engage the thoughts slightly.

Cudgel one's brains. To think very earnestly.

Deliberate. To weigh in the mind.

Digest. To think out; to settle systematically in the mind.

Discuss. To reason upon.

Dream. To have ideas during sleep; to think idly.

Engross the thoughts. To entirely occupy the mind.

Fatuity. Imbecility; idiocy. See SAGACITY-INCAPACITY.

Incogitancy. Want of thought.

Inunderstanding. Void of understanding.

Thoughtlessness. Lack of thought or attention. See HEED-DISREGARD.

Vacancy. State of being empty of thought or stupid.

VACANCY—*Verbs.*

Dismiss from the mind.
Dismiss from the thoughts. } To pay no attention to. See REFLECTION.

Divert the mind. To turn aside the thoughts.

Indulge in reverie. To indulge in listless musing. See HEED-DISREGARD.

Not think.
Not think of. } To be free from the mind. See REFLECTION.

Put away thought. To relieve the mind from labor.

Relax the mind. To release the mind from effort.

Unbend the mind. To free the mind from care or labor.

VACANCY—*Adjectives.*

Absent. Of wandering mind. See HEED-DISREGARD.

Diverted. Turned away from labor or study, as by amusement.

Incogitable. Not capable of being known.

Inconsiderate. Thoughtless; heedless.

Irrational. Not possessed of reasoning powers. See SAGACITY-INCAPACITY.

Narrow-minded. Of confined views. See DECISION-MISJUDGMENT.

Not to be thought of. Impossible.

Off one's mind. Free from care.

Thoughtless. Heedless.

Unconsidered. Not considered or regarded.

Undreamt of. Not thought of.

Unideal. Destitute of ideas.

Unintellectual. Lacking intellect.

Unoccupied. Not possessed.

Unthinking. Lacking thought.

Unthought of. Not thought of.

Vacant. Idle; thoughtless.

VACANCY—*Phrases.*

Absence d'esprit [F.]. Absence of mind.

Bayer aux corneilles [F.]. To gape at the crows; *i. e.,* to gape idly upwards into vacancy.

Pabulum pictura pascit inani [L.]. He feeds his mind with an empty picture.

REFLECTION—*Verbs—Continued.*

Entertain an idea. To have a notion or impression. See CONCEPTION.

Enter the mind. To engage the thoughts.

Excogitate. To strike out by thinking.

Fancy. To portray in the mind; to be pleased with. See FANCY.

Fasten itself on the mind. To take a permanent place in the thoughts.

Flash across the mind. To engage the thoughts for an instant.

Flash on the mind. To come suddenly to the thoughts.

Flit across the brain. To pass quickly through the mind.

Float in the mind. To linger idly in the thoughts.

Get into one's head. Occupy a place in the thoughts.

Hammer at. To work at steadily in the mind.

Harbor an idea. To have a purpose or plan of action. See CONCEPTION.

Have in one's mind. To hold in one's thoughts.

Make an impression. To produce an effect on the mind.

Meditate.
Muse. } To think upon; turn over in the mind.

Nurture an idea. To keep an object occupying the mind. See CONCEPTION.

Occupy the mind. To engage the thoughts.

Occur. To come to the mind.

Pass in the mind. To occur in the thoughts.

Penetrate into the mind. To pass into or affect the thoughts.

Perpend. To weigh carefully in the mind.

Ponder. To think attentively about.

Present itself. To introduce itself into the mind.

Rack one's brains. To exert one's mind to the utmost.

Ransack one's brains. To search one's mind thoroughly.

Realize. To impress on the mind as real.

Reconsider. To review in the mind.

Reflect. To think seriously; revolve in the mind.

Revolve in the mind. To think deliberately upon.

Ruminate. To muse; meditate.

Run in one's head. To stay in one's thoughts.

REFLECTION—Verbs—*Continued*.

Run over in the mind. To think over hurriedly in review

Set one's brain to work. To make one think.

Set one's wits to work. To make one's mind exert itself.

Sink into the mind. To impress in the thoughts.

Sleep upon. To sleep before rendering a decision upon something.

Speculate. To pursue inquiries and theories in one's mind.

Strike one. To impress one's mind.

Study. To endeavor to learn by mental application, to inspect thoughtfully.

Suggest itself. To introduce itself to the thoughts.

Take counsel. To be advised. See Advice.

Take counsel of one's pillow. To think over after retiring.

Take into consideration. To take into one's thoughts.

Take into one's head. To form a notion in one's mind.

Think. To produce or form by mental processes.

Trow. To suppose; to think.

Turn over in the mind. To deliberate upon.

Weigh. To estimate the worth of.

REFLECTION—*Adjectives*.

Contemplative. Given to thoughtful consideration.

Deep musing. Thinking deeply. See Heed.

Deliberative. Pertaining to deliberation or careful consideration.

In the mind. In thought.

Introspective. Looking within.

Lost in thought. Absent-minded. See Heed-Disregard.

Meditative. Disposed to meditation or contemplative thought.

Museful. Deeply thoughtful.

Pensive. Thoughtful; sad.

Philosophical. Belonging to philosophy

Platonic. Pertaining to the Greek philosopher Plato; purely spiritual.

Reflective. Meditative.

Sedate. Calm; sober· contemplative.

Speculative. Given to speculation. See *Nouns*.

Studious. Given to earnest study.

Thinking. Reviewing in mind. See *Verbs*.

Thoughtful. Given to thought; meditative.

Under consideration. In the thought of.

Wistful. Marked by earnest thought.

REFLECTION—*Phrases*.

En toute chose il faut considerer le fin [F.]. In everything one must consider the end.

The head running upon.

The head turning upon.

The mind being on the stretch.

The mind running upon.

The mind turning upon.

Vivere est cogitare [L.]. To live is to think.

Volk der Dichter und Denker [G.]. Nation of poets and thinkers Germans.

---

re-flec'-tive. Thoughtful. Reflection-Vacancy.

re-flect'-or. Mirror. Optical Instruments.

re-flex'. A turning back. Impetus-Reaction.

re'-flex''. Image; reflexed. Advance-Retrogression, Copy-Model.

re-flex'-ion. Copy; turning backward. Copy-Model, Impetus-Reaction, Light-Darkness, Resonance-Nonresonance.

re-flex'-ive-ly. In a reflexive manner. Advance-Retrogression

ref'-lu-ence. A flowing back. Advance-Retrogression.

ref'-lu-ent. Flowing back. Advance-Retrogression.

re'-flux''. A flowing back. Advance-Retrogression, Impetus-Reaction, Increase-Decrease, River-Wind.

re-foc'-il-late. To invigorate. Weariness-Refreshment.

re-foc''-il-la'-tion. Refreshment. Strength-Weakness, Weariness-Refreshment.

re-form'. To change for the better. Betterment-Deterioration, Conversion-Reversion.

ref''-or-ma'-tion. Reform. Betterment-Deterioration.

re-form'-a-to-ry. Place for reforming young criminals. Betterment-Deterioration, School.

Re-formed'. Noting the Churches organized by Protestants in the 16th century under the direction of Zwingli and Calvin. Orthodoxy-Heterodoxy.

re-form'-er. One who advocates reform. Betterment-Deterioration.

re-found'. To put on a new basis. Conversion-Reversion.

re-frac'-tion. Deviation. Aim-Aberration, Light-Darkness, Sight-Dimsightedness.

re-frac'-to-ry. Uncontrollable. Bigotry-Apostasy, Difficulty-Facility, Insubordination-Obedience, Reprisal-Resistance.

re-frain'. To forbear. Action-Passiveness, Moderation-Selfindulgence, Quest-Evasion, Recurrence; **refrain from laughter,** Lightheartedness-Dejection; **refrain from voting,** Choice-Neutrality.

re-frain'. Something repeated. Recurrence.

re-frain'-ing. Avoiding. Quest-Evasion.

re-fresh'. To reinvigorate; to repair. Alleviation-Aggravation, Betterment-Deterioration, Heating-Cooling, Pleasurableness-Painfulness, Renovation-Relapse, Strength-Weakness, Weariness-Refreshment; **refresh the memory,** Remembrance-Forgetfulness, Weariness-Refreshment.

re-freshed'. Reinvigorated. Weariness-Refreshment.

re-fresh'-ing. Pleasant. Pleasurableness-Painfulness, Sensuality-Suffering.

re-fresh'-ment. That which refreshes. Alleviation-Aggravation, Betterment-Deterioration, Nutriment-Excretion, Pleasure-Pain, Renovation-Relapse, Sensuality-Suffering.

re'-frig'-er-ate. To cool. Heating-Cooling.

re-frig''-er-a'-tion. A cooling. Feeling-Insensibility, Heating-Cooling.

re-frig'-er-a''-tor. A cooler. Oven-Refrigerator.

re-frig'-er-a-to''-ry. Cooling. Oven-Refrigerator

reft. Stolen away. Union-Disunion.

ref'-uge. Shelter. Escape, Refuge-Pitfall, Security-Insecurity.

REFUGE—PITFALL.

Anchor. An iron instrument which keeps a floating vessel from drifting.

Anchorage. A place suitable for anchoring vessels.

Ark. That which preserves and keeps in safety; or refuge from floods.

Asylum. A place of refuge.

Ballast. Any heavy substance put in the hold of a vessel to steady it.

Breakwater. Any structure which affords protection against the waves.

Ambush. A lying in concealment in order to attack by surprise.

Bank. A shoal; a sand-bar.

Breakers. Waves broken into foam by rocks or sand-bars underneath.

Breakers ahead. Dangers ahead.

Coral reef. Limestone formations produced by the coral-polyp.

Dangerous person. One ready or likely to do harm or injury.

Death in the pot. Figurative expression for an enterprise fraught with danger.

REFUGE—PITFALL—*Continued.*

Check. That which restrains or guards from danger.
Cork jacket. A jacket used as an aid in swimming.
Covert. Something that shelters or defends.
Embankment. Any bank thrown up as a protection.
Fastness. A secure retreat.
Fort. A stronghold.
Grapline. A small anchor.
Grappling-iron. A hooked iron used to hold a vessel or other object.
Harbor. A refuge for ships.
Harbor of refuge. A place of security and shelter.
Hedge. A small anchor.
Haven. A place of anchorage for ships.
Hiding-place. A refuge.
Home. A place of peace and rest.
Jetty. Any structure intended to counteract the action of tides or currents.
Jury-mast. A temporary mast.
Keep. A stronghold.
Lee-wall. A wall to protect shipping from the wind.
Life-boat. A boat specially designed for saving lives in time of shipwreck.
Lightning-rod. A metallic conductor of electricity used as a protection against lightning.
Mainstay. A chief support or dependence.
Means of escape. Anything by which one gains safety.
Mole. A breakwater built to protect a harbor.
Parachute. An apparatus used in descending from a balloon.
Pier. A mass of masonry used as a support.
Plank. Anything that sustains or upholds.
Quay. A wharf or artificial landing-place on the shore of a harbor.
Refuge. A place or means of protection or shelter.
Refuge for the destitute. A place of safety.
Retreat. A place to which one may retire for safety.
Roadstead. A place of anchorage off shore without harbor protection.
Safeguard. That which keeps in safety.
Safety-lamp. A lamp so constructed as to prevent the ignition of gases.
Safety-valve. A valve to permit the escape of excessive steam.
Sanctuary. A place to which fugitives from justice might flee as a refuge from arrest.
Sanctum sanctorum [L.]. The Holy of Holies; hence, a place of inviolate safety.
Screen. Anything that shields against external injury or danger.
Sea-port. A harbor on the sea-coast.
Sheet-anchor. One of the large anchors of a ship.
Shelter. That which shields or protects from danger.
Shield. A defensive armor.
Stepping-stone. Any means of advance or escape.
Support. That which preserves from falling or perishing.
Swimming-belt. A belt to prevent one from sinking.
Umbrella. A shelter from the rain; a little shade.
Vent-peg. A peg for stopping a vent.
Wall. A barrier constructed for defense.
Ward. Any means of defense or protection.
Wing. A fortification; a jetty.

REFUGE—*Verbs*

Find refuge, etc.
Find safety, etc. } To be free from danger.

Firebrand. A piece of wood or other substance kindled and partly burned; a dangerous person.
Flat. A shoal; a strand.
Fly-trap. A trap for catching flies.
Goodwin Sands. Dangerous shoals about five miles off the coast of Kent, England, drifted up at the building of Tenterden Steeple, and so reported to have been caused by it.
Hornet's-nest. A figurative expression for a swarm of petty troubles.
Iron-bound coast. A rocky dangerous coast.
Latency. The condition of being concealed; hence, hidden danger.
Maelstrom. A famous whirlpool off the coast of Norway; hence, any power or influence that ruins.
Pitfall. A pit partly concealed and used as a trap.
Precipice. A very steep declivity; hence, a dangerous situation.
Quicksands. A bed of sand in which a body readily sinks of its own weight.
Reefs. Chains of rocky formation in the ocean lying at or near the water's surface.
Rocks. That which causes disaster and wreck, as reefs.
Rocks ahead. Danger.
Sands. A sand-bar; a shoal.
Sandy foundation. A place of insecure footing.
Shallows. Waters of little depth; shoals.
Shelf. A steep-sided rock or sand-bar in a body of water.
Shoals. Sand-banks or bars in shallow water.
Slippery ground. Ground on which it is difficult to stand.
Snags. Any hidden obstacles.
Snake in the grass. A snake in hiding; hence, hidden danger.
Sunken rocks. Rocks beneath the surface; hidden danger.
Sword of Damocles. Damocles's sword was suspended over his head by a single hair; hence, threatening peril.
Trap. Any means by which one falls into danger unawares.
Trap-door. A concealed door.
Ugly customer. A troublesome or dangerous person.
Volcano. Typical of uncertain and extreme peril.
Washout. Excavation made by water.
Wolf at the door. Figurative expression for poverty and want.

PITFALL—*Phrases.*

Latet anguis in herba [L.]. A snake lies hidden in the grass. [Virgil, Eclogues, iii, 93.]
Le chat qui dort [F.]. The sleeping cat.
Proximus ardet Ucalegon [L.]. [The house of] Ucalegon burns near at hand. [Virgil, Æneid, ii, 312.]

REFUGE—VERBS—*Continued.*

Seek refuge.
Seek safety. } To flee from danger.
Take refuge. To find refuge in some place.
Throw oneself into the arms of. To entrust oneself to the protection of.

REFUGE—*Phrases.*

Bibere venenum in auro [L.]. To drink poison from a golden cup.
Valet anchora virtus [L.]. Virtue is an effectual anchor.

---

ref''-u-gee'. One who flees. ESCAPE, QUEST-EVASION, WAYFARER-SEAFARER.
re-ful'-gence. Splendor. LIGHT-DARKNESS.
re-ful'-gent. Shining. LIGHT-DARKNESS.
re-fund'. To pay back. SETTLEMENT-DEFAULT.
re-furb'-ish. To brighten anew. PREPARATION-NON-PREPARATION.
re-fu'-sal. Act of refusing; option. ASSERTION-DENIAL, BUYING-SALE, CHOICE-NEUTRALITY, PROFFER-REFUSAL, READINESS-RELUCTANCE.
ref'-use. Worthless stuff. INCREMENT-REMNANT, USEFULNESS-USELESSNESS.
re-fuse'. To decline. ASSERTION-DENIAL, CONSEQUENCE-INSIGNIFICANCE, PROFFER-REFUSAL, READINESS-RELUCTANCE; **refuse assent,** ASSENT-DISSENT, PROFFER-REFUSAL; **refuse to associate with,** SOCIABILITY-PRIVACY; **refuse to believe,** CREDULOUSNESS-SKEPTICISM, FAITH-MISGIVING; **refuse to hear,** CAREFULNESS-CARELESSNESS.

re-fused'. Denied. PROFFER-REFUSAL.
re-fu'-sing. Denying. PROFFER-REFUSAL.
re-fu'-ta-ble. Capable of being refuted. PROOF-DISPROOF.
ref''-u-ta'-tion. Disproof. EVIDENCE-COUNTEREVIDENCE, PROOF-DISPROOF.
re-fute'. To disprove. PROOF-DISPROOF.
re-gain'. To gain again. GAIN-LOSS; **regain breath,** WEARINESS-REFRESHMENT.
re'-gal. Royal. RULE-LICENSE.
re-gale'. Feast; to delight. ENTERTAINMENT-WEARINESS, NUTRIMENT-EXCRETION, PLEASURABLENESS-PAINFULNESS, SENSUALITY-SUFFERING, WEARINESS-REFRESHMENT.
re-gale'-ment. Refreshment. NUTRIMENT-EXCRETION, WEARINESS-REFRESHMENT.
re-ga'-li-a. Royal insignia. SCEPTER.
re-gal'-i-ty. Sovereignty. RULE-LICENSE.

re-gard′. Reference; esteem. APPROVAL-DISAPPROVAL, CONNECTION - INDEPENDENCE, DECISION - MISJUDGMENT, HEED-DISREGARD, LOVE-HATE, REGARD-DISRESPECT, REPUTATION-DISCREDIT, SIGHT-BLINDNESS; **have regard to,** HEED-DISREGARD; **merit regard,** CONSEQUENCE-INSIGNIFICANCE; **pay regard to,** FAITH-MISGIVING, REPUTATION - DISCREDIT; **regard as,** FAITH-MISGIVING.

REGARD—DISRESPECT.

Admiration. Wonder combined with approbation.
Approbation. Expression of approval or satisfaction with.
Attention. An act of courtesy or gallantry.
Consideration. Thoughtful and kindly feeling or treatment.
Courtesy, etc. Politeness originating in kindliness and exercised habitually. See POLITENESS.
Deference. Respectful yielding, as to another's opinion, wishes, or judgment.
Devoirs [F.]. Regards or respect.
Devotion, etc. Strong attachment expressing itself in earnest service. See GODLINESS.
Duty. An act of respect.
Egards [F.]. Regards; respects.
Esteem. Favorable opinion, as that based on moral worth.
Estimation. An opinion or judgment of the value or worth of.
Fealty. Devoted fidelity.
Homage. Respect exhibited by outward action; a promise to be another's man.
Honor. Consideration due or paid on account of some worth or excellence
Obsequiousness. Slavish submission. See PRESUMPTION-OBSEQUIOUSNESS.
Regard. Particular attention or notice from a feeling of interest.
Regards. Courteous greeting or message.
Respect. A just regard for and appreciation of the worth of others.
Respects. Expression of consideration, esteem, or compliment.
Reverence. A feeling of profound respect, often mingled with awe and affection.
Veneration. The highest degree of respect and reverence.

REGARD—*Associated Nouns.*

Bow. An inclination of the body or head forward and downward, as in courtesy.
Genuflexion. A bending of the knee, as an act of courtesy.
Kneeling. A falling on the knees.
Kow-tow [Chinese]. A Chinese form of obeisance in which an inferior kneels and touches the ground with his forehead.
Obeisance. Bowing or bending of the knee in courtesy.
Presenting arms. Saluting by holding weapons perpendicularly in front of the body.
Prostration. The act of casting oneself down in humility or reverence.
Salaam. An Oriental salutation performed by bowing the head and body very low, with the palm of the right hand on the forehead.
Salute. A display of military, naval, or other official honors out of respect for a person, a nation, a day, etc.

REGARD—*Verbs.*

Awe. To impress with reverential fear.
Bear respect for. To hold in esteem; honor.
Bend the knee to. To do obeisance to.
Bow to. To show respect for.
Command respect. To stand high in public estimation.
Dazzle. To bewilder or charm, as with brilliant prospects.
Defer to. To submit to the opinion of another, or to authority.
Do homage to. To treat with reverential regard.
Do honor to. To confer distinction upon.
Do the honors. To act as host or hostess.
Entertain respect for. To hold in the mind with favor.
Esteem, etc. To regard as having worth or excellence. See APPROVAL.
Fall down before. To prostrate oneself in worship.
Hail. To give greeting to; salute.
Hallow. To honor as sacred.
Hold in reverence. To worship; venerate.
Honor. To treat with deference and submission.
Impose. To lay hands on, as in confirmation.
Inspire respect. To call forth or prompt respect for.
Keep one's distance. To refrain from familiarity; stand aloof.
Kiss the hem of one's garment. To regard with the greatest reverence.
Kneel to. To make obeisance; worship.
Look up to. To respect; regard with deference.
Make room. To open a space, way, or passage.
Observe due decorum. To treat with respect or attention.
Overawe. To restrain by fear or by superior influence.

Discourtesy. Rudeness of behavior or language; incivility. See POLITENESS-IMPOLITENESS.
Disesteem. }
Disestimation. } Lack of esteem; inclination to dislike.
Dishonor. Want or loss of honor; disgrace.
Disparagement, etc. A lessening of value or excellence. See ADULATION-DISPARAGEMENT, APPROVAL-DISAPPROVAL.
Disrespect. Want of respect; discourtesy.
Irreverence. Want of veneration or reverence.
Vilipendency. Disesteem.

DISRESPECT—*Nouns of Expression.*

Affront. An open insult or indignity.
Contumely. An act or statement exhibiting haughtiness and contempt. "The oppressor's wrong, the proud man's contumely." [Shakespeare, *Hamlet*, III, i.]
Derision. Contempt shown by laughter.
Fling. A sarcastic expression.
Flout. A mocking or jeering.
Gibe. An expression of sarcasm and ridicule.
Gleek. A jesting or jeering.
Hiss. A manifestation of contempt and disapproval.
Hoot. A cry uttered in derision.
Indignity. An act or action designed to abase.
Insult. An expression of insolence or discourtesy.
Irony, etc. Sarcasm. See SOCIETY-DERISION.
Irrision. A laughing at some one.
Jeer. A taunting and derisive word or speech.
Mockery. A speech or action of contempt or scorn.
Neglect. Omission to pay due attention or civility.
Outrage. A gross insult.
Practical joking. Joking involving some rude action.
Quip. A sarcastic taunt or remark.
Sarcasm. A scornful or taunting expression.
Scoff. }
Scoffing. } An expression of contempt, mockery, or ridicule.
Scurrility. Low or vile abusiveness.
Sibilation. A hissing sound, uttered in contempt.
Slap in the face. A direct rebuff or insult.
Slight. Any contemptuous or neglectful action.
Sneer. A grimace of contempt or derision.
Spretæ injuria formæ [L.]. The insult of slighted beauty. [Virgil, *Æneid,* i, 27.]
Superciliousness, etc. Conduct or action showing haughty and careless contempt; raising the eyebrows. See REGARD-SCORN.
Taunt. A bitterly sarcastic speech or remark.
Wipe. A sarcastic remark.

DISRESPECT—*Verbs.*

Affront. To insult openly; treat with insolence.
Be discourteous, etc. To be impolite or rude. See POLITENESS-IMPOLITENESS.
Be disrespectful, etc. To be wanting in respect; be uncivil. See *Adjectives.*
Bite the thumb. To make a gesture of contempt; defy.
Browbeat. To daunt or depress by haughty and stern looks.
Burlesque, etc. To represent mockingly or ludicrously. See SOCIETY-DERISION.
Call names. To use opprobrious epithets to.
Deride. To make the object of mockery or ridicule.
Desecrate. To divert from a sacred to a common use.
Dishonor. To subject to indignities; insult.
Disparage, etc. To speak slightingly of one. See APPROVAL-DISAPPROVAL.
Disregard. To slight as unworthy of regard or notice.
Drag through the mud. To disgrace one.
Fleer. To jeer at; treat disrespectfully.
Fling dirt. To make sneering remarks.
Flout. To mock; treat with contempt.
Fool. To make a fool of; impose upon.
Gibe. To cast reproaches and sneering expressions at.
Gird. To lash with sneers or reproaches.
Gleek. To banter; jeer at.
Have a fling at. To hurl a severe or contemptuous remark.
Have in derision. To regard with scorn.
Hiss. To express contempt for by hissing.

REGARD—DISRESPECT—*Continued.*

REGARD—Verbs—*Continued.*

Pay attention to. To be courteous to; court.
Pay homage to. To do reverence to.
Pay respect to, etc. To have deferential regard for. See *Nouns.*
Pay tribute to. To render what is due to worth, affection, or duty
Present arms. To show a soldier-like respect.
Prostrate oneself. To bow in humble reverence.
Regard. To treat as something of peculiar value, sanctity, or the like.
Render honor to. To show distinction or respect toward.
Respect. To view or consider with some degree of reverence.
Revere. To regard with worshipful reverence.
Reverence. To regard with respect and affection mingled with fear.
Salute. To accost in welcome or reverence.
Show courtesy, etc. To treat with courtesy. See POLITENESS.
Stand upon ceremony. To regard formalities; not to be familiar or bold.
Think much of it. To esteem it highly.
Venerate. To regard with the highest degree of respect and reverence.
Worship, etc. To reverence with supreme respect and veneration. See DEVOTION.

REGARD—*Adjectives.*

Bare-headed. Uncovered from respect.
Cap in hand. Obsequiously; submissively.
Ceremonious. Formally respectful.
Decorous. Suitable for the occasion; becoming.
Deferential. Respectful.
Emeritus [L.]. Retired from active service, but retained in an honorary position.
In deference to. With respectful submission.
In high esteem. }
In high estimation. } Regarded as having worth or excellence.
Obsequious. Promptly obedient or submissive; compliant.
On one's knees. Worshipful.
Prostrate, etc. To bow in humble reverence. See OBSEQUIOUSNESS.
Respected, etc. Looked upon with respect. See *Verbs.*
Respectful. Marked by outward civility; courteous.
Respecting, etc. Having regard for. See *Verbs.*
Reverential. Expressing reverence.
Saving your grace. }
Saving your presence. } Excepting those present.
Time-honored. Observed or honored from former times.
Venerable. Worthy of the highest respect.
With all respect. }
With due respect. } With a feeling of regard or attention; respectfully.
With the highest respect. }

REGARD—*Interjections.*

All hail!
Esto perpetua [L.]. Let it [the country] endure forever. [Blackstone, I, 145.]
Hail!
May your shadow never be less!
Salva sit reverentia [L.]. May your regard be preserved.

DISRESPECT—Adjectives—*Continued from Column 2.*

Supercilious, etc. Exhibiting haughty contempt or indifference. See REGARD-SCORN.
Unenvied. Exempt from the envy of others.
Unregarded. Slighted, deemed unworthy of notice.
Unrespected. Not honored or esteemed.
Unsaluted. Not greeted.
Unworshiped. Not worshiped or adored.

DISRESPECT—*Adverbs.*

Disrespectfully, etc. In a disrespectful manner. See *Adjectives.*

SCORN.

Byword. A phrase person, etc., that has become an object of derision.
Contempt. The feeling with which one regards that which is esteemed mean, vile, or worthless.
Contemptuousness, etc. Manifestation of contempt; haughtiness; insolence. See *Adjectives.*
Contumely. Insulting rudeness in speech or manner.
Derision, etc. Contempt shown by laughter. See REGARD-DISRESPECT

Hold in derision. To treat scornfully.
Hold in disrespect, etc. To look upon contemptuously. See REGARD-SCORN.
Hoot. To cry or shout in contempt.
Indulge in personalities. To give free course to personal remarks.
Insult. To treat with indignity or insolence.
Jeer. To speak in a deriding, mocking manner.
Laugh at. To make fun of.
Laugh in one's sleeve. To laugh secretly, or so as not to be observed.
Laugh to scorn, etc. To treat with mockery and contempt. See REGARD-SCORN.
Lead one a dance. To cause to follow aimlessly.
Make a fool of. To render ridiculous.
Make an April fool of. To sportively impose upon on the first of April.
Make faces. To distort the countenance; mock.
Make game of. To make sport of; mock.
Make mouths. To make wry faces, as in derision.
Misprize. To slight or undervalue.
Mob. To attack in a disorderly crowd.
Mock. To laugh at; mimic in contempt.
Niggle. Trifle with; mock.
Outrage. To treat with violence; do violence in words.
Overlook. To fail to see or observe; slight.
Pass by. To disregard; neglect.
Play a practical joke. To have fun with.
Pluck by the beard. To treat rudely or discourteously.
Point at. To treat with scorn by directing attention to.
Push aside. To hasten unceremoniously.
Ridicule. To laugh at mockingly or disparagingly.
Roast. To banter severely.
Run the rig upon. To do something strange and unbecoming.
Scoff. To treat with ridicule or contempt.
Scout. To sneer at; reject disdainfully.
Set at naught. To treat as of no account.
Set down. To humiliate.
Slight. To manifest intentional neglect or disregard of
Smoke. To ridicule to the face; quiz.
Sneer. To speak or utter with contempt.
Snigger. To laugh slyly; laugh in one's sleeve.
Speak slightingly of. To converse about in a contemptuous manner.
Take by the beard. To seize in contempt.
Tar and feather. To smear with tar and cover with feathers, as a punishment or an indignity.
Taunt. To reproach with severe or insulting words.
Throw dirt. To abuse or slander.
Toss in a blanket. To make sport of.
Treat with disrespect, etc. To act contemptuously toward.
Trifle with. To play the fool with; mock.
Turn into ridicule. To make the subject of satirical remarks.
Turn one's back upon. To treat with contempt; slight.
Twit. To annoy by reminding of something unpleasant.
Vilipend. To value lightly; slight.

DISRESPECT—*Adjectives.*

Aweless. Void of respectful fear.
Contumelious. Rude and sarcastic in speech.
Derisive. Mocking; ridiculing.
Disparaging, etc. Belittling. See ADULATION-DISPARAGEMENT.
Disregarded. Intentional neglect.
Disrespectful. Wanting in respect.
Insulting, etc. Conveying an insult. See *Verbs.*
Irreverent. Wanting in respect to superiors.
Rude. Characterized by rough discourtesy; impolite.
Sarcastic. Bitterly ironical; taunting.
Scurrile. }
Scurrilous. } Grossly offensive or vulgar.

(Continued on Column 1.)

REGARD—SCORN.

Despiciency. A looking down; despection.
Despisal. A despising; contempt.
Despisedness. State of being despised.
Disdain. A blended feeling of superiority and dislike; proud contempt.
Scorn. That disdain which springs from the opinion of the utter meanness and unworthiness of the object.
Scornful eye. A look expressing scorn or disdain.
Slight. The manifestation of a moderate degree of contempt, as by neglect or oversight.

REGARD—SCORN—*Continued.*

Smile of contempt. A sneer.
Sneer. The manifestation of contempt by turning up the nose or laughing ironically.
Sovereign contempt. The utmost contempt.
Spurn. Disdainful rejection; contemptuous treatment.
Vilipendency. Slight; disparagement.

SCORN—*Verbs.*

Care nothing for. To disregard.
Contemn. To look upon as mean and despicable.
Curl up one's lip. To express dislike for.
Damn with faint praise. To condemn by giving only slight praise. [Pope, *Prologue to Satires*, 201.]
Despise. To look down upon with scorn.
Disdain. To recoil from with pride or scorn.
Disregard. To neglect to take notice of; slight.
Esteem of small or no account. To be regarded as unworthy.
Esteem slightly. To look upon negligently.
Feel contempt for. To despise.
Fling to the winds, etc. To disregard. See CHOICE-REJECTION.
Flout. To treat with contempt; jeer.
Hiss. To express contempt by hisses; condemn by hissing.
Hold cheap. To regard as unworthy.
Hold in contempt. } To treat as mean, vile, or worthless.
Hold in disrespect. }
Hold up to scorn. To expose to ridicule.
Hoot. To cry or shout in contempt.
Kick. To show hostility; spurn.
Laugh at, etc. To make an object of ridicule; deride. See REGARD-DISRESPECT.
Laugh in one's sleeve. To be full of inward merriment while outwardly demure.
Laugh to scorn. To treat with mockery and contempt.
Look down upon. To treat with indifference or contempt.
Make light of. To treat as of little consequence; slight.
Not care a straw, etc. To look upon as a mere trifle. See CONSEQUENCE-INSIGNIFICANCE.
Not mind. To regard as of no consequence.
Pass by, etc. To slight. See CAREFULNESS-CARELESSNESS.
Point the finger of scorn. To expose to ridicule or shame.
Pooh-pooh. To treat with derision or contempt; make light of.
Scoff at. To treat with insolent scorn.
Scorn. To treat as unworthy or contemptible.
Scout. To reject disdainfully; treat with contempt.
Send away with a flea in the ear. To despatch with an unexpected reply or unwelcome hint.
Set at naught. To contemn; despise.
Set no more by. To pay no attention to.
Shrug one's shoulders. To draw up the shoulders by way of expressing dislike, etc.

Slight. To omit due respect for.
Snap one's fingers at. To express scorn for.
Sneer at. To utter with a contemptuous expression.
Sneeze at. To despise; treat lightly.
Spurn. To treat with scornful rejection.
Take no account of. To take no notice of.
Think nothing of. To regard as unworthy.
Think small beer of. To hold in contempt.
Toss the head. To throw up the head in contempt.
Traiter de haut en bas [F.] To drag down in estimation; treat with contempt.
Trample under foot. } To treat with contempt.
Trample upon. }
Tread upon. To set the foot on in contempt.
Turn a cold shoulder upon. } To reject or disregard
Turn one's back upon. }
Turn up one's nose at. To express contempt for.
Underestimate, etc. To set too low a value on. See OVERVALUATION-UNDERVALUATION.
View with a scornful eye. To express scorn for.
Whistle at. To regard as unworthy.

SCORN—*Adjectives.*

Bumptious. Full of offensive self-conceit.
Cavalier. Haughty; slighting; supercilious.
Contemptible. Worthy of scorn or disdain.
Contemptuous. Showing contempt or disdain.
Contumelious. Haughtily reproachful; insolent.
Cynical. Snarling; having the qualities of a surly dog.
Derisive. Mocking; ridiculing.
Despicable. That should be despised; contemptible.
Despised, etc. Considered as mean or worthless. See *Verbs.*
Disdainful. Full of disdain; scornful.
Downtrodden. Abused by superior power; treated with contempt.
Haughty. Proud and disdainful.
Pitiable. } Contemptible; paltry. See CONSEQUENCE-INSIGNIFI-
Pitiful, etc. } CANCE.
Scornful. Full of scorn or contempt.
Supercilious. Overbearing; arrogant.
Unenvied. Contemptible.
Withering. Blighting.

SCORN—*Adverbs.*

Contemptuously, etc. With scorn or disdain. See *Adjectives.*

SCORN—*Interjections.*

A fig for, etc. See CONSEQUENCE-INSIGNIFICANCE; **away with! bah! fiddle-de-dee! hang it! never mind!**

---

re-gard′-ful. Having regard. CAREFULNESS-CARELESSNESS, HEED-DISREGARD.
re-gard′-less. Lacking regard. HEED-DISREGARD, SENSITIVENESS-APATHY.
re-gards′. Esteem. POLITENESS-IMPOLITENESS, REGARD-DISRESPECT.
re-gat′-ta. Boat-race. ENTERTAINMENT-WEARINESS, STRIFE-PEACE.
re′-ge-late. To unite by freezing again. HEATING-COOLING.
regem aut fatuum nasci oportet, aut [L.] (rī′-jem aut fat′-yu-um nas′-sai op-or′-tet, aut). It behooves one to be born either king or fool. SAGACITY-INCAPACITY.
re′-gen-cy. Government of a regent. COMMISSION-ABROGATION.
re-gen′-er-a-cy. Regeneration. RENOVATION-RELAPSE.
re-gen′-er-ate. To reproduce; reformed. GODLINESS-UNGODLINESS, RENEWAL, RENOVATION-RELAPSE.
re-gen′-er-a″-ted. Born again. GODLINESS-UNGODLINESS.
re-gen″-er-a′-tion. State of being regenerated. DIVINITY, GODLINESS-UNGODLINESS, RENEWAL, RENOVATION-RELAPSE; **baptismal regeneration,** CEREMONIAL.
re-gen′-e-sis. Renewal. RENEWAL, RENOVATION-RELAPSE.

re′-gent. A kind of ruler. CHIEF-UNDERLING, PRESIDENT-MEMBER, REPRESENTATIVE.
re′-gent-ship. The office of a regent. COMMISSION-ABROGATION.
regibus esse manus, an nescis longas [L.] (rej′-i-bus es′-sî mê′-nus, an nes′-sis lon′-gas). Do you not know that kings have far-reaching hands? RULE-LICENSE.
reg′-i-cide. Killing of a king. LIFE-KILLING.
ré″-gime′. Government. CONDITION-SITUATION, CONDUCT, RULE-LICENSE.
reg′-i-men. Diet. NUTRIMENT-EXCRETION, REMEDY-BANE.
reg′-i-ment. Body of soldiers. BELLIGERENT, GATHERING-SCATTERING.
reg″-i-men′-tals. Uniform. DRESS-UNDRESS.
re′-gion. District. EXTENSION-DISTRICT.
reg′-is-ter. Record. CHRONOLOGY-ANACHRONISM, MARK-OBLITERATION, ORGANIZATION-DISORGANIZATION, RECORD, RECORDER.
reg′-is-trar. Recorder. RECORDER.
reg′-is-tra-ry. A registrar. RECORDER.
reg″-is-tra′-tion. Enrolment. MARK-OBLITERATION.
reg′-is-try. A register. CHRONOLOGY-ANACHRONISM, MARK-OBLITERATION.
règle, en [F.] (rêgl, an·). According to rule. DUENESS-UNDUENESS.

reg'-let. A strip used for making space between lines in printing. WRITING-PRINTING.

reg'-nant. Reigning. DOMINANCE-IMPOTENCE, RULE-LICENSE.

regni, anno [L.] (reg'-nai, an'-no). In the year of the reign. DURATION-NEVERNESS.

re-gorge'. To vomit. TAKING-RESTITUTION.

re-grade'. To deteriorate. ADVANCE-RETROGRESSION.

re-grate'. To buy extensively. HOLDING-EXEMPTION.

re-gra'-tor. Huckster. DEALER.

re'-gress. A turning back. ADVANCE-RETROGRESSION.

re-gres'-sion. Backward movement. ADVANCE-RETROGRESSION, CONVERSION-REVERSION.

re-gress'-ive. Returning. ADVANCE-RETROGRESSION.

re-gret'. Sorrow. CONTENTEDNESS-DISCONTENTEDNESS, CONTENTEDNESS-REGRET, REPENTANCE-OBDURACY.

re-gret'-ful. Causing regret. CONTENTEDNESS-DISCONTENTEDNESS, CONTENTEDNESS-REGRET, DISCONTENTMENT.

re-gret'-ta-ble. Causing regret. CONTENTEDNESS-REGRET.

re-gret'-ted. Sorry for. **To be regretted,** CONTENTEDNESS-REGRET.

re-gret'-ting. Sorrowing. CONTENTEDNESS-REGRET.

re-growth'. New growth. RENEWAL, RENOVATION-RELAPSE.

re-guer'-don. To reward. RECOMPENSE-PUNITION.

reg'-u-lar. Uniform. CONVENTIONALITY-UNCONVENTIONALITY, ENTIRETY-DEFICIENCY, HABIT-DESUETUDE, NATURE-ART, ORGANIZATION-DISORGANIZATION, PERIODICITY-IRREGULARITY, PROPORTION-DEFORMITY, REGULARITY-IRREGULARITY, UNIFORMITY-MULTIFORMITY; **by regular intervals,** REGULARITY-IRREGULARITY; **regular return,** PERIODICITY-IRREGULARITY.

reg''-u-lar'-i-ty. Evenness. NATURE-ART, PERIODICITY-IRREGULARITY, REGULARITY-IRREGULARITY, UNIFORMITY-DIVERSITY, UNIFORMITY-MULTIFORMITY.

REGULARITY—IRREGULARITY.

Arrangement. The state of being in definite or proper order.
Array. Proper or regular arrangements.
Course. The state of being in regular sequence.
Discipline. Systematic training or subjection to authority.
Disposition. The act of arranging or ordering.
Economy. The practical adjustment or organization of affairs, etc.
Even tenor. A regular course or manner of progress.
Gradation. Orderly or continuous succession or arrangement.
Lucidus ordo [L.]. Lucid arrangement.
Method. A general and established way or proceeding.
Music of the spheres. A harmony produced by the movements of the heavenly bodies, audible to the gods only. "There's not the smallest orb which thou behold'st, but in his motion like an angel sings." [Shakespeare, *Merchant of Venice*, V, 1.]
Order. Arrangement according to some definite method.
Orderliness, etc. The state of being in order. See *Adjectives.*
Place, etc. Position in relative order. See STATION.
Progression. A proceeding in course or order.
Rank. A series of objects arranged in a line or row.
Regularity. The state of being according to rule.
Routine. A detailed method of procedure.
Series, etc. The state of being arranged in a given order. See CONTINUITY.
Subordination. Habitual submission to an authority.
Symmetry. Due arrangement or balancing of the parts or elements of a whole.
System. Arrangement in orderly combination.
Uniformity. Sameness; regularity.

REGULARITY—*Verbs.*

Arrange itself. To come into an orderly state.
Become in order.⎫
Be in order.⎭ To be in succession. See *Adjectives.*
Draw up. Lo put in array.
Fall in. To come into order, as a soldier falls into line.
Fall into one's place.⎫
Fall into rank.⎭ To get into a regular order.
Form. To mold; put in definite regular form.
Place itself. To arrange, or fall into position.
Rally round. To arrange around.
Range itself.⎫
Take one's place.⎬ To take one's place in a regular order.
Take rank.⎭

REGULARITY—*Adjectives.*

Arranged, etc. According to some definite order. See ORGANIZATION.
Businesslike. Prompt and orderly.
Correct. Exact; perfectly in order.
En règle [F.]. In order.
In apple-pie order. In perfect order
In its proper place.⎫
In order.⎭ In regular arrangement.
In trim. In order.
Methodical. According to method; orderly
Neat. Well-arranged.
Orderly. Having care for arrangement and method.
Regular. According to rule.
Shipshape. Well-arranged; in good order.

Complexity.⎫ The state or quality of being complex. See *Adjectives.*
Complexness, etc.⎭
Complication. The act, process, or result of being complicated.
Concordia discors [L.]. Discordant harmony and wit. [Horace, *Epistles*, I, xii, 19.]
Confusedness, etc. The state of being confused. See *Adjectives.*
Confusion. A disorderly mixture.
Convulsion. An irregular and violent commotion.
Derangement, etc. Disorder; confusion. See ORGANIZATION.
Disarray. Loss of regular order.
Discord. Variance or strife due to lack of agreement. See HARMONY-DISCORD.
Disturbance. A disordered condition.
Disunion. A condition of disagreement.
Embroilment. Disturbance; strife.
Entanglement. The state of being entangled.
Ferment. Excitement or agitation. See AGITATION.
Huddle. A confused crowd or collection.
Implication. An entanglement.
Intricacy. The quality of being entangled or perplexed.
Intrication. Entanglement.
Involution. The state of being involved or rolled up.
Irregularity. Lack of conformity, rule, or method.
Jumble. Disorder.
Litter. A state of disorder.
Lumber. Piled up or disordered.
Mere mixture. A collection of things without connection.
Mess. A state of disorder.
Muddle. A mixed or confused condition.
Network. An entanglement.
Omnium gatherum [L.]. A mixture of all things.
Perplexity. The quality of being intricate or complicated.
Pother. An excitement mingled with confusion.
Pudder. Pother.
Raveling. An entanglement.
Riot. A tumultuous disturbance of the public peace.
Row. A noisy quarrel.
Rudis indigestaque moles [L.]. A rude undigested mass. [Ovid, *Metamorphoses*, i, 7.]
Rumpus. A row.
Saturnalia. A season of general license and revelry.
Scramble. Any disorderly performance.
Slattern. A woman, negligent and slovenly in dress.
Sleave. Knotted or matted silk.
Slut. A slovenly woman.
Stour. A battle or conflict.
To-do. Confusion or bustle.
Trouble. A state of distress or perplexity.
Tumult. The commotion, disturbance, or agitation of a multitude.
Turmoil. Confused motion.
Untidiness, etc. State of being untidy. See *Adjectives.*
Uproar. Violent disturbance and clamor.
Whirlwind. A violent wind-storm. See RIVER-WIND.
Wilderness. A growth of rank and wild vegetation.

IRREGULARITY—*Denotations.*

Anarchism. The theory that teaches a state of political and social confusion.
Anarchy. Absence or utter disregard of government.

REGULARITY—IRREGULARITY—*Continued.*

REGULARITY—ADJECTIVES—*Continued.*

Symmetrical.   Well-ordered; in due balancing arrangement.
Systematic.   Pertaining to orderly combination or arrangement.
Tidy.   Neat; well-arranged.
Unconfused, etc.   Not disordered.   See ORGANIZATION.
Uniform.   Harmonious; well-ordered.
Well-regulated.   Well-ordered.

REGULARITY—*Adverbs, etc.*

At stated periods, etc.   In due recurrent order; periodically.   See PERIODICITY.
By clockwork.   Regularly.
By regular gradations. ⎫
By regular intervals. ⎬ According to some plan or arrangement.
By regular stages. ⎥
By regular steps. ⎭
Gradatim [L.].   Step by step.
In its turn.   Successively.
In order.   Regularly.
In turn.   Successively.
Methodically, etc.   In an orderly manner.   See *Adjectives.*
Seriatim [L.]. ⎫
Step by step. ⎭ In order.

REGULARITY—*Phrases.*

Natura non facit saltum [L.].   Nature makes no leaps.   [Leibnitz.]

IRREGULARITY—ADJECTIVES—*Continued from Column 2.*

Inextricable.   Involved in such a manner as to make disentanglement difficult.
Intricate.   Complicated; complex.
Involved.   Intricate; entangled.
Irreducible.   Not to be restored to normal order or condition.
Irregular.   Out of order.
Knotted.   Difficult to loosen; intricately intertwined.
Orderless.   Out of order; confused; disordered.
Out of gear. ⎫
Out of joint. ⎬
Out of order. ⎥ Irregular.
Out of place. ⎭
Out of sorts.   Ill-humored; indisposed.
Perplexed.   Confused; complicated; difficult to unravel.
Promiscuous.   Consisting of parts confusedly mingled.
Raveled.   Intricately and confusedly involved.
Riotous, etc.   Pertaining to turbulent and boisterous conduct.   See TURBULENCE.
Shapeless, etc.   Chaotic; formless.   See FORM.
Slovenly.   Disorderly in dress.
Straggling.   Striving; struggling.
Tangled.   Intertwined in a confused mass.
Topsy-turvy, etc.   Disordered; confused; upside down.   See REVERSAL.
Troublous.   Tumultuous.
Unarranged, etc.   Disordered.   See ORGANIZATION.
Unmethodical.   Without method.
Unsymmetric.   Out of harmonious proportion.
Unsystematic.   Out of orderly arrangement and combination.
Untidy.   Lacking tidiness.

IRREGULARITY—*Adverbs, etc.*

At cross-purposes.   In an antagonistic manner.
At sixes and sevens.   In confusion and disorder.
By fits and snatches.   Disjointedly.
By starts.   Irregularly.
Harum-scarum.   In extreme disorder and confusion.
Helter-skelter.   With disorderly haste.
Higgledy-piggledy.   In a confused or disordered state.
In a ferment.   In a state of confusion or uproar.
Irregularly, etc.   In a confused manner.   See *Adjectives.*
Pell-mell.   Confusedly; helter-skelter.
Upside down, etc.   Topsy-turvy.   See REVERSAL.

IRREGULARITY—*Phrases.*

Chaos is come again.   Original confusion has come again.
Hysteron proteron [Gr.].   The last first.
The cart before the horse.   In reverse order.

IRREGULARITY—DENOTATIONS—*Continued.*

Anomaly, etc.   Anything that deviates from a rule, type, or form.   See CONVENTIONALITY.
Babel.   The tower during the building of which occurred the confusion of tongues.
Cahotage [F.].   The jolting of a carriage.
Chaos.   The first state of the universe.
Disjecta membra [L.].   Scattered parts.   [Horace, *Satires*, I, iv, 62.]
Farrago.   A confused mixture.
Fracas.   A noisy confused tumult.
Hash.   A mixture made up of material used before.
Hodge-podge. ⎫
Hotch-pot. ⎬ A commixture of property to secure an equitable
Hotch-potch. ⎭ division; any confused mixture.
Imbroglio.   A troublesome complication of affairs.
Jungle.   A tangled or impenetrable swamp.
Knot.   An intertwining of the parts of one or more ropes, cords, etc.
Labyrinth.   A place full of windings.
Mash.   A mass of something beaten into a soft state.
Medley.   A composition of different songs or parts of songs.
Mêlée [F.].   A confused fight.

IRREGULARITY—*Figurative Nouns.*

All the fat in the fire.   A foolish step that has been taken from which results must follow.
Bear-garden.   A place of disorder and tumult.
Bedlam broke loose.   A scene of uproar and wild madness.
Bull in a china shop.   A state of great confusion.
Confusion worse confounded.   The greatest confusion.
Devil to pay.   Serious or unforeseen perplexity.
Diable à quatre [F.].   The very devil.
Donnybrook Fair.   A village in Ireland noted for its good-natured rioting at the annual fair held there.
Fortuitous concourse of atoms.   Accidental and unexpected combination of atoms.
Gordian knot.   The knot tied by Gordius and severed by Alexander the Great to win Asia; any perplexing tangle.
Hell broke loose.   Great confusion.
Most admired disorder.   The greatest confusion.
Pretty kettle of fish.   A confused and disordered state of affairs.
Pretty piece of business.   An ironical way of saying a poor or confused work.
Pretty piece of work.   A confusion.
Rough and tumble.   A confused or disordered state.
Spill and pelt.   A tumbling and rolling together.
Tangled skein.   A very confused and disordered mass, like a tangled skein of silk.
Wheels within wheels.   A complication of circumstances.

IRREGULARITY—*Verbs.*

Be disorderly, etc.   To be confused.   See *Adjectives.*
Derange, etc.   To put in disorder.   See ORGANIZATION.
Ferment.   To stir; agitate.
Play at cross-purposes.   To work with conflicting purposes.
Put out of order.   To confuse.
Ravel, etc.   To become diffused; disordered.   See CROSSING.
Ruffle.   To make disordered.
Rumple.   To ruffle; wrinkle.

IRREGULARITY—*Adjectives.*

Anarchical.   Lawless; confused; disordered.
Anomalous, etc.   Irregular; out of regular matter.   See CONVENTIONALITY.
Chaotic.   Like chaos; disordered; jumbled.
Complex.   Consisting of various parts; involved.
Complexed.   Confused.
Complicated.   Woven together.
Confused.   Disordered; indiscriminately mixed.
Deranged, etc.   Put out of order.   See ORGANIZATION.
Desultory.   Incoherent; not connected.
Disjointed.   Out of proper order or sequence.
Dislocated.   Disordered.
Disorderly.   Out of the normal or regular way.
Entangled.   Confused so as to make extrication difficult.
Immethodical.   Out of order.
Indiscriminate.   Confused; mingled.

(*Continued on Column 1.*)

---

reg'-u-lars.   Standing army.   BELLIGERENT.
reg'-u-late.   To control.   HARMONY-DISCORD, MANAGEMENT, ORGANIZATION-DISORGANIZATION.

reg"-u-la'-tion.   Rule.   LAW-LAWLESSNESS, PRECEPT.
re-gur'-gi-tate.   To pour back.   ADVANCE-RETROGRESSION, RIVER-WIND, TAKING-RESTITUTION.

re-gur″-gi-ta′-tion. A rushing back. ADVANCE-RETRO-GRESSION, RIVER-WIND.

re″-ha-bil′-i-tate. To restore RENOVATION-RELAPSE, TAKING-RESTITUTION.

re″-ha-bil′-i-ta′-tion. Reinstatement. RENOVATION-RELAPSE, TAKING-RESTITUTION.

re-hears′-al. A recital. ACCOUNT, PREPARATION-NON-PREPARATION, RECURRENCE.

re-hearse′. To repeat. ACCOUNT, ACTING, PREPARATION-NONPREPARATION, RECURRENCE-TRIAL.

Reichs′-rath″ [G.]. Assembly. COUNCIL.

reign. Rule. DOMINANCE-IMPOTENCE, PLEASURE-PAIN, RULE-LICENSE; **reign of terror,** HARSHNESS-MILDNESS, SANGUINENESS-TIMIDITY, TYRANNY-ANARCHY.

re″-im-burse′. To repay. SETTLEMENT-DEFAULT, TAKING-RESTITUTION.

re′-im-burse′-ment. Repayment. SETTLEMENT-DEFAULT.

rein. Check. CONNECTIVE, RELEASE-PRISON; **rein in,** RELEASE-RESTRAINT, SWIFTNESS-SLOWNESS.

rein′-deer″. Kind of deer. CONVEYER.

re infecta [L.] (rî in-fect-′ta). The business being unfinished. BRAVERY-COWARDICE, TRANSCURSION-SHORTCOMING.

rein′-less. Uncontrolled. RULE-LICENSE.

reins. Control. GUARD-PRISONER, MANAGEMENT, SCEPTER; **give reins to the imagination,** FANCY; **give the reins to,** DIFFICULTY-FACILITY, RULE-LICENSE; **hold the reins,** MANAGEMENT; **take the reins,** MANAGEMENT, RULE-LICENSE.

re″-in-stall′. To install again. RENOVATION-RELAPSE.

re″-in-state′. To restore. RENOVATION-RELAPSE.

re″-in-state′-ment′. Reestablishment. RENOVATION-RELAPSE.

re″-in-vest′. To invest again. TAKING-RESTITUTION.

re″-in-vest′-ment. A second occupation. TAKING-RESTITUTION.

re″-in-vig′-or-ate. To revive. RENOVATION-RELAPSE, WEARINESS-REFRESHMENT.

Reis Effendi. Chancellor of Turkish Empire. MANAGER.

Reise glückliche [G.] (rai′-se glük′-liн-e). Prosperous journey to you. ARRIVAL-DEPARTURE.

re-it′-er-ate. To repeat. RECURRENCE.

re-it″-er-a′-tion. Repetition. RECURRENCE.

re-ject′. To refuse. ADMISSION-EXPULSION, CHOICE-REJECTION, INCLUSION-OMISSION, PROFFER-REFUSAL.

re″-jec-ta′-ne-ous. Rejected. CHOICE-REJECTION.

re-ject′-ed. Excluded. CHOICE-REJECTION, LOVE-HATE, PROFFER-REFUSAL.

re-jec′-tion. Act of rejecting. ADMISSION-EXPULSION, CHOICE-REJECTION, INCLUSION-OMISSION, QUEST-EVASION.

re″-jec-ti′-tious. Deserving rejection. CHOICE-REJECTION.

re-joice′. To be glad. ENTERTAINMENT-WEARINESS, JUBILATION-LAMENTATION; **rejoice in,** PLEASURE-PAIN; **rejoice in the name of,** NAME-MISNOMER; **rejoice the heart,** LIGHTHEARTEDNESS-DEJECTION, PLEASURABLENESS-PAINFULNESS.

re-joi′-cing. Feeling glad. ENTERTAINMENT-WEARINESS, JUBILATION-LAMENTATION, LIGHTHEARTEDNESS-DEJECTION.

re-join′. To reunite. ARRIVAL-DEPARTURE, GATHERING-SCATTERING, INVESTIGATION-ANSWER.

re-join′-der. Reply. INVESTIGATION-ANSWER, LITIGATION.

re-ju″-ve-nes′-cence. Renewal of youth. RENOVATION-RELAPSE.

re-kin′-dle. To kindle again. EXCITATION, HEATING-COOLING.

re-lapse′. Return to a former state. CONVERSION-REVERSION, RENOVATION-RELAPSE.

re-late′. To tell; to refer. ACCOUNT, CONNECTION-INDEPENDENCE.

re-la′-ted. Akin. RELATIONSHIP.

re-la′-tion. Kinship; account. ACCOUNT, RELATIONSHIP.

re-la′-tion-ship. Connection. RELATIONSHIP.

RELATIONSHIP

Affiliation. Intimate association.
Agnation. Relationship through male lines only.
Alliance. Matrimonial connection between families.
Aunt. The sister of one's father or mother; also, the wife of one's uncle.
Blood. Relationship because of descent from a common ancestor.
Brother. A son having common parents with another or others.
Brotherhood. The state of being sons of the same parents.
Connection. A distant kindred tie resulting from matrimony.
Consanguinity. Relationship proceeding from a common ancestry.
Cousin. One, not a brother or sister, yet related by reason of common ancestry, such as the child of one's uncle and aunt.
Cousin german. A first or full cousin.
Cousinhood. The state of being cousins.
Cousin, once removed. A first cousin's child; a second cousin.
Cousin, twice removed. A first cousin's grandchild.
Distant relation. One whose connection is far removed.
Enate. Relative on the mother's side.
Family. A group of persons connected by some sign of kinship.
Family-connection. Relationship through the same family.
Family-tie. The sign of one's relation to his family.
Filiation. A child's relation to its parents.
First cousin. The child of one's uncle or aunt.
Fraternity. The state of brotherhood.
Generation. The people descended from a common ancestor.
Kindred. Relationship by common origin.
Kinsfolk. Persons who have common family ties.
Kinsman. One of the same family.
Kith and kin. Friends and relatives.
Lineage. Consanguine descent from a common progenitor.
Near relation. One closely related.
Nephew. A brother's or sister's son.
Nepotism. Excessive attachment to relatives, causing favoritism.
Next of kin. The nearest relative.
Niece. A brother's or sister's daughter.
One's own flesh and blood. Children.
Parentage. The relation of parent to offspring.
Paternity. The state of being a father.
Race. The descendants of a common ancestor.
Relation. One connected by blood or marriage.
Relationship. The state of being related.
Relative. Same as relation.
Second cousin. The child of a first cousin.
Sept, etc. A group of related persons. See PARENTAGE.
Sib. One related by blood.
Side. Ancestry through one parent as distinguished from that traced through another.
Sister. A daughter having parents common to another or others.
Sisterhood. The state of being sisters.
Stirps. A family of common descent.
Stock. A series of descendants of the same ancestor.
Ties of blood. Relationship.
Uncle. The brother of one's father or mother, or an aunt's husband.

RELATIONSHIP—*Verbs.*

Be akin to.
Be consanguineous to. } To be a relative of. See *Adjectives.*
Be related to.
To claim kindred with. } To claim descent from the same ancestor. See *Nouns.*
To claim relationship with.

RELATIONSHIP—*Adjectives.*

Affiliated. Intimately associated.
Agnate. Having the same male ancestor.
Akin. Of the same family.
Allied. Bound by common family ties.
Closely allied. } Closely connected by blood or marriage.
Closely related.
Cognate. Having common blood.
Collateral. Indirectly descended from the same ancestor.
Consanguineous. Lineally descended from a common ancestor.
Distantly allied. } Connected by blood or marriage.
Distantly related.

Family. Of or pertaining to the family.
Fraternal. Brotherly
German. Related as sisters and brothers.
Intimately allied. }
Intimately related. } Closely connected by blood or marriage.
Kindred. Of the same family.
Nearly allied. }
Nearly related. } Of one family.
Of the blood. Related.
Related. Connected by blood or marriage.
Remotely allied. }
Remotely related. } Of the same family.

rel'-a-tive. Pertaining; a kinsman. Connection-Independence, Relationship.
rel'-a-tive-ly. In a relative manner. Comparison, Connection-Independence.
re-la'-tor. Accuser. Account, Justification-Charge.
re-lax'. To diminish tension or severity; to repose.

Activity-Indolence, Cohesion-Looseness, Compassion - Ruthlessness, Dueness - Undueness, Hardness-Softness, Release-Restraint, Rule-License, Strength-Weakness, Swiftness-Slowness, Toil-Relaxation; **relax one's efforts,** Action-Passiveness; **relax the mind,** Reflection-Vacancy.
re"-lax-a'-tion. Diversion; remission of rigor. Activity-Indolence, Cohesion-Looseness, Duty-Dereliction, Entertainment-Weariness, Rule-License, Turbulence-Calmness.
re-laxed'. Loose. Cohesion-Looseness, Rule-License, Strength-Weakness.
re-lay'. Supply. Materials, Store.
re-lease'. To free in any sense. Duty-Immunity, Engagement-Release, Exculpation-Conviction, Leave-Prohibition, Life-Death, Pardon-Vindictiveness, Release-Restraint, Security, Settlement - Default, Taking - Restitution; **deed of release,** Fighting-Conciliation.

RELEASE—RESTRAINT.

Absolution. An acquittal; a declaration that an accused person is innocent.
Acquittal, etc. A deliverance from a charge; release. See Exculpation.
Acquittance. The act of discharging from a debt.
Affranchisement. The act of liberating from servitude or dependence.
Deliverance, etc. The act of freeing from restraint. See Rescue.
Discharge. The act of relieving from anything that oppresses.
Disengagement. The act of releasing or setting free.
Dismissal. The act of sending away or permitting to go.
Emancipation. The act of setting free from subjection, slavery, or the like.
Enfranchisement. The act of freeing from slavery or servitude.
Enlargement. The act of setting free from servitude, confinement, or the like.
Escape, etc. Deliverance from restraint or injury. See Escape.
Extrication. The act of freeing from perplexities.
Liberation. The act of setting free.
Manumission. The act of liberating a slave from bondage.
Redemption. Release; rescue; deliverance.
Release. The act of liberating or freeing from any restraint.

Release—Verbs.

Absolve, etc. To free from any bond. See Exculpation.
Acquire one's liberty, etc. To obtain one's freedom. See Liberty.
Affranchise. To make free.
Break loose. To shake off restraint.
Break prison. To free oneself from prison.
Cast adrift. To send off in an aimless state.
Clear. To acquit, free from the imputation of guilt.
Deliver, etc. To set at liberty; release; free from restraint. See Rescue.
Deliver oneself from. To free oneself from any burden, trouble or restraint.
Disband. To set free.
Discharge. To acquit; exonerate.
Disengage. To release or set free from.
Disentangle. To extricate from confusion or perplexity.
Disenthrall. To release from slavery.
Dismiss. To give permission to depart or go away.
Emancipate. To set free from slavery by a voluntary act.
Enfranchise. To set free from servitude or bondage.
Enlarge. To release from confinement or restraint.
Escape, etc. To avoid or flee from danger or restraint. See Escape.
Extricate. To free from difficulties.
Free. To set at liberty; clear.
Gain one's liberty. To be freed from restraint.
Get clear of. To be released from.
Get rid of. To disengage oneself from.
Let go. }
Let loose. }
Let out. } To release or free.
Let slip. }
Liberate. To set free from restraint.
Loose, etc. To release from anything. See Union-Disunion.
Loosen. To free from restraint.
Manumit. To free from slavery.
Obtain one's liberty. To gain freedom.

Arrest. Hindrance; restraint.
Arrestation. The act of arresting
Blockade. The investment of a port by a hostile naval force.
Captivity. The state of being a prisoner; subjection; bondage.
Care. Responsible charge or oversight.
Charge. Keeping; custody.
Check-rein. A looped rein to keep a horse's head up.
Coarction. Restraint of liberty.
Coercion, etc. The act of restraining. See Coercion.
Cohibition. Hindrance; restraint.
Confinement. Restraint of liberty by force.
Constraint. Any power which restrains from acting.
Control. Restraining or directing influence.
Corral. An enclosed space for keeping cattle.
Curb. Anything that restrains or controls. See Release-Prison.
Custody. Restraint of liberty; confinement.
Discipline. Systematic training or subjection to authority.
Durance. Imprisonment.
Durance vile. Disagreeable personal restraint.
Duress. Restraint of liberty.
Entombment. Burial.
Hackamore. A raw-hide halter.
Hindrance, etc. The act of checking or retarding in progress or motion. See Obstruction.
Imprisonment. The state of being confined in a prison.
Incarceration. The act of imprisoning.
Keep. A dungeon.
Lettres de cachet [F.]. A secret letter containing orders for arrest and imprisonment without trial.
Limbo. A place of confinement.
Limitation. A restriction.
Mancipation. Involuntary servitude.
Monopoly. An exclusive license which limits the number of people engaged in a particular work.
Prisoner, etc. A person held in restraint. See Keeper-Prisoner.
Prohibition, etc. The act of hindering or preventing some act. See Leave-Prohibition.
Protection. Preservation from harm or danger.
Repression. The act of restraining.
Restraint. The act of hindering or holding in check.
Restriction. The act of restraining.
Restringency. The act or state of being confined.
Vise. A clasping device.

Restraint—Verbs.

Arrest. To obstruct, check, or hinder the motion or progress of anything.
Bethrall. To reduce to bondage.
Bind hand and foot. To confine completely; make utterly helpless.
Bolt in. To fasten; restrain within.
Bottle up. To shut in or close up, as in a bottle.
Box up. To enclose, as in a box.
Bridle. To restrain; check; curb.
Button up. To fasten with a button.
Cage. To confine and shut up, as in a cage.
Captivate. To subdue; take by force.
Cast into prison. To throw into prison.
Check. To put sudden or continued restraint upon.
Clap under hatches. To confine below deck.

RELEASE—Verbs—*Continued*.

Relax. To relieve; make less rigorous.
Release. To set free from restraint.
Render free. To make free.
Set at liberty. }
Set free. } To give freedom to.
Shake off the yoke. To throw off bondage or servitude.
Slip the collar. To escape from servitude.
Tear asunder one's bonds. To free oneself from servitude or restraint.
Turn adrift. To send away in an aimless condition.
Unbar. To open; unfasten.
Unbind. To set free from shackles.
Unbolt. To unfasten; remove the bolt from.
Unchain. To free from servitude.
Unclog. To free from encumbrances.
Unclose. To open.
Uncork. To draw the cork from.
Unentangle. To disentangle.
Unfetter, etc. To set at liberty; free from restraint. See RELEASE-RESTRAINT.
Unhand. To let go.
Unloose. To make loose
Untie, etc. To unfasten. See UNION.
'Vade in pace [L.]. Go in peace.

RELEASE—*Adjectives*.

Liberated, etc. Made free; freed. See *Verbs*.
Out of harness, etc. Liberated; freed. See LIBERTY.

RELEASE—*Interjections*.

Let me go!
Unhand me! Let me go!

RESTRAINT—Verbs—*Continued from Column 2.*

Send to prison. To deprive of liberty.
Sent up. Sent to prison.
Shackle. To tie or confine the limbs so as to prevent free motion.
Shut in. To enclose.
Shut up. To close.
Smother. To suppress; deprive of activity.
Sprag. To stop the motion of the wheels with a stick.
Subjugate, etc To subdue or bring under the power of. See LIBERTY-SUBJECTION.
Suppress. To restrain; keep in check.
Swaddle. To bind tightly with clothes.
Swathe. To bind with a bandage.
Take a captive. }
Take a prisoner. }
Take charge of. } To get under one's power or control.
Take into custody. }
Take up. To seize; arrest.
Tether. To confine within certain limits by a chain or rope.
Throw into prison. To imprison.
Tie down. To fasten so as to prevent from rising; restrain.
Tie one's hands. To deprive of freedom of action.
Tie up. To confine; restrain.
Trammel. To confine; shackle.
Wall in. To enclose with a wall.
Withhold. To hold back or keep from action.

RESTRAINT—*Adjectives*.

"Cabined, cribbed, confined." Closely restrained. [Shakespeare, *Macbeth*, III, iv.]
Coactive, etc. Serving to constrain. See COERCION.
Cohibitive. Restraining.
Constrained. Chained; secured with bonds.
Hidebound. Closely confined.
Ice-bound. Totally surrounded by ice.
Imprisoned, etc. Confined in prison. See *Verbs*.
In custody, etc. Under guard. See KEEPER-PRISONER.
In lob's pound. Held playfully between the legs and feet of an adult: said of a child.
In swaddling-clothes. In the band wrapped around infants. [*Luke*, ii, 7.]
Jammed in. Wedged in.
Laid by the heels. Fettered; shackled.
On parole. Bound by one's word of honor.
Put up. Imprisoned.
Restrained. Held in check; hindered.
Restringent. Restrictive.

RESTRAINT—Verbs—*Continued*.

Clap up. To dispose of hastily.
Cloister. To shut up closely within a cloister.
Close the door upon. To confine within or keep out.
Coerce, etc To restrain by force. See COERCION.
Cohibit. To restrain.
Commit. To put into charge of.
Commit to prison. To put into prison.
Confine. To restrain within limits.
Control. To restrain; govern; check.
Coop. To shut up or confine within a narrow compass.
Cork up. To stop up with a cork.
Curb. To subject; restrain; confine.
Debar, etc. To shut out or exclude from entrance. See OBSTRUCTION.
Encage. To confine in a cage.
Enchain. To confine; restrain.
Enclose, etc. To confine on all sides. See CONFINEMENT.
Enthrall. To enslave.
Entomb. To shut up in a tomb.
Entrammel. To entangle.
Fasten, etc. To secure; make fast. See UNION.
Fetter. To confine with chains.
Forge fetters. To place under restraint.
Gag. To stop up the mouth so as to hinder speaking.
Give in charge. }
Give in custody. } To put under the care of another.
Handcuff. To manacle the hands.
Hem in. To confine.
Hobble. To fasten the legs together loosely.
Hold. To impose restraint upon.
Hold back. To restrain.
Hold fast. To deprive one of freedom.
Hold from. To restrain.
Hold in. To restrain; curb.
Hold in check. To keep in restraint.
Hold in leading-strings. To keep in a state of dependence.
Hold in leash. To hold under control.
Hold within bounds. To hold in check.
Immure. To enclose within walls.
Impound. To restrain within limits.
Imprison. To confine in a prison.
Incage. To confine in a cage or any narrow limits.
Incarcerate. To imprison or confine.
Inhibit. To restrain; hold back.
Inthrall. To enslave.
Keep a tight hand on. To use unyielding firmness.
Keep back. }
Keep from. }
Keep in. } To restrain.
Keep in check. }
Keep within bounds. }
Keep under. To keep subdued or subject.
Lay under hatches. To put below deck.
Lay under restraint. To deprive of freedom of action.
Lead captive. }
Lead into captivity. } To place one in subjection.
Lock up. To imprison.
Make a captive of. }
Make a prisoner of. } To take into one's power.
Manacle. To fasten the hands.
Mew up. To confine, as in an enclosure.
Muzzle. To restrain from doing injury.
Pen. To shut up in a small enclosure.
Picket. To fasten with a pointed stick, or enclose with narrow, pointed boards.
Pin down. To fasten with a pin.
Pinion. To restrain by binding the arms.
Prohibit, etc. To forbid; hinder. See LEAVE-PROHIBITION.
Pull in. To arrest.
Put in a straight waistcoat. To fasten into a dress of strong materials used to restrain raving maniacs and the like
Put in irons. To put in chains.
Put into bilboes. To put into a kind of shackle used on shipboard to confine prisoners or captives.
Put under restraint. To deprive of freedom.
Rail in. To enclose with rails
Rein in. To restrain or control.
Repress. To check; restrain.
Restrain. To hold back or in check
Secure. To confine effectually.

Continued on Column 1.

RESTRAINT—Adjectives—*Continued*.

Stiff. Rigid; inflexible
Strait-laced. Having the bodice or stays tightly laced.
Under hatches. Confined below deck.
Under lock and key. Under restraint or in prison.

Under restraint. Deprived of freedom.
Weather-bound. Detained by unfavorable weather.
Wedged in. Fastened in tightly.
Wind-bound. Delayed by contrary winds.

RELEASE—PRISON.

Prison.

Bastile. A famous French prison destroyed by a popular uprising, July 14, 1789.
Black Hole. A dungeon in Calcutta, India, in which 146 British subjects were confined, of whom 123 died of asphyxia.
Bridewell. A house of correction for the confinement of disorderly persons in London.
Cage. A place of confinement.
Cell. A small room in a prison.
Coop. An enclosure for small animals; a prison.
Den. A cavern or recess that is the haunt of animals.
Donjon. The strongest room in a fortress.
Dungeon. A dark underground cell for close confinement.
Fleet. A famous prison in London.
Fold. A pen for domestic animals.
Fortress. A large, strong, and permanent prison, usually for military offenders.
Gaol. Jail.
Guard-room. A room for the detention of prisoners.
Hold. A place of security.
House of correction. A place of confinement for disorderly persons.
House of detention. A place for the temporary detention of offenders.
Hulks. Old, unseaworthy vessels used as prisons.
Jail. A building or place for the confinement of arrested or sentenced persons.
Keep. The strongest room in a castle or prison.
King's Bench. A division of the high court of justice in England.
Limbo. A place of restraint.
Lockup. A place for the temporary restraint of prisoners.
Marshalsea. A famous jail in London.
Newgate. A well-known English prison.
Oubliette [F.]. A dungeon having an opening at the top.
Panopticon. A prison so constructed as to allow the inspector to watch all the prisoners without being seen.
Pen. A small enclosure for animals.
Penal settlement. A place to which offenders or criminals are banished.
Penitentiary. A prison or place of punishment.
Pound. A place where stray animals are kept.
Prison. A place of confinement for persons in legal custody.
Prison-house. A prison.
Queen's Bench. A division of the high court of justice in England, during a queen's reign.
Quod. A prison.
Sponging-house. A house where debtors were temporarily lodged.
Station.
Station-house. } A place for the temporary confinement of prisoners.
Stronghold. A fortified place
Toll-booth. A jail or prison.
Watch-house. A guard-house; a night lockup.

Prison—*Nouns of Instrument*.

Band. That which securely binds a person.
Bandage. Any band used to bind together.

Bar. A piece of wood used as a barrier or obstruction.
Barricade. An obstruction closing a street, etc.
Barrier. Something that bars, or keeps out.
Bearing-rein. A rein used to make a horse hold up his head.
Bilboes. Fetters.
Bit. The mouthpiece of a bridle used to control and guide a horse.
Bolt. A sliding bar for fastening a door.
Bond. That which binds two objects together.
Brake. A device for retarding the motion of a vehicle.
Bridle. The head-harness of a horse used for controlling it.
Chain. A string of metal links used to bind connect, etc.
Collar. An iron band for the neck of a convict, or slave, or animal.
Cord. A string for binding things together.
Curb. A chain or strap fastened to a bridle-bit to control a horse.
Drag, etc. Anything used to impede progress. See Obstruction.
Enclosure, etc. That which encloses. See Inclosure.
Fence. A barrier of rails, boards, wire, or the like, enclosing a field.
Fetter. A chain or shackle by which the feet of a person or animal are fastened together.
Gag. An appliance for silencing a person by obstructing the vocal organs.
Guy, etc. A rope, rod, or chain for holding a mast. See Connection.
Gyve. A fetter for confining the limbs of a prisoner.
Halter. A strap or rope for leading or confining an animal.
Handcuff. A device for holding the hands together.
Harness. An equipment put upon a draft-animal.
Irons. Shackles for the feet.
Leading-string. Strings by which children are supported when beginning to walk.
Lock. A device for fastening a door.
Manacle. A metallic instrument for confining the hands.
Martingale. A strap for holding down a horse's head.
Muzzle. A covering for an animal's snout to prevent biting.
Padlock. A detachable lock.
Paling. A strip of wood used to form a fence.
Palisade. A strong, high fence used as a fortification.
Picket. A strip of wood used for making fences.
Pinion. A band for the arm.
Rail. A long bar of wood or iron.
Rein. }
Reins. } A strap for controlling a horse.
Shackle. A ring or clasp for restraining a limb.
Shaffle. A shackle.
Stocks. A frame by which the legs and arms of common offenders were confined.
Straight waistcoat. A garment of strong canvas for confining the arms of lunatics, etc.
Tether. A rope for fastening an animal.
Trammel. A fetter, shackle, or bond.
Wall. A structure of stone for enclosing a space.
Yoke. A frame or cross-bar for coupling draft-animals.

re-leased'. Freed. Life-Death.
re-leas''-ee'. The recipient of an instrument of release. Giving-Receiving, Holder.
rel'-e-gate. Banish. Admission-Expulsion, Inclusion-Omission, Transfer.
rel''-e-ga'-tion. Removal. Admission-Expulsion, Transfer.
re-lent'. To yield. Compassion-Ruthlessness, Hardness-Softness, Turbulence-Calmness.
re-lent'-less. Unpitying. Charitableness-Malevolence, Determination-Vacillation, Favorite-Anger, Harshness-Mildness, Pardon-Vindictiveness, Repentance-Obduracy.
rel'-e-van-cy. Pertinence. Connection-Independence, Harmony-Discord.
rel'-e-vant. Pertinent. Connection-Independence, Harmony-Discord, Ratiocination-Instinct.

relève [F.] (re-lêv'). A course removed from a table. Nutriment-Excretion.
re-li''-a-bil'-i-ty. Trustworthiness. Certainty-Doubt.
re-li'-a-ble. Trustworthy. Certainty-Doubt, Faith-Misgiving.
re-li'-ance. Confidence; hope. Faith-Misgiving, Sanguineness-Hopelessness.
rel'-ic. Keepsake. Increment-Remnant, Mark-Obliteration, Remembrance-Forgetfulness.
rel'-ics. Corpse; something remaining from a saint. Ceremonial, Life-Corpse.
rel'-ict. Widow. Marriage-Divorce.
re-lief'. Projection; alleviation. Alleviation-Aggravation, Convexity-Concavity, Obstruction-Help; **bas-relief,** Convexity-Concavity, Sculpture; **in strong relief,** Manifestation-La-

TENCY, RENOVATION-RELAPSE, VISIBILITY-INVISI-BILITY, WEARINESS-REFRESHMENT.

re-lieve'. To help; to comfort. ALLEVIATION-AGGRA-VATION, BETTERMENT-DETERIORATION, DIFFICULTY-FACILITY, OBSTRUCTION-HELP, REMEDY-BANE.

re-liev'-ing. Giving help. ALLEVIATION-AGGRAVA-TION.

religieuse [F.] (re-lī''-zhiuz'). Nun. MINISTRY-LAITY.

re-lig'-ion. System of worship. GODLINESS-UNGODLI-NESS, ORTHODOXY - HETERODOXY; **under the mask of religion,** CEREMONIAL.

re-lig'-ion-ism. Affected religion. GODLINESS-UN-GODLINESS.

re-lig'-ion-ist. An adherent of a religion. CERE-MONIAL.

re-lig'-ious. Devout. GODLINESS-UNGODLINESS, THEOLOGY, UPRIGHTNESS - DISHONESTY; **overrelig-ious,** AUSTERITY; **religious education,** EDUCATION-MISTEACHING; **religious persuasion,** THEOLOGY; **re-ligious sects,** CHURCH, ORTHODOXY-HETERODOXY.

re-lig'-ious-ly. In reference to religion. **Religiously exact,** ORTHODOXY-HETERODOXY.

re-lin'-quish. To abandon. KEEPING-RELINQUISH-MENT, QUEST-ABANDONMENT; **relinquish a purpose,** BIGOTRY-APOSTASY; **relinquish hope,** SANGUINE-NESS-HOPELESSNESS; **relinquish life,** LIFE-DEATH.

re-lin'-quished. Given up. KEEPING-RELINQUISH-MENT, QUEST-ABANDONMENT.

re-lin'-quish-ing. Giving up. QUEST-ABANDONMENT.

re-lin'-quish-ment. Giving up. BIGOTRY-APOSTASY, KEEPING-RELINQUISHMENT, USE-DISUSE.

rel'-i-qua-ry. Repository. CEREMONIAL, CONTENTS-RECEIVER.

reliquiæ [L.] (re-lic'-wi-î) Fossil organisms. LIFE-CORPSE.

rel'-ish. To enjoy. CONDIMENT, DESIRE-DISTASTE, PALATABLENESS - UNPALATABLENESS, PLEASURE-PAIN, SENSUALITY-SUFFERING.

re-lu'-cent. Gleaming. DIAPHANEITY-OPAQUENESS, LIGHT-DARKNESS.

re-luc'-tance. Unwillingness. DESIRE-DISTASTE, MOTIVE-CAPRICE, READINESS-RELUCTANCE.

re-luc'-tant. Unwilling. READINESS-RELUCTANCE.

re-luc'-tate. To hesitate. REPRISAL-RESISTANCE.

re''-luc-ta'-tion. Reluctance. REPRISAL-RESISTANCE.

re-lume'. Rekindle. HEATING-COOLING, LIGHT-DARKNESS.

re-ly'. Depend on. FAITH-MISGIVING, SANGUINE-NESS-HOPELESSNESS.

rem acu tetigisti [L.] (rem ê'-ciu tet''-i-jis'-tai). You have touched the thing with a needle. ADAGE-NON-SENSE, DIFFERENTIATION-INDISCRIMINATION, HAR-MONY-DISCORD.

re-main'. To be left; to continue. DURATION-NEVER-NESS, INCREMENT-REMNANT, LASTINGNESS-TRAN-SIENTNESS, MOVEMENT-REST, MUTATION-PERMA-NENCE, PRESENCE-ABSENCE; **remain firm,** MUTA-BILITY-STABILITY; **remain in one's mind,** REMEM-BRANCE-FORGETFULNESS; **remain in possession of the field,** SUCCESS FAILURE; **remain** *in situ*, MOVE-MENT-REST; **remain neuter,** DETERMINATION-VACIL-LATION; **remain on one's hands,** EXCESS-LACK.

re-main'-der. Surplus. ANTECEDENCE-SEQUENCE, EXCESS-LACK, INCREMENT-DECREMENT, PROPERTY; **in remainder,** ANTECEDENCE-SEQUENCE.

re-main'-der-man''. Receiver of an estate in re-mainder. HOLDER.

re-main'-ing. Left over. INCREMENT-REMNANT.

re-mains'. Something left; corpse. INCREMENT-REMNANT, LIFE-CORPSE, MARK-OBLITERATION; **or-ganic remains,** ORGANIZATION - DISORGANIZATION.

re-mand'. Recommit. EARLINESS-LATENESS, OR-DER.

rem'-a-net. A deferred trial. INCREMENT-REMNANT.

re-mark'. To say. ASSERTION-DENIAL, HEED-DIS-REGARD; **worthy of remark,** CONSEQUENCE-INSIG-NIFICANCE.

re-mark'-a-ble. Worthy of notice. CONSEQUENCE-INSIGNIFICANCE, CONVENTIONALITY-UNCONVENTION-ALITY, MAGNITUDE-SMALLNESS, REPUTATION-DIS-CREDIT.

re-me'-di-a-ble. Curable. REMEDY-BANE, RENOVA-TION-RELAPSE.

re-me'-di-al. Curative. BETTERMENT-DETERIORA-TION, REMEDY-BANE, RENOVATION-RELAPSE.

rem'-e-di-less. Not curable. SANGUINENESS-HOPE-LESSNESS.

remedio sino para la muerte, para todo hay [Sp.] (rê-mê'-dî-o sî'-no par'-a la mu-er'-tê, par'-a to'-do a-î'). There is remedy for all things except death. CERTAINTY-DOUBT, REMEDY-BANE.

REMEDY—BANE.

Aconite. A medicinal plant.
Catholicon. A supposed remedy for all diseases; a panacea.
Certain cure. A medicine, or the like, which works a certain cure.
Cure. That which heals or restores to health.
Drug. Any substance used as medicine.
Help. Remedy or relief, but not complete cure.
Manicure. The care and treatment of the hands and finger-nails.
Medicament. Any healing application; a medicine.
Medicine. Any substance possessing remedial or curative qualities.
Palliative. That which alleviates or partially cures.
Panacea. A remedy professing to cure all diseases or ills; a catholicon.
Perfect cure. A medicine or the like which rids of all trouble or sick-ness.
Radical cure. A thorough going entire cure; also, a cure effected by resorting to extreme measures.
Remedy. Anything which is used either to relieve or cure bodily dis-ease or ailment.
Sovereign remedy. A remedy efficacious in the highest degree.

REMEDY—*Nouns of Agent.*

Accoucheur. A professional assistant in childbirth.
Accoucheuse. A midwife.
Æsculapius. The god of medicine; hence, a physician.
Apothecary. A druggist; especially one skilled in pharmacy.
Aurist. One specially skilled in the treatment of the ear.
Doctor. One who practises medicine.
Dresser. One who assists in surgery.
Druggist. One who deals in or compounds drugs.

Appendicitis. An inflammation of the appendix of the cæcum.
Bane. Any cause of ruin or lasting injury.
Curse. An evil or calamity.
Demon. An evil spirit.
Evil. Something that harms or hurts.
Hurtfulness. The condition of causing harm or injury.
Painfulness. The condition or state of suffering pain.
Pest. A plague; a pestilence.
Scourge. A plague.
Toxicology. The branch of medical science which treats of poisons, their effects, etc.

BANE—*Nouns of Cause.*

Aconite. A medicinal plant, the extract of which is a poison.
Antimony. A metal possessing poisonous properties.
Arsenic. A poisonous element.
Azote. Nitrogen.
Bed-sore. A sore from lying on the bed.
Belladonna. A very poisonous medicinal plant and extract; **deadly nightshade.**
Bramble. Any rough prickly shrub.
Brier. A plant with rough prickly stems; a bramble.
Cancer. A malignant growth of new tissue.
Canker. An ulcerous sore; also a disease of trees.
Canker-worm. A variety of caterpillar, destructive to fruit-trees.
Damnosa hereditas [L.]. Evil or pernicious heredity.
Dry-rot. A rotting caused by fungi.
Fang. A long tooth, especially the tooth of a serpent.

REMEDY—BANE—*Continued.*

REMEDY—Nouns of Agent—*Continued.*

Galen. An early writer on medicine.
General practitioner. One who practises all branches of medicine.
Hippocrates. "The Father of Medicine."
Leech. One who professes the art of medicine; a doctor.
Medical attendant. One who assists in medical treatment.
Medical practitioner. One who engages in medicine as a profession.
Midwife. A woman who assists in childbirth.
Monthly nurse. A nurse who attends women during the period of their confinement.
Nurse. One who cares for the sick or wounded.
Oculist. One skilled in the treatment of the eyes.
Operator. One who takes the leading part in a surgical operation.
Pharmacopolist. A druggist.
Physician. A doctor; especially one legally authorized to practise medicine.
Red Cross Society. A society organized for the succor of the sick and wounded in war.
Sister. Usually a member of an organization for attending the sick and needy.
Surgeon. One who treats diseases or injuries by mechanical operations.

REMEDY—*Nouns of Cause.*

Alterant. An alterative.
Alterative. A medicine that causes a gradual improvement of the health.
Antidote. A remedy that will counteract the effects of poison.
Antiseptic. Any agent or medicine used to prevent putrefaction.
Arquebuscade. A lotion for wounds from a harquebus, and for sprains and bruises.
Asafetida. A bitter, offensive medical compound.
Balm. A soothing remedy.
Balsam. A medicinal preparation used for healing purposes.
Bandage. A strip of cloth used in dressing wounds, etc.
Bleeding. The surgical operation of drawing blood from the veins.
Blood-letting. Bleeding.
Bolus. A large pill.
Boneset. A bitter herb used for curing colds.
Carminative. Any substance used for removing gas from the stomach.
Cataplasm. A poultice.
Catnip. An herb used as a remedy.
Cerate. An unctuous compound used for wounds and blisters.
Cold water cure. Large and frequent drafts of cold water taken as medicine.
Collyrium. An eye-wash or eye-salve.
Compress. Folded cloth or the like used in making pressure.
Cordial. Any preparation used to stimulate and give new vigor.
Corrective. A restorative.
Cosmetic. Any preparation used to improve the appearance of the skin.
Counter-poison. An antidote.
Cupping. The process of drawing blood to any place by creating a vacuum at that point.
Depilatory. A preparation for removing hairs.
Dietary. A system of diet.
Dose. The quantity of medicine to be taken at one time.
Draft. A dose.
Electuary. A medicine mixed with some sweet substance.
Elixir. An alcoholic preparation holding small quantities of medicine in solution; also, any invigorating compound.
Elixir vitæ. An imaginary liquor for prolonging life.
Embrocation. A liquid remedy to be applied externally; a liniment.
Emetic. Any substance used to produce vomiting.
Epithem. Any external application, except a salve or plaster, as a poultice or lotion.
Epsom salts. A cathartic.
Febrifuge. Any medicine that is efficacious against fever.
Galenicals. Those medicines which are prepared by infusion and decoction, as distinguished from those which are chemically prepared.
Healing art. The art of medicine.
Jonquil. A medicinal plant.
Leech. A small animal used for drawing blood.
Leechcraft. The art of healing.
Lenitive. Any application that allays pain or suffering.
Licorice. A tree from which a juice, used for coughs and colds, is obtained.
Lincture. Medicine taken by licking or sucking.
Liniment. A liquid preparation to be applied by rubbing.
Lithagogue. A medicine supposed to have the power of expelling calculous matter with the urine.

BANE—Nouns of Cause—*Continued.*

Fungus. A morbid granulated growth, as proud flesh.
Hellebore. A medicinal plant whose roots act as a powerful cathartic and narcotic: among the ancients, a specific for madness.
Hemlock. An extremely poisonous herb.
Henbane. A plant poisonous to fowls; stinking nightshade: it is used for the same purposes as belladonna.
Leaven. Any substance that causes fermentation.
Malaria. Infected air; also, the disease produced by breathing it.
Mephitis. Noxious exhalations.
Miasma. Infectious germs floating in the air; also, the air made noxious by their presence.
Mildew. Several varieties of fungi.
Moth. An insect that gradually eats or destroys.
Moth and rust. [Bible.]
Nettle. A plant covered with minute, poisonous, stinging hairs.
Nicotine. The poison in tobacco.
Nightshade. A variety of medicinal plants, said to be poisonous.
Nux vomica. A poisonous seed containing brucin and strychnin.
Poison. Any noxious or pernicious substance.
Prussic acid. An extremely poisonous liquid compound.
Rust. A chemical action destroying metals or plants.
Sewer-gas. Foul air from a sewer.
Sting. The bite of an insect.
Strychnin. A powerful poison.
Tang. A projecting part of an object by which it is fastened to a handle.
Tartar emetic. A tartrate of antimony and potassium; strongly cathartic and even fatally poisonous in its effects.
Thorn. A spine.
Torpedo. An explosive cartridge or shell.
Upas-tree. A Javanese tree, the juice of which is a virulent poison.
Venom. The poisonous liquid secreted by certain animals, as serpents.
Viper. An extremely venomous snake.
Virus. A morbid poison; a medium for communicating an infectious disease.
White elephant. A costly and worthless possession.
Worm. A creeping or crawling animal.
Yarrow. An astringent herb.

BANE—*Adjectives.*

Baneful, etc. Having poisonous or deadly qualities. See *Nouns.*
Poisonous, etc. Having the qualities of a poison. See *Nouns.*

BANE—*Phrase.*

Bibere venenum in auro [L.]. To drink poison from a gold cup.

REMEDY—Nouns of Cause—*Continued.*

Lotion. A liquid preparation for healing or cleansing.
Massage. A system of treatment consisting of manipulating a part or all of the body by kneading.
Médecine expectante [F.]. Expectant medicine; so called from expecting more from nature than from art.
Medical treatment. The application of medicines.
Mithridate. An antidote against poison, from Mithridates, "The Pontic monarch of old days, who fed on poisons, and they were a nutriment." [Byron, *The Dream.*]
Nepenthe. A drug reputed among the ancients to banish pain and sorrow.
Nostrum. A medicine whose composition is kept secret; a quack medicine.
Oil. Medicine for external application.
Ointment. An oily preparation to be applied externally
Operation. The application of instruments for removing diseased parts.
Pepastic. Any remedy which tends to bring a disease to maturity.
Philosopher's stone. A soluble stone, the red tincture of which was reputed to prolong life and restore youth.
Phlebotomy. Blood-letting.
Physic. Medicine in general; specifically, a cathartic.
Pill. A medical substance prepared in globular form for swallowing whole.
Plaster. A topical application spread upon linen, silk, or the like, adhesive to the body.
Pledget. A wad of cotton or the like placed over a wound or sore to keep out the air, absorb the discharges, etc.
Potion. A dose of liquid medicine.
Poultice. A mollifying remedy of meal or the like, for bruises and inflammations.

REMEDY—Nouns of Cause—*Continued.*

Prescription. A formula for the compounding and administering of a medicine.
Prophylactic. A medicine used to ward off disease.
Ptisan. A weak, aqueous medicine.
Receipt. Recipe.
Recipe. A written formula giving directions for the mixing of some preparation, especially of a medicine.
Redress. A relief or remedy.
Regimen. Any process or remedy intended to gradually bring about beneficial results.
Restorative. Any medicine that restores health and vigor.
Roborant. Any strengthening medicine; a tonic.
Salve. A thick, adhesive ointment.
Sassafras. A tree, the bark of whose roots is used as a medicine.
Sedative. A medicine for allaying pain.
Simple. A medicinal plant or the extraction.
Sinapism. A mustard plaster.
Specific. A medicine for a particular disease.

Splint. Thin piece of wood bound on a fracture to keep the bones in place.
Stethoscope. An instrument for listening to the sounds made in the body.
Surgical operation. The application of mechanical means to cure a wound or disease.
Theriac. An antidote to the bite of venomous animals.
Traumatic. Any remedy or application effective in the curing of wounds.
Treatment. The manner of applying remedies in disease.
Tuberculin. A liquid used in examining cattle suspected of tuberculosis.
Vaccinate. To inoculate with vaccine virus.
Varicella. Properly chicken-pox.
Venesection. Blood-letting.
Vis medicatrix [L.]. Medical power.
Vis naturæ [L.] The capability of living tissue to overcome disease or injury.
Vulnerary. Any application for healing external wounds.

REMEDY—*Nouns of Place.*

Dispensary. A place where medicines are compounded and dealt out.
Hospice. A place in which sick travelers are cared for.
Hospital. A place or institution where the sick or wounded are cared for.
Infirmary. A hospital; especially a small hospital where free treatment is given.
Lazaretto. A hospital for diseased persons, like Lazarus, especially those affected with contagious diseases; a pest-house.

Lazar-house. A lazaretto.
Lock hospital. A place for the treatment of venereal diseases.
Maison de santé [F.]. A private hospital, an insane retreat.
Pest-house. A hospital for the treatment of infectious diseases.
Pump-room. The drinking-place at a mineral spring.
Sanatorium. A health resort.
Spa. A mineral spring or its locality.

REMEDY—*Scientific Nouns*

Acology. That branch of medicine which treats of remedies.
Allopathy. That system of remedial treatment which seeks to cure disease by producing a condition incompatible with the disease; opposed to homeopathy. "And poisons must, as Galen held, by counter-poisons be expelled."
Chirurgery. Surgery.
Dentistry. The science which deals with the treatment of the teeth.
Dietetics. That branch of medicine or hygiene which treats on diet.
Homeopathy. That system of medical treatment which seeks to cure a disease by administering medicine which would produce this same disease in a healthy condition; opposed to allopathy. *Similia similibus curantur.*
Hydropathy. Water-cure.
Materia medica [L.]. Medicines in the broadest sense; all substances or remedies used to cure or heal.

Midwifery. Obstetrics.
Obstetrics. That branch of medical science which treats on pregnancy and parturition.
Orthopedia. The science which treats on the correcting and preventing of bodily deformities.
Orthopraxy. Orthopedia.
Pharmaceutics. The science of pharmacy.
Pharmacology. The entire science of medicines, as to their nature, effects, etc.
Pharmacy. That branch of medical science which treats on the preparation of medicines and drugs.
Posology. The science of quantitative dosing.
Surgery. That branch of medical science which treats on the curing of wounds or diseases by the application of mechanical means.
Therapeutics. The science of remedies; ecology.

REMEDY—*Verbs.*

Apply a remedy, etc. To apply something to effect a cure.
Attend. To wait upon, as a sick person.
Bleed. To let blood.
Cup. To draw the blood to one spot.
Doctor. To give medical treatment.
Dose. To give medicine; usually more than is needful.
Drench with physic. To give physic in large quantities.
Dress the wound. To cleanse and cover with antiseptic applications.
Embrocate. To rub with oil.

Let blood. To bleed.
Minister to. To attend.
Nurse. To attend upon a sick person.
Palliate. To relieve but not cure.
Physic. To give a physic to.
Plaster. To apply a plaster.
Prevent, etc. To keep disease away from a person.
Relieve. To cure wholly or in part.
Restore. To bring back to a former condition of health or soundness.

REMEDY—*Adjectives.*

Abstersive. Having cleansing qualities.
Alexipharmic. Serving to counteract poison.
Alexiteric. Serving to ward off contagion.
Alimentary. Nutritious.
Alterative. Tending to cause a gradual change
Analeptic. Reinvigorating.
Anodyne. Soothing.
Balsamic. Having the qualities of balsam. See *Nouns.*
Chirurgical. Surgical.
Corrective. Tending to restore
Corroborant. Invigorating.
Curable. Susceptible of cure.
Demulcent. Soothing.
Depuratory. Fitted to purify.
Detergent. Having cleansing qualities.
Detersive. Detergent.
Dietetic. Relating to the diet.
Disinfectant. Having power to destroy the germs of infectious disease.
Emollient. Producing a soothing effect.
Epulotic. Having healing qualities; cicatrizing.
Febrifugal. Efficacious against fever

Healing. Tending to cure.
Hypnotic. Sleep-producing.
Lenitive. Palliating; soothing.
Medical. Pertaining to medicine or the science of medicine; also, possessing curative properties.
Medicinal. Possessing curative properties.
Narcotic. Stupor-producing.
Neurotic. Efficacious in nervous diseases.
Nutritious. Nourishing.
Nutritive. Having nutritious properties.
Palliative. Giving relief.
Paregoric. Soothing pain.
Peptic. Of aid in digestion.
Prophylactic. Efficacious in warding off disease.
Remediable. Curable.
Remedial. Having curative properties.
Restorative. Tending to cure or restore to health
Salutiferous. Health-giving.
Sanative. Tending to cure or heal.
Sanatory. Health-giving.
Sedative. Having the power of soothing or calming as the nerves.
Therapeutic. Curative.

REMEDY—Adjectives—*Continued*.

Tonic. Invigorating; bracing.
Traumatic. Efficacious in the cure of wounds

Vulnerary. Tending to cure wounds or external injuries See Vul-
NERARY.

REMEDY—*Phrases*.

Aux grands maux les grands remèdes [F.]. To desperate evils, desperate remedies.
Dios que da la llaga da la medicina [Sp.]. God who sends the wound

sends the cure.
Para todo hay remedio sino para la muerte [Sp.]. There is a remedy
for all things except death.

re-mem'-ber. To recall. Remembrance-Forgetfulness.
re-mem'-bered. Preserved in the memory. Remembrance-Forgetfulness.

re-mem'-ber-ing. Keeping in mind. Remembrance-
Forgetfulness.
re-mem'-brance. Memory. Remembrance-Forgetfulness.

REMEMBRANCE—FORGETFULNESS.

Artificial memory. The power of reproducing past knowledge, which
has been cultivated by a series of rules or precepts.
Memoria technica [L.]. A memory trained by rules and precepts to
remember particular subjects.
Memory. The mental power of reproducing past knowledge.
Recognition. Knowing as identical with something previously
known.
Recollection. The operation by which ideas are revived in the mind.
Recurrence. The act of coming back or returning to the mind.
Remembrance. A holding in mind, or bringing to mind.
Rememoration. A recalling by the faculty of memory.
Reminiscence. A statement or narration of remembered experience.
Retention. } The power or capacity of the mind to keep knowl-
Retentiveness. } edge.
Retrospect. } A view or contemplation of something past.
Retrospection. }
Tenacity. That quality of memory which holds or keeps knowledge.
Veteris vestigia flammæ [L.] The traces of old fire; flashes of
memory.

REMEMBRANCE—*Denotations*.

Afterthought. A thought that comes later than its expected time.
Art of memory. A system of rules devised for strengthening the
memory.
Capacious memory. A memory that is able to retain much.
Commemoration. A memorial.
Correct memory. A memory that is able to retain facts just as
received.
Exact memory. } A correct memory.
Faithful memory. }
Flapper. Anything used to jog the memory.
Green memory. A memory that is able to retain things correctly.
Hint. An indirect allusion or suggestion.
Keepsake. Anything kept to remember the giver.
Memento. A hint or memorial to awaken memory.
Memorabilia. Things worthy to be remembered.
Memorandum. A record of things to be remembered.
Memorial. Something designed to keep in remembrance a person,
event, place, etc.
Mnemonics. The art or science of artificial memory.
Mnemosyne. The goddess of memory.
Mnemotechnics. A system of principles and formulas designed to
assist the memory.
Phrenotypics. A system of rules or formulas for developing the
memory.
Prompting. An impulse or suggestion.
Prompt memory. A memory that readily recalls past events.
Ready memory. A memory that at once recalls past experiences.
Relic. Something kept as a memento.
Reminder. Anything serving to remind.
Retentive memory. A memory that easily retains past experiences.
Souvenir. Something that serves to recall the past.
Suggestion. A hint.
Tablets of the memory. Figuratively, the memory. [Shakespeare,
"table," *Hamlet*, I, v.]
Tenacious memory. A memory that retains past experiences for a
long time.
Things to be remembered. Notable events.
Token of remembrance. A memento.
Trustworthy memory. A correct memory.

REMEMBRANCE—*Verbs*.

Commemorate. To call to remembrance by a special act or observ-
ance.
Con. To study with care and attention.
Memorialize. To address or petition by a memorial.

Decay of memory. Tendency to forget past experiences.
Failing memory. A memory that fails to retain past events.
Failure of memory. Forgetfulness
Forgetfulness, etc. The state of being liable to let slip from the mind.
See *Adjectives*.
Insensibility, etc. Lack of an impressible memory.
Insensibility to the past. Forgetfulness.
Lapse of memory. Failure to remember past events.
Loose memory. A memory that cannot recall past events correctly.
Obliteration, etc. The state of being forgotten. See Mark-Oblit-
ERATION.
Obliteration of the past. Forgetfulness.
Oblivion. The state of having utterly passed out of memory
Short memory. A memory that remembers only very recent events.
Treacherous memory A memory that cannot be relied upon.
Waters of Lethe. } Forgetfulness.
Waters of oblivion. }

FORGETFULNESS—*Verbs*.

Be forgetful, etc. To fail to remember See *Adjectives*.
Cast behind one's back. To forget intentionally.
Come in at one ear and go out at the other. To forget.
Consign to oblivion. To forget.
Consign to the tomb of the Capulets. To consign to oblivion.
[*Romeo and Juliet*.]
Die away from the memory. } To be forgotten.
Discharge from the memory. }
Efface from the memory, etc. To lose the power of recalling. See
Mark-Obliteration.
Escape from the memory. } To fail to recall.
Fade from the memory. }
Fall into oblivion. To forget.
Forget. To let slip from the memory.
Forget one's own name. To have a very poor memory, like Mon-
taigne.
Have a short memory. To be able to recall only very recent events.
Have no head. To be unable to remember anything at all.
Have on the tip of one's tongue. To forget what one was about to
say.
Let bygones be bygones, etc. To forgive and forget. See Pardon.
Lose. To forget unintentionally.
Lose sight of. To forget to take into consideration.
Sink into oblivion. } To be forgotten.
Slip from the memory. }
Think no more of, etc. To be lost from the memory. See Heed-
Disregard.
Unlearn. To forget something learned.
Wean one's thoughts from. To forget by making a strong effort.

FORGETFULNESS—*Adjectives*.

Buried in oblivion. Forgotten for all time.
Bygone. Long past and forgotten.
Clean forgotten. Entirely forgotten.
Forgetful. Liable to let slip out of mind.
Forgotten. Slipped from the memory.
Gone out of one's head. } Not remembered.
Gone out of one's recollection. }
Insensible, etc. Lacking an impressible memory.
Insensible to the past. Forgetful of the past.
Lethean. Producing forgetfulness.
Mindless. Having no recollection of.
Oblivious. Forgetful.
Out of mind. Forgotten for the time being.
Past recollection. That cannot be recalled.
Sunk in oblivion. Forgotten for all time.
Unremembered. Not retained in the memory.

REMEMBRANCE—FORGETFULNESS—*Continued*.

REMEMBRANCE—Verbs—*Continued*.

Mind. To fix the mind or thoughts on.
Prompt. To assist or induce the action of the memory.
Rankle. To linger in the mind and grow violent. See PARDON-VINDICTIVENESS.
Recall. To call back to mind.
Recognize. To perceive the identity of with something previously known.
Recollect. To recover the knowledge of.
Remember. To come into the mind again, as previously perceived, known, or felt.
Remind. To bring to notice.
Renew. To restore to freshness of memory
Retrace. To go over again in the mind.
Review. To reconsider or reexamine.
Suggest. To introduce indirectly to the thoughts. See ENLIGHTENMENT

REMEMBRANCE—*Verbal Expressions*.

Bear in the memory; bear in the mind; bear in the remembrance; bear in the thoughts; be deeply impressed with; be in one's memory; be in one's mind; be in one's thoughts; bethink oneself; bottle up in the memory; bring back to the memory; bring to mind; bring to remembrance; burden the memory with; call to mind; call to remembrance; call up; carry in the memory; carry in the mind; carry in the remembrance; carry in the thoughts; carry one's thoughts back; commit to memory; con over; dwell in one's memory; dwell in one's mind; dwell in one's thoughts; embalm in one's memory; engrave in one's memory; enshrine in one's memory; fan the embers; fix in the memory; flap the memory; flash across the memory; flash on one's mind; get by heart; get by rote; grave in the memory; haunt one's memory; haunt one's mind; haunt one's thoughts; have at one's fingers' ends; have by heart; have in the memory; have in the mind; have in the remembrance; have in the thoughts; hold in the memory; hold in the mind; hold in the remembrance; hold in the thoughts; impress the memory; impress the mind; impress the thoughts; imprint in the memory; *infandum renovare dolorem* [L.], to revive unspeakable grief; jog the memory; keep in mind; keep in the memory; keep in the remembrance; keep in the thoughts; keep in view; keep the memory alive; keep the wound green; keep up the memory of; know by heart; know by rote; learn by heart; learn by rote; live in one's memory; live in one's mind; live in one's thoughts; load the memory with; look back; look back upon; look backwards; make a note of; not be able to get it out of one's head; put in mind; put in remembrance; rake up the past; recall to mind; recall to remembrance; recur to the mind; redeem from oblivion; refresh the memory; remain in one's memory; remain in one's mind; remain in one's thoughts; repeat as a parrot; repeat by heart; repeat by rote; retain in the memory; retain in the mind; retain in the remembrance; retain in the thoughts; retain the memory of; retain the remembrance of; rip up; rivet in the memory; rub up the memory; run in the head; say by heart; say by

FORGETFULNESS—*Phrases*.

Non mi recordo [It.]. I do not remember.
The memory being at fault.⎫
The memory deserting one. ⎬Weak of memory; forgetful.
The memory failing one.   ⎭

REMEMBRANCE—Verbal Expressions—*Continued*.

rote; say one's lesson; sink in the mind; stamp in the memory; store in the memory; store the memory with; stuff the memory with; summon up; *tangere ulcus* [L.], to touch the wound; task the memory; tax the memory; think upon; trace back; trace backwards; treasure up in the memory.

REMEMBRANCE—*Adjectives*

Fresh. In the memory
Green. Unforgotten.
Green in remembrance.
Indelible. Not to be blotted out.
Memorable. Worthy to be remembered.
Mindful. Regarding with thoughtful care.
Pent up in one's memory.⎫
Present to the mind.   ⎬ Remembered.
Remembered.
Remembering.   ⎫
Retained in the memory.⎬Known by memory   See *Verbs*
Unforgotten. Remembered.
Uppermost in one's thoughts.
Within one's memory. See *Nouns*.

REMEMBRANCE—*Adverbs*.

By heart. From memory; quickened by feeling.
By rote. By mere repetition.
In memoriam [L.]. In memory of.
In memory of. Serving as a memento.
Memoriter [L.]. From memory.
Suggestive. Likely to recall something else.
Without book. From memory.

REMEMBRANCE—*Phrases*

Absens hæres non erit [L.]. The absent man will not be heir.
Beatæ memoriæ [L.]. Of blessed memory.
Forsan hæc olim meminisse juvabit [L.]. Perhaps it will even be pleasant hereafter to remember these things. [Virgil, *Æneid*, i, 203.[
Littera scripta manet [L.]. The written word remains.
Manet alta mente repostum [L.]. It remains deeply fixed in the mind. [Virgil, *Æneid*, i, 26.]
Memoriâ in æternâ [L.]. In everlasting remembrance.
Mendacem memorem esse oportet [L.]. A liar needs to have a good memory. [Quintilian, *Institutes*, IV, ii, 91.]
Vox audita perit, littera scripta manet [L.]. The spoken word perishes, the written word remains.

---

re-mem'-bran-cer. A token; recorder RECORDER, REMEMBRANCE-FORGETFULNESS.
re-mem'-bran-ces. Tokens of friendship. POLITENESS-IMPOLITENESS.
re-mem''-o-ra'-tion. Recollection. REMEMBRANCE-FORGETFULNESS
rem''-i-gra'-tion. Return. ADVANCE-RETROGRESSION, ARRIVAL-DEPARTURE, ENTRANCE-EXIT.
re-mind'. To bring to mind. REMEMBRANCE-FORGETFULNESS; **that reminds me,** OPPORTUNENESS-UNSUITABLENESS.
re-mind'-er. Something that calls to mind. REMEMBRANCE-FORGETFULNESS.
rem''-i-nis'-cence. Recollection REMEMBRANCE-FORGETFULNESS.
rem''-i-nis-cen'-tial. Reminiscent REMEMBRANCE-FORGETFULNESS
re-mise'. To relinquish. DUTY-IMMUNITY.
re-miss'. Negligent. ACTIVITY-INDOLENCE, CAREFULNESS-CARELESSNESS READINESS-RELUCTANCE, RULE-LICENSE.
re-mis'-sion. Forgiveness, relaxation. DISCONTINUANCE-CONTINUANCE, PARDON-VINDICTIVENESS, RULE-LICENSE, TURBULENCE-CALMNESS.
re-miss'-ness. Neglect ACTIVITY-INDOLENCE

re-mit'. To abate; pardon, send money. ACTION-PASSIVENESS, DIAPHANEITY-OPALESCENCE, DISCONTINUANCE-CONTINUANCE, PARDON-VINDICTIVENESS, TAKING-RESTITUTION, TURBULENCE-CALMNESS.
re-mit'-tance. Payment. MONEY, SETTLEMENT-DEFAULT.
re-mit'-tent. Periodic. PERIODICITY-IRREGULARITY.
re-mit'-ter. One who remits. TAKING-RESTITUTION.
rem'-nant. Remainder. INCREMENT-REMNANT.
re-mod'-el. To rearrange. BETTERMENT-DETERIORATION, CONVERSION-REVERSION, REVOLUTION.
re-mol'-li-ent. Softening. HARDNESS-SOFTNESS, TURBULENCE-CALMNESS.
re-mon'-strance. Reproof. APPROVAL-DISAPPROVAL, MOTIVE-DEHORTATION.
re-mon'-strate. To urge reasons against. APPROVAL-DISAPPROVAL, MOTIVE-DEHORTATION.
rem'-o-ra. Kind of sucking-fish; stagnation. COHESION-LOOSENESS, OBSTRUCTION-HELP.
re-morse'. Anguish. REPENTANCE-OBDURACY.
re-morse'-less. Lacking remorse. PARDON - VINDICTIVENESS, REPENTANCE-OBDURACY.
re-mote'. Distant; unconnected. CONNECTION-INDEPENDENCE, REMOTENESS-NEARNESS: **remote age,**

Future-Past; **remote cause,** Cause-Effect; **re-** **re-mote′-ness.** The state of being distant. Remote-
mote future, Future-Past.   ness-Nearness.

REMOTENESS—NEARNESS.

Dispersion. State of being scattered far and wide.
Distance. Remoteness of a place; period of time.
Elongation. Extension; protraction, separation.
Far cry to. A great distance.
Farness. The state of being afar off: remote.
Longinquity. Greatness of distance.
Long range. A long distance.
Reach. A long unbroken stretch.
Remoteness. A great distance from a specified point.
Removedness. The state of being separated by a long distance.
Space. An interval between points or objects.

REMOTENESS—*Denotations.*

Antipodes. A place or region on the opposite side of the earth.
Aphelion. The point in an orbit of a planet farthest from the sun.
Background. That part in a picture which is behind the principal objects represented.
Echimeter. An instrument for measuring distances between objects near the horizon.
Foreign parts. Regions in another country.
Giant's stride. A long distance
Horizon. The line on the earth's surface that bounds the view.
Ne plus ultra [L.]. The farthest point, the limit.
Offing. That part of the visible sea distant from shore, beyond anchorage-ground.
Outlier. That which is without or beyond the main body.
Outpost. The station held by a body of troops at a distance from the main body
Outskirts. A place or situation on or near the border.
Parallax. The distance between the directions of a body from the earth's center and from a point of observation on its surface.
Span. The entire distance covered by anything.
Stride. A long measured step.
Ultima Thule [L.]. The most remote land of the world. [Virgil, *Georgics*, i 30.]

REMOTENESS—*Verbs.*

Be distant. Separated; far away.
Extend to. To reach to; stretch to.
Get to. Arrive at; attain.
Go to. Travel toward.
Keep at a distance. To be far removed from.
Range. To reach out in an unbroken space.
Reach to. To extend to a distance.
Remain at a distance. Stay away; go no nearer.
Spread. To extend over some area.
Stand aloof. Keep away from.
Stand away. To be removed from.
Stand clear of. To be distant from.
Stand off. Keep at a distance.
Stretch away. To fade from view.
Stretch to. Cause to extend.

REMOTENESS—*Adjectives.*

Antipodean. Pertaining to those on the opposite side of the earth.
Distal. Remote from the origin or center.
Distant. Separated.
Far. A long way off; remote.
Far away. Distant.
Far off. Remote.
Hyperborean. Most northern; beyond the frozen north.
Inaccessible. Unapproachable; not to be reached.
Incontiguous. Not in contact; separate.
Out of the way. Secluded; hard to find.
Remote. Distant; far away.
Stretching to. Reaching far out.
Telescopic. To be seen only by a telescope.
Tramontane. Beyond the mountains.
Transalpine. Beyond the Alps.
Transatlantic. Beyond the Atlantic.
Transmarine. Across the sea.
Transmontane. Across the mountain.
Ulterior. Further; beyond.
Ultramontane. Beyond the mountain.
Ultramundane. Beyond the world.
Unapproachable. } Gigantic; awe-inspiring: not to be reached.
Unapproached. }

Adjacency. State of lying close by.
Approach. A coming near.
Bow-shot. The distance to which an arrow may be sent from a bow.
Contiguity. Nearness, proximity.
Convergence. The state of coming nearer to.
Ear-shot. The distance at which sounds may be heard
Gun-shot. The range or reach of a gun.
Hairbreadth. The width of a hair.
Nearness. State of being near.
Pistol-shot. The range of a pistol.
Propinquity. Close relation.
Proximity. Nearness in time, place, or relation.
Short cut. The shortest distance.
Short distance. The nearest way.
Short step. A short distance
Stone's throw. The distance to which a stone may be thrown.

NEARNESS—*Denotations.*

Alentours [F.]. The grounds round.
Banlieue [F.]. The outskirts.
Borderer. One who dwells near the border of a country.
Borderland. Land on the border of two adjoining countries.
Bystander. One who stands by.
Confines. Borderlands.
Environs. The surrounding region.
Neighbor. One who lives near another.
Neighborhood The region lying near where one resides.
Perihelion. The point in the orbit of a planet where it is nearest to the sun.
Purlieus. The outskirts of any place.
Span. The extreme space over which the hand can be expanded.
Suburbs. A region or place adjacent to a city.
Vicinage. Neighboring places.
Vicinity. Neighborhood.
Whereabouts. The place in or near which a person or thing is.

NEARNESS—*Verbs.*

Adjoin. Border upon; append.
Approximate. To come nearer to.
Be near. To be only a short distance from.
Border upon. To touch or come in contact with.
Bring near. To come close to. See Approach.
Burn. To approach very near to a concealed object.
Clasp. To take hold of; seize.
Cling to. Adhere; embrace.
Converge. To come near to. See Concentration.
Crowd. To bring together closely. See Gathering.
Draw near. To come close to.
Hang about. To cling to.
Hang upon the skirts of. Follow closely.
Huddle. To cling close to.
Hug. To embrace; clasp in the arms tightly.
Hover over. To hang over.
Place side by side. To place in contact.
Stand by. To stand by the side of.
Tread on the heels of. Follow up too closely.
Trench on. Encroach.
Verge upon. To come next to.

NEARNESS—*Adjectives.*

At hand. Close to.
Adjacent. Contiguous.
Adjoining. Lying next; bordering.
Close. Near by.
Close at hand. Near
Handy. Convenient; close at hand.
Home. Nearest to.
Intimate. Confidential, familiar.
Near. Close by.
Near at hand. Not remote; neighborly
Near run. Almost deprived of.
Near the mark. Close to.
Neighboring. Closely associated.
Nigh. Near; being close by.
Proximal. } Near to; next.
Proximate. }

NEARNESS—*Adverbs.*

About. Nearly
Alongside. Side by side.

REMOTENESS—NEARNESS—*Continued.*

REMOTENESS—ADJECTIVES—*Continued.*

Wide of. Far from the mark.
Yon. }
Yonder. } At a distance.

REMOTENESS—*Adverbs, etc.*

Abroad. In distant lands; widely.
Afar. }
Afar off. } At a great distance.
A good way off. Quite a distance removed.
A great way off. }
A long way off. } Far; remote.
Aloof. Away from.
Apart. Isolated; aside; separate.
À perte de vue [F.]. Out of sight.
Asunder. Apart; separated from one another.
At arm's length. At a distance as long as the arm.
Away. Far from.
Beyond. On the other side; out of reach.
Clear of. Separated from.
Far and wide. Comprehensively; broadly.
Far away. At a distance.
Far off. Remote; at a great distance.
Farther. At a greater distance.
From pole to pole. Covering the whole world.
Further. More remote; farther.
Longo intervallo [L.]. With a long interval.
Nobody knows where. Out of sight.
Off. At a distance from.
Out of hearing. So far as not to hear a sound from.
Out of reach. Unattainable.
Out of the sphere. Out of the proper field of action.
Out of the way. Separated from.
Outre mer [F.] Beyond the sea.

---

re-mo′-tion. Act of removing. TRANSFER.
re-mov′-al. Change of place. ADDITION-SUBTRACTION, ARRIVAL-DEPARTURE, ESTABLISHMENT-REMOVAL, INJECTION-EJECTION, TRANSFER.
re-move′. To take or go away or back; course; class. ADDITION-SUBTRACTION, APPROACH-WITHDRAWAL, ARRIVAL-DEPARTURE, ENTITY-NONENTITY, ESTABLISHMENT-REMOVAL, INJECTION-EJECTION, INSTRUCTOR-PUPIL, NUTRIMENT-EXCRETION, STATION; **remove the mask,** EXPOSURE-HIDINGPLACE.
re-mov′-ed-ness. State of being removed. REMOTENESS-NEARNESS.
re-mu′-gi-ent. Rebellowing. CRY-ULULATION.
re-mu′-ner-ate. To repay. RECOMPENSE-PUNITION, USEFULNESS-USELESSNESS.
re-mu″-ner-a′-tion. Compensation. RECOMPENSE-PUNITION.
re-mu′-ner-a-tive. Profitable. GAIN-LOSS, USEFULNESS-USELESSNESS.
re-mu′-ner-a-to″-ry. Compensating. RECOMPENSE-PUNITION.
Re-nais″-sance′. Revival. RENOVATION-RELAPSE.
re-nas′-cent. Revived. RENEWAL.
ren-con′-ter. To encounter. INTERSPACE-CONTACT, STRIFE-PEACE.
ren-coun′-ter. To meet by surprise. ARRIVAL-DEPARTURE, INTERSPACE-CONTACT, STRIFE-PEACE.
rend. To separate. UNION-DISUNION; **rend the air,** CRY-ULULATION, LOUDNESS-FAINTNESS; **rend the heart-strings,** PLEASURABLENESS-PAINFULNESS.
ren′-der. To alter; to translate; to give. CONVERSION-REVERSION, GIVING-RECEIVING, INTERPRETATION-MISINTERPRETATION, TAKING-RESTITUTION; **render an account,** ACCOUNT, ENLIGHTENMENT-SECRECY; **render a service,** USEFULNESS-USELESSNESS.
ren′-dez-vous. Meeting place GATHERINGPLACE, GATHERING-SCATTERING.
ren-di′-tion. Translation; surrender. INTERPRETATION-MISINTERPRETATION, TAKING-RESTITUTION.
ren′-e-gade. Deserter. BIGOTRY-APOSTASY, CONVERSION-REVERSION, PATRIOTISM-TREASON, UPRIGHTNESS-ROGUE.

NEARNESS—ADVERBS—*Continued.*

Approximately. }
Approximatively. } Nearly.
Beside. By the side of.
Hereabouts. In this place.
Near. At a short distance from.
Nigh. Near.
Roughly. Approximately.
Thereabouts. About.
Well-nigh. Nearly.

NEARNESS—*Adverbial Phrases.*

As good as; at close quarters; at no great distance; at one's door; at one's elbow; at one's feet; at one's finger ends; at one's side; at the heels of; at the point of; bordering upon; but a step to; cheek by jowl; close to; close upon; fast by; hard by; in juxtaposition; in preference of; in round numbers; in sight of; in the environs; in the way; next door to; not far from; on the confines of; on the skirts of; on the tip of one's tongue; on the verge of; side by side; *tête-à-tête* [F.], head to head; under one's nose; verging to; within an ace; within a stone's throw; within call; within ear-shot; within hearing; within reach; yard-arm to yard-arm.

REMOTENESS—ADVERBS, ETC.—*Continued.*

Over the border. Beyond the verge.
Over the hills and far away. At a great distance from.
To the ends of the earth. To the most remote places.
To the uttermost parts. Farthest away.
Wide apart. Far from one another.
Wide asunder. Thrown far apart.
Wide away. Far distant.
Wide of the mark. Not near to the spot aimed at.

---

re-new . To repeat; to restore; to begin again. DOUBLING-HALVING, RECURRENCE, REMEMBRANCE-FORGETFULNESS, RENEWAL, RENOVATION-RELAPSE; **renew one's strength,** WEARINESS-REFRESHMENT.
re-new′-al. Revival. DOUBLING-HALVING, RECURRENCE, RENEWAL, RENOVATION-RELAPSE.

RENEWAL.

Apotheosis. The act of placing a mortal among the gods; deification.
Generation. Act of begetting or reproducing. See CREATION.
Multiplication. Act of increasing in number.
New edition. A reissue of a publication.
Palingenesia. A new birth.
Phenix. A sacred bird fabled to burn itself on an altar and then rise afresh from the ashes.
Reanimation. The condition of living again.
Reappearance. The act or process of coming into view again.
Regeneration. See sub *Verbs.*
Regenesis. Renewal.
Regrowth. A growing again.
Renewal. The act of renewing or restoring.
Renovation. The act of making over again.
Reprint. An edition of an already printed work that is a verbatim copy of the original.
Reproduction. The process by which life is continued from one generation to another. See *Verbs*
Restoration. The act of restoring to a former place or condition.
Resurrection. A rising again from the dead.
Resuscitation. Revival from apparent death.
Revival. Resuscitation; a giving of new life or vigor.
Revivification. Act of recalling to life.

RENEWAL—*Verbs.*

Crop up. To spring up; sprout
Multiply. To increase in number.
Put into the crucible. To remold.
Reanimate. To renew the life of.
Refashion. To form into shape a second time.
Regenerate. To give new birth or strength.
Renew. To make new again; to restore to a former condition.
Renovate. To repair or make good again what has fallen into a bad condition.
Repeat. To say or do over again.
Reproduce. To bring forward or exhibit afresh.
Restore. To bring back to life.
Resuscitate. To revive from apparent death.

Revive. To inspire with new life and vigor.
Revivify. To revive: revivify is more intense than revive.
Spring up like mushrooms. To grow up very rapidly.
Stir the embers. To put new force and vigor into.

RENEWAL—Adjectives.

Reappearing. Showing forth again. See *Verbs.*
Renascent. Revived; reanimated.
Reproducing. Bringing forth new life. See *Verbs.*
Reproductive. Employed in reproduction.

ren'-i-form. Kidney-shaped. CURVATION-RECTILINE-ARITY.

re-ni'-tence. Reluctance; offering resistance; elastic. COOPERATION - OPPOSITION, HARDNESS - SOFTNESS, READINESS-RELUCTANCE, REPRISAL-RESISTANCE.

re-ni'-ten-cy. Renitence. ELASTICITY-INELASTICITY, LIGHT-DARKNESS.

re-ni'-tent. Resisting. COOPERATION-OPPOSITION, ELASTICITY-INELASTICITY, REPRISAL-RESISTANCE.

re-nounce'. To disown. BIGOTRY-APOSTASY, DUTY-DERELICTION, HEALTHINESS-SICKNESS, KEEPING-RELINQUISHMENT, QUEST-ABANDONMENT.

renovare dolorem infandum [L.] (ren-o-vê'-rî do-lo'-rem infan'-dum). To revive unspeakable grief. CONTENTEDNESS-REGRET.

ren'-o-vate. To renew. RENEWAL, RENOVATION-RELAPSE.

ren'-o-va"-ted. Renewed. NOVELTY-ANTIQUITY.

ren"-o-va'-tion. Renewal. NOVELTY-ANTIQUITY, RENEWAL, RENOVATION-RELAPSE.

RENOVATION—RELAPSE.

Cicatrization. A healing of an ulcer by inducing the formation of connective tissue.
Convalescence. A progressive recovering of health after sickness.
Curableness. State of being able to be restored.
Cure. A complete restoration to health and strength.
Disinfection. A purification from infecting matter.
Healing. The act or process of healing, or of restoring to a former state of health. See *Verbs.*
Instauration. Restoration after decay; renewal.
New birth. The beginning of a new condition in the spiritual life.
Palingenesis. A second birth into a higher life.
Phenix. A fabled bird said to arise anew from its own burning.
Reaction. A tendency to a former state, be it good or evil.
Reanimation. The infusion of new life, vigor, etc.
Réchauffé [F.] Anything warmed anew.
Reclamation. A bringing into a better state.
Reconstruction. A making again; a restoration.
Reconversion. A second conversion.
Recovery. The act of gaining again, as one's health.
Recruitment. A building up anew with fresh supplies. See *Verbs.*
Rectification. The act or operation of making right.
Recure. A second cure.
Recurrence. The act of recurring, or of resorting. See *Verbs.*
Redemption. A rescue from sin and its consequences; a recovery; a buying back. See RESCUE.
Redintegration. Restoration to a whole and sound state.
Reestablishment. An establishment anew; a restoration.
Refreshment. The act of refreshing or of reinvigorating. See WEARINESS-REFRESHMENT.
Regeneracy. State of being regenerated or of being born into a new-life.
Regenerateness. State of being regenerated.
Regeneration. Act of being renewed spiritually.
Regenesis. State of being born or produced again.
Regrowth. New growth.
Rehabilitation. Restoration to former state.
Reinstatement. A putting back in a place previously occupied.
Rejuvenescence. A renewal of youth.
Relief. A freeing wholly or in part from an evil or hardship. See ALLEVIATION.
Renaissance. A new birth; specifically the revival of letters and art at the end of the medieval period.
Renovation. A making as good as new; a purification.
Reorganization. An organizing anew.
Repair. A restoration to a sound condition after decay, lapse, or injury.
Reparation. The act of repairing, as of an injury; an indemnification.
Replacement. A putting back in place; a substitution in the place of.
Reproduction. Act of producing again; a bringing back of what previously existed or was known. See RENEWAL.
Restitution. The act of putting back something that was taken away, a making good of a loss, an indemnification. See TAKING-RESTITUTION.
Restoral. A restoration.
Restoration. The act of bringing back to a former state; a reconstruction out of existing materials into its former condition.
Resumption. A beginning again after cessation; a taking into possession again after relinquishment.
Résumption [F.] A resumption.
Resuscitation. A restoration to life; revivification.
Retrieval. Restoration to an improved condition from one of loss or disaster; a remedying of the evil consequences of an action.

Backset. A taking back.
Backsliding. A falling back, as in religion.
Deterioration. The process of deteriorating, of growing worse. See BETTERMENT-DETERIORATION.
Falling back. A falling into sickness or the like. See *Verbs.*
Lapse. A gradual falling away; a slip.
Recidivation. A backsliding.
Recrudescence. An increased severity of a disease after a temporary remission.
Relapse. A falling back, especially in a former state of sickness or wickedness.
Retrogradation. The act of retrograding, or of moving backwards. See ADVANCE-RETROGRESSION.
Tabescence. A state of emaciation.

RELAPSE—Verbs.

Fall again. } To relapse.
Fall back. }
Fall off. To withdraw; apostatize. See BETTERMENT-DETERIORATION.
Lapse. To fall back or away.
Recividate. To backslide.
Relapse. To turn back into a former state.
Retrograde. To move backward. See ADVANCE-RETROGRESSION.
Return. To turn back; come to the same place.
Sink back. } To relapse.
Slide back. }

RENOVATION—Continued.

Reviction. A return to life.
Revival. The act of reviving or of renewing interest in any subject.
Revivification. A giving of new life spirit, or energy to.
Reviviscence. A renewal of life.
Rifacimento [It.] Renewal; reestablishment.
Sanation. The act of healing.
Second youth. A renewal of youth; a feeling of becoming younger.
Tinkering. A mending or patching.

RENOVATION—Nouns of Agent.

Cobbler. One who repairs shoes.
Tinker. An itinerant repairer in small metal utensils.
Vis medicatrix [L.] A healing force. See REMEDY.

RENOVATION.—Verbs.

Be oneself again. To recover from an injury or sickness.
Bind up wounds. To dress the wounds.
Botch. To repair in an imperfect and clumsy manner.
Break of. To cure of.
Bring round. To restore, as from a sickness.
Calk. To make tight, as the seams of a boat, by filling with waste matter.
Careen. To make a vessel lean over on one side so that the other may be repaired.
Caulk. To calk
Cicatrize. To cause to heal by inducing a formative tissue.
Cobble. To mend or repair coarsely.
Come round. } To restore to health.
Come round to oneself. }
Come to. To revive, as from a swoon.
Come to life again. To revive.
Come to oneself. To recover your senses.
Correct. To make right what is wrong.
Cure. To restore to soundness or health; to heal.

RENOVATION—Verbs—*Continued.*

Darn. To repair a hole by filling with yarn.
Doctor. To repair; take medical advice.
Do up. To make fresh and clean.
Fill up. }
Fill up the ranks. } To recruit.
Fine draw. To repair a hole or rent by filling up with new thread so carefully that it is almost imperceptible.
Get over. To recover.
Get round. To become well.
Get round about. To be able to move about, after a sickness.
Get the better of. To overcome a weakness.
Get well. To be restored.
Heal. To restore to health; make sound, as an injury.
Heelpiece. To provide with a heelpiece.
Live again. To recover from sickness.
Make all square. To make sound.
Make good. To indemnify.
Make whole. To restore.
Medicate. To treat with medicine.
Patch up. To fix a broken or torn part.
Physic. To give medicine to.
Place in statu quo. To put in the position in which it was.
Plaster up. To conceal the defects of, as by plastering.
Pull through. To recover, but with difficulty.
Put back. To reinstate.
Put in complete repair. To repair; restore; renew.
Put in order. To arrange. See ORGANIZATION.
Put in repair. }
Put right. }
Put straight. } To repair; restore; renew.
Put through repair. }
Put to rights. }
Rally. To recover strength and vigor; to restore to discipline, as a demoralized army.
Reanimate. To call back to life; reinvigorate.
Reappear. To appear again.
Rebuild. To build again after destruction or decay.
Recall to life. To revive.
Reclaim. To call back; restore land to use; reform.
Reconstitute. To constitute again.
Reconstruct. To rebuild.
Reconvert. To convert again.
Recoup. To gather strength as compensation for what was lost; reimburse. See TAKING-RESTITUTION.
Recover. To get again; regain health after sickness.
Recruit. To repair with fresh supplies; renew in strength, vigor, etc.
Rectify. To make right what is wrong.
Recure. To cure again.
Redeem. To purchase back; rescue from bondage, as of sin.
Redintegrate. To restore to soundness or wholeness.
Redress. To set right a wrong.

Reestablish. To establish again.
Reestate. To reestablish.
Refit. To equip again.
Refresh. To make fresh; relieve from fatigue. See WEARINESS-REFRESHMENT.
Regenerate. To give new life to; make a change for the better.
Rehabilitate. To invest with some right or office formerly possessed; restore to former position or privileges.
Reinforce. To strengthen with new force.
Reinstall. To place again in former state or possession.
Reinstate. To place in a former position.
Reinvigorate. To invigorate anew.
Remedy. To cure; repair.
Renew. To make new; give new life to.
Renovate. To render as good as new.
Reorganize. To reduce again to an organized condition.
Repair. To mend or restore after partial destruction.
Replace. To put back in place.
Reproduce. To produce again. See RENEWAL.
Rescue. To deliver from danger or disaster. See RESCUE.
Reseat. To seat again.
Restore. To cause to assume a former condition; reproduce.
Resume. To begin after cessation; take back.
Resuscitate. To restore to life.
Retouch. To touch again; renew.
Retrieve. To remedy the evil consequences of.
Return to the original state. To replace or renew.
Revive. To return to life; reanimate.
Revivify. To give new life or vigor to.
Right itself. To free from fault, etc.
Right oneself. To make well.
Rise again. To recover from disaster.
Rise from one's ashes. To rise from degradation.
Rise from the grave. To come to a new life.
Set on one's legs. To reestablish.
Set right. }
Set straight. } To put in order; restore.
Set to rights. }
Set up. To establish in business.
Skin over. To cover as with a skin.
Splice. To join or unite, as the ends of rope; restore to former condition of wholeness.
Stanch. }
Staunch. } To check the flow of blood.
Stop a gap. To fix or repair.
Survive. To outlive; exist in force or operation. See LASTINGNESS.
Tinker. To repair clumsily.
Vamp. }
Vamp up. } To furnish with a vamp; repair.
Warm up. To animate.
Weather the storm. To survive.

RENOVATION—*Adjectives.*

Convalescent. Recovering health.
Curable. Capable of being cured.
Curative. Tending to cure diseases.
In a fair way. Convalescing.
None the worse. Recovered from danger.
Recoverable. Able to recover.
Recuperative. Tending to recovery.
Redivivus [L.]. Renewed.
Remediable. Capable of being remedied.
Remedial. Intended for a remedy.

Reparative. }
Reparatory. } Tending to recover.
Restorable. Capable of being restored.
Restorative. Tending to restore.
Restored. }
Restoring. } Made well or strong. See *Verbs.*
Sanable. Curable.
Sanative. Sanatory; healing.
Sanatory. Promotive of health

RENOVATION—*Adverbs, etc.*

As you were. As in a former condition.

In statu quo [L.]. In the former condition.

RENOVATION—*Phrases.*

Médecin, guéris-toi toi-même [F.] Physician, heal thyself.
Revenons à nos moutons [F.]. Let us return to our [sheep] subject.

Vestigia nulla retrorsum [L.]. No footsteps backward. [Horace, Epistles I, i, 74.]

re-nown'. Fame. REPUTATION-DISCREDIT.
re-nowned'. Famous. REPUTATION-DISCREDIT.
re-nown'-less. Unfamous. REPUTATION-DISCREDIT.
rent. Hole; pay for use of something. BUYING-SALE, INTERSPACE-CONTACT, LOAN-BORROWING, OUTLAY-INCOME, UNION-DISUNION.
rent'-age. Rent. OUTLAY-INCOME.
rent'-al. Revenue. OUTLAY-INCOME.
rent'-er. Tenant. HOLDER.

rent'-free''. Not paying rent. COSTLINESS-CHEAPNESS.
rent'-roll''. Income. OUTLAY-INCOME, PROPERTY.
rents. Houses rented. DWELLER-HABITATION.
re-nun''-ci-a'-tion. Denial; abandonment. BIGOTRY-APOSTASY, COMMISSION-ABROGATION, DUTY-DERELICTION, QUEST-ABANDONMENT.
reo absente [L.] (rĭ'-o ab-sen'-tĭ). In the absence of the defendant. LITIGATION.

re-or''-gan-i-za'-tion. The act of reorganizing. RENOVATION-RELAPSE.

re-or'-gan-ize. To organize again. BETTERMENT-DETERIORATION, CONVERSION-REVERSION, RENOVATION-RELAPSE.

re-pair'. To mend; to renew. ATONEMENT, BETTERMENT-DETERIORATION, RENOVATION-RELAPSE, TAKING-RESTITUTION, WEARINESS-REFRESHMENT; **out of repair,** BETTERMENT-DETERIORATION; **repair to,** TRAVELING-NAVIGATION.

rep''-a-ra'-tion. Satisfaction. ATONEMENT, RECOMPENSE-PUNITION, RENOVATION-RELAPSE, TAKING-RESTITUTION.

re-par'-a-tive. Serving to repair. RENOVATION-RELAPSE.

re-par'-a-to-ry. Reparative. RECOMPENSE-PUNITION, RENOVATION-RELAPSE.

rep''-ar-tee'. Witty reply. INVESTIGATION-ANSWER, WITTINESS-DULNESS.

rep''-ar-tee'-ist. One ready at repartee. WAG.

re''-par-ti'-tion. Redivision. ASSIGNMENT.

re-pass'. To pass again. **Pass and repass,** TRANSMISSION, VIBRATION.

re-past'. Meal. NUTRIMENT-EXCRETION.

re-pay'. To pay back; to recompense. RECOMPENSE-PUNITION, SETTLEMENT-DEFAULT.

re-pay'-ment. Reimbursement. SETTLEMENT-DEFAULT.

re-peal'. To revoke. COMMISSION-ABROGATION.

re-peat'. To reproduce; to do or say again. ASSERTION-DENIAL, DOUBLING-HALVING, HABIT-DESUETUDE, IMITATION-ORIGINALITY, RECURRENCE, REMEMBRANCE-FORGETFULNESS, RENEWAL; **repeat by rote,** REMEMBRANCE-FORGETFULNESS.

re-peat'-ed. Done or occurring often. FREQUENCY-RARITY, RECURRENCE.

re-peat'-ed-ly. Often. FREQUENCY-RARITY, RECURRENCE.

re-peat'-er. Watch; firearm. CHRONOLOGY-ANACHRONISM, WEAPON.

re-pel'. To force back; refuse. ATTACK-DEFENSE, ATTRACTION-REPULSION, DESIRE-DISTASTE, LOVE-HATE, MOTIVE-DEHORTATION, PLEASURABLENESS-PAINFULNESS, PROFFER-REFUSAL, REPRISAL-RESISTANCE, SOCIABILITY-PRIVACY.

re-pel'-lent. Repulsive. BEAUTY-UGLINESS, DESIRE-DISTASTE, NUTRIMENT-EXCRETION, PLEASURABLENESS-PAINFULNESS, REPRISAL-RESISTANCE.

re-pel'-ling. Thrusting back. ATTRACTION-REPULSION.

re-pent'. To feel sorrow for wrong done. CONTENTEDNESS-REGRET, REPENTANCE-OBDURACY.

re-pent'-ance. Regret. BIGOTRY-APOSTASY, REPENTANCE-OBDURACY.

REPENTANCE—OBDURACY.

Acknowledgment. The act of acknowledging or confessing.

Apology, etc. A formal acknowledgment of error or wrong, etc. See ATONEMENT.

Awakened conscience. Acknowledgment of wrong-doing.

Compunction. Pain occasioned by a sense of guilt.

Compunctious visitings of nature. Pricks of conscience.

Confession, etc. The acknowledgment of faults or sins, etc. See EXPOSURE.

Contrition. Deep sorrow and penitence for sin.

Death-bed repentance. Repentance at the last moment.

Pangs of conscience. Uneasiness occasioned by guilt. See *Nouns.*

Penance, etc. Punishment or suffering, voluntary or imposed, submitted to as an expression of repentance. See ATONEMENT.

Penitence. Sorrow for sins.

Prickings of conscience. Pangs of conscience. See *Nouns.*

Qualms of conscience. Compunction.

Recantation, etc. The act of taking back openly, etc. See BIGOTRY-APOSTASY.

Regret, etc. Pain of mind arising from some past experience or occurrence. See CONTENTEDNESS-REGRET.

Remorse. Anguish of conscience produced by the recollection of guilt.

Repentance. Sincere sorrow for sin, accompanied by a turning away from sin.

Resipiscence. Wisdom, derived from experience.

Self-accusation. Act of being accused by one's own conscience.

Self-condemnation. Condemnation by one's own judgment.

Self-humiliation. The state of being humbled by oneself.

Self-reproach. }
Self-reproof. } Censure by one's own conscience.

Stings of conscience.]
Touch of conscience.]
Twinge of conscience. } Compunctions. See *Nouns.*
Twitch of conscience.]
Voice of conscience.]

REPENTANCE—*Denotations.*

A sadder and a wiser man. A penitent person.

Magdalen. The woman described by Luke as a demoniac from whom seven devils were cast out.

Penitent. One sorry for sin.

Prodigal son. A repentant person.

REPENTANCE—*Nouns of Place.*

Cutty-stool. A seat in the old Scottish churches, where offenders were made to sit to receive rebuke from the minister.

Locus pænitentiæ [L.] The place of repentance.

Stool of repentance. The cutty-stool.

REPENTANCE—*Verbs.*

Acknowledge. To admit what we have said or done, good or bad.

Beg pardon, etc. To apologize See ATONEMENT

Hardness of heart. The state of being without sympathy or pity.

Impenitence. The state of being impenitent.

Induration. Lack of feeling.

Irrepentance. Want of repentance.

Obduracy. Invincible hardness of heart.

Recusance. The state of being obstinate in refusal.

Seared conscience. A conscience not susceptible to moral influences.

OBDURACY—*Verbs.*

Be impenitent. To be hardened to sin. See *Adjectives.*

Die and make no sign. To die impenitent.

Die game. To maintain an unyielding spirit to the end

Harden the heart. To become unsympathetic.

Steel the heart. To harden the heart.

OBDURACY—*Adjectives.*

Graceless. Lacking in grace; depraved.

Hardened. Wanting in feeling; confirmed in error.

Impenitent. Not penitent.

Incorrigible. Beyond hope of reclaiming.

Irreclaimable. Not able to be reclaimed.

Lost. Hardened beyond recovery.

Obdurate. Stubbornly impenitent.

Recusant. Obstinate in refusal.

Relentless. Unyielding.

Remorseless. Wanting in remorse.

Seared. Hardened.

Shriftless. Without absolution.

Unatoned. Not expiated.

Uncontrite. Not having deep sorrow for sin.

Unreclaimed. Not reformed.

Unreformed. Not improved morally.

Unrepentant. Not repentant.

Unrepented. Not sorry for sin. See *Verbs.*

REPENTANCE—*Verbs—Continued.*

Be penitent. } To express sorrow for one's own wrong-doing. See
Be sorry for. } *Adjectives.*

Confess, etc. To admit our faults, etc. See EXPOSURE.

Cry *peccavi* [L.] To cry I have sinned.

Humble oneself. To bring oneself low; to humiliate oneself.

Knock under, etc. To acknowledge oneself conquered, etc. See YIELDING.

Learn by experience. To learn of wrong by committing wrong.

Own oneself in the wrong. To confess.

Plead guilty. To present the answer of guilty.

Put on the new man. To be regenerated.

Recant, etc. To take back openly, etc. See BIGOTRY-APOSTASY.

REPENTANCE—Verbs—*Continued.*

Reclaim. To cause to reform morally.
Regret, etc. To have pain of mind on account of some past experience, etc. See CONTENTEDNESS-REGRET.
Repent. To feel sincere sorrow for and to turn away from sin.
Repent in sackcloth and ashes, etc. To sincerely repent. See ATONEMENT. [Bible.]
Rue. To extremely regret.

Sing *de profundis.* To sing out of the depths; hence, to be penitent. To sing the canticle beginning "*De profundis.*"
Sing *miserere.* To implore compassion in song. To sing the canticle beginning "*Miserere.*"
Think better of. To have a higher regard for.
Turn from sin. To repent.
Turn over a new leaf. To begin to live better.

REPENTANCE—*Adjectives.*

Conscience-smitten. Feeling regret or remorse.
Conscience-stricken. Having a feeling of remorse.
Contrite. Humbly penitent.
Not hardened. Ready to turn from sin.
Penitent. Feeling sorrow on account of sins or offenses.
Penitential. Pertaining to penitence.
Penitentiary. Relating to penance or expressing penitence.

Reclaimed. Freed from sin. See *Verbs.*
Repentant. Showing sorrow for sin.
Repenting. Expressing sorrow for wrong done. See *Verbs.*
Self-accusing. Accused by one's conscience.
Self-convicted. Convicted by one's consciousness or acts.
Unhardened. Not confirmed in wickedness.

REPENTANCE—*Phrases.*

Erubuit, salva res est [L.]. He blushes, all is safe. [Terence, *Brothers,* IV, v, 9.]

Mea culpa [L.]. Through my fault.
Peccavi [L.]. I have sinned.

re-pent'-ant. Penitent. REPENTANCE-OBDURACY.
re-pent'-ing. Deeply regretting. REPENTANCE-OB-DURACY.
re''-per-cuss'. To drive back. IMPETUS-REACTION.
re''-per-cus'-sion. Rebound. IMPETUS-REACTION.
rep''-er-toire'. List. ACTING.
repertorium [L.] (rep-er-to'-ri-um). A catalogue. STORE.
rep'-er-to''-ry. Repository. STORE.
rep'-e-tend''. Repeated decimal. NUMBER, RECURRENCE.
re''-pe-ti'-tion. Act of repeating. CRASH-DRUMMING, DISCONTINUANCE-CONTINUANCE, FREQUENCY-RARITY, IMITATION-ORIGINALITY, RECURRENCE, RHETORIC, UNIFORMITY-DIVERSITY.
re''-pe-ti'-tion-al. Iterative. RECURRENCE.
re''-pe-ti'-tion-a-ry. Repetitional. RECURRENCE.
re-pine'. To be sad; to complain. CONTENTEDNESS-DISCONTENT, LIGHTHEARTEDNESS-DEJECTION, PLEASURABLENESS-PAINFULNESS.
re-pi'-ning. Sorrowing. CONTENTEDNESS-DISCONTENTMENT, CONTENTEDNESS-REGRET.
re-place'. To substitute; to restore. CHEMISTRY, COMMUTATION-PERMUTATION, ESTABLISHMENT-REMOVAL, RENOVATION-RELAPSE.
re-place'-ment. Reinstatement. CHEMISTRY, RENOVATION-RELAPSE.
re-plen'-ish. To fill again. ENTIRETY-DEFICIENCY, PROVISION-WASTE.
re-plete'. Full. ENOUGH, ENTIRETY-DEFICIENCY, EXCESS-LACK.
re-ple'-tion. Fulness. ENOUGH, EXCESS-LACK, REPLETION.
re-plev'-in. Recovery of property by law. GAIN-LOSS, LOAN-BORROWING, TAKING-RESTITUTION.
re-plev'-y. Recovery. GAIN-LOSS, TAKING-RESTITUTION.
rep''-li-ca'-tion. Reply. INVESTIGATION-ANSWER, LITIGATION.
re-ply'. To answer. INVESTIGATION-ANSWER, JUSTIFICATION-CHARGE.
répondre en Normand [F.] (rê-pon·dr' an· nor-man·). To answer in French. TRUTHFULNESS-FALSEHOOD.
re-port'. Noise; rumor; account. ACCOUNT, CRASH-DRUMMING, DECISION-MISJUDGMENT, ENLIGHTENMENT-SECRECY, MARK-OBLITERATION, PUBLICITY, TIDINGS-MYSTERY; **good report,** REPUTATION-DISCREDIT; **report progress,** ENLIGHTENMENT-SECRECY; **through evil report and good report,** PERSISTENCE-WHIM.
re-port'-ed. Stated. ENLIGHTENMENT-SECRECY.
re-port'-er. Bearer of news; journalist. ENLIGHTEN-

MENT-SECRECY, MESSENGER, MISSIVE-PUBLICATION.
re-ports'. Judicial opinions. LITIGATION.
re-pose'. To rest; confide in. HURRY-LEISURE, MOVEMENT-REST, TOIL-RELAXATION; **repose confidence in,** FAITH-MISGIVING; **repose on,** EVIDENCE-COUNTER-EVIDENCE, SUSPENSION-SUPPORT; **repose on one's laurels,** DISCONTINUANCE-CONTINUANCE, MOVEMENT-REST.
re-pos'-ing. Resting. TOIL-RELAXATION.
re-pos'-it. Deposit. ESTABLISHMENT-REMOVAL.
re''-po-si'-tion. A deposit. ESTABLISHMENT-REMOVAL.
re-pos'-i-to-ry. Storeroom. STORE.
repostum manet alta mente [L.] (rep-os'-tum mê'-net al'-ta men'-tî). It remains fixed deeply in the mind. PARDON-VINDICTIVENESS.
repoussé [F.] (re-pu''-sê'). Recoiling. CONVEXITY-CONCAVITY.
rep''-re-hend'. To chide. APPROVAL-DISAPPROVAL, REPUTATION-DISCREDIT.
rep''-re-hen'-si-ble. Deserving reproof. APPROVAL-DISAPPROVAL, GOODNESS-BADNESS, INNOCENCE-GUILT, VICE-VIRTUE.
rep''-re-hen'-sion. Reproof. APPROVAL-DISAPPROVAL.
rep''-re-sent'. To act as agent for; to portray. COMMISSION-ABROGATION, DELINEATION-CARICATURE, ENLIGHTENMENT-SECRECY, IMITATION-ORIGINALITY, MANIFESTATION-LATENCY, REPRESENTATIVE, SIGN; **represent to oneself,** FANCY.
rep''-re-sen-ta'-tion. A showing or drawing. ACTING, COPY-MODEL, DELINEATION-CARICATURE, ENLIGHTENMENT-SECRECY, NATURE-ART, SIGN.
rep''-re-sent'-a-tive. Deputy. AGENT, COMMUTATION-PERMUTATION, DELINEATION-CARICATURE, PRESIDENT-MEMBER, REPRESENTATIVE, SIGN; **representative of the people,** COUNCIL; **representative of the press,** MESSENGER, MISSIVE-PUBLICATION.

REPRESENTATIVE.

Alter ego [L.]. Another self.
Commissioner. One who bears a commission or warrant from some authority to act in its behalf. See CONSIGNEE.
Delegate. One sent for another or for a body who elected him.
Deputy. An assistant; a substitute.
Lieutenant. One who takes his superior's place during absence.
Locum tenens [L.]. One occupying the place.
Next friend. One designated by law to act for another.
Proxy. One delegated to act for another.
Representative. A substitute; one elected to carry out the wishes of his constituents.
Secondary. One deputed to carry out the wishes of another.
Substitute. A proxy; a lieutenant.
Surrogate. A delegate; one who presides over the probates of wills and testaments.

Vicar. A substitute in office.
Vice. Second in rank; logical successor to a superior
Warden. A keeper; a guardian.

REPRESENTATIVE—*Denotations.*

Archon. The first of the nine chief magistrates in ancient Athens.
Chancellor. The chief secretary of a Roman emperor; the chief justice in England.
Consul. A government's guardian of its trade and seamen in foreign ports.
Minister. One who represents a government at the court of some foreign country.
Plenipotentiary. A government representative at a foreign court who is entrusted with full power to act and negotiate for his government.
Prefect. A Roman officer who had charge of a particular department of work.
Premier. The responsible head of the English cabinet. See **MANAGER.**
Proconsul. One who takes the place of the consul; a governor of a province.
Provost. The appointed head of some college, university, or English city.
Regent. The temporary ruler in the minority, absence, or disability of the king; an overseer.
Tsung li Yamun. A Chinese foreign office.
Vicar. One authorized to act instead of another, especially in religious functions.
Vicegerent. One deputed to perform the functions of another; substitute governor or ruler.
Viceroy. A ruler acting in the place of a sovereign. See **CHIEF.**
Vizier. A councilor of state.

REPRESENTATIVE—*Verbs.*

Ablegate. To commission.
Accredit. To invest with authority.
Answer for. To be one's proxy.
Appear for. To be one's substitute.

Be deputy. To be a lieutenant.
Represent. To stand or speak in the place of another.
Stand for. To bear the responsibility of.
Stand in the shoes of. To fill another's place.
Stand in the stead of. To be a deputy; a proxy.
Walk in the shoes of. To follow the same course.

REPRESENTATIVE—*Adjectives.*

Accredited to. Bearing a warrant to deal with.   See *Verbs.*
Acting. Taking the part of another.
Vice. In the place of. See *Nouns.*
Viceregal. Pertaining to a viceroy.

REPRESENTATIVE—*Adverb.*

In behalf of. On account of.

rep″-re-sent′-ed. Portrayed. DELINEATION-CARICATURE.
rep″-re-sent′-ing. Portraying. DELINEATION-CARICATURE, LIKENESS-UNLIKENESS.
re-press′. To restrain. RELEASE-RESTRAINT; repress one's feelings, EXCITABILITY-INEXCITABILITY; repress a smile, LIGHTHEARTEDNESS-DEJECTION.
re-pres′-sion. Restraint. COOPERATION-OPPOSITION, RELEASE-RESTRAINT.
re-priev′-al. Suspension. RESCUE.
re-prieve′. To relieve from danger; to defer punishment. ESCAPE, EXCULPATION-CONVICTION, PARDON-VINDICTIVENESS, RESCUE.
rep″-ri-mand′. Reproof. APPROVAL-DISAPPROVAL.
re-print′. To print anew. RENEWAL.
re′-print″. Copy. COPY-MODEL.
re-pri′-sal. Retaliation. REPRISAL-RESISTANCE, TAKING-RESTITUTION.

REPRISAL—RESISTANCE.

A game at which two can play. Reprisal.
A Roland for an Oliver. Tit for tat. [Rival heroes of romance.]
Blow for blow. Like for like.
Compensation. That which makes good the lack or variation of something else. See **COMPENSATION.**
Counterblast. An answering argument.
Counterplot. A plot opposing another plot.
Counterproject. A plan to overcome another plan.
Counterstroke. A plan in opposition to another plan.
Diamond cut diamond. A contest between intellects well matched.
Give and take. The giving of like for like.
Measure for measure. Like for like.
Quid pro quo [L.]. Something for something.
Reaction. Any action in resistance or response to the influence of another action or power. See **IMPETUS-REACTION.**
Reciprocation. A mutual giving and returning. See **INTERDEPENDENCE.**
Recrimination. The return of one accusation with another.
Reprisal. A taking by way of retaliation.
Retaliation. The return of like for like.
Retort. A censure or argument returned
Retribution. The act of requiting actions whether good or bad.
Revenge. The return of an injury received.
The biter bit. A giving or inflicting upon one what he inflicted upon us.
Tit for tat. Retort or retaliation in kind.

REPRISAL—*Verbs.*

Be even with. To have retaliation.
Be hoist on one's own petard. Blown up by his own mine. [Shakespeare, *Hamlet,* III. iv.]
Be quits. Be even with.
Cap. To follow up with something more remarkable than what has been done.
Catch a Tartar. To encounter a person who proves too strong for the assailant.
Exchange fisticuffs. To combat with the fists.
Give and take. To retaliate.
Give a *quid pro quo.* To give something for something.
Give as much as one takes. To retaliate in kind.
Pay back. To retaliate; to revenge.
Pay in one's own coin. } To return like treatment for like treatment.
Pay in the same coin. }
Pay off. To retaliate; to recompense.

Barring out. Shutting out from.
Front. The manner of confronting a person.
Insurrection. An organized and armed resistance.
Jacquerie. The peasant insurrection in France in 1358.
Kicking. Opposition. See *Verbs.*
Levée en masse [F.]. A rising in force.
Lockout. The shutting up of a place of business by the employers to punish the employees.
Opposition. The act of opposing or resisting. See **ANTAGONISM.**
Oppugnation. Opposition or resistance.
Rebuff. A sudden repulse.
Recalcitration. The act of making forcible resistance.
Reluctation. Repugnance; resistance.
Renitence. State of making resistance.
Repulse. Act of repelling or state of being repelled.
Resistance. The act of resisting or making opposition.
Riot. A disturbance by a large number of persons. See **REGULARITY-IRREGULARITY.**
Stand. A standing firmly or with decision.
Strike. A quitting of work by a body of laborers for the purpose of compelling employers to yield to their demands.
Turnout. A strike.

RESISTANCE—*Verbs.*

Bear up against. To oppose; to offer resistance.
Be proof against. To be capable of successful resistance.
Breast the wave. }
Breast the wave. } To resist manfully.
Confront. To offer resistance face to face.
Die hard. To resist till death.
Draw up a round robin. To resist by written petition with the signatures thereto in a circle, so as not to disclose who signed first.
Face. To resist to the face.
Fly in the face of. To offer defiant resistance.
Grapple with. To contend with.
Hold one's ground. To continue one's resistance.
Hold one's own. To maintain a successful resistance.
Hold out. To continue resisting.
Keep at bay. To keep an opponent at a standstill.
Kick. }
Kick against. } To offer resistance to.
Kick against the pricks. To resist that which cannot be overcome.
Lift the hand against. To oppose. See **ATTACK.**
Make a riot. To cause turbulent and disorderly resistance.

REPRISAL—RESISTANCE—*Continued.*

REPRISAL—Verbs—*Continued.*

Pay off old scores. To revenge old injuries.
Reciprocate. To give and return mutually. See Commutation-Permutation.
Retaliate. To return like for like.
Retort. To return an argument or incivility.
Return the compliment. To give back a compliment in return.
Serve one right. To treat one as he deserves.
Throw a stone in one's garden. Figurative for to do one an injury.
Turn the tables upon. To give a formerly successful opponent fully the worst of it.
Turn upon. To cause to operate on or against; to return.

REPRISAL—Adjectives.

Retaliating.
Retaliative. } Returning like for like. See *Verbs.*
Retaliatory.

REPRISAL—Adverbs, etc.

En revanche [F.]. In return; in revenge.
In retaliation. In return for. See *Nouns.*

REPRISAL—Phrases.

Ab alio expectes, alteri quod feceris [L.]. Expect to receive such treatment as you have given. [Publius Cyrus, 2.]
À beau jeu, beau retour [F.]. Tit for tat.
Litem . . . lite resolvit [L.]. He settles strife by strife. [Horace, *Satires,* II, iii, 103.]
Mutato nomine de te fabula narratur [L.]. The name being changed the story applies to you. [Horace, *Satires,* I, i, 69.]
Par pari refero [L.]. I return like for like. [Terence, *Eunuch,* III, i, 55.]
Suo sibi gladio hunc jugulo [L.]. Fight him with his own weapons.
Tu quoque [L.]. You also.
You're another.

RESISTANCE—Adjectives—*Continued from Column 2.*

Resistant.
Resisting. } Having the power of resistance. See *Nouns.*
Resistive.
Stubborn. Inflexible in resistance; intractable.
Unconquerable. Not to be conquered. See Strength.
Unconquered. Not overcome.
Unyielding. Not yielding; of persistent resistance. See Bigotry.
Up in arms. In armed resistance.

RESISTANCE—Interjections.

Hands off! keep off!

RESISTANCE—Verbs—*Continued.*

Make a stand. To offer resistance.
Make head against. To resist successfully.
Not submit. To fight against. See Yielding.
Oppose. To resist; withstand. See Antagonism.
Prendre le mors aux dents [F.]. To take the bit between the teeth; to run recklessly into danger.
Present a front. To make resistance.
Recalcitrate. To kick against. See *Nouns.*
Reluctate. To struggle against.
Repel. To force or keep back, physically or mentally.
Repugn. To fight against; resist.
Repulse. To repel resolutely or harshly.
Resist. To oppose, strive against, or obstruct, whether by inertness or active force.
Revolt. To shock; repel. See Order.
Rise up in arms. To fight against. See Strife.
Sell one's life dearly. To resist death desperately.
Show a bold front. To make a show of brave resistance. See Bravery.
Stand. To take a stand for resistance.
Stand firm. To be unshaken by resistance.
Stand one's ground. To hold one's position against opposition.
Stand out. To make successful resistance.
Stand the brunt of. To withstand the bulk of opposition.
Stand up against. To place oneself in opposition to; to resist.
Stem the tide. To make way in opposition to some obstruction, as the tide.
Stem the torrent. To make way in opposition to some strong obstruction, as the torrent.
Strike. To refuse to work until certain demands are satisfied.
Strive against. To oppose.
Take one's stand. To take position for resistance.
Take the bit between the teeth. To resist, assert independence of control, as an unruly horse.
Turn out. To strike, as mill-hands leaving their shop.
Withstand. To make forcible resistance.

RESISTANCE—Adjectives.

Indomitable. Not to be subdued. See Determination.
Proof against. Unyielding to force.
Recalcitrant. Refusing compliance or submission.
Refractory. Displaying resistance. See Insubordination.
Renitent. Offering resistance to any influence or force.
Repellent. Serving, tending, or having power to repel. See *Verbs.*
Repulsive. Exciting such feelings that one is repelled.

(Continued on Column 1.)

---

re-prise'. Captured property. Taking-Restitution.
re-proach'. To blame; disgrace. Approval-Disapproval, Justification-Charge, Reputation-Discredit.
re-proach'-ful. Causing reproach. Approval-Disapproval.
re-proach'-ful-ly. In a reproachful manner. Approval-Disapproval.
rep'-ro-bate. An abandoned person; to disapprove. Approval-Disapproval, Godliness-Ungodliness, Good Man-Bad Man, Virtue-Vice.
rep''-ro-ba'-tion. Censure; state of being abandoned. Approval-Disapproval, Godliness-Ungodliness.
re''-pro-duce'. To produce again. Imitation-Originality, Recurrence, Renewal, Renovation-Relapse.
re''-pro-duced'. Produced again. Renewal.
re''-pro-duc'-tion. The act of reproducing. Biology, Copy-Model, Imitation-Originality, Recurrence, Renewal, Renovation-Relapse.
re''-pro-duc'-tive. Pertaining to reproduction. Renewal.
re-proof'. Censure. Approval-Disapproval.
re-prove'. To upbraid. Approval-Disapproval.
re-prov'-er. One who reproves. Flatterer-Defamer.
rep'-tile. Kind of animal; abject person. Fauna-Flora, Good Man-Bad Man, Presumption-Obsequiousness, Uprightness-Rogue.
re-pub'-lic. Kind of government. Humanity, Rule-License; **republic of letters,** Knowledge-Ignorance, Language.
republica, vivat [L.]. (rî-pub'li-ca vai'vat). Long live the republic. Approval-Disapproval, Reputation-Discredit.
re-pub'-li-can. Pertaining to a republic. Gentility-Commonalty, Rule-License.
re-pub'-lic-an-ism. Republican form of government. Rule-License.
re-pu'-di-ate. To disavow. Assent-Dissent, Assertion-Denial, Choice-Rejection, Commission-Abrogation, Duty-Dereliction, Inclusion-Omission, Observance-Nonobservance, Settlement-Default.
re-pu''-di-a'-tion. Act of repudiating. Assertion-Denial, Choice-Rejection, Commission-Abrogation, Inclusion-Omission, Observance-Nonobservance, Settlement-Default.
re'-pugn. To oppose. Reprisal-Resistance.
re-pug'-nance. Aversion. Desire-Distaste, Harmony-Discord, Love-Hate.
re-pug'-nant. Distasteful. Desire-Distaste, Harmony-Discord, Motive-Dehortation, Readiness-Reluctance.
re-pulse'. To resist; a defeat. Attraction-Repulsion, Impetus-Reaction, Proffer-Refusal, Reprisal-Resistance, Success-Failure.
re-pul'-sion. A throwing backward. Attraction-Repulsion.

re-pul'-sive. Offensive. ATTRACTION-REPULSION, BEAUTY-UGLINESS, DESIRE-DISTASTE, LOVE-HATE, PALATABLENESS-UNPALATABLENESS, PLEASURABLE-NESS-PAINFULNESS, POLITENESS-IMPOLITENESS, REPRISAL-RESISTANCE.

re-pur'-chase. To purchase back. BUYING-SALE.

rep'-u-ta-ble. Honorable. REPUTATION-DISCREDIT, UPRIGHTNESS-DISHONESTY.

rep'-u-ta-ble-ness. Good report. REPUTATION-DISCREDIT, UPRIGHTNESS-DISHONESTY.

rep''-u-ta'-tion. Repute. REPUTATION-DISCREDIT.

REPUTATION—DISCREDIT.

Account. Importance or worth in the eyes of others.
Approbation. Sanction; commendation.
Aura popularis [L.]. The breeze of popular favor.
Celebrity. Great distinction, renown. See REPUTATION.
Credit. Reputation derived from the confidence of others.
Dignity. High rank; distinction.
Distinction. High rank or estimation.
Éclat [F]. Brilliancy: splendor.
Fair name. A good reputation.
Fame. The applause of the many.
Famousness. The condition of having fame.
Figure. Distinction.
Glory. Great distinction or eminence given to a man because of some exceptional achievement or exploit.
Good name. ⎫
Good report. ⎬ Honorable reputation.
Good repute. ⎭
Grandeur. Imposing dignity or greatness.
High repute. Excellent reputation.
Honor. High esteem or regard paid to true worth.
Illustriousness. The condition of being illustrious. See *Adjectives*.
Luster. Brilliant distinction; glory.
Majesty. Exalted dignity: usually applied to the rank of sovereigns.
Mark. ⎫
Name. ⎬ Distinction; eminence.
Nobility. High rank; loftiness of character.
Notability. The quality of being worthy of note; distinction.
Note. ' Importance.
Notoriety. The state or quality of being notorious. See *Adjectives*.
Popularity. The quality or condition of being held in high esteem by the common people.
Prestige. Importance or reputation based on past success.
Queenliness. The state, quality, or dignity of a queen.
Regard. Good reputation; more personal and more deserved than respect.
Renown. Lasting and well-deserved fame.
Reputableness. The condition of being of good reputation.
Reputation. The estimation in which one is held by others; good character or standing.
Repute. Reputation; regard.
Respect. Honor and esteem.
Respectability. Good repute.
Solemnity. Formal dignity.
Splendor. Conspicuous greatness; glory.
Stateliness. The condition of being imposing or dignified.
Sublimity. The quality of inspiring a feeling of awe; grandeur.
Talk of the town. A conspicuous person.
The bubble reputation. Reputation regarded as transient or fleeting. "Seeking the bubble reputation even in the cannon's mouth." [Shakespeare, *As You Like It*, ii, 7.]
Vogue. Fashion; prevailing usage.

REPUTATION—*Denotations*.

Chief. The person highest in authority.
Choice and master spirits of the age. Most distinguished and influential people of an age.
Classman. An honor-man in the English universities.
Constellation. An assemblage of brilliant persons.
Cynosure. An object to which all eyes are turned.
Élite [F.] Select persons.
First fiddle. The leading personage.
Flower. The choicest or most select person.
Galaxy. An assemblage of noted persons; a collection of stars, a milky way.
Great card. A prominent person.
Hero. A man of courage or noble qualities; a demigod.
Lion. Any prominent or notable person much sought after in society.
Man of mark. A distinguished person.
Man of rank. A person of a high class.
Mirror. An exemplary personage.
Notability. Distinguished persons.
Paragon. A man whose life is worth copying after.
Pearl. The select.

Abjectness. The condition of being cast down in spirit.
A long farewell to all one's greatness. A sinking into disfavor. [Shakespeare, *Henry VIII*, III, ii.]
Argumentum ad verecundiam [L.]. The argument for modesty or shame.
Bad favor. Bad reputation; also, ill favor.
Badge of infamy. Any mark or outward token of dishonor or disgrace.
Bad name. Bad reputation.
Bad odor. ⎫
Bad repute. ⎬ See BAD NAME.
Bar sinister. A mark diagonally across a shield from sinister chief to dexter base, erroneously considered a mark of bastardy.
Baseness. See *Adjectives*.
Bend sinister. The bar sinister.
Blot. A spot or stain on one's reputation.
Blot in one's escutcheon. A mark of disrepute. [Browning, drama.]
Blur. A blot.
Brand. Any mark of disgrace or infamy.
Burning shame. Shame that excites intense feeling.
Byword of reproach. A common subject or cause of reproach.
Champain. A mark of dishonor on a shield.
Crying shame. One that calls for immediate vengeance.
Debasement. The condition of being of low moral character.
Dedecoration. The condition of being disgraced.
Defilement. Anything that injures one's reputation. See *Verbs*.
Degradation. The condition of being reduced in rank or standing.
Derogation. The act of injuring or seeking to injure another's reputation.
Disapprobation. The condition of being displeased, or the act of expressing unfavorable criticism.
Discredit. Impaired reputation.
Disgrace. A condition of dishonor or reproach.
Dishonor. Lack of honor; shame; reproach.
Disrepute. The condition of having a bad name or reputation.
Humiliation. The condition of being humbled or put to shame.
Ichabod. The glory is departed. [Whittier, *Webster*.]
Ignominy. Public disgrace or dishonor.
Ill favor. Bad favor.
Ill name. A bad name.
Ill odor. A bad or questionable reputation.
Ill repute. A bad reputation.
Imputation. The act of imputing or charging with evil.
Infamy. Entire loss of all honor and reputation, usually accompanied with public disgrace.
Ingloriousness. Disgrace.
Obloquy. The condition of being in odium or disgrace; also, censorious language.
Odium. The condition of being disliked or hated.
Opprobrium. Scornful disgrace; infamy.
Point champain. A point on a shield serving as a mark of disgrace.
Pollution. The condition of being impure or debased.
Reproach. A cause or condition of disgrace or dishonor.
Scandal. Reproach or disgrace brought about by improper conduct.
Scandalum magnatum [L.]. Defamation of persons of rank and dignity.
Scarlet letter. A mark of disgrace. [Hawthorne, a romance.]
Sense of shame. A feeling of shame.
Shame. The condition of being a cause of or subject to reproach; dishonor; disgrace.
Slur. A slight reproach or disgrace.
Spot. A stain or blemish.
Stain. A slight blemish or reproach on one's character.
Stigma. Any mark or token of infamy or disgrace; also, any stain or reproach on one's character.
Taint. A very slight stain or blemish.
Tarnish. A blemish or spot.
Turpitude. Extreme baseness and depravity.
Vileness. The condition of being morally base and depraved.

DISCREDIT—*Verbs*.

Be a reproach to. To make one infamous.
Be base. To be disgraced.
Be conscious of disgrace. To feel low or vile.

REPUTATION—DISCREDIT—*Continued*.

REPUTATION—Denotations—*Continued*.

Pillar of the church.   A distinguished person of the church.
Pillar of the state.   An eminent statesman. "With grave aspect he rose, and in his rising seemed a pillar of state." [Milton, *Paradise Lost*, ii, 300.]
Pink.   The choicest.
Rara avis [L.].   A rare bird.
Somebody.   A person of some distinction.
Star. }
Sun. }   A conspicuous person.
Worthy.   A person of distinction.

REPUTATION—*Nouns of Cause*.

Aggrandizement.   Exaltation or increase of honor or power.
Ascent.   Rising to eminence or power.
Brevet rank.   Honorary promotion.
Canonization.   The enrolling of a person in the calendar of saints.
Caste.   Rank or standing in society.
Celebration.   The act or occasion of giving honor or praise.
Condition.   One's rank or position in society.
Consecration.   The act of separating to a sacred use. See *Verbs*.
Dedication.   A setting apart to sacred uses. See *Verbs*.
Degree.   Class or rank; also, any distinction conferred indicating marked excellence.
Dignification.   The act of exalting or adding honor.
Elevation.   The act of elevating. See *Verbs*.
Eminence.   Distinction; very high standing.
Enshrinement.   The act of enshrining. See *Verbs*.
Enthronement.   The act of enthroning. See *Verbs*.
Exaltation.   The act of giving dignity and praise to. See *Verbs*.
Glorification.   The act of glorifying. See *Verbs*.
Greatness.   The condition of being distinguished or celebrated.
Height.   Elevation of condition; high standing.
High mightiness.   The quality or condition of being extremely mighty or powerful.
Immortality.   The condition of being exempt from oblivion.
Immortal name.   Everlasting repute.
Importance.   The condition of being of influence or consequence.
Locus standi [L.].   One's rank or station.
Magni nominis umbra [L.].   The shadow of a great name. [Lucan, of Pompey, *Pharsalia*, 1, 135.]
Memory.   The condition of being remembered.
Niche in the temple of fame.   Rank among distinguished persons.
Order.   Rank, class, or degree.
Pas [F.]   Standing.
Place.   Position; rank.
Position.   Rank or station.
Position in society.   Rank.
Posthumous fame.   Fame which comes after death.
Precedence.   The condition of standing first.
Preeminence.   The condition of being preeminent. See *Adjectives*.
Primacy.   The condition of being first in excellence or importance.
Rank.   Station or position; also distinction or eminence.
Standing.   Rank.
Station.   Place in society.
Status.   Relative position or rank.
Supereminence.   The condition of surpassing all others in excellence.
Superexaltation.   Elevation far above the common degree.
Top of the ladder. }
Top of the tree. }   Highest fame.

REPUTATION—*Nouns of Indication*.

Aureola.   The halo of glory surrounding Christ and the saints.
Blaze of glory.   A visible representation of power or distinction.
Blushing honors.   Great and roseate honors. [Shakespeare, *Henry VIII*, III, ii.]
Feather in one's cap.   An expression to indicate success in some difficult undertaking.
Halo.   A circlet of light around the head of a sacred personage.
Halo of glory.   Representation of rank.
Honor.   A title or other mark of distinction conferred.
Laurels.   Marks of honor and distinction.
Nimbus.   A halo.
Ornament.   A mark of distinction, as a badge.

REPUTATION—*Verbs*.

Accredit.   To put confidence in as worthy of trust.
Acquire honor.   To get honor by one's own efforts.
Aggrandize.   To make great in honor, power, etc.
Bear away the bell.   To win the prize, as in a race.
Bear the bell.   To be the leader.
Bear the palm.   To be the winner in any contest.
Be conscious of glory.   To be proud or haughty.

DISCREDIT—Verbs—*Continued*.

Beggar.   To reduce to a low condition; impoverish.
Be inglorious, etc.   To be disgraced. See *Adjectives*.
Blot.   To impair or stain one's reputation.
Brand.   To mark with disgrace or infamy.
Bring low.   To debase or degrade.
Cast a slur upon. }
Cast dishonor upon. }   To disgrace.
Cast into the shade.   To render another obscure by one's own success and good name.
Cause shame, etc.   To dishonor.
Cut a poor figure.   To make a poor appearance; also, to have poor success.
Cut a sorry figure.   To cut a poor figure.
Debase.   To reduce to a low moral condition.
Defame.   To openly make charges against another's character.
Defile.   To tarnish or corrupt the good name of another.
Degrade.   To lose or cause another to lose reputation or standing.
Derogate from.   To injure one's name or reputation.
Discompose.   To stir up or agitate by denunciations against.
Disconcert.   To disturb the self-possession of.
Discredit.   To cast discredit upon.
Disgrace.   To bring reproach or shame upon.
Disgrace oneself.   To commit a base deed.
Dishonor.   To deprive of rightful honor; also, to bring reproach upon.
Drag through the mire.   To disgrace.
Earn a bad name.   To commit unworthy deeds.
Eclipse.   To surpass so as to obscure.
Expel.   To dismiss in disgrace.
Expose oneself.   To render oneself liable to charges that will be injurious to his reputation.
Fall from one's high estate.   To fall from favor or honor.
Fling dishonor upon.   To disgrace.
Go away with a flea in one's ear.   To be upbraided or reproached.
Have a bad name.   To be disreputable.
Heap dirt upon.   To abuse with reproachful or vile language.
Hold up to shame.   To openly reproach or disgrace.
Impute shame to.   To make shameful charges against.
Incur disgrace.   To make oneself subject to shame or reproach.
Keep in the background.   To keep out of sight or favor.
Laugh on the wrong side of the mouth.   To feel regret or disappointment after exultation.
Leave in the background.   To keep out of sight.
Look blue.   To feel disappointed, like a bilious, melancholy man.
Look foolish.   To feel as if one were dishonored.
Look like a fool.   To feel dishonored.
Lose caste.   To lose standing or rank.
Make a sorry face.   To meet with disappointment
Obscure.   To hide; to eclipse.
Outshine.   To surpass.
Overshadow.   To render insignificant by comparison.
Pale one's ineffectual fire.   To become discouraged by failure. [Shakespeare, *Hamlet*, I, v (of the glow-worm at dawn).]
Play second fiddle.   To be subordinate in importance or position.
Post.   To openly reproach or make charges against.
Push into a corner.   To get out of the view of the people.
Put a halter round one's neck.   To incur dishonor or disgrace.
Put down.   To lower another's rank or reputation.
Put in the background. }
Put into a corner. }   To put out of sight or favor.
Put one's nose out of joint.   To humiliate another's pride, especially by supplanting him in favor or position.
Put out.   To dismiss in disgrace; to expel.
Put out of countenance.   To abash or confound.
Put to shame.   To disgrace.
Put to the blush.   To put to shame or confusion.
Recede into the hole.   To withdraw into obscurity.
Recede into the shade.   To retire from view on account of dishonor.
Reflect dishonor upon.   To dishonor.
Reprehend.   To blame or find fault with.
Send to Coventry.   To shut out from social intercourse.
Shame.   To bring reproach upon; also, to reproach.
Show up.   To expose the bad parts of one's character.
Slink away.   To withdraw in disgrace.
Slur.   To injure the character of another by disparaging remarks.
Snub.   To treat with contemptuous neglect.
Stain.   To disgrace.
Stigmatize.   To brand with some mark of reproach or infamy.
Sully.   To tarnish a good name.
Taint.   To slightly impair or tarnish a good name.
Take down a peg.   To lower one in his own esteem or in the esteem of others; humiliate.

REPUTATION—DISCREDIT—*Continued.*

REPUTATION—Verbs—*Continued.*

Be distinguished, etc. To be set apart by marks of honor and esteem. See *Adjectives.*
Be proud of. To feel proud because of.
Be run after. To be sought after because of one's position or wealth.
Be vain of. To feel vainglorious.
Blazon. To publish or make widely known.
Blow the trumpet. To proclaim great or famous.
Cast into the shade. To make another obscure by one s own greatness.
Come into vogue. To come into fashion.
Come to the front. To be conspicuous.
Confer honor on. To confer some mark of distinction upon.
Consecrate. To enroll as a god or saint; canonize.
Crown with laurel. To indicate honor or high merit.
Cut a dash. To make a big display.
Cut a figure. } To cut a dash.
Cut a splash. }
Dedicate to. To inscribe to as a mark of honor or respect, as a book.
Deify. To enroll among the gods; to canonize.
Devote to. To attach oneself to as a mark of respect or honor.
Dignify. To exalt or give honor to.
Do honor to. To show esteem for, or confer distinction upon.
Eclipse. To surpass; outshine.
Elevate. To raise in standing; to promote.
Emulate. To strive to equal or excel.
Ennoble. To make more noble; exalt.
Enshrine. To preserve or cherish.
Enthrone. To make preeminent.
Exalt. To pay high honor to.
Exalt one's horn. To act in a haughty or arrogant manner.
Exalt to the skies. To honor in the highest degree possible.
Exult. To rejoice over success.
Figure. To be prominent or conspicuous.
Flaunt. To make an ostentatious display.
Flourish. To be prosperous.
Gain golden opinions. To gain the favor or good report of the people.
Gain honor. }
Gain laurels. } To gain a position of rank and distinction.
Gain spurs. }
Give honor to. To do honor to.
Glitter. To shine: usually said of passing popularity.
Glorify. To ascribe glory and honor to.
Hand one's name down to posterity. To be honored.
Have a run. To be popular for a short time; usually said of a play.
Honor. To show esteem or reverence for; also to bestow marks of esteem.
Immortalize. To make immortal.
Inscribe. To leave a lasting influence or impression.
Lead the way. To stand at the head; to be first.
Leave one's mark. To have done something worthy of note.
Lionize. To give great attention to.
Live. To be unperishing in influence or memory.
Look up to. To respect or honor
Make a dash. To cut a dash.
Make a figure. }
Make a noise. }
Make a noise in the world. }
Make a splash. } To attract notice or attention.
Make some noise. }
Make some noise in the world. }
Nobilitate. To make noble.
Outjump. To surpass.
Outrival. To overcome a rival.
Outshadow. } To surpass in distinction.
Outshine. }
Outvie. } To outrank.
Overshadow. }
Pass one's examinations. To be entitled to honor.
Pay honor to. To regard with respect.
Pay regard to. To regard.
Play first fiddle. To be the leader; to hold the first positions.
Raise one's head. To better one's condition; also, to show oneself proud.
Redound to one's honor. To contribute to one s honor.
Reflect honor on. To contribute or add honor: usually said of some act.
Render honor to. To do honor to.
Rival. To strive to equal or excel; to emulate.
Shed a luster on. To add splendor and renown
Shine. To be popular or famous.

DISCREDIT—Verbs—*Continued.*

Take down a peg lower. }
Take down a peg or two. } To take down a peg.
Take the shine out of. To cast disfavor upon.
Tarnish. To injure one's reputation.
Throw dishonor upon. To dishonor.
Throw into the shade. To cast disfavor upon.
Throw off one's center. To throw into confusion by making defamatory charges against.
Trample under foot. }
Tread under foot. } To dishonor.
Upset. To throw into confusion and disgrace.
Vilify. To defame by making base charges against.
Wear a halter round one's neck. To put a halter round one's neck.

DISCREDIT—*Adjectives.*

Abject. Sunk to a very low condition.
Arrant. Notoriously bad; shameless.
At a discount. Of questionable reputation.
Base. Of low moral character.
Beggarly. Of little or no standing or worth.
Blown upon. Having a tainted or impaired reputation.
Dedecorous. Disgraceful.
Degrading. Tending to injure or lower.
Derogatory. Defamatory or injurious.
Despicable. Mean; contemptible.
Dirty. Of low reputation.
Discreditable. Injurious to reputation; disgraceful.
Disgraced. In bad repute.
Disgraceful. Bringing disgrace; shameful.
Disreputable. Causing ill repute.
Down in the world. Disgraced.
Downtrodden. Dishonored.
Humiliating. Dishonored. See *Verbs.*
Ignominious. Marked with ignominy; shameful.
In bad repute. Disgraced.
Infamous. Of exceedingly bad repute.
Infra dignitatem [L.]. Below one's dignity.
Inglorious. Without glory; also, disgraceful; shameful.
In the background. } In ill favor.
In the shade. }
Loaded with shame. Disgraced.
Low. Base of reputation.
Mean. Of contemptible reputation.
Nameless. Without fame or distinction.
Notorious. Widely known as of bad reputation.
Opprobrious. Offensively reproachful.
Out at elbows. In bad circumstances.
Out of countenance. Abashed; confounded.
Out of fashion. } Deprived of rank or honor.
Out of favor. }
Out of repute. Not favored.
Outrageous. Shocking; extremely disgraceful.
Overcome. Surpassed; outrivaled.
Pitiful. Awakening pity.
Questionable. Of suspicious or doubtful character.
Renownless. Without renown.
Ribald. Coarsely indecent or obscene.
Scandalous. Disgraceful.
Scrubby. Of an inferior kind; low; mean.
Shabby. Low; contemptible.
Shameful. Bringing reproach or disgrace.
Shocking. Extremely surprising or offensive in conduct or character.
Shorn of its beams. } Deprived of honor. [Milton, *Paradise Lost,*
Shorn of one's glory. } i, 596.]
Too bad.
Unable to show one's face. Disgraced.
Unbecoming. Unbefitting.
Under a cloud. } In ill favor.
Under an eclipse. }
Unglorified. Without glory or worship.
Unhonored. Disgraced.
Unknown to fame. Not honored.
Unmentionable. Too shameful to mention.
Unnoted. Unhonored.
Unnoticed. Neglected.
Unworthy. Base; low.
Vile. Base; of the lowest character or reputation.

DISCREDIT—*Interjections.*

Fie! For shame!
For shame!
O tempores! O mores! [L.] O the times! O the customs!

REPUTATION—DISCREDIT—*Continued.*

REPUTATION—Verbs—*Continued.*

Shine forth. To come suddenly into prominence.
Signalize. To render distinguished or noteworthy.
Sing praises to. To honor.
Star it. To act as the most distinguished person.
Surpass. To excel; to outrival.
Take one's degree. To earn and accept a degree.
Take precedence. To stand first
Take the wall of. To get the better of; to take the side of a walk next the wall and so furthest from the gutter.
Throw into the shade. To cast into the shade.
Win golden opinions. To gain the favor of the people.
Win laurels.
Win spurs. } To gain honor.

REPUTATION—*Adjectives.*

Ære perennius [L.]. More enduring than bronze.
At the head of. First.
At the top of the tree. Most conspicuous.
August. Inspiring awe or reverence.
Bright. Illustrious or glorious.
Brilliant. Celebrated; illustrious.
Celebrated. Distinguished; known far and wide.
Conspicuous. Very prominent.
Creditable. Deserving credit.
Deathless. Immortal.
Dignified. Stately; majestic.
Distingué [F.]. Distinguished.
Distinguished. Noted; eminent.
Eminent. Standing high as compared with those about.
Famed. Spoken of.
Famous. Celebrated; renowned.
Far-famed. Known in many regions.
Fashionable. Conforming to the prevailing form or style.
Foremost. Standing at the head.
Full-blown. In a state of maturity or perfection.
Glorious. Resplendent with honor or glory.
Grand. Preeminent in ability or character; worthy of the highest respect.
Great. Standing among the foremost; eminent, distinguished.
Heaven-born. Lofty and exalted.
Heroic. Bold; brave; illustrious.
High. Distinguished; exalted.
Honorable. Worthy of esteem and honor.
Honored. Regarded or treated with honor or reverence.
Honorific. Conferring, or tending to, honor.
Illustrious. Greatly distinguished; full of glory or honor.
Immortal. Of undying fame or renown.
Imperishable. Enduring; immortal.
Imposing. Grandly impressive; commanding.
In every one's mouth. Widely spoken of.
In favor. Esteemed; held in high regard.
In good odor. In good esteem.
In high favor. Noted.
In the ascendent. Having commanding power or influence.
In the front rank.
In the zenith. } Most distinguished.
Lordly. Having the character or mien of a lord, grand; dignified.
Majestic. Exhibiting majesty; stately; grand.
Never-fading. Immortal.
Noble. Exalted in rank or character.
Notable. Worthy of note or regard.
Noted. Well-known; celebrated.
Notorious. Widely known: usually in a bad sense.
Of note. Of reputation or distinction.
Of the first water. Of the first excellence, as a diamond.
Peerless. Without an equal.
Popular. In favor with the masses.
Preeminent. Standing first.
Princely. Of the highest rank or ability.
Prominent. Of note; attracting attention.
Proud. Worthy of admiration; splendid

DISCREDIT—Interjections—*Continued.*

Ough!
Proh pudor [L.]. O for shame!
Shame!

DISCREDIT—*Phrases.*

Giuoco di mano giuoco di villano [It.]. Practical jokes are the jokes of low folks.
Sic transit gloria mundi [L.]. Thus passes away the glory of the world.
To one's shame be it said.
Tout est perdu hors l'honneur [F.]. All is lost save honor. [Francis I. of France.]

REPUTATION—Adjectives—*Continued.*

Radiant. Full of splendor or glory.
Remarkable. Extraordinary; distinguished.
Renowned. Of well-deserved and lasting fame.
Reputable. Of good reputation.
Respectable. Of good reputation; also, of moderate excellence.
Sacred. Worthy of reverence and veneration.
Sans peur et sans reproche. [F]. Without fear and without reproach.
Solemn. Impressive; awe-inspiring.
Splendid. Very good; excellent, brilliant.
Stately. Dignified; majestic.
Sublime. Distinguished by the noblest traits; of solemn grandeur; awe-inspiring.
Supereminent. Highest of all.
Superior. Of higher standing or excellence.
Talked of. Conspicuous.
Time-honored. Claiming veneration because of long observance in the past.
To the front. Leading.
Transcendent. Very excellent; surpassing.
Worshipful. Worthy of honor or reverence.

REPUTATION—*Interjections.*

All hail!
Ave! Hail!
Glory be to!
Hail!
Honor be to!
Long life to!
Viva [It.]. Live! long live!
Vive [F.]. Live! long live!

REPUTATION—*Phrases.*

Al hombre bueno no le busquen abolengo [Sp.]. No one explores a good man's pedigree.
Aucun chemin de fleurs ne conduit à la gloire [F.]. There is no pathway of flowers that leads to glory.
Aut Cæsar aut nullus [L.]. Either Cæsar or no one. [Motto of Cæsar Borgia.]
Avito viret honore [L.]. He flourishes in ancestral honor.
Fama semper vivat [L.]. May his fame live forever.
Fame volat [L.]. Fame flies.
Honor virtutis præmium [L.]. Honor is the reward of virtue. [Cicero, *Brutus*, 81.]
None but himself could be his parallel.
Not to know him argues oneself unknown.
One's name being in every mouth.
One's name living forever.
Palmam qui meruit ferat [L.]. Let him who has won bear the palm. [Nelson's motto.]
Sic itur ad astra [L.]. Such is the way to the stars.
Vivat respublica [L.]. Long live the republic.
Vivit post funera virtus [L.]. Virtue lives after death.
Voilà le soleil d'Austerlitz [F.]. Behold the sun of Austerlitz. [Napoleon.]

---

re-pute'. Opinion held by others of oneself. Approval-Disapproval, Reputation-Discredit.
re-quest'. Something asked for. Investigation-Answer, Petition-Expostulation; **in request,** Mutation-Permanence, Need; **request permission,** Leave-Prohibition.
re-quest'-ing. Asking. Petition-Expostulation.

re'-qui-em. Dirge. Jubilation-Lamentation, Movement-Rest.
requies, nec mora nec [L.] (rec'-qui-îz, nec mo'-ra nec). Neither delay nor rest. Activity-Indolence.
requiescat in pace [L.] (rec''-qui-es'-cat in pê'-sî). May he rest in peace. Fighting-Conciliation.
re-quire'. To demand; to need. Coercion, Due-

NESS - UNDUENESS, DUTY - DERELICTION, EXCESS-LACK, NEED, ORDER, PRICE-DISCOUNT; **require explanation,** CLEARNESS-OBSCURITY, NEED.

re-quire'-ment. Need; demand. NEED.

req'-ui-site. Necessity. NEED.

req''-ui-si'-tion. Request; requirement. NEED, ORDER, PETITION-EXPOSTULATION; **put in requisition,** ORDER, USE-MISUSE.

re-quis'-i-tive. Necessary. INVESTIGATION-ANSWER.

re-quis'-i-to-ry. Embodying a requisition. INVESTIGATION-ANSWER.

re-qui'-tal. Thanks; recompense. RECOMPENSE-PUNITION, THANKFULNESS-THANKLESSNESS.

re-quite'. To reward. RECOMPENSE-PUNITION.

re-scind'. To shorten; to make void. BIGOTRY-APOSTASY, COMMISSION-ABROGATION, PROFFER-REFUSAL, UNION-DISUNION.

re-scis'-sion. The act of rescinding. COMMISSION-ABROGATION, UNION-DISUNION.

re'-script. Decree; reply. INVESTIGATION-ANSWER, MISSIVE-PUBLICATION, ORDER, WRITING-PRINTING.

res'-cu-a-ble. Capable of rescue. RESCUE.

res'-cue. To deliver; to save. CONSERVATION, OBSTRUCTION-HELP, RENOVATION-RELAPSE, RESCUE.

RESCUE.

Deliverance. Freedom from danger.
Extrication. A disentanglement.
Gaol delivery. The release of prisoners whom the grand jury does not indict.
Liberation. A freeing from restraint. See RELEASE.
Redeemableness. The quality of being able to be redeemed.
Redemption. Saving from sin.
Reprieval. Suspension of punishment for a short time.
Reprieve. Temporary withdrawing of a sentence whereby execution is suspended.
Rescue. A saving from danger, peril, or violence.
Respite. Postponement of a penalty.
Riddance. Deliverance, freedom from objectionable things.
Salvation. Act of saving; deliverance from destruction or danger.

RESCUE—Verbs.

Be rid of. To free from.
Bring off. To clear from condemnation.
Bring through. To save the life of a patient.
Come to the rescue. To arrive in time to save.
Deliver. To set free; take out of danger.
Extricate. To free from entanglement.
Get rid of. To have deliverance from.
Get the wheel out of the rut. To lift the carriage to the open road.
Ransom. To secure the release of.
Redeem. To buy back.
Rescue. To bring from danger to safety. See *Nouns*.
Retrieve. To remedy the evil consequences of.
Rid. To free from.
Save. To rescue; free.
Snatch from the jaws of death. To barely take from the jaws of death.
Tirer d'affaire [F.]. To get out of trouble.

RESCUE—Adjectives.

Extricable. Able to be disentangled.
Redeemable. Able to be redeemed.
Rescuable. Able to be rescued.
Saved. Freed from danger. See *Verbs*.

RESCUE—Interjection.

To the rescue.

re-search'. Inquiry. INVESTIGATION-ANSWER.

re-seat'. To restore. RENOVATION-RELAPSE.

re-sec'-tion. A cutting off. UNION-DISUNION.

re-seiz'-er. To take into custody lands that have been unlawfully taken possession of. LITIGATION, TAKING-RESTITUTION.

re-sell'. To sell again. BUYING-SALE.

re-sem'-blance. Similarity. LIKENESS-UNLIKENESS, UNIFORMITY-DIVERSITY.

re-sem'-ble. To be like. LIKENESS-UNLIKENESS.

re-sent'. To be indignant at. FAVORITE-ANGER.

re-sent'-ful. Disposed to resent. FAVORITE-ANGER.

re-sent'-ment. Indignation. CHARITABLENESS-MALEVOLENCE, FAVORITE-ANGER.

res''-er-va'-tion. Keeping something back. ENLIGHTENMENT-SECRECY; **mental reservation,** AMBIGUITY, ENLIGHTENMENT-SECRECY, TRUTHFULNESS-FABRICATION; **with a reservation,** ADDITION-SUBTRACTION.

re-serv'-a-to-ry. Depository. CONTENTS-RECEIVER, STORE.

re-serve'. To save; coyness; exception. CONCEIT-DIFFIDENCE, EARLINESS-LATENESS, ENLIGHTENMENT-SECRECY, KEEPING-RELINQUISHMENT, STORE, TALKATIVENESS-TACITURNITY, USE-MISUSE; **in reserve,** OCCURRENCE-DESTINY, PREPARATION-NONPREPARATION; **reserve forces,** BELLIGERENT; **reserve oneself,** CONCEIT-DIFFIDENCE.

re-served'. Modest. CONCEIT-DIFFIDENCE; **reserved fund,** STORE.

re-serves'. Auxiliary troops. BELLIGERENT.

res'-er-voir''. Receptacle. GULF-PLAIN, STORE.

res'-i-ance. Residence. DWELLER-HABITATION.

res'-i-ant. Resident. PRESENCE-ABSENCE.

re-side'. To dwell. PRESENCE-ABSENCE.

res'-i-dence. Dwelling-place. DWELLER-HABITATION.

res'-i-dent. Dweller; representative. CONSIGNEE, DWELLER-HABITATION, PRESENCE-ABSENCE.

res''-i-den'-tia-ry. Resident. DWELLER-HABITATION, MINISTRY, PRESENCE-ABSENCE.

re-sid'-u-al. Remaining. INCREMENT-REMNANT.

re-sid'-u-a-ry. Residual. INCREMENT-REMNANT.

res'-i-due. Remainder. INCREMENT-REMNANT.

re-sid'-u-um. Residue; rabble. CLEANNESS-FILTHINESS, GENTILITY-COMMONALTY, INVESTIGATION-ANSWER.

re-sign'. To give up. COMMISSION-RETIREMENT, KEEPING-RELINQUISHMENT, YIELDING; **resign one's being,** LIFE-DEATH; **resign one's breath,** LIFE-DEATH; **resign oneself,** EXCITABILITY-INEXCITABILITY, YIELDING.

res''-ig-na'-tion. Act of giving up; submissiveness. COMMISSION-ABROGATION, CONTENTEDNESS-DISCONTENTMENT, EXCITABILITY - INEXCITABILITY, INSUBORDINATION - OBEDIENCE, KEEPING - RELINQUISHMENT, QUEST-ABANDONMENT, SELFRESPECT-HUMBLENESS, YIELDING.

re-signed'. Yielding. CONTENTEDNESS-DISCONTENT, DISCONTINUANCE-CONTINUANCE, EXCITABILITY-INEXCITABILITY, YIELDING.

re-sil'-i-ence. Elasticity. ADVANCE-RETROGRESSION, ELASTICITY-INELASTICITY.

re-sil'-i-ent. Elastic. ADVANCE-RETROGRESSION, ELASTICITY-INELASTICITY.

res'-in. Stuff exuding from plants. PULPINESS-ROSIN.

res'-in-ous. Of the nature of resin. ROSIN.

res''-i-pis'-cence. Wisdom. REPENTANCE-OBDURACY.

res ipsa loquitur [L.] (rîz ip'-sa loq'-wi-tur). The thing itself speaks. MANIFESTATION-LATENCY.

re-sist'. To oppose. PROFFER-REFUSAL, REPRISAL-RESISTANCE.

re-sist'-ance. Opposition. ANTAGONISM-CONCURRENCE, ATTACK - DEFENSE, COOPERATION - OPPOSITION, REPRISAL-RESISTANCE.

résistance, pièce de [F.] (rê-zis''-tan·s', pî·es de). The principal dish. NUTRIMENT-EXCRETION, REPRISAL-RESISTANCE.

re-sist'-ant. Opposing. ANTAGONISM-CONCURRENCE.

re-sist'-ing. Obstinate. INSUBORDINATION-OBEDIENCE, REPRISAL-RESISTANCE, TOUGHNESS-BRITTLENESS.

re-sist'-ive. Offering opposition. REPRISAL-RESISTANCE.

re-sist'-less. Irresistible. STRENGTH-WEAKNESS, VOLI-TION-OBLIGATION.

res'-o-lute. Bold; determined. BRAVERY-COWARD-ICE, DETERMINATION-VACILLATION.

res'-o-lute-ly. Perseveringly. DETERMINATION-VAC-ILLATION.

res'-o-lute-ness. Perseverance. BRAVERY-COWARD-ICE, DETERMINATION-VACILLATION.

res"-o-lu'-tion. Bravery; analysis; determination; decision; change of chords in music. BIGOTRY-APOSTASY, BRAVERY - COWARDICE, COMPOSITION-RESOLUTION, CONCEPTION - THEME, CONVERSION-REVERSION, DESIGN, DETERMINATION-VACILLATION, INVESTIGATION - ANSWER, MELODY - DISSONANCE, PRESIDENT-MEMBER, PURPOSE-LUCK, TOIL-RELAX-

ATION, VIGOR-INERTIA; **dogged resolution,** BIGOTRY-APOSTASY.

re-solv'-a-ble. Able to be analyzed. **Resolvable into,** CONVERSION-REVERSION, EQUALITY-INEQUALITY.

re-solve'. To determine; to melt; to interpret. DE-TERMINATION-VACILLATION, DISCOVERY, INTERPRE-TATION - MISINTERPRETATION, INVESTIGATION - AN-SWER, LIQUEFACTION-VOLATILIZATION, PREDETERMI-NATION-IMPULSE, PURPOSE-LUCK; **resolve into,** CON-VERSION-REVERSION; **resolve into elements,** COM-POSITION-RESOLUTION.

re-solved'. Determined. DETERMINATION-VACILLA-TION.

res'-o-nance. The quality of sounding. LOUDNESS-FAINTNESS, RESONANCE-NONRESONANCE, SOUND-SILENCE.

RESONANCE—NONRESONANCE.

Reflection. The act of throwing sound back from any surface.
Resonance. A prolongation or reenforcement of sound by means of sympathetic vibration.
Reverberation. The act of returning or sending a sound back; an echo; a reecho.
Ring. A sound produced by a bell or other sonorous body.
Ringing. The act of sounding. See *Verbs.*
Tintinnabulation. The ringing of a bell. [Poe.]

RESONANCE—*Denotations.*

Baritone. A male voice higher than bass and lower than tenor.
Bass. The lowest tones of the voice.
Bass note. A low note.
Basso [It.]. A bass part in music.
Basso-profundo. The lowest bass voice.
Contralto. The musical part between soprano and tenor.
Deep note. A low note
Flat note. A note below a certain pitch.
Grave note. A note very low in pitch.
Low note. A note of low pitch.
Profundo. The deepest bass.

RESONANCE—*Verbs.*

Chime. To ring in harmony or unison.
Chink. To produce a short, sharp sound as of metals striking together.
Clink. To make a short, sharp, slightly ringing sound.
Echo. To give back or repeat a sound.
Gingle. To jingle.
Guggle. To gurgle.
Gurgle. To make a murmuring sound.
Jingle. To produce a sharp, tinkling sound, as of a little bell.
Plash. To make the sound of rapidly falling water.
Reecho. To echo again.
Resound. To give forth a deep heavy sound; also, to echo.
Reverberate. To send back a sound; also, to reecho time and again.
Ring. To give forth a resonant sound, as of a bell.
Ring in the ear. To have a tingling sensation in the ear produced by irritation of the auditory nerve from within.
Tink. To make a tinkling sound.

Cracked bell. A bell which has a crack in it, and will therefore not be resonant.
Damper. Any means for stopping the vibrations.
Dead sound. One in which there is no resonance.
Muffled drums. Drums so covered as to deaden the sound.
Non-resonance. The quality of not tending to prolong and reenforce the sound by sympathetic vibration.
Thud. A dull heavy sound.
Thump. A heavy and rather dull sound.

NONRESONANCE—*Verbs.*

Damp the reverberations. To damp the sound.
Damp the sound. To check the vibrations; to deaden the sound.
Sound dead. To have a non-resonant sound.
Stop the reverberations. To stop the sound.
Stop the sound. To prevent resonance by interfering with the sym-pathetic vibrations.

NONRESONANCE—*Adjectives.*

Dead. Non-resonant.
Non-resonant. Without the quality of sending back or prolonging sound.

RESONANCE—VERBS—*Continued.*

Tinkle. To give forth a series of slight, sharp, clear sounds, as of a sheep-bell.

RESONANCE—*Adjectives.*

Deep-mouthed. Having a loud and sonorous voice.
Deep-sounding. Low and bass.
Deep-toned. Of a low tone.
Gruff. Having or giving forth a rough sound.
Hollow. Resembling the sound reverberated from a cavity.
Resonant. Tending to prolong and reenforce sound by sympathetic vibration.
Resounding. Ringing. See *Verbs.*
Sepulchral. Unnaturally low or hollow in tone.
Tinnient. Emitting a clear tinkling sound.
Tintinnabulary. Ringing or sounding like a bell.

RESONANCE—SIBILATION

SIBILATION.

Hiss. A prolonged sound of *s* made by forcing the breath between the tongue and teeth; a sibilation.
Sibilation. A hissing sound, such as that produced by a goose or serpent.
Sternutation. The act of sneezing.

SIBILATION—*Denotations*

Goose. A fowl which utters a hissing sound.
High note. A note marking a tone of many vibrations.
Serpent. A crawling animal which hisses.

SIBILATION—*Verbs.*

Buzz. To make a humming, sibilant sound, as a bee.
Fizz. To make a hissing noise.
Fizzle. To make a hissing noise, as of wet wood burning.

Hiss. To utter a prolonged sound of *s* through the teeth.
Huzz. To buzz; murmur.
Rustle. To make a series of quick gentle sounds, as of leaves blown by the wind.
Sneeze. To produce a sound by convulsively and spasmodically driving the breath through the nose.
Snuffle. To make a noise by forcing the breath through the ob-structed nasal passages.
Swish. To move with a whistling sound.
Wheeze To breathe hard and with an audible sound.
Whistle. To make a shrill musical sound by forcing the breath through the contracted lips.
Whiz. A sibilant sound slightly sonant.

SIBILATION—*Adjectives*

Hissing. Making a hissing sound. See *Verbs*
Sibilant. Making a hissing sound.
Wheezy. Making a whistling sound

res′-o-nant. Sonorous. RESONANCE-NONRESONANCE, SOUND-SILENCE.

re-sorb′. Reabsorb. ADMISSION-EXPULSION.

re-sort′. Gathering-place; haunt. CONCENTRATION-RADIATION, DWELLER-HABITATION, GATHERING-PLACE, GATHERING-SCATTERING; **last resort,** VOLITION-OBLIGATION; **resort to,** PRESENCE-ABSENCE, TRAVELING-NAVIGATION, USE-DISUSE.

re-sound′. To ring out. LOUDNESS-FAINTNESS, RESONANCE-NONRESONANCE; **resound praises,** APPROVAL-DISAPPROVAL.

re-sound′-ing. Echoing. RESONANCE-NONRESONANCE.

re-sour′-ces. Means; wealth. AFFLUENCE-PENURY, MEANS, PROPERTY, PROVISION-WASTE.

re-spect′. Esteem; connection. CONNECTION-INDEPENDENCE, OBSERVANCE-NONOBSERVANCE, POLITENESS-IMPOLITENESS, REGARD-DISRESPECT, REPUTATION-DISCREDIT; **in no respect,** ASSERTION-DENIAL, MAGNITUDE-SMALLNESS; **with respect to,** CONNECTION-INDEPENDENCE.

re-spect′′-a-bil′-i-ty. State of being respectable. MEDIOCRITY, REPUTATION-DISCREDIT, UPRIGHTNESS-DISHONESTY.

re-spect′-a-ble. Worthy of esteem. CONSEQUENCE-INSIGNIFICANCE, REPUTATION-DISCREDIT, UPRIGHTNESS-DISHONESTY.

re-spect′-ed. Esteemed. REGARD-DISRESPECT.

re-spect′-ful. Polite. REGARD-DISRESPECT; **respectful distance,** QUEST-EVASION, RECKLESSNESS-CAUTION.

re-spect′-ing. Regarding. REGARD-DISRESPECT.

re-spect′-ive. Pertaining to each of several or more. ASSIGNMENT, UNIVERSALITY-PARTICULARITY.

re-spect′-ive-ly. Severally. ASSIGNMENT, UNIVERSALITY-PARTICULARITY.

re-spect′-less. Regardless. HEED-DISREGARD.

re-spects′. Compliments. POLITENESS-IMPOLITENESS, REGARD-DISRESPECT.

re-sperse′. To scatter. GATHERING-SCATTERING.

re-sper′-sion. A scattering. GATHERING-SCATTERING.

respicere finem [L.] (re-spic′-er-î fai′-nem). To look to the end. PREVISION.

res′′-pi-ra′-tion. Breathing. LIFE-DEATH.

re-spire′. To breathe; to rest. ANATOMY, LIFE-DEATH, RIVER-WIND, WEARINESS-REFRESHMENT.

res′-pite. Delay; rest. DISCONTINUANCE-CONTINUANCE, DURATION-NEVERNESS, EARLINESS-LATENESS, EXCULPATION-CONVICTION, RESCUE, TOIL-RELAXATION.

re-splen′-dent. Splendid. BEAUTY-UGLINESS, LIGHT-DARKNESS.

re-spond′. To answer; act in sympathy with. EMOTION, HARMONY-DISCORD, INVESTIGATION-ANSWER.

re-spond′-ent. One who answers; defendant. INVESTIGATION-ANSWER, JUSTIFICATION-CHARGE.

re-sponse′. Answer; a kind of repetition in music. ADDRESS-RESPONSE, AMITY-HOSTILITY, DEVOTION-IDOLATRY, EMOTION, VARIANCE-ACCORD.

re-spon′′-si-bil′-i-ty. Trust; duty. DUTY-DERELICTION.

re-spon′-si-ble. Accountable. DUTY-DERELICTION.

re-spon′-sive. Ready to answer. INVESTIGATION-ANSWER.

rest. Remainder; pause; repose; to be supported. ACTION-PASSIVENESS, DISCONTINUANCE-CONTINUANCE, INCREMENT-REMNANT, LIFE-DEATH, MELODY-DISSONANCE, MOVEMENT-REST, MUTATION-PERMANENCE, SUSPENSION-SUPPORT, TOIL-RELAXATION; **at rest,** CONTENTEDNESS-DISCONTENTMENT; **rest and be thankful,** ACTION-PASSIVENESS, CONTENTEDNESS-DISCONTENTMENT, TOIL-RELAXATION; **rest assured,** FAITH-MISGIVING, SANGUINENESS-HOPELESSNESS; **rest on,** SUSPENSION-SUPPORT; **rest on one's oars,** ACTION-PASSIVENESS, DISCONTINUANCE-CONTINUANCE,

TOIL-RELAXATION; **rest satisfied,** CONTENTEDNESS-DISCONTENTMENT; **rest upon,** EVIDENCE-COUNTEREVIDENCE, FAITH-MISGIVING; **rest with,** DUTY-DERELICTION; **set at rest,** CERTAINTY-DOUBT, COMPLETION-NONCOMPLETION, CONTRACT, INVESTIGATION-ANSWER; **set one's mind at rest,** EXCITABILITY-INEXCITABILITY, PLEASURABLENESS-PAINFULNESS; **set the question at rest,** DECISION-MISJUDGMENT, PROOF-DISPROOF.

res′-tau-rant. Eating-house. DWELLER-HABITATION

restaurateur [F.] (rê′′-sto′′-ra′′-tur′). Keeper of a restaurant. PROVISION-WASTE.

reste, au [F.] (rest, o). Besides. ADDITION-SUBTRACTION.

rest′-ful. Quiet. MOVEMENT-REST

rest′-iff. Restive. BIGOTRY-APOSTASY, FAVORITE-MOROSENESS, FAVORITE-QUARRELSOMENESS, INSUBORDINATION-OBEDIENCE, PROFFER-REFUSAL, READINESS-RELUCTANCE.

rest′-ing. Being supported; enjoying repose. **Resting-place,** ARRIVAL-DEPARTURE, MOVEMENT-REST, SUSPENSION-SUPPORT.

res′′-ti-tu′-tion. Giving back. RENOVATION-RELAPSE, TAKING-RESTITUTION.

rest′-ive. Restless; rebellious. BIGOTRY-APOSTASY, FAVORITE-MOROSENESS, INSUBORDINATION-OBEDIENCE, PROFFER-REFUSAL, READINESS-RELUCTANCE.

rest′-less. Uneasy; active; agitated. ACTIVITY-PASSIVENESS, AGITATION, EXCITABILITY-INEXCITABILITY, MOVEMENT-REST, MUTABILITY-STABILITY, SANGUINENESS-TIMIDITY, STRENGTH-WEAKNESS.

rest′-less-ness. Uneasy. ACTIVITY-INDOLENCE, AGITATION, EXCITABILITY-INEXCITABILITY, MOVEMENT-REST, MUTABILITY-STABILITY.

re-stor′-a-ble. Capable of being restored. RENOVATION-RELAPSE.

re-stor′-al. Restoration. RENOVATION-RELAPSE.

res′′-to-ra′-tion. Revival. RENOVATION-RELAPSE.

re-stor′-a-tive. Tending to restore. ALLEVIATION-AGGRAVATION, HEALTHINESS-UNHEALTHINESS, REMEDY-BANE.

re-store′. To revive; to replace. CONVERSION-REVERSION, REMEDY-BANE, RENEWAL, RENOVATION-RELAPSE, TAKING-RESTITUTION; **restore equilibrium,** EQUALITY-INEQUALITY; **restore harmony,** FIGHTING-CONCILIATION; **restore to health,** HEALTH-SICKNESS.

re-stored′. Renewed. RENOVATION-RELAPSE.

re-stor′-ing. Giving back. RENOVATION-RELAPSE, TAKING-RESTITUTION.

re-strain′. To hold back. ENLARGEMENT-DIMINUTION, INSUBORDINATION-OBEDIENCE, LEAVE-PROHIBITION, RELEASE-RESTRAINT.

re-strain′-a-ble. Controllable. INSUBORDINATION-OBEDIENCE.

re-strained′. Curbed. RELEASE-RESTRAINT.

re-straint′. Restriction. COERCION, EXCITABILITY-INEXCITABILITY, RELEASE-RESTRAINT; **self-restraint,** DETERMINATION-VACILLATION, EXCITABILITY-INEXCITABILITY, MODERATION-SELFINDULGENCE.

re-strict′. To restrain. LEAVE-PROHIBITION, OBSTRUCTION-HELP, RELEASE-RESTRAINT.

re-stric′-tion. Limitation. LEAVE-PROHIBITION, OBSTRUCTION-HELP.

re-strict′-ive. Limiting. LEAVE-PROHIBITION.

re-strin′-gen-cy. Astringency. RELEASE-RESTRAINT.

re-strin′-gent. Restrictive. RELEASE-RESTRAINT.

rest′-y. Restive. BIGOTRY-APOSTASY.

re-sult′. Outcome. CAUSE-EFFECT. COMPLETION-NONCOMPLETION, DECISION-MISJUDGMENT, INCREMENT-REMNANT.

re-sult′-ance. A resultant. CAUSE-EFFECT.

re-sult′-ant. Effect. CAUSE-EFFECT. COMPOSITION-RESOLUTION.

re-sume′. To take up again. BEGINNING-END, MU-
TATION-PERMANENCE, RECURRENCE, RENOVATION-
RELAPSE, TAKING-RESTITUTION.

résumé [F.] (rê-zü-mê′). Summary. DIGEST.

re-sump′-tion. Act of taking up again. RENOVA-
TION-RELAPSE, TAKING-RESTITUTION.

re-su″-pi-na′-tion. The state of lying. ERECTNESS-
FLATNESS.

res″-ur-rec′-tion. Rising from the dead; renewal.
HEAVEN-HELL, RENEWAL.

re-sus′-ci-tate. To revive. RENEWAL, RENOVATION-
RELAPSE.

re-sus″-ci-ta′-tion. Act of reviving. HEAVEN-HELL,
RENEWAL, RENOVATION-RELAPSE.

re-ta′-ble. An altar-piece. SUSPENSION-SUPPORT.

re-tail′. To gossip; to sell. BUYING-SALE, ENLIGHT-
ENMENT-SECRECY, EXCHANGE, GATHERING-SCATTER-
ING.

re′-tail. Selling. BUYING-SALE, EXCHANGE.

re-tail′-er. One who retails. DEALER.

re-tain′. To hold. KEEPING-RELINQUISHMENT, MU-
TABILITY-STABILITY; **retain one's reason,** SANENESS-
LUNACY; **retain the memory,** REMEMBRANCE-FOR-
GETFULNESS.

re-tain′-er. Servant. CHIEF-UNDERLING.

re-tain′-ing. Holding back. KEEPING-RELINQUISH-
MENT.

re-take′. To take back. TAKING-RESTITUTION.

re-tal′-i-ate. To return like for like. COMMUTATION-
PERMUTATION, REPRISAL-RESISTANCE.

re-tal′-i-at-ing. Revenging. REPRISAL-RESISTANCE.

re-tal″-i-a′-tion. Return of like for like. PARDON-
VINDICTIVENESS, REPRISAL-RESISTANCE.

re-tal′-i-a-tive. Given to revenge. REPRISAL-RESIST-
ANCE.

re-tal′-i-a-to-ry. Retaliative. REPRISAL-RESISTANCE.

re-tard′. To hinder. EARLINESS-LATENESS, OB-
STRUCTION-HELP, SWIFTNESS-SLOWNESS.

re″-tar-da′-tion. Hindrance. EARLINESS-LATENESS,
OBSTRUCTION-HELP, SWIFTNESS-SLOWNESS.

re-tard′-ment. Retardation. OBSTRUCTION-HELP.

retch. To heave. ADMISSION-EXPULSION.

re-tec′-tion. Act of disclosing. EXPOSURE-HIDING-
PLACE.

re-ten′-tion. Keeping. HOLDING-EXEMPTION, KEEP-
ING-RELINQUISHMENT.

re-ten′-tive. Retaining. KEEPING-RELINQUISHMENT;
retentive memory, REMEMBRANCE-FORGETFULNESS.

re-ten′-tive-ness. Power of holding. REMEMBRANCE-
FORGETFULNESS.

ret′-i-cence. Reserve in speech. ENLIGHTENMENT-
SECRECY.

ret′-i-cent. Reserved. ENLIGHTENMENT - SECRECY,
TALKATIVENESS-TACITURNITY.

ret′-i-cle. Part of a telescope. CROSSING.

re-tic′-u-lar. Meshy. CROSSING.

re-tic″-u-la′-tion. Network. CIRCLE-WINDING, CROSS-
ING.

ret′-i-cule. Network. CONTENTS-RECEIVER.

re′-ti-form. Like a network. CROSSING.

ret′-i-na. Part of the eye. ANATOMY, SIGHT-BLIND-
NESS.

ret′-i-nue. Retainers; results. CHIEF-UNDERLING, CON-
TINUITY - INTERRUPTION, PREDECESSOR - CONTINUA-
TION.

re-tire′. To recede; to give up office; to go into priv-
acy. ADVANCE-RETROGRESSION, APPROACH-WITH-
DRAWAL, ARRIVAL-DEPARTURE, COMMISSION-RETIRE-
MENT, CONCEIT-DIFFIDENCE, CONVEXITY-CONCAV-
ITY, QUEST-EVASION, SOCIABILITY-PRIVACY; **retire
from sight,** APPEARANCE-DISAPPEARANCE, ENLIGHT-
ENMENT-SECRECY; **retire into the shade,** INCREASE-
DECREASE, SUPREMACY-SUBORDINACY.

re-tired′. Secluded. SOCIABILITY-PRIVACY.

re-tire′-ment. Seclusion. COMMISSION-RETIREMENT,
SOCIABILITY-PRIVACY.

re-tir′-ing. Bending backward; not showy. BLUE-
NESS-ORANGE, CONVEXITY-CONCAVITY.

re-told′. Told over. RECURRENCE.

re-tort′. Receptacle; sharp reply. CHEMISTRY, CON-
TENTS-RECEIVER, INVESTIGATION-ANSWER, LIQUE-
FACTION - VOLATILIZATION, OVEN - REFRIGERATOR,
PROOF-DISPROOF, REPRISAL-RESISTANCE, WITTI-
NESS-DULNESS.

re-touch′. To modify. RENOVATION-RELAPSE.

re-trace′. To trace back; to recite. REMEMBRANCE-
FORGETFULNESS; **retrace one's steps,** BIGOTRY-APOS-
TASY.

re-tract′. To recant; to draw back. BIGOTRY-APOS-
TASY, COMMISSION-ABROGATION, COMMISSION-RE-
TIREMENT, DETERMINATION-VACILLATION, OBSERV-
ANCE-NONOBSERVANCE.

re″-trac-ta′-tion. Retraction. BIGOTRY-APOSTASY,
ESTABLISHMENT-REMOVAL.

re-trac′-tion. Act of taking back. ASSERTION-DENIAL,
BIGOTRY-APOSTASY, COMMISSION-ABROGATION.

re-treat′. To withdraw; secluded spot; moving back-
ward. ADVANCE-RETROGRESSION, APPROACH-WITH-
DRAWAL, COMMISSION-ABROGATION, DWELLER-HABI-
TATION, ESCAPE, EXPOSURE-HIDINGPLACE, QUEST-
EVASION, REFUGE-PITFALL, YIELDING; **beat a retreat,**
QUEST-EVASION, YIELDING.

re-treat′-ing. Bending backward. CONVEXITY-CON-
CAVITY.

re-trench′. To curtail. ADDITION-SUBTRACTION, GEN-
EROSITY - FRUGALITY, LENGTH - SHORTNESS, LOAN-
BORROWING.

re-trench′-ment. Act of retrenching. ADDITION-SUB-
TRACTION, GENEROSITY-FRUGALITY, LENGTH-SHORT-
NESS.

re-trib′-ute. To pay back. SETTLEMENT-DEFAULT.

ret″-ri-bu′-tion. Punishment; retaliation. RECOM-
PENSE-PUNITION, REPRISAL-RESISTANCE, SETTLE-
MENT-DEFAULT.

re-trib′-u-tive. Retaliative. RECOMPENSE-PUNITION.

re-triev′-a-ble. Recoverable. RENOVATION-RELAPSE.

re-triev′-al. Restoration. GAIN-LOSS.

re-trieve′. To recover. GAIN-LOSS, RENOVATION-RE-
LAPSE, RESCUE.

re-triev′-er. Kind of dog. FAUNA-FLORA.

re″-tro-ac′-tion. Action backward. ADVANCE-RETRO-
GRESSION, COOPERATION-OPPOSITION, IMPETUS-RE-
ACTION.

re″-tro-act′-ive. Designed to react. FUTURE-PAST.

re″-tro-cede′. To cede or give back. ADVANCE-RETRO-
GRESSION.

re″-tro-ces′-sion. The act of ceding back. ADVANCE-
RETROGRESSION, APPROACH-WITHDRAWAL.

ret″-ro-gra-da′-tion. Movement backward. ADVANCE-
RETROGRESSION, RENOVATION-RELAPSE.

ret′-ro-grade. To recede; to deteriorate. ADVANCE-
RETROGRESSION, BETTERMENT - DETERIORATION,
RENOVATION-RELAPSE.

re″-tro-gres′-sion. Deterioration; a receding. AD-
VANCE-RETROGRESSION, BETTERMENT-DETERIORA-
TION.

re″-tro-gres′-sive. Moving backward. ADVANCE-RET-
ROGRESSION.

re-trorse′. Bent backward. CONVERSION-REVERSION,
PLICATURE.

ret′-ro-spect. Looking back on past things. REMEM-
BRANCE-FORGETFULNESS.

ret″-ro-spec′-tion. A looking back on the past. FU-
TURE-PAST, MIND-IMBECILITY, REMEMBRANCE-FOR-
GETFULNESS.

ret″-ro-spec′-tive. Referring to the past. FUTURE-
PAST.

ret″-ro-spec′-tive-ly. Pertaining to the past. FUTURE-PAST.

re″-tro-ver′-sion. A tipping backward. REVERSAL.

re″-tro-vert′. To turn back. REVERSAL.

re-trude′. To thrust back. ATTRACTION-REPULSION.

re-tund′. To render dull. SHARPNESS-BLUNTNESS.

re-turn′. Repetition; backward movement; restoration; reply; gain. ACCOUNT, ADVANCE-RETROGRESSION, ARRIVAL-DEPARTURE, COMMISSION-ABROGATION, CONVERSION-REVERSION, ENLIGHTENMENT-SECRECY, GAIN-LOSS, IMPETUS-REACTION, INVESTIGATION-ANSWER, MARK, OUTLAY-INCOME, PERIODICITY-IRREGULARITY, PROPERTY, RECOMPENSE-PUNITION, RECORD, RECURRENCE, RENOVATION-RELAPSE; in return, COMPENSATION; return thanks, DEVOTION-IDOLATRY, THANKFULNESS-THANKLESSNESS; return the compliment, COMMUTATION-PERMUTATION, REPRISAL-RESISTANCE; return to the original state, RENOVATION-RELAPSE.

re-un′-ion. Coming together again. UNION-DISUNION.

réunion [F.] (rê-ü-ni-on′). Meeting. GATHERING-SCATTERING, VARIANCE-ACCORD.

réunion, point de [F.] (rê-ü-ni-on″, pwan· de). A gathering point. GATHERINGPLACE.

réunion social [F.] (rê-ü-ni-on″, so-sî-al′). A social gathering. SOCIABILITY-PRIVACY.

revanche, en [F.] (re-van·sh′, an·). In return. REPRISAL-RESISTANCE.

re-veal′. To disclose. EXPOSURE-HIDINGPLACE; reveal itself, VISIBILITY-INVISIBILITY.

re-veal′-ment. Revelation. EXPOSURE-HIDINGPLACE.

rev″-eil-le′. The morning-call to soldiers in camp. SIGN.

reveiller le chat qui dort, ne pas [F.] (rê-ve-yĕ′ le sha kî dor, ne pa). Do not arouse the sleeping cat. RECKLESSNESS-CAUTION, WARNING.

rev′-el. To make merry; to carouse. ENTERTAINMENT-WEARINESS, MODERATION-VOLUPTUARY; revel in, SENSUALITY-SUFFERING.

rev″-e-la′-tion. Something revealed. EXPOSURE-HIDINGPLACE, REVELATION-PSEUDOREVELATION

REVELATION—PSEUDOREVELATION.

Afflatus [L.]. A supernatural elevation of soul accompanying a divine revelation.

Inspiration. Supernatural divine influence, as exerted upon sacred teachers and writers, by which divine authority was given to their writings.

Revelation. The act or process of revealing by divine agency, or the state of being revealed; that which has been revealed, as the doctrines of the Bible.

REVELATION—*Denotations.*

Acts. The record of the deeds of the apostles, written by St Luke.

Apocalypse. The revelation recorded in the last book of the New Testament.

Apocrypha. A collection of fourteen books, included in the Septuagint and Vulgate versions of the Bible.

Ecclesiastes. One of the books of the Old Testament attributed to Solomon.

Epistles. The writings of the apostles.

Evangelists. The four Gospels.

Gospel. The announcement of the salvation of men through the death of Christ.

Gospels. The four memoirs of Christ in the New Testament.

Hagiographa. All the books of the Old Testament not reckoned in the Law or the Prophets.

Hagiology. A compilation of the lives of saints.

Hierographa. Sacred writings.

Holy Scriptures. The Bible.

Holy Writ. The writings of inspired writers.

Inspired writing. A writing inspired by God.

Leviticus. The book of the law of the Old Testament.

Major Prophets. The Old Testament books containing the prophecies of Isaiah, Jeremiah, Ezekiel, and Daniel.

Masorah. A collection of criticisms and marginal notes on the Old Testament.

Minor Prophets. The works of the prophets of the Old Testament, excluding the Major Prophets.

Mishna. The first part of the Talmud.

New Testament. That part of the Scriptures written after the Advent.

Octateuch. The eight first books of the Old Testament.

Old Testament. That part of the Scriptures written before the Advent.

Pentateuch. The five first books of the Bible.

Revelations. The last book of the New Testament.

Septuagint. A Greek version of the Old Testament made between 280 and 130 B.C.

Talmud. The body of Jewish civil and canonical law not comprised in the Pentateuch.

Thalmud. The Talmud.

The Bible. The sacred Scriptures as received by the Christian Church.

The Jewish Law. The books of the Talmud and the Pentateuch.

The Law. The Pentateuch.

The Prophets. The books of the Old Testament written by the prophets.

The Scriptures. Holy writings.

Pseudo-revelation. The act or process of revealing falsely, or that which has been falsely revealed.

PSEUDOREVELATION—*Denotations.*

Baal. The supreme divinity of the Phenician and Canaanitish nations.

Babism. The principles of the Babi.

Book of Mormon. The book containing the Mormon revelation and faith.

Buddha. A deified religious teacher of the Buddhists.

Confucius. The great Chinese philosopher and teacher.

Dagon. The national god of the Philistines.

Edda. The religious mythological book of the old Scandinavian tribes.

Gautama. The founder of the Hindu Nyaya philosophy.

Golden calf. An image for worship. See DEVOTION-IDOLATRY.

Gotama. Gautama.

Mahomet. The founder of Mohammedanism.

Moloch. A Phenician god.

Purana. Sanskrit sacred writings.

Shaster. The Brahminical institutes of laws, letters, and religions.

The Alcoran. The Koran.

The Koran. The Mohammedan Bible.

Vedas. The holy books of the Hindus.

Zend-Avesta. The sacred writings of the religion of Zoroaster.

Zoroaster. The founder of the Irano-Persian religion.

REVELATION—DENOTATIONS—*Continued.*

Vulgate. St. Jerome's Latin version of the Bible, used by Roman Catholics.

Word. ⎫ The Bible.
Word of God. ⎭

REVELATION—*Nouns of Agent.*

Apostle. One of the twelve chosen witnesses sent forth by Christ to proclaim the revelations of his gospel; any person zealously advocating any doctrine.

Disciple. One who believes the teaching of another, or adopts and follows some doctrine, as disciples of Christ.

Evangelist. One of the four writers of the Gospels.

Holy men of old. The prophets.

Inspired penmen. Sacred writers.

Prophet. One who delivers divine revelations. See SOOTHSAYER.

Saint. A holy, godly, or sanctified person.

The Apostolical Fathers. Clement of Rome. Barnabas, Hermes, Ignatius, Polycarp, contemporaries with the apostles.

The Fathers. The founders of the Christian Church.

REVELATION—*Adjectives.*

Apocalyptic. Pertaining to or like the Apocalypse or any prophetic revelation.

Apostolic. ⎱ Of or pertaining to an apostle or the apostles. See
Apostolical. ⎰ *Nouns.*

Biblical. Pertaining to the Bible.

Canonical. Belonging to the canon of Scripture.

REVELATION—Adjectives—*Continued.*

Ecclesiastical. Of or pertaining to the Church.
Evangelical. Of or pertaining to the gospel or the four Gospels.
Evangelistic. Evangelical.
Inspired. Communicated, imparted, or guided by inspiration.
Prophetic. Of or pertaining to a prophet or prophecy.

Rev-e-la'-tions. The last book of the Bible. REVELA-TION-PSEUDOREVELATION.
rev'-el-er. One who revels. ENTERTAINMENT-WEARI-NESS, TEETOTALISM-INTEMPERANCE.
rev'-el-ing. Carousing; rejoicing. ENTERTAINMENT-WEARINESS, JUBILATION-LAMENTATION, REGULAR-ITY-IRREGULARITY.
rev'-el-ry. Noisy festivity. ENTERTAINMENT-WEARI-NESS, MODERATION-SELFINDULGENCE.
rev'-els. A revel. ENTERTAINMENT-WEARINESS, MOD-ERATION-SELFINDULGENCE.
re-ven'-di-cate. To reclaim. GAIN-LOSS, JUBILATION-LAMENTATION, ORDER.
re-ven''-di-ca'-tion. A lawsuit. ORDER.
re-venge'. Avenge. FAVORITE-ANGER, PARDON-VIN-DICTIVENESS, REPRISAL-RESISTANCE; **breathe re-venge,** FAVORITE-ANGER, PARDON-VINDICTIVENESS.
re-venge'-ful. Disposed to revenge. PARDON-VINDIC-TIVENESS.
re-venge'-ment. Retribution. PARDON-VINDICTIVE-NESS.
revenons à nos moutons [F.] (re-ve-non· a no mu-ton·'). Let us resume our subject. ADVANCE-RETROGRES-SION, RENOVATION-RELAPSE.
rev'-e-nue. Income. OUTLAY-INCOME.
re-ver'-ber-ate. To reecho. IMPETUS-REACTION, RES-ONANCE-NONRESONANCE.
re-ver''-ber-a'-tion. Act of resounding or reflecting. CRASH-DRUMMING, IMPETUS-REACTION, RESONANCE-NONRESONANCE.
re-ver'-ber-a-to''-ry. Reverberative. OVEN-REFRIGER-ATOR.
re-vere'. To esteem highly. GODLINESS-UNGODLINESS, REGARD-DISRESPECT, TITLE.
rev'-er-ence. To respect; to adore. CHURCH, GODLI-NESS-UNGODLINESS, REGARD-DISRESPECT, TITLE.
rev'-er-enced. Respected. SAGE-FOOL.
rev'-er-end. Venerable. CHURCH, TITLE.
rev'-er-ent. Devout. DEVOTION-IDOLATRY, GODLI-NESS-UNGODLINESS.
rev''-er-en'-tial. Showing reverence. REGARD-DISRE-SPECT.
rev'-er-ie. Day-dream. FANCY, HEED-DISREGARD, MIND-IMBECILITY.
re-vers'-al. Change. BIGOTRY-APOSTASY, REVERSAL.

REVERSAL

Anastrophe [Gr.]. An inversion of the natural order of words.
Anastrophy. Anastrophe.
Contraposition, etc. A placing opposite. See LATERALITY-CON-TRAPOSITION.
Contrariety, etc. The state or quality of being opposite or contrary. See CONTRAST.
Culbute [F.]. Summersault.
Eversion. The state of being turned back or outward; the act of everting.
Hypallage. A figure consisting of a transference of attributes from their proper subjects to others.
Hyperbaton [L.]. A transposition of words from their grammatical order.
Hysteron-proteron [Gr.]. A figure in which the natural order of the sense is reversed.
Introversion. The act of turning inward, or the state of being turned inward.
Inversion. The act of inverting, or turning over and backward, or the state of being inverted; transposition.
Metastasis [Gr.]. In theology, a spiritual change; in medicine, a change in the location of a disease.

Sacred. Set apart or dedicated to religious use; esteemed especially dear to Deity.
Scriptural. Of or pertaining to Biblical revelations.
Textuary. Contained in the text; serving as a text.
Theopneustic. Given by inspiration of the Spirit of God.

Metathesis [Gr.]. Transposition, as of the letters or syllables of a word.
Overturn. The act of overturning, or the state of being overturned or subverted.
Palindrome. A word or words that read the same forward or back-ward.
Parenthesis. The curved lines which enclose a parenthetic word or phrase.
Pirouette [F.]. A rapid whirling on the toes in dancing.
Pronation and supination. The act of turning the hand palm down-ward and upward.
Retroversion. A turning or bending backward; also, the state of being turned or bent backward.
Reversal. The act of reversing; the causing to move or face in an opposite direction; a change or overthrowing.
Reversion. The act of returning or coming back; that which reverts or returns; a return toward some ancestral type or character; the returning of an estate to a grantor or his heirs, by operation of law, after the grant has terminated.
Revulsion. A sudden reaction; a sudden and complete change.
Somersault. } A leap in which a person turns heels over head and
Somerset. } lights on his feet.
Subversion. Overthrow; ruin.
Summerset. Somerset.
Synchysis [Gr.] A derangement or confusion of any kind; as, of words in a sentence.
Tmesis [Gr.]. The separation of the parts of a compound word by the intervention of one or more words.
Transposition. The act of transposing or the state of being trans-posed.
Turn of the tide. Change of the tide.

REVERSAL—*Verbs.*

Be inverted, etc. To be set upside down. See *Adjectives.*
Capsize. Upset or overturn, as a boat.
Culbuter [F.]. Throw down head over heels.
Introvert. Turn within; turn in, as one part within another.
Invert. Turn inside out or upside down; reverse.
Overset. To turn over.
Overturn. Upset; turn over; capsize.
Retrovert. Tip or turn back.
Reverse. Turn back, to the contrary or upside down; change to the former or to a contrary condition or state.
Subvert. Overthrow from the foundation; utterly destroy.
Transpose. Reverse the order or change the place of.
Upset. Overturn; to be upset.
Upturn. Turn up or over; overturn.

REVERSAL—*Verbal Expressions.*

Go about; go over; go round; go to the right-about; put the cart before the horse; tilt over; topple over; turn about; turn around; turn over; turn the tables; turn topsy-turvy; turn to the right-about; wheel about; wheel round; wheel to the right-about.

REVERSAL—*Adjectives*

Bottom upwards. } Reversed.
Inside out. }
Inverse. Opposed in order or effect; inverted.
Inverted, etc. Turned in a contrary direction, etc. See *Verbs.*
Keel upwards. Overturned.
On one's head. Upside down.
Opposite, etc. Standing, situated, or placed in front of or over against. See LATERALITY-CONTRAPOSITION.
Reverse, etc. Turned backward, etc. See CONTRAST.
Sens dessus dessous [F.]. Upside down.
Supine. Lying on the back.
Topheavy. Having the top or upper part too heavy for the lower part; hence, liable to turn or tip over.
Topsy-turvy. Upside down.
Upside down. With the upper side down.
Wrong side out. With the inside out.
Wrong side up. With the bottom up.

REVERSAL—*Adverbs, etc.*

Head over heels.
Heels over head.
Hirdie-girdie. Topsy-turvy.
Inversely, etc. In an inverse order or manner. See *Adjectives*

re-verse'. Opposite side or order; misfortune; to annul. ANTERIORITY-POSTERIORITY, COMMISSION-ABROGATION, ENTERTAINMENT WEARINESS, LATERALITY-CONTRAPOSITION, REVERSAL, SAMENESS-CONTRAST, WELFARE-MISFORTUNE.

re-verse'-less. Not reversible. MUTABILITY-STABILITY.

re-vers'-i-ble. Capable of being reversed. DETERMINATION-VACILLATION.

re-ver'-sion. A going back. ALIENATION, ANTECEDENCE-SEQUENCE, CONVERSION-REVERSION, HOLDING-EXEMPTION, PROPERTY, REVERSAL, TAKING-RESTITUTION.

re-ver'-sion-er. One entitled to an estate in reversion. HOLDER.

re-ver'-sis. A game of cards. ENTERTAINMENT-WEARINESS.

re-vert'. To turn back; repeat. ADVANCE-RETROGRESSION, CONVERSION-REVERSION, RECURRENCE, TAKING-RESTITUTION; **revert to,** HEED-DISREGARD.

re-vest'. To clothe again. TAKING-RESTITUTION.

re-vic'-tion. Revival. RENOVATION-RELAPSE.

re-view'. To reconsider; to examine; discussion. BETTERMENT-DETERIORATION, DECISION-MISJUDGMENT, ESSAY, HEED-DISREGARD, INVESTIGATION-ANSWER, POMP, REMEMBRANCE-FORGETFULNESS.

re-view'-er. One who reviews. DECISION-MISJUDGMENT.

re-vile'. To vilify. APPROVAL-DISAPPROVAL, GODLINESS-UNGODLINESS.

re-vi'-ler. One who reviles. FLATTERER-DEFAMER.

re-vi'-sal. A revision. HEED-DISREGARD.

re-vise'. To review or correct. BETTERMENT-DETERIORATION, COPY-MODEL, DESIGN, HEED-DISREGARD, WRITING-PRINTING.

re-vi'-sing bar'-ris-ter. A kind of English judge. JUDGE.

re-vi'-sion. Act of revising. EMBELLISHMENT-DISFIGUREMENT, HEED-DISREGARD; **under revision,** PREPARATION-NONPREPARATION.

re-vis'-it. To visit again. PRESENCE-ABSENCE.

re-vi'-val. Renewal; religious awakening. DEVOTION-IDOLATRY, RENEWAL, RENOVATION-RELAPSE, WEARINESS-REFRESHMENT.

re-vi'-val-ist. One who helps in revivals. CHURCH.

re-vive'. To reanimate; to restore. EXCITATION, LIFE-DEATH, RENEWAL, RENOVATION-RELAPSE, STRENGTH-WEAKNESS.

re-viv'-i-fy. To restore life to. RENEWAL, RENOVATION-RELAPSE.

rev''-i-vis'-cence. A renewing of life. RENOVATION-RELAPSE.

rev'-o-ca-ble. Capable of being revoked. DETERMINATION-VACILLATION.

rev''-o-ca'-tion. The act of revoking. BIGOTRY-APOSTASY, COMMISSION-ABROGATION, PROFFER-REFUSAL.

rev'-o-ca-to''-ry. Recalling. BIGOTRY-APOSTASY.

revoir, au [F.] (o re-vwar'). Adieu. ARRIVAL-DEPARTURE.

re-voke'. To disavow; to rescind. ASSERTION-DENIAL, BIGOTRY-APOSTASY, COMMISSION-ABROGATION.

re-voke'-ment. Revocation. BIGOTRY-APOSTASY, COMMISSION-ABROGATION.

re-volt'. To shock; rebel. APPROVAL-DISAPPROVAL, INSUBORDINATION-OBEDIENCE, PLEASURABLENESS-PAINFULNESS, REPRISAL-RESISTANCE; **revolt against,** LOVE-HATE; **revolt at the idea,** ASSENT-DISSENT.

re-volt'-ing. Repugnant. PLEASURABLENESS PAINFULNESS, SANGUINENESS-TIMIDITY.

rev''-o-lu'-tion. Rotation; change. CREATION-DESTRUCTION, MUTATION-PERMANENCE, PERIODICITY-IRREGULARITY, REVOLUTION, REVOLUTION-EVOLUTION.

REVOLUTION.

Bouleversement [F.]. An overturning.
Break-up. A scattering of parts.
Cataclysm. A sudden and overwhelming change.
Clean sweep. An entire change.
Convulsion. A violent disturbance of existing order.
Counter-revolution. A movement working against another movement.
Coup d'état [F.]. A violent measure in state affairs.
Destruction. A bringing to naught; devastation. See CREATION-DESTRUCTION.
Earthquake. A sudden undulation of a part of the earth's surface.
Explosion. A sudden breaking apart or shattering.
Jerk. A sudden arrest of motion.
Jump. A sudden change of position.
Leap. A sudden change.
Legerdemain. A deceptive performance. See TRUTHFULNESS-FRAUD.
Organic change. A complete change.
Plunge. A sudden leap.
Radical change. A movement causing great changes.
Revolution. A radical and usually sudden change, as in governmental or social conditions.
Revulsion. A strong or sudden change, as of feelings.
Spasm. A sudden action or effort.
Start. A sudden movement.
Storm. A great change of the existing order of things.
Subversion. Overthrow; ruin.
Sudden change. A change occurring without warning
Sweeping change. A movement that changes everything.
Throe. A violent effort.
Transilience. A leap across from one thing to another

REVOLUTION—*Verbs.*

Break with the past. To change one's course of life.
Change the face of. To make different.
New-model. To remodel.
Recast. To fashion anew by changing form, style, or arrangement.
Remodel. To put into new shape.
Revolutionize. To effect a radical or entire change in the character, government, or affairs of.
Strike out something new. To work out or devise promptly a new scheme.
Unsex. To rob of qualities or traits distinctively belonging to a sex.

REVOLUTION—*Adjective.*

Unrecognizable. Incapable of being recognized

REVOLUTION—EVOLUTION.

Circination. A spherical motion.
Circulation. The act of moving in a circle or in a course which brings the moving body to the place where its motion began.
Circumgyration. The act of turning, rolling, or whirling round.
Circumrotation. The act of rolling or revolving round as a wheel.
Circumvolution. The act of winding.
Convolution. The act of rolling anything upon itself.
Gyration. The act of turning or whirling, as round a fixed center.
Pirouette [F.] A whirling or turning on the toes in dancing.
Revolution. The act of revolving or turning round on an axis or a center.
Rotation. The act of rotating or turning, as a wheel or a solid body on its axis.
Turbination. The act of spinning or whirling as a top.
Verticity. The quality of turning.
Volutation. A rolling of a body.

Development. Gradual advancement or growth through a series of progressive changes.
Eversion. The state of being turned back or outward. See REVERSAL.
Evolution. The act of unfolding or unrolling; hence, in the progress of growth development.
Unfolding. The act of bringing out by successive development.

EVOLUTION—*Verbs.*

Develop. To unfold gradually; hence, to bring through a succession of states or stages, each of which is preparatory to the next.
Disentangle. To free from entanglement.
Evolve. To unfold or unroll.
Uncoil. To unwind or open.
Unfold. To open the folds of.
Unfurl. To unfold; to expand.

REVOLUTION—EVOLUTION—*Continued.*

REVOLUTION—*Denotations.*

Charybdis. A dangerous whirlpool off the coast of Sicily.
Cyclone. An atmospheric disturbance accompanied by spiral winds.
Dizzy round. Continued movement in a circle.
Eddy. A backward-circling current of water.
Gurge. A whirlpool.
Ixion. The king of the Lapithæ, bound in hell to an endlessly revolving wheel.
Maelstrom. A noted whirlpool off the coast of Norway.
Roll. That which is rolled up.
Surge. A large swelling wave that seems to roll back upon itself.
Tornado. A whirling wind-storm.
Trochilics. The science of rotary motion.
Vertigo. Dizziness.
Vortex A mass of whirling or rotating fluid.
Whir. A sound produced by a rapidly rotating instrument.
Whirl. A swift rotating motion.
Whirlpool. An eddy where water moves with a gyrating sweep.

REVOLUTION—*Nouns of Agent.*

Arbor. A framework supporting vines, etc.
Axis. A line on which something rotates.
Axle. A cross-bar on which a wheel rotates.
Bobbin. A small spool on which thread is wound.
Caster. A small roller or wheel on which an article of furniture moves.
Fly-wheel. A heavy wheel which by its revolution gives a uniform motion to machinery.
Gimbals. A contrivance for allowing a suspended object to tip freely.
Hinge. A connection between two parts so that one part will turn upon the other.
Jack. A device for turning or revolving objects.
Mandrel. A shaft or spindle on which an object may be fixed for rotation.
Pin. A bar of wood or metal used as an axis.
Pivot. A short shaft on which something rotates.
Pole. The end of an axis: an axis.
Roller. That upon which something rolls.
Rolling stone. A stone in a revolving motion.
Screw. A cylindrical piece of metal for holding things together.
Spindle. A short slender rod on which thread, etc., is wound.
Swivel. A coupling device that permits either half to rotate independently of the other.
Teetotum. A four-sided top.
Top. A rotating toy.
Wheel. A circular framework turning on an axis
Whirligig. Any toy that revolves on an axis.
Wind-mill. A machine turned by the wind.

REVOLUTION—*Verbs.*

Bowl. To roll along.
Box the compass. The name the thirty-two points of the compass in their order.

EVOLUTION—VERBS—*Continued.*

Unravel. To disentangle.
Unroll. To open, as what is rolled.
Untwine. To untwist; to disentangle.
Untwist. To separate and open.
Unwind. To wind off; to untwist.

EVOLUTION—*Adjectives.*

Evolved. }
Evolving. } Rolling off. See *Verbs.*

REVOLUTION—VERBS—*Continued.*

Circulate. To move in a circle; to move round and return to the same point.
Circumvolve. To roll round; to revolve.
Furl. To wrap or roll closely, as a sail.
Gyrate. To revolve round a central point.
Gyre. To turn round; to gyrate.
Revolve. To turn or roll round on.
Roll. To cause to revolve by turning over and over; to wrap round on itself.
Roll along. To revolve on an axis.
Roll up. To roll on an axis.
Rotate. To turn round on an axis.
Spin. To cause to turn round rapidly; to whirl.
Spin like a teetotum. } To spin on an axis.
Spin like a top. }
Troll. To roll round.
Trundle. To roll along.
Turn. To move round.
Turn round. To turn on an axis.
Twirl. To move or turn round rapidly.
Wallow. To roll oneself about as in mire.
Welter. To roll; to tumble about, as in blood.
Wheel. To turn round on an axis.
Whirl. To turn round rapidly.

REVOLUTION—*Adjectives.*

Circumrotatory. Turning, rolling, or whirling round.
Gyratory. Revolving; whirling around.
Rotary.)
Rotating. } Turning round, as a wheel on its axis. See *Verbs.*
Rotatory.)
Trochilic. Having power to draw out or turn round.
Vertiginous. Turning round; rotary.
Vortical. Of or pertaining to a vortex or vortices in form or motion; whirling.
Vorticose. Vortical; whirling.

REVOLUTION—*Adverbs etc.*

Head over heels. After a tumbling and overturned manner.
Like a horse in a mill. Turning in a circle.
Round and round. Repeatedly turned round.

---

rev″-o-lu′-tion-ize. To change completely. REVOLUTION.
re-volve′. To rotate. PERIODICITY-IRREGULARITY, REVOLUTION EVOLUTION; **revolve in the mind,** REFLECTION-VACANCY.
re-volv′-er. Small gun. WEAPON.
re-vul′-sion. Sudden change; recoil. CONVERSION-REVERSION, IMPETUS-REACTION, REVERSAL, REVOLUTION.
re-ward′. Recompense. RECOMPENSE - PUNITION, TITLE.
re-word′. To say again. RECURRENCE.
rex vivat [L.] (rex vai′-vat). Long live the king. APPROVAL-DISAPPROVAL.
rey′-nard. The fox. CRAFT-ARTLESSNESS, FAUNA-FLORA.
rez de chaussée [F.] (rêd″-sho″-sê′). The ground floor CONTENTS-RECEIVER, HEIGHT-LOWNESS.
rhab-dol′-o-gy. Method of calculation. NUMBERING.
Rhad″-a-man′-thus. Judge; son of Zeus. HEAVEN-HELL, JUDGE.
rhap-sod′-i-cal. Disconnected. PERIODICITY-IRREGULARITY.

rhap′-so-dist. Versifier. FANCY, SANENESS-MANIAC.
rhap′-so-dy. Senseless talk; irregular musical composition. ADAGE-NONSENSE, CONTINUITY-INTERRUPTION, FANCY.
rhe′-o-tome. An instrument which interrupts an electrical current. ELECTRICITY.
rhet′-o-ric. The art of discourse. NATURE-ART, RHETORIC, SPEECH-INARTICULATENESS; **flowers of rhetoric,** SIMPLICITY-FLORIDNESS.

RHETORIC.

Composition. Act of composing, of putting together into literary form, that which is composed.
Description. A portrayal in language.
Discourse. A formal communication of thought.
Disquisition. A systematic discourse or treatment of any subject.
Dissertation. A presentation of a subject in argumentative form.
Essay. A brief composition on a given subject.
Fine writing. Composition showy in appearance or high-flown in style.
Rhetoric. Science and art of effective discourse.

RHETORIC—*Associated Nouns.*

Accent. A greater force of voice placed upon a syllable or phrase of word

Allegory. A figure of speech in which something is described by means of something resembling it.

Amplification. The act of making clearer.

Anacoluthon. Want of grammatical sequence in a sentence.

Analogy. Conformity of words to the rules of a language.

Anapest. A metrical foot consisting of two short and one long syllable.

Antistrophe. The repetition of words in an inverse order

Antithesis. A contrast of words or sentiments.

Apheresis. A dropping of a letter or syllable from the beginning of a word.

Apocope. A cutting off of the last letter or syllable from a word.

Aposiopesis. A figure of speech in which a speaker breaks off suddenly, as if unwilling or unable to state what was in his mind.

Apostrophe. A figure of speech in which the absent is addressed as though present.

Balanced sentence. A sentence having corresponding parts or sentiments.

Bombast. High-sounding words.

Climax. A figure in which the parts of a discourse are so arranged that each succeeding rises above the preceding in impressiveness.

Common meter. Four iambic verses making a stanza the first and third each having four feet, the second and fourth, three.

Dactyl. A metrical foot of one long and two short syllables, or one accented followed by two unaccented; a finger, one long part followed by two short.

Dialect. The form of speech of a limited region or people.

Dieresis. The separation of one syllable into two.

Dimeter. A verse of two meters.

Doubt. A question.

Elegance. Beauty of expression, etc.

Ellipsis. The omission of one or more words.

Emphasis. A stress of utterance placed upon words.

Encomium. A speech of praise.

Epenthesis. The insertion of a letter or sound in the body of a word.

Eulogy. A speech in commendation of a person.

Euphemism. A figure in which a harsh or indelicate word is softened.

Euphuism. An affectation of elegance of language.

Fable. A figure of speech describing one thing under the name of another.

Figure. A mode of expressing ideas by words which suggest images or pictures.

Foot. A combination of syllables constituting a metrical element in a verse.

Force. Vigor of expression.

Hexameter. A verse of six feet, the first four of which may be either dactyls or spondees, the fifth a dactyl, and the sixth a spondee.

Humor. That quality of speech or thought which produces laughter.

Hypallage. A figure consisting of a transference of attributes from their proper subjects to others.

Hyperbaton. A figure in which the natural order of words is inverted

Hyperbole. A figure in which the expression is an evident exaggeration of the meaning intended.

Hysteron-proteron. A figure in which the natural order of the sense is reversed; the cart before the horse.

Iambic. A metrical foot of one short and one long syllable, or one unaccented followed by an accented.

Illustration. A comparison or example intended to make clear.

Image. Anything represented to the mind by a picture.

Interrogation. The act of questioning.

Inversion. A change of the usual order of words or phrases.

Irony. Humor, ridicule, or sarcasm.

Long meter. Iambic verses or lines of four feet each.

Loose sentence. A sentence whose parts are disconnected.

Metaphor. A compressed simile.

Metaphorical expression. An expression transferring the relation between one set of objects to another set.

Meter. Rhythmical arrangement of syllables or words into verses, stanzas, etc.

Metonymy. A figure in which one word is put for another that suggests it.

Monometer. A rhythmical series consisting of a single meter

Narration. A part of a discourse

Oration. An elaborate discourse.

Ornament. That which embellishes or adorns.

Panegyric. A formal or elaborate oration in honor of a dead person.

Paragoge. The addition of a letter or syllable at the end of a word.

Paragraph. A distinct part of a discourse or writing.

Paronomasia. A pun.

Pentameter. A verse of five feet.

Periodic sentence. A well-proportioned, harmonious sentence.

Personification. A figure of speech in which an inanimate object is represented as animate.

Perspicuity. Clearness of expression.

Phrase. A short pithy expression.

Phraseology. A mode or form of speech.

Pictorial language. Figurative language.

Pleonasm. Unnecessary use of words.

Poetry. Rhythmical language.

Prose. Writing without metrical structure.

Prosopopeia. A figure in which the speaker personates another.

Prosthesis. The addition of a letter or letters to a word.

Provincialism. An offense against purity of language

Pun. The witty use of a word in two senses.

Repetition. A form of figurative energy that permits the repeating of words, otherwise not permitted.

Rhythm. Movement in musical time, with periodical recurrence of accent.

Rime. Correspondence of sound in the terminating words or syllables of two or more verses.

Sarcasm. An ironical expression.

Sentence. A related group of words expressing a thought.

Sententiousness. Quality of being witty.

Short meter. A stanza usually consisting of four iambic lines.

Simile. A word or phrase by which one thing is likened to another.

Slang. The use of expressions not approved by good taste.

Stanza. A group of rimed lines.

Strength. Vigor or force of style.

Style. The proper expression of thought in language.

Symbol. A sign or representation of an idea.

Synalepha. A contraction of syllables by suppressing a vowel or diphthong at the end of a word.

Synaphea. A connection between one colon and another of a metrical period.

Syncope. The elision of a syllable from the middle of a word.

Syncrisis. A comparison of opposite persons or things.

Synecdoche. A kind of metonymy in which a part is put for the whole or a whole for a part.

Synonym. A word having the same meaning as another.

Systole. The shortening of a syllable that is naturally long.

Taste. A correct choice of words.

Tautology. Unnecessary repetition.

Tetrameter A verse of four meters.

Thesis. An essay on a particular subject.

Treatise. A composition written on a definite theme.

Trimeter. A verse of three meters.

Trochee. A metrical foot of one long or accented followed by one short or unaccented syllable.

Trope. The use of a word or expression in a changed sense.

Unity. The principle of composition according to which one idea controls the whole.

Verbosity. Unnecessary use of words.

Verse. A line consisting of a certain number of metrical feet.

Vigor. Force of style.

Vision. The representation of absent things as present.

Wit. The perception and expression of unexpected and amusing relations.

Zeugma. A figure by which an adjective or verb, which agrees with a nearer word, is referred to another more remote.

RHETORIC—*Adjectives.*

Allegorical. Describing by resemblances.

Anapestic. Composed of anapests.

Dactylic. Pertaining to a foot consisting of a long followed by two short syllables.

Descriptive. Affording description.

Dialectic. Relating to a given and provincial mode of speech.

Elliptical. Shortened.

Humorous. Suited to excite laughter or amusement.

Hyperbolic. Pertaining to rhetorical exaggeration; exaggerating.

Iambic. Of a foot having a short followed by a long syllable.

Interrogative. Denoting inquiry

Ironical. Covertly sarcastic.

Metaphorical. Figurative.

Narrative. Given to narration.

Ornamental. Serving to adorn.

Prosaic. Pertaining to prose; dul.

Rhythmical. Pertaining to rhythm.

Sarcastic. Relating to taunting and contemptuous language.

Symbolic. Pertaining to something that serves to represent another thing.

Synonymous. Being similar or equivalent in meaning or force.

Tautologic. Pleonastic; redundant.

Trochaic. Relating to a foot consisting of a long followed by a short syllable or an accented followed by an unaccented.

Witty. Good at repartee; having humor.

rhe-tor′-ic-al. Declamatory. SIMPLICITY-FLORIDNESS, SPEECH-INARTICULATENESS.

rhet″-o-ri′-cian. A master of rhetoric. SPEECH-INAR-TICULATENESS.

rheum. Discharge from the mouth or nose. LIQUID-GAS, NUTRIMENT-EXCRETION, WATER-AIR.

rhi′-no. Money. MONEY.

rhi-noc′-e-ros hide. Insensibility. SENSITIVENESS-APATHY, SENSUALITY-SUFFERING.

rhomb. Mathematical figure ANGULARITY.

rhom′-bic. In the form of a rhomboid. **Rhombic dodecahedron,** MINERALOGY.

rhom″-bo-he′-dral. Consisting of rhombohedrons. MINERALOGY.

rhom′-boid. A mathematical figure. ANGULARITY.

rhom-boi′-dal. Having the character of a rhomboid. ANGULARITY.

rhom′-bus. Rhomb. ANGULARITY.

rhumb. Geographic line. AIM-ABERRATION.

rhyme. Rhythmical repetition of sound. LIKENESS-UNLIKENESS, MELODY-DISSONANCE, POETRY-PROSE.

rhyme′-less. Without rhyme. POETRY-PROSE.

rhy′-mer. A maker of rhymes. POETRY-PROSE

rhyme′-ster. A maker of poor rhymes. POETRY-PROSE.

rhym′-ing. Making rhymes. POETRY-PROSE.

rhym′-ist. A rhymer. POETRY-PROSE.

rhythm. Orderly succession of beats of sound. MELODY-DISSONANCE, PERIODICITY-IRREGULARITY, POETRY-PROSE, RECURRENCE, RHETORIC.

rhyth′-mi-cal. Having rhythm. MELODY-DISSONANCE, PERIODICITY - IRREGULARITY, PURITY - CRUDENESS, RHETORIC.

rib. Bone; ridge; wife. CONVEXITY - CONCAVITY, MATRIMONY-CELIBACY, SUSPENSION-SUPPORT.

rib′-ald. Vulgar. PURITY-IMPURITY, REPUTATION-DISCREDIT, TASTE-VULGARITY.

rib′-ald-ry. Coarse language. PURITY - IMPURITY, TASTE-VULGARITY.

rib′-and. Ribbon. LAMINA-FIBER.

ribbed. Ridged. GROOVE.

rib′-bon. Strip of cloth. CONNECTIVE, LAMINA-FIBER, TITLE.

rib′-roast″. Beating. RECOMPENSE-PUNITION.

rich. Wealthy; elegant; tasteful; copious. AFFLUENCE-PENURY, BEAUTY-UGLINESS, COLOR-ACHROMATISM, EMBELLISHMENT-DISFIGUREMENT, ENOUGH, PALATABLENESS - UNPALATABLENESS, SIMPLICITY-FLORIDNESS; **rich man,** AFFLUENCE-PENURY.

rich′-es. Wealth. AFFLUENCE-WEALTH.

richesses, embarras de [F.] (ri-shes′, an′-ba-ra′ de). The plague of riches. AFFLUENCE-WEALTH, EXCESS-LACK.

rich′-ly. In a rich manner. MAGNITUDE-SMALLNESS; **richly deserve,** DUENESS-UNDUENESS.

rich′-ness. The state of being rich. EMBELLISHMENT-DISFIGUREMENT, TERSENESS-PROLIXITY.

rick. Stack. GATHERING-SCATTERING, STORE.

rick′-ets. A disease of early childhood. HEALTH-SICKNESS.

rick′-et-y. Tottering. BEAUTY-UGLINESS, STRENGTH-WEAKNESS.

ric″-o-chet′. Bounding. IMPETUS-REACTION.

ricordo, non mi [It.] (rî-cor′-do, non mî). I do not remember. REMEMBRANCE-FORGETFULNESS.

rid. To free. RESCUE; **get rid of,** ADMISSION-EXPULSION, GAIN-LOSS, KEEPING-RELINQUISHMENT, RELEASE-RESTRAINT, RESCUE.

rid′-dance. Deliverance. GAIN-LOSS, KEEPING-RELINQUISHMENT, RESCUE.

rid′-dle. To perforate; to sift, puzzle. APERTURE-CLOSURE, CLEANNESS-FILTHINESS, CLEARNESS-OBSCURITY, ORGANIZATION-DISORGANIZATION, TIDINGS-MYSTERY.

rid′-dled. Perforated. APERTURE-CLOSURE.

ride. To travel; to be borne on something. HEIGHT-

LOWNESS, TRAVELING-NAVIGATION; **ride and tie,** PERIODICITY-IRREGULARITY, TRAVELING-NAVIGATION; **ride at anchor,** MOVEMENT-REST; **ride full tilt at,** ATTACK-DEFENSE, QUEST-EVASION; **ride hard,** SWIFTNESS-SLOWNESS; **ride one's hobby,** QUEST-EVASION; **ride out the storm,** SECURITY-INSECURITY; **ride roughshod,** HARSHNESS-MILDNESS, LAW-LAWLESSNESS, PRESUMPTION-OBSEQUIOUSNESS, TURBULENCE-CALMNESS; **ride the whirlwind,** DETERMINATION-VACILLATION.

rideau, lever de [F.] (ri-do′, le-vĕ′ de). To raise the curtain. ACTING.

ridentem dicere verum [L.] (ri-den′-tem dis′-er-î vî′-rum). To speak the truth in a joking manner. LIGHTHEARTEDNESS-DEJECTION, WITTINESS-DULNESS.

ri′-der. One who rides; addition. INCREMENT-REMNANT, WAYFARER-SEAFARER.

rideret Heraclitus [L.] (rai-dî′-ret her-a-clai′-tus). Heraclitus would laugh. SOCIETY-LUDICROUSNESS.

ridge. Elevation. BREADTH-NARROWNESS, CONVEXITY-CONCAVITY, HEIGHT-LOWNESS.

rid′-i-cule. Derision. RESPECT-DISRESPECT, SOCIETY-DERISION, WITTINESS-DULNESS.

ri-dic′-u-lous. Laughable. ADAGE-NONSENSE, CONSEQUENCE-INSIGNIFICANCE, SAGACITY-INCAPACITY, SOCIETY-LUDICROUSNESS.

ri-dic′-u-lous-ness. Laughableness. SOCIETY - LUDICROUSNESS.

ri′-ding. Traveling; road. EXTENSION-DISTRICT, TRAVELING-NAVIGATION.

ri-dot′-to. Entertainment. ENTERTAINMENT-WEARINESS, SOCIABILITY-PRIVACY.

rifacimento [It.] (rî-fa″-chî-men′-to). A remaking. RECURRENCE, RENOVATION-RELAPSE.

rife. Current. DOMINANCE-IMPOTENCE, TIDINGS-MYSTERY, UNIVERSALITY-PARTICULARITY.

riff′-raff″. Rubbish; rabble. CLEANNESS-FILTHINESS, GENTILITY-COMMONALTY, GOOD MAN-BAD MAN.

ri′-fle. Gun; to pillage. THEFT, WEAPON.

ri′-fled can′-non. Cannon having spiral grooves in the bore. WEAPON.

ri′-fle-man. One who uses a rifle. BELLIGERENT, PUSH-PULL.

ri′-fler. Robber. ROBBER.

ri′-fles. Soldiers armed with rifles. BELLIGERENT.

ri′-fle-shoot″-ing. Marksmanship. ENTERTAINMENT-WEARINESS.

rift. Split. INTERSPACE-CONTACT, UNION-DISUNION.

rig. Clothing; joke; strumpet; to fit out. DRESS-UNDRESS, ENTERTAINMENT-WEARINESS, PREPARATION-NONPREPARATION, PURITY-RAKE; **rig the market,** EXCHANGE; **run the rig upon,** REGARD-DISRESPECT.

rig″-a-doon′. Dance. ENTERTAINMENT-WEARINESS.

rig′-ging. Tackle; dress. CONNECTIVE, DRESS-UNDRESS, INSTRUMENT; **running rigging,** CONNECTIVE; **standing rigging,** CONNECTIVE.

rig′-gish. Lewd. PURITY-IMPURITY.

right. Not left; straight; correct; proper; privilege. CURVATION-RECTILINEARITY, DUENESS-UNDUENESS, DUTY-DERELICTION, PROPERTY, RIGHT-LEFT, RIGHT-WRONG, RULE-LICENSE, TRUTH-ERROR, UPRIGHTNESS-DISHONESTY, VIRTUE-VICE; **bill of right,** LITIGATION; **by right,** DUENESS - UNDUENESS; **have a right to,** DUENESS-UNDUENESS; **hit the right nail on the head,** DISCOVERY, SKILL-UNSKILFULNESS; **in one's right mind,** SAGACITY-INCAPACITY, SANENESS-LUNACY; **in the right place,** PROPRIETY-IMPROPRIETY; **keep the right path,** VIRTUE-VICE; **right about,** ADVANCE-RETROGRESSION; **right ahead,** ANTERIORITY-POSTERIORITY; **right and left,** ENVIRONMENT-INTERPOSITION, EXTENSION-DISTRICT, LATERALITY-CONTRAPOSITION; **right angle,** ANGULARITY, ERECTNESS-FLATNESS; **right as a trevet,** FAULTLESS-

NESS - FAULTINESS; **right ascension,** ASTRONOMY, DIFFERENTIATION-INDISCRIMINATION; **right away,** DISCONTINUANCE-CONTINUANCE; **right hand,** AN-TAGONIST-ASSISTANT, MIGHT - IMPOTENCE, RIGHT-LEFT; **right itself,** RENOVATION-RELAPSE; **right line,** CURVATION-RECTILINEARITY; **right man in the right place,** HARMONY-DISCORD; **right owner,** HOLDER; **right thing to do,** DUTY-DERELICTION; **right word in the right place,** PURITY-CRUDENESS; **set right,** EN-LIGHTENMENT-SECRECY, EXPOSURE-HIDINGPLACE, RENOVATION-RELAPSE; **step in the right direction,** USEFULNESS-USELESSNESS.

RIGHT—LEFT.

Dexter. The right side.
Dextrality. The quality of being right-handed.
Offside. On the right side (of two side by side).
Right. The side opposed to the left.
Right hand. The right side.
Starboard. The right-hand side of a vessel as regarded by one standing on the deck facing the bow.

RIGHT—*Adjectives.*

Ambidextral. Able to use both hands with equal skill.
Dextral. On the right. See *Nouns.*
Right-handed. On the right side. See *Nouns.*

Larboard. The left-hand side of a ship to one facing the bow
Left. Opposed to right.
Left hand.⎫ The left side.
Near side.⎭
Port. Opening in the side of a ship.
Sinister. On the side of the left hand; bad; unfortunate.
Sinistrality. The quality of being left-handed.

LEFT—*Adjectives.*

Left-handed. Capable of using the left hand better than the right.
Sinistral. Toward the left.

RIGHT—WRONG.

Clear stage. A record or course free from wrong-doing.
Duty. That which one is bound by moral obligation to do See DUTY.
Equitableness. Fairness and just dealing. See *Adjectives.*
Equity. Equality of rights.
Even-handed justice. Strict uprightness.
Fair field. Just dealing for all parties.
Fitness. Suitableness. See *Adjectives.*
Give and take. Dealing like for like.
Honor. A nice sense of what is right. See UPRIGHTNESS.
Impartiality. Freedom from bias.
Justice. Conformity to the principles of righteousness and rectitude in all things.
Law. A rule of action to enforce justice. See LAW.
Lex talionis [L.] The law of like for like
Measure for measure.
Right. Conformity to the constitution of man and the will of God, or to justice and equity
Scales of justice. Figuratively. the dealings of justice.
Summum jus [L.] The extreme of justice.
Suum cuique [L.] To each one his own.
Virtue. Cordial conformity of an act to the moral law. See VIRTUE.
What ought to be.⎫ Duty.
What should be.⎭

RIGHT—*Nouns of Agent.*

Astræa. Goddess of innocence and daughter of justice.
Nemesis. The goddess of retribution.
Themis. The patroness of existing rights.

RIGHT—*Verbs.*

Audire alteram partem [L.] To hear the other side.
Be right. To be according to justice. See *Adjectives.*
Deserve. To be worthy of recompense. See DUENESS.
Do justice to. To administer righteous equity to.
Give and take. To average gains and losses.
Give every one his due. To do justice to every one.
Give the devil his due. To do justice to one hated and despised.
Hold the scales even. To preserve justice impartially.
Put the saddle on the right horse. To impute blame where it is rightly deserved.
Recompense. To give or render a just equivalent to. See RECOMPENSE.
See fair play. To see justice done.
See justice done. To see equity shown.
See one righted. To turn from wrong.
Serve one right. To befall one justly.
Stand to reason. To be rightly consistent with reason.

RIGHT—*Adjectives.*

As it ought to be.⎫ Right.
As it should be. ⎭
Deserved. Accordant with justice.
Equable. Equal and uniform at all times.
Equal. Just; equitable.
Equitable. Distributing equal justice.
Even-handed. Impartial; just.
Fair. Equitable; just.
Fit. Conforming to a standard of right. See DUENESS.
Good. Worthy; righteous.

Favor. An act of kindness, as distinguished from one inspired by justice.
Favoritism. A disposition to prefer one person over another.
Foul play. Conduct intended to take another at an unfair advantage.
Grievance. A wrong done and suffered.
Iniquity. Want of rectitude; wrong-doing.
Injustice. Violation of the rights of another or others.
Leaning. Departing from a course of justice.
Malum in se [L.] Bad in itself.
Nepotism. Favoritism to relatives.
Partiality. Inclination to favor one party more than another.
Party spirit. Zeal for party.
Sham. Any trick, fraud, or device that deludes and disappoints.
Undueness. Impropriety or lawlessness. See DUENESS-UNDUE-NESS.
Unfairness. The quality of being unfair. See *Adjectives.*
Unlawfulness. Opposition to law. See LAW-LAWLESSNESS.
Unreasonableness. The state of being without or beyond reason.
What ought not to be.⎫ That which is contrary to right or justice.
What should not be. ⎭
Wrong. Not according to the laws of good morals, whether divine or human.

WRONG—*Figurative Expressions.*

A custom more honored in the breach than in the observance. An unjust custom. [Shakespeare, *Hamlet,* I. iv.]
Robbing Peter to pay Paul. To take from one as deserving as the person to whom it is given. See *Verbs.*
The wolf and the lamb.

WRONG—*Verbs.*

Be inequitable. To be unjust. See *Adjectives.*
Be wrong. Not to be right. See *Adjectives.*
Do wrong. Not to do according to justice. See *Nouns.*
Encroach. To enter gradually into the rights of another.
Favor. To show partiality for.

WRONG—*Verbal Expressions.*

Give an inch and take an ell; impose upon; lean towards; reap where one has not sown; rob Peter to pay Paul.

WRONG—*Adjectives.*

Bad. Wanting good qualities, whether physical or moral.
Doli capax [L.] Capable of committing a wrong.
Illegal. Not according to law. See LAW-LAWLESSNESS.
Immoral. Inconsistent with rectitude, purity, or good morals. See VIRTUE-VICE.
Improper. Not proper; unfit.
Inequitable. Not according to equitable principles; unfair.
Iniquitous. Unjust; wicked.
In the wrong. Holding a wrong or unjustifiable position as regards another person.
In the wrong box. In error.
Objectionable. Liable to objection because of wrong.
One-sided. Pertaining to, having, or considering only one side.
Partial. Favoring one party or side.
Too bad. Wrong.
Unallowable. Not to be allowed.
Unequal. Not equal; inequitable; unjust.

RIGHT—WRONG—*Continued.*

RIGHT—Adjectives—*Continued.*

Just. Impartial; equitable, righteous.
Justifiable. Capable of being justified.
Lawful. Conformable to law; rightful. See PROFFER; LAW.
Legitimate. Accordant with law; rightful.
Reasonable. Governed by right reason; just.
Right. According to the law and will of God or conformity to the standard of truth and justice.
Rightful. Righteous; just.

RIGHT—*Adverbs, etc.*

In equity. With equity; righteously.
In justice. With justice; equitably.
In reason. With reason; impartially.
Rightly. According to justice. See *Adjectives*
Upon even terms. Equally.
Without distinction of persons.
Without regard to persons. } Impartially.
Without respect to persons.

RIGHT—*Interjection.*

All right!

RIGHT—*Phrases.*

À bon droit [F.]   With justice.
Au bon droit [F.]   Of good right.

WRONG—Adjectives—*Continued*

Unequitable. Not equitable, fair, or just.
Unfair. Showing partiality or prejudice.
Unfit. Not fit; improper; wanting suitable qualifications, physical or moral.
Unjust. Not acting or disposed to act according to justice.
Unjustifiable. Not capable of being justified or proved to be right.
Unjustified. Not according to justice. See DUENESS-UNDUENESS.
Unwarrantable. Not justifiable; unjust, improper.
Wrong. Not physically or morally right; not according to moral or divine law.
Wrongful. Injurious; unjust.

WRONG—*Adverb.*

Wrongly. Not according to justice.

WRONG—*Phrase*

It will not do.

RIGHT—PHRASES—*Continued.*

Dieu défend le droit [F.]   God defend the right.
Dieu et mon droit [F.]   God and my right.
Justitiæ soror incorrupta Fides [L.]   Uncorrupt Faith, sister of Justice.
Justitia virtutum regina [L.]   Justice is queen of the virtues

right'-a-bout''. To the right-about. ADVANCE-RETROGRESSION, AIM-ABERRATION, PROFFER-REFUSAL; **go to the right-about,** BIGOTRY-APOSTASY, CIRCUITION, REVERSAL; **send to the right-about,** ADMISSION-EXPULSION, CHOICE-REJECTION, PROFFER-REFUSAL; **turn to the right-about,** AIM-ABERRATION, REVERSAL.
right'-eous. Just. VIRTUE-VICE; **righteous overmuch,** GODLINESS-UNGODLINESS; **the righteous,** GODLINESS-UNGODLINESS.
right'-eous-ness. Rectitude. **Lord our Righteousness,** DIVINITY; **Sun of Righteousness,** DIVINITY.
right'-ful. Having right. RIGHT-WRONG; **rightful owner,** HOLDER.
right hand. Help; strength. ANTAGONIST-ASSISTANT, MIGHT-IMPOTENCE, RIGHT-LEFT; **not let the right hand know what the left is doing,** ENLIGHTENMENT-SECRECY; **right hand of friendship,** AMITY-HOSTILITY.
right'-hand''-ed. Using the right hand more easily than the left. RIGHT-LEFT.
right'-ly. With right. **Be rightly reserved,** RECOMPENSE-PUNITION.
right'-mind''-ed. Just. UPRIGHTNESS-DISHONESTY, VIRTUE-VICE.
rights. Order. **Put to rights,** RENOVATION-RELAPSE; **set to rights,** ORGANIZATION-DISORGANIZATION; **stand on one's rights,** LIBERTY-SUBJECTION.
rig'-id. Stiff; severe. CONVENTIONALITY-UNCONVENTIONALITY, HARDNESS-SOFTNESS, HARSHNESS-MILDNESS, TRUTH-ERROR.
rig'-ma-role. Frivolous. MEANING-JARGON.
rig'-or. Strictness; harshness. HARSHNESS-MILDNESS, TRUTH-ERROR.
rigor mortis [L.] (rai'-gor mor'-tis). The stiffness of death. LIFE-DEATH.
rig'-or-ous. Severe. HARSHNESS-MILDNESS, PARDON-VINDICTIVENESS, TRUTH-ERROR.
Rigs'-dag. Assembly. COUNCIL.
rile. To vex. FAVORITE-ANGER, LOVE-HATE, PLEASURABLENESS-PAINFULNESS.
rilievo [It.] (rî-lyê'-vo). Relief. CONVEXITY-CONCAVITY, SCULPTURE.
rill. Stream. RIVER-WIND.
rim. Edge. BORDER.
rime. Similarity of sounds. LIKENESS-UNLIKENESS. POETRY-PROSE; **without rime or reason,** ADAGE-NONSENSE, BIGOTRY-WHIM, MOTIVE-CAPRICE, RHETORIC.
rime. Frost; chink. ADVANCE-RETROGRESSION, INTERSPACE-CONTACT.

rime'-less. Lacking rime. POETRY-PROSE.
ri'-mer. A tool for shaping the rimes of a ladder. PERFORATOR-STOPPER.
rime'-ster. Inferior poet. POETRY-PROSE. See RHYMESTER.
rim'-ple. To wrinkle. PLICATURE.
rind. Skin. COVER-LINING.
ring. Amulet; circle; arena; sound; clique. ASSOCIATION, CIRCLE-WINDING, LISTS, LOUDNESS-FAINTNESS, RESONANCE-NONRESONANCE, SUSPENSION-SUPPORT; **in a ring fence,** CONFINEMENT, ENCLOSURE; **ring in the ear,** LOUDNESS-FAINTNESS, RESONANCE-NONRESONANCE; **ring the changes,** MUTABILITY-STABILITY, MUTATION-PERMANENCE, RECURRENCE; **ring the tocsin,** ALARM; **ring with the praises of,** APPROVAL-DISAPPROVAL; **rub the ring,** DEVOTION-MAGIC.
ring'-ing. Giving forth a resonant sound. RESONANCE-NONRESONANCE.
ring'-lead''-er. Chief. INSUBORDINATION-OBEDIENCE, MANAGER.
ring'-let. Small ring. CIRCLE-WINDING, SMOOTHNESS-ROUGHNESS.
rink. Floor. ENTERTAINMENT-WEARINESS
rinse. To cleanse. CLEANNESS-FILTHINESS.
rins'-ings. Liquid used in rinsing. CLEANNESS-FILTHINESS.
ri'-ot. Tumult. INSUBORDINATION-OBEDIENCE, ORGANIZATION-DISORGANIZATION, REGULARITY-IRREGULARITY, REPRISAL-RESISTANCE, TURBULENCE-CALMNESS, TYRANNY-ANARCHY, VARIANCE-ACCORD; **riot in,** SENSUALITY-SUFFERING; **run riot,** ACTIVITY-INDOLENCE, EXCESS-LACK, EXCITABILITY-INEXCITABILITY, INSUBORDINATION-OBEDIENCE, MODERATION-SELFINDULGENCE.
ri'-ot-er. One who riots. INSUBORDINATION-OBEDIENCE.
ri'-ot-ous. Boisterous. INSUBORDINATION-OBEDIENCE, REGULARITY-IRREGULARITY, TURBULENCE-CALMNESS.
rip. Depraved person. GOOD MAN-BAD MAN, PURITY-RAKE; **rip open,** APERTURE-CLOSURE; **rip up,** EXCITATION, REMEMBRANCE-FORGETFULNESS, UNION-DISUNION.
ri-pa'-ri-an. Pertaining to a river-bank. OCEAN-LAND.
ripe. Aged; matured. COMPLETION-NONCOMPLETION, INFANCY-AGE, MANHOOD.

ri'-pen. To mature; to be perfected. BETTERMENT-DETERIORATION, COMPLETION - NONCOMPLETION, FAULTLESSNESS - FAULTINESS, PREPARATION - NON-PREPARATION; **ripen into,** CONVERSION-REVERSION.

ri-post'. Repartee. INVESTIGATION-ANSWER.

rip'-ple. To be wavy; to babble. AGITATION, LOUD-NESS - FAINTNESS, RIVER - WIND, SMOOTHNESS-ROUGHNESS.

rip'-rap''. Broken stones for making walls. SUSPEN-SION-SUPPORT.

rire, pour [F.] (rîr, pur). Laughable. SOCIETY-LUDI-CROUSNESS.

rise. To ascend; to advance; to grow; to take up arms; to begin. ACTIVITY-INDOLENCE, ADVANCE-RETROGRESSION, ASCENT-DESCENT, HEIGHT-LOW-NESS INCREASE-DECREASE, INSUBORDINATION-OBE-DIENCE, PARALLELISM-INCLINATION; **rise again,** REN-OVATION-RELAPSE; **rise from,** CAUSE-EFFECT; **rise in arms,** FIGHTING-CONCILIATION, INSUBORDINA-TION-OBEDIENCE; **rise in price,** COSTLINESS-CHEAP-NESS; **rise in the world,** WELFARE-MISFORTUNE; **rise up,** ELEVATION-DEPRESSION.

ris''-i-bil'-i-ty. Tendency to laughter. JUBILATION-LAMENTATION.

ris'-i-ble. Laughable. JUBILATION-LAMENTATION, SOCIETY-LUDICROUSNESS.

ri'-sing. Growing. **Rising generation,** ASCENT-DE-SCENT, INFANCY-AGE, PARALLELISM-INCLINATION, PARENTAGE - PROGENY; **rising ground,** HEIGHT-LOWNESS, PARALLELISM-INCLINATION; **rising of the**

curtain, APPEARANCE-DISAPPEARANCE; BEGINNING-END, INSUBORDINATION-OBEDIENCE; **worship of the rising sun,** PRESUMPTION-OBSEQUIOUSNESS.

risk. Venture. PURPOSE - LUCK, SECURITY - INSECU-RITY; **at any risk,** DETERMINATION-VACILLATION.

risum teneatis, amici [L.] (rai'-sum tê''-ni-ê'-tis, a-mai'-sai). Can you, my friends, forbear laughing. SOCIETY-LUDICROUSNESS.

rit bien qui rit le dernier, il [F.] (rit bi-an-' ki rit le dêr-niê', il). He laughs best who laughs last. RECKLESS-NESS-CAUTION.

rite. Ceremony. CEREMONIAL, LAW-LAWLESSNESS; **funeral rite,** LIFE-FUNERAL.

ritornello [It.] (rî''-tor-nel'-lo). Refrain. RECUR-RENCE.

rit'-u-al. Ceremony. CEREMONIAL, POMP.

rit'-u-al-ism. The use of ritual. CEREMONIAL, ORTHO-DOXY-HETERODOXY.

rit'-u-al-ist. One devoted to a ritual. CEREMONIAL, ORTHODOXY-HETERODOXY.

rit''-u-al-is'-tic. Adhering to rituals. CEREMO-NIAL.

ri'-val. To compete with. ANTAGONISM-CONCURRENCE, ANTAGONIST-ASSISTANT, BELLIGERENT, GOODNESS-BADNESS, REPUTATION-DISCREDIT, STRIFE-PEACE.

ri'-val-ry. Act of rivaling. ANTAGONISM-CONCURRENCE, PARDON-ENVY, STRIFE-PEACE.

rive. Split. UNION-DISUNION.

riv'-el. Shrivel. PLICATURE.

riv'-er. Stream. RIVER-WIND.

RIVER—WIND.

Anerithmon gelasma [Gr.]. Innumerable laughter: said of the waves of the sea.

Beck. A small brook.

Billow. A great wave or surge of the sea or other water.

Body of water. An area of water, as a lake or the like.

Bore. A high crested roaring wave, caused by the rushing of a flood tide up a river.

Breakers. A wave breaking into foam against the shore.

Brook. A stream of water smaller than a river or creek.

Brooklet. A small brook.

Burn. A small stream.

Cascade. A fall of water over a precipice.

Cataclysm. A sweeping flood of water.

Catadupe. A waterfall, originally of the Nile.

Cataract. A great fall of water over a precipice.

Chopping sea. Rough, short, noisy waves.

Confluence. The running together of two or more streams of water.

Corrivation. The flowing of different streams into one.

Coulee. A river of lava.

Course. The path of a stream.

Cross sea. A sea in which the waves run in contrary directions.

Current. A body of moving water.

Débâcle [F.]. A violent rush or flood of waters.

Defluxion. A discharge of waters.

Deluge. A great flood of water.

Downpour. A heavy fall of rain.

Drenching rain. A rain that thoroughly soaks.

Driving rain. A rain driven by the wind.

Drizzle. Rain falling slowly and in very small drops.

Dropping. Falling drop by drop. See *Verbs.*

Eager. A wave moving up a river.

Eddy. A current of water moving in a circular direction.

Effluence. A flowing out. See ENTRANCE-EXIT.

Fall. A rush of water down a precipice.

Flood. A great flow of water.

Flow. A stream of water.

Flowing. Moving along, as a stream. See *Verbs.*

Flush. A sudden overflow of water.

Flux. The setting in of the tide toward the shore.

Fount.
Fountain. } The source of a stream of water.

Fresh. A stream or spring of fresh water.

Freshet. An overflowing of a stream caused by heavy rain.

Full tide. The high tide.

Geyser. A boiling spring which throws forth jets of water.

Ghyll.
Gill. } A stream flowing in a narrow valley.

Afflation. A blowing or breathing.

Afflatus [L.]. A breath or blast of wind.

Air. A gentle wind.

Aura. A subtle emanation from a substance.

Bise [F.]. A cold northerly wind prevalent in Switzerland and parts of France.

Blast. A violent gust of wind.

Blirt. A gust of wind and rain.

Blizzard. A furious blast of wind and snow.

Blow.
Blowing. } A heavy gale.

Boreas. The north wind.

Breath. A light breeze.

Breath of air. A gentle wind.

Breeze. A light, gentle wind.

Capful of wind. A light puff of wind.

Catching of the breath. A drawing of air into the lungs.

Cave of Eolus. The home of the god of the winds.

Current. A body of air moving in a certain direction.

Cyclone. A violent wind-storm, with spiral inward currents.

Dirty sky. A cloudy sky indicative of high winds.

Dirty weather. Weather of high winds blowing the dust.

Draft. A current of wind.

Drift. A violent movement of air.

Efflation. That which is blown forth.

Eluvium. A wind-drift.

Eolus. The god of winds.

Fanning. The act of stirring up the air. See *Verbs.*

Flatus.
Fresh breeze. } A puff of wind.

Gale. A strong current of air.

Gust. A sudden squall.

Half a gale. A high wind.

Harmattan. A dry, hot wind prevalent on the Atlantic coast of Africa.

Hiccough. A spasmodic drawing in of the breath.

Hiccup. Hiccough.

Hurricane. A high wind-storm of the tropics.

Inflation. State of being filled or blown up with air.

Insufflation. The act of breathing upon.

Keen blast. A piercing wind.

Levanter. A strong easterly wind prevalent on the Mediterranean.

Mare's-tail. A long cirrus tail indicative of rain.

Mistral. A cold northwest wind blowing in southern France.

Monsoon. A wind blowing six months in one direction and six months in another.

RIVER—WIND—Continued.

Ground-swell. A broad deep swell of the ocean, caused by a continued gale.
Gullet. A channel for water
Gurge. A whirlpool.
Gush. A sudden flowing of water from an enclosed space.
Heavy sea. A strong, violent sea.
High tide. The greatest flow of the tide.
Huger. A wave moving up a river
Indraft. A flow of water setting inward.
Inundation. An overflow.
Jet. A sudden rush of water, as from a pipe.
Jet d'eau [F.]. A jet of water
Lin. }
Linn. } A pool or waterfall.
Long sea. A smooth sea.
Maelstrom. A celebrated whirlpool on the coast of Norway
Mizzle. Fine rain or mist.
Niagara. A celebrated American cataract.
Overflow. A sudden rising of a stream over its banks.
Plash. A small pool of standing water.
Predominance of Aquarius. A heavy and continued rainfall.
Profluence. A course of a stream.
Race. The current of water that turns a water-wheel.
Rain. }
Rainfall. } The falling of water from the clouds.
Rapids. The part of a river where the water moves with great swiftness.
Reach. An extended portion of water.
Reflux. The ebbing or flowing back of a stream.
Regurgitation. A pouring back by the orifice of entrance.
Reign of St. Swithin. The forty days after St. Swithin's day, July 15, said by popular superstition to be rainy days if it rains on that date.
Rill. A very small brook.
Rillet. A little rill.
Ripple. A little wave.
River. A large stream of water flowing in a channel.
Rivulet. A small river.
Rollers. Long heavy waves that roll in upon the coast.
Rough sea. A stormy sea.
Runnel. A small brook.
Running water. A stream.
Rush. A rapidly moving stream.
Scud. A slight, sudden shower.
Serein. A mist or very fine rain.
Short sea. A sea with small waves
Shower. A fall of rain.
Sike. A stream that is usually dry in summer.
Sluice. A stream flowing through a flood-gate.
Splash. Water thrown from a puddle.
Spout. A jet of water.
Spring. A source of a stream of water.
Spring tide. The high tide.
Spurt. A sudden gushing forth of water.
Squirt. A sudden jetting of water
Stillicidium [L.]. Falling rain.
Stream. Flowing water.
Streamlet. A small stream.
Surf. The swell of the sea which breaks upon the shore.
Surge. A large wave or billow.
Swash. A dashing or splashing of water
Swell. A succession of large waves.
Tide. The alternate rising and falling of the waters of the ocean.
Torrent. A violent stream of water.
Tributary. A stream of water flowing into another stream.
Undercurrent. A current below the surface of water.
Vortex. A stream with a whirling or circular motion.
Waterfall. A fall of water over a precipice.
Waterspout. The throwing up of water into a long column by a violent wind.
Wave. An advancing ridge or swell on the surface of the sea.
Whirlpool. An eddy or vortex of water.
White horses. White-topped waves.

RIVER—*Associated Nouns.*

Force-pump. A pump adapted for delivering water at a considerable height.
Hydrant. A discharge pipe for water.
Irrigation. The operation of causing water to flow over lands. See WATER.
Pump. A machine for raising water.
Rain-gage. An apparatus that measures the amount of rainfall.
Syringe. A small hand-pump for throwing a stream of liquid.

Perflation. The act of blowing through.
Puff. A wind which produces ruffs.
Rough weather. High wind.
Samiel. The simoom.
Simoom. }
Simoon. } A hot, dry, dust-laden wind of Arabia.
Sirocco. An oppressive wind blowing from the Libyan deserts.
Sneezing. A violent emission of air through the nose. See *Verbs.*
Squall. A sudden gust of wind.
Sternutation. The act of sneezing.
Stiff breeze. A violent wind.
Storm. A violent disturbance of the air accompanied by wind.
Stream. A steady current of air.
Stress of weather. Continued bad weather.
Sufflation. The act of inflating.
Tempest. A furious storm.
Tornado. A violent whirling wind.
Trade-wind. A steady wind blowing in the torrid zone.
Tramontane. An Italian north wind.
Typhoon. A violent whirlwind occurring in the Chinese Sea.
Undercurrent. A current under or below another current of air.
Ventilation. The process of replacing foul air with pure air
Ventosity. Windiness.
Whiff. A sudden gust of wind.
Whirlwind. A violent wind-storm.
Wind. A current of air in motion.
Windiness. Tendency or state of being windy. See *Adjectives.*
Zephyr. The west wind.

WIND—*Nouns of Instrument.*

Air-pump. A pump for exhausting air from an enclosed space.
Bellows. An instrument for producing a current of air.
Blow-pipe. A tube for directing a jet of air into a fire.
Fan. An instrument used for producing currents of air.
Lungs. The organs of the body into which the air is drawn
Pipe. Any wind-instrument of music.
Punkah. A machine for fanning a room.
Ventilator. A contrivance for effecting ventilation.

WIND—*Scientific Nouns.*

Aerodynamics. The science which treats of the air and other gaseous bodies under the action of force and their mechanical effects.
Anemography. A description of the winds.
Anemometer. An instrument for measuring the force and velocity of the winds.
Vane. A contrivance fixed on an elevated place for showing which way the wind blows.
Weathercock. A vane.
Wind-gage. An anemometer.

WIND—*Verbs.*

Blow. To produce a current of air.
Blow a hurricane. }
Blow great guns. } To blow furiously.
Blow hard. To blow violently.
Blow up. To fill with air.
Breathe. To inhale and exhale air.
Cough. To expel air from the lungs or air-passages in a noisy or violent manner.
Fan. To move the air with a fan.
Gasp. To respire convulsively.
Inflate. To swell or distend with air or gas.
Issue. To pass or flow out.
Perflate. To blow through.
Puff. To blow in puffs or whiffs.
Respire. To take breath again; breathe.
Sneeze. A sudden and forcible ejection of air chiefly through the nose.
Sniff. }
Sniffle. } To draw air audibly up the nose.
Snuff. }
Snuffle. } To draw in forcibly through the nose.
Stream. To float in the wind.
Ventilate. To admit pure currents of air.
Waft. To float lightly on the air.
Wheeze. To breathe hard and with an audible sound.
Whiff. }
Whiffle. } To expel air suddenly from the mouth.

WIND—*Adjectives.*

Blowing. Causing the air to be in motion. See *Verbs.*
Blustering. Exhibiting noisy violence, as the wind.

RIVER—WIND—*Continued.*

RIVER—Associated Nouns—*Continued*

Watering-cart. A sprinkling-cart.
Watering-pot. A pot for sprinkling water.

RIVER—*Scientific Nouns.*

Hydraulicostatics. } That branch of mechanics which treats of fluids
Hydraulics. } in motion.
Hydrodynamics. The principles of dynamics as applied to water and other fluids.
Hyetography. The branch of physical science which treats of the geographical distribution of rain.
Hyetology. That branch of meteorology which treats of rain.

RIVER—*Verbs.*

Babble. To make a continuous murmuring noise, as shallow water running over stones.
Bubble. To run with a gurgling noise, as if forming bubbles.
Dam. To obstruct or restrain the flow of.
Dam up. To make a dam or pool. See Aperture-Closure.
Deluge. To overflow with water.
Discharge itself. To flow from.
Disembouge. To pour out or discharge at the mouth, as a stream
Distil. To fall in drops.
Drain into. To flow into.
Drench. To soak. See Water.
Dribble. To fall in drops or small drops or a quick succession of drops.
Drip. To let fall in drops.
Drizzle. To rain slightly in very small drops.
Drop. To pour or let fall in drops.
Fall. To find its outlet; discharge its waters.
Fall into. To flow into.
Flow. To change place, or circulate, as a liquid.
Flow into. To empty the water from.
Flow out. To flow from.
Flow over. To run over the banks.
Guggle. To gurgle.
Gurgle. To run or flow in a broken, irregular, noisy current.
Gush. To flow copiously.
Inundate. To cover with a flood.
Irrigate. To moisten with running or dropping water.
Issue. To flow out.
Jet. To spout; to emit in a stream.
Meander. To wind, turn, or twist. "Where Meander's amber waves in lingering labyrinths creep." [Gray, *Progress of Poesy*, II, 3.]
Murmur. To make a low, continued noise like a stream of water.
Obstruct. To hinder from passing; impede. See Obstruction.
Ooze. To flow gently.
Open into. To flow into.
Overflow. To flow over; cover with, or as with, water.
Percolate. To cause to pass through fine interstices, as a liquid.
Plash. To dabble in water; splash.
Pour. To cause to flow in a stream.
Pour out. To flow with a strong stream.
Pour with rain. To rain very heavily.
Purl. To run swiftly round, as a small stream flowing among stones or other obstructions.
Rain cats and dogs. A figurative expression for very heavy rain.
Rain hard. To rain very much.

WIND—Adjectives—*Continued.*

Boisterous. Acting with noisy turbulence. See Turbulence.
Breezy. Characterized by, or having breezes; airy.
Flatulent. Affected with flatus or gases generated in the alimentary canal; windy.
Gusty. Subject to gusts or squalls.
Pulmonary. } Of or pertaining to the lungs.
Pulmonic. }
Squally. Disturbed often with sudden or violent gusts of wind.
Stormy. Characterized or proceeding from a storm.
Tempestuous. Of or pertaining to a tempest.
Windy. Accompanied or characterized by wind.

RIVER—Verbs—*Continued.*

Rain in torrents. To pour.
Rain pitchforks. A figurative expression for heavy rain.
Regurgitate. To throw or pour back.
Roll. To move as waves or billows, with alternate swell and depression.
Run. To flow, as a liquid.
Set in. To flow in.
Shower down. To rain.
Spill. To suffer to fall or run out of a vessel.
Spirtle. To spurt.
Spit. To eject; throw out; belch.
Splash. To dabble in water.
Spout. To throw out in a jet.
Spurt. To gush out violently or suddenly in a stream.
Sputter. To throw out anything, as saliva from the mouth, in little jets.
Stanch. To stop the flowing of.
Stream. To send forth in a current or stream.
Swash. To dash or flow noisily.
Swirl. To form eddies.
Trickle. To flow in a small gentle stream.
Trill. To flow in a small stream, or in drops rapidly succeeding each other.
Well. To issue forth, as water from the ground

RIVER—*Adjectives.*

Affluent. Flowing abundantly.
Diffluent. Flowing apart or off.
Flowing. Running along, as a stream. See *Verbs*.
Fluent. Flowing or capable of flowing.
Fluvial. } Belonging to rivers.
Fluviatile. }
Meandering. }
Meandrous. } Flowing in windings. See *Verbs*.
Meandry. }
Pluvial. Of or pertaining to rain.
Profluent. Flowing forward.
Rainy. Abounding with rain.
Showery. Abounding with frequent showers of rain.
Stillicidous. Falling in drops.
Streamy. Abounding with streams or with running water.
Tidal. Of or pertaining to tides.

---

riv'-et. To fasten. Connective, Union-Disunion; **rivet in the memory**, Remembrance-Forgetfulness; **rivet the attention**, Excitation, Heed-Disregard; **rivet the eyes upon**, Sight-Blindness; **rivet the yoke**, Harshness-Mildness.
riv'-et-ed. Fixed. Mutability-Stability
riv'-u-let. Stream. River-Wind.
rix-a'-tion. Brawl. Variance-Accord.
road. Direction; street. Aim-Aberration, Dweller-Habitation, Way; **on the high road to**, Advance-Retrogression, Aim-Aberration, Sanguineness-Hopelessness; **on the road**, Advance-Retrogression, Aim-Aberration, Approach-Withdrawal, Transfer; **road to ruin**, Creation-Destruction, Security-Insecurity, Welfare-Misfortune.
road'-book". Guide-book. Traveling-Navigation.
roads. Anchorage. Dweller-Habitation, Gulf-Plain.

road'-stead. Anchorage. Dweller-Habitation, Refuge-Pitfall.
road'-ster. Traveling horse. Conveyer.
road'-way". Way. Way.
roam. Range. Traveling-Navigation.
roan. Horse; sorrel. Conveyer, Gray-Brown.
roar. To laugh; to rage; to make a loud noise. Cry-Ululation, Jubilation-Lamentation, Loudness-Faintness, Turbulence-Calmness.
roar'-ing. Prosperous. Magnitude-Smallness; **roaring trade**, Success-Failure, Welfare-Misfortune.
roast. To cook; to ridicule. Heating-Cooling, Regard-Disrespect, Society-Derision; **rib-roast**, Recompense-Punition; **roast and boiled**, Nutriment-Excretion; **roast an ox**, Heat-Cold, Solemnization.
roast'-ing. Heating. Chemistry.

rob. Jelly; to steal. PULPINESS-OILINESS, THEFT; **rob Peter to pay Paul,** COMPENSATION, THEFT.

rob'-ber. Thief. ROBBER.

ROBBER.

Artful Dodger. Sobriquet of a young thief in Dickens's *Oliver Twist*.
Bandit. An outlawed thief; highwayman.
Blackleg. A swindler at gambling games.
Brigand. One of a set of thieves banded secretly together in mountain or forest.
Buccaneer.⎫ A sea-robber.
Buccanier.⎭
Burglar. A nocturnal housebreaker and thief.
Bushranger. An escaped convict or criminal living in the bush.
Card-sharper. One who cheats at cards.
Chevalier d'industrie [F.]. A thief.
Coiner. A maker of counterfeit coin.
Corsair. A sea-thief; a pirate vessel.
Cracksman. A burglar.
Cutpurse. One who thieves from the person, formerly by cutting the purse.
Dacoit. One of a band of Indian thieves.
Defaulter. One who fails to account for money entrusted to him.
Depredator. One who plunders.
Duffer. A hawker of sham goods.
Falcon. A bird of prey.
Fence. One who knowingly receives stolen goods.
Filcher. One guilty of petty theft.
Filibuster. A buccaneer.
Footpad. A thief or highwayman who robs on foot.
Forger. One guilty of theft by forgery.
Freebooter. A wandering thief.
Harpy. An extortioner; a plunderer.
Highwayman. One who robs on the highway.
Homo trium literarium [L.]. A man of three letters, *i. e.*, *fur*, thief.
Housebreaker. One who breaks into a house with thieving intent.
Land-shark. One who cheats in land dealing.
Leg. Blackleg.
Light-fingered gentry. A sobriquet of the pickpockets.
Magsman. A swindler of countrymen and simple folk.
Marauder. A roving, plundering thief.
Miquelet. A bandit.
Moss-trooper. A name given to the border marauders between England and Scotland.
Peculator. One who embezzles.
Picaroon. A plunderer of wrecks.
Pickeerer.⎫ A pirate.
Picqueerer.⎭
Pickpocket. A thief who steals from the pocket.
Pickpurse. A purse thief.
Pilferer. A petty thief.
Pillager. One who thieves and plunders openly.
Pirate. A sea-thief.
Plagiarist. A thief of the ideas or language of another.
Poacher. One who steals game.
Privateer. A vessel or its commander licensed by government to plunder an enemy's ships.
Ranger. A roving thief.
Rapparee. A wild Irish thief.
Receiver of stolen goods. A thief's accomplice.
Rifler. A pillager; plunderer.
Robber. A thief; plunderer.
Rook. A thieving cheat; a swindler.
Rover. A wandering robber; a pirate.
Shark. An artful thief; a sharper.
Sharper. A cheat in bargaining or gambling.
Shoplifter. One who thieves in a shop.
Skittle-sharper. One who cheats in the game of skittles.
Smuggler. One who brings goods into a country secretly to avoid duties.
Spoiler. A thief; a plunderer.
Sturdy beggar. A name applied to a foraging soldier.
Swell-mob. That class of well-dressed pickpockets who mix with crowds to do their work.
Swindler. A cheat; an artful defrauder.
Thief. One who steals.
Thimble-rigger. A thieving trickster.
Thug. Formerly a member of an Indian association for robbery and murder, hence, a murderous robber.
Trickster. A player of tricks: a cheat.
Viking. A sea-thief of the Northmen.
Welsher. A professional gambler who does not pay if he loses.
Wrecker. One who wrecks and plunders ships.

ROBBER—*Figurative Expressions.*

Autolycus. A rogue in Shakespeare's *Winter's Tale*.
Bedouin. A member of a thieving Arabian tribe.
Bill Sykes. A brutal thief in Dickens's *Oliver Twist*.
Claude Duval. A noted highwayman, the hero of some novels and ballads.
Dick Turpin. A notorious English highwayman.
Greek. A thief or rogue, as was often the Greek.
Jack Sheppard. A notorious English robber, the hero of a novel of his name by Ainsworth.
Jeremy Diddler. A type of swindler in Kennedy's farce, *Raising the Wind*.
Jonathan Wild. An English robber, the hero of novels by Fielding and Defoe.
Macheath. The principal character in Gay's *Beggars' Opera*, a wild and dissolute robber.
Paul Jones. A Scottish-American naval hero.
Robert Macaire. A thief and villain of French comedy.

rob'-ber-y. Plunder. THEFT.
robe. Garment. CANONICALS, DRESS-UNDRESS.
robes. Costume. Robes of state, SCEPTER.
Rob'-in Good'-fel''-low. An elf. JOVE-FIEND.
rob'-o-rant. Strengthening. REMEDY-BANE.
ro-bust'. Rugged. HEALTH-SICKNESS, STRENGTH-WEAKNESS.
roc. Bird of prey. CONVENTIONALITY-UNCONVENTIONALITY.
Ro''-ci-nan'-te. The steed of Don Quixote. CONVEYER.
rock. To sway; stone; reef. HARDNESS-SOFTNESS, MUTABILITY-STABILITY, OCEAN-LAND, OSCILLATION, REFUGE-PITFALL; **build on a rock,** MUTABILITY-STABILITY; **rock ahead,** SECURITY-INSECURITY; **rock-oil,** PULPINESS-OIL; **split upon a rock,** SUCCESS-FAILURE.
rock'-et. Kind of fireworks. ASCENT-DESCENT, LUMINARY-SHADE, SIGN, SWIFTNESS-SLOWNESS, WEAPON; **go up like a rocket and come down like a stick,** SUCCESS-FAILURE.
rock'-ing-chair. Chair set on rockers. SUSPENSION-SUPPORT.
rocks. Mass of stony matter. REFUGE-PITFALL.
ro-co'-co. Anything quaint. NOVELTY-ANTIQUITY.
rod. Pole; whip; measure; twig. DEVOTION-CHARM, MEASURE, MENSURATION, RECOMPENSE-SCOURGE, SUSPENSION-SUPPORT; **kiss the rod,** YIELDING; **rod in pickle,** JUSTIFICATION-CHARGE, MINISTRY-LAITY, PARDON-VINDICTIVENESS, PREPARATION-NONPREPARATION, RECOMPENSE-PUNITION; **rod of empire,** RULE-LICENSE, SCEPTER; **sounding-rod,** DEEPNESS-SHALLOWNESS.
rod'-o-mont. A braggart. BRAWLER.
rod''-o-mon-tade'. Bragging. BRAGGING, MEANING-JARGON.
roe. Deer; spawn of fishes. FAUNA-FLORA.
Roent'-gen ray. A ray penetrating but invisible. X RAY.
ro-ga'-tion. Request; litany DEVOTION-IDOLATRY, PETITION-EXPOSTULATION.
rogue. Knave; trickster. GOOD MAN-BAD MAN, GULL-DECEIVER, UPRIGHTNESS-ROGUE; **rogue's march,** ADMISSION-EXPULSION.
rogu'-er-y. Knavery; waggery. UPRIGHTNESS-DISHONESTY
rogu'-ish. Mischievous. ENTERTAINMENT-WEARINESS.
roi est mort, vive le roi, le [F.] (rwa ê mor, vîv le rwa, le). The king is dead, long live the king. JUBILATION-LAMENTATION.
roi le veut, le [F.] (rwa le vu, le). The king wills it. COMMAND, RULE-LICENSE.
roil. To render muddy; to vex. CLEANNESS-FILTHINESS, FAVORITE-ANGER.
roist'-er. To bluster. BRAWLER, PRESUMPTION-OBSEQUIOUSNESS.

roist'-er-ing. Blustering. PRESUMPTION - OBSEQIOUS-NESS.

Roland for an Oliver. Hero for hero; tit for tat. EXCHANGE, REPRISAL-RESISTANCE.

rôle [F.] (rol). Character. ACTING, CONDUCT, DESIGN, OCCUPATION.

roll. List; anything round; to smooth; to sway; to flow; to sound. CIRCLE-WINDING, CRASH-DRUMMING, LAMINA-FIBER, MARK-OBLITERATION, MOVEMENT-REST, RECORD, REVOLUTION, RIVER-WIND, ROUNDNESS, SMOOTHNESS-ROUGHNESS, VIBRATION; **roll along,** REVOLUTION-EVOLUTION; **roll in,** ENOUGH, EXCESS-LACK; **roll in riches,** AFFLUENCE-PENURY; **roll in the dust,** SUCCESS-FAILURE; **roll into one,** UNION-DISUNION; **roll in wealth,** AFFLUENCE-PENURY; **roll of parchment,** MEASURE; **roll on,** MOVEMENT-REST, PERIOD-PROGRESS; **roll on the ground,** JUBILATION-LAMENTATION; **roll up,** REVOLUTION-EVOLUTION; **roll up in,** DRESS-UNDRESS; **strike off the roll,** COMMISSION-ABROGATION, RECOMPENSE-PUNITION.

roll'-call". Calling of names. NUMBERING.

roll'-er. Rod; something that rotates; towel; bandage. CONNECTIVE, REVOLUTION-EVOLUTION, ROUNDNESS, SMOOTHNESS-ROUGHNESS.

roll'-ers. Waves. RIVER-WIND.

rol'-lick. To frolic. LIGHTHEARTEDNESS-DEJECTION.

rol'-lick-er. One who frolics. JUBILATION-LAMENTATION.

rol'-lick-ing. Frolicking. LIGHTHEARTEDNESS-DEJECTION, PRESUMPTION-OBSEQUIOUSNESS.

roll'-ing-pin". A cylinder with handle at each end to roll out dough, etc. ROUNDNESS; **rolling-stock,** CONVEYANCE-VESSEL, CRASH-DRUMMING; **rolling stone,** REVOLUTION-EVOLUTION.

rolls. Register. **Master of the rolls,** JUDGE-RECORDER; **rolls court,** TRIBUNAL.

Roma deliberat, Saguntum perit, dum [L.] (ro'-ma de-lib'-er-at sag-un'-tum per-it, dum). While Rome deliberates, Saguntum perishes. DESTRUCTION, SWIFTNESS-SLOWNESS.

Ro'-man Cath'-o-lic. Religious denomination. ORTHODOXY-HETERODOXY.

ro-mance'. Fanciful story. ACCOUNT, ADAGE-NONSENSE, FANCY, TRUTHFULNESS-FABRICATION, TRUTHFULNESS-FALSEHOOD.

ro-man'-cer. Writer of romance. FANCY.

Ro'-man-ism. Principles of the Romish Church. ORTHODOXY-HETERODOXY.

Ro'-man-ist. Roman Catholic. ORTHODOXY-HETERODOXY.

Romanorum, ultimus [L.] (ro-ma-no'-rum ul'-tim-us). Last of the Romans. BEGINNING-END, FUTURE-PAST.

ro-man'-tic. Fanciful. FANCY, SENSITIVENESS-APATHY.

ro-man'-ti-cism. Romantic style. FANCY.

Romanus sum, civis [L.] (ro-mê'-nus sum, sai'-vis). I am a Roman citizen. DUENESS-UNDUENESS.

Rom'-a-ny. Pertaining to the Gipsies. WORD-NEOLOGY.

Rome. Church of Rome. ORTHODOXY-HETERODOXY, **do as the Romans do,** CONVENTIONALITY-UNCONVENTIONALITY.

Ro'-mish. Relating to Rome. ORTHODOXY-HETERODOXY.

romp. To frisk. ENTERTAINMENT-WEARINESS, TURBULENCE-CALMNESS.

romp'-ish. Inclined to romp. ENTERTAINMENT-WEARINESS.

ron-deau'. Poem. POETRY-PROSE.

ron'-do. Kind of musical composition. MUSIC.

ron'-ion. A scurvy person. GOOD MAN-BAD MAN.

rood. A measure. LENGTH-SHORTNESS.

roof. Dwelling; cover. COVER-LINING.

roof'-less. Without roof or shelter. DRESS-UNDRESS.

rook. Trickster. ROBBER, THEFT.

rook'-er-y. Breeding place for birds; shabby tenement. CLEANNESS-FILTHINESS, DWELLER-HABITATION.

room. Open space; occasion; apartment. CONTENTS-RECEIVER, EXTENSION-DISTRICT, OPPORTUNENESS-UNSUITABLENESS, PRETEXT; **assembly-room,** ENTERTAINMENT-WEARINESS; **in the room of,** COMMUTATION-PERMUTATION; **make room for,** APERTURE-CLOSURE, REGARD-DISRESPECT.

room'-age. Space. EXTENSION-DISTRICT.

room'-y. Convenient. EXTENSION-DISTRICT.

roost. Perch. DWELLER-HABITATION, PRESENCE-ABSENCE.

roost'-er. Male chicken. FAUNA-FLORA.

root. Cause; derivation; base; part of a plant. CAUSE-EFFECT, ESTABLISHMENT-REMOVAL, NUMBER, TOP-BOTTOM, WORD-NEOLOGY; **cut up root and branch,** CREATION-DESTRUCTION; **lie at the root of,** CAUSE-EFFECT, INVESTIGATION-ANSWER; **pluck up by the roots,** INJECTION-EJECTION; **root and branch,** ENTIRETY-DEFICIENCY; **root out,** ADMISSION-EXPULSION, DISCOVERY, INJECTION-EJECTION; **strike at the root of,** ATTACK-DEFENSE; **take root,** DOMINANCE-IMPOTENCE, ESTABLISHMENT-REMOVAL, HABIT-DESUETUDE.

root'-ed. Fixed. ESTABLISHMENT-REMOVAL, HABIT-DESUETUDE, MUTABILITY-STABILITY, NOVELTY-ANTIQUITY; **deep-rooted,** AFFECTIONS, HABIT-DESUETUDE; **rooted antipathy,** DESIRE-DISTASTE; **rooted belief,** FAITH-MISGIVING.

rope. Cord; license; whip. CONNECTIVE, INSTRUMENT, LAMINA-FIBER, LIBERTY-SUBJECTION, RECOMPENSE-SCOURGE; **give enough rope,** RULE-LICENSE; **rope of sand,** COHESION-LOOSENESS, POSSIBILITY-IMPOSSIBILITY, STRENGTH-WEAKNESS; **rope's end,** RECOMPENSE-SCOURGE.

rope'-dan"-cer. Performer on a tight rope. ADEPT-BUNGLER.

rope'-dan"-cing. Performance on a tight rope. SKILL-UNSKILFULNESS.

rope'-walk". A long shed used for spinning rope-yarn. WORKSHOP.

ro'-py. Stringy. LAMINA-FIBER, VISCIDITY-FOAM.

roqu'-e-laure. Cloak. DRESS-UNDRESS.

ro'-ral. Dewy. DAMPNESS-DRYNESS.

ro'-rid. Dewy. DAMPNESS-DRYNESS.

rosâ, sub [L.] (ro'-sa, sub). Privately. ENLIGHTENMENT-SECRECY.

ro'-sa-ry. String of beads. CEREMONIAL.

ros'-cid. Dewy. DAMPNESS-DRYNESS.

Ros'-ci-us. A noted Roman actor. ACTING.

rose. Kind of flower; perforated nozzle. BEAUTY-UGLINESS, PATRIOTISM-TREASON, PERFUME-STENCH, REDNESS-GREENNESS, WATERCOURSE-AIRPIPE; **bed of roses,** SENSUALITY-SUFFERING, WELFARE-MISFORTUNE; **under the rose,** ENLIGHTENMENT-SECRECY; **welcome as the roses in June,** PLEASURABLENESS-PAINFULNESS, SOCIABILITY-PRIVACY.

rose, couleur de [F.] (roz, cu-lur' de). Rose-color. GOODNESS-BADNESS, REDNESS-GREENNESS, SANGUINENESS-HOPELESSNESS, WELFARE-MISFORTUNE.

ro'-se-ate. Rosy. REDNESS-GREENNESS, SANGUINENESS-HOPELESSNESS.

rose'-col"-ored. REDNESS-GREENNESS, SANGUINENESS-HOPELESSNESS.

ro-sette'. Ornament. EMBELLISHMENT-DISFIGUREMENT.

rose'-wa"-ter. Sentimental. ADULATION-DISPARAGEMENT, TURBULENCE-CALMNESS; **not made with rose-water,** DIFFICULTY-FACILITY.

Ro"-si-cru'-ci-an. Pertaining to the Rosicrucians. DEVOTION-MAGICIAN, GULL-DECEIVER, ORTHODOXY-HETERODOXY.

ros'-in. Residue from distillation of turpentine. Friction-Lubrication, Pulpiness-Rosin.

ros'-ter. Register. Record.

ros'-trum. Platform; beak. Anteriority-Posteriority, School.

ro'-sy. Like a rose. Redness-Greenness; **rosy wine,** Beauty-Ugliness, Teetotalism-Intemperance.

ro'-sy-cheeked". Having red cheeks. Beauty-Ugliness.

rot. To decay. Betterment-Deterioration, Cleanness-Filthiness, Health-Sickness.

ro'-ta. Routine. Periodicity-Irregularity.

ro'-ta-ry. Turning around its axis. Revolution-Evolution.

ro'-tate. To turn on its axis. Revolution-Evolution.

ro'-ta"-ting. Turning around its axis. Revolution-Evolution.

ro-ta'-tion. Alternation; motion around its own axis. Periodicity-Irregularity, Revolution-Evolution.

ro'-ta-to-ry. Going in a circle. Revolution-Evolution.

rote. Repetition. **By rote,** Remembrance-Forgetfulness; **know by rote,** Knowledge-Ignorance, Remembrance-Forgetfulness; **learn by rote,** Education-Learning, Remembrance-Forgetfulness.

rot'-gut". Cheap whisky. Goodness-Badness, Nutriment-Excretion.

Roth'-schild. English banking-house. Labor-Capital.

rot'-ten. Decayed; not trustworthy. Betterment-Deterioration, Cleanness-Filthiness, Goodness-Badness, Health-Sickness, Strength-Weakness; **rotten at the core,** Faultlessness-Faultiness, Health-Sickness, Truthfulness-Fraud.

rot'-ten-ness. Decay. Betterment-Deterioration.

rot'-ting. Decomposing. Cleanness-Filthiness.

rotulorum, custos [L.] (rot-yu-lo'-rum, cus'-tos) Keeper of the rolls. Recorder.

ro-tund'. Spherical. Roundness.

ro-tun'-da. Circular building. Dweller-Habitation.

ro-tund'-i-ty. Roundness. Circle-Winding, Roundness.

roturier [F.] (ro-tü-riê'). Plebeian. Gentility-Commonalty.

roué [F.] (ru-ê'). Rake. Good Man-Bad Man.

rouge [F.] (ruzh). Red. Redness-Greenness.

rouge. Red cosmetic. Redness-Greenness.

rouge-et-noir [F.] (ruzh"-ê-nwɑr'). Red and black. Purpose-Luck.

rough. Uneven; rude; jarring; not well prepared; astringent; ruffian. Beauty-Ugliness, Belligerent, Benefactor-Evildoer, Brawler, Cacophony, Form-Formlessness, Gentility-Commonalty, Good Man-Bad Man, Palatableness-Unpalatableness, Preparation-Nonpreparation, Politeness-Impoliteness, Pungency, Smoothness-Roughness, Sweetness-Acidity, Turbulence-Calmness; **rough-and-tumble,** Regularity-Irregularity; **rough copy,** Preparation-Nonpreparation, Writing-Printing; **rough diamond,** Craft-Artlessness, Gentility-Commonalty, Goodness-Badness, Taste-Vulgarity; **rough draft,** Design; **rough guess,** Hypothesis; **rough it,** Toil-Relaxation; **rough sea,** River-Wind; **rough side of the tongue,** Approval-Disapproval; **rough weather,** River-Wind, Turbulence-Calmness.

rough'-cast". Rude model. Design, Form-Formlessness, Preparation-Nonpreparation.

rough'-en. Become rough. Preparation-Nonpreparation, Smoothness-Roughness.

rough'-hew". To shape roughly. Form-Formlessness, Preparation-Nonpreparation.

rough'-hewn". Roughly shaped. Smoothness-Roughness.

rough'-ly. Nearly. Remoteness-Nearness.

rough'-ness. Unevenness. Cacophony, Palatableness-Unpalatableness, Pungency, Smoothness-Roughness, Strength-Weakness.

rough'-rid"-er. One who breaks horses to the saddle. In the army, a riding-master's assistant. Wayfarer-Seafarer.

rough'-shod". Shod with armed shoes; overbearing. Ride roughshod over, Harshness-Mildness.

rou"-lade'. Musical flourish. Music.

rou"-leau'. A roll; coin; bundle. Gathering-Scattering, Money, Roundness.

rou-lette'. Game of chance. Purpose-Luck.

round. Series; period; step; musical composition; circular. Assertion-Denial, Circle-Winding, Continuity-Interruption, Curvation-Rectilinearity, Music, Occupation, Periodicity-Irregularity, Roundness, Strife-Peace, Suspension-Support; **all round,** Environment-Interposition; **bring round,** Renovation-Renewal; **come round,** Bigotry-Apostasy, Fighting-Conciliation, Motive-Caprice, Periodicity-Irregularity, Renovation-Relapse; **dizzy round,** Revolution-Evolution; **get round,** Renovation-Relapse; **go one's rounds,** Traveling-Navigation; **go round,** Circle-Winding, Revolution-Evolution; **go the rounds,** Circuition, Publicity; **go the same round,** Recurrence; **in round numbers,** Medium, Remoteness-Nearness; **round a corner,** Revolution-Evolution; **round and round,** Periodicity-Irregularity, Revolution-Evolution; **round game,** Entertainment-Weariness; **round like a horse in a mill,** Habit-Desuetude; **round number,** Multiplicity-Paucity; **round of pleasures,** Entertainment-Weariness, Sensuality-Suffering; **round of the ladder,** Station; **round of visits,** Sociability-Privacy; **round robin,** Approval-Disapproval, Petition-Expostulation, Toughness-Brittleness; **round sum,** Affluence-Penury, Money; **round terms,** Phrase; **round trot,** Swiftness-Slowness.

round'-a-bout". Circuitous; dance; merry-go-round. Aim-Aberration, Entertainment-Weariness, Environment-Interposition, Midcourse-Circuit, Revolution-Evolution, Terseness-Prolixity; **roundabout phrases,** Terseness-Prolixity; **roundabout way,** Midcourse-Circuit.

round'-ed. Well-developed. Circle-Winding; **rounded periods,** Purity-Crudeness, Simplicity-Floridness.

roun'-del-ay. Melody. Poetry-Prose.

round'-house". Building for sheltering engines. Release-Prison.

round'-let. Little circle. Circle-Winding.

round'-ness. The state of being round. Circle-Winding, Roundness.

ROUNDNESS.

Bell-shape. The shape of a bell.
Conoid. Cone-shaped.
Cylindricity. The quality or condition of being cylindrical.
Cylindroid. The shape of a cylinder.
Egg-shape. The shape of an egg.
Globosity. Sphericity, roundness.
Pear-shape. The shape of a pear.
Rotundity. The state or quality of being rotund; roundness.
Roundness. See *Adjectives*.
Sphericity. }
Spheroidity. } The quality or state of being spherical, roundness.

ROUNDNESS—*Denotations*.

Ball. A spherical body of any dimension.
Barrel. A cylindrical vessel bulging in the middle, made of wooden staves held together by hoops.

Boulder.
Bowlder. } A rounded stone or rock.
Bulb. A spheroidal underground leaf-bud.
Bullet. A leaden ball shot from a gun.
Clew. A round bunch.
Column. A vertical shaft, commonly cylindrical.
Cone. A solid figure that tapers from a circular base to a point.
Cylinder. A solid with curved bounding surfaces.
Drop. A small round portion of anything.
Drum. A cylindrical musical instrument.
Ellipsoid. A solid, every plane section of which is a circle or ellipse.
Globe. A spherical representation of the earth's surface.
Globule. A small globe.
Knob. A rounded protuberance.
Knot. An intertwining of the parts of a rope, etc.
Marble. A small, spherical solid of baked clay, glass, etc.
Oblate spheroid. A sphere slightly flattened at the poles.
Oblong spheroid. A body almost spherical, having one axis a little longer than another.
Pea. A small round fruit of the pea.
Pellet. A bullet; a ball
Pelote [F.]. A ball.
Pill. A medicine put up in a solid, circular form.
Pommel. A knob at the front of a saddle.
Roll. That which is rolled up.
Roller. A cylindrical shaft on which something is rolled.
Rolling-pin. A roller with a handle at each end for rolling out dough, etc.
Rouleau [F.]. A little roll.
Rundle. The round of a ladder.
Sphere. A solid bounded by a curved surface, every point of which is equally distant from the center.
Spheroid. A body having nearly the form of a sphere.
Spherule. A small sphere.
Vesicle. A small bladder-like cavity or cell.

ROUNDNESS—*Verbs.*

Form into a sphere. To make round.
Give rotundity. To make round. See *Nouns.*
Render spherical. To make round. See *Adjectives.*
Roll into a ball. To collect into a sphere.
Round. To make round.
Sphere. To form into roundness.

ROUNDNESS—*Adjectives.*

Bead-like. Round, like a bead.
Bell-shaped. In the form of a bell.
Bulbous. Bulb-like in shape or structure.
Campaniform.
Campaniliform. } Bell-shaped.
Campanulate.
Columnar. Having the form of a column.
Conic. Having the form of a geometrical cone.
Conical. Cone-shaped.
Cylindric.
Cylindrical. } Having the form of a cylinder.
Cylindroid.
Egg-shaped. Having the shape of an egg.
Fungiform. Shaped like a fungus or mushroom.
Gibbous. Swelling by a regular curve or surface.
Globated.
Globose.
Globous. } Having the form of a globe; spherical.
Globular.
Lumbriciform. Resembling an earthworm in form.
Moniliform. Jointed or constricted, at regular intervals, so as to resemble a string of beads.
Oviform.
Ovoid. } Egg-shaped.
Pear-shaped. Having the form of a pear.
Pyriform. Pear-shaped.
Rotund. Round; circular; spherical.
Round. Having every portion of the surface or of the circumference equally distant from the center. See CIRCLE.
Round as a ball.
Round as a billiard-ball.
Round as a cannon-ball.
Round as an apple.
Round as an orange.
Spherical. Round, like a sphere.
Spheroidal. Almost a sphere.
Teres atque rotundus [L.]. Smooth and round.

round'–shoul''–dered. Having drooping shoulders. PROPORTION-DEFORMITY.
roup. To auction. BUYING-SALE.
rouse. Mirth; to arouse. EXCITATION, MOTIVE-CAPRICE; **rouse oneself,** ACTIVITY-INDOLENCE.
rous'–ing. Exciting. VIGOR-INERTIA.
rout. To overcome; rabble; uproar. AGITATION, GENTILITY-COMMONALTY, SOCIABILITY-PRIVACY, SUCCESS-FAILURE; **put to the rout, rout out,** CLEANNESS-FILTHINESS.
route. Way. WAY; **en route,** TRANSFER, TRAVELING-NAVIGATION; **en route for,** ADVANCE-RETROGRESSION.
rou''–tine'. Regular course. HABIT-DESUETUDE, OCCUPATION, PERIODICITY-IRREGULARITY, REGULARITY-IRREGULARITY, UNIFORMITY-DIVERSITY, UNIFORMITY-MULTIFORMITY.
rove. To wander. AIM-ABERRATION, TRAVELING-NAVIGATION.
ro'–ver. Wanderer; pirate. ROBBER, WAYFARER-SEAFARER.
ro'–ving. Roaming about. TRAVELING-NAVIGATION.
row. To propel; street; series. CONTINUITY-INTERRUPTION, DWELLER-HABITATION, TRAVELING-NAVIGATION; **row in the same boat,** SOLITUDE-COMPANY.
row. Quarrel. REGULARITY-IRREGULARITY, TURBULENCE-CALMNESS, VARIANCE-ACCORD.
row'–dy. Rough. BRAWLER, CITY, GOOD MAN-BAD MAN, TASTE-VULGARITY.
row'–dy-ism. Conduct of a rowdy. TASTE-VULGARITY.
row'–el. Spur. MOTIVE-CAPRICE, SHARPNESS-BLUNTNESS.
row'–er. One who rows. WAYFARER-SEAFARER.
row'–lock. Socket. SUSPENSION-SUPPORT.
roy'–al. Kingly. RULE-LICENSE; **royal way,** DIFFICULTY-FACILITY, WAY.
Roy'–al Ac'a-de-mi-ci-an. Member of the Royal Academy. ARTIST.
roy'–al-ist. Supporter of a royal dynasty. RULE-LICENSE
roy'–al-ty. Sovereignty. RULE-LICENSE.
royne. Scab. NUTRIMENT-EXCRETION.
Roz-i-nan'-te. Don Quixote's charger. CONVEYER.
ruade [F.] (rü-ad'). Wincing. ATTACK-DEFENSE, IMPETUS-REACTION.
ruat cœlum [L.] (ru'-at si'-lum). Let the heavens fall. CHARITABLENESS-CURSE.
rub. Difficulty; friction. DIFFICULTY-FACILITY, FRICTION-LUBRICATION, PLEASURABLENESS-PAINFULNESS, WELFARE-MISFORTUNE; **rub down,** ENLARGEMENT-DIMINUTION, FRIABILITY; **rub down with an oaken towel,** RECOMPENSE-PUNITION; **rub off,** MARK-OBLITERATION; **rub off corners,** CONVENTIONALITY-UNCONVENTIONALITY; **rub on,** ADVANCE-RETROGRESSION, EXCITABILITY-INEXCITABILITY, SWIFTNESS-SLOWNESS; **rub one's eyes,** ASTONISHMENT-EXPECTANCE; **rub one's hands,** JUBILATION-LAMENTATION; **rub out,** MARK-OBLITERATION; SOLIDITY-RARITY; **rub up,** BETTERMENT-DETERIORATION; **rub up the memory,** REMEMBRANCE-FORGETFULNESS.
rub'–a-dub''. The sound of a drum. CRASH-DRUMMING.
rub'–ber. A game. ENTERTAINMENT-WEARINESS.
rub'–bing. Moving over. FRICTION-LUBRICATION.
rub'–bish. Waste. CONSEQUENCE-INSIGNIFICANCE, MEANING-JARGON, USEFULNESS-USELESSNESS.
rub'–ble. Fragments. USEFULNESS-USELESSNESS.
ru-bes'-cence. Redness. REDNESS-GREENNESS.
Ru'-bi-con. River boundary of Italy. BOUNDARY; **pass the Rubicon,** BEGINNING-END, CHOICE-NEUTRALITY, TRANSCURSION-SHORTCOMING.

ru'-bi-cund. Red. REDNESS-GREENNESS.

ru''-bi-cun'-di-ty. Ruddiness. REDNESS-GREENNESS.

ru''-bi-fi-ca'-tion. A making red. REDNESS-GREEN-NESS.

ru'-bi-form. Reddish. REDNESS-GREENNESS.

ru'-bi-fy. To redden. REDNESS-GREENNESS.

ru-bi'-go. Rust. CLEARNESS-FILTHINESS.

ru'-bric. Rule. CEREMONIAL-PRECEPT.

ru'-bri-cate. To redden. REDNESS-GREENNESS.

ru'-by. Red; gem. EMBELLISHMENT-DISFIGURE-MENT, GOODNESS-BADNESS, REDNESS-GREENNESS.

ruck. Wrinkle. PLICATURE.

ruc-ta'-tion. Forcing of gas from the stomach. AD-MISSION-EXPULSION.

rud'-der. Device for directing a boat. MANAGEMENT.

rud'-der-less. Deprived of a rudder. MIGHT-IMPO-TENCE.

rud'-dle. Redness. REDNESS-GREENNESS.

rud'-dy. Red. BEAUTY-UGLINESS, REDNESS-GREEN-NESS.

rude. Rough; misshapen; ignorant; impolite. BEAUTY-UGLINESS, FORM-FORMLESSNESS, GENTIL-ITY-COMMONALTY, KNOWLEDGE-IGNORANCE, POLITE-NESS-IMPOLITENESS, PURITY-CRUDENESS, REGARD-DISRESPECT, TASTE-VULGARITY, TURBULENCE-CALMNESS; rude health, HEALTH-SICKNESS.

ru'-di-ment. Beginning. BEGINNING-END, CAUSE-EFFECT, GREATNESS-LITTLENESS.

ru''-di-men'-tal. Initial. BEGINNING-END, GREAT-NESS-LITTLENESS, PREPARATION-NONPREPARATION.

ru''-di-men'-ta-ry. Abortive. GREATNESS-LITTLE-NESS.

ru'-di-ments. Fundamental principles. BEGINNING-END, KNOWLEDGE-IGNORANCE, SCHOOL.

rudis indigestaque moles [L.] (ru'-dis in-di-ges'-ta-quî mo'-lîs). A rude and undigested mass. FORM-FORM-LESSNESS, REGULARITY-IRREGULARITY.

rue. To be sorry for. CONTENTEDNESS-REGRET, PALATABLENESS-UNPALATABLENESS, REPENTANCE-OBDURACY.

rue'-ful. Woful. LIGHTHEARTEDNESS-DEJECTION, PLEASURABLENESS-PAINFULNESS.

ruff. Ruffle. DRESS-UNDRESS.

ruf'-fi-an. Lawless fellow. BENEFACTOR-EVILDOER, GOOD MAN-BAD MAN.

ruf'-fi-an-ism. Lawlessness. CHARITABLENESS-MA-LEVOLENCE.

ruf'-fle. To fold; to anger; to roughen. EMOTION, EXCITABILITY-INEXCITABILITY, EXCITATION, FAVOR-ITE-ANGER, ORGANIZATION-DISORGANIZATION, PLEAS-URABLENESS-PAINFULNESS, PLICATURE, REGULAR-ITY-IRREGULARITY, SMOOTHNESS-ROUGHNESS.

ru'-fous. Dull-red. REDNESS-GREENNESS.

rug. Thick covering. COVER-LINING, SUSPENSION-SUPPORT.

rug'-ged. Rough; stern. BEAUTY-UGLINESS, DIF-FICULTY-FACILITY, FORM-FORMLESSNESS, POLITE-NESS-IMPOLITENESS, SMOOTHNESS-ROUGHNESS.

ru'-gose. Wrinkled. SMOOTHNESS-ROUGHNESS.

ru-gos'-i-ty. Roughness. SMOOTHNESS-ROUGHNESS.

ru'-gous. Wrinkled. SMOOTHNESS-ROUGHNESS.

ru'-in. Destruction; misfortune. AFFLUENCE-PENURY, APPROVAL-DISAPPROVAL, CREATION-DE-STRUCTION, GOOD-EVIL, SUCCESS-FAILURE, WEL-FARE-MISFORTUNE.

ru''-in-a'-tion. Ruin. WELFARE-MISFORTUNE.

ru'-ined. Impoverished. SANGUINENESS-HOPELESS-NESS.

ru'-in-ous. Baneful. MAKER-DESTROYER, MEDIOC-RITY, PLEASURABLENESS-PAINFULNESS.

ru'-in-ous-ness. A ruinous state. WELFARE-MISFOR-TUNE.

ru'-ins. Remains. INCREMENT-REMNANT.

rule. Method, measure; decision; authority. DE-CISION-MISJUDGMENT, HABIT-DESUETUDE, LAW-LAWLESSNESS, LENGTH-SHORTNESS, LIBERTY-SUB-JECTION, MANAGEMENT, MENSURATION, PRECEPT, PRESIDENT-MEMBER, RULE-LICENSE, UNIFORMITY-MULTIFORMITY; absence of rule, SKILL-UNSKILFUL-NESS; as a rule, HABIT-DESUETUDE; by rule, CON-VENTIONALITY-UNCONVENTIONALITY; golden rule, PRECEPT; obey rules, CONVENTIONALITY-UNCONVEN-TIONALITY; rule of three, NUMBERING; rule of thumb, RATIOCINATION-INSTINCT, SKILL-UNSKILFUL-NESS, TRIAL, VENTURE; rule with a rod of iron, TYRANNY-ANARCHY.

RULE—LICENSE.

Absoluteness. Unlimited power.

Absolutism. The principle of absolute power.

Accession. Induction to an office or government.

Administration. The act of administering or conducting affairs.

Authoritativeness. The state of being authoritative, or of command-ing credit or obedience.

Authority. Lawful right to exercise power or rule.

Body politic. Collective body of people carrying on government.

Chiefdom. Headship; dominion.

Command. The act of ordering with authority.

Commission. The granting of certain powers to another to exercise. See COMMISSION.

Control. The restraining power.

Credit. The influence derived from character, or from standing in the community.

Despotism. The exercise of absolute, unlimited power

Dictation. Arbitrary commanding.

Divine right. Exercise of authority as if appointed by God.

Domination. The act of exercising authority; control.

Dominion. Supreme authority or rule.

Dynastic rights. The rights of a given family to rule.

Empery. Sovereignty.

Empire. Supreme control.

Government. The act of governing or of causing to obey the will of. See MANAGEMENT.

Grasp. Possession taken and kept by force.

Grip. Act of holding fast, of controlling.

Gripe. A very firm grip.

Headship. The chief place, government.

Heteronomy. Subjection of a community to the state.

Hold. Power of keeping.

Abdication. A voluntary surrender of power.

Anarchy. Want of government, disorder.

Brutum fulmen [L.]. A harmless stroke of lightning.

Dead letter. A law that exists in verbal form, but is not enforced.

Deposition. A deprivation of power.

Dethronement. A driving out of power.

Freedom. Absence of everything that impedes the exercise of one's will. See LIBERTY.

Insubordination. Refusal to submit to lawful authority. See IN-SUBORDINATION.

Interregnum. Suspension of executive authority through a change of government.

Laxity. The state of being lax, remiss, or careless.

Laxness. Laxity.

License. Defiance of natural restraints, and reckless indulgence of all passions or desires.

Licentiousness. Wanton license of action.

Looseness. Slackness in power or virtuous restraint.

Loosening. A making loose.

Lynch-law. The infliction of punishment without a trial or after trial by a self-appointed body of men.

Misrule. A bad rule or government.

Nihilism. The doctrine of the Nihilists, a secret organization organized for the destruction of political, religious, and social institutions.

Relaxation. Abatement of severity.

Remission. Relaxation of authority; cessation of activity.

Slackness. Inattention to business; looseness.

Toleration. Allowance of what is partially disapproved. See HARSHNESS-MILDNESS.

Usurpation. Taking possession of power without right.

RULE—LICENSE—*Continued.*

Influence. The exercise of control over the actions of others.
Installation. The act of inducting into an office.
Jurisdiction. Lawful power to exercise official authority.
Lordship. The authority of a lord.
Masterdom. The state of being master.
Mastership. The control; supreme power.
Mastery. The superiority; the dominion.
Palatine. Ruler of a palatinate.
Pantisocracy. A government of all by all.
Paternalism. The theory of government after the manner of a father.
Patronage. A fatherly guardianship.
Permission. Consenting; allowing. See Leave.
Power. The right of holding dominion over.
Preponderance. An outweighing in authority.
Prerogative. A peculiar power.
Prestige. Power derived from past accomplishments.
Reach. The power of attainment; extent of mental activity.
Right. A lawful claim to anything. See Dueness.
Rule. Government; control.
Seigniority. The power of a lord.
Seigniory. Seigniority.
Sovereignty. The state of a sovereign; supreme authority.
Supremacy. The possession of highest power.
Suzerainty. Authority superior to another.
Sway. A moving backward and forward; hence, a ruling; a controlling.

Rule—*Nouns of Agency.*

Cabinet. A body of men acting as advisers and administrating the several departments of government. See Council.
Deputy. One delegated to exercise specific powers for another or others.
Dictator. One who exercises arbitrary power.
Director. One who gives orders, or controls.
Judicature. Power of administering law. See Jurisdiction.
Person in authority. The master, the ruler. See Chief.
Posse comitatus [L.]. A body of men deputized by the sheriff to assist in the preservation of order.
Proconsul. An ancient Roman ruler of subject provinces.
Protector. One who defends; a guardian.

Rule—*Nouns of Result.*

Aristarchy. Rule by best men.
Aristocracy. Government by the best.
Autocracy. Government of an autocrat.
Autonomy. Self-government.
Beadledom. Petty and stupid officialism.
Bumbledom. Pompous authority.
Bureaucracy. Government by bureaus, or departments.
Caliphate. Government by a caliph.
Constitutional government. A government in which the officers are controlled by a written constitution.
Constitutional monarchy. A monarchy administered according to the provisions of a constitution.
Consulship. The authority or government of a consul.
Demagogy. The practise of a demagogue, ruling by popular methods.
Democracy. Government by the people.
Dictatorship. Government by a dictator.
Dinarchy. Government by two equal rulers.
Duarchy. Government by two persons.
Duumvirate. Government exercised by two officers in union.
Dynasty. A series of sovereigns who govern a country, all belonging to one family.
Electorate. The body of people who vote in an election; the country ruled by an elector.
Empire. An extensive tract of country ruled by an emperor.
Feodality. Condition of being feudal.
Feudalism. The system by which lands were held on condition of military service.
Feudal system. Feudalism.
Gynæocracy.
Gynocracy. } Gynarchy.
Gynarchy. Government by women.
Hegemony. Leadership; preponderant authority.
Heterarchy. A government by a foreigner.
Imperium in imperio [L.]. A government within a government.
Kinghood. The state of being a king.
Kingship. Kingly rank or dignity.
Limited monarchy. A monarchy where the royal prerogatives are limited by a constitution or otherwise.
Magistracy. Rank, state, or dignity of a magistrate.

License—*Verbs.*

Abdicate. To yield up voluntarily, as a throne.
Act on one's own responsibility.
Act without authority. } To do without legal authority.
Act without instructions.
Be lax. To exercise no power over. See *Adjectives.*
Depose. To remove from an office, etc.
Dethrone. To deprive of a throne.
Gerrymander. To mark off the voting districts so that the map of them looks like a salamander, as did Gov. Gerry of Massachusetts.
Give a loose to. To give free vent to.
Give rope enough.
Give the reins to. } To permit to act without restraint.
Go beyond the length of one's tether. To go beyond one's authority.
Have one's fling.
Have one's swing. } To act without restraint.
Hold a loose rein.
Laisser aller [F.]. Let it go.
Laisser faire [F.]. Let it be as it will.
Misrule. To rule badly.
Relax. To make loose.
Tolerate. To allow what one disapproves.
Usurp authority. To seize wrongfully upon authority.

License—*Adjectives.*

Adespotic. Not despotic.
Anarchical. Without government; confused.
Lax. Loose; not firm.
Licensed. Allowed to do or perform with authority.
Loose. Lax in power, etc.
Reinless. Without reins or checks.
Relaxed. Made loose.
Remiss. Not attending to one's duties. See Carefulness-Carelessness.
Slack. Loose; careless.
Unauthorized. Unsanctioned.
Unbridled. Without a bridle; without checks.
Weak. Yielding to influence; not strong.

RULE—Nouns of Result—*Continued.*

Magistrature. A magistracy.
Military government. A government conducted by military officers.
Military power. A country having a powerful military force.
Mob-law. Law administered by the mob; irregular law.
Mobocracy. Government lawlessly administered by the mob.
Monarchy. A government by a single person.
Ochlocracy. Government by the mob.
Oligarchy. A government by the few.
Pashawlic. Jurisdiction of a pasha.
Petticoat government. A government by the women.
Prefecture. The governmental department ruled by a prefect.
Presidency. The chief executive office of a republic.
Presidentship. The rank or dignity of a president.
Proconsulship. The position of a proconsul.
Protectorate. Protection imposed by a larger state upon a smaller.
Protectorship. Government under a protector.
Regality. A sovereignty.
Regime. A manner or system of administration.
Reign. Dominion; royal power; time of the exercise of the power.
Republic. A government in which the people rule.
Republicanism. The system or principles of a republican form of government.
Royalty. The character of a king; royal authority.
Seneschalship. The rank or dignity of a seneschal, or an officer who directed feasts, etc., in medieval times.
Slavocracy. The slave-holding people as a political power.
Socialism. Various theories for the reorganization of society so that individual action may be supplanted and cooperation substituted.
Stratocracy. Military despotism.
Thearchy. A government by God.
Triarchy. A government by three.
Triumvirate. A coalition of three men to exercise sovereign power jointly.
Vox populi [L.]. Voice of the people.

Rule—*Nouns of Place.*

Headquarters. Place where sovereign power resides.
Realm. The dominions of ruler or king.
Seat of authority. The place from which authority emanates.

RULE—Nouns of Place—*Continued*.

Seat of government. The place where the governmental business has its headquarters.

State. A body politic exercising jurisdiction over a given **territory** and its inhabitants.

RULE—*Figurative Nouns*.

Clutches. A powerful grip.
Fangs. Teeth of a serpent.
Iron sway. Rough, despotic rule. See HARSHNESS.

Rod of empire. Insignia of power. [Gray, *Elegy in a Country Churchyard*.]
Talons. The claws of a bird.

RULE—*Verbs*.

Administer. To carry into effect; direct; govern.
Ascend the throne. To begin to rule.
Assume authority.
Assume command. } To take power into one's hands.
Assume the reins of government. } See *Nouns*.
Authorize. To confer the power of doing upon; deputize. See LEAVE.
Be at the head of. To be the ruler.
Be governed by. To be ruled by.
Be in an office. To have legal authority.
Be in the power of. }
Be master of. } To rule over.
Be master of the situation. To have control of.
Bend to one's will. To comply with.
Be seated on the throne. To possess power.
Carry with a high hand. To rule despotically.
Command. To bid to do with authority.
Control. To have an influence over; direct.
Dictate. To command haughtily and arbitrarily. See ORDER.
Dominate. To rule over, as a lord.
Exercise authority. }
Exert authority. } To rule.
Fill an office. To exert power.
Gain a hold upon. To be able to exercise some influence over.
Get the upper hand. Get the best of.
Get the whip hand. To obtain control of; to be master of.
Give the law to. To control thought.
Govern. To cause to obey one's will. See MANAGEMENT.
Have authority.
Have it all one's way.
Have on the hip.
Have the ball at one's feet.
Have the game in one's own hand. } To exert influence or power over.
Have the upper hand.
Have the whip hand.
Have under one's thumb.
Hold an office.
Hold a post. } To have legal authority to exercise power.
Hold authority.

Hold in hand. To exert influence over.
Hold one's own. To maintain one's power.
Keep under. To hold the mastery.
Lay down the law. To assert one's authority.
Lead. To guide; control.
Lead by the nose. To lead as one wishes.
Lord it over. To rule despotically.
Make a puppet of. To subordinate.
Mount the throne. To assume power.
Occupy a post. }
Occupy the throne. } To have legal authority to exercise power.
Overawe. To check by superior authority.
Override. To ride over; treat contemptuously.
Overrule. To rule over.
Play first fiddle. To be leader; be conspicuous.
Possess authority. }
Possess the throne. } To have power.
Preponderate. To outweigh in influence.
Preside over. To be moderator of; act as ruler over others.
Reign. To hold the power of sovereign.
"Ride the whirlwind and direct the storm." To rule supremely. [Addison, *The Campaign*.]
Rule. To exercise controlling power.
Rule the roost. To exert authority.
Rule with a rod of iron. To rule harshly.
Set the fashion. To establish the rule.
Sway. To swing backwards and forwards; to rule.
Sway the scepter. To rule.
Take the command.
Take the lead.
Take the reins. } To exercise authority.
Take the reins into one's hand.
Turn round one's little finger. To exercise power as one wishes.
Warrant. To guarantee the authority, credit, or authenticity of. See DUENESS.
Wear the breeches. To rule; govern in a family.
Wear the crown. To be the ruler.
Wield authority. }
Wield the scepter. } To rule.

RULE—*Adjectives*.

Absolute. Having no limitations; unrestricted.
Administrative. Capable of carrying into effect.
Arbitrary. Acting according to his own will; despotic.
Aristocratic. Of or pertaining to an aristocracy; haughty.
At one's command. Under one's rule.
At the head. Ruling.
Authoritative. Having authority; exercising power.
Authorized. Commanded; sanctioned.
Autocratic. Characteristic of an autocrat.
Clothed with authority. Invested with power.
Compulsory. Making use of compulsion; enforced. See COERCION.
Dominant. Exercising chief power; predominant.
Dynastic. Pertaining or concerned in a dynasty.
Executive. Carrying into effect; charged with execution.
Ex officio [L.]. By virtue of office.
Feudal. Relating to a fee, founded on tenures by military service.
Gubernatorial. Of or concerning a governor.
Hegemonic. Pertaining to a hegemony or leadership.
Hegemonical. Same as hegemonic.
Imperative. Containing a demand; positive.
Imperatorial. Pertaining to an imperator; commanding.
Imperial. Pertaining to an emperor; having power.
Imperious. Having qualities and attributes of an emperor; haughty; exclusive.
Influential. Having influence; controlling.

In one's grasp. }
In one's power. } Under one's authority.
In the ascendent. Ruling.
Kingly. Like a king.
Masterful. Showing mastery.
Monarchical. Pertaining to a monarchy; regal; imperial.
Official. Given with authority; authoritative.
Oligarchic. Pertaining to a government in the hands of a few.
Overruling. Ruling over; predominating.
Paramount. Superior to all; preeminent, superior in authority.
Peremptory. Not admitting of debate or question; final in opinion; dogmatic.
Predominant. Superior in power.
Preponderant. Overcoming.
Princely. Having the qualities of a prince.
Regal. Belonging to a king; royal.
Regnant. Ruling.
Republican. Suitable to a republic; harmonious to the principles of a republic.
Royal. Pertaining to a king; kingly.
Royalist. Favoring monarchy.
Ruling. Exercising authority; governing. See *Verbs*.
Sovereign. Supreme in power or authority; imperial.
Stringent. Exact in the exercise of power; severe.
Supreme. Highest in anything.
Under control.

RULE—*Adverbs, etc*.

At one's pleasure. As one wishes.
By a dash of the pen. }
By the stroke of the pen. } By the authority of one's name.

By the authority of. In virtue of power.
De par le roi [F.]. In the king's name.

RULE—Adverbs, etc.—*Continued.*

Ex cathedra [L.]. After the manner of one speaking from a seat or office.
Ex mero motu [L.]. From his own free will.
In the hands of. Under one's power.

In the name of. By one's authority.
In virtue of. By the authority.
Under the auspices of. Under the protection of one.

RULE—*Phrases.*

Cada uno tiene su alguazil [Sp.]. Everybody has his governor.
Every inch a king. [*King Lear*, IV, iii.]
Jus divinum [L.]. Divine law.
Jus nocendi [L.].
L'homme propose et Dieu dispose [F.]. Man proposes and God disposes.

Le roi le veut [F.]. The king wills it.
Licentia vatum [L.]. Poetic license.
Regibus esse manus, an nescio longas [L.]. Do you not know that kings have far-reaching hands?
Regnant populi [L.]. The people rule. [Motto of Arkansas.]
The gray mare the better horse.

ru'-ler. Sovereign. Chief-Underling.
ru'-ling. Controlling. Rule-License; **ruling passion,** Affections, Bigotry-Apostasy.
rum. Strange. Society-Ludicrousness.
rum'-ble. To rattle. Crash-Drumming.
ru'-mi-nate. To chew; to muse. Mind-Imbecility, Reflection-Vacancy.
ru'-mi-na'-tion. Chewing the cud. Nutriment-Excretion.
rum'-mage. To bustle. Investigation-Answer.
rum'-mer. Drinking-glass. Contents-Receiver.
ru'-mor. Report. Publicity, Tidings-Mystery.
rump. Buttocks. Anteriority-Posteriority.
rum'-ple. To wrinkle. Organization-Disorganization, Plicature, Regularity-Irregularity, Smoothness-Roughness.
rum'-pus. Disturbance. Regularity-Irregularity, Turbulence-Calmness, Variance-Accord.
run. Generality; series; motion; to flow; to smuggle. Discontinuance-Continuance, Entrance-Exit, Habit-Desuetude, Law-Lawlessness, Liquefaction-Volatilization, Movement-Rest, Occurrence-Destiny, Period-Progress, Quest-Evasion, Recurrence, River-Wind, Theft, Universality-Particularity; **have a run,** Reputation-Discredit, Society-Ludicrousness, Traveling-Navigation; **have run of,** Liberty-Subjection; **he that runs may read,** Clearness-Obscurity, Manifestation-Latency; **near run,** Remoteness-Nearness; **race is run,** Completion-Noncompletion; **run abreast,** Equality-Inequality; **run a chance,** Likelihood-Unlikelihood, Purpose-Luck; **run after,** Desire-Distaste, Quest-Evasion, Reputation-Discredit; **run against,** Antagonism-Concurrence, Attack-Defense, Cooperation-Opposition, Impetus-Reaction; **run amuck,** Attack-Defense, Excitability-Inexcitability, Life-Killing, Turbulence-Calmness; **run a race,** Conduct, Quest-Evasion, Strife-Peace, Swiftness-Slowness; **run a rig,** Entertainment-Weariness; **run a risk,** Security-Insecurity; **run at,** Attack-Defense; **run a tilt at,** Attack-Defense, Strife-Peace; **run away,** Approach-Withdrawal, Quest-Evasion, Remedy-Bane; **run away with,** Taking-Restitution, Theft; **run away with a notion,** Credulousness-Skepticism, Decision-Misjudgment; **run back,** Advance-Retrogression; **run counter to,** Antagonism-Concurrence; **run down,** Adulation-Disparagement, Approval-Disapproval, Attack-Defense, Goodness-Badness, Quest-Evasion; **run dry,** Provision-Waste; **run foul of,** Impetus-Reaction; **run hard,** Difficulty-Facility, Security-Insecurity, Success-Failure; **run high,** Magnitude-Smallness, Turbulence-Calmness; **run in,** Environment-Interposition; **run in a race,** Action-Passiveness; **run in one's head,** Hypothesis, Reflection-Vacancy, Remembrance-Forgetfulness; **run into** Conversion-Reversion; **run into danger,** Recklessness-Caution, Security-Insecurity; **run into debt,** Affluence-Penury, Credit-Debt, Loan-Borrowing; **run its course,** Completion-Noncompletion, Future-Past, Period-Progress; **run like mad,** Swiftness-Slowness; **run low,** Increase-Decrease; **run mad,** Excitability-Inexcitability, Excitation, Saneness-Lunacy; **run mad after,** Desire-Distaste; **run of luck,** Rationale-Luck, Welfare-Misfortune; **run of things,** Occurrence-Destiny; **run on,** Discontinuance-Continuance; **run on in a groove,** Habit-Desuetude; **run out,** Beginning-End, Entrance-Exit, Future-Past, Novelty-Antiquity, Reversal; **run out on,** Terseness-Prolixity; **run over,** Account, Digest, Excess-Lack, Heed-Disregard, Numbering; **run parallel,** Cooperation-Opposition; **run riot,** Activity-Passiveness, Excess-Lack, Gull-Hyperbole, Insubordination-Obedience, Moderation-Voluptuary, Turbulence-Calmness; **run rusty,** Readiness-Reluctance; **run smooth,** Difficulty-Facility, Welfare-Misfortune; **run the eye over,** Education-Learning, Sight-Blindness; **run the fingers over,** Touch; **run the gauntlet,** Bravery-Cowardice, Determination-Vacillation; **run the rig upon,** Regard-Disrespect; **run through,** Dominance-Impotence, Entrance-Exit, Extravagance-Avarice, Life-Killing, Outlay-Income, Presence-Absence, Uniformity-Diversity; **run to seed,** Betterment-Deterioration, Infancy-Age; **run to waste,** Provision-Waste; **run up,** Creation-Destruction, Increase-Decrease, Price-Discount; **run up an account,** Credit-Debt, Price-Discount; **run up bills,** Credit-Debt, Price-Discount, Settlement-Default; **run upon,** Need; **run upon a bank,** Outlay-Income, Settlement-Default; **run wild,** Excitability-Inexcitability, Turbulence-Calmness; **time runs,** Duration-Neverness.
run'-a-gate. Deserter of a cause; vagabond. Bravery-Cowardice, Good Man-Bad Man, Insubordination-Obedience, Quest-Evasion.
run'-a-way". Fugitive. Quest-Evasion.
run'-dle. Rung; something rotating on its own axis. Circle-Winding, Roundness.
rund'-let. Small barrel. Contents-Receiver.
rune. A poem; letter. Devotion-Charm, Poetry-Prose, Writing-Printing.
ru'-ner. An early Gothic bard. Poetry-Prose.
rung. Step of a ladder. Suspension-Support.
ru'-nic. Inscribed with runes. Writing-Printing.
run'-nel. Rivulet. River-Wind.
run'-ner. Messenger. Messenger, Wayfarer-Seafarer.
run'-ning. Continuous. Continuity-Interruption; **running account,** Accounts; **running commentary,** Essay; **running fight,** Strife-Peace; **running hand,** Writing-Printing; **running over,** Excess-Lack; **running water,** River-Wind; **the mind running upon,** Reflection-Vacancy; **the mind running upon other things,** Heed-Disregard.
runt. Dwarf. Greatness-Littleness.

ru-pee'. Coin. VALUES.

rup'-ture. The act of bursting; disagreement. UNION-DISUNION, VARIANCE-ACCORD.

ru'-ral. Pertaining to the country. COUNTRY, DO-MESTICATION-AGRICULTURE, DWELLER-HABITATION

ru'-ral-ist. A rustic. SOCIABILITY-PRIVACY.

ruse. Trick. CRAFT-ARTLESSNESS.

rush. Crowd; haste; pressure; herb. CONSEQUENCE-INSIGNIFICANCE, FAUNA-FLORA, GATHERING-SCAT-TERING, HURRY-LEISURE, RIVER-WIND, SWIFTNESS-SLOWNESS, TURBULENCE-CALMNESS; **make a rush at,** ATTACK-DEFENSE; **rush in medias res,** DETERMINA-TION-VACILLATION; **rush into print,** WRITING-PRINT-ING; **rush on destruction,** RECKLESSNESS-CAUTION, **rush to a conclusion,** CREDULOUSNESS-SKEPTICISM, DECISION-MISJUDGMENT; **rush upon,** QUEST-EVASION.

rus in urbe [L.] (rʊs in ʊr'-bĭ). The country in the city. DWELLER-HABITATION, SOCIABILITY-PRIVACY.

rush'-light''. Kind of candle. DIMNESS, LUMINARY-SHADE.

rusk. A kind of light, sweetened bread. NUTRIMENT-EXCRETION.

Russe, montagne [F.] (rüs, mon'-tɑny'). Russian moun-tain. ENTERTAINMENT-WEARINESS.

rus'-set. Reddish. GRAY-BROWN, REDNESS-GREEN-NESS.

Rus'-sian. Pertaining to Russia. **Russian Bear,** PA-TRIOTISM-TREASON.

Rus'-sian bath. A kind of bath. OVEN-REFRIGERATOR.

rust. A coating; to be diseased; to become dull. AC-TIVITY-INDOLENCE, BETTERMENT-DETERIORATION, CHEMISTRY, REDNESS-GREENNESS, REMEDY-BANE; **moth and rust,** BETTERMENT-DETERIORATION; **rust of antiquity,** NOVELTY-ANTIQUITY.

rus'-tic. Rural. COUNTRY, DOMESTICATION-AGRICUL-TURE, DWELLER-HABITATION, GENTILITY-COMMON-ALTY, TASTE-VULGARITY.

rus'-ti-cate. To send into the country; to suspend. RECOMPENSE-PUNITION, SOCIABILITY-PRIVACY

rus''-ti-ca'-tion. Act of rusticating. SOCIABILITY-PRI-VACY.

rus-tic'-i-ty. Awkwardness. POLITENESS-IMPOLITE-NESS, TASTE-VULGARITY.

rusticus expectat dum defluat amnis [L.] (rʊs'-ti-cʊs ex-pec'-tat dum def'-lu-at am'-nis). The country-man waits while the river flows away. SANGUINE-NESS-HOPELESSNESS.

rust'-i-ness. State of being rusty. ACTIVITY-INDO-LENCE.

rus'-tle. To sound. RESONANCE-NONRESONANCE.

rust'-y. Covered with rust; decayed; dull; unskilful, surly. ACTIVITY-INDOLENCE, BETTERMENT-DETERI-ORATION, CLEANNESS-FILTHINESS, FAVORITE-MO-ROSENESS, SKILL-UNSKILFULNESS; **run rusty,** READI-NESS-RELUCTANCE.

rut. Furrow; habit. GROOVE, HABIT-DESUETUDE.

ruth. Compassion. COMPASSION-RUTHLESSNESS.

ruth'-ful. Sorrowful. COMPASSION-RUTHLESSNESS.

ruth'-less. Unpitying. CHARITABLENESS - MALEVO-LENCE, COMPASSION-RUTHLESSNESS, PARDON-VIN-DICTIVENESS.

ruth'-less-ness. Want of compassion. PARDON-VIN-DICTIVENESS.

ru'-ti-lant. Glittering. LIGHT-DARKNESS.

rut'-tish. Lustful. PURITY-IMPURITY.

ry'-ot. Peasant. CHIEF-UNDERLING, GENTILITY-COM-MONALTY, HOLDER.

S

Sab'-a-oth. Armies. Belligerent.

Sab''-ba-ta'-ri-an. A Christian who observes Sunday with strictness. Austerity, Ceremonial, Godliness-Ungodliness.

Sab''-ba-ta'-ri-an-ism. Doctrines of the Sabbatarians. Godliness-Ungodliness.

Sab'-bath. The seventh day of the week. Ceremonial, Toil-Relaxation.

Sab'-bath–break''-er. One who profanes the Sabbath. Godliness-Ungodliness.

Sab'-ba-tism. The keeping of the Sabbath. Godliness-Ungodliness.

Sa-bel'-li-an-ism. The doctrine of a modal Trinity. Orthodoxy-Heterodoxy.

Sa'-bi-an. One of an ancient Persian sect. Devotion-Idolatry, Orthodoxy-Heterodoxy.

Sa'-bi-an-ism. Worship peculiar to the Sabians. Orthodoxy-Heterodoxy.

saber que haber, más vale [Sp.] (sɑ-ber' kê ɑ-ber', mas val'-ê). Wisdom is better than wealth. Affluence-Penury, Sagacity-Incapacity.

sa'-ber. A heavy sword. Life-Killing, Weapon.

sa'-ble. Black, mourning color. Dress-Undress, Whiteness-Blackness.

sabreur [F.] (sɑ-brur'). A slasher. Belligerent, Life-Killing.

sab'-u-lous. Gritty, like sand. Friability.

sac. A cavity or pouch. Contents-Receiver.

sac''-cha-rif'-er-ous. Producing sugar. Sweetness-Acidity.

sac'-cha-rine. Having the qualities of sugar. Sweetness-Acidity.

sac'-cu-lar. Sac-shaped. Contents-Receiver.

sac'-cu-la''-ted. Pouched. Contents-Receiver.

sac'-cule. A little sac. Contents-Receiver.

sac''-er-do'-tal. Priestly. Church.

sac''-er-do'-tal-ism. Character or methods of the priesthood. Ceremonial.

sach'-el. A small hand-bag. Contents-Receiver.

sa'-chem. An Indian chief. Chief-Underling.

sa''-chet'. A small bag for perfumed powder. Perfume-Stench.

sack. A bag; to plunder or pillage. Contents-Receiver, Gain-Loss, Taking-Restitution, Theft; **give the sack to,** Admission-Expulsion.

sack'-age. Pillage. Theft.

sack'-but. A musical instrument. Musical Instruments.

sack'-cloth''. Haircloth worn in penance. **Sackcloth and ashes,** Atonement, Austerity, Ceremonial, Jubilation-Lamentation.

sac'-ra-ment. A rite ordained as a sign of spiritual grace. Ceremonial.

sac''-ra-men-ta'-ri-an. One who regards the sacraments as channels of divine grace. Orthodoxy-Heterodoxy.

sa-cra'-ri-um. The sanctuary of a church. Fane.

sa'-cred. Set apart to religious use. Divinity, Godliness-Ungodliness, Reputation-Discredit, Revelation-Pseudorevelation.

sa-crif'-ic-a-to-ry. Offering sacrifice. Atonement.

sac'-ri-fice. An offering to God; a loss incurred in behalf of another; a victim; to give up as an offering or tribute. Atonement, Creation-Destruction, Devotion-Idolatry, Giving-Receiving; **at any sacrifice,** Determination-Vacillation; **fall a sacrifice,** Pleasure-Pain; **make a sacrifice,** Unselfishness-Selfishness; **self-sacrifice,** Unselfishness-Selfishness.

sac'-ri-ficed. Lost without return. Success-Failure.

sac''-ri-fi'-cial. Pertaining to sacrifice. Atonement.

sac'-ri-lege. Act of profaning any sacred thing. Godliness-Ungodliness.

sac'-ris-tan. An officer having charge of the sacred vessels in a church. Ministry-Laity.

sac'-ris-ty. A vestry in a church. Fane.

sa'-crum. Bone. Anatomy.

sad. Sorrowful; unfortunate; heavy; firm; of dark color. Faultlessness-Faultiness, Gray-Brown, Lightheartedness-Dejection, Magnitude-Smallness, Pleasurableness-Painfulness; **sad disappointment,** Expectation-Disappointment; **sad dog,** Good Man-Bad Man; **sad times,** Welfare-Misfortune; **sad work,** Skill-Unskilfulness.

sad'-den. To make sad or mournful. Lightheartedness-Dejection, Pleasurableness-Painfulness.

sad'der and wi'ser man. A repentant man. Repentance-Obduracy.

sad'-dle. To load; a seat to support a rider. Suspension-Support; **in the saddle,** Preparation-Nonpreparation; **saddle on,** Addition-Subtraction, Union-Disunion; **saddle on the right horse,** Decision, Right-Wrong, Skill-Unskilfulness, Uprightness-Dishonesty; **saddle on the wrong horse,** Truth-Error; **saddle with,** Addition-Subtraction, Duty-Dereliction, Establishment-Removal, Justification-Charge, Obstruction-Help.

sad'-dle–bags''. Bags connected by a strap and slung over an animal's back. Contents-Receiver, Suspension-Support.

Sad'-du-cee. A Jewish sect. Orthodoxy-Heterodoxy.

sad'-ly. Sorrowfully. Lightheartedness-Dejection.

sad'-ness. Sorrow. Lightheartedness-Dejection; **in sadness,** Assertion-Denial.

safe. Free from harm or danger; a strong chest for keeping valuables. Contents-Receiver, Security-Insecurity; **on the safe side,** Recklessness-Caution; **safe and sound,** Conservation, Health-Sickness, Security-Insecurity; **safe-conduct,** Instrumentality, Security-Insecurity; **safe-conscience,** Duty-Dereliction, Innocence-Guilt; **safe-keeping,** Conservation.

safe'-guard''. Convoy. Attack-Defense, Refuge-Pitfall, Security-Insecurity.

safe'-ty. Freedom from risk or danger. Security-Insecurity; **safety-lamp,** Chemistry; **safety-valve,** Refuge-Pitfall.

saf'-fron. Orange color. Yellowness-Purple.

sag. To bend downward in the middle. Curvation-Rectilinearity, Parallelism-Inclination.

sa-ga'-cious. Quick and shrewd to apprehend. Prevision, Sagacity-Incapacity.

sa-gac'-i-ty. Readiness and accuracy of judgment. Prevision Sagacity-Incapacity.

SAGACITY—INCAPACITY.

Acumen. Quickness of intellectual apprehension, insight, or discernment.

Acuteness, etc. Fine and penetrating perception, etc. See *Adjectives.*

Aplomb [F.]. Self-possession; assurance resulting from self-confidence.

Ballast. That which gives stability to character or which makes the mind equable.

Caliber. Degree of individual capacity or power.

Capacity. Adequate mental power to receive, understand, endure, or accomplish.

Common sense. Practical understanding; sound judgment.

Compass of thought. Limit of understanding.

Comprehension. The act or power of grasping ideas, facts, etc., with the mind.

Cunning, etc. Knowledge coupled with manual skill, etc. See CRAFT.

Depth. Profundity of thought or feeling.

Discernment. Mental power of perceiving or discriminating.

Discrimination, etc. The act or power of distinguishing or discriminating, etc. See DIFFERENTIATION.

Due sense of. Adequate appreciation of.

Enlarged views. Increased intellectual perception.

Enlargement of mind. Increased power to think, feel, or will.

Esprit [F.]. Spirit; wit.

Foresight, etc. Prudence, etc. See PREVISION.

Geist [G.]. Spirit; mind.

Genius. Exalted intellectual power, marked by an extraordinary faculty for original creation, expression, or achievement.

Good judgment. Good sense.

Good sense. Normal power of mind or understanding.

Grasp of intellect. Power of comprehension.

Gumption. Ready perception; quick-wittedness.

Inspiration. The inbreathing or imparting of an idea, emotion, or influence; lofty thought, emotion, or creative power.

Intellect, etc. See MIND.

Intelligence. The act or state of knowing; readiness of comprehension.

Judgment. The faculty of judging or deciding correctly.

Mother wit. Inherent or natural wit.

Nous. Reason as repetition of the divine activity, the life of intellect, understanding and talent: sometimes used humorously.

Parts. Faculties; talents.

Penetration. Acuteness; discernment.

Perspicacity. Mental discernment or penetration.

Perspicacy. Perspicacity.

Plain sense. Simple, ordinary intelligence or judgment.

Profundity. Depth of thought.

Prudence, etc. Good judgment in practical affairs, etc. See RECKLESSNESS-CAUTION.

Quick parts. Talents.

Rationality. Reasoning power.

Reach of thought. Depth of thought.

Reason. The entire mental or rational nature of man as distinguished from the intelligence of the brute.

Reasonableness, etc. The quality of being reasonable, or of having the faculty of reason, etc. See *Adjectives.*

Refinement, etc. Fineness or delicacy of thought, etc. See TASTE.

Sagacity. Ready and accurate discernment and judgment.

Sapience. Wisdom or knowledge.

Self-possession. Full possession or control of one's powers or faculties; presence of mind.

Sense. Normal power of mind or understanding sound or natural judgment.

Sobriety. Calmness; gravity; seriousness, coolness.

Solidity. Soundness strength, validity.

Subtlety. Intellectual acuteness, sagacity, or insight.

Tact, etc. Intuitive appreciation of what is right, proper, or fit in any given case, etc. See SKILL.

Talent, etc. Superior mental endowments or capacities, mental ability in general, as a loan on which interest is to be paid. [*Matthew* xxv, 19.] See SKILL.

Understanding. The faculty by which one understands; in general, the sum of the mental powers by which knowledge is acquired, retained, and extended.

Vigilance, etc. Alertness, etc. See CAREFULNESS.

Wisdom. Knowledge, and the capacity to make due use of it.

Wit. Mind; intellect, sense.

SAGACITY—*Denotations.*

A bright thought. A thought showing quick intelligence.

Not a bad idea. An idea or plan from an acute or active mind.

Act of folly, etc. An act showing deficiency of understanding. See SKILL-UNSKILFULNESS.

Anility. Old-womanishness; dotage.

Apartments to let. Want of intellect or knowledge; emptiness of mind. [An advertising card for a fool's forehead.]

Babyhood. The state of infancy; incapacity.

Bias, etc. Prejudice; partiality, etc. See DECISION-MISJUDGMENT.

Clouded perception. Darkened or obscured power of discerning or understanding.

Conceit. Self-flattering opinion.

Dotage. Feebleness of mind, due to old age.

Driveling. Senseless talk; twaddle.

Dull understanding. Slowness of perception or thought; stupidity.

Eccentricity, etc. Deviation from the customary line of conduct; oddity, etc. See SANENESS-LUNACY.

Extravagance, etc. Prodigality of expression or imagination, etc. See ADAGE-NONSENSE.

Fatuity. Imbecility; idiocy.

Folly. The state of being foolish.

Foolishness, etc. The character or quality of being foolish, etc. See *Adjectives.*

Frivolity. The quality or condition of being frivolous; triviality.

Giddiness, etc. Foolish levity or imprudence, etc. See HEED-DISREGARD.

Hebetude. Stupidity.

Idiocy. Absence of sense and intellect.

Idiotism. Lack of knowledge or mental capacity.

Imbecility. Weakness or feebleness of mind.

Incapacity. Lack of intellectual power.

Incompetence, etc. Want of intellectual ability, etc. See SKILL-UNSKILFULNESS.

Inconsistency. Want of stability; changeableness.

Ineptitude. Absurdity; nonsense.

Infatuation, etc. Folly, etc. See SANENESS-LUNACY.

Irrationality. The quality or state of being void of reason or foolish.

Lip-wisdom. Wise talk without practise, or unsupported by experience.

Meanest capacity. Extreme poverty of mental power.

Nugacity. Trifling talk or behavior.

One's weak side. The side or aspect of a person's character or disposition by which he is most easily affected or influenced.

Poor head. Slowness of perception or understanding.

Poverty of intellect. Want of intellect.

Puerility. The state of being childish or silly.

Rashness, etc. The state or quality of being rash or reckless, etc. See RECKLESSNESS.

Second childishness. Anility; weakness of intellect.

Shallowness. Quality of being not intellectually deep.

Short-sightedness. Quality of being of limited intellect, heedlessness.

Silliness. The quality or state of being weak of intellect; folly; stupidity

Simplicity. Weakness of intellect, silliness.

Sophistry, etc. Fallacious reasoning, etc. See RATIOCINATION-CASUISTRY

Stolidity. Dulness of intellect; stupidity.

Stupidity. Extreme dulness of perception or understanding.

Trifling. Triviality; frivolity.

Vacancy of mind. Emptiness of mind.

Want of intellect, etc. Absence of the power of perception or thought. See MIND.

Want of intelligence, etc. Absence of ability to understand. See SAGACITY.

INCAPACITY—*Verbs.*

Be imbecile, etc. Be mentally impotent, etc. See *Adjectives.*

Dote. Lavish extravagance or foolish fondness; be in one's dotage.

Drivel. Be weak or silly in talk or conduct.

Have no brains. Want intelligence.

Have no sense, etc. See SAGACITY.

Not see an inch beyond one's nose. Be dull of intellect; be stupid.

Play the fool. Be foolish.

Play the monkey. Act grotesquely.

Radoter [F.]. Talk stuff or nonsense.

Ramble, etc. Act or talk aimlessly, etc. See SANENESS-LUNACY.

Stultify oneself, etc. Make a fool of oneself, etc. See SKILL-UNSKILFULNESS.

Take leave of one's senses. Act or talk senselessly.

Talk nonsense, etc. To talk without sense. See ADAGE-NONSENSE.

Trifle. Dally; toy.

SAGACITY--INCAPACITY—*Continued.*

SAGACITY—*Figurative Nouns.*

Brains. The intelligence or mental power of which the brain is held to be the seat.

Eagle eye. }
Eagle glance } Keen power of apprehension.

Eye of a hawk. }
Eye of a lynx. } Keen mental perception.

Fire of genius. Liveliness or intensity of thought or action.

Head. Understanding.

Head-piece. The head; hence, the wits.

Heaven-born genius Natural capacity independent of tuition and training.

Long head. Shrewdness.

Soul. Reason.

Upper story. The head; hence the intellect.

SAGACITY—*Verbs.*

Be intelligent, etc. Be distinguished or marked by intelligence, etc. See *Adjectives.*

Catch an idea. Understand an idea or thought.

Discern, etc. Perceive; see as distinct; recognize, etc. See SIGHT.

Discriminate. Note the differences between; differentiate; distinguish.

Foresee, etc. Discern beforehand, etc. See PREVISION.

Have one's wits about one. Have one's mental faculties active.

Know what's what, etc. Be intelligent, etc. See SKILL.

Listen to reason. Be reasonable or sensible.

Penetrate. Pierce to the meaning of; discern.

See at a glance. Detect instantly.

See far into. Understand; comprehend.

See through. Understand.

See through a millstone. See through a difficult matter.

See with half an eye. See through at a careless glance.

Take a hint. To be able to act upon the slightest suggestion.

Take a joke. To recognize the intended playfulness of words or actions.

Take an idea. To grasp the meaning of words or the object of actions, etc.

Understand, etc. Take in or make out the meaning of; comprehend, etc. See CLEARNESS.

SAGACITY—*Adjectives.*

Abnormis sapiens [L.]. Abnormally wise.

Acuminous. Sharp in intellect.

Acute, etc. Having fine and penetrating discernment, etc. See ACTIVITY.

Alive. Sensitive to; easily impressed.

Alive to, etc. Susceptible to, etc. See KNOWLEDGE.

Arch, etc. Cunning or sly, etc. See CRAFT.

Argute. Sagacious; subtle; shrewd.

Astute. Critically discerning; sagacious.

Awake. In a state of action or vigilance.

Bright. Possessing or showing quick intelligence; quick-witted.

Calculating. Given to contrivance or forethought.

Canny. Shrewd; prudent.

Clear-eyed. Seeing clearly; having a clear mental vision.

Clear-headed. Having a clear understanding; intelligent.

Clear-sighted. Discerning.

Clear-witted. Understanding; intelligent.

Clever, etc. Possessing quickness of intellect; expert etc. See SKILL.

Considerate. Thoughtful; reflective.

Cool. Self-controlled; self-possessed.

Cool-headed. Not easily excited; free from passion.

Deep. Of penetrating intellect; sagacious.

Discerning. Acute; shrewd.

Equitable. Characterized by fairness.

Expedient, etc. Tending to promote a proposed object, etc. See PROPRIETY.

Fair. Characterized by frankness, honesty, candor, or impartiality.

Far-sighted etc. Of good judgment regarding the remote effects of actions; sagacious, etc. See PREVISION.

Fox-like. Cunning; artful.

Hard-headed. Having sound judgment; shrewd.

Heaven-born. Born with one.

Heaven-directed Directed by divine power.

Impartial. Unbiased; fair.

In advance of one's age. Far-sighted.

In one's right mind Sane.

Intelligent. Distinguished for intelligence; discerning.

Judicious Proceeding with discretion; wise; prudent.

Keen. Acute of mind; penetrating.

INCAPACITY—*Adjectives.*

Addle-headed. }
Addle-pated. } Dull-witted; stupid; with brain like an addled egg.

Anile. Old-womanish; imbecile.

Apish. Apelike; silly.

Asinine. Like an ass; stupid; obstinate.

Babbling. Talking idly.

Babish. Childish.

Babyish. Childish; simple.

Beef-headed. Having a head like a cow's; stupid.

Beef-witted. Having the intelligence of a cow.

Beetle-headed. Dull; stupid.

Bewildered, etc. Greatly perplexed, etc. See CERTAINTY-DOUBT.

Bigoted, etc. Obstinately and blindly attached to some creed, opinion, etc. See BIGOTRY.

Blatant. Noisy; blustering.

Blockish. Deficient in understanding; stupid.

Blunder-headed. Blundering; stupid.

Blunt. Slow of wit; dull.

Blunt-witted. Dull; stupid.

Bœotian. Dull; obtuse, as the Athenians esteemed the natives of Bœotia to be.

Bœotic. Bœotian.

Borné [F.] Narrow-minded.

Bovine. Sluggish; dull, as a cow.

Brainless. Without understanding.

Childish. Like a child; puerile.

Childlike. Like a child.

Clod-pated. Stupid; dull.

Dim-sighted. Lacking clear perception.

Doltish. Stupid; dull.

Driveling. Silly; weak; speaking twaddle.

Dull. Slow of perception; sluggish.

Dull as a beetle. Figurative degree of dulness.

Dull-brained. Stupid; doltish.

Dull-witted. Stupid.

Eccentric, etc. Peculiar; erratic, etc. See SANENESS-LUNACY.

Extravagant, etc. Immoderate; fantastic, etc. See ADAGE-NONSENSE.

Fat-headed. Dull of apprehension.

Fatuous. Feeble in mind; weak; silly; stupid.

Fat-witted. Dull; stupid.

Feather-brained. Weak; giddy

Feeble-minded. Weak in intellectual power.

Foolish. Wanting in judgment.

Frivolous, etc. Trivial; silly, etc. See CONSEQUENCE-INSIGNIFICANCE.

Giddy, etc. Characterized by foolish levity or imprudence, etc. See HEED-DISREGARD.

Gross-headed. Thick-skulled; stupid.

Half-witted. Weak in intellect; silly.

Having no head, etc. See sub SAGACITY.

Heavy. Sluggish of mind.

Idiotic. Like an idiot, imbecile.

Idle. Slothful; sluggish.

Ill-advised. Injudicious.

Ill-devised. Not well planned.

Ill-imagined. Not well imagined.

Ill-judged. Injudicious; foolish.

Imbecile. Having feeble mental faculties.

Improper. Not proper or right under the circumstances.

Inapprehensible. Unintelligible.

Inapt, etc. Unsuitable, etc. See SKILL-UNSKILFULNESS.

Inconsistent Incongruous; contradictory.

Inept. Silly; useless; absurd.

Inexpedient, etc. Unwise; inadvisable; indiscreet, etc. See PROPRIETY IMPROPRIETY.

Infantile. }
Infantine. } Childish.

Injudicious. Wanting in sound judgment; indiscreet.

Insensate. Destitute of sense; stupid.

Insulse. Insipid; dull, stupid.

Irrational. Not according to reason; absurd.

Lack-brained. Deficient in understanding; witless

Lean-witted. Having little sense.

Maggoty-headed. Capricious.

Mindless. Not imbued with intellectual powers; unthinking.

Muddle-headed. Stupid.

Muddy-headed. Dull; stupid.

Narrow-minded, etc. Illiberal; mean, etc. See DECISION-MISJUDGMENT.

Nonsensical. Without sense; absurd; foolish.

Not bright, etc. Dull of intellect. See SAGACITY.

SAGACITY—INCAPACITY—*Continued.*

SAGACITY—Adjectives—*Continued.*

Keen-eyed. Having a keen mental vision.
Keen-sighted. Discerning.
Keen-witted. Intelligent; sharp.
Long-headed. Having unusual sagacity.
Long-sighted. Having great foresight.
Needle-witted. Sharp-witted.
Nimble-witted. Quick to discern.
Of unwarped judgment. Impartial.
Oracular. Authoritative; dogmatical.
Pas si bête [F.]. Not such a fool.
Penetrating. Acute; discerning; sagacious.
Perspicacious. Of acute discernment.
Piercing. Penetrating; keen.
Politic. Sagacious in promoting a policy; discreet.
Profound. Deep intellectually.
Provident, etc. Prudent in preparing for future exigencies, etc. See PREPARATION.
Prudent, etc. Practically wise; discreet, etc. See RECKLESSNESS-CAUTION.
Quick. Animated; ready; brisk.
Quick-eyed. Quick to discern.
Quick of apprehension. Of an active mind.
Quick-sighted. Having acute discernment.
Quick-witted. Having ready wit.
Rational. Endowed with reason; judicious.
Reasonable. Governed by reason; agreeable to reason.
Reflecting. Contemplative.
Sagacious. Of keen penetration and judgment; shrewd; far-sighted.
Sage. Prudent; grave; sagacious.
Sapient. Wise; discerning.
Sensible. Possessing sense or reason; intelligent.
Sharp. Marked by keenness of perception or discernment.
Sharp as a needle. Very keen of intellect.
Sharp-eyed.
Sharp-sighted. } Having acute perception or discernment.
Sharp-witted. Having a nicely discerning mind.
Shrewd. Astute; sharp-witted.
Sober. Self-possessed; staid.
Solid. Manifesting strength and firmness.
Sound. Having all the faculties complete and in normal action or relation.
Staid. Of a steady and sober character.
Strong-headed. Having strength of mind.
Strong-minded. Having a firm and vigorous intellect.
Thoughtful. Given to thought; meditative.
Unbiased. Impartial.
Unbigoted. Unprejudiced; tolerant.
Undazzled. Unconfused.
Unperplexed. Free from perplexity.
Unprejudiced. Free from prejudice.
Unprepossessed. Free from prepossession.
Watchful, etc. Circumspect; observant, etc. See CAREFULNESS.
Well-advised.
Well-judged. } Intelligent.
Wide-awake. Keen; alert.
Wise. Having knowledge; prudent.
Wise as a serpent. [Biblical.])
Wise as Solomon. [Hebrew.] } Degrees of wisdom.
Wise as Solon [Greek.])
Wise in one's generation. Wise in comparison with others. [Seneca, *Claudius* I, i]

SAGACITY—*Phrases.*

Aut regem aut fatuum nasci oportet [L.]. It behooves one to be born either a king or a fool.
Flosculi sententiarum [L.]. Flowerets of wisdom.

sag'-a-more. An Indian chief. CHIEF-UNDERLING, PRESIDENT-MEMBER.
sage. A wise man; wise and prudent. SAGACITY-IN-

INCAPACITY—Adjectives—*Continued.*

Obtuse. Dull intellectually; stupid.
Pig-headed. Stupidly obstinate.
Prosaic. Dull; uninteresting.
Puerile. Boyish; childish; silly.
Puzzle-headed. Having the head full of confused notions.
Rash, etc. Overhasty in counsel or action, etc. See RECKLESSNESS.
Reasonless. Destitute of reason; unreasonable.
Ridiculous. Unworthy of consideration; absurd and laughable.
Sappy. Silly.
Senseless. Without sense; foolish.
Shallow. Lacking intellectual depth.
Shallow-brained. Weak in intellect; foolish.
Shallow-pated. Shallow-brained.
Short-sighted. Unable to understand things deep; of limited intellect.
Short-witted. Having little wit; not wise.
Silly. Destitute of ordinary good sense; simple; foolish.
Simple, etc. Not wise or clever, etc. See CREDULOUSNESS.
Sleeveless. Unreasonable; profitless.
Soft. Somewhat weak in intellect.
Sottish. Very foolish from habitual drunkenness.
Spoony. Weak-minded.
Stolid. Impassible, dull, or stupid.
Stupid. Very slow of apprehension or understanding; dull-witted.
Thick-skulled. Stupid.
Undiscerning. Wanting discernment.
Unenlightened. Lacking knowledge or intelligence.
Ungifted. Being without native gifts or endowments
Unintellectual. Without intellect.
Unintelligent. Lacking intelligence; ignorant.
Unphilosophical. Not rational; unwise.
Unreasonable. Irrational; not agreeable to reason.
Unreasoning. Not reasoning; not having reasoning faculties.
Unteachable. Not teachable; indocile.
Unwise. Not wise; injudicious; foolish.
Useless, etc. Having, or being of, no use, etc. See USEFULNESS-USELESSNESS.
Vacant. Empty of thought; stupid.
Wanting. Absent; lacking; soft.
Weak. Feeble of mind; foolish.
Weak-headed. Not possessing intellectual strength.
Weak in the upper story. Figurative for weak-headed.
Weak-minded. Feeble-minded; foolish, idiotic.
Without reason. Lacking the faculty of reason.
Witless. Destitute of wit or understanding; indiscreet.

INCAPACITY—*Phrases.*

Davus sum, non Œdipus [L.] I am Davus, not Œdipus; a simple servant, not a solver of sphinx's puzzles.
Mal entendu [F.]. Ill-advised.

SAGACITY—*Phrases*—*Continued.*

Gnothi seauton [Gr.]. Know thyself. [Inscription on the temple of Apollo at Delphi.]
Les affaires font les hommes [F.]. Experience of affairs makes men.
Más vale saber que haber [Sp.]. Wisdom is better than wealth.
Más vale ser necio que porfiado [Sp.]. Better to be stupid than stubborn.
Nosce te [L.]. Know thyself.
Nullum magnum ingenium sine mixtura dementiæ fuit [L.]. No great genius was ever born without a mixture of madness. [Seneca from Aristotle.]

CAPACITY, SAGE-FOOL, SCHOLAR-DUNCE; sage maxim, ADAGE-NONSENSE.

SAGE—FOOL.

Authority. One from whom may be obtained a correct opinion upon a given subject
Bigwig. A person of importance.
Esprit fort [F.]. A freethinker.
Expert, etc. One having special skill. See ADEPT.
Long-head. A man of keen discernment; astute man.
Luminary. One able to shed light upon a subject.

Addlehead. One easily muddled.
Ass. An obstinate, stupid fellow.
Babbler. One continually saying foolish things.
Baby. A man of babyish thoughts.
Badaud [F.]. A saunterer; a booby.
Beetlehead. Densely stupid man.
Block. A man of slow, thick comprehension.

SAGE—FOOL—*Continued.*

Magi.　The learned and priestly caste of the Medes and Persians.
Magnus Apollo [L.].　Great Apollo, the god of wisdom.
Man of learning, etc.　An educated person.　See SCHOLAR.
Master-mind.　A man of extraordinary intellectual ability.
Master spirit of the age.　A man who leads in thought and intellectual ability.
Nestor.　The wisest of the Greek chiefs before Troy; an adviser or counselor.
Oracle.　A man of undoubted wisdom.
Sage.　A venerable man of broad practical wisdom.
Second Daniel.　A man like Daniel; a prudent, sagacious man.
Shining light.　A man of brilliant scholarship.
Solomon.　The wise king of Israel.
Solon.　An ancient lawgiver of Sparta; one of the seven wise men of Greece.
Thinker.　One of finely-educated powers of thinking.
Wiseacre.　One who affects great wisdom.
Wise man.　A man of great learning.
Wizard.　One supposed to have secret power.　See DEVOTION-MAGICIAN.

SAGE—*Adjectives.*

Emeritus.　Honorably relieved from duty.
Reverenced.　Regarded with profound respect.
Venerable.　Exciting reverential feelings.

SAGE—*Phrases.*

Barbâ tenus sapientes [L.].　Sage as far as the beard.
L'hypocrisie est un hommage que le vice rend à la vertu [F.].　Hypocrisy is a homage that vice pays to virtue.

FOOL—*Continued from Column 2.*

Old fógy.　An old-fashioned fellow.
Old woman.　A weakling or coward.
One who did not invent gunpowder.　One who did not know enough to invent gunpowder.
One who will not set the Thames on fire.　A person who will not startle the world with his intellectual doings.
Owl.　A dull, slow person.
Pretty fellow.　A contemptible person.
Put.　A clownish fellow
Qui n'à pas inventé la poudre [F.].　One who did not invent powder.
Radoteur [F.].　A dotard.
Sawney.　A simpleton; from a Scotch proper name. [Alexander, Sandy.]
Shallowbrain.　A person of weak intellect.
Simpleton.　One unable to learn.
Sop.　A person easily won over or pacified.
Sot.　A person foolish from drunkenness.
Stick.　A stiff, stupid person.
Stock.　An object of contempt on account of ignorance.
Thickskull.　A dull, stupid person.
Tomfool.　An idiot or silly person.
Tom-noddy.　A weak-minded person.
Tony.　A simpleton.
Trifler.　One who trifles and knows nothing better.
Un sot à triple étage [F.].　A fool to the third power; a very great fool.
Wiseacre.　One pretending but lacking wisdom.
Wise men of Gotham.　Fools; from Gotham, England; noted for its simplicity.
Witling.　One having little wit; a pretender to wit.
Zany.　A clown; a fool.

FOOL—*Phrases.*

Fortuna favet fatuis [L.].　Fortune favors fools.
Les fous font les festins, et les sages les mangent [F.].　Fools make feasts and wise men eat them.
Locos y niños dicen la verdad [Sp.].　Children and fools speak the truth.
Nomina stultorum parietibus hærent [L.].　Fools' names are stuck on house-walls.

Blockhead.　A dull-witted or stupid person.
Booby. }
Bull-calf. } A dull, stupid fellow.
Bullhead.　A thick-headed person.
Buzzard.　A dull coward.
Calf.　An effeminate coward; a young person without wit or courage.
Changeling.　A child left by fairies in exchange for a good child they steal.
Child.　A man of childish thoughts.
Clod.　Dull, stupid fellow.
Clodhopper.　An awkward fellow.
Clodpate. }
Clodpoll. } A stupid fellow.
Clotpate.　A clodpate.
Clotpoll.　A clodpoll.
Crone.　An old, withered, foolish person, generally a woman.
Dizzard.　A blockhead.
Dolt.　A stupid person.
Donkey.　Figuratively, a person with the stupid nature of an ass.
Doodle.　A simple idler.
Dotard.　A foolishly fanciful person, on account of age or extravagant affection.
Driveler.　Idle talker.
Dullard.　A dull or stupid person.
Dullhead.　One slow to learn or perceive.
Dunce, etc.　An ignorant, ridiculous person.　See SCHOLAR-DUNCE.
Dunderhead. }
Dunderpate. } A blockhead.
Fool.　One lacking common sense or the power to learn.
Gaby.　One who gabs.
Giddyhead.　A foolish, reckless person.
Gobemouche [F.].　A simple, credulous person.
Goose.　A silly creature.
Goose-cap.　A silly person.
Gowk.　An awkward fool.
Greenhorn, etc.　One who has not learned.　See GULL.
Grosshead.　A thick-headed person.
Half-wit.　A person of weak mind.
Hoddy-doddy.　A foolish, awkward person.
Hoodlum.　A young rowdy.
Idiot.　One who lacks the power of knowing and learning.
Imbecile.　One of feeble mind.
Infant.　One knowing no more than an infant.
Innocent.　One harmlessly foolish.
Jobbernowl.　A blockhead.
Jolterhead. }
Jolthead. } A dunce.
Lack-brain. }
Lack-wit. } A person of weak mind.
Loggerhead.　A stupid or thick-headed person.
Looby.　Lubber.
Loon.　A dull, stupid person.
Lout.　Awkward fool.
Lown.　A loon.
Lubber, etc.　A bungling, ignorant fellow.　See ADEPT-BUNGLER.
Madman, etc.　A person who is insane.　See SANENESS-MANIAC.
Men of Bœotia.　Foolish people: from Bœotia, Greece, noted for the ignorance of its inhabitants.
Milksop.　A soft, silly fellow.
Moon-calf.　A stupid fellow.
Natural *niais* [F.].　A born fool.
Nincompoop.　A foolish or silly person.
Ninny. }
Ninnyhammer. } A foolish person.
Nizy.　A simpleton.
No conjurer.　A person not of the strongest wits.
Noddy.　A dunce; a fool.
Nonny.　A ninny.
Noodle.　A stupid or silly person.
Numps.　A blockhead.
Numskull.　A dunce.
Oaf.　A dolt or simpleton.

(*Continued on Column 1.*)

Sag″-it-ta′-ri-us.　A constellation.　ASTRONOMY.
sag′-it-ta-ry.　A centaur.　CONVENTIONALITY-UNCONVENTIONALITY.
Sa-ha′-ra.　A great desert in Africa.　FERTILITY-STERILITY.
sa′-hib.　A Moslem title.　GENTILITY-COMMONALTY.

said.　Previously mentioned.　ANTECEDENCE-SEQUENCE, PRECEDENCE-SUCCESSION, RECURRENCE; **it is said,** TIDINGS-MYSTERY; **more easily said than done,** DIFFICULTY-FACILITY; **thou hast said,** ASSENT-DISSENT.
sail.　To travel by water; to begin a voyage; **part of a**

ship. ARRIVAL-DEPARTURE, CONVEYANCE-VESSEL, TRAVELING-NAVIGATION; easy sail, TURBULENCE-CALMNESS; sail before the wind, WELFARE-MISFORTUNE; sail near the wind, SKILL-UNSKILFULNESS; sail too near the wind, RECKLESSNESS-CAUTION, SECURITY-INSECURITY; shorten sail, SWIFTNESS-SLOWNESS; take in sail, TURBULENCE-CALMNESS; take the wind out of one's sails, OBSTRUCTION-HELP; too much sail, RECKLESSNESS-CAUTION; under sail, TRAVELING-NAVIGATION.

sail'-er. A vessel that sails. CONVEYANCE-VESSEL.

sail'-ing. Setting forth on a voyage. TRAVELING-NAVIGATION; plain sailing, DIFFICULTY-FACILITY; sailing vessel, CONVEYANCE-VESSEL.

sail'-ma"-ker. One who manufactures sails. AGENT.

sail'-or. A seaman. WAYFARER-SEAFARER; fair weather sailor, ADEPT-BUNGLER.

saint. A holy or godly person; holy. ANGEL-SATAN, GODLINESS - UNGODLINESS, GOOD MAN - BAD MAN, REVELATION-PSEUDOREVELATION; tutelary saint, SECURITY-INSECURITY.

Saint El'mo's fire. A globular light, sometimes seen at night on the spar of a ship. PHENOMENON.

saint'-like". Like a saint. GODLINESS-UNGODLINESS.

saint'-ly. Like a saint. GODLINESS-UNGODLINESS, VIRTUE-VICE.

Saint Mon'day. Monday of Easter week. ENTERTAINMENT-WEARINESS.

saint sa chandelle, a chaque [F.] (san· sa shan·-del', a shak). To every saint his candle. DUENESS-UNDUENESS.

sais quoi, je ne [F.] (sê kwa, zhe ne). I know not what; something indefinite. WORD-NEOLOGY.

sake. Purpose of accomplishing or attaining. For goodness' sake, PETITION-EXPOSTULATION; for the sake of, MOTIVE-CAPRICE, OBSTRUCTION-HELP.

sa-laam'. An Oriental salutation. POLITENESS-IMPOLITENESS, REGARD-DISRESPECT.

sa'-la-ble. Fit to be sold. BUYING-SALE.

sa-la'-cious. Lustful. PURITY-IMPURITY.

sa-lac'-i-ty. Lustful quality. PURITY-IMPURITY.

sal'-ad. A vegetable mixed with meats. MIXTURE-HOMOGENEITY; salad oil, PULPINESS-OIL.

sal'-a-man"-der. A lizard-like reptile; an iron poker. OVEN-REFRIGERATOR.

sal'-a-ry. Pay or wages. LABOR-CAPITAL, RECOMPENSE-PUNITION.

sale. Exchange of property for money or its equivalent. BUYING-SALE; bill of sale, SECURITY; for sale, BUYING-SALE, EXCHANGE, PROFFER-REFUSAL.

sal"-e-bros'-i-ty. Quality of being uneven. SMOOTHNESS-ROUGHNESS.

sal'-e-brous. Uneven. SMOOTHNESS-ROUGHNESS.

sales'-man. One who sells goods. DEALER.

sa'-li-ent. Standing out prominently. CONSEQUENCE-INSIGNIFICANCE, CONVEXITY-CONCAVITY, MANIFESTATION-LATENCY, SHARPNESS-BLUNTNESS; salient angle, ANGULARITY; salient points, CONSEQUENCE-INSIGNIFICANCE.

sa'-line. Salty. PUNGENCY.

sa-li'-va. Spittle. FRICTION-LUBRICATION, NUTRIMENT-EXCRETION.

sal"-i-va'-tion. Ptyalism. NUTRIMENT-EXCRETION.

salle-à-manger [F.] (sal'-a-man·"-zhê'). Dining-room. CONTENTS-RECEIVER.

sal'-low. An unhealthy yellowish color. COLOR-ACHROMATISM, YELLOWNESS-PURPLE.

sal'-ly. A sudden attack; sudden overflow of spirits. ARRIVAL - DEPARTURE, ATTACK - DEFENSE, WITTINESS-DULNESS.

sal'-ly-port". A gate or passage for attacking parties. ATTACK-DEFENSE, ENTRANCE-EXIT.

sal"-ma-gun'-di. A dish of chopped meat with dressing. MIXTURE-HOMOGENEITY.

salm'-on–col'-ored. A reddish orange color. REDNESS-GREENNESS.

sa"-lon'. Drawing-room. CONTENTS-RECEIVER.

sa-loon'. An apartment or hall devoted to some specific use; a place where liquor is retailed. CITY-COUNTRY, CONTENTS-RECEIVER.

salt. Sodium chlorid, used as a seasoning or preservative; wittiness; a compound. CHEMISTRY, CONDIMENT, CONSEQUENCE-INSIGNIFICANCE, CONSERVATION, MONEY, PUNGENCY, WITTINESS-DULNESS; below the salt, GENTILITY-COMMONALTY; salt of the earth, GOOD MAN-BAD MAN, GOODNESS-BADNESS; salt water, OCEAN-LAND; worth one's salt, USEFULNESS-USELESSNESS.

sal-ta'-tion. Act of jumping. SPRING-DIVE.

sal'-ta-to-ry. Moving by leaps. AGITATION, SPRING-DIVE.

saltimbanco [It.] (sal"-tim-ban'-co). A vender of quack medicines. GULL-DECEIVER.

salto, di [It.] (sal'-to, dî). At a leap. SPRING-DIVE.

salto in salto, di [It.] (sal'-to in sal'-to, dî). With leap after leap. SPRING-DIVE.

salt"-pe'-ter. Niter; a component of gunpowder. PUNGENCY.

saltum, per [L.] (sal'-tum, per). By leaps. AGITATION, CONTINUITY-INTERRUPTION.

sa-lu'-bri-ous. Wholesome. HEALTHINESS-UNHEALTHINESS.

sa-lu'-bri-ty. Healthfulness. HEALTHINESS-UNHEALTHINESS.

sal'-u-ta-ry. Beneficial. GOODNESS-BADNESS, HEALTHINESS-UNHEALTHINESS.

sal"-u-ta'-tion. Greeting. ADDRESS-RESPONSE, POLITENESS-IMPOLITENESS.

sa-lute'. To greet with a sign of welcome or respect. ADDRESS-RESPONSE, BLANDISHMENT, POLITENESS-IMPOLITENESS, REGARD-DISRESPECT, SOLEMNIZATION.

salute, alla vostra [It.] (sa-lu'-tê, al'-la vos'-tra). To your health. POLITENESS-IMPOLITENESS, SOCIABILITY-PRIVACY.

sal"-u-tif'-er-ous. Health-giving. HEALTHINESS-UNHEALTHINESS, REMEDY-BANE.

salva res est [L.] (sal'-va rîz est) It is safe. SECURITY-INSECURITY.

salva sit reverentia [L.] (sal'-va sit rev-er-en'-shi-a). Let there be due reverence. REGARD-DISRESPECT.

sal'-va-ble. Capable of being saved or redeemed. INNOCENCE-GUILT.

sal'-vage. Compensation allowed for saving a ship. GAIN-LOSS, PRICE-DISCOUNT, RECOMPENSE-PUNITION.

sal-va'-tion. Deliverance from impending evil or destruction. CONSERVATION, DIVINITY, GODLINESS-UNGODLINESS, RESCUE; work out one's salvation, DEVOTION-IDOLATRY.

salve. A thick adhesive ointment. ALLEVIATION-AGGRAVATION, REMEDY-BANE.

sal'-ver. A tray. CONTENTS-RECEIVER.

sal'-vo. A discharge of artillery; a saving clause. CONVENTIONALITY - UNCONVENTIONALITY, CRASH-DRUMMING, JUSTIFICATION-CHARGE, MODIFICATION-PRETEXT, SOLEMNIZATION; salvo of artillery, SOLEMNIZATION.

Sa-mar'-i-tan. A native of Samaria; a humane person. Good Samaritan, BENEFACTOR-EVILDOER, CHARITABLENESS-MALEVOLENCE.

same. Not different. SAMENESS-CONTRAST, SYNONYM-ANTONYM; all the same to, SENSITIVENESS-APATHY; at the same time, COEXISTENCE - COMPENSATION; go over the same ground, RECURRENCE; in the same boat, ANTAGONISM-CONCURRENCE; in the same breath, COEXISTENCE, ETERNITY-INSTANTANE-

ITY; **of the same mind,** ASSENT-DISSENT; **on the same tack,** ANTAGONISM-CONCURRENCE.

same'-ness. Lack of change or variety. LIKENESS-UNLIKENESS, SAMENESS-CONTRAST.

SAMENESS—CONTRAST.

Actual thing. Identical thing.
Alter ego [L.]. Another self. See LIKENESS.
Coalescence. Blending; the act of becoming identical.
Coincidence. The act of agreeing or becoming identical.
Convertibility. Capability of being made identical.
Equality, etc. The state of being of the same value or magnitude, etc. See EQUALITY.
Facsimile. An exact copy. See COPY.
Idem [L.]. The same.
Identification. The process of making identical.
Identity. The state of being identical.
Ipsissima verba [L.]. The very words. See TRUTH.
Monotony. The use of identically the same tone or pitch.
No other. }
One and the same. } The identical one.
Oneself. One's identical self.
Same. The identical thing or person.
Sameness. Lack of variety.
Self. That which has distinct individuality.
Selfness. Individuality; separate identity.
Self-same. The identical person or thing.
Tautology, etc. Needless repetition of identical words or ideas, etc. See sub REPETITION.
Very same. Identically the same.
Very thing. Identically the thing.

SAMENESS—Verbs.

Be identical, etc. Be exactly the same, etc. See *Adjectives.*
Coalesce. Become identical.
Coincide. To have the same condition or quality.
Identify. Prove to be the same or identical.
Recognize the identity of. To see the likeness between.
Render identical. }
Render the same. } To make alike.
Treat as identical. }
Treat as the same. } To treat as if equal or the same.

SAMENESS—Adjectives.

Coalescent. Agreeing.
Coincident. Occurring at identically the same time.
Coinciding. Having identically the same condition or quality.
Cotidal. Indicating simultaneity in tides.
Equivalent, etc. Identical in value, etc. See EQUALITY.
Identical. Precisely the same.
Ilk. Identical.
Indistinguishable. Showing no difference.
Much of a muchness. Very similar.
Much the same. Identical in many respects.
One. }
Self. } Identical.
Self-same. The very same.
The same, etc. The identical, etc. See *Nouns.*
Unaltered. Not modified.

SAMENESS—Adverbs, etc.

Identically, etc. In the same manner, etc. See *Adjectives.*
On all fours. Corresponding identically.

CONTRAST—Continued from Column 2.

CONTRAST—Adverbs, etc.

Contra [L.]. Opposed to.
Contrarily, etc. In opposition, etc. See sub *Adjectives.*
Contrariwise. Oppositely.
Nay rather. On the contrary.
On the contrary. In opposition.
On the other hand, etc. In opposition, etc. See COMPENSATION
Per contra [L.]. Oppositely.
Vice versa [L.]. Terms being exchanged

Antagonism, etc. Active mutual opposition, etc. See ANTAGONISM.
Antithesis. The balancing of contrasted words or thoughts.
Contradiction. Opposition; something said oppositely to what has been said.
Contrariety. The quality of being opposite.
Contrast Oppositeness between things which have similar qualities.
Inversion, etc. The state of being inverted or the act of transposing, etc. See REVERSAL.
Oppositeness. State of being opposite or contrary.

CONTRAST—Denotations.

Foil. Anything serving by contrast to adorn or set off to advantage something different or superior.
The antipodes. Places situated on the opposite sides of the earth.
The converse. That which exists in a reciprocal or converse relation to something.
The inverse. That which is opposed in order or effect.
The opposite. One who or that which is in marked contrast.
The other extreme. That which opposes or is adverse.
The reverse. That which is directly opposite or contrary.

CONTRAST—Verbs.

Antagonize, etc. Oppose, etc. See ANTAGONISM.
Be contrary, etc. Be opposite, etc. See *Adjectives.*
Contradict. Oppose.
Contrast with. Set in opposition with.
Contravene. Obstruct; oppose.
Differ *toto cœlo.* To be directly opposite.
Invert. To place in an opposite position.
Oppose. Resist.
Reverse. To move in an opposite way.
Turn the tables. An expression taken from the changes of fortune in gambling; change to an opposite condition.

CONTRAST—Adjectives.

Antagonistic. Opposing.
Antipodean. Relating to the opposite side of the world.
Antithetical. Directly opposite.
As opposite as black and white. }
As opposite as fire and water. }
As opposite as light and darkness. } Directly opposite.
As opposite as the poles. }
At cross purposes. Having opposite purposes.
Conflicting. Opposing.
Contradictory. Contradictory statements cannot be both true.
Contrariant. Opposed; antagonistic.
Contrarious. Showing oppositeness; repugnant.
Contrary. Opposite; adverse.
Contrasted. Opposed; placed in comparison.
Converse. Turned about so that opposite parts are changed about.
Counter. Opposing.
Dead against. Vigorously opposed to.
Diametrically opposite. Opposite as the two extremities of a diameter.
Differing *toto cœlo.* Directly opposite.
Hostile, etc. Opposed, etc. See ANTAGONISM.
"Hyperion to a satyr." [Shak.] Hyperion was the god of the sun and noted for his beauty; a satyr is part man, part goat : hence, as opposite as beauty and ugliness. [*Hamlet,* I, ii.]
Inconsistent. Self-opposing; not agreeing with each other.
Just the other way. Exactly opposite.
Negative. Opposite of positive.
No such thing. Not this, but the opposite or the other.
Opposed. Contrary; opposite; adverse.
Opposing. Contrary; antagonistic.
Opposite. Contrary; different.
Quite the contrary. }
Quite the reverse. } Quite the opposite.
Reverse. Opposite.
Tout au contraire [F.]. Quite the opposite.

(*Continued on Column* 1.)

---

sa'-mi-el. The simoom. RIVER-WIND.
Sam'-ma-el. A demon. ANGEL-SATAN.
sam'-pan. A Chinese boat. CONVEYANCE-VESSEL.
sam'-ple. A portion representative of the whole. CONVENTIONALITY-UNCONVENTIONALITY

Sam'-son. A Biblical strong man. STRENGTH-WEAKNESS.
san'-a-ble. Curable. RENOVATION-DETERIORATION.
sana, mens [L.] (sē'-na, mens). A sound mind. SANENESS-LUNACY.

sana mens in corpore sano [L.] (sê'-nɑ mens in cor'-por-î sê-no). Sound mind in a sound body. PLEASURE-PAIN.

sa-na'-tion. A healing. RENOVATION-RELAPSE.

san'-a-tive. Having power to heal. HEALTHINESS-UNHEALTHINESS, REMEDY-BANE.

san''-a-to'-ri-um. A health retreat. REMEDY-BANE.

san'-a-to-ry. Healing. HEALTH-SICKNESS, REMEDY-BANE.

sanc''-ti-fi-ca'-tion. Act of setting apart as holy. DIVINITY, GODLINESS-UNGODLINESS.

sanc'-ti-fied. Consecrated. GODLINESS-UNGODLINESS.

sanc'-ti-fy. To make holy. DIVINITY, GODLINESS-UNGODLINESS.

sanc''-ti-mo'-ni-ous. Affecting piety. REVELATION-PSEUDOREVELATION.

sanc''-ti-mo'-ni-ous-ness. Affected piety. GODLINESS-UNGODLINESS.

sanc'-ti-mo-ny. Affected saintliness. GODLINESS-UNGODLINESS.

sanc'-tion. Ratification. APPROVAL-DISAPPROVAL, DUENESS-UNDUENESS, LEAVE-PROHIBITION.

sanc'-tioned. Ratified. DUENESS-UNDUENESS.

sanc'-ti-tude. Sacred character. GODLINESS-UNGODLINESS.

sanc'-ti-ty. Spiritual purity. GODLINESS-UNGODLINESS.

sanc'-tu-ar''-y. A holy or sacred place. FANE, REFUGE-PITFALL.

sanc'-tum. A sacred spot; a private room. CONTENTS-RECEIVER; **sanctum sanctorum,** DWELLER-HABITATION, FANE, SOCIABILITY-PRIVACY.

sand. Rock material coarser than dust. FRIABILITY; **built upon sand,** SECURITY-INSECURITY; **sow the sand,** USEFULNESS-USELESSNESS.

san'-dal. A kind of shoe. DRESS-UNDRESS.

sand'-blind''. Partially blind. SIGHT-BLINDNESS.

San''-de-ma'-ni-an. A Christian sect. ORTHODOXY-HETERODOXY.

sand'-i-ness. The state or quality of containing sand. FRIABILITY.

sand'-pa''-per. Paper coated with sand used for smoothing. SMOOTHNESS-ROUGHNESS.

sands. Stretches of sandy beach. REFUGE-PITFALL.

sand'-storm''. A high wind which carries sand along. FRIABILITY.

sand'-wich-wise''. Like a sandwich. ENVIRONMENT-INTERPOSITION.

sandy. Of the color of sand. FRIABILITY, YELLOWNESS-PURPLE.

sane. Mentally sound. SANENESS-LUNACY.

sane'-ly. In a sane manner. SANENESS-LUNACY.

sane'-ness. Soundness of mind. SANENESS-LUNACY.

SANENESS—LUNACY.

Lucid interval. A period of mental clearness.
Lucidity. The condition or quality of being lucid.
Mens sana [L.]. Sound mind.
Rationality. The state or quality of being rational.
Sanity. The state or quality of being sane.
Senses. Intellectual powers of perception.
Sober senses. Rational powers of mind.
Sobriety. The state or quality of being sober.
Sound mind. A mind not enfeebled or deranged.
Soundness, etc. The quality of being sound.

SANENESS—*Verbs.*

Become sane, etc. To come into the full possession of one's senses. See *Adjectives.*
Be sane, etc. To be mentally sound. See *Adjectives.*
Bring to one's senses. Cause to think rationally.
Come to one's senses. Begin to think rationally.
Render sane, etc. To cause to be free from mental derangement. See *Adjectives.*
Retain one's reason. } To continue in the full possession of will and
Retain one's senses. } reason.
Sober. To cause to think seriously
Sober down. To become sober.

SANENESS—*Adjectives.*

Compos mentis [L.]. Of a sound mind.
In one's right mind. Having power to think rightly.
In one's sober senses. Free from mental derangement.
In possession of one's faculties. Having power to think.
Of sound mind. Not enfeebled or deranged.
Rational. Having the power of reasoning.
Reasonable. Having the faculty of reasoning.
Sane. Having power to reason; mentally sound.
Self-possessed. In control of one's faculties.
Sober. Not swayed by excitement or passion.
Sober-minded. Having a cool, dispassionate mind.
Sound. Having the faculties of the mind in normal action and relation.
Sound-minded. Of such degree of mental capacity as makes a person responsible for his acts.

SANENESS—*Adverbs.*

Sanely, etc. In a sane manner.

LUNACY—*Continued from Column 2.*

Rabies. Hydrophobia or dog madness, as in man.
Rats in the upper story. A lack of mental power.
Raving. Insanity accompanied by wild and incoherent utterances.
Screw loose. A mental deficiency.
Siriasis. Sunstroke. [Sirius the Dog Star.]

Aberration. Partial insanity.
Abnormal mind. A mind not performing the proper functions
Amentia. Total absence of mental power.
Bee in one's bonnet. Something wrong in the mental faculties.
Calenture of the brain. A delirious, fanciful state of the mind.
Coup de soleil [F.]. Sunstroke.
Craze. An intense, impassionate, insane desire or liking for something.
Delirium. An irrational temporary condition of the mind accompanied by hallucinations.
Delusion. A false conception and persistent belief, unconquerable by reason.
Demency. Dementia.
Dementation. Loss of power to reason.
Dementia. Unsoundness of mind, with loss of power of coherent thought.
Derangement. Unbalanced reason.
Dipsomania. Uncontrollable passion for drink.
Diseased mind. A mind that fails in its normal action.
Disordered intellect. } Mental derangement.
Disordered reason. }
Dizziness. A feeling of whirling and confusion in the head.
Dotage, etc. Weakness of mind from old age. See MIND-IMBECILITY.
Eccentricity. Peculiarity of intellect.
Fanaticism. Fierce, extravagant zeal or conduct.
Frenzy. Great agitation approaching distraction.
Furor. Overpowering rage.
Hallucination. Mistaken perception of what does not exist.
Hypochondriasis, etc. Disorder of mind causing melancholy views, especially of health.
Hysteria. Violent nervous excitement, accompanied by paroxysms of laughing and crying.
Incoherence. A lack of connection or reasonableness of thought
Infatuation. An insane passion or love for anything.
Insanity. Morbid condition of mind from disease, with loss of power of rational thought and action.
Kleptomania. An uncontrollable desire and inclination to steal
Lunacy. Intermittent insanity.
Lycanthropy. Madness with belief that one is a wolf.
Madness, etc. The quality of being mad. See *Adjectives.*
Mania. Raving insanity.
Melancholia. A depressing, gloomy state of mind, sometimes verging upon insanity.
Mental alienation. Entire or partial loss of mental power.
Monomania. Mental derangement with reference to one craze.
Oddity. Erratic difference of conduct from what is normal or common.
Phrenitis. } Frenzy
Phrensy. }

(*Continued on Column* 1.)

LUNACY—*Continued.*

Slate loose. Mental deficiency.
Sunstroke. Disturbance of the brain caused by excessive heat, especially of the sun.
Swimming. Dizziness.
Tile loose. Mental deficiency.

Twist. Distinctive character or peculiarity.
Unsound mind. A mind unable to perform its normal functions.
Unsoundness. Deficiency of mental stability.
Vertigo. Giddiness.
Wandering. Deliriousness.

LUNACY—*Verbs.*

Addle the wits To confuse.
Avoir le diable au corps [F.]. To have a devil.
Become insane, etc. To lose control of one's mental faculties. See *Adjectives.*
Befool. To delude.
Be insane, etc. To be mentally deranged. See *Adjectives.*
Dementate. Deprive of reason.
Derange the head. To make crazy.
Dote. To be weak-minded from old age.
Drivel, etc. To be silly and foolish. See MIND-IMBECILITY.
Drive mad. To make crazy.
Go mad. To become insane.
Have a devil. To be crazy.
Have a screw loose. To be mentally deficient.
Infatuate. To inspire with passion too obstinate to be controlled by reason.

Lose one's faculties. To become weak-minded.
Lose one's head, etc. To lose presence of mind. See CERTAINTY-DOUBT.
Lose one's reason. }
Lose one's senses. } To lose control of one's reason and judgment.
Lose one's wits. }
Madden. To make or render mad.
Ramble. To talk foolishly and incoherently.
Rave. To talk wildly and violently.
Render mad. To make crazy.
Run mad. To become insane.
Turn one's head. To affect mentally.
Turn the brain. To craze.
Wander. To be out of one's mind.

LUNACY—*Adjectives.*

Aliéné [F.]. Mad.
Bereft of reason. Crazy.
Beside oneself Not in usual mental condition.
Bewildered, etc. Confused or uncertain in mind. See CERTAINTY-DOUBT.
Corybantic. Frenzied, like the priests of Cybele.
Cracked. Having mental defects.
Crack-brained. Weak-minded.
Crazed. Rendered crazy.
Crazy. Disordered in intellect; lacking power of rational thought.
Daft. Weak-minded.
Delirious. In a state of delirium.
Demented. Lacking power to reason.
Distracted. Wildly confused.
Distraught. Distracted.
Dithyrambic. Passionately or wildly lyrical.
Doting. Characterized by dotage.
Eccentric. Very peculiar in thought and ideas.
Fanatical. Characterized by fanaticism.
Far-gone. Almost hopelessly insane.
Flighty. Slightly delirious.
Frantic. Wildly distracted, as by fear or grief.
Frenetic. Frenzied.
Frenzied. Affected with frenzy.
Giddy. Light-headed.
Haggard. Weakened by great anxiety of mind.
Hypped. Offended or melancholy.
Hyppish. Hypped.
Imbecile. Weak-minded.
Incoherent. Talking aimlessly.
Infatuated. Filled with an uncontrollable passion.
Insane. Showing symptoms of insanity.
Insensate. Showing a lack of sense.
Light-headed. Wanting soundness of mind.
Lunatic. Subject to lunacy; moonstruck.
Mad. Disordered in mind and bereft of self-control.
Mad as a hatter. }
Mad as a March hare. } Very mad.
Mad-brained Crazy.
Maddened. Made insane. See *Verbs.*
Maniacal. Affected with mania.
Mazed. Bewildered.

Moonstruck. Lunatic.
Non compos mentis [L.]. Not of sound mind.
Not in one's right mind. Crazy.
Not right Mentally wrong.
Not right in one's head. }
Not right in one's mind. } Mentally deranged; crazy.
Not right in one's upper story. }
Not right in one's wits. }
Odd. Having peculiar or strange ideas.
Of unsound mind, etc. Crazy. See *Nouns.*
Out of one's mind. }
Out of one's senses. } Unable to control one's will and judgment.
Out of one's wits. }
Phrenetic. Frenetic.
Phrensied. Frenzied.
Possessed. Beyond self-control.
Possessed with a devil. Mad.
Rabid. Affected with rabies; raging mad.
Rambling. Uttering incoherent words.
Raving. Past reason or being reasoned with.
Reasonless. Bereft of reason.
Scatter-brained. With little brains.
Shatter-brained. }
Shatter-pated. } Disordered in mind.
Silly, etc. Lacking good common sense.
Stark staring mad. Wholly and completely destitute of all power of rational thought or action.
Touched. Mentally affected.
Touched in one's head. }
Touched in one's mind. }
Touched in one's upper story. } Slightly insane.
Touched in one's wits. }
Unhinged. Not mentally sound.
Unsettled in one's mind. Deranged.
Vertiginous. Affected with dizziness.
Wandering. Without control of one's mental faculties. See *Verbs.*
Wild. Mad beyond control.
Wrong in one's head. }
Wrong in one's mind. }
Wrong in one's upper story. } Mentally weak.
Wrong in one's wits. }

LUNACY—*Adverbs, etc.*

Like one possessed. Wildly; furiously.

LUNACY—*Phrases.*

Ira furor brevis est [L.]. Anger is a brief madness.
Tête-exaltée [F.]. To be crack-brained.

Tête-montée [F.]. To be crack-brained.
The mind having lost its balance.

SANENESS—MANIAC.

MANIAC.

Automaniac. One who has worked himself into insanity.
Bedlamite. A madman or inmate of Bedlam, the hospital of St. Mary of Bethlehem in London.
Candidate for Bedlam. A person who should be sent to Bedlam; a crazy person.

Dipsomaniac. One who has an uncontrollable desire for strong drink.
Don Quixote. The hero of Cervantes's romance, *Don Quixote;* a country gentleman who becomes half-crazed by reading romances of chivalry.
Dreamer, etc. One who forms projects but does not act. See FANCY.

SANENESS—MANIAC—*Continued.*

Energumen. One who is possessed by evil spirits.
Enthusiast. One who is passionately devoted to a person, principle, or object.
Exalté [F.]. An enthusiast.
Fanatic. One who is moved by a frenzy of enthusiasm.
Fanatico [It.]. A fanatic.
High-flier. One who is extravagant in his opinions or pretensions.
Hypochondriac, etc. One who is affected with a mental disorder which causes gloom and melancholy. See LIGHTHEARTEDNESS-DEJECTION.
Idiot, etc. One destitute of normal intellectual powers. See SAGE-FOOL.
Kleptomaniac. One who has an uncontrollable passion for stealing.

Knight errant. One of the wandering knights who in the Middle Ages went forth in search of adventures fitted to exhibit their military skill or chivalry toward women.
Lunatic. A person bereft of reason; moonstruck.
Madcap. A person who acts in a rash or giddy manner.
Madman. A person deranged or frantic.
Maniac. A person raving with madness.
Monomaniac. A person affected with insanity confined to one idea or object.
Raver. A madman.
Rhapsodist. One who expresses himself with exaggeration of sentiment.
Seer. One who sees visions of imaginary objects.

sang″-froid′. Cold blood; steadiness of nerve. EXCITABILITY-INEXCITABILITY, RECKLESSNESS-CAUTION, SENSITIVENESS-APATHY.
san′-gui-na-ry. Bloody. LIFE-KILLING.
san′-guine. Hopeful; red. FANCY, FAITH-MISGIVING, REDNESS-GREENNESS, SANGUINENESS-HOPE-LESSNESS; sanguine expectation, EXPECTATION-SURPRISE, SANGUINENESS-HOPELESSNESS; sanguine imagination, FANCY.
san′-guine-ness. Hopefulness. SANGUINENESS-HOPELESSNESS.

SANGUINENESS—HOPELESSNESS.

Affiance. Trust; confidence; reliance.
Anticipation, etc. A previous view or impression of something that will happen afterwards. See EXPECTATION.
Aspiration. The act of strongly desiring.
Assumption. The act of taking anything for granted.
Assurance. The state of being full of confidence or trust.
Bright prospect. A cheerful reason for hoping.
Buoyancy. Cheerfulness; confidence.
Cheer. The state of being in a state of good spirits.
Confidence. The act of confiding or trusting.
Desire, etc. A strong natural longing or craving for something. See DESIRE.
Enthusiasm. Ardent and eager interest for some cause, study, or the like.
Faith, etc. Intellectual conviction. See FAITH.
Fervent hope. Eager, ardent hope.
Good auspices. Favorable omens.
Good omens. Favorable signs or indications.
Good prospects. A cheerful and hopeful lookout.
Hope. A desire for some good accompanied by a belief that it is attainable.
Hopefulness. The state of being full of hope.
Hopes. Prospects.
Optimism. The doctrine that everything is ordered for the best.
Optimist. One who believes in optimism.
Presumption. The act of believing on probable evidence.
Promise. Ground for hope.
Reassurance. Confirmation repeated.
Reliance. The state of having confidence or trust.
Sanguine expectation. Hopeful expectation.
Sanguineness. The state of being full of hope and confidence.
Secureness. Confidence of safety.
Security. The state or condition of being free from trouble, anxiety or the like.
Trust. Confidence in.
Utopist. One who believes in a state or place of ideal perfection.
Well-grounded hope. Hope founded on a good basis.

SANGUINENESS—*Figurative Nouns.*

Airy hopes. Expectation without solid foundation.
Anchor. That on which we place dependence for safety.
Balm in Gilead. Anything that soothes the mind. [Bible.]
Beam of hope. A ray or gleam of hope.
Bit of blue sky. A slight ground of hope.
Bottom of Pandora's box. Hope.
Castles in the air. A visionary project.
Châteaux en Espagne [F.]. Castles in Spain; a baseless scheme.
Clear sky. A promising outlook.
Dawn of hope. The beginning of promise.
Day-dream. A vain fancy or speculation.
Dream of Alnaschar. A visionary project. [*Arabian Nights.*]
Flash of hope. A sudden promise of success.
Fond hope. Longing or yearning.
Fool's paradise. The region of vanity and nonsense.
Gleam of hope. ⎫ A sudden, slight ground for success.
Glimmer of hope. ⎭
Golden dreams. Eminently auspicious hopes.
Heart of grace. Courage.

Dashed hopes. Broken hopes.
Despair. Utter loss of hope.
Desperation. The state of despair or hopelessness.
Despondency, etc. Abandonment of hope. See LIGHTHEARTED-NESS-DEJECTION.
Forlorn hope. Lost hope.
Hope deferred. Hope delayed.
Hopelessness, etc. The state of being without hope. See *Adjectives.*
Pessimism. The view of looking at the bad side of everything or considering the world the worst possible world.
Pessimist. One who believes in pessimism.
Vain expectations, etc. Hopes that cannot be attained. See EXPECTATION-DISAPPOINTMENT.

HOPELESSNESS—*Figurative Nouns.*

Airy hopes, etc. Hopes founded on no foundation. See SANGUINENESS.
Bad business. ⎫ Work causing loss or injury.
Bad job. ⎭
Bird of bad omen. ⎫ Any unfavorable indication.
Bird of ill omen. ⎭
Black spots in the horizon. Unfavorable indications.
Cave of despair. Figuratively, a feeling of utter hopelessness.
Enfant perdu [F.]. The lost child.
Gloomy spots on the horizon. Unfavorable signs.
Job's comforter. A tactless person who, under pretense of sympathy, insinuates rebukes.
Slough of despond. A position of hopelessness.

HOPELESSNESS—*Verbs.*

Abandon all hope. To give up hope.
Crush one's hope. To break down one's hope.
Dash one's hopes. To ruin one's hopes.
Despair. To give up all hope.
Despond, etc. To lose hope or courage. See LIGHTHEARTEDNESS-DEJECTION.
Destroy one's hopes. To set one's hopes at naught.
Disconcert. To break the composure of a person.
Drive to despair. To impel to loss of hope.
Falter. To hesitate; lose hope.
Give over. To abandon completely.
Give up. To yield.
Give up all hope. To yield to despair.
Hope against hope. To be in a state of despair.
Inspire to despair, etc. To infuse despair into. See *Nouns.*
Jeter le manche après la cognée [F.]. To throw the helve after the hatchet; to give up the last possible hope.
Lose all hope. To give up all hope.
Relinquish all hope. To renounce all hope.
Relinquish the hope of. To give up all hope of attaining.
Yield to despair. To give up to despair.

HOPELESSNESS—*Adjectives.*

At one's last gasp, etc. Deprived of all hope. See LIFE-DEATH.
Au désespoir [F.]. In despair.
Beyond remedy. Not capable of being remedied.
Broken-hearted. Crushed with grief or despair.

SANGUINENESS—HOPELESSNESS—*Continued.*

SANGUINENESS—Figurative Nouns—*Continued.*

Heaven. The place of supreme blessedness.
Le pot au lait [F.]. The pot of milk.
Mainstay, etc. Main support. See Suspension-Support.
Millennium. The period of the reigning of Christ on earth.
Mirage, etc. A false hope or expectation. See Sight-Dimsighted-ness.
Ray of hope. A slight gleam of hope.
Sheet-anchor. The best hope or refuge.
Silver lining of the clouds. A bright prospect. [Milton, *Comus*, 221.]
Staff. That which upholds.
Star of hope. A favorable omen.
Utopia. An imaginary island enjoying the greatest perfection in politics, laws, and the like. [More.]

SANGUINENESS—*Verbs.*

Anticipate. To expect or look ahead towards.
Assure. To render confident.
Augur well. To portend favorably.
Be hopeful, etc. To be sanguine or full of hope. See *Adjectives.*
Be in a fair way. To be in a favorable condition.
Be of good cheer. } Sanguine or hopeful.
Be of good heart. }
Bid fair. To offer a good prospect.
Buoy up. To keep from sinking into despondency.
Catch at a straw. To hope against hope.
Cheer. To encourage; make hopeful.
Cherish hope, etc. To entertain hope. See *Nouns.*
Cling to hope, etc. To adhere to hope. See *Nouns.*
Confide. To trust; have confidence.
Embolden. To make bold; encourage.
Encourage. To inspire with hope; to hearten.
Encourage hope, etc. To inspire hope. See *Nouns.*
Entertain hope, etc. To cherish hope. See *Nouns.*
Expect, etc. To look forward to something which is expected to happen. See Expectation.
Feed hope, etc. To encourage hope. See *Nouns.*
Feel assured. } To feel hopeful.
Feel confident. }
Feel hope, etc. To be conscious of hope. See *Nouns.*
Flatter. To encourage with false hopes.
Flatter oneself. To deceive oneself with false hopes.
Foster hope, etc. To cherish or encourage hope. See *Nouns.*
Give hope, etc. To impart hope. See *Nouns.*
Harbor hope, etc. To entertain hope. See *Nouns.*
Hold out hope, etc. To extend or offer hope. See *Nouns.*
Hope. To cherish something good with the expectation of obtaining it.
Hope against hope. To hope when all ground for hope is gone.
Hope for, etc. To desire; long for. See Desire.
Hope for the best. To desire the best.
Indulge hope, etc. To harbor hope. See *Nouns.*
Inspire hope, etc. To fill with hope. See *Nouns.*
Keep one's spirits up. To maintain a state of cheerfulness or hopefulness.
Lay the flattering unction to one's soul. To please with false hopes. [Shakespeare, *Hamlet*, III, iv.]
Lean upon. To depend upon for support.
Live in hope, etc. To be in a state of hope. See *Nouns.*
Look on the bright side of. To look at things in a favorable light.
Look up. To seek with the hope of finding.
Make the best of it. To reduce to the least possible inconvenience.
Nourish hope, etc. To support or encourage hope. See *Nouns.*
Pin one's faith upon, etc. To put one's faith in. See Faith.
Pin one's hope upon, etc. To put one's hope in. See Faith.
Presume. To believe by anticipation.
Promise. To give reason to expect; afford hopes.
Promise oneself. To have strong confidence.
Put a bold face upon. }
Put a good face upon. } To look favorably upon something unpleasant.
Put the best face upon. }
Put one's trust in. To place one's confidence in.
Raise expectations.
Raise hope, etc. To arouse hope. See *Nouns.*
Reassure. To restore courage or hope.
Reckon one's chickens before they are hatched. To confidently expect to obtain something which one never may obtain.
Rely on. To have confidence in.
Rest assured. } To remain hopeful. See *Adjectives.*
Rest confident. }
See land. To have cause for hope.
Take heart. To gain confidence.

HOPELESSNESS—Adjectives—*Continued.*

Clouded over. Made gloomy.
Cureless. Beyond all hope of living.
Despairing. Being without hope.
Desperate. Beyond hope; desponding.
Forlorn. Abandoned; lost.
Given over. Completely abandoned.
Given up. Ceasing from effort.
Hopeless. Despairing; without hope.
Ill-omened. Unfortunate.
Immedicable. Incurable.
Immitigable. Not capable of being appeased.
Impracticable, etc. Incapable of being practised. See Possibility-Impossibility.
Inauspicious. Unfavorable; unlucky.
Inconsolable, etc. Grieved beyond comfort. See Lighthearted-ness-Dejection.
Incorrigible. Bad beyond correction.
Incurable. Not to be cured.
In despair. Without hope.
Irreclaimable. Incapable of being reclaimed.
Irrecoverable. Not capable of being restored or remedied.
Irredeemable. Incapable of being redeemed or recovered.
Irremediable. Incapable of being cured.
Irreparable. Not capable of being recovered.
Irretrievable. Incurable.
Irreversible. Irrevocable.
Irrevocable. Incapable of being recalled.
Not to be thought of. Not to be considered.
Out of the question. Not worthy of consideration.
Past cure. }
Past hope. } With no chance of recovery.
Past mending. }
Past recall. }
Remediless. Not capable of being remedied.
Ruined. Seriously damaged or impaired.
Threatening. Menacing.
Undone. Ruined in reputation or morals.
Unpromising. Not affording a favorable aspect.
Unpropitious. Unfavorable.

HOPELESSNESS—*Phrases.*

Its days are numbered.
Lasciate ogni speranza voi ch'entrate [It.]. All hope abandon, ye who enter here. [Dante. Inscription over the gate of hell.]
The worst come to the worst.

SANGUINENESS—Verbs—*Continued.*

Take heart of grace. To be encouraged.
Tell a flattering tale. To tell a deceitful story.
Trust. To confide in; hope.
View on the sunny side. To look upon in a favorable light.
Voir en couleur de rose [F.]. To see in rose-color or a favorable light.

SANGUINENESS—*Adjectives.*

Auspicious. Favorable; hopeful.
Bright. Cheerful; encouraging.
Buoyant. Lively; cheerful.
Buoyed up. Kept from despondency.
Cheering. Encouraging.
Confident. Having trust; trustful.
Couleur de rose [F.]. Rose-colored.
De bon augure [F.]. Of good omen.
Elated. Filled with confidence and hope.
Encouraging. Furnishing ground to hope for success.
Enthusiastic. Eager and zealous in the pursuit of an object.
Exempt from despair. }
Exempt from distrust. }
Exempt from fear. } To remove doubt or want of faith.
Exempt from suspicion. }
Exultant. Triumphant.
Fearless. Without fear.
Flushed. Elated; animated with joy.
Free from despair. }
Free from distrust. } To remove causes of hopelessness or want of
Free from fear. } expectation.
Free from suspicion. }
Full of promise. Likely to fulfil expectations.
Hoping, etc. Having confidence or a desire for something good. See *Verbs.*
Hopeful. Full of expectation.

SANGUINENESS—Adjectives—Continued.

In good heart. In a state of confidence or kindliness.
In hopes, etc. Hoping. See *Nouns*.
Inspiriting. Encouraging; animating.
Looking up. Hoping.
Of good omen. Propitious; favorable.
Of promise. Tending to cause hope.
On the highroad to. On the way to success or completion.
Probable. Likely.
Promising. Affording hopes.
Propitious. Favorable; hopeful.
Reassuring. Restoring confidence to.
Roseate. Full of roses; blooming; promising.

Rose-colored. Alluring.
Sanguine. Full of hope; not desponding.
Secure, etc. Free from care, anxiety, or the like; confident. See FAITH.
Self-reliant. Having confidence in oneself.
Undespairing. Not despairing; hopeful.
Unsuspecting. Not distrusting.
Unsuspicious. Not suspicious.
Utopian. Involving imaginary perfection.
Within sight of land. } In a hopeful condition.
Within sight of shore. }

SANGUINENESS—Adverbs.

Hopefully, etc. In a hopeful manner. See *Adjectives*.

SANGUINENESS—Interjection.

Godspeed! Success to you!

SANGUINENESS—Phrases.

Ægroto dum anima est spes esse dicitur [L.]. When there is life to the sick man, there is said to be hope. [Cicero, *Atticus*, 9, 10.]
All is for the best. "All things work together for good." [Bible.]
Ante victoriam ne canas triumphum [L.]. Do not chant your triumph before you conquer.
At spes non fracta [L.]. But hope is not broken.
Dum spiro, spero [L.]. While I breathe, I hope. [Motto of South Carolina.]
En Dieu est ma fiance [F.]. In God is my trust.
Expertus metuit [L.]. Having had experience, he fears.
"**Hope told a flattering tale.**" Hope inspired one with a false and deceitful prospect. [*The Universal Songster.*]
In hoc signo spes mea [L.]. In this sign is my hope.

In hoc signo vinces [L.]. In this sign thou wilt conquer. [Motto of Emperor Constantine.]
La speranza é il pan de' miseri [It.]. Hope is the bread of the wretched.
Latet scintillula forsan [L.]. Perhaps a small spark may lie hid.
Never say die. Never give up hope.
Nil desperandum [L.]. Never despair. [Horace, *Odes*, I, vii, 27.]
Rusticus expectat dum defluit amnis [L.]. The rustic waits until the river shall have flowed by. [Horace, *Epistles*, I, ii, 42.]
Spero meliora [L.]. I hope for better things.
The wish being father to the thought. A striving for what one desires. [Shakespeare, *Henry IV*, II, iv, 5.]
Voilà le soleil d'Austerlitz [F.]. Behold the sun of Austerlitz. [Napoleon.]

SANGUINENESS—TIMIDITY.

TIMIDITY.

Abject fear, etc. Fear that reduces one to a low degraded state. See BRAVERY-COWARDICE.
Affright. Sudden and great fear or terror.
Affrightment. Affright; terror.
Ague fit. A state of shaking, as from terror.
Alarm. An apprehension of sudden danger which springs from a sense of immediate danger.
Anxiety. Concern about some future event which disturbs the mind.
Apprehension. A sense of danger or fear of something remote but approaching.
Apprehensiveness, etc. The state or quality of being fearful. See *Adjectives*.
Awe. Dread or fear inspired by something great, terrible, or sublime.
Care. Fear for safety or prosperity.
Cold sweat. A chilling feeling caused by fear.
Consternation. Fear which confounds the faculties and incapacitates them for considering.
Despair, etc. Utter hopelessness, or fear for a result. See SANGUINENESS-HOPELESSNESS.
Despondency. Depression of the mind.
Diffidence. Fear caused by lack of confidence in one's powers.
Dismay. A helpless sinking of heart caused by fright or some calamity.
Disquietude. Uneasiness; anxiety.
Dread. Terror aroused by the anticipation of a great evil.
Fear. An emotion excited by the expectation of evil and accompanied with a desire to escape it.
Fear and trembling. The emotion and physical effect excited by the expectation of something evil.
Fearfulness, etc. The state of being fearful. See *Adjectives*.
Flutter. Agitation of the mind arising from fear, etc.
Fright. An emotion excited by a sudden apprehension of danger.
Heart-quake. } Fear.
Heart-sinking. }
Hesitation. Doubt caused by fear of consequences. See DETERMINATION-VACILLATION.
Horror. A painful emotion of dread, fear, and abhorrence.
Inquietude. The state of being disturbed either in body or mind.
Intimidation. The state of being frightened.
Misgiving. The state of being deprived of confidence.
Mistrust, etc. Want of confidence. See FAITH-MISGIVING
Mortal funk. A shrinking back through fear.
Nervousness. State or quality of being timid.
Palpitation. A rapid pulsation of the heart caused by fear.
Panic. A sudden fright affecting numbers at once.

Perturbation. Agitation of mind caused by fear.
Qualm. A sudden attack of pain or distress.
Quivering. A trembling, as from fear.
Restlessness, etc. Uneasiness caused by evil. See *Adjectives*.
Scare. Sudden fright produced by a trifling cause.
Shaking. A trembling or quaking.
Solicitude. Uneasiness of mind occasioned by fear of evil.
Suspicion. A feeling of mistrust or fear.
Terror. Sudden abject fear.
Throbbing heart. A mark of fear.
Timidity. The state or quality of wanting courage to face a danger.
Trembling. An involuntary shaking with fear.
Tremor. A shivering or shaking as with fear.
Trepidation. A state of terror or alarm.
Want of confidence. Timidity.

TIMIDITY—Nouns of Cause.

Bête noir [F.]. A black beast.
Bugaboo. Anything imaginary that causes needless fright.
Bugbear. Something causing needless fright.
Enfant terrible [F.]. Terrible child; one that annoys by ill-timed remarks.
Few faw fum. A mysterious jargon to awe the foolish or ignorant. [*Jack the Giant Killer.*]
Gorgon. One of three fabled sisters, with snaky hair and of terrific aspect, the sight of whom turned the beholder to stone.
Hobgoblin, etc. A frightful goblin. See CONCEIT.
Hurlothrumbo. The chief character in a whimsical play entitled *Hurloth rumbo, or the Supernatural.*
Morm. A false terror.
Nightmare. A fiend supposed to cause trouble in sleep.
Raw head and bloody bones. Sights that inspire fear and terror.
Reign of Terror. A period of bloodshed and anarchy, especially in the French Revolution.
Scarecrow. Anything terrifying without danger.
Stampede. Any sudden flight or dispersion in consequence of a panic.
Terrorism. A mode of government by terror or intimidation.

TIMIDITY—Verbs.

Abash. To destroy the self-possession of.
Affright. To fill with sudden fear.
Alarm. To surprise with the apprehension of danger; to call to arms.
Appall. To depress with fear so that the mind shrinks.
Apprehend. To fear.
Astound. To strike dumb with surprise; to thunderstrike.
Awe. To strike with reverence and fear.

TIMIDITY—*Continued.*

Be afraid, etc. To be fearful. See *Adjectives.*
Blanch. To cause to become white, as from fear or terror.
Browbeat. To bear down or intimidate with a stern or haughty look.
Bully. To insult in a more blustering than courageous manner.
Cow. To depress with fear.
Cower. To bend down with fear.
Crouch. To stoop lowly and with meanness or fear.
Cry "wolf." To give a false alarm. [Æsop's fable.]
Daunt. To restrain by fear.
Deter. To prevent by fear.
Discourage. To deprive of confidence, to dishearten.
Dismay. To bring into a state of deep and gloomy apprehension.
Disquiet. To make uneasy or disturb the tranquillity of.
Distrust, etc. To have no confidence in. See FAITH-MISGIVING.
Excite awe. To arouse awe.
Excite fear. To arouse fear.
Eye askance. To look upon with doubt.
Falter. To tremble.
Fear. To be in apprehension of evil.
Flinch. To withdraw from pain or danger.
Flutter. To throw into confusion.
Fly, etc. To run away from danger or alarm. See QUEST-EVASION.
Fright. To alarm with danger.
Frighten. To disturb with fear.
Fright from one's propriety. To disturb with fear so that one neglects or transgresses propriety.
Fright out of one's senses.
Fright out of one's seven senses. } To frighten that one does not know what to do.
Fright out of one's wits.
Funk. To shrink back from fear.
Give an alarm. To notify of danger.
Grow pale. To become white from fear.
Harrow upon the soul. To torment or harass the soul.
Haunt. To inhabit as a ghost.
Have qualms, etc. To have scruples of conscience. See *Nouns.*
Hesitate, etc. To waver; be uncertain as to the outcome. See DETERMINATION-VACILLATION.
Horrify. To fill with horror and dread.
Inspire awe. To fill with or cause awe.
Inspire fear. To fill with or cause fear.
Intimidate. To make timid or fill with fear.
Let "I dare not" wait upon "I would." Do not say "I would," but " I dare not."
Make one's blood run cold. To cause one to be very much frightened.
Make one's flesh creep. To frighten one very much.
Make one's hairs stand on end. To cause one to be much terrified.
Make one's teeth chatter. To terrify.
Make one tremble, etc. To cause one to quake.
Not dare to say one's soul is one's own. To be very much frightened.
Overawe. To restrain by awe or fear.
Petrify. To become stone from fear.
Prey on the mind. To trouble the mind.
Put in bodily fear. To put in fear of bodily injury.
Put in fear. To bring into a condition of fear.
Quail. To sink into dejection.
Quake. To shake with fear.
Quaver. To tremble.
Quiver. To tremble or quake.
Raise an alarm. To create a feeling of danger.
Raise apprehensions. To raise causes for fear.
Scare. To frighten.
Shake. To tremble; quiver.
Shake all over. To tremble very much.
Shake like an aspen-leaf. To be thoroughly frightened.
Shiver. To quake or tremble.
Shiver in one's shoes. To tremble from fright.
Shrink. To recoil from in fear or horror.
Shudder. To tremble with horror or fear.
Shy. To start aside suddenly from fright.
Sit upon thorns. To be in a state of apprehension or nervous excitement.
Skulk, etc. To get out of the way of danger in a sneaking, cowardly manner. See BRAVERY-COWARDICE.
Sound an alarm. To give notice of danger.
Stand aghast. To stand stupefied with sudden fright.
Stand in awe of. To be in fear of.
Start. To move suddenly, as from surprise, pain, or fear.
Startle. To excite by sudden alarm.
Stop one's breath. To cause one's breath to cease.
Strike all of a heap. To surprise or frighten utterly.
Strike an awe into. To fill with awe.
Strike terror. To cause terror.
Take alarm. To become alarmed.

Take away one's breath. To frighten utterly.
Take fright. To become frightened.
Terrify. To fill with terror or fear.
Terrorize. To strike with terror.
Threaten, etc. To hold up as a terror. See CHARITABLENESS-MENACE.
Tremble. To shake from fear.
Tremble all over. To be much frightened.
Tremble like an aspen-leaf. To be frightened so as to tremble very much.
Turn pale. To become pale.
Unman. To deprive of courage.
Weigh on the mind. To burden or trouble the mind.
Wince. To shrink from.

TIMIDITY—*Adjectives.*

Afraid. Somewhat impressed with fear.
Afraid of one's own shadow. Needlessly or excessively afraid.
Aghast. Stupefied with sudden horror or fright.
Alarming. Causing apprehension of danger.
Apprehensive. Fearful of or expecting danger.
Awe-inspiring. Filling with awe.
Awestricken.
Awestruck. } Impressed with awe.
Awful. Frightful; horrible.
Breathless. Out of breath, as from fright or violent exercise.
Coy. Shrinking from approach.
Diffident. Not self-reliant; suspicious.
Dire. Horrible; dreadful; dismal.
Direful. Dreadful; terrible.
Dread. Exciting apprehension or great fear.
Dreadful. Inspiring dread or fear.
Faint-hearted. Not courageous; timorous.
Fearful. Inspiring horror or fear.
Fearing, etc. Being filled with fear. See *Verbs.*
Fearsome. Easily frightened; timid.
Fell. Fierce; barbarous.
Fidgety. Restless; nervous; uneasy.
Formidable. Adapted to cause fear or shrinking from.
Frightened, etc. Excited by fright. See *Verbs.*
Frightened to death. Very much frightened.
Ghastly. Horrible; shocking; dreadful.
Haunted with the fear of. Continually fearing something.
Horrible. Inspiring horror.
Horrid. Disagreeable; horrible.
Horrific. Causing horror.
Horror-stricken.
Horror-struck. } Impressed with awe.
In a fright, etc. Frightened. See *Nouns.*
In fear, etc. Fearing. See *Nouns.*
In hysterics. In a state of excessive nervous excitement, as hysteria.
Inspiring fear, etc. Causing or filling with fear. See *Nouns.*
More frightened than hurt. Very much frightened, but little hurt.
Nervous. Having weak nerves; easily excited.
Pale as a ghost.
Pale as ashes. } Thoroughly overcome by fright.
Pale as death.
Panic-stricken.
Panic-struck. } Impressed or filled with panic.
Perilous, etc. Full of risk; dangerous. See SECURITY-INSECURITY.
Portentous. Foreshadowing ill.
Redoubtable. Formidable; dreadful.
Restless. Uneasy; disturbed.
Revolting, etc. Shocking; offensive. See PLEASURABLENESS-PAINFULNESS.
Shaky. Trembling.
Shocking. Striking with horror.
Terrible. Exciting terror; dreadful.
Terrific. Adapted to excite great fear or dread.
Terror-stricken.
Terror-struck. } Impressed with terror.
Timid. Wanting courage; easily frightened.
Timorous. Fearful of danger.
Tremendous. Adapted to excite dread or fear.
Tremulous. Shaking; quivering.
White as a sheet. Pale from fear.

TIMIDITY—*Adverb.*

In terrorem [L.]. In terror.

TIMIDITY—*Phrases.*

"Angels and ministers of grace defend us." [Shakespeare, *Hamlet,* I, iv.]

TIMIDITY—*Continued.*

Ante tubam trepidat [L.]. He trembles even before the trumpet sounds.

Expertus metuit [L.]. Having experienced, he fears. [Horace, *Epistles*, I, xviii, 87.]

Horresco reperens [L.]. I shudder to relate.

Obstupui steteruntque comæ et vox faucibus hæsit [L.]. I was amazed, and my hair stood on end and my voice clung in my throat. [Virgil, *Æneid*. iii, 204.]

One's heart failing one. One's courage leaving one. Virgil, *Æneid*, ii, 774.]

san-guin′-o-lent. Bloody. LIFE-KILLING.

San′-he-drim. The supreme council of the Jewish nation. CHURCH, COUNCIL.

sa′-ni-es. Discharge from an ulcer. LIQUID-GAS.

sanitaire, cordon [F.] (sa-ni-têr′, cor-don·′). A guard to prevent the spread of disease. CONSERVATION, SECURITY-INSECURITY.

san′′-i-ta′-ri-an. Relating to the public health. HEALTHINESS-UNHEALTHINESS.

san′′-i-ta′-ri-um. A health retreat. HEALTHINESS-UNHEALTHINESS.

san′-i-ta-ry. Relating to preservation of health. HEALTHINESS-UNHEALTHINESS.

san′-i-ty. Soundness of mind. HEALTH-SICKNESS, SANENESS-LUNACY.

sans [F.] (san·). Without. PRESENCE-ABSENCE.

sans cérémonie [F.] (san· sê-rê-mo-nî′). Without ceremony. AMITY-HOSTILITY, SOCIABILITY-PRIVACY.

sans culotte [F.] (san·′′ cü′′-lot′). Without breeches; one of a revolutionary mob. GENTILITY-COMMONALTY, INSUBORDINATION-OBEDIENCE.

sans facon [F.] (san· fa-son·′). Without fashion. CONCEIT-DIFFIDENCE, EMBELLISHMENT-SIMPLICITY, SOCIABILITY-PRIVACY.

sans pareil [F.] (san· pa-rey′). Without an equal. SUPREMACY-SUBORDINACY.

sans peur et sans reproche [F.] (san· pur ê san· reprosh′). Without fear and without reproach. FAULTLESSNESS-FAULTINESS, REPUTATION-DISCREDIT, UPRIGHTNESS-DISHONESTY.

sans souçi [F.] (san· su′′-sî′). Without care. CONTENTEDNESS-DISCONTENTMENT, PLEASURE-PAIN, SENSITIVENESS-APATHY.

San′-skrit. The oldest Indo-European language. NOVELTY-ANTIQUITY.

santé, maison de [F.] (san·-tê′, mê-zon·′ de). An insane retreat. REMEDY-BANE.

Santiago [Sp.] (san-tî-a′-go). St. James; a Spanish battle-cry. PATRIOTISM-TREASON.

santo diavolo vecchio, giovine [It.] (san′-to dî-a-vo′-lo vech′-î-o, jo-vî′-nê). Young saint, old devil. GODLINESS-UNGODLINESS.

san′-ton. A Mohammedan hermit. MINISTRY-LAITY, SOCIABILITY-PRIVACY.

sap. The juice of plants; to wear away gradually; to undermine. ATTACK-DEFENSE, BETTERMENT-DETERIORATION, CONVEXITY-CONCAVITY, CREATION-DESTRUCTION, LIQUID-GAS, SUBJECTIVENESS-OBJECTIVENESS; **sap the foundations,** BETTERMENT-DETERIORATION, CREATION-DESTRUCTION.

sap′-id. Having flavor. SAVOR-TASTELESSNESS.

sa′-pi-ent. Wise. SAGACITY-INCAPACITY.

sapienti, sat est, dictum [L.] (sê-pi-en′-tai, sat est, dic′-tum). A word to the wise is sufficient. ENOUGH, HEED-DISREGARD.

sapientes, tenus barba [L.] (sê-pi-en′-tîz, tî′-nus bar′-ba). Sages as far as the beard. SAGE-FOOL.

sap′-less. Destitute of sap. DAMPNESS-DRYNESS, STRENGTH-WEAKNESS.

sap′-ling. A young tree. INFANT-VETERAN.

sap′′-o-na′-ceous. Soapy. PULPINESS-OILINESS.

sap′′-o-rif′-ic. Imparting a taste. SAVOR-TASTELESSNESS.

sap′-per. A soldier employed in making trenches; a wood-turning tool. BELLIGERENT, CONVEXITY-CONCAVITY.

sap′-pers and mi′-ners. Soldiers employed in undermining. PREPARATION-NONPREPARATION.

Sap′-phic. A verse or stanza in poetry. POETRY-PROSE.

sap′-phire. A gem of a blue color. BLUENESS-ORANGE, EMBELLISHMENT-DISFIGUREMENT.

sap′-py. Full of sap; young; silly. INFANCY-AGE, LIQUID-GAS, SAGACITY-INCAPACITY.

sara, sara, che [It.] (sa′-ra, sa′-ra, kê). What will be, will be. VOLITION-OBLIGATION.

sar′-a-band. A Spanish dance. ENTERTAINMENT-WEARINESS.

sar′-casm. A scornful or taunting expression. ADULATION-DISPARAGEMENT, APPROVAL - DISAPPROVAL, REGARD-DISRESPECT, RHETORIC.

sar-cas′-tic. Keen or taunting. ADULATION-DISPARAGEMENT, POLITENESS-IMPOLITENESS, REGARD-DISRESPECT, RHETORIC, SOCIETY-DERISION.

sar-co′-ma. A tumor. CONVEXITY-CONCAVITY.

sar-coph′-a-gus. A stone coffin. LIFE-FUNERAL.

sar′′-cu-la′-tion. Raking together. MULTIPLICITY-PAUCITY.

sard. A blood-red gem. EMBELLISHMENT-DISFIGUREMENT.

Sar′′-da-na-pa′-lus. A king of ancient Assyria. MODERATION-VOLUPTUARY.

sar-don′-ic. Sneering; mocking. ADULATION-DISPARAGEMENT, APPROVAL-DISAPPROVAL; **sardonic grin,** APPROVAL-DISAPPROVAL, JUBILATION-LAMENTATION, SOCIETY-DERISION.

sar′-do-nyx. A variety of onyx. EMBELLISHMENT-DISFIGUREMENT.

sark. A shirt. DRESS-UNDRESS.

sar-to′-ri-al. Pertaining to a tailor. DRESS-UNDRESS.

sash. An ornamental band around the waist. CIRCLE-WINDING.

sas′-sa-fras. A tree of the laurel family whose roots are used as a stimulant. PERFUME-STENCH, REMEDY-BANE.

Sa′-tan. The devil. ANGEL-SATAN.

sa-tan′-ic. Devilish. ANGEL-SATAN, CHARITABLENESS-MALEVOLENCE, VIRTUE-VICE.

Sa′-tan-ism. Satanic doctrine. ANGEL-SATAN.

satch′-el. A small hand-bag. CONTENTS-RECEIVER.

sate. To satisfy the appetite. DESIRE-REPLETION.

sat′-el-lite. A secondary planet; a servant. ANTAGONIST-ASSISTANT, ASTRONOMY, CHIEF-UNDERLING, LEADING - FOLLOWING, SOLITUDE-COMPANY, UNIVERSE.

sa′-ti-ate. Gratify to the utmost. DESIRE-REPLETION, PLEASURABLENESS-PAINFULNESS.

sa′-ti-at′′-ed. Well satisfied; surfeited. DESIRE-REPLETION.

sa-ti′-e-ty. State of being satisfied to the utmost. DESIRE-REPLETION, ENOUGH.

sat′-in. A silk fabric with glossy surface. SMOOTHNESS-ROUGHNESS.

sat′-ire. Keenness of wit and ridicule. APPROVAL-DISAPPROVAL, SOCIETY-DERISION.

sa-tir′-ic-al. Ridiculing. ADULATION-DISPARAGEMENT, APPROVAL-DISAPPROVAL.

sat′-i-rist. A writer of satires. FLATTERER-DEFAMER.

sat′-i-rize. Ridicule. APPROVAL-DISAPPROVAL, SOCIETY-DERISION.

satis, eheu jam [L.] (sê′-tis î′-hiu jam). Alas, it is sufficient. DESIRE-REPLETION.

sat″-is-fac′-tion Making of amends, reparation, or payment. ATONEMENT, CONTENTEDNESS - DISCONTENTMENT, DESIRE-REPLETION, DUTY-DERELICTION, ENOUGH, OBSERVANCE-NONOBSERVANCE, PLEASURE-PAIN, SETTLEMENT-DEFAULT, STRIFE-PEACE; **hail with satisfaction,** APPROVAL-DISAPPROVAL.

sat″-is-fac′-to-ri-ly. Giving satisfaction. FAITH-MISGIVING, GOOD-EVIL.

sat″-is-fac′-to-ry. Answering fully all requirements. CONTENTEDNESS-DISCONTENTMENT, ENOUGH, FAITH-MISGIVING, GOODNESS-BADNESS, PLEASURABLENESS-PAINFULNESS.

sat′-is-fied″. Contented. CONTENTEDNESS - DISCONTENTMENT, FAITH-MISGIVING.

sat′-is-fy. To cause to have enough; to free from doubt; to pay a debt. CONSENT, CONTENTEDNESS-DISCONTENTMENT, DESIRE-REPLETION, ENOUGH, FAITH-MISGIVING, INVESTIGATION-ANSWER, OBSERVANCE-NONOBSERVANCE, PLEASURABLENESS-PAINFULNESS, RECOMPENSE - PUNITION, SETTLEMENT - DEFAULT; **satisfy an obligation,** DUTY-DERELICTION; **satisfy oneself,** FAITH-MISGIVING.

satis superque [L.] (sē′tis siu-per′-quî). Enough and more. EXCESS-LACK.

sa′-trap. Governor of a Persian province. CHIEF-UNDERLING.

sat′-u-rate. To fill to the utmost extent. DAMPNESS-DRYNESS, DESIRE - REPLETION, ENTIRETY - DEFICIENCY.

sat″-u-ra″-ted. Filled with. DAMPNESS-DRYNESS, MAGNITUDE-SMALLNESS.

sat″-u-ra″-tion. Full impregnation. DESIRE - REPLETION, ENTIRETY-DEFICIENCY.

Sat′-urn. A planet. ASTRONOMY.

Sat″-ur-na′-li-a. The Roman feast of Saturn; season of revelry. ENTERTAINMENT-WEARINESS, MODERATION-SELFINDULGENCE, REGULARITY-IRREGULARITY.

Sa-tur′-ni-an. Characterized by virtue and happiness. INNOCENCE-GUILT, PLEASURABLENESS-PAINFULNESS; **Saturnian age,** WELFARE-MISFORTUNE.

Saturnia regna [L.] (sa-tur′-ni-a reg′-na). Saturnian reign. PLEASURE-PAIN, WELFARE-MISFORTUNE.

sat′-ur-nine. Gloomy disposition. LIGHTHEARTEDNESS-DEJECTION.

sat′-yr. An ugly woodland deity; a lascivious person. BEAUTY-UGLINESS, JOVE-FIEND, PURITY-RAKE.

sauce. An appetizing dressing for food; insolent language. CHARITABLENESS-CURSE, CONDIMENT, INCREMENT-REMNANT, MIXTURE-HOMOGENEITY; **pay sauce for all,** SETTLEMENT-DEFAULT.

sauce′-box″. A saucy person. BRAWLER, PRESUMPTION-OBSEQUIOUSNESS.

sauce′-pan″. A small cooking pan. CONTENTS-RECEIVER.

sauce piquante [F.] (sos pi-kan·t′). Cutting language. PLEASURABLENESS-PAINFULNESS.

sau′-cer. A small dish; widely opened eyes. CONTENTS-RECEIVER; **saucer eyes,** SIGHT-BLINDNESS.

sau′-ci-ness. Impudence. PRESUMPTION-OBSEQUIOUSNESS.

sau′-cy. Impertinently bold. POLITENESS-IMPOLITENESS, PRESUMPTION-OBSEQUIOUSNESS.

saun′-ter. To walk in an aimless manner. SWIFTNESS-SLOWNESS, TRAVELING-NAVIGATION.

saute aux yeux, cela [F.] (sot oz yu, se-la′). That leaps to the eyes. MANIFESTATION-LATENCY.

sau′-vage. Of a wild and untamed nature. SOCIABILITY-PRIVACY.

sauve qui peut [F.] (sov kî pu). Escape who can. ALARM, BRAVERY - COWARDICE, HURRY - LEISURE, QUEST-EVASION.

sav′-age. A man of the woods; uncivilized, brutal; fierce; cruel. BENEFACTOR-EVILDOER, BRAVERY-COWARDICE, CHARITABLENESS - MALEVOLENCE, FAVORITE - ANGER, GENTILITY - COMMONALTY, TASTE-VULGARITY, TURBULENCE-CALMNESS.

sav′-age-ry. Cruelty. CHARITABLENESS-MALEVOLENCE.

sa-van′-na. A tract of level land. GULF-PLAIN.

sa″-vant′. A professional scientist. KNOWLEDGE-IGNORANCE, SCHOLAR-DUNCE.

save. Keep from injury or evil; make allowance for; except. ADDITION - SUBTRACTION, CONSERVATION, CONVENTIONALITY-UNCONVENTIONALITY, GENEROSITY-FRUGALITY, INCLUSION - OMISSION, RESCUE, STORE; **God save,** DEVOTION-IDOLATRY, DIVINITY; **save and except,** ADDITION-SUBTRACTION, CONVENTIONALITY-UNCONVENTIONALITY; **save money,** GENEROSITY-FRUGALITY; **save one's bacon,** ESCAPE; **save the necessity,** DUTY-IMMUNITY; **save us,** OBSTRUCTION-HELP.

save′-all″. A contrivance for preventing waste. GENEROSITY-FRUGALITY.

saved. Preserved. RESCUE.

sa′-ving. Preservation from loss or danger; frugal; excepting. GENEROSITY-FRUGALITY; **saving clause,** MODIFICATION.

sa′-ving-ness. Frugality. GENEROSITY-FRUGALITY.

sa′-vings. Money saved from expenditure. GENEROSITY-FRUGALITY, STORE.

Sa′-viour. One who saves; Christ. BENEFACTOR-EVILDOER, DIVINITY.

savoir faire [F.] (sa-vwar′ fêr). To know how to do. SKILL-UNSKILFULNESS, SOCIETY-LUDICROUSNESS.

savoir gré [F.] (sa-vwar′ grê). To take it kindly. THANKFULNESS-THANKLESSNESS.

savoir vivre [F.] (sa-vwar′ vîvr). Good breeding. SKILL - UNSKILFULNESS, SOCIABILITY-PRIVACY, SOCIETY - LUDICROUSNESS.

sa′-vor. Quality that affects taste and smell. SAVOR-TASTELESSNESS; **savor of,** LIKENESS-UNLIKENESS; **savor of the reality,** PROPERTY.

SAVOR—TASTELESSNESS.

After-taste. A taste succeeding eating or drinking.
Degustation. A tasting.
Flavor. That quality which affects the taste.
Gust. The sense of tasting.
Gustation. The act of tasting.
Gusto. Keen enjoyment; relish.
Sapidity. Tastefulness.
Sapor. Taste; the power of affecting the organs of taste.
Savor. Flavor; taste.
Smack. } A taste or flavor, such as to suggest the quality of some-
Smatch. } thing tasted.
Tang. A strong or specific taste.
Taste. A certain sensation excited by some bodies when applied to the tongue and palate.
Tasting. The act of taking a taste.
Twang. A disagreeable after-taste left in the mouth.

Insipidity. The quality of being tasteless.
Tastelessness. The quality or state of having no distinctive **flavor.** See *Adjectives.*

TASTELESSNESS—*Verb.*

Be tasteless. Be without taste.

TASTELESSNESS—*Adjectives.*

Fade [F.]. Flat; tasteless.
Flat. Lacking taste.
Gustless. Without taste.
Ingustible. Having no taste.
Insipid. Tasteless.
Mawkish. Disgusting; insipid.
Mild. Having little taste.
Milk and water. Weak-tasting.

SAVOR—TASTELESSNESS—*Continued.*

SAVOR—*Nouns of Agent.*

Palate. An organ of taste.
Stomach. An organ of digestion.
Tongue. An organ of taste.
Tooth. An instrument of mastication.

SAVOR—*Verbs*

Flavor. To communicate a quality of taste to.
Savor. To have a particular taste.
Smack. To have a taste.
Smack the lips. To make a noise by separating the lips after tasting anything.
Smatch. To have a taste.
Taste. To try the flavor of.
Tickle the palate. To agreeably affect the taste. See PALATABLENESS.
Twang. To leave a disagreeable taste in the mouth.

TASTELESSNESS—ADJECTIVES—*Continued.*

Savorless. Tasteless.
Stale. Old to the taste.
Tasteless. Without a particular flavor
Untasted. Not having been tasted.
Vapid. Insipid.
Void of taste. Tasteless.
Weak. Defective in stimulative properties.
Wishy-washy. Very much diluted and weak to the taste.

SAVOR—*Continued.*

SAVOR—*Adjectives.*

Gustable. Pleasant to the taste.
Gustatory. Pertaining to the taste.
Palatable. Agreeable to the taste. See PALATABLENESS.
Sapid. Affecting the taste.
Saporific. Having the power to produce taste.
Strong. Forcibly affecting the taste.

sa'-vor-i-ness. Pleasant taste or smell. PALATABLENESS-UNPALATABLENESS.
sa'-vor-less. Tasteless. SAVOR-TASTELESSNESS.
sa'-vor-y. Palatable. PALATABLENESS-UNPALATABLENESS.
saw. A cutting tool; to cut with a saw; a worn-out saying. ADAGE-NONSENSE, INDENTATION, UNION-DISUNION; **saw the air,** SIGN.
saw'-der. Flattery. **Soft sawder,** ADULATION-DISPARAGEMENT, PRETEXT.
saw'-dust''. Fragments of wood cut out by a saw. FRIABILITY.
saw'-ney. A simpleton. SAGE-FOOL.
sax'-horn''. A brass wind-instrument. MUSICAL INSTRUMENTS.
Sax'-on. Pure idiomatic English. PURITY-CRUDENESS, SIMPLICITY-FLORIDNESS.
say. To utter words; suppose; testimony. ASSERTION-DENIAL, MAGNITUDE-SMALLNESS, SPEECH-INARTICULATENESS; **have one's say,** ASSERTION-DENIAL, SPEECH-INARTICULATENESS; **say by heart,** REMEMBRANCE-FORGETFULNESS; **say no,** ASSENT-DISSENT; **say nothing,** TALKATIVENESS-TACITURNITY; **say one's prayers,** DEVOTION-IDOLATRY; **say to oneself,** CONVERSATION-MONOLOGUE; **say what comes uppermost,** PREDETERMINATION-IMPULSE; **that is to say,** INTERPRETATION-MISINTERPRETATION; **what do you say to that,** ASTONISHMENT-EXPECTANCE; **you don't say so,** ASTONISHMENT-EXPECTANCE.
say'-ing. A statement; a maxim. ADAGE-NONSENSE, ASSERTION-DENIAL.
sbir'-ro. Italian police officer. JUDICATURE.
scab. A non-union workman. CONVENTIONALITY-UNCONVENTIONALITY.
scab'-bard. Sheath of a sword. CONTENTS-RECEIVER; **throw away the scabbard,** DETERMINATION-VACILLATION, FIGHTING-CONCILIATION.
scab'-by. Full of scabs; mean; vile. UPRIGHTNESS-DISHONESTY.
sca'-brous. Rough. SMOOTHNESS-ROUGHNESS.
scaf'-fold. An elevated structure. PREPARATION-NONPREPARATION, RECOMPENSE-SCOURGE, SUSPENSION-SUPPORT.
scaf'-fold-ing. A scaffold about a structure in course of preparation. PREPARATION-NONPREPARATION.
scagl-io'-la. Polished plasterwork, imitating marble or granite. TRUTHFULNESS-FRAUD.
scald. To burn with a hot liquid; a Scandinavian bard. HEATING-COOLING, POETRY-PROSE.
scale. To climb; an instrument for weighing; a graded series; to divide into portions. ASCENT-DESCENT, CONTINUITY-INTERRUPTION, COVER-LINING, HEAVINESS-LIGHTNESS, LAMINA-FIBER, MELODY-DISSONANCE, MENSURATION, STATION; **hold the scales,** DE-

CISION-MISJUDGMENT; **hold the scales even,** RIGHT-WRONG; **scales falling from the eyes,** SIGHT-BLINDNESS; **scales of justice,** RIGHT-WRONG; **scale the heights,** ASCENT-DESCENT; **scale the walls,** ATTACK-DEFENSE; **turn the scale,** CONVERSION-REVERSION, DOMINANCE-IMPOTENCE, EVIDENCE-COUNTEREVIDENCE, MOTIVE-CAPRICE.
sca-lene'. In geometry a triangle no two of whose sides are equal. ANGULARITY, PROPORTION-DEFORMITY.
scal'-lop. A semicircular curve in ornamental work. CIRCLE-WINDING, INDENTATION.
scalp. To denude. DRESS-UNDRESS.
scal'-pel''. A surgeon's knife. SHARPNESS-BLUNTNESS.
sca'-ly. Laminar. COVER-LINING, LAMINA-FIBER.
scam'-ble. To scatter. UNION-DISUNION.
scamp. A confirmed rogue. CAREFULNESS-CARELESSNESS, GOOD MAN-BAD MAN.
scamped. Performed carelessly or dishonestly. TRUTHFULNESS-FRAUD.
scam'-per. To run rapidly. SWIFTNESS-SLOWNESS; **scamper off,** QUEST-EVASION.
scamp'-ish. Rascally. VIRTUE-VICE.
scan. To examine carefully; to divide into metrical feet. HEED-DISREGARD, INVESTIGATION-ANSWER, KNOWLEDGE-IGNORANCE, POETRY-PROSE, SIGHT-BLINDNESS.
scan'-dal. Evil reports. ADULATION-DISPARAGEMENT, JUSTIFICATION-CHARGE, REPUTATION-DISCREDIT, TIDINGS-MYSTERY, VIRTUE-VICE.
scandaleuse, chronique [F.] (scan'-da-luz', cro-nĭk'). Chronicle of scandals. ADULATION-DISPARAGEMENT.
scan'-dal-ize. To bring into reproach. APPROVAL-DISAPPROVAL.
scan'-dal-ized. Brought into reproach. APPROVAL-DISAPPROVAL.
scan'-dal-mon-ger. One who spreads evil reports. TIDINGS-MYSTERY.
scan'-dal-ous. Disgraceful. REPUTATION-DISCREDIT, VIRTUE-VICE.
scandalum magnatum [L.] (scan'-dal-um mag-nê'-tum). Defamation of persons of rank and dignity. ADULATION-DISPARAGEMENT, JUSTIFICATION-CHARGE, REPUTATION-DISCREDIT.
scan'-dent. Climbing. ASCENT-DESCENT.
scant. Small in measure or quantity. BREADTH-NARROWNESS, EXCESS-LACK, GREATNESS-LITTLENESS, MAGNITUDE-SMALLNESS, MULTIPLICITY-PAUCITY.
scant'-i-ness. Meagerness. ENOUGH.
scant'-ling. A piece of timber; a set of dimensions; a rough sketch. BREADTH-NARROWNESS, COPY-MODEL, GREATNESS-LITTLENESS, MAGNITUDE-SMALLNESS, MULTIPLICITY-PAUCITY.
scant'-y. Small in quantity or number. BREADTH-NARROWNESS, EXCESS-LACK, GREATNESS-LITTLE-

NESS, MAGNITUDE - SMALLNESS, MULTIPLICITY - PAU-
CITY.

scape. To escape. ESCAPE.

scape'-goat". The sacrificial goat; a person made to bear the blame of another. ATONEMENT, COMMUTA-TION-PERMUTATION.

scape'-grace". An incorrigible fellow. GOOD MAN-BAD MAN, RECKLESSNESS-CAUTION.

scapin [F.] (sca-pan·'). A knave. GULL-DECEIVER, UPRIGHTNESS-ROGUE.

scap'-u-la. Shoulder-blade. ANATOMY.

scap'-u-lar. Pertaining to the scapula. **Scapular fossa,** ANATOMY

scap'-u-la-ry. Pertaining to the scapula, a garment of certain orders of monks. VESTMENTS.

scar. A mark left by an injury; indentation made by the waves. EMBELLISHMENT-DISFIGUREMENT, MARK-OBLITERATION, OCEAN-LAND.

scar'-a-mouch". A boastful, cowardly person. WAG.

scarce. Not plentiful; to be absent. EXCESS-LACK, FREQUENCY-RARITY; **make oneself scarce,** PRESENCE-ABSENCE, QUEST-EVASION.

scarce'-ly. Not quite; hardly. MAGNITUDE-SMALL-NESS; **scarcely any,** MULTIPLICITY-PAUCITY; **scarcely anything,** CONSEQUENCE-INSIGNIFICANCE; **scarcely ever,** FREQUENCY-RARITY.

scar'-ci-ty. Rarity. ENOUGH.

scare. To frighten. SANGUINENESS-TIMIDITY.

scare'-crow". Anything set up to scare birds from crops. BEAUTY-UGLINESS, SANGUINENESS-TIMIDITY.

scarf. A woven sash worn about the head and neck; a sash. DRESS-UNDRESS, VESTMENTS.

scarf'-skin". The outer layer of the skin. COVER-LINING.

scar'-i-fy. To scratch or make small incisions in. INDENTATION, PLEASURABLENESS-PAINFULNESS.

scar'-let. Bright red color. REDNESS-GREENNESS; **scarlet woman** [*Revelation* xvii, 4, 5], ORTHODOXY-HETERODOXY.

scarp. A steep slope. ATTACK-DEFENSE, PARALLEL-ISM-INCLINATION.

scath. To injure severely. BETTERMENT-DETERIORA-TION, GOODNESS-BADNESS.

scath'-ful. Injurious. GOODNESS-BADNESS.

scath'-less. Free from harm or injury. FAULTLESS-NESS-FAULTINESS.

scat'-ter. To throw around. CONCENTRATION-RADIA-TION, GATHERING-SCATTERING, ORGANIZATION-DIS-ORGANIZATION; **scatter to the winds,** CREATION-DE-STRUCTION, PROOF-DISPROOF.

scat'-ter-brained". Without concentration of mind. HEED-DISREGARD, SANENESS-LUNACY.

scat'-ter-ing. Dispersion. GATHERING-SCATTERING.

scat'-ter-ling. A vagrant. WAYFARER-SEAFARER.

scav'-en-ger. A street-cleaner. CLEANNESS-FILTHI-NESS.

scene. A locality; place represented on the stage; a display of passion. ACTING, APPEARANCE-DIS-APPEARANCE, EXCITABILITY-INEXCITABILITY, PAINT-ING; **scene of action,** LISTS.

scene'-paint"-er. One who paints scenes for theaters. ARTIST.

scene'-paint"-ing. Art of painting scenery. PAINT-ING.

sce'-ner-y. Appearance, view. APPEARANCE-DIS-APPEARANCE.

scen'-ic. Picturesque; pertaining to stage scenery or setting. ACTING.

scen-og'-ra-phy. Art of making drawings in perspec-tive. PAINTING.

scent'. Odor; to trace by the sense of smell; to per-ceive through some faint evidence. DISCOVERY, FAITH-MISGIVING, KNOWLEDGE-IGNORANCE, MARK-OBLITERATION, ODOR-INODOROUSNESS SIGN; **get**

scent of, ENLIGHTENMENT-SECRECY; **on the right scent,** INVESTIGATION-ANSWER; **on the scent,** INVES-TIGATION-ANSWER, QUEST-EVASION; **put on a new scent,** AIM-ABERRATION; **scent from afar,** PRE-VISION; **throw off the scent,** QUEST-EVASION.

scent'-bag". A scent-gland in an animal. PERFUME-STENCH.

scent'-ed. Perfumed. PERFUME-STENCH.

scent'-less. Without odor. ODOR-INODOROUSNESS.

scep'-ter. A staff or baton, as an emblem of au-thority. SCEPTER; **sway the scepter,** RULE-LICENSE.

SCEPTER.

Badge of authority. Anything that designates authority.

Baton. A rod or staff showing authority.

Cap of maintenance. Scarlet cap of velvet borne before English sov-ereigns at coronation.

Chair. The seat of one having power or authority.

Coronet. Crown of inferior rank.

Crown. The head-piece of a sovereign denoting his power.

Dais. A raised platform for the seats of those in power.

Decoration. Anything worn or carried as a designation of honor or authority.

Diadem. A crown.

Divan. A room of state.

Emblem. A flag or badge of office.

Ensign of authority. A distinguishing mark, as of rank or office.

Ermine. The official robe of a judge.

Fasces [L.]. A bundle of rods borne by lictors in ancient Rome, desig-nating authority.

Flag, etc. A piece of cloth, plain or otherwise, used as a standard or emblem of authority. See INDICATION.

Helm. The responsibility or office of government.

Insignia of authority. Things as badges, ribbons, etc., used as marks of distinction or office.

Key. A position or condition conveying authority or power.

Mace. A club-shaped staff symbolic of authority over a legislative body.

Mantle. A royal robe.

Musnud. A raised seat of honor.

Pall. A mantle; a Y-shaped figure designating the authority of a bishop.

Portfolio. The office of a cabinet minister.

Purple. A purple garment worn by kings; hence, kingly power.

Regalia. Whatever designates royalty.

Reins, etc. Restraint exercised by a governing power. See RE-LEASE-PRISON.

Robes of state. A garment worn as a badge of office or rank.

Rod of empire. The authority exercised by sovereignty. [Gray, *Elegy in a Country Churchyard.*]

Scepter. An ornamented staff symbolic of sovereignty.

Seal. That which confirms or ratifies authority.

Signet. A sovereign's private seal.

Staff. An emblem of authority; a baton or scepter.

Staff of office. A staff indicative of authority.

Talisman. Something that gives secret and wonderful power.

Throne. A royal chair of state.

Tiara. A head-dress showing princely rank.

Title, etc. An appellation of honor or authority; right to govern. See TITLE.

Toga. A Roman outer garment, the garb of the Roman senators.

Truncheon. Official badge of earl marshal of England.

Wand. A staff designating authority.

Woolsack. The cushion of the Lord Chancellor of England.

scep'-tic, or **skep'-tic.** A doubter of divine revelation. CREDULOUSNESS - SKEPTICISM, GODLINESS - DISBE-LIEF, ORTHODOXY-HETERODOXY.

scep'-tic-al, or **skep'-tic-al.** Like a skeptic. CREDULOUS-NESS-SKEPTICISM, GODLINESS-DISBELIEF.

scep'-ti-cism, or **skep'-ti-cism.** Attitude of doubt. CREDULOUSNESS - SKEPTICISM, FAITH - MISGIVING, GODLINESS-DISBELIEF.

sched'-ule. A list of times, prices, etc. RECORD.

sche'-ma-tist. A schemer. DESIGN.

scheme. A plan, or plot. DELINEATION-CARICATURE.

sche'-mer. One who devises schemes or plans. DE-SIGN.

sche'-mist. A schemer. DESIGN.

scher'-if. Chief administrative officer of a county CHIEF-UNDERLING, GENTILITY-COMMONALTY.

scher'-zo. A sportive movement in music. MUSIC.

sche'-sis. Disposition or condition. CONDITION-SITUATION.

schism. A splitting up in a Church. ASSENT-DISSENT, ORTHODOXY-HETERODOXY, VARIANCE-ACCORD.

schis-mat'·ic. Sectary. ASSENT-DISSENT, ORTHODOXY-HETERODOXY.

schis-mat'-ic-al. Promotive of division. ORTHODOXY-HETERODOXY

schis-mat'-i-cism. ORTHODOXY-HETERODOXY.

schism'-less. Free from division. ORTHODOXY-HETERODOXY.

schist'-ose. Having the quality of splitting or cleaving readily. LAMINA-FIBER.

schis-tos'-i-ty. The quality of splitting easily. GEOLOGY.

schis'-tous. Secondary foliation. LAMINA-FIBER.

schol'-ar. A person of high attainments; one acquiring knowledge. INSTRUCTOR - PUPIL, SCHOLAR-DUNCE.

SCHOLAR—DUNCE.

Academician. A member of an academy of art, etc.
Academist. An academic philosopher.
Admirable Crichton. A noted Scotch scholar and linguist.
Antiquarian. An antiquary.
Antiquary. A student of some particular subject of antiquity.
Archeologist. A student of archeology, the general science of antiquities.
Bas-bleu [F.]. A literary woman.
Bibliomaniac. One having a passion for collecting books.
Bigwig. An important person.
Bluestocking. A literary pedantic woman.
Bookworm. One who spends all his time with books.
Clerk. In the middle age, a learned person.
Connoisseur. One having a thorough knowledge of some fine art.
Criminologist. Student of criminals.
Dilettante [F.]. A dabbler in art, etc.
Doctor. One who has received the highest degree in a college or university, especially of medicine.
Doctrinaire. An impractical theorist.
Don. A person of or affecting importance.
Dr. Pangloss. A person who speaks all tongues; a philosopher and optimist.
Glossographer. One who writes explanatory notes.
Glossologist. One versed in the science of language.
Gownsman. A professional man who wears a gown.
Graduate. One who has graduated from a school of learning.
Grammarian One skilled in grammar.
Helluo librorum [L.]. Bookworm.
Homo multarum literarum [L.]. A man of many letters.
Illuminati. Persons professing special endowments.
Learned man. A man of education.
Learned Theban. A wise and learned man.
Lexicographer. One skilled in compiling of dictionaries.
Licentiate. One licensed to practise a profession.
Linguist. One knowing several languages or skilled in the science of language.
Literary man. A man versed in or devoted to literature.
Literati. Men of letters.
Litterateur. One studying language as a profession.
Mæcenas. A patron of art; the patron of the Roman poet Horace.
Man of education.
Man of learning. } A man developed and informed by study.
Man of letters. A man of literary culture.
Master of arts. One graduated in a classical course of study.
Mezzofanti. A linguist: after an Italian of that name.
Moonshee. A teacher, especially a Mohammedan teacher of languages.
Pantologist. One skilled in pantology.
Pedagogue. A teacher of young people.
Pedant. One making needless show of learning.
Penologist. Student of crime and criminals.

Agrammatist. A dunce.
Charlatan. One who makes extravagant pretensions of knowledge.
Dabbler. One having only superficial knowledge.
Dunce. A dull-witted person.
Fool. One having no sense or judgment; an idiot.
Greenhorn, etc. One lacking knowledge from experience. See GULL
Half scholar. A partially educated person.
Ignoramus. An ignorant, pretentious person.
Lubber. A bungling, inexperienced person.
No scholar. A man of no mental capacity.
Novice. One who is just learning.
Pedant, etc. A person who makes needless display of his learning. See SCHOLAR.
Sciolist. One pretending scientific knowledge.
Smatterer. A dabbler.
Tyro. A novice. See EDUCATION-PUPIL.
Wooden spoon. A dunce.

DUNCE—*Adjectives*.

Bookless. Unscholarly.
Ignorant, etc. Having no knowledge. See KNOWLEDGE-IGNORANCE.
Shallow. With only superficial knowledge.

SCHOLAR—*Continued*.

Philologist. One skilled in philology.
Philomath. One who loves learning.
Philosopher. A student of philosophy.
Professor. A teacher of the higher branches of learning.
Pundit. A learned man or one who makes pretensions to learning.
Sage. A man of well-known, thorough, and experienced learning and wisdom.
Savant. A man of exceptional learning.
Scholar. A man of exceptional literary ability and attainments.
Schoolboy. A boy attending school.
Schoolman. A theologian of the Middle Ages.
Scientist. One skilled in science.
Soph. A sophomore; a sophister.
Sophist. A member of a Greek school of philosophy.
Sophister. In England, one in the later years of a university course.
Wrangler. A man of high rank in English University of Cambridge.

SCHOLAR—*Adjectives*.

Brought up at the feet of Gamaliel. Having had the advantages of an excellent education. [Paul.]
Learned, etc. Trained and informed by study. See KNOWLEDGE.

SCHOLAR—*Phrases*.

Artium Baccalaureus [L.]. Bachelor of Arts: abbrev. A. B.
Artium Magister [L.]. Master of Arts: abbrev. A. M.

schol'-ar-ly. Indicative of great learning. EDUCATION-LEARNING.

schol'-ar-ship. The sum of mental attainments of a person. EDUCATION-LEARNING, KNOWLEDGE-IGNORANCE.

scho-las'-tic. Pertaining to scholars, education, or schools. EDUCATION-LEARNING, EDUCATION-MISTEACHING, KNOWLEDGE-IGNORANCE, SCHOOL.

scho'-li-ast. A commentator INTERPRETER-MISINTERPRETER.

scho'-li-um. An explanatory marginal note. ADAGE-NONSENSE, INTERPRETATION-MISINTERPRETATION.

school. An educational institution; a large multitude; pupils in an educational institution; disciples of a teacher or system. EDUCATION-MISTEACHING, FAITH-MISGIVING, GATHERING-SCATTERING, KNOWLEDGE-IGNORANCE, PAINTING, SCHOOL; **go to school,** EDUCATION-LEARNING; **school board,** SCHOOL; **send to school,** EDUCATION-MISTEACHING.

SCHOOL.

Abecedary. A primer.
Academy. A school of higher learning.
Alma mater [L.]. The name given by students to their college.
Ambo. A pulpit; a reading-desk.
Amphitheater. An oval or circular building with rising tiers of seats about an open space.

Boarding-school. A school at which the scholars board.

Board-school. A school managed by a school board.

British and Foreign School. An English school not supported by the Church.

Chair. A seat of office, as the chair of a professor.

Class. A number of students of the same rank in a school.

Cocker. An English authority on mathematics.

College. A society incorporated for study in the higher branches.

Collegiate school. A school under the auspices of a college.

Council of education. A body of persons having control of educational matters.

Crèche [F.]. A public nursery for poor children.

Dame's school. A school presided over by a woman, often old and with little education.

Day-school. A school taught during the day, where the pupils are not boarded.

Denominational school. A school presided over by some religious sect.

Desk. An inclined table used in schools.

Forum. A tribunal; a court.

Grammar. A treatise on the elements or principles of any science for use in schools.

Grammar-school. A school in which Latin and Greek grammar is taught.

Gymnasium. A school for physical exercise.

Hornbook. In early times, the book on which children learned their letters; a board with figures, letters and the Lord's Prayer on it, covered with thin transparent horn, and framed.

Hustings. A platform.

Infant-school. A school in which infants are taught.

Institute. } A society established for the furtherance of some par-
Institution. } ticular object.

Kindergarten [G.]. A school for small children in which object lessons are taught.

Lecture-room. A room used for lecture delivery.

Lectureship. The office of a lecturer.

Lindley Murray. An American grammarian; an authority on English grammar.

Lyceum. An intermediate classical school.

Manual. A handbook.

Middle-class school. A school founded for the higher education of the middle classes.

National school. Schools supported by government.

Nursery. A playroom for children.

Palæstra [Gr.]. A place for athletic exercises.

Platform. A place raised above the floor for speakers.

Preparatory school. A school which prepares for college.

Primary school. An elementary school.

Primer. An elementary reading-book.

Professorship. The office of a professor.

Propaganda [L.]. A system for spreading a doctrine.

Pulpit. A reading-stand in a church.

Readership. The office of a reader.

Reading-desk. A desk at which reading is done.

Reformatory. A school for the reformation and education of young criminals.

Rostrum. A platform from which a speaker addresses his audience.

Rudiments. The beginning of learning.

School. An institution of learning.

School board. A body of managers elected to provide adequate means of instruction for all children under their jurisdiction.

School-book. A book to be studied at school.

Seminary. Any school for the education of young people along the line of their future employment.

Stage. A platform for presenting speakers to the public.

Text-book. A book used in schools as a standard for some particular study.

Theater. A building used for dramatic representations.

Tribune. An elevated place from which a speaker addresses his audience.

University. An establishment for instruction in all the branches of science and literature.

Vade mecum [L.]. Go with me; constant companion; a guide-book.

Varsity. Colloquial for university.

School—*Adjectives*

Academic. Pertaining to an academy. See *Nouns*

Baccalaureate. Relating to the degree of bachelor.

Collegiate. Pertaining to a college. See *Nouns*.

Educational. Pertaining to education.

Scholastic. Pertaining to scholars. See *Nouns*.

School—*Adverb*.

Ex cathedra [L.]. Officially.

school'–book". A text-book. SCHOOL.

school'–boy". A boy attending school, or in the period of school life. INFANT-VETERAN, INSTRUCTOR-PUPIL; familiar to every schoolboy, KNOWLEDGE-IGNORANCE.

school'–days". Period of school life. INFANCY-AGE.

school'–fel"-low. Schoolmate. FRIEND-FOE.

school'–ing. Education. EDUCATION-MISTEACHING.

school'–man. A theologian of the Middle Ages. SCHOLAR-DUNCE, THEOLOGY.

school'–mas"-ter. A man who teaches school. INSTRUCTOR-PUPIL; schoolmaster abroad, EDUCATION-MISTEACHING, KNOWLEDGE-IGNORANCE.

school'–mis"-tress. A woman who teaches school. INSTRUCTOR-PUPIL.

school'–room". A room in which pupils meet for instruction. CONTENTS-RECEIVER.

schoon'–er. A sailing vessel. CONVEYANCE-VESSEL.

sci'–a-graph". A shadow picture made by X rays. X RAYS.

sci-ag'–ra-phy. Finding the time by observing shadows; correct shading. LIGHT-DARKNESS, PAINTING.

sci-at'–ic. A nerve. ANATOMY.

sci'–ence. Systematized knowledge. KNOWLEDGE-IGNORANCE, NATURE-ART, SKILL-UNSKILFULNESS.

sci"–en-tif'–ic. Agreeing with the rules and principles of science. SKILL-UNSKILFULNESS, TRUTH-ERROR.

sci'–en-tist. One devoted to scientific study. RATIOCINATION-INSTINCT.

scim'–i-tar. A curved sword. WEAPON.

scin-til'–la. A spark; the smallest particle. LIGHT-DARKNESS, LUMINARY-SHADE, MAGNITUDE-SMALLNESS.

scin'–til-lant. Sparkling. LIGHT-DARKNESS.

scin'–til-late. Sparkle. LIGHT-DARKNESS.

scin"–til-la'–tion. A twinkling; sparkle of wit. HEAT-COLD, LIGHT-DARKNESS, WITTINESS-DULNESS.

scintillula forsan, latet [L.] (sin-til'–liu-la for'–san, lê'–tet). A spark of life may perhaps be hidden. SANGUINENESS-HOPELESSNESS.

sci'–o-lism. Quackery. KNOWLEDGE-IGNORANCE.

sci'–o-list. One who pretends to have scientific knowledge. SCHOLAR-DUNCE.

sci-om'–a-chy. Visionary warfare. ADAGE-NONSENSE.

sci'–o-man"-cy. Divination by shades of departed spirits. PROPHECY.

sci'–on. A twig; a child or descendant. INFANT-VETERAN, PARENTAGE-PROGENY, WHOLE-PART.

scire facias [L.] (sai'–rî fê'–shi-as). Cause to be known. INVESTIGATION-ANSWER.

scire quid valeant humeri [L.] (sai'–rî quid vê'–li-ant hiu'–mer-ai). To know what your shoulders can bear. SKILL-UNSKILFULNESS.

scis'–sile. Scrap. UNION-DISUNION.

scis'–sion. Act of cutting. UNION-DISUNION.

scis'–sors. A cutting implement. SHARPNESS-BLUNTNESS; scissors and paste, CHOICE-NEUTRALITY.

scis'–sure. A lengthwise cut. INTERSPACE-CONTACT.

scle-rot'–ic coat. Part of the eye. ANATOMY.

scobs. Waste made by sawing. FRIABILITY.

scoff. Expression of contempt, mockery, or ridicule. GODLINESS-UNGODLINESS, REGARD-DISRESPECT, SOCIETY-DERISION; scoff at, APPROVAL-DISAPPROVAL, REGARD-SCORN.

scoff'–er. Mocker. GODLINESS-UNGODLINESS.

scoff'–ing. Mocking. REGARD-DISRESPECT, SOCIETY-DERISION.

scold. To reprove harshly; an habitual scolder. APPROVAL-DISAPPROVAL, CHARITABLENESS-CURSE, FAVORITE-QUARRELSOMENESS.

scold'–ing. Reproving. APPROVAL-DISAPPROVAL.

scol'–lop. A semicircular curve in ornamental work. EMBELLISHMENT-DISFIGUREMENT.

sconce. To fine; covering for the head; brains; a candlestick. ATTACK-DEFENSE, LUMINARY-SHADE, MIND-IMBECILITY, RECOMPENSE-PENALTY, TOP-BOTTOM.

scoop. A shovel-like implement for scooping. CONVEXITY-CONCAVITY, PERFORATOR-STOPPER.

scopa nuova spazza bene, una [It.] (sco'-pa nu-o'-va spats'-a bê'-nê, u'-na). A new broom sweeps clean. ENTIRETY-DEFICIENCY, NOVELTY-ANTIQUITY.

scope. Range of action or view; purpose. EXTENSION-INEXTENSION, LIBERTY-SUBJECTION, MEANING-JARGON, QUANTITY-MEASURE.

scorch. To burn on the surface. HEATING-COOLING.

scorch'-ing. Very hot. TURBULENCE-CALMNESS.

score. To mark; to incur debts; an account or reckoning; notes in a musical composition; twenty. ACCOUNTS, CREDIT-DEBT, FIVE-QUINQUESECTION, GROOVE, MUSIC, NUMBERING, RECORD, SIGN; **on the score of,** CONNECTION-INDEPENDENCE, MOTIVE-CAPRICE.

scores. Many. MULTIPLICITY-PAUCITY

sco'-ri-æ. Fragments of lava; ashes. CLEANNESS-FILTHINESS, HEATING-COOLING.

sco''-ri-fi-ca'-tion. Smelting of ore with lead for the purpose of collecting small quantities of a metal. HEATING-COOLING.

sco'-ri-fy. To reduce to ashes. HEATING-COOLING.

scorn. Contempt. REGARD-SCORN.

scorn'-ful. Disdainful. REGARD-SCORN.

scor'-pi-on. A reptile with a poisonous sting; constellation. ASTRONOMY, BENEFACTOR-EVILDOER, PLEASURABLENESS-PAINFULNESS; **chastise with scorpions,** HARSHNESS-MILDNESS.

scorse. To trade. EXCHANGE.

scot. A tax. RECOMPENSE-PENALTY.

scotch. To cut or scratch. BETTERMENT-DETERIORATION, INDENTATION; **scotch the snake,** COMPLETION-NONCOMPLETION, EXCESS-LACK, MIGHT-IMPOTENCE; **scotch the wheel,** OBSTRUCTION-HELP.

Scotch'-man. A native of Scotland: noted for shrewdness. CRAFT-ARTLESSNESS.

scot'-free'. Unharmed; exempt from taxation. COSTLINESS-CHEAPNESS, DUTY-IMMUNITY, LIBERTY-SUBJECTION; **escape scot-free,** ESCAPE; **let off scot-free,** EXCULPATION-CONVICTION.

scot'-o-my. Defective field of vision. SIGHT-DIMSIGHTEDNESS.

Scot'-ti-cism. A Scottish idiom. WORD-NEOLOGY

scoun'-drel. A rascal. GOOD MAN-BAD MAN.

scour. To traverse thoroughly; to rub or scrub. CLEANNESS-FILTHINESS, FRICTION-LUBRICATION, SWIFTNESS-SLOWNESS; **scour the country,** TRAVELING-NAVIGATION; **scour the plain,** SWIFTNESS-SLOWNESS.

scourge. To whip; torment; a lash. PLEASURABLENESS-PAINFULNESS, RECOMPENSE-PUNITION, RECOMPENSE-SCOURGE, REMEDY-BANE; **scourge of the human race,** BENEFACTOR-EVILDOER.

scour'-ings. Particles worn off by rubbing. USEFULNESS-USELESSNESS.

scout. To watch carefully; to reject with contempt; a person sent out to watch an enemy. CHIEF-UNDERLING, CHOICE-REJECTION, MESSENGER, REGARD-DISRESPECT, REGARD-SCORN, SECURITY-INSECURITY, TRIAL, WARNING.

scow. A flat-bottomed boat. CONVEYANCE-VESSEL.

scowl. Lowering of the brows in anger or strong disapproval. APPROVAL-DISAPPROVAL, FAVORITE-ANGER, FAVORITE-QUARRELSOMENESS, JUBILATION-LAMENTATION, POLITENESS-IMPOLITENESS.

scowl'-ing. Gloomy. FAVORITE-MOROSENESS.

scrab'-ble. To make unmeaning marks. MEANING-JARGON, WRITING-PRINTING.

scrag. Thin or lean. MAGNITUDE-SMALLNESS.

scrag'-gy. Thin; rough. GREATNESS-LITTLENESS, SMOOTHNESS-ROUGHNESS.

scram'-ble. To struggle in a disorderly manner; to climb; to contend for. ASCENT-DESCENT, DIFFICULTY-FACILITY, HURRY-LEISURE, QUEST-EVASION, REGULARITY-IRREGULARITY, STRIFE-PEACE, UNION-DISUNION.

scram'-bling. Rushing. HURRY-INDOLENCE.

scranch. To crunch. FRIABILITY.

scran'-nel. Slight. CONSEQUENCE-INSIGNIFICANCE.

scrap. A small fragment. MAGNITUDE-SMALLNESS.

scrap'-book''. A book in which pictures, scraps, or the like are kept. DIGEST.

scrape. To rub; to gather together; to play discordantly; to drag the feet in making a bow. ADDITION-SUBTRACTION, DIFFICULTY-FACILITY, ENGRAVING, ENLARGEMENT-DIMINUTION, FRIABILITY, FRICTION-LUBRICATION, POLITENESS-IMPOLITENESS, SUCCESS-FAILURE; **scrape together,** GAIN-LOSS, GATHERING-SCATTERING.

scratch. To tear or mark the surface with something sharp or rough; to erase; to draw or write awkwardly. DELINEATION-CARICATURE, FRICTION-LUBRICATION, GOOD-EVIL, GOODNESS-BADNESS, GROOVE, PAINTING, WRITING-PRINTING; **come to the scratch,** BRAVERY-COWARDICE, STRIFE-PEACE; **mere scratch,** DEEPNESS-SHALLOWNESS; **old scratch,** ANGEL-SATAN; **scratch out,** MARK-OBLITERATION; **scratch the head,** INVESTIGATION-ANSWER; **up to the scratch,** BRAVERY-COWARDICE.

scrawl. Irregular writing. WRITING-PRINTING

screak. A sharp scream. CRY-ULULATION.

scream. A loud cry. CRY-ULULATION, JUBILATION-LAMENTATION.

screech. A shrill, harsh cry. CRY-ULULATION.

screech'-owl''. An owl that screeches instead of hooting. CRY-ULULATION.

screen. To shield from observation; to pass through a sieve; any means of shelter. ACTING, APERTURE-CLOSURE, ATTACK-DEFENSE, CLEANNESS-FILTHINESS, ENLIGHTENMENT-SECRECY, EXPOSURE-HIDING-PLACE, LUMINARY-SHADE, ORGANIZATION-DISORGANIZATION, REFUGE-PITFALL, SECURITY-INSECURITY; **screen from sight,** SIGHT-BLINDNESS, SIGHT-DIMSIGHTEDNESS.

screw. A piece of metal threaded, to hold boards together; a propeller in a vessel; a miser. CONNECTIVE, EXTRAVAGANCE-AVARICE, INSTRUMENT, REVOLUTION-EVOLUTION, TRAVELING-NAVIGATION, UNION-DISUNION; **put on the screw,** COERCION, HARSHNESS-MILDNESS; **screw loose,** FAULTLESSNESS-FAULTINESS, OBSTRUCTION-HELP, SANENESS-LUNACY, SKILL-UNSKILFULNESS, VARIANCE-ACCORD; **screw one's courage to the sticking place,** BRAVERY-COWARDICE; **screw up,** PREPARATION-NONPREPARATION, STRENGTH-WEAKNESS, UNION-DISUNION; **screw up the eyes,** SIGHT-DIMSIGHTEDNESS.

screw'-driv''-er. A tool for fastening a screw INSTRUMENT.

screwed. Drunk. TEETOTALISM-INTEMPERANCE.

screw'-steam''-er. A vessel driven by screw propellers. CONVEYANCE-VESSEL.

scrib'-ble. Careless writing. WRITING-PRINTING.

scrib'-bler. A careless writer. MISSIVE-PUBLICATION.

scribe. A clerk; a Jewish writer of the records. MINISTRY-LAITY, RECORDER, WRITING-PRINTING.

scribendi, cacoëthes [L.] (scri-ben'-dai, cac-o-i'-thîz). Passion for writing. WRITING-PRINTING.

scrim'-mage. Rough-and-tumble contest. STRIFE-PEACE, VARIANCE-ACCORD.

scrimp. Scanty; short. EXCESS-LACK, EXTRAVAGANCE-AVARICE, LENGTH-SHORTNESS.

scrip. A wallet. CONTENTS-RECEIVER.

scripta, lex [L.] (scrip′-ta, lex). Written law; statute law. LAW-LAWLESSNESS.

scriptæ, literæ [L.] (scrip′-tî, lit′-er-î). Written letters. WRITING-PRINTING.

Scrip′-tur-al. Relating to the Holy Scriptures. ORTHODOXY-HETERODOXY, REVELATION-PSEUDOREVELATION.

Scrip′-ture. The sacred writings of Christianity. CERTAINTY-DOUBT, REVELATION-PSEUDOREVELATION.

scriv′-en-er. One who draws deeds, contracts, etc. ADVOCATE, WRITING-PRINTING.

scrof′-u-la. A chronic disease of the lymphatic glands. HEALTH-SICKNESS.

scroll. A roll of written parchment; ornament. ARCHITECTURE, MARK-OBLITERATION.

scrub. To clean by rubbing; inferior persons. CLEANNESS-FILTHINESS, FRICTION-LUBRICATION, GENTILITY-COMMONALTY.

scrub′-by. Stunted; mean; worthless. CONSEQUENCE-INSIGNIFICANCE, EXTRAVAGANCE-AVARICE, GENTILITY-COMMONALTY, GREATNESS-LITTLENESS, REPUTATION-DISCREDIT, UPRIGHTNESS-DISHONESTY.

scru′-ple. Doubt; reluctance; an apothecaries' weight; a small quantity. CAREFULNESS-CARELESSNESS, FAITH-MISGIVING, HEAVINESS-LIGHTNESS, MAGNITUDE-SMALLNESS, MOTIVE-CAPRICE, READINESS-RELUCTANCE, UPRIGHTNESS-DISHONESTY.

scru″-pu-los′-i-ty. A scruple. READINESS-RELUCTANCE, UPRIGHTNESS-DISHONESTY.

scru′-pu-lous. Cautious; exact. CAREFULNESS-CARELESSNESS, CREDULOUSNESS-SKEPTICISM, DESIRE-PARTICULARNESS, READINESS-RELUCTANCE, TRUTH-ERROR, TRUTHFULNESS-FALSEHOOD, UPRIGHTNESS-DISHONESTY.

scru′-pu-lous-ness. Preciseness. READINESS-RELUCTANCE, UPRIGHTNESS-DISHONESTY.

scru-ta′-tor. An examiner. INVESTIGATION-ANSWER.

scru″-ti-neer′. A scrutinizer. INVESTIGATION-ANSWER.

scru′-ti-nize. Investigate minutely. HEED-DISREGARD, REFLECTION-VACANCY.

scru′-ti-ny. Close observation or examination. HEED-DISREGARD, INVESTIGATION-ANSWER.

scru″-toir′. A writing-desk. CONTENTS-RECEIVER.

scud To move swiftly; light clouds. RAIN-WIND, SWIFTNESS-SLOWNESS, TRAVELING-NAVIGATION, VISCIDITY-FOAM; **scud under bare poles,** DIFFICULTY-FACILITY.

scud′-dle. Scurry. SWIFTNESS-SLOWNESS.

scuf′-fle. To struggle roughly. STRIFE-PEACE.

scull. To row with a single oar; the skull. MIND-IMBECILITY, TRAVELING-NAVIGATION.

scull′-cap″. A light cap fitting tightly on the head DRESS-UNDRESS.

scul′-ler-y. A room where cooking utensils are kept. CONTENTS-RECEIVER.

scul′-lion. A kitchen servant. CHIEF-UNDERLING.

sculpsit [L.] (sculp′-sit) He sculptured it. ENGRAVING.

sculp′-tor. A maker of statues. ARTIST.

sculp′-ture. A work carved in stone, bronze, etc. FORM-FORMLESSNESS, NATURE-ART, SCULPTURE.

sculp′-tured. Carved in stone. SCULPTURE.

SCULPTURE.

Alto-rilievo [It.]. High relief.

Anaglyph. A figure in relief.

Bas-relief. Sculpture in which the figures are but little raised above the background.

Basso-rilievo [It.]. Bas-relief.

Carving, etc. Decorative sculpture. See *Verbs.*

High-relief. Sculptured work which stands out prominently from background.

Insculpture. A sculpture.

Intaglio. Incised or sunk engraving.

Low-relief. Bas-relief.

Mezzo-rilievo [It.]. Half relief.

Relief. The projection of sculptured work above the background.

Rilievo [It.]. Relief.

Sculpture. The art of sculpturing; a sculptured work or figure; the art of fashioning figures out of stone or other solid materials by carving or chiseling.

SCULPTURE—*Denotations.*

Bronze. An artistic production in bronze.

Cameo. Any small engraved or carved work in relief.

Cast. An object founded or run in a mold, as of metal, plaster, wax, etc.

Ceramic ware. Articles of porcelain and pottery in general.

China. Porcelain or porcelain-ware, so called because originally brought from China.

Earthenware. Anything made of clay and baked in a kiln or dried in the sun.

Glyptotheca. A museum or cabinet of engraved or sculptured work.

Intaglio. A gem with incised carving.

Laocoon. An antique group in marble representing the death of a Trojan priest and his two sons.

Marble. A stone used for building or ornament.

Medal. A piece of metal engraved with a figure, scene, etc.

Medallion. Subjects painted, drawn, engraved, or sculptured.

Porcelain. A glazed pottery.

Pottery. Any kind of clay-ware molded in a plastic condition and then hardened by fire.

Statuary. Statues.

Statue. A plastic work representing a figure in marble or bronze.

Terra-cotta. A species of hard pottery much used in building ornamentation and in statuary.

SCULPTURE—*Place.*

Glyptotheca. A sculpture gallery.

SCULPTURE—*Verbs.*

Carve. To cut figures upon.

Cast. To fashion by molding.

Chisel. To carve with a chisel.

Cut. To shape or fashion with a sharp instrument.

Model. To make or fashion in the form of something.

Mold. To make into a certain form in or as in a mold.

Sculpture. To grave or carve out of stone, wood, or metal; to make or form by cutting or carving or casting in metal.

SCULPTURE—*Adjectives.*

Anaglyptic. Pertaining to an anaglyph, or figure in relief.

Ceramic. Pertaining to pottery.

Ceroplastic. Pertaining to wax-molding.

In relief. Raised above the background.

Marble, etc. Made of marble.

Parian. Like the marble statuary of Paros, an island in the Ægean Sea.

Sculptured, etc. Carved or decorated. See *Verbs.*

Xanthian. Relating to Xanthus, a town in Lycia, famous for the sculptures found there.

scum. Surface impurities on liquids. CLEANNESS-FILTHINESS; **scum of society,** GENTILITY-COMMONALTY; **scum of the earth,** GOOD MAN-BAD MAN.

scup′-per. A hole in a vessel's side. WATERCOURSE-AIRPIPE.

scurf. Waste scarf-skin. CLEANNESS-FILTHINESS.

scurf′-i-ness. Scabbiness. CLEANNESS-FILTHINESS.

scurf′-y. Scabby. CLEANNESS-FILTHINESS.

scur′-rile. Vulgar. ADULATION-DISPARAGEMENT, REGARD-DISRESPECT.

scur-ril′-i-ty. Vulgarity. ADULATION-DISPARAGEMENT, REGARD-DISRESPECT.

scur′-ril-ous. Grossly indecent. ADULATION-DISPARAGEMENT, REGARD-DISRESPECT, SOCIETY-DERISION.

scur′-vy. Of little account; base. CONSEQUENCE-INSIGNIFICANCE, EXCESS-LACK, UPRIGHTNESS-DISHONESTY, VIRTUE-VICE.

scut. A short tail. ANTERIORITY-POSTERIORITY.

scutch′-eon. An emblazoned shield. SIGN, TITLE.

scu′-ti-form. Shield-shaped. LEVELNESS.

scut'-tle. To destroy, to hurry, a coal-bucket. CONTENTS-RECEIVER, CREATION-DESTRUCTION, SWIFTNESS-SLOWNESS; **scuttle along,** HURRY-LEISURE.

scu'-tum. A shield used by the Romans. SECURITY-INSECURITY.

Scyl'-la and Cha-ryb'-dis. A dangerous rock and whirlpool. **Between Scylla and Charybdis,** DIFFICULTY-FACILITY, SECURITY-INSECURITY.

Scyllam qui vult vitare Charybdim, incidit in [L.] (sil'-lam quai vult vi-tê'-rî ca-rib'-dim, in'-si-dit in). He falls into Scylla who wishes to avoid Charybdis. SKILL-UNSKILLFULNESS.

scythe. A mowing implement. ANGULARITY, SHARPNESS-BLUNTNESS.

'sdeath. An exclamation. APPROVAL-DISAPPROVAL, FAVORITE-ANGER.

sea. Many; a body of water. MULTIPLICITY-PAUCITY, OCEAN-LAND; **at sea,** CERTAINTY-DOUBT, OCEAN-LAND; **go to sea,** ARRIVAL-DEPARTURE; **heavy sea,** AGITATION; **sea of doubt,** CERTAINTY-DOUBT; **sea of troubles,** DIFFICULTY-FACILITY, WELFARE-MISFORTUNE.

sea'-beach". A beach. OCEAN-LAND.

sea'-board". The seacoast. OCEAN-LAND.

sea'-coast". Seashore. OCEAN-LAND.

sea'-far"-er. A seaman. WAYFARER-SEAFARER.

sea'-far"-ing. Following the life of a seaman. TRAVELING-NAVIGATION.

sea'-fight". A naval battle. STRIFE-PEACE.

sea'-girt". Surrounded by sea. SWAMP-ISLAND.

sea'-go"-ing. Fitted for or accustomed to the sea. OCEAN-LAND, TRAVELING-NAVIGATION.

sea'-green". Of the color of the sea. OCEAN-LAND, REDNESS-GREENNESS.

seal. A stamp; evidence; completion; security. APERTURE-CLOSURE, COMPLETION-NONCOMPLETION, CONTRACT, COPY-MODEL, DETERMINATION-VACILLATION, EVIDENCE-COUNTEREVIDENCE, SECURITY, SIGN, **break the seal,** EXPOSURE-HIDINGPLACE; **seal of secrecy,** ENLIGHTENMENT-SECRECY; **seal one's infamy,** UPRIGHTNESS-DISHONESTY; **seal the doom of,** CREATION-DESTRUCTION; **seal the lips of,** TALKATIVENESS-TACITURNITY; **seal up,** ENLIGHTENMENT-SECRECY, RELEASE-RESTRAINT.

sealed. Stamped or finally finished. **Hermetically sealed,** APERTURE-CLOSURE; **one's fate is sealed,** VOLITION-OBLIGATION; **sealed book,** CLEARNESS-OBSCURITY, KNOWLEDGE-IGNORANCE, TIDINGS-MYSTERY

seals. Marks of office or distinction. SCEPTER.

seam. A line of junction. UNION-DISUNION.

sea'-maid". A sea-nymph. JOVE-FIEND.

sea'-man. A sailor. WAYFARER-SEAFARER.

sea'-man-ship. The skill of a seaman. CONDUCT, SKILL-UNSKILLFULNESS.

sea'-mark. Any beacon or lighthouse. SIGN.

seam'-less. Without seam. WHOLE-PART.

seam'-stress. A needlewoman. AGENT.

sé"-ance'. A session.

sea'-piece. A marine picture. PAINTING.

sea'-port. A harbor. REFUGE-PITFALL.

sear. To dry or burn; to harden. DAMPNESS-DRYNESS, HEATING-COOLING, SENSITIVENESS-APATHY; **fall into the sear and yellow leaf,** BETTERMENT-DETERIORATION.

search. To inquire into. INVESTIGATION-ANSWER.

search'-ing. Severe. HARSHNESS-MILDNESS, PLEASURABLENESS-PAINFULNESS.

search'-less Not to be found out. CLEARNESS-OBSCURITY.

sea'-ser"-pent. A kind of sea-monster. CONVENTIONALITY-UNCONVENTIONALITY

sea'-sick"-ness. An illness on shipboard caused by the rolling of the vessel. HEALTH-SICKNESS.

sea'-side". The seashore. OCEAN-LAND.

sea'-son. To mix or savor; prepare; preserve. CONSERVATION, DURATION-NEVERNESS, HABIT-DESUETUDE, MIXTURE-HOMOGENEITY, PREPARATION-NON PREPARATION, PUNGENCY.

sea'-son-able. Fit or timely. HARMONY-DISCORD, OPPORTUNENESS-UNSUITABLENESS.

sea'-song". Rhythmic motion of the waves. POETRY-PROSE.

sea'-son-ing. That which gives relish. CONDIMENT, HABIT-DESUETUDE, MIXTURE-HOMOGENEITY, PUNGENCY, VIGOR-INERTIA.

seat. To locate; a place; abode. DWELLER-HABITATION, ESTABLISHMENT-REMOVAL, POSITION, PRESIDENT-MEMBER, SUSPENSION-SUPPORT; **judgment-seat,** TRIBUNAL; **seat of government,** RULE-LICENSE; **seat of war,** LISTS.

seat'-ed. Established. **Firmly seated,** MUTABILITY-STABILITY.

sea'-wor"-thy. Fit for a sea voyage. FAULTLESSNESS-FAULTINESS.

se-ba'-ceous. Fatty. PULPINESS-OILINESS.

se-cede'. To withdraw; disobey. ASSENT-DISSENT, INSUBORDINATION-OBEDIENCE.

se-ce'-der. One who secedes. INSUBORDINATION-OBEDIENCE, ORTHODOXY-HETERODOXY.

se-cern'. To secrete. NUTRIMENT-EXCRETION.

se-ces'-sion. Voluntary withdrawal. GATHERING-PLACE, QUEST-EVASION.

se-clu'-sion. Retirement. QUEST-ABANDONMENT, SOCIABILITY-PRIVACY.

sec'-ond. Following the first; a musical term; a division of time; to aid. ANTAGONISM-CONCURRENCE, DOUBLING-HALVING, ETERNITY-INSTANTANEITY, MEASURE, MELODY-DISSONANCE, MUSIC, OBSTRUCTION-HELP, PERIOD-PROGRESS; **one's second self,** LIKENESS-UNLIKENESS; **play or sing a second,** MUSICIAN; **play second fiddle,** INSUBORDINATION-OBEDIENCE, LIBERTY-SUBJECTION, REPUTATION-DISCREDIT; **second best,** FAULTLESSNESS-FAULTINESS; **second childhood,** INFANCY-AGE; **second edition,** RECURRENCE; **second nature,** HABIT-DESUETUDE; **second sight,** DEVOTION-MAGIC, PREVISION; **second thoughts,** BETTERMENT-DETERIORATION, PREDECESSOR-CONTINUATION, REFLECTION-VACANCY; **second to none,** SUPREMACY-SUBORDINACY; **second youth,** RENOVATION-RELAPSE.

sec'-ond-ar'-y. The one following; an inferior. FAULTLESSNESS-FAULTINESS, REPRESENTATIVE, SUPREMACY-SUBORDINACY; **secondary education,** EDUCATION-MISTEACHING; **secondary evidence,** EVIDENCE-COUNTEREVIDENCE.

sec'-ond-er. A supporter. ANTAGONIST-ASSISTANT.

sec'-ond-hand". Used before; not new or original. BETTERMENT-DETERIORATION, GIVING-RECEIVING, IMITATION-ORIGINALITY, NOVELTY-ANTIQUITY

sec'-ond-ly. In the second place. DOUBLING-HALVING.

sec'-ond-rate". Of inferior quality, rank, etc. FAULTLESSNESS-FAULTINESS, SUPREMACY-SUBORDINACY.

se'-cre-cy. Privacy. ENLIGHTENMENT-SECRECY.

se'-cret. Something hidden, an underlying reason. ENLIGHTENMENT-SECRECY, INTERPRETATION-MISINTERPRETATION, MANIFESTATION-LATENCY, TIDINGS-MYSTERY; **in the secret,** KNOWLEDGE-IGNORANCE; **keep a secret,** TALKATIVENESS-TACITURNITY; **secret motive,** MOTIVE-CAPRICE; **secret passage,** WAY; **secret place,** EXPOSURE-HIDINGPLACE; **secret session,** PRESIDENT-MEMBER; **secret writing,** WRITING-PRINTING.

sec"-re"-taire'. A writing-desk. CONTENTS-RECEIVER.

sec'-re-tar"-y. A clerk; director; assistant. ANTAGONIST-ASSISTANT, CHIEF-UNDERLING, CONSIGNEE, MANAGER, RECORDER, WRITING-PRINTING.

se-crete'. To separate; conceal. ADMISSION-EXPULSION, ENLIGHTENMENT-SECRECY.

se-cre'-tion. Any substance secreted. BIOLOGY, NUTRIMENT-EXCRETION.

se-cre'-tive. Given to secreting. ENLIGHTENMENT-SECRECY.

se'-cret-ly. Clandestinely. ENLIGHTENMENT-SECRECY.

se'-cret-ness. Obscurity. ENLIGHTENMENT-SECRECY.

sect. A school. DIVISION; **religious sect,** ORTHODOXY-HETERODOXY.

sec-ta'-ri-an. A heretic; one of a sect. ANTAGONIST-ASSISTANT, ASSENT-DISSENT, ORTHODOXY-HETERODOXY.

sec-ta'-ri-an-ism. Undue denominationalism. ORTHODOXY-HETERODOXY.

sect'-a-rism. Sectarianism. ORTHODOXY-HETERODOXY.

sect'-a-ry. Dissenter. ORTHODOXY-HETERODOXY.

sec'-tion. A division or part. BELLIGERENT, DIVISION, MISSIVE-PUBLICATION, UNION-DISUNION, WHOLE-PART.

sec'-tion-al. Local. WHOLE-PART.

sec'-tor. A part of a circle. CIRCLE-WINDING, WHOLE-PART.

sec'-u-lar. Occurring at long intervals; worldly. FIVE-QUINQUESECTION, MINISTRY-LAITY, PERIODICITY-IRREGULARITY; **secular education,** EDUCATION-MIS-TEACHING.

sec'-u-lar-ism. Worldliness. ORTHODOXY-HETERODOXY.

sec'-u-lar-ist. A worldly person. MINISTRY-LAITY.

sec'-u-lar-ize. Make worldly. MINISTRY-LAITY.

secula seculorum, in [L.] (sec'-yu-la sec-yu-lo'-rum, in). From age to age. ETERNITY-INSTANTANEITY.

secundum artem [L.] (sê-cun'-dum ar'-tem). According to rule. CONVENTIONALITY-UNCONVENTIONALITY, SKILL-UNSKILFULNESS.

se-cure'. To make fast or certain; get; safe. EARLINESS-LATENESS, ENGAGEMENT-RELEASE, FAITH-MISGIVING, GAIN-LOSS, KEEPING-RELINQUISHMENT, RELEASE-RESTRAINT, SANGUINENESS-TIMIDITY, SECURITY-INSECURITY, UNION-DISUNION; **secure an object,** SUCCESS-FAILURE; **secure from danger,** PATRIOTISM-TREASON.

se-cure'-ness. Safety. SANGUINENESS-HOPELESSNESS.

se-cu'-ri-ty. Safety; a pledge; confidence. ENGAGEMENT-RELEASE, SANGUINENESS-TIMIDITY, SECURITY, SECURITY-INSECURITY; **lend on security,** LOAN-BORROWING.

SECURITY.

Acceptance. An agreement to pay a draft or the like according to its terms.

Acquittance. A paper showing release from debt.

Assurance. Insurance of life or property.

Attested copy. A copy certified as true by signature.

Authentication. The act of attesting.

Bail. Security given that a prisoner shall appear at a given time and place for trial.

Bill. A bill of exchange; a promissory note.

Bill of exchange. An order from one person to a second to pay money to a third, to be charged to account of drawer.

Bill of sale. A declaration in writing of transfer of property.

Bond. A paper in which one person is bound to pay a sum to another at a certain time.

Caution. In Scotland, security or person giving security for performance of obligation.

Certificate. A transferable security as to ownership in a stock company, or the like.

Charter, etc. A document from a government conferring privileges. See CONTRACT.

Charter-poll. A charter executed by one party only, and having its edges polled or cut even instead of being indented.

Codicil. Supplementary explanation or change in a will.

Covenant. A written sealed agreement; action to recover damages for breach of contract.

Covenant of indemnity. A sealed agreement to make satisfaction for any loss sustained.

Debenture. A written acknowledgment of debt with provision for payment.

Deed. A written, sealed, and delivered instrument of transference or contract.

Deed of indemnity. A sealed instrument making satisfaction for damages sustained.

Deed-poll. A deed executed by only one party, and having the edge of the parchment cut even or polled instead of being indented.

Deposit. That which is given as a security.

Discharge. A paper granting release from an obligation.

Doquet. A warrant.

Earnest. Payment in part as guarantee of future payment in full.

Execution. The judicial writ by which a judgment is carried into effect.

Gage. That which is given as security for some act

Guarantee. A guaranty.

Guaranty. Anything that assures or makes certain.

Handsel. Earnest-money as indication of good faith.

Hostage. A person given or held as a pledge in war for performance of treaty or the like.

Hypothecation. A lien given to a creditor on movable property without passing possession of same.

Indenture. A sealed contract in duplicate, each party keeping a counterpart.

Indorsement. Any writing on the back of a document.

Indorser. One who indorses.

Instrument. A document acknowledging or certifying a claim or terms of a contract.

I O U. An acknowledgment of debt; in England, in writing.

Last will and testament. A will.

Lien. A claim on property for debt.

Mainpernor. One who is surety for a prisoner to produce him before court to answer charges.

Mortgage. An estate held by conveyance, or a claim upon an estate, which conveyance or claim will become void upon the performance of a certain condition.

Muniment. A written record as a defense to a title or to an estate.

Paper. Any written or printed document or statement.

Parchment. A formal writing on parchment.

Parole, etc. An oral statement or pledge, especially of a prisoner that he will not escape. See ENGAGEMENT.

Pawn. Personal property pledged to secure a loan.

Personal security. Acknowledgment of debt by personal liability of maker.

Pignoration. The contract of pawning personal property.

Pledge. Anything given as security for performance of contract.

Plight. A solemn pledge.

Probate. Legal proof or process of proving; specifically, of a will.

Promissory note. A written promise to pay a certain sum at a specified time for value received.

Quittance. A release from debt; a receipt.

Real security. Property given as security.

Receipt. A written acknowledgment of payment of money or delivery of property.

Recognizance. An acknowledgment on the record of an obligation; specifically, an obligation of record before a court to do some particular act.

Record, etc. A written memorial by an authorized person of the evidence of some act. See MARK.

Release. A written instrument which sets free from obligation or relinquishes a claim or interest.

Seal. Any document, as a warrant executed with a seal.

Security. Written promise of payment of debt; anything given as a pledge.

Settlement. Conveyance of property making provision for the future.

Signature. The name or something representing the name of a person written by himself or another authorized as an acknowledgment of agreement.

Specialty. Any document sealed and delivered.

Sponsion. The act of becoming security for another.

Sponsor. One who becomes responsible for the acts or obligations of another.

Sponsorship. The state of being a sponsor.

Stake. Anything put at a risk in a competition or enterprise.

Stamp. A mark or printed or stamped device put upon a taxable commodity to signify that the tax is paid.

Surety. One who or that which gives security; a security.

Testament. A will; strictly, bequeathing personal property only.

Tie. Any legal bond or obligation.

Title-deed. A document showing right to ownership of property.

Vadium. A pledge of property for debt or loan,

Verification. An oath appended to a document, declaring the facts therein to be true.

Voucher. Any material thing that alleges that an act has been done; especially with reference to the loaning of money.

Warrant. A judicial written instrument giving an officer authority to arrest.

Warranty. An assurance by seller that property is as represented, an instrument granting authority to do certain acts in a deed whereby grantor binds himself and heirs to secure estate to grantee.

Will. An instrument in which a man makes disposition of his property in effect after his death

SECURITY—*Verbs*

Accept. To acknowledge the validity or receipt of

Assure. To insure, as against loss.

Execute. To make a document unquestionably valid by fulfilling all requirements of the law.

Give bail. } To promise to be responsible for the acts of a person,
Give security. } as paying money, appearance at court, etc.

Give substantial bail. To give good security.

Go bail. To act as surety by giving bail.

Grant a lease. To give a right to possession and profits of property for a certain period.

Guarantee. To become responsible for the payment or performance of; assure against loss or damages.

Hold a lease. To hold lands, etc., for a term of years.

Hold in pledge. To hold as security.

Hypothecate. To pledge personal property as security for debt.

Impawn. To give as a pawn.

Impignorate. To pawn.

Indorse. To guarantee payment by writing one's name on the back of.

Insure. To contract to pay a certain sum to, in case of loss or death.

Lend on security, etc. To give on sufficient security to repay. See LOAN.

Let. To lease or rent for a consideration.

Mortgage. To give as security for performance of an obligation, conveyance to become void upon fulfilment of same.

Pawn. To give as a pawn.

Seal, etc. To set a seal to; to confirm. See EVIDENCE.

Sett. To attach or affix, as a signature.

Sign. To attach one's name to, as a proof of genuineness. See EVIDENCE.

Spout. To pawn or pledge.

Stamp. To put a stamp upon.

Take a lease. To take possession of a property for a term of years.

Underwrite. To execute an insurance policy.

Warrant. To guarantee the character or quality of.

SECURITY—*Phrase.*

Bonis avibus [L.]. Under good auspices.

SECURITY—INSECURITY

Auspices. Friendly or favoring protection.

Coast clear. An open safe way.

Confidence. A feeling of safety.

Custody. Entrusted care or oversight of a person or thing.

Danger over. } Freedom from danger.
Danger past. }

Escape, etc. Flight from confinement or danger See ESCAPE

Escort. Special or distinctive protection.

Garrison. A body of troops protecting a town.

Guard. Careful protection from injury or attack.

Guardianship. The duty or condition of being a guardian.

Impregnability. The state of not being able to be harmed by attack.

Invulnerability. The condition of being incapable of being hurt or injured.

Invulnerableness. Invulnerability

Precaution. Forethought; the act of preparing for future or unexpected danger.

Preservation. The act of being kept from injury.

Protection. Preservation from loss, injury, or annoyance.

Quarantine. Enforced isolation of persons with contagious diseases; protection against contagious disease.

Refuge. Avoidance of danger or distress

Safe-keeping. Freedom from danger.

Safety. The condition or state of being safe.

Security. The state of being secure

Storm blown over. Danger past

Surety. Positive safety

Tutelage. The duty to keep under watch, as of a guardian; the condition of being under a tutor.

Wardenship. The duty or jurisdiction of a warden

Wardship. The care of a ward or pupil.

SECURITY—*Nouns of Agency*

Anchor. A large weight or hook for securing a ship or boat.

Bandog. A fierce watch-dog.

Cerberus. A careful guardian: from Cerberus, the watch-dog of Hades.

Chaperon. A female guardian of young unmarried women

Convoy. A force of ships or men for protection in transit.

Cordon sanitaire [F.]. Troops stationed for the purpose of stopping the spreading of disease.

Custodian. One having the custody of anything.

Duenna. An elderly woman who keeps careful watch over a young woman.

Escort. A guard of honor or favor.

Garrison. A force of soldiers stationed in a fort.

Genius loci [L.]. A mythical protecting deity of a locality

Guard. Anything that protects from injury.

Guardian. One having the care or protection of another; especially in a legal sense.

Guardian angel. An angel having special care of a person; hence, any one devoted to the care of another.

Means of escape. } Any way or means by which a person escapes danger
Means of safety. }

Alarm, etc. Excitement caused by sudden fear of danger. See ALARM.

Apprehension, etc. Anxiety caused by fear of future. See SANGUINENESS-TIMIDITY.

Breakers ahead. Danger ahead.

Cause for alarm. Anything that causes fear.

Clouds gathering. Threatening danger.

Clouds in horizon. Premonition of danger.

Danger. The condition of being exposed to injury or risk.

Defenselessness, etc. The state of being defenseless, etc.

Exposure, etc. The condition of being exposed. See CONTINGENCY.

Facilis descensus Averni [L.]. The easy descent to Avernus, the lower world. [Virgil, *Æneid*, vi, 126.]

Forlorn hope, etc. A hopeless condition or enterprise. See SANGUINENESS-HOPELESSNESS.

Hairbreadth escape. Very narrow escape.

Hazard. Liability to encounter danger.

Heel of Achilles. A vulnerable spot. [The water of the Styx did not touch the heel by which he was held.]

Insecurity. Lack of security.

Instability, etc. The quality of being easily overthrown. See MUTABILITY.

Jeopardy. The state of being under great risk.

Leap in the dark, etc. Foolish exposure to danger. See RECKLESSNESS.

Peril. Exposure to imminent and very great danger.

Precariousness. The condition of being under great risk.

Risk. Liability to suffer loss or injury

Road to ruin. A dangerous course.

Rock ahead. Danger ahead.

Slipperiness. The quality of being slippery or dangerous.

Source of danger, etc. Anything from which danger arises. See REFUGE-PITFALL.

Storm brewing. Danger threatening.

Venture. A doubtful undertaking.

Vulnerability. The quality of being vulnerable.

Vulnerable point. A place easily attacked or injured. [The arrow of Paris pierced the heel of Achilles.]

Warning, etc. That which foretells of danger See WARNING.

INSECURITY—*Verbs.*

Adventure. To risk losing

Be exposed to danger. }
Be in danger, etc. } To be in a dangerous position. See *Nouns.*
Being in danger, etc. }

Compromise. Put in a position of risk of loss or injury

Encounter danger. To be in a dangerous condition.

Endanger. Make liable to injury or harm.

Engage in a forlorn hope. To attempt to do what seems impossible.

Expose to danger. To place in a position full of risk.

Feel ground sliding from under one. To feel insecure.

Hang by a thread. Be in a very dangerous position, as over a precipice.

SECURITY—INSECURITY—*Continued.*

SECURITY—Nouns of Agency—*Continued.*

Palladium. A safeguard; especially of a community: from the image of Pallas in ancient Troy, on which the safety of the city was supposed to depend.
Policeman. A civil officer for the protection of a town or district.
Preserver. Anything that preserves.
Protector. Anything that protects.
Safe-conduct. A passport ensuring security from danger.
Safeguard. Anything that keeps in safety.
Safety-valve. A valve on a boiler, allowing escape of steam when pressure is too great.
Scout. A person sent out to reconnoiter.
Scutum. Kind of shield.
Security. That which makes secure.
Sentinel. A soldier stationed on guard.
Sentry. A sentinel.
Shield. A broad piece of metal for defense; anything that shelters or defends.
Third person. A person who is present as a mediator or peacemaker.
Tutelary deity. A deity or angel supposed to have special watch or care over one.
Tutelary god. } A tutelary deity.
Tutelary saint. }
Warden. One who keeps guard; especially in a prison.
Warder. One who wards or watches over.
Watch-dog. A dog kept for protection of property.
Watchman. One who keeps watch, especially over property and at night.

SECURITY—*Verbs.*

Bear a charmed life. To be miraculously preserved from harm.
Be safe, etc. To be free from harm or injury. See *Adjectives.*
Convoy. To act as a convoy.
Cover. To defend from or make provision for danger.
Double reef topsails. To make perfectly safe and secure.
Ensconce. To set down in a safe place.
Escape. To get away or free from harm.
Escort. To act as an escort.
Fence round. To put defenses around.
Find shelter. To go to a place of safety.
Flank. To guard the flank.
Garrison. To fit out with soldiers.
Guard, etc. To protect from injury or attack. See ATTACK-DEFENSE.
House. To protect by putting under shelter, as a house.
Intrench. To protect by putting a trench around.
Keep one's head above water. To be safe in time of danger or trouble.
Light on one's feet. To come safely through a dangerous experience.
Make assurance doubly sure, etc. To be sure of perfect safety. See RECKLESSNESS-CAUTION.
Make safe. To free from danger.
Mount guard. To be on guard duty.
Nestle. To take shelter fondly, as a bird in its nest.
Patrol. To guard by marching around, as on a beat.
Preserve. To keep and hold in safety.
Protect. To ward off danger or attack from.
Render safe. To place in security.
Ride out the storm. To successfully resist and ward off threatened danger; as a good ship.
Save one's bacon. To keep self and property from harm.
Screen. To surround with something for protection.
Secure, etc. To free and keep from injury or risk. See RELEASE-RESTRAINT.
Seek safety. To look for a place of security.
Shelter. To keep safe by surrounding or covering.
Shroud. To conceal or hide.
Take care of, etc. To protect. See CAREFULNESS-CARELESSNESS.
Take charge of. To take under one's care.
Take precautions, etc. Be on the watch for danger. See PREPARATION.
Take shelter, etc. To go to a place of safety. See REFUGE.
Take up a loose thread. To take away the slightest liability to danger.
Tide over. To carry safely over a crisis.
Ward. To keep or cast off, as of danger.
Watch. Keep guard over.
Weather the storm. To come out of threatened injury in safety.

SECURITY—*Adjectives.*

Above water. Out of danger.
Achillean. Invulnerable, like Achilles who had been dipped in the Styx.

INSECURITY—Verbs—*Continued.*

Have the chances against one. } To be in such a position that a person cannot succeed.
Have the odds against one. }
Have to run for it. Be compelled to exert oneself to escape danger.
Hazard. Run a risk.
Imperil. Put in position of great danger.
Incur danger. Expose oneself to danger.
Jeopard. To put in jeopardy.
Jeopardize. To place in great danger.
Lay a trap for, etc. To attempt to draw into a dangerous position. See TRUTHFULNESS-FRAUD.
Lay oneself open to, etc. Expose oneself to. See CONTINGENCY.
Lean on a broken reed. To have a poor protection.
Live in a glass house. To be poorly protected.
Place in danger, etc. } To risk. See *Nouns.*
Put in danger, etc. }
Risk. Run a chance of loss or injury.
Run a risk. To be liable to loss or injury.
Run into danger. To expose to harm or injury.
Run one hard. Press upon with danger.
Run the gauntlet, etc. To take a chance of injury. See BRAVERY.
Sail too near the wind, etc. To foolishly go near danger. See RECKLESSNESS.
Set at hazard. To put out at a venture.
Sit on a barrel of gunpowder. To be in a very dangerous position.
Sleep on a volcano. To be in great danger unconsciously.
Stake. To put out at a risk.
Stand on a volcano. To be in great danger.
Threaten danger. To promise harm to. See CHARITABLENESS-MENACE.
Totter. To be on the point of falling.
Trust to a broken reed. To put faith in a dangerous support.
Venture. To undertake or put out at a great risk.

INSECURITY—*Adjectives.*

Adventurous. Full of risk.
Alarming, etc. Causing alarm. See SANGUINENESS-TIMIDITY.
At bay. Without way of escape.
At stake. Attended with risk.
At the last extremity. In the greatest danger.
Aux abois [F.]. At bay.
Between Scylla and Charybdis. Surrounded by great peril.
Between the hammer and the anvil. Liable to meet violent death.
Between two fires. In very great danger.
Built upon sand. Having no foundation.
Critical. Attended by peril.
Crumbling. Going to decay.
Dangerous. Accompanied by danger.
Defenseless. Without means of defense.
Endangered, etc. Placed in danger. See *Verbs.*
Explosive. Liable to explode.
Exposed. Without protection.
Expugnable. Capable of being taken by storm.
Fenceless. Undefended.
Fraught with danger. Very dangerous.
Guardless. Without a guard.
Guideless. Without a guide.
Hanging by a thread, etc. In great peril. See *Verbs.*
Harborless. Without place of refuge.
Hazardous. Exposed to risk.
Helpless. Without means of help.
Ill-omened. Foretelling danger.
In a bad way. In a critical condition.
In danger, etc. Liable to injury. See *Nouns.*
In question. Uncertain.
Insecure. Lacking security.
In the lion's den. In the midst of the greatest peril.
Nodding to its fall, etc. About to perish. See CREATION-DESTRUCTION.
Not out of the wood. Still in danger.
Off one's guard, etc. Not on the lookout for danger. See EXPECTATION-SURPRISE.
Ominous. Portending evil.
On a lee shore. Near the rocks.
On a sandy basis. Without a firm foundation.
On slippery ground. In a perilous position.
On the brink. Dangerously situated.
On the edge. In the greatest danger.
On the rocks. Almost certain to be destroyed.
On the verge of a precipice. } In a very dangerous position.
On the verge of a volcano. }
On the wrong side of the wall. In danger from a falling wall.
Open to, etc. Exposed to. See CONTINGENCY.

SECURITY—INSECURITY—*Continued*.

SECURITY—Adjectives—*Continued*.

At anchor. Secure from injury.
Bailable. Able to be bailed.
Cavendo tutus [L.]. Safe by taking heed.
Defensible. Capable of being defended.
Fire-proof. Incapable of being destroyed by fire.
Guardian. Charged with the duty of guarding.
Harmless. Incapable of inflicting injury.
High and dry. Out of harm's way.
Imperdible. That cannot be destroyed.
Impregnable. That cannot be injured by attack.
Inexpugnable. That cannot be successfully attacked.
In safety. }
In security. } Free from danger
Insurable. Capable of being insured.
Invulnerable. Incapable of being wounded.
Not dangerous, etc. Free from danger. See SECURITY-INSECURITY.
On sure ground. }
On the safe side. }
Out of danger. } Free from harm or danger
Out of harm's way. }
Out of the meshes. Out of danger of being caught; out of the net.
Panoplied, etc. Completely protected, as by armor.
Preservative, etc. Able to preserve. See PRESERVATION.
Proof against. Capable of resisting.
Protected, etc. Rendered safe. See *Verbs*.
Protecting, etc. Able to protect.
Safe. In a position where harm cannot be done.
Safe and sound, etc. Free from all harm or injury. See PRESERVATION.
Scathless, etc. Unharmed. See FAULTLESSNESS.
Seaworthy. Capable of successfully resisting the dangers of the sea.
Secure. Not liable to be exposed to injury or attack.
Snug. Closely protected.
Sure. Certainly protected.
Tenable. That can be defended.
Trustwrothy, etc. That can be depended upon. See UPRIGHTNESS.
Tutelary. Having guardianship over.
Unassailable. That cannot be assailed.
Unattackable. That cannot be successfully attacked.
Under cover. Protected.
Under lock and key. Protected by lock and key.
Under the shade of. Under the protection of.
Under the shadow of one's wing. Under the careful protection of.
Under the shield of. }
Under the wing of. } In one's charge or care.
Unhazarded. Not placed in danger of loss or injury.
Unmolested. Not disturbed or attacked.
Unthreatened. Not in the way of danger.
Water-proof. That cannot be injured by water.
Weather-proof. That cannot be harmed by destructive force of weather.

INSECURITY—Adjectives—*Continued*.

Parlous. Perilous.
Periculous. Perilous.
Perilous. Attended by peril.
Precarious. Subject to risk or danger.
Ramshackle.. Going to pieces.
Reduced to the last extremity. About to be destroyed.
Shaky. Uncertain and fraught with danger.
Slippery. Liable to prove dangerous; risky.
Slippy. Slippery.
Threatening, etc. Portending evil. See CHARITABLENESS-MENACE.
Ticklish. Involving risk.
Top-heavy. Heavy at top and liable to fall.
Tottering. Going to ruin.
Trembling in the balance. Uncertain and fearful.
Tumble-down. Gone to ruin.
Unadmonished. Not forewarned.
Unadvised. Not advised.
Under fire. In danger of being shot.
Unprepared, etc. Not ready for danger. See PREPARATION-NON-PREPARATION.
Unprotected, etc. Exposed to danger See SECURITY.
Unsafe, etc. See sub SAFETY.
Unshielded. Unprotected.
Unstable. Not characterized by certainty.
Unsteady. Shaky.
Untrustworthy. Not to be risked.
Unwarned. Not knowing of danger ahead.
Vulnerable. Capable of being wounded or destroyed by attack.
Waterlogged. Soaked with water; liable to sink.
With a halter around one's neck. In imminent danger of death.

INSECURITY—*Phrases*.

Incidit in Scyllam qui vult vitare Charybdin [L.]. He who tries to escape one peril encounters another.
Nam tua res agitur paries dum proximus ardet [L.]. Your own property is in peril when your neighbor's house burns.

SECURITY—*Continued*.

SECURITY—Adverbs, *etc*.

Ex abundante cautela [L.]. Strict precaution.
With impurity. Without harm.

SECURITY—*Phrases*.

À couvert [F.]. Under cover.
All's well.
Dieu vous garde [F.]. God guard you.
Salva res est [L.]. The matter is safe.
Suave mari magno, e terra alterius spectare laborem [Lucretius, ii, 1], etc. [L.]. Sweet, in a great sea, to view from land another's struggle. Pleasant when one is safe to watch another in danger.
Via trita, via tuta [L.]. The beaten path, the safe path.

---

se-dan'-chair". A closed chair carried on poles. CONVEYANCE-VESSEL.
se-date'. Grave. EXCITABILITY-INEXCITABILITY, LIGHTHEARTEDNESS-DEJECTION, REFLECTION-VACANCY.
sed'-a-tive. Soothing; a medicine. ACTIVITY-INDOLENCE, REMEDY-BANE, TURBULENCE-CALMNESS.
sed'-en-ta-ry. Lacking in activity. MOVEMENT-REST.
sedge. A grass-like herb. FAUNA-FLORA.
sed'-i-ment. Settlings. CLEANNESS-FILTHINESS.
sed'-i-men'-ta-ry. Of the nature of sediment. INCREMENT-REMNANT; **sedimentary rocks,** GEOLOGY.
se-di'-tion. Covert acts against government. INSUBORDINATION-OBEDIENCE, PATRIOTISM-TREASON.
se-di'-tious. Turbulent. INSUBORDINATION-OBEDIENCE, PATRIOTISM-TREASON.
se-duce'. To entice into wrong. LOVE-HATE, MOTIVE-DEHORTATION, PURITY-IMPURITY.
se-duce'-ment. Enticement into wrong. MOTIVE-CAPRICE.
se-duc'-er. One who entices. MOTIVE-CAPRICE, PURITY-RAKE.
se-duc'-ing. Enticing. PLEASURABLENESS-PAINFULNESS.
se-duc'-tion. Enticements of evil. DESIRE-DISTASTE,

MOTIVE-CAPRICE, PLEASURABLENESS-PAINFULNESS, PURITY-IMPURITY.
se-duc'-tive. Enticing. MOTIVE-CAPRICE, PLEASURABLENESS-PAINFULNESS.
se-duc'-tor. Seducer. MOTIVE-CAPRICE.
sed'-u-lous. Diligent. ACTIVITY-INDOLENCE, DESIRE-DISTASTE.
see. To look; believe or know; a bishopric. CHURCH, FAITH-MISGIVING, HEED-DISREGARD, KNOWLEDGE-IGNORANCE, SIGHT-BLINDNESS; **see after,** CAREFULNESS-CARELESSNESS; **see at a glance,** SAGACITY-INCAPACITY; **see daylight,** CLEARNESS-OBSCURITY, DISCOVERY; **see double,** TEETOTALISM-INTEMPERANCE; **see fit,** READINESS-RELUCTANCE, VOLITION-OBLIGATION; **see justice done,** RIGHT-WRONG; **see land,** SANGUINENESS-HOPELESSNESS; **see one's way,** CLEARNESS-OBSCURITY, DIFFICULTY-FACILITY, KNOWLEDGE-IGNORANCE, OBSTRUCTION-HELP, PREVISION, SKILL-UNSKILFULNESS; **see service,** FIGHTING-CONCILIATION; **see sights,** INQUISITIVENESS-INDIFFERENCE; **see the light,** LIFE-DEATH, PUBLICITY; **see through,** DISCOVERY, SAGACITY-INCAPACITY; **see to,** CAREFULNESS-CARELESSNESS, HEED-DISREGARD, MANAGEMENT; **we shall see,** EXPECTATION-SURPRISE.

seed. Something small; a cause; posterity; grain. CAUSE-EFFECT, FRIABILITY, MAGNITUDE-SMALLNESS, PARENTAGE-PROGENY; **run to seed,** BETTERMENT-DETERIORATION, INFANCY-AGE; **sow the seed,** PREPARATION-NONPREPARATION.

seed'-ling. A plant grown from a seed. INFANT-VETERAN.

seed'-plot". A nursery. DOMESTICATION - AGRICULTURE, FERTILITY-STERILITY.

seed'-time" of life. Childhood. INFANCY-AGE.

seed'-y. In bad condition. AFFLUENCE-PENURY, BETTERMENT - RELAPSE, CREATION - DESTRUCTION, HEALTH-SICKNESS, WEARINESS-REFRESHMENT.

see'-ing. Perceiving. SIGHT-BLINDNESS.

see'ing that. Since this is so. CONDITION-SITUATION, RATIOCINATION-INSTINCT.

seek. To inquire into; search; ask. INVESTIGATION-ANSWER, PETITION-EXPOSTULATION, PROFFER-REFUSAL, QUEST-ABANDONMENT; **seek safety,** SECURITY-INSECURITY.

seek'-sor"-row. A self - tormentor. LIGHTHEARTEDNESS-DEJECTION.

seel. To roll, as a vessel. SUSPENSION-SUPPORT.

Seelen dulden still, grosse [G.] (sê'-len dul'-den shtill, gros'-se). Great souls suffer in silence. SOUND-SILENCE, UNSELFISHNESS-SELFISHNESS.

seem. To appear. APPEARANCE-DISAPPEARANCE; **as it seems good to,** VOLITION-OBLIGATION

seem'-ing. Apparently so. APPEARANCE-DISAPPEARANCE.

seem'-ing-ly. Apparently. APPEARANCE - DISAPPEARANCE, LIKELIHOOD-UNLIKELIHOOD.

seem'-less. Not comely; undue. BEAUTY-UGLINESS, DUENESS-UNDUENESS.

seem'-li-ness. Propriety. DUTY-DERELICTION.

seem'-ly. Fitting; comely. BEAUTY-UGLINESS, DUENESS-UNDUENESS, PROPRIETY-IMPROPRIETY.

seer. One gifted with prophetic vision. DEVOTION-MAGICIAN, INFANT-VETERAN, SANENESS-MANIAC, SOOTHSAYER.

see'-saw". A kind of sport. VIBRATION.

seethe. To be hot; to be excited. EXCITATION, HEAT-COLD, HEATING-COOLING.

seeth'-ing cal'-dron. A boiling caldron. OVEN-REFRIGERATOR.

se-gar'. A cigar. PUNGENCY.

seg'-ment. A section. WHOLE-PART.

seg'-ni-tude. Inactivity. ACTIVITY-INDOLENCE.

seg'-ni-ty. Inactivity. ACTIVITY-INDOLENCE.

s'égosiller [F.] (sê-go-zï-yê'). To cry aloud. CRY-ULULATION.

seg'-re-gate. Not related; to set apart. CONNECTION-INDEPENDENCE, INCLUSION-OMISSION, UNION-DISUNION.

seg'-re-ga"-ted. Not connected. COHESION-LOOSENESS.

seg"-re-ga'-tion. Isolation. INCLUSION - OMISSION UNION-DISUNION.

seigneur, grand [F.] (sê-niur' gran·). A great lord. PRESUMPTION-OBSEQUIOUSNESS, SELFRESPECT-HUMBLENESS.

sei'-gnior. A lord; sir. CHIEF-UNDERLING, PRESUMPTION-OBSEQUIOUSNESS.

sei'-gnior-i-ty. Authority; possession. HOLDING-EXEMPTION, PROPERTY, RULE-LICENSE.

sei'-gnior-y. Lordship. RULE-LICENSE.

seine. A fish-net. ENCLOSURE.

sei'-sin. Possession; property. HOLDING-EXEMPTION, PROPERTY.

seis-mom'-e-ter. An instrument for measuring earthquakes. IMPETUS-REACTION.

seize. To take. TAKING-RESTITUTION, THEFT; **seize an opportunity.** OPPORTUNENESS-UNSUITABLENESS.

seized with. Affected with. EMOTION, HEALTH-SICK-

sei'-zure. Taking possession of by law. TAKING-RESTITUTION.

se-junc'-tion. Disjunction. UNION-DISUNION.

sel'-dom. Not often. FREQUENCY-RARITY.

sel'-dom-ness Rarity. FREQUENCY-RARITY.

se-lect'. To choose. CHOICE-REJECTION, GOODNESS-BADNESS.

self. The individual. SAMENESS-CONTRAST, UNIVERSALITY-PARTICULARITY; **self-abasement,** SELFRESPECT-HUMBLENESS; **self-abnegation,** UNSELFISHNESS - SELFISHNESS; **self-accusation,** REPENTANCE-OBDURACY; **self-accusing,** REPENTANCE-OBDURACY; **self-admiration,** CONCEIT-DIFFIDENCE; **self-admiring,** CONCEIT-DIFFIDENCE; **self-applauding,** CONCEIT-DIFFIDENCE; **self-applause,** CONCEIT-DIFFIDENCE; **self-approbation,** CONCEIT - DIFFIDENCE; **self-called,** NAME-MISNOMER; **self-christened,** NAME-MISNOMER; **self-command,** DETERMINATION-VACILLATION, MODERATION-SELFINDULGENCE, RECKLESSNESS-CAUTION; **self-communing,** REFLECTION-VACANCY; **self-complacency,** CONCEIT-DIFFIDENCE, LIGHTHEARTEDNESS-DEJECTION; **self-conceit,** CONCEIT-DIFFIDENCE; **self-condemnation,** REPENTANCE-OBDURACY; **self-confidence,** CONCEIT-DIFFIDENCE; **self-confident,** CONCEIT-DIFFIDENCE; **self-conquest,** MODERATION-SELFINDULGENCE, PERSISTENCE-WHIM; **self-conscious,** SOCIETY-AFFECTATION; **self-consultation,** REFLECTION-VACANCY; **self-control,** DETERMINATION-VACILLATION, EXCITABILITY-INEXCITABILITY, MODERATION-SELFINDULGENCE, UNSELFISHNESS - SELFISHNESS; **self-convicted,** REPENTANCE-OBDURACY; **self-conviction,** FAITH-MISGIVING, NUMBER; **self-council,** REFLECTION-VACANCY; **self-deceit,** TRUTH-ERROR; **self-deception,** CREDULOUSNESS-SKEPTICISM, TRUTH-ERROR; **self-defense,** ATTACK-DEFENSE; **self-denial,** DETERMINATION-VACILLATION, DEVOTION-IDOLATRY, MODERATION - SELFINDULGENCE, UNSELFISHNESS-SELFISHNESS, VIRTUE-VICE; **self-denying,** UNSELFISHNESS - SELFISHNESS; **self-devoted,** UNSELFISHNESS-SELFISHNESS; **self-discipline,** DEVOTION-IDOLATRY; **self-esteem,** CONCEIT-DIFFIDENCE; **self-evident,** CERTAINTY-DOUBT, MANIFESTATION-LATENCY; **self-examination,** DEVOTION - IDOLATRY; **self-existent,** ENTITY-NONENTITY; **self-existing,** ENTITY-NONENTITY; **self-flattering,** CONCEIT-DIFFIDENCE; **self-glorification,** CONCEIT-DIFFIDENCE; **self-glorious,** CONCEIT-DIFFIDENCE; **self-government,** DETERMINATION-VACILLATION, LIBERTY-SUBJECTION; **self-gratulation,** CONCEIT-DIFFIDENCE; **self-help,** SKILL-UNSKILFULNESS; **self-humiliation,** REPENTANCE-OBDURACY; **self-immolation,** DEVOTION-IDOLATRY; **self-indulgence,** MODERATION-SELFINDULGENCE; UNSELFISHNESS - SELFISHNESS; **self-indulgent,** UNSELFISHNESS-SELFISHNESS; **self-instruction,** EDUCATION-LEARNING; **self-interest,** UNSELFISHNESS-SELFISHNESS; **self-interested,** UNSELFISHNESS-SELFISHNESS; **self-knowledge,** CONCEIT-DIFFIDENCE; **self-laudation,** CONCEIT - DIFFIDENCE; **self-love,** UNSELFISHNESS-SELFISHNESS; **self-luminous,** LUMINARY-SHADE; **self-opinionated,** CONCEIT - DIFFIDENCE; **self-opinioned,** BIGOTRY-APOSTASY, DECISION-MISJUDGMENT, SAGACITY - INCAPACITY; **self-possessed,** DETERMINATION-VACILLATION, RECKLESSNESS-CAUTION, SANENESS-LUNACY; **self-possession,** DETERMINATION-VACILLATION, EXCITABILITY - INEXCITABILITY, RECKLESSNESS - CAUTION; **self-praise,** CONCEIT - DIFFIDENCE; **self-preservation,** REPRISAL - RESISTANCE; **self-reliance,** BRAVERY-COWARDICE, DETERMINATION-VACILLATION, SANGUINENESS - HOPELESSNESS; **self-reproach,** REPENTANCE-OBDURACY; **self-reproof,** REPENTANCE-OBDURACY; **self-respect,** GENTILITY-COMMONALTY, SELFRESPECT-HUMBLENESS; **self-restraint,** DETERMINATION - VACILLATION, EXCITABILITY-INEXCITABILITY, MODERATION - SELFINDULGENCE;

self - sacrifice, UNSELFISHNESS - SELFISHNESS ; self-sacrificing, UNSELFISHNESS - SELFISHNESS; self-satisfied, CONCEIT - DIFFIDENCE; self - seeking, UN-SELFISHNESS - SELFISHNESS; self - styled, NAME-MISNOMER; self-sufficiency, CONCEIT - DIFFIDENCE; self - sufficient, CONCEIT - DIFFIDENCE; self - taught, KNOWLEDGE - IGNORANCE; self - tormentor, LIGHT-HEARTEDNESS-DEJECTION, self-will, BIGOTRY-APOS-TASY; self-willed, BIGOTRY - APOSTASY; self-worship, UNSELFISHNESS-SELFISHNESS.

self'-ish-ness. Seek ng one s own interest. CONCEIT-DIFFIDENCE, EXTRAVAGANCE-AVARICE, UNSELFISH-NESS-SELFISHNESS.

SELFRESPECT—HUMBLENESS.

Arrogance. Extreme self-assertion, claiming much for self and granting little to others. See PRESUMPTION.
Dignity. Stately impressiveness of character.
Haughtiness. Thinking highly of self and poorly of others. See Adjectives.
Hauteur. Disdainful spirit.
Mens sibi conscia recti [L.]. A mind conscious of rectitude. [Virgil *Æneid*, i, 604.]
Pride. Honorable self-respect; a sense of one's superiority
Self-respect. Respect for oneself, laudable self-esteem.
Vainglory. Excessive vanity.

SELFRESPECT—Denotations.

Crest. The helm or head, as typical of a high spirit; pride.
Fine gentleman. }
Fine lady. } A person aiming at show or effect.
High-flier. One who is extravagant in opinions or manners.
High notions. Extravagance of opinions or pretensions.
Proud man. A man showing too great self-esteem.

SELFRESPECT—Verbs.

"Bear like the Turk no rival [brother] near the throne." To allow no possible rival. [Pope (of Addison). *To Arbuthnot*, 197.]
Be proud. To have self-respect. See Adjectives.
Be proud of. To have a regard or esteem for.
Boast. To talk highly of oneself; brag. See BRAGGING.
Bridle. To express pride or scorn by holding up the head and drawing in the chin.
Carry with a high hand. To conduct overbearingly.
Give oneself airs. To assume affectation. See PRESUMPTION.
Glory in. To take pride in.
Hold one's head high. }
Hold up one's head. } To be proud.
Hug oneself. To congratulate oneself.
Lift up one's head. To exhibit one's pride.
Look big. To have an appearance of pride.
Look one in the face. To have his full respect.
Mount on one's high horse. To have much self-esteem.
Not hide one's light under a bushel. } To make a show of one's capa-
Not put one's talent in a napkin. } bilities.
Not to think small beer of oneself. To think well of oneself.
Perk oneself up. To bear oneself loftily.
Pique oneself. To pride or value.
Presume. To go beyond what is warranted.
Pride oneself on. To indulge in pride or self-esteem.
Put a good face on. To assume a false appearance.
Rear up one's head. }
Ride the high horse. } To show off.
Set one's back up. To assume a haughty attitude.
Stalk abroad. To walk boldly about.
Stand upon. To value; insist upon.
Strut. To walk with show; to walk Spanish.
Swagger. To boast loudly.
Take a pride in. To esteem highly.
Take the wall. To take the advantageous side.
Toss the head. To express pride in oneself or scorn for something else.

SELFRESPECT—Adjectives.

Arrogant. Having excessive, offensive pride. See PRESUMPTION.
Baronial. Having the character of a baron; lordly.
Bloated with pride. Swollen with pride.
Blown. Swollen; distended.
Bumptious. Full of odious self-conceit.
Consequential. Having the air of importance.
Dignified. Having a stately impressiveness.
Disdainful. Full of disdain; scornful.
En grand seigneur [F.]. In the manner of a great lord.
Fine. Showy; pretentious.
Flushed. Excited; animated.
Haughty. Proud and scornful.
High. Conceited.
High and mighty. Powerful and proud.

Abasement. The condition of being brought low in condition or feeling.
Affability. Courteousness combined with ease in conversation. See POLITENESS.
Blush. A suffusion of the cheeks with red, as from a sense of modesty.
Condescension. Courteousness to inferiors.
Confusion. Loss of self-possession.
Humbleness. State of being humble, or of thinking poorly of oneself.
Humiliation. Reduction to a lower state; mortification.
Humility. Modest estimate of one's worth; willingness to take a lower place than merit deserves.
Let down. A lowering of one's personal opinion.
Lowlihood. }
Lowliness. } State of being lowly, of being low in rank.
Lowness. State of being low.
Meekness. State of being meek, or of being not easily provoked, or resentful.
Modesty. Unwillingness to put oneself forward; absence of overweening confidence in one's abilities.
Mortification. Subduing of the passions by penance.
Resignation. The state of being submissive to a superior.
Self-abasement. Degradation by one's own act; humiliation from consciousness of guilt, etc.
Sense of disgrace. }
Sense of shame. } A feeling of a lowering in public estimation.
Set-down. A set-back; a humiliation.
Submission. Conformity to the will of another; resignation.
Suffusion. An overspreading, as of blushes.
Verecundity. Modesty.

HUMBLENESS—Verbs.

Abase. To bring low.
Abash. To disconcert by depriving of self-possession.
Ashame. To make ashamed; to confuse by knowledge of guilt.
Be conscious of disgrace. To have a feeling of shame.
Be conscious of shame. To be ashamed.
Be humble. To think lowly of oneself. See Adjectives.
Blush for. To feel shame for.
Blush up to the eyes. To blush all over.
Carry coals. To bear indignities tamely.
Cast into shade. To eclipse; subdue. See REPUTATION-DISCREDIT.
Change color. To blush.
Color up. To change color; be abashed.
Condescend. To be courteous to inferiors.
Confuse. To throw the mind in perplexity by a feeling of inferiority.
Crush. To overcome completely, as by a feeling of littleness.
Deign. To stoop to an inferior.
Demean oneself. To conduct oneself with modesty.
Disgrace. To bring shame upon; reject from favor.
Draw in one's horns. To retract; withdraw.
Drink the cup of humiliation to the dregs. To humble oneself.
Feel. To be conscious of some state or sensation of wrong or impropriety.
Feel ashamed. } Confused by a conviction of some wrong action or
Feel shame. } impropriety.
Feel small. To feel ignoble and mean.
Frown down. To disapprove by looks; rebuke.
Get a set-down. To be humiliated.
Hang one's head. To feel disgraced.
Hide one's diminished head. }
Hide one's face. } To retire in disfavor or disgrace.
Humble. To make humble; lower the pride of.
Humble oneself. To think lowly of oneself.
Humiliate. To reduce the pride or self-respect of.
Let down. To lower in esteem, consideration, etc.
Look foolish. To express by appearance the feeling of impropriety.
Lower one's note. }
Lower one's tone. } To diminish one's consequence.
Make one sing small. To subdue one's self-consequence.
Mortify. To bring one's passions into subjection; to humble.
Not dare to show one's face. To be retired in disgrace.
Not have a word to say for oneself. To be overcome by a sense of guilt.

SELFRESPECT—HUMBLENESS—*Continued.*

SELFRESPECT—ADJECTIVES—*Continued.*

High-flown. Proud; pretentious.
High-handed. Carried on in an overbearing manner.
High-mettled. Full of mettle or spirit; proud.
High-minded. Foolish and proud.
High-plumed. Abundantly decorated.
High-souled. Magnanimous.
High-toned. Aristocratic.
Imperious. Haughtily commanding; imperative.
In buckram. In a stiff manner.
Lofty. Elevated in manner or mien; proud.
Lofty-minded. High-minded; characterized by pride.
Lordly. Like a lord; haughty; domineering.
Magisterial. Having the manners of a master.
Mighty.
On one's high horses. ⎱
On one's high ropes. ⎰ Haughty.
On one's tight ropes. ⎰
On stilts. Pompous; haughty.
Overweening. Characterized by arrogance.
Perked up. Being exalted; carrying oneself proudly.
Prim. Very neat and stiff.
Proud. Having an undue sense of one's importance.
Proud as a peacock. ⎱
Proud as Lucifer. ⎰ Showy and proud.
Proud-crested. Proudly presumptuous.
Puffed up. Swollen, as with self-importance.
Purse-proud. Arrogant, due to money.
Starch. Stiff and rigid.
Stately. , Evincing dignity; dignified.
Stiff. Haughty.
Stiff-necked. Unyielding; insubordinate.
Strait-laced. Stiff and straight, especially in morals.
Stuck up. Proud; haughty.
Supercilious. Haughty with pride; with raised eyebrows.
Swollen. Inflated or distended, as with one's consequence.
Unblushing. Not blushing; bold. See CONCEIT.
Vainglorious. Excessive in boasting; vaunting.

SELFRESPECT—*Adverb.*

With head erect. Proudly.

SELFRESPECT—*Phrase.*

Odi profanum vulgus et arceo [L.]. I hate the profane crowd and I
shun them. [Horace, *Odes*, III, i, 1.]

HUMBLENESS—ADJECTIVES—*Continued from Column 2.*

Unoffended. Not offended.
Verecund. Modest; shy.

HUMBLENESS—*Adverbs.*

On all fours. ⎱
On one's feet. ⎰ Submissively.
Under correction. Reproved.
With bated breath. In fear.
With bended knees. Humbly.
With downcast eyes. In shame.
With due deference. Honorably.

HUMBLENESS—*Phrases.*

À pobreza no hay vergüenza [Sp.]. Poverty has no shame.
I am your obedient servant.
I am your very humble servant.
My service to you.

self'-same". Identical. SAMENESS-CONTRAST.
sell. To exchange; deceive. ADAGE-NONSENSE, BUY-
ING-SALE, TRUTHFULNESS-FABRICATION, TRUTHFUL-
NESS-FALSEHOOD; sell for, PRICE-DISCOUNT; sell off,
BUYING-SALE; sell oneself, UPRIGHTNESS-DISHON-
ESTY; sell one's life dearly, FIGHTING-CONCILIATION,
REPRISAL-RESISTANCE; sell out, BUYING-SALE.
sell'-er. One who sells. BUYING-SALE, DEALER.
selon les règles [F.] ´se-lon·' lê rêgl). According to rule.
CONVENTIONALITY-UNCONVENT ONALITY.
sel'-vedge. A finished edge. BORDER.
sem'-a-phore. A signal apparatus. SIGN.

HUMBLENESS—VERBS—*Continued.*

Put out of countenance. To be confused.
Put to the blush. To cause shame to.
Redden. To make red; to blush.
Render humble. To lower one's respect for self.
Send away with a flea in one's ear. To send away with a caution or
rebuff.
Set-down. To humble in a rough way.
Sing small. To have a lowly opinion of oneself.
Snub. To rebuff; to treat contemptuously.
Sober down. To become serious and grave.
Stare out of countenance. To cause confusion of countenance.
Stoop. To yield to another.
Stoop to conquer. To condescend to conquer. [Goldsmith, *She
Stoops to Conquer.*]
Strike dumb. To confound.
Submit. To yield to the power or bearing of another. See YIELD-
ING.
Submit with good grace. To yield gracefully. See EXCITABILITY-
INEXCITABILITY.
Take down. To humble; to abash.
Take down a peg. ⎱
Take down lower. ⎰ To lower one's opinion of self.
Take shame to oneself. To humble oneself for another's sake.
Teach one his distance. To show one his place; show one's estimate
of.
Throw into the shade. To eclipse; to subdue.
Tread down. To humble or disgrace.
Vouchsafe. To grant with condescension.
Yield the palm. To acknowledge superiority.

HUMBLENESS—*Adjectives.*

Abashed. Deprived of self-possession.
Affable. Courteous and ready to converse. See POLITENESS.
Ashamed. Feeling shame; abashed by guilt.
Bowed down. Caused to stoop, as with grief or shame.
Brow-beaten. Intimidated by rough manner or address.
Chapfallen. Having the lips or jaw drooping.
Condescending. Courteous to inferiors.
Crestfallen. Having the crest lowered; dejected.
Dashed. Checked; confounded.
Down in the mouth. Chapfallen; depressed in countenance.
Down on one's knees. In humble attitude.
Down on one's marrow-bones. Down on one's knees.
Dumfounded. Confused with astonishment.
Flabbergasted. Struck with wonder.
Humble. Not thinking highly of oneself.
Humbled. Lowered in one's self-esteem. See *Verbs.*
Humbled in the dust. Greatly humbled.
Humble-minded. Having an humble mind.
Lowly. Having low rank.
Meek. Gentle and submissive in disposition.
Modest. Unwilling to push oneself forward unduly. See CONCEIT-
DIFFIDENCE.
Out of countenance. Downcast.
Resigned. Submissive to superiors.
Servile. Having the spirit of a slave; cringing. See PRESUMPTION-
OBSEQUIOUSNESS.
Shorn of one's glory. Deprived of one's occasion of glory See
REPUTATION-DISCREDIT.
Sober-minded. Serious and grave.
Submissive. Willing to obey or conform to the will of another. See
YIELDING.

(*Continued on Column* 1.)

sem'-blance. Apparent likeness. COPY-MODEL, IMI-
TATION-ORIGINALITY, LIKELIHOOD-UNLIKELIHOOD,
LIKENESS-UNLIKENESS; wear the semblance of, AP-
PEARANCE-DISAPPEARANCE.
se"-mei-ol'-o-gy. The science of signs. INTERPRETA-
TION-MISINTERPRETATION, SIGN.
se"-mei-ot'-ics. The science of signs. SIGN.
sem'-i. Half. DOUBLING HALVING.
sem"-i-bar-ba'-ri-an. Half-civilized BENEFACTOR-
EVILDOER.
sem'-i-breve". A whole note. MELODY-DISSONANCE.
sem'-i-cir"-cle. A half-circle. CIRCLE-WINDING.
sem"-i-cir'-cu-lar. CURVATION-RECTILINEARITY

sem'-i-co''-lon. A mark of punctuation. MUTATION-PERMANENCE.

sem''-i-di-aph'-a-nous. Half transparent. DIAPHANEITY OPAQUENESS.

sem''-i-flu'·id. Partly fluid. VISCIDITY-FOAM.

sem''-i liq' uid. Semifluid. VISCIDITY-FOAM.

sem''-'-li-quid'-i-ty. Partially fluid. VISCIDITY-FOAM.

sem'-'-i-lu'-nar Crescent-shaped. CURVATION-RECTILINEARITY.

sem'-i-nal. Germinal. CAUSE-EFFECT.

sem'--na-ry. A school. SCHOOL.

sem''-i-na'-tion. The act of sowing. PREPARATION-NONPREPARATION.

sem''-i-o-pa'-cous. Semiopaque. D.APHANEITY-OPALESCENCE.

sem''-i-o-paque'. Translucent. DIAPHANEITY-OPALESCENCE.

sem''-i pel-lu'-cid. Semitransparent. DIAPHANEITY-OPALESCENCE.

sem'-i-qua '-ver. A sixteenth note. MELODY-DISSONANCE.

Sem-it'-ic. Pertaining to the descendants of Shem. ETHNOLOGY.

sem'-i-tone. Half a tone. MELODY-DISSONANCE.

sem''-i-trans-par'-en-cy. Partial transparency. DIAPHANEITY-OPAQUENESS.

sem''-i-trans-par'ent. Imperfectly transparent. DIAPHANEITY-OPAQUENESS.

semper, in utrumque [L.] (sem'-per, in yu-trum'-quî). Always prepared. PREPARATION-NONPREPARATION.

sem''-pi-ter'-nal. Everlasting. ETERNITY-INSTANTANEITY.

sem''-pi-ier'-ni-ty. Everlastingness. ETERNITY - INSTANTANEITY.

sempre l'ora, è [It.] (sem'-prê lo'-ra, e). It is always time. OPPORTUNENESS-UNSUITABLENESS.

semp'-stress. A seamstress. AGENT, DRESS-UNDRESS.

sem'-stress. A seamstress. AGENT.

sen. Coin. VALUES.

sen'-a-ry. Pertaining to six. FIVE-QUINQUESECTION.

sen'-ate. A legislative assembly. COUNCIL.

sen'-ate-house''. A legislative chamber. TRIBUNAL.

sen'-a-tor. A member of a senate. ADVICE, COUNCIL, PRESIDENT-MEMBER.

sen-a-to'-ri-al. Pertaining to a senator. COUNCIL.

sen'-a-tor-ship. The office of a senator. MANAGEMENT.

senatus consultum [L.] (sen-ê'-tus con-sul'-tum). A decree of the senate. ORDER.

send. To impel; transfer. PUSH-PULL, TRANSFER; **send adrift,** ADMISSION-EXPULSION; **send a letter to,** MISSIVE-PUBLICATION; **send away,** ADMISSION-EXPULSION, ATTRACTION-REPULSION, COMMISSION-ABROGATION; **send for,** ORDER; **send forth,** PUBLICITY, PUSH-PULL; **send off,** ADMISSION-EXPULSION, ATTRACTION-REPULSION, COMMISSION-ABROGATION, PUSH-PULL; **send out,** ADMISSION-EXPULSION; **send word,** ENLIGHTENMENT SECRECY.

senes, bis pueri [L.] (sî'-nîz, bis piu'-er-ai). Old men are children twice. INFANCY-AGE.

se-nes' cence. Aging. INFANCY-AGE.

sen'-ə-schal. A steward. CHIEF-UNDERLING, MANAGER.

sen'-e-schal-ship. The office of a seneschal.

se'-nile. Imbecile. INFANCY-AGE.

se'-nior. One older; a superior. CHIEF-UNDERLING, INFANCY-AGE.

seniores priores [L.] (sî-ni-o'-rîz pri-o'-rîz). The foremost fathers. LEADING-FOLLOWING, PRECEDENCE-SUCCESSION.

se''-ni-or'-i-ty. Priority of age or rank. INFANCY-AGE, NOVELTY ANTIQUITY.

se non è vero, è ben trovato [It.] (sê non e vê'-ro, ê ben tro-va'-to). If it is not true, it is well feigned. TRUTHFULNESS-FABRICATION.

se-ñor'. Mister. TITLE.

sen-sa'-tion. Feeling; a surprise. ASTONISHMENT-EXPECTANCE, EMOTION, FEELING-INSENSIBILITY; **sensation drama,** ACTING; **sensation of touch,** TINGLING-NUMBNESS.

sen-sa'-tion-al. Tending to cause feeling. EXCITATION, FORCE-WEAKNESS.

sense. Good judgment; meaning. MEANING-JARGON, SAGACITY-INCAPACITY; **accept in a particular sense,** INTERPRETATION-MISINTERPRETATION; **deep sense,** EMOTION; **in no sense,** NAME-MISNOMER; **sense of duty,** DUTY-DERELICTION.

sense'-less. Without feeling or good sense. ADAGE-NONSENSE, FEELING-INSENSIBILITY, MEANING-JARGON, SAGACITY-INCAPACITY.

sen'-ses. The five senses; soundness of mind. FEELING-INSENSIBILITY, MIND-IMBECILITY, SANENESS-LUNACY.

sen''-si-bil-i'-ty. The power to feel or know. MATERIALITY-SPIRITUALITY, SAGACITY-INCAPACITY.

sen'-si-ble. Capable of feeling. HEATING-COOLING, SENSITIVENESS-APATHY.

sen'-si-ble-ness. Feeling. SENSITIVENESS-APATHY.

sen'-si-bly. With feeling. SENSITIVENESS-APATHY.

sen'-si-tive. Easily affected. FEELING-INSENSIBILITY, SENSITIVENESS-APATHY.

sen'-si-tive-ness. State of having feeling. SENSITIVENESS-APATHY.

SENSITIVENESS—APATHY.

Affectibility. The state or quality of being capable of being affected.

Excitability, etc. The state or quality of being easily excited. See sub *Adjectives*.

Fastidiousness, etc. The quality of being easily repelled or disgusted. See *Adjectives*.

Impressibility. The state or quality of being impressible.

Mobility. The state or quality of being mobile.

Moral sensibility. The quality or state of being sensible of moral distinctions.

Physical sensibility, etc. State or quality of being susceptible to physical influences. See FEELING.

Sensibility. The capacity of receiving impressions from external objects.

Sensibleness. Capability of being acted on through the emotions or feelings.

Sensitiveness. The state or quality of being sensitive.

Sentimentalism. An excessive sentimental spirit.

Sentimentality. Affectation of fine, tender feeling.

Softness. The state or quality of being yielding or impressible. See *Adjectives*.

Susceptibility. The state or quality of being susceptible.

Apathy. A lack of emotion or feeling.

Callousness. The state or quality of being callous.

Cold. Lack of warmth or feeling.

Cold-blood. Languid condition of passions.

Cold-fit. An attack of disease producing a loss of sensation or emotion.

Cold-heart. Want of sympathy.

Coldness. The state or quality of being cold.

Coma. A condition of profound insensibility.

Deadness. The condition of being wholly unaffected by outside influences.

Dry eyes. Lack of sympathy.

Dulness. The state of being dull.

Frigidity. Coldness.

Heart of stone. A heart not susceptible to sympathetic influence.

Hebetude. Obtuseness; dulness.

Impassibility. Insensibility to suffering or pain.

Impassibleness. Impassibility.

Imperturbation, etc. Freedom from anxiety or excitement. See EXCITABILITY.

Inappetency. Lack of natural affection or desire.

SENSITIVENESS—APATHY—*Continued.*

Susceptibleness. The quality of being brought under a specified power or influence. See *Adjectives.*
Susceptivity. Susceptibility.
Tenderness. The quality of being sensitive to impressions. See *Adjectives.*
Vivaciousness.}
Vivacity. } Fulness of life and spirit. See *Adjectives.*

SENSITIVENESS—*Nouns of Place.*

Sore place. }
Sore point. } A distressing and painful subject of discourse, etc.
Where the shoe pinches. A sensitive spot or subject.

SENSITIVENESS—*Verbs.*

Be sensitive. To be capable of being acted on through the emotions.
"Die of a rose in aromatic pain." To be exceedingly sensitive. [Pope, *Essay on Man*, i, 200.]
Have a sensitive heart. }
Have a tender heart. } To be easily moved to pity.
Have a warm heart. }
Shrink. To decline or draw back on account of fear or sensitiveness.
Take to heart. To grieve over or be sensitive about.
Touch to the quick. To stir the feelings of, deeply or harshly.
Treasure up in the heart. To cherish fondly or with feeling.

SENSITIVENESS—*Adjectives.*

Alive to. Attentive; open to impressions.
Enthusiastic. Having the feelings or sympathies intensely aroused in approval.
Excitable, etc. Capable of having the feelings greatly agitated; very nervous. See EXCITABILITY.
Expressive. Give forcible expression to the feelings.
Fastidious, etc. Hard to please; oversensitive.
Gushing. Weakly sentimental.
High-flying. Extravagant in feelings and action.
Impassionable. Capable of being strongly affected by passion.
Impressible. Capable of being affected by an impression.
Impressionable. Susceptible of or subject to impression.
Lively. Full of animation or feeling.
Mettlesome. High-spirited.
Mobile. Easy or slow of expression of feeling.
Oversensitive. Too sensitive.
Romantic. Inspiring imaginary or ideal thoughts.
Sensible. Capable of sensation or emotion.
Sensitive. Easily or strongly affected by outside influences.
Sentimental. Given to or inspiring tender or extravagant emotions.
Soft. Foolishly sentimental or impressible.
Soft-hearted. Pitiful.
Spirited. Having considerable spirit or vivacity.
Susceptible. Capable of being influenced.
Susceptive. That receives or tends to receive an impression.
Tender as a chicken. Very tender.
Tender-hearted. Easily moved to pity.
Thin-skinned. Very easily affected or impressed.
Tremblingly alive. Sensible to even the slightest influence.
Vivacious. Full of lively spirit and feeling.
Warm-hearted. Sympathetic.
Without skin. Very sensitive.

SENSITIVENESS—*Adverbs, etc.*

Sensibly. Easily affected.
To the inmost core. Feelingly.
To the quick. To one's feelings.

SENSITIVENESS—*Phrase.*

Mens æqua in arduis [L.]. Equanimity in difficulties. [Inscription on portrait at Calcutta of Warren Hastings.]

APATHY—ADJECTIVES—*Continued from Column 2*

Callous. Hardened in feeling.
Careless. Having no care or consideration.
Case-hardened. Made insensible to external influences. See *Verbs.*
Chloroformed. Under the influence of chloroform; insensible. See *Verbs.*
Cold. Lacking feeling or sympathy.
Cold as charity. Very unsympathetic.
Cold blooded. }
Cold hearted. } Unfeeling.
Comatose. Relating to or affected with coma.
Dead to. Not affected by; indifferent to.
Deaf to. Paying no heed to.
Disregarding. Paying no attention to. See *Verbs.*

Inertia. Indisposition to motion or activity.
Inertness. Habitual want of activity or inclination to move.
Insensibility. The state or quality of being insensible.
Insensibleness. Insensibility.
Insouciance, etc. [F.]. Indifference. See UNCONCERN
Lethargy. Morbid drowsiness.
Lukewarmness. The state or quality of being lukewarm
Marble. Lack of compassion.
Moral insensibility. Incapability to distinguish right and wrong.
Neutrality. Indifference.
Nonchalance. Coolness; indifference.
Numbness, etc. The state or quality of being numb. See FEELING-INSENSIBILITY.
Obstupefaction. Stupefaction.
Palsy. Paralysis.
Paralysis. Loss or diminution of power of having emotion.
Phlegm. Lack of interest.
Quietism. Calmness or tranquillity of mind.
Recklessness. The state or quality of being rashly indifferent.
Sang froid [F.]. Coolness; calmness in time of excitement.
Sleep, etc. A state or period of suspension of sensory activity. See ACTIVITY-INDOLENCE.
Stock and stone. Insensibility.
Stoicism. A real or pretended indifference to feeling.
Stupefaction. The act of stupefying or state of being stupefied.
Stupor. Great suspension or diminution of sensibility or feeling.
Supineness. The state or quality of being supine.
Suspended animation. Loss of feeling.
Torpidity. The quality or state of being torpid.
Torpor. A state of inactivity accompanied by partial or total insensibility.
Trance. A condition, like death, in which there is total suspension of sensible powers.
Unconcern. Want of sympathy or anxiety.
Vegetation. The act or state of vegetating.
Vis inertiæ [L.]. Inertness; resistance to feeling.

APATHY—*Verbs.*

Assify. To make stupid or dull.
Be insensible. To be without feeling.
Benumb. Render numb.
Blunt. Make blunt.
Brutalize. To make brutal and unfeeling.
Brutify. To make like a brute; to render senseless.
Case-harden. To make insusceptible to good influences.
Chloroform. Put under influence of chloroform; render insensible.
Deaden. To render as dead.
Disregard. Give no thought or attention to
Feel no interest in. To be unaffected by.
Harden. Render hard or unfeeling.
Harden the heart. To be pitiless.
Have a rhinoceros hide. To be totally unimpressionable.
Have no desire for. }
Have no interest in. } To have no feeling toward.
Hebetate. Render obtuse; stupefy.
Inure. Harden by use.
Nil admirari [L.]. To be disturbed by nothing.
Not care. To pay no attention to.
Not care a straw for. To be wholly undisturbed by. See CONSEQUENCE-INSIGNIFICANCE.
Not mind. To disregard.
Not to be affected by. To be insensible to.
Numb. Benumb.
Obtund. To blunt or deaden.
Paralyze. Destroy or impair the power of sensation.
Render callous. }
Render insensible. } To make insensible.
Sear. To make callous or hard.
Set at naught, etc. }
Show insensibility. } Disregard; have no feeling for
Steel. To render very insensible or obdurate.
Stun. To render insensible by a blow
Stupefy. Deprive of sensibility.
Take no interest in. To be unaffected by.
Turn a deaf ear to. Disregard. See HEED-DISREGARD
Vegetate. To live in a state of continual insensibility.

APATHY—*Adjectives.*

Anaesthetic. Producing or characterized by insensibility.
Apathetic. Characterized by apathy.
Blind to. Wholly indifferent to.

(*Continued on Column* 1.)

APATHY—Adjectives—*Continued.*

Dull. Not quick in sensibility.
Flat. Lacking keen sensibility; dull.
Frigid. Cold.
Half-hearted. Only partially interested; lacking spirit.
Hard. Unyielding; unsympathetic.
Hardened. Rendered insensible to outside influences. See *Verbs*.
Heartless. Without pity or feeling for.
Impassible. Insensible to suffering.
Impassive. Unaffected by suffering; not exhibiting emotion.
Imperturbable. Incapable of being disturbed.
Impervious. Impenetrable to effect or feeling.
Inattentive, etc. Not giving attention to. See HEED-DISREGARD.
Indifferent. Exhibiting no interest.
Inert. Characterized by inertness.
Insensible. Devoid of feeling, emotion, or sympathy.
Insouciant [F.]. Indifferent; careless.
Insusceptible. Incapable of being influenced or moved.
Inured. Hardened. See *Verbs*.
Languid. Wanting in interest or spirit.
Leucophlegmatic. Relating to or affected with a dropsical feeling or condition.
Lukewarm. Not enthusiastic; indifferent.
Maudlin. Foolishly affectionate.
Mindless. Unmindful; careless.
Neglectful, etc. Full of or indicating neglect. See CAREFULNESS-CARELESSNESS.
Nonchalant [F.]. Lacking interest.
Numb. Destitute wholly or partially of the power of sensation or feeling.
Numbed. Insensible to. See *Verbs*.
Obtuse. Not keen; dull in feeling.
Pachydermatous. Thick-skinned.
Palsy-stricken. Having lost sensation.
Passionless. Lacking passion or emotion.
Phlegmatic. Not easily roused to feeling.
Pococurante. Caring little.

Proof against. Capable of resisting successfully; impervious to.
Regardless. Exhibiting no regard; neglectful.
Sans souci [F.]. Without care.
Sleepy, etc. Drowsy; lacking spirit. See ACTIVITY-INDOLENCE
Sluggish. Slow of emotion or feeling.
Soulless. Without soul; lacking human feeling.
Spiritless. Lacking spirit or liveliness of feeling.
Steeled against. Having no feeling toward. See *Verbs*.
Stupefied. Incapable of emotion. See *Verbs*.
Supine. Having no interest or care; indolent.
Tame. Lacking in interest or animation.
Thick-skinned. Not sensitive.
Torpid. Having lost partially or wholly the power of sensibility; sluggish.
Unaffected. Having the feelings unmoved.
Unambitious. Lacking ambition, energy or spirit.
Unanimated. Not roused; lacking spirit and life.
Unblushing. Having no sense or feeling of shame.
Unconcerned. Not concerned or interested.
Unconscious. Passing without noticing.
Unexcited. Not agitated or deeply stirred in feeling.
Unfeeling. Not conscious of the feelings of others; unsympathetic.
Unfelt. Not exciting feeling.
Unimpressed. Not affected by an impression.
Unimpressible. }
Unimpressionable. } That cannot have an impression made upon.
Uninspired. Without emotions.
Unmoved. Not aroused to compassion.
Unruffled. Not agitated.
Unshocked. Not having the emotions deeply stirred.
Unstirred. Not aroused or agitated.
Unstruck. Not suddenly impressed.
Unsusceptible. Not subject to or liable to be affected.
Untouched. Not having the sympathies or feelings aroused.
Vegetative. Living in a state of habitual indifference.

APATHY—*Adverbs, etc.*

Æquo animo [L.]. With unruffled mind.
In cold blood. In a heartless, brutal manner.
Insensibly, etc. Without feeling.
With dry eyes. Without any sympathy or feeling.

Without being impressed. }
Without being moved. } Insensibly.
Without being touched. }
With withers unwrung. Unsympathetically. [Shakespeare. *Hamlet*, III, ii.]

APATHY—*Phrases.*

It cannot be helped.
It is all one to.
It is all the same to.

It is of no consequence.
Never mind.
Nothing coming amiss.

sen'-sor. Producing sensation. EMOTION.
sen-so'-ri-al. Pertaining to the senses. EMOTION.
sen-so'-ri-um. The nervous system. MIND-IMBECILITY.
sen'-so-ry. Conveying sensation. EMOTION, MIND-IMBECILITY.
sen'-su-al. Licentious. MODERATION-SELFINDULGENCE,

PLEASURABLENESS-PAINFULNESS, SENSUALITY-SUFFERING.
sen'-su-al-ist. A sensual person. MODERATION-VOLUPTUARY.
sen"-su-al'-i-ty. Carnality. MODERATION-SELFINDULGENCE.

SENSUALITY—SUFFERING.

Animal gratification. } Sensual enjoyment.
Bodily enjoyment. }
Comfort. Ease or rest of body.
Creature comforts. Enjoyments which satisfy the base nature of man
Ease. Relief from labor or effort; relaxation.
Gusto. Keen enjoyment.
Happiness, etc. Joyful satisfaction, etc. See PLEASURE.
Luxuriousness. State of living in luxury.
Physical pleasure. Sensual pleasure.
Pleasure. Agreeable sensations; gratification of the senses.
Round of pleasure. A continued course of enjoyment.
Sensuality. The state of being sensual; free enjoyment of sensual or carnal pleasures.
Sensual pleasure. }
Sensuous pleasure. } Pleasures of sense and appetite.
Titillation. A tickling sensation or any pleasurable sensation.

SENSUALITY—*Nouns of Cause.*

Bed of down. } Figuratively, anything that affords ease, enjoyment,
Bed of roses. } and pleasure.
Bonne bouche [F.]. A sweet morsel,

Ache. Continued pain.
Aching. A continuous pain.
Agony. Pain so extreme as to cause writhings or contortions of the body.
Anguish. Extreme pain of body or mind.
Bodily pain. Physical suffering, in distinction from mental suffering.
Burning pain. A pain producing a sensation of a burn.
Discomfort. Lack of comfort; uneasiness.
Dolor. Pain; distress.
Gnawing pain. A pain producing the sensation as of a biting.
Malaise [F.]. Uneasiness.
Mental suffering, etc. Suffering of the mind. See PLEASURE-PAIN.
Pain. Any uneasy sensation of the body; bodily suffering.
Physical pain. }
Physical suffering. } Bodily pain.
Piercing pain. The sensation as of pricking with a needle.
Sharp pain. Extreme pain.
Shooting pain. Sensation as of something darting from place to place.
Soreness. Painfulness.

SENSUALITY—SUFFERING—*Continued.*

SENSUALITY—Nouns of Cause—*Continued.*

Clover. Pleasant circumstances.
Cup of Circe, etc. The enchanting cup, etc. See MODERATION-SELFINDULGENCE.
Dainty, etc. An exquisite article of cookery, etc. See PALATABLE-NESS.
Délice [F.]. A delicacy.
Dissipation. An extravagant course of life.
Feast. A banquet.
Lap of luxury. Figuratively, a condition of enjoyment and plenty.
Luxury. Something which pleases the senses and is expensive or rare.
Melody. A sweet succession of sounds.
Pillow, etc. Anything used to support the head of one when sleeping, usually a case filled with feathers or down, etc. See SUSPENSION-SUPPORT.
Purple and fine linen. Dress that is emblematic of royalty.
Refreshment. That which refreshes; an article of food or drink.
Regale. A banquet.
Source of pleasure, etc. Anything that affords enjoyment. See PLEASURABLENESS.
Treat. An entertainment given as an expression of regard.
Velvet. A silk fabric with a short, close nap of erect threads; hence, anything affording ease and comfort.

SENSUALITY—*Verbs.*

Bask in. To lie in the warmth of.
Bask in the sunshine. To enjoy oneself.
Enjoy. To be delighted with.
Experience pleasure. To enjoy oneself. See *Nouns.*
Faire ses choux gras [F.]. To delight in.
Feast on. To eat sumptuously of.
Feel pleasure. To enjoy oneself. See *Nouns.*
Give pleasure, etc. To delight. See PLEASURABLENESS.
Gloat on. }
Gloat over. } To gaze on with passionate desire.
Live in comfort. To enjoy oneself. See *Nouns.*
Live on the fat of the land. To live in luxury.
Luxuriate in. To freely indulge in.
Receive pleasure. To derive enjoyment from. See *Nouns.*
Relish. To receive pleasure from.
Revel in. To indulge without restraint.
Riot in. To indulge in luxury, feasting, and the like to excess.
Smack the lips. To make a noise with the lips after tasting, signifying enjoyment.
Swim in. To excessively indulge in.
Wallow in. To indulge in in a beastly manner.

SENSUALITY—*Adjectives.*

Agreeable, etc. Pleasant to the senses, etc. See PLEASURABLENESS.
At ease. Comfortable.
Comfortable. Affording comfort.
Comforting. Enjoying. See *Nouns.*
Cordial. Tending to revive or invigorate.
Cosy. }
Cozy. } Comfortable; easy.
Enjoying. Delighting in See *Verbs.*
Fragrant, etc. Having a sweet smell, etc. See PERFUME.
Genial. Contributing to the enjoyment of life.
Grateful. Giving pleasure to the senses.
In comfort. At ease.
Lovely, etc. Delightful, etc. See BEAUTY.
Luxurious. Relating to luxury; voluptuous.
Melodious, etc. Pleasant to the senses by a sweet succession of sounds, etc.
Palatable, etc. Pleasant to the taste, etc. See PALATABLENESS.
Refreshing. Reanimating.
Sensual. Given to the pleasures of sense and appetite.
Sensuous. Pertaining to the senses.
Snug. Convenient or comfortable.
Sweet, etc. Having a pleasant taste; agreeable to the senses, etc. See SWEETNESS.
Voluptuous. Given to the enjoyment of luxury and pleasure; excessively indulgent in sensual gratifications.

SENSUALITY—*Adverbs, etc.*

At one's ease. In enjoyment.
In comfort. Comfortably. See *Nouns.*
On a bed of roses. In ease and luxury. See *Nouns.*

Sufferance. The bearing of pain.
Suffering. Pain endured or injury incurred.
Throbbing pain. A sensation as of something beating in the body.
Throe. Extreme pain.

SUFFERING—*Denotations.*

Ache. Continued pain.
Convulsion. An unnatural, violent, and involuntary contraction of the muscular parts of the body.
Cramp. A spasmodic and painful involuntary contraction of a muscle.
Crick. A painful spasmodic affection of a muscle rendering it difficult to move the part.
Cut. A wound made by cutting.
Ephialtes. The nightmare.
Gripe. Pinching and spasmodic pain in the intestines
Headache. Pain in the head.
Hurt. A bodily injury causing pain.
Martyr. One who is put to death for his religion.
Nightmare. A condition in sleep characterized by frightful and oppressive dreams.
Pang. A fit of extreme pain and anguish.
Shoot. A sudden fit of pain.
Smart sore. A painful sore.
Sore. A rupture of the skin and flesh.
Spasm. An involuntary contraction of the muscles.
Stitch. An acute pain like the piercing of a needle.
Thrill. A sensation as of being pierced with something sharp.
Throb. A violent beating. See AGITATION.
Twinge. A darting local pain of momentary continuance.
Twitch. A short sharp contraction of the muscles.
Toad under a harrow. Figuratively, a sensation as of being crushed.

SUFFERING—*Nouns of Agent.*

Cruciation. The act of torturing.
Crucifixion. The act of nailing a person to a cross to put him to death.
Martyrdom. The suffering of death on account of adherence to the Christian faith.
Rack. An engine of torture.
Torment. That which gives pain or misery.
Torture. The act of torturing or producing pain.
Vivisection. The dissection of an animal while alive.

SUFFERING—*Verbs.*

Ache. To be in continued pain.
Agonize. To suffer violent pain or anguish.
Bite. To cause sharp, cutting pain.
Bleed. To die by violence.
Break on the wheel. To suffer excruciating pain.
Chafe. To be irritated or vexed.
Convulse. To shake with irregular spasms in grief or pain.
Cruciate. To torment.
Crucify. To fasten to a cross in order to put to death.
Excruciate. To cause to suffer agonizing pain.
Experience pain. }
Feel pain. } To suffer. See *Nouns.*
Flog, etc. To inflict punishment by means of a rod or whip, etc. See RECOMPENSE-PUNITION.
Fret. To irritate or be agitated.
Gall. To vex or chafe.
Give pain. To cause to suffer. See *Nouns.*
Gnaw. To corrode or fret away.
Grate. To irritate.
Grate on the ear, etc. To give pain to the ear by harsh sounds. See CACOPHONY.
Gripe. To distress or pinch.
Hurt. To do bodily injury to.
Inflict pain. To cause suffering to.
Lancinate. To tear or lacerate.
Make a wry face. Show signs of pain.
Pain. To afflict with uneasy sensations; to distress.
Pierce. To penetrate, as with a sharp instrument; to affect deeply.
Pinch. To oppress or distress.
Prick. To puncture, as with a pin; to sting.
Put to the rack. To torture with the rack. See *Nouns.*
Rack. To afflict with great pain.
Shoot. To throb with pain.
Sit on pins and needles. }
Sit on thorns. } To be in a very painful position.
Smart. To feel a pricking pain.
Sting. To pain sharply.

SUFFERING—Verbs—*Continued*.

Suffer. To feel pain; to undergo punishment.
Suffer pain. To feel pain. See *Nouns*.
Tingle. To have a quick thrilling pain.
Torment. To afflict; to harass.
Torture. To vex; to put on the rack.
Tweak. To twitch.

Twinge. To affect with a darting local pain.
Twitch. To snatch or pluck with a quick motion.
Undergo pain. To suffer. See *Nouns*
Wince. To shrink, as from pain.
Wring. To distress or torment.
Writhe. To twist or distort.

SUFFERING—*Adjectives*.

Aching. Paining continually. See *Verbs*.
In a state of pain. Suffering.
In pain. Suffering. See *Nouns*.
Pained. Hurt physically or mentally. See *Verbs*.

Painful. Causing physical uneasiness or distress.
Raw. Deprived of skin; galled.
Sore. Inflamed; painful.

sen'-su-ous. Affecting the senses. EMOTION, FEELING-INSENSIBILITY, SENSUALITY-SUFFERING.

sen'-tence. A statement; final judgment. ADAGE-NONSENSE, ASSERTION-DENIAL, DECISION-MISJUDGMENT, EXCULPATION-CONVICTION, PHRASE, RHETORIC.

sen-ten'-tious. Pithy. FORCE - WEAKNESS, SIMPLICITY-FLORIDNESS.

sen-ten'-tious-ness. Pithiness. FORCE-WEAKNESS, RHETORIC.

sen'-ti-ent. Having the power of sense. EMOTION, FEELING-INSENSIBILITY.

sen'-ti-ment. Delicate feeling; opinion. ADAGE-NONSENSE, CONCEPTION-THEME, FAITH-MISGIVING.

sen''-ti-men'-tal. Emotional; affected ONLOOKER, SENSITIVENESS-APATHY, SOCIETY-AFFECTATION.

sen''-ti-men'-tal-ism. Too great regard for sentiment. SENSITIVENESS-APATHY.

sen''-ti-men-tal'-i-ty. Too great regard for sentiment. SENSITIVENESS-APATHY.

sen'-ti-nel. } A guard. GUARD-PRISONER, SECURITY-
sen'-try. } INSECURITY, WARNING.

sep'-a-rate. To part; scatter. DIFFERENTIATION-INDISCRIMINATION, DOUBLING-HALVING, INCLUSION-OMISSION, INTERSPACE-CONTACT, MATRIMONY-DIVORCE, UNION - DISUNION; **separate into elements,** COMPOSITION-RESOLUTION; **separate maintenance,** MATRIMONY-DIVORCE; **separate the chaff from the wheat,** CHOICE-NEUTRALITY, DIFFERENTIATION-INDISCRIMINATION.

sep'-a-rate-ly. In a separate manner. UNION-DISUNION.

sep'-a-rate-ness. State of being separate. UNION-DISUNION.

sep''-a-ra'-tion. Division. CONCENTRATION - RADIATION, INCLUSION-OMISSION, MATRIMONY-DIVORCE, UNION-DISUNION.

sep'-a-ra-tist. A dissenter. ORTHODOXY-HETERODOXY

se'-pi-a. A pigment. GRAY-BROWN.

se''-po-si'-tion. The act of setting aside. INCLUSION-OMISSION, UNION-DISUNION.

se'-poy. A native East-Indian soldier. BELLIGERENT.

sept. A clan. DIVISION, PARENTAGE PROGENY, RELATIONSHIP.

sep-ten'-tri-on-al. Northern. LATERALITY-CONTRAPOSITION.

sep-tet'. A group of seven singers. MUSIC.

sep'-tic. Putrid. HEALTHINESS-UNHEALTHINESS.

sep-tic'-i-ty. The quality of being putrid. HEALTH-SICKNESS.

Sep'-tu-a-gint. The Greek translation of the Hebrew of the Old Testament made by seventy select translators. REVELATION-PSEUDOREVELATION.

sep'-tum. A partition. ENVIRONMENT-INTERPOSITION.

sep'-ul-cher. A tomb. LIFE-FUNERAL; **whited sepulcher,** TRUTHFULNESS-FRAUD.

sep-ul'-chral. Dismal; hollow in sound. CACOPHONY, LIFE-FUNERAL, RESONANCE-NONRESONANCE, VOCALIZATION-MUTENESS.

sep'-ul-ture. Burial. LIFE-FUNERAL.

se-qua'-cious. Following. HARDNESS-SOFTNESS, PRECEDENCE-SUCCESSION, TOUGHNESS-BRITTLENESS.

se-quac'-i-ty. Pliancy. HARDNESS-SOFTNESS, TOUGHNESS-BRITTLENESS.

se'-quel. A concluding portion. ANTECEDENCE-SEQUENCE, INCREMENT-REMNANT, PREDECESSOR-CONTINUATION.

se-que'-la. A morbid condition. INCREMENT-REMNANT.

se'-quence. The act of following, ANTECEDENCE-SEQUENCE, LEADING-FOLLOWING, PRECEDENCE-SUCCESSION; **logical sequence,** RATIOCINATION-INSTINCT.

se'-quent. Succeeding. INCREMENT-REMNANT.

sequentia, et [L.] (sec-wen'-shi-a, et). And the things following. PRECEDENCE-SUCCESSION.

se-ques'-ter. To take away from; seclude. ENLIGHTENMENT-SECRECY, RECOMPENSE-PENALTY, TAKING-RESTITUTION.

se-ques'-tered. Secluded. SOCIABILITY-PRIVACY.

se-ques'-trate. To seize. EXCULPATION-CONVICTION, RECOMPENSE-PENALTY, TAKING-RESTITUTION.

seq''-ues-tra'-tion. Seizure. RECOMPENSE-PENALTY.

sé''-rac'. A block of ice. HEAT-COLD.

se-ra'-glio. A harem. PURITY-IMPURITY.

ser'-aph. An angel. ANGEL-SATAN, GOOD MAN-BAD MAN.

ser-aph'-ic. Angelic. ANGEL-SATAN, GODLINESS-UNGODLINESS, PLEASURABLENESS - PAINFULNESS, VIRTUE-VICE.

ser'-a-phim. Angels. ANGEL-SATAN.

ser''-a-phi'-na. A musical instrument. MUSICAL INSTRUMENTS.

ser-as'-kier. A Turkish official. CHIEF - UNDERLING.

sere and yellow leaf. INFANCY-AGE, SEAR. [Shakespeare, *Macbeth*, V, i.]

se-rein'. A mist. DAMPNESS-DRYNESS.

ser''-e-nade'. A song; compliment. BLANDISHMENT, MUSIC, POLITENESS-IMPOLITENESS.

se-rene'. Clear; calm CONTENTEDNESS-DISCONTENTMENT, DIAPHANEITY-OPAQUENESS, EXCITABILITY-INEXCITABILITY; **serene highness,** TITLE.

se-ren'-i-ty. Calmness. CONTENTEDNESS-DISCONTENTMENT, EXCITABILITY-INEXCITABILITY.

serf. A peasant. CHIEF UNDERLING, GENTILITY-COMMONALTY.

serf'-dom. Slavery. LIBERTY-SUBJECTION.

ser'-geant. A military officer. CHIEF-UNDERLING.

se'-ri-al. Continued; a continued story. CONTINUITY-INTERRUPTION, MISSIVE-PUBLICATION, PERIODICITY-IRREGULARITY.

se''-ri-a'-tim. One after another; slowly. CONTINUITY - INTERRUPTION, REGULARITY - IRREGULARITY, SWIFTNESS-SLOWNESS, UNVIERSALITY-PARTICULARITY.

se'-ri-es. A regular order. CONTINUITY-INTERRUPTION, NUMBER, REGULARITY-IRREGULARITY.

sérieux, **take** *au* (o sê-riu'). To take seriously WITTINESS-DULNESS.

se″-ri-o-com′-ic. Combined mirth and gravity. SO-CIETY-LUDICROUSNESS.

se′-ri-ous. Important; grave. CONSEQUENCE-INSIGNIFICANCE, DETERMINATION-VACILLATION, LIGHTHEARTEDNESS-DEJECTION, MAGNITUDE-SMALLNESS.

se′-ri-ous-ly. Earnestly. ASSERTION-DENIAL, DETERMINATION-VACILLATION, MAGNITUDE-SMALLNESS.

se′-ri-ous-ness. Earnestness. CONSEQUENCE-INSIGNIFICANCE.

seris, tibi metis, tibi [L.] (tib′-i sī′-ris, tib′-i mĭ′-tis). For yourself you sow, for yourself you reap. GATHERING-SCATTERING, RECOMPENSE-PUNITION.

ser′-jeant. A lawyer. **Common serjeant,** JUDGE; **serjeant at law,** ADVOCATE.

ser′-mon. A religious discourse. CEREMONIAL, EDUCATION - MISTEACHING, ESSAY, SPEECH - INARTICULATENESS; **funeral sermon,** LIFE-FUNERAL.

ser′-mon-ize. Preach. CEREMONIAL, EDUCATION-MISTEACHING, SPEECH-INARTICULATENESS.

ser′-mon-i″-zer. A tedious adviser. TALKATIVENESS-TACITURNITY.

se-roon′. A fruit-crate. GATHERING-SCATTERING.

se-ros′-i-ty. The condition of being watery. LIQUID-GAS, WATER-AIR.

se′-rous. Pertaining to serum. LIQUID-GAS.

ser′-pent. A snake; winding; wise; a deceiver; an evil one. BENEFACTOR-EVILDOER, CIRCLE-WINDING, FAUNA-FLORA, GOOD MAN-BAD MAN, GULL-DECEIVER, MUSICAL INSTRUMENTS, RESONANCE-SIBILATION, UPRIGHTNESS-ROGUE; **great sea-serpent,** FANCY; **the old serpent,** ANGEL-SATAN.

ser-pen′-ti-form. Snake-like. CIRCLE-WINDING.

ser′-pen-tine. Winding. CIRCLE-WINDING.

ser′-ra″-ted. Notched like a saw. ANGULARITY, INDENTATION.

ser′-ried. Crowded. GATHERING-SCATTERING, SOLIDITY-RARITY.

se′-rum. Watery fluid. LIQUID-GAS, WATER-AIR.

serus in cœlum redeas [L.] (sī′-rus in cī′-lum red′-ĭ-as). Late return thou to the skies. LOVE-HATE, POLITENESS-IMPOLITENESS.

serv′-ant. A helper. AGENT, ANTAGONIST-ASSISTANT, CHIEF-UNDERLING, CONSIGNEE; **servant of all work,** AGENT, CHIEF UNDERLING.

serve. To wait upon; be a soldier; assist; obey. ACTION-PASSIVENESS, CHIEF-UNDERLING, FIGHTING-CONCILIATION, INSUBORDINATION-OBEDIENCE, LIBERTY - SUBJECTION, OBSTRUCTION - HELP, OCCUPATION, USEFULNESS-USELESSNESS; **serve an apprenticeship,** EDUCATION-MISTEACHING, PREPARATION-NONPREPARATION; **serve as a substitute,** COMMUTATION-PERMUTATION; **serve faithfully,** INSUBORDINATION-OBEDIENCE; **serve one right,** RECOMPENSE-PUNITION, REPRISAL-RESISTANCE, RIGHT-WRONG; **serve one's turn,** USEFULNESS-USELESSNESS; **serve out,** RECOMPENSE-PUNITION; **serve with a writ,** LITIGATION.

serv′-ice. Use; warfare; slavery; worship. CEREMONIAL, FIGHTING-CONCILIATION, GOOD-EVIL, LIBERTY-SUBJECTION, OCCUPATION, USE-DISUSE, USEFULNESS-USELESSNESS, WORSHIP-IDOLATRY; **at one's service,** PROFFER-REFUSAL; **press into the service,** USE-DISUSE; **render a service,** CHARITABLENESS-MALEVOLENCE, OBSTRUCTION - HELP, USEFULNESS-USELESSNESS.

serv′-ice-a-ble. Useful. GOODNESS-BADNESS, USEFULNESS-USELESSNE S.

serv′-ile. Abject. ADULATION-FLATTERY, PRESUMPTION-OBSEQUIOUSNESS, SELFRESPECT-HUMBLENESS.

ser-vil′-i-ty. Abject; flattering. ADULATION-DISPARAGEMENT, PRESUMPTION-OBSEQUIOUSNESS.

serv′-i-tor. An attendant. CHIEF-UNDERLING.

serv′-i-tor-ship. The office of a servitor. LIBERTY-SUBJECTION.

serv′-i-tude. Slavery. LIBERTY - SUBJECTION; **penal servitude,** RECOMPENSE-PUNITION.

ses′-a-me, open. A charm which opened the door of the robbers' cave in the *Arabian Nights.* APERTURE-CLOSURE, DEVOTION-CHARM, SIGN.

ses′-qui. One-half more. SOLITUDE-COMPANY.

ses′-qui-ped″-al. A foot and a half long. SIMPLICITY-FLORIDNESS.

ses″-qui-ped-a′-li-an. Very long. LENGTH-SHORTNESS, SIMPLICITY-FLORIDNESS.

sesquipedalia verba [L.] (ses″-qui-ped-ê′-li-a ver′-ba). Words a foot and a half long. SIMPLICITY-FLORIDNESS.

sess. A tax. PRICE-DISCOUNT.

ses′-sile. Attached by the base. COHESION-LOOSENESS.

ses′-sion. A sitting. COUNCIL.

ses′-sions. The sitting of a certain court. TRIBUNAL.

ses-ter′-ti-um. Roman money. VALUES.

ses-ter′-ti-us. Roman coin. VALUES.

set. Union; group; to sharpen; fixed; placed; ready. AIM-ABERRATION, ASCENT-DESCENT, ASSOCIATION, COHESION-LOOSENESS, CONDITION-SITUATION, DIVISION, ESTABLISHMENT-REMOVAL, GATHERING-SCATTERING, HABIT-DESUETUDE, INCLINATION, MUTABILITY-STABILITY, ORDER, PREPARATION-NONPREPARATION, SHARPNESS-BLUNTNESS, SOLIDITY-RARITY, UNION-DISUNION; **make a dead set at,** ATTACK-DEFENSE; **set about,** BEGINNING-END, ENTERPRISE, QUEST-EVASION; **set abroach,** BEGINNING-END, GATHERING-SCATTERING; **set afloat,** CAUSE-EFFECT; **set against,** ANTAGONISM-CONCURRENCE, COOPERATION - OPPOSITION, FAVORITE - ANGER, LOVE - HATE, VARIANCE-ACCORD; **set against one another,** COMPARISON; **set agoing,** BEGINNING-END, IMPETUS-REACTION, OBSTRUCTION-HELP, PUSH-PULL; **set an example,** COPY-MODEL, MOTIVE-CAPRICE, VIRTUE-VICE; **set apart,** CHOICE-REJECTION, INCLUSION-OMISSION, PROVISION-WASTE, UNION-DISUNION; **set a price,** PRICE; **set aside,** ASSERTION-DENIAL, CAREFULNESS-CARELESSNESS, CHOICE-REJECTION, COMMISSION-ABROGATION, DUTY-DERELICTION, ESTABLISHMENT-REMOVAL, HEED-DISREGARD, INCLUSION-OMISSION, KEEPING-RELINQUISHMENT, OBSERVANCE-NONOBSERVANCE, PROFFER-REFUSAL, USE-DISUSE; **set at ease,** ALLEVIATION-AGGRAVATION, CONTENTEDNESS-DISCONTENTMENT; **set at hazard,** SECURITY-INSECURITY; **set at naught,** ANTAGONISM-CONCURRENCE, CHOICE-REJECTION, DEFIANCE, DUTY-DERELICTION, OBSERVANCE-NONOBSERVANCE, OVERVALUATION-UNDERVALUATION, SENSITIVENESS-APATHY; **set a trap for,** TRUTHFULNESS-FRAUD; **set at rest,** BEGINNING-END, CERTAINTY-DOUBT, COMPLETION-NONCOMPLETION, CONTRACT, DECISION-MISJUDGMENT, INVESTIGATION-ANSWER; **set before,** CHOICE-REJECTION, ENLIGHTENMENT-SECRECY; **set before oneself,** PURPOSE-LUCK; **set by,** STORE; **set by the ears,** FAVORITE-ANGER, LOVE-HATE; **set foot on,** ENTRANCE-EXIT; **set forth,** ACCOUNT, ASSERTION-DENIAL, MANIFESTATION-LATENCY; **set forward,** ARRIVAL-DEPARTURE, ENTERPRISE; **set free,** LIBERTY-SUBJECTION, RELEASE-RESTRAINT, UNION-DISUNION; **set going,** IMPETUS - REACTION, OBSTRUCTION - HELP, PUSH-PULL; **set in,** BEGINNING-END, RIVER-WIND; **set in motion,** MOVEMENT-REST, USE-DISUSE; **set in order,** ORGANIZATION-DISORGANIZATION; **set in towards,** APPROACH-WITHDRAWAL; **set no store by,** OVERVALUATION-UNDERVALUATION, REGARD-SCORN; **set off,** ARRIVAL-DEPARTURE, BEAUTY-UGLINESS, BETTERMENT-DETERIORATION, COMPENSATION, POMP, PRICE-DISCOUNT; **set on,** DESIRE-DISTASTE, MOTIVE-CAPRICE; **set on a cast,** PURPOSE-LUCK; **set one's affections on,** LOVE-HATE; **set one's back up,** SELFRESPECT-HUM-

BLENESS; **set one's cap at,** BLANDISHMENT, DESIRE-DISTASTE, LOVE-HATE; **set one's face against,** ANTAGONISM-CONCURRENCE, APPROVAL-DISAPPROVAL, PROFFER-REFUSAL; **set one's heart upon,** DESIRE-DISTASTE, DETERMINATION-VACILLATION; **set one's seal to,** EVIDENCE-COUNTEREVIDENCE; **set one's teeth,** DETERMINATION-VACILLATION; **set one's wits to work,** REFLECTION-VACANCY; **sct on fire,** EXCITATION, HEATING-COOLING; **set on foot,** BEGINNING-END, CAUSE-EFFECT; **set on its legs,** CHANGEABLENESS-STABILITY; **set on one's lcgs,** OBSTRUCTION-HELP, STRENGTH-WEAKNESS; **set out,** ARRIVAL-DEPARTURE, BEAUTY-UGLINESS, BEGINNING-END, ORGANIZATION-DISORGANIZATION; **set over,** COMMISSION-ABROGATION; **set phrase,** PHRASE; **set purpose,** PURPOSE-LUCK; **set right,** EDUCATION-MISTEACHING, ENLIGHTENMENT-SECRECY, EXPOSURE-HIDINGPLACE, JUSTIFICATION-CHARGE, RENOVATION-RELAPSE; **set sail,** ARRIVAL-DEPARTURE; **set store by,** IMPORTANCE-INSIGNIFICANCE; **set straight,** CURVATION-RECTILINEARITY, FIGHTING-CONCILIATION; **set the eyes on,** SIGHT-BLINDNESS; **set the fashion,** CREATION-DESTRUCTION, DOMINANCE-IMPOTENCE, PRECEDENCE-SUCCESSION, RULE-LICENSE, SOCIETY-LUDICROUSNESS; **set the seal on,** COMPLETION-NONCOMPLETION; **set the table in a roar,** ENTERTAINMENT-WEARINESS; **set-to,** ENTERPRISE, FIGHTING-CONCILIATION, STRIFE-PEACE; **set to music,** MUSICIAN; **set too high a value upon,** OVERVALUATION-UNDERVALUATION; **set to rights,** ORGANIZATION-DISORGANIZATION; **set to work,** BEGINNING-END, ENTERPRISE, ORDER, USE-DISUSE; **set up,** BEGINNING-END, CAUSE-EFFECT, CREATION-DESTRUCTION, ELEVATION-DEPRESSION, ERECTNESS-FLATNESS, OBSTRUCTION-HELP, RENOVATION-RELAPSE, STRENGTH-WEAKNESS, SUCCESS-FAILURE, WELFARE-MISFORTUNE; **set upon,** ATTACK-DEFENSE, DESIRE-DISTASTE, PURPOSE-LUCK; **set up shop,** ENTERPRISE; **set watch,** CAREFULNESS-CARELESSNESS.

set down. To record; rebuke. APPROVAL-DISAPPROVAL, MARK-OBLITERATION, REGARD-DISRESPECT, SELFRESPECT-HUMBLENESS; **give one a set-down,** PROOF-DISPROOF; **set down as,** FAITH-MISGIVING; **set down for,** FAITH-MISGIVING; **set down for hearing,** LITIGATION; **set down in writing,** MARK-OBLITERATION; **set down to,** RATIONALE-LUCK.

se-ta'-ceous. Bristly. SMOOTHNESS-ROUGHNESS.

se'-tose''. Bristly. SMOOTHNESS-ROUGHNESS.

se'-tous. Bristly. SMOOTHNESS-ROUGHNESS.

sett. A lease. SECURITY, LOAN-BORROWING.

set-tee'. A seat. SUSPENSION-SUPPORT.

set'-ter. A hunting-dog. FAUNA-FLORA.

set'-tle. To put in order; fix; descend; agree. ASCENT-DESCENT, CHOICE-REJECTION, CONSENT, DECISION-MISJUDGMENT, ESTABLISHMENT-REMOVAL, LIFE-KILLING, MOVEMENT-REST, MUTABILITY-STABILITY, ORGANIZATION-DISORGANIZATION, SETTLEMENT-DEFAULT, SUCCESS-FAILURE, SUSPENSION-SUPPORT, VOLITION-OBLIGATION; **settle accounts,** ACCOUNTS, SETTLEMENT-DEFAULT; **settle down,** ESTABLISHMENT-REMOVAL, MUTABILITY-STABILITY, TURBULENCE-CALMNESS; **settle into,** CONVERSION; **settle matters,** FIGHTING-CONCILIATION; **settle preliminaries,** PREPARATION-NONPREPARATION; **settle property,** KEEPING-RELINQUISHMENT; **settle the question,** PROOF-DISPROOF; **settle to sleep,** ACTIVITY-INDOLENCE; **settle upon,** GIVING-RECEIVING; **settle with,** SETTLEMENT-DEFAULT.

set'-tled. Ended. BEGINNING-END, MUTABILITY-STABILITY; **account settled,** ACCOUNTS; **settled opinion,** FAITH-MISGIVING; **settled purpose,** PURPOSE-LUCK.

set'-tle-ment. Newly settled country; dirt; an agreement; property. CLEANNESS-FILTHINESS, CONSENT, CONTRACT, DWELLER-HABITATION, ESTABLISHMENT-REMOVAL, PROPERTY, SECURITY; **strict settlement,** KEEPING-RELINQUISHMENT, PROPERTY.

SETTLEMENT—DEFAULT.

Acknowledgment. The act of avowing or confessing to a charge or report.

Acquittance. Release from an obligation or debt.

Arrangement. The adjustment of a contention, etc.

Clearance. The act of clearing from debt, responsibility, obligation, etc.

Defrayment. The act of satisfying with payment.

Discharge. A release from anything.

Instalment. A limited payment of money at different times.

Liquidation. A complete payment or settlement.

Money paid. Payment or part payment of a debt. See OUTLAY.

Pay. Compensation for services rendered.

Payment. The act of paying; the compensation itself.

Quittance. Discharge as from a debt, etc.

Ready money. Cash; money that may be used at once. See MONEY.

Receipt. An acknowledgment of money paid.

Receipt in full of all demands. An acknowledgment satisfying all demands.

Reckoning. The act of computing; arrangement of accounts for settlement.

Reimbursement. Making good a debt; a refunding.

Release. Discharge from obligation or responsibility.

Remittance. Transmission of money in payment to a distance.

Repayment. A paying back of what is due.

Retribution. The giving of what is due for good or evil.

Satisfaction. The act of paying off, or making amends.

Settlement. The act of settling, of liquidating a debt.

Stake. A pledge.

Voucher. A document which vouches the truth of accounts.

SETTLEMENT—Nouns of Agent.

Liquidator. One who settles the accounts of a company that has failed. See TREASURER.

Payer. One who pays.

Application of the sponge. Destruction of a debt.

Bankruptcy. State of being bankrupt or unable to pay one's debts.

Defalcation. An embezzlement of money held in trust.

Default. A failure or neglect in some duty or requirement.

Dishonored bills. Notes or bills of exchange on which payment has been refused when due or presented.

Failure. Suspension of payment.

Fieri facias. A legal term directing an execution to be issued against the goods of a debtor.

Insolvency. State of being unable to pay one's debts at the proper time.

Insufficiency. Want of enough to meet one's obligations. See EXCESS-LACK.

Non-payment. Neglect of payment.

Protest. In law, the necessary proceedings to force an unwilling indorser to make good dishonored commercial paper.

Protested bills. Notes or bills of exchange whose payment has been refused.

Repudiation. Refusal to fulfil an obligation or a contract.

Run upon a bank. A succession of pressing demands for obligations due.

Waste-paper bonds. Written obligations or promises to pay which are worthless.

Whitewashing. A freeing from debts.

DEFAULT—Nouns of Agent.

Bankrupt. One who is unable to make payment of a just debt when due and demanded of him.

Defaulter. One who fails to account for moneys with which he is entrusted.

Insolvent debtor. A debtor whose property is taken to be divided among his creditors.

Lame duck. On the stock exchange one who cannot fulfil his contracts.

Levanter. An absconder.

Man of straw. A fraudulent surety.

SETTLEMENT—DEFAULT—*Continued.*

SETTLEMENT—*Verbs.*

Account with. To give a reckoning
Acknowledge. To admit or confess.
Acquit oneself of. To free or clear of.
Balance accounts with. To adjust accounts; settle.
Be even with. To repay in full
Be quits with. To make mutual settlement of demands.
Cash. To dismiss by paying up in full.
Clear. To free from obligations.
Clear off old scores. To settle old accounts.
Come down with. ⎫
Come down with the dust. ⎬ To pay money.
Defray. To make payment; bear the expense of.
Discharge. To free oneself of.
Disgorge. To make give forth; discharge.
Do the needful. To pay up.
Expend. To pay out. See OUTLAY.
Fork out. To hand over.
Grease the palm. To bribe.
Honor a bill. To acknowledge and pay a bill.
Lay down. To pay.
Liquidate. To pay off.
Make compensation. To pay, as for damages suffered.
Make payment. To pay
Make repayment. To pay a second time; to pay for something received.
Pay. To satisfy for service rendered property received, etc.
Pay all demands in full. To satisfy all claims upon.
Pay at sight. To pay as soon as an obligation is incurred.
Pay down. To pay what has been promised.
Pay for all. To pay in full.
Pay in advance. To pay before an obligation is incurred.
Pay in full To satisfy all claims against.
Pay one's footing. To pay the amount of one's obligation.
Pay one's shot. To pay for what one has received in service , loan, etc.
Pay one's way. To pay for one's passage from place to place.
Pay on the nail. ⎫
Pay ready money. ⎬ To pay at once.
Pay same for all. To deal with all alike.
Pay the costs. To pay an amount fixed by court for damages sustained etc
Pay the piper. To bear the cost expense, or trouble.
Pay up. To pay one's debts.
Pay up old debts. To pay a long-standing obligation.
Put down. To pay.
Quit. To release or discharge from an obligation.
Quit scores. To settle accounts; pay up.
Reckon with. To open an account with.
Redeem. To buy back.
Refund. To repay.
Reimburse To make payment of an equivalent.
Repay. ⎫
Retribute. ⎬ To pay back.
Satisfy. To free from obligation.
Satisfy all demands. To satisfy all claims against.
Settle. To adjust differences or accounts.
Settle accounts with. To free from obligation.
Settle with.
Shell out. To pay.
Square accounts with. To pay in full.
Strike a balance. To find out the difference between the debit and credit sides of an account.
Tickle the palm. To bribe.
Wipe off old scores. To pay long-standing obligations.

DEFAULT—NOUNS OF AGENT—*Continued.*

Stag. One who bids on an allotment of stocks, not intending to take the shares unless he can sell them at a profit.
Welsher. A sharper; a cheat.

DEFAULT—*Verbs.*

Apply the sponge. To efface, as a debt.
Become bankrupt. ⎫ To be unable to pay one's debts; to break one's
Become insolvent. ⎬ bench.
Be gazetted. To be announced officially as a debtor.
Break. To make bankrupt.
Button up his pockets. To decline payment.
Dishonor. To refuse to acknowledge, as a bill, debt, etc.
Draw the purse-strings. To refuse to pay.
Fail. To become bankrupt.
Fly kites. To issue fictitious commercial money.
Get whitewashed. Get freed from debt.
Not pay. To continue in debt. See CREDIT-DEBT.
Nullify. To make null or void.
Pay over the left shoulder. To default payment.
Pay under protest. To pay after notice of refusal to pay.
Protest. To declare publicly against the justice, equity, or right of.
Repudiate. To refuse to fulfil a contract or agreement.
Run up bills. To run into debt.
Stop payment. To refuse payment on a note or bill.
Swindle. To cheat; to get money by fraud or trickery. See sub THEFT.

DEFAULT—*Adjectives.*

Bankrupt. Unable to pay one's debts.
Beggared. Reduced to a beggar; impoverished. See AFFLUENCE-PENURY.
Behindhand. In arrear.
Gazetted. Officially announced as a debtor.
Gratis. Freely. See COSTLINESS-CHEAPNESS.
In arrear In debt.
In debt. Owing.
Insolvent. Unable to meet the claims of one's creditors.
In the gazette. Publicly announced as a debtor.
Minus. Lacking
Not paying. Defaulting
Unable to make both ends meet. To be in debt.
Unpaid. Owing. See CREDIT-DEBT.
Unremunerated. Without pay.
Worse than nothing. Worthless.

SETTLEMENT—*Continued.*

SETTLEMENT—*Adjectives.*

All straight. Paid in full.
Never indebted. Never going in debt.
Out of debt. ⎫
Owing nothing. ⎬ Free from obligation
Paid. Free from claims upon. See *Verbs.*
Paying Freeing from debt.
Unowed. Free from debt

SETTLEMENT—*Adverbs, etc.*

Money down Paid at once.
On the nail. At once
To the tune of. To the amount of.

---

set′-tler. One who settles. DWELLER-HABITATION.
set′-tlor. Law term. GIVING-RECEIVING.
sev′-en. A number. FIVE-QUINQUESECTION; **in seven-league boots,** SWIFTNESS-SLOWNESS; **wake the seven sleepers,** LOUDNESS-FAINTNESS.
sev′-enth. Next in order after the sixth. FIVE-QUINQUESECTION.
sev′-en-ty. A number. FIVE-QUINQUESECTION.
sev′-er. To separate. UNION-DISUNION.
sev′-er-al. A few; separate. MULTIPLICITY-FEWNESS, PLURALITY-FRACTION, UNIVERSALITY-PARTICULARITY; **several times,** RECURRENCE.
sev′-er-al-ize. To distinguish. DIFFERENTIATION-INDISCRIMINATION.

sev′-er-al-ly. Individually. UNION-DISUNION, UNIVERSALITY-PARTICULARITY.
sev′-er-al-ty. Tenancy. UNION-DISUNION.
se-vere′. Painful; harsh; critical; grave. APPROVAL-DISAPPROVAL, EMBELLISHMENT-SIMPLICITY, HARSHNESS-MILDNESS, PLEASURABLENESS-PAINFULNESS, PROPORTION-DEFORMITY, SIMPLICITY-FLORIDNESS, VIGOR INERTIA.
se-vere′-ly. In a severe manner. HARSHNESS-MILDNESS, MAGNITUDE-SMALLNESS.
se-ver′-i-ty. The quality of being severe. FORCE-WEAKNESS, HARSHNESS-MILDNESS, TURBULENCE-CALMNESS, VIGOR-INERTIA.
sew. To unite with a thread. UNION-DISUNION.

sew'-age. Refuse. CLEANNESS-FILTHINESS, NUTRI-MENT-EXCRETION.

sewed up. Drunk. TEETOTALISM-INTEMPERANCE.

sew'-er. Drain. CLEANNESS-FILTHINESS, WATER-COURSE-AIRPIPE.

sew'-er-age. Sewers. CLEANNESS-FILTHINESS.

sew'-er-gas". Gas formed in sewers. REMEDY-BANE.

sew'-ing-silk". Silk thread. LAMINA-FIBER.

sex. Difference between male and female; woman. DIVISION, MALE-FEMALE; **fair sex,** MALE-FEMALE.

sex"-a-ge-na'-ri-an. One over sixty years of age. IN-FANT-VETERAN.

sex-ag'-e-na-ry. Pertaining to sixty. FIVE-QUINQUE-SECTION.

sex"-a-ges'-i-mal. Founded on the number sixty. FIVE-QUINQUESECTION.

sex'-tant. Astronomical instrument. ANGULARITY, ASTRONOMY, CIRCLE-WINDING.

sex'-ton. Church-janitor. LIFE-FUNERAL, MINISTRY-LAITY.

sex'-tu-ple. Sixfold. FIVE-QUINQUESECTION.

sey'-id. An Arabian chief. CHIEF-UNDERLING.

shab'-bi-ness. State of being shabby. UPRIGHTNESS-DISHONESTY.

shab'-by. Paltry; torn; trifling. BETTERMENT-DE-TERIORATION, CONSEQUENCE-INSIGNIFICANCE, EX-TRAVAGANCE-AVARICE, REPUTATION-DISCREDIT, UP-RIGHTNESS-DISHONESTY.

shab"-by-gen-teel'. Affecting gentility. TASTE-VUL-GARITY.

shack'-le. To hamper; to bind. CONNECTIVE, OB-STRUCTION-HELP, RELEASE-PRISON, RELEASE-RE-STRAINT.

shade. Degree; shadow; screen; ghost. COLOR-ACHRO-MATISM, ENLIGHTENMENT-SECRECY, EXPOSURE-HIDINGPLACE, JOVE-FIEND, LIFE-CORPSE, LIGHT-DARKNESS, LUMINARY-SHADE, MAGNITUDE-SMALL-NESS, PAINTING, QUANTITY-MEASURE; **distribution of shade,** LIGHT-DARKNESS; **into the shade,** ENLIGHTEN-MENT-SECRECY, REPUTATION-DISCREDIT; **shadow of a shade,** DIMNESS, MAGNITUDE-SMALLNESS; **throw all else into the shade,** CONSEQUENCE-INSIGNIFICANCE; **throw into the shade,** ENLIGHTENMENT-SECRECY, REPUTATION-DISCREDIT, SELFRESPECT-HUMBLENESS, TRANSCURSION-SHORTCOMING; **thrown into the shade,** REPUTATION-DISCREDIT, SUPREMACY-SUBOR-DINACY; **under the shade of,** SECURITY-INSECURITY; **without a shade of doubt,** CERTAINTY-DOUBT.

shades. Plural of shade. **Shades below,** HEAVEN-HELL; **shades of death,** LIFE-DEATH; **shades of differ-ence,** VARIATION; **shades of evening,** DIMNESS.

sha'-ding. Making darker. LIGHT-DARKNESS; **shad-ing off,** QUANTITY-MEASURE.

shad'-ow. Shade; dream; type; ghost; slight degree. COPY-MODEL, FANCY, JOVE-FIEND, LEADING-FOL-LOWING, LIGHT-DARKNESS, LUMINARY-SHADE, MAG-NITUDE-SMALLNESS, SOLITUDE-COMPANY, SUBSTANCE-NULLITY, THICKNESS-THINNESS; **fight with a shadow,** SKILL-UNSKILFULNESS; **follow as a shadow,** LEADING-FOLLOWING; **may your shadow never be less,** APPROV-AL-DISAPPROVAL, POLITENESS-IMPOLITENESS, RE-GARD-DISRESPECT; **partial shadow,** DIMNESS; **shad-ow forth,** DELINEATION-CARICATURE, DIMNESS, PROPHECY, TROPE; **shadow of coming events,** PROPH-ECY; **take the shadow for the substance,** CREDULOUS-NESS-SKEPTICISM, SKILL-UNSKILFULNESS, TRUTH-ER-ROR; **under the shadow of one's wing,** SECURITY-INSE-CURITY; **without a shadow of turning,** MUTATION-PERMANENCE; **worn to a shadow,** BETTERMENT-DE-TERIORATION, BREADTH-NARROWNESS.

shad'-ow-y. Obscure; unreal. SUBSTANCE-NULLITY, VISIBILITY-INVISIBILITY.

shaft. Weapon; handle; column; tunnel. APER-TURE-CLOSURE, DEEPNESS-SHALLOWNESS, INSTRU-MENT, SUSPENSION-SUPPORT, WATERCOURSE-AIR-PIPE, WEAPON.

shag. A rough mass. SMOOTHNESS-ROUGHNESS.

shag'-ged. Rough; shaggy. SMOOTHNESS-ROUGHNESS.

shag'-gy. Rough. SMOOTHNESS-ROUGHNESS.

sha-green'. Skin of fishes. COVERING-LINING.

shah. Ruler. CHIEF-UNDERLING.

shake. To totter; to trill; to weaken; to fear. AGI-TATION, BETTERMENT-DETERIORATION, CRASH-DRUMMING, EMOTION, EXCITATION, HEAT-COLD, MOTIVE-CAPRICE, MUSICIAN, MUTABILITY-STABILITY, SANGUINENESS-TIMIDITY, STRENGTH-WEAKNESS, VI-BRATION; **shake hands,** AMITY-HOSTILITY, FIGHTING-CONCILIATION, PARDON-VINDICTIVENESS, POLITE-NESS-IMPOLITENESS; **shake off,** ADMISSION-EXPUL-SION; **shake off the yoke,** RELEASE-RESTRAINT; **shake one's faith,** FAITH-MISGIVING; **shake one's sides,** JUBILATION-LAMENTATION; **shake the head,** APPROVAL-DISAPPROVAL, ASSENT-DISSENT, ASSER-TION-DENIAL, PROFFER-REFUSAL; **shake to pieces,** CREATION-DESTRUCTION; **shake up,** AGITATION.

shake'-down". Bed. SUSPENSION-SUPPORT.

sha'-ken. Past participle of shake. STRENGTH-WEAK-NESS.

shakes. Importance. **No great shakes,** CONSEQUENCE-INSIGNIFICANCE, FAULTLESSNESS-FAULTINESS, GEN-TILITY-COMMONALTY.

sha'-king. Present participle of shake. AGITATION.

shak'-o. Cap. ATTACK-DEFENSE, DRESS-UNDRESS.

shak'-y. Weak; fearful. SANGUINENESS-TIMIDITY, SE-CURITY-INSECURITY, STRENGTH-WEAKNESS.

shale. Kind of rock. GEOLOGY.

shal'-lop. Boat. CONVEYANCE-VESSEL.

shal'-low. Not deep; lacking intelligence. CONSE-QUENCE-INSIGNIFICANCE, DEEPNESS-SHALLOWNESS, KNOWLEDGE-IGNORANCE, SAGACITY-INCAPACITY, SCHOLAR-DUNCE; **shallow pretext,** PRETEXT; **shallow profundity,** SOCIETY-AFFECTATION.

shal'-low-brain". Dunce. SAGE-FOOL.

shal'-low-ness. Lack of depth. DEEPNESS-SHALLOW-NESS, SAGACITY-INCAPACITY.

shal'-low-pa"-ted. Having no depth of affections. SAGACITY-INCAPACITY.

shal'-lows. Shoal. REFUGE-PITFALL.

sham. Deception. TRUTHFULNESS-FABRICATION, TRUTHFULNESS-FALSEHOOD, TRUTHFULNESS-FRAUD; **sham fight,** STRIFE-PEACE.

sha'-man. Exorcist. DEVOTION-MAGICIAN.

sha'-man-ism. Divination. DEVOTION-MAGIC.

sham'-ble. Saunter. AGITATION, SWIFTNESS-SLOW-NESS.

sham'-bles. Slaughter-house. LIFE-KILLING.

sham'-bling. Shuffling. AGITATION.

shame. Disgrace. APPROVAL-DISAPPROVAL, PURITY-IMPURITY, REPUTATION-DISCREDIT, RIGHT-WRONG; **cry shame upon,** APPROVAL-DISAPPROVAL; **false shame,** SOCIETY-AFFECTATION; **for shame,** REPUTA-TION-DISCREDIT; **sense of shame,** LOVE-HATE, REPU-TATION-DISCREDIT; **shame the devil,** UPRIGHTNESS-DISHONESTY; **to one's shame be it spoken,** REPUTA-TION-DISCREDIT.

shame'-faced". Abashed. CONCEIT-DIFFIDENCE.

shame'-ful. Scandalous. REPUTATION-DISCREDIT, VIRTUE-VICE.

shame'-less. Lacking shame. PRESUMPTION-OBSE-QUIOUSNESS, PURITY-IMPURITY, VIRTUE-VICE.

sham-poo'. To lather, rub, and wash thoroughly. CLEANLINESS-FILTHINESS.

sham'-rock. The emblem of Ireland. PATRIOTISM-TREASON, SIGN.

shan'-dred-han. An Irish cart. CONVEYANCE-VESSEL.

shang"-hai'. To induce a person by some trick to return within the jurisdiction of the officer who wishes to arrest him. TRUTHFULNESS-DECEPTION.

shank. Shaft. INSTRUMENT, SUSPENSION-SUPPORT.

shank's mare. Afoot. TRAVELING-NAVIGATION.

shan'-ty. Hut. DWELLER-HABITATION.

shape. Form; aspect. APPEARANCE-DISAPPEARANCE, FORM-FORMLESSNESS; **shape one's course,** ACTION-PASSIVENESS, AIM-ABERRATION, CONDUCT, QUEST-EVASION; **shape out a course,** DESIGN.

shape'-less. Not well formed. BEAUTY-UGLINESS, FORM-FORMLESSNESS, REGULARITY-IRREGULARITY.

shape'-li-ness. State of being well formed. PROPORTION-DEFORMITY.

shape'-ly. Well formed. BEAUTY-UGLINESS, PROPORTION-DEFORMITY.

share. Portion; to take part in. ASSIGNMENT, PARTICIPATION, WHOLE-PART; **share and share alike,** PARTICIPATION.

share'-hold''-er. Partner. PARTICIPATION.

shar'-er. One who holds a share. PARTICIPATION.

shark. Sharper. ROBBER.

sharp. Not blunt; painful; censorious; sagacious; musical note. ACTIVITY-INDOLENCE, APPROVAL-DISAPPROVAL, CACOPHONY, CRAFT-ARTLESSNESS, EMOTION, FEELING-INSENSIBILITY, MELODY-DISSONANCE, PLEASURABLENESS-PAINFULNESS, POLITENESS-IMPO-LITENESS, PUNGENCY, SAGACITY-INCAPACITY, SHARPNESS-BLUNTNESS, SKILL-UNSKILFULNESS, TURBULENCE-CALMNESS, VIGOR-INERTIA; **look sharp,** ACTIVITY-INDOLENCE, CAREFULNESS-CARELESSNESS; **sharp appetite,** DESIRE-DISTASTE; **sharp contest,** STRIFE-PEACE; **sharp ear,** HEARING-DEAFNESS; **sharp eye,** SIGHT-BLINDNESS; **sharp fellow,** ADEPT-BUNGLER, CAREFULNESS-CARELESSNESS; **sharp frost,** HEAT-COLD; **sharp lookout,** CAREFULNESS-CARELESSNESS, EXPECTATION-SURPRISE; **sharp pain,** SENSUALITY-SUFFERING; **sharp practise,** CRAFT-ARTLESSNESS, HARSHNESS-MILDNESS, UPRIGHTNESS-DISHONESTY; **sharp set,** DESIRE-DISTASTE.

sharp'-en. To make sharp. EXCITATION, FEELING-INSENSIBILITY, SHARPNESS-BLUNTNESS, TURBULENCE-CALMNESS, VIGOR-INERTIA; **sharpen one's tools,** PREPARATION-NONPREPARATION; **sharpen one's wits,** EDUCATION-MISTEACHING.

sharp'-en-er. One who or that which sharpens. SHARPNESS-BLUNTNESS.

sharp'-er. Scoundrel. ROBBER.

sharp'-ness. The state of being sharp. CACOPHONY, PUNGENCY, SHARPNESS-BLUNTNESS, SKILL-UNSKILFULNESS.

SHARPNESS—BLUNTNESS.

Acuity. Sharpness; acuteness.

Acumination. The state or quality of tapering or ending in a point.

Sharpness, etc. The quality or state of being sharp, etc.

Spinosity. The state or character of having spines or thorns.

SHARPNESS—*Denotations.*

Adz. A carpenter's tool with a thin arching blade.

Aiguille [F.]. A sharp mountain peak.

Antler. The horn of a stag.

Arête [F.]. An abrupt mountain spur.

Ax. A sharp tool of steel for cutting wood.

Barb. The point that stands backward in an arrow, etc.

Beard. The barb, or sharp point of an arrow.

Bill. A beak of a bird; a weapon of war.

Bill-hook. A knife with a hooked point used in pruning.

Bistoury. A slender knife used in surgery.

Blade. The cutting part of an instrument.

Bodkin, etc. An instrument of steel, for making holes, etc. See PERFORATOR.

Bramble. Any rough prickly shrub.

Brier. The sharp prickles of a plant.

Bristle. A short stiff hair.

Chevaux de frise [F.]. A piece of timber filled with iron spikes to defend a passage.

Cleaver. A butcher's cutting tool.

Cog. A tooth on a wheel for imparting or receiving motion.

Comb. An instrument with teeth for arranging the hair.

Cone. A solid body with a circular base and tapering to a point.

Colter. A knife attached to the beam of a plow.

Crag. A sharp-pointed rock.

Crest. The summit of a hill or mountain ridge.

Cusp. The point of a crescent moon.

Cutlery. Edged or cutting instruments.

Cutter. An instrument for cutting.

Cutting-edge. An edge or blade for cutting.

Edge-tool. A tool with a sharp edge.

Hatchet. A small ax.

Hedgehog. A small animal covered with sharp spines.

Horn. A hard projecting organ growing from the heads of certain animals.

Knife. A small tool having one or more blades.

Knife-edge. A blade.

Lancet. A sharp-pointed surgical instrument.

Mattock. An implement for digging.

Needle. A sharp-pointed steel instrument.

Nib. The point of a pen.

Paring-knife. A knife for paring fruit.

Peak. The top of a mountain.

Penknife. A small pocket-knife.

Pick. An instrument for digging.

Pickax. An ax with a point at one end.

Pike. A long shaft with a pointed steel head.

Pin. A small, pointed piece of brass or other metal for holding clothes together.

BLUNTNESS

Bluntness, etc. The state or quality of being blunt. See *Adjectives.*

BLUNTNESS—*Verbs.*

Be blunt, etc. To be dull or without a point or edge. See *Adjectives.*

Dull. Render less sharp.

Obtund. To render blunt or dull.

Render blunt. To make dull.

Retund. To render blunt or obtuse.

Take off the edge. Render an edge less keen.

Take off the point. To deprive of sharpness.

Turn. To blunt by turning over a fine edge or point.

BLUNTNESS—*Adjectives.*

Bluff. Abrupt; broad and flat.

Blunt. Having a thick edge or lacking an acute point; not sharp or piercing.

Dull. Not sharp or keen; having a blunt edge or point.

Obtuse. Blunt or rounded at the extremity, as a leaf.

SHARPNESS—*Denotations—Continued.*

Plowshare. The part of a plow which cuts the earth.

Point. A sharp point of land.

Porcupine. An animal covered with long sharp quills.

Prick. } A small sharp point.
Prickle. }

Pyramid. A solid having a polygon for its base and tapering to a point.

Ratchet. A click for holding a ratchet-wheel.

Razor. A keen-edged knife for shaving hair.

Rowel. A small wheel of a spur.

Scalpel. A small surgical knife.

Scissors. A cutting instrument of two blades.

Scythe. An instrument for mowing grass.

Shears. A large scissors.

Sickle. A reaping instrument.

Snag. A tooth projecting beyond the rest.

Spiculum. A minute granule, or point.

Spike. A large nail.

Spine. A sharp projection on any part of an animal.

Spire. A tapering body.

Spit. A long, slender, pointed rod.

Spoke. A projecting handle on a steering-wheel.

Spur. An implement fastened to a boot for urging on a horse.

Steeple. A spire.

Sugar-loaf. A mass of sugar in the shape of a cone; anything so shaped.

Sword, etc. An edged instrument of war. See WEAPON.

Tag. A metallic binding at the end of a string.

Thistle. A prickly plant.

SHARPNESS—DENOTATIONS—*Continued*.

Thorn. A pointed projection from a plant.
Tooth. Anything resembling the tooth of an animal.

Tusk. A long, protruding tooth.
Wedge. A tapering piece of wood or metal.

SHARPNESS—*Nouns of Agency*.

Emery. A very hard substance, usually mixed with magnetic iron, used for grinding very hard substances.
Grindstone. A flat circular stone, on an axle, for grinding tools.
Hone. A fine-grained stone or metal for sharpening cutting instruments, as a razor.

Sharpener. One who or that which sharpens.
Steel. An instrument of steel for sharpening knives.
Strop. A strip of leather for sharpening a razor.
Whetstone. A stone used for whetting, or sharpening, edge tools.

SHARPNESS—*Verbs*.

Aculeate. To make sharp or pointed, like a prickle
Barb. To furnish with barbs.
Be sharp, etc. To have a point or edge. See *Adjectives*.
Bristle with. To appear as though covered with bristles.
Cut, etc. To separate the parts of, with a sharp instrument. See UNION-DISUNION.
Grind. To sharpen by friction.
Point. To file or cut to an acute end.

Render sharp, etc. See *Adjectives*.
Set. To bend the teeth of a saw in alternate directions.
Sharpen. To make sharp.
Spiculate. To shape like a spicule.
Strop. To sharpen, as a razor by rubbing on a strop.
Taper to a point. To be sharp.
Whet. To sharpen on a whetstone

SHARPNESS—*Adjectives*.

Acicular. Having points like a needle.
Aciform. Shaped like a needle.
Aculeated. Having a sharp point; armed with prickles. See *Verbs*.
Acuminated. Brought to a point.
Acute. Having a sharply tapering point.
Arrow-headed. Pointed like an arrow
Arrowy. Sharp like an arrow.
Barbed. Provided with barbs.
Briery. Covered with briers.
Bristling. Standing like, or appearing as if covered with, bristles.
Conical. Shaped like a cone.
Corniculate. Having horns, or projections like small horns.
Cornute. Having, or shaped like, horns.
Cornuted. Cornute.
Craggy, etc. With numerous crags. See SMOOTHNESS-ROUGHNESS.
Cusped. Furnished with cusps.
Cuspidate. Having a sharp end like the point of a spear.
Cuspidated. Cuspidate.
Cutting. Adapted to cut.
Denticulated. Notched into small toothlike projections.
Dentiform. Tooth-shaped.
Digitated. Having finger-like processes.
Ensiform. Sword-shaped.
Fusiform. Spindle-shaped.
Keen. With fine edge or point.
Keen as a razor. Very keen.
Knife-edged. With an edge like a knife.
Mucronate. Ending abruptly in a sharp point.
Mucronated. Mucronate.
Muricated. Full of sharp points.
Needle-pointed.⎫ Pointed like a needle.
Needle-shaped.⎭
Odontoid. Tooth-shaped.

Peaked. Ending in a point from a wider base.
Pectinated. Having narrow divisions arranged like the teeth of a comb.
Pointed. Coming to a point; sharp. See *Verbs*
Prickly. Covered with prickles.
Pyramidal. In the form of a pyramid.
Salient. Standing out prominently; projecting.
Set. To bend the teeth of a saw slightly, every alternate one being bent to one side, so that the opening made may be wider. See *Verbs*.
Sharp. Having a thin edge or acute point capable of cutting or piercing.
Sharp as a needle.⎫ Very sharp.
Sharp as a razor.⎭
Sharp-edged. Keen; cutting.
Sharpened. Made to have a point or edge. See *Verbs*.
Snaggy. Full of snags.
Spiked. Furnished with spikes.
Spiky. Like a spike; having sharp points or spikes.
Spindle-shaped. Thick in the middle and tapering to both ends.
Spinous. Having spines; prickly.
Spiny. Full of spines.
Spurred. Furnished with spurs; having shoots like spurs.
Star-like. Having points like a star.
Stellated. Pointed like a star.
Stelliform. Star-shaped.
Studded. Filled with studs or little points.
Tapering. Becoming gradually smaller toward one end.
Thistly. Full of or resembling thistles.
Thorny. Rough with or like thorns.
Toothed. Furnished with teeth.
Two-edged. Having two edges.

---

sharp'-shoot"-er. Marksman. BELLIGERENT, PUSH-PULL.
sharp'-shoot"-ing. Marksmanship. ATTACK-DEFENSE.
shas'-ter. Brahman institutions. REVELATION-PSEUDOREVELATION.
shat'-ter. To ruin. CREATION-DESTRUCTION, MIGHT-IMPOTENCE, UNION-DISUNION.
shat'-ter-brained". Heedless. SANENESS-LUNACY.
shat'-tered. Weakened. MIGHT-IMPOTENCE, STRENGTH-WEAKNESS, WEARINESS-REFRESHMENT.
shat'-ter-ing. Present participle of shatter. STRENGTH-WEAKNESS.
shat'-ter-pa"-ted. Of trifling intellect. SANENESS-LUNACY.
shat'-ter-y. Brittle. STRENGTH-WEAKNESS.
shave. To smooth; to slice; to cheat. ENLARGEMENT-DIMINUTION, FRIABILITY, LAMINA-FIBER, LENGTH-SHORTNESS, SMOOTHNESS-ROUGHNESS, TRUTHFULNESS-FABRICATION.
shav'-ing. Slice. BREADTH-NARROWNESS, LAMINA-FIBER, MAGNITUDE-SMALLNESS.
shawl. Garment. DRESS-UNDRESS.
she. Feminine pronoun. MALE-FEMALE.
sheaf. Bundle. GATHERING-SCATTERING.

shear. To clip close. ENLARGEMENT-DIMINUTION, LENGTH-SHORTNESS, TAKING-RESTITUTION.
shears. Scissors. SHARPNESS-BLUNTNESS.
sheath. Case. COVER-LINING, CONTENTS-RECEIVER.
sheathe. Cover. DRESS-UNDRESS, TURBULENCE-CALMNESS; **sheathe the sword,** FIGHTING-CONCILIATION.
sheath'-ing. Covering. COVER-LINING.
sheave. The wheel of a pulley-block. SUSPENSION-SUPPORT.
shed. To cast off; to turn off; building. ADMISSION-EXPULSION, COVER-LINING, DWELLER-HABITATION, GATHERING-SCATTERING, GIVING-RECEIVING; **shed a luster on,** REPUTATION-DISCREDIT; **shed blood,** LIFE-KILLING; **shed light upon,** LIGHT-DARKNESS; **shed tears,** JUBILATION-LAMENTATION.
sheen. Brightness. LIGHT-DARKNESS.
sheen'-y. Shining. LIGHT-DARKNESS.
sheep. Animal. FAUNA-FLORA.
sheep'-dog". Kind of dog. DOMESTICATION-AGRICULTURE, FAUNA-FLORA.
sheep'-fold". Shelter for sheep. ENCLOSURE.
sheep'-ish. Abashed. CONCEIT-DIFFIDENCE.
sheep's'-eye". An oblique glance, amorously bashful.

Cast a sheep's eye, BLANDISHMENT, CONCEIT-DIFFI-DENCE, DESIRE-DISTASTE.

sheer. Mere. ENTIRETY-DEFICIENCY, MAGNITUDE-SMALLNESS, MIXTURE-HOMOGENEITY; **sheer off,** APPROACH-WITHDRAWAL, QUEST-EVASION.

sheet. Layer; cover. COVER-LINING, LAMINA-FIBER, MISSIVE-PUBLICATION; **balance-sheet,** OUTLAY-INCOME; **sheet of fire,** HEAT-COLD; **sheet of water,** GULF-PLAIN; **white sheet,** ATONEMENT; **winding-sheet,** LIFE-FUNERAL.

sheet'–an"-chor. Anchor. BETTERMENT-DETERIORATION, MEANS, REFUGE-PITFALL.

sheet'–light"-ning. Kind of lightning. LUMINARY-SHADE.

sheik. Arab chief. CHIEF-UNDERLING, MINISTRY-LAITY.

shek'-el. Hebrew coin. VALUES.

shelf. Ledge; support. REFUGE-PITFALL, SUSPENSION-SUPPORT; **on the shelf,** ACTION-PASSIVENESS, MIGHT-IMPOTENCE, USE-DISUSE.

shell. Cover; bomb; to bombard. ATTACK-DEFENSE, COVER-LINING, LIFE-FUNERAL, WEAPON; **shell out,** OUTLAY-INCOME, SETTLEMENT-DEFAULT.

shell'–fish". Fish having a shell. FAUNA-FLORA.

shel'-ter. Refuge. REFUGE-PITFALL, SECURITY-INSECURITY; **shelter oneself under plea of,** PRETEXT.

shel'-tie. Pony. CONVEYER.

shelve. To postpone; to slope. CAREFULNESS-CARELESSNESS, ESTABLISHMENT-REMOVAL, PARALLELISM-INCLINATION, USE-DISUSE.

shelved. Retired. CAREFULNESS-CARELESSNESS.

shelv'-ing beach. Sloping beach. PARALLELISM-INCLINATION.

shend. To reproach. BETTERMENT-DETERIORATION.

Shep'-herd. Jesus Christ. **The Good Shepherd,** DIVINITY.

shep'-herd. Keeper of sheep; pastor. CITY-COUNTRY, DOMESTICATION-AGRICULTURE, MANAGER, MINISTRY-LAITY.

shep'-herd-ess. Female shepherd. CITY-COUNTRY.

shep'-herd's dog. A collie; a sheep-dog. FAUNA-FLORA.

Shep'-pard. Jack Sheppard. ROBBER.

shere. To shear. MAGNITUDE-SMALLNESS.

sher'-iff. Officer. JUDICATURE.

shib'-bo-leth. Watchword. SIGN.

shield. Buckler; refuge. ATTACK-DEFENSE, COVER-LINING, REFUGE-PITFALL, SECURITY-INSECURITY, SIGN, TITLE; **look only at one side of the shield,** DECISION-MISJUDGMENT; **reverse of the shield,** ANTERIORITY-POSTERIORITY, EVIDENCE-COUNTEREVIDENCE; **under the shield of,** SECURITY-INSECURITY.

shield'-ing. Present participle of shield. ATTACK-DEFENSE.

shift. To change; pretext; turn; chemise. AIM-ABERRATION, COMMUTATION-PERMUTATION, CONVERSION-REVERSION, CRAFT-ARTLESSNESS, DRESS-UNDRESS, MOVEMENT-REST, MUTABILITY-STABILITY, MUTATION-PERMANENCE, PRETEXT, TRANSFER, TRUTHFULNESS-FABRICATION; **last shift,** DESIGN, VOLITION-OBLIGATION; **left to shift for oneself,** SOCIABILITY-PRIVACY; **make a shift with,** COMMUTATION-PERMANENCE, USE-DISUSE; **put to one's shifts,** AFFLUENCE-PENURY, DIFFICULTY-FACILITY; **shift for oneself,** CONDUCT, LIBERTY-SUBJECTION; **shift off,** EARLINESS-LATENESS; **shift one's ground,** BIGOTRY-APOSTASY; **shift one's quarters,** MOVEMENT-REST; **shift the scene,** MUTATION-PERMANENCE; **shift to and fro,** MUTABILITY-STABILITY.

shift'-ing. Changing from place to place. ALIENATION, CONVERSION, LASTINGNESS-TRANSIENTNESS, MOVEMENT-REST, TRANSFER; **shifting sands,** MUTABILITY-STABILITY; **shifting trust or use,** ALIENATION.

shift'-less. Not thrifty. PREPARATION-NONPREPARATION, REPENTANCE-OBDURACY, SKILL-UNSKILFULNESS.

shil-la'-lah. Cudgel. WEAPON.

shil'-ling. Coin. MONEY.

shil'-ly-shal"-ly. To waver. DETERMINATION-VACILLATION, REPUTATION-DISCREDIT.

shim'-mer. To glimmer. LIGHT-DARKNESS.

shin'-dy. Row. STRIFE-PEACE.

shine. To give light; to be eminent. BEAUTY-REPUTATION, LIGHT-DARKNESS, REPUTATION-DISCREDIT; **shine in conversation,** CONVERSATION-MONOLOGUE; **shine forth,** REPUTATION-DISCREDIT; **shine upon,** LIGHT-DARKNESS, OBSTRUCTION-HELP; **take the shine out of,** REPUTATION-DISCREDIT.

shin'-gle. Gravel. FRIABILITY.

shin'-ing. Giving forth light; prominent. **Shining light,** BEAUTY-UGLINESS, LIGHT-DARKNESS, SAGE-FOOL.

shi'-ny. Glossy. LIGHT-DARKNESS.

ship. Vessel; to put or get onto a ship. CONTENTS-RECEIVER, CONVEYANCE-VESSEL, CONVEYER, TRANSFER, TRAVELING-NAVIGATION; **one's ship coming in,** AFFLUENCE-PENURY; **ship of the line,** BELLIGERENT; **take ship,** ARRIVAL-DEPARTURE, TRAVELING-NAVIGATION.

ship'-board". Vessel. **On ship-board,** CONVEYANCE-VESSEL.

ship'-load". Cargo. CONTENTS-RECEIVER, MAGNITUDE-SMALLNESS.

ship'-man. Sailor. WAYFARER-SEAFARER.

ship'-mate". Sailor. FRIEND-FOE.

ship'-ment. Something shipped. CONTENTS-RECEIVER, TRANSFER.

ship'-pen. Stall. DWELLER-HABITATION.

ship'-ping. Tonnage. CONVEYANCE-VESSEL.

ship'-shape". Orderly. CONVENTIONALITY-UNCONVENTIONALITY, REGULARITY-IRREGULARITY, SKILL-UNSKILFULNESS.

ship'-wreck". Ruin. CREATION-DESTRUCTION, SUCCESS-FAILURE.

shire. County. EXTENSION-DISTRICT.

shirk. To slight. INSUBORDINATION-OBEDIENCE, QUEST-EVASION.

shirk'-er. One who evades work or obligation. QUEST-EVASION.

shirt. Garment. DRESS-UNDRESS.

shive. Cork. LAMINA-FIBER, MAGNITUDE-SMALLNESS.

shiv'-er. To shatter; to quiver. AGITATION, CREATION-DESTRUCTION, HEAT-COLD, LAMINA-FIBER, MAGNITUDE-SMALLNESS, SANGUINENESS-TIMIDITY, TOUGHNESS-BRITTLENESS, UNION-DISUNION; **go to shivers,** CREATION-DESTRUCTION; **shiver in one's shoes,** SANGUINENESS-TIMIDITY.

shiv'-er-ing. Shaking from cold. HEAT-COLD.

shiv'-er-y. Easily broken. FRIABILITY, TOUGHNESS-BRITTLENESS.

shoal. Shallow; throng. DEEPNESS-SHALLOWNESS, GATHERING-SCATTERING, MULTIPLICITY-FEWNESS.

shoals. Sand-banks. DEEPNESS-SHALLOWNESS, REFUGE-PITFALL; **surrounded by shoals,** DIFFICULTY-FACILITY.

shoal'-y. Abounding in shoals. DEEPNESS-SHALLOWNESS.

shock. A sheaf; a concussion; a sensation; to pain; to disgust. AGITATION, APPROVAL-DISAPPROVAL, DESIRE-DISTASTE, EMOTION, EXCITATION, EXPECTATION-SURPRISE, GATHERING-SCATTERING, IMPETUS-REACTION, PLEASURE-PAIN, PLEASURABLENESS-PAINFULNESS, TURBULENCE-CALMNESS, VARIANCE-ACCORD.

shock'-ing. Painful; fearful; disgusting. BEAUTY-UGLINESS, GOODNESS-BADNESS, LOVE-HATE, PLEASURABLENESS-PAINFULNESS, REPUTATION-DISCREDIT, SANGUINENESS-TIMIDITY, TASTE-VULGARITY; **in a shocking temper,** FAVORITE-MOROSENESS.

shock'-ing-ly. Disgustingly. MAGNITUDE-SMALLNESS.

shod. Having shoes. DRESS-UNDRESS.

shod'-dy. Cloth. USEFULNESS-USELESSNESS.

shoe. Foot-wear; a support; a break. DRESS-UNDRESS, OBSTRUCTION-HELP, SUSPENSION-SUPPORT; **stand in the shoes of,** COMMISSION-ABROGATION, REPRESENTATIVE; **where the shoe pinches,** ANTAGONISM-CONCURRENCE, DIFFICULTY-FACILITY, GOODNESS-BADNESS, PLEASURABLENESS-PAINFULNESS, SENSITIVENESS-APATHY.

shoe'-ma"-ker. A cobbler. DRESS-UNDRESS.

shog. A jog. TURBULENCE-CALMNESS.

shoot. To kill; offspring; to dart; to grow; to execute; to pain. ENLARGEMENT-DIMINUTION, EXCULPATION-PUNITION, LIFE-KILLING, PARENTAGE-PROGENY, PUSH-PULL, SENSUALITY-SUFFERING, SWIFTNESS-SLOWNESS; **shoot ahead,** ADVANCE-RETROGRESSION; **shoot ahead of,** TRANSCURSION-SHORTCOMING; **shoot at,** ATTACK-DEFENSE; **shoot out beams,** LIGHT-DARKNESS; **shoot up,** CONVEXITY-CONCAVITY, QUANTITY-MEASURE; **teach the young idea to shoot,** EDUCATION-MISTEACHING.

shoot'-er. One who or that which shoots. PUSH-PULL.

shoot'-ing. Hunting. LIFE-KILLING, QUEST-EVASION; **shooting pain,** SENSUALITY-SUFFERING; **shooting star,** ASTRONOMY, UNIVERSE.

shoot'-ing-coat. A garment. DRESS-UNDRESS.

shop. To buy; a store. BUYING-SALE, MARKET; **keep a shop,** EXCHANGE, OCCUPATION; **shut up shop,** BEGINNING-END, DISCONTINUANCE-CONTINUANCE, QUEST-ABANDONMENT, TOIL-RELAXATION; **smell of the shop,** EMBELLISHMENT-VULGARITY.

shop'-keep"-er. A tradesman. DEALER.

shop'-lift"-er. A thief. ROBBER.

shop'-lift"-ing. Thievery. THEFT.

shop'-man. A shopkeeper. DEALER.

shop'-mate". A comrade. FRIEND-FOE.

shop'-ping. Buying. BUYING-SALE, EXCHANGE.

shore. Border; land; a support. ATTACK-DEFENSE, BORDER, OCEAN-LAND, SUSPENSION-SUPPORT; **hug the shore,** APPROACH-WITHDRAWAL; **on shore,** GULF-PLAIN; **shore up,** SUSPENSION-SUPPORT.

shore'-less. Boundless. EXTENSION-DISTRICT.

shorn. Cut short; deprived. GAIN-LOSS, LENGTH-SHORTNESS, TOP-BOTTOM; **shorn of its beams,** DIMNESS, GENTILITY-COMMONALTY; **shorn lamb,** PLEASURE-PAIN.

short. Not long; brittle; uncivil. ENTIRETY-DEFICIENCY, GREATNESS-LITTLENESS, LENGTH-SHORTNESS, POLITENESS-IMPOLITENESS, TERSENESS-PROLIXITY, TOUGHNESS-BRITTLENESS, TRANSCURSION-SHORTCOMING; **at short notice,** EARLINESS-LATENESS, LASTINGNESS-TRANSIENTNESS; **come short of,** EXCESS-LACK, SUPREMACY-SUBORDINACY; **in short,** DIGEST, LENGTH-SHORTNESS, TERSENESS-PROLIXITY; **make short work of,** ACTIVITY-INDOLENCE, COMPLETION-NONCOMPLETION, CREATION-DESTRUCTION, DETERMINATION-VACILLATION, EXCULPATION-PUNITION, HURRY-LEISURE, SUCCESS-FAILURE; **short allowance,** EXCESS-LACK; **short breath,** WEARINESS-REFRESHMENT; **short by,** LENGTH-SHORTNESS; **short commons,** EXCESS-LACK, FASTING-GLUTTONY; **short cut,** CURVATION-RECTILINEARITY, MIDCOURSE-CIRCUIT; **short distance,** REMOTENESS-NEARNESS; **short life and merry,** ENTERTAINMENT-WEARINESS; **short measure,** ENTIRETY-DEFICIENCY; **short meter,** RHETORIC; **short of,** ADDITION-SUBTRACTION, ENLARGEMENT-DIMINUTION, EXCESS-LACK, HURRY-LEISURE, MAGNITUDE-SMALLNESS, SUPREMACY-SUBORDINACY; **short sea,** RIVER-WIND.

short'-breathed". Short-winded. WEARINESS.

short'-com"-ing. Deficiency; shortage. COMPLETION-NONCOMPLETION, ENTIRETY-DEFICIENCY, EXCESS-LACK, FAULTLESSNESS-FAULTINESS, HARMONY-DISCORD, SUPREMACY-SUBORDINACY, TRANSCURSION-SHORTCOMING.

short'-en. To curtail. ENLARGEMENT-DIMINUTION, INCREASE-DECREASE, LENGTH-SHORTNESS; **shorten sail,** SWIFTNESS-SLOWNESS.

short'-en-ing. That which shortens. DIGEST, LENGTH-SHORTNESS.

short'-hand". Stenography. WRITING-PRINTING.

short'-hand"-ed. Lacking men. FAULTLESSNESS-FAULTINESS.

short'-horn". An ox. FAUNA-FLORA.

short'-lived". Dying young. LASTINGNESS-TRANSIENTNESS.

short'-ly. Soon. EARLINESS-LATENESS, LENGTH-SHORTNESS.

short'-ness. Smallness. LENGTH-SHORTNESS; **for shortness' sake,** TERSENESS-PROLIXITY.

short'-sight"-ed. Lacking foresight. SIGHT-DIMSIGHTEDNESS.

short'-sight"-ed-ness. Myopic; foolish; imprudent. ADAGE-NONSENSE, DECISION-MISJUDGMENT, SAGACITY-INCAPACITY, SIGHT-DIMSIGHTEDNESS.

short'-wind"-ed. Breathless; fatigued. STRENGTH-WEAKNESS, WEARINESS-REFRESHMENT.

short'-wit"-ted. Unwise. SAGACITY-INCAPACITY.

shot. A missile; variegated; a guess; bullets; price; reward. FIGHTING-CONCILIATION, HYPOTHESIS, PRICE-DISCOUNT, PUSH-PULL, RECOMPENSE-PUNITION, VARIEGATION, WEAPON; **bad shot,** ADEPT-BUNGLER; **exchange shots,** STRIFE-PEACE; **good shot,** ADEPT-BUNGLER, PUSH-PULL; **have a shot at,** ATTACK-DEFENSE; **like a shot,** ETERNITY-INSTANTANEITY; **not have a shot in one's locker,** AFFLUENCE-PENURY; **off like a shot,** QUEST-EVASION; **random shot,** PURPOSE-LUCK, TRIAL; **round shot,** WEAPON; **shot in the locker,** MEANS.

shot'-free. Scot-free. COSTLINESS-CHEAPNESS.

should be. Ought. **No better than she should be,** PURITY-IMPURITY; **what should be,** RIGHT-WRONG.

shoul'-der. A support; a projection; to shove. CONVEXITY-CONCAVITY, IMPETUS-REACTION, SUSPENSION-SUPPORT; **broad-shouldered,** STRENGTH-WEAKNESS; **cold shoulder,** ATTRACTION-REPULSION; **have on one's shoulders,** OCCUPATION; **on the shoulders of,** ELEVATION-DEPRESSION, HEIGHT-LOWNESS, INSTRUMENTALITY; **rest on the shoulders of,** DUTY-DERELICTION; **shoulder a musket,** FIGHTING-CONCILIATION; **shoulder arms,** PREPARATION-NONPREPARATION; **shoulder to shoulder,** ANTAGONISM-CONCURRENCE, ASSOCIATION; **shoulder to the wheel,** DETERMINATION-VACILLATION, ENTERPRISE, TOIL-RELAXATION; **shrug the shoulders,** YIELDING; **take upon one's shoulders,** ENTERPRISE.

shoul'-der-knot". An epaulet. EMBELLISHMENT-DISFIGUREMENT.

shout. To cry; to rejoice. CRY-ULULATION, JUBILATION-LAMENTATION, LOUDNESS-FAINTNESS.

shove. Push. IMPETUS-REACTION; **give a shove to,** OBSTRUCTION-HELP.

shov'-el. A scoop. CLEANNESS-FILTHINESS, CONTENTS-RECEIVER, CONVEYANCE-VESSEL, OVEN-REFRIGERATOR, TRANSFER; **put to bed with a shovel,** LIFE-FUNERAL; **shovel away,** ADMISSION-EXPULSION.

shov'-el-hat. A hat. VESTMENTS.

shov'-el-ing. Present participle of shovel. TRANSFER.

show. An exhibition; to demonstrate; to manifest; appearance; to appear. APPEARANCE-DISAPPEARANCE, EVIDENCE-COUNTEREVIDENCE, HEED-DISREGARD, MANIFESTATION-LATENCY, POMP, PROOF-DISPROOF, SOCIETY, VISIBILITY-INVISIBILITY; **dumb show,** SIGN; **make a show,** POMP, TRUTHFULNESS-

FALSEHOOD; mere show, TRUTHFULNESS-FALSE-HOOD; peep-show, ENTERTAINMENT-WEARINESS; **show a light pair of heels,** QUEST-EVASION; **show cause,** ENLIGHTENMENT-SECRECY; **show fight,** AT-TACK-DEFENSE, BRAVERY-COWARDICE, DEFIANCE; **show in front,** TRANSCURSION-SHORTCOMING; **show itself,** VISIBILITY-INVISIBILITY; **show off,** BRAGGING, POMP; **show of similarity,** LIKELIHOOD-UNLIKELI-HOOD, LIKENESS-UNLIKENESS; **show one's cards,** EX-POSURE-HIDINGPLACE; **show one's colors,** MANIFES-TATION-LATENCY, SIGN; **show one's face,** EXPOSURE-HIDINGPLACE, MANIFESTATION-LATENCY, PRES-ENCE-ABSENCE; **show one's hand,** EXPOSURE-HID-INGPLACE; **show one's teeth,** DEFIANCE; **show up,** APPROVAL-DISAPPROVAL, JUSTIFICATION-CHARGE, MANIFESTATION-LATENCY, REPUTATION-DISCREDIT, SOCIETY-DERISION, VISIBILITY-INVISIBILITY.

show'-er. A rain; abundance. GATHERING-SCATTER-ING, RIVER-WIND; **shower down,** ENOUGH, RIVER-WIND; **shower down upon,** GENEROSITY-FRUGALITY, GIVING-RECEIVING.

show'-er-y. Abounding with showers. RIVER-WIND.

show'-ing. Appearance. EVIDENCE-COUNTEREVI-DENCE, MANIFESTATION-LATENCY.

show'-man. An exhibitor. INTERPRETER.

show'-y. Noticeable. BEAUTY-UGLINESS, COLOR-ACHROMATISM, EMBELLISHMENT-DISFIGUREMENT, POMP.

shrap'-nel. A shell. WEAPON.

shred. A bit; a filament. LAMINA-FIBER, MAGNI-TUDE-SMALLNESS.

shrew. A vixen. FAVORITE-QUARRELSOMENESS.

shrew'-ish. Resembling a shrew FAVORITE-QUAR-RELSOMENESS.

shrewd. Sagacious. CRAFT-ARTLESSNESS, KNOWL-EDGE-IGNORANCE, SAGACITY-INCAPACITY.

shriek. A cry. CRY-ULULATION.

shriev'-al-ty. Office of sheriff. JURISPRUDENCE.

shrieve. Sheriff. JURISPRUDENCE.

shrift. Confession; absolution. ATONEMENT, EX-POSURE-HIDINGPLACE.

shrift'-less. Obdurate. LOUDNESS-FAINTNESS, RE-PENTANCE-OBDURACY.

shrill. Piercing. CACOPHONY.

shrimp. A dwarf. GREATNESS-LITTLENESS.

shrine. A tomb; a temple. FANE, LIFE-FUNERAL.

shrink. To contract; to recoil. ADVANCE-RETRO-GRESSION, APPROACH-WITHDRAWAL, ENLARGEMENT-DIMINUTION, INCREASE-DECREASE, QUEST-EVASION, READINESS-RELUCTANCE, SENSITIVENESS-APATHY; **shrink from,** DESIRE-DISTASTE, LOVE-HATE, SAN-GUINENESS-TIMIDITY.

shrink'-ing. Present participle of shrink. ENLARGE-MENT-DIMINUTION, INCREASE-DECREASE, READI-NESS-RELUCTANCE.

shrive. To absolve. ATONEMENT.

shriv'-el. To shrink. ENLARGEMENT-DIMINUTION.

shriv'-eled. Shrunken. BREADTH-NARROWNESS.

shroud. A winding-sheet; to conceal; protection. AT-TACK-DEFENSE, ENLIGHTENMENT-SECRECY, LIFE-FUNERAL, SECURITY-INSECURITY; **shrouded in mystery,** CLEARNESS-OBSCURITY.

shrub. A plant. DOMESTICATION-AGRICULTURE, FAUNA-FLORA.

shrug. A movement. SIGN; **shrug the shoulders,** AP-PROVAL-DISAPPROVAL, ASSENT-DISSENT, CONTENT-EDNESS-DISCONTENTEDNESS, DESIRE-DISTASTE, RE-GARD-DISRESPECT, YIELDING.

shrunk. Contracted; little. ENLARGEMENT-DIMINU-TION, GREATNESS-LITTLENESS.

shud'-der. To shiver; to tremble. HEAT-COLD, SAN-GUINENESS-TIMIDITY; **make one shudder,** PLEASUR-ABLENESS-PAINFULNESS; **shudder at,** DESIRE-DIS-TASTE, LOVE-HATE.

shud'-der-ing. Having or causing a shudder. DESIRE-DISTASTE.

shuf'-fle. To derange; to shamble; an artifice; be irreso-lute; be evasive. AGITATION, BIGOTRY-APOSTASY, COMMUTATION-PERMUTATION, DETERMINATION-VAC-ILLATION, MIXTURE-HOMOGENEITY, MUTABILITY-STABILITY, MUTATION-PERMANENCE, ORGANIZATION-DISORGANIZATION, SWIFTNESS-SLOWNESS, TRUTH-FULNESS-FABRICATION, TRUTHFULNESS-FALSEHOOD, UPRIGHTNESS-DISHONESTY; **patience and shuffle the cards,** EXCITABILITY-INEXCITABILITY; **shuffle off,** QUEST-EVASION; **shuffle off this mortal coil,** LIFE-DEATH; **shuffle on,** TRAVELING-NAVIGATION; **shuffle the cards,** BEGINNING-END, MUTATION-PERMANENCE, PREPARATION-NONPREPARATION, PURPOSE-LUCK.

shuf'-fler. A deceiver. GULL-DECEIVER.

shuf'-fling. Done with a shuffle; prevaricating. AGI-TATION, COMMUTATION-PERMUTATION, ORGANIZA-TION-DISORGANIZATION, TRUTHFULNESS-FALSEHOOD, UPRIGHTNESS-DISHONESTY.

shun. To avoid. DESIRE-DISTASTE, QUEST-EVASION.

shunt. To turn aside. AIM-ABERRATION, TRANSFER.

shunt'-ed. Shelved. CAREFULNESS-CARELESSNESS.

shut. To close. APERTURE-CLOSURE, APPROACH-WITHDRAWAL, TRANSFER; **shut in,** RELEASE-RE-STRAINT; **shut one's ears,** CREDULOUSNESS-SKEPTI-CISM, HEARING-DEAFNESS; **shut oneself up,** SOCIA-BILITY-PRIVACY; **shut one's eyes to,** CAREFULNESS-CARELESSNESS, CREDULOUSNESS-SKEPTICISM, HEED-DISREGARD, LEAVE-PROHIBITION, OBSERVANCE-NON-OBSERVANCE; **shut out,** INCLUSION-OMISSION, LEAVE-PROHIBITION; **shut the door,** APERTURE-CLOSURE, LEAVE-PROHIBITION; **shut the door in one's face,** PROFFER-REFUSAL; **shut the door upon,** SOCIABILITY-PRIVACY; **shut the eyes,** SIGHT-BLINDNESS; **shut the gates of mercy,** COMPASSION-RUTHLESSNESS; **shut up,** APERTURE-CLOSURE, PROOF-DISPROOF, RELEASE-RESTRAINT; **shut up shop,** BEGINNING-CONTINUANCE, DISCONTINUANCE-CONTINUANCE, QUEST-ABANDON-MENT, TOIL-RELAXATION.

shut'-ter. A blind. LUMINARY-SHADE.

shut'-tle-cock". A plaything. DETERMINATION-VACIL-LATION.

shy. Modest; fearful; to fling; to swerve. ADVANCE-RETROGRESSION, AIM-ABERRATION, BRAVERY-COW-ARDICE, CONCEIT-DIFFIDENCE, PUSH-PULL, QUEST-EVASION, SANGUINENESS-TIMIDITY; **fight shy of,** QUEST-EVASION; **have a shy at,** ATTACK-DEFENSE; **shy cock,** BRAVERY-COWARDICE; **shy of,** DESIRE-DIS-TASTE, FAITH-MISGIVING, READINESS-RELUCTANCE, RECKLESSNESS-CAUTION; **shy of belief,** CREDULOUS-NESS-SKEPTICISM.

Si-a-mese' twins. United twins, 1811–1874. DUALITY.

sib. A kinsman. RELATIONSHIP.

Si-be'-ri-a. A part of Russia. HEAT-COLD.

Si-be'-ri-an. Of or pertaining to Siberia. HEAT-COLD.

sib'-i-lant. Hissing. RESONANCE-SIBILATION.

sib"-i-la'-tion. A hiss; disrespect; disapprobation. APPROVAL-DISAPPROVAL, REGARD-DISRESPECT, RES-ONANCE-NONRESONANCE.

sib'-yl. An oracle. BEAUTY-UGLINESS, JOVE-FIEND, SOOTHSAYER.

sib'-yl-line. Oracular. PROPHECY; **sibylline leaf,** SOOTHSAYER.

sic [L.] (sic). Thus. SAMENESS-CONTRAST, TRUTH-ERROR.

sic omnes, si [L.] (sic om'-niz, sai). Would they all were so! . GOOD MAN-BAD MAN.

sic transit gloria mundi [L.] (sic tran'-sit glo'-ri-a mun'-dai). Thus passes away the glory of the world. LASTINGNESS-TRANSIENTNESS, WELFARE-MISFOR-TUNE.

sic volo, sic jubeo [L.] (sic vo'-lo, sic jiub'-i-o). As I will, I command. ORDER, VOLITION-OBLIGATION.

sic vos non vobis [L.] (sic vos non vo'-bis). Thus not for yourself you toil. THEFT.

sic'-ci-ty. Dryness. DAMPNESS-DRYNESS.

sick. Ill. HEALTH-SICKNESS; **make one sick,** DESIRE-DISTASTE, PLEASURABLENESS-PAINFULNESS; **sick at heart,** LIGHTHEARTEDNESS-DEJECTION; **sick of,** DESIRE-DISTASTE, DESIRE-REPLETION, ENTERTAINMENT-WEARINESS; **visitation of the sick,** CEREMONIAL.

sick'-cham"-ber. Sick-room. HEALTH-SICKNESS.

sick'-en. To disgust; to nauseate; to become ill. DESIRE-DISTASTE, ENTERTAINMENT-WEARINESS, HEALTH-SICKNESS, PALATABLENESS-UNPALATABLENESS, PLEASURABLENESS-PAINFULNESS.

sick'-en-er. Overdose. DESIRE-DISLIKE, EXCESS-LACK, PLEASURABLENESS-PAINFULNESS.

sick'-en-ing. Causing to sicken. PALATABLENESS-UNPALATABLENESS, PLEASURABLENESS-PAINFULNESS.

sick'-le. A tool. ANGULARITY, SHARPNESS-BLUNTNESS.

sick'-ly. Weak. STRENGTH-WEAKNESS.

sick'-ness. Illness. HEALTH-SICKNESS.

sick'-room. A sick-chamber. HEALTH-SICKNESS.

side. Party; face; lineage. ASSOCIATION, BORDER, LATERALITY-CONTRAPOSITION, RELATIONSHIP; **at one's side,** REMOTENESS-NEARNESS; **from side to side,** VIBRATION; **look only at one side of the shield,** DECISION-MISJUDGMENT; **on one side,** PARALLELISM-INCLINATION, PROPORTION-DEFORMITY; **on one's side,** LATERALITY-CONTRAPOSITION, VARIANCE-ACCORD; **pass from one side to another,** BIGOTRY-APOSTASY; **side by side,** ASSOCIATION, LATERALITY-CONTRAPOSITION, REMOTENESS-NEARNESS, SOLITUDE-COMPANY; **side with,** ANTAGONISM-CONCURRENCE, OBSTRUCTION-HELP, VARIANCE-ACCORD; **take up a side,** RATIOCINATION-INSTINCT; **wrong side up,** REVERSAL.

side'-arms. Weapons. WEAPONS.

side'-blow. A thrust. CRAFT-ARTLESSNESS.

side'-board. A cabinet. CONTENTS-RECEIVER.

side'-drum. A musical instrument. MUSICAL INSTRUMENTS.

side'-ling. Sloping. AIM-ABERRATION, LATERALITY-CONTRAPOSITION.

side'-long. Oblique. LATERALITY-CONTRAPOSITION, PARALLELISM-INCLINATION.

sid"-er-a'-tion. A stroke. MIGHT-IMPOTENCE.

si-de'-re-al. Starry. ASTRONOMY, UNIVERSE.

sid'-er-ite. A mineral. ATTRACTION-REPULSION.

sid'-er-o-man"-cy. Divination. PROPHECY.

side'-sad"-dle. A saddle. SUSPENSION-SUPPORT.

side'-scene. A curtain. ACTING.

sides'-man. A churchwarden. MINISTRY-LAITY.

side'-walk". A path. WAY.

side'-ways". Oblique; lateral. LATERALITY-CONTRAPOSITION, PARALLELISM-INCLINATION.

side'-wind. An indirect attack. CRAFT-ARTLESSNESS, MIDCOURSE-CIRCUIT, PARALLELISM-INCLINATION.

si'-dle. To deviate; to move sidewise. AIM-ABERRATION, LATERALITY-CONTRAPOSITION.

siege. An investment. ATTACK-DEFENSE; **lay siege to,** ATTACK-DEFENSE; **state of siege,** FIGHTING-CONCILIATION.

siege'-train. A military train. WEAPON.

sies'-ta. A nap. ACTIVITY-INDOLENCE.

sieve. To sort; to clean; a utensil. APERTURE-CLOSURE, CLEANNESS-FILTHINESS, ORGANIZATION-DISORGANIZATION; **pour water into a sieve,** EXTRAVAGANCE-AVARICE, PROVISION-WASTE; **stop one hole in a sieve,** EXTRAVAGANCE-AVARICE.

sift. To clean; to sort; to simplify; to scrutinize. CLEANNESS-FILTHINESS, DIFFERENTIATION-INDISCRIMINATION, INVESTIGATION-ANSWER, MIXTURE-HOMOGENEITY, ORGANIZATION-DISORGANIZATION; **sift the chaff from the wheat,** CHOICE-REJECTION.

sift'-ing. Separating into fine parts. INVESTIGATION-ANSWER, MIXTURE-HOMOGENEITY.

sigh. A deep breath. JUBILATION-LAMENTATION; **sigh for,** DESIRE-DISTASTE.

sigh'-ing like a fur'-nace. BLANDISHMENT.

sight. A view; a prodigy; vision; quantity. APPEARANCE-DISAPPEARANCE, BEAUTY-UGLINESS, MAGNITUDE-SMALLNESS, MULTIPLICITY-PAUCITY, PHENOMENON, SIGHT-BLINDNESS; **at sight,** EARLINESS-LATENESS, SIGHT-BLINDNESS; **dim sight,** SIGHT-DIMSIGHTEDNESS; **in sight,** VISIBILITY-INVISIBILITY; **in sight of,** REMOTENESS-NEARNESS, SIGHT-BLINDNESS, VISIBILITY-INVISIBILITY; **keep in sight,** CAREFULNESS-CARELESSNESS, HEED-DISREGARD; **within sight of shore,** SANGUINENESS-HOPELESSNESS.

SIGHT—BLINDNESS.

Bird's-eye view. A view at a glance.

Clear glance.
Clear sight. } A view free from obstruction or impediment.
Commanding view.

Conspection.
Conspectuity. } The faculty of seeing.

Contemplation. The act of looking forward to.

Coup d'oeil [F.]. A glance.

Discernment. The power of seeing.

Eagle glance.
Eagle sight. } Keen power of sight.

Espial. The act of espying.

Espionage. Secret watching.

Eyesight. The sense of seeing.

Gaze. A continued look.

Glance. A swift survey by the eye.

Glimpse. A short, hurried view.

Inspection. Careful looking into.

Introspection. A looking inward.

Ken. A view.

Leer. An indirect glance.

Look. A sight; a view.

Ocular demonstration.
Ocular inspection. } Proof or examination by eyesight.

Peep. A sly look.

Penetrating glance.
Penetrating sight. } A look through.

Periscope. A general comprehensive view.

Perlustration. The act of viewing all over.

Ablepsy. Blindness.

Amaurosis. Loss of sight without organic effect.

Blindness. Without the power of seeing.

Cataract. Opacity of the crystalline lens.

Cecity. Without sight.

Dimsightedness. The state of having obscure sight. See SIGHT-DIMSIGHTEDNESS.

Execation. The act of making blind.

Prestriction. Want of sight. [Milton.]

Teichopsia. A temporary blindness, as though one saw a wall.

Xanthocyanopia. A form of color-blindness, in which yellow and blue only are seen.

BLINDNESS—*Denotation.*

Noctograph. A kind of writing-frame for the blind.

BLINDNESS—*Verbs.*

Avert the eyes. To turn away the eyes.

Be blind to. To be without sight.

Blind. To deprive of sight.

Blindfold. To cover the eyes.

Blink at. To shut one's eyes to.

Close the eyes. To bring together the eyelids.

Dazzle. To blind for a moment by light.

Have the eyes bandaged. To have a soft cloth fastened upon the eyes.

Hoodwink. To blindfold.

Jeter de la poudre aux yeux [F.]. To throw dust into the eyes.

Look another way. To avoid with the eyes.

SIGHT—BLINDNESS—*Continued.*

Perspicacity. Acuteness of sight.
Piercing glance. ⎫
Piercing sight. ⎬ A look that sees through.
Quick glance. ⎫
Quick sight. ⎬ A sharp, sudden look.
Reconnaissance. An examination of territory or an enemy's position.
Regard. A view; a gaze.
Sharp glance. ⎫
Sharp sight. ⎬ A keen, piercing look.
Short sight. Ability to see but a short distance.
Sight. Perception of objects by the eye.
Sightseeing. The act of seeing sights.
Speculation. Examination by the eye.
Stare. A fixed look with eyes wide open.
Survey. A general view.
View. Examination by the eye.
Vision. The act of seeing external objects.
Watch. Close observation.

SIGHT—*Denotations.*

Autopsy. Examination of a dead body for the purpose of ascertaining the cause of death.
Catopsis. Science of reflection.
Optics. That branch of physical science which treats of the nature and properties of light.

SIGHT—*Nouns of Cause.*

Clear eye. An eye able to perceive clearly.
Eagle eye. An eye with the power of sight of an eagle.
Eye. The organ of sight or vision.
Naked eye. The eye unassisted by glasses.
Organs of vision. The eye.
Penetrating eye. An eye or sight that sees through.
Piercing eye. An eye that seems to be able to see through things.
Quick eye. An eye of very ready-perceptive power.
Sharp eye. An eye of keen vision.
Unassisted eye. The eye without glasses.

SIGHT—*Organs of Sight.*

Cornea. The transparent outer coat of the eyeball.
Eye. The organ of sight.
Iris. The colored curtain about the pupil of the eye.
Orbs. Eyes.
Pupil. The central part of the front eye.
Retina. The inner coat of the eye.
Visual organs. The eye and its parts.
White. The white covering of the eye.

SIGHT—*Nouns of Place.*

Amphitheater. A circular or oval building with rising tiers of seats.
Arena. The oval space in the center of an amphitheater.
Belvedere. An open, upper story of an Italian house.
Field of view. As far as the eye can see.
Gazebo. A summer house with an extended view.
Horizon. The range of vision; where the earth and sky seem to meet.
Loophole. A hole in a fortification for observation, etc.
Point of view. The standpoint from which anything is seen.
Theater. A house where plays are to be seen.
Vista. A prospect.
Watch-tower. A tower in a fortified wall for a sentinel.

SIGHT—*Figurative Nouns.*

Argus. A hundred-eyed giant.
Basilisk. A creature the look of whose eye was fatal.
Cat A person of very keen sight.
Cockatrice A serpent with a fatal eye.
Eagle. A person of very keen sight.
Evil eye. A person whose eye inflicts injury by some magical influence.
Goggle-eye. A person having prominent and distorted or rolling eyes.
Gooseberry-eye. A person having large round, rolling eyes.
Lynx. A person of keen sight.

SIGHT—*Verbs.*

Be a spectator of. To be one who sees.
Behold. To apprehend by vision.
Bend one's looks upon. To direct one's eyes toward.
Cast a glance. To cause the eyes to be directed for a moment.
Cast the eyes on. To cause the eyes to look at.
Catch a glimpse of. To see for an instant indistinctly.
Catch a sight of. To see plainly for a moment.

BLINDNESS—Verbs—*Continued.*

Lose sight of. To permit to escape from view.
Not look. Not to perform the operation of seeing.
Not see. Not to understand.
Put one's eyes out. To blind by injuring the eye.
Render blind. To cause one to be mentally or physically blind.
Screen from sight.
Shut the eyes. To close the lids.
Shut the eyes to. Purposely to overlook.
Throw dust into one's eyes. To mislead by confusing statements.
Turn away the eyes. To avert the face.
Wink. To close the eye for a moment.
Wink at. To overlook.

BLINDNESS—*Adjectives.*

Blind. Without sight.
Blind as a bat. Very blind.
Blind as a beetle. Entirely blind.
Blind as a buzzard. Sightless.
Blind as a mole. Not able to see.
Blind as an owl. Able to see little.
Blinded. Made blind.
Dark. Not to be seen.
Dimsighted. Having poor sight.
Eyeless. Without the organs of sight.
Sightless. Without the sense of sight.
Sand-blind. Half blind.
Stark-blind. Entirely without sight.
Stone-blind. Sightless.
Undiscerning. Not able to distinguish.
Visionless. Without ability to see.

BLINDNESS—*Adverbs.*

Blindfold. Unable to see.
Blindly. In the manner of the blind.
Darkly. Dimly.

SIGHT—Verbs—*Continued.*

Cock the eye. To turn the eye in a knowing way.
Command a view of. Obtain a wide view.
Contemplate. To consider carefully.
Descry. To recognize through obscurity.
Direct the eyes to. To turn the eyes in the direction of.
Discern. To recognize objects as distinct from others.
Discover. To detect.
Distinguish. To perceive as different.
Espy. To see suddenly.
Eye. To scrutinize.
Fix the eyes upon. To look closely at.
Gaze. To look earnestly at.
Get a glimpse of. To obtain an indistinct view of.
Get a sight of. To obtain a view of.
Glance on. To look at suddenly.
Glance over. To examine carelessly.
Glance round. To dart the look about suddenly.
Glare. To gaze fiercely.
Gloat. To look steadily, exhibiting evil triumph.
Gloat on. To look on with evil satisfaction.
Goggle. To roll the eyes staringly.
Have a glimpse of. To have a momentary look.
Have a sight of. To have a distinct view for a moment.
Have in sight. To see.
Inspect. To examine critically.
Ken. To see, to know.
Leer. To look slyly.
Lift up the eyes. To look up.
Look. To direct the gaze for the purpose of seeing.
Look about one. To be observant.
Look askance. To use an indirect glance.
Look at. To direct the sight to.
Look full in the face. To look boldly.
Look hard at. To gaze with steadfastness.
Look intently. To look fixedly.
Look on. To be a spectator.
Look over. To examine hastily.
Look round. To see in all directions.
Look upon. To regard.
Make out. To decipher.
Observe. To discern.
Ogle. To look with impudence.
Open one's eyes. To put away mistaken ideas.
Peep. To look furtively.

SIGHT—Verbs—Continued.

Peer. To look inquiringly.
Perceive. To receive knowledge through the senses.
Play at bo-peep. To peep from concealment and hide again.
Pore over. To read with absorbing interest.
Pry. To look into with curiosity.
Recognize. To know at sight.
Reconnoiter. To examine by the eye for military purposes.
Rivet the eyes upon. To look fixedly at.
Run the eye over. To glance hastily over.
Run the eye through. To look through pages rapidly.
Scan. To observe closely.
See. To perceive by the eye.
See at a glance. To understand quickly.
See sights. To visit objects of interest.
See with one's own eyes. To know from one's own observation.

Set the eyes on. To behold.
Sight. To bring into the field of observation.
Speculate. To have in view.
Spy. To see from concealment.
Squint. To look with half-closed eyes.
Stare. To look fixedly.
Strain one's eyes. To overtask the eyes.
Survey. To look around.
Take a peep. To take one short look.
Turn one's looks upon. To examine carefully.
Turn the eyes on. To observe.
View. To look.
Watch. To observe attentively.
Watch for. To wait expectantly.
Witness. To see with the eye.

SIGHT—Adjectives.

Argus-eyed. Hundred-eyed; watchful.
Clear-sighted. Of keen physical or intellectual vision.
Eagle-eyed. Far-sighted and keen-sighted.
Hawk-eyed. Having piercing eyes.
Keen-eyed. Sharp-sighted.
Lynx-eyed. Having acute sight.
Ocular. Pertaining to the eye.

Ophthalmic. Of or pertaining to the organ of vision.
Optic. Of or pertaining to the eye.
Optical. Of or pertaining to the science of optics.
Seeing. Having knowledge by the eye.
Visible. Capable of being seen.
Visual. Connected with the sense of sight.

SIGHT—Adverbs, etc.

At a glance. Immediately.
At first sight. Without consideration.
At sight. As soon as seen.
At the first blush. At the first view.

In sight of. Before.
Prima facie [L.]. At first appearance.
Visibly. Obviously.
With one's eyes open. On one's guard.

SIGHT—Interjection.

Look! Behold!

SIGHT—Phrase.

The scales falling from one's eyes. Becoming enlightened.

SIGHT—DIMSIGHTEDNESS.

DIMSIGHTEDNESS.

Color-blindness. Inability to distinguish between colors.
Confusion of vision. Indistinctness of vision.
Dimsight. Obscureness of vision.
Dimsightedness. The state of having obscure sight.
Distortion. A defect in seeing.
Double sight. A condition of the eyes which makes one see two images.
Dull sight. Indistinct vision.
Failing sight. Failing of the power of seeing.
Half sight. Indistinct vision.
Imperfect vision. Defective eyesight.
Limitations of vision. Defects of sight.
Long sight. A condition of the eyes which makes one see things at a distance better than at hand.
Looming. Indistinct and magnified appearance of objects.
Near sight. Vision of less range than normal.
Purblindness. Near-sightedness.
Short sight. Vision of less range than normal.

DIMSIGHTEDNESS—Denotations.

Albino. A person with pink eyes which are day-blind.
Apparition. An imaginary object.
Blinkard. One who blinks.
Blinker. Something to keep off the light.
Cast in the eye. A twist of the eye.
Cataract. Opacity of the crystalline lens.
Fallacies of vision. Deceptive appearances.
False light. A deceptive light.
Ghost. A spirit supposed to be of a dead person.
Goggle-eyes. Large, staring eyes.
Ignis fatuus. The will-o'-the-wisp.
Illusion. An imaginary appearance.
Lens. An instrument of glass for aiding or correcting sight.
Magic lantern. A lantern that throws pictures on a screen.
Magic mirror. A mirror whose images deceive.
Mirage. An optical effect showing images on the clouds.
Mirror. A looking-glass.
Nystagmus. A rapid involuntary oscillation of the eyeballs.
Phantasm. An imaginary appearance.
Screen. That which cuts off the light.
Specter. An imaginary appearance.
Specter of the Brocken. The shadow of a person seen from the Brocken Mountain.

Squint. A defect of the eyes when their axes are differently directed.
Swivel-eye. An eye that rolls in the socket.
Vision. An imaginary appearance.
Winking. An involuntary movement of the eyelids.

DIMSIGHTEDNESS—Scientific Nouns.

Anamorphosis. A distorted image which seems correct when seen in an anamorphoscope.
Astigmatic sight. Sight affected by astigmatism.
Astigmatism. Defect of eye such that the rays of light converge in a line.
Chromato-pseudo-blepsis [L.]. Affection of eye that causes images to be blurred by colors.
Daltonism. Color-blindness, especially red-blindness.
Deceptio visus [L.]. Deception of the vision.
Lippitude. Chronic ophthalmia, gummy eyelids.
Myopia. Near-sightedness.
Nictalopy. Day-blindness.
Nictation. Nervous involuntary winking.
Ophthalmia. Inflammation of the eye.
Phantasma. A day-dream.
Phasma. A phantasm.
Presbyopia. Long-sightedness incident to age.
Scotomy. A defect in the field of vision.
Spectrum. The image of a ray of light broken up into its component colors.
Strabism. Strabismus.
Strabismus. When the eyes turn inward.
Virtual image. An image formed by the imaginary prolongation of rays.

DIMSIGHTEDNESS—Verbs.

Be dimsighted. To have obscure sight.
Blink. To wink the eyes.
Dazzle. To blind by too much light.
Glare. To look fixedly.
Glower. To look threateningly.
Have a film over the eyes. To have a temporarily imperfect sight.
Have a mist before the eye. To have the sight clouded.
Have a mote in the eye. To have the vision obscured by a speck.
Look askance. To use an indirect glance.
Look askant. To look askance.
Loom. To appear to come gradually nearer.
Nictitate. To wink involuntarily.
Screw up the eyes. To close the eyelids partially.

SIGHT—DIMSIGHTEDNESS—*Continued.*

See double. To see two images.
See through a glass darkly. Not to understand clearly.
See through a prism. To see in many colors.
Squint. To have the eyes out of their normal position.
Wink. To close the eyelids.

DIMSIGHTEDNESS—*Adjectives.*

Astigmatic. Pertaining to astigmatism.
Blear. Having bloodshot appearance.
Blear-eyed. With bloodshot eyes.
Blind as a bat. Very blind.
Blind of one eye. Being without sight in one of the visual organs.

Dimsighted. Seeing obscurely.
Goggle-eyed. Having staring eyes.
Gooseberry-eyed. Having large round eyes.
Half-blind. Partially able to see.
Monoculous. One-eyed.
Moon-eyed. Having an eye affected by the moon.
Mope-eyed. Short-sighted.
Myopic. Near-sighted.
One-eyed. Having one good eye.
Presbyopic. Long-sighted; far-sighted.
Purblind. Near-sighted.
Winking. Closing and opening the eye suddenly.

sight'-less. Blind; invisible; unsightly. BEAUTY-UGLINESS, SIGHT-BLINDNESS, VISIBILITY-INVISIBILITY.
sight'-ly. Comely. BEAUTY-UGLINESS.
sights. Objects seen. See sights, INQUISITIVENESS-INDIFFERENCE, SIGHT-BLINDNESS.
sight'-see"-ing. Observation. SIGHT-BLINDNESS.
sight'-se"-er. A spectator. INQUISITIVENESS-INDIFFERENCE, ONLOOKER.
sig'-il. A seal; a sign. CONTRACT, SIGN.
sig-moid'-al. Like S. CIRCLE-WINDING.
sign. To attest; a mark; an indication; a prodigy; to engage. CONTRACT, EVIDENCE-COUNTEREVIDENCE, MARK-OBLITERATION, PHENOMENON, PORTENT, SECURITY, SIGN, WRITING-PRINTING; **give sign of,** MANIFESTATION-LATENCY; **make no sign,** TALKATIVENESS-TACITURNITY; **signs of the times,** PORTENT-WARNING; **signs of the zodiac,** UNIVERSE.

SIGN.

SIGN—*Subjective Nouns.*

Indication. The act of pointing out or manifesting.
Semeiology. The science of signs; in medicine, the science of the symptoms of disease.
Semeiotics. Semeiology.
Symbolism. The act of symbolizing or using types; representation by symbols.
Symbolization. The act of indicating by means of symbols.
Telegraphy. The art or process of sending messages by telegraph.

SIGN—*Objective Nouns.*

Address. A person's name and place of residence.
Address-card. A card having an address written on it.
Advertisement, etc. A notice to the public, as in a daily paper. See PUBLICITY.
Alarm, etc. Anything, as a signal, indicating danger. See ALARM.
Alarum. An alarm; an alarm-clock.
Ancient. An ensign or flag; one who bears a flag.
Annotation. A commentary on any written work.
Armorial bearings. Ensigns armorial of a family indicating rank and distinction.
Arms. Same as armorial bearings.
Asterisk. A star (*) used by printers or writers for reference.
Attestation. Subscription of a person to a written document to witness its genuineness.
Autograph. Signature written by oneself.
Autography. The process of writing in facsimile, as a signature.
Badge. A token or decoration indicating honor, rank, etc.
Balize. A sea beacon or landmark consisting of a raised pole or frame.
Bandrol. A small flag, banner, or streamer.
Banner. A suspended piece of cloth or other fabric bearing some motto or device.
Banneret. A title or rank bestowed for heroic deeds.
Bannerol. A banderole; a banner carried at funerals and placed over the tomb.
Battle-cry. A cry of the soldiers on entering a battle or fight.
Beacon. Any visible and prominent object set on shores, etc., as a warning to mariners.
Beck. Indication of command, desire, or inquiry given by nodding the head or otherwise.
Bell. A hollow metallic instrument which when struck by a hammer gives forth a sound, used for various purposes, as to indicate the hour, etc.

Bill. A statement from creditor to debtor indicating amount of money due.
Billet. A ticket given by an officer to a soldier indicating where to lodge.
Bill-head. The heading on papers used for bills.
Blue light. A light used as a signal in military operations and at sea.
Blue peter. A blue flag having a white square in the center, used at sea in signaling boats to return.
Brand. A trade-mark; a mark of crime.
Bugle-call. A playing on the bugle to order soldiers to advance, retreat, etc.
Bunting. Material used for making flags.
Burgee. A swallow-tailed flag.
Byplay. A diversion from the main action of a play.
Cairn. A pile of stones heaped up as a landmark.
Call. Any form of summons; an instrument for giving a signal.
Calumet. A pipe used by the North-American Indians for smoking tobacco at conferences as an indication of peace.
Card. A piece of cardboard bearing an address, advertisement, published statement, or the like.
Carte de visite [F.] A visiting card.
Catchword. The last words of an actor considered as indicating the entrance of another actor.
Cedilla. A mark indicating the soft sound of *c.*
Characteristic. That which indicates distinction in features, character, etc.
Check. A tag put on baggage so that the owner may identify his property; a written order on a bank.
Chevron. A device like the letter V worn by non-commissioned officers.
Chirology. The art and practise of using the hands in conversation as the deaf and dumb do.
Cipher. The character o, indicating zero.
Clew. Anything which suggests the solution of difficulty or mystery.
Cloven hoof. Figurative for a devilish character, Satan being dramatically represented as having cloven hoofs.
Clue. A clew.
Coat of arms. A person's armorial bearings.
Cock. A contrivance for indicating which way the wind blows.
Cockade. A badge usually worn on the hat as an indication of military service.
Colors. A badge, flag, or ensign.
Counter. A piece of wood or other substance used for counting, as in games.
Counterfoil. Part of a tally, formerly in the exchequer, in the keeping of an officer of that court, the other part, called the stock, being in the possession of the person who had lent the king money on that account.
Countermark. A mark in addition to those already existing, in order to give security.
Countersign. A private word or phrase known only to partizans; a watchword.
Credentials, etc. Certificates showing that a person is invested with the authority claimed by him. See EVIDENCE.
Cresset. A frame or vessel filled with combustible material and mounted to serve as a beacon.
Crest. The ornament on a helmet which distinguishes and indicates the rank of the wearer.
Criterion. A test by which is determined the correctness of a conclusion.
Cry. Call; a party watchword.
Cue. A catchword.
Cynosure. An object which attracts the attention of everybody.
Dactylology. The use of the finger-alphabet.
Dactylonomy. Art of counting with the fingers.
Dash. A mark used in punctuation to indicate a sudden break, stop, or transition in a sentence, etc.
Device. A fanciful design used to indicate the historical situation or the desire of the person who adopts it.

Diagnostic. A symptom which indicates the nature of a disease.

Directing post. A post used to indicate direction.

Direction. A prescription or order giving authoritative instruction; an address.

Divining-rod. A rod, commonly of witch-hazel, used by certain persons to indicate the position of water or metals under ground.

Docket. A calendar indicating the cases to be called at any time of court.

Dot. A point, in music, put after a rest or note to make that note or rest half as long again.

Dumb show. A form of communication consisting of signs and gestures.

Duplicate. A copy; a transcript.

Eagle. · The national emblem of the United States.

Emblem. A typical designation.

Endorsement. **Indorsement.** { Writing on the back of a note or paper to make it valid for transference, to secure the payment of a note, draft, and the like.

Ensign. A flag or banner indicating distinction.

Epaulet. A shoulder-strap worn by an officer.

Epigraph. An inscription carved in a stone to indicate whom the stone memorializes; the superscription to a chapter or a book.

Escutcheon. The surface on which armorial bearings are displayed.

Exponent. In algebra, a symbol indicating a power.

Exposition, etc. An explanation or interpretation of the meaning of something. See INTERPRETATION.

Favor. A token of respect or regard.

Feature. The cast or appearance of the human face; a marked characteristic.

Fiery cross. A cross constructed of two firebrands, formerly, in Scotland, carried by a runner as a signal for the clan to take up arms.

Figure. A representation of the form of a person or object.

Figurehead. An image on the prow of a vessel indicating directly or emblematically the name of the vessel.

Finger-post. A guide-post having on it an index finger.

Flag. A cloth bearing some device used to indicate nationality, party, etc.

Flagstaff. A pole on which a flag is raised.

Fool's cap. A cap with bells worn by professional jesters.

Footfall. A footstep by which one recognizes a person.

Freemasonry. The institutions of Freemasons; hence, sympathy and community of interests.

Gage, etc. A standard measurement. See MENSURATION.

Garland. A wreath of flowers, leaves, etc., used as a token of victory or joy.

Gesticulation. Movement of the body or some part of the body to illustrate speech.

Gesture. Motion, especially of the hands, indicative or expressive of some idea or emotion.

Glance. A quick or passing look indicative of surprise, anger, etc.

Gonfalon. A flag which hangs from a crosspiece instead of from a staff or mast.

Guide. One who or that which points out the way.

Guide-board. Board showing distances and directions to places.

Guide-post. A post with a board bearing directions for travelers, usually erected at the joining of highways.

Guidon. Guide-flag carried by cavalry.

Hall-mark. In the United Kingdom, the official stamp of the assay offices on gold and silver articles attesting their purity.

Hand. The pointer of a clock.

Hand-post. A guide-post.

Handwriting. The form of writing peculiar to any person.

Hatchment. Armorial bearings of a deceased person indicating rank, sex, etc.

Heading. A title of a chapter, etc.

Headlight. A light at a locomotive's front to light up the track at night.

Heraldry. A coat of arms indicative of rank, dignity, etc.; also, the art of blazoning armorial bearings.

Hint, etc. An indirect allusion. See ENLIGHTENMENT.

Impress. Stamp; characteristic.

Impression. A mark or stamp indicating influence from without.

Imprint. That part of the title-page of a book which gives the publisher's name with the time and place of issue; an impress or mark.

Index. Anything used to indicate; an alphabetical list of subjects discussed in a book.

Indicator. One who or that which indicates; an instrument so contrived as to indicate the position or condition of something, as the amount of steam in a boiler.

Indice. Index.

Insignia. Badges, etc., used by societies to indicate official distinction.

Italics. Kind of type in which the letters slope toward the right· used to indicate emphasis, importance, etc.

Jack. A national flag showing the canton or union, not the fly.

Jotting. Brief annotation.

Key. That which discloses or opens something.

Knocker. Kind of door-bell.

Labarum. An ecclesiastical banner; a moral guide.

Label. A slip, as of paper, attached to an article and bearing an inscription to indicate its contents, character, etc.

Landmark. A fixed object serving to indicate the boundary of a tract of land.

Leer. A sly oblique look expressive of sinister or lustful intent.

Letter. A character used to represent a sound; a written statement to identify or introduce a person.

Lighthouse. A tower or the like bearing a lamp on the top and erected on a shoal, etc., to guide seamen by night.

Line. A mark drawn by a pen or pencil to indicate division.

Lineament. A characteristic mark or line; a feature.

Livery. A dress distinguishing any organization.

Loadstar. **Lodestar.** } A guiding star.

Love-knot. A knot tied by lovers in pledge of constancy.

Mark. A character for identification; a number to indicate a student's grade; an object serving to indicate the way; a guide; a badge.

Means of recognition. That which serves to indicate identity.

Mile-post. A post, or one of a series of posts, set up at a roadside to indicate distance from a given point.

Mile-stone. A stone set up for the same purpose as a mile-post.

Mot de guerre [F.] A watchword.

Mot de passe [F.] A password.

Motto. An expressive word or pithy sentence suggestive of some guiding principle.

Name. The distinctive appellation by which a person or thing is indicated or pointed out.

Nick. One of a series of slight cuts, as in a stick, to indicate a score or tally.

Nod. A quick forward and downward motion of the head indicative of assent, friendly salutation, drowsiness, etc.

Notch. A nick, as in a stick, to record a score or tally.

Note. A mark or sign used to indicate or call attention to something.

Notification, etc. See sub INFORMATION. Notice given in writing or by signs. See ENLIGHTENMENT.

Nudge. A gentle push, as with the elbow, in order to call attention or convey intimation.

Omen, etc. A prophetic sign. See PORTENT.

Open sesame. A magical conjuration by which secret doors are opened and entrance gained; as to the robbers' cave of the forty thieves in the *Arabian Nights*.

Oriflamme. The ancient royal ensign of France; any royal banner.

Pantomime. A series of gestures or postures employed to express ideas or convey information.

Paraph. A flourish with the pen at the end of a signature, used in the Middle Ages as a safeguard against forgery.

Passe-parole [F.]. A password.

Password. A word to be given by a person before he may pass.

Pattern, etc. Something used as a copy. See COPY-MODEL.

Pendant. A naval flag.

Pennant. A small flag used chiefly on naval vessels.

Pennon. A small swallow-tailed flag borne by a knight of the Middle Ages on his lance and displaying his personal device.

Pharos. A lighthouse or beacon.

Pillars of Hercules. Two hills on opposite sides of the Straits of Gibraltar; figuratively, used to indicate the boundary of the world.

Point. Any mark to indicate punctuation; in printing, a period.

Pointer. One who or that which points, as a hand on a clock.

Pole-star. The brilliant star, near the north pole, which guides the mariner.

Post. The place where anything is stopped, placed, or fixed.

Posy. A sentiment in poetry; especially a motto on a ring.

Prefiguration, etc. Representation by types, figures, etc. See PROPHECY.

Print. The impression taken from type.

Proof, etc. Conclusive evidence; convincing argument. See TRIAL.

Rallying cry. A battle-cry to reunite scattering or downhearted soldiers.

Record, etc. An authorized register of past achievements, personal history, etc. See MARK.

Red letter. A letter used in old calendars to mark the saints' days.

Representation, etc. Anything which serves as a sign or symbol, etc. See DELINEATION.

Reveille. Beat of drums at daybreak, after which the sentries do not challenge.

Rocket. An artificial firework which is projected through the air for various purposes, as for signaling.

Scent. The odor left by an animal on the ground, which indicates, as to a dog, the course of pursuit.

Sceptre, etc. A baton carried by a sovereign indicative of authority, etc. See SCEPTER.

Score. A notch or mark made for the purpose of account.

Scratch. In athletics, the line from which contestants start.

Scutcheon. Escutcheon.

Seal. An instrument for making an impression, as on wax or wafer; also, the impression made; any mark or substance affixed to a document to indicate that it is authentic or must not be tampered with.

Seamark. Any elevated object on land which serves as a beacon to mariners.

Semaphore. An apparatus for giving signals by the use of lanterns, flags, etc.

Shibboleth. A party cry or watchword.

Shield. A piece of defensive armor, commonly carried on the arm.

Shrug. A drawing up of the shoulders in a sudden movement indicative of dislike, dread, doubt, or the like.

Sigil. A seal or signature.

Sign. An action indicative of thought, desire, or command; a board plate, or the like, generally containing an inscription and used to indicate a place of business, etc.

Signal. A sign used for conveying information, distance.

Signal-post. A post for displaying signals.

Signature. A person's name in his own handwriting written as a sign of agreement or acknowledgment.

Sign-board. A board placed on or before a shop, office, etc., on which some notice is written.

Signet. A seal; in England, one of the royal seals.

Sign manual. In England, the royal signature written at the top of state papers.

Sign-post. A post on which a sign is suspended.

Staff. A stick used as an emblem of authority.

Stamp. An official mark or device required by law to be affixed to certain papers as an indication that the government dues are paid.

Standard. That which is established by authority as a measure of extent, quality, quantity, or value.

Stars and Stripes. Popular term for the flag of the United States.

Streak. A long, irregular mark, line, or stripe; a not very marked trait.

Streamer. A flag ensign, etc., which floats in the wind.

Stripe. A regular streak; marked quality or character.

Stroke. A mark or line made by one movement of an instrument, as a pencil.

Sublineation. A mark of a line or lines under a word to indicate its importance, emphatic position, etc.

Superscription. An address on a letter.

Supporters. Figures of living objects placed on either side of an escutcheon.

Tally. A score or mark; a mark used to indicate tale or number.

Telegraph. An apparatus for transmitting signals or messages.

Telltale. A device for giving information, as a watchman's clock.

Tessera. A small piece of wood, bone, or the like, used as a ticket of admission to theaters in ancient Rome and for various other purposes.

Test, etc. Criterion, etc. See TRIAL.

Tick. A mark employed in checking off something.

Ticket. A card with writing on it indicating that the holder is entitled to something.

Tilde. A diacritical sign used in writing the Spanish language.

Title. An inscription serving as a name for designating something, as a literary production.

Token A sign; indication.

Totem. An emblem used by savages.

Touch. That which serves as a test.

Trace. A mark or impression which indicates the passage of any person or thing.

Trade-mark. A symbol, mark, etc., used, as by merchants, to designate and distinguish goods.

Trait. A characteristic feature or quality.

Tricolor. A flag of three colors: the national standard of France.

Trophy, etc. Something taken from an enemy and treasured up in proof of victory, etc. See TROPHY.

Trumpet-call. A call by the sound of the trumpet.

Type. Something that indicates or is emblematic.

Underlining. Marking with a line underneath.

Uniform. A distinguishing dress worn by persons of some body or rank.

Union jack. A flag, containing the union, but not the fly.

Vane. A flag or thin plate turning with the wind and indicating its direction.

Varvel. A metal ring bearing the owner's name attached to the jesses of a hawk.

Vexillum. A standard used by the Romans; often a battle signal.

Visiting card. A small card used in visiting, which bears the name, and sometimes the address, of the person presenting it.

Voucher. A book, paper, or document that serves to attest an alleged act, as to attest the receipt of money; one who vouches for another.

Warning, etc. Indication of danger, etc. See WARNING.

Watchfire. A fire kindled at night as a signal.

Watchtower. A tower on which a sentinel is placed to look out for the approach of danger.

Watchword. A password.

Weathercock. A vane.

Wink. A hint given by winking.

Witness. One who or that which gives evidence.

Word of command. An order.

Zeitgeist [G.] The spirit of the time.

SIGN—*Verbs.*

Argue. Bring forth reasons for or against; debate

Attest. Confirm, as by a signature or oath.

Beck. Give a signal by nodding, moving hand, etc.

Beckon. Call by gesture; make a mute signal.

Betoken. To be an indication of.

Chalk. Mark with chalk to indicate something.

Connotate. Indicate as additional.

Connote. Indicate; enlarge the definition of a word; descriptive qualities.

Dash. Erase by a dash or stroke.

Denote. Mark out plainly or indicate the objects to which a word may be applied.

Docket. Indorse; put a tag on.

Dot. Mark or indicate by a dot or dots.

Earmark. Crop or slit the ear, as of sheep, for identification.

Engrave. Represent by means of incisions or inscriptions on wood, stone, etc.

Gesticulate. Illustrate by gestures.

Glance. Indicate or hint by a quick or passing look.

Impress. Mark by pressure.

Imprint. Mark or stamp by pressure or by means of type, plate stamps, etc.

Indicate. Show; point out; suggest.

Label. Mark with a label.

Leer. Look obliquely, with malicious, lustful, or equivocal intent.

Mark. Put a mark on as an indication of something.

Nod. Indicate or signify by a nod.

Note. Set down in writing for future reference; denote; designate.

Nudge. Touch or push gently, as with the elbow, in order to attract attention.

Print. Take the impression from type.

Represent. Serve as a sign or symbol of.

Score. Mark with a cut or cuts as in wood; keep tally of.

Seal. Put a seal on to indicate verification or authenticity.

Shrug. Draw up the shoulders to indicate dislike, surprise, doubt, etc.

Sign. Affix one's signature to, mark.

Signalize. Signal or make signals.

Spot. Mark for recognition.

Stamp. Put a stamp on. See *Nouns.*

Stereotype. Make stereotype plates for.

Symbolize. Use symbols.

Testify, etc. Serve as evidence; give testimony, etc. See EVIDENCE.

Ticket. Put a ticket on for identification.

Trace. Search out proofs or indications.

Typify, etc. Indicate by a type, be a type of, etc. See PROPHECY.

Underline, etc. Draw a line underneath to indicate importance, etc., as to underline a word, etc. See CONSEQUENCE.

Wink. Make a sign by drawing the eyelids together.

SIGN—*Verbal Expressions.*

Bear the impress of, etc. (see *Nouns*); **beat the drum; be the sign of,** etc. (see *Nouns*); **call attention to,** etc. (see HEED); **give an alarm; give a signal; give notice,** etc. (see ENLIGHTENMENT); **give the cue,** etc. (see ENLIGHTENMENT); **hang out a banner,** etc. (see *Nouns*), **hang out a signal; hoist a banner,** etc. (see *Nouns*); **hold up the finger; hold up the hand; make a sign,** etc. (see *Nouns*); **put a mark; put an indication; raise a cry; raise the finger; raise the hand; saw the air; show one's colors; sound an alarm; sound the trumpets; stand for; suit the action to the word; tip the wink; unfurl a banner,** etc. (see *Nouns*); **wave a banner,** etc. (see *Nouns*); **wave a kerchief; wave the hand.**

SIGN—*Adjectives.*

Armorial. Relating to heraldry.

Characteristic. Distinguishing; marking.

Connotative. Implying something added to a definition, so that it will apply to fewer objects.

Demonstrative. Having the power to indicate.

Denotable. Capable of being indicated.

Denotative. Marking off, designating objects to which a definition is to apply.

Diacritical. That distinguishes; distinctive.

Diagnostic. Indicating the nature of a disease.

Emblematic. Serving as a sign or emblem.

Exponential. Relating to exponents.

Indelible. That cannot be removed or blotted out.

Indicated, etc. Pointed out, etc. See *Verbs.*

Indicating, etc. Marking out, etc. See *Verbs.*

Indicative. Pointing out; giving intimation.

Indicatory. Serving to show; indicating.

Individual, etc. Indicating singleness, etc. See UNIVERSALITY-PARTICULARITY.

Known by. Indicated or distinguished by.

Marked. Designated; indicated.

Pantomimic. Representing by dumb show.

Pathognomonic. Indicating a disease with certainty.

Pointed. Marked by a point or points, as to designate the pauses in a sentence.

Recognizable by. Capable of being recognized by, as by a mark or sign.

Representative. Indicative of a class.

Symbolic. Indicating by a symbol.

Symptomatic. Indicating the existence of something other than itself.

Typical. Representing something by a sign, model, form, etc.

SIGN—*Adverbs, etc.*

In dumb show. By means of pantomime.

In token of. As a sign of.

Symbolically, etc. By means of symbols, etc. See *Adjectives.*

SIGN—*Phrases.*

Ecce signum [L.]. Behold the sign! here is the proof.

Ex pede Herculem [L.]. We recognize a Hercules from the foot; that is, we judge of the whole from the specimen.

Ex ungue leonem [L.]. The lion is recognized by his claw.

L'Étoile du Nord [F.]. The North Star.

Vide ut supra [L.]. See what is given above.

Vultus ariete fortior [L.]. Valor is stronger than the battering-ram.

sig'-nal. Remarkable; sign. CONSEQUENCE-INSIGNIFICANCE, MAGNITUDE-SMALLNESS, SIGN; **give the signal,** ORDER; **signal of distress,** ALARM.

sig'-nal-ize. To make noteworthy. REPUTATION, SIGN, SOLEMNIZATION.

sig'-nal-ly. Greatly. MAGNITUDE-SMALLNESS.

sig'-nal-post". Post from which signals are displayed. SIGN, WARNING.

sig'-na-ture. Name; mark. CONTRACT, EVIDENCE-COUNTEREVIDENCE, MARK-OBLITERATION, SECURITY, SIGN, WRITING-PRINTING.

sign'-board". Board giving directions. SIGN.

sig'-net. Seal. CONTRACT, SCEPTER, SIGN; **writer to the signet,** ADVOCATE.

sig-nif'-i-cance. Expressiveness; importance. CONSEQUENCE-INSIGNIFICANCE, MEANING-JARGON.

sig-nif'-i-cant. Important. CONSEQUENCE-INSIGNIFICANCE.

sig"-nif-i-ca'-tion. That which is signified. MEANING-JARGON.

sig-nif'-i-ca-tive. Symbolical. MEANING-JARGON.

sig-nif'-i-ca-to"-ry. Having significance. MEANING-JARGON.

sig'-ni-fies. Amounts to. **What signifies,** CONSEQUENCE-INSIGNIFICANCE.

sig'-ni-fy. To mean. CONSEQUENCE-INSIGNIFICANCE, ENLIGHTENMENT - SECRECY, MEANING - JARGON, PROPHECY.

sign man'-u-al. Signature. SIGN, WRITING-PUBLICATION.

signo spes mea, in hoc [L.] (sig'-no spîz mî'-a, in hoc). In this sign is my hope. SANGUINENESS-HOPELESSNESS.

signo vinces, in hoc [L.] (sig'-no, vin'-sîz, in hoc). In this sign thou wilt conquer. SANGUINENESS-HOPELESSNESS.

si'-gnor. Sir. TITLE.

sign'-paint"-er. One who paints signs. ARTIST.

sign'-paint"-ing. DELINEATION-CARICATURE.

sign'-post". Post supporting a sign-board. SIGN.

signum, ecce [L.] (sig'-num, ec'-sî). Behold the sign. SIGN.

sike. Rill. RIVER-WIND.

si'-lence. To refute; quietness. ENLIGHTENMENT-SECRECY, MANIFESTATION-LATENCY, MIGHT-IMPOTENCE, MOVEMENT-REST, PROOF-DISPROOF, SOUND-SILENCE, SUCCESS-FAILURE, TALKATIVENESS-TACITURNITY, VOCALIZATION-MUTENESS.

silence du peuple est la leçon des rois, le [F.] (si-lan's' dü pupl ê la le-son'' dê rwa, le). The silence of the people is the lesson of kings. RECKLESSNESS-CAUTION, WARNING.

si'-lent. Still. MOVEMENT-REST, TALKATIVENESS-TACITURNITY, VOCALIZATION-MUTENESS.

silentio, sub [L.] (si-len'-shi-o, sub). In silence. VOCALIZATION-MUTENESS.

si'-lent-ly. In a silent manner. HEED-DISREGARD, MANIFESTATION-LATENCY, SOUND-SILENCE.

sil"-hou-ette'. Picture. OUTLINE, PAINTING.

sil'-i-ca. Chemical substance. CHEMISTRY.

sil'-i-quose. Like a pod. CONTENTS-RECEIVER.

silk. Cloth. HARDNESS-SOFTNESS, SMOOTHNESS-ROUGHNESS; **make a silk purse out of a sow's ear,** POSSIBILITY-IMPOSSIBILITY; **silk gown,** ADVOCATE.

silk'-en. Made of or like silk. SMOOTHNESS-ROUGHNESS.

silk'-en re-pose'. Soft rest. TOIL-RELAXATION.

silk'-i-ness. The qualities of silk. MODERATION-SELFINDULGENCE.

silk'-y. Like silk. SMOOTHNESS-ROUGHNESS.

sill. Foundation. SUSPENSION-SUPPORT.

sil'-li-ness. State or quality of being silly. SAGACITY-INCAPACITY.

sil'-ly. Simple. CREDULOUSNESS-SKEPTICISM, SAGACITY-INCAPACITY, SANENESS-LUNACY.

silt. Dirt. CLEANNESS-FILTHINESS.

sil'-ver. Bright; gray; coin; metal. CHEMISTRY, GRAY-BROWN, LIGHT-DARKNESS, MONEY, WHITENESS-BLACKNESS; **bait with a silver hook,** MOTIVE-CAPRICE; **silver lining of the cloud,** SANGUINENESS-HOPELESSNESS.

sil'-ver-toned". Clear. MELODY-DISSONANCE.

sil'-ver-y. Containing or resembling silver, in luster, hue, or sound. GRAY-BROWN, MELODY-DISSONANCE, WHITENESS-BLACKNESS.

simagrée [F.] (si-ma-grê'). Grimace. SOCIETY-AFFECTATION.

sim'-i-lar. Like. SYNONYM-ANTONYM.

sim"-i-lar'-i-ty. Likeness. DIVISION, LIKENESS-UNLIKENESS; **similarity of form,** FORM-FORMLESSNESS.

sim'-i-le. Rhetorical figure. COMPARISON, LIKENESS-UNLIKENESS, RHETORIC, TROPE.

similibus, et sic de [L.] (sim-il'-i-bus, et sic dî). And so of the like. LIKENESS-UNLIKENESS.

si-mil'-i-tude. Resemblance. COMPARISON, COPY-MODEL, LIKENESS-UNLIKENESS.

sim'-mer. To boil. AGITATION, EXCITATION, HEAT-COLD, HEATING-COOLING.

sim'-mer-ing. Boiling. EXCITABILITY-INEXCITABILITY.

Si'-mon. Credulous person. **Simple Simon,** GULL-DECEIVER.

Si'-mon Pure. The genuine or true. TRUTH-ERROR.

Si'-mon Sty-li'-tes. An ascetic. SOCIABILITY-PRIVACY.

si-moom'. A hot wind. HEAT-COLD, RIVER-WIND.

sim'-o-ny. Traffic. LAW-LAWLESSNESS.

sim'-per. Smirk. JUBILATION-LAMENTATION, SOCIETY-AFFECTATION.

sim'-ple. Credulous; pure; easy. CRAFT-ARTLESS-NESS, CREDULOUSNESS - SKEPTICISM, EMBELLISHMENT - SIMPLICITY, MAGNITUDE - SMALLNESS, MIXTURE-HOMOGENEITY, REMEDY-BANE, SAGACITY-INCAPACITY, SIMPLICITY-FLORIDNESS; **simple meaning,** INTERPRETATION - MISINTERPRETATION, MEANING-JARGON.

Sim'-ple Si'-mon. Credulous person. GULL-DECEIVER.

sim'-ple-heart''-ed. Frank. TRUTHFULNESS-FALSEHOOD.

sim'-ple-ness. The quality of being simple. CRAFT-ARTLESSNESS, MIXTURE-HOMOGENEITY.

sim'-ple-ton. Silly person. SAGE-FOOL.

simplex munditiis [L.] (sim'-plex mun-dish'-i-is). Of simple elegance. EMBELLISHMENT-SIMPLICITY.

sim-plic'-i-ty. Simpleness. EMBELLISHMENT-SIMPLICITY, NATURE-ART, SAGACITY-INCAPACITY, SIMPLICITY-FLORIDNESS.

SIMPLICITY—FLORIDNESS.

Plainness. The state of being plain. See *Adjectives*.
Severity. Exactness; strictness.
Simplicity. State of being simple or not complex.

SIMPLICITY—*Denotations*.

Household words. Words most commonly used.
Plain English.
Plain terms. } Language that may be readily understood.
Saxon English. Pure idiomatic English.

SIMPLICITY—*Verbs*.

Call a spade "a spade." To speak in plain, unequivocal terms.
Come to the point. To speak directly.
Plunge *in medias res* [L.]. To plunge into the midst of things; to begin the story or discussion at once without introduction.

SIMPLICITY—*Adjectives*.

Chaste. Free from barbarisms or vulgarisms: simple.
Dry. Void of that which interests or amuses; plain.
Homely. Unpolished; plain.
Homespun. Simple or plain in style.
Monotonous, etc. Wanting in change or variety, etc. See FORCE-WEAKNESS.
Neat. Free from that which is unbecoming or inappropriate.
Plain. Without ornament or embellishment.
Pure. Unmixed; clear; simple.
Saxon. Pertaining to the Anglo-Saxon language.
Severe. Rigidly adherent to a standard.
Simple. Clear; direct.
Unadorned. Not adorned.
Unornamented. Plain.
Unvaried. Monotonous.
Unvarnished. Without embellishment.

SIMPLICITY—*Adverbs, etc.*

In common parlance. In simple diction or phrase.
In plain English.
In plain terms. } In simplest and most direct language.
In plain words.
Point-blank. In a plain or direct manner.

FLORIDNESS—ADJECTIVES—*Continued from Column 2.*

Fustian. Pompous; inflated.
Grandiloquent. Speaking in pompous language.
Grandiose. Marked by affectation of grandeur.
High-flowing. Extravagant.
High-flown. Bombastic.
High-sounding. Ostentatious.
Inflated. Puffed up; pompous.
Johnsonian. Resembling the style of Dr. Johnson; pompous.
Magniloquent. Speaking in a lofty style.
Mouthy. Loquacious.
Ornamented. Decorated. See *Verbs*.
Ornate. Finely finished; polished.
Pedantic. Affectedly learned.
Pompous. Showy, boastful.
Rhetorical. Exhibiting rhetoric; figurative.
Rich. Highly ornate; abounding in beauty.
Sententious. Terse and pithy in expression.
Sesquipedal. Measuring a foot and a half; applied to long words.
Sesquipedalian. Using very long words.
Sonorous. High-sounding.
Stilted. Pompous.
Swelling. Inflated; puffed up.
Tumid. High-sounding; pompous.
Turgescent. Becoming inflated.
Turgid. Vainly ostentatious.

FLORIDNESS—*Adverbs, etc.*

Ore rotundo [L.]. With round mouth; with swelling eloquence.

Altiloquence. Lofty speech. See *Adjectives*.
Declamation. Rhetorical delivery; noisy or bombastic public speaking.
Elegance, etc. The quality of being elegant; fine polish, etc. See PURITY.
Floridness. The state of being rhetorically embellished.
Ornament. That which embellishes or contributes to the beauty of
Teratology. Affectation of sublimity.
Turgescence. Empty pompousness.
Turgidity. The quality of being turgid.
Well-rounded periods. Highly rhetorical language.

FLORIDNESS—*Denotations*.

Alexandrine. A kind of English verse consisting of twelve syllables.
Alliteration. The recurrence of the same sound at the beginning of successive words or at short intervals.
Antithesis. A contrast of words or sentiments occurring in the same sentence.
Big-sounding words. Arrogant or pompous speech.
Bombast. Extravagant language on unimportant subjects.
Euphemism. A figure of speech in which a mild term is put for something disagreeable.
Figurativeness. Abundance of figures of speech. See TROPE.
Fine writing. Writing expressing refinement or cultivation.
Flourish. Language used for display or ornament.
Flowers of rhetoric.
Flowers of speech. } Figures of speech.
Fustian. An inflated style of speaking or writing.
High-sounding words. Arrogant and pompous expressions.
Inflation. Bombastic or conceited speech.
Inversion. The placing of words before their subjects for the purpose of emphasis.
Macrology. A superfluity of words.
Minerva Press. A printing house in London in the eighteenth century, noted for the publication of sentimental novels.
Paronomasia. A play on words.
Pretension. Affectation in speaking or writing.
Prose run mad. A poetical style of writing.
Rant. Bombastic or windy declaratory talking.
Sesquipedalia verba [L.]. Words a foot and a half long.

FLORIDNESS—*Nouns of Agent*.

Euphemist. One who uses euphemisms.
Euphuist. A user of euphuism.
Phrasemonger. A wordy writer or speaker.

FLORIDNESS—*Verbs*.

Ornament. To embellish or adorn.
Overcharge. To exaggerate.
Overlay with ornament. To use figures, etc., very freely.
Smell of the lamp. To be laboriously wrought out.

FLORIDNESS—*Adjectives*.

Alliterative. Containing alliteration.
Altiloquent. High-sounding; talking big; bombastic.
Antithetical. Having opposition of words or sentiments.
Artificial, etc. Affected, etc. See PURITY-CRUDENESS.
Beautified, etc. Made beautiful or ornate, etc. See EMBELLISHMENT.
Big-sounding. Talking loudly or pretentiously.
Bombastic. Characterized by bombast.
Declamatory. Of or pertaining to declamation.
Euphemism. Softened in expression or rendered less offensive.
Euphuistic. Relating to euphuism.
Figurative, etc. Containing figures, etc. See TROPE.
Flaming. Very ardent.
Flashy. Showy, but empty.
Florid. Highly ornate.
Flowery. Abounding in figures.
Frothy. Empty.

(*Continued on Column* 1.)

sim'-pli-fy. To make simple. CLEARNESS-OBSCURITY, EMBELLISHMENT-SIMPLICITY, MIXTURE-HOMOGENEITY.

sim'-ply. Alone. MAGNITUDE-SMALLNESS, MIXTURE-HOMOGENEITY, SOLITUDE-COMPANY; **more simply,** INTERPRETATION-MISINTERPRETATION.

sim'-u-late. Imitate; to counterfeit. IMITATION-ORIGINALITY, TRUTHFULNESS-FALSEHOOD.

sim'-u-la''-ting. Imitating. LIKENESS-UNLIKENESS.

sim''-u-la'-tion. Imitation. IMITATION-ORIGINALITY.

sim''-ul-ta'-ne-ous. Done at the same time. COEXISTENCE.

sim''-ul-ta'-ne-ous-ness. State or quality of being simultaneous. COEXISTENCE.

sin. Wickedness. DUTY-DERELICTION, GODLINESS-UNGODLINESS, INNOCENCE-GUILT, VIRTUE-VICE.

sin'-a-pism. Mustard plaster. REMEDY-BANE.

since. Because; after. ANTECEDENCE-SEQUENCE, CONDITION-SITUATION, RATIOCINATION-INSTINCT, RATIONALE-LUCK.

sin-cere'. Honest. CRAFT-ARTLESSNESS, EMOTION, TRUTHFULNESS-FALSEHOOD.

sin-cer'-i-ty The quality of being sincere. TRUTHFULNESS-FALSEHOOD.

sine. Mathematical term. PARALLELISM-INCLINATION.

sine cura [L.] (sai'-nî kiu'-ra). Without care. CONTENTEDNESS-DISCONTENTMENT.

sine die [L.] (sai'-nî dai'-î). Without a day. DURATION-NEVERNESS, EARLINESS-LATENESS.

sine ictu [L.] (sai'-nî ic'-tiu). Without a stroke. MIGHT-IMPOTENCE.

sine qua non [L.] (sai'-nî qua non). Without which, not. CONSEQUENCE-INSIGNIFICANCE, NEED, TERMS.

si'-ne-cure. Having no duties. ACTION-PASSIVENESS; **no sinecure,** ACTIVITY-INDOLENCE.

sin'-ew. Strength. STRENGTH-WEAKNESS.

sin'-ew-less. Weak. MIGHT-IMPOTENCE.

sin'-ews of war. Resources. MONEY.

sin'-ew-y. Strong. STRENGTH-WEAKNESS.

sin'-ful. Wicked. VIRTUE-VICE.

sin'-ful-ly. In a sinful manner. VIRTUE-VICE.

sin'-ful-ness. The state or quality of being sinful. INNOCENCE-GUILT.

sing. To utter a song. JUBILATION-LAMENTATION, MUSICIAN, POETRY-PROSE; **sing Io triumphe,** BRAGGING; **sing out,** CRY-ULULATION; **sing praises,** APPROVAL-DISAPPROVAL, DEVOTION-IDOLATRY, REPUTATION-DISCREDIT; **sing small,** SELFRESPECT-HUMBLENESS.

singe. Scorch. HEATING-COOLING.

sing'-er. One who sings. MUSICIAN.

sin'-gle. Alone. MATRIMONY-CELIBACY, MIXTURE-HOMOGENEITY, SOCIABILITY-PRIVACY, SOLITUDE-COMPANY; **ride at single anchor,** RECKLESSNESS-CAUTION; **single combat,** STRIFE-PEACE; **single fit,** CONTINUITY-INTERRUPTION; **single out,** CHOICE-NEUTRALITY.

sin'-gle—hand''-ed. Unaided. DIFFICULTY-FACILITY, OBSTRUCTION-HELP, SOLITUDE-COMPANY.

sin'-gle—mind''-ed. Frank. CRAFT-ARTLESSNESS.

sin'-gle-ness. State of being single. **Singleness of heart,** CRAFT-ARTLESSNESS, MATRIMONY-CELIBACY, UPRIGHTNESS-DISHONESTY; **singleness of purpose,** CRAFT-ARTLESSNESS, PERSISTENCE-APOSTASY.

sin'-gle—stick''. Cudgel. STRIFE-PEACE.

sin'-gly. Individually. SOLITUDE-COMPANY.

sing'-song''. Monotonous talking. MELODY-DISSONANCE.

sin'-gu-lar. Odd; lone. CONVENTIONALITY-UNCONVENTIONALITY, SOLITUDE-COMPANY, UNIVERSALITY-PARTICULARITY.

sin''-gu-lar'-i-ty. Oddity. CONVENTIONALITY-UNCONVENTIONALITY, UNIVERSALITY-PARTICULARITY.

sin'-gu-lar-ly. In a singular manner. MAGNITUDE-SMALLNESS.

sin'-is-ter. Left; bad. GOODNESS-BADNESS, RIGHT-LEFT, VIRTUE-VICE; **bar sinister,** FAULTLESSNESS-FAULTINESS, REPUTATION-DISCREDIT.

sin'-is-tral. Pertaining to the left. RIGHT-LEFT.

sin''-is-tral'-i-ty. Sinistral state. RIGHT-LEFT.

sin'-is-trous. Sinistral. FAVORITE-MOROSENESS.

sink. To go down; to ruin; to fail; privy. ASCENT-DESCENT, CAREFULNESS-CARELESSNESS, CLEANNESS-FILTHINESS, CREATION-DESTRUCTION, ELEVATION-DEPRESSION, ENLIGHTENMENT-SECRECY, LIGHTHEARTEDNESS-DEJECTION, PLEASURE-PAIN, SPRING-DIVE, SUCCESS-FAILURE, · WEARINESS-REFRESHMENT, WELFARE-MISFORTUNE; **sink back,** RENOVATION-RELAPSE; **sink in the mind,** EXCITATION, REFLECTION-VACANCY, REMEMBRANCE-FORGETFULNESS; **sink into oblivion,** REMEMBRANCE-FORGETFULNESS; **sink into the grave,** LIFE-DEATH; **sink money,** OUTLAY-INCOME; **sink of corruption,** CLEANNESS-FILTHINESS; **sink of iniquity,** VIRTUE-VICE; **sink or swim,** CERTAINTY-DOUBT, PERSISTENCE-WHIM.

sink'-ing. Going down. Heart sinking, LIGHTHEARTEDNESS-DEJECTION; **sinking fund,** TREASURY.

sin'-less. Without sin. VIRTUE-VICE.

sin'-ner. Wicked man. GOOD MAN-BAD MAN, VIRTUE-VICE.

sin'-ning. Doing wrong. UPRIGHTNESS-DISHONESTY.

sin'-of''-fer-ing. Sacrifice. ATONEMENT.

sin''-u-a'-tion. A winding. CIRCLE-WINDING.

sin''-u-os'-i-ty. Quality or state of being sinuous. CIRCLE-WINDING, CURVATION-RECTILINEARITY.

sin'-u-ous. Curved. CIRCLE-WINDING.

si'-nus. Recess. CONVEXITY-CONCAVITY.

sip. Taste. MAGNITUDE-SMALLNESS, NUTRIMENT-EXCRETION.

si'-phon. Tube. WATERCOURSE-AIRPIPE.

sip'-pet. An eatable. NUTRIMENT-EXCRETION.

sir. Man. MALE-FEMALE, TITLE; **sir Oracle,** SOLITUDE-COMPANY.

sir-dar'. Leader. CHIEF-UNDERLING.

sire. Old man. PARENTAGE-PROGENY.

si'-ren. Singer; seducer; sea-nymph; musical instrument. BENEFACTOR-EVILDOER, DEVOTION-MAGICIAN, JOVE-FIEND, MOTIVE-CAPRICE, MUSICAL INSTRUMENTS, MUSICIAN, OCEAN-LAND; **siren strains,** MUSIC; **song of the sirens,** MOTIVE-CAPRICE.

si-ri'-a-sis. Sunstroke. SANENESS-LUNACY.

Sir'-i-us. Dog-star. LUMINARY-SHADE.

sir'-loin''. A loin of beef, especially the upper portion. NUTRIMENT-EXCRETION.

si-roc'-co. Simoom. HEAT-COLD, RIVER-WIND.

sir'-rah. Sir. GOOD MAN-BAD MAN.

sis'-ter. Female of the same association or born of the same parents. LIKENESS-UNLIKENESS, RELATIONSHIP, REMEDY-BANE.

sis'-ter-hood. Body of females. ASSOCIATION, RELATIONSHIP; **frail sisterhood,** PURITY-RAKE.

sis'-ter-ly. Like a sister. CHARITABLENESS-MALEVOLENCE.

sis'-ters. Plural of sister. **Sisters three,** VOLITION-OBLIGATION; **weird sisters,** DEVOTION-MAGICIAN.

Sis'-y-phus. Son of Eolus. **Task of Sisyphus,** DIFFICULTY-FACILITY, USEFULNESS-USELESSNESS.

sit. To rest on the haunches. **Sit down,** ARRIVAL-DEPARTURE, ELEVATION-DEPRESSION, ERECTNESS-FLATNESS, ESTABLISHMENT-REMOVAL; **sit in judgment,** DECISION-MISJUDGMENT, JUDICATURE, LITIGATION; **sit on,** SUSPENSION-SUPPORT; **sit on thorns,** PLEASURE-PAIN, SANGUINENESS-TIMIDITY, SENSUALITY-SUFFERING.

site. Location. POSITION.

sit'-ting. Incubation; session. COUNCIL, PREPARA-

TION-NONPREPARATION; **sitting up late,** EARLINESS-LATENESS, TOIL-RELAXATION.

sit'-ting–room". Room. CONTENTS-RECEIVER.

situ, in [L.] (sai'-tiu, in) In position. MOVEMENT-REST, POSITION.

sit'-u-ate. To locate. ESTABLISHMENT-REMOVAL.

sit"-u-a'-tion. Location; condition. CONDITION-SITUATION, ESTABLISHMENT-REMOVAL, OCCUPATION, OCCURRENCE-DESTINY, POSITION; **out of a situation,** ESTABLISHMENT-REMOVAL.

Si'-va. A god. JOVE-FIEND.

six. A number. FIVE-QUINQUESECTION; **six of one and half a dozen of the other,** EQUALITY-INEQUALITY.

six'-es and sev'-ens. Disorder. **At sixes and sevens,** REGULARITY-IRREGULARITY, VARIANCE-ACCORD.

sixth. Next in order after the fifth. FIVE-QUINQUE-SECTION.

six'-ty. Six times ten. FIVE-QUINQUESECTION.

si'-zar. Undergraduate. CHIEF-UNDERLING.

size. Largeness; glue; to arrange. CONNECTIVE, GREATNESS-LITTLENESS, MAGNITUDE-SMALLNESS, ORGANIZATION-DISORGANIZATION, QUANTITY-MEASURE, VISCIDITY-FOAM.

skate. To move. CONVEYANCE-VESSEL, TRAVELING-NAVIGATION.

ska'-ting. A kind of sport. ENTERTAINMENT-WEARINESS.

skean. Dagger. WEAPON.

ske-dad'-dle. To scamper. QUEST-EVASION.

skein. Roll. CROSSING; **tangled skein,** REGULARITY-IRREGULARITY.

skel'-et-on. Corpse; frame; outline. DESIGN, INCREMENT-REMNANT, LIFE-CORPSE, SUSPENSION-SUPPORT, WHOLE-PART; **reduced to a skeleton,** BETTERMENT-DETERIORATION; **skeleton in a closet,** GOODNESS-BADNESS, PLEASURABLENESS-PAINFULNESS.

skep'-tic. Doubter of religion. CREDULOUSNESS-SKEPTICISM.

sketch. Outline. ACCOUNT, DELINEATION-CARICATURE, DESIGN, FORM-FORMLESSNESS, PAINTING.

sketch'-er. Artist. ARTIST.

sketch'-y. Incomplete. COMPLETION-NONCOMPLETION, ENTIRETY-DEFICIENCY, FORCE-WEAKNESS.

skew. Perverted. PARALLELISM-INCLINATION.

skew'-er. To fasten. CONNECTIVE.

skid. Brake; support. OBSTRUCTION-HELP, SUSPENSION-SUPPORT.

skies. Heaven. **Exalt to the skies,** REPUTATION-DISCREDIT; **praise to the skies,** ADULATION-DISPARAGEMENT.

skiff. Boat. CONVEYANCE-VESSEL.

skil'-ful. Having skill. CRAFT-ARTLESSNESS.

skil'-ful-ly. In a skilful manner. SKILL-UNSKILFULNESS.

skil'-ful-ness. State or quality of being skilful. SKILL-UNSKILFULNESS.

skill. Dexterity. SKILL-UNSKILFULNESS; **acquisition of skill,** EDUCATION-LEARNING; **game of skill,** ENTERTAINMENT-WEARINESS.

SKILL—UNSKILFULNESS.

Ability. The state or quality of being able.

Address. Skilful management.

Adroitness. The quality of being adroit.

Ambidexterity. The state or quality of being able to use both hands equally well.

Ambidextrousness. Ambidexterity.

Aptitude. The state or quality of being apt.

Aptness. Aptitude.

Callidity. Acuteness of discernment.

Capability. The state or quality of being capable.

Capacity. Power of receiving; ability to do.

Capacity for. Ability to do.

Cleverness. The quality or state of being clever.

Competence. The quality or state of being competent.

Craft. Skill in a particular employment.

Craftiness, etc. The state or quality of being skilful in a craft. See CRAFT.

Curiosa felicitas [L.]. Studied felicity.

Dexterity. The quality of being dexterous.

Dexterousness. Dexterity.

Discretion, etc. The quality of being discreet. See RECKLESSNESS-CAUTION.

Endowment. Gift of nature: a talent.

Excellence. Superiority in skill.

Expertness. The quality of being expert.

Facility. Ease or quickness in performance.

Faculty. Power to do, natural or acquired.

Felicity. A pleasing faculty or accomplishment.

Finesse. Subtility practised for gain.

Genius. Individual character; superior power.

Genius for. Special taste for.

Gift. Special talent.

Habilitation. Qualification.

Ingenuity. Quickness in producing something new.

Intelligence, etc. Readiness of comprehension. See SAGACITY.

Invention, etc. Skill in contriving something new. See FANCY.

Knack. Aptness in doing.

Knowledge of the world. Ability to get along in different conditions.

Management. Skilful treatment.

Mastership. Mastery.

Mastery. Supremacy; complete understanding.

Mother wit. Natural intelligence.

Panurgy. Skill in all kinds of work.

Parts. Qualities or talents.

Practical knowledge. Knowledge put to good use in doing things.

Proficiency. The state or quality of being proficient.

Qualification. An enabling quality or endowment.

Disqualification. Lack of qualification.

Folly. The state or quality of being foolish.

Inability. Lack of ability.

Incompetence.} Lack of ability.
Incompetency.}

Indexterity. Lack of dexterity.

Indiscretion. Lack of discretion.

Inexperience. Lack of experience.

Infelicity. The state or quality of being infelicitous.

Quackery. Pretentious and ignorant practise.

Stupidity, etc. The quality or state of being stupid. See SAGACITY-INCAPACITY.

Thoughtlessness, etc. Lack of thought or care; heedlessness. See HEED-DISREGARD.

Unproficiency. Lack of proficiency.

Unskilfulness. Lack of skilfulness.

Want of skill, etc. Inability to do. See SKILL.

UNSKILFULNESS—*Denotations.*

Absence of rule. Lack of any regular method of working.

Act of folly. The result of a ruinous undertaking or enterprise.

Bad job. A work that shows lack of skill.

Balourdise [F.]. A blunder.

Blunder, etc. A heedless or stupid mistake. See TRUTH-ERROR.

Botch. A bungled piece of work.

Botchery. Bungling work.

Bungler, etc. One who works badly or clumsily. See ADEPT-BUNGLER.

Bungling. Clumsy and faulty work.

Etourderie [F.]. A thoughtless act.

Failure, etc. Anything done imperfectly or attempted unsuccessfully. See SUCCESS-FAILURE.

Fool, etc. A person lacking in common sense or judgment. See SAGE-FOOL.

Gaucherie [F.]. A blunder.

Impolicy. Unsuitableness to the end proposed.

Maladministration. Vicious administration of public office.

Misapplication. Devotion to a purpose not intended or improper.

Misconduct. Bad behavior.

Misdirection. A pointing or leading the wrong way.

Misfeasance. The doing of a lawful act in an unlawful or improper manner.

Misgovernment. Poorly administered government.

Mismanagement. Unskilful management.

Misrule. Unjust rule or government.

Much ado about nothing. Unnecessary activity in trifling matters. [Shakespeare.]

SKILL—UNSKILFULNESS—*Continued.*

Readiness, etc. Facility; aptitude. See ACTIVITY.
Savoir faire [F.]. Ability; skill.
Self-help. Ability to do without outside aid.
Sharpness. The state or quality of being sharp.
Skilfulness. The quality of being skilful.
Skill. Familiar knowledge of an art or science accompanied by dexterity of performance.
Sleight. Artful skill.
Sleight of hand, etc. A feat so dexterous that the manner of performance escapes detection. See TRUTHFULNESS-FRAUD.
Tact. Skill in doing the right and fitting thing.
Talent. Ability to learn and practise.
Talents. Capabilities; natural or acquired endowments; loans from the Lord, which draw interest. [*Matthew* xxv, 25.]
Technicality. The quality or state of being technical.
Technical knowledge. Knowledge of useful or mechanical arts.
Turn. Distinctive character or disposition.
Turn for. Aptness for.
World wisdom. Practical skill.

SKILL—*Denotations.*

Accomplishment. An acquirement or attainment that tends to perfect or equip in character, manners, etc.
Acquirement. Some mental or physical power or attribute which is not a natural gift or talent.
Art. Facility resulting from practise.
Attainment. An acquisition of a personal character, as scholarship, etc.
Chef d'œuvre [F.]. A masterpiece.
Coup de maître [F.]. A master-stroke.
Forte. That for which one has a special faculty, or in which he chiefly excels.
Good stroke, etc. A decisive accomplishment. See DESIGN.
Horsemanship. Equestrian skill.
Marksmanship. The skill or art of shooting.
Masterpiece. A superior production.
Proficient. An expert; an adept.
Rope-dancing. The art of dancing or performing on a tight rope.
Science. Knowledge gained and verified by exact observation.
Seamanship. Knowledge and skill in the art of navigation.
Technology. The science of the facts and principles of the industrial arts.
Tour de force [F.]. A feat of skill.
Trick. A peculiar skill or knack.
Yankee. An American noted for shrewdness, like the northern sea captain; the modern Ulysses.

SKILL—*Verbs.*

Be master of. To be able to do in the very best way.
Be skilful. To be able to accomplish. See *Adjectives.*
Excel in. Surpass others in.
Have a turn for. To have a special capability for.

SKILL—*Verbal Expressions.*

Cut one's coat according to one's cloth; exercise one's discretion; feather the oar; have all one's wits about one; have cut one's eye-teeth; have cut one's wisdom teeth; have one's hand in; hit the right nail on the head; know a hawk from a handsaw; know on which side one's bread is buttered; know what one is about; know what's o'clock; know what's what; live by one's wits; look after the main chance; make a hit; make a virtue of necessity; make hay while the sun shines, etc. (see OPPORTUNENESS); make the most of; play one's best card; play one's cards well; profit by; put the saddle on the right horse; sail near the wind; *savoir vivre* [F.], to know how to live; *scire quid valeant humeri quid ferre recusent* [L.] to know what one's shoulders can and what they cannot bear: see one's way; see where the wind lies; see which way the wind blows; stoop to conquer: take advantage of.

SKILL—*Adjectives.*

Able. Having sufficient or superior power.
Accomplished. Having accomplishments.
Adroit. Skilful in use of bodily or mental powers.
A good hand at. Having some skill in.
Alive to. Understanding thoroughly.
Ambidextrous. Skilful in both hands.
Apt. Especially fitted; quick to learn.
Artistic. Showing taste or skill.
At home in. Thoroughly familiar with.
Au fait [F.]. Well instructed.
Businesslike. Like one who transacts business well.
Capable. Possessing adequate power; fully competent.
Clever. Possessing quick active intellect.
Competent. Fulfilling all requirements; qualified.

UNSKILFULNESS—DENOTATIONS—*Continued.*

Petticoat government. Government by women.
Rule of thumb. Any primitive method, roughly practical rather than scientific.
Sad work. Work poorly done.
Screw loose. Something wanting or improper in the arrangement of anything.
Sprat sent out to catch a whale. Figuratively, useless work.
Too many cooks. Unnecessary workers.
Wild-goose chase. Fruitless undertaking.

UNSKILFULNESS—*Verbs.*

Be unskilful, etc. To be unable to do rightly. See *Adjectives.*
Bitch. To botch.
Blunder. To make a stupid mistake.
Boggle. Work in a clumsy manner; make a botch of.
Botch. Put together clumsily, make a thing badly.
Bungle. To perform in a blundering manner.
Fail, etc. To lack ability. See SUCCESS-FAILURE.
Flounder. To progress or perform awkwardly on account of some deficiency.
Fumble. To handle clumsily.
Hobble. To do something in a lame, unskilful manner.
Misapply. Apply wrongly.
Misconduct. } To lead wrongly.
Misdirect. }
Mismanage. To conduct poorly.
Missend. To send to the wrong place.
Mistake, etc. To understand wrongly. See TRUTH-ERROR.
Stumble. Act in a blundering manner.
Trip. Commit an error.

UNSKILFULNESS—*Verbal Expressions.*

Act foolishly; aim at a pigeon and kill a crow; begin at the wrong end; be in the wrong box; bring the house about one's ears; burn one's fingers; catch a Tartar; catch at straws; commit oneself; cut blocks with a razor; cut one's own throat; do things by halves, etc. (see COMPLETION-NONCOMPLETION); fall into a trap; fight with a shadow; get the dirty end of the stick; get the wrong sow by the ear; go further and fare worse; go on a fool's errand; go on a sleeveless errand; grasp at a shadow; have too many eggs in one basket; have too many irons in the fire; hold a farthing candle to the sun, etc. (see RECKLESSNESS); kill the goose which lays the golden eggs; knock one's head against a stone wall; lock the stable door when the horse is stolen, etc. (see OPPORTUNENESS-UNSUITABLENESS); lose one's cunning; lose one's head; lose one's way; make a fool of oneself; make a hash of; make a mess of; make a sad work of; make two bites of a cherry; miss one's way; not know one's own interest; not know on which side one's bread is buttered; not know what one is about; not see an inch beyond one's nose; overshoot the mark; pay dear for one's whistle; play at cross purposes; play Puck; play the fool; play tricks with; pursue a wild-goose chase; put a square thing in a round hole; put new wine into old bottles; put oneself out of court; put one's foot in it; put the cart before the horse; put the saddle on the wrong horse; quarrel with one's bread and butter; reckon without one's host; run one's head against a stone wall; stand in one's own light; strain at a gnat and swallow a camel; stultify oneself; take the dirty end of the stick; take the shadow for the substance, etc. (see CREDULOUSNESS); take the wrong sow by the ear; throw a stone in one's own garden; trust to a broken reed.

UNSKILFULNESS—*Adjectives.*

Adrift. In a confused state.
At fault. In the wrong.
Awkward. Not skilful or graceful in action.
Bungling. Inclined to bungle.
Clumsy. Lacking dexterity and grace.
Disqualified. Not having the necessary qualifications.
Foolish. Wholly lacking in ability or intelligence.
Gauche [F.]. Left-handed.
Gawky. Very awkward.
Giddy, etc. Lacking judgment. See HEED-DISREGARD.
Green. Lacking knowledge from experience.
Heavy-handed. Clumsy.
Ill-advised. Badly advised.
Ill-conducted. Poorly managed.
Ill-contrived. Badly planned.
Ill-devised. Unskilfully planned.
Ill-imagined. } Not well planned.
Ill-judged. }
Ill-qualified. Not fitted for.
Inactive. Not active. See ACTIVITY-INDOLENCE.

SKILL—UNSKILFULNESS—*Continued.*

SKILL—Adjectives—*Continued.*

Conversant, etc. Having precise and familiar knowledge. See KNOWLEDGE.
Crack. Of superior excellence.
Cunning, etc. Knowing and skilful. See CRAFT.
Cut out for. Specially adapted to.
Dædalian. Ingenious, like Dædalus.
Deft. Apt; fit; neat.
Dexterous. Skilful with hands or body, especially the right hand.
Discreet. Having excellent powers of discernment.
Efficient. Fully qualified and able to perform successfully.
Endowed. Furnished with endowments.
Experienced. Skilful from experience.
Expert. Taught by practise; very skilful.
Felicitous. Characterized by felicity.
Fine-fingered. Skilful in the use of the fingers.
Finished. Of the highest degree of perfection.
Fit for. Adapted to; ready for.
Fitted. Qualified.
Fitted for. Able to do.
Gain. Suitable; dexterous.
Gifted. Having many gifts.
Good at. Skilful in doing.
Hackneyed. Much used.
Handy. Skilful in use of the hand.
Ingenious. Characterized by ingenuity.
Initiated. Instructed in first principles.
In practise. Used.
In proper cue. In practise.
Inventive, etc. Quick at contriving. See FANCY.
Masterful. Showing mastery.
Masterly. Having thorough knowledge and superior skill.
Master of. Having attained great skill in.
Neat-handed. Skilful in hands.
Not to be caught with chaff. To have skill or experience.
Practised. Experienced.
Prepared. Made suitable; qualified.
Primed. Instructed beforehand.
Proficient. Possessed of considerable skill; well advanced in knowledge.
Qualified. Having the necessary qualifications.
Quick. Of acute, active capabilities.
Ready. Quick in action; expert.
Scientific. Well versed in science; remarkably skilled.
Sharp, etc. Of keen discernment and excellent skill. See SAGACITY.
Shipshape. Well arranged.
Shrewd. Able and clever in practise.
Skilful. Characterized by skill.
Skilled. Having knowledge and dexterity in applying.
Smart, etc. Accomplishing quick results; efficient. See ACTIVITY.
Statesmanlike. Having the wisdom of a statesman.
Surefooted. Not liable to err.
Talented. Having many talents.
Technical. Skilled in mechanical and useful arts.
Thoroughbred. Of long and thorough practise.
Trained. Well taught by practise.
Up in. Informed about; versed in.
Up to. Prepared for; able to perform.
Up to snuff. Knowing; acute.
Up to the mark. Fulfilling the requirements.
Well up in. Skilled.
Workmanlike. Having the characteristics of a good workman.

SKILL—Adverbs, etc.

Artistically. In an artistic manner.
Secundum artem [L.]. According to art.
Skilfully. In a skilful manner.
Suo marte [L.]. By his own force of arms.
To the best of one's abilities, etc. See TOIL.

UNSKILFULNESS—Adjectives—*Continued.*

Inapt. Unhandy.
Incompetent. Unfit.
Inconsiderate, etc. Regardless of what should be considered. See CAREFULNESS-CARELESSNESS.
Inexperienced. Without practise.
Inexpert. Unskilful.
Infelicitous. Not felicitous; lacking in fitness; unlucky.
Inhabile. Incompetent; unskilful.
Left-handed. Clumsy.
Lubberly. Like a lubber.
Maladroit. Lacking adroitness.
Misadvised. Wrongly advised.
Misconducted. } Badly led.
Misguided. }
Out of practise. Untrained to.
Penny-wise and pound-foolish, etc. Careful in small matters, careless in important affairs. See PERSISTENCE-WHIM.
Quackish. Characterized by quackery.
Raw. Of no experience.
Rusty. Having lost skill for want of practise.
Shiftless. Wanting in energy or ability.
Slatternly. Untidy; slovenly.
Slovenly. Negligent and disorderly.
Stupid, etc. Lacking intelligence and skill. See SAGACITY-INCAPACITY.
Unaccustomed. Not familiar.
Unadvised. Not advised.
Unapt. Not fitted for.
Unconversant, etc. See KNOWLEDGE-IGNORANCE.
Unfit. Not adapted to.
Unguided. Without a leader or example.
Unhandy. That cannot be well used.
Uninitiated. Not trained to.
Unqualified. Unable to do.
Unskilful, etc. Without special ability. See SKILL.
Unstatesmanlike. Without the characteristics of a statesman.
Unteachable. That cannot be taught.
Untractable. That cannot be trained.
Untrained, etc. Without practise. See EDUCATION.
Unused. Not familiar.
Wild. Untrained; careless.

UNSKILFULNESS—Phrases.

Il se noyerait dans une goutte d'eau [F.]. He would drown himself in a glass of water.
Incidit in Scyllam qui vult vitare Charybdin [L.]. He encounters Scylla who wishes to escape Charybdis.
One's fingers being all thumbs.
Out of the frying-pan into the fire.
The right hand forgets its cunning.

SKILL—Adverbs—*Continued.*

Well, etc. Properly. See GOOD.
With consummate skill. Very well.
With skill. Showing ability.

SKILL—Phrases.

Ars celare artem [L.]. It is true art to conceal art.
Artes honorabit [L.]. He will honor the arts.
Celui qui veut, celui-là peut [F.]. Who has the will, he has the skill.
Es bildet ein Talent sich in der Stille, sich ein Charakter in dem Strom der Welt [G.]. Talent is built up in quiet, character in the stream of the world.
Materiam superabat opus [L.]. The workmanship was better than the material. [Ovid, *Metamorphoses*, II, 5.]

---

skilled. Expert. SKILL-UNSKILFULNESS; **skilled workman,** LABOR-CAPITAL.
skil'-let. Stew-pan. CONTENTS-RECEIVER.
skim. Move; remove; haste. CAREFULNESS-CARELESSNESS, DIGEST, HEED-DISREGARD, SWIFTNESS-SLOWNESS, TRAVELING-NAVIGATION.
skim'-mer. A flat ladle for skimming. INSTRUMENT.
skin. Integument; coat. COVER-LINING, DRESS-UNDRESS, OUTSIDE-INSIDE, UNION-DISUNION; **mere skin** and bones, BREADTH-NARROWNESS; **skin a flint,** EXTRAVAGANCE-AVARICE, POSSIBILITY-IMPOSSIBILITY; **skin over,** RENOVATION-RELAPSE; **wet to the skin,** DAMPNESS-DRYNESS; **with a whole skin,** CONSERVATION; **without skin,** SENSITIVENESS-APATHY.
skin'-deep". Superficial. DEEPNESS-SHALLOWNESS, OUTSIDE-INSIDE.
skin'-flint". A miser. EXTRAVAGANCE-AVARICE.
skinned. Having a skin; also, having the skin removed. **Thick-skinned,** FEELING-INSENSIBILITY,

Sensitiveness - Apathy; **thin - skinned,** Feeling-Insensibility.

skin'-ny. Lean. Breadth-Narrowness, Cover-Lining.

skip. Leap; pass. Carefulness-Carelessness, Jubilation-Lamentation, Spring-Dive.

skip'-jack". Upstart. Gentility-Commonalty, Welfare-Misfortune.

skip'-per. Master. Chief-Underling, Wayfarer-Seafarer.

skip'-pet. A round flat box. Contents-Receiver.

skip'-ping-ly. With skips. Continuity - Interruption.

skips, by. By bounds. Continuity-Interruption

skir'-mish. Fighting. Strife-Peace.

skir'-mish-er. Soldier. Belligerent.

skirt. Border; dress. Border, Dress-Undress, Environment-Interposition, Increment-Remnant, Laterality-Contraposition, Suspension-Support.

skirt'-dance". A dance in which the performer waves her skirt to the movements of the body Entertainment-Weariness.

skirt'-ing. Skirts. Border, Laterality-Contraposition.

skirts. Border. Beginning-End; **hang upon the skirts of,** Leading-Following, Remoteness-Nearness; **on the skirts of,** Remoteness-Nearness.

skit. Jest; jade; reflection. Adulation-Disparagement, Purity-Rake, Society-Laughingstock.

skit'-tish. Timid; capricious. Bravery-Cowardice, Conceit - Diffidence, Excitability - Inexcitability, Persistence-Whim.

skit'-tles. Ninepins. Entertainment-Weariness.

skit'-tle sharp'-er. Cheat. Robber.

skulk. Lurk. Bravery-Cowardice, Enlightenment-Secrecy, Sanguineness-Timidity.

skulk'-ing. Lurking. Enlightenment-Secrecy.

skull. Cranium. Mind-Imbecility.

skull'-cap" Cap. Dress-Undress.

skunk. Animal. Perfume-Stench.

skur'-ry. Hurry. Hurry-Leisure.

sky. Vault; heaven; cloud. Dampness-Dryness, Top-Bottom, Universe, Volition-Obligation.

sky"-as-pir'-ing. Pious. Desire-Distaste.

sky'-blue". Azure. Blueness-Orange.

sky'-lark". Bird. Ascent-Descent.

sky'-lark"-ing. Frolicking. Entertainment-Weariness.

sky'-light". Window. Aperture-Closure.

sky'-rock"-et. Rocket. Ascent-Descent.

sky'-scra"-per. Building. Top-Bottom.

slab. Plank; mire; plate. Gulf-Plain, Lamina-Fiber, Levelness, Mark-Obliteration, Suspension-Support, Viscidity-Foam.

slab'-ber. Saliva; drivel. Admission-Expulsion, Cleanness-Filthiness.

slack. Loose; slake; cool; abate; sluggish; inactive. Activity-Indolence, Cohesion-Looseness, Combustible, Excess-Lack, Heating-Cooling, Readiness - Reluctance, Rule - License, Strength-Weakness, Swiftness-Slowness, Vigor-Inertia.

slack'-en. Loose; abate; hinder. Cohesion-Looseness, Obstruction-Help, Swiftness-Slowness, Toil-Relaxation, Turbulence-Calmness.

slack'-en-ing. Flowing slowly. Swiftness-Slowness.

slack'-ness. Remissness. Rule-License.

slade. The sole of a plow. Convexity-Concavity.

slag. Refuse. Chemistry, Cleanness-Filthiness, Heating-Cooling.

slake. Assuage; satisfy. Desire-Repletion, Pleasurableness-Painfulness, Turbulence-Calmness; **slake one's appetite,** Moderation-Selfindulgence.

slam. Bang; shut. Crash-Drumming, Impetus-Re-

action; **slam the door in one's face,** Antagonism-Concurrence, Proffer-Refusal.

slam'-mer-kin. Slattern. Cleanness-Filthiness.

slan'-der. Defame. Adulation-Disparagement.

slan'-der-er. Defamer. Flatterer-Defamer.

slan'-der-ous. Calumnious. Adulation-Disparagement.

slang. Inelegant language. Purity - Crudeness, Rhetoric, Taste-Vulgarity, Word-Neology.

slant. Slope. Parallelism-Inclination.

slant'-wise. Obliquely. Parallelism-Inclination.

slap. Strike; punish. Approval-Disapproval, Eternity-Instantaneity, Exculpation-Punition, Recompense-Punition, Traveling-Navigation; **slap in the face,** Antagonism-Concurrence, Approval-Disapproval, Attack-Defense, Favorite-Anger, Regard-Disrespect; **slap in the forehead,** Investigation-Answer.

slap'-dash". Carelessness. Eternity-Instantaneity, Hurry-Leisure.

slash. Cut. Union-Disunion.

slash'-ing. Random. Force-Weakness.

slate. Stone. Cover-Lining, Writing-Printing; **slate loose,** Saneness-Lunacy.

slate'-col"-ored. Gray. Gray-Brown.

slates. Roofing. Cover-Lining.

sla'-ting. Roofing. Cover-Lining.

slat'-tern. Untidy; wasteful person. Cleanness-Filthiness, Length-Shortness, Regularity-Irregularity, Taste-Vulgarity.

slat'-tern-ly. Unskilfully. Skill-Unskilfulness.

slaugh'-ter. Slaying. Life-Killing.

slaugh'-ter—house". Life-Killing.

slaugh'-ter-ing. Slaying. Life-Killing.

slaugh'-ter-ous. Murderous. Life-Killing.

slave. Work; serf. Chief-Underling, Presumption-Obsequiousness, Toil-Relaxation; **a slave to,** Liberty-Subjection.

sla'-ver. Vessel; Conveyance-Vessel.

slav'-er. Drivel; flatter. Admission-Expulsion, Adulation-Disparagement, Cleanness-Filthiness.

sla'-ver-y. Subjection; work. Liberty-Subjection, Presumption-Obsequiousness, Toil-Relaxation.

slave'-trade". The practise of selling or trading slaves. Buying-Sale.

sla'-vish. Servile. Presumption-Obsequiousness.

sla-voc'-ra-cy. Slave-holding interests as a political power. Rule-License.

Sla-von'-ic. Pertaining to the Slavs. Ethnology.

slay. Kill. Life-Killing.

slay'-er. One who slays. Life-Killing.

sleave. Ravel; knotted. Regularity-Irregularity.

sled. A snow-vehicle. Conveyance-Vessel.

sledge. Sled. Conveyance-Vessel.

sledge'-ham"-mer. Heavy hammer. Impetus-Reaction; **with a sledge,** Activity-Indolence, Creation-Destruction.

sleek. Smooth; trim. Beauty-Ugliness, Smoothness-Roughness.

sleep. Rest. Activity-Indolence, Feeling-Insensibility, Movement-Rest, Sensitiveness-Apathy, Toil-Relaxation; **last sleep,** Life-Death; **not have a wink of sleep,** Excitability-Inexcitability; **rock to sleep,** Turbulence-Calmness; **send to sleep,** Entertainment-Weariness; **sleep at one's post,** Activity-Indolence; **sleep upon,** Earliness-Lateness, Reflection-Vacancy; **sleep with one eye open,** Carefulness-Carelessness.

sleep'-er. Beam. Suspension-Support; **wake the seven sleepers,** Loudness-Faintness.

sleep'-ful. Sleepy. Activity-Indolence.

sleep'-ing. Resting in sleep. Movement-Rest.

sleep'-ing part'-ner. Silent partner. Activity-Indolence.

sleep'-less. Wakeful. ACTIVITY-INDOLENCE.
sleep'-less-ness. Wakefulness. ACTIVITY-INDOLENCE.
sleep'-y. Drowsy. ACTIVITY-INDOLENCE, SENSITIVE-NESS-APATHY.
sleet. Snow and rain. HEAT-COLD.
sleeve. Arm; skein. CROSSING, DRESS-UNDRESS; **hang on the sleeve,** CHIEF-UNDERLING; **in one's sleeve,** EN-LIGHTENMENT-SECRECY; **laugh in one's sleeve,** JUBI-LATION - LAMENTATION, SOCIETY - DERISION; **wear one's heart upon his sleeve,** CRAFT-ARTLESSNESS, MANIFESTATION-LATENCY.
sleeve'-less. Fruitless. PERSISTENCE-WHIM, SAGACITY-INCAPACITY; **sleeveless errand,** SKILL-UNSKILFULNESS.
sleigh. Sled. CONVEYANCE-VESSEL.
sleight. Skill. SKILL-UNSKILFULNESS; **sleight of hand,** TRUTHFULNESS-FRAUD.
slen'-der. Frail; trifling. BREADTH-NARROWNESS, CONSEQUENCE-INSIGNIFICANCE, MAGNITUDE-SMALL-NESS; **slender means,** AFFLUENCE-PENURY.
sleuth. The track of man or beast as followed by the scent. CRAFT-ARTLESSNESS.
slice. Cut; piece. LAMINA-FIBER, UNION-DISUNION, WHOLE-PART.
slide. Movement, slip; default. ASCENT-DESCENT, MOVEMENT-REST, PERIOD-PROGRESS, SMOOTHNESS-ROUGHNESS, TRAVELING-NAVIGATION; **slide back,** RENOVATION-RELAPSE; **slide in,** ENVIRONMENT-IN-TERPOSITION; **slide into,** CONVERSION-REVERSION.
slide'-valve". A sliding piece in the steam-chest of a steam-engine. PERFORATOR-STOPPER.
sli'-ding. Coasting. ENTERTAINMENT-WEARINESS.
sli'-ding pan'-el. Panel capable of sliding. TRUTHFUL-NESS-FRAUD.
sli'-ding rule. Slide-rule. NUMBERING.
slight. Little; meager; shirk; frail; overlook. CARE-FULNESS-CARELESSNESS, DUTY-DERELICTION, FORCE-WEAKNESS, MAGNITUDE-SMALLNESS, OVERVALUA-TION-UNDERVALUATION, REGARD-DISRESPECT, RE-GARD - SCORN, SKILL - UNSKILFULNESS, SOLIDITY-RARENESS.
slight'-ly. In a slight manner. CONSEQUENCE-INSIG-NIFICANCE, MAGNITUDE-SMALLNESS.
slight'-made". Frail. BREADTH-NARROWNESS.
sli'-ly. Slyly. CRAFT-ARTLESSNESS, TRUTHFULNESS-FALSEHOOD.
slim. Narrow. BREADTH-NARROWNESS.
slime. Filth; viscid. CLEANNESS-FILTHINESS, VIS-CIDITY-FOAM.
sling. Suspend; throw; weapon. PUSH-PULL, SUS-PENSION-SUPPORT, WEAPON.
slink. Sneak. BRAVERY-COWARDICE, ENLIGHTEN-MENT-SECRECY; **slink away,** QUEST-EVASION, REPU-TATION-DISCREDIT.
slip. Piece; pass; strip; glide; mistake; counterfeit; err; vice. ASCENT-DESCENT, INNOCENCE-GUILT, LAMINA - FIBER, MAGNITUDE - SMALLNESS, MONEY, PERIOD-PROGRESS, SUCCESS-FAILURE, TRUTH-ERROR, VIRTUE-VICE, WORKSHOP; **give one the slip,** ESCAPE; **let slip,** GAIN-LOSS, KEEPING-RELINQUISHMENT, RELEASE-RESTRAINT; **let slip the dogs of war,** FIGHT-ING-CONCILIATION; **slip away,** QUEST-EVASION; **slip cable,** QUEST-EVASION; **slip in,** ENTRANCE-EXIT; **slip of the pen,** GRAMMAR-SOLECISM, TRUTH-ERROR; **slip of the tongue,** GRAMMAR-SOLECISM, SPEECH-IN-ARTICULATENESS, TRUTH-ERROR; **slip the collar,** ESCAPE, RELEASE-RESTRAINT; **slip the memory,** REMEMBRANCE-FORGETFULNESS; **slip through the fingers,** ESCAPE, OPPORTUNENESS-UNSUITABLENESS, SUCCESS-FAILURE; **slip 'twixt cup and lip,** EXPECTA-TION-DISAPPOINTMENT, SUCCESS-FAILURE.
slip'-per. Shoe. DRESS-UNDRESS; **hunt the slipper,** ENTERTAINMENT-WEARINESS.
slip'-per-i-ness. Quality of being slippery. SECURITY-INSECURITY.

slip'-per-y. Smooth; elusive. BIGOTRY - APOSTASY, CERTAINTY-DOUBT, DIFFICULTY-FACILITY, LASTING-NESS - TRANSIENTNESS, PULPINESS - OILINESS, SECU-RITY - INSECURITY, SMOOTHNESS - ROUGHNESS, UP-RIGHTNESS-DISHONESTY; **slippery ground,** REFUGE-PITFALL.
slip'-shod". Slovenly. FORCE-WEAKNESS.
slip'-slop". Weak; blunder. ADAGE-NONSENSE, FORCE-WEAKNESS, GRAMMAR-SOLECISM.
slit. Slash; crack. GROOVE, INTERSPACE-CONTACT, UNION-DISUNION.
sliv'-er. Splinter. MAGNITUDE-SMALLNESS, WHOLE-PART.
slob. A careless person. ACTIVITY-INDOLENCE.
slob'-ber. Drivel; foul. ADMISSION-EXPULSION, CLEANNESS-FILTHINESS, WATER-AIR.
sloe. Fruit. WHITENESS-BLACKNESS.
slo'-gan. Battle-cry. FIGHTING-CONCILIATION.
sloop. Vessel. CONVEYANCE-VESSEL; **sloop of war,** BELLIGERENT.
slop. Spill; dirty water. ADMISSION-EXPULSION, CLEANNESS-FILTHINESS, WATER-AIR.
slope. Incline; run. PARALLELISM-INCLINATION. QUEST-EVASION.
slope'-ness. Obliqueness. PARALLELISM-INCLINA-TION.
slope'-wise. Obliquely. PARALLELISM-INCLINATION.
slo'-ping. Bending down. PARALLELISM - INCLINA-TION.
slop'-py. Moist; marsh. DAMPNESS - DRYNESS, SWAMP-ISLAND.
slops. Clothes. DRESS-UNDRESS.
slosh. Splash. CLEANNESS-FILTHINESS.
slot. A slit. APERTURE-CLOSURE.
sloth. Laziness. ACTIVITY-INDOLENCE, VIGOR-INER-TIA.
sloth'-ful. Lazy. ADEPT-BUNGLER.
slouch. Droop; bungler. ACTIVITY-INDOLENCE, HEIGHT - LOWNESS, PARALLELISM - INCLINATION, SWIFTNESS-SLOWNESS.
slouch'-ing. Ungainly. BEAUTY-UGLINESS.
slough. Mire; swamp. CLEANNESS-FILTHINESS, DIFFICULTY-FACILITY, SWAMP-ISLAND, WELFARE-MISFORTUNE; **Slough of Despond,** LIGHTHEARTED-NESS-DEJECTION, PLEASURE-PAIN, SANGUINENESS-HOPELESSNESS, WELFARE-MISFORTUNE.
slov'-en. Bungler. ADEPT-BUNGLER.
slov'-en-li-ness. Carelessness. CAREFULNESS-CARE-LESSNESS, CLEANNESS-FILTHINESS.
slov'-en-ly. Negligent; dirty. CAREFULNESS-CARE-LESSNESS, CLEANNESS-FILTHINESS, REGULARITY-IR-REGULARITY, SKILL-UNSKILFULNESS, TASTE-VUL-GARITY.
slow. Not quick; sluggish; inert. ACTIVITY-INDO-LENCE, EARLINESS - LATENESS, ENTERTAINMENT-WEARINESS, HURRY - LEISURE, SWIFTNESS - SLOW-NESS, TURBULENCE - CALMNESS, VIGOR - INERTIA, WITTINESS-DULNESS; **be slow to,** COMPLETION-NON-COMPLETION, PROFFER-REFUSAL, READINESS-RELUC-TANCE; **by slow degrees,** QUANTITY - MEASURE; **march in slow time,** SWIFTNESS-SLOWNESS; **slow movement,** MUSIC.
slow'-coach". Dull person. ACTIVITY - INDOLENCE, ADEPT-BUNGLER, SWIFTNESS-SLOWNESS.
slow'-ly. In a slow manner. EARLINESS-LATENESS.
slow'-ness. Inactivity. SWIFTNESS-SLOWNESS.
slub'-ber. Soil. CLEANNESS-FILTHINESS.
slub"-ber-de-gul'-lion. Wretch. GENTILITY - COMMON-ALTY.
sludge. Mire. CLEANNESS-FILTHINESS.
slug. Slow; bullet. ACTION-PASSIVENESS, ACTIVITY-INDOLENCE, SWIFTNESS-SLOWNESS, WEAPON.
slug'-gard. Drone. ACTIVITY-INDOLENCE, SWIFT-NESS-SLOWNESS.

slug'-gard-ize. To make sluggish. ACTIVITY-INDOLENCE.

slug'-gish. Slow. ACTIVITY-INDOLENCE, SENSITIVE-NESS-APATHY, SWIFTNESS-SLOWNESS, VIGOR-INERTIA.

slug'-gish-ness. Laziness. ACTIVITY-INDOLENCE.

sluice. Gate; channel. BOUNDARY, ENTRANCE-EXIT, RIVER-WIND, WATERCOURSE-AIRPIPE; **open the sluice,** ADMISSION-EXPULSION.

slum. Low quarter. CITY, CLEANNESS-FILTHINESS.

slum'-ber. Sleep. ACTIVITY-INDOLENCE.

slum'-ber-er. One who slumbers. ACTIVITY-INDOLENCE.

slur. Conceal; disparage; stigma. JUSTIFICATION-CHARGE, REPUTATION-DISCREDIT; **slur over,** CAREFULNESS-CARELESSNESS, OVERVALUATION-UNDERVALUATION.

slush. Snow and water; mud. CLEANNESS-FILTHINESS, SWAMP-ISLAND, VISCIDITY-FOAM.

slut. Defile; wench; bitch. CLEANLINESS-FILTHINESS, PURITY-RAKE, REGULARITY-IRREGULARITY.

slut'-tish. Dirty. CLEANNESS-FILTHINESS.

sly. Stealthy. CRAFT-ARTLESSNESS, ENLIGHTENMENT-SECRECY.

sly'-boots". A sly person or animal. CRAFT-ARTLESSNESS.

sly'-ness. Quality of being sly. ENLIGHTENMENT-SECRECY.

smack. Boat. CONVEYANCE-VESSEL.

smack. Taste; kiss; slap. BLANDISHMENT, IMPETUS-REACTION, MAGNITUDE-SMALLNESS, MIXTURE-HOMOGENEITY, RECOMPENSE-PUNITION, SAVOR-TASTELESSNESS; **smack of,** LIKENESS-UNLIKENESS; **smack the lips,** JUBILATION-LAMENTATION, LIKENESS-UNLIKENESS, PALATABLENESS-UNPALATABLENESS, SAVOR-TASTELESSNESS, SENSUALITY-SUFFERING.

small. Little; lacking. GREATNESS-LITTLENESS, MAGNITUDE-SMALLNESS, SUPREMACY-SUBORDINACY; **become small,** ENLARGEMENT-DIMINUTION; **esteem of small account,** REGARD-SCORN; **feel small,** SELF-RESPECT-HUMBLENESS; **not think small beer of oneself,** CONCEIT-DIFFIDENCE, SELFRESPECT-HUMBLENESS; **of small account,** CONSEQUENCE-INSIGNIFICANCE; **on a small scale,** GREATNESS-LITTLENESS, MAGNITUDE-SMALLNESS; **small arms,** WEAPON; **small by degrees,** INCREASE-DECREASE; **small chance,** LIKELIHOOD-UNLIKELIHOOD; **small coin,** MONEY; **small fry,** CONSEQUENCE-INSIGNIFICANCE, GENTILITY-COMMONALTY, GREATNESS-LITTLENESS; **small matter,** CONSEQUENCE-INSIGNIFICANCE; **small number,** MULTIPLICITY-PAUCITY; **small part,** WHOLE-PART; **small talk,** CONVERSATION-MONOLOGUE, TALKATIVENESS-TACITURNITY.

small'-bore". Gun. WEAPON.

small'-clothes". Breeches. DRESS-UNDRESS.

smal'-ler. Less. ENLARGEMENT-DIMINUTION, SUPREMACY-SUBORDINACY.

small'-ness. Littleness. MAGNITUDE-SMALLNESS, SUPREMACY-SUBORDINACY.

small'-pox". Variola. HEALTH-SICKNESS.

smalls. Small-clothes. DRESS-UNDRESS.

smalt. Paint. BLUENESS-ORANGE.

smart. Hurt; airs; clever; forceful. ACTIVITY-INDOLENCE, BEAUTY-UGLINESS, EMBELLISHMENT-DISFIGUREMENT, FEELING, PLEASURE-PAIN, SENSUALITY-SUFFERING, SKILL-UNSKILFULNESS, WITTINESS-DULNESS; **smart pace,** SWIFTNESS-SLOWNESS; **smart saying,** WITTINESS-DULNESS; **smart under,** FEELING.

smart'-en. Improve. EMBELLISHMENT-DISFIGUREMENT.

smart'-mon"-ey. Damages. RECOMPENSE-PENALTY.

smart'-ness. Quality of being smart. ACTIVITY-INDOLENCE, WITTINESS-DULNESS.

smash. Crush; fail. CREATION-DESTRUCTION, SUCCESS-FAILURE.

smatch. Taste. SAVOR-TASTELESSNESS.

smat'-ter-er. Superficial. SCHOLAR-DUNCE.

smat'-ter-ing. Slight knowledge. KNOWLEDGE-IGNORANCE.

smear. Bedaub. CLEANNESS-FILTHINESS, COVER-LINING.

smell. Odor. ODOR-INODOROUSNESS; **bad smell,** PERFUME-STENCH; **smell of the lamp,** PREPARATION-NONPREPARATION, SIMPLICITY-FLORIDNESS; **smell powder,** FIGHTING-CONCILIATION.

smell'-feast". Epicure. PRESUMPTION-OBSEQUIOUSNESS.

smel'-ling. Giving off odor. ODOR-INODOROUSNESS, PERFUME-STENCH.

smel'-ling-bot"-tle. Salts. PERFUME-STENCH.

smelt. Fuse. HEATING-COOLING, PREPARATION-NONPREPARATION.

smick'-er. Amorous. JUBILATION-LAMENTATION.

smile. Expression. JUBILATION-LAMENTATION, LIGHTHEARTEDNESS-DEJECTION; **raise a smile,** ENTERTAINMENT-WEARINESS, OBSTRUCTION-HELP; **smile at,** SOCIETY-DERISION; **smile of contempt,** REGARD-SCORN; **smile of fortune,** WELFARE-MISFORTUNE; **smile upon,** BLANDISHMENT, OBSTRUCTION-HELP, POLITENESS-IMPOLITENESS.

smirch. Soil. CLEANNESS-FILTHINESS, WHITENESS-BLACKNESS.

smirk. Smile. JUBILATION-LAMENTATION.

smite. Hit; punish. EXCITATION, GOOD MAN-BAD MAN, PLEASURABLENESS-PAINFULNESS, RECOMPENSE-PUNITION.

smith. Blacksmith. AGENT.

smith'-y. A blacksmith shop. WORKSHOP.

smi'-ting. Striking. LIGHTHEARTEDNESS-DEJECTION.

smit'-ten. Struck. LOVE-HATE; **smitten with,** MOTIVE-CAPRICE.

smock. Garment. DRESS-UNDRESS.

smock'-faced". Effeminate. BRAVERY-COWARDICE.

smock'-frock". Blouse. DRESS-UNDRESS.

smoke. Dust; vapor; heat. CLEANNESS-FILTHINESS, CONSEQUENCE-INSIGNIFICANCE, DISCOVERY, FAITH-MISGIVING, FRIABILITY, HEAT-COLD, LIQUEFACTION-VOLATILIZATION, PUNGENCY, REGARD-DISRESPECT; **end in smoke,** SUCCESS-FAILURE, TRANSCURSION-SHORTCOMING; **smoke the calumet of peace,** FIGHTING-CONCILIATION.

smoke'-stack". An upright pipe for discharging gases from a boiler-furnace. WATERCOURSE-AIRPIPE.

smo'-king. Giving forth smoke. HEAT-COLD; **smoking hot,** HEAT-COLD; **smoking room,** CONTENTS-RECEIVER.

smo'-ky. Of the color of smoke. CLEANNESS-FILTHINESS.

smold'-er. Smoke. HEAT-COLD, MANIFESTATION-LATENCY, VIGOR-INERTIA.

smold'-er-ing. Smoking. VIGOR-INERTIA.

smooth. Even; regular; easy. ADULATION-DISPARAGEMENT, DIFFICULTY-FACILITY, ERECTNESS-FLATNESS, SMOOTHNESS-ROUGHNESS, TURBULENCE-CALMNESS, UNIFORMITY-DIVERSITY; **smooth down,** TURBULENCE-CALMNESS; **smooth over,** TURBULENCE-CALMNESS; **smooth sailing,** DIFFICULTY-FACILITY; **smooth the bed of death,** CHARITABLENESS-MALEVOLENCE, OBSTRUCTION-HELP; **smooth the ruffled brow of care,** ALLEVIATION-AGGRAVATION; **smooth the way,** DIFFICULTY-FACILITY; **smooth water,** DIFFICULTY-FACILITY.

smooth'-bore". Firearm. WEAPON.

smooth'-ly, go on. Go without rocking. DIFFICULTY-FACILITY, TURBULENCE-CALMNESS.

smooth'-ness. Without roughness. FRICTION-LUBRICATION, LEVELNESS, SMOOTHNESS-ROUGHNESS.

SMOOTHNESS—ROUGHNESS.

Gloss. The brightness of a smooth surface.
Lubrication. The act of making slippery.
Lubricity. The slipperiness of a smooth surface.
Polish. A smooth bright surface.
Smoothness, etc. The quality of being smooth, etc. See *Adjectives.*

Smoothness—*Denotations*

Asphalt. A bituminous composition used for pavements, roofs, etc.
Blackboard. A large slate or broad board painted black, for writing upon with chalk.
Bowling green. A level lawn for playing bowls.
Byssus. A kind of flax of which fine linen is made.
Down. The fine soft under-plumage of birds.
Flag. A broad, thick, flat stone suitable for pavements.
Floss. The silk of Indian corn and some other plants.
Fur. The short, fine coat covering the skin of many mammals.
Glass. A very smooth, transparent compound of silica.
Ice. Frozen water.
Plush. A cloth of wool or cotton, having longer projecting fibers than velvet.
Satin. A silk fabric with a glossy surface.
Silk. A fine, glossy, fibrous substance produced by the silk-worm.
Slide. A glass that slides in a frame in front of a magic lantern.
Velvet. A silk fabric having on one side a thick, smooth nap.
Velveteen. A cotton fabric with a pile like velvet.
Wood-pavement. Long smooth boards used as a walk.

Smoothness—*Nouns of Agent.*

Burnisher. A tool used in polishing.
Emery-paper. Paper covered with ground emery, used in polishing.
Roller. Cylinder arranged to revolve on its own axis, used to smooth surfaces.
Sand-paper. Paper covered with sand, used in polishing.
Steam-roller. Large roller for smoothing street surfaces.
Turpentine and beeswax. A preparation used for polishing furniture.

Smoothness—*Verbs.*

Burnish. Make smooth and bright.
Calender. Press between rollers.
File. Smooth with a file.
Glaze. Render glass-like.
Hot-press. Apply pressure and heat to obtain a glossy surface.
Iron. Smooth with an iron instrument.
Level. Make even.
Lubricate. Make slippery. See words associated with PULPINESS-OIL.
Macadamize. Make a smooth, hard road, according to plans invented by Mr. MacAdam.
Mangle. Smooth with the rolling-press, called a mangle.
Mow. Smooth by cutting the grass.
Plane. Smooth by cutting off the surface.
Polish. Make smooth and glossy.
Roll. Level with a roller.
Shave. Smooth by cutting off closely the surface or covering.
Smooth. Make even.

Smoothness—*Adjectives.*

Downy. Covered with down.
Even. Without irregularities in surface.
Glabrous. Smooth; hairless.
Glassy. Like glass.
Glossy. Smooth and bright.
Lanate. Woolly.
Level. Smooth. See ERECTNESS-FLATNESS.
Lubricous. Smooth and slippery.
Oily. Like oil.
Plane. Flat. See LEVELNESS.
Polish. Smooth.
Polished, etc. Made smooth or glossy. See *Verbs.*
Silken. Made of silk.
Silky. Like silk.
Sleek. With a bright and even surface.
Slippery. Causing anything to slip; hard to adhere to.
Slippery as an eel. Very hard to hold.
Smooth. Having an even, regular surface.

Arborescence. The resemblance to a tree in minerals, etc.
Asperity. The state or quality of being rough or harsh.
Corrugation. The state of being corrugated.
Grain. Degree of roughness.
Nodosity. The quality of being knotty.
Plumosity. The state of being feathered.
Ripple. A slight wave on the surface of water.
Roughness, etc. The quality of being uneven, etc. See *Adjectives.*
Rugosity. The quality of being wrinkled, corrugated.
Salebrosity. The quality of being rugged, uneven.
Texture. Minute structure or arrangement of threads, as of cloth.
Tooth. A ridge or roughness on a veneer.

Roughness—*Denotations.*

Beard. The hair on a man's face.
Brush. An implement made of bristles, hair, broom-corn, etc., for sweeping.
Bur. A rough or prickly seed-vessel, as of the chestnut.
Cilia. The hairs or hair-like growths on a cell, organ, or parts of the body.
Crest. A projecting growth on the top of an animal's head.
Curl. Anything coiled, especially a ringlet of hair.
Feather. The appendages growing out of the skin of a bird.
Fimbria. A fringe or fringe-like structure.
Floccule. A loose tuft, like wool.
Fringe. An ornamental trimming.
Hair. The outgrowth from the skin of animals.
Imperial. A pointed tuft of hair on the chin.
Lock. A tuft of hair.
Mane. The long hair growing on the neck of a horse.
Moss. A delicate, low-growing plant.
Mustache. The growth of hair on the upper lip of men.
Nap. The projecting fibers of thread on the surface of flannel, silk.
Panache. A plume or bunch of feathers used as a head-dress.
Pile. Hair, collectively.
Plumage. The feathers of a bird.
Plume. A long, ornamental feather.
Ringlet. A long spiral lock of hair.
Shag. A rough coat or bunch of hair.
Toupee. A small tuft of hair.
Tress. A lock or curl of human hair.
Tuft. A collection or bunch of small flexible things held together at the base.
Villi. The short hair-like growths on the membranes of the body.
Whisker. The hair that grows on the sides of a man's face.
Wool. The hair obtained from the sheep.

Roughness—*Verbs.*

Be rough, etc. To have small ridges or points on the surface. See *Adjectives.*
Corrugate. To contract into ridges.
Crisp. Roughen with slight undulations.
Crumple. Press into wrinkles.
Render rough, etc. To cause to have inequalities on the surface. See *Adjectives.*
Roughen. Make rough.
Ruffle. Gather into folds.
Rumple. Make irregular or uneven.

Roughness—*Verbal Expressions.*

Go against the grain; set on edge; stroke the wrong way.

Roughness—*Adjectives.*

Arborescent, etc. Like a tree. See PROPORTION.
Asperous. Rough; uneven.
Bearded. Having a beard.
Befringed. Fringed.
Bushy. Like a bush.
Ciliated. Having movable hair-like processes.
Cragged. } Having many crags.
Craggy. }
Crankling. Bent; twisted.
Crinite. Having or like long weak hairs.
Crinose. Hairy.
Crisp. Having waves or curls.
Feathery. Like or having feathers.
Filamentous. Like or having threads or filaments.
Fimbriated. Having a fringe.
Fringed. Furnished with a fringe.
Gnarled. Full of knots.
Hairy. Covered with or like hair.
Hirsute. Covered with hairs or bristles.

SMOOTHNESS—ROUGHNESS—*Continued.*

SMOOTHNESS—ADJECTIVES—*Continued.*

Smooth as glass. ⎫
Smooth as ice. ⎬ Figurative degrees of smoothness.
Smooth as oil. ⎪
Smooth as velvet. ⎭
Soft. Yielding to the touch.
Unwrinkled. Without furrows.
Velvety. Like velvet.

ROUGHNESS—ADJECTIVES—*Continued from Column 2.*

Setaceous. Covered with or like setæ or bristles.
Setose. ⎫
Setous. ⎬ Having stiff hairs.
Shagged. Covered with a coarse thick growth.
Shaggy. Covered with or like rough hair.
Tomentous. Covered with matted woolly hairs.
Tufted. Having a tuft or crest.
Uneven. Not even.
Unpolished. ⎫
Unsmooth. ⎬ Rough.
Villous. Covered with short soft hairs.
Well-wooded. Thickly covered with trees.
Woolly. Covered with or like wool.

ROUGHNESS—*Adverb.*

Against the grain. Roughly.

smooth'-tongued". Flattering. ADULATION-DISPAR-
AGEMENT, TRUTHFULNESS-FALSEHOOD.
smoth'-er. Prevent; kill; hide. ENLIGHTENMENT-
SECRECY, LIFE-KILLING, RELEASE-RESTRAINT, TUR-
BULENCE-CALMNESS, VOCALIZATION-MUTENESS.
smudge. Soil; soot. CLEANNESS-FILTHINESS, EM-
BELLISHMENT-DISFIGUREMENT.
smug. Trim. SOCIETY-AFFECTATION.
smug'-gle. Importing. ENVIRONMENT-INTERPOSI-
TION, LAW-LAWLESSNESS, THEFT.
smug'-gler. Law-breaker. ROBBER.
smug'-gling. Illicit importing. LAW-LAWLESSNESS.
smut. Black; soot. CLEANNESS-FILTHINESS, PU-
RITY-IMPURITY, SOLIDITY-RARITY.
smutch. Stain. CLEANNESS-FILTHINESS, WHITENESS-
BLACKNESS.
smut'-ty. Obscene in language. CLEANNESS-FILTHI-
NESS, PURITY-RAKE.
snack. Share; bite. MAGNITUDE-SMALLNESS, NU-
TRIMENT-EXCRETION.
snacks. Shares. PARTICIPATION.
snacks, go. Share. PARTICIPATION.
snaf'-fle. Bridle. RELEASE-PRISON.
snag. Branch; projection. OBSTRUCTION-HELP, REF-
UGE-PITFALL, SHARPNESS-BLUNTNESS, SMOOTHNESS-
ROUGHNESS.
snag'-gy. Full of snags. SHARPNESS-BLUNTNESS.
snags. Projections. REFUGE-PITFALL.
snail. Mollusk. SWIFTNESS-SLOWNESS.
snail'-like. Slow. SWIFTNESS-SLOWNESS.
snake. Serpent; person. BENEFACTOR-EVILDOER,
FAUNA-FLORA; scotch the snake, EXCESS-LACK;
snake in the grass, BENEFACTOR-EVILDOER, EN-
LIGHTENMENT-SECRECY, GOODNESS-BADNESS, GULL-
DECEIVER, MANIFESTATION-SECRECY, REFUGE-PIT-
FALL, UPRIGHTNESS-ROGUE.
snake'-like. Serpent-like. CIRCLE-WINDING.
snak'-y. Insinuating. CIRCLE-WINDING.
snap. Strike; break; flip; emit; energy. CRASH-
DRUMMING, FAVORITE-ANGER, NUTRIMENT-EXCRE-
TION, POLITENESS-IMPOLITENESS, TOUGHNESS-BRIT-
TLENESS, UNION-DISUNION; snap at, PLEASURABLE-
NESS-PAINFULNESS, TAKING-RESTITUTION; snap of
the fingers, CONSEQUENCE-INSIGNIFICANCE; snap
one's fingers at, DEFIANCE, PRESUMPTION-OBSE-
QUIOUSNESS, REGARD-SCORN; snap one up, APPRO-
VAL-DISAPPROVAL; snap the thread, CONTINUITY-IN-
TERRUPTION; snap up, TAKING-RESTITUTION.

ROUGHNESS—ADJECTIVES—*Continued.*

Hispid. Rough with bristles.
Knotted. Having knots.
Lanate. ⎫
Lanated. ⎬ Woolly.
Lanuginose. ⎫
Lanuginous. ⎬ Woolly or downy.
Leafy. Full of leaves.
Like quills upon the fretful porcupine. Covered with long sharp
quills. [Shakespeare, *Hamlet*, I, v.]
Pappous. Having down.
Pilous. Hairy.
Plumigerous. Furnished with plumage.
Plumose. Bearing plumes or processes.
Prickly, etc. Having prickles. See SHARPNESS.
Rough. Having an uneven, irregular surface.
Rough as a bear. ⎫
Rough as a nutmeg-grater. ⎬ Figurative degrees of roughness.
Rough-hewn. Roughly shaped.
Rugged. Having a surface full of points or bristles.
Rugose. ⎫
Rugous. ⎬ Full of wrinkles.
Salebrous. Rugged; uneven.
Scabrous. Roughened with little points.
Scraggy. Rough with irregular points.

(Continued on Column 1.)

snap'-drag"-on. Sport. ENTERTAINMENT-WEARI-
NESS.
snap'-pish. Tart. FAVORITE-QUARRELSOMENESS.
snare. Trap. TRUTHFULNESS-FRAUD.
snarl. Growl; quarrel. CHARITABLENESS-MENACE,
CRY-ULULATION, FAVORITE-ANGER, POLITENESS-IM-
POLITENESS.
snarl'-ing. Growling. POLITENESS-IMPOLITENESS.
snatch. Catch; bit. MAGNITUDE-SMALLNESS, TAK-
ING-RESTITUTION; snatch a grace beyond the reach of
art, BEAUTY-UGLINESS; snatch at, QUEST-EVASION,
TAKING-RESTITUTION; snatch a verdict, CRAFT-ART-
LESSNESS, TRUTHFULNESS-FRAUD; snatch from one's
grasp, TAKING-RESTITUTION; snatch from the jaws of
death, RESCUE.
sneak. Conceal; fear; cringe. BRAVERY-COWARDICE,
ENLIGHTENMENT-SECRECY, GOOD MAN-BAD MAN,
PRESUMPTION-OBSEQUIOUSNESS, UPRIGHTNESS-DIS-
HONESTY, UPRIGHTNESS-ROGUE; sneak off, QUEST-
EVASION; sneak out of, QUEST-EVASION.
sneak'-ing. Acting stealthily. BRAVERY-COWARDICE,
PRESUMPTION-OBSEQUIOUSNESS, UPRIGHTNESS-DIS-
HONESTY.
sneer. Grimace; insinuate. APPROVAL-DISAPPROVAL,
REGARD-DISRESPECT, REGARD-SCORN.
sneered at, not to be. Of value. CONSEQUENCE-IN-
SIGNIFICANCE.
sneeze. Blow; snuff. RESONANCE-SIBILATION, RIV-
ER-WIND; sneeze at, REGARD-SCORN.
snick. Snip. MAGNITUDE-SMALLNESS, WHOLE-PART.
sniff. Perception; inhalation; smell. DISCOVERY,
ODOR-INODOROUSNESS, RIVER-WIND.
snif'-fle. Snuffle. RIVER-WIND.
snig'-ger. Laugh. DUTY-DERELICTION, JUBILATION-
LAMENTATION, SOCIETY-DERISION.
snig'-gle. Ensnare. TRUTHFULNESS-FRAUD.
snip. Clip; piece; tailor. DRESS-UNDRESS, MAGNI-
TUDE-SMALLNESS, UNION-DISUNION.
snip'-pet. Piece. MAGNITUDE-SMALLNESS.
snip'-snap". Dialogue. VARIANCE-ACCORD.
snip"-snap"-snov'-em. A game. ENTERTAINMENT-
WEARINESS.
sniv'-el. Cry. JUBILATION-LAMENTATION.
sniv'-el-ing. Crying. PRESUMPTION-OBSEQUIOUSNESS.
snob. Vulgar; servile. GENTILITY-COMMONALTY, PRE-
SUMPTION-OBSEQUIOUSNESS, TASTE-VULGARITY.
snob'-bish. Pertaining to a snob. GENTILITY-COM-
MONALTY, TASTE-VULGARITY.

snob'-bish-ness. Pretense. ADULATION-DISPARAGEMENT.

snood. Fillet. CIRCLE-WINDING, DRESS-UNDRESS.

Snooks, Mr. A nobody. GENTILITY-COMMONALTY.

snooze. Doze. ACTIVITY-INDOLENCE.

snore. Hoarseness. ACTIVITY-INDOLENCE, CRY-ULULATION, SIGHT-BLINDNESS.

snort. Sound. CRY-ULULATION.

snout. Muzzle. CONVEXITY-CONCAVITY.

snow. Vessel. CONVEYANCE-VESSEL.

snow. Precipitation; white. HEAT-COLD, WHITENESS-BLACKNESS.

snow'-ball''. Ball of snow. GATHERING-SCATTERING.

snow'-drift''. Pile. GATHERING-SCATTERING, HEAT-COLD.

snow'-plow''. A plow-like apparatus for clearing railway-tracks of snow. INSTRUMENT.

snow'-shoe''. A network of sinews fixed in a frame, and used for walking on snow. DRESS-UNDRESS.

snub. Check; pug; slight. APPROVAL-DISAPPROVAL, LENGTH-SHORTNESS, OBSTRUCTION-HELP, PRESUMPTION-OBSEQUIOUSNESS, REPUTATION-DISCREDIT, SELFRESPECT-HUMBLENESS.

snub'-nosed''. Pug. PROPORTION-DEFORMITY.

snuff. Scent; inhale; tobacco. DISCOVERY, ODOR-INODOROUSNESS, PUNGENCY, RIVER-WIND; **go out like the snuff of a candle,** LIFE-KILLING; **snuff out,** CREATION-DESTRUCTION, LIGHT-DARKNESS; **snuff up,** ADMISSION-EXPULSION, ODOR-INODOROUSNESS, SWEETNESS-ACIDITY; **up to snuff,** CRAFT-ARTLESSNESS, SKILL-UNSKILFULNESS.

snuff'-col''-or. Yellowish. GRAY-BROWN.

snuf'-fing, want. Impudent. PRESUMPTION-OBSEQUIOUSNESS.

snuf'-fle. Breathe; cant. GODLINESS-UNGODLINESS, RESONANCE-SIBILATION, RIVER-WIND, SPEECH-INARTICULATENESS.

snuff'-y. Soiled. CLEANNESS-FILTHINESS.

snug. Covered; cozy; trim. APERTURE-CLOSURE, CONTENTEDNESS-DISCONTENTMENT, PREPARATION-NONPREPARATION, SECURITY-INSECURITY, SENSUALITY-SUFFERING, SOCIABILITY-PRIVACY; **keep snug,** ENLIGHTENMENT-SECRECY, SOCIABILITY-PRIVACY; **make all snug,** PREPARATION-NONPREPARATION.

snug'-ger-y. Den. DWELLER-HABITATION.

snug'-ness. Coziness. PLEASURE-PAIN.

so. Very; like; therefore. LIKENESS-UNLIKENESS, MAGNITUDE-SMALLNESS, RATIOCINATION-INSTINCT, WAY; **so be it,** ASSENT-DISSENT, CONSENT; **so far so good,** APPROVAL-DISAPPROVAL, GOOD-EVIL; **so let it be,** ACTION-PASSIVENESS, ASSENT-DISSENT; **so much the better,** CONTENTEDNESS-DISCONTENTMENT, JUBILATION-LAMENTATION; **so much the worse,** ALLEVIATION-AGGRAVATION, CONTENTEDNESS-DISCONTENTMENT; **so to speak,** LIKENESS-UNLIKENESS, TROPE.

soak. Steep; saturate; guzzle. DAMPNESS-DRYNESS, INJECTION-EJECTION, TEETOTALISM-INTEMPERANCE, WATER-AIR; **soak up,** DAMPNESS-DRYNESS.

soak'-er. A heavy drinker. TEETOTALISM-INTEMPERANCE.

So-and-so, Mr. Imaginary. WORD-NEOLOGY.

soap. Cleanser. FRICTION-LUBRICATION, VISCIDITY-FOAM.

soap'-y. Flattering. ADULATION-DISPARAGEMENT, PRESUMPTION-OBSEQUIOUSNESS, PULPINESS-OILINESS.

soar. Rise; aspire. ASCENT-DESCENT, HEIGHT-LOWNESS, MAGNITUDE-SMALLNESS, TRANSCURSION-SHORTCOMING, TRAVELING-NAVIGATION.

soar'-ing. Rising. HEIGHT-LOWNESS.

sob. Weep. JUBILATION-LAMENTATION.

so'-ber. Moderate; grave; modest. EXCITABILITY-INEXCITABILITY, LIGHTHEARTEDNESS-DEJECTION, MODERATION-SELFINDULGENCE, SAGACITY-INCAPACITY, SANENESS-LUNACY, TEETOTALISM-INTEMPERANCE, TURBULENCE-CALMNESS; **in sober sadness,** ASSERTION-DENIAL; **sober down,** SANENESS-LUNACY, SELFRESPECT-HUMBLENESS, TURBULENCE-CALMNESS; **sober senses,** SANENESS-LUNACY; **sober truth,** TRUTH-ERROR, TRUTHFULNESS-FALSEHOOD.

so''-ber-mind'-ed. Self-controlled. EXCITABILITY-INEXCITABILITY, SANENESS-LUNACY, SELFRESPECT-HUMBLENESS.

so-bri'-e-ty. Moderateness. EXCITABILITY-INEXCITABILITY, MODERATION-SELFINDULGENCE, TEETOTALISM-INTEMPERANCE, TURBULENCE-CALMNESS.

so''-bri''-quet'. Nickname. NAME-MISNOMER.

soc. Franchise. JUDICATURE.

soc'-age. Tenure. HOLDING-EXEMPTION.

so''-called'. Styled. NAME-MISNOMER, TRUTHFULNESS-FRAUD.

so''-cia-bil'-i-ty. Quality of being fond of society. SOCIABILITY-PRIVACY.

SOCIABILITY—PRIVACY.

Cheer. A general spirit of good feeling.

Clubbism. Fondness for clubs and club-life.

Companionship. The state of being a companion.

Comradeship. The state of being a comrade.

Consociation. An act of coming together to form a society.

Consortship. Partnership, as of husband and wife.

Conviviality. Mirth and good-comradeship of a feast.

Esprit de corps [F.]. A spirit of common sympathy.

Familiarity. The state or quality of being familiar.

Festivity. Social enjoyment.

Good-fellowship. Friendly intercourse.

Heartiness. The state or quality of being earnest and sincere.

Hospitality. Kind treatment of strangers or guests.

Intercommunity. Harmonious communion.

Intercourse. Frequent association.

Jollity. The quality of being jolly.

Joviality. The quality of being jovial.

Merrymaking. Merriment; jollity.

Savoir vivre [F.]. Good manners.

Sociability. ⎫
Sociableness. ⎭ The quality of being sociable.

Social intercourse. Interchange of thought and feeling.

Sociality. The quality of being social.

Urbanity, etc. Refined courtesy. See POLITENESS.

Welcomeness. The quality of being welcome.

Anthrophobia. Hatred of the society of man.

Banishment. The act of banishing or state of being banished.

Cut. ⎫
Cut direct. ⎭ Refusal to recognize.

Dead cut. Complete cut.

Delitescence. The state of being concealed or hidden.

Depopulation. The act of depopulating or state of being depopulated.

Desertion. The act of forsaking, as a duty, party, or friend.

Desolation. The act of making or state of being desolate.

Dissociability. Lack of sociability.

Domesticity. The state of being domestic.

Estrangement from the world. Entire separation from worldly pleasures and activities.

Exclusion. The act of excluding or state of being excluded.

Excommunication. The act of excommunicating or state of being excommunicated.

Exile. Banishment from home or country by civil authority.

Inhospitableness, etc. The quality of being inhospitable.

Inhospitality. Same as inhospitableness.

Isolation. The act of making or state of being isolated.

Loneliness. The state or feeling of being lonely.

Ostracism. Banishment in general.

Privacy. The state of being private.

Proscription. The act of proscribing or state of being proscribed.

SOCIABILITY—PRIVACY—*Continued.*

SOCIABILITY—*Nouns of Agency.*

Bon enfant [F]. A good fellow.
Good fellow.
Jolly fellow. } A person full of life and mirth.

SOCIABILITY—*Associated Nouns.*

Afternoon party. A party held between noon and sunset.
Appointment. An agreement to meet.
Assembly, etc. A number of persons met together for social enjoyment. See GATHERING.
Assignation. An appointment to meet.
At home. At one's own abode.
Ball. A formal evening assembly for dancing.
Call. A brief social visit.
Circle of acquaintance. The list of persons with whom one is acquainted.
Club, etc. An organization of persons who meet for social intercourse. See ASSOCIATION.
Conversazione [It.]. A meeting for conversation.
Coterie. A circle of persons who meet, as for social entertainment.
Dish of tea. The drink served at a social gathering.
Drum. A social gathering, formerly a noisy party.
Entertainment. The act of receiving and caring for guests.
Evening party. A party held after sunset.
Family circle. The members of a family.
Festival, etc. A public entertainment. See ENTERTAINMENT.
Festive board. A feast.
Garden-party. An open-air party
Greeting. Salutation on meeting.
Hearty reception. Pleasant manner of receiving.
Housewarming. An entertainment in honor of the entry of a family into a new home.
Interview. A formal or appointed consultation. See CONVERSATION.
Kettledrum. A somewhat informal ladies' afternoon party.
Levee. A morning reception.
Matinee. An entertainment or reception formerly held in the morning, but now usually in the afternoon.
Morning call. A call made before noon.
Morning party. A party held before noon.
Partie carrée [F.]. A party of two men and two women.
Party. A company of persons assembled for social entertainment.
Reception. The act of receiving, or welcoming guests.
Ridotto [It.] A musical and dancing entertainment.
Round of visits. Visits upon all of one's acquaintances.
Rout. A disorderly assembly.
Social circle. The people with whom one is intimately acquainted.
Social gathering.
Social reunion. } A company of persons met for social entertainment.
Society. The fashionable portion of a community.
Soirée [F.]. An evening party.
Sorosis. A woman's club.
Tea-party. A social gathering at which tea is served.
The feast of reason and the flow of soul. A social and literary gathering. [Pope, *Satires,* I, ii, 127.]
Tryst. An appointment to meet.
Trysting-place. A place agreed upon for meeting.
Visit. The act of coming to see a person.
Visitant. One who visits.
Visiting. Coming to see a person.
Warm reception. A pleasant manner of receiving.
Welcome. A hearty greeting given.
Welcome reception. A cordial reception.

SOCIABILITY—*Verbs.*

Consort. To join, as in sympathy; live together.
Embrace. To clasp in the arms.
Entertain. To care or provide amusement for.
Fraternize. To mingle as companions.
Join. To bring together; to associate with.
Know. Be familiarly acquainted with.
Receive. Extend a welcome to.
Visit. Make a visit with.
Welcome. Extend a welcome to

SOCIABILITY—*Verbal Expressions.*

Associate with; be acquainted, etc.; bear one company; be at home; be at home with; beat up one's quarters; be sociable, etc.; call at; call upon; club together; crack a bottle with; do the honors; drop in; eat off the same trencher; feel at home with; give a party; give a warm reception to; hang out; interchange cards; interchange visits; keep company with; keep open house; kill the fatted calf;

Recess. Cessation from employment.
Reclusion. Retirement from the world.
Retirement. The act of retiring or state of being retired.
Rus in urbe [L.] Country in city
Rustication. The act of rusticating or state of being rusticated.
Seclusion. The act of secluding or state of being secluded.
Snugness. The state of being snug
Solitariness, etc. The state of being solitary. See SOLITUDE
Solitude. The state of being solitary.
Voluntary exile. Withdrawal from society of one's own accord.

PRIVACY—*Denotations.*

Anchoret.
Anchorite. } A person who has withdrawn himself from the world for religious seclusion.
Castaway. One who is cast out from his family or from society.
Cell. A hermit s hut or cave.
Cenobite. A monk as distinguished from a religious recluse.
Closet cynic. A pessimistic person who has withdrawn from society.
Convent, etc. A house occupied by a body of monks or nuns. See FANE.
Country-seat. A retired home in the country.
Darby and Joan. The subjects of Woodfall's ballad, *The Happy Old Couple.*
Diogenes. The most famous of the cynic philosophers.
Disciple of Zimmerman. A follower of Johann Zimmerman, who taught withdrawal from the world.
Hermit. One who abandons society and lives alone.
Hermitage. The retreat of a hermit.
Howling wilderness. Wild and dismal country.
Outcast. One who is cast out from home or country.
Pariah. A Hindu outcast.
Pilgarlic. A sneaking, chicken-hearted fellow.
Recluse. One who lives in retirement or seclusion.
Ruralist. One who leads a rural life.
Sanctum sanctorum [L.]. The holy of holies.
Santon. A Mohammedan hermit.
Simeon Stylites. The first of the pillar-saints. He stood continually on the top of a pillar for his last 30 years, near Antioch, 459.
Solitaire. A hermit or recluse.
Timon of Athens. A misanthrope. [Shakespeare, *Timon of Athens.*]
Troglodyte. A cave-dweller, figuratively, a hermit.
Wilderness, etc. A wild, unsettled country. See FERTILITY-STERILITY

PRIVACY—*Verbs.*

Abandon, etc. To forsake or give up utterly. See QUEST-ABANDONMENT.
Banish. To cause to leave one's country by a judicial decree; drive from a certain place.
Blackball. To vote against; to ostracize.
Cut. Refuse to recognize.
Cut off from. Deprive of the privileges or use of
Deny oneself. Refuse oneself a gratification.
Depopulate. Remove the inhabitants from.
Dispeople. Depopulate.
Exclude. To shut or keep out purposely or forcibly.
Excommunicate. To cut off from membership.
Exile. Cause to go into exile.
Expatriate. To drive from one's fatherland.
Ostracize. Subject to ostracism or banishment from Athens by a vote with an oyster-shell.
Outlaw. Drive from the protection of the law.
Proscribe. Declare to be a public enemy and outside the aid of the law.
Repel. Keep at a distance.
Retire. Withdraw and remain in private.
Rusticate. To live in the country.
Seclude oneself. Remove and keep oneself apart from others.
Unpeople. Depopulate.

PRIVACY—*Verbal Expressions.*

Aller planter ses cohux [F.], to retire into the country; **be secluded; creep into a corner; cut dead; draw a cordon round; hold oneself aloof; hold oneself in the background; keep at arm's length; keep in the background; keep oneself aloof; keep snug; live secluded; look cool upon; refuse to acknowledge; refuse to associate with; retire from the world; send to Coventry; shut oneself up; shut the door upon; stand aloof; stand in the background; take the veil; turn one's back upon.**

SOCIABILITY—PRIVACY—*Continued.*

SOCIABILITY—Verbal Expressions—*Continued.*

leave a card; live at free quarters; look in; look one up; make acquaintance with, etc. (see Amity); make advances; make free with; make oneself at home with; pay a visit; receive hospitality; receive with open arms; sort with; walk hand in hand with.

SOCIABILITY—*Adjectives.*

Acquainted. Personally known; having mutual knowledge.
Chatty. Familiar and gossipy.
Clubable. Liking club-life and able to play a part in it.
Companionable. Capable of being, or inclined to be, a pleasing companion.
Conversable. Disposed to converse.
Conversational. Given to conversation.
Convivial. Devoted to feasting; jovial.
Cosey.
Cosy. } Contented and sociable.
Cozy.
Entertained. Treated as a guest. See *Verbs.*
Familiar. Having intimate personal knowledge.
Festal. Pertaining to a festival or feast; merry; festive.
Festive. Pertaining to a feast; joyous.
Fête [F.] Festive.
Free and easy. At home.
Gregarious. Going or inclined to go in blocks or companies.
Hail fellow well met. On very familiar or cordial terms.
Homiletical. Conversable.
Hospitable. Entertaining pleasantly.
International. Pertaining to two or more nations.
Jolly. Full of or expressing life and mirth.
Jovial. Possessing or expressing mirth and good-fellowship.
Neighborly. Disposed to cultivate acquaintance.
On visiting terms. Acquainted.
Sociable. Inclined to seek society· agreeable in company.
Social. Pertaining to society; sociable.
Welcome. Cordially received.
Welcome as a rose in May. Well received.

SOCIABILITY—*Adverbs, etc.*

Alla vostra salute [It.] To your health.
Arm in arm. Sociably.
À votre santé [F.] To your health.
En famille [F.] In the family.
In the family circle. Familiarly.
Sans ceremonie [F.] Without ceremony; familiarly.
Sans façon [F.] Informally.

PRIVACY—*Continued from Column 2.*

PRIVACY—*Phrases.*

Magna civitas, magna solitudo [L.] A great city, a great solitude.
Noli me tangere [L.] Don't touch me.

PRIVACY—*Adjectives.*

Abandoned. Left alone. See *Verbs.*
Banished. Driven from home or country. See *Verbs.*
Bye. Situated apart or aside.
Cynical. Sneering or criticizing others.
Delitescent. Concealed; in retirement.
Derelict. Deserted or abandoned.
Deserted. Abandoned permanently or without consideration.
Deserted in one's utmost need. Left when help is most needed.
Desolate. Deprived of inhabitants; made lonely.
Dissocial. Not inclined to be social.
Domestic. Pertaining to or liking home duties.
Estranged. Distant in interest; made a stranger.
Forlorn. Without hope; forsaken; lost.
Friendless. Without a friend.
Homeless. Without a home.
Incommunicative. Reserved.
Inconversable. Not conversable.
Inhospitable. Not hospitable.
Isolated. Detached from others.
Kithless. Without kith.
Left to shift for oneself. Deserted.
Lonely. Deserted by human beings.
Lonesome. Sad because of loneliness.
Lorn. Without kindred or friends; lost, forlorn.
Outcast. Rejected as unworthy.
Out of the way. }
Out of the world. } Retired from society.
Private. Removed from public view.
Retired. In privacy. See *Verbs.*
Sauvage [F.] Savage; unsociable.
Secluded. Apart from others.
Sequestered. Withdrawn into obscurity or solitude.
Single. Having no companion.
Snug. Not exposed to notice.
Solitary. Living or being alone; unfrequented by human beings.
Stay-at-home.
Tenantless. Without a tenant.
The world forgetting, by the world forgot. Living in privacy. [Pope, *Eloise*, 207.]
Unclubable. Not clubable.
Under a cloud. With an injured reputation.
Unfrequented. Not resorted to or crowded with people.
Unfriended. Not helped by friends.
Unhabitable. Not fit to be inhabited.
Uninhabited. Not dwelt in.
Unintroduced. Not made known to.
Uninvited. Not having had one's presence requested.
Unsociable. Not sociable.
Unsocial. Not social.
Unvisited. Not visited.
Unwelcome. Not welcome.

(*Continued on Column 1.*)

---

so'-cia-ble. Social; carriage. Conveyance-Vessel, Sociability-Privacy.
so'-cia-ble-ness. Companionableness. Sociability-Privacy.
so'-cial. Friendly; loving mankind. Humanity, Sociability-Privacy; **social circle,** Sociability-Privacy; **social evil,** Purity-Impurity; **social gathering,** Sociability-Privacy; **social science,** Humanitarianism-Misanthropy.
so'-cial-ism. Polity; ownership; government. Humanitarianism - Misanthropy, Participation, Rule-License, Tyranny-Anarchy.
so'-cial-ist. One who advocates socialism. Participation.
so''-ci-al'-i-ty. Sociability. Sociability-Privacy.
so-ci'-e-ty. Mankind; association; fashionable. Association, Humanity, Sociability-Privacy, Society-Affectation, Society-Dandy, Society-Derision, Society-Laughingstock, Society-Ludicrousness; **position in society,** Reputation-Discredit.

SOCIETY—LUDICROUSNESS.

Air. Impression made by a person's appearance.
Arbiter elegantiarum [L.] An authority in matters of taste.
Beau monde [F.] World of society.
Bienseance [F.] Propriety.
Bon ton [F.] Highest fashion.
Breeding. Manner and conduct as a result of birth and training.
Civilization. An improved condition of man.
Civilized life. Life among the most advanced peoples.
Conventions of society. Rules of polite society.
Court. Council and retinue of a king, usually the model of fashions.
Custom. General usage.
Decorum. Quality of being suitable to character, time, or occasion.

Absurdity. Anything nonsensical or ridiculous.
Anticlimax. A falling off in the importance of ideas.
Bathos. A ridiculous anticlimax.
Bombast. Extravagant language on unimportant subjects.
Buffoonery. Coarse jokes and antic gestures.
Burlesque. A ludicrous imitation, either written or acted.
Comedy. A trivial, amusing drama.
Comicality. That which is comical.
Doggerel verses. Rude burlesque poetry.
Drollery. That which is laughable and odd.
Extravagance. Something beyond the limits of truth.
Farce. Something absurdly exaggerated.

SOCIETY—LUDICROUSNESS—Continued.

Demeanor.   Bearing as indicative of a temper of the mind.
Drawing-room.   A room appropriated for the reception of company.
Dress.   Attention to apparel.
Élite [F.].   Choicest part of society.
Etiquette.   Ceremonial code of polite society.
Fashion.   Recognized custom in small matters.
Fashionable world.   The people who follow the fashions closely
Form.   Conventional rules of society.
Formality.   Adherence to the conventional rules of society.
Gay world.   The people of leisure and fashion.
Gentility.   Characteristics of one well bred.
Gentlemanliness.   Conduct of a well-bred man.
Glass of fashion.   One whom or that which is copied after in matters of dress, etc.   [Shakespeare, *Hamlet*, III, i.]
Go.   Fashion or mode.
Good society.   The fashionable portion of a community.
Height of fashion.   The very latest fashion.
High life.   Life of the well-bred and fashionable.
Leader of fashion.   One who initiates the fashions.
Manners.   Habitual behavior in respect to etiquette and politeness.
Man of fashion. }
Man of the world. }   One who adjusts himself to the fashions.
Mode.   The fashion.
Pink of fashion.   Latest fashion.
Point of etiquette.   A rule of polite society.
Polite society.   The most refined portion of a community.
Prevailing taste.   The style; the fashion.
Propriety.   Accordance with recognized principles rules, and customs.
Punctilio.   Exactness in the observance of etiquette.
Rage.   Fashion.
Savoir faire [F.].   Good manners.
Show.   Outward display.
Society.   Fashionable portion of a community.
Star of fashion.   A very fashionable person.
Style.   Manner or form approved as elegant or fashionable.
Ton [F.].   Fashion.
Town.   The center of fashion.
Upper ten thousand.   The fashionable set.
"Vanity Fair."   World of fashion.   [Bunyan, Thackeray.]
Woman of fashion. }
Woman of the world. }   One who adjusts herself to the fashions.
World.   People of fashion.

SOCIETY—Verbs.

Be fashionable.   To be in style.
Behave oneself.
Be the rage.   To be very fashionable.
Bring into fashion.   To lead others to use or do.
Conform to the fashion.   To be stylish.
Cut a figure in society.   To be popular in society.
Fall in with the fashion. }
Follow the fashion. }   To be fashionable.
Give a tone to society.   To raise the standard of society.
Go with the stream.   To follow the fashion.
Have a run.   To be fashionable for a short time.
Keep one's carriage. }
Keep up appearances. }   To be fashionable.
Pass current.   To be generally accepted.
Savoir faire [F.].   To know just what to do.
Savoir vivre [F.].   To have good manners.
Set the fashion.   To initiate the fashion.

SOCIETY—Adjectives.

Admissible in society. }
Admitted in society. }   Fit for good society.
À la mode [F.].   According to a certain fashion.
Civil.   Observant of the proprieties of speech and manner.
Comme il faut [F.].   As it should be.
Conventional.   Growing out of custom.
Courtly.   Having the refinement becoming to a court.
Dashing.   Showy and gay.
Dégagé [F.].   Easy and unconstrained.
Distingué [F.].   Noticeable; attractive.
En grand tenue [F.].   In full dress.
Fashionable.   According to the fashion.
Fast.   Given up to extravagant and sensuous pleasures.
Genteel.   Suited to the station of a gentleman.
Gentlemanlike. }
Gentlemanly. }   Becoming a well-bred man.
In court dress.
In evening dress.   In full dress.

Frippery.   Second-hand finery.
Laughing-stock.   A butt for literature.
Monstrosity.   Something greatly exaggerated.
Oddity.   Anything that creates laughter.
Ridiculousness.   Quality of being ridiculous.

LUDICROUSNESS—Verbs.

Be ridiculous.   To create laughter by one's actions.
Commit an absurdity.   To do something nonsensical.
Make a fool of oneself.   To do something foolish.
Make one laugh.   To act foolishly.
Pass from the sublime to the ridiculous.   To pass from something worthy to something laughable.
Play the fool.   To act a foolish part.

LUDICROUSNESS—Adjectives.

Awkward.   Ungraceful in action.
Baroque.   Fantastical in style.
Bizarre.   Odd in manner or appearance.
Bombastic.   Marked by bombast.
Burlesque.   Having the qualities of burlesque.
Comic. }
Comical. }   Adapted to produce mirth.
Contemptible.   Worthy of contempt or ridicule.
Doggerel.   Weak, trivial, or absurd: said of verse.
Droll. }
Drollish. }   Laughable and odd.
Eccentric.   Departing from the ordinary modes and customs.
Extravagant.   Beyond the limits of truth.
Fanciful.   Irregular and extravagant in opinion or taste.
Fantastic.   Absurdly fanciful.
Farcical.   Absurdly exaggerated.
Funny.   Laughable.
Gimcrack.   Cheap and showy.
Grotesque.   Misshapen or ludicrously odd.
Inflated.   Bombastic; pompous.
Ironical.   Characterized by irony.
Laughable.   Very ludicrous.
Ludicrous.   Tending to produce laughter.
Mock heroic.   Burlesque in heroic style.
Monstrous.   Greatly exaggerated.
Odd.   Unmatched; not common.
Outlandish.   Strange and uncouth.
Out of the way.   Uncommon.
Outre [F.].   Overstrained.
Pour rire [F.].   Laughable.
Preposterous.   Utterly absurd.
Quaint.   Pleasingly odd.
Queer.   Out of the common way.
Quizzical.   Absurd and puzzling.
Ridiculous.   Contemptible and funny.
Risible.   Mirthful.
Rum.   Odd; queer: used contemptuously.
Serio-comic.   Combining mirth and gravity.
Stilted.   Artificial and elevated in manner or style.
Strange.   New or foreign to the observer.
Tragi-comic.   Of a mixture of grave and comic scenes.
Whimsical. }
Whimsical as a dancing bear. }   Producing laughter.

LUDICROUSNESS—Phrases.

Du sublime au ridicule il n'v a qu'un pas [F.].   From the sublime to the ridiculous there is but a step.   [Napoleon.]
Rideret Heraclitus [L.].   Heraclitus would laugh.
Risum teneatis, amici [L.].   Can you, my friends, forbear laughing?   [Horace, *Ars Poetica*, 5.]

SOCIETY—ADJECTIVES—Continued.

In fashion.   According to style.
In full dress.   Dressed properly for formal, social occasions.
Janty. }
Jaunty. }   Showy and at ease.
Ladylike.   Becoming to a woman of good breeding.
Modish.   Fashionable.
Newfangled.   New and novel.
Polished.   Possessing the elegancies of speech and manners.
Polite.   Observing the proprieties, and careful of the comfort of others.
Presentable.   Fit for society.
Recherché [F.].   Nice to an extreme.
Refined.   Devoid of anything coarse; cultivated.
Stylish.   According to approved style.

Thoroughbred. Showing the qualities of good breeding.
Unembarrassed. Not disturbed in the presence of others.
Well-behaved. Conducting oneself properly.

Well-bred. Trained to good manners.
Well-mannered. Well-bred.
Well-spoken. Cultivated in speech.

Society—Adverbs, etc.

Fashionable. According to fashion.

For fashion's sake. According to fashion.

Society—Phrases.

À la française [F.]. In French style.
À l'américaine [F.]. In American style.
À l'anglaise [F.]. In the English style.
À la parisienne [F.]. In the Parisian style.

Autre temps, autre mœurs [F.]. Change of time, change of manners.
Chaque pays a sa guise [F.]. Each country has its style.
Y á Roma por todo [Sp.]. To Rome for everything.

SOCIETY—DANDY

DANDY

Beau. A dandy.
Blade. A rake.
Blood. A gay, showy man.
Buck. A dashing fellow.
Carpet-knight. An effeminate man averse to manly sports.
Coquette. Vain girl, trifling in love.
Coxcomb. Vain, showy fellow.
Dandiprat. A dapperling.
Dandy. A man, dainty in attire and manners.
Exquisite. A dandy.
Fast man. One given over to dissolute pleasures.
Fine gentleman. }
Fine lady. } Persons given to display.
Fop. A dandy.

Fribble. A trifler.
Jackadandy. An insignificant fop.
Jackanape. An impertinent fellow.
Jemmy. A spruce young fellow.
Jemmy Jessamy. A showy, vain person.
Macaroni. A fop.
Man about town. Fashionable idler.
Man-milliner. An effeminate man.
Petit-maître [F.]. Coxcomb.
Popinjay. A chattering coxcomb.
Prig. Pert, conceited fellow.
Puppy. Conceited, finely dressed young man.
Spark. Dressy man, fond of gallantry.
Swell. A dandy.

SOCIETY—AFFECTATION.

AFFECTATION.

Acting a part. Making pretension to something one is not.
Affectation. }
Affectedness. } Assuming what is not real, or unnatural.
Airs. Show of pride or vanity.
Boasting. Ostentatious talk about oneself.
Buckram. Stiffness of manner.
Charlatanism. Boasting. See BRAGGING.
Conceit. Overestimation of oneself.
Coquetry. Vain trifling in love.
Coxcombry. Practises and arts of a coxcomb.
Dandyism. Manners and dress of a dandy.
Demureness. Affected modesty.
Euphuism. Affectation of elegance in writing.
False shame. Affected shame.
Foppery. Fastidiousness in dress and deportment.
Formality. Strict observance of rules of etiquette and good style.
Grimace. Hypocritical expression of interest or feeling.
Man-millinery. Effeminacy.
Mannerism. Characteristic peculiarities carried to success.
Mauvaise honte [F.]. False modesty.
Minauderie [F.]. False shame.
Mock modesty. Assumed modesty.
Pedantry. Vain and uncalled-for display of knowledge.
Précieuse ridicule [F.]. One of the ridiculous fine ladies of Molière.
Precisianism. Overpreciseness.
Pretense. Holding forth as true what is unreal.
Pretension. Assertion or display of a quality as possessed.
Profundity. Depth of knowledge.
Prudery. Excessive or affected scrupulousness in speech or conduct.
Puppyism. The manners and actions of a puppy.
Purism. Affectation of rigid purity in use of words.
Quackery. The boastful pretensions of a quack.
Sentimentalism. Indulgence in displays of exaggerated feelings.
Shallow profundity. An affected learning, etc.
Simagree. A grimace.
Stiffness. State of formality and constraint.
Teratology. Affectation of sublimity.

AFFECTATION—Nouns of Agent.

Actor. One who assumes a character that is not real.
Affector. One given to studied pretense or attempt.
Bas bleu [F.]. A bluestocking.
Bluestocking. A pedantic and undomestic literary woman.
Charlatan. One who makes unwarranted pretensions to knowledge.
Coquette. A woman who endeavors to attract admiration and advances in love, merely to gratify her vanity.
Doctrinaire. One whose views are derived from theories rather than from facts.
Euphuist. One who indulges in euphuism.

Flatterer. One who tries to please or gain favor by a complimentary speech or conduct.
Grimacer. One who is in the habit of distorting his features in affectation.
Lump of affectation. A very pretentious person.
Mannerist. A person addicted to one manner or style.
Pedagogue. A conceited, narrow-minded teacher.
Pedant. A scholar who makes needless display of his learning.
Performer. One who acts a part.
Petit-maître [F.]. A fop; a dude.
Poetaster. A mere rimer or verse-maker.
Prig. A conceited person who assumes superior learning, virtue, etc.
Prude. A woman who makes an affected display of modesty.
Purist. One who is overparticular as to purity of literary style.
Puritan. One who is scrupulously strict in his religious life.

AFFECTATION—Verbs.

Act a part. To assume a character which one is not.
Affect. Assume what is not real or unnatural.
Attitudinize. Assume affected attitudes.
Boast. Talk ostentatiously about oneself.
Coquet. To trifle vainly in love.
Flirt a fan. To draw attention to.
Give oneself airs. To make a show of pride or vanity.
Mince. To speak imperfectly with affected softness.
Overact. To perform to excess.
Overdo. To exaggerate, as manners or style.
Pose. To assume an attitude for effect.
Put on. To affect.
Simper. To smile in a silly, affected manner.

AFFECTATION—Adjectives.

Ad captandum [L.]. For the purpose of pleasing or attracting.
Affected. Having assumed what is not real or unnatural.
Artificial. Unnatural; feigned.
Big-sounding. Bombastic; pompous.
Conceited. Having a high estimation of oneself.
Coxcombical. Foppish.
Dandified. Foppish.
Demure. Affectedly modest.
Euphuistic. Affectedly elegant in writing.
Finical. }
Finikin. } Foppish.
Foppish. Vain and overnice in dress and deportment.
Formal. Strictly observing rules of etiquette.
Full of affectation. Affected.
Maniéré [F.]. Affected.
Mincing. Spoken imperfectly and with affected softness.
Namby-pamby. Weakly sentimental.
Not natural. Unnatural.
Overacted. Performed to excess.

SOCIETY—AFFECTATION—*Continued.*

AFFECTATION—Adjectives—*Continued.*

Overdone. } Exaggerated; too elaborate.
Overwrought. }
Pedantic. Like a pedant.
Pragmatical. Unduly busy.
Pretentious. Attempting to pass for more than one's real value.
Priggish. Like a prig.
Prim. Minutely or affectedly nice or formal.
Prudish. Affectedly modest.
Puritanical. Scrupulously strict in morals or religion.
Quakerish. Scrupulous in dress.
Self-conscious. Unduly conscious of one's own acts.

Sentimental. Indulging in displays of exaggerated feelings.
Simpering. Smiling in a silly or affected manner.
Smug. Affectedly nice.
Stagey. Bombastic in style or manner.
Starchy. Stiff and precise.
Stiff. Formal and not easy.
Stilted. Artificially elevated in manner.
Theatrical. Pompous.
Tire à quatre epingles [F.]. To touch with the point of a needle.
Unnatural. In an assumed manner.

SOCIETY—DERISION.

DERISION.

Badinage. Delicate, refined gossip.
Banter. Good-natured wit at the expense of another.
Buffoonery. Low jests and ridiculous pranks.
Burlesque. A ludicrous imitation.
Caricature. A picture giving a grotesque exaggeration of features or peculiarities.
Chaff. Coarse witticisms.
Derision. Hostile, scornful laughter.
Farce. A ridiculous proceeding.
Grin. A sneering smile.
Horse-play. Boisterous play.
Irony. A use of words in which the meaning is contrary to the literal sense.
Irrision. Derision.
Mockery. Derisive mimicry.
Parody. A trivial imitation, keeping the style, but changing the subject.
Persiflage. Frivolous, bantering talk or writing.
Practical joke. A joke which is done, not said.
Quib. } A gibe.
Quip. }
Quiz. An absurd, puzzling question.
Quizzing. A ridiculous hoax.
Raillery. Satirical merriment.
Ridicule. Contemptuous laughter.
Sardonic grin. Forced, sarcastic grin.
Sardonic smile. Forced, sarcastic smile.
Satire. A formal, derisive composition.
Scoffing. Contempt for serious matters, expressed in word, look, or deed.
Skit. A short, trivial satire.
Squib. A mild lampoon.
Travestie. } An imitation of a subject in a trivial or grotesque style.
Travesty. }

Fool to the top of one's bent. To heartily play the fool.
Grin at. To look at grinning.
Joke. To indulge in jokes.
Laugh at. To express one's feelings by laughter.
Laugh in one's sleeve. Laugh on the sly.
Make a fool of. To cause someone to appear ridiculous.
Make a fool of oneself. To place oneself in a ridiculous position.
Make an April fool of. To play a joke on someone on April 1st.
Make fun of. To make fun at someone's expense.
Make game of. To make the butt of a play or game.
Make merry with. To have pleasure together.
Parody. To write a parody on.
Play the fool. Act a foolish part.
Play tricks upon. To make the object of practical jokes.
Play upon. Make sport of.
Poke fun at. Make sport of.
Quiz. To ask absurd puzzling questions.
Raise a laugh. To cause laughter.
Rally. To use raillery.
Ridicule. To contemptuously hold up to laughter.
Roast. To ridicule severely.
Satirize. To treat with satire.
Scoff. To treat things serious with contempt.
Show up. To expose.
Smile at. To express slight contempt with a smile.
Snigger. To laugh in a suppressed manner.
Tehee. A restrained laughter.
Travesty. To imitate a subject in a trivial or grotesque style.
Turn into ridicule. To make laughable.
Twit. Tease with something discreditable.

DERISION—*Adjectives.*

Burlesque. In the style of burlesque.
Derisive. } Characterized by derision.
Derisory. }
Hudibrastic. Coarsely satirical like *Hudibras.*
Ironical. Mockingly sarcastic.
Mock. Containing derisive mimicry.
Quizzical. Characterized by quizzes.
Sarcastic. Containing covert, bitter, personal satire.
Scurrilous. Low and indecent.

DERISION—*Verbs.*

Banter. To be good-naturedly witty at another's expense.
Burlesque. To imitate in burlesque.
Caricature. To sketch with grotesque exaggerations of features or peculiarities.
Chaff. To indulge in coarse witticisms.
Deride. To laugh at in hostile scorn.
Fleer. To mock with the looks.
Fool. To deceive.

DERISION—*Adverbs, etc.*

In ridicule, etc. Scornfully. See *Nouns.*

SOCIETY—LAUGHINGSTOCK.

LAUGHINGSTOCK.

April fool. Subject of practical joke on April 1st.
Buffoon. A practiser of buffoonery.
Butt. The one against whom criticism, satire, or jokes are aimed.
Comedian. Humorous actor.
Fair game. One easily made a laughing-stock.
Game. One made sport of.
Gazing-stock. One who attracts attention by a queer appearance.
Jest. }
Jesting-stock. } Object of jest or laughter.
Laughing-stock. }
Monkey. One who plays tricks like a monkey.

Odd fish. An odd person.
Oddity. A singular person.
Old fogy. An elderly person, unsympathetic with the young.
Original. A person of unique character or genius.
Pantomimist. One who acts by gesticulation only.
Queer fish. A queer man.
Quiz. One who puts absurd, puzzling questions.
Square toes. An old-fashioned, formal person.

LAUGHINGSTOCK—*Phrase.*

Dum vitant stulti vitia, in contraria currunt [L.]. Fools while avoiding a vice run into its opposite.

so-cin'-i-an-ism. Doctrine. ORTHODOXY - HETERODOXY.
so''-ci-o-log'-ic-al. Pertaining to sociology. ETHNOLOGY.
so''-ci-ol'-o-gist. One versed in sociology. ETHNOLOGY.
so''-ci-ol'-o-gy. Science of society. ETHNOLOGY.

sock. Stocking; shoe. ACTING, DRESS-UNDRESS.
sock'-et. Cavity. CONTENTS-RECEIVER, CONVEXITY-CONCAVITY.
so'-cle. Base. SUSPENSION-SUPPORT.
So-crat'-ic meth'-od. Dialectics. INVESTIGATION-ANSWER.

sod. Sward. Gulf-Plain; **beneath the sod,** Life-Funeral.

so-dal'-i-ty. Brotherhood. Amity-Hostility, Association.

sod'-den. Soaked; boiled. Dampness-Dryness, Heating-Cooling.

so'-di-um. An element. Chemistry.

so'-fa. Seat. Suspension-Support.

sof'-fit. Ceiling. Architecture.

so'-fi. Pantheist. Ministry-Laity, Orthodoxy-Heterodoxy.

soft. Impressible; smooth; gentle; mild; pleasing; weak; fool. Bravery-Cowardice, Compassion-Ruthlessness, Credulousness-Skepticism, Dampness-Dryness, Discontinuance-Continuance, Hardness-Softness, Harshness-Mildness, Loudness-Faintness, Sagacity-Incapacity, Sensitiveness-Apathy, Smoothness-Roughness, Sound-Silence, Strength-Weakness, Swamp-Island, Turbulence-Calmness; **own to the soft impeachment,** Exposure-Hidingplace; **soft music,** Music; **soft sawder,** Adulation-Disparagement, Pretext; **soft soap,** Adulation-Disparagement, Pulpiness-Rosin; **soft tongue,** Politeness-Impoliteness; **soft words,** Politeness-Impoliteness.

sof'-ten. Impressible; smooth; gentle; mild; pleasing; weak; fool. Alleviation-Aggravation, Bravery-Cowardice, Compassion-Ruthlessness, Credulousness-Skepticism, Dampness-Dryness, Discontinuance-Continuance, Hardness-Softness, Harshness-Mildness, Justification-Charge, Loudness-Faintness, Sagacity-Incapacity, Sensitiveness-Apathy, Smoothness-Roughness, Sound-Silence, Strength-Weakness, Swamp-Island, Turbulence-Calmness.

sof'-ten down. To relieve. Alleviation-Aggravation.

sof'-ten-ing. Making soft. Alleviation-Aggravation, Hardness-Softness, Justification-Charge.

sof'-ten-ing of the brain. Degeneration. Might-Impotence.

sof'-ter sex. Woman. Male-Female.

soft'-heart''-ed. Tender-hearted. Compassion-Ruthlessness, Sensitiveness-Apathy.

soft'-ling. Voluptuary. Creation-Destruction.

soft'-ness. Gentleness. Hardness-Softness, Motive-Caprice, Sensitiveness-Apathy.

soft''-spo'-ken. Gentle. Politeness-Impoliteness.

sog'-gy. Moist. Dampness-Dryness.

so-ho'. Hallo; hunting cry. Address-Response, Heed-Disregard, Quest-Evasion.

soi''-di''-sant'. Self-styled. Assertion-Denial, Bragging, Conceit-Diffidence, Gull-Deceiver, Name-Misnomer, Truthfulness-Fabrication.

soil. Ground; stain; country. Beauty-Ugliness, Cleanness-Filthiness, Extension-District, Ocean-Land; **till the soil,** Domestication-Agriculture, Preparation-Nonpreparation.

soiled. Befouled. Cleanness-Filthiness.

soil'-i-ness. Tarnish. Cleanness-Filthiness.

soil'-ure. Soiling. Cleanness-Filthiness.

soir, bon [F.] (swar, bon·). Good evening. Politeness-Impoliteness,

soirée [F.] (swa''-rê'). Evening party. Sociability-Privacy.

so'-journ. Residence. Dweller-Habitation, Presence-Absence.

so'-journ-er. Resident. Dweller-Habitation.

sol'-ace. Cheer; pleasure. Alleviation-Aggravation, Entertainment-Weariness; **solace oneself with,** Pleasure-Pain.

so'-lar. Pertaining to the sun. Astronomy, Universe; **solar prominences,** Astronomy; **solar system,** Universe.

so-la'-ti-um. Compensation. Recompense-Punition

Sol'-dan. Sultan. Chief-Underling.

sold'-er. Alloy; unite. Cohesion-Looseness, Connective, Union-Disunion.

sold'-er-ing. Uniting. Cohesion-Looseness.

sol'-dier. Fighter. Belligerent.

sol'-dier-like''. Martial. Fighting-Conciliation.

sol'-dier-ship. State of a soldier. Fighting-Conciliation.

sol'-dier-y. A body of soldiers. Bravery-Cowardice.

sol'-do. Coin. Values.

sold to the dev''-il. Lost. Good Man-Bad Man.

sole. Alone; bottom. Solitude-Company, Suspension-Support, Top-Bottom; **feme-sole,** Matrimony-Celibacy.

sol'-e-cism. Impropriety. Grammar-Solecism, Ratiocination-Casuistry.

sol'-e-cize. To do improperly. Grammar-Solecism.

soleil, coup de [F.] (so-lêye', cu de). Sunstroke. Heating-Cooling, Saneness-Lunacy.

sol'-emn. Awe-inspiring; sacred; grave. Assertion-Denial, Consequence-Insignificance, Devotion-Idolatry, Godliness-Ungodliness, Lightheartedness-Dejection, Pomp, Reputation-Discredit; **solemn mockery,** Pomp; **solemn silence,** Sound-Silence.

so-lem'-ni-ty. Reverence. Ceremonial, Lightheartedness-Dejection; **funereal solemnity,** Life-Funeral.

sol''-em-ni-za'-tion. Celebration. Solemnization.

SOLEMNIZATION.

Celebration. A demonstration of respect or rejoicing on account of or in memory of.

Commemoration. A solemn demonstration in memory of some person or event.

Solemnization. A reverential ceremony.

Solemnization—*Denotations.*

Bonfire. A large fire in the open air in honor of some person or event.

Colors flying. Flags waving in celebration of some event.

Coronation. The ceremony of crowning a monarch.

Fanfare [F.]. A flourish of trumpets.

Fête. A festival; a holiday. See Pomp.

Feu de joie [F.] A bonfire.

Flourish of trumpets. A blast from many trumpets.

Harvest home. A feast after the harvest has been gathered.

Illumination. The act of lighting up for festal purposes.

Inauguration. The ceremony of investing persons with public office.

Installation. The ceremony of placing in office.

Jubilation. The act of rejoicing.

Jubilee. A season of rejoicing or festivity.

Lord Mayor's show. The installation of the lord mayor into office.

Ovation. An expression of popular homage and applause.

Pæan. A song of joy or triumph.

Presentation. The ceremony attending the offering of a complimentary gift.

Red-letter day. A day of notable festivity.

Salute. A display of military, naval, or other official honors.

Salvo. } A salute given by firing all the guns at one time.
Salvo of artillery.

Te Deum [L.]. A Latin hymn of praise. See Devotion.

Triumph. Joy and gratulation on account of great success.

Triumphal arch. An arch commemorating some great event.

Trophy. A memento of victory or success. See Trophy.

Solemnization—*Verbs.*

Celebrate. To honor by ceremonies of joy or respect.

Chair. To triumphantly carry in a chair.

Commemorate. To recall by fitting ceremonies the memory of some person or event.

Do honor to. To show marks of respect or regard for.

Drink to. To drink to one's health or honor.

Hallow. To hold in sacred memory; to treat reverently.

Hob and nob. To drink socially.

Hold jubilee. To celebrate.

Inaugurate. To seat in office with formal ceremonies.

Install. To place in charge or office with the usual ceremonies.

Keep. To observe suitably.

Kill the fatted calf. To rejoice with a great feast. [Bible.]
Mark with a red letter. To have a notable celebration.
Pledge. To drink the health of.
Rejoice. To celebrate. See JUBILATION.
Roast an ox. To celebrate with a feast.
Signalize. To mark with distinction.
Solemnize. To make revered by religious ceremonies.
Toast. To drink to the honor or health of.

SOLEMNIZATION—*Adjectives.*

Celebrated, etc. Marked with particular ceremony. See *Verbs.*
Celebrating, etc. Honoring. See *Verbs.*
Commemorative. Tending to keep fresh in memory.
Immortal. Never to die.
Solemnized. Celebrated. See *Verbs.*

SOLEMNIZATION—*Adverbs, etc.*

In commemoration of. }
In honor of. } In respect to the memory of.

SOLEMNIZATION—*Interjections.*

All hail!
Hail!
Io pæan! [L.] Shout huzza!
Io triumphe! [L.] Behold the triumphant!
See the conquering hero comes!

SOLEMNIZATION—*Phrase.*

Magister ceremoniarium [L.]. Master of ceremonies.

sol'-em-nize. To perform with honors. SOLEMNIZA-
TION.
sol'-en-oid. A form of magnet. ELECTRICITY.

sol''-fa'. Choir-leader. MUSICIAN.
sol-feg'-gio. Singing. MUSIC.
so-lic'-it. Ask; entreat. DESIRE-DISTASTE, MOTIVE-
CAPRICE, PETITION-EXPOSTULATION; solicit the attention, HEED-DISREGARD.
so-lic'-it-ant. Solicitous. DESIRE-DISTASTE.
so-lic''-i-ta'-tion. Making petition. MOTIVE-CAPRICE,
PETITION-EXPOSTULATION.
so-lic'-it-or. Attorney; one who solicits. ADVOCATE,
CONSIGNEE, PETITIONER.
so-lic'-it-ous. Anxious; uneasy. DESIRE-DISTASTE.
so-lic'-i-tude. Uneasiness; anxiety. CAREFULNESS-
CARELESSNESS, DESIRE-DISTASTE, PLEASURE-PAIN,
SANGUINENESS-TIMIDITY.
sol'-id. Compact; strong; substantial. CERTAINTY-
DOUBT, ENTIRETY-DEFICIENCY, KNOWLEDGE-IGNO-
RANCE, PERSISTENCE-WHIM, SAGACITY-INCAPACITY,
SOLIDITY-RARITY, TRUTH-ERROR.
sol''-i-dar'-i-ty. Oneness. ASSOCIATION, ENTIRETY-
DEFICIENCY.
sol'-i-date. To make solid. SOLIDITY-RARITY.
sol''-i-da'-tion. A making solid. SOLIDITY-RARITY.
so-lid''-i-fi-ca'-tion. Reduction to a solid. SOLIDITY-
RARITY.
so-lid'-i-fied. Made solid. SOLIDITY-RARITY.
so-lid'-i-fy. Unify. SOLIDITY-RARITY.
so-lid'-i-ty. Property of being solid. ENTIRETY-DE-
FICIENCY, SAGACITY-INCAPACITY, SOLIDITY-RARITY.

SOLIDITY—RARITY.

Consistence. An indefinite degree of density or hardness.
Densely. Closeness of molecules forming the body.
Impenetrability. The quality that two bodies cannot occupy the
same space at the same time.
Impermeability. The quality of being so closely put together as to
allow nothing to pass through.
Imporosity. The quality of having no pores; compactness.
Incompressibility. Quality of not being able to be forced to occupy
less volume.
Indiscerptibility. Inseparability.
Indissolvableness. The quality of being incapable of being broken
up by any chemical process.
Indivisibility. The quality of being inseparable.
Solidity. The state of being dense, compact, or hard.
Solidness. The quality of being firm or dense.
Spissitude. The quality of being dense or compact from evapora-
tion.

SOLIDITY—*Nouns of Instrument.*

Areometer An instrument to measure specific gravity of fluids.
Hydrometer. An instrument to test specific gravity of liquids,
especially spirituous and saline liquids.

SOLIDITY—*Denotations.*

Block A solid piece of wood, metal, or other material.
Bone. The solid framework of the body.
Cake. A hardened mass of anything.
Cartilage. An elastic animal tissue or gristle.
Clot. A hardened mass of an evaporated liquid, as of blood.
Coagulum. A clot of blood or serum.
Concrete. Ground rock cemented.
Conglomerate. An irregular solid mass of particles.
Curd. The coagulated portion of milk.
Deposit. The solid substance that falls to the bottom of a liquid.
Gristle. Cartilage.
Knot. A hard, gnarled portion of a tree.
Lump. A shapeless mass of matter.
Mass. A solid body of concrete matter.
Precipitate. The solid portions in a liquid which settle to the
bottom.
Solid body. A hard and firm substance.
Specific gravity. The force by which bodies are drawn to the center
of the earth.
Stone. A piece of rock.

SOLIDITY—*Nouns of Cause.*

Coagulation. The thickening of the blood by evaporation.
Cohesion. The attraction by which molecules in a body are held
together.

Absence of solidity. The quality of being soft or yielding. See
SOLIDITY.
Compressibility. The quality of being compressible.
Dilatation. The act of dilating, or of expanding on all sides.
Ether. A very rare gas above the atmosphere. See LIQUID-GAS.
Expansion. An increasing in amount, size, etc.
Inflation. A filling up, as with air; expansion.
Rarefaction. The act of making rare.
Rarity. State or quality of being rare or rarefied.
Sponginess. State of being spongy, or of being elastic and com-
pressible.
Subtility. State of being subtile, or of being rare or rarefied.
Subtilization. The act of rendering subtile.
Tenuity. State of being thin; rare, or subtile.

RARITY—*Verbs.*

Dilate. To spread out in all directions; puff out.
Expand. To enlarge; increase the scope of.
Rarefy. To make rare.
Subtilize. To make subtile.

RARITY—*Adjectives.*

Cavernous. Filled with small cavities or cells· having a porous
texture.
Compressible. Capable of being pressed into a smaller space.
Fine. Not coarse; tenuous; subtile.
Flimsy. Having no substantial texture.
Light. Lacking density or weight. See HEAVINESS-LIGHTNESS.
Rare. Occurring but seldom; thinly scattered.
Rarefied. Made rare. See *Verbs.*
Slight. Slender in build or construction; delicate.
Spongy. Like a sponge; elastic; porous. See CONVEXITY-CON-
CAVITY.
Subtile. Characterized by rarity; rarefied.
Tenuous. Characterized by thinness; rare.
Thin. Having little body; loose in structure.
Uncompact. Not compact; not close or firm in structure.
Uncompressed. Not compressed.
Unsubstantial. Having no solid, strong texture; chimerical.

SOLIDITY—*Nouns of Cause—Continued.*

Concretion. Process of uniting.
Condensation. Putting into a more compact form.
Consolidation. The act of bringing together; make solid, firm.
Constipation. The formation of a solid mass.
Crystallization. The process of assuming definite form; like crystals
of various substances.

SOLIDITY—Nouns of Cause—*Continued.*

Inspissation. Thickening a fluid by boiling; evaporation.
Petrifaction. Process of making like rock. See HARDNESS.
Precipitation. The process of solidifying one of the component parts of a liquid by introducing a new substance

Solidation. Causing to become solid, firm.
Solidification. The quality which some liquids have of assuming a more rigid form on cooling.
Thickening. Something put into a liquid to make it thicker

SOLIDITY—*Verbs.*

Become solid. To become hard or firm. See *Adjectives.*
Be dense. To be closely packed together. See *Adjectives.*
Be solid. To be hard or firm. See *Adjectives.*
Cake. To mold into a solid mass.
Candy. To harden by crystallization.
Clot. To thicken; to coagulate.
Coagulate. To clot; become thick.
Cohere. To cleave; hold firmly.
Compress. To make more compact; to press together.
Concrete. To unite; to form into a mass.
Condense. To press together, to lessen.
Congeal. To grow hard; solid.
Consolidate. To unite firmly. See *Nouns.*
Constipate. To crowd together; to stop up.
Crystallize. To form into crystals.
Curd. To coagulate; thicken.

Curdle. To change to curd.
Fix. To set; establish; make firm.
Incrassate. To thicken by introducing another substance, or evaporating a thinner.
Inspissate. To bring to a greater degree of thickness.
Petrify. To turn to stone. See HARDNESS.
Precipitate. To form a solid at the bottom of a liquid. See *Nouns.*
Ram down. To pack tightly.
Render solid. To make firm or hard.
Set. To congeal; solidify.
Solidate. } To become solid. See *Nouns.*
Solidify. }
Squeeze. To press; to compress.
Take a set. To become firm.
Thicken. To congeal; coagulate.

SOLIDITY—*Adjectives.*

Close. Dense; compact.
Coherent } Clinging firmly together. See COHESION.
Cohesive. }
Compact. Molecules not far apart.
Concrete. Hard and firm. See HARDNESS.
Constipated. Pressed together or condensed. See *Verbs.*
Crystalline. Like crystal; hard.
Crystallizable. Able to be reduced to crystal forms.
Dense. Closely crowded, firm; solid.
Gnarled. Full of knots, or hard protuberances.
Grumous. Thick; concrete; clotted.
Impenetrable. That cannot be penetrated.
Impermeable. Not permitting passage through.
Imporous. Destitute of pores.
Incompressible. That cannot be pressed together.
Indiscerptible. } That cannot be separated into parts.
Indissolvable. }
Indissoluble. Not capable of being reduced to a liquid state.
Indivisible. Not to be divided.

Infrangible. Not able to be broken.
Infusible. Not capable of melting
Insoluble. Not to be dissolved.
Knotted. Full of knots.
Knotty. Gnarled; full of hard protuberances.
Lumpish. Heavy; bulky.
Massive. Huge; weighty.
Serried. Compacted, as in rows.
Solid. Hard and firm.
Solidified. Rendered hard.
Stuffy. Strong; hard to breathe.
Substantial. Solid; firm; stable
Thick. } Closely put together; strong.
Thickset. }
Undissolved. Not dissolved.
Unmelted. Not melted.
Unliquefied. Not reduced to a liquid state.
Unthawed. Not changed from a frozen state to a liquid state.

so′-lid-ness. State of being solid. SOLIDITY-RARITY.
so-lil′-o-quize. To talk to oneself. CONVERSATION-MONOLOGUE, SPEECH-INARTICULATENESS.
so-lil′-o-qui″-zing. Talking to oneself. SPEECH-INARTICULATENESS.
so-lil′-o-quy. Monologue. CONVERSATION-MONOLOGUE, SPEECH-INARTICULATENESS.

sol″-i-taire′. Game; recluse. ENTERTAINMENT-WEARINESS, SOCIABILITY-PRIVACY.
sol′-i-ta-ri-ness. Loneliness. SOCIABILITY-PRIVACY.
sol′-i-ta-ry. Alone. SOCIABILITY-PRIVACY, SOLITUDE-COMPANY.
sol′-i-tude. Alone. SOCIABILITY-PRIVACY, SOLITUDE-COMPANY.

SOLITUDE—COMPANY.

Ace. A single mark or spot on a card or die.
Individual. A single person, animal, or thing.
Individuality. The state of pertaining to one particular person or thing.
Isolation. The state of being in a detached position. See UNION-DISUNION.
None else. Only a single person.
No other. A single person or thing.
One. A single individual.
Oneness. The state of being one only.
Solitude. The state of being alone.
Unification. The act of causing to be a unit or one.
Unit. A single person or thing.
Unity. The state of being indivisibly one.

Accompaniment. The state of having several things or ideas associated.
Adjunct. A person or thing accompanying another subordinately.
Association. The state of accompanying another or others.
Coefficiency. Working together to produce the same effect.
Coexistence. Existence together at the same time.
Companionship. The state of accompanying another or others.
Company. The state of being together with another or others.
Concomitance. The state of existing or occurring at the same time.
Context. The portions of a discourse connected with a passage quoted.
Copartnership. The state of being a sharer in business.
Partnership. Accompaniment of another in business.

SOLITUDE—*Verbs.*

Be alone. To be without company.
Be one. To be a single person or thing.
Dine with Duke Humphrey. To go without a dinner; to spend the dinner hour walking in St. Paul's, London, by the tomb of Duke Humphrey.
Isolate. To place in a detached position. See UNION-DISUNION.
Render one. To cause to be one.
Unite. To join two or more into one. See COMPOSITION.

SOLITUDE—*Adjectives.*

Alone. Without company.
Apart. By itself.

COMPANY—*Nouns of Agent.*

Accessory. One who assists in a subordinate position.
Associate. One who accompanies as an equal.
Attendant. One who accompanies to serve.
Classman. One of a class.
Classmate. A member of the same class.
Coefficient. Any agent that accompanies another in action.
Colleague. An associate, as in office.
Companion. One who or that which accompanies another or others.
Concomitant. That which exists or occurs at the same time with something else.
Consort. An equal associate.
Copartner. One who accompanies in business.
Cortége [F.]. A train of attendants.

SOLITUDE—Adjectives—*Continued*.

Azygous. Occurring singly.
Compact. United closely together.
Desolate. Made solitary by violent means.
Dreary. Solitary in a forlorn manner.
First and last. Only.
Indiscerptible. That cannot be deprived of its unity by separation of parts.
Individual. Single.
Insecable. Incapable of being divided by a cutting instrument.
Inseverable. Incapable of being divided by force.
Insular. Standing alone.
Irresolvable. That cannot be divided into its constituent parts.
Isolated. Placed in a detached position.
Kithless. Alone; without kindred.
Lone. Without any thing or person possessing similar qualities.
Lonely. Alone from lack of company.
Lonesome. Wanting the society of human beings.
Odd. Without a like.
One. Being a unit.
Single. Separated from others.
Single-handed. Alone; without assistance.
Singular. Confined to one.
Sole. Being the only one.
Solitary. Lacking life or society.
Solus. Sole.
Unaccompanied. Having no companions.
Unattended. Having no attendants.
Unique. Without another of the same kind.
Unrepeated. Not done again.

SOLITUDE—*Adverbs, etc.*

Alone. Singly.
Apart. In an isolated condition.
By itself. With only one thing itself in consideration.
In the abstract. Apart from all material considerations.
In the singular number. Concerning only one person or thing.
One and a half. Scarcely one.
One at a time. }
One by one. } Singly and in order.
Only. Without another or others.
Per se [L.]. By itself.
Sesqui [L.]. By the ratio one, as 3 to 2, 5 to 4, etc.
Simply. Of itself.
Singly. By itself.

SOLITUDE—*Phrases.*

Du fort au faible [F.]. Strong and weak take together.
Natura il fece, e poi roppe la stampa [It.]. Nature made him and then broke the mold.

COMPANY—*Continued from Column* 2.

COMPANY—*Phrases.*

Noscitur a sociis [L.]. He is known by his company.
Virtutis fortuna comes [L.]. Fortune is the companion of virtue.

COMPANY—Nouns of Agent—*Continued*.

Escort. A guard accompanying a person or property.
Fellow. An associate of equal rank.
Hanger-on. One who accompanies in a servile manner.
Partner. One who takes part or is associated with another.
Satellite. An obsequious or servile follower or attendant.
Shadow. An inseparable companion.
Spouse. An associate in marriage.

COMPANY—*Verbs.*

Accompany. To go with as an associate.
Associate with. To be in company with.
Attend. To wait upon as an inferior.
Bear company. To accompany.
Bring in its train. To have attendant results.
Coexist. To exist together at the same time.
Couple with. To associate with.
Go hand in hand with. To accompany in an intimate manner.
Hang on. To accompany persistently.
Keep company. To accompany.
Row in the same boat. To be closely associated with.
Synchronize. To concur in point of time.
Wait on. To serve as an attendant.

COMPANY—*Adjectives.*

Accessory. Aiding the principal design, or assisting subordinately the chief agent.
Accompanying. Going along with as a companion or attendant.
Associated with. Joined.
Attendant. Following or accompanying.
Concomitant. Occurring together at the same time.
Coupled with. United.
Fellow. Associated in action, location, or position.
Joint. Involving the combined action of two or more.
Obbligato [It.]. A necessary accessory.
Twin. Being one of a pair.

COMPANY—*Adverbs, etc.*

Along with. In company with.
And. In addition.
Arm in arm. Accompanying with arms interlocked.
Cheek by jole. }
Cheek by jowl. } With cheeks together.
Collectively. In a general mass or body.
Hand in hand. Accompanying with hands joined.
Herewith. Along with this.
In a body. Collectively.
In company with. Accompanying.
Side by side. Closely joined.
Therewith. Along with that.
Together. In company.
Together with. In union with.
With. In the company or companionship of; jointly.
Withal. With the rest.

(Continued on Column 1.)

---

sol″-mi-za′-tion. Singing. MUSICIAN.
so′-lo. One voice. MUSIC.
Sol′-o-mon. King; sage. SAGACITY-INCAPACITY, SAGE-FOOL.
So′-lon. Sage. SAGACITY-INCAPACITY, SAGE-FOOL.
sol′-stice. Point of greatest declination of the sun. ASTRONOMY.
sol″-u-bil′-i-ty. Capacity of being dissolved. LIQUID-GAS.
sol′-u-ble. Dissolvable. LIQUEFACTION-VOLATILIZATION, LIQUID-GAS.
sol′-u-ble-ness. State of being soluble. LIQUID-GAS.
solus [L.] (so′-lus). Alone. SOLITUDE-COMPANY.
so-lu′-tion. Liquid; answer. INTERPRETATION-MISINTERPRETATION, INVESTIGATION-ANSWER, LIQUEFACTION-VOLATILIZATION; **solution of continuity,** CONTINUITY-INTERRUPTION.
solve. Clear. DISCOVERY, INTERPRETATION-MISINTERPRETATION, INVESTIGATION-ANSWER, LIQUEFACTION-VOLATILIZATION.
sol′-ven-cy. Capable of being dissolved, as debts. AFFLUENCE-PENURY.

sol′-vent. Assets; fluid. AFFLUENCE-PENURY, LIQUEFACTION-VOLATILIZATION.
so-mat′-ic. Of a body. MATERIALITY-SPIRITUALITY.
so-mat′-ics. Organic bodies. MATERIALITY-SPIRITUALITY.
som′-ber. Dark; gloomy. GRAY-BROWN, LIGHT-DARKNESS, LIGHTHEARTEDNESS-DEJECTION, WHITENESS-BLACKNESS.
som′-brous. Somber. LIGHT-DARKNESS.
some. Quantity; number. MAGNITUDE-SMALLNESS, PLURALITY-FRACTION, QUANTITY-MEASURE; **at some other time,** TIME; **in some degree,** MAGNITUDE-SMALLNESS, QUANTITY-MEASURE; **in some place,** EXTENSION-PLACE; **somebody,** CONSEQUENCE-INSIGNIFICANCE, HUMANITY, REPUTATION-DISCREDIT; **some ten or a dozen,** MULTIPLICITY-PAUCITY; **some time ago,** FUTURE-PAST; **some time or other,** TIME.
some′-how. In some way. INSTRUMENTALITY.
some′-how or oth′-er. In some way. INSTRUMENTALITY, RATIONALE-LUCK.
some′-one. A person. HUMANITY.
som′-er-sault. Reversal. REVERSAL.
som′-er-set. A somersault. REVERSAL.

some'-thing. Particular. MAGNITUDE-SMALLNESS, MATERIALITY-SPIRITUALITY, SUBSTANCE-NULLITY; **something else,** VARIATION; **something like,** LIKENESS-UNLIKENESS; **something or other,** CERTAINTY-DOUBT.

some'-times". At some time. FREQUENCY-RARITY.

some'-what". More or less. CONSEQUENCE-INSIGNIFICANCE, MAGNITUDE-SMALLNESS.

some'-where". In some place. EXTENSION-PLACE; **somewhere about,** MAGNITUDE-SMALLNESS.

som-nam'-bu-lism. Sleep-walking. MEANING-JARGON, TRAVELING-NAVIGATION.

som-nam'-bu-list. Walker; dreamer. FANCY, WAYFARER-SEAFARER.

somnia ægri, vana [L.] (som'-ni-ɑ ī'-graī, vê'-nɑ). A sick man's empty dreams. FANCY.

som-nif'-er-ous. Narcotic; sleep. ACTIVITY-INDOLENCE, ENTERTAINMENT-WEARINESS.

som-nif'-ic. Producing sleep. ACTIVITY-INDOLENCE.

som'-no-lence. Drowsiness. ACTIVITY-INDOLENCE.

som'-no-lent. Drowsy. ACTIVITY-INDOLENCE.

son. Male child. PARENTAGE-PROGENY.

so-na'-ta. Composition. MUSIC.

Sonderbund [G.] (son'-der-bund). Band. CONTRACT.

song. Music; ballad. MUSIC, POETRY-PROSE; **death-song,** JUBILATION-LAMENTATION, LIFE-DEATH; **for a mere song,** COSTLINESS-CHEAPNESS; **love-song,** POETRY-PROSE; **no song, no supper,** PRICE-DISCOUNT; **old song,** CONSEQUENCE-INSIGNIFICANCE.

songes, tous, sont mensonges [F.] (son·zh, tu, son· man·son·zh'). Dreams all are lies all. FANCY, TRUTHFULNESS-FALSEHOOD.

song'-ster. Singer. MUSICIAN.

song'-sters. Singers. **Feathered songsters,** MUSICIAN.

so-nif'-er-ous. Sound. SOUND-SILENCE.

son'-net. Poem. POETRY-PROSE.

son"-net-eer'. Composer. POETRY-PROSE.

so"-no'-rif'-ic. Producing sound. SOUND-SILENCE.

so-no'-rous. Sounding; loud. LOUDNESS-FAINTNESS, SIMPLICITY-FLORIDNESS, SOUND-SILENCE.

so-no'-rous-ness. A sounding. SOUND-SILENCE.

son'-ship. State of being a son. PARENTAGE-PROGENY.

sons of. Identified with. **Sons of Belial,** GODLINESS-UNGODLINESS; **sons of God,** ANGEL-SATAN.

son'-tag. A woman's cape. DRESS-UNDRESS.

soo'-fee. A pantheist. ORTHODOXY-HETERODOXY.

soo'-fee-ism. Pantheism. ORTHODOXY-HETERODOXY.

soon. Shortly; early. EARLINESS-LATENESS, FUTURE-PAST, LASTINGNESS-TRANSIENTNESS; **too soon for,** PERIODICITY-IRREGULARITY.

soon'-er. Before. **Sooner or later,** FUTURE-PAST, TIME; **sooner said than done,** DIFFICULTY-FACILITY.

soot. Black; carbon. CLEANNESS-FILTHINESS, WHITENESS-BLACKNESS.

sooth. Truth. PROPHECY; **in good sooth,** TRUTHFULNESS-FALSEHOOD.

soothe. Calm; soften. ADULATION-DISPARAGEMENT, ALLEVIATION-AGGRAVATION, TURBULENCE-CALMNESS.

sooth'-ing. Faint. LOUDNESS-FAINTNESS

sooth'-say". Divination. PROPHECY.

sooth'-say"-er. Diviner. DEVOTION-MAGICIAN, SOOTHSAYER.

SOOTHSAYER.

Aruspex. } A soothsayer or diviner.
Aruspice. }

Augur. An official in Rome who foretold future events by the interpretation of omens.

Cassandra. A prophetess, daughter of Priam and Hecuba, whose predictions, always true, were never credited.

Delphian oracle. The oracle of Apollo at Delphi.

Fortune-teller. One who pretends to foretell future events of a person's life.

Geomancer. One who foretells events by means of circles or points drawn on the ground or on paper.

Haruspice. A soothsayer.

Interpreter, etc. One who unfolds or explains anything. See INTERPRETER.

Monitor. One who advises or reproves by way of caution.

Old Moore. A fortune-teller.

Oracle. One of infallible knowledge or authority.

Prophet. One who foretells the future.

Pythia. The priestess of Apollo who uttered his oracles at Delphi.

Pythian oracle. The oracle of Apollo at Delphi.

Python. A soothsayer or soothsaying spirit.

Pythoness. The priestess of the Delphic oracle.

Seer. A prophet; one who foretells future events.

Sibyl. A woman that prophesied under the supposed inspiration of some deity, and delivered her oracles in a frenzied state.

Sibylline leaves. Fragmentary writings easily scattered, mixed, or lost.

Soothsayer. One who claims to have supernatural power to foretell future events.

Sorcerer, etc. One who uses preternatural powers. See DEVOTION-MAGICIAN.

Sphinx. A female monster of Thebes who strangled all passers-by unable to guess a riddle she proposed.

Tiresias. A blind Theban seer.

Witch. One who deals with evil spirits, usually a woman.

Zadkiel. The pseudonym of a noted English astrologer.

sooth'-say"-ing. Prophecy. PROPHECY.

soot'-y. Black. CLEANNESS-FILTHINESS, WHITENESS-BLACKNESS.

sop. Piece; concession; morsel. MAGNITUDE-SMALLNESS, MOTIVE-CAPRICE, NUTRIMENT-EXCRETION, RECOMPENSE-PUNITION, SAGE-FOOL; **sop in the pan,** MOTIVE-CAPRICE; **sop to Cerberus,** HEED-DISREGARD.

soph. Sophomore. INSTRUCTOR-PUPIL, SCHOLAR-DUNCE.

so'-phi. Pantheist; king. CHIEF-UNDERLING, MINISTRY-LAITY.

soph'-ism. Fallacy. ADAGE-NONSENSE, RATIOCINATION-CASUISTRY.

soph'-ist. Philosopher. GULL-DECEIVER, SCHOLAR-DUNCE.

soph'-ist-er. Student. INSTRUCTOR-PUPIL, SCHOLAR-DUNCE.

so-phis'-tic-al. Fallacious. RATIOCINATION-CASUISTRY.

so-phis'-ti-cate. Delude; impure. BETTERMENT-DETERIORATION, MIXTURE-HOMOGENEITY.

so-phis'-ti-ca"-ted. Adulterated. TRUTHFULNESS-FRAUD.

so-phis"-ti-ca'-tion. A corruption. MIXTURE-HOMOGENEITY.

soph'-ist-ry. Casuistry. ADAGE-NONSENSE, EDUCATION-LEARNING, RATIOCINATION-CASUISTRY, SAGACITY-INCAPACITY.

soph'-o-more. In schools and colleges having a four-year course, a student of the second year. EDUCATION-MISTEACHING.

so"-por-if'-er-ous. Bringing sleep ACTIVITY-INDOLENCE.

so"-por-if'-ic. Sleep-producing. ACTIVITY-INDOLENCE, ENTERTAINMENT-WEARINESS.

so'-por-ous. Soporific. ACTIVITY-INDOLENCE.

so-pra'-no. Voice. CACOPHONY.

sor'-cer-er. Wizard. DEVOTION-MAGICIAN, SOOTHSAYER.

sor'-cer-y. Magic. DEVOTION-MAGIC.

sor'-des. Discharge. CLEANNESS-FILTHINESS.

sor'-det. Mute. MUSICAL INSTRUMENTS.

sor'-did. Mean; mercenary. DESIRE-DISTASTE, EXTRAVAGANCE-AVARICE.

sor'-dine. Damper. MUSICAL INSTRUMENTS.

sore. Tender; trouble. CONTENTEDNESS-DISCONTENTMENT, FAVORITE-ANGER, HEALTH-SICKNESS, PLEASURABLENESS-PAINFULNESS, PLEASURE-PAIN, SENSUALITY-SUFFERING; **sore place,** SENSITIVENESS-APATHY; **sore subject,** FAVORITE-ANGER, PLEASURABLENESS-PAINFULNESS.

sore'-ly. Greatly. MAGNITUDE-SMALLNESS.

sore'-ness. A tenderness. CONTENTEDNESS-DISCONTENTMENT, FAVORITE-ANGER, SENSUALITY-SUFFERING.

s'orienter [F.] (so-ri-an'-tê'). To find one's bearings. AIM-ABERRATION.

so-ri'-tes. Syllogism. RATIOCINATION-INSTINCT.

so-ror'-i-cide. One who kills a sister. LIFE-KILLING.

so-ro'-sis. A woman's club. SOCIABILITY-PRIVACY, UNION-DISUNION.

sor'-rel. Herb. REDNESS-GREENNESS.

sor'-row. Grief. PLEASURE-PAIN; **give sorrow words,** JUBILATION-LAMENTATION.

sor'-row-ful. Full of sorrow. JUBILATION-LAMENTATION, PLEASURE-PAIN.

sor'-row-ing. Grieving. JUBILATION-LAMENTATION, PLEASURE-PAIN.

sor'-ry. Grieved; poor. CONSEQUENCE-INSIGNIFICANCE, GENTILITY-COMMONALTY, PLEASURE-PAIN; **be sorry for,** COMPASSION-RUTHLESSNESS, REPENTANCE-OBDURACY; **cut a sorry figure,** REPUTATION-DISCREDIT; **in a sorry plight,** SUCCESS-FAILURE; **make a sorry face,** REPUTATION-DISCREDIT; **sorry sight,** LIGHTHEARTEDNESS-DEJECTION, PLEASURABLENESS-PAINFULNESS.

sort. Kind; degree; classify. DIVISION, ORGANIZATION-DISORGANIZATION, QUANTITY-MEASURE; **sort with,** SOCIABILITY-PRIVACY.

sort'-a-ble. Suitable. HARMONY-DISCORD.

sort'-ance. Agreement. HARMONY-DISCORD.

sortes [L.] (sor'-tîz) Lots. PURPOSE-LUCK, RATIONALE-LUCK.

sortes Virgilianæ [L.] (sor'-tîz vir-jil''-i-ê'-nî). Virgilian lots. DEVOTION-MAGIC, PURPOSE-LUCK.

sor'-tie. Sally. ATTACK-DEFENSE.

sor'-ti-lege. Lots; sorcery. DEVOTION-MAGIC, PROPHECY.

sor'-ti-leg-y. Sortilege. PURPOSE-LUCK.

sort'-ing. Arranging. ORGANIZATION-DISORGANIZATION.

sor-ti'-tion. Casting lots. PURPOSE-LUCK.

sorts, out of. Indisposed. FAVORITE-MOROSENESS, HEALTH-SICKNESS.

so'-so''. Mediocre. CONSEQUENCE-INSIGNIFICANCE, FAULTLESSNESS-FAULTINESS, MAGNITUDE-SMALLNESS.

sot. Stupid; drunkard. SAGE-FOOL, TEETOTALISM-INTEMPERANCE.

sot à triple étage [F.] (sot a tripl ê-tazh') A most egregious fool. SAGE-FOOL.

sot'-tish. Dull; drunk. SAGACITY-INCAPACITY, TEETOTALISM-INTEMPERANCE.

sotto voce [It.] (sot'-to vo'-chê). Softly. ENLIGHTENMENT-SECRECY, LOUDNESS-FAINTNESS, VOCALIZATION-MUTENESS.

sou [F.] (su). Coin. MONEY.

sou, qui n'a pas le [F.] (su, ki na pa le). Who has not a sou. AFFLUENCE-PENURY.

sou''-brette'. Actress; maid. CHIEF-UNDERLING.

sough. Drain; sewer. FAULTLESSNESS-FAULTINESS, MIND-IMBECILITY.

soul. Essence; identity. AFFECTIONS, HUMANITY, MIND-IMBECILITY, SAGACITY-INCAPACITY, SUBJECTIVENESS-OBJECTIVENESS; **flow of soul,** CONVERSATION-MONOLOGUE; **have one's whole soul in his work,** TOIL-RELAXATION; **not a soul,** PRESENCE-ABSENCE; **not dare to say one's soul is his own,** LIBERTY-SUBJECTION, SANGUINENESS-TIMIDITY; **soul of wit,** TERSENESS-PROLIXITY.

soul'-less. Unfeeling; inactive. ACTIVITY-INDOLENCE, SENSITIVENESS-APATHY.

soul'-sick''. Anxious. LIGHTHEARTEDNESS-DEJECTION.

soul'-stir''-ring. Feeling. EXCITATION, FEELING.

soul'-sub-du''-ing. A calming. EXCITATION.

sound. Right; whole; deep; complete; noise; distance. CONVENTIONALITY-UNCONVENTIONALITY, DEEPNESS-SHALLOWNESS, FAULTLESSNESS-FAULTINESS, GOODNESS-BADNESS, GULF-PLAIN, HEALTH-SICKNESS, INVESTIGATION-ANSWER, MAGNITUDE-SMALLNESS, MENSURATION, MUTABILITY-STABILITY, ORTHODOXY-HETERODOXY, SAGACITY-INCAPACITY, SANENESS-LUNACY, SOUND-SILENCE, STRENGTH-WEAKNESS, TRUTH-ERROR; **catch a sound,** HEARING-DEAFNESS; **full of sound and fury,** MEANING-JARGON, PRESUMPTION-OBSEQUIOUSNESS; **safe and sound,** CONVERSATION, HEALTH-SICKNESS; **sound a retreat,** ADVANCE-RETROGRESSION; **sound asleep,** ACTIVITY-INDOLENCE; **sound a trumpet,** ALARM, PUBLICITY; **sound mind,** SANENESS-LUNACY; **sound of limb,** HEALTH-SICKNESS; **sound of wind,** HEALTH-SICKNESS; **sound reasoning,** RATIOCINATION-INSTINCT; **sound sleep,** ACTIVITY-INDOLENCE; **sound the alarm,** ALARM, SANGUINENESS-TIMIDITY, SIGN, WARNING; **sound the horn,** MUSICIAN; **sound the note of preparation,** PREPARATION-NONPREPARATION; **sound the praises of,** APPROVAL-DISAPPROVAL.

SOUND—SILENCE.

Accent. Stress of voice on a particular syllable of a word.
Audibility. The state or quality of being audible.
Birr. A whirring or buzzing sound.
Cadence. Modulation of the voice, as in poetry or music.
Intonation. Modulation of the voice in speaking.
Noise. A sound of any kind, especially a confused or disagreeable kind.
Resonance, etc. The quality of being resonant; the act of resounding. See RESONANCE.
Sonorousness, etc. The quality of being loud and full-sounding, etc.
Sound. The sensation produced through the organs of hearing.
Strain. A portion of a musical composition.
Tone. Sound in relation to volume, duration, quality, and pitch.
Twang. A sharp ringing sound; nasal modulation of the voice.
Voice, etc. Sound produced by the vocal organs. See VOCALIZATION.

Sound—Scientific Nouns.

Acoustics. Branch of physics treating of the phenomena and laws of sound.
Diacoustics. The science of the refraction of sounds.
Diaphonics. Diacoustics.
Phonetics. The science of articulate sound.
Phonics. Phonetics.
Phonography. The art or science of writing by sound.
Phonology. The science of human vocal sounds and their relations.

Awful silence. } A silence that fills one with awe and fear.
Dead silence. }
Deathlike silence. A silence resembling the silence of death.
Hush. Profound silence.
Lull. Momentary quiet.
Muteness, etc. The state or quality of being mute. See VOCALIZATION-MUTENESS.
Peace. A state of quiet or tranquillity.
Silence. The state or quality of being silent; absence of sound.
Solemn silence. Impressive or awe-inspiring silence.
Stillness, etc. The state or quality of being still. See MOVEMENT-REST.

SILENCE—Verbs.

Be silent. To be without sound.
Hold one's tongue, etc. Refrain from speaking. See TALKATIVENESS-TACITURNITY.
Hush. Be or cause to be quiet.
Muffle. Deaden the sound of.
Muzzle. Put to silence.
Put to silence. } To prevent all sound. See VOCALIZATION-MUTENESS.
Render silent. }
Silence. Compel to keep silent.
Stifle. To silence by force.
Still. Make quiet; hush.
Stop. Cease or cause to cease from speaking.

SOUND—SILENCE—*Continued*

Sound—*Verbs*.

Emit sound. } To produce vibrations which are perceived by the
Give out sound. } ear.
Make a noise. To produce a disagreeable sound.
Produce sound. To affect the organ of hearing.
Resound, etc. To emit a loud, prolonged sound. See RESONANCE.
Sound. To make a sound upon or cause to resound.

Sound—*Adjectives*.

Audible. Capable of being heard.
Distinct. Clearly and easily heard.
Phonetic. Relating to or representing articulate sounds or speech.
Resonant. Sending back or capable of sending back or of prolonging sound.
Soniferous. Producing or conducting sound.
Sonorific. Producing sound.
Sonorous. Loud and full-sounding.
Sounding. Giving forth a sound.
Stertorous. Having a snoring sound.

Sound—*Phrase*.

Forensis strepitus [L.]. The clamor of the forum.

SILENCE—PHRASES—*Continued from Column 2.*

One might hear a pin drop.
Tacent, satis laudant [L.]. They are silent, they give enough praise.

Silence—*Adjectives*.

Awful. Inspiring or manifesting awe.
Deathlike. Silent, like the silence of death.
Hushed, etc. Made quiet. See *Verbs.*
Inaudible, etc. Incapable of being heard. See LOUDNESS-FAINTNESS.
Mute, etc. Uttering no word or sound. See VOCALIZATION-MUTENESS.
Noiseless. Without noise.
Silent. Making no sound; not speaking; still.
Silent as the grave. Silent, like the silence of death.
Soft. Not loud or harsh.
Solemn. Impressive; awe-inspiring.
Soundless. Without sound.
Still. Making no sound; silent.
Stilly Still; subdued in sound.

Silence—*Adverbs, etc.*

Silently, etc. Without making any sound.
Sub silentio [L.]. In silence.

Silence—*Interjections*.

Chut! hush! *pax* [L.]. Peace; silence! soft! tush! tut! whist!

Silence—*Phrases*.

Grosse Seelen dulden still [G.]. Great souls suffer in silence.
One might hear a feather drop.

(*Continued on Column 1.*)

---

sound'-mind''-ed. Strong of mind. SANENESS-LUNACY.
sound'-ing. Sonorous. Sounding big, SIMPLICITY-FLORIDNESS; sounding brass, MEANING-JARGON.
sound'-ing-board''. Board in instrument. MUSICAL INSTRUMENTS.
sound'-ings. Depth. DEEPNESS-SHALLOWNESS.
sound'-less. Silent; unfathomable. DEEPNESS-SHALLOWNESS, SOUND-SILENCE.
sound'-ness. Healthiness; freedom from injury. HEALTH-SICKNESS, MUTABILITY-STABILITY, ORTHODOXY-HETERODOXY, SANENESS-LUNACY.
soup. Liquid. NUTRIMENT-EXCRETION, VISCIDITY-FOAM.
soupçon [F.] (sup-son'). Taste. MAGNITUDE-SMALLNESS, MIXTURE-HOMOGENEITY.
soupe maigre [F.] (sup mêgr). Fish soup. FASTING-GLUTTONY.
sour. Acid; morose. ALLEVIATION-AGGRAVATION, CONTENTEDNESS-DISCONTENTMENT, FAVORITE-QUARRELSOMENESS, POLITENESS-IMPOLITENESS, SWEETNESS-ACIDITY; sour grapes, POSSIBILITY-IMPOSSIBILITY, PRETEXT; sour the temper, PLEASURABLENESS-PAINFULNESS.
source. Cause; beginning. BEGINNING-END, CAUSE-EFFECT.
sour'-det. Damper. MUSICAL INSTRUMENTS.
sourdine, à la [F.] (sur-dîn', a la). Softly. ENLIGHTENMENT-SECRECY, LOUDNESS-FAINTNESS.
soured. Spoiled. CONTENTEDNESS-DISCONTENTMENT.
sour'-ish. Somewhat sour. SWEETNESS-ACIDITY.
sour'-ness. Acidity. SWEETNESS-ACIDITY.
souse. Drench. SPRING-DIVE, WATER-AIR.
sous tous les rapports [F.] (su tu lê ra-por'). In all respects. ENTIRETY-DEFICIENCY, TRUTH-ERROR.
south. Direction. AIM-ABERRATION; north and south, LATERALITY-CONTRAPOSITION.
South-ern. Direction. LATERALITY-CONTRAPOSITION; Southern Cross, UNIVERSE.
sou''-ve-nir'. Keepsake. REMEMBRANCE-FORGETFULNESS.
sov'-er-eign. Ruler; royal; superior. CHIEF-UNDERLING, RULE-LICENSE, STRENGTH-WEAKNESS, SUPREMACY-SUBORDINACY; sovereign contempt, REGARD-SCORN; sovereign remedy, REMEDY-BANE.
sov'-er-eign-ty. Dominion. DIVINITY, RULE-LICENSE.

sow. Pig; female. DOMESTICATION-AGRICULTURE, FAUNA-FLORA, GATHERING-SCATTERING, MALE-FEMALE; get the wrong sow by the ear, DECISION-MISJUDGMENT, SKILL-UNSKILFULNESS, SUCCESS-FAILURE, TRUTH-ERROR.
sow. sow broadcast, scatter; farm. EXTRAVAGANCE-AVARICE, GATHERING-SCATTERING; sow dissension, LOVE-HATE, VARIANCE-ACCORD; sow one's wild oats, BETTERMENT-DETERIORATION, ENTERTAINMENT-WEARINESS, MODERATION-SELFINDULGENCE, VIRTUE-VICE; sow the sand, USEFULNESS-USELESSNESS; sow the seed, PREPARATION-NONPREPARATION; sow the seeds of, CAUSE-EFFECT, EDUCATION-MISTEACHING.
sow'-ing. Scattering. PREPARATION-NONPREPARATION.
spa. Spring. DWELLER-HABITATION, REMEDY-BANE.
space. Distance; period; degree. DURATION-NEVERNESS, EXTENSION-INEXTENSION, MELODY-DISSONANCE, REMOTENESS-NEARNESS; celestial spaces, UNIVERSE.
spa'-cious. Ample in room. EXTENSION-INEXTENSION, GREATNESS-LITTLENESS.
spad. Spade. CONVEYANCE-VESSEL.
spade. Implement. CONVEYANCE-VESSEL; call a spade a spade, CRAFT-ARTLESSNESS, SIMPLICITY-FLORIDNESS.
spade'-hus''-band-ry. Gardening. DOMESTICATION, AGRICULTURE.
spa'-hi. Cavalry. BELLIGERENT.
span. Link; measure. CONNECTIVE, DURATION-NEVERNESS, LASTINGNESS-TRANSIENTNESS, LENGTH-SHORTNESS, MENSURATION, REMOTENESS-NEARNESS, UNION-DISUNION.
span'-drel. Decoration. ARCHITECTURE.
span'-gle. Glitter; tin-foil. EMBELLISHMENT-DISFIGUREMENT, LIGHT-DARKNESS.
span'-iel. Dog; sycophant. FAUNA-FLORA, PRESUMPTION-OBSEQUIOUSNESS.
spank. Slap; go fast. RECOMPENSE-PUNITION, SWIFTNESS-SLOWNESS.
spank'-er. Something large. GREATNESS-LITTLENESS.
spank'-ing. Swift. GREATNESS-LITTLENESS; spanking pace, SWIFTNESS-SLOWNESS.
spar. Pole; box; wrangle. STRIFE-PEACE, SUSPENSION-SUPPORT, VARIANCE-ACCORD.

spare. Forbear; allow; reserve; thin; scanty. AC-TION-PASSIVENESS, BREADTH-NARROWNESS, DUTY-IMMUNITY, EXCESS-LACK, GENEROSITY-FRUGALITY, GIVING - RECEIVING, KEEPING - RELINQUISHMENT, MODERATION - SELFINDULGENCE, QUEST - EVASION, STORE, USE-DISUSE; **enough and to spare,** ENOUGH; **not a moment to spare,** ACTIVITY-INDOLENCE; **spare diet,** FASTING-GLUTTONY; **spare no expense,** GENEROSITY-FRUGALITY; **spare no pains,** TOIL-RELAXATION; **spare room,** EXTENSION-INEXTENSION; **spare time,** HURRY-LEISURE; **to spare,** EXCESS-LACK.

spared. Alive. **Be spared,** LIFE-DEATH; **it cannot be spared,** NEED.

spar″-ge-fac′-tion. Sprinkling. GATHERING-SCATTERING, WATER-AIR.

spar′-ing. Little; economy; frugal. EXTRAVAGANCE-AVARICE, GENEROSITY - FRUGALITY, MAGNITUDE-SMALLNESS, MODERATION - SELFINDULGENCE; **sparing of praise,** APPROVAL-DISAPPROVAL; **sparing of words,** TALKATIVENESS-TACITURNITY; **with a sparing hand,** EXTRAVAGANCE-AVARICE; **with no sparing hand,** ENOUGH.

spar′-ing-ly. In a sparing manner. GENEROSITY-FRUGALITY.

spark. Glisten; light; top. HEAT-COLD, LIGHT-DARKNESS, LUMINARY-SHADE, MAGNITUDE-SMALLNESS, PRESUMPTION-OBSEQUIOUSNESS, WAG; **as the sparks fly upwards,** HABIT-DESUETUDE; **vital spark,** LIFE-DEATH.

spark′-le. Glisten; effervesce. LIGHT-DARKNESS, VISCIDITY-FOAM.

spark′-ling. Brilliant. BEAUTY-UGLINESS, EXCITATION, FORCE-WEAKNESS, LIGHT-DARKNESS, LIGHT-HEARTEDNESS-DEJECTION, VISCIDITY-FOAM, WITTINESS-DULNESS; **with sparkling eyes,** PLEASURE-PAIN.

spar′-ring. Boxing. STRIFE-PEACE.

sparse. Scattered. GATHERING-SCATTERING.

Spar′- ta - cus. Gladiator. INSUBORDINATION - OBEDIENCE.

spasm. Convulsion; pain. AGITATION, REVOLUTION, SENSUALITY-SUFFERING, TURBULENCE-CALMNESS.

spas-mod′-ic. Convulsive; violent. CONTINUITY-INTERRUPTION, LASTINGNESS-TRANSIENTNESS, MUTABILITY-STABILITY, PERIODICITY-IRREGULARITY, TURBULENCE-CALMNESS.

spat. Spawn. PARENTAGE-PROGENY.

spat′-ter. Splash. CLEANNESS-FILTHINESS.

spat′-ter-dash″. Legging. DRESS-UNDRESS.

spat′-u-la. Spoon. CONTENTS - RECEIVER, CONVEYANCE-VESSEL.

spav′-ined. Halting. HEALTH-SICKNESS.

spawn. Eggs. CLEANNESS-FILTHINESS, PARENTAGE-PROGENY.

speak. Utter. SPEECH-INARTICULATENESS; **speak for,** JUSTIFICATION - CHARGE; **speak for itself,** CLEARNESS - OBSCURITY, EVIDENCE - COUNTEREVIDENCE, MANIFESTATION - LATENCY; **speak ill of,** ADULATION - DISPARAGEMENT, APPROVAL - DISAPPROVAL ; **speak low,** VOCALIZATION - MUTENESS; **speak of,** MEANING - JARGON, PUBLICITY, SPEECH - INARTICULATENESS; **speak one fair,** POLITENESS-IMPOLITENESS; **speak out,** CRAFT-ARTLESSNESS, EXPOSURE-HIDINGPLACE, MANIFESTATION-LATENCY; **speak softly,** VOCALIZATION-MUTENESS; **speak to,** ADDRESS-RESPONSE; **speak up,** CRY-ULULATION, LOUDNESS-FAINTNESS; **speak up for,** JUSTIFICATION-CHARGE; **speak volumes,** EVIDENCE-COUNTEREVIDENCE; **speak well of,** APPROVAL-DISAPPROVAL.

speak′-er. Orator; officer. INTERPRETER, MANAGER, PRESIDENT-MEMBER, SPEECH-INARTICULATENESS.

speak′-ing. Conversing; **much speaking.** TALKATIVENESS-TACITURNITY; **on speaking terms,** AMITY-HOSTILITY; **speaking likeness,** DELINEATION-CARICATURE; **way of speaking,** TROPE.

speak′-ing-trum″-pet. Trumpet for shouting orders. HEARING-DEAFNESS.

spear. Weapon. APERTURE - CLOSURE, MOVEMENT-REST, WEAPON.

spear′-man. Warrior. BELLIGERENT.

spe′-cial. Express. UNIVERSALITY - PARTICULARITY; **special pleader,** ADVOCATE; **special pleading,** PRETEXT, RATIOCINATION-CASUISTRY.

speciale gratia [L.] (spe-shi-ê′-lî grê′-shi-α). With special favor. LEAVE-PROHIBITION.

spécialité [F.] (spê-si-α-li-tê′). A speciality. UNIVERSALITY-PARTICULARITY.

spec″-i-al′-i-ty. Peculiarity. UNIVERSALITY-PARTICULARITY.

spe′-cial-ty. Deed. SECURITY.

spe′-cie. Coin. MONEY.

spe′-ci-es. Group. APPEARANCE-DISAPPEARANCE, DIVISION ; **human species,** HUMANITY.

spe-cif′-ic. Particular. QUEST-EVASION, UNIVERSALITY-PARTICULARITY; **specific gravity,** CHEMISTRY, HEAVINESS-LIGHTNESS, SOLIDITY-RARITY.

spec″-i-fi-ca′-tion. Detail. ACCOUNT.

spe-cif′-ic-ness. Exactness. UNIVERSALITY-PARTICULARITY.

spec′-i-fy. Tell; state. ENLIGHTENMENT-SECRECY, NAME-MISNOMER, UNIVERSALITY-PARTICULARITY.

spec′-i-men. Sample. CONVENTIONALITY-UNCONVENTIONALITY.

spe′-cious. Plausible. ADULATION - DISPARAGEMENT, BEAUTY-UGLINESS, JUSTIFICATION-CHARGE, LIKELIHOOD-UNLIKELIHOOD, RATIOCINATION-INSTINCT.

spe′-cious-ness. Plausibility. RATIOCINATION-INSTINCT.

speck. Particle. EMBELLISHMENT-DISFIGUREMENT, MAGNITUDE-SMALLNESS.

speck′-le. Spot; variegate. EMBELLISHMENT-DISFIGUREMENT, VARIEGATION.

speck′-led. Spotted. VARIEGATION.

spec′-ta-cle. Exhibition; sight. ACTING, CONCEIT-DIFFIDENCE, GULL-DECEIVER, PHENOMENON.

spec′-ta-cles. Eye-glasses. OPTICAL INSTRUMENTS

spec-tac′-u-lar. Display. POMP.

spec′-ta-tor. Eye-witness. ONLOOKER.

spec′-ter. Apparition. BEAUTY-UGLINESS, JOVE-FIEND, SIGHT-DIMSIGHTEDNESS.

spec′-tral. Ghostly. JOVE-FIEND.

spec′-tro-scope. Analyzer. ASTRONOMY, CHEMISTRY, COLOR-ACHROMATISM, OPTICAL INSTRUMENTS.

spec′-trum. Image. COLOR - ACHROMATISM, SIGHT-DIMSIGHTEDNESS, VARIEGATION.

spec′-u-late. Consider; view; invest. EXCHANGE, HYPOTHESIS, MARK-OBLITERATION, PURPOSE-LUCK, SIGHT-BLINDNESS, VENTURE.

spec″-u-la′-tion. Opinion; cards. ENTERTAINMENT-WEARINESS, EXCHANGE, HYPOTHESIS, MARK-OBLITERATION, PURPOSE-LUCK, RATIONALE-LUCK, SIGHT-BLINDNESS, TRIAL, VENTURE.

spec′-u-la-tive. Reflective. HYPOTHESIS, REFLECTION-VACANCY.

spec′-u-la″-tor. One who speculates. LABOR-CAPITAL.

spec′-u-lum. Instrument. OPTICAL INSTRUMENTS.

speculum, veluti in [L.] (spec′-yu-lum, vel′-yu-tai in). As in a looking-glass. VISIBILITY-INVISIBILITY.

sped. Finished. COMPLETION-NONCOMPLETION.

speech. Language. SPEECH-INARTICULATENESS; **figure of speech,** GULL-HYPERBOLE, MEANING-JARGON, TROPE; **parts of speech,** GRAMMAR-SOLECISM.

SPEECH—INARTICULATENESS.

Allocution, etc. A formal exhortation or address. See AD-DRESS.

Brogue, etc. A dialectic pronunciation, especially the Irish manner of pronouncing English. See WORD-NEOLOGY.

SPEECH—INARTICULATENESS—*Continued.*

Declamation. A set speech intended for recitation from memory in public.
Delivery. Mode of utterance or articulation.
Effusion. A pouring forth of speech.
Faculty of speech. The power of expressing thought in spoken words.
Formal speech. A dignified and impressive speech.
Harangue. An extemporaneous and forcible speech to a public assembly.
Interlocution, etc. Alternate speaking. See CONVERSATION.
Lecture. A formal or methodical discourse intended for instruction.
Locution. A manner of speaking.
Oral communication. Conveyance of thought in spoken words.
Oration. An elaborate or formal public speech.
Oratory. The ability so to speak in public as to please, arouse, convince, or persuade.
Palaver. Vain and idle speech.
Parlance. Mode of speech.
Parole. In law, an oral statement.
Peroration. The conclusion of a speech.
Prattle. Childish speech.
Prolation. The act of uttering articulate sounds.
Recitation. The act of repeating from memory in public.
Say. What one has said or has to say.
Sermon. A discourse by a clergyman upon some religious topic.
Soliloquy, etc. A talking to oneself. See CONVERSATION-MONO-LOGUE.
Speech. The expression of thought in spoken words.
Speechifying. Making speeches.
Talk. Verbal interchange of ideas.
Tirade. A prolonged declamatory outpouring of censure or dislike.
Verbal intercourse. Conversation.
Word of mouth. Direct oral communication.

SPEECH—*Associated Nouns.*

Burst of eloquence. A sudden breaking forth into lofty and impassioned speech.
Command of words. Mastery of the use of language.
Copia verborum [L.]. An abundance of words.
Elocution. The art of correct intonation, inflection and gesture in public speaking.
Eloquence. The art, power, or act of speaking in language expressing strong feeling, so as to move or convince.
Facundity. Readiness of speech.
Flow of language. ⎫ A copious outpouring of words.
Flow of words. ⎭
Gift of the gab. Fluency in speaking.
Grandiloquence. Pompous or bombastic speaking.
Multiloquence. Talkativeness.
Power of speech. Great or telling force or effect of speech.
Rhetoric. The art of discourse.
Usus loquendi [L.]. Usage in speaking.

SPEECH—*Nouns of Agent.*

Cicero. Roman, a copious and grateful orator.
Demosthenes. Greek, a condensed and powerful orator.
Hermes. The messenger of the gods; one who speaks the highest truth divinely like Plato.
Improvisatore [It.]. An extemporaneous speaker.
Interlocutor. One who takes part in a conversation.
Mouthpiece. One who gives the opinions of another in his speech.
Orator. A public speaker.
Oratress. ⎫ A female orator.
Oratrix. ⎭
Patterer. A childish talker.
Platform-orator. A public political speaker.
Prolocutor. A person who speaks for another.
Rhetorician. An artificial speaker.
Speaker, etc. One who engages in public speaking. See *Verbs.*
Speechmaker. One given to public speaking.
Spokesman. One delegated by others to speak for them.
Stump orator. ⎫ A public political speaker.
Stump speaker. ⎭

SPEECH—*Verbs*

Be eloquent, etc. To be able to express emotion or feeling in lofty speech. See *Adjectives.*
Be on one's legs. To speak in a standing position.
Blurt out. To speak abruptly and without consideration.
Break silence. To speak.
Breathe. To speak in a low voice.
Come out with. To disclose by speaking of.
Declaim. To speak in a rhetorical manner.
Deliver. To speak formally.
Deliver a speech. To speak with formality or officially.

Broken accents. Words hindered by imperfect utterance.
Broken sentences. Sentences disjointed by imperfect utterance.
Broken voice. A voice made indistinct by sobs or imperfect utterance.
Drawl. Slow and lazy utterance.
Falsetto, etc. The high, artificial tones of the voice. See VOCALIZA-TION-MUTENESS.
Hesitation, etc. Uncertain utterance. See *Verbs.*
Impediment in one's speech. A natural failing in the organs of speech.
Inarticulateness. Indistinctness of utterance.
Lapsus linguæ [L.]. A slip of the tongue.
Lisp. To speak imperfectly and timidly. "I lisped in numbers, for the numbers came." [Pope, *Satires, Prologue,* 127.]
Nasal accent. The manner of speaking through the nose.
Nasal tone. The sound of voice when speaking through the nose.
Slip of the tongue. An unintentional expression.
Stammering etc. The habit of faltering and halting in pronouncing. See *Verbs.*
Tardiloquence. The habit of speaking slowly.
Titubancy. The habit of wavering while speaking.
Traulism. A stammering.
Twang. A sharp, nasal sound.
Whisper, etc. A low and soft utterance of the voice. See LOUD-NESS-FAINTNESS.

INARTICULATENESS—*Verbs.*

Balbucinate. ⎫ To stammer.
Balbutiate. ⎭
Be unable to put two words together. To stammer or halt in speaking.
Clip one's words. To be too short in pronouncing one's words.
Croak. To speak in a complaining tone.
Drawl. To speak slowly and lazily.
Falter. To speak in a weak and hesitating manner.
Gibber. To talk incoherently.
Hammer. To speak in sharp, short breaks.
Haw. To hesitate in speaking.
Hesitate. To be slow in speaking.
Hum and haw. To drawl in a nasal tone.
Jabber. To speak rapidly and without meaning.
Lisp. To speak *p* and *z* like *th*; to speak like a child.
Maund. ⎫ To speak in an incoherent and complaining manner.
Maunder. ⎭
Mince. To cut up one's words in speaking.
Mispronounce. To articulate incorrectly.
Missay. To speak poorly.
Mouth. To speak in an unnaturally big voice.
Muffle. To speak without clear articulation.
Mumble. To speak low and indistinctly.
Mump. To speak brokenly.
Murder the king's English. ⎫
Murder the language. ⎬ To mar or spoil correct or pure language.
Murder the queen's English. ⎭
Mutter. To speak in an indistinct and complaining tone.
Snuffle. To talk through the nose in a whimpering tone.
Speak thick. To speak without proper intervals of articulation.
Speak through the nose. To utter with a nasal twang.
Splutter. To speak with confused articulation.
Sputter. To speak in a hasty and indistinct tone.
Stammer. To speak with hesitation.
Stutter. To speak with involuntary repetitions.
Whisper, etc. To speak in a low, soft voice without vibration of the vocal cords. See LOUDNESS-FAINTNESS.

INARTICULATENESS—*Adjectives.*

Guttural. Coming from the throat.
Inarticulate. With no distinction of syllables.
Nasal. Pronounced through the nose.
Stammering, etc. Hesitating in speech. See *Verbs.*
Tremulous. Unsteady in speech.

INARTICULATENESS—*Adverb.*

Sotto voce [It.]. Softly See LOUDNESS-FAINTNESS.

SPEECH—*Verbs—Continued*

Discourse. To give an oral exposition of a subject.
Escape one's lips. To disclose a secret by accident.
Expatiate etc. To speak at length. See TERSENESS-PROLIXITY.
Fall from the lips. ⎫ To be uttered unconsciously.
Fall from the mouth. ⎭
Flourish. To speak in an elaborate manner.
Give tongue. To clamor in an unreasonable manner.

Give utterance to. To express in words.
Harangue. To make a forcible, public speech.
Have a tongue in one's head. To be able to talk with great ease.
Have at the end of one's tongue. ⎫
Have at the tip of one's tongue. ⎬ To be ready to speak of.
Have one's say. To have one's turn to express an opinion.
Have on one's lips. To be ready to speak about with ease.
Have the gift of the gab, etc. To have the ability to talk much. See *Nouns.*
Hold forth. To speak in public.
Lecture. To deliver a discourse in public.
Let fall. To be uttered carelessly.
Lift one's voice. To speak up.
Make a speech, etc. To speak in public. See *Nouns.*
Open one's lips. ⎫
Open one's mouth. ⎬ To speak.
Outspeak. To speak with greater effect than.
Pass one's lips. To be uttered.
Pour forth. To speak in a profuse manner.
Pronounce. To utter in a formal manner.
Put in a word or two. To mingle in a conversation.

Raise one's voice. To speak.
Rant. To speak vehemently and extravagantly.
Rap out. To utter suddenly and violently.
Recite. To speak something committed to memory.
Say. To express as an opinion in words.
Say one's say. To give one's opinion in turn.
Sermonize. To speak in a solemn and tiresome manner.
Soliloquize, etc. To talk to oneself. See Conversation-Monologue.
Speak of. To mention.
Speak one's mind. To give one's opinion fearlessly.
Speak to, etc. To address. See Address.
Speechify. To make a speech.
Spout. To recite in an oratorical or pompous manner.
Stump. To travel over, delivering electioneering speeches.
Talk. To interchange thoughts in words.
Talk together, etc. To converse. See Conversation.
Tell. To relate in words.
Utter. ⎫
Utter forth. ⎬ To give expression to in words.
Wag the tongue. To be loquacious.

SPEECH—*Adjectives.*

Declamatory. Given to speaking in a rhetorical style.
Elocutionary. Pertaining to the art of public speaking.
Eloquent. Having the power of expressing strong emotions in an elevated and effective manner.
Grandiloquent, etc. Given to speaking in a pompous manner. See Simplicity-Floridness.
Lingual. Pertaining to the use of the tongue in speaking.
Not written. Spoken.
Oral. Uttered by the mouth.

Oratorical. Becoming an eloquent public speaker.
Outspoken. Expressing a decided opinion for or against.
Phonetic. Pertaining to the articulate sounds made by the human voice.
Rhetorical. Eloquent in an artificial manner.
Speaking, etc. Expressing thoughts in words. See *Verbs.*
Spoken, etc. By word of mouth. See *Verbs.*
Talkative, etc. Given to talking a great deal. See Talkativeness.
Unwritten. Spoken.

SPEECH—*Adverbs, etc.*

By word of mouth. By direct oral communication.
From the lips of. Received by actual speech of.

Orally, etc. By word of mouth. See *Adjectives.*
Viva voce [L.]. By spoken word, orally.

SPEECH—*Phrases*

Quoth he.

Said he.

speech'-i-fy. Speaking. Speech-Inarticulateness.
speech'-i-fy-ing. Making speeches. Speech-Inarticulateness.
speech'-less. Mute. Vocalization-Muteness.
speech'-mak''-er. Speaker. Speech-Inarticulateness.
speed. Help; velocity. Activity-Indolence, Obstruction-Help, Success-Failure, Swiftness-Slowness; **Godspeed,** Charitableness-Malevolence; **with breathless speed,** Hurry-Leisure.
speed'-i-ly. Soon. Earliness-Lateness.
speed'-y. Quick. Swiftness-Slowness.
spell. Letter; charm; tell. Devotion-Charm, Duration-Neverness, Education-Learning, Letter, Motive-Caprice, Toil-Relaxation, Volition-Obligation; **cast a spell,** Devotion-Magic, Volition-Obligation; **knurr and spell,** Entertainment-Weariness; **spell out,** Interpretation-Misinterpretation.
spell'-bound''. Fascinated. Astonishment-Expectance, Motive-Caprice, Volition-Obligation.
spell'-ing. Naming the letters. Letters.
spence. Larder. Store.
spen'-cer. Overcoat. Dress-Undress.
spend. Pay; exhaust; lose; waste. Admission-Expulsion, Buying-Sale, Giving-Receiving, Outlay-Income, Provision-Waste; **spend freely,** Generosity-Frugality; **spend one's time in,** Occupation; **spend time,** Duration-Neverness; **spend time in,** Activity-Indolence.
spend'-thrift''. Prodigal. Extravagance-Avarice.
spent. Exhausted. Strength-Weakness, Weariness-Refreshment.
speranza é il pan de miseri, la [It.] (spê-ran'-tsa ê il pan dê mî'-ser-î, la). Hope is the bread of the wretched.

sper''-ma-ce'-ti. Stearin. Pulpiness-Oiliness.
sper'-ma-ry. Testicle. Biology.
sper-mat'-ic. Fructifying. Fertility-Sterility.
sper'-ma-tize. Emit seed. Fertility-Sterility.
spero, dum spiro [L.] (spî'-ro, dum spai'-ro). While I breathe, I hope. Sanguineness-Hopelessness.
spero meliora [L.] (spî'-ro mel-i-o'-ra). I hope for better things. Sanguineness-Hopelessness.
spes esse dicitur, ægroto dum anima est [L.] (spîz es'-sî dis'-i-tur, î-gro'-to dum an'-im-a est). While there is life to a sick man, there is said to be hope. Sanguineness-Hopelessness.
spes non fracta, at [L.] (spîz non frac'-ta, at). But hope is not broken. Sanguineness-Hopelessness.
spes sibi quisque [L.] (spîz sib'-i quis'-quî). Each one a hope for himself. Determination-Vacillation.
spew. Vomit. Admission-Expulsion.
sphac'-el-us. Gangrene. Health-Sickness.
sphe-noi'-dal. Pertaining to the sphenoid. Mineralogy.
sphere. Solid; ball; province. Extension-District, Extension-Inextension, Occupation, Quantity-Measure, Roundness, Universe.
spher'-ic-al. Globular. Circle-Winding, Roundness.
sphe'-roid. Almost a sphere. Roundness.
spher'-ule. Globule. Roundness.
spher'-y. Celestial. Universe.
sphinx. Monster; oracle; person. Ambiguity, Conventionality-Unconventionality, Soothsayer, Tidings-Mystery.
spi'-al. Spy. Warning.
spice. Aromatic; smack; taste. Condiment, Magnitude-Smallness, Mixture-Homogeneity, Pungency

spicilegium [L.] (spis-î-le′-ji-um). Gleaning. DIGEST, GATHERING-SCATTERING.

spick and span. New. NOVELTY-ANTIQUITY.

spic′-u-late. Sharp-pointed. SHARPNESS-BLUNTNESS.

spic′-u-lum. Spicule. SHARPNESS-BLUNTNESS.

spi′-cy. Pungent; piquant. EXCITATION, PERFUME-STENCH, PUNGENCY.

spig′-ot. Plug. PERFORATOR-STOPPER.

spike. Nail; pierce. APERTURE-CLOSURE, PERFORATOR-STOPPER, SHARPNESS-BLUNTNESS; **spike guns,** MIGHT-IMPOTENCE, OBSTRUCTION-HELP, USEFULNESS-USELESSNESS.

spike′-bit″. Bit shaped like a spike. PERFORATOR-STOPPER.

spiked. Nailed. SHARPNESS-BLUNTNESS.

spik′-y. Full of spikes. SHARPNESS-BLUNTNESS.

spill. Filament; plug; shed; waste; throw. ADMISSION-EXPULSION, COMBUSTIBLE, EXTRAVAGANCE-AVARICE, LAMINA-FIBER, PERFORATOR-STOPPER, PROVISION-WASTE, RIVER-WIND; **spill and pelt,** MEDIUM, REGULARITY-IRREGULARITY; **spill blood,** FIGHTING-CONCILIATION.

spin. Twist; reject. CHOICE-REJECTION, REVOLUTION-EVOLUTION; **spin a long yarn,** GULL-HYPERBOLE, TERSENESS-PROLIXITY; **spin out,** EARLINESS-LATENESS, LASTINGNESS-TRANSIENTNESS, LENGTH-SHORTNESS, TERSENESS-PROLIXITY.

spin′-dle. Rod. REVOLUTION-EVOLUTION.

spin′-dle-shanks″. Slender legs. BREADTH-NARROWNESS.

spin′-dle-shaped″. Fusiform. SHARPNESS-BLUNTNESS.

spin′-drift. Spoondrift. VISCIDITY-FOAM.

spine. Projection. SHARPNESS-BLUNTNESS.

spin′-el. Mineral. EMBELLISHMENT-DISFIGUREMENT.

spin′-et. Harpsichord; thicket. FAUNA-FLORA, MUSICAL INSTRUMENTS.

spin′-na-ker. A sail carried on the mainmast of racing vessels. CONVEYANCE-VESSEL.

spin′-ney. Copse. FAUNA-FLORA.

spi-nos′-i-ty. Thorniness. CLEARNESS-OBSCURITY, FAVORITE-MOROSENESS, POLITENESS-IMPOLITENESS, SHARPNESS-BLUNTNESS.

spi′-nous. Prickly. SHARPNESS-BLUNTNESS.

spin′-ster. Old maid. MATRIMONY-CELIBACY.

spi′-ny. Thorny. SHARPNESS-BLUNTNESS.

spir′-a-cle. Aperture. WATERCOURSE-AIRPIPE.

spi′-ral. Winding. CIRCLE-WINDING.

spire. Point; send upward. ARCHITECTURE, ASCENT-DESCENT, HEIGHT-LOWNESS, SHARPNESS-BLUNTNESS.

spir′-it. Essence; rational being; energy; influence; meaning; ghost. ACTIVITY-INDOLENCE, AFFECTIONS, BRAVERY-COWARDICE, FORCE-WEAKNESS, JOVE-FIEND, MATERIALITY-SPIRITUALITY, MEANING-JARGON, MIND-IMBECILITY, SUBJECTIVENESS-OBJECTIVENESS, TOIL-RELAXATION; **bad spirit,** JOVE-FIEND; **evil spirit,** ANGEL-SATAN; **keep one's spirit up,** SANGUINENESS-HOPELESSNESS; **master spirit,** TOIL-RELAXATION; **spirit up,** EXCITATION, MOTIVE-CAPRICE; **unclean spirit,** ANGEL-SATAN; **with life and spirit,** ACTIVITY-INDOLENCE.

Spir′-it, the Ho′-ly. Deity. DIVINITY.

spir′-it-ed. Animated. ACTIVITY-INDOLENCE, BRAVERY-COWARDICE, FORCE-WEAKNESS, LIGHTHEARTEDNESS-DEJECTION, SENSITIVENESS-APATHY, UNSELFISHNESS-SELFISHNESS.

spir′-it-ful. Full of spirit. BRAVERY-COWARDICE, LIGHTHEARTEDNESS-DEJECTION.

spir′-it-less. Dead; listless. BRAVERY-COWARDICE, LIGHTHEARTEDNESS-DEJECTION, SENSITIVENESS-APATHY.

spi″-ri-to′-so. Animated. MUSIC.

spir′-it-rap′-ping. Communication. DEVOTION-MAGIC.

spir′-its. Liquor. LIGHTHEARTEDNESS-DEJECTION, NUTRIMENT-EXCRETION.

spir′-it-stir′-ring. Soul-stirring. EXCITATION.

spir′-i-tu-al. Incorporeal; pure. DIVINITY, GODLINESS-UNGODLINESS, MATERIALITY-SPIRITUALITY, MIND-IMBECILITY; **spiritual director,** MINISTRY-LAITY; **spiritual existence,** GODLINESS-UNGODLINESS.

spir′-i-tu-al-ism. Belief; state. DEVOTION-MAGIC, MATERIALITY-SPIRITUALITY, MIND-IMBECILITY.

spir′-i-tu-al-ist. One who believes in spiritualism. MATERIALITY-SPIRITUALITY.

spir″-i-tu-al′-i-ty. Freedom from worldliness. MATERIALITY-SPIRITUALITY.

spir′-i-tu-al-ize. Make spiritual. SPIRITUALITY, RATIOCINATION-INSTINCT.

spirituelle [F.] (spir″-i-tu-el′). Fine qualities. WITTINESS-DULNESS.

spirt. Spurt; eject; hasten. APPROACH-WITHDRAWAL, HURRY-LEISURE, RIVER-WIND, TOIL-RELAXATION.

spir′-tle. Scatter; splash. GATHERING-SCATTERING, RIVER-WIND.

spis′-si-tude. Thickness. SOLIDITY-RARITY, VISCIDITY-FOAM.

spit. Saliva; flurry; point. ADMISSION-EXPULSION, APERTURE-CLOSURE, RIVER-WIND, SHARPNESS-BLUNTNESS; **spitfire,** FAVORITE-QUARRELSOMENESS.

spite. Bitterness. CHARITABLENESS-MALEVOLENCE; **in spite of,** ANTAGONISM-CONCURRENCE, COOPERATION-OPPOSITION, HARMONY-DISCORD; **in spite of one's teeth,** ANTAGONISM-CONCURRENCE, COERCION, READINESS-RELUCTANCE.

spite′-ful. Maliciousness. CHARITABLENESS-MALEVOLENCE, LOVE-HATE.

spit′-tle. Saliva. NUTRIMENT-EXCRETION.

splanch-nol′-o-gy. Study of viscera. TEXTURE.

splash. Spatter; parade. CLEANNESS-FILTHINESS, POMP, RIVER-WIND, STREAM; **make a splash,** POMP, REPUTATION-DISCREDIT.

splay′-foot″-ed. Flatness. PROPORTION-DEFORMITY.

spleen. Malice; organ; temper. FAVORITE-MOROSENESS, LIGHTHEARTEDNESS-DEJECTION, LOVE-ANGER, LOVE-HATE; **harbor spleen,** CHARITABLENESS-MALEVOLENCE.

spleen′-less. Without spite. CHARITABLENESS-MALEVOLENCE.

spleen′-y. Irritable. FAVORITE-MOROSENESS.

splen′-did. Shining; magnificent. BEAUTY-UGLINESS, LIGHT-DARKNESS, POMP, REPUTATION-DISCREDIT.

splen′-dor. Richness; preeminence; bright. BEAUTY-UGLINESS, LIGHT-DARKNESS, POMP, REPUTATION-DISCREDIT.

sple-net′-ic. Peevish. FAVORITE-MOROSENESS, LIGHTHEARTEDNESS-DEJECTION.

splice. Unite; fix. CROSSING, ENVIRONMENT-INTERPOSITION, RENOVATION-RELAPSE, UNION-DISUNION; **splice the main brace,** TEETOTALISM-INTEMPERANCE.

spliced, be. Married. MATRIMONY-CELIBACY.

splint. Support. REMEDY-BANE, SUSPENSION-SUPPORT.

splint′-er. Sliver; piece. LAMINA-FIBER, MAGNITUDE-SMALLNESS, TOUGHNESS-BRITTLENESS, UNION-DISUNION.

splin′-ter-y. Full of splinters. TOUGHNESS-BRITTLENESS.

split. Part; disrupt; laugh. DOUBLING-HALVING, JUBILATION-LAMENTATION, SUCCESS-FAILURE, TOUGHNESS-BRITTLENESS, UNION-DISUNION, VARIANCE-ACCORD; **split hairs,** DIFFERENTIATION-INDISCRIMINATION, RATIOCINATION-INSTINCT; **split one's sides,** JUBILATION-LAMENTATION; **split the difference,** COMPOSITION, MEDIUM; **split the ears,** CACOPHONY, LOUDNESS-FAINTNESS; **split the head,** CACOPHONY, LOUDNESS-FAINTNESS; **split upon a rock,** SUCCESS-FAILURE.

split'-ting. Dividing. TOUGHNESS-BRITTLENESS.

splut'-ter. Speak; bustle. ADMISSION-EXPULSION, HURRY-LEISURE, SPEECH-INARTICULATENESS, VIGOR-INERTIA.

spoil. Booty; waste; injure. BETTERMENT-DETERIORATION, HARSHNESS-MILDNESS, OBSTRUCTION-HELP, PLUNDER, REPLETION, THEFT; **spoil sport**, OBSTRUCTION-HELP; **spoil trade**, ANTAGONISM-CONCURRENCE.

spoiled child. Petted. FAVORITE-ANGER, REPLETION; **spoiled child of fortune**, WELFARE-MISFORTUNE.

spoil'-er. Robber. ROBBER.

spoil'-ing. Wasting. BETTERMENT-DETERIORATION.

spoke. Wheel; obstruct. LENGTH-SHORTNESS, OBSTRUCTION-HELP, SHARPNESS-BLUNTNESS; **put a spoke in one's wheel**, DIFFICULTY-FACILITY, MIGHT-IMPOTENCE, OBSTRUCTION-HELP.

spo'-ken. Uttered orally. SPEECH-INARTICULATENESS.

spokes'-man. Speaker. INTERPRETER, SPEECH-INARTICULATENESS.

spolia opima [L.] (spo'-li-a op-ai'-ma). The richest spoils. PLUNDER.

spo'-li-ate. Plunder. THEFT.

spo''-li-a'-tion. Plundering. GOOD-EVIL, THEFT.

spon'-dee. Foot. POETRY-PROSE.

sponge. Animal; parasite; dampen; dry. CLEANNESS-FILTHINESS, DAMPNESS-DRYNESS, TEETOTALISM-INTEMPERANCE, THEFT; **apply the sponge**, MARK-OBLITERATION, SETTLEMENT-DEFAULT; **sponge out**, MARK-OBLITERATION.

spon'-gi-ness. Porosity. SOLIDITY-RARITY.

spong'-ing-house. Prison. RELEASE-PRISON.

spon'-gi-ous. Spongy. CONVEXITY-CONCAVITY.

spon'-gy. Soft; porous. CONVEXITY-CONCAVITY, HARDNESS-SOFTNESS.

spon'-sion. Surety. SECURITY.

spon'-sor. Responsible; god-father. EVIDENCE-COUNTEREVIDENCE, SECURITY; **be sponsor for**, DUTY-DERELICTION, ENGAGEMENT-RELEASE.

spon'-sor-ship. Being sponsor. SECURITY.

spon''-ta-ne'-i-ty. Quality of being spontaneous. VOLITION-OBLIGATION.

spon-ta'-ne-ous. Impulsive; willing. LIBERTY-SUBJECTION, NATURE-ART, PREDETERMINATION-IMPULSE.

spon-ta'-ne-ous-ness. State of being spontaneous. IMPULSE, READINESS-RELUCTANCE, VOLITION-OBLIGATION.

spon'-toon. Demi-pike. WEAPON.

spook. Ghost. JOVE-FIEND.

spoon. Utensil; love. BLANDISHMENT, CONTENTS-RECEIVER, CONVEYANCE-VESSEL, INSTRUMENT; **born with a silver spoon in one's mouth**, WELFARE-MISFORTUNE.

spoon'-ful. Small amount. MAGNITUDE-SMALLNESS, QUANTITY-MEASURE.

spoon'-meat''. Pap. NUTRIMENT-EXCRETION.

spoon'-y. Love-sick. BLANDISHMENT, SAGACITY-INCAPACITY.

spo-rad'-ic. Separate. GATHERING-SCATTERING.

spore. Germ. FRIABILITY.

sport. Pastime. ENTERTAINMENT-WEARINESS, LIFE-KILLING, POMP, QUEST-EVASION; **in sport**, ENTERTAINMENT-WEARINESS, WITTINESS-DULNESS; **sport of fortune**, WELFARE-MISFORTUNE; **the sport of**, LIBERTY-SUBJECTION.

sport'-ing. Engaging in field-sports. ENTERTAINMENT-WEARINESS, LIFE-KILLING, QUEST-EVASION, STRIFE-PEACE; **sporting dog**, FAUNA-FLORA.

sport'-ive. Frolicsome. ENTERTAINMENT-WEARINESS, LIGHTHEARTEDNESS-DEJECTION.

sports'-man. Sporting man. ENTERTAINMENT-WEARINESS, LIFE-KILLING, QUEST-EVASION.

spor'-tu-la-ry. Living on alms. GIVING-RECEIVING.

spor'-tule. Spore. FRIABILITY.

spot. Place; stain. CLEANNESS-FILTHINESS, EMBELLISHMENT-DISFIGUREMENT, EXTENSION-PLACE, POSITION, REPUTATION-DISCREDIT, SIGN; **on the spot**, EARLINESS-LATENESS, ETERNITY-INSTANTANEITY, PRESENCE-ABSENCE, TIME.

spot'-less. Clean; flawless. BEAUTY-UGLINESS, CLEANNESS-FILTHINESS, FAULTLESSNESS-FAULTINESS, INNOCENCE-GUILT.

spots in the sun, see. Fastidious. PARTICULARNESS.

spot'-ted. Stained. BETTERMENT-DETERIORATION, VARIEGATION.

spot'-ti-ness. State of being spotted. BETTERMENT-DETERIORATION, VARIEGATION.

spot'-ty. Spotted. VARIEGATION.

spou'-sal. Nuptial. MATRIMONY-CELIBACY.

spouse. Husband; wife. MATRIMONY-CELIBACY, SOLITUDE-COMPANY.

spouse'-less. Unmarried. MATRIMONY-CELIBACY.

spout. Speak; opening; pawn. ACTING, ENTRANCE-EXIT, RIVER-WIND, SECURITY, SPEECH-INARTICULATENESS, WATERCOURSE-AIRPIPE.

sprag. An instrument for chocking the wheels of a coal-car. INSTRUMENT, RELEASE-RESTRAINT.

sprain. Strain. MIGHT-IMPOTENCE, STRENGTH-WEAKNESS.

sprawl. Prostrate. ASCENT-DESCENT, ERECTNESS-FLATNESS, LENGTH-SHORTNESS.

spray. Sprig; foam. VISCIDITY-FOAM, WHOLE-PART.

spread. Cover; expand; table. CONCENTRATION-RADIATION, ENLARGEMENT-DIMINUTION, EXTENSION-INEXTENSION, GATHERING-SCATTERING, INCREASE-DECREASE, NUTRIMENT-EXCRETION, PUBLICITY; **spread abroad**, PUBLICITY; **spread a shade**, LIGHT-DARKNESS; **spread canvas**, TRAVELING-NAVIGATION; **spread out**, ENLARGEMENT-DIMINUTION; **spread sail**, TRAVELING-NAVIGATION; **spread to**, REMOTENESS-NEARNESS; **spread the toils**, TRUTHFULNESS-FRAUD.

spree. Frolic. ENTERTAINMENT-WEARINESS.

spretæ injuria formæ [L.] (spri'-ti in-jiu'-ri-a for'-mi). The insult to her slighted beauty. ADULATION-DISPARAGEMENT, BEAUTY-UGLINESS, REGARD-DISRESPECT.

sprig. Sprout. SUSPENSION-SUPPORT, WHOLE-PART.

spright'-ful. Lively. LIGHTHEARTEDNESS-DEJECTION.

spright'-ly. Animated. ENTERTAINMENT-WEARINESS.

spring. Time; leap; water; instrument. ARRIVAL-DEPARTURE, CAUSE-EFFECT, ELASTICITY-INELASTICITY, IMPETUS-REACTION, INSTRUMENT, MORNING-EVENING, RIVER-WIND, SPRING-DIVE, STORE, STRENGTH-WEAKNESS, SWIFTNESS-SLOWNESS; **spring a leak**, BETTERMENT-DETERIORATION, FAULTLESSNESS-FAULTINESS; **spring a mine**, ATTACK-DEFENSE, CREATION-DESTRUCTION, EXPECTATION-SURPRISE; **spring a project**, DESIGN; **spring back**, ELASTICITY-INELASTICITY, IMPETUS-REACTION; **spring from**, CAUSE-EFFECT; **springs of action**, HABIT-DESUETUDE; **spring to one's feet**, ELEVATION-DEPRESSION; **spring up**, ASCENT-DESCENT, BEGINNING-END, ENLARGEMENT-DIMINUTION, OCCURRENCE-DESTINY, VISIBILITY-INVISIBILITY; **spring upon**, TAKING-RESTITUTION.

SPRING—DIVE.

Bound. A leap; a spring.
Caper. A frolicsome leap or spring.

Dip. The act of plunging momentarily into a liquid.
Dive. A plunge, head foremost, into water.

SPRING--DIVE--*Continued.*

Capriole. A leap that a horse makes with all fours, upwards only, without advancing.

Caracole. A half-turn which a horseman makes.

Curvet. A leap of a horse when he raises both his fore legs at once, and, as his fore legs are falling, raises his hind legs.

Dance. The leaping tripping, or measured stepping of one who dances.

Demivolt. A half-vault; a particular leap of a horse.

Falcade. The action of a horse when he springs alternately on hind and fore feet.

Gambade.} A curveting or prank.
Gambado.}

Hop. A leap on one leg.

Hop, skip, and jump. A game in which one covers as much ground as possible by a hop, skip, and jump in succession.

Jump. A springing free from the ground by the muscular action of feet and legs.

Leap. A spring in which both feet are off the ground.

Saltation. A leaping.

Spring. A leap; a jump.

Vault. A leap or bound.

SPRING--*Denotations.*

Buck.} The male of fallow deer, antelopes, goats, etc.
Buck-jump.}

Chamois. A small species of antelope, possessing remarkable agility.

Flea. An insect destitute of wings, but having the power of leaping energetically.

Frog. An amphibious animal which swims rapidly and takes long leaps on land.

Goat. A horned ruminant, remarkable for its leaping ability.

Grasshopper. A jumping winged insect.

Jerboa. A small jumping rodent.

Kangaroo. A species of jumping marsupials.

SPRING--*Verbs.*

Bob. To move in a short jerky manner.

Bounce. To spring or leap quickly.

Bound. To move forward by leaps or bounds.

Caper. To leap in a sprightly manner.

Caracole. To wheel or turn.

Curvet. To leap or spring, as a horse.

Cut capers. To frolic; caper.

Dance. To leap or move in measured steps, usually to the accompaniment of music.

Dance oneself off one's legs. To dance very rapidly.

Flounce. To throw the body and limbs one way and the other.

Foot it. To dance; skip.

Frisk, etc. To leap; gambol. See ENTERTAINMENT.

Hop. To leap on one leg.

Jump about, etc. To spring or leap about. See AGITATION.

Jump over the moon. To leap very high.

Jump up. To raise both feet off the ground at once.

Diver. One who dives.

Ducking, etc. The act of dipping or plunging suddenly into water and then quickly withdrawing. See *Verbs.*

Header. A plunge or dive into the water, head foremost.

Plunge. To drive oneself into the water.

DIVE--*Verbs.*

Bathe, etc. To wash the body by immersing in water. See WATER.

Dip. To plunge into water.

Dive. To descend or plunge into water.

Douse. To thrust into water.

Duck. To dip into water.

Engulf. To swallow up.

Founder. To fill with water.

Get out of one's depth. To get into water that is too deep for one.

Go down like a stone.} To sink to the bottom of the water.
Go to the bottom.}

Make a plunge. To throw oneself into water.

Plump. To plunge like a mass of dead matter.

Plunge. To dive; thrust oneself into water.

Send to the bottom. To sink.

Sink. To go to the bottom.

Souse. To plunge into water.

Submerge. To put under water.

Submerse. To submerge.

Take a header.} To leap head foremost.
Take a plunge.}

Wallow. To roll or tumble about heavily, as in mire.

Welter. To rise and fall as waves.

SPRING--*Verbs--Continued.*

Leap. To jump; spring.

Ramp. To leap; bound; prance.

Skip. To leap and bound, as a goat.

Spring. To bound; jump.

Start. To move with a sudden leap or jump.

Trip. To move or walk with light, quick steps.

Trip it on the light fantastic toe. To dance.

Vault. To leap over.

SPRING--*Adjectives.*

Frisky. Jumping with lightness.

Leaping, etc. Jumping. See *Verbs.*

Saltatory. Leaping; springing.

SPRING--*Adverbs, etc.*

Di salto [It.]. At a leap.

On the light fantastic toe. In a dancing manner.

SPRING--*Phrase*

Di salto in salto [It.]. With leap after leap.

---

spring'-bal''-ance. A device for weighing. HEAVINESS-LIGHTNESS.

springe. A snare. TRUTHFULNESS-FRAUD.

spring e'-qui-nox. Crossing of the earth's equator by the sun on March 21st. ASTRONOMY.

spring'-gun''. A gun worked by a spring. TRUTHFULNESS-FRAUD.

spring'-i-ness. Elasticity. ELASTICITY-INELASTICITY.

sprin'-gle. A snare. TRUTHFULNESS-FRAUD.

spring'-net''. A snare. TRUTHFULNESS-FRAUD.

spring'-tide''. The high tide which occurs twice every month; any great flood of feeling. ENTIRETY-DEFICIENCY, HEIGHT-LOWNESS, INFANCY-AGE, MAGNITUDE-SMALLNESS, RIVER-WIND.

spring'-y. Elastic. ELASTICITY-INELASTICITY.

sprin'-kle. A falling in drops; a small quantity. ADDITION-SUBTRACTION, CEREMONIAL, GATHERING-SCATTERING, MIXTURE-HOMOGENEITY, VARIEGATION, WATER-AIR.

sprin'-kling. A small, scattering quantity. MAGNITUDE-SMALLNESS, MIXTURE-HOMOGENEITY.

sprit. A small spar; a sprout. PARENTAGE-PROGENY, SUSPENSION-SUPPORT.

sprite. A fairy or goblin. JOVE-FIEND.

sprit'-sail. A sail extended by a sprit. CONVEYANCE-VESSEL.

sprout. A new shoot or bud. ENLARGEMENT-DIMINUTION, INCREASE-DECREASE, PARENTAGE-PROGENY; **sprout from,** CAUSE-EFFECT.

spruce. Neat; trim. BEAUTY-UGLINESS, CLEANNESS-FILTHINESS.

sprue. A projection from a casting. CLEANNESS-FILTHINESS.

sprung. Cracked or strained. BETTERMENT-DETERIORATION, FAULTLESSNESS-FAULTINESS.

spry. Agile. ACTIVITY-INDOLENCE, LIGHTHEARTEDNESS-DEJECTION.

spud. A spade-like implement. CONVEYANCE-VESSEL.

spume. Froth. VISCIDITY-FOAM.

spunk. Courage. BRAVERY-COWARDICE.

spun out. Protracted. LASTINGNESS-TRANSIENTNESS, TERSENESS-PROLIXITY.

spur. A goading instrument worn on the heel; instigation. CONVEXITY-CONCAVITY, MOTIVE-CAPRICE, SHARPNESS-BLUNTNESS; **on the spur of the moment,** EARLINESS-LATENESS, ETERNITY-INSTANTANEITY, OPPORTUNENESS-UNSUITABLENESS, PREDETERMINA-

TION-IMPULSE; **win spurs,** REPUTATION-DISCREDIT, SUCCESS-FAILURE.

spu'-ri-ous. Not genuine. DUENESS-UNDUENESS, TRUTH-ERROR, TRUTHFULNESS-FALSEHOOD, TRUTHFULNESS-FRAUD.

spurn. To reject with scorn. REGARD-SCORN, UNCONCERN.

spurred. Wearing spurs. SHARPNESS-BLUNTNESS.

spurt. An increase of energy for a short time. HURRYLEISURE, LASTINGNESS - TRANSIENTNESS, PREDETERMINATION-IMPULSE, RIVER-WIND, SWIFTNESSSLOWNESS, TOIL-RELAXATION.

spu'-ta. Saliva. NUTRIMENT-EXCRETION.

sput'-ter. To emit in a scattering manner; to stammer. ADMISSION-EXPULSION, RIVER-WIND, SPEECH-INARTICULATENESS, VIGOR-INERTIA.

spy. To explore; to see secretly. ENLIGHTENMENTSECRECY, INVESTIGATION - ANSWER, MESSENGER, ONLOOKER, SIGHT-BLINDNESS, WARNING.

spy'-glass''. A small terrestrial telescope. OPTICAL INSTRUMENTS.

squab. Fat and short. BREADTH-NARROWNESS, GREATNESS-LITTLENESS, LENGTH-SHORTNESS, SUSPENSION-SUPPORT.

squab'-ble. To quarrel. VARIANCE-ACCORD.

squab'-by. Short and fat. LENGTH-SHORTNESS.

squad. A small group of persons, as soldiers. BELLIGERENT, GATHERING-SCATTERING.

squad'-ron. An assemblage of war-vessels; a company of soldiers. BELLIGERENT.

squal'-id. Having a mean, poverty-stricken appearance. BEAUTY-UGLINESS, CLEANNESS-FILTHINESS.

squall. A loud outcry; a burst of wind. CRY-ULULATION, RIVER-WIND, TURBULENCE-CALMNESS, VARIANCE-ACCORD.

squall'-er. One who squalls. BEAUTY-UGLINESS.

squal'-or. The filth of thriftless poverty. CLEANNESSFILTHINESS.

squa'-mous. Scaly. COVER-LINING, LAMINA-FIBER.

squan'-der. To spend wastefully. EXTRAVAGANCEAVARICE, PROVISION-WASTE, USE-MISUSE.

squan'-dered. Spent. EXTRAVAGANCE-AVARICE.

squan'-der-ing. Spending. EXTRAVAGANCE-AVARICE.

square. A figure having four equal sides and four right angles; an open space in a town; true; just. AGREEMENT - DISAGREEMENT, ANGULARITY, COMPENSATION, DUENESS-UNDUENESS, DWELLER-HABITATION, ERECTNESS-FLATNESS, QUATERNITY, STRIFE-PEACE; **make all square,** RENOVATION-RELAPSE; **on the square,** UPRIGHTNESS-DISHONESTY; **put a square thing into a round hole,** SKILL-UNSKILFULNESS; **square accounts,** ACCOUNTS, SETTLEMENT-DEFAULT; **square chain,** MEASURE; **square foot,** MEASURE; **square inch,** MEASURE; **square inches,** EXTENSION-DISTRICT; **square link,** MEASURE; **square mile,** MEASURE; **square rod,** MEASURE; **square the circle,** POSSIBILITY-IMPOSSIBILITY; **square up,** PAINTING; **square with,** HARMONY-DISCORD; **square yards,** EXTENSION-DISTRICT.

square'-toes''. A precise person. SOCIETY-LAUGHINGSTOCK.

squash. To beat or press into a soft mass. CREATIONDESTRUCTION, HARDNESS-SOFTNESS, IMPETUS-REACTION, RESONANCE-SIBILATION, SWAMP-ISLAND, VISCIDITY-FOAM.

squash'-y. Mashed into a soft mass. SWAMP-ISLAND, VISCIDITY-FOAM.

squat. To crouch in a sitting posture; short and thick. BREADTH-NARROWNESS, ESTABLISHMENT-REMOVAL, GREATNESS-LITTLENESS, HEIGHT-LOWNESS, LENGTHSHORTNESS, SPRING-DIVE.

squat'-ter. One who settles on land without right. DWELLER-HABITATION.

squaw. An American Indian woman. MALE-FEMALE, MATRIMONY-CELIBACY.

squeak. A sharp, penetrating sound. CRY-ULULATION.

squeal. A shrill cry. CRY-ULULATION.

squeam'-ish. Easily shocked. DESIRE-PARTICULARNESS, HEALTH-SICKNESS, READINESS-RELUCTANCE.

squea'-sy. Sick at the stomach; nauseating. DESIREPARTICULARNESS.

squeez'-a-ble. That may be squeezed. CONSENT.

squeeze. To compress. ENLARGEMENT-DIMINUTION, POLITENESS - IMPOLITENESS, SOLIDITY - RARITY; **squeeze out,** GIVING-RECEIVING, INJECTION-EJECTION.

squeez'-ing. Compressing. ENLARGEMENT-DIMINUTION.

squelch. To disconcert. CREATION-DESTRUCTION.

squib. To discharge; a lampoon. CRASH-DRUMMING, SOCIETY-DERISION.

squint. Looking askance. SIGHT-DIMSIGHTEDNESS.

squire. An esquire; a lawyer or prominent citizen. OBSTRUCTION-HELP, CHIEF-UNDERLING, GENTILITYCOMMONALTY.

squire'-ar''-chy. A body of squires. GENTILITYCOMMONALTY.

squir-een'. An Irish landlord. GENTILITY-COMMONALTY.

squir'-rel. A rodent. ACTIVITY - INDOLENCE, SWIFTNESS-SLOWNESS.

squirt. To spurt forth. ADMISSION-EXPULSION, RIVER-WIND.

S. S. C. Solicitor Supreme Court. ADVOCATE.

stab. To pierce with a pointed weapon. APERTURECLOSURE, BETTERMENT-DETERIORATION, GOODNESSBADNESS, LIFE-KILLING.

sta-bil'-i-tate. To establish firmly. MUTABILITY-STABILITY.

sta-bil'-i-ty. Steadiness. MUTABILITY-STABILITY, MUTATION-PERMANENCE.

sta'-ble. A building for the occupancy of horses; fixed. DWELLER-HABITATION, MUTABILITY-STABILITY, MUTATION-PERMANENCE; **lock the stable door when the steed is stolen,** OPPORTUNENESS-UNSUITABLENESS, SKILL-UNSKILFULNESS, USEFULNESS-USELESSNESS; **stable equilibrium,** MUTABILITY-STABILITY.

stab'-lish. To settle. MUTABILITY-STABILITY.

stab'-lish-ment. Settlement. MUTABILITY-STABILITY.

stac-ca'-to. Marked by abrupt, sharp emphasis. MUSIC.

stack. A systematic pile or heap. GATHERING-SCATTERING, STORE.

stad'-dle. A prop. SUSPENSION-SUPPORT.

stade. A wharf. CONVEXITY-CONCAVITY.

stadt'-hold''-er. A governor. CHIEF-UNDERLING.

staff. A stick carried for some special purpose; a body of officers; a musical scale. ASSOCIATION, CHIEFUNDERLING, COUNCIL, MELODY-DISSONANCE, SANGUINENESS - HOPELESSNESS, SCEPTER, SIGN, SUSPENSION - SUPPORT, WEAPON; **pastoral staff,** VESTMENTS; **staff-officer,** CHIEF-UNDERLING; **staff of life,** LIFE-DEATH, NUTRIMENT-EXCRETION; **staff of office,** SCEPTER.

stag. A male, especially of the deer. FAUNA-FLORA, MALE-FEMALE, SETTLEMENT-DEFAULT.

stage. A platform; the theater; a station; a degree of advancement; a vehicle. ACTING, CONVEYANCEVESSEL, DURATION-NEVERNESS, FAUNA - FLORA, LAMINA-FIBER, LISTS, POSITION, QUANTITY-MEASURE, SCHOOL, STATION, SUSPENSION-SUPPORT; **come upon the stage,** VISIBILITY-INVISIBILITY; **go off the stage,** APPEARANCE-DISAPPEARANCE, ARRIVAL-DEPARTURE; **on the stage,** ACTING, MANIFESTATIONLATENCY; **stage business,** ACTING; **stage-coach,** CONVEYANCE-VESSEL; **stage direction,** PRECEPT; **stage effect,** POMP; **stage-manager,** ACTING; **stage-play,**

ACTING; **stage-player**, ACTING; **stage trick**, POMP; **stage whisper**, VOCALIZATION-MUTENESS.

sta'-ger. An actor. ACTING, AGENT; **old stager**, ADEPT-BUNGLER, INFANT-VETERAN.

sta'-ger-y. Exhibition. ACTING.

stage'-wag-on. A wagon serving as a stage-coach. CONVEYANCE-VESSEL.

stage'-y. Theatrical. ACTING.

stag'-ger. To reel; to waver. AGITATION, ASTONISH-MENT - EXPECTANCE, EXCITATION, EXPECTATION-SURPRISE, FAITH-MISGIVING, MOTIVE-CAPRICE, OSCIL-LATION, SWIFTNESS-SLOWNESS; **stagger belief**, FAITH-MISGIVING; **stagger like a drunken man**, DETERMINA-TION-VACILLATION.

stag'-ger-ing. Giddy. AGITATION.

stag'-gers. Giddy sensation. AGITATION.

Stag'-i-rite. A native of Stageira, especially Aristotle. TASTE-VULGARITY.

stag'-nan-cy. A stagnant condition. MOVEMENT-REST.

stag'-nant. Standing still. MOVEMENT-REST.

stag'-nate. To be or become stagnant. MOVEMENT-REST.

stag-na'-tion. An inaction. MOVEMENT-REST.

sta'-gy. Belonging to or befitting the stage. ACTING, SOCIETY-AFFECTATION.

staid. Sedate. EXCITABILITY-INEXCITABILITY, LIGHT-HEARTEDNESS - DEJECTION, SAGACITY - INCAPACITY.

staid'-ness. Sedateness. EXCITABILITY-INEXCITABIL-ITY

stain. A spot; a moral taint. BETTERMENT-DETERI-ORATION, CLEANNESS-FILTHINESS, COLOR-ACHRO-MATISM, EMBELLISHMENT-DISFIGUREMENT, REPUTA-TION-DISCREDIT; **stain-paper**, WRITING-PRINTING.

stained. Discolored; soiled. **Travel-stained**, TRAV-ELING-NAVIGATION.

stain'-less. Without stain. CLEANNESS-FILTHINESS, INNOCENCE-GUILT, UPRIGHTNESS-DISHONESTY.

stair. A step, or a series of steps. WAY.

stair'-case''. A flight of steps. WAY.

stair'-way''. A staircase. WAY.

stake. A post; something wagered. CONNECTIVE, HURRY-LEISURE, PROPERTY, PURPOSE-LUCK; **at stake**, PURPOSE-LUCK, SECURITY-INSECURITY.

sta-lac'-tite. An icicle-like form in which certain minerals are deposited. COVER-LINING.

sta-lag'-mite. A deposition on the floor of a cavern. COVER-LINING.

stale. Having lost freshness. BETTERMENT-DETERI-ORATION, NOVELTY-ANTIQUITY, SAVOR-TASTELESS-NESS; **stale, flat, and unprofitable**, USEFULNESS-USELESSNESS; **stale news**, TIDINGS-MYSTERY.

stale'-mate''. A situation in chess resulting in a drawn game. SUCCESS-FAILURE.

stalk. To approach stealthily or in a dignified manner. TRAVELING-NAVIGATION; **stalk abroad**, SELFRE-SPECT-HUMBLENESS, UNIVERSALITY-PARTICULARITY.

stalk'-ing-horse''. A horse behind which a hunter conceals himself in stalking game. EXPOSURE-HIDINGPLACE, PRETEXT.

stall. A stable; booth; seat. ACTING, ARCHITECTURE, CHURCH, CONTENTS-RECEIVER, DWELLER-HABITA-TION, FANE, SUSPENSION-SUPPORT; **finger-stall**, COVER-LINING.

stal'-lion. An uncastrated male horse. CONVEYER, MALE-FEMALE.

stal'-wart. Brawny. GREATNESS - LITTLENESS, STRENGTH-WEAKNESS.

stam'-i-na. Strength. PERSISTENCE-WHIM, STRENGTH-WEAKNESS.

stam'-mel. Red. REDNESS-GREENNESS.

stam'-mer-ing. Halting utterance. SPEECH-INARTIC-ULATENESS.

stamp. An impressed mark; kind; label. COMPLE-TION-NONCOMPLETION, CONDITION - SITUATION, DI-VISION, ENGRAVING, FORM-FORMLESSNESS, SECURITY, SIGN; **stamp in the memory**, REMEMBRANCE-FORGET-FULNESS; **stamp out**, CREATION-DESTRUCTION, HEAT-ING-COOLING; **stamp the foot**, FAVORITE-ANGER.

stam-pede'. A sudden, tumultuous movement of a crowd. SANGUINENESS-TIMIDITY.

stanch. To stop or check the flow of ; staunch a flow. DETERMINATION-CAPRICE, HEALTH-SICKNESS, RENO-VATION-RELAPSE, RIVER-WIND.

stan'-chion. A timber support. SUSPENSION-SUPPORT.

stanch'-less. Incapable of being stanched or stopped. EXCITABILITY-INEXCITABILITY.

stand. To rest in an erect position; to keep firm; to stop; to halt; to endure; to continue in force. APER-TURE-CLOSURE, BRAVERY-COWARDICE, DIFFICULTY-FACILITY, EMOTION, ENTITY-NONENTITY, EXCITA-BILITY-INEXCITABILITY, LASTINGNESS - TRANSIENT-NESS, MUTATION-PERMANENCE, PRESENCE-ABSENCE, REPRISAL-RESISTANCE, STATION, SUSPENSION-SUP-PORT; **at a stand**, ACTION-PASSIVENESS; **come to a stand**, DIFFICULTY-FACILITY; **make a stand**, ANTAGO-NISM-CONCURRENCE, STRIFE-PEACE; **stand a chance**, LIKELIHOOD-UNLIKELIHOOD, POSSIBILITY - IMPOSSI-BILITY; **stand aghast**, ASTONISHMENT-EXPECTANCE; **stand aloof**, ACTION-PASSIVENESS, POLITENESS-IM-POLITENESS, PROFFER - REFUSAL, QUEST - EVASION, RECKLESSNESS-CAUTION, **stand at attention**, EXPEC-TATION-SURPRISE; **stand at ease**, HEED-DISREGARD; **stand by**, ATTACK - DEFENSE, OBSTRUCTION - HELP, REMOTENESS - NEARNESS; **stand committed**, GUARD-PRISONER; **stand fair for**, LIKELIHOOD-UNLIKELI-HOOD; **stand fire**, BRAVERY-COWARDICE; **stand firm**, DETERMINATION-VACILLATION, MUTABILITY-STABIL-ITY, REPRISAL-RESISTANCE; **stand first**, BEGINNING-END; **stand for**, BEGINNING-END, COMMISSION-ABRO-GATION, PROFFER-REFUSAL, REPRESENTATIVE, SIGN; **stand forth**, VISIBILITY-INVISIBILITY; **stand in need of**, NEED; **stand in the shoes of**, COMMISSION-ABRO-GATION, COMMUTATION-PERMUTATION, REPRESENTA-TIVE; **stand in the way of**, OBSTRUCTION-HELP; **stand no nonsense**, DETERMINATION-VACILLATION; **stand of arms**, WEAPON; **stand off**, APPROACH-WITH-DRAWAL; **stand on**, SUSPENSION-SUPPORT; **stand one in**, PRICE-DISCOUNT; **stand one in good stead**, USE-FULNESS-USELESSNESS; **stand one's ground**, CONSER-VATION, REPRISAL - RESISTANCE; **stand on one's rights**, LIBERTY-SUBJECTION; **stand out**, BIGOTRY-APOSTASY, CONVEXITY-CONCAVITY, REPRISAL-RE-SISTANCE, VISIBILITY-INVISIBILITY; **stand over**, EARLINESS-LATENESS; **stand still**, DIFFICULTY-FA-CILITY, MOVEMENT-REST, MUTATION-PERMANENCE; **stand the brunt**, ATTACK-DEFENSE; **stand the hazard of the die**, PURPOSE-LUCK; **stand the proof**, GOOD-NESS-BADNESS; **stand the test**, GOODNESS-BADNESS, TRUTH-ERROR; **stand to one's engagement**, OB-SERVANCE-NONOBSERVANCE; **stand to reason**, CER-TAINTY-DOUBT, DUENESS-UNDUENESS, MANIFESTA-TION-LATENCY, PROOF-DISPROOF; **stand up**, ELEVA-TION-DEPRESSION, ERECTNESS-FLATNESS; **stand well in the opinion of**, APPROVAL-DISAPPROVAL; **take one's stand**, DETERMINATION-VACILLATION, DUENESS-UN-DUENESS, REPRISAL-RESISTANCE; **take one's stand upon**, ASSERTION - DENIAL, PRETEXT, RATIOCINA-TION-INSTINCT.

stand'-ard. Serving as a model. COPY-MODEL, FAULTLESSNESS - FAULTINESS, GOODNESS - BADNESS, MENSURATION, QUANTITY-MEASURE, SIGN, UNI-FORMITY-MULTIFORMITY.

stand'-ard-bear''-er. One who carries the flag or ensign; the leader. BELLIGERENT.

stand'-ing. Relative position; station; permanent. BELLIGERENT, CONDITION-SITUATION, LASTINGNESS-TRANSIENTNESS, MUTATION - PERMANENCE, POSI-

TION, QUANTITY-MEASURE, REPUTATION-DISCREDIT; **standing army,** BELLIGERENT; **standing committee,** PRESIDENT-MEMBER; **standing dish,** MUTATION-PERMANENCE, UNIFORMITY-MULTIFORMITY; **standing jest,** WITTINESS-DULNESS; **standing order,** HABIT-DESUETUDE, LAW-LAWLESSNESS; **standing water,** GULF-PLAIN.

stand'-point". A point of view. POSITION.

St. An'-drew. Patron saint of Scotland. PATRIOTISM-TREASON.

stand'-still. Halt. MUTATION-PERMANENCE.

stand up. To be upright. ELEVATION-DEPRESSION, ERECTNESS-FLATNESS; **stand up against,** REPRISAL-RESISTANCE; **stand-up fight,** STRIFE-PEACE; **stand up for,** APPROVAL-DISAPPROVAL, JUSTIFICATION-CHARGE.

stan'-na-ry court. Courts for administering justice among the tinners. TRIBUNAL.

stan'-za. A group of rimed lines. POETRY-PROSE, RHETORIC.

sta'-ple. A metal fastening; a principal commodity; a mart. CONNECTIVE, EXCHANGE, MARKET, MATERIALS, TEXTURE, WHOLE-PART; **staple commodity,** MERCHANDISE.

star. One of the minor luminous heavenly bodies; a star-shaped ornament of honor; a person of brilliant qualities. ACTING, ASTRONOMY, EMBELLISHMENT-DISFIGUREMENT, GENTILITY-COMMONALTY, LUMINARY-SHADE, REPUTATION-DISCREDIT, TITLE, VOLITION-OBLIGATION; **star in the ascendant,** SUCCESS-FAILURE, WELFARE-MISFORTUNE; **star it,** ACTING, POMP, REPUTATION-DISCREDIT; **star of fashion,** SOCIETY-LUDICROUSNESS; **star-spangled banner,** PATRIOTISM-TREASON.

star'-board. The right side of a vessel facing the bow. RIGHT-LEFT.

starch. A granular substance used for stiffening cloth; prim; precise. HARDNESS-SOFTNESS, SELFRESPECT-HUMBLENESS, SOCIETY-AFFECTATION, VISCIDITY-FOAM.

star'' cham''-ber. An ancient high court. TRIBUNAL.

starched. Farinaceous. POMP.

starch'-ed-ness. Stiffness. SOLEMNIZATION.

stare. A steady, fixed gaze. ASTONISHMENT-EXPECTANCE, INQUISITIVENESS-INDIFFERENCE, SIGHT-BLINDNESS; **death stares one in the face,** LIFE-DEATH; **make one stare,** ASTONISHMENT-EXPECTANCE; **stare one in the face,** MANIFESTATION-LATENCY, OCCURRENCE-DESTINY; **stare out of countenance,** POLITENESS-IMPOLITENESS, PRESUMPTION-OBSEQUIOUSNESS, SELFRESPECT-HUMBLENESS.

stare super antiquas vias [L.] (stê'-rî siu'-per an-ti'-quas vai'-as). To stand above the old ways. ACTION-PASSIVENESS, CONSERVATION, DISCONTINUANCE-CONTINUANCE, HABIT-DESUETUDE.

star'-ga''-zer. A man who gazes at the stars. UNIVERSE.

star'-ga''-zing. The act of attentively observing the stars; abstraction. UNIVERSE.

star'-ing. Gazing with fixed attention. VISIBILITY-INVISIBILITY.

stark. Stiff; stubborn; completely. ENTIRETY-DEFICIENCY, HARDNESS-SOFTNESS, MAGNITUDE-SMALLNESS.

stark''-star'-ing. With wide open eyes. MAGNITUDE-SMALLNESS, MANIFESTATION-LATENCY.

star'-light''. The light given by the stars. LIGHT-DARKNESS.

star'-like''. Resembling a star. SHARPNESS-BLUNTNESS.

star'-ry. Set with stars; lighted by stars. UNIVERSE.

stars. Celestial bodies. UNIVERSE; **bless one's stars,** THANKFULNESS-THANKLESSNESS; **stars and stripes,** SIGN; **stars in the firmament,** MULTIPLICITY-PAUCITY.

start. To move suddenly; to begin; a setting out. ARRIVAL-DEPARTURE, ASTONISHMENT-EXPECTATION, BEGINNING-END, BETTERMENT-DETERIORATION, EXPECTATION-SURPRISE, HYPOTHESIS, IMPETUS-REACTION, OCCURRENCE-DESTINY, PROFFER-REFUSAL, PUSH-PULL, REVOLUTION, SANGUINENESS-TIMIDITY, SPRING-DIVE; **get the start,** LEADING-FOLLOWING, SUCCESS-FAILURE; **give a start to,** IMPETUS-REACTION; **have the start,** ANTECEDENCE-SEQUENCE, EARLINESS-LATENESS, LEADING-FOLLOWING; **start a doubt,** FAITH-MISGIVING; **start afresh,** BEGINNING-END; **start a question,** INVESTIGATION-ANSWER; **start game,** QUEST-EVASION; **start off,** ARRIVAL-DEPARTURE; **start up,** ASCENT-DESCENT, LAMINA-FIBER, VISIBILITY-INVISIBILITY.

start'-ing. Setting out. **Starting-hole,** PRETEXT; **starting-point,** ARRIVAL-DEPARTURE, BEGINNING-END, RATIOCINATION-INSTINCT.

start'-le. To alarm; to arouse suddenly. ASTONISHMENT-EXPECTATION, EXCITATION, EXPECTATION-SURPRISE, FAITH-MISGIVING, SANGUINENESS-TIMIDITY.

start'-ling. Causing to start. EXPECTATION-SURPRISE.

start'-lish. Easily startled. EXCITABILITY-INEXCITABILITY.

starts. Sudden quick and startled movements. **By fits and starts,** PERSISTENCE-WHIM.

star-va'-tion. The act of starving or of being starved. EXCESS-LACK, FASTING-GLUTTONY.

starve. To perish with cold or hunger. AFFLUENCE-PENURY, EXTRAVAGANCE-AVARICE, FASTING-GLUTTONY, HEAT-COLD, HEATING-COOLING.

starved. Reduced to a state of extreme hunger. BREADTH-NARROWNESS, EXCESS-LACK, FASTING-GLUTTONY, HEAT-COLD.

starve'-ling. A person or animal that is starved. AFFLUENCE-PENURY, BREADTH-NARROWNESS, EXCESS-LACK.

state. Condition of a being at any given time; rank; quality; a body politic. ASSERTION-DENIAL, CONDITION-SITUATION, ENLIGHTENMENT-SECRECY, HUMANITY, POMP, PROPERTY, RULE-LICENSE, UNIVERSALITY-PARTICULARITY; **robes of state,** SCEPTER; **secretary of state,** MANAGER; **state of affairs,** OCCURRENCE-DESTINY; **state of facts,** ACCOUNT, LITIGATION; **state of siege,** FIGHTING-CONCILIATION; **state paper,** MARK-OBLITERATION; **stateroom,** CONTENTS-RECEIVER.

state'-craft". The art of conducting state affairs. MANAGEMENT.

sta'-ted per'-i-ods. Fixed or appointed times. **At stated periods,** PERIODICITY-IRREGULARITY, POMP, REGULARITY-IRREGULARITY.

state'-li-ness. Dignity. REPUTATION-DISCREDIT.

state'-ly. Lofty; dignified. POMP, REPUTATION-DISCREDIT, SELFRESPECT-HUMBLENESS.

state'-ment. The act of stating. ACCOUNT, ASSERTION-DENIAL, ENLIGHTENMENT-SECRECY.

state'-mon"-ger. One versed in politics. MANAGER.

States' Gen'-er-al. A political assembly. COUNCIL.

states'-man. A political leader of distinguished ability. MANAGER.

states'-man-like". Resembling a statesman. SKILL-UNSKILFULNESS.

states'-man-ship. The qualifications, duties, or employments of a statesman. CONDUCT, MANAGEMENT.

stat'-ics. A branch of mechanics, treating of bodies at rest. HEAVINESS-LIGHTNESS, STRENGTH-WEAKNESS.

sta'-tion. A place where anything stands; post assigned; office. ESTABLISHMENT-REMOVAL, EX-

TENSION - PLACE, POSITION, QUANTITY - MEASURE, RELEASE-PRISON, REPUTATION-DISCREDIT, STATION.

STATION.

Degree. The point or step of progression to which a person has arrived. QUANTITY-MEASURE.
Footing. Established position.
Grade. A step or degree in any series, rank, or order; relative position.
Link. A division of a chain in land-measuring used to mark position.
Mark. A sign to mark position.
Pas [F.]. A step; a pace used to define the position of an object.
Peg. A small pointed piece of wood used to mark position.
Period. A limit; a bound; an end.
Pitch. Technically, the distance between two points.
Place. A particular point or position; position in life.
Point. A particular place or position.
Position. The situation in which a thing is placed.
Range. The area over which anything moves.
Rank. Relative position or degree.
Remove. The space through which anything is removed.
Round of the ladder. Figurative for position in life.
Scale. A system of notation in which the successive places determine the value of figures.
Stage. A definite position in a development.
Stand. Position; place.
Standing. Relative position.
Station. Social position; the spot or place where anything stands.
Status [L.]. Relative position or rank.
Step. An advance position.
Term. A dividing mark of position.

STATION—Verbs.

Fall into a place. |
Find a place. |
Hold a place.   } To be in a certain rank or position. See *Nouns.*
Occupy a place. |

sta′-tion-a-ry. Remaining in one place or position. MOVEMENT-REST, MUTATION-PERMANENCE.
sta′-tion-er″-y. Writing materials. WRITING-PRINTING.
sta′-tion-house″. The district headquarters of police and place of confinement. RELEASE-PRISON.
sta′-tist. A statistician. MANAGER.
sta-tis′-tic-al. Relating to statistics. NUMBERING.
sta-tis′-tics. Systematized numerical facts collectively. MARK-OBLITERATION, NUMBERING, OUTLAY-INCOME, RECORD.
statu pupillari, in [L.] (stět′-yu piu-pil-lê′-ri, in). In infancy. INFANCY-AGE.
statu quo, in [L.] (stê-tiu quo, in). In the former state. MUTATION-PERMANENCE, RENOVATION-RELAPSE.
statu quo ante bellum, in [L.] (stê-tiu quo an′-tî bel′-lum′). As it was before the war. MUTATION-PERMANENCE.
stat′-u-a-ry. Art of carving statues; a maker, also a collection of statues. ARTIST, SCULPTURE.
stat′-ue. A plastic work representing a human or animal figure. ARTIST, DELINEATION - CARICATURE; **still as a statue,** MOVEMENT-REST.
stat″-u-ette′. A small statue. DELINEATION-CARICATURE.
stat′-ure. The natural height of an animal body. HEIGHT-LOWNESS.
sta′-tus. Relative position or rank. CONDITION-SITUATION, POSITION, REPUTATION-DISCREDIT.
stat′-u-ta-ble. Relating to a statute. LAW-LAWLESSNESS.
stat′-ute. A law; an edict; legal. LAW-LAWLESSNESS, PRECEPT; **statute law,** LAW-LAWLESSNESS; **statute mile,** QUANTITY-MEASURE.
stat′-u-to-ry. Relating to a statute. LAW-LAWLESSNESS.
staunch. Strong and firm; sound; hearty. DETERMINATION - VACILLATION, HEALTH - SICKNESS,

RENOVATION-RELAPSE, UPRIGHTNESS-DISHONESTY; **staunch belief,** FAITH-MISGIVING.
stave. A part of a psalm as sung in churches; to ward off, as with a staff. MELODY-DISSONANCE, MUSIC, STRIFE-PEACE; **stave in,** APERTURE-CLOSURE, CONVEXITY-CONCAVITY; **stave off,** EARLINESS-LATENESS, OBSTRUCTION-HELP.
stay. To remain; to stop; to check. DISCONTINUANCE-CONTINUANCE, EARLINESS-LATENESS, MOVEMENT-REST, MUTATION-PERMANENCE, OBSTRUCTION-HELP, PRESENCE-ABSENCE, SUSPENSION-SUPPORT; **stay at home,** SOCIABILITY-PRIVACY; **stay away,** PRESENCE-ABSENCE; **stay one's hand,** DISCONTINUANCE-CONTINUANCE, QUEST-ABANDONMENT, TOIL-RELAXATION.
stayed. Staid; settled; sober. EXCITABILITY-INEXCITABILITY, LIGHTHEARTEDNESS-DEJECTION, SAGACITY-INCAPACITY.
stays. An old form of corsets. DRESS-UNDRESS.
St. Da′-vid. Patron saint of Wales. PATRIOTISM-TREASON.
stead. Place or room; turn. CONSEQUENCE-INSIGNIFICANCE; **in the stead of,** COMMISSION-ABROGATION, COMMUTATION-PERMUTATION, REPRESENTATIVE; **stand one in good stead,** USEFULNESS-USELESSNESS.
stead′-fast. Constant. DETERMINATION - WHIM, STRENGTH-WEAKNESS; **steadfast belief,** FAITH-MISGIVING; **steadfast thought,** HEED-DISREGARD.
stead′-i-ness. Stability in position. DETERMINATION-VACILLATION.
stead′-y. Stable in position; constant in mind or conduct. DETERMINATION - VACILLATION, MUTABILITY-STABILITY, PERIODICITY-IRREGULARITY, PERSISTENCE-WHIM, RECKLESSNESS-CAUTION, UNIFORMITY-MULTIFORMITY.
steak. A slice of meat. NUTRIMENT-EXCRETION.
steal. To take unlawfully and secretly. TAKING-RESTITUTION, THEFT; **steal along,** ENLIGHTENMENT-SECRECY, SWIFTNESS-SLOWNESS; **steal a march,** ACTIVITY-INDOLENCE, ANTECEDENCE-SEQUENCE, CRAFT-ARTLESSNESS, EARLINESS-LATENESS, LEADING-FOLLOWING, TRANSCURSION-SHORTCOMING, TRUTHFULNESS-FRAUD; **steal away,** QUEST-EVASION; **steal on the ear,** LOUDNESS-FAINTNESS; **steal upon one,** EXPECTATION-SURPRISE.
steal′-ing. The act of taking secretly and unlawfully. GAIN-LOSS, THEFT.
stealth. A secret or clandestine act. ENLIGHTENMENT-SECRECY; **do good by stealth,** CONCEIT-DIFFIDENCE.
stealth′-i-ly. In a concealed manner. ENLIGHTENMENT-SECRECY.
stealth′-i-ness. A stealing away. ENLIGHTENMENT-SECRECY.
stealth′-y. Moving or acting secretly or slyly. CRAFT-ARTLESSNESS, ENLIGHTENMENT - SECRECY, RECKLESSNESS-CAUTION.
steam. The elastic vapor of boiling water; an exhalation. LIQUEFACTION-VOLATILIZATION, LIQUID, TRAVELING-NAVIGATION, VISCIDITY-FOAM; **get the steam up,** EXCITATION, PREPARATION-NONPREPARATION; **steam up,** VIGOR-INERTIA; **under sail and steam,** SWIFTNESS-SLOWNESS; **under steam,** TRAVELING-NAVIGATION
steam′-boat″. A boat propelled by steam. CONVEYANCE-VESSEL.
steam′-en″-gine. An engine that derives its motive force from the action of steam. TRAVELING-NAVIGATION; **steam-engine to crack a nut,** EXCESS-LACK, PROVISION-WASTE, USE-MISUSE.
steam′-er. A steamship. CONVEYANCE-VESSEL.
steam′-ing. Making steam. LIQUEFACTION-VOLATILIZATION.

steam'-rol"-ler. A roller propelled by steam. TRAVELING-NAVIGATION.

steam'-ship". A ship propelled by steam. CONVEYANCE-VESSEL.

ste'-ar-in. The harder ingredient of animal fat. PULPINESS-OILINESS.

steed. A horse. CONVEYER.

steel. Iron combined with a small portion of manganese. CHEMISTRY, HARDNESS - SOFTNESS, SENSITIVENESS - APATHY, SHARPNESS - BLUNTNESS, STRENGTH-WEAKNESS, WEAPON; **steel oneself,** DETERMINATION-VACILLATION; **steel plate,** ENGRAVING; **steel the heart,** REPENTANCE-OBDURACY.

steeled a-gainst'. Hardened against. DETERMINATION-VACILLATION, SENSITIVENESS-APATHY.

steel'-en-grav'-ing. Engraving done on a steel plate. ENGRAVING.

steel'-yard. A device for weighing.

steep. To soak in a liquid; greatly inclined. PARALLELISM-INCLINATION, WATER-AIR.

steeped in. Imbued with. **Steeped in iniquity,** VIRTUE-VICE; **steeped in misery,** PLEASURE-PAIN.

stee'-ple. A spire. ARCHITECTURE, HEIGHT-LOWNESS, SHARPNESS-BLUNTNESS.

stee'-ple-chase". A race on horseback across country. QUEST-EVASION, SWIFTNESS-SLOWNESS.

steep'-ness. Sharpness. PARALLELISM-INCLINATION.

steeps. Hills. HEIGHT-LOWNESS.

steer. To direct; to guide. MANAGEMENT; **steer clear,** AIM-ABERRATION, QUEST-EVASION; **steer for,** AIM-ABERRATION; **steer one's course,** CONDUCT.

steer'-age. Pilotage. AIM-ABERRATION, MANAGEMENT.

steer'-ing. Directing. AIM-ABERRATION.

steers'-man. One who steers. · MANAGER, WAYFARER-SEAFARER.

steers'-mate". A man who steers. MANAGER.

steg'-a-nog'-ra-phy. The art of writing in cipher. CLEARNESS - OBSCURITY, ENLIGHTENMENT-SECRECY, WRITING-PRINTING.

stel'-lar. Of or pertaining to the stars. UNIVERSE.

stel'-la"-ted. Resembling a star. SHARPNESS-BLUNTNESS.

stel'-li-form. Star-shaped. SHARPNESS-BLUNTNESS.

ste-log'-ra-phy. The art of writing or inscribing characters on pillars. WRITING-PRINTING.

stem. The principal body of a tree or plant; the stock of a family; the forward part of a vessel. ANTAGONISM-CONCURRENCE, ANTERIORITY-POSTERIORITY, CAUSE-EFFECT, PARENTAGE-PROGENY; **stem the tide,** ANTAGONISM-CONCURRENCE, DISCONTINUANCE-CONTINUANCE, REPRISAL-RESISTANCE, SUCCESS-FAILURE; **stem the torrent,** REPRISAL-RESISTANCE, SUCCESS-FAILURE; **stem to stern,** LENGTH-SHORTNESS.

stench. A foul smell. PERFUME-STENCH.

sten'-cil. A metal plate used in marking letters or patterns. PAINTING.

sten-og'-ra-phy. The art of writing in shorthand. WRITING-PRINTING.

Sten'-tor. A person of powerful voice. CRY-ULULATION, LOUDNESS-FAINTNESS.

sten-to'-ri-an. Extremely loud. CRY - ULULATION, LOUDNESS-FAINTNESS.

step. A pace; a stair; a small space; progression. ACTION-PASSIVENESS, DESIGN, MENSURATION, MOVEMENT-REST, STATION, SUSPENSION-SUPPORT, TRAVELING-NAVIGATION; **but a step,** REMOTENESS-NEARNESS; **dance the back-step,** ADVANCE-RETROGRESSION; **not stir a step,** MOVEMENT-REST; **step by step,** CONTINUITY - INTERRUPTION, QUANTITY - MEASURE, REGULARITY-IRREGULARITY, SWIFTNESS-SLOWNESS; **step forward,** ADVANCE-RETROGRESSION; **step in,** MEDIATION; **step in the right direction,** USEFULNESS-USELESSNESS; **step into,** GAIN-LOSS; **step into the**

shoes of, ANTECEDENCE-SEQUENCE, COMMUTATION-PERMUTATION, GAIN-LOSS, PRECEDENCE-SUCCESSION; **step of time,** PERIOD-PROGRESS; **step on,** SUSPENSION-SUPPORT; **step short,** SWIFTNESS-SLOWNESS; **take a decisive step,** CHOICE-NEUTRALITY, DETERMINATION-VACILLATION.

steppe. A vast plain devoid of forest. GULF-PLAIN.

step'-ping-stone". A stone affording a foot-rest; anything by means of which one advances. CONNECTIVE, INSTRUMENTALITY, PREPARATION-NONPREPARATION, REFUGE-PITFALL.

steps. Paces; stairs. WAY; **find one's steps,** AIM-ABERRATION, QUEST-EVASION, TRAVELING-NAVIGATION; **flight of steps,** ASCENT-DESCENT; **retrace one's steps,** ADVANCE-RETROGRESSION; **take steps,** CONDUCT, DESIGN, PREPARATION-NONPREPARATION; **tread in the steps of,** IMITATION-ORIGINALITY, LEADING-FOLLOWING.

ster"-co-ra'-ceous. Of or pertaining to dung. CLEANNESS-FILTHINESS.

ster"-e-og'-ra-phy. Perspective. WRITING-PRINTING.

ster"-e-om'-e-try. The art of measuring and computing the cubical contents of bodies and figures. MENSURATION.

ster'-e-o-scope. An optical instrument. OPTICAL INSTRUMENTS.

ster"-e-o-scop'-ic. Of or pertaining to a stereoscope.

ster'-e-o-type. A plate of type-metal, resembling the surface of a page of type. ENGRAVING, SIGN, WRITING-PRINTING.

ster'-e-o-typed. Formed into or printed from stereotype plates. HABIT-DESUETUDE.

ster'-ile. Barren. FERTILITY-STERILITY.

ste-ril'-i-ty. Barrenness. FERTILITY-STERILITY.

ster"-il-i-za'-tion. Process of sterilizing. BIOLOGY.

ster'-ling. Of standard weight or quality; genuine; pure. TRUTH-ERROR, VIRTUE-VICE; **sterling coin,** MONEY.

stern. Severe; harsh. ANTERIORITY-POSTERIORITY, HARSHNESS, SOCIABILITY-PRIVACY; **stern necessity,** TRUTH-ERROR, VOLITION-OBLIGATION.

stern'-most. Farthest in the rear. ANTERIORITY-POSTERIORITY.

stern'-ness. Severity. POLITENESS-IMPOLITENESS.

ster"-nu-ta'-tion. The act of sneezing. RESONANCE-NONRESONANCE, RIVER-WIND.

stern'-way". Backward motion of a vessel. TRAVELING-NAVIGATION.

ster'-tor-ous. Hoarsely breathing; snoring. VOCALIZATION-MUTENESS.

steth'-o-scope. An apparatus of auscultation. REMEDY-BANE.

stet pro ratione voluntas [L.] (stet pro rê-shi-o'-nî voî-un'-tas). The wish stands for the thought. VOLITION-OBLIGATION.

ste'-ve-dore". One whose business is that of stowing or unloading the hold of vessels. TRAVELING-NAVIGATION.

stew. To boil slowly and gently; stewed food; mental agitation. DIFFICULTY-FACILITY, EMOTION, EXCITABILITY-INEXCITABILITY, HEAT-COLD, HEATING-COOLING, NUTRIMENT-EXCRETION, PLEASURE-PAIN, PURITY-IMPURITY; **in a stew,** FAVORITE-ANGER.

stew'-ard. A person in charge of an establishment. MANAGER, TREASURER.

stew'-ard-ship. The office of a steward. CONDUCT, MANAGEMENT.

stew'-pan". A pan used for stewing. OVEN-REFRIGERATOR.

St. George. Patron saint of England. PATRIOTISM-TREASON.

stich'-o-man"-cy. Divinations from lines taken at hazard from books. PROPHECY.

stick. A small shoot of a tree; a rod; to cling; **to stop.**

ADEPT-BUNGLER, APERTURE-CLOSURE, COHESION-LOOSENESS, DISCONTINUANCE-CONTINUANCE, MOVEMENT-REST, SAGE-FOOL, SCOURGE, SUSPENSION-SUPPORT, WEAPON; **dirty end of the stick,** SKILL-UNSKILFULNESS; **give the stick to,** EXCULPATION-PUNITION; **stick at,** FAITH-MISGIVING, READINESS-RELUCTANCE; **stick at nothing,** ACTIVITY-INDOLENCE, DETERMINATION-VACILLATION, DIFFICULTY-FACILITY, RECKLESSNESS-CAUTION; **stick fast,** DIFFICULTY-FACILITY, MOVEMENT-REST, MUTABILITY-STABILITY; **stick in,** INJECTION-EJECTION; **stick in one's gizzard,** FAVORITE-ANGER, PLEASURABLENESS-PAINFULNESS; **stick in the mud,** SUCCESS-FAILURE, TRANSCURSION-SHORTCOMING; **stick in the throat,** DESIRE-DISTASTE, PLEASURABLENESS-PAINFULNESS, TALKATIVENESS-TACITURNITY, VOCALIZATION-MUTENESS; **stick law,** EXCULPATION-PUNITION; **stick out,** CONVEXITY-CONCAVITY; **stick to,** DETERMINATION-VACILLATION, DISCONTINUANCE - CONTINUANCE, TOIL - RELAXATION; **stick up,** ELEVATION-DEPRESSION, ERECTNESS-FLATNESS; **stick up for,** APPROVAL-DISAPPROVAL, JUSTIFICATION-CHARGE, OBSTRUCTION-HELP.

stick'-i-ness. Adhesion. COHESION-LOOSENESS, VISCIDITY-FOAM.

stick'-ing. Adhering. COHESION-LOOSENESS.

stick'-le. To contend about trifling matters. BIGOTRY-APOSTASY, EXCHANGE, READINESS-RELUCTANCE; **stickle for,** EXCHANGE, STRIFE-PEACE.

stick'-ler. One who stickles. BIGOTRY-APOSTASY, HARSHNESS-MILDNESS.

stick'-y. Adhesive. COHESION-LOOSENESS, VISCIDITY-FOAM.

stiff. Rigid; obstinate; severe. BEAUTY-UGLINESS, HARDNESS-SOFTNESS, HARSHNESS-MILDNESS, POMP, PURITY-CRUDENESS, RELEASE-RESTRAINT, SELFRESPECT - HUMBLENESS, SOCIETY - AFFECTATION; **stiff breeze,** RIVER-WIND.

stiff'-en. To make or become stiff or stiffer. HARDNESS-SOFTNESS.

stiff'-head'-ed. Obstinate. BIGOTRY-APOSTASY.

stiff'-heart'-ed. Stubborn. BIGOTRY-APOSTASY.

stiff'-necked. Stubborn. BIGOTRY-APOSTASY, SELFRESPECT-HUMBLENESS.

stiff'-ness. The quality or state of being stiff. MUTABILITY-STABILITY, PURITY-CRUDENESS, SOCIETY-AFFECTATION.

sti'-fle. To smother; to conceal. ENLIGHTENMENT-SECRECY, LIFE-KILLING, SOUND-SILENCE.

sti'-fled. Smothered. LOUDNESS-FAINTNESS.

sti'-fling. Suffocating. HEAT-COLD.

stig'-ma. A mark of infamy. REPUTATION-DISCREDIT.

stig'-ma-tize. To mark with a stigma. APPROVAL-DISAPPROVAL, JUSTIFICATION-CHARGE, REPUTATION-DISCREDIT.

stile. A set of steps for passing a fence. OBSTRUCTION-HELP, WAY; **help a lame dog over a stile,** OBSTRUCTION-HELP.

sti-let'-to. A small dagger. PERFORATOR-STOPPER, WEAPON.

still. Silent; inert; a distillery. COMPENSATION, LIQUEFACTION-VOLATILIZATION, MOVEMENT-REST, OVEN - REFRIGERATOR, SOUND - SILENCE, TURBULENCE-CALMNESS; **in still water,** VARIANCE-ACCORD; **still-born,** LIFE-DEATH, SUCCESS-FAILURE; **still less,** EVIDENCE-COUNTEREVIDENCE; **still life,** MATERIALITY-SPIRITUALITY, PAINTING.

still'-hunt". To pursue noiselessly. QUEST-EVASION.

stil"-li-cid'-i-ous. Falling in drops. RIVER-WIND.

stil"-li-cid'-i-um. The flow of urine drop by drop. RIVER-WIND.

still'-ness. Quiet. MOVEMENT-REST, SOUND-SILENCE.

still'-y. Soft. SOUND-SILENCE.

stilt'-ed. Artificially elevated in manner. BRAGGING,

ELEVATION - DEPRESSION, SIMPLICITY - FLORIDNESS, SOCIETY-AFFECTATION, SOCIETY-LUDICROUSNESS.

stilts. Wooden bars devised to raise the foot above the ground in walking. SUSPENSION-SUPPORT; **on stilts,** BRAGGING, ELEVATION-DEPRESSION, GULL-HYPERBOLE, PARALLELISM, SELFRESPECT-HUMBLENESS.

stim'-u-late. To animate. EXCITATION, MOTIVE-CAPRICE, PLEASURABLENESS-PAINFULNESS, TRUTHFULNESS-FRAUD, TURBULENCE-CALMNESS, VIGOR-INERTIA.

stim'-u-lus. An incentive. MOTIVE-CAPRICE.

sting. To affect with a sharp sensation, as if from a sting. EXCITATION, FAVORITE-ANGER, PLEASURABLENESS-PAINFULNESS, REMEDY-BANE, SENSUALITY-SUFFERING, TINGLING-NUMBNESS.

stin'-gi-ness. Niggardliness. EXTRAVAGANCE-AVARICE.

sting'-ing. Piercing; pungent. PLEASURABLENESS-PAINFULNESS, PUNGENCY.

stin'-go. Strong liquor. NUTRIMENT-EXCRETION.

stin'-gy. Niggardly. EXCESS-LACK, EXTRAVAGANCE-AVARICE.

stink. Foul odor. CLEANNESS-FILTHINESS, PERFUME-STENCH; **stink in the nostrils,** DESIRE-DISTASTE, LOVE-HATE, PLEASURABLENESS-PAINFULNESS.

stink'-ing. Having a foul odor. PERFUME-STENCH.

stink'-pot". A pot containing something that stinks; the musk-turtle. PERFUME-STENCH.

stint. Proportion allotted. BOUNDARY, EXCESS-LACK, EXTRAVAGANCE-AVARICE, QUANTITY-MEASURE.

stint'-ed. Restrained. EXCESS-LACK.

stint'-less. Without limit. ENOUGH.

sti'-pend. Salary. RECOMPENSE-PENALTY.

sti-pen'-di-a-ry. Receiving a stipend; one who receives a stipend. GIVING-RECEIVING, LIBERTY-SUBJECTION.

stip'-ple. A method of engraving or painting. ENGRAVING, PAINTING, VARIEGATION; **stipple engraving,** ENGRAVING.

stip'-u-late. To particularize. CONTRACT, TERMS; **stipulate for,** STRIFE-PEACE.

stip"-u-la'-tion. An agreement. ENGAGEMENT-RELEASE, TERMS.

stir. To move; agitation. ACTIVITY-INDOLENCE, AGITATION, EXCITATION, MOVEMENT-REST, VIGOR-INERTIA; **make a stir,** ACTIVITY-INDOLENCE, CONSEQUENCE-INSIGNIFICANCE; **stir about,** ACTIVITY-INDOLENCE; **stir a question,** INVESTIGATION-ANSWER, RATIOCINATION-INSTINCT; **stir one's stumps,** ACTIVITY-INDOLENCE, SWIFTNESS-SLOWNESS, TRAVELING-NAVIGATION; **stir the blood,** EXCITATION, FAVORITE-ANGER; **stir the feelings,** EXCITATION; **stir the fire,** HEATING-COOLING; **stir up,** EXCITATION, MIXTURE-HOMOGENEITY, TURBULENCE-CALMNESS; **stir up dissension,** VARIANCE-ACCORD.

stirps. A race; family. CAUSE-EFFECT, PARENTAGE-PROGENY, RELATIONSHIP.

stir'-ring. Active. ACTIVITY-INDOLENCE, CONSEQUENCE-INSIGNIFICANCE, OCCURRENCE-DESTINY; **stirring news,** TIDINGS-MYSTERY.

stir'-rup. A kind of ring, for supporting a horseman's foot. SUSPENSION-SUPPORT; **with a foot in the stirrup,** ARRIVAL-DEPARTURE.

stir'-rup-cup". A parting cup taken after mounting. ARRIVAL-DEPARTURE.

stir'-rups. A ring for support. SUSPENSION-SUPPORT.

stitch. To sew or unite together; a sharp pain. ACTION-PASSIVENESS, SENSUALITY-SUFFERING, UNION-DISUNION; **stitch in time,** EARLINESS-LATENESS; **stitch of work,** TOIL-RELAXATION.

stive. To cram; stifle. HEATING-COOLING.

sti'-ver. A small Dutch coin. MONEY.

stoat. The ermine. PERFUME-STENCH.

stoc-ca'-do. A stab. REPRISAL-RESISTANCE.

stock. Stem; race; a cravat; supply; standard; capital. CAUSE-EFFECT, CONSANGUINITY, DRESS-UNDRESS, HABIT-DESUETUDE, LABOR-CAPITAL, MAGNITUDE-SMALLNESS, MATERIALS, MERCHANDISE, MONEY, PARENTAGE - PROGENY, PROPERTY, PROVISION-WASTE, QUANTITY-MEASURE, SAGE-FOOL, STORE; **in stock,** HOLDING-EXEMPTION; **laughing-stock,** SOCIETY-LAUGHINGSTOCK; **lay in a stock,** PROVISION-WASTE; **stock exchange,** LABOR-CAPITAL; **stock in trade,** MERCHANDISE, PROPERTY, READINESS-RELUCTANCE, STORE; **stock-still,** MOVEMENT - REST; **stock with,** PROVISION - WASTE; **take stock,** ACCOUNTS, HEED-DISREGARD.

stock-ade'. A fortifying fence. ATTACK-DEFENSE.

stocked. Supplied. **Well stocked,** ENOUGH.

stock' ing. A covering for the foot and leg. DRESS-UNDRESS.

stock'–job''–bing. Speculating in stocks. EXCHANGE.

stocks. An apparatus formerly used for holding and punishing petty criminals. RECOMPENSE-SCOURGE, RELEASE-PRISON, TREASURY; **on the stocks,** OCCUPATION, PREPARATION-NONPREPARATION; **stocks and stones,** MATERIALITY-SPIRITUALITY, SENSITIVENESS-APATHY.

sto'-ic-al. Impassive. EXCITABILITY-INEXCITABILITY, UNSELFISHNESS-SELFISHNESS.

sto'-i-cism. Stoical indifference to pleasure or pain. EXCITABILITY-INEXCITABILITY, MODERATION-SELF-INDULGENCE, SENSITIVENESS-APATHY, UNSELFISHNESS.

sto'-ker. One who tends an engine fire. WAYFARER-SEAFARER.

stole. An ecclesiastical vestment. VESTMENTS.

sto'-len. Taken by stealth. THEFT; **stolen away,** ESCAPE; **stolen goods,** PLUNDER.

stol'-id. Dull or stupid. SAGACITY-INCAPACITY, WITTINESS-DULNESS.

sto-lid'-i-ty. Impassibility. SAGACITY-INCAPACITY.

stom'-ach. The principal organ of digestion; appetite; desire. CONTENTS-RECEIVER, DESIRE-DISTASTE, EXCITABILITY-INEXCITABILITY, SAVOR-TASTELESSNESS; **not have the stomach to,** READINESS-RELUCTANCE; **stomach of an ostrich,** FASTING-GLUTTONY; **turn the stomach,** PLEASURABLENESS-PAINFULNESS.

stom'-ach-er. An ornament or support to the breast. DRESS-UNDRESS.

stone. A mass of hard mineral matter; a gem; English legal weight of 14 pounds; to pelt or kill with stones. ATTACK-DEFENSE, ENGRAVING, EXCULPATION-PUNITION, HARDNESS-SOFTNESS, HEAVINESS-LIGHTNESS, LIFE-FUNERAL, LIFE-KILLING, MATERIALS, MEASURE, SOLIDITY-RARITY, WEAPON; **cast the first stone at,** JUSTIFICATION-CHARGE; **corner-stone,** CONSEQUENCE-INSIGNIFICANCE; **heart of stone,** CHARITABLENESS-MALEVOLENCE, SENSITIVENESS-APATHY; **keystone,** CONSEQUENCE-INSIGNIFICANCE; **mark with a white stone,** CONSEQUENCE - INSIGNIFICANCE; **musical stones,** MUSICAL INSTRUMENTS; **no stone unturned,** INVESTIGATION-ANSWER, TOIL-RELAXATION; **philosopher's stone,** MIGHT-IMPOTENCE, REMEDY-BANE; **precious stone,** GOODNESS-BADNESS; **stepping-stone,** WAY; **stone of Sisyphus,** USEFULNESS-USELESSNESS; **throw a stone at,** APPROVAL-DISAPPROVAL, JUSTIFICATION - CHARGE, REPRISAL - RESISTANCE; **throw a stone in one's own garden,** REPRISAL-RESISTANCE, SKILL-UNSKILFULNESS; **throw stones at,** ATTACK-DEFENSE, CHARITABLENESS-MALEVOLENCE; **tombstone,** LIFE-FUNERAL.

stone'-blind''. Totally blind. SIGHT-BLINDNESS.

stone'–col''-ored. Bluish gray. GRAY-BROWN.

stone'-deaf''. Completely deaf. HEARING-DEAFNESS.

stone's throw. The distance a stone may be thrown by hand. REMOTENESS-NEARNESS.

stone'-ware. A variety of pottery. HEATING-COOLING.

sto'-ny. Abounding in stone. HARDNESS-SOFTNESS.

sto'–ny–heart''-ed. Hard-hearted; unfeeling. CHARITABLENESS-MALEVOLENCE, PARDON-VINDICTIVENESS.

stool. A seat. SUSPENSION-SUPPORT; **between two stools,** DIFFICULTY-FACILITY, SUCCESS-FAILURE; **stool of repentance,** REPENTANCE-OBDURACY.

stoop. To lean; to condescend. ASCENT-DESCENT, ELEVATION - DEPRESSION, PARALLELISM - INCLINATION, PRESUMPTION-OBSEQUIOUSNESS, SELFRESPECT-HUMBLENESS, UPRIGHTNESS-DISHONESTY; **stoop to conquer,** CRAFT-ARTLESSNESS, SELFRESPECT-HUMBLENESS, SKILL-UNSKILFULNESS.

stop. To obstruct; to stay; to bring from motion to rest. ACTION-PASSIVENESS, APERTURE-CLOSURE, BEGINNING - END, CONSEQUENCE - INSIGNIFICANCE, DISCONTINUANCE - CONTINUANCE, LEAVE - PROHIBITION, MOVEMENT-REST, OBSTRUCTION-HELP, SOUND-SILENCE; **put a stop to,** DISCONTINUANCE-CONTINUANCE, OBSTRUCTION-HELP; **stop a flow,** RIVER-WIND; **stop a gap,** RENOVATION-RELAPSE; **stop payment,** SETTLEMENT-DEFAULT; **stop short,** DISCONTINUANCE-CONTINUANCE, MOVEMENT-REST; **stop short of,** TRANSCURSION-SHORTCOMING; **stop the breath,** LIFE-KILLING; **stop the ears,** HEARING-DEAFNESS; **stop the mouth,** PROOF-DISPROOF, VOCALIZATION-MUTENESS; **stop the sound,** RESONANCE-NONRESONANCE; **stop the way,** OBSTRUCTION-HELP; **stop up,** APERTURE-CLOSURE.

stop'-cock''. A faucet having a stop or valve. PERFORATOR-STOPPER.

stop'-gap''. That which stops a gap. COMMUTATION-PERMUTATION, PERFORATOR-STOPPER.

stop'-page. A stopping or arresting progress. DISCONTINUANCE-CONTINUANCE, OBSTRUCTION-HELP.

stop'-per. One that stops or hinders; that which fills a vent. APERTURE-CLOSURE, OBSTRUCTION-HELP, PERFORATOR-STOPPER.

stop'-ping. A hindering. DISCONTINUANCE-CONTINUANCE, PERFORATOR-STOPPER.

stop'-ple. A stopper. PERFORATOR-STOPPER.

stor'-age. Act of storing. STORE.

store. A source of supplies; a place where goods are sold. MARKET, STORE; **in store,** HOLDING-EXEMPTION, OCCURRENCE-DESTINY, PREPARATION-NONPREPARATION; **lay in a store,** PROVISION-WASTE; **set no store,** OVERVALUATION-UNDERVALUATION; **set store by,** APPROVAL-DISAPPROVAL, CONSEQUENCE-INSIGNIFICANCE; **store in the memory,** REMEMBRANCE-FORGETFULNESS; **store of knowledge,** KNOWLEDGE-IGNORANCE.

STORE.

Accumulation. That which is stored up.

Bonne bouche [F.]. A nice amount stored up

Budget. A stock or store.

Conservation. The act of preserving or keeping.

Corps de reserve [F.]. A part of an army held in reserve.

Crop. The product of what is planted.

Fund. A sum of money stored up for a specific purpose.

Harvest. That which is reaped.

Heap, etc. A collection of things stored together. See GATHERING.

Hoard. Something gathered and stored away.

Lumber. Disused articles stored away.

Milch-cow. A cow giving milk.

Mine. A productive supply of anything.

Mow. A heap of hay or sheaves stored in a barn.

Nest-egg. A sum of money stored away.

Relay, etc. A supply stored up for anticipated use. See PROVISION.

Reserve. Something held back for future use.

Reserved fund. A fund laid aside for future use.

Rick. A stack or pile of grain in the open air.

Savings. Sums stored up.

Stack. A large pile of grain, hay, or straw.

Stock. The capital of a company represented by shares held by individuals.

Stock in trade. Goods employed by a merchant in his business.

Storage.
Storing. } The act of depositing in a store or warehouse.
Store. Something laid up for future need.
Supply. Sufficiency of things for use or want.
Treasure. Riches stored up.
Vintage. The produce of the vine for one season.

STORE—*Nouns of Place.*

Armory. A place where instruments of war are deposited.
Arsenal. A public place for the storage of arms.
Bank, etc. A place where money is kept. See TREASURY.
Budget. A bag or sack.
Buttery. An apartment where butter, milk and other provisions are kept.
Cache. A hole in the ground for preserving provisions.
Cistern. A hollow place for storing water.
Coffer, etc. A chest for keeping money or valuables. See CONTENTS-RECEIVER.
Conservatory. A place for preserving anything from loss or decay.
Depository. A place where anything is deposited for sale or keeping.
Depot. A place of deposit for the storing of goods.
Dock. An artificial basin used for the reception of vessels.
Entrepôt [F.]. A storehouse.
Fount.
Fountain. } An artificial basin for water.
Gallery. A room for keeping works of art.
Garner. A storehouse for grain.
Gasometer. An apparatus for holding gas.
Granary. A place for storing grain.
Larder. A room where food is kept.
Lode. A vein or bed of ore.
Magazine. A room for storing military supplies.
Menagerie. A place where animals are kept.
Mill-pond. A pond which supplies water for a mill.
Museum. A place where curiosities are kept.
Pond. A basin for storing water.
Portfolio. A portable case for holding loose papers.
Promptuary. That from which supplies are drawn.
Quarry. A cavern or pit where stone is taken from the earth.
Quiver. A sheath for carrying arrows.
Répertorium [L.]. A repertory.
Repertory. A place in which things are stored in an orderly manner.
Repository. A place where things may be laid up for safety.
Reservatory. A place for storing things.
Reservoir. An artificial place for storing water.
Spence. A pantry.
Spring. Any source of supply from which a stream proceeds.
Storecloset.
Storehouse. } A place for the deposit of goods.
Storeroom.
Tank. An artificial receptacle for liquids.
Thesaurus. A depository of knowledge; a treasury
Vein. That which contains useful minerals or ores.
Warehouse. A storehouse for goods.
Well. A hole sunk into the earth so as to supply water.
Well-spring. A source of continual water supply.

STORE—*Verbs.*

Accumulate. To store up by degrees.
Amass. To store up to a great degree.
Collect, etc. To gather together. See GATHERING.
Deposit. To give over for safe-keeping.
File. To preserve in a systematic order.
Fund. To store up money in a fund.
Garner. To store in a granary.
Garner up. To store, as grain.
Harvest. To collect and store in a place of safety.
Heap. To collect and store together in a pile.
Heap up. To amass.
Hoard.
Hoard up. } To store up secretly and selfishly
Hold back. To reserve.
Husband.
Husband one's resources. } To use with economy
Keep.
Keep back. } To take care of.
Lay apart. To put away for future use.
Lay by. To deposit for future use.
Lay in, etc. To store up as a provision for the future. See PROVISION.
Lay in store, etc. To store up. See *Adjectives.*
Lay up. To store away carefully for future use.
Load. To heap upon.
Preserve, etc. To store in safety. See CONSERVATION.

Put by. To lay aside for future need.
Put up. To store away; to preserve
Reserve. To hold back for future use.
Save.
Save up. } To store what would otherwise be lost.
Set apart. To put aside for future use.
Set by. To put on one side for safe-keeping.
Stack. To store without any systematic arrangement.
Store.
Store up. } To put into keeping for future use.
Stow.
Stow away. } To put away compactly for future use.
Treasure up. To store up with great care.

STORE—*Adjectives.*

In ordinary. Stored up for constant service.
In reserve. Held back for future use.
In store. In readiness for use.
Spare. Held back for use or need; additional.
Stored, etc. Heaped up; kept. See *Verbs.*
Supernumerary. More than is needed at the present time.

STORE—*Phrase.*

Adde parvum parvo, magnus acervus erit [L.]. Add little to little, a great heap will be.

store'-clos''-et. Storing place. STORE.
stored. Treasured up. STORE.
store'-house''. Warehouse. STORE.
store'-room''. A warehouse. STORE.
store'-ship''. A vessel carrying naval stores. BELLIGERENT, CONVEYANCE-VESSEL.
storge [Gr.] (stor-gê)'). Love; affection. LOVE-HATE.
sto'-ried. Told in a story. ACCOUNT.
stor'-ing. A putting away for use. STORE.
storm. A violent disturbance of the atmosphere; a violent agitation. AGITATION, ATTACK-DEFENSE, EXCITABILITY - INEXCITABILITY, FAVORITE - ANGER, GATHERING-SCATTERING, REVOLUTION, RIVER-WIND, TURBULENCE-CALMNESS; **ride the storm,** TRAVELING-NAVIGATION; **storm brewing,** SECURITY-INSECURITY; **storm in a tea-cup,** GULL-HYPERBOLE, OVERVALUATION-UNDERVALUATION; **take by storm,** SUCCESS-FAILURE, TAKING-RESTITUTION.
storm'-ing. Taking by storm. ATTACK-DEFENSE.
storm'-y. Boisterous. RIVER-WIND.
Stor'-thing. The Norwegian parliament. COUNCIL.
sto'-ry. A tale; a division in a building. ACCOUNT, CONTENTS-RECEIVER, LAMINA-FIBER, TRUTHFULNESS-FABRICATION; **as the story goes,** TIDINGS-MYSTERY; **the old story,** LOVE-HATE.
sto'-ry-tel''-ler. One who tells stories; a liar. GULL-DECEIVER.
stound. Astonishment; amazement. ASTONISHMENT-EXPECTANCE.
stoup. A vessel for holding liquids. CONTENTS-RECEIVER.
stour. A conflict. REGULARITY-IRREGULARITY.
stout. Strong of structure; bulky. BRAVERY-COWARDICE, GREATNESS-LITTLENESS, STRENGTH-WEAKNESS
stout'-heart''-ed. Courageous. BRAVERY-COWARDICE.
stout'-ness. Strength. STRENGTH-WEAKNESS.
stove. An apparatus holding a fire; broken in. OVEN-REFRIGERATOR; **stove in,** CONVEXITY-CONCAVITY.
stow. To pack closely. ENLARGEMENT-DIMINUTION, ESTABLISHMENT-REMOVAL, STORE.
stow'-age. A stowing. ESTABLISHMENT-REMOVAL, EXTENSION-PLACE.
St. Pat'-rick. Patron saint of Ireland. PATRIOTISM-TREASON.
stra'-bism. Squinting. SIGHT-DIMSIGHTEDNESS.
stra-bis'-mus. Squinting. SIGHT-DIMSIGHTEDNESS.
strad'-dle. To stand or walk with the legs far apart. TRAVELING-NAVIGATION.
strag'-gle. To stray. AIM-ABERRATION, TRAVELING-NAVIGATION.

strag'-gling. Wandering aimlessly about. REGULARITY-IRREGULARITY, UNION-DISUNION.

straight. Direct; upright. AIM-ABERRATION, CURVATION-RECTILINEARITY, ERECTNESS-FLATNESS, MIDCOURSE-CIRCUIT; **all straight,** AFFLUENCE-PENURY, SETTLEMENT-DEFAULT; **straight arch,** ARCHITECTURE; **straight course,** MIDCOURSE-CIRCUIT; **straight descent,** PARENTAGE-PROGENY; **straight sailing,** DIFFICULTY-FACILITY.

straight'-en. To make straight. CURVATION-RECTILINEARITY.

straight'-forth''. Immediately. EARLINESS-LATENESS.

straight'-for'-ward. Undeviating. AIM-ABERRATION, CRAFT-ARTLESSNESS, TRUTHFULNESS-FALSEHOOD, UPRIGHTNESS-DISHONESTY.

straight''-for'-wards. Undeviating. AIM-ABERRATION.

straight'-ness. State or quality of being straight. CURVATION-RECTILINEARITY.

straight'-way''. Immediately. EARLINESS-LATENESS.

strain. To draw with force; to exert to the utmost; to sprain. AGENCY, CLEANNESS-FILTHINESS, ENTRANCE-EXIT, GULL-HYPERBOLE, MUSIC; OVERVALUATION-UNDERVALUATION, POETRY-PROSE, SOUND-SILENCE, STRENGTH-WEAKNESS, STYLE, TOIL-RELAXATION, TRANSCURSION-SHORTCOMING, TURBULENCE-CALMNESS, VOCALIZATION-MUTENESS, WEARINESS-REFRESHMENT; **strain a point,** DUENESS-UNDUENESS, GULL-HYPERBOLE, OBSERVANCE-NONOBSERVANCE, TRANSCURSION-SHORTCOMING; **strain at a gnat and swallow a camel,** BIGOTRY-APOSTASY, SKILL-UNSKILFULNESS; **strain every nerve,** TOIL-RELAXATION; **strain one's eyes,** SIGHT-BLINDNESS; **strain one's invention,** FANCY; **strain the meaning,** INTERPRETATION-MISINTERPRETATION; **strain the throat,** CRY-ULULATION.

strained. Injured by exertion. TOIL-RELAXATION.

strait. Distress; narrow passage of water; interval. DIFFICULTY-FACILITY, GULF-PLAIN, INTERSPACE-CONTACT.

strait'-ened. Poor. AFFLUENCE-PENURY, DIFFICULTY-FACILITY.

strait'-hand''-ed. Parsimonious. EXTRAVAGANCE-AVARICE.

strait'-laced''. Fastidious; restricted; rigid in opinion. DESIRE-PARTICULARNESS, HARSHNESS-MILDNESS, RELEASE-RESTRAINT, SELFRESPECT-HUMBLENESS.

strait'-waist''-coat. A restraint; a means of restraint. RELEASE-RESTRAINT.

strand. A beach. OCEAN-LAND.

strand'-ed. Left helpless; run aground. DIFFICULTY-FACILITY, MUTABILITY-STABILITY, PLEASURE-PAIN, SUCCESS-FAILURE.

strange. Remarkable; unrelated; queer. ASTONISHMENT-EXPECTANCE, CONNECTION-INDEPENDENCE, CONVENTIONALITY-UNCONVENTIONALITY, SOCIETY-LUDICROUSNESS; **strange bedfellows,** VARIANCE-ACCORD; **strange to say,** ASTONISHMENT-EXPECTANCE.

strange'-ly. Wonderfully. MAGNITUDE-SMALLNESS.

stran'-ger. A foreigner. CONSTITUENT-ALIEN; **a stranger to,** KNOWLEDGE-IGNORANCE.

stran'-gle. To throttle; to kill; to repress. ENLARGEMENT-DIMINUTION, LIFE-KILLING, MIGHT-IMPOTENCE.

stran'-gu-la''-ted. Suffocated by constriction of the throat. ENLARGEMENT-DIMINUTION.

stran''-gu-la'-tion. Act of strangling. ENLARGEMENT-DIMINUTION, LIFE-KILLING.

strap. To fasten; a strip of leather; to beat; an instrument of punishment. CONNECTIVE, RECOMPENSE-SCOURGE, UNION-DISUNION.

strap-pa'-do. A military punishment. RECOMPENSE-PUNITION.

strap'-per. A large person or thing. GREATNESS-LITTLENESS.

strap'-ping. Big and strong. GREATNESS-LITTLENESS, STRENGTH-WEAKNESS.

strap'-work''. Ornamentation. EMBELLISHMENT-DISFIGUREMENT.

strat'-a-gem. An artifice in war; a secret plot; a deceptive design CRAFT-ARTLESSNESS, DESIGN, TRUTHFULNESS-FRAUD.

stra-teg'-ic. Artful; designing. CRAFT-ARTLESSNESS.

stra-teg'-ic-al. Artful CONDUCT, DESIGN, FIGHTING-CONCILIATION.

stra-teg'-ics. Science of strategy CONDUCT.

strat'-e-gist. One versed in strategy. ADEPT-BUNGLER, DESIGN, MANAGER.

strat'-e-gy. Use of artifice; science of military position. CONDUCT, FIGHTING-CONCILIATION.

strath. An open valley. CONVEXITY-CONCAVITY.

strath'-spey''. A Scottish dance. ENTERTAINMENT-WEARINESS.

strat''-i-fi-ca'-tion. The process of laying in layers. GEOLOGY, LAMINA-FIBER, TEXTURE.

strat'-i-fied. Laid in layers. LAMINA-FIBER; **stratified rocks,** GEOLOGY.

strat'-i-form. Formed like a stratum. LAMINA-FIBER.

stra-toc'-ra-cy. Military despotism. OUTSIDE-INSIDE, RULE-LICENSE.

stra'-tum. A layer. ERECTNESS-FLATNESS, GEOLOGY, LAMINA-FIBER.

stra'-tus. A thin layer of cloud. VISCIDITY-FOAM.

straw. A dry ripened stalk of grain; the collection of such stalks; an insignificant thing. CONSEQUENCE-INSIGNIFICANCE, GATHERING-SCATTERING, HEAVINESS-LIGHTNESS; **care not a straw,** REGARD-SCORN, SENSITIVENESS-APATHY, UNCONCERN; **catch at straws,** CREDULOUSNESS-SKEPTICISM, OVERVALUATION-UNDERVALUATION, RECKLESSNESS-CAUTION, SANGUINENESS-HOPELESSNESS, SKILL-UNSKILFULNESS, USE-MISUSE; **in the straw,** CREATION-DESTRUCTION; **man of straw,** GENTILITY-COMMONALTY, SETTLEMENT-DEFAULT, SUBSTANCE-NULLITY, TRUTHFULNESS-FRAUD; **not worth a straw,** CONSEQUENCE-INSIGNIFICANCE, USEFULNESS-USELESSNESS; **straw to show the wind,** TRIAL; **the eyes drawing straw,** ACTIVITY-INDOLENCE.

straw'-col''-ored. Pale-yellow. YELLOWNESS-PURPLE.

stray. To wander; irregular. AIM-ABERRATION, CONVENTIONALITY-UNCONVENTIONALITY, GATHERING-SCATTERING.

streak. A long stripe; a whim; a dash. BREADTH-NARROWNESS, GROOVE, LENGTH-SHORTNESS, LIGHT-DARKNESS, SIGN, VARIEGATION.

streaked. Marked by streaks. CROSSING, VARIEGATION.

stream. To pour forth; to move with a trail of light; a watercourse. ENOUGH, GATHERING-SCATTERING, LIGHT-DARKNESS, MOVEMENT-REST, RIVER-WIND, STREAM; **against the stream,** ANTAGONISM-CONCURRENCE; **stream of events,** OCCURRENCE-DESTINY; **stream of time,** PERIOD-PROGRESS; **with the stream,** ADVANCE-RETROGRESSION, ASSENT-DISSENT, CONVENTIONALITY-UNCONVENTIONALITY, DIFFICULTY-FACILITY, PRESUMPTION-OBSEQUIOUSNESS, SOCIETY-LUDICROUSNESS, VARIANCE-ACCORD.

STREAM.

Stream. A steady flow of air or water See RIVER-WIND.

STREAM—*Verbs.*

Blow, etc. To move in a steady stream. See RIVER-WIND.
Flow, etc. To move in a steady stream. See RIVER.

stream'-er. A flag. SIGN.

stream'-ing. Loose; dispread. COHESION-LOOSENESS, GATHERING-SCATTERING.

stream'-let. A rivulet. RIVER-WIND.

stream'-y. Full of streams. RIVER-WIND.

street. A public way with buildings on the sides. CITY-COUNTRY, DWELLER-HABITATION, EXTENSION-DISTRICT, WAY; **in the streets,** MANIFESTATION-LATENCY; **on the streets,** PURITY-IMPURITY.

street ar'-ab. Outcast. CITY-COUNTRY.

strength. Power; force; toughness; animality. ANIMALITY - VEGETABILITY, MAGNITUDE - SMALLNESS, MIGHT-IMPOTENCE, QUANTITY-MEASURE, RHETORIC, STRENGTH - WEAKNESS, TOUGHNESS - BRITTLENESS, VIGOR-INERTIA; **put all one's strength into,** TOIL-RELAXATION; **strength of mind,** DETERMINATION-VACILLATION; **tower of strength,** ATTACK-DEFENSE.

STRENGTH—WEAKNESS.

Brute force. Great strength without reason.

Elasticity. Power of resistance to or recovery from depression or overwork.

Energy etc. The power to do work. See VIGOR.

Force. Acting and effective strength.

Lustihood. Healthy and vigorous strength.

Main force. Sheer force.

Muscle. Powerful strength.

Nerve. Great self-reliance.

Physical force. Bodily strength.

Physique. The bodily structure of a person.

Pith. Concentrated strength.

Pithiness. The state of possessing nervous energy or force.

Power. etc The ability to exercise strength. See MIGHT.

Sinew. That which supplies strength.

Spring. That by which action or motion is produced.

Stamina. Supporting strength.

Stoutness, etc. The state of being vigorously strong. See *Adjectives.*

Strength. Inherent muscular energy.

Strengthening. A giving or increasing strength.

Tension. Great physical or intellectual effort.

Thews and sinews. Muscular strength.

Tone. State of mind or body.

Tonicity. The state of being healthful and vigorous.

Vigor. Active physical or mental strength.

Virility. Manly strength.

Vitality. The state of having animate strength.

STRENGTH—*Denotations.*

Acrobat. One who practises rope-dancing, high-vaulting, or other feats of strength.

Adamant. A stone imagined to be of impenetrable hardness.

Antæus. A giant whose strength was renewed every time that he touched the earth, his mother.

Athlete. One trained to contend in exercises requiring great physical agility and strength.

Atlas. A god represented as bearing up the pillars of heaven.

Cedar. A tree whose wood is remarkable for its durability

Cyclops. One of a race of giants having but one eye in the middle of the forehead. [Homer, *Odyssey*.]

Giant refreshed. A person of great strength.

Goliath. A Philistine giant slain by David.

Gymnast. One who practises gymnastic exercises.

Heart of oak. Courage, spirit.

Hercules. A mythological hero celebrated for his great strength.

Iron. A hard metallic element.

Iron grip. A grip holding like an iron band.

Oak. A tree whose wood is noted for its strength and durability.

Samson. A Biblical character celebrated for his strength.

Steel. A variety of iron.

Tower of strength. A source of strength.

STRENGTH—*Nouns of Cause.*

Athleticism. Training for athletic games.

Athletics. The art of training for athletic exercises.

Feats of strength. Striking acts of strength which develop the muscles.

Gymnastics. Athletic or disciplinary exercises.

Invigoration. The act of giving vigor or strength to.

Refocillation. Restoration of strength by refreshment.

Refreshment. Restoration of strength or spirit.

STRENGTH—*Scientific Nouns.*

Dynamics. That branch of mechanics which treats of the action of forces producing or changing motion.

Statics. That branch of mechanics which treats of bodies held at rest by the forces acting on them.

STRENGTH—*Verbs.*

Be strong, etc. To have great physical power. See *Adjectives.*

Be stronger. To have more power than.

Adynamia. Lack of strength resulting from disease.

Asthenia. General debility.

Atony. Abnormal weakness.

Cachexia.⎫
Cachexy.⎭ General bad health resulting from malnutrition.

Debility. Undue weakness in the vital functions.

Declension of strength. The gradual coming on of weakness.

Decrepitude. Weakness resulting from age.

Delicacy. Constitutional weakness.

Effemination. The state of becoming weak like a woman.

Enervation. Weakness resulting from nervous troubles.

Failure of strength. Gradual weakness.

Feminality. The state of lacking manly strength.

Flaccidity. Lack of firmness.

Fragility. The state of being liable to fail.

Impotence, etc. The state of wanting power. See MIGHT-IMPOTENCE.

Inactivity, etc. Lack of power to act. See ACTIVITY-INDOLENCE.

Infirmity. The state of being feeble.

Invalidation. The state of being weakened by ill-health.

Languor. Weakness resulting from the exhaustion of strength.

Loss of strength. Weakness resulting from any cause.

Relaxation. A weakening of the normal condition of the body.

Weakness. Lack of physical strength.

WEAKNESS—*Denotations.*

House of cards. A weak, unsubstantial structure.

Infant, etc. A child in the first period of life. See INFANT.

Reed. A slender grass-like plant.

Rope of sand. A weak and useless barrier.

Softling. A soft, effeminate person.

Thread. A very small twist of flax, wool, cotton, etc.

Weakling. A weak or feeble creature.

Youth, etc. The period of existence before maturity. See INFANCY.

WEAKNESS—*Nouns of Cause.*

Sprain. Lameness or weakness caused by excessive exertion or wrenching of a muscle.

Strain. An excessive and hurtful exertion of the muscles.

WEAKNESS—*Verbs.*

Be weak, etc. To lack physical strength. See *Adjectives.*

Blunt the edge of. To dull the sensibilities of.

Cramp. To weaken by confining and contracting.

Cripple. To weaken by depriving of an essential part.

Crumble. To decay bit by bit.

Debilitate. To weaken the vital functions.

Decimate. To destroy a large portion of.

Decline. To diminish in strength.

Deprive of strength. To make weak.

Dilute. To weaken by admixture with something.

Enervate. To weaken the nervous power of.

Enfeeble. To reduce the strength of.

Extenuate. To weaken the force of, as a statement.

Fade. To lose vigor and beauty.

Fail. To become weak steadily.

Flag. To grow languid.

Give way. To yield to superior force.

Halt. To be imperfect.

Have one leg in the grave. To be weak and dying.

Impoverish. To weaken by exhausting the resources of.

Languish. To lose strength and animation.

Limp. To walk lamely.

Mettre de l'eau dans son vin [F.]. To put water in his wine; to dilute.

Reduce. To bring to a lower condition.

Reduce in strength.⎫
Reduce the strength of.⎭ To weaken.

STRENGTH—WEAKNESS—*Continued.*

STRENGTH—Verbs—*Continued.*

Brace. To strengthen by giving a support.
Brace up one's loins. To prepare for action.
Case-harden. To strengthen against external good influences.
Fortify. To give strength to.
Gird up one's loins. To prepare for action.
Give strength, etc. To cause to have power. See *Nouns.*
Harden. To give great endurance to.
Invigorate. To strengthen with new energy.
Nerve. To give strength to bear trying circumstances.
Overmatch. To surpass in strength.
Recruit. To give fresh strength to.
Reenforce, etc. To give new strength to. See RENOVATION.
Refect. To refresh by food.
Refresh, etc. To renew worn-out strength. See WEARINESS-REFRESHMENT.
Render strong. To give strength to.
Set on one's legs. To renew one's strength.
Steel. To give unyielding strength to.
Strengthen. To make strong.
Sustain. To assist with supporting strength.
Validate. To make strong and powerful.
Vivify. To animate with new strength.

STRENGTH—*Adjectives.*

Able-bodied. Having a strong body.
Adamantine. Too strong to be subdued.
All-powerful. Having the strength to do everything.
Athletic. Strong from exercise.
Atlantean. Of gigantic strength.
Brawny. Having large and strong muscles.
Broad-shouldered. Having strong and well-developed shoulders.
Cyclopean. Very strong and savage.
Deep-rooted. Deep-seated.
Forcible. Having active power.
Gigantic. Of great and unusual strength
Hard. Possessing great endurance.
Hardy. Strong to endure fatigue.
Herculean. Of remarkable strength.
Impregnable. That cannot be influenced by strength.
Incontestable. Too evident to be questioned
Indomitable. Too strong to be subdued.
Inextinguishable. Too strong to be repressed
In fine feather. Elated on account of the possession of strength.
In full force. ⎫
In full swing. ⎬ With unrestrained force.
In high feather. Conscious of strength.
In the plenitude of power. With the greatest fulness of power.
Invincible. That cannot be overcome by strength.
Irresistible. That cannot be opposed by strength.
Like a giant refreshed. With great strength.
Made of iron. Very strong to endure.
Male. Of superior strength.
Manful. Having the strong and courageous nature of a man.
Manlike. Possessing the strength of a man.
Manly. Strong in a manner becoming a man.
Masculine. Strong and vigorous.
Mighty. Very forcible.
More than a match for. Superior in strength.
Muscular. Having strong muscles.
Overpowering. Bearing down by superior strength.
Overwhelming. Crushing with sudden and irresistible force.
Potent. Having power to accomplish a result.
Powerful. Possessing strength and influence.
Proof against. Too strong to be influenced by.
Puissant. Strong and mighty.
Resistless. Too strong to be withstood.
Robust. Having perfect strength.
Sinewy. Strong and vigorous.
Sound as a roach. Perfectly sound.
Sovereign. Possessing the greatest strength,
Stalwart. Strong in frame.
Stout. Possessing muscular strength.
Strapping. Physically well-developed.
Strong. Having great physical power.
Strong as a horse. ⎫
Strong as a lion. ⎬ Figurative degrees of strength.
Strong as brandy. ⎭
Stubborn. Obstinately headstrong.
Sturdy. Exhibiting rugged strength.
Thick-ribbed. Having a sturdy constitution.
Unallayed. Not diminished.

WEAKNESS—Verbs—*Continued.*

Relax. To weaken in one's efforts.
Render weak, etc. To deprive of strength. See *Adjectives.*
Shake. To lessen the steadiness of.
Sprain. To twist the ligaments about a joint.
Strain. To weaken by overexertion.
Totter. To become weak and unstable.
Tremble. To quiver involuntarily from weakness.
Unbrace. To lose one's muscular power.
Unman, etc. To destroy the virility of. See MIGHT-IMPOTENCE.
Unnerve. To remove the strength and courage of.
Weaken. To grow or make weak.

WEAKNESS—*Adjectives.*

Adynamic. Weak as a result of disease.
Aidless. Weak from want of assistance.
Asthenic. Weak from general debility.
Broken. Having one's strength seriously impaired.
Cranky. Aged and feeble.
Crazy. Mentally weak.
Creachy. Old and weak.
Debile. Weak in the vital functions.
Decayed. Reduced in strength.
Decrepit. Weak from old age.
Defenseless, etc. Without strength to ward off danger. See MIGHT-IMPOTENCE.
Drooping. Growing faint from any cause.
Dull. Weak in the power of understanding.
Effeminate. Marked by womanly weakness.
Effete. Worn out with age.
Evanid. Too weak to be permanent.
Faint. Lacking vigor.
Faintish. Somewhat faint.
Feeble. Lacking energy.
Feminate. Weak as a woman.
Flaccid. Unnaturally soft and weak.
Flimsy. Showy and weak.
Fragile. Easily broken.
Frail. Too weak to resist external influences.
Gimcrack. Showy and worthless.
Gingerbread. Unstable.
Impotent, etc. Wanting power. See MIGHT-IMPOTENCE.
Infirm. Not sound or stable.
Laid low. Overcome, as by disease.
Lame. Weakened by an injury.
Languid. Weak from listlessness.
Languishing. Having lost strength and animation.
Nervous. Having weak nerves.
On its last legs. About to fail entirely.
Palsied, etc. Not able to control one's movements. See MIGHT-IMPOTENCE.
Poor. Lacking in vigor.
Powerless. Too weak to produce an effect.
Pulled down. Weakened in vigor.
Relaxed. Having become weak in energy.
Rickety. Weak enough to fall from lack of stability.
Rotten. Weak and untrustworthy.
Sapless. Lacking spirit and energy.
Seedy. Worn out.
Shaken. Having the strength impaired.
Shaky. Of doubtful strength.
Shattered. Deprived of health.
Shattery. Liable to be shattered.
Short-winded. Affected with shortness of breath.
Sickly, etc. Liable to be affected by disease. See HEALTHINESS-SICKNESS.
Slack. Too weak to be active.
Soft. Lacking courage and manliness.
Spent. Exhausted.
Strengthless. Weak.
The worse for wear. Worn out.
Tottering, etc. About to fall. See *Verbs.*
Unaided. ⎫
Unassisted. ⎬ Weak, with no other strength to depend on.
Unnerved. Deprived of nerve force or strength.
Unstrengthened, etc. Made weak. See STRENGTH.
Unstrung. Relaxed.
Unsubstantial. Having no real strength.
Unsupported. Not upheld.
Washy. Lacking substance and strength.
Wasted. Weakened by constant loss.
Weak. Lacking physical strength.

STRENGTH—WEAKNESS—*Continued.*

STRENGTH—ADJECTIVES—*Continued*

Unconquerable. Not to be overcome by force.
Unexhausted. Not having all its strength used up.
Unquenchable. That cannot be suppressed.
Unshaken. Not weakened in strength.
Unweakened. Not made feeble.
Unwithered. Not having lost its freshness and strength.
Unworn. Having lost none of its strength from use.
Valid. Having strength founded on truth.
Vigorous. Strong in an active and lively manner.
Virile. Strong like a mature male.
Well-knit. Having a strong and compact frame
Wiry. Thin and strong.

STRENGTH—*Adverbs, etc.*

By force, etc. By using strength. See *Nouns.*
By main force, etc. By compulsion. See COERCION.
Strongly, etc. With power. See *Adjectives.*

STRENGTH—*Phrases.*

Blut und Eisen [G.]. Blood and iron.
Cœlitus mihi vires [L.]. My strength is from heaven.
Du fort au faible [F.]. Strong and weak take together.
En habiles gens [F.]. The able men.

strength'-en. To become strong. INCREASE-DECREASE.
strength'-en-ing. Making strong. STRENGTH-WEAKNESS.
strength'-less. Weak. STRENGTH-WEAKNESS.
stren'-u-ous. Earnest; insistent. ACTIVITY-INDOLENCE, PERSISTENCE-WHIM, TOIL-RELAXATION.
Strephon and Chloe. Two lovers. BLANDISHMENT.
stress. Special significance; pressure; emphasis. CONSEQUENCE-INSIGNIFICANCE, DIFFICULTY - FACILITY, NEED, TOIL-RELAXATION, VOCALIZATION-MUTENESS; **by stress of,** VOLITION-OBLIGATION; **lay stress on,** CONSEQUENCE-INSIGNIFICANCE, RATIOCINATION-INSTINCT; **stress of circumstances,** COERCION; **stress of weather,** RIVER-WIND.
stretch. To distend; to exaggerate; to exert to the utmost. DUENESS - UNDUENESS, ENLARGEMENT-DIMINUTION, GULL - HYPERBOLE, LENGTH - SHORTNESS, TOIL-RELAXATION; **at a stretch,** CONTINUITY-INTERRUPTION; **mind on the stretch,** REFLECTION-VACANCY; **on the stretch,** TOIL-RELAXATION; **stretch a point,** CONVENTIONALITY-UNCONVENTIONALITY, DUENESS - UNDUENESS, DUTY - IMMUNITY, GULL-HYPERBOLE, HARSHNESS-MILDNESS, LEAVE-PROHIBITION, OBSERVANCE-NONOBSERVANCE, TRANSCURSION-SHORTCOMING; **stretch away to,** REMOTENESS-NEARNESS; **stretch forth one's hand,** ACTION-PASSIVENESS, TAKING - RESTITUTION; **stretch of the imagination,** FANCY, GULL-HYPERBOLE; **stretch the meaning,** INTERPRETATION - MISINTERPRETATION; **stretch to,** LENGTH-SHORTNESS, REMOTENESS-NEARNESS; **upon the stretch,** HEED-DISREGARD.

WEAKNESS—ADJECTIVES—*Continued.*

Weak as a baby.
Weak as a cat.
Weak as a chicken. } Figurative expressions for degrees of physical weakness.
Weak as a child.
Weak as a rat.
Weak as gingerbread.
Weak as milk and water. } Figurative expressions for the lack or weakness of a distinguishing or essential element.
Weak as water.
Weak as water-gruel.
Weakly. Inclined to be weak.
Weather-beaten. Weakened by exposure.
Withered. Having lost freshness and power.
Womanly. Weak as a woman.
Worn. Weakened by continuous use.

WEAKNESS—*Phrase.*

Non sum qualis eram [L.]. I am not what I was.

STRENGTH—PHRASES—*Continued.*

Ex vi termini [L.]. By force of the expression.
Flecti, non frangi [L.]. You can bend but you cannot break
Our withers are unwrung.

stretch'-er. A frame for carrying the bodies of persons; a support. CONVEYANCE-VESSEL, SUSPENSION-SUPPORT.
strew. To scatter. GATHERING-SCATTERING.
stri'-æ. } Furrows; variegation. GROOVE, VARIEGA-
stri-a'-ted. } TION.
strick'-en. Afflicted. PLEASURE-PAIN; **stricken in years,** INFANCY - AGE; **terror-stricken,** SANGUINENESS-TIMIDITY.
strict. Exact; harsh; orthodox; conscientious. CONVENTIONALITY - UNCONVENTIONALITY, HARSHNESS-MILDNESS, ORTHODOXY-HETERODOXY, TRUTH-ERROR, UPRIGHTNESS-DISHONESTY; **strict inquiry,** INVESTIGATION-ANSWER; **strict interpretation,** INTERPRETATION-MISINTERPRETATION; **strict search,** INVESTIGATION-ANSWER; **strict settlement,** PROPERTY.
strict'-ly speak'-ing. Being exact. INTERPRETATION-MISINTERPRETATION, TRUTH-ERROR.
strict'-ness. Exactness. HARSHNESS - MILDNESS, ORTHODOXY-HETERODOXY.
stric'-ture. Censure; contraction; hindrance. APPROVAL - DISAPPROVAL, BREADTH - NARROWNESS, OBSTRUCTION-HELP.
stride. A step; to span with a stride. MOVEMENT-REST, REMOTENESS-NEARNESS, TRAVELING-NAVIGATION.
strides, make. To advance. ADVANCE - RETROGRESSION; **rapid strides,** SWIFTNESS-SLOWNESS.
stri'-dor. A harsh noise. CACOPHONY.
strife. Fighting; angry contention. STRIFE-PEACE, VARIANCE-ACCORD.

STRIFE—PEACE.

Action. A military engagement.
Affair. An unimportant military engagement.
Affair of honor. A duel.
Affrayment. A public brawl or fight.
Agonism. A contention for a prize.
Appeal to arms, etc. A resort to fighting as a final means. See FIGHTING.
Athletics. Games and sports that depend wholly or partly on physical strength.
Battle. A combat or conflict between two hostile forces.
Battle-royal. A battle hotly contested.
Belligerency. The state of being engaged in legitimate war.
Bone of contention, etc. A subject of contention or quarrel. See VARIANCE.
Bout. A single round or turn, as at a game.

Amity, etc. Friendly relations, etc. See AMITY.
Harmony, etc. Hearty cooperation, etc. See VARIANCE-ACCORD.
Neutrality. State of inaction for or against something; state of peace.
Pacification. Act of making peaceful.
Peace. Freedom from strife.
Tranquillity, etc. Quietness, etc. See MOVEMENT-REST.
Truce, etc. Suspension of hostilities for a time, etc. See FIGHTING-CONCILIATION.

PEACE—*Associated Nouns.*

Calumet of peace. The pipe of peace.
Pipe of peace. A pipe smoked in turn by the Indians to express friendship.

STRIFE—PEACE—*Continued.*

Boxing. The act or practise of sparring.
Brabble. A paltry dispute.
Brigue. Strife; contention.
Broil. A noisy quarrel.
Brush. A short, spirited fight.
Bull-fight. A combat in an arena between men and bulls.
Bush-fighting. Fighting under the cover of bushes or trees.
Clash of arms. A conflict.
Collision. A violent contact of forces or views.
Colluctation. A struggling together.
Combat. A contest conducted by blows.
Combativeness. Quickness to engage in conflict or dispute.
Competition. Striving for something that is sought by another at the same time.
Concours [F.]. A conflict.
Conflict. A struggle to resist or overcome.
Contention. Strife; dispute.
Contest. A struggle for supremacy.
Contestation. Dispute; strife.
Controversy. Debate or disputation.
Corrivalry. } Rivalry.
Corrivalship. }
Death-struggle. A struggle in which one of the parties is put to death.
Debate. Argumentation for and against.
Digladiation. A combat with swords.
Duel. A combat fought with deadly weapons between two persons.
Duello [It.]. The practise of duelling.
Encounter. A hostile meeting.
Engagement. An entering into or being in conflict.
Event. A proceeding in a series of games or sports.
Fight. An attempt by adversaries to overcome, injure, or destroy each other.
Fisticuffs. A pugilistic encounter.
Fracas, etc. A general fight. See VARIANCE.
Fray. A disturbance of the peace.
Free-fight. A fight engaged in by a number of persons.
Games of skill, etc. Contests for recreation, amusement, or profit. See ENTERTAINMENT.
Gladiatorship. The occupation of a gladiator.
Gymnastics. Exercises in a gymnasium.
Handicap. A race or contest in which inferiors are given certain advantages.
Hand-to-hand fight. A contest or struggle in which the contestants are so close as to touch each other.
Hard knocks. Blows with the fist or a weapon.
Heat. A single course or division of a race.
High words. A quarrel.
Horse-racing. A running race of mounted horses.
Hostile meeting. A conflict.
Joust. A tilting-match between mounted knights with blunt lances.
Litigation. A controversy that must be decided upon evidence.
Logomachy. A wordy contest without deeds.
Luctation. A struggle for success.
Match. A contest of skill or strength.
Mélée. A general hand-to-hand fight.
Mill. A pugilistic combat.
Monomachy. A duel.
Naumachia. A mock sea-fight.
Naval engagement. A battle between ships.
Opposition, etc. Attempt to obstruct or defeat. See ANTAGONISM.
Paper war. A dispute carried on in printed articles in newspapers.
Passage d'armes [F.]. A passage of arms.
Passage of arms. A personal encounter.
Pitched battle. A battle carried on by armies set in orderly array and fully prepared.
Polemics. The art of controversy or disputation.
Prize-fighting. A fight between professional pugilists for a wager or prize.
Pugilism. The practise of fighting with the fists.
Pugnacity. Quarrelsome disposition.
Quarter-staff. A contest carried on with stout sticks or staves about 6½ feet long.
Race. A competitive trial of speed.
Regatta. A series of rowing or sailing races.
Rencontre [F.]. An encounter.
Rencounter. A sudden hostile collision.
Rivalry. Competition.
Round. A single bout of wrestlers or pugilists.
Running fight. A fight engaged in while running or chasing.
Scramble. A rude, disorderly struggle or strife.
Scrimmage. A rough-and-tumble contest.

PEACE—ASSOCIATED NOUNS—*Continued.*

Piping times of peace. The times of pipe-music rather than of martial music.
Quiet life. A life of retirement and peace.

PEACE—*Verbal Expressions.*

Be at peace; keep the peace, etc. (see VARIANCE-ACCORD); make peace, etc. (see FIGHTING-CONCILIATION).

PEACE—*Adjectives.*

Bloodless. Not attended by the shedding of blood.
Calm. Free from violent agitation or noise.
Halcyon. Calm, in an interval among storms.
Pacific. Disposed to make peace.
Peaceable. Not disposed to engage in quarrels, etc.
Peaceful. Exempt from commotion.
Tranquil. Not agitated.
Untroubled. Not troubled.

PEACE—*Phrases.*

The lion lies down with the lamb.
The storm blown over.

STRIFE—*Continued.*

Scuffle. A disorderly struggle carried on by grappling, pulling, pushing, etc.
Sea-fight. A fight between ships.
Set-to. A bout at fighting, or any mode of contest.
Sham fight. A pretended or mock fight.
Sharp contest. A hotly contested struggle.
Shindy. A riotous conflict with sticks or cudgels.
Single combat. A duel.
Single-stick. A bout with cudgels.
Skirmish. A light engagement between small parties.
Spar. The act of sparring.
Sparring. The practise of boxing.
Sporting. The act of engaging in field-sports.
Sports. Athletic or outdoor games.
Stand-up fight. A hand-to-hand fight.
Steeplechase. A race on horseback in which fences, ditches, and other obstacles must be leaped.
Strife. Angry contention; hostile struggling.
Struggle. A labored contest against opposition or difficulty.
Struggle for life or death. A struggle in which one's life may be lost.
Tauromachy. Bull-fighting.
Tilt. A mock contest with lances.
Tilting. Tilt.
Tournament. A pageant in which two opposing parties of men in armor contended with blunted weapons.
Tourney. A tournament.
Triangular duel. A fight engaged in by three persons.
Tug of war. A contest in which a number of persons at one end of a rope pull against a similar number at the other end.
Tussle. A disorderly struggle.
Velitation. A slight skirmish or contest.
War of words. A wordy dispute.
Wrestling. The sport in which two persons contest, each attempting to throw the other to the ground.

STRIFE—*Associated Nouns.*

Armageddon. A plain in Palestine noted for Israelitish victories and disasters.
Deeds of arms. Remarkable achievements in war.
Derby day. The day of the annual horse-race instituted by the Earl of Derby, in 1780.
Feats of arms. Notable warlike achievements.
Field-day. A day devoted to athletic sports.
List. A jousting-field.
Satisfaction. That which is accepted as a reparation.
Turf. The race-course.

STRIFE—*Verbs.*

Box. To spar.
Clapperclaw. To scold vehemently.
Contend. To strive against another.
Contest. To enter a contest.
Emulate. To have a desire to excel.
Encounter. To meet in combat.
Fence. To use the sword in the practise of the art of attack and defense.
Fib. To pummel with short, quick blows.
Fight, etc. To strive for victory, etc. See FIGHTING.
Justle. To strike against each other.

STRIFE—Verbs—*Continued*.

Oppose, etc. To set some force against, etc. See ANTAGONISM.
Outvie. To excel.
Reluct. To struggle against anything.
Scramble. To strive eagerly for something.
Skirmish. To fight slightly.
Spar. To contest with boxing-gloves.
Square. To quarrel or fight.

Stave. To fight with staves.
Strive. To contend.
Struggle. To strive desperately.
Tilt. To contend with lances on horseback.
Tussle. To scuffle.
Wrangle, etc. To quarrel angrily, etc. See VARIANCE.
Wrestle. To try to put each other down.

STRIFE—*Verbal Expressions*.

Appeal to arms, etc. (see FIGHTING); bandy with; break the peace; buckle with; close with; come to blows; come to the scratch; compete with; contend for; contend with; cope with; couch one's lance; engage with; enter the lists; exchange blows; exchange fisticuffs; exchange shots; fall foul of; give satisfaction; go to loggerheads; grapple with; have a brush with, etc. (see Nouns); have a tilt with; insist upon; join issue; lay about one; make a point of; measure swords; meet hand to hand; pitch into; race with; run a race; run a tilt at; set-to; stickle for; stipulate for; take up the cudgels; take up the gauntlet; take up the glove; try conclusions with; vie with.

STRIFE—*Adjectives*.

At issue. Disputing.
At loggerheads. Quarreling.
At war. Engaged in fighting.
Bellicose. Disposed to make war.
Belligerent. Engaged in legitimate warfare.
Combative. Desirous of combating.
Competitive. Marked by competition.
Contending etc. Struggling with. See *Verbs*.
Contentious. Fond of contention.
Gladiatorial. Pertaining to gladiators.

Palestric. } Pertaining to wrestling.
Palestrical. }
Pugilistic. Pertaining to pugilism.
Pugnacious. Disposed to fight.
Quarrelsome, etc. Inclined to quarrel, etc. See FAVORITE-QUARRELSOMENESS.
Rival. Having opposing interests.
Together by the ears. Struggling.
Unpeaceful. Not peaceful.
Warlike, etc. Eager to carry on war, etc. See FIGHTING.

STRIFE—*Phrases*.

A verbis ad verbera [L.]. From words to blows.
A word and a blow.
Commune periculum concordiam parit [L.]. Common danger produces concord.

Lis litem generat [L.]. Strife breeds strife.
Litem lite resolvit [L.]. He settles strife by strife.
Mars gravior sub pace latet [L.]. A more serious war lurks under the peace.

strike. To hit; resist; arouse; punish; surprise; quitting of work; geologic term. AGENCY, ASTONISHMENT-EXPECTANCE, EXCITATION, GEOLOGY, IMPETUS-REACTION, INSUBORDINATION-OBEDIENCE, LABOR-CAPITAL, RECOMPENSE-PUNITION, REPRISAL-RESISTANCE; **strike a balance,** EQUALITY-INEQUALITY, MEDIUM, SETTLEMENT-DEFAULT; **strike a bargain,** CONTRACT, EXCHANGE; **strike a blow,** ACTION-PASSIVENESS; **strike a light,** HEATING-COOLING, LIGHT-DARKNESS; **strike all of a heap,** EXCITATION, SANGUINENESS-TIMIDITY; **strike at,** ATTACK-DEFENSE, IMPETUS-REACTION; **strike at the root of,** CREATION-DESTRUCTION; **strike dumb,** VOCALIZATION-MUTENESS; **strike hard,** VIGOR-INERTIA; **strike home,** ATTACK-DEFENSE, VIGOR-INERTIA; **strike in with,** ASSENT-DISSENT, CRAFT-ARTLESSNESS, IMITATION-ORIGINALITY; **strike off,** INCLUSION-OMISSION; **strike off the roll,** ADMISSION-EXPULSION, COMMISSION-ABROGATION, RECOMPENSE-PUNITION; **strike one,** REFLECTION-VACANCY; **strike one's flag,** YIELDING; **strike out,** CREATION-DESTRUCTION, DESIGN, FANCY, INCLUSION-OMISSION, MARK-OBLITERATION; **strike out something new,** FANCY, REVOLUTION; **strike root,** MUTABILITY-STABILITY; **strike sail,** SWIFTNESS-SLOWNESS; **strike tents,** ARRIVAL-DEPARTURE; **strike terror,** SANGUINENESS-TIMIDITY; **strike the eye,** HEED-DISREGARD; **strike the first blow,** ATTACK-DEFENSE; **strike the iron while it is hot,** OPPORTUNENESS-UNSUITABLENESS; **strike the lyre,** MUSICIAN; **strike the mind,** HEED-DISREGARD; **strike up,** MUSICIAN; **strike with wonder,** ASTONISHMENT-EXPECTANCE.
strik'-ing. Very noticeable. MANIFESTATION-LATENCY; **striking likeness,** ASTONISHMENT-EXPECTANCE, DELINEATION-CARICATURE, LIKENESS-UNLIKENESS.
strik'-ing-ly. Impressively. MAGNITUDE-SMALLNESS.
string. A tie; cord; fiber; continuation. CONNECTIVE, CONTINUATION-INTERRUPTION, LAMINA-FIBER, MELODY-DISSONANCE, UNION-DISUNION; **string together,** CONTINUITY-INTERRUPTION, ORGANIZATION-DISORGANIZATION.
stringed in'stru-ments. Instruments with vibrating strings. MUSICAL INSTRUMENTS.
strin'-gen-cy. Strictness. HARSHNESS-MILDNESS.
strin'-gent. Vigorous; severe. COERCION, HARSHNESS-MILDNESS, RULE-LICENSE, VIGOR-INERTIA.
strings, leading-. Guidance. INSTRUCTOR-PUPIL; **pull the strings,** DOMINANCE-IMPOTENCE, MANAGEMENT; **two strings to one bow,** MEANS.
string'-y. Fibrous; tough. LAMINA-FIBER, TOUGHNESS-BRITTLENESS.
strip. A long thin piece; to take away. BREADTH-NARROWNESS, DRESS-UNDRESS, LAMINA-FIBER, TAKING-RESTITUTION, THEFT.
stripe. A long thin mark; a blow. LENGTH-SHORTNESS, RECOMPENSE-PUNITION, SIGN, VARIEGATION.
strip'-ling. A mere youth. INFANT-VETERAN.
stripped. Poor. AFFLUENCE-PENURY.
strive. To labor; contend. STRIFE-PEACE, TOIL-RELAXATION, VENTURE; **strive against,** REPRISAL-RESISTANCE, STRIFE-PEACE.
stroke. A movement; tracing; sudden ill-health; an act. ACTION-PASSIVENESS, DESIGN, GOOD-EVIL, HEALTH-SICKNESS, HURRY-LEISURE, IMPETUS-REACTION, PLEASURABLENESS-PAINFULNESS, SIGN, SUCCESS-FAILURE; **at a stroke,** ETERNITY-INSTANTANEITY; **good stroke,** DESIGN; **stroke of policy,** DESIGN; **stroke of the pen,** ORDER, WRITING-PRINTING; **stroke of time,** ETERNITY-INSTANTANEITY; **stroke of work,** TOIL-RELAXATION; **stroke the wrong way,** SMOOTHNESS-ROUGHNESS.
stroll. To ramble. TRAVELING-NAVIGATION.
stroll'-ing play'-er. A traveling actor. ACTING.
strong. Powerful; energetic; tough; pungent. ASTONISHMENT-EXPECTANCE, EMOTION, MAGNITUDE-SMALLNESS, PERFUME-STENCH, PUNGENCY, SAVOR-TASTELESSNESS, STRENGTH-WEAKNESS, TOUGHNESS-BRITTLENESS, VIGOR-INERTIA; **by a strong arm,** COERCION; **smell strong of,** PERFUME-INODOROUS-

NESS; **strong accent,** VOCALIZATION-MUTENESS; **strong argument,** RATIOCINATION-INSTINCT; **strong language,** FORCE-WEAKNESS; **strong point,** RATIOCINATION-INSTINCT; **strong pull,** TOIL-RELAXATION; **with a strong hand,** DETERMINATION-VACILLATION, RATIOCINATION-INSTINCT, TOIL-RELAXATION.

strong'–head''–ed. Of a strong mind. SAGACITY-INCAPACITY.

strong'–hold''. A fortified place. ATTACK-DEFENSE, RELEASE-PRISON, TREASURY.

strong'–mind''–ed. Of vigorous intellect. SAGACITY-INCAPACITY, SANGUINENESS-HOPELESSNESS.

strong'–room''. A treasure house. TREASURY.

strong'–scent''–ed. Very odorous. ODOR-INODOROUSNESS.

strong'–smel''–ling. Loud in odor. PERFUME-STENCH.

strong'–willed''. Resolute. DETERMINATION-VACILLATION.

strop. A razor-strap. SHARPNESS-BLUNTNESS.

stro'–phe. A division of a lyric. POETRY-PROSE.

strow. To scatter. GATHERING-SCATTERING.

struck. Hit; beat. IMPETUS-REACTION, RECOMPENSE-PUNITION; **awestruck,** ASTONISHMENT-EXPECTANCE, SANGUINENESS-TIMIDITY; **struck all of a heap,** ASTONISHMENT-EXPECTANCE, EMOTION; **struck down,** SUCCESS-FAILURE; **struck with,** LOVE-HATE.

struc'–tur–al. Pertaining to structure. CONDITION-SITUATION; **structural geology,** GEOLOGY.

'struc'–ture. A combination of related parts. CREATION-DESTRUCTION, DWELLER-HABITATION, ORGANIZATION-INORGANIZATION, PROPORTION-DEFORMITY, TEXTURE.

strug'–gle. Toil; conflict. DIFFICULTY-FACILITY, STRIFE-PEACE, TOIL-RELAXATION.

strum. To make noisy music. MUSICIAN.

strum'–pet. A harlot. PURITY-RAKE.

strut. To walk haughtily; to boast. BRAGGING, POMP, SELFRESPECT-HUMBLENESS, TRAVELING-NAVIGATION; **strut and fret one's hour upon a stage,** ACTING, LIFE-DEATH.

strych'–nin. A poison. REMEDY-BANE.

stub'–bed. Short and thick. LENGTH-SHORTNESS.

stub'–ble. Remains of grain-stalks. INCREMENT-REMNANT, USEFULNESS-USELESSNESS.

stub'–born. Enduring; obstinate. BIGOTRY-APOSTASY, DIFFICULTY-FACILITY, HARDNESS-SOFTNESS, REPRISAL-RESISTANCE, STRENGTH-WEAKNESS, TOUGHNESS-BRITTLENESS; **stubborn fact,** ENTITY-NONENTITY.

stub'–born–ness. Obstinacy. TOUGHNESS-BRITTLENESS.

stub'–by. Blunt. LENGTH-SHORTNESS.

stuc'–co. A plaster. CONNECTIVE, COVER-LINING.

stuck. (See STICK.) Fast; in difficulty. **Stuck fast,** DIFFICULTY-FACILITY, MUTABILITY-STABILITY.

stuck'–up''. Haughty. SELFRESPECT-HUMBLENESS.

stud. A hanging-peg; horses. CONVEXITY-CONCAVITY, CONVEYER, SUSPENSION-SUPPORT.

stud'–ded. Thickly set. MULTIPLICITY-PAUCITY, SHARPNESS-BLUNTNESS, VARIEGATION.

stu'–dent. A learner. INSTRUCTOR-PUPIL.

studia in mores, abeunt [L.] (stud'–i–a in mo'–rîz, ab'–î–unt). One's habitual pursuits pass over into character. HABIT-DESUETUDE.

stud'–ied. Planned. PREDETERMINATION-IMPULSE, VOLITION-OBLIGATION.

stu'–di–o. An artist's workroom. CONTENTS-RECEIVER, PAINTING, WORKSHOP.

stu'–di–ous. Given to study; earnest. EDUCATION-LEARNING, PURPOSE-LUCK, REFLECTION-VACANCY.

stu'–di–ous–ly. In a studious manner. PURPOSE-LUCK.

stud'–y. A subject; room; thought; close attention; first sketch. CONTENTS-RECEIVER, COPY-MODEL, EDUCATION-LEARNING, ESSAY, HEED-DISREGARD, INVESTIGATION-ANSWER, PAINTING, PURPOSE-LUCK, REFLECTION-VACANCY; **study nature not books,** NATURE-ART.

stuff. Matter; cloth; nonsense; trash; to overeat; press into. ADAGE-NONSENSE, CONSEQUENCE-INSIGNIFICANCE, CONTENTS-RECEIVER, COVER-LINING, ENLARGEMENT-DIMINUTION, FASTING-GLUTTONY, MATERIALITY-SPIRITUALITY, MATERIALS, MEANING-JARGON, SUBSTANCE-NULLITY; **stuff and nonsense,** CONSEQUENCE-INSIGNIFICANCE, MEANING-JARGON, SUBSTANCE-NULLITY; **stuff in,** INJECTION-EJECTION; **stuff the memory with,** REMEMBRANCE-FORGETFULNESS; **stuff up,** APERTURE-CLOSURE, TRUTHFULNESS-FRAUD; **such stuff as dreams are made of,** FANCY, SUBSTANCE-NULLITY.

stuff'–ing. That which fills or closes. CONTENTS-RECEIVER, COVER-LINING, PERFORATOR-STOPPER.

stuff'–y. Badly ventilated. HEAT-COLD, SOLIDITY-RARITY.

stul'–ti–fied. Made a fool of. SUCCESS-FAILURE.

stul'–ti–fy. To make a fool of. COOPERATION-OPPOSITION; **stultify oneself,** SKILL-UNSKILFULNESS.

stul–til'–o–quent. Talking foolishly. ADAGE-NONSENSE.

stul–til'–o–quy. Foolish talk. ADAGE-NONSENSE.

stultorum parietibus hærent, nomina [L.] (stul–to'–rum pê'–ri–et'–i–bus hî'–rent, nom'–i–na). Fools' names are stuck on house-walls. PUBLICITY, SAGE-FOOL.

stum'–ble. To fall; blunder; fail. AGITATION, ASCENT-DESCENT, SKILL-UNSKILFULNESS, SUCCESS-FAILURE, TRUTH-ERROR; **stumble on,** DISCOVERY, RATIONALE-LUCK.

stum'–bling–block''. A hindrance. DIFFICULTY-FACILITY, OBSTRUCTION-HELP.

stump. The part left; a soft bar used in painting; to canvass. INCREMENT-REMNANT, PAINTING, SMOOTHNESS-ROUGHNESS, SPEECH-INARTICULATENESS, WHOLE-PART; **stir your stumps,** ACTIVITY-INDOLENCE; **stump along,** SWIFTNESS-SLOWNESS; **worn to the stump,** BETTERMENT-DETERIORATION.

stump or'–a–tor. A political canvasser. SPEECH-INARTICULATENESS.

stump'–y. Short. LENGTH-SHORTNESS, PROPORTION-DEFORMITY.

stun. To render senseless; deafen; astound. ASTONISHMENT-EXPECTANCE, EXCITATION, EXPECTATION-SURPRISE, FEELING-INSENSIBILITY, HEARING-DEAFNESS, LOUDNESS-FAINTNESS, SENSITIVENESS-APATHY.

stung. Wounded. **Stung to the quick,** EXCITATION.

stunned. Deafened. HEARING-DEAFNESS.

stunt. To check the growth of. LENGTH-SHORTNESS.

stunt'–ed. Small. ENLARGEMENT-DIMINUTION, GREATNESS-LITTLENESS.

stupe. A bandage. ALLEVIATION-AGGRAVATION.

stu''–pe–fac'–tion. Stupor. ASTONISHMENT-EXPECTANCE, EXCITABILITY-INEXCITABILITY, SENSITIVENESS-APATHY.

stu'–pe–fied. Astounded. SENSITIVENESS-APATHY.

stu'–pe–fy. To dull the feelings; astound. ASTONISHMENT-EXPECTANCE, FEELING-INSENSIBILITY, SENSITIVENESS-APATHY.

stu–pen'–dous. Large; wonderful. ASTONISHMENT-EXPECTANCE, GREATNESS-LITTLENESS, MAGNITUDE-SMALLNESS.

stu'–pid. Dull; tiresome; credulous. CREDULOUSNESS-SKEPTICISM, DECISION-MISJUDGMENT, ENTERTAINMENT-WEARINESS, SAGACITY-INCAPACITY, WITTINESS-DULNESS.

stu–pid'–i–ty. Slowness of apprehension. SAGACITY-INCAPACITY, SKILL-UNSKILFULNESS, WITTINESS-DULNESS.

stu′-por. Astonishment; insensibility. ASTONISH-MENT-EXPECTANCE, SENSITIVENESS-APATHY.

stu-pra′-tion. Rape. PURITY-IMPURITY.

stur′-dy. Strong; resolute. PERSISTENCE - WHIM, STRENGTH-WEAKNESS; **sturdy beggar,** PETITIONER, ROBBER.

stut′-ter. To stammer. SPEECH-INARTICULATENESS.

sty. A pig-pen. CLEANNESS-FILTHINESS, DWELLER-HABITATION.

Styg′-i-an. Dark; infernal. HEAVEN-HELL, LIGHT-DARKNESS, VIRTUE-VICE; **cross the Stygian ferry,** LIFE-DEATH; **Stygian creek,** HEAVEN-HELL; **Stygian shore,** LIFE-DEATH.

style. Manner or method; title; diction; fashion. BEAUTY - UGLINESS, CHRONOLOGY - ANACHRONISM, CONDITION - SITUATION, ENGRAVING, NAME - MISNO-MER, PAINTING, RHETORIC, SOCIETY - LUDICROUS-NESS, STYLE, WRITING-PRINTING.

STYLE.

Authorship. The state, quality, or function of an author.

Choice of words. Mastery shown in the use of language.

Command of language, etc. Power to use good language. See SPEECH.

Composition. General structural arrangement of a literary production.

Diction. The use or manner of using words.

La morgue litteraire [F.] Literary style.

Literary power. Ability to write well.

Manner. Characteristic style.

Mode of expression. The way in which a thought or sentiment is expressed.

Pen of a ready writer. Easy flowing style.

Phraseology. Choice and arrangement of words and phrases.

Ready pen. Good quality of composition.

Strain. Prevailing manner of expression or thought.

Style. Distinctive and characteristic diction; suitable choice and mode of expressing thought.

Wording. Mode of expressing in words.

STYLE—*Verbs.*

Express by words, etc. To set forth or declare. See PHRASE.

Write. To compose or produce a literary work.

style est l'homme même, le [F.] (stîl ê lom mem, le). The style is the man himself. UNIVERSALITY-PARTICULARITY, WRITING-PRINTING.

sty′-let. A little style. PERFORATOR-STOPPER, WEAP-ON.

sty′-lish. Having style. SOCIETY-LUDICROUSNESS.

Sty-li′-tes, Sim′-e-on. Syrian ascetic. SOCIABILITY-PRIVACY.

styp′-tic. Efficacious in stopping hemorrhage. SWEET-NESS-ACIDITY.

sua′-si-ble. Persuadable. READINESS-RELUCTANCE.

sua′-sion. Persuasion. MOTIVE-CAPRICE.

sua′-sive. Persuasive. MOTIVE-CAPRICE.

suave, mari magno [L.] (swê′-vî mê′-rai mag′-no). Sweet, when on the great sea. SECURITY-INSECU-RITY.

suaviter in modo [L.] (swav′-i-ter in mo′-do). Gently in manner. EXCITABILITY - INEXCITABILITY, POLITE-NESS-IMPOLITENESS.

suav′-i-ty. Urbanity. POLITENESS-IMPOLITENESS.

sub. Under. SUPREMACY-SUBORDINACY.

sub-ac′-id. Moderately acid. SWEETNESS-ACIDITY.

sub-ac′-tion. Reduction. FRIABILITY.

su′-bah-dar. A viceroy. CHIEF-UNDERLING.

sub-al′-pine. Alpestrine. HEIGHT-LOWNESS.

sub-al′-tern. A military officer below a captain. BEL-LIGERENT, CHIEF-UNDERLING, GENTILITY - COMMON-ALTY, SUPREMACY-SUBORDINACY.

sub-a′-que-ous. Under water. DEEPNESS-SHALLOW-NESS.

sub-as′-tral. Earthly. UNIVERSE.

sub′′-au-di′-tion. Supplying what is not expressed. ENLIGHTENMENT-SECRECY.

sub′′-com-mit′-tee. Under - committee. COUNCIL, PRESIDENT-MEMBER.

sub-con′-tra-ry. Somewhat contrary. LATERALITY-CONTRAPOSITION.

sub′′-cu-ta′-ne-ous. Hypodermic. OUTSIDE-INSIDE.

sub′-dean′′. Under-deacon. MINISTRY-LAITY.

sub′′-di-chot′-o-my. A subdivision. DOUBLING-HALV-ING.

sub′′-di-ti′-tious. Foisted in. COMMUTATION-PERMU-TATION.

sub′′-di-vide′. To divide into smaller parts. UNION-DISUNION.

sub′′-di-vi′-sion. A separation into smaller parts. BELLIGERENT, WHOLE-PART.

sub′-do-lous. Somewhat sly. CRAFT-ARTLESSNESS.

sub-dom′-i-nant. The tone below the dominant. MEL-ODY-DISSONANCE.

sub-du′-al. Subjugation. SUCCESS-FAILURE.

sub-duct′. To remove. ADDITION-SUBTRACTION.

sub-duc′-tion. A removal. ADDITION-SUBTRACTION.

sub-due′. To tame; to overcome. SUCCESS-FAILURE, TURBULENCE-CALMNESS.

sub-dued′. Rendered gentle. EXCITABILITY-INEXCI-TABILITY.

sub′-ed′′-i-tor. Under-editor. MISSIVE-PUBLICATION.

sub′′-i-ta′-ne-ous. Sudden. ETERNITY - INSTANTANE-ITY.

su′-bi-to. Suddenly. ETERNITY-INSTANTANEITY.

sub-ja′-cent. Directly underneath. HEIGHT-LOW-NESS.

sub′-ject. Theme; anything or any person subject; liable. CHIEF - UNDERLING, CONCEPTION - THEME, CONTINGENCY, LIBERTY-SUBJECTION, MEANING-JAR-GON; **subject matter,** COMPARISON, MEANING-JARGON; **subject of dispute,** VARIANCE-ACCORD; **subject of inquiry,** INVESTIGATION-ANSWER; **subject of thought,** CONCEPTION-THEME; **subject to,** CERTAINTY-DOUBT, MODIFICATION; **subject to examination,** INVESTIGA-TION-ANSWER.

sub-jec′-ted. Subdued. LIBERTY-SUBJECTION.

sub-jec′-tion. State of being subject. INSUBORDINA-TION-OBEDIENCE, LIBERTY-SUBJECTION, VOLITION-OBLIGATION.

sub-jec′-tive. Within the mind. MATERIALITY-SPIR-ITUALITY, MIND-IMBECILITY, SUBJECTIVENESS-OB-JECTIVENESS.

sub-jec′-tive-ness. State of being subjective. SUB-JECTIVENESS-OBJECTIVENESS.

SUBJECTIVENESS—OBJECTIVENESS.

Aspects. Look, or particular appearance of the face.

Backbone. Something likened to a backbone in position or function.

Capability, etc. The quality of being capable; intellectual power or ability, etc. See MIGHT.

Capacity. The power of receiving and holding; adequate mental power to receive, understand, endure, or accomplish.

Character. The peculiar quality, or the sum of qualities, by which a person or a thing is distinguished from others.

Constitution. The state of being; natural condition; the aggregate of all one's inherited physical qualities.

Crasis. A mixture of constituents, as of the blood; temperament.

Accident. Any non-essential circumstance, accompaniment, or attribute.

Extraneousness, etc. The quality of being outside a thing and not naturally pertaining to it, etc. See CONSTITUENT-ALIEN.

Extrinsicality. The state or quality of being extrinsic.

Non ego [L.] Not I; the objective.

Objectiveness. The state, quality, or relation of being objective.

OBJECTIVENESS—*Adjectives.*

Accidental. Non-essential; not necessarily belonging.

Adscititious. Supplemental; additional.

SUBJECTIVENESS—OBJECTIVENESS—*Continued.*

Declensions. In grammar, the inflections of nouns, adjectives, etc., according to the grammatical cases.

Diagnostics. That part of medicine which has to do with ascertaining the nature of diseases by means of their symptoms or signs.

Diathesis. Bodily constitution or condition.

Ego [L.] I.

Egohood. Personality.

Endowment. Any gift, as talent, with which a person is endowed by nature.

Essence. That in which the real character of a thing consists or which constitutes its nature; that which makes a thing what it is.

Essentialness, etc. The quality of being essential, etc. See *Adjectives.*

Essential part. Indispensable part.

Features. The cast or structure of anything, or of any part of a thing; the whole turn or style of the body.

Gist. The main point, as of a question; the pith of a matter.

Grain. Temper; natural disposition.

Habit. A tendency toward an action or condition, which by repetition has become spontaneous; an action or condition so induced; habitual course of action or conduct.

Heart. The central or vital part of interest.

Humor. Characteristic mood; frame of mind.

Idiocrasy, etc. That temperament, or state of constitution, which is peculiar to a person, etc. See INCLINATION.

Idiosyncrasy. A constitutional peculiarity.

Important part, etc. A part which is necessary. See CONSEQUENCE.

Inbeing. Inherence; inherent existence.

Incarnation. A striking exemplification in person or act; personification.

Inherence. The state of being inherent or intrinsic.

Inhesion. The condition of inhering or being fixed in something; inherence.

Intrinsicality. The quality of being intrinsic; essentialness.

Lifeblood. Figurative for that which gives strength and energy.

Marrow. The essence or best part.

Moods. The manner in which the action, being, or state expressed by a verb is stated or conceived, whether as actual, doubtful, etc.; denoted by the form of the verb.

Nature. Character; constitution or quality of mind or character; inherent or essential qualities or attributes.

Peculiarities, etc. Special and distinctive characteristics or habits, etc. See UNIVERSALITY-PARTICULARITY.

Pith. Vital or essential part; that which contains the strength or life.

Principle. Fundamental substance or energy; a fundamental truth; a governing law of conduct; in chemistry any original inherent constituent, which characterizes a substance, or gives it its essential properties.

Quality. That which makes a being or thing such as it is; essential property.

Quiddity. That which a thing is; essence; nature.

Quintessence. The most essential part of anything.

Sap. The juice of plants; hence, any fluid or humor essential to life or health; essential element.

Soul. The incorporeal nature of man; the essence, heart, or animating principle of anything.

Spirit. The part of man that has intelligence and is invisible and incorporeal; animating principle· peculiar character or quality.

Subjectiveness. The quality of proceeding from or taking place within the thinking subject; the quality of being related to the mind or mental world in distinction from the outward or material.

Temper. Disposition of mind; quality of mind with reference to the passions, emotions, or affections.

Temperament. A special type of mental constitution due to natural characteristics; constitution; make-up.

Type. Something that is emblematic; the ideal representation combining essential characteristics, as of a species.

SUBJECTIVENESS—*Verbs.*

Be born so. Have from birth a certain character.

Be in the blood. Be natural to one; be inherited.

Be intrinsic, etc. Be inherent; pertain to the nature of a thing or person, etc. See *Adjectives.*

Run in the blood. To be characteristic of all the family.

SUBJECTIVENESS—*Adjectives.*

Bred in the bone. Intrinsic; inherent.

Characteristic, etc. Distinguishing; marking, etc. See UNIVERSALITY-PARTICULARITY.

Congenital. Born with one; existing from birth.

OBJECTIVENESS—ADJECTIVES—*Continued.*

Adventitious. Added extrinsically; not essentially inherent.

Ascititious. Supplemental; not inherent.

Derived from without. Acquired; not natural.

Extraneous, etc. Not belonging to, or dependent upon a thing; not essential, etc. See CONSTITUENT-ALIEN.

Extrinsic. Not contained in or belonging to a body; external; unessential.

Extrinsical. Extrinsic.

Implanted. Planted for the purpose of growth; inculcated.

Incidental. Happening, as an occasional event; accidental; casual.

Ingrafted. Introduced; set deeply.

Modal. Characterized by form or manner, irrespective of matter or substance.

Non-essential. Not essential.

Objective. Pertaining to an object; outward; external.

Outward, etc. Pertaining to the exterior of an object; external, etc. See OUTSIDE.

OBJECTIVENESS—*Adverbs, etc.*

Accidentally. In no essential manner.

Extrinsically, etc. Outwardly; externally, etc. See *Adjectives.*

SUBJECTIVENESS—ADJECTIVES—*Continued.*

Congenite. Inborn; congenital.

Connate. Existing from birth.

Derived from within. Inborn.

Essential. Important in the highest degree; containing the essence of a substance.

Fixed. Settled; established; unalterable.

Fundamental. Indispensable; basal; primary.

Hereditary. Deriving by inheritance; passing naturally from parent to child.

Immanent. Inherent; intrinsic; subjective.

Implanted. Deeply fixed; instilled.

Inborn. Implanted by nature; innate.

Inbred. Developed from and in the nature; innate.

Incarnate. Embodied in flesh.

Incurable. Remediless.

Indigenous. Native; inherent.

Ineradicable. Incapable of being rooted out.

Ingenerate. Generated within; inborn.

Ingenite. Inbred; inherent.

Ingrained. Worked into the mental or moral constitution of; infixed deeply.

Inherent. Permanently existing in something; innate.

Inherited. Received by birth; derived from ancestors.

Innate. Inborn; natural; native.

Instinctive. Derived from, or prompted by, instinct; natural.

Internal, etc. Inward; inherent, etc. See OUTSIDE-INSIDE.

In the grain, etc. Infixed deeply, etc. See *Nouns.*

Intrinsic. Inward; inherent; essential; genuine; real.

Intrinsical. Intrinsic.

Invariable. Not given to variation or change; always uniform.

Inward. Seated in the mind, heart, spirit, or soul.

Inwrought. Worked into any fabric so as to form a part of its texture.

Natural. Pertaining to the constitution of a thing; essential; characteristic.

Normal. According to an established rule or principle; natural.

Radical. Original; fundamental; thoroughgoing.

Running in the blood. Inherited.

Subjective. Proceeding from or taking place within the thinking subject.

Thoroughbred. Bred from the best blood through a long line; hence, high-spirited, courageous, etc.

To the manner born. Familiar with something from birth. [Shakespeare, *Hamlet*, I, iv.]

Virtual. Being in essence or effect, but not in form or appearance.

SUBJECTIVENESS—*Adverbs, etc.*

At bottom. At the foundation or basis; in reality.

Au fond [F.] At bottom.

En effet [F.] In effect.

Fairly. Clearly; openly; distinctly.

In effect. In fact; in substance.

In the main. For the most part.

Intrinsically, etc. Essentially; really; truly. See *Adjectives.*

Practically. Really; in practise or use.

Substantially. In substance; essentially.

Virtually. To all intents and purposes; practically.

sub-join'. To attach. ADDITION-SUBTRACTION.

sub'-ju-gate. To subdue. LIBERTY-SUBJECTION, RELEASE-RESTRAINT, SUCCESS-FAILURE.

sub''-ju-ga'-tion. Act of subjugating. APPROVAL-DISAPPROVAL, EXCITATION, LIBERTY-SUBJECTION, SUCCESS-FAILURE.

sub-junc'-tive. Pertaining to a mood. ADDITION-SUBTRACTION.

sub''-lap-sa'-ri-an. After the fall. ORTHODOXY-HETERODOXY.

sub-la'-tion. Removal. ADDITION-SUBTRACTION, NUTRIMENT-EXCRETION.

sub''-le-va'-tion. Elevation. ELEVATION-DEPRESSION.

sub''-lieu-ten'-ant. Under-lieutenant. CHIEF-UNDERLING.

sub'-li-mate. To elevate; to vaporize. ELEVATION-DEPRESSION, HEAVINESS-LIGHTNESS, LIQUEFACTION-VOLATILIZATION.

sub''-li-ma'-tion. Elevating. ELEVATION-DEPRESSION.

sub-lime'. Lifted up; exalted; noble; majestic. BEAUTY-UGLINESS, FORCE-WEAKNESS, HEIGHT-LOWNESS, LIQUEFACTION-VOLATILIZATION, REPUTATION-DISCREDIT, UNSELFISHNESS-SELFISHNESS; **from the sublime to the ridiculous,** SOCIETY-LUDICROUSNESS.

sublime au ridicule, il n'y a qu'un pas du [F.] (su-blîm' o ri-di-cül, il ni a kun' pa dü). From the sublime to the ridiculous there is but a step. SOCIETY-LUDICROUSNESS.

sub-lim''-i-fi-ca'-tion. Act of making sublime. BEAUTY-UGLINESS.

sub-lim'-i-ty. Grandeur. BEAUTY-UGLINESS, FORCE-WEAKNESS, UNSELFISHNESS-SELFISHNESS.

sub-lin''-e-a'-tion. An underlining. SIGN.

sub'-lu-na-ry. Beneath the moon. UNIVERSE.

sub''-ma-rine'. Existing under the sea. DEEPNESS-SHALLOWNESS.

sub-me'-di-ant. The sixth of a scale. MELODY-DISSONANCE.

sub-merge'. To plunge under water; to deluge. CREATION-DESTRUCTION, INJECTION-EJECTION, SPRING-DIVE, WATER-AIR.

sub-merged'. Plunged under water. DEEPNESS-SHALLOWNESS, SPRING-DIVE.

sub-mer'-gence. Inundation. INJECTION-EJECTION.

sub-merse'. To grow under water. SPRING-DIVE.

sub-mer'-sion. Act of submerging. DEEPNESS-SHALLOWNESS, INJECTION-EJECTION.

sub-min''-is-tra'-tion. Act of subministering. OBSTRUCTION-HELP.

sub-mis'-sion. Obedience; meekness. EXCITABILITY-INEXCITABILITY, INSUBORDINATION-OBEDIENCE, SELFRESPECT-HUMBLENESS, YIELDING.

sub-miss'-ive. Yielding; obedient. DIFFICULTY-FACILITY, EXCITABILITY-INEXCITABILITY, INSUBORDINATION-OBEDIENCE, SELFRESPECT-HUMBLENESS, YIELDING.

sub-miss'-ive-ness. Obedience. INSUBORDINATION-OBEDIENCE.

sub-mit'. To yield. EXCITABILITY-INEXCITABILITY, INSUBORDINATION-OBEDIENCE, LIBERTY-SUBJECTION, SELFRESPECT-HUMBLENESS, YIELDING.

sub-mit' to ar''-bi-tra'-tion. To come together for consideration. COMPOSITION.

sub-mon'-ish. To warn. ADVICE.

sub''-mo-ni'-tion. Mild rebuke. ADVICE.

sub-mul'-ti-ple. An aliquot part. NUMBER.

sub-or'-di-nate. Secondary; inferior; subject. CONSEQUENCE-INSIGNIFICANCE, LIBERTY-SUBJECTION, PRESIDENT-MEMBER, SUPREMACY-SUBORDINATION.

sub-or''-di-na'-tion. State of being subordinate. LIBERTY-SUBJECTION, REGULARITY-IRREGULARITY.

sub-orn'. To instigate to perjury; to procure a criminal act. BUYING-SALE, MOTIVE-CAPRICE.

sub-pœ'-na. A judicial writ. LITIGATION, ORDER.

sub-rep'-tion. A fraudulent procuring. GAIN-LOSS, TRUTHFULNESS-FALSEHOOD.

sub-scribe'. To engage oneself; to pledge; to promise to give. ASSENT-DISSENT, CONTRACT, GIVING-RECEIVING, OBSTRUCTION-HELP, OUTLAY-INCOME.

sub-scrip'-tion. A giving. GIVING-RECEIVING.

sub'-se-quence. A following. ANTECEDENCE-SEQUENCE.

sub'-se-quent. Following in time or order. ANTECEDENCE-SEQUENCE, PRECEDENCE-SUCCESSION.

sub'-se-quent-ly. In a subsequent time. ANTECEDENCE-SEQUENCE, PRECEDENCE-SUCCESSION.

sub-serve'. To administer to. INSTRUMENTALITY, OBSTRUCTION-HELP, USEFULNESS-USELESSNESS.

sub-serv'-i-ence. Act of subserving. INCLINATION, OBSTRUCTION-HELP, USEFULNESS-USELESSNESS.

sub-serv'-i-en-cy. Condition of being subservient. INSTRUMENTALITY, PRESUMPTION-OBSEQUIOUSNESS.

sub-serv'-i-ent. Being of service; truckling. INCLINATION, INSTRUMENTALITY, OBSTRUCTION-HELP, USE-DISUSE, USEFULNESS-USELESSNESS.

sub-side'. To quiet down; to sink down. ASCENT-DESCENT, INCREASE-DECREASE.

sub-si'-dence. A sinking down. ASCENT-DESCENT, INCREASE-DECREASE.

sub-sid'-i-a-ry. In an inferior capacity; auxiliary. CHIEF-UNDERLING, INCLINATION, OBSTRUCTION-HELP, USE-DISUSE.

sub'-si-dize. To aid with money. OUTLAY-INCOME.

sub'-si-dy. An aid. GIVING-RECEIVING, OUTLAY-INCOME.

sub-sist'. To have existence; to continue. ENTITY-NONENTITY, LIFE-DEATH, MUTATION-PERMANENCE.

sub-sist'-ence. That on which one subsists. NUTRIMENT-EXCRETION.

sub'-soil''. The undersoil. OCEAN-LAND, OUTSIDE-INSIDE.

sub'-stance. Essence; body; matter; nature; property. AFFLUENCE-PENURY, CONSEQUENCE-INSIGNIFICANCE, MATERIALITY-SPIRITUALITY, QUANTITY-MEASURE, SUBSTANCE-NULLITY, TEXTURE; **in substance,** DIGEST; **man of substance,** AFFLUENCE-PENURY.

SUBSTANCE—NULLITY.

A being. Whatever has consciousness.

An existence. That which is

Article. A particular commodity or substance.

Body. A mass of living or dead matter.

Creature. Every living being except God.

Flesh and blood. Human nature.

Hypostasis. A groundwork; a fundamental principle.

Matter. That which occupies space.

Object. Something perceived by sight.

Person. A human being.

Plenum [L.] Fulness of matter in space.

Something Some matter indefinitely conceived or stated.

Stuff. Raw material.

Blank. An empty surface.

Cipher. The character o representing, by itself, nothing; a person or thing of no importance.

Hollowness. The state of being an empty space in a rigid body.

Inanity. Mental vacuity.

Insubstantiality. Unsubstantiality.

Mockery. Vain imitation; false show.

Naught. Nothing, cipher, zero.

Ne'er a one. } Not a person.
Never a one. }

Nihility. State of being nothing.

Nil. Nothing.

Nobody. Not a person.

SUBSTANCE—NULLITY—*Continued.*

Substance. Any particular kind of matter.
Substantiality. State of being substantial; substance.
Substratum. A layer or stratum lying beneath.
Thing. Any separable or distinguishable object of thought.
World. The earth and all it contains.

SUBSTANCE—*Adjectives.*

Bodily. Corporeal; pertaining to the body.
Hypostatic. Constituting a distinct personality or substance.
Personal. Pertaining to a particular person.
Substantial. Having real existence; actual.
Substantive. Lasting; relating to what is essential.
Tangible. Perceptible by touch; capable of being possessed.

SUBSTANCE—*Adverbs.*

Bodily. In the form of a body; in one mass.
Essentially. With reference to the essence of a thing.
Substantially, etc. In substance; essentially. See *Adjectives.*

NULLITY—VERBS—*Continued from Column 2.*

Melt away. To change from a solid to a liquid by heat; to become lost in something else, as a view.
Vanish. To disappear suddenly or in an irregular manner.

NULLITY—*Adjectives.*

Airy. Unsubstantial; fanciful.
Baseless. Without foundation.
Blank. Empty.
Dreamy. Indistinct; appropriate to dreams.
Empty. Having nothing in it.
Ethereal. Having the nature of ether; spirit-like
Eviscerated. Deprived of the entrails.
Groundless. Without cause, reason, or proper support; false.
Having no foundation. Baseless.
Hollow. Having a cavity within
Inane. Displaying mental vacuity.
Nominal. In name only; trivial.
Null. Of no legal force or effect.
Shadowy. Unreal; unsubstantial.
Ungrounded. Groundless.
Unsubstantial. Not substantial.
Vacant. Empty or unengaged, though usually not so.
Vacuous. Containing no matter.
Visionary. Impracticable; existing in imagination only
Without foundation. Having nothing to rest upon.

NULLITY—*Phrase.*

There's nothing in it.

None in the world. Nothing or nobody.
Nonentity. A non-existence.
No one. Not a person.
No such thing. Nothing.
Not a particle. Nothing at all.
Nothing. No thing.
Nothing at all. Nothing.
Nothingness. State of being nothing.
Nothing on earth. }
Nothing whatever. } Nullity.
Nullity. That which is of no effect; want of existence or force.
Thing of naught. Nothing.
Unsubstantiality. Want of substance.
Void. Empty space; emptiness in a figurative sense.
Zero.

NULLITY—*Denotations.*

Air. The gases surrounding the earth.
All moonshine. Empty nonsense.
All stuff and nonsense. Empty talk without sense.
All talk. Talk without meaning.
Baseless fabric of a vision. Lack of reality. [Shakespeare, *Tempest*, IV, i.]
Bubble. A cohesive liquid filled with air or other gas.
Dream. Thoughts or images passing through the mind in sleep.
Flash in the pan. An explosion of the powder in the pan of a flint-lock musket that does not discharge the weapon.
Fool's paradise. A place in the world of spirits formerly considered as the abode of vanity and nonsense.
Ignis fatuus [L.]. The will-o'-the-wisp.
John Doe and Richard Roe. Fictitious plaintiffs in old law pleadings.
Man of straw. One put forward as an irresponsible tool or fraudulent surety.
Nominis umbra [L.]. The shadow of a name.
Phantom. Something that exists only in appearance.
Shadow. Something having a false appearance of reality.
Such stuff as dreams are made of. Passing images. [Shakespeare, *Tempest*, iv, i.]
Thin air. Empty nonsense.
Vox et preterea nihil [L.]. Sound without sense.

NULLITY—*Verbs.*

Disappear. To go out of sight.
Dissolve. To become disseminated through a liquid; to come to an end.
Evaporate. To change into a vapor; to dissipate.
Fade. To disappear gradually, as a color.

(*Continued on Column* 1.)

---

sub-stan'-tial. Actual; strong; solid; real. ENTITY-NONENTITY, MATERIALITY-SPIRITUALITY, SOLIDITY-RARITY, SUBSTANCE-NULLITY, TRUTH-ERROR; **substantial meaning,** MEANING-JARGON.
sub-stan''-ti-al'-i-ty. State of being substantial. MATERIALITY-SPIRITUALITY, SUBSTANCE-NULLITY.
sub-stan'-tial-ly. In a substantial manner. SUBJECTIVENESS-OBJECTIVENESS, SUBSTANCE-NULLITY, WHOLE-PART; **substantially true,** TRUTH-ERROR.
sub-stan'-ti-ate. To establish the truth. DUENESS-UNDUENESS, EVIDENCE-COUNTEREVIDENCE, TRUTH-ERROR.
sub'-stan-tive. Expressing existence. ENTITY-NONENTITY, SUBSTANCE-NULLITY, TRUTH-ERROR.
sub'-sti-tute. One who takes the place of another. ALIENATION, COMMUTATION-PERMUTATION, REPRESENTATIVE, SUBSTITUTE.

SUBSTITUTE.

Deputy. One authorized to act for or in place of another. See REPRESENTATIVE.
Substitute. One who or that which takes the place of another. See COMMUTATION.

---

sub''-sti-tu'-tion. A substituting. CHEMISTRY, COMMUTATION-PERMUTATION.
sub-stra'-tum. That which is spread under; the subsoil. LAMINA-FIBER, MATERIALITY-SPIRITUALITY,
OUTSIDE-INSIDE, SUBSTANCE-NULLITY, SUSPENSION-SUPPORT, TOP-BOTTOM.
sub-struc'-ture. A foundation. TOP-BOTTOM.
sub-sul'-to-ri-ly. In a spasmodic manner. AGITATION.
sub-sul'-to-ry. Moving spasmodically. AGITATION.
sub-sul'-tus. Convulsive twitching. AGITATION.
sub-tend'. To extend opposite to. LATERALITY-CONTRAPOSITION.
sub'-ter-fuge. A false excuse. CRAFT-ARTLESSNESS, RATIOCINATION-CASUISTRY, TRUTHFULNESS-FABRICATION.
sub''-ter-ra'-ne-an. Under the earth's surface. DEEPNESS-SHALLOWNESS.
sub''-ter-rene'. Under the earth. DEEPNESS-SHALLOWNESS.
sub'-tile. Fine; not gross. HEAVINESS-LIGHTNESS, SOLIDITY-RARITY, TEXTURE.
sub-til'-i-ty. Thinness. SOLIDITY-RARITY.
sub''-til-i-za'-tion. Act of making subtile. SOLIDITY-RARITY.
sub'-til-ize. To refine. RATIOCINATION-CASUISTRY, SOLIDITY-RARITY.
sub'-tle. Sly in design; delicate. CRAFT-ARTLESSNESS, MAGNITUDE-SMALLNESS.
sub'-tle-ty. Artifice. RATIOCINATION-CASUISTRY, SAGACITY-INCAPACITY.
sub-tract'. To deduct. ADDITION-SUBTRACTION, INCREASE-DECREASE, NUMBERING.
sub-trac'-ted. Deducted. ADDITION-SUBTRACTION.

sub-trac'-tion. A deducting. ADDITION-SUBTRACTION, NUMBERING, TAKING-RESTITUTION.

sub-tract'-ive. Serving to diminish. ADDITION-SUBTRACTION.

sub'-tra-hend''. That to be subtracted. ADDITION-SUBTRACTION, NUMBER.

sub-treas'-u-ry. A branch of the treasury of the United States. TREASURY.

sub'-urb. The outer part of a city. DWELLER-HABITATION, ENVIRONMENT-INTERPOSITION, REMOTENESS-NEARNESS.

sub'-urbs. Outer parts. DWELLER-HABITATION, ENVIRONMENT-INTERPOSITION.

sub-ven'-tion. Aid; a subsidy. GIVING-RECEIVING, OBSTRUCTION-HELP, PROVISION-WASTE, SUSPENSION-SUPPORT.

sub-ver'-sion. An overthrow. CREATION-DESTRUCTION, ELEVATION-DEPRESSION, REVERSAL, REVOLUTION.

sub-ver'-sive. Destructive. CREATION-DESTRUCTION.

sub-vert'. To destroy; overturn. CREATION-DESTRUCTION, ELEVATION-DEPRESSION, EVIDENCE-COUNTEREVIDENCE, REVERSAL.

suc''-ce-da'-ne-um. A substitute. COMMUTATION-PERMUTATION.

suc-ceed'. To come in place of another; to follow in order; to pursue; to prosper. ALIENATION, ANTECEDENCE-SEQUENCE, PRECEDENCE-SUCCESSION, SUCCESS-FAILURE; **succeed to,** GAIN-LOSS.

suc-ceed'-ing. Prospering. SUCCESS-FAILURE.

suc-cess'. Prosperous issue. SUCCESS-FAILURE, WELFARE-MISFORTUNE.

SUCCESS—FAILURE.

Advance. Forward movement; progress. See ADVANCE.

Advantage over. The condition more favorable to success.

Ascendancy. The controlling influence or power.

Bold stroke. A sudden and courageous movement or effort.

Checkmate. The final position in a game of chess by which the game is won.

Conquest. Acquisition by force.

Continued success. Success without interruption.

Coup de maître [F.]. A master-stroke.

Expugnation. Act of taking by assault.

Fortunate hit. } A stroke of luck; fortunate achievement.
Fortunate stroke. }

Good fortune. Something good, coming as if by chance.

Good hit. } A decisive accomplishment.
Good stroke. }

Half the battle. Half of success.

Hit. A stroke of luck.

Lucky hit. } A favorable action.
Lucky stroke. }

Master of the position. } One who has the results of a condition or
Master of the situation. } event under control.

Master-stroke. A stroke showing the greatest ability or genius.

Mastery. Superior skill; superiority in a contest; victory in war.

Prize. The reward given to the victor.

Proficiency. An advanced state of acquirement See SKILL

Profit. Any accession or increase of good. See GOOD.

Speed. Rate of progress.

Stroke. A sudden, effective action.

Subdual. Act of subduing.

Subjugation. Act of bringing into a state of submission. See LIBERTY-SUBJECTION.

Success. Attainment of the object proposed.

Successfulness. The condition of being successful.

Time well spent. Time in which success is gained.

Triumph. A glorious victory.

Trump-card. A winning card; a good stroke.

Upper hand. The advantage.

Victory. A gaining of superiority in war, struggle, or combat.

Walkover. Easy or unopposed success.

Whip-hand. Advantage.

Success—*Nouns of Agent.*

Conqueror. One who conquers or overcomes.

Victor. One who overcomes another in any kind of contest.

Success—*Verbs.*

Accomplish. To bring to pass. See COMPLETION.

Answer. } To be sufficient for.
Answer the purpose. }

Attain an object. To get an object by effort.

Attain a point. To get to a point by effort.

Avail. To be of benefit in accomplishing.

Baffle. To defeat the designs or efforts of. See OBSTRUCTION.

Bear away the bell. To capture a prize.

Bear fruit. To have results.

Beat. To gain the victory.

Beat hollow. To surpass greatly.

Be successful. To obtain what one desires.

Be triumphant. Be gloriously victorious.

Break the back of. } Break the force or strength of.
Break the neck of. }

Capsize. To upset or overturn.

Abortion. Failure before maturity.

Abortive attempt. } An attempt to accomplish before the plans are
Abortive effort. } mature.

Affaire flambée [F.]. A desperate situation.

Bankrupt. } Failure to pay one's debts. See SETTLEMENT-DE-
Bankruptcy. } FAULT.

Beating. The act of defeating; defeat.

Blow. A sudden loss or misfortune

Blunder. A heedless or stupid mistake.

Botchery. Imperfect and bungled work.

Breakdown. A falling to pieces.

Brutum fulmen [L.]. A harmless thunderbolt.

Checkmate. Complete arrest; final defeat, as in playing chess.

Claudication. A limping.

Collapse. Utter failure.

Dead failure. A complete failure.

Death-blow. Something causing ruin.

Defeat. The act of being thwarted in object or purpose

Discomfiture. A defeat that confounds.

Downfall. Loss of position, fame, power, influence.

Drubbing. A sound thrashing.

Explosion. Destruction; refutation, as of theories.

Failure. An unsuccessful attempt, or work.

Fall. Termination of power.

False step. A movement that causes failure.

Fault. Something ill done.

Faute. A fault.

Faux pas [F.]. A false step.

Fiasco. A failure, especially of a play.

Flash in the pan. Something which lasts only a moment, as that of a gun; an abortive attempt.

Foolsmate. In chess, a certain way of checkmating which ought to be prevented easily by a good player.

Footfall. A blunder.

Frustration. State of not attaining or securing what is sought.

Ineffectual attempt. } An attempt or effort that fails.
Ineffectual effort. }

Inefficaciousness, etc. } Inability to produce the desired results. See
Inefficacy. } *Adjectives.*

Labor in vain. Labor which necessarily can produce no results. See USEFULNESS-USELESSNESS.

Lame and impotent conclusion. A failure.

Losing game. A plan sure to fail.

Lurch. A difficult situation.

Mess. A confusion; botchery.

Miscarriage. An unfortunate result; a failure, as of a plan.

Mishap. An evil accident. See WELFARE-MISFORTUNE.

Miss. A failure to find, succeed, etc.

No go. A failure.

Non-fulfilment. } Inability to achieve the desired result
Non-success. }

Nonsuit. Abandonment of a suit by the plaintiff.

Omission. Something left out.

Oversight. An error due to inattention.

Overthrow. The act of throwing down by force or violence.

Perdition. Utter destruction.

Quietus. Death; rest; repose. "Who would bear the whips and scorns of time, when he himself might his quietus make with a bare bodkin." [Shakespeare, *Hamlet*, III, i.]

Rebuff. A sudden, often contemptuous, rejection.

Repulse. A decided refusal; rejection; denial, etc

Rout. A disastrous defeat.

SUCCESS—FAILURE—*Continued.*

SUCCESS—VERBS—*Continued.*

Carry all before one. To have unimpeded and uniform success.
Carry an object. } To gain an object or point by contest or adroit
Carry a point. } movement.
Carry by storm. To carry by a violent and rapid assault.
Carry the day. To win the contest of that day.
Carry the palm. To be superior.
Carry the prize. Win the prize.
Chain victory to one's car. To be a victor.
Checkmate. To defeat by a skilful maneuver.
Circumvent. To gain an advantage over artfully.
Come off successful. To accomplish one's desire.
Come off well. To do creditably in a contest.
Come off with colors flying. To be triumphant.
Confound. To benumb or confuse the mind.
Conquer. To gain possession of by force.
Contrive to. To manage to do.
Crown with success. To reward.
Defeat. Overcome; overthrow; beat.
Discomfit. To defeat so as to confound.
Distance. To outrun.
Do. Injure; flog; kill; defeat.
Do for. To be sufficient for.
Do wonders. To do remarkable deeds.
Drive. To strive to accomplish.
Drive a roaring trade. To carry on a large trade.
Drive into a corner. To force into a desperate situation.
Drive to the wall. To force into an extremity; to force to yield.
Drown. To overwhelm, as if with water.
Drub. To beat.
Elude. To baffle the search of.
Find one's account in. To find profitable.
Find one's way. To succeed somehow.
Floor. Defeat; vanquish in debate.
Gain an advantage. }
Gain an object. }
Gain a point. } To get what one strives for
Gain a victory. }
Gain one's end. } To accomplish one's purpose.
Gain one's ends. }
Gain the ascendancy. To overcome.
Gain the best of. } To defeat.
Gain the better of. }
Gain the day. Win the contest of that day
Gain the palm. } To win a reward.
Gain the prize. }
Gain the start of. }
Gain the upper hand. } Get the advantage of.
Gain the whip-hand. }
Gather the benefit. }
Gather the fruit. } To secure reward.
Gather the harvest. }
Get in the harvest. To reap successful results.
Get over a difficulty. } To overcome.
Get over an obstacle. }
Get the ascendancy of. }
Get the best of. } To defeat in contest or debate.
Get the better of. }
Get the start of. }
Get the upper hand of. } Get the advantage of.
Get the whip-hand of. }
Have it all one's own way. Be too powerful for one's opponent.
Have one on the hip. Have one at one's mercy.
Have the ascendancy. To control.
Have the ball at one's feet. To have under one's control.
Have the best of. } To be ahead of.
Have the better of. }
Have the game in one's hands. To be able to control the result.
Have the start of. }
Have the upper hand of. } To have an advantage over.
Have the whip-hand of. }
Hit it. To be successful in coming upon.
Hit the mark. To have the intended result.
Hit the right nail on its head. To say or do exactly the right thing.
Keep one's head above water. Keep from being overcome by difficulties.
Lick. To overcome in a contest.
Make a hit. To make a favorable stroke.
Make head against. Make progress against.
Make one's fortune. Acquire wealth or position.
Make one's way. To succeed by persistent effort.
Make profit. To gain. See GAIN.
Make progress. To advance. See ADVANCE.

Ruin. Irretrievable injury.
Scrape. An embarrassing situation resulting from one's own acts.
Slip. An unintentional error or fault.
Slip 'twixt cup and lip. A slip at the last moment.
Smash. The act of suddenly breaking into many pieces.
Split. A schism.
Stalemate. A standstill, especially in chess.
Stumble. A false step; a blunder.
Subjugation. Submission. See LIBERTY-SUBJECTION.
Successlessness. Quality of being unsuccessful.
Titubation. The act of stumbling or rocking to and fro.
Trip. A misstep or stumble.
Vain attempt. }
Vain effort. } An attempt or effort that comes to nothing.
Victim. A person who is swindled or duped.
Wreck. Shattered condition.
Wrong step. A movement that causes failure.

FAILURE—*Verbs.*

Abort. To fail of development.
Be all over with. }
Be all up with. } To be beyond all hope of recovery.
Be defeated, etc. To be overcome. See SUCCESS.
Be unsuccessful, etc. To fail to achieve one's object. See *Adjectives.*
Bitch it. To make a blunder of; to botch it.
Bite the dust. To suffer an humiliating defeat.
Breakdown. To fail in health or strength.
Break one's back. To ruin one.
Bring to naught. To cause to be unsuccessful.
Collapse. To fail utterly.
Come off ill. To be unsuccessful in a contest.
Come off second best. To be second in a contest.
Come to grief. To turn out unfortunately. See WELFARE-MISFORTUNE.
Come to nothing. To fail; accomplish nothing.
Dash one's head against a stone wall. To make a foolish attempt. [Stonewall Jackson.]
Dash one's hopes. To destroy one's hopes. See EXPECTATION-DISAPPOINTMENT.
Defeat the purpose. To cause to fail.
Do by halves. To do imperfectly.
Do in vain. To do something which necessarily can produce no results.
Drown. To be overwhelmed, as if with water.
End in smoke. Fail.
Explode. To be found false or incorrect.
Fail. To prove useless or disappointing.
Fall. To lose power, position, influence, etc.
Fall a prey to. To become the prey of.
Fall between two stools. To try to do two things at once, and fail in both.
Fall flat. To fail to interest or impress.
Fall short of. To do less than.
Fall still-born. To be doomed from the start.
Fall through. }
Fall to the ground. } To fail.
Falter. To show physical or moral hesitancy.
Flash in the pan. To be momentary and abortive, as in the pan of an old gun.
Flounder. To stumble or struggle.
Founder. To be ruined, as if like a sinking ship.
Get into a mess. }
Get into a scrape. } To get into a position from which it is difficult to get out.
Get into trouble. }
Get the wrong sow by the ear. To hit upon the wrong person or thing.
Go amiss. To go improperly or erroneously.
Go cross. To go perversely or contrarily.
Go hard with. To be a strain or burden on.
Go on a wrong tack. To take a wrong turn.
Go on ill. To progress poorly.
Go to pot. To go to destruction.
Go to the dogs. To go to ruin.
Go to the wall. To be pressed to an extremity; to fail in business.
Go to wrack and ruin. To fail completely. See CREATION-DESTRUCTION.
Go up like a rocket and come down like a stick. To make a brilliant but unsuccessful attempt.
Go wrong. To turn out unfortunately.
Halt. To be in doubt; to stop suddenly.
Hang fire. To suffer a delay.

SUCCESS—FAILURE—*Continued.*

SUCCESS—VERBS—*Continued.*

Make short work of. To defeat quickly.
Make the enemy bite the dust. To defeat severely.
Manage to. To bring about.
Master. To bring under control; overpower.
Nick it. To strike at the lucky moment.
Nonplus. To stop by embarrassment.
Nonsuit. To order the dismissal of a suit.
Obtain an advantage. ⎫
Obtain a victory. ⎬ To win.
Outdo. Surpass; excel.
Outflank. To get the better of by a like maneuver.
Outgeneral. To surpass in the advantageous disposition of forces.
Outmaneuver. To surpass in the use of means at hand.
Outvote. To have more votes than.
Outwit. Defeat by greater cunning or ingenuity.
Overcome. To defeat.
Overcome a difficulty. ⎫
Overcome an obstacle. ⎬ To succeed.
Overmaster. To obtain control over by force.
Overmatch. ⎫
Overpower. ⎬ To be too powerful or skilful for.
Overreach. To obtain an advantage over by trickery or deception.
Override. To overcome as if by trampling under the feet of one's horse.
Overset. To cause the downfall of.
Overthrow. To throw over on the side.
Prevail. To gain the victory or superiority over.
Prosper. To cause to succeed. See WELFARE.
Put an extinguisher upon. To quench, to smother.
Put down. To repress; crush.
Put *hors de combat* [F.] To injure so as to be unfit for fight.
Put one's nose out of joint. To defeat one's plans or purposes.
Put out of court. To defeat in a lawsuit.
Put to flight. To compel to flee.
Put to rout. To defeat utterly.
Quell. To crush; put down; subdue.
Reap the benefit of. ⎫
Reap the fruit of. ⎬ To derive gain or success from.
Reap the harvest of. ⎭
Reduce. To bring into subjection.
Remain in possession of the field. To be undefeated.
Roll in the dust. To inflict an humiliating defeat.
Rout. To defeat disastrously.
Run hard. To pursue closely.
Secure an object. ⎫
Secure a point. ⎬ To accomplish one's purpose.
Se tirer d'affaire [F.]. To get out of a thing successfully.
Settle. To bring to a conclusion.
Shipwreck. To bring to ruin.
Silence. To cause to be silent or inactive.
Sink. To ruin, as if by sinking.
Speed. To hasten toward a conclusion.
Stalemate. To bring to a standstill as in chess.
Stem the current. ⎫
Stem the tide. ⎬ To counteract a tremendous influence or force.
Stem the torrent. ⎭
Strive to some purpose. To meet with a measure of success.
Subdue. To obtain dominion over by force.
Subjugate. To conquer and retain under continued pressure.
Succeed. To attain the object proposed.
Surmount a difficulty. ⎫
Surmount an obstacle. ⎬ To overcome.
Surpass. To defeat in a contest.
Swamp. To overwhelm, as to sink into a swamp.
Take. To capture by force.
Take by storm. To take by violent and rapid assault.
Take effect. To have effect.
Take the wind out of one's adversary's sails. To strip him of his resources.
Tell. To produce a marked effect.
Tide over. To surmount.
Trample under foot. To administer an humiliating defeat
Trip the heels of. ⎫
Trip up. ⎬ To cause to make a misstep; to cause to fail.
Triumph. To gain a glorious victory.
Trump. To impose upon; deceive.
Turn a corner. To get out of trouble.
Turn out well. To succeed.
Turn to account. ⎫
Turn to good account. ⎬ To derive advantage from. See USE.
Turn up trumps. To turn out well, as in playing cards.
Upset. To spoil; disarrange; overthrow.

FAILURE—VERBS—*Continued.*

Have the ground cut out from under one. To lose one's main support.
Have the worst of it. To be defeated; to be beaten in a bargain.
Hobble. To walk with a limp.
Jump out of the frying-pan into the fire. To go from one evil to a greater.
Knock one's head against a stone wall. Make a foolish attempt.
Labor in vain. To perform labor necessarily fruitless.
Lick the dust. To be defeated to humiliation.
Limp. To walk lamely.
Lose. To be defeated; to incur a loss.
Lose ground. To fall off or decline.
Lose one's balance. To be deprived of one's support.
Lose one's labor. To labor ineffectually.
Lose the day. To be defeated.
Make a blunder. ⎫
Make a botch of. ⎬ To make a stupid and awkward mistake.
Make a mess of. ⎪
Make a slip. ⎭
Make nothing of. To fail to comprehend.
Make vain efforts. To try to do what cannot be done.
Miscarry. To fail; turn out unfortunately.
Miss. To go wrong; to fail of.
Miss fire. To fail to discharge, as a firearm.
Miss one's aim. To fail to accomplish what one strives for.
Miss one's footing. To slip or fall.
Miss stays. To fail in an endeavor to tack, as a ship.
Miss the mark. To fail to attain one's object, as the archer or gunner.
Not have a leg to stand on. Have no support or further resort.
Not succeed, etc. To fail. See SUCCESS.
Reckon without one's host. To neglect important matters in deciding.
Roll the stone of Sisyphus. To perform useless labor.
Run aground. To come to a standstill.
Run one's head against a stone wall. To make a foolish attempt.
Sink. To fall or fail slowly.
Slip. Lose one's footing.
Slip through one's fingers. To lose unconsciously.
Sow the wind and reap the whirlwind. To do what is sure to receive a severe recompense.
Split upon a rock. To go to ruin.
Stick in the mud. To come to a standstill.
Stumble. To make a misstep.
Succumb. To sink as if under a burden.
Take an ugly turn. To go very wrong.
Take a wrong turn. To go wrong.
Take nothing by one's motion. To work in vain.
Titubate. To rock to and fro.
Toil in vain. To work without result.
Topple down. To fall. See ASCENT-DESCENT.
Trip. To make a misstep.
Tumble. To roll or fall down by losing one's footing.
Turn out ill. To be unsuccessful.
Wash a blackamoor white. To try to do the impossible. [Bible.]
Work ill. To be unsuccessful.

FAILURE—*Adjectives.*

Abortive. Failing before maturity.
Addle. Good for nothing; weak; idle.
Aground. At a standstill.
All up with. Without hope or resource.
At fault. Having the fault.
Bankrupt. Unable to pay one's debts, having broken one's bank. See SETTLEMENT-DEFAULT.
Befooled. Swindled; cheated; gulled.
Bootless. Without profit or advantage.
Borne down. Having sunk, as if under a great weight.
Broken. Crushed in feeling or spirit.
Broken down. Ruined or wrecked, financially or physically
Capsized. Upset, as a boat.
Cast away. Wrecked; wasted.
Crossed. Hindered; obstructed.
Dashed. Checked or discouraged.
Dead beat. Thoroughly defeated.
Décousu [F.]. Ripped.
Defeated, etc. Beaten; overcome. See SUCCESS.
Destroyed. Overthrown; torn down; knocked to pieces.
Disconcerted. Confused so as to falter.
Dished. Ruined; cheated; badly used.
Done for. Useless; wrecked; ruined.
Done up. Tired out; badly used.
Downtrodden. Oppressed.

SUCCESS—FAILURE—*Continued.*

SUCCESS—Verbs—*Continued.*

Vanquish. To defeat utterly and hopelessly.
Victimize. To make the victim of a fraud.
Walk over the course. To win easily by going through the form.
Weather a point. To gain anything against opposition.
Weather the storm. To endure the opposition.
Win an object. }
Win a point. } To obtain one's desire.
Win one's spurs. To perform one's first noteworthy deed.
Win one's way. To get along by one's own efforts.
Win the battle. To gain success.
Win the day. Win the contest of the day.
Win the palm. }
Win the prize. } To be successful.
Work one's way. To defray expenses by one's own labor.
Work well. To work successfully.
Work wonders. To do remarkable work.
Worst. Defeat.

Success—*Adjectives.*

Crowned with success. Rewarded with success.
Effective. Producing effect.
Felicitous. Happy in operation or effect.
Flushed with success. Animated or elated by success.
In full swing. In full operation.
In the ascendant. Dominant in influence or power.
Prosperous. Succeeding in efforts to gain what is desirable   See WELFARE.
Set up. Caused to develop.
Succeeding, etc. Accomplishing one's object. See *Verbs.*
Successful. Enjoying success.
Triumphant. Gloriously victorious.
Unbeaten, etc. Always successful. See *Verbs.*
Victorious. Having gained a victory.
Well-spent. So as to produce results.

Success—*Adverbs, etc.*

A merveille [F.]. Marvelously.
Beyond all hope. Hopelessly.
In triumph. Successfully.
Successfully, etc. Favorably. See *Adjectives.*
Swimmingly. Easily and gracefully.
To one's heart's content. As much as one desires.
To some good purpose. }
To some purpose. } So as to produce successful results.
With flying colors. In triumph.

Success—*Phrases.*

Bis vincit qui se vincit in victoria [L.]. He twice conquers who conquers himself in victory.
Chacun est l'artisan de sa fortune [F.] Every man is the architect of his own fortune.
Dies faustus [L.]. Lucky day.
Faber est quisque fortunæ suæ [L.] Every man is the architect of his own fortune.
Flectere si nequeo superos, Acheronta movebo [L.] If I fail to bend the powers above, I will move Acheron.
Fronte capillato, post est occasio calva [L.]. Opportunity, though she has hair in front, is bald behind.
Omne tulit punctum [L.]. He has gained every point.
Omnia vincit amor [L.]. Love conquers all things.
One's star in the ascendant.
The day being one's own.
Veni, vidi, vici [L.]. I came, I saw, I conquered.
Vincit qui patitur [L.]. He conquers who endures.
Vincit qui se vincit [L.]. He conquers who conquers himself

FAILURE—Adjectives—*Continued.*

Failing, etc. Wasting away. See *Verbs.*
Flambé [F.]. Singed; blazed.
Foiled. Rendered ineffectual by counteraction.
Foundered. Wrecked.
Fruitless. Without results.
Frustrated. Having failed in attainment.
Grounded. At a standstill.
Hobbling. Limping.
Hoist on [with] one's own petard. Injured by one's own act. [Shakespeare. *Hamlet*, III, iv.]
In a sorry plight. In a complicated situation.
Ineffective. Not producing a decided effect.
Ineffectual. Not producing the result intended.
Inefficacious. Not producing or doing any good.
Inefficient. Lacking in ability or skill or power.
Insufficient. Lacking in quantity or degree.
Knocked on the head. Defeated; destroyed.
Lame. Having a halt in the gait.
Left in the lurch. Left in an embarrassing situation, as a ship.
Lost. Not won, gained, or enjoyed.
Nonsuited. Having one suit dismissed in court.
Out of one's reckoning. Not according to one's plan.
Overborne. Crushed.
Overwhelmed. Overpowered.
Played out. Worn out.
Ruined. Irretrievably injured.
Ruined root and branch. Thoroughly ruined.
Sacrificed. Lost in pursuing an object.
Shipwrecked. Ruined.
Still-born. Doomed from the start.
Stranded. Helpless; without resources.
Struck down. Suddenly wrecked, ruined, or killed.
Stultified. Given an appearance of foolishness.
Successless. Without success.
Swamped. Overturned, as a boat.
Thrown away. Wasted.
Thrown off one's balance. Confused; discomposed; disconcerted.
Thrown on one's back. In a well-nigh hopeless position.
Thrown on one's beam ends. In a serious or hopeless predicament.
Tripping. Almost falling.
Unattained. Not attained. See SUCCESS.
Unavailing. Not availing. See SUCCESS.
Uncompleted. Not finished. See COMPLETION-NONCOMPLETION.
Undone. Ruined; brought to grief.
Unfortunate. Unsuccessful. See WELFARE-MISFORTUNE.
Unhinged. Unsettled.
Unhorsed. Defeated; repulsed.
Unsuccessful. Not successful.
Victimized. Swindled or duped.
Wide of the mark. Far from correct, or from one's object or purpose.
Wrecked. Disabled; nearly ruined.

FAILURE—*Adverbs, etc.*

In vain. Necessarily to no purpose.
Re infecta [L.]. The business being unfinished.
To little or no purpose. With few results.
Unsuccessfully, etc. With failure. See *Adjectives.*

FAILURE—*Phrases.*

All is lost.
Dies infaustus [L.]. Unlucky day.
Parturiunt montes, nascetur ridiculus mus [L.]. The mountains are in labor, a ridiculous mouse will be born. [Horace, *Art of Poetry*, 139.]
The bubble has burst.
The devil to pay.
The game is up.
Tout est perdu hors l'honneur [F.]. All is lost save honor. [Francis I. of France.]

---

suc-cess'-ful. Prosperous. SUCCESS-FAILURE.
suc-cess'-ful-ness. Prosperousness. SUCCESS-FAILURE.
suc-ces'-sion. A succeeding; series; right of acceding to station of father. ALIENATION, COMMUTATION-PERMUTATION, CONTINUITY-INTERRUPTION, PRECEDENCE-SUCCESSION, RECURRENCE; **in quick succession,** FREQUENCY-RARITY; **in regular succession,** PERIODICITY-IRREGULARITY; **succession of ideas,** RE-
FLECTION-VACANCY; **succession of time,** PERIOD-PROGRESS.
suc-ces'-sive. Consecutive. PRECEDENCE-SUCCESSION.
suc-ces'-sive-ness. Consecutiveness. PRECEDENCE-SUCCESSION.
suc-cess'-less. Unprosperous. SUCCESS-FAILURE.
suc-ces'-sor. Succeeder. ANTECEDENCE-SEQUENCE, PREDECESSOR-CONTINUATION.
suc-cinct'. Terse. TERSENESS-PROLIXITY.

suc'-cor. To help. OBSTRUCTION-HELP.

suc'-cors. Helps. OBSTRUCTION-HELP.

suc'-co-tash. A dish of corn and beans. NUTRIMENT-EXCRETION.

suc'-cu-ba. A female demon. JOVE-FIEND.

suc'-cu-bus. A demon. JOVE-FIEND.

suc'-cu-lent. Juicy. LIQUID-GAS, NUTRIMENT-EXCRETION, VISCIDITY-FOAM.

suc-cumb'. To sink down; to die; to yield. SUCCESS-FAILURE, WEARINESS-REFRESHMENT, YIELDING.

suc-cus'-sion. A shaking. AGITATION.

such. Of that kind; like. **Such a one,** HUMANITY; **such as,** LIKENESS-UNLIKENESS; **such being the case,** CONDITION-SITUATION; **such like,** LIKENESS-UNLIKENESS.

such'-wise''. In a given condition. CONDITION-SITUATION.

suck. To draw in; to absorb. ADMISSION-EXPULSION, GIVING-RECEIVING, NUTRIMENT-EXCRETION; **suck in,** ADMISSION-EXPULSION; **suck the blood of,** TAKING-RESTITUTION.

suck'-er. That which sucks. APERTURE-CLOSURE.

suck'-ing. Drawing into the mouth. ADMISSION-EXPULSION.

suck'-le. To give suck to. OBSTRUCTION-HELP.

suck'-ling. An unweaned animal. INFANT-VETERAN

suc'-tion. A drawing by exhausting the air. ADMISSION-EXPULSION, MIGHT-IMPOTENCE.

su'-da-ry. A sweat-cloth. CLEANNESS-FILTHINESS.

su-da'-tion. Excessive sweat. NUTRIMENT-EXCRETION.

su'-da-to-ry. Sudorific. OVEN-REFRIGERATOR.

sud'-den. Quick; unexpected; abrupt. EARLINESS-LATENESS, ETERNITY-INSTANTANEITY, EXPECTATION-SURPRISE, LASTINGNESS-TRANSIENTNESS; **sudden and quick in quarrel,** FAVORITE-MOROSENESS; **sudden burst,** EXPECTATION-SURPRISE; **sudden death,** LIFE-DEATH; **sudden thought,** PREDETERMINATION-IMPULSE.

sud'-den-ly. Quickly. EARLINESS-LATENESS, ETERNITY-INSTANTANEITY, LASTINGNESS-TRANSIENTNESS.

sud'-den-ness. Quickness. EARLINESS-LATENESS, ETERNITY-INSTANTANEITY, LASTINGNESS-TRANSIENTNESS.

su''-dor-if'-ic. Sweat-producing. HEAT-COLD.

suds. Soapy water. VISCIDITY-FOAM; **in the suds,** DIFFICULTY-FACILITY, LIGHTHEARTEDNESS-DEJECTION.

sue. To prosecute; to beg. LITIGATION, PETITION-EXPOSTULATION.

su'-et. Fatty tissues of kine. PULPINESS-OIL.

suf'-fer. To feel pain; to undergo; to permit; to endure. EMOTION, EXCITABILITY-INEXCITABILITY, HEALTH-SICKNESS, LEAVE-PROHIBITION, PLEASURE-PAIN, SENSUALITY-SUFFERING; **suffer for,** RECOMPENSE-PUNITION; **suffer punishment,** RECOMPENSE-PUNITION.

suf'-fer-ance. Permission. EMOTION, EXCITABILITY-INEXCITABILITY, PLEASURE-PAIN; **tenant on sufferance,** HOLDER.

suf'-fer-er. One who suffers. PLEASURE-PAIN.

suf'-fer-ing. Allowing. EMOTION, PLEASURE-PAIN, SENSUALITY-SUFFERING.

suf-fice'. To be sufficient. ENOUGH.

suf-fi'-cien-cy. Adequacy. ENOUGH.

suf-fi'-cient. Adequate. ENOUGH.

suf-fi'-cient-ly. Adequately. ENOUGH.

suf'-fix. A formative element at the end of a word. INCREMENT-REMNANT, LETTER, PRECEDENCE-SUCCESSION, PREDECESSOR-CONTINUANCE.

suf-fla'-tion. Inflation. RIVER-WIND.

suf'-fo-cate. To kill by stopping respiration. EXCESS-LACK, LIFE-KILLING.

suf'-fo-ca''-ting. Becoming choked. HEAT-COLD, PERFUME-STENCH.

suf''-fo-ca'-tion. Stoppage of respiration. LIFE-DEATH, LIFE-KILLING.

suf'-fra-gan. An auxiliary bishop. MINISTRY-LAITY.

suf'-frage. The right of voting. CHOICE-NEUTRALITY.

suf-fuse'. To overspread. MIXTURE-HOMOGENEITY.

suf-fu'-sion. An overspreading, as with blushes. EMOTION, MIXTURE-HOMOGENEITY, SELFRESPECT-HUMBLENESS.

sug'-ar. A sweet, crystalline substance. CHEMISTRY, CONVEXITY-CONCAVITY, SWEETNESS-ACIDITY.

sug'-ar-loaf. Conical. SHARPNESS-BLUNTNESS.

sug-gest'. To hint; insinuate. ADVICE, ENLIGHTENMENT-SECRECY, HYPOTHESIS, REMEMBRANCE-FORGETFULNESS; **suggest a question,** INVESTIGATION-ANSWER; **suggest itself,** FANCY, HYPOTHESIS, REFLECTION-VACANCY.

suggestio falsi [L.] (suj-jes'-ti-o fal'-sai). A hint of falsehood. TRUTHFULNESS-FABRICATION, TRUTHFULNESS-FALSEHOOD.

sug-ges'-tion. An indication; a diffident proposal. ADVICE, DESIGN, ENLIGHTENMENT-SECRECY, HYPOTHESIS, MEANING-JARGON, REMEMBRANCE-FORGETFULNESS.

sug-gest'-ive. Stimulating to thought. ACCOUNT, MEANING-JARGON, REMEMBRANCE-FORGETFULNESS.

su'-i-ci''-dal. Self-destructive. CREATION-DESTRUCTION, LIFE-KILLING.

su'-i-cide. Killing of oneself. LIFE-KILLING.

sui generis [L.] (siu''-ai jen'-er-is). Of one's own kind. CONVENTIONALITY-UNCONVENTIONALITY.

suis, et j'y reste, j'y [F.] (sui, ê zhi rest, zhi). Here I am and here I stay. DETERMINATION-VACILLATION, MUTATION-PERMANENCE.

suisse [F.] (suis). A priest. MINISTRY-LAITY.

Suisse, point d'argent point de [F.] (suis, pwan' darzhan' pwan' de). No penny, no paternoster. PRICE-DISCOUNT.

suit. A courtship; to correspond; a series or set; to agree. BLANDISHMENT, CONTINUITY-INTERRUPTION, DIVISION, DRESS-UNDRESS, HARMONY-DISCORD, LITIGATION, PROPRIETY-IMPROPRIETY; **do suit and service,** INSUBORDINATION-OBEDIENCE; **follow suit,** IMITATION-ORIGINALITY; **lawsuit,** LITIGATION; **love suit,** LOVE-HATE; **suit the action to the word,** EARLINESS-LATENESS, SIGN; **suit the occasion,** PROPRIETY-IMPROPRIETY.

suit'-a-ble. Opportune. HARMONY-DISCORD; **suitable season,** OPPORTUNENESS-UNSUITABLENESS.

suite'. Attendants; a set. CHIEF-UNDERLING, CONTINUITY-INTERRUPTION, PREDECESSOR-CONTINUATION; **suite of rooms,** CONTENTS-RECEIVER.

suit'-or. A legal applicant; a wooer; petitioner. LITIGATION, LOVE-HATE, PETITIONER.

sul'-ca''-ted. Grooved. GROOVE.

sul'-cus. A narrow channel. GROOVE.

sulk. In bad humor. LIGHTHEARTEDNESS-DEJECTION, POLITENESS-IMPOLITENESS.

sulks. Bad humor. FAVORITE-MOROSENESS; FAVORITE-QUARRELSOMENESS.

sulk'-y. A two-wheeled vehicle; sullen; sour; obstinate; morose. BIGOTRY-APOSTASY, CONTENTEDNESS-DISCONTENTMENT, CONVEYANCE-VESSEL, FAVORITE-MOROSENESS, FAVORITE-QUARRELSOMENESS, LIGHTHEARTEDNESS-DEJECTION.

sul'-len. Obstinate; sour; gloomy; ill-humored. BIGOTRY-APOSTASY, CHARITABLENESS-MALEVOLENCE, FAVORITE-MOROSENESS, LIGHTHEARTEDNESS-DEJECTION, POLITENESS-IMPOLITENESS.

sul'-len-ness. Gloominess. FAVORITE-MOROSENESS.

sul'-ly. To injure the purity of. CLEANNESS-FILTHINESS, REPUTATION-DISCREDIT.

sul'-phur. A pale-yellow substance. COMBUSTIBLE.

sul'-phur-col''-ored. Yellowish. YELLOWNESS-PURPLE.

sul'-tan. A Mohammedan ruler. CHIEF-UNDERLING.

sul'-ta-na. Wife of sultan. CHIEF-UNDERLING.

sum. Any amount of money; the whole. MONEY, NUMBER; **sum and substance,** CONSEQUENCE-INSIGNIFICANCE, DIGEST, MEANING-JARGON; **sum up,** ACCOUNT, DIGEST, NUMBERING.

sum'-less. Incalculable. INFINITY.

sum'-ma-ri-ly. In a summary manner. EARLINESS-LATENESS, TERSENESS-PROLIXITY.

sum'-ma-rize. To epitomize. DIGEST.

sum'-ma-ry. An epitome; on the spot; offhand, in law; concise. DIGEST, EARLINESS-LATENESS, LASTINGNESS-TRANSIENTNESS, LAW-LAWLESSNESS, LENGTH-SHORTNESS, TERSENESS-PROLIXITY; **summary of facts,** ACCOUNT.

sum-ma'-tion. Addition. NUMBERING.

sum'-mer. Warm portion of the year; bright period. HEAT-COLD, MORNING-EVENING, SUSPENSION-SUPPORT; **summer equinox,** ASTRONOMY; **summer lightning,** LUMINARY-SHADE.

sum'-mer-house''. A country-seat. CONTENTS-RECEIVER.

sum'-mer-set. A somersault. REVERSAL.

sum'-mit. A top. FAULTLESSNESS-FAULTINESS, TOP-BOTTOM.

sum'-mit-y. Like a summit. TOP-BOTTOM.

sum'-mon. To command to appear; to call. LITIGATION, ORDER; **summon up,** EXCITATION, REMEMBRANCE-FORGETFULNESS; **summon up courage,** BRAVERY-COWARDICE.

sum'-mons. A call. LITIGATION.

summum bonum [L.] (sum'-mum bo'-num). The highest good. GOOD-EVIL, PLEASURE-PAIN.

summum jus [L.] (sum'-mum jus). The highest right. RIGHT-WRONG.

sump. A foul, swampy pool. CLEANNESS-FILTHINESS, SWAMP-ISLAND.

sump'-ter–horse. A pack-horse. CONVEYER.

sump'-ter–mule. A pack-mule. CONVEYER.

sump'-tu-a-ry. Pertaining to expense. MONEY, OUTLAY-INCOME.

sump'-tu-ous. Luxurious. POMP.

sum to'-tal. The whole. WHOLE-PART.

sun. A heavenly body; something of importance. ASTRONOMY, HEAT-COLD, LIGHT-DARKNESS, LUMINARY-SHADE, REPUTATION-DISCREDIT, UNIVERSE; **as the sun at noonday,** CERTAINTY-DOUBT, LIGHT-DARKNESS, MANIFESTATION-SECRECY; **bask in the sun,** SENSUALITY-SUFFERING; **farthing candle to the sun,** USEFULNESS-USELESSNESS; **going down of the sun,** MORNING-EVENING, SKILL-UNSKILLFULNESS; **Sun of Righteousness,** DIVINITY; **sun oneself,** HEATING-COOLING; **under the sun,** EXTENSION-DISTRICT, UNIVERSE.

sun'-beam''. A ray of the sun. LIGHT-DARKNESS; **sunbeams from cucumbers,** POSSIBILITY-IMPOSSIBILITY.

sun'-bow''. A rainbow formed by the sun. VARIEGATION.

sun'-burn''. Discoloration of the skin caused by the sun. HEATING-COOLING.

sun'-burnt''. Discolored by the sun. GRAY-BROWN.

Sun'-day. First day of the week. **Sunday, Monday,** etc., PERIODICITY-IRREGULARITY; **Sunday's best,** EMBELLISHMENT-DISFIGUREMENT, POMP.

sun'-der. To break apart. UNION-DISUNION.

sun'-di''-al. A measuring device. CHRONOLOGY-ANACHRONISM.

sun'-down''. Sunset. MORNING-EVENING.

sun'-dry. Various. MULTIPLICITY-PAUCITY.

sunk. Fallen; subsided; depressed; declined; decreased; immersed; destroyed. ASCENT-DESCENT, CAREFULNESS-CARELESSNESS, CLEANNESS-FILTHINESS, CREATION-DESTRUCTION, DEEPNESS-SHALLOWNESS, ELEVATION-DEPRESSION, ENLIGHTENMENT-SECRECY, LIGHTHEARTEDNESS-DEJECTION, PLEASURE-PAIN, SPRING-DIVE, SUCCESS-FAILURE, WEARINESS-REFRESHMENT, WELFARE-MISFORTUNE; **sunk fence,** ATTACK-DEFENSE; **sunk in iniquity,** VIRTUE-VICE; **sunk in oblivion,** EXPECTATION-SURPRISE, REMEMBRANCE-FORGETFULNESS.

sunk'-en rocks. Rocks beneath the water. REFUGE-PITFALL.

sun'-less. Cheerless. LIGHT-DARKNESS.

sun'-light''. The light of the sun. LIGHT-DARKNESS.

sun'-ny. Resembling the sun; lighthearted. HEAT-COLD, LIGHTHEARTEDNESS-DEJECTION, LUMINARY-SHADE.

sun'-ny side. Bright side. PLEASURABLENESS-PAINFULNESS; **view the sunny side,** SANGUINENESS-HOPELESSNESS.

sun'-paint''-ing. Photography. PAINTING.

sun'-rise''. The morning. MORNING-EVENING.

sun'-set''. The twilight. MORNING-EVENING; **at sunset,** EARLINESS-LATENESS.

sun'-shade''. An awning. COVER-LINING, LUMINARY-SHADE.

sun'-shine''. Shining light; a cheering influence. LIGHT-DARKNESS, LIGHTHEARTEDNESS-DEJECTION, PLEASURE-PAIN, WELFARE-MISFORTUNE.

sun'-stroke''. A sudden prostration occasioned by the sun. HEATING-COOLING, SANENESS-LUNACY.

suo periculo [L.] (siu'-o per-ic'-yu-lo). At his own peril. DUTY-DERELICTION.

suo sibi gladio hunc jugulo [L.] (siu'-o sib'-i glê'di-o hunc jug'-yū-lo). I cut this with his own sword. PROOF-DISPROOF, REPRISAL-RESISTANCE.

sup. A mouthful of food. MAGNITUDE-SMALLNESS, NUTRIMENT-EXCRETION; **sup full of horrors,** PLEASURE-PAIN.

su'-per. One in excess. ACTING.

su'-per-a-ble. That which can be overcome. POSSIBILITY-IMPOSSIBILITY.

su''-per-a-bound'. Overabundant. EXCESS-LACK.

su''-per-a-bun'-dance. Overabundance. EXCESS-LACK.

su''-per-a-bun'-dant. Overabundant. EXCESS-LACK.

su''-per-add'. To add over. ADDITION-SUBTRACTION.

su''-per-ad-di'-tion. Addition to addition. ADDITION-SUBTRACTION.

su''-per-an'-nu-a''-ted. Incapacitated by years. INFANCY-AGE.

su''-per-an'-nu-a'-tion. Incapacity by age. INFANCY-AGE.

su-perb'. Imposing. BEAUTY-UGLINESS.

su''-per-car'-go. An agent sent by owners of cargo. MANAGER.

supercherie [F.] (sŭ-persh-rî'). A cheat. TRUTHFULNESS-FRAUD.

su''-per-cil'-i-ous. Arrogant; proud; haughty. PRESUMPTION-OBSEQUIOUSNESS, REGARD-DISRESPECT, REGARD-SCORN, SELFRESPECT-HUMBLENESS.

su''-per-cil'-i-ous-ness. Arrogance. REGARD-DISRESPECT.

su''-per-em'-i-nence. Overeminence. GOODNESS-BADNESS, REPUTATION-DISCREDIT.

su''-per-er'-o-ga'-tion. Something superfluous. EXCESS-LACK, USEFULNESS-USELESSNESS.

su''-per-ex''-al-ta'-tion. Excessive exaltation. REPUTATION-DISCREDIT.

su''-per-ex'-cel-lence. Overexcellence. GOODNESS-BADNESS.

su''-per-ex'-cel-lent. Overexcellent. GOODNESS-BADNESS.

su''-per-fe-ta'-tion. A double fetation. ADDITION-SUBTRACTION, FERTILITY-STERILITY.

su''-per-fi'-cial. Cursory; shallow; unlearned; pertaining to the surface. DECISION-MISJUDGMENT, DEEPNESS-SHALLOWNESS, KNOWLEDGE-IGNORANCE.

Outside-Inside, superficial extent, Extension-District, Thickness-Thinness.

su″-per-fi′-ci-es. A surface. Outside-Inside.

su′-per-fine″. Very fine. Goodness-Badness.

su″-per-flu′-ence Overabundance. Excess-Lack.

su″-per-flu′-i-tant. Floating on the surface. Ascent-Descent.

su″-per-flu′-i-ty. More than needed. Excess-Lack, Increment-Remnant.

su-per′-flu-ous. Unnecessary. Increment-Remnant, Usefulness-Uselessness.

su″-per-hu′-man. Beyond human power. Divinity, Faultlessness-Faultiness.

su″-per-im-pose′. To put on above. Cover-Lining.

su″-per-imposed′. Put on above. Height-Lowness.

su″-per-in-cum′-bent. Resting on something else. Heaviness-Lightness, Height-Lowness.

su″-per-in-duce′. To superadd. Cause-Effect, Creation-Destruction, Mutation-Permanence.

su″-per-in-tend′. To manage. Management.

su″-per-in-tend′-ence. Management. Management.

su″-per-in-tend′-ent. One who manages. Manager, President-Member.

su-pe′-ri-or. Higher; upper; preferable; a chief. Consequence-Insignificance, Enlargement-Diminution, Goodness-Badness, Manager, Reputation-Discredit, Supremacy-Subordinacy.

su-pe″-ri-or′-i-ty. State of being superior. Equality-Inequality, Precedence-Succession, Supremacy-Subordinacy.

su″-per-junc′-tion. Joining together. Addition-Subtraction.

su-per′-la-tive. Consummate. Adjective, Supremacy-Subordinacy.

su-per′-la-tive-ly. Of the highest degree. Magnitude-Smallness, Supremacy-Subordinacy.

su-per′-la-tive-ly good. Supremely good. Goodness-Badness.

su-per′-nal. Higher; celestial. Heaven-Hell, Top-Bottom.

su″-per-na′-tant. Swimming above. Ascent-Descent, Height-Lowness.

su″-per-nat′-u-ral. Beyond the natural. Divinity, Jove-Fiend; **supernatural aid,** Obstruction-Help.

su″-per-nu′-mer-a-ry. Superfluous; one who fills the place of another. Acting, Excess-Lack, Increment-Remnant, Store.

su″-per-pose′. To lay upon. Addition-Subtraction, Cover-Lining.

su″-per-po-si′-tion. Act of placing over. Addition-Subtraction, Cover-Lining.

su″-per-sat′-u-rate. To add beyond saturation. Excess-Lack.

su″-per-sat′-u-rat-ed. Thoroughly filled. Excess-Lack.

su″-per-sat″-u-ra′-tion. Overabundance. Excess-Lack.

su″-per-scrip′-tion. Address on a letter. Sign, Writing-Printing.

su″-per-sede′. To displace; to render unnecessary. Commutation-Permutation, Keeping-Relinquishment, Use-Disuse.

su″-per-sti′-tion. A false religion. Orthodoxy-Heterodoxy.

su″-per-sti′-tious. Influenced by superstitions. Credulousness-Skepticism, Orthodoxy-Heterodoxy.

su″-per-stra′-tum. An upper stratum. Outside-Inside.

su″-per-struc′-ture. Any upper structure. Completion-Noncompletion.

su″-per-va-ca′-ne-ous. Unnecessary. Excess-Lack.

su″-per-vene′. To happen; to come as something additional. Addition-Subtraction, Antecedence-Sequence, Occurrence-Destiny.

su″-per-ve′-ni-ent. Following closely. Reputation-Discredit.

su″-per-vise′. To superintend. Management.

su″-per-vi′-sion. Overseeing. Management.

su″-per-vi′-sor. A superintendent. Manager.

su″-pi-na′-tion. Act of turning palm upwards. Erectness-Flatness.

su-pine′. Lying on the back; inactive; sloping. Activity-Indolence, Carefulness-Carelessness, Erectness-Flatness, Reversal, Sensitiveness-Apathy.

su-pine′-ness. Inactivity. Carefulness-Carelessness, Heed-Disregard, Indifference, Sensitiveness-Apathy.

sup-ped′-i-tate. To supply. Provision-Waste.

sup′-per. Last meal of the day. Nutriment-Excretion.

sup-plant′. To displace. Commutation-Permutation.

sup′-ple. Easily bent; submissive. Hardness-Softness, Presumption-Obsequiousness.

sup′-ple-ment. A supplying of a deficiency. Addition-Subtraction, Increment-Remnant, Whole-Part.

sup′-ple-to″-ry. Supplementing. Addition-Subtraction.

sup′-pli-ant. Beseeching; one who supplicates. Petitioner, Petition-Expostulation.

sup′-pli-cate. To beseech in prayer. Compassion-Ruthlessness, Devotion-Idolatry, Petition-Expostulation.

sup″-pli-ca′-tion. Entreaty. Worship-Idolatry.

sup-plies′. That which is supplied; store. Materials, Money, Obstruction-Help.

sup-ply′. To provide; to give. Giving-Receiving, Provision-Waste, Store; **supply aid,** Obstruction-Help; **supply deficiencies,** Entirety-Deficiency; **supply the place of,** Commutation-Permutation.

sup-port′. An aid; sustenance; to endure; to defend; to show to be true; to help; to keep from falling. Agency, Conservation, Emotion, Evidence-Counterevidence, Excitability-Inexcitability, Instrument, Justification-Charge, Obstruction-Help, Refuge-Pitfall; **support life,** Life-Death.

sup-port′-ers. An heraldic device. Sign.

sup-po′-sa-ble. That may be assumed. Hypothesis.

sup-pose′. To believe. Hypothesis.

sup-po′-sing. Assuming for argument. Hypothesis, Modification.

sup″-po-si′-tion. Conjecture. Hypothesis.

sup-pos″-i-ti′-tious. Spurious. Entity-Nonentity, Hypothesis, Truthfulness-Fabrication.

sup-pos′-i-tive. Implying supposition. Hypothesis, Particle.

sup-press′. To crush; to conceal; to restrain from utterance. Creation-Destruction, Enlightenment-Secrecy, Release-Restraint, Vocalization-Muteness.

sup-pres′-sion. Hiding. Enlightenment-Secrecy.

sup-pres′-sion of the truth. Enlightenment-Secrecy, Truthfulness-Falsehood.

suppressio veri [L.] (sup-presh′-i-o vī′-rai). Suppression of the truth. Truthfulness-Falsehood.

sup″-pu-ra′-tion. The making of pus. Cleanness-Filthiness.

sup″-pu-ta′-tion. Reckoning. Numbering.

sup-pute′. To reckon. Numbering.

su″-pra-lap-sa′-ri-an. A theological doctrine. Orthodoxy-Heterodoxy.

su″-pra-mun′-dane. Supernatural. Uprightness-Dishonesty.

su-prem′-a-cy. State of being supreme. Rule-License, Supremacy-Subordinacy.

SUPREMACY—SUBORDINACY.

Advantage. A condition favorable to success.
Climax. The highest point in an ascending progress.
Culmination. The condition of having arrived at its highest point.
Excess. That which passes the required limit.
Greatness. Strength or extent of intellectual faculties.
Majority. More than half.
Maximum. Highest degree attainable.
Ne plus ultra [L.]. The furthermost point; the pillars of Hercules.
Nulli secundus [L.]. Second to none.
Partiality. Special fondness.
Personal superiority. Superiority of one's abilities, aside from one's views.
Preeminence. Distinction above others of eminence.
Preponderance. }
Preponderation. } Superiority of weight, influence, power, etc.
Prevalence. The act of gaining superiority, or the condition of being superior.
Primus inter pares [L.]. First among equals.
Superiority. The quality of surpassing in quantity, quality, or degree.
Supremacy. The quality of being highest in power, authority, or influence.
Surplus. The amount above what is necessary.
Transcendence. Superior excellence.
Vantage-ground. Advantageous place or condition.

SUPREMACY—Denotations.

Benjamin's mess. The largest share. [*Genesis* xliii, 24.]
Captain. One at the head of or who has command over others.
Lion's share. The whole or an unduly large proportion of anything; the whole, according to the fable of his hunting excursion.
Nobility. The body of persons under an hereditary government ranked above the common people.
Tricumia [Gr.]. A mighty wave.
Triton among the minnows. A giant among pigmies.

SUPREMACY—Verbs.

Bear the palm. To come off victorious.
Beat. To win from.
Beat all others. To win from all others.
Beat hollow. To win from easily.
Become larger. To grow; increase.
Be superior. To surpass in quantity, quality, or degree.
Cap. To surpass.
Come first. To be ahead of.
Come to a head. To come to a crisis.
Culminate. To arrive at the highest point of progress.
Cut out. To supersede.
Eclipse. To surpass so as to obscure.
Exceed. To go beyond in measure, degree, quantity, or quality.
Excel. To go beyond in good qualities and laudable actions.
Get ahead of. To surpass.
Have the advantage. To excel in any way.
Have the upper hand. Have the advantage.
Have the whip-hand. Have the advantage of.
Kick the beam. To touch the highest point.
O'ertop. To surpass.
Outbalance. To exceed.
Outdo. Surpass.
Outherod. To surpass in violence or cruelty.
Outrank. To take higher rank than.
Outrival. To surpass in excellence.
Outstrip. To leave behind.
Outweigh. To exceed in value, influence, or importance.
Overbalance. Exceed in importance, etc.
Overmatch. To be too powerful for; to subdue.
Overpass. To go beyond or away from.
Override. To outride; to pass.
Overtop. To surpass.
Overweigh. Outweigh.
Pass. To go by.
Play first fiddle. To take the most important part in anything. See CONSEQUENCE.
Precede. To go before in rank, place, or importance.
Predominate. To have controlling influence.
Preponderate. To outweigh.
Prevail. To gain the mastery or upper hand.
Put one's nose out of joint. To defeat; to gain an advantage over.
Render larger. To increase in size.
Surpass. To go beyond in anything admitting of degree, especially in a specified particular.

Commonalty. The quality of being commonplace.
Deficiency. State of being below what is required.
Inferiority. State of being lower in rank or quality.
Minimum. The least possible amount, degree, etc.
Minority. The smaller of two groups into which a group or number is divided.
Shortcoming. A coming short of the expected amount.
Smallness. The quality or state of being small. See MAGNITUDE-SMALLNESS.
Subordinacy. Inferiority of rank; subjection to a superiority.

SUBORDINACY—Verbs.

Become smaller. To decrease in size, etc.
Be inferior. To be lower in excellence, quality, or rank.
Come short of. }
Fall short of. } To be below an expected amount or standard.
Hide its diminished head. To retire defeated.
Not come up to. }
Not pass up to. } To be short of expectations.
Play second fiddle. To take a subordinate part.
Render smaller. To decrease in size, etc.
Retire into the shade. To be eclipsed.
Want. To be without.
Yield the palm. To be defeated.

SUBORDINACY—Adjectives.

Deficient. Below what is required.
Diminished. Reduced in degree, quantity, etc.
Inferior. Lower in rank or quality.
Least. In the lowest or smallest degree.
Less. }
Lesser. } Of slighter consequence.
Lower. }
Lowest. } Having less than the usual rate, amount, etc.
Minor. Less in importance or value.
Minus. Deprived of; lacking.
Not fit to hold a candle to. Greatly inferior to.
Reduced. Brought to an inferior state.
Secondary. Not of greatest importance, etc.
Second-rate. Second in size, rank, etc.
Small. Of little importance. See MAGNITUDE-SMALLNESS.
Smaller. }
Smallest. } Of little consequence.
Sub. Secondary.
Subaltern. Inferior in rank or position.
Subordinate. Belonging to an inferior order in classification.
Thrown into the shade. Eclipsed.
Unimportant. Not important.
Weighed in the balance and found wanting. Not up to a standard.

SUBORDINACY—Adverbs, etc.

At a disadvantage. Under unfavorable conditions.
At a low ebb. In a low condition.
At the bottom of the scale. Lowest in rank, etc.
Below par. }
Below the mark. } Below the standard.
Less. In inferior or smaller degree.
Short off. }
Under. }
Under par. } Below the standard.
Under the mark. }

SUPREMACY—Verbs—Continued.

Take precedence. To take the front as the more honorable place; to have right of previous consideration.
Take the shine out of. To outshine; eclipse.
Throw into the shade. To eclipse.
Top. To surpass.
Transcend. To be superior in excellence; to climb over.
Turn the scale. To give superiority or success.

SUPREMACY—Adjectives.

Beyond compare. }
Beyond comparison. } Easily first, highest, or best.
Crowning. Completing; most perfect.
Culminating. Arriving at its highest point.
Distinguished. Having a reputation.
Enlarged. Made larger.
Exceeding, etc. Greater than what is usual or sufficient. See *Verbs*.
Facile princeps [L.]. Indisputably first.
First-rate. Of the best kind or class.
Foremost. First in place, rank, or dignity.

SUPREMACY—Adjectives—*Continued.*

Great. Powerful; uncommonly gifted.
Greater. More powerful.
Greatest. Most powerful.
Higher. More advanced.
Incomparable. Beyond compare.
Increased. Made larger, etc.
Inimitable. Beyond imitation.
Major. Greater in number, quantity, or extent.
Matchless. Without equal.
More than a match for. Superior to.
Ne plus ultra [L.]. Nothing further.
None such. Incomparable.
Nulli secundus [L.]. Second to none.
Paramount. Of highest consideration, value, dignity, or rank.
Peerless. Matchless.
Preeminent. Distinguished above others of eminence.
Sans pareil [F.]. Without equal.

Second to none. First.
Sovereign. Efficacious in the highest degree.
Superior. Surpassing in quantity, quality, or degree.
Superlative. The very highest.
Supreme. Highest, greatest, or most excellent.
Transcendent. } Superior in excellence.
Transcendental. }
Ultra. Exceeding moderation or propriety; extreme.
Unapproached. Far superior.
Unequaled. } Not to be compared with.
Unparagoned. }
Unparalleled. Without a similar case.
Unrivaled. Without a rival.
Unsurpassed. Not overcome.
Utmost. In the highest degree.
Vaulting. Surpassing.
Without parallel. Unparalleled.

SUPREMACY—*Adverbs, etc.*

Above all. Before every other consideration.
Above par. Above face value; above the standard.
Above the mark. Above the standard.
A fortiori [L.]. } With stronger reason.
At its height. }
At the top of the scale. At the highest point.
Beyond. Surpassing.
Egregiously. Extraordinarily; in a bad sense.
Eminently. In the highest possible manner or degree. See *Adjectives.*
Especially. Very particularly.
Even. Exactly.
In advance of. Ahead.
Kat exochen [Gr.]. Par excellence.
More. Of a greater quantity, etc.
Of all things. } Eminently.
Over. }

Over and above. With supremacy.
Over the mark. Above the standard.
Par excellence. By way of eminence.
Particularly. In an uncommon degree.
Peculiarly. In a manner characteristic of the individual.
Preeminently. Supremely. See *Adjectives.*
Principally. For the most part.
Prominently. In a well-known way.
Still more. In a higher degree.
Superlatively. } In the highest degree. See *Adjectives.*
Supremely. }
Surpassingly. Much excelling. See *Adjectives.*
The most. In the highest degree.
To crown all. To make complete.
Upwards of. Exceeding.
Yea. Not only so, but more so.

SUPREMACY—*Phrase.*

We shall not look upon his like again.

su-preme'. Highest in rank, power, or importance. RULE-LICENSE, SUPREMACY-SUBORDINACY, TOP-BOTTOM; **Supreme Being,** DIVINITY.
su-preme'-ly. Chiefly. SUPREMACY-SUBORDINACY.
sur-bate'. To bruise. BETTERMENT-BRUISE.
sur-bat'-ed. Made sore. WARNING.
sur-cease'. To cease entirely. DISCONTINUANCE-CONTINUANCE.
sur-charge'. An excessive charge. EXCESS-LACK; **surcharge and falsify,** ACCOUNTS.
sur'-cin"-gle. A girdle. CONNECTIVE.
sur'-coat". An outer coat. DRESS-UNDRESS.
surd. An irrational number; a consonant sound. HEARING-DEAFNESS, NUMBER.
sure. Certain; trustworthy; stable. CERTAINTY-DOUBT, FAITH-MISGIVING, SECURITY-INSECURITY; **make sure against,** PREPARATION-NONPREPARATION; **make sure of,** INVESTIGATION-ANSWER, TAKING-RESTITUTION; **on sure ground,** SECURITY-INSECURITY; **to be sure,** ASSENT-DISSENT, CERTAINTY-DOUBT; **you may be sure,** ASSERTION-DENIAL.
sure'-foot"-ed. Liable not to stumble. CAREFULNESS-CARELESSNESS, RECKLESSNESS-CAUTION, SKILL-UNSKILFULNESS.
sure'-ly. Certainly. ASTONISHMENT-EXPECTANCE.
sure'-ty. Security for payment. CERTAINTY-DOUBT, SECURITY, SECURITY-INSECURITY.
surf. Foamy swell of the sea. RIVER-WIND, VISCIDITY-FOAM.
sur'-face. The exterior part; external appearance. OUTSIDE-INSIDE, TEXTURE; **lie on the surface,** CLEARNESS-OBSCURITY, MANIFESTATION-LATENCY; **skim the surface,** CAREFULNESS-CARELESSNESS.
Sur'-face, Jo'-seph. An extravagant fellow. GULL-DECEIVER.
sur'-feit. To feed to excess; to satiate. EXCESS-LACK, REPLETION.

surge. To rise high; billow; a heavy rolling; a mass of rolling water. ASCENT-DESCENT, GATHERING-SCATTERING, REVOLUTION-EVOLUTION, RIVER-WIND.
sur'-geon. A medical officer. REMEDY-BANE.
sur'-ger-y. A healing of diseases by manual operation. REMEDY-BANE.
surgit amari aliquid [L.] (sur'-jit am-ê'-rai al'-i-quid). Something bitter rises. FAULTLESSNESS-FAULTINESS.
sur'-ly. Cross; rude; crabbed. CHARITABLENESS-MALEVOLENCE, FAVORITE-MOROSENESS, POLITENESS-IMPOLITENESS.
sur-mise'. To suppose. FAITH-MISGIVING, HYPOTHESIS.
sur-mount'. To mount upon; to rise superior to; to pass over. ASCENT-DESCENT, HEIGHT-LOWNESS, TRANSCURSION-SHORTCOMING.
sur-mount'-a-ble. Capable of being surmounted. POSSIBILITY-IMPOSSIBILITY.
sur'-name'. A family name. NAME-MISNOMER.
sur-pass'. To exceed; to go beyond; to excel. ENLARGEMENT-DIMINUTION, REPUTATION-DISCREDIT, SUCCESS-FAILURE, SUPREMACY-SUBORDINACY, TRANSCURSION-SHORTCOMING.
sur-pass'-ing. Excelling. SUPREMACY-SUBORDINACY, TRANSCURSION-SHORTCOMING.
sur'-plice. A clerical vestment. VESTMENTS.
sur'-plus. That which remains after use. EXCESS-LACK, INCREMENT-REMNANT, SUPREMACY-SUBORDINACY.
sur'-plus-age. Excess. EXCESS-LACK.
sur-prise'. A surprising; wonder. ASTONISHMENT-EXPECTANCE, CRAFT-ARTLESSNESS, EXPECTATION-SURPRISE.
sur-prised'. Astonished. ASTONISHMENT-EXPECTANCE, EXPECTATION-SURPRISE.
sur-pris'-ing. Causing wonder. ASTONISHMENT-EXPECTANCE.

sur-pris'-ing-ly. Wonderfully. MAGNITUDE - SMALL-NESS.

sur"-re-but'-ter. A plaintiff's reply to a rebutter. IN-VESTIGATION-ANSWER, LITIGATION.

sur"-re-join'-der. A plaintiff's answer to a rejoinder. INVESTIGATION-ANSWER, LITIGATION.

sur-ren'-der. To yield to another. KEEPING-RELIN-QUISHMENT, YIELDING; **surrender one's life,** LIFE-DEATH.

sur"-rep-ti'-tious. Clandestine. ENLIGHTENMENT-SECRECY, TRUTHFULNESS-FRAUD, TRUTHFULNESS-FABRICATION.

sur'-ro-gate. A substitute. REPRESENTATIVE.

sur-round'. To encompass; to enclose. CONFINE MENT, ENVIRONMENT-INTERPOSITION.

sur-round'-ing. Lying about. ENVIRONMENT-INTER-POSITION.

sur-round'-ings. Environment. **Amidst such and such surroundings,** ENVIRONMENT-INTERPOSITION, POSITION.

sursum corda [L.] (sur'-sum cor'-da). **Lift up your hearts.** DEVOTION-IDOLATRY.

sur-tout'. An overcoat. DRESS-UNDRESS.

sur-veil'-lance. A spying supervision. CAREFULNESS-CARELESSNESS, MANAGEMENT; **under surveillance,** JUSTIFICATION-CHARGE.

sur-vene'. To come in addition. OCCURRENCE-DES-TINY.

sur-vey'. To look over carefully. SIGHT-BLINDNESS, VISIBILITY-INVISIBILITY.

sur-vey'-ing. Measuring. MENSURATION.

sur-vey'-or. One who surveys. MANAGER.

sur-vi'-val. Outliving. INCREMENT-REMNANT, LAST-INGNESS-TRANSIENTNESS.

sur-vi'-vance. Outliving. INCREMENT - REMNANT, LASTINGNESS-TRANSIENTNESS.

sur-vive'. To outlive; to outlast. INCREMENT-REM-NANT, LASTINGNESS-TRANSIENTNESS, MUTATION-PERMANENCE.

sur-vi'-ving. Living. INCREMENT-REMNANT.

sus-cept"-i-bil-'i-ty. Liability; sensitiveness; tenden-cy; an easy yielding. CONTINGENCY, FAVORITE-QUARRELSOMENESS, INCLINATION, MIGHT-IMPO-TENCE, MOTIVE - CAPRICE, SENSITIVENESS - APATHY.

sus-cep'-ti-ble. Yielding readily; easily irritated. FA-VORITE-QUARRELSOMENESS, SENSITIVENESS-APATHY.

sus-cep'-ti-ble-ness. Sensitiveness. SENSITIVENESS-APATHY.

sus-cep'-tive. Susceptible. SENSITIVENESS-APATHY.

sus-cep-tiv'-i-ty. Quality of being susceptive. SEN-SITIVENESS-APATHY.

sus-cip'-i-en-cy. Act of receiving. GIVING-RECEIV-ING.

sus-cip'-i-ent. One who receives. GIVING-RECEIV-ING.

sus'-ci-tate. To arouse. CAUSE-EFFECT, CREATION-DESTRUCTION, EXCITATION, TURBULENCE - CALM-NESS.

sus"-ci-ta'-tion. Rousing. EXCITATION.

sus-pect'. To surmise; to mistrust. FAITH-MISGIV-ING, HYPOTHESIS.

sus-pect'-ed. Distrusted. JUSTIFICATION-CHARGE.

sus-pect'-less. Without suspicions. FAITH-MISGIV-ING.

sus-pend'. To cease; to delay; to hang. DISCON-TINUANCE - CONTINUANCE, EARLINESS - LATENESS, SUSPENSION-SUPPORT.

sus-pend'-ed. Hanging. SUSPENSION-SUPPORT.

sus-pend'-ed an"-i-ma'-tion. SENSITIVENESS-APATHY.

sus-pense'. Uncertainty; vacillation; cessation; anxi-ety. CERTAINTY-DOUBT, DETERMINATION-VACILLA-TION, DISCONTINUANCE-CONTINUANCE, EXPECTA-TION-SURPRISE; **in suspense,** CERTAINTY - DOUBT, VIGOR-INERTIA.

sus-pen'-sion. The act of suspending. DISCONTINU-ANCE-CONTINUANCE, MELODY-DISSONANCE, SUSPEN-SION-SUPPORT; **suspension of arms,** FIGHTING-CON-CILIATION.

SUSPENSION—SUPPORT.

Dependency. The state of relying upon something or someone.
Hanging. The act of suspending.
Pendency. The state of being pendent, or hanging down loosely.
Suspension. The act of suspending, or of causing to hang down.

SUSPENSION—*Denotations.*

Button. A knob or disk of bone metal, etc., for fastening one part of a garment to another.
Fastening. etc. A fastener, as a bolt, catch, etc. See CONNECTIVE.
Flap. A broad, loosely hanging part or attachment.
Hangnail. Skin partially torn from its attachment near the root of a finger-nail.
Hook. A device of a bent piece of metal serving to catch or hold another piece.
Horse. A device used to support anything.
Knob. A rounded handle.
Nail. A piece of metal driven into wood, from which things are sus-pended.
Peg. A wooden pin thrust into a hole and left projecting, upon which something may be fastened.
Pendulum. A body suspended by a rod or cord from a fixed point, and free to swing to and fro.
Pigtail. A cue or plait of hair.
Ring. A circle of metal from which things may be suspended.
Skirt. That part of a dress that hangs below the waist.
Spar. A round timber or pole on which to extend a sail.
Staple. A U-shaped piece of metal used as a fastener.
Stud. An ornamental button.
Tail. The part of an animal prolonged beyond the rest of the body
Tenterhook. A sharp hook for stretching cloth.
Train. Something pulled along with and in the track of another.

SUSPENSION—*Scientific Nouns.*

Pedicel. A stalk supporting a single flower.
Pedicle. A stalk supporting leaves or flowers.
Peduncle. A stalk that supports the flower or fruit

Base. Foundation; that upon which anything is placed as **a sup-port.**
Basis. That upon which anything rests; a support.
Bearing. That which endures or sustains something.
Block. A support of any kind, as a solid piece of metal or wood upon which hammering or chopping is done.
Caudex. The trunk or persistent support of a plant.
Floor. The part of a room on which the furniture is placed. See TOP-BOTTOM.
Footing. A firm spot for the feet; a small foundation.
Foundation. That upon which anything is established.
Fulcrum. The support of a lever.
Ground. The solid earth; hence, a base; a starting-point.
Groundwork. That which gives a foundation or a support.
Hold. The act of holding; a controlling influence.
Landing. } A place for going on or off vessels.
Landing-place. }
Landing-stage. A structure at a wharf for landing goods or pas-sengers.
Locus standi [L.]. A place for standing.
Platform. A support used for speakers.
Point d'appui [F.]. Point of support.
Pou sto [Gr.]. Where I may stand; what Archimedes wanted **to** move the world with a lever.
Purchase. In mechanics, an advantage for leverage.
Rest. That upon which anything can be supported.
Resting-place. A place for stopping.
Stage. The place on which orators speak, plays are performed, **etc.**
Substratum. That which is spread under and supports.
Subvention. The act of subvening, or of giving aid.
Support. That which bears the weight of.
Sustentation. Support of life.

SUPPORT—*Denotations.*

Abutment. A supporting structure to sustain lateral pressure.
Aid, etc. Anything that helps or supports. See OBSTRUCTION-HELP.

SUSPENSION—SUPPORT—*Continued.*

SUSPENSION—*Verbs.*

Append. To hang or fasten to.
Be pendent. To hang from. See *Adjectives.*
Daggle. To trail as in the dust.
Dangle. To hang loosely.
Depend. To hang to in a subordinate character.
Fasten to. To cause to become fixed to.
Flap. To move about while hanging loosely.
Flow. To hang loose, like hair.
Hang. To fasten to something for support; suspend
Hitch. To fasten to; make fast, as a horse.
Hook up. To fasten to.
Sling. To suspend as in a sling; hang up with rope and tackle
Suspend. To cause to hang; make hang.
Swag. To swing heavily.
Swing. To vibrate; wave backwards and forwards.
Trail. To draw along loosely, as the train of a dress.

SUSPENSION—*Adjectives.*

Caudate. Having a tail.
Dependent. Hanging down; relying upon; unable to exist without something else.
Flowing. Floating loosely, like hair.
Hanging. Fastened to something else. See *Verbs.*
Having a peduncle. Having a stem. See *Nouns.*
Loose. Not fastened; swinging.
Pedunculate. Having a peduncle.
Pendent. Hanging downward and fastened by one end.
Pendulous. Hanging; swinging.
Pensile. Pendent and hanging.
Suspended. Hanging by one end   See *Verbs.*
Tailed. Having a tail.

SUPPORT—Denotations—*Continued from Column 2.*

Mantel.
Mantelpiece. } A shelf above a fireplace,
Mantel-shelf.
Mat. A covering for the floor.
Mattress. A stuffed tick used as a bed.
Morris-chair. A reclining armchair.
Mullion. A division piece between the lights of windows.
Musnud. A dais or raised seat. [Anglo-Indian.]
Ottoman. A cushioned seat.
Outrigger. A part projecting beyond a vessel or machine for support.
Pack-saddle. A saddle to which packages are attached for carrying.
Paillasse [F.] A straw mattress.
Pallet. A bed of straw.
Panel. A piece of wood set in a door.
Pedestal. A base or support for a column, statue, etc.
Pedicle A short stalk.
Pediment. A triangular piece surrounding a door or screen.
Peg, etc. A wooden pin for fastening articles together. See Suspension.
Perch. A pole serving as a roost for birds.
Persides. Descendants of Perseus, a Grecian hero who changed Atlas into a mountain.
Pilaster. A right-angled column.
Pillar. A firm, upright, separate support.
Pillion. A pad behind a saddle on which a second person may ride.
Pillow. A head-rest.
Pivot. A pin or short staff upon which something turns.
Plinth. A square stone on which a column or statue stands.
Pommel. A wooden block for pressing and working skins.
Post. An upright piece of timber used as a support.
Prop. That which sustains a weight.
Rack. A frame for hanging clothes.
Ratlings. The rounds of a rope ladder.
Retable. An altar-piece.
Rib. One of the parts of the framework of the chest.
Rip-rap. Broken stones for making foundations of walls.
Rocking-chair. A chair having the legs set on rockers.
Rod. A long stick for the support of a light weight.
Round. The rung of a ladder.
Rowlock. A device for supporting an oar.
Rug. A covering for the floor.
Rung. One of the rounds of a ladder or chair.
Saddle. A seat of leather for riding horseback.
Saddle-bag. A pouch suspended from a saddle.
Scaffold. A temporary structure about a building.

SUPPORT—Denotations—*Continued*

Alpenstock. A long pointed staff, shod with iron, used for mountain climbing.
Anvil. A heavy block of iron or steel on which metals may be hammered.
Arbor. A wooden framework for supporting vines.
Arch. A structure supported at the sides or ends only.
Armchair. A chair with side supports for the arms.
Atlantes. Columns or pillars in the shape of male human figures.
Atlas. A mythological character who supported the heavens upon his shoulders.
Axis. A line on which something rotates.
Axle. A cross-bar on which a wheel-turns.
Axletree. An axle.
Backbone. The spinal or vertebral column.
Baluster. A small pillar supporting a hand-rail.
Balustrade. A railing formed of a range of balusters supporting a hand-rail.
Bandage. A strip of cloth for binding wounds.
Banister. An upright supporting a hand-rail.
Bar. A long piece of wood forming a barrier.
Baton. An official staff.
Beam. A long horizontal piece of wood for supporting weight.
Bed. An article of furniture used to rest or sleep on.
Bedding. The furnishings for a bedstead.
Bedstead. A framework for supporting a bed.
Bench. A long wooden seat.
Berth. A bed in a vessel, sleeping-car, etc.
Board. A table.
Bolster. A long underpillow for a bed.
Boom. A spar for holding a sail.
Bracket. A frame for supporting a shelf, etc.
Buttress. A structure built against a wall to strengthen it.
Caryatides. A supporting column shaped like a female figure.
Chair. A single seat with four legs and a back.
Clothes-horse. A frame for hanging clothes while drying.
Colstaff. A pole on which a large water vessel is carried.
Columella. A little rod, pillar, or central axis.
Column. A vertical shaft for the support of a building, etc.
Console. A bracket whose supporting brace is in the form of a reverse scroll.
Corbel. An ornamental bracket.
Corner-stone. A stone uniting two walls at the corner of a building.
Cot. A light bedstead.
Couch. A structure on which to rest or sleep.
Counter. A table or bench on which goods are exposed for sale.
Cradle. A child's rocking or swinging bed.
Crib. A child's bed with side railings.
Crutch. A staff used as a support in walking.
Cushion. A soft seat.
Dais. A raised platform for a seat.
Desk. A table adapted for writing.
Divan. A cushioned place for reclining.
Dresser. A kitchen table on which food is prepared.
Easel. A frame for holding a picture.
Easy-chair. A cushioned armchair.
Elbow-chair. An armchair.
Faldstool. A cushioned stool on which worshipers kneel.
Fauteuil [F.] An upholstered armchair.
Flange. A projecting rim used to strengthen an object.
Footstool. A stool for supporting the feet.
Form. } A long seat in the nave of a church.
Frame.
Framework. The supporting and formative parts of a structure.
Fulciment. A prop, fulcrum, or pivot.
Girder. The principal horizontal beam which supports a structure.
Hammock. A swinging couch hung by the ends.
Hassock. A thick mat or cushion to kneel on.
Heel. That part of a shoe that supports the back of the foot.
Hercules. A mythological character noted for his strength.
Hob. A projecting frame on the side of a fireplace.
Horse. Anything used as a support.
Jamb. A side post of a door, window, etc.
Joist. One of the horizontal timbers that supports a floor.
Keystone. The stone which locks the members of an arch together.
Lap. The part of a substance that extends over another.
Ledge. A shelf upon which articles can be laid.
Leg. A limb of an animal used for support.
Lintel. The horizontal top piece of a doorway or window.
Litter. A stretcher used for carrying sick or wounded.
Mainstay. A chief support or dependence.

(*Continued on Column 1.*)

SUPPORT—Denotations—*Continued*.

Seat. That on which one sits.
Settee. A long seat with a back.
Settle. A long seat with high back and arms.
Shaft. A column or pillar.
Shake-down. A makeshift bed
Shank. The shaft of a column.
Sheave. The pully of a window- or door-hanger.
Shelf. A board set horizontally into a wall and supported by brackets.
Shoe. An outer covering for the foot
Shore. A beam to support a wall.
Shoulder. That part which supports.
Side-saddle. A saddle for the use of women.
Sill. The horizontal member forming the foundation of a structure
Skeleton. The bony framework of the body.
Skid. One of a pair of parallel timbers to support a cannon.
Slab. A flat piece of metal or stone used as a base.
Sleeper. A heavy beam of wood used as a support for a roadway.
Socle. A plain square block supporting a statue.
Sofa. A long upholstered seat with a back, and raised head.
Sole. The bottom of a shoe.
Splint. A thin flat piece of wood for holding broken bones in place.
Sprit. A small spar.
Squab. A stuffed cushion.
Staddle. Anything that serves as a foundation or support.
Staff. A stick used in climbing or walking.
Stall. A seat in a choir.
Stanchion. An upright bar or timber forming a principal support.
Stand. A structure upon which persons or things may stand.
Stay. That which supports.
Step. A door-step.

Stick. A long piece of wood used in walking.
Stilts. Slender poles or stilts with projections to support the feet above the ground in walking.
Stirrup. The loops suspended from the sides of a saddle, to support the feet.
Stool. A seat without a back.
Stretcher. A frame for carrying injured persons.
Summer. A heavy horizontal timber or girder.
Supporter. A support for some portion of the body.
Table. An article of furniture with a flat top and three or more legs.
Tabouret. A small seat without arms or back.
Tea-poy. A small table for holding a tea-service.
Terra firma [L.]. Solid land.
Tester. A flat canopy over a tomb.
Throne. The seat of a monarch.
Tie-beam, etc A timber that serves as a tie, as between walls. See CONNECTIVE.
Transom. } A cross-beam
Trave. }
Travis. A bar or beam.
Trestle. A beam or bar supported by four divergent legs.
Trevet. A trivet.
Tripod. A small three-legged stand.
Trivet. A tripod.
Trunnion. The frame supporting the axis of a cannon.
Truss. A collection of timbers supporting a roof or bridge.
Vertebra. One of the portions of the backbone.
Woolsack. The seat of the Lord Chancellor as the presiding officer of the House of Lords in England.
Zocle. An unmolded base supporting a wall.

SUPPORT—*Verbs*.

Abut on. To meet with, project to.
Afford foundation. } To form the base or foundation of.
Afford support. }
Aid. To support. See OBSTRUCTION-HELP.
Back up. To give strength to, maintain.
Bandage. To give support with a bandage. See UNION.
Base. To put upon, as a foundation.
Bear. } To rest on for support.
Bear on. }
Be based on. To rest on.
Bestraddle. To bestride.
Bestr'de. To set astride.
Be supported. To have a support.
Bolster up. To support, as with a bolster.
Bottom. To put upon a bottom of a foundation.
Carry. To bear or support
Embed. To support n surrounding matter, imbed.
Found. To establish.
Furnish foundation. } To fix upon a base.
Furnish support. }
Give foundation } To establish
Give support. }
Ground. To fix as in the ground.
Have at one's back. To have support
Hold. } To strengthen
Hold up. }
Imbed. To fix, as in a bed; embed.

Incline on. To lean for support.
Keep on foot To maintain in an active condition.
Lean on. To depend for support.
Lend foundation. } To strengthen.
Lend support. }
Lie on. To depend upon for support.
Loll on. To lie on or recline carelessly
Maintain. To keep; support.
Prop. To keep from falling by some prop.
Recline on. To lean on.
Repose on. To lay back on.
Rest on. To be supported by.
Shore up. To prop up with a leaning timber.
Shoulder. To put upon the shoulder; sustain.
Sit on. To rest upon.
Stand on. } To be supported by.
Step on. }
Supply foundation } To strengthen.
Supply support }
Support. To bear; endure; maintain
Sustain. To hold up; support.
Underpin. To support from below.
Underprop. To prop up from below.
Underset. To support by placing under.
Upbear. To support from below.
Uphold. To keep from overthrow

SUPPORT—*Adjectives*.

Fundamental. Pertaining to a foundation; essential.
Supported. Kept from falling. See *Verbs*.

Supporting. Holding up. See *Verbs*.

SUPPORT—*Adverbs*.

Astraddle. } With one leg on each side of
Astride. }

sus-pi'-cion. Conjecture; doubt; mistrust. CREDULOUSNESS-SKEPTICISM, FAITH-MISGIVING, HYPOTHESIS, KNOWLEDGE-IGNORANCE, SANGUINENESS-TIMIDITY; **under suspicion,** JUSTIFICATION-CHARGE.
sus-pi'-cious. Questionable. FAITH-MISGIVING.
sus-pi'-cious-ness. Mistrust. CREDULOUSNESS-SKEPTICISM.
sus"-pi-ra'-tion. A sighing. JUBILATION-LAMENTATION.
sus-tain'. To uphold; to help; to prove; to establish; to keep up courage; to suffer. AGENCY, CONSERVATION, DISCONTINUANCE-CONTINUANCE, EMOTION,

OBSTRUCTION-HELP, STRENGTH-WEAKNESS, SUSPENSION-SUPPORT.
sus-tained' note. Prolonged note. MELODY-DISSONANCE.
sus'-te-nance. Food. NUTRIMENT-EXCRETION.
sus"-ten-ta'-tion. Support of life; maintenance. CONSERVATION, NUTRIMENT-EXCRETION, OBSTRUCTION-HELP, SUSPENSION-SUPPORT.
su"-sur-ra'-tion. A whispering. LOUDNESS-FAINTNESS.
sut'-ler. A small, military trader. DEALER, PROVISION-WASTE.

sut-tee'. Immolation of widow upon husband's funeral pyre. DEVOTION-IDOLATRY, LIFE - KILLING, UNSELFISHNESS-SELFISHNESS.

su'-ture. Junction of two surfaces. UNION-DISUNION.

suum cuique [L.] (siu'-um kai'-quî). Let each have his own. PROPERTY, RIGHT-WRONG, TAKING-RESTITUTION.

su'-ze-rain. One having paramount authority. CHIEF-UNDERLING.

su'-ze-rain''-ty. Supreme authority. RULE-LICENSE.

swab. One who uses a swab; a utensil used to clean the bore of a cannon. ADEPT-BUNGLER, CLEANNESS-FILTHINESS, DAMPNESS-DRYNESS.

swad'-dling–clothes''. Winding - clothes for children. In swaddling-clothes, INFANT - VETERAN, LIBERTY-SUBJECTION, RELEASE-RESTRAINT.

swag. Plunder; a swaying; low; a hanging cluster. ASCENT - DESCENT, CURVATION - RECTILINEARITY, PARALLELISM-INCLINATION, PLUNDER, SUSPENSION-SUPPORT, VIBRATION.

swag'–bel''–lied. Corpulent. ENLARGEMENT - DIMINUTION.

swage. To assuage. TURBULENCE-CALMNESS.

swag'-ger. To strut; to boast noisily. BRAGGING, PRESUMPTION-OBSEQUIOUSNESS, SELFRESPECT-HUMBLENESS.

swag'-ger-er. One who swaggers. BRAWLER.

swag'-ger-ing. Bragging. PRESUMPTION - OBSEQUIOUSNESS.

swain. A lover; a gallant; a rustic. CITY-COUNTRY, GENTILITY-COMMONALTY, LOVE-HATE, MALE-FEMALE.

swale. Marshy ground. BETTERMENT - DETERIORATION.

swal'-low. To receive; to receive credulously; to take food. ADMISSION-EJECTION, CREDULOUSNESS-SKEPTICISM, EXCITABILITY-INEXCITABILITY, FAITH-MISGIVING, NUTRIMENT-EXCRETION; swallow the bait, GULL-DECEIVER, READINESS-RELUCTANCE; swallow the leek, BIGOTRY-APOSTASY, YIELDING; swallow up, CREATION - DESTRUCTION, PROVISION - WASTE, TAKING-RESTITUTION, USE-DISUSE.

swamp. To sink; a swamp; to be overwhelmed. CREATION-DESTRUCTION, SUCCESS-FAILURE, SWAMP-ISLAND.

SWAMP—ISLAND.

Bog. Wet, soft, and spongy ground, where the soil is composed mainly of decayed vegetable matter.

Fen. Low land overflowed or partially covered with water, but growing sedge, coarse grasses, etc.

Marish. ⎫ A tract of low, wet land commonly covered with coarse
Marsh. ⎬ vegetation.
Morass. ⎭

Moss. A low, wet ground containing peat.

Mud. Moist and soft earth.

Quagmire. Soft wet land which yields or shakes under the feet.

Slough. A hole filled with mud and mire.

Slush. Soft, sloppy material.

Squash. Soil that is soft and easily crushed.

Sump. A pool of water thick with mud.

Swamp. Soft, low ground soaked with water but not covered.

Wash. A piece of ground sometimes covered with water and sometimes left dry.

SWAMP—*Adjectives*.

Boggy. Having the nature of a bog.
Fenny. Having the nature of a fen.
Marsh. ⎫ Having the nature of a marsh.
Marshy. ⎭
Moorish. ⎫ Having the nature of a moor.
Moory. ⎭

Ait. A little island in a river or lake.

Archipelago. A number of islands taken together.

Atoll. A ring-shaped coral island.

Breaker. A wave broken into foam against the shore.

Eyot. A little island in a river or lake.

Holm. An islet in a river.

Island. A portion of land entirely surrounded by water.

Islander. One who lives on an island.

Isle. An island; chiefly a poetical word.

Islet. A small island.

Reef. A ridge of rocks lying at or near the surface of the water.

ISLAND—*Adjectives*.

Insular. Pertaining to an island.

Sea-girt. Surrounded by water, as an island.

SWAMP—ADJECTIVES—*Continued*

Muddy. ⎫
Paludal. ⎪
Plashy. ⎪
Poachy. ⎬ Soft and wet
Quaggy. ⎪
Sloppy. ⎪
Soft. ⎪
Squashy. ⎭
Swampy. Having the nature of a swamp.

swamped. Overwhelmed with difficulties. SUCCESS-FAILURE.

swamp'-y. Low and wet. DAMPNESS-DRYNESS.

swan'-pan''. A Chinese form of abacus. NUMBERING.

swap. To strike; exchange. COMMUTATION-PERMUTATION, IMPETUS-REACTION.

sward. Turf. GULF-PLAIN.

swarm. A congregated multitude. ENOUGH, EXCESS-LACK, GATHERING-SCATTERING, MULTIPLICITY-PAUCITY.

swarm'-ing. Gathering together. GATHERING-SCATTERING.

swart. Being of a dark hue. WHITENESS-BLACKNESS.

swarth'-ness. Darkness of color. WHITENESS-BLACKNESS.

swarth'-y. Having a dark hue. WHITENESS-BLACKNESS.

swash. To spill in considerable quantity; wash violently against. RIVER-WIND, WATER-AIR.

swash'–buck''–ler. A swaggering ruffian. BELLIGERENT, BRAWLER.

swash'-y. Dashing; splashy. DAMPNESS-DRYNESS.

swathe. To wrap in a bandage; confine. DRESS-UNDRESS, RELEASE-RESTRAINT, UNION-DISUNION.

sway. To wave or swing; govern; lean to one side; have influence over. AGITATION, DOMINANCE - IMPOTENCE, MIGHT-IMPOTENCE, MOTIVE-CAPRICE, PARALLELISM-INCLINATION, RULE-LICENSE; sway to and fro, MUTABILITY-STABILITY.

sweal. To burn away slowly. BETTERMENT-DETERIORATION.

swear. To vow; affirm upon oath; utter profanity. ASSERTION-DENIAL, CHARITABLENESS-CURSE, ENGAGEMENT-RELEASE, GODLINESS-UNGODLINESS, PRESUMPTION-OBSEQUIOUSNESS; just enough to swear by, MAGNITUDE-SMALLNESS; swear at, CHARITABLENESS-CURSE; swear a witness, ENGAGEMENT-RELEASE; swear by, ASSERTION-DENIAL, FAITH-MISGIVING; swear false, TRUTHFULNESS-FALSEHOOD.

swear'-ing. Cursing. ASSERTION-DENIAL.

sweat. Sensible perspiration; hard labor; toil. ENTRANCE-EXIT, HEAT-COLD, NUTRIMENT-EXCRETION, TOIL-RELAXATION, WEARINESS-REFRESHMENT; cold sweat, DESIRE-DISTASTE, SANGUINENESS-TIMIDITY; in a cold sweat, HEATING-COOLING; sweat of one's brow, TOIL-RELAXATION.

sweat-ing. Perspiring. ENTRANCE-EXIT.

Swe''–den–bor'–gi–an. Pertaining to a Church founded

by Emanuel Swedenborg, a Swedish mystic. OR-THODOXY-HETERODOXY.

sweep. To clean with a broom; the motion of a long stroke; a curve; extent; one who sweeps; to draw something along. AIM-ABERRATION, CLEANNESS-FILTHINESS, CURVATION-RECTILINEARITY, EXTENSION-INEXTENSION, SWIFTNESS-SLOWNESS, THEFT; **make a clean sweep of,** ADMISSION-EXPULSION, CLEANNESS-FILTHINESS; **sweep along,** MOVEMENT-REST; **sweep away,** ADMISSION-EXPULSION, COMMISSION-ABROGATION, CREATION-DESTRUCTION, KEEPING-RELINQUISHMENT; **sweep off,** ADMISSION-EXPULSION; **sweep out,** ADMISSION-EXPULSION, CLEANNESS-FILTHINESS; **sweep the chords,** MUSICIAN.

sweep'-ing. Comprehensive; affecting a large area. ENTIRETY-DEFICIENCY, UNIVERSALITY-PARTICULARITY, WHOLE-PART; **sweeping change,** REVOLUTION.

sweep'-ings. Refuse. CLEANNESS-FILTHINESS, USEFULNESS-USELESSNESS.

sweep'-stakes". A gambling arrangement at races. GAIN-LOSS, OUTLAY-INCOME.

sweet. Pleasing to the sense of taste; having the taste of sugar; harmonious; gentle; fresh; lovely. CLEANNESS-FILTHINESS, COLOR-ACHROMATISM, LOVE-HATE, MELODY-DISSONANCE, PLEASURABLENESS-PAINFULNESS, SWEETNESS-ACIDITY; **look sweet upon,** BLANDISHMENT, DESIRE-DISTASTE, LOVE-HATE; **sweet smell,** PERFUME-STENCH; **sweet tooth,** DESIRE-DISTASTE, DESIRE-PARTICULARNESS; **sweet wine,** SWEETNESS-ACIDITY; **sweet words,** POLITENESS-IMPOLITENESS.

sweet'-en. To make sweet or more endurable. PLEASURABLENESS-PAINFULNESS, SWEETNESS-ACIDITY.

sweet'-en-ed. Made sweet. SWEETNESS ACIDITY.

sweet'-heart". A lover or the person loved. FAVORITE-ANGER, LOVE-HATE.

sweet'-meat". A confection. SWEETNESS-ACIDITY.

sweet'-ness. The quality of being sweet. SWEETNESS ACIDITY.

SWEETNESS—ACIDITY

Dulcification. The act of sweetening.
Dulcitude. Sweetness.
Dulcoration. Act of sweetening.
Sweetness. The quality of being pleasant to the taste, or tasting like sugar.

SWEETNESS—*Denotations.*

Bon-bon. A sugar-plum.
Caramel. A confection, variously colored and flavored.
Cavendish. A brand of tobacco sweetened with molasses.
Comfit. A fruit preserved with sugar and dried.
Confection. An article of confectionery.
Confectionery. The sweetmeats collectively.
Confiture. A confection.
Conserve. A sweetmeat in which fruits are preserved with sugar.
Edulcorator. Anything which sweetens.
Grocery. An article of household supplies for the table, as sugar, etc.
Honey. A sweet, syrupy secretion, derived by bees from the nectar of flowers.
Honeysuckle. A variety of sweet-scented shrub.
Hydromel. A liquor consisting of honey diluted with water.
Jam. A conserve of fruit prepared by thorough cooking and stewing with sugar.
Jujube. A sweetmeat of gum-arabic sweetened and flavored.
Julep. A drink composed of brandy or whisky, sugar, cracked ice, and green mint.
Licorice. The root of a plant used as a flavoring in confectionery, etc.
Liqueur. An alcoholic cordial sweetened and flavored with aromatic substances.
Lollypop. A kind of taffy.
Manna. A sweetish substance obtained from incisions in the stems of various trees and shrubs.
Marmalade. A preserve or confection made by boiling the pulp of fruit with sugar.
Mead. } A fermented liquor composed of honey and boiling water.
Metheglin. }
Molasses. A viscid dark-colored liquor obtained from sugar.
Nectar. Any especially sweet and delicious drink.
Pastry. Articles of food, as pies and tarts.
Pie. Prepared food of fruit and shortened dough.
Plum. A fruit.
Preserve. A cooked fruit kept from fermenting by boiling with sugar.
Pudding. A dish of fruit, milk, eggs, etc., sweetened and flavored.
Puff. A light tart or cake filled with some sweet substance.
Sugar. A sweet crystalline compound derived from the sugar-cane.
Sugar-candy. Crystallized sugar.
Sugar-plum. A bon-bon or small sweetmeat.
Sweetmeat. A confection, jelly, or sweet food.
Sweets. Confections.
Sweet wine. Wine in which all the sugar has not passed off into alcohol.
Syrup. A thick, sweet liquid.
Taffy. A sweetmeat of brown sugar and molasses.
Tart. A piece of pastry containing fruit or jam.
Treacle. The syrup obtained in refining sugar.

Acetous fermentation. Fermentation that changes alcohol, etc., to vinegar.
Acidity. The quality of being sharp to the taste.
Sourness. Mild acidity, the quality of being sour

ACIDITY—*Denotations.*

Acid. Any sour substance.
Alum. A chemical compound used as an astringent in medicine.
Crab. A small sour apple.
Verjuice. The sour juice of green fruit.
Vinegar. An acid liquid obtained from cider or wine.

ACIDITY—*Verbs.*

Acidify. To convert into acid.
Acidulate. To make acid in a moderate degree.
Be sour. To be of a mildly acid taste.
Render sour. Make sour.
Turn sour. Become sour.
Set the teeth on edge. To feel a sensation in the teeth on eating sour things.

ACIDITY—*Adjectives.*

Acerb. Sour and bitter.
Acescent. Readily turning sour.
Acetic. Pertaining to vinegar, so
Acetose. } Causing acetification
Acetous. }
Acid. Containing acid.
Acidulated. Tinged with acid
Acidulous. Slightly sour.
Crabbed. Rough or harsh to the taste.
Hard. Acid, as hard cider.
Rough. Astringent, applied to wine, etc.
Sour. Mildly acid.
Sour as vinegar. Very sour.
Sourish. Acidulous.
Styptic. Having the quality of restraining hemorrhage.
Subacid. Moderately acid.
Tart. Having a sharp, sour taste.

SWEETNESS—*Continued.*

SWEETNESS—*Verbs.*

Be sweet. To be agreeable to the sense of taste.
Candy. To conserve in sugar.
Dulcify. }
Dulcorate. } To sweeten.
Edulcorate. }
Mull. To enrich with spices.
Render sweet. } To make sweet.
Sweeten. }

SWEETNESS—*Adjectives.*

Candied. Conserved into sugar.
Dulcet. Having a delicate, luscious taste.
Edulcorant. Sweetening.
Honeyed. Sweet.
Lush. Full of juice

SWEETNESS—ADJECTIVES—*Continued*.

Luscious. Excessively sweet.
Melliferous. Producing honey; flowing with honey.
Nectareous. Of the nature of nectar.
Sacchariferous. Producing sugar.
Saccharine. Pertaining to or like sugar.

Sweet. Pleasant to the taste tasting like sugar.
Sweet as a nut. ⎫
Sweet as honey. ⎬ Figurative degrees of sweetness.
Sweet as sugar. ⎭
Sweetened, etc. See *Verbs*.

SWEETNESS—*Phrase*.

Eau sucrée [F.]. Sweetened water.

sweets. Confections; pastry. NUTRIMENT-EXCRE-TION, PLEASURABLENESS-PAINFULNESS, SWEETNESS-ACIDITY.
sweet′–scent″-ed. Sweet-smelling. PERFUME-STENCH.
swell. To expand; grow violent; a billow; the increase and succeeding decrease of a musical note; a fop. APPROVAL-DISAPPROVAL, CITY-COUNTRY, EMOTION, ENLARGEMENT-DIMINUTION, GENTILITY-COMMONALTY, LOUDNESS-FAINTNESS, PRESUMPTION-OBSEQUIOUSNESS, RIVER-WIND, SOCIETY-DANDY; **ground swell,** AGITATION; **swell out,** TERSENESS-PROLIXITY; **swell over,** CONVEXITY-CONCAVITY; **swell the ranks of,** ADDITION-SUBTRACTION; **swell with rage,** FAVORITE-ANGER.
swell′-ing. The act of expanding; a protuberance;

bombastic; increasing. CONVEXITY-CONCAVITY, ENLARGEMENT-DIMINUTION, EXCITATION, SIMPLICITY-FLORIDNESS.
swell′–mob″. Well-dressed pickpockets collectively. ROBBER.
swel′-ter. To be oppressed with heat. HEAT-COLD.
swel′-tered. Oppressed with heat. HEAT-COLD.
swel′-ter-ing. Sweating. HEAT-COLD.
swerve. To turn aside; deviate; fluctuate. AIM-ABERRATION, BIGOTRY-APOSTASY, MUTATION-PERMANENCE, READINESS-RELUCTANCE.
swerv′-ing. Turning from a course. AIM-ABERRATION.
swift. Rapid. SWIFTNESS-SLOWNESS.
swift′-ness. The quality of being swift. SWIFTNESS-SLOWNESS.

SWIFTNESS—SLOWNESS.

Acceleration. Increased velocity.
Celerity. Quickness of motion.
Dash. Sudden and quick forward motion.
Eagle-speed. The swiftness of an eagle.
Expedition. State of moving or going swiftly.
Flight. ⎫
Flying. ⎬ Movement by means of wings; motion as if by wings.
Full gallop. Full speed.
Haste. Voluntary quickness of motion.
Lively pace. ⎫
Lively rate. ⎬ Full rate of speed.
Pernicity. Swiftness.
Rapidity. Swiftness of motion or progress.
Rattling pace. ⎫
Rattling rate. ⎬ Lively or surprising rate of speed.
Run. A going rapidly by.
Rush. Extraordinary haste.
Scamper. The act of running hastily.
Smart pace. ⎫
Smart rate. ⎬ Quick rate of speed.
Spanking pace. ⎫
Spanking rate. ⎬ Swift and dashing rate of speed.
Speed. The act or state of going swiftly.
Spurt. An increase of speed for a short time.
Swiftness. The quality of moving quickly.
Swift pace. ⎫
Swift rate. ⎬ Rapid rate of speed.
Velocity. Rapid motion; swiftness.

SWIFTNESS—*Denotations*.

Amble. A method of motion in quadrupeds in which but one foot supports the body at a time.
Antelope. A ruminant noted for its swiftness.
Arrow. A slender weapon shot by a bow.
Cannon-ball. A shot fired from a cannon.
Canter. Quadrupedal locomotion like a walk but quicker.
Chase. The practise of hunting game with horses and dogs.
Courser. A fast running horse.
Dart. A pointed weapon thrown with the hand.
Doe. A deer notable for its swiftness.
Eagle. A large bird of prey noted for its swift flying powers.
Electricity. A form of energy acting very quickly.
Express train. A fast train which carries express matter.
Gallop. A very rapid quadrupedal motion in which an animal springs from a fore foot and lands upon the diagonal hind foot.
Gazelle. A small antelope.
Greyhound. A tall, slender, swift hunting dog.
Hand gallop. A gallop held in check by the hand.
Hare. A small animal noted for its swiftness.
Light. Radiant energy characterized by rapidity of motion.
Lightning. A flash of light due to electrical discharge from the clouds.

Claudication. A limping.
Creeping. A moving slowly, as on hands and knees.
Delay. A suspension of progress.
Dog-trot. A slow trot.
Inactivity. State or quality of being inactive; sluggishness.
Jog-trot. An easy pace.
Languor. A state of listless indolence.
Lentor. Sluggishness.
Mincing steps. A slow rate of motion.
Retardation. ⎫
Slackening. ⎬ A lessening of velocity.
Slow march. A slow movement.
Slowness. The state or quality of being slow.
Slow time. Small velocity.

SLOWNESS—*Denotations*.

Dawdle. A loiterer.
Drawl. Slow, lengthened utterance.
Lingerer. One who delays action.
Loiterer. One who has a slow and lingering movement
Slow-coach. A slow-moving, dull person.
Slow-back. An idler.
Slow-goer. One who goes slowly, a careful person.
Sluggard. A drone; a person habitually lazy or idle.
Snail. One who makes a slow rate of progress.
Tortoise. A testudinate reptile of slow movements; a turtle.

SLOWNESS—*Verbs*.

Apply the brake. To check the speed.
Bundle on. To send away unceremoniously.
Check. To restrain the speed of.
Claudicate. To limp.
Clip the wings. To cut the wing-feathers; to check ambition.
Crawl. To move slowly with the body to the ground.
Creep. To crawl with slow movements, upon hands and knees
Curb. To check or control.
Dawdle. To loiter or move lazily.
Drag. To pull along against considerable resistance.
Drawl. To move slowly.
Falter. To be or seem to be tottering or undecided.
Flag. To move weakly.
Grovel. To creep or crawl with face to the ground.
Halt. To cause to stop.
Hang fire. To delay in exploding or blasting.
Hobble. To walk with a limp.
Jog on. To move with a slow, trotting motion.
Lag. To stay or fall behind; loiter.
Limp. To walk lamely.
Linger. To protract or to pass waitingly.
Loiter. To spend time idly.
Lose ground. To fall behind.
Lumber. To move heavily.

SWIFTNESS—SLOWNESS—*Continued.*

SWIFTNESS—Denotations—*Continued.*

Log. A device for showing the speed of a vessel.
Log-line. The line of a log attached to the ship.
Quicksilver. Mercury, characterized by breaking up into small particles which move very freely.
Race-horse. A horse trained to run races.
Squirrel. A small animal that moves very quickly.
Steeplechase. A race across country in which fences, ditches, etc., must be leaped.
Telegraph. An electrical apparatus for sending and receiving messages.
Torrent. A swift stream of water.
Trot. Quadrupedal motion in which each pair of diagonal legs is alternately put forward.
Velo. A velocity of one foot per second
Wind. The air in motion.

Swiftness—*Figurative Nouns.*

Ariel. A spirit of the air or of water; hence, a very swift person. [Bible, Shakespeare, Milton, Pope.]
Camilla. A swift-footed servant of Diana; hence, a swift person. [Virgil.]
Harlequin. A buffoon practised in sleight of hand; hence, an active person.
Mercury. The messenger of the gods; hence, a very active person.

Swiftness—*Verbs.*

Accelerate. To increase speed.
Amble. To go with a gentle pace.
Be violent. To be in a hurry.
Bolt. To make a sudden dash
Boom. To advance with a rush.
Bound. To leap.
Bowl along. To move along on wheels.
Brush. To move lightly and quickly.
Carry sail. To sail fast.
Clap spurs to one's horse. To urge on forcibly.
Crowd sail. To carry as much sail as possible to increase speed.
Cut along. To move along rapidly.
Cut away. To break away.
Dart. To move swiftly; like a dart.
Dash forward. To rush violently forward.
Dash off. To go hastily.
Dash on. To hurry on.
Fisk. To run or bustle about.
Flit. To fly rapidly from one place to another.
Fly. To pass rapidly through the air.
Fly on the wings of the wind. To go with the highest speed.
Gain ground. To make headway.
Gallop. To run or move with speed.
Get over the ground. To go with great speed.
Go ahead. To push forward.
Go off like a shot. To start suddenly.
Hasten. To drive or urge forward.
Hie. To pass over with haste.
Hurry. To move or act rapidly, or more and more rapidly.
Keep pace with. To go at the same speed.
Keep up. Not to fall behind.
Make forced marches. To make as long marches as possible.
Make haste. To act with quickness and despatch.
Make rapid strides. To progress rapidly.
Make the best of one's way. To make as much progress as possible.
March in double time. To march at rate of 180 36-inch steps a minute.
March in quick time. To march in six-eighth or two-quarter time.
Mend one's pace. To go faster.
Move quickly. To hurry.
Outstrip. To surpass; outrun.
Outstrip the wind. To go surpassingly fast.
Post. To travel with post-horses; hasten.
Put on. To hasten motion.
Put one's best leg foremost. To go as fast as possible.
Quicken. To increase the activity of.
Quicken one's pace. To walk more rapidly
Race. To run swiftly; contend in a race.
Ride hard. To ride rapidly.
Run. To move or go swiftly.
Run a race. To compete in a running contest.
Run like mad. To run in a furious manner.
Rush. To move impetuously.
Scamper. To hasten from alarm or danger.
Scour. To move, pass, or run swiftly.

SLOWNESS—Verbs—*Continued.*

March in funeral procession. To proceed solemnly and slowly.
March in slow time. To march with slow and measured tread.
Mince. To proceed with precise steps.
Moderate. To reduce from a great or excessive activity.
Move slowly. To act with deliberation.
Plod. To trudge with slow and steady steps.
Put on the drag. To check the speed of.
Reduce the speed. To go with lessened velocity.
Reef. To lessen speed by reducing extent of sail.
Rein in. To hold in check with reins.
Relax. To slacken speed.
Retard. To diminish the velocity of.
Rub on. To exist somehow, in spite of difficulties.
Saunter. To walk in a leisurely, aimless or lazy way
Shamble. To walk with a shuffling gait.
Shorten sail. To take in or reef part of the sails.
Shuffle. To move scraping the feet along.
Slacken. To retard motion.
Slacken one's pace. To walk with less rapidity.
Slacken speed. To retard the velocity.
Slouch. To move with a clownish gait.
Slug. To move slowly or lie idly; be sluggish or lazy.
Stagger. To move unsteadily from one side to the other.
Steal along. To move along gradually or stealthily.
Step short. To take steps of fifteen inches each.
Strike sail. To take in sail suddenly.
Stump along. To walk heavily and stiffly.
Take in sail. To reef part of the sails.
Take one's time. To move leisurely.
Toddle. To walk with short and unsteady steps.
Totter. To walk unsteadily or feebly.
Trail. To be drawn along.
Traipse. To gad about in an idle manner.
Trudge. To make one's way laboriously.
Wabble. To oscillate or sway unsteadily from side to side.
Waddle. To rock or sway from side to side when walking.
Worm one's way. To crawl along slowly.

Slowness—*Adjectives.*

Creeping. Proceeding on hands and knees.
Deliberative. Of or pertaining to being slow and careful in decision.
Dilatory. Characterized by delay.
Easy. Causing no disquiet or discomfort.
Gentle. Moderate in action.
Gradual. Moving slowly and regularly.
Imperceptible. } That cannot be perceived.
Insensible. }
Languid. Indisposition to physical exertion.
Leisurely. Not hasty; deliberate.
Slack. Retarded.
Slow. Having relatively small velocity.
Slow-paced. Moving or walking slowly.
Sluggish. Having little power of motion.
Snail-like. Having a slow or sluggish movement.
Tardy. Having a slow movement.
Tardigrade. Slow in pace or movement like one of the Tardigrada.

Slowness—*Adverbs, etc.*

Adagio [It.]. Slowly but more rapidly than largo.
At a foot's pace. At a slow or walking pace.
At a funeral pace. With solemn step and slow.
At a snail's pace. At a very slow movement or pace.
At half-speed. With half velocity.
Bit by bit. Little by little; gradually.
By degrees. Little by little.
By inches. Gradually.
By little and little. Gradually; slowly.
By slow degrees. Gradually; by slow steps.
Consecutively. In a logical sequence.
Gradatim [L.]. By degrees; a step at a time.
Gradually. By degrees or steps; slowly.
Handpassibus æquis [L.]. With steps not equal [to his precedessors]. [Virgil, Æneid, II, 724.]
Inch by inch. By small degrees or steps.
In slow time. More slowly than usual.
Larghetto [It.]. In a time not so slow as largo.
Largo [It.]. In slow musical time.
Leisurely. Deliberately.
Little by little. A little at a time; gradually.
Piano [It.]. With slight force.
Seriatim [L.]. One after another.

SWIFTNESS—SLOWNESS—*Continued.*

SWIFTNESS—Verbs—*Continued.*

Scour the plain. To pass over a plain quickly.
Scud. To move swiftly over, as if in haste.
Scuddle. To run hastily.
Scuttle. To scurry.
Set off at a score. To start from scratch; to start.
Shoot. To dart along swiftly.
Skim. To move lightly and swiftly over a surface.
Spank. To move briskly; at a gait between a trot and a gallop.
Speed. To advance with speed.
Spring. To move suddenly.
Stir one's stumps. To walk or run rapidly.
Sweep. To pass with speed or force along some surface.
Tear. To rush on violently.
Trip. To move quickly with light and nimble steps.
Troll. To move around.
Trot. To hurry.
Whisk. To move quickly, lightly and suddenly.
Wing one's way. To move by, or as by the aid of wings.

SWIFTNESS—*Adjectives.*

Active. Quick.
Agile. Able to move or act quickly.
Eagle-winged. Having an eagle's wings
Eagly. Swift as an eagle.
Electric. Spirited.
Expeditious. Accomplished with energy and speed.
Express. Pertaining to quick or special conveyance· quick.
Fast. That moves or acts rapidly.
Fleet. Moving or capable of moving swiftly.
Flying Intended or adapted to swift or easy motion.
Galloping Progressing rapidly.
Light-footed. Nimble in running or dancing.
Light-legged. Swift of foot.
Light of heel. Nimble in running
Mercurial. Swift, like Mercury.
Nimble. Showing easy quickness.
Nimble-footed. Able to run swiftly.
Quick. Characterized by rapidity of movement or action.
Quick as lightning. }
Quick as thought. } Very rapid
Rapid. Having great speed.
Speedy. Moving swiftly.
Swift. Moving with high velocity.
Swift as an arrow. Very swift.
Swift as a thought. Momentary
Telegraphic. Pertaining to the telegraph; swift, as by telegraph
Winged. Passing swiftly.

SLOWNESS—Adverbs, etc.—*Continued.*

Slowly. With small velocity.
Step by step. By gradual advance.
Under easy sail. Leisurely.
With clipped wings. With retarded flight.
With mincing steps. With nice or exact steps.

SLOWNESS—*Phrase.*

Dum Roma deliberat, Saguntum perit [L.]. While Rome deliberates Saguntum perishes.

SWIFTNESS—*Continued.*

SWIFTNESS—*Adverbs, etc.*

Apace. At a good and rapid pace.
À pas de géant [F.]. With giant strides.
As fast as one can lay legs to the ground. Very rapidly.
As fast as one's heels will carry one. As fast as possible.
As fast as one's legs will carry one. At full speed.
At a great rate. At a fast pace.
At full speed. As rapidly as possible.
At railway speed. Very rapidly.
At the top of one's speed. As fast as one can.
Full drive. With all one's strength or speed.
Full gallop. With horse at full speed.
In double-quick time. With a rapid march
In full sail. With greatest speed.
In seven-league boots. With great rapidity.
Instantaneously. Immediately.
On eagle's wing. With rapid flight.
Post-haste. With the speed of the post; rapidly.
Swiftly. In a swift manner.
Tantivy. With all speed.
Trippingly. Lightly and nimbly.
Under press of canvas. Under all possible sail.
Under press of sail. Under as much sail as the wind will permit
Under press of sail and steam. As fast as it is possible to go.
Velis et remis [L.]. With sails and oars.
Ventre à terre [F.]. At full speed.
Whip and spur. With forcible and exacting urgency.
With giant strides. With rapid progress.
With haste. Hastily.
With rapid strides. With long, rapid and sweeping steps.
With speed. Rapidly.

SWIFTNESS—*Phrases.*

Epea pter? vente [Gr.]. Winged words.
Tempus fugit [L.]. Time flies.
Vires acquiret eundo [L.]. He acquires power or speed by going.

---

swig. A drunkard; a deep draft of liquor; a tackle having diverging falls. NUTRIMENT-EXCRETION, PUSH-PULL, TEETOTALISM-INTEMPERANCE.

swill. To drink greedily; inebriate; liquid food for animals. MODERATION - SELFINDULGENCE, NUTRIMENT-EXCRETION, TEETOTALISM-INTEMPERANCE.

swim. To move through water by natural means of propulsion; float; seem buoyed up. ASCENT-DESCENT, HEAVINESS-LIGHTNESS, TRAVELING-NAVIGATION; **swim against the stream,** DIFFICULTY-FACILITY; **swim in,** ENOUGH, SENSUALITY-SUFFERING; **swim with the stream,** ACTIVITY-INDOLENCE, ASSENT-DISSENT, CONVENTIONALITY-UNCONVENTIONALITY, VARIANCE-ACCORD; **swim with the tide,** CONVENTIONALITY, WELFARE-MISFORTUNE.

swim'-ming. Overflowing. SANENESS - LUNACY, SIGHT-DIMSIGHTEDNESS, TRAVELING-NAVIGATION.

swim'-ming-belt''. A belt serving to buoy up a person in water. REFUGE-PITFALL.

swim'-ming-ly. With continued success. DIFFICULTY-FACILITY, SUCCESS-FAILURE, WELFARE-MISFORTUNE.

swin'-dle. To cheat; steal. SETTLEMENT-DEFAULT, THEFT, TRUTHFULNESS-FRAUD.

swin'-dler. One who cheats. GULL-DECEIVER, TRUTHFULNESS-FRAUD.

swine. An omnivorous suoid mammal. FAUNA-FLORA; **cast pearls before swine,** PROVISION-WASTE,

USEFULNESS-USELESSNESS; **swine of Epicurus,** MODERATION-VOLUPTUARY.

swine'-herd''. A tender of swine. CHIEF-UNDERLING.

swing. To oscillate; turn on a pivot; be hanged; the influence to put in motion; the sweep of a moving body; an instrument of amusement. AGENCY, ENTERTAINMENT - WEARINESS, EXTENSION - INEXTENSION, LIBERTY-SUBJECTION, SUSPENSION-SUPPORT, VIBRATION; **full swing,** ACTIVITY-INDOLENCE, SUCCESS-FAILURE; **give full swing,** DIFFICULTY-FACILITY, LIBERTY-SUBJECTION; **have one's swing,** RULE-LICENSE.

swinge. To whip. EXCULPATION-PUNITION.

swing'-ing. Very large. MAGNITUDE-SMALLNESS.

swi'-nish. Grossly gluttonous; beastly. FASTING-GLUTTONY, MODERATION-SELFINDULGENCE; **swinish multitude,** GENTILITY-COMMONALTY.

swink. To toil hard. TOIL-RELAXATION.

swirl. To cause to whirl along in irregular eddies. CIRCLE-WINDING, RIVER-WIND.

swish. A hissing sound. RESONANCE-SIBILATION.

switch. To strike with something slender and flexible; a flexible twig. RECOMPENSE-PUNITION, RECOMPENSE-SCOURGE.

Swith'-in, reign of St. A period of rain. RIVER-WIND.

swiv'-el. A coupling device; a cannon. REVOLUTION-EVOLUTION, WEAPON.

swiv'-el–eye''. A squint-eye. Sight-Dimsighted-ness.

swoll'-en. Expanded; proud. Enlargement-Diminution, Selfrespect-Humbleness.

swoon. A fainting-fit. Might-Impotence, Weariness-Refreshment.

swoop. To sweep down and seize. Ascent-Descent, Taking-Restitution; **at one fell swoop,** Eternity-Instantaneity, Taking-Restitution, Turbulence-Calmness.

swop. To exchange. Exchange.

sword. A keen-edged weapon. Weapon; **at the point of the sword,** Coercion, Fighting-Conciliation, Harshness-Mildness, Liberty-Subjection, Sharpness-Bluntness; **draw the sword,** Fighting-Conciliation; **flash one's sword,** Fighting-Conciliation; **measure swords,** Fighting-Conciliation, Strife-Peace; **put to the sword,** Life-Killing; **sword in hand,** Fighting-Conciliation, Preparation-Nonpreparation; **sword of Damocles,** Refuge-Pitfall; **turn sword into plowshare,** Fighting-Conciliation.

swords'-man. One skilful with the sword. Belligerent.

Syb'-a-rite. A voluptuary. Moderation-Voluptuary.

Syb'-a-ri''-tism. Voluptuousness. Moderation-Self-indulgence.

syc'-o-phan-cy. Obsequious and mean flattery. Adulation-Disparagement, Presumption-Obsequiousness.

syc'-o-phant. A servile flatterer. Flatterer-Defamer, Presumption-Obsequiousness, Uprightness-Rogue.

sy''-co-phan'-tic. Fawning. Adulation-Disparagement, Presumption-Obsequiousness.

sy'-en-ite. A kind of granite. Blueness-Orange.

Sykes, Bill. A thief and murderer in Dickens's *Oliver Twist.* Robber.

syl-lab'-ic. Consisting of syllables. Letter.

syl'-la-ble. A single vocal sound. Letter; **breathe not a syllable,** Enlightenment-Secrecy.

syl'-la-bus. The outline of a subject; schedule of contents. Digest, Record.

syl'-lo-gism. Mediate reasoning in logical form. Digest.

sylph. A fairy. Jove-Fiend.

sylph'-ic. Like a sylph. Jove-Fiend.

sylph'-id. A little sylph. Jove-Fiend.

sylph'-like. Like a sylph. Jove-Fiend.

syl'-van. Forest-like. Fauna-Flora.

sym'-bol. A sign or mark representing something. Mineralogy, Number, Sign.

sym-bol'-ic. Represented by symbols. Mineralogy, Sign.

sym-bol'-ic-al-ly. Represented by symbols. Sign.

sym'-bol-ism. Representation by symbols. Sign.

sym''-bol-i-za'-tion. Act of representing by symbols. Sign.

sym'-bol-ize. To represent by symbols; treat as figurative. Delineation-Caricature, Sign.

sym-met'-ric-al. Having harmonious proportions. Beauty-Ugliness, Equality-Inequality, Proportion-Deformity, Regularity-Irregularity.

sym'-met-ry. Harmony of the parts of a body. Beauty-Ugliness, Center, Equality-Inequality, Mineralogy, Proportion-Deformity, Regularity-Irregularity; **want of symmetry,** Proportion-Deformity, Regularity-Irregularity.

sym''-pa-thet'-ic. Having a like feeling with another. Amity-Hostility, Charitableness-Malevolence, Compassion-Ruthlessness, Love-Hate.

sym'-pa-thi''-zer. A partizan. Charitableness-Malevolence, Compassion-Ruthlessness, Friend-Foe.

sym'-pa-thy. Fellow-feeling; pity; harmony; accord. Affections, Amity-Hostility, Charitableness-Malevolence, Compassion-Ruthlessness, Condolence, Emotion, Felicitation, Variance-Accord.

sym-pho'-ni-ous. Harmonious. Melody-Dissonance.

sym'-pho-nize. To be in harmony. Melody-Dissonance.

sym'-pho-ni''-zing. Harmonizing. Melody-Dissonance.

sym'-pho-ny. Harmony of mingled sounds; a musical composition. Music, Predecessor-Continuation, Variance-Accord.

sym'-phy-sis. The union of parts normally separate. Union-Disunion.

sym-po'-si-um. A conversational feast. Entertainment-Weariness.

symp'-tom. A sign which points out the existence of something. Sign.

symp''-to-mat'-ic. Indicative. Sign.

symp''-to-ma-tol'-o-gy. That branch of medicine which treats of symptoms. Interpretation-Misinterpretation.

syn'-a-gogue. A Jewish place of worship. Fane.

syn''-a-le'-pha. Suppression of a vowel. Rhetoric.

syn''-a-phei'-a. Kind of metrical flow. Rhetoric.

syn'-chro-nal. One of two or more events happening simultaneously. Synchronism.

syn-chron'-ic-al. Coincidence in time. Synchronism.

syn'-chro-nism. Coincidence in time of different events. Coexistence.

syn-chron'-is-ti-cal. Happening at the same time. Synchronism.

syn'-chro-nize. To assign the same date to. Solitude-Company, Synchronism.

syn'-chro-nous. Coincident. Synchronism.

syn'-chy-sis. A derangement of any sort. Reversal.

syn''-co-pa'-tion. Contraction by syncope; to begin on an unaccented part of a measure and end on an accented part. Melody-Dissonance.

syn'-co-pe. The elision of a vowel or syllable from the middle of a word; a fainting-fit; the beginning of a tone on an unaccented part of a measure and ending on an accented part. Melody-Dissonance, Might-Impotence, Rhetoric, Terseness-Prolixity, Weariness-Refreshment.

syn-cret'-ic. Blending parties or systems. Organization-Disorganization.

syn'-cre-tism. An attempt to blend different philosophic schools and religious sects into one system. Harmony-Discord, Orthodoxy-Heterodoxy.

syn''-cre-tis'-tic. Pertaining to syncretism. Organization-Disorganization.

syn'-cri-sis. Contrast. Rhetoric.

syn'-dic. A civil magistrate. Chief-Underling, Judge.

syn'-di-cate. A combination of capitalists. Council.

syn-ec'-do-che. A figure of speech. Rhetoric, Trope.

syn'-er-gism. The combined efforts of the human being and divine grace in the salvation of the soul. Orthodoxy-Heterodoxy.

syn'-od. An ecclesiastical council. Church, Council.

syn'-o-nym. A word having the same or nearly the same meaning as another. Interpretation-Misinterpretation, Meaning-Jargon, Rhetoric, Synonym-Antonym

SYNONYM—ANTONYM.

Equivalent. Expression carrying the same meaning as another.
Equivalent term. } A word or phrase expressing the same thought as
Equivalent word. } another
Synonym. Word having nearly the same meaning as another.
Variant. Strict synonym; word differing from another only in form of spelling.
Words of same meaning. Expressions of the same thought.

SYNONYM—*Associated Nouns.*

Homonym. A word differing in meaning from another, but having the same sound.
Homonymy. Sameness of sound or name, with diversity of sense.
Synonymicon. A dictionary of synonyms.
Synonymics. }
Synonymity. } The state of being synonymous.
Synonymy. }

SYNONYM—*Verb.*

Synonymize. To express by equivalent words; give the synonyms of.

SYNONYM—*Adjectives.*

Alike. Having likeness in any respect.
Correspondent. } Alike in meaning.
Corresponding. }
Equivalent. } Having equal power or force.
Equipollent. }

syn″-o-nym′-ic. Synonymous. SYNONYM-ANTONYM.
syn″-o-nym′-i-con. Book of synonyms. SYNONYM-ANTONYM.
syn″-o-nym′-ics. Synonymy. SYNONYM-ANTONYM.
syn″-o-nym′-i-ty. State of being synonymous. SYNONYM-ANTONYM.
syn-on′-y-mize. Give synonyms of. SYNONYM-ANTONYM.
syn-on′-y-mous. Having a close relation to each other. EQUALITY-INEQUALITY, INTERPRETATION-MISINTERPRETATION, MEANING-JARGON, RHETORIC, SYNONYM-ANTONYM.
syn-on′-y-my. Sameness of meaning. SYNONYM-ANTONYM.
syn-op′-sis. A summary; a general view. DIGEST, ORGANIZATION-DISORGANIZATION, RECORD.
syn-op′-tic. Containing or being a synopsis. DIGEST.
syn-o′-vi-a. The fluid secreted in the interior of the joints to keep them moist and lubricated. FRICTION-LUBRICATION, VISCIDITY-OIL.
syn-tac′-tic. Relating to grammatical construction. GRAMMAR-SOLECISM.
syn-tag′-ma. An orderly arrangement. ORGANIZATION-DISORGANIZATION.
syn′-tax. The part of grammar which treats of the sentence and its construction. GRAMMAR-SOLECISM.

SYNONYM—ANTONYM.

Antithesis. The placing of words or clauses in contrast.
Antonym. A word whose meaning is opposite that of another.
Counter-term. A term or word which is the opposite of another in meaning.
Opposite term. A word or phrase expressing a contrary meaning.

ANTONYM—*Adjectives.*

Antithetic. } Placed in contrast.
Antithetical. }
Different. Not the same.
Not identical. Having different meanings.
Opposed in meaning. Expressing different thoughts.

SYNONYM—ADJECTIVES—*Continued.*

Identical. Exactly the same.
Interchangeable. Capable of being used the one for the other.
Of similar meaning. } Expressing the same thought.
Of the same meaning. }
Same. Not different.
Similar. Alike in respect to certain aspects of the meaning of a word.
Synonymic. Of, or pertaining to synonyms.
Synonymous. Expressing the same.

syn-tax′-is. A joint. ORGANIZATION-DISORGANIZATION.
syn′-the-sis. The putting together of different things to form a whole. COMPOSITION-RESOLUTION, RATIOCINATION-INSTINCT.
syn-thet′-ic. Pertaining to synthesis. COMPOSITION-RESOLUTION, RATIOCINATION-INSTINCT.
syr′-inge. An instrument for withdrawing or ejecting a liquid. RIVER-WIND, WATER-AIR.
syr′-up. A thick, sweet liquid. SWEETNESS-ACIDITY.
sys′-tem. Orderly arrangement; plan. DESIGN, REGULARITY-IRREGULARITY; **system of knowledge,** KNOWLEDGE-IGNORANCE; **system of opinions,** FAITH-MISGIVING.
sys″-tem-at′-ic. Methodical. ORGANIZATION-DISORGANIZATION, REGULARITY-IRREGULARITY.
sys″-tem-at′-ic-al-ly. Methodically. REGULARITY-IRREGULARITY.
sys′-tem-a-tize. To reduce to a system. DESIGN, ORGANIZATION-DISORGANIZATION.
sys′-to-le. The regular contraction of the heart; shortening of a syllable. ENLARGEMENT-DIMINUTION, RHETORIC.
syz′-y-gy. The times of both new and full moon. ASTRONOMY, INTERSPACE-CONTACT.

T

T, to a T. Exactly. TRUTH-ERROR.

tab'-ard. A heavy, coarse garment. DRESS-UNDRESS.

tab'-by. Marked with spots; a gossip. CONVERSATION-MONOLOGUE, VARIEGATION.

tab''-e-fac'-tion. Emaciation. ENLARGEMENT-DIMINUTION.

ta-ber'-na. A tent; booth. DWELLER-HABITATION.

tab'-er-na-cle. A tent; a temple. DWELLER-HABITATION, FANE.

ta-bes'-cence. A state of emaciation. RENOVATION-RELAPSE.

tab'-id. Wasted by disease; shrunken. BETTERMENT-DETERIORATION, BREADTH-NARROWNESS, ENLARGEMENT-DIMINUTION, HEALTH-SICKNESS.

ta'-ble. A piece of furniture; fare; a systematized synopsis; layer. LAMINA-FIBER, LEVELNESS, NUTRIMENT-EXCRETION, ORGANIZATION-DISORGANIZATION, SUSPENSION-SUPPORT, WRITING-PRINTING; **on the table,** PREPARATION-NONPREPARATION; **table of the Lord,** FANE; **turn the tables,** REVERSAL; **under the table,** ENLIGHTENMENT-SECRECY, TEETOTALISM-INTEMPERANCE.

ta''-bleau'. A picturesque representation; a list. ACTING, APPEARANCE-DISAPPEARANCE, PAINTING, RECORD.

table d'hôte [F.] (tɑbl dot). A common table at a hotel. NUTRIMENT-EXCRETION.

ta'-ble-land''. A plateau. ERECTNESS-FLATNESS, GULF-PLAIN.

ta'-ble-spoon''. A large spoon for table use. CONTENTS-RECEIVER.

ta'-ble-talk''. Conversation at table. CONVERSATION-MONOLOGUE, TIDINGS-MYSTERY.

tab'-let. A pad; a flat surface for an inscription. LAMINA-FIBER, LEVELNESS, MARK-OBLITERATION, WRITING-PRINTING.

tab'-lets. Pads; records; **Tablets of the memory,** REMEMBRANCE-FORGETFULNESS.

ta'-ble-turn''-ing. Mysterious movement of tables. DEVOTION-MAGIC.

ta'-ble-ware''. Ware for table use. CONTENTS-RECEIVER.

ta-bli'-er. An apron. DRESS-UNDRESS.

tab-li'-num. The record-room of an old Roman house. CONTENTS-RECEIVER.

ta''-boo'. To ostracize; to mark as sacred. DEVOTION-MAGIC, LEAVE-PROHIBITION.

ta'-bor. A small drum. MUSICAL INSTRUMENTS.

tab'-o-rine. A tabor. MUSICAL INSTRUMENTS.

tab'-ou-ret. A stool. SUSPENSION-SUPPORT.

tab'-ou-rine. A drum. MUSICAL INSTRUMENTS.

tab'-ret. A small drum. MUSICAL INSTRUMENTS.

tabula rasa [L.] (tab'-yu-lɑ rê'-sɑ). The mind in its earliest state. DIFFICULTY-FACILITY, ENTITY-NONENTITY, KNOWLEDGE-IGNORANCE, MARK-OBLITERATION, PRESENCE-ABSENCE.

tab'-u-lar. Computed with a mathematical table. NUMBERING.

tab'-u-late. To arrange systematically. CONTINUITY-INTERRUPTION, ORGANIZATION-DISORGANIZATION.

tab''-u-la'-tion. Systematic arrangement. MARK-OBLITERATION.

ta-chyg'-ra-phy. Stenography. WRITING-PRINTING.

tacent, satis laudant [L.] (tê'-sent, sê'-tis lau'-dant).

They are silent, they give enough praise. APPROVAL-DISAPPROVAL, SOUND-SILENCE.

tac'-it. Inferred; silent. CLEARNESS-OBSCURITY, MANIFESTATION-LATENCY.

tac'-i-turn. Silent. ENLIGHTENMENT-SECRECY.

tac''-i-tur'-ni-ty. Reticence. TALKATIVENESS-TACITURNITY.

Tac'-i-tus. Roman historian. TERSENESS-PROLIXITY.

tack. A small nail; to change one's course. AIM-ABERRATION, CONNECTIVE, MUTATION-PERMANENCE, UNION-DISUNION, WAY; **go upon another tack,** BIGOTRY-APOSTASY; **tack to,** ADDITION-SUBTRACTION; **tack together,** UNION-DISUNION; **wrong tack,** SUCCESS-FAILURE.

tack'-le. To grapple with; equipment. CONNECTIVE, ENTERPRISE, INSTRUMENT, MANAGEMENT.

tack'-ling. Tackle collectively, or material for it. INSTRUMENT.

tack'-tack''. A quickly repeated beat. RECURRENCE.

tact. Adroitness. DIFFERENTIATION-INDISCRIMINATION, SAGACITY-INCAPACITY, SKILL-UNSKILFULNESS, TASTE-VULGARITY, TINGLING; **want of tact,** TASTE-VULGARITY.

tac'-tic-al. Strategic. CRAFT-ARTLESSNESS.

tac-ti'-cian. An expert in tactics. ADEPT-BUNGLER.

tac'-tics. Adroit management. CONDUCT, FIGHTING-CONCILIATION.

tac'-tile. Tangible. TOUCH.

tac-til'-i-ty. State or quality of being tactile. TOUCH.

tac'-tion. State of contact. TOUCH.

tac'-tu-al. Tangible. TOUCH.

tad'-pole''. A stage in the growth of a frog. INFANT-VETERAN.

tædium vitæ [L.] (tî'-di-um vai'-tî). Irksomeness. ENTERTAINMENT-WEARINESS, LIGHTHEARTEDNESS-DEJECTION.

tael. A Chinese monetary unit. MONEY, VALUES.

taf'-fe-ta. A silk-and-linen fabric. DRESS-UNDRESS, MATERIALS.

taf'-fy. A sweet candy; sweet words. ADULATION-DISPARAGEMENT, NUTRIMENT-EXCRETION, SWEETNESS-ACIDITY.

tag. To join; to label. ADDITION-SUBTRACTION, BEGINNING-END, CONNECTIVE, MAGNITUDE-SMALLNESS, PREDECESSOR-CONTINUATION, SHARPNESS-BLUNTNESS.

tag-li-o'-ni. A style of overcoat. DRESS-UNDRESS.

tag'-rag''. A fluttering rag. **Tag-rag and bobtail,** GENTILITY-COMMONALTY.

tag'-tail''. A hanger-on. PRESUMPTION-OBSEQUIOUSNESS.

tail. The hindmost part of an animal. ANTERIORITY-POSTERIORITY, BEGINNING-END, INCREMENT-REMNANT, PREDECESSOR-CONTINUATION, SUSPENSION-SUPPORT; **estate tail,** PROPERTY; **tail off,** INCREASE-DECREASE; **turn tail,** QUEST-EVASION.

tail'-age. To tax. PRICE-DISCOUNT.

tail'-coat''. A dress coat. DRESS-UNDRESS.

tailed. Having a tail. SUSPENSION-SUPPORT.

tail'-end''. The hind part of anything. BEGINNING-END.

tai'-lor. A maker of men's clothes. AGENT, DRESS-UNDRESS.

tai'-lor-ing. The work of a tailor. DRESS-UNDRESS, POMP.

tail'-piece". An appendage. EMBELLISHMENT-DISFIGUREMENT, ENGRAVING, PREDECESSOR-CONTINUATION.

tail'-race". A mining instrument. WATERCOURSE-AIRPIPE.

taint. To corrupt. BETTERMENT-DETERIORATION, CLEANNESS - FILTHINESS, FAULTLESSNESS - FAULTINESS, HEALTH-SICKNESS, REPUTATION-DISCREDIT.

taint'-ed. Corrupted. BETTERMENT-DETERIORATION, CLEANNESS - FILTHINESS, FAULTLESSNESS - FAULTINESS, HEALTH-SICKNESS, PERFUME-STENCH.

taint'-less. Pure. CLEANNESS-FILTHINESS.

tain'-ture. Stain; taint. CLEANNESS-FILTHINESS.

taj. A head-dress. DRESS-UNDRESS.

take. To gain possession of. CLEARNESS-OBSCURITY, FAITH-MISGIVING, GIVING-RECEIVING, KNOWLEDGE-IGNORANCE, NUTRIMENT-EXCRETION, PLEASURABLENESS-PAINFULNESS, SUCCESS-FAILURE, TAKING-RESTITUTION; give and take, REPRISAL-RESISTANCE, RIGHT-WRONG; take aback, EXPECTATION-SURPRISE; take a course, CONDUCT, QUEST-EVASION; take action, ACTION-PASSIVENESS; take a disease, HEALTH-SICKNESS; take advice, ADVICE; take after, IMITATION-ORIGINALITY, LIKENESS-UNLIKENESS; take a hint, SAGACITY-INCAPACITY; take a leaf out of another's book, IMITATION-ORIGINALITY; take a lease, LOAN-BORROWING; take a liberty, LIBERTY-SUBJECTION; take a likeness, DELINEATION-CARICATURE; take an account of, NUMBERING; take an ell, PRESUMPTION-OBSEQUIOUSNESS; take an infection, HEALTH-SICKNESS; take a peep, SIGHT-BLINDNESS; take aside, ADDRESS-RESPONSE; take a turn, MUTATION-PERMANENCE; take *au serieux*, BEAUTY-UGLINESS; take away, ADDITION-SUBTRACTION, ESTABLISHMENT-REMOVAL, SUBSTANCE-NULLITY, TAKING-RESTITUTION; take away life, LIFE-KILLING; take back again, TAKING-RESTITUTION; take by surprise, EXPECTATION-SURPRISE; take by the button, ADDRESS-RESPONSE; take by the hand, ASTONISHMENT-EXPECTANCE, OBSTRUCTION-HELP; take care, RECKLESSNESS-CAUTION; take care of, ATTACK-DEFENSE, CAREFULNESS-CARELESSNESS, SECURITY-INSECURITY; take comfort, ALLEVIATION-AGGRAVATION, CONTENTEDNESS-DISCONTENTMENT; take coolly, EXCITABILITY-INEXCITABILITY; take down, ACTION-PASSIVENESS, APPROVAL-DISAPPROVAL, ELEVATION - DEPRESSION, MARK-OBLITERATION, NUTRIMENT-EXCRETION, REPUTATION-DISCREDIT, SELFRESPECT-HUMBLENESS; take easily, EXCITABILITY-INEXCITABILITY; take effect, AGENCY, OCCURRENCE-DESTINY, SUCCESS-FAILURE; take exception, APPROVAL-DISAPPROVAL, MODIFICATION; take fire, FAVORITE-ANGER, HEATING-COOLING; take flight, ARRIVAL-DEPARTURE, QUEST-EVASION; take for, FAITH-MISGIVING; take for better or for worse, CHOICE-NEUTRALITY, MATRIMONY-CELIBACY; take for gospel, CREDULOUSNESS-SKEPTICISM, FAITH-MISGIVING; take for granted, FAITH-MISGIVING, HYPOTHESIS; take from, ADDITION-SUBTRACTION, TAKING-RESTITUTION; take heart, CONTENTEDNESS-DISCONTENTMENT, LIGHTHEARTEDNESS-DEJECTION; take heed, RECKLESSNESS-CAUTION; take hold of, COHESION-LOOSENESS, TAKING-RESTITUTION; take hold of the mind, FAITH-MISGIVING; take ill, CONTENTEDNESS-DISCONTENTMENT; take in, ADMISSION-EXPULSION, CLEARNESS-OBSCURITY, GIVING-RECEIVING, INCLUSION-OMISSION, LENGTH-SHORTNESS, TRUTHFULNESS-FRAUD; take in an idea, SAGACITY-INCAPACITY; take in good part, CHARITABLENESS-MALEVOLENCE, CONTENTEDNESS-DISCONTENTMENT, EXCITABILITY-INEXCITABILITY, PLEASURE-PAIN, POLITENESS-IMPOLITENESS; take in hand, EDUCATION-MISTEACHING, ENTERPRISE, OBSTRUCTION-HELP; take in sail, SWIFTNESS-SLOWNESS; take into account, ADMISSION-EXCLUSION, DIFFERENTIATION-INDISCRIMI-

NATION, MODIFICATION; take into consideration, DIFFERENTIATION - INDISCRIMINATION, INVESTIGATION-ANSWER, REFLECTION-VACANCY; take into custody, RELEASE-RESTRAINT; take into one's head, DESIRE-DISTASTE, FAITH-MISGIVING, HYPOTHESIS, PERSISTENCE-WHIM, PURPOSE-LUCK; take it, FAITH-MISGIVING, HYPOTHESIS; take its course, DISCONTINUANCE-CONTINUANCE, OCCURRENCE-DESTINY; take its rise, BEGINNING-END, CAUSE-EFFECT; take leave of, POLITENESS-IMPOLITENESS, QUEST-ABANDONMENT; take measures, DESIGN; take money, CONDUCT, OUTLAY-INCOME; take no care of, CAREFULNESS-CARELESSNESS; take no denial, BIGOTRY-APOSTASY, COERCION; take no interest in, SENSITIVENESS-APATHY; take no note of, CAREFULNESS-CARELESSNESS; take no note of time, CHRONOLOGY-ANACHRONISM; take no notice, HEED-DISREGARD; take off, CREATION-DESTRUCTION, DRESS-UNDRESS, ESTABLISHMENT-REMOVAL, IMITATION-ORIGINALITY, PRICE-DISCOUNT; take off one's hands, GIVING-RECEIVING; take off the hat, POLITENESS-IMPOLITENESS; take on, CONTENTEDNESS-DISCONTENTMENT, LIGHTHEARTEDNESS-DEJECTION; take on credit, FAITH-MISGIVING; take one at one's word, CONSENT, CONTRACT; take one's chance, PURPOSE-LUCK, VENTURE; take one's choice, CHOICE-NEUTRALITY; take oneself off, ARRIVAL-DEPARTURE; take one's fancy, DESIRE-DISTASTE, PLEASURABLENESS-PAINFULNESS; take one's oath, ASSERTION-DENIAL; take one with another, MEDIUM; take on trust, CREDULOUSNESS-SKEPTICISM, FAITH-MISGIVING; take out, INJECTION-EJECTION, MARK-OBLITERATION; take part with, ANTAGONISM-CONCURRENCE; take pattern by, IMITATION-ORIGINALITY; take pen in hand, WRITING-PRINTING; take place, OCCURRENCE-DESTINY; take possession of, TAKING-RESTITUTION; take precedence, LEADING-FOLLOWING, PRECEDENCE-SUCCESSION, SUPREMACY-SUBORDINACY; take root, ESTABLISHMENT-REMOVAL, MUTABILITY-STABILITY; take ship, TRAVELING-NAVIGATION; take steps, ACTION-PASSIVENESS, CONDUCT, DESIGN, PREPARATION-NONPREPARATION; take stock, NUMBERING; take the chair, PRESIDENT-MEMBER; take the consequences, CAUSE-EFFECT; take the good the gods provide, CONTENTEDNESS-DISCONTENTMENT; take the lead, BEGINNING-END, PRECEDENCE-SUCCESSION, RULE-LICENSE; take the place of, COMMUTATION-PERMUTATION; take the shine out of, SUPREMACY-SUBORDINACY; take things as they come, ACTIVITY-INDOLENCE, EXCITABILITY-INEXCITABILITY; take time, DURATION-NEVERNESS, EARLINESS-LATENESS, HURRY-LEISURE; take time by the forelock, EARLINESS-LATENESS; take to, DESIRE-DISTASTE, HABIT-DESUETUDE, LOVE-HATE, PLEASURE-PAIN, QUEST-EVASION, USE-DISUSE; take to heart, CONTENTEDNESS-DISCONTENTMENT, PLEASURE-PAIN; take to pieces, ACTION-PASSIVENESS, UNION-DISUNION; take up, APPROVAL-DISAPPROVAL, CHOICE-NEUTRALITY, ELEVATION-DEPRESSION, ENTERPRISE, ESSAY, INVESTIGATION-ANSWER, LOAN-BORROWING, QUEST-EVASION, RELEASE-RESTRAINT; take up a case, RATIOCINATION-INSTINCT; take up an inquiry, INVESTIGATION-ANSWER; take up arms, FIGHTING-CONCILIATION; take up money, LOAN-BORROWING; take up one's abode, DWELLER-HABITATION, ESTABLISHMENT-REMOVAL; take up one's pen, WRITING-PRINTING; take upon oneself, DUTY-DERELICTION, ENGAGEMENT-RELEASE, ENTERPRISE; take up the cudgels, ATTACK-DEFENSE, FIGHTING-CONCILIATION, STRIFE-PEACE; take up with, CONTENTEDNESS-DISCONTENTMENT. USE-DISUSE; take warning, WARNING; take wing, ARRIVAL-DEPARTURE.

ta'-ken. Past participle of take. Be taken, LIFE-DEATH; be taken ill, HEALTH - SICKNESS; be taken with, LOVE-HATE.

ta'-ker. One who takes. Taking-Restitution.
ta'-king. Contagious; attractive. Healthiness-Un-

TAKING—RESTITUTION

Abduction. Act of taking away wrongfully.
Ablation. Act of taking from. as amputation.
Abruption. A sudden breaking
Abstraction. Act of removing; theft.
Ademption. A taking away.
Apprehension. The act of taking hold of.
Appropriation. The act of taking apart for a particular use.
Bereavement. Act or state of being bereaved, particularly by the death of a friend.
Caption. Act of taking unawares; imposition.
Capture. Act of taking forcibly.
Catch. The act of grasping or seizing.
Clutch. A seizure, or attempt at seizure, as if with claws.
Confiscation. Act of taking by forfeiture.
Deglutition. Act of swallowing.
Deprehension. A seizing or taking away.
Deprivation. Act of depriving, or state of being deprived.
Deprivement. Deprivation.
Dispossession. The taking away of possession.
Distraint. The act of taking security for a debt.
Distress. In law, synonymous with distraint.
Divestment. The act of taking away from.
Eviction. The act of taking away; alienating, as property. See Admission-Expulsion.
Extortion. Taking by violence, threats, or compulsion.
Grip. The act of grasping firmly. See Keeping.
Haul. A pulling with force.
Prehension. Act of laying hold of, or grasping.
Prensation. The act of seizing.
Rapacity. Disposition to seize by violence or greedy methods.
Reception. The act of receiving.
Recovery. The act of recovering or regaining. See Gain.
Reprisal. Forcible seizure of anything by way of retaliation
Reprise. A retaliatory seizure.
Resumption. The act of taking again.
Scramble. A struggle to seize something.
Seizure. The act of taking forcibly.
Sequestration. The act of seizing. particularly for government service; confiscation.
Subtraction. A taking away from something.
Swoop. Any sudden approach, as for seizing.
Take. The act of taking in any sense. See *Verbs.*
Taking. Act of one who takes.
Theft. The act of stealing. See Theft.
Vampirism. The practise of extortion or of preying upon others.
Wrench. A twisting from

Taking—*Nouns of Agent.*

Captor. One who takes captive
Kidnapper. Man-stealer.
Reseizer. One who seizes again.
Taker. One who takes.

Taking—*Verbs.*

Abduct. To take away wrongfully.
Absorb. To take up, as by suction. See Admission.
Abstract. To take away.
Accept. To take an offer.
Accroach. To draw to oneself.
Adeem. To take away. as in law.
Appropriate. To take for some particular use.
Assume. To take upon oneself.
Bag. To seize, capture.
Bear away. } To remove.
Bear off. }
Bereave. To take away from.
Capture. To take by force.
Carry away. } To take from
Carry off. }
Catch. To take hold of.
Catch at. To attempt to take.
Catch hold of. To grasp.
Catch up. To pick up suddenly.
Clap one's hands on. To seize with the hands
Clasp. To hold firmly.
Claw. To tear or scratch at. as with the claws or nails.
Clench. To take a firm grasp.
Clinch. To take with a tight grip
Clutch. To seize with the hand.

Atonement. The act by which restitution is made.
Recovery. The getting or gaining of something previously had.
Recuperation. Act of recovery.
Reddition. A returning.
Redemption. The act of regaining possession of by the payment of a price.
Rehabilitation. A restitution to a former position. See Renovation.
Reinvestment. Act of repeating an investment.
Release. To make restitution from debt.
Rendition. Act of yielding possession.
Reparation. Restitution for a wrong.
Replevin. The recovery of the possession of goods by a personal action at law.
Restitution. Act of returning what has been taken
Restoration. Act of restoring.
Return. A rendering back.
Reversion. The returning of an estate to the grantor.

Restitution—*Noun of Agent.*

Remitter. One making remittance for payment.

Restitution—*Verbs.*

Bring back. } To place in a former place.
Carry back. }
Disgorge. To make restitution, as for dishonesty.
Give back. } To give to the rightful owner.
Give up. }
Let go. To lose one's hold upon.
Recoup. To make restitution for a loss.
Recover. To gain restitution by judicial proceedings. See Gain.
Redeem. To recover; to rescue.
Regorge. To throw back again.
Regurgitate. To surge back.
Rehabilitate. To restore to a former position.
Reimburse. To pay back; restore.
Reinvest. To invest again.
Remit. To relax, to restore.
Render. To give to.
Render up. To give up an account.
Repair. To make a restoration of. See Renovation.
Restore. To make restitution for what has been lost.
Return. To give back in restitution.
Revert. To turn back.
Revest. To make restitution of position or office.
Take back again. To take what one had before.
Unclutch. To release from clutching.

Restitution—*Adjectives.*

Recuperative. Pertaining to recovery. See Renovation.
Restoring. Giving up. See *Verbs.*

Restitution—*Phrase.*

Suum cuique [L.] To each one his own.

TAKING—Verbs—*Continued.*

Collar. To take by the collar.
Confiscate. To take as a forfeit under legal authority.
Crimp. To seize;
Crop. To pull off; pluck.
Cull. To gather; collect.
Deduct. To take away from. See Addition-Subtraction
Deprive of. To take away.
Despoil. To take away from by force.
Dip one's hands into. To take a part in.
Displume. To take off plumes; hence, to strip of honors.
Dispossess. To deprive of occupancy.
Distrain. To seize goods.
Divest. To take off.
Drain. To draw off gradually.
Drain to the dregs. To take all of anything.
Draw. To take along after, take from.
Draw off. To take from.
Dry. To take moisture from.
Ease one of. To relieve.
Eat out of house and home. To ruin by gluttony.
Embrace. To take in the arms
Exhaust. To take away the whole of anything

TAKING—Verbs—*Continued.*

Extort. To take by force; to twist out.
Fasten upon. Take firm hold of.
Fleece. To take away from under a pretext.
Gather. To take together; unite; assemble. See Gain.
Get hold of. To grasp.
Grab. To take with a sudden grasp.
Grapple. To seize closely.
Grip. To take with forcible grasp.
Gripe. To hold close.
Gut. To take out the entrails.
Help oneself to. To take what one wishes.
Hook. To take by stealth.
Hurry off with. To seize hurriedly.
Impropriate. To take for private use
Impoverish. To take away the strength richness, or fertility of.
Intercept. To take from its course.
Jump at. To take eagerly
Kidnap. To take one away by force.
Lay by the heels. To put in the stocks; hence, to imprison.
Lay fast hold of. To seize securely.
Lay hold of. To seize.
Lay one's hands on. To find.
Lay under contribution. To assess.
Lay violent hands on. To seize by force.
Levy. To raise or collect.
Make a grab at. To grasp at suddenly
Make a long arm. To reach for.
Make free with. To treat with freedom.
Make sure of. To make certain.
Nab. To take with a sudden grasp.
Nip up. To steal.
Oust. To take away. See Admission-Expulsion.
Pluck. To take from.
Pocket. To take secretly.
Possess oneself of. To take in one's possession.
Pounce upon. To seize eagerly.
Put into one's pocket. Generally, by stealth.
Ravish. To take away violently.
Reach. To try to take.
Reap. To obtain; take as a reward.
Reave. To take by violence.
Receive. To take, as offered.
Recover. To take back. See Gain.
Resume. To take again, or back.
Retake. To take again.

Retrench. To lessen; deprive of. See Length-Shortness.
Run away with. To steal.
Sack. To plunder.
Scramble for. To seize at eagerly.
Seize. To take forcibly
Sequester. To take from the owner for a time.
Sequestrate. To take apart from others
Shear. To take off by cutting with shears
Snap at. To suddenly seize at
Snap up. To seize up suddenly
Snatch. To take quickly.
Snatch at. To seize at hastily.
Snatch from one's grasp. To take from one who is holding.
Spring upon. To start upon suddenly.
Steal. To take by theft. See Theft.
Stretch forth one's hand. To reach for.
Strip. To take off.
Suck. To take in by sucking.
Suck like a leech. To take away one's substance, as a leech does blood.
Suck the blood of. To extort a figurative expression.
Swallow up. To cause to disappear.
Swoop down upon. } To approach, as if for seizing.
Swoop to. }
Take. To gain possession of, to seize.
Take away. } To remove from.
Take away from. }
Take by assault. } To take by force.
Take by storm. }
Take by the throat. To seize violently.
Take firm hold of. Grasp securely.
Take from. To take from the ownership of.
Take hold of. To hold with the hand.
Take off.
Take possession of. To take into one s ownership.
Take prisoner. To make captive.
Tear away from. } To take by force.
Tear from. }
Throttle. To seize by the throat.
Usurp. To take without right
Whip up. To seize by force
Wrench from. } Take from violently.
Wrest from. }
Wring from. To take by extortion.

Taking—*Adjectives.*

Bereft. Lost. See Gain-Loss.
Parasitic. Living on another, and taking nourishment therefrom.
Predaceous. Living by prey.
Predal. Plundering.
Predatorial. } Pillaging.
Predatory. }

Prehensile. Seizing; adapted to grasp.
Privative. Causing privation.
Rapacious. Wont to take by violence.
Raptorial. Seizing.
Ravenous. Hungry to rage.
Taking. Alluring; attracting. See *Verbs*

Taking—*Adverb.*

At one fell swoop. At one stroke of adversity.

Taking—*Phrase.*

Give an inch and take an ell.

tal'-a-poin. A Buddhist priest. Ministry-Laity.
ta-la'-ri-a. Winged boots or sandals. Dress-Undress.
tal'-bo-type. A method of photography. Painting.
tale. A recital; a reckoning. Account, Numbering; **thereby hangs a tale,** Manifestation-Latency; **twice-told tales,** Entertainment-Weariness.
tale'-bear''-er. A meddling informer. Tidings-Mystery.
tal'-ent. A superior faculty. Skill-Unskilfulness; **bury one's talent in a napkin,** Enlightenment-Secrecy; **not put one's talent in a napkin,** Selfrespect-Humbleness.
talent sich in der Stille, es bildet ein, sich ein Charakter in dem Strom der Welt [G.] (tal'-ent siH in der stil'-lê, es bil'-det ain, siH ain ca-rak'-ter in dem strom der velt). Talent is built up in quiet, character in the stream of the world. Movement-Rest, Skill-Unskilfulness.
tales'-man. A person summoned to make up a jury where the panel is exhausted. Litigation

talionis, lex [L.] (lex tê-li-o'-nis). Law of retaliation. Reprisal-Resistance, Right-Wrong.
tal'-i-ped. Club-footed. Proportion-Deformity.
tal'-is-man. A charm. Devotion-Charm, Scepter.
tal''-is-man'-ic. Magical. Devotion-Magic.
talk. To converse; rumor. Conversation-Monologue, Speech - Inarticulateness, Substance-Nullity, Tidings-Mystery; **small talk,** Conversation - Monologue, Talkativeness - Taciturnity; **talk against time,** Action-Passiveness, Duration-Neverness, Lastingness-Transientness; **talk at random,** Ratiocination-Instinct, Talkativeness-Taciturnity; **talk big,** Bragging, Charitableness-Menace, Presumption-Obsequiousness; **talk glibly,** Talkativeness-Taciturnity; **talk nonsense,** Adage-Nonsense, Regularity-Irregularity; **talk of,** Publicity, Purpose-Luck; **talk of the town,** Conversation - Monologue, Reputation - Discredit; **talk oneself out of breath,** Talkativeness-Taciturnity; **talk over,** Conversation-Monologue,

Motive-Caprice; **talk together**, Conversation-Monologue, Speech-Inarticulateness; **talk to in private**, Address-Response; **talk to oneself**, Conversation-Monologue.

talk′-a-tive. Given to talking. Speech-Inarticulateness, Talkativeness-Taciturnity.

talk′-a-tive-ness. Loquaciousness. Talkativeness-Taciturnity.

TALKATIVENESS—TACITURNITY.

Babel. A confused mixture of voices. [Bible.]
Bavardage [F.]. Chatter.
Bibble-babble. Foolish chatter.
Cackle. Idle talk.
Cacoëthes loquendi [L.] A rage for speaking
Caquet [F.] Prating.
Caquetterie [F.]. Chattering.
Chatter. Sounds like those of a magpie or monkey.
Clack. Continual talk.
Copia verborum [L.]. Flow of words.
Flippancy. Empty, trifling talk.
Flow. Continuous talk
Flowing tongue. Ready talk.
Flow of words. A continuous talking.
Fluency. Rapidity or readiness of speech
Flux de bouche [F.] Garrulity.
Flux de mots [F.]. Talkativeness.
Gab. Unmeaning talk.
Gabble. Loud or rapid talk without meaning.
Garrulity. The quality of being characterized by long and prosy talk
Gibble-gabble. Chatter.
Gift of the gab. Readiness of speech. See Speech.
Gossip. The tattle of a gossip. See Conversation.
Jabber. Rapid talk.
Jaw. Impudent talk.
Loquaciousness.⎫ The habit or practise of talking continually or
Loquacity. ⎭ excessively.
Much speaking. A great deal of talking.
Multiloquence. The use of many words.
Prate. Trifling talk.
Prattle. Childish talk.
Rattle. Noisy, rapid talk.
Small talk, etc. Gossip. See Conversation.
Talkativeness, etc. The quality or condition of being much given to talking. See *Adjectives*.
Twaddle.⎫ Silly talk
Twattle. ⎭
Verbosity, etc. The use of more words than necessary. See Terseness-Prolixity.
Volubility. Garrulity; great fluency of speech.

TALKATIVENESS—*Denotations*.

Babbler. One who babbles.
Blabber. A telltale.
Blatherskite. A blustering, talkative fellow.
Chatterbox.⎫ One who talks incessantly and idly
Chatterer. ⎭
Driveler. An idle talker.
Jay. ⎫ One who is always talking.
Magpie. ⎭
Moulin à paroles [F.] A mill of words, hence, a chatterbox.
Parrot.⎫ An incessant talker, like a parrot.
Poll. ⎭
Proser. One who talks tediously.
Ranter. A noisy talker.
Sermonizer. One who is always preaching to.
Talker. One who talks all the time.

TALKATIVENESS—*Verbs*.

Babble. To talk thoughtlessly and foolishly.
Be hoarse with talking. To have talked so much as to become hoarse.
Be loquacious, etc. To be talkative. See *Adjectives*.
Chatter. To talk idly, carelessly, and with undue rapidity.
Clack. To utter words continually in a short, sharp manner.
Din in the ears, etc. To cause a resounding in the ears, as by excessive and loud talking. See Recurrence.
Expatiate, etc. To be copious in argument. See Terseness-Prolixity.
Gabble. Meaningless, loud, and rapid talking.
Gossip, etc. To tell idle and often untrue or malicious tales about people. See Conversation,
Jabber. To speak rapidly and indistinctly
Jaw. To scold.
Outtalk. To exceed in talking.
Palaver. To use idle and deceitful talk.
Patter. To repeat in a low, muttering voice.

Costiveness. Coldness of manner.
Curtness. Shortness.
Man of few words. A taciturn man.
Muteness. The quality or state of being silent.
Obmutescence. The state of keeping silence.
Pauciloquy. The utterance of few words.
Reserve. Restraint of freedom in words and action.
Reticence, etc. The state of observing continued silence. See Enlightenment-Secrecy.
Silence. Forbearance from speech.
Taciturnity. Reserve in speaking or habitual silence.

TACITURNITY—*Verbs*.

Be silent, etc. To be indisposed to talk. See *Adjectives*.
Close the lips. ⎫ To keep silent.
Close the mouth. ⎭
Hold one's jaw. ⎫
Hold one's peace. ⎬ To be silent.
Hold one's tongue. ⎭
Keep a secret, etc. To preserve a secret. See Enlightenment-Secrecy.
Keep one's tongue between one's teeth. To preserve silence.
Keep silence. To remain still.
Lay the finger on the lips. A gesture for silence.
Make no sign. To be quiet.
Not have a word to say. To remain silent.
Not let a word escape one. To remain perfectly quiet.
Not speak, etc. To be silent. See Speech.
Place the finger on the lips. A gesture for silence.
Put a bridle on one's tongue. To restrain or keep one's speech in check.
Put a padlock on the lips. ⎫ To silence.
Put a padlock on the mouth. ⎭
Render mute, etc. To make silent. See Vocalization-Muteness.
Say nothing. ⎫
Seal the lips. ⎬ To remain silent.
Seal the mouth. ⎭
Stick in one's throat. To be difficult to utter.

TACITURNITY—*Adjectives*.

Close. Silent.
Close-tongued. Cautious in speaking.
Costive. Cold in manner; reserved.
Curt. Short.
Dumb, etc. Unable to speak. See Vocalization-Muteness.
Inconversable. Unsocial; reserved.
Mum. Silent.
Mute. Held from speaking.
Reserved. Restrained from freedom of words.
Reticent, etc. Inclined to keep silent. See Enlightenment-Secrecy.
Silent. Not speaking.
Silent as a post. ⎫ Figurative degrees of silence. See Sound-
Silent as a stone. ⎬ Silence.
Silent as the grave. ⎭
Sparing of words. Taciturn.
Taciturn. Naturally or habitually silent.

TACITURNITY—*Interjections*.

Chut [F.] Hush! Hist! hush! mum! silence! tush! tut!

TACITURNITY—*Phrases*.

Cave quid dicis, quando, et cui [L.]. Beware what you say, when, and to whom.
Volto sciolto e pensieri stretti [It.]. Countenance open and thoughts closed.

TALKATIVENESS—Verbs—*Continued*.

Pour forth. To speak very fast and loud.
Prate. To talk much and foolishly.
Prattle. To be loquacious on trifling or foolish subjects.
Prose. To tell or relate tediously
Rattle. To speak in a noisy, clattering manner.
Rattle on. To continue talking noisily.
Talk at random. To talk without any definite aim or purpose.

Talk glibly. To talk fluently.
Talk nonsense, etc. To talk about trifles. See ADAGE-NONSENSE.
Talk oneself hoarse. To talk so much that one becomes hoarse.

Talk oneself out of breath. To talk much and fast.
**Twaddle. } **To talk in an idle or silly manner.
Twattle. }

TALKATIVENESS—*Adjectives.*

Chattering, etc. Talking idly and rapidly. See *Verbs.*
Chatty, etc. Talkative. See SOCIABILITY.
Declamatory, etc. Pretentious and rhetorical. See SPEECH
Flippant. Having a voluble tongue.
Fluent. Ready in the use of words; flowing.
Garrulous. Talkative.
Glib. Smooth; voluble.
Largiloquent. Speaking in a boastful manner.

Linguacious. Talkative; loquacious.
Long-tongued. Given to gossip.
Long-winded. Tedious in speech or argument.
Loquacious. Given to continual talking.
Multiloquent. Very talkative.
Open-mouthed. Clamorous.
Talkative. Given to much talking.
Voluble. Moving with ease in speaking.

TALKATIVENESS—*Adverbs, etc.*

Glibly, etc. In a glib, fluent manner. See *Adjectives.*
Off the reel. Volubly; fluently.

Trippingly on the tongue. Speaking in a light, smooth manner.
[*Hamlet*, III, ii.]

TALKATIVENESS—*Phrases.*

Furor loquendi [L.]. Rage for speaking.
The tongue running fast.

The tongue running loose.
The tongue running on wheels.

talked. Past tense of talk. **Talked of,** REPUTATION-DISCREDIT.
talk'-er. One who talks. TALKATIVENESS-TACITURNITY.
talk'-ing. Present participle of talk. **Fine talking,** BRAGGING, OVERVALUATION-UNDERVALUATION.
tall. High. HEIGHT-LOWNESS; **tall talk,** BRAGGING.
tal'-lage. Taxation. PRICE-DISCOUNT.
tal'-lies. Records; scores. NUMBERING.
tal'-low. An animal fat. PULPINESS-ROSIN.
tal'-low-faced". Having the appearance of tallow. COLOR-ACHROMATISM.
tal'-ly. To conform; to score. CREDIT-DEBT, HARMONY-DISCORD, RECORD, SIGN; **tally with,** CONVENTIONALITY-UNCONVENTIONALITY.
tal'-ly-ho". The huntsman's cry to hounds. QUEST-EVASION.
tal'-ly-man. One who keeps a shop on the instalment plan. DEALER.
tal'-ma. A style of long cloak. DRESS-UNDRESS.
Tal'-mud. The body of Jewish law not comprised in the Pentateuch. REVELATION-PSEUDOREVELATION.
tal'-ons. Claws. KEEPING-RELINQUISHMENT, RULE-LICENSE.
ta'-lus. Fragments. GEOLOGY.
tam'-bour. A small drum. MUSICAL INSTRUMENTS.
tam"-bou-rine'. A musical instrument. MUSICAL INSTRUMENTS.
tame. Docile; to subdue. DOMESTICATION-AGRICULTURE, EDUCATION-MISTEACHING, EXCITABILITY-INEXCITABILITY, FORCE-WEAKNESS, LIBERTY-SUBJECTION, SENSITIVENESS-APATHY, TURBULENCE-CALMNESS, VIGOR-INERTIA.
tame'-less. Incapable of being tamed. CHARITABLENESS-MALEVOLENCE.
ta'-ming. Present participle of tame. DOMESTICATION-AGRICULTURE.
Tam'-ma-ny. A political organization in New York City. ASSOCIATION.
tam"-o'-shan"-ter. A cap. DRESS-UNDRESS.
tam'-per. To meddle. **Tamper with,** ACTIVITY-INDOLENCE, BETTERMENT-DETERIORATION, MOTIVE-CAPRICE, MUTATION-PERMANENCE.
tam'-tam". A kind of drum. MUSICAL INSTRUMENTS.
tan. A reddish-brown color. GRAY-BROWN.
tan'-dem. A team in which the draft animals are hitched, one before the other; at length. CONVEYANCE-VESSEL, LENGTH-SHORTNESS.
tang. A foreign flavor in anything. REMEDY-BANE, SAVOR-TASTELESSNESS.
tan'-gent. Touching. INTERSPACE-CONTACT; **fly off**

at a tangent, AIM-ABERRATION, CONCENTRATION-RADIATION, EXCITABILITY-INEXCITABILITY.
tan-gen'-tial. Pertaining to or moving in a tangent. INTERSPACE-CONTACT.
tangere ulcus [L.] (tan'-jer-î ul'-cus). To touch a sore. REMEMBRANCE-FORGETFULNESS.
tan'-gi-ble. Perceptible by touch. ENOUGH, MATERIALITY-SPIRITUALITY, SUBSTANCE-NULLITY, TOUCH, TRUTH-ERROR, USEFULNESS-USELESSNESS.
tan'-gle. To intertwine in a confused mass. CROSSING, ORGANIZATION-DISORGANIZATION.
tan'-gled. Confusedly intertwined. REGULARITY-IRREGULARITY; **weave a tangled web,** DIFFICULTY-FACILITY.
tank. Receptacle for a fluid. STORE.
tank'-ard. A large drinking-cup. CONTENTS-RECEIVER.
tanned. Colored a reddish-brown. GRAY-BROWN.
tan'-ner. One whose business is to tan hides. AGENT.
tan'-ner-y. A place where leather is tanned. WORKSHOP.
tant mieux [F.]. (tan· miu). So much the better. JUBILATION-LAMENTATION.
tant s'en faut [F.] (tan· san· fo). So far from. ASSENT-DISSENT.
tant soit peu [F.] (tan· swa pu). As small as possible. MAGNITUDE-SMALLNESS.
tantæ animis cælestibus iræ [L.] (tan'-tî an'-i-mis si'les'-ti-bus ai'-rî). Anger so great in heavenly minds. FAVORITE-ANGER.
tan-ta-li-za'-tion. State or quality of being tantalized. MOTIVE-CAPRICE.
tan'-ta-lize. Harass. DESIRE-DISTASTE, EXPECTATION-DISAPPOINTMENT, MOTIVE-CAPRICE.
tan'-ta-liz"-ing. Annoying. DESIRE-DISTASTE, EXCITATION.
Tan'-ta-lus. Son of Zeus, said to have been placed in water, but unable to reach it to quench his thirst. **Torment of Tantalus,** DESIRE-DISTASTE, EXPECTATION-SURPRISE.
tan'-ta-mount". Having equivalent value. EQUALITY-INEQUALITY, MEANING-JARGON.
tan-tar'-a. A quick succession of sounds from a horn or trumpet. CRASH-DRUMMING.
tantas componere lites [L.] (tan'-tas com-pon'-er-î lai'-tis). To settle such great quarrels. FIGHTING-CONCILIATION.
tanti [L.] (tan'-tai). Of such importance. CONSEQUENCE-INSIGNIFICANCE.
tan-tiv'-y. Swift. SWIFTNESS-SLOWNESS.
tan'-trum. A fit of passion. FAVORITE-ANGER.

tap. To strike gently; to draw liquid from a cask. ADMISSION-EXPULSION, APERTURE-CLOSURE, CRASH-DRUMMING, ENTRANCE-EXIT, IMPETUS-REACTION, PERFORATOR-STOPPER; **turn on the tap,** ADMISSION-EXPULSION.

tape. A narrow strip of woven fabric. LAMINA-FIBER.

ta'-per. To lessen gradually; a small candle. BREADTH-NARROWNESS, LUMINARY-SHADE; **taper to a point,** SHARPNESS-BLUNTNESS.

tap'-es-try. A textile fabric used for ornamentation. EMBELLISHMENT-DISFIGUREMENT, PAINTING.

tapinois, en [F.] (an· ta-pi-nwa'). Stealthily. ENLIGHTENMENT-SECRECY.

tap''-i-o-ca. A nutritious starch obtained from the roots of a Brazilian plant. NUTRIMENT-EXCRETION.

ta'-pis. A table-cover. **On the tapis,** CONCEPTION-THEME, DESIGN, OCCURRENCE-DESTINY, PURPOSE-LUCK.

tap–root. The principal descending root of a plant. CAUSE-EFFECT.

tap'-ster. A bartender. CHIEF-UNDERLING.

tar. A viscous liquid obtained by the distillation of wood; a sailor. COVER-LINING, PULPINESS-ROSIN, WAYFARER-SEAFARER; **tar and feather,** RECOMPENSE-PUNITION, REGARD-DISRESPECT.

ta'-ra''-did'le. Nonsensical talk. ADAGE-NONSENSE, TRUTHFULNESS-FABRICATION.

tar-boosh'. A cap worn in Moslem countries. DRESS-UNDRESS.

tardi che mai, è meglio [It.] (tar'-dî kê ma'-î, ê mê'-lyo). It is better late than never. EARLINESS-LATENESS.

tar'-di-grade. Slow in movement. SWIFTNESS-SLOWNESS.

tar-dil'-o-quence. High-sounding speech. ADAGE-NONSENSE, SPEECH-INARTICULATENESS.

tar'-di-ness.. State or quality of being tardy. EARLINESS-LATENESS.

tar'-dy. Late; slow. EARLINESS-LATENESS, SWIFTNESS-SLOWNESS.

tare. An allowance made to the·purchaser by deducting the weight of receptacle containing goods. **Tare and tret,** PRICE-DISCOUNT.

tares. Weeds. USEFULNESS-USELESSNESS.

tar'-get. A mark to be shot at. PURPOSE-LUCK.

tar'-iff. A schedule of duties. PRICE-DISCOUNT.

tar'-la-tan. A muslin for women's wear. DRESS-UNDRESS.

tarn. A small lake. LAKE-PLAIN.

tar'-nish. Loss of luster. CLEANNESS-FILTHINESS, COLOR-ACHROMATISM, EMBELLISHMENT-DISFIGUREMENT, REPUTATION-DISCREDIT.

tar'-pan. A Russian horse. CONVEYER.

tar-pau'-lin. A water-proof canvas. COVER-LINING.

tar'-ry. Await; abide. EARLINESS-LATENESS, LASTINGNESS-TRANSIENTNESS, MUTATION-PERMANENCE, PULPINESS-ROSIN; **tarry for,** EXPECTATION-SURPRISE.

tar'-sus. Ankle. ANATOMY.

tart. Having a sour taste; severe; a kind of pastry. POLITENESS-IMPOLITENESS, SWEETNESS-ACIDITY.

tar'-tan. A Scotch plaid fabric. VARIEGATION.

tar'-tane. A sailing vessel. CONVEYANCE-VESSEL.

Tar'-tar. A fierce Turkish barbarian; a person of a savage temper. FAVORITE-QUARRELSOMENESS; **catch a Tartar,** GULL-DECEIVER, REPRISAL-RESISTANCE, SKILL-UKSKILFULNESS.

tar'-tar. An incrustation that forms on the teeth; an emetic. CLEANNESS-FILTHINESS, REMEDY-BANE.

Tar'-ta-rus. Hades. HEAVEN-HELL.

tart'-ness. State or quality of being tart. FAVORITE-QUARRELSOMENESS.

Tar-tufe'. A character in one of Molière's comedies; a hypocrite. GODLINESS-UNGODLINESS, GULL-DECEIVER, TRUTHFULNESS-FALSEHOOD.

Tar-tuf'-ish Hypocritical. TRUTHFULNESS-FALSEHOOD.

ta-sim'-e-ter. Electrical apparatus. ELECTRICITY.

task. Toil; to overtax with labor; a lesson to be learned. EDUCATION-MISTEACHING, OCCUPATION, ORDER, USE-DISUSE, WEARINESS-REFRESHMENT; **hard task,** DIFFICULTY-FACILITY; **set a task,** ORDER; **take to task,** APPROVAL-DISAPPROVAL; **task the memory,** REMEMBRANCE-FORGETFULNESS.

task'-mas''-ter. One who assigns tasks. MANAGER, TYRANNY-ANARCHY.

tas'-sel. A pendent ornament. EMBELLISHMENT-DISFIGUREMENT.

tas'-set. A piece of an armor for the thigh. WEAPON.

taste. Flavor; a sample; the æsthetic faculty; one of the five senses. EMOTION, PUNGENCY, SAVOR-TASTELESSNESS, TASTE-VULGARITY; **man of taste,** TASTE-VULGARITY; **to one's taste,** LOVE-HATE, PALATABLENESS-UNPALATABLENESS, PLEASURABLENESS-PAINFULNESS, RHETORIC.

TASTE—VULGARITY.

Æsthetics. The science of the beautiful in nature and art

Cultivated taste. A taste improved by refinement.

Cultivation. Advancement in intellectual condition

Culture. The refinement of the moral and intellectual nature of man.

Delicacy. The quality of being agreeable to the taste.

Dilettanteism. The state or quality of being an admirer of the fine arts.

Elegance. That which pleases the taste by its perfect qualities.

Esthetics. The science of the beautiful.

Fine art. Art applied to the production of the beautiful.

Finesse [F.] Artifice; fineness.

Good taste. A taste that is correct in its choices.

Grace. A quality which commends its possessor to the taste of others

Gust. The sense of tasting.

Gusto [It. and Sp.] A keen relish; taste.

Nicety. Great delicacy of taste. See DIFFERENTIATION.

Polish. Refinement; elegancy of taste.

Refined taste. Educated taste.

Refinement. Purity of taste.

Tact. Tasteful discrimination in action.

Taste. Nice perception in relishing the good and the beautiful.

To prepon [Gr.] The fit; the becoming.

Virtù [It.] A taste for the fine arts.

TASTE—*Nouns of Agent.*

Amateur. One who practises an art for the love of it.

Arbiter elegantiarum [L] An umpire in matters of taste.

Awkwardness. An ungraceful bearing.

Bad joke. A morally or intellectually evil speech or action.

Bad taste. Carelessness of manner in respect to what is in accordance with good usage.

Barbarism. Vulgarity of manners or ways of living.

Blackguardism. Lowness; baseness.

Boorishness. Rudeness; clownishness See *Adjectives.*

Brutality. State or quality of being brutal.

Coarseness. The state of being vulgar.

Gaucherie [F] Clumsiness.

Gaudiness. The quality of being decorated with showy trinkets.

Gothicism. Rudeness of manners.

Homeliness. Lack of beauty or refinement.

Ill-breeding. Bad training.

Indecorum. Act of violating good manners.

Low life. Life vulgar and degraded.

Lowness. Meanness or vulgarity of condition.

Mauvais gout [F] Bad taste.

Mauvais plaisanterie [F.] A bad joke.

Mauvais ton [F.] Bad tone; ill-breeding.

Misbehavior. Vulgar or improper behavior.

Ribaldry. Vulgar conduct or speech.

Rowdyism. The conduct of a rowdy.

Rusticity. The state of being rustic; awkwardness.

Slang. Inelegant and vulgar language not authorized. See WORD-NEOLOGY.

Tawdriness. Showiness.

Trickery. The art of dressing up.

TASTE—Nouns of Agent—*Continued.*

Aristarchus. A noted Greek critic.
Connoisseur [F.]. A critical judge of art.
Conoscente [It.]. An art critic.
Corinthian. A citizen of Corinth, and hence a master of taste.
Critic. One who discerns the beauties or faults in literature and art
Dilettante. A lover of fine arts.
Euphemist. One who uses good taste in his choice of words.
Judge. A critic; a connoisseur.
Man of taste. One who exercises good taste in all things.
Stagirite. An appellation of Aristotle from the place of his birth, Stagira.
Virtuoso. One skilled in the fine arts.

TASTE—*Figurative Noun.*

Caviare to the general. [From *Hamlet.*] A delicacy made from fish-roes too refined for the common taste. So Shakespeare characterizes by it a play above the taste of the vulgar.

TASTE—*Verbs.*

Appreciate. To value duly.
Criticize. To judge critically.
Discriminate. To note differences.
Judge. To decide on the merits or demerits of anything.

TASTE—*Adjectives.*

Æsthetic. Pertaining to the science of taste.
After one's fancy. To one's taste.
Artistic. Pertaining to art.
Attic. Marking such elegance of taste as characterized Attica in Greece; classic; elegant.
Chaste. Showing good taste by freedom from extravagance.
Classical. In correct and refined taste; conforming to ancient Greece or Rome.
Comme il faut [F.]. As it should be.
Cultivated. Cultured; refined by good taste.
Dainty. Of exquisite taste.
Elegant. Refined; pleasing to good taste. See Purity.
Euphemistic. Using fair words.
In good taste. Refined.
Pure. Refined; classic.
Refined. Cultivated.
Tasteful. Displaying good taste.
Tasty. In conformity to good taste.
To one's mind. } Agreeable to one.
To one's taste. }
Unaffected. Natural.

TASTE—*Adverb.*

Elegantly. In an elegant manner. See *Adjectives.*

TASTE—*Phrases.*

Chacun a son gout [F.]. Every man to his taste.
Nihil tetigit quod non ornavit [L.]. He touched nothing which he did not adorn. [From Dr. Johnson's epitaph on Goldsmith.]

VULGARITY—Adjectives—*Continued from Column 2.*

Particular. Odd; singular.
Provincial. Showing the vulgar manners of a province.
Ribald. Low; vulgar; base.
Rowdy. Vulgarly showy and pretentious.
Rude. Lacking good taste.
Rustic. Rude; unpolished; countrified.
Savage. Beastly; cruel; barbarous; living in the woods.
Shabby-genteel. Trying vulgarly to achieve gentility.
Shocking. Obnoxious to good taste. See Pleasurableness-Painfulness.
Slovenly. Vulgarly neglectful and untidy. See Cleanness-Filthiness.
Snobbish. Making a vulgar pretension to gentility.
Tawdry. Vulgarly showy.
Tramontane. Lying beyond the mountains; hence, foreign and vulgar.
Tricked out. Vulgarly overdressed.
Unbeseeming. Not fitting to good taste.
Uncivil. Of vulgar manners. See Politeness-Impoliteness.
Unclassical. Not of classic taste.
Uncombed. With hair vulgarly neglected.
Uncourtly. Not pleasing to court taste.
Uncouth. Awkward; ungainly.

Vandalism. The barbarous spirit or conduct of vandals.
Vulgarism. Coarseness of manners; vulgarity.
Vulgarity. State or quality of being vulgar. See *Adjectives.*
Want of tact. Without discernment.

VULGARITY—*Denotations.*

Clinquant [F.]. Tinsel; false glitter.
False ornament. Assumed or designed finery.
Finery. Excessive or showy decoration.
Frippery. Second-hand finery.
Gewgaw. Showy trifles.
Tinsel. Something more gay and showy than valuable.

VULGARITY—*Nouns of Agent.*

Bœotian. Like the Bœotians—dull, stupid.
Cad. A mean vulgar person.
Clown. A person with vulgar manners.
Cub. A contemptuous name for a young child.
Dowdy. A vulgar looking woman.
Frump. A vulgar, old-fashioned female.
Gent. Vulgar substitution for gentleman.
Goth. One lacking taste.
Hoyden. A rude and vulgar person.
Parvenu [F.]. A vulgar upstart. See Gentility-Commonalty.
Rough diamond. Figurative for a person with uncouth manners but good heart.
Slattern. A vulgar, slovenly woman.
Snob. A vulgar pretender to gentility.
Tomboy. A vulgar, romping girl.
Unlicked cub. Ignorant, untrained person.
Vandal. One who wilfully destroys any work of art or literature.

VULGARITY—*Verbs.*

Be vulgar. To be ill-bred. See *Adjectives.*
Misbehave. To behave vulgarly.
Smell of the shop. To carry vulgar evidences of trade.
Talk shop. To converse vulgarly about business to the exclusion of more refined topics.

VULGARITY—*Adjectives.*

Affected. Pretending to possess what is not natural. See Society-Affectation.
Awkward. Ungraceful in bearing.
Barbaric. Uncivilized; crude.
Barbarous. Uncultivated; rude.
Bedizened. Vulgarly adorned.
Blackguard. Befitting a blackguard. See *Nouns.*
Boorish. Vulgar; clownish.
Brutish. Resembling brutes in nature.
Clownish. With the vulgarity and rudeness of a clown.
Coarse. Low and vulgar.
Contra bonos mores [L.]. Against good manners.
Countrified. Rustic-mannered.
Doggerel. Versified vulgarly in sense or rhythm.
Dowdy. Vulgar-looking.
Extravagant. Beyond the limits of good taste.
Gaudy. Gay beyond good taste.
Gingerbread. Too fancifully made.
Gothic. Having the vulgar manners of a Goth.
Gross. Coarse; indelicate; vulgar.
Heathenish. Rude; uncivilized.
Heavy. Slow; dull; inanimate.
Home-bred. Plain; rude; lacking the polish of travel.
Homely. Plain; rude; coarse.
Homespun. Homely; rude.
Horrid. Exciting horror; hideous; frightful.
Ill-bred. Badly brought up or trained.
Ill-mannered. Of vulgar manners.
In bad taste. In violation of good taste.
Incondite. Rude; unpolished.
Indecorous. Violating good manners.
Low. Below the standard of good taste. See Gentility-Commonalty.
Meretricious. Vulgar; tawdry.
Monstrous. Inspiring disgust.
Newfangled. Novel in a depreciative sense. See Conventionality-Unconventionality.
Obsolete. Out of use.
Obtrusive. Tending to thrust into undue prominence.
Odd. Peculiar, not in good taste.
Outlandish. Of strange and vulgar action.

(Continued on Column 1.)

VULGARITY—Adjectives—*Continued.*

Underbred. Of vulgar manners.
Unfashionable. Not in fashionable taste.
Unfeminine. Not feminine in manner.
Ungenteel. Impolite; vulgar.
Ungentlemanlike. }
Ungentlemanly. } Not becoming a gentleman's good taste.
Ungraceful. Without form or beauty. See Beauty-Ugliness.
Unkempt. Uncombed; rough; offensive to good taste.

Unladylike. Not becoming a lady's good taste.
Unlicked. Ungainly; unpolished.
Unpolished. Of vulgar manners; without refinement.
Unpresentable. Not fit for presentation.
Unrefined. Of vulgar manners
Unseemly. Not becoming to good taste.
Untamed. Not domesticated.
Vulgar. Unrefined: coarse; rude.

taste'-ful. Possessing good taste. Taste-Vulgarity.
taste'-less. Having no flavor. Savor-Tastelessness.
ta'-sty. Savory. Palatableness-Unpalatableness, Savor-Tastelessness.
tâtonner [F.] (ta-to-nê'). To grope. Trial.
tatonnement [F.] (ta-ton-man·'). Groping. Trial.
tat'-ter. A hanging shred. Magnitude-Smallness.
tat''-ter-de-mal'-ion. A ragged fellow. Gentility-Commonalty.
tat'-ters. Ragged clothing. Dress-Undress; **tear to tatters,** Creation-Destruction, Union-Disunion.
Tat'-ter-sall's. A market for the sale and exchange of horses. Market.
tat'-tle. Idle talk; to blab. Conversation-Monologue.
tat'-tler. A telltale. Conversation-Monologue, Tidings-Mystery.
tat-too'. To mark with indelible pigments; a continuous drumming. Crash-Drumming, Order, Variegation.
taught. Past participle of teach; firm. Education-Misteaching, Union-Disunion; **teach one's grandmother,** Excess-Lack, Presumption-Obsequiousness.
taunt. To denounce with scorn. Justification-Charge, Regard-Disrespect.
tau-rom'-a-chy. Bull-fighting. Strife-Peace.
Tau'-rus. A constellation. Astronomy.
taut. Firmly drawn. Excess-Lack.
tau''-to-log'-ic. Repetitious. Rhetoric.
tau-tol'-o-gy. Unnecessary repetition. Recurrence, Rhetoric, Sameness-Contrast, Terseness-Prolixity, Usefulness-Uselessness.
tau-toph'-o-ny. Repetition of the same sound. Recurrence.
tav'-ern. A public house. Dweller-Habitation.
taw'-dri-ness. Quality of being tawdry. Taste-Vulgarity.
taw'-dry. Gaudy. Taste-Vulgarity.
taw'-ny. Brownish-yellow. Gray-Brown, Yellowness-Purple.
tax. Assessment; to subject to a severe strain; to censure. Accounts, Coercion, Investigation-Answer, Justification-Charge, Order, Petition-Expostulation, Price-Discount, Use-Disuse, Weariness-Refreshment; **tax one's energies,** Toil-Relaxation; **tax the memory,** Remembrance-Forgetfulness.
tax-a'-tion. Imposing a tax. Price-Discount.
tax'-i-der''-my. The art of preserving dead animals. Zoology-Botany.
tax'-is. Arrangement. Organization-Disorganization.
tax-on'-o-my. The science of classification. Organization-Disorganization.
taz'-za. An ornamental cup. Contents-Receiver.
Te De'-um. An ancient hymn. Devotion-Idolatry, Sanguineness-Hopelessness, Solemnization, Thankfulness-Thanklessness.
te fabula narratur, de [L.] (tî fab'-yu-la nar-rê'-tur, dî). The story is told about you. Exculpation-Conviction, Reprisal-Resistance.
tea. A beverage. Nutriment-Excretion.
teach. To instruct. Education-Misteaching; **teach**

one's grandmother, Excess-Lack, Presumption-Obsequiousness.
teach'-a-ble. Capable of being taught. Education-Learning.
teach'-er. One who teaches. Advice, Instructor-Pupil, President-Member.
teach'-ing. The act of a teacher; doctrine. Education-Misteaching; **false teaching,** Education-Misteaching, Ratiocination-Instinct.
tea'-cup''. A cup for tea. **Storm in a teacup,** Gull-Hyperbole, Overvaluation-Undervaluation.
team. Two or more beasts of burden harnessed together. Continuity-Interruption.
team'-ster. One who drives a team as an occupation. Manager.
tea'-par''-ty. A social gathering at which a light repast is served. Sociability-Privacy.
tea'-poy. A small table for holding a tea-service. Suspension-Support.
tear. To rend. Excitability-Inexcitability, Jubilation-Lamentation, Swiftness-Slowness, Turbulence-Calmness, Union-Disunion; **tear asunder one's bonds,** Release-Restraint; **tear away from,** Taking-Restitution; **tear oneself away,** Quest-Evasion; **tear one's hair,** Jubilation-Lamentation; **tear out,** Injection-Ejection; **tear to pieces,** Creation-Destruction, Union-Disunion; **tear up,** Creation-Destruction.
tear'-ful. Causing tears. Jubilation-Lamentation.
tears. Drops of the liquid moistening the eye. **Draw tears,** Pleasurableness-Painfulness; **shed tears,** Jubilation-Lamentation; **tears in one's eyes,** Excitation, Lightheartedness-Dejection.
tease. To irritate in a petty way. Charitableness-Malevolence, Pleasurableness-Painfulness.
teas'-er. One who teases. Difficulty-Facility.
teas'-ing. Harassing. Pleasurableness-Painfulness.
tea'-spoon''. A small spoon. Contents-Receiver.
teat. A nipple. Convexity-Concavity.
tea''-ta'-ble. A table on which tea is served. **Tea-table talk,** Conversation-Monologue.
technica, memoria [L.] (tec'-ni-ca, mem-o'-ria). An ingenious memory. Remembrance-Forgetfulness.
tech'-nic-al. Pertaining to a particular art, science, or the like. Conventionality-Unconventionality, Skill-Unskilfulness; **technical education,** Education-Misteaching; **technical knowledge,** Skill-Unskilfulness; **technical term,** Name-Misnomer.
tech''-ni-cal'-i-ty. Anything technical; a quibbling nicety. Precept, Skill-Unskilfulness, Universality-Particularity, Word-Neology.
tech''-nique'. Manner of artistic performance. Music.
tech-nol'-o-gy. Theoretical knowledge. Skill-Unskilfulness.
tech'-y. Peevishly sensitive. Favorite-Quarrelsomeness.
ted. To spread loosely for drying. Gathering-Scattering.
te'-di-ous. Causing weariness. Entertainment-Weariness; **while away the tedious hours,** Action-Passiveness.

te'-di-um. Wearisomeness. ENTERTAINMENT-WEARINESS.

teem. To be full; to be pregnant. CREATION-DESTRUCTION, ENOUGH, FERTILITY-STERILITY; **teem with,** MULTIPLICITY-PAUCITY.

teem'-ful. Prolific. FERTILITY-STERILITY.

teem'-ing. To be full. GATHERING-SCATTERING, MULTIPLICITY-PAUCITY.

teem'-less. Barren. FERTILITY-STERILITY.

'teens. The numbers whose names end in teen. FIVE-QUINQUESECTION, INFANCY-AGE; **in one's 'teens,** FIVE-QUINQUESECTION, INFANCY-AGE, INFANT-VETERAN.

tee'-pee. One of the conical lodges of the North-American Indians. DWELLER-HABITATION.

teeth. The hard structures in the jaw for chewing food. FRIABILITY, INSTRUMENT, KEEPING-RELINQUISHMENT; **armed to the teeth,** ATTACK-DEFENSE, FIGHTING-CONCILIATION, PREPARATION-NONPREPARATION;

between the teeth, LOUDNESS-FAINTNESS; **cast in one's teeth,** JUSTIFICATION-CHARGE; **chattering of teeth,** HEAT-COLD; **grind one's teeth,** FAVORITE-ANGER; **have cut one's eye-teeth,** CRAFT-ARTLESSNESS, SKILL-UNSKILFULNESS; **in spite of one's teeth,** ANTAGONISM-CONCURRENCE, COERCION; **in the teeth of,** ANTAGONISM-CONCURRENCE, DEFIANCE, DIFFICULTY-FACILITY; **make one's teeth chatter,** HEATING-COOLING, SANGUINENESS-TIMIDITY; **set one's teeth,** DETERMINATION-VACILLATION; **set the teeth on edge,** CACOPHONY, FRICTION-LUBRICATION, PLEASURABLENESS-PAINFULNESS, SWEETNESS-ACIDITY; **show one's teeth,** DEFIANCE, FAVORITE-ANGER.

tee-to'-tal. Entire. MODERATION-SELFINDULGENCE.

tee-to'-tal-er. One pledged to entire abstinence from all intoxicating drinks. FASTING-GLUTTONY, MODERATION-SELFINDULGENCE.

tee''-to'-tal-ism. Total abstinence. MODERATION-SELFINDULGENCE, TEETOTALISM-INTEMPERANCE.

TEETOTALISM—INTEMPERANCE.

Sobriety. The state or quality of being sober

Teetotalism. Total abstinence from the use of intoxicants.

TEETOTALISM—Denotations.

Abstainer. One who abstains from the use of intoxicating liquors

Band of Hope. A temperance organization.

Good Templar. A member of the Good Templar temperance organization.

Prohibitionist. One who favors the prohibition of the sale of alcoholic liquors.

Teetotaler. One pledged to entire abstinence from all intoxicating drinks.

Teetotalist. A teetotaler.

Water-drinker. One who abstains entirely from intoxicating liquors.

White ribboner. A teetotaler.

TEETOTALISM—Verb.

Take the pledge. Make a written agreement not to use intoxicants

TEETOTALISM—Adjectives.

Sober. Moderate in or abstinent from the use of intoxicants; not under the influence of liquor.

Sober as a judge. Perfectly sober

INTEMPERANCE—Denotations—Continued from Column 2.

Devotee of Bacchus. A drunken reveler.

Dram-drinker. One who drinks too freely.

Drunkard. One whose habit is to get drunk.

Gin-drinker. A drunkard.

Hard drinker. One who drinks habitually.

Love-pot. One who likes alcoholic liquors.

Reveler. One who engages in drunken feasts.

Soaker. A hard drinker.

Sot. A person stupefied by excessive drinking.

Sponge. One who drinks liquor as a sponge takes up water.

Thirsty soul. A person who always wants to drink.

Tippler. An habitual drunkard.

Toper. One who drinks frequently to excess.

Toss-pot. A toper.

Tun. A drunkard.

Wine-bibber. An habitual drinker of strong drink.

INTEMPERANCE—Verbs.

Be drunk. To be under the influence of liquor.

Befuddle. To confuse, as with liquor.

Bib. To drink.

Booze.
Bouse. } To drink alcoholic liquors to excess.

Carouse. Drink in a boisterous manner.

Drink. To take spirituous liquors, especially in excess.

Fuddle. Make stupid with drink.

Fuzzle. Fuddle.

Get drunk. To be under the influence of liquor.

Guzzle. To drink much or frequently.

Inebriate. Be or become intoxicated.

Liquor. To supply with liquor.

Lush. To be drunk.

Alcoholism. A morbid condition resulting from use of alcoholic beverages.

Bibacity. Addiction to drink.

Bibulous. Addicted to drink immoderately.

Dipsomania. Uncontrollable craving for drink.

Drinking, etc. Practise of using alcoholic liquors. See Verbs.

Drunkenness, etc. The state of being drunk.

Ebriety. Intoxication produced by liquor.

Ebriosity. Habitual intoxication.

Inebriation. The act of inebriating or state of being inebriated.

Inebriety. The state of being inebriated.

Insobriety. Want of sobriety.

Intemperance. Habitual and excessive indulgence in alcoholic drinks.

Intoxication. The act of making, or state of being, drunk.

Oinomania. Dipsomania.

Temulency. Extreme drunkenness.

Wine-bibbing. Habitual and excessive drinking of wine.

INTEMPERANCE—Associated Nouns.

Bacchanalia. Drunken revelry.

Bacchanals. Drunken revelries.

Compotation. A drinking together; a carouse.

Delirium tremens. Mental derangement caused by excessive drinking.

Deep potations.

Potation. The act of drinking.

INTEMPERANCE—Nouns of Cause

Alcohol. A colorless liquid, the intoxicating principle of wines and liquors.

Alcoholic drinks. Drinks that cause drunkenness.

Beer, etc. An alcoholic beverage made from starchy substances. See NUTRIMENT.

Blue ruin. Bad gin, rum, or the like.

Champagne. A kind of wine.

Cup. Any intoxicating drink.

Dram. A drink of spirits.

Drink. Alcoholic liquor.

Drop. A small amount of liquor.

Drop too much. A drink that makes one drunk.

Flowing bowl. A bowl full of wine or liquor.

Gin. An aromatic alcoholic liquor made from grain flavored with juniper berries.

Grog. Intoxicating drink of any kind.

Libation. Liquor or wine poured out for drinking.

Port wine. A wine made from Concord grapes.

Punch. Wine flavored or sweetened, usually with lemon or orange.

Punch-bowl. Figuratively, drink.

Rosy wine. Alcoholic drink.

Whiskey. Strong spirits distilled from corn.

INTEMPERANCE—Denotations.

Bacchanal.
Bacchanalian. } One who indulges in drunken revels.
Bacchante.

Bibber. One given to drinking too freely.

Carouser. One who engages in drunken revels.

(Continued on Column 1.)

INTEMPERANCE—Verbs—*Continued.*

Make one drunk, etc. To put under the influence of liquor. See *Adjectives.*
Soak. To drink intemperately.
Sot. To make stupid with drink.
Swig. To drink in long drafts.

Swill. To drink to excess.
Tipple. To drink strong liquors habitually.
Tope. To become a toper.
Toss off, etc. Take a glass of liquor at one draft. See NUTRIMENT.

INTEMPERANCE—*Verbal Expressions denoting excessive drinking.*

Crack a bottle; drain the cup; drink deep; drink hard; drink like a fish; get into one's head; go to the ale; go to the public house; have one's swill; liquor up; pass the bottle; sacrifice at the shrine of Bacchus; see double; splice the main brace; take a drop too much; take a glass too much; take a hair of the dog that bit you; take a whet; take to drinking; wet one's whistle.

INTEMPERANCE—*Adjectives.*

Addicted to drink. Drinking habitually.
Beery. Affected by beer.
Bibacious. Given to drinking.
Crapulous. Sick from drunkenness.
Drunk. Under the influence of intoxicating liquor, with no normal mental control.
Drunken. Under alcoholic influence. See *Verbs.*
Ebrious. Drunken.
Fuddled. Confused with liquor. See *Verbs.*
Flustered. Befuddled with drink.
Given to drink. Drinking habitually.
Groggy. Stupid or unsteady from drink.
In a state of intoxication. Drunk.
Inebriate. Drunken.

Inebriated. Drunk. See *Verbs.*.
Inebrious. Drunken or producing drunkenness.
Intoxicated. Made drunk.
Maudlin. Made foolish by drinking.
Muddled. Confused by drink.
Muzzy. Dazed from drinking.
Pot-valiant. Courageous from drink.
Sottish. Like a sot.
Temulent. } Extremely drunk.
Temulentive. }
Tipsy. Partially drunk.
The worse for liquor. Drunk.
Toping, etc. Habitually drinking.

INTEMPERANCE—*Figurative and Slang Adjectives and Phrases meaning drunk.*

Addicted to the bottle; boozy; corned; cut; dead drunk; disguised; drunk as a fiddler; drunk as a lord; drunk as an owl; drunk as a piper; drunk as a wheelbarrow; drunk as Chloe; drunk as David's sow; elevated; flush; flushed; fou; fresh; given to the bottle; glorious; half seas over; having had a drop too much; in liquor; in one's. cups; *inter forcula* [L.] in the cups; lushy; mellow; merry; nappy; obfuscated; overcome; overtaken; potulent; primed; raddled; screwed; sewed up; tight; topheavy; three sheets in the wind; under the table; whittled.

INTEMPERANCE—*Phrase.*

Nunc est bibendum [L.]. Now it must be drunk.

tee-to'-tal-ist. One pledged to entire abstinence from all intoxicating drinks. FASTING-GLUTTONY.
tee"-to-tum. A top. ENTERTAINMENT-WEARINESS, REVOLUTION-EVOLUTION.
tegitur timor, audendo magnus [L.] (tej'-i-tur tai'-mor, au-den'-do mag'-nus). Great fear is covered by a show of daring. BRAVERY-COWARDICE.
teg'-u-ment. Any outer covering. COVER-LINING.
teg"-u-men'-ta-ry. Consisting of teguments. COVER-LINING.
te-hee'. Titter. SOCIETY-DERISION.
tei-chop'-si-a. A temporary blindness. SIGHT-BLINDNESS.
tei'-no-scope. An instrument to correct dispersion. OPTICAL INSTRUMENTS.
tekel upharsin [Chal.] (ti'-kel yu-far'-sin). Thou art weighed in the balance and found wanting. WARNING.
tel'-e-gram. A message by telegraph. TIDINGS-MYSTERY.
tel'-e-graph. An electric apparatus for transmitting messages. MESSENGER, SIGN, SWIFTNESS-SLOWNESS; by telegraph, HURRY-LEISURE.
tel"-e-graph'-ic. Pertaining to the telegraph. SWIFTNESS-SLOWNESS.
tel'-e-graph-y. The art of telegraphing. PUBLICITY, SIGN.
tel"-e-ki-ne'-sis. A psychical force capable of moving heavy bodies without physical contact.
tel-em'-e-ter. An apparatus for measuring distances on the earth's surface. MENSURATION.
tel"-e-o-log'-ic-al. Relating to order. PURPOSE-LUCK.
tel"-e-ol'-o-gy. The doctrine of design. PURPOSE-LUCK.
tel-ep'-a-thy. Thought-transference. MATERIALITY-SPIRITUALITY.
tel'-e-phone. An instrument for reproducing sound at a distance. HEARING-DEAFNESS.

tel'-e-scope. An optical instrument. ASTRONOMY, OPTICAL INSTRUMENTS.
tel"-e-scop'-ic. Visible only with the aid of a telescope. ASTRONOMY, REMOTENESS-NEARNESS.
tel'-esm. A charm. DEVOTION-CHARM.
tell. To relate; to bid; to decide; to tattle; to count; to produce an effect. ACCOUNT, DOMINANCE-IMPOTENCE, ENLIGHTENMENT-SECRECY, EVIDENCE-COUNTEREVIDENCE, EXPOSURE-HIDINGPLACE, NUMBERING, SPEECH-INARTICULATION, SUCCESS-FAILURE; let me tell you, ASSERTION-DENIAL; tell a lie, TRUTHFULNESS-FALSEHOOD; tell a piece of one's mind, EXPOSURE-HIDINGPLACE; tell fortunes, PROPHECY; tell how, RATIONALE-LUCK; tell its own tale, CLEARNESS-OBSCURITY, MANIFESTATION-LATENCY; tell of, EVIDENCE-COUNTEREVIDENCE, MEANING-JARGON; tell off, NUMBERING; tell one plainly, ENLIGHTENMENT-SECRECY; tell one's beads, CEREMONIAL, DEVOTION-IDOLATRY; tell tales, EXPOSURE-HIDINGPLACE; tell the cause of, INTERPRETATION-MISINTERPRETATION; tell the truth, TRUTHFULNESS-FALSEHOOD; who can tell, CERTAINTY-DOUBT.
tell'-er. A bank officer. ENLIGHTENMENT-SECRECY, TREASURER.
tell'-ing. Producing a great effect; striking. CONSEQUENCE-INSIGNIFICANCE, EXCITATION; with telling effect, DOMINANCE-IMPOTENCE, VIGOR-INERTIA.
tell'-tale". Tattling; a tattler; an indicator. EXPOSURE-HIDINGPLACE, SIGN, TIDINGS-MYSTERY, UPRIGHTNESS-ROGUE.
tel-lu'-ric. Pertaining to the earth. UNIVERSE.
telum imbelle [L.] (ti'-lum im-bel'-li). Unwarlike weapon. MIGHT-IMPOTENCE.
tem"-er-a'-ri-ous. Rash; headstrong. RECKLESSNESS-CAUTION.
te-mer'-i-ty. Recklessness. RECKLESSNESS-CAUTION.
tem'-per. To mitigate; passion; disposition. AFFECTIONS, CONDITION-SITUATION, FAVORITE-QUARRELSOMENESS, HARDNESS-SOFTNESS, PREPARATION-NON-

PREPARATION, SUBJECTIVENESS-OBJECTIVENESS, TURBULENCE-CALMNESS; **command of temper,** EX-CITABILITY-INEXCITABILITY; **lose one's temper,** FAVORITE-ANGER; **out of temper,** FAVORITE-MO-ROSENESS; **temper the wind to the shorn lamb,** ALLEVIATION-AGGRAVATION; **trial of temper,** EX-CITATION.

tem'-pe-ra. Painting in distemper. PAINTING.

tem'-per-a-ment. A system of tuning musical instruments; constitution. AFFECTIONS, INCLINATION, MELODY-DISSONANCE, SUBJECTIVENESS-OBJECTIVE-NESS.

tem'-per-ance. Habitual moderation. MODERATION-SELFINDULGENCE, TURBULENCE-CALMNESS.

tem'-per-ate. Mild; observing self-control. EXCITA-BILITY-INEXCITABILITY, MODERATION-SELFINDUL-GENCE, TURBULENCE-CALMNESS.

tem'-per-a-ture. Degree of heat or cold. HEAT-COLD; **increase of temperature,** HEATING-COOLING; **reduction of temperature,** HEATING-COOLING.

tem'-pered. Brought to a proper temper. TURBU-LENCE-CALMNESS.

tem'-pest. A violent wind. EXCITABILITY-INEXCITA-BILITY, RIVER-WIND, TURBULENCE-CALMNESS, VI-BRATION.

tem''-pes-tiv'-i-ty. Seasonableness. OPPORTUNENESS-UNSUITABLENESS.

tem'-pest-tossed. Storm-beaten. EXCITATION.

tem-pes'-tu-ous. Stormy. RIVER-WIND.

tempete dans un verre d'eau [F.] (tan·-pêt' dan·z un·vêr do). Tempest in a glass of water. AGITATION, CONSEQUENCE-INSIGNIFICANCE.

tempi passati [L.] (tem'-pai pas-sê'-tai). Times gone by. FUTURE-PAST, NOVELTY-ANTIQUITY.

Tem'-plar. A member of a great military order. **Good Templar,** TEETOTALISM-INTEMPERANCE.

tem'-ple. A place of worship; a part of the human anatomy. ANATOMY, DWELLER-HABITATION, FANE, LATERALITY-CONTRAPOSITION; **temple of the Holy Ghost,** ORTHODOXY-HETERODOXY.

tempora mutantur et nos mutamur in illis [L.] (tem'-po-ra miu-tan'-tur et nos miu-tê'-mur in il'-lis). Times are changed and we change with them. MU-TATION-PERMANENCE.

tempora! O mores! O [L.] (tem'-po-ra, o mo'-rîz, o). O times! O customs! APPROVAL-DISAPPROVAL, JUBILATION-LAMENTATION, REPUTATION-DISCREDIT, UPRIGHTNESS-DISHONESTY, VIRTUE-VICE.

tem'-po-ral. Secular; pertaining to the temple. ANATOMY, LASTINGNESS-TRANSIENTNESS, MINISTRY-LAITY; **lords temporal and spiritual,** GENTILITY-COMMONALTY.

tem''-po-ral'-i-ty. The laity. MINISTRY-LAITY.

tem'-po-ra-ry. To be used for a short time only. LASTINGNESS-TRANSIENTNESS; **temporary chairman,** PRESIDENT-MEMBER.

tempore, dextro [L.] (tem'-po-rî, dex'-tro). At a lucky moment. PURPOSE-LUCK.

tempori parendum [L.] (tem'-po-rai pê-ren'-dum). One must yield to the times. OBSERVANCE-NON-OBSERVANCE.

tem''-po-ri-za'-tion. The act of temporizing. CRAFT-ARTLESSNESS.

tem'-po-rize. To procrastinate; to parley. CRAFT-ARTLESSNESS, EARLINESS-LATENESS, LASTINGNESS-TRANSIENTNESS.

temps, autre, autre mœurs [F.] (tan·, otr, otr murs). Change of times, change of manners. SOCIETY-LUDICROUSNESS.

tempt. To try; to attempt; to allure. DESIRE-DIS-TASTE, MOTIVE-CAPRICE, VENTURE; **tempt fortune,** PURPOSE-LUCK, VENTURE; **tempt Providence,** PRE-SUMPTION-OBSEQUIOUSNESS, RECKLESSNESS-CAU-TION.

temp-ta'-tion. Enticing to evil. DESIRE-DISTASTE.

tempt'-er. One who tempts. ANGEL-SATAN, MOTIVE-CAPRICE; **voice of the tempter,** MOTIVE-CAPRICE.

tempt'-ing. Enticing. MOTIVE-CAPRICE.

tempus fugit [L.] (tem'-pus fiu'-jit). Time flies. SWIFT-NESS-SLOWNESS, TIME.

tem'-u-len-cy. Extreme drunkenness. TEETOTALISM-INTEMPERANCE.

tem'-u-lent. Drunken. TEETOTALISM-INTEMPERANCE.

tem'-u-lent-ive. Given to drink. TEETOTALISM-IN-TEMPERANCE.

ten. A numeral. FIVE-QUINQUESECTION; **ten to one,** LIKELIHOOD-UNLIKELIHOOD; **ten thousand,** ΓIVE-QUINQUESECTION.

ten'-a-ble. Capable of being held. SECURITY-INSE-CURITY.

te-na'-cious. Tough. COHESION-LOOSENESS, TOUGH-NESS-BRITTLENESS.

te-nac'-i-ty. Firmness; persistency. BIGOTRY-APOS-TASY, COHESION-LOOSENESS, DETERMINATION-VACIL-LATION, EXTRAVAGANCE-AVARICE, KEEPING-RELIN-QUISHMENT, REMEMBRANCE-FORGETFULNESS, TOUGH-NESS-BRITTLENESS; **tenacity of purpose,** PERSIST-ENCE-APOSTASY.

te-nac'-u-lum. Surgical forceps. KEEPING-RELIN-QUISHMENT.

ten'-an-cy. Occupancy. HOLDING-EXEMPTION.

ten'-ant. A lessee. DWELLER-HABITATION, HOLDER, PRESENCE-ABSENCE.

ten'-ant-less. Unoccupied. PRESENCE-ABSENCE, SOCIABILITY-PRIVACY.

tenax propositi [L.] (tî'-nax pro-pos'-it-ai). Tenacious of a purpose. DETERMINATION-VACILLATION, UP-RIGHTNESS-DISHONESTY.

tend. Have a bent; give heed to. CHIEF-UNDER-LING, DOMESTICATION-AGRICULTURE, INCLINATION, OBSTRUCTION-HELP; **tend towards,** AIM-ABERRA-TION.

tend'-ence. Inclination. LIBERTY-SUBJECTION.

tend'-en-cy. Inclination. AIM-ABERRATION, INCLINA-TION, PURPOSE-LUCK.

ten'-der. Offer; delicate; vessel; susceptible. BEL-LIGERENT, COMPASSION-RUTHLESSNESS, CONVEY-ANCE-VESSEL, HARDNESS-SOFTNESS, LOVE-HATE, MAGNITUDE-SMALLNESS, PROFFER-REFUSAL, SENSI-TIVENESS-APATHY; **tender age,** INFANCY-AGE; **tender conscience,** DUTY-DERELICTION; **tender heart,** CHARITABLENESS-MALEVOLENCE, COMPASSION-RUTH-LESSNESS, SENSITIVENESS-APATHY; **tender mercies,** CHARITABLENESS-MALEVOLENCE, GOOD MAN-BAD MAN, HARSHNESS-MILDNESS; **tender one's resigna-tion,** COMMISSION-RETIREMENT; **tender passion,** LOVE-HATE; **tender to,** OBSTRUCTION-HELP.

ten'-der-foot''. A newcomer. CONSTITUENT-ALIEN.

Ten'-der-loin''. A police district of New York City. CITY, VIRTUE-VICE.

ten'-der-ness. Kindness. CHARITABLENESS-MALEVO-LENCE, COMPASSION-RUTHLESSNESS, LOVE-HATE.

tend'-ing. Inclining. INCLINATION.

ten'-don. An end of a muscle. CONNECTIVE.

ten'-dril. The part of a plant which attaches itself to another body. CIRCLE-WINDING, CONNECTIVE, IN-FANT-VETERAN, LAMINA-FIBER.

ten-e'-bri-ous. Gloomy. LIGHT-DARKNESS.

ten'-e-ment. Dwelling; property. EXTENSION-DIS-TRICT, PROPERTY; **tenement of clay,** LIFE-CORPSE.

ten'-et. A principle of belief. FAITH-MISGIVING.

tenez [F.] (te-nê'). Hold; wait. DISCONTINUANCE-CONTINUANCE.

ten'-fold''. In tens. FIVE-QUINQUESECTION.

ten'-nis. A game. ENTERTAINMENT-WEARINESS.

ten'-or. The highest adult male voice; nature; a musical instrument; career; intent. AIM-ABERRATION, CACOPHONY, CONDITION-SITUATION, MEANING-JARGON, MUSICAL INSTRUMENTS, QUANTITY-MEASURE; **pursue the noiseless tenor of one's way,** CONCEIT-DIFFIDENCE.

ten'-pen''-ny. A certain size of nails. INSTRUMENT.

ten'-pins''. A game played in a bowling-alley. ENTERTAINMENT-WEARINESS.

ten'-pound''-er. A cannon discharging a ten-pound ball. WEAPON.

tense. Stretched tight; a form of the verb to indicate time. HARDNESS-SOFTNESS, VERB; **aorist tense,** VERB; **future tense,** VERB; **future perfect tense,** VERB; **imperfect tense,** VERB; **past tense,** VERB; **past perfect tense,** VERB; **pluperfect tense,** VERB; **present tense,** VERB; **present perfect tense,** VERB; **preterite tense,** VERB.

ten'-sile. Capable of extension. ELASTICITY-INELASTICITY.

ten'-sion. The act of stretching or straining. LENGTH-SHORTNESS, STRENGTH-WEAKNESS.

ten'-sure. A stretching. LENGTH-SHORTNESS.

tent. A shelter of canvas; to cover with a tent. COVER-LINING, DWELLER-HABITATION; **pitch one's tent,** ARRIVAL - DEPARTURE, ESTABLISHMENT - REMOVAL.

ten'-ta-cle. A feeler. KEEPING-RELINQUISHMENT.

ten'-ta-tive. Conjecture. TRIAL, VENTURE.

tente d'abri [F.] (tɑnt· dɑ-brī'). A shelter-tent. COVER-LINING.

tent'-ed. Occupied by tents. **Tented field,** FIGHTING-CONCILIATION.

ten'-ter-hook''. A hook for stretching cloth. SUSPENSION-SUPPORT; **on tenter-hooks,** EXPECTATION-SURPRISE.

tenth. The ordinal of ten. FIVE-QUINQUESECTION.

tenths. Plural of tenth. PRICE-DISCOUNT.

tent'-peg''-ging. A British military game. ENTERTAINMENT-WEARINESS.

tents. Shelters of canvas. **To your tents, O Israel,** FIGHTING-CONCILIATION.

tenue, en grande [F.] (te-nü', ɑn· grɑn·d). In full dress. DRESS-UNDRESS, EMBELLISHMENT-DISFIGUREMENT, POMP.

ten-u'-i-ty. Thin; rare. BREADTH-NARROWNESS, MAGNITUDE-SMALLNESS, SOLIDITY-RARITY.

ten'-ure. Possession; being held. DUENESS-UNDUENESS, HOLDING-EXEMPTION, PROPERTY.

tep''-e-fac'-tion. Lukewarmness. HEATING-COOLING.

teph'-ro-man''-cy. Divination. PROPHECY.

tep'-id. Lukewarm. HEAT-COLD.

ter''-a-tol'-o-gy. The science of monstrosities. BRAGGING, CONVENTIONALITY-UNCONVENTIONALITY, ELECTRICITY, PROPORTION-DEFORMITY, SIMPLICITY-FLORIDNESS, SOCIETY-AFFECTATION.

ter'-ce-ron'. A person having one-third negro and two-thirds white blood. MIXTURE-HOMOGENEITY.

ter''-e-bra'-tion. The act of boring in surgery. APERTURE-CLOSURE.

teres atque rotundus [L.] (tĭ'-rĭz at'-quĭ ro-tun'-dus). Smooth and round. ROUNDNESS.

teres atque rotundus, in seipso totus [L.] (tĭ'-rĭz at'-quĭ ro-tun'-dus, in sĭ'-ip''-so to'-tus). Altogether smooth and round. FAULTLESSNESS-FAULTINESS.

ter''-gi-ver-sa'-tion. Evasion; fickleness. ADVANCE-RETROGRESSION, MUTATION-PERMANENCE, PERSISTENCE-WHIM.

term. A technical word; a period of time; place in a series. BEGINNING-END, BOUNDARY, DURATION-NEVERNESS, NAME-MISNOMER, PROPERTY, WORD-NEOLOGY.

ter'-ma-gant. Violently abusive. FAVORITE-QUARRELSOMENESS.

ter'-mi-nal. Limit. BEGINNING-END, BOUNDARY; **terminal moraine,** GEOLOGY.

ter'-mi-nate. To finish. BEGINNING-END.

ter''-mi-na'-tion. The act of terminating; end. BOUNDARY.

ter'-mi-na''-tor. Boundary. ASTRONOMY.

termine, mezzo [It.] (ter'-mi-nê, med'-zo). Half the time. MIDCOURSE-CIRCUIT.

termini, ex vi [L.] (ter'-mi-nai, ex vai). By force of expression. STRENGTH-WEAKNESS.

ter''-mi-nol'-o-gy. The science of terms. WORD-NEOLOGY.

ter'-mi-nus. The final goal. ARRIVAL-DEPARTURE, BEGINNING-END, BOUNDARY, COMPLETION-NONCOMPLETION.

term'-less. Unlimited. INFINITY.

terms. Conditions. BEGINNING-END, BOUNDARY, CONDITION-SITUATION, DURATION-NEVERNESS, FIGHTING-CONCILIATION, NAME-MISNOMER, PROPERTY, RATIOCINATION-INSTINCT, STATION, TERMS, WORD-NEOLOGY; **bring to terms,** FIGHTING-CONCILIATION; **come to terms,** ASSENT-DISSENT, CONSENT, CONTRACT, FIGHTING-CONCILIATION, YIELDING; **couch in terms,** PHRASE; **in no measured terms,** FORCE-WEAKNESS; **on friendly terms,** AMITY-HOSTILITY.

TERMS.

Articles. Portions of a contract, account, treaty, or the like.

Articles of agreement. Conditions, or terms of agreement.

Casus fœderis [L.] The basis of an agreement or treaty.

Clauses. Separate portions of a legal paper, writing, or sentences.

Conditions. Terms specified.

Covenant. A written and sealed agreement between two or more persons to do or not to do some act.

Obligation. The binding power of a vow, promise, or contract.

Provisions. A previous agreement.

Proviso. An article or clause, as in a contract, introducing a condition.

Sine qua non [L.] An indispensable condition.

Stipulation. A material article of an agreement.

Terms. The specific parts of a contract which, if agreed upon, bind the parties.

Ultimatum. Final condition.

TERMS—*Verbs.*

Bind. To subject to a definite legal obligation.

Come to terms. To agree upon conditions. See CONTRACT.

Insist upon. To be persistent in one's demands or claims.

Make a point of. To make a special resolve about.

Make it a condition. Make it a necessary provision.

Make terms. To make an agreement.

Stipulate. To specify as being a condition of an agreement.

Tie up. To confine; to restrain.

TERMS—*Adjectives.*

Conditional. Made or granted on certain definite terms.

Fenced. Secured.

Guarded. On condition.

Hedged in. Surrounded.

Provisional. Provided for present service; temporary.

TERMS—*Adverbs, etc.*

Conditionally. See MODIFICATION.

On condition. Having conditions attached.

Pro re natâ [L.] According to the circumstances.

Provisionally. Having conditions attached.

ter'-na-ry. Consisting of three. TRIPLICATION-TRISECTION.

ter'-ni-on. Triad. TRIALITY.

Terp-sich'-o-re. The muse of dancing. ENTERTAINMENT-WEARINESS, MUSICIAN.

ter quaterque beatus [L.] (ter qua-ter'-quĭ bĭ-ê'-tus). Thrice and four times happy. PLEASURE-PAIN.

terra firma [L.] (ter'-ra fir'-ma). Solid land. OCEAN-LAND, SUSPENSION-SUPPORT.

terra incognita [L.] (ter'-ra in-cog'-ni-ta). Unknown land. KNOWLEDGE-IGNORANCE, TIDINGS-MYSTERY.

ter'-race. A raised level with sloping sides; houses occupying such a position. DWELLER-HABITATION, ERECTNESS-FLATNESS.

ter'-ra-cot''-ta. A species of pottery. HEATING-COOLING, SCULPTURE.

ter-ra'-que-ous. Containing both land and water. UNIVERSE.

terre verte [F.] (tar vert). Green earth. REDNESS-GREENNESS.

ter-rene'. Earthy. UNIVERSE, OCEAN-LAND.

ter'-re-ous. Earthy. UNIVERSE.

ter-res'-tri-al. Pertaining to the earth. UNIVERSE.

ter-res'-tri-ous. Terrestrial. UNIVERSE.

ter'-ri-ble. Appalling. SANGUINENESS-TIMIDITY.

ter'-ri-bly. Awe-inspiring. MAGNITUDE-SMALLNESS.

ter'-ri-er. A dog; a land-survey; an augur. FAUNA-FLORA, PERFORATOR-STOPPER, RECORD.

ter-rif'-ic. Very alarming. PLEASURABLENESS-PAINFULNESS, SANGUINENESS-TIMIDITY.

ter'-ri-fy. To fill with terror. SANGUINENESS-TIMIDITY.

ter-rine'. An earthenware jar, containing some table delicacy, sold with its contents. CONTENTS-RECEIVER.

ter''-ri-to''-ri-al. Pertaining to a territory. EXTENSION-DISTRICT, OCEAN-LAND.

ter'-ri-to''-ry. A nation's domain. EXTENSION-DISTRICT, PROPERTY.

ter'-ror. Extreme fright. SANGUINENESS-TIMIDITY; **king of terrors,** LIFE-DEATH; **reign of terror,** HARSHNESS-MILDNESS, PLEASURE-PAIN.

terrorem, in [L.] (ter-ro'-rem, in). In terror. CHARITABLENESS-MENACE, SANGUINENESS-TIMIDITY.

ter'-ror-ism. The state of extreme fright. PRESUMPTION-OBSEQUIOUSNESS, SANGUINENESS-TIMIDITY.

ter'-ror-ist. One who governs by intimidation. BENE-FACTOR - EVILDOER, BRAVERY - COWARDICE, BRAWLER.

ter'-ror-ize. To reduce to a state of terror. SANGUINENESS-TIMIDITY.

terse. Short and pointed. TERSENESS-PROLIXITY.

terse'-ness. Briefness and comprehensiveness. TERSENESS-PROLIXITY.

TERSENESS—PROLIXITY.

Abridgment. That which diminishes; a reduction.

Brevity. Shortness.

Compression. The state of being brought within narrow limits. See ENLARGEMENT-DIMINUTION.

Conciseness. Brevity in speaking or writing.

" The soul of wit." Brevity. [Shakespeare, *Hamlet*, II, ii.]

TERSENESS—*Denotations.*

Ellipsis. The omission of a word or words necessary to complete a sentence.

Epitome. A concise statement of the main points of a work. See DIGEST.

Laconism. A brief and sententious manner of expression, like that of the Laconians or Spartans.

Monostich. A composition of one verse; an epigram.

Syncope. The elision of a vowel or syllable from the middle of a word.

Tacitus. A Roman historian celebrated for his profound thought and terse style.

TERSENESS—*Verbs.*

Abridge. To shorten. See LENGTH-SHORTNESS.

Abstract. To epitomize or reduce. See DIGEST.

Be concise. To express in a few words.

Come to the point. To speak in as few words as possible.

Condense. To make more close, compact, or dense. See ENLARGEMENT-DIMINUTION.

TERSENESS—*Adjectives*

Brief. In few words.

Close. Concise; to the point.

Compact. Consolidated.

Compendious. Abridged. See DIGEST.

Concise. Expressed in few words.

Crisp. Short.

Curt. Characterized by brevity.

Elliptical. Having a part omitted.

Epigrammatic. Concise; pointed.

Exact. Precisely or definitely conceived or stated.

Laconic. Expressing much in a few words.

Neat. Free from admixture.

Pithy. Having concentrated force and energy.

Pregnant. Implying more than expressed.

Quaint. Prim.

Short. Brief.

Succinct. Characterized by pithiness and brevity.

Summary. Condensed to the utmost practicable degree.

Terse. Free of superfluous words.

To the point. Spoken directly.

Trenchant. Effective; penetrating.

TERSENESS—*Adverbs.*

Briefly. In few words.

Concisely In a few words.

Ambages. A circumlocution.

Amplification. Diffusive description or discussion.

Battology. Unnecessary repetition in speaking or writing.

Circumlocution. Indirect or roundabout expression.

Cloud of words. Words in such numbers as to obscure the meaning.

Copia verborum [L]. An abundance of words.

Diffuseness. A copious use of words.

Dilating. Writing diffusely or at length.

Flow of words. Copiousness of words.

Penny-a-lining. Furnishing matter to a journal at so much a line.

Periphrase. Periphrasis.

Periphrasis. The art of saying little in many words.

Perissology. Superabundance of words.

Pleonasm. The use of more words than needed to express a thought.

Polylogy. Talkativeness.

Prolixity. The state or quality of being drawn out by minute detail.

Redundance. Superabundance.

Richness. The condition of being full of good thoughts. See SIMPLICITY-FLORIDNESS.

Roundabout phrases. Phrases characterized by indirectness.

Tautology. Unnecessary repetition, whether in word or sense.

Thrice-told tale. Tale told many times

Verbiage. The use of many words without necessity.

Verbosity. The state or quality of using wearisome and unnecessary number of words.

PROLIXITY—*Nouns of Cause.*

Episode. A separate incident introduced into a story to give variety

Expletive. A word or syllable not necessary to the sense.

Exuberance. Copiousness.

PROLIXITY—*Verbs.*

Amplify. To enlarge by addition or discussion.

Battre la campagne [F] To beat about the bush.

Beat about the bush. To approach a subject in a roundabout way.

Branch out. To enlarge, amplify, or diverge from the main subject.

Descant. To discourse at length or in detail.

Diffuse. To be prolix.

Digress. To turn aside from the main subject and dwell for a time upon incidental matters.

Dilate. To enlarge upon.

Draw out. To prolong.

Dwell on. To expatiate.

Enlarge. To express oneself at length or diffusely.

Expand. To enlarge without increasing the substance.

Expatiate. To discuss copiously or with many words.

Harp upon. To revert to some subject incessantly.

Inflate. To cause to be extended or bombastic.

Insist upon. To be persistent.

Launch out. To expatiate in language.

Maunder. To talk incoherently or foolishly.

Perorate. To deliver a grandiloquent oration.

Prose. To speak or discourse prosily or tediously.

Protract. To cause to occupy a longer time than usual.

TERSENESS—PROLIXITY—*Continued.*

TERSENESS—Adverbs—*Continued.*

For shortness' sake.
In a few words.
In a word.
In brief.
In short.
It comes to this.   In short.
Summarily.   In a condensed manner.
The long and short of it is.
To be brief.
To come to the point.
To cut the matter short.   To speak in a few words.
To make a long story short.   In a few words.

PROLIXITY—Adjectives—*Continued from Column 2.*

Pleonastic.   Characterized by the use of superfluous words.
Profuse.   Characterized by overabundance.
Prolix.   Unduly extended by the use of needless words.
Prosing.   Speaking or discoursing prosily or tediously.
Protracted.   To cause to occupy a longer time than is usual.
Rambling.   Talking aimlessly.
Roundabout.   Characterized by indirect methods.
Spun out.   Drawn out to undue length.
Verbose.   Containing an unnecessary number of words.
Wordy.   Expressed in many words.

PROLIXITY—*Adverbs, etc.*

About it and about it.   In many words.
At large.   Without speaking directly.
Diffusely.   In a diffuse manner.
In extenso [L.]   In full.

PROLIXITY—Verbs—*Continued*

Ramble.   To talk in a careless, aimless manner.
Rant.   To speak vehemently without corresponding force of thought or feeling.
Run out on.   To expatiate.
Spin a long yarn.   To relate a long story.
Spin out.   To protract.
Swell out.   To make large.

PROLIXITY—*Adjectives.*

Ambagious.   Characterized by circumlocution.
Circumlocutory.   Roundabout.
Copious.   Employing more expression and illustration.
Diffuse.   Characterized by redundance or prolixity.
Digressive.   Given to or characterized by digression.
Discursive.   Wandering away from the point or theme.
Episodic.   Pertaining to or of the nature of an episode.
Excursive.   Disconnected and rambling.
Exuberant.   Marked by great plentifulness.
Flatulent.   Pretentious without substance or reality.
Frothy.   Empty.
Largiloquent.   Speaking in an inflated or boastful manner.
Lengthy.   Not brief.
Long.   Continued to a great length.
Long drawn out.   Long-winded.
Longsome.   Extended in length.
Long-spun.   Protracted.
Long-winded.   Continuing for a long time in speaking or writing.
Maundering.   Incoherent.
Periphrastic.   Expressed in a roundabout manner.

(*Continued on Column 1.*)

ter'-tian.   Recurring on the third day.   PERIODICITY-IRREGULARITY.
ter'-ti-a-ry.   Third in number.   TRIALITY.
Ter'-ti-a-ry pe'-ri-od.   Geologic period.   GEOLOGY.
tertium quid [L.] (ter'-shi-um quid).   A third something.   COMPOSITION-RESOLUTION, CONVENTIONALITY-UNCONVENTIONALITY, LIKENESS-UNLIKENESS, MIXTURE-HOMOGENEITY.
tes'-sel-la"-ted.   Constructed in mosaic style.   EMBELLISHMENT-DISFIGUREMENT, VARIEGATION.
tes'-se-ra.   One of a set of dice.   SIGN.
tes'-se-ræ.   Stones for mosaic pavements; dice.   SIGN, VARIEGATION.
test.   Critical trial.   SIGN, TRIAL.
testa, voce di [It.] (tes'-ta, vo'-chê di).   The head-voice.   CACOPHONY.
tes'-ta-ment.   A covenant.   SECURITY.
Tes-ta-ment.   One of the two volumes of Scripture.   REVELATION-PSEUDOREVELATION.
tes-ta'-mur.   A certificate that one has passed an examination at an English university.   EVIDENCE-COUNTEREVIDENCE.
teste valgono più che una sola, due [It.] (tes'-tê valgo'-no pi'-u kê u'-na so'-la, du'-ê).   Two heads are better than one.   COOPERATION-OPPOSITION.
tes'-ter.   A canopy over a bed; a coin.   MONEY, SUSPENSION-SUPPORT.
tes"-ti-fi-ca'-tion.   Act of testifying.   SUSPENSION-SUPPORT.
tes'-ti-fy.   To affirm positively.   EVIDENCE-COUNTEREVIDENCE, SIGN.
tes"-ti-mo'-ni-al.   A formal token of regard.   MARK-OBLITERATION.
tes'-ti-mo-ny.   A sworn statement.   EVIDENCE-COUNTEREVIDENCE.
test'-tube".   A vessel used in making chemical tests.   CHEMISTRY, TRIAL.
tes'-ty.   Snappish.   FAVORITE-QUARRELSOMENESS.
tet"-ar-to-he'-drism.   A form of crystal.   MINERALOGY.
tetch'-y.   Peevishly sensitive.   FAVORITE-QUARRELSOMENESS.
tête-à-tête [F.] (têt'-a-têt').   A private conversation.

CONVERSATION-MONOLOGUE, DUALITY, REMOTENESS-NEARNESS.
tête baissée, donner [F.] (têt bê-sê', do-nê').   To undertake rashly.   RECKLESSNESS-CAUTION.
tête d'armée [F.] (têt dar-mê').   Head of the army.   CHIEF-UNDERLING.
tête exaltée [F.] (têt eg-zal-tê').   Insanity.   SANENESS-LUNACY.
tête montée [F.] (têt mon'-tê').   Insanity.   EXCITABILITY-INEXCITABILITY, SANENESS-LUNACY.
teth'-er.   Restrain; something used to check.   ESTABLISHMENT-REMOVAL, RELEASE-PRISON, RELEASE-RESTRAINT, UNION-DISUNION; go beyond the length of one's tether, RULE-LICENSE.
teth'-ered.   Restrained.   MUTABILITY-STABILITY.
tet'-ra-chord.   A scale series of half an octave.   MELODY-DISSONANCE.
tet'-ract-ic.   The quality of having four rays.   QUATERNITY.
tet'-rad.   A collection of four.   QUATERNITY.
tet-rag'-o-nal.   Forming a certain kind of symmetry.   MINERALOGY; tetragonal prism, MINERALOGY; tetragonal pyramid, MINERALOGY; tetragonal system, MINERALOGY.
tet"-ra-he'-dral.   Like a tetrahedron.   MINERALOGY.
tet"-ra-he'-dron.   A solid bounded by four faces.   ANGULARITY.
tet"-ra-hex"-a-he'-dron.   Form of crystal.   MINERALOGY.
tet'-rarch.   The governor of one part of a country divided into four governments.   CHIEF-UNDERLING.
Teu-ton.   A German.   ETHNOLOGY.
text.   The original words of an author; topic; the body of matter as distinguished from a paraphrase.   CONCEPTION-THEME, COPY-MODEL, MEANING-JARGON, WRITING-PRINTING.
text'-book".   A manual.   DIGEST, SCHOOL.
tex'-tile.   Pertaining to weaving.   CROSSING, TEXTURE.
tex'-tu-a-ry.   Authoritative; one versed in the Scriptures.   ORTHODOXY-HETERODOXY, REVELATION-PSEUDOREVELATION.

tex'-ture. Structural order. EMBELLISHMENT-DIS-FIGUREMENT, MIXTURE-HOMOGENEITY, SMOOTHNESS-ROUGHNESS, TEXTURE.

TEXTURE.

Anatomy. The study of the structure of organisms.
Architecture. The science of designing and constructing structures.
Carcass. The frame or structure of anything.
Cleavage. The act of splitting or dividing the texture of anything.
Compages [L.]. A structure of many united parts.
Constitution. An established system of related parts.
Construction. The act of building; structure.
Contexture. Anything composed of interwoven materials.
Intertexture. What is interwoven.
Organization. That which is brought into structural connection.
Stratification. That which is of stratified structure.
Structure. A combination of parts in relation to each other.
Texture. Structural order of anything.

TEXTURE—*Nouns of Cause.*

Coarseness of grain. Textile materials not closely interwoven.
Fabric. Structure; texture.
Fineness of grain. Of finely woven texture.
Frame. Structure.
Framework. A structure for enclosing anything.
Grain. An essential element in the structure of anything.
Mold. Anything which serves to regulate the structure of.
Nap. The edge of woven cloth. See SMOOTHNESS-ROUGHNESS.
Organism. Organic structure.
Parenchyma [Gr.]. The tissue outside the blood-vessels and derived from the blood.
Staple. The principal element in anything.
Stuff. The material of which anything is made.
Substance. That of which a thing consists.
Surface. The exterior part of anything that has length and breadth.
Tissue. A light textile fabric.
Tooth. One of the wires in a carding instrument used in the manufacture of textile fabrics.
Warp and weft. In weaving textile fabrics, the threads lengthwise and crosswise.
Warp and woof. Same as warp and weft.
Web. That which is woven.

TEXTURE—*Scientific Nouns.*

Adenography. That part of anatomy which treats of the structure of the glands.
Adenology. The doctrine of the glands.
Angiography. A description of the vessels of the human body.
Angiology. The doctrine of the vessels of the human body.
Histology. That branch of biology that treats of the structure of the tissues of organisms.

Myology. The science which treats of the structure of the muscular system.
Neurology. The science of the nervous system.
Organology. That branch of biology treating of the structure of the organs of the body.
Osteology. The science of the bones.
Splanchnology. The doctrine of the viscera.

TEXTURE—*Adjectives.*

Anatomic. Pertaining to anatomy. See *Nouns.*
Anatomical. Same as anatomic.
Coarse. Of rough structure.
Coarse-grained. Composed of large or rough structural elements.
Delicate. Of fine, light texture.
Filmy. Of gauzy, unsubstantial texture.
Fine. Of light and delicate texture.
Fine-grained. Composed of fine and light structural elements.
Gossamery. Of fine and filmy substance.
Homespun. Spun at home; hence, coarse and rough.
Organic. Consisting of organs.
Structural. Pertaining to the structure.
Subtile. Of very fine texture.
Textile. Formed by weaving.
Textural. Of or pertaining to texture. See *Nouns.*

Tha'-is. A courtezan of Alexander the Great. PURITY-RAKE.
tha'-ler. Coin. VALUES.
Tha-li'-a. The muse of comedy. ACTING.
thalatta! thalatta! [Gr.] (thα'-lat-ta thα'-lat-tα). The sea! the sea! JUBILATION-LAMENTATION.
Thal'-mud. Talmud; the Jewish law not comprised in the Pentateuch. REVELATION-PSEUDOREVELATION.
Thames. A river in England. **Never set the Thames on fire,** ADEPT-BUNGLER, POSSIBILITY-IMPOSSIBILITY, SAGE-FOOL.
thane. One of the old nobility in the king's service. GENTILITY-COMMONALTY.
thank. To express gratitude. THANKFULNESS-THANKLESSNESS; **no thank you,** PROFFER-REFUSAL; **thank one's stars,** JUBILATION-LAMENTATION; **thank you for nothing,** THANKFULNESS-THANKLESSNESS.
thank'-ful. Sensible of kindness received and disposed to acknowledge it. THANKFULNESS-THANKLESSNESS; **rest and be thankful,** ACTION-PASSIVENESS, CONTENTEDNESS-DISCONTENTMENT, MOVEMENT-REST.
thank'-ful-ness. Gratitude. THANKFULNESS-THANKLESSNESS.

THANKFULNESS—THANKLESSNESS.

Feeling of obligation. A feeling of being constrained to return kindnesses shown.
Gratitude. A feeling of appreciation for favors shown.
Thankfulness. The outward expression of gratitude.

THANKFULNESS—*Nouns of Means.*

Acknowledgment. The act of expressing thanks.
Benediction. An expression of blessing, prayer, or kind wishes.
Giving thanks. Thanksgiving.
Grace. The exercise of love, kindness, mercy, and favor.
Grace after meat. } A prayer of thanksgiving for the blessings of
Grace before meat. } food.
Pæan. A song of praise.
Praise. The tribute of gratitude and honor rendered to God.
Recognition. The act of gratefully recognizing services bestowed.
Requital. Return, good or bad, for anything done.
Te Deum [L.]. A Latin hymn of praise. See DEVOTION.
Thank-offering. A gift given to show one's gratitude.
Thanks. Expression of gratitude.
Thanksgiving. A formal expression of thanks.

THANKFULNESS—*Verbs.*

Acknowledge. To own with gratitude.
Be grateful. To feel appreciation for favors shown.
Be under obligation. To be constrained to return some kindness or courtesy.
Bless one's stars. To be grateful for one's good luck.
Fall on one's knees. To give thanks to God.

Ingratitude. A lack of appreciation for favors received.
Oblivion of benefits. The entire forgetting of benefits received.
Thanklessness. The quality of not expressing gratitude.

THANKLESSNESS—*Denotations.*

Benefits forgot. Favor for which one expresses no gratitude.
Thankless office. } That which one does for which he receives no re-
Thankless task. } ward or gratitude.

THANKLESSNESS—*Verbs.*

Be ungrateful, etc. To be marked by ingratitude. See *Adjectives.*
Forget benefits. To be ungrateful after a short time.
Look a gift-horse in the mouth. To be doubtful about the value of a gift.

THANKLESSNESS—*Adjectives.*

Forgotten. Treated with ingratitude.
Ill-requited. Treated with ingratitude when some recompense was deserved.
Ingrate. Ungrateful, so as to return evil for good.
Insensible of benefits. Naturally devoid of gratitude.
Thankless. Not feeling or expressing gratitude.
Unacknowledged. Not having received thanks.
Ungrateful. Not feeling gratitude.
Unmindful. Not keeping benefits in mind with gratitude
Unrequited. Not having received any recompense of gratitude.
Unrewarded. Not having received the due reward of gratitude.

THANKFULNESS—THANKLESSNESS—*Continued*.

THANKFULNESS—Verbs—*Continued*.

Feel under an obligation. To feel constrained to return some kindness or courtesy.
Give thanks. To express gratitude, usually in prayer.
Lie under an obligation. To be under an obligation.
Never forget. To be grateful forever.
Not look a gift-horse in the mouth. To be grateful for a gift without doubting its value.
Offer thanks. To express gratitude, usually in prayer.
Overflow with gratitude. To be grateful in a very great degree.
Render thanks. To express gratitude in words.
Requite. To return something good out of gratitude.
Return thanks. To express gratitude, especially for something before prayed for.
Savoir gré [F.] To take kindly.
Tender thanks. To present thanks to any one.
Thank. To express gratitude.
Thank one's stars. To express gratitude for one's good fortune.

THANKFULNESS—*Adjectives*.

Beholden. Owing gratitude.
Grateful. Full of gratitude.

thank'-less. Not feeling gratitude. PLEASURABLE-NESS-PAINFULNESS, THANKFULNESS-THANKLESSNESS.
thank'-less-ness. State of being thankless. THANKFUL-NESS-THANKLESSNESS.
thank'-of"-fer-ing. An offering expressive of gratitude. THANKFULNESS-THANKLESSNESS.
thanks. Gratitude. THANKFULNESS-THANKLESSNESS; **thanks to,** RATIONALE-LUCK.
thanks'-giv"-ing. The expression of gratitude. DEVOTION-IDOLATRY, THANKFULNESS-THANKLESSNESS.
that. A demonstrative pronoun having reference to a definite person or thing. UNIVERSALITY-PARTICULARITY; **at that time,** TIME; **that being so,** CONDITION-SITUATION; **that is,** TIME; **that is to say,** INTERPRETATION-MISINTERPRETATION, MEANING-JARGON, UNIVERSALITY-PARTICULARITY.
thatch. A covering of reeds or the like. COVER-LINING.
thau'-ma-trope. An optical toy. OPTICAL INSTRUMENTS.
thau'-mat-ur"-gist. A magician. DEVOTION-MAGICIAN.
thau'-mat-ur"-gy. Magic. ASTONISHMENT-EXPECTANCE, DEVOTION-MAGICIAN.
thaw. Melt. COMPASSION-RUTHLESSNESS, EXCITABILITY-INEXCITABILITY, HEAT-COLD, HEATING-COOLING, LIQUEFACTION-VOLATILIZATION.
the'-ar-chy. Government by a supreme deity. DIVINITY, RULE-LICENSE.
the'-a-ter. A playhouse; the scene of any event. ACTING, ENTERTAINMENT-WEARINESS, LISTS, SCHOOL, SIGHT-BLINDNESS, TRIBUNAL.
théâtre, coup de [F.] (tê-atr', cu de). A stage trick. ACTING, APPEARANCE-DISAPPEARANCE, PHENOMENON, POMP.
théâtre, jeu de [F.] (tê-atr', zhu de). Dumb show. APPEARANCE-DISAPPEARANCE, PHENOMENON.
the-at'-ric. Pertaining to a theater. ACTING.
the-at'-ric-al. Pertaining to the theater; done for effect. ACTING, POMP, SOCIETY-AFFECTATION.
The'-ban. A native of Thebes. **Learned Theban,** SCHOLAR-DUNCE.
the'-ca. A sheath or case. COVER-LINING.
theft. Larceny. THEFT, TRUTHFULNESS-FRAUD.

THEFT.

Abstraction. Stealing so as not to be noticed.
Appropriation. Taking another's property for one's own use without consent.
Blackmail. Money extorted from persons by threats of exposure.
Brigandage. Highway robbery.
Buccaneering. Robbery on the high seas.
Burglary. Breaking into a dwelling-house at night for the purpose of stealing.

THANKLESSNESS—Adjectives—*Continued*.

Unthanked. Having received no expression of gratitude.
Unthankful. Not possessing or expressing gratitude.
Wanting in gratitude. Lacking in gratitude.

THANKLESSNESS—*Phrases*.

Et tu Brute [L.]. Thou too, Brutus. [Julius Cæsar.]
Thank you for nothing.

THANKFULNESS—*Adjectives*—*Continued*.

Indebted to. Full of gratitude towards for a service rendered.
Obliged. Pleased in a grateful manner.
Thankful. Full of thanks.
Under obligation. Owing gratitude to.

THANKFULNESS—*Interjections*.

Gramercy! heaven be praised! many thanks! much obliged! thank heaven! thanks! thank you!

Direption. The act of carrying away something stolen.
Embezzlement. The fraudulent appropriation of entrusted funds to one's own use.
Filibustering. Carrying on an unlawful military expedition for plunder.
Filibusterism. The conduct of filibusters.
Foray. A sudden raid for plunder.
Fraud. Theft accomplished by deliberate deception.
Housebreaking. Entering into a house in the daytime with the intention of stealing.
Larceny. Stealing the personal property of another.
Latrociny. Theft.
Peculation. Fraudulent appropriation of public money to one's own use.
Petty larceny. The stealing of goods of or under a fixed small value.
Pillage. Robbing on a large and thorough scale.
Piracy. Forcible seizure without lawful authority on the high seas.
Plagiarism. Literary theft.
Plagiary. A literary thief.
Plunder. The act of removing another's property with force.
Privateering. Lawful depredation on the high seas.
Rape. The carrying away of property by violence.
Rapine. Seizure by superior force.
Razzia. A military incursion for pillage.
Robbery. The act of stealing openly and with violence.
Sack. }
Sackage. } The act of storming and plundering.
Shoplifting. Petty theft from a store under a pretense of buying.
Spoliation. Robbery that takes away the value.
Stealing. Taking the property of another without his consent.
Theft. The act of stealing secretly and without violence.
Thievery. The practise of stealing by stealth.

THEFT—*Denotations*.

Alsatia. A slang name for Whitefriars, London, a noted den of thieves.
Den of Cacus. The cave of a noted thief in mythology.
Den of thieves. A thieves' quarter.

THEFT—*Nouns of Cause*.

Cleptomania. A morbid propensity to steal.
Cleptomaniac. One who steals involuntarily.
Kidnapper. Man-stealer.
Rapacity. An overwhelming desire to plunder.
Thievishness. The state of being addicted to stealing.

THEFT—*Nouns of Agency*.

Letters of marque. Licenses given to privateers to seize vessels belonging to the enemy.
License to plunder.

THEFT—*Verbs*.

Abduct. To take away wrongfully.
Abstract. To steal so as not to be noticed.
Bag. To seize property without permission.
Bilk. To cheat by taking advantage of.
Borrow of Peter to pay Paul. To take from one person to help another; originally, taking the revenue from St. Peter's (Westminster Abbey) to pay the cost of building St. Paul's, London.

Cabbage. To steal small amounts at a time.
Carry off. }
Convey away. } To take away without the owner's consent.
Crib. To take small things secretly.
Crimp. To decoy and then rob.
Defraud. To withhold someone's property by deliberate deception. See TRUTHFULNESS-FRAUD.
Despoil. To take away from by force.
Disregard the distinction between *meum* **and** *tuum.* To disregard the distinction between mine and thine.
Embezzle. To fraudulently appropriate entrusted funds for one's own use.
Filch. To pilfer cunningly.
Fleece. To take all one's money away by fraud.
Forage. To take away provisions for military use.
Gut. To plunder thoroughly.
Kidnap. To steal a child.
Levy blackmail. To extort money by threats of exposure.
Lift cattle. To steal cattle.
Live by one's wits. To live by tricks and expedients.
Loot. To take booty in a captured city.
Make off with. To take away with no one's consent or knowledge.
Maraud. To make an incursion for plunder.
Mulct. To deprive of money by fining unjustly.
Nim. To steal by trickery.
Obtain under false pretenses. To get money by making false representations of what it will be used for.
Palm. To cheat by imposing upon.
Peculate. To fraudulently appropriate public funds to one's own use.
Pickeer. To pillage in skirmishing parties.
Pigeon. To swindle by imposing upon one's credulity.
Pilfer. To steal articles of trifling value.
Pillage. To rob on a large and thorough scale.
Pirate. To practise piracy.
Plagiarize. To commit a literary theft.
Pluck. To deprive of everything of value.
Plunder. To remove another's property with force.
Poach. To hunt unlawfully or steal.
Prig. In slang, to steal.
Purloin. To take by theft.
Ransack. To pillage entirely.
Rifle. To remove everything that could be plundered.
Rob. To steal with open violence.
Rob Peter to pay Paul. To take from one person to help another.
Rook. To cheat.
Run. To evade legal restrictions on imported goods.
Run away with. }
Run off with. } To steal.
Sack. To storm and plunder.
Seize. To take by force.
Set a thief to catch a thief. To catch by secret methods.
Smuggle. To take merchandise into a country unlawfully
Spoil. To rob thoroughly by violence.
Spoliate. To practise robbery.
Sponge. To get from another by a mean trick.
Steal. To take another's property without his consent.
Strip. To deprive of entirely.
Sweep. To make a sudden and thorough depredation.
Swindle. To take from by fraud.
Thieve. To steal in a stealthy manner.
Walk off with. To steal.

THEFT—*Adjectives.*

Furacious. }
Furtive. } Stealing.
Light-fingered. Adept at picking pockets.
Piratical. Pertaining to piracy.
Predaceous. Living by preying upon others.
Predal. Practising robbery.
Predatorial. Thieving.
Predatory. Characterized by plundering.
Raptorial, etc. Adapted for seizing prey. See THEFT.
Stolen, etc. Taken by theft. See *Verbs.*
Tnieving, etc. See *Verbs.*
Thievish. Inclined to thieve.

THEFT—*Phrase.*

Sic vos non vobis [L.] Thus you toil, not for yourselves.

the'-ism. Belief in God. GODLINESS-UNGODLINESS, ORTHODOXY-HETERODOXY.
the'-ist. A believer in God. THEOLOGY.
the-is'-tic. Pertaining to theism. DIVINITY.

theme. Subject; an essay. CONCEPTION-THEME, ESSAY.
The'-mis. A goddess personifying custom, justice, law, and peace. RIGHT-WRONG.
then. At that time; therefore. DURATION-NEVERNESS, RATIOCINATION-INSTINCT, TIME.
thence. From that place; after that time; therefore. ARRIVAL-DEPARTURE, FUTURE-PAST, RATIOCINATION-INSTINCT, RATIONALE-LUCK.
thence''-forth'. Thereafter. FUTURE-PAST.
thence''-for'-ward. From that time on. FUTURE-PAST.
the'-oc'-ra-cy. A government directly by God. CHURCH, DIVINITY.
the''-o-crat'-ic. Pertaining to theocracy. CHURCH, DIVINITY.
the-od'-o-lite. A surveying instrument. ANGULARITY.
the-og'-o-ny. The generation of the gods. THEOLOGY.
the-o-lo'-gi-an. One versed in theology. THEOLOGY.
the-o-log'-i-cal. Of or pertaining to theology. THEOLOGY.
theologicum, *odium* [L.] (thĭ''-ol-oj'-i-cum, o'-di-um). The hate excited by theological views. CHURCH, DECISION-MISJUDGMENT, GODLINESS-UNGODLINESS.
the'-o-logue. A theological student. THEOLOGY.
the-ol'-o-gy. The branch of religious science which treats of God. THEOLOGY.

THEOLOGY.

Articles. A statement of the points of doctrine of the English Church.
Caucasian mystery. Mystery of the Caucasian peoples.
Confession of faith. A formulary comprising the Articles of Faith.
Creed. A definite summary of what is believed in religious matters. See FAITH.
Declaration of faith. Open expression of faith.
Divinity. The science of divine things.
Hagiography. The last of the three Jewish divisions of the Old Testament.
Hagiology. The history of the sacred writings.
Monotheism. The doctrine or belief of one God only.
Profession of faith. Public avowal of faith.
Religion. A system of faith and worship.
Religious denomination. A collection of individuals of the same religion.
Religious persuasion. A creed or belief of religion.
Religious sect. A party united in some settled tenets of religion.
Theogony. That branch of heathen theology which taught the origin of their deities.
Theology. The science of the Christian religion.
Theosophy. The system of philosophy which professes to attain to a knowledge of God by direct intuition.

THEOLOGY—*Nouns of Agent.*

Canonist. One skilled in ecclesiastical law.
Divine. One learned in divinity.
Schoolman. One versed in school divinity.
Theologian. }
Theologue. } One versed in theology.

THEOLOGY—*Adjectives.*

Denominational. Pertaining to a denomination. See *Nouns.*
Religious. Pertaining to religion. See *Nouns.*
Sectarian. Attached to the beliefs of a denomination. See ORTHODOXY-HETERODOXY.
Theological. Relating to theology. See *Nouns.*

the'-o-man''-cy. Divination by oracles. PROPHECY.
the-op'-a-thy. Religious emotion. GODLINESS-UNGODLINESS.
the''-op-neus'-tic. Divine inspiration. REVELATION-PSEUDOREVELATION.
the-or'-bo. A lute. MUSICAL INSTRUMENTS.
the'-o-rem. A true proposition, not self-evident. ADAGE-NONSENSE, CONCEPTION-THEME, HYPOTHESIS.
the'-o-ret'-ic-al. Based on speculation. HYPOTHESIS.
the'-o-rize. Speculate. HYPOTHESIS, RATIONALE-LUCK.
the'-o-ry. A plan based on true principles. CONCEPTION-THEME, HYPOTHESIS, KNOWLEDGE-IGNORANCE, RATIONALE-LUCK.

the-os'-o-phy. Mystical speculation applied to deduce a philosophy of the universe. THEOLOGY.

ther-a-peu'-tic. Pertaining to therapeutics. REMEDY-BANE.

ther-a-peu'-tics. The treatment of disease. REMEDY-BANE.

there. In that place. POSITION, PRESENCE-ABSENCE.

there'-a-bouts". Approximately. MAGNITUDE-SMALLNESS, POSITION, REMOTENESS-NEARNESS.

there-aft'-er. Afterward. ANTECEDENCE-SEQUENCE.

there-by'. In consequence of that. INSTRUMENTALITY, MANIFESTATION-LATENCY; **thereby hangs a tale,** CAUSE-EFFECT, CONNECTION-INDEPENDENCE.

there'-fore. For this or that reason. MOTIVE-CAPRICE, RATIOCINATION-INSTINCT, RATIONALE-LUCK.

there-in'. In this or that. OUTSIDE-INSIDE.

there-of'. Of this or that. CONNECTION-INDEPENDENCE.

there"-to-fore'. Before this or that. ANTECEDENCE-SEQUENCE.

there"-up-on'. Upon that; in consequence of that. ANTECEDENCE-SEQUENCE, DURATION-NEVERNESS.

there-with'. With this or that; at the same time. MEANS, SOLITUDE-COMPANY.

the'-ri-ac. Medicinal. REMEDY-BANE.

ther'-mal. Pertaining to heat. HEAT-COLD.

ther'-mic. Thermal. HEAT-COLD.

ther-mol'-o-gy. A discourse on heat. HEAT-COLD.

ther-mom'-e-ter. An instrument for measuring temperature. HEAT-COLD, THERMOMETER.

THERMOMETER.

Calorimeter. Any apparatus for measuring heat.
Fahrenheit. A thermometer scale in which the freezing point is 32°.
Pyrometer. An instrument for measuring high heat.
Thermometer. An instrument for measuring temperature.
Thermoscope. An instrument for marking change in temperature.

ther'-mo-scope. An instrument for detecting differences in temperatures. THERMOMETER.

ther-mot'-ics. The science of heat. HEAT-COLD.

Ther-si'-tes. The most scurrilous of the Greeks before Troy. FLATTERER-DEFAMER.

the-sau'-rus. A storehouse; a lexicon. STORE, WORD-NEOLOGY.

the'-sis. A theme; a proposition to be maintained by argument. CONCEPTION-THEME, ESSAY, HYPOTHESIS, RHETORIC.

Thes'-pi-an. Pertaining to Thespis, the father of Greek tragedy. ACTING.

Thes'-pis. The founder of the Greek drama. ACTING.

The'-tis. A Nereid; the mother of Achilles. OCEAN-LAND.

the'-ur"-gist. A magician. DEVOTION-MAGICIAN.

the'-ur"-gy. Magic. DEVOTION-MAGIC.

thews. Muscles. **Thews and sinews,** STRENGTH-WEAKNESS.

thick. Compactly arranged; dense; stupid; intimate. AMITY-HOSTILITY, BREADTH-NARROWNESS, CLEANNESS-FILTHINESS, DIAPHANEITY-OPAQUENESS, GATHERING-SCATTERING, MULTIPLICITY-PAUCITY, SOLIDITY-RARITY, VISCIDITY-FOAM; **come thick,** MULTIPLICITY-PAUCITY; **in the thick of,** ACTION-PASSIVENESS, ENVIRONMENT-INTERPOSITION; **lay it on thick,** ADULATION-DISPARAGEMENT, COVER-LINING, EXCESS-LACK; **thick of the action,** ACTIVITY-INDOLENCE; **thick of the fray,** FIGHTING-CONCILIATION; **through thick and thin,** ENTIRETY-DEFICIENCY, PERSISTENCE-WHIM, TURBULENCE-CALMNESS.

thick'-com"-ing. Coming densely or fast. FREQUENCY-RARITY, MULTIPLICITY-PAUCITY, RECURRENCE; **thick-coming fancies,** FANCY.

thick'-en. To become thick. BREADTH-NARROWNESS, ORGANIZATION-INORGANIZATION, SOLIDITY-RARITY.

thick'-en-ing. The act or process of making thick; that which thickens. SOLIDITY-RARITY, VISCIDITY-FOAM.

thick'-ens. Becomes thick. **The plot thickens,** ACTIVITY-INDOLENCE.

thick'-et. A thick growth of trees or underbrush. FAUNA-FLORA.

thick'-ness. The quality of being thick. BREADTH-NARROWNESS.

thick'-ribbed". Having thick ribs. STRENGTH-WEAKNESS; **thick-ribbed ice,** HEAT-COLD.

thick'-set". Having a short, thick body; dense. BREADTH-NARROWNESS, LENGTH-SHORTNESS, SOLIDITY-RARITY.

thick'-skinned". Having a thick skin; dull. FEELING-INSENSIBILITY, SENSITIVENESS-APATHY.

thick'-skull". A blockhead. SAGACITY-INCAPACITY, SAGE-FOOL.

thief. One who steals. BENEFACTOR-EVILDOER, GOOD MAN-BAD MAN, ROBBER; **like a thief in the night,** ENLIGHTENMENT-SECRECY, EXPECTATION-SURPRISE, UPRIGHTNESS-DISHONESTY; **set a thief to catch a thief,** THEFT.

thiev'-er-y. The practise of thieving. THEFT.

thieves. Robbers. **Thieves' Latin,** WORD-NEOLOGY.

thim'-ble. A protection for the finger in sewing; a tubular piece of metal through which a bolt passes. ATTACK-DEFENSE, CONTENTS-RECEIVER.

thim'-ble-ful. As much as a thimble will hold. MAGNITUDE-SMALLNESS.

thim'-ble-rig". Trickery. TRUTHFULNESS-FRAUD.

thim'-ble-rig"-ger. A trickster. TRUTHFULNESS-FRAUD.

thin. Lean; sparse; rare; to make sparse. ADDITION-SUBTRACTION, BREADTH-NARROWNESS, EXCESS-LACK, GREATNESS-LITTLENESS, MULTIPLICITY-PAUCITY, SOLIDITY-RARITY; **thin end of the wedge,** BEGINNING-END, CRAFT-ARTLESSNESS.

thing. Any inanimate substance. MATERIALITY-SPIRITUALITY, SUBSTANCE-NULLITY; **just the thing,** DUENESS-UNDUENESS; **the thing,** DUTY-DERELICTION; **thing of naught,** SUBSTANCE-NULLITY; **thing to do,** OCCUPATION.

things. Inanimate substances; events; clothes. DRESS-UNDRESS, OCCURRENCE-DESTINY, PROPERTY; **as things go,** CONDITION-SITUATION, HABIT-DESUETUDE, OCCURRENCE-DESTINY.

thing'-um-bob. A thing. WORD-NEOLOGY.

thing'-um-my. A thing. WORD-NEOLOGY.

think. To produce by mental process; to believe. FAITH-MISGIVING, REFLECTION-VACANCY; **as one thinks proper,** VOLITION-OBLIGATION; **reason to think,** LIKELIHOOD-UNLIKELIHOOD; **think aloud,** CONVERSATION-MONOLOGUE, CRAFT-ARTLESSNESS; **think better of,** BETTERMENT-DETERIORATION, PERSISTENCE-WHIM; **think fit,** READINESS-RELUCTANCE, VOLITION-OBLIGATION; **think highly,** APPROVAL-DISAPPROVAL; **think ill,** APPROVAL-DISAPPROVAL; **think likely,** EXPECTATION-SURPRISE, LIKELIHOOD-UNLIKELIHOOD; **think no more of,** HEED-DISREGARD, PARDON-VINDICTIVENESS, REMEMBRANCE-FORGETFULNESS; **think of,** PURPOSE-LUCK; **think out,** HEED-DISREGARD; **think twice,** DETERMINATION-VACILLATION, RECKLESSNESS-CAUTION; **think upon,** REMEMBRANCE-FORGETFULNESS.

think'-er. One who thinks deeply. SAGE-FOOL.

think'-ing. Mental action. REFLECTION-VACANCY; **thinking principle,** MIND-IMBECILITY.

thin'-ness. The quality of being thin. BREADTH-NARROWNESS.

thin'-skinned". Having a thin skin; sensitive. Desire - Particularness, Favorite - Quarrelsomeness, Feeling-Insensibility, Sensitiveness-Apathy.

third. The ordinal of three. Melody-Dissonance, Triplication-Trisection; **third heaven,** Heaven-Hell; **third part,** Triplication - Trisection; **third person,** Security-Insecurity; **third power,** Triality.

third'-ly. In the third place. Triplication-Trisection.

thirst. Crave. Desire-Distaste; **thirst for knowledge,** Inquisitiveness-Indifference.

thirst'-i-ness. State of being thirsty. Desire-Distaste.

thirst'-y. Eagerly desirous. Desire-Distaste; **thirsty soul,** Teetotalism-Intemperance.

thir'-teen". The sum of ten and three. Five-Quinquesection.

thir'-teenth'. The ordinal of thirteen. Five-Quinquesection.

thir"-ty-nine'. One less than forty. **Thirty-nine Articles,** Faith-Misgiving, Orthodoxy-Heterodoxy.

thir"-ty-one'. One more than thirty; a game of cards. Entertainment-Weariness.

this. What is here present. Universality-Particularity; **at this time of day,** Time; **this, that, or the other,** Variation.

this'-tle. A prickly plant. Sharpness - Bluntness.

this'-tle-down". The pappus of the thistle. Heaviness-Lightness.

thith'-er. To that place. Aim-Aberration.

thong. A strip of leather used for fastening; the lash of a whip. Connective, Recompense-Scourge.

Thor. A heathen god. Jove-Fiend.

tho'-rax. Trunk. Anatomy.

thorn. A sharp-pointed process from a branch; a vexation. Pleasurableness - Painfulness, Remedy-Bane, Sharpness-Bluntness; **plant a thorn,** Charitableness-Malevolence, Pleasurableness-Painfulness; **thorn in the flesh,** Pleasurableness-Painfulness; **thorn in the side,** Goodness-Badness, Pleasurableness-Painfulness.

thorns. Sharp-pointed processes from a branch. **On thorns for,** Desire-Distaste; **sit on thorns,** Pleasure-Pain, Sanguineness-Timidity, Sensuality-Suffering.

thorn'-y. Bearing thorns; vexatious. Difficulty-Facility, Sharpness-Bluntness.

thor'-ough. Complete. Completion-Noncompletion, Entirety-Deficiency.

thor'-ough-bass". A bass part in singing with shorthand marks to indicate the general harmony. Melody-Dissonance.

thor'-ough-bred. Bred from the purest stock; high-spirited. Conveyer, Skill-Unskilfulness, Society - Ludicrousness, Subjectiveness - Objectiveness.

thor'-ough-fare". A frequented way; an outlet. Aperture-Closure, Magnitude-Smallness, Way.

thor'-ough-go"-ing. Efficient. Entirety-Deficiency.

thor'-ough-ly. In a thorough way. **Do thoroughly,** Completion-Noncompletion.

thor'-ough-paced". Thoroughgoing. Magnitude-Smallness.

thorp. A village. City-Country, Dweller-Habitation.

though. Notwithstanding; even if. Antagonism-Concurrence, Compensation, Modification.

thought. The process of thinking. Conception-Theme, Heed-Disregard, Magnitude-Smallness, Reflection-Vacancy; **give a thought to,** Heed-Disregard; **not to be thought of,** Choice-Rejection, Dueness-Undueness, Leave-Prohibition. Prof-

fer-Refusal; **organ of thought,** Mind-Imbecility; **quick as thought,** Swiftness-Slowness; **seat of thought,** Mind-Imbecility; **subject of thought,** Conception-Theme; **thought of,** Conception-Theme; **want of thought,** Heed-Disregard; **who could have thought it,** Expectation-Surprise.

thought'-ful. Meditative; circumspect. Carefulness - Carelessness, Reflection - Vacancy, Sagacity-Incapacity.

thought'-ful-ness. State or quality of being full of thought. Reflection-Vacancy.

thought'-less. Heedless. Carefulness - Carelessness, Heed-Disregard, Preparation-Nonpreparation, Reflection-Vacancy.

thought'-less-ness. State or quality of lacking thought. Recklessness-Caution, Reflection-Vacancy.

thoughts. Cogitations. **Thoughts elsewhere,** Heed-Disregard; **thoughts that breathe,** Force-Weakness, Reflection-Vacancy.

thou'-sand. Ten hundred; a large number. Five-Quinquesection, Multiplicity-Paucity; **one in a thousand,** Good Man-Bad Man, Goodness-Badness.

thou'-sandth. An ordinal numeral. Five-Quinquesection.

thral'-dom. Servitude. Liberty-Subjection.

thrall. A slave. Liberty-Subjection.

thrash. To beat. Recompense-Punition.

Thra'-so. The name of a braggart soldier in Terence's *Eunuch.* Brawler.

thra-son'-ic. Boastful. Bragging, Presumption-Obsequiousness.

thread. A slender cord; to arrange on a thread; to pick one's way. Continuity - Interruption, Lamina - Fiber, Organization - Disorganization, Strength - Weakness, Transmission; **hang by a thread,** Security-Insecurity; **life hangs by a thread,** Life-Death; **not have a dry thread,** Dampness-Dryness; **thread one's way,** Transmission, Traveling-Navigation; **worn to a thread,** Betterment-Deterioration.

thread'-bare". Worn so that the threads show; clad in old garments. Betterment - Deterioration, Dress-Undress.

thread'-like. Resembling thread. Breadth-Narrowness, Lamina-Fiber.

thread'-pa"-per. A thin paper for rolling up thread. Breadth-Narrowness.

threat. Menace. Charitableness-Menace, Defiance.

threat'-en. Utter menaces; to be ominous. Charitableness - Curse, Charitableness - Menace, Defiance, Future - Past, Occurrence - Destiny, Sanguineness - Hopelessness, Security - Insecurity.

threat'-en-ing. Menacing. Charitableness-Menace, Sanguineness-Hopelessness.

three. One more than two. Triplication - Trisection; **go through three hundred and sixty degrees,** Circuition; **sisters three,** Volition-Obligation; **three sheets in the wind,** Teetotalism - Intemperance, Triality; **three times three,** Approval-Disapproval, Five-Quinquesection.

three'-fold". Triple. Triplication-Trisection.

three'-score". Sixty. Five-Quinquesection; **three-score years and ten,** Infancy-Age.

three'-tailed". Having three tails. **Three-tailed bashaw,** Chief-Underling, Gentility-Commonalty.

threne. A dirge. Jubilation-Lamentation.

thren'-o-dy. A dirge. Jubilation-Lamentation.

thresh. To beat. Investigation-Answer, Recompense-Punition.

thresh'-old. The entrance of a building; a starting-point. Beginning-End, Border; **at the threshold,**

REMOTENESS-NEARNESS; **threshold of an inquiry,** IN-VESTIGATION-ANSWER.

thrice. Three times. TRIPLICATION - TRISECTION; **thrice happy,** PLEASURE-PAIN; **thrice-told tale,** TERSE-NESS-PROLIXITY.

thrid. To pass through. TRANSMISSION.

thrift. Care and prudence in managing one's resources; vigorous growth. GAIN-LOSS, GENEROSITY-FRU-GALITY, WELFARE-MISFORTUNE.

thrift'-less. Extravagant; not thriving. EXTRAVA-GANCE-AVARICE.

thrill. To cause to tremble; extreme emotion. EMO-TION, EXCITATION, SENSUALITY-SUFFERING, TING-LING-NUMBNESS.

thrill'-ing. Exciting. PLEASURABLENESS-PAINFULNESS.

thrive. To prosper. GATHERING-SCATTERING, WEL-FARE-MISFORTUNE.

thri'-ving. Prospering. WELFARE-MISFORTUNE.

throat. The pharynx; any orifice. APERTURE - CLO-SURE, WATERCOURSE-AIRPIPE; **cut the throat,** LIFE-KILLING; **force down the throat,** HARSHNESS-MILD-NESS; **stick in one's throat,** TALKATIVENESS - TACI-TURNITY, VOCALIZATION - MUTENESS; **take by the throat,** TAKING-RESTITUTION.

throb. To pulsate. AGITATION, EMOTION, SENSUAL-ITY-SUFFERING.

throb'-bing. Pulsating. **Throbbing heart,** SANGUINE-NESS-TIMIDITY; **throbbing pain,** SENSUALITY-SUF-FERING.

throe. A violent pang; agony. AGITATION, REVOLU-TION, SENSUALITY-SUFFERING, TURBULENCE-CALM-NESS; **birth-throe,** CREATION-DESTRUCTION.

throne. A monarch's chair of state. DWELLER-HABI-TATION, SCEPTER, SUSPENSION-SUPPORT; **ascend the throne,** RULE-LICENSE; **occupy the throne,** RULE-LICENSE; **throne of God,** HEAVEN-HELL.

throng. A multitude. GATHERING-SCATTERING.

throt'-tle. To obstruct; to choke. APERTURE-CLO-SURE, LIFE - KILLING, MIGHT - IMPOTENCE, TAKING-RESTITUTION.

through. All the way; going from one end or side to or beyond the other; by means of; complete. AGEN-CY, AIM-ABERRATION, CAUSE-EFFECT, INSTRUMEN-TALITY, MEANS; **get through,** AGENT, COMPLETION-NONCOMPLETION; **go through one,** EXCITATION; **through thick and thin,** ENTIRETY-DEFICIENCY, PER-SISTENCE-WHIM, TOIL-RELAXATION, TURBULENCE-CALMNESS; **wet through,** DAMPNESS-DRYNESS.

through-out'. In every part. DURATION-NEVERNESS, ENTIRETY-DEFICIENCY, WHOLE-PART; **throughout the world,** EXTENSION-DISTRICT.

throw. To hurl. IMPETUS-REACTION, PUSH-PULL, SWIFTNESS-SLOWNESS, TOIL-RELAXATION; **throw a tub to catch a whale,** TRUTHFULNESS-FRAUD; **throw a veil over,** ENLIGHTENMENT-SECRECY; **throw away,** CHOICE - REJECTION, KEEPING - RELINQUISHMENT, PROVISION-WASTE; **throw away the scabbard,** FIGHT-ING-CONCILIATION, PERSISTENCE-WHIM; **throw cold water on,** MOTIVE-DEHORTATION; **throw doubt upon,** FAITH-MISGIVING; **throw down,** CREATION-DESTRUC-TION, ELEVATION-DEPRESSION; **throw good money after bad,** EXTRAVAGANCE-AVARICE; **throw in,** EN-VIRONMENT-INTERPOSITION; **throw into the shade,** CONSEQUENCE - INSIGNIFICANCE, ENLIGHTENMENT-SECRECY, INCREASE-DECREASE, SUPREMACY-SUB-ORDINACY, TRANSCURSION-SHORTCOMING; **throw off,** ADMISSION - EXPULSION; **throw off all disguise,** EXPOSURE-HIDINGPLACE; **throw off one's guard,** CRAFT-ARTLESSNESS; **throw off the mask,** EXPO-SURE-HIDINGPLACE; **throw off the scent,** EDUCATION-MISTEACHING, QUEST-EVASION; **throw of the dice,** RATIONALE - LUCK; **throw oneself at the feet of,** PETITION-EXPOSTULATION, YIELDING; **throw one-**

self into the arms of, AMITY-HOSTILITY, REFUGE-PITFALL, SECURITY - INSECURITY; **throw on paper,** WRITING-PRINTING; **throw open,** ADMISSION-EXPUL-SION, APERTURE-CLOSURE; **throw out,** ADMISSION-EXPULSION, PUSH-PULL; **throw out a feeler,** TOUCH, TRIAL; **throw out a hint,** ENLIGHTENMENT-SECRECY; **throw out a suggestion,** HYPOTHESIS; **throw out of gear,** ORGANIZATION-DISORGANIZATION, UNION-DIS-UNION; **throw over,** CREATION-DESTRUCTION; **throw overboard,** ADMISSION-EXPULSION, CHOICE-REJEC-TION, COMMISSION - ABROGATION, CREATION - DE-STRUCTION, INCLUSION-OMISSION; **throw up,** ADMIS-SION-EXPULSION, COMMISSION-RETIREMENT; **throw up one's cap,** BRAGGING; **throw up the game,** QUEST-ABANDONMENT.

thrown. Hurled. **Thrown out,** DIFFICULTY-FACIL-ITY.

thrum. To play on an instrument without expression. MUSICIAN.

thrush. A song-bird. MUSICIAN.

thrust. To shove with force; a sharp onset; a breaking of the supports in a mine. ATTACK-DEFENSE, GE-OLOGY, IMPETUS-REACTION; **thrust down one's throat,** COERCION; **thrust in,** INJECTION-EJECTION; **thrust one's nose in,** ACTIVITY-INDOLENCE; **thrust upon,** GIVING-RECEIVING.

thud. A dull, heavy sound. CRASH-DRUMMING, RES-ONANCE-NONRESONANCE.

thug. Cutthroat. LIFE-KILLING, ROBBER, TYRANNY-ANARCHY.

thug'-gism. Secret murder by thugs. LIFE-KILLING, TYRANNY-ANARCHY.

thumb. The short, thick digit on the human hand. ANATOMY, TOUCH; **bite the thumb,** REGARD-DISRE-SPECT; **one's fingers all thumbs,** SKILL-UNSKILFUL-NESS; **rule of thumb,** RATIOCINATION-INSTINCT, TRIAL, VENTURE; **thumb over,** EDUCATION-MISTEACHING; **thumbscrew,** RECOMPENSE-SCOURGE; **under one's thumb,** LIBERTY-SUBJECTION.

thump. To pound; a dull sound. IMPETUS-REACTION, RECOMPENSE - PUNITION, RESONANCE - NONRESO-NANCE.

thump'-er. One who or that which thumps. GREAT-NESS-LITTLENESS.

thump'-ing. Huge. GREATNESS - LITTLENESS, MAG-NITUDE-SMALLNESS.

thun'-der. The sound that accompanies lightning; a startling threat. CHARITABLENESS-MENACE, LOUD-NESS-FAINTNESS, PHENOMENON, TURBULENCE-CALM-NESS; **look black as thunder,** CONTENTEDNESS-DIS-CONTENTMENT, FAVORITE-ANGER; **thunder against,** APPROVAL - DISAPPROVAL, CHARITABLENESS - CURSE; **thunder at the top of one's voice,** CRY-ULULATION; **thunder forth,** PUBLICITY; **thunder of applause,** AP-PROVAL-DISAPPROVAL; **thunders of the Vatican,** CHARI-TABLENESS-CURSE.

thun''-der-a'-tion. An exclamation of surprise or em-phasis. APPROVAL-DISAPPROVAL.

thun'-der-bolt''. An electric discharge. EXCULPA-TION-PUNITION, PHENOMENON, WEAPON.

thun'-der-clap''. The sound of thunder. EXPEC-TATION-SURPRISE, LOUDNESS-FAINTNESS, PHENOME-NON.

thun'-der-ing. Unusually great. GREATNESS-LITTLE-NESS.

thun'-der-storm''. A storm accompanied by thunder. TURBULENCE-CALMNESS.

thun'-der-struck''. Amazed. ASTONISHMENT-EXPECT-ANCE.

thu'-ri-fer. A censer-bearer. VESTMENTS.

thu-rif'-er-ous. Bearing incense. PERFUME-STENCH.

thu''-ri-fi-ca'-tion. The act of burning incense. CERE-MONIAL, PERFUME-STENCH.

thus. In this way. CONDITION-SITUATION, RATIOCINA-TION-INSTINCT; **thus far,** BOUNDARY, MAGNITUDE-SMALLNESS.

thwack. To strike with something flat. IMPETUS-RE-ACTION, RECOMPENSE-PUNITION.

thwart. Transverse; to foil. ANTAGONISM-CONCUR-RENCE, CROSSING, OBSTRUCTION-HELP.

ti-a′-ra. The pope's crown. SCEPTER, VESTMENTS.

tib′-i-a. Bone in the leg. ANATOMY.

tib′-i-al. Pertaining to the tibia. ANATOMY.

Tib's eve. Never. DURATION-NEVERNESS.

tick. A tapping noise; credit; to check. CRASH-DRUMMING, CREDIT-DEBT, SIGN, VIBRATION; **go on tick,** CREDIT-DEBT, **tick off,** MARK-OBLITERATION.

tick′-et. Label. SIGN; **ticket of leave,** LEAVE-PRO-HIBITION; **ticket-of-leave man,** GOOD MAN-BAD MAN, GUARD-PRISONER.

tick′-le. Tingle; amuse. ENTERTAINMENT-WEARI-NESS, PLEASURABLENESS-PAINFULNESS, TINGLING-NUMBNESS; **tickle the fancy,** ENTERTAINMENT-WEARINESS, PLEASURABLENESS-PAINFULNESS; **tickle the palate,** PALATABLENESS - UNPALATABLENESS, SAVOR-TASTELESSNESS; **tickle the palm,** GIVING-RE-CEIVING, SETTLEMENT-DEFAULT.

tick′-lish. Difficult; delicate; unsteady. CERTAINTY-DOUBT, DIFFICULTY-FACILITY, SECURITY-INSECU-RITY.

ti-dal. Pertaining to the tides. ASTRONOMY.

tid′-bit″. A bit or morsel. GOODNESS-BADNESS, PLEASURABLENESS-PAINFULNESS.

tide. Rise and fall of the waters of the ocean. AS-TRONOMY.

tide. The periodic rise and fall of waters. ENOUGH, OCEAN-LAND, RIVER-WIND, WELFARE-MISFORTUNE; **against the tide,** ANTAGONISM-CONCURRENCE; **drift with the tide,** DIFFICULTY-FACILITY; **go with the tide,** CONVENTIONALITY-UNCONVENTIONALITY; **high tide,** HEIGHT-LOWNESS, RIVER-WIND; **stem the tide,** AN-TAGONISM-CONCURRENCE; **swim with the tide,** WEL-FARE-MISFORTUNE; **tide of events,** OCCURRENCE-DESTINY; **tide of time,** PERIOD-PROGRESS; **tide over,** ACTION-PASSIVENESS, DURATION-NEVERNESS, EARLINESS-LATENESS, SECURITY-INSECURITY, SUC-CESS-FAILURE; **turn of the tide,** INVERSION, TOP-BOTTOM.

ti′-di-ness. The quality or state of being tidy. CARE-FULNESS-CARELESSNESS.

ti′-dings. News. TIDINGS-MYSTERY.

TIDINGS—MYSTERY.

Advice. A speaking to, as to conduct; counsel.

Aviso [Sp.]. Information.

Bruit [F.]. Report; rumor.

Budget of information. ⎫ News gathered or communicated at one
Budget of news. ⎭ time.

Bulletin. An announcement of news.

Communication. News sent from one person or place to another.

Despatch. News sent by telegraph or messenger.

Embassy. A mission.

Errand. A message.

Fame. Public report.

Fresh news. The latest happenings.

Glad tidings. Good news.

Hearsay. Common talk.

Information. Acquired or derived knowledge.

Intelligence. Communicated information.

Message. News received by despatch or messenger.

News. Account of anything that has occurred.

Old news. ⎫ News commonly or generally known.
Old story. ⎭

On dit [F.]. They say; rumor.

Oui dire [F.]. Hearsay.

Piece of information. ⎫ Part of an account of a recent occurrence.
Piece of news. ⎭

Report. That which is generally noised about.

Rumor. An unverified report passing from mouth to mouth.

Scandal. An utterance injurious to the reputation of others.

Stale news. ⎫ Information generally known.
Stale story. ⎭

Stirring news. Information which excites or stirs up people.

Table-talk. Rumor passed about during meals.

Talk. Report; rumor.

Telegram. News sent by despatch.

Tidings. Previously unknown or uncertain information.

Tittle-tattle. Idle, trifling talk.

Topic of the day. The latest news.

Town-talk. Subject of conversation of the town generally.

Word. Communication.

TIDINGS—*Nouns of Agent.*

Gossip. An idle tattler.

Narrator, etc. One who tells or relates. See ACCOUNT.

Newsmonger. One who employs much time in hearing and telling news.

Scandal-monger. One who spreads defamatory reports about people.

Talebearer. One who tells tales that may create mischief.

Tattler. An idle talker.

Telltale. An informer of another's private concerns.

TIDINGS—*Figurative Nouns.*

Buzz. Indistinct rumor; gossip.

Canard [F.]. A fabricated sensational report.

Anagram. A new word formed from the letters of another word.

Arcanum. Secret; mystery.

Asian mystery. A mystery of an Asiatic character.

Charade. A scene which represents a syllable of a word and ends by representing the word itself.

Conundrum. A riddle founded on some odd resemblance.

Crux criticorum [L.]. The puzzle of critics.

Dead secret. A perfect secret.

Enigma. Dark saying; anything obscure.

Latency, etc. State of being concealed. See MANIFESTATION-LATENCY.

Logogriph. A word-puzzle in which the original word is discovered from various combinations of letters found in it.

Monogram. Private mark of an artist; intertexture of two or more letters.

Mystery. Something kept secret for a time, to be afterwards re-vealed.

Paradox, etc. A statement seemingly absurd in its terms. See DIFFICULTY.

Problem. Any perplexing question demanding settlement. See INVESTIGATION.

Profound secret. A deep secret.

Puzzle. Something that tries the ingenuity.

Rebus. A riddle in which words are represented by pictures whose names resemble them.

Riddle. Anything ambiguous; a puzzling question.

Secret. Something undiscovered or unknown.

Secrets of the prison-house. Happenings in a prison. [*Hamlet*, I, iv.]

Unintelligibility, etc. Quality of not being understood.

MYSTERY—*Denotations.*

Hyrcanian wood. An impenetrable wood in the region of the Cas-pian Sea.

Labyrinth. A place full of windings.

Le dessous des cartes [L.]. The underside of the cards.

Maze. A place from which it is difficult to get out.

Nut to crack. Something obscure to be explained.

Sealed book. A mystery.

Sphinx. An enigmatical person.

Terra incognita [L.]. Unknown ground. See KNOWLEDGE-IGNO-RANCE.

MYSTERY—*Adjectives.*

Secret, etc. Secluded; hidden; occult. See MANIFESTATION-LA-TENCY.

TIDINGS—FIGURATIVE NOUNS—*Continued*

Cry. Public reports or complaints; fame.

Eavesdropping. Catching the private conversation of others.

Flying rumor. Sensational report, passing from mouth to mouth.

Idea afloat. News.

News-stirring. Rumor or report.

TIDINGS—*Continued.*

TIDINGS—*Verbs.*

Rumor, etc. To circulate by report. See **PUBLICITY**. | **Transpire,** etc. To become public. See **EXPOSURE**.

TIDINGS—*Adjectives.*

Afloat. In motion or circulation: used of rumor, etc.
All over the town. Pertaining to rapidly spreading news.
Current. Circulating; general.
Currently reported. An account or statement, circulating in general.
Currently rumored. An unverified report, spreading widely.
Floating. Temporary or fluctuating news.
Going about. Circulating in general.

In circulation. Going around.
In every one's mouth. Widespread.
Many-tongued. Ready with the tongue to circulate anything.
Publicly reported. Something noised about openly.
Publicly rumored. Rumor spreading in an open manner.
Rife. Prevalent; current.
Rumored. Generally spoken of.

TIDINGS—*Adverbs, etc.*

As the story goes.
As the story runs.
As they say.
It is said.
} Expressions used in the sense of "According to report or rumor."

ti'-dy. Neat; a cover for the back of a chair. CLEANNESS-FILTHINESS, EMBELLISHMENT-DISFIGUREMENT, GOODNESS-BADNESS, ORDER-DISORDER.

tie. Bind; reaching the same total; low shoes; a bow or the like worn at the neck. CONNECTION-INDEPENDENCE, CONNECTIVE, DRESS-UNDRESS, DUTY-DERELICTION, EQUALITY-INEQUALITY, SECURITY, UNION-DISUNION; **nuptial tie,** MATRIMONY-CELIBACY; **ride and tie,** TRAVELING-NAVIGATION; **ride down,** COERCION, OBSTRUCTION-HELP, RELEASE-RESTRAINT; **tie oneself,** ENGAGEMENT-RELEASE; **ties of blood,** RELATIONSHIP; **tie the hands,** MIGHT-IMPOTENCE, RELEASE-RESTRAINT; **tie up,** RELEASE-RESTRAINT, TERMS.

tie'-beam". A timber that serves as a tie. CONNECTIVE, SUSPENSION-SUPPORT.

tied. Fastened; bound. **Tied up,** CREDIT-DEBT.

tier. A row. CONTINUITY-INTERRUPTION, LAMINA-FIBER.

tierce. A third standard thrust in fencing. **Carte and tierce,** ATTACK-DEFENSE.

tiff. A slight altercation; be peevish. FAVORITE-ANGER, VARIANCE-ACCORD.

tif'-fing. A light meal. NUTRIMENT-EXCRETION.

ti'-ger. A wild animal; a roistering knave. BENEFACTOR-EVILDOER, BRAVERY-COWARDICE, CHARITABLENESS-MALEVOLENCE, CHIEF-UNDERLING, GOOD MAN-BAD MAN, TURBULENCE-CALMNESS.

tight. Closely and firmly together; stretched; intoxicated. APERTURE-CLOSURE, BEAUTY-UGLINESS, TEETOTALISM-INTEMPERANCE, UNION-DISUNION; **keep a tight hand on,** RELEASE-RESTRAINT; **on one's tight ropes,** SELFRESPECT-HUMBLENESS; **tight grasp,** HARSHNESS-MILDNESS; **tight hand,** HARSHNESS-MILDNESS.

tight'-en. To make tight. ENLARGEMENT-DIMINUTION, UNION-DISUNION.

tight'-fist"-ed. Parsimonious. EXTRAVAGANCE-AVARICE.

tight'-ness. State or quality of being tight. UNION-DISUNION.

tights. A skin-fitting garment. DRESS-UNDRESS.

ti'-gress. A female tiger. MALE-FEMALE.

tike. A boor. GENTILITY-COMMONALTY.

til'-bur-y. A conveyance. CONVEYANCE-VESSEL.

til'-de. A sign used in writing the Spanish language. MARK-OBLITERATION, SIGN.

tile. A piece of baked clay; a high hat. COVER-LINING, DRESS-UNDRESS; **tile loose,** SANENESS-LUNACY.

ti'-ling. A tile-covered surface. COVER-LINING.

till. To cultivate; a money-drawer; until. CONTENTS-RECEIVER, DOMESTICATION-AGRICULTURE, DURATION-NEVERNESS, TREASURY; **till doomsday,** ETERNITY-INSTANTANEITY; **till now,** FUTURE-PAST; **till the**

soil, DOMESTICATION-AGRICULTURE, PREPARATION-NONPREPARATION.

till'-age. Land cultivation. DOMESTICATION-AGRICULTURE.

till'-er. A means of guidance; a money-box. INSTRUMENT, TREASURY; **tiller of the soil,** DOMESTICATION-AGRICULTURE, GENTILITY-COMMONALTY.

till'-ing. Present participle of till. PREPARATION-NONPREPARATION.

tilt. To tip; to contend with the lance; a canvas cover. ASCENT-DESCENT, COVER-LINING, PARALLELISM-INCLINATION, PUSH-PULL, STRIFE-PEACE; **full tilt,** ACTIVITY-INDOLENCE, AIM-ABERRATION, HURRY-LEISURE; **ride full tilt at,** ATTACK-DEFENSE, QUEST-EVASION; **run a tilt at,** ATTACK-DEFENSE; **tilt over,** REVERSAL; **tilt up,** ELEVATION-DEPRESSION; **tilt with,** STRIFE-PEACE.

tilt'-ed. Inclined. PARALLELISM-INCLINATION.

tilt'-ing. A medieval sport. ENTERTAINMENT-WEARINESS.

tilt'-yard". A place for tilting. LISTS.

tim'-ber. Wood for building purposes; trees. FAUNA-FLORA, MATERIALS.

tim'-bre. The quality of a tone. MELODY-DISSONANCE.

tim'-brel. A musical instrument. MUSICAL INSTRUMENTS.

time. Duration. DURATION-NEVERNESS, ETERNITY-INSTANTANEITY, HURRY-LEISURE, OCCURRENCE-DESTINY; **against time,** HURRY-LEISURE; **at times,** FREQUENCY-RARITY; **course of time,** PERIOD-PROGRESS; **employ one's time in,** OCCUPATION; **glass of time,** DURATION-NEVERNESS; **in time,** EARLINESS-LATENESS, OCCURRENCE-DESTINY, PERIOD-PROGRESS; **measure time,** CHRONOLOGY-ANACHRONISM; **no time,** EARLINESS-LATENESS, ETERNITY-INSTANTANEITY; **no time to lose,** HURRY-LEISURE, NEED; **no time to spare,** HURRY-LEISURE; **ravages of time,** BETTERMENT-DETERIORATION, DURATION-NEVERNESS; **slow time,** SWIFTNESS-SLOWNESS; **take time,** ACTION-PASSIVENESS, ACTIVITY-INDOLENCE, SWIFTNESS-SLOWNESS; **there being times when,** FREQUENCY-RARITY; **time after time,** RECURRENCE; **time being,** TIME; **time drawing on,** FUTURE-PAST; **time enough,** EARLINESS-LATENESS; **time gone by,** OPPORTUNENESS-UNSUITABLENESS; **time hanging on one's hands,** ACTION-PASSIVENESS, ENTERTAINMENT-WEARINESS, HURRY-LEISURE; **time has been,** FUTURE-PAST; **time immemorial,** FUTURE-PAST; **time of day,** ETERNITY-INSTANTANEITY; **time of life,** DURATION-NEVERNESS, INFANCY-AGE, TIME; **time out of mind,** FUTURE-PAST; **time to come,** FUTURE-PAST; **time to spare,** HURRY-LEISURE; **time up,** LASTINGNESS-TRANSIENTNESS, OPPORTUNENESS-UNSUITABLENESS; **time was,** FUTURE-PAST; **true time,** ETERNITY-INSTANTANEITY; **waste time,** ACTIVITY-INDOLENCE.

TIME.

Age. A particular period as distinguished from others.
Aorist. Indefinite past time.
Crisis. A time of great danger or uncertainty.
Day. The time of sunlight.
Different time. Time of a period as distinguished from another.
Epoch. An interval of time regarded as a whole.
Existing time. The present time; now.
Hour. A portion of a day.
Nineteenth century. The nineteenth hundred of years after the birth of Christ, 1801-1900.
Nonce. The present.
Other time. A period of time as distinguished from another.
The present day.
The present junction.
The present moment. } Time now existing.
The present occasion.
The present time.
The times. Lapse of time considered with reference to events taking place.
Time being. The present.
Time of life. The length of time that one lives.

TIME—Adjectives.

Actual. Existing at the present time.
Aoristic. Expressing completed action without any limitation.
Current. Belonging to the present time or passing period.
Existing. Being or continuing to be.
Instant. Now passing; current.
Present. Occurring in the present period; current.
That is. Now.

TIME—Adverbs.

Already. Previously to some mentioned time.
Now. Presently.
Then. At some past time.
To-day. In the present.
Upon. At a time.
When. At what time.
Whenever. }
Whensoever. } At whatever time.

TIME—Adverbial Phrases.

At a different time; at another time; at any time; at present; at some other time; at that instant; at that moment; at that time; at the present time; at this moment; at this time; at this time of day; at various times; at which instant; at which moment; at which time; but now; even now; for the nonce; for the time; for the time being; just now; now-a-days; once upon a time; one fine morning; one of these days; on that occasion; on the nail; on the present occasion; on the spot; on the spur of the moment; on the spur of the occasion; on which occasion; *pro hac vice* [L.]; for this occasion; some fine morning; some of these days; sometime or other; sooner or later; to the present day; to this day; until now; upon which.

time'-ful. Opportune. OPPORTUNENESS-UNSUITABLE-NESS.
time'-hon''-ored. Venerable as of long existence. NOVELTY-ANTIQUITY, REGARD-DISRESPECT, REPUTATION-DISCREDIT.
time'-keep''-er. One who or that which keeps time. CHRONOLOGY-ANACHRONISM.
time'-less. Untimely. OPPORTUNENESS-UNSUITABLE-NESS.

time'-ly. In proper time. EARLINESS-LATENESS, OPPORTUNENESS-UNSUITABLENESS.
timeo Danaos [L.] (tim'-î-o dan'-ê-os). I fear the Greeks. FAITH-MISGIVING, RECKLESSNESS-CAUTION.
time'-piece''. A clock or watch. CHRONOLOGY-ANACHRONISM.
time'-pleas''-er. A time-server. PERSISTENCE-WHIM.
times. Portions of duration. OCCURRENCE-DESTINY, TIME; **hard times,** WELFARE-MISFORTUNE; **many times,** FREQUENCY-RARITY.
time'-serv''-er. One who adapts his opinions and manners to the times. PRESUMPTION-OBSEQUIOUS-NESS.
time'-serv''-ing. Yielding to the apparent demands of the times, without reference to principle. CRAFT-ARTLESSNESS, PERSISTENCE-WHIM, PRESUMPTION-OBSEQUIOUSNESS, UNSELFISHNESS-SELFISHNESS, UPRIGHTNESS-DISHONESTY.
time'-worn''. Impaired by time. BETTERMENT-DETERIORATION, INFANCY-AGE, NOVELTY-ANTIQUITY.
tim'-id. Shy. BRAVERY-COWARDICE, CONCEIT-DIFFIDENCE, SANGUINENESS-TIMIDITY.
ti-mid'-i-ty. The quality or state of being timid. CERTAINTY-DOUBT, CONCEIT-DIFFIDENCE, PERSISTENCE-APOSTASY, SANGUINENESS-TIMIDITY.
ti'-mist. One who beats time for others. PERSISTENCE-WHIM.
ti-moc'-ra-cy. A kind of government in which honors are distributed according to a rating of property. AFFLUENCE-PENURY.
Ti'-mon. An Athenian called "the Misanthrope." Timon of Athens, AFFLUENCE-PENURY, HUMANITARIANISM-MISANTHROPY, SOCIABILITY-PRIVACY.
tim'-or-ous. Lacking courage. BRAVERY-COWARDICE, CONCEIT-DIFFIDENCE, SANGUINENESS-TIMIDITY.
tim'-o-thy. A fodder-grass. DOMESTICATION-AGRICULTURE.
tin. To incase in tins; money; metal. CHEMISTRY, CONSERVATION, MONEY.
tinct. To tinge. COLOR-ACHROMATISM.
tinc-to'-ri-al. Pertaining to color. COLOR-ACHROMATISM.
tinc'-ture. To impart a slight tint to. COLOR-ACHROMATISM, MAGNITUDE-SMALLNESS, MIXTURE-HOMOGENEITY.
tinc'-tured. To affect slightly with some sentiment or influence. AFFECTIONS.
tin'-der. Something very inflammable for kindling fire from a spark; easily angered. COMBUSTIBLE, FAVORITE-QUARRELSOMENESS.
tinge. To imbue with a faint trace of color. COLOR-ACHROMATISM, MAGNITUDE-SMALLNESS, MIXTURE-HOMOGENEITY.
tin'-gent. Capable of tingeing. COLOR-ACHROMATISM.
tin'-gle. To produce a prickly, stinging sensation. EMOTION, SENSUALITY-SUFFERING, TINGLING-NUMBNESS; **make the ears tingle,** FAVORITE-ANGER.
tin'-gling. Producing a prickly, stinging sensation. TINGLING-NUMBNESS.

TINGLING—NUMBNESS.

Aura. A sensation as of vapor or cold air rising from the body toward the head.
Formication. An itching sensation like the creeping of ants.
Itching, etc. A tickling, irritating sensation.
Tingling. A prickly, stinging sensation; the act of tingling.
Titillation. The act of titillating.

TINGLING—Verbs.

Creep. To have the sensation as of something creeping on the skin.
Itch. To have a peculiar irritation or titillation of the skin.
Prick. To cause to be or have the sensation of being stung or pierced with a sharp point or points.
Prickle. To prick slightly.

Numbness, etc. The state of being numb. See FEELING-INSENSIBILITY.
Pins and needles. A kind of numbness, though accompanied by minute prickling sensations, as in the hand and foot.

NUMBNESS—Verbs.

Benumb, etc. To cause to be numb. See FEELING-INSENSIBILITY.

NUMBNESS—Adjectives.

Benumbed, etc. Without feeling. See *Verbs.*
Impalpable. Imperceptible to the touch; specifically, ground so fine that no grit can be felt.
Intangible. Incapable of being perceived by the sense of touch.
Numb. Lacking the power of sensation.

Sting. To feel or cause to feel a smarting, painful sensation, as from a sting.

Thrill. To feel or cause to feel a quivering tingling sensation.

Tickle. To excite the nerves, but not painfully; have such a sensation.

Tingle. To have or produce a prickly, stinging sensation.

Titillate. To excite a tickling or pleasant sensation in.

TINGLING—*Adjectives.*

Itching, etc. Tingling. See *Verbs.*

tink. A single tinkle. Resonance-Nonresonance.

tink'-er. A mender. Health-Sickness, Renovation-Relapse.

tink'-er-ing. Present participle of tinker. Renovation-Relapse.

tin'-kle. To give a faint, metallic sound. Loudness-Faintness, Resonance-Nonresonance.

tin'-kling. Giving faint, metallic sounds. **Tinkling cymbal,** Meaning-Jargon.

tin'-ni-ent. Emitting a clear, tinkling sound. Resonance-Nonresonance.

tin'-sel. Thin, glittering bits of metal for ornamentation. Embellishment-Disfigurement, Light-Darkness, Taste-Vulgarity, Truthfulness-Fraud.

tint. Hue. Color-Achromatism.

tin''-ta-mar'. A loud and hideous noise. Loudness-Faintness.

tin''-tin-nab'-u-la-ry. Characterized by ringing or tinkling. Resonance-Nonresonance.

ti'-ny. Very small. Greatness-Littleness.

tip. Tilt; a fee; the top; to cover the tip of. Beginning-End, Cover-Lining, Giving-Receiving, Top-Bottom; **on tiptoe,** Expectation-Surprise, Height-Lowness; **tip the wink,** Enlightenment-Secrecy, Sign.

tip'-cat''. A boys' game. Entertainment-Weariness.

tip'-pet. A covering for the neck. Dress-Undress.

tip'-ple. To drink habitually. Nutriment-Excretion, Teetotalism-Intemperance.

tip'-pler. One who drinks habitually, but not to excess. Teetotalism-Intemperance.

tip'-staff''. A court officer. Judicature.

tip'-sy. Unsteady. Teetotalism-Intemperance.

tip'-top'. The very top; the best of its kind. Goodness-Badness, Top-Bottom.

ti-rade'. A declamatory outpouring, as of censure. Approval-Disapproval, Speech-Inarticulateness.

tire. Weary. Desire-Repletion, Entertainment-Weariness, Pleasurableness-Painfulness, Weariness-Refreshment.

tiré à quatre épingles [F.] (ti-rê' α kɑtr êpan·gl'). Finespun. Society-Affectation, Taste-Vulgarity.

tired'-ness. State or quality of being tired. Weariness-Refreshment.

tirer d'affaire, se [F.] (ti-rê' dɑ-fêr', se). To deliver from the affair; to get out of trouble. Rescue, Success-Failure.

Ti-re'-si-as. A blind seer. Soothsayer.

tire'-some. Wearisome. Entertainment-Weariness, Pleasurableness-Painfulness, Weariness-Refreshment.

Tis-iph'-o-ne. One of the Eumenides. Turbulence-Calmness.

tis'-sue. Any light textile fabric; an elementary fabric of which an organ in the human body is composed. Crossing, Gathering-Scattering, Texture, Whole-Part.

tit. A small horse. Conveyer, Greatness-Littleness; **tit for tat,** Reprisal-Resistance.

Ti'-tan. A demigod, the incarnation of natural forces. Jove-Fiend.

tit'-bit''. A bit or morsel. Condiment, Pleasurableness-Painfulness.

tithe. A tenth; a ratable tax. Five-Quinquesection, Price-Discount.

tit-il-late. Excite pleasurably. Desire-Distaste, Entertainment-Weariness, Tingling-Numbness.

tit''-il-la'-tion. The act of exciting pleasurably. Sensuality-Suffering, Tingling-Numbness.

ti'-tle. A claim; name; appellation. Dueness-Undueness, Name-Misnomer, Property, Scepter, Sign, Title.

TITLE.

Handle to one's name. Slang for title.

Honor. Respectful regard or veneration; hence, any outward token of such feeling.

Knighthood. The character or dignity of a knight; the rank or honor accompanying the title. See Gentility.

Title. An appellation significant of office or honor.

TITLE—*Denotations.*

Esquire. A title given to any man as a mark of respect.

Excellency. A title of honor bestowed upon high officials.

Grace. A title of honor applied to a duke, duchess, or archbishop.

Highness. A title of honor belonging to persons of princely rank.

His honor. } A title of honor applied to a judge.
Honor.

Lordship. A title of honor applied to a lord.

Master. A title given to a boy as a mark of respect.

Mein Herr [G.]. Dear sir.

Mr. Mister; a title of respect applied to a man.

Mynheer [Dutch]. A title of address in Holland.

Reverence. } A title of respect applied to clergymen.
Reverend.

Señor [Sp.]. Sir.

Serene Highness. The title of princes in Germany and France.

Signor [It.]. Sir.

Sir. A title of respect applied to any man.

Worship. A title of honor applied to clergymen, nobility, magistrates, etc.

Your honor. A title belonging to a judge.

TITLE—*Associated Nouns.*

Arms. The ensigns armorial of a family; marks of dignity and honor, descending from father to son.

Bays. Honorary garlands of laurel leaves bestowed as prizes.

Blue ribbon. The ribbon worn by members of the Order of the Garter; hence, a distinction, a prize.

Cockade. A badge, generally worn upon the hat, indicating military or naval service.

Colors. An ensign, flag, or badge.

Cordon [F.]. A cord or ribbon given as a badge of honor.

Coronet. A crown denoting various degrees of rank less than sovereign.

Cross. An ornament in the form of a cross worn as a mark of honor.

Crown. A decorated head-piece worn or displayed as a mark of sovereign power.

Decoration. A badge bestowed as a mark of honor.

Epaulet. } A fringed ornament worn on the shoulder as a mark
Epaulette [F.]. of military rank.

Feather. } An honor or mark of distinction.
Feather in one's cap.

Garland. A wreath worn as a mark of honor.

Garter. The distinguishing badge of the highest ranked order of knighthood in Great Britain.

Laurel. A crown of laurel bestowed as a prize; hence, honor distinction.

Livery. The peculiar dress appropriated as a distinctive mark of honor or service.

Medal. A small ornamental disk of metal conferred as a mark of honor.

Order. A body of persons with some common honorary distinction.

Palm. A symbol of success or triumph.

Reward. That which is given in return for some service or attainment. See Recompense.

Riband.
Ribbon. } A mark of honor consisting of a bow or streamer of ribbon.

Scutcheon. A shield for armorial bearings.

Shield. An escutcheon on which heraldry is depicted.

Star. A figure having radiating points used as an emblem of distinction or honor.

Wreath. A twisted band of leaves or flowers bestowed upon a person as a mark of distinction.

ti'-tled. Having a title, as of nobility. GENTILITY-COMMONALTY.

ti'-tle–deed". The instrument by which the title is evidenced. SECURITY.

ti'-tle–page". The page containing the title. BEGINNING-END.

tit'-ter. To giggle. JUBILATION-LAMENTATION.

tit'-tle. A jot; iota. MAGNITUDE-SMALLNESS; **to a tittle,** TRUTH-ERROR.

tit'-tle-tat"-tle. To chatter foolishly. CONVERSATION-MONOLOGUE, TIDINGS-MYSTERY.

tit'-u-ban-cy. The quality of staggering; stumbling. SPEECH-INARTICULATENESS.

tit'-u-bate. To stumble. ASCENT-DESCENT, SUCCESS-FAILURE.

tit'-u-ba'-tion. A reeling. ASCENT-DESCENT.

tit'-u-lar. Nominal. NAME-MISNOMER, WORD-NEOLOGY.

tiv'-o-li. A game like bagatelle. ENTERTAINMENT-WEARINESS.

tme'-sis. The separation of the elements of a compound word by an intervening word. REVERSAL.

to. In the direction of. AIM-ABERRATION; **lie to,** ACTION-PASSIVENESS; **to a certain degree,** MAGNITUDE-SMALLNESS; **to a great extent,** MAGNITUDE-SMALLNESS; **to all intents and purposes,** ENTIRETY-DEFICIENCY, EQUALITY-INEQUALITY; **to a man,** UNIVERSALITY-PARTICULARITY; **to and fro,** VIBRATION; **to a small extent,** MAGNITUDE-SMALLNESS; **to be sure,** ASSENT-DISSENT; **to come,** FUTURE-PAST, OCCURRENCE-DESTINY; **to crown all,** CONSEQUENCE-INSIGNIFICANCE, SUPREMACY-SUBORDINACY; **to do,** REGULARITY-IRREGULARITY; **to some extent,** QUANTITY-MEASURE; **to the credit of,** CREDIT-DEBT; **to the end of time,** ETERNITY-INSTANTANEITY; **to the full,** ENTIRETY-DEFICIENCY; **to the letter,** IMITATION-ORIGINALITY; **to the point,** HARMONY-DISCORD; **to the purpose,** HARMONY-DISCORD; **to this day,** TIME; **to wit,**

ENLIGHTENMENT-SECRECY, UNIVERSALITY-PARTICULARITY.

toad. A tailless amphibian. EMBELLISHMENT-UGLINESS, GOODNESS-BADNESS, PRESUMPTION-OBSEQUIOUSNESS; **toad under a harrow,** SENSUALITY-SUFFERING.

toad'-eat"-er. A fawning parasite. FLATTERER-DEFAMER, PRESUMPTION-OBSEQUIOUSNESS.

toad'-eat"-ing. Practising flattery. ADULATION-DISPARAGEMENT.

toad'-stool". A poisonous mushroom. FAUNA-FLORA.

toad'-y. An obsequious flatterer. PRESUMPTION-OBSEQUIOUSNESS.

toast. To drink to the health of; to brown over a fire. HEATING-COOLING, SOLEMNIZATION.

to-bac'-co. A plant used for smoking. PUNGENCY.

to-bog'-gan. A sled-like vehicle used for coasting. CONVEYANCE-VESSEL.

to'-by. A mug. CONTENTS-RECEIVER.

toc-ca'-ta. A touch-piece. MUSIC.

toc'-sin. An alarm. ALARM.

tod. A weight of about twenty-eight pounds. HEAVINESS-LIGHTNESS.

to–day'. The present day. TIME.

tod'-dle. To walk as a little child. SWIFTNESS-SLOWNESS, TRAVELING-NAVIGATION.

tod'-dy. A beverage. NUTRIMENT-EXCRETION.

toe. One of the digits of the foot. ANATOMY, TOP-BOTTOM; **on the light fantastic toe,** ENTERTAINMENT-WEARINESS, SPRING-DIVE.

toes. The digits of the foot. **Turn up the toes,** LIFE-DEATH.

toft. A homestead. PROPERTY.

to'-ga. The outer garment of a Roman citizen. DRESS-UNDRESS, SCEPTER; **assume the toga virilis,** MANHOOD.

to-geth'-er. Conjointly. COEXISTENCE, SOLITUDE-COMPANY; **come together,** CONCENTRATION-RADIATION; **get together,** GATHERING-SCATTERING; **hang together,** ANTAGONISM-CONCURRENCE; **lay heads together,** ADVICE; **together with,** ADDITION-SUBTRACTION, SOLITUDE-COMPANY.

tog'-ger-y. Clothes. DRESS-UNDRESS.

togs. Clothes. DRESS-UNDRESS.

toil. Arduous labor. ACTIVITY-INDOLENCE, TOIL-RELAXATION.

TOIL—RELAXATION.

Ado. Unnecessary and troublesome work.

A strong pull, a long pull, and a pull all together. Hard labor.

Dead lift. Labor without mechanical aid.

Drudgery. Wearisome work.

Duty. That which one is bound to do.

Effort. The putting forth of strength voluntarily to perform something.

Energy. The power to do work.

Exercise.
Exercitation. } Physical or other activity for developing the body.

Exertion. The exercise of any power.

Fagging. Exhaustion caused by severe exertion.

Gymnastics. Method of taking exercise.

Hammering. The act of striking with the hammer.

Hard work. Labor.

Harvest time. The time of labor.

Heft. The act of heaving.

Labor. Hard work.

Limæ labor [L.]. Labor of revising a literary work.

Manual labor. Work with the hands.

Operoseness. The state of being fraught with labor.

Pains. Tedious exertion.

Pull. A drawing.

Resolution. Determination to effect something by toil.

Slavery. Drudgery.

Spell. A required amount of work.

Spirt.
Spurt. } A short, energetic exertion.

Halt. A cessation of movement.

Pause. A rest; a stop.

Recess. A period of rest from employment.

Relaxation. Diversion from regular or severe duties.

Repose. Rest.

Respite. Temporary rest from labor.

Rest. Cessation from activity.

Silken repose. Soft repose.

Sleep. A state of repose.

RELAXATION—*Nouns of Time.*

Breathing time. A time of rest.

Day of rest. A period of repose; a sabbath.

Dies non [L.]. A legal holiday.

Holiday. A day of exemption from labor.

Lord's day. The first day of the week, the day of Christ's resurrection; by many united with the Sabbath.

Red-letter day. A Church holiday.

Sabbath. The seventh day of the week, the rest-day of the Jews.

Vacation. A stated period for rest.

RELAXATION—*Verbs.*

Pause. To make a short stop.

Recline. To lie down.

Relax. To indulge in recreation.

Repose. To take complete rest.

Rest. To be inactive.

TOIL—RELAXATION—*Continued.*

Stitch of work. A particular piece of work.
Strain. A severe taxing of the powers.
Stress. A specific force tending to produce a strain.
Stretch. Effort to lengthen.
Stroke of work. A particular labor.
Struggle. A violent effort.
Sweat of one's brow. Result of labor.
Swink. Labor.
Throw. The act of throwing.
Toil. Grievous work.
Toil and trouble. Labor.
Travail. Pain in childbirth.
Trouble. Annoyance of putting forth effort.
Tug. To pull against great resistance.
Uphill work. Very difficult work.
Warm work. Work which causes one to sweat.
Wear and tear. Use by work.
Work. The production of motion against resistance.

TOIL—*Verbs.*

Drudge. To do irksome or menial work.
Fag. To become weary from drudgery.
Labor. To work hard.
Moil. To work in a drudging manner.
Ply. To be constantly employed.
Pull. To draw.
Slave. To drudge.
Strain. To make effort to the limit of endurance.
Strive. To make an effort.
Sweat. To work hard, so as to perspire.
Toil. To work so as to strain or exhaust one's strength.
Tug. To pull against great resistance.
Work. To do something.

TOIL—*Verbal Expressions.*

Bend the bow; bestir oneself (see ACTIVITY); buckle to; burn the candle at both ends; do all in one's power; do all one can; do as much as in one lies; do double duty; do one's best; do one's utmost; do the best one can; do the work; do what lies in one's power; drag a lengthened chain; exert oneself; exert one's energies; fall to work; fight one's way; go all lengths; go through fire and water (see DETERMINATION); hammer at; have one's whole soul in the work; labor day and night; lay about one; leave no stone unturned; make a long arm; move heaven and earth; play one's best card; ply the oar; put all one's strength into; put forth a strong arm; put forth one's strength; put one's best leg forward; put one's right leg forward; redouble one's efforts; rough it; set one's shoulder to the wheel (see DETERMINATION); sit up; spare no efforts; spare no pains; stick to (see PERSISTENCE); strain every nerve; stretch a long arm; take pains; take the laboring oar; take trouble; tax one's energies; trouble oneself; try one's best; try one's utmost; tug at the oar; use exertion; use one's best endeavor; use one's utmost endeavor; wade through; work day and night; work double hours; work double tides; work hard; work like a cart-horse; work like a coal-heaver; work like a galley-slave; work like a horse; work one's way.

TOIL—*Adjectives.*

Elaborate. Done or prepared with great pains.
Energetic. Active.

RELAXATION—VERBS—*Continued.*

Slacken. To ease up.
Unbend. To relieve tension.

RELAXATION—*Verbal Expressions.*

Go to bed; go to rest; go to sleep (see ACTIVITY-INDOLENCE); lie down; lie fallow (see ACTION-PASSIVENESS); recline on a bed of down; recline on an easy chair; rest and be thankful; rest upon one's oars; shut up shop; stay one's hand; take a holiday; take breath (see REFRESHMENT); take one's ease; take rest.

RELAXATION—*Adjectives.*

Reposing. In a state of complete rest.
Unstrained. Not strained.

RELAXATION—*Adverb.*

At rest. Enjoying leisure.

TOIL—ADJECTIVES—*Continued.*

Gymnastic. Pertaining to gymnastics.
Hard at work. Laboring.
Hard-working. Making great efforts.
Herculean. Requiring great strength.
Laboring. Burdened, or moving with difficulty or pain. See *Verbs.*
Laborious. Requiring a great amount of labor.
On the stretch. At work.
Operose. Attended with much labor.
Painstaking. Working with care.
Palestric. Pertaining to gymnastic games and exercises.
Strained. Exerted to the limit of endurance.
Strenuous. Vigorous and persevering.
Toilsome. Marked by toil.
Troublesome. Attended with trouble.
Uphill. Requiring unceasing efforts.
Wearisome. Making weary.

TOIL—*Adverbs.*

Laboriously. With much labor.
Lustily. With vigor.

TOIL—*Adverbial Expressions.*

By the sweat of one's brow; hammer and tongs; heart and soul; *manibus pedibusque* [L.], with hands and feet, with all one's might; *suo marte* [L.], with his own strength; through thick and thin (see PERSISTENCE), tooth and nail; to the best of one's abilities; *totis viribus* [L.], with all possible strength; *unguibus et rostro* [L.], with claws and beak with determination; *vi et armis* [L.], with force and arms; with all one's might; with a strong hand; with might and main; with much ado; with sledge-hammer.

TOIL—*Phrases.*

Aide-toi, le ciel t'aidera [F.]. Help yourself, and heaven will help you.
Buen principio, la mitad es hecha [Sp.]. Well begun is half done.
Cosa ben fatta è fatta due volte [It.]. A thing well done is twice done.
Manu forti [L.]. With the strong hand.
Ora et labora [L.]. Pray and work.

---

toil'-er. Laborer. LABOR-CAPITAL.
toi'-let''. The process of dressing. DRESS-UNDRESS.
toilette [F.] (twa-let'). The process of dressing. DRESS-UNDRESS.
toilette, en grande [F.] (twa-let, an· gran·d). Well dressed. EMBELLISHMENT-DISFIGUREMENT.
toils. Snares. TRUTHFULNESS-FRAUD.
toil'-some. Accompanied with fatigue. DIFFICULTY-FACILITY, TOIL-RELAXATION.
toil'-worn''. Worn by toil. WEARINESS-REFRESHMENT.
to'-ken. A sign. SIGN; **give token,** MANIFESTATION-LATENCY; **token of remembrance,** REMEMBRANCE-FORGETFULNESS.
told. Bade. **Do what one is told,** INSUBORDINATION-OBEDIENCE.
tol''-de-rol'-loll. An expression of joy. JUBILATION-LAMENTATION.
To-le'-do. A sword from Toledo, Spain. WEAPON.

tol'-er-a-ble. Passably good. CONSEQUENCE-INSIGNIFICANCE, CONTENTEDNESS-DISCONTENTMENT, FAULTLESSNESS-FAULTINESS, GOODNESS-BADNESS, MAGNITUDE-SMALLNESS.
tol'-er-a-bly. Passably well. **Get on tolerably,** MEDIOCRITY.
tol'-er-ance. The character or state of being tolerant. HARSHNESS-MILDNESS, LEAVE-PROHIBITION.
tol'-er-ate. To suffer to remain. LEAVE-PROHIBITION, RULE-LICENSE.
tol'-er-a'-tion. Tolerating that which is not wholly approved. CHARITABLENESS-MALEVOLENCE, HARSHNESS-MILDNESS, LEAVE-PROHIBITION, RULE-LICENSE.
toll. To sound slowly; tax. CRASH-DRUMMING, PRICE-DISCOUNT; **toll the knell,** LIFE-FUNERAL.
toll'-booth''. A market; jail. MARKET, RELEASE-PRISON.
toll'-ing. Present participle of toll. LIFE-FUNERAL.

tom'-a-hawk. A battle-ax. WEAPON.

to-ma'-to. A plant bearing an edible fruit. DOMESTICATION-AGRICULTURE, NUTRIMENT-EXCRETION.

tomb. A sepulcher. LIFE-FUNERAL; **lay in the tomb,** LIFE-FUNERAL; **tomb of the Capulets,** REMEMBRANCE-FORGETFULNESS.

tombé des nues [F.] (ton·-bê' de nü). Fallen from the clouds. ASTONISHMENT-EXPECTANCE, CONVENTIONALITY-UNCONVENTIONALITY.

tom'-boy". A boisterous girl. TASTE-VULGARITY.

tomb'-stone". A stone marking a place of burial. LIFE-FUNERAL.

tom'-cat". A male cat. FAUNA-FLORA, MALE-FEMALE.

tome. A volume. MISSIVE-PUBLICATION.

to-men'-tous. Covered with woolly hair. SMOOTHNESS-ROUGHNESS.

tom'-fool". A silly person. SAGE-FOOL.

tom"-fool'-er-y. Nonsensical behavior. ADAGE-NONSENSE, ENTERTAINMENT-WEARINESS, POMP, WITTINESS-DULNESS.

Tom'-my At'-kins. A British soldier. BELLIGERENT.

tom"-nod'-dy. A blockhead. SAGE-FOOL.

to-mor'-row. The morrow. FUTURE-PAST; **to-morrow and to-morrow,** PERIOD-PROGRESS, RECURRENCE.

tom'-pi-on. An inking-pad. PERFORATOR-STOPPER.

Tom Thumb. A dwarf. GREATNESS-LITTLENESS.

tom'-tit". A titmouse. GREATNESS-LITTLENESS.

tom'-tom". A drum. FIGHTING-CONCILIATION, MUSICAL INSTRUMENTS.

ton. A measure of weight; the style. HEAVINESS-LIGHTNESS, MEASURE, SOCIETY-LUDICROUSNESS.

ton, bon [F.] (ton·, bon·). The fashionable world. SOCIETY-LUDICROUSNESS.

to-nal'-i-ty. A system of tones; a scheme of colors. LIGHT-DARKNESS, MELODY-DISSONANCE.

tone. To harmonize; the timbre of an instrument; mood. AFFECTIONS, COLOR-ACHROMATISM, CONDITION-SITUATION, INCLINATION, MELODY-DISSONANCE, SOUND-SILENCE, STRENGTH-WEAKNESS, WAY, WHITENESS-BLACKNESS; **give a tone to,** SOCIETY-LUDICROUSNESS; **tone down,** COLOR-ACHROMATISM, LIGHT-DARKNESS, TURBULENCE-CALMNESS; **tone of voice,** VOCALIZATION-MUTENESS.

ton'-ga. A two-wheeled cart of British India. CONVEYANCE-VESSEL.

tongs. A pair of pivoted levers, often used in handling hot objects. KEEPING-RELINQUISHMENT, OVEN-REFRIGERATOR.

tongue. The organ of speech and of taste. CONVEXITY-CONCAVITY, LANGUAGE, SAVOR-TASTELESSNESS; **bite the tongue,** PUNGENCY; **bridle one's tongue,** SPEECH-INARTICULATENESS, TALKATIVENESS-TACITURNITY; **give tongue,** VOCALIZATION-MUTENESS; **have a tongue in one's head,** SPEECH-INARTICULATENESS; **hold one's tongue,** ENLIGHTENMENT-SECRECY, SOUND-SILENCE, TALKATIVENESS-TACITURNITY; **keep one's tongue between one's teeth,** TALKATIVENESS-TACITURNITY; **on the tip of one's tongue,** MANIFESTATION-LATENCY, REMEMBRANCE-FORGETFULNESS, REMOTENESS-NEARNESS, SPEECH-INARTICULATENESS; **slip of the tongue,** GRAMMAR-SOLECISM, SPEECH-INARTICULATENESS, TRUTH-ERROR; **tongue cleave to the roof of one's mouth,** ASTONISHMENT-EXPECTANCE; **tongue of land,** OCEAN-LAND; **tongue running loose,** TALKATIVENESS-TACITURNITY; **wag the tongue,** SPEECH-INARTICULATENESS.

tongue'-less. Without a tongue; mute. VOCALIZATION-MUTENESS.

tongue'-tied". Abnormal shortness of the fillet of the tongue. VOCALIZATION-MUTENESS.

ton'-ic. Bracing; the key-note in music. HEALTHINESS-UNHEALTHINESS, MELODY-DISSONANCE, REMEDY-BANE.

ton mauvais [F.] (ton· mo-vê'). Ill-breeding. TASTE-VULGARITY.

to-nic'-i-ty. Health. STRENGTH-WEAKNESS.

ton'-nage. The capacity of a vessel. GREATNESS-LITTLENESS.

ton'-sils. Organs in the throat. WATERCOURSE-AIRPIPE.

ton'-sure. The shaved part of a priest's head. VESTMENTS.

ton-tine'. A life annuity. OUTLAY-INCOME.

to'-ny. A simpleton. SAGE-FOOL.

To'-ny Lump'-kin. One of Goldsmith's characters in *She Stoops to Conquer.* GENTILITY-COMMONALTY.

too. Also; more than sufficiently. ADDITION-SUBTRACTION, EXCESS-LACK; **have too much of,** DESIRE-REPLETION; **in a too great degree,** MAGNITUDE-SMALLNESS; **make too much of,** OVERVALUATION-UNDERVALUATION; **too bad,** APPROVAL-DISAPPROVAL, REPUTATION-DISCREDIT, RIGHT-WRONG; **too clever by half,** CRAFT-ARTLESSNESS; **too far,** EXCESS-LACK; **too hot to hold one,** PLEASURABLENESS-PAINFULNESS; **too late,** EARLINESS-LATENESS; **too late for,** EARLINESS-LATENESS, OPPORTUNENESS-UNSUITABLENESS; **too little,** EXCESS-LACK; **too many,** EXCESS-LACK; **too much,** EXCESS-LACK, MODERATION-SELFINDULGENCE; **too much for,** POSSIBILITY-IMPOSSIBILITY; **too much of a good thing,** DESIRE-REPLETION; **too soon,** EARLINESS-LATENESS; **too soon for,** OPPORTUNENESS-UNSUITABLENESS; **too true,** CONTENTEDNESS-REGRET, JUBILATION-LAMENTATION.

tool. An instrument. ANTAGONIST-ASSISTANT, INSTRUMENT, MANAGEMENT, PRESUMPTION-OBSEQUIOUSNESS; **edge tool,** SHARPNESS-BLUNTNESS; **mere tool,** AGENT.

tooth. One of the hard structures of the jaw; a cog; palate; something resembling a tooth. ANATOMY, CONNECTIVE, CONVEXITY-CONCAVITY, INDENTATION, SAVOR-TASTELESSNESS, SHARPNESS-BLUNTNESS, SMOOTHNESS-ROUGHNESS, TEXTURE; **sweet tooth,** DESIRE-DISTASTE, DESIRE-PARTICULARNESS; **tooth and nail,** ATTACK-DEFENSE, TOIL-RELAXATION, TURBULENCE-CALMNESS.

toothed. Supplied with teeth. INDENTATION, SHARPNESS-BLUNTNESS.

tooth'-ful. Toothsome. PALATABLENESS-UNPALATABLENESS.

tooth'-some". Having a pleasant taste. PALATABLENESS-UNPALATABLENESS.

top. The highest part; a toy. COVER-LINING, REVOLUTION-EVOLUTION, SUPREMACY-SUBORDINACY, TOP-BOTTOM; **at the top of one's speed,** SWIFTNESS-SLOWNESS; **at the top of one's voice,** CRY-ULULATION, LOUDNESS-FAINTNESS; **at the top of the tree,** REPUTATION-DISCREDIT, TOP-BOTTOM; **fool to the top of one's bent,** TRUTHFULNESS-FRAUD; **from top to toe,** ENTIRETY-DEFICIENCY, LENGTH-SHORTNESS; **sleep like a top,** ACTIVITY-INDOLENCE; **top of the ladder,** REPUTATION-DISCREDIT; **top to bottom,** ENTIRETY-DEFICIENCY.

TOP—BOTTOM

Acme. The top or highest point.
Apex. The point or summit, as of a pyramid, mountain, etc.
Brow. The upper edge of a steep slope.
Cap. A covering at the top of anything.

Base. The part of an object on which the remainder rests.
Basement. The lower story of a building.
Basis. The fundamental principle; chief component part: foundation of a pillar or statue.

TOP—BOTTOM—*Continued.*

Climax. The point of greatest development; a ladder.
Crest. The highest ridge of a mountain; top of anything.
Crown. A perfect type; top; summit; crest.
Crowning point.
Culminating point. } The highest point.
Culmination. The condition of having arrived at the highest point.
End. The terminal point.
Fountain-head. Source.
Head. Upper part or beginning, as of a stream, valley; highest position, as of a party, army, etc.
Height. The utmost degree in anything.
Heights. Elevation of land; elevation of condition, as the heights of fame.
High places. High government offices.
Knob. A hard, round ball or protuberance, usually at the end of something.
Maximum. The greatest degree possible.
Meridian. The culminating point; the middle of the day.
Ne plus ultra [L.]. Uttermost point.
Nib. The point, as of a pen, crowbar, etc.
Noddle. The head: used contemptuously.
Peak. A projecting edge or point, as of a roof, mountain, etc.
Pinnacle. A height; a topmost point.
Pitch. Degree of elevation.
Summit. The highest part or top, as of a hill; highest degree.
Summity. Summit; perfection.
Tip. The point of something slender or small.
Tip-top. The very top.
Top. The upper extremity of anything.
Turn of the tide. The meridian; the height.
Turning-point. The important point or moment.
Utmost height. The highest point.
Vertex. The highest point, as of a dome or the sky.
Zenith. The point in the heavens directly overhead; the culminating point.

Top—*Denotations.*

Architrave. A beam supporting a roof.
Attic. A half story next to the roof.
Capital. The upper member of a column.
Ceiling. The overhead covering of a room.
Coping-stone. The top stone of a wall.
Cornice. The projection along the top of a building.
Crow's-nest. An elevated point of view.
Entablature. A projecting frieze or cornice.
Frieze. A projection of a building below the cornice.
Garret. That part of a house directly under the roof.
Housetop. The roof of a house.
Hurricane-deck. The highest deck about amidships.
Loft. A room under the roof.
Pate. The top of the head.
Pediment. A piece surmounting a door.
Pole. The extremity of an axis.
Quarter-deck. Part of the deck of a war-vessel.
Scone. A projecting candlestick.
Sky. The blue vault overhead.
Skyscraper. A tall building.
Topgallantmast. The mast above the topmast.
Truck. The upper extremity of a mast.
Upper story. A room or floor near the roof.
Water-parting. } The ridge of land from which water flows in different directions.
Watershed. }
Zoophorous [G.] A frieze.

Top—*Verbs.*

Crown. To place upon the top, like a crown.
Culminate. To arrive at the highest point of progress.

---

to'-paz. A mineral. EMBELLISHMENT-DISFIGUREMENT, YELLOWNESS-PURPLE.
top'–boot". A boot with a high top. DRESS-UNDRESS.
tope. A shrine; to drink excessively. FANE, FAUNA-FLORA, LIFE-FUNERAL, TEETOTALISM-INTEMPERANCE.
to'-per. An habitual drunkard. TEETOTALISM-INTEMPERANCE.
top'–full". Brimful. ENTIRETY-DEFICIENCY.
top"-gal'-lant. The parts of a deck that are higher than the rest. TOP-BOTTOM; **topgallantmast**, HEIGHT-LOWNESS, TOP-BOTTOM.

Bottom. Lowest part of anything.
Caudex. The trunk, as of a tree.
Foot. The last of a series or scale.
Footing. A place to stand, walk, or work on.
Foundation. The hidden structure upon which a building or machine rests.
Ground. That upon which we base belief, feeling, or action.
Groundwork. That which furnishes support for anything.
Plinth. A block of stone on which a column rests.
Root. That which furnishes support or is the origin of anything.
Sole. The part on which a thing rests in standing.
Substratum. A stratum immediately beneath another.
Substructure. The foundation; opposed to superstructure.
Toe. Lower end or projection of something.

Bottom—*Denotations.*

Bilge. The flat part of a ship's bottom.
Carpet. Floor-covering.
Dado. A flat surface between a base and surbase molding.
Deck. A platform or floor of a vessel.
Earth. The ground under foot.
Flag. A flat stone used for pavement.
Ground-floor. The floor next to the ground.
Hold. The part of a ship below the deck.
Hoof. The horny sheath encasing the feet of animals.
Keel. The lowest member of the framework of a vessel.
Nadir. The point of a celestial sphere directly beneath one.
Pavement. }
Paving. } The surface walked on.
Wainscot. A lining along the bottom of a wall.

Bottom—*Adjectives.*

Based on. Resting upon.
Bottom. Pertaining to the bottom.
Built on. }
Founded on. } Having under.
Fundamental. Constituting the foundation.
Grounded on. Built upon.
Nethermost. }
Undermost. } Lowest.

TOP—*Verbs—Continued.*

Overtop. To rise above the top of.
Top. To cover on the top.

Top—*Adjectives.*

Capital. First in importance.
Culminating, etc. Attaining the highest point. See *Verbs.*
Head. Pertaining to what is at the head of.
Highest. The topmost.
Meridian. }
Meridional. } See *Nouns.*
Polar. Pertaining to the axile extremities of the earth.
Supernal. Pertaining to heavenly regions or things.
Supreme. Highest, greatest, or most excellent.
Tip-top. Highest; best.
Top. Pertaining to the top.
Topgallant. Between the topmast and the royalmast.
Topmost. Pertaining to the very top.
Uppermost. The highest.

Top—*Adverbs, etc.*

A-top. On the top; above.
At the top of a tree. At the highest point.

Top—*Phrases.*

En flûte [F.]. With guns on the upper deck only.
Fleur d'eau [F.]. Even with the surface of the water.

---

top'-heav"-y. Ill-proportioned; tipsy. EQUALITY-INEQUALITY, REVERSAL, SECURITY-INSECURITY, TEETOTALISM-INTEMPERANCE.
To'-phet. Hell. HEAVEN-HELL.
top'-ic. A theme for discourse. CONCEPTION-THEME; **topic of the day**, TIDINGS-MYSTERY.
top'-ic-al. Local. POSITION.
to'-ping. Drinking excessively. TEETOTALISM-INTEMPERANCE.
top'-knot". A crest on the top of the head. EMBELLISHMENT-DISFIGUREMENT.

top'-mast. The mast next above the lower mast. HEIGHT-LOWNESS.

top'-most''. At the very top. TOP-BOTTOM.

top''-o-graph'-i-cal. Pertaining to topography. POSITION.

to-pog'-ra-phy. Physical features. GEOLOGY, POSITION.

top'-ple. To totter and fall. CREATION-DESTRUCTION, EQUALITY-INEQUALITY, REVERSAL, SUCCESS-FAILURE; **topple down,** ASCENT-DESCENT; **topple over,** ASCENT-DESCENT, EQUALITY-INEQUALITY.

top'-sail''. The sail next above the lowest. **Topsail schooner,** CONVEYANCE-VESSEL.

top'-saw''-yer. One who occupies a superior position. ADEPT-BUNGLER, CONSEQUENCE-INSIGNIFICANCE.

top''-sy-tur'-vy. Upside down. REGULARITY-IRREGULARITY, REVERSAL.

tor. A high hill. HEIGHT-LOWNESS.

torch. A flambeau. COMBUSTIBLE, LUMINARY-SHADE; **apply the torch,** EXCITATION, HEATING-COOLING; **light the torch of war,** FIGHTING-CONCILIATION; **torch of Hymen,** MATRIMONY-CELIBACY.

tor'-ment. Agony. PLEASURABLENESS-PAINFULNESS, PLEASURE-PAIN, SENSUALITY-SUFFERING; **place of torment,** HEAVEN-HELL.

Tormes, Lazarillo de [It.] (tor'-mês, läts-a-rîl'-lo dê). One of de Mendoza's characters. UPRIGHTNESS-ROGUE.

torn. Severed; rent. SWIFTNESS-SLOWNESS, TURBULENCE-CALMNESS, UNION-DISUNION, VARIANCE-ACCORD.

tor-na'-do. A violent storm. REVOLUTION-EVOLUTION, RIVER-WIND.

tor-pe'-do. A device containing an explosive. ACTIVITY-INDOLENCE, BENEFACTOR-EVILDOER, REMEDY-BANE, WEAPON.

tor-pes'-cent. Becoming torpid. ACTIVITY-INDOLENCE.

tor'-pid. Sluggish. ACTIVITY-INDOLENCE, SENSITIVENESS-APATHY, VIGOR-INERTIA.

tor-pid'-i-ty. State or quality of being torpid. ACTIVITY-INDOLENCE.

tor'-por. Stupor. ACTIVITY-INDOLENCE, SENSITIVENESS-APATHY, VIGOR-INERTIA.

torque. A necklace. EMBELLISHMENT-DISFIGUREMENT.

tor''-re-fac'-tion. Drying by heat. HEATING-COOLING.

tor'-re-fy. Expose to extreme heat. HEATING-COOLING.

tor'-rent. A cascade. RIVER-WIND, SWIFTNESS-SLOWNESS, TURBULENCE-CALMNESS; **rain in torrents,** RIVER-WIND.

tor'-rid. Very sultry. HEAT-COLD.

tor'-sion. The state of being twisted. CIRCLE-WINDING.

tort. Any wrongful act. DUENESS-UNDUENESS.

tort et à travers, à [F.] (tort ê a tra-vêr', a). At cross-purposes. ADAGE-NONSENSE, DETERMINATION-VACILLATION, HARMONY-DISCORD.

tor'-tile. Coiled. CIRCLE-WINDING.

tor'-tious. Of the nature of a tort. DUENESS-UNDUENESS.

tor'-tive. Twisted. CIRCLE-WINDING.

tor'-toise. A turtle. SWIFTNESS-SLOWNESS.

tor'-toise–shell''. The shell of the sea-turtle. VARIEGATION.

tor'-tu-ous. Twisting; erratic. CIRCLE-WINDING, UPRIGHTNESS-DISHONESTY.

tor'-ture. Extreme suffering. CHARITABLENESS-MALEVOLENCE, PLEASURABLENESS-PAINFULNESS, PLEASURE-PAIN, RECOMPENSE-PUNITION, SENSUALITY-SUFFERING; **torture a question,** RATIOCINATION-INSTINCT.

tor'-vi-ty. Severity of countenance. FAVORITE-MOROSENESS.

To-ry. A member of one of the old English political parties. ASSOCIATION.

toss. To throw; agitate. AGITATION, ORGANIZATION-DISORGANIZATION, PUSH-PULL, VIBRATION; **toss in a blanket,** REGARD-DISRESPECT; **toss off,** NUTRIMENT-EXCRETION, TEETOTALISM-INTEMPERANCE; **toss on one's pillow,** EXCITABILITY-INEXCITABILITY; **toss overboard,** CHOICE-REJECTION; **toss the head,** PRESUMPTION-OBSEQUIOUSNESS, REGARD-SCORN, SELF-RESPECT-HUMBLENESS; **toss up,** PURPOSE-LUCK, RATIONALE-LUCK.

toss'-pot''. A drunkard. TEETOTALISM-INTEMPERANCE.

to'-tal. Complete amount. WHOLE-PART; **total abstinence,** AUSTERITY, MODERATION-SELFINDULGENCE; **total eclipse,** LIGHT-DARKNESS.

to-tal'-i-ty. The state of being whole or entire. WHOLE-PART.

to'-tal-ly. Completely. ENTIRETY-DEFICIENCY, WHOLE-PART.

to'-tal-ness. Totality. WHOLE-PART.

to'-tem. An object used by savages as an emblem of individual or clan. SIGN.

totidem verbis [L.] (tot'-i-dem ver'-bis). In so many words. IMITATION-ORIGINALITY, TRUTH-ERROR.

toties quoties [L.] (to'-shi-îz quo'-shi-îz). As often as. FREQUENCY-RARITY.

totis viribus [L.] (to'-tis vir-i-bus). With all his might. TOIL-RELAXATION.

toto, in [L.] (to'-to, in). Entirely. ENTIRETY-DEFICIENCY.

toto cælo [L.] (to'-to sî'-lo). By the whole heaven. ENTIRETY-DEFICIENCY.

tot'-ter. To waver. AGITATION, BETTERMENT-DETERIORATION, MUTABILITY-STABILITY, SECURITY-INSECURITY, STRENGTH-WEAKNESS, SWIFTNESS-SLOWNESS, VARIATION; **totter to its fall,** BETTERMENT-DETERIORATION, CREATION-DESTRUCTION.

tot'-ter-ing. About to fall. BETTERMENT-DETERIORATION, SECURITY-INSECURITY, STRENGTH-WEAKNESS.

touch. To be in contact with; to affect. ACTION-PASSIVENESS, COMPASSION-RUTHLESSNESS, CONNECTION-INDEPENDENCE, EXCITATION, FAVORITE-QUARRELSOMENESS, GIVING-RECEIVING, INTERSPACE-CONTACT, MAGNITUDE-SMALLNESS, MIXTURE-HOMOGENEITY, MUSICIAN, SIGN, TOUCH, TRIAL; **touch and go,** DIFFICULTY-FACILITY, EARLINESS-LATENESS, ETERNITY-INSTANTANEITY, MUTABILITY-STABILITY; **touch the guitar,** MUSICIAN; **touch the hat,** POLITENESS-IMPOLITENESS; **touch the heart,** EXCITATION; **touch on,** MEANING-JARGON; **touch to the quick,** SENSITIVENESS; **touch up,** BETTERMENT-DETERIORATION; **touch upon,** ESSAY.

TOUCH.

Feeling. The sense of touch; hence, general sensation.

Manipulation. The art of working by hand.

Palpability. The quality of being perceptible to the touch.

Palpation. The act of feeling.

Tact. Touch; perception.

Tactility. Capable of being touched or felt.

Taction. The act of touching.

Touch. The act of touching or being in contact; the sense of feeling.

TOUCH—*Nouns of Agent.*

Antenna. A movable organ of touch attached to the heads of insects.

Feeler. One of the sense organs of certain animals used in testing animals by touch.

Finger. One of the five terminating members of the hand, the chief organs of touch.

Forefinger. The finger next to the thumb.

Hand. That part of the fore limb attached to the lower extremity of the forearm, adapted for grasping.
Paw. The hand of an animal.
Thumb. The first digit of the human hand, which differs from the others in having but two phalanges.

TOUCH—*Verbs.*

Feel. To perceive, as by the touch.
Finger. To touch or handle with the fingers.
Fumble. To handle clumsily.
Grabble. To feel with the hands.
Grope. To search out by feeling in the dark.
Handle. To touch or feel with the hands.
Manipulate. To handle skilfully.
Pass the fingers over. To feel lightly with the fingers.
Paw. To touch or scrape with the feet or paws.
Run the fingers over. To touch lightly and quickly with the fingers.
Throw out a feeler. A proposal or observation thrown out to touch the feelings of others.
Thumb. To feel with the thumb.
Touch. To come in contact with.
Tweedle. To handle lightly.
Twiddle. To touch lightly.
Wield. To manage; to handle.

TOUCH—*Adjectives.*

Lambent. Touching lightly.
Palpable. Perceptible by touch or feeling.
Tactile. Of or pertaining to touch.
Tactual. Tangible.
Tangible. Perceptible by touch or the senses

touched. Affected; slightly insane. CLEANNESS-FILTHINESS, COMPASSION-RUTHLESSNESS, SANENESS-LUNACY; **touched in the wind**, HEALTH-SICKNESS; **touched with**, EMOTION.
touch'-ing. Affecting. INTERSPACE-CONTACT, PLEASURABLENESS-PAINFULNESS.
touch'-stone''. A testing-stone. TRIAL.
touch'-wood''. A combustible wood used as tinder. COMBUSTIBLE, FAVORITE-QUARRELSOMENESS.
touch'-y. Irascible. FAVORITE-QUARRELSOMENESS.
tough. Laborious; susceptible of great tension; a rowdy. CITY-COUNTRY, COHESION-LOOSENESS, DIFFICULTY-FACILITY, TOUGHNESS-BRITTLENESS.
tough'-ness. Tenacity. COHESION-LOOSENESS, TOUGHNESS-BRITTLENESS.

TOUGHNESS—BRITTLENESS.

Cohesion. The state of holding tightly together. See COHESION.
Sequacity. State of being pliable.
Strength. The ability to withstand the application of force without tearing apart.
Stubbornness. Tenacity of will. See BIGOTRY.
Tenacity. The quality of a body by which it resists being pulled or forced apart.
Toughness. Quality of being susceptible to great strain or tension without breaking.

TOUGHNESS—*Denotations.*

Cartilage. An elastic animal tissue of firm consistence.
Gristle. Cartilage.
Leather. The skin or hide of an animal tanned or dressed for use.

TOUGHNESS—*Verbs.*

Be tenacious. To be difficult to pull apart.
Resist fracture. To overcome a power that tries to break.

TOUGHNESS—*Adjectives.*

Cartilaginous. Tenacious, like cartilage.
Coriaceous. Resembling leather in tenacity.
Gristly. Tough, like gristle.
Leathery. Of the tenacity of leather.
Resisting. Withstanding; tenacious.
Sequacious. Ductile and pliable, as wire. See *Nouns.*
Stringy. Sinewy; fibrous.
Strong. Having the power to withstand force without tearing apart.
Stubborn. Of tenacious purpose. See BIGOTRY.
Tenacious. Holding fast; adhesive.
Tough. Not separated easily.
Tough as whit-leather. Extremely tenacious and hard to separate.

BRITTLENESS—ADJECTIVES—*Continued from Column 2.*

Lacerable. Capable of being torn.
Shivery. Easily falling into pieces.
Short. Brittle· friable.
Splintery. Breaking into splinters.
Splitting. Causing to split; bursting. See *Verbs.*

Brittleness. State of being brittle. See *Adjectives.*
Fissility. The quality of being fissile, or easily split into layers. See *Adjectives.*
Fragility. Liability to be broken.
Frangibility. The quality of being easily broken.
Friability. The state of being brittle and reducible to powder.

BRITTLENESS—*Denotations.*

House of cards. } Anything that is very liable to fall or break to
House of glass. } pieces.

BRITTLENESS—*Verbs.*

Be brittle. To be liable to break. See *Adjectives.*
Break. Separate into parts.
Break short. To break violently; snap.
Burst. To break open violently.
Crack. To break partially.
Crumble. To break into small pieces.
Crumble into dust. }
Crumble to dust. } To break and grind into dust.
Fall to pieces. To break into small parts.
Fly. To part violently; to burst into pieces.
Give way. To break, as under a weight.
Live in a glass house. Figurative for being open to attack; such persons should not throw stones.
Shiver. To break suddenly into small pieces.
Snap. To break with a sudden crack.
Splinter. To split into fragments.
Split. To tear apart longitudinally.

BRITTLENESS—*Adjectives.*

Brittle. Liable to break.
Brittle as glass. As easy to break as glass.
Crimp. Crumbled easily; brittle.
Crisp. Easily crumbled.
Fissile. Easily split.
Fragile. Easily broken.
Frail. So constituted as to be broken easily.
Frangible. Capable of being broken.
Gimcrack. Cheap, showy, and frail.

(Continued on Column 1.)

toujours perdrix [F.] (tu-zhur' per-dri'). Always partridges; no change. DESIRE-REPLETION, ENTERTAINMENT-WEARINESS, RECURRENCE.
tou-pee'. A little tuft. SMOOTHNESS-ROUGHNESS.
tour. A journey. TRAVELING-NAVIGATION.
tour'-ist. One who makes a tour. WAYFARER-SEAFARER.
tour'-na-ment. A contest. ENTERTAINMENT-WEARINESS, STRIFE-PEACE.
tour'-ni-quet. A medical instrument for stopping the flow of blood. PERFORATOR-STOPPER.
tour-nure'. Outline. APPEARANCE-DISAPPEARANCE, OUTLINE.

tournure, belle [F.] (tur-nür', bel). Beautiful form. BEAUTY-UGLINESS.
tours de force [F.] (tur de fors). A feat of strength or skill. ACTION-PASSIVENESS, CRAFT-ARTLESSNESS, POMP, SKILL-UNSKILFULNESS.
tous les rapports, sous [F.] (tu lê ra-por', su). In all respects. TRUTH-ERROR.
touse. To stir up, as a row. PUSH-PULL.
tou'-sle. To tangle; confuse. ORGANIZATION-DISORGANIZATION.
tout. To solicit patronage. PETITION-EXPOSTULATION.

tout-à-l'heure [F.] (tut'-a-lur'). Instantly. ETERNITY-INSTANTANEITY.

tout au contraire [F.] (tut o con'-trêr'). Everything to the contrary. ASSERTION-DENIAL, SAMENESS-CONTRAST.

tout court [F.] (tu cur). To be at a stand. MOVEMENT-REST.

tout ensemble [F.] (tut an'-san·bl'). The whole. WHOLE-PART.

tout outrance [F.] (tut u-tran·s'). To the utmost. MAGNITUDE-SMALLNESS.

tout'-er. One who solicits patronage. CONSIGNEE, FLATTERER-DEFAMER, PETITIONER.

tow. To drag through the water. PUSH-PULL; **take in tow,** OBSTRUCTION-HELP, PUSH-PULL.

to'-ward-ly. Docile. DIFFICULTY-FACILITY.

to-wards. Leading to; facing. AIM-ABERRATION; **draw towards,** ATTRACTION-REPULSION; **move towards,** APPROACH-WITHDRAWAL.

tow'-el. A cloth for drying; to thrash. CLEANNESS-FILTHINESS, RECOMPENSE-PUNITION.

tow'-er. A very tall structure; to soar; a citadel. ARCHITECTURE, ASCENT-DESCENT, ATTACK-DEFENSE, CREATION-DESTRUCTION, DWELLER-HABITATION, HEIGHT-LOWNESS, MUTABILITY-STABILITY; **tower of strength,** ATTACK-DEFENSE, DOMINANCE-IMPOTENCE.

tow'-er-ing. Lofty. GREATNESS-LITTLENESS, HEIGHT-LOWNESS, MAGNITUDE-SMALLNESS; **towering passion,** FAVORITE-ANGER.

town. A collection of dwellings. CITY-COUNTRY, DWELLER-HABITATION, SOCIETY-LUDICROUSNESS; **all over the town,** TIDINGS-MYSTERY; **man about town,** SOCIETY-DANDY; **on the town,** PURITY-IMPURITY; **talk of the town,** CONVERSATION-MONOLOGUE, REPUTATION-DISCREDIT; **town hall,** TRIBUNAL; **town talk,** CONVERSATION-MONOLOGUE, TIDINGS-MYSTERY.

town'-ship. A division of a county. EXTENSION-DISTRICT, MEASURE.

towns'-man. A fellow citizen. DWELLER-HABITATION.

tow'-path". A path along any body of water, used by horses, etc., in towing boats. WAY.

tox'-ic. Pertaining to poison. HEALTHINESS-UNHEALTHINESS.

tox"-i-col'-o-gy. The science of poisons. REMEDY-BANE.

tox-oph'-i-lite. One devoted to archery. PUSH-PULL.

toy. A plaything; to trifle; dalliance. BLANDISHMENT, CONSEQUENCE-INSIGNIFICANCE, ENTERTAINMENT-WEARINESS; **toy dog,** FAUNA-FLORA.

toy'-shop". A shop for the sale of toys. ENTERTAINMENT-WEARINESS.

tracasserie [F.] (tra-cas-rî'). Treachery. VARIANCE-ACCORD.

trace. To follow. DELINEATION-CARICATURE, DISCOVERY, INVESTIGATION-ANSWER, MARK-OBLITERATION, SIGN; **trace back,** FUTURE-PAST, REMEMBRANCE-FORGETFULNESS; **trace out,** DISCOVERY; **trace to,** RATIONALE-LUCK; **trace up,** INVESTIGATION-ANSWER.

tra'-ce-ry. Ornamental work of ramifying lines. ARCHITECTURE, CROSSING, CURVATION-RECTILINEARITY, EMBELLISHMENT-DISFIGUREMENT.

tra'-ces. Parts of a set of harness. CONNECTIVE.

tra'-che-a. The windpipe. WATERCOURSE-AIRPIPE.

tra'-cing. That which is traced. DELINEATION-CARICATURE.

track. To trace; trail. INVESTIGATION-ANSWER, MARK-OBLITERATION, WAY.

track'-less. Untrodden. DIFFICULTY-FACILITY, EXTENSION-DISTRICT.

tract. An extended area; a short treatise. ESSAY, EXTENSION-DISTRICT, MISSIVE-PUBLICATION; **tract of time,** PERIOD-PROGRESS.

tract'-a-ble. Docile; readily worked. DIFFICULTY-FACILITY, HARDNESS-SOFTNESS, READINESS-RELUCTANCE.

Trac-ta'-ri-an. A member of the High-church party in England. ORTHODOXY-HETERODOXY.

Trac-ta'-ri-an-ism. The doctrines of the Tractarians. ORTHODOXY-HETERODOXY.

tract'-ate. A short treatise. ESSAY, MISSIVE-PUBLICATION.

trac-ta'-tion. Discussion. ESSAY.

trac'-tile. Ductile. HARDNESS-SOFTNESS, PUSH-PULL.

trac-til'-i-ty. Ductility. HARDNESS-SOFTNESS.

trac'-tion. The act of drawing. AIM-ABERRATION, PUSH-PULL.

trade. Exchange; mercantile traffic. EXCHANGE, OCCUPATION; **drive a trade,** OCCUPATION; **learn one's trade,** EDUCATION-LEARNING; **trade with,** EXCHANGE; **tricks of the trade,** CRAFT-ARTLESSNESS; **two of a trade,** ANTAGONISM-CONCURRENCE.

trade'-mark". A mark to distinguish a merchant's goods. SIGN.

tra'-der. One who trades. DEALER.

trades'-man. A shopkeeper. DEALER.

trade'-un"-ion. An association of workmen. ASSOCIATION.

trade'-wind". A wind on the sea which is sought by traders. RIVER-WIND.

tra-di'-tion. The transmission of knowledge by word of mouth. ACCOUNT, NOVELTY-ANTIQUITY.

tra-di'-tion-al. Belonging to tradition. ACCOUNT, NOVELTY-ANTIQUITY.

tra-di'-tion-a-ry. Founded on tradition. ACCOUNT.

tra-duce'. To slander. ADULATION-DISPARAGEMENT.

tra-du'-cer. One who slanders. FLATTERER-DEFAMER.

traf'-fic. Trade. EXCHANGE.

tra-ge'-di-an. An actor. ACTING.

tra"-ge"-dienne'. An actress of tragedy. ACTING.

trag'-e-dy. A drama in which a fatal event occurs. ACTING, GOOD-EVIL.

trag'-ic. Pertaining to tragedy. ACTING.

trag'-ic-al. Involving death. PLEASURABLENESS-PAINFULNESS.

trag"-i-com'-e-dy. A drama of tragic and comic scenes. ACTING.

trag"-i-com'-ic. That which is both tragic and comic. SOCIETY-LUDICROUSNESS.

trail. To follow; to drag after; a track. INVESTIGATION-ANSWER, MARK-OBLITERATION, ODOR-INODOROUSNESS, PREDECESSOR-CONTINUATION, PUSH-PULL, SUSPENSION-SUPPORT, SWIFTNESS-SLOWNESS; **follow in the trail of,** LEADING-FOLLOWING; **trail of a red herring,** MOTIVE-CAPRICE.

train. To educate; discipline; anything drawn out; a retinue. ACTING, ANTERIORITY-POSTERIORITY, CONTINUITY-INTERRUPTION, CONVEYANCE-VESSEL, DOMESTICATION-AGRICULTURE, EDUCATION-MISTEACHING, HABIT-DESUETUDE, LEADING-FOLLOWING, PREDECESSOR-CONTINUATION, PREPARATION-NONPREPARATION, PUSH-PULL, SUSPENSION-SUPPORT; **bring in its train,** MOTIVE-CAPRICE; **in the train of,** CHIEF-UNDERLING, LEADING-FOLLOWING; **in train,** PREPARATION-NONPREPARATION; **lay a train,** DESIGN, PREPARATION-NONPREPARATION; **put in train,** PREPARATION-NONPREPARATION; **siege-train,** WEAPON; **train of reasoning,** RATIOCINATION-INSTINCT; **train of thought,** REFLECTION-VACANCY.

train'-band". A militia organization. BELLIGERENT.

train'-bear"-er. An attendant who carries the train. CHIEF-UNDERLING.

trained. Educated. SKILL-UNSKILFULNESS.

train'-er. One who trains. DOMESTICATION-AGRICULTURE, INSTRUCTOR-PUPIL, WAYFARER-SEAFARER.

train'-ing. Education. EDUCATION-MISTEACHING,

HABIT-DESUETUDE, PREPARATION-NONPREPARATION.

train'-oil''. Oil from the fat of whales. PULPINESS-OIL.

traipse. A saunter. SWIFTNESS-SLOWNESS.

trait. A characteristic. ACCOUNT, APPEARANCE-DISAPPEARANCE, SIGN, UNIVERSALITY-PARTICULARITY.

trai'-tor. A betrayer. INSUBORDINATION-OBEDIENCE, UPRIGHTNESS-ROGUE.

tra-jec'-tion. A throwing over or through. ADMISSION-EXPULSION.

tra-ject'-o-ry. The path of a projectile. WAY.

tral''-a-ti'-tious. Legendary. TROPE.

tra-lin'-e-ate. To deviate. AIM-ABERRATION.

tra-lu'-cent. Allowing light to pass through. DIAPHANEITY-OPAQUENESS.

tram. A street-car. CONVEYANCE-VESSEL.

tram'-mel. An impediment. OBSTRUCTION-HELP, RELEASE-PRISON, RELEASE-RESTRAINT; **cast trammels off,** RELEASE-RESTRAINT.

tra-mon'-tane. Beyond the mountains. CONSTITUENT-ALIEN, REMOTENESS-NEARNESS, RIVER-WIND, TASTE-VULGARITY.

tramp. To walk with heavy steps; to wander; a vagabond. GENTILITY-COMMONALTY, TRAVELING-NAVIGATION, WAYFARER-SEAFARER; **on the tramp,** MOVEMENT-REST.

tramp'-er. One who or that which tramps. WAYFARER-SEAFARER.

tram'-ple. Tread under foot. **Trample in the dust,** CREATION-DESTRUCTION, ELEVATION-DEPRESSION; **trample out,** CREATION DESTRUCTION; **trample under foot,** CREATION-DESTRUCTION, DUTY-DERELICTION, HARSHNESS-MILDNESS, OBSERVANCE-NONOBSERVANCE, PRESUMPTION-OBSEQUIOUSNESS, REGARD-SCORN, REPUTATION-DISCREDIT, SUCCESS-FAILURE; **trample upon,** GOODNESS-BADNESS, HARSHNESS-MILDNESS.

tram'-road''. A street-railroad. WAY.

tram'-way''. A street-railroad. WAY.

trance. A state of insensibility. ACTIVITY-INDOLENCE, FANCY, SENSITIVENESS-APATHY.

tranchant [F.] (tran'-shan'). Decisive. DETERMINATION-VACILLATION.

tran'-quil. Quiet. STRIFE-PEACE, TURBULENCE-CALMNESS, VARIANCE-ACCORD; **tranquil mind,** EXCITABILITY-INEXCITABILITY.

tran''-quil-i-za'-tion. The act of tranquilizing, or state of being tranquilized. TURBULENCE-CALMNESS.

tran'-quil-ize. To soothe. FIGHTING-CONCILIATION, TURBULENCE-CALMNESS.

tran-quil'-li-ty. A state of rest. MOVEMENT-REST, STRIFE-PEACE.

trans-act'. To do business. ACTION-PASSIVENESS, CONDUCT; **transact business,** OCCUPATION; **transact business with,** EXCHANGE.

trans-ac'-tion. The management of an affair. ACTION-PASSIVENESS, CONDUCT, OCCURRENCE-DESTINY.

trans-ac'-tions. The reports of societies. **Transactions of,** MARK-OBLITERATION.

trans-al'-pine. Across the Alps. REMOTENESS-NEARNESS

trans-an''-i-ma'-tion. Transmigration of souls. MUTATION-PERMANENCE.

trans''-at-lan'-tic. Across the Atlantic. REMOTENESS-NEARNESS.

trans-ca'-len-cy. The property of conducting heat. HEATING-COOLING.

tran-scend'. To surpass. FAULTLESSNESS-FAULTINESS, GOODNESS-BADNESS, MAGNITUDE-SMALLNESS, SUPREMACY-SUBORDINACY, TRANSCURSION-SHORTCOMING.

tran-scend'-ence. Act or quality of surpassing. FAULTLESSNESS-FAULTINESS, TRANSCURSION-SHORTCOMING.

tran-scend'-en-cy. Surpassing eminence. EXCESS-LACK.

tran-scend'-ent. Surpassing. REPUTATION-DISCREDIT, SUPREMACY-SUBORDINACY.

tran''-scen-den'-tal. Of very high degree. CLEARNESS-OBSCURITY, UNIVERSALITY-PARTICULARITY.

tran''-scen-den'-tal-ism. That which is vague. CLEARNESS-OBSCURITY, MIND-IMBECILITY.

trans'-co-late. To filter. ENTRANCE-EXIT.

tran-scribe'. To copy. IMITATION-ORIGINALITY, WRITING-PRINTING.

tran'-script. A copy. COPY-MODEL, WRITING-PRINTING.

tran-scrip'-tion. A copying. COPY-MODEL, IMITATION-ORIGINALITY, WRITING-PRINTING.

trans-cur'-sion. Overrunning. TRANSCURSION-SHORTCOMING.

TRANSCURSION—SHORTCOMING.

Encroachment. Intrusion on the rights of another.

Extravagation. A wandering beyond limits.

Infringement. Act of infringing; transgression.

Redundance. Excess; superabundance. See EXCESS.

Transcendence. Exaggeration.

Transcursion. A passage over bounds.

Transgression. The act of passing beyond any law.

Transilience. A leap from one thing to another.

Trespass. Infringement; transgression.

TRANSCURSION—*Verbs.*

Beat. To surpass.

Beat hollow. To greatly surpass.

Come to the front. To take the most advanced position.

Distance. To greatly excel.

Encroach. To enter gradually or stealthily into the possessions of another.

Exceed. To go beyond; surpass.

Go beyond. To surpass; overreach.

Go by. To pass over; omit.

Infringe. To encroach upon.

Intrench on. To trespass on.

Leave in the lurch. To leave behind; to forsake.

Leave in the rear. To leave behind; to surpass

Outdo. To excel; surpass.

Outgo. To go beyond.

Outjump. To surpass in jumping.

Outleap. To surpass in leaping.

Outride. To surpass in riding.

Defalcation. A deducting; fraudulent appropriation of money.

Default. A failure in an obligation or duty.

Failure. The act of failing; non-performance. See SUCCESS-FAILURE.

Falling short. A proving deficient. See *Verbs.*

Imperfection. Lack of completeness. See FAULTLESSNESS-FAULTINESS.

Incompleteness. Want of completeness; a deficiency in some of its parts. See ENTIRETY-DEFICIENCY.

Insufficiency. Want of sufficiency; inadequateness. See EXCESS-LACK.

Labor in vain. A labor that accomplishes nothing.

Leeway. A gradual falling behind or away from a set course.

No go. No use.

Non-completion. Failure of completion. See COMPLETION-NON-COMPLETION.

Shortcoming. A failure in duty; a failing of the usual quantity.

SHORTCOMING—*Verbs.*

Break down. To fail in an undertaking.

Cave in. To yield.

Collapse. To fall in or fail.

Come short. } To be deficient.
Come short of. }

Come to nothing. To fail completely.

End in smoke. To fail.

Fail. To prove inadequate; to be found wanting.

Fall short. } To prove deficient.
Fall short of. }

TRANSCURSION—SHORTCOMING—*Continued*.

TRANSCURSION—Verbs—*Continued*.

Outrival. To surpass or excel in rivalry
Outrun. To surpass in running.
Outstep. To surpass in stepping.
Outstrip. To excel; surpass.
Overgo. To exceed; surpass.
Overjump. To omit.
Overlap. To lie or be folded partly upon.
Overleap. To leap over; hence, to omit.
Overpass. To omit; disregard.
Overreach. To reach too far; cheat.
Override. To supersede.
Overshoot the mark. To venture too far.
Overskip. To jump over.
Overstep. To transgress.
Pass. To go by.
Pass the Rubicon. To take a decisive step.
Shoot ahead of. To outstrip, surpass.
Show in front. To be in the lead.
Soar. To fly aloft. See ASCENT.
Steal a march upon. To gain an advantage stealthily.
Strain. To carry beyond the proper limit.
Strain a point. To exceed one s duty.
Stretch a point. To carry beyond the truth.
Surmount. To overcome; surpass.
Surpass. To excel, go beyond in anything good or bad.
Throw into the shade. To surpass utterly.
Transcend. To go beyond; excel.
Transgress. To pass beyond; infringe.
Trench upon. To encroach upon.
Trespass. To pass beyond a limit; transgress.

TRANSCURSION—*Adjective*.

Surpassing. Going beyond. See *Verbs*.

TRANSCURSION—*Adverbs, etc*.

Ahead. At the head; in advance.
Beyond the mark. Without the limit.

---

tran′-sept. A part of a cruciform church. FANE.
trans-fer′. To remove from one place to another. ESTABLISHMENT-REMOVAL.
trans′-fer. A removal from one place, person, or condition to another. ALIENATION, TRANSFER.

TRANSFER.

Amotion. Removal, as from office.
Carriage. A transportation.
Carrying. The act of transporting from one place to another.
Cartage. }
Carting. } Carriage or conveyance as in a cart.
Conduction. Transmission; transportation.
Contagion. Transference of disease.
Convection. The act of conveying.
Conveyance. Transportation; transmission.
Deportation. The act of transferring.
Dispersion. The act of dispersing. See GATHERING-SCATTERING.
Displacement. The act of transferring from its place.
Dodging. Transference with a sudden start.
Draft. The act of drawing.
Drift. A driving or carrying onward by a current.
Elocation. A transference from the usual place of residence; displacement.
Extradition. The surrender by a government of a person accused of crime to a government within whose jurisdiction the crime was committed.
Ferry. A system for the regular transportation of passengers.
Freight. Transportation as by freight.
Gestation. The act of carrying young in the uterus.
Metastasis [Gr.] A transference of a disease from one part to another.
Metathesis [Gr.] A transfer of letters or sounds for the sake of euphony
Passage. Movement from one place to another.
Portage. Carriage, especially of boats or stores.
Porterage. Transportation.
Relegation. The act of transferring to an obscure position.
Remotion. Transference.
Removal. The act of removing.
Shifting. Transfer of place, form, or character.

SHORTCOMING—Verbs—*Continued*.

Fall through. }
Fall to the ground. } To fail.
Keep within bounds. }
Keep within compass. } To limit or restrain.
Keep within the mark. }
Lose ground. To fall back.
Miss stays. To fail in an attempt to tack a ship.
Miss the mark. To fail to accomplish.
Not reach. To fail in an attempt.
Stick in the mud. To be hindered or defeated in one's attempts.
Stop short. }
Stop short of. } To fail after almost accomplishing.
Want. To be insufficient; fall short.

SHORTCOMING—*Adjectives*.

Deficient. Lacking in necessary qualities.
Minus. Deprived of.
Out of depth. Beyond one's power.
Perfunctory. Done carelessly; negligent. See CAREFULNESS-CARELESSNESS.
Short. }
Short of. } Deficient in.
Unreached. Unattained.

SHORTCOMING—*Adverbs, etc*.

Behindhand. Behind a proper stage of progress; late.
Far from it. Failing.
Re infecta [L.] The work being unfinished.
To no purpose. Without accomplishing anything.
Within bounds. }
Within compass. } Limited; restrained.
Within the mark. }

SHORTCOMING—*Phrase*.

The bubble bursts.

Shipment. The act of shipping anything.
Shoveling. Moving or gathering with a shovel. See *Verbs*.
Traction. The act of drawing or state of being drawn. See PUSH-PULL.
Transfer. The act of removing or causing to pass from one person or place to another. See ALIENATION.
Transference. Transfer.
Transit. The act of carrying across or through.
Transition. Passage from one place, condition, or action to another.
Translation. Transference from one language to another.
Translocation. A transfer of things from one place to another.
Transmission. The act of passing from one to another.
Transplantation. The act of transferring and planting in another place.
Transport. A transfer from one place to another.
Transportation. Carriage of persons or commodities from one place to another.
Transposition. Transfer of things, each in the place of another. See COMMUTATION-PERMUTATION.
Transumption. The act of taking from one place to another.
Vection. }
Vectitation. } The act of carrying.
Vecture. }
Wafting. A carrying, as by the air or water.

TRANSFER—*Verbs*

Bear. To convey; carry.
Bring. To convey or carry toward the place where the speaker is.
Carry. To transfer from one place to another.
Carry over. To transport.
Conduct. To manage; carry on.
Consign. To transfer into the care of another.
Convey. To transfer from one to another; transport.
Convoy. To convey.
Decant. To transfer gently, as liquor.
Delegate. To transfer or entrust authority or right to act.
Deliver. To transfer from evil or injury.
Displace. To transfer from its place.
Draft off. To draw off.
Drag. To pull along by main force.
Embark. To go on board a boat.
Ferry over. To convey on a float over a body of water.
Fetch. To bring.

Fetch and carry. To perform menial tasks, as a dog.
Hand forward. To transmit.
Ladle. To transfer with a ladle.
Pass forward. To advance.
Reach. To transfer to another; extend to.
Relegate. To transfer; send into exile.
Send. To cause to be transferred.
Shift. To transfer from one place to another.
Ship. To transfer by carriage on a ship.
Shovel. To transfer by shoveling.
Shunt. To transfer to one side.
Throw. To fling hurl, or cast forth. See PUSH.
Transfer. The act of removing from one place to another.
Transfuse. To transfer by pouring, as a fluid.
Transmit. To send through or hand down; transfer.
Transplace. To transfer from one place to another.
Transplant. To transfer and plant in another place.
Transport. To transfer or carry from one place to another.
Transpose. To change in place or order.
Transpossess. To change from one ownership to another. See COMMUTATION-PERMUTATION.
Turn over to. To put in other control.
Waft. To transfer gently and lightly with a fluctuating motion in a buoyant medium.

TRANSFER—*Adjectives.*

Contagious. Transferable by contact.
Drifted. Carried along gently or unconsciously.
Efferent. Carrying outward.
Movable. Capable of being transferred.
Portable. Readily removed from one place to another.
Portative. Capable of carrying.
Transferred. Removed to another place. See *Verbs.*

TRANSFER—*Adverbs, etc.*

As one goes. On the way.
By the way. Along one's route or way.
Chemin faisant [F.] By the way.
En passant [F.] In passing.
En route [F.] On the way.
From hand to hand. From one person to another.
From pillar to post. Hither and thither.
In mid-progress. In the midst of the way.
In transitu [L.] On the passage.
On the road.⎫
On the way. ⎬Going from one place to another.
On the wing.⎭

trans-fer′-ence. The act of transferring. MUTATION-PERMANENCE, TRANSFER.
trans-fig″-ur-a′-tion. The act of being made glorious. CEREMONIAL, MUTATION-PERMANENCE.
trans-fig′-ure. To make glorious. MUTATION-PERMANENCE.
trans-fix′. To pierce through. APERTURE-CLOSURE.
trans-fixed′. Impaled. MUTABILITY-STABILITY.
trans-form′. Metamorphose. MUTATION-PERMANENCE.
trans″-for-ma′-tion. A change. ACTING.
trans-fuse′. To pour from one vessel to another. MIXTURE-HOMOGENEITY, TRANSFER; **transfuse the sense of,** INTERPRETATION-MISINTERPRETATION.
trans-fu′-sion. A pouring out. MIXTURE-HOMOGENEITY.
trans-gress′. To overpass; violate. DUTY-DERELICTION, OBSERVANCE-NONOBSERVANCE, TRANSCURSION-SHORTCOMING, VIRTUE-VICE.
trans-gres′-sion. Sin. DUTY-DERELICTION, INNOCENCE-GUILT, TRANSCURSION-SHORTCOMING.
transi de froid [F.] (tran′-si′ de-frwa). Benumbed with cold. HEAT-COLD.
tran′-sient. Passing. LASTINGNESS-TRANSIENTNESS, MUTABILITY-STABILITY.
tran′-sient-ness. The quality of being transient. LASTINGNESS-TRANSIENTNESS, MUTABILITY-STABILITY.
tran-sil′-i-ence. A leap to. REVOLUTION, TRANSCURSION-SHORTCOMING.
trans′-it. Passage; surveying instrument. ASTRONOMY, CONVERSION-REVERSION, MENSURATION, MOVEMENT-REST, TRANSFER.

transit gloria mundi, sic [L.] (tran′-sit glo′-ri-ɑ mun′-dai, sic). So passes the glory of the world. REPUTATION-DISCREDIT, WELFARE-MISFORTUNE.
trans-i′-tion. Change. CONVERSION, TRANSFER.
trans-i′-tion-al. Transient; changing. CONVERSION-REVERSION, MOVEMENT-REST, MUTATION-PERMANENCE.
trans′-i-tive. Expressing action. LASTINGNESS-TRANSIENTNESS.
trans′-i-to-ry. Short-lived. LASTINGNESS-TRANSIENTNESS.
transitu, in [L.] (tran′-si-tiu, in). On the passage. ADVANCE-RETROGRESSION, LASTINGNESS-TRANSIENTNESS, TRANSFER, TRAVELING-NAVIGATION, WAY.
trans-late′. To interpret; to transform. CHURCH, INTERPRETATION-MISINTERPRETATION.
trans-la′-tion. The act of translating. CHURCH, HEAVEN-HELL, INTERPRETATION-MISINTERPRETATION, TRANSFER.
trans″-lo-ca′-tion. A shifting of position. DIAPHANEITY-OPAQUENESS, TRANSFER.
trans-lu′-cence. The quality of allowing light to pass through. DIAPHANEITY-OPAQUENESS.
trans-lu′-cen-cy. The state of being translucent. DIAPHANEITY-OPAQUENESS.
trans″-ma-rine′. Beyond the sea. REMOTENESS-NEARNESS.
trans″-mi-gra′-tion. The act of transmigrating. CONVERSION-REVERSION, MUTATION-PERMANENCE.
trans-mis′-sion. Sent across. ALIENATION, TRANSFER, TRANSMISSION.

TRANSMISSION.

Egress. A going out, as of a building. See ENTRANCE-EXIT.
Infiltration. The transmission of liquid through a cleansing material.
Ingress. A coming in. See CONCENTRATION-RADIATION.
Intercurrence. A running between.
Interpenetration. Mutual penetration.
Journey. A passage from one place to another. See TRAVELING.
Opening. The act of opening.
Passage. A going through or over.
Penetration. A passing into the interior parts of.
Permeation. An entrance into the pores of.
Transmission. The act of passing across.
Transudation. The act of passing through, as of a membrane.
Voyage. A passage through the water, as in a ship.

TRANSMISSION—*Nouns of Means.*

Conduit. A means for transmitting water.
Path. A beaten walk. See WAY.

TRANSMISSION—*Scientific Nouns.*

Endosmose. The passage of a fluid or gas from an outside vessel to one within it.
Exosmose. The opposite of endosmose; the passage of a liquid or gas from an inner vessel to one without.

TRANSMISSION—*Verbs.*

Cross. To pass from one side to another.
Enfilade. To rake crosswise with shot.
Ford. To cross a river at a shallow spot.
Pass. To move from one place to another.
Penetrate. To go into; go through, as the pores.
Perforate. To pierce with holes. See APERTURE.
Permeate. To pass through the pores.
Thread. To pass through a narrow place, as a thread through a needle's eye.
Thrid. To thread.
Transmit. To send across.
Transverse. To change from prose to verse.
Traverse. To move back and forth, or across.
Work. To make progress or pass through a change.

TRANSMISSION—*Verbal Expressions.*

Clear the course; cut across; cut one's way through; find its vent; find its way; force a passage; force one's way; go across; go over; go over the ground; go through; make a passage; make one's way; make way; pass and repass; pass over; pass through; thread one's way through; work one's way through; worm one's way through.

TRANSMISSION—*Adjectives.*

Intercurrent. Running amongst.
Passing. Going from point to point. See *Verbs.*

TRANSMISSION—*Adverb.*

En passant [F.]. In passing. See TRANSFER.

trans-mit'. To send through or across. **Transmit light,** DIAPHANEITY-OPAQUENESS.

trans-mog'-ri-fy. To transform. MUTATION-PERMANENCE.

trans''-mu-ta'-tion. Changing the state of. CONVERSION-REVERSION, MUTATION-PERMANENCE.

tran'-som. A window above a door. SUSPENSION-SUPPORT.

trans-par'-ence. The property of transmitting light. DIAPHANEITY-OPAQUENESS.

trans-par'-en-cy. The property of being transparent. DIAPHANEITY-OPAQUENESS.

trans-par'-ent. Easy to see through. CLEARNESS-OBSCURITY, DIAPHANEITY-OPAQUENESS.

tran-spic'-u-ous. Transparent; obvious. CLEARNESS-OBSCURITY, DIAPHANEITY-OPAQUENESS.

trans-pierce'. To pierce through. APERTURE-CLOSURE.

tran-spire'. Exhale; become known. EXPOSURE-HIDINGPLACE, LIQUEFACTION-VOLATILIZATION, MANIFESTATION-LATENCY, TIDINGS-MYSTERY.

trans-place'. To remove. TRANSFER.

trans-plant'. To plant in another place. TRANSFER.

tran-splen'-dent. Resplendent in the highest degree. LIGHT-DARKNESS.

trans-pon'-tine. Beyond the bridge. REMOTENESS-NEARNESS.

trans-port'. To carry across; enraptured; a government vessel. BELLIGERENT, CONVEYANCE-VESSEL, PLEASURABLENESS-PAINFULNESS, PLEASURE-PAIN, RECOMPENSE-PUNITION, TRANSFER; **transport of love,** LOVE-HATE.

trans''-por-ta'-tion. Conveyance. EXCULPATION-PUNITION.

trans-pose'. Interchange; to play on a different key. COMMUTATION-PERMUTATION, MELODY-DISSONANCE, REVERSAL, TRANSFER.

trans''-po-si'-tion. A change of position. COMMUTATION-PERMUTATION, ESTABLISHMENT-REMOVAL, REVERSAL.

tran''-sub-stan''-ti-a'-tion. A change of substance. CEREMONIAL, MUTATION-PERMANENCE.

tran''-su-da'-tion. Passage through the pores. ENTRANCE-EXIT, TRANSMISSION.

tran-sude'. To pass through the pores. ENTRANCE-EXIT.

tran-sume'. To convert. MUTATION-PERMANENCE.

tran-sump'-tion. The act of transporting. TRANSFER.

trans-ver'-sal. Running across. PARALLELISM-INCLINATION.

trans-verse'. Athwart. CROSSING, PARALLELISM-INCLINATION.

trans-verse'-ly. Lying athwart. CROSSING.

trans-ver'-sion. A crossing over. CROSSING.

trant'-er. A pedler. CONVEYER.

trap. A snare; a carriage. ACTING, APERTURE-CLOSURE, CONVEYANCE-VESSEL, CRAFT-ARTLESSNESS, EXPOSURE-HIDINGPLACE, REFUGE-PITFALL, TRUTHFULNESS-FRAUD; **fall into a trap,** GULL-DECEIVER, SKILL-UNSKILFULNESS; **lay a trap for,** SECURITY-INSECURITY, TRUTHFULNESS-FRAUD; **trap, bat, and ball,** ENTERTAINMENT-WEARINESS.

tra-pan'. A snare. TRUTHFULNESS-FRAUD.

trap'-door''. A door in a floor. APERTURE-CLOSURE, REFUGE-PITFALL, TRUTHFULNESS-FRAUD.

trapes. A tramp. ADEPT-BUNGLER.

trap''-e-zo-he'-dral. Like a trapezohedron. MINERALOGY.

trap'-pings. Adornments. DRESS-UNDRESS, EMBELLISHMENT-DISFIGUREMENT, INCREMENT-REMNANT, INSTRUMENT.

Trap'-pist. A member of a Cistercian order. MINISTRY-LAITY.

traps. Personal effects. DRESS-UNDRESS, PROPERTY.

trash. Rubbish. CONSEQUENCE-INSIGNIFICANCE, MEANING-JARGON, USEFULNESS-USELESSNESS.

trash'-y. Worthless. CONSEQUENCE-INSIGNIFICANCE, FORCE-WEAKNESS, MEANING-JARGON.

trau'-lism. A stammering. SPEECH-INARTICULATENESS.

trau-mat'-ic. Pertaining to medication for wounds. REMEDY-BANE.

trav'-ail. Labor in childbirth; hard labor. CREATION-DESTRUCTION, TOIL-RELAXATION.

trave. A shackle. SUSPENSION-SUPPORT.

trav'-el. To journey. TRAVELING-NAVIGATION; **travel out of the record,** RATIOCINATION-INSTINCT.

trav'-el-ing. Making a tour. TRAVELING-NAVIGATION.

TRAVELING—NAVIGATION.

Airing. A walk or ride in the open air.
Ambulation. The act of walking.
Campaigning. Serving with an army on its marches, etc.
Circuit. A journeying round.
Constitutional. A walk taken for one's health or constitution.
Countermarching. A marching back.
Course. Career of journeying.
Demigration. A journey out of.
Discursion. A journeying about.
Drive. A trip in a carriage.
Emigration. A journey out of.
Equitation. Riding on horseback.
Excursion. A pleasure journey.
Expedition. A journey for some purpose.
Flit. A journeying rapidly about.
Flitting. Act of journeying rapidly.
Gadding. Journeying idly.
Grand tour. Very extensive journey.
Immigration. A journeying into.
Intermigration. A journeying between.
Jaunt. A short journey.
Journey. Period of travel.
March. A journey on foot and in time, as of soldiers.
Marching. Traveling on foot.
Migration. Act of journeying.
Noctambulation. Walking in sleep.

Aeronautics. That branch of aerostatics that treats of navigating the air.
Aerostatics. That branch of pneumatics that treats of the mechanical properties of airs and gases not in motion.
Aerostation. Art of raising and supporting bodies by means of the air.
Aquatics. Water sports.
Balloonery. Aeronautics.
Ballooning. Air-voyaging by balloons.
Boating. Navigation by boats.
Circumnavigation. A sailing around.
Cruise. A voyage at sea.
Flight. Act of flying.
Flying. Act of flight.
Headway. Forward movement of a vessel.
Leeway. The lateral drift of a vessel.
Natation. Art of swimming.
Navigation. Art of navigating. See *Verbs.*
Passage. A voyage.
Periplus [L.]. A sailing around.
Sail. Passage in a sailing vessel.
Sternway. The backward motion of a vessel.
Swimming. Navigation by natural means.
Volitation. Act of flying.
Voyage. A journey by water.
Yachting. Sailing in a yacht.

TRAVELING—NAVIGATION—*Continued.*

Nomadism. Tendency to journey.
Outing. A holiday journeying.
Perambulation. A walking about for pleasure.
Peregrination. Journey to foreign lands.
Pererration. A rambling journey.
Pilgrimage. A long journey, often to some sacred place.
Procession. Act of journeying.
Promenade. A walk for pleasure or exercise.
Ramble. An aimless journey.
Ride.
Riding. } An excursion on horseback or in a vehicle.
Roving. Aimless journeying.
Saunter. A walking about idly or in a leisurely manner.
Somnambulism. A walking in sleep.
Stalk. A high, proud, stately step or walk.
Stroll. An idle and leisurely walk.
Tour. A journey of extent.
Tramp. A foot journey or excursion.
Travel.
Traveling. } Act of traveling. See *Verbs.*
Trip. A short journey.
Turn. A walk to and fro.
Vagabondage. The condition of a vagabond.
Vagabondism. State of continual journeying with no definite home.
Vagrancy. Act of wandering idly.
Walk. A moving on the feet with a slow pace.
Wayfaring. Journeying.

TRAVELING—*Nouns of Agent.*

Baedeker. Guide-book for travelers.
Bradshaw. Bradshaw's Railway Guides.
Caravan. A desert convoy; any company on a journey.
Cavalcade. A parade.
Column. A body of troops in marching order.
Cortege. A train of attendants on a journey.
Feet. The parts of the limbs below the ankles.
File. Row of men in marching order.
Guide. A leader on a journey.
Handbook. A small guide-book.
Horsemanship. Skill in managing horses.
Itinerary. A plan of a journey.
Jog-trot. A slow, jolting gait.
Legs. Limbs of an animal body used in locomotion.
Locomotive. A steam-engine.
Manège [F.]. Art of horsemanship.
Murray. Murray's Guide-book.
Pegs.
Pins. } Slang for legs.
Plan. A design or method of a journey.
Ride and tie. Walking and riding alternately as two persons do sharing the same horse.
Road-book. A guide-book for roads.
Steam-engine. Engine deriving its power from steam.
Traveler. One who travels. See WAYFARER.
Trek. An organized migration.
Trolley. A grooved metal wheel for rolling on a trolley-wire to convey the current to the car.
Trotters. Horses that trot.
Vehicle. A contrivance for carrying on a journey. See CONVEYANCE.

TRAVELING—*Verbs.*

Amble. To move with a swaying motion.
Bend one's course. To change the direction of one's way.
Bend one's steps. To direct one's way.
Betake oneself to. To journey to.
Bowl along. To move along smoothly.
Bundle. To depart on a journey hastily.
Canter. To move in a canter.
Caracoler. To move in caracoles.
Circumambulate. To walk round about.
Course. To run through or over.
Defile. To journey in file.
Drive. To journey onward by force.
Emigrate. To journey from one country to another.
Expatiate. To give free range to.
File off. To move off in file.
Find one's way. Ascertain one's course.
Fisk. To run about.
Flit. To journey rapidly.
Foot it. To journey on foot.
Frisk. To move lightly.
Gad.
Gad about. } To journey idly about.

NAVIGATION—*Nouns of Agency.*

Balloon. A device for sailing the air. See CONVEYANCE-VESSEL.
Canvas. A strong fabric used for sails.
Fin. A membranous extension serving to propel or steer a fish.
Fish's tail. That part of a fish by which it steers itself.
Flipper. A limb used in swimming.
Mariner. One who navigates a ship.
Oar. A wooden instrument used in propelling a boat.
Paddle. Resembling an oar, but used without rowlocks.
Pinion. A wing of a bird.
Sail. A piece of canvas used to catch the wind and propel a vessel.
Screw. A steam-vessel propelled by a screw.
Ship. A large vessel.
Wing. The fore limb of a bird designed for flight.

NAVIGATION—*Verbs.*

Be wafted. Be carried gently along.
Boom. To move by means of a spar or boom.
Buffet the waves. To sail against the waves, as a boxer meets his foe
Buffet the wind. Sail against the wind.
Carry sail. To be propelled by the wind.
Circumnavigate. To sail around.
Coast. To sail near the coast.
Course. To sail over a route.
Cruise. To sail over or through.
Dive. To plunge headlong into the water.
Drift. To carry along as by currents of water.
Effleurer. To skim the surface of.
Float. To move with the current.
Flutter. To move with quick-beating motions of the wings.
Fly. To pass through the air by use of wings.
Gather way.
Get under way. } To begin to move, as a ship.
Have way on.
Hover. To pause in air with fluttering wing.
Hug the land. To sail close to the land.
Hug the shore. To sail close to the shore.
Kedge. To move a vessel by hauling on a grounded anchor
Luff. To steer closer to the wind.
Make sail. To set sail.
Navigate. To journey by ship.
Paddle. To propel with a paddle.
Plow the deep.
Plow the main.
Plow the ocean. } To sail the sea.
Plow the waves.
Ply the oar. To work steadily with the oar.
Pull. To row.
Punt. To propel a boat with a pole.
Put to sea. To begin a voyage.
Ride the storm. To withstand the gale.
Row. To propel by oars.
Sail. To navigate.
Scud. To move rapidly before the wind.
Scull. To propel with an oar or oars.
Skim. To move lightly over.
Soar. To sail on wings through the air.
Spread canvas.
Spread sail. } To set sail to the wind.
Steam. To move by steam.
Swim. To propel oneself through the water by natural means.
Take a flight. To move as by wings.
Take ship. To begin a voyage.
Take wing. To fly.
Wade. To pass through water by walking on the bottom.
Walk the waters. To sail. "She walks the waters like a thing of life and seems to dare the elements to strife." [Byron, *Corsair*, 1, 3.]
Warp. To move a vessel by hauling on a rope.
Wing one's flight.
Wing one's way. } To move as on wings.

NAVIGATION—*Adjectives.*

Aerostatic. Pertaining to aerostatics. See *Nouns.*
Afloat. In a floating condition.
Coasting. Sailing along the coast.
Maritime. Pertaining to the sea.
Nautical. Pertaining to navigation.
Naval. Pertaining to ships or navy.
Navigable. Capable of navigation. See *Verbs.*
Sailing. That which sails. See *Verbs.*
Seafaring. Following the sea.
Seagoing. Going by sea.
Volant. Flying.

TRAVELING—NAVIGATION—*Continued.*

TRAVELING—Verbs—*Continued*

Gallop. To move at a gallop. See SWIFTNESS-SLOWNESS.
Glide. To move onward rapidly.
Go. To move from one place to another.
Go a journey. To travel.
Go one's rounds. To go over a regular course.
Go out for a walk. To walk leisurely.
Go to. To travel to a place.
Have a run. To continue in motion.
Hie to. Hurry to.
Hover. To wander about.
Jog on. To move on with slow, trotting movement.
Journey. To go on a journey.
Make one's way. To progress on a journey.
March. To move together on foot.
March in procession. To move together for display.
Migrate. To move from one country to another.
Nomadize. To live as a nomad, or wanderer.
Pace. To move with even steps.
Pace up and down. Pace forth and back.
Paddle. To use a paddle, as in a boat without rowlocks.
Patrol. To go the rounds of, as a sentry.
Peg on. To move on slowly and steadily.
Peragrate. To journey over or through.
Perambulate. To walk through.
Peregrinate. To wander; to emigrate.
Pick one's way. To choose one's course.
Plod. To walk heavily.
Plow one's way. To go forward with great difficulty.
Prance. To move about struttingly.
Promenade. To walk for pleasure.
Prowl. To wander about stealthily.
Ramble. To wander aimlessly.
Range. To journey along a course.
Repair to. To betake oneself to.
Resort to. To go frequently to.
Ride. To journey through or over in any way.
Roam. To wander over.
Rove. To roam over.
Saunter. To walk aimlessly.
Scour the country. To search the country thoroughly.
Shuffle on. To move along scraping the feet.
Skate. To move on skates.
Skim. To move over lightly.
Slide. To move along easily and swiftly.
Stalk. To pace in a dignified manner, or stealthily.
Step. To move by taking steps.
Stir one's stumps. To move hastily.
Straddle. To stretch the legs far apart.
Straggle. To wander aimlessly.
Stride. To pass over with a stride.
Stroll. To wander idly.
Strut. To walk pompously.
Stump. To travel from place to place making political speeches
Take a journey. To journey.
Take a walk. To walk leisurely.
Take horse. To travel on horseback.
Take the air. To take a walk in the open air.
Take wing. To fly.

NAVIGATION—*Adverbs, etc.*

On the wing. Flying.
Under canvas. } Moving by sail-power.
Under sail.
Under steam. Moving by steam.
Under way. Moving, or beginning to move.

NAVIGATION—*Phrase.*

Bon voyage [F.]. Prosperous voyage to you.

TRAVELING—Verbs—*Continued.*

Thread one's way. To make one's way slowly and with difficulty.
Toddle. To walk unsteadily.
Tramp. To walk heavily.
Travel. To journey over.
Traverse. To journey across.
Traverse the country. To travel extensively.
Tread. To step or walk.
Tread a path. To step in a path.
Trot. To journey at a trot.
Trudge. To journey laboriously.
Wag on. To move quickly on.
Walk. To journey with the gait called a walk.
Wander. To journey at random.
Wend. To journey on.
Wend one's way. To journey over one's course.

TRAVELING—*Adjectives.*

Ambulatory. Pertaining to walking.
Circumforanean. } Journeying from house to house.
Circumforaneous.
Discursive. Journeying from the point; digressive.
Gadding. Roaming about idly.
Itinerant. Journeying from place to place.
Locomotive. Moving from place to place.
Migratory. Roving; wandering.
Mundivagant. Wandering over the world.
Nomadic. Pertaining to nomads.
Noctivagant. Night-wandering.
Peripatetic. Moving from place to place.
Rambling. Aimlessly moving.
Roving. Wandering.
Traveling. Journeying. See *Verbs.*
Travel-stained. Soiled by travel.
Vagrant. Wandering from place to place.
Wayfaring. Journeying.
Wayworn. Fatigued by journeying.

TRAVELING—*Adverbs, etc.*

By the marrow-bone stage. On the knees.
En route [F.]. On the way.
In transitu [L.]. On the way.
On foot. Walking.
On horseback. Traveling by horse.
On shank's mare. On foot.

TRAVELING—*Interjection.*

Come along!

---

trav'-el-er. One who travels; a commercial agent. CONSIGNEE, TRAVELING-NAVIGATION, WAYFARER-SEAFARER; **traveler's tale,** GULL-HYPERBOLE,TRUTH-FULNESS-FABRICATION; **tricks upon travelers,** CRAFT-ARTLESSNESS, TRUTHFULNESS-FRAUD.

trav'-erse. Crosswise; to wander over; to deny. ASSERTION-DENIAL, OBSTRUCTION-HELP, TRANS-MISSION, TRAVELING-NAVIGATION.

travestie [F.] (trɑ-ves-tī'). Disguise. COPY-MODEL, SOCIETY-DERISION, SUBJECTIVENESS-OBJECTIVENESS.

trav'-es-ty. Burlesque. COPY-MODEL, IMITATION-ORIGINALITY, INTERPRETATION - MISINTERPRETA-TION, SOCIETY-DERISION.

trav'-is. A crosspiece. SUSPENSION-SUPPORT.

trawl. To drag, as a net. TRIAL.

trawl'-er. A vessel engaged in trawling. CONVEY-ANCE-VESSEL.

tray. A flat utensil. CONTENTS-RECEIVER.

treach'-er-ous. Untrustworthy. PATRIOTISM-TREA-SON, UPRIGHTNESS-DISHONESTY; **treacherous mem-ory,** REMEMBRANCE-FORGETFULNESS.

treach'-er-y. Perfidy; treason. TRUTHFULNESS-FRAUD, UPRIGHTNESS-DISHONESTY.

trea'-cle. Molasses. SWEETNESS-ACIDITY.

tread. To walk on. MOVEMENT-REST, TRAVELING-NAVIGATION; **tread a path,** QUEST-EVASION, TRAVEL-ING-NAVIGATION; **tread down,** HARSHNESS-MILD-NESS, LIBERTY-SUBJECTION, PRESUMPTION-OBSEQUI-OUSNESS, SELFRESPECT-HUMBLENESS; **tread in the steps of,** IMITATION-ORIGINALITY, LEADING-FOLLOW-ING; **tread on the heels of,** APPROACH-WITHDRAWAL, LEADING-FOLLOWING, QUEST-EVASION; **tread the beaten track,** CONVENTIONALITY-UNCONVENTIONAL-ITY, HABIT-DESUETUDE; **tread the boards,** ACTING; **tread the stage,** ACTING; **tread under foot,** CREATION-DESTRUCTION, HARSHNESS-MILDNESS, LIBERTY-SUB-

JECTION, PRESUMPTION-OBSEQUIOUSNESS, REGARD-SCORN, REPUTATION-DISCREDIT; **tread upon,** GOODNESS-BADNESS.

tread'-le. A lever to impart motion to a machine. INSTRUMENT.

tread'-mill". A mechanism rotated by treading persons, usually as a punishment. RECOMPENSE-SCOURGE.

trea'-son. Betrayal. INSUBORDINATION-OBEDIENCE, PATRIOTISM-TREASON, UPRIGHTNESS-DISHONESTY.

treas'-ure. To prize; valuables. GOODNESS-BADNESS, MONEY, STORE; **treasure-trove,** GOOD-EVIL; **treasure up in the memory,** REMEMBRANCE-FORGETFULNESS.

treas'-ur-er. One who has charge of money. CONSIGNEE, TREASURER.

TREASURER.

Accountant. One skilled in keeping accounts.
Accountant-general. The principal accountant in a mercantile or banking house; formerly, an officer in chancery.
Almoner. One who dispenses alms and charity.
Banker. One who keeps a bank; a trafficker in money.
Bursar. A treasurer, or money-keeper.
Bursary. The treasury of a college or university.
Cambist. One who deals in notes and bills of exchange; a banker.
Cashier. A cash- or money-keeper.
Cash-keeper. A cashier.
Chancellor of the Exchequer. The minister of finance in the British cabinet.
Depositary. One entrusted with something for safe-keeping.
Financier. One skilled or occupied in monetary affairs.
Fiscal. A financial secretary or minister.
Fiscal agent. Disbursing officer of the treasury.
Liquidator. One who settles accounts.
Minister of finance. One engaged in the administration of a government's financial affairs.
Money-changer. A broker who deals in money.
Paymaster. One who regularly pays wages or reward.
Purser. Formerly, the name of a naval paymaster.
Purse-bearer. One who carries another's purse.
Questor. A public treasurer.
Receiver. An officer appointed to receive public money, or settle an estate or business.
Steward. A person appointed to administer affairs in general and also financial matters.
Teller. A person who receives and pays out money in a bank.
Treasurer. One who has the care of a treasury, who receives, keeps and disburses public money.
Trustee. A person who holds property in trust for another.

treas'-ur-y. Place where money is kept. TREASURY

TREASURY.

Bank. An establishment which trades in money, and holds it in custody.
Breeches pocket. A pocket for carrying money.
Bursary. The treasury of a college or monastery.
Chest. A box for treasuring money. See CONTENTS-RECEIVER.
Coffer. A strong box for use as a treasury.
Depository. A place where anything is treasured up. See STORE.
Exchequer. The treasury of a state.
Fisc. A treasury.
Hanaper. A receptacle for treasuring valuables.
Money-bag. A bag for holding money.
Money-box. A box for holding money.
Pocket. A pouch attached to a garment for carrying money and other articles.
Porte-monnaie [F.]. A small book for holding money in the pocket.
Purse. Anything for carrying money on the person.
Purse-strings. The cords for drawing up the mouth of a purse.
Safe deposit vault. A strong place for keeping valuables.
Strong-box. A box used as a treasury and strengthened to resist assault.
Stronghold. A fortified place for treasuring anything.
Strong-room. A room fortified for use as a treasury.
Subtreasury. A branch of the United States Treasury.
Till.
Tiller. } A drawer for holding money.
Treasury. A place for keeping valuables in safe custody.

TREASURY—*Associated Nouns.*

Consols. A governmental security of Great Britain.
Crédit Mobilier [F.]. A French financial institution.
Parliamentary funds.
Parliamentary securities. } Government indebtedness represented by certificates issued to creditors.
Parliamentary stocks.
Public funds.
Public securities. } Government indebtedness represented by certificates.
Public stocks.
Sinking-fund. A fund instituted and invested in such wise that its gradual accumulations will enable it to wipe out a debt at maturity.
Stocks. Shares of capital.

treat. Pleasure; bargain; manage. CONDUCT, CONTRACT, ENTERTAINMENT-WEARINESS, PLEASURE-PAIN, PLEASURABLENESS-PAINFULNESS, SENSUALITY-SUFFERING; **treat of,** ESSAY; **treat oneself to,** PLEASURE-PAIN; **treat well,** CHARITABLENESS-MALEVOLENCE.

trea'-tise. An extended written exposition. ESSAY, RHETORIC.

treat'-ment. Conduct; painting. CONDUCT, PAINTING, REMEDY-BANE; **ill-treatment,** GOODNESS-BADNESS; **medical treatment,** REMEDY-BANE.

treat'-y. A formal compact between nations. CONTRACT.

treb'-le. Triple; soprano. CACOPHONY, TRIPLICATION-TRISECTION; **childish treble,** VOCALIZATION-MUTENESS.

treb'-le-ness. State of being triple. TRIPLICATION-TRISECTION.

treb'-ly. Triply. TRIPLICATION-TRISECTION.

tree. Gibbet; a perennial woody plant; lineage. FAUNA-FLORA, MAKER-DESTROYER, RECOMPENSE-SCOURGE; **as the tree falls,** OCCURRENCE-DESTINY; **top of the tree,** REPUTATION-DISCREDIT, TOP-BOTTOM; **tree of knowledge,** KNOWLEDGE-IGNORANCE, SCHOLAR-DUNCE; **up a tree,** DIFFICULTY-FACILITY.

tre'-foil. A three-leafed ornament. ARCHITECTURE.

trek. An organized migration. CONSTITUENT-ALIEN, TRAVELING-NAVIGATION.

trel'-lis. A cross-barred lattice. CROSSING.

trem'-ble. Quiver. AGITATION, EMOTION, HEAT-COLD, MUTABILITY-STABILITY, SANGUINENESS-TIMIDITY, STRENGTH-WEAKNESS; **make one tremble,** SANGUINENESS-TIMIDITY.

trem'-bling. Quivering. **Trembling in the balance,** CERTAINTY-DOUBT, SANGUINENESS-TIMIDITY, SECURITY-INSECURITY; **trembling to its fall,** CREATION-DESTRUCTION, STRENGTH-WEAKNESS.

trem'-bling-ly a-live'. Scarcely alive. SENSITIVENESS-APATHY.

tre-men'-dous. Alarming. PLEASURABLENESS-PAINFULNESS, SANGUINENESS-TIMIDITY.

tre-men'-dous-ly. With great violence. MAGNITUDE-SMALLNESS.

trem'-or. A quick vibratory movement. AGITATION, EMOTION, SANGUINENESS-TIMIDITY.

trem'-u-lous. Quivering. AGITATION, DETERMINATION-VACILLATION, SANGUINENESS-TIMIDITY, TALKATIVENESS-TACITURNITY.

trench. Furrow. GROOVE; **trench on,** DUENESS-UNDUENESS, REMOTENESS-NEARNESS, TRANSCURSION-SHORTCOMING.

trench'-ant. Penetrating; biting; keen. APPROVAL-DISAPPROVAL, ASSERTION-DENIAL, CONSEQUENCE-INSIGNIFICANCE, DETERMINATION-VACILLATION, EMOTION, FELICITATION, STRENGTH-WEAKNESS, TERSENESS-PROLIXITY, VIGOR-INERTIA.

trench'-er. Platter. CONTENTS-RECEIVER, LAMINA-FIBER.

trench'-es. Long irregular ditches about three feet deep, used to cover the advance of an army. **Open the trenches,** ATTACK-DEFENSE.

trend. Tendency. Aim-Aberration, Dominance-Impotence.

tren'-nel''. A wooden nail. Connective.

trep-an'. Snare; rock-boring tool. Perforator-Stopper, Truthfulness-Fraud.

trep''-i-da'-tion. Agitation from fear. Agitation, Emotion, Excitability-Inexcitability, Sanguineness-Timidity.

tres'-pass. Go beyond; transgress. Innocence-Guilt, Transcursion-Shortcoming, Virtue-Vice.

tress. Plait of hair. Smoothness-Roughness.

tres'-tle. A carpenter's horse. Suspension-Support.

trev'-et. Three-legged stool. Suspension-Support.

trey. The three-spot of cards. Triality.

tri'-ad. Trivalent. Triality.

tri-ag'-on-al. Three-cornered. Angularity.

tria juncta in uno [L.] (trai'-α junc'-tα in yu'-no). Three things joined in one. Triality, Union-Disunion.

tri'-al. Affliction; effort; proof. Difficulty-Facility, Investigation - Answer, Litigation, Pleasurableness - Painfulness, Pleasure-Pain, Recompense-Punition, Trial, Venture; **trial of temper,** Excitation.

TRIAL.

Assay. Analysis of an ore to ascertain its ingredients.

Analysis, etc. Resolution of anything into its elements. See Investigation.

Criterion. Established rule for testing.

Crucial test. A test that determines absolutely the truth or falsity of a statement or theory.

Diagnostic. The distinguishing symptom of a disease.

Empiricism. Practise of medicine from experience without the aid of science.

Essay, etc. A test of one's powers by doing something. See Venture.

Experiment. Means taken to arrive at truth.

Experimentum crucis [L.]. The trial of the cross; a severe test.

Leap in the dark. A step taken in ignorance of the consequences.

Ordeal. Ancient trial of guilt.

Probation. Examination; period of trial of one's ability or qualities.

Proof. That which establishes a truth.

Random shot. An attempt without definite aim or intention.

Rule of thumb. A method of measurement, roughly practical rather than scientific.

Speculation. Intellectual examination.

Tâtonnement [F.]. Supposition; groping.

Tentative method. A method used in making a trial.

Test. Decisive trial.

Trial. Partial test made in any manner.

Verification. Confirmation.

Trial—*Nouns of Agent.*

Adventurer. One who seeks his fortune in new or untried fields.

Analyst. } One who analyzes, especially in chemistry or mathe-
Analyzer. } matics.

Experimentalist. }
Experimenter. } One who makes experiments, especially scientific experiments.
Experimentist. }

Trial—*Nouns of Agency.*

Check. Any mark or register used as a means of verification or identification.

Crucible. A pot or vessel for melting metals or minerals.

Feeler. One who or that which feels; a trial venture.

Messenger balloon. A balloon used for investigating in warfare.

Pilot balloon. A small balloon sent up before a larger one, to show the direction and velocity of the wind.

Pilot-engine. A locomotive piloting a train.

Pyx. A receptacle for coins selected for trial at the British mint.

Reagent. Any substance used to ascertain the nature or composition of another by means of their mutual chemical action.

Scout. A person sent out to observe and get information of an enemy in war.

Straws to show the wind. Straws held up in the air to show by their movements the direction of the wind.

Test-tube. A thin glass tube used in making chemical tests.

Touchstone. A fine-grained stone, usually schist or jasper, used to test the fineness of gold alloys.

Trial—*Verbs.*

Angle. To fish; scheme.

Assay. To make an analysis of an ore.

Essay, etc. To try one's powers. See Essay.

Experiment. To use a process of finding out truth.

Explore. To search. See Investigation.

Fumble. To endeavor in an unskilful manner.

Grope. To feel about in darkness.

Prove. To establish a truth.

Rehearse. To recite for practise.

Tâtonner [F.]. To grope.

Test. To give a decisive trial.

Touch. To perceive with the feeling.

Trawl. To fish with a long line.

Try. To give or make a trial.

Verify. To show to be correct.

Trial—*Verbal Expressions.*

Aller â tâtons [F.], to find one's way by groping; beat about for; beat the bushes; bob for; bring to the proof; bring to the test; cast about for; cast one's net; consult the barometer; experiment upon; feel for; feel one's way; feel the pulse; fish for; give a trial to; grope for; grope one's way; make an experiment; make a trial of; practise upon; put out a feeler; put to the proof; put to the test; put upon trial; see how the land lies; see how the wind blows; send up a pilot balloon; subject to trial; submit to the proof; submit to the test; throw out a feeler; try one's fortune, etc. (see Venture); try one's strength.

Trial—*Adjectives.*

Analytic. Pertaining to an analysis.

Docimastic. Proving by experiments.

Empirical. Based on experiment without regard to science.

Experimental. Pertaining to experiments.

On one's trial. Undergoing a test.

Probationary. }
Probative. } Serving for trial.
Probatory. }

Tentative. Essaying.

Under probation. On trial.

tri-al'-i-ty. Union of three in one. Triality.

TRIALITY.

Triality. State of being three.

Trinity. Used in theology to denote the union of three persons in one Godhead.

Triality—*Denotations.*

Cube. The product of three equal factors.

Leash. Three creatures of the same kind, as greyhounds, foxes, etc.

Ternion. A group or congregation of three.

Third power. A number multiplied by itself three times.

Three. The sum of two and one.

Trey. A card or die having three spots.

Triad. A group of three persons or things.

Tricuspid. A valve or tooth having three cusps or points.

Trinomial. An algebraic expression consisting of three terms connected by plus or minus signs.

Trio. A musical composition for three performers.

Triphthong. Three vowels combined to produce one sound.

Triplet. One of three children born at one birth.

Triality—*Adjectives.*

Tertiary. Third in number.

Three. Consisting of one more than two; a cardinal number.

Triform. Having a triple form.

Trinal. Threefold.

Trinomial. Consisting of three terms.

Triune. Three in one.

Triality—*Phrases.*

Tria juncta in uno [L.]. Three joined in one.

tri'-a-log. Discourse between three people. Conversation-Monologue.

tri'-an''-gle. A plane figure bounded by three sides. Angularity, Musical Instruments, Recompense-Scourge.

tri-an'-gu-lar. Three-sided or cornered. Angularity; **triangular duel,** Strife-Peace.

tri-ar-chy. Government by a triumvirate. Rule-License.

Tri-as'-sic pe'-ri-od. Geologic period. Geology.

tribe. Class; division. DIVISION, ETHNOLOGY, GATH-ERING-SCATTERING, PARENTAGE-PROGENY.

trib''-u-la'-tion. Sorrow. PLEASURE-PAIN.

tri-bu'-nal. Court of justice. JUDICATURE, TRIBUNAL.

TRIBUNAL.

Areopagus. The highest judicial tribunal of ancient Athens.

Assize. A sitting or session of a court.

Bar. The legal profession.

Bar of justice. Any tribunal.

Bench. The judge's seat in court; hence, the judge or judges constituting a court or tribunal.

Board. A table at which a council sits; hence, a council convened for business.

Board of greencloth. A board of the royal household controlling the commissariat.

Bureau. A body of officials in a particular department.

Burghmote. A borough court.

County court. A court whose jurisdiction is limited to a county.

Court. A tribunal constituted to try cases and administer justice.

Court baron. An inferior court of civil jurisdiction.

Court-leet. A court of record held once a year.

Court-martial. A court consisting of military or naval officers.

Court of admiralty. A court with jurisdiction over maritime questions.

Court of appeal. A court of review.

Court of arbitration. A court for the hearing and determining a controversy between two parties.

Court of Arches. The court of appeal of the Archbishop of Canterbury.

Court of assize. The session of the judges of superior courts.

Court of chancery. An equity court.

Court of common council. Municipal legislative body.

Court of common pleas. An inferior court having civil and criminal jurisdiction.

Court of error. A court of record.

Court of exchequer. A superior court of law and equity.

Court of justice. A court of a justice of the peace.

Court of King's Bench. The highest court of common law in England.

Court of law. A court where law is administered.

Court of oyer and terminer. Criminal courts.

Court of piepoudre. An ancient court of record in England.

Court of probate. A court for the probation of wills.

Court of record. A court whose proceedings are preserved in writing.

Divan. A council of state in Oriental countries.

Divorce court. A court having jurisdiction over divorce cases.

Dock. A place in court where an accused person stands.

Drumhead. } A court-martial called to try offenses on
Drumhead court-martial. } the battle-field.

Durbar. A court of a native prince of India.

Eyre. The court held on circuit by judges.

Forum. An assembly empowered to hear and decide causes.

Guild. An association of persons engaged in kindred pursuits for mutual aid and protection.

High court of appeal. The highest court to which appeal can be made from a lower court.

High court of judicature. The highest court of justice.

Hustings. An English court.

Inquisition. A court for the examination and punishment of heretics.

Judgment seat. A court; a tribunal.

Judicature. A court of justice.

Judicial committee of the privy council. A court composed of members of the privy council.

Jury-box. The place where the jury is seated.

Justice-seat. The seat of a judge in court, hence, a court.

Lord justice's court. A Scotch supreme court.

Mercy-seat. A place where mercy is dispensed.

Palatine court. A court of a local prince.

Petty sessions. } A court for the trial of minor offenses.
Police court. }

Quarter sessions. A general court of criminal jurisdiction.

Rolls court. A court whose proceedings are kept on rolls.

Senate-house. The meeting place of the senate.

Sessions. Courts of justice.

Stannary court. Courts for the administration of justice among the tinners of Cornwall.

Star Chamber. A high court of the king's ministers.

Superior courts of Westminster. Appellate court of the highest rank in England

Theater. A place where assemblies meet

Townhall. A hall where the town-meeting is held.

Tribunal. A court of justice.

Vice-chancellor's court. A court presided over by a vice-chancellor.

Ward-mote. A court held in the ward of a city.

Witness box. The place where witnesses stand in court.

Woolsack. The seat of the Lord Chancellor of England in the House of Lords.

TRIBUNAL—Adjectives.

Appellate. Capable of being appealed to a higher tribunal.

Judicial. Pertaining to a court or tribunal.

TRIBUNAL—Phrases.

Accedas ad curiam [L.]. You may go to the court.

Die Weltgeschichte ist das Weltgericht [G.]. World-history is a world-tribunal.

trib'-une. Rostrum; judge. JUDGE, PRESIDENT-MEMBER, SCHOOL.

trib'-u-ta-ry. Contributory. GIVING-RECEIVING, RIVER-WIND.

trib'-ute. Donation; reward. GIVING-RECEIVING, OUTLAY-INCOME, RECOMPENSE-PENALTY; **pay tribute to,** APPROVAL-DISAPPROVAL, REGARD-DISRESPECT.

trice. Instant. ETERNITY-INSTANTANEITY; **trice up,** UNION-DISUNION.

tri-chot'-o-mous. Divided into three parts. TRIPLICATION-TRISECTION.

tri-chot'-o-my. Division into three parts. TRIPLICATION-TRISECTION.

tri'-chro-ism. The property possessed by some crystals of exhibiting different colors in three different directions when viewed by transmitted light. VARIEGATION.

trick. Deception; skill; habit. CRAFT-ARTLESSNESS, DESIGN, GAIN-LOSS, HABIT-DESUETUDE, SKILL-UNSKILFULNESS, TRUTHFULNESS-FALSEHOOD; **play tricks,** CRAFT-ARTLESSNESS, ENTERTAINMENT-WEARINESS, SKILL-UNSKILFULNESS, SOCIETY-DERISION; **trick of fortune,** EXPECTATION-DISAPPOINTMENT; **tricks of the trade,** CRAFT-ARTLESSNESS; **trick out,** EMBELLISHMENT - DISFIGUREMENT, TASTE - VULGARITY.

trick'-er-y. Deceit; finery. CRAFT-ARTLESSNESS, TASTE-VULGARITY, TRUTHFULNESS-FRAUD.

trick'-le. Ooze. ENTRANCE-EXIT, RIVER-WIND.

trick'-ster. Deceiver. GULL-DECEIVER, ROBBER.

trick'-sy. Playful; ornamental. BEAUTY-UGLINESS, CRAFT - ARTLESSNESS, EMBELLISHMENT - DISFIGUREMENT, LIGHTHEARTEDNESS-DEJECTION.

trick'-y. Deceiving. TRUTHFULNESS-FRAUD.

tri-clin'-ic sys'-tem. Class of crystals. MINERALOGY.

tri'-col''-or. Three-colored flag. PATRIOTISM-TREASON, SIGN, VARIEGATION.

tri-cus'-pid. Having three points. TRIALITY.

tri'-cy-cle. Three-wheeled conveyance. CONVEYANCE-VESSEL.

tri'-dent. Three-pronged weapon, the emblem of Neptune. OCEAN-LAND.

tri-en'-ni-al. Occurring every three years. FAUNA-FLORA, PERIODICITY-IRREGULARITY.

tri'-fid. Three-cleft. TRIPLICATION-TRISECTION.

tri'-fle. Of little importance; to neglect. CAREFULNESS-CARELESSNESS, CONSEQUENCE-INSIGNIFICANCE, MAGNITUDE-SMALLNESS, SAGACITY-INCAPACITY; **not stick at trifles,** PERSISTENCE-WHIM; **not to be trifled with,** COERCION; **trifle time away,** ACTIVITY-INDOLENCE; **trifle with,** CAREFULNESS-CARELESSNESS, REGARD-DISRESPECT, TRUTHFULNESS-FRAUD.

tri'-fler. Jester. CAREFULNESS-CARELESSNESS, SAGE-FOOL.

tri'-fling. Frivolous; insignificant. CAREFULNESS-CARELESSNESS, CONSEQUENCE-INSIGNIFICANCE, SAGACITY-INCAPACITY, WITTINESS-DULNESS.

tri'-form. Triple-shaped. TRIALITY.

trig'-a-my. State of having three husbands or wives at the same time. MATRIMONY-CELIBACY.

trig'-ger. Finger-piece of a gun-lock. INSTRUMENT; **draw the trigger,** FIGHTING-CONCILIATION.

Trig'-ger, Sir Lu'-ci-us O'. A principal personage in Sheridan's *Rivals*, noted for fighting. BRAWLER.

tri'-gon. A triangle. ANGULARITY.

trig″-o-nal. Triangular. ANGULARITY.

trig″-o-nom'-e-try. A branch of mathematics. ANGULARITY.

trikumia [Gr.] (tri-kü-mĭ'-α). The third or largest wave. SUPREMACY-SUBORDINACY.

tri-lat'-er-al. Three-sided. ANGULARITY, LATERALITY-CONTRAPOSITION, PROPORTION-DEFORMITY.

tril'-o-gis-tic. Pertaining to a trilogy. TRIPLICATION-TRISECTION.

tril'-o-gy. A series of three dramas having the same general subject. ACTING.

trill. To sing with a quavering voice; flow in drops. CRASH-DRUMMING, MUSICIAN, RIVER-WIND.

tril'-lion. A million millions. FIVE-QUINQUESECTION.

trim. Condition; costume; adorn; chastise. APPROVAL-DISAPPROVAL, BEAUTY-UGLINESS, BIGOTRY-APOSTASY, CLEANNESS-FILTHINESS, CONDITION-SITUATION, DETERMINATION-VACILLATION, DRESS-UNDRESS, EMBELLISHMENT-DISFIGUREMENT, EQUALITY-INEQUALITY, EXCULPATION-PUNITION, FORM-FORMLESSNESS, TRUTHFULNESS-FALSEHOOD; **in trim,** REGULARITY-IRREGULARITY.

trim-e-ter. Verse of three measures. RHETORIC.

trim'-mer. Fickle person. BIGOTRY-APOSTASY, UPRIGHTNESS-ROGUE.

trim'-ming. Adornment. BIGOTRY-APOSTASY, BORDER, EMBELLISHMENT-DISFIGUREMENT, UPRIGHTNESS-DISHONESTY.

tri'-nal. Threefold. TRIALITY.

trine. Triple. TRIPLICATION-TRISECTION.

trin'-i-ty. Union of three. TRIALITY.

Trin'-i-ty, Ho'-ly. Godhead. DIVINITY.

trin'-ket. Trifle; ornament. CONSEQUENCE-INSIGNIFICANCE, EMBELLISHMENT-DISFIGUREMENT.

trink geld [G.] (trink gelt). A tip. GIVING-RECEIVING.

tri-no'-mi-al. Having three terms. TRIALITY.

tri'-o. Three. MUSIC, TRIALITY.

trip. Err; journey; fail. ASCENT-DESCENT, INNOCENCE-GUILT, SKILL-UNSKILFULNESS, SPRING-DIVE, SUCCESS-FAILURE, SWIFTNESS-SLOWNESS, TRUTH-ERROR, TRAVELING-NAVIGATION, VIRTUE-VICE; **trip up,** SUCCESS-FAILURE, TRUTHFULNESS-FRAUD.

trip'-ar-tite. Threefold. TRIPLICATION-TRISECTION.

trip'-ar-ti'-tion. Division into three parts. TRIPLICATION-TRISECTION.

triph'-thong. The vowels or vowel-characters combined to produce one sound. LETTER, TRIALITY.

trip'-le. Treble. TRIPLICATION-TRISECTION; **triple crown,** VESTMENTS.

trip'-let. Three units combined. POETRY-PROSE, TRIALITY.

trip'-li-cate. Treble. TRIPLICATION-TRISECTION.

trip'-li-ca″-tion. Act of making threefold. TRIPLICATION-TRISECTION.

TRIPLICATION—TRISECTION.

Trebleness. The state of being treble.
Trine. A triad.
Triplication. The act of trebling.
Triplicity. The state of being triple.

TRIPLICATION—*Verbs.*

Cube. To raise to the third power.
Treble. To multiply by three.
Triple. To make threefold.
Triplicate. To make three times as many.

TRIPLICATION—*Adjectives.*

Tern. Threefold.
Ternary. Proceeding by threes.
Third. The ordinal of three.
Threefold. Made up of three.
Treble. Multiplied by three.
Trilogistic. Made up of a series of three dramas.
Triple. Increased threefold.
Triplicate. Made thrice as much.

TRIPLICATION—*Adverbs, etc.*

In the third place. Coming after two that have gone before.
Thirdly. In the third place.

Third. One of three equal parts of anything.
Third part. A third.
Trichotomy.
Tripartition. } Division into three parts.
Trisection.

TRISECTION—*Verbs.*

Divide into three parts. } To divide into three parts.
Trisect.

TRISECTION—*Adjectives.*

Trichotomous. Divided into threes.
Trifid. Three-cleft.
Tripartite. Threefold.
Trisected. Divided into three parts. See *Verbs.*
Trisulcate. Having three forks.

TRIPLICATION—ADVERBS, ETC.—*Continued.*

Threefold. Trebly.
Three times. Threefold.
Thrice. Three times.
Trebly. In a threefold manner or quantity. See *Adjectives.*

tri-plic'-i-ty. Trinity. TRIPLICATION-TRISECTION.

tri'-pod. Three-legged stool. CHEMISTRY, SUSPENSION-SUPPORT.

tripotage [F.] (tri-po-tαzh'). Medley. CONVERSATION-MONOLOGUE.

trip'-ping. Quick. ACTIVITY-INDOLENCE, PURITY-CRUDENESS, SUCCESS-FAILURE, TRUTH-ERROR; **caught tripping,** KNOWLEDGE-IGNORANCE.

trip'-ping-ly on the tongue. Rapid but clear enunciation. TALKATIVENESS-TACITURNITY.

Trip-to'-le-mus. Patron of agriculture in Greek mythology. DOMESTICATION-AGRICULTURE.

tri'-reme. An ancient galley. CONVEYANCE-VESSEL.

tri'-sect. To divide into three parts. TRIPLICATION-TRISECTION.

tri-sect'-ed. Ternately divided. TRIPLICATION-TRISECTION.

tri-sec'-tion. Division into three parts. TRIPLICATION-TRISECTION.

tris-oc″-ta-he'-dron. Kind of crystal. MINERALOGY.

trist. Sad. LIGHTHEARTEDNESS-DEJECTION.

trist'-ful. Sorrowful. LIGHTHEARTEDNESS-DEJECTION.

tri-sul'-cate. Three-grooved. GROOVE, TRIPLICATION-TRISECTION.

trite. Common. HABIT-DESUETUDE, KNOWLEDGE-IGNORANCE; **trite saying,** ADAGE-NONSENSE.

tri'-the-ism. Doctrine of the existence of three separate and distinct gods. ORTHODOXY-HETERODOXY.

Tri'-ton. A fabled sea demigod. OCEAN-LAND; **Triton among the minnows,** CONSEQUENCE-INSIGNIFICANCE, GREATNESS-LITTLENESS, SUPREMACY-SUBORDINACY.

trit'-u-ra″-tion. Pulverization. FRIABILITY.

trium literarum homo [L.] (trαi'-um lit-er-ê'-rum hom'-o). A man of three letters, [L.], *fur,* a thief. ROBBER.

tri'-umph. Success; to celebrate. BRAGGING, JUBILATION-LAMENTATION, SOLEMNIZATION, SUCCESS-FAILURE, WELFARE-MISFORTUNE.

tri-um'-phant. Exultant. JUBILATION-LAMENTATION, SUCCESS-FAILURE.

tri-um'-vi-rate. Coalition of three men to rule. RULE-LICENSE.

tri'-une. Three in one. TRIPLICATION-TRISECTION.

Tri'-une God. The Godhead. DIVINITY.

triv'-et. A three-legged stool. OVEN-REFRIGERATOR, SUSPENSION-SUPPORT; **right as a trivet,** DUENESS-UNDUENESS, FAULTLESSNESS-FAULTINESS.

triv'-i-al. Trifling. CONSEQUENCE-INSIGNIFICANCE, MEANING-JARGON, USEFULNESS-USELESSNESS.

triv-i-al'-i-ty. Something insignificant. CONSEQUENCE-INSIGNIFICANCE.

troat. To cry as a buck in rutting time. CRY-ULULATION.

tro'-car. Surgical instrument used in dropsy. PERFORATOR-STOPPER.

tro-cha'-ic. Composed of or pertaining to trochees. POETRY-PROSE, RHETORIC.

tro'-chee. A foot composed of a long and a short, or accented and unaccented, syllable. POETRY-PROSE, RHETORIC.

tro-chil'-ic. Pertaining to rotary motion. REVOLUTION-EVOLUTION.

tro-chil'-ics. The science of rotary motion. REVOLUTION-EVOLUTION.

trod'-den. Trampled underfoot. **Downtrodden,** LIBERTY-SUBJECTION; **well trodden,** HABIT-DESUETUDE, USE-DISUSE.

trog'-lo-dyte''. One living in seclusion. SOCIABILITY-PRIVACY.

troll. Roll; move rapidly; a fairy. JOVE-FIEND, REVOLUTION-EVOLUTION, SWIFTNESS-SLOWNESS.

trol'-ley. A grooved-metal wheel for running on a trolley-wire. ELECTRICITY, TRAVELING-NAVIGATION.

trol'-lop. Prostitute. PURITY-RAKE.

trom'-bone. Musical instrument. MUSICAL INSTRUMENTS.

troop. Soldiers; an assemblage. BELLIGERENT, GATHERING-SCATTERING; **raise troops,** FIGHTING-CONCILIATION.

troop'-er. Cavalryman. BELLIGERENT; **lie like a trooper,** TRUTHFULNESS-FALSEHOOD; **swear like a trooper,** CHARITABLENESS-MENACE.

troop-ship. Ship for troops. BELLIGERENT.

trop, de [F.] (tro, de). Not wanted. EXCESS-LACK.

trope. Figure of speech. RHETORIC, TROPE.

TROPE.

Adumbration. The faint sketch or outlines of a figure.

Allegory. The setting forth of one subject under the guise of another.

Allusion. An indirect reference to something supposed to be known.

Anagogue. The spiritual or mystical application of words.

Antonomasia. The substitution of a title or epithet for a proper noun.

Apologue. A tale or fable with a moral.

Application. The part of a sermon or discourse in which the principles set forth are applied to practical uses.

Catachresis. The use of one word wrongly for another or the wresting of a word from its true significance.

Colloquialism. An expression used in common conversation, but not in formal discourse or writing.

Enallage. The substitution of one part of speech, gender, etc., for another.

Fable. A brief story or tale intended to impart a moral, especially one introducing animals and the like as speaking.

Façon de parler [F.]. Manner of speaking.

Figurativeness. Abundance of figures of speech. See *Adjectives.*

Figure. Pictorial or poetic language used for the sake of a more pleasing and powerful effect.

Figure of speech. A rhetorical figure.

Image. A picture or illustration, frequently taken from sensible objects, and used to illustrate a subject.

Imagery. Rhetorical embellishment in writing or speaking.

Irony. The use of a mode of speech the meaning of which is contrary to the literal sense.

Metalepsis. A compound figure consisting in uniting two or more tropes in one word.

Metaphor. A figure in which the relation of one object to another is shown by asserting it to be that object.

Metonymy. A trope consisting in putting one word for another suggested by it.

Parable. A short fictitious narrative teaching some important truth or lesson.

Personification. A figure by which an inanimate object or abstract idea is represented as having life.

Phrase, etc. A manner or style of expression, etc. See *Phrase.*

Prosopopeia. A figure of speech in which the speaker personates another.

Simile. A figure of speech in which two things, strongly resembling each other in some point or points, are compared.

Synecdoche. A figure in which a part of anything is put for the whole.

Trope. The use of a word or expression in a different sense from the one properly belonging to it.

Type. A figurative representation of something to come.

Way of speaking. A customary or habitual manner, mode, or style of expression.

TROPE—*Verbs.*

Adumbrate. To shadow forth in outline.

Allegorize. To use allegory.

Allude to. To refer to indirectly or by suggestion.

Apply. To have some reference or analogy.

Employ metaphor. To use figurative language. See *Nouns.*

Personify. To represent an inanimate object as a rational being.

Shadow forth. To represent typically.

TROPE—*Adjectives.*

Allegorical. Belonging to or pertaining to an allegory.

Allusive. Figurative; containing an allusion.

Anagogical. Having a spiritual or mystical meaning.

Catachrestical. Twisted from its natural sense or meaning; far-fetched.

Colloquial. Used in familiar conversation.

Figurative. Employed in a sense not literal.

Ironical. Characterized by irony.

Metaphorical. Relating to metaphor; figurative.

Parabolic. Having the nature of a parable.

Tralatitious. Handed down or transmitted.

Typical. Representing by form or resemblance· symbolical.

TROPE—*Adverbs, etc.*

As it were. In a manner.

So to express oneself.

So to say. } If one may say or speak thus.

So to speak.

TROPE—*Phrase.*

Mutato nomine de te fabula narratur [L.]. The name being changed, the story is related of you. [Horace, *Satires*, I, i, 69.]

Tro-phon'-i-us, cave of. Cave where the oracle of Trophonius was. LIGHTHEARTEDNESS-DEJECTION.

tro'-phy. Memento of success or defeat. MARK-OBLITERATION, SIGN, SOLEMNIZATION, TROPHY.

TROPHY.

Bays. The leaves of the laurel used in wreaths conferred as prizes to the victors in various contests.

Chaplet. A garland or wreath worn as a trophy of victory.

Civic crown. A Roman trophy bestowed on a soldier who had saved the life of a citizen in battle.

Crown. A decorative circlet for the head worn as a mark of kingly or sovereign power.

Decoration. A badge or medal worn as a trophy of distinction and honor. See TITLE.

Feather in one's cap. A mark of distinction. See TITLE.

Flying colors. A trophy or mark of victory. See POMP.

Garland. A wreath or chaplet worn as a trophy or mark of honor.

Insignia. Trophies or marks of office or honor. See SIGN.

Laurel. }

Laurels. } The ancient trophy of honor and victory.

Medal. A trophy of merit.

Monumentum ære perennius [L.]. A monument more enduring than bronze. [Horace, *Odes*, III, xxx, 1]

Palm. A branch or leaf of the palm-tree, an ancient trophy of victory.

Prize. That which is obtained or offered as a trophy or reward of victory.

Triumph. An ancient Roman procession of great magnificence in honor of a victorious general, the highest military honor obtainable.

Triumphal arch. An arch commemorative of a triumph. See SOLEMNIZATION.

Trophy. A memorial in commemoration of some victory or honor.

Wreath. A garland or chaplet, a trophy of honor or victory.

trop'-ic-al. Torrid. HEAT-COLD.

trot. Run. SWIFTNESS-SLOWNESS, TRAVELING-NAVIGATION; **trot out,** MANIFESTATION-LATENCY, POMP.

troth. Promise; faith. ASSERTION-DENIAL, ENGAGEMENT, FAITH-UNBELIEF, TRUTHFULNESS-FALSEHOOD; **by my troth,** ASSERTION-DENIAL, TRUTHFULNESS-FALSEHOOD; **plight one's troth,** BLANDISHMENT.

troth'-less. False; dishonorable. TRUTHFULNESS-FALSEHOOD, UPRIGHTNESS-DISHONESTY.

trot'-ters. Feet. TRAVELING-NAVIGATION.

trot'-toir. Sidewalk. WAY.

trou'-ba-dour''. A lyric poet of the 13th century. POETRY-PROSE.

troub'-le. Difficulty; pain; disorder. DIFFICULTY-FACILITY, ORGANIZATION-DISORGANIZATION, PLEASURABLENESS-PAINFULNESS, PLEASURE-PAIN, REGULARITY-IRREGULARITY, TOIL-RELAXATION, WELFARE-MISFORTUNE; **bring into trouble,** GOODNESS-BADNESS; **get into trouble,** SUCCESS-FAILURE; **in trouble,** GOOD-EVIL; **take trouble,** TOIL-RELAXATION; **trouble one for,** PETITION-DEPRECATION; **trouble oneself,** TOIL-RELAXATION; **trouble one's head about,** ACTIVITY-INDOLENCE, HEED-DISREGARD.

troub'-led wa'-ters, fish in. Labor under a disadvantage. DIFFICULTY-FACILITY.

troub'-le-some. Difficult; painful. DIFFICULTY-FACILITY, PLEASURABLENESS-PAINFULNESS, TOIL-RELAXATION.

troub'-lous. Tumultuous. REGULARITY-IRREGULARITY, TURBULENCE-CALMNESS; **troublous times,** VARIANCE-ACCORD.

trough. A wooden vessel for holding or conveying water. CONVEXITY-CONCAVITY, GROOVE, WATERCOURSE-AIRPIPE.

trounce. Punish. APPROVAL-DISAPPROVAL, EXCULPATION-PUNITION.

troupe. A theatrical company. GATHERING-SCATTERING.

trou'-sers. A man's garment. DRESS-UNDRESS.

trous''-seau'. A bride's outfit. DRESS-UNDRESS.

trout. A fresh-water fish. FAUNA-FLORA.

trouvaille [F.] (tru-vaiy'). Godsend. GAIN-LOSS.

trouvère [F.] (tru-vêr'). Troubadour. POETRY-PROSE.

tro'-ver. The finding of anything. DISCOVERY, GAIN-LOSS, LAW-LAWLESSNESS.

trow. Think; believe; know. FAITH-MISGIVING, KNOWLEDGE-IGNORANCE, REFLECTION-VACANCY.

trow'-el. A tool for spreading mortar. CONTENTS-RECEIVER.

trow'-sers. Same as trousers. DRESS-UNDRESS.

troy weight. A weight chiefly used in weighing gold, silver, and jewelry. HEAVINESS-LIGHTNESS.

tru'-ant. Absent; to idle. ACTIVITY-INDOLENCE, PRESENCE-ABSENCE, QUEST-EVASION, UPRIGHTNESS-ROGUE.

truce. Armistice. DISCONTINUANCE-CONTINUANCE, FIGHTING-CONCILIATION, STRIFE-PEACE; **flag of truce,** FIGHTING-CONCILIATION, MEDIATION.

tru''-ci-da'-tion. Act of killing. LIFE-KILLING.

truck. Barter; vehicle. CONVEYANCE-VESSEL, EXCHANGE, TOP-BOTTOM.

truck'-le to. Submit; flatter. ADULATION-DISPARAGEMENT, PRESUMPTION-OBSEQUIOUSNESS, YIELDING.

truc'-u-lence. Barbarity; cruelty. CHARITABLENESS-MALEVOLENCE.

tru'-cu-lent. Savage. CHARITABLENESS-MALEVOLENCE.

trudge. Walk slowly. SWIFTNESS-SLOWNESS, TRAVELING-NAVIGATION.

truditur dies die [L.] (triu'-di-tur dai'-îz dai'-î). It is hurried day by day. PERIOD-PROGRESS.

true. Real; honorable; accurate. APPROVAL-DISAPPROVAL, ASSENT-DISSENT, CURVATION-RECTILINEARITY, ENTITY-NONENTITY, NATURE-ART, OBSERVANCE-NONOBSERVANCE, THEOLOGY, TRUTH-ERROR, TRUTHFULNESS-FALSEHOOD; **see in its true colors,** DISCOVERY; **true bill,** JUSTIFICATION-DISPARAGEMENT, LITIGATION; **true meaning,** MEANING-JARGON; **true nature,** LIKENESS-UNLIKENESS; **true saying,** ADAGE-NONSENSE; **true to oneself,** PERSISTENCE-WHIM.

true'-heart''-ed. Sincere. TRUTHFULNESS-FALSEHOOD, UPRIGHTNESS-DISHONESTY.

true'-love''. One really beloved. LOVE-HATE.

true'-lov''-er's knot'. A kind of double knot. BLANDISHMENT, LOVE-HATE.

true'pen''-ny. Honest fellow. UPRIGHTNESS-DISHONESTY.

tru'-ism. Axiom. ADAGE-NONSENSE, MEANING-JARGON.

trull. Prostitute. PURITY-RAKE.

tru'-ly. Very; correctly; honestly. ASSENT-DISSENT, ASSERTION-DENIAL, MAGNITUDE-SMALLNESS, TRUTH-ERROR, TRUTHFULNESS-FALSEHOOD.

trump. Perfect; honorable. FAULTLESSNESS-FAULTINESS, GOOD MAN-BAD MAN, SUCCESS-FAILURE, UPRIGHTNESS-DISHONESTY; **trump card,** DESIGN, SUCCESS-FAILURE; **trump up,** JUSTIFICATION-CHARGE, TRUTHFULNESS-FALSEHOOD; **turn up trumps,** SUCCESS-FAILURE.

trumped up. Forged. TRUTHFULNESS-FABRICATION, TRUTHFULNESS-FRAUD.

trump'-er-y. Trash. CONSEQUENCE-INSIGNIFICANCE, MEANING-JARGON.

trump'-et. A wind musical instrument. BRAGGING, FIGHTING-CONCILIATION, MUSICAL INSTRUMENTS; **ear-trumpet,** HEARING-DEAFNESS; **flourish of trumpets,** BRAGGING, POMP, SOLEMNIZATION; **penny trumpet,** CACOPHONY; **sound of trumpet,** ALARM; **speaking-trumpet,** HEARING-DEAFNESS; **trumpet blast,** LOUDNESS-FAINTNESS; **trumpet-call,** ORDER, SIGN; **trumpet forth,** PUBLICITY.

trump'-et-er. One who sounds a trumpet; boaster. BRAGGING, MESSENGER, MUSICIAN.

trump'-et-toned. Tone like a trumpet. CACOPHONY.

trump'-et-tongued. Loud. LOUDNESS-FAINTNESS, PUBLICITY.

trun'-cate. Maimed. FORM-FORMLESSNESS, LENGTH-SHORTNESS.

trun'-ca-ted. Maimed. ENTIRETY-DEFICIENCY.

trun'-cheon. Weapon; staff of office; instrument of punishment. ATTACK-DEFENSE, RECOMPENSE-SCOURGE, SCEPTER, WEAPON.

trun'-dle. Roll. PUSH-PULL, REVOLUTION-EVOLUTION.

trunk. Origin; main body; box. ANATOMY, CAUSE-EFFECT, CONTENTS-RECEIVER, PARENTAGE-PROGENY, WHOLE-PART.

trunk'-hose. Short wide breeches. DRESS-UNDRESS.

trun'-nion. A knob projecting on each side of a gun and helping support it on the cheeks of the cannon. SUSPENSION-SUPPORT.

truss. Support; tie. GATHERING-SCATTERING, SUSPENSION-SUPPORT, UNION-DISUNION.

trust. Combination; credit; belief; property. CREDIT-DEBT, EXPECTATION-SURPRISE, FAITH-UNBELIEF, LABOR-CAPITAL, PROPERTY, SANGUINENESS-HOPELESSNESS; **trust to a broken reed,** SECURITY-INSECURITY, SKILL-UNSKILFULNESS; **trust to the chapter of accidents,** PURPOSE-LUCK.

trus-tee'. Steward. CONSIGNEE, HOLDER, TREASURER.

trust'-less. Unreliable. UPRIGHTNESS-DISHONESTY.
trust'-wor"-thy. Reliable. CERTAINTY-DOUBT, FAITH-MISGIVING, REMEMBRANCE-FORGETFULNESS, SECURITY-INSECURITY, TRUTHFULNESS-FALSEHOOD, UPRIGHTNESS-DISHONESTY.
trust'-y. Trustworthy. UPRIGHTNESS-DISHONESTY.
truth. Veracity. ORTHODOXY-HETERODOXY, TRUTH-ERROR, TRUTHFULNESS-FALSEHOOD, UPRIGHTNESS-DISHONESTY; **arrive at the truth,** DISCOVERY; **in truth,** ASSERTION-DENIAL, CERTAINTY-DOUBT, TRUTHFULNESS-FALSEHOOD; **love of truth,** TRUTHFULNESS-FALSEHOOD; **of a truth,** ASSERTION-DENIAL, TRUTHFULNESS-FALSEHOOD; **prove the truth,** JUSTIFICATION-CHARGE; **religious truth,** ORTHODOXY-HETERODOXY; **speak the truth,** EXPOSURE-HIDINGPLACE, TRUTHFULNESS-FALSEHOOD.

TRUTH—ERROR.

Accuracy. Exact conformity to truth.
Authenticity. The quality of being established for truth.
Clockwork precision. A regular and continued exactness.
Delicacy. Perfection in detail and harmony in adjustment.
Exactitude. The quality of being exactly conformable to truth.
Exactness. The quality of perfectly conforming to a standard.
Exact preciseness. Strict or perfect exactness. See *Adjectives.*
Exact truth. Perfect conformity to reason.
Fact. Anything done; anything knowable by the senses.
Gospel. That which is held to be infallibly true.
Honest truth. Truth expressed openly and frankly.
Incontestable. Not to be disputed,
Intrinsic truth. Truth that is natural and inherent.
Ipsissima verba [L.]. The very words.
Just the truth. The exact truth.
Mathematical precision. The accuracy of mathematics.
Naked truth. Simple and evident truth.
Nature. That which is conformed to nature or to truth and reality. See SUBJECTIVENESS.
Not an illusion. Not an unreal image or appearance, but the real.
Nuda veritas [L.]. The naked truth.
Orthodoxy. Soundness in the true faith. See ORTHODOXY.
Orthology. The right naming or correct description of things.
Plain matter of fact. Fact plainly evident to the senses.
Plain truth. Truth that is readily seen or understood.
Preciseness. Strict accuracy or exactness.
Precision. The quality of being strictly true.
Punctuality. The quality of being punctual or exact.
Realism. The depicting of persons and scenes as they truthfully are.
Reality. The state or quality of being real; something true or genuine. See ENTITY.
Real Simon pure. The genuine article.
Rigor. Exactness without indulgence.
Sober truth. Expression or statement not swayed by excitement or passion.
Stern truth. Truth that inspires fear.
The truth, the whole truth, and nothing but the truth. The exact truth, and nothing more.
The very thing. The exact thing.
Truth. The state or character of being true; fact seen in the light of reason.
Unalloyed truth. Absolute truth.
Unqualified truth.} The true story or statement.
Unvarnished tale.}
Veracity. The state of being truthful.
Verity. A true statement; something really existent.

TRUTH—*Verbs.*

Be the case. Be the facts what they may.
Be true. To conform to a standard. See *Adjectives.*
Get at the truth. To find out what is true. See DISCOVERY.
Hold good. Remain as true.
Hold true. Remain truthful.
Hold water. To stand true after examination.
Prove true. To establish the truth by evidence. See *Adjectives.*
Render true. To make conformable to a standard. See *Adjectives.*
Stand the test. Remain true after examination.
Substantiate. To establish as true by substantial evidence.

TRUTH—*Adjectives.*

Accurate. Conforming exactly to truth.
Actual. Something real or actually existing. See ENTITY.
Authentic. According with the facts; trustworthy; reliable.
Categorically true. True without qualification.
Certain. Established as fact or truth. See CERTAINTY.
Constant. Steady in purpose; faithful.
Correct. In accordance with what is true.
Curious. Eager for information.
Definite. Having precise limits; known with exactness.
Delicate. Nice in discrimination.
Exact. Strictly observant of truth.
Ex officio [L.]. By virtue of office.

Bias. A prejudice or predilection. See DECISION-MISJUDGMENT.
Blot. A disfiguring spot or stain.
Blunder. A stupid error.
Botchery. Bungling work. See SKILL-UNSKILFULNESS.
Bubble. Anything unsubstantial; a delusion.
Bull. A ridiculous contradiction in terms.
Clerical error. A mistake in copying or writing.
Corrigendum. A thing or word to be corrected.
Cross-purposes. Contrary purposes; misunderstanding.
Delusion. Erroneous impression or belief.
Dream. A vague notion. See FANCY.
Erratum [L.]. An error, especially in writing or printing.
Error. A wandering from the truth; something done, **said,** or believed wrongly.
Fable. A brief story or tale feigned or invented to embody a moral. See TRUTHFULNESS-FABRICATION.
Fallacy. Deception or false appearance, nature, or quality.
False idea.}
False impression.} An erroneous notion.
False light. A light intended to mislead or deceive. See SIGHT-DIMSIGHTEDNESS.
Falsism. A self-evident falsity.
Fault. A slight error in conduct; defect.
Flaw. Something in an instrument rendering it invalid.
Hallucination. An impression not founded on fact. See SANENESS-LUNACY.
Heresy. A doctrinal view or belief at variance with recognized standards. See ORTHODOXY-HETERODOXY.
Illusion. Any misleading appearance.
Inexactness. The want of precision. See *Adjectives.*
Lapsus lingua [L.]. A slip of the tongue.
Laxity. Want of exactness or precision; looseness.
Loose thread. A statement or reasoning not exact or precise.
Misapprehension. A mistake in apprehending.
Miscomputation. Erroneous reckoning. See DECISION-MISJUDGMENT.
Misconception. An erroneous notion or understanding of a thing.
Misconstruction. An erroneous interpretation of words or things. See INTERPRETATION-MISINTERPRETATION.
Misleading. Leading into error. See *Verbs.*
Misprint. An error in printing.
Misreport. An erroneous report.
Miss. Mistake; error.
Misstatement. An erroneous representation, verbal or written.
Mistake. The act of taking something to be other than it is.
Mists of error. Anything that dims the mental vision.
Misunderstanding. A mistake as to meaning or motive.
Non sequitur [L.]. It does not follow. See RATIOCINATION-CASUISTRY.
Oversight. An error due to inattention.
Quid pro quo [L.]. Something for something; an equivalent.
Self-deceit. Self-deception.
Self-deception. Deception concerning oneself, proceeding from one's own error.
Slip. An error or fault.
Slip of the pen. A lapse in writing.
Slip of the tongue. A lapse in speech.
Stumble. A blunder or false step. See SUCCESS-FAILURE.
Trip. A false step; a blunder.

ERROR—*Verbs.*

Be at cross-purposes. To disagree. See DECISION.
Be deceived. To be misled. See GULL.
Be erroneous. To be mistaken. See *Adjectives.*
Beguile. To deceive; delude.
Be in error. To be wrong. See *Adjectives.*
Be in the wrong. To be in error.
Be mistaken. To take something to be what it is not. See *Verbs.*
Blunder. To err egregiously.
Deceive. To mislead by deluding. See TRUTHFULNESS-FRAUD.
Deceive oneself. To cause oneself to err.
Delude. To lead into error; beguile.

TRUTH—Adjectives—*Continued.*

Faithful.   Firmly adhering to the truth.

Fine.   Excellent or admirable in quality, character, form, or appearance.

Genuine.   Belonging to the original or true stock.

In its true colors.   As it truly is.

Just.   Agreeing with a required standard; true.

Legitimate.   Having the sanction of law or custom.

Literal.   True as to fact or detail.

Mathematical.   Demonstrably true or correct.

Natural.   True to nature.

Nice.   Fitted or adjusted exactly true; accurate.

Official.   Pertaining to an office or public trust.

Orthodox.   Holding the faith commonly accepted as true.   See Orthodoxy.

Particular.   Exact in performance or requirement.

Precise.   Strictly accurate.

Punctual.   Exact as.to appointed time.

Pure.   Free from mixture; truly genuine.

Real.   Being in true accordance to appearance or claim; genuine.

Realistic.   Conformable to the principles and methods of realism. See *Nouns.*

Religiously exact.   Conscientiously observant of truth.

Right.   According to fact or truth.

Rigid.   Strict; exact.

Rigorous.   Exacting; logically accurate.

Scientific.   Agreeing with the rules or principles of science; hence accurate; exact.

Scrupulous.   Exact; precise.   See Uprightness.

Solid.   Characterized by reality; substantial or satisfactory.

Sound.   Founded in truth.

Sterling.   True; genuine.

Strict.   Exacting; rigidly observed.

Substantial.   Of true worth and importance.

Substantially true.   Essentially true.

Tangible.   Perceptible by touch or by the senses.

True.   Conformable to fact in the light of reason.

True as gospel.   Absolutely truthful.

True to the letter.   True in every particular.

Unadulterated.   Genuine; pure.

Unaffected.   Simple; true to nature.

Uncolored.   True; without prejudice or exaggeration.

Unconfuted.   Not confuted or proved false; hence, true.

Undisguised.   Not covered with a disguise; hence, open, frank, truthful.

Undistorted.   Not distorted, as by falsehood.

Unerring.   Certain; of true insight.

Unexaggerated.   Not exaggerated; hence, truthful.

Unflattering.   Not coloring the truth to please.

Unideal.   Not ideal; real.

Unimagined.   Not imagined, conceived, or formed in idea.

Unimpeachable.   Not capable of being impeached or called in question.

Unrefuted.   Not capable of being refuted; hence, truthful.

Unromantic.   Contrary to romance.

Unsophisticated.   Simple; pure.

Unvarnished.   Not artfully embellished; plain.

Valid.   Sufficiently supported by actual fact.

Veracious.   Observant of truth.   See Truthfulness.

Veritable.   Agreeable to truth.

Well-defined.   Having the precise limit well-marked.

Well-founded. }
Well-grounded. }   Founded on good and true reasons.

TRUTH—*Adverbs, etc.*

Actually.   In truth.

Ad amussim [L.].   Accurately; exactly.

Ad unguem [L.].   To a hair; exactly.

At all events.   In all probability.

At any rate.   Certainly.

Au pied ae la lettre [F.].   Literally.

Certainly.   With certainty.   See Certainty.

Chapter and verse.   Accurately.

Exactly.   Strictly.   See *Adjectives.*

In all respects.   In every regard.

Indeed.   In fact.

In effect.   In fact or reality.   See Subjectiveness.

In every respect.   In every regard; entirely.

In reality.   In truth or fact.

Ipsissimis verbis [L.].   The very words.

Literally.   Exactly in fact or detail.

Literatim [L.].   Letter for letter; literally.

Neither more nor less.   Exactly.

ERROR—Verbs—*Continued*

Dream.   To think of things which have only an imaginary reality. See Fancy.

Err.   To mistake in judgment or opinion; wander from the right way.

Fail.   To prove inadequate or defective.   See Success-Failure.

Fall into an error.   To be wrong.

Falsify.   To represent falsely.

Give a false idea. }
Give a false impression. } To mislead.

Go astray.   To go into error.

Labor under an error.   To have a false idea.   See *Nouns.*

Lead astray.   To lead into error.

Lead into error.   To mislead.

Lie.   To utter falsehood with intention to lead into error.   See Truthfulness-Falsehood.

Lie under an error.   To be mistaken.   See *Nouns.*

Lose oneself.   To be uncertain of one's views.   See Certainty-Doubt.

Misapprehend.   To form an erroneous apprehension of.

Miscalculate.   To calculate erroneously.   See Decision-Misjudgment.

Misconceive.   To have an erroneous understanding of anything.

Miscount.   To make erroneous reckoning.

Misguide.   To lead or guide into error.

Misinform.   To give erroneous information to.   See Education-Misteaching.

Mislead.   To guide into error.

Misreckon.   To compute erroneously.

Misstate.   To make an erroneous representation of.

Mistake.   To take in error.

Misunderstand.   To take in an erroneous sense.

Play at cross-purposes.   To disagree.   See Interpretation-Misinterpretation.

Put the saddle on the wrong horse.   To ascribe blame erroneously.

Receive a false impression.   To misunderstand.

Reckon without one's host.   To reckon the cost of entertainment without consulting one's host; hence, to neglect important facts in reaching a conclusion.

Stumble.   To confound; puzzle.

Take the shadow for the substance.   To take something to be what it is not.   See Credulousness.

Take the wrong sow by the ear.   To hit upon the wrong person or thing.   See Skill-Unskilfulness.

Trip.   To cause to fail, catch in a mistake.

ERROR—*Adjectives.*

Aberrant.   Wandering into error.

All in the wrong.   Wholly in error.

Apocryphal.   Of doubtful authenticity, spurious.

Astray.   Wandering into error or evil.   See Certainty-Doubt.

At cross-purposes.   In disagreement.   See Interpretation-Misinterpretation.

Beside the mark.   Away from the mark, or in error.

Controvertible.   Not too evident to exclude difference of opinion.

Deceitful.   Tending to mislead or ensnare.   See Truthfulness-Falsehood.

Delusive.   Apt to lead into error.

Devoid of truth.   Not possessing truth.

Erroneous.   Marked by error.

Exploded.   Having had the falsity or error of shown.

Fallacious.   Of, pertaining to, or involving a fallacy or error.

False.   Contrary to truth or fact; erroneously believed to exist.

Groundless.   Without foundation in truth.

Heretical.   At variance with or subversive of accepted views or beliefs.   See Orthodoxy-Heterodoxy.

Ideal.   Consisting of, pertaining to, or existing in ideas.   See Fancy.

Illogical.   Of erroneous reasoning.   See Ratiocination-Casuistry.

Illusive.   Deceiving by false show.

Illusory.   Tending to lead into error by false appearances.

Inaccurate.   Not accurate; erroneous.

Incorrect.   In error; faulty.

Indefinite.   Not definite, determinate, or precise.   See Certainty-Doubt.

In error.   Wrong.   See *Nouns.*

Inexact.   Not precisely true.

In the wrong box.   Erroneously placed.

Mistaken.   Wrong in judgment.   See *Verbs.*

Mock.   False; counterfeit.

On a false scent. }
On the wrong scent. } Tracing anything erroneously.

TRUTH—ERROR—*Continued.*

TRUTH—Adverbs, etc.—*Continued.*

Sic [L.]. So; thus; literally reproduced.
Sous tous les rapports [F.]. In all respects.
Strictly speaking. Speaking exactly; in strict observance to truth.
To a hair.
To a nicety.
To an inch.
To a T. } Exactly.
To a title.
To a turn.
To the letter.
Totidem verbis [L.]. In so many words.
Truly. In conformity with truth or reality. See *Adjectives.*
Verbatim [L.]. In the exact words.
Verbatim et literatim [L.]. Word for word and letter for letter.
Verily. Truly.
With truth. Truthfully. See Truthfulness.
Word for word. In the exact words.

TRUTH—*Phrases.*

En suivant la verité [F.]. In following the truth.
Ex facto jus oritur [L.]. The law arises out of fact.
Locos y niños dicen la verdad [Sp.]. Children and fools speak the truth.
Rem acu tetigisti [L.]. You have hit the thing exactly.
The fact is.
The truth is. } This is the truth.

Truth', Spir'-it of. God. Divinity.

ERROR—Adjectives—*Continued.*

Out.
Out in one's reckoning. } Mistaken.
Perverted. Turned to error.
Refuted. Proved in error.
Spurious. Not genuine; false. See Truthfulness-Fraud.
Tripping. Blundering. See *Verbs.*
Unauthenticated. Not shown to be genuine.
Under an error. Mistaken. See *Nouns.*
Unexact. Not correct or accurate.
Ungrounded. Without foundation in truth.
Unreal. Not real.
Unsound. Not founded on truth or correct principles.
Unsubstantial. Not real; not having substance. See Substance-Nullity.
Unsustainable. Not capable of being sustained or supported.
Untrue. Not according to truth.
Untrustworthy. Not worthy of being trusted.
Wide of the mark.
Wide of the truth. } Far from being true.

ERROR—*Adverbs.*

More or less. To a greater or less degree of truth.

ERROR—*Phrase.*

Errare est humanum [L.]. To err is human.

truth'-ful-ness. Veracity. Truthfulness-Falsehood.

TRUTHFULNESS—FALSEHOOD.

Artlessness. The quality or state of being without deceit. See Craft-Artlessness.
Bona fide [L.]. Good faith.
Candor. Freedom from mental reservation; openness.
Conjurer. One who confirms another's testimony.
Fact. Concrete truth; a true or correct statement. See Truth.
Fidelity. Faithfulness in the discharge of duty, or of obligation.
Frankness. The quality of being frank; ingenuousness.
Honest truth. The unreserved truth.
Honesty. Character or quality of being honest; uprightness.
Ingenuousness. The quality or state of being open in character, frankness.
Light of truth. Unobscured truth.
Love of truth. A delight in what is true.
Plain-dealing. Frankness and sincerity; straightforward honesty.
Probity. Strict honesty, able to withstand tests. See Uprightness.
Sincerity. The state or quality of being free from deceit; truthfulness.
Sober truth. Truth which must be considered seriously.
The truth, the whole truth, and nothing but the truth. The unvarnished truth in its entirety and nothing more.
Truth. The state or character of being true in being, knowledge, or speech.
Truthfulness. The quality of speaking the truth.
Unvarnished tale. A true description or story.
Veracity. The quality or state of being truthful or observant of truth.

TRUTHFULNESS—*Verbs.*

Make a clean breast of. To confess all.
Not deceive. Not to mislead by falsehood. See Truthfulness-Fraud.
Not lie. Not to utter a statement to deceive. See Truthfulness-Falsehood.
Paint in its true colors. To describe without reservation or equivocation.
Show oneself in one's true colors. To expose one's real self.
Speak by the card. To speak from exact knowledge.
Speak one's mind. To speak out frankly.
Speak the truth. To give utterance to what is true.
Tell the truth. Not to speak falsehoods; to speak what you know.

TRUTHFULNESS—*Adjectives.*

As good as one's word. Reliable; possessing quality of keeping a promise.
Bona fide [L.]. In good faith; without deceit.
Candid. Sincere in speech; straightforward; clear; white.
Frank. Free from concealment; open in manner.

Artfulness. Deceitfulness.
Charlatanism.
Charlatanry. } Undue or fraudulent pretensions to skill.
Deceit. The quality of being deceptive.
Falsehood. The quality of being deceitful.
Falseness. The quality of being untrue.
Falsism. An assertion the falsity of which is plainly apparent.
Falsity. The quality of being false; characterized by deception.
Hollowness. Deceitfulness.
Hypocrisy. The acting of a false part.
Insincerity. The lack of the quality of being sincere.
Mealy-mouthedness. Speaking with insincerity.
Unfairness. Dishonesty; fraud. See Uprightness-Dishonesty.

FALSEHOOD—*Nouns of Agent.*

Bam. A cheat.
Buncome. Inflated or bombastic speech-making only for effect.
Bunkum. Buncome.
Cajolery. The act or practise of making delusive speech.
Cant. The hypocritical use of speech to appear pious.
Covin. A secret agreement to defraud another.
Crocodile tears. Simulated or pretended weeping.
Deception. The act of deceiving or misleading another by spoken or acted falsehood. See Truthfulness-Fraud.
Dissembling. Concealing; a giving the semblance of something to
Dissimulation. The act or practise of feigning; deceit.
Distortion. A straining or perversion of meaning.
Double-dealing. The act of being treacherous or deceitful.
Duplicity. The act of speaking differently with different persons in relation to the same things; double-dealing.
Equivocation. The act of equivocating for the purpose of deceit.
Evasion. The act, means, or result of evading, eluding, or avoiding.
Exaggeration. The act of representing with extravagance. See Gull-Hyperbole.
Fabrication. That which is invented; a concoction; a falsehood.
False coloring. Specious appearance.
False swearing. Perjury.
Falsification. The act or process of falsifying; the representing of anything to be what it is not.
Fencing. The act of avoiding making disclosures.
Flam. A false pretense; sham; falsehood; lie.
Flattery. Insincere complimentary language or conduct.
Flim-flam. The process of cheating a person by confusing him so that he pays out more change than he ought.
Forgery. The act of falsely making or altering writing with intent to defraud.
Fraud. An act of deliberate deception for gain.
Gammon. An imposition or hoax.

TRUTHFULNESS—FALSEHOOD—*Continued.*

TRUTHFULNESS—ADJECTIVES—*Continued.*

Guileless   Free from guile; artless; frank.
Honest.   Free from fraud, equitable; fair.
Ingenuous   Free from reserve, disguise, equivocation, or dissimulation.
Open.   Without reserve or false pretense.
Open-hearted.   Showing the thoughts and intentions plainly.
Outspoken.   Plain-spoken; frank; speaking out freely and frankly.
Pure.   Free from moral defilement.
Scrupulous.   Cautious in action for fear of doing wrong.
Simple-hearted.   Open; sincere.
Sincere.   Acting and speaking the truth; without alloy.
Straightforward.   Free from prevarication or concealment.
True.   Conformable to reality or fact and law.
True-blue.   Of uncompromising principles.
True-hearted.   Loyal; faithful, honest; sincere.
Trustworthy.   Worthy of confidence.
Truthful.   Habitually speaking the truth.
Unaffected.   Not showing affectation; sincere; real.
Undisguised.   Not concealed by false appearances.
Undissembling.   True.   See TRUTHFULNESS-FALSEHOOD.
Unfeigned.   Not hypocritical; real.
Unperjured.   Free from perjury; not forsworn.
Unreserved.   Holding nothing back; frank.
Veracious.   Habitually disposed to speak the truth.
Veridical.   Truth-telling; veracious.

TRUTHFULNESS—*Adverbs, etc.*

As the dial of the sun.   Without deviation.
As the needle to the pole   Directly.
Bona fide [L.].   In good faith; without deceit.
By my troth.   Of a truth.   See ASSERTION.
Cartes sur table [F.].   The cards upon the table; openly.
From the bottom of one's heart.   Truly.
Honor bright.   An expletive used to emphasize an affirmation.
In foro conscientiæ [L.].   In the forum of conscience.
In good earnest.   In reality.
In good sooth.   Truly.
In good truth.   In sound reason.
In plain words.   In simple language
In sooth.   In truth.
In truth.   In the language of reason.
Of a truth.   Assuredly.
Sooth to say.   In truth
Troth.   In truth.
Truly.   In conformity with reason.
Unfeignedly.   Without hypocrisy; really.
With no nonsense.   Truthfully and seriously.
Without equivocation.   With nothing but the plain meaning.
With truth.   Without falsifying.

TRUTHFULNESS—*Phrases.*

Audacter et sincere [L.].   Bravely and sincerely.
Dichtung und Wahrheit [G.]   Fiction and truth.
Di il vero e affronterai il diavolo [It.].   Speak the truth and you will shame the devil.
Esto quod esse videris [L.].   Be what you seem to be.
Magna est veritas et prævalet [L.].   Great is truth and it prevails.
Veritas odium parit [L.].   Truth engenders hatred.
Veritatis simplex oratio est [L.].   The language of truth is simple.
Verite sans peur [F.].   Truth without fear.

FALSEHOOD—VERBS—*Continued from Column 2*

Falsify.   To make deceptive or delusive, to misrepresent
Feign.   To make a false show of
Fence.   To talk in defense, not openly.
Fib.   To tell a harmless untruth; to tell a white lie.
Forge.   To make false or alter writing with intent to defraud.
Forswear.   To swear falsely, commit perjury
Garble.   To change with evil intent, pervert, falsify.
Get up.   To make up; to disguise.
Give a color to.   To invest with the appearance of truth or reality
Give a false coloring upon.   To make to appear more beautiful.
Give a gloss.   To make to have a greater brilliancy.
Gloss over.   To excuse; to give a false appearance to.
Hang out false colors.   To use a flag without right.
Hatch.   To make up.
Hold out false colors.   To hold out dishonest inducements.
Invent.   To fabricate in the mind; concoct; devise.
Lie.   To speak knowingly and wrongly that which is not true.
Lie like a conjurer.   To falsify with skill.

FALSEHOOD—NOUNS OF AGENT—*Continued.*

Guile.   The act of deceiving; the disposition to deceive.
Humbug.   Any person or thing calculated or intended to deceive.
Hypocrisy.   The acting of a false part.
Il volto sciolto i pensieri stretti [It]   Countenance open and thoughts closed.
Invention.   Mental fabrication or concoction.
Jesuitism.   Deceptive practises, subtle distinctions, or political duplicity.
Jesuitry.   The methods or principles professed by Jesuits.
Judas kiss.   The act of betraying under guise of friendship.
Lip homage.   Homage rendered by the lips only
Lip service.   Service in profession as opposed to practise
Lying.   The practise of telling falsehoods.
Machiavelism.   The justification of the means by the end.
Malingering.   The act of feigning or inducing sickness or injury to avoid duty
Mendacity.   A lie, a falsehood.
Mere outside.   That which is superficial.
Mere show.   That which is done for effect.
Misrepresentation.   The act or instance of misrepresenting.
Misstatement.   A wrong or false statement or account.   See TRUTH-ERROR.
Mouth honor.   An insincere expression of esteem or respect.
Mystification.   The act of artfully perplexing.
Organized hypocrisy.   Continued falsehood or deception.   See UPRIGHTNESS-DISHONESTY.
Perfidy.   The act of violating faith or allegiance.
Perjury.   The giving of false testimony under oath.
Perversion.   Diversion from the true meaning.
Perversion of truth.   Misapplication of truth.
Pharisaism.   Formality self-righteousness or hypocrisy
Pretending.   The act of making a pretense.
Pretense.   The act of making a false assumption.
Prevarication.   The act of making misleading statements to deceive.
Quackery.   Fraudulent practise.
Sham.   That which or the one who is a deception
Shuffling.   Evading the truth, prevaricating.
Simulation.   The act of assuming a false form, appearance, character, or condition.
Subreption.   Procuring of some favor or reward by fraudulent concealment
Suggestio falsi [L.]   A suspicion of falsity.
Suppression of truth.   The keeping back or hiding truth.
Suppressio veri [L]   The suppression of truth.

FALSEHOOD—*Verbs.*

Act a part.   To appear to be what one is not.
Affect.   To do for effect, assume, put on.
Ambiguas in vulgum spargere voces [L]   To spread doubtful rumors among the populace
Assume.   To put on deceitfully.
Be a liar.   To practise falsehood
Bear false witness.   To give untrue evidence.
Beat about the bush.   To approach a subject in a roundabout way.
Be false.   To appear to be what it is not.
Belie.   To represent falsely, misrepresent
Blague.   To humbug.
Blow hot and cold.   To vacillate; be inconsistent or irresolute.
Cant.   To make hypocritical use of speech to appear pious.
Clean the outside of the platter.   To appear in a false light.
Color.   To make to appear in a false and specious light
Commend the poisoned chalice to the lips.   To be treacherous. ·[Shakespeare *Macbeth*, I, vii]
Concoct.   To scheme
Cook.   To tamper with or garble for the purpose of deceiving.
Coquet.   To deceive in love.
Counterfeit.   To make a copy of to deceive; to feign.
Cry "Wolf!"   To frighten with imaginary terrors.   [Æsop, *Fable.*]
Deceive.   To mislead by or as by falsehood or deceit
Disguise.   To change the appearance of, so as to deceive.
Dissemble.   To conceal as by a false appearance or pretense.
Dissimulate.   To give a false appearance to; to feign.
Distort.   To interpret falsely; to give a strained meaning to
Dress up.   To put on disguise.
Embroider.   To embellish with additions.
Equivocate.   To use words of double meaning to deceive
Exaggerate.   To describe or represent with extravagant additions.
Fabricate.   To invent fancifully or falsely.
Faire pattes de velours [F.]   To make claws of velvet; to be deceitful.

(*Continued on Column* 1.)

FALSEHOOD—VERBS—*Continued*.

Lie like a trooper. To be an inveterate liar.

Make a show of. To make a pretense; to make an appearance without reality.

Make-believe. To pretend.

Malinger. To feign or induce sickness to avoid service or shirk duty.

Mince the truth. To affect extreme delicacy in discussing things.

Miscite. To cite erroneously.

Misquote. To quote wrongly or incorrectly.

Misreport. To make a false report; slander.

Misrepresent. To make false or wrong representations concerning.

Misstate. To state wrongly or falsely.

Palter. To deal in a trifling manner; to equivocate.

Palter to the understanding. To attempt to confuse.

Pass off for. To give out or circulate as genuine.

Perjure oneself. To swear falsely.

Pervert. To turn from its right meaning.

Play a double game. To have one line of action openly for the purpose of concealing another or the real line.

Play a part. To feign.

Play false. To act falsely.

Play fast and loose. To be tricky or untrustworthy.

Play the hypocrite. To make false professions of one's belief.

Pretend. To act or speak as if the facts were other than they are.

Prevaricate. To use ambiguous language for the purpose of deceiving.

Put a false coloring upon. To make more attractive than reality.

Put a false construction upon. To make a wrong interpretation of.

Put a gloss on. To cover over.

Put on. To assume.

Put on the mask. To conceal.

Quibble. To evade the plain truth by artifice.

Repondre en Normand [F.]. To reply like a Norman; to answer evasively.

Romance. To indulge in false or visionary fabrications.

Sail under false colors. To pass for what one is not.

Say the grapes are sour. To give an untrue reason for not taking something. [Æsop, *Fable*.]

Sham. To make a false pretense of.

Sham Abraham. To feign sickness.

Shuffle. Evasive or tricky course of behavior.

Simulate. To assume the mere appearance or form of without the reality.

Speak falsely. To tell untruths.

Swear false. To give false witness.

Tell a lie. Utter a falsehood. See TRUTHFULNESS-FABRICATION.

Trim. To practise double-dealing.

Trump up. To make up or invent for a fraudulent purpose.

Varnish. To give a fair coloring to by words; to gloss over.

Varnish right and puzzle wrong. To put on a false or deceitful appearance.

FALSEHOOD—*Adjectives*.

Affected. Assumed falsely or in outward semblance only. See AFFECTATION.

Artful. Produced or characterized by craft or cunning.

Canting. Said in a hypocritical way.

Collusive. Fraudulently concerted or devised.

Collusory. Plotting secretly with evil design.

Covinous. Fraudulent; collusive.

Deceitful. Characterized by deception; tricky. See TRUTHFULNESS-FRAUD.

Dishonest. Destitute of integrity or good faith; untrustworthy.

Disingenuous. Wanting in openness and honesty.

Double-dealing. Treacherous; deceitful.

Double-faced. Deceitful; hypocritical.

Double-handed. Deceitful; deceptive.

Double-hearted. False; deceitful.

Double-minded. Unsettled; unstable.

Double-tongued. Characterized by duplicity of speech.

Evasive. Tending to deceive.

Faithless. Untrue to promise or obligation; deceptive; unfaithful.

False. Contrary to truth; erroneous; not accordant with fact.

Falsified. Misrepresented.

Forsworn. Perjured.

Fraudulent. Based on, proceeding from, or characterized by fraud.

Hollow. Insincere; empty or vacant, as if containing nothing.

Hypocritical. Characterized by hypocrisy.

Insincere. Acting, speaking, or appearing falsely to deceive.

Janus-faced. Double-faced.

Jesuitical. Using crafty or insidious arts or methods.

Machiavellian. Crafty or cruel in politics; treacherous.

Mealy-mouthed. Speaking with insincerity.

Mendacious. Addicted to lying; falsifying.

Parthis mendacior [L.]. More deceitful than Parthians.

Perfidious. Violating good faith. See UPRIGHTNESS-DISHONESTY.

Pharisaical. Observing the form but neglecting the spirit of religion.

Plausible. Seeming likely to be true though open to doubt.

Smooth-faced. Having a bland expression to deceive.

Smooth-spoken. Using plausible and flattering speech.

Smooth-tongued. Using easy speech.

Spurious. Not genuine; false.

Tartuffish. Hypocritical.

Trothless. Faithless; treacherous.

Truthless. Not agreeing with fact.

Uncandid. Not frank.

Unfair. Not honest.

Uningenuous. Not free from reserve, disguise, equivocation or dissimulation.

Untrue. Not corresponding with fact.

Unveracious. Not habitually disposed to speak the truth.

FALSEHOOD—*Adverbs, etc.*

A la Tartufe [F.]. Like Tartufe; hypocritically. [Molière.]

Falsely. In a false manner; dishonestly.

Slyly. In a sly manner; artfully. See CRAFT.

With a double tongue. With duplicity.

FALSEHOOD—*Phrases*.

Blandæ mendacia linguæ [L.]. Falsehood of a smooth tongue.

Falsus in uno, falsus in omnibus [L.]. False in one point, false in all.

Tous songes sont men songes [F.]. Dreams all are lies all.

TRUTHFULNESS—FABRICATION.

FABRICATION.

Bosh. Empty words.

Bounce. An audacious lie.

Canard. A fabricated sensational statement.

Canterbury tale. A story told by a traveler to pass away the time, like those told in Chaucer by prilgrims to the shrine of Thomas a Becket, at Canterbury.

Clap-trap. Language or conduct designed only to evoke applause.

Cock-and-bull story. A highly improbable story.

Concealment. Hidden knowledge.

Crammer. A lie.

Deception. An act that deceives. See TRUTHFULNESS-FRAUD.

Disguise. False speech.

Empty words. Words without sense or meaning.

Evasion. The act, means, or result of avoiding by artifice.

Exaggeration. Extravagant statements. See GULL-HYPERBOLE.

Fable. A story feigned or invented to embody a moral.

Fabrication. That which is feigned or fabricated; a falsehood.

Falsehood. An intentional untruth.

False plea. A false pretense or pretext.

False statement. A wrong recital of facts.

False story. An invention or fabrication.

Falsification. The telling or acting of falsehood.

Fib. An untruth told without evil intent.

Fiction. That which is feigned or imagined.

Forgery. Something made in false and fraudulent imitation of something genuine.

Gloss. A deceptive show.

Half-truth. An assertion that is true as far as it goes, but conceals part of the truth.

Hum. A trick; a cheat.

Invention. Mental fabrication.

Irony. The use of words designed to convey a meaning opposite to the literal sense.

Judas kiss. A hypocritical and deceitful mark of affection. [Bible.]

Lie. A statement made with intention to deceive.

Make-believe. A pretense.

TRUTHFULNESS—FABRICATION—*Continued.*

Mare's nest. A discovery that seems important, but turns out to be a hoax.

Mental reservation. A withholding of truth or knowledge.

Misrepresentation. A wrong or false representation.

Misstatement. A wrong or false statement or account.

Moonshine. Pretense.

Myth. A fictitious narrative presented as historical.

Nursery tale. A story or fable to amuse children.

Perversion. Diversion from the true meaning.

Pious fraud. A deception intended to bring about a good result.

Pretense.⎫ That which is advanced or displayed for the purpose of
Pretext.⎬ concealing or misrepresenting.

Profession. A pretense.

Romance. A form of prose fiction.

Sell. A trick, joke, or swindle.

Sham. A fraudulent show.

Shave. A fabricated report.

Shift. An artful trick.

Shuffle. An evasive or tricky course of behavior.

Story. A real or fictitious narrative of events; a lie.

Subterfuge. Evasion.

Suggestio falsi [L.]. A suggestion of falsity.

Tarradiddle. A false statement.

Thing devised by the enemy. A trap or deception.

Thing that is not. A fabrication.

Traveler's tale. An exaggerated story.

Trumped-up statement. A statement made up or invented for a fraudulent purpose.

Trumped-up story. A story invented for a fraudulent purpose.

Untrue statement. A false statement.

Untrue story. A story not conforming to fact.

White lie. A false statement made without intention of malice.

Whopper. A big lie.

FABRICATION—*Verb.*

Have a false meaning. To be deceitful.

FABRICATION—*Adjectives.*

Ben trovato [It.]. Well invented.

Elusory. Tending to deceive one's expectations.

Fabricated. Contrived without ground or reason.

Fabulous. Belonging to fable; fictitious.

Factitious. Created by art as opposed to nature.

False. Contrary to truth; erroneous; artificial.

False as dicer's oaths. Very false.

Far from the truth. False.

Fictitious. Substituted for something real.

Forged. Made in false and fraudulent imitation of something which if genuine would be legal.

Illusory. Deceiving or intending to deceive.

Invented. Fabricated in the mind; concocted.

Ironical. Disguising the real meaning.

Soi-disant [F.]. Pretended.

Supposititious. Put in the place or made to represent the person of another, to deceive or defraud.

Surreptitious. Accomplished by secret and illegitimate or improper means.

Trumped up. To make up or invent for a fraudulent purpose.

Unfounded. Resting on no solid foundation of truth or reason.

Untrue. Not corresponding with fact.

Void of foundation. Without any element of truth.

Without foundation. Without any element of truth.

FABRICATION—*Phrases.*

All in my eye and Betty Martin.

Se non è vero è ben trovato [It.]. If not true, 'tis well feigned.

TRUTHFULNESS—FRAUD.

FRAUD.

Deceit. Intentional deception or the attempt.

Deception. The act of deceiving by falsehood, spoken or acted.

Delusion. The state of being deceived or led astray.

Falsehood. Intentional and moral deviation from fact or truth. See TRUTHFULNESS-FALSEHOOD.

Falseness. The quality of being false. See TRUTHFULNESS-FALSEHOOD.

Fraud. An act of deliberate deception practised with the object of securing something to the prejudice of another.

Guile. The act of deceiving or the disposition to deceive.

Imposition. The act of imposing; a trick of deception.

Imposture. Deception by means of false pretenses.

Misrepresentation. An act or an instance of misrepresenting.

Untruth. A falsehood. See TRUTHFULNESS-FABRICATION.

FRAUD—*Nouns of Cause.*

Ambush. Unseen peril or snare of any kind. See EXPOSURE-HIDINGPLACE.

Artful dodge. A crafty device.

Artifice. A subtle or deceptive art in contriving. See CRAFT.

Bait. Anything used on a hook, or in a snare, trap, or the like, to allure a fish or animal.

Baited trap. A trap ready for action.

Birdlime. A sticky substance smeared on twigs to catch small birds.

Bite. A sharp trick or fraud; a cheat.

Blind. Something intended to deceive or mislead or to conceal an ulterior purpose.

Bubble. Something true in appearance only.

Card-sharping. Cheating at cards.

Catch. An artful and entangling device; trick.

Cheat. Imposture; fraud.

Chicane. A sort of trickery that has a show of honesty.

Chicanery. The use of mean or paltry subterfuges.

Circumvention. A forestalling by artifice; stratagem.

Cobweb. A snare or entanglement.

Coggery. The act of flattering.

Collusion. Fraudulent cooperation.

Conjuration. Magical expression.

Conjuring. Planning by conspiracy.

Copy. A reproduction or imitation. See COPY.

Counterfeit. Something made fraudulently to resemble what is true and genuine.

Covin. A secret agreement to defraud or injure another.

Cozenage. Deceit; fraud.

Decoy. Anything that allures or is intended to allure.

Decoy-duck. A duck or an imitation of one, used to decoy wild ducks.

Disguise. That which alters the appearance of.

Disguisement. The changing the appearance of a person by an unusual costume.

Escamoterie [F.]. Jugglery.

False bottom. A bottom which conceals a secret drawer or place in which to deposit valuables.

False colors. False pretenses.

False jewelry. Paste jewelry.

Feint. Any sham, pretense, or deceptive movement.

Fetch. A stratagem by which one thing is brought about, though another was seemingly intended; an artifice.

Forgery. The act of falsely making or materially altering with intent to defraud any writing.

Fraud. The act of deliberate deception practised with the object of procuring something at the expense of another.

Fraudulence. The quality of being fraudulent.

Fraudulency. Fraudulence.

Gin. Artifice of any sort.

Guet-à-pens [F.]. Ambush; lying in wait.

Gullery. Trickery; fraud; cheating.

Hocus. A person who deceives by some trickery.

Hocus-pocus. A conjurer's trick.

Hook. Something that catches or snares.

Ignis fatuus [L.]. A phosphorescent light over marshes. See LUMINARY.

Illusion. An unreal image presented to the senses. See TRUTH-ERROR.

Ingannation. Deception; fraud.

Jockeyship. Deceitful tactics.

Juggle. A trick, imposture, or deception.

Jugglery. Delusive speech or action.

Juggling. Jugglery, in any sense.

Knavery. Deceitfulness in dealing.

Legerdemain. A deceptive performance that depends upon manual skill or dexterity.

Lie. A statement made with intention to deceive. See TRUTHFULNESS-FABRICATION.

Magic. Sleight of hand; legerdemain. See DEVOTION-MAGIC.

Make-believe. A mere pretense; sham.

Mask. Anything used to cover or disguise the features.

Masked battery. A concealed or disguised battery.

Masquerade. A social party composed of persons masked and costumed so as to be disguised.

Meshes. Anything that entangles, snares, or constrains.

TRUTHFULNESS—FRAUD—Continued.

Mine. A cavity for an explosive charge, sometimes dug stealthily.

Mirage. An optical illusion, so that images are seen in the sky. See SIGHT-DIMSIGHTEDNESS.

Mockery. A false show; a deceitful appearance.

Mockery, delusion, and snare. A disappointing effort.

Mouse-trap. A trap for catching mice.

Mummery. A masked performance.

Net. An open fabric of twine used to ensnare.

Noose. A loop furnished with a running knot, as in a snare.

Paint. A coloring matter used as a cosmetic; rouge.

Paste. A vitreous composition used for making false gems.

Pattes de velours [F.]. Claws of velvet.

Pitfall. A pit slightly covered for concealment and intended to entrap wild beasts and men.

Plant. A trick; dodge; imposition; swindle.

Practical joke. A trick or joke involving some action, usually rude.

Prestidigitation. The practise of sleight of hand.

Prestigiation. Prestidigitation; legerdemain.

Reach. An artifice or device to effect a purpose or obtain an advantage.

Scagliola. Plasterwork in imitation of marble.

Sham. A false pretense; fraudulent show.

Sleight of hand. Skill in performing tricks in juggling.

Sliding panel. A movable panel that conceals a secret space.

Snare. A trap or gin.

Springe. A noose fastened to a bent sapling.

Spring-gun. Gun set to be discharged when an animal or trespasser treads upon something in front of it.

Springle. A snare.

Spring-net. A net that closes with a spring.

Stratagem. A shrewd maneuver designed to deceive or outwit an enemy.

Supercherie [F.]. Imposture; deception; fraud.

Swindle. The act or process of cheating.

Theft. Stealing; the act of thieving. See THEFT.

Thimblerig. Gambling game in which three thimble-shaped cups and a ball or pea are used.

Tinsel. Superficial adornment and brilliancy.

Toils. Net; snare.

Trap. A device for entrapping game and other animals.

Trap-door. A door to cover opening in floor, cellarway, deck, or flat roof.

Treachery. Treacherous conduct. See UPRIGHTNESS-DISHONESTY.

Trick. A device for getting the advantage by deception.

Trickery. Stratagem in an unfavorable sense.

Tricks upon travelers. Frauds practised upon travelers.

Wile. An act or a means of cunning deception.

FRAUD—*Figurative Nouns.*

Borrowed plumes. Another's clothes.

Cornish hug. A grip in which one wrestler held the other on the breast; hence, deceitful dealing.

Man of straw. A false argument made by a speaker for the purpose of proving it false.

Painted sepulcher. A hypocrite. [Bible.]

Tub to the whale. A concession or sop.

White sepulcher. A hypocrite.

Wolf in sheep's clothing. A treacherous person. [Bible.]

FRAUD—*Verbs.*

Abuse. To wrong in speech; to speak disparagingly.

Bait the hook. To put bait on the hook.

Balk. To stop short and refuse to proceed; to quibble.

Bamboozle. To deceive or impose upon; to practise deceit.

Befool. To lead astray; to delude.

Beguile. To mislead or get the better of by guile; deceive; delude.

Betray. To prove unfaithful to.

Bilk. To take advantage of; to cheat; to swindle.

Bite. To cause loss by fraud; cheat; trick.

Blear. To close one's eyes to.

Blind. To render incapable of discernment.

Blindfold. To mislead; to deceive.

Blind one's eye. To obscure to the eye or understanding; to deceive.

Cajole. To impose on or dupe by flattering speech.

Catch. To take by stratagem; ensnare.

Catch in a trap. To entrap; ensnare.

Cheat. To deceive or defraud in a bargain.

Chouse. To cheat or swindle.

Circumvent. To gain advantage over another by fraud.

Cog. To mislead or deceive by wheedling or flattery.

Cog the dice. To load for cheating.

Come over. To circumvent; get the better of. See MOTIVE.

Conjure. To plan by conspiracy.

Cozen. To cheat in a petty way; swindle.

Cully. To impose upon; trick.

Deceive. To mislead by falsehood or deceit.

Decoy. To lead or lure by some inducement.

Defraud. To take or withhold something from by fraud.

Delude. To persuade to believe error.

Diddle. To cheat by trickery; outwit; overreach.

Dissemble. To give the appearance of something else to. See TRUTHFULNESS-FALSEHOOD.

Divert. To turn from the proper channel.

Do. To swindle; cheat; defraud.

Dupe. To take advantage of the credulity or weakness of.

Ensnare. To take by craft; to allure by artifice.

Entangle. To catch in a snare; to bewilder.

Entrap. To take captive by trick or artifice.

Escamoter [F.]. To juggle; to conjure.

Fake. To cheat.

Flatter. To encourage with hopes and beliefs that may be false.

Fob off. To get rid of by cunning; dispose of by artifice.

Foist off. To palm off; to cheat.

Foist upon. To put something improperly upon; to chea .

Fool. To impose upon; to gull; to cheat; to deceive.

Fool to the top of one's bent. To deceive one to the limi or one s capacity.

Forelay. To lie in wait for.

Gammon. To impose upon by improbable stories.

Gerrymander. To divide voting districts unfairly so as to keep political control, as Gov. Gerry divided Massachusetts so as to look like a salamander.

Gild the pill. To gloss over something disagreeable.

Give the go-by to. To overlook purposely but apparently unintentionally.

Gull. To play upon the credulity or simplicity of.

Hoax. To deceive or play a trick upon for amusement.

Hocus. To deceive by some trick, as in jugglery.

Hoodwink. To deceive as if by blinding.

Hook in. To secure by allurement or artifice.

Hum. To impose upon; cajole.

Humbug. To deceive, as by false pretenses.

Illaqueate. To ensnare or entangle.

Impose upon. To pass off falsely as true and genuine.

Insnare. To take by craft; to allure by artifice.

Intrap. To take captive by trick or artifice.

Inveigle. To persuade into some unwise act by deceptive arts or flattery.

Jilt. To discard after encouraging.

Jockey. To deceive in a bargain.

Juggle. To deceive by trick or artifice.

Keep the word of promise to the ear and break it to the hope. To break one's promise. [Shakespeare, *Macbeth*, V, viii.]

Kidnap. To carry off any human being from his own country or jurisdiction forcibly, by fraud, into another.

Lay a snare for. To lie in wait for.

Lay a trap for. To make use of stratagems.

Leave in the lurch. To abandon through trickery.

Let in. To defraud; to cheat.

Lie. To speak knowingly and wrongly that which is not true. See TRUTHFULNESS-FALSEHOOD.

Lime. To daub with birdlime; hence, to entangle, to ensnare.

Live by one's wits. To have no settled means of subsistence.

Lure. To invite by fair and false promises.

Make a fool of. To put in a false and ridiculous position.

Make an April fool of. To perpetrate a practical joke on the first of April upon a person.

Make an ass of. To make one act foolishly.

Make game of. To jest about, as opposed to being in earnest.

Make things pleasant. To make things seem better than they are.

Misinform. To give false information. See MISTEACHING.

Mislead. To lead into a wrong path; deceive. See ERROR.

Mystify. To confuse designedly; artfully perplex.

Nab. To catch or seize suddenly and unexpectedly.

Nick. To shorten, especially deceitfully.

Nousel. To nousle.

Nousle. To ensnare, to entrap.

Obtain money under false pretenses. To obtain money under wilful misrepresentations; to swindle.

Outmaneuver. To surpass in intrigue.

Outreach. To overreach; to cheat.

Outwit. To defeat by greater cunning; to overreach; to cheat.

Overreach. To obtain an advantage over by deception.

Palm off. }
Palm upon. } To impose fraudulently upon.

TRUTHFULNESS—FRAUD—*Continued.*

Play a practical joke upon one. To trick or joke one with rudeness for amusement.

Play at hide-and-seek. To evade an open answer.

Play a trick. To indulge in a practical joke.

Play off. To feign or pretend.

Play one false. To act falsely.

Play upon. To impose upon for amusement or profit.

Pluck. To strip of anything valuable; cozen or swindle.

Practise chicanery. To do trickery that has a show of legality and honesty.

Practise on one's credulity. To take advantage of one's readiness to believe without sufficient evidence.

Practise upon. To carry out by secret devices.

Put a good face upon. To make to appear to advantage.

Put upon. To impose upon; to deceive.

Sell. To impose upon or cause to believe what is not so.

Send on a fool's errand. To send on a foolish or fruitless enterprise.

Set a snare for. To place a snare in position to get.

Set a trap for. To make ready to catch.

Snatch a verdict. To gain a verdict which does not rightly belong to one.

Sniggle. To entrap in a net; ensnare; to catch eels.

Spread the toils. To lay plans to catch.

Springe. To catch in a springe.

Steal a march upon. To make a march unexpectedly and secretly to an enemy's disadvantage.

Stuff up. [Slang.] To impose on the credulity of.

Swindle. To cheat or defraud grossly or with deliberate artifice.

Take in. To cheat; to dupe.

Throw a tub to a whale. To offer something worthless for something good.

Throw dust into the eyes. To deceive by confusing statements.

Trapan. Trepan.

Trepan. To snare; to trick; to inveigle.

Trick. To induce by trickery; delude; inveigle.

Trifle with. To deceive; to cheat.

Trip up. To cause to lose balance, stumble, or fall by entangling or throwing up the feet: used figuratively.

Victimize. To make the victim of a fraud or swindle.

Waylay. To watch insidiously for the passing of.

FRAUD—*Adjectives.*

Ad captandum [L.]. To catch; for catching.

Adulterated. Rendered counterfeit.

Artificial. Produced by art to imitate nature.

Bastard. Not genuine; false; spurious.

Bogus. Counterfeit; fraudulent; spurious.

Brummagem. Cheap and showy, spurious; bogus.

Catchpenny. Cheap; poor: showy; deceptive in appearance.

Colorable. Specious; plausible: deceptive.

Contraband. Falling under public edict.

Counterfeit. Made to resemble something else; pretended.

Covinous. Collusive; fraudulent.

Cunning. Having or exercising craft or shrewdness. See CRAFT.

Deceitful. Characterized by deception.

Deceived. Misled by falsehood or deceit.

Deceiving. Misleading.

Deceptious. Calculated to deceive.

Deceptive. Having power or tendency to deceive.

Delusive. Misleading; deceptive.

Delusory. Tending to mislead; deceptive.

Disguised. Changed in appearance by unusual arrangement of hair by mask, or by dress.

Elusive. Fallacious; using deception to escape.

Factitious. Proceeding from or created by art as opposed to nature; artificial.

Feigned. Simulated; pretended.

Fraudulent. Based on, proceeding from, or characterized by fraud.

Illegitimate. Spurious; not genuine.

Illusive. Deceiving or misleading by allusion or false appearance.

Illusory. Deceiving or tending to deceive, as by false appearance.

Insidious. Treacherous.

Make-believe. Pretended; imagined.

Meretricious. Deceitfully and artfully attractive.

Mock. Merely imitating the reality; counterfeit; assumed.

Pinchbeck. Made of pinchbeck; not genuine; cheap.

Prestigiatory. Juggling; delusive.

Prestigious. Of or pertaining to sleight of hand; deceptive.

Pretended. Affected; counterfeited.

Pseudo. False.

Rotten at the core. Apparently good but bad in reality.

Scamped. Made dishonestly.

Sham. Not genuine or real; pretended. See TRUTHFULNESS-FALSE-HOOD.

Simulated. Assumed; having a false appearance.

So-called. Called, but perhaps doubtfully so.

Sophisticated. Obscure with specious reasoning.

Spurious. Not proceeding from the proper source or from the source pretended; not genuine; counterfeit.

Surreptitious. Accomplished by secret and improper means.

Tinsel. Superficially brilliant.

Tricky. Deceitful; knavish.

Trumped-up. Invented for a fraudulent purpose.

Unsound. Not sound; defective; unreal.

Untrue. Lacking truth; false. See TRUTHFULNESS-FABRICATION.

FRAUD—*Adverbs, etc.*

Over the left. [Slang.] Just the reverse; reversely; not at all.

Under color of. Under an appearance of.

Under false colors. Under false pretenses.

Under the garb of. Under the appearance of.

FRAUD—*Phrases.*

Falsi crimen [L.]. The crime of forgery.

Fraus est celare fraudem [L.]. It is a fraud to conceal a fraud.

Fronti nulla fides [L.]. No reliance on the face.

Lupus in fabula [L.]. The wolf in the story.

Ne es oro todo loque reluce [Sp.]. All is not gold that glitters.

---

truth'-less. Dishonest. TRUTHFULNESS-FALSEHOOD.

tru''-ti-na'-tion. Act of weighing. HEAVINESS-LIGHTNESS.

try. Strive; examine; attempt; use. DECISION-MISJUDGMENT, LITIGATION, TRIAL, VENTURE, USE-DISUSE; **try a case,** JUDGE; **try a cause,** DECISION-MISJUDGMENT; **try a prisoner,** JUDGE; **try conclusions,** RATIOCINATION-INSTINCT, STRIFE-PEACE, VARIANCE-ACCORD; **try one,** DIFFICULTY-FACILITY; **try one's hand,** VENTURE; **try one's luck,** PURPOSE-LUCK, VENTURE; **try one's temper,** EXCITATION; **try one's utmost,** TOIL-RELAXATION; **try the patience,** DIFFICULTY-FACILITY, PLEASURABLENESS-PAINFULNESS.

try'-ing. Severe. DIFFICULTY-FACILITY, WEARINESS-REFRESHMENT.

tryst. A secret meeting. SOCIABILITY-PRIVACY.

tryst'-ing-place'. A secret meeting place. GATHERING-PLACE, SOCIABILITY-PRIVACY.

tsar. The title of the ruler of Russia. CHIEF-UNDERLING.

Tsung li Ya'-mun. The Chinese Foreign Office. REPRESENTATIVE.

tu quoque [L.] (tiu quo'-quî). Thou also. REPRISAL-RESISTANCE; *tu quoque* argument, EVIDENCE-COUNTEREVIDENCE, JUSTIFICATION-CHARGE, PROOF-DISPROOF.

tub. An open wooden vessel. CONTENTS-RECEIVER; **tub to a whale,** PRETEXT, TRUTHFULNESS-FRAUD.

tubam trepidat, ante [L.] (tiu'-bam trep'-i-dat, an'-tî). He trembles even before the trumpet sounds. BRAVERY-COWARDICE.

tube. A hollow cylinder. APERTURE-CLOSURE.

tu'-ber-cle. A small rounded eminence. CONVEXITY-CONCAVITY.

tu-ber'-cu-lin. A liquid used in examination of cattle suspected of tuberculosis. REMEDY-BANE.

tu-ber'-cu-lous. Tubercular. CONVEXITY-CONCAVITY.

tu''-ber-os'-i-ty. A protuberance. CONVEXITY-CONCAVITY.

tu'-ber-ous. Resembling or bearing tubes. CONVEXITY-CONCAVITY.

tub-man. One of the two most experienced barristers in the Court of Exchequer. ADVOCATE.

tu'-bu-lar. Cylindrical. APERTURE-CLOSURE; **tubular bridge,** ARCHITECTURE.

tu'-bu-la''-ted. Provided with a tube. APERTURE-CLOSURE.

tu'-bule. A minute tube. APERTURE-CLOSURE.

tu'-bu-lous. Tubular. CONVEXITY-CONCAVITY.

tuck. A fold; rapier. BELLIGERENT, PLICATURE; **tuck in,** ESTABLISHMENT-REMOVAL, INJECTION-EJECTION, NUTRIMENT-EXCRETION.

tuck'-er. Maker of tucks. DRESS-UNDRESS.

tuft. A collection of small flexible things fastened together at base. GATHERING-SCATTERING, SMOOTH-NESS-ROUGHNESS.

tuft'-ed. Bearing a tuft. SMOOTHNESS-ROUGHNESS.

tuft'-hunt'-er. Toady. PRESUMPTION-OBSEQUIOUS-NESS, UNSELFISHNESS-SELFISHNESS.

tuft'-hunt'-ing. Toadying. ADULATION-DISPARAGE-MENT, ASSERTION - DENIAL, PRESUMPTION - OBSE-QUIOUSNESS.

tug. Small ship; pull; effort. CONVEYANCE-VESSEL, PUSH-PULL, TOIL-RELAXATION; **tug of war,** ENTER-TAINMENT - WEARINESS, FIGHTING - CONCILIATION, STRIFE-PEACE.

tu-i'-tion. Instruction. EDUCATION-MISTEACHING.

tu'-lip. A beautiful flower. POMP, VARIEGATION.

tum'-ble. Derange; agitate; fall. AGITATION, ASCENT-DESCENT, CREATION-DESTRUCTION, ORGANIZATION-DISORGANIZATION, SUCCESS-FAILURE; **rough-and-tumble,** REGULARITY-IRREGULARITY; **tumble-down,** SECURITY-INSECURITY.

tum'-bler. Acrobat; drinking-glass without a foot. ACTING, CONTENTS-RECEIVER, WAG.

tum'-brel. A covered cart. CONVEYANCE-VESSEL.

tu''-me-fac'-tion. A swelling. ENLARGEMENT-DIMINU-TION.

tu'-mid. Enlarged; bombastic. ENLARGEMENT-DIMI-NUTION, SIMPLICITY-FLORIDNESS.

tu'-mor. Swelling. CONVEXITY-CONCAVITY, ENLARGE-MENT-DIMINUTION.

tu'-mor-ous. Having tumors. CONVEXITY-CONCAV-ITY.

tu'-mult. Disorder; hurly-burly. AGITATION, EXCITA-BILITY - INEXCITABILITY, INSUBORDINATION - OBEDI-ENCE, REGULARITY-IRREGULARITY.

tu-mul'-tu-a-ry. Disorderly. TURBULENCE-CALMNESS.

tu-mul''-tu-a'-tion. Commotion. AGITATION.

tu-mul'-tu-ous. Disorderly. TURBULENCE-CALMNESS.

tu'-mu-lus. A sepulchral mound. LIFE-FUNERAL.

tun. Large cask; drunkard. CONTENTS-RECEIVER, GREATNESS - LITTLENESS, TEETOTALISM - INTEMPER-ANCE.

tu'-na-ble. Musical. MELODY-DISSONANCE.

tund. A flogging. RECOMPENSE-PUNITION.

tun'-dra. A rolling-plain of Russia and Siberia. GULF-PLAIN.

tune. Melody. MELODY-DISSONANCE, MUSIC; **in tune,** MELODY-DISSONANCE; **out of tune,** BETTERMENT-DETERIORATION, CONVENTIONALITY-UNCONVENTION-ALITY, FAULTLESSNESS-FAULTINESS, HARMONY-DIS-CORD, MELODY-DISSONANCE; **put in tune,** PREPARA-TION-NONPREPARATION, VARIANCE-ACCORD; **to the tune of,** PRICE-DISCOUNT, QUANTITY-MEASURE, SET-TLEMENT-DEFAULT.

tune'-ful. Melodious. MELODY-DISSONANCE, POETRY-PROSE; **tuneful nine,** MUSICIAN, POETRY-PROSE.

tune'-less. Rhythmless. MELODY-DISSONANCE.

tung'-sten. An element. CHEMISTRY.

tu'-nic. A body-garment. DRESS-UNDRESS.

tu'-ni-cle. Ecclesiastical vestment. VESTMENTS.

tu'-ning. Present participle of tune. PREPARATION-NONPREPARATION.

tu'-ning-fork''. A steel instrument used by musicians. MUSICAL INSTRUMENTS.

tun'-nage. The weight of goods carried in a boat or ship. GREATNESS-LITTLENESS.

tun'-nel. An artificial subterranean passageway. APERTURE - CLOSURE, CONVEXITY - CONCAVITY, WA-TERCOURSE-AIRPIPE, WAY.

tup. Ram. FAUNA-FLORA, MALE-FEMALE.

Tu-ra'-ni-an. One not of the Aryan or Semitic fami-lies. ETHNOLOGY.

tur'-ban. An Oriental head-dress. DRESS-UNDRESS.

tur'-ba-ry. A place for digging peat. FAUNA-FLORA.

tur'-bid. Muddy. CLEANNESS-FILTHINESS, DIAPHA-NEITY-OPAQUENESS.

tur'-bi-na''-ted. Tapered from a broad base to an apex. CIRCLE-WINDING.

tur''-bi-na'-tion. The act of whirling, as a top. REVO-LUTION-EVOLUTION.

tur'-bu-lence. Disorder; tumult. AGITATION, EXCITA-BILITY-INEXCITABILITY, TURBULENCE-CALMNESS.

TURBULENCE—CALMNESS.

Bluster. Noisy talk.
Boisterousness. Uproariousness.
Bounce. Boastful exaggeration.
Callithump. Noise made with horns as at a serenade.
Convulsion. An irregular and violent commotion.
Detonation. A loud report.
Devil to pay. Great confusion or mischief.
Displosion. Explosion.
Dissilience. The act of flying apart with a noise.
Ebullition. A boiling or bubbling.
Effervescence. Bubbling without boiling.
Exacerbation. Increased severity.
Exasperation. Roughening and irritating.
Ferment. Excitement or agitation.
Fit. Impulsive and irregular exertion or action.
Fury. Violent action or agitation.
Impetuosity. Action characterized by sudden and violent energy.
Inclemency. Severity of climate or weather.
Le diable à quatre [F.]. The devil to pay.
Malignity. Violent enmity.
Orgasm. Immoderate excitement.
Outbreak. A sudden and violent breaking forth.
Outburst. A violent issue of passion.
Outrage. Violent rage.
Paroxysm. A sudden and violent excitement or emotion.
Passion. Intense or overpowering feeling.
Rage. Violent anger expressed in furious speech.
Riot. A disturbance by a mob.
Rough weather. Stormy or tempestuous weather.
Row. A noisy disturbance or quarrel.
Rumpus. A disorderly disturbance.

Ariston metron [Gr.]. A mean is best.
Assuagement. A causing to be less violent, harsh, or severe.
Calmness. The state or quality of being calm, in any sense.
Contemperation. Moderation.
Gentleness. Softness and sweetness of disposition.
Golden mean. A wise moderation.
Juste milieu [F.]. Golden mean.
Lenity. Mildness of temper. See HARSHNESS-MILDNESS.
Measure. Moderation.
Mental calmness. The state or quality of being undisturbed in mind.
Mitigation. Diminution of anything harmful, harsh, or severe.
Moderating. Becoming less intense and violent.
Moderation. The quality of not being extreme.
Pacification. The act of making peace.
Quiet. The state of being quiet, or a quiet condition.
Relaxation. Remission of rigor or restraint.
Remission. The act of refraining from exacting, as a penalty.
Sobriety. Moderateness of temper, mind, or conduct.
Temperateness. The quality of observing moderation.
Tranquilization. The state of being composed.

CALMNESS—*Nouns of Agency.*

Anodyne. An agent that relieves pain by blunting or diminishing sensibility.
Balm. Any soothing medicinal palliative.
Demulcent. A substance supposed to be able to protect the tissues from the action of irritant or acrid humors.
Lenitive. A medicine or application that has the quality of easing pain.
Lullaby. A strain sung to soothe a child to sleep.

TURBULENCE—CALMNESS—*Continued*

Rush. A struggle or rough-and-tumble contest.

Severity. An extreme degree of that by which the feelings may be affected. See HARSHNESS-MILDNESS.

Spasm. A sudden or convulsive action or effort.

Strain. A violent effort or exertion.

Throe. Extreme struggling anguish.

Turbulence. The state or condition of being violently disturbed

Turmoil. Confused motion; disturbance.

Uproar. Violent disturbance and noise.

Vehemence. Great force or impetuosity.

Violence The quality, character, or state of being violent.

TURBULENCE—*Nouns of Cause.*

Beldame. A hag.

Blast. A violent movement of the air.

Blow up. A raising into the air by an explosion.

Brute force. Unintelligent force.

Burst. A sudden explosion.

Coup de main [F.]. A blow of the hand; a surprise

Discharge. A shooting or firing.

Earthquake. A vibration or sudden undulation of a portion of the earth's crust.

Eruption. A breaking forth with violence.

Explosion. A sudden breaking apart, shattering, or bursting in pieces by internal pressure.

Ferocity. The state or quality of being ferocious.

Fire-eater. A restless, daring person, always wanting to fight.

Force Strength or energy of body or mind.

Hysterics. Nervous or convulsive fits of a certain kind

Madcap. A rash person.

Might. Force or power of any kind

Shock. A violent collision of bodies

Shog. A shove to one side.

Squall. A sudden burst of wind.

Torrent. A stream of water flowing with great velocity

Volley. A simultaneous discharge of many missiles

TURBULENCE—*Figurative Nouns*

Alecto. One of the three Furies.

All the fat in the fire. The mischievous step has been taken.

Demon. An evil spirit.

Dragon. A fabulous monster, like a winged lizard or serpent

Megæra. One of the Furies.

Storm. A disturbance of the atmosphere with whirling motion of the air.

Tempest. An extensive and violent wind.

Thunderstorm. A local storm accompanied by lightning and thunder,

Tiger. A large, ferocious cat-like animal.

Tisiphone. One of the Furies.

Volcano. An opening in the earth from which is ejected smoke, stones, lava, etc.

Wild beast. An untamed animal

Zulu. A South-African savage.

TURBULENCE—*Verbs.*

Accelerate. To cause to act or move more quickly.

Add fuel to the flame. To increase bad feeling by giving more cause for it.

Aggravate. To irritate.

Bear down. To overthrow or crush by force.

Be violent. To be characterized by force and rudeness

Blow up. To raise into the air by explosion.

Bluster. To blow fitfully with violence and noise

Boil. To be agitated by heat.

Boil over. To run over the top of a vessel on account of violent agitation by heat or other cause.

Bounce. To drive against anything suddenly and violently

Break out. To take or force out by breaking.

Break the peace. To violate the public peace.

Burst. To break or rend by force or violence.

Burst out. To come forth suddenly.

Come in like a lion. To come in with bluster, as does the month of March.

Convulse. To cause spasms in; to disturb violently

Detonate. To explode with a sudden report.

Detonize. To cause to explode.

Discharge. To send forth a missile by explosion

Displode. To explode.

Effervesce. To give off bubbles of gas.

Exacerbate. To make more sharp, severe, or virulent

Exasperate. To irritate in a high degree.

Excite. To produce agitation or great stir in.

Explode. To cause to burst in pieces by force from within

CALMNESS—NOUNS OF AGENCY—*Continued.*

Milk. The whitish liquid secreted by the mammary glands of female mammals.

Moderator. One who or that which moderates, or restrains.

Opiate. Medicine containing opium; something inducing sleep.

Opium. A milky exudation from the unripe capsules of the poppy.

Poppy. A plant of the genus Papaver, from which opium is obtained.

Poppy or Mandragora. Papaver or nightshade; mandrake.

Rose-water. A fragrant toilet and pharmaceutical water made by distillation of rose-petals or of rose-oil with water.

Sedative. A medicine having a soothing or tranquilizing tendency

CALMNESS—*Verbs.*

Accoy. To calm; soothe.

Allay. To calm the violence or reduce the intensity of.

Alleviate. To make less burdensome or less hard to bear.

Appease. To soothe or satisfy the cravings, pangs, or pain of.

Assuage. To cause to be less harsh, violent, or severe.

Attemper. To reduce or modify by or as by mixture.

Be moderate. Free from undue violence, rigor, or excitement.

Blunt. To take off the sharp edge or point of.

Calm. To bring into repose, mental or physical

Chasten. To moderate or restrain.

Check. To restrain by force or suddenly

Compose. To bring into a state of repose

Contemper. To modify by admixture.

Cool. To render less excited or excitable.

Curb. To restrain; to hold in subjection.

Damp. To slacken or lessen the intensity of.

Deaden. To diminish the acuteness, vigor, or intensity of

Dull. To diminish the violence or strength of.

Go out like a lamb. To go out gently, as does the month of March.

Hush. To repress the noise of.

Keep the peace. To refrain from violation of the public peace

Keep within bounds. To keep under restraint

Keep within compass. To be moderate.

Lay. To cause to lie.

Lenify. To mitigate; assuage; soothe

Lessen. To diminish or reduce.

Lull. To put into a state of rest or quiet.

Mettre de l'eau dans son vin [F.]. To put water into wine.

Mitigate. To make milder or more endurable.

Moderate. To reduce from a great or excessive degree, amount, or activity, to a more reasonable.

Mollify. To reduce the harshness or asperity of

Obtund. To render blunt or dull.

Pacify. To reduce to quiet.

Palliate. To reduce the severity, violence, or painfulness of

Pour balm into. To soothe.

Pour oil on the troubled waters. To make things harmonious.

Pour oil on the waves. To calm trouble.

Quell. To cause to subside.

Quiet. To bring to a state of rest or quiet.

Rebate. To make a deduction of or abatement from

Relent. To grow more gentle or mild.

Remit. To make less tense or violent.

Restrain. To hold in check. See RELEASE-RESTRAINT.

Roar as gently as a sucking dove. To speak gently. [Shakespeare, *Midsummer Night's Dream*, I, ii.]

Rock to sleep. To move in or as in a cradle until slumber is induced.

Settle down. To cease from agitation.

Sheathe. To render milder; dull.

Slacken. To render less in degree, strength, or violence.

Slake. To lessen the force of in any way.

Smooth. To make calm; mollify.

Smooth down. To make level.

Smooth over To soften the worst features of

Smother. To suppress.

Sober. To cause to become sober, mild, or thoughtful

Sober down. To recover from intoxication.

Soften. To make less harsh, severe, violent, or offensive.

Soothe. To reduce from excitement to a quiet or normal state.

Still. To cause to be still, calm, or quiet.

Subdue. To render mild and gentle.

Swage. To assuage; to cause to be less violent, harsh, or severe.

Take in sail. To proceed with less rapidity.

Take off the edge. To make smooth.

Tame. To bring into subjection or obedience.

Temper. To reduce in violence or intensity.

Throw a wet blanket over. To discourage a project.

Throw cold water on. To discourage.

TURBULENCE—CALMNESS—Continued.

TURBULENCE—Verbs—Continued.

Fan the flame. To irritate.
Ferment. To produce fermentation in.
Flare. To become suddenly heated or excited.
Flash. To burst or break forth with a flood of flame or light.
Fly. To move suddenly or with violence.
Fly out. To burst into passion.
Foam. To froth.
Foment. To cherish and promote by excitements.
Fulminate. To explode with a violent report.
Fume. To express irritation or anger.
Go off. To explode.
Incite. To move to action.
Inflame. To cause to burn.
Infuriate. To render furious or mad.
Irritate. To increase the action or violence of.
Kick up a row. To cause a disturbance.
Kindle. To cause to burn.
Lash. To strike or beat upon as with a lash.
Lash into fury. To arouse ungovernable rage.
Let fly. To utter, throw, or discharge violently.
Let off. To discharge or explode.
Madden. To inflame with passion.
Make a riot. To create great wildness and turbulence.
Make a row. To start a disturbance.
Oleum addere camino [L.]. To add oil to the fire.
Outherod Herod. To surpass in cruelty, wickedness, or crime. [Bible.]
Quicken. To increase the activity or sprightliness of.
Rage. To be furious with anger.
Raise a storm. To stir up confusion.
Rampage. To dash about violently.
Render violent. To cause to be violent.
Ride roughshod. To act in an overbearing manner.
Riot. To make a disturbance consisting of wild and turbulent conduct.
Roar. To utter boisterously or with prolonged resounding noise.
Romp. To play boisterously.
Run amuck. To rush through the streets frantically attacking all that comes in the way.
Run high. To be very rough, as waves of the sea.
Run riot. To go to excess.
Run wild. To fall into loose and vicious habits.
Rush. To drive or push with violent haste or swiftness.
Rush head foremost. To rush precipitately.
Rush headlong. To run recklessly.
Sharpen. To make more acute, severe, intense, or eager.
Shock. To shake by a sudden collision.
Spread like wild-fire. To spread rapidly.
Stimulate. To rouse to activity or to quickened action.
Stir up. To rouse to action or feeling.
Storm. To give vent boisterously to rage or passion.
Strain. To put in action to the utmost point of one's ability.
Suscitate. To excite; to rouse.
Tear. To remove violently by pulling.
Thunder. To make a noise suggestive of thunder.
Urge. To press forcibly in any direction.
Wreak. To inflict.

TURBULENCE—Adjectives.

Abrupt. Involving unexpected changes.
Acute. Violent; not chronic.
Bluff. Blustering.
Blustering. Windy; disagreeable; swaggering.
Boisterous. Exhibiting tumultuous violence and fury.
Brusque. Blunt or rough in manner.
Convulsive. Spasmodic.
Desperate. Without care for danger or safety; without hope.
Detonating. Causing to explode with a sudden and loud report.
Disorderly. Lacking due order or arrangement.
Ebullient. In a bubbling or boiling condition.
Excited. Stirred up.
Explosive. Liable to explode or to cause explosion.
Extravagant. Exceeding just or ordinary limits.
Ferocious. Of a wild, fierce, or savage nature.
Fierce. Having or showing a furious cruel nature.
Fierce as a tiger. Very fierce.
Fiery. Showing excessive warmth or vehemence of mood or temperament.
Flaming. Tending to excite.
Frantic. Manifesting excessive excitement.
Frenzied. Violently agitated.
Furious. Overcome with rage or passion.
Headstrong. Not easily restrained.

CALMNESS—Verbs—Continued.

Tone down. To subdue; soften.
Tranquilize. To soothe; to compose.
Weaken. To render weak or less vigorous. See STRENGTH-WEAKNESS.

CALMNESS—Adjectives.

Anodyne. Having power to allay pain.
Bland. Of a soft and balmy quality.
Calm. Free from disturbance or agitation.
Cool. Exercising self-control.
Demulcent. An application soothing to an irritated surface.
Gentle. Moderate in action.
Halcyon. Calm and peaceful, as the ocean, while Halcyon broods.
Hypnotic. Tending to produce sleep. See ACTIVITY-INDOLENCE.
Lenient. Of merciful disposition. See HARSHNESS-MILDNESS.
Lenitive. Having the power or tendency to allay pain or mitigate suffering.
Measured. Restrained within bounds.
Mild. Moderate in action or disposition.
Mild as mother's milk. Very gentle.
Milk and water. Weak and vacillating.
Moderate. Keeping or kept within reasonable limits.
Oily. Pertaining to, containing, or resembling oil.
Pacific. Having a peaceful nature or character.
Palliative. Serving to mitigate or relieve.
Peaceable. Inclined to peace.
Peaceful. Undisturbed; tranquil.
Quiet. Being in a state of repose.
Reasonable. Characterized by moderation.
Remollient. Having a soothing effect.
Sedative. Having a soothing or tranquilizing tendency.
Slow. Having no spirit or liveliness.
Smooth. Calm and unruffled.
Sober. Moderate in or abstinent from the use of intoxicating drink.
Soft. Expressive of mildness.
Still. Being at rest.
Tame. Lacking in interest or animation.
Temperate. Observing moderation in the indulgence of the appetites.
Tempered. Moderated.
Tranquil. Free from and unaffected by agitation or disturbance.
Unexciting. Not exciting.
Unirritating. Not exciting anger.
Unruffled. Tranquil.
Untroubled. Rid of trouble.

CALMNESS—Adverbs, etc.

At half-speed. Slow.
Gingerly. In a cautious, scrupulous, or fastidious manner.
In reason. With justice.
Moderately. Within reasonable limits.
Piano [It.]. With slight force.
Under easy sail. Not rapidly.
Within bounds. Within limits.
Within compass. Within moderate bounds.

CALMNESS—Phrase.

Est modus in rebus [L.]. There is a limit in things.

TURBULENCE—Adjectives—Continued.

Hot. Characterized by heat, ardor, or animation.
Hysteric. Convulsive.
In hysterics. Having nervous or convulsive fits of a certain kind.
Impetuous. Rushing with force and violence.
Incontrollable. Incapable of being controlled, restrained, or governed.
Infuriate. Furiously angry.
Insuppressible. Not to be suppressed or concealed.
Irrepressible. Not capable of being repressed.
Meteoric. Having the nature of meteors.
Obstreperous. Making a great outcry or disturbance.
Outrageous. Heedless of authority or decency.
Raging. Acting with passionate or unrestrained violence.
Rampant. Exceeding all bounds.
Ravening. Seeking eagerly for prey.
Red-hot. Heated to redness; very enthusiastic.
Riotous. Guilty of riot or tumultuous disorder.
Rough. Characterized by rude or violent action.
Rude. Characterized by abrupt or rough discourtesy.
Savage. Of a wild and untamed nature, like the wild man of the woods.

TURBULENCE—Adjectives—*Continued*

Scorching. Very hot.
Sharp. Impetuous or fiery.
Spasmodic. Abnormally sudden and irregular.
Stormy. Characterized by or proceeding from violent agitation or fury.
Tameless. Untamable.
Troublous. Marked by commotion or tumult
Tumultuary. Characterized by tumult.
Tumultuous. Disorderly.
Turbulent. Being in violent agitation or commotion
Unappeasable. Not to be quieted, calmed, or pacified
Unbridled. Unrestrained.
Uncontrollable. Ungovernable.
Unextinguished. Uncontrolled.
Ungentle. Wild, turbulent, harsh, refractory

Ungovernable. Not capable of being governed, ruled, or restrained.
Unmitigable. Not capable of being alleviated.
Unmitigated. Not softened in severity or harshness.
Unquelled. Not quieted.
Unquenched. Not put an end to
Unrepressed. Not held in check.
Unruly. Not submissive to rule.
Uproarious. Accompanied by or making uproar
Vehement. Acting with great force.
Violent. Characterized by intense force, rudeness, and rapidity.
Volcanic. Resembling a volcano.
Warm. Showing excitement.
Waspish. Irascible; having a nature like a wasp.
Wild. Affected with or originating violent disturbances.

TURBULENCE—*Adverbs, etc*

À outrance [F.]. To the bitter end.
À toute outrance [F.]. With every rigor; quite mercilessly
Amain. Forcibly.
At one fell swoop. Altogether.
At the point of the bayonet.
At the point of the sword. } With extreme force.
By force. Violently.
By main force. By full force.
By storm. Completely

Head foremost. Precipitately.
Headlong. Without deliberation.
In desperation. Recklessly.
Through thick and thin. Steadfastly; resolutely.
Tooth and nail. With all possible strength or effort
With a vengeance. With great force or violence.
With might and main. With utmost endeavor.
Vi et armis [L.]. By force and arms.
Violently. In a forcible manner

TURBULENCE—*Phrase*

Furor arma ministrat [L.]. Rage supplies arms.

tur'-bu-lent. Disorderly. TURBULENCE-CALMNESS.
Turc-ism. Turkish religion ORTHODOXY-HETERODOXY.
tu-reen'. A deep table-dish. CONTENTS-RECEIVER.
turf. Fuel; grass-plot. COMBUSTIBLE, ENTERTAINMENT - WEARINESS, FAUNA - FLORA, GULF - PLAIN, LISTS, PURPOSE-LUCK, STRIFE-PEACE.
turf'-man. A man identified with horse-racing. ENTERTAINMENT-WEARINESS.
tur-ges'-cence. State of being turgid. ENLARGEMENT-DIMINUTION, EXCESS-LACK.
tur'-gid. Bloated. EXCESS - LACK, ENLARGEMENT-DIMINUTION, POMP, PURITY-CRUDENESS, SIMPLICITY-FLORIDNESS.
tur-gid'-i-ty. State of being turgid. ENLARGEMENT-DIMINUTION, GREATNESS - LITTLENESS, SIMPLICITY-FLORIDNESS.
tur-gid-ness. State of being turgid ENLARGEMENT-DIMINUTION.
Turk. Ottoman. MATRIMONY-CELIBACY; **grand Turk,** CHIEF-UNDERLING; **"bear like the Turk no rival near the throne,"** SELFRESPECT-HUMBLENESS.
Turk'-ish bath". A hot bath. OVEN-REFRIGERATOR.
turlupinade [F.] (tür'-lü-pi-nɑd') Puns. WITTINESS-DULNESS.
tur'-moil. Agitation; tumult. AGITATION, REGULARITY-IRREGULARITY, TURBULENCE-CALMNESS.
turn. To revolve; alter; shape; crisis; emotion. ADVANCE-RETROGRESSION, AFFECTIONS, AIM-ABERRATION, CONDITION-SITUATION, CIRCUITION, CURVATION-RECTILINEARITY, DESIRE-DISTASTE, EMOTION, FORM-FORMLESSNESS, INCLINATION, MUTATION-PERMANENCE, OPPORTUNENESS-UNSUITABLENESS, PERIODICITY - IRREGULARITY, REVOLUTION - EVOLUTION, SHARPNESS - BLUNTNESS, SKILL - UNSKILFULNESS, TRAVELING-NAVIGATION; **by turns,** COMMUTATION-PERMUTATION, INTERDEPENDENCE, PERIODICITY-IRREGULARITY; **come in its turn,** PERIODICITY - IRREGULARITY; **do a good turn,** CHARITABLENESS-MALEVOLENCE, GOODNESS-BADNESS; **each in its turn,** COMMUTATION-PERMUTATION; **give one a turn,** EXCITATION, OBSTRUCTION-HELP; **ill-turn,** CHARITABLENESS-MALEVOLENCE, PARDON-VINDICTIVENESS; **in turn,** CONTINUITY-INTERRUPTION, PERIODICITY-IRREGULARITY, POSITION, REGULARITY-IRREGULARITY;

meet one at every turn, PURPOSE-LUCK, **one's luck turns,** WELFARE-MISFORTUNE; **serve one's turn,** USEFULNESS-USELESSNESS; **take a favorable turn,** BETTERMENT-DETERIORATION, SUCCESS-FAILURE, WELFARE-MISFORTUNE; **to a turn,** TRUTH-ERROR; **turn a corner,** CIRCUITION, MUTATION-PERMANENCE, SUCCESS-FAILURE; **turn a deaf ear to,** CAREFULNESS-CARELESSNESS, CREDULOUSNESS-SKEPTICISM, HEARING-DEAFNESS, HEED-DISREGARD, PROFFER-REFUSAL; **turn adrift,** ADMISSION-EXPULSION, GATHERING-SCATTERING; **turn and turn about,** COMMUTATION-PERMUTATION, MUTABILITY-STABILITY; **turn and twist,** CIRCLE-WINDING; **turn a penny,** GAIN-LOSS; **turn aside,** AIM-ABERRATION, COMMISSION-ABROGATION, HEED - DISREGARD, MOTIVE - DEHORTATION, MUTATION-PERMANENCE, OBSTRUCTION-HELP, RELEASE-RESTRAINT; **turn away,** ADMISSION-EXPULSION, COMMISSION-ABROGATION, QUEST-EVASION, SIGHT-BLINDNESS, YIELDING; **turn back,** ADVANCE-RETROGRESSION, CONVERSION-REVERSION; **turn color,** EMOTION; **turn down,** PLICATURE; **turn for,** SKILL-UNSKILFULNESS; **turn from,** REPENTANCE-OBDURACY; **turn in,** ACTIVITY-INDOLENCE; **turn inside out,** EXPOSURE-HIDINGPLACE; **turn into,** BUYING-SALE, CONVERSION-REVERSION, INTERPRETATION-MISINTERPRETATION, SOCIETY-DERISION; **turn of expression,** PHRASE; **turn off,** ADMISSION-EXPULSION, RECOMPENSE-PUNITION; **turn of mind,** AFFECTION; **turn of the cards,** RATIONALE-LUCK; **turn of the table,** RATIONALE-LUCK; **turn of the tide,** CONVERSION-REVERSION; **turn one's attention from,** HEED-DISREGARD; **turn one's back upon,** ADVANCE-RETROGRESSION, ANTAGONISM-CONCURRENCE, ATTRACTION-REPULSION, CONCEPTION-THEME, PROFFER-REFUSAL, REGARD-DISRESPECT, REGARD-SCORN, SOCIABILITY-PRIVACY; **turn one's hand to,** ENTERPRISE, OCCUPATION; **turn on one's heel,** CIRCUITION, POLITENESS-IMPOLITENESS, QUEST-EVASION; **turn on the tap,** ADMISSION-EXPULSION; **turn out,** ADMISSION-EXPULSION, COMMISSION-ABROGATION, CONVEYANCE-VESSEL, CONVERSION-REVERSION, DRESS-UNDRESS, OCCURRENCE-DESTINY, OUTSIDE-INSIDE, POMP, SUCCESS-FAILURE; **turn over,** GIVING-RECEIVING; **turn over a new leaf,** BETTERMENT-DETERIORATION, BIGOTRY-APOSTASY, MUTATION-PERMANENCE, RE-

PENTANCE-OBDURACY; **turn over in the mind,** RE-FLECTION-VACANCY; **turn over the leaves,** EDUCA-TION-LEARNING, HEED-DISREGARD; **turn over to,** CONCEIT-DIFFIDENCE, TRANSFER; **turn round,** AD-VANCE-RETROGRESSION, BIGOTRY-APOSTASY, CIRCUI-TION, REVERSAL, REVOLUTION-EVOLUTION, RULE-LICENSE; **turn tail,** ADVANCE-RETROGRESSION, BRAVERY-COWARDICE, QUEST-EVASION ; **turn the brain,** SANENESS-LUNACY; **turn the corner,** AIM-ABER-RATION, BETTERMENT-DETERIORATION, MUTATION-PERMANENCE; **turn the eyes upon,** SIGHT-BLINDNESS; **turn the head,** ASTONISHMENT-EXPECTANCE, EXCITA-TION, LOVE-HATE; **turn the house out of the window,** VARIANCE-ACCORD; **turn the mind to,** HEED-DISRE-GARD; **turn the other cheek,** YIELDING; **turn the scale,** CAUSE-EFFECT, CONVERSION-REVERSION, DOMINANCE-IMPOTENCE, EQUALITY-INEQUALITY, EVIDENCE-COUNTEREVIDENCE, MOTIVE-CAPRICE, MUTATION-PERMANENCE, SUPREMACY-SUBORDINACY; **turn the stomach,** DESIRE-DISTASTE, PALATABLE-NESS-UNPALATABLENESS; **turn the tables,** REPRISAL-RESISTANCE, SAMENESS-CONTRAST; **turn the tide,** CONVERSION-REVERSION; **turn to account,** GAIN-LOSS, USE-DISUSE; **turn to good account,** BETTER-MENT-DETERIORATION, SUCCESS-FAILURE; **turn top-sy-turvy,** ORGANIZATION-DISORGANIZATION, REVER-SAL; **turn under,** PLICATURE; **turn up,** CONCEIT-DIF-FIDENCE, EXPECTATION-SURPRISE, OCCURRENCE-DESTINY, RATIONALE-LUCK, VISIBILITY-INVISIBIL-ITY; **turn upon,** CAUSE-EFFECT, REPRISAL-RESIST-ANCE; **turn up one's eyes,** ASTONISHMENT-EXPECT-ANCE, GODLINESS-UNGODLINESS; **turn up one's nose at,** DESIRE-DISTASTE, REGARD-SCORN, UNCONCERN.

turn-coat". Renegade. BIGOTRY-APOSTASY, PATRIOT-ISM-TYRANNY.

turned' of. Passed beyond; years old. INFANCY-AGE.

turned off'. Hanged. PUNITION.

turn'-ing. Act of one who turns. CIRCUITION.

turn'-ing-point". Crisis. ADVANCE-RETROGRESSION, BEGINNING-END, BOUNDARY, CAUSE-EFFECT, CONDI-TION-SITUATION, CONVERSION-REVERSION, OPPOR-TUNENESS-UNSUITABLENESS, TOP-BOTTOM.

turn'-key". Jailer. GUARD-PRISONER.

turn'-pike" road. Toll-road. WAY.

turn'-screw". Screw-driver. INSTRUMENT.

turn'-spit". A small dog. FAUNA-FLORA.

turn'-stile". A revolving X-shaped gate. ARCHITEC-TURE, OBSTRUCTION-HELP.

turn'-tip"-pet. A turncoat. BIGOTRY-APOSTASY.

tur'-pen-tine and bees'-wax". A polishing compound. SMOOTHNESS-ROUGHNESS.

Tur'-pin, Dick. A notorious English robber. ROBBER.

tur'-pi-tude. Depravity. REPUTATION-DISCREDIT, UPRIGHTNESS-DISHONESTY.

tur-quoise'. A sky-blue or apple-green stone. BLUE-NESS-ORANGE, EMBELLISHMENT-DISFIGUREMENT.

tur'-ret. Tower. ARCHITECTURE, HEIGHT-LOWNESS.

tur'-ret-ship. Monitor. BELLIGERENT.

tur'-tle. Chelonian. PALATABLENESS-UNPALATABLE-NESS.

tur'-tle-doves". Birds noted for their affection. LOVE-HATE.

Tus'-can. Pertaining to Tuscany. **Tuscan capital,** ARCHITECTURE; **Tuscan order,** ARCHITECTURE.

tush. Expression of contempt. CONSEQUENCE-INSIG-NIFICANCE, SOUND-SILENCE, TALKATIVENESS-TACI-TURNITY.

tusk. A long-pointed tooth. SHARPNESS-BLUNTNESS.

tus'-sle. Struggle. STRIFE-PEACE.

tut. Exclamation of impatience. APPROVAL-DISAP-PROVAL, CONSEQUENCE-INSIGNIFICANCE, SOUND-SILENCE, TALKATIVENESS-TACITURNITY.

tutaris aut perfice, aut non [L.] (tiu-tê'-ris aut per-fi-sî, aut non). Either do not attempt or else achieve. COMPLETION-NONCOMPLETION, VENTURE.

tu'-tel-age. Guardianship; act of tutoring. EDUCA-TION-LEARNING, EDUCATION-MISTEACHING, IN-STRUCTOR-PUPIL, LIBERTY-SUBJECTION, SECURITY-INSECURITY.

tu'-te-la-ry. Protective. SECURITY-INSECURITY; **tutelary genius,** ANTAGONIST-ASSISTANT, JOVE-FIEND; **tutelary god,** SECURITY-INSECURITY; **tute-lary saint,** BENEFACTOR-EVILDOER, FRIEND-FOE, SECURITY-INSECURITY.

tu'-tor. To teach; an instructor. EDUCATION-MIS-TEACHING, FEELING-INSENSIBILITY, INSTRUCTOR-PUPIL.

tu'-tor-age. The occupation of a tutor EDUCATION-MISTEACHING.

tutus cavendo [L.] (tiu'-tus ca-ven'-do). Protected. SECURITY-INSECURITY.

tuum est [L.] (tiu'-um est). It is thine. HOLDING-EXEMPTION.

tu"-yere'. Pipe through which air is forced into a forge. OVEN-REFRIGERATOR.

twad'-dle. Nonsense. ADAGE-NONSENSE, TALKA-TIVENESS-TACITURNITY, MEANING-JARGON.

twain. Two. DUALITY; **in twain,** UNION-DISUNION.

twang. Unpleasant taste; sharp nasal modulation of the voice. CACOPHONY, PUNGENCY, SAVOR-TASTE-LESSNESS, SOUND-SILENCE, TALKATIVENESS-INAR-TICULATION.

twat'-tle. Idle talk. MEANING-JARGON, TALKATIVE-NESS-TACITURNITY.

tweak. Twist sharply. SENSUALITY-SUFFERING; **tweak the nose,** PLEASURABLENESS-PAINFULNESS.

twee'-dle. To play a violin or bagpipe. TOUCH, MUSICIAN.

twee'-dle-dum and twee'-dle-dee. Two things between which there is the slightest possible difference. MUSIC.

twelfth. Second in order after the tenth. FIVE-QUINQUESECTION.

twelve. A cardinal numeral. FIVE-QUINQUESEC-TION.

twen'-ti-eth. One of twenty equal parts; the ordinal of twenty. FIVE-QUINQUESECTION.

twen'-ty. Twice ten. FIVE-QUINQUESECTION.

twen'-ty-five". The sum of twenty and five. FIVE-QUINQUESECTION.

twen'-ty-four". The sum of twenty and four. FIVE-QUINQUESECTION.

twen'-ty-fourth". One of twenty-four equal parts; the ordinal of twenty-four. FIVE-QUINQUESECTION.

twice. Two times. DOUBLING-HALVING.

twice-told tale. Stale. ENTERTAINMENT-WEARINESS, RECURRENCE.

twid'-dle. Toy idly. TOUCH.

twig. A small branch. WHOLE-PART; **hop the twig,** LIFE-DEATH.

twi'-light. A faint light. DIMNESS, MORNING-EVE-NING.

twill. A woven cloth. CROSSING, CIRCLE-WINDING, PLICATURE.

twin. Similar; duplicate. DOUBLING-HALVING, DUAL-ITY, LIKENESS-UNLIKENESS; **twin crystals,** MINER-ALOGY.

twine. Twist spirally; strong string. CROSSING, CIR-CLE-WINDING, LAMINA-FIBER; **twine round,** EN-VIRONMENT-INTERPOSITION, UNION-DISUNION.

twinge. Pinch. SENSUALITY-SUFFERING.

twin'-kle. A moment; gleam. DIMNESS, ETERNITY-INSTANTANEITY, LIGHT-DARKNESS.

twin'-kling. The act of one who twinkles; a moment. ETERNITY-INSTANTANEITY; **in the twinkling of an eye,** ETERNITY-INSTANTANEITY.

twins. Two born at one birth. DUALITY.

twire. Flash. AGITATION.

twirl. Revolve. CIRCLE-WINDING, CIRCUITION, REVOLUTION-EVOLUTION.

twist. Wind; contort; prejudice; thread. AIM-ABERRATION, CIRCLE-WINDING, CIRCUITION, CROSSING, DECISION-MISJUDGMENT, DESIRE-DISTASTE, FAULTLESSNESS-FAULTINESS, LAMINA-FIBER, PARALLELISM-INCLINATION, PROPORTION-DEFORMITY, SANENESS-LUNACY, UNION-DISUNION.

twist'-ed. Crooked spirally. CIRCLE-WINDING.

twit. Reproach. APPROVAL-DISAPPROVAL, JUSTIFICATION-CHARGE, REGARD-DISRESPECT, SOCIETY-DERISION.

twitch. Pull; a sudden pain. PUSH-PULL, SENSUALITY-SUFFERING.

twit'-ter. Tremble; tremulous note of a bird. AGITATION, CRY-ULULATION, EMOTION, MUSICIAN.

'twixt. Between. ENVIRONMENT-INTERPOSITION.

two. One more than one. DUALITY; **fall between two stools,** SUCCESS-FAILURE; **game at which two can play,** REPRISAL-RESISTANCE; **in two places at once,** POSSIBILITY-IMPOSSIBILITY; **kill two birds with one stone,** ACTIVITY-INDOLENCE; **make two bites of a cherry,** FASTING-GLUTTONY, MIDCOURSE-CIRCUIT, SKILL-UNSKILFULNESS; **two dozen,** FIVE-QUINQUESECTION; **two meanings,** AMBIGUITY; **two of a trade,** ANTAGONISM-CONCURRENCE; **two or three,** PLURALITY-FRACTION; **twoscore,** FIVE-QUINQUESECTION; **two strings to one's bow,** MEANS; **unable to put two words together,** TALKATIVENESS-INARTICULATION.

two-edged. Cutting both ways. SHARPNESS-BLUNTNESS.

two'-fold''. Double. DOUBLING-HALVING.

two'-pen''-ny–half–pen'-ny. Unimportant. CONSEQUENCE-INSIGNIFICANCE.

two'-sid''-ed. Having two sides. DOUBLING-HALVING.

ty-coon'. A title assumed by the shogun of Japan about 1854. CHIEF-UNDERLING.

tyg. A three-handled drinking-cup. CONTENTS-RECEIVER.

tyke. Churl. GENTILITY-COMMONALTY.

tym'-bal. Kettle-drum. MUSICAL INSTRUMENTS.

tym'-pan-um. Middle ear. HEARING-DEAFNESS.

tym'-pa-ny. Conceit. ENLARGEMENT-DIMINUTION.

type. Image; letter used in printing. COPY-MODEL, DIVISION, FORM-FORMLESSNESS, LETTER, LIKENESS-UNLIKENESS, PROPHECY, SIGN, SUBJECTIVENESS-OBJECTIVENESS, TROPE, WRITING-PRINTING.

type'-wri''-ter. A machine for producing printed characters as a substitute for writing. WRITING-PRINTING.

ty'-phoid. An infectious fever. HEALTH-SICKNESS.

ty-phoon'. Cyclone; hurricane. RIVER-WIND.

typ'-ic-al. Symbolical. CONVENTIONALITY-UNCONVENTIONALITY, SIGN, TROPE, UNIVERSALITY-PARTICULARITY.

typ'-i-fy. Signify by an image. PROPHECY, SIGN.

ty''-po-graph'-ic-al. Pertaining to typography. WRITING-PRINTING.

ty-pog'-ra-phy. Art of printing. WRITING-PRINTING.

ty-ran'-nic-al. Like a tyrant. HARSHNESS-MILDNESS, TYRANNY-ANARCHY.

ty-ran'-nic-al-ly. Despotically. TYRANNY-ANARCHY.

tyr'-an-nize. Domineer over. HARSHNESS-MILDNESS.

tyr'-an-nous. Despotic. TYRANNY-ANARCHY.

tyr'-an-ny. Despotism. HARSHNESS-MILDNESS, PRESUMPTION-OBSEQUIOUSNESS, TYRANNY-ANARCHY.

TYRANNY—ANARCHY.

Absoluteness. Absolute power.
Absolutism. The principles of despotism.
Arbitrariness. The quality of ruling according to one's own will.
Autocracy. Absolute rule by a single person.
Cæsarism. Government by one person with unrestricted powers.
Despotism. Government by an absolute and irresponsible ruler.
Dictatorship. High-handed and absolute rule by a single person.
Imperialism. Government in which all power is concentrated in one person.
Nepotism. Favoritism to relatives.
Oppression. Government without consideration for the rights of the governed.
Personal government. Government by one person.
Tyranny. Cruel government by an absolute ruler.

TYRANNY—Nouns of Agent.

Absolute ruler. A ruler not limited or restrained by any power or authority.
Autocrat. A supreme ruler whose power is unrestrained and irresponsible.
Czar. An absolute monarch.
Despot. One who rules without constitutional check or restraint.
Dictator. A person having absolute powers of government.
Man on horseback. A person in authority.
Oppressor. One who abuses power or authority.
Pasha. An Ottoman governor.
Pharaoh. One of the ancient rulers of Egypt.
Taskmaster. One who loads with heavy burdens.
Tyrant. One who rules oppressively or cruelly.

TYRANNY—Verbs.

Domineer. To rule arrogantly and absolutely.
Lord. To rule over with entire authority.
Tyrannize. To rule cruelly and absolutely.
Usurp. To rule without legal authority.

TYRANNY—Verbal Expressions.

Act the tyrant; carry matters with a high hand; exercise oppression; keep in subjection; lord it over; rule with a rod of iron.

Anarchism. Absolute freedom from laws.
Anarchy. State of society having no laws and absolute individual freedom.
Communism. Government with community of property and an equitable division of labor.
Lynch-law. The practise of inflicting capital punishment upon suspected criminals without legal authority.
Nihilism. The principles of a Russian secret society holding that all existing governments should be overthrown.
Socialism. The theory that governments should depend on cooperative, not individual action.
Thuggism. A system of organized assassination practised by a secret society of India.

ANARCHY—Nouns of Agent.

Anarchist. One who would use violence to destroy the existing civil and social order of things.
Assassin. One who kills secretly or treacherously; hashish eater.
Communist. One who is in favor of the abolition of all private property, by force or violence if necessary.
Czolgosz. The anarchist assassin of President McKinley.
Haymarket gang. A body of Chicago anarchists.
Luddite. One of an organization of English workingmen, formed to destroy labor-saving machinery.
Molly Maguires. A secret society in the coal regions of Pennsylvania formed to resist the officers of the law.
Nihilist. A Russian anarchist.
Petroleur [F.]. An incendiary who uses petroleum; specifically, at the time of the Commune of Paris.
Thug. One of an organization of religious assassins in India.

ANARCHY—Associated Nouns.

Assassination. Killing secretly or treacherously.
Commune. The revolutionary body which controlled the city of Paris in 1871.
Reign of Terror. The period of the French Revolution from May, 1793, to August, 1794, during which thousands of persons were guillotined.
Riot. A disturbance by a mob.
Tumult. The commotion or disturbance of a multitude.

TYRANNY—ANARCHY—*Continued*

TYRANNY—*Adjectives.*

Absolute.　Governing without any restraints.
Autocratic.　Pertaining to a government by one person of unlimited powers.
Cruel.　Governing so as to inflict injury upon the governed.
Despotic.　Ruling like an absolute monarch.
High-handed.　Governing in an arbitrary and overbearing manner.
Imperious.　Given to commanding in an arrogant manner.
Irresponsible.　Careless of the responsibilities of government.
Tyrannical.　Like a tyrant.
Tyrannous.　In the manner of a tyrant.

TYRANNY—*Adverbs.*

Absolutely.　Without restraint.
Arbitrarily.　According to one's own pleasure or caprice.
Despotically.　With unlimited power.
Tyrannically.　With unjust exercise of power.

ANARCHY—*Verbs.*

Assassinate.　To kill by surprise or secret assault.
Raise an uproar.　To bring about a public disturbance.
Raise the red flag.　To raise the standard of anarchy.
Riot.　To make a tumultuous disturbance of the peace.

ANARCHY—*Adjectives.*

Anarchic.
Anarchical. } Holding to the principles of anarchy.
Anarchistic.　Striving to overturn all law and order.
Communistic.　Believing in holding property in common.
Insubordinate.　Hard to govern.
Nihilistic.　Following the practise of nihilism.
Ungovernable.　That cannot be ruled.
Unruly.　Disposed to violate the laws.

ty'-rant.　A despot; severe ruler.　CHIEF-UNDERLING, HARSHNESS-MILDNESS, SCHOLAR-DUNCE, TYRANNY-ANARCHY.

ty'-ro.　A novice.　BENEFACTOR - EVILDOER, INSTRUCTOR-PUPIL.

U

u′-ber-ous. Fruitful. FERTILITY-STERILITY.

uberrima fides [L.] (yu-ber′-ri-ma fai′-dîz). Fullest faith. FAITH-MISGIVING.

u′-ber-ty. Fruitfulness. FERTILITY-STERILITY.

u-bi′-e-ty. Omnipresence. PRESENCE-ABSENCE.

U-biq″-ui-ta′-ri-an. Believer in bodily presence of Christ in the Eucharist. ORTHODOXY-HETERODOXY.

u-biq′-ui-ta-ry. Omnipresent. PRESENCE-ABSENCE.

u-biq′-ui-tous. Omnipresent. PRESENCE-ABSENCE.

u-biq′-ui-tous-ness. Omnipresence. PRESENCE-ABSENCE.

u-biq′-ui-ty. Whereness. EXTENSION-DISTRICT, PRESENCE-ABSENCE.

Ucalegon proximus ardet [L.] (yu-cal′-î-gon prox′-i-mus ard′-et). Ucalegon's house will burn next REFUGE-PITFALL. [At the burning of Troy, Virgil, *Æneid*, ii, 312.]

ud′-der. Milk-bag. CONTENTS-RECEIVER.

u-dom′-e-ter. Rain-gage. MENSURATION.

ugh. An exclamation of repugnance or disgust. DESIRE-DISTASTE.

ug′-li-ness. Unsightly. BEAUTY-UGLINESS, PROPORTION-DEFORMITY.

ug′-ly. Ill-looking. BEAUTY-UGLINESS; **ugly customer,** APPROVAL-DISAPPROVAL, BENEFACTOR-EVILDOER, GOOD MAN-BAD MAN, REFUGE-PITFALL, SUCCESS-FAILURE.

uh′-lan. A cavalryman and lancer. BELLIGERENT.

u-kase′. A decree of the Russian government. ORDER.

ul′-cer. An open sore. HEALTH-SICKNESS, PLEASURABLENESS-PAINFULNESS.

U′-le-ma. The body of Moslem lawyers who interpret the Koran. JUDGE, MINISTRY-LAITY.

u-lig′-i-nous. Slimy. VISCIDITY-FOAM.

ul′-lage. Wantage. CONTENTS-RECEIVER.

ul″-la—lul′-la. Lament for the dead. JUBILATION-LAMENTATION.

ul′-ster. A very long, loose overcoat. DRESS-UNDRESS.

ul-te′-ri-or. Following; more remote. CONSTITUENT-ALIEN, FUTURE-PAST, REMOTENESS-NEARNESS.

ultima ratio regum [L.] (ul′-ti-ma rê′-shi-o rî′-gum). Last argument of kings; war. COERCION.

ultima Thule [L.] (ul′-ti-ma thiu′-lî). The most remote land in the world. REMOTENESS-NEARNESS.

ul′-ti-mate. Final. BEGINNING-END.

ul′-ti-mate-ly. Finally. EARLINESS-LATENESS, FUTURE-PAST.

ul″-ti-ma′-tum. A last offer. CERTAINTY-UNCERTAINTY, ORDER, PURPOSE-LUCK, TERMS.

ultimo [L.] (ul′-ti-mo). In the last month. FUTURE-PAST.

ultimus regum [L.] (ul′-ti-mus rî′-gum). The last of the kings. FIGHTING-CONCILIATION.

ultra [L.] (ul′-tra). Beyond. MAGNITUDE-SMALLNESS, SUPREMACY-SUBORDINACY.

ultra, ne plus [L.] (ul′-tra, nî plus). Nothing beyond; nothing better. BOUNDARY, COMPLETION-NONCOMPLETION, ENTIRETY-DEFICIENCY, FAULTLESSNESS-FAULTINESS, TOP-BOTTOM.

ultra crepidam ne sutor [L.] (ul′-tra crep′-i-dam, nî siu-tor). Let not the shoemaker leave his last. POSSIBILITY-IMPOSSIBILITY.

ul″-tra-ma-rine′. Beyond the sea; a blue pigment. BLUENESS-ORANGE.

ul″-tra-mon′-tane. Beyond the mountains; a believer in ultramontanism. CHURCH, CONSTITUENT-ALIEN, ORTHODOXY-HETERODOXY, REMOTENESS-NEARNESS.

ul″-tra-mon′-ta-nism. Support of the pope; the view of those beyond the Alps. CHURCH.

ul″-tra-mun′-dane. Beyond the world. REMOTENESS-NEARNESS.

u″-lu-la′-tion. A howling. CRY-ULULATION.

U-lys′-ses. A king of Ithaca. CRAFT-ARTLESSNESS.

um-bil′-i-cal. Central; pertaining to the umbilicus. ANATOMY, CENTER.

um″-bi-li′-cus. The navel. CENTER.

um′-bra. The portion of a shadow from which the direct light is entirely cut off. LIGHT-DARKNESS.

umbra magni nominis [L.] (um′-bra mag′-nai nom′-i-nis). The shadow of a great name. BETTERMENT-DETERIORATION.

um′-brage. Shadow. FAVORITE-ANGER, LOVE-HATE, LUMINARY-SHADE; **take umbrage,** FAVORITE-ANGER.

um-bra′-geous. Shady. LIGHT-DARKNESS, LUMINARY-SHADE.

um-brel′-la. A device for protection against sun or rain. COVER-LINING, LUMINARY-SHADE, REFUGE-PITFALL.

um′-pire. A judge. DECISION-MISJUDGMENT, JUDGE.

una voce [L.] (yu′-na vo′-sî). With one voice. ASSENT-DISSENT.

un″-a-bashed′. Undaunted. BRAVERY-COWARDICE, CONCEIT-DIFFIDENCE, PRESUMPTION-OBSEQUIOUSNESS.

un″-a-ba′-ted. Continued. MAGNITUDE-SMALLNESS.

un-a′-ble. Incompetent. MIGHT-IMPOTENCE; **unable to say "no,"** DETERMINATION-VACILLATION.

un″-ac-cept′-a-ble. Unpleasing. PLEASURABLENESS-PAINFULNESS.

un″-ac-com′-mo-dat-ing. Disagreeable. FAVORITE-MOROSENESS, HARMONY-DISCORD, PLEASURABLENESS-PAINFULNESS, POLITENESS-IMPOLITENESS.

un″-ac-com′-pa-nied. Unattended. SOLITUDE-COMPANY.

un″-ac-com′-plished. Lacking accomplishments. COMPLETION-NONCOMPLETION.

un″-ac-count′-a-ble. Extraordinary. CLEARNESS-OBSCURITY, CONVENTIONALITY-UNCONVENTIONALITY, DUTY-IMMUNITY, LAW-LAWLESSNESS.

un″-ac-cus′-tomed. Unusual; unused. CONVENTIONALITY-UNCONVENTIONALITY, HABIT-DESUETUDE, SKILL-UNSKILFULNESS.

un″-a-chiev′-a-ble. Unattainable. POSSIBILITY-IMPOSSIBILITY.

un″-ac-knowl′-edged. Not recognized. ASSENT-DISSENT, THANKFULNESS-THANKLESSNESS.

un″-ac-quaint′-ed. Not familiar with. KNOWLEDGE-IGNORANCE.

un″-ac-quired′. Not gained. HOLDING-EXEMPTION.

un″-ad-mon′-ished. Unwarned. SECURITY-INSECURITY.

un″-a-dorned′. Plain. SIMPLICITY-FLORIDNESS; **unadorned beauty,** BEAUTY-UGLINESS.

un″-a-dul′-ter-a-ted. Pure. MIXTURE-HOMOGENEITY, TRUTH-ERROR.

un″-ad-ven′-tur-ous. Cautious. RECKLESSNESS-CAUTION.

un″-ad-vi′-sa-ble. Imprudent. GOODNESS-BADNESS, PROPRIETY-IMPROPRIETY.

un″-ad-vised′. Not warned. SECURITY-INSECURITY, SKILL-UNSKILFULNESS.

un″-af-fect′-ed. Natural; real. BIGOTRY-APOSTASY, EMBELLISHMENT-SIMPLICITY, PURITY-CRUDENESS, TASTE-VULGARITY, TRUTH-ERROR, TRUTHFULNESS-FALSEHOOD.

un″-af-flict′-ed. Not troubled. CONTENTEDNESS-REGRET.

un-aid′-ed. Not assisted. STRENGTH-WEAKNESS.

un″-a-larmed′. Calm. BRAVERY-COWARDICE.

un-a′-lien-a-ble. Untransferable. DUENESS-UNDUENESS.

un″-al-layed′. Aroused. STRENGTH-WEAKNESS.

un″-al-lied′. Not united. CONNECTION-INDEPENDENCE.

un″-al-low′-a-ble. Intolerable. RIGHT-WRONG.

un″-al-lowed′. Not tolerated. DUENESS-UNDUENESS.

un″-al-loyed′. Pure. Mixture-Homogeneity, Pleasure-Pain; **unalloyed happiness,** PLEASURE-PAIN; **unalloyed truth,** TRUTH-ERROR.

un″-al-lur′-ing. Not tempting. UNCONCERN.

un-al′-ter-a-ble. Unchangeable. MUTABILITY-STABILITY.

un-al′-tered. Unchanged. MUTABILITY-STABILITY, SAMENESS-CONTRAST.

un″-a-mazed′. Not bewildered. ASTONISHMENT-EXPECTANCE.

un″-am-big′-u-ous. Clear. CLEARNESS-OBSCURITY.

un″-am-bi′-tious. Having no desire for. SENSITIVENESS-APATHY, UNCONCERN.

un-a′-mi-a-ble. Churlish. CHARITABLENESS-MALEVOLENCE.

un-an′-i-ma″-ted. Unmoved. SENSITIVENESS-APATHY.

u″-na-nim′-i-ty. Harmoniousness. ANTAGONIST-ASSISTANT, ASSENT-DISSENT, VARIANCE-ACCORD.

u-nan′-i-mous. Harmonious. ASSENT-DISSENT.

u-nan′-i-mous-ly. Harmoniously. ASSENT-DISSENT.

un″-an-nexed′. Disunited. UNION-DISUNION.

un-an′-swer-a-ble. Clear; free; irresponsible. LAW-LAWLESSNESS, PROOF-DISPROOF.

un-an′-swered. Not replied to. PROOF-DISPROOF.

un″-an-tic′-i-pa″-ted. Unforeseen. EXPECTATION-SURPRISE.

un″-ap-palled′. Not terrified. BRAVERY-COWARDICE.

un″-ap-par′-ent. Dubious. ENLIGHTENMENT-SECRECY.

un″-ap-peas′-a-ble. Not to be allayed. TURBULENCE-CALMNESS.

un″-ap-plied′. Not utilized. USE-MISUSE.

un-ap″-pre-hend′-ed. Unperceived. KNOWLEDGE-IGNORANCE.

un-ap″-pre-hen′-sive. Without fear. BRAVERY-COWARDICE.

un″-ap-prized′. Uninformed. KNOWLEDGE-IGNORANCE.

un″-ap-proach′-a-ble. Inaccessible. INFINITY, REMOTENESS-NEARNESS.

un″-ap-proached′. Not excelled. REMOTENESS-NEARNESS, SUPREMACY-SUBORDINACY.

un″-ap-pro′-pri-a-ted. Unused. KEEPING-RELINQUISHMENT.

un″-ap-proved′. Not justified. APPROVAL-DISAPPROVAL.

un-apt′. Incongruous; impotent; unskilful. HARMONY-DISCORD, MIGHT-IMPOTENCE, SKILL-UNSKILFULNESS.

un-armed′. Having no means of defense. MIGHT-IMPOTENCE.

un″-ar-ranged′. Unprepared; disordered. PREPARATION-NONPREPARATION, REGULARITY-IRREGULARITY

un″-ar-rayed′. Unadorned. EMBELLISHMENT-SIMPLICITY.

un-as″-cer-tained′. Not found out. CERTAINTY-DOUBT, KNOWLEDGE-IGNORANCE.

un-asked′. Voluntary. OBSTRUCTION-HELP, READINESS-RELUCTANCE.

un″-as-pir′-ing. Indifferent; modest. CONCEIT-DIFFIDENCE, DESIRE-DISTASTE.

un″-as-sail′-a-ble. Impregnable. SECURITY-INSECURITY.

un″-as-sailed′. Not assaulted. LIBERTY-SUBJECTION.

un″-as-sem′-bled. Scattered. GATHERING-SCATTERING.

un″-as-sist′-ed. Weak; unaided. OBSTRUCTION-HELP, STRENGTH-WEAKNESS; **unassisted eye,** SIGHT-BLINDNESS.

un″-as-so′-ci-at-ed. Separate. UNION-DISUNION.

un″-as-sum′-ing. Modest. CONCEIT-DIFFIDENCE.

un″-a-toned′. Not expiated. REPENTANCE-OBDURACY.

un″-at-tached′. Not connected. UNION-DISUNION.

un″-at-tack′-a-ble. Unassailable. SECURITY-INSECURITY.

un″-at-tain′-a-ble. Unachievable. POSSIBILITY-IMPOSSIBILITY.

un″-at-tained′. Unachieved. SUCCESS-FAILURE.

un″-at-tempt′-ed. Not undertaken. QUEST-EVASION.

un″-at-tend′-ed. Alone. SOLITUDE-COMPANY; **unattended to,** CAREFULNESS-CARELESSNESS.

un″-at-test′-ed. Not witnessed. EVIDENCE-COUNTEREVIDENCE.

un″-at-tract′-ed. Indifferent. UNCONCERN.

un″-at-tract′-ive. Without pleasing qualities. UNCONCERN.

un″-au-then′-tic. Untrustworthy. CERTAINTY-DOUBT.

un″-au-then′-ti-ca′-ted. Unattested; uncertain. CERTAINTY-DOUBT, EVIDENCE-COUNTEREVIDENCE, TRUTH-ERROR.

un″-au-thor′-i-ta-tive. Uncertain. CERTAINTY-DOUBT.

un-au′-thor-ized. Unsanctioned; unjustified. DUENESS-UNDUENESS, LAW-LAWLESSNESS, LEAVE-PROHIBITION.

un″-a-vail′-ing. Useless. SUCCESS-FAILURE, USEFULNESS-USELESSNESS.

un″-a-venged′. Unpunished. PARDON-VINDICTIVENESS.

un″-a-void′-a-ble. Certain. CERTAINTY-DOUBT, VOLITION-OBLIGATION.

un″-a-vowed′. Unacknowledged. ASSENT-DISSENT.

un″-a-wak′-ened. Not aroused. ACTIVITY-INDOLENCE.

un″-a-ware′. Ignorant; unexpecting. EXPECTATION-SURPRISE, KNOWLEDGE-IGNORANCE.

un″-a-wares′. Ignorant. KNOWLEDGE-IGNORANCE.

un-awed′. Fearless. BRAVERY-COWARDICE.

un-bal′-anced. Unequal. EQUALITY-INEQUALITY.

un-bar′. To remove a bar. RELEASE-RESTRAINT.

un-bashed′. Undismayed. BRAVERY-COWARDICE.

un-bear′-a-ble. Insufferable. PLEASURABLENESS-PAINFULNESS.

un-beat′-en. Uncommon. NOVELTY-ANTIQUITY.

un-beau′-te-ous. Plain. BEAUTY-UGLINESS.

un-beau′-ti-fied. Unadorned. BEAUTY-UGLINESS.

un″-be-com′-ing. Incongruous; disreputable. DUENESS-UNDUENESS, HARMONY-DISCORD, REPUTATION-DISCREDIT, UPRIGHTNESS-DISHONESTY; **unbecoming a gentleman,** POLITENESS-IMPOLITENESS.

un″-be-fit′-ting. Incongruous. HARMONY-DISCORD, UPRIGHTNESS-DISHONESTY.

un″-be-got′-ten. Not procreated. ENTITY-NONENTITY.

un″-be-guile′. Undeceive; disclose. ENLIGHTENMENT-SECRECY, EXPOSURE-HIDINGPLACE.

un″-be-gun′. Not started; not prepared. BEGINNING-END, PREPARATION-NONPREPARATION.

un″-be-lief′. Lack of faith. FAITH-MISGIVING, GODLINESS-DISBELIEF.

un″-be-liev′-er. A doubter. CREDULOUSNESS-SKEPTICISM, FAITH-MISGIVING, GODLINESS-DISBELIEF.

un″-be-liev′-ing. Doubting. CREDULOUSNESS-SKEPTICISM, FAITH-MISGIVING, GODLINESS-DISBELIEF.

un″-be-lov′-ed. Not dear to the heart. LOVE-HATE.

un-bend′. Straighten; repose. CURVATION-RECTILINEARITY, TOIL-RELAXATION; **unbend the mind,** REFLECTION-VACANCY.

un-bend′-ing. Hard. HARDNESS-SOFTNESS.

un″-be-nev′-o-lent. Unkind. CHARITABLENESS-MALEVOLENCE.

un″-be-nign′. Ill-disposed. CHARITABLENESS-MALEVOLENCE.

un-bent′. Straight. CURVATION-RECTILINEARITY.

un″-be-seem′-ing. Vulgar. TASTE-VULGARITY, UPRIGHTNESS-DISHONESTY.

un″-be-sought′. Unasked. PETITION-EXPOSTULATION.

un″-be-trayed′. Not misled. UPRIGHTNESS-DISHONESTY.

un″-be-wailed′. Unmourned. APPROVAL-DISAPPROVAL.

un-bi′-ased. Unprejudiced. LIBERTY-SUBJECTION, SAGACITY-INCAPACITY.

un-bid′-den. Not ordered. INSUBORDINATION-OBEDIENCE, VOLITION-OBLIGATION.

un-big′-ot-ed. Not stubbornly attached to a creed or opinion. SAGACITY-INCAPACITY.

un-bind′. Detach; loosen. RELEASE-RESTRAINT, UNION-DISUNION.

un-blam′-a-ble. Not culpable. INNOCENCE-GUILT.

un-blamed′. Unaccused. INNOCENCE-GUILT.

un-blem′-ished. Untainted. FAULTLESSNESS-FAULTINESS, INNOCENCE-GUILT.

un-blenched′. Unflinched. BRAVERY-COWARDICE.

un-blench′-ing. Unflinching. BRAVERY-COWARDICE.

un-blend′-ed. Not combined. MIXTURE-HOMOGENEITY.

un-blest′. Unfortunate; not approved. APPROVAL-DISAPPROVAL, WELFARE-MISFORTUNE; **unblest with,** HOLDING-EXEMPTION.

un-blown′. Not in bloom. PREPARATION-NONPREPARATION.

un-blush′-ing. Proud. CONCEIT-DIFFIDENCE, PRESUMPTION-OBSEQUIOUSNESS, SELFRESPECT-HUMBLENESS, SENSITIVENESS-APATHY.

un-boast′-ful. Modest. CONCEIT-DIFFIDENCE.

un-bod′-ied. Incorporeal. MATERIALITY-SPIRITUALITY.

un-boiled′. Not made ready. PREPARATION-NONPREPARATION.

un-bolt′. To unfasten. RELEASE-RESTRAINT.

un-book′-ish. Not theoretical. KNOWLEDGE-IGNORANCE.

un-born′. Being of a future generation. ENTITY-NONENTITY, OCCURRENCE-DESTINY.

un-bor′-rowed. Not lent. LOAN-BORROWING.

un-bos′-om one-self. To confide. EXPOSURE-HIDINGPLACE.

un-bought′. Not purchased; honorable. COSTLINESS-CHEAPNESS, EXCHANGE, SALE, UNSELFISHNESS-SELFISHNESS, UPRIGHTNESS-DISHONESTY.

un-bound′. Free. LIBERTY-SUBJECTION, DUTY-IMMUNITY.

un-bound′-ed. Limitless. INFINITY.

un-brace′. Weaken; loose. HEALTH-SICKNESS, STRENGTH-WEAKNESS.

un-braced′. Unnerved. HEALTH-SICKNESS.

un-breathed′. Secret. ENLIGHTENMENT-SECRECY.

un-bred′. Vulgar. POLITENESS-IMPOLITENESS.

un-bribed′. Honorable; disinterested. UNSELFISHNESS-SELFISHNESS, UPRIGHTNESS-DISHONESTY.

un-bri′-dled. Unrestrained; free. LIBERTY-SUBJECTION, RULE-LICENSE, TURBULENCE-CALMNESS.

un-bro′-ken. Entire; unviolated. CONTINUITY-INTERRUPTION, UPRIGHTNESS-DISHONESTY, WHOLE-PART.

un-bruised′. Unbroken. WHOLE-PART.

un-buck′-le. Loosen. UNION-DISUNION.

un-bur′-den Free from a load. **Unburden one's mind,** EXPOSURE-HIDINGPLACE.

un-bur′-ied. Uninterred. LIFE-CORPSE.

un-bus′-ied. Indolent. ACTIVITY-INDOLENCE.

un-but′-toned. Loosened. LIBERTY-SUBJECTION.

un-cal′-cu-la″-ting. Thoughtless. RECKLESSNESS-CAUTION.

un-called′ for. Unnecessary. EXCESS-LACK, USE-DISUSE, USEFULNESS-USELESSNESS.

un-can′-did. Insincere. CHARITABLENESS-MALEVOLENCE, TRUTHFULNESS-FALSEHOOD.

un-can′-ny. Weird. BEAUTY-UGLINESS, JOVE-FIEND.

un″-ca-non′-ic-al. Not characteristic of the canon of Scripture. ORTHODOXY-HETERODOXY.

un-cared′ for. Neglected; disliked. CAREFULNESS-CARELESSNESS, DESIRE-DISTASTE, LOVE-HATE, UNCONCERN.

un-caught′. Free. LIBERTY-SUBJECTION.

un-caused′. Accidental. RATIONALE-LUCK.

un-ceas′-ing. Continuous. ETERNITY-INSTANTANEITY.

un-cen′-sured. Unpunished. APPROVAL-DISAPPROVAL.

un-cer″-e-mo′-ni-ous Informal. CONCEIT-DIFFIDENCE, POLITENESS-IMPOLITENESS.

un-cer′-tain. Irregular; doubtful. CERTAINTY-DOUBT, PERIODICITY-IRREGULARITY; **in an uncertain degree,** MAGNITUDE-SMALLNESS.

un-cer′-tain-ty. State of being uncertain. CERTAINTY-DOUBT, CLEARNESS-OBSCURITY, DETERMINATION-VACILLATION, DIFFERENTIATION-INDISCRIMINATION.

un-chain′. To loosen. RELEASE-RESTRAINT, UNION-DISUNION.

un-chained′. Free. LIBERTY-SUBJECTION.

un-chal′-lenged. Not challenged; not called in question. ASSENT-DISSENT, DUENESS-UNDUENESS.

un-change′-a-ble. Firm. BIGOTRY-APOSTASY, CERTAINTY-DOUBT, MUTABILITY-STABILITY, PERSISTENCE-WHIM.

un-change′-a-ble-ness. Stability. MUTABILITY-STABILITY.

un-changed′. The same. MUTATION-PERMANENCE.

un-char′-i-ta-ble. Not beneficent. CHARITABLENESS-MALEVOLENCE.

un-char-i-ta-ble-ness. Unkindness. CHARITABLENESS-MALEVOLENCE.

un-char′-tered. Undue; illegal. DUENESS-UNDUENESS, LAW-LAWLESSNESS.

un-chaste′. Impure. PURITY-IMPURITY.

un″-chas-tised′. Unpunished. EXCULPATION-CONVICTION.

un-checked′. Free. LIBERTY-SUBJECTION.

un-cheer′-ful. Sad. LIGHTHEARTEDNESS-DEJECTION.

un-cheer′-y. Sad. LIGHTHEARTEDNESS-DEJECTION.

un-cheq′-uered. Unrestrained. MUTATION-PERMANENCE.

un-chiv′-al-ric. Not generous. UPRIGHTNESS-DISHONESTY.

un-chris′-tian. Pagan. GODLINESS-DISBELIEF, ORTHODOXY-HETERODOXY.

un′-cial. Consisting of a form of letters prevalent from the 4th to 8th century. WRITING-PRINTING.

un′-cin-a″-ted. Hooked at the end. ANGULARITY.

un-cir′-cum-scribed″. Unrestricted. EXTENSION-INEXTENSION.

un-cir′-cum-spect. Incautious. CAREFULNESS-CARELESSNESS.

un-civ′-il. Discourteous; ill-bred. POLITENESS-IM-POLITENESS, TASTE-VULGARITY.

un-civ′-il-ized. Unrefined. GENTILITY-COMMONALTY, POLITENESS-IMPOLITENESS.

un-claimed′. Not demanded. LIBERTY-SUBJECTION.

un-clas′-sic-al. Unrefined. TASTE-VULGARITY.

un′-cle. A father's or mother's brother; the husband of an aunt. RELATIONSHIP; **my uncle's,** LOAN-BOR-ROWING.

un-clean′. Dirty. CLEANNESS-FILTHINESS, PURITY-IMPURITY; **unclean spirit,** ANGEL-SATAN, JOVE-FIEND.

un-clean′-ly. Filthy. CLEANNESS-FILTHINESS.

un-clean′-ness. Dirtiness. CLEANNESS-FILTHINESS, PURITY-IMPURITY.

un-clipped′. Not curtailed. WHOLE-PART.

un-clog′. Unobstruct. DIFFICULTY - FACILITY, RE-LEASE-RESTRAINT.

un-close′. Open. APERTURE-CLOSURE, RELEASE-RESTRAINT.

un-closed′. Open. APERTURE-CLOSURE.

un-cloud′-ed. Clear; visible. LIGHT-DARKNESS, VISI-BILITY-INVISIBILITY.

un-club′-ha-ble. Not genial. SOCIABILITY-PRIVACY.

un-clutch′. To loose from a firm grasp. TAKING-RES-TITUTION.

un-coif′. To take off a coif. DRESS-UNDRESS.

un-coil′. To straighten; evolve. REVOLUTION-EVO-LUTION.

un-col′-ored. True; without color. COLOR-ACHRO-MATISM, TRUTH-ERROR.

un-combed′. Dirty; vulgar. CLEANNESS-FILTHINESS, TASTE-VULGARITY.

un″-com-bined′. Not blended; loose. COHESION-LOOSENESS, MIXTURE-HOMOGENEITY.

un″-come-at′-a-ble. Unattainable. POSSIBILITY-IMPOSSIBILITY.

un-come′-ly. Homely. BEAUTY-UGLINESS.

un-com′-fort-a-ble. Wretched. PLEASURABLENESS-PAINFULNESS, PLEASURE-PAIN.

un″-com-menced′. Not begun. BEGINNING-END.

un″-com-mend′-a-ble. Blamable; bad. APPROVAL-DISAPPROVAL, INNOCENCE-GUILT, VIRTUE-VICE.

un″-com-men′-su-ra-ble. Inadapted. HARMONY-DIS-CORD.

un-com′-mon. Rare. CONVENTIONALITY - UNCONVEN-TIONALITY.

un-com′-mon-ly. Odd. MAGNITUDE-SMALLNESS.

un″-com-mu′-ni-ca″-ted. Not made known. KEEPING-RELINQUISHMENT.

un″-com-mu′-ni-ca-tive. Not ingenuous. ENLIGHT-ENMENT-SECRECY.

un″-com-pact′. Not dense. SOLIDITY-RARITY.

un″ - com - pas′ - sion - ate. Unmerciful. COMPASSION-RUTHLESSNESS.

un″-com-pelled′. Not coerced. LIBERTY - SUBJEC-TION.

un″-com-ple′-ted. Unfinished. COMPLETION-NON-COMPLETION, ENTIRETY-DEFICIENCY, SUCCESS-FAIL-URE.

un-com-pli′-ant. Unyielding. INSUBORDINATION-OBEDIENCE.

un″-com-ply′-ing. Disobedient. INSUBORDINATION-OBEDIENCE, PROFFER-REFUSAL.

un″-com-pound′-ed. Simple. MIXTURE - HOMOGE-NEITY.

un″-com-pressed′. Not condensed. HEAVINESS-LIGHTNESS, SOLIDITY-RARITY.

un″-com-pro-mis′-ing. Severe. CONVENTIONALITY-UNCONVENTIONALITY, HARSHNESS-MILDNESS.

un″-con-ceal′-a-ble. Not secretable. ENLIGHTEN-MENT-SECRECY.

un″-con-ceived′. Uncreated; unintelligible. CLEAR-NESS-OBSCURITY, ENTITY-NONENTITY.

un″-con-cern′. Indifference. DESIRE-DISTASTE, SEN-SITIVENESS-APATHY.

UNCONCERN.

Anorexy. Want of appetite, without a loathing for food.

Apathy. A calmness, indolence. or state of indifference; incapable of being roused to active interest. See SENSITIVENESS-APATHY.

Coldness. The quality of being wanting in ardor zeal, or passion.

Disdainfulness. A feeling of contempt and aversion. See REGARD-SCORN.

Inappetency. Want of desire.

Inattention. Want of attention or failure to pay attention. See HEED-DISREGARD.

Indifference. Unconcern; absence of anxiety or interest in respect to what is presented to the mind.

Insouciance [F.]. Carelessness; heedlessness.

Neutrality. State of taking no part on either side.

Nonchalance [F.]. Coolness; indifference.

Recklessness. Utter carelessness or heedlessness. See RECKLESS-NESS.

Supineness. Carelessness or inattention. See ACTIVITY-INDOLENCE.

Unconcern. Absence of anxiety or care.

Want of earnestness. Absence of hearty endeavor or eagerness.

Want of interest. The absence of excitement of feeling.

UNCONCERN—*Verbs*

Be cold. ⎫
Be indifferent. ⎬ To feel no interest, anxiety, or care respecting any-
Be lukewarm. ⎭ thing. See *Adjectives.*

Care nothing about. To be indifferent about.

Care nothing for. To be cold or distant.

Have no desire. To have no longing or wish for. See DESIRE.

Have no relish for. To lack fondness for.

Have no taste for. To have no intellectual relish or fondness for.

Not care a straw about. ⎫ To have the least possible care or concern
Not care a straw for. ⎬ for. See CONSEQUENCE-INSIGNIFICANCE.

Not care. ⎫
Not mind. ⎬ To give no attention or heed to.

Set at naught. To regard as of no value or account. See OVER-VALUATION-UNDERVALUATION.

Spurn. To drive back or away; treat with contempt. See REGARD-SCORN.

Stand neuter. To take no part on either side.

Take no interest. To be unaffected by excitement of feeling. See SENSITIVENESS-APATHY.

UNCONCERN—*Adjectives*

All one to. Making no difference to.

Careless. Indifferent.

Cold. Distant; reserved.

Cool. Chilling: apathetic.

Cool as a cucumber. Entirely unaffected by.

Devil-may-care. Let the devil care, not I.

Easy-going. Reckless; inactive.

Frigid. Cold; wanting feeling.

Half-hearted. Lacking zeal or earnestness

Impartial. Not favoring one more than another.

Indifferent. Feeling no interest anxiety, or care.

Insipid. Wanting in spirit, life. or animation. See SAVOR-TASTE-LESSNESS.

Insouciant. Heedless

Lackadaisical. Indolently sentimental.

Listless. Languid; spiritless.

Lukewarm. Neither for nor against.

Phlegmatic. Dull; sluggish.

Pococurante. Caring little.

Unalluring. Not tempting.

Unambitious. Not desirous of advancement

Unaspiring. Listless; unprogressive.

Unattracted. Disinterested.

Uncared for. Unheeded.

Unconcerned. Easy in mind, not anxious.

Undesirable. Not cared for.

Undesired. Not wanted.

Undesiring. Wishing little for.

Unsolicitous. Not anxious for.

Unvalued. Regarding as worthless.

Unwished. Not desirable.

Vain. Worthless. unimportant.

UNCONCERN—*Adverb.*

For aught one cares. Not caring at all.

UNCONCERN—*Interjection.*

Never mind!

un″-con-cerned′. Indifferent. SENSITIVENESS-APATHY, UNCONCERN.

un″-con-coct′-ed. Not planned. PREPARATION-NONPREPARATION.

un″-con-demned′. Not proved wrong. EXCULPATION-CONVICTION.

un″-con-di′-tion-al. Without limitations; free. CONSENT, ENGAGEMENT-RELEASE. ENTIRETY-DEFICIENCY, LEAVE-PROHIBITION, LIBERTY-SUBJECTION.

un″-con-du′-cing. Not helping. DOMINANCE-IMPOTENCE.

un″-con-du′-cive. Not aiding. DOMINANCE-IMPOTENCE.

un″-con-duct′-ing to. Not contributing to. DOMINANCE-IMPOTENCE.

un″-con-fined′. Unrestricted. LIBERTY-SUBJECTION.

un″-con-firmed′. Unfixed. CERTAINTY-DOUBT.

un″-con-form′-a-ble. Inconsistent. CONNECTION-INDEPENDENCE, CONVENTIONALITY-UNCONVENTIONALITY, HARMONY-DISCORD, PERSISTENCE-WHIM.

un″-con-form′-a-bly. Inconsistently. CONVENTIONALITY-UNCONVENTIONALITY.

un″-con-form′-i-ty. Irregularity. CONVENTIONALITY-UNCONVENTIONALITY, HARMONY-DISCORD, LAW-LAWLESSNESS, UNIFORMITY-DIVERSITY.

un″-con-fused′. Orderly; not dark. CLEARNESS-OBSCURITY, REGULARITY-IRREGULARITY.

un″-con-fu′-ted. Not proved wrong. PROOF-DISPROOF, TRUTH-ERROR.

un″-con-gealed′. Not made solid. LIQUID-GAS.

un″-con-ge′-nial. Unsympathetic. HARMONY-DISCORD, HEALTHINESS-UNHEALTHINESS.

un″-con-nect′-ed. Discontinuous; illogical. CONNECTION-INDEPENDENCE, CONTINUITY-INTERRUPTION, RATIOCINATION-INSTINCT.

un-con′-quer-a-ble. Unyielding. PERSISTENCE-WHIM, REPRISAL-RESISTANCE, STRENGTH-WEAKNESS; **unconquerable will,** DETERMINATION-VACILLATION.

un-con′-quered. Not subdued. REPRISAL-RESISTANCE.

un-con″-sci-en′-tious. Unscrupulous. GOOD MAN-BAD MAN.

un-con′-scion-a-ble. Unjust. MAGNITUDE-SMALLNESS, VIRTUE-VICE.

un-con′-scious. Unaware; not felt to exist. KNOWLEDGE-IGNORANCE, SENSITIVENESS-APATHY, VOLITION-OBLIGATION.

un-con′-scious-ness. Stupor. KNOWLEDGE-IGNORANCE.

un″-con-sent′-ing. Not agreeing with. ASSENT-DISSENT, PROFFER-REFUSAL, READINESS-RELUCTANCE.

un″-con-sid′-ered. Unthought of. REFLECTION-VACANCY.

un″-con-sol′-a-ble. Not to be comforted. LIGHTHEARTEDNESS-DEJECTION.

un″-con-sol′-i-da″-ted. Disunited. COHESION-LOOSENESS.

un-con′-so-nant. Discordant. HARMONY-DISCORD.

un″-con-spic′-u-ous. Not obvious. VISIBILITY-INVISIBILITY.

un-con″-sti-tu′-tion-al. Undue; illegal. DUENESS-UNDUENESS, LAW-LAWLESSNESS.

un″-con-strained′. Free; unabashed. CONCEIT-DIFFIDENCE, LIBERTY-SUBJECTION.

un″-con-sumed′. Remaining. INCREMENT-REMNANT.

un″-con-test′-ed. Undisputed. CERTAINTY-DOUBT.

un-con″-tra-dict′-ed. Undenied. ASSENT-DISSENT.

un-con-trite′. Not penitent. REPENTANCE-OBDURACY.

un-con-trol′-la-ble. Violent; excitable. EXCITABILITY-INEXCITABILITY, TURBULENCE-CALMNESS, VOLITION-OBLIGATION.

un″-con-trolled′. Unrestrained. EXCITABILITY-INEXCITABILITY, LIBERTY-SUBJECTION.

un-con″-tro-vert′-ed. Undenied. ASSENT-DISSENT.

un″-con-ven″-tion-al. Informal. CONVENTIONALITY-UNCONVENTIONALITY.

un″-con-ven″-tion-al′-i-ty. Informality. CONVENTIONALITY-UNCONVENTIONALITY.

un-con′-ver-sant. Ignorant. KNOWLEDGE-IGNORANCE, SKILL-UNSKILFULNESS.

un″-con-vert′-ed. Irreligious; not transformed. ASSENT-DISSENT, GODLINESS-DISBELIEF.

un″-con-vinced′. Not persuaded. ASSENT-DISSENT.

un-cooked′. Not prepared for food by the action of heat. PREPARATION-NONPREPARATION.

un-cop′-ied. Not duplicated. IMITATION-ORIGINALITY.

un-cork′. To take out a cork. RELEASE-RESTRAINT.

un-cor-rupt′. Upright. UPRIGHTNESS-DISHONESTY.

un″-cor-rupt′-ed. Honest. UNSELFISHNESS-SELFISHNESS, UPRIGHTNESS-DISHONESTY.

un-count′-ed. Not reckoned. CERTAINTY-DOUBT.

un-cour′-te-ous. Inaffable. POLITENESS-IMPOLITENESS.

un-cour′-te-ous-ness. Impoliteness. POLITENESS-IMPOLITENESS.

un-court′-ly. Inelegant. POLITENESS-IMPOLITENESS, TASTE-VULGARITY.

un-couth′. Outlandish. BEAUTY-UGLINESS, PURITY-CRUDENESS, TASTE-VULGARITY.

un-cov′-er. To denude, disclose, or bow. APERTURE-CLOSURE, DRESS-UNDRESS, EXPOSURE-HIDINGPLACE, POLITENESS-IMPOLITENESS.

un″-cre-a′-ted. Not made. ENTITY-NONENTITY.

un-crit′-ic-al. Not faultfinding. APPROVAL-DISAPPROVAL.

un-cropped′. Uncut. WHOLE-PART.

un-crown′. To take off a crown. COMMISSION-ABROGATION.

unc′-tion. That characteristic of speech which awakens deep sympathetic feeling; divine grace. DIVINITY, EXCITATION, GODLINESS-UNGODLINESS, SENSITIVENESS-APATHY; **extreme unction,** CEREMONIAL; **lay the flattering unction to one's soul,** ALLEVIATION-AGGRAVATION, CONCEIT-DIFFIDENCE, SANGUINENESS-HOPELESSNESS.

unc″-tu-os′-i-ty. Greasiness. PULPINESS-OILINESS.

unc′-tu-ous. Greasy; sympathetic. ADULATION-DISPARAGEMENT, GODLINESS-UNGODLINESS, PULPINESS-OILINESS.

unc′-tu-ous-ness. Greasiness; flattery. ADULATION-FLATTERY, FRICTION-LUBRICATION, PULPINESS-OILINESS.

un-culled′. Not collected apart. KEEPING-RELINQUISHMENT, USE-DISUSE.

un-cul′-pa-ble. Faultless. INNOCENCE-GUILT.

un-cul″-ti-va′-ted. Ignorant; unprepared. KNOWLEDGE-IGNORANCE, PREPARATION-NONPREPARATION.

un-curbed′. Free. LIBERTY-SUBJECTION.

un-curl′. To straighten. CURVATION-RECTILINEARITY.

un-cus′-tom-a-ry. Unusual. CONVENTIONALITY-UNCONVENTIONALITY.

un-cut′. Undivided. WHOLE-PART.

un-damped′. Dry. DAMPNESS-DRYNESS.

un-da′-ted. Without date; waving. CHRONOLOGY-ANACHRONISM, CIRCLE-WINDING.

un-daunt′-ed. Unsubdued. BRAVERY-COWARDICE.

un-daz′-zled. Bewildered. SAGACITY-INCAPACITY.

un″-de-bauched′. Honorable. UPRIGHTNESS-DISHONESTY.

un″-de-ceive′. Inform; disclose. ENLIGHTENMENT-SECRECY, EXPOSURE-HIDINGPLACE.

un″-de-ceived′. Knowing. KNOWLEDGE-IGNORANCE.

un″-de-cid′-ed. Irresolute; doubtful. CERTAINTY-DOUBT, CHOICE-ABSENCE OF CHOICE, DETERMINATION-VACILLATION, INVESTIGATION-ANSWER; **leave undecided,** CHOICE-NEUTRALITY.

un″-de-ci′-pher-a-ble. Obscure. CLEARNESS - OBSCURITY.

un-decked′. Unadorned. EMBELLISHMENT - SIMPLICITY.

un-de″-com-posed′. Not separated. MIXTURE-HOMOGENEITY.

un″-de-faced′. Unimpaired. BEAUTY-UGLINESS.

un″-de-fend′-ed. Unprotected. YIELDING.

un″-de-filed′. Chaste; honorable. INNOCENCE-GUILT, PURITY-IMPURITY, UPRIGHTNESS-DISHONESTY.

un″ de-fi′-na-ble. Uncertain; unintelligible. CERTAINTY-DOUBT, CLEARNESS-OBSCURITY, MEANING-JARGON.

un″-de-fined′. Limitless. CERTAINTY-DOUBT, VISIBILITY-INVISIBILITY.

un″-de-formed′. Not misshapen. BEAUTY - UGLINESS.

un″-de-mol′-ished. Not destroyed. WHOLE-PART.

un″-de-mon′-stra-ble. Incapable of positive proof. FAITH-MISGIVING.

un″-de-mon′-strat-ed. Not proved. CERTAINTY-DOUBT.

un″-de-mon′-stra-tive. Not convincing; inexcitable. EXCITABILITY-INEXCITABILITY.

un″-de-ni′-a-ble. True. CERTAINTY-DOUBT.

un-de-plored′. Unlamented. LOVE-HATE.

un-de-praved′. Not corrupt. UPRIGHTNESS-DISHONESTY.

un-de-prived′. Not dispossessed. KEEPING-RELINQUISHMENT.

un′-der. Less than; subordinate. DEEPNESS-SHALLOWNESS, LIBERTY-SUBJECTION, SUPREMACY-SUBORDINACY; **range under,** ADMISSION-EXCLUSION; **under age,** INFANCY-AGE; **underagent,** CONSIGNEE; **under breath,** LOUDNESS-FAINTNESS; **under cover,** COVER-LINING, ENLIGHTENMENT - SECRECY, SECURITY-INSECURITY; **under full strength,** FAULTLESSNESS-FAULTINESS; **under lock and key,** RELEASE-RESTRAINT, SECURITY-INSECURITY; **under one's control,** INSUBORDINATION-OBEDIENCE; **under one's eyes,** VISIBILITY-INVISIBILITY; **under press of,** COERCION; **under protest,** ASSENT-DISSENT, COERCION, READINESS-RELUCTANCE; **under restraint,** RELEASE-RESTRAINT; **under seal,** EVIDENCE-COUNTEREVIDENCE; **under the circumstances,** CONDITION-SITUATION; **under the head of,** CONNECTION-INDEPENDENCE; **under the mark,** MAGNITUDE-SMALLNESS, SUPREMACY-SUBORDINACY; **under the sun,** ENTITY-NONENTITY, UNIVERSE; **under way,** ADVANCE-RETROGRESSION, MOVEMENT-REST, TRAVELING-NAVIGATION.

un″-der-bid′. To bid lower than. EXCHANGE.

un′-der-bred′. Ot impure breed. TASTE-VULGARITY.

un′-der-cloth″-ing. Clothes designed for underwear. DRESS-UNDRESS.

un′-der-cur″-rent. A hidden tendency; a current, as of water or air, below another current. ANTAGONISM-CONCURRENCE, CAUSE-EFFECT, ENLIGHTENMENT-SECRECY, RIVER-WIND.

un″-der-es′-ti-mate. To undervalue. DECISION-MISJUDGMENT, OVERVALUATION-UNDERVALUATION, REGARD-SCORN.

un″-der-es″-ti-ma′-tion. Too low a valuation. OVERVALUATION-UNDERVALUATION.

un″-der-foot′. Low. HEIGHT-LOWNESS; **tread underfoot,** HARSHNESS-MILDNESS.

un″-der-go′. To exist under. OCCURRENCE-DESTINY; **undergo a change,** CONVERSION-REVERSION; **undergo pain,** PLEASURE-PAIN, SENSUALITY-SUFFERING.

un″-der-grad′-u-ate. A student of a university or college who has not taken the bachelor's degree. INSTRUCTOR-PUPIL.

un′-der-ground″. Beneath the surface of the ground; secret. DEEPNESS-SHALLOWNESS, ENLIGHTENMENT-SECRECY, HEIGHT-LOWNESS, MANIFESTATION-LATENCY.

un′-der-hand″. Acting in a treacherously secret manner. CRAFT-ARTLESSNESS, ENLIGHTENMENT-SECRECY, MANIFESTATION-LATENCY; **underhand dealing,** ENLIGHTENMENT-SECRECY.

un″-der-les-see′. One who holds a sublease. HOLDER.

un″-der-let′. To sublet. LOAN-BORROWING.

un″-der-lie′. To be answerable for; to lie below ENLIGHTENMENT-SECRECY, HEIGHT-LOWNESS.

un″-der-line′. To underscore. CONSEQUENCE-INSIGNIFICANCE, SIGN.

un′-der-ling. A subordinate. CHIEF-UNDERLING, GENTILITY-COMMONALTY.

un″-der-lin′-ing. Scoring. SIGN.

un″-der-mine′. To weaken; a cave. BETTERMENT-DETERIORATION, CONVEXITY - CONCAVITY, CRAFT-ARTLESSNESS, OBSTRUCTION-HELP.

un-der-mined′. Weakened. BETTERMENT-DETERIORATION.

un′-der-most″. Lowest. TOP-BOTTOM.

un′-der-neath′. Below. HEIGHT-LOWNESS.

un″-der-paid′. Insufficiently paid. GENEROSITY-FRUGALITY.

un″-der-pin′. To support with a prop. SUSPENSION-SUPPORT.

un″-der-plot″. A trick. DESIGN.

un″-der-prop′. To put a prop under. SUSPENSION-SUPPORT.

un″-der-rate′. To rate too low. OVERVALUATION-UNDERVALUATION.

un″-der-reck′-on. To rate too low. OVERVALUATION-UNDERVALUATION.

un′-der-sec′-re-tar″-y. An official. CHIEF-UNDERLING.

un-der-sell′. To sell cheaper than another. BUYING-SALE.

un-der-set′. To support. SUSPENSION-SUPPORT.

un-der-sign′. To subscribe. EVIDENCE-COUNTEREVIDENCE.

un-der-sized′. Small. GREATNESS-LITTLENESS.

un″-der-stand′. To comprehend. CLEARNESS - OBSCURITY, ENLIGHTENMENT-SECRECY, KNOWLEDGE-IGNORANCE, MANIFESTATION-LATENCY, SAGACITY-INCAPACITY; **understand by,** INTERPRETATION-MISINTERPRETATION, MEANING-JARGON; **understand one another,** ANTAGONISM - CONCURRENCE, VARIANCE-ACCORD.

un″-der-stand′-ing. Comprehension. MIND - IMBECILITY, SAGACITY-INCAPACITY; **come to an understanding,** ASSENT-DISSENT, CLEARNESS-OBSCURITY, CONTRACT, FIGHTING-CONCILIATION, VARIANCE - ACCORD; **good understanding,** AMITY-HOSTILITY, VARIANCE-ACCORD; **with the understanding,** MODIFICATION.

un″ - der - stood′. Comprehended; customary. ENLIGHTENMENT-SECRECY, HABIT-DESUETUDE.

un′-der-strap″-per. An underling. CHIEF-UNDERLING.

un″-der-take′. To attempt. BEGINNING-END, ENGAGEMENT-RELEASE, ENTERPRISE, OCCUPATION.

un′-der-ta′-ker. One who oversees funerals. LIFE-FUNERAL.

un′-der-ta′-king. Task. ENGAGEMENT-RELEASE, ENTERPRISE, OCCUPATION, PURPOSE-LUCK.

un′-der-tone″. A subdued tone. LOUDNESS-FAINTNESS.

un″-der-val′-ue. Underrate. OVERVALUATION - UNDERVALUATION.

un″-der-val′-u-ing. Underrating. OVERVALUATION-UNDERVALUATION.

un'-der-waist'-coat''. A garment. DRESS-UNDRESS.

un'-der-wood''. Coppice. FAUNA-FLORA.

un''-der-write'. To insure. CONTRACT, ENGAGEMENT-RELEASE, SECURITY.

un'-der-wri''-ter. An insurer. CONSIGNEE.

un''-de-scribed'. Not outlined. CONVENTIONALITY-UNCONVENTIONALITY.

un''-de-served'. Unjust. DUENESS-UNDUENESS.

un''-de-serv'-ing of be-lief. FAITH-MISGIVING.

un''-de-signed'. Chance. PURPOSE-LUCK.

un''-de-sign'-ing. Not cunning. CRAFT-ARTLESSNESS.

un''-de-si-ra-bil'-i-ty. Impropriety. PROPRIETY-IMPROPRIETY.

un''-de-si'-ra-ble. Inexpedient; painful. DESIRE-DISTASTE, PLEASURABLENESS-PAINFULNESS, PROPRIETY-IMPROPRIETY.

un''-de-si''-ra-ble-ness. Impropriety. PROPRIETY-IMPROPRIETY.

un''-de-sired'. Not longed for. DESIRE-DISTASTE, PLEASURABLENESS-PAINFULNESS.

un''-de-si'-rous. Having no desire. DESIRE-DISTASTE.

un''-de-spair'-ing. Hopeful. SANGUINENESS-HOPELESSNESS.

un''-de-stroyed'. Not ruined. ENTITY-NONENTITY, MUTATION-PERMANENCE, WHOLE-PART.

un''-de-ter''-mi-na'-tion. Fickleness. DETERMINATION-VACILLATION.

un''-de-ter'-mined. Uncertain. CERTAINTY-DOUBT, CLEARNESS-OBSCURITY, DETERMINATION-VACILLATION, INVESTIGATION-ANSWER, RATIONALE-LUCK.

un''-de-vel'-oped. Latent. ENLIGHTENMENT-SECRECY.

un-de'-vi-a''-ting. Direct; persevering. AIM-ABERRATION, CURVATION-RECTILINEARITY, MUTABILITY-STABILITY, PERSISTENCE-WHIM.

un''-de-vout'. Not pious. GODLINESS-DISBELIEF.

un''-di-gest'-ed. Crude. PREPARATION-NONPREPARATION.

un-dig'-ni-fied. Not honored. UPRIGHTNESS-DISHONESTY.

un''-di-min'-ished. Entire; not lessened. INCREASE-DECREASE, MAGNITUDE-SMALLNESS, WHOLE-PART.

un''-di-rect'-ed. Erratic. AIM-ABERRATION, PURPOSE-LUCK.

un''-dis-cern'-i-ble. Imperceptible. CLEARNESS-OBSCURITY, VISIBILITY-INVISIBILITY.

un''-dis-cern'-ing. Unobserving. HEED-DISREGARD. SAGACITY-INCAPACITY, SIGHT-BLINDNESS.

un''-dis-closed'. Hidden. ENLIGHTENMENT-SECRECY, MANIFESTATION-LATENCY.

un''-dis-cov'-er-a-ble. Indiscernible. CLEARNESS-OBSCURITY.

un''-dis-cov'-ered. Unexposed. MANIFESTATION-LATENCY.

un''-dis-guised'. True; manifest. MANIFESTATION-LATENCY, TRUTH-ERROR, TRUTHFULNESS-FALSEHOOD.

un''-dis-mayed'. Fearless. BRAVERY-COWARDICE.

un''-dis-posed' of. Kept. KEEPING-RELINQUISHMENT, USE-DISUSE.

un''-dis-put'-ed. Undenied. CERTAINTY-DOUBT.

un''-dis-sem'-bling. Upright. TRUTHFULNESS-FALSEHOOD.

un''-dis-solved'. Entire; dense. SOLIDITY-RARITY, WHOLE-PART.

un''-dis-tin'-guish-a-ble. Inseparable. DIFFERENTIATION-INDISCRIMINATION.

un''-dis-tin'-guished. Not separated. DIFFERENTIATION-INDISCRIMINATION.

un''-dis-tort'-ed. Straight. CURVATION-RECTILINEARITY, TRUTH-ERROR.

un''-dis-tract'-ed. Unbewildered. HEED-DISREGARD.

un''-dis-turbed'. Quiet; unexcited. EXCITATION, HURRY-LEISURE, MOVEMENT-REST.

un''-di-vi'-ded. Complete. ENTIRETY-DEFICIENCY, WHOLE-PART.

un-do'. Destroy; take apart. ACTION-PASSIVENESS, CONVERSION-REVERSION, COOPERATION-OPPOSITION, CREATION-DESTRUCTION, UNION-DISUNION.

un-do'-ing. Ruin. WELFARE-MISFORTUNE.

un-done'. Ruined. ACTION-PASSIVENESS, PLEASURE-PAIN, SANGUINENESS-HOPELESSNESS, SUCCESS-FAILURE, WELFARE-MISFORTUNE.

un-doubt'-ed. Positive. CERTAINTY-DOUBT.

un-draped'. Uncovered. DRESS-UNDRESS.

un-dread'-ed. Not feared. BRAVERY-COWARDICE.

un-dreamt' of. Unthought of. REFLECTION-VACANCY.

un-dress'. Disrobe. DRESS-UNDRESS, EMBELLISHMENT-SIMPLICITY, PREPARATION-NONPREPARATION.

un-dressed'. Unprepared. DRESS-UNDRESS, PREPARATION-NONPREPARATION.

un-dried'. Green; wet. DAMPNESS-DRYNESS.

un-drilled'. Not trained. PREPARATION-NONPREPARATION.

un-droop'-ing. Persevering. PERSISTENCE-WHIM.

un-due'. Unnecessary. DUENESS-UNDUENESS.

un-due'-ness. Excessiveness. DUENESS-UNDUENESS.

un'-du-late. To move like a wave. CIRCLE-WINDING, VIBRATION.

un''-du-la'-tion. A wave. CIRCLE-WINDING, VIBRATION.

un'-du-la-to''-ry. Wavy. CIRCLE-WINDING, VIBRATION.

un-du'-te-ous. Negligent. VIRTUE-VICE.

un-du'-ti-ful. Disrespectful. VIRTUE-VICE.

un-dy'-ing. Everlasting. DISCONTINUANCE-CONTINUANCE, ETERNITY-INSTANTANEITY, MUTABILITY-STABILITY.

une aile, ne battre que d' [F.] (ün êl, ne batr ke d'). To sleep at one's post. ACTIVITY-INDOLENCE.

un-earned'. Not merited. DUENESS-UNDUENESS.

un-earth'. Disinter; reveal; eject. ADMISSION-EXPULSION, DISCOVERY, INVESTIGATION-ANSWER, LIFE-FUNERAL.

un-earth'-ly. Supernatural. DIVINITY, GODLINESS-UNGODLINESS, HEAVEN-HELL, JOVE-FIEND, MATERIALITY-SPIRITUALITY.

un-eas'-i-ness. Worry. PLEASURE-PAIN.

un-eas'-y. Disturbed. PLEASURE-PAIN.

un-ed'-i-fy''-ing. Not instructive, especially with regard to morals. EDUCATION-MISTEACHING.

un''-ed-u-ca'-ted. Ignorant. KNOWLEDGE-IGNORANCE, PREPARATION-NONPREPARATION.

un''-em-bar'-rassed. Unhindered. DIFFICULTY-FACILITY, SOCIETY-LUDICROUSNESS.

un''-em-bod'-ied. Spiritual. MATERIALITY-SPIRITUALITY.

un''-em-ployed'. Unused; inactive. ACTION-PASSIVENESS, USE-DISUSE.

un''-en-cum'-bered. Free. DIFFICULTY-FACILITY, DUTY-IMMUNITY.

un''-en-deared'. Unbeloved. LOVE-HATE.

un-end'-ing. Everlasting. ETERNITY-INSTANTANEITY.

un''-en-dowed'. Unequipped. MIGHT-IMPOTENCE; unendowed with reason, MIND-IMBECILITY.

un''-en-du'-ra-ble. Intolerable. PLEASURABLENESS-PAINFULNESS.

un''-en-joyed'. Not enjoyed. ENTERTAINMENT-WEARINESS.

un''-en-light'-ened. Ignorant; foolish. KNOWLEDGE-IGNORANCE, SAGACITY-INCAPACITY.

un''-en-slaved'. Free. LIBERTY-SUBJECTION.

un-en'-ter-pris''-ing. Not energetic. RECKLESSNESS-CAUTION.

un-en''-ter-tain'-ing. Not diverting. WITTINESS-DULNESS.

un''-en-thralled'. Unrestrained. LIBERTY-SUBJECTION.

un″-en-ti′-tled. Undeserving. DUENESS-UNDUENESS.

un-en′-vied. Despised. REGARD-DISRESPECT, REGARD-SCORN.

un-e′-qual. Not uniform. EQUALITY-INEQUALITY, VARIATION; **unequal to,** EXCESS-LACK.

un-e′-qualed. Surpassing. SUPREMACY-SUBORDINACY.

un″-e-quipped′. Unarrayed. PREPARATION-NONPREPARATION.

un-eq′-ui-ta-ble. Unjust. RIGHT-WRONG.

un″-e-quiv′-o-cal. Definite. CERTAINTY-DOUBT, CLEARNESS-OBSCURITY, MAGNITUDE-SMALLNESS.

un″-e-quiv′-o-cal-ly. Definitely. MAGNITUDE-SMALLNESS.

un-err′-ing. Certain; not wayward. CERTAINTY-DOUBT, INNOCENCE-GUILT, TRUTH-ERROR.

un″-es-sayed′. Not tried. USE-DISUSE.

un″-es-sen′-tial. Unnecessary. CONSEQUENCE-INSIGNIFICANCE.

un″-es-tab′-lished. Unfounded. ESTABLISHMENT-REMOVAL.

un-e′-ven. Diverse; rough. EQUALITY-INEQUALITY, SMOOTHNESS-ROUGHNESS, UNIFORMITY-DIVERSITY.

un-e′-ven-ness. Inequality. EQUALITY-INEQUALITY, UNIFORMITY-DIVERSITY.

un″-e-vent′-ful. Not momentous. CONSEQUENCE-INSIGNIFICANCE.

un″-ex-act′. Involved. TRUTH-ERROR.

un″-ex-ag′-ger-a″-ted. Precise. TRUTH-ERROR.

un″-ex-am′-ined. To inspect with care. CAREFULNESS-CARELESSNESS.

un″-ex-am′-pled. Without a parallel. CONVENTIONALITY-UNCONVENTIONALITY.

un″-ex-cep′-tion-a-ble. Good; excellent. DUENESS-UNDUENESS, FAULTLESSNESS-FAULTINESS, INNOCENCE-GUILT.

un″-ex-ci′-ta-ble. Not easily excited. EXCITABILITY-INEXCITABILITY, SENSITIVENESS.

un″-ex-ci′-ted. Calm. EMOTION-APATHY, EXCITABILITY-INEXCITABILITY.

un″-ex-ci′-ting. Not stirring. TURBULENCE-CALMNESS.

un-ex′-e-cu″-ted. Unenforced. COMPLETION-NONCOMPLETION.

un″-ex-empt′. Liable. CONTINGENCY.

un-ex′-er-cised. Undeveloped. PREPARATION-NONPREPARATION, USE-DISUSE.

un″-ex-ert′-ed. Unused. VIGOR-INERTIA.

un″-ex-haust′-ed. Not weakened. ENOUGH, STRENGTH-WEAKNESS.

un″-ex-pand′-ed. Not spread out. BREADTH-NARROWNESS, ENLARGEMENT-DIMINUTION.

un″-ex-pect′-ed. Sudden. CONVENTIONALITY-UNCONVENTIONALITY, EARLINESS-LATENESS, EXPECTATION-SURPRISE.

un″-ex-pect′-ed-ly. Suddenly. EXPECTATION-SURPRISE.

un″-ex-pen′-sive. Cheap. COSTLINESS-CHEAPNESS.

un″-ex-plain′-a-ble. Unintelligent. CLEARNESS-OBSCURITY.

un″-ex-plained′. Not elucidated. CLEARNESS-OBSCURITY, KNOWLEDGE-IGNORANCE, MANIFESTATION-LATENCY.

un″-ex-plored′. Unknown; hidden. CAREFULNESS-CARELESSNESS, KNOWLEDGE-IGNORANCE, MANIFESTATION-LATENCY.

un″-ex-posed′. Hidden. MANIFESTATION-LATENCY.

un″-ex-pressed′. Not uttered. ASSERTION-DENIAL.

un″-ex-press′-ive. Unutterable. MEANING-JARGON.

un″-ex-tend′-ed. Not enlarged. MATERIALITY-SPIRITUALITY.

un-ex-tin′-guished. Unquenched; not destroyed. HEAT-COLD, TURBULENCE-CALMNESS.

un-fa′-ded. Without any change in color. COLOR-ACHROMATISM.

un-fa′-ding. Unchanging. ETERNITY-INSTANTANEITY.

un-fail′-ing. Certain. MUTATION-PERMANENCE.

un-fair′. Unjust. RIGHT-WRONG, TRUTHFULNESS-FALSEHOOD, UPRIGHTNESS-DISHONESTY.

un-fair′-ness. Unjustness. RIGHT-WRONG, TRUTHFULNESS-FALSEHOOD, UPRIGHTNESS-DISHONESTY.

un-faith′-ful. Perfidious. UPRIGHTNESS-DISHONESTY.

un-fal′-ter-ing. Firm. PERSISTENCE-WHIM.

un″-fa-mil′-iar. Formal. CONVENTIONALITY-UNCONVENTIONALITY.

un-fash′-ion-a-ble. Not in accordance with fashion. CONVENTIONALITY-UNCONVENTIONALITY, TASTE-VULGARITY.

un-fash′-ioned. Unwrought; formless. FORM-FORMLESSNESS, PREPARATION-NONPREPARATION.

un-fast′-en. To loosen. UNION-DISUNION.

un-fath′-om-a-ble. Infinite; too deep for measurement. CLEARNESS-OBSCURITY, DEEPNESS-SHALLOWNESS, INFINITY.

un-fath′-omed. Unmeasured. DEEPNESS-SHALLOWNESS.

un-fa′-vor-a-ble. Adverse. ANTAGONISM-CONCURRENCE, OBSTRUCTION-HELP, OPPORTUNENESS-UNSUITABLENESS; **unfavorable chance,** LIKELIHOOD-UNLIKELIHOOD.

un-feared′. Undreaded. BRAVERY-COWARDICE.

un-fea′-si-ble. Impracticable. POSSIBILITY-IMPOSSIBILITY.

un-fed′. Not supplied with food. EXCESS-LACK, FASTING-GLUTTONY.

un-feel′-ing. Heartless. FEELING-INSENSIBILITY, SENSITIVENESS-APATHY.

un-feigned′. Real. TRUTHFULNESS-FALSEHOOD.

un-felt′. Not perceived. SENSITIVENESS-APATHY.

un-fem′-i-nine. Effeminate. MALE-FEMALE, TASTE-VULGARITY.

un-fer′-tile. Unproductive. FERTILITY-STERILITY.

un-fet′-ter. Free. LIBERTY-SUBJECTION, RELEASE-RESTRAINT.

un-fet′-tered. Freed. LIBERTY-SUBJECTION.

un-fin′-ished. Not done. COMPLETION-NONCOMPLETION, ENTIRETY-DEFICIENCY.

un-fit′. Unsuitable. DUENESS-UNDUENESS, HARMONY-DISCORD, MIGHT-IMPOTENCE, PROPRIETY-IMPROPRIETY, RIGHT-WRONG.

un-fit′-ness. Unsuitableness. HARMONY-DISCORD, PROPRIETY-IMPROPRIETY.

un-fit′-ted. Not ready. PREPARATION-NONPREPARATION.

un-fit′-ting. Inappropriate. HARMONY-DISCORD.

un-fix′. Undo. UNION-DISUNION.

un-fixed′. Changeable. MUTABILITY-STABILITY.

un-flag′-ging. Resolute. PERSISTENCE-WHIM.

un-flam′-ma-ble. Capable of being cooled. HEATING-COOLING.

un-flat′-ter-ing. True. CRAFT-ARTLESSNESS, TRUTH-ERROR.

un-fledged′. Immature. INFANT-VETERAN, PREPARATION-NONPREPARATION.

un-flinch′-ing. Firm. BRAVERY-COWARDICE, DETERMINATION-VACILLATION, PERSISTENCE-WHIM.

un-fold′. To make known; to straighten. CURVATION-RECTILINEARITY, EXPOSURE-HIDINGPLACE, INTERPRETATION-MISINTERPRETATION, REVOLUTION-EVOLUTION; **unfold a tale,** ACCOUNT.

un-fold′-ing. Disclosing. REVOLUTION-EVOLUTION.

un″-for-bid′. Allowed. LEAVE-PROHIBITION.

un″-for-bid′-den. Unprohibited. LEAVE-PROHIBITION.

un-forced′. Willing; free. LIBERTY-SUBJECTION, READINESS-RELUCTANCE.

un″-fore-seen′. Unexpected. EXPECTATION-SURPRISE.

un-for′-feit-ed. Not given up. KEEPING-RELINQUISHMENT.

un″-for-giv′-ing. Relentless. THANKFULNESS-VIN-DICTIVENESS.

un″-for-got′-ten. Remembered. REMEMBRANCE-FOR-GETFULNESS.

un-formed′. Shapeless. FORM-FORMLESSNESS, PREPA-RATION-NONPREPARATION.

un-for′-ti-fied. Pure; powerless. MIGHT-IMPOTENCE, MIXTURE-HOMOGENEITY.

un-for′-tu-nate. Unlucky; unhappy. OPPORTUNE-NESS-UNSUITABLENESS, PLEASURE-PAIN, PURITY-RAKE, SUCCESS-FAILURE, WELFARE-MISFORTUNE; **unfortunate woman,** PURITY-RAKE.

un-found′-ed. False. TRUTHFULNESS - FABRICATION.

un-fre′-quent. Rare. FREQUENCY-RARITY.

un″-fre-quent′-ed. Rarely visited. SOCIABILITY - PRI-VACY.

un-fre′-quent-ly. Seldom. FREQUENCY-RARITY.

un-friend′-ed. Wanting friends. MIGHT-IMPOTENCE, SOCIABILITY-PRIVACY.

un-friend′-li-ness. Unfavorableness. AMITY-HOSTIL-ITY.

un-friend′-ly. Hostile. AMITY - HOSTILITY, ANTAGO-NISM - CONCURRENCE, CHARITABLENESS - MALEVO-LENCE.

un-frock′. To deprive of a privilege. COMMISSION-AB-ROGATION, EXCULPATION-PUNITION.

un-fro′-zen. Warm. HEAT-COLD.

un-fruit′-ful. Barren. FERTILITY-STERILITY.

un-fruit′-ful-ness. Barrenness. USEFULNESS-USELESS-NESS.

un″-ful-filled′. Not performed. DUENESS-UNDUENESS, OBSERVANCE-NONOBSERVANCE.

un-furl′. To unfold. REVOLUTION-EVOLUTION; **unfurl a flag,** MANIFESTATION-LATENCY, SIGN.

un-fur′-nished. Divested. EXCESS-LACK, PREPARA-TION-NONPREPARATION.

un-gain′-ly. Uncouth. BEAUTY-UGLINESS, POLITENESS-IMPOLITENESS.

un-gal′-lant. Uncourteous. POLITENESS - IMPOLITE-NESS.

un-gar′-nished. Undecked. EMBELLISHMENT - SIM-PLICITY.

un-gath′-ered. Uncollected. USE-DISUSE.

un-gen′-er-ous. Selfish. EXTRAVAGANCE - AVARICE, UNSELFISHNESS-SELFISHNESS.

un-gen′-er-ous-ly. Selfishly. UNSELFISHNESS-SELFISH-NESS.

un-ge′-ni-al. Morose. HEALTHINESS-UNHEALTHINESS.

un″-gen-teel′. Boorish. POLITENESS-IMPOLITENESS.

un-gen′-tle. Violent; rude. POLITENESS-IMPOLITE-NESS, TURBULENCE-CALMNESS.

un-gen′-tle-man-like″. Uncourteous. POLITENESS-IM-POLITENESS, TASTE-VULGARITY, UPRIGHTNESS-DIS-HONESTY.

un-gen′-tle-man-ly. Uncourteous. POLITENESS-IMPO-LITENESS, TASTE-VULGARITY, UPRIGHTNESS-DISHON-ESTY.

un-gift′-ed. Being without native gifts. SAGACITY-IN-CAPACITY.

un-glor′-i-fied. Unhonored. REPUTATION-DISCREDIT.

un-glue′. To open; to separate. COHESION-LOOSE-NESS.

un-god′-li-ness. Impiety. GODLINESS-DISBELIEF.

un-god′-ly. Wicked. GODLINESS-DISBELIEF.

un-gov′-ern-a-ble. Wild. EXCITABILITY - INEXCITA-BILITY, INSUBORDINATION-OBEDIENCE, TURBULENCE-CALMNESS, TYRANNY-ANARCHY.

un-gov′-erned. Unrestricted. LIBERTY-SUBJECTION.

un-grace′-ful. Clumsy; awkward. BEAUTY-UGLINESS, PURITY-CRUDENESS, TASTE-VULGARITY.

un-gra′-cious. Uncivil; unfriendly. CHARITABLENESS-MALEVOLENCE, POLITENESS-IMPOLITENESS.

un″-gram-mat′-ic-al. Based on the principles of gram-mar. GRAMMAR-SOLECISM.

un-grant′-ed. Refused. PROFFER-REFUSAL.

un-grate′ ful. Thankless. THANKFULNESS-THANKLESS-NESS.

un-grat′-i-fied. Unpleased. CONTENTEDNESS-DISCON-TENTMENT.

un-ground′-ed. Unfounded. SUBSTANCE-NULLITY, TRUTH-ERROR.

un-grudg′-ing. Liberal. GENEROSITY-FRUGALITY.

un-guard′-ed. Neglected; spontaneous. CAREFUL-NESS-CARELESSNESS, PREDETERMINATION-IMPULSE, PREPARATION-NONPREPARATION; **in an unguarded moment,** CAREFULNESS-CARELESSNESS, EXPECTA-TION-SURPRISE.

unguem, ad [L.] (un-gwem, ad). Exactly. FAULTLESS-NESS-FAULTINESS, TRUTH-ERROR.

un′-guent. An ointment. PULPINESS-OIL.

unguibus et rostro [L.] (un′-gwi-bus et ros′-tro). With claws and beak, tooth and nail, hammer and tongs. TOIL-RELAXATION.

un-guid′-ed. Wandering. KNOWLEDGE - IGNORANCE, PREDETERMINATION - IMPULSE, SKILL - UNSKILFUL-NESS.

un-guilt′-y. Innocent. INNOCENCE-GUILT.

un-hab′-it-a-ble. Not suitable to be dwelt in. PRES-ENCE-ABSENCE.

un″-ha-bit′-u-a″-ted. Unaccustomed. HABIT-DESUE-TUDE.

un-hack′-neyed. New. HABIT-DESUETUDE.

un-hal′-lowed. Impious. GODLINESS-DISBELIEF, GOD-LINESS-UNGODLINESS.

un-hand′. To release. RELEASE-RESTRAINT.

un-hand′-seled. Untilled. NOVELTY-ANTIQUITY.

un-hand′-some. Unbecoming. UPRIGHTNESS-DISHON-ESTY.

un-hand′-y. Clumsy. SKILL-UNSKILFULNESS.

un-hap′-pi-ness. Sadness. PLEASURE-PAIN.

un-hap′-py. Sad. LIGHTHEARTEDNESS - DEJECTION, PLEASURE-PAIN, WELFARE-MISFORTUNE; **make un-happy,** PLEASURABLENESS-PAINFULNESS.

un-har′-bored. Without shelter. ESTABLISHMENT-REMOVAL.

un-har′-dened. Tender; innocent; penitent. COMPAS-SION-RUTHLESSNESS, INNOCENCE-GUILT, REPENT-ANCE-OBDURACY.

un″-har-mo′-ni-ous. Unmusical. HARMONY-DISCORD, MELODY-DISSONANCE.

un-har′-ness. Liberate. RELEASE-RESTRAINT.

un-hatched′. Not formed. PREPARATION-NONPREPA-RATION.

un-haz′-ard-ed. Unattempted. SECURITY-INSECURITY.

un-health′-i-ness. Sickness. HEALTH-SICKNESS.

un-health′-y. Unsound. HEALTH-SICKNESS, HEALTHI-NESS-UNHEALTHINESS, LIFE-KILLING.

un-heard′ of. Improbable; wonderful. ASTONISHMENT-EXPECTANCE, CONVENTIONALITY-UNCONVENTIONAL-ITY, EXPECTATION-SURPRISE, KNOWLEDGE - IGNO-RANCE, LIKELIHOOD-UNLIKELIHOOD.

un-heed′. Inattention. CAREFULNESS-CARELESSNESS.

un-heed′-ed. Neglected. CAREFULNESS-CARELESSNESS.

un-heed′-ing. Neglecting. HEED-DISREGARD.

un-hes′-i-ta″-ting. Not vacillating. DETERMINATION-VACILLATION, FAITH-MISGIVING.

un-hewn′. Unfashioned. FORM-FORMLESSNESS, PREP-ARATION-NONPREPARATION.

un-hin′-dered. Free. LIBERTY-SUBJECTION.

un-hinge′. Derange. MIGHT-IMPOTENCE, ORGANIZA-TION-DISORGANIZATION.

un-hinged′. Deranged; deprived of support. MIGHT-IMPOTENCE, SANENESS-LUNACY, SUCCESS-FAILURE.

un-ho′ly. Sinful. GODLINESS-DISBELIEF.

un-hon′-ored. Unesteemed. REPUTATION-DISCREDIT.

un-hoped′. Unexpected. EXPECTATION-SURPRISE.

un-horsed′. Unseated. SUCCESS-FAILURE.

un-hos′-tile. Friendly. AMITY-HOSTILITY.

un-house′. To take from under cover   ADMISSION-EX-PULSION.

un-housed′. Taken from under cover.   ESTABLISH-MENT-REMOVAL.

un-hurt′. Unharmed. CONSERVATION.

u′-ni-corn. A fabulous animal having the head and body of a horse with a single straight horn on the forehead. CONVENTIONALITY - UNCONVENTIONALITY, CONVEYANCE-VESSEL.

un″-i-de′-al. Real; not existing in thought. ENTITY-NONENTITY, REFLECTION-VACANCY, TRUTH-ERROR.

u″-ni-fi-ca′-tion. Act of uniting. COMPOSITION-RESO-LUTION, SOLITUDE-COMPANY.

u′-ni-form. Regular; harmonious. DRESS-UNDRESS, MIXTURE-HOMOGENEITY, PROPORTION-DEFORMITY, REGULARITY-IRREGULARITY, SIGN, UNIFORMITY-DI-VERSITY, UNIFORMITY-MULTIFORMITY.

u′-ni-form″-i-ty. Regularity. FORM-FORMLESSNESS, HARMONY-DISCORD, LIKENESS-UNLIKENESS, REGU-LARITY-IRREGULARITY, UNIFORMITY-DIVERSITY,UNI-FORMITY-MULTIFORMITY.

UNIFORMITY—DIVERSITY

Accordance. Considerable resemblance.
Agreement. Entire sameness. See HARMONY.
Conformity. Correspondence in form manner, or use. See CON-VENTIONALITY.
Connaturality. ⎫
Connaturalness. ⎬ The state of being the same by nature.
Consistency. Uniformity of things or statements.
Constancy. Uniformity of affections.
Even tenor. Uniform run, as of conduct.
Homogeneity. ⎫
Homogeneousness. ⎬ Uniformity of material or structure.
Homology. The state of being similar in structure and properties.
Monotony. Tiresome uniformity.
Regularity. Uniformity according to rule.
Routine. A uniform method of procedure.
Uniformity. The state of being the same in characteristic qualities.

UNIFORMITY—Verbs.

Accord with. To have similar feelings. See HARMONY.
Assimilate. To transform to uniformity in matter or structure.
Become uniform. To grow uniform.
Be uniform. To be of the same form.
Conform to. To act in uniformity with. See CONVENTIONALITY.
Dress. To adjust to a uniform line
Level. To bring to a common state.
Render uniform. To make to agree.
Run through. To pervade with uniformity.
Smooth. To give a uniform evenness to.

UNIFORMITY—Aajectives.

Connatural. Having a uniform nature.
Consistent. Characterized by harmony between things or state-ments.
Even. Free from great roughness.
Homogeneous. Composed of uniform material.
Homologous. Composed of similar material.
Invariable. Absolutely uniform in occurrence
Monotonous. Uniform in a tiresome manner.
Of a piece. Of the same sort.
Uniform. Having always the same form, manner, or character.

Diversity. A striking and essential difference.
Irregularity. A departure from uniformity in violation of all rules.
Multiformity. The state of having many forms. See UNIFORMITY-MULTIFORMITY.
Roughness. The state of being uneven. See SMOOTHNESS-ROUGH-NESS.
Unconformity. Difference in form or manner.
Unevenness. The state of being not uniformly plane.

DIVERSITY—Adjectives.

All kinds of. ⎫
All manners of. ⎬ Widely differing examples of.
All sorts of. ⎭
Diversified. Differing essentially.
Irregular. Departing from the usual or proper form.
Of various kinds. Of many different shapes, forms, styles, etc.
Rough. Characterized by a lack of uniformity in surface.
Uneven. Not uniformly plane.
Varied. Not uniform in all its parts.

DIVERSITY—Adverbs, etc.

Here, there, and everywhere. In various parts; widely separated.
In all manner of ways. Variously.

UNIFORMITY—Continued

UNIFORMITY—Adverbs, etc.

Always. Constantly during a certain period; uniformly
By clockwork. In a mechanically uniform manner
In harmony. In uniform accord.
Invariably. Uniformly without exception.
Never otherwise. Uniformly the same.
Uniformity. Without variation or diversity
Uniformly with. In a manner having the same general characteris-tics as something else.
Without exception. In an absolutely uniform manner.

UNIFORMITY—Phrase.

Ab uno disce omnes [L.]. From one learn all.

UNIFORMITY—MULTIFORMITY.

Clockwork precision. Exact uniformity of action.
Conformity. Correspondence in form, manner or character. See CONVENTIONALITY.
Constancy. The state or quality of being constant or steadfast.
Formula. A fixed or conventional method in which anything is to be done, arranged, or said.
Key-note. The fundamental tone of the chord, to which all the modulations of the piece are referred.
Model. That by which a thing is to be measured; standard.
Model condition. ⎫
Model state. ⎬ A condition or state after a model or pattern.
Natural condition. ⎫
Natural state. ⎬ A form or state according to nature.
Nature. Conformity to that which is natural.
Normal condition. ⎫ Accordance with an established norm, rule, or
Normal state. ⎬ principle.
Order of things. Customary mode of procedure.
Ordinary condition. ⎫
Ordinary state. ⎬ Accordance with customary or usual rule.
Precedent. An authoritative example. See COPY-MODEL.
Principle. A settled rule of action by which all action is regulated.
Punctuality. The quality or state of being punctual. See TRUTH.
Regularity. The condition or quality of being regular.
Routine. Any regular course of action or procedure rigidly adhered to by mere force of habit See HABIT.

Diversity. Multiplicity of difference; a state of difference.
Multifariousness. Multiplied diversity. See *Adjectives*.
Multiformity. Diversity of forms; variety of appearances in same thing.
Omniformity. The condition or quality of having every form.
Variety. Intermixture or succession of different things.

MULTIFORMITY—Adjectives.

All manner of. Every sort of.
And what not. Having very many different things.
De omnibus rebus et quibusdam aliis [L.]. Concerning all things and certain things beside.
Desultory. Jumping or passing from one thing to another without order or rational connection.
Different. Of various or contrary nature, form, or quality.
Divers. Different in kind or species.
Diversified. Distinguished by various forms.
Epicene. Common to both sexes.
Et hoc genus omne [L.]. And everything of the sort.
Heterogeneous Differing in kind; having unlike qualities
Indiscriminate. Not making any distinction.
Irregular. Not conforming to a law, method, or usage, recognized as the general rule.
Manifold. Various in kind or quality.

UNIFORMITY—MULTIFORMITY—*Continued*.

Rule. To establish or settle by, or as by, a rule   See PRECEPT.
Standard. That which is established as a rule or model.
Standing order. An order or regulation requiring conformity to.
Uniformity. Conformity to a pattern or rule.

UNIFORMITY—*Denotations*.

Law. A rule of being or of conduct, established by an authority able to enforce its will.
Law of the Medes and Persians. A strict, unchangeable law.
Procrustean law. Production of conformity by violent means.
Standing dish. A dish of food served very frequently.

UNIFORMITY—*Adjectives*.

According to rule. Uniformly. See CONVENTIONALITY.
Constant. Remaining unchanged, or invariable.
Customary. Established by common usage. See HABIT.
Regular. Conformed to a rule.

MULTIFORMITY—ADJECTIVES—*Continued*.

Many-sided. Versatile; having an aptitude for many unlike pursuits.
Mosaic. Composed of various materials.
Motley. Heterogeneously made or mixed up.
Multifarious. Made up of many differing parts.
Multifold. Many times doubled; manifold· numerous.
Multiform. .Having many forms, shapes, or appearances.
Multigenerous. Having many kinds.
Of all sorts and kinds.} Of all known forms, shapes, styles, etc.
Of every description. }
Omnifarious. Of all varieties, forms, or kinds.
Omniform. Having every form or shape.
Omnigruous. Consisting of all kinds.
Variform. Having different shapes or forms.

UNIFORMITY—ADJECTIVES—*Continued*

Steady. Regular, constant; uniform.
Uniform. Having always the same form, manner, or degree.

u″-ni-form′-ly. Evenly. UNIFORMITY-DIVERSITY.
un″-il-lu′-min-a″-ted. Dark. LIGHT-DARKNESS.
un″-im-ag′-in-a-ble. Wonderful. ASTONISHMENT-EXPECTANCE, LIKELIHOOD-UNLIKELIHOOD, POSSIBILITY-IMPOSSIBILITY.
un″-im-ag′-in-a-tive. Not creative. WITTINESS-DULNESS.
un″-im-ag′-ined. Unthought. ENTITY-NONENTITY, TRUTH-ERROR.
un″-im-i-ta′-ted. Uncopied. IMITATION-ORIGINALITY.
un″-im-paired′. Uninjured. CONSERVATION.
un″-im-pas′-sioned. Not fervent. EXCITABILITY-INEXCITABILITY.
un″-im-peach′-a-ble. Certain; trustworthy. APPROVAL-DISAPPROVAL, CERTAINTY-DOUBT, DUENESS-UNDUENESS, INNOCENCE-GUILT, TRUTH-ERROR.
un″-im-peached′. Trusted. APPROVAL-DISAPPROVAL, INNOCENCE-GUILT.
un″-im-por′-tance. Meanness. CONSEQUENCE-INSIGNIFICANCE.
un″-im-por′-tant. Trifling. CONSEQUENCE-INSIGNIFICANCE, SUPREMACY-SUBORDINACY.
un″-im-pressed′. Uninfluenced. JUBILATION-LAMENTATION.
un″-im-press′-i-ble. Unsusceptible. SENSITIVENESS-APATHY.
un″-im-pres′-sion-a-ble. Unsusceptible. SENSITIVENESS-APATHY.
un″-im-proved′. Not made better. BETTERMENT-DETERIORATION.
un″-in-creased′. Not multiplied. INCREASE-DECREASE.
un″-in-cum′-bered. Unhindered. DIFFICULTY-FACILITY, DUTY-IMMUNITY.
un″-in-duced′. Uninfluenced. MOTIVE-CAPRICE.
un″-in-fect′-ed. Uncorrupted. CLEANNESS-FILTHINESS.
un″-in-fec′-tious. Not contagious. HEALTHINESS-UNHEALTHINESS.
un″-in-flam′-ma-ble. Not readily ignited. HEATING-COOLING.
un-in′-flu-enced. Unswayed; obstinate. BIGOTRY-APOSTASY.
un-in″-flu-en′-tial. Without influence; inactive. DOMINANCE-IMPOTENCE, VIGOR-INERTIA.
un″-in-formed′. Untaught. KNOWLEDGE-IGNORANCE.
un″-in-ge′-nious. Not skilful in contriving. TRUTHFULNESS-FALSEHOOD.
un″-in-hab′-it. To go away from home. PRESENCE-ABSENCE, SOCIABILITY-PRIVACY.
un″-in-hab′-it-a-ble. Unfit to live in. PRESENCE-ABSENCE, SOCIABILITY-PRIVACY.

un″-in-hab′-it-ed. Vacant. PRESENCE-ABSENCE, SOCIABILITY-PRIVACY.
un″-in-i′-ti-a″-ted. Uninstructed. KNOWLEDGE-IGNORANCE, SKILL-UNSKILFULNESS.
un-in′-jured. Perfect; healthy. CONSERVATION, FAULTLESSNESS-FAULTINESS, HEALTH-SICKNESS.
un″-in-ju′-ri-ous. Not hurtful. HEALTHINESS-UNHEALTHINESS.
un″-in-quis′-i-tive. Indifferent. INQUISITIVENESS-INDIFFERENCE.
un″-in-spired′. Unanimated. SENSITIVENESS - APATHY.
un″-in-struct′-ed. Unlearned. KNOWLEDGE - IGNORANCE.
un′-in″-tel-lec′-tu-al. Unintelligent. REFLECTION-VACANCY, SAGACITY-INCAPACITY.
un″-in-tel′-li-gent. Unreasoning. SAGACITY - INCAPACITY.
un″-in-tel′-li-gi-bil′-i-ty. Ignorance. CLEARNESS-OBSCURITY, TIDINGS-MYSTERY.
un″-in-tel′-li-gi-ble. Not capable of being understood. CLEARNESS - OBSCURITY, PERSPICUITY - OBSCURITY; **render unintelligible,** EDUCATION-MISTEACHING, TIDINGS-MYSTERY.
un″-in-tend′-ed. Accidental. PURPOSE-LUCK.
un″-in-ten′-tion-al. Accidental. PURPOSE-LUCK, RATIONALE-LUCK, VOLITION-OBLIGATION.
un″-in-ten′-tion-al-ly. Accidentally. PURPOSE-LUCK.
un-in′-ter-est-ed. Unattracted. ENTERTAINMENT-WEARINESS.
un-in′-ter-est-ing. Dull. WITTINESS-DULNESS.
un-in′-ter-mit′-ting. Continuing; persistent. CONTINUITY-INTERRUPTION, DISCONTINUANCE-CONTINUANCE, LASTINGNESS-TRANSIENTNESS, PERSISTENCE-WHIM.
un″-in″-ter-rupt′-ed. Continuous; unremitting. CONTINUITY-INTERRUPTION, DISCONTINUANCE-CONTINUANCE, ETERNITY-INSTANTANEITY.
un-in′-tro-duced″. Unacquainted with. SOCIABILITY-PRIVACY.
un″-in-ured′. Unaccustomed. HABIT-DESUETUDE.
un″-in-vent′-ed. Hidden. ENLIGHTENMENT-SECRECY.
un″-in-ves′-ti-ga″-ted. Not inquired into. KNOWLEDGE-IGNORANCE.
un″-in-vi′-ted. Unasked. SOCIABILITY-PRIVACY.
un″-in-vi′-ting. Unalluring. PLEASURABLENESS-PAINFULNESS.
un′-ion. Coalescence; league; state of wedlock. ANTAGONISM-CONCURRENCE, ASSOCIATION, COMPOSITION-RESOLUTION, COOPERATION-OPPOSITION, HARMONY-DISCORD, LABOR-CAPITAL, MATRIMONY-CELIBACY, UNION-DISUNION, VARIANCE-ACCORD.

UNION—DISUNION.

Accouplement. The act of coupling or uniting.
Alligation. The act of tying together or attaching by some bond.
Anastomosis. Union or connection, as of arteries or veins.
Annexation. }
Annexion. } The process of attaching, adding, or appending.
Annexment. The act of annexing.
Articulation. The act of putting together with a joint or joints.
Assemblage. State of being assembled. See GATHERING.
Astriction. Act of joining together.
Attachment. Act or state of attaching.
Combination. Junction to produce a whole
Commissure. A joint, seam, or closure.
Communication. Connection.
Compagination. Act of joining together.
Concatenation. A joining together like a chain.
Confluence. The meeting or junction of two or more streams.
Conjugation. The act of uniting or combining.
Conjunction. State of being joined together.
Connection. The act of joining or fastening together.
Hinge. A joint by which two parts of anything are connected to permit turning on one another.
Infibulation. Act of fastening, as with a buckle or string.
Inosculation. Union by continuity; the junction or connection of vessels, or passages, so that their contents pass from one to the other.
Joinder. The joining or uniting of things together.
Joining. A bringing together.
Joint. A joining of two parts so as to admit of motion.
Jointure. A joining; a joint.
Ligation. The tying or binding together.
Link. A part of a connected series.
Marriage. Union in wedlock.
Meeting. A coming together.
Miter. A junction effected by two beveled ends or edges.
Mortise. A union of two pieces of timber.
Pivot. A union of two things which admits of free motion of one upon another.
Reunion. Coming together again.
Seam. A joining of pieces of cloth by sewing.
Stitch. A joining by sewing.
Suture. The uniting of the parts of a wound by stitching.
Symphysis. The union or coalescence of bones.
Union. The act of uniting or joining two or more things into one.
Vincture. A binding.

UNION—Nouns of Quality.

Closeness. State or quality of being closely joined.
Coherence. State or quality of cohering.
Tightness. State or quality of being tightly joined.

UNION—Verbs.

Accouple. To join; couple.
Affix. To join to something.
Associate. To join together.
Attach. To unite to something.
Bandage. To fasten with a bandage.
Be joined. To be fastened together.
Belay. To fasten, as with a rope.
Bind. To fasten together.
Bind together. To fasten, as with a bandage.
Bind up. To fasten or tie, as with a bandage.
Bolt. To fasten with a bolt.
Brace. To strengthen with a brace.
Bracket. To join with a brace.
Braid. To bind with a braid.
Bridge over. To join with a bridge.
Buckle. To fasten with a buckle.
Button. To fasten with a button.
Chain. To fasten with a chain.
Clamp. To join, as with a clamp.
Clap together. }
Clap up. } To fasten.
Clasp. To hold in encircling grasp.
Clinch. To secure; grapple.
Cohere. To hold together. See COHESION.
Conjoin. To join together.
Connect. To join; unite; combine.
Couple. To join together in a pair.
Dovetail. To join by interlacing.
Embody. To collect in a whole.
Enchase. To incase as a jewel.
Enlink. To link together.
Entangle. To tangle together.

Abjunction. Separation by means of joints.
Abruption. A sudden break.
Abscission. State of being removed.
Abstractedness. State of being separated or disconnected.
Abstraction. Act of abstracting, separating, or withdrawing.
Apportionment. A proportionate division.
Avulsion. Forcible separation.
Breach. A gap or opening made by breaking.
Break. An opening; breach.
Cæsura [L.]. A break in the middle of a foot of poetry.
Cleavage. Act of cleaving or splitting.
Compartition. A division of parts.
Crack. A partial separation of parts.
Decomposition. The act or process of resolving a compound body into its elementary parts.
Detachment. Act of detaching.
Diduction. Separation made by withdrawal of one part from another.
Dilaceration. Act of tearing apart.
Diremption. A forcible separation.
Disassociation. Severance from association.
Discerption. A tearing to pieces.
Disconnection. Disassociation; separation.
Discontinuity. Disunion of parts.
Disengagement. State of being disengaged; at liberty.
Disintegration. Act of breaking into pieces.
Disjecta membra [L.]. Disunited limbs.
Disjunction. Process of disjoining.
Dislocation. Act of displacing.
Dismemberment. Act of separating limb from limb.
Dispersion. Act of dispersing, or scattering the parts of.
Disruption. Act of breaking apart.
Dissection. The act of dividing for the purpose of critical examination.
Disseverance. Separation.
Disunion. State of being disunited.
Disunity. Severance; separation.
Division. Act of dividing.
Divorce. A legal dissolution of the marriage contract.
Divulsion. Act of pulling apart.
Elision. The cutting off of a vowel for the sake of meter or euphony.
Fissure. A narrow opening made by the parting of any substance.
Fracture. Act of breaking.
Incision. The act of cutting into a substance.
Inconnection. Disconnection.
Insulation. Detachment from other objects.
Isolation. The act of placing by itself or alone.
Laceration. Act of tearing apart raggedly; mangling.
Luxation. A disconnection at a joint.
Oasis. A fertile spot in a desert.
Off-cut. A surplus margin cut from paper.
Parting. The act of dividing or separating.
Rescission. The act of annulling or making void.
Resection. Act of cutting off.
Rupture. State of being burst; act of rupturing.
Scission. Act of cutting.
Section. A separation; division.
Segregation. Separation from others.
Sejunction. The act of disjoining.
Separateness. State of being separate.
Separation. The act of parting or dividing in any manner.
Seposition. The act of setting aside.
Severalty. A state of separation from the rest, or from all others.
Severance. The act of dividing.
Slit. A long, narrow opening.
Split. A breach or separation.
Subdivision. The act of separating a part into smaller parts.

DISUNION—Denotations.

Anatomy. The art of separating the different parts of an organized body to discover their situation, structure, and economy.
Cutting instrument. An instrument for cutting or separating into parts.
Oasis. A fertile spot in a desert.
Outlier. One who resides in a different place from his business.

DISUNION—Verbs.

Abscind. To cut off
Anatomize. To cut apart for anatomical examination; dissect.
Apportion. To divide proportionally.
Be disjoined. To be apart.
Break. To separate into parts.
Break up. To fall to pieces.

UNION—DISUNION—*Continued.*

UNION—VERBS—*Continued.*

Entwine. To twine round.
Fasten. To make fast.
Fetter. To fasten with fetters.
Fix. To fasten firmly.
Fix together. To join.
Fuse together. To join, as by melting.
Gird. To bind around; to encircle.
Graft. To incorporate; unite completely.
Grapple. To hold together with a hook.
Hang together. } To be joined.
Hang up. }
Harness. To put harness on.
Hasp. To fasten with a hasp.
Hinge. To attach by hinges.
Hitch. To fasten; to become entangled.
Hold together. To be united.
Hook. To fasten with a hook.
Impact. To press closely together.
Ingraft. To graft in; to incorporate.
Inosculate. To unite by continuity.
Interlace. To join by twisting together.
Interlink. To join by uniting links.
Interlock. To join, as by a lock.
Intertwine. To wind about.
Intertwist. To twist up with.
Interweave. To mingle together, as by weaving.
Intwine. To twine or twist together.
Jam. To press together.
Join. To bind together.
Knit. To join closely.
Lace. To fasten with cords.
Lash. To tie with lashing.
Latch. To fasten with a latch.
Lay together. To place side by side.
Lay up. To put away for future use.
Leash. To bind with a leash.
Link. To join by links.
Lock. To fasten with a lock; to hold securely.
Lump together. To gather in one mass.
Make fast. To fasten securely. See *Adjectives.*
Marry. To join by wedlock. See sub WED.
Miter. To unite with a miter joint.
Moor. To secure; to fasten, as a ship.
Mortise. To join together with a mortise and tenon.
Nail. To fasten with a nail.
Picket. To enclose within a fence.
Piece together. To fasten by joining pieces.
Piece up. To join the pieces or parts of anything.
Pin. To fasten with a pin.
Pinion. To bind or confine the wings of.
Put together. To unite.
Rabbet. To unite in a close joint.
Reembody. To reunite in one whole.
Rivet. To fasten with rivets.
Roll into one. To unite in a whole.
Saddle on. To load; to burden.
Screw. To tighten with screws.
Screw up. To tighten by screwing.
Secure. To make secure; fasten.
Set. To become fixed or settled.
Sew. To fasten with thread and needle.
Solder. To unite by solder.
Span. To join by reaching from one side to the other.
Splice. To unite in one piece.
Stitch. To join together with stitches.
Strap. To fasten with a strap.
String. To fasten with a string.
Swathe. To bind or wrap up.
Tack. } To fasten by tacks.
Tack together. }
Tether. To fasten with a tether.
Tie. To fasten with cord or lash.
Tighten. To fasten closely.
Trice up. To raise or tie up with a rope.
Truss. To support by truss; to fasten.
Twine round. To intertwist.
Twist. To unite by intertexture of parts.
Unite. To join together to form one whole.
Wedge. To fasten with a wedge.
Weld together. To press or beat into a permanent union.
Yoke. To join with a yoke.

DISUNION—VERBS—*Continued.*

Burst. To break forcibly and with a loud report.
Carve. To cut in design.
Chip. To break off a small piece.
Chop. To cut; to sever.
Circumcise. To cut off the foreskin.
Cleave. To cut through; split.
Come off. To be loosed from something to which it is joined.
Come to pieces. To be separated into parts.
Comminute. To reduce to small parts.
Crack. To break apart; to split.
Cranch. }
Craunch. } To crush with the teeth.
Crunch. }
Cut. To make an incision; divide as with a knife.
Cut adrift. } To break off from a fastening.
Cut off. }
Cut up. To break to pieces.
Detach. To disconnect; separate.
Disband. To release from service.
Disbranch. To divest of branches.
Discind. To divide.
Disconnect. To sever connection.
Disengage. To break the engagement of.
Disentangle. To free from entanglement.
Disintegrate. To break into pieces.
Disjoin. To separate; divide.
Disjoint. To divide at the joints.
Dislocate. To put out of place.
Dismember. To divide limb from limb.
Dispair. To part a pair.
Dispart. To set apart.
Disperse. To scatter apart.
Dissect. To cut for the purpose of examination.
Dissever. To disjoin; separate.
Dissociate. To break the association of; disconnect.
Disunite. To separate; disjoin.
Divellicate. To pull in pieces.
Divide. To separate into parts.
Divorce. To set apart; sunder.
Fall off. To drop away from.
Fall to pieces. To drop apart.
Gash. To cut into.
Get loose. To obtain freedom.
Hack. To cut aimlessly.
Hackle. To tear apart.
Haggle. To cut poorly; mangle.
Hash. To cut into bits.
Hew. To cut into shape.
Incide. To cut or break up.
Incise. To cut into.
Insulate. To separate from others.
Isolate. To place alone.
Keep apart. To prevent a union or joining.
Lacerate. To tear in a mangling manner.
Leave. To go away from; sever communication with.
Loose. To set free; release.
Mangle. To mutilate, as by cutting.
Mince. To chop into bits.
Nib. To cut a point on a pen.
Nip. To pinch; clip off.
Part. To separate; sever; divide.
Part company. To break up the company.
Peel off. To tear or strip off.
Pick to pieces. } To break apart.
Pull to pieces. }
Rend. To make forcible division.
Rend asunder. To divide apart forcibly.
Rend in twain. To divide into two parts forcibly.
Rescind. To cut off; repeal.
Rip up. To tear up violently.
Rive. To tear apart forcibly.
Rupture. To break or burst apart.
Saw. To cut with a saw.
Scramble. To put hurriedly together.
Segregate. To separate or isolate from others.
Separate. To sever connection.
Set apart. To remove alone.
Set free. To grant liberty to.
Sever. To put apart; disjoin.
Shatter. To break violently; smash.
Shiver. To shake or vibrate.

UNION—DISUNION—*Continued.*

UNION—*Adjectives.*

Close. Nearly attached; compact.
Compact. United closely.
Conjoint. Associated.
Conjunct. Joined together.
Corporate. Collective.
Fast. Held firmly; secure.
Firm. Solid; closely united.
Hand in hand. United by clasping hands.
Indissoluble. Impossible of being dissolved.
Insecable. Not capable of being cut.
Inseparable. Not to be separated.
Inseverable. Not capable of division.
Intervolved. Involved one within another.
Joined. Brought together.
Joint. Done by two or more working together
Secure. Fastened.
Set. Fixed in position.
Taught.
Taut. } Secure; tight.
Tight. Firmly held together.

UNION—*Adverbs, etc.*

Fast. Firmly; securely.
Firmly. Securely.
In conjunction with. Together.
Intimately. Closely connected.
Jointly. Together.

UNION—*Phrase.*

Tria juncta in uno [L.]. Three joined in one.

DISUNION—*Continued from Column 2.*

Straggling. Wandering aimlessly.
Unannexed. Not joined to anything else.
Unassociated. Alone.
Unattached. Separate.

DISUNION—*Adverbs, etc.*

Abstractedly. In an abstract manner. See *Adjectives.*
Adrift. In a drifting state.
Apart. Separately; aside.
Asunder. Apart.
In the abstract. In the general.
In twain. In two parts.
One by one. Singly; apart.
Separately. Alone.
Severally. Apart from others.

DISUNION—Verbs—*Continued.*

Skin. To strip the skin from.
Slash. To cut with a long stroke.
Slice. To cut into thin parts.
Slit. To make a long cut.
Snap. To break short.
Snip. To cut lightly; clip.
Splinter. To split into splinters.
Split. To rend apart.
Subdivide. To divide into parts.
Sunder. To break apart violently.
Take to pieces. To break.
Tear. To pull apart; rend.
Tear piecemeal. To tear piece by piece.
Tear to tatters. To rend to rags.
Throw out of gear. To disconnect the machinery so as to stop its action.
Unbind. To release from bonds.
Unchain. To release from chains.
Undo. To take apart.
Unlock. To release the lock.
Unloose. To disconnect.
Unpack. To remove as from a pack.
Unravel. To separate the connected or united parts of.
Whittle. To gradually cut away.
Wrench. To twist forcibly.

DISUNION—*Adjectives.*

Abstract. General; abstruse.
Adrift. In a drifting state.
Apart. Separate; aside.
Asunder. Apart.
Discontinuous. Not continued.
Discrete. Disconnected; distinct.
Disjoined. Separated; disunited.
Disjunctive. Helping to disjoin.
Disparate. Dissimilar.
Distinct. Separate from all others.
Divisible. Capable of division.
Far between. Much space intervening.
Free. Exempt; possessing liberty.
Insular. Pertaining to an island.
Isolated. Set apart; alone.
Loose. Not fastened tightly.
Multipartite. Having many parts.
Reft. Torn apart.
Rift. Split open.
Scissile. Capable of being cut.
Separate. Disjoined; apart.

(*Continued on Column 1.*)

un′-ion jack′. The canton of a flag used separately as a flag; flag of England. PATRIOTISM-TREASON, SIGN.
un′-ion-pipes′. A musical instrument similar to the trombone. MUSICAL INSTRUMENTS.
u-nique′. Uncommon; alone; original. CONVENTION-ALITY - UNCONVENTIONALITY, IMITATION - ORIGINAL-ITY, LIKENESS-UNLIKENESS, SOLITUDE-COMPANY.
un-ir″-ri-ta′-ting. Calm. TURBULENCE-CALMNESS.
u′-ni-son. Harmony. HARMONY-DISCORD, MELODY-DISSONANCE, VARIANCE-ACCORD.
u′-ni-so″-nance. Harmony. MELODY-DISSONANCE.
u′-ni-so″-nant. Harmonious. MELODY - DISSONANCE.
u′-nit. A body or group considered as a single whole. SOLITUDE-COMPANY.
U″-ni-ta′-ri-an. A member of any religious body that rejects the doctrine of the Trinity. ORTHODOXY-HET-ERODOXY

u-nite′. To combine; associate. ASSOCIATION, COMPO-SITION - RESOLUTION, CONCENTRATION - RADIATION, COOPERATION-OPPOSITION, GATHERING-SCATTERING, SOLITUDE-COMPANY, UNION-DISUNION; **unite one's efforts,** ANTAGONISM-CONCURRENCE; **unite with,** AN-TAGONISM-CONCURRENCE.
u-ni′-ted. Combined. COHESION-LOOSENESS, VARI-ANCE-ACCORD.
u′-ni-ty. Singleness; harmony. ENTIRETY-DEFICIENCY, RHETORIC, SOLITUDE-COMPANY, VARIANCE-ACCORD, WHOLE-PART; **unity of time,** SYNCHRONISM.
U′-ni-ty, Trin′-i-ty in. The union in one God of the Father, Son, and Holy Spirit. DIVINITY.
u″-ni-ver′-sal. Entire. UNIVERSALITY-PARTICULAR-ITY; **universal church,** THEOLOGY; **universal favor-ite,** FAVORITE-ANGER.
u″-ni-ver-sal′-i-ty. Generality. UNIVERSALITY-PAR-TICULARITY.

UNIVERSALITY—PARTICULARITY.

Catholicism. Universality.
Catholicity. The quality of being universal or large-minded.
Generality. The quality of pertaining to a genus or kind.
Generalization. The process of forming general principles.
Miscellaneousness. The state of being a general mixture.
Prevalence. The quality of being very general in occurrence.
Universality. The quality of being entirely general.

Characteristic. A distinguishing specialty.
Distinctive feature. A feature that marks a difference.
Idiocrasy. A special peculiarity of constitution.
Idiosyncrasy. An eccentricity special to some person.
Individuality. That quality which distinguishes one person or thing from another.
Individuity. Special existence.

UNIVERSALITY—PARTICULARITY—*Continued*.

UNIVERSALITY—*Denotations*.

All hands. Everybody.
All sorts. Persons or things of all qualities.
All the world and his wife. Everybody.
Anybody. Any one out of an indefinite number of persons.
Drag-net. A net dragged along the bottom of the water, in which many things are caught.
Everybody.⎫
Everyone.⎭ Every person.
Miscellany. A mass or mixture of various things.
N or M. Either the one thing or the other; everything.
Run. That which continues in a certain course or series.

UNIVERSALITY—*Verbs*.

Be general, etc. To comprehend many species or individuals.
Be going about. To be in general circulation as a matter of conversation.
Generalize. To infer a general law from a set of particulars.
Prevail. To be generally accepted.
Render general. To make to be generally accepted.
Stalk abroad. To be general in a bad sense.

UNIVERSALITY—*Adjectives*.

All. The whole number or quantity of anything.
All over. Generally distributed.
Besetting Generally troubling.
Broad. General in scope.
Catholic.⎫
Catholical.⎭ General in the widest sense.
Collective. Gathered into a general mass.
Common. General in occurrence.
Comprehensive. Of general application.
Covered with. Overspread with.
Customary. According to general usage. See HABIT.
Ecumenical. Generally applying to the habitable earth.
Encyclopedical. Including the entire circle of knowledge and information.
Epidemic Generally prevailing.
Every. Each individual of a whole collection.
General. Wide in meaning or scope.
Generic. Having a general comprehension or application.
Impersonal. Not relating to a particular person or thing.
Pan-American. All American.
Panharmonic. Accompanied by universal consent.
Panslavic. Pertaining to all the Slavic peoples.
Prevailing. Very general.
Prevalent. Most generally current.
Rife. Of general abundance.
Sweeping. General in comprehension.
Transcendental. Very high in degree.
Universal. Relating to the universe in general.
Unspecified. Not mentioned particularly.
Wide-spread. General over a great area.
World-wide. General throughout the world.

UNIVERSALITY—*Adverbs, etc*.

Always. At all times.
For better for worse. Under every circumstance. good or bad.
For the most part. With reference to the larger part of a thing.
Generally. In most cases.
Generally speaking. Speaking with general application.
In general. Usually.
In the long run. In the end.
One and all. So as to include every one.
Speaking generally. Speaking of a large class.
To a man. Entirely inclusive.
Whatever.⎫
Whatsoever.⎭ Being this or that; anything that may be.

PARTICULARITY—ADVERBS, ETC —*Continued from Column 2*

Seriatim. One after the other.
Severally. With a separate and distinct existence.
Specially In a particular manner.
That is to say.
To wit.
Videlicet. Namely.
Viz.

PARTICULARITY—*Phrases*.

Ad hominem [L.]. To a man.
In propria persona [L.]. In person
Le style est l'homme même [F.]. The style is the man himself.
Pro hac vice [L.]. For this occasion.
Pro re nata [L.]. For a special emergency.

Mannerism. Constant clinging to some specialty.
Particularity. An individual specialty.
Peculiarity. A specialty belonging to only one person or thing.
Personality. That which distinguishes a person.
Singularity. A specialty peculiar to one person or thing.
Spécialité [F.]. A special branch.
Specialty. That which specially characterizes a person or thing.
Specificness. The quality of being explicit.

PARTICULARITY—*Denotations*.

Counts. Particular allegations or charges in a declaration.
Details. Particulars; items.
Herself. Her own true or real character.
Himself. His own true or proper character.
I. The speaker as distinguished from others.
I myself. The speaker or writer as distinguished from everybody else.
Item. A separate particular.
Itself. An article as distinguished from other things.
Lection. A reading.
Myself. The speaker distinguished from others.
Particulars. Individual facts, points, or circumstances that may be considered separately.
Reading. Force of a word or passage presented by a documentary authority.
State. Condition or quality.
Technicality. That which is peculiar to any trade or profession.
Trait. A distinguishing or marked feature.
Version. An account or description from a particular point of view.

PARTICULARITY—*Verbs*.

Come to the point. To arrive at the special point under discussion.
Descend to particulars. To describe with special reference to details.
Designate. To give a special name to anything.
Determine. To give a special form to anything.
Enter into details. To report minutely.
Individualize. To distinguish from others by special qualities.
Particularize. To give special details.
Realize. To bring into actual existence.
Specialize. To give anything a specific character.
Specify. To state fully and clearly.

PARTICULARITY—*Adjectives*.

Appropriate. Specially apt.
Certain. Established as a fact.
Characteristic. Distinguished by some specialty.
Definite. Known with exactness.
Determinate. Specially limited.
Diagnostic. Indicating the nature of. as of a disease.
Endemic. Peculiar to a specified country or people.
Esoteric. Fitted only for the enlightened.
Especial. Exceptionable among others of the same kind.
Exclusive. Having a tendency to shut out.
Idiomatic. Peculiar to a certain language or dialect.
Individual. Pertaining to a particular person or thing.
Original. Belonging to the beginning.
Partial. Favoring one side.
Particular. Peculiar to something specified.
Party. Favoring one party.
Peculiar. Having a character exclusively its own.
Personal. Pertaining to a particular person.
Private. Not common or general.
Proper. Specially adapted.
Respective. Having relation to a particular person or thing.
Several. Considered distinctly as an individual or as individuals.
Singular. Consisting of only one part.
Special. For a particular purpose.
Specific. Possessing a peculiar property.
That. A specific object in the distance.
This. A specific object near at hand.
Typical. Pertaining to a class or kind.
Yon. At a distance but in sight.
Yonder. At a distance in the direction indicated by a gesture.

PARTICULARITY—*Adverbs, etc*.

Apiece. For each one.
Bit by bit. Piecemeal.
Each. One of two.
Each to each. Separately.
For my part. According to one's own desire.
In detail.⎫
In particular.⎭ Part by part.
Namely. That is to say.
One by one. One at a time.
Respectively. Considered singly.

(*Continued on Column 1.*)

u'-ni-verse. The world. UNIVERSE.

UNIVERSE.

Aerolite. A meteorite.
Apollo. The god of the sun; hence, figuratively, the sun.
Asteroids. The small planets whose orbits lie between Mars and Jupiter.
Canopy of heaven. The sky.
Cassiopeia's Chair. A group of six stars, in Cassiopeia, resembling a chair.
Celestial spaces. The apparent distances between heavenly bodies.
Charles's Wain. The seven brightest stars in Ursa Major.
Chromosphere. The outer cloudy envelope around the sun.
Comet. A heavenly body consisting of a star-like body with a long tail.
Constellation. A cluster or group of fixed stars, or division of the heavens.
Cosmos. The universe, so named from the perfection of its arrangement.
Creation. The product of God's creative power; the universe.
Diana. Figuratively, the moon.
Earth. The globe or planet which we inhabit.
Empyrean. The highest heaven, or the seat of Deity.
Falling star. A star-like, luminous meteor that darts swiftly across some portion of the sky.
Firmament. The sky or heavens.
Galactic circle. The great circle of the heavens to which the galaxy most nearly conforms.
Galaxy. The Milky Way.
Globe. The earth.
Great Bear. The constellation Ursa Major.
Heavenly bodies. The bodies appearing in the sky.
Heavens. The place where the sun, moon, and stars appear.
Macrocosm. The visible system of worlds; the universe.
Megacosm. Macrocosm.
Meteor. A mass of stone or iron or other substance that falls to the earth.
Microcosm. A little world.
Midgard. In Norse mythology, the earth the abode of men.
Milky Way. The luminous tract or belt which is seen at night stretched across the heavens.
Moon. The celestial orb which revolves round the earth.
Music of the spheres. The music made by heavenly bodies in their courses.
Nature. The universe.
Nebulæ. A gauzy, cloud-like appearance amongst the stars.
Orb of day. The sun.
Orb of night. The moon.
Orion's belt. A large and bright constellation on the equator between the stars Aldebaran and Sirius.
Phœbus. Figuratively, the sun.
Photosphere. The luminous spherical envelope of the sun.
Planet. A celestial body which revolves about the sun.
Planetoid. A small planet revolving in the space between Mars and Jupiter.
Pleiades. A cluster of seven small stars in the neck of the constellation Taurus.
Satellite. A secondary planet which revolves about another planet.
Shooting star. A falling star.
Signs of the zodiac. The twelve divisions of the ecliptic or zodiac.
Sky. The apparent arch or vault overhead.
Solar system. The sun with the group of celestial bodies which revolve round it.
Southern Cross. A constellation of the southern hemisphere containing several bright stars so related in position as to resemble a cross.
Sphere. A celestial globe, as the sun, planet, etc.
Starry heaven. The sky adorned with stars.
Starry host. The body of stars.
Stars. The innumerable luminous bodies seen in the heavens.
Sun. The luminous orb seen in the heavens during the day.
Terraqueous globe. A globe like the earth consisting of land and water.
Vault of heaven. The sky.
Via lactea [L.] The Milky Way.
Welkin. The visible regions of the air; the cloud region.
Zodiac. An imaginary belt in the heavens extending 8 degrees on each side of the ecliptic.

UNIVERSE—*Scientific Nouns.*

Astronomer. One given to the study of the heavenly bodies.
Astronomy. The science that treats of everything connected with the heavenly bodies
Colures. The two circles which pass through the four cardinal points of the ecliptic and intersect at the poles.
Cosmogony. A doctrine or an account of the creation or of the system of the universe.
Cosmography. The science which treats of the universe.
Cosmology. The general science of the universe, in all its parts, laws, etc.
Ecliptic. The apparent path of the sun in the heavens in a year.
Eidouranion [Gr.]. A representation of the heavens.
Equator. The great circle in which the plane of the earth's equator cuts the celestial sphere.
Geodesy, etc. The determination of the magnitude and figure of the earth. See MENSURATION.
Observatory. A building for making observations of the heavenly bodies.
Orbit. The path in space along which a heavenly body moves about its center of attraction.
Orrery. A machine for exhibiting the relative motions and positions of the members of the solar system.
Star-gazer. One who studies the stars.
Star-gazing. The act of studying the stars.
Uranography. That branch of astronomy which treats of the constellations and the stars that form them.
Uranology. The knowledge of the heavens.
Zodiac. An imaginary belt in the heavens extending 8 degrees on each side of the ecliptic.

UNIVERSE—*Adjectives.*

Astral. Pertaining to the stars; starry.
Celestial. Pertaining to the sky or heaven.
Cosmical. Relating to the universe and all visible nature.
Earthly. Pertaining to this world.
Geotric. Belonging to earth; terrestrial.
Heavenly. Resembling heaven; celestial.
Heliacal. Emerging from or passing into the light of the sun.
Lunar. Pertaining to the moon.
Mundane. Pertaining to the world; worldly.
Nebular. Of or relating to nebulæ.
Sideral. } Relating to the stars; measured by the apparent motion
Sidereal. } of the stars.
Solar. Pertaining to the sun; measured by its apparent revolution.
Sphery. Like a sphere or star.
Starry. Adorned with or resembling stars.
Stellar. Of or pertaining to the stars; astral.
Subastral. Beneath the stars or heavens.
Sublunary. Situated under the moon.
Telluric. Pertaining to the earth, or procured from it.
Terraqueous. Consisting of land and water.
Terrene. Pertaining to the earth; earthy.
Terreous. Consisting of earth.
Terrestrial. Pertaining to the terraqueous globe; existing on the earth.
Terrestrious. Earthy; being or living on the earth.
Under the sun. Anywhere on earth.
Uranic. Celestial; astronomical.

UNIVERSE—*Adverbs, etc.*

Earthward. Toward the earth.
Here below. On earth.
In all creation. Anywhere.
On the face of the globe. On the earth's surface.
Under the sun. In this world.

UNIVERSE—*Phrase.*

Die Weltgeschichte ist das Weltgericht [G.]. World-history is a world-tribunal.

u''-ni-ver'-si-ty. An educational institution for superior instruction. SCHOOL; **go to the university,** EDUCATION-LEARNING.

un-just'. Unfair. RIGHT-WRONG.

un-jus'-ti-fi''-a-ble. Wrong. JUSTIFICATION-CHARGE, RIGHT-WRONG, VIRTUE-VICE.

un-jus'-ti-fied. Wrong. DUENESS-UNDUENESS, RIGHT-WRONG.

un-kempt'. Disheveled. CLEANNESS-FILTHINESS, TASTE-VULGARITY.

un-ken'-nel. Eject; disclose. ADMISSION-EXPULSION, EXPOSURE-HIDINGPLACE.

un-kind'. Harsh. CHARITABLENESS-MALEVOLENCE; **unkindest cut of all,** PLEASURE-PAIN.

un-kind'-ness. Harshness. CHARITABLENESS-MALEVOLENCE.

un-knight'-ly. Not gallant. UPRIGHTNESS-DISHONESTY.

un-know'-a-ble. Hidden. CLEARNESS-OBSCURITY.

un-know'-ing. Ignorant. KNOWLEDGE-IGNORANCE.

un-known'. Ignorant; latent. ENLIGHTENMENT-SECRECY, KNOWLEDGE-IGNORANCE; **unknown quantities,** KNOWLEDGE-IGNORANCE; **unknown to fame,** GENTILITY-COMMONALTY, REPUTATION-DISCREDIT.

un-la'-bored. Easy; not ready. PREPARATION-NONPREPARATION, PURITY-CRUDENESS.

un-lade'. Remove. ADMISSION-EXPULSION.

un-la'-dy-like". Rough. POLITENESS-IMPOLITENESS, TASTE-VULGARITY.

un''-la-ment'-ed. Unmourned. APPROVAL-DISAPPROVAL, LOVE-HATE.

un-law'-ful. Illegal; unjust. DUENESS-UNDUENESS, LAW-LAWLESSNESS.

un-law'-ful-ness. Wrong. LAW-LAWLESSNESS, RIGHT-WRONG.

un-learn'. Forget. REMEMBRANCE-FORGETFULNESS.

un-learned'. Uneducated. KNOWLEDGE-IGNORANCE.

un-leav'-ened. Unimbued. PREPARATION-NONPREPARATION.

un-less'. Except. CONDITION-SITUATION, CONVENTIONALITY-UNCONVENTIONALITY, MODIFICATION.

un-let'-tered. Unlearned. KNOWLEDGE-IGNORANCE; **unlettered Muse,** PURITY-CRUDENESS.

un-li'-censed. Prohibited. LEAVE-PROHIBITION.

un-licked'. Not properly formed. GENTILITY-COMMONALTY, PREPARATION-NONPREPARATION, TASTE-VULGARITY; **unlicked cub,** FORM-FORMLESSNESS, GENTILITY-COMMONALTY, POLITENESS-IMPOLITENESS, TASTE-VULGARITY.

un-like'. Different. LIKENESS-UNLIKENESS.

un-like'-li-hood. Improbability. LIKELIHOOD-UNLIKELIHOOD.

un-like'-ly. Improbable. LIKELIHOOD-UNLIKELIHOOD.

un-like'-ness. Dissimilarity. LIKENESS-UNLIKENESS.

un-lim'-ber. Stiff. HARDNESS-SOFTNESS.

un-lim'-it-ed. Great; infinite; free. INFINITY, LIBERTY-SUBJECTION, MAGNITUDE-SMALLNESS; **unlimited space,** EXTENSION-DISTRICT.

un-liq'-ue-fied. Solid. SOLIDITY-RARITY.

un-live'-ly. Dull. LIGHTHEARTEDNESS-DEJECTION, WITTINESS-DULNESS.

un-load'. Disencumber; discharge. ADMISSION-EXPULSION, DIFFICULTY-FACILITY, ESTABLISHMENT-REMOVAL.

un-load'-ed. Disencumbered. DIFFICULTY-FACILITY.

un-lock. Unfasten. DISCOVERY, UNION-DISUNION.

un-looked' for. Unexpected. EXPECTATION-SURPRISE.

un-loose'. Unfasten. RELEASE-RESTRAINT, UNION-DISUNION.

un-loved'. Hated. LOVE-HATE.

un-love'-ly. Plain. BEAUTY-UGLINESS.

un-luck'-y. Ill-starred; bad. GOODNESS-BADNESS, OPPORTUNENESS-UNSUITABLENESS, PLEASURABLENESS-PAINFULNESS, WELFARE-MISFORTUNE.

un-made'. Taken to pieces. ENTITY-NONENTITY.

un-maimed'. Not crippled. HEALTH-SICKNESS.

un-make'. Destroy. CONVERSION-REVERSION.

un-man'. Deprive of manly strength; dishearten. LIGHTHEARTEDNESS-DEJECTION, MIGHT-IMPOTENCE, SANGUINENESS-HOPELESSNESS, STRENGTH-WEAKNESS.

un-man'-age-a-ble. Unwieldy; perverse. DIFFICULTY-FACILITY, PROPRIETY-IMPROPRIETY.

un-man'-ly. Effeminate; dishonorable. MALE-FEMALE, UPRIGHTNESS-DISHONESTY.

un-manned'. Dejected; cowardly. BRAVERY-COWARDICE, LIGHTHEARTEDNESS-DEJECTION.

un-man'-nered. Boorish. POLITENESS-IMPOLITENESS.

un-man'-ner-ly. Misbehaved. POLITENESS-IMPOLITENESS.

un-marked'. Disregarded. CAREFULNESS-CARELESSNESS.

un-marred'. Sound. CONSERVATION, HEALTH-SICKNESS.

un-mar'-ried. Not united in wedlock. MATRIMONY-CELIBACY.

un-mask'. Reveal. EXPOSURE-HIDINGPLACE.

un-matched'. Different. DEVIATION, LIKENESS-UNLIKENESS, VARIATION.

un-mean'-ing. Senseless. ADAGE-NONSENSE, MEANING-JARGON.

un-mean'-ing-ness. Meaninglessness. MEANING-JARGON.

un-meant'. Unintelligible. MEANING-JARGON.

un-meas'-u-ra-ble. Infinite. INFINITY.

un-meas'-ured. Very great. DIFFERENTIATION-INDISCRIMINATION, ENOUGH, INFINITY.

un-med'-i-ta"-ted. Unthought of. PREDETERMINATION-IMPULSE.

un-meet'. Improper. DUENESS-UNDUENESS.

un-mel'-lowed. Imperfect. PREPARATION-NONPREPARATION.

un''-mel-o'-di-ous. Discordant. MELODY-DISSONANCE.

un-melt'-ed. Solid. SOLIDITY-RARITY.

un-men'-tion-a-ble. Dishonorable. REPUTATION-DISCREDIT.

un-mer'-ci-ful. Pitiless. COMPASSION-RUTHLESSNESS.

un-mer'-it-ed. Undeserved. DUENESS-UNDUENESS.

un''-meth-od'-ic-al. Erratic. REGULARITY-IRREGULARITY.

un-mind'-ful. Heedless. CAREFULNESS-CARELESSNESS, HEED-DISREGARD, THANKFULNESS-THANKLESSNESS.

un-min'-gled. Separate. MIXTURE-HOMOGENEITY.

un-missed'. Unheeded. CAREFULNESS-CARELESSNESS.

un''-mis-ta'-ka-ble. Manifest. CERTAINTY-DOUBT, CLEARNESS-OBSCURITY, MANIFESTATION-LATENCY.

un-mit'-i-ga-ble. Unallayable. TURBULENCE-CALMNESS.

un-mit'-i-ga"-ted. Very great; unassuaged. ENTIRETY-DEFICIENCY, MAGNITUDE-SMALLNESS, TURBULENCE-CALMNESS.

un-mixed'. Separate. MIXTURE-HOMOGENEITY.

un''-mo-lest'-ed. Safe; content. CONTENTEDNESS-DISCONTENTMENT, SECURITY-INSECURITY.

un-mon'-eyed. Poor. AFFLUENCE-PENURY.

un-mourned'. Unlamented. LOVE-HATE.

un-moved'. Quiescent. BIGOTRY-APOSTASY, MOVEMENT-REST, SENSITIVENESS-APATHY.

un-mu'-sic-al. Harsh. MELODY-DISSONANCE; **unmusical voice,** VOCALIZATION-MUTENESS.

un-muz'-zled. Unrestrained. LIBERTY-SUBJECTION.

un-named'. Nameless. NAME-MISNOMER.

un-nat'-u-ral. Affected; heartless. CHARITABLENESS-MALEVOLENCE, CONVENTIONALITY-UNCONVENTIONALITY, SOCIETY-AFFECTATION.

un-nec'-es-sa-ry. Not required. EXCESS-LACK, PROPRIETY-IMPROPRIETY, USEFULNESS-USELESSNESS.

un-need'-ed. Unrequired. USEFULNESS-USELESSNESS.

un-neigh'-bor-ly. Not sociable. POLITENESS-IMPOLITENESS.

un-nerve'. To weaken. MIGHT-IMPOTENCE, STRENGTH-WEAKNESS.

un-nerved'. Powerless; dejected. LIGHTHEARTEDNESS-DEJECTION, MIGHT-IMPOTENCE, STRENGTH-WEAKNESS.

un-no'-ted. Unheeded; unhonored. CAREFULNESS-CARELESSNESS, REPUTATION-DISCREDIT.

un-no'-ticed. Unheeded; unhonored. CAREFULNESS-CARELESSNESS, REPUTATION-DISCREDIT.

un-num'-bered. Innumerable. INFINITY.

un-nur'-tured. Not nourished. PREPARATION-NONPREPARATION.

un''-o-beyed'. Uncomplied with. INSUBORDINATION-OBEDIENCE.

un″-ob-jec′-tion-a-ble. Without exception. GOODNESS-BADNESS, INNOCENCE-GUILT, RENOVATION-RELAPSE.

un″-ob-nox′-ious. Not odious. GOODNESS-BADNESS.

un′-ob-scured′. Bright. LIGHT-DARKNESS.

un″-ob-serv′-ant. Inattentive. HEED-DISREGARD.

un″-ob-served′. Disregarded. CAREFULNESS-CARELESSNESS.

un″-ob-struct′-ed. Clear. DIFFICULTY-FACILITY, LIBERTY-SUBJECTION.

un″-ob-tain′-a-ble. Incapable of being acquired. POSSIBILITY-IMPOSSIBILITY.

un″-ob-tained′. Not secured. HOLDING-EXEMPTION.

un″-ob-tru′-sive. Modest. CONCEIT-DIFFIDENCE.

un-oc′-cu-pied. Vacant; idle. ACTION-PASSIVENESS, ACTIVITY-INDOLENCE, PRESENCE-ABSENCE, REFLECTION-VACANCY.

un′-of-fend′-ed. Unaroused. EXCITABILITY-INEXCITABILITY, SELFRESPECT-HUMBLENESS.

un′-of-fi′-cial. Unauthorized. LAW-LAWLESSNESS.

un-oft′-en. Rarely. FREQUENCY-RARITY.

un-o′-pened. Not begun. PREPARATION-NONPREPARATION.

un″-op-posed′. Unresisted. ANTAGONISM-CONCURRENCE.

un-or′-gan-ized. Not systematic. PREPARATION-NONPREPARATION; **unorganized matter,** PULPINESS-ROSIN.

un-or″-na-ment′-al. Plain. BEAUTY-UGLINESS.

un-or″-na-ment′-ed. Simple. EMBELLISHMENT-SIMPLICITY, SIMPLICITY-FLORIDNESS.

un-or′-tho-dox. Not Trinitarian. ORTHODOXY-HETERODOXY.

uno saltu **[L.] (yu′-no sal′-tiu).** At one leap. ETERNITY-INSTANTANEITY.

un-os″-ten-ta″-tious. Modest. CONCEIT-DIFFIDENCE.

un-owed′. Paid. SETTLEMENT-DEFAULT.

un-owned′. Ownerless. KEEPING-RELINQUISHMENT.

un″-pa-cif′-ic. Stormy; pugnacious. FIGHTING-CONCILIATION, VARIANCE-ACCORD.

un-pac′-i-fied. Not calmed. VARIANCE-ACCORD.

un-pack′. Loosen; take out. ADMISSION-EXPULSION, UNION-DISUNION.

un-paid′. Owed. COSTLINESS-CHEAPNESS, CREDIT-DEBT.

un-pal′-a-ta-ble. Unsavory. PALATABLENESS-UNPALATABLENESS, PLEASURABLENESS-PAINFULNESS.

un-par′-a-goned. Unrivaled. FAULTLESSNESS-FAULTINESS, GOODNESS-BADNESS, SUPREMACY-SUBORDINACY.

un-par′-al-leled. Unsurpassed; without exception. CONVENTIONALITY-UNCONVENTIONALITY, DEVIATION, FAULTLESSNESS-FAULTINESS, GOODNESS-BADNESS, SUPREMACY-SUBORDINACY.

un-par′-don-a-ble. Unexcusable; wicked. JUSTIFICATION-CHARGE, VIRTUE-VICE.

un-par″-lia-men′-ta-ry lan′-guage. Uncourteous or foul speech. CHARITABLENESS-CURSE, POLITENESS-IMPOLITENESS.

un-pass′-a-ble. Impenetrable. APERTURE-CLOSURE.

un-pas′-sion-ate. Calm. EXCITABILITY-INEXCITABILITY.

un-pa″-tri-ot′-ic. Without patriotism. HUMANITARIANISM-MISANTHROPY.

un-peace′-ful. Contentious. FIGHTING-CONCILIATION, STRIFE-PEACE.

un-peo′-ple. Depopulate. ADMISSION-EXPULSION, SOCIABILITY-PRIVACY.

un″-per-ceived′. Unnoticed. CAREFULNESS-CARELESSNESS, KNOWLEDGE-IGNORANCE.

un″-per-formed′. Undone. COMPLETION-NONCOMPLETION.

un-per′-jured. Truthful. TRUTHFULNESS-FALSEHOOD, UPRIGHTNESS-DISHONESTY

un′-per-plexed′. Unembarrassed. SAGACITY-INCAPACITY.

un′-per-sua′-da-ble. Obstinate. BIGOTRY-APOSTASY, MOTIVE-DEHORTATION.

un″-per-turbed′. Calm. EXCITABILITY-INEXCITABILITY.

un-phil″-o-soph′-ic-al. Irrational. SAGACITY-INCAPACITY.

un-pierced′. Unpenetrated. APERTURE-CLOSURE.

un-pit′-ied. Not sympathized with. APPROVAL-DISAPPROVAL.

un-pit′-y-ing. Relentless. COMPASSION-RUTHLESSNESS.

un-placed′. Unassigned. ESTABLISHMENT-REMOVAL.

un-plagued′. Undisturbed. CONTENTEDNESS-DISCONTENTMENT.

un-pleas′-ant. Disagreeable. PALATABLENESSS-UNPALATABLENESS, PLEASURABLENESS-PAINFULNESS.

un-pleas′-ing. Disagreeable. PLEASURABLENESS-PAINFULNESS.

un″-po-et′-ic-al. Inartistic; plain. CRAFT-ARTLESSNESS, POETRY-PROSE.

un-pol′-ished. Clumsy; rough. POLITENESS-IMPOLITENESS, PREPARATION-NONPREPARATION, SMOOTHNESS-ROUGHNESS, TASTE-VULGARITY.

un-po-lite′. Rude. POLITENESS-IMPOLITENESS.

un-pop′-u-lar. Disliked. DESIRE-DISTASTE, PLEASURABLENESS-PAINFULNESS.

un-pop″-u-lar′-i-ty. Disfavor. LOVE-HATE.

un-por′-tioned. Disinherited. AFFLUENCE-PENURY.

un′-pos-sessed′. Uncontrolled. HOLDING-EXEMPTION.

un-prec′-e-dent-ed. Unexampled. CONVENTIONALITY-UNCONVENTIONALITY, FREQUENCY-RARITY, LIKENESS-UNLIKENESS.

un-prej′-u-diced. Unbiased. SAGACITY-INCAPACITY.

un″-pre-med′-i-ta-ted. Unthought of. PREDETERMINATION-IMPULSE, PREPARATION-NONPREPARATION, PURPOSE-LUCK.

un″-pre-pared′. Not ready. PREPARATION-NONPREPARATION, SECURITY-INSECURITY.

un-pre″-pos-sessed′. Not preoccupied. SAGACITY-INCAPACITY.

un-pre″-pos-sess′-ing. Unattractive. BEAUTY-UGLINESS.

un″-pre-sent′-a-ble. Not worthy of being offered. TASTE-VULGARITY.

un″-pre-tend′-ing. Modest. CONCEIT-DIFFIDENCE.

un″-pre-ten′-tious. Modest. CONCEIT-DIFFIDENCE.

un″-pre-vent′-ed. Free. LIBERTY-SUBJECTION.

un-prin′-ci-pled. Knavish. VIRTUE-VICE.

un-priv′-i-leged. Unfavored. DUENESS-UNDUENESS.

un-prized′. Unvalued. OVERVALUATION-UNDERVALUATION.

un″-pro-claimed′. Unannounced. ENLIGHTENMENT-SECRECY.

un″-pro-duced′. Uncreated. ENTITY-NONENTITY.

un″-pro-duct′-ive. Useless. FERTILITY-STERILITY, USEFULNESS-USELESSNESS.

un″-pro-duct′-ive-ness. Barrenness. FERTILITY-STERILITY.

un″ pro-fi′-cien-cy. Inadeptness. SKILL-UNSKILFULNESS.

un-prof′-it-a-ble. Useless. FERTILITY-STERILITY, GOODNESS-BADNESS, PROPRIETY-IMPROPRIETY, USEFULNESS-USELESSNESS.

un-prof′-it-a-ble-ness. Uselessness. FERTILITY-STERILITY.

un″-pro-lif′-ic. Barren. FERTILITY-STERILITY.

un-prom′-is-ing. Unfavorable. SANGUINENESS-HOPELESSNESS.

un-prompt′-ed. Uninstigated. PREDETERMINATION-IMPULSE.

un″-pro-pi′-tious. Unfavorable; ill-timed. ANTAGONISM-CONCURRENCE, OPPORTUNENESS-UNSUITABLENESS, SANGUINENESS-HOPELESSNESS.

un-pros'-per-ous. Unfortunate. WELFARE-MISFORTUNE.

un''-pro-tect'-ed. Insecure. SECURITY-INSECURITY.

un-proved'. Not demonstrated. RATIOCINATION-INSTINCT.

un''-pro-vid'-ed. Unsupplied; unprepared. EXCESS-LACK, PREPARATION-NONPREPARATION.

un-pub'-lished. Unproclaimed. ENLIGHTENMENT-SECRECY.

un-punc'-tu-al. Tardy; untimely. EARLINESS-LATENESS, OPPORTUNENESS-UNSUITABLENESS, PERIODICITY-IRREGULARITY.

un-punc''-tu-al'-i-ty. Tardiness. PERIODICITY-IRREGULARITY.

un-pun'-ished. Unconvicted. EXCULPATION-CONVICTION.

un-pur'-chased. Unbought. BUYING-SALE.

un-pur'-i-fied. Dirty. CLEANNESS-FILTHINESS.

un-pur'-posed. Accidental. PURPOSE-LUCK.

un''-pur-sued'. Unfollowed. QUEST-ABANDONMENT.

un-qual'-i-fied. Incompetent; unentitled. CERTAINTY-DOUBT, DUENESS-UNDUENESS, ENTIRETY-DEFICIENCY, MIGHT-IMPOTENCE, PREPARATION-NONPREPARATION, SKILL-UNSKILFULNESS; **unqualified truth,** TRUTH-ERROR.

un-quelled'. Unabated. TURBULENCE-CALMNESS.

un-quench'-a-ble. Unextinguishable. DESIRE-DISTASTE, STRENGTH-WEAKNESS.

un-quenched'. Unextinguished. HEAT-COLD, TURBULENCE-CALMNESS.

un-ques'-tion-a-ble. Certain. CERTAINTY-DOUBT.

un-ques'-tion-a-bly. Certainly. ASSENT-DISSENT.

un-ques'-tion-ed. Undoubted. ASSENT-DISSENT, CERTAINTY-DOUBT.

un-qui'-et. Restless. AGITATION, EXCITABILITY-INEXCITABILITY, MOVEMENT-REST.

un-rav'-el. Separate; unfold. COMPOSITION-RESOLUTION, CURVATION-RECTILINEARITY, DIFFICULTY-FACILITY, DISCOVERY, INTERPRETATION-MISINTERPRETATION, ORGANIZATION-DISORGANIZATION, REVOLUTION-EVOLUTION, UNION-DISUNION.

un-reached'. Unattained. TRANSCURSION-SHORTCOMING.

un-read'. Ignorant. KNOWLEDGE-IGNORANCE.

un-read'-y. Unprepared. PREPARATION-NONPREPARATION.

un-real'. Imaginary. ENTITY-NONENTITY, FANCY, TRUTH-ERROR.

un-rea'-son-a-ble. Unjust. COSTLINESS-CHEAPNESS, DECISION-MISJUDGMENT, POSSIBILITY-IMPOSSIBILITY, RATIOCINATION-INSTINCT, RIGHT-WRONG, SAGACITY-INCAPACITY.

un-rea'-son-a-ble-ness. Impropriety. OPPORTUNENESS-UNSUITABLENESS.

un-rea'-son-ing. Prejudiced. DECISION-MISJUDGMENT.

un''-re-claimed'. Unconverted. REPENTANCE-OBDURACY.

un-rec'-og-ni''-za-ble. Unacknowledgable. REVOLUTION.

un-rec'-on-ciled. Not harmonized. VARIANCE-ACCORD.

un''-re-cord'-ed. Unmarked. MARK-OBLITERATION.

un-re-count'-ed. Untold. INCLUSION-OMISSION.

un''-re-duced'. Undiminished. MAGNITUDE-SMALLNESS.

un''-re-fined'. Vulgar. TASTE-VULGARITY.

un''-re-flect'-ing. Heedless. HEED-DISREGARD.

un'-re-formed'. Not reclaimed from vice. REPENTANCE-OBDURACY.

un''-re-freshed'. Weary. WEARINESS-REFRESHMENT.

un''-re-fut'-ed. Not disproved. PROOF-DISPROOF, TRUTH-ERROR.

un''-re-gard'-ed. Unobserved. CAREFULNESS-CARELESSNESS, REGARD-DISRESPECT.

un''-re-gen'-er-a-cy. State of being unregenerate. NATURE-ART.

un''-re-gen'-er-ate. Wicked. GODLINESS-UNGODLINESS, NATURE-ART.

un-reg'-is-tered. Unrecorded. MARK-OBLITERATION.

un-reined'. Unrestrained. LIBERTY-SUBJECTION.

un''-re-la'-ted. Not connected. CONNECTION-INDEPENDENCE.

un''-re-lent'-ing. Merciless. COMPASSION-RUTHLESSNESS, PARDON-VINDICTIVENESS.

un''-re-li'-a-ble. Untrustworthy. CERTAINTY-DOUBT.

un''-re-lieved'. Troubled. ALLEVIATION-AGGRAVATION.

un''-re-marked'. Unnoticed. CAREFULNESS-CARELESSNESS.

un''-re-mem'-bered. Forgotten. REMEMBRANCE-FORGETFULNESS.

un''-re-mit'-ting. Continuous. CONTINUITY-INTERRUPTION, LASTINGNESS-TRANSIENTNESS, PERSISTENCE-WHIM.

un''-re-moved'. Left. ESTABLISHMENT-REMOVAL.

un''-re-mu'-ner-a-ted. Unrewarded. SETTLEMENT-DEFAULT.

un''-re-newed'. Not reestablished. MUTATION-PERMANENCE.

un''-re-pealed'. Unrevoked. MUTATION-PERMANENCE.

un''-re-peat'-ed. Single. MULTIPLICITY-PAUCITY, SOLITUDE-COMPANY.

un''-re-pent'-ant. Unhumbled. REPENTANCE-OBDURACY.

un-re-pent'ed. Not contrite. REPENTANCE-OBDURACY.

un''-re-pin'-ing. Uncomplaining. CONTENTEDNESS-DISCONTENTMENT.

un''-re-plen'-ished. Unfilled. EXCESS-LACK.

un''-re-pressed'. Unrestrained. TURBULENCE-CALMNESS.

un''-re-proached'. Upright. INNOCENCE-GUILT.

un''-re-proved'. Not censured. INNOCENCE-GUILT.

un''-re-quit'-ed. Not reciprocated. CREDIT-DEBT, THANKFULNESS-THANKLESSNESS.

un''-re-sent'-ed. Forgiven. PARDON-VINDICTIVENESS.

un''-re-served'. Frank. CRAFT-ARTLESSNESS, ENLIGHTENMENT-SECRECY, TRUTHFULNESS-FALSEHOOD.

un''-re-sist'-ed. Obeyed. INSUBORDINATION-OBEDIENCE.

un''-re-sist'-ing. Submissive. EXCITABILITY-INEXCITABILITY, YIELDING.

un''-re-solved'. Not fixed. DETERMINATION-VACILLATION.

un''-re-spect'-ed. Disregarded. REGARD-DISRESPECT.

un-rest'. Uneasiness. MOVEMENT-REST, MUTABILITY-STABILITY.

un''-re-stored'. Fatigued. WEARINESS-REFRESHMENT.

un''-re-strained'. Free. DIFFICULTY-FACILITY, LIBERTY-SUBJECTION.

un''-re-strict'-ed. Unlimited. LIBERTY-SUBJECTION, MAGNITUDE-SMALLNESS.

un''-re-tract'-ed. Undenied. ASSERTION-DENIAL.

un''-re-venged'. Pardoned. PARDON-VINDICTIVENESS.

un''-re-versed'. Unchanged. DISCONTINUANCE-CONTINUANCE.

un''-re-voked'. Unannulled. DISCONTINUANCE-CONTINUANCE.

un''-re-ward'-ed. Not compensated. CREDIT-DEBT, THANKFULNESS-THANKLESSNESS.

un-rhymed'. Inharmonious. POETRY-PROSE.

un-rid'-dle. Interpret. DISCOVERY, EXPOSURE-HIDINGPLACE.

un-rig'. Dismantle. USEFULNESS-USELESSNESS.
un-right'-eous. Wrong. VIRTUE-VICE.
un-rip'. To cut open. APERTURE-CLOSURE.
un-ripe'. Unready. PREPARATION - NONPREPARA-TION.
un-ri'-valed. Unexcelled. SUPREMACY-SUBORDINACY.
un-roll'. Open. MANIFESTATION-LATENCY, REVOLUTION-EVOLUTION.
un''-ro-man'-tic. Prosaic. TRUTH-ERROR.
un-root'. Eradicate. INJECTION-EJECTION.
un-ruf'-fled. Calm. EXCITABILITY-INEXCITABILITY, MOVEMENT-REST, SENSITIVENESS-APATHY, TURBULENCE-CALMNESS.
un-ru'-ly. Stubborn. BIGOTRY-APOSTASY, INSUBORDINATION-OBEDIENCE, TURBULENCE-CALMNESS, TYRANNY-ANARCHY.
un-sad'-dle. Depose. COMMISSION-ABROGATION.
un-safe'. Perilous. SECURITY-INSECURITY.
un-said'. Unuttered. MANIFESTATION-LATENCY.
un-sa'-la-ble. Useless. COSTLINESS-CHEAPNESS, SALE, USEFULNESS-USELESSNESS.
un''-sa-lu'-ted. Unnoticed. REGARD-DISRESPECT.
un-sanc'-ti-fied. Unholy. GODLINESS - DISBELIEF, GODLINESS-UNGODLINESS.
un-sanc'-tioned. Unapproved. DUENESS - UNDUENESS.
un-sa'-ted. Unsatisfied. DESIRE-DISTASTE.
un-sat'-is-fac''-to-ry. Inexpedient; displeasing. CONTENTEDNESS-DISCONTENTMENT, GOODNESS-BADNESS, PLEASURABLENESS - PAINFULNESS, PROPRIETY - IMPROPRIETY.
un-sat'-is-fied. Rash; discontented. CONTENTEDNESS-DISCONTENTMENT, RECKLESSNESS-CAUTION.

un-sa'-vor-i-ness. Tastelessness. PALATABLENESS-UNPALATABLENESS, PUNGENCY.
un-sa'-vor-y. Distasteful. PALATABLENESS-UNPALATABLENESS, PUNGENCY.
un-say'. Recant. BIGOTRY-APOSTASY.
un-scanned'. Unmeasured. CAREFULNESS - CARELESSNESS.
un-scathed'. Uninjured. HEALTH-SICKNESS.
un-schooled'. Uneducated. KNOWLEDGE-IGNORANCE.
un-sci''-en-tif'-ic. Illogical. RATIOCINATION - INSTINCT.
un-scoured'. Dirty. CLEANNESS-FILTHINESS.
un-scrip'-tur-al. Contrary to the Word of God. ORTHODOXY-HETERODOXY.
un-scru'-pu-lous. Unprincipled. UPRIGHTNESS-DISHONESTY.
un-seal'. Disclose. EXPOSURE-HIDINGPLACE.
un-searched'. Unexamined. CAREFULNESS-CARELESSNESS.
un-sea'-son-a-ble. Ill-timed. HARMONY-DISCORD, OPPORTUNENESS-UNSUITABLENESS.
un-sea'-soned. Unusual; unprepared. HABIT-DESUETUDE, PREPARATION-NONPREPARATION.
un-seat'. Remove from office. COMMISSION-ABROGATION.
un-seem'-ly. Inexpedient; vulgar. BEAUTY-UGLINESS, DUENESS - UNDUENESS, PROPRIETY - IMPROPRIETY, TASTE-VULGARITY, VIRTUE-VICE.
un-seen'. Invisible. VISIBILITY-INVISIBILITY.
un-scl'-dom. Often. FREQUENCY-RARITY.
un-self'-ish. Liberal. UNSELFISHNESS-SELFISHNESS.
un-self'-ish-ness. Liberality. CHARITABLENESS-MALEVOLENCE, UNSELFISHNESS-SELFISHNESS.

UNSELFISHNESS—SELFISHNESS.

Benevolence. Love of mankind, accompanied with a desire to promote their happiness. See CHARITABLENESS.
Charity. Free giving to others.
Chivalrous spirit. A feeling or disposition raised above what is low, mean, or ungenerous.
Chivalry. The spirit or manners of knighthood.
Devotion. Ardent love or affection.
Disinterestedness. The state of being unmoved by personal interest or advantage. See *Adjectives.*
Elevation. The condition of mind of being above what is low or mean.
Exaltation. Elevation of character.
Free-hearted. Generous; kindly.
Generosity. The quality of being noble.
Heroism. Qualities of a hero as bravery courage, unselfishness, etc.
Labor of love. Work for the pleasure of the work, or love of others.
Liberalism. Principles of freedom from prejudice.
Liberality. The quality of generosity.
Loftiness of purpose. Elevation , nobility of purpose.
Magnanimity. That quality or combination of qualities which enables one to disdain injustice meanness, and revenge , large-mindedness.
Martyrdom. The laying down one s life for a cause.
Self-abnegation. Self-denial.
Self-control. Restraint exercised over oneself.
Self-denial. A foregoing of one's own welfare for others.
Self-immolation. Self-sacrifice.
Self-sacrifice. The quality of denying the enjoyment of one s own interest.
Stoicism. Indifference to pleasure or pain.
Sublimity. The quality of being distinguished by lofty or noble traits.
Suttee. The burning of a widow on the funeral pyre of her husband.

UNSELFISHNESS—*Verbs.*

Be disinterested. To be free from selfish motives. See *Adjectives.*
Do as one would be done by. To treat or deal with others as we wish to be treated.
Lay one's head on the block. To die for a cause.
Make a sacrifice. To devote with loss or suffering.
Put oneself in the place of others. To undertake another's work , to imagine oneself to be in another's place.

Amour propre [F.]. Self-love. See CONCEIT.
Charity that begins at home. Love or good-will that embraces first the circle of one's own family.
Egoism. Excessive love of self.
Egotism. Speaking and writing overmuch of oneself.
Illiberality. Narrow-mindedness.
Ingrate. An ungrateful person.
Ingratitude. Insensible to favors received.
Meanness. The condition or quality of being mean or stingy.
Nepotism. Favoritism shown to relatives, especially in public service.
Self-indulgence. Cringing to selfish desires and inclinations
Self-interest. The interest in oneself.
Selfishness. Exclusive regard to one's own interest or happiness.
Self-love. Tendency to seek one's own advantage.
Self-worship. Idolizing oneself.
Worldliness. A passion for temporal gain and enjoyments. See *Adjectives.*
World-wisdom. Devotion to worldly interests only.

SELFISHNESS—*Nouns of Agent.*

Dog in the manger. A person who prevents others from enjoying what would be an advantage to them, but is none to him.
Egoist. One who has a very exalted opinion of himself.
Egotist. One who parades the love of himself openly.
Fortune-hunter. One who seeks to acquire wealth by marriage.
Jobber. One who turns public office to private advantage.
Monopolist. One who gains sole control of.
Nepotist. One who practises nepotism
Time-server. One who obsequiously complies with the ruling power.
Tuft-hunter. A hanger-on to noblemen, or persons of quality.
Worldling. One devoted to this world and its enjoyments.

SELFISHNESS—*Verbs.*

Be selfish. To care only for oneself. See *Adjectives.*
Coddle oneself. To treat with too great tenderness.
Consult one's own pleasure. To regard one's own pleasure in doing or not doing a thing.
Consult one's own wishes. To care only for self, regardless of others.
Feather one's nest. To provide selfishly for the future.
Give an inch and take an ell. To take ore than belongs to one.
Have an eye to the main chance. To look out for one's own interest.
Indulge oneself. To cater to pride, selfishness, etc.

UNSELFISHNESS—SELFISHNESS—*Continued*.

UNSELFISHNESS—*Adjectives*.

Chivalrous. Sacrificing; self-denying; knightly.
Disinterested. Free from selfish motives.
Elevated.
Exalted. } Noble-minded. See *Nouns*.
Generous. Liberal in giving.
Great. Philanthropic; large-hearted.
Handsome. Noble; exhibiting a feeling of generosity.
Heroic. Brave; courteous; unselfish.
High. Exalted in action.
High-minded. Of lofty purpose.
Large-hearted. Full of brotherly sympathy.
Liberal. Broad in views or sympathies. See *Nouns*.
Lofty. Elevated in purpose.
Magnanimous. Raised above what is low, mean, or ungenerous; great-minded.
Noble. Grand; having a contempt for everything mean.
Noble-minded. Honorable; magnanimous.
Princely. Exercising the qualities of a prince.
Self-denying. Giving up one's own desires for the good of others. See *Verbs*.
Self-devoted. Unselfish.
Self-sacrificing. Losing or suffering for another. See *Verbs*.
Spirited. Bold; courageous.
Stoical. Indifferent to pain or pleasure.
Sublime. Lofty; noble.
Unbought. Not influenced by bribery or favor.
Unbribed. Full of integrity; upright.
Uncorrupted. Above the influence of bribes. See UPRIGHTNESS.
Unselfish. Free from the feeling or regard for one's own comfort or advantage alone.

UNSELFISHNESS—*Phrases*.

Canis in præsepi [L.]. Dog in the manger.
Grosse Seelen dulden still [G.]. Great souls suffer in silence.
Non nobis solum [L.]. Not for ourselves merely.

SELFISHNESS—*Continued from Column 2.*

SELFISHNESS—*Phrase*.

Après nous le deluge [F.]. After us the deluge.

un-sep'-ar-a''-ted. Joined. COHESION-LOOSENESS.
un-ser'-vice-a-ble. Useless. USEFULNESS - USELESSNESS.
un-serv'-i-ent. Insubordinate. USEFULNESS - USELESSNESS.
un-set'-tle. Derange. ORGANIZATION-DISORGANIZATION.
un-set'-tled. Uncertain; changeable. CERTAINTY-DOUBT, ESTABLISHMENT - REMOVAL, MUTABILITY-STABILITY; **unsettled in one's mind,** SANENESS-LUNACY.
un-set'-tle-ment. Vacillation. DETERMINATION-VACILLATION.
un-sev'-ered. Uncut. WHOLE-PART.
un-sex'. Unwoman. REVOLUTION.
un-sha'-ded. Clear. MANIFESTATION-LATENCY.
un-sha'-ken. Resolute. STRENGTH-WEAKNESS; **unshaken belief,** FAITH-MISGIVING.
un-shape'-ly. Ugly. BEAUTY-UGLINESS.
un-sha'-pen. Deformed. FORM-FORMLESSNESS.
un-shared'. Not shared. HOLDING-EXEMPTION.
un-sheathe'. To draw from a sheath. **Unsheathe the sword,** FIGHTING-CONCILIATION.
un-shield'-ed. Exposed. SECURITY-INSECURITY.
un-shift'-ing. Unchanging. DISCONTINUANCE-CONTINUANCE.
un-ship'. Remove. ADMISSION-EXPULSION.
un-shocked'. Unshaken by horror. SENSITIVENESS-APATHY.
un-shorn'. Unclipped. WHOLE-PART.
un-short'-ened. Undiminished in length. LENGTH-SHORTNESS.
un-shrink'-ing. Courageous. BRAVERY-COWARDICE, DETERMINATION-VACILLATION.

SELFISHNESS—VERBS—*Continued*.

Know on which side one's bread is buttered. To look after one's own interests.
Look after one's own interests. To care only for self.
Please oneself. Gratify; suit one's own taste.
Take care of number one. To be selfish; prejudiced.

SELFISHNESS—*Adjectives*.

Alieni appetens, sui profusus [L.]. Lavish of his own property while coveting that of others.
Centered in self. Narrow; prejudiced.
Covetous. Greedy. See EXTRAVAGANCE-AVARICE.
Earthly. Material; gross.
Earthly-minded. Limited to earthly things.
Egotistic.
Egotistical. } Pertaining to self-love.
Illiberal. Not generous.
Interested. Biased; caring for self only.
Mean. Low; stingy.
Mercenary. Greedy for gain; close-fisted.
Mundane. Worldly.
Narrow-minded. Unsympathetic; bigoted.
Self-indulgent. Pleasing only one's own wishes.
Self-interested. Self-centered.
Selfish. Considering only one's own comfort and advantage.
Self-seeking. Seeking self-interest.
Time-serving. Changing one's opinions according to one's advantage. See *Nouns*.
Ungenerous. Not generous; illiberal.
Unspiritual. Carnal-minded.
Venal. Capable of being bought for money.
Worldly. Worldly-minded; worldly-wise.
Worldly-minded.
Worldly-wise. } Caring for present gain and enjoyment.
Wrapt up. Altogether devoted to.

SELFISHNESS—*Adverbs, etc.*

From interested motives. Selfishly.
To gain some private ends. For one's own advantage.
Ungenerously. Selfishly. See *Adjectives*.

(Continued on Column 1.)

un-sift'-ed. Untried. CAREFULNESS-CARELESSNESS.
un-sight'-ly. Deformed. BEAUTY-UGLINESS.
un-singed'. Not scorched. CONSERVATION.
un-skil'-ful. Unclever. SKILL-UNSKILFULNESS.
un-skil'-ful-ness. Awkwardness. SKILL-UNSKILFULNESS, USEFULNESS-USELESSNESS.
un-slaked'. Unabated. DESIRE-DISTASTE.
un-sleep'-ing. Wakeful; active. ACTIVITY-INDOLENCE, PERSISTENCE-WHIM.
un-smooth'. Rough. SMOOTHNESS-ROUGHNESS.
un-so'-cia-ble. Disagreeable. SOCIABILITY-PRIVACY.
un-so'-cial. Disagreeable. SOCIABILITY-PRIVACY.
un-soiled'. Unpolluted. CLEANNESS-FILTHINESS.
un-sold'. Not sold. HOLDING-EXEMPTION.
un-sol'-dier-like. Cowardly. BRAVERY-COWARDICE.
un''-so-lic'-i-tous. Unconcerned. UNCONCERN.
un-solved'. Unexplained. MANIFESTATION-LATENCY.
un''-so-phis'-ti-ca''-ted. Artless; simple. CRAFT-ARTLESSNESS, MIXTURE-HOMOGENEITY, TRUTH-ERROR.
un-sought'. Unasked. PETITION-EXPOSTULATION, QUEST-EVASION.
un-sound'. Irrational; erroneous. FAULTLESSNESS-FAULTINESS, RATIOCINATION-INSTINCT, TRUTH-ERROR, TRUTHFULNESS-FRAUD; **unsound mind,** SANENESS-LUNACY.
un-sound'-ness. Aberration. SANENESS-LUNACY.
un-sown'. Unplanted. PREPARATION-NONPREPARATION.
un-spar'-ing. Liberal; severe; abundant. ENOUGH, GENEROSITY - FRUGALITY, HARSHNESS - MILDNESS; **with an unsparing hand,** EXTRAVAGANCE - AVARICE.
un-speak'-a-ble. Unutterable. ASTONISHMENT-EXPECTANCE, MAGNITUDE-SMALLNESS.

un-spec'-i-fied. Not particularly mentioned. UNIVERSALITY-PARTICULARITY.

un-spent'. Unused. USE-DISUSE.

un-spied'. Unknown. ENLIGHTENMENT-SECRECY.

un-spir'-it-u-al. Worldly. MATERIALITY-SPIRITUALITY, UNSELFISHNESS-SELFISHNESS.

un-spot'-ted. Clean; beautiful; innocent. BEAUTY-UGLINESS, CLEANNESS - FILTHINESS, INNOCENCE-GUILT.

un-sta'-ble. Irresolute. MUTABILITY-STABILITY, SECURITY-INSECURITY; **unstable equilibrium,** MUTABILITY-STABILITY.

un-staid'. Fickle. MUTABILITY-STABILITY.

un-stained'. Pure. CLEANNESS-FILTHINESS, UPRIGHTNESS-DISHONESTY.

un-states'-man-like". Untrained. SKILL - UNSKILFULNESS.

un-stead'-fast. Not firm. DETERMINATION-VACILLATION.

un-stead'-y. Irresolute. DETERMINATION-VACILLATION, MUTABILITY-STABILITY, SECURITY-INSECURITY.

un-stint'-ed. Abundant. ENOUGH.

un-stint'-ing. Liberal. ENOUGH.

un-stirred'. Passive. EXCITABILITY-INEXCITABILITY, SENSITIVENESS-APATHY.

un-stopped'. Continued. APERTURE-CLOSURE, DISCONTINUANCE-CONTINUANCE.

un-stored'. Unreplenished. EXCESS-LACK.

un-strained'. Turbid; relaxed. CLEANNESS-FILTHINESS, TOIL - RELAXATION; **unstrained meaning,** MEANING-JARGON.

un-strength'-ened. Unsupported. STRENGTH-WEAKNESS.

un-struck'. Unimpressed. SENSITIVENESS-APATHY.

un-strung'. Weak. STRENGTH-WEAKNESS.

un-stud'-ied. Natural. CAREFULNESS-CARELESSNESS.

un-sub'-ject. Free. LIBERTY-SUBJECTION.

un"-sub-miss'-ive. Stubborn. INSUBORDINATION-OBEDIENCE.

un"-sub-serv'-i-ence. Inexpediency. USEFULNESS-USELESSNESS.

un"-sub-serv'-i-ent. Useless; inexpedient. PROPRIETY-IMPROPRIETY, USEFULNESS-USELESSNESS.

un"-sub-stan'-tial. Unreal; weak; rare. ENTITY-NONENTITY, FANCY, SOLIDITY - RARITY, STRENGTH-WEAKNESS, SUBSTANCE-NULLITY, TRUTH-ERROR.

un"-sub-stan"-ti-al'-it-y. Want of existence. PLURALITY-ZERO, SUBSTANCE-NULLITY.

un"-suc-cess'-ful. Fruitless. SUCCESS-FAILURE.

un"-suc-cess'-ive. Not consecutive. CONTINUITY-INTERRUPTION.

un-suit'-a-ble. Incongruous. HARMONY - DISCORD; **unsuitable time,** OPPORTUNENESS-UNSUITABLENESS.

un-suit'-ed. Inopportune; inharmonious. HARMONY-DISCORD, OPPORTUNENESS-UNSUITABLENESS.

un-sul'-lied. Unstained. CLEANNESS-FILTHINESS, UPRIGHTNESS-DISHONESTY.

un-sung'. Not sung. MANIFESTATION-LATENCY.

un"-sup-plied'. Unprovided with. EXCESS-LACK.

un"-sup-port'-ed. Weak. STRENGTH-WEAKNESS; **unsupported by evidence,** EVIDENCE-COUNTEREVIDENCE.

un"-sup-pressed'. Unrestrained. MUTATION-PERMANENCE.

un"-sur-mount'-a-ble. Unconquerable. POSSIBILITY-IMPOSSIBILITY.

un"-sur-passed'. Unexcelled. MAGNITUDE - SMALLNESS, SUPREMACY-SUBORDINACY.

un"-sus-cep'-ti-ble. Insusceptible. EXCITABILITY-INEXCITABILITY, SENSITIVENESS-APATHY.

un"-sus-pect'-ed. Unthought of. FAITH-MISGIVING, MANIFESTATION-LATENCY.

un"-sus-pect'-ing. Hopeful. FAITH-MISGIVING, SANGUINENESS-HOPELESSNESS.

un"-sus-pi'-cious. Unsuspecting. FAITH-UNBELIEF, SANGUINENESS-HOPELESSNESS.

un"-sus-tain'-a-ble. Erroneous. TRUTH-ERROR.

un-sweet'. Sour. PALATABLENESS-UNPALATABLENESS.

un-swept'. Dirty. CLEANNESS-FILTHINESS.

un-swerv'-ing. Direct; persevering. AIM-ABERRATION, CURVATION-RECTILINEARITY, PERSISTENCE-WHIM.

un"-sym-met'-ric. Irregular. PROPORTION-DEFORMITY, REGULARITY-IRREGULARITY.

un-sys'-te-mat"-ic. Irregular. PROPORTION-DEFORMITY, REGULARITY-IRREGULARITY.

un-taint'-ed. Pure; healthy; honorable. CLEANNESS-FILTHINESS, HEALTH-SICKNESS, UPRIGHTNESS-DISHONESTY.

un-talked' of. Secret. MANIFESTATION-LATENCY.

un-tamed'. Unsubdued. CHARITABLENESS-MALEVOLENCE, TASTE-VULGARITY.

un-tarn'-ished. Honorable. UPRIGHTNESS-DISHONESTY.

un-tast'-ed. Not tasted. SAVOR-TASTELESSNESS.

un-taught'. Ignorant. KNOWLEDGE - IGNORANCE, PREPARATION-NONPREPARATION.

un-taxed'. Not taxed. COSTLINESS-CHEAPNESS.

un-teach'. To cause to forget what has been taught. EDUCATION-MISTEACHING.

un-teach'-a-ble. Foolish; unskilful. SAGACITY-INCAPACITY, SKILL-UNSKILFULNESS.

un-ten'-a-ble. Illogical. MIGHT-IMPOTENCE, RATIOCINATION-INSTINCT, YIELDING.

un-ten"-ant-ed. Uninhabited. HOLDING-EXEMPTION, PRESENCE-ABSENCE.

un-thanked'. Not received with gratitude. THANKFULNESS-THANKLESSNESS.

un-thank'-ful. Ungrateful. THANKFULNESS-THANKLESSNESS.

un-thawed'. Frozen. HEAT-COLD, SOLIDITY-RARITY.

un-think'-ing. Careless. REFLECTION - VACANCY, VOLITION-OBLIGATION.

un-thought' of. Neglected. CAREFULNESS-CARELESSNESS, REFLECTION-VACANCY.

un-threat'-ened. Not threatened. SECURITY - INSECURITY.

un-thrift'-i-ness. Indolence. EXTRAVAGANCE - AVARICE.

un-thrift'-y. Prodigal. EXTRAVAGANCE-AVARICE, PREPARATION-NONPREPARATION.

un-throne'. Dethrone. COMMISSION-ABROGATION.

un-ti'-dy. Slovenly; disordered. CLEANNESS-FILTHINESS, REGULARITY-IRREGULARITY.

un-tie'. Liberate. LIBERTY-SUBJECTION; **untie the knot,** DIFFICULTY-FACILITY.

un-til'. Up to. DURATION-NEVERNESS; **until now,** TIME.

un-tilled'. Uncultivated. PREPARATION-NONPREPARATION.

un-time'-ly. Ill-timed. OPPORTUNENESS-UNSUITABLENESS; **untimely end,** LIFE-DEATH.

un-tinged'. Simple. MIXTURE-HOMOGENEITY.

un-tired'. Unexhausted. WEARINESS-REFRESHMENT.

un-tir'-ing. Persisting. PERSISTENCE-WHIM.

un-ti'-tled. Without a title. GENTILITY-COMMONALTY.

un-told'. Countless; latent. CERTAINTY-DOUBT, ENLIGHTENMENT-SECRECY, INFINITY, MANIFESTATION-LATENCY.

un-touched'. Unused; insensible. SENSITIVENESS-APATHY, USE-DISUSE.

un-to'-ward. Vexatious; unfortunate. GOODNESS-BADNESS, OPPORTUNENESS-UNSUITABLENESS, PLEASURABLENESS-PAINFULNESS, WELFARE-MISFORTUNE.

un-traced'. Unmarked. MANIFESTATION-LATENCY.

un-tracked'. Unmarked. MANIFESTATION-LATENCY.

un-tract'-a-ble. Stubborn; unskilful. BIGOTRY-APOSTASY, SKILL-UNSKILFULNESS.

un-trained'. Unskilled. HABIT-DESUETUDE, PREPARATION-NONPREPARATION, SKILL-UNSKILFULNESS.

un-tram'-meled. Unimpeded. DIFFICULTY-FACILITY, LIBERTY-SUBJECTION.

un''-trans-la'-ta-ble. Incapable of being differently rendered. INTERPRETATION-MISINTERPRETATION.

un''-trans-la'-ted. Unchanged. INTERPRETATION-MISINTERPRETATION.

un-trav'-eled. Having never seen foreign countries. MOVEMENT-REST.

un-treas'-ured. Deprived. EXCESS-LACK.

un-tried'. New; undecided. INVESTIGATION - ANSWER, NOVELTY-ANTIQUITY.

un-trimmed'. Simple; new. EMBELLISHMENT-SIMPLICITY, PREPARATION-NONPREPARATION.

un-trod'-den. New; impervious. APERTURE-CLOSURE, NOVELTY-ANTIQUITY, USE-DISUSE.

un-troub'-led. Quiet. STRIFE-PEACE, TURBULENCE-CALMNESS.

un-true'. Erroneous. ADAGE-NONSENSE, TRUTHFULNESS - FABRICATION, TRUTHFULNESS - FALSEHOOD, TRUTHFULNESS-FRAUD.

un-trust'-worth-y. Uncertain; dangerous. CERTAINTY-DOUBT, SECURITY-INSECURITY, TRUTH-ERROR, UPRIGHTNESS-DISHONESTY.

un-truth'. Falsehood. TRUTHFULNESS-FALSEHOOD.

un-tu'-na-ble. Discordant. MELODY-DISSONANCE.

un-turned'. Straight. CURVATURE-RECTILINEARITY.

un-tu'-tored. Untaught. CRAFT-ARTLESSNESS, KNOWLEDGE-IGNORANCE, PREPARATION-NONPREPARATION.

un-twine'. Untwist. REVOLUTION-EVOLUTION.

un-twist'. Separate. REVOLUTION-EVOLUTION.

un-used'. Unaccustomed; awkward. HABIT-DESUETUDE, SKILL-UNSKILFULNESS.

un-u'-su-al. Uncommon. CONVENTIONALITY-UNCONVENTIONALITY, HABIT-DESUETUDE.

un-u'-su-al-ly. Very. MAGNITUDE-SMALLNESS.

un-ut'-ter-a-ble. Inexpressible. ASTONISHMENT-EXPECTANCE, MAGNITUDE-SMALLNESS.

un-val'-ued. Undesired; underrated. LOVE-HATE, OVERVALUATION-UNDERVALUATION, UNCONCERN.

un-van'-quished. Unconquered. LIBERTY - SUBJECTION.

un-va'-ried. Unchanged. DISCONTINUANCE-CONTINUANCE, FORCE-WEAKNESS, SIMPLICITY-FLORIDNESS.

un-var'-nished. Plain. EMBELLISHMENT-SIMPLICITY, FORCE-WEAKNESS, TRUTH-ERROR; **unvarnished tale,** TRUTH-ERROR, TRUTHFULNESS-FALSEHOOD.

un-var'-y-ing. Unchanging. DISCONTINUANCE-CONTINUANCE.

un-veil'. Disclose. EXPOSURE-HIDINGPLACE.

un-veil'-ing. Disclosure. EXPOSURE-HIDINGPLACE.

un-ven'-ti-la''-ted. Not purified by a free current of air. APERTURE-CLOSURE.

un'-ve-ra'-cious. Untruthful. TRUTHFULNESS-FALSEHOOD.

un-versed'. Untaught. KNOWLEDGE-IGNORANCE.

un-vexed'. Undisturbed. CONTENTEDNESS - DISCONTENTMENT.

un-vi'-o-la''-ted. Pure. UPRIGHTNESS-DISHONESTY.

un-vis'-it-ed. Solitary. SOCIABILITY-PRIVACY.

un-wak'-ened. Unaroused. ACTIVITY-INDOLENCE.

un-war'-like. Not military. BRAVERY-COWARDICE.

un-warmed'. Cold. HEAT-COLD.

un-warned'. Uncautioned. EXPECTATION-SURPRISE, SECURITY-INSECURITY.

un-warped' judg'-ment. Unbiased judgment. SAGACITY-INCAPACITY.

un-war'-rant-a-ble. Unjust. LAW - LAWLESSNESS, RIGHT-WRONG.

un-war'-rant-ed. Illogical; undue; illegal. DUENESS-UNDUENESS, LAW-LAWLESSNESS, RATIOCINATION-INSTINCT.

un-wa'-ry. Incautious. CAREFULNESS-CARELESSNESS.

un-washed'. Dirty. CLEANNESS-FILTHINESS; **great unwashed,** GENTILITY-COMMONALTY.

un-wa'-sted. Ample. ENOUGH.

un-watch'-ful. Heedless. CAREFULNESS - CARELESSNESS.

un-wa'-ver-ing. Firm. PERSISTENCE-WHIM.

un-weak'-ened. Strong. STRENGTH-WEAKNESS.

un-wea'-ried. Assiduous. ACTIVITY-INDOLENCE, PERSISTENCE-WHIM, WEARINESS-REFRESHMENT.

un-wed'-ded. Unmarried. MATRIMONY-CELIBACY.

un-weed'-ed gar'-den. Not clear of weeds. PREPARATION-NONPREPARATION.

un-weet'-ing. Ignorant. KNOWLEDGE-IGNORANCE.

un-weighed'. Unconsidered. CAREFULNESS-CARELESSNESS.

un-wel'-come. Disagreeable. PLEASURABLENESS-PAINFULNESS.

un-well'. Sick. HEALTH-SICKNESS.

un-whole'-some. Diseased. HEALTHINESS-UNHEALTHINESS.

un-wield'-y. Ponderous; awkward. BEAUTY-UGLINESS, DIFFICULTY - FACILITY, GREATNESS - LITTLENESS, HEAVINESS-LIGHTNESS, PROPRIETY-IMPROPRIETY.

un-will'-ing. Reluctant. ASSENT-DISSENT, READINESS-RELUCTANCE.

un-will'-ing-ly. Reluctantly. READINESS - RELUCTANCE.

un-will'-ing-ness. Disinclination. READINESS - RELUCTANCE.

un-wind'. Separate. REVOLUTION-EVOLUTION.

un-wiped'. Not wiped. CLEANNESS-FILTHINESS.

un-wise'. Foolish. SAGACITY-INCAPACITY.

un-wished'. Undesired. DESIRE-DISTASTE.

un-with'-ered. Unfaded. STRENGTH-WEAKNESS.

un-wit'-ting. Ignorant; involuntary. KNOWLEDGE-IGNORANCE, VOLITION-OBLIGATION.

un-wit'-ting-ly. Inadvertently. PURPOSE-LUCK.

un-wom'-an-ly. Unbecoming a woman. MALE-FEMALE.

un-wont'-ed. Unusual. CONVENTIONALITY-UNCONVENTIONALITY, HABIT-DESUETUDE.

un-world'-ly. Spiritually-minded. UPRIGHTNESS-DISHONESTY.

un-worn'. Unimpaired. STRENGTH-WEAKNESS.

un-wor'-shiped. Dishonored. REGARD-DISRESPECT.

un-worth'-y. Base. REPUTATION-DISCREDIT, VIRTUE-VICE; **unworthy of belief,** REVELATION-PSEUDOREVELATION; **unworthy of notice,** CONSEQUENCE-INSIGNIFICANCE.

un-wrap'. Straighten. CURVATION-RECTILINEARITY.

un-wrink'-led. Smooth. SMOOTHNESS-ROUGHNESS.

un-writ'-ten. Oral; hidden; obliterated. ENLIGHTENMENT - LATENCY, MARK - OBLITERATION, SPEECH-INARTICULATION.

un-wrought'. Not manufactured. PREPARATION-NONPREPARATION.

un-yield'-ing. Tough; firm. BIGOTRY-APOSTASY, HARDNESS-SOFTNESS, REPRISAL-RESISTANCE.

up. Erect; aloft; effervescing. ERECTNESS - FLATNESS, EXCITATION, HEIGHT-LOWNESS, VISCIDITY-FOAM; **all up with,** CREATION-DESTRUCTION, FAILURE, WELFARE-MISFORTUNE; **prices looking up,** COSTLINESS-CHEAPNESS; **the game is up,** WELFARE-MISFORTUNE; **time up,** LASTINGNESS-TRANSIENTNESS; **up and at them,** ATTACK-DEFENSE; **up and doing,** ACTIVITY-INDOLENCE; **up and down,** VIBRATION; **up in,** SKILL-UNSKILFULNESS; **up in arms,** ACTIVITY-INDOLENCE, ATTACK-DEFENSE, FIGHTING-CONCILIATION, OPPOSITION-CONCURRENCE, PREPARATION- NONPREPARATION, REPRISAL - RESISTANCE; **up on end,** ERECTNESS-FLATNESS; **up to,** BRAVERY-COWARDICE, DURATION-NEVERNESS, KNOWLEDGE-IGNORANCE, MIGHT-IMPOTENCE, SKILL-UNSKILFULNESS; **up to one's ears** EXCESS-LACK; **up to one's**

eyes, Excess-Lack; **up to snuff**, Craft-Artlessness; **up to the brim**, Entirety-Deficiency; **up to the mark**, Dueness-Undueness, Enough, Equality-Inequality, Goodness - Badness, Skill - Unskilfulness; **up to this time**, Duration - Neverness, Future-Past.

u'-pas-tree''. A tall Javanese tree having an acrid milky juice which contains a virulent poison. Remedy-Bane.

up-bear'. Support; elevate. Elevation-Depression, Suspension-Support.

up-braid'. Reproach. Approval-Disapproval.

up-braid'-ing. Reproach. Approval-Disapproval.

up-cast'. Directed up. Elevation-Depression.

up-grow'. Grow up. Height-Lowness.

up-growth'. Development; ascent. Ascent - Descent, Enlargement-Diminution.

up-heave'. Raise aloft. Elevation-Depression.

up'-hill''. Ascent; laborious. Parallelism-Inclination, Toil-Relaxation.

up''-hill'. Difficult. Ascent-Descent, Difficulty-Facility.

up-hoist'. Elevate. Elevation-Depression.

up-hold'. Support; defend. Approval-Disapproval, Discontinuance - Continuance, Divinity, Evidence - Counterevidence, Obstruction - Help, Suspension-Support.

up-hold'-er. Defender. Antagonist-Assistant.

up-hol'-ster-y. The business of an upholsterer. Instrument.

up'-land. Highland. Height-Lowness.

up'-lands. Highlands. Height-Lowness.

up-lift'. Elevate. Elevation-Depression.

up-on'. On; after. **Upon my honor**, Assertion-Denial; **upon my oath**, Assertion-Denial; **upon which**, Antecedence-Posteriority, Future-Past, Time.

up'-per. Above. Gentility - Commonalty, Height-Lowness, **upper hand**, Dominance - Impotence, Rule-License, Success-Failure; **upper story**, Mind-Imbecility, Sagacity-Incapacity, Top-Bottom; **upper ten thousand**, Gentility-Commonalty, Society-Ludicrousness.

up'-per-most. Highest. Top-Bottom; **say what comes uppermost**, Predetermination - Impulse; **uppermost in mind**, Conception-Theme, Heed-Disregard, Reflection-Vacancy; **uppermost in one's thoughts**, Remembrance-Forgetfulness.

up-raise'. Lift up. Elevation-Depression.

up-rear'. Elevate. Elevation-Depression.

up-right'. Erect. Erectness-Flatness, Uprightness-Dishonesty.

up-right'-ness. Erectness. Uprightness-Dishonesty.

UPRIGHTNESS—DISHONESTY.

Bona fide [L.]. Good, genuine faith or sincerity.

Candor. A disposition to treat with fairness and sincerity.

Constancy. Fixedness of mind; firmness in one's attachments or loyalty.

Delicacy. Nice propriety in conduct or manners; a careful consideration of others.

Dignity. Stately impressiveness in bearing or air. See Reputation.

Equity. A giving to every man his dues impartially and freely and as much to one as another.

Fairness. A showing of no partiality or favoritism. See *Adjectives.*

Fair-play. Fair or just opportunity.

Faith. Fidelity to duty or obligations; good faith.

Faithfulness. The quality of being firm in the keeping of promises or the discharge of duties. See *Adjectives.*

Fidelity. Staunchness in loyalty or in performance of duties, etc.

Good faith. Wholesome, sound faith or loyalty.

Grace. An inherent gift of beauty, physical or moral.

Honesty. Fairness and uprightness in dealing with others; freedom from fraud or deceit.

Honor. A delicate sense of what is just, true, etc.

Impartiality. Freedom from bias; equitableness.

Incorruptibility. Inflexible adherence to right conduct.

Incorruption. Absence of corruption.

Integrity. Moral soundness; complete rectitude.

Justice. A giving to each what he deserves.

Loyalty. Constant faithfulness in any trust.

Nicety. Delicacy.

Point. Exactness.

Principle. An established, fixed rule of right action.

Probity. Tested integrity; tried honesty.

Punctilio. Strictness and carefulness in observance of etiquette.

Punctuality. A habit of being punctual, observance of promptness.

Purity. Freedom from moral defilement.

Rectitude. Straightforwardness in conduct or morals.

Respectability. } State of being respectable, of having a good name
Respectableness. } and fair morals. See *Adjectives.*

Scruple. Hesitation regarding moral questions or duties.

Scrupulosity. Same as scrupulousness.

Scrupulousness. State of being scrupulous. See *Adjectives.*

Singleness of heart. Freedom from duplicity.

Trustworthiness. State of being worthy of trust. See *Adjectives.*

Truth. Sincerity.

Uprightness. Moral correctness and rectitude. See *Adjectives.*

Veracity. Habitual observance of truth. See Truthfulness.

UPRIGHTNESS—*Denotations.*

A fair field and no favor. A fair chance.

Argumentum ad verecundiam [L.]. An argument appealing to one's modesty.

Abjection. State of being abject; despicableness.

Apostasy. Desertion or abandonment of party or principles. See Obstruction-Help.

Bad faith. Faithlessness.

Barratry. An unlawful act committed by the master of a ship, whereby the owner sustains injury.

Baseness. State of being base; of being low in rank; meanness. See *Adjectives.*

Betrayal. A violation of confidence or trust.

Breach of faith. A betrayal of confidence or implied trust.

Breach of promise. Failure to keep a promise to marry.

Breach of trust. Violation by fraud or omission of any duty imposed upon a trustee.

Corruption. Loss of integrity; wickedness.

Debasement. A lowering of value; deterioration in purity.

Deviation from rectitude. Guiltiness.

Disgrace. A condition of reproach or shame. See Reputation-Discredit.

Dishonesty. Want of honesty; insincerity; fraud.

Dishonor. Want of honor; degradation.

Disloyalty. Want of loyalty; inconstancy.

Double-dealing. Treachery; deception.

Faithlessness. State of being without faith or constancy. See *Adjectives.*

Fishy transaction. A doubtful or incredible business, like a fish-story.

Foul play. Conduct that is intended to take others at an unfair advantage.

Fraud. Deception purposely practised to gain an advantage. See Truthfulness-Fraud.

Heads I win, tails you lose. An artful trick.

High treason. Treachery toward a sovereign or government.

Improbity. Want of probity; dishonesty.

Infidelity. Lack of fidelity; lack of faith.

Jobbery. Practise of low intriguing.

Jobbing. A working for one's advantage under the pretense of doing for others.

Judas kiss. A hypocritical and deceitful mark of affection. [Bible.]

Knavery. Small dishonesty, roguery, like that of a body-servant.

Laxity. Want of firmness; licentiousness.

Lying. Telling what is untrue. See Truthfulness-Falsehood.

Mala fides [L.]. Bad faith.

Moral turpitude. Inherent moral baseness.

Mouth honor. Flattery. See Adulation.

Nepotism. Undue distinction in favor of relatives.

Non-observance. Neglect to fulfil or observe.

Perfidiousness. The state of being perfidious. See *Adjectives.*

Perfidy. The state of violating faith; faithlessness.

Prodition. Treachery.

Punica fides [L.]. Punic faith.

Punic faith. Faith of the Carthaginians as seen at Rome; treachery.

Rascality. State of being a rascal; low trickery.

UPRIGHTNESS—DISHONESTY—*Continued.*

UPRIGHTNESS—Denotations—*Continued.*

Brick. A first-rate fellow.
Clean hands. Marks of uprightness.
Court of honor. A person or council adjudicating a question of honor as to privileges of conduct.
Fidus Achates [L.]. Faithful Achates. [Virgil.] Brotherly.
Galantuomo [It.]. A gentleman.
Gentleman. A man of honor.
Man of his word. } A man whose verbal promise binds him as much
Man of honor. } as an oath.
Point of honor. A question of honor affecting a detail of conduct.
Preux chevalier [F.]. A valiant knight.
Tender conscience. A conscience easily touched.
True Briton. An honorable man.
Truepenny. An honest fellow.
Trump. A very satisfactory person.

UPRIGHTNESS—*Verbal Expressions.*

Audire alteram partem [L.], to hear the other side; **be as good as one's promise; be as good as one's word;** be honorable (see *Adjectives*); **deal fairly; deal honorably; deal impartially; deal squarely;** do one's duty (see VIRTUE); **give and take; give the devil his due; keep faith with; keep one's promise; keep one's word; make a point of; not fail; put the saddle on the right horse; redeem one's pledge; redound to one's honor; show a proper spirit; speak the truth** (see TRUTHFULNESS); **tell the truth and shame the devil;** *vitam impendere vero* [L.], to risk one's life for the truth.

UPRIGHTNESS—*Adjectives.*

As good as one's word. Reliable.
Candid. Free from bias or prejudice.
Chivalrous. Having the qualities of an ancient knight; gallant.
Conscientious. Governed by conscience, or by the sense of right and wrong.
Constant. Steady in purpose; faithful.
Constant as the Northern Star. Always steady.
Correct. Free from wrong; consonant with what is right.
Equitable. Characteristic of equity; conforming to the principles of equity
Even-handed. Impartial.
Fair. Showing no partiality; just.
Fair and above board. Impartial and open.
Faithful. Trusty in any duty or position.
Fide et fiducia [L.]. By fidelity and confidence.
Frank Candid and sincere.
Gentlemanlike. Suited to a gentleman; honorable.
High-minded. Magnanimous.
High-principled. Furnished with good principles.
High-spirited. Full of spirit.
Honest Fair and straightforward in dealings with others: free from deceit.
Honest as daylight. Very honest.
Honorable. Conforming to what honor would demand; having excellent motives.
Impartial. Showing no favors: disinterested.
Incorruptible. Incapable of being corrupted or defiled.
Innocent. Without fault. See INNOCENCE.
Integer vitæ scelerisque purus [L.]. Unimpaired in vigor and free from crime. [Horace, *Odes*, I, xxii, 1.]
Inviolable. Not to be injured or profaned.
Inviolate. Not violated.
Jealous of honor. Earnestly guarding honor.
Just. Conformable to the principles of law or justice.
Justus et tenax propositi [L.]. A just man and one tenacious of his purpose. [Horace, *Odes*, III, iii, 1.]
Loyal. Constant and reliable in the performance of duties.
Nice. Refined in habits or manner.
Open and above board. Dealing fair.
Open-hearted. Disclosing one's thoughts; candid and kind.
Overscrupulous. Scrupulous to excess.
Punctilious. Very nice in regard to etiquette.
Punctual. Exact in respect to the appointed time.
Pure. Free from corruption or moral depravity.
Religious. Given to religion; pious; strict.
Reputable. Having a good reputation; honorable.
Respectable. Deserving respect: having fair excellence.
Right. In accordance with the will of God or the moral law.
Right-minded. Having an honest mind.
Sans peur et sans reproche [F.]. Without fear and without reproach.
Scrupulous. Hesitating to violate conscience.
Square. Rendering justice; just.
Stainless. Without stain or crime.

Roguery. Practise of a rogue; mischievousness.
Shabbiness. Meanness; despicableness.
Sharp practise. Artful dealing.
Shuffle. }
Shuffling. } Changing one's position; prevaricating.
Treachery. Conduct that is treacherous; fairness in appearance, but wicked in character.
Trimming. Double-dealing.
Turpitude. Inherent vileness or baseness.
Unfairness. Want of impartiality. See *Adjectives*.
Venality. State of being venal or purchasable.
Villainy. Depravity; conduct of a villain.

DISHONESTY—*Verbs.*

Be dishonest. To be destitute of integrity or good faith. See *Adjectives*.
Betray. To break faith; to violate promises.
Break one's faith. }
Break one's promise. } To be faithless or dishonest.
Break one's word. }
Degrade oneself. To lower in purity; debase.
Demean oneself. To conduct oneself meanly.
Derogate oneself. To lessen one's value.
Disgrace oneself. To bring shame upon oneself.
Dishonor oneself. To deprive of honor.
Forswear. To swear falsely.
Go over to the enemy. To be a traitor.
Grovel. To creep on the earth; take pleasure in what is low.
Jilt. To be capricious; discard, as a lover.
Live by one's wits. To have no steady means of maintenance.
Lose caste. To lose social position; to be degraded.
Play false. To be dishonest with.
Sail near the wind. On the verge of falsehood.
Seal one's infamy. To be forever disgraced.
Sell oneself. To take bribes.
Shuffle. To go from one side to another; to prevaricate. See TRUTHFULNESS-FALSEHOOD.
Sneak. To act cowardly; to behave meanly.
Stoop. To condescend to meanness.

DISHONESTY—*Adjectives.*

Abject. Sunk to a mean condition; groveling.
Arrant. Very bad; notoriously depraved.
Base. Low in rank or character; mean.
Base-minded. Low in thoughts; ignoble.
Beneath one. Unworthy of.
Blackguard. Suited to a blackguard; low; vile.
Contemptible. Worthy of disdain; despicable.
Corrupt. Of an impure character; depraved.
Crooked. Not straight in character or morals; **dishonest.**
Dark. Concealed; mysterious.
Dead to honor. Debased.
Debased. Lowered in character or purity.
Degraded. Made mean; lowered in moral purity.
Derogatory. Detracting; injurious to one's reputation.
Dirty. Morally filthy; vile.
Disgraceful. Full of disgrace; causing disgrace. See REPUTATION-DISCREDIT.
Dishonest. Wanting honesty; deceptive.
Dishonorable. Bringing dishonor; discreditable.
Disingenuous. Not frank, sincere, or candid.
Disloyal. Lacking loyalty; faithless.
Double-faced. Deceitful.
Double-tongued. Having duplicity of speech.
Faithless. Not observing one's obligations; untrustworthy.
False. Not true or faithful; deceptive.
False-faced. Hypocritical.
False-hearted. False in character or disposition.
Fishy. Doubtful; improbable; foul.
Foul. Offensive to the moral sense; unfair.
Fraudulent. Practising fraud; deceitful. See TRUTHFULNESS-FRAUD.
Groveling. Crawling on the earth; mean; base.
Ignominious. Deserving ignominy or public disgrace.
Indign. Unworthy.
Infamous. Having a bad reputation: having no honor.
Infra dignitatem [L.]. Beneath one's dignity.
Inglorious. Without glory or honor.
Insidious. Lying in wait to do harm; stealthy in doing harm; wily.
Knavish. Like a knave; roguish; dishonest.
Little. Small in dignity; contemptible.
Lost to shame. Utterly depraved.

UPRIGHTNESS—DISHONESTY—*Continued.*

UPRIGHTNESS—Adjectives—*Continued.*

Staunch. Firm and steadfast in principle.
Straightforward. Going in a straight path; frank. See CRAFT-ART-LESSNESS.
Strict. Conforming scrupulously to a principle.
Supramundane. Situated above our world; celestial.
Tender-conscienced. Having a sensitive conscience.
To be depended upon. Honorable.
True. Conformable to fact; steady in respect to principles and friendships.
True as the needle to the north. Upright.
True-blue. Of inflexible principles; loyal.
True-hearted. Of a true and loyal heart.
True to one's colors. Uncompromisingly loyal.
True to the core. Honorable to the heart.
Trusty. Faithful to duty.
Trustworthy. Worthy of trust or confidence.
Unbetrayed. Having no trust or confidence violated.
Unbought. Uncorrupted.
Unbribed. Not corrupted with money or rewards.
Unbroken. Not having lost credit.
Uncorrupt.
Uncorrupted. } Free from bribery.
Undebauched. Not corrupt in morals.
Undefiled. Not polluted or filthy.
Undepraved. Not made worse; uncorrupted.
Unperjured. Not swearing to what one knows is untrue.
Unstained. Not stained; untouched by crime.
Unsullied. Untarnished; unspoilt.
Untainted. Not infected by a physical or moral taint.
Untarnished. Not tarnished; without its purity destroyed.
Unviolated. Not broken; unprofaned.
Unworldly. Not worldly; spiritual.
Upright. Correct in morals or conduct.
Veracious. Disposed to speak the truth from habit. See TRUTH-FULNESS.
Virtuous. Characterized by virtue. See VIRTUE.

UPRIGHTNESS — Adverb.

Honorably. With honor. See *Adjectives.*

UPRIGHTNESS—Phrases.

Ab ulla fraude [L.]. Without fraud.
Bene qui latuit bene vixit [L.]. He who has lived obscure has lived well. [Ovid, *Tristia,* III, iv, 25.]
Bona fide [L.]. In good faith.
Bonne foi [F.]. Good faith.
Cassis tutissima virtus [L.]. The safest helmet is virtue.
Conscia mens recti [L.]. A mind conscious of rectitude. [Ovid.]
Constantia, basis virtutum [L.]. Constancy is the basis of the virtues.
Foro conscientia [L.]. In the realm of conscience.
Gentilhomme [F.]. Gentleman.
Honesta mors turpi vitâ potior [L.]. Honorable death is better than base life. [Tacitus, *Agricola,* xxxiii, 25.]
Honor bright. In good faith.
Loyal en tout [F.]. Loyal in everything.
Loyauté me oblige [F.]. Loyalty binds me.
On the square. With exactness and fairness.
Parole d'honneur [F.]. Word of honor.
Probitas laudatur et alget [L.]. Integrity is praised and freezes. [Juvenal, I, 74.]
With clean hands. Guiltless.

DISHONESTY—Adjectives—*Continued*

Low-minded. Entertaining low sentiments and base motiv
Low-thoughted. Having low thoughts.
Machiavellian. Relating to Machiavelli; unscrupulous.
Mean. Ignoble in character; without honor.
Mongrel. Of mixed breed: ofttimes used as an epithet of contempt.
Of bad faith.
One-sided. Having only one side; partial; unfair.
Paltry. Trifling; contemptible.
Perfidious. Violating one's obligations; faithless.
Perjured. Having sworn falsely.
Pettifogging. Conducting in a mean and tricky manner.
Rascally. Worthy of a rascal; base.
Recreant. Apostate; crying for mercy; craven.
Scabby. Full of scabs; mean; vile.
Scrubby. Stunted; small and mean.
Scurvy. Covered with scabs; contemptible.
Shabby. Ill-dressed; despicable.
Slippery. Evading one; tricky.
Sneaking. Acting with cowardice; cringing.
Time-serving. Complying to the demands of the times without regard to principle.
Tortuous. Having twists; hence, erratic.
Treacherous. Having good appearance, but bad by nature.
Trothless. Without good faith; not keeping a pledge.
Trustless. Not worthy of trust; faithless.
Truthless. Faithless.
Unbecoming.
Unbefitting. } Not befitting; not suitable.
Unbeseeming. Not becoming or proper.
Unchivalric. Unbecoming an ideal knight; ungallant.
Unconscientious. Not governed by conscience.
Undignified. Without dignity.
Unfair. Marked by dishonesty or fraud.
Unfaithful. Manifesting absence of faith.
Ungentlemanlike.
Ungentlemanly. } Unbefitting the manner of a gentleman.
Unhandsome. Ungenerous; ungracious.
Unknightly.
Unmanly. } Without gallant or noble qualities.
Unscrupulous. Without any scruple or caution.
Untrustworthy. That cannot be depended on.
Venal. Capable of being bribed.
Vile. Low; mean.
Wicked. Evil in principle; sinful.

DISHONESTY—Adverbs, etc.

By crooked paths. Deceitfully.
Dishonestly. In a dishonest manner.
Like a thief in the night. Secretly; treacherously.
Mala fides [L.]. In bad faith.

DISHONESTY—Interjection.

O tempora! O mores! [L.]. O times! O customs! [Cicero, *Catiline,* i, 1.]

DISHONESTY—Phrases.

Male parta, male dilabuntur [L.]. Gains ill-gotten are ill made away with. [Nævius.]
Venalis populus, venalis curia patrum [L.]. Venal the people, venal the council of the fathers.

UPRIGHTNESS—ROGUE.

ROGUE.

Arch-traitor. A chief traitor.
Bad man. One who is opposed to all that is good and acts accordingly. See GOOD MAN-BAD MAN.
Betrayer. One who betrays.
Blackguard. A vile, abusive person. See GOOD MAN-BAD MAN.
Catiline. A conspirator: from Catiline, the Roman conspirator made famous by Cicero.
Conspirator. One who secretly plots a crime.
Jerry Sneak. A watch-snatcher.
Judas. A friend who betrays. from Judas, betrayer of Christ.
Knave. A sly, dishonest fellow.
Lazarillo de Tormes [It.]. A sneak: after a noted one of that name.
Mischief-maker. One who stirs up trouble.
Rascal. A tricky, contemptible person.
Recreant. A faithless person.

Renegade. One who deserts a party or faith. See BIGOTRY-APOSTASY.
Reptile. A sneaking or morally repulsive person.
Rogue. A man of no principle or honesty.
Scapin. An intriguing person: after a scheming valet of that name in comedy.
Serpent. An insinuating, artful person.
Snake in the grass. A treacherous man who hides his evil designs.
Sneak. A crafty coward.
Sycophant. A base flatterer. See PRESUMPTION-OBSEQUIOUSNESS.
Telltale. One who tattles.
Traitor. One who betrays a trust.
Trimmer. One who deserts principle for gain.
Truant. One who shirks a duty.
Wolf in sheep's clothing. A treacherous man who puts on an appearance of good.

up-rise'. Uprising. ASCENT-DESCENT.

up-ris'-ing. Insurrection. INSUBORDINATION-OBEDIENCE.

up'-roar''. Tumult. LOUDNESS-FAINTNESS, REGULARITY-IRREGULARITY, TURBULENCE-CALMNESS.

up-roar'-i-ous. Excitable. EXCITABILITY-INEXCITABILITY, LOUDNESS-FAINTNESS, TURBULENCE-CALMNESS.

up-root'. Eradicate. INJECTION-EJECTION.

ups and downs of life. Successes and reverses. OCCURRENCE-DESTINY, WELFARE-MISFORTUNE.

up-set'. Arouse; destroy; disconcert. CREATION-DESTRUCTION, ELEVATION-DEPRESSION, EXCITATION, REPUTATION-DISCREDIT, REVERSAL, SUCCESS-FAILURE.

up-shot'. Result. CAUSE-EFFECT, COMPLETION-NONCOMPLETION, DECISION-MISJUDGMENT.

up-side' down. Topsy-turvy. REGULARITY-IRREGULARITY, REVERSAL.

up'-stairs''. An upper story of a house. HEIGHT-LOWNESS.

up'-start''. Parvenu. GENTILITY-COMMONALTY, WELFARE-MISFORTUNE.

up-turn'. Upset. REVERSAL, TOP-BOTTOM.

up'-wards. Toward a higher place; more. HEIGHT-LOWNESS, PLURALITY-FRACTION, SUPREMACY-SUBORDINACY.

u-ram'-ic. Pertaining to the heavens. UNIVERSE.

u''-ra-nog'-ra-phy. Astronomy. UNIVERSE.

u-ran'-o-lith. Meteorite. ASTRONOMY.

u''-ra-nol'-o-gy. Astronomy. UNIVERSE.

ur'-ban. Civic. DWELLER-HABITATION.

ur-bane'. Courteous. CITY-COUNTRY, POLITENESS-IMPOLITENESS.

ur-ban'-i-ty. Courteousness. CITY, SOCIABILITY - PRIVACY.

urbis conditæ anno [L.] (ur'-bis con'-di-tî an'-no). In the year when the city was founded; time from which the Romans reckoned time. DURATION-NEVERNESS.

ur'-ce-us. Water-jug. CONTENTS-RECEIVER.

ur'-chin. A mischievous boy. GOOD MAN-BAD MAN, GREATNESS-LITTLENESS, INFANT-VETERAN, JOVE-FIEND.

urge. Impel; beg. HURRY-LEISURE, IMPETUS-REACTION, MOTIVE-CAPRICE, PETITION-EXPOSTULATION, TURBULENCE-CALMNESS.

ur'-gen-cy. Hurry; need; importance. CONSEQUENCE-INSIGNIFICANCE, HURRY-LEISURE, NEED.

ur'-gent. Important; solicitous. CONSEQUENCE-INSIGNIFICANCE, HURRY-LEISURE, NEED, PETITION-EXPOSTULATION.

urn. Vase, used by ancients to hold ashes of the dead. CONTENTS-RECEIVER, LIFE-FUNERAL, OVEN-REFRIGERATOR; **cinerary urn,** LIFE-FUNERAL.

Ur'-sa Ma'-jor. The Great Bear; constellation. ASTRONOMY.

u'-sage. Custom; use. HABIT-DESUETUDE, USE-DISUSE.

u'-sance. Time allowed in certain countries for the payment of bills of exchange drawn on those countries. CREDIT-DEBT.

use. Habit; employ. HABIT-DESUETUDE, PROPERTY, PROVISION-WASTE, USE-DISUSE, USEFULNESS-USELESSNESS; **be of use to,** CHARITABLENESS-MALEVOLENCE; **in use,** USE-DISUSE; **make good use of,** BETTERMENT-DETERIORATION; **use aright,** DUENESS-UNDUENESS; **use one's discretion,** CHOICE-NEUTRALITY, VOLITION-OBLIGATION; **use one's endeavor,** VENTURE; **use up,** USE-DISUSE.

USE—DISUSE.

Adhibition. Application.

Agency. Means of action. See AGENCY.

Appliance. The act of putting to use.

Application. The act or process of bringing into actual use.

Avail. Use for a practical purpose.

Consumption. Use resulting in entire destruction.

Disposal. Assigning to a use.

Disposition. The act of using for a particular purpose.

Employ. Fixed or regular service.

Employment. The act of making use of as an instrument or agent.

Exercise. ⎫
Exercitation. ⎭ A carrying out into use.

Recourse. Use of efforts, labor, or art to a certain purpose.

Resort. The use of something as a means.

Service. The act or quality of being of use.

Usage. The act of using.

Use. The act of employing for the accomplishment of a purpose.

Usefulness. The state of serving for a purpose. See USEFULNESS.

Usufruct. The right of using something belonging to another without wasting its substance.

Utilization. The act of making useful.

Wear. Consumption by use.

USE—Verbs.

Absorb. To use up entirely.

Adhibit. To put to use.

Apply. To use for a particular purpose.

Avail oneself of. To use to one's own advantage.

Betake oneself to. To have recourse to.

Bring into play. To begin to make use of.

Bring to bear upon. To use effectively upon.

Call forth. To bring forth into use.

Call into play. To bring into use.

Consecrate. To set apart solemnly for sacred use.

Consume. To destroy gradually by use.

Convert to use. To turn to use.

Dedicate. To set apart for any use.

Devote. To surrender completely for some use.

Dispose of. To make over for some one's use.

Draw forth. To call into use.

Abstinence. The practise of keeping from using certain things.

Desuetude. The cessation of use. See HABIT-DESUETUDE.

Disuse. Want or neglect of use.

Forbearance. Not using what there is a desire to use.

Relinquishment. A cessation of use without the intention of resuming. See QUEST-ABANDONMENT.

DISUSE—Verbs.

Abstain. To not use at all.

Cast overboard. To throw away.

Cast to the dogs. To throw away contemptuously.

Cast to the winds. To throw away as something of little weight or importance.

Discard. To turn away as undesirable. See ADMISSION-EXPULSION.

Dismantle. To render useless by depriving of essential parts. See USEFULNESS-USELESSNESS.

Dismiss. To put out of some position.

Dispense with. To do without.

Disuse. To cease to use or practise.

Do without. To use not at all.

Forbear. To disuse something for which one has a liking.

Give warning. To give notice of dismissal.

Have done with. To cease intercourse with.

Heave overboard. To get rid of.

Keep back. To hold back from use.

Lay aside. ⎫
Lay by. ⎭ To store up for future use.

Lay on the shelf. To retire ignominiously.

Lay up. To store up for future use.

Lay up in a napkin. To store up to no advantage. [Bible.]

Lay up in ordinary.

Leave off. ⎫
Let alone. ⎭ To desist from.

Lie unemployed. To go without employment.

Make away with. To destroy.

Neglect. To disuse through carelessness or oversight.

Not touch. ⎫
Not use. ⎭ Not to handle or deal with.

Put aside. To store up for future use.

USE—DISUSE—*Continued.*

USE—Verbs—*Continued.*

Employ. To use an instrument or agent.
Enlist into the service. To come into one's employ.
Exercise. To use actively in order to train or develop.
Exert. To put into active use.
Expend. To use for a great purpose.
Fall back upon. To return to the use of.
Handle. To use the hands upon.
Have recourse to. To turn to for use in exigency or trouble.
Lay one's hands on. To make use of.
Make a cat's paw of. To employ as an agent for one's own purpose.
Make a handle of. To make use of a person.
Make a shift with. To use as a last recourse.
Make the best of. ⎫ To use to the best advantage.
Make the most of. ⎭
Make use of. To use as an agent or a means.
Manipulate. To use with the hands.
Mold. To form into a particular shape.
Play. To use without special aim.
Play off. To put in exercise.
Ply. To use with diligence.
Practise. To perform regularly.
Press into the service. To force into use.
Profit by. Gain something useful by.
Put in action. ⎫ To begin to make active use of.
Put in operation. ⎭
Put in practise. To make use of.
Put into requisition. To make the use of necessary.
Put to task. To put to use.
Put to use. To make use of.
Recur to. To betake oneself to.
Render useful. To make useful. See USEFULNESS.
Resort to. To have recourse to.
Set in motion. To put in operation.
Set to work. To put to work.
Swallow up. To occupy.
Take advantage of. To make the best use of.
Take to. To resort to.
Take up with. To be contented to use.
Task. To impose labor upon.
Tax. To subject to severe labor.
Try. To undertake to use.
Turn to account. To use to advantage.
Turn to use. To apply to use.
Use To employ for the accomplishment of a purpose.

DISUSE—Verbs—*Continued.*

Remain unemployed. To continue without employment.
Reserve. To keep back for the present.
Set aside. To put aside for future use.
Shelve. To postpone indefinitely.
Spare. To refrain from using or spending.
Supersede. To take the place of.
Throw aside. To part with. See QUEST-ABANDONMENT.
Throw overboard. To get rid of.
Waive. To relinquish temporarily.

DISUSE—*Adjectives.*

Disused. Not used.
Done with. Finished.
Not required. Unnecessary.
Not used. Not in service.
Unapplied. Not used according to the intention.
Uncalled for. Not required or needed.
Unculled. Not gathered.
Undisposed of. Not distributed or bestowed.
Unemployed. Not used for any purpose.
Unessayed. Unattempted.
Unexercised. Not yet put into use.
Ungathered. Not collected.
Unspent. Not wasted by use.
Untouched. Not meddled with.
Untrodden. Not used by people in walking.

USE—Verbs—*Continued.*

Use up. To consume.
Utilize. To turn to a practical use.
Wear. To consume away by use.
Wield. To use with great effect.
Work. To make use of labor on.
Work up. To use in the process of manufacture.

USE—*Adjectives.*

In use. Made use of at the present time.
Subservient. Adapted for an especial use. See INSTRUMENTALITY.
Used. Made use of.
Useful. Serving a use. See USEFULNESS.
Well-worn. ⎫ Much used.
Well-trodden. ⎭

USE—MISUSE.

MISUSE.

Abuse. Misuse in an unnatural manner.
Desecration. The misuse of sacred things.
Misapplication. The act of devoting to a wrong use.
Misappropriation. Wrongful use.
Misemployment. Misuse for a bad purpose.
Misusage. Ill-treatment.
Misuse. A wrong use.
Profanation. An irreverent use of sacred things.
Prostitution. Misuse for vile or bad purposes.
Waste. Misuse of money in an extravagant manner. See PROVISION-WASTE.

MISUSE—*Verbs*

Abuse. To misuse in an unnatural manner.
Desecrate. To misuse sacred things as common.
Misapply. To devote to a wrong use.
Misappropriate. To use for a wrong purpose.
Misemploy. To misuse for a bad purpose.

Misuse. To put to a wrong use.
Overtask. To require too much labor from.
Overtax. To misuse some one by imposing a severe strain.
Overwork. To misuse by giving too much work to.
Profane. To misuse sacred things in an irreverent manner.
Prostitute. To misuse for vile or bad purposes.
Squander. To misuse money in a profusely extravagant manner. See EXTRAVAGANCE.
Waste. To use money with foolish extravagance.

MISUSE—*Adjectives.*

Misused, etc. Devoted to wrong use. See *Adjectives.*

MISUSE—*Phrases.*

Catch at a straw.
Cut blocks with a razor.
Employ a steam-engine to crack a nut.
Ludere cum sacris [L.]. To sport with things sacred.

---

used up. Wearied. BETTERMENT-DETERIORATION, DESIRE-REPLETION, LIGHTHEARTEDNESS-DEJECTION, WEARINESS-REFRESHMENT.
used to. Accustomed. HABIT-DESUETUDE.
use′-ful. Helpful; beneficial. GOOD-EVIL, HEALTH-SICKNESS, INCLINATION, INSTRUMENTALITY, USE-DISUSE, USEFULNESS-USELESSNESS; **render useful,** USE-DISUSE, USEFULNESS-USELESSNESS.
use′-ful-ness. Utility; benefit. CONSEQUENCE-INSIGNIFICANCE, USE-DISUSE, USEFULNESS-USELESSNESS.

USEFULNESS—USELESSNESS.

Adequacy. The quality of coming up to the point of utility.
Applicability. The quality of being fit to be used for a particular purpose.
Avail. Advantage.
Common weal. The general welfare.

Abusefulness. Lack of usefulness.
Disservice. Injury; harm.
Futility. The quality of producing no valuable result.
Inadequacy. The quality of being too insufficient to be useful. See EXCESS-LACK.

USEFULNESS—USELESSNESS—*Continued*.

Cui bono [L.]. For what good? For whose good? The fundamental inquiry of utilitarians.

Efficacy. Power to produce effects having utility.

Efficiency. The relative amount of utility of anything.

Function. The special phase in which something possesses utility. See BUSINESS.

Help. Utility which one person gives another. See OBSTRUCTION-HELP.

Money's worth. Full degree of utility; exchangeable value.

Productiveness. The quality of possessing utility for producing. See FERTILITY.

Service. Any work resulting in utility for another.

Stead. Considerable utility.

Step in the right direction. A useful action.

Subservience. The state of helping as a subordinate. See INSTRUMENTALITY.

Use. The quality of gratifying human desires.

Usefulness. The quality of serving for a purpose.

Utilitarianism. Devotion to the greatest good of the greatest number.

Utility. Fitness to gratify human desire.

Utilization. The state of being made to serve some practical purpose. See USE.

Value. Utility, power to gratify human desires.

Worth. Quality of anything which renders it useful. See GOODNESS.

USEFULNESS—*Verbs*.

Act a part. To be of some degree of utility. See ACTION.

Answer a purpose. To serve for use.

Answer one's turn. To possess utility for a personal end.

Avail. To be of use for a purpose.

Bear fruit. To possess utility in production. See CREATION.

Benefit. To be useful to.

Bestead. To be of use to.

Be the making of. To be of great use in developing.

Be useful. To be full of use or advantage.

Bring grist to the mill. To bring gain or profit.

Conduce. To tend to be useful. See LIABILITY.

Discharge a function. To perform a duty.

Do a good service. To be of great use to.

Do a service. To be of use to.

Find one's account in. } To find one's gain or profit in.
Find one's advantage in. }

Help. To furnish assistance.

Perform a function. To perform a duty.

Profit. To be of material use.

Reap the benefit of. To get an advantage from. See BETTERMENT.

Remunerate. To repay justly.

Render a good service. To be of great use to another.

Render a service. To be of use to another.

Render useful. To cause to be useful. See USE.

Serve. To be of use for.

Serve a purpose. To be of use for an end.

Serve one's turn. To be of temporary personal use.

Stand one in good stead. To be of considerable advantage for.

Subserve. To serve in an inferior capacity. See INSTRUMENTALITY.

USEFULNESS—*Adjectives*.

Adaptable. Capable of being adjusted to some use.

Adequate. Equal to what is required.

Advantageous. Affording utility. See GOODNESS.

Applicable. Capable of being brought into actual use.

At hand. Available for immediate use.

Available. Capable of being used.

Commodious. Well suited to the purpose for which made.

Conducive. Tending to be useful.

Effective. Producing a decided consequence.

Effectual. Capable of producing an effect.

Efficacious. Possessing the quality of being efficient.

Efficient. Actively operative.

Expedient. Useful in promoting a desired end. See PROPRIETY-IMPROPRIETY.

Gainful. Producing profit.

Good for. Useful for.

Handy. Convenient for use.

Of all work. Adapted for all kinds of work.

Of use. Advantageous.

Proficuous. Proficient or useful.

Profitable. Producing profit.

Prolific. Producing in abundance. See FERTILITY.

Remunerative. Making a proper profit.

Serviceable. That can be used for a purpose.

Subservient. Serving as a subordinate. See INSTRUMENTALITY.

Inanity. The quality of being devoid of sense.

Inaptitude. Unfitness for use.

Inefficacy. Want of power to produce the proper or desired result.

Inefficiency. The quality of being incapable of effective action. See MIGHT-IMPOTENCE.

Ineptitude. The quality of being unfit for use.

Inutility. The quality of being useless.

Labor in vain. Useless labor.

Labor lost.

Labor of Sisyphus. Never-ending useless labor.

Lost labor. } Useless labor.
Lost trouble. }

Mere farce. Something inconsequential.

Nugacity. Trifling talk or behavior.

Sleeveless errand. A useless errand.

Supererogation. Doing more than is called for. See EXCESS.

Tautology. Unnecessary repetition. See REPETITION.

Triviality. The quality of being almost useless. See CONSEQUENCE-INSIGNIFICANCE.

Unfruitfulness. The quality of not producing any results. See CREATION.

Unskilfulness. Lack of skill. See MIGHT-IMPOTENCE.

Unsubservience. The quality of not being subordinately useful.

Uselessness, etc. Incapability of serving any beneficial purpose. See *Adjectives*.

Vanitas vanitatum [L.]. Vanity of vanities. [Bible.]

Vanity. The quality of being unproductive of any useful results.

Wild-goose chase. The pursuit of something impossible to attain.

Work of Penelope. Never-ending useless labor; she raveled by night what she wove by day. [Homer, *Odyssey*.]

Worthlessness. The quality of having no utility or value.

USELESSNESS—*Denotations*.

Blunt tool. A tool whose edge has become dull.

Broken meat. Meat left over a meal.

Button-top. A knob like a button on the end of a foil that makes it useless as a weapon.

Caput mortuum [L.]. A deadhead; worthless residue.

Cast-off clothes. Clothes no longer wanted or used.

Débris. Accumulated fragments; ruins.

Dregs. Worthless residuum. See CLEANNESS-FILTHINESS.

Dust-hole. A place where dust collects.

Fruges consumere natus [L.]. Born merely to consume the fruits of the earth. See ACTIVITY-INDOLENCE. [Horace, *Epistles*, I, ii, 27.]

Leavings. Things left.

Litter. Waste materials scattered about.

Lumber. Discarded household goods.

Odds and ends. Fragments, remnants, and scraps.

Offscourings. Rejected matter.

Orts. Leavings of little value.

Rags. Worn or shabby clothing.

Refuse. Anything discarded as worthless.

Rubbish. Waste, refuse, or rejected matter.

Rubbish-heap. A collection of rejected or refuse matter.

Rubble. Rough irregular pieces of broken stone.

Scourings. Material rubbed off in rubbing or scouring.

Shoddy. Fiber remanufactured from shredded rags.

Stubble. The stubs of grain-stalks after the grain has been cut.

Sweepings. A collection of particles swept up.

Tares. Weeds that grow among wheat.

Trash. Worthless or waste matter of any kind.

Waste. Something rejected or not needed.

Waste paper. Paper that cannot be used.

Weeds. Plants that are injurious to crops.

USELESSNESS—*Verbs*.

Battre l'eau avec un baton [F.]. To beat the water with a stick; do useless work.

Bay the moon. To bark at the moon; waste breath in idle vaunting. "I had rather be a dog and bay the moon, than such a Roman." [Shakespeare, *Julius Cæsar*, IV, iii.]

Beat the air. To make useless motions.

Be useless, etc. To be of no service. See *Adjectives*.

Carry coals to Newcastle. To render a useless service by giving something superfluous. See REDUNDANCY.

Cast pearls before swine. To waste. [*Matthew* vii, 6.]

Clip the wings. To deprive of power of service.

Cripple. To render useless by maiming.

Disable. To render useless by making incapable of service.

Dismantle. To render useless by stripping of equipments.

Dismast. To deprive of masts.

Dismount. To throw down, as a rider from a horse, or a cannon from its mounting.

USEFULNESS—USELESSNESS—*Continued.*

USEFULNESS—Adjectives—*Continued.*

Subsidiary. Giving aid in an inferior capacity. See Obstruction-Help.
Tangible. Capable of being possessed or realized.
Useful. Serving a use or purpose.
Valuable. Possessing qualities that are useful.
Worth one's salt. Of some service or advantage.

Usefulness—*Adverbs, etc.*

Pro bono publico [L.]. For the public good.
Usefully, etc. With advantage.

USELESSNESS—Adjectives—*Continued from Column 2*

Inoperative. Not acting so as to produce an effect.
Inservient. } Useless.
Inutile. }
Leading to no end. Without any aim.
Not worth a straw. } Entirely useless.
Not worth having. }
Not worth powder and shot. Not worth an effort.
Obsolete. Gone out of general use.
Of no avail. Useless. See Usefulness.
Of no earthly use. Entirely worthless.
Past work. Useless from exertion in the past. See Deterioration.
Priceless. Useless because of great price.
Profitless. Void of gain or advantage.
Stale flat, and unprofitable. [*Hamlet*, I, iii.]
Subservient. Useful in an inferior capacity.
Superfluous. More than is useful. See Excess.
Thrown away. Of too little value to have been kept. See Provision-Waste.
Unavailing. Not having the desired effect.
Uncalled for. Not required or needed.
Unexceeded. Not surpassed.
Unnecessary. Not required under the circumstances.
Unproductive. Of no use in bringing forth. See Fertility-Sterility.
Unprofitable. Producing no improvement or advantage.
Unsalable. Not capable of being sold.
Unserviceable. Not capable of being put to service.
Unservient. Useless.
Unsubservient. Not of use in an inferior capacity.
Vain. Having no useful results.
Valueless. Of so little use as to have no value.
Worthless. Without any value.

Uselessness—*Adverbs, etc.*

To little or no purpose.)
To little purpose. } Uselessly.
To no purpose.)
Uselessly, etc. Being of no use. See *Adjectives.*

Uselessness—*Phrases.*

Actum ne agas [L.]. Do not do what is done. [Terence.]
Chercher une aiguille dans une botte de foin [F.]. To look for a needle in a haystack.
Cui bono [L.]. Of what good; for whose good.
Tanto buon che val niente [It.]. So good as to be worth nothing.
What's the good.

USELESSNESS—Verbs—*Continued.*

Disqualify. To render useless by depriving of qualifications.
Donner un coup d'epee dans l'eau [F.]. To strike the water with a sword; to perform a useless action.
Drop a bucket into an empty well. To seek where there is no chance of finding.
Fail. To prove inadequate. See Success-Failure.
Fish in the air. To attempt a useless task.
Go a begging. To be superfluous. See Excess.
Hold a farthing candle to the sun. To enter into a useless competition. "How commentators each dark passage shun and hold their farthing candle to the sun." [Young, *Love of Fame.* vii, 97.]
Kick against the pricks. To make useless opposition. [Bible.]
Labor in vain. To perform useless work.
Lame. To disable in a limb. See Betterment-Deterioration.
Lash the waves. To do useless work.
Lock the stable door when the steed is stolen. To take precautions too late. See Opportuneness-Unsuitableness.
Milk the ram. To attempt a useless task.
Preach to the winds. To speak in vain.
Put out of gear. To render useless by putting out of working condition.
Render useless. To make incapable of use.
Roll the stone of Sisyphus. To be engaged in a never-ending useless task.
Se battre contre des moulins [F.]. To fight against windmills; to attempt the impossible. [*Don Quixote.*]
Seek after impossibilities. To seek what cannot be found.
Sow the sand. To devote one's energies uselessly, as Ulysses did.
Speak to the winds. To speak with no possibility of influencing any one.
Spike guns. To render guns useless by stopping their vents.
Strive after impossibilities. To make an effort for what cannot be attained.
Unrig. To render useless by removing the rigging.
Use vain efforts. Make useless attempts.
Wash a blackamoor white. To attempt the impossible.
Whistle jigs to a mile-stone. To make an idle and useless attempt.

Uselessness—*Adjectives.*

Abortive. Brought forth prematurely. See Preparation-Non-preparation.
Bootless. Of no advantage or use.
Dear at any price. Of little value or use.
Effete. Worn out and incapable of further use.
Empty. Without force or use.
Fit for the dust-hole. Useless enough to be thrown away.
Fruitless. Unproductive of good results.
Futile. Of no avail.
Gainless. Producing no profit.
Good for nothing. Of absolutely no use.
Hors de combat [F.]. Unfit for further use.
Ill-spent. Spent to no advantage.
Inadequate. Not sufficient for use.
Inane. Wanting in understanding.
Incompetent. Unable to do what is required.
Ineffectual. Not productive of effect.
Inefficacious. Not capable of producing the desired or proper effect.
Inefficient. Not capable of effective action.
Inept Not suitable for a purpose.

(Continued on Column 1.)

---

use'-less. Worthless. Sagacity-Incapacity, Usefulness-Uselessness.
use'-less-ness. Inutility. Usefulness-Uselessness.
use'-less-ly. In vain. Usefulness-Uselessness.
u'-ser. One who uses. **Right of user,** Property.
ush'-er. Servant; one who conducts persons to their seats; under-teacher. Admission-Expulsion, Chief-Underling, Instructor-Pupil, Politeness-Impoliteness; **usher in,** Beginning-End, Leading-Following, Precedence-Succession, Prophecy; **usher into the world,** Creation-Destruction.
usque ad nauseam [L.] (us'-qui ad nau-'shi-am). To the point of very nauseation. Desire-Distaste, Entertainment-Weariness.
us''-tu-la'-tion. Drying. Heating-Cooling.

u'-su-al. Customary. Conventionality-Unconventionality, Habit-Desuetude.
u'-su-fruct. Use. Use-Disuse.
u'-su-rer. Money-lender who charges an illegal rate. Credit-Debt, Dealer, Extravagance-Avarice, Loan-Borrowing.
u-su'-ri-ous. Practising usury. Extravagance-Avarice.
u-surp'. Seize illegally. Dueness-Undueness, Harshness-Mildness, Taking-Restitution; **usurp authority,** Rule-License.
u''-sur-pa'-tion. Forcible seizure of kingly power. Dueness-Undueness, Harshness-Mildness, Presumption-Obsequiousness, Rule-License.
u-surped'. Seized. Dueness-Undueness.

u-surp′-er. An impostor. DUENESS-UNDUENESS

u′-su-ry. Exorbitant interest. CREDIT-DEBT.

u-ten′-sil. A useful article. CONTENTS-RECEIVER, IN-STRUMENT.

uti possidetis [L.] (yu′-tɑi pos-sid-ĭ′-tis). Right of pos-session. HOLDING-EXEMPTION, KEEPING-RELIN-QUISHMENT, MUTATION-PERMANENCE.

u-til″-i-ta′-ri-an. Pertaining to utilitarianism. HUMANI-TARIANISM-MISANTHROPY.

u-til″-i-ta′-ri-an-ism. Usefulness. HUMANITARIANISM-MISANTHROPY.

u-til′-i-ty. Usefulness. GOOD-EVIL, PROPRIETY-IMPRO-PRIETY, USEFULNESS-USELESSNESS; **general utility,** ACTING.

u″-til-i-za′-tion. Using. USE-DISUSE, USEFULNESS-USELESSNESS.

u′-til-ize. Make use of. USE-DISUSE.

ut′-most. Of the highest degree. SUPREMACY-SUBORDI-NACY; **deserted in one's utmost need,** AFFLUENCE-PENURY; **do one's utmost,** TOIL-RELAXATION; **in one's utmost need,** WELFARE-MISFORTUNE; **utmost height,** TOP-BOTTOM.

U-to′-pi-a. An imaginary island having a perfect social and political system: described by Sir Thomas More. FANCY, SANGUINENESS-HOPELESSNESS.

U-to′-pi-an. Fanciful. FANCY, SANGUINENESS-HOPE-LESSNESS.

U-to′-pi-an-ism. Quality of being visionary. FANCY.

U-to′-pist. A dreamer. SANGUINENESS-HOPELESSNESS.

u′-tri-cle. Sac-like cavity found in the labyrinth of the internal ear. CONTENTS-RECEIVER.

ut′-ter. Extreme; issue; speak. EXPOSURE-HIDING-PLACE, GATHERING-SCATTERING, MAGNITUDE-SMALL-NESS, MONEY, PUBLICITY, TALKATIVENESS-INARTICU-LATENESS, VOCALIZATION-MUTENESS.

ut′-ter-ance. Expression. VOCALIZATION-MUTENESS.

ut′-ter-ly. Completely. ENTIRETY-DEFICIENCY.

ut′-ter-most. Farthest. MAGNITUDE-SMALLNESS; **to the uttermost parts of the earth,** EXTENSION-DIS-TRICT, REMOTENESS-NEARNESS.

ux-o′-ri-ous. Extravagantly devoted to one's wife, or to wives, like that "uxorious king," Solomon. [Milton, *Paradise Lost,* i, 444.] LOVE-HATE.

V

va'-can-cy. Emptiness. Excess-Lack, Mind-Imbecility, Presence-Absence.

va'-cant. Empty; stupid; void. Excess-Lack, Meaning-Jargon, Presence-Absence, Reflection-Vacancy, Sagacity-Incapacity, Substance-Nullity; **vacant hour,** Hurry-Leisure; **vacant mind,** Sagacity-Incapacity.

va'-cate. Displace. Arrival-Departure, Commission-Retirement, Establishment-Removal, Presence-Absence.

va-ca'-tion. Repose. Toil-Relaxation.

vac'-ci-nate. To inoculate with virus of cowpox. Remedy-Bane.

vac'-cine. Virus of cowpox. Fauna-Flora.

vache [F.] (vash). A milch cow. Contents-Receiver.

vac'-il-late. Be irresolute. Determination-Vacillation, Mutability-Stability, Vibration.

vac'-il-la''-ting. Wavering. Determination-Vacillation.

vac''-il-la'-tion. Unsteadiness. Bigotry-Apostasy, Certainty-Doubt, Mutability-Stability, Vibration.

vac'-u-ate. To empty. Arrival-Departure.

va-cu'-i-ty. Emptiness. Presence-Absence.

vac'-u-ous. Empty. Presence-Absence, Substance-Nullity.

vac'-u-um. Emptiness. Presence-Absence.

vade in pace [L.] (vē'-dî in pê'sî). Depart in peace. Release-Restraint.

vade mecum [L.] (vê'-dî mî'-cum). Go with me; guidebook. Enlightenment-Secrecy, School.

va'-di-um. Property pledged as security. Security.

væ victis [L.] (vî vic'-tis). Woe to the vanquished. Charitableness-Menace, Fighting-Conciliation.

vag'-a-bond, Wanderer; rogue. Gentility-Commonalty, Good Man-Bad Man, Wayfarer-Seafarer.

vag'-a-bond''-age. Worthlessness. Traveling-Navigation.

vag'-a-bond''-ism. Vagabondage. Traveling-Navigation.

va-ga'-ry. Caprice. Adage-Nonsense, Entertainment-Weariness, Fancy, Persistence-Whim.

va-gi'-tus. First cry of new-born infant. Infant-Veteran, Cry-Ululation.

va'-gran-cy. The state of a vagrant. Aim-Aberration, Traveling-Navigation.

va'-grant. Vagabond; wandering. Aim-Aberration, Mutability-Stability, Traveling-Navigation, Wayfarer-Seafarer.

vague. Uncertain; obscure. Certainty-Doubt, Clearness-Obscurity, Perspicuity-Obscurity, Ratiocination-Instinct; **vague suggestion,** Hypothesis.

vague'-ness. The state or quality of being vague. Certainty-Doubt, Meaning-Jargon, Perspicuity-Obscurity.

vail. Veil; donation; reward. Environment-Interposition, Exculpation-Punition, Giving-Receiving.

vain. Showy; worthless. Conceit-Diffidence, Entity-Nonentity, Reputation-Discredit, Unconcern Usefulness-Uselessness; **labor in vain,** Success-Failure, Transcursion-Shortcoming, Usefulness-Uselessness; **take a name in vain,** Politeness-Impoliteness; **use vain efforts,** Usefulness-Uselessness; **vain attempt,** Success-Failure; **vain expectations,** Expectation-Disappointment.

vain-glo'-ri-ous. Boastful. Bragging, Conceit-Diffidence, Selfrespect-Humbleness.

vain-glo'-ry. Empty pride. Conceit-Diffidence, Selfrespect-Humbleness.

vain'-ly. With vanity. Selfrespect-Humbleness.

vai'-vode. A liege prince. Chief-Underling.

va'-kass. Vestment used in the Armenian Church. Vestments.

va-keel'. An Oriental commissioner Chief-Underling.

vak'-ka. Canoe. Conveyance-Vessel.

val'-ance. Damask. Border.

vale. Valley. Convexity-Concavity; **vale of years,** Infancy-Age.

valeat quantum [L.] (vê'-li-at quan'-tum). What it is worth. Evidence-Counterevidence.

valeat quantum valere potest [L.] (vê'-li-at quan'-tum va-li'-rî po'-test). Let it pass for what it is worth. Differentiation-Indiscrimination.

val''-e-dic'-tion. Farewell. Arrival-Departure, Politeness-Impoliteness.

val''-e-dic'-to-ry. Bidding farewell. Arrival-Departure.

val'-en-tine. A lover or love-token on St. Valentine's day, February 14. Blandishment.

val'-et. Body-servant. Chief-Underling.

valet anchora virtus [L.] (vê'-let an'-ko-ra vir'-tus). Virtue an effectual anchor. Refuge-Pitfall.

valet de chambre [F.] (va-lê' de shan·br'). Body-servant. Chief-Underling.

valet de place [F.] (va-lê' de plas). Courier. Enlightenment-Secrecy, Interpreter.

valete et plaudite [L.] (va-li'-tî et plau'-di-tî). Farewell and applaud. Approval-Disapproval.

val''-e-tu''-di-na'-ri-an. Invalid. Health-Sickness, Healthiness-Unhealthiness.

val''-e-tu''-di-na'-ri-an-ism. Infirmity. Health-Sickness.

val''-e-tu'-di-na-ry. An infirm person. Healthiness-Unhealthiness.

Val-hal'-la. Hall of the slain. Heaven-Hell.

val'-iant. Brave. Bravery-Cowardice.

val'-id. Sound. Enough, Might-Impotence, Mutability-Stability, Strength-Weakness, Truth-Error; **valid reasoning,** Ratiocination-Instinct.

val'-id-ate. To ratify. Might-Impotence, Strength-Weakness.

va-lid'-i-ty. Strength. Might-Impotence.

va-lise'. Traveling-bag. Contents-Receiver.

val'-ley. Depression. Convexity-Concavity; **valley of the shadow of death,** Life-Death.

val'-lum. Rampart. Attack-Defense.

valoir, se faire [F.] (va-lwar', se fêr). To maintain dignity. Bragging.

val'-or. Courage. Bravery-Cowardice.

valorem, ad [L.] (va-lo'-rem, ad). According to value. Price-Discount.

val'-or-ous. Brave. Bravery-Cowardice.

val'-u-a-ble. Worth. GOODNESS-BADNESS, USEFUL-NESS-USELESSNESS.

val"-u-a'-tion. Estimated worth. DECISION-MIS-JUDGMENT, MENSURATION, PRICE-DISCOUNT.

val'-ue. Worth; import. APPROVAL-DISAPPROVAL, CONSEQUENCE-INSIGNIFICANCE, DISCOVERY, GOODNESS - BADNESS, MENSURATION, PRICE - DISCOUNT, USEFULNESS - USELESSNESS; **of priceless value,** COSTLINESS - CHEAPNESS; **set a value upon,** MENSURATION, OVERVALUATION - UNDERVALUATION; **value received,** OUTLAY-INCOME.

val'-ues. Measures of worth. VALUES.

VALUES.

Abas. A Persian silver coin, worth 4½ cents.
Argentine. A gold coin of Argentina, worth $4.85.
As. A Roman copper coin, worth 1 cent.
Bolivar. A silver coin of Venezuela, worth 97 cents.
Cash. A Chinese coin, worth 1-11 of a cent.
Centavo. A Mexican nickel-copper coin, worth 1 cent.
Commassee. An Arabian coin, worth 1¼ cents.
Condor. A coin of Chili and Ecuador, worth about nine dollars.
Copeck. A Russian coin, worth 2-3 of a cent.
Crown. An Austrian coin, worth 24¼ cents; an English coin, worth $1.21; a Portuguese coin, worth $10.78
Cuarto. A Spanish coin, worth ¾ of a cent.
Decime. A French coin, worth 2 cents.
Decimo. A coin of Spanish-speaking countries, worth about 4 cents.
Denarius. An ancient Roman coin, worth 10 asses.
Derham. A coin of Morocco, worth 7½ cents.
Dime. A coin of the United States, worth 10 cents.
Dinar. A Servian coin, worth 19½ cents.
Dinero. A Peruvian coin, worth 9 7-10 cents.
Diwani. An Arabic coin, worth 1 cent.
Dollar. A coin of the United States, worth 100 cents.
Dubbelt-je. A Dutch coin, worth 4 cents.
Ducat. An Austrian coin, worth $2.28.
Eagle. A coin of the United States, worth $10.00.
Farthing. An English coin, worth ½ a cent.
Florin. An Austrian coin, worth 48½ cents; an English coin, worth 48½ cents; a Bavarian coin, worth 41 cents; a Dutch coin, worth 40 cents.
Franc. A French coin, worth 19½ cents.
Groschen. A German coin, worth 2⅓ cents.
Guinea. An English coin, worth $5.09¼.
Heller. An Austrian coin, worth ¼ of a cent; a German coin, worth ¼ of a cent.
Hidalgo. A Mexican coin, worth $10.00.
Krone. An Austrian coin, worth 27 cents.
Lira. An Italian coin, worth 19½ cents.
Marengo. An Italian coin of 20 francs.
Nickel. A coin of the United States, of 5 cents value.
Peseta. A South-American coin, worth 19½ cents.
Pfennig. A German coin, worth ¼ of a cent.
Rupee. An Indian coin, worth 77 cents.
Sen. A Japanese coin, worth 1 cent.
Sestertium. A Roman coin, worth $42.04.
Sestertius. An old Roman coin, worth 4½ cents.
Shekel. A Hebrew coin, worth 60 cents.
Soldo. An Italian coin, worth 1 cent.
S vereign. An English gold coin, worth $4.85½.
Tael. A Chinese coin, worth $1.40.
Thaler. A German coin, worth 71½ cents.

val'-ue-less. Worthless. USEFULNESS-USELESSNESS.
valve. Opening; covering. PERFORATOR-STOPPER, WATERCOURSE-AIRPIPE; **safety-valve,** ESCAPE, REFUGE-PITFALL, SECURITY-INSECURITY.
vam'-brace. Armor for forearm. ATTACK-DEFENSE.
vamp. Repair; improvise. MUTATION-PERMANENCE, RENOVATION-RELAPSE; **vamp up,** BETTERMENT-DE-

TERIORATION, PREPARATION-NONPREPARATION, RENOVATION-RELAPSE.
vam'-pire. Outcast; extortioner. BENEFACTOR-EVILDOER, JOVE-FIEND.
vam'-pir-ism. Extortion; belief. DEVOTION-MAGIC, TAKING-RESTITUTION.
van. Vehicle; front. ANTERIORITY-POSTERIORITY, BEGINNING-END, CONVEYANCE-VESSEL, PUSH-PULL; **in the van,** ANTERIORITY-POSTERIORITY, LEADING-FOLLOWING.
van'-cou"-ri-er. A forerunner. PREDECESSOR-CONTINUATION.
van'-dal. Rude; plunderer. BENEFACTOR-EVILDOER, GENTILITY-COMMONALTY, TASTE-VULGARITY.
van'-dal-ism. Wanton destruction. TASTE-VULGARITY.
Van-dyke'. Beard; collar. INDENTATION.
Van'-dyke' brown. Color. GRAY-BROWN.
vane. Weather-cock. RIVER-WIND, SIGN.
van'-foss". Ditch. ATTACK-DEFENSE.
van'-guard. Advance-guard. ANTERIORITY-POSTERIORITY.
va-nil'-la. Kind of plant. NUTRIMENT-EXCRETION.
van'-ish. Disappear. LASTINGNESS-TRANSIENTNESS, MUTABILITY-STABILITY, SUBSTANCE-NULLITY.
van'-ish-ing-point". Intersection. GREATNESS-LITTLENESS, MAGNITUDE-SMALLNESS.
van'-i-ty. Futility; conceit. CONCEIT-DIFFIDENCE, CONSEQUENCE-INSIGNIFICANCE, FAITH-MISGIVING, OVERVALUATION-UNDERVALUATION, USEFULNESS-USELESSNESS.
Van'-i-ty Fair. Fashion. SOCIETY-LUDICROUSNESS.
van'-quish. Conquer. SUCCESS-FAILURE.
van'-tage-ground". Position. DOMINANCE-IMPOTENCE, HEIGHT-LOWNESS, MIGHT-IMPOTENCE, SUPREMACY-SUBORDINACY.
vap'-id. Insipid. SAVOR-TASTELESSNESS; **vapid style,** FORCE-WEAKNESS.
va'-por. Mist; swagger; fantasy. BRAGGING, FANCY, LIQUID-GAS, PRESUMPTION-OBSEQUIOUSNESS, VISCIDITY-FOAM; **vapor bath,** OVEN-REFRIGERATOR.
va'-por-er. Braggart. BRAWLER.
vap'-or-er. One who or that which vapors, or converts into vapor. LIQUEFACTION-VOLATILIZATION.
va'-por-ing. Boasting. BRAGGING, PRESUMPTION-OBSEQUIOUSNESS.
vap'-o-ri"-za-ble. Capable of being converted into vapor. LIQUEFACTION-VOLATILIZATION.
va"-por-i-za'-tion. State of being vaporized. LIQUEFACTION-VOLATILIZATION.
vap'-o-rize. To convert into vapor. LIQUEFACTION-VOLATILIZATION.
va'-por-ous. Misty. DIAPHANEITY-OPAQUENESS, LIQUID-GAS, VISCIDITY-FOAM.
va'-por-ous-ness. The state or quality of being vaporous. LIQUEFACTION-VOLATILIZATION.
va'-pors. Depression. LIGHTHEARTEDNESS-DEJECTION.
va'-ri-a-ble. Changeable; fickle. MUTABILITY-STABILITY; **variable star,** ASTRONOMY.
va'-ri-ance. Conflict; change. HARMONY-DISCORD, VARIANCE-ACCORD, VARIATION; **at variance,** AMITY-HOSTILITY, HARMONY-DISCORD, VARIANCE-ACCORD; **at variance with,** ANTAGONISM-CONCURRENCE, ASSENT-DISSENT, HARMONY-ACCORD.

VARIANCE—ACCORD

Altercation. Dispute carried on with heat and anger.
Brabble. A broil; a wrangle.
Brawl. A noisy quarrel.
Breach. A violation of the law.
Breach of the peace. Disturbance of the public peace.

Accord. Agreement; harmony of opinion.
Agreement. The act of being in accord. See HARMONY.
Alliance. A formal treaty or agreement.
Amity. Friendly or peaceful relations. See AMITY.
Bonds of harmony. Peaceful relations.

VARIANCE—ACCORD—*Continued.*

Breeze. A disturbance or quarrel.
Broil. A noisy disturbance.
Brouillerie [F.]. Strife; contention.
Casus belli [L.]. That which causes war.
Clash. Opposition of views and opinions; beginning of armed strife.
Commotion. A public disturbance. See AGITATION.
Contentiousness. Quarrelsomeness.
Cross-purposes. Opposition without intention.
Difference. Variation of opinion.
Disaccord. Disagreement.
Disagreement. Difference of opinion or sentiment; a falling out. See HARMONY-DISCORD.
Discord. Dissension; opposition.
Disputant. One who disputes.
Dispute. Difference of opinion.
Disrupture. A breaking off of friendly relations.
Dissension. Discord; strife.
Dissidence. Disagreement; withdrawal from the established religion.
Dissonance. A mingling of inharmonious sounds.
Disturbance. An interruption of a state of peace or quiet. See REGULARITY-IRREGULARITY.
Disunion. Separation; dissension.
Division. Difference in opinion or feeling.
Embranglement. Confusion; entanglement.
Embroilment. Implication in some strife.
Enmity. Hostile or unfriendly disposition. See AMITY-HOSTILITY.
Faction. Tumult; discord.
Feud. Hate between parties, usually leading to bloodshed.
Fracas. A noisy quarrel; an uproar.
Hate. Strong aversion with a desire that evil should befall a person. See LOVE-HATE.
Hubbub. Confusion of voices.
Imbroglio. A serious misunderstanding.
Jangle. A quarrel; a word-battle.
Jar. A crash; a dissension.
Jarring. A clashing of interests.
Jostling. A crowding or bumping together.
Litigation. A contest at law.
Misunderstanding. Disagreement; difference of opinion.
Odds. Quarrel; strife.
Open rupture. Open hostility or war.
Outbreak. The beginning of armed strife.
Quarrel. Strife; contention.
Question at issue. A question causing difference of opinion. See INVESTIGATION.
Racket. A confused, clattering noise.
Riot. Disturbance of the public peace by an unlawful assembly.
Rixation. A brawl; quarrel.
Row. A turbulent disturbance.
Rumpus. A great confusion.
Rupture. Breach of peace or concord between individuals; open hostility between nations.
Schism. Breach of unity among people of the same religious faith. See ASSENT-DISSENT.
Scrimmage. A general confusion.
Shock. An encountering with violence.
Split. A breach or separation, as in a political party.
Squabble. A quarrel; a brawl.
Squall. A cry of fright or anger.
Strife. Violent contention; fight. See STRIFE.
Tiff. A slight altercation or contention.
Tracasserie [F.]. Difficulty; shuffle.
Variance. Difference.
Warfare. Contest carried on by enemies.
Words. Verbal contention.
Wrangling. A noisy quarrel.

VARIANCE—*Associated Nouns.*

Apple of discord. A subject of contention and envy; a golden apple inscribed "Let the most beautiful have me," thrown among the guests at the marriage of Peleus and Thetis, and claimed by Juno, Minerva, and Venus; whence came the Trojan war, Homer, and "the glory that was Greece and the grandeur that was Rome." [Poe. *To Helen.*]
Battle-ground. A place where a battle is fought.
Bear-garden. Any place where riotous conduct is common.
Bone of contention. A subject of contention or dispute.
Bone to pick. A dispute to be settled.
Brand of discord. Anything that stirs up strife.
Cat-and-dog life. A quarrelsome, contentious life.
Cross questions and crooked answers. Contention.

Conciliation. The act of winning the friendship of.
Concord. Union; cordial feeling.
Entente cordiale [F.]. Cordial understanding.
Good understanding. Kindly feeling toward one another.
Happy family. Persons in entire harmony or agreement.
Harmony. Agreement; friendship.
League. A close connection or union. See ASSOCIATION.
Peace. A state of reconciliation after strife or enmity. See STRIFE-PEACE.
Peacemaker. One who effects a reconciliation between unfriendly parties.
Rapprochement [F.]. Reconciliation.
Response. Sympathy; concord.
Reunion. Renewed union or harmony.
Sympathy. The quality of being affected by the state or condition of another; fellow-feeling. See LOVE.
Symphony. Concord; harmony; agreeable blending of any kind.
Unanimity. The state of being of one mind or of one opinion.
Union. League; confederation.
Unison. Concord; harmony.
Unity. A state of general good feeling or understanding.

ACCORD—*Verbs.*

Accord. To bring to an agreement. See *Nouns.*
Agree. To be of one mind or opinion. See HARMONY.
Assent. To express agreement with a statement or matter of opinion. See ASSENT.
Be concordant. To be agreeable or harmonious.
Be pacified. To be brought into a peaceful state. See FIGHTING-CONCILIATION.
Chime in with. To agree with; support the same measures.
Come round. To come into agreement with another's views.
Come to an understanding. To come to agree; reach a settlement.
Enter into the feelings of. To have feelings in common.
Enter into the ideas of. To share another's ideas.
Fall in with. To ally; associate oneself with.
Fraternize. To make brotherly.
Go hand in hand. To be an equal participant with another.
Go with. To agree.
Go with the stream. To make one's opinions or the like agree with the opinions of the majority.
Harmonize with. To bring in accordance with.
Hurler avec les loups [F.]. To howl with the wolves; when in Rome do as the Romans do.
Keep in good humor. To adapt oneself to the feelings of another.
Keep the peace. To live on friendly terms.
Meet half-way. To make mutual concession.
Pull together. To act in harmony. See ANTAGONISM-CONCURRENCE.
Put in tune. To harmonize.
Put up one's horses together. To associate; be on friendly terms with.
Reciprocate. To return favors.
Remain at peace. To continue in friendly relations.
Render accordant. To set in harmony.
Run parallel. To have like views and aims. See ANTAGONISM-CONCURRENCE.
Side with. To agree with; take the part of.
Sing in chorus. To be on intimate terms.
Swim with the stream. To make one's views conform with the views of the majority.
Sympathize with. To feel the sorrows and misfortunes of others.
Understand one another. To have like thoughts and feelings.

ACCORD—*Adjectives.*

Agreeing. In accord.
Allied. Akin; joined.
At one with. On good terms.
At peace. Friendly.
Banded together. United for a common purpose. See ASSOCIATION.
Cemented. Closely united.
Conciliatory. Pacific.
Concordant. Agreeing. See *Verbs.*
Congenial. Kindred; sympathetic.
Fraternal. Brotherly.
Friendly. Living as friends. See AMITY.
Harmonious. Agreeing in thought or purpose.
In accord. Agreeing.
In still water. Free from strife.
Of one mind. Agreeing in thought. See ASSENT.
Tranquil. At peace; free from strife. See STRIFE-PEACE.
United. Of like views or purposes.

VARIANCE—ACCORD—*Continued.*

VARIANCE—Associated Nouns—*Continued.*

Declaration of war. Public announcement of intention to begin open strife.
Disputed point. A question that causes dispute.
Division in the camp. Difference in opinion or feeling between different factions.
Donnybrook Fair. A famous annual Irish fair, exciting much contention and confusion.
Family jars. Slight disagreement between members of a family.
Ground of quarrel. A cause of contention.
High words. Angry contention in words.
House divided against itself. An organization disturbed by internal disputes. [*Mark* iii, 25.]
Kilkenny cats. Two cats in an Irish story, which fought till nothing was left but their tails.
Piece of work. That which causes strife.
Polemics. The art or practise of disputation or controversy.
Screw loose. Something out of order; anything that may cause discord.
Snip-snap. A tart dialogue with quick replies.
Strange bedfellows. Persons of entirely different kinds and opinions. ["Misery acquaints a man with strange bedfellows." Shakespeare, *Tempest,* II, i.]
Subject of dispute. Anything that causes quarreling.
Troublous times. Times of strife or warfare.
Vexata quæstio [L.] A vexed question.
Vexed question. Anything that causes discussion or contest.

VARIANCE—*Verbs.*

Be discordant. To clash or be at variance. See *Nouns.*
Bicker. To wrangle; exchange blows.
Brangle. To dispute contentiously.
Brawl. To quarrel noisily. See *Nouns.*
Break squares with. To fall out.
Break with. To differ in opinions; dissolve partnership or friendship.
Clash. To meet in opposition. See *Nouns.*
Come amiss. To take offense at. See Harmony-Discord.
Conflict. To come into serious opposition.
Controvert. To contradict; meet in opposition. See Assertion-Denial.
Declare war. To make known publicly that hostilities exist between two nations.
Differ. To disagree.
Disagree. To be at variance in opinions.
Dispute. To argue; question an assertion or proposition.
Dissent. To differ in opinion. See Assent-Dissent.
Disunite. To become separated. See *Nouns.*
Embroil. To get into difficulty.
Entangle. To ensnare; entrap.
Fall foul of. To attack; assault.
Fall out. To break friendships.
Fasten a quarrel on. To stir up to anger or dispute; give cause for strife.
Fish in troubled waters. [As the best place for catching fish.] To take advantage of disturbance and trouble to gain one's end. [Matthew Henry, *Psalm* lx.]
Get into hot water. To experience bitter opposition.
Have a bone to pick with. To quarrel with.
Have a crow to pluck with. To settle a difference with.
Have no measures with. To have no dealings with.
Have words with. To quarrel.
Jangle. To wrangle or quarrel.
Jar. To bring into unpleasant relations.
Join issue. To take different positions; oppose.
Jostle. To crowd; hustle.
Kick up a dust. To stir up confusion.
Kick up a row. To start a fight.
Litigate. To contend at law. See *Nouns.*
Live like cat and dog. To fight all the time.
Misunderstand one another. Not to know one another's motives.
Nag. To tease in a petty way.
Part company with. To break up friendly associations.

va′-ri-ant. Different form. Synonym-Antonym.
va′-ri-a″-tion. Modification; alteration. Deviation, Music, Mutation - Permanence, Number, Variation.

Accord—*Adverbs, etc.*

Hand in hand. In union; peacefully.
In concert with. In concord with; united.
On one's side. Favoring one's cause.
With one voice. In agreement. See Assent.

Accord—*Phrase.*

Commune periculum concordiam parit [L.]. Common danger produces concord.

VARIANCE—Verbs—*Continued*

Pick a quarrel. To look for trouble.
Pit against. To set in opposition.
Pull different ways. To controvert; oppose.
Put in issue. To make contrary; cause to disagree.
Quarrel. To violate agreement; dispute angrily or violently.
Set against. Diametrically opposed.
Set at odds.   } To cause to quarrel.
Set together by the ears.
Sow dissension. To cause ill-feeling or hatred.
Spar. To contest in words; wrangle. See Strife.
Split. Separate; sunder.
Squabble. To wrangle.
Stir up dissension. To cause quarrel.
Try conclusions. To st ive with.
Turn house out of window. To raise a great row.
Widen the breach. To cause greater ill-feeling.
Wrangle. To jangle; quarrel.

VARIANCE—*Adjectives.*

Ajar. Out of harmony.
At cross-purposes. To act counter to one another without intending it.
At daggers drawn. Ready to fight.
At feud. At enmity.
At high words. Strongly enraged.
At issue. In controversy.
At loggerheads. Quarreling, as thick heads.
At odds. At variance.
At sixes and sevens. } Disagreeing.
At variance.
Controversial. Pitted against in defending some cause.
Disagreeing. Differing in opinion. See Harmony-Discord.
Discordant. Clashing; opposing. See *Nouns.*
Disputatious. Ready to argue.
Dissentient. Declaring dissent. See Assent-Dissent.
Disunited. Separated; put apart.
Embroiled. Entangled in a broil or quarrel. See *Verbs.*
Factious. Pugnacious; quarrelsome; opposed to law.
Gladiatorial. Eager for a combat.
In hot water. In trouble; in difficulties.
Litigant. Contending in law.
Litigious. Given to the practise of contending in law.
On bad terms. Unfriendly; jangling.
Out of tune. Out of harmony; discordant.
Pettifogging. Subject to artful tricks, as in law.
Polemic. Disposed to argue or dispute.
Quarrelsome. Easily provoked to contest. See *Verbs.*
Together by the ears. Quarreling.
Torn. Divided by violent measures.
Unpacific. Not peaceful.
Unpacified. Fighting.
Unreconciled. At variance.
Up in arms. Fighting against.

VARIANCE—*Phrases.*

Mars gravior sub pace latet [L.]. A more serious war lurks under the peace.
No love lost between them.
Non nostrum tantas componere lites [L.]. It is not for us to settle such grave offenses. [Virgil, *Eclogues,* III, 108.]
Quot homines tot sententiæ [L.]. Many men, many minds. [Terence, *Phormio,* II, iv, 14.]

VARIATION.

Contradistinction. Distinction by opposite qualities.
Delicate distinction. } Degrees of distinction.
Fine distinction.

Difference. The state or quality of being unlike.

Different thing. Something differing from another thing in essential qualities.

Disagreement, etc. Failure to agree or correspond. See HARMONY-DISCORD.

Discrimination, etc. The act of noting differences or distinctions. See DIFFERENTIATION.

Disparity, etc. Difference in any respect. See EQUALITY-INEQUALITY.

Dissimilarity, etc. Unlikeness; difference. See LIKENESS-UNLIKENESS.

Distinction. The act of pointing out the difference between things; an exactly defined difference.

Diversity. The state of differing essentially one from another.

Modes and tenses. Verb forms used to express different manners and times of action.

Modification. The act of making somewhat different; the result of so acting.

Nice distinction. ⎱ Degrees of distinction.
Subtle distinction. ⎰

This, that, or the other. This thing or a different thing.

Variance. Altering of condition; difference that causes dispute.

Variation. Difference in the form, position, or state of a thing at different times.

Variety. A number of different things in the same group.

VARIATION—*Figurative Nouns.*

Another pair of shoes. ⎱ Things entirely different.
Apple of another tree. ⎰

Nuance [F.]. A shade or tint.

Shade of difference. A slight difference.

VARIATION—*Verbs.*

Ablude. Differ.

Be different, etc. Be unlike, etc. See *Adjectives.*

Contrast. Put in comparison to show difference.

Differ. Be unlike.

Differ *longo intervallo* [L.]. To differ by a long interval. [Virgil, *Æneid*, V, 320.]

Differ *toto cælo* [L.]. To be entirely different. [Macrobius, *Saturnalia*, III, xii, 10.]

Discriminate. Point out differences between.

Divaricate. Separate into two branches; diverge.

Mismatch. Match things unsuited to each other.

Modify, etc. To change. See MUTATION.

Vary. Be different in form, position, or state at different times; cause to so differ.

VARIATION—*Adjectives.*

All manner of. All the different kinds of.

Characteristic. Showing the distinctive qualities of.

Dædal. ⎱ Intricately made, like the work of Dædalus.
Dedal. ⎰

Different. Unlike.

Differing, etc. Being unlike, etc. See *Verbs.*

Discriminative. Making sharply defined differences.

Distinctive. Showing sharply defined differences.

Distinguishable. Capable of being differentiated.

Divers. Of different kinds; differing.

Diverse. Distinct; different.

Diversified. Made different; variegated.

Heterogeneous. Made up of different kinds.

Modified. Made somewhat different.

Not the same. Different.

Other. Different.

Something else. Something different.

Unequal. Of different magnitudes.

Unmatched. Having no equal or match.

Varied. Made different.

Variform, etc. Of different form. See UNIFORMITY-MULTIFORMITY.

Various. Diverse.

Widely apart. Very different.

VARIATION—*Adverbs.*

Differently, etc. In a different manner, etc. See *Adjectives.*

VARIATION—*Phrase.*

Il y a fagots et fagots [F.]. There are fagots and fagots; things that are alike in name differ in quality.

---

var″-i-cel′-la. An eruptive disease. HEALTH-SICKNESS.

var′-i-cose″. Affected with varix. HEALTH-SICKNESS.

va′-ried. Changed. DEVIATION, UNIFORMITY-DIVERSITY, VARIATION.

va′-ri-e-gate. To diversify in external appearance. VARIEGATION.

va″-ri-e-ga′-tion. Variegating. VARIEGATION.

VARIEGATION.

Iridescence. Exhibition of a play of changeable colors.

Maculation. The act of spotting.

Play of colors. A variation or changing of colors.

Spottiness. State or quality of being full of spots.

Variegation. The act of diversifying by employing different tints or hues.

VARIEGATION—*Denotations.*

Butterfly. A species of insect occurring in many different colors.

Chameleon. A lizard which has the power of changing its color.

Check. A woven or painted design in colored squares.

Checkers. ⎱ A game played on a board with squares of alternate
Chequers. ⎰ colors.

Chess-board. A board used in the game of chess, having eight rows of alternate light and dark squares, eight in each row.

Harlequin. A clown dressed in many-colored clothes.

Iris. The rainbow; an appearance resembling the rainbow.

Joseph's coat. A coat of many colors. [Bible.]

Leopard. A large savage animal with black spots along the back and sides. [Lion Pard.]

Mackerel. A fish covered with bright yellow circular spots.

Mackerel sky. A sky flecked with small white clouds.

Marble. A hard building-stone occurring in variegated colors.

Marquetry. Inlaid work of wood, stone, or ivory.

Mosaic. A decoration made with variously colored pieces of glass, stone, etc. [Dear to the Muses.]

Mother-of-pearl. The variously colored internal layer of several kinds of shells.

Opal. A mineral presenting a peculiar play of colors.

Parquetry. Wooden mosaic.

Patchwork. Work composed of pieces of various colors.

Peacock. A bird whose feathers are marked with bands of blue, green, and golden colors.

Plaid. A piece of cloth of checkered material.

Polychrome. A picture or statue in several colors.

Rainbow. An arch exhibiting all the colors of the spectrum, formed by the refraction and reflection of the sun's rays in drops of falling rain.

Spectrum. The colored rays of which light is composed, separated by the refraction of a prism.

Sunbow. A rainbow.

Tartan. Woolen cloth checkered or cross-barred with narrow bands of various colors.

Tesseræ [L.]. Small pieces of marble, glass, earthenware, etc. used by the ancients as mosaic.

Tortoise-shell. The variously colored shell of a species of tortoise used for ornamental work.

Tricolor. A three-colored flag.

Tulip. A plant bearing beautiful, variegated flowers.

Zebra. A South-African wild horse, remarkable for having its white or yellowish-white body marked with brown or black bands.

VARIEGATION—*Scientific Nouns.*

Dichroism. The property of transmitting color in two directions.

Striæ. Thread-like lines of color.

Trichroism. The property of transmitting colors in three directions.

VARIEGATION—*Verbs.*

Bespeckle. To mark with speckles or spots.

Bespot. To mark with spots.

Besprinkle. To sprinkle or scatter over.

Be variegated. To be of various colors.

Braid. To weave or intwine together, as threads of different colors.

Checker. ⎱ To diversify with different colors, scenes, etc.
Chequer. ⎰

Damascene. To ornament with waving lines, Damascus work.

Dot. To mark with small spots.

Embroider. To ornament with needlework.

Engrail. To variegate or spot, as with hail.

Inlay. To insert, as pieces of wood, pearl, ivory, etc., in a groundwork of some other material.

Maculate. To mark with spots.

Quilt. To sew in lines or patterns.

Speckle. To mark with small spots of a different color from that of the rest of the surface.

Stipple. To engrave by means of dots.

Streak. To variegate with lines of a different color

Stripe. To form with lines of different colors.
Tattoo. To color, as the flesh, by pricking in coloring matter which cannot be washed out.
Variegate. To mark with different colors.

VARIEGATION—*Adjectives*

Barred. Marked with bars of colors
Bicolored. Of two colors
Brind. }
Brinded. } Of a gray or tawny color with streaks of a darker hue.
Brindled. }
Chatoyant [F.]. Having a changeable, varying luster like that of a cat's eye in the dark.
Checkered. Marked with alternate squares of different colors
Clouded. Variegated with colors.
Cymophanous. Having a wavy light
Dædal. Artistic.
Dappled. Marked with spots of different shades of color
Dichromatic. Having two colors.
Divers-colored. Of many colors.
Embroidered. Ornamented with needlework.
Flea-bitten. White, flecked with minute spots of a bay or sorrel
Flecked. }
Fleckered. } Streaked; speckled.
Freckled. Marked with small discolored spots.
Gorge de pigeon [F.] Shot, in color; like throat of a dove
Grizzled. Sprinkled or mixed with gray.
Iridescent. Having colors like the rainbow.
Kaleidoscopic. Variegated.
Listed. Striped.
Many-colored. }
Many-hued. } Showing a variety of colors.
Marbled. Stained or veined like marble.
Mosaic. Formed by uniting pieces of different colors.
Motley. Consisting of different colors.
Mottled. Spotted.
Nacreous. Like mother-of-pearl.
Of all manner of colors. }
Of all the colors of the rainbow. } Having very many different colors.
Opalescent. }
Opaline. } Having changeable colors like those of the opal.
Paned. Provided with panes, as of different colors.
Party-colored. Colored with different tints.
Pearly. Showing changeable colors, as a pearl.
Pepper-and-salt. Sprinkled with white and dark spots.
Piebald. Having spots and patches of black and white.
Pied. Variegated with spots of different colors.
Plaid. Checkered or marked with bars or stripes.
Polychromatic. Many-colored.
Powdered. Sprinkled, as with powder
Punctuated. Dotted with spots.
Shot. Woven as to produce an effect of variable tints.
Speckled. Marked with small spots of a different color from that of the rest of the surface.
Spotted. }
Spotty. } Marked with spots.
Striated. Marked with fine lines of color.
Studded. Set thickly, as with studs.
Tabby. Diversified in color.
Tesselated. Formed of little squares of different colors.
Tortoise-shell. Of variegated colors.
Tricolored. Three-colored.
Variegated. Having marks or patches of different colors
Veined. Streaked.
Venous. Marked with veins.
Versicolored. Of different colors.
Watered. Diversified with wave-like lines.

va-ri′-et-y. Diversity; collection; kind. CONVENTIONALITY-UNCONVENTIONALITY, DIVISION, UNIFORMITY-MULTIFORMITY, VARIATION.
va′-ri-form. Of different shapes. UNIFORMITY-MULTIFORMITY.
va-ri′-o-la. Smallpox. HEALTH-SICKNESS.
va″-ri-om′-e-ter. Scientific instrument. MENSURATION.
va″-ri-o′-rum. Having correlated notes. DIGEST.
va′-ri-ous. Diverse. MULTIPLICITY-PAUCITY, VARIATION; **at various times,** TIME; **in various places,** EXTENSION-PLACE.
var′-let. Menial. GOOD MAN-BAD MAN.
var′-min. Troublesome fellow. GOOD MAN-BAD MAN.

var′-nish. Resin; gloss; polish. COVER-LINING, EMBELLISHMENT-DISFIGUREMENT, JUSTIFICATION-CHARGE, PAINTING, PULPINESS-ROSIN, RATIOCINATION-INSTINCT, TRUTHFULNESS-FALSEHOOD.
var′-si-ty. University. SCHOOL.
var′-vel. Ring worn by a hawk, bearing its owner's name. SIGN.
va′-ry. Modify; disagree; change. DEVIATION, LIKENESS-UNLIKENESS, MUTABILITY-STABILITY, MUTATION-PERMANENCE, VARIATION.
va sans dire, cela [F.] (va san· dîr, se-la′). That goes without saying. CERTAINTY-DOUBT, MANIFESTATION-LATENCY.
vas′-cu-lar. Having vessels. APERTURE-CLOSURE, CONTENTS-RECEIVER, WATERCOURSE-AIRPIPE.
vas′-cu-lum. Vessel. CONTENTS-RECEIVER.
vase. Vessel. CONTENTS-RECEIVER.
vas′-sal. Retainer. CHIEF-UNDERLING.
vas′-sal-age. Servitude. LIBERTY-SUBJECTION.
vast. Great; massive. GREATNESS-LITTLENESS, MAGNITUDE-SMALLNESS, EXTENSION-INEXTENSION; **vast learning,** KNOWLEDGE-IGNORANCE.
vast′-y deep. Ocean. GREATNESS-LITTLENESS, OCEAN-LAND.
vat. Vessel. CONTENTS-RECEIVER.
Vat′-i-can. Papal residence; government. AUSTERITY, FANE; **thunders of the Vatican,** CHARITABLENESS-CURSE.
vat′-i-cide. One who kills a prophet. LIFE-KILLING.
va-tic′-i-nal. Foretelling. PROPHECY.
va-tic′-i-nate. To foretell. PROPHECY.
va-tic″-i-na′-tion. Prophecy. PROPHECY.
vatum, genus irritabile [L.] (vē′-tum, jī′-nus ir-ri-tab′-i-lī). The irritable race of bards. POETRY-PROSE.
vaude′-ville. Entertainment. ACTING.
vault. Leap; cellar; arch. CONTENTS-RECEIVER, CURVATION-RECTILINEARITY, LIFE-FUNERAL, SPRING-DIVE; **vault of heaven,** UNIVERSE.
vault′-ed. Arched. CURVATION-RECTILINEARITY, LEVELNESS.
vault′-ing. Superior. DESIRE-DISTASTE, SUPREMACY-SUBORDINACY.
vaunt. Boast. BRAGGING.
vaunt′-ed. Boasted. BRAGGING.
vaunt′-ing-ly. Boastfully. BRAGGING.
vaurien [F.] (vo-ri-an′). Worthless fellow. GOOD MAN-BAD MAN.
vav′-a-sor. Vassal. GENTILITY-COMMONALTY, HOLDER.
veal. The meat of a calf. NUTRIMENT-EXCRETION.
vectigalia nervos esse reipublicæ [L.] (vec-ti-gē′-li-a ner′-vos es′-sî rî″-ai-pub′-li-sî). Revenues are the sinews of the commonwealth. OUTLAY-INCOME.
vec′-tion. Carrying. TRANSFER.
vec″-ti-ta′-tion. A carrying. TRANSFER
vect′-ure. Carrying. TRANSFER.
Vedas. The four holy books of the Hindus REVELATION-PSEUDOREVELATION.
ve-dette′. Sentinel. WARNING.
ve′-dro. Liquid measure. QUANTITY-MEASURE.
veer. Change. ADVANCE-RETROGRESSION, AIM-ABERRATION, BIGOTRY-APOSTASY, MUTATION-PERMANENCE.
veer′-ing. Turning. ADVANCE-RETROGRESSION.
ve′-ga. A plain. GULF-PLAIN.
veg″-e-ta-bil′-i-ty. Vegetable nature. FAUNA-FLORA.
veg′-e-ta-ble. Plant. FAUNA-FLORA; **vegetable kingdom,** FAUNA-FLORA; **vegetable life,** ANIMALITY-VEGETABILITY; **vegetable oil,** PULPINESS-OILINESS; **vegetable physiology,** ZOOLOGY-BOTANY.
veg″-e-ta′-ri-an. One who lives on vegetables. MODERATION-SELFINDULGENCE.
veg″-e-ta′-ri-an-ism. The theory and practise of living wholly on vegetables. MODERATION-SELFINDULGENCE.

veg′-e-tate. Grow; live passively. ACTIVITY-INDO-LENCE, ENLARGEMENT-DIMINUTION, ENTITY-NON-ENTITY, SENSITIVENESS-APATHY.

veg′-e-ta-tion. Plant life. MOVEMENT-REST, SENSI-TIVENESS-APATHY.

veg′-e-ta″-tive. Growing, or having the power of growing, as plants. SENSITIVENESS-APATHY

veg′-e-tous. Vigorous. FAUNA-FLORA.

ve′-he-mence. Impetuosity; fervor. EXCITABILITY, FEELING, TURBULENCE-CALMNESS.

ve′-he-ment. Eager; ardent. EXCITABILITY-INEX-CITABILITY, FORCE-WEAKNESS, TURBULENCE-CALM-NESS.

ve′-hi-cle. Carriage; medium. CONVEYANCE-VESSEL, INSTRUMENTALITY, TRAVELING-NAVIGATION.

veil. Curtain; concealment. COVER-LINING, DRESS-UNDRESS, ENLIGHTENMENT-SECRECY, EXPOSURE-HIDINGPLACE, LUMINARY-SHADE; **draw aside the veil,** EXPOSURE-HIDINGPLACE; **take the veil,** CHURCH, SOCIABILITY-PRIVACY.

veiled. Concealed. VISIBILITY-INVISIBILITY.

vein. Quality; stripe. AFFECTIONS, BREADTH-NAR-ROWNESS, INCLINATION, LAMINA-FIBER, READI-NESS-RELUCTANCE, STORE; **in the vein,** READINESS-RELUCTANCE; **not in the vein,** READINESS-RELUC-TANCE.

veined. Streaked. VARIEGATION.

veldt. Open country. GULF-PLAIN.

velis et remis [L.] (vī′-lis et rī′-mis) With sails and oars. SWIFTNESS-SLOWNESS.

vel″-i-ta′-tion. Skirmish. STRIFE-PEACE.

vel-le′-i-ty. Desire. VOLITION-OBLIGATION.

vel′-li-cate. Twitch. AGITATION.

vel′-li-ca″-ting. Twitching. PUNGENCY.

vel′-lum. Parchment. WRITING-PRINTING.

ve′-lo. Velocity of one foot per second. MENSURA-TION, SWIFTNESS-SLOWNESS.

veloce [It.] (vê-lo′-chê). Swiftly. MUSIC.

ve-loc′-i-pede. Vehicle. CONVEYANCE-VESSEL.

ve-loc′-i-ty. Rapidity. LASTINGNESS-TRANSIENT-NESS, MOVEMENT-REST, SWIFTNESS-SLOWNESS; **an-gular velocity,** ACTIVITY-INDOLENCE, ANGULARITY, HURRY-LEISURE.

veluti in speculum [L.] (vel′-yu-tai in spec′-yu-lum) As in a looking-glass. LIKENESS-UNLIKENESS, MOVEMENT-REST, VISIBILITY-INVISIBILITY.

vel′-vet. Fabric; soft. SENSUALITY-SUFFERING, SMOOTHNESS-ROUGHNESS; **on velvet,** DIFFICULTY-FACILITY.

vel″-vet-een′. Kind of cloth. SMOOTHNESS-ROUGH-NESS.

vel′-vet-y. Made of velvet or like velvet. SMOOTH-NESS-ROUGHNESS.

vena [L.] (vī′-na). Vein. WATERCOURSE-AIRPIPE.

ve′-nal. Purchasable; sordid; pertaining to the blood. ANATOMY, EXTRAVAGANCE-AVARICE, PRICE-DIS-COUNT, UNSELFISHNESS-SELFISHNESS, UPRIGHT-NESS-DISHONESTY.

ve-nal′-i-ty. Mercenariness. EXTRAVAGANCE-AVA-RICE, UPRIGHTNESS-DISHONESTY.

ve-na′-tion. Hunting. QUEST-EVASION.

vend. Sell. BUYING-SALE.

ven-dee′. Buyer. BUYING-SALE.

vend′-er. Seller. BUYING-SALE.

ven-det′-ta. Feud. PARDON-VINDICTIVENESS.

vend′-i-ble-ness. Salable. BUYING-SALE.

vend-i-bil′-i-ty. The state of being vendible. BUYING-SALE.

vend′-i-ble. Vendibility. BUYING-SALE.

ven″-di-ta′-tion. Exposition for sale. BRAGGING.

ven′-dor. Seller. BUYING-SALE.

ven-due′. Auction. BUYING-SALE.

ve-neer′. Coating; polish. COVER-LINING, LAMINA-FIBER.

ven″-e-na′-tion. Poisoning. BETTERMENT-DETERIO-RATION.

venenum in auro, bibere [L.] (vī-nī′-num in au′-ro, bib′-î-rî). To drink poison from a gold cup. REF-UGE-PITFALL, REMEDY-BANE.

ven′-er-a-ble. Aged; estimable. INFANCY-AGE, NOV-ELTY-ANTIQUITY, REGARD-DISRESPECT, SAGE-FOOL.

ven′-er-ate. To reverence. REGARD-DISRESPECT.

ven″-er-a′-tion. Respect; piety. GODLINESS-UNGOD-LINESS, REGARD-DISRESPECT.

ven′-er-y. Chase; indulgence. LIFE-KILLING, PURITY-IMPURITY, QUEST-EVASION.

ven″-e-sec′-tion. Blood-letting. ADMISSION-EXPUL-SION, REMEDY-BANE.

Ve-ne′-tian blinds. Shade. WATERCOURSE-AIRPIPE.

venge′-ance. Revenge. PARDON-VINDICTIVENESS; **cry to heaven for vengeance,** RIGHT-WRONG; **with a vengeance,** MAGNITUDE-SMALLNESS, TURBULENCE-CALMNESS.

venge′-ful. Vindictive. PARDON-VINDICTIVENESS.

ve′-ni-a-ble. Pardonable. JUSTIFICATION-CHARGE.

ve′-ni-al. Pardonable. INNOCENCE-GUILT, JUSTIFI-CATION-CHARGE.

veniam petimusque damusque vicissim [L.] (vî′-ni-am pet-i-mus′-quî da-mus′-quî vai-sis′-sim). We both seek pardon and on the other hand give it. PARDON-VINDICTIVENESS.

venienti occurrere morbo [L.] (vî-ni-en′-tai oc-cur′-er-î mor′-bo). To meet disease coming. PREPARATION-NONPREPARATION.

ve-ni′-re. Kind of legal writ. LITIGATION.

ven′-i-son. Flesh of deer. PALATABLENESS-UNPALA-TABLENESS.

veni, vidi, vici [L.] (vî′-nai, vai′-dai, vai′-sai). I came, I saw, I conquered. ACTIVITY-INDOLENCE, SUCCESS-FAILURE.

ven′-om. Poison. CHARITABLENESS-MALEVOLENCE, REMEDY-BANE.

ven′-om-ous. Noxious; baneful. CHARITABLENESS-MALEVOLENCE, GOODNESS-BADNESS, HEALTHINESS-UNHEALTHINESS, POLITENESS-IMPOLITENESS.

ve′-nous. Marked with veins. VARIEGATION.

vent. To utter; hole. APERTURE-CLOSURE, BUYING-SALE, ENTRANCE-EXIT, EXPOSURE-HIDINGPLACE, PERSPICUITY-OBSCURITY, WATERCOURSE-AIRPIPE; **find vent,** ENTRANCE-EXIT, PERSPICUITY-OBSCURITY, PUBLICITY, TRANSMISSION; **give vent to,** ADMISSION-EXPULSION, EXPOSURE-HIDINGPLACE; **vent one's rage,** FAVORITE-ANGER; **vent one's spleen,** FAVORITE-ANGER.

ven′-ter. Abdomen. CONTENTS-RECEIVER.

ven′-ti-duct. Air-passage. WATERCOURSE-AIRPIPE.

ven′-ti-late. Air; render pure. BEGINNING-END, CLEANNESS-FILTHINESS, ESSAY, RIVER-WIND, WATER-AIR; **ventilate a question,** INVESTIGATION-ANSWER, RATIOCINATION-INSTINCT.

ven″-ti-la′-tion. The act of ventilating, or the state of being ventilated. INVESTIGATION-ANSWER, RATI-OCINATION-INSTINCT, RIVER-WIND, WATER-AIR.

ven″-ti-la′-tor. Air-passage. RIVER-WIND, WATER-COURSE-AIRPIPE.

ven-tos′-i-ty. Windiness. RIVER-WIND.

vent′-peg. Safety-valve. PERFORATOR-STOPPER, PER-SPICUITY-OBSCURITY, REFUGE-PITFALL.

ventre à terre [F.] (van·tr a têr). Belly to ground. SWIFTNESS-SLOWNESS.

ven′-tri-cle. Chamber of heart. CONTENTS-RE-CEIVER.

ven-tric′-u-lar. Of or pertaining to a ventricle. CON-TENTS-RECEIVER.

ven-tril′-o-quism. Voice. VOCALIZATION-MUTENESS.

ven-tril′-o-quist. One who speaks in such a manner that his voice seems to come from some distant or different place. VOCALIZATION-MUTENESS.

ven'-ture. Risk; undertake. Bravery-Cowardice, Purpose-Luck, Security-Insecurity, Venture; **I'll venture to say,** Assertion-Denial.

VENTURE.

Adventure. A dangerous or uncertain undertaking.
Attempt. An effort to effect something.
Coup d'essai [F.]. A first attempt.
Début [F.]. The first appearance before the public.
Endeavor. A continued attempt.
Essay. An attempt or effort made.
Probation. Any proceeding designed to test character, qualifications, attainments, etc.
Speculation. A more or less risky investment of money.
Trial. A proving or testing by experience or use.
Venture. An undertaking attended with risk.

Venture—*Verbs*.

Adventure. To venture.
Attempt. To make an effort to do.
Endeavor. To make continuous attempts.
Essay. To make weak attempts.
Experiment. To make tests.
Push. To press forward with continued and unwearied effort.
Speculate. To invest money or do business on great risks.
Strive. To make an effort.
Tempt. To test.
Try. To exercise power to observe the result.
Venture. To risk with good chances of gaining.

Venture—*Verbal Expressions*.

Do one's best (see Toil); feel one's way; grope one's way; **make a bold push; make an attempt; pick one's way; take one's chances; tempt fortune; try hard; try one's fortune; try one's hand; try one's luck; use one's best endeavor; use one's endeavor.**

Venture—*Adjectives*.

Empirical. Not resting on a scientific basis.
Essaying. Making weak attempts. See *Verbs*.
Experimental. Hazardous.
Probationary. Undergoing trial.
Tentative. Hazardous, with the hope of good resulting.

Venture—*Adverbs, etc.*

At a venture. Without seeing the result.
By rule of thumb. Judging roughly.
Experimentally. By way of trial. See *Adjectives*.
If one may be so bold. If one may venture.
On trial. Undergoing a test.

Venture—*Phrases*.

Aut non tentaris aut perfice [L.]. Either do not attempt or else achieve. [Ovid, *Ars amatoria*, I, 389.]
Chi non s'arrischia non guadagua [It.]. Nothing venture, nothing have.

ven'-ture-some. Bold. Bravery-Cowardice, Recklessness-Caution.
vent'-ur-ous. Venturesome. Bravery-Cowardice, Recklessness-Caution.
Ve'-nus. The goddess of love, beauty, a planet. Astronomy, Beauty-Ugliness, Love-Hate.
ve ra'-cious. Truthful. Truth-Error, Truthfulness-Falsehood, Uprightness-Dishonesty.
ve-ran'-da. A portico. Architecture, Contents-Receiver.
verb. A part of speech which asserts, declares, or predicates. Verb; **primitive verb,** Verb; **principal verb,** Verb; **reflexive verb,** Verb; **regular verb,** Verb; **strong verb,** Verb; **substantive verb,** Verb; **transitive verb,** Verb; **weak verb,** Verb

VERB

Verb. A part of speech which asserts, declares, or predicates something.

Verb—*Kinds*

Adjective verb. One that can form the copula and the predicate of a proposition.
Auxiliary verb. One used to assist in the conjugation of another.
Common verb. One that can form the copula and the predicate of a proposition.

Copulative verb. One that predicates an adjective or noun.
Defective verb. One wanting in some of its forms.
Derived verb. One made up of two or more other words.
Impersonal verb. One with no logical subject conceived of or expressed.
Intransitive verb. One that denotes a complete act or state.
Irregular verb. One which forms its parts irregularly.
Neuter verb. An intransitive verb.
Primitive verb. One not derived from other words.
Principal verb. The main verb when an auxiliary is used.
Reflexive verb. Verb followed by a reflexive pronoun.
Regular verb. One that forms its past tense and past participle by adding *d* or *ed* to the present.
Strong verb. An irregular verb.
Substantive verb. One that can form the copula of a proposition.
Transitive verb. One denoting an act as affecting some object.
Weak verb. Regular verb.

Verb—*Attributes*.

Mode. The verb-form used to express action, etc., in a particular manner.
  Imperative. Mode of command.
  Indicative. Mode of simple assertion or question.
  Infinitive. Mode used as a noun.
  Participle. Mode used as an adjective.
  Potential. Mode used to express possibility, necessity, or duty.
  Subjunctive. Mode used to express a condition.
Number. Form of a verb dependent upon the number of the subject.
Person. Form of a verb dependent upon the person of the subject.
Tense. Form of the verb to indicate time, or the continuance or completedness of the action, being, or state.
  Aorist. A Greek tense expressing a completed action as a simple occurrence.
  Future. Tense denoting future time.
  Future perfect. Tense denoting action complete before some future time.
  Imperfect. The past tense.
  Past. Tense denoting past time.
  Past perfect. Tense denoting action complete before some past time.
  Perfect. The present perfect.
  Pluperfect. The past perfect.
  Present. Tense denoting present time.
  Present perfect. Tense denoting an action complete at the present time.
  Preterite. The past tense.
Voice. The relation of the subject of a verb to the action expressed.
  Active. Voice where the subject is acting.
  Passive. Voice where the subject is acted upon.

Verb—*Associated Nouns*.

Conjugation. Inflection of a verb.
Emphatic form. Form with auxiliary *do*, used for emphasis.
Inflection. The changes undergone by words to express their relations and attributes.
Interrogative form. Form with auxiliary *do* preceding the subject, used in asking questions.
Progressive form. Form with *be* joined to present participle, used to indicate action as going on.
Verbal adjective. Participle which has lost its verbal force.

ver'-bal. Spoken. Word-Neology; **verbal intercourse,** Conversation-Monologue, Speech-Inarticulateness; **verbal quibble,** Adage-Nonsense, Wittiness-Dulness.
ver'-bal-ly. Orally. Word-Neology.
ver-ba'-ri-an. Word coiner. Word-Neology.
ver-ba'-tim. Word for word. Imitation-Originality, Truth-Error, Word-Neology.
ver'-bi-age. Wordiness. Meaning-Jargon, Terseness-Prolixity.
verbis, ad verbera [L.] (ver'-bis, ad ver'-bĭ-ra) From words to blows. Strife-Peace.
verbis, totidem [L.] (ver'-bis, tot'-i-dem). In so many words. Truth-Error.
verborum, copia [L.] (ver-bo'-rum, co'-pi-a). An abundance of words. Speech-Inarticulateness, Talkativeness-Taciturnity, Terseness-Prolixity.
ver-bose'. Wordy. Terseness-Prolixity.
ver-bos'-i-ty. Prolixity. Rhetoric, Talkativeness-Taciturnity, Terseness-Prolixity.

verbum sapienti [L.] (ver'-bum sê-pi-en'-tai) A word to the wise. ENLIGHTENMENT-SECRECY.

verbum sat sapienti [L] (ver'-bum sat sê-pi-en'-tai). A word to the wise is sufficient. ADVICE, WARNING.

ver'-dant. Green. FAUNA-FLORA, REDNESS-GREENNESS.

verd"-an-tique'. Ancient green, ornaments of stone. REDNESS-GREENNESS.

ver'-dict. Decision DECISION-MISJUDGMENT, LITIGATION; **snatch a verdict,** CRAFT-ARTLESSNESS, TRUTHFULNESS-FRAUD

ver'-di-gris. Paint. REDNESS-GREENNESS.

ver'-di-ter. Paint. REDNESS-GREENNESS.

ver-dun'. Dueling-rapier. WEAPON.

ver'-dure. Vegetation. FAUNA-FLORA, REDNESS-GREENNESS.

ver'-e̲-cund. Shy. CONCEIT-DIFFIDENCE, SELFRESPECT-HUMBLENESS.

verecundiam, argumentum ad [L.] (ver-î-cun'-di-am, ar-giu-men'-tum ad). Argument appealing to modesty. CONCEIT-DIFFIDENCE, REPUTATION-DISCREDIT.

ver"-e-cun'-di-ty. Modesty. CONCEIT-DIFFIDENCE, SELFRESPECT-HUMBLENESS.

verein [G.] (fer-ain'), Association. ASSOCIATION.

verge. Brink. AIM-ABERRATION, BORDER, BOUNDARY, INCLINATION, REMOTENESS-NEARNESS.

ver'-gent. Nearing an end. BEGINNING-END.

ver'-ger. Mace-bearer. MINISTRY-LAITY.

ver-gette'. Pallet. PAINTING.

ve-rid'-ic-al. Truthful. TRUTHFULNESS-FALSEHOOD.

ver'-i-est. Degree. MAGNITUDE-SMALLNESS.

ver"-i-fi-ca'-tion. Confirmation. SECURITY, TRIAL.

ver'-i-fy. Substantiate; fulfil. DISCOVERY, EVIDENCE-COUNTEREVIDENCE, PROOF, TRIAL.

ver'-i-ly. Truly. TRUTH-ERROR.

ver"-i-si-mil'-i-tude. Likelihood LIKELIHOOD-UNLIKELIHOOD.

ver'-i-ta-ble. True. TRUTH-ERROR.

veritas, et praevalet, magna est [L.] (ver'-i-tas, et prev'-ê-let, mag'-na est). Great is truth, and it prevails. TRUTHFULNESS-FALSEHOOD.

veritas, nuda [L.] (ver'-i-tas, niu'-da) Naked truth. TRUTH-ERROR.

veritas odium parit [L.] (ver'-i-tas o'-di-um pê'-rit). Truth engenders hatred. TRUTHFULNESS-FALSEHOOD.

veritatis simplex oratio est [L.] (ver"-i-tê'-tis sim'-plex o-rê'-shi-o est). The language of the truth is simple. EMBELLISHMENT-SIMPLICITY, TRUTHFULNESS-FALSEHOOD.

vérité, en suivant la [F.] (vê-ri-tê', an'' swî-van'' la) In following the truth. TRUTH-ERROR.

vérité, palais de [F.] (vê-ri-tê', pa-lê' de). Palace of truth. CRAFT-ARTLESSNESS.

vérité sans peur [F.] (vê-ri-tê' san pur). Truth without fear. TRUTHFULNESS-FALSEHOOD.

ver'-i-ty. Truthfulness. TRUTH-ERROR.

ver'-juice. Sour juice. SWEETNESS-ACIDITY.

ver"-mi-cel'-li. Wheat paste. NUTRIMENT-EXCRETION.

ver-mic'-u-lar. Worm-like CIRCLE-WINDING, FAUNA-FLORA.

ver'-mi-form. Worm-shaped. CIRCLE-WINDING.

ver-mil'-ion. Red color. REDNESS-GREENNESS.

ver'-min. Animal; low person. CLEANNESS-FILTHINESS, FAUNA-FLORA, GENTILITY-COMMONALTY.

ver-nac'-u-lar. Mother tongue. DWELLER-HABITATION, HABIT-DESUETUDE, LANGUAGE, OUTSIDE-INSIDE.

ver'-nal. Spring. MORNING-EVENING, NOVELTY-ANTIQUITY; **vernal equinox,** ASTRONOMY.

ver'-ni-er. Scale. GREATNESS-LITTLENESS; **vernier scale,** MENSURATION.

ver non semper viret [L.] (ver non sem'-per vai'-ret). Spring does not always flourish. OPPORTUNENESS-UNSUITABLENESS.

vero e affronterai il diavolo, di il [It.] (vê-ro ê af-fron-têr'-ai îl dî-a-vo'-lo, dî îl). Speak the truth and you will shame the devil. JOVE-FIEND, TRUTHFULNESS-FALSEHOOD.

ve-ron'-i-ca. Handkerchief. DEVOTION-CHARM.

vero, vitam impendere [L.] (vî-ro, vai'-tam im-pen'-di-rî). To pay down one's life for truth. ASSERTION-DENIAL, UPRIGHTNESS-DISHONESTY.

verrons, nous [F.] (ve-ron'', nu). We shall see. EXPECTATION-SURPRISE.

ver'-sa-tile. Many-sided. MUTABILITY-STABILITY.

ver"-sa-til'-i-ty. Aptness to change. MUTABILITY-STABILITY.

verse. Line. POETRY-PROSE, RHETORIC, WHOLE-PART.

versed in. Know. KNOWLEDGE-IGNORANCE.

ver'-si-col"-or. Variegated. VARIEGATION.

ver"-si-fi-ca'-tion. Metrical composition. POETRY-PROSE.

ver'-si-fi-er. One who versifies. POETRY-PROSE.

ver'-si-fy. Write poetry. POETRY-PROSE.

ver'-sion. Translation; opinion. INTERPRETATION-MISINTERPRETATION, UNIVERSALITY-PARTICULARITY.

ver'-sus. Against. AIM-ABERRATION, ANTAGONISM-CONCURRENCE.

vert. Green. REDNESS-GREENNESS.

ver'-te-bra. Portion of the spinal column. SUSPENSION-SUPPORT.

ver'-tex. Apex. TOP-BOTTOM.

ver'-tic-al. Upright. ANATOMY, ERECTNESS-FLATNESS.

ver'-tic-al-ly. In a vertical manner. ERECTNESS-FLATNESS.

ver"-ti-cal'-i-ty. Verticalness. ERECTNESS-FLATNESS.

ver-tic'-i-ty. Turning. REVOLUTION-EVOLUTION.

ver-tig'-i-nous. Whirling. REVOLUTION, SANENESS-LUNACY

ver'-ti-go. Dizziness. REVOLUTION-EVOLUTION, SANENESS-LUNACY.

verve. Spirit, imagination. FANCY, FEELING, FORCE-WEAKNESS.

ver'-y. True; extremely. MAGNITUDE-SMALLNESS; **very best,** GOODNESS-BADNESS; **very image,** DELINEATION-CARICATURE; **very likely,** LIKELIHOOD-UNLIKELIHOOD; **very many,** MULTIPLICITY-PAUCITY; **very minute,** ETERNITY-INSTANTANEITY; **very much,** MAGNITUDE-SMALLNESS; **very picture,** LIKENESS-UNLIKENESS; **very small,** MAGNITUDE-SMALLNESS; **very thing,** HARMONY-DISCORD, SAMENESS-CONTRAST, TRUTH-ERROR; **very true,** ASSENT-DISSENT; **very well,** ASSENT-DISSENT, CONTENTEDNESS-DISCONTENTMENT.

ves'-i-cal. Bladder. COVER-LINING, IMITATION-ORIGINALITY, ROUNDNESS.

ve-sic'-u-lar. Air-bladders. APERTURE-CLOSURE, CONTENTS-RECEIVER.

ves'-pers. Evening service. DEVOTION-IDOLATRY.

ves'-per-tine. Evening. MORNING-EVENING.

ves'-sel. Receptacle; craft. APERTURE-CLOSURE, CONVEYANCE-VESSEL, CONTENTS-RECEIVER.

vest. Garment; put on. DRESS-UNDRESS, ESTABLISHMENT-REMOVAL; **vest in,** GIVING-RECEIVING, HOLDING-EXEMPTION.

ves'-ta. Match. COMBUSTIBLE.

ves'-tal. Priestess of Vesta vowed to chastity. PURITY-IMPURITY.

vest'-ed. Held; legal. LAW-LAWLESSNESS, MUTABILITY-STABILITY; **vested in,** ESTABLISHMENT-REMOVAL; **vested interest,** DUENESS-UNDUENESS, PROPERTY.

ves'-ti-bule. Entrance. BEGINNING-END, CONTENTS-RECEIVER.

ves'-tige. Trace. MARK-OBLITERATION.

vestigia nulla retrorsum [L.] (ves-tij'-i-ɑ nuĺ-lɑ rî-tror'-sum). No footsteps backward. ADVANCE-RETRO-GRESSION, DISCONTINUANCE-CONTINUANCE, PERSIST-ENCE-WHIM.

vest'-ments. Dress. DRESS-UNDRESS, VESTMENTS.

VESTMENTS.

Alb. A long, rich, linen vestment, with close sleeves, worn by priests over the cassock and amice.

Alba. An alb.

Amice. A fine, white, linen collar with hood attached worn by priests.

Apron. A part of a bishop's dress worn in front.

Bands. A pair of linen strips suspended from the neck in front, and worn with clerical vestments.

Biretta. A square cap worn by Roman Catholic officials.

Calote. } A skull-cap worn by Roman Catholic ecclesiasts.
Calotte. }

Canonicals. The official robes of clergymen.

Capouch. A hood or cowl peculiar to the Capuchin monks.

Cardinal's hat. A red hat worn by cardinals.

Cassock. A long, plain, close-fitting garment worn under vestments by clergymen of the Roman Catholic and Anglican Churches.

Chasuble. A sleeveless outer-garment hanging low in front and behind, with a cross on the back, worn by priests.

Cope. A long vestment worn over the alb by Roman Catholic clergymen on solemn occasions.

Costume. All the garments worn at one time. See DRESS.

Cowl. A hooded garment, or the hood alone, worn by monks.

Crosier. A staff with the head crooked, or mounted with a cross; a mark of the office of bishop or archbishop.

Dalmatic. A tunic with wide sleeves, worn over the alb and cassock by deacons during mass or communion.

Fannel. } A cloth used for handling holy vessels or the offertory
Fanon. } bread.

Frock. A long, loose-sleeved robe worn by monks.

Gown. A long, loose robe worn by clergymen, judges, professors, and students.

Hood. A flexible head-covering, as those worn by monks.

Lawn-sleeves. The sleeves of a bishop's vestments in the Anglican Church.

Miter. A tall, double-peaked cap worn by Church dignitaries.

Mozetta. A cape worn by various dignitaries of the Roman Catholic Church.

Pall. A covering for a chalice, made of a square piece of cardboard faced with embroidered linen.

Pallium. A vestment of the pope and sometimes of the archbishops.

Pastoral staff. A staff carried as a mark of ecclesiastical authority by archbishops, etc.; the head is usually curved, but sometimes bears a cross.

Pontificals. The dress and other distinctive insignia of a pontiff, as a bishop.

Robe. The chasuble of former days.

Scapulary. A cloak with hood used mostly as a working dress by monks of certain orders.

Scarf. A light and ornamented garment worn loosely over the shoulders.

Shovel-hat. A broad-brimmed hat turned up at the sides, and with a front projection, worn by clergymen of the Church of England.

Stole. A narrow band, having the ends fringed, worn by clergymen of the Roman Catholic, Oriental, and Anglican Churches while participating in public services.

Surplice. A loose white vestment with flowing sleeves, worn by Anglican, Moravian, and Roman Catholic clergymen, also by the members of vested choirs.

Thurifer. One who bears incense.

Tiara. The triple crown of the pope.

Tonsure. The shaving of the head or a part of it when entering the priesthood or a monastic order

Triple crown. A tiara.

Tunicle. A short vestment worn over an alb by deacons in solemn ceremonies.

Vakass. A vestment of the Armenian Church.

Vestments. An official garment of clergymen.

ves'-try. Room; council. CHURCH, COUNCIL, FANE.

ves'-ture. Clothing. DRESS-UNDRESS.

ve-su'-vi-an. Volcanic. COMBUSTIBLE.

vet'-er-an. Old; soldier. ADEPT-BUNGLER, BELLIG-ERENT, INFANT-VETERAN

vet'-er-i-na-ry art. Healing animals. DOMESTICA-TION-AGRICULTURE.

veteris vestigia flammæ [L.] (vet'-ê-ris ves-tij'-i-ɑ flam'-mî). The traces of the old flame. HABIT-DESUETUDE, REMEMBRANCE-FORGETFULNESS.

ve'-to. Interdict. LEAVE-PROHIBITION.

vetturino [It.] (vet"-tu-rî'-no). Driver. MANAGER, WAYFARER-SEAFARER.

vex. Annoy. PLEASURABLENESS-PAINFULNESS.

vexata quæstio [L.] (vex-ɑ'-tɑ ques'-ti-o). Vexed question. DIFFICULTY-FACILITY, VARIANCE-AC-CORD.

vex-a'-tion. Irritation. PLEASURE-PAIN, PLEASURA-BLENESS-PAINFULNESS; **vexation of spirit,** CONTENT-EDNESS-DISCONTENTMENT, PLEASURE-PAIN.

vex-a'-tious. Troublesome. PLEASURABLENESS-PAINFULNESS.

vexed ques'-tion. Difficulty. DIFFICULTY-FACILITY, VARIANCE-ACCORD.

vex'-il-la-ry. Standard-bearer. CHIEF-UNDERLING.

vex'-il-lum. Flag. SIGN.

vi'-bro-scope. Instrument for measuring vibrations. VIBRATION.

vi et armis [L.] (vai et ɑr'-mis). By force and arms. COERCION, TOIL-RELAXATION, TURBULENCE-CALM-NESS.

via [L.] (vai'-ɑ). By way. AIM-ABERRATION, WAY.

via lactea [L.] (vai lac'-tî-ɑ). Milky Way. UNIVERSE.

via tentanda est [L.] (vai'-ɑ ten-tan'-dɑ est). A way must be attempted. DETERMINATION-VACILLATION.

via trita, via tuta [L.] (vai'-a trai'-tɑ, vai'-ɑ tiu'-tɑ). The beaten path, the safe path. SECURITY-INSECURITY

vi'-a-duct. Bridge. WAY.

vi'-al. Glass vessel. CONTENTS-RECEIVER.

vi'-als. Vessels. **Vials of hate,** LOVE-HATE; **vials of wrath,** FAVORITE-ANGER.

vi'-ands. Food. NUTRIMENT-EXCRETION.

vi-at' i-cum. Provision; rite. CEREMONIAL, PROVI-SION-WASTE.

vi'-brate. Swing. VIBRATION, **vibrate between two extremes,** MUTABILITY-STABILITY.

vi'-bra-tile. Adapted to, or used in, vibratory motion. VIBRATION.

vi-bra'-tion. Oscillation. VIBRATION

VIBRATION.

Alternation. Return from one condition, place, or state to another and back again.

Beat. A regular recurrent throb or pulsation.

Coming and going. A motion hither and thither.

Dance. A series of rhythmic bodily movements and steps

Dodge. A motion from side to side.

Ebb and flow. A rising and falling, as the water of the ocean.

Fluctuation. A state of irregular passing backward and forward

Flux and reflux. A continuous flowing in and out.

Libration. The act or state of oscillating.

Lurch. A sudden swaying or rolling to one side, as a ship.

Motion of a pendulum. A motion to and fro.

Nutation. A constant oscillation or nodding of the head.

Oscillation. The act or state of swinging in a to and fro motion.

Pulsation. The act of moving with rhythmical impulses.

Pulse. The rhythmic beating of the arteries due to the passage of blood-waves.

See-saw. Any up and down movement.

Shake. A short and abruptly checked movement, such as up and down, from side to side, etc.

Swing. To and fro vibrating motion.

Undulation. Motion in wave form.

Ups and downs. Variations of fortune.

Vacillation, etc. Moving in a wavering motion. See DETERMINA-TION-VACILLATION.

Vibration. A swinging or oscillating motion

Vibratiuncle. A slight vibration.

Vibroscope. A device for registering vibrations.

Wag. Motion from side to side.

Wave. The rising and falling of the waters of the ocean.

VIBRATION—*Verbs*.

Alternate. To occur in turns.
Beat. To pulsate; vibrate.
Bob. To move with a jerky motion.
Bob up and down. To move regularly up and down.
Brandish. To shake or wave defiantly, as a sword.
Come and go. To go back and forth.
Courtesy. ⎫ A gesture of respect or honor made by bending the knees
Curtsy. ⎭ so as to drop the body and then raising it again.
Curvet. To leap or bound.
Dance. To move in a rhythmic motion usually to time marked by music.
Dangle. To hang so as to swing loosely.
Ebb and flow. To rise and fall regularly.
Flicker. To move unsteadily or in a wavering manner.
Flounder. To move unsteadily.
Flourish. To wave or swing about; brandish.
Fluctuate. To move to and fro in an irregular manner.
Libate. To pour out a liquid.
Move up and down. To move in regular motions one after the other.
Nod. To bend forward and downward.
Oscillate. To vibrate to and fro.
Pass and repass. To go back and forth.
Pitch. To rise and fall as a ship.
Play. To move with quick, capricious motion, as a sunbeam
Pulsate. To beat with regular rhythmic motion.
Quake. To tremble; vibrate.
Quaver. ⎫ To move with a trembling or quavering motion.
Quiver. ⎭
Reel. To move unsteadily.
Rock. To move from side to side.
Roll. To undulate or fluctuate, as waves.
Shake. To move to and fro in quick, sudden movements.
Stagger. To move from side to side in an unsteady manner.
Swag. A swaying, wabbling motion.
Swagger. To move with a swaying motion.
Swing. To move to and fro with an oscillating motion.
Tick. To make a small, recurring, clicking sound.
Toss. To move with a quick, jerky motion.
Totter. To move or walk unsteadily; waver.
Undulate. To move in a wave-like motion.
Vacillate, etc. To move in an irresolute manner. See DETERMINA-TION-VACILLATION.
Vibrate. To move back and forth, as a pendulum.
Wabble. To move unsteadily.
Wag. To sway; oscillate; move in opposite directions.
Waggle. To move in unsteady, quick motions.
Wamble. To move to and fro in an irregular manner.
Wave. To move with an undulatory motion.
Wiggle. To move to and fro in a quick, squirming manner.

VIBRATION—*Adjectives*.

Libratory. Oscillating; balancing.
Oscillating, etc. Moving to and fro. See *Verbs*.
Oscillatory. ⎫ Moving like a pendulum.
Pendulous. ⎭
Pulsatory, etc. In a pulsating manner. See *Nouns*.
Undulating. Rising and falling like waves
Vibratile. Vibratory.
Vibratory. Moving to and fro.

VIBRATION—*Adverbs, etc.*

Backward and forward. Toward and away.
From side to side. Here and there.
In and out. To and fro.
Like buckets in a well. Swinging up and down.
See-saw. Up and down.
To and fro. Hither and thither.
Up and down.
Wibble-wabble. Unsteady.
Zigzag. In a sharp-angled manner.

vi-bra'-ti-un"-cle. A small vibration. VIBRATION.
vi'-bra-to-ry. Changeable. MUTABILITY-STABILITY, VIBRATION.
vic'-ar. Substitute; clergyman. GOODNESS-BADNESS, MINISTRY-LAITY, REPRESENTATIVE; **vicar of Bray,** BIGOTRY-APOSTASY, PRESUMPTION-OBSEQUIOUSNESS.
vic'-ar-age. Residence. FANE.
vi-ca'-ri-ate. Office. CHURCH.
vi-ca'-ri-ous. Substituted. COMMUTATION-PERMU-TATION.

vic'-ar-ship. Office. CHURCH.
vice. Substitute; vise; wickedness. INSTRUMENT, KEEPING-RELINQUISHMENT, RIGHT-WRONG, TEE-TOTALISM-INTEMPERANCE, VIRTUE-VICE.
vice'-ad''-mi-ral. Naval officer. CHIEF-UNDERLING.
vice'—chan'-cel-lor. Judge. JUDGE; **vice-chancellor's court,** TRIBUNAL.
vice—ge'-ren-cy. Office. COMMISSION-ABROGATION.
vice-ge'-rent. Deputy. CONSIGNEE, REPRESENTA-TIVE.
vice'—pres'-i-dent. Assistant presiding officer. MAN-AGER, PRESIDENT-MEMBER.
vice-re'-gal. Vice-royal. REPRESENTATIVE.
vice'-roy. Ruler. CHIEF-UNDERLING, REPRESENTA-TIVE.
vi-ces'-i-mal. Occurring by twenties; **vi-ges'-i-mal.** FIVE-QUINQUESECTION.
vi'-ce ver'-sa. Interchanged. COMMUTATION-PERMU-TATION, INTERDEPENDENCE, SAMENESS-CONTRAST.
vic'-i-nage. Vicinity. REMOTENESS-NEARNESS.
vi-cin'-i-ty. Proximity. REMOTENESS-NEARNESS.
vi'-cious. Corrupt. APPROVAL-DISAPPROVAL, JUSTI-FICATION-CHARGE, VIRTUE-VICE; **render vicious,** BETTERMENT-DETERIORATION; **vicious reasoning,** RATIOCINATION-CASUISTRY.
vi'-cious-ness. Wickedness. VIRTUE-VICE.
vi-cis'-si-tude. Change. MUTABILITY-STABILITY.
vic'-tim. Sacrifice; sufferer. GULL-DECEIVER, PLEAS-URE PAIN, SUCCESS-FAILURE.
vic'-tim-ize. Dupe; kill. GOODNESS-BADNESS, LIFE-KILLING, SUCCESS-FAILURE, TRUTHFULNESS-FRAUD.
vic'-tim-ized. Duped. PLEASURE-PAIN, SUCCESS-FAILURE.
victis, væ [L.] (**vic'-tis, vî**). Wo to the conquered. CHARITABLENESS-MENACE, FIGHTING-CONCILIATION.
vic'-tor. Winner. SUCCESS-FAILURE.
vic-to'-ri-a. Carriage. CONVEYANCE-VESSEL.
victoriam ne canas triumphum, ante [L.] (**vic-to'-ri-am nî kê'-nas trai-um'-fum, an'-tî**). Do not chant your triumph before you conquer. RECKLESSNESS-CAU-TION, SANGUINENESS-HOPELESSNESS.
vic-to'-ri-ous. Having conquered in battle or contest. SUCCESS-FAILURE.
vic'-to-ry. Overcoming. SUCCESS-FAILURE.
vict'-ual. Food. PROVISION-WASTE.
vict'-ual-er. One who furnishes victuals or provisions. PROVISION-WASTE.
vict'-uals. Food. NUTRIMENT-EXCRETION.
vide et crede [L.] (**vai'-dî et crî'-dî**). See and believe. FAITH-MISGIVING.
vi-del'-i-cet. Namely. INTERPRETATION-MISINTER-PRETATION, UNIVERSALITY-PARTICULARITY.
vide ut supra [L.] (**vai'-dî ut siu-pra**). See what is given above. SIGN.
vi-du'-i-ty. Widowhood. MATRIMONY-DIVORCE.
vie. Contend. GOODNESS-BADNESS; **vie with,** STRIFE-PEACE.
vielle [F.] (**vi-el'**). Hurdy-gurdy. MUSICAL INSTRU-MENTS.
view. Look; opinion; painting; end. APPEARANCE-DISAPPEARANCE, CONCEPTION-THEME, DELINEATION-CARICATURE, FAITH-MISGIVING, HEED-DISREGARD, PURPOSE-LUCK, SIGHT-BLINDNESS; **bring into view,** MANIFESTATION-LATENCY; **come into view,** VISIBIL-ITY-INVISIBILITY; **commanding view,** SIGHT-BLIND-NESS; **in view,** EXPECTATION-SURPRISE, LIGHT-DARK-NESS, PURPOSE-LUCK, VISIBILITY-INVISIBILITY; **keep in view,** CAREFULNESS-CARELESSNESS, HEED-DISRE-GARD; **on view,** APPEARANCE-DISAPPEARANCE; **pre sent to the view,** APPEARANCE-DISAPPEARANCE; **view as,** FAITH-MISGIVING; **view in a new light,** BET-TERMENT - DETERIORATION; **view things** *en couleur de rose,* LIGHTHEARTEDNESS - DEJECTION; **with a view to,** PURPOSE-LUCK.

view'-less. Sightless. VISIBILITY-INVISIBILITY.
vi-ges'-i-mal. Twentieth. FIVE-QUINQUESECTION.
vig'-il. Watch. CAREFULNESS-CARELESSNESS.
vig'-i-lance. Watchfulness. ACTIVITY-INDOLENCE, CAREFULNESS - CARELESSNESS, RECKLESSNESS - CAUTION, SAGACITY-INCAPACITY.
vig'-i-lant. Watchful. CAREFULNESS-CARELESSNESS.
vig'-ils. Devotions. DEVOTION-IDOLATRY.

vign-ette'. Ornament; picture. EMBELLISHMENT-DISFIGUREMENT, ENGRAVING.
vig'-or. Force; capacity; energy. ACTIVITY-INDOLENCE, DETERMINATION-VACILLATION, HEALTH-SICKNESS, RHETORIC, STRENGTH-WEAKNESS, TURBULENCE-CALMNESS, VIGOR-INERTIA.
vigueur de dessus [F.] (vi-gur' de de-su'). Strength from on high. HEAVEN-HELL.

VIGOR—INERTIA.

Acrimony. Deep-seated bitterness.
Acritude. Bitterness of feeling.
Activity. The state of being active.
Agitation. The arousing into action.
Bustle. Excited activity.
Causticity. The quality of sharp and penetrating spite.
Ebullition. State of highly aroused emotions.
Edge. Sharpness.
Effervescence. Great excitement.
Elasticity. The quality of returning to a condition when forced from it.
Energy. Power to do work.
Excitation. The act of getting excited. See EXCITATION.
Exertion. The putting forth of effort. See TOIL.
Ferment. A substance which produces fermentation.
Fermentation. The act or process of fermenting.
Force. That which changes motion or state of a thing.
Go. Energy.
Harshness. The quality of being disagreeable to the ear.
High pressure. Exhausting activity.
Intensity. Relative strength or degree of a quality or force.
Keenness. The state of being keen or intense. See *Adjectives*.
Perturbation. A temporary agitation.
Physical energy. The energy of the human body.
Poignancy. Acuteness.
Point. Directness of application.
Pungency. Quality of piercing.
Resolution. Deliberate determination. See DETERMINATION.
Seasoning. Something which gives zest or relish.
Severity. The quality of being severe.
Splutter. Confused noise.
Stir. Commotion.
Strength. Power.
Vigor. Strength resulting from a sound natural condition.
Virulence. Extreme noxiousness or bitterness.
Voluntary energy. Energy or force freely exerted.

VIGOR—*Denotations.*

Cantharides. A Spanish fly, dried and used in medicine as a blister externally, and internally an irritant.
Quicksilver. A metal characterized by great freedom of movement of its molecules.

VIGOR—*Verbs.*

Energize. To give energy to.
Excite. To rouse up.
Exert. To make effort.
Inflame. To make very zealous. See TURBULENCE.
Intensify. To make more active or severe.
Kindle. To stir up.
Sharpen. To make more acute.
Stimulate. To move to greater activity.
Strike. To hit or rush against with force.

VIGOR—*Verbal Expressions.*

Give energy (see *Nouns*); **make an impression; strike hard; strike home; strike into; wind up** (see STRENGTH).

VIGOR—*Adjectives.*

Active. Lively.
Acute. Sharp in perception and understanding.
Brisk. Moving, acting, or taking place with quickness.
Caustic. Spitefully sharp; burning.
Corrosive. Rusting.
Deep-dyed. Of great intensity.
Double-distilled. Purified twice.
Double-edged. Having two edges.
Double-shotted. Heavily loaded, as a gun.
Drastic. Acting with vigor; purging.
Energetic. Acting with force.
Escharotic. Destructive to human tissues.
Forcible. Possessing force.

Dulness. Lack of quickness of mental powers. See *Adjectives*
Inaction. } Absence of action.
Inactivity. }
Inertia. }
Inertion. } Tendency to continue in a state.
Inertness. }
Inexcitability. The quality of not being easily excited.
Irresolution. The trait of being unfirm in resolution. See DETERMINATION-VACILLATION.
Languor. Chronic listlessness of body.
Latency. The state of lying hidden or undeveloped.
Mental inertness. Lack of mental activity.
Obstinacy. Stubbornness.
Permanence. Ability to remain stable or to last. See MUTATION-PERMANENCE.
Quiescence. Freedom from emotion or agitation. See MOVEMENT-REST.
Sloth. Laziness; unreadiness to work.
Torpor. Continued inactiveness from numbness.
Vis inertiæ [L.] Inertia.

INERTIA—*Verbs.*

Be inert. To be slow in motion.
Hang fire. To be slow in taking effect.
Smolder. To be in a latent state, as fire.

INERTIA—*Adjectives.*

Blunt. Dull.
Dead. Lifeless.
Dormant. Possessing inherent activity in a quiescent state.
Dull. Lacking in quickness of mental powers.
Flat. Not interesting.
Heavy. Sluggish.
Inactive. Not active.
Inert. Not changing its condition.
Latent. Undeveloped.
Lifeless. Lacking in energy.
Passive. Not active.
Slack. Moving in a sluggish manner.
Slow. Not moving fast.
Sluggish. Showing a lack of energy.
Smoldering. In a latent state.
Tame. Spiritless.
Torpid. Continuously inactive from cold. See under INACTIVITY.
Unexerted. Not exerted.
Uninfluential. Not having influence.

INERTIA—*Adverbs, etc.*

In abeyance. Dormant.
Inactively. Not active. See *Adjectives.*
In suspense. Refraining from activity.

VIGOR—ADJECTIVES—*Continued.*

Harsh. Severe.
Incisive. Cutting.
Intense. Violent.
Irritating. Tending to provoke anger.
Keen. Penetrating.
Mordant. Biting.
Poignant. Painful to the spirit.
Potent. Having power. See MIGHT.
Racy. Striking and pleasing.
Rousing. Stirring to action.
Severe. Merciless.
Sharp. Cutting.
Stringent. Severe in operation.
Strong. Having strength.
Trenchant. Cutting deeply.
Virulent. Exhibiting envenomed hostility.
Vivid. Intense.

VIGOR—*Continued*.

VIGOR—*Adverbs, etc.*

Fortiter in re [L]. Firmly in the act. Strongly. With strength. See *Adjectives*.

With telling effect. Acting forcibly.

VIGOR—*Phrases*.

The steam is up.

Vires acquirit eundo [L.]. It gains strength as it goes.

vig'-or-ous. Strong; lusty. FORCE-WEAKNESS, HEALTH-SICKNESS, STRENGTH-WEAKNESS.

vi-ha'-ra. A Buddhist temple. FANE.

vi'-king. Pirate. ROBBER.

vile. Base; sinful; odious. CONSEQUENCE-INSIGNIFICANCE, GENTILITY-COMMONALTY, GOODNESS-BADNESS, PLEASURABLENESS-PAINFULNESS, REPUTATION-DISCREDIT, UPRIGHTNESS-DISHONESTY, VIRTUE-VICE.

vile fano, ne [L.] (vai'-lî fê'-no, nî). Let there be nothing vile in the temple. FANE, GODLINESS-UNGODLINESS.

vile'-ness. Baseness. REPUTATION-DISCREDIT.

vil''-i-fi-ca'-tion. Act of vilifying or defaming. ADULATION-DISPARAGEMENT,

vil'-i-fy. Defame; degrade. ADULATION-DISPARAGEMENT, APPROVAL-DISAPPROVAL, REPUTATION-DISCREDIT.

vil'-i-pend. Depreciate; vilify; despise. ADULATION-DISPARAGEMENT, APPROVAL-DISAPPROVAL, REGARD-DISREGARD.

vil''-i-pend'-en-cy. Disparagement. REGARD-SCORN.

vil'-la. Country-seat. DWELLER-HABITATION.

vil'-lage. Small town. CITY-COUNTRY, DWELLER-HABITATION; **village green**, CITY-COUNTRY; **village talk**, CONVERSATION-MONOLOGUE.

vil'-lag-er. Rustic. DWELLER-HABITATION.

vil'-lain. Knave; peasant. CHIEF-UNDERLING, GENTILITY-COMMONALTY, GOOD MAN-BAD MAN.

vil'-lain-age. The state of a villain. HOLDING-EXEMPTION.

vil'-lain-ous. Vile. GOODNESS-BADNESS, VIRTUE-VICE; **villanous saltpeter**, WEAPON.

vil'-lain-y. Depravity. UPRIGHTNESS-DISHONESTY.

vil'-lein. A serf. CHIEF-UNDERLING.

vil'-len-age. Serfdom. HOLDING-EXEMPTION, LIBERTY-SUBJECTION.

vil'-li. Outgrowths. SMOOTHNESS-ROUGHNESS.

vil'-lous. Nappy. SMOOTHNESS-ROUGHNESS.

vi'-na. Musical instrument. MUSICAL INSTRUMENTS.

vin''-ai-grette'. Bottle. PERFUME-STENCH.

vina non bisogna frasca, al buon [It.] (vî'-na non bî-so'-nya fras'-ka, al bu'-on). Good wine needs no bush. JUSTIFICATION-CHARGE.

vin'-ci-ble. Conquerable. MIGHT-IMPOTENCE.

vincit qui patitur [L.] (vin'-sit quai pat-i-tur). He conquers who endures. SUCCESS-FAILURE.

vincit qui se vincit [L.] (vin'-sit quai sî vin'-sit). He conquers who conquers himself. SUCCESS-FAILURE.

vincit qui se vincit in victoria, bis [L.] (vin'-sit quai sî vin'-sit in vic-to'-ri-a, bis). He twice conquers who conquers himself in victory. SUCCESS-FAILURE.

vinc'-ture. Binding. UNION-DISUNION

vinculo matrimonii, separatio a [L.] (vin'-kiu-lo mat-ri-mo'-ni-ai, sep-a-rê'-shi-o ê). Separation from the bonds of matrimony. MATRIMONY-DIVORCE.

vin d'honneur [F.] (van· do-nur'). Wine of honor. ARRIVAL-DEPARTURE, POLITENESS-IMPOLITENESS.

vin'-di-cate. Defend. JUSTIFICATION-CHARGE; **vindicate aright**, DUENESS-UNDUENESS.

vin'-di-ca''-ted. Justified. JUSTIFICATION-CHARGE.

vin'-di-ca''-ting. Present participle of vindicate. JUSTIFICATION-CHARGE.

vin''-di-ca'-tion. Defense. EVIDENCE-COUNTEREVIDENCE, JUSTIFICATION-CHARGE.

vin-dic'-a-tive. Tending to vindicate. JUSTIFICATION-CHARGE.

vin'-di-ca''-tor. Avenger. JUSTIFICATION-CHARGE, PARDON-VINDICTIVENESS.

vin-dic'-tive. Revengeful. FAVORITE-QUARRELSOMENESS, PARDON-VINDICTIVENESS.

vin-dic'-tive-ness. Revengefulness. PARDON-VINDICTIVENESS.

vin-e-a. Shelter. ATTACK-DEFENSE.

vin'-e-gar. Acid liquid. SWEETNESS-ACIDITY; **vinegar aspect**, BEAUTY-UGLINESS.

vine'-yard. Plantation. CITY-COUNTRY, DOMESTICATION-AGRICULTURE.

vingt-un [F.] (van·t'-un·). Cards. ENTERTAINMENT-WEARINESS.

vint'-age. Harvest. DOMESTICATION-AGRICULTURE, STORE.

vint'-ner. Wine-dealer. DEALER.

vi'-ol. Violin. MUSICAL INSTRUMENTS.

vi'-o-la. The alto or tenor violin. MUSICAL INSTRUMENTS.

vi'-o-late. Break; profane. DUENESS-UNDUENESS, DUTY-DERELICTION, INSUBORDINATION-OBEDIENCE, OBSERVANCE-NONOBSERVANCE, PURITY-IMPURITY; **violate a law**, CONVENTIONALITY-UNCONVENTIONALITY; **violate a usage**, HABIT-DESUETUDE; **violate the law**, LAW-LAWLESSNESS.

vi'-o-la-ting. Outraging. OBSERVANCE-NONOBSERVANCE.

vi''-o-la'-tion. Transgression. DUENESS-UNDUENESS, DUTY-DERELICTION, INSUBORDINATION-OBEDIENCE, OBSERVANCE-NONOBSERVANCE, PURITY-IMPURITY.

vi'-o-lence. Fury. EXCITABILITY-INEXCITABILITY, FAVORITE-ANGER, LAW-LAWLESSNESS, TURBULENCE-CALMNESS; **do violence to**, GOODNESS-BADNESS, OBSERVANCE-NONOBSERVANCE, DUENESS-UNDUENESS.

vi'-o-lent. Forcible. EXCITABILITY-INEXCITABILITY, TURBULENCE-CALMNESS; **violent death**, FAVORITE-ANGER, LIFE-DEATH, LIFE-KILLING; **in a violent degree**, MAGNITUDE-SMALLNESS; **lay violent hands on**, TAKING-RESTITUTION.

vi'-o-lent-ly. Forcibly. TURBULENCE-CALMNESS.

vi'-o-let. Flower. YELLOWNESS-PURPLE.

vi''-o-lin'. Instrument. MUSICAL INSTRUMENTS.

vi''-o-lin'-ist. Musician. MUSICIAN.

vi''-o-lon-cel'-lo. Bass violin. MUSICAL INSTRUMENTS.

violone [It.] (vî''-o-lo'-nê). The largest instrument of the bass-viol kind. MUSICAL INSTRUMENTS.

vi'-per. Snake; snake-like. BENEFACTOR-EVILDOER, FAUNA-FLORA, GOOD MAN-BAD MAN, REMEDY-BANE.

vi-ra'-go. Vixen. FAVORITE-QUARRELSOMENESS.

vi'-rent. Green. REDNESS-GREENNESS.

vires acquiret eundo [L.] (vai'-rîz ac-quai'-ret î-un'-do). It acquires strength by going. INCREASE-DECREASE, SWIFTNESS-SLOWNESS, VIGOR-INERTIA.

vi-res'-cence. Greenness. REDNESS-GREENNESS.

Virgilianæ, sortes [L.] (vir-jil''-i-ê-nî, sor'-tîz). Virgilian lot. PURPOSE-LUCK.

vir'-gin. Maid; fresh; pure. INFANT-VETERAN, MATRIMONY-CELIBACY, NOVELTY-ANTIQUITY, PURITY-IMPURITY; **virgin soil**, KNOWLEDGE-IGNORANCE, PREPARATION-NONPREPARATION.

vir'-gin-als. Instrument. MUSICAL INSTRUMENTS.

vir-gin′-i-ty.   Maidenhood.   MATRIMONY-CELIBACY, PURITY-IMPURITY.

viribus totis [L.] (vir′-i-bus to′-tis).   With the whole force.   TOIL-RELAXATION.

vi-rid′-i-ty.   Greenness.   REDNESS-GREENNESS.

vir′-ile.   Sturdy; masculine.   MALE-FEMALE, MANHOOD, STRENGTH-WEAKNESS.

vi-ril′-i-ty.   The quality of being virile.   MANHOOD, STRENGTH-WEAKNESS.

vir-tu′.   Taste in the fine arts.   TASTE-VULGARITY.

vir′-tu-al.   Essential; actual.   ENTITY-NONENTITY, SUBJECTIVENESS - OBJECTIVENESS;   **virtual image,** SIGHT-DIMSIGHTEDNESS.

vir′-tu-al-ly.   Essentially.   SUBJECTIVENESS-OBJECTIVENESS.

vir′-tue.   Excellence; chastity; merit; valor.   BRAVERY-COWARDICE, GOODNESS-BADNESS, MIGHT-IMPOTENCE, PURITY-IMPURITY, RIGHT-WRONG, VIRTUE-VICE; **by virtue of,** INSTRUMENTALITY, MIGHT-IMPOTENCE; **in virtue of,** RULE-LICENSE; **make a virtue of necessity,** CHOICE-NEUTRALITY, COMPOSITION, EXCITABILITY-INEXCITABILITY, SKILL-UNSKILFULNESS, YIELDING.

VIRTUE—VICE.

Cardinal virtues.   Prudence, justice, temperance, and fortitude.

Credit.   Reputation derived from the confidence of others.

Desert.   Right to reward.

Discharge of duty.   Faithful performance.   See DUTY.

Ethics.   The science of human duty.

Excellence.   The state or property of possessing eminent virtues.

Fulfilment of duty.   Faithful performance.

Good action.   A course worthy of commendation.

Good behavior.   Conformity to rules of conduct.

Innocence.   Freedom from taint.   See INNOCENCE.

Integrity.   Moral soundness.   See UPRIGHTNESS.

Merit.   Excellence or goodness that entitles to honor or reward.

Morality.   The rules of moral duties.

Moral rectitude.   Rightness of character, intention, or life.

Morals.   The doctrines or the practise of the duties of life.

Nobleness.   Exaltation of character.

Performance of duty.   Execution or completion of duty.

Self-control.   The power of having one's faculties and inclinations under control.   See DETERMINATION.

Rectitude.   Uprightness; strict honesty.

Self-denial.   Forbearance to gratify one's own feelings.

Virtue.   Moral excellence.

Virtuousness.   The state or character of being virtuous.

Well-doing.   Acting according to what is right.

Well-spent life.   A life lived in conformity with ethical laws.

Worth.   Value of moral or personal qualities.

VIRTUE—*Verbs.*

Acquit oneself well.   To conduct oneself well.

Act well.   To behave well.

Act well one's part.   To perform well the part.

Be on one's best behavior.   To deport oneself as well as possible.

Be on one's good behavior.   To be under trial in which something depends upon good behavior.

Be virtuous.   To show moral virtue or excellence.

Command one's passions.   To have control of one's feelings or emotions.

Discharge one's duty.   To relieve oneself by the performance of one's duty.

Do one's duty.   To act as one ought.

Fight the good fight.   To live a good life.

Fulfil one's duty.   To accomplish what one is morally bound to do.

Keep in the right path.   To live virtuously.

Master one's passions.   To control the physical impulses.

Perform one's duty.   To do what one is morally bound to do.

Practise virtue.   To endeavor to lead a blameless life.

Redeem one's pledge.   To live abstemiously.   See DUTY.

Set a good example.   To live so as to be a good model.

Set an example.   To make one worthy to be copied.

VIRTUE—*Adjectives.*

Above all praise.   Superlatively good.

Admirable.   Having qualities to excite approbation, esteem, or reverence.

Angelic.   Of the nature of angels.

Beyond all praise.   Surpassing praise.

Commendable.   Deserving of approbation or praise.

Correct.   Free from error.

Creditable.   Deserving or possessing reputation or esteem.

Desertful.   Meritorious.

Deserving.   Being entitled to.

Duteous.   Performing that which is due.

Dutiful.   Controlled by a sense of duty.

Excellent.   Excelling or surpassing others in virtue, or the like.

Exemplary.   Serving as a pattern or model.

Godlike.   Of superior excellence.

Good.   Possessing moral excellence or virtue.

Atrocity.   Shocking cruelty or wickedness.

Backsliding.   A return to wrong or vicious ways.

Besetting sin.   A sin that habitually presses upon one.

Brutality.   Inhumanity; savageness.

Cannibalism.   The practise of eating human flesh.

Corruption.   Perversion of moral principles.   See BETTERMENT-DETERIORATION.

Crime.   A violation of divine or human law.

Criminality.   The quality or state of being criminal; guiltiness.   See INNOCENCE-GUILT.

Crying sin.   A notorious or heinous sin.

Defect.   Moral imperfection.

Deficiency.   Imperfection.

Demerit.   That which deserves blame.

Demoralization.   Loss of morals.

Depravity.   Low state of moral character.

Error.   Violation of duty.

Evil courses.   Wicked ways.

Evil-doing.   Mischief.

Failing.   Imperfection; fault.

Failure.   Omission; non-performance.

Fault.   An offense less serious than a crime.

Flagrancy.   Atrocity; enormity.

Foible.   A personal weakness or failing.

Frailty.   A moral infirmity.

Gusto picaresco [Sp.].   A roguish taste.

Hardness of heart.   The quality of being impenitent of sin.

Immorality.   An immoral act or practise.

Imperfection.   Fault or blemish.

Impropriety.   An unsuitable or improper act.

Indecorum.   That in behavior which violates the rules of civility or etiquette.

Infamy.   A quality which exposes to disgrace.

Infirmity.   A personal frailty or failing.

Iniquity.   Gross injustice.

Knavery.   The practises of a knave.

Laxity.   Looseness of morals.

Looseness of morals.   Lack of strictness in matters of morality.

Lowest dregs of vice.   The lowest possible condition of vice or low living.

Obliquity.   Deviation from moral rectitude.

Peccability.   Liability to sin.

Pollution.   Uncleanness or impurity.

Pravity.   Moral corruption.

Profligacy.   A state of being abandoned in moral principle and in vice.

Scandal.   Defamatory talk; disgrace.

Sin.   Transgression of the law of God.

Sink of iniquity.   A resort of dissolute and depraved persons.

Tenderloin.   A resort of low, depraved people.

Vice.   Immoral conduct or habit.

Viciousness.   Corruption in principles or conduct.

Want of ballast.   Lack of stability of character.

Want of principle.   Lack of moral rectitude.

Weakness.   Want of moral strength.

Weakness of the flesh.   Liability to sin.

Weak side.   Tendency to commit sin.

Wickedness.   Immorality; sinfulness.

Wrong-doing.   Sinning.

Wrong side.   Tendency to crime.

VICE—*Noun of Agent.*

Sinner.   One who has transgressed the law of right or duty.

VICE—*Figurative Nouns.*

Adam.   The one who brought sin into the world.

Alsatian den.   A vile resort of Whitefriars, London.

VIRTUE—Adjectives—*Continued.*

Heaven-born. Born in heaven.
Innocent. Not tainted with sin.
Laudable. Worthy of praise; commendable.
Matchless. Having no equal.
Meritorious. Deserving of reward or honor.
Moral. Relating to duty or obligation.
Noble. Above whatever is low, mean, degrading, or dishonorable.
Peerless. Matchless.
Praiseworthy. Commendable.
Pure. Free from moral defilement or guilt.
Right. According with truth and duty.
Righteous. According with, or performing that which is right.
Right-minded. Having a right or honest mind.
Saintlike. Resembling a saint.
Saintly. Becoming a holy person.
Seraphic. Angelic.
Sterling. Of excellent quality.
Virtuous. Possessing or exhibiting virtue.
Well-intentioned. Having upright intentions or honorable purposes.
Worthy. Having worth or excellence.

VIRTUE—*Adverbs, etc.*

E merito [It.]. According to merit.
Virtuously. In conformity with the moral law.

VIRTUE—*Phrases.*

Cassis tutissima virtus [L.]. The safest helmet is virtue.
Justitia virtutum regina [L.]. Justice is queen of the virtues.
Virtus semper viridis [L.]. Virtue is ever flourishing.
Virtus sola nobilitat [L.]. Virtue alone ennobles.
Virtus vincit invidiam [L.]. Virtue prevails over envy.
Virtutis fortuna comes [L.]. Fortune is the companion of virtue.
Vivit post funera virtus [L.]. Virtue lives after death.

VICE—Adjectives—*Continued from Column 2.*

Imperfect. Morally defective.
Improper. Indecent.
Incarnate. Having the nature of flesh.
Incorrect. Not according to morality.
Incorrigible. Bad beyond correction.
Indecorous. Unbecoming.
Indefensible. Not capable of being justified.
Indiscreet. Wanting in discretion.
Inexcusable. Not able to be justified.
Inexpiable. Not able to be softened or appeased by atonement.
Infamous. Of the worst reputation.
Infernal. Resembling hell.
Infirm. Weak; feeble.
Iniquitous. Unjust; wicked.
Irreclaimable. Incapable of being reclaimed.
Irremissible. Unpardonable.
Lawless. Not held in check by moral law or the laws of man.
Lax. Easy or indulgent in principles.
Lost in iniquity. Hardened by wickedness.
Lost to virtue. Ruined morally.
Malevolent. Wishing evil. See CHARITABLENESS-MALEVOLENCE.
Mephistophelian. Fiendish. [Goethe, *Faust.*]
Misbegotten. Begotten out of wedlock; despicable.
Miscreated. Created amiss.
Naughty. Guilty of improper conduct.
Nefarious. Extremely wicked.
Obdurate. Persistent in sin.
Of a deep dye. Deeply impregnated with: usually in a bad sense.
Past praying for. Lost in sin.
Profligate. Lost in vice.
Recreant. Unfaithful to one's duty.
Reprehensible. Worthy of blame.
Reprobate. Lost to all sense of duty.
Satanic. Devilish.
Scampish. Rascally.
Scandalous. Shocking to morality.
Scurvy. Mean, low, or contemptible.
Shameful. Disgraceful; infamous.
Shameless. Having no sense of shame.
Sinful. Contrary to the laws of God.
Sinister. Evil; malevolent; left-handed.
Sinning. Transgressing divine law.
Steeped in iniquity. Impregnated with wickedness.

VICE—Figurative Nouns—*Continued.*

Cloven foot. The foot of the devil.
Offending Adam. Man's wicked nature.
Old Adam. Depraved human nature.

VICE—*Verbs.*

Be vicious. To violate moral principles.
Brutalize. To make brutal or to become brutal.
Commit sin. To do sin.
Corrupt. To change from good to bad. See BETTERMENT-DETERIORATION.
Demoralize. To cause a loss of morality.
Deviate from the line of duty. To turn aside from duty.
Deviate from the path of virtue. Not to do what one ought. See VIRTUE.
Do amiss. To do wrong.
Err. To deviate from morality.
Fall. To sink in sin or error.
Forget oneself. To be guilty of unworthy conduct.
Go astray. To go out of the right way; to sin.
Hug a fault. To hold fast to a fault.
Hug a sin. To continue to commit a sin.
Lapse. To fail in duty or moral conduct.
Misbehave. To behave badly.
Misconduct oneself. To behave improperly.
Misdemean oneself. To conduct oneself badly.
Misdo. To act wrongly.
Offend. To sin against.
Render vicious. To make corrupt in conduct or principles.
Sin. To commit a sin.
Slip. To fall into fault or error.
Sow one's wild oats. To indulge in the follies and excesses in which young people indulge.
Take a wrong course. To stray from the path of rectitude.
Transgress. To sin.
Trespass. To violate a law of God.
Trip. To commit an error.

VICE—*Adjectives.*

Abandoned. Extremely wicked.
Accursed. Worthy of the curse; detestable.
Atrocious. Full of enormous wickedness.
Base. Low in morals.
Black. Without moral light or goodness.
Blameworthy. Worthy of censure.
Contra bonos mores [L.]. Contrary to good manners.
Corrupt. Changed from good to bad.
Criminal. Pertaining to crime.
Culpable. Worthy of blame.
Deep in iniquity. Sunk low in wickedness.
Degrading. Causing loss in estimation, character, or reputation.
Demoniacal. Pertaining to or resembling evil spirits.
Demoralized. Having suffered a loss of moral principles.
Demoralizing. Causing a loss of morality.
Depraved. Corrupted.
Desertless. Without merit.
Diabolic. }
Diabolical. } Pertaining to the devil; devilish.
Discreditable. Injurious to reputation.
Disgraceful. Causing shame.
Disorderly. Not regulated by the restraints of morality.
Disreputable. Injurious to the reputation.
Dissolute. Given up to vicious pleasures.
Evil-disposed. Disposed to wickedness.
Evil-minded. Disposed to mischief or sin.
Facinorous. Very wicked; atrocious.
Felonious. Malicious.
Fiendlike. Like an infernal being.
Flagitious. Disgracefully criminal.
Flagrant. Notorious.
Foul. Loathsome; impure.
Frail. Not able to withstand temptations to evil.
Graceless. Depraved.
Grave. Serious.
Gross. Obscene; impure.
Heartless. Cruel.
Heinous. Odious; enormous.
Hell-born. Born in hell.
Hellish. Fit for hell; detestable.
Ill-conditioned. Not well-circumstanced.
Immoral. Contrary to divine law.

(*Continued on Column 1.*)

VICE—Adjectives—Continued.

Stygian. Infernal; from the river Styx
Sunk in iniquity. Lost in sin.
Uncommendable. Unworthy of praise.
Unconscionable. Inordinately excessive.
Unduteous. Not rendering the respect or obedience due.
Undutiful. Not submissive to superiors.
Unjustifiable. Not capable of being justified.
Unpradonable. That may not be pardoned.
Unprincipled. Destitute of conscientious scruples.
Unrighteous. Wicked; sinful.

Unseemly. Not becoming.
Unworthy. Improper; wrong.
Vicious. Addicted to immorality.
Vile. Morally base, despicable, or loathsome.
Villainous. Very wicked or vile.
Virtueless. Destitute of moral excellence.
Weak. Lacking in moral vigor
Wicked. Given to vice or sin.
Worthless. Without virtue.
Wrong. Violating moral law

VICE—Adverbs, etc

Sinfully. Wickedly.
Without excuse. Without justification.

Wrong. In a wrong manner.

VICE—Interjection.

O tempora! O mores! [L.] O times! O customs!

VICE—Phrases.

Alitur vitium vivitque tegendo [L.]. Vice is nourished and lives by concealment.
Ex delicto [L.]. From the crime.
I frutti proibiti sono i piu dolci [It.]. The forbidden fruits are sweetest.

L' hypocrisie est un hommage que le vice rend à la vertu [F.]. Hypocrisy is a homage that vice pays to virtue.
Vitiis nemo sine nascitur [L.]. No one is born free from faults.

vir'-tue-less. Without virtue. VIRTUE-VICE.
vir''-tu-o'-so. Adept. TASTE-VULGARITY.
vir'-tu-ous. Good; chaste. INNOCENCE-GUILT, PURITY-IMPURITY, UPRIGHTNESS-DISHONESTY, VIRTUE-VICE.
vir'-tu-ous-ly. In a virtuous manner. VIRTUE-VICE.
vir'-tu-ous-ness. State or character of being virtuous. VIRTUE-VICE.
virtus ariete fortior [L.] (vir'-tus ar''-i-ê'-té for'-shi-or). Virtue is stronger than a battering-ram. BRAVERY-COWARDICE.
virtus, cassis tutissima [L.] (vir'-tus, cas'-sis tiu-tis'-si-ma). The safest helmet is virtue. UPRIGHTNESS-DISHONESTY, VIRTUE-VICE.
virtus, gaudet tentamine [L.] (vir'-tus, gau'-det ten-tam'-i-nî) Virtue rejoices in trial. WELFARE-MISFORTUNE.
virtus milia scuta [L.] (vir'-tus mil'-i-a skiu'-ta). Virtue is a thousand shields. BRAVERY-COWARDICE.
virtus semper viridis [L.] (vir'-tus sem'-per vir'-i-dis). Virtue is always flourishing. VIRTUE-VICE.
virtus sola nobilitate [L.] (vir'-tus so'-la no-bil-i-tê'-tî) Virtue alone ennobles. VIRTUE-VICE.
virtus vincit invidiam [L.] (vir'-tus vin'-sit in-vid'-i-am). Virtue prevails over envy. BRAVERY-COWARDICE, VIRTUE-VICE.
virtutis fortuna comes [L.] (vir-tiu'-tis for-tiu'-na co'-mîz). Fortune is the companion of virtue. SOLITUDE-COMPANY, VIRTUE-VICE.
vir'-u-lence. Bitterness; poisonousness. CHARITABLENESS-MALEVOLENCE, FAVORITE-ANGER, GOODNESS-BADNESS, HEALTHINESS-UNHEALTHINESS, POLITENESS-IMPOLITENESS, VIGOR-INERTIA.

vir'-u-lent. Very active in doing injury. CHARITABLENESS-MALEVOLENCE, FAVORITE-ANGER, FRIEND-FOE, HEALTHINESS-UNHEALTHINESS, VIGOR-INERTIA.
virum volitare per ora [L.] (vai'-rum vol-i-tê'-ri' per o'ra). To fly through the mouths of men. PUBLICITY.
vi'-rus. Poison; germ. HEALTH-SICKNESS, REMEDY-BANE.
vis a tergo [L.] (vis ê ter'-go) Force from behind. PUSH-PULL.
vis-à-vis [F.] (vîz''-a-vî'). Face to face. ANTERIORITY-POSTERIORITY, CONVEYANCE-VESSEL, LATERALITY-CONTRAPOSITION.
vis comica [L.] (vis com'-i-ca). Comic talent. WITTINESS-DULNESS.
vis conservatrix [L.] (vis con-ser-vê'-trix). Preservative power. CONSERVATION.
vis inertiæ [L.] (vis in-er'-shi-î). Force at rest. MIGHT-IMPOTENCE, SENSITIVENESS-APATHY, VIGOR-INERTIA.
vis medicatrix [L.] (vis med-i-kê'-trix). The power of healing. REMEDY-BANE, RENOVATION-RELAPSE.
vis mortua [L.] (vis mor'-tiu-a). The power of death. LIFE-DEATH.
vis viva [L.] (vis vai'-va) Living force. MIGHT-IMPOTENCE.
vi'-sa. Signature. ASSENT-DISSENT
vis'-age. Face; aspect. ANTERIORITY-POSTERIORITY, APPEARANCE-DISAPPEARANCE.
vis'-ce-ra. Intestines. OUTSIDE-INSIDE.
vis'-cid. Sticky. VISCIDITY-FOAM.
vis-cid'-i-ty. Stickiness. VISCIDITY-FOAM.

VISCIDITY—FOAM.

Adhesiveness, etc. The quality of being adhesive. See COHESION
Crassitude. The quality or state of being crass or thick.
Glutinosity. The quality or state of being glutinous, like glue.
Gummosity. The state or quality of being gummy.
Lentor. Viscidity.
Mucosity. The quality or state of being mucous.
Semiliquidity. The state or quality of being semiliquid.
Spissitude. Thickness; viscosity.
Stickiness, etc. The state or quality of being sticky.
Viscidity. The state or quality of being viscid.
Viscosity. The state or quality of being viscous.

VISCIDITY—Nouns of Agency.

Incrassation. The act or process of thickening or the state of being thick.
Inspissation. The act or process of inspissating.
Thickening. The process of making or becoming thick.

Barm. Froth rising on fermented liquors, used for yeast.
Bubble. A vesicle of cohesive liquid filled with air.
Cirro-cumulus. A kind of cloud arranged in well-defined roundish heaps.
Cirro-stratus. Horizontal masses, undulated masses of clouds; separate or in small groups.
Cirrus. A kind of cloud composed of fibers; parallel or extending in all directions.
Cloud. A mass of visible vapor floating in the air
Cloudiness. The condition of being cloudy.
Cumulo-stratus. A form of cloud between cumulus and stratus.
Cumulus. A cloud of irregularly rounded heaps.
Dirty sky. A sky filled with dark, threatening clouds.
Foam. A collection of minute bubbles forming a whitish mass from fermentation or agitation.
Fog. A cloud lying close to the earth composed of finer particles than mist.

VISCIDITY—FOAM—*Continued.*

VISCIDITY—*Denotations.*

Albumen. The white of an egg.
Beeswax. The wax secreted by bees used in making their cells.
Cream. The rich, oily part which collects on the surface of milk.
Emulsion. The white, milky pulp of bitter almonds.
Gelatin. Glutinous material obtained from animal tissues by long boiling.
Glair. The white of an egg.
Glue. A hard, brittle, brownish gelatin obtained by boiling to a jelly the skins, hoofs, etc., of animals.
Gluten. The viscid, tenacious substance which gives adhesiveness to dough.
Gum. A vegetable secretion of many trees.
Jelly. The juice of fruits or meats boiled with sugar to an elastic consistence.
Lava. The molten matter poured out of the crater of a volcano.
Marsh, etc. A tract of soft, wet land. See SWAMP.
Milk. The white fluid secreted by the mammary glands of female animals.
Moisture, etc. Exuding fluid. See DAMPNESS.
Mucilage. An aqueous solution of gum.
Mucus. A viscid fluid secreted by mucous membranes.
Mud. Earth and water mixed so as to be soft and adhesive.
Ooze. Earth so wet as to flow gently.
Phlegm. Viscid mucus secreted in abnormal quantities in the respiratory and digestive passages.
Pituite. Mucus; phlegm.
Protein. The basis of all albuminous substances.
Size. Any viscous substance.
Slime. Soft, moist earth or clay.
Slush. A mixture of snow and water.
Soup. A liquid food made by boiling meat and vegetables.
Squash. Something soft and easily crushed.
Starch. A vegetable substance extracted from potatoes, corn, etc., and used as a food and paste; stiffening.
Wax. A fatty solid substance produced by bees.

VISCIDITY—*Verbs.*

Beat up. To thicken by continual stirring.
Churn. To agitate milk by stirring to produce butter.
Incrassate. To thicken; specifically, in pharmacy.
Inspissate. To thicken, as a fluid, by boiling.
Mash. To change from solid to semiliquid state by crushing or by infusing in hot water, as in brewing.
Squash. To beat or press into a pulp.
Thicken. To make thick or thicker.

VISCIDITY—*Adjectives.*

Albuminous. Like albumen; thick and oily.
Amylaceous. Like starch.
Clammy. Viscous and sticky.
Clotted. Coagulated or thickened, as blood.
Curdled. Changed into a curd, as milk; thickened.
Emulsive. Like, or capable of making like, emulsion.
Gelatine. } Like gelatin; similar to jelly; jelly-like.
Gelatinous. }
Glutinous. Resembling glue; viscid and sticky.
Half-frozen. } Half-solid.
Half-melted. }
Lacteal. } Pertaining to or resembling milk.
Lactean. }
Lacteous. Milk-like.
Lactescent. Having a milky consistency.
Lactiferous. Containing or producing milk or a milky fluid.
Lentous. Tenacious and viscid.
Mastic. Sticky and adhesive.
Milky. Made of, containing, or resembling milk.
Mucid. Mucilaginous; slimy.
Mucilaginous. Like mucilage; sticky and soft.
Mucous. Like mucus; slimy; viscous.
Muculent. Resembling mucus.
Muddy. Containing mud; thick.
Pituitous. Pertaining to a body secreting mucus; like mucus.
Ropy. Stringy and viscous.
Semifluid. } Fluid, but thick and viscous.
Semiliquid. }

Froth. Minute bubbles resulting from fermentation on liquids, or at the mouth from great agitation.
Haze. Very fine particles suspended in the air, with little or no moisture, causing dimness.
Head. The mass of foam rising on the top of a glass of liquor.
Lather. Foam formed by mixing soap and water.
Mackerel sky. A cirro-cumulus cloud-formation, suggesting the form of a fish.
Mare's-tail. Long, fibrous cirrus-clouds indicating rain.
Messenger. A cloud that foretells a storm.
Mist. A collection of watery drops near the earth, less dense or of larger drops than fog.
Nebula. A luminous cloud-like object in the sky.
Nebulosity. Mistiness; haziness.
Nimbus. A rain cloud.
Rack. Thin, flying clouds.
Scud. Light clouds or sea-foam driven by the wind.
Spindrift. Spray blown from the crests of waves.
Spray. Particles of water scattered by wind or other force.
Spume. Froth from fermentation or agitation of a liquid.
Steam. Water in the form of vapor, especially that generated by boiling.
Stratus. A very low, thin layer of cloud.
Suds. Soapy water, especially if frothy; something resembling soapy water.
Surf. The foam thrown up on the beach by the sea-waves.
Vapor. Moisture in the atmosphere, especially if visible.
Woolpack. A cumulus cloud.
Yeast. The froth of new beer or other liquor; froth or spume.

FOAM—*Scientific Noun.*

Nephelognosy. The department of meteorology that treats of the clouds.

FOAM—*Nouns of Agency.*

Bubbling, etc. Formation of vapor or foam. See *Verbs.*
Effervescence. The escape of bubbles of gas from a liquid, otherwise than by boiling.
Fermentation. The process of undergoing an effervescent change; the decomposition of an organic substance caused by a ferment.

FOAM—*Verbs.*

Boil. To cause bubbles to escape from, generally by heating; bubble up.
Bubble. To form bubbles in; to produce bubbles, as a liquid.
Effervesce. To give off bubbles of gas.
Ferment. To cause fermentation in; undergo fermentation.
Foam. To be or become covered or filled with foam; cause to foam.
Froth. To cause to foam; throw off froth.
Guggle. To gurgle.
Gurgle. To flow with a bubbling, noisy current or sound.
Mantle. To become covered, as with foam.
Sparkle. To effervesce with glistening bubbles.

FOAM—*Adjectives.*

Bubbling, etc. Giving off bubbles.
Cloudy, etc. Covered with or resembling clouds.
Effervescent. In a state of effervescence.
Frothy. Covered or filled with froth.
Mousseux [F.]. Foaming; sparkling.
Nappy. Strong; effervescent.
Nebulous. Cloudy; indistinct.
Overcast. Covered, as the sky with clouds.
Sparkling. Effervescent. See *Verbs.*
Up. Rising, as in a cloud.
Vaporous. Full of or resembling vapor.

VISCIDITY—*Adjectives—Continued.*

Slab. Mucilaginous.
Slabby. Thick; viscous.
Sticky. Adhering to a surface; thick and adhesive.
Succulent. Juicy; specifically, of plants.
Thick. Having considerable density or thickness.
Uliginous. Slimy; miry.
Viscid. Adhesive; semifluid; viscous.
Viscous. Having a glutinous consistency; viscid.

---

vis-cos'-i-ty. Viscidity. VISCIDITY-FOAM.
vis'-count. Noble. REPUTATION-DISCREDIT.
vis'-cous. Tenacious. VISCIDITY-FOAM.

vise. Clamp. RELEASE-RESTRAINT.
Vish'-nu. God. JOVE-FIEND.
vis"-i-bil'-i-ty. Visibleness. VISIBILITY-INVISIBILITY.

VISIBILITY—INVISIBILITY.

Conspicuity. The quality of being bright.
Conspicuousness. The quality of attracting the eye.
Distinctness. The quality of being clearly seen.
Perceptibility. The state of being cognizable.
Visibility. The state of being visible.

VISIBILITY—*Nouns of Agency.*

Appearance. Act of coming into view. See APPEARANCE.
Manifestation. Act of making plain to the eye. See MANIFESTATION.

VISIBILITY—*Nouns of Cause.*

Exposure. The state of being exposed to observation.
Ocular demonstration. Proof of eye that precludes denial.
Ocular evidence. The evidence of the eye.
Ocular proof. The establishment of fact by the evidence of the eye.

VISIBILITY—*Nouns of Place.*

Exposure. The place where anything can be seen.
Field of view. The space within which objects can be seen.

VISIBILITY—*Verbs.*

Appear. To come within sight.
Appear to one's eyes. To seem.
Arise. To come up into view.
Attract the attention. To become conspicuous. See HEED.
Become visible. To pass into a state of visibility.
Betray itself. To show what is not evident.
Be visible. To be able to be seen.
Break through the clouds. To become evident.
Burst forth. To come out suddenly.
Burst upon the sight. To come suddenly within reach of the eye.
Burst upon the view. To come suddenly within sight.
Catch the eye. To attract the attention.
Come forth. To come from concealment.
Come forward. To come to a nearer position; to offer oneself.
Come in sight. To appear.
Come into view. To put in an appearance.
Come out. To be made public.
Come upon the stage. To come upon the scene of action.
Crop out. To become partly visible.
Crop up. To appear above the surface.
Discover itself. To show itself.
Expose itself. To lay itself open.
Expose to view. To be placed in sight. See MANIFESTATION.
Float before the eyes. To be suspended in full view.
Glare. To shine with brilliancy.
Glimmer. To send out flickering rays.
Heave in sight. To come within view, as a ship.
Live in a glass house. To be open to countercharge.
Loom. To rise gradually to an impressive position.
Make its appearance. To come into view.
Manifest itself. To make its presence known.
Meet the eye. To become discernible.
Open to the view. To become a wider view.
Peep out. To be seen partially.
Peer out. To appear.
Present itself. To come into view.
Produce itself. To bring itself into view.
Reappear. To come into sight after absence.
Reveal itself. To make itself known.
See the light of day. To come into the daylight from a dark place.
Show. To cause to be seen.
Show itself. To appear.
Show its face. To put in an appearance.
Show up. To expose, as a fraud.
Speak for itself. See MANIFESTATION.
Spring out. To come into view.
Spring up. To arise suddenly.
Stand forth. To stand before.
Stand out. To be prominent; to be in relief.
Stand up. To stand erect.
Turn up. To put in an appearance.

VISIBILITY—*Adjectives.*

Apparent. Easily seen.
Autoptical. Based upon the evidence of one's own eyes
À vue d'œil [F.]. By the eye.
Before one. In one's presence.
Before one's eyes. In one's presence.
Clear. Distinct.
Conspicuous. In very plain sight.
Definite. Clear.
Discernible. Capable of being perceived.

Concealment. The state of being hidden.
Delitescence. Seclusion.
Imperceptibility. Indistinguishability.
Indistinctness. The lack of perspicuity.
Invisibility. The quality of not being in sight.
Latency. The state of being hidden. See MANIFESTATION-LATENCY.
Mystery. That which is very obscure.
Non-appearance. Failure to come to sight.

INVISIBILITY—*Verbs.*

Be hidden. To be put out of sight. See MANIFESTATION-LATENCY.
Be invisible. To be so as not to be seen.
Conceal. To keep purposely from sight. See ENLIGHTENMENT-SECRECY.
Escape notice. To slip from the observation.
Hide. To secrete. See ENLIGHTENMENT-SECRECY.
Lose sight of. To fail to take note of.
Lurk. To lie hidden to attack or to escape notice.
Not see. To overlook.
Put out of sight. To hide.
Render invisible. To make impossible to be seen.

INVISIBILITY—*Adjectives.*

À perte de vue [F.]. Out of sight.
Behind the curtain. In secret.
Behind the scenes. Where one has inside information
Blurred. Indistinct.
Confused. Mixed.
Covert. Secret.
Dark. Not easily seen.
Dim. Shadowy.
Eclipsed. Cast into the shadow.
Ill-defined. Badly outlined.
Ill-marked. With indistinct marks.
Imperceptible. Not to be seen.
Inconspicuous. So as not to attract attention.
Indefinite. With uncertain boundaries.
Indiscernible. Not capable of being discerned.
Indistinct. Not clearly perceptible.
Indistinguishable. Incapable of being separated by the eye.
Invisible. Not to be seen.
Misty. Made indistinct, as if by mist.
Mysterious. Obscure.
Non-apparent. Not evident.
Not in sight. Out of sight.
Obscure. Less bright.
Out of focus. Not in focus.
Out of sight. Out of the field of vision.
Shadowy. Lacking clearness.
Sightless. Without sight.
Unapparent. Not apparent.
Unconspicuous. Not conspicuous.
Undefined. Not defined, with uncertain boundaries.
Under an eclipse. Overshadowed.
Undiscernible. Not capable of being discerned
Unseen. Not visible. See SIGHT.
Veiled. Shielded from sight.
Viewless. Invisible.

INVISIBILITY—*Phrase.*

Celare fraudem fraus est [L.]. It is a fraud to conceal a fraud.

VISIBILITY—ADJECTIVES—*Continued.*

Distinct. Easily perceived.
En évidence [F.]. In evidence; conspicuous.
Exposed to view. Laid open to sight.
Glaring. Reflecting a brilliant light.
In bold relief. Giving the appearance of standing out from the background.
In focus. Giving a sharp image.
In full view. Entirely in sight.
In one's eye. Imaginary.
In relief. Projecting upon a plane.
In sight. In view of the eye.
In strong relief. Distinctly outlined.
In view. In the plane of sight.
Obvious. Plainly evident.
Oculis subjecta fidelibus [L.]. Examined by trustworthy eyes.
Palpable. That may be touched; obvious.
Panoramic. Pertaining to an extended view.
Perceivable. Capable of being seen, physically or mentally,

VISIBILITY—Adjectives—Continued.

Perceptible. Which may be seen.
Periscopic. Viewing on all sides.
Plain. Clear.
Recognizable. Able to be recognized.
Staring. Gazing fixedly.
Stereoscopic. Pertaining to the stereoscope.

Unclouded. Not obscure.
Under one's eye. Under one's direction.
Visible. Perceivable by the eye.
Well-defined. Clearly bounded.
Well-marked. Plainly marked.

VISIBILITY—Adverbs.

Before one's eyes. In front of one.
In sight of. Within the range of vision.

Veluti in speculum [L.]. As in a looking-glass.
Visibly. In a visible manner.

vis'-i-ble. Apparent. SIGHT-BLINDNESS, VISIBILITY-INVISIBILITY; **become visible,** APPEARANCE-DISAPPEARANCE; **be visible,** APPEARANCE-DISAPPEARANCE; **darkness visible,** LIGHT-DARKNESS.

vis'-i-bly. In a visible manner. SIGHT-BLINDNESS, VISIBILITY-INVISIBILITY.

vi'-sion. Sight; dream; fancy. FANCY, JOVE-FIEND, RHETORIC, SIGHT-BLINDNESS, SIGHT-DIMSIGHTEDNESS; **organ of vision,** SIGHT-BLINDNESS.

vi'-sion-a-ry. Dreamer; imaginary. FANCY, ORTHODOXY-HETERODOXY, POSSIBILITY-IMPOSSIBILITY, SUBSTANCE-NULLITY.

vi'-sion-less. Sightless. SIGHT-BLINDNESS.

vis'-it. Sojourn. ARRIVAL-DEPARTURE, POLITENESS-IMPOLITENESS, SOCIABILITY-PRIVACY; **visit upon,** RECOMPENSE-PUNITION.

vis'-it-ant. Visitor. ARRIVAL-DEPARTURE, SOCIABILITY-PRIVACY.

vis''-it-a'-tion. Visit. HEALTH-SICKNESS, PLEASURE-PAIN, WELFARE-MISFORTUNE; **visitations of Providence,** DIVINITY; **visitations of the sick,** CEREMONIAL.

vis--it-ing. Calling. **Visiting card,** SIGN; **on visiting terms,** AMITY-HOSTILITY, SOCIABILITY-PRIVACY.

vis'-it-or. Guest; official. FRIEND-FOE, MANAGER.

vis'-or. Mask. EXPOSURE-HIDINGPLACE.

vis'-ta. View. APERTURE-CLOSURE, APPEARANCE-DISAPPEARANCE, EXPECTATION-SURPRISE, SIGHT-BLINDNESS.

vis'-u-al. Visible. SIGHT-BLINDNESS; **visual organ,** SIGHT-BLINDNESS.

vi''-ta-bil'-i-ty. Quality of being vital. LIFE-DEATH.

vitæ, elixir [L.] (vai'-tî, î-lix'-ir). The elixir of life. REMEDY-BANE.

vi'-tal. Living; necessary. CONSEQUENCE-INSIGNIFICANCE, LIFE-DEATH.

vi-tal'-i-ty. Vital force. LIFE-DEATH, MUTABILITY-STABILITY, STRENGTH-WEAKNESS.

vi'-tal-ize. Animate. LIFE-DEATH.

vi'-tals. Parts necessary for life. OUTSIDE-INSIDE.

vitam impendere vero [L.] (vai'-tam im-pen'-der-î vî'-ro). To stake one's life for the truth. ASSERTION-DENIAL, UPRIGHTNESS-DISHONESTY.

vi'-ti-ate. Debase. BETTERMENT-DETERIORATION.

vi'-ti-at''-ed. Contaminated. HEALTH-SICKNESS.

vi''-ti-a'-tion. Depravation. BETTERMENT-DETERIORATION.

vitiis nemo sine nascitur [L.] (vish'-i-is nî'-mo sai'-nî nas'-si-tur). No one is born free from faults. VIRTUE-VICE.

vitium vivatque tegendo, alitur [L.] (vish''-i-um vai-vat'-quî ti-jen'-do, al'-it-ur). Vice is nourished and lives by concealment. ENLIGHTENMENT-SECRECY, VIRTUE-VICE.

vit'-re-ous. Glassy. DIAPHANEITY-OPAQUENESS, HARDNESS-SOFTNESS.

vit''-ri-fi-ca'-tion. Vitrifaction. HARDNESS-SOFTNESS.

vit'-ri-fy. Fuse into glass. HARDNESS-SOFTNESS.

vit'-rite. Hard glass. DIAPHANEITY-OPAQUENESS.

vi-tu'-per-ate. Upbraid. APPROVAL-DISAPPROVAL.

vi-tu''-per-a'-tion. Abuse; blame. APPROVAL-DISAPPROVAL.

vi-tu'-per-a-tive. Abusive. APPROVAL-DISAPPROVAL.

vi-tu'-per-a''-tor. Fault-finder. FLATTERER-DEFAMER.

vi'-va. Live. APPROVAL-DISAPPROVAL, REPUTATION-DISCREDIT.

vi-va'-ce. Lively. MUSIC.

vi-va'-cious. Active. ACTIVITY-INDOLENCE, LIGHT-HEARTEDNESS-DEJECTION, SENSITIVENESS-APATHY.

vi-va'-cious-ness. Quality of being vivacious. SENSITIVENESS-APATHY.

vi-vac'-i-ty. Liveliness. ACTIVITY-INDOLENCE.

vivamus, dum vivimus [L.] (vai-vê'-mus, dum viv'-i-mus). Let us live while we live. ENTERTAINMENT-WEARINESS.

vivandière [F.] (vî''-van·dyêr'). Woman sutler. DEALER.

vi-va'-ri-um. Habitation. DOMESTICATION-AGRICULTURE.

viva voce [L.] (vai'-va vo'-sî). By spoken word. SPEECH-INARTICULATENESS.

vive la bagatelle [F.] (vîv la ba-ga-tel'). Success to trifling. ENTERTAINMENT-WEARINESS.

vive memor lethi [L.] (vai'-vî mi'-mor lî'-thai). Live mindful of death. ADVICE, WARNING.

vivendi causa [L.] (vai-ven'-dai cau'-sa). With the cause of living. LIFE-DEATH.

vivere est cogitare [L.] (viv'-i-rî est coj''-i-tê'-rî). To live is to think. REFLECTION-VACANCY.

vivere, non est, sed valere, vita [L.] (viv'-e-rî, non est, sed va-lî'-rî, vai'-ta). Not to live, but to be well, is life. HEALTH-SICKNESS, LIFE-DEATH.

vive, valeque [L.] (vai'-vî, va-lî'-quê). Life and health to you! farewell! ARRIVAL-DEPARTURE.

viv'-id. Intense. COLOR-ACHROMATISM, CONSCIOUSNESS-INSENSIBILITY, LIGHT-DARKNESS, VIGOR-INERTIA.

vi-vif'-i-cate. To animate. LIFE-DEATH.

viv''-i-fi-ca'-tion. Revival. LIFE-DEATH.

viv'-i-fied. Animated. LIFE-DEATH.

viv'-i-fy. Animate. LIFE-DEATH, STRENGTH-WEAKNESS.

viv'-i-fy-ing. Animating. LIFE-DEATH.

viv''-i-sec'-tion. Dissection. CHARITABLENESS-MALEVOLENCE, SENSUALITY-SUFFERING.

vivit post funera virtus [L.] (vai'-vit post fiu'-ni-ra vir'-tus). Virtue lives after death. REPUTATION-DISCREDIT, VIRTUE-VICE.

vivre, savoir [F.] (vîvr, sa-vwar'). Good breeding. SOCIETY-LUDICROUSNESS.

vix'-en. Shrew; fox. FAUNA-FLORA, FAVORITE-QUARRELSOMENESS, MALE-FEMALE.

viz. Namely. INTERPRETATION-MISINTERPRETATION, UNIVERSALITY-PARTICULARITY.

vi-zier'. Official. MANAGER, REPRESENTATIVE.

viz'-or. Mask. EXPOSURE-HIDINGPLACE.

vobis, sic vos non [L.] (vo'-bis, sic vos non). Thus you do not labor for yourselves. THEFT.

vo'-ca-ble. Sound. WORD-NEOLOGY.

vo-cab'-u-la-ry. List. WORD-NEOLOGY.

vo'-cal. Oral. MUSIC, VOCALIZATION-MUTENESS.

vo'-cal-ism. Exercise of the vocal organs. MUSIC.

vo'-cal-ist. Singer. MUSICIAN.

vo-cal'-i-ty. Quality of being vocal. VOCALIZATION-MUTENESS.

vo''-cal-iz-a'-tion. Sound. VOCALIZATION-MUTENESS.

VOCALIZATION—MUTENESS.

Accent. Stress of voice on a particular word or syllable.

Accentuation. The act of accenting or giving stress to words.

Articulate sound. The sound of the voice that can be heard.

Articulation. Distinct utterance.

Broad accent. Speech that is strongly marked by a peculiar accent.

Clearness. The quality of being clear or easily understood.

Clearness of articulation. The quality by which speech is easily understood.

Cry. A loud utterance.

Delivery. The style of utterance.

Distinctness. Quality of being easily understood.

Emphasis. Special stress of voice in speaking or reading.

Enunciation. The mode of utterance of vocal sounds.

Ejaculation. The uttering of brief exclamations.

Euphony. Agreeableness of sound.

Exclamation. An emphatic expression.

Fine voice. A voice that is clearly heard.

Foreign accent. A stress of voice peculiar to a particular language.

Gastriloquism. Ventriloquism.

Good voice. A voice that is distinctly heard or understood.

Intonation. Modulation of the voice in speaking.

Melody. Vocalization that is agreeable to the ear.

Musical voice. A voice that is agreeable to the ear. See MELODY.

Native accent. A stress of voice peculiar to a particular place.

Polyphonism. Multiplicity of sounds.

Powerful voice. A voice able to be heard at a great distance.

Prolation. Pronunciation; utterance.

Pronunciation. The act or manner of speaking words.

Pure accent. An accent or method of speech free from any peculiarity.

Sound. A sensation caused by the voice, etc., received through the ear. See SOUND.

Sound of voice. The vibrations caused by the voice striking the ear. See SOUND.

Stage whisper. A loud whisper.

Strain. The prevailing note of a song, etc.

Stress. The relative force with which sound is uttered.

Strong accent. A very apparent peculiarity of pronunciation.

Tone. The character of a sound.

Tone of voice. The character of the sound of the voice.

Utterance. Vocal expression.

Ventriloquism. The speaking of tones in such a manner that the sound seems to come from some other source than the speaker.

Vocality. Utterance.

Vocalization. The act of uttering.

Vociferation. Vehement utterance of the voice.

Voice. A sound produced by the vocal organs.

VOCALIZATION—*Nouns of Agency.*

Bellows. A machine for producing a current of air.

Lungs. The organs of respiration used in producing vocal sound.

Organ. An instrument for producing musical sounds.

VOCALIZATION—*Associated Nouns.*

Homonym. A word which has a sound similar to another word.

Orthoepy. The science or art of correct pronunciation.

Phonology. The science of human vocal sounds.

Science of voice. Knowledge of the properties, characteristics, etc., of the human voice.

VOCALIZATION—*Verbs.*

Accentuate. To give emphasis to.

Articulate. To utter sounds in distinct syllables.

Aspirate. To make harsh or uneven sound.

Breathe. To utter with breath only.

Cry. To utter a sound in loud and vehement tone.

Deliver. To utter articulate sounds or vocal tones.

Ejaculate. To speak vehemently and briefly.

Enunciate. To utter with organs of speech.

Give tongue. To bark.

Give utterance. To speak.

Mouth. To enunciate in a loud, unnatural, and constrained manner.

Prolate. To pronounce or utter with a drawl.

Pronounce. To give articulate utterance to.

Rap out. To express by means of raps.

Utter. To give out or send forth with audible sound.

Vocalize. To utter with the voice; make sonant.

Whisper in the ear. To speak with caution into the ear.

VOCALIZATION—*Adjectives.*

Articulate. Clearly enunciated.

Distinct. Clear.

Absence of voice. The quality of being unable to speak.

Aphonia. Loss of the power of articulation.

Aphony. Loss of voice.

Childish treble. Speech that pipes and whistles, "his big manly voice, turning again toward childish treble, pipes and whistles in his sound." [Shakespeare, *As You Like It*, II, vii.]

Dumbness. State or quality of being dumb or unable to speak.

Dysphony. Difficulty in uttering articulate sounds.

Falsetto. Artificial tones of the voice.

Harsh voice. A discordant or disagreeable voice. See CACOPHONY.

Muteness. Inability to speak.

Obmutescence. Loss of speech.

Raucity. Hoarseness.

Silence. Absence of sound or speech.

Unmusical voice. A harsh, disagreeable voice. See DISSONANCE.

Want of voice. Lack of the power of speech.

MUTENESS—*Nouns of Agent.*

Dummy. }
Mute. } One who is unable to speak.

MUTENESS—*Verbs.*

Cut one short. To cause one to stop speaking.

Drown the voice. To overwhelm the voice by other sounds.

Dumfounder. To strike dumb; confound.

Gag. To silence by force.

Keep silence. To keep still and mute. See TALKATIVENESS-TACITURNITY.

Muffle. To deaden the sound of.

Muzzle. To put to silence; prevent from utterance.

Put to silence. To make silent.

Render mute. To render speechless by refutation of argument.

Render silent. To be made speechless.

Silence. To compel to keep silent or still.

Smother. To cover up or suppress.

Speak low. To speak with little volume to the voice.

Speak softly. To speak in low tones.

Stick in the throat. To be unable to speak.

Stop one's mouth. To cause one to stop speaking.

Strike dumb. Deprive of speech.

Suppress. To withhold from expression or utterance.

Whisper. To utter in a whisper.

MUTENESS—*Adjectives.*

Aphonous. Affected with or characterized by aphony.

Breathless. Intense or eager, as if holding the breath.

Croaking. Harsh; guttural.

Deaf and dumb. Without ability to hear or speak.

Deaf-mute. Dumb in consequence of deafness.

Dry. Uninteresting; unattractive.

Dumb. Unable to make articulate sounds.

Hoarse. Harsh and rough in sound.

Hoarse as a raven. With a croaking voice.

Hollow. Resembling sound reverberated from a cavity.

Husky. Not clear; hoarse.

Inarticulate. Not produced in distinct intelligible syllables.

Inaudible. That cannot be heard or is very difficult to hear.

Mum. Saying nothing; silent.

Mute. Uttering no word or sound.

Mute as a fish. Voiceless.

Mute as a mackerel. Dumb.

Mute as a stock-fish. Without utterance.

Muzzled. Put to silence.

Raucous. Hoarse.

Sepulchral. Unnaturally low and hollow in tone.

Silent. Not making any sound or noise.

Speechless. Being without faculty of speech.

Taciturn. Habitually silent or reserved.

Tongueless. Speechless; silent.

Tongue-tied. Having the speech impeded by tongue-tie.

Voiceless. Having no voice or speech.

Wordless. Having no words; dumb.

MUTENESS—*Adverbs, etc.*

In a broken voice. With disconnected utterance.

In a cracked voice. In a broken voice.

In a low tone. Softly.

Sotto voce [It.]. In a low voice; softly.

With bated breath. With the voice checked through fear, awe, etc.

With the finger on the lips. With silence.

MUTENESS—*Phrase.*

Vox faucibus hæsit [L.]. The voice stuck in the throat. [Virgil, *Æneid*, ii, 774.]

VOCALIZATION—Adjectives—*Continued.*

Ejaculatory. Exclamatory.
Euphonious. Well-sounding.
Oral. Uttered through the mouth.

Phonetic. Belonging or relating to sounds made by the human voice or articulate sounds.
Stertorious. Accompanied by a snoring sound.
Vocal. Pertaining or relating to the voice or oral utterance.

vo'-cal-ize. Voice. VOCALIZATION-MUTENESS.
vo-ca'-tion. Occupation. OCCUPATION.
voce, *sotto* [It.] (vo'-chê, sot'-to). In a low voice. LOUDNESS-FAINTNESS, SPEECH-INARTICULATION, VOCALIZATION-MUTENESS.
vo-cif''-er-a'-tion. Shout. CRY-ULULATION, LOUDNESS-FAINTNESS, VOCALIZATION-MUTENESS.
vogue. Fashion; rumor. HABIT-DESUETUDE, REPUTATION-DISCREDIT, SOCIETY-LUDICROUSNESS.
vogue la galère [F.] (vog la ga-lêr'). Forward, come what may. ENTERTAINMENT-WEARINESS, PERSISTENCE-WHIM.
voice. Tone; speech; report; speaker; a property of verbs. CHOICE-NEUTRALITY, CRY-ULULATION, DECISION-MISJUDGMENT, SOUND-SILENCE, VOCALIZATION-MUTENESS; **active voice,** VERB; **give one's voice for,** ASSENT-DISSENT; **make one's voice heard,** DOMINANCE-IMPOTENCE; **passive voice,** VERB; **raise one's voice,** ASSERTION-DENIAL, CRY-ULULATION, SPEECH-INARTICULATION; **still small voice,** DUTY-DERELICTION, LOUDNESS-FAINTNESS; **voice against,** ANTAGONISM-CONCURRENCE, ASSENT-DISSENT; **voice of conscience,** REPENTANCE-OBDURACY; **voice of the charmer,** FLATTERER-DEFAMER; **voice of the tempter,** MOTIVE-CAPRICE; **want of voice,** VOCALIZATION-MUTENESS; **warning voice,** WARNING.
voice'-less. Without voice. VOCALIZATION-MUTENESS.
void. Nullify; evacuate; empty. ADMISSION-EXPULSION, COOPERATION-OPPOSITION, SUBSTANCE-NULLITY; **null and void,** LAW-LAWLESSNESS; **void of foundation,** TRUTHFULNESS-FABRICATION; **void of suspicion,** FAITH-MISGIVING.

voiturier [F.] (vwa-tü-riê'). Wagoner. WAYFARER-SEAFARER.
volante [Sp.] (vo-lan'-tê). Carriage. TRAVELING-NAVIGATION.
volat irrevocabile verbum, semel emissum [L.] (vo'-lat ir-rev-o-cab'-i-lî ver'-bum, sî'-mel î-mis'-sum). Once sent forth the word flies irrevocable. PUBLICITY.
vol'-a-tile. Vaporized; fickle; changeable. DETERMINATION - VACILLATION, HEAVINESS - LIGHTNESS, LIQUEFACTION-VOLATILIZATION, LIQUID-GAS, PERSISTENCE-WHIM.
vol''-a-til'-i-ty. The quality of being volatile. HEAVINESS-LIGHTNESS, LIQUEFACTION-VOLATILIZATION, LIQUID-GAS.
vol'-a-til-ize''. To render volatile. LIQUEFACTION-VOLATILIZATION.
vol'-a-til-ized''. Rendered volatile. LIQUEFACTION-VOLATILIZATION.
vol-au-vent [F.] (vol''-o-van·'). Meat pie. NUTRIMENT-EXCRETION.
vol-can'-ic. Bursting; heat; stirred. COMBUSTIBLE, EXCITABILITY-INEXCITABILITY, HEAT-COLD, HEATING-COOLING, TURBULENCE-CALMNESS.
vol-ca'-no. Violence; heat; eruption. GEOLOGY, OVEN-REFRIGERATOR, REFUGE-PITFALL, TURBULENCE-CALMNESS; **on a volcano,** SECURITY-INSECURITY.
volitare per ora, virum [L.] (vol-i-tê'-rî per o'-ra, vai'-rum). To speak through the mouths of men. [Virgil, *Georgics*, iii, 9.] PUBLICITY.
vol''-i-ta'-tion. Flight. TRAVELING-NAVIGATION.
vo-li'-tion. Will. VOLITION-OBLIGATION.

VOLITION—OBLIGATION.

Conation. An attempt; endeavor.
Determination, etc. Firm resolution; fixed purpose. See DETERMINATION.
Discretion. Prudence; wise conduct; liberty of acting without control.
Frame of mind. State of mind. See READINESS.
Freedom, etc. State of being free; liberty; independence. See LIBERTY.
Free will. That which acts without constraint.
Intention, etc. Determination to act in a particular manner. See PURPOSE.
Option. Selection; right of choice. See CHOICE.
Originality. The quality of being productive of new thoughts or combinations of thoughts.
Pleasure. That which the will dictates or prefers.
Predetermination, etc. Purpose formed beforehand. See PREDETERMINATION.
Self-control. Restraint exercised over oneself. See DETERMINATION.
Spontaneity. Quality of proceeding without compulsion.
Spontaneousness. State of acting of one's own accord.
Velleity. An inactive or indolent wish or inclination.
Volition. The power of willing; any act or exercise of will.
Voluntariness. State of acting from choice.
Will. Something resolved or determined upon.
Will and pleasure. Resolution; preference.
Wish. Something desired; eager or longing desire.

VOLITION—*Noun of Source.*

Mind. That which thinks, feels, and wills; the soul.

VOLITION—*Verbs.*

Determine, etc. To resolve; come to a decision. See DETERMINATION.
Do of one's own accord, etc. To exercise one's own will.
Do upon one's own authority. To act without restraint.

Adverse fate. }
Adverse necessity. } A contrary or unfavorable lot or life.
Anagka [Gr.]. Force; constraint; necessity.
Astral influence. The astrological power which governs one's life.
Blind impulse. A hidden or unseen restraining power.
Book of Fate. A book of judgments or decrees.
Compulsion, etc. Constraint of will or action. See COERCION.
Dernier ressort [F.] The last resource.
Destination. The act of fixing by destiny or by an authoritative decree.
Destiny. A resistless power or agency conceived as determining the future.
Dire fate. }
Dire necessity. } An evil or dreadful outcome.
Doom. Judgment.
Election. Divine choice.
Fatalism. The doctrine of an inevitable necessity for all things.
Fatality. The state of proceeding from destiny; necessity superior to free and rational control.
Fate. Appointed lot or life.
Fates. The three goddesses who were supposed to determine the course of human life.
Foredoom. Sentence or doom decreed in advance.
Foreordination. The ordering of all things beforehand by the Creator.
Fortune. That which falls or is to befall one.
God's will. An interruption of the usual course of events, in which God's purpose is recognized.
Hard fate. }
Hard necessity. } A lot or life difficult to bear or endure.
Hobson's choice. A choice without an alternative.
Ides of March. A fateful day. [Shakespeare, *Julius Cæsar*.]
Imperious fate. }
Imperious necessity. } Lot or event that cannot be controlled.
Inevitableness, etc. Certainty of happening. See *Adjectives*.
Inexorable fate. }
Inexorable necessity. } Unchangeable or relentless course.

VOLITION—OBLIGATION—*Continued*.

VOLITION—Verbs—*Continued*.

Do what one chooses. To be independent; be free to act. See LIBERTY.
Exercise one's discretion. To be free in the exercise of judgment.
Have a will of one's own. To exercise one's power of choice.
Have it all one's own way. To dictate; order with authority.
Have it one's own way. To do as one pleases.
Have one's will. To decide for oneself.
List. To desire or choose; prefer.
Originate, etc. To produce what is new; create. See CAUSE.
See fit. To be disposed; purpose.
Settle, etc. To bring to a conclusion; decide; determine. See CHOICE.
Take one's own course. To decide without help.
Take the law into one's own hands. To make a decision upon one's own authority.
Take upon oneself. To assume; undertake a responsibility.
Think fit. To resolve; purpose.
Use one's discretion. To decide of one's own free will; choose for oneself.
Volunteer. To offer or bestow voluntarily.
Will. To resolve; determine upon.

VOLITION—*Adjectives*.

Autocratic. Having absolute power; irresponsible.
Discretional. } Left to the control of one's own judgment.
Discretionary. }
Free, etc. Having liberty to follow one's own inclinations or choice. See LIBERTY.
Intended, etc. Engaged; betrothed. See PURPOSE.
Minded, etc. Having an inclination; disposed. See READINESS.
Optional. Depending on choice; elective.
Original, etc. Produced by one's own mind or thought. See CAUSE.
Prepense, etc. Considered beforehand; premeditated. See PREDETERMINATION.
Spontaneous. Acting of one's own accord; done without compulsion.
Unbidden, etc. Not commanded; unsought; not invited. See ORDER.
Volitional. Pertaining to willing or choosing.
Voluntary. Done with deliberation and purpose.
Wilful. Done by design; governed by the will.

VOLITION—*Adverbs, etc.*

A discrétion [F.]. At discretion; without limit.
À volonté [F.]. At pleasure.
Ad arbitrium [L.]. At will.
Ad libitum. [L.]. } At pleasure.
Al piacere. [It.]. }
As it seems good to. } As one judges.
As one thinks proper. }
At pleasure. } When one wishes.
At will. }
By choice. By one's own will. See CHOICE.
Deliberately. Not sudden or rash. See PREDETERMINATION.
Ex mero motu [L.]. Of one's own free will.
Of one's own accord. }
Of one's own free will. } Voluntarily.
Out of one's own head. }
Proprio ex mero motu [L.]. By one's own free will.
Purposely. With an object in view. See PURPOSE.
Suo ex mero motu [L.]. With his own free will.
Voluntarily. Of one's own free will. See *Adjectives*.

VOLITION—*Phrases*.

A beneplacito [It.]. } At pleasure.
À volonté [F.]. }
A vostro beneplacito [It.]. At your pleasure; as you will.
Beneficium accipere libertatem est vendere [L.]. To accept a favor is to sell your liberty.
Deus vult [L.]. God wills.
Liberum arbitrium [L.]. Free will.
Sic volo, sic jubeo [L.]. Thus I will, thus I command.
Stat pro ratione voluntas [L.]. My will stands in place of reason.
Was man nicht kann meiden, muss man willig leiden [G.]. What can't be cured must be endured.

OBLIGATION—Adjectives—*Continued from Column 2*.

Involuntary. Independent of will or choice.
Irresistible. Incapable of being successfully opposed.
Irrevocable. That cannot be recalled or revoked.

Involuntariness. Want of will or choice.
Iron fate. } Unrelenting fate.
Iron necessity. }
Kismet. Fate.
Last resort. } Last means or effort to escape from an evil impending.
Last shift. }
Lot. The part which falls to one, as it were by chance, or without his planning.
Necessaries. Things that one cannot do without. See NEED.
Necessitation. The state of being made necessary; compulsion.
Necessity. The quality or state of being necessary or absolutely requisite.
Obligation. Any power which binds one.
Parcæ [L.]. The three goddesses of fate.
Pis aller [F.]. A last shift; a makeshift.
Planet. A star, as influencing the fate of men.
Predestination. The doctrine that God has determined that certain persons shall be conformed to the image of His Son. [*Romans* viii, 29.]
Preordination. Foreordination.
Sisters three. The Fates.
Sky. The sky, as influencing the fate of men.
Spell. A charm. See DEVOTION-CHARM.
Star. A planet supposed to influence one's destiny.
Stars. A configuration of the planets supposed to influence fortune.
Stern fate. } Unchanging or unrelenting fate.
Stern necessity. }
Subjection, etc. The state of being under the power or control of another. See LIBERTY-SUBJECTION.
What must be. That which is decreed by fate.
Wheel of fortune. Fate.
Will of heaven. That which cannot be controlled by human power.

OBLIGATION—*Nouns of Agent*.

Automaton. A self-moving figure or machine that imitates the actions of living beings.
Fatalist. One who maintains that all things happen by inevitable necessity.
Necessarian. } One who holds the doctrine of philosophical necessity.
Necessitarian. }

OBLIGATION—*Verbs*.

Be destined. To appoint or fix unalterably.
Be doomed. To be consigned to death or ruin; be condemned.
Be driven into a corner. To compel to assent.
Be fated. To be subject to inevitable necessity; be decreed by fate.
Be in for. To be marked for future recognition.
Be one's fate, etc. To be one's lot or destiny. See *Nouns*.
Be one's fate to. To be destined; foredetermined.
Be pushed to the wall. To be forced to an extremity.
Be unable to help. To be beyond one's power to aid.
Be under the necessity of. To be obliged or compelled.
Cast a spell, etc. To fascinate; exercise irresistible power over. See DEVOTION-MAGIC.
Compel, etc. To drive on forcibly; oblige. See COERCION.
Destine. To fix unalterably; set or appoint to a use.
Devote. To set apart by a solemn act; consign over.
Doom. To fix irrevocably the fate of.
Foredoom. To doom beforehand.
Have no alternative. } To be obliged to accept things as they are.
Have no choice. }
Lie under a necessity. To be subject to an irresistible power.
Necessitate. To render unavoidable; force; oblige.
Predestine. To decree beforehand.
Preordain. To appoint beforehand; predetermine.

OBLIGATION—*Adjectives*.

Automatic. Not voluntary; instinctive.
Avoidless. Not to be evaded; inevitable.
Blind. Unseen; unintelligible; compelling.
Compulsory, etc. Not voluntary; not of choice. See COERCION.
Destined, etc. Appointed unalterably to any state or condition. See *Verbs*.
Elect. Chosen; consecrate; invested with office.
Fated. Assigned with a certain fate; doomed.
Impulsive, etc. Having the power of driving or impelling. See PREDETERMINATION-IMPULSE.
Inevitable. Unavoidable; admitting of no evasion.
Inexorable. Incapable of being moved by entreaty or prayer; unyielding.
Instinctive. Determined by natural impulse or propensity; spontaneous.

(*Continued on Column* 1.)

OBLIGATION—ADJECTIVES—*Continued.*

Mechanical. Done involuntarily, by mere force of habit.
Necessary. That cannot be otherwise, inevitable.
Needful, etc. Needed or requisite, as for some purpose. See NEED.
Resistless. That cannot be effectually opposed.
Spellbound. Bound as by a spell or charm.
Unavoidable. That cannot be shunned; certain.

Unconscious. Not knowing; unaware.
Uncontrollable. Beyond control; ungovernable; irresistible.
Unintentional, etc. Done or happening without design. See PURPOSE-LUCK.
Unthinking. Not heedful; thoughtless.
Unwitting. Ignorant; unaware; unconscious.

OBLIGATION—*Adverbs.*

Bon gré, mal gré [F.]. With a good or bad grace; willing or unwilling.
By stress of. Under compulsion.
Coûte que coûte [F.]. Come what may; at whatever cost.
Ex necessitate rei [L.]. From the urgency of the case.
Faute de mieux [F.]. For lack of something better.
If need be. Should it be necessary.
Necessarily, etc. By inevitable consequence. See *Adjectives.*

Needs must. Must of necessity.
Nolens volens [L.]. Whether he will or not.
Of course. By consequence.
Of necessity. By necessary consequence; by compulsion.
Perforce, etc. By force. See COERCION.
Will he nill he. Whether he will or will not; without choice.
Willing or unwilling. Compelled by force.

OBLIGATION—*Phrases.*

Actum me invito factus, non est meus actus [L.]. An act done against my will is not my act.
Che sarà, sarà [It.]. Whatever will be, will be.
Diis aliter visum [L.]. The gods have judged otherwise.
Fata obstant [L.]. The Fates oppose.
It cannot be helped.
It is written.
It must be.
It must be so.
It must have its way.
It must needs be.

It must needs be so.
It must needs have its way.
It will be.
It will be so.
It will have its way.
Jacta est alea [L.]. The die is cast.
One's days are numbered.
One's fate is sealed.
The die is cast.
There is no help for it.
There is no helping it.

---

vo-li′-tion-al. Belonging or relating to the volition. VOLITION-OBLIGATION.

Volk der Dichter und Denker [G.] (folk der diн′-ter und den′-ker). Nation of poets and thinkers· the Germans. POETRY-PROSE, REFLECTION-VACANCY.

vol′-ley. Discharge; number. ATTACK-DEFENSE, CRASH-DRUMMING, GATHERING-SCATTERING, TURBULENCE-CALMNESS.

volo sic jubeo, sic [L.] (vol′-o sic jiu′-bî-o, sic). Thus I will, thus I order. ORDER, VOLITION-OBLIGATION.

volonté, à [F.] (vo-lon·-tê′, a). At pleasure. VOLITION-OBLIGATION.

vol-ta′-ic. Produced by chemical action. **Voltaic cell,** ELECTRICITY; **voltaic electricity,** ELECTRICITY; **voltaic pile,** ELECTRICITY.

vol′-ta-ism. Form of electricity developed by chemical action. MIGHT-IMPOTENCE.

vol″-ti-geur′. Vaulter. BELLIGERENT.

volt′-me″-ter. An instrument for measuring a current of electricity. ELECTRICITY.

volto sciolto i pensieri stretti, il [It.] (vol-to schi′-ol-to î pên-sî′-êr-î strêt′-tî, îl). The countenance open, but the thought closely concealed. TRUTHFULNESS-FALSEHOOD.

vol″-u-bil′-i-ty. Quality of being talkative. TALKATIVENESS-TACITURNITY.

vol′-u-ble. Ready in speech. TALKATIVENESS-TACITURNITY.

vol′-ume. Mass; book. GREATNESS-LITTLENESS, MAGNITUDE-SMALLNESS, MISSIVE-PUBLICATION; **speak volumes,** CLEARNESS-OBSCURITY, ENLIGHTENMENT-SECRECY, EVIDENCE-COUNTEREVIDENCE; **volume of smoke,** FRIABILITY.

vo-lu′-mi-nous. Copious. GREATNESS-LITTLENESS.

vol-un-ta′-ri-ness. Willingness. READINESS-RELUCTANCE, VOLITION-OBLIGATION.

vol-un-ta′-ri-ly. Willingly. VOLITION-OBLIGATION.

vol′-un-ta-ry. Will; purposed. GIVING-RECEIVING, READINESS-RELUCTANCE, VOLITION-OBLIGATION.

voluntas, stet pro ratione [L.] (vo-lun′-tas, stet pro rê-shi-o′-nî). Let the will stand for reason. VOLITION-OBLIGATION.

vol″-un-teer′. Offer; serve; soldier. BELLIGERENT, ENTERPRISE, PROFFER-REFUSAL, READINESS-RELUCTANCE, VOLITION-OBLIGATION.

voluptas, est quædam flere [L.] (vo-lup′-tas, est quî′-dam flî-rî). There is in weeping a certain pleasure. PLEASURE-PAIN.

voluptas, sua cuique [L.] (vo-lup′-tas, siu′-a kai′-quî). To each, his own pleasure. DESIRE-DISTASTE.

voluptas, trahit sua quemque [L.] (vo-lup′-tas, trê-hit siu′-a quem′-quî). His own pleasure draws each man. MODERATION-SELFINDULGENCE.

vo-lup′-tu-a-ry. Sensualist. MODERATION-VOLUPTUARY, PURITY RAKE.

vo-lup′-tu-ous. Sensual; fulness. MODERATION-SELFINDULGENCE, PLEASURABLENESS-PAINFULNESS, PURITY-IMPURITY, SENSUALITY-SUFFERING.

vo-lup′-tu-ous-ness. Luxuriousness. MODERATION-SELFINDULGENCE.

vol″-u-ta′-tion. Wallowing. REVOLUTION-EVOLUTION.

vo-lute′. Scroll. ARCHITECTURE, CIRCLE-WINDING.

vom′-it. Puke. ADMISSION-EXPULSION.

vo-mi′-tion. The act or power of vomiting. ADMISSION-EXPULSION.

vom′-i-to-ry. Producing vomiting. APERTURE-CLOSURE, ENTRANCE-EXIT.

voo′-doo. To bewitch. DEVOTION-CHARM.

vo-ra′-cious. Hungry; rapacious. DESIRE-DISTASTE, FASTING-GLUTTONY.

vo-rac′-i-ty. Greediness of appetite. DESIRE-DISTASTE, FASTING-GLUTTONY.

vorstellen [G.] (for′-stel″-len). To represent. FANCY.

Vorstellung [G.] (for′-stel″-lung). Perception. FANCY.

vor′-tex. Whirlpool; rotation. AGITATION, REVOLUTION-EVOLUTION, RIVER-WIND.

vor′-ti-cal. Whirling. REVOLUTION-EVOLUTION.

vor′-ti-cose. Rotating rapidly. REVOLUTION-EVOLUTION.

vo′-ta-ry. Devotee; votive. ANTAGONIST-ASSISTANT, DECISION-MISJUDGMENT, DESIRE-DISTASTE.

vote. Will; ballot. ASSERTION-DENIAL, CHOICE-NEUTRALITY, PRESIDENT-MEMBER; **vote for,** ASSENT-DISSENT.

vo′-ter. One who votes. ASSERTION-DENIAL, CHOICE-NEUTRALITY.

vot′-ing. Present participle of vote. CHOICE-NEUTRALITY; **voting machine,** INSTRUMENT.

votis, hoc erat in [L.] (vo′-tis, hoc î′-rat in). This was in my prayers. DESIRE-DISTASTE.

vo'-tive. Vowed. ENGAGEMENT-RELEASE; **votive of-fering,** DEVOTION-IDOLATRY.

voto, ex [L.] (vo'-to, ex). According to one's vow. DEVOTION-IDOLATRY, ENGAGEMENT-RELEASE.

vo'-to-graph. Vote-recorder. INSTRUMENT.

vouch. Confirm. ASSERTION-DENIAL; **vouch for,** EVIDENCE-COUNTEREVIDENCE.

vouch'-er. Writing; security. EVIDENCE-COUNTEREVIDENCE, SECURITY, SETTLEMENT-DEFAULT, SIGN.

vouch-safe'. Grant; deign; assure. CONSENT, LEAVE-PROHIBITION, PETITION-EXPOSTULATION, SELFRESPECT-HUMBLENESS.

vouch-safe'-ment. A gift or grant in condescension. LEAVE-PROHIBITION.

vow. Promise; devote. ASSERTION-DENIAL, DEVOTION-IDOLATRY, ENGAGEMENT-RELEASE; **take vows,** CHURCH.

vow'-el. A character representing a vocal sound. LETTER.

vox audita perit, littera scripta manet [L.] (vox audai'-ta pî-rit, lit'-ter-a scrip'-ta mê'-net). The voice heard perishes, the letter written remains. MUTATION-PERMANENCE, REMEMBRANCE-FORGETFULNESS.

vox et præterea nihil [L.] (vox et prî-ter'-î-a nai'-hil). Talk and nothing else. BRAGGING, CONCEIT-DIFFIDENCE, MEANING-JARGON, MIGHT-IMPOTENCE, SUBSTANCE-NULLITY.

vox faucibus hæsit [L.] (vox fau'-si-bus hî'-sit). The voice stuck in his throat. ASTONISHMENT-EXPECTANCE, SANGUINENESS-TIMIDITY, VOCALIZATION-MUTENESS.

vox populi [L.] (vox pop'-yu-lai). The voice of the people. ASSENT-DISSENT, CHOICE-NEUTRALITY, PUBLICITY, RULE-LICENSE.

voy'-age. Travel. ASCENT-DESCENT, MOVEMENT-REST, TRAVELING-NAVIGATION.

voyage, bon [F.] (vwa-yazh', bon·). Prosperous voyage to you. ARRIVAL-DEPARTURE, TRAVELING-NAVIGATION.

voy'-a-ger. Navigator. WAYFARER-SEAFARER.

vraisemblance [F.] (vrê-san·-blan·s'). Truth. LIKELIHOOD-UNLIKELIHOOD.

vue d'oeil, à [F.] (vü duy, a). At sight. EARLINESS-LATENESS, VISIBILITY-INVISIBILITY.

Vul'-can. A god; planet. AGENT, ASTRONOMY.

vul'-gar. Common. GENTILITY-COMMONALTY, POLITENESS-IMPOLITENESS, TASTE-VULGARITY; **vulgar tongue,** LANGUAGE.

vul'-gar-ism. Grossness of manners. TASTE-VULGARITY.

vul-gar'-i-ty. Commonness. POLITENESS-IMPOLITENESS, TASTE-VULGARITY.

Vul'-gate. Bible. REVELATION-PSEUDOREVELATION.

vulgus, ad captandum [L.] (vul'-gus, ad cap-tan'-dum). To catch the rabble. TRUTHFULNESS-FRAUD.

vulgus ignobile [L.] (vul'-gus ig-no'-bi-lî). The ignoble common people. GENTILITY-COMMONALTY.

vul'-ner-a-bil'-i-ty. State of being vulnerable. SECURITY-INSECURITY.

vul'-ner-a-ble. Assailable. SECURITY-INSECURITY.

vul'-ner-a-ry. Application. REMEDY-BANE.

vulnus, æternum servans sub pectore [L.] (vul'-nus, î-ter'-num ser'-vans sub pec'-to-rî). Keeping the eternal wound under his breast. PARDON-VINDICTIVENESS.

vulnus, immedicabile [L.] (vul'-nus im-med-i-cab'-i-lî). Incurable wound. GOOD-EVIL.

vul'-pine. Sly. CRAFT-ARTLESSNESS.

vul'-ture. Bird; evil-doer. BENEFACTOR-EVILDOER, HARSHNESS-MILDNESS.

vultus est index animi [L.] (vul'-tus est in'-dex an'-i-mai). The countenance is the index of the soul. SIGN.

W

wab′-ble. To go slowly; oscillate. AIM-ABERRATION, DESIRE-DISTASTE, SWIFTNESS-SLOWNESS, VIBRATION.

Wacht am Rhein [G.]. (vɑʜt ɑm rɑin). National song of Germany. PATRIOTISM-TREASON.

wad. Stuffing. COVER-LINING.

wad′-die. War-club. WEAPON.

wad′-ding. Lining; stopper. COVER-LINING, HARDNESS-SOFTNESS, HEATING-COOLING, PERFORATOR-STOPPER.

wad′-dle. To move clumsily. SWIFTNESS-SLOWNESS.

wade. To walk through water. TRAVELING-NAVIGATION; **wade in blood,** LIFE-KILLING; **wade through,** TEACHING-LEARNING, TOIL-RELAXATION.

wa′-fer. Cement; a small, thin disk. BREADTH-NARROWNESS, CONNECTIVE, LAMINA-FIBER.

waf′-fle. Kind of cake. NUTRIMENT-EXCRETION.

waf′-fle-i″-rons. Cooking utensils. HEATING-COOLING.

waft. To carry lightly. RIVER-WIND, TRANSFER.

waf′-ture. Conveyance. TRANSFER.

wag. To oscillate; a joker. AGITATION, VIBRATION, WAG; **wag on,** ADVANCE-RETROGRESSION, TRAVELING-NAVIGATION.

WAG.

Acrobat. One who practises rope-dancing, vaulting, etc.

Bel esprit [F.]. A person of wit.

Bon diable. A devilish good-natured fellow.

Buffoon. A man who makes a practise of amusing tricks and jokes.

Caricaturist. One who represents or draws with ridiculous exaggeration.

Charlatan. A quack.

Clown. The fool or buffoon in a play.

Diseur de bon mots [F.]. A sayer of good things.

Drolle de corps [F.]. The buffoon of the crowd.

Epigrammatist. One who uses sharp, witty sayings.

Farceur [F.]. A jester; a wag.

Gaillard [F.]. A merry fellow.

Gipsy. One of a vagabond tribe making their living by fortune-telling, etc. In Europe in 1417, from India. Gypsy means Egypt.

Grimacier [F.]. One who amuses by a distortion of the features.

Harlequin. A buffoon dressed in party-colored clothes.

Humorist. One who displays a genial and droll form of wit.

Jack-a-dandy. A little, foppish, impertinent fellow.

Jack in the green. A clown.

Jack-pudding. A buffoon.

Jester. A court fool.

Joe Miller. A worn-out joke.

John. A name sometimes used humorously when applied to an awkward person.

Life of the party. A wit.

Madcap. A person of wild behavior.

Merry-andrew. One whose business is to make sport for others.

Mime. An actor in a ridiculous play.

Motley fool. A jester in many colored clothes.

Mountebank. A boastful or false pretender.

Pantaloon. A buffoon in pantomimes.

Pickle-herring. A merry-andrew.

Posture-maker. An acrobat or contortionist.

Punch. The buffoon of a puppet-show.

Punchinello. A character in an Italian puppet show, whence English Punch; a buffoon.

Punster. One skilled in punning.

Reparteeist. One skilled in repartee.

Scaramouch. A character in Italian comedy.

Spark. A brisk, showy, gay man.

Tumbler. One who plays tricks by various motions of the body.

Wag. A man full of sport and humor.

Wearer of the cap and bells.⎫ A clown; a jester.
Wearer of the motley.⎭

Wit. A man of humor.

Wit-cracker. A humorist.

Witling. A pretended wit.

Wit-snapper. One who affects repartee.

Wit-worm. One who feeds on wit.

Zany. A buffoon.

wa′-ger. A bet; strife. PURPOSE-LUCK; **wager of battle,** FIGHTING-CONCILIATION; **wager of law,** EVIDENCE-COUNTEREVIDENCE.

wa′-ges. Payment for service. LABOR-CAPITAL, PRICE-DISCOUNT, RECOMPENSE-PUNITION.

wag′-ger-y. Drollery. WITTINESS-DULNESS.

wag′-gish. Drollish. LIGHTHEARTEDNESS-DEJECTION, WITTINESS-DULNESS.

wag′-gish-ness. Jocoseness. WITTINESS-DULNESS.

wag′-gle. To wag. AGITATION, VIBRATION.

Wag-ne′-ri-an. Pertaining to Richard Wagner. MUSIC.

wag′-on. A heavy, four-wheeled vehicle. CONVEYANCE-VESSEL.

wag′-on-er. A wagon-driver. WAYFARER-SEAFARER.

wag″-on-ette′. A kind of carriage. CONVEYANCE-VESSEL.

wag′-on-load″. Enough to fill a wagon. MAGNITUDE-SMALLNESS.

wag′-on-train″. Train of wagons. CONVEYANCE-VESSEL.

Wa-ha′-bi. A Mohammedan sect. ORTHODOXY-HETERODOXY.

Wahrheit und Dichtung [G.] (vɑr′-hait unt diʜ′-tung). Truth and fiction. FANCY, POETRY-PROSE.

waif. A Godsend. GOOD-EVIL.

waifs and es-trays′. Outcasts. GATHERING-SCATTERING, WAYFARER-SEAFARER.

wail. A moan. JUBILATION-LAMENTATION.

wain. A wagon. CONVEYANCE-VESSEL.

wain′-scot. A lining for inner walls. COVER-LINING, TOP-BOTTOM.

waist. The small part of the trunk. BREADTH-NARROWNESS.

waist′-coat. A garment for the waist. DRESS-UNDRESS; **put in a strait-waistcoat,** RELEASE-RESTRAINT.

wait. To tarry; a delay; to serve. ACTION-PASSIVENESS, EARLINESS-LATENESS; **lie in wait for,** EXPOSURE-HIDINGPLACE, PREPARATION-NONPREPARATION; **wait impatiently,** EARLINESS-LATENESS; **wait on company,** OBSTRUCTION-HELP, SOLITUDE-COMPANY; **wait to see how the wind blows,** BIGOTRY-APOSTASY; **wait upon,** CHIEF-UNDERLING, POLITENESS-IMPOLITENESS.

wait′-er. Attendant. CHIEF-UNDERLING.

wait′-ing. Delay. EXPECTATION-SURPRISE; **be kept waiting,** EARLINESS-LATENESS.

wait′-ing-maid. A female attendant. CHIEF-UNDERLING.

wait′-ress. Female attendant. CHIEF-UNDERLING.

waits. Christmas carolers. MUSICIAN.

waive. To give up; relinquish temporarily. CHOICE-NEUTRALITY, EARLINESS-LATENESS, USE-DISUSE.

wai′-wode. A liege prince. CHIEF-UNDERLING.

wake. To rouse; a death-watch; track left by a ship. ANTERIORITY-POSTERIORITY, ENTERTAINMENT-WEARINESS, EXCITATION, LIFE-FUNERAL, MARK-OBLITERATION, PREDECESSOR-CONTINUATION; **enough to wake**

the dead, Loudness-Faintness; **follow in the wake of,** Imitation-Originality, Leading-Following; **wake the thoughts,** Heed-Disregard; **wake up,** Excitation.

wake'-ful. Alert. Carefulness-Carelessness.

wake'-ful-ness. Tendency to keep awake. Activity-Indolence.

wak'-en. To arouse. Excitation.

wald'-grave. Title of German nobility. Gentility-Commonalty.

wale. Ridge. Convexity-Concavity.

Wal-hal'-la. Hall of the slain. Heaven-Hell.

walk. To move slowly on the feet; conduct; business; way; pasture. Conduct, Extension - District, Lists, Movement-Rest, Occupation, Traveling-Navigation; **walk in the shoes of,** Imitation-Originality, Representative; **walked off one's legs,** Weariness-Refreshment; **walk off with,** Theft; **walk of life,** Occupation; **walk one's chalks,** Arrival-Departure, Quest-Evasion; **walk over the course,** Difficulty-Facility, Success-Failure; **walk the earth,** Life-Death.

walk'-er. One who walks. Wayfarer-Seafarer.

walk'-ing gen'-tle-man. A traveling actor. Acting.

walk'-o''-ver. Success. Success-Failure.

wall. A continuous, upright structure; a defense; a barrier. Attack-Defense, Cover-Lining, Enclosure, Erectness - Flatness, Guard - Prisoner, Obstruction-Help, Refuge-Pitfall; **driven to the wall,** Difficulty-Facility; **go to the wall,** Creation-Destruction, Life - Death, Success - Failure; **pushed to the wall,** Volition-Obligation; **take the wall,** Reputation-Discredit, Selfrespect-Humbleness; **wall in,** Release-Restraint; **wooden walls,** Attack-Defense, Belligerent.

wal'-let. A pocketbook. Contents-Receiver.

wal'-lop. To flog. Agitation.

wal'-low. To roll; to revel indecently. Height-Lowness, Revolution, Spring-Dive; **wallow in pleasures,** Enough, Excess-Lack, Sensuality-Suffering; **wallow in riches,** Affluence-Penury; **wallow in the mire,** Cleanness-Filthiness, Moderation-Selfindulgence.

Walls'-end. A grade of coal. Combustible.

Wall Street slang. Slang of brokers. Word-Neology.

wal'-nut. Kind of nut. Nutriment-Excretion.

waltz. Music in triple measure; a dance. Entertainment-Weariness, Music.

wam'-ble. To roll unsteadily; to be disturbed with nausea. Desire-Distaste, Determination-Vacillation, Mutability-Stability, Vibration.

wam'-pum. Indian money. Money.

wan. Pale; sad. Color-Achromatism, Lightheartedness-Dejection.

wand. A rod indicating authority or function. Charm, Scepter; **wave a wand,** Magic.

wan'-der. To journey; to deviate; to be delirious. Aim-Aberration, Movement-Rest, Saneness-Lunacy, Traveling-Navigation; **the attention wanders,** Heed-Disregard.

wan'-der-er. A rover. Wayfarer-Seafarer.

wan'-der-ing. Stray. Aim-Aberration, Conventionality - Unconventionality, Saneness - Lunacy; **wandering Jew,** Wayfarer-Seafarer.

wane. To decrease; to decline. Betterment-Deterioration, Enlargement-Diminution, Increase-Decrease, Infancy-Age; **one's star on the wane,** Welfare-Misfortune; **wax and wane,** Mutation-Permanence.

wa'-ning. Decreasing. Enlargement - Diminution, Infancy-Age.

want. Lack. Affluence-Penury, Desire-Distaste, Excess-Lack, Need, Supremacy-Subordinacy, Transcursion-Shortcoming.

want'-ing. Lacking; imbecile. Entirety-Deficiency, Presence-Absence, Sagacity-Incapacity; **found wanting,** Adulation-Disparagement, Faultlessness-Faultiness, Innocence-Guilt.

want'-less. Lacking nothing. Enough.

want'-on. Unrestrained. Carefulness-Carelessness, Conventionality-Unconventionality, Entertainment - Weariness, Liberty - Subjection, Persistence-Whim, Purity-Impurity, Recklessness-Caution.

wap'-en-take. A Saxon court. Extension-District.

war. Fighting. Fighting-Conciliation; **at war,** Harmony-Discord, Strife-Peace; **at war with,** Antagonism-Concurrence, Fighting-Conciliation; **declare war,** Variance-Accord; **man-of-war,** Weapon; **seat of war,** Lists; **war of words,** Conversation-Monologue, Strife-Peace.

war'-ble. To sing in trills. Musician.

war'-bled. Trilled. Musician.

war'-cry''. A rallying-cry. Alarm, Defiance, Fighting-Conciliation.

ward. A charge; a district; protection. Attack-Defense, Chief-Underling, City-Country, Extension-District, Refuge-Pitfall, Release-Restraint, Security-Insecurity, Whole-Part; **ward off,** Attack - Defense, Obstruction - Help, Guard-Prisoner; **watch and ward,** Carefulness-Carelessness.

war'-dance''. A dance before going to war. Defiance.

ward'-en. A guardian. Chief-Underling, Representative, Security-Insecurity.

ward'-er. A guard; a perforator. Guard-Prisoner, Perforator-Stopper, Security-Insecurity.

ward'-mote. A ward meeting. Tribunal.

ward'-robe. Apparel. Dress-Undress.

ward'-ship. Guardianship. Security-Insecurity.

ware. Wary; merchandise. Merchandise, Warning.

ware'-house''. A storehouse. Market, Store.

ware'-room''. Storage-room. Market.

war'-fare''. Fighting. Fighting-Conciliation, Variance-Accord.

war'-horse''. A charger. Belligerent.

war'-like. Delighting in war. Fighting-Conciliation, Strife-Peace.

war'-lock. A wizard. Devotion-Magician.

warm. To make hot; passionate; wealthy; to flog. Affluence-Penury, Blueness-Orange, Emotion, Excitation, Favorite-Quarrelsomeness, Heat-Cold, Heating-Cooling, Recompense - Punition, Redness - Greenness, Turbulence - Calmness, Yellowness-Purple; **warm bath,** Oven-Refrigerator; **warm imagination,** Fancy; **warm man,** Affluence-Penury; **warm reception,** Attack-Defense, Sociability-Privacy; **warm the cockles of the heart,** Pleasurableness-Painfulness; **warm up,** Betterment-Deterioration, Renovation-Relapse; **warm work,** Toil-Relaxation.

warm'-heart''-ed. Kind. Amity-Hostility, Charitableness-Malevolence, Emotion, Sensitiveness-Apathy.

warm'-ing. Heating. Heating-Cooling.

warm'-ing-pan''. A heater; a deputy. Commutation-Permutation, Oven-Refrigerator, Preparation-Nonpreparation.

warmth. Vigorous language. Emotion, Favorite-Anger, Force-Weakness, Heat-Cold, Redness-Greenness.

warn. To caution. Alarm, Motive-Dehortation, Prophecy, Warning; **warn off,** Leave-Prohibition.

warn'-er. One who warns. Warning.

warn'-ing. Caution; omen. Advice, Portent, Recklessness-Caution, Sign, Warning; **give warning,** Keeping-Relinquishment, Refuge-Pitfall, Use-

Disuse; **warning voice**, Alarm, Refuge-Pitfall, Warning.

WARNING.

Admonition. A warning containing instruction for future guidance.
Alarm, etc. An outcry or information to announce danger. See Alarm.
Caution. Prudence in regard to danger.
Cautiousness, etc. The quality of being cautious. See Recklessness-Caution.
Caveat [L.]. In law, an intimation to stop proceedings; a warning.
Contraindication. In medicine, a symptom which forbids the usual treatment.
Dehortation. Advice or counsel against anything; discussion.
Lesson. A formal reproof; a reprimand; a rebuff.
Monition. Instruction given by way of caution.
Notice, etc. Intimation beforehand; warning. See Enlightenment.
Prediction. A declaration of a future event; a prophecy See Prophecy.
Premonishment. Previous warning or information.
Premonition. Previous notice of something yet to occur; forewarning.
Warning. Caution against danger.

Warning—Nouns of Agent.

Advanced-guard. Detachment of troops which precedes the main body.
Bandog. A large fierce dog, usually kept chained.
Beacon. A signal or mark as a guide to mariners.
Bird of ill omen. A warning of danger or misfortune.
Bivouac. A night-watch of a force to prevent surprise.
Cassandra. One whose predictions or warnings no one believes. [Homer.]
Clouds on the horizon. Signs of danger or warning.
Death-watch. A small insect whose sound is supposed to presage death.
Fog-horn. } A horn, etc., that sounds an alarm in thick weather.
Fog-signal. }
Gathering clouds. Signs of warning.
Guide-board. A board having upon it information as to the road.
Guidon. A small flag used to direct the movement of troops.
Handwriting on the wall. A warning. [Bible.]
House-dog. A dog kept to guard the house.
Lighthouse. A building on a dangerous shore to warn sailors.
Monitor. One who instructs in regard to duty; an American battleship.
Mother Carey's chickens. A name given by sailors to the storm-petrels.
Patrol. A detachment whose duty is to preserve order and repress disorders.
Picket. A guard on a camp's outskirts to warn against an enemy's approach.
Rear-guard. A body of troops to guard the rear of an army.
Scout. One sent ahead to gain information concerning an enemy.
Sentinel. One who guards or warns.
Sentry. A soldier placed on guard to give notice of any approaching danger.
Signal-post. A post for displaying flags, lamps, etc., as signals.
Signs of the times. Occurrences which indicate coming events.
Spial. One who watches closely, so as to give warning.
Spy. One who covertly obtains and gives information.
Stormy petrel. A black sea-bird prophetic of a storm.
Vedette. An outpost to give warning of an enemy and its movements.
Warning voice. A sound calling attention to impending danger.
Watch. One who guards or gives warning of danger.
Watch and ward. One who is vigilant by night and day; a very careful watch.
Watch-dog. A dog kept to give warning of danger approaching premises or property.
Watchman. One whose vocation is to watch or guard.
Watch-tower. A tower from which a sentinel gives warning of approaching danger,
Yellow flag. A flag that indicates disease on shipboard.

Warning—Verbs.

Admonish. To warn of a fault; reprove gently.
Beware. To regard with caution; be wary of.
Caution. To give notice of danger; to warn
Croak. To forebode evil.
Dehort. To dissuade; warn not to undertake.
Forewarn. To caution beforehand; instruct in advance

Gardez [F.]. Take care.
Give notice. To notify; inform in advance.
Give warning. To caution against anything that may prove injurious.
Keep watch and ward, etc To be vigilant by night and day. See Carefulness.
Menace. To threaten; indicate the danger or risk of.
Premonish. To admonish beforehand.
Prewarn. To warn beforehand.
Put on one's guard. To make known beforehand; inform previously.
Sound the alarm. To apprise of danger; summon to meet danger.
Take heed at one's peril. To be careful or cautious at one's own risk
Take warning. To be on one's guard; take heed.
Ware. To guard oneself; beware of.
Warn. To put on guard against danger; caution.

Warning—Adjectives.

Admonitive. } Serving to warn or reprove.
Admonitory. }
Cautionary. Conveying a warning.
Monitory. Giving warning or advice.
On one's guard. On the lookout for danger or attack; cautious. See Recklessness-Caution.
Premonitory. Giving previous warning or notice.
Warned, etc. Made aware; notified; informed. See Verbs.
Warning, etc. Cautioning against danger. See Verbs.

Warning—Adverbs.

In terrorem, etc. [L.]. As a warning. See Charitableness-Menace.

Warning—Interjections

Beware! mind! mind what you are about! take care! take care what you are about! ware!

Warning—Phrases.

Caveat actor [L.]. Let the doer beware.
Cave quid dicis, quando, et cui [L.]. Beware what you say, when, and to whom.
Fœnum habet in cornu [L.]. He has hay upon his horns; beware of him.
Le silence du peuple est la leçon des rois [F.]. The silence of the people is the lesson of kings.
Ne reveillez pas le chat qui dort [F.] One must not arouse the sleeping lion
Verbum sat sapienti [L.] A word to the wise is sufficient.

warp. Bend; deviate; bias. Aim-Aberration, Betterment-Deterioration, Decision-Misjudgment, Enlargement - Diminution, Mutation - Permanence, Proportion-Deformity, Traveling-Navigation; **warp and weft**, Texture.
war'-paint. Paint put on the body before going to war. Preparation-Nonpreparation.
warped. Bent. Faultlessness-Faultiness.
war'-rant. To justify; a bond; an order. Assertion-Denial, Dueness-Undueness, Engagement, Evidence-Counterevidence, Justification-Charge, Leave-Prohibition, Money, Order, Rule-License, Security; **death-warrant**, Exculpation-Conviction, Life - Death, Life - Killing; **I'll warrant you**, Assertion-Denial, Faith-Misgiving.
war'-rant-ed. Justified. Dueness-Undueness.
war-rant'-y. Security; authorization. Dueness-Undueness, Engagement, Evidence-Counterevidence, Leave-Prohibition, Security.
war'-ren. A place for keeping small game. Fertility-Sterility.
war'-rior. A soldier. Belligerent.
wart. A small excrescence. Convexity-Concavity.
wa'-ry. Cautious. Carefulness-Carelessness, Caution.
was ich nicht weiss, macht mich nicht heiss [G.] (vas ih niht vais, maht mih niht hais). What I do not know does not make me glow; nought out of sight wakes appetite. Knowledge-Ignorance.
wash. To cleanse; to overlay; to color; a marsh.

CLEANNESS-FILTHINESS, COLOR-ACHROMATISM, COV-ER-LINING, PAINTING, SWAMP-ISLAND, WATER-AIR; **wash down**, NUTRIMENT-EXCRETION; **wash one's hands of,** COMMISSION-RETIREMENT, DUTY-DERELIC-TION, KEEPING-RELINQUISHMENT, PROFFER-REFU-SAL, QUEST-ABANDONMENT; **wash out,** COLOR-ACHRO-MATISM, MARK-OBLITERATION.

wash'-er-wom''-an. A woman who washes. CLEAN-NESS-FILTHINESS.

wash'-house. A small house where the washing is done. CLEANNESS-FILTHINESS, OVEN-REFRIGERATOR.

wash'-ing. Cleansing. WATER-AIR.

wash'-out''. Erosion. CREATION-DESTRUCTION, REF-UGE-PITFALL.

wash'-y. Weak. FORCE-WEAKNESS, MEANING-JAR-GON, STRENGTH-WEAKNESS.

wasp. An insect. BREADTH-NARROWNESS; **bring a wasp's nest about one's ears,** WELFARE-MISFOR-TUNE.

wasp'-ish. Snappish. FAVORITE-QUARRELSOMENESS, POLITENESS-IMPOLITENESS, TURBULENCE-CALMNESS.

was'-sail. Liquor; carousal. ENTERTAINMENT-WEARI-NESS, MODERATION-SELFINDULGENCE, NUTRIMENT-EXCRETION.

waste. To decrease; destroy; loss; unproductive; a plain. BETTERMENT-DETERIORATION, CREATION-DESTRUCTION, ENLARGEMENT-DIMINUTION, EXTEN-SION-DISTRICT, EXTRAVAGANCE-AVARICE, FERTILITY-STERILITY, GAIN-LOSS, GULF-PLAIN, INCREASE-DE-CREASE, PROVISION-WASTE, USE-DISUSE, USEFUL-NESS-USELESSNESS; **run to waste,** BETTERMENT-DE-TERIORATION, EXCESS-LACK; **waste time,** ACTION-PASSIVENESS, ACTIVITY-INDOLENCE, DURATION-NEV-ERNESS, OPPORTUNENESS-UNSUITABLENESS; **watery waste,** OCEAN-LAND.

wa'-sted. Weak; deteriorated. BETTERMENT-DETERI-ORATION, PROVISION-WASTE, STRENGTH-WEAKNESS.

waste'-ful. Prone to waste. EXTRAVAGANCE-AVARICE. PROVISION-WASTE.

waste'-pa''-per. Soiled paper; of no force. MIGHT-IM-POTENCE, SETTLEMENT-DEFAULT.

waste'-pipe. A pipe to carry off waste. WATERCOURSE-AIRPIPE.

waste'-thrift. A spendthrift EXTRAVAGANCE-AVA-RICE

wa'-sting. Wasteful. **Wide-wasting,** GOODNESS-BAD-NESS, PROVISION-WASTE.

wast'-rel. A waif. WAYFARER-SEAFARER.

watch. A clock; a guard; to observe. CAREFULNESS-CARELESSNESS, CHRONOLOGY-ANACHRONISM, EXPEC-TATION-SURPRISE, GUARD-PRISONER, HEED-DISRE-GARD, SECURITY-INSECURITY, SIGHT-BLINDNESS, WARNING; **death-watch,** LIFE-DEATH, WARNING; **on the watch,** EXPECTATION-SURPRISE, HEED-DISRE-GARD, REFLECTION-VACANCY; **watch and ward,** CARE-FULNESS-CARELESSNESS, KEEPER-PRISONER, WARN-ING; **watch for,** CAREFULNESS-CARELESSNESS, EX-PECTATION-SURPRISE, SIGHT-BLINDNESS.

watch'-dog. A dog that guards property. FAUNA-FLORA, GUARD-PRISONER, SECURITY-INSECURITY, WARNING.

watch'-et. Pale blue. BLUENESS-ORANGE.

watch'-fire. A fire used for a signal. SIGN.

watch'-ful. Careful. CAREFULNESS-CARELESSNESS, HEED-DISREGARD, SAGACITY-INCAPACITY.

watch'-ful-ness. Vigilance. CAREFULNESS-CARELESS-NESS.

watch'-glass. A cup. CONTENTS-RECEIVER.

watch'-house. A guard-house. RELEASE-PRISON, **in the watch-house,** JUSTIFICATION-CHARGE.

watch'-man. A guard. GUARD-PRISONER, SECURITY-INSECURITY, WARNING.

watch'-tow''-er. A tower upon which a sentinel is placed. SIGHT-BLINDNESS, SIGN, WARNING.

watch'-word. A countersign; a rallying-cry. FIGHT-ING-CONCILIATION, SIGN.

wa'-ter. A colorless liquid. CHEMISTRY, DEEPNESS-SHALLOWNESS, TRANSPARENCY-OPAQUENESS; WA-TER-AIR; **back water,** ADVANCE-RETROGRESSION; **cast one's bread upon the waters,** PROVISION-WASTE; **depth of water,** DEEPNESS-SHALLOWNESS; **great waters,** OCEAN-LAND; **hold water,** PROOF-DISPROOF; **keep one's head above water,** SECURITY-INSECURITY; **land covered with water,** GULF-PLAIN; **of the first water,** GOODNESS-BADNESS; **pour forth like water,** EXTRAVAGANCE-AVARICE; **pour water into a sieve,** PROVISION-WASTE; **running water,** RIVER-WIND; **throw cold water on,** TURBULENCE-CALMNESS, WIT-TINESS-DULNESS; **walk the waters,** RIVER-WIND

WATER—AIR.

Deluge, etc. A flood. See RIVER.
Diluent. That which dilutes; any medicine that thins the blood.
Flood tide. } The rising water.
High water. }
Lymph. A colorless fluid in animal bodies, found in the lymphatics
Rheum. Any thin watery discharge from the mucous membrane of the head.
Serosity. Quality or state of being serous.
Serum. A thin watery substance which separates from the body when coagulated.
Water. A colorless liquid compound, made up of oxygen and hydrogen.

WATER—*Nouns of Operation.*

Affusion. Act of pouring upon a person or thing.
Balneation. Act of bathing.
Bath. Operation of cleaning the body by the application of water.
Dilution. Operation of making more liquid.
Douche [F.]. A bath given by a forcible jet of water against the body.
Humectation. Act of wetting or moistening, as in medicine.
Immersion. Act of plunging into a liquid until covered.
Infiltration. Operation of passing into the pores or textures of a body.
Irrigation. Operation of causing water to flow over land to increase its productivity.
Lotion. A bathing or washing; a medicinal wash.
Maceration. Act of softening by steeping in a liquid.
Mersion. Act of plunging into a liquid until covered.
Spargefaction. Act of sprinkling.
Washing, etc. Act of cleansing with water.

Air, etc. The gaseous mixture of oxygen and nitrogen surrounding the earth. See LIQUID-GAS.
Atmosphere. The whole mass of air, clouds, and vapor surrounding the earth.
Atmospheric air. The air existing in the atmosphere
Blue. } The mass of atmosphere surrounding the earth.
Blue sky. }
Cloud. A collection of visible vapor suspended in the upper atmos-phere.
Common air. The air we breathe.
Open. } The air out of doors.
Open air. }
Sky. } The apparent arch or vault of heaven.
Welkin. }

AIR—*Nouns of Instrument.*

Aerometer. An instrument for finding the weight of the atmosphere or other gases.
Aneroid. The air-barometer consisting of a small metallic box nearly exhausted of air.
Barometer. An instrument for indicating atmospheric pressure.
Baroscope. An instrument showing the changes in the weight of the atmosphere.
Endiometer. An instrument for the measurement of gases.
Weathercock. That which shows by its turning the direction of the wind; a vane.
Weather-gage. An instrument for measuring atmospheric pressure
Weather-glass. An instrument which indicates the condition of the weather.

WATER—AIR—Continued.

WATER—Verbs.

Add water. To pour water in; dilute.
Affuse. To pour upon; sprinkle as with a liquid.
Bathe. To cleanse the body with water.
Be watery, etc. To be moist; be abounding with water. See *Adjectives*.
Dabble. To play in water; throw and splash water about.
Deluge. To overflow with water; inundate.
Dilute. To reduce the strength of, as with water.
Dip. To plunge into a liquid and withdraw again.
Douse. To thrust into water.
Drench. To wet through and through; soak.
Drown. To overwhelm in water.
Duck. To plunge suddenly into water.
Gargle. To wash the mouth and throat with a liquid agitated by air from the wind-pipe.
Immerge. To plunge into or under a fluid.
Immerse. To dip entirely under a fluid.
Inject. To force a fluid in by mechanical or physical means.
Inundate. To cover with water; flood.
Irrigate. To water land by artificial means.
Lave. To wash with water; bathe.
Macerate. To soften the parts of a substance by steeping in a liquid.
Merge. To sink into a fluid; be swallowed up or lost.
Moisten, etc. To wet in a small degree; make damp. See DAMPNESS.
Pickle. To preserve, as with brine.
Plunge. To thrust into water or other fluid substance.
Reek. To steam; exhale; emit vapor.
Slobber. To drip saliva or other fluid from the mouth; drivel.
Slop. To spill a liquid upon; soil with a liquid spilled.
Soak. To wet thoroughly; saturate; enter gradually into the pores.
Souse. To plunge suddenly into water.
Splash. To dash water about; soil with a liquid dashed about.
Sprinkle. To scatter a liquid in drops or small particles.
Steep. To soak in a liquid; imbue.
Submerge. To put under water; drown.
Swash. To dash noisily, as water.
Syringe. To wash or clean with a syringe.
Wash. To cleanse with water or other liquid.
Water. To supply with water; wet.
Wet. To saturate with water; dip in a liquid.

WATER—Adjectives.

Aquatic. Living in the water or much on it.
Aqueous. Watery; pertaining to water.
Balneal. Pertaining to a bath.
Diluent. Weakening the strength of by mixing with water; diluting.
Diluted, etc. Made thinner or weaker. See *Verbs*.
Drenching, etc. Soaking; wetting thoroughly. See *Verbs*.
Lymphatic. Pertaining to lymph; absorbent.
Watery. Containing a great deal of water.
Weak. Feeble; yielding to pressure.
Wet, etc. Damp; rainy; saturated with a liquid. See DAMPNESS.

WATER—Phrase.

The waters are out.

AIR—Scientific Nouns.

Aerography. A treatise on the atmosphere and its phenomena.
Aerology. The science which treats of the air, its nature and uses.
Aeronautics. The science of sailing in the air by mechanical means.
Aeroscopy. The observation of the state and variations of the atmosphere.
Aerostation. Science of ascending in air-balloons.
Climatology. A science which treats of the different climates of the earth.
Isobar. A line connecting places of the same barometric pressure.
Meteorology. The science which treats of atmospheric phenomena especially in reference to weather and climate.

AIR—Noun of Agent.

Aeronaut. An aerial navigator.

AIR—Nouns of Operation.

Exposure to the air. Laying open to the operation of the air.
Exposure to the weather. Submitting anything to the action of the weather.
Ventilation. Supplying buildings with regular quantities of fresh air.

AIR—Nouns of Condition.

Climate. The condition of a place or country with reference to the prevailing weather.
Rise and fall of barometer. Indicative of atmospheric instability.
Weather. Atmospheric conditions or changes at a given time.

AIR—Verbs.

Air. To expose to the air; dry.
Fan, etc. To cool and refresh by moving the air. See RIVER-WIND.
Ventilate. To supply with fresh air.

AIR—Adjectives.

Aerial. Belonging to the air; high.
Aeriform. Having the nature or form of air; not solid.
Airy. Light like air; high in the air.
Atmospheric. Pertaining to the atmosphere.
Containing air. Holding air
Effervescent. Gently giving off bubbles of gas
Flatulent. Windy; affected with gas in the stomach
Meteorological. Relating to the atmosphere and its phenomena.
Weatherwise. Skilful in foreseeing the changes of the weather.
Windy, etc. Abounding with wind; airy. See RIVER-WIND.

AIR—Adverbs, etc.

À la belle étoile [F.] Under the stars; in the open air
Al fresco [It.] In the open air
In the open air. Out of doors, outside.
Sub dio [L.] Out in the open air.
Sub Jove [L.] Under the heavens.

---

wa'-ter-col''-or. A paint mostly water. PAINTING; **water-color drawing,** PAINTING.

wa'-ter-course''. A river. WATERCOURSE-AIRPIPE.

WATERCOURSE—AIRPIPE.

Adit. A nearly horizontal opening to a mine by which entrance and exit is had.
Adjutage. } A tube through which water is discharged.
Ajutage. }
Aorta. The great artery of the body.
Aquage. A mill-stream before it enters its pond.
Aqueduct. An artificial channel for conveying water.
Canal. An artificial water-channel designed for navigation.
Catch-drain. A ditch along the side of a hill to catch the surface-water.
Channel. The bed where a stream runs.
Cloaca. A sewer.
Conduit. A pipe or channel for conveying water.
Dike. A channel for water made by digging.
Ditch. A trench for draining wet land.
Drain. A channel, a watercourse.
Duct. A tube or canal by which water is conveyed.
Emunctory. An organ for removing fluid waste matter.
Flood-gate. A gate for shutting out or releasing a body of water.
Force-pump. A pump for drawing and forcing a liquid.

Air-pipe. } A pipe for conveying a current of air.
Air-tube. }
Blow-hole. A nostril in the top of a whale's head, a hole in the ice to which whales, seals, etc , come to breathe.
Blowpipe. A tube for directing a jet of air into a flame.
Bronchia [L.] The tube which carries air to the lungs.
Bronchus [L.] A subdivision of the bronchia.
Chimney. A smoke flue.
Flue. An enclosed passage for establishing and directing a current of air.
Funnel. A smoke flue or pipe.
Larynx. The upper part of the windpipe.
Louvre. An opening in ancient buildings for the escape of smoke.
Nozzle. A projecting vent or air-tube
Pipe. A tube for directing a current of air.
Shaft. A long passage for the admission or outlet of air.
Smokestack. A pipe serving as a chimney on a locomotive, steam-vessel, etc.
Spiracle. A small aperture in an animal or vegetable body by which air is inhaled and exhaled.

WATERCOURSE—AIRPIPE—*Continued.*

Funnel. A vessel for conveying liquids into a close vessel.

Gargoyle. } An ornamental water-spout.
Gurgoyle. }

Gully. A hollow worn in the earth by a current of water.

Gullyhole. The opening through which gutters discharge surface-water.

Gutter. A small channel at the roadside for carrying off surface water.

Headrace. The part of a channel above a water-wheel.

Hose. A flexible pipe of India rubber for conveying water

Kennel. The watercourse of a street.

Lock. An enclosure in a canal with gates at each end, used in raising or lowering boats from one level to another.

Lock-weir. A waste-weir for a canal.

Main. A principal water-pipe as distinguished from others.

Moat. A deep trench around a castle, sometimes filled with water.

Pantile. A tile with a curved surface for carrying off the water.

Passage. A channel or course. See WAY.

Penstock. The barrel of a wooden pump.

Pipe. A long tube for carrying water.

Pore. One of the minute orifices in the body through which perspiration comes

Race. A channel for a current of water.

Rose. A perforated nozzle.

Scupper. A channel for carrying off the water from a ship.

Sewer. A channel for carrying waste matter.

Siphon. A pipe or bent tube of two branches by which a liquid can be transferred from a lower level.

Sluice. A passage for water with a sliding gate.

Throat. The passage by which the air passes to the windpipe.

Tonsils. The two glandular organs situated in the throat.

Trachea. The windpipe.

Venetian blinds. Blinds with slats so attached that they may be turned so as to let in or exclude light.

Vent. A hole or passage for air.

Ventiduct. An underground ventilating passage.

Ventilator. A contrivance for effecting the passage of currents of air.

Weasand. The windpipe.

Windpipe. The passage for the breath from the larynx to the lungs.

WATERCOURSE—*Continued.*

Sough. A small drain.

Spout. A discharging pipe or orifice.

Tail-race. The part of a race below the water-wheel.

Trough. A long, hollow vessel for holding water.

Tunnel. An underground channel.

Valve. A lid, or cover for an aperture.

Vena [L.]. A vein.

Waste-pipe. A pipe for carrying off fluid waste matter.

Water-gate. A gate by which water may be confined or released.

Water-pipe. A tube or pipe for carrying water.

Water-works. The system of pipes, etc., connected with the carrying of water.

Weir. An artificial obstruction to direct the course of water.

WATERCOURSE—*Adjectives.*

Vascular. Consisting of tubes or vessels.

---

wa'-ter-cure''. Hydropathy. REMEDY-BANE.

wa'-ter-dog''. A water-spaniel. FAUNA-FLORA.

wa'-ter-drink''-er. An abstainer. TEETOTALISM-INTEMPERANCE.

wa'-tered. Variegated; inflated. VARIEGATION; **watered stock,** LABOR-CAPITAL.

wa'-ter-fall''. A cascade. RIVER-WIND.

wa'-ter-glass''. A substance used in painting. PAINTING.

wa'-ter-gru''-el. Gruel made with water. STRENGTH-WEAKNESS.

wa'-ter-ing. Supplying water. **Watering-cart,** RIVER-WIND; **watering-place,** DWELLER-HABITATION; **watering-pot,** RIVER-WIND.

wa'-ter-logged''. Water-soaked; unmanageable. MIGHT-IMPOTENCE, OBSTRUCTION-HELP, SECURITY-INSECURITY.

wa'-ter-man. A boatman. WAYFARER-SEAFARER.

wa'-ter-part''-ing. Watershed. TOP-BOTTOM.

wa'-ter-pipe''. A pipe for conveying water. APERTURE-CLOSURE, RIVER-WIND.

wa'-ter-proof''. Impervious. DAMPNESS-DRYNESS, DRESS-UNDRESS, SECURITY-INSECURITY.

wa'-ters. Waters of bitterness. PLEASURABLENESS-PAINFULNESS, SUPREMACY-SUBORDINACY; **waters of oblivion,** REMEMBRANCE-FORGETFULNESS.

wa'-ter-shed''. A water divide. TOP-BOTTOM.

wa'-ter-span''-iel. A kind of dog. FAUNA-FLORA.

wa'-ter-spout''. A column of spray. RIVER-WIND.

wa'-ter-tight''. Impervious. APERTURE-CLOSURE, DAMPNESS-DRYNESS.

wa'-ter-wheel''. Wheel run by water. INSTRUMENT.

wa'-ter-work''. A system for furnishing water RIVER-WIND.

wa'-ter-y. Wet. DAMPNESS-DRYNESS, WATER-AIR; **watery eyes,** JUBILATION-LAMENTATION; **watery grave,** LIFE-DEATH.

watt. Electrical unit. ELECTRICITY

wat'-tle. To interweave. CROSSING.

Wat Ty'-ler. An English rebel. INSUBORDINATION-OBEDIENCE.

wave. To oscillate; sinuous; billow. CIRCLE-WINDING, OCEAN-LAND, VIBRATION; **wave a banner,** SIGN; **wave a wand,** WORSHIP-MAGIC; **waves of water,** RIVER-WIND.

wa'-ver. To reel. DETERMINATION-VACILLATION, MUTABILITY-STABILITY.

wa'-ver-er. A vacillating person. DETERMINATION-VACILLATION.

waves. Curved ridges. OCEAN-LAND; **buffet the waves,** ANTAGONISM-CONCURRENCE, DIFFICULTY-FACILITY, TRAVELING-NAVIGATION; **lash the waves,** USEFULNESS-USELESSNESS; **plow the waves,** TRAVELING-NAVIGATION.

wa'-vy. Ruffled. CIRCLE-WINDING.

wax. To grow; a soft substance. CONVERSION, ENLARGEMENT-DIMINUTION, HARDNESS-SOFTNESS, INCREASE-DECREASE, PULPINESS-ROSIN; **close as wax,** ENLIGHTENMENT-SECRECY; **wax and wane,** MUTATION-PERMANENCE.

wax'-work''. Wax figures. DELINEATION-CARICATURE.

wax'-y. Slippery; angry. FAVORITE-ANGER, PULPINESS-OILINESS.

way. A road; a habit; space. APERTURE-CLOSURE, EXTENSION-DISTRICT, HABIT-DESUETUDE, QUANTITY-MEASURE, WAY; **by the way,** PURPOSE-LUCK, TRANSFER; **by way of,** AIM-ABERRATION, WAY; **fall in the way of,** PRESENCE-ABSENCE; **fight one's way,** FIGHTING-CONCILIATION, QUEST-EVASION, TOIL-RELAXATION; **find its way,** TRANSMISSION; **gather way,** TRAVELING-NAVIGATION; **get into the way of,** HABIT-DESUETUDE; **go one's way,** ARRIVAL-DEPARTURE; **go your way,** ADMISSION-EXPULSION; **have one's own way,** DIFFICULTY-FACILITY, LIBERTY-SUBJECTION; **have way on,** TRAVELING-NAVIGATION; **in a bad way,** HEALTH-SICKNESS, SECURITY-INSECURITY; **in a way,** FAVORITE-ANGER, PLEASURE-PAIN, VOLITION-OBLIGATION; **in the way near,** REMOTENESS-NEARNESS; **in the way of,** ANTAGONISM-CONCURRENCE, DIFFICULTY-FACILITY, EDUCATION-MISTEACHING, OBSTRUCTION-HELP; **it must have its way,** BIGOTRY-APOSTASY, VOLITION-OBLIGATION; **let it have its way,** ACTION-PASSIVENESS; **long way off,** REMOTENESS-NEARNESS; **make one's way,** ADVANCE-RETROGRESSION, SUCCESS-FAILURE, TRANSMISSION, TRAVELING-NAVIGATION, WELFARE-MISFORTUNE; **make way,** TRANSMISSION; **make way for,** AIM-ABERRATION, APERTURE-CLOSURE, COMMUTATION-PERMUTATION, DIFFICULTY-FACILITY, POLITENESS-IMPOLITENESS, QUEST-EVASION; **not know which way to turn,** CERTAINTY-

DOUBT; **on the way**, ADVANCE-RETROGRESSION, TRANSFER; **place in one's way**, PROFFER-REFUSAL; **put in the way of**, EDUCATION-MISTEACHING, POSSIBILITY-IMPOSSIBILITY; **see one's way**, DIFFICULTY-FACILITY, KNOWLEDGE-IGNORANCE; **show the way**, MANAGEMENT; **under way**, ADVANCE-RETROGRESSION, ARRIVAL-DEPARTURE, MOVEMENT-REST, TRAVELING-NAVIGATION; **way in**, ENTRANCE-EXIT; **way of speaking**, TROPE; **way of thinking**, FAITH-MISGIVING; **way out**, ENTRANCE-EXIT; **wing one's way**, TRAVELING-NAVIGATION.

WAY.

Adit. An entrance or passage.
Aisle. A passage into which the pews of a church open.
Alley. A narrow passage or way.
Artery. A continuous channel of communication, as of blood from the heart.
Avenue. A way or opening for entrance into a place.
Back-door. } An indirect way.
Back-stairs. }
Beat. A round or course which is frequently gone over.
Beaten path. } A way worn by use.
Beaten track. }
Bridge. A structure to make a passageway across a stream of water.
Bridle-path. }
Bridle-road. } A way for saddle-horses and pack-horses, as distinguished from the way for vehicles.
Bridle-track. }
Broad highway. A public way.
Bypath. }
Byroad. } An obscure or private way.
Byway. }
Canal, etc. A channel for navigation. See WATERCOURSE.
Carrefour [F.]. A carriageway.
Causeway. A way or road across a wet or marshy ground.
Channel. A means of passing.
Coach road. A way or road where coaches are driven.
Corridor. A gallery or passageway in a building.
Course. The ground or path traversed.
Covert way. A covered way or passage.
Cross-path. }
Cross-road. } An obscure road intersecting or avoiding the main road.
Cross-way. }
Cut. A passage made by cutting or digging.
Door. An opening in the wall of a house.
Drawbridge. A bridge, the whole or part of which may be raised, lowered, or turned aside.
Ferry. A place where persons or things are carried across a river in a ferryboat.
Flags. Flat stones used for paving.
Flight of stairs. A series of steps leading from one landing to another.
Foot-bridge. A narrow bridge for foot-passengers only.
Foot-path. A narrow path for pedestrians only.
Ford. A place in a river where it may be crossed on foot.
Gangway. A passage into any enclosed space.
Gateway. A passage through a fence or wall. See APERTURE.
Highway. A public road or way.
Highways and byways. Public and private ways.
Horse-path. }
Horse-road. } A way for horses, as distinguished from the way for vehicles.
Horse-track. }
King's highway. The public road.
Ladder. A frame for ascent and descent.
Lane. A passageway between hedges or fences which is not used as a highroad.
Line of road. } A road or route.
Line of way. }
Lobby. A passage or hall of communication.
Means of access. A course or passage.
Occupation road. A road connecting the parts of an estate separated by a railroad, canal, etc.
Orbit. The path of a heavenly body.
Pass. }
Passage. } An opening, road, or track available for passing.
Path. }
Pathway. } A way, course, or track in which anything moves.

Pavement. A floor of solid material, making a hard and convenient surface for travel.
Pipe. A passageway for liquid, air, etc. See OPENING.
Plank. A road-surface formed of planks.
Pontoon. A flat-bottomed boat used to support the roadway in the construction of floating bridges.
Private road. A road used only by particular persons.
Queen's highway. The public road.
Railroad. } A road or way consisting of steel rails adjusted for the wheels of vehicles.
Railway. }
Road. A public passage for persons, animals, and vehicles.
Roadway. A part of a road traveled by carriages.
Route. The course or way which is traveled or passed.
Royal road. A public way.
Secret passage. A way known to but few.
Short cut. A way that shortens the ordinary distance. See MID-COURSE.
Sidewalk. A walk for foot-passengers at the side of a street.
Stair. A series of steps leading from one landing to another.
Staircase. } A flight of stairs with their supporting framework, etc.
Stairway. }
Stepping-stone. A means of progress or advancement.
Steps. Walk; passage.
Stile. A step or set of steps for crossing a fence.
Street. A public highway. See DWELLER-HABITATION.
Tack. The direction of a vessel in regard to the trim of her sails.
Thoroughfare. An unobstructed way open to the public.
Tow-path. A path traveled by men or animals in towing boats.
Track. A path or course laid out for a race, etc.
Trajectory. A curve which a body describes in space.
Tramroad. } A road prepared for easy transit of trams or wagons.
Tramway. }
Trottoir [F.]. A sidewalk.
Tunnel. An underground passage.
Turnpike. A road obstructed by a gate or bar for the purpose of collecting toll.
Viaduct. A bridge crossing a valley or gorge.
Walk. A frequented track.
Way. A passage.

WAY—*Nouns of Method.*

Fashion. Mode of conduct.
Form. The established way of proceeding.
Gait. Carriage of the body while moving; mode of walking.
Guise. Outward appearance.
Manner. Mode of acting or doing anything.
Method. Regular mode of procedure or manner of doing anything.
Mode. Manner of acting or being.
Modus operandi [L.]. Manner of operating.
Procedure, etc. The method or manner of proceeding or moving forward. See CONDUCT.
Tone. Distinctive style or tendency.
Way. Course of action.
Wise. Manner of being or acting.

WAY—*Adverbs, etc.*

After this fashion. In this manner.
Anyhow. In any way at all.
By way of. Passing.
By what mode. In what manner.
How. In what way.
In this way. In this manner.
In transitu, etc. [L.]. On the passage; by the way, etc. See CIRCLE.
In what manner. } How
In what way. }
One way or another. In some manner.
On the highroad to. Going to.
So. In this way.
Somehow or other, etc. In some way. See INSTRUMENTALITY.
Via [L.]. By the way of.

WAY—*Phrase.*

Hæ tibi erunt artes [L.]. These shall be your arts.

Way. Course of life. **The Way.** DIVINITY.
way'-far''-er. A traveler. WAYFARER-SEAFARER.

WAYFARER—SEAFARER

Adventurer. One who travels in search of adventure.
Alpine Club. A company formed for travel in the Alps.
Arab. A native of Arabia: applied to a homeless wanderer because the Arabs are nomadic.

A. B. Abbreviation for able-bodied seaman.
Able seaman. One able to fulfil the ordinary duties of seamanship.
Aerial navigator. One who navigates in the air.
Aeronaut. An aerial navigator.

WAYFARER—SEAFARER—*Continued.*

Argonaut. One who sailed in the Argo.
Ariel. A spirit of the air. [Bible. Shakespeare, *Tempest.*]
Bird of passage. Birds which come and go with the seasons.
Bohemian. A French name for Gipsies, supposed to be Hussites.
Breaker. A man who travels about breaking horses.
Cab-driver.
Cabman. } One who drives a cab.
Carter. A man who drives a cart.
Cavalier. A military man serving on horseback.
Charioteer. One who drives a chariot.
Coachman. One who drives a coach or carriage.
Comet. A heavenly body appearing irregularly and traveling in parabolic curves, or in a few instances in elliptical orbits of great eccentricity.
Condottiere [It.]. One of a class of mercenary military travelers.
Courier. A messenger carrying letters or despatches.
Drayman. A man who attends a dray.
Driver. One who drives.
Emigrant. One who travels from his home-country to settle in another.
Engine-driver.
Engineer. } One who manages an engine.
Equestrian. A traveler on horseback.
Excursionist. One who travels on an excursion.
Explorer. One who travels for discovery.
Fireman. A man who tends the fires of a steam-engine.
Foot-passenger. One who travels on foot.
Foundling. A child found without parent or owner.
Fugitive. One who travels from danger.
Gadabout. One who travels about without business.
Gadling. An idle gadabout.
Gipsy. One of a wandering Hindu race supposed to be Egyptians.
Guard. One who has charge of a railway train.
Hadji. A Mussulman who has traveled on the sacred pilgrimage to Mecca.
Horseman. One who rides on horseback.
Iris. In Greek divinity, the messenger of the gods.
Itinerant. One who travels from place to place.
Jehu. One who drives furiously. [Bible.]
Jockey. A professional rider of horses in races.
Landloper. One without a home, who travels from one part of the land to the other.
Loafer. An idle lounger.
Mercury. The messenger of the gods; the god of merchants.
Mountaineer. A mountain-dweller or traveler.
Nomad. One of a race of people with no fixed abode who travel continually attending their flocks.
Palmer. A traveling pilgrim to holy places.
Passenger. A wayfarer; a traveler.
Pedestrian. A traveler on foot.
Peregrinator. A traveler into foreign countries.
Peripatetic. A follower of Aristotle, who taught his philosophy while walking about.
Pilgrim. A traveler, especially from his own country to some holy place.
Post-boy. One who rides post-horses.
Postillion. One who rides the first pair of horses of a coach.
Rambler. A wayfarer; a rover.
Refugee. One who flees for safety.
Rider. One who rides; a horseman.
Rough-rider. A daring rider; one who breaks horses.
Rover. A wayfarer; a wanderer about.
Runner. One who runs.
Scatterling. A vagabond.
Somnambulist. One who walks in his sleep.
Stoker. A fireman.

Balloonist. One who navigates the air in a balloon.
Bargee. One of the crew of a barge.
Bargeman. The manager of a barge.
Bluejacket. A sailor, from the color of his jacket.
Boatman. One who manages a boat.
Boatswain. A ship officer of the lower rank.
Cockswain. The one who steers a boat, or who has charge of it under an officer.
Coxwain. Cockswain.
Crew. The company of seamen who man a ship.
Ferryman. One in charge of a ferry.
Gondolier. The rower of a gondola.
Icarus. A legendary Greek character who flew through the air on wings fastened with wax until, coming too near the sun, they melted, and he fell into the Icarian sea and was drowned.
Jack tar. A sailor, so called from his tarred hands and clothes.
Jolly. A sailor's nickname.
Lighterman. One who manages a lighter, a large open barge.
Longshoreman. A laborer employed along the shore in loading and unloading vessels.
Man-of-war's man. A sailor employed on a man-of-war.
Marine. A soldier serving on board ships in naval engagements
Mariner. A seaman or sailor.
Middy.
Midshipman. } A petty officer in the navy.
Navigator. A sailor.
Oar.
Oarsman. } One who rows with an oar.
Pilot. A steersman of a ship.
Rower. One who rows or manages an oar
Sailor. A mariner; a seaman.
Seafarer.
Seafaring man. } A man following the business of a seaman.
Seaman.
Shipman. A sailor.
Skipper. A sea-captain.
Steersman. One who directs the course of a ship
Tar. A sobriquet of a sailor.
Waterman. One who manages water-craft.

———

WAYFARER—*Continued*

Straggler. A wandering traveler; a vagabond.
Tourist. One who travels for pleasure.
Trainer. One who trains another, as for a race.
Tramp.
Tramper. } A wandering beggar; a vagabond.
Traveler. One who journeys from place to place; a wayfarer.
Vagabond. An idle wayfarer.
Vagrant. A vagabond; a tramp.
Vetturino [It.]. One who drives an Italian four-wheeled carriage.
Voiturier [F.]. A carriage-driver.
Voyager. One who travels over water.
Wagoner. One who drives a wagon.
Waifs and estrays. Wanderers; castaways.
Walker. One who travels by walking.
Wanderer. A roving traveler.
Wandering Jew. A legendary character who struck Christ on His way to the cross and was condemned by Him to wander about the earth until His second coming.
Wastrel. A wandering, neglected child.
Wayfarer. A traveler; a passenger.
Whip. A coachman.
Zingaro. A Gipsy.

---

way'-far"-ing. Traveling. Traveling-Navigation.
way"-lay'. To attack or rob. Craft-Artlessness, Truthfulness-Fraud.
way'-less. Pathless. Aperture-Closure.
ways. Manner. Conduct; **in all manner of ways,** Aim-Aberration; **ways and means,** Means, Money.
way'-wode. A liege prince. Chief-Underling.
way'-worn. Fatigued by travel. Traveling-Navigation, Weariness-Refreshment.
weak. Feeble; infirm. Compassion-Ruthlessness, Consequence - Insignificance, Determination-Vacillation, Force-Weakness, Ratiocination-Instinct, Rule-License, Sagacity-Incapacity, Sa-

vor-Tastelessness, Strength-Weakness, Virtue-Vice, Water-Air; **expose one's weak point,** Proof-Disproof; **weak point,** Faultlessness-Faultiness, Ratiocination-Instinct; **weak side,** Sagacity-Incapacity, Virtue-Vice.
weak'-en. To enfeeble. Evidence-Counterevidence, Increase-Decrease, Might-Impotence, Strength-Weakness, Turbulence-Calmness.
weak'-er ves'-sel. Woman. Male-Female.
weak–head'-ed. Dull. Sagacity-Incapacity.
weak–heart'-ed. Timorous. Bravery-Cowardice.
weak'-ling. Feeble person. Strength-Weakness.
weak'-ly. Sickly. Strength-Weakness.

weak'-ness. Feebleness. Determination-Vacillation, Strength-Weakness, Virtue-Vice; **weakness of the flesh,** Virtue-Vice.

weal. Welfare. Good-Evil, **common weal,** Good-Evil, Humanity, Usefulness-Uselessness.

weald. A forest. Fauna-Flora.

wealth. Property. Affluence-Penury, Gain-Loss, Money, Property.

wealth'-y. Rich. Affluence-Penury.

wean. To change or detach. Faith-Misgiving, Habit-Desuetude; **wean from,** Motive-Dehortation; **wean one's thoughts from,** Remembrance-Forgetfulness.

wean'-ling. A child newly weaned. Infant-Veteran.

weap'-on. An instrument for fighting. Weapon.

WEAPON

Adaga. An Asiatic parrying-weapon.

Air-gun. A gun in which the elastic force of condensed air is used to discharge the ball.

Ammunition. Articles used in charging firearms

Apparatus belli [L.]. Materials of war.

Arm. A weapon of offense or defense.

Armament. All the cannon and small arms of a fortification collectively.

Armature. Whatever is worn or used for the protection and defense of the body.

Armor. Any covering worn to protect one's person in battle. See Attack-Defense.

Armory. A place where arms and instruments of war are kept. See Store.

Arms. Instruments or weapons of offense or defense.

Armstrong gun. A wrought-iron breech-loading cannon; invented by Sir William Armstrong.

Arquebuse [G.]. A sort of hand-gun having a primitive trigger.

Arrow. A weapon to be shot from a bow.

Artillery. Implements for warfare; heavy cannon.

Assagai.
Asseguai. } A light spear used by South-African tribes.

Ataghan.
Atâghan. } A long knife, or short saber; used by Mohammedan nations.

Ax. A weapon with a steel edge or blade.

Back-plate. An armorial plate on the back.

Ball. A solid projectile of lead or iron to be discharged from a firearm.

Ball-cartridge. A cartridge containing a ball, as distinguished from a blank which contains only powder.

Ballister. A crossbow.

Ballistics. The art of hurling stones or missile weapons with an engine. See Push.

Bar-shot. A double-headed shot, consisting of a bar with a ball at each end.

Baselard. A dagger or short sword.

Basilisk. An old-fashioned cannon.

Bat. A club used for offense or defense.

Battering-ram. An engine used in ancient times to beat down the walls of besieged places.

Battering-train. A train of artillery for siege operations.

Battery. Two or more pieces of artillery in the field.

Battle-ax. A kind of broadax formerly used as an offensive weapon.

Bayonet. A pointed instrument of the dagger kind fitted on the end of a musket or rifle.

Bilbo. A long bar or bolt of iron with sliding shackles, and a lock at the end, to confine the feet of prisoners.

Bill. An ancient weapon consisting of a hook-shaped blade on a staff.

Billy. A policeman's club.

Blade. The flat, cutting part of an edged weapon.

Bludgeon. A short club, used as a weapon.

Blunderbuss. A short muzzle-loading gun with large bore and flaring mouth.

Bolo. A sword-like knife used by Filipinos

Bolt. A shaft or missile shot from a crossbow or catapult.

Bomb. A hollow projectile of iron containing an explosive material

Boomerang. A curved wooden missile having the quality of returning to the thrower.

Bouche à feu [F.]. A cannon.

Bow. An elastic weapon, used to discharge an arrow.

Bowie-knife. A hunting-knife having a curved edge, a two-edged point and thick back, a hilt, cross-piece, and sheath.

Brand. A sword. so called from its flashing brightness.

Breech-loader. A firearm in which the load is inserted at the breech.

Brickbat. A piece of a brick.

Broadsword. A sword with a broad cutting blade and obtuse point.

Brown-bess. An old flint-lock musket.

Bullet. A small projectile discharged from a firearm.

Caliver. An early form of hand-gun.

Cane. A walking-stick.

Canister-shot. A shot for cannon, in which a number of lead or iron balls are enclosed in a case fitting the gun.

Cannon. A firearm for discharging heavy shot with great force.

Cannon-shot. A shot used in cannon.

Carbine. A short light musket or rifle.

Carcass. A hollow case or shell, filled with combustibles, to be thrown from a mortar.

Carronade. A kind of short cannon, used more for breaking or smashing than piercing.

Cartouche [F.]. A roll or case of paper holding a charge for a firearm.

Cartridge. A complete charge for a firearm.

Catapult. An engine for throwing stones, arrows, spears, etc.

Chain-shot. Two cannon-balls united by a short chain.

Chassepot [F.]. A kind of breech-loading, center-firing rifle.

Cimeter. A saber with a much-curved blade having the edge on the convex side.

Claymore. A heavy two-handed and double-edged broadsword.

Club. A stout stick or staff.

Cold steel. An instrument of steel.

Congreve. A kind of lucifer match.

Congreve rocket. A weapon by which balls and combustibles are discharged to a great distance.

Creese. A Malayan dagger or short sword.

Crossbow. A weapon used in discharging arrows, formed by placing a bow crosswise on a stock.

Cudgel. A short thick stick used as a club.

Culverin. A long cannon of the 16th century.

Cutlass. A short heavy sword-like weapon.

Dagger. A short, edged and pointed weapon, for stabbing.

Dart. A pointed missile weapon.

Deadly weapon. A weapon, the wound of which causes death.

Dirk. A dagger or poniard.

Djerrid. A blunt javelin used in military games in Moslem countries.

Dudgeon. A dagger with a hilt of box-tree wood.

Enfield rifle. A British rifle, named after its inventor.

Falchion. A sword with a broad and slightly curved blade.

Falconet. A small cannon of the 16th century.

Ferrara. A sword bearing the mark of one of the Ferrara family of Italy.

Field-piece. A cannon mounted on wheels.

Firearms. A gun, pistol, or any weapon from which a shot is discharged by the force of an explosive.

Fire-ball. A ball filled with powder or other combustibles.

Firelock. An old form of gun in which the priming was ignited by a spark.

Flobert. A small rifle designed for target-shooting.

Foil. A slender and pliable sword with a button on the end, used in fencing.

Fowling-piece. A light smooth-bore shot gun used for bird-shooting.

Fusil [F.]. A musket.

Gaff. A pointed iron hook at the end of a pole.

Gatling gun. A machine gun, consisting of a cluster of barrels revolved by a crank, which fires automatically.

Gisarm. A weapon with a scythe-shaped blade, mounted on a long staff.

Glaive. A weapon like a hook fastened to the end of a pole.

Glave. Glaive.

Good sword. A figurative expression for a sword.

Grape.
Grape-shot. } A cluster of cast-iron shot to be shot from a cannon.

Grenade. An explosive shell, intended to be thrown by hand.

Gun. A metal tube for firing projectiles by the force of an explosive.

Gun-cotton. An explosive made of the salt of nitric acid.

Gun-flint. A piece of flint fitted to the hammer on a flint-lock musket.

Gun-lock. Mechanism by which the charge in a gun is fired.

Gunnery. The practise of using artillery.

Gun of position. A heavy field-piece not designed to execute quick movements.

Gunpowder. An explosive made of a mixture of niter, charcoal and sulfur.

Haguebut. An old harquebus.

Halberd. A weapon in the form of a battle-ax and pike at the end of a long staff.

Handstaff. A stick carried in the hand for defense.

Hanger. A short cut-and-thrust sword.

Harpoon. A missile weapon, consisting of a barbed head and a shank.

Harquebus. A firearm, the predecessor of the musket.

Heavy gun. A cannon.

Howitzer. A short light cannon for throwing shells at a low elevation.

Infernal machine. A machine or apparatus maliciously designed to explode, and destroy life and property.

Javelin. A short, light spear, used as a missile weapon.

Jingal. A small portable piece of ordnance mounted on a swivel.

Krag-Jorgensen rifle. A 22-calibre magazine army gun.

Knuckle-duster. An iron instrument to cover the knuckles when striking a blow.

Kris. A Malay dagger.

Krupp gun. A wrought steel breech-loading cannon: named after its inventor, Herr Krupp.

Lancaster gun. A rifled cannon, named after its inventor.

Lance. A long shaft with a spear head, used as a thrusting weapon.

Langrage shot. An old form of canister-shot.

Langrel shot. A shot formerly used at sea for tearing sails and rigging.

Lee rifle. A style of gun used in the English army.

Life-preserver. An apparatus to save one from drowning.

Lochaber ax. An ax formerly used by the Scottish Highlanders.

Lyddite (from Lydd, England). A powerful explosive made by boiling carbolic acid with an equal quantity of oil of vitriol, which, after washing, becomes picric acid; when this composition unites with oxide it forms lead picrate, forming an explosive.

Mace. A medieval steel war-club.

Machete. A Cuban weapon, resembling a corn-knife; also for cutting cane.

Machine gun. A mounted breech-loading gun with reservoir for cartridges, fired by turning a crank.

Martini-Henry rifle. A rifle in which the magazine is in a tube parallel with and either beneath or above the barrel.

Match-lock. A musket fired by means of a match.

Maxim gun. A mounted magazine gun invented by Maxim.

Melinite. } Same as lyddite.
Peroxilene. }

Minie rifle. A rifle invented by a Frenchman by the name of Miniè.

Missile. A weapon to be thrown or discharged.

Mitraille [F.]. Shot or bits of iron used in loading cannon.

Mitrailleur [F.]. One who serves a mitrailleuse.

Mitrailleuse [F.]. A breech-loading machine gun consisting of a number of barrels fitted together, so arranged that they can be fired simultaneously.

Mortar. A short heavy gun for throwing bombs at a high elevation.

Musket. A kind of firearm used by infantry.

Musketoon. A short musket.

Musketry. Small guns collectively.

Muzzle-loader. A gun that receives the load at the muzzle instead of the breech.

Naked sword. An unsheathed sword.

Needle-gun. A firearm loaded at the breech with a cartridge which is discharged by driving a slender needle into it.

Ordnance. A general name for all kinds of weapons and their appliances used in war.

Ox-goad. A goad for driving oxen.

Paixhan gun. A howitzer for the horizontal firing of heavy shells: named after its inventor, General Paixhan.

Panoply. A full set of armor.

Park. A collective body of siege or field artillery.

Parrot gun. A large-bore cannon, unrifled.

Partizan. A pike having lateral projections; a halberd.

Pederero [Sp.]. A short piece of chambered ordnance.

Petard. A conical iron case filled with powder and fired by a slow match.

Petronel. A hand-cannon of the 15th century.

Piece. A firearm.

Pike. A long shaft or pole, having a metal point, used in medieval warfare.

Pistol. A short firearm having a stock to fit the hand and a short barrel or barrels.

Pistolet. A small pistol.

Poleax. An old weapon consisting of an ax set on a pole.

Poniard. A small dagger with a slender triangular or square blade.

Powder. An explosive substance consisting of niter, charcoal, and sulfur.

Powder and shot. A charge for a gun.

Priming. A little powder or combustible used to explode powder

Projectile. A bullet fired from a gun.

Quarter-staff. A long and stout staff formerly used as a weapon; so called because in holding it one hand was placed at the end and the other between the middle and the end.

Rapier. A light, long, and narrow sword for thrusting.

Reed. An arrow or javelin.

Repeater. A firearm discharged many times in quick succession.

Revolver. A firearm having a revolvable chambered cylinder, so that it may be fired several times without reloading.

Rifle. A firearm having spiral grooves in the surface of the bore for imparting rotation to the projectile and increasing the accuracy of the weapon.

Rifled cannon. A cannon bored like a rifle.

Rocket. A firework that ascends by the reaction of combustion-gases.

Round shot. A solid spherical projectile for ordnance.

Saber. A heavy one-edged sword used by cavalry.

Scimitar. A sword of extreme curve.

Shaft. The stock of a weapon, without the head.

Shell. A hollow metallic projectile filled with an explosive.

Shillalah. A stout cudgel.

Shot. A solid ball or bullet that is not intended to fit the bore of a gun.

Shrapnel. A shell filled with bullets, and having a bursting-charge to explode it at any given point in its flight.

Side-arms. Weapons worn at the side, as sword, bayonet, etc.

Siege-train. Artillery adapted for attacking fortified places.

Skean. A knife or short dagger used among the Highlanders of Scotland.

Sling. An instrument for throwing stones or other missiles.

Slug. An irregularly shaped piece of metal used as a bullet.

Small arms. Muskets, rifles, pistols, etc., in distinction from cannon.

Small bore. A firearm having a small internal cylindrical cavity

Smoothbore. A firearm whose bore is without spiral grooves.

Snider rifle. A rifle invented by Snider.

Spear. A weapon of a sharp-pointed head on a long shaft.

Spontoon. A half-pike or halberd.

Staff. A stick carried in the hand for defense.

Stand of arms. A complete set for one soldier.

Steel. Any weapon of steel.

Stick. Any long and comparatively slender piece of wood.

Stiletto. A dagger with a slender, rounded, and pointed blade.

Stone. Rock discharged from a catapult or crossbow.

Stylet. A slender pointed instrument.

Swivel. A small piece of ordnance turning on a point.

Sword. An offensive weapon having a long, sharp-pointed blade with a cutting edge or edges.

Sword bayonet. A bayonet which can be used as a sword.

Sword stick. A cane sword.

Tasset. One of the overlapping metal plates used in an armor to protect the thighs.

Ten-pounder. A cannon which discharges a ten-pound ball.

Thunderbolt. Shot resembling thunder in its suddenness and effectiveness.

Toledo. A sword made at Toledo in Spain.

Tomahawk. A war-hatchet of the American Indians.

Torpedo. A shell or cartridge to be exploded by electricity or by stepping on it.

Truncheon. A military staff of command.

Trusty sword. A sword as a reliance in combat.

Tuck. A long, narrow sword.

Verdun. A dueling-rapier of the 16th century.

Villanous saltpeter. Gunpowder. [Shakespeare, *Henry IV*, I, i, 3.}

Waddie. A war-club.

Weapon. Anything used in destroying, defeating, or injuring an enemy.

Westley Richards rifle. Kind of rifle.

Whinyard. A sword or hanger.

Whitworth gun. A form of rifled cannon and small arms used in the British army.

Wind-gun. A gun whose discharging force is condensed air.

Yatachan. } A long knife, or short saber common among Mohamme-
Yataghan. } dan people.

WEAPON—*Phrases.*

En flûte [F.]. With guns on the upper deck only.

Nervos belli pecuniam infinitam [L.]. The sinews of war [are] unlimited money

weap'-on-less. Without a weapon. MIGHT-IMPOTENCE.

wear. To decrease; use; to deflect; garments. AIM-ABERRATION, DRESS-UNDRESS, INCREASE-DECREASE, USE-DISUSE; **wear and tear,** BETTERMENT-DETERIORATION, PROVISION - WASTE, TOIL - RELAXATION; **wear away,** BETTERMENT-DETERIORATION, DISCONTINUANCE-CONTINUANCE; **wear off,** DISCONTINUANCE-CONTINUANCE, HABIT-DESUETUDE; **wear on,** PERIOD-

Progress; **wear out**, Betterment-Deterioration, Weariness-Refreshment; **wear the breeches**, Rule-License.

wear'-i-ness. Ennui. Desire-Repletion, Entertainment-Weariness, Lightheartedness-Dejection, Pleasure-Pain, Toil-Relaxation.

WEARINESS—REFRESHMENT.

Anhelation. State of being out of breath.
Collapse. Extreme depression of vital powers, as a result of over-exertion.
Deliquium. Faintness.
Drowsiness. Disposition to sleep.
Exhaustion. Fatigue, so that further exertion for the time is impossible.
Fainting. Sudden loss of consciousness.
Faintness. Disposition to swoon.
Fatigation. Weariness.
Fatigue. Painful lack of strength, from exertion.
Lassitude. Chronic fatigue.
Lipothymy. A fainting fit.
Prostration. Great depression.
Shortness of breath. Condition of the lungs when exertion makes respiration hard.
Sweat. Matter given off by the skin, especially during exertion.
Swoon. Apparent suspension of vital functions and mental powers.
Syncope. A fainting or swooning.
Tiredness. Reduction of strength by exertion.
Weariness. Painful lack of strength from continued strain.
Yawning. Expressing fatigue by opening the mouth.

Weariness—*Verbs.*

Be fatigued. To be very weary.
Blow. To breathe hard from quick movements.
Droop. To lose vigor and spirit.
Drop. To become faint.
Exhaust. To cause to be in a state of exhaustion.
Faint. To swoon.
Fatigue. To tire.
Flag. To become tired.
Gasp. To breathe convulsively, as from exhaustion.
Harass. To weary with annoyances.
Irk. To weary: used impersonally.
Jade. To weary with repetition of same thing.
Knock up. To utterly exhaust.
Lose breath.
Lose wind. } To feel shortness of the breath from exertion.
Overburden.
Overstrain.
Overtask. } To make tired.
Overtax.
Overwork.
Pant. To breathe in short labored breaths.
Prostrate. To depress greatly.
Puff. To breathe hard.
Sink. To lose strength slowly.
Strain. To injure by overexertion.
Succumb. To become prostrate.
Swoon. To become weak and lose consciousness.
Task. To overtax.
Tax. To impose a severe strain.
Tire. To reduce strength by exertion.
Wear out. To exhaust.
Weary. To fatigue by a long-continued strain.
Yawn. To open the mouth as an expression of fatigue.

Weariness—*Adjectives.*

Altered. Changed; tired.
Anhelose. Short-breathed.
Battered. Worn out.
Blown. Winded from overexertion.
Breathless. Panting.
Broken-winded. Having disordered respiration.
Dog weary. Very weary.
Done up. Used up.
Drooping. Having little vigor left.
Drowsy. Disposed to sleep.
Exhausted. Unable to do further work for a time.
Faint. Inclined to swoon.
Fatigued. Painfully tired.
Fatiguing. Tiring.
Footsore. Having sore feet from walking.
Haggard. Gaunt and careworn.
Hors de combat [F.]. Disabled.
Irksome. Annoying from long continuance.

Bait. Refreshment taken on a journey.
Bracing. A strengthening.
Recovery of strength. Refreshment.
Refection. Refreshment.
Refocillation. Restoration of strength by refreshment.
Refreshment. Renewal of strength.
Regalement. Refreshment on sumptuous fare.
Relief. Freedom from duty or care.
Repair. Recovery of strength.
Restoration. Bringing back to normal condition.
Revival. Restoration of one for a time lifeless.

Refreshment—*Verbs.*

Air. To refresh.
Brace. To restore tone or vigor.
Breathe. To pause for breath.
Come to oneself. To revive.
Draw breath. To pause to breathe.
Fan. To cool by stirring up currents of air.
Feel like a giant refreshed. To feel the very best.
Freshen up. To become vigorous.
Gather breath. To pause to breathe.
Get better. Improve in health.
Pick up. Become sprightly.
To raise one's head. To recover from exhaustion.
Recover breath. To become rested.
Recover strength. To become strong again.
Recruit. Recover strength.
Refocillate. Restore by refreshment.
Refresh. To renew the strength.
Regain breath. To pause to breathe.
Regain strength. To grow strong again.
Reinvigorate. To renew the vigor.
Renew strength. To become stronger.
Repair. To restore to sound condition that which was damaged.
Respire. To enjoy rest.
Take a long breath. Pause a short while to breathe.
Take breath. To pause to breathe.

Refreshment—*Adjectives.*

Recuperated. Restored to strength.
Refreshed, etc. Recovered. See *Verbs.*
Refreshing. Strengthening.
Untired.
Unwearied. } Not worn out.

Weariness—Adjectives—*Continued*

Knocked up. Greatly fatigued.
More dead than alive. Utterly exhausted.
On one's last legs. Almost exhausted.
Out of breath.
Out of wind. } Breathless.
Overfatigued.
Overspent. } Greatly fatigued.
Overtired. Fatigued.
Played out. Tired.
Prostrate. Weary; thrown down.
Puffing and blowing. Breathless.
Pulled down. In poor health from continued strain.
Ready to drop. Too weary to stand.
Seedy. Old and worn out.
Shattered. Broken in health.
Short-breathed. Affected with anhelation.
Short of breath.
Short of wind. } Breathless.
Short-winded. Affected with anhelation.
Spent. Exhausted.
Surbated. Harassed.
Tired to death. Exhausted.
Tiresome. Causing fatigue from its regularity.
Toilworn. Haggard.
Trying. Hard to endure.
Unrefreshed.
Unrestored. } Not recovered from fatigue.
Used up. Exhausted.

WEARINESS—Adjectives—*Continued.*

Walked off one's legs. Unable to walk farther.
Wayworn. Wearied by traveling.
Wearisome. Causing weariness from regularity or repetition.
Weary. Fatigued by a long strain.

Weatherbeaten. Showing exposure to the weather.
Windless. Breathless.
Worn. Gaunt and spiritless.
Worn out. Exhausted.

wear'-ing. Wearisome. ENTERTAINMENT-WEARINESS; **wearing apparel,** DRESS-UNDRESS; **wearing of the green,** PATRIOTISM-TREASON.
wear'-i-some. Laborious; fatiguing. PLEASURABLE-NESS-PAINFULNESS, TOIL-RELAXATION, WEARINESS-REFRESHMENT.
wear'-y. Fatigued; vexed. ENTERTAINMENT-WEARI-NESS, LIGHTHEARTEDNESS-DEJECTION, PLEASURE-PAIN, WEARINESS-REFRESHMENT; **weary, flat, stale, and unprofitable,** WITTINESS-DULNESS; **weary waste,** GULF-PLAIN.
wea'-sand. Windpipe. APERTURE-CLOSURE, WATER-COURSE-AIRPIPE.
wea'-sel a-sleep'. **Catch a weasel asleep,** ACTIVITY-IN-DOLENCE, POSSIBILITY-IMPOSSIBILITY.
weath'-er. Condition of the atmosphere. WATER-AIR; **weather permitting,** MODIFICATION, POSSIBILITY-IM-POSSIBILITY; **weather the storm,** ESCAPE, MUTABIL-ITY-STABILITY, RENOVATION-RELAPSE, SECURITY-INSECURITY, SUCCESS-FAILURE.
weath'-er–beat"-en. Seasoned; damaged. BET-TERMENT-DETERIORATION, STRENGTH-WEAKNESS, WEARINESS-REFRESHMENT.
weath'-er–bound". Detained by the weather. RE-LEASE-RESTRAINT.
weath'-er-cock". A weather-vane. BIGOTRY-APOSTASY, MUTABILITY-STABILITY, RIVER-WIND, SIGN, WATER-AIR.
weath'-ered. Seasoned. BETTERMENT-DETERIORATION.
weath'-er-gage". Weather indicator. WATER-AIR.
weath'-er-glass". A weather indicator. WATER-AIR.
weath'-er-proof". Healthy; secure. HEALTH-SICK-NESS, SECURITY-INSECURITY.
weath'-er-wise". Predicting weather. PREVISION, WATER-AIR.
weave. To make; to interlace. CREATION-DESTRUC-TION, CROSSING; **weave a tangled web,** DIFFICULTY-FACILITY.
wea'-zen. Shriveled. GREATNESS-LITTLENESS.
web. An intersection; texture. CROSSING, TEXTURE.
wed. To marry. MATRIMONY-CELIBACY.
wed'-ded. Married. MATRIMONY-CELIBACY; **wedded pair,** MATRIMONY-CELIBACY; **wedded to,** FAITH-MIS-GIVING, HABIT-DESUETUDE, LOVE-HATE; **wedded to an opinion,** BIGOTRY-APOSTASY, DECISION-MISJUDG-MENT.
wed'-ding. A marriage. MATRIMONY-CELIBACY.
wedge. A piece of wood; to press. ANGULARITY, IN-STRUMENT, SHARPNESS-BLUNTNESS, UNION-DIS-UNION; **thin edge of the wedge,** BEGINNING-END, CRAFT-ARTLESSNESS, ENVIRONMENT-INTERPOSITION; **wedge in,** ENVIRONMENT-INTERPOSITION.
wedge'-shaped". Like a wedge. ANGULARITY.
wed'-lock. Marriage. MATRIMONY-CELIBACY.
Wednes'-day. Fourth day of the week. PERIODICITY-IRREGULARITY.
wee. Little. GREATNESS-LITTLENESS.
weed. To exclude; to clean; a plant; tobacco. CLEAN-NESS-FILTHINESS, CONSEQUENCE-INSIGNIFICANCE,
DOMESTICATION-AGRICULTURE, FAUNA-FLORA, IN-CLUSION-OMISSION, MULTIPLICITY-PAUCITY, PUN-GENCY; **weed out,** ADMISSION-EXPULSION, INJECTION-EJECTION.
weeds. Plants; dress. DRESS-UNDRESS, JUBILATION-LAMENTATION, MATRIMONY-DIVORCE, USEFULNESS-USELESSNESS.
weed'-y. Thin; trifling. BREADTH-NARROWNESS, CON-SEQUENCE-INSIGNIFICANCE.
week. Seven days. MEASURE, PERIOD-PROGRESS.
week'-ly. Once a week. PERIODICITY-IRREGULARITY.
ween. To think. DECISION-MISJUDGMENT, FAITH-MIS-GIVING, KNOWLEDGE-IGNORANCE.
weep. To lament. COMPASSION-RUTHLESSNESS, JU-BILATION-LAMENTATION.
weep'-ing. Crying. JUBILATION-LAMENTATION.
weet. To know. DECISION-MISJUDGMENT, KNOWL-EDGE-IGNORANCE.
weet'-less. Thoughtless. KNOWLEDGE-IGNORANCE.
weft. Warp and weft. TEXTURE.
weigh. To ponder; lift; depress; influence. DOMI-NANCE-IMPOTENCE, ELEVATION-DEPRESSION, HEAVI-NESS-LIGHTNESS, MIND-IMBECILITY, SPRING-DIVE; **weigh anchor,** ARRIVAL-DEPARTURE; **weigh care-fully,** DIFFERENTIATION-INDISCRIMINATION; **weigh down,** GOODNESS-BADNESS, LIBERTY-SUBJECTION; **weigh heavy on,** GOODNESS-BADNESS; **weigh on the heart,** PLEASURABLENESS-PAINFULNESS; PLEASURE-PAIN; **weigh on the mind,** CONTENTEDNESS-REGRET, LIGHTHEARTEDNESS-DEJECTION, PLEASURABLENESS-PAINFULNESS, SANGUINENESS-TIMIDITY; **weigh with,** MOTIVE-CAPRICE.
weigh'-bridge". Platform scales. HEAVINESS-LIGHT-NESS.
weigh'-ing. Determining weight. CHEMISTRY, HEAVI-NESS-LIGHTNESS.
weight. Influence; gravity; importance. CONSE-QUENCE-INSIGNIFICANCE, DOMINANCE-IMPOTENCE, HEAVINESS-LIGHTNESS; **attach weight to,** FAITH-MISGIVING; **carry weight,** DOMINANCE-IMPOTENCE, EVIDENCE-COUNTEREVIDENCE; **drag weight,** OB-STRUCTION-HELP; **have weight,** EVIDENCE-COUNTER-EVIDENCE; **throw one's weight into the scale,** DOMI-NANCE-IMPOTENCE.
weight'-less. Light. LIGHTNESS-HEAVINESS.
weight'-y. Heavy; important. DOMINANCE-IMPO-TENCE, HEAVINESS-LIGHTNESS.
weir. A dam. OBSTRUCTION-HELP, WATERCOURSE-AIRPIPE.
weird. Unearthly; a spell. DEVOTION-CHARM, DEVO-TION-MAGIC, JOVE-FIEND; **weird sisters,** DEVOTION-MAGICIAN.
wel'-come. A reception; grateful. AMITY-HOSTILITY, ARRIVAL-DEPARTURE, POLITENESS-IMPOLITENESS, PLEASURABLENESS-PAINFULNESS, SOCIABILITY-PRI-VACY.
weld. To join. COHESION-LOOSENESS, UNION-DIS-UNION.
wel'-fare. Prosperity. WELFARE-MISFORTUNE.

WELFARE—MISFORTUNE.

Affluence. An abundant supply. See AFFLUENCE
Blessings. Things that promote one's welfare.
Godsend. An unexpected stroke of good fortune.
Good fortune.⎫ Prosperity as reached partly by chance and partly
Good luck. ⎭ by effort.
Luck Prosperity regarded as coming by chance.

Accident. An unfortunate occurrence without any one's direct in-tention.
Adverse fortune. ⎫
Adverse hap. ⎪ A calamity; a misfortune; an adversity.
Adverse lot. ⎬
Adverse luck. ⎭

WELFARE—MISFORTUNE—*Continued.*

Prosperity. Successful progress in any business or enterprise.
Run of luck. A continuance of good fortune.
Success. Favorable or prosperous termination of anything attempted.
Thrift. Success and advance in the acquisition of property.
Welfare. Enjoyment of the blessings of life.
Well-being. Welfare; prosperity.

WELFARE—*Denotations.*

Enfant gâté [F.]. A spoiled child.
Lucky dog. A fortunate person.
Made man. A man to whom success has come by labor.
Mushroom. One who rises suddenly from a low condition in life.
Parvenu. A man newly risen into notice.
Skipjack. An upstart.
Spoiled child of fortune. A person who has always been fortunate.
Upstart. One who has risen suddenly, as from low life to fortune and honor.

WELFARE—*Figurative Nouns.*

Bed of roses. A life of ease and happiness.
Bright days.⎫
Fair weather.⎬ Good fortune.
Fat of the land. Riches.
Flood. A condition of prosperity.
Golden age.⎫
Golden time.⎬ A time of great well-being
Halcyon days. Days of repose and happiness, like those while Halcyone broods her young.
High tide. A favorable condition of fortune.
Loaves and fishes. Wealth. [Bible.]
Milk and honey. Riches. [Bible.]
Palmy days. Prosperous days.
Piping times. Times of peace, characterized by the music of the pipe rather than of the drum and fife.
Roaring trade. Success in business.
Saturnian age. The golden age, when Saturn ruled.
Saturnia regna [L.]. The rule of Saturn.
Smiles of fortune. Good luck.
Sunshine. Good fortune.
Tide. Success.

WELFARE—*Verbs.*

Bask in the sunshine. To be prosperous; enjoy life under benign influences.
Bear a charmed life. To be lucky and fortunate always.
Bear fruit. To be of advantage to.
Be prosperous. To succeed in one's objects. See *Adjectives.*
Bloom. To be in a state of freshness and beauty.
Blossom. To flourish and prosper.
Blow. To cause to bloom.
Drive a roaring trade. To conduct a profitable business.
Drop into a good thing. To fall into a lucrative position.
Fall on one's feet.⎫
Fall on one's legs.⎬ To be in a favorable situation.
Fatten. To make fat; become rich.
Feather one's nest. To marry a rich woman.
Flourish. To be prosperous or thriving.
Flower. To come to finest condition.
Fructify. To make fruitful.
Get on in the world. To be fairly prosperous.
Go on smoothly.⎫
Go on swimmingly.⎬ To be favorable and successful.
Go on well.⎭
Have a fine time of it.⎫
Have a good time of it.⎬ To be happy. See *Nouns.*
Have a run.⎫
Have a run of fortune.⎬ To have a continuous occurrence of.
Have a run of luck.⎭
Have the good fortune. To obtain one's desire.
Keep oneself afloat.⎫ To be in a safe condition in respect to
Keep one's head above water.⎬ finances.
Lift one's head. To better one's condition or standing.
Light on one's feet.⎫
Light on one's legs.⎬ To be in a favorable condition.
Live in clover.⎫
Live on the fat of the land.⎬ To be wealthy.
Make one's fortune.⎫
Make one's way.⎬ To succeed.
Prosper. To make successful; be successful.
Raise one's head. To make more important or prominent.
Rise in the world. To increase one's fortune.
Run on all fours. To go like a quadruped on all four feet; hence, not to be crippled or embarassed for money or resources.

Adversity. A condition of affliction, of hardship, or misery
Affliction. The act of afflicting; dire distress of body or mind　See PLEASURABLENESS-PAINFULNESS.
Backcast. Anything which brings misfortune upon one.
Bad fortune.⎫
Bad hap.⎬ Misfortune; calamity
Bad lot.⎪
Bad luck.⎭
Bad times. Times of misfortune.
Blast.⎫
Blight.⎬ Anything that destroys the prospects or fortunes.
Broken fortune. Shattered, blasted fortune.
Calamity. Something causing distress; sudden misfortune often overwhelming.
Care. Trouble caused by onerous duties.
Casualty. A fatal accident.
Catastrophe. A final event, generally disastrous
Contretemps [F.]. An untoward accident.
Cross. An affliction or misfortune regarded as a test.
Curse. Calamity invoked.
Hardship. That which is hard to bear; an adversity.
Disaster. A sudden, crushing misfortune.
Downfall. A sudden descent from rank or state, reputation or happiness.
Evil. Anything that lessens the happiness of an individual; that which harms or injures. See GOOD-EVIL.
Evil dispensation. The harmful dealing out, as by a higher power.
Extremity. An extreme degree of pain, or suffering.
Failure. That which does not succeed. See SUCCESS-FAILURE.
Fall. Destruction, downfall, ruin.
Falling. Termination of greatness or power. See *Verbs.*
Hard case.⎫
Hard fortune.⎪
Hard hap.⎪
Hard life.⎬ An adverse, unfortunate condition.
Hard lines.⎪
Hard lot.⎪
Hard luck.⎭
Hardship. That which is hard to bear, as toil, privation, etc
Hard times. Times of misfortune.
Ill fortune.⎫
Ill hap.⎬ Misfortune.
Ill lot.⎪
Ill luck.⎭
Infliction. Anything inflicted; a punishment; a calamity.
Load. That which burdens or oppresses.
Misadventure. Mischance; misfortune.
Mischance. A happening that is bad or full of ill luck.
Misfortune. Bad fortune; any untoward, adverse event.
Mishap. Anything that happens unluckily.
Pressure. Oppressive weight or influence.
Reverse. A partial defeat; a misfortune
Rub. A cause of uneasiness.
Ruin. Anything that defeats the accomplishment of a given object.
Ruination. The act of ruining.
Ruinousness. Causing ruin. See *Adjectives.*
Sad times. Times of grief and sadness.
Trial. An affliction that tries a man.
Trouble. Anything that disturbs or annoys.
Undoing. Bringing into poverty or disgrace or disaster.
Visitation. Retributive calamity.

MISFORTUNE—*Figurative Nouns.*

Bitter pill. Something offensive or harmful which must be accepted or endured.
Cloud.⎫
Dark cloud.⎬ An indication of misfortune; a misfortune.
Evil day. A day of misfortune.
Evil genius. An evil spirit supposed to preside over a man's destiny.
Evil star. A planet supposed to influence one's destiny.
Frowns of fortune. Ill fortune.
Gathering clouds. Failure.
Hell upon earth. A condition of great mental torment.
Ill wind. Unfavorable turn of affairs.
Iron age. A low condition of fortune.
Losing game. Misfortune.
Peck of trouble. A great trouble.
Pressure of the times. Anything that puts one into difficulty.
Rainy day. A period of misfortune.
Sea of trouble. Troubles resembling the sea in vastness. [Shakespeare, *Hamlet.*]

WELFARE—MISFORTUNE—*Continued.*

WELFARE—Verbs—*Continued.*

Run smooth.
Run smoothly. } To go on favorably.
Sail before the wind. } To go on safely and successfully.
Swim with the tide. }
Take a favorable turn. To change for the better.
Thrive. To prosper by economy and care.
Work one's way. To labor and overcome difficulties.

WELFARE—*Adjectives.*

Agreeable. Pleasant or grateful to one. See PLEASURABLENESS.
At one's ease. Without trouble or anxiety.
Auspicious. Giving promise of success or prosperity.
Born under a lucky star.
Born with a silver spoon in one's mouth. } Lucky.
Buoyant. Lighthearted; cheerful.
Couleur de rose [F.]. Rose-color; with beauty and attractiveness.
Fortunate. Receiving some unforeseen good or blessings; favored of fortune.
Halcyon. Calm and peaceful, as the sea while the halcyon broods.
In a fair way. Having good prospects of success.
In full feather. }
In high feather. } In full spirits; having plenty of money.
In good case. Well-circumstanced.
In luck. Fortunate; unexpectedly successful.
Lucky. Favored by luck; meeting with success.
Palmy. Flourishing; prosperous.
Propitious. Helping to success; having favoring influence or tendency.
Prosperous. Successful in those things which men desire, tending to gain.
Providential. Effected by divine direction.
Rich. Having an abundance of money. See AFFLUENCE.
Set up. Raised from disaster to a sufficient fortune.
Thriving. Successful through economy and care. See *Verbs.*
Well-off. }
Well-to-do. } Prosperous.
Well-to-do in the world. }

WELFARE—*Adverbs, etc.*

As good luck would have it. Fortunately.
Beyond all hope. Successful beyond one's expectations.
Prosperously. With good fortune.
Swimmingly. Fortunately.

WELFARE—*Phrases.*

All for the best.
Chacun est l'artisan de sa fortune [F.]. Every man is the architect of his own fortune.
Felicitas multos habet amicos [L.]. Prosperity has many friends.
One's course runs smooth.
One's star in the ascendant.

MISFORTUNE—Adverbs, etc.—*Continued from Column 2.*

If the worst comes to worse. Seemingly hopeless.
Out of the frying-pan into the fire. From bad to worse.

MISFORTUNE—*Phrases.*

Amici probantur rebus adversis [L.]. Friends are tested by adversity.
Bien vengas, mal, si vienes solo [Sp.]. You are welcome, misfortune, if you come alone.
Fiel, pero desdichado [Sp.]. Faithful but unfortunate.
Gaudet tentamine virtus [L.]. Virtue rejoices in trial.
Ingentes stupent curæ leves loquuntur [L.]. Trivial anxieties talk, great one stand mute.
One's doom is sealed.
One's luck fails.
One's luck turns.
One's star is on the wane.
Tant va la cruche à l'eau qu'a le fin elle se casse [F.]. The water-jug holds as much as it is broken off from the top.
The game is up.
The ground trembles under one's feet.
Ver non semper viret [L.]. Spring does not always flourish.

---

wel'-kin. The sky. UNIVERSE, WATER-AIR.
well. A cistern; good; healthy; to flow. APPROVAL-DISAPPROVAL, ASSENT-DISSENT, CAUSE-EFFECT,

MISFORTUNE—Figurative Nouns—*Continued.*

Slough of despond. A condition of despondency and wretchedness. [Bunyan, *Pilgrim's Progress.*]
The sport of fortune. Man as subject to all the changes of fortune.
Times out of joint. Unfavorable or unsuccessful times.
Ups and downs of life. Changes of fortune.

MISFORTUNE—*Verbs.*

Be all over with. }
Be all up with. } To be in a ruined condition.
Be ill off. To be badly in want.
Bring a hornet's nest about one's ears. }
Bring a wasp's nest about one's ears. } To get into trouble.
Bring down one's gray hairs with sorrow to the grave. [*Genesis* 42, 38.]
Come to grief. To meet with calamity or accident.
Decay. To go from a prosperous to a disastrous condition.
Decline. To tend to a less perfect state; take a downward direction
Fall. To decline in wealth, importance, etc.
Fall from one's high estate. To be degraded in rank, fortune, etc.
Fall on evil. To meet with misfortune.
Fall on evil days. To meet with evil days.
Go down hill. To be in a bad way.
Go down in the world. To fall into misfortune.
Go hard with. To result disastrously to.
Go on ill. To continue ill.
Go to rack and ruin. To decay completely.
Go to the dogs. Go to ruin.
Have seen better days. To be in a state of misfortune.
Not prosper. To fail. See *Adjectives.*
Sink. To ruin; destroy.

MISFORTUNE—*Adjectives.*

Adverse. Opposed; antagonistic.
Badly off. Unfortunate.
Behindhand. Behind in progress.
Born under an evil star. }
Born with a wooden ladle in one's mouth. } Unlucky.
Calamitous. Full of calamity.
Clouded. Unfavorable.
Decayed. Declined or failed.
Deplorable. Lamentable.
Devoted. Doomed to evil.
Dire. Extremely calamitous.
Disastrous. Causing disaster.
Down in the world. Unfortunate.
Hapless. Having no luck; luckless.
Ill-fated. }
Ill-off. }
Ill-omened. } Unfortunate; calamitous.
Ill-starred. }
Improsperous. Not prosperous.
In a bad way. }
In adverse circumstances. }
In an evil plight. } Unfortunate; having ill fortune
In one's utmost need. }
In trouble. }
Luckless. Having no luck.
On its last legs. On the point of ruin or disaster.
On the road to ruin. Failing.
On the wane. Decreasing in prosperity, power etc.
Out of luck. Unfortunate.
Planet-struck. Affected by the influence of the planets; moonstruck.
Poor. Without money or resources. See AFFLUENCE-PENURY.
Ruinous. Tending to ruin; calamitous.
Unblest. Not blest; accursed.
Under a cloud. Unfavorable.
Undone. Ruined; brought to grief.
Unhappy. Not happy.
Unfortunate. Having ill fortune.
Unlucky. Not lucky.
Unprosperous. Not prosperous.
Untoward. Inconvenient; unfortunate.

MISFORTUNE—*Adverbs, etc.*

As ill luck would have it. Unfortunately.
From bad to worse. Failing.

(*Continued on Column* 1.)

DEEPNESS-SHALLOWNESS, ENTRANCE-EXIT, GOOD-EVIL, GULF-PLAIN, MAGNITUDE-SMALLNESS, PROVISION-WASTE, REMEDY-BANE, RIVER-WIND, SKILL-

UNSKILFULNESS, USEFULNESS-USELESSNESS; **act well**, VIRTUE-VICE; **all's well**, SECURITY-INSECURITY; **drop a bucket into an empty well**, USEFULNESS-USELESSNESS; **get well**, RENOVATION-RELAPSE; **get on well**, WELFARE-MISFORTUNE; **let well alone**, ACTION-PASSIVENESS, PUSH-PULL; **think well of**, APPROVAL-DISAPPROVAL; **treat well**, CHARITABLENESS-MALEVOLENCE: **turn out well**, SUCCESS-FAILURE; **well and good**, ASSENT-DISSENT, CONSENT, CONTENTEDNESS-DISCONTENTMENT; **well done**, APPROVAL-DISAPPROVAL; **well enough**, FAULTLESSNESS-FAULTINESS, MAGNITUDE-SMALLNESS; **well out**, ENTRANCE-EXIT; **well over**, EXCESS-LACK; **well up in**, SKILL-UKSKILFULNESS; **well with**, AMITY-HOSTILITY; **work well**, SUCCESS-FAILURE.

well'-a-day. Grief; wonder. ASTONISHMENT-EXPECTANCE, JUBILATION-LAMENTATION.

well'-ad-vised''. Prudent. SAGACITY-INCAPACITY.

well'-af-fect''-ed. Kindly disposed. AMITY-HOSTILITY.

well'-a-way. Alas. JUBILATION-LAMENTATION.

well'-be-haved''. Mannerly. POLITENESS-IMPOLITENESS, SOCIETY-LUDICROUSNESS.

well'-be''-ing. Prosperity; happiness. PLEASURE-PAIN, WELFARE-MISFORTUNE.

well'-be-loved''. Dear. LOVE-HATE.

well'-born''. Of good lineage. GENTILITY-COMMONALTY.

well'-bred''. Courteous. SOCIETY-LUDICROUSNESS.

well'-com-posed''. Beautiful. BEAUTY-UGLINESS.

well'-de-fined''. Visible; exact; determined. PREDETERMINATION-IMPULSE, TRUTH-ERROR, VISIBILITY-INVISIBILITY.

well'-de-vised''. Shrewdly planned. PREDETERMINATION-IMPULSE.

well'-dis-posed''. Inclined. OBSTRUCTION-HELP.

well'-do''-ing. Virtue. VIRTUE-VICE.

well'-drawn''. Graphic. ACCOUNT.

well'-ed''-u-ca''-ted. Learned. KNOWLEDGE-IGNORANCE.

well'-fa''-vored. Comely. BEAUTY-UGLINESS.

well'-formed. Shapely. BEAUTY-UGLINESS.

well'-fed. Sleek. GREATNESS-LITTLENESS.

well'-found''-ed. Certain; probable. CERTAINTY-DOUBT, ENTITY-NONENTITY, LIKELIHOOD-UNLIKELIHOOD; **well-founded belief**, FAITH-MISGIVING, TRUTH-ERROR.

well'-ground''-ed. Informed; probable. ENTITY-NONENTITY, KNOWLEDGE-IGNORANCE, LIKELIHOOD-UNLIKELIHOOD, TRUTH-ERROR.

well'-grouped''. Arranged in a good manner. BEAUTY-UGLINESS.

well'-in-formed''. Educated. KNOWLEDGE-IGNORANCE.

Well'-ing-ton. A style of boot. DRESS-UNDRESS.

well'-in-ten''-tioned. Kind; virtuous. CHARITABLENESS-MALEVOLENCE, VIRTUE-VICE.

well'-judged''. Skilfully adapted. SAGACITY-INCAPACITY.

well'-knit''. Strong. MIGHT-IMPOTENCE.

well'-known''. Habitual; commonplace. HABIT-DESUETUDE, KNOWLEDGE-IGNORANCE.

well'-laid''. Carefully thought out. PREDETERMINATION-IMPULSE.

well'-made''. Beautiful. BEAUTY-UGLINESS.

well'-man''-nered. Courteous. POLITENESS-IMPOLITENESS, SOCIETY-LUDICROUSNESS.

well'-marked''. Visible. VISIBILITY-INVISIBILITY.

well'-mean''-ing. Kind. CHARITABLENESS-MALEVOLENCE.

well'-meant''. Kind. CHARITABLENESS-MALEVOLENCE.

well'-met''. Greeting. POLITENESS-IMPOLITENESS.

well'-na''-tured. Friendly. CHARITABLENESS-MALEVOLENCE.

well'-nigh. Almost; near. MAGNITUDE-SMALLNESS, REMOTENESS-NEARNESS.

well'-off. Prosperous; rich. AFFLUENCE-PENURY, WELFARE-MISFORTUNE.

well'-pro-por''-tioned. Shapely. BEAUTY-UGLINESS.

well'-pro-vi''-ded. Stored. ENOUGH.

well'-reg''-u-la-ted. Adjusted; cautious. CONVENTIONALITY-UNCONVENTIONALITY, RECKLESSNESS-CAUTION, REGULARITY-IRREGULARITY.

well'-set. Stout. PROPORTION DEFORMITY.

well'-spent. Successful; virtuous. SUCCESS-FAILURE, VIRTUE-VICE.

well'-spo''-ken. Genteel. SOCIETY-LUDICROUSNESS.

well'-spring''. Source. STORE.

well'-stocked''. Stored. ENOUGH.

well'-ta''-sted. Savory. PALATABLENESS-UNPALATABLENESS.

well'-timed. Opportune. OPPORTUNENESS-UNSUITABLENESS.

well'-to-do''. Prosperous; rich. AFFLUENCE-PENURY, WELFARE-MISFORTUNE.

well'-turned pe'-ri-ods. Elegant sentences. PURITY-CRUDENESS.

well'-weighed''. Pondered. PREDETERMINATION-IMPULSE.

well'-wish''-er. A friend. FRIEND-FOE.

well'-wood''-ed. Covered with forests. SMOOTHNESS-ROUGHNESS.

well'-worn''. Shoddy. USE-DISUSE.

Wels'-bach lamp. Kind of gas-lamp. CHEMISTRY.

welsh'-er. A swindler. ROBBER, OUTLAY-INCOME.

welt. Seam-covering. BORDER.

wel'-ter. To roll; to plunge. REVOLUTION-EVOLUTION, SPRING-DIVE; **welter in one's blood**, LIFE-KILLING.

Weltgeschichte ist das Weltgericht, die [G.] (velt''-ge-shiн'-tê ist das velt''-gê-riн', dî). World-history is a world-tribunal. ACCOUNT, TRIBUNAL, UNIVERSE.

wem. A spot. EMBELLISHMENT-DISFIGUREMENT.

wen. A protuberance. CONVEXITY-CONCAVITY, EMBELLISHMENT-DISFIGUREMENT.

wench. A girl; a woman; a prostitute. INFANT-VETERAN, MALE-FEMALE, PURITY-RAKE.

wench'-ing. Libertinism. PURITY-IMPURITY.

wend. To walk. TRAVELING-NAVIGATION.

were. As you were, RENOVATION-RELAPSE.

wer'-gild''. Fine. RECOMPENSE-PENALTY.

Wes'-ley-an. A follower of John and Charles Wesley. ORTHODOXY-HETERODOXY.

west. A direction. AIM-ABERRATION, LATERALITY-CONTRAPOSITION.

west'-ern. Pertaining to the west. LATERALITY-CONTRAPOSITION.

wet. Moist. DAMPNESS-DRYNESS, WATER-AIR; **just enough to wet one's feet**, DEEPNESS-SHALLOWNESS; **wet blanket**, ENTERTAINMENT-WEARINESS, LIGHTHEARTEDNESS-DEJECTION, MOTIVE-DEHORTATION, OBSTRUCTION-HELP, WITTINESS-DULNESS; **wet one's whistle**, NUTRIMENT-EXCRETION, TEETOTALISM-INTEMPERANCE.

whack. To strike. IMPETUS-REACTION.

whack'-ing. Large. GREATNESS-LITTLENESS.

whale. An animal. GREATNESS-LITTLENESS; **sprat to catch a whale**, SKILL-UNSKILFULNESS; **tub to a whale**, PRETEXT, TRUTHFULNESS-FRAUD.

whale'-bone. A substance. ELASTICITY-INELASTICITY.

wha'-ler. A ship. CONVEYANCE-VESSEL.

whal'-lop. To flog. RECOMPENSE-PUNITION.

whap. To flop. IMPETUS-REACTION.

wharf. A pier. DWELLER-HABITATION, MARKET, WORKSHOP.

wharf'-age. Wharf rent. PRICE-DISCOUNT.

what. An expression of inquiry or surprise. ASTONISHMENT-EXPECTANCE, INVESTIGATION-ANSWER; **and what not**, MULTIPLICITY-PAUCITY, UNIFORMITY-MULTIFORMITY: **know what's what**, DIFFERENTIATION-

INDISCRIMINATION, SAGACITY-INCAPACITY, SKILL-UNSKILFULNESS; **what d' ye call 'em**, WORD-NEOLOGY; **what in the world**, ASTONISHMENT-EXPECTANCE, CONVENTIONALITY-UNCONVENTIONALITY; **what is the reason**, INVESTIGATION-ANSWER; **what next**, INQUISITIVENESS-INDIFFERENCE; **what on earth**, ASTONISHMENT-EXPECTANCE, CONVENTIONALITY-UNCONVENTIONALITY; **what's his name**, WORD-NEOLOGY; **what signifies**, CONSEQUENCE-INSIGNIFICANCE.

what-ev'-er. No matter what. UNIVERSALITY-PARTICULARITY; **whatever may happen**, CERTAINTY-DOUBT, OCCURRENCE-DESTINY.

what"-so-ev'-er. Whatever. GATHERING-SCATTERING.

wheal. A ridge. CONVEXITY-CONCAVITY.

wheat. A cereal. DOMESTICATION-AGRICULTURE; **winnow the chaff from the wheat**, CHOICE-NEUTRALITY.

whee'-dle. To coax; to flatter. ADULATION-DISPARAGEMENT, BLANDISHMENT, MOTIVE-CAPRICE.

whee'-dling. Deceiving. ADULATION-DISPARAGEMENT.

wheel. A circle; to turn; the rack. ADVANCE-RETROGRESSION, AIM-ABERRATION, CIRCLE-WINDING, CIRCUITION, INSTRUMENT, RECOMPENSE-REWARD, REVOLUTION-EVOLUTION; **break on the wheel**, PLEASURABLENESS-PAINFULNESS, RECOMPENSE-PUNITION, SENSUALITY-SUFFERING; **get the wheel out of the rut**, RESCUE; **scotch the wheel**, OBSTRUCTION-HELP; **wheel about**, AIM-ABERRATION, REVERSAL; **wheel and axle**, INSTRUMENT; **wheel around**, BIGOTRY-APOSTASY, REVERSAL; **wheel of fortune**, MUTABILITY-STABILITY, RATIONALE-LUCK, VOLITION-OBLIGATION.

wheel'-bar"-row. A conveyance. CONVEYANCE-VESSEL.

wheel'-chair. A conveyance. CONVEYANCE-VESSEL.

wheels within wheels. Entangled; machinery. INSTRUMENT, REGULARITY-IRREGULARITY.

wheel'-work. Machinery. INSTRUMENT.

wheel'-wright". Wagon-maker. AGENT.

wheeze. To blow; to hiss. RESONANCE-SIBILATION, RIVER-WIND.

wheez'-y. Husky. RESONANCE-SIBILATION.

whelm. To submerge. EXCESS-LACK.

whelp. A pup; a son; a rogue. FAUNA-FLORA, GOOD MAN-BAD MAN, INFANT-VETERAN.

when At what time. DURATION-NEVERNESS, INVESTIGATION-ANSWER; **in the time when**, DURATION-NEVERNESS.

whence. From where; wherefore. ARRIVAL-DEPARTURE, INVESTIGATION-ANSWER, RATIOCINATION-INSTINCT, RATIONALE-LUCK.

when-ev'-er. At whatever time. TIME.

when"-so-ev'-er. Whenever. TIME.

where. In what place. INVESTIGATION-ANSWER, PRESENCE-ABSENCE; **where am I**, ASTONISHMENT-EXPECTANCE.

where'-a-bouts". Situation; near. REMOTENESS-NEARNESS, SITUATION.

where-as'. Because; when in truth. CONNECTION-INDEPENDENCE, RATIOCINATION-INSTINCT.

where-by'. By which. INSTRUMENTALITY.

where'-fore. Because; why. INVESTIGATION-ANSWER, MOTIVE-CAPRICE, RATIOCINATION-INSTINCT, RATIONALE-LUCK.

where-in'. In which. OUTSIDE-INSIDE.

where'-ness. Presence. PRESENCE-ABSENCE.

where"-up-on'. After which. DURATION-NEVERNESS, FUTURE-PAST.

wher-ev'-er. Where. EXTENSION-DISTRICT, EXTENSION-PLACE.

where-with'. Means; money. MEANS, MONEY.

where"-with-al'. That which is necessary. MEANS, MONEY.

wher'-ret. A blow. PLEASURABLENESS-PAINFULNESS.

wher'-ry. A boat. CONVEYANCE-VESSEL.

whet. To sharpen; to excite; a dram. EXCITATION, MOTIVE-CAPRICE, NUTRIMENT-EXCRETION, SHARPNESS-BLUNTNESS; **take a whet**, TEETOTALISM-INTEMPERANCE; **whet the appetite**, DESIRE-DISTASTE; **whet the knife**, PREPARATION-NONPREPARATION.

wheth'-er or not. CHOICE-NEUTRALITY.

whet'-stone". Stone used to sharpen tools. SHARPNESS-BLUNTNESS.

which. At which time. TIME; **know which is which**, DIFFERENTIATION-INDISCRIMINATION.

whiff. A gust. EXCITABILITY-INEXCITABILITY, RIVER-WIND.

whif'-fle. To puff. RIVER-WIND.

Whig. Political party. ASSOCIATION.

while. When. DURATION-NEVERNESS; **in a while**, EARLINESS-LATENESS; **while away time**, ACTION-PASSIVENESS, DURATION-NEVERNESS, ENTERTAINMENT-WEARINESS; **while speaking of**, CONNECTION-INDEPENDENCE, OPPORTUNENESS-UNSUITABLENESS; **worth while**, PROPRIETY-IMPROPRIETY.

whi'-lom. Formerly. FUTURE-PAST.

whilst. While. DURATION-NEVERNESS.

whim. A fancy; a caprice. DESIRE-DISTASTE, FANCY, PERSISTENCE-WHIM, WITTINESS-DULNESS.

whim'-per. A whine. JUBILATION-LAMENTATION.

whim'-si-cal. Freakish. AGITATION, PERSISTENCE-WHIM, SOCIETY-LUDICROUSNESS, WITTINESS-DULNESS.

whim'-si-cal'-i-ty. Freakishness. WITTINESS-DULNESS.

whim'-sy. A whim. DESIRE-DISTASTE, FANCY.

whim'-wham. A whim; a toy. CONSEQUENCE-INSIGNIFICANCE, PERSISTENCE-WHIM.

whin. Furze. FAUNA-FLORA.

whine. To cry; to complain. CRY-ULULATION, JUBILATION-LAMENTATION.

whin'-yard. A weapon. WEAPON.

whip. To flog; to strike; to urge; a director; a coachman; to agitate. AGITATION, EXCULPATION-PUNITION, HURRY-LEISURE, IMPETUS-REACTION, MANAGER, MOTIVE-CAPRICE, RECOMPENSE-SCOURGE, VARIANCE-ACCORD, WAYFARER-SEAFARER; **whip and spur**, SWIFTNESS-SLOWNESS; **whip away**, ARRIVAL-DEPARTURE; **whip-hand**, RULE-LICENSE, SUCCESS-FAILURE; **whip in**, INJECTION-EJECTION; **whip off**, ARRIVAL-DEPARTURE; **whip on**, HURRY-LEISURE; **whip up**, TAKING-RESTITUTION.

whip'-cord". A strong cord. LAMINA-FIBER.

whip'-per-in". A manager. MANAGER.

whip'-per-snap"-per. A whipster. INFANT-VETERAN.

whip'-ping-post". A post for whipping culprits. RECOMPENSE-SCOURGE.

whip'-ster. A shallow fellow. INFANT-VETERAN.

whir. To whirl; to buzz. CRASH-DRUMMING, REVOLUTION-EVOLUTION.

whirl. To rotate. REVOLUTION-EVOLUTION.

whirl'-i-gig. A toy. REVOLUTION-EVOLUTION.

whirl'-pool. A revolving vortex; a commotion. AGITATION, REVOLUTION-EVOLUTION, RIVER-WIND.

whirl'-wind. A vortex of wind; disorder. AGITATION, REGULARITY-IRREGULARITY, RIVER-WIND; **reap the whirlwind**, CAUSE-EFFECT, SUCCESS-FAILURE; **ride the whirlwind**, DETERMINATION-VACILLATION, RULE-LICENSE.

whisk. To move; to flourish; to mix. AGITATION, CIRCUITION, SWIFTNESS-SLOWNESS.

whisk'-er. Beard. SMOOTHNESS-ROUGHNESS.

whisk'-et. A basket. CONTENTS-RECEIVER.

whis'-ky. A spirituous liquor. LIQUID-GAS.

whis'-per. A faint sound; to tell. ENLIGHTENMENT-SECRECY, LOUDNESS-FAINTNESS, MANIFESTATION-LATENCY, SPEECH-INARTICULATION; **stage whisper**, VOCALIZATION-MUTENESS; **whisper about**, ENLIGHTENMENT-SECRECY, EXPOSURE-HIDINGPLACE,

PUBLICITY; **whisper in the ear,** VOCALIZATION-MUTE-NESS.

whist. Hush; a game. ENTERTAINMENT-WEARINESS, SOUND-SILENCE.

whis'-tle. To hiss; to pipe; a pipe. MUSICAL INSTRUMENTS, MUSICAIN, RESONANCE-SIBILATION; **clean as a whistle,** CLEANNESS-FILTHINESS, ENTIRETY-DEFICIENCY, FAULTLESSNESS-FAULTINESS; **pay too dear for one's whistle,** COSTLINESS-CHEAPNESS, PROPRIETY-IMPROPRIETY, SKILL-UNSKILFULNESS; **wet one's whistle,** NUTRIMENT-EXCRETION, TEETOTALISM-INTEMPERANCE; **whistle at,** REGARD-SCORN; **whistle for,** DESIRE-DISTASTE, PETITION-EXPOSTULATION; **whistle for want of thought,** ACTION-PASSIVENESS; **whistle jigs to a mile-stone,** USEFULNESS-USELESSNESS.

whit. A bit. MAGNITUDE-SMALLNESS

white. A color. COLOR-ACHROMATISM, WHITENESS-BLACKNESS; **mark with a white stone,** APPROVAL-DISAPPROVAL, CONSEQUENCE-INSIGNIFICANCE; **stand in a white sheet,** ATONEMENT; **white as a sheet,** SANGUINENESS-TIMIDITY, WHITENESS-BLACKNESS; **white feather,** BRAVERY-COWARDICÆ; **white flag,** FIGHTING-CONCILIATION; **white frost,** HEAT-COLD; **white heat,** HEAT-COLD; **white horses,** RIVER-WIND; **white lie,** AMBIGUITY, ENLIGHTENMENT-SECRECY, PRETEXT, TRUTHFULNESS-FABRICATION; **white liver,** BRAVERY-COWARDICE; **white livered,** BRAVERY-COWARDICE; **white of the eye,** SIGHT-BLINDNESS.

White'-chap''-el cart. A two wheeled shop-cart. CONVEYANCE-VESSEL.

whi'-ten. To make white. WHITENESS-BLACKNESS.

white'-ness. Color. WHITENESS-BLACKNESS.

WHITENESS—BLACKNESS.

Whiteness, etc. Quality of being white; white color. See *Adjectives.*

WHITENESS—*Denotations.*

Alabaster. A hard white and translucent stone.
Argent. Silver.
Chalk. A soft earthy substance of a white color.
Eburin. A composition of dust of ivory with a cement.
Ivory. The hard white substance constituting the tusks of the elephant.
Lily. A plant bearing a white flower.
Milk. The white fluid secreted by the mammary glands of female animals.
Paper. A substance, usually white, in the form of thin leaves, intended to be written on.
Silver. A whitish metal.
Snow. Watery particles frozen into white transparent crystals.

WHITENESS—*Nouns of Operation.*

Albification. Act or process of making white.
Etiolation. Act of becoming white by excluding the light of the sun or by disease.

WHITENESS—*Verbs.*

Be white, etc. To possess the color of pure snow. See *Adjectives.*
Blanch. To whiten by depriving of color, either permanently or temporarily.
Bleach. To deprive of color permanently, as linen.
Etiolate. To whiten by excluding the light of the sun.
Render white, etc. To make or cause to be white. See *Adjectives.*
Silver. To cover or coat with silver.
Whiten. To make white in general; overspread with white coloring-matter.
Whitewash. To cover with a liquid composition of slaked lime.

WHITENESS—*Adjectives*

Argent. Like or made of silver.
Argentine. Pertaining to silver; silvery.
Blanched, etc. Colorless. See *Verbs.*
Blonde [F.] Fair; of a light yellow.
Candid. White; sincere; frank.
Canescent. Tending to become white.
Chalky. Like chalk.
Creamy. Like or full of cream.
Fair. Free from any dark hue; spotless.
High in tone. In painting, brilliant coloring.
Hoar. }
Hoary. } White or gray with age; grayish-white.
Light. Not dark or obscure; whitish.
Like ivory, etc. Having the color of ivory. See *Nouns.*
Milk-white. White as milk.
Niveous. Snowy; resembling snow.
Pearly. Like pearls.
Silvery. Having a silver-like luster.
Snow-white. White as snow.
Snowy. White, like snow.
White. Having the hue or color of pure snow.
Whitish. White in a moderate degree.
White as a lily.
White as a sheet. } Expressions signifying a high degree of
White as driven snow. } whiteness.
White as silver. }

Black. A destitution of all color.
Blackness, etc. The quality of being black, or destitute of color. See *Adjectives.*
Color. The hue or appearance that a body presents to the eye.
Dark color. A hue which is not reflective of light.
Darkness, etc. The want of physical light; obscurity. See LIGHT-DARKNESS.
Lividity. The state of being of a black-and-blue color.
Swarthiness. Duskiness or darkness of complexion.

BLACKNESS—*Denotations.*

Blackamoor. A negro or negress.
Blue-black. Liege black, used as a pigment.
Charcoal. Impure carbon prepared by burning wood, etc.
Chiaroscuro [It.]. A drawing in black and white.
Coal. A black, solid, combustible substance dug from the earth.
Crow. A bird whose feathers are very black.
Darky. A negro.
Ebony. A hard, black wood.
Ethiop. A negro.
India ink. A mixture of lampblack and gum.
Ink. A fluid, commonly black, used in writing.
Ivory-black. Carbonized ivory used as a pigment.
Jet. A variety of lignite of a velvet-black color.
Lampblack. Carbon from burning oil.
Man of color. A negro.
Negro. A black man.
Nigger. A negro: in vulgar derision.
Pitch. A thick, black substance obtained by boiling tar.
Printers' ink. }
Printing-ink. } A very black ink made of lampblack and linseed-oil.
Raven. A black bird similar to the crow.
Sable. Black clothing.
Sloe. The blackthorn tree.
Smut. Soot or coal-dust.
Soot. A black substance from burning fuel.
Tone. The general effect of a picture produced by a combination of light and shade.
Writing-ink. Ink used in writing.

BLACKNESS—*Nouns of Operation.*

Infuscation. The act of darkening or blackening.
Nigrification. The act of making black.

BLACKNESS—*Verbs*

Be black, etc. To be destitute of color. See *Adjectives.*
Blacken. To make black.
Blot. To spot or stain with ink or other coloring matter.
Blotch. To blacken or spot; daub.
Darken, etc. To make dark or destitute of light. See LIGHT-DARKNESS.
Denigrate. To blacken thoroughly; sully or defame.
Infuscate. To darken; obscure.
Render black, etc. To make destitute of color. See *Adjectives.*
Smirch. To smear with something which stains or makes dirty.
Smutch. To blacken with soot, smoke, or coal.

BLACKNESS—*Adjectives.*

Atramentous. Inky; black, like ink.
Black. Absolutely destitute of color.

BLACKNESS—Adjectives—*Continued.*

Black as a shoe.
Black as a tinker's pot.
Black as jet.
Black as midnight.
Black as my hat.
Black as November.
Black as thunder. } Figurative degrees of blackness; expressions denoting intense blackness

Coal-black.}
Jet-black. } Black as coal or jet; deep-black.

Dark. Absolutely destitute of light.
Dingy. Soiled; tarnished; dirty; dark brown.
Dusky. Not luminous; partially dark.
Ebon. Like ebony in color; black.
Ethiopic. Applied to the negro race as inhabiting Africa.
Fuliginous. Smoke-colored; sooty.
Gray, etc. Of a white color tempered with black; hoary. See GRAY.
Inky. Of or like ink.

Jetty. Black as jet.
Low in tone. In painting, not very brilliant coloring.
Low-toned. In painting, a softened or less pronounced effect.
Murky. That which is at once dark, obscure, and gloomy.
Nigrescent. Growing black; approaching blackness.
Nocturnal, etc. Pertaining to night; nightly. See LIGHT-DARKNESS.
Obscure, etc. That from which light is more or less cut off. See LIGHT-DARKNESS.
Of the deepest dye. Very black.
Pitchy. Like pitch in color; dark; dismal.
Sable. Of the color of a sable's fur; black.
Somber. Cloudy; gloomy; melancholy.
Sooty. Resembling soot; black, like soot.
Swart. Being of a dark hue; moderately black.
Swarthy. Being of a dusky complexion; tawny or black.

BLACKNESS—*Adverb.*

In mourning. In black to express sorrow or grief.

white'-wash". To paint; acquit; justify. CLEANNESS-FILTHINESS, COVER-LINING, EMBELLISHMENT-DISFIGUREMENT, EXCULPATION-CONVICTION, JUSTIFICATION-CHARGE, WHITENESS-BLACKNESS.
white'-washed". Washed white. **Get whitewashed,** SETTLEMENT-DEFAULT.
white'-wash"-er. A flatterer. FLATTERER-DEFAMER.
white'-wash"-ing. Coating with lime. JUSTIFICATION-CHARGE, SETTLEMENT-DEFAULT.
white'-y-brown. A color. GRAY-BROWN.
whith'-er. To what place. AIM-ABERRATION, INCLINATION, INVESTIGATION-ANSWER.
whi'-tish. Gray. WHITENESS-BLACKNESS.
whit'-leath-er. Tough leather. TOUGHNESS-BRITTLENESS.
Whit'-Mon-day. A holiday. ENTERTAINMENT-WEARINESS.

Whit'-sun-tide". A holy week. CEREMONIAL.
whit'-tle. To cut. UNION-DISUNION.
whit'-tled. Drunk. TEETOTALISM-INTEMPERANCE.
whiz. To buzz. RESONANCE-SIBILATION.
who. An interrogative and relative pronoun. INVESTIGATION-ANSWER; **who would have thought,** ASTONISHMENT-EXPECTANCE, EXPECTATION-SURPRISE.
whoa. Stop. MOVEMENT-REST.
whole. Entire; healthy. HEALTH-SICKNESS, WHOLE-PART; **go the whole hog,** COMPLETION-NONCOMPLETION, DETERMINATION-VACILLATION; **make whole,** RENOVATION-RELAPSE; **on the whole,** DECISION-MISJUDGMENT, RATIOCINATION-INSTINCT; **the whole time,** DURATION-NEVERNESS; **whole truth,** EXPOSURE-HIDINGPLACE, TRUTH-ERROR, TRUTHFULNESS-FALSEHOOD.

WHOLE—PART.

Aggregate. A sum or mass of particulars.
All. The numerical totality of a body; the whole number.
Alpha and Omega. The first and the last. [Greek letters.]
Be all and end all. The entirety.
Bulk. The greater part; the mass.
Collectiveness. The state of being gathered into a mass or body; combination.
Completeness. The state of wanting no part or element; perfection.
Embodiment. The act of forming into a whole out of a number of individuals or units.
Ensemble [F.]. The parts of a thing taken or viewed as a whole.
Entirety. The state of being undivided.
Gross amount. The total amount without deduction.
Indiscerptibility. The condition of not being separable into parts.
Indivisibility. The state of being indivisible.
Integer. The whole of anything; an entire entity.
Integration. The act of making entire.
Integrity. Unbroken state; moral soundness.
Length and breadth of. The whole extent.
Lion's share. The largest portion of, or the whole.
One and all. The entirety.
Sum. The entire quantity; the whole of anything.
Sum total. The whole amount of several totals taken together.
The long and the short. The whole of the matter.
The whole. The entire assembly or collection of the parts of a thing.
Total. Complete in amount, as to quantity.
Totality. The whole sum or amount; completeness.
Totalness, etc. The quality or state of being total. See *Adjectives.*
Tout ensemble [F.]. The whole taken together; general effect.
Unity, etc. State of being one; oneness. See SOLITUDE.
Whole. That in which no part is wanting.

WHOLE—*Partitive Nouns.*

Almost all. The greater part.
Best part. The largest portion.
Essential part. The most necessary part.
Greater part. The larger part. See CONSEQUENCE.
Main part. The principal part.

Any. One or more persons, things, or portions out of a number.
Aught. Anything; any part, even the smallest.
Bit. A small piece or fragment of anything.
Component part. A part entering into the composition of anything. See CONSTITUENT.
Division. The act of separating into parts; that which divides
Fraction. One of the several equal parts of a whole or unity.
Fragment. A broken part of a whole.
Instalment. One of a series of proportionate payments to be continued until the claim is discharged.
Member. Part of an aggregate or whole.
Parcel. A portion of anything taken separately.
Part. Something less than the whole.
Particle. A minute part or portion of matter.
Piece. A part separated from the whole in any manner, generally evenly.
Portion. A part viewed with reference to an individual or some purpose to which it is to be applied.
Section. A part cut or separate from the rest.
Segment. A part cut off; one of the parts into which a body naturally divides itself.
Share, etc. A part or portion of a thing owned by several individuals in common. See ASSIGNMENT.
Subdivision. The part of a larger part.

PART—*Denotations.*

Arm. The upper limb of the human body.
Article. A distinct proposition or statement in a series of statements.
Bow. The forward part of a ship.
Branch. A bough of a tree.
Bush. A branching shrub.
Cantle. The hind bow of a saddle.
Cantlet. A small fragment cut or broken off.
Chapter. A division of a book or treatise.
Chip. A small piece cut or broken off.
Clause. A distinct part of a composition.
Collop. A small slice of meat.

WHOLE—PART—*Continued.*

WHOLE—Partitive Nouns—*Continued.*

Major part.⎫
Nearly all.⎬ The greater part.
Principal part. The most necessary portion.

WHOLE—Denotations.

Benjamin's mess. Benjamin's share. [*Genesis* xliii, 34]
Body. The entire physical part of man or other animals.
Bole. The trunk or body of a tree.
Compasses [L.]. A system or structure of many parts united.
Hulk. The body of an old ship or decked vessel.
Hull. The body of a vessel exclusive of the rigging, etc.
Lump. A mass of things thrown together.
Mass. An aggregation of matter into one coherent whole.
Skeleton. The framework of an animal body.
Staple. A principal commodity or production.
Tissue. One of the elementary fabrics of which an organ is composed.
Trunk. The main body or stock of a tree

WHOLE—Verbs.

Aggregate. To pile up, used of numbers and amounts. See GATHERING.
Amass. To bring together materials that make a mass.
Amount to. To rise up to in the whole.
Come to. To amount to; have a total of.
Constitute a whole. To make up a whole.
Embody. To collect into a whole; incorporate.
Form a whole. To go to make up a whole.
Integrate. To renew; to make a thing entire.

WHOLE—Adjectives.

Complete, etc. Wanting no part or element. See COMPLETION.
Entire. Perfect and undiminished unity.
Indiscerptible. That cannot be destroyed by separation of parts.
Indissoluble.⎫ Not to be melted or liquefied; incapable of separa-
Indissolvable.⎭ tion.
Individual. Existing as one entity; not to be divided; single.
Indivisible. That cannot be divided or separated.
Integral. Comprising all the parts; unbroken parts or numbers.
One. A single number; forming a whole.
Seamless. Having no seam; woven throughout.
Sweeping. Including many in a single act or assertion.
Total. Complete in amount, used in reference to quantity.
Unbroken.
Unbruised.
Unclipped.
Uncropped.
Uncut.
Undemolished.
Undestroyed.⎬ Adjectives expressing completeness or entirety
Undiminished.
Undissolved.
Undivided.
Unsevered.
Unshorn.
Whole. Containing all the parts.
Wholesale. Buying and selling in large quantities only

WHOLE—Adverbs, etc.

All. In compounds, wholly, completely, or perfectly.
All in all. Everything.
All put together. Wholly.
Altogether. Wholly; entirely.
Bodily. In one mass; all together; completely
Collectively. In a mass or body; unitedly.
En bloc [F.]. In a lump.
En masse [F.]. In a body.
Entirely. In the whole; completely.
Every inch. Entirely; completely.
In a body. All together; collectively.
In extenso [L.]. In the extended form; at full length.
In gross.
In lump.
In the aggregate.⎬ Entirely
In the long run.
In the main.
In the mass.
On the whole. Taking all things into consideration.
Substantially. In substance; essentially.
Throughout. Everywhere; in every part.
Totally, etc. In a total manner; completely. See COMPLETELY
Wholesale. In bulk or quantity; indiscriminately.
Wholly. In all the parts; entirely

PART—Denotations—*Continued.*

Compartment. One of the parts into which an enclosed space is divided.
Count. A separate and distinct charge in a pleading or indictment.
County. A civil division of a state or kingdom. See EXTENSION-DISTRICT.
Cut. A part cut off.
Cutting. A piece cut off or out, as from a newspaper, etc.
Debris. Accumulated fragments.
Department. A part or portion of something as extensive or complete. See DIVISION.
Detachment. A body of troops drawn off from the main body.
Detritus. Loose fragments or particles of rock.
Dividend. A number or quantity to be divided into equal parts.
Dose. The quantity of medicine prescribed to be given at one time.
Excerpta [L.]. Extracts or selections from written or printed matter.
Frustum. That which is left of a pyramid or cone after cutting off the upper part.
Item. A separate article or entry in an account.
Joint. The place where two or more things are joined together.
Lamina, etc. A thin plate or scale split off. See LAMINA.
Leaf. A single division of a folded sheet of paper.
Leaflet. A little leaf.
Limb. A branch of a tree growing out from the trunk.
Link. One of the rings or loops of which a chain is made.
Lobe. The lower part of the ear.
Lobule. A small lobe.
Lump. A shapeless mass of matter.
Morsel, etc. A small piece of food. See MAGNITUDE-SMALLNESS.
Octant. The eighth part of a circle.
Oddments. Things left over.
Odds and ends. Fragments; remnants.
Offshoot. Something that branches off from the parent stock.
Paragraph. A passage in a written or printed discourse.
Particular. A separate matter or item.
Passage. A separate portion of a discourse, treatise, or writing.
Ramification. Subdivisions of roots or branches.
Scale. A rudimentary leaf, as those covering the leaf-buds.
Scion. A piece cut from a twig, a shoot of a tree, or plant.
Sector. A part of a circle bounded by two radii and an arc.
Slice. A thin broad piece cut off from a larger body.
Spray. Water or other liquid dispersed in particles.
Sprig. A shoot or sprout of a tree or plant.
Stump. That portion of the trunk of a tree left standing after the tree is felled.
Twig. A small shoot or branch of a tree.
Verse. A single line of poetry.
Ward. A territorial division of a city.
Wing. The fore limb of a bird; a building attached to another building.

PART—Verbs.

Break, etc. To separate or divide by force. See DISUNION.
Divide. To part a thing into two or more pieces.
Part. To remove from contact or contiguity; cause to sunder.
Partition, etc. To divide into distinct parts. See ASSIGNMENT.

PART—Adjectives

Aliquot. That measures or divides exactly.
Divided, etc. Parted; separated; distributed. See *Verbs.*
Fractional. Comprising a part or the parts of a unit.
Fragmentary. Composed of broken pieces.
In compartments. Composed of distinct parts or divisions.
Multifid. Having many clefts or divisions.
Sectional. Made up of several distinct parts.

PART—Adverbs

Bit by bit. Piecemeal; by portions at a time.
By driblets. In small sums.
By inches. By slow degrees; gradually.
By instalments. By partial payments.
By snatches. In a disconnected way; by fits and starts.
Drop by drop. Drop succeeding drop; slowly.
Foot by foot. Gradually; surely.
Inch by inch. By small degrees or steps.
In detail. Item by item; with particularity.
In lots. In distinct portions.
In part. In some degree; partly.
Part by part. Gradually and carefully.
Partially. Not totally; in part.
Partly. Not wholly; in some measure or degree.
Piecemeal. Piece by piece; by degrees.

whole'-sale". On a large scale; abundant. ENOUGH, EXCHANGE, MAGNITUDE-SMALLNESS, WHOLE-PART.

whole'-some. Healthful. HEALTHINESS-UNHEALTHINESS.

whol'-ly. Entirely. ENTIRETY-DEFICIENCY, WHOLE-PART.

whoop. A yell. CRY-ULULATION; war-whoop, DEFIANCE, FIGHTING-CONCILIATION.

whop. To flog. EXCULPATION-PUNITION.

whop'-per. Remarkable. GREATNESS-LITTLENESS, TRUTHFULNESS-FABRICATION.

whop'-ping. Huge. GREATNESS-LITTLENESS.

whore. A prostitute. PURITY-RAKE.

whore'-dom. Harlotry. PURITY-IMPURITY.

whore'-mon"-ger. A whoremaster. PURITY-RAKE.

why. Reason; inquiry; surprise. ASSERTION-DENIAL, CAUSE-EFFECT, INVESTIGATION-ANSWER, MOTIVE-CAPRICE, RATIONALE-LUCK.

wib'-ble-wab"-ble. To oscillate. VIBRATION.

wick. Fuel; light. COMBUSTIBLE, LUMINARY-SHADE.

wick'-ed. Bad. UPRIGHTNESS-DISHONESTY, VIRTUE-VICE; the wicked, GODLINESS-UNGODLINESS, GOOD MAN-BAD MAN; the wicked one, ANGEL-SATAN, GODLINESS-UNGODLINESS.

wick'-ed-ness. Sinfulness. VIRTUE-VICE.

wick'-er. Withe. CROSSING.

wick'-et. A gate. APERTURE-CLOSURE, BEGINNING-END.

wide. Broad: BREADTH-NARROWNESS; in the wide world, EXTENSION-DISTRICT; wide apart, VARIATION; wide as a church door, BREADTH-NARROWNESS; wide asunder, REMOTENESS-NEARNESS; wide awake, ACTIVITY-INDOLENCE, ASSENT-DISSENT, CAREFULNESS-CARELESSNESS, DRESS-UNDRESS; wide away, REMOTENESS-NEARNESS; wide berth, LIBERTY-SUBJECTION; wide of, REMOTENESS-NEARNESS; wide of the mark, AIM-ABERRATION, REMOTENESS-NEARNESS, SUCCESS-FAILURE, TRUTH-ERROR; wide of the truth, TRUTH-ERROR; wide open, APERTURE-CLOSURE, ENLARGEMENT-DIMINUTION; wide world, UNIVERSE.

wide'-ly. To a wide extent. MAGNITUDE-SMALLNESS; widely apart, VARIATION.

wi'-den. To broaden. BREADTH-NARROWNESS, ENLARGEMENT-DIMINUTION; widen the breach, FAVORITE-ANGER, VARIANCE-ACCORD.

wide'-spread". Great; dispersed. ENLARGEMENT-DIMINUTION, EXTENSION-DISTRICT, GATHERING-SCATTERING, MAGNITUDE-SMALLNESS, UNIVERSALITY-PARTICULARITY.

wid'-ow. A woman who has lost her husband by death. MATRIMONY-DIVORCE.

wid'-ow-er. A man whose wife is dead and who is not married again. MATRIMONY-DIVORCE.

wid'-ow-hood". State of a widow. MATRIMONY-DIVORCE.

width. Breadth. BREADTH-NARROWNESS.

wield. To use; to handle; to brandish. AGITATION, TOUCH, USE-DISUSE; wield authority, RULE-LICENSE; wield the scepter, RULE-LICENSE; wield the sword, FIGHTING-CONCILIATION.

wield'-y. Manageable. DIFFICULTY-FACILITY.

wife. A spouse. MALE-FEMALE, MATRIMONY-DIVORCE.

wife'-less. Unmarried. MATRIMONY-CELIBACY.

wig. A head-dress. DRESS-UNDRESS.

wig'-ging. A rebuke. APPROVAL-DISAPPROVAL.

wight. A person. MALE-FEMALE.

wig'-wam. A tent. DWELLER-HABITATION.

wild. Uncultivated; passionate; shy; unskilled; a plain. EXCITABILITY-INEXCITABILITY, EXCITATION, FAVORITE-ANGER, FERTILITY-STERILITY, GULF-PLAIN, HEED-DISREGARD, MODIFICATION-SELFINDULGENCE, QUEST-EVASION, RECKLESSNESS-CAUTION, SANENESS-LUNACY, SKILL-UNSKILFULNESS,

TURBULENCE-CALMNESS; run wild, EXCITABILITY-INEXCITABILITY; sow one's wild oats, BETTERMENT-DETERIORATION, ENTERTAINMENT-WEARINESS, MANHOOD, MODERATION-SELFINDULGENCE, VIRTUE-VICE; wild animals, FAUNA-FLORA; wild beast, BENEFACTOR-EVILDOER, TURBULENCE-CALMNESS; wild fancy, FANCY; wild-goose chase, PERSISTENCE-WHIM, SKILL-UNSKILFULNESS, USEFULNESS-USELESSNESS; wild imagination, FANCY.

Wild, Jonathan. A thief; a rascal. GOOD MAN-BAD MAN, ROBBER.

wil'-der-ness. A waste; a solitude; a confusion. EXTENSION-DISTRICT, FERTILITY-STERILITY, REGULARITY-IRREGULARITY, SOCIABILITY-PRIVACY.

wild'-fire. A combustible. HEAT-COLD; run like wild-fire, PUBLICITY; spread like wild-fire, DOMINANCE-IMPOTENCE, ENLARGEMENT-DIMINUTION, GATHERING-SCATTERING, PUBLICITY, TURBULENCE-CALMNESS.

wild'-ness. An uncultivated state. EXTENSION-INEXTENSION.

wile. A machination. CRAFT-ARTLESSNESS, TRUTHFULNESS-FRAUD.

wil'-ful. Voluntary; obstinate. BIGOTRY-APOSTASY, VOLITION-OBLIGATION.

will. A testament; volition; determination. GIVING-RECEIVING, PERSISTENCE-WHIM, SECURITY, VOLITION-OBLIGATION; at will, VOLITION-OBLIGATION; have one's own will, VOLITION-OBLIGATION; make one's will, LIFE-DEATH; tenant at will, HOLDER; will and will not, DETERMINATION-VACILLATION; will be, OCCURRENCE-DESTINY; will for the deed, COMPOSITION, JUSTIFICATION-CHARGE; will he nill he, VOLITION-OBLIGATION; will of heaven, VOLITION-OBLIGATION; will you, PETITION.

will'-ing. Favorably disposed. ASSENT-DISSENT, READINESS-RELUCTANCE.

will'-ing-ly. Without reluctance. ASSENT-DISSENT, READINESS-RELUCTANCE.

will'-ing-ness. Readiness. DESIRE-DISTASTE, READINESS-RELUCTANCE.

will'-o'-the-wisp". Ignis fatuus; imp. JOVE-FIEND, LUMINARY-SHADE.

wil'-low. A tree; an emblem of sorrow. JUBILATION-LAMENTATION.

wilt'-ed. Withered. BETTERMENT-DETERIORATION.

wi'-ly. Subtle. CRAFT-ARTLESSNESS.

wim'-ble. An auger. PERFORATOR-STOPPER.

wim'-ple. A veil. DRESS-UNDRESS.

win. Succeed; get. GAIN-LOSS, SUCCESS-FAILURE; win golden opinions, APPROVAL-DISAPPROVAL; win laurels, REPUTATION-DISCREDIT; win over, CONTENTEDNESS-DISCONTENTMENT, FAITH-MISGIVING, MOTIVE-CAPRICE; win the affections, BLANDISHMENT, LOVE-HATE; win the heart, LOVE-HATE, PLEASURABLENESS-PAINFULNESS.

wince. To shrink; to flinch. EMOTION, EXCITABILITY-INEXCITABILITY, PLEASURE-PAIN, SANGUINENESS-TIMIDITY, SENSUALITY-SUFFERING.

winch. To lift. ELEVATION-DEPRESSION, INSTRUMENT.

win'-cing. Shrinking back. EXCITABILITY-INEXCITABILITY.

wind. A blast; life. CIRCUITION, LIFE-DEATH, OCEAN-LAND, STRENGTH-WEAKNESS, SWIFTNESS-SLOWNESS; against the wind, AIM-ABERRATION, ANTAGONISM-CONCURRENCE; before the wind, AIM-ABERRATION; cast to the winds, CHOICE-REJECTION, KEEPING-RELINQUISHMENT, USE-DISUSE; close to the wind, AIM-ABERRATION; fair wind, DIFFICULTY-FACILITY; get wind, PUBLICITY; hit between wind and water, BETTERMENT-DETERIORATION; in the wind, OCCURRENCE-DESTINY; in the wind's eye, AIM-ABERRATION; lose wind, WEARINESS-REFRESHMENT; outstrip the wind, SWIFTNESS-SLOWNESS; preach to the winds, USEFUL-

NESS-USELESSNESS; **raise the wind**, GAIN-LOSS; **sail near the wind**, AIM-ABERRATION, SKILL-UNSKILFUL-NESS, UPRIGHTNESS-DISHONESTY; **scatter to the winds**, COMMISSION-ABROGATION; **see how the wind blows**, AIM-ABERRATION, BIGOTRY-APOSTASY, PRE-VISION, SKILL-UNSKILFULNESS, TRIAL; **see where the wind lies**, SKILL-UNSKILFULNESS, TRIAL; **short-wind-ed**, WEARINESS-REFRESHMENT; **sport of winds and waves**, AGITATION; **sound of wind and limb**, HEALTH-SICKNESS; **take the wind out of one's sails**, MIGHT-IMPOTENCE, OBSTRUCTION-HELP; **to the four winds**, EXTENSION-DISTRICT; **touched in the wind**, HEALTH-SICKNESS; **what's in the wind**, INVESTIGATION-AN-SWER; **wind ahead**, ANTAGONISM-CONCURRENCE; **wind and weather permitting**, MODIFICATION, POSSI-BILITY-IMPOSSIBILITY.

wind. To coil; to deviate. AIM-ABERRATION, CIRCLE-WINDING, CIRCUITION; **wind round the heart**, LOVE-HATE; **wind up**, COMPLETION-NONCOMPLETION, PREPARATION-NONPREPARATION, STRENGTH-WEAK-NESS; **wind up accounts**, ACCOUNTS.

wind'-bound. Delayed. OBSTRUCTION-HELP, RE-LEASE-RESTRAINT.

wind'-fall''. Good fortune. GOOD-EVIL.

wind'-gage. An indicator. RIVER-WIND.

wind'-gun. Air-gun. WEAPON.

wind'-i-ness. The state of being windy RIVER-WIND.

wind'-ing. A bend; a coil. CIRCLE-WINDING, MID-COURSE-CIRCUIT; **winding up**, COMPLETION-NON-COMPLETION.

wind'-ing-sheet''. A shroud. LIFE-FUNERAL.

wind'-lass. A machine. ELEVATION-DEPRESSION.

wind'-less. Puffed. WEARINESS-REFRESHMENT.

wind'-mill''. A mill run by the wind. REVOLUTION-EVOLUTION.

win'-dow. An opening. APERTURE-CLOSURE; **make the windows shake**, LOUDNESS-FAINTNESS.

wind'-pipe''. The trachea. WATERCOURSE-AIRPIPE.

wind'-ward. Toward the wind. AIM-ABERRATION, LATERALITY-CONTRAPOSITION.

wind'-wards. Windward. AIM-ABERRATION.

wind'-y. Stormy. RIVER-WIND, WATER-AIR.

wine. A beverage. NUTRIMENT-EXCRETION; **put new wine into old bottles**, SKILL-UNSKILFULNESS.

wine'-bib''-ber. One who drinks wine to excess. TEE-TOTALISM-INTEMPERANCE.

wine'-bib''-bing. Tippling. TEETOTALISM-INTEMPER-ANCE.

wine'-cool''-er. A refrigerator. OVEN-REFRIGERATOR.

wing. A pinion; a part; a side; a flare; to fly. ACT-ING, BELLIGERENT, INSTRUMENT, LATERALITY-CON-TRAPOSITION, REFUGE-PITFALL, TRAVELING-NAVIGA-TION, WHOLE-PART; **clip the wings**, OBSTRUCTION-HELP, SWIFTNESS-SLOWNESS; **lend wings to**, OB-STRUCTION-HELP; **on the wing**, ARRIVAL-DEPARTURE, MOVEMENT-REST, TRANSFER, TRAVELING-NAVIGA-TION; **on the wings of the wind**, SWIFTNESS-SLOW-NESS; **take wing**, ARRIVAL-DEPARTURE, TRAVELING-NAVIGATION; **under the wing of**, SECURITY-INSECU-RITY; **wing one's flight**, ARRIVAL-DEPARTURE, TRAV-ELING-NAVIGATION; **wing one's way**, SWIFTNESS-SLOWNESS, TRAVELING-NAVIGATION; **with wings**, AC-TIVITY-INDOLENCE.

winged. Rapid. SWIFTNESS-SLOWNESS.

wink. To nictitate; to signify. SIGHT-BLINDNESS, SIGHT-DIMSIGHTEDNESS, SIGN; **tip the wink**, EN-LIGHTENMENT-SECRECY, SIGN; **wink at**, CAREFUL-NESS-CARELESSNESS, LEAVE-PROHIBITION, PARDON-VINDICTIVENESS, SIGHT-DIMSIGHTEDNESS; **wink of sleep**, ACTIVITY-INDOLENCE.

wink'-ing. Blinking. SIGHT-DIMSIGHTEDNESS.

win'-ning. Pleasing; courteous. LOVE-HATE, PLEAS-URABLENESS-PAINFULNESS. POLITENESS-IMPOLITE-NESS.

win'-nings. Profits. GAIN-LOSS.

win'-now. To sift; to clean. CHOICE-NEUTRALITY, CLEANNESS-FILTHINESS, INCLUSION-OMISSION. IN-VESTIGATION-ANSWER, MIXTURE-HOMOGENEITY; **win-now the chaff from the wheat**, CHOICE-NEUTRALITY, DIFFERENTIATION-INDISCRIMINATION.

win'-some. Genial. LIGHTHEARTEDNESS-DEJECTION, PLEASURABLENESS-PAINFULNESS.

win'-ter. A season; cold. ASTRONOMY, HEAT-COLD, MORNING-EVENING; **winter garden**, DOMESTICATION-AGRICULTURE; **winter of our discontent**, CONTENTED-NESS-DISCONTENTMENT.

win'-try. Cold. HEAT-COLD

wipe. To rub; to strike. CLEANNESS-FILTHINESS, DAMPNESS-DRYNESS, PLEASURABLENESS-PAINFUL-NESS, RECOMPENSE-PUNITION; **give one a wipe**, AP-PROVAL-DISAPPROVAL; **wipe away**, MARK-OBLITERA-TION; **wipe off**, MARK-OBLITERATION; **wipe off old scores** ATONEMENT, SETTLEMENT-DEFAULT; **wipe out**, MARK-OBLITERATION; **wipe the eyes**, ALLEVIA-TION-AGGRAVATION; **wipe the tears**, ALLEVIATION-AGGRAVATION, COMPASSION-RUTHLESSNESS.

wire. A filament; telegraph. CONNECTIVE, LAMINA-FIBER, MESSENGER; **pull the wires**, MANAGEMENT.

wire'-drawn. Strained. LAMINA-FIBER, LENGTH-SHORTNESS

wire'-less. Not using a wire. **Wireless telegraphy**, ELECTRICITY.

wire'-pull''-er. An intriguer. MANAGER.

wire'-worm. A worm. BENEFACTOR-EVILDOER.

wir'-y. Strong LAMINA-FIBER, STRENGTH-WEAK-NESS.

wis. To think. HYPOTHESIS.

wis'-dom. Knowledge. ADAGE-NONSENSE, MIND-IM-BECILITY; **have cut one's wisdom teeth**, SKILL-UN-SKILFULNESS; **worldly wisdom**, RECKLESSNESS-CAU-TION.

wise. Intelligent; manner. SAGACITY-INCAPACITY, WAY; **in such wise**, CONDITION-SITUATION; **merry and wise**, WITTINESS-DULNESS; **wise in one's own conceit**, CONCEIT-DIFFIDENCE; **wise man**, SAGE-FOOL; **wise maxim**, ADAGE-NONSENSE; **word to the wise**, ADVICE.

wise'-a''-cre. A simpleton. SAGE-FOOL.

wish. Desire. DESIRE-DISTASTE, PURPOSE-LUCK, VO-LITION-OBLIGATION; **do what one wishes**, LIBERTY-SUBJECTION; **wish at the bottom of the Red Sea**, CON-TENTEDNESS-DISCONTENTMENT; **wish joy**, FELICITA-TION; **wish the father to the thought**, CREDULOUS-NESS-SKEPTICISM, DECISION-MISJUDGMENT, DESIRE-DISTASTE, SANGUINENESS-HOPELESSNESS; **wish well**, CHARITABLENESS-MALEVOLENCE.

wish'-ful. Having a desire. DESIRE-DISTASTE.

wish'-ing-cap''. A talisman. DEVOTION-CHARM.

wish'-wash''. Nonsense. MEANING-JARGON.

wish'-y-wash''-y. Feeble; unimportant. CONSE-QUENCE-INSIGNIFICANCE, FORCE-WEAKNESS, SAVOR-TASTELESSNESS.

wis'-ket. A basket. CONTENTS-RECEIVER.

wisp. A broom. GATHERING-SCATTERING.

wist'-ful. Pensive; wishful. CAREFULNESS-CARELESS-NESS, DESIRE-DISTASTE, EMOTION, REFLECTION-VA-CANCY.

wist'-ful-ly. Desirously. DESIRE-DISTASTE.

wit. Humor; wisdom; intellect; a humorist. ENTER-TAINMENT-WEARINESS, MIND-IMBECILITY, RHETORIC, SAGACITY-INCAPACITY, WAG, WITTINESS-DULNESS; **at one's wit's end**, CERTAINTY-DOUBT, DIFFICULTY-FACILITY; **mother-wit**, SAGACITY-INCAPACITY; **soul of wit**, TERSENESS-PROLIXITY; **to wit**, INTERPRETA-TION-MISINTERPRETATION.

wit'-an. Members of a witenagemot. COUNCIL.

witch. A sorceress; a hag; a spell. BEAUTY-UGLINESS, DEVOTION-MAGICIAN, SOOTHSAYER.

witch'-craft. Sorcery. DEVOTION-MAGIC.

witch'-er-y. Witchcraft; fascination. DEVOTION-MAGIC, MOTIVE-CAPRICE, PLEASURABLENESS-PAINFULNESS.

wit'-crack''-er. A joker. WAG.

wit'-en-a-ge-mot''. A Saxon Senate. COUNCIL.

with. Added; mixed; accompanying; means; a ligature. ADDITION-SUBTRACTION, CONNECTIVE, MEANS, MIXTURE-HOMOGENEITY, SOLITUDE-COMPANY; go with, COOPERATION-OPPOSITION; with all its parts, ENTIRETY-DEFICIENCY; with a vengeance, ENTIRETY-DEFICIENCY, MAGNITUDE-SMALLNESS; with a witness, ENTIRETY-DEFICIENCY, MAGNITUDE-SMALLNESS; with regard to, CONNECTION-INDEPENDENCE.

with-al'. With; enough. ADDITION-SUBTRACTION, ENOUGH, SOLITUDE-COMPANY.

with-draw'. To recede; subduct. ADDITION-SUBTRACTION, ADVANCE-RETROGRESSION, APPROACH-WITHDRAWAL, ARRIVAL-DEPARTURE, PRESENCE-ABSENCE; withdraw from, BIGOTRY-APOSTASY, DESIRE-DISTASTE, QUEST-ABANDONMENT.

with-draw'-al. The act of withdrawing. ADVANCE-RETROGRESSION, APPROACH-WITHDRAWAL, BIGOTRY-APOSTASY, QUEST-ABANDONMENT.

withe. A ligature. CONNECTIVE.

with'-er. To perish. BETTERMENT-DETERIORATION, ENLARGEMENT-DIMINUTION; wither one's hopes, LIGHTHEARTEDNESS-DEJECTION.

with'-ered. Blighted. SECURITY-INSECURITY, STRENGTH-WEAKNESS.

with'-er-ing. Harsh. ADULATION-DISPARAGEMENT, HARSHNESS-MILDNESS, PLEASURABLENESS-PAINFULNESS, REGARD-SCORN.

with'-ers. Binders. CONVEXITY-CONCAVITY; withers unwrung, STRENGTH-WEAKNESS.

with-hold' To retain. ENLIGHTENMENT-SECRECY, EXTRAVAGANCE-AVARICE, KEEPING-RELINQUISHMENT, LEAVE-PROHIBITION, RELEASE-RESTRAINT; withhold one's assent, PROFFER-REFUSAL.

with'-in. Inside. OUTSIDE-INSIDE; derived from within, SUBJECTIVENESS-OBJECTIVENESS; keep within, OUTSIDE-INSIDE; place within, OUTSIDE-INSIDE; within an ace of, MAGNITUDE-SMALLNESS; within bounds, MAGNITUDE-SMALLNESS, QUALITY-MEASURE, RELEASE-RESTRAINT, TRANSCURSION-SHORTCOMING, TURBULENCE-CALMNESS; within call, REMOTENESS-NEARNESS; within compass, MODERATION-SELFINDULGENCE, TRANSCURSION-SHORTCOMING, TURBULENCE-CALMNESS; within one's memory, REMEMBRANCE-FORGETFULNESS; within reach, DIFFICULTY-FACILITY, REMOTENESS-NEARNESS; within the mark, TRANSCURSION-SHORTCOMING.

with-out'. Unless; exterior; lacking. ADDITION-SUBTRACTION, CONDITION-SITUATION, CONVENTIONALITY-UNCONVENTIONALITY, ENVIRONMENT-INTERPOSITION, HOLDING-EXEMPTION, OUTSIDE-INSIDE, PRESENCE-ABSENCE; derived from without, SUBJECTIVENESS-OBJECTIVENESS; not be able to do without, NEED; without a dissenting voice, ASSENT-DISSENT; without a leg to stand on, MIGHT-IMPOTENCE; without alloy, PLEASURE-PAIN; without a rap, AFFLUENCE-PENURY; without a shadow of turning, MUTATION-PERMANENCE; without ballast, DETERMINATION-VACILLATION, VIRTUE-VICE; without ceasing, FREQUENCY-RARITY; without ceremony, CONCEIT-DIFFIDENCE; without charge, COSTLINESS-CHEAPNESS; without end, ETERNITY-INSTANTANEITY, INFINITY; without exception, UNIFORMITY-DIVERSITY; without excuse, VIRTUE-VICE; without fail, CERTAINTY-DOUBT, PERSISTENCE-WHIM; without fear of contradiction, ASSERTION-DENIAL; without God, GODLINESS-DISBELIEF; without limit, INFINITY; without measure, INFINITY; without notice, EXPECTATION-SURPRISE; without number, INFINITY; without parallel, SUPREMACY-SUBORDINACY; without reason, SAGACITY-INCAPACITY; without reference to, CONNECTION-INDEPENDENCE; without regard to, CONNECTION-INDEPENDENCE; without reluctance, READINESS-RELUCTANCE; without reserve, MANIFESTATION-LATENCY; without rime or reason, ADAGE-NONSENSE, MOTIVE-CAPRICE; without stint, ENOUGH; without warning, EXPECTATION-SURPRISE.

with-stand'. To oppose. ANTAGONISM-CONCURRENCE, COOPERATION-OPPOSITION, REPRISAL-RESISTANCE.

with'-y. A rope. CONNECTIVE.

wit'-less. Foolish. KNOWLEDGE-IGNORANCE, SAGACITY-INCAPACITY.

wit'-ling. A fool; a wag. SAGE-FOOL, WAG.

wit'-ness. A spectator; to observe; testimony. EVIDENCE-COUNTEREVIDENCE, ONLOOKER, SIGHT-BLINDNESS, SIGN; bear witness, EVIDENCE-COUNTEREVIDENCE; call to witness, EVIDENCE-COUNTEREVIDENCE.

wit'-ness-box''. Witness-stand. TRIBUNAL.

wits. Intelligence. MIND-IMBECILITY; all one's wits about one, SAGACITY-INCAPACITY, SKILL-UNSKILFULNESS; live by one's wits, CRAFT-ARTLESSNESS, SKILL-UNSKILFULNESS, THEFT, TRUTHFULNESS-FRAUD, UPRIGHTNESS-DISHONESTY; one's wits gone a woolgathering, SAGACITY-INCAPACITY; out of one's wits, PLEASURABLENESS-PAINFULNESS; set one's wits to work, DESIGN, FANCY, REFLECTION-VACANCY.

wit'-snap''-per. A witmonger. WAG.

wit'-ti-cism. A jest. WITTINESS-DULNESS.

wit'-ti-ness. Humor. WITTINESS-DULNESS.

WITTINESS—DULNESS.

Atticism. Concise and elegant expression.

Attic salt.
Attic wit. } Refined classical wit.

Badinage [F.]. Playful raillery.

Banter. Wit at the expense of another.

Broad humor. Humor that extends beyond the bounds of decency or propriety.

Buffoonery. Low drollery.

Comicality, etc. The quality of being comical or laughable. See SOCIETY-LUDICROUSNESS.

Concetto [It.]. Affected wit.

Drollery. Humor.

Espieglerie [F.]. Roguish bantering.

Esprit [F.]. Wit.

Facetiæ [L.]. Wittiness in speaking or writing.

Facetiousness. The quality of being witty or humorous.

Flash.
Flash of merriment. } A sudden burst of wit.
Flash of wit.

Fooling. Playfulness in speech.

Fun. Mirth and enjoyment derived therefrom.

Dulness. Slowness and heaviness of intellect.

Flatness. Lack of interest or animation; deadness.

Heaviness. Despondency; grief; languidness.

Infestivity, etc. Want of cheerfulness and mirth, as at entertainments. See LIGHTHEARTEDNESS-DEJECTION.

Stupidity, etc. Extreme dulness of perception and understanding; dull foolishness. See SAGACITY-INCAPACITY.

Want of originality. Dulness; stupidity.

DULNESS—*Denotations.*

Conte à dormir debout [F.]. An idle, silly story.

Heavy book. An uninteresting book.

Matter of fact. Plain statement of facts.

Platitude. A dull or commonplace statement.

Prose. Dull language or discourse.

DULNESS—*Verbs.*

Be caught napping. To catch unawares or unprepared.

Be dull, etc. To be slow of understanding. See *Adjectives.*

Damp. To depress or discourage; dispirit.

Depress. To render languid or dull; deject.

WITTINESS—DULNESS—*Continued*

Humor. The quality which gives to ideas a ludicrous turn, and tends to excite laughter.
Feu d'esprit [F.]. A play of wit.
Jocoseness.⎫
Jocosity.⎬ The quality of being jocose, or given to jokes and jesting.
Jocularity.⎭ ing.
Plaisanterie [F.]. Pleasantry; jesting.
Pleasantry. The spirit of playful and jocose merriment.
Ready wit. Quick perception and expression of amusing analogies.
Salt. Wit.
Smartness. Exhibition of keen wit.
Tomfoolery. Nonsensical behavior.
Trifling. Playfulness.
Vis comica [L.]. Comic talent.
Waggery. Mischievous merriment.
Waggishness. The quality of being waggish or frolicsome.
Whimsicality. The quality of being freakier or capricious.
Wit. The ready perception and happy expression of amusing relations causing delight and surprise.
Wittiness. The quality of being witty.

WITTINESS—*Denotations.*

Anagram. The letters of a word or phrase so transposed as to make a different word or phrase.
Bon mot [F.]. A witty repartee.
Bright thought.⎫ A thought or expression that causes delight and
Brilliant idea.⎭ surprise.
Broad farce. A short comedy whose incidents go beyond the bounds of propriety or decency.
Capital joke. An excellent joke.
Conceit. A quaint or humorous fancy.
Conundrum, etc. A riddle founded upon some odd resemblance between odd things. See TIDINGS-MYSTERY.
Crank. A fantastic turn of speech.
Cream of the jest. The most laughable part of an expression.
Double acrostic. A poem in which the initial and final letters of the lines form words.
Double entendre [F.]. A word or phrase with a double meaning, one of which is somewhat obscene. See AMBIGUITY.
Dry joke. A lifeless, spiritless joke.
Epigram. A bright thought tersely and sharply expressed.
Fancy. A conceit or whim.
Farce. A short comedy whose humor is due to exaggeration of effects.
Happy thought. A thought that surprises and delights.
Harlequinade [F.]. A kind of pantomime. See ACTING.
Idle conceit. A droll lazy turn of speech.
Jest. Something ludicrous meant only to excite laughter.
Jest-book. A collection of jests, jokes, and diverting stories.
Feu de mot [F.]. A play on words.
Joe Miller. A stale joke, as from Joe Miller's jest book.
Joke. Something said or done for the purpose of exciting a laugh.
Merry thought. A thought causing delight or enjoyment; a wish bone.
Mot [F.]. A witty saying.
Mot pour rire [F.]. A jest or joke.
Nugæ canoræ [L.]. Mere singsong without meaning.
Old joke. A joke often repeated.
Play of words.⎫
Play upon words.⎬ An ingenious and witty turn given to words.
Point. A turn of expression that gives agreeable surprise.
Pun. A witty use of a word in two senses.
Punning. The practise of using puns.
Quibble. A petty evasion in speaking.
Quid pro quo [L.]. A tit for tat.
Quiddity. A trifling subtlety.
Quip. A sarcastic taunt or remark.
Quips and cranks. Sarcastic repartee.
Quirk. A bright retort.
Quodlibet [L.]. A nice point; a subtlety.
Repartee. Ready and witty reply.
Retort. A keen or sharp rejoinder.
Ridicule. Language calculated to make a person or thing the object of contemptuous humorous disparagement. See SOCIETY-DERISION.
Sally. A sudden outflow of jocosity or raillery.
Scintillation. A sparkling or flashing, as of speech.
Smart saying. A sharp answer.
Standing jest.⎫
Standing joke.⎬ A joke often repeated.
Turlupinade [F.]. A silly joke or jest.
Verbal quibble. A juggle with words.
Whim. A peculiar fancy.

DULNESS—VERBS—*Continued.*

Fall flat upon the ear. To fail to excite interest.
Lay a wet blanket on. To cause to become discouraged; throw a damper on.
Prose. To write or say in a dull or commonplace manner.
Render dull, etc. To make or cause to become dull. See *Adjectives*.
Take *au sérieux* To take in earnest; take serious offense at.
Throw cold water on. To dampen one's spirits; discourage.

DULNESS—*Adjectives.*

Commonplace. Neither new nor striking; ordinary.
Dull. Without spirit; slow of understanding; not cheerful.
Dull as ditch-water. Stupid and inactive.
Dry as dust. Dull and prosy.
Flat. Lacking spirit or interest; dull; insipid.
Flat-brained. Dull.
Humdrum. Monotonous; commonplace; stupid.
Insulse. Dull; insipid.
Matter of fact. Treating of facts or realities; ordinary.
Melancholic, etc. Depressed in spirits; dejected. See LIGHTHEARTEDNESS-DEJECTION.
Monotonous. Continued with dull uniformity; unvaried.
Plodding. Diligent but slow.
Pointless. Without any sharpness or keenness.
Prosaic. Resembling prose; dull; uninteresting.
Prosing. Dull and tedious minuteness in speech or writing.
Prosy. Like prose; dull; tedious.
Slow. Dull, as in understanding; not lively.
Stolid, etc. Heavy; foolish; calm and unmoved. See SAGACITY-INCAPACITY.
Stupid. Deficient in understanding; sluggish; foolish.
Unentertaining. Not amusing; giving no delight.
Unimaginative. Dull; stupid.
Uninteresting. Not capable of exciting or attracting the mind.
Unlively. Not lively; dull.
Weary, flat, stale, and unprofitable. Tiresome; irksome.

DULNESS—*Phrase.*

Davus sum, non Œdipus [L.]. I am Davus [a common man], not Œdipus [who guessed the riddle of the Sphinx].

WITTINESS—*Denotations—Continued.*

Witticism. A bright, brilliant saying or sentiment.
Word-play. Discussion turning chiefly on the meaning and use of words.

WITTINESS—*Verbs.*

Banter, etc. To make sport of; joke. See SOCIETY-DERISION.
Crack a joke. To tell with spirit.
Cut jokes. To be witty and sociable.
Jest. To divert by words or actions for the sake of others' enjoyment.
Joke. To be merry in words or actions for one's own sake.
Joke at one's expense. To make merry with one; rally one.
Make fun of. To ridicule; deride; make sport of.
Make merry. To be jovial or joyful; feast.
Perpetuate a joke.⎫
Perpetuate a pun.⎬ To keep cracking the same joke or pun.
Retort. To make a severe reply; throw back a spiteful rejoinder.
Ridentem dicere verum [L.]. To speak the truth, though laughing.
Set the table in a roar, etc. To entertain with lively jests and jokes. See ENTERTAINMENT.

WITTINESS—*Adjectives.*

Attic. Pertaining to Attica; witty.
Ben trovato [It.]. Well-feigned or invented.
Comic, etc. Relating to comedy; raising mirth. See SOCIETY-LUDICROUSNESS.
Epigrammatic. Pertaining to epigram; witty; pointed.
Facetious. Sprightly with wit and good-humor; gay.
Full of point. Very witty or humorous; full of stinging epigram.
Humorous. Fitted to excite laughter; fanciful.
Jocose. Given to jokes and jesting; merry; sportive.
Jocular. Being in a joking mood; making jokes.
Merry and wise. Laughingly discreet and judicious.
Nimble-witted. Having a ready wit; quick-witted.
Playful, etc. Full of play; sportive. See ENTERTAINMENT.
Pleasant. Conducive to merriment; gay; lively.
Quick-witted. Having a keen and sharp discernment; sharp-witted.
Smart. Impertinently or pretentiously witty.

WITTINESS—Adjectives—*Continued*

Sparkling. Brilliant; vivacious; lively.
Spirituel [F.]. Intellectual; witty.
Sprightly. Lively; brisk; animated; gay.

Waggish. Mischievous in sport; frolicsome.
Whimsical. Full of odd fancies; capricious.
Witty. Having or displaying wit; droll; facetious.

WITTINESS—*Adverbs, etc.*

In jest. For the sake of raising a laugh.
In joke. With no serious intention.

In play. Not in earnest.
In sport. For fun.

WITTINESS—*Phrase.*

Adhibenda est in jocando moderatio [L.]. Moderation is to be observed in joking.

wit'-ting-ly. Knowingly. PURPOSE-LUCK.
wit'-tol. A cuckold. PURITY-RAKE.
wit'-ty. Humorous. ENTERTAINMENT-WEARINESS, RHETORIC, WITTINESS-DULNESS.
wive. To marry. MATRIMONY-CELIBACY.
wive'-less. Unmarried. MATRIMONY CELIBACY.
wiz'-ard. A sorcerer; a sage. ADEPT-BUNGLER, DEVOTION-MAGICIAN, SAGE-FOOL.
wiz'-en. Shrunken; a throat. APERTURE-CLOSURE, ENLARGEMENT-DIMINUTION.
wiz'-ened. Shrunken. ENLARGEMENT-DIMINUTION.
wo. Pain. PLEASURE-PAIN; **wo betide,** CHARITABLENESS-CURSE, COMPASSION-RUTHLESSNESS; **wo is me,** JUBILATION - LAMENTATION; **wo to,** CHARITABLENESS-CURSE.
wo'-be-gone". Sorrowful. LIGHTHEARTEDNESS - DEJECTION, PLEASURE-PAIN.
wo'-ful. Direful. GOODNESS - BADNESS, PLEASURABLENESS-PAINFULNESS.
wold. A down. GULF-PLAIN.
wolf. A ravenous beast. DESIRE-DISTASTE; **cry wolf,** ALARM, SANGUINENESS-TIMIDITY, TRUTHFULNESS-FALSEHOOD; **hold the wolf by the ears,** DIFFICULTY-FACILITY; **keep the wolf from the door,** LIFE-DEATH; **unable to keep the wolf from the door,** LIFE-DEATH; **wolf and the lamb,** RIGHT-WRONG; **wolf at the door,** AFFLUENCE - PENURY, REFUGE - PITFALL; **wolf in sheep's clothing,** GULL-DECEIVER, TRUTHFULNESS-FRAUD, UPRIGHTNESS-ROGUE.
wom'-an. A female; an adult. MALE-FEMALE, MANHOOD; **woman of the town,** PURITY-IMPURITY.
wom'-an-hood. State of being a woman. MALE-FEMALE, MANHOOD.
wom'-an-ish. Effeminate. MALE-FEMALE.
wom'-an-kind. Women collectively. MALE-FEMALE.
wom'-an-ly. Feminine; weak. MALE-FEMALE, MANHOOD, STRENGTH-WEAKNESS.
womb. Origin; interior. CAUSE-EFFECT, OUTSIDE-INSIDE; **womb of time,** FUTURE-PAST, OCCURRENCE-DESTINY.
won'-der. A prodigy; surprise. ASTONISHMENT-EXPECTANCE, CLEARNESS-OBSCURITY, CONVENTIONALITY-UNCONVENTIONALITY, EXPECTATION-SURPRISE, PHENOMENON; **do wonders,** ACTIVITY-INDOLENCE, SUCCESS-FAILURE; **for a wonder,** ASTONISHMENT-EXPECTANCE; **nine days' wonder,** CONSEQUENCE-INSIGNIFICANCE; **not wonder,** EXPECTATION-SURPRISE; **wonders of the world,** PHENOMENON; **wonder whether,** CERTAINTY-DOUBT, HYPOTHESIS, KNOWLEDGE-IGNORANCE.
won'-der-ful. Marvelous. ASTONISHMENT-EXPECTANCE, CONVENTIONALITY.
won'-der-ful"-ly. Remarkably. ASTONISHMENT-EXPECTANCE, MAGNITUDE-SMALLNESS.
won'-der-ment. Emotion of wonder. ASTONISHMENT-EXPECTANCE, PHENOMENON.
won'-der-work"-ing. Magical. ASTONISHMENT-EXPECTANCE.
won'-drous. Wonderful. ASTONISHMENT-EXPECTANCE.
wont. Accustomed. HABIT-DESUETUDE; **wont do it,** APPROVAL-DISAPPROVAL.
wont'-ed. Commonly done. HABIT-DESUETUDE.

woo. To court; to entreat. BLANDISHMENT, DESIRE-DISTASTE.
woo'-er. A lover. LOVE-HATE.
wood. A forest; a material. FAUNA-FLORA, MATERIALS; **not out of the woods,** DIFFICULTY-FACILITY, SECURITY-INSECURITY.
wood'-cut". An engraving. ENGRAVING.
wood'-cut"-ter. A woodchopper. DOMESTICATION-AGRICULTURE, FAUNA-FLORA.
wood'-ed. Covered with wood. **Well wooded,** SMOOTHNESS-ROUGHNESS.
wood'-en. Made of wood. MATERIALS; **wooden horse,** RECOMPENSE-SCOURGE; **wooden spoon,** SCHOLAR-DUNCE; **wooden walls,** ATTACK-DEFENSE, WEAPON.
wood'-en-gra"-ving. A woodcut. ENGRAVING.
wood'-land. Forest. CITY-COUNTRY.
wood'-lands. Forests. FAUNA-FLORA.
wood'-note. A song. CRY-ULULATION.
wood'-pave"-ment. Pavement made of wood. SMOOTHNESS-ROUGHNESS.
wood-y. Sylvan. FAUNA-FLORA.
woo'er. A lover. LOVE-HATE.
woof. Warp and woof. TEXTURE.
woo'ing. Courting. BLANDISHMENT.
wool. Flocculent; warm. HEAT-COLD, SMOOTHNESS-ROUGHNESS; **much cry and little wool,** BRAGGING, EXPECTATION - DISAPPOINTMENT, OVERVALUATION-UNDERVALUATION.
wool'-gath"-er-ing. Idle reveries. **Wits gone woolgathering,** HEED-DISREGARD.
wool'-ly. Hairy. SMOOTHNESS-ROUGHNESS.
wool'-pack". A cloud. VISCIDITY-FOAM.
wool'-sack". A pillow; authority; a tribunal. SCEPTER, SUSPENSION-SUPPORT, TRIBUNAL.
word. A vocable; a promise; a command; intelligence; a maxim; a phrase. ADAGE-NONSENSE, ASSERTION-DENIAL, DIVINITY, ENGAGEMENT-RELEASE, ORDER, PHRASE, REVELATION - PSEUDOREVELATION, TIDINGS-MYSTERY, WORD-NEOLOGY; **as good as one's word,** COMPLETION-NONCOMPLETION, OBSERVANCE-NONOBSERVANCE, TRUTHFULNESS-FALSEHOOD, UPRIGHTNESS-DISHONESTY; **in a word,** TERSENESS-PROLIXITY; **give the word,** ORDER; **keep one's word,** OBSERVANCE-NONOBSERVANCE, UPRIGHTNESS-DISHONESTY; **man of his word,** UPRIGHTNESS-DISHONESTY; **not a word to say,** SELFRESPECT-HUMBLENESS, TALKATIVENESS-TACITURNITY; **password,** FIGHTING-CONCILIATION, SIGN; **put in a word,** SPEECH-INARTICULATION; **take at one's word,** CONSENT, FAITH-MISGIVING; **upon my word,** ASSERTION-DENIAL; **watchword,** FIGHTING-CONCILIATION; **word and a blow,** FAVORITE - QUARRELSOMENESS, HURRY -LEISURE, STRIFE-PEACE; **word for word,** IMITATION-ORIGINALITY, TRUTH-ERROR; **word in the ear,** ADDRESS-RESPONSE, ENLIGHTENMENT-SECRECY; **word it,** PHRASE; **word of command,** FIGHTING-CONCILIATION, ORDER, SIGN; **word of honor,** ENGAGEMENT-RELEASE; **word of mouth,** SPEECH-INARTICULATION; **words of same meaning,** SYNONYM-ANTONYM; **word to the wise,** ADVICE, CLEARNESS-OBSCURITY, ENLIGHTENMENT-SECRECY.

WORD—NEOLOGY.

Derivative. A word formed from another word, or which takes its origin from a root.

Etymon. An original or primitive word; a root.

Name, etc. The distinctive word or term by which a person or thing is designated or known. See NAME.

Phrase, etc. Any term or characterization, in one word or several. See PHRASE.

Root. A word from which other words are formed; a primitive form of speech.

Term. A word or expression denoting something peculiar to an art or science.

Vocable. A word, especially regarded in relation merely to its qualities of sound.

Word. An articulate sound, or combination of sounds, expressing an idea.

WORD—*Scientific Nouns.*

Derivation. The tracing of a word from its primitive form and meaning.

Etymology. That department of philology which treats of the derivation and growth of words and inflections.

Glossology. A department of anthropology relating to the classification of languages; comparative philology.

Lexicography. The art of compiling a lexicon.

Orismology. The science of definitions and defining, especially scientific terms.

Paleology, etc. The study of antiquity or antiquities. See LANGUAGE.

Part of speech, etc. One of the classes into which words are divided. See GRAMMAR.

Terminology. The science of a correct use and distribution of terms.

WORD—*Collective Nouns.*

Concordance. An index of words or topics in a book, as the Bible.

Delectus [L.]. An elementary text-book for students in Greek or Latin.

Dictionary. A book containing the words of a language, arranged alphabetically, with their meanings.

Glossary. A lexicon of the obsolete, obscure, or foreign words of a work.

Gradus [L.]. A dictionary of quantities in prosody.

Index. An alphabetical list of matters discussed, showing where each is to be found.

Lexicon. A dictionary of words of a foreign language.

Thesaurus. A repository of words or knowledge.

Vocabulary. A collection of words, especially of a particular author, arranged and defined alphabetically.

WORD—*Nouns of Agent.*

Glossographer. One who defines and explains terms; a commentator.

Verbarian. A word-coiner.

WORD—*Adjectives.*

Conjugate. Applied to words from the same root.

Derivative. Taken or formed from another word.

Literal. According to the letter or exact words.

Nominal. Pertaining to a name or term; giving the meaning of a word.

Paronymous. Of like derivation; kindred.

Titular. Existing in name or title only.

Verbal. Not written; relating to words only.

WORD—*Adverbs.*

Verbally, etc. By words uttered; orally. See *Adjectives.*

Verbatim [L.]. Word for word. See TRUTH.

WORD—*Phrase*

Epea pteroente [Gr.]. Winged words.

NEOLOGY—*Continued from Column 2.*

NEOLOGY—*Adjectives.*

Archaic. No longer in common use; out of use.

Colloquial. Peculiar to common speech as distinguished from literary.

Neologic.
Neological. } Introducing new words or new meanings of words.

Obsolete, etc. Gone out of use; out of date. See NOVELTY-ANTIQUITY.

Abuse of language.
Abuse of terms. } Improper use of words or expressions.

Americanism. A word or phrase peculiar to the people of the United States.

Antiphrasis. The use of a word or phrase in a sense exactly opposite to its natural meaning.

Archaism. A word or expression no longer in common use.

Argot [F.]. The peculiar phraseology of any class.

Babel. Confused unintelligible speech.

Barbarism. The use of words or forms not in approved usage.

Billingsgate. Rough or foul language.

Black letter. The old English alphabetic character.

Brogue. Any dialect pronunciation of English, especially that of the Irish people.

Broken English. English with a mixture of some other language.

By-word. A word or phrase that has become an object of derision.

Cant. Slang or provincial jargon.

Clinch. A pun.

Colloquialism, etc. A form of speech used only or chiefly in conversation. See TROPE.

Confusion of tongues. A confused speech.

Corruption. Departure from what is pure and correct in the use of language.

Dialect. The forms of speech that are peculiar to a people of a particular district.

Dog Latin. Barbarous or mongrel Latin.

Double entendre [F.]. A word or phrase capable of double interpretation.

Flash tongue. Thieves' jargon.

Gallicism. A French idiom.

Gibberish. Speech that is so rapid, confused, or disguised as to be unintelligible.

Gipsy lingo. The language used by the wandering tribes of Gipsies.

Hibernicism. An Irish idiom.

Jargon. Confused, unintelligible speech.

Je ne sais quoi [F.]. Something indefinite.

Lingo. Language rendered slightly unintelligible by peculiar expression.

Lingua franca [It.]. Mixed language spoken by Europeans in the East.

Macaronics. A confused jumble of words.

Missaying. A wrong saying.

Monkish Latin. Latin like that used by the middle age monks.

Mr. So-and-so. Somebody indefinite.

Neologism. The use of new words or phrases.

Neology. The introduction and use of new words and phrases.

Newfangled expressions. Expressions not commonly used.

Paragram. A play on words.

Paronomasia. A pun.

Patois [F.]. Provincial dialect.

Pedler's French. The lingo of pedlers.

Pidgin-English. A jargon of English intermixed with Chinese, Portuguese, and Malay words: *Pidgin English* means *Business English.*

Play upon words. The use of words in more than one meaning.

Plindrome. A word which reads the same backward and forward.

Provincialism. A form of speech peculiar to a province.

Pseudology. Falsehood.

Pseudonym. An assumed name. See NAME-MISNOMER.

Romany. Gipsy dialect.

Scotticism. A Scotch idiom.

Slang. Inelegant and unauthorized popular language.

St. Giles's Greek. Form of speech used in St. Giles, the center of London.

Technicality. Quibbling nicety as to speech.

Thieves' Latin. Thieves' dialect.

Thingumbob.
Thingummy. } A thing: applied indefinitely to any object.

Wall Street slang. Expressions in use on the stock markets.

What d' ye call 'em.
What's his name. } Indefinite persons or things.

Word-play. Disputation over the meaning of words. See WITTINESS.

NEOLOGY—*Nouns of Agent.*

Coiner of words. One who makes new words.

Neologist. An innovator in language.

NEOLOGY—*Verb.*

Coin words. To make or invent new words.

(Continued on Column 1.)

Word. The Christ. DIVINITY; **Word of God,** REVELATION-PSEUDOREVELATION.

word'-ing. Phraseology. STYLE.

word'-less. Speechless. VOCALIZATION-MUTENESS.

word'-play. Wit; jugglery. AMBIGUITY, WITTINESS-DULNESS, WORD-NEOLOGY.

words. A quarrel. VARIANCE-ACCORD; **bandy words,** CONVERSATION-MONOLOGUE; **bitter words,** APPROVAL-DISAPPROVAL; **choice of words,** STYLE; **command of words,** FORCE-WEAKNESS, TALKATIVENESS-TACITURNITY; **express by words,** LANGUAGE, PHRASE, STYLE; **flow of words,** SPEECH-INARTICULATION, TALKATIVENESS-TACITURNITY; **mere words,** MEANING-JARGON, RATIOCINATION-INSTINCT; **no words can paint,** PHENOMENON; **play of words,** WITTINESS-DULNESS; **put into words,** PHRASE; **war of words,** CONVERSATION-MONOLOGUE, STRIFE-PEACE; **words that burn,** FORCE-WEAKNESS; **words with,** APPROVAL-DISAPPROVAL.

word'-y. Prolix. TERSENESS-PROLIXITY.

work. Product; operation; book; business; ornament; exertion; to pass. ACTION-PASSIVENESS, AGENCY, CAUSE-EFFECT, EMBELLISHMENT-DISFIGUREMENT, MISSIVE-PUBLICATION, OCCUPATION, TOIL-RELAXATION, TRANSMISSION, USE-DISUSE; **earth-work,** ATTACK-DEFENSE; **field-work,** ATTACK-DEFENSE; **hard work,** DIFFICULTY-FACILITY, WEARINESS-REFRESHMENT; **piece of work,** CONSEQUENCE-INSIGNIFICANCE, VARAINCE-ACCORD; **stick to work,** PERSISTENCE-WHIM; **stitch of work,** TOIL-RELAXATION; **stroke of work,** TOIL-RELAXATION; **work a change,** MUTATION-PERMANENCE; **work against time,** HURRY-LEISURE; **work at,** ACTION-PASSIVENESS, ACTIVITY-INDOLENCE, AGENCY, OCCUPATION; **work for,** OBSTRUCTION-HELP; **work hard,** DIFFICULTY-FACILITY, TOIL-RELAXATION; **work ill,** SUCCESS-FAILURE; **work in,** ENVIRONMENT-INTERPOSITION; **work of art,** BEAUTY-UGLINESS, EMBELLISHMENT-DISFIGUREMENT; **work of fiction,** ACCOUNT; **work one's way,** ADVANCE-RETROGRESSION, ASCENT-DESCENT, SUCCESS-FAILURE, TOIL-RELAXATION, WELFARE-MISFORTUNE; **work out,** COMPLETION-NONCOMPLETION, CONDUCT; **work out one's salvation,** DEVOTION-IDOLATRY; **work up,** EXCITATION, PREPARATION-NONPREPARATION, USE-DISUSE; **work up into a passion,** FAVORITE-ANGER; **work up into form,** FORM-FORMLESSNESS; **work upon,** DOMINANCE-IMPOTENCE, EXCITATION, MOTIVE-CAPRICE; **work well,** DIFFICULTY-FACILITY, SUCCESS-FAILURE; **work wonders,** ACTIVITY-INDOLENCE, SUCCESS-FAILURE.

work'-a-day". A week-day; toiling. ACTIVITY-INDOLENCE, OCCUPATION.

work'-er. Laborer. AGENT.

work'-house. A workshop. WORKSHOP.

work'-ing. Active; acting. ACTIVITY-INDOLENCE, AGENCY; **working bee,** AGENT; **working man,** AGENT; **working order,** PREPARATION-NONPREPARATION; **working towards,** INCLINATION.

work'-man. A mechanic. AGENT.

work'-man-like". Orderly. SKILL-UNSKILFULNESS.

work'-man-ship. Skill; production. ACTION-PASSIVENESS, CREATION-DESTRUCTION.

works. Deeds. **Board of works,** COUNCIL; **good works,** CHARITABLENESS-MALEVOLENCE; **works of the mind,** REFLECTION-VACANCY.

work'-shop. A workhouse. WORKSHOP.

WORKSHOP.

Atelier [F.]. The workroom of a painter or sculptor.

Bureau [F.]. The office of an ambassador, state secretary, etc., for business.

Cabinet. A private room in which consultations are held.

Dock. An artificial basin for the reception of vessels.

Dockyard. A storage place for all kinds of naval stores and timber for ship-building.

Factory. A place where goods are manufactured.

Forge. A place for heating and beating into shape iron or any other metal.

Foundery. } An establishment in which articles are cast from metal.
Foundry. }

Furnace. An enclosed fireplace for obtaining a high degree of heat.

Hive. A place in which bees dwell and store honey; hence, any place of industry.

Hive of industry. A place full of activity.

Hotbed. A bed of rich earth, protected by glass, for promoting plant growth.

Hothouse. A structure kept warm artificially for the forced growth of flowers, etc., or the shelter of exotics.

Kitchen. The place where food is cooked.

Laboratory. A place fitted up for conducting scientific experiments, or similar work.

Loom. A simple machine in which cloth is woven.

Manufactory. A place where anything is manufactured.

Mill. A building fitted up with the machinery requisite for a factory, working crude metal, etc.

Mint. A place for the legal manufacture and issue of the coin of a country.

Nailery. Manufactory where nails are made.

Nursery. A place where trees, shrubs, etc., are raised for sale or transplanting.

Officina gentium [L.]. Workshop of nations, in which nations are produced.

Ropewalk. Shed used for the spinning of rope-yarn.

Slip. A marine railway dock.

Smithy. Forge.

Studio [It.]. An artist's study or workshop.

Tannery. A workshop for tanning hides.

Wharf. A landing-place, as of timber or masonry, for vessels and their cargoes.

Workhouse. } A place where any manufacture or hand-work is carried on.
Workshop. }

Yard. An enclosure within which any work or business is carried on.

WORKSHOP—*Nouns of Instrument*

Alembic. An apparatus of glass or metal, formerly used in distilling.

Caldron. A large kettle or boiler.

Crucible. A pot for melting metals or minerals.

Emeril. A glazier's diamond.

Matrix [L.]. A mold in which anything is cast or shaped.

work'-wom"-an. A laborer. AGENT.

world. Immensity; the universe; mankind; fashion; events. EXTENSION-DISTRICT, HUMANITY, MAGNITUDE-SMALLNESS, OCCURRENCE-DESTINY, SOCIETY-LUDICROUSNESS, UNIVERSE; **all the world over,** EXTENSION-DISTRICT; **as the world goes,** HABIT-DESUETUDE; **a world of,** MULTIPLICITY-PAUCITY; **citizen of the world,** HUMANITARIANISM-MISANTHROPY; **come into the world,** LIFE-DEATH; **follow to the world's end,** INSUBORDINATION-OBEDIENCE; **for all the world,** MOTIVE-CAPRICE; **give to the world,** PUBLICITY; **knowledge of the world,** SKILL-UNSKILFULNESS; **man of the world,** ADEPT-BUNGLER, SOCIETY-LUDICROUSNESS; **not for the world,** DECISION-MISJUDGMENT, PROFFER-REFUSAL, READINESS-RELUCTANCE; **organized world,** ORGANIZATION-INORGANIZATION; **Prince of this world,** ANGEL-SATAN; **rise in the world,** WELFARE-MISFORTUNE; **throughout the world,** EXTENSION-DISTRICT; **world and his wife,** MULTIPLICITY-PAUCITY; **world forgetting by the world forgot,** SOCIABILITY-PRIVACY; **world of good,** GOOD-EVIL, GOODNESS-BADNESS; **world to come,** OCCURRENCE-DESTINY; **world without end,** ETERNITY-INSTANTANEITY.

world'-li-ness. State of being worldly. UNSELFISHNESS-SELFISHNESS.

world'-ling. A miser; a railer. GODLINESS-UNGODLINESS, UNSELFISHNESS-SELFISHNESS.

world'-ly. Selfish; irreligious. GODLINESS-DISBELIEF, UNSELFISHNESS-SELFISHNESS.

world'-wide. Great; universal. EXTENSION-DISTRICT, MAGNITUDE-SMALLNESS, UNIVERSALITY-PARTICULARITY.

world'–wis"–dom. Shrewdness; selfishness. RECKLESS-NESS-CAUTION, SKILL-UNSKILFULNESS, UNSELFISH-NESS-SELFISHNESS.

worm. An animal; a bane; a spire. CIRCLE-WINDING, FAUNA-FLORA, GREATNESS-LITTLENESS, REMEDY-BANE; **worm in,** ENVIRONMENT-INTERPOSITION; **worm oneself,** ENTRANCE-EXIT, LOVE-HATE; **worm one's way,** SWIFTNESS-SLOWNESS, TRANSMISSION; **worm out,** DISCOVERY; **worm that never dies,** HEAVEN-HELL.

worm'–eat"–en. Perforated. BETTERMENT-DETERIORATION.

worm'–wood". A drug. **Wormwood and gall,** DESIRE-DISTASTE, PALATABLENESS-UNPALATABLENESS, PLEASURABLENESS-PAINFULNESS.

worn. Damaged; fatigued. BETTERMENT-DETERIORATION, STRENGTH-WEAKNESS, WEARINESS-REFRESHMENT; **well worn,** USE-DISUSE; **worn out,** BETTERMENT-DETERIORATION, ENTERTAINMENT-WEARINESS, WEARINESS-REFRESHMENT.

wor'–ried. Harassed. PLEASURE-PAIN.

wor'–ry. Vexation; to vex; to harass. CHARITABLE-NESS-MALEVOLENCE, PLEASURABLENESS-FAINFUL-NESS, PLEASURE-PAIN.

wor'–ry-ing. Fretting. PLEASURABLENESS-PAINFUL-NESS.

worse. Deteriorated; aggravated. ALLEVIATION-AGGRAVATION, BETTERMENT-DETERIORATION; **worse for wear,** STRENGTH-WEAKNESS.

wor'–ship. A title; adoration. DEVOTION-IDOLATRY, PRESUMPTION-OBSEQUIOUSNESS, REGARD-DISRESPECT, TITLE; **demon worship,** DEVOTION-IDOLATRY; **fire worship,** DEVOTION-IDOLATRY; **his worship,** JUDGE; **idol worship,** DEVOTION-IDOLATRY; **place of worship,** FANE; **worship Mammon,** AFFLUENCE-PENURY; **worship the rising sun,** PRESUMPTION-OBSEQUIOUSNESS.

wor'–ship-er. One who worships. DEVOTION-IDOLATRY.

wor'–ship-ful. Honorable. REPUTATION-DISCREDIT.

wor'–ship-ing. Revering. DEVOTION-IDOLATRY.

worst. To defeat. FIGHTING-CONCILIATION; **do one's worst,** BETTERMENT-DETERIORATION, CHARITABLE-NESS-MALEVOLENCE; **do your worst,** CHARITABLE-NESS-MENACE, DEFIANCE; **have the worst of it,** SUCCESS-FAILURE; **make the worst of it,** OVERVALUATION-UNDERVALUATION; **worst come to the worst,** CERTAINTY-DOUBT, GOODNESS-BADNESS, SANGUINE-NESS-HOPELESSNESS, WELFARE-MISFORTUNE.

worth. Value; virtue; wealth. GOODNESS-BADNESS, HOLDING-EXEMPTION, PRICE-DISCOUNT, USEFUL-NESS-USELESSNESS, VIRTUE-VICE; **pennyworth,** PRICE-DISCOUNT; **what one is worth,** PROPERTY; **worth much,** AFFLUENCE-PENURY; **worth one's salt,** USEFULNESS-USELESSNESS; **worth the money,** COST-LINESS-CHEAPNESS; **worth while,** PROPRIETY-IM-PROPRIETY.

worth'–less. Trifling; useless; profligate. CONSE-QUENCE-INSIGNIFICANCE, USEFULNESS-USELESSNESS, VIRTUE-VICE.

wor'–thy. Virtuous; estimable. GOOD MAN-BAD MAN, REPUTATION-DISCREDIT, VIRTUE-VICE; **worthy of,** DUENESS-UNDUENESS; **worthy of belief,** FAITH-MIS-GIVING; **worthy of blame,** APPROVAL-DISAPPROVAL; **worthy of notice,** CONSEQUENCE-INSIGNIFICANCE; **worthy of remark,** CONSEQUENCE-INSIGNIFICANCE.

wot. Think. KNOWLEDGE-IGNORANCE.

would. Wishing. **Would fain,** DESIRE-DISTASTE; **would that,** DESIRE-DISTASTE.

would'–be". Pretentious. DUENESS-UNDUENESS, PRE-SUMPTION-OBSEQUIOUSNESS.

wound. Injury; insult. BETTERMENT-DETERIORA-TION, FAVORITE-ANGER, GOOD-EVIL, PLEASURABLE-NESS-PAINFULNESS; **keep the wound green,** PARDON-

VINDICTIVENESS; **wound the feelings,** PLEASURABLE-NESS-PAINFULNESS.

wrack. Ruin. CREATION-DESTRUCTION; **go to wrack and ruin,** AFFLUENCE-PENURY, CREATION-DESTRUC-TION, SUCCESS-FAILURE.

wraith. A ghost. JOVE-FIEND.

wran'–gle. To quarrel; to debate. RATIOCINATION-INSTINCT, STRIFE-PEACE, VARIANCE-ACCORD.

wran'–gler. An opponent; a scholar; a disputer. AN-TAGONIST-ASSISTANT, RATIOCINATION-INSTINCT, SCHOLAR-DUNCE.

wran'–gling. Quarreling. RATIOCINATION-INSTINCT, VARIANCE-ACCORD.

wrap. To cover. COVER-LINING, DRESS-UNDRESS.

wrapped in. Absorbed. HEED-DISREGARD; **wrapped in clouds,** ENLIGHTENMENT-SECRECY; **wrapped in self,** UNSELFISHNESS-SELFISHNESS; **wrapped in thought,** HEED-DISREGARD.

wrap'–per. A covering. COVER-LINING, DRESS-UN-DRESS, ENCLOSURE.

wrap'–ping. Covering. COVER-LINING.

wrap'–ras"–cal. A garment. DRESS-UNDRESS.

wrath. Anger. FAVORITE-ANGER.

wrath'–ful. Very angry. FAVORITE-ANGER.

wreak. To inflict. HARSHNESS-MILDNESS, TURBU-LENCE-CALMNESS; **wreak one's anger,** PARDON-VIN-DICTIVENESS; **wreak one's malice on,** CHARITABLE-NESS-MALEVOLENCE.

wreath. A woven band; a trophy; an ornament; an honor; a circle. CIRCLE-WINDING, CROSSING, EM-BELLISHMENT-DISFIGUREMENT, TITLE, TROPHY.

wreathe. To weave. CIRCLE-WINDING, CROSSING.

wreath'–y. Spiral. CIRCLE-WINDING.

wreck. Ruin; to damage; to defeat. BETTERMENT-DETERIORATION, CREATION-DESTRUCTION, INCRE-MENT-REMNANT, SUCCESS-FAILURE.

wrecked. Destroyed totally. SUCCESS-FAILURE.

wreck'–er. Robber. ROBBER.

wrench. To twist; to take from. CIRCUITION, INJEC-TION-EJECTION, PUSH-PULL, TAKING-RESTITUTION, UNION-DISUNION.

wrest. To distort. PROPORTION-DEFORMITY; **wrest from,** TAKING-RESTITUTION; **wrest the sense,** INTER-PRETATION-MISINTERPRETATION.

wres'–tle. To contend. STRIFE-PEACE.

wrest'–ler. One who wrestles. BELLIGERENT.

wrest'–ling. Contending. STRIFE-PEACE.

wretch. A sufferer; a sinner. GOOD MAN-BAD MAN, PLEASURE-PAIN.

wretch'–ed. Worthless; bad; unhappy. CONSEQUENCE-INSIGNIFICANCE, GOODNESS-BADNESS, PLEASURE-PAIN.

wretch'–ed-ness. Unhappiness. PLEASURE-PAIN.

wretch'–ed-ly. Very small. MAGNITUDE-SMALLNESS.

wrig'–gle. To twist; to be agitated. VIBRATION-AGI-TATION; **wriggle into,** ENTRANCE-EXIT; **wriggle out of,** ESCAPE.

wright. An artificer. AGENT.

wring. To twist; to torture. CIRCLE-WINDING, CLEAN-NESS-FILTHINESS, PLEASURABLENESS-PAINFULNESS, SENSUALITY-SUFFERING; **wring from,** COERCION, IN-JECTION-EJECTION, TAKING-RESTITUTION; **wring one's hands,** JUBILATION-LAMENTATION; **wring the heart,** PLEASURABLENESS-PAINFULNESS.

wring'–ing wet. Drenched. DAMPNESS-DRYNESS.

wrin'–kle. A crease. CIRCLE-WINDING, PLICATURE.

wrin'–kled. Aged. INFANCY-AGE.

wrist. A part of the arm. KEEPING-RELINQUISHMENT.

wrist'–band. Part of a sleeve. DRESS-UNDRESS.

writ. An order. LITIGATION, ORDER.

Writ. Scripture. **Holy Writ,** REVELATION-PSEUDOREVE-LATION.

write. To inscribe. STYLE, WRITING-PRINTING; **write down,** INCLUSION-OMISSION, WRITING-PRINTING;

write out, WRITING-PRINTING; write upon, ESSAY; write word, ENLIGHTENMENT-SECRECY.

wri'-ter. A scrivener; an author. MISSIVE-PUBLICATION, WRITING-PRINTING; dramatic writer, ACTING; pen of a ready writer, STYLE; writer to the Signet, ADVOCATE.

writhe. To twist; be in pain. AGITATION, PROPORTION-DEFORMITY, SENSUALITY-SUFFERING.

wri'-ting. Inscription; books. MISSIVE-PUBLICATION, WRITING-PRINTING; put in writing, MARK-OBLITERATION; writing in cipher, WRITING-PRINTING.

WRITING—PRINTING.

Autograph. Writing done with one's own hand.
Bad hand. Incorrect or illegible writing.
Barbouillage [F.]. A scrawl; a scribble.
Bold hand. Prominent and easily read writing.
Cacoëthes scribendi [L.]. An incurable passion for writing.
Cacography. Bad writing.
Calligraphy. Fair or elegant penmanship.
Cerography. The art of writing on a waxed copper plate.
Chirography. The art of writing.
Composition. Anything written.
Copy. A reproduction or imitation, as of a writing.
Coup de plume [F.]. An attack in writing.
Crabbed hand. Writing that is irregular in form.
Cramped hand. Writing that is small and contracted and irregular in form.
Cursive hand. Writing in which the letters or characters are joined together.
Dash of the pen. A hasty writing.
Fair copy. Regular and flowing writing.
Fist. Handwriting.
Flowing hand. Writing that seems to move as a stream.
Good hand. Legible writing.
Graphology. Studying character from the handwriting.
Griffonage [F.]. Scrawl; scribbling.
Hand. Writing.
Handwriting. Writing done by the hand.
Hectograph. A pad for multiplying copies of writing.
Holograph. Writing entirely by the hand of the person in whose name it is issued.
Illegible hand. Writing that is difficult to read or cannot be read
Ill-formed letters. Irregular writing.
Inscription, etc. The act of marking with written characters. See MARK.
Legible hand. Writing that can be easily read.
Line. A row of written words.
Literæ scriptæ [L.]. Written letters.
Manuscript. Writing done by the hand.
Mimeograph. Writing traced so as to make copies.
Monograph. A written account of a single thing.
MS. Abbreviation for manuscript.
Pattes de mouche [F.]. Fly's feet; scribbling.
Pen and ink. Writing.
Pencraft. The art of composing or writing.
Penmanship. Style or manner of writing.
Pot-hooks and hangers. A scrawled writing.
Quill-driving. Writing with a quill.
Rescript. An imperial writing or decree.
Rough copy. Writing hastily done.
Running hand. Writing in which the letters or characters are joined together.
Scribble, etc. Hasty, careless writing. See *Verbs*.
Signature. The name of a person written by himself.
Sign-manual. The personal signature of a person.
Stelography. The art of writing or inscribing characters on pillars.
Stroke of the pen. Hasty writing.
Superscription, etc. The act of writing on the outside or upper part of. See SIGN.
These presents. Writings or documents now present or referred to.
Transcript. A copy.
Transcription, etc. A copying. See COPY.
Type-writer. Manutyper.
Writing, etc. The forming of characters or letters in order to record ideas for the information of others. See *Verbs*.

WRITING—*Nouns of Instrument.*

Foolscap. Writing-paper folded to make pages about 13 by 8 inches.
Goose-quill. A quill from a goose's wing, used for writing with.
Ink-bottle. } A bottle or plant for ink.
Ink-plant. }
Marble. A stone for some inscription.
Paper. A thin substance in the form of sheets, used for writing on.
Papyrus. The writing paper of the ancient Egyptians, made from the papyrus-plant.
Parchment. Sheep or goat-skin polished with pumice-stone for writing upon.
Pen. An instrument for writing with fluid ink.

Block-printing. A mode of printing from engraved boards by means of a sheet of paper laid on the inked surface and rubbed with a brush.
Composition. The setting up of type and arranging it for printing.
Manutype. Printing done with a typewriter by hand.
Plate-printing, etc. The process of printing from an engraved plate or plates. See ENGRAVING.
Printing. The art of making and issuing matter for reading by means of type and the printing-press.
Type-printing. The process of printing from raised type.

PRINTING—*Associated Nouns.*

Column. One of two or more vertical series of lines.
Context. The whole text of a book.
Copy. A reproduction or imitation, as of writing, printing, etc.
Folio, etc. A book with the pages folded once. See MISSIVE-PUBLICATION.
Head-line. A line of type set above the text to which it refers.
Impression. The imprint of types, illustrations, etc.
Letterpress. Printed matter from type.
Note. A brief comment appended to the text of a work.
Offcut. The part cut off from a printed page.
Page. One side of a leaf of a book.
Print. Printed matter.
Proof. A first print.
Pull. An impression made by pulling the lever of a hand-press.
Revise. A proof for revision.
Text. The body of matter on a written or printed page.
The press. Persons engaged in newspaper work collectively.

PRINTING—*Nouns of Instrument.*

Aprotype. Close type.
Block letter. Type cut from wood.
Bourgeois. A kind of type between long primer and brevier.
Brevier. A size of type between bourgeois and minion.
Capitals, etc. Large letters or type. See LETTER.
Electrotype. A facsimile plate made by electrotypy for use in printing.
Font. }
Fount. } A complete assortment of printing-type of one size.
Minionette. A very small size of type.
Pi. }
Pie. } A mass of type confusedly mixed or unsorted.
Pica. A size of type six lines to an inch in depth of body.
Reglet. Wooden strip for making space between lines.
Stereotype. A metal plate cast from a mold taken from one or more pages of movable types, for subsequent use in printing from.
Type. The shape or form of an alphabetic letter in metal.
Typewriter. A machine for producing printed characters.

PRINTING—*Nouns of Agent.*

Compositor. One who sets types, and puts them into pages and forms.
Manutyper. One who prints with a typewriter.
Printer. One who prints on paper, as books, newspapers, etc.
Printer's devil. The youngest apprentice in a printing-office, who does all of the dirty work.
Reader. A corrector of the press.

PRINTING—*Scientific Nouns.*

Typography. The art of composing and printing from types.

PRINTING—*Verbs.*

Appear in print. To come before the public; be published.
Bring out. To publish; bring into notice.
Compose. To arrange type in a composing-stick for printing; set types.
Enface. To print on the face of.
Go to press. To be in the course of printing.
Pass through the press. To be printed.
Print. To form or copy by pressure, as from type or engraved plate.
Publish, etc. To print and offer for sale. See PUBLICITY.
Put to press. To start to print.
Rush into print. To hurry the publication.
See through the press. To keep to the publication of something.

WRITING—PRINTING—*Continued.*

WRITING—Nouns of Instrument—*Continued.*

Pencil. A pointed strip of graphite, slate or similar metal, often enclosed in wood.
Pillar. A monument for inscription.
Quill. An instrument for writing.
Slate. A thin plate of stone for writing upon.
Stationery. Paper, pens, ink, and other materials employed in writing.
Style. A pointed metal instrument for writing on tablets covered with wax.
Table. A slab of stone, wood, metal, or the like for writing.
Tablet. A small table or flat surface for an inscription.
Tabula. A writing-table.
Vellum. A fine parchment made from the skins of calves, kids, and lambs.

WRITING—Nouns of Means.

Arrow-heads. Alphabetic characters the elements of which consist of strokes resembling arrow-heads.
Cuneiform character. A character or letter having a wedge-like appearance, found in old Persian inscriptions.
Hieroglyphic. The picture-writing of ancient Egypt.
Letter, etc. A mark or character representing a sound or an element of speech. See LETTER.
Ogham. A kind of shorthand writing or cipher, in use among the ancient Irish.
Runes. Characters of an early alphabet of the Germans, Anglo-Saxons or Scandinavians.
Uncial writing. Consisting of a form of letters found in manuscripts from the 4th to the 8th century.

WRITING—Nouns of Agent.

Amanuensis. One who copies manuscript or writes from dictation.
Clerk. An employee who keeps accounts or does writing.
Copyist. One who does copying.
Penman. A person considered with regard to his handwriting.
Quill-driver. One who works with a pen.
Scribe. One who writes; an official or public writer.
Scrivener. One whose business is to draw contracts or prepare writings.
Secretary. One who attends to correspondence, etc.
Transcriber. One who writes from a copy.
Writer. One who writes, or engages in literary composition.
Writer for the press, etc. One who writes for newspapers or periodicals. See MISSIVE-PUBLICATION.

WRITING—Scientific Nouns.

Brachygraphy. Art or practise of writing in short compass.
Contraction. The shortening of a word in writing.
Cryptography. Art of writing in secret characters.
Logography. Art of reporting speeches in longhand by several reporters, each taking down a few words in succession.
Pasigraphy. Any system of universal writing.
Phonography. A system of shorthand writing.
Polygraphy. The art of writing in various ciphers.
Secret writing. A system of writing known only to those concerned.
Shorthand. A rapid system of writing by means of contractions and simple characters.
Steganography. The art of writing in cipher.
Stenography. Art of writing by the use of contractions or arbitrary symbols.
Tachygraphy. Any ancient stenographic system.
Writing in cipher. A secret system of writing.

PRINTING—*Adjectives.*

In type. Ready to print.
Printed, etc. Impressed with letters. See *Verbs.*
Typographical, etc. Pertaining to the art of printing. See *Nouns.*

WRITING—*Continued.*

WRITING—Noun of Source.

Authorship Source from which a work proceeds.

WRITING—*Verbs.*

Compose. To write, as an author.
Copy. To write from an original.
Dash off. To write hastily.
Dictate. To communicate orally something to be written by an amanuensis.
Dip one's pen in ink. To engage temporarily in writing.
Draw up. To compose in due form; form in writing.
Enface. To write on the face of.
Engross. To copy or write in a large hand.
Indite. To put into words or writing; compose.
Inscribe. To write or engrave on anything.
Interline. To write between the lines.
Pen. To commit to writing, indite.
Scrabble. To make irregular or crooked letters in writing.
Scratch. To write awkwardly.
Scrawl. To write hastily or improperly.
Scribble. To write carelessly and illegibly.
Shed ink. To write.
Sign, etc. To write one's name to. See EVIDENCE.
Spill ink. To waste one's time in writing.
Stain paper. To write: used in derision.
Take pen in hand. }
Take up the pen. } To begin writing.
Throw on paper. To write hurriedly.
Transcribe. To write over again; copy.
Write. To express by means of forming letters and words.
Write down, etc. To record; put into writing. See MARK.
Write fair. To write distinctly or legibly.
Write out. To write a full statement of.

WRITING—*Adjectives.*

Cuneiform. Wedge-shaped; said of cuneiform letters.
Demotic. Simplified form of the Egyptian hieroglyphic characters.
Hieroglyphical. Expressive of some meaning by pictures or figures.
In black and white. In writing or print.
In writing.
Runic. Pertaining to rune or runes.
Uncial. Pertaining to uncial letters.
Under one's hand. Attested or confirmed by writing one's name.
Writing, etc. See *Verbs.*
Written, etc. Reduced to writing. See *Verbs.*

WRITING—*Adverbs, etc.*

Currente calamo [L.]. Offhand; with great rapidity; with running pen.
Pen in hand. Ready for writing.

WRITING—*Phrases.*

Audacter et sincere [L.]. Boldly and sincerely.
Le style est l'homme même [F.]. The style is the man himself.

---

writ'-ten. Marked down. WRITING-PRINTING; **it is written,** VOLITION-OBLIGATION.
wrong. Evil; improper. CHARITABLENESS-MALEVOLENCE, GOOD-EVIL, GOODNESS-BADNESS, RIGHT-WRONG, VIRTUE-VICE; **begin at the wrong end,** SKILL-UNSKILFULNESS; **go wrong,** SUCCESS-FAILURE; **in the wrong,** RIGHT-WRONG, TRUTH-ERROR; **in the wrong place,** PROPRIETY-IMPROPRIETY; **own oneself in the wrong,** REPENTANCE-OBDURACY; **wrong box,** DIFFICULTY-FACILITY, RIGHT-WRONG, SKILL-UNSKILFULNESS; **wrong course,** VIRTUE-VICE; **wrong in one's head,** SANENESS-LUNACY; **wrong side of the wall,** SECURITY-INSECURITY; **wrong side out,** REVERSAL; **wrong side up,** REVERSAL; **wrong sow by the ear,** SKILL-UNSKILFULNESS, SUCCESS-FAILURE; **wrong step,** SUCCESS-FAILURE.
wrong'-do''-er. A culprit. BENEFACTOR-EVILDOER, GOOD MAN-BAD MAN.

wrong'-do-ing. Mischief. VIRTUE-VICE.
wrong'-ful. Injurious. RIGHT-WRONG.
wrong'-head-ed. Obstinate. DECISION-MISJUDGMENT.
wrong'-ly. Not rightly. RIGHT-WRONG.
wrought. Worked. **Highly wrought,** COMPLETION-NONCOMPLETION, PREPARATION-NONPREPARATION; **wrought iron,** HARDNESS-SOFTNESS; **wrought out,** COMPLETION-NONCOMPLETION; **wrought up,** EMOTION, EXCITATION, FAVORITE-ANGER.
wry. Oblique; distorted. PARALLELISM-INCLINATION, PROPORTION-DEFORMITY; **wry face,** APPROVAL-DISAPPROVAL, BEAUTY-UGLINESS, CONTENTEDNESS-DISCONTENTMENT, JUBILATION-LAMENTATION, SENSUALITY-SUFFERING.
wynd. An alley. DWELLER-HABITATION.
wy'-vern. A dragon. CONVENTIONALITY-UNCONVENTIONALITY.

X

xa-nor′-phi-ca. Stringed instrument. MUSICAL IN-STRUMENTS.

xan′-the-in. Yellow pigment. YELLOWNESS-PURPLE.

Xan′-thi-an. Relating to Xanthus. SCULPTURE.

xan′-thic. Having a yellow color. YELLOWNESS-PURPLE.

xanth″-o-cy″-an-o′-pi-a. Form of color-blindness. SIGHT-DIMSIGHTEDNESS, YELLOWNESS-PURPLE.

xan-thop′-si-a. Kind of color-blindness. SIGHT-DIM-SIGHTEDNESS, YELLOWNESS-PURPLE.

xan′-those. Yellow pigment. YELLOWNESS-PURPLE.

Xan′-thous. Mongolian. YELLOWNESS-PURPLE.

Xan-tip′-pe. The wife of Socrates. FAVORITE-QUARREL-SOMENESS.

xe′-bec. A small vessel. CONVEYANCE-VESSEL.

xen″-o-do-chi′-um. Room. DWELLER-HABITATION.

xen″-o-gen′-e-sis. The fancied production of an organism of one kind by an organism of another. CREA-TION-DESTRUCTION.

xe-roph′-a-gy. The eating of dry food. FASTING-GLUT-TONY.

xiph-op′-a-gus. Double monster. CONVENTIONALITY-UNCONVENTIONALITY, PHENOMENON.

X ray. A Roentgen ray, called X as an unknown quantity.

X RAY.

Bocquerel rays. Rays of force acting like Roentgen rays, given off by certain substances without electrical stimulus.

Cathode. The point at which electricity flows from Crookes's tube.

Crookes's tube. An electrical receiver, by which Roentgen rays are produced.

Fluoroscope. A radiant image of something passed through by X rays which fall upon a prepared surface of fluorescent materials.

Photographic film. Films prepared to take an image from rays directed upon them.

Radiograph. A sciagraph or fluoroscope.

Roentgen ray photograph. A sciagraph.

Roentgen rays. Rays starting from the point where cathode rays strike the surface of Crookes's tube; they will pass through most solid bodies, and are invisible, but produce chemical effects upon certain substances so as to make radiographs of the objects they pass through. They are named from their discoverer

Sciagraph. A shadow picture made by Roentgen rays upon a photographic film.

xy′-lo-graph. A wood-engraving. ENGRAVING.

xy-log′-ra-phy. Wood-engraving. ENGRAVING.

xy-lo′-phone. Musical instrument. MUSICAL INSTRU-MENTS.

x, y, z. An unknown quantity. KNOWLEDGE-IGNO-RANCE.

Y

yacht. A pleasure-craft. CONVEYANCE-VESSEL.

yacht'-ing. The act of sailing a yacht. TRAVELING-NAVIGATION.

ya'-ger. A sharpshooter. BELLIGERENT.

Ya-hoo'. A low person. CRAFT-ARTLESSNESS, GENTILITY-COMMONALTY.

yak. Bison. FAUNA-FLORA.

yam. Kind of sweet potato. FAUNA-FLORA.

ya'-ma. A god. JOVE-FIEND.

yank. To pull. PUSH-PULL.

Yan'-kee. A New Englander. CRAFT-ARTLESSNESS, SKILL-UNSKILFULNESS.

Yan'-kee Doo'-dle. Popular American tune. ENTERTAINMENT-WEARINESS, PATRIOTISM-TREASON.

yap. To yelp. CRY-ULULATION.

yard. An enclosure; a measure of length. DWELLER-HABITATION, LENGTH-SHORTNESS, MEASURE, WORKSHOP.

yard'-arm" to yard'-arm". From end to end of a yard. REMOTENESS-NEARNESS.

yard'-man. Laborer in the railroad yards. CHIEF-UNDERLING.

yare. Prompt. ACTIVITY-INDOLENCE.

yarn. A fibrous material; a story. GULL-HYPERBOLE, LAMINA-FIBER; **mingled yarn,** MIXTURE-HOMOGENEITY; **spin a long yarn,** GULL-HYPERBOLE, TERSENESS-PROLIXITY.

yarr. To snarl. CRY-ULULATION.

yar'-row. An astringent herb. REMEDY-BANE.

yat'-a-ghan. A sword. WEAPON.

yaup. To yelp. CRY-ULULATION.

yaw. To steer wildly. AIM-ABERRATION.

yawl. A small vessel; a howl. CONVEYANCE-VESSEL, CRY-ULULATION.

yawn. To open. ACTIVITY-INDOLENCE, APERTURE-CLOSURE, ENTERTAINMENT-WEARINESS, WEARINESS-REFRESHMENT.

yawn'-ing. A wide opening. APERTURE-CLOSURE, INTERSPACE-CONTACT, WEARINESS-REFRESHMENT; **yawning gulf,** INTERSPACE-CONTACT.

y-clept'. Named. NAME-MISNOMER.

yea. Yes; more so. ASSENT-DISSENT, SUPREMACY-SUBORDINACY.

yean. To bring forth. CREATION-DESTRUCTION.

year. A period of time. DURATION-NEVERNESS, PERIOD-PROGRESS; **all the year round,** LASTINGNESS-TRANSIENTNESS; **since the year one,** NOVELTY-ANTIQUITY; **tenant from year to year,** HOLDER; **year after year,** RECURRENCE.

year'-book. Book published annually. PERIODICITY-IRREGULARITY.

year'-ling. Being a year old. INFANT-VETERAN.

year'-ly. Once a year. PERIODICITY-IRREGULARITY.

yearn. To desire anxiously. LIGHTHEARTEDNESS-DEJECTION, PLEASURE-PAIN; **yearn for,** COMPASSION-RUTHLESSNESS, DESIRE-DISTASTE.

yearn'-ing. Act or state of longing. COMPASSION-RUTHLESSNESS, DESIRE-DISTASTE, LOVE-HATE.

years. Plural of year. DURATION-NEVERNESS, INFANCY-AGE; **in years,** INFANCY-AGE; **tenant for years,** HOLDER; **years ago,** FUTURE-PAST; **come to years of discretion,** MANHOOD; **years old,** INFANCY-AGE.

yeast. The foam or froth of fermenting beer or other liquor. HEAVINESS-LIGHTNESS, VISCIDITY-FOAM.

yell. A sharp loud cry. CRY-ULULATION.

yel'-low. A color of the spectrum between green and orange. YELLOWNESS-PURPLE; **yellow flag,** WARNING; **yellow and red,** BLUENESS-ORANGE.

yel'-low-eyed". Having yellow eyes. PARDON-VINDICTIVENESS.

yel'-low-ness. The state or quality of being yellow. YELLOWNESS-PURPLE.

YELLOWNESS—PURPLE.

Aureolin. A golden yellow.

Cadmium yellow. An intense yellow.

Claude tint. The tint in Claude Lorrain's pictures.

Gamboge. A brownish yellow.

Indian yellow. A pigment of a bright yellow color.

Lemon yellow. Bright yellow, like a lemon.

Orpiment. A pearly lemon yellow.

Xanthein. A yellow pigment.

Xanthocyanopia. A form of color-blindness.

Xanthopsia. The state of seeing yellow as the color of every object.

Xanthose. A yellow pigment.

Yellow. One of the seven prismatic colors, resembling gold, but brighter.

Yellow ocher. A natural yellow pigment of iron.

YELLOWNESS—Denotations.

Crocus. A plant bearing large yellow flowers.

Jaundice. A disease characterized by yellowness of the skin.

London fog. The thick yellow fog peculiar to London.

Saffron. The dried orange-colored stigmas of the saffron plant.

Topaz. A whitish-yellow mineral.

YELLOWNESS—Adjectives.

Amber-colored. Of a semi-transparent yellow, like amber.

Aureate. Of a golden yellow.

Citrine. Green-yellow, like a citron.

Citron-colored. Green-yellow, as citron.

Cream-colored. Rich yellow, as cream.

Creamy. Of a rich yellow color, resembling cream.

Amethyst. A purple-violet color.

Aniline dyes. Dyes used to give various shades of purple.

Bishop's purple. The color of the vestments of a cardinal bishop.

Blue and red. The colors going to make up purple.

Lividity. Lividness. The state or quality of having an extremely dark-purple color.

Purple. The color resulting from a blending of violet and red.

Purpure. The term used for purple in heraldry.

PURPLE—Verb.

Empurple. To tinge or color with purple.

PURPLE—Adjectives.

Lavender. Of a very pale purple color.

Lilac. Of a pale purple color, like the lilac.

Livid. Of an extremely dark purple color.

Mauve. Of a delicate purple color.

Plum-colored. Of a rich reddish-purple.

Puce. Of a dark-brownish purple color.

Purple. Colored with purple.

Violet. Of a dark blue, inclining to red and not quite purple.

YELLOWNESS—ADJECTIVES—Continued.

Fallow. Of a pale brownish-yellow color, like a fallow deer.

Flavous. Bright yellow.

Fulvid. Fulvous. Reddish yellow.

YELLOWNESS—Adjectives—*Continued.*

Gold-colored. Yellow, of the color of gold.
Golden. Yellow, of a color resembling gold.
Jaundiced. Made sickly yellow by the jaundice.
Lemon-colored. Bright yellow, as a lemon.
Luteous. Of a muddy-yellow color.
Primrose-colored. Of a pale greenish-yellow color.
Saffron-colored. Of a deep reddish-yellow color.
Sallow. Of an unhealthy yellowish color.
Straw-colored. Pale yellow, like straw.

Sulfur-colored. Pale yellow, like sulfur.
Tawny. Brownish yellow.
Xanthic. Of a predominantly yellow color.
Xanthous. Pertaining to the yellow type of mankind.
Yellow. Of the color of the spectrum, between green and orange.
Yellow as a crow's foot. ⎫
Yellow as a guinea. ⎬ Figurative expressions for degrees of yellowness.
Yellow as a quince. ⎭

yel'-lows. Jealousy. PARDON-JEALOUSY.
yelp. A sharp cry. CACOPHONY, CRY-ULULATION.
yeo'-man. A farmer. DOMESTICATION-AGRICULTURE, MALE-FEMALE; **yeoman of the guard,** BELLIGERENT.
yeo'-man-ry. A home guard of cavalry. BELLIGERENT.
yerk. To jerk. IMPETUS-REACTION.
yes. Just so. ASSENT-DISSENT, ASSERTION-DENIAL, CONSENT, READINESS-RELUCTANCE.
yes'-ter-day. The day preceding to-day. FUTURE-PAST; **of yesterday,** NOVELTY-ANTIQUITY.
yet. Besides; eventually; heretofore. ANTECEDENCE-SEQUENCE, COMPENSATION, CONVENTIONALITY-UNCONVENTIONALITY, DURATION-NEVERNESS, FUTURE-PAST, MODIFICATION.
yeux doux [F.] (yu du). Soft eyes. BLANDISHMENT.
yeux doux, faire les [F.] (yu du fâr lê). To ogle. BLANDISHMENT.
yew. An ornamental tree. FAUNA-FLORA.
yield. To furnish in return; to give up. CONSENT, GIVING, HARDNESS-SOFTNESS, KEEPING-RELINQUISHMENT, OUTLAY-INCOME, PRICE, YIELDING; **yield one's breath,** LIFE-DEATH; **yield the palm,** SELFRESPECT - HUMBLENESS, SUPREMACY - SUBORDINACY; **yield to despair,** SANGUINENESS - HOPELESSNESS; **yield to temptation,** MOTIVE-CAPRICE; **yield up the ghost,** LIFE-DEATH.
yield'-ance. The act of yielding. CONSENT.
yield'-ing. Disposed to yield. CONSENT, DIFFICULTY-FACILITY, HARDNESS-SOFTNESS, YIELDING.

YIELDING.

Backdown. A yielding; a retraction.
Capitulation. A yielding to an enemy upon stipulated terms.
Cession. The yielding of possessions to another.
Non-resistance. Yielding without opposition.
Obedience, etc. Habitual yielding to superior authority. See OBEDIENCE.
Resignation. Habitual yielding to circumstances over which one has no control.
Submission. The act of yielding to power or authority.
Surrender. The act of yielding to another because of his superior force.
Yielding. Giving in to the will of another.

YIELDING—*Associated Nouns.*

Courtesy. ⎫ An act of civility or reverence made by a dropping of
Curtsy. ⎬ the body with a bending of the knees.
Genuflection. A bending of the knee.
Homage. Profession of fealty to a sovereign.
Kneeling. A bending of the knees in submission.
Kowtow. A Chinese form of obeisance.
Obeisance. An expression of deference or respect.
Prostration. The act of bowing in humility.

YIELDING—*Verbs.*

Avaler les couleuvres [F.] To put up with mortifications.
Beat a retreat. To give the signal for a retreat.
Be at one's feet. To humbly submit to.
Bend. To yield.
Bend before the storm. To yield to circumstances over which one has no control.
Bend down. To yield entirely.
Bend the knee. ⎫ To yield.
Bend the neck. ⎭
Bend to one's yoke. To submit to another's control.
Bite the dust. To submit with the utmost humility.

Bow submission. Submit with obeisance.
Bow to. To submit to.
Capitulate. To surrender on certain conditions.
Cave in. To yield unexpectedly from lack of support.
Cede. To yield the control of.
Come to terms. To submit to a compromise.
Courtesy. To perform an act of respectful submission.
Craven. To cause to yield in a cowardly manner.
Crouch before. To submit because of fear.
Curtsy. Courtesy.
Deliver up one's arms. To surrender.
Draw in one's horns. To give in. See SELFRESPECT-HUMBLENESS.
Eat dirt. ⎫ To have to submit in a very humiliating fashion.
Eat humble pie. ⎭
Eat the leek. To have to retract slanderous statements.
Fall on one's knees. To take an humble and suppliant position.
Give ground. To yield under pressure.
Give in. To yield to a just demand.
Give up. To yield as hopeless.
Give way. To yield to superior authority.
Grin and abide. To submit with forced cheerfulness.
Gulp down. To yield with aversion.
Haul down one's flag. To give a sign of submission.
Kiss the rod. To submit humbly to punishment.
Kneel. To bend the knee as a sign of submission.
Kneel to. To humbly submit to.
Knock under. ⎫
Knuckle down. ⎬ To acknowledge oneself beaten.
Knuckle to. ⎪
Knuckle under. ⎭
Lay down. To relinquish.
Lick the dust. To submit abjectly.
Lower one's flag. To give a sign of submission.
Make a virtue of necessity. To make a pretense of submitting voluntarily when one has to.
Make the best of. To submit with the best possible grace.
Obey, etc. To submit to superior authority. See INSUBORDINATION-OBEDIENCE.
Pay homage to. To submit with reverential regard.
Pocket the affront. To submit to an insult with good grace.
Reel back. To fall back as a sign of being beaten.
Resign. To yield with confidence.
Resign oneself. To submit passively to circumstances over which one has no control.
Retreat. To retire from a position before held.
Shrug the shoulders. To submit with dissatisfaction.
Strike one's colors. To lower one's colors as a sign of surrender.
Strike one's flag. To surrender.
Submit. To yield to power or authority.
Submit with good grace. To submit with an air of graciousness.
Succumb. To yield after resisting.
Suffer judgment by default. To submit to accusations without attempting to disprove them.
Surrender. To yield to another because of his superior strength.
Surrender at discretion. To surrender unconditionally.
Swallow the leek. To be compelled to undergo humiliation.
Swallow the pill. To submit to something unpleasant.
Throw oneself at the feet of. To submit to in an humble and suppliant manner.
Truckle. To yield in an obsequious manner.
Turn the other cheek to. To submit to personal insults without getting offended.
Yield. To give in to the will of another.

YIELDING—*Adjectives.*

Down on one's marrow-bones. Extremely humble.
Downtrodden. Unjustly and cruelly oppressed.
Humble. Given to habitual submission.
Indefensible. That cannot be defended.
Non-resisting. Submitting to everything.
On one's bending knee. Humble and suppliant.
Pliant, etc. Submitting easily. See HARDNESS-SOFTNESS.

Resigned. Given to acquiescing without resistance.
Submissive Given to yielding to the will of others.
Surrendering, etc. See *Verbs.*
Undefended. Having no means of protection against others
Unresisting. Yielding without the slightest opposition
Untenable. That cannot be upheld.

YIELDING—*Phrases.*

Amen, etc. See ASSENT.
Da locum melioribus [L.]. Give place to your betters
Have its own way.
It can't be helped.
Tempori parendum [L.] One must yield to the times

yo"–ho'. Heed. HEED-DISREGARD.
yoicks. To urge on by crying "yoicks," QUEST-EVASION.
yoke. A bond of connection. CONNECTIVE, DUALITY, LIBERTY-SUBJECTION, UNION-DISUNION; **rivet the yoke,** HARSHNESS-MILDNESS.
yo'-kel. A countryman. ADEPT-BUNGLER, GENTILITY-COMMONALTY.
yoke'-mate". A companion under the yoke. MATRIMONY-CELIBACY.
yon. } In that place. REMOTENESS - NEARNESS,
yon'-der. } UNIVERSALITY-PARTICULARITY.
yolk The yellow of an egg. NUTRIMENT-EXCRETION.

yore. Old time. FUTURE-PAST.
York'-shire-man. A native of Yorkshire. CRAFT-ARTLESSNESS.
you. The person, animal, or thing (as personified) addressed. You don't say so, ASTONISHMENT-EXPECTANCE; **you're another,** REPRISAL-RESISTANCE.
young. Pertaining to youth; immature. INFANCY-AGE, NOVELTY-ANTIQUITY. LOVE-HATE.
young'-er. A young person. INFANCY-AGE.
young'-ster. A child. INFANT-VETERAN.
youn'-ker. A youngster. INFANT-VETERAN.
youth. The state or condition of being young; a young man. INFANCY-AGE, INFANT-VETERAN, NOVELTY-ANTIQUITY, STRENGTH-WEAKNESS.
youth'-ful. Pertaining to youth. INFANCY-AGE.
youth'-hood. The condition of being young. INFANCY-AGE.
Yule. Christmas-time. CEREMONIAL, ENTERTAINMENT-WEARINESS, PERIODICITY-IRREGULARITY.
Yule can'-dle. Candle burned at the Yule feast. PORTENT.
Yule log. Log burned Christmas eve. ENTERTAINMENT-WEARINESS.
Yule'-tide". Christmas-time. PERIODICITY-IRREGULARITY.

Z

Zad'-ki-el. In Jewish lore, an angel. SOOTHSAYER.

zaf'-fer. Blue pigment. BLUENESS-ORANGE.

Zam'-bo. The child of a mulatto and a negro, or an Indian and a negro. MIXTURE-HOMOGENEITY.

zam-bom'-ba. Spanish instrument. MUSICAL INSTRUMENTS.

Zam'-i-el. In rabbinical lore, a demon. ANGEL-SATAN.

za'-ny. A buffoon; a fool. SAGE-FOOL.

zapaiero a tu zapato [Sp.] (thɑ-pɑ-ter'-o ɑ tu thɑ-pɑ'-to). Shoemaker, mind thy shoe. PRESUMPTION-OBSEQUIOUSNESS.

zarf. Oriental cup-holder. CONTENTS-RECEIVER.

zeal. Fervor. ACTIVITY-INDOLENCE, DESIRE - DISTASTE, DETERMINATION-VACILLATION, EMOTION.

zeal'-ot. One who is full of zeal. ACTIVITY-INDOLENCE, BIGOTRY-APOSTASY, DETERMINATION-VACILLATION.

zeal'-ot-ry. The conduct of a zealot. BIGOTRY-APOSTASY.

zeal'-ous. Fervent. ACTIVITY-INDOLENCE, EMOTION.

ze'-bra. An ass-like animal. VARIEGATION.

ze'-bu. Indian ox. FAUNA-FLORA.

zeitgeist [G.] (tsɑit'-gɑist). The spirit of the times. SIGN.

zem-in'-dar. An East-Indian landlord. HOLDER.

zem-in'-da-ry. The system of land tenure under a zemindar. PROPERTY.

zen-a'-na. East-Indian harem. DWELLER-HABITATION.

Zend''-A-ves'-ta. The sacred books of Zoroaster. REVELATION-PSEUDOREVELATION.

ze'-nith. The point in the heavens directly overhead; the culminating point. ASTRONOMY, MAGNITUDE-SMALLNESS, TOP-BOTTOM; **in the zenith,** MAGNITUDE-SMALLNESS, REPUTATION-DISCREDIT.

zeph'-yr. The west wind. RIVER-WIND.

ze'-ro. A cipher; naught. PLURALITY-ZERO, SUBSTANCE-NULLITY.

zest. Agreeable excitement of the mind accompanying exercise, mental or physical. PALATABLENESS-UNPALATABLENESS, PLEASURE-PAIN.

ze-tet'-ic. A seeker. INVESTIGATION-ANSWER.

zeug'-ma. Figure of speech. RHETORIC.

Zeus. Greek god. JOVE-FIEND.

zig'-zag''. Having a series of short alternating turns from side to side. AIM-ABERRATION, ANGULARITY, EMBELLISHMENT-DISFIGUREMENT, MIDCOURSE-CIRCUIT, PARALLELISM-INCLINATION, VIBRATION.

Zim'-mer-mann. A Swiss philosopher. **Disciple of** Zimmermann, SOCIABILITY-PRIVACY.

zinc. An element. CHEMISTRY.

zinc'-ite. Zinc ore. CHEMISTRY.

zinc'-o-graph. An etching on zinc. ENGRAVING.

zinc-og'-ra-phy. The art of etching on zinc. ENGRAVING.

zinc-ol'-y-sis. A chemical action. CHEMISTRY.

Zin'-ga-ra. Gipsy. GULL-DECEIVER, WAYFARER-SEAFARER.

Zinn'-i-a. An ornamental flower. FAUNA-FLORA.

Zi'-on. Church of Christ; the heavenly Jerusalem. HEAVEN-HELL, ORTHODOXY-HETERODOXY.

zir'-con. A mineral. EMBELLISHMENT-DISFIGUREMENT.

zo'-cle. A pedestal. SUSPENSION-SUPPORT.

zo'-di-ac. An imaginary belt encircling the heavens. ASTRONOMY, OUTLINE, UNIVERSE.

zo-di'-a-cal. Pertaining to the zodiac. ASTRONOMY.

zo-di'-a-cal light. A disk of faint light surrounding the sun. LUMINARY-SHADE.

zoe mou, sas agapo [Gr.] (zo'-ê mu, sɑs ɑg-ɑ-po'). My life, I love thee. BLANDISHMENT, LOVE-HATE.

Zo'-i-lus. A Greek critic. FLATTERER-DEFAMER.

zoll'-ver-ein''. A union of German states. ASSOCIATION, CONTRACT.

zonam perdidit [L.] (zo'-nam per'-di-dit). He has lost his purse. AFFLUENCE-PENURY.

zone. A belt or area delimited from others. CIRCLE-WINDING, EXTENSION - DISTRICT, LAMINA - FIBER, OUTLINE.

zo-og'-ra-phy. The branch of zoology that describes animals. ZOOLOGY-BOTANY.

zo''-o-hy-gi-an'-tics. The science of medicine for animals. DOMESTICATION-AGRICULTURE.

zo-ol'-a-try. Animal worship. DEVOTION-IDOLATRY.

zo''-o-log'-ic-al. Pertaining to zoology. FAUNA-FLORA; **zoological garden,** DOMESTICATION-AGRICULTURE.

zo-ol'-o-gist. A specialist in zoology. FAUNA-FLORA.

zo-ol'-o-gy. The science which treats of animals. ORGANIZATION-INORGANIZATION, ZOOLOGY-BOTANY.

ZOOLOGY—BOTANY.

Anatomy. The science treating of the structure and organization of living things.

Animal physiology. The science treating of the vital functions of animals.

Anthropology. The science of man in general.

Comparative anatomy. The science comparing the structure and organization of one living thing with another or others.

Comparative physiology. The science comparing the vital functions of one animal with those of another or of others.

Entomology. That branch of zoology that treats of insects.

Entomotomy. That branch of anatomy that treats of insects.

Helminthology. That branch of zoology that treats of worms.

Helminthotomy. That branch of anatomy that treats of worms.

Herpetology. That branch of zoology that treats of reptiles and amphibians.

Herpetotomy. That branch of anatomy that treats of reptiles and amphibians.

Ichthyology. That branch of zoology that treats of fishes.

Algology. The branch of botany that treats of sea-weeds.

Botany. The science of the structure and functions of plants.

Dendrology. The branch of botany that treats of trees.

Fungology. The branch of botany that treats of fungi.

Mycology. The science of fungi.

Phytography. Descriptive botany.

Phytology. See BOTANY.

Phytotomy. Vegetable anatomy.

BOTANY—*Associated Nouns.*

Botanic garden, etc. A place where plants are grown. See DOMESTICATION-AGRICULTURE.

Flora. The goddess of flowers; flowers.

Herbarium. A collection of pressed plants arranged for scientific study.

Hortus siccus [L.]. A dry garden; a herbarium.

Pomona. The goddess of fruits; fruits.

ZOOLOGY—BOTANY—*Continued*.

Ichthyotomy. The branch of anatomy that treats of fishes.
Malacology. The branch of zoology that treats of mollusks.
Malacotomy. The branch of anatomy that treats of mollusks.
Morphology. The science treating of the form and structure of animals and plants.
Ophiology. The branch of herpetology that treats of serpents.
Ophiotomy. The branch of anatomy that treats of serpents.
Ornithology. The branch of zoology that treats of birds.
Ornithotomy. The branch of anatomy that treats of birds.
Oryctology. The study of skeletons and fossils dug out of the earth.
Paleontology. The science of fossils found in the crust of the earth.
Taxidermy. The art of preparing and preserving the skins of animals so that the shape and appearance of the animal may be represented.
Zoography. A description of animals with their forms and habits.
Zoology. The science of the structure and functions of all animals.
Zoonomy. The science of the laws of animal life as distinguished from those of vegetable life.
Zootomy. The dissection of animals.

ZOOLOGY—*Nouns of Agent*.

Zoologist, etc. A student of zoology. See *Nouns*.

zo-on′-o-my. The laws of animal life. ZOOLOGY-BOTANY.

zo-oph′-o-rus. A frieze with figures of animals carved upon it. TOP-BOTTOM.

zo′-o-phyte. An animal forming branching or tree-like colonies. FAUNA-FLORA.

zo″-o-thap′-sis. Premature burial. LIFE-FUNERAL.

zo-ot′-o-my. The dissection of animals. ZOOLOGY-BOTANY.

Zo″-ro-as′-ter. One of the great religious teachers of the East. REVELATION-PSEUDOREVELATION.

BOTANY—*Nouns of Agent*.

Botanist, etc. A student of botany. See *Nouns*.
Herbalist. One skilled in the study of plants.
Herbarist.
Herbist. } A herbalist.
Herborist.

BOTANY—*Verbs*.

Botanize. To study plant-life.
Herborize. To search for plants.

BOTANY—*Adjectives*.

Botanical, etc. Pertaining to botany. See *Nouns*

ZOOLOGY—*Continued*.

ZOOLOGY—*Adjectives*.

Zoological, etc. Pertaining to zoology. See *Nouns*.

Zou-ave′. A light-armed French infantryman. BELLIGERENT.

zounds. God's wounds: a corruption used as an exclamation. ASTONISHMENT-EXPECTANCE, FAVORITE-ANGER.

Zu′-lu. South-African savage. GENTILITY-COMMONALTY, BENEFACTOR-EVILDOER, TURBULENCE-CALMNESS.

zy-mot′-ic. Morbific fermentation. HEALTH-SICKNESS, HEALTHINESS-UNHEALTHINESS.

Supplement To

MARCH'S THESAURUS-DICTIONARY

by

R. A. GOODWIN

INTRODUCTION TO THE SUPPLEMENT

This Supplement lists and defines some 1800 words and phrases that have come into general use since the turn of the twentieth century. These include many vigorous and expressive creations of informal language (*behind the eight ball, clobber, cloak-and-dagger, debunk, in the groove, pin-up, slap-happy, snafu, zip, zoom,* and many others), scientific and technical terms that have aroused popular interest (*hormones, vitamins, inferiority complex, existentialism, surrealism, relativity, mass-energy equation, neutrons, radio-astronomy, transistor, turboprop,* etc.), terms that have a flourishing metaphoric life beyond their basic technical meaning (*spark plug, nose dive, chain reaction,* and others), and a great miscellany of terms reflecting new ways of living and turbulent twentieth-century history (*broadcast, picture tube, hardtop, streamline, king-size, horse opera, soap opera, roadblock, brain washing, witch hunt, flying saucer, New Deal, gremlins, foxhole, iron curtain, bait advertising, plastic surgery, quisling, deepfreeze,* and so on).

This new material is, for the most part, handled in much the same way as the basic material in the original Thesaurus. Since, however, many of the terms are technical in some degree, and since in many cases the entries involve extensions of meaning of words that appear in the original book, the entries in the Supplement are defined more fully and precisely than was done in the original work. Furthermore, some innovations were necessary in order to key the new material effectively to the material in the original Thesaurus. These are discussed in the following paragraphs.

HOW TO USE THE SUPPLEMENT

(1). In many cases it is not the word itself but the meaning that is new. This fact is indicated in the Supplement by placing an asterisk (*) immediately before the entry. For instance, in the entry:

*in-trigue'. To interest, fascinate, excite the curiosity of. EXCITATION. the asterisk indicates that the word **intrigue** also appears in the original Thesaurus and that what is specifically new in the Supplement is the new meaning.

Similarly, a word that is in the original may be entered, with an asterisk, in the Supplement in order to list and define a new phrase in which it appears. For instance, the entry ***green** appears in the Supplement, not with any new meaning of the word itself but in order to list and define the phrases **green light** and **green thumb**.

(2.) Cross-references, in caps and small caps, at the end of the entries tell the headings of the word lists where synonyms, antonyms, and associated terms are gathered. A cross-reference ordinarily refers back to the original Thesaurus. For instance, in the entry:

husk'-y. Rugged, strong, strongly built. STRENGTH-WEAKNESS. the words STRENGTH-WEAKNESS indicate that in the original Thesaurus there is a list of terms, under that title, relating to strength and weakness.

(3.) The symbol # before a cross-reference indicates that the word list in which it and related terms appear is in the Supplement. The lists that appear in the Supplement alone are AUTOMOBILE, AVIATION, ELECTRONICS, MOTION PICTURES, NUCLEAR PHYSICS, and RADIO-TELEVISION. For example, in the entry:

tel'-e-cast''. To broadcast by television; a television broadcast. #RADIO-TELEVISION. the symbol # indicates that the list of words relating to radio and television is grouped under the heading RADIO-TELEVISION in the Supplement.

In the entry: **em-plane'.** To get aboard an airplane, to go away in an airplane. ARRIVAL-DEPARTURE, #AVIATION you are referred both to older words dealing with arrival and departure, generally, under the heading ARRIVAL-DEPARTURE in the main part of the book, and to the aviation terms under the heading AVIATION in the Supplement.

(4.) In a number of instances where the Supplement contains a significant number of additional synonyms or associated terms for one of the word lists that appear in the original Thesaurus, the heading of that list is repeated in the Supplement with a list of the new terms of the Supplement that relate to the same subject. These headings in the Supplement are identified by the asterisk (*). For instance, the original Thesaurus contains a list of words under the heading SUCCESS-FAILURE. A fair number of new terms of that category have accumulated in the Supplement, and they are listed under the heading *SUCCESS-FAILURE at its alphabetical position in the Supplement. That is, to find all of the words on this topic, consult both the original SUCCESS-FAILURE list in the original Thesaurus and the supplementary list at the heading *SUCCESS-FAILURE in the Supplement.

SYMBOLS

To recapitulate what is said about the use of symbols in the foregoing explanation:

* before a word entry (e.g., *in-trigue') means that the word also appears in the original Thesaurus; before the title of a word list (e.g., *SUCCESS-FAILURE) it means that there is also a word list under the same heading in the original work.

before a cross-reference (e.g., #AVIATION) means that the word list appears in the Supplement only.

Supplement To

MARCH'S THESAURUS-DICTIONARY

A

A-bomb. Atomic bomb; specifically, the fission bomb. #NUCLEAR PHYSICS, WEAPON.

*ab-stract'. Relating to art which does not attempt to depict external realities but creates effects through handling of the materials (e.g., geometric forms or musical tones) alone. DELINEATION-CARICATURE, NATURE-ART.

*ab-strac'-tion. A product of abstract art. DELINEATION-CARICATURE, NATURE-ART.

*ac"-a-dem'-ic. Academic freedom, freedom to teach what the teacher believes is true, without interference or threat of discharge, EDUCATION-MISTEACHING, LIBERTY-SUBJECTION.

ac-cel'-er-a"-tor. A device for regulating the speed of an automobile, #AUTOMOBILE; **atomic accelerator,** any of several devices for accelerating atomic particles to high speeds as projectiles for disintegrating or transmuting atomic nuclei, #NUCLEAR PHYSICS; **linear accelerator,** an atomic accelerator in which protons or other particles are accelerated in crossing the gaps in a line of tubular electrodes.

*ace. A fighter pilot who has shot down at least five (in World War I, three) enemy planes; a leader, an expert; excelling, first-class. #AVIATION, BELLIGERENT, GOODNESS-BADNESS, SKILL-UNSKILLFULNESS.

*ac'-id. Acid test, a test of authenticity, a severe test, TRIAL.

ack'-ack". Anti-aircraft fire; anti-aircraft guns. ATTACK-DEFENSE, #AVIATION, WEAPON.

ac'-ti-vate. To treat (various substances) so as to make possible or to improve certain chemical, filtering, or sewage-disposal operations; to make radioactive; to bring (a military unit) to active status by assigning the necessary personnel and equipment. CHEMISTRY, FIGHTING-CONCILIATION, #NUCLEAR PHYSICS.

ac'-tiv-ism. A policy of vigorous action or of demanding action; any philosophical position in which activity is a basic pinciple. ACTION-PASSIVENESS.

*ACTIVITY-INDOLENCE

ACTIVITY

Razzle-dazzle. Fast and bewildering or spectacular action or performance.
Workout. A strenuous exertion; practice or exercise.

ACTIVITY—Nouns of Agent

Ball of fire. A person of great energy and brisk action.
Eager beaver. An enthusiastic or zealous person; one who volunteers for extra work.
Go-getter. An enterprising, aggressive, generally successful person.
Live wire. An active and enterprising person.
Spark plug. A person who inspires others, or stirs them to activity, or is the leading spirit.

ACTIVITY—Verbs

Butt in. To interfere, intrude.
High-pressure. To compel; to advertise or sell by energetic and insistent methods.
Horn in. To intrude, interfere, meddle.
Kibitz. To interfere, meddle.
Play ball. To start or get on with the game; to get busy.

ACTIVITY—Adjectives

High-pressure. Energetic, insistent.
Peppy. Energetic, lively, brisk, spirited.
Zippy. Energetic, brisk, lively, vigorous.

INDOLENCE

Featherbedding. Requiring the hiring of men who will be idle at least part of the time.

INDOLENCE—Nouns of Agent

Barfly. A person who loiters in barrooms.
Gold-brick, gold-bricker. A shirker.
Playboy. A man whose principal interest is in play or love-making or dissipation.
Slacker. A person who shirks or evades work or a duty or responsibility.
Zombie. A person who shows no animation, drive, intelligence, or will; a group or institution which has no initiative or powers.

INDOLENCE—Verbs

Putter. To potter, idle, trifle, dawdle; to move (about) aimlessly or ineffectually.

ad. Advertisement. *PUBLICITY.

*ADAGE-NONSENSE

NONSENSE

Baloney. Nonsense.
Bilge. Nonsense, foolishness.
Blooper. An error, usually amusing and often embarrassing, made in some public utterance.
Boner. A blunder, a foolish error.
Bromide. A trite saying.
Bull. Idle talk.
Bunk. Buncombe, nonsense.
Corn. Stereotyped, trite, tiresomely sentimental stories, behavior, etc.
Double talk. Nonsense containing enough sensible words to seem serious; deceptive or ambiguous statements.

Gobbledygook. Pompous, stilted, and involved language.
Hogwash. Nonsense, idle talk.
Hokum. Nonsense, bunk.
Hooey. Nonsense.
Spoonerism. An accidental mix-up of parts of two or more words.
Tommyrot. Nonsense, bosh, rubbish, foolishness.

NONSENSE—Adjectives

Screwball. Eccentric, irrational, erratic, unconventional, zany.
Screwy. Irrational, eccentric, absurd, preposterous.
Wacky, whacky. Eccentric, unconventional, irrational,

ad'-dict. A person addicted to some habit, such as the use of drugs. HABIT-DESUETUDE.

ad"-lib'. To extemporize (e.g. lines of a play, music, or remarks in any public appearance). PREDETERMINA-TION-IMPULSE, PREPARATION-NONPREPARATION.

ad'-man". A person engaged in advertising. * PUBLICITY.

*aer'-i-al. An antenna. #RADIO-TELEVISION.

a-fi"-cio-na'-do. A fan, devotee. * APPROVAL-DISAP-PROVAL, DESIRE-DISTASTE.

af'-ter-bur"-ner. A device for injecting and burning additional fuel in the hot exhaust gases from a turbojet engine and thus increasing speed. #AVIATION.

af'-ter-ef-fect". An effect that appears some time after its cause; a secondary effect that follows the principal effect. CAUSE-EFFECT.

agent provocateur [F.]. An agent employed to incite a suspected person or group to commit an offense for which he or they may be punished. *ENLIGHTENMENT-SECRECY.

ai'-ler-on. A hinged portion of the wing of an airplane which can be moved to control the balance of the plane. #AVIATION.

*air. Relating to aircraft and aviation, e.g., *air attack, air base, air-borne, air fleet, air mail, air map, air route,* #AVIATION; relating to radio or television, #RADIO-TELEVISION; **air conditioning,** treatment of air (most often, by cooling and drying) so as to de-liver it to a room or building at desired temperature and humidity, DAMPNESS-DRYNESS, HEATING-COOLING; **air foil,** any part of an airplane, such as a wing, aileron, or rudder, which because of surface presented to the air helps to lift or hold up or control the movement of the plane, #AVIATION; **air force,** part of a country's military establishment which operates and maintains aircraft, #AVIATION, BELLIGERENT; **air lane,** a route through the air over which aircraft are operated, especially a route with favorable air conditions, #AVIA-TION; **air line** or **airline,** a company operating air-planes for transportation of passengers and cargo; the system of routes over which such a company's planes are operated, #AVIATION; **air liner,** a passenger air-plane operated by an air line, #AVIATION; **air pocket,** any local condition of the air which makes an airplane drop suddenly, #AVIATION, WATER-AIR; **air raid,** an attack, usually a bombing attack, by enemy aircraft, #AVIATION, ATTACK-DEFENSE; **air-raid shelter,** a place provided and designated for refuge during an air raid, REFUGE-PITFALL, SECURITY-INSECURITY; **air speed,** the speed of an aircraft in relation to the air through which it moves, #AVIATION, SWIFTNESS-SLOW-NESS; **on the air,** broadcast or being broadcast by radio or television, #RADIO-TELEVISION.

air'-craft". Airplanes and airships; an airplane or an airship, #AVIATION, CONVEYANCE-VESSEL; **aircraft car-rier,** a vessel which is a floating base for aircraft, #AVIATION, BELLIGERENT, CONVEYANCE-VESSEL.

air'-field". A tract of land where airplanes land and take off. #AVIATION.

air'-lift". Transportation by air; especially, maintenance of a supply line by air where other transportation is impossible. #AVIATION, TRANSFER.

air'-plane". A heavier-than-air vehicle which travels through the air. #AVIATION, CONVEYANCE-VESSEL.

air'-port". A place for aircraft to land and to take off, with facilities for loading and unloading passengers and cargo and for servicing the aircraft. #AVIATION, AR-RIVAL-DEPARTURE.

air'-ship". A lighter-than-air vehicle with machinery for driving and steering it through the air. #AVIATION, CONVEYANCE-VESSEL.

air'-sick". Ill as a result of flying in an aircraft. #AVIATION, HEALTH-SICKNESS.

air'-strip". A runway for airplanes; a strip of land, often prepared under emergency conditions, for use as a landing field in wartime. #AVIATION.

*air'-tight'. Having no weak points or loopholes (in a defense, an argument, or the like). ATTACK-DEFENSE, SECURITY-INSECURITY.

air'-way". A designated route for an airplane flight; a channel of a certain frequency for use by a desig-nated radio or television station. #AVIATION, #RADIO-TELEVISION.

*a-lert'. An air-raid alarm, or the period while it lasts; to warn against an air raid; to warn or give notice of some expected event. ALARM, SECURITY-INSECURITY, WARNING.

*al'-i-bi. An excuse; to make an excuse for. JUSTIFI-CATION-CHARGE, PRETEXT.

*all. All in, very tired, exhausted, MIGHT-IMPOTENCE, WEARINESS-REFRESHMENT; **all-out,** using all one's abilities and resources. COMPLETION-NONCOMPLETION, TOIL-RELAXATION.

al-ler'-gic. Having an allergy; finding another person or some thing unpleasant or objectionable. * APPROVAL-DISAPPROVAL, DESIRE-DISTASTE, HEALTH-SICKNESS.

al'-ler-gy. Abnormal sensitiveness (resulting in asthma, hay fever, hives, or other disorder) to certain foods, pollen, hair, or other substances, or to physical condi-tions or emotional or mental states. HEALTH-SICKNESS, REMEDY-BANE.

*al'-pha. Alpha particle, one of the particles given off in the radioactive decay of heavy elements such as radium and uranium (the nucleus of a helium atom), #NUCLEAR PHYSICS.

A.M. Amplitude modulation, the older and more common method of sending radio signals (the other is F.M.). #RADIO-TELEVISION.

a-mi'-no ac'-ids. Organic compounds which are the main components of proteins. BIOLOGY, CHEMISTRY.

am-phib'-i-an. Amphibious; an airplane capable of taking off from and landing on either land or water. #AVIATION.

*an'-gel. A financial backer, especially of a theatrical venture. LABOR-CAPITAL, OBSTRUCTION-HELP.

*an'-gle. A point of view or special interest, as in a news story or business transaction; to write a news story so as to serve one's point of view or special interest. DECISION-MISJUDGMENT.

*an'-i-ma"-ted. Animated cartoon, a motion picture made by photographing a series of drawings, #MOTION PICTURES.

*an"-i-ma'-tion. The making of an animated cartoon. #MOTION PICTURES.

An'-nie Oak'-ley. A complimentary ticket or pass. GIVING-RECEIVING.

an-noun'-cer. A person who makes announcements on radio and television programs, especially to identify the station, introduce performers, and make explanatory comments. #RADIO-TELEVISION.

*an-ten'-na. An apparatus, usually of wire or wires, for sending or receiving the waves by which radio and television signals are transmitted. #RADIO-TELEVISION.

an"-ti-air'-craft". Used for defense against enemy air-planes. ATTACK-DEFENSE, #AVIATION.

an"-ti-bi-ot'-ic. A substance obtained from living orga-nisms (notably fungi and bacteria), used in the treat-ment or prevention of disease. BIOLOGY, REMEDY-BANE.

an'-ti-bod"-y. A substance formed in the body and found chiefly in the blood, which combats a disease by attack-ing a bacterium, virus, or other parasite, or its poison. ANATOMY, BIOLOGY.

an'-ti-freeze". A liquid with a low freezing point used in the cooling system of an internal-combustion engine to keep the cooling liquid from freezing in cold weather. #AUTOMOBILE.

an"-ti-his'-ta-mine. A drug used in the treatment of the symptoms of allergy and the common cold. REMEDY-BANE.

apartheid. A policy of racial discrimination and segregation in South Africa. INCLUSION-OMISSION.

ap-pease'-ment. A policy of conciliation even at the expense of some moral principle, in the hope of avoiding aggression or war. PRESUMPTION-OBSEQUIOUS-NESS, VARIANCE-ACCORD.

*APPROVAL—DISAPPROVAL

APPROVAL

Blurb. A highly laudatory announcement.
Oscar. A statuette awarded annually in the motion-picture industry.
Plug. A favorable mention.
Pulitzer prize. A prize awarded annually for journalistic or literary work.

APPROVAL—*Associated Nouns*

Aficionado. A fan, devotee.
Fan. An ardent admirer.
Rooter. A supporter, booster, adherent.

APPROVAL—*Verbs*

Go overboard for. To be wildly enthusiastic about, to approve without reservation.
Plug. To advertise or publicize persistently; to help popularize (a song) by repeated use.
Root for. To cheer, applaud, encourage, support.

APPROVAL—*Adjectives*

Sold on. In favor of, convinced of.

DISAPPROVAL

Kickback. An objection, an unfavorable reaction.
Raspberry, razzberry. An expression of disapproval, dislike, etc.
Razz. Disapproval, criticism, derision.

DISAPPROVAL—*Verbs*

Bawl out. To scold, reprimand.
Pan. To criticize severely.
Raise the roof. To protest or complain vehemently.
Razz. To criticize, deride, tease.
Smear. To malign, vilify, besmirch, defame, slander.
Take a dim view of. To disapprove, suspect, be skeptical or pessimistic about.

DISAPPROVAL—*Adjectives, Phrases*

Allergic. Finding another person or some thing unpleasant or objectionable.
In Dutch. In disfavor, in trouble.
In the doghouse. Out of favor.

art'-y. Claiming to be artistic; too demonstrative in attention to art. NATURE-ART, SOCIETY-AFFECTATION.

a-so'-cial. Not social; withdrawing from contact with other people; self-centered; inconsiderate of others. SOCIABILITY-PRIVACY, UNSELFISHNESS-SELFISHNESS.

*as-sem'-bly. Assembly line, machines and workmen placed so that a product is assembled in successive steps as it passes from one to another, LABOR-CAPITAL, WORK-SHOP.

as"-tro-nom'-i-cal, as"-tro-nom'-ic. Astoundingly large, like the numbers commonly used in astronomy. MAGNITUDE-SMALLNESS.

*at'-om. Atom bomb or atomic bomb, a bomb in which the explosion is caused by the release of energy in a nuclear reaction: the term usually means a fission bomb rather than a fusion bomb, #NUCLEAR PHYSICS, WEAPONS.

*a-tom'-ic. Relating to atoms (e.g., *atomic nuclei*), atomic energy (e.g., *atomic power*), or atomic bombs (e.g., *atomic warfare*); atomic age, the era dating from the discovery of means of utilizing atomic energy; atomic energy, the energy obtained from nuclear reactions; atomic number, a number (corresponding to the number of electrons rotating around the nucleus of an atom) determining the chemical identity of the element (e.g. the atomic number of uranium is 92, the atomic number of radium is 88); atomic weight, a number (e.g. for uranium 238.07) expressing the weight of an element in relation to oxygen (atomic weight 16). CHEMISTRY, #NUCLEAR PHYSICS.

a-ton'-al. Not organized in accordance with a musical key or tonal center. MELODY-DISSONANCE, MUSIC.

au'-di-o. Relating to sound, especially to record-playing equipment or the sound apparatus of a television set. HEARING-DEAFNESS, #RADIO-TELEVISION, SOUND-SILENCE.

au-di'-tion. A trial performance of a speaker, singer, or instrumentalist; to give (such a person) a tryout. TRIAL.

*au"-to-mat'-ic. Automatic pilot, an automatic device for keeping an airplane level and flying on a straight course, #AVIATION.

au"-to-ma'-tion. Automatic control; operation of machinery with special devices which regulate the operation to meet prescribed requirements and to respond to changing conditions. LABOR-CAPITAL, WORKSHOP.

*au'-to-mo-bile". #AUTOMOBILE.

AUTOMOBILE

Accelerator. A device for regulating speed.
Balloon tire. A tire or large dimensions and low pressure.
Car. An automobile.
Carburetor. An apparatus for mixing air and gasoline to make the fuel mixture.
Chassis. The supporting framework, including wheels and machinery.
Choke. A device for reducing air supply to a carburetor to enrich the fuel mixture when starting the engine.
Convertible. An automobile with a folding top.
Coupé. An enclosed, two-door, essentially single-seated body type.
Dashboard. A panel with gauges and instruments.
Duck. A military truck and barge to travel either on land or on water.
Fender. The guard over a wheel.
Flivver. A small, cheap automobile.
Fluid drive. A hydraulic drive that eliminates manual gear shifting.
Gearshift. A device for connecting a motor to any of several sets of gears.
Half-track. A military vehicle with caterpillar tracks in place of rear wheels.

Hardtop. A body style with fixed top but no post between front and rear windows.
High. The high or fastest gear.
Hood. The hinged cover over an engine.
Hot rod. An automobile specially prepared for high speed.
Jalopy. An automobile which is old and in poor condition.
Jeep. A small, rugged, powerful military automobile, or civilian car patterned after it.
Jitney. A bus or automobile which carries passengers for a small fare.
Knee action. A type of suspension of the front wheels permitting each wheel to move up and down independently.
Limousine. A large, luxurious automobile.
Low. The lowest or slowest gear.
Overdrive. A gear arrangement which under certain conditions maintains speed with less power consumption.
Pickup. A small truck with open body for light hauling.
Roadster. An open automobile with a single seat.
Rumble seat. A folding extra seat behind the enclosed seat.
Sedan. A closed body type having front and rear seats in a single compartment.
Spark plug. A device which emits a spark and explodes the fuel mixture.

AUTOMOBILE—*Continued*

Speedometer. An instrument indicating the speed.

Station wagon. An enclosed body type with a long rear section for seats or for light hauling.

Tonneau. An enclosed rear part of a body containing the passenger seats; a body including such a compartment.

Touring car. An open automobile with front and rear seats and often a folding top.

Tractor. A self-propelled work vehicle; a truck unit for pulling trailers.

Trailer. A vehicle for hauling loads, pulled by an automobile, truck, or tractor; a vehicle containing living quarters, pulled by an automobile.

Wheelbase. The length between front and rear axles.

Automobile—*Verbs*

Backfire. To explode prematurely or in the wrong place.

Hitchhike. To travel by asking for rides on a highway.

Honk. To sound an automobile horn.

Knock. To make a noise indicating wear or faulty operation in an engine.

Motor. To travel by or ride in an automobile.

Recap. To renovate a worn tire by affixing new rubber over the worn surface.

Retread. To renovate a worn tire by removing the old rubber surface and placing new rubber over the old fabric.

Soup up. To make alterations so as to increase power and speed.

Thumb. To hitchhike, to solicit rides by signaling with the thumb.

Automobile—*Associated Terms*

Antifreeze. A liquid used to keep the cooling liquid from freezing.

Automotive. Pertaining to motor vehicles.

au″-to-mo′-tive. Self-propelling; pertaining to motor vehicles. #Automobile.

Back-seat driver. A person who insists on giving instructions to the driver.

Blowout. The bursting of a tire.

Camelback. A compound of reclaimed or synthetic rubber and a small amount of natural rubber used for retreading or recapping tires.

Car pool. An arrangement to take turns driving to work or to public transportation.

Carport. An automobile shelter adjoining a house.

Carsick. Ill from riding in a motorcar.

Drag race. A short race (usually with souped-up motors) which is largely a test of acceleration.

Filling station, gas station, service station. A place where gasoline and oil are sold and other services provided.

Flat tire. A pneumatic tire which has been deflated.

Gas. Gasoline.

Hit-and-run driver. A driver involved in an accident who leaves without giving aid or reporting the accident.

Hitting on all four (six, eight) (cylinders). Working smoothly and efficiently.

Honk. The sound of an automobile horn.

Joy ride. A pleasure ride, especially a wild and irresponsible ride.

Knock. A noise indicating wear or faulty operation in an engine.

Motorcade. A procession of automobiles.

Octane. A constituent of petroleum.

Octane number. A measure of the quality of gasoline.

Pickup. Acceleration.

Recap. A recapped tire (see *Verbs*).

Retread. A retreaded tire (see *Verbs*).

Road hog. A person who takes more of the road than he should.

a″-vi-a′-tion. The operation of heavier-than-air flying machines. #Aviation.

AVIATION

Afterburner. A device for increasing speed of a turbojet engine.

Aileron. A hinged portion of a wing.

Air. Relating to aircraft and aviation.

Aircraft. Airplanes and airships; an airplane or an airship.

Airfield. A tract of land where planes land and take off.

Air foil. A part which helps to lift, hold up, or control movement of a plane.

Air lane. A route over which aircraft are operated.

Airlift. Transportation by air, especially where other transportation is impossible.

Air line, airline. A company operating airplanes, or its system of routes.

Air liner. A passenger plane operated by an air line.

Airplane, plane. A heavier-than-air vehicle which travels through the air.

Airport. A place for aircraft to land and take off, with facilities for loading and unloading and for servicing the aircraft.

Airship. A lighter-than-air vehicle.

Air speed. Speed in relation to the air.

Airstrip. A runway; a strip of land for use as a landing field in wartime.

Airway. A designated route.

Amphibian. A plane which can take off from and land on either land or water.

Automatic pilot, gyropilot. An automatic device for keeping a plane level and on a straight course.

Aviation. The operation of heavier-than-air flying machines.

Barrel roll. A complete rotation on the long axis.

Beam. A radio signal indicating the course.

Blimp. A small airship.

Blind flying, instrument flying. Flying entirely on information supplied by instruments.

Ceiling. The height to which a certain plane can climb; the highest point above the earth from which the ground can be seen.

Chassis. The supporting framework (the main landing gear) of a plane.

Cockpit. A small space containing the pilot's seat and usually seats for one or several other persons.

Condensation trail, contrail. The visible trail or vapor left in the wake of jet-propelled airplanes.

Contact flying. Flying with the surface below in view.

Deicer. A device for preventing or removing formation of ice on airplanes.

Drone. An airplane without a pilot and controlled by radio signals.

Equitime point. The point at which a pilot may choose (as in case of trouble) either to turn back or to go on.

Flap. A hinged addition to a wing which can be set at different angles.

Flight. Operation of an aircraft; a trip in an aircraft; a recurring trip in the regular operation of an air line; a tactical unit of two or more planes.

Flying field. A landing place which does not have all the facilities of an airport.

Flying fortress. A large bomber and fighter plane.

Fuselage. The body of an airplane, not including wings and tail.

Glider. An aircraft similar to an airplane but having no motor.

Gondola. A car suspended from a dirigible balloon.

Grasshopper. A small, unarmed plane for scouting and directing artillery fire.

Ground crew. Workmen who service and repair airplanes.

Ground loop. A sharp, unexpected turn while moving over the ground.

Hangar. A shed sheltering planes or airships.

Heading. The direction in which a plane is headed.

Helicopter. An aircraft lifted and moved by a propeller rotating in a horizontal plane.

Heliport. An airport for helicopters.

Howgozit curve. A graph giving the pilot a summary of information on distance, elapsed time, and fuel consumption.

Hydroplane, seaplane. An airplane equipped to take off from and to land on water.

Immelmann turn. A maneuver in which an airplane makes a U turn in a vertical plane by making a half loop and then righting the plane.

Jalopy. An airplane which is old and in poor condition.

Jato, JATO. Jet-assisted take-off, the addition of rocket units to assist an airplane in taking off.

Jet. A stream of heated air and combustion gases ejected to the rear to provide thrust, as in *jet aircraft, jet-assisted take-off, jet engine, jet plane, jet-propelled, jet propulsion;* a jet airplane.

Landing gear. Wheels or pontoons which support an airplane in landing and while it remains on land or water.

AVIATION—Continued

Landing strip. A long, narrow runway on which airplanes take off and land.

Monoplane. An airplane supported by a single pair of wings.

Nose dive. A sudden fall with the fore part pointed toward the earth.

Off the beam. Off the course.

On the beam. On course.

Power dive. A dive with the engines running.

Pulse-jet engine. A jet engine operating in rapid cycles of explosions from build-up of pressure in a chamber where air and fuel are mixed.

Ram jet. A jet engine in which forward motion rams air into the combustion chamber where fuel is added and the mixture ignited in a continuous operation.

Rocket engine. An engine propelling an aircraft or missile by ejection of expanded hot gases and carrying its own oxygen.

Rotor. An assembly of rotating blades or other parts which lifts an aircraft such as a helicopter.

Runway. A level strip of ground on which planes land and take off.

Slip stream. The stream of air pushed back by the propeller.

Tail spin. A steep fall or descent with nose down and the tail moving in circles.

Three-point landing. A perfect landing.

Turbojet. A jet engine with a turbine and an air compressor.

Turboprop. A jet engine which drives a propeller.

Undercarriage. Landing gear.

Zeppelin. A large dirigible airship.

Zoom. A sudden climb.

AVIATION—Nouns of Agent

Ace. A fighter pilot who has shot down at least five enemy planes.

Aviator, flier, flyer. A person who operates an airplane.

Copilot. The assistant pilot.

Pilot. A person who operates or is qualified to operate an aircraft; the person in command of a flight.

AVIATION—Verbs

Bail out. To jump from an airplane in a parachute.

Bank. To tip a plane toward one side when making a turn.

Buzz. To fly a plane very low over (a field, a building, etc.).

Conk out. To fail (said of an engine).

Crab. To head toward the side from which the wind is blowing to avoid being blown off course.

Emplane. To get aboard or go away in an airplane.

Feather. To change the pitch of (a propeller) so that it turns without moving the airplane.

Ferry. To fly an airplane to a point where it is to be delivered.

Flatten out. To bring a plane to a horizontal position; to take a horizontal position.

Fly. To operate or ride in an aircraft.

Give it the gun. To speed up.

Glide, volplane. To come down slowly without using the motor.

Ground. To keep an aircraft or flyer from leaving the ground; to take away a pilot's license.

Gun. To open the throttle so as to increase speed.

Hedge-hop. To fly a plane close to the ground.

Nose over. To turn over in a forward motion.

Pancake. To level off a short distance above the ground and land flat in a quick vertical drop.

Peel off. To veer away from a formation to make a dive or to land.

Pressurize. To keep the air pressure inside (an airplane) up to normal by means of a compressor.

Rev. To change the speed of (a motor or engine).

Rev down. To decrease the speed of.

Rev up. To increase the speed of.

Solo. To fly an airplane alone.

Stall. To lose the speed necessary to fly or to fly under control.

Take off. To go up into the air.

Taxi. To move about or run on the ground or water.

Zoom. To climb suddenly and steeply; to make (an airplane) zoom.

AVIATION—Associated Terms

Ack-ack. Anti-aircraft fire or guns.

Aircraft carrier, flattop. A vessel which is a floating base for aircraft.

Air force. Part of a military establishment operating and maintaining aircraft.

Air pocket. A local condition of the air which makes a plane drop suddenly.

Air raid. An attack by enemy aircraft.

Airsick. Ill as a result of flying.

Anti-aircraft. Used for defense against enemy planes.

Blackout. Fainting under some conditions of flight.

Dive bombing. Releasing a bomb or bombs from an airplane which dives at a steep angle toward its target.

Dry run. A practice bombing flight on which no bombs are actually dropped.

Glide bombing. Bombing while descending at a shallow angle.

Gremlins. Elves or gnomes who get the blame when things go wrong.

Hump. A mountain range that must be crossed on an airplane route.

Mach number. The ratio of speed in relation to the speed of sound.

O'clock. Referring to an imaginary clock dial as a means of indicating direction.

Oxygen mask. A device supplying additional oxygen to aviators flying at great heights in thin atmosphere.

Rev. A revolution (of a motor or engine).

Rip cord. A cord pulled to open a parachute.

Skywriting. The forming of letters or figures in the sky with smoke or vapor ejected from an airplane.

---

a'-vi-a"-tor. A person who operates an airplane. #AVIATION.

A.W.O.L. or **AWOL.** Absent without leave. PRESENCE-ABSENCE.

*****ax'-is.** An alignment of several countries for mutual support and furtherance of common interests; the Axis, in World War II, the alliance opposing the United States and its allies. ANTAGONISM-CONCURRENCE, ASSOCIATION, COOPERATION-OPPOSITION, INTERDEPENDENCE.

B

Bab'-bitt. The main character in a novel of that name by Sinclair Lewis; a businessman whose thought and action are bounded by middle-class respectability and the goal of business success. CONVENTIONALITY-UNCONVENTIONALITY, MEDIOCRITY.

ba'-by-sit". To stay with a child during a short absence of its parents.

back'-drop". Curtain at the rear of a stage; background. ACTING, ANTERIORITY-POSTERIORITY.

back'-fire". To explode (in a gasoline engine) prematurely or in the wrong place; to get an unexpected and wrong result. #AUTOMOBILE, CAUSE-EFFECT, *SUCCESS-FAILURE.

*****back'-log".** A reserve or accumulation of unfilled orders, work, or the like. COMPLETION-NONCOMPLETION, ENTIRETY-DEFICIENCY.

back'-seat" driv'-er. A person who is not driving but insists on giving instructions to the driver. ADVICE, #AUTOMOBILE, COOPERATION-OPPOSITION.

back'-stage'. Behind the scenes, concealed from public view. ACTING, *ENLIGHTENMENT-SECRECY, MANIFESTATION-LATENCY.

back'-track". To go back, withdraw. ADVANCE-RETROGRESSION, APPROACH-WITHDRAWAL.

*****ba'-con.** Bring home the bacon, to succeed, *SUCCESS-FAILURE.

*****bag.** Hold the bag, be left holding the bag, to be left empty-handed; to be left to suffer the consequences, *GULL-DECEIVER; in the bag, sure, certain, CERTAINTY-DOUBT.

*bail. Bail out, to jump from an airplane in a parachute, #AVIATION, ESCAPE.

*bait. Bait advertising, advertising an article at a very low price with no true intent to sell it but to sell a more expensive article to anyone who responds, BUYING-SALE, *PUBLICITY, *TRUTHFULNESS-FRAUD.

*ball. Ball of fire, an intensely hot luminous sphere formed in an atomic explosion; a person of great energy and brisk action, *ACTIVITY-INDOLENCE, MIGHT-IMPOTENCE, #NUCLEAR PHYSICS, *SUCCESS-FAILURE; play ball, to start or go on with the game; to get busy; to cooperate, work together, *ACTIVITY-INDOLENCE, ANTAGONISM-CONCURRENCE, BEGINNING-END, ENTERTAINMENT-WEARINESS, OCCUPATION.

bal-lis'-tic mis'-sile. A rocket designed to carry a load of explosive, an engine to propel it a long distance in a trajectory high above the earth, and a control mechanism to guide it to an enemy target. WEAPON.

*bal-loon'. Balloon tire, a tire of large dimensions and air at low pressure, #AUTOMOBILE.

ball'-point" pen. A pen in which ink is applied by means of a tiny rotating ball instead of a sharp fixed point. WRITING-PRINTING.

bal'-ly-hoo. Noisy or sensational advertising or publicity; to advertise or attract attention in such a manner; uproar. EXCITATION, LOUDNESS-FAINTNESS, *PUBLICITY, TURBULENCE-CALMNESS.

ba-lo'-ney. Nonsense. *ADAGE-NONSENSE, MEANING-JARGON, *TRUTHFULNESS-FALSEHOOD.

Bam-boo' Cur'-tain. The barrier of aloofness between Communist China and the free world. ANTAGONISM-CONCURRENCE, UNION-DISUNION.

*band. Climb aboard or get on the band wagon, to join or change to the winning or apparently winning side, MUTATION-PERMANENCE, *SUCCESS-FAILURE.

*bank. To tip an airplane toward one side when making a turn. #AVIATION.

bar'-fly". A person who loiters in barrooms. *ACTIVITY-INDOLENCE, MODERATION-SELF-INDULGENCE, TEETOTALISM-INTEMPERANCE.

*bar'-rel. Barrel roll, a complete rotation of an airplane on the axis of its length, #AVIATION.

*bat. Go to bat for, to fight on behalf of; to defend, ATTACK-DEFENSE, OBSTRUCTION-HELP.

bath'-y-sphere. A steel sphere with glass windows in which men can be lowered to great depths to study deep-sea life and conditions.

*bat'-tle. Battle fatigue, combat fatigue: an emotional disorder associated with participation in battle, *SANENESS-LUNACY.

bat'-ty. Crazy; queer. *SAGACITY-INCAPACITY, *SANENESS-LUNACY.

*bawl. Bawl out, to scold, reprimand, *APPROVAL-DISAPPROVAL.

beach'-head". A position on an enemy shore seized at the start of an invasion. ENTRANCE-EXIT, LISTS.

*beam. A radio signal indicating the course for an airplane or a vessel; on the beam, on course, on the right track, right; off the beam, off the course, wrong. AIM-ABERRATION, #AVIATION, RIGHT-WRONG, *TRUTH-ERROR.

*beau'-ty. Beauty parlor or beauty shop, an establishment where women get treatments for the care of their hair, skin, and hands, BEAUTY-UGLINESS, CONSERVATION.

be'-bop". A kind of jazz music. MELODY-DISSONANCE, MUSIC.

*bell. Ring the bell, to succeed, to win a prize, *SUCCESS-FAILURE.

be'-ta rays. One of the products of disintegration of a radioactive substance, now identified as high-speed electrons and positrons. #NUCLEAR PHYSICS.

be'-ta-tron. A doughnut-shaped atomic accelerator producing electron beams of high energy and X rays of very high penetrating power. #NUCLEAR PHYSICS.

bev'-a-tron. An atomic accelerator generally similar to the synchrotron but producing streams of protons or other particles at energies measured in billions of electron volts. #NUCLEAR PHYSICS.

*bilge. Nonsense, foolishness. *ADAGE-NONSENSE, MEANING-JARGON.

bi"-o-log'-i-cal war'-fare". A threatened kind of warfare in which living organisms, especially disease germs, would be used against the enemy. FIGHTING-CONCILIATION.

*birth. Birth control, limitation of conception in order to control the number of children a woman will have, CREATION-DESTRUCTION.

*black. Black market, unlawful trade in goods that are under governmental restriction of supply, price, or the like, LAW-LAWLESSNESS, LEAVE-PROHIBITION; in the black, showing a profit, out of debt, GAIN-LOSS.

black'-out". Putting out or covering the lights of a city or region as a protection against an air raid; fainting, especially of an airplane pilot under some conditions of flight. ATTACK-DEFENSE, #AVIATION, HEALTH-SICKNESS.

blimp. A small airship. #AVIATION, CONVEYANCE-VESSEL.

*blind. Blind date, a date between persons who do not know each other, arranged by a third person, KNOWLEDGE-IGNORANCE, SOCIABILITY-PRIVACY; blind flying, flying an airplane without seeing out, depending entirely on information supplied by instruments, #AVIATION, VISIBILITY-INVISIBILITY.

blip. The image on a radar screen. #ELECTRONICS.

blitz. A sudden, overwhelming attack; to attack suddenly and violently; blitzkrieg (German), "lightning war," blitz. ATTACK-DEFENSE, ETERNITY-INSTANTANEITY.

bloc. A group, especially of nations or of members of a legislature, united for some particular goal. ASSOCIATION.

*blood. Blood bank, a place where blood or blood plasma is stored; blood or blood plasma kept in storage, REMEDY-BANE.

bloop'-er. An error, usually amusing and often embarrassing, made in some public utterance. *ADAGE-NONSENSE, DIFFICULTY-FACILITY, *TRUTH-ERROR.

blow'-out". The bursting of a pneumatic tire. #AUTOMOBILE.

*blue. Blue chip, a poker chip of highest value; a stock highly valued by investors, GOODNESS-BADNESS, LABOR-CAPITAL.

blue'-print". A special kind of photograph much used for copying drawings; a thorough and detailed plan; to plan. DELINEATION-CARICATURE, DESIGN.

blue"-sky' law". A law regulating the sale of stocks and bonds. LABOR-CAPITAL, LAW-LAWLESSNESS.

blurb. Advertising matter on the dust jacket of a book; any highly laudatory announcement. *APPROVAL-DISAPPROVAL, *PUBLICITY.

*board. Across the board, in betting on horse races, (a bet) to win, place, or show; across-the-board, comprehensive, all-inclusive, PURPOSE-LUCK, UNIVERSALITY-PARTICULARITY.

Bol'-she-vik. A member of the radical (centralist) faction of the Russian Social Democratic Party, which in 1918 became the Communist Party; generally, an extreme radical. TYRANNY-ANARCHY.

bone'-head". A stupid person, blockhead. *SAGE-FOOL.

bon'-er. A blunder, a foolish error. *ADAGE-NONSENSE, *TRUTH-ERROR.

boob. A fool, a stupid person. *SAGE-FOOL.

*boo'-by. Booby trap, a practical joke arranged to surprise some unwary person; a bomb arranged to explode when a soldier touches some apparently harmless object; any trap for the unsuspecting, ATTACK-DEFENSE, CRAFT-ARTLESSNESS, SOCIETY-DERISION, *TRUTHFUL-NESS-FRAUD.

boo'-gie-woo'-gie. A style of jazz music or of jazz piano playing. MELODY-DISSONANCE, MUSIC.

***book.** **Book club,** a company which supplies selected books at regular intervals to its subscribers, MISSIVE-PUBLICATION.

***boom.** **Boom and bust,** periods of prosperity alternating with periods of depression, AFFLUENCE-PENURY, WELFARE-MISFORTUNE.

boon'-dog"-gling. Useless or unnecessary work, especially such work paid for out of public funds. USEFUL-NESS-USELESSNESS.

***brain.** **Brain trust,** derogatory term for administrative officers or political advisers chosen because of their academic specialties or other expert knowledge, AD-VICE, *SAGE-FOOL; **brain washing,** intensive retraining to make a person accept the ideas of a controlling group; menticide; especially, such a process carried out in Communist China, COERCION, EDUCATION-MIS-TEACHING.

***brass.** High-ranking military officers; the top officials of any organization. BELLIGERENT, CHIEF-UNDERLING, MANAGER.

***break.** A chance, an opportunity, a bit of good luck, RATIONALE-LUCK; **break down,** to analyze, INVESTI-GATION-ANSWER; **break even,** to come out with neither profit nor loss, GAIN-LOSS.

breed'-er. An atomic reactor which produces fissionable material for use in other processes, i.e., which produces more such material than it consumes in its own operation. #NUCLEAR PHYSICS.

broad'-cast". To send out by radio or television; to announce or distribute widely. *PUBLICITY, #RADIO-TELEVISION.

bro'-mide. A sedative drug; a trite saying. *ADAGE-NONSENSE, REMEDY-BANE.

brush'-off". An unceremonious refusal or dismissal. COMMISSION-ABROGATION, PROFFER-REFUSAL.

***buck.** **Pass the buck,** to shift blame or responsibility to another person, DUTY-DERELICTION, OBSERVANCE-NONOBSERVANCE, QUEST-EVASION.

build'-up". Building up, development; a planned program of favorable publicity to make a person or thing well known and popular. CREATION-DESTRUCTION, *PUBLICITY.

***bull.** Idle talk; **bull session,** a gathering for informal talk. *ADAGE-NONSENSE, BRAGGING, CONVERSATION-MONOLOGUE.

bunk. Buncombe, nonsense. *ADAGE-NONSENSE, BRAGG-ING, MEANING-JARGON, *TRUTHFULNESS-FALSEHOOD.

burp. A belch; to belch; to hold (a baby) over one's shoulder and pat its back to help it expel gas. ADMIS-SION-EXPULSION.

***butt.** **Butt in,** to interfere, intrude, *ACTIVITY-INDO-LENCE, COOPERATION-OPPOSITION.

buy'-er's strike. A general refusal of consumers to buy an article while they feel the price is too high. BUYING-SALE, READINESS-RELUCTANCE.

***buzz.** To fly an airplane very low over (a field, a building, etc.), #AVIATION; **buzz bomb,** the pulse-jet robot bomb (V-1 weapon) launched by the Germans against England in the spring of 1944, WEAPON.

by'-line". A line stating the name of the writer at the beginning of a newspaper or magazine article. MISSIVE-PUBLICATION, REPUTATION-DISCREDIT.

by'-pass". An alternative section of a highway permitting a motorist to avoid congested traffic, a city, or some other obstacle. CONTINUITY-INTERRUPTION, TRANSMISSION, WAY.

C

ca-lyp'-so. A style of songs improvised by natives of the British West Indies, especially Trinidad. MUSIC.

cam'-el-back". A compound of reclaimed or synthetic rubber and a small amount of natural rubber, used for retreading or recapping tires. #AUTOMOBILE, ELAS-TICITY-INELASTICITY.

cam'-ou-flage. The disguising of a vessel, camp, or other military target by painting or other means to deceive the enemy; disguise, deception; to disguise, deceive. *ENLIGHTENMENT-SECRECY, *TRUTHFULNESS-FABRICATION, *TRUTHFULNESS-FALSEHOOD.

***can'-did.** **Candid camera,** a small camera particularly suited to taking candid photographs, OPTICAL INSTRU-MENTS; **candid photograph,** an unposed snapshot, DELINEATION-CARICATURE, LIKENESS-UNLIKENESS.

canned. Preserved; stereotyped, trite, CONSERVATION, HABIT-DESUETUDE; **canned heat,** a kind of alcoholic paste, packed in a can, which can furnish a small flame for cooking or heating water, COMBUSTIBLE; **canned music,** music played from a record, MUSIC.

can'-ni-bal-ize. To dismantle (a vehicle or other machine) in order to get parts for repairing other vehicles or machines. CREATION-DESTRUCTION, RENO-VATION-RELAPSE.

***cap'-tive.** Owned by and producing for a single large user rather than for the open market (e.g., *captive mine, captive plant*), HOLDING-EXEMPTION, PROPERTY; **captive audience,** people in a public vehicle or other place who have to listen to music or announcements which they may not welcome, LIBERTY-SUBJECTION, *PUBLICITY.

***car.** An automobile, #AUTOMOBILE; **car pool,** an arrangement between neighbors to take turns driving the whole group to work or to public transportation, ASSOCIATION, #AUTOMOBILE, TRAVELING-NAVIGATION.

car'-bu-re"-tor. An aparatus for mixing air and gaso-line to make the fuel mixture for an internal-combustion engine. #AUTOMOBILE, INSTRUMENT.

car'-port". An automobile shelter, with open sides, adjoining a house. #AUTOMOBILE, DWELLER-HABITA-TION.

car'-ry-back". A credit on income taxes because of over-payment or losses not accounted for in a previous year. ACCOUNTS, PRICE-DISCOUNT.

car'-sick". Ill as a result of riding in a motorcar or train. #AUTOMOBILE, HEALTH-SICKNESS.

***cash.** **Cash and carry,** the slogan of retail stores which do not give credit and do not make deliveries, BUYING-SALE, CREDIT-DEBT.

cat'-er-pil'-lar trac'-tor. A tractor moving on two endless belts that pass over cogged drive wheels (a trademark: Caterpillar); a **caterpillar crane** or **caterpillar tank** or the like is a machine similarly equipped. INSTRUMENT.

ca-thar'-sis. In psychoanalysis, the release of sup-pressed emotion by reliving an experience in the imagination, especially by talking about it. *MIND-IMBECILITY, RELEASE-RESTRAINT.

***ceil'-ing.** The height to which a certain airplane can climb; the highest point above the earth from which the ground can be seen, generally the height of the lowest cloud; an upper limit on prices, rent, wages, or the like. #AIRPLANE, HEIGHT-LOWNESS, RELEASE-RESTRAINT.

***cel'-lar.** **In the cellar,** in last place (in a baseball or other sports league), *SUCCESS-FAILURE.

cel'-lo-phane. A transparent, waterproof, flexible wrap-ping material (a trademark: Cellophane). COVER-LINING, MATERIALS.

*chain. Chain reaction, atomic fission which releases the neutrons needed to produce further fission and make the process continuous and self-maintaining; any succession of interrelated causes and effects, CAUSE-EFFECT, #NUCLEAR PHYSICS.

*chan'-nel. A frequency band over which radio or television signals are transmitted. #RADIO-TELEVISION.

chas'-sis. The supporting framework of an automobile (including wheels and machinery), an airplane (the main landing gear), a coast-artillery gun (the frame along which the carriage moves), or a radio or television set (the base which holds the tubes and other operating parts). #AUTOMOBILE, #AVIATION, #RADIO-TELEVISION, WEAPON.

check'-off". The withholding of union dues by an employer from employees' pay for payment to the union. LABOR-CAPITAL.

cheese'-cake". Photographs, especially newspaper photographs, of a pretty girl in some pose which displays her legs. BEAUTY-UGLINESS, *PUBLICITY.

chi'-chi". Overly stylish or ornate; arty. SOCIETY-AFFECTATION, SOCIETY-LUDICROUSNESS.

chi'-ro-prac"-tic. A therapeutic method involving manipulation of the vertebrae. REMEDY-BANE.

*choke. A device for reducing the air supply to a carburetor to enrich the fuel mixture when startnig the engine. #AUTOMOBILE, INSTRUMENT.

cho'-rine. A girl in the chorus of a musical play or entertainment. ACTING.

cin'-e-ma. A motion picture; a motion-picture theater; the motion-picture art and industry. #MOTION PICTURES.

cin"-e-ma-tog'-ra-phy. The making of motion pictures. #MOTION PICTURES.

*cit'-y. City manager, a professional administrator employed to direct a city government, MANAGER.

*civ'il. Civil defense, civilian services organized to minimize casualties and destruction from air attacks and the special weapons of modern warfare, ATTACK-DEFENSE.

clas'-si-fied. Withheld from public knowledge; secret. *ENLIGHTENMENT-SECRECY.

*clean. Come clean, to confess, tell the whole truth, *ENLIGHTENMENT-SECRECY, EXPOSURE-HIDINGPLACE, *TRUTHFULNESS-FALSEHOOD.

*cloak. Cloak-and-dagger, involving intrigue and danger (said of a story, a diplomatic or military assignment, or a person, usually ironically or whimsically), *ENLIGHTENMENT-SECRECY, RECKLESSNESS-CAUTION.

clob'-ber. To overwhelm, defeat decisively; to maul. OBSTRUCTION-HELP, *SUCCESS-FAILURE.

closed'-end". See open-end.

close'-up". A scene in a motion picture in which a person or thing is photographed at close range and is seen in intimate detail; an intimate view or detailed exposition. INTERPRETATION-MISINTERPRETATION, #MOTION PICTURES, VISIBILITY-INVISIBILITY.

clout . To hit hard (especially, a baseball). IMPETUS-REACTION.

clo'-ver-leaf". A highway intersection where one road passes over the other and all connections are made by short loops with right-hand turns. CROSSING, WAY.

co-ax'-i-al ca'-ble. A cable, consisting of electric conductors surrounding a central wire inside a tube and separated by insulation, used for sending telegraph or telephone messages or for carrying radio or television signals to a point where they will be broadcast. ELECTRICITY, #RADIO-TELEVISION.

*co'-balt. Cobalt bomb, (1) a projected hydrogen bomb—the deadliest weapon yet conceived—with a cobalt case which upon explosion of the bomb would be strewn over enormous areas as a radioactive cobalt dust. #NUCLEAR PHYSICS, WEAPON; (2) a machine which con-

tains radioactive cobalt and emits high-energy gamma radiation, used in treatment of deep-seated cancerous growths, #NUCLEAR PHYSICS, REMEDY-BANE.

*cock'-pit". In some airplanes, a small space containing the pilot's seat and usually seats for one or several other persons. #AVIATION.

*cock'-tail". Cocktail lounge, a drinking place where patrons sit at tables or in lounging chairs and where food is not served except as snacks, DWELLER-HABITATION.

*cof'-fee. Coffee break, a short rest period allowed during working hours, especially when coffee may be drunk on the premises or nearby, TOIL-RELAXATION.

*cold. Cold war, a period of hostility between nations (or groups of nations) expressed in any sort of opposition other than military action, FIGHTING-CONCILIATION, STRIFE-PEACE.

*col-lab'-o-ra"-tor. A person who voluntarily assists an enemy who has invaded his country. PATRIOTISM-TREASON.

col-lage'. An abstract artistic production made by pasting together bits of paper or other flat substances, perhaps with lines or forms added by the artist. DELINEATION-CARICATURE, NATURE-ART.

*col-lec'-tive. In Socialist theory or operation, a group of workers who jointly operate and divide the income from a shop, farm or other unit, ASSOCIATION; collective agreement, a contract between an employer (or group of employers) and a labor union, CONTRACT, LABOR-CAPITAL; collective bargaining, negotiation between an employer (or group) and a union concerning wages and other conditions of employment, CONTRACT, LABOR-CAPITAL; collective farm, a farm, especially a farm created in the Soviet Union by the pooling of individual landholdings, operated collectively, ASSOCIATION, DOMESTICATION-AGRICULTURE; collective security, an agreement between nations to join in mutual defense and use their conbined resources to resist an aggressor nation, ANTAGONISM-CONCURRENCE, ASSOCIATION, SECURITY-INSECURITY.

*colo'-nel. Colonel Blimp, a British cartoon character who has become the stock epithet for an elderly Englishman who is pompous, extremely conservative, and not very bright, NOVELTY-ANTIQUITY, SIMPLICITY-FLORIDNESS, WITTINESS-DULLNESS.

col'-umn-ist. A person who writes regular contributions, such as reports on a particular subject or comment in an individual style, for a newspaper. MISSIVE-PUBLICATION.

*com'-bat. Combat fatigue, battle fatigue, an emotional disorder associated with participation in battle, *SANENESS-LUNACY.

com'-bine. A machine which cuts, threshes, and cleans grain in a continuous operation. DOMESTICATION-AGRICULTURE, INSTRUMENT.

*com'-ic. Comics, comic strips and cartoons, especially those published as newspaper features; comic book, a booklet containing a collection of comic strips or telling a story in a series of cartoons; comic strip, a sequence of cartoons telling a story, often continued from one issue of a newspaper to the next. MISSIVE-PUBLICATION, WITTINESS-DULLNESS.

com-man'-do. A unit of men specially trained to make a quick, carefully planned raid into enemy territory (in World War II); one of the raiders in such a unit. ATTACK-DEFENSE, BELLIGERENT.

*com'-men-ta"-tor. A person who makes explanatory comments on the news, especially on radio and television. INTERPRETER, #RADIO-TELEVISION.

com-mer'-cial. An advertisement broadcast before, during, or after a radio or television program. *PUBLICITY, #RADIO-TELEVISION.

com'-mis-sar. A commissioner; the head of a governmental department or bureau (a **comissariat**) in the Soviet Union. CHIEF-UNDERLING.

*com-mu'-ni-ty. **Community chest,** a campaign for collecting in a single solicitation funds to be divided among a number of charitable organizations serving the same community, CHARITABLENESS-MALEVOLENCE, GIVING-RECEIVING.

com-pan'-ion-ate mar'riage. A suggested form of "trial marriage" recognizing birth control and easy divorce if there are no children. MATRIMONY-CELIBACY, TRIAL.

*com-pat'-i-ble. Describing a system of color television broadcasts which can be received, but without color, without any change in ordinary receiving sets. #RADIO-TELEVISION.

*com"-pen-sa'-tion. The exaggeration of abilities and favorable traits to offset weaknesses and unfavorable traits of personality. COMPENSATION, MIGHT-IMPOTENCE, *MIND-IMBECILITY.

com'-plex. A group of ideas and feelings, largely repressed and in the unconscious mind, which account for some abnormality of behavior. *MIND-IMBECILITY, RELEASE-RESTRAINT.

*con"-cen-tra'-tion. **Concentration camp,** a place, usually tightly fenced and closely guarded, for the imprisonment of political prisoners or prisoners of war or the internment of enemy aliens, RELEASE-PRISON.

*con"-den-sa'-tion. **Condensation trail,** the visible trail or vapor left in the wake of jet-propelled airplanes, #AVIATION.

con-di'-tioned. Trained, accustomed, inured, EDUCATION-MISTEACHING; **conditioned reflex** or **response,** a response to a stimulus which does not cause that response except after a process of learning through association with an adequate stimulus, *MIND-IMBECILITY.

*cone. **Ice-cream cone,** a cone of pastry holding a ball of ice cream. NUTRIMENT-EXCRETION.

conk out. To fail (said of an engine, especially an airplane engine). #AVIATION, *SUCCESS-FAILURE.

*con-struc'-tion. A three-dimensional work of abstract art (sculpture, wire figure, geometrical model, etc.). DELINEATION-CARICATURE, NATURE-ART.

*con'-tact. To get in touch with (a person); a connection, CONNECTION-INDEPENDENCE, FRIEND-FOE; **contact flying,** the opposite of blind flying (instrument flying), i.e., flying with the surface below in view, #AVIATION, VISIBILITY-INVISIBILITY.

con-tain'-ment. In international politics, an effort to block the expansion of an enemy or rival, or of his influence, beyond his own borders. INCLUSION-OMISSION, RELEASE-RESTRAINT.

*con"-ti-nu'-i-ty. The detailed plan and directions for making a motion picture; the script for the spoken part of a radio or television program. #MOTION PICTURES, #RADIO-TELEVISION.

con'-trail". The condensation trail of a jet plane. #AVIATION.

*con-vert'-i-ble. An automobile with a folding top. #AUTOMOBILE.

cook'-out". The cooking and serving of a meal out of doors. ENTERTAINMENT-WEARINESS, NUTRIMENT-EXCRETION.

co'-pi'-lot. The assistant pilot of an airplane. #AVIATION.

*corn. Corny music, stories, behavior, or the like. *ADAGE-NONSENSE, TASTE-VULGARITY.

corn'-y. Stereotyped, trite, tiresomely sentimental. HABIT-DESUETUDE, TASTE-VULGARITY.

cor'-ti-sone. A hormone obtained from the adrenal gland or produced synthetically, sometimes used in the treatment of arthritis and other diseases, especially inflammations. REMEDY-BANE.

cos'-mic rays. High-energy radiation entering the earth's atmosphere from interstellar space. ASTRONOMY, #NUCLEAR PHYSICS, UNIVERSE.

cos'-mo-tron. A very powerful synchrotron which will accelerate protons or other particles to energies of several billion electron volts. #NUCLEAR PHYSICS.

co'-star". To present (two or more actors, who usually already are stars) in important roles in the same production; to appear as a star along with another in the same production. ACTING, #MOTION PICTURES.

*count'-er. **Under the counter,** surreptitious(ly), illicit(ly), contrary to government regulation. *ENLIGHTENMENT-SECRECY, LAW-LAWLESSNESS, *TRUTHFULNESS-FRAUD.

coun"-ter-in-tel'-li-gence. A military service which tries to prevent the enemy from obtaining information. *ENLIGHTENMENT-SECRECY.

coun'-ter-word". A word which has been overworked and so loosely used that it appears in many contexts as a substitute for a word of more precise meaning. HABIT-DESUETUDE, WORD-NEOLOGY.

cou-pé'. An enclosed, two-door, essentially single-seated automobile body style. #AUTOMOBILE.

*cov'-er. **Cover charge,** a fixed charge added to the charge for food and drinks in a restaurant or night club, PRICE-DISCOUNT.

*crab. To head (an airplane) toward the side from which the wind is blowing to avoid being blown off course, making the plane seem to be moving sideways. AIM-ABERRATION, #AVIATION.

*crack. **Crack down,** to take firm action to prevent or punish violations, RECOMPENSE-PUNITION; **crackup,** to crash; to go to pieces, to lose one's health or sanity, HEALTH-SICKNESS, IMPETUS-REACTION, *SANENESS-LUNACY.

crack'-pot". Cracked-brained, eccentric, impractical; a crack-brained person. *SAGACITY-INCAPACITY, *SAGE-FOOL.

*crash. To get into (a party, public spectacle, or the like) without being invited or without paying; **crash the gate,** to get in without paying or being invited. ENTRANCE-EXIT, *TRUTHFULNESS-FRAUD.

*crime. **Crime wave,** a widespread increase in the occurrence of crime, VIRTUE-VICE.

*crit'-i-cal. **Critical size,** the amount of uranium or plutonium in which a chain reaction will cause an atomic explosion, #NUCLEAR PHYSICS, QUANTITY-MEASURE.

cross'-fil'-ing. Registering a candidate in the primary elections of more than one party, as is permitted in certain states. CHOICE-NEUTRALITY.

cross'-word" puz'-zle. A puzzle in which words, to be supplied according to definitions furnished as clues, are filled into interlocking horizontal and vertical spaces. ENTERTAINMENT-WEARINESS.

*crys'-tal. **Crystal detector,** a radio device in which alternating current is changed into direct current with the aid of a crystal; **crystal pickup,** a phonograph part in which a crystal helps turn mechanical motion (of the needle in the groove) into electrical signals; **crystal set,** a radio set with a crystal detector instead of tubes. HEARING-DEAFNESS, #RADIO-TELEVISION.

cub'-ism. A method of abstract art making large use of cubical and other geometrical forms. DELINEATION-CARICATURE, NATURE-ART.

*cuff. **Off the cuff,** impromptu, not prepared in advance, PREDETERMINATION-IMPULSE; **on the cuff,** on credit, CREDIT-DEBT.

cu'-rie. A unit of measure for radioactivity, being the quantity of a radioactive substance which decays at a stated rate. MEASURE, #NUCLEAR PHYSICS.

*cut. A share, especially of profit or plunder, ASSIGNMENT, WHOLE-PART; **cut back,** to reduce (an expenditure, employment, or the like), ENLARGEMENT-DIMINUTION.

cut'-back". A reduction in a motion picture, novel, or the like, a shift from one course of events to another, especially to one which occurred earlier in time. Account, Enlargement-Diminution, #Motion Pictures.

cy"-ber-net'-ics. The comparative study of the mechanisms that control the functioning of electronic computers and the human brain and nervous system. #Electronics, *Mind-Imbecility.

cy'-clo-tron. An apparatus in which protons or other atomic particles are accelerated (to be used as projectiles in nuclear experiments) in moving through a spiral path in a magnetic field. #Nuclear Physics.

D

dash'-board". A panel in front of the driver's seat in an automobile, with gauges and instruments. #Automobile.

***day'-light".** **Daylight-saving time,** time one hour (usually) ahead of standard time, adopted in some places during summer months in order to have more daylight hours for work and play, Light-Darkness, Time.

D-day. The day set for beginning a military operation. Beginning-End, Opportuneness-Unsuitableness.

DDT. A powerful insecticide (initials of the components of its full chemical name). Remedy-Bane.

dead'-line". Time limit. Beginning-End.

dead'-pan". Without facial expression; with deliberate or mock seriousness, as a style of comedy; expressing no emotion. Acting, Emotion, Sensitiveness-Apathy.

de-bunk'. To take the "bunk" (nonsense, romantic legends, false claims) away from (a person, a thing). Motive-Dehortation, *Truthfulness-Falsehood.

***de-cay'.** Disintegration of a radioactive substance. #Nuclear Physics.

de-cel'-er-ate. To slow down. Swiftness-Slowness.

dec'-i-bel. A unit for measuring the loudness of sounds. Measure, Sound-Silence.

de"-con-tam'-i-nate. To clear of radioactivity, poison gas, or other pollution. Cleanness-Filthiness.

de"-con-trol'. To remove from governmental control (of supply or prices). Release-Restraint, Rule-License.

deep'-freeze'. Storage for indefinite length of time at very low temperature; **Deepfreeze,** a box for such storage (a trademark). Conservation, Heating-Cooling, Oven-Refrigerator.

de-feat'-ist. A person who accepts the idea of defeat when it is still possible to fight or to resist. Sanguineness-Hopelessness.

***de-fense'.** **Defense mechanism,** unconscious mental process by which a person avoids facing a disagreeable situation or painful fact; the behavior reflecting such processes, Compensation, *Mind-Imbecility.

de-flate'. To let air or gas out of; to reduce (prices or an inflated currency). Enlargement-Diminution, Money.

de-fla'-tion. Deflating; a process or period in which prices fall and the value of money rises. Enlargement-Diminution, Money.

de-frost'. To thaw out; to clear of snow or ice. Heating-Cooling.

de-gauss'. To demagnetize (a magnetized substance); to equip (a ship) with protection against magnetic mines. Electricity.

de-ic'-er. A device for preventing or removing formation of ice on airplanes. #Aviation, Heating-Cooling.

***de-men'-tia.** **Dementia praecox,** a mental disorder (a form of schizophrenia), victims of which are usually very young people, *Saneness-Lunacy.

de-mil'-i-tar-ize. To free from military control; to take away military personnel or armaments. Fighting-Conciliation.

de-mote'. To reduce in rank. Betterment-Deterioration, Elevation-Depression.

de-na'-tion-al-ize. To return (nationalized property) to private owners. Taking-Restitution.

de-na'-zi-fy. To rid of nazi ideas or influences.

den"-dro-chro-nol'-o-gy. The study of tree rings as a system of dating archeological finds by the wood preserved in them. Chronology-Anachronism.

***dent.** **Make a dent (in** or **on),** to make an impression; to make progress, Advance-Retrogression, Feeling-Insensibility.

***depth.** **Depth bomb** or **depth charge,** an explosive charge dropped from a ship or airplane to destroy submarines or other underwater targets, Weapon.

de-sen'-si-tize. To make less sensitive or insensitive. Feeling-Insensibility, Sensitiveness-Apathy.

de-ster'-i-lize. To put into useful service (something previously withdrawn, especially gold as the basis of a country's currency). Money, Renovation-Relapse.

deu-te'-ri-um. Heavy hydrogen, an isotope with almost twice the weight of ordinary hydrogen. Chemistry, #Nuclear Physics.

deu'-ter-on. The nucleus of the deuterium atom, containing one neutron in addition to one proton (the hydrogen atom contains one proton). #Nuclear Physics.

de-val'-u-ate or **de-val'-ue.** To reduce or take away the value (especially of a currency). Increase-Decrease, Money.

de"-vi-a'-tion-ist. A member or former member of the Communist Party who deviates from the strict line of the party doctrine; a person who deviates from any official doctrine. Insubordination-Obedience, Mutability-Stability.

di'-al. To call on a dial telephone; **dial telephone,** a telephone with a dial by which the user makes his call without the aid of an operator. Hearing-Deafness.

di"-a-net'-ics. A theory of mental treatment based on the idea that a person can be taken back in memory to a time before the injury which caused the disorder. *Mind-Imbecility, Remedy-Bane.

di'-a-ther"-my. The passing of electric currents through the body to generate heat for treating diseases or injuries. Remedy-Bane.

dick. A detective. *Enlightenment-Secrecy, Judicature.

dic'-ta-phone. A machine for recording and reproducing speech, especially for transcription by a stenographer (a trademark: Dictaphone). Hearing-Deafness.

dic'-to-graph. A sensitive and easily concealed telephonic device frequently used for listening to or recording conversations (a trademark: Dictograph). Hearing-Deafness.

Die'-sel en'-gine. An internal-combustion engine in which the explosive mixture of fuel and air is ignited by heat of compression. Instrument.

***dim.** **Take a dim view of,** to disapprove, suspect, be skeptical or pessimistic about, *Approval-Disapproval, Faith-Misgiving.

dim'-out". A partial covering or reduction of lighting as a protection against air raids; a partial blackout. Attack-Defense.

dim'-wit". A slow-thinking or stupid person. *Sage-Fool, Wittiness-Dulness.

di-nette'. A small dining room or dining space. Contents-Receiver.

di-rec'-tive. An order or instruction, especially by governmental or military authorities. ORDER.

dis"-as-sem'-ble. To take apart. GATHERING-SCATTERING, UNION-DISUNION.

dis-cog'-ra-phy. A list, often with comments, of phonograph records of one composer or performer, or other classification; the study of musical recording. HEARING-DEAFNESS, MUSIC.

dis'-co-phile. A collector of phonograph records; an ardent student of recorded music. GATHERING-SCATTERING, HEARING-DEAFNESS, MUSIC, SCHOLAR-DUNCE.

*__dis'-count.__ **Discount house,** a store which sells goods at prices generally lower than the manufacturers' list prices, DEALER, PRICE-DISCOUNT.

*__dis-crim'-i-na'-tion.__ Different treatment, especially denial of rights or privileges because of a person's color, national origin, or religion. AMITY-HOSTILITY, EQUALITY-INEQUALITY.

*__disk.__ A phonograph record; **disk jockey,** the announcer on a radio program consisting chiefly of phonograph records. HEARING-DEAFNESS, #RADIO-TELEVISION.

*__dis-placed'.__ **Displaced person,** a war refugee or person deported for enforced labor, especially one of the numerous such persons gathered into refugee camps after World War II, PRESENCE-ABSENCE, QUEST-EVASION, WAYFARER-SEAFARER.

*__dis-qual'-i-fy.__ To take away the right to participate in a sport, or to cancel the effect of participating, as for breaking rules. INCLUSION-OMISSION.

dith'-er. A state of agitation, confusion, or apprehension. AGITATION.

*__dive.__ **Dive bombing,** releasing a bomb or bombs from an airplane which dives at a steep angle toward its target, ATTACK-DEFENSE, #AVIATION.

Dix'-ie-crat. A member of the States' Rights Party formed in 1948 by Southern Democrats who refused to support the Democratic Party platform and candidates.

doc"-u-men'-ta-ry. A motion picture, play, radio or television program, or literary or artistic work aiming principally to impart factual information. ACCOUNT, #MOTION PICTURES, #RADIO-TELEVISION.

dog'-fight". A free-for-all fight between individual fighter planes. FIGHTING-CONCILIATION.

dog'-gy. Well dressed; stylish; showy. SOCIETY-LUDICROUSNESS.

dog'-house". **In the doghouse,** out of favor, *__Approval-Disapproval.__

do'-gie. A motherless calf in a herd. INFANT-VETERAN.

do'-good"-er. Term of ridicule for a reformer or humanitarian (inferring blundering or ineffectuality). BETTERMENT-DETERIORATION, HUMANITARIANISM-MISANTROPHY, MIGHT-IMPOTENCE.

*__dol'-lar.__ **Dollar-a-year man,** a person who takes a government appointment at a nominal salary, usually $1 a year, OBSTRUCTION-HELP; **dollar diplomacy** a nickname for a foreign policy which its opponents claim has the object of creating business opportunities. CRAFT-ARTLESSNESS; **dollar gap,** a shortage of dollars in a country which imports more goods from than it exports to the United States, MONEY.

dol'-ly. A low platform on wheels, for moving heavy loads short distances; a similar device used for moving a motion-picture camera about. CONVEYANCE-VESSEL, #MOTION PICTURES.

doo'-dad. A word replacing the name of anything that does not readily come to mind; a trivial ornament. CONSEQUENCE-INSIGNIFICANCE, EMBELLISHMENT-DISFIGUREMENT.

*__doo'-dle.__ To scribble or draw figures absent-mindedly while talking or thinking. WRITING-PRINTING.

doo'-dle-bug". The buzz bomb (robot bomb). WEAPON.

*__dou'-ble.__ A substitute who takes the place of a motion-picture star for dangerous stunts or for actions requiring a special skill the actor does not have, #MOTION PICTURES, SUBSTITUTE; **double feature,** a motion-picture program with two full-length films, #MOTION PICTURES; **double image,** in surrealism, a figure which can be interpreted as a representation of two different objects at the same time, DELINEATION-CARICATURE, NATURE-ART; **double take,** a delayed perception of and reaction to the full meaning (usually humorous) of something heard or seen, CONCEPTION-THEME, KNOWLEDGE-IGNORANCE; **double talk,** speech that is essentially nonsense but contains enough sensible words and phrases to seem to be serious; deceptive or ambiguous statements, *__Adage-Nonsense,__ AMBIGUITY, MEANING-JARGON, *__Truthfulness-Fabrication.__

down'-beat". The conductor's motion indicating the first accent in a measure; the first accented note in a measure. MUSIC.

down'-grade". To reduce in rank or importance. BETTERMENT-DETERIORATION, ELEVATION-DEPRESSION.

DP or D.P. A displaced person. PRESENCE-ABSENCE, QUEST-EVASION, WAYFARER-SEAFARER.

*__drag.__ **Drag race,** a short race between automobiles (usually with souped-up motors) which is largely a test of acceleration, #AUTOMOBILE, QUEST-EVASION.

*__drag'-net".__ An extensive police operation to bring in criminals or suspects. JUDICATURE, QUEST-EVASION.

*__drain.__ **Down the drain,** lost, wasted, GAIN-LOSS, PROVISION-WASTE.

Dram'-a-mine. A drug used principally against seasickness or air-sickness (a trademark). REMEDY-BANE.

*__dream.__ **Dream up,** to invent or conceive, in a flight of fancy (especially, some startling original creation), DESIGN, FANCY, REFLECTION-VACANCY.

*__drive.__ An impelling force; energy, initiative; an organized effort for some special purpose such as to raise money. COOPERATION-OPPOSITION, DETERMINATION-VACILLATION, VIGOR-INERTIA.

drive'-in". An open-air theater where customers see a motion picture from their automobiles; any place where customers may be served while seated in their automobiles. DWELLER-HABITATION, #MOTION PICTURES.

*__driv'-er.__ **In the driver's seat,** in control, at the head of any organization, MANAGEMENT, RULE-LICENSE.

*__drone.__ An airplane without a pilot and controlled by radio signals, as from another airplane; a vessel remotely controlled by radio. #AVIATION, CONVEYANCE-VESSEL.

*__dry.__ **Dry run,** a practice bombing flight on which no bombs are actually dropped; a rehearsal or simulated performance, #AVIATION, TRIAL, VENTURE; **not dry behind the ears,** immature, gullible, *__Gull-Deceiver,__ INFANCY-AGE, NOVELTY-ANTIQUITY.

*__dub.__ To transfer sound from one phonograph record to another, usually of a different kind; **dub in,** to add sound to a motion picture or to make changes in a motion-picture sound track, #MOTION PICTURES.

*__duck.__ A military truck and barge equipped to travel either on land or on water. #AUTOMOBILE, CONVEYANCE-VESSEL.

duct'-less glands. Glands which secrete hormones directly into the blood stream; endocrine glands. ANATOMY.

dude ranch. A ranch which takes vacationers as paying guests. DWELLER-HABITATION, ENTERTAINMENT-WEARINESS.

dug'-out". A rough shelter formed by digging a hole in the ground or the side of a hill and (in trench warfare) covering it with logs or the like; a shelter at the side of a baseball field for players who are not on the field. REFUGE-PITFALL.

dumb'-bell". A stupid person. *__Sage-Fool.__

dunk. To dip (bread or pastry) into soup or a beverage before eating. NUTRIMENT-EXCRETION.

Dun'-kirk. A hasty retreat in the face of disaster (from the British evacuation at Dunkirk in 1940). ADVANCE-RETROGRESSION, APPROACH-WITHDRAWAL, WELFARE-MISFORTUNE.

*__du'-plex.__ A house built to be occupied by two families; **duplex apartment,** an apartment with rooms on two floors of a building. DWELLER-HABITATION.

*__dust.__ **Dust bowl,** a large area in the western part of the United States subject to excessive drought and severe wind erosion of cultivated land. CREATION-DESTRUCTION, DAMPNESS-DRYNESS, FERTILITY-STERILITY.

* __Dutch.__ **In Dutch,** in disfavor, in touble, *APPROVAL-DISAPPROVAL, DIFFICULTY-FACILITY.

E

*__ea'-ger.__ **Eager beaver,** an enthusiastic or zealous person, especially a person who volunteers for extra work, *ACTIVITY-INDOLENCE, READINESS-RELUCTANCE.

*__ech'-e-lon.__ Arrangement of ships or airplanes in a formation resembling a series of steps; one of the units of a military force, named with regard to relative distance from the front (*assault, reconnaissance, rear,* etc.); one of the levels in a steplike organization of command, as in the phrase *top echelons.* ATTACK-DEFENSE, ORGANIZATION-DISORGANIZATION.

*__ech'-o.__ A radio wave, sent out by a radar transmitter, reflected back from an object. #ELECTRONICS.

ec'-to-morph. A person of light and delicate type of body build, with relatively long limbs, light muscling, and body surface large in comparison to body mass.

edg'-y. On edge, irritable. EMOTION, EXCITABILITY-INEXCITABILITY, FAVORITE-QUARRELSOMENESS.

ed"-i-to'-ri-al-ize. To mix the writer's opinions with the facts in a news report. DECISION-MISJUDGMENT, EDUCATION-MISTEACHING.

egg'-head". A disparaging nickname for an intellectual. *SAGE-FOOL, SCHOLAR-DUNCE.

*__e'-go.__ Conceit, egotism; in psychoanalysis, the part of a person's mental make-up corresponding to his conscious experience and activities (contrasting with the *id* and the *superego*). *MIND-IMBECILITY, SUBJECTIVE-NESS-OBJECTIVENESS.

e"-go-cen'-tric. Self-centered. CONCEIT-DIFFIDENCE.

*__eight.__ **Eight ball,** a black pool ball bearing the number 8; a small microphone that can pick up sounds from all directions, #RADIO-TELEVISION; **behind the eight ball,** in a difficult situation, at a disadvantage, DIFFICULTY-FACILITY, WELFARE-MISFORTUNE.

Ein'-stein e-qua'-tion. See **mass-energy equation.**

E-lec'-tra com'-plex. A complex resulting from a girl's unconscious and, according to psychoanalysis, sexual attachment to her father and antagonism toward her mother, creating emotional disturbance when it persists beyond childhood. *MIND-IMBECILITY.

*__e-lec'-tric.__ **Electric eye,** a photoelectric cell, so called because can control an electric current in response to changes in the light reaching the cell, #ELECTRONICS; **electric** or **electronic organ,** an organ in which sound is produced by electronic devices instead of pipes, MUSICAL INSTRUMENTS.

e-lec"-tro-mag-net'-ic waves. Vibrations or wave motions traveling with the speed of light and requiring, so far as is known, no material medium for their transmission; they include gamma rays, X rays, ultraviolet light, visible light, infrared light (heat radiation), and radio (including radar and television) waves, distinguished from one another by the frequency of their vibrations.

e-lec'-tron. A particle bearing a charge of negative electricity; one or more electrons revolve around the nucleus of the atom, balancing the positive charges of the protons; the behavior of the electron is involved in chemical reactions, electricity, and magnetism, the production of electromagnetic waves, and the fission, fusion, or radioactive decay of the nucleus of the atom, #NUCLEAR PHYSICS; **electron volt,** a unit of energy used in nuclear physics (especially in *million electron volts* or *billion electron volts*), e.g., to express the energy imparted to a particle in an atomic accelerator or the energy expended or released in a nuclear reaction, MEASURE, #NUCLEAR PHYSICS.

e-lec"-tron'-ic. Relating to electrons or electronics, #ELECTRONICS, #NUCLEAR PHYSICS; **electronic brain,** a machine performing complex calculations by means of electrical circuits, vacuum tubes, and related devices, #ELECTRONICS, NUMBERING.

e-lec"-tron'-ics. The study of vacuum tubes, photoelectric cells, and the like, and their applications. #ELECTRONICS.

ELECTRONICS

Blip, pip. The image on a radar screen.

Cybernetics. The comparative study of the mechanisms that control the functioning of electronic computers and the human brain and nervous system.

Echo. A radio wave, sent out by a radar transmitter, reflected back from an object.

Electric eye, photoelectric cell. A device in which the action of light produces or controls an electric current.

Electronic. Relating to electrons or electronics.

Electronic brain. A machine performing complex calculations by means of electrical circuits, vacuum tubes, and related devices.

Electronics. The study of vacuum tubes, photoelectric cells, and the like, and their applications.

Ghost. Abnormal echoes on a radar screen.

Grid. A wire loop or coil which controls the passage of electrons between the filament and the plate in a vacuum tube.

Image converter. An electronic device to increase the power of a telescope.

Loran. An electronic device enabling the navigator of an airplane or ship to determine its position from radio signals sent out from two stations.

Proximity fuse. A miniature radio device in the nose of a projectile which causes it to explode at a determined distance from the target.

Radar. An instrument which detects and locates objects by means of radio waves sent out by and reflected back to it.

Scan. To inspect an area by swinging a radar antenna through a certain angle.

Thermion. An ion or electron emitted by a hot body.

Thermionic emission. Emission of electrons from an incandescent filament, etc.

Thermionic valve. British term for vacuum tube.

Transistor. A crystal device smaller and more durable than and serving much the same purposes as the vacuum tube.

Tube, vacuum tube. A glass bulb enclosing electrodes in a near vacuum, used to modify or control a flow of electricity.

em-cee'. M. C., master of ceremonies. ACTING, #RADIO-TELEVISION.

em'-pa-thy. Projection of the imagination into another person's feelings and motives, as in appreciation of a work of art; unconscious identification of oneself with another person, especially in behaving or imagining oneself behaving as the other person would. DECISION-MISJUDGMENT, *MIND-IMBECILITY.

em-plane'. To get aboard an airplane, to go away in an airplane. ARRIVAL-DEPARTURE, #AVIATION.

en'-do-crine glands. Ductless glands (glands which secrete hormones directly into the blood stream). ANATOMY.

en'-do-morph. A person of the rounded type of body structure with relatively large abdomen, smooth contours, short limbs, and small bones.

*ENLIGHTENMENT—SECRECY

ENLIGHTENMENT

Hand-out. An official statement, news release, etc.
The lowdown. The whole truth, the real facts, a confidential report.
Pipe line. A channel through which information is received.
Tip. A hint, suggestion, warning, secret information.
Tip-off. A warning, secret information.

ENLIGHTENMENT—*Nouns of Agent*

Dick. A detective.
Gumshoe. A detective.
Legman. A newspaper reporter or other person who gathers information.

ENLIGHTENMENT—*Verbs*

Come clean. To confess, tell the whole truth.
Rubber. To gape, stare; to eavesdrop.
Spill. To let out, divulge, disclose, make known, tell.
Tip, tip off. To give a hint, suggestion, warning, or secret information.

ENLIGHTENMENT—*Adjectives*

Unclassified. Not secret, open, publicly revealed.

*en-rich. To increase the nutritional value of (a food) by adding vitamins or minerals. NUTRIMENT-EXCRETION.

e-phed'-rine. A drug used to relieve colds, hay fever, asthma, and the like. REMEDY-BANE.

eq'-ui-time" point. In a long flight, especially over an ocean, the point at which a pilot may choose (as in case of trouble) either to turn back or to go on. #AVIATION.

*eq'-ui-ty. The value of property in excess of charges against it; the common stock of a corporation, as distinguished from bonds and preferred stock, LABOR-CAPITAL, PROPERTY; **equity capital,** money invested in common stocks, LABOR-CAPITAL.

er'-satz. Substitute, imitation, inferior. FAULTLESSNESS-FAULTINESS, *TRUTHFULNESS-FABRICATION.

es'-ca-la"-tor. A moving stairway (an endless belt which forms a series of steps as it moves up or down an incline; a trademark), ELEVATION-DEPRESSION, WAY; **escalator clause,** in a labor contract, a provision for automatic increases or decreases in pay if living costs (as shown by an official index) go up or down, LABOR-CAPITAL.

*es-cape'. Relief from boredom or from facing reality; **escape literature,** literary works which afford such an escape from reality. ACCOUNT, ALLEVIATION-AGGRAVATION.

es-ca"-pee'. A person who has escaped from one of the countries under Communist control. ESCAPE.

es-cap'-ism. Habitual avoidance of boredom or unpleasant realities through the imagination or by a diversion such as reading or watching motion pictures; fiction, motion pictures, or other work which provides such a diversion. ALLEVIATION-AGGRAVATION, *MIND-IMBECILITY.

eth"-no-cen'-trism. The belief or tendency to believe that one's own race, nation, or group is inherently superior to all others. CONCEIT-DIFFIDENCE, UNSELFISHNESS-SELFISHNESS.

eu-pho'-ri-a. A feeling of well-being; often an unfounded or exaggerated feeling of well-being from mental disorder, use of drugs, or other cause. CONTENTEDNESS-DISCONTENTMENT, LIGHTHEARTEDNESS-DEJECTION, PLEASURE-PAIN.

SECRECY

Agent provocateur [F.]. An agent employed to incite a suspected person or group to commit a punishable offense.
Camouflage. Disguise, deception.
Counterintelligence. A military service which tries to prevent the enemy from obtaining information.
Joker. A provision in a contract with consequences not immediately apparent.
Smoke screen. Any action, etc., intended to conceal the truth.

SECRECY—*Verbs*

Camouflage. To disguise, deceive.
Gumshoe. To go around quietly and stealthily.
Hush-hush. To suppress or silence.

SECRECY—*Adjectives, Adverbs*

Backstage. Behind the scenes, concealed from public view.
Classified. Withheld from public knowledge, secret.
Cloak-and-dagger. Involving danger and intrigue.
Hush-hush. Done or made quietly or secretly.
Incommunicado. Deprived of communication with other persons.
Off the record. Not to be published or quoted, in confidence.
Tight-lipped. Not talking, uncommunicative, secretive.
Top-secret. Highly secret or confidential.
Under the counter. Surreptitious(ly), illicit(ly).

eu-then'-ics. The study of means of improving living conditions as a means of improving the human race. BETTERMENT-DETERIORATION.

e-vac'-u-ee". A person who is removed from a place of danger, as from a large city in wartime. SECURITY-INSECURITY.

ex'-cess–prof'-its tax. A tax on business profits that exceed the average profit during a preceding period, or a certain return on investment (typically levied in wartime or other inflationary period). PRICE-DISCOUNT.

*ex-co'-ri-ate. To flay with words, censure, denounce bitterly. APPROVAL-DISAPPROVAL, CHARITABLENESS-CURSE.

ex"-is-ten'-tial-ism. A philosophy, influential in contemporary literature (notably fiction and drama) and religion, holding that man is made by his experience rather than by a common quality of human nature; as a reaction from rationalism it holds that man is free and must make decisions in the recurrent crises that confront him, but in contrast to idealism it offers no end except annihilation. ENTITY-NONENTITY, *MIND-IMBECILITY.

*ex-pan'-sive. Effusive, demonstrative, unrestrained. EXCITABILITY-INEXCITABILITY, LIGHTHEARTEDNESS-DEJECTION, SPEECH-INARTICULATENESS.

ex-pan'-sive-ness. An abnormal feeling of well-being and exaggerated idea of one's importance. CONCEIT-DIFFIDENCE, CONTENTEDNESS-DISCONTENTMENT, PLEASURE-PAIN.

*ex-pect'-ant. Going to have a child (*expectant mother* or *father*). FERTILITY-STERILITY.

ex-pend'-a-ble. In military use, denoting supplies which are used up in service, hence, troops or equipment which may be sacrificed in order to achieve a desired result. PROVISION-WASTE.

ex-pres'-sion-ism. A theory or practice of art (painting, drama, and others) which aims at expression of the artist's emotions and sensations rather than objective portrayal of scenes, situations, and the like. DELINEATION-CARICATURE, NATURE-ART.

ex-press'-way". A highway built for high-speed traffic, especially by avoiding cross traffic and stops. WAY.

ex"-tra-sen'-so-ry. Beyond the range of ordinary sense

perception; **extrasensory perception,** perception in a way not explained by the normal senses, as in clairvoyance or telepathy. MATERIALITY-SPIRITUALITY.

ex″-tro-ver′-sion. Interest in and direction of one's activities toward other persons and things outside of oneself. *MIND-IMBECILITY, SOCIABILITY-PRIVACY, UNSELFISHNESS-SELFISHNESS.

ex′-tro-vert″. A person whose interests are largely in other persons and external things rather than his own thoughts and feelings. *MIND-IMBECILITY, SOCIABILITY-PRIVACY, UNSELFISHNESS-SELFISHNESS.

*eye. **Eye rhyme,** a rhyme of words which are spelled alike but pronounced differently, as *fear* and *wear,* POETRY-PROSE.

eye′-some. Handsome, beautiful. BEAUTY-UGLINESS.

F

*face. **Face up to,** to confront; to meet (a challenge); to admit the existence of (unpleasant problems), ANTAGONISM-CONCURRENCE, BRAVERY-COWARDICE, KNOWLEDGE-IGNORANCE.

face′-lift″-ing. Surgery to remove wrinkles and otherwise improve the appearance of the face; any improvement of appearance or removal of evidences of age. BEAUTY-UGLINESS, REMEDY-BANE, RENOVATION-RELAPSE.

*fa-cil′-i-ty. Equipment, buildings or other physical means of doing something, e.g. *housing facilities, facilities for washing.* MEANS.

*fade. **Fade in,** (in motion pictures, radio, or television) to become gradually more distinct in visibility or audibility; **fade out,** (in motion pictures, radio, or television) to disappear gradually from sight or hearing, (generally) to disappear. #MOTION PICTURES, #RADIO-TELEVISION, VISIBILITY-INVISIBILITY.

*fair. **Fair Deal,** the social and economic policies of the administration of President Harry S. Truman, essentially a continuation of the New Deal of President Franklin D. Roosevelt, RULE-LICENSE; **fair employment,** employment without discrimination because of racial origin, religion, sex, or other ground unrelated to ability, INCLUSION-OMISSION, LABOR-CAPITAL, LIBERTY-SUBJECTION.

fair′-haired′ boy. A favorite. FAVORITE-ANGER.

fair′-trade′. To fix retail prices by a fair-trade agreement; **fair-trade agreement,** a contract between a manufacturer and one or more retailers, authorized by the laws of some states, by which the manufacturer fixes minimum retail selling prices of his products. BUYING-SALE, PRICE-DISCOUNT, RELEASE-RESTRAINT.

Fa′-lange. The fascist party which was victorious in the Spanish Civil War of 1936–39 and which since then has controlled the government of Spain. RULE-LICENSE.

Fa-lan′-gist. A member of the Falange. RULE-LICENSE.

*fall. **Fall for,** to be deceived by, to accept (a false account); to fall in love with, *GULL-DECEIVER, LOVE-HATE; **fall guy,** a scapegoat, COMMUTATION-PERMUTATION.

fall′-out″. The radioactive dust or particles that come to earth, sometimes over a large area, after the explosion of an atomic bomb. #NUCLEAR PHYSICS.

*fan. An enthusiast for a sport; an ardent admirer of an actor, player, singer, or other public figure, *APPROVAL-DISAPPROVAL, DESIRE-DISTASTE; **fan mail,** mail received from fans by a public figure, MISSIVE-PUBLICATION.

*farm. A minor-league baseball team owned by or connected with a major-league team and serving as a training ground or reservoir of players for the major-league club. ENTERTAINMENT-WEARINESS

far″-mer-ette′. A girl or woman farm worker, especially one who takes the place of a man in a period of labor shortage such as exists in wartime. DOMESTICATION-AGRICULTURE.

fas′-cism. A political movement advocating, or system of government practicing, tight governmental control of industry and labor and suppression of opposition from competing political parties or otherwise. RULE-LICENSE, TYRANNY-ANARCHY.

fas′-cist. A person who advocates or practices fascism, especially a member of a party advocating fascism or a supporter of a government practicing it; **Fascisti,** members of a fascist party which took control of Italy in 1922. RULE-LICENSE, TYRANNY-ANARCHY.

*fast. **Fast time,** daylight-saving time, TIME.

FBI. Federal Bureau of Investigation, a bureau in the United States Department of Justice which investigates and gathers evidence of violation of Federal laws, except laws (such as tax laws and postal laws) assigned to other organizations. JUDICATURE.

feath′-er. To change the pitch of (an airplane propeller) so that the propeller turns without pulling the airplane (as in idling or coming to a stop). #AVIATION.

feath′-er-bed″-ding. Requiring (by union rule or labor contract) the hiring of men who will be idle at least part of the time, as when labor is replaced by machines or when each worker's activities are specialized within narrow limits. *ACTIVITY-INDOLENCE, LABOR-CAPITAL, USEFULNESS-USELESSNESS.

fea′-ture. The principal film in a motion-picture program; a full-length film. #MOTION PICTURES.

feed′-back″. The action of a regulating device in an automatic control system, such as the thermostat which "feeds back" to the heating unit information about the temperature of the room. RELEASE-RESTRAINT.

fel′-low trav′-el-er. A sympathizer, especially a person who is not a member but follows the principles of the Communist Party. ASSENT-DISSENT, FRIEND-FOE.

femme fatale [F.]. An irresistibly seductive woman. MOTIVE-CAPRICE.

fend′-er. The guard over a wheel of a motor vehicle. #AUTOMOBILE.

*fer′-ry. To fly an airplane to the point where it is to be delivered to a purchaser or user. #AVIATION, TRANSFER.

fe′-ver. **Fever therapy,** the treatment of disease by causing a rise of temperature in the body, REMEDY-BANE.

Fi′-ber-glas″. Fine flexible glass threads made into insulating material, a fabric or a building material (a trademark). MATERIALS.

*fifth. **Fifth column,** persons who aid their country's enemy, especially in preparing the way for an invasion and by collaborating after an invasion, PATRIOTISM-TREASON.

fif′-ty-fif′ty. Equally, in equal parts. EQUALITY-INEQUALITY.

*fight′-ing. **Fighting chance,** a chance of success but against formidable odds, POSSIBILITY-IMPOSSIBILITY.

*fill-ing. **Filling station,** a business place where gasoline and oil are sold at retail and, usually, other services provided for motor vehicles and motorists, #AUTOMOBILE.

*film. A motion picture; to photograph (a motion picture). #MOTION PICTURES.

*fin. A five-dollar bill. VALUES.

fi-na′-gle. To deceive, to cheat; to get by craft or slyness, to wangle. CRAFT-ARTLESSNESS, *TRUTHFULNESS-FRAUD.

fi-nal-ize. To complete; to give final form to. COMPLETION-NONCOMPLETION.

fin′-ger-print″. An impression of the lines and whorls on a person's finger tips, useful in identification.

fin'-ick-y. Finical, overnice, too precise, fussy. DESIRE-PARTICULARNESS, PERSISTENCE-WHIM.

fink. A strikebreaker; an informer. BENEFACTOR-EVIL-DOER, GOOD MAN-BAD MAN, LABOR-CAPITAL.

*fis'-sile. Capable of nuclear fission, especially fission through the action of slow or low-energy neutrons. #NUCLEAR PHYSICS.

fis'-sion. The pocess in which an atom, especially a heavy element (uranium or plutonium), absorbs a free neutron and splits into other elements, with the release of enormous amounts of energy, #NUCLEAR PHYSICS; **fission bomb,** an atomic bomb in which the explosive force results entirely from nuclear fission, #NUCLEAR PHYSICS, WEAPON.

fis'-sion-a-ble. Fissile. #NUCLEAR PHYSICS.

*five. Five percenter, a person who for a fee (5%) obtains government contracts for his clients, AGENT, MEDIATION; **five-year plan,** a comprehensive scheme of goals to be achieved in five years or less, specifically **(Five-Year-Plan),** such a plan for economic development of the Soviet Union: several such plans have been decreed, the first beginning in 1928, DESIGN.

*fix-a'-tion. An abnormal attachment (as to one's mother or father, or to a period of one's life or something connected with it) which interferes with proper psychological and emotional development. LOVE-HATE, *MIND-IMBECILITY.

flak. The fire of anti-aircraft cannon. ATTACK-DEFENSE, #AVIATION, WEAPON.

*flame. Flame thrower, a weapon which throws a stream of spray of burning oil, WEAPON.

*flap. A hinged addition to an airplane wing which can be set at different angles to aid in taking off or landing. #AVIATION.

*flap'-per. A young girl, especially one who is frivolous or flippant or unconventional (a term much used in the 1920's). INFANT-VETERAN, MALE-FEMALE.

*flash. Flash bulb, a bulb which gives a brief bright light for taking photographs, LUMINARY-SHADE; **flash burn,** a severe burn from the intense heat liberated in an explosion, HEAT-COLD; **flash gun,** a device for setting off a flash bulb and the camera shutter at the same time.

flash'-back". In a motion picture, novel, or the like, a scene or sequence inserted to relate something that happened before the main course of the story. ACCOUNT, #MOTION PICTURES.

*flat. Flat tire, a pneumatic tire which has been deflated; a tiresome or uninteresting person, #AUTOMOBILE, ENTERTAINMENT-WEARINESS.

*flat'-ten. Flatten out, to bring (an airplane) to a horizontal position after a climb or a dive; to take a horizontal position, #AVIATION.

flat'-top". An aircraft carrier. #AVIATION, BELLIGERENT, CONVEYANCE-VESSEL.

fli'-er or **fly'-er.** A person who flies an airplane. #AVIATION.

*flight. The operation of an aircraft; a trip in an aircraft; an airplane trip made as a recurring unit (identified by number) of the operation of an air line; a tactical unit of two or more airplanes. #AVIATION, TRAVELING-NAVIGATION.

fliv'-ver. A small, cheap automobile, especially (in their days) the Model T or the Model A Ford. #AUTOMOBILE, CONVEYANCE-VESSEL.

*floor. A minimum established for prices or wages, PRICE-DISCOUNT; **floor show,** a program of music, singing, dancing, or other entertainment provided in a place where food and drinks are served, ENTERTAINMENT-WEARINESS.

*flop. To fail; a failure. *SUCCESS-FAILURE.

flop'-house". A place where the bare essentials for staying overnight are provided at a very low charge. DWELLER-HABITATION.

fluff. To make a mistake in speaking or reading (lines in a play or the like), or to miss a cue. ACTING, SKILL-UNSKILFULNESS.

*flu'-id. Unsettled, changeable, in flux. MUTABILITY-STABILITY; **fluid drive,** a hydraulic device which varies the gear ratio in an automotive power transmission without manual shifting, #AUTOMOBILE.

flu"-o-res'-cent lamp. A glass tube in which ultraviolet light produced inside the tube is changed into visible light by a fluorescent inner coating, with smaller consumption of electricity than in incandescent lamps. LUMINARY-SHADE.

fluor'-i-date. To add small quantities of fluorine compounds to drinking water, with the aim of reducing tooth decay in children. REMEDY-BANE.

fluor'-i-dize. To treat with a fluorine compound (especially, teeth, with the aim of preventing decay). REMEDY-BANE.

*fly. To operate an aircraft; to ride in an aircraft. #AVIATION, TRAVELING-NAVIGATION.

*fly'-ing. Flying bomb, a robot bomb (buzz bomb), WEAPON; **flying field,** a place where airplanes may land and take off, and be serviced, but not as large as or with all the facilities of an airport, ARRIVAL-DEPARTURE, #AVIATION; **flying fortress,** a large armored airplane built and equipped both for fighting and for bombing, #AVIATION, BELLIGERENT; **flying saucer,** any of various phenomena reportedly seen over the United States (or, less often, elsewhere) in recent years, often described as resembling a saucer or disk and usually as traveling at great height and great speed, FANCY, PHENOMENON.

fly'-way". An aerial path regularly followed by birds in their migration. WAY.

F.M. Frequency modulation, a method of radio transmission in which static is almost eliminated but which can be received only a short distance from the sending station as compared with A.M. #RADIO-TELEVISION.

*foam. Foam rubber, rubber prepared with a spongy texture making it appropriate for upholstery, cushions and the like, MATERIALS.

*fold or **fold up.** To fail, collapse, go out of existence (said especially of a play or business enterprise). *SUCCESS-FAILURE.

fold'-ing mon'-ey. Paper money. MONEY.

folk'-ways". The customs and habits which serve as guides of conduct of a social group; loosely, folklore. HABIT-DESUETUDE, JOVE-FIEND.

fool'-proof". Safe or certain in spite of mishandling or misjudgment. SECURITY-INSECURITY.

foot'-age. Amount of film, measured in linear feet, in a motion-picture sequence; amount of wood, measured in board feet. MENSURATION, #MOTION PICTURES.

*form. Form letter, a letter (reproduced mechanically or copied from a standard form) which can be used over and over or sent to many people at the same time, MISSIVE-PUBLICATION.

*for'-ti-fy. To enrich (a food) by adding vitamins or minerals. NUTRIMENT-EXCRETION.

*foul. Foul up, to entangle, ensnarl, confuse, mix up, ORGANIZATION-DISORGANIZATION.

Four-H clubs or **4-H clubs.** A national system of youth clubs to improve "head, heart, hands, and health": through these clubs children in rural areas receive instruction and carry out individual projects in agriculture and home economics. ASSOCIATION.

fox'-hole". A small pit for one or sometimes two soldiers, often dug hastily and under fire, serving as protection and firing position in a battle. REFUGE-PITFALL.

*frame. To conspire to put blame on (an innocent person), JUSTIFICATION-CHARGE; **frame of reference,** a set of standards developed in an individual's experience which serve as a basis for his ideas and judgments, CONCEPTION-THEME, *MIND-IMBECILITY.

frame'-up". A plot or fraudulent scheme, especially one to fix blame on an innocent person or one to decide the winner of a contest. DESIGN, JUSTIFICATION-CHARGE.

*frat'-er-nize. To associate on friendly terms with an enemy or with civilians in an occupied country; to have illicit sexual relations with a woman of an occupied country. AMITY-HOSTILITY, PURITY-IMPURITY.

*free. Free association, in psychoanalysis, a technique in which a person is asked either to state the idea that comes to mind when each word on a list is read, or to tell the continuous series of ideas that begin with reaction to some word, *MIND-IMBECILITY; **free enterprise,** operation of private business with a minimum of control by the government (as opposed to socialism, communism and fascism), LIBERTY-SUBJECTION; **the free world,** the countries not included within the Communist group, LIBERTY-SUBJECTION.

*free'-dom. **The four freedoms,** the fundamental aspects of freedom as stated by President Franklin D. Roosevelt: freedom of speech, freedom of worship, freedom from want, and freedom from fear, LIBERTY-SUBJECTION.

free'-way". An expressway, superhighway. WAY.

*freeze. To fix or immobilize, usually by government order, e.g., to prevent increase or decrease of prices or wages, or to prohibit sale of stocks of some commodity except on specific authorization. RELEASE-RESTRAINT.

freez'-er. A cabinet in which foods can be frozen and in which frozen foods can be stored. CONSERVATION, OVEN-REFRIGERATOR.

Freud'-i-an. Relating to the teaching and practice (psychoanalysis) of Sigmund Freud. *MIND-IMBECILITY.

*fringe. Marginal, peripheral, secondary, additional, ADDITION-SUBTRACTION, INCREMENT-REMNANT; **fringe benefits,** in a labor contract, benefits other than the money paid as wages (e.g., insurance or pensions), LABOR-CAPITAL.

frog'-man". An underwater swimmer with equipment enabling him to stay underwater for long periods, especially for scouting or placing explosives in naval warfare. BELLIGERENT, SPRING-DIVE.

*front. A person chosen as head of an organization in order to add respectability or prestige or to conceal the identity of the persons who really control it, COMMUTATION-PERMUTATION, *GULL-DECEIVER; **Communist front,** an organization not connected, or not formally connected, with the Communist Party which carries out some of the aims of that party, TYRANNY-ANARCHY.

fud'-dy–dud"-dy. An overcritical or ineffectual or old-fashioned person. MIGHT-IMPOTENCE, *SAGE-FOOL.

Füh'-rer or **Fueh'-rer.** Title, meaning "leader," given to Adolf Hitler as head of the German government during the nazi period, 1933 to 1945. CHIEF-UNDERLING.

fun"-da-men'-tal-ism. A movement among American Protestants based upon the doctrine that the Bible is literally true in every respect, such as (especially) the account of the creation of the world. CONVENTIONALITY-UNCONVENTIONALITY, ORTHODOXY-HETERODOXY.

fu'-se-lage. The body of an airplane, as distinguished from wings and tail attached to it. #AVIATION.

*fu'-sion. The combining of nuclei of atoms of light elements to form nuclei of heavier elements, with the release of tremendous amounts of energy, #NUCLEAR PHYSICS; **fusion bomb,** a bomb in which the explosive and other destructive effects are due principally to fusion of atomic nuclei but in part also to the explosion of an atomic (fission) bomb to generate the tremendously high temperature needed to accomplish fusion, WEAPON.

fu'-tur-ism. A theory and practice in art, including literature and music, beginning shortly before World War I, which rejected traditional ideas and methods and aimed at a dynamic representation of the machine-age world. NATURE-ART.

G

gaffe. A social blunder, a faux pas. SOCIETY-LUDICROUSNESS, *SUCCESS-FAILURE.

gag'-man". A person who writes jokes, devises comic situations, or the like, especially for radio and television comedians. #RADIO-TELEVISION, WAG.

gam'-ma glob'-u-lin. A portion of the human blood containing many antibodies; it can be extracted and used as an inoculation against certain diseases. ANATOMY, REMEDY-BANE.

gam'-ma rays. Electromagnetic waves similar to but shorter than X rays, emitted in the disintegration of a radioactive substance or in the reactions occurring when cosmic rays enter the earth's atmosphere. #NUCLEAR PHYSICS.

*gang. **Gang up on,** to attack or oppose in a gang, ATTACK-DEFENSE, GATHERING-SCATTERING.

gang'-ster. A member of a gang, especially a gang of criminals or bullies; a criminal or a bully. BENEFACTOR-EVILDOER, GOOD MAN-BAD MAN.

*gas. Gasoline, #AUTOMOBILE; **gas mask,** a device covering mouth and nose and containing a filter to enable a person to breathe the air after a poison-gas attack, ATTACK-DEFENSE; **gas station,** a place where gasoline is sold at retail, a filling station, #AUTOMOBILE; **poison gas,** any gas used or prepared for use in warfare to kill or disperse enemy troops, ATTACK-DEFENSE.

*gate. **Gate crasher,** a person who gets into a sports event or other spectacle without a ticket, ENTRANCE-EXIT, *GULL-DECEIVER.

Gauleiter [G.]. The head of a district in Germany during the nazi regime; a subordinate or henchman. CHIEF-UNDERLING.

*gear. To connect by gears; to coordinate or harmonize (with), to adjust or subordinate (to); **gear up,** to speed up (e.g., for greater industrial production). CONNECTIVE, HARMONY-DISCORD, SWIFTNESS-SLOWNESS.

gear'-shift". A device for connecting a motor to any of several sets of gears providing different speeds. #AUTOMOBILE, CONNECTIVE.

Gei'-ger count'-er. A device for detecting and indicating the amount of radiation from radioactive substances or in cosmic-ray reactions. #NUCLEAR PHYSICS.

gene. A unit of heredity in the germ plasm which is connected with the development of a specific character. BIOLOGY, CAUSE-EFFECT, SUBJECTIVENESS-OBJECTIVENESS.

gen'-o-cide. A deliberate program of extermination of a people, such as the systematic killing of Jews in Europe by the nazis. LIFE-KILLING.

*gen'-tle-man. **Gentleman's agreement** or **gentlemen's agreement,** an informal agreement, fulfillment of which depends upon the good faith of the parties rather than enforcement by legal procedures, CONTRACT, ENGAGEMENT-RELEASE, VARIANCE-ACCORD.

ge"-o-pol'-i-tics. The study of geography in relation to a country's foreign policy; specifically, the nazi doctrine attempting to justify expansion of the Germans into the productive and strategically vital parts of the Eurasian continent. CONDUCT.

ger″-i-at′-rics. A branch of medicine dealing with the health and ailments of aged people. INFANCY-AGE, REMEDY-BANE.

***germ.** Germ warfare, the spreading of disease germs among the population of an enemy country, FIGHTING-CONCILIATION.

ger′-mi-cide. Any substance used to kill germs, especially disease germs. REMEDY-BANE.

ger″-on-tol′-o-gy. The study of the phenomena and problems of old age. INFANCY-AGE.

Ge-stalt′ psy-chol′-o-gy. A school of psychology based on the principle that mental processes and behavior must be studied in whole configurations rather than in isolated individual phenomena. *MIND-IMBECILITY.

Ge-sta′-po. The secret police in Germany during the nazi regime; any secret police or other organization which operates secretly, arbitrarily, and ruthlessly. JUDICATURE, TYRANNY-ANARCHY.

***ges′-ture.** Any statement or action aimed at a certain effect or suggesting an intention, e.g., *a gesture of friendship.* MANIFESTATION-LATENCY, PROFFER-REFUSAL.

***ghost.** A secondary image or bright spot in an optical instrument (with a defective lens); a secondary or multiple image on a television screen; abnormal echoes on a radar screen; a ghost writer; to ghost-write, ANTAGONIST-ASSISTANT, #ELECTRONICS, MISSIVE-PUBLICATION, OPTICAL INSTRUMENTS, #RADIO-TELEVISION, WRITING-PRINTING; **ghost town,** a town or city which has been abandoned by all or almost all of its inhabitants, PRESENCE-ABSENCE, SOCIABILITY-PRIVACY; **ghost writer,** a person who writes speeches delivered by another person or things published under another person's name, ANTAGONIST-ASSISTANT, MISSIVE-PUBLICATION, WRITING-PRINTING.

ghost′-write″. To write speeches, books, articles, and the like for another person who delivers or publishes them as his own. MISSIVE-PUBLICATION, WRITING-PRINTING.

G.I. or **GI.** An enlisted man in the United States Army; relating to servicemen or former servicemen; government issue, or conforming to military regulations. BELLIGERENT.

gig′-o-lo. A man hired as a dancing partner or escort for a woman; a man who is supported by a woman. GOOD MAN-BAD MAN, PURITY-RAKE, SOLITUDE-COMPANY.

gim′-mick. Any small device (often used instead of referring to the article by its real name); a device used to control a prize wheel, or a device used in a magical trick; any trick or stratagem; a premium offer or similar advertising or sales inducement. CONSEQUENCE-INSIGNIFICANCE, CRAFT-ARTLESSNESS, USEFULNESS-USELESSNESS.

give′-a-way″. An article given away or sold at nominal cost to promote sales; a radio or television program in which prizes are given to members of the audience or other selected participants in a contest. GIVING-RECEIVING, #RADIO-TELEVISION.

glam′-or-ize. To adorn (by dress, cosmetics, and the like) so as to make glamorous and alluring; to glorify. BEAUTY-UGLINESS, EMBELLISHMENT-DISFIGUREMENT.

***glide.** In aviation, to come down slowly without using the motor, ASCENT-DESCENT, #AVIATION; **glide bombing,** bombing from an airplane which is descending toward the target at a shallower angle than in dive bombing, ATTACK-DEFENSE, #AVIATION.

glid′-er. An aircraft similar to an airplane but having no motor. #AVIATION, CONVEYANCE-VESSEL.

glob′-al. World-wide, relating to the whole world. EXTENSION-INEXTENSION, MAGNITUDE-SMALLNESS, UNIVERSALITY-PARTICULARITY.

globe′-trot″-ter. A person who travels extensively about the world for sightseeing or on business. WAYFARER-SEAFARER.

G′-man″. An agent of the FBI. JUDICATURE.

***goat.** Get one's goat, to anger or annoy or tease a person, CHARITABLENESS-MALEVOLENCE, PLEASURABLENESS-PAINFULNESS.

gob. A sailor in the United States Navy. BELLIGERENT.

gob′-ble-dy-gook″. Pompous, stilted, and involved language. *ADAGE-NONSENSE, MEANING-JARGON.

go′-get″-ter. An enterprising, aggressive, and generally successful person. *ACTIVITY-INDOLENCE, *SUCCESS-FAILURE.

***gold.** Gold digger, a girl or woman who uses her charms to get money or expensive attentions from men, MOTIVE-CAPRICE, UNSELFISHNESS-SELFISHNESS.

gold′-brick″. To avoid work or duties, as by pretending illness; a shirker, especially in the army or navy. *ACTIVITY-INDOLENCE, QUEST-EVASION.

gold′-brick″-er. A gold-brick, a shirker. *ACTIVITY-INDOLENCE, QUEST-EVASION.

***gon′-do-la.** A car suspended from a dirigible baloon to carry motors, crew, and passengers. #AVIATION.

goo. A thick, sticky liquid or semifluid; a sweet, sticky substance. COHESION-LOOSENESS, VISCIDITY-FOAM.

***good.** Good Neighbor Policy, a policy of the United States, formulated in 1933, of encouraging friendly political and economic relations with and between the other countries of North and South America. AMITY-HOSTILITY.

***goods.** Catch with the goods, to catch with stolen goods, to catch in the act of committing a crime, DISCOVERY; **get** or **have the goods on,** to find out or know some evidence of (a person's) guilt, DISCOVERY. JUSTIFICATION-CHARGE, KNOWLEDGE-IGNORANCE.

goo′-ey. Thick and sticky (sometimes, also, sweet). COHESION-LOOSENESS, VISCIDITY-FOAM.

goof. A silly or stupid person. SAGE-FOOL; **goof off,** to do idle or silly things; to shirk or avoid work, QUEST-EVASION, *SAGE-FOOL.

goof′-y. Silly, foolish, stupid. *SAGACITY-INCAPACITY.

goon. A ruffian hired to terrorize or intimidate, especially to get control of a labor union or to break a strike; a ruffian, a stupid or brutal person. BENEFACTOR-EVILDOER, GOOD MAN-BAD MAN, LABOR-CAPITAL.

goop. A boor, a person with bad manners; a silly person. GENTILITY-COMMONALTY, POLITENESS-IMPOLITENESS, *SAGE-FOOL.

***grade.** Grade A, first class, GOODNESS-BADNESS; **grade separation,** the construction of a highway so that it passes over or under another highway or a railway rather than crossing at grade level. WAY; **make the grade,** to reach the top of an uphill road; to reach any goal; to meet a required standard, *SUCCESS-FAILURE.

***grand.** A thousand dollars. VALUES.

***grand′-fa″-ther.** Grandfather clause, in a law abolishing or restricting some activity, an exemption for persons engaged in that activity before a specified date (originally, a clause in measures intended to disfranchise Negro voters exempting those whose fathers or grandfathers had voted), HOLDING-EXEMPTION.

***grass′-hop″-per.** A small, unarmed airplane used for scouting and for directing the fire of artillery. #AVIATION, BELLIGERENT.

***grass.** Grass roots or grass-roots, the people of the United States living in the country or in small towns; grass-roots, arising from or representing the common people. CITY-COUNTRY, HUMANITY.

***grave′-yard.** Graveyard shift, the working hours in a factory between 11 P.M. or midnight and the day shift, LIGHT-DARKNESS.

***gra′-vy.** Profit obtained without or with little effort. GAIN-LOSS, OUTLAY-INCOME.

***gray.** Gray market, trade, at exorbitant prices, in goods which are scarce but not under the restrictions that give rise to a black market, COSTLINESS-CHEAP-NESS, TAKING-RESTITUTION.

*great. **Great White Way,** the brightly lighted theater district on Broadway in New York City, CITY-COUNTRY, ENTERTAINMENT-WEARINESS.

*green. **Green light,** a traffic signal authorizing motorists or a railroad train to proceed; authorization to proceed with any project, LEAVE-PROHIBITION; **green thumb,** exceptional ability and luck in the growing of plants; a person who has such ability and luck, SKILL-UNSKILFULNESS.

grem'-lins. Elves or gnomes who get the blame when things go wrong, especially with airplanes. #AVIATION, JOVE-FIEND.

grid. A grating, gridiron, or network; the lead electrode in a storage battery; a wire loop or coil which controls the passage of electrons between the filament and the plate in a vacuum tube. CROSSING, ELECTRICITY, #ELECTRONICS.

*grill. To question minutely and severely. INVESTIGATION-ANSWER.

*gripe. To complain. CONTENTEDNESS-DISCONTENTMENT, JUBILATION-LAMENTATION.

*groove. **In the groove,** in top form, especially in playing jazz music, FAULTLESSNESS-FAULTINESS, MELODY-DISSONANCE.

grouch. A sulky, discontented mood; a sulky, grumbling person; to be sulky, nag, complain. CONTENTEDNESS-DISCONTENTMENT, FAVORITE-QUARRELSOMENESS.

grouch'-y. Peevish, discontented, grumbling. CONTENTEDNESS-DISCONTENTMENT, FAVORITE-QUARRELSOMENESS.

*ground. To keep an aircraft or a flier from leaving the ground; to take away a pilot's license, #AVIATION, LEAVE-PROHIBITION; **ground crew,** workmen who service and repair airplanes before and after flights, #AVIATION; **ground loop,** a sharp unexpected turn of an airplane while moving over the ground, in taking off, landing or taxiing, AIM-ABERRATION, #AVIATION.

grouse. To grumble, complain. CONTENTEDNESS-DISCONTENTMENT, JUBILATION-LAMENTATION.

guar"-an-teed' an'-nu-al wage. A labor agreement providing for compensation during unemployment if a worker's earnings fall below a specified amount. LABOR-CAPITAL, RECOMPENSE-PUNITION.

*guid'-ed. **Guided missile,** a self-propelling missile such as a rocket or robot bomb which is guided to a target by radio signals, or a radar device, or control mechanisms set before the missile is launched, WEAPON.

guin'-ea pig. Any person or thing used as a subject for experimentation or observation. TRIAL.

*GULL—DECEIVER

GULL

Fall for. To be deceived by; to accept (a false account).
Hold the bag, be left holding the bag, hold the sack. To be left empty-handed, to be left to suffer the consequences.
Not dry behind the ears. Immature, gullible.

DECEIVER

Front. A person chosen as head of an organization to add respectability or prestige or to conceal the identity of the persons who really control it.
Gate crasher. A person who gets in without a ticket.
Phony. A faker, pretender, impostor.
Ringer. A contestant whose identity and abilities are not revealed; a person who enters a group or activity under a false claim or concealment of his real interest.

gum'-shoe". To go around quietly and stealthily; a detective. *ENLIGHTENMENT-SECRECY.

*gun. To open the throttle (of a motor, especially an airplane motor) so as to increase speed; **give it the gun,** to speed up. #AVIATION, SWIFTNESS-SLOWNESS.

gun'-man. A person who uses a gun in committing a crime, an armed desperado; a hired killer. BENEFACTOR-EVILDOER, GOOD MAN-BAD MAN, LIFE-KILLING.

gy"-ni-at'-rics. A branch of medicine dealing with the treatment of women's diseases. REMEDY-BANE.

gy"-ro-com'-pass. A compass with a motor-driven wheel, the axis of which points to true north. MENSURATION.

gy"-ro-pi'-lot. Same as automatic pilot. #AVIATION.

gy"-ro-sta'-bi-liz"-er. A device for stabilizing a vessel by counteracting its roll. MUTABILITY-STABILITY.

H

hair'-do". The way a girl's or woman's hair is arranged. DRESS-UNDRESS, EMBELLISHMENT-DISFIGUREMENT.

hair'-pin" bend or turn. A U-shaped bend or turn in a railroad track or a highway. WAY.

*half. **Half life,** a measure of radioactivity of a radioactive element or isotope: energy is lost at a constantly diminishing rate; in any half-life period half of the atoms decay; half of those that are left decay in another period of the same length, and so on, #NUCLEAR PHYSICS.

half'-track". A motor vehicle used in the army, having wheels in front and caterpillar tracks in back. #AUTOMOBILE.

hal"-i-to'-sis. Bad breath. PERFUME-STENCH.

*ham. A poor actor or an actor who overacts; an amateur radio operator. ACTING, #RADIO-TELEVISION.

ham'-burg"-er. Ground beef; a sandwich of grilled hamburger meat. NUTRIMENT-EXCRETION.

*ham'-mer. **Hammer and sickle,** an emblem representing the worker and the peasant, used on the flag of the Soviet Union, SIGN.

hand'-out". An official statement, news release, or the like given to the press by a government agency, a business organization, or other source of news. *ENLIGHTENMENT-SECRECY, *PUBLICITY.

hand'-set". A telephone instrument in which both the receiver and the mouthpiece are contained in a case held in the hand. HEARING-DEAFNESS.

hang'-ar. A shed sheltering airplanes or airships. #AVIATION, DWELLER-HABITATION.

hang'-o"-ver. A survival, something remaining from an earlier time; the aftereffect of drinking too much alcoholic liquor at one time. INCREMENT-REMNANT, TEETOTALISM-INTEMPERANCE.

*hap'-py. Exhilarated, irresponsible, obsessed (in combinations, e.g. *bomb-happy, power-happy, trigger-happy,* cf. **slap-happy**). EXCITABILITY-INEXCITABILITY, *SAGACITY-INCAPACITY.

*hard. **Hard core,** the central, essential, permanent part of any thing or group, CONSEQUENCE-INSIGNIFICANCE.

hard'-boiled'. Unimpressionable, tough, rough. POLITENESS-IMPOLITENESS, SENSITIVENESS-APATHY.

hard'-top". An automobile body style with a fixed top but resembling a convertible in lack of a post between front and rear windows. #AUTOMOBILE.

has'-sle. A mix-up, muddle; a wrangle, quarrel. ORGANIZATION-DISORGANIZATION, REGULARITY-IRREGULARITY, VARIANCE-ACCORD.

hat'-chet-man". A writer or politician who undertakes

to destroy or damage opponents by violent accusations, often on personal or collateral issues. FLATTERER-DEFAMER, JUSTIFICATION-CHARGE.

hay'-mak"-er. In boxing, a powerful, swinging blow. IMPETUS-REACTION.

hay'-wire". Wire used in bailing hay, also for making impromptu repairs to vehicles and other machinery; makeshift, inferior, FAULTLESSNESS-FAULTINESS, LAMINA-FIBER, REGULARITY-IRREGULARITY; **go haywire,** to get out of order, to become confused, to go crazy, FAULTLESSNESS-FAULTINESS, ORGANIZATION-DISORGANIZATION, *SANENESS-LUNACY.

H-bomb. The hydrogen bomb. #NUCLEAR PHYSICS, WEAPON.

***head'-ache".** A cause of worry or trouble. PLEASURABLENESS-PAINFULNESS, PLEASURE-PAIN.

***head'-ing.** The direction in which an airplane is headed. AIM-ABERRATION, #AVIATION.

***hear'-ing.** **Hearing aid,** a device, small enough to be worn on the person, for amplifying sound for persons with defective hearing. HEARING-DEAFNESS.

heart'-land". In geopolitics, an area (the northern sweep of the Eurasian land mass) believed to be economically self-sufficient, potentially invulnerable, and able to dominate the world. EXTENSION-DISTRICT.

Heav'-i-side" lay'-er (or Kennelly-Heaviside layer). A layer of the upper atmosphere which reflects radio waves and thus makes it possible to receive radio (but not F.M. or television) signals at great distances from the broadcasting station. #RADIO-TELEVISION, WATER-AIR.

***heav'-y.** **Heavy hydrogen,** deuterium, an isotope with almost twice the weight of ordinary hydrogen; **heavy water,** a liquid similar to water but containing deuterium (heavy hydrogen) atoms in place of hydrogen: small quantities are present in water and can be separated from it; it can be used as a moderator in nuclear reactions. CHEMISTRY, #NUCLEAR PHYSICS.

hedge'-hop". To fly an airplane close to the ground. #AVIATION, TRAVELING-NAVIGATION.

hel'-i-cop"-ter. A heavier-than-air aircraft which is lifted and moved by a propeller rotating in a horizontal plane. #AVIATION, CONVEYANCE-VESSEL.

hel'-i-port". An airport for helicopters. ARRIVAL-DEPARTURE, #AVIATION.

hel'-lion. A mischievous person, a troublemaker. BENEFACTOR-EVILDOER, GOOD MAN-BAD MAN.

hep. Knowing, well informed. KNOWLEDGE-IGNORANCE.

het'-er-o-dyne". Relating to a system for reducing the high frequencies of radio signals to a much lower frequency (the difference between the frequency of the incoming waves and that of a second current which is combined with it) which can be more efficiently handled in the receiving apparatus. #RADIO-TELEVISION.

hi'-fi'. High-fidelity (said of phonograph or radio equipment, sound, etc.; see **high fidelity**). #RADIO-TELEVISION, SOUND-SILENCE.

***high.** A peak or high point (of achievement, prices, etc.); the high or fastest gear of a motor vehicle, #AUTOMOBILE, FAULTLESSNESS-FAULTINESS, HEIGHT-LOWNESS; **high fidelity,** in phonograph and radio operation, the reproduction of sound in all or approximately all audible frequencies and with the least possible distortion, #RADIO-TELEVISION, SOUND-SILENCE.

high'-brow". A person of outstanding intellectual and cultural interests (usually said somewhat derisively); pertaining to or characterized by intellect and culture. KNOWLEDGE-IGNORANCE, SOCIETY-AFFECTATION, TASTE-VULGARITY.

high'-en'-er-gy phys'-ics. Nuclear physics. #NUCLEAR PHYSICS.

high"-er-up'. A person in a higher position or rank. CHIEF-UNDERLING, CONSEQUENCE-INSIGNIFICANCE.

high'-hat'. Snobbish; a snob; to snub, treat snobbishly. PRESUMPTION-OBSEQUIOUSNESS, SELF-RESPECT-HUMBLENESS, SOCIETY-AFFECTATION.

high'-light". The most brightly illuminated part of a picture; the most conspicuous or interesting part of a scene, an event, etc.; to emphasize, to make prominent. CONSEQUENCE-INSIGNIFICANCE.

high'-pres'-sure. Energetic, insistent (in compelling action, as in advertising and selling); to compel; to advertise or sell by energetic and insistent methods. *ACTIVITY-INDOLENCE, COERCION, DETERMINATION-VACILLATION, MOTIVE-CAPRICE, *PUBLICITY.

high'-tail". To run fast; **high-tail it,** to start out at full speed. HURRY-LEISURE, SWIFTNESS-SLOWNESS.

hi'-jack" or **high'-jack".** To rob or take by force, especially liquor or other commodity which is being transported unlawfully. THEFT.

hike. A long walk, a tramp, a march; to take a long walk, to tramp, to march; to raise, to increase; an increase. INCREASE-DECREASE, TRAVELING-NAVIGATION.

hill'-bil"-ly. A person who lives in or comes from the backwoods or mountainous places, especially in the South. DWELLER-HABITATION, GENTILITY-COMMONALTY.

***hit.** **Hit-and-run driver,** a driver who is involved in an automobile accident and drives away without giving aid or reporting the accident, #AUTOMOBILE, DUTY-DERELICTION; **hitting on all four** (or **six** or **eight**) (**cylinders**), working smoothly and efficiently, #AUTOMOBILE, SKILL-UNSKILFULNESS, USEFULNESS-USELESSNESS.

hitch'-hike". To travel by asking for rides in automobiles or trucks that come along on a highway. #AUTOMOBILE, PETITION-EXPOSTULATION, TRAVELING-NAVIGATION.

ho'-bo. A tramp, vagrant. WAYFARER-SEAFARER.

hog'-tie". To tie (a pig's or other animal's) four feet together; to restrain, prevent movement or action. RELEASE-RESTRAINT.

***hog'-wash".** Nonsense, idle talk. *ADAGE-NONSENSE, CONVERSATION-MONOLOGUE.

ho'-kum. Nonsense, bunk; either low comedy or sentimental elements of a story or play. *ADAGE-NONSENSE, *GULL-HYPERBOLE.

***hold'-ing.** **Holding company,** a corporation formed to hold stocks (and sometimes bonds) of other corporations, especially corporations which it thus controls, LABOR-CAPITAL.

***home.** **Home economics,** the science and art of managing a household, especially as organized for a school course, CONDUCT.

ho-mog'-e-nized milk. Milk in which the fat particles are distributed evenly and emulsified. MIXTURE-HOMOGENEITY.

honk. The cry of a wild goose; a similar sound, especially the sound of an automobile horn; to make such a sound. #AUTOMOBILE, CRY-ULULATION.

hooch. Alcoholic liquor. TEETOTALISM-INTEMPERANCE.

***hood.** The hinged cover over an automobile engine. #AUTOMOBILE.

hoo'-ey. Nonsense. *ADAGE-NONSENSE, MEANING-JARGON.

hoof'-er. A professional dancer. ACTING.

hook'-up". A connection or combination, especially the arrangement and connection of the parts of a radio receiver, or the cable connection of a number of radio or television stations for broadcasting the same program. #RADIO-TELEVISION, UNION-DISUNION.

hoo'-li-gan. A hoodlum, member of a gang of street ruffians. BENEFACTOR-EVILDOER, GOOD MAN-BAD MAN.

hoop'-la". Excitement, great activity; ballyhoo. Excit-ability-Inexcitability, Loudness-Faintness, *Pub-licity.

*hope. Hope chest, a chest for a collection of articles a young woman acquires in expectation of using them after she marries, Contents-Receiver.

hopped up. Stimulated with drugs; stimulated, excited. Excitation.

*hor"-i-zon'-tal. Horizontal union, a labor union made up of workers in the same craft even though they work in different industries, Labor-Capital.

hor'-mone. One of various substances secreted into the blood stream by the ductless glands which have a power-ful effect on growth, health, personality, and behavior. Anatomy, Biology.

*horn. Horn in, to intrude, interfere, meddle, *Activ-ity-Indolence, Cooperation-Opposition.

*horse. Horse opera, a motion picture or radio or television play based on cowboy adventures in the West, Account, #Motion Pictures, #Radio-Television; horse trade, a political bargain, a compromise, Ex-change, Mediation.

horse'-and-bug'gy. Old-time, old-fashioned, antiquated. Novelty-Antiquity.

*hos'-tel. A unit in a chain of inexpensive lodgings maintained for young people on hikes or bicycle tours. Dweller-Habitation.

*hot. Radioactive, #Nuclear Physics; hot rod, an automobile which has been specially prepared for high speed by removal of fenders or other parts and by alter-ing the motor, #Automobile, Swiftness-Slowness; hot war, war (as contrasted with cold war, in which there is no military action), Fighting-Conciliation, Strife-Peace.

*house. Clean house, to cleanse, get rid of corruption, inefficiency, or other bad conditions, Admission-Expul-sion, Cleanliness-Filthiness; house organ, a peri-odical published by a business company or other organi-zation either to publicize its products or services or to inform and stimulate its employees, Missive-Publica-tion, *Publicity.

how-go'-zit curve. A graph evolved as an airplane progresses in a long flight, giving the pilot a summary of information on distance traveled, elapsed time, and fuel consumption. #Aviation, Sign.

*huck'-ster. An advertising man. *Publicity.

*hud'-dle. A football maneuver in which the players form a tight group to receive signals for the next play; a conference, especially an intimate or secret one. Council, Gathering-Scattering.

*hump. A mountain range that must be crossed on an airplane route, #Aviation, Height-Lowness; over the hump, past a difficult period or crucial test, Comple-tion-Noncompletion, Security-Insecurity.

*hunch. An intuitive feeling, a premonition. Prophecy.

*hur'-dle. A frame set up as a barrier in a race; an obstacle or difficulty; to jump over a hurdle; to over-come (an obstacle or difficulty). Obstruction-Help, *Success-Failure.

hush'-hush". Done or made quietly or secretly; to sup-press or silence. *Enlightenment-Secrecy.

husk'-y. Rugged, strong, strongly built. Strength-Weakness.

hy"-dro-e-lec'-tric. Relating to the production of elec-tricity from water power. Electricity.

*hy'-dro-gen. Hydrogen bomb, a bomb in which im-mense energy is released by the fusion of hydrogen atoms at high temperature generated by explosion of a fission bomb, #Nuclear Physics, Weapon.

hy'-dro-plane". An airplane equipped to take off from and to land on water. #Aviation, Conveyance-Vessel.

hy"-dro-pon'-ics. The growing of plants without soil, by immersing the roots in water containing nutritive materials in solution. Domestication-Agriculture.

hyp"-no-ther'-a-py. The treatment of mental or other ailments by methods involving hypnotism. Remedy-Bane.

I

i-con'-o-scope. A vacuum tube in a television camera which converts the image into the waves which are broadcast. #Radio-Television.

id. In psychoanalysis, the part of a personality which is instinctive and unconscious and underlies the conscious mental processes. *Mind-Imbecility, Subjectiveness-Objectiveness.

*i"-de-ol'-o-gy. A way of thinking, the complex of ideas and doctrines making up and associated with a social or political movement. Faith-Misgiving, Knowl-edge-Ignorance.

if'-fy. Conditional, doubtful, indefinite. Certainty-Doubt.

*im'-age. Image converter, an electronic device to increase the power of a telescope, #Electronics, Opti-cal Instruments.

im'-ag-ism. A movement in poetry aiming at expression in precise images; the movement was a reaction against romanticism and convention and its products are often in free verse. Poetry-Prose.

im-bal'-ance. Lack of balance, especially, faulty coor-dination of eye muscles or of the activity of the endo-crine glands. Health-Sickness.

Im'-mel-mann" turn. A maneuver in which an airplane makes a U turn in a vertical plane by making a half loop and then righting the plane. #Aviation.

im-mo'-bi-lize. To make immobile; to take (coined money) out of circulation. Money, Mutability-Sta-bility.

in"-com-mu"-ni-ca'-do. Deprived of communication with other people (while imprisoned). *Enlighten-ment-Secrecy, Release-Restraint.

*in-fe"-ri-or'-i-ty. Inferiority complex, in psychol-ogy, a neurotic condition resulting from a feeling of inferiority, expressed in defensive or compensatory or aggressive behavior; also popularly an inferiority feel-ing; inferiority feeling, a feeling of weakness or inferiority, real or imagined, not amounting to a neuro-sis. Equality-Inequality, *Mind-Imbecility, Su-premacy-Subordinacy.

in"-fra-red' rays. Heat waves, electromagnetic waves with longer wave length than the red part of visible light. Heat-Cold, Light-Darkness.

in'-group". A group of persons united by mutual ac-ceptance and enjoyment of similar privileges, from which outsiders are excluded. Association, Inclu-sion-Omission.

*in"-hi-bi'-tion. The stopping or restraining of some mental function by some other function or circumstance. *Mind-Imbecility, Release-Restraint.

ink'-blot" test. See Rorschach test. *Mind-Imbe-cility.

in-op'-er-a-ble. Not suitable for or in condition for a surgical operation. Health-Sickness.

in"-sti-tu'-tion-al ad'-ver-tis"-ing. Advertising in-tended to build good will and prestige rather than to stimulate immediate sales. *Publicity.

in"-sti-tu'-tion-al-ize. To confine (a person) in an institution. Release-Restraint.

*in'-stru-ment. Instrument flying, see blind flying, #Aviation.

in'-su-lin. A hormone secreted by the pancreas which controls the amount of sugar in the blood; an extract of this hormone obtained from the pancreas of slaughtered animals and used in the treatment of diabetes (a trademark: Insulin). ANATOMY, REMEDY-BANE.

*in-tel′-li-gence. **Intelligence quotient,** a measure of intelligence, obtained by dividing a person's mental age (as shown by tests) by his age in years (but age over 16 is usually not counted) and multiplying by 100 to eliminate the decimal point; **intelligence test,** a test employed to determine a person's intelligence, especially a test giving results from which the intelligence quotient is computed. *MIND-IMBECILITY, *SAGACITY-INCAPACITY, TRIAL.

in-tel″-li-gent′-si-a. People thought to be or claiming to be the most intelligent and enlightened element of a population; intellectuals. *SAGE-FOOL, SCHOLAR-DUNCE.

in′-ter-com″ or **in′-ter-com-mu″-ni-ca′-tion sys′-tem.** A telephone apparatus for communication between persons in an airplane, a building or other restricted space. HEARING-DEAFNESS.

*in-trigue′. To interest, fascinate, excite the curiosity of. EXCITATION.

*in″-tro-ver′-sion. The direction of a person's interests to his own thoughts and feelings rather than to persons and things around him. *MIND-IMBECILITY, SOCIABILITY-PRIVACY, UNSELFISHNESS-SELFISHNESS.

in′-tro-vert″. A person whose interests are largely in his own thoughts and feelings rather than in the world around him. *MIND-IMBECILITY, SOCIABILITY-PRIVACY, UNSELFISHNESS-SELFISHNESS.

i′-on. An atom or group of atoms which has an electric charge because its electrical neutrality has been disrupted by gain or loss of an electron or electrons. CHEMISTRY, ELECTRICITY.

i′-on-ize. To change (a substance) from a state of electrical balance (neutrality) to a condition in which some atoms or groups of atoms are positively charged (positive ions) and some are negatively charged (negative ions), as when certain solids go into solution, or when high-energy radiation passes through a gas, or in certain nuclear reactions. CHEMISTRY.

i-on′-o-sphere″. A region of thin and highly ionized air constituting the upper part of the atmosphere, beyond the stratosphere. WATER-AIR.

IQ or **I.Q.** Intelligence Quotient. *MIND-IMBECILITY, *SAGACITY-INCAPACITY.

*i′-ron. **Iron Curtain,** the barrier of aloofness and secrecy blocking contacts between the Soviet Union and its satellites and the free world, ANTAGONISM-CONCURRENCE, UNION-DISUNION; **iron lung,** an apparatus for supplying artificial respiration to a person who cannot breathe naturally, as in some cases of infantile paralysis. REMEDY-BANE.

*is′-land. **Island universe,** a galaxy, any of the gigantic star clusters like the galaxy containing the sun and the earth, ASTRONOMY, UNIVERSE.

*i′-so-bar. One of two or more isotopes which have the same mass number (total number of protons and neutrons in the nucleus) but different atomic number (number of protons) and hence belong to different elements, e.g. mercury-204 and lead-204. CHEMISTRY, #NUCLEAR PHYSICS.

i″-so-la′-tion-ism. Political doctrine of opposing United States participation in international affairs. UNION-DISUNION.

i′-so-tope. One of two or more atomic forms which have the same atomic number (number of protons in the nucleus) and hence are forms of the same element, but differ in mass number (total of protons and neutrons in the nucleus) and in nuclear stability or radioactivity, e.g. uranium-235 and uranium-238. CHEMISTRY, #NUCLEAR PHYSICS.

*i′-vo-ry. **Ivory tower,** a figurative expression for withdrawal (especially of an artist or writer) from the practical realities of life. APPROACH-WITHDRAWAL.

J

jack′-pot″. A cumulative stake in various games or the highest prize that can be won in a slot machine; **hit the jackpot,** to win a jackpot; to have a stroke of very good luck or make any highly successful move. GAIN-LOSS, RATIONALE-LUCK, *SUCCESS-FAILURE.

ja-lop′-y. An automobile or airplane which is old and in poor condition. #AUTOMOBILE, #AVIATION, CONVEYANCE-VESSEL.

*jam. A tight spot, a predicament, a difficult situation; to make (radio or radar signals) unintelligible by broadcasting other signals on the same wave length, CONDITION-SITUATION, DIFFICULTY-FACILITY, OBSTRUCTION-HELP, #RADIO-TELEVISION; **jam session,** a gathering at which musicians improvise jazz for their own entertainment, MUSIC.

jam′-packed′. Tightly packed, filled to capacity or overflowing. ENOUGH, ENTIRETY-DEFICIENCY.

ja′-to or **JATO.** Jet-assisted take-off, the addition to an airplane of rocket units to assist it in taking off. #AVIATION.

jay′-walk″. To cross a street in any improper way, especially at any place other than the crosswalks at street intersections. MIDCOURSE-CIRCUIT.

jazz. A kind of lively music characterized especially by syncopation, MELODY-DISSONANCE, MUSIC; **jazz** or **jazz up,** to enliven, to make spirited and informal, EXCITATION.

jaz′-zy. Like jazz, lively, informal. EXCITABILITY-INEXCITABILITY.

jeep. A small but rugged and powerful military automobile, or civilian automobile patterned after it. #AUTOMOBILE, CONVEYANCE-VESSEL.

jell. To take definite form. SOLIDITY-RARITY.

*jet. A stream of heated air and combustion gases ejected to the rear, thereby providing the thrust to propel an aircraft or a rocket; in phrases, referring to this type of power, e.g. *jet aircraft, jet-assisted take-off* (see **jato**), *jet engine, jet plane, jet-propelled, jet propulsion*; **jet** can also mean a jet airplane, #AVIATION; **jet stream,** an air current high (6 to 10 miles) above the earth and traveling at high speed from west to east, RIVER-WIND.

jinx. A person or thing which is said to bring bad luck; to bring bad luck to. GOOD-EVIL, GOODNESS-BADNESS, WELFARE-MISFORTUNE.

jit′-ney. A nickel; a bus or automobile which carries passengers, usually over a regular route, for a small fare, originally a nickel. #AUTOMOBILE, CONVEYANCE-VESSEL, VALUES.

jit′-ter-bug″. A person who is excited by jazz music and expresses his feeling in exaggerated dance movements and gestures; to dance in such a fashion. ENTERTAINMENT-WEARINESS.

jit′-ters. Extreme uneasiness, nervousness. SANGUINENESS-TIMIDITY.

jit′-ter-y. Uneasy, nervous. SANGUINENESS-TIMIDITY.

jive. Jazz music of particular fervor and enthusiasm; to dance to such music; a special jargon associated with devotees of such music. ENTERTAINMENT-WEARINESS, MEANING-JARGON, MUSIC, WORD-NEOLOGY.

*jok′-er. A provision in a document such as a law or a contract which makes some important addition or exception which is not immediately apparent. *ENLIGHTENMENT-SECRECY.

*joy. **Joy ride,** a pleasure ride in an automobile, especially a wild and irresponsible ride; a spree, #AUTOMOBILE, ENTERTAINMENT-WEARINESS, TRAVELING-NAVIGATION.

*juic′-y. Interesting, lively, spicy. EXCITATION, PLEASURABLENESS-PAINFULNESS.

juke box. An automatic phonograph which plays records when coins are deposited in a slot. ENTERTAINMENT-WEARINESS.

juke joint. A place for drinking and eating, especially a small establishment where music is furnished by a juke box. ENTERTAINMENT-WEARINESS.

*****jump. Get (or have) the jump on,** to get an earlier start than, to have an advantage over, to steal a march on, LEADING-FOLLOWING, SUPREMACY-SUBORDINACY.

*****jun′-ior. Junior college,** a college which covers only the first two years of a four-year college course; **junior high school,** a school which takes over some of the instruction otherwise given in the upper grades (seventh and eighth) of elementary school and the first year of high school. SCHOOL.

K

ka″-mi-ka′-ze. A Japanese suicide pilot: in World War II flew their planes with large cargoes of explosives onto targets, especially ships. BELLIGERENT, PATRIOTISM-TREASON.

*****key′-note″. Keynote speech,** a speech at the opening of a political convention outlining problems and policies.

key′-not″-er. A person who makes a keynote speech.

khak′-i. Dull yellowish-brown; a stout twilled cloth of this color, of cotton or sometimes wool, used especially for uniforms. GRAY-BROWN, MATERIALS.

kib′-itz. To look on at a card game and offer unasked advice; to interfere, meddle. *ACTIVITY-INDOLENCE, COOPERATION-OPPOSITION.

kick′-back″. An objection, an unfavorable reaction; money paid (often surreptitiously) to an employer, a foreman, or other person who assisted one in obtaining employment or making a sale. *APPROVAL-DISAPPROVAL, PRICE-DISCOUNT, RECOMPENSE-PUNITION.

kil′-o-cy″-cle. A thousand cycles; one thousand cycles per second, a unit used especially in radio as a measure of the frequency of electromagnetic waves. MEASURE, #RADIO-TELEVISION.

kil′-o-ton″. A measure of the explosive force of an atomic bomb, equal to the energy released by one thousand tons of TNT. MEASURE, #NUCLEAR PHYSICS.

ki-mo′-no. A woman's loose dressing gown with long sleeves and a sash, patterned after a Japanese garment so named. DRESS-UNDRESS.

kin′-e-scope. The picture tube in a television receiver: a vacuum tube which converts the broadcast signals into images (a trademark: Kinescope); a motion picture which records the images received on such a tube. #RADIO-TELEVISION.

king′-fish″. A person in a dominating position in any group or community. CHIEF-UNDERLING, MANAGER.

king′-pin″. The most important person of a group or part of a thing. CHIEF-UNDERLING, CONSEQUENCE-INSIGNIFICANCE.

king′-size″ or **king′-sized″.** Longer or larger than an ordinary or standard size. MAGNITUDE-SMALLNESS.

*****kitch′-en. Kitchen police,** soldiers to assist army cooks, wash dishes, etc.: their work, often assigned as a disciplinary measure, CHIEF-UNDERLING, RECOMPENSE-PUNITION.

kitch″-en-ette′. A small, compact kitchen. CONTENTS-RECEIVER.

kit′-ty. The pool to which all players contribute in a card game; a pool or fund to which several persons contribute for a common purpose. MONEY, PURPOSE-LUCK.

Ki-wa′-ni-an. A member of a Kiwanis club.

Ki-wa′-nis Club. A unit in an organization of clubs of business and professional men, formed to further civic interests, good business practices, and good fellowship. ASSOCIATION.

klieg (or kleig) light. A very bright arc light used in making motion pictures or lighting a scene for a television camera. LUMINARY-SHADE, #MOTION PICTURES.

*****knee. Knee action,** a type of suspension of the front wheels of an automobile permitting each wheel to move up and down independently of the other, #AUTOMOBILE.

*****knock.** A tapping or pounding noise indicating wear or faulty operation in an engine; to make such a noise. #AUTOMOBILE.

knock′-out″. A blow which knocks a boxer down and leaves him unable to go on with the fight; a highly successful or very attractive person or thing. BEAUTY-UGLINESS, IMPETUS-REACTION, *SUCCESS-FAILURE.

know′-how″. Expert skill and knowledge, especially in technology. KNOWLEDGE-IGNORANCE, SKILL-UNSKILFULNESS.

kol-khoz′. A collective farm (in Russia). DOMESTICATION-AGRICULTURE.

K.P. Kitchen Police. CHIEF-UNDERLING, RECOMPENSE-PUNITION.

ku-lak′. In Russian history, a prosperous peasant or farmer, especially one who employed other peasants and, in the Soviet period, one who opposed collectivization. GENTILITY-COMMONALTY, HOLDER.

L

la-gniappe′. A small present given with a purchase; something extra. ADDITION-SUBTRACTION, EXCESS-LACK, GIVING-RECEIVING.

*****land′-ing. Landing gear,** wheels or pontoons which support an airplane in landing and while it remains on land or water; **landing strip,** a long, narrow runway on which airplanes take off and land. #AVIATION.

*****league. League of Nations,** the association of nations organized in 1919, after the end of World War I, and dissolved in 1946, after the formation of the United Nations, ASSOCIATION.

Lebensraum [G.]. "Living space": in Nazi ideology, the space (to be acquired, when necessary, by expansion into neighbors' lands) required for a country, and specifically Germany, to be economically self-sufficient. EXTENSION-INEXTENSION.

left′-ist. A member or adherent or any political party or faction variously described as socialist, communistic, radical, liberal or progressive, especially any which proposes radical political and social changes.

*****leg. Leg work,** work which requires much walking; the work of a legman, OCCUPATION.

*****le″-gion-naire′.** A member of the American Legion, an organization made up of veterans of the United States Army or Navy.

leg′-man″. A newspaper reporter who goes to the site or source of a story to gather the facts for another writer or for himself; an assistant who run errands, especially to gather information, for his employer. *ENLIGHTENMENT-SECRECY, MESSENGER, MISSIVE-PUBLICATION.

lend′-lease′. A system of mutual assistance in World War II, in which the United States furnished food and war materials to its allies in exchange ior materials and services they could provide, especially the use of military, air, and naval bases; a mutually advantageous exchange. OBSTRUCTION-HELP.

*****li″-ai-son′.** Contact or communication maintained between different units of a military force, or between any different groups of organizations. CONNECTION-INDEPENDENCE.

*lib'-er-ty. **Liberty ship,** a type of freighter built in large numbers in the United States during World War II, Conveyance-Vessel.

li-bi'-do. Sexual desire or drive; in psychoanalysis, the instinctual cravings and drives generally, the vital impulse or driving force of the personality. Desire-Distaste, *Mind-Imbecility.

*lie. **Lie detector,** an apparatus used to indicate whether a person under examination is telling the truth: it measures and records slight physical changes when a person is emotionally disturbed, as when telling a lie, *Mind-Imbecility.

*life. **Life line,** a rope thrown to a person in danger of drowning or shot to a vessel in distress; a route on which a country depends for contact with outlying colonies or the like, or for transportation of vital supplies, Security-Insecurity; **the life of Riley,** a life of ease, abundance, and pleasure, Pleasure-Pain.

life'-sav"-er. A person who saves another, or others, from drowning; a person or thing which saves someone from some difficulty. Obstruction-Help, Security-Insecurity.

*limb. **Out on a limb,** in some risky or vulnerable position, Security-Insecurity; **go out on a limb,** to take a definite stand on some debatable issue, Ratiocination-Instinct.

li'-men. A threshold, in psychology or physiology: a dividing point between stimuli or differences which can be perceived and those which cannot. *Mind-Imbecility.

lim'-er-ick. A form of whimsical verse with rhyme scheme aabba, and ordinarily three strong accents in first, second, and fifth lines and two in the third and fourth. Poetry-Prose.

lim'-ou-sine. A large, luxurious automobile with a closed body in which the driver's seat is ordinarily separated from the passengers' space. #Automobile, Conveyance-Vessel.

*lin'-e-ar. **Linear accelerator,** see **accelerator.** #Nuclear Physics.

*liq'-ui-date. To abolish, get rid of (a custom, institution, or the like); to get rid of, to put to death (a person or persons, especially political enemies). Admission-Expulsion, Recompense-Punition.

*live. In radio and television: performed at the time of the broadcast, that is, not played from a recording, transcription, or film, #Radio-Television; **live wire,** a wire carrying electricity; an active and enterprising person, *Activity-Indolence, Electricity.

lo-bot'-o-my. A surgical operation severing some of the nerve tracts of the brain, to relieve certain mental disorders. *Mind-Imbecility, Remedy-Bane.

*lo-ca'-tion. Any place, away from the studio, where scenes for a motion picture are photographed. #Motion Pictures.

long'-hair". A composer, player, or devotee of classical music; **longhair** or **long-haired,** relating (disparagingly or ironically) to classical music, intellectual tastes and activities, or theory. *Sagacity-Incapacity, Taste-Vulgarity.

long'-play'-ing. Said of microgroove phonograph record made to be played at 33⅓ revolutions per minute.

lo'-ran. An electronic apparatus which enables the navigator of an airplane or ship to determine its position from radio signals sent out from two stations. #Electronics, Position.

*lot. A studio and grounds connected with it where motion pictures are made. #Motion Pictures.

loud'-speak'-er. A device which converts electrical signals into sound in a radio, phonograph, or similar apparatus. Hearing-Deafness.

*low. A low point (of achievement, prices, etc.); the low or slowest gear of a motor vehicle. #Automobile, Faultlessness-Faultiness, Height-Lowness.

low'-brow". A person with little or no interest in intellectual and artistic matters. Knowledge-Ignorance, Taste-Vulgarity.

low'-down". **The low-down,** the whole truth, the real facts, especially a confidential report, *Enlightenment-Secrecy, Knowledge-Ignorance, *Truth-Error.

lu"-mi-nes'-cence. Cold light: emission of light by a chemical or electrical process rather than by incandescence. Luminary-Shade.

lunch"-eon-ette'. A lunchroom or restaurant where light lunches are furnished. Dweller-Habitation.

*lyr'-ic. **Lyrics,** the words for a song; the words for the musical numbers of a show. Music, Poetry-Prose.

M

Mach num'-ber. The ratio of the speed of a body (airplane, rocket, etc.) in relation to the speed of sound; **Mach One,** the speed of sound. #Aviation, Measure, Swiftness-Slowness.

Mae West. A lifesaving vest, inflatable from cartridges of carbon dioxide, worn by aviators flying over water. Security-Insecurity.

mag-net'-ic. **Magnetic tape (or wire),** tape (or wire) used in sound recording by converting the sound to magnetization of varying intensity; the sound is "played back" by the reverse process, Hearing-Deafness.

*main. **Main Street,** a general term for the small towns of the United States, especially of the Midwest (from a novel of that name by Sinclair Lewis), City-Country, Dweller-Habitation.

main'-stream". In the main stream of development, e.g., *mainstream literature.* Consequence-Insignificance.

*main'-te-nance. **Maintenance of membership,** a provision in a labor agreement which, while not requiring the employer to hire union workers only, requires him to discharge union workers if they leave the union, Labor-Capital.

*ma'-jor. The principal subject or course of study in a student's work for a college degree; to specialize, to do the greater part of one's college work (in a certain study or course). Education-Learning, Universality-Particularity.

mal"-ad-just'-ed. Badly adjusted; not in proper adjustment to one's environment (usually with implication of a resulting emotional disturbance). Conventionality-Unconventionality, *Mind-Imbecility, Regularity-Irregularity.

man'-da-tar"-y or man'-da-to"-ry. A country which had (under the League of Nations) a mandate over some former enemy territory. Rule-License.

*man'-date. Under the League of Nations, a commission given to one nation to administer the affairs of some part of former enemy territory; the territory covered by such a commission. Rule-License.

man'-ic–de-pres'-sive psy-cho'-sis. A mental illness in which periods of great excitement alternate with periods of melancholia, and perhaps with periods of sanity. *Saneness-Lunacy.

maquis. [F.] The French guerrilla groups opposing the Germans during the occupation of France in World War II; a member of any of these groups. Belligerent, Patriotism-Treason.

mar'-a-thon. A long-distance race; a contest of endurance (e.g. *dance marathon*). Lastingness-Transientness.

mar"-i-jua'-na or mar"-i-hua'-na. The hemp plant; a narcotic prepared from dried hemp leaves and flowers and smoked in cigarettes. Remedy-Bane.

ma-ri'-na. A commercial yacht basin with facilities for anchoring or tying up private pleasure craft and often with sleeping accommodations, restaurants, amusements, and the like, for boatowners. DWELLER-HABITATION.

mas'-och-ism. An abnormality consisting in deriving pleasure, especially sexual pleasure, from suffering physical pain. PLEASURE-PAIN, *SANENESS-LUNACY.

***mass. Mass number,** a whole number identifying an isotope of an element, e.g. 235 in uranium-235: it is the whole number closest to the atomic weight (for uranium 1235 the atomic weight is 235.11704); it is also the number of protons and neutrons combined in an atom of the isotope, #NUCLEAR PHYSICS.

mass'–en'-er-gy e-qua'-tion. Albert Einstein's equation, $E = mc^2$, expressing the equivalence and convertibility of mass and energy: energy (in ergs) is equivalent to mass (in grams) multiplied by the square of the speed of light (in centimeters per second); from this equation the energy released in a nuclear reaction can be calculated from the decrease in mass. #NUCLEAR PHYSICS.

***mas'-ter. Master of ceremonies,** a person who introduces the speakers and performers in an entertainment program, as at a dinner or night club or on radio or television, ACTING, #RADIO-TELEVISION.

***mas'-ter-mind".** To work out a clever and successful plan for; to direct, to control from behind the scenes. MANAGEMENT.

mav'-er-ick. An unbranded animal, especially an unbranded calf, in a herd of cattle (formerly, the property of anyone who found it); a politician who acts independently of regular parties or factions; any person who rejects the authority or discipline of a group; a stray or unmarked object. CONVENTIONALITY-UNCONVENTIONALITY, GATHERING-SCATTERING, INFANT-VETERAN.

May'-day". An international radio (spoken) distress signal used by ships and aircraft. ALARM, #RADIO-TELEVISION, SIGN.

M.C. or **m.c.** Master of ceremonies. ACTING, #RADIO-TELEVISION.

Mc-Coy'. The McCoy or **the real McCoy,** the genuine article or person, the real thing, GOODNESS-BADNESS, *TRUTH-ERROR.

***meas'-ure. Measure up to,** to meet the qualifications or expectations for, SKILL-UNSKILFULNESS.

***mech'-a-nism.** A mental process by which an inner conflict is eliminated or lessened, or socially acceptable behavior is substituted for repressed wishes or drives (see also **defense mechanism**). *MIND-IMBECILITY.

mech'-a-nize. To replace hand labor or use of animals in (a process or industry) with machinery; to provide (a military unit) with armored transport and mobile fighting equipment.

meg'-a-cy"-cle. A million cycles; a million cycles per second, a measure of frequency used especially in radio. MEASURE, #RADIO-TELEVISION.

meg"-a-lo-ma'-ni-a. A mental disorder characterized by exaggerated ideas of one's importance, powers, or the like; an exaggerated fondness for doing things on a grand scale. CONCEIT-DIFFIDENCE, *SANENESS-LUNACY, SELF-RESPECT-HUMBLENESS.

meg'-a-ton". A measure of the explosive force of an atomic bomb, equal to the energy released by a million tons of TNT. MEASURE, #NUCLEAR PHYSICS.

meld. To merge, to combine. COMPOSITION-RESOLUTION.

mel'-on. A large profit or other accumulation of money for distribution among stockholders or other participants; **cut a melon** or **split a melon,** to divide such profits or other accumulation. GAIN-LOSS, LABOR-CAPITAL, PARTICIPATION.

Men-de'-li-an-ism or **Men'-del-ism.** The science of the function of genes in heredity, inaugurated by the experiments of Gregor Mendel. BIOLOGY.

***men'-tal. Mental age,** a measure of a person's mental development, determined by an individual test and the average age of normal children who show comparable results in the same test, *MIND-IMBECILITY, *SAGACITY-INCAPACITY.

men'-ti-cide. The application of mental and physical tortures, drugs, suggestion, and other techniques to destroy a person's beliefs and force him to accept new ones; brain-washing. COERCION, EDUCATION-MISTEACHING.

***mer'-chan-dise.** To promote the sale of (an article or service) by advertising and special inducements, special schemes for distribution, or the like. BUYING-SALE, *PUBLICITY.

merg'-er. Merging or combination of two or more businesses, interests, etc.; a combination of two or more corporations in which one corporation survives and absorbs the other or others. COMPOSITION-RESOLUTION.

mes'-o-morph. A person of the athletic type of body structure characterized by relative prominence of bone, muscle, and connective tissue, with evenly proportioned limbs and chest volume greater than abdominal volume.

mes'-on. An atomic particle, of positive, negative, or neutral electric charge, formed in the collision of cosmic rays with atomic nuclei or produced artificially in a cyclotron: it has a very short life, being transformed into another particle or radiation. #NUCLEAR PHYSICS.

met"-a-gal'-ax-y. All of the physical universe outside of our own galaxy. ASTRONOMY, UNIVERSE.

mev. Million electron volts, a measure of energy released in a nuclear reaction. MEASURE, #NUCLEAR PHYSICS.

Mick'-ey or **Mick'-ey Finn.** A drink of liquor to which a soporific or knockout drug has been added. FEELING-INSENSIBILITY, TEETOTALISM-INTEMPERANCE.

mi'-cro-film". A film on which many pages or sheets of books, newspapers, business records, and the like can be photographed and preserved in small space. RECORD.

mi'-cro-groove". The fine groove, very closely spaced, of a phonograph record made to be played at comparatively slow speeds (usually 33⅓ or 45 revolutions per minute).

mi'-cro-wave". An electromagnetic wave of very short wave length (very high frequency) in the range including television and radar and lying between the radio and the infrared bands. #RADIO-TELEVISION.

mid'-dle–of–the–road'. Moderate, avoiding extremes. MODERATION-SELF-INDULGENCE.

mid'–Vic-to'-ri-an. Relating to the era of roughly 1850–90, the middle period of Queen Victoria's reign; old-fashioned, conservative in tastes and ideas, and strict in morals. CONVENTIONALITY-UNCONVENTIONALITY.

Mid'-west' or **Mid'-dle West'.** The part of the United States between the Allegheny Mountains and the Rockies and north of the Ohio River and the southern boundaries of Missouri and Kansas. EXTENSION-DISTRICT.

mike. Microphone. HEARING-DEAFNESS, #RADIO-TELEVISION.

***milk. Milk run,** a routine bombing or reconnaissance flight, in which no serious opposition or damage is expected; any routine operation, ATTACK-DEFENSE, HABIT-DESUETUDE.

***mill.** To tramp around in a circle (of cattle); **mill** or **mill around,** to move around aimlessly or in confusion. AIM-ABERRATION, MOVEMENT-REST.

milque'-toast". A timid, retiring, ineffectual person (resembling the comic-strip character Caspar Milquetoast). BRAVERY-COWARDICE, MIGHT-IMPOTENCE.

mim'-e-o-graph". A machine using a stencil to make copies of typewritten, written, or drawn material; to make copies with such a machine. WRITING-PRINTING.

MIND

Catharsis. The release of suppressed emotion by reliving an experience in the imagination.

Compensation. The exaggeration of abilities and favorable traits to offset weaknesses and unfavorable traits.

Complex. A group of ideas and feelings, largely repressed and in the unconscious mind, which account for some abnormality of behavior.

Conditioned reflex, conditioned response. A response acquired through association with an adequate stimulus.

Defense mechanism. An unconscious mental process by which a person avoids facing a disagreeable situation or painful fact; the behavior reflecting such processes.

Ego. The part of a person's mental make-up corresponding to his conscious experience and activities.

Electra complex. A complex resulting from a girl's unconscious attachment to her father and antagonism toward her mother.

Empathy. Unconscious identification of oneself with another person.

Escapism. Habitual avoidance of boredom or unpleasant realities through the imagination or by a diversion.

Extroversion. Interest in and direction of one's activities toward other persons and things outside of oneself.

Extrovert. A person whose interests are largely in other persons and external things.

Fixation. An abnormal attachment which interferes with proper psychological and emotional development.

Frame of reference. A set of standards serving as a basis for one's ideas and judgments.

Free association. A technique in which a person is asked either to state the idea that comes to mind when each word on a list is read, or to tell the continuous series of ideas that begin with reaction to some word.

Id. The part of a personality which is instinctive and unconscious.

Inferiority complex. A neurotic condition resulting from a feeling of inferiority.

Inferiority feeling. A feeling of inferiority, not amounting to a neurosis.

Inhibition. The stopping or restraining of some mental function by some other function or circumstances.

Inkblot test, Rorschach test. A psychological test based on identification of and reactions to a set of ink blots.

Intelligence quotient, IQ, I.Q. A measure of intelligence, obtained by dividing mental age by age in years.

Intelligence test. A test of intelligence, especially one giving results from which the intelligence quotient is computed.

Introversion. The direction of a person's interests to his own thoughts and feelings.

Introvert. A person whose interests are largely in his own thoughts and feelings.

Libido. Sexual desire or drive; the instinctual cravings and desires, the vital impulse or driving force of the personality.

Lie detector. An apparatus used to indicate whether a person under examination is telling the truth.

Limen. A threshold.

Lobotomy. A surgical operation to relieve certain mental disorders.

Mechanism. A mental process by which an inner conflict is eliminated or lessened, or socially acceptable behavior is substituted for repressed wishes or drives.

Mental age. A measure of a person's mental development.

Narcissism. An early stage of a person's development in which (according to psychoanalysis) the sexual object is the self, or retention or recurrence of this stage beyond its normal period.

Oedipus complex. A complex resulting from a boy's unconscious attachment to his mother and antagonism toward his father.

Overcompensation. An exaggerated process of compensation for some psychological lack or defect.

Personal equation. Allowance for the fact that individuals differ in capacities, reactions, etc.

Stream of consciousness. An individual's conscious thought processes regarded as a continuous flow.

Sublimation. The unconscious deflection of an unsatisfactory or socially unacceptable desire into some expression which is satisfactory and socially approved; replacement of overt expression of sexual desire by nonsexual behavior.

Superego. The part of the personality formed by external authority.

Superiority feeling, superiority complex. An exaggerated feeling of self-importance.

Threshold. A dividing point between stimuli or differences which can be perceived and those which cannot.

Trauma. An injury or wound, either physical or psychic, or the condition resulting from it.

Unconditioned reflex, unconditioned response. A response produced by its normal or natural stimulus.

The unconscious. All of a person's mental make-up which does not enter into consciousness but which influences his behavior.

Wishful thinking. Mental activity governed by one's wishes rather than by realistic consideration of the facts and circumstances.

MIND—*Philosophical and Scientific Terms*

Cybernetics. The comparative study of the mechanisms that control the functioning of electronic computers and the human brain and nervous system.

Dianetics. A theory of mental treatment based on the idea that a person can be taken back in memory to a time before the injury which caused the disorder.

Gestalt psychology. A school based on the principle that mental processes and behavior must be studied in whole configurations.

Parapsychology. A branch of psychology dealing with investigation of phenomena such as telepathy, clairvoyance, extrasensory perception, and spiritualism.

Psychiatry. The branch of medicine dealing with mental ailments.

Psychoanalysis. A method of investigating mental behavior and of treating mental ailments, and a system of psychological theory: particular emphasis is placed on the unconscious mind.

Psychosomatic medicine. The investigation and treatment of physical disorders induced by or related to mental and emotional disturbances.

Psychotherapy. The treatment of disorders, especially mental or nervous disorders, by psychological methods.

Relativism. A theory of knowledge or ethics holding that the basis of judgment is relative to the person and the circumstances.

Surrealism. A movement in art and literature influenced by psychoanalysis.

MIND—*Verbs*

Rationalize. To justify one's irrational, improper, or questionable actions, emotions, or ideas by ascribing rational and proper motives or interpretations.

MIND—*Adjectives*

Freudian. Relating to the teaching and practice (psychoanalysis) of Sigmund Freud.

Maladjusted. Not in proper adjustment to one's environment.

Psychosomatic. Relating both to mind and to body.

---

*min'-er-al. **Mineral wool,** a fibrous material made from molten slag, used as an insulating material, MATERIALS.

*min'-i-a-ture. **Miniature camera,** a small camera using film of 35 millimeters or less, OPTICAL INSTRUMENTS.

*mi'-nor. A secondary subject or course of study in a student's college work; to follow such a subject or course. EDUCATION-LEARNING, UNIVERSALITY-PARTICULARITY.

mis-brand'. To label or mark falsely or deceptively. *TRUTHFULNESS-FALSEHOOD.

mis'-fit". A maladjusted person; a person who does not meet the standards of his group, his position, or the like. CONVENTIONALITY-UNCONVENTIONALITY, *SAGE-FOOL.

*miss. **Miss America,** the winner of a beauty contest held every year to select the holder of this title, BEAUTY-UGLINESS; **miss the boat** or **miss the bus,** to let an opportunity slip by, to make a wrong decision, OPPORTUNENESS-UNSUITABLENESS, *TRUTH-ERROR.

mix'-er. A social occasion for getting people acquainted; **mixer** or **good mixer,** a person who gets along easily and quickly with others. SOCIABILITY-PRIVACY.

mix'-up". Confusion, misunderstanding, snarl; a fight, melee. REGULARITY-IRREGULARITY, STRIFE-PEACE.

mo'-bile. An abstract art construction of rings and

other solid movable parts suspended on wires in a form designed to suggest motion. DELINEATION-CARICATURE.

mob'-ster. A member of a criminal gang; a gangster. BENEFACTOR-EVILDOER, GOOD MAN-BAD MAN.

mock'-up". A model of an airplane or other machine, usually in light and cheap materials and either full-sized or reduced in scale, used for teaching the construction and operation of the machine; an assembly (for study and test) of parts made for a proposed machine such as a new model of an automobile. COPY-MODEL.

*mod'-el. A person employed to wear garments so as to display them to prospective buyers; to display in such fashion. DRESS-UNDRESS, MANIFESTATION-LATENCY.

*mod'-er-a"-tor. A substance (such as graphite or heavy water) used in an atomic reactor to slow down (without absorbing) neutrons to the speed required to maintain a chain reaction. #NUCLEAR PHYSICS.

*mod'-ern-ism. Any of several trends of liberal interpretation of the Bible and church teachings, especially interpretation in accordance with scientific discoveries and theories. ORTHODOXY-HETERODOXY.

mod"-ern-is'-tic. Modern, especially relating to a rather conspicuously severe art form or product resulting from unyielding rejection of old forms. DELINEATION-CARICATURE, NOVELTY-ANTIQUITY.

mo-nad'-nock. An isolated hill or peak rising from a plain, the result of erosion of less resistant rock around it. GEOLOGY, HEIGHT-LOWNESS.

Mon'-gol-ism. A physical malformation, marked by a broad, flattened skull and closely set, slanting eyes, which is usually accompanied by mental deficiency. PROPORTION-DEFORMITY, *SAGACITY-INCAPACITY.

*mon'-i-tor. To listen to radio broadcasts from other countries, especially to gather military and propaganda information in wartime; to listen to radio or television to check the programs or the technical quality of the broadcast; to watch or check (any process). DISCOVERY, KNOWLEDGE-IGNORANCE.

mon'-o-plane. An airplane supported by a single pair of wings. #AVIATION.

mon-tage'. A composite picture, or the combination of different pictures into a composite; in motion pictures, a rapid succession of short scenes; in radio, the introduction of different voices or other sounds with a little overlapping or in quick succession. DELINEATION-CARICATURE, #MOTION PICTURES, #RADIO-TELEVISION.

mo'-res. Customs which have a definite and well-established moral value and on which much of a people's law is based. HABIT-DESUETUDE, LAW-LAWLESSNESS, SOCIETY-LUDICROUSNESS.

*morgue. A newspaper's file of clippings, photographs, and other reference material. MISSIVE-PUBLICATION, RECORD.

mo'-ron. Technically, a person with an IQ of 50 to 70 (in adults, a mental age of 8 to 12); loosely, a feeble-minded person, a stupid person, a fool. *SAGE-FOOL.

mo-ron'-ic. Relating to a moron; stupid, foolish, *SAGACITY-INCAPACITY.

mor-ti'-cian. An undertaker. LIFE-FUNERAL.

mo-tel'. A building or group of cabins beside or near a highway, providing overnight sleeping accommodations for motorists. DWELLER-HABITATION.

*moth. **Moth ball,** a ball of naphthalene (a white crystal prepared from coal tar) which protects wool and other fabrics from moths, CONSERVATION; **moth-ball fleet,** United States naval vessels taken out of service and treated and sealed to protect them against rust, etc., while held for possible future use.

*moth'-er. **Mother's Day,** the second Sunday in May. PERIODICITY-IRREGULARITY.

*mo'-tion. **Motion picture,** a series of pictures photographed on a film and projected onto a screen in such rapid succession that the eye does not perceive any break and the images appear to move; a succession of photographed scenes arranged to tell a story or otherwise entertain or instruct. #MOTION PICTURES.

MOTION PICTURES

Animated cartoon. A motion picture made by photographing a series of drawings.

Animation. The making of an animated cartoon.

Cinema. A motion picture; a motion-picture theater; the motion-picture art and industry.

Cinematography. The making of motion pictures.

Close-up. A scene in which a person or thing is photographed at close range.

Continuity. The detailed plan and directions for making a motion picture.

Co-star. To present (two or more stars) in the same production; to appear as a star along with another star.

Cutback. A shift from one course of events to another, especially to one earlier in time.

Documentary. A motion picture aiming principally to impart factual information.

Dolly. A platform on wheels for moving a motion-picture camera about.

Double. A substitute who takes the place of a star for dangerous stunts or for actions requiring a special skill the star does not have.

Double feature. A program with two full-length films.

Drive-in. An open-air theater where customers see a motion picture from their automobiles.

Dub in. To add sound to a motion picture or to make changes in a sound track.

Fade in. To become gradually more distinct.

Fade out. To disappear gradually.

Feature. The principal film in a program; a full-length film.

Film. A motion picture; to photograph.

Flashback. A scene or sequence inserted to relate something that happened before the main course of the story.

Footage. Amount of film in a motion-picture sequence.

Horse opera. A motion picture based on a cowboy adventures in the West.

Klieg light, kleig light. A very bright arc light used in making motion pictures.

Location. Any place, away from the studio, where scenes for a motion picture are photographed.

Lot. A studio and grounds connected with it where motion pictures are made.

Montage. A rapid succession of short scenes.

Motion picture. A series of pictures projected in such rapid succession that the images appear to move; a succession of photographed scenes arranged to tell a story or otherwise entertain or instruct.

Movie, moving picture. A motion picture.

Newsreel. A motion picture reporting current news.

Oscar. One of the statuettes awarded each year for outstanding performances and achievements in making moving pictures.

Pan. To swing (a camera) to follow movements or to get a panoramic effect.

Photogenic. Easy to photograph well, coming out well in photographic reproduction.

Photoplay. A motion-picture play.

Preview. A showing of a motion picture to a private audience before its public showing.

Preview, prevue, trailer. A selection of scenes from a motion picture shown in another program as a sample to arouse interest in it.

Quickie. A motion picture produced quickly and cheaply.

Retake. A retaking of a scene; a scene which is photographed a second time.

Rushes. Prints made immediately after scenes are photographed and shown for inspection.

Scenario. An outline of the plot of a motion picture, with essential details about the scenes, characters, and action.

Screen. A surface on which motion pictures are displayed; motion pictures, the motion-picture industry; to show on a screen; to photograph; to adapt (a story, play, etc.) for making a motion picture.

MOTION PICTURES—*Continued*

Screenplay. A story or adaptation written in form for making a motion picture.

Screenwriter. A writer of scenarios, screenplays, or scripts.

Script. A screenplay with detailed instructions and directions for use in filming a motion picture.

Shoot. To photograph, film.

Slow motion. A way of taking or showing a motion picture so that action seems much slower than it actually occurred.

Stand-in. A person hired to stand in the place of a star while the lights, camera, etc., are being gotten ready.

Starlet. A young actress who is given much publicity in minor roles because she is thought to have a chance of becoming a star.

Talkie, talking picture. A motion picture accompanied by sound.

Technicolor. A process of making color motion pictures.

3-D. Stereoscopic, giving the effect or illusion of three dimensions.

Travelogue. A motion picture describing travels.

---

mo'-ti-vate. To act as a motive, to impel; to provide with a motive. MOTIVE-CAPRICE.

*****mo'-tor.** To travel by or ride in an automobile, #AUTOMOBILE, TRAVELING-NAVIGATION; **motor court,** a motel, especially a group of cabins for overnight accommodation of motorists, DWELLER-HABITATION.

mo'-tor-cade. A procession of automobiles. #AUTOMOBILE, TRAVELING-NAVIGATION.

mo'-tor-ize. To equip with a motor; to equip with motor vehicles.

mov'-ie. A motion picture. #MOTION PICTURES.

*****mov'-ing.** **Moving picture,** a motion picture, #MOTION PICTURES; **moving staircase** or **moving stairway,** an escalator: an endless belt which forms a series of steps as it moves up or down an incline, ELEVATION-DEPRESSION, WAY.

muck'-rake". To make sensational charges of corruption; to seek out and expose, especially in newspaper articles, corruption in politics, business, etc. JUSTIFICATION-CHARGE.

mul'-ti-graph. A machine for printing circulars or the like from type assembled on a drum (a trademark: Multigraph); to print with such a machine. WRITING-PRINTING.

Mu'-nich. An appeasement on shameful terms (from the Munich Pact of 1938 at which England and France agreed to the seizure of part of Czechoslovakia by Germany). PRESUMPTION-OBSEQUIOUSNESS, UPRIGHTNESS-DISHONESTY, VARIANCE-ACCORD.

*****mu'-ral.** A painting on a wall of a building. DELINEATION-CARICATURE, PAINTING.

*****mus'-cle.** To shove, IMPETUS-REACTION; muscle in, to force one's way into a business, a labor union, a racket, etc., ADVANCE-RETROGRESSION, ENTRANCE-EXIT.

*****mush'-room.** To take the shape of a mushroom by spreading and flattening; to spread out or grow up rapidly. ENLARGEMENT-DIMINUTION.

mu'-tant. An animal or plant differing from its parents as a consequence of mutation of inheritable characters. BIOLOGY, #MUTATION-PERMANENCE.

mutt. A cur, a mongrel dog; a fool, a stupid person. MIXTURE-HOMOGENEITY, *SAGE-FOOL.

N

*****name.** Famous, well known, e.g., *name artists, name brands.* REPUTATION-DISCREDIT.

na'-palm. A chemical which thickens gasoline; gasoline thickened into a jelly used in incendiary bombs and flame-throwing weapons. WEAPON.

na-prap'-a-thy. A therapeutic method employing massage and based on the theory that diseases are caused by strains and disorders of connective tissue and ligaments. REMEDY-BANE.

nar-cis'-sism. Exaggerated self-love; extreme and abnormal admiration of one's own body and concern with one's own interests; in psychoanalysis, an early stage of a person's development in which the sexual object is the self, or the retention or recurrence of this stage beyond its normal period. CONCEIT-DIFFIDENCE, *MIND-IMBECILITY.

NATO. North Atlantic Treaty Organization, an organization of European and American nations pledged by treaty to collective resistance to attack on any member. ASSOCIATION.

Na'-zi. A member or adherent of the National Socialist German Workers' Party in Germany under Adolf Hitler from 1921 to 1945, or an adherent of Nazism at a later time or another country. RULE-LICENSE, TYRANNY-ANARCHY.

na'-zism or **na'-zi-ism.** Fascism as developed in Germany under the Nazis, or a similar movement later or elsewhere: the doctrine and practice or goals have included totalitarian government, state control of industry and of cultural activities, personal dictatorship by a *Führer,* belief in racial differences and domination of supposedly inferior races by supposedly superior ones (with extreme anti-Semitism), and establishment of world domination by force. RULE-LICENSE, TYRANNY-ANARCHY.

*****near.** **Near beer,** a beverage like beer but containing little or no alcohol, TEETOTALISM-INTEMPERANCE.

*****neck.** To hug around the neck, to embrace in amorous play, to caress, to pet. BLANDISHMENT.

*****nee'-dle.** To annoy or to goad into action by teasing, heckling, or ridiculing. CHARITABLENESS-MALEVOLENCE, MOTIVE-CAPRICE.

neg'-a-tiv-ism. A tendency to resist suggestions or to do the opposite of what is suggested or commanded; any philosophical position which is essentially negative, such as agnosticism, skepticism, or denial of reality. COOPERATION-OPPOSITION, ORTHODOXY-HETERODOXY, PROFFER-REFUSAL.

ne'-o-prene. A synthetic rubber: one of the plastic compounds resembling, and used as, a substitute for natural rubber. MATERIALS.

NEP or **Nep.** The New Economic Policy (in the Soviet Union).

nep'-man. A person who engaged in private trade in the Soviet Union under the New Economic Policy. DEALER.

nep-tu'-ni-um. A transuranic element (Number 93) artificially produced by the transmutation of uranium in a nuclear reactor: the short-lived isotope neptunium-239 decays at once to yield plutonium. CHEMISTRY, #NUCLEAR PHYSICS.

nerv'-y. Bold, brash, impudent. PRESUMPTION-OBSEQUIOUSNESS.

*****net'-work".** A number of radio or television stations joined by cables so that a program from a single source may be broadcast from all or any of them. #RADIO-TELEVISION.

neu"-ras-the'-ni-a. A neurosis marked by physical and mental fatigue, often accompanied by physical symptoms such as insomnia or loss of appetite and by phobias, inability to concentrate, or other mental disturbance. HEALTH-SICKNESS, *SANENESS-LUNACY.

neu-ro'-sis. Any of various mental disorders which are not due to physical impairment and which, as contrasted to psychoses, are milder, involve a partial rather than a general change in personality, and are recognized as abnormal by the patient. *SANENESS-LUNACY.

*****neu-rot'-ic.** Suffering from a neurosis; behaving in some way which suggests a mental disorder. *SAGACITY-INCAPACITY.

neu'-tral-ism. A national policy of neutrality in the face of tension or conflict between two other countries or alignments of countries. CHOICE-NEUTRALITY.

neu-tri'-no. A particle, without electrical charge, which is one of the products of radioactive decay: its existence was suggested by a loss of energy not otherwise accounted for, and its discovery was announced in 1956. #NUCLEAR PHYSICS.

neu'-tron. A particle which is one of the constituents of the nucleus of the atom in all elements except normal hydrogen: it carries no electrical charge and has a mass slightly greater than that of the proton. #NUCLEAR PHYSICS.

nev'-er–nev'-er land. An imaginary place of perfection, pleasure, and freedom from care (allusion to Never-Never Land in James M. Barrie's *Peter Pan*). FANCY.

*new. **New Deal,** the social and economic legislative program of the administration of President Franklin D. Roosevelt; **New Economic Policy,** a policy followed in the Soviet Union from 1921 to approximately 1928 (gradually abandoned after that time), relaxing the strict application of socialism, especially to permit private operation of small industries and businesses and to allow the peasants to sell surplus grain on the open market; **new look,** a striking change in appearance or organization (first used of a sweeping change in styles of women's clothing in 1947), NOVELTY-ANTIQUITY, RENOVATION-RELAPSE; **New Order,** the reorganization of government, industry, and living conditions proposed and partly accomplished in Germany and its conquered territories under the nazis.

news'-cast". A news broadcast on radio or television. #RADIO-TELEVISION, TIDINGS-MYSTERY.

news'-reel". A motion picture reporting current news. #MOTION PICTURES, TIDINGS-MYSTERY.

news'-wor"-thy. Of sufficient novelty and interest to be reported in the newspapers. CONSEQUENCE-INCONSEQUENCE.

ni'-a-cin or **nic"-o-tin'-ic ac'-id.** A vitamin (of the vitamin-B complex) found in protein foods (lean meat, milk, eggs, and others): lack of it causes pellagra. BIOLOGY, REMEDY-BANE.

Ni'-ke. An anti-aircraft rocket missile guided by signals from the ground. WEAPON.

nit'-wit". A dunce, a foolish person. *SAGE-FOOL.

no man's land. A strip of land lying between the positions, especially trenches, of hostile forces; a tract of land no one claims or to which no one has a clear title. EXTENSION-INEXTENSION, INTERSPACE-CONTACT, LISTS.

non"-co-op"-er-a'-tion. Failure or refusal to cooperate; especially, political opposition by refusal to pay taxes, take part in political activities, or otherwise support the government in power. COOPERATION-OPPOSITION.

non"-ob-jec'-tive or **non"-rep-re-sen-ta'-tion-al.** Not portraying or representing physical realities; abstract. DILINEATION-CARICATURE, NATURE-ART.

non'-stop". Without a stop. DISCONTINUANCE-CONTINUANCE.

*nose. **Nose dive,** a sudden fall of an airplane, with the fore part pointed toward the earth; any sudden, sharp drop, ASCENT-DESCENT, #AVIATION; **nose over,** to turn over in a forward direction (said especially of an airplane on the ground), #AVIATION, REVERSAL.

*nos-tal'-gia. A wistful longing for something in the past or for faraway places. DESIRE-DISTASTE.

nos-tal'-gic. Arousing a feeling of nostalgia; feeling nostalgia. DESIRE-DISTASTE, PLEASURABLENESS-PAINFULNESS.

nouveau riche [F.]. A person who has recently become rich, especially, such a person who delights in showing his wealth or uses it in a tasteless manner. AFFLUENCE-PENURY, SOCIETY-AFFECTATION, TASTE-VULGARITY.

no'-vo-caine or **no'-vo-cain.** A chemical compound used as local anaesthetic in medicine and dentistry (a trademark: Novocain). REMEDY-BANE.

nu'-cle-ar. Pertaining to a nucleus, especially the nucleus of the atom (often used as synonymous with *atomic*); **nuclear energy,** the energy obtained from nuclear reactions; **nuclear fission,** the process in which an atom, especially of a heavy element, absorbs a free neutron and splits into other elements; **nuclear fusion,** the combining of nuclei of atoms of light elements to form nuclei of heavier elements; **nuclear physics,** the science dealing with the composition and behavior of atoms, especially their nuclei; **nuclear reaction,** a process (fission, fusion, radiation) in which the nucleus of an atom is changed by absorption or emission of one or more particles. #NUCLEAR PHYSICS.

NUCLEAR PHYSICS

A-bomb, atom bomb, atomic bomb. A bomb in which the explosion is caused by the release of energy in a nuclear reaction.

Activate. To make radioactive.

Alpha particle. One of the products of radioactive decay.

Atomic. Relating to atoms, atomic energy, or atomic bombs.

Atomic accelerator. An apparatus for accelerating particles for disintegrating or transmuting nuclei.

Atomic age. The era since the discovery of means of utilizing atomic energy.

Atomic energy. The energy obtained from nuclear reactions.

Atomic number. A number (same as the number of electrons in the atom) determining the chemical identity of an element.

Ball of fire. An intensely hot luminous sphere formed in an atomic explosion.

Beta particle. One of the products of disintegration of a radioactive substance.

Betatron. An accelerator producing electron beams of high energy and X-rays of high penetrating power.

Bevatron. An accelerator producing streams of protons or other particles at billions of electron volts.

Breeder. A reactor which produces fissionable material for use in other processes.

Chain reaction. Atomic fission which releases the neutrons needed to produce further fission and make the process continuing and self-maintaining.

Cobalt bomb. (1) A projected hydrogen bomb with a cobalt case which would become radioactive cobalt dust. (2) A machine containing radioactive cobalt, used in treatment of cancer.

Cosmic rays. High-energy radiation entering the atmosphere from interstellar space.

Cosmotron. A powerful synchrotron to accelerate protons and other particles to several billion electron volts.

Critical size. The amount of uranium or plutonium in which a chain reaction will cause an atomic explosion.

Curie. A measure of radioactivity, the quantity which decays at a stated rate.

Cyclotron. An apparatus in which protons or other particles are accelerated in moving through a spiral path in a magnetic field.

Decay. Disintegration of a radioactive substance.

Deuterium, heavy hydrogen. An isotope of hydrogen with almost twice the weight of ordinary hydrogen.

Deuteron. The nucleus of the deuterium atom.

Einstein equation, mass-energy equation. The equation $E=mc^2$ expressing the equivalence and convertibility of mass and energy.

Electron. A particle bearing a charge of negative electricity.

Electron volt. A unit of energy.

Electronic. Relating to electrons or electronics.

Fall-out. The radioactive dust or particles that come to earth after the explosion of an atomic bomb.

Fissile, fissionable. Capable of nuclear fission.

Fission, nuclear fission. The process in which an atom absorbs a free neutron and splits into atoms of other elements.

Fusion, nuclear fusion. The combining of nuclei to form nuclei of heavier elements.

Gamma rays. Electromagnetic waves emitted in radioactive disintegration or in cosmic-ray reactions.

NUCLEAR PHYSICS—*Continued*

Geiger counter. A device for detecting and indicating the amount of radiation.

Half life. A measure of radioactivity: the period in which half of the atoms decay (at a constantly diminishing rate).

H-bomb, hydrogen bomb. A bomb in which immense energy is released by the fusion of hydrogen atoms.

Heavy water. A liquid containing heavy hydrogen in place of hydrogen, used as a moderator.

High-energy physics. Nuclear physics.

Hot. Radioactive.

Isobar. One of two or more isotopes which have the same mass number but belong to different elements.

Isotope. One of two or more forms of the same element which differ in mass number.

Kiloton. Explosive force equal to energy released by a thousand tons of TNT.

Linear accelerator. An accelerator in which protons or other particles are accelerated in crossing the gaps in a line of tubular electrodes.

Mass number. A whole number identifying an isotope: the number of protons and neutrons in the atom.

Megaton. Explosive force equal to the energy released by a million tons of TNT.

Meson. An atomic particle formed in the collision of cosmic rays with atomic nuclei or produced in a cyclotron.

Mev. Million electron volts.

Moderator. A substance used to slow down neutrons to the speed required to maintain a chain reaction.

Neptunium. A transuranic element (Number 93) artificially produced by transmutation of uranium.

Neutrino. A particle without electrical charge which is one of the products of radioactive decay.

Neutron. One of the constituents of the nucleus of the atom in all elements except normal hydrogen.

Nuclear. Pertaining to the nucleus of the atom.

Nuclear energy. The energy obtained from nuclear reactions.

Nuclear physics, nucleonics. The science dealing with the composition and behavior of atoms, especially their nuclei.

Nuclear reaction. A process in which the nucleus of an atom is changed by absorption or emission of one or more particles.

Nucleon. A proton or neutron.

Nuclide. An isotope or an element which has no isotopes.

Photon. A quantum of light energy.

Pile. Earlier name for a nuclear reactor.

Plutonium. A transuranic element (Number 94) artificially produced from uranium in nuclear reactors.

Positron. An atomic particle formed transiently in certain nuclear reactions.

Protium. The common isotope of hydrogen.

Proton. A positively charged particle contained in the nucleus of the atom.

Quantum. One of the minute "bundles" in which the energy of electromagnetic waves is radiated.

Radioactive. Disintegrating by emission of particles and (usually) gamma rays; relating to radioactivity.

Radioactivity. Spontaneous disintegration of nuclei of atoms.

Radiocarbon. A radioactive isotope of carbon.

Radioisotope. A radioactive isotope, especially one produced artificially in nuclear reactors.

Reactor. An assembly of fissile material and a moderator, with controls and protective walls, for producing controlled atomic reactions.

Synchrocyclotron. A modification of the cyclotron which will produce beams of protons or other particles at much higher energies.

Synchrotron. An atomic accelerator which accelerates electrons to a speed almost as great as that of light.

Thermonuclear. Relating to the high temperatures generated in atomic reactions and required in order to bring about atomic fusion; relating to atomic fusion or the fusion bomb.

Tracer. A radioactive isotope employed in biological or chemical investigations or experiments.

Tritium. An isotope of hydrogen heavier than deuterium.

Triton. The nucleus of a tritium atom.

Uranium. A radioactive metallic element important as a source of atomic energy.

nu′-cle-on. A proton or neutron in the nucleus of an atom. #NUCLEAR PHYSICS.

nu″-cle-on′-ics. Nuclear physics. #NUCLEAR PHYSICS.

nu′-clide. An isotope or element differing from all other isotopes or elements in the make-up of its nucleus: an isotope of an element which has two or more isotopes; an element which has no isotopes. #NUCLEAR PHYSICS.

nud′-ism. The belief (and practice in special camps or where otherwise possible) in going without clothing as a measure of natural and healthful living. DRESS-UNDRESS.

*nui′-sance. Nuisance tax, a tax which is a particular annoyance to the taxpayer because it makes him pay small amounts on frequent occasions, PRICE-DISCOUNT.

*nurs′-er-y. Nursery school, a school for children too young to start in kindergarten, SCHOOL.

*nut. A crazy or queer person. *SAGE-FOOL.

nut′-ty. Crazy, queer. *SAGACITY-INCAPACITY.

ny′-lon. A strong, durable artificial fabric used to make stockings, clothing, bristles, and other articles, MATERIALS; **nylons,** nylon stockings, DRESS-UNDRESS.

O

oc″-cu-pa′-tion-al ther′-a-py. The use of exercises, crafts, or light work to relieve or to assist recovery from certain injuries or physical or mental ailments. REMEDY-BANE.

o′clock. Referring to an imaginary clock dial as a means of indicating direction (especially with relation to an airplane): 12 o'clock is straight ahead, 3 o'clock is directly to the right, etc. AIM-ABERRATION, #AVIATION.

oc′-tane. A constituent (in a number of forms) of petroleum; **octane number,** a measure of the quality of a gasoline in terms of likelihood of producing a knock in the engine: the higher the number, the less likelihood of producing a knock. #AUTOMOBILE, MEASURE.

*Oed′-i-pus. Oedipus complex, a complex resulting from a boy's unconscious and, according to psychoanalysis, sexual attachment to his mother and antagonism toward his father, creating emotional disturbance when it persists beyond childhood; sometimes, similar attachment of a girl to her father and antagonism toward her mother (this also called *Electra complex*), LOVE-HATE, *MIND-IMBECILITY.

off′-beat″. Out of the ordinary, unconventional. CONVENTIONALITY-UNCONVENTIONALITY.

off′-set″. A printing process in which the ink is transferred from a flat form to a rubber roller which then applies it to the paper. WRITING-PRINTING.

O′-kie. A migratory farm worker; originally, one who had lost his own farm in Oklahoma or elsewhere in the Dust Bowl in the 1930's. WAYFARER-SEAFARER.

one′-track″ mind. Inability to give attention to anything except one matter of all-absorbing interest. BIGOTRY-APOSTASY, DECISION-MISJUDGMENT, HEED-DISREGARD, PERSISTENCE-WHIM.

one′-way″. Going one way only, passable in one direction only, e.g., *one-way street.* AIM-ABERRATION, WAY.

*o′-pen. Open city, an undefended city with no power to oppose occupation by an enemy and supposedly immune, under international law, from enemy fire or bombardment, ATTACK-DEFENSE, SECURITY-INSECURITY.

o′pen-end″. Arranged for modification in amount or in specific details: an *open-end contract* for supplying materials, etc., is flexible as to exact amounts: an *open-end investment trust* is one in which the capitalization fluctuates freely with the purchase, or sale of shares by participants (in a *closed-end investment trust* the capitalization is fixed); an *open-end radio transcription* is a recorded program with open spaces where commercials may be added. MUTABILITY-STABILITY.

*op'-po-site. **Opposite number,** a person who has the same rank, title, duties, or the like in another organization or situation, LIKENESS-UNLIKENESS.

op'-ti-mal. Best, most favorable. FAULTLESSNESS-FAULTINESS, GOODNESS-BADNESS.

op'-ti-mum. Best, most favorable: the most favorable point, amount, conditions, or the like. FAULTLESSNESS-FAULTINESS, GOODNESS-BADNESS.

or'-thi-con. An improved camera tube in a television broadcasting apparatus which is replacing the iconoscope (a trademark: Orthicon). #RADIO-TELEVISION.

or"-tho-don'-tia. A branch of dentistry concerned with straightening and other correction of teeth, especially in children. REMEDY-BANE.

or-thop'-tic ex'-er-cis"-es. Exercises, with the aid of prisms, for strengthening and correcting muscles of the eye. REMEDY-BANE.

Os'-car. One of the statuettes awarded each year for outstanding performances and achievements in the making of motion pictures. *APPROVAL-DISAPPROVAL, #MOTION PICTURES, TROPHY.

Oui'-ja board. A board bearing letters, numbers and symbols, and a traveler on which the user or users place their finger tips and which spells out a message without voluntary control: used as a game or in spiritualist demonstrations (a trademark: Ouija). DEVOTION-MAGIC, ENTERTAINMENT-WEARINESS.

out'-group". With respect to any in-group, all people who are not included within it. INCLUSION-OMISSION.

*out'-go"-ing. Affable, interested in other people, of or like an extrovert. SOCIABILITY-PRIVACY, UNSELFISHNESS-SELFISHNESS.

out'-size". Unusually large: an uncommon or unusually large size; an outsize garment. GREATNESS-LITTLENESS, MAGNITUDE-SMALLNESS.

o'-ver-all". Including everything, total. ENTIRETY-DEFICIENCY, UNIVERSALITY-PARTICULARITY, WHOLE-PART.

*o'-ver-board". **Go overboard (for),** to be wildly enthusiastic (about) to approve without reservation, *APPROVAL-DISAPPROVAL.

o"-ver-com"-pen-sa'-tion. An exaggerated process of compensation for some psychological lack or defect. *MIND-IMBECILITY.

o'-ver-drive". An automobile gear arrangement, above high gear, which engages automatically under favorable conditions and maintains speed with less power consumption. #AUTOMOBILE.

o'-ver-pass". A bridge which carries a highway over another highway, a railroad, a canal, or some other structure. WAY.

ox"-y-a-cet'-y-lene. Composed of or relating to a mixture of oxygen and acetylene, COMBUSTIBLE; **oxyacetylene torch,** a tool using a very hot oxyacetylene flame to weld or cut metals, INSTRUMENT.

ox'-y-gen. **Oxygen mask,** a device supplying additional oxygen for breathing to aviators flying at great heights in thin atmosphere, or to mountain climbers, #AVIATION, SECURITY-INSECURITY; **oxygen tent,** a small enclosure over the head of a patient in a hospital bed, filled with oxygen to help the patient in certain conditions when breathing is difficult, REMEDY-BANE.

P

pac'-i-fism. Opposition to all forms of military action; the belief that international disputes should and can be settled by peaceful methods. FIGHTING-CONCILIATION, STRIFE-PEACE.

*pack'-age. A combination, sold at a flat price, of items which might otherwise be purchased separately, e.g., a tour, a radio show made up of different acts, or certain machinery installations, COMPOSITION-RESOLUTION, WHOLE-PART; **package deal,** a deal which has to be accepted in its entirety or not at all; a deal in which bad features have to be accepted along with the good, CONTRACT, EXCHANGE, WHOLE-PART; **package store,** a store in which alcoholic liquor is sold in closed containers to be taken away from the store and not consumed there, MARKET.

pal"-o-mi'-no. A horse of cream or golden or silver-yellow color, with lighter mane and tail and white markings, bred especially in the West; a color resembling that of the palomino horse. CONVEYOR, YELLOWNESS-PURPLE.

*pan. To criticize severaly; to swing (a motion-picture camera) from side to side or up and down to follow movements or to get a panoramic effect. ADULATION-DISPARAGEMENT, *APPROVAL-DISAPPROVAL, #MOTION PICTURES.

pan'-cake". Of an airplane: to level off a short distance above the ground and land flat in a quick vertical drop. ASCENT-DESCENT, #AVIATION.

pan"-chro-mat'-ic. Sensitive to light of all colors (e.g., photographic film). LIGHT-DARKNESS.

*pan'-el. **Panel heating,** see **radiant heating.** HEATING-COOLING.

pan'-han-dle. To beg on the streets or from door to door. PETITION-EXPOSTULATION.

pan'-zer. German for "armor": a panzer unit in the German Army in World War II was a tank unit. BELLIGERENT.

par"-a-psy-chol'-o-gy. A division of psychology which deals with investigation of phenomena outside of normal experience such as telepathy, clairvoyance, extrasensory perception, and spiritualism. DEVOTION-MAGIC, MATERIALITY-SPIRITUALITY, *MIND-IMBECILITY.

par'-a-troops". Specially trained soldiers who can be transported by air and landed by parachute behind enemy lines or into a battle area. BELLIGERENT.

*par'-i-ty. A standard, worked out by a formula prescribed by law, for stating what prices for farm products would be if they had risen from the period 1910-14 in the same ratio as farmers' costs and expenses; **parity payments,** payments to farmers from public funds to bring farmers' income up to parity or a specified percentage of parity. EQUALITY-INEQUALITY, RECOMPENSE-PUNITION.

par'-lay. To multiply possible winnings by using the winnings from a successful bet as the stake on another bet; to make strikingly successful use of (one's talents, possessions, or the like); to expand (a small business, into a very large one). DOUBLING-HALVING, ENLARGEMENT-DIMINUTION, *SUCCESS-FAILURE.

pe"-di-a-tri'-cian. A doctor who specializes in pediatrics. REMEDY-BANE.

pe"-di-at'-rics. A branch of medicine dealing with the care of babies and children and the treatment of children's diseases. REMEDY-BANE.

*peel. **Peel off,** of an airplane, to veer away from a formation to make a dive or to land, APPROACH-WITHDRAWAL, #AVIATION.

pe'-ne-plain" or pe'-ne-plane". An area of gently rolling hills, resulting from the wearing down of old mountains or hills almost to a plain. GEOLOGY, GULF-PLAIN, HEIGHT-LOWNESS.

pen"-i-cil'-lin. An antibiotic drug prepared from a fungus (penicillium) mold, effective in treatment of some diseases or preventing infections because it checks growth of certain bacteria. REMEDY-BANE.

*pen'-ta-gon. **The Pentagon,** a building in Arlington, Virginia, which is headquarters for the National Military Establishment. ATTACK-DEFENSE.

*pent'-house". An apartment or small house built on the roof of an apartment building or office building. DWELLER-HABITATION.

pep. Energy, vigor, high spirits, briskness. LIGHTHEARTEDNESS-DEJECTION, VIGOR-INERTIA.

pep'-py. Eergetic, lively, brisk, spirited. *ACTIVITY-INDOLENCE, LIGHTHEARTEDNESS-DEJECTION, VIGOR-INERTIA.

*per'cent'-age. Advantage, profit. GAIN-LOSS, USEFULNESS-USELESSNESS.

per-fec'-tion-ist. A person who insists on perfection in every detail of something done by or for him. CAREFULNESS-CARELESSNESS, FAULTLESSNESS-FAULTINESS.

*per'-i-scope. A tube with prisms or mirrors at the two ends, enabling a person to look from a point above his eye level or where direct vision is impossible, e.g., permitting a person in a submarine to see from a point above the water. OPTICAL INSTRUMENT.

*per'-ma-nent or per'-ma-nent wave. A wave set in hair by a special process and lasting for several months. EMBELLISHMENT-DISFIGUREMENT.

persona grata [L.]. A person who is acceptable or welcome; especially, a diplomatic representative acceptable to the country to which he is assigned. FRIEND-FOE.

persona non grata [L.]. A person who is not acceptable or not welcome; especially, a diplomat not acceptable to the country to which he is assigned. FRIEND-FOE.

*per'-son-al. Personal equation, in scientific observation, the time lag between an individual's perception and his recording of the event; generally, allowance for the fact that individuals differ in capacities, reactions, judgment, responsibility, etc., DECISION-MISJUDGMENT, *MIND-IMBECILITY, VARIATION.

*pet. To engage in hugging, kissing, and fondling; to caress, to neck. BLANDISHMENT.

pho'-ny. False, counterfeit, fake, fraudulent; a fake, a sham; a faker, a pretender, an impostor. *GULL-DECEIVER, *TRUTHFULNESS-FRAUD.

pho"-to-e-lec'-tric. Relating to production of electrical effects by the action of light; photoelectric cell, a device in which the action of light produces or controls an electric current, especially, a vacuum tube used as a control device in many industrial operations and in the reproduction of sound from the sound track of a motion-picture film. ELECTRICITY, #ELECTRONICS.

pho'to fin'-ish. A finish of a horse race so close that the winner can be determined only by a photograph of the horses crossing the finish line; a very close outcome of any contest. BEGINNING-END, REMOTENESS-NEARNESS.

*pho"-to-gen'-ic. Easy to photograph well, coming out well in photographic reproduction, especially in motion pictures. BEAUTY-UGLINESS, #MOTION PICTURES.

pho"-to-mon-tage'. The combination of two or more photographs into a single photograph; a composite photograph. DELINEATION-CARICATURE.

pho'-ton. A quantum of light energy: the particle of energy in which light and X-rays and gamma rays are radiated (the energy increases with the frequency of the vibration). LIGHT-DARKNESS, #NUCLEAR PHYSICS.

pho'-to-play". A motion-picture play. #MOTION PICTURES.

pho'-to-stat. An inexpensive photographic reproduction, made by a special camera, used for making exact copies of documents, drawings, maps, printed pages, etc. COPY-MODEL.

pho"-to-syn'-the-sis. The process by which green plants manufacture carbohydrates from carbon dioxide and water from the air with the aid of energy and sunlight. BIOLOGY.

pick'-up". Acceleration (of a motor vehicle); a small truck with open body for light hauling; a companion

informally acquired, especially for making love; a device in a phonograph for changing the mechanical vibrations of the needle (stylus) in the record grooves to electrical impulses. #AUTOMOBILE, CONVENTIONALITY-UNCONVENTIONALITY, CONVEYANCE-VESSEL, HEARING-DEAFNESS, SWIFTNESS, SLOWNESS.

*pic'-ture. Picture tube, kinescope: a vacuum tube which converts signals received in a television set into images, #RADIO-TELEVISION; picture window, a large window, usually in an outside wall of a living room, which gives a wide view of the exterior to occupants of the room, APERTURE-CLOSURE, VISIBILITY-INVISIBILITY.

pig'-gy-back". Relating to the carrying of one vehicle on another, especially when a loaded truck trailer is hauled on a railroad flatcar to a point near the place where the truck is to deliver its load. TRANSFER.

pik'-er. A person who is laughed at for gambling or speculating with small amounts of money; a stingy or timid person who does things in a small way; a shirker. BRAVERY-COWARDICE, EXTRAVAGANCE-AVARICE, SOCIETY-LAUGHINGSTOCK.

*pile. Earlier name for nuclear reactor: the first reactors included piles of uranium rods and graphite bars. #NUCLEAR PHYSICS.

*pi'-lot. A person who operates or is qualified to operate an aircraft; the person in command of an aircraft on a flight. #AVIATION, CHIEF-UNDERLING.

pin'-ball". A game board studded with pins which interfere with movement of a ball which a player tries to drive into holes or pockets. ENTERTAINMENT-WEARINESS.

pinch'-hit'. In baseball, to bat in place of another player in a spot when a hit is badly needed; generally, to take the place of another person in any emergency. COMMUTATION-PERMUTATION.

*pink. Moderately radical; a person of somewhat radical (often communistic) political views. CONVENTIONALITY-UNCONVENTIONALITY.

pin'-point". Minutely detailed and precise, e.g., pinpoint bombing; to show exact location on a map; to determine accurately and precisely; to hit with great accuracy. *TRUTH-ERROR, UNIVERSALITY-PARTICULARITY.

pin'-up". A picture of a pretty girl (especially an actress, singer, or other young woman publicly known), displayed on the wall in an admirer's room, in a barracks, etc.; a girl whose picture is so displayed, or a girl whose picture should be so displayed, a very attractive girl. BEAUTY-UGLINESS, FAVORITE-ANGER.

pip. The image on a radar screen (also called blip). #ELECTRONICS.

*pipe. To send radio or television programs by wire or coaxial cable to another location for broadcasting, #RADIO-TELEVISION; pipe down, to stop talking, be quiet, TALKATIVENESS-TACITURNITY; pipe dream, a fantastic scheme, impractical plan, impossible story, etc., such as might occur to a person as a result of smoking opium, FANCY; pipe line, a line of pipe through which water, oil, gas, or other fluid is moved; a channel through which information, especially secret information, is received; the chain of dealers and transporters who handle a commodity before it reaches consumers (especially, referring to commodities in the pipe line or quantities needed to fill the pipe line), *ENLIGHTENMENT-SECRECY, TRANSFER, WAY.

*plane. An airplane. #AVIATION.

*plas'-tic. Plastic surgery, surgery for repairing injured or deformed parts of the body, especially by the transfer of tissue from elsewhere in the body or from another person. REMEDY-BANE, RENOVATION-RELAPSE.

*plat'-i-num. Platinum blonde, a woman or girl with silvery blond hair, COLOR-ACHROMATISM.

play'-boy". A man whose principal interest is play or love-making or dissipation and who has the leisure and means to indulge his desires. *ACTIVITY-INDOLENCE, GOOD MAN-BAD MAN, PLEASURABLENESS-PAINFULNESS, PURITY-RAKE.

*plug. A favorable mention of a product or idea in some public utterance such as a newspaper article or a radio or television program; to advertise or publicize (a product, etc.) persistently; to help popularize (a song) by repeated use. *APPROVAL-DISAPPROVAL, *PUBLICITY.

*plum'-met. To plunge, drop, fall straight down. ASCENT-DESCENT.

plunk. To put (down), throw (down), or drop firmly or with a noise; to fall heavily, to plump. ASCENT-DESCENT, IMPETUS-REACTION.

plu-to'-ni-um. A transuranic element (Number 94), artificially produced from uranium in nuclear reactors: the isotope plutonium-239 is of great importance in the production of atomic energy since it undergoes fission when bombarded by slow neutrons. CHEMISTRY, #NUCLEAR PHYSICS.

ply'-wood". A board made by gluing together several thin layers of wood, strengthened by running the grain of alternate layers in opposite directions. MATERIAL.

*poc'-ket. Pocket battleship, a small battleship conforming to regulation of tonnage under a treaty but with larger guns than a cruiser, BELLIGERENT.

po-di'-a-try. A branch of medicine dealing with treatment of ailments of the feet. REMEDY-BANE.

po'-grom. An organized raid on or massacre of Jews in Czarist Russia; an organized attack on any minority population. ATTACK-DEFENSE, CHARITABLENESS-MALEVOLENCE.

poi'-lu. Nickname for a French soldier in World War I. BELLIGERENT.

pok'-er face. An expressionless face, especially a face which reveals no information or emotion. MANIFESTATION-LATENCY, SENSITIVENESS-APATHY.

*po-lice'. Police dog, a German shepherd dog: a large, strong dog somewhat like a wolf in appearance, FAUNA-FLORA; police state, a country in which political, economic, cultural, and personal liberties are strictly curtailed by totalitarian control and police supervision, LIBERTY-SUBJECTION, RULE-LICENSE, TYRANNY-ANARCHY.

Po-lit'-bu"-ro. A committee of the Communist party of the Soviet Union which determines policies of the party and thus, indirectly, of the country. RULE-LICENSE.

*poll. Public-opinion poll, a survey of public opinion on some topic, or an estimate of the outcome of a pending election, made by compiling and analyzing answers from a representative sample of the population, INVESTIGATION-ANSWER.

poll'-ster. A person who conducts public-opinion polls (used with some connotation of skepticism or ridicule). INVESTIGATION-ANSWER.

Pol"-ly-an'-na. The heroine of a novel by Eleanor H. Porter; a person who finds something to be cheerful about under all circumstances, an unshakable and unvarying optimist. SANGUINENESS-HOPELESSNESS.

*por'-tal. Portal-to-portal pay, payment of wages for all of the time spent on the employer's premises, including time spent going from the entrance to the place of actual work (e.g., a mine) and return, RECOMPENSE-PUNITION.

pos'-i-tron. An atomic particle of the same mass as an electron but with a positive charge, not existing in ordinary matter but formed transiently in certain nuclear reactions. #NUCLEAR PHYSICS.

*pow'-er. Power dive, in aviation, a dive with the engines of the plane running, #AVIATION.

prag'-ma-tism. A philosophical position holding that

the meaning of a conception or the truth or falsity of a proposition lies in its practical consequences. KNOWLEDGE-IGNORANCE.

pre'-fab". Prefabricated; a prefabricated house. DWELLER-HABITATION.

pre-fab'-ri-cate. To manufacture and assemble parts of (especially, a house), in sectional units which can be quickly erected at a building site. CREATION-DESTRUCTION.

*pref"-er-en'-tial. Preferential shop, a place of employment giving preference in hiring, promoting, etc., to union members, LABOR-CAPITAL.

pre-mière'. The first public performance of a play, a movie, or the like. BEGINNING-END.

pre-par'-ed-ness. Preparation for war, by the training of men and the assembling of war materials, in the hope of discouraging attack or of having an adequate defense if war occurs. PREPARATION-NONPREPARATION.

pres'-sur-ize. To keep the air pressure inside (an airplane) up to normal by means of a compressor when flying at high altitudes. #AVIATION.

pre'-view. A showing of a motion picture or other spectacle to a private audience before its public showing; preview or prevue, a selection of scenes from a motion picture shown in another program as a sample to arouse interest in it. #MOTION PICTURES.

primp. To dress with extreme care and nicety; to fuss over details of one's personal appearance; to prink. DRESS-UNDRESS, EMBELLISHMENT-DISFIGUREMENT, POMP.

*print'-ed. Printed circuit, an electrical circuit made by affixing a flat pattern in conductive material on a nonconductive base, ELECTRICITY.

pris'-sy. Overly prim and precise, fussy; affectedly refined, easily shocked. SELF-RESPECT-HUMBLENESS, SOCIETY-AFFECTATION.

pro'-ti-um. Ordinary hydrogen: the common isotope of hydrogen, as distinguished from deuterium (heavy hydrogen) and tritium. CHEMISTRY, #NUCLEAR PHYSICS.

pro'-ton. The positively charged particle contained (in varying numbers for the different elements) in the nucleus of the atom. #NUCLEAR PHYSICS.

*prox-im'-i-ty. Proximity fuse, a miniature radio device in the nose of a projectile (such as an anti-aircraft shell) which by means of signals sent out and reflected back causes the shell to explode at a determined distance from the target, #ELECTRONICS.

psy-chi'-a-try. The branch of medicine dealing with the study and treatment of mental ailments. *MINDIMBECILITY, REMEDY-BANE.

psy"-cho-a-nal'-y-sis. A method of investigating mental behavior and of treating mental ailments, and a system of psychological theory: particular emphasis is placed on the unconscious mind as the seat of the drives for a person's behavior and of conflicts underlying mental disturbances. *MIND-IMBECILITY, REMEDY-BANE.

psy"-cho-neu-ro'-sis. A neurosis: this term stresses the concept of a neurosis as a mental ailment not due to a physical impairment. *SANENESS-LUNACY.

psy'-cho-path. A psychopathic personality; loosely, a person afflicted with a mental ailment. BENEFACTOR-EVILDOER, GOOD MAN-BAD MAN, *SAGE-FOOL.

psy"-cho-path'-ic. Relating to mental diseases; afflicted with a mental disease, *SAGACITY-INCAPACITY; psychopathic personality, a person with emotional instability and socially disturbing behavior but not, in general, the definite mental disorder of a neurosis or psychosis: included are some alcoholics, delinquents, and criminals; also, the personality of such a person, BENEFACTOR-EVILDOER, GOOD MAN-BAD MAN, *SAGE-FOOL.

psy-cho'-sis. A severe mental disorder involving loss of mind or complete derangement of mental activity, sometimes with and sometimes without underlying physical cause. *SANENESS-LUNACY.

psy"-cho-so-mat'-ic. Relating both to mind and to body, especially to the interdependence of certain mental, emotional, and bodily disorders. HEALTH-SICKNESS, *MIND-IMBECILITY; **pycshosomatic medicine,** the investigation and treatment of physical disorders induced by or related to mental and emotional disturbances, *MIND-IMBECILITY, REMEDY-BANE.

psy"-cho-ther'-a-py. The treatment of disorders, especially mental or nervous disorders, by psychological methods. *MIND-IMBECILITY, REMEDY-BANE.

***pub'-lic.** **Public relations,** activities of a business organization or governmental or military agency or the like, either in public actions or in preparation of matter for publication or for presentation on radio or television programs or otherwise, aimed at making the organization or agency better known and fostering a good public opinion of it, *PUBLICITY.

*PUBLICITY

Ad. Advertisement.

Adman. A person engaged in advertising.

Bait advertising. Advertising an article at a very low price with intent to sell a more expensive article.

Ballyhoo. Noisy or sensational advertising.

Blurb. Advertising matter on the dust jacket of a book; any highly laudatory announcement.

Build-up. A planned program of favorable publicity to make a person or thing well known and popular.

Captive audience. People in a public vehicle or other place who have to listen to music or announcements they may not welcome.

Cheesecake. Photographs, especially newspaper photographs, of a pretty girl in some pose which displays her legs.

Commercial. An advertisement before, during, or after a radio or television program.

Handout. An official statement, news release, etc.

Hoopla. Ballyhoo.

House organ. A periodical published to publicize products and services or to inform and stimulate employees.

Huckster. An advertising man.

Institutional advertising. Advertising to build good will and prestige rather than to stimulate immediate sales.

Plug. A favorable mention.

Public relations. Public actions or preparation of matter for publication or for radio or television to make an organization better known and foster a good public opinion of it.

Skywriting. The forming of letters and figures in the sky with smoke or vapor ejected from an airplane.

Sponsor. A business organization which pays the cost of a radio or television program to advertise its products or services.

Throwaway. An advertising leaflet, circular, publication, or the like, given on the streets or from house to house.

Want ad. A small advertisement grouped with others of the sort, offering or asking for employment or services or merchandise.

Wirephoto. A system for sending photographs by wire; a photograph transmitted by this system.

PUBLICITY—*Verbs*

Ballyhoo. To advertise or attract attention in a noisy or sensational manner.

Broadcast. To announce or distribute widely.

High-pressure. To advertise or sell by energetic and insistent methods.

Merchandise. To promote sale by advertising and special inducements, special schemes for distribution, or the like.

Plug. To advertise or publicize persistently; to help popularize (a song) by repeated use.

Publicize. To make publicly known, to give publicity to, to get publicity for, to advertise.

pub'-li-cize. To make publicly known, to give publicity to, to get publicity for, to advertise. *PUBLICITY.

pul"-chri-tu'-di-nous. Beautiful, BEAUTY-UGLINESS.

Pu'-litz-er Prize. One of a number of prizes presented annually for the outstanding accomplishments in several categories of journalistic and literary work in the United States. *APPROVAL-DISAPPROVAL, TROPHY.

pul'-mo"-tor. A machine for supplying oxygen or air to the lungs and maintaining respiration of a person who has almost drowned, is asphyxiated, or otherwise cannot breathe (a trademark: Pulmotor). REMEDY-BANE.

***pulp.** A magazine printed on cheap, rough paper (made from wood pulp), especially such a magazine publishing sensational and trivial but widely popular fiction. MISSIVE-PUBLICATION.

pulse'-jet" en'-gine. A jet engine (without compressor or turbine) operating in rapid cycles of explosions resulting from build-up of pressure in a chamber where air and fuel are mixed, accompanied by the loud buzzing noise which gave the nickname *buzz bomb* to a German missile in which such an engine was used. #AVIATION.

***punch.** **Punch line,** the line in a play, dialogue, speech, article, cartoon, or the like, which contains the point of a joke or clinches an argument, MEANING-JARGON, RHETORIC, WITTINESS-DULNESS.

punch'-drunk". Injured by blows on the head in prizefighting; groggy, shaky, unsteady, staggering, dizzy. AGITATION.

***punk.** Very poor, inferior, bad, wretched, worthless; a petty lawbreaker, delinquent, or gangster. CONSEQUENCE-INSIGNIFICANCE, FAULTLESSNESS-FAULTINESS, GOOD MAN-BAD MAN.

***purge.** The elimination of disloyal or suspected members or persons from a political party, governmental office, etc.; to eliminate disloyal or suspected persons from (a party, etc.). ADMISSION-EXPULSION.

push'-o"-ver. Something very easy to do, an aim which offers no difficulties; a person very easy to defeat or persuade. DIFFICULTY-FACILITY, READINESS-RELUCTANCE.

pus'-sy-foot". To move softly and cautiously, to proceed quietly and craftily, to avoid committing oneself, to evade an issue; a person who acts in such a manner. CRAFT-ARTLESSNESS, QUEST-EVASION.

Putsch [G.]. A revolt, insurrection, uprising, especially of brief duration and minor consequences. INSUBORDINATION-OBEDIENCE, REPRISAL-RESISTANCE.

put'-ter. To potter, idle, trifle, dawdle; to move (about) aimlessly or ineffectually. *ACTIVITY-INDOLENCE.

***pyr'-a-mid.** To raise or increase or enlarge (wages, costs, profits, market operations, etc.) in a succession of expanding steps. DOUBLING-HALVING, ENLARGEMENT-DIMINUTION.

py"-ro-ma'-ni-a. A form of insanity marked by an urge to set things on fire. HEATING-COOLING, *SANENESS-LUNACY.

Q

***quan'-tum.** One of the minute but definite "bundles" in which, according to present theory, the energy of electromagnetic waves is radiated: the energy of a quantum varies with the frequency of vibration and thus is very low for radio waves and very high for X rays and gamma rays. #NUCLEAR PHYSICS.

ques"-tion-naire'. A list of questions, usually a standard list or form used in connection with application for some privilege or in gathering information. INVESTIGATION-ANSWER.

quick'-freeze'. To freeze (food, for storage and handling) in a rapid process which does not break the cell walls and thus checks loss of flavor. CONSERVATION, HEATING-COOLING.

quick'-ie. Something hastily done or made; especially, a motion picture produced quickly and cheaply. HURRY-LEISURE, #MOTION PICTURES.

quis'-ling. A traitor who collaborates with an enemy preparing to invade his country. PATRIOTISM-TREASON.

quiz. To question, interrogate, examine by questioning; an examination, a set of questions, INVESTIGATION-ANSWER; **quiz program,** a radio or television program in which contestants are offered prizes for correctly answering a set of questions, #RADIO-TELEVISION.

quiz'-mas"-ter. The person who conducts a quiz program. INVESTIGATION-ANSWER.

R

*race. Race suicide, the tendency toward extinction of a people when it allows the birth rate to fall below the death rate, CREATION-DESTRUCTION.

rac'-ism. A belief that some races are superior to others and (usually) that a superior race should dominate an inferior one; racial prejudice; discriminatory treat-ment or persecution based on such beliefs and prejudices. BIGOTRY-APOSTASY, EQUALITY-INEQUALITY.

*rack'-et. A dishonest scheme, a trick, dodge, or fraud; an organized illegal activity, especially one which preys on legitimate business and organized labor by violence and threats; (jocularly) an occupation. LAW-LAWLESS-NESS, OCCUPATION, UPRIGHTNESS-DISHONESTY.

rack"-e-teer'. A person engaged in a racket, especially as a member of a criminal gang which extorts money from a business or controls a labor union or other organization by violence or threats; to engage in a racket. BENEFACTOR-EVILDOER, GOOD MAN-BAD MAN.

ra'-dar. An instrument which detects and locates objects by means of radio waves sent out by and reflected back to it. #ELECTRONICS.

*ra'-di-ant. Radiant heating, the heating of a room or building by heat radiated from walls, floors, or other surfaces which are warmed by electric coils or hot water, steam, or hot air circulating through pipes or ducts (also called *panel heating*), HEATING-COOLING.

ra'-di-o. The transmission of sound, especially speech and music, by electromagnetic waves; an apparatus for receiving radio waves and reproducing the sound. #RADIO-TELEVISION.

RADIO-TELEVISION

Aerial, antenna. An apparatus for sending or receiving the waves by which signals are transmitted.

Air. Relating to radio or television.

Airway. A channel of a certain frequency for use by a designated station.

A.M. Amplitude modulation, the more common method of radio transmission.

Announcer. A person who makes announcements, especially to identify the station, introduce performers, and make explanatory comments.

Audio. Relating to the sound apparatus of a television set.

Broadcast. To send out by radio or television.

Channel. A frequency band over which signals are transmitted.

Chassis. The base which holds the tubes and other operating parts of a receiving set.

Coaxial cable. A cable used for sending signals to any point where they will be broadcast.

Commentator. A person who makes explanatory comments on the news.

Commercial. An advertisement broadcast before, during, or after a program.

Compatible. Describing a system of color television broadcasts which can be received without color by ordinary receiving sets.

Continuity. The script for the spoken part of a program.

Crystal detector. A radio device in which alternating current is changed into direct current with the aid of a crystal.

Crystal set. A radio with a crystal detector instead of tubes.

Disk jockey. The announcer on a radio program consisting chiefly of phonograph records.

Documentary. A program aiming principally to impart factual information.

Emcee, M.C., m.c., master of ceremonies. A person who introduces the speakers and performers in a program.

Fade in. To become gradually more distinct in visibility or audibility.

Fade out. To disappear gradually from sight or hearing.

F.M. Frequency modulation, a method of radio transmission.

Gagman. A person who writes jokes, devises comic situations.

Ghost. A secondary or multiple image on a television screen.

Giveaway. A program in which prizes are given to members of the audience or other selected participants in a contest.

Ham. An amateur radio operator.

Heaviside layer. A layer of the upper atmosphere which reflects radio waves.

Heterodyne. Relating to a system for reducing incoming radio signals to a lower frequency for efficient handling in the receiving set.

Hi-fi. High-fidelity.

High fidelity. Reproduction of sound in all or approximately all audible frequencies and with least possible distortion.

Hookup. The arrangement and connection of the parts of a radio receiver; the cable connection of a number of stations for broadcasting the same program.

Iconoscope. A vacuum tube in a television camera which converts the image into the waves which are broadcast.

Jam. To make (radio signals) unintelligible by broadcasting other signals on the same wave length.

Kilocycle. One thousand cycles per second, a measure of frequency of waves.

Kinescope. The picture tube; a motion picture which records the images received on such a tube.

Live. Performed at the time of the broadcast; not played from a recording, transcription, or film.

Mayday. A distress signal used by ships and aircraft.

Megacycle. A million cycles per second, a measure of frequency.

Microwave. A wave in the range including television and radar.

Mike. Microphone.

Montage. The introduction of different voices or other sounds with a little overlapping or in quick succession.

Network. A number of stations joined by cables.

Newscast. A news broadcast.

On the air. Broadcast or being broadcast.

Orthicon. An improved camera tube.

Picture tube. A vacuum tube which converts signals received in a television set into images.

Pipe. To send programs by wire or coaxial cable to another station.

Quiz program. A program in which contestants are offered prizes for correctly answering a set of questions.

Radio. The transmission of sound by electromagnetic waves; an apparatus for receiving radio waves and reproducing the sound.

Rebroadcast. To broadcast material that has been broadcast before; to broadcast a program received from another station.

Scan. To pass a beam of electrons over the image in a television camera in order to produce electrical signals by which the image is broadcast; to pass a beam of electrons over the surface of a picture tube in order to reproduce an image that has been broadcast.

Screen. The surface of a picture tube.

Script. The text of a program with dialogue and directions.

Sign off. To announce the end of broadcasting.

Signature. A musical phrase or other sound which regularly precedes or follows a program and is part of its identification.

$64 question. A crucial question (from a radio program).

Snow. A confusion of small spots on a television screen resulting from electrical disturbances in the atmosphere.

Soap opera. A daytime serial story, usually dealing in a highly emotional or melodramatic way with family life and domestic problems.

S O S. A signal of distress.

Sponsor. A business organization which pays the cost of a program for advertising purposes.

RADIO-TELEVISION—*Continued*

Spot announcement. A brief announcement in the interval between one program and another.

Static. Miscellaneous noises produced by electrical disturbances in the atmosphere.

Station break. A pause in a program or between programs to announce the identity of the station.

Superheterodyne. Relating to a type of heterodyne radio reception in which the incoming wave is changed to a fixed frequency for ease and efficiency of amplification and detection.

Telecast. To broadcast by television; a television broadcast.

Telegenic. Suitable for telecasting, making a good appearance on television.

Telethon. A protracted television program soliciting contributions to a fund.

Teleview. To see or watch by television.

Television. Broadcasting of images by radio waves.

Transcribe. To make a phonograph record of (music, etc.) for reproduction by radio.

Transcription. A phonograph record made for a broadcast; the use of such a record.

TV. Television.

UHF, U.H.F., ultrahigh frequency. Any broadcasting frequency of 300 megacycles or more.

VHF, V.H.F., very high frequency. Any broadcasting frequency between 30 and 300 megacycles.

Video. Television; relating to television.

Walkie-talkie. A light, portable radio for sending and receiving.

ra″-di-o-ac′-tive. Disintegrating by emission of particles and (usually) gamma rays; relating to radioactivity. #Nuclear Physics.

ra″-di-o-ac-tiv′-i-ty. Spontaneous disintegration of nuclei of atoms by emission of charged particles and (usually) gamma rays, as occurs in some isotopes of heavy elements (radium, uranium, and others) found in nature and in other isotopes and other elements as a result of nuclear reactions. #Nuclear Physics.

ra″-di-o-as-tron′-o-my. A new branch of astronomy which records and studies radiation in those radio wave lengths which reach the earth from space outside the earth's atmosphere, thus supplementing information concerning the nature of the universe furnished by visible light. Astronomy.

ra″-di-o-car′-bon. A radioactive isotope of carbon (carbon-14) : a small amount is formed in nature and the amount found in wood, charcoal, bone, and the like, tells the age of archeological finds or recent geological strata ; it is also produced in reactors and used as a tracer in biological and chemical studies. Chemistry, Chronology-Anachronism, #Nuclear Physics.

ra″-di-o-i′-so-tope. A radioactive isotope, especially one produced artificially in nuclear reactors : such isotopes of various elements are designated by the combining form radio-, e.g., *radioiodine, radiophosphorus, radiosodium.* Chemistry, #Nuclear Physics.

ra′-di-um. A highly radioactive element found in small quantities in uranium ores. Chemistry.

ra′-don. A radioactive but chemically inert gas formed in the disintegration of radium and other radioactive elements. Chemistry.

rag′-time″. An early form (or forerunner) of jazz music, with syncopation in the melody but regular accents in the accompaniment ; the rhythm of such music. Melody-Dissonance, Music.

***rain.** **Rain check,** a check or ticket stub good another time if a baseball game or other outdoor event is stopped by rain ; a promise that an invitation or privilege once declined will be available some other time, Earliness-Lateness.

rake′-off″. A share, commission, or rebate, especially one obtained improperly or illegally ; an unearned share or profit. Assignment, Gain-Loss.

***ram.** **Ram jet,** a type of jet engine adapted to pilotless aircraft or guided missiles : it must be launched or brought to operating speed by another unit ; forward motion rams air into the combustion chamber, where fuel is added, and the mixture ignited in a continuous operation, and expulsion of the expanded gases provides the forward thrust, #Aviation.

ranch. A large property, especially in the West, devoted to pasturing and raising cattle, horses, or sheep ; a large farm, especially for a particular crop or product, such as a *fruit ranch* or a *chicken ranch,* Domestication-Agriculture ; **ranch house,** a dwelling house on a ranch ; a single-story, low-roofed style of house design which became popular in the United States in the 1940's, Dweller-Habitation.

***rank.** **Pull rank,** to take advantage, especially unfair advantage, of one's rank to obtain privileges, settle disputes arbitrarily, etc. (mainly in military slang), Rule-License, Supremacy-Subordinacy.

***rap.** **Beat the rap,** to escape conviction or punishment, Escape, Quest-Evasion ; **take the rap,** to accept the blame, to bear the punishment, to pay the penalty, Recompense-Punition.

rasp′-ber″-ry or **razz′-ber″-ry.** A blatant sound made by vibrating the tongue between the lips, to express disapproval, dislike, derision, or contempt ; any expression of disapproval, etc. *Approval-Disapproval, Cry-Ululation.

***rat.** **Rat race,** an endless scramble and confusion, great activity without much purpose or accomplishment, exhausting but unescapable routine, Regularity-Irregularity, Toil-Relaxation.

ra′-tion-al-ize. To justify one's irrational or improper or questionable actions, emotion, or ideas by ascribing (often unconsciously) motives or interpretations that are rational and proper. Justification-Charge, *Mind-Imbecility, Pretext.

rat′-tle-brain″. A giddy, flighty, silly, or frivolous person ; an empty-headed, talkative person, an idle chatterer. *Sage-Fool, Talkativeness-Taciturnity.

ray′-on. A fiber made from cellulose ; a fabric made from such fiber, often made to resemble silk, wool, or cotton. Materials.

razz. To criticize ; to deride, laugh at, make fun of ; to banter, tease ; disapproval, criticism, derision. *Approval-Disapproval, Charitableness-Malevolence, Society-Derision.

raz′-zle-daz″-zle. Fast and bewildering or spectacular action or performance ; tricky, confusing ; flashy, showy. *Activity-Indolence, Craft-Artlessness, Pomp, *Truthfulness-Fraud.

re-ac′-tor. An assembly of fissile material and a moderator, with controls and protective walls, for production of other fissile materials, artificially radioactive materials, or atomic power. #Nuclear Physics.

re′-al-tor. A real-estate dealer, especially one who is associated with the National Association of Real Estate Boards. Dealer.

re-broad′-cast″. To broadcast material that has been broadcast before ; to broadcast a radio or television program received from another station. #Radio-Television.

re′-cap″. To renovate a worn tire by fixing a new strip of rubber over the worn surface ; a tire so renovated. #Automobile, Renovation-Relapse.

***re-ces′-sion.** A decrease in business activity, less severe and shorter than a depression. Betterment-Deterioration, Increase-Decrease, Welfare-Misfortune.

***rec′-ord.** A disk or cylinder on which sound is recorded, Hearing-Deafness ; **off the record,** not for the official record, not to be published or quoted, in confidence, *Enlightenment-Secrecy, Manifestation-Latency.

*red. **Red**, a communist, anarchist, or other radical or revolutionary; communistic, anarchistic, radical, or revolutionary; relating to the Soviet Union or its inhabitants; an inhabitant of the Soviet Union, Insubordination-Obedience, Tyranny-Anarchy; **in the red**, losing money; in debt, Credit-Debt, Gain-Loss; **red light**, a traffic signal directing a train or automobiles to stop, Leave-Prohibition; **red-light district**, an area in which there are many houses of prostitution, City-Country, Purity-Impurity, Virtue-Vice.

red'-bait"-ing. Denunciation or verbal attacks on a person or group accused or suspected of politically radical activities, especially membership in or sympathy with the aims of the Communist party. Adulation-Disparagement, Justification-Charge, Reputation-Discredit.

red'-cap". A porter at a railroad or bus station or the like. Conveyer.

reef'-er. A marijuana cigarette. Remedy-Bane.

re-for'-est. To replant (an area from which trees have been removed) with trees. Renovation-Relapse.

re-fresh'-er course. A course of instruction reviewing a subject in which the student has had previous instruction or experience. Remembrance-Forgetfulness.

Reich. Germany or the German state, especially, **Third Reich**, the fascist regime in Germany from 1933 to 1945.

rel'-a-tiv-ism. A theory of knowledge or ethics holding that the basis of judgment is relative to the person and the circumstances. Connection-Independence, Knowledge-Ignorance, *Mind-Imbecility.

rel"-a-tiv'-i-ty. A basic principle of physics formulated by Albert Einstein: space and time and motion are nowhere absolute but can only be observed in relation to the observer: the principle and its consequences have been essential to advancement in understanding of the atom and have led to new conceptions of the structure of the universe. Knowledge-Ignorance.

*re-mote'. **Remote control**, control of an electrical apparatus, radio, television set, or airplane or other vehicle from a distance by means of radio signals, Management.

*rest. **Rest cure**, treatment of nervous disorders or other ailments by complete rest, usually along with some special care, Toil-Relaxation.

*re-straint'. **Restraint of trade**, business actions which tend to create a monopoly, maintain artificial price levels, or otherwise interfere with free competition or free movement of goods, Exchange, Labor-Capital.

re'-take". A retaking, as of a picture or a scene in a motion picture; a scene which is photographed a second time. #Motion Pictures.

re-tread'. To renovate a worn tire by removing the old rubber surface and placing a new rubber surface over the old fabric; **re'-tread"**, a retreaded tire. #Automobile, Renovation-Relapse.

rev. A revolution (of a motor or engine); to change the speed of (a motor or engine), especially, **rev up**, to increase the speed of; **rev down** to decrease the speed of. #Aviation, Swiftness-Slowness.

re-vamp'. To patch up again, repair; to reconstruct, renovate, refashion. Renovation-Relapse.

re-volv'-ing fund. A fund of money available for recurrent withdrawals and maintained by steady payments or repayments, such as a loan fund or certain governmental funds for special purposes. Money.

re-vue' or re-view'. A musical show made up of songs, dances, and skits, often burlesquing or satirizing current events, fads, or entertainments. Acting.

re'-write. A newspaper story written by a rewrite man; **rewrite man**, one who writes a story in form for publication from a first draft written by someone else or from information furnished (often by telephone) by a reporter. Missive-Publication.

rhu'-barb. A dispute among players during a baseball game; a dispute or conflict involving much heat and loose talk. Regularity-Irregularity, Turbulence-Calmness, Variance-Accord.

*rib. To make fun of, ridicule, banter, tease. Society-Derision.

ri'-bo-fla"-vin. A vitamin of the vitamin-B group, found in eggs, milk, liver, yeast, leafy vegetables, and some other foods, which is necessary for growth (also called *vitamin B₂, vitamin G*, or lactoflavin). Biology, Remedy-Bane.

*ride. To tease, ridicule, criticize, harass, torment, oppress, or tyrannize; in jazz music, to play with free variations and improvisations, Charitableness-Malevolence, Melody-Dissonance, Society-Derision; **take for a ride**, to take (an unsuspecting or abducted victim) away in an automobile and kill; to betray, victimize, hoax, or swindle, Life-Killing, *Truthfulness-Fraud, Uprightness-Dishonesty.

right'-ist. A conservative or reactionary in politics.

ring'-er. A contestant in a game, race, etc., whose participation is unfair or dishonest because his identity, experience, or abilities are not revealed; a person who enters a group or activity under some false claim or concealment of his real interest, *Gull-Deceiver; **ringer or dead ringer**, a person or thing which looks very much like another person or thing, Likeness-Unlikeness.

ring'-side". The space or seats immediately around the ring at a prize fight or circus; a place from which one can have a close or intimate view. Entertainment-Weariness, Remoteness-Nearness, Visibility-Invisibility.

*rip. **Rip cord**, a cord which is pulled to open a parachute, #Aviation.

ritz'-y. Luxurious, elegant; smart, fashionable; ostentatious. Conceit-Diffidence, Society-Affectation, Taste-Vulgarity.

*road. **Hit the road**, to start traveling, get started, set out, Arrival-Departure; **road company**, a touring theatrical company, Acting; **road hog**, a person who takes more of the road than he should, especially in driving over the center of the road, #Automobile, Unselfishness-Selfishness; **road show**, a traveling theatrical show, Acting.

road'-block". A barricade built across a road for holding back an enemy invasion; a patrol established at a point on a road with the aim of catching escaping criminals; an obstacle, impediment. Attack-Defense, Obstruction-Help, Release-Restraint.

*road'-ster. An open automobile with a single cross seat, and occasionally a rumble seat. #Automobile.

ro'-bot. A machine built in the form of a human being and functioning to some extent like a human (in the play *R.U.R.* by Karel Capek and in science fiction); a mechanical device with automatic controls which substitutes for a man in any work; an automaton; a person who works or acts mechanically and without thinking. *Sage-Fool, Volition-Obligation; **robot bomb**, the self-propelled bomb used by the Germans against England in the spring of 1944 (also called the *buzz bomb* or the *flying bomb*), Weapon.

*rock. **Rock wool**, a fibrous material made from molten rock or slag, used as an insulating or sound-proofing material, Materials.

*rock'-et. To rise or move like a rocket, to rise steeply and fast; relating to rocket engines, e.g., *rocket-propelled, rocket propulsion*, Ascent-Descent; **rocket bomb**, a bomb self-propelled to its target by means of a rocket engine, especially the V-2 weapon used by the Germans against England in the late summer of 1944, Weapon; **rocket engine**, an engine adapted to high-speed aircraft and self-propelled missiles, in which air and fuel are ignited in a combustion chamber and forward thrust is obtained from ejection of the expanded hot gases through exhaust tubes: the rocket carries its own oxygen supply and thus the height it can reach is not limited to the earth's atmosphere, #Aviation, Weapon.

ro'-de-o. A roundup of cattle for branding, counting, etc.; a public entertainment demonstrating skills in riding, lassoing, and other activities of the cowboy and the ranch; loosely, any public contest in which contestants are gathered to display skills or attainments. Entertainment-Weariness, Gathering-Scattering.

Rog'-er. A signal in radio operation, especially in aviation, meaning "message received [and understood]"; all right, O.K. Right-Wrong.

*roll. Roll back, to reduce (prices) to an earlier level by government order, Increase-Decrease.

roll'-back". Reduction of prices to an earlier level by government order. Increase-Decrease.

roman à clef [F.]. A novel with a key, i.e., a novel depicting real persons and real events but in fictional treatment and with changed names. Account.

*ro-mance'. A romantic experience, a love affair. Love-Hate.

roman-fleuve [F.]. A long novel or novel in several volumes which follows a family through several generations or a group or community through a long series of changes and developments; a saga novel. Account.

*roof. Raise the roof, to create a disturbance, to have a noisy celebration, to applaud or cheer boisterously, to be demonstratively angry, to protest or complain vehemently, *Approval-Disapproval, Favorite-Anger, Turbulence-Calmness.

rook'-ie. A new recruit (in the army, in baseball, etc.); a beginner, a novice. Instructor-Pupil.

room-ette'. A small single bedroom on some railroad sleeping cars. Contents-Receiver.

*root. Root for, to cheer for or support an athletic team or contestant; to applaud, encourage, support, *Approval-Disapproval, Obstruction-Help.

root'-er. A person who cheers for or supports a team or contestant; a supporter, a booster, an adherent. Antagonist-Assistant, *Approval-Disapproval, Desire-Distaste, Obstruction-Help.

Ror'-schach test. A psychological test in which a person is shown cards with ink blots and is scored for personality traits, imagination, and general intelligence according to his identification of the figures, details reported, time consumed, emotional reactions, etc. *Mind-Imbecility, Trial.

*ro'-ta-ry. A traffic circle: an intersection at which all traffic from and to any of the roads moves in one direction around a central plot, Crossing, Way; Rotary Club, a club of business and professional men, a unit in an international organization formed with the objects of community service and promoting understanding and good will among nations, Association.

ro"-to-gra-vure'. A process of printing from copper cylinders into which pictures and text have been engraved; rotogravure or roto section, a special section of a newspaper printed by rotogravure. Missive-Publication, Writing-Printing.

ro'-tor. The rotating part of a dynamo or motor; an upright metal cylinder rotated by a small motor to catch the wind and drive a ship; an assembly of rotating blades or other parts which lifts an aircraft such as a helicopter, #Aviation, Instrument. Revolution-Evolution; rotor ship, a ship propelled by one or more rotors, Conveyance-Vessel.

rough'-house". Rough, disorderly, or rowdy conduct; boisterous play; to take part in roughhouse; to handle roughly or boisterously. Turbulence-Calmness.

rough'-neck". A rough, uncouth, or coarse person; a boor; a rowdy, a ruffian. Gentility-Commonalty.

*round. Round the clock, night and day, continuing through the 24 hours of the day, Continuity-Interruption.

*rub'-ber. To gape, stare, or gaze in curiosity; to eavesdrop, *Enlightenment-Secrecy, Expectation-Surprise, Sight-Blindness; rubber check, a check which bounces, i.e., is returned by the bank because it is not covered by money on deposit, *Truthfulness-Fraud, Usefulness-Uselessness; rubber stamp, a person who, or an office or other group which, approves another's action or endorses another's views without independent thought, Liberty-Subjection, *Sage-Fool.

rub'-ber-neck". To stretch or twist one's neck to see persons or things, to stare, to gaze; a person who gapes or stares, a sightseer, a tourist, Expectation-Surprise, Sight-Blindness; rubberneck bus, a vehicle which hauls people on sightseeing tours, Conveyance-Vessel.

rub"-ber-stamp'. To approve another's action or endorse another's views without independent thought. Assent-Dissent, Insubordination-Obedience.

ruck'-us. An uproar, disturbance, noisy confusion, fracas. Turbulence-Calmness, Variance-Accord.

*rug'-ged. Rugged individualist, a person who is tenaciously devoted to individual independence in all personal, economic, and social matters and resists governmental participation or interference in these matters, Liberty-Subjection.

rum'-ba. A dance of complex rhythm, of Cuban Negro origin; the music for this dance. Entertainment-Weariness.

*rum'-ble. Rumble seat, in some types of automobiles formerly popular, a folding extra seat behind the regular enclosed seat, occupants of which are exposed to the open air, Anteriority-Posteriority, #Automobile.

*rum'-pus. Rumpus room, a room, usually in the basement of a house, set aside and furnished for games and other recreation, Entertainment-Weariness.

rum'-run"-ner. A person who smuggles alcoholic liquor into a country, or a vessel engaged in the smuggling of liquor. Law-Lawlessness, Robber.

run'-a-round". Deliberate avoidance or evasion, evasive answers, equivocation: chiefly in the phrases *give* (someone) *the runaround* and *get the runaround*. Ratiocination-Casuistry, *Truthfulness-Falsehood.

run'-way. A level and usually paved strip of ground on which airplanes land and take off. #Aviation.

*rush. Rushes, prints of motion-picture scenes made immediately after the scenes are photographed and shown for inspection by the director and others, #Motion Pictures.

S

sab'-o-tage. Damage or destruction of production or transportation facilities or the like by agents or sympathizers of a country's enemy; damage behind the lines in a country occupied by an enemy; damage or destruction of other people's property as a means of attack or reprisal; to damage, destroy, wreck, ruin, or obstruct. Creation-Destruction, Obstruction-Help, Patriotism-Treason.

*sack. Hold the sack, to be left empty-handed; to be left to suffer the consequences. *Gull-Deceiver.

sad'-ism. An abnormality consisting in deriving pleasure, especially sexual pleasure, from inflicting pain on other people; enjoyment of tormenting or torturing or seeing other people suffer; persistent and extreme cruelty. Charitableness-Malevolence, *Mind-Imbecility, Pleasure-Pain, *Saneness-Lunacy.

*sad. Sad sack, a soldier fresh out of civilian life who is bewildered by army life and blunders into constant trouble or is the butt of tricks or abuse (a comic-strip character); an ineffective, bewildered, blundering, gullible, or persistently unlucky person, MIGHT-IMPOTENCE, *SAGE-FOOL, SOCIETY-LAUGHING-STOCK.

sa'-ga. A lengthy account of exciting and heroic deeds and happenings; **saga novel,** a *roman-fleuve:* a long novel or novel in several volumes which follows a family through several generations or a group or community through a long series of changes and developments. ACCOUNT.

*SAGACITY—INCAPACITY

SAGACITY

Intelligence quotient, IQ, I.Q. A measure of intelligence.
Intelligence test. A test of intelligence, especially one giving . sults from which the IQ is computed.
Mental age. A measure of mental development.

SAGACITY—*Adjectives*

Longhair, long-haired. Relating (disparagingly or ironically) to classical music, intellectual tastes and activities, or theory.

INCAPACITY

Mongolism. A physical malformation usually accompanied by mental deficiency.

INCAPACITY—*Adjectives*

Batty. Crazy, queer.
Crackpot. Crack-brained, eccentric, impractical.
Goofy. Silly, foolish, stupid.
Happy. Exhilarated, irresponsible, obsessed (e.g., *bomb-happy, power-happy, trigger-happy*).
Moronic. Stupid, foolish.
Neurotic. Suffering from a neurosis; behaving in some way which suggests a neurosis.
Nutty. Crazy, queer.
Psychopathic. Afflicted with a mental disease.
Screwy. Crazy, crack-brained, irrational, eccentric, absurd, preposterous.
Slap-happy. Irrational, silly, crazy; irresponsible, carefree.
Wacky, whacky. Eccentric, unconventional, erratic, irrational, crazy.

*SAGE—FOOL

SAGE

Brain trust. Derogatory term for administrative officers or political advisers chosen because of their academic specialties or other expert knowledge.
Egghead. A disparaging nickname for an intellectual.
Intelligentsia. People thought to be or claiming to be the most intelligent and enlightened element; intellectuals.

FOOL

Bonehead. A stupid person, blockhead.
Boob. A fool, a stupid person.
Crackpot. A crack-brained person.
Dim-wit. A slow-thinking or stupid person.
Dumbbell. A stupid person.
Fuddy-duddy. An overcritical or ineffectual or old-fashioned person.
Goof. A silly or stupid person.
Goop. A silly person; a boor.
Misfit. A person who does not meet the standards of his group, his position, etc.

Moron. A person with an IQ of 50 to 70; a feeble-minded person, a stupid person, a fool.
Mutt. A fool, a stupid person.
Nitwit. A dunce, a foolish person.
Nut. A crazy or queer person.
Psychopath. A physchopathic personality; a person afflicted with a mental ailment.
Psychopathic personality. A person with emotional stability and socially disturbing behavior but not, in general, the mental disorder of a neurosis or psychosis.
Rattlebrain. A giddy, flightly, silly, or frivolous person; an empty-headed, talkative person, an idle chatterer.
Robot. A person who works or acts mechanically and without thinking.
Rubber stamp. A person who endorses another's action or views without independent thought.
Sad Sack. An ineffective, bewildered, blundering, gullible, or persistently unlucky person.
Screwball. A person with eccentric, irrational, erratic, or unconventional ideas or behavior.
Zombie. A person who shows no animation, drive, intelligence, or will, a dull or stupid person.

sales re-sist'-ance. Reluctance to buy an article or service someone is trying to sell. BUYING-SALE, READINESS-RELUCTANCE.

sales talk. A prepared set of statements and arguments used in persuading a person to buy something; persuasion, alluring argument. BUYING-SALE, MOTIVE-CAPRICE.

sales tax. A tax upon sales (in the United States usually retail sales) or gross receipts from sales. PRICE-DISCOUNT.

Salk vac'-cine. A vaccine used as a safeguard against infantile paralysis. REMEDY-BANE.

salt'-y. Witty, provocative, sharp, piquant, racy. WITTINESS-DULNESS.

*sal'-vage. The reclaiming, restoration, or utilization of property damaged or in danger of damage from shipwreck, fire, waste, etc.; property so saved and used; to reclaim, restore, or utilize damaged or threatened property. PROVISION-WASTE, RENOVATION-RELAPSE.

sam'-ba. A lively dance adopted from Brazil but originating in Africa. ENTERTAINMENT-WEARINESS.

*SANENESS—LUNACY

LUNACY

Battle fatigue, combat fatigue. An emotional disorder associated with participation in battle.
Dementia praecox. A form of schizophrenia, victims of which are usually very young people.
Manic-depressive psychosis. A mental illness in which periods of great excitement alternate with periods of melancholia.
Masochism. An abnormality consisting in deriving pleasure from suffering pain.
Megalomania. A mental disorder characterized by exaggerated ideas of one's importance, powers, or the like.
Neurasthenia. A neurosis involving fatigue, insomnia, loss of appetite, phobias, or the like.
Neurosis. A mental illness without physical impairment and not of the severity of a psychosis.
Psychoneurosis. A neurosis.

Psychosis. A severe mental disorder; loss of mind; complete derangement of mental activity.
Pyromania. A form of insanity marked by an urge to set things on fire.
Sadism. An abnormality consisting in deriving pleasure from inflicting pain.
Schizoid. Relating to or resembling schizophrenia.
Schizophrenia. A severe mental disorder involving disorganization, hallucinations, delusions, incoherence, or dissociation between intellect and emotions.
Shell shock. A term used during and after World War I for neuroses connected with combat or military service.

LUNACY—*Verbs*

Crack up. To go to pieces, to lose one's health or sanity.
Go haywire. To become confused, to go crazy.

San'-for-ize. To preshrink: to treat (cotton or linen fabrics) by a patented process to eliminate shrinkage of garments in use. Conservation, Mutation-Permanence.

***scan.** To pass a beam of electrons over the image in a television camera in order to produce electrical signals by which the image is broadcast; to pass a beam of electrons over the surface of a picture tube in order to reproduce an image which has been broadcast. #Electronics, #Radio-Television.

sce-nar'-i-o. An outline of a play, opera, or the like; an outline of the plot of a motion picture, with essential details about the scenes, characters, and action. Account, #Motion Pictures.

***sched'-ule.** To plan, arrange, or list (something to be done or to occur) for a certain time. Design, Order.

schiz'-oid. Relating to or resembling schizophrenia. *Saneness-Lunacy.

schiz"-o-phre'-ni-a. A mental disorder, effects and symptoms of which include severe emotional disorganization, withdrawal from reality, hallucinations and delusions, incoherence in thought processes, and dissociation between the intellect and the emotions. *Saneness-Lunacy.

schmaltz. Fulsome, cloying, and conventional sweetness and sentimentality in music, literature, or art. Melody-Dissonance, Simplicity-Floridness.

***sci'-ence.** Science fiction, novels and stories of fantasy suggested by scientific facts or imagining future scientific developments, Account, Fancy.

scorched-earth pol'-i-cy. A strategic plan of destruction of crops, food supplies, industrial plants, and transportation and communication facilities in the path of an invading army. Attack-Defense, Creation-Destruction.

***scout.** Good scout, a good fellow, a friendly and helpful person, Good Man-Bad Man.

scrag'-gly. Rough, irregular, ragged; shaggy, unkempt; jagged. Smoothness-Roughness.

scram. To get out, go out, go away. Admission-Expulsion, Approach-Withdrawal.

***scream.** Something hilariously funny; a compellingly amusing person. Society-Ludicrousness, Wag, Wittiness-Dulness.

***screen.** A surface on which motion pictures are displayed; the surface of a television picture tube; motion pictures, the motion-picture industry; to show (a motion picture) on a screen; to photograph (a motion picture); to adapt (a story, play, etc.) for making a motion picture. #Motion Pictures, #Radio-Television.

screen'-play". A story, or adaptation of a novel, a play, or the like, written in form for making a motion picture, with dialogue and directions. #Motion Pictures.

screen'-writ"-er. A person who writes scenarios, screenplays, or scripts for motion pictures. #Motion Pictures.

screw'-ball". A person with eccentric, irrational, erratic, or unconventional ideas or behavior; zany; eccentric, irrational, erratic, unconventional. *Adage-Nonsense, Conventionality-Unconventionality, *Sage-Fool, Society-Laughingstock.

screw'-y. Crazy, crack-brained, irrational, eccentric, absurd, preposterous. *Adage-Nonsense, Conventionality-Unconventionality, *Sagacity-Incapacity, Skill-Unskilfulness.

script. The manuscript of a play or of an actor's part, used in rehearsing a play; a screenplay with detailed instructions and directions for use in filming a motion picture; the text of a radio or television program with dialogue and directions. Acting, #Motion Pictures, #Radio-Television.

scrounge. To hunt for food, drinks, or other things

and get them by pilfering or by begging; to pilfer, steal; to cadge. Petition-Expostulation, Provision-Waste, Theft.

scum'-my. Low, worthless, mean, despicable, scurvy. Consequence-Insignificance, Reputation-Discredit.

scut'-tle-butt". Rumors, gossip. Conversation-Monologue, Talkativeness-Taciturnity, Tidings-Mystery.

sea'-plane". An airplane equipped to take off from and to land on water, a hydroplane. #Aviation, Conveyance-Vessel.

***se-cu'-ri-ty.** Security Council, a commission of the United Nations in continuous session and charged with maintaining peace, especially by settlement of international disputes and action to prevent aggression, Association, Council.

se-dan'. A closed automobile body type having front and rear seats for four or more persons, including the driver, in a single compartment. #Automobile.

se-lect"-ee'. A person drafted for military service. Belligerent.

Se-lec'-tive Serv'-ice. A compulsory military service system established in the United States in 1940. Belligerent.

***sell.** To win acceptance or approval of (especially, an idea or a person); sell on, to convince (a person) of the merits of (a person or thing); sold on, in favor of, convinced of. *Approval-Disapproval, Education-Misteaching, Faith-Misgiving, Motive-Caprice.

se-man'-tics. (1) The study of meaning and changes of meanings of words and other speech forms; (2) the study of the relations between signs and symbols and what they mean or denote; (3) the study of human behavior as it is affected by the use of words and signs. Knowledge-Ignorance, Meaning-Jargon, Word-Neology.

***serv'-ice.** To keep (a machine) in operating condition by inspection, adjustments, repairs, etc.; to serve, Obstruction-Help; service station, an establishment where gasoline and oil are sold and air, water, and repairs are provided for automobiles, #Automobiles.

serv'-ice-man". A member of the army, navy, or air force, Belligerent; serviceman or service man, a person who services household appliances or public utility or machinery installations.

ser"-vo–mech'-a-nism. An automatic control device which includes a servo-motor. Instrument.

ser'-vo–mo"-tor. An electric motor which controls the operation of a machine in response to signals received automatically from the working part of the mechanism. Instrument.

set'-up". A match or contest with an inferior opponent so that victory is easy and certain; an undertaking which has been deliberately made easy or success made certain. Difficulty-Facility, Readiness-Reluctance.

***sex.** Sex appeal, physical qualities which attract persons of the opposite sex. Beauty-Ugliness, Love-Hate, Pleasurableness-Painfulness.

sex'-y. Sexually attractive or exciting; concerned with sex. Beauty-Ugliness, Pleasurableness-Painfulness.

shag'-gy–dog' sto'-ry. A humorous anecdote in which a succession of trivial or apparently irrelevant details leads up to a nonsensical or eccentric ending. Wittiness-Dulness.

***shake.** Shake down, to extort money from, to get money from by threat of violence, blackmail, or other reprisal, Coercion, Taking-Restitution.

***shake'-down".** An extortion. Coercion, Taking-Restitution.

shake'-out". A reorganization which causes some persons to lose their offices or jobs; a process or period of economic adjustment regarded as comparatively mild and comparatively brief, in which there is some reduction of prices, some business failures, or some unemployment. BETTERMENT-DETERIORATION, WELFARE-MISFORTUNE.

Shan'-gri-La'. A remote idyllic land invented by James Hilton in his novel *Lost Horizon*; an earthly paradise, a utopia. FANCY.

*sheik. A masterful and irresistible lover. LOVE-HATE.

*shell. Shell shock, a term used during and after World War I for neuroses connected with combat or military service, *SANENESS-LUNACY.

shel-lac'. To beat, drub, maltreat; to defeat completely and decisively. OBSTRUCTION-HELP, *SUCCESS-FAILURE.

shim'-my. A once popular dance involving much shaking of the body; a vibration or wobble caused by looseness or faulty adjustment, as of automobile wheels; to shake, vibrate, wobble. AGITATION, ENTERTAINMENT-WEARINESS, VIBRATION.

*shock. Shock troops, troops chosen for an attack because of superior training and fitness, BELLIGERENT, GOODNESS-BADNESS; shock wave, a wave of high air pressure caused by impact of air and an airplane or other body moving at a speed greater than the velocity of sound, RIVER-WIND.

shoe'-string. On a shoestring, with a small amount of money, AFFLUENCE-PENURY, DIFFICULTY-FACILITY.

shoo'-in". An easy winner, a sure winner. *SUCCESS-FAILURE.

*shoot. To photograph (motion pictures), to film. #MOTION PICTURES.

short"-change'. To give less than the right amount of change; to cheat, defraud. *TRUTHFULNESS-FRAUD.

shot'-gun" mar'-riage or **shot'-gun" wed'-ding.** A marriage or wedding which is forced upon the groom or upon the couple because of sexual indiscretions; a forcible union in which there is at least one reluctant party. COERCION, MATRIMONY-CELIBACY.

shut'-in". A person confined to the house by illness or injury. HEALTH-SICKNESS, RELEASE-RESTRAINT.

side'-kick". Partner, close friend, companion. FRIEND-FOE.

side'-step". To step aside from, avoid, dodge, evade. AIM-ABERRATION, QUEST-EVASION, RATIOCINATION-CASUISTRY.

side'-swipe". To strike with a broadside glancing blow. IMPETUS-REACTION.

*sign. Sign off, to announce the end of broadcasting, as at the end of the day or to relinquish the channel to another station; to end a conversation, BEGINNING-END, #RADIO-TELEVISION.

*sig'-na-ture. A musical phrase or other sound which regularly precedes or follows a radio program, thus is part of its identification. #RADIO-TELEVISION.

sit'-down" strike. A strike in which the workers remain in and keep possession of the place of work until the strike is ended. LABOR-CAPITAL, REPRISAL-RESISTANCE.

$64 ques'-tion. A crucial question (from a radio program in which $64 was the reward for answering the last in a series of questions; more recently, a television program has introduced the *$64,000 question*). DIFFICULTY-FACILITY, INVESTIGATION-ANSWER, #RADIO-TELEVISION.

*skid. Skid row, a run-down part of a city with cheap eating, drinking, and sleeping places, frequented by derelicts, vagrants, and transient laborers, AFFLUENCE-PENURY, CITY-COUNTRY, WELFARE-MISFORTUNE.

*skin. Skin diver, a diver who carries apparatus enabling him to breathe under water but no special suit to withstand underwater pressures; a frogman, SPRING-DIVE.

sky'-rock"-et. To go up like a rocket, to rise steeply and rapidly. ASCENT-DESCENT.

sky'-writ"-ing. The forming of letters or figures in the sky with smoke or vapor ejected from an airplane. #AVIATION, *PUBLICITY.

slack'-er. A person who shirks or evades work or a duty or responsibility; especially, a person who evades military service in time of war. *ACTIVITY-INDOLENCE, QUEST-EVASION.

*slant. A point of view, attitude, tendency; a special interest, bias, angle; to write or speak for a special audience or with a special interest; to write (news) from a personal point of view or with a bias. DECISION-MISJUDGMENT.

slap'-hap"-py. Injured or dazed by blows on the head, punch-drunk, dizzy; irrational, silly, crazy; irresponsible, carefree, elated. AGITATION, LIGHTHEARTEDNESS-DEJECTION, *SAGACITY-INCAPACITY, *SANENESS-LUNACY.

slap'-stick". A pair of sticks fastened so as to slap together with a bang when a person is hit with it, formerly much used in low comedy; a style of comedy depending greatly on roughness and horseplay to get laughs. ACTING, SOCIETY-LUDICROUSNESS.

slick. A magazine printed on smooth, glossy paper, especially one with large circulation and broad popular appeal (contrasted, as a market for a writer's output, with *pulp*). MISSIVE-PUBLICATION.

*slip. Slip stream, the stream of air pushed back from the propeller of an airplane, #AVIATION.

*slow. Slow motion, a way of taking or of showing a motion picture so that action seems much slower than as it actually occurred, #MOTION PICTURES. slow-motion, moving at less than usual speed, abnormally slow. SWIFTNESS-SLOWNESS.

*smear. To attack or harm a person's reputation; to malign, vilify, besmirch, defame, slander. ADULATION-DISPARAGEMENT, *APPROVAL-DISAPPROVAL, REPUTATION-DISCREDIT.

smog. A mixture of smoke and fog. WATER-AIR.

*smoke. Smoke screen, a screen of smoke produced to hide military operations or a military target; any action, speech, etc., intended to conceal a true state of facts, ATTACK-DEFENSE, *ENLIGHTENMENT-SECRECY, *TRUTHFULNESS-FABRICATION.

sna-fu'. "Situation normal—all fouled up"; disordered, snarled, confused; a muddle, mix-up; to mix up, snarl, entangle, throw into disorder or confusion. ORGANIZATION-DISORGANIZATION, REGULARITY-IRREGULARITY.

snide. Maliciously insinuating, slyly derogatory. ADULATION-DISPARAGEMENT, MANIFESTATION-LATENCY.

snip'-py. Made up of snips, fragmentary; brief, curt; sharp, insolent, supercilious. REGARD-DISRESPECT, WHOLE-PART.

snoot'-y. Snobbish, conceited, haughty. CONCEIT-DIFFIDENCE, PRESUMPTION-OBSEQUIOUSNESS.

*snow. A profusion of small spots on a television screen resulting from electrical disturbances in the atmosphere. #RADIO-TELEVISION.

*soap. Soap opera, a daytime radio or television serial story, usually dealing in a highly emotional or melodramatic way with family life and domestic problems, ACCOUNT, #RADIO-TELEVISION.

*so'-cial. Social security, broadly, all direct Federal payments and Federal contributions to state funds for support of the aged, the disabled, the unemployed, and others without income or support; in a narrower sense, a Federal system of old-age pensions paid from a fund supported by payments by employees and employers. HUMANITARIANISM-MISANTHROPY.

*soil. Soil bank, land withdrawn from agricultural use by agreement between the owners and the government in order to avoid excess production and to conserve natural resources, DOMESTICATION-AGRICULTURE.

*so'-lo. A flight without an instructor, as a stage in a training program; to fly an airplane alone. #AVIATION.

so'-nar. An apparatus for locating objects and measuring distances under water by means of the reflection of high-frequency sound waves. HEARING-DEAFNESS, SOUND-SILENCE.

son'-ic. Relating to sound or to the speed of sound in air; **sonic barrier** or **sound barrier,** the point at which an airplane or missile attains the same speed as sound. SOUND-SILENCE, SWIFTNESS-SLOWNESS.

S O S. An international signal of distress, in wireless telegraphy, used by ships and airplanes; a call for help. ALARM, #RADIO-TELEVISION, SIGN.

*****sound. Sound barrier,** see **sonic barrier,** SOUND-SILENCE, SWIFTNESS-SLOWNESS; **sound track,** a band along the edge of a motion-picture film on which the speech and other sounds accompanying the picture are recorded, #MOTION PICTURES, SOUND-SILENCE.

*****soup. Soup up,** to increase effectiveness of; especially, to make alterations or adjustments so as to increase power and speed of (an automobile engine), #AUTOMOBILE, BETTERMENT-DETERIORATION, SWIFTNESS-SLOWNESS.

so'-vi-et. In Russia, a council or assembly, COUNCIL; **Soviet,** Russian, relating to the Soviet Union; **Soviet Russia,** (1) the Soviet Union, or (2) a republic in the Soviet Union including most of what was formerly Russia in Europe; **Soviet Union,** the successor to the Russian Empire, now organized into sixteen republics.

space'-ship". A hypothetical aircraft for travel outside the earth's atmosphere. FANCY.

space'-time'. Space and time combined into a four-dimensional manifold, especially in certain operations in mathematics, physics, and astronomy connected with the theory of relativity.

*****spark.** To stimulate, animate, inspire, stir, fire with zeal, EXCITATION, MOTIVE-CAPRICE: **spark plug,** a device in an internal-combustion engine which emits a spark which explodes the fuel mixture; a person who inspires others, or stirs them to activity, or is the leading spirit of an undertaking, *ACTIVITY-INDOLENCE, AUTOMOBILE, MOTIVE-CAPRICE.

speed-om'-e-ter. An instrument which indicates the speed of a vehicle. #AUTOMOBILE, MENSURATION.

*****spill.** To let (a secret) leak out, divulge, disclose, make known, tell. *ENLIGHTENMENT-SECRECY, EXPOSURE-HIDINGPLACE, MANIFESTATION-LATENCY.

*****splin'-ter. Splinter group** or **splinter party,** a group or party split off from an older organization, especially referring to one of a number of dissenting factions, VARIANCE-ACCORD, WHOLE-PART.

split'-lev"-el. Describing a house design in which no floor level extends the entire length of the house, the rooms at one end being on a level above or below the level of the rooms at the other end. DWELLER-HABITATION.

*****spon'-sor.** A business organization which pays the cost of a radio or television program to advertise its products or services. *PUBLICITY, #RADIO-TELEVISION.

spoof. To joke, fool, trick, deceive; a trick, hoax, deception. SOCIETY-DERISION, *TRUTHFULNESS-FRAUD.

spoon'-er-ism. An accidental mix-up of initial sounds or other parts of two or more words, such as saying *well-boiled icicle* for *well-oiled bicycle.* *ADAGE-NONSENSE, *TRUTH-ERROR, WORD-NEOLOGY.

*****sport'-ing.** Involving a fair risk of winning or losing, as in sports, e.g., *sporting chance* or *sporting offer.* POSSIBILITY-IMPOSSIBILITY, RATIONALE-LUCK.

*****spot. On the spot,** in trouble or difficulty, in an embarrassing or difficult situation; in danger, especially of death, DIFFICULTY-FACILITY, SECURITY-INSECURITY; **put on the spot,** to put (someone) in a difficult or embarrassing or dangerous position; to mark for death, to murder, CHARITABLENESS-MALEVOLENCE, GOODNESS-BADNESS, LIFE-KILLING; **spot announcement,** a brief announcement in the interval between one radio or television program and another, #RADIO-TELEVISION; **spot**

check, observation or sampling at one or more spots to study an operation, mass opinions, etc.; an investigation made without warning, INVESTIGATION-ANSWER.

spot'-light". A strong light giving prominence to a person, group, or scene on a stage; an automobile light capable of casting a powerful beam in any direction; a prominent or conspicuous position; public notice or attention. CONSEQUENCE-INSIGNIFICANCE, LUMINARY-SHADE, REPUTATION-DISCREDIT.

*****square. Square shooter,** an honorable, honest, fair person, GOOD MAN-BAD MAN.

*****stab. Make a stab at** (or **for**), to try to reach or accomplish (something), AIM-ABERRATION, PURPOSE-LUCK, VENTURE.

*****stall.** To stop, bring or be brought to a standstill (as when an engine is overloaded); (of an airplane) to lose the speed necessary to fly or to fly under control; to delay, play for time, put off; to evade, deceive; an evasion, trick, excuse, or pretext. #AVIATION, DISCONTINUANCE-CONTINUANCE, EARLINESS-LATENESS, PRETEXT, QUEST-EVASION.

stand'-in". A person who is hired to stand in the place of a star while the lights, camera, etc., are being gotten ready for filming a scene. #MOTION PICTURES, SUBSTITUTE.

star'-let. A young motion-picture actress who is given much publicity in minor roles because she is thought to have a chance of becoming a star. ACTING, #MOTION PICTURES.

stash. To put away, put in a cache, hide in a safe place, store for future use. STORE.

stat'-ic. Miscellaneous noises produced in a radio receiving set produced by electrical disturbances in the atmosphere. ELECTRICITY, #RADIO-TELEVISION, SOUND-SILENCE.

*****sta'-tion. Station break,** a pause in a radio or television program or between programs to announce the identity of the broadcasting station, #RADIO-TELEVISION; **station wagon,** an enclosed automobile body type in which a long rear section may either hold seats or be used for light hauling, #AUTOMOBILE.

stat'-ism. A governmental theory and practice in which political and economic powers are concentrated in the hands of a highly centralized government. RULE-LICENSE.

*****stem. Stem from,** to originate, spring, derive, or develop from, to have one's origin in, CAUSE-EFFECT.

*****step. Step up,** to increase, raise; to speed up, intensify, INCREASE-DECREASE, SWIFTNESS-SLOWNESS.

ster"-e-o-phonic. Describing a method of sound projection from two or more loudspeakers to give a three-dimensional effect. SOUND-SILENCE.

*****stick. Stick up,** to hold up with a gun, to rob, THEFT.

*****stick'-y.** Oppressively humid (e.g., weather). DAMPNESS-DRYNESS.

stooge. A person who assists a comedian by feeding him lines and being the butt of his jokes; a person who performs ignominious or menial tasks for another; a subservient person, a foil, a flatterer, a hanger-on; to act as a stooge. ACTING, ANTAGONIST-ASSISTANT, PRESUMPTION-OBSEQUIOUSNESS, SOCIETY-LAUGHINGSTOCK.

strafe. To fire on (troops or other targets on the ground) with machine guns in low-flying airplanes; to shell or bombard heavily; to harass. ATTACK-DEFENSE, CHARITABLENESS-MALEVOLENCE.

strat'-o-sphere. An upper region of the atmosphere beginning about seven miles above the earth. WATER-AIR.

*****stream. Stream of consciousness,** an individual's conscious thought processes regarded as a continuous flow rather than as separate actions, *MIND-IMBECILITY; **stream-of-consciousness novel,** a novel in which the story is told by representing the flow of thoughts of one or more of the characters, ACCOUNT.

stream'-line". To shape a body (e.g., an automobile or a vessel) to the flow of fluid (air or water) around it so as to reduce frictional resistance; to simplify, make more efficient; to modernize, bring up to date. BETTER-MENT-DETERIORATION.

stream'-lin"-er. A streamlined train. CONVEYANCE-VESSEL.

strep"-to-my'-cin. An antibiotic drug similar to penicillin, used in treating tuberculosis and certain other bacterial diseases. REMEDY-BANE.

*stride. **Hit one's stride,** to reach one's usual or expected speed, efficiency, or performance, *SUCCESS-FAILURE.

stuffed shirt. A person of pompous behavior and imposing appearance but of no real worth or importance. SOCIETY-AFFECTATION.

*stunt. A feat, especially a feat of skill, strength, cleverness, or daring done for excitement or entertainment; an unusual enterprise or performance; a device or trick; to do stunts. CRAFT-ARTLESSNESS, SKILL-UN-SKILFULNESS.

styl'-ize. To make (a work of art) conform to a particular style or rules; to shape or perform in accordance with an artificial convention. CONVENTIONALITY-UN-CONVENTIONALITY, FORM-FORMLESSNESS.

sty'-mie. In golf, the blocking of a ball by another which lies on the putting green between it and the hole; to block, impede, obstruct. OBSTRUCTION-HELP.

sub'-deb". A young girl who has not yet made but will soon make a formal debut into society. INFANT-VET-ERAN, MALE-FEMALE.

*sub"-li-ma'-tion. The unconscious deflection of an unsatisfactory or socially unacceptable desire into some expression which is satisfactory and socially approved; specifically, in psychoanalysis, the replacement of overt expression of sexual desire by nonsexual behavior. *MIND-IMBECILITY.

sub-mar'-gin-al. Unproductive, unprofitable; especially, of land: not worth cultivating. CONSEQUENCE-INSIGNI-FICANCE, FERTILITY-STERILITY.

sub-son'-ic. Less than or slower than the speed of sound in air. SOUND-SILENCE, SWIFTNESS-SLOWNESS.

sub-ur'-ban-ite. A person who lives in a suburb. DWEL-LER-HABITATION.

sub-ur'-bi-a. The suburbs of a large city; a collective term for suburbanites or for suburban life. CITY-COUNTRY, DWELLER-HABITATION.

sub'-way. An underground railway providing public transportation in a metropolitan area. CONVEYANCE-VESSEL, WAY.

*SUCCESS—FAILURE

SUCCESS

V-Day. Day of victory.
Walkaway. An easy victory.
Wow. A hit, a sensational success.

SUCCESS—Nouns of Agent

Ball of fire. A person of great energy and brisk action.
Go-getter. An enterprising, aggressive, and generally successful person.
Knockout. A highly successful person or thing.

SUCCESS—Verbs

Bring home the bacon. To succeed.
Climb aboard the band wagon, get on the band wagon. To join or change to the winning or apparently winning side.
Clobber. To overwhelm, defeat decisively, maul.
Go over the top. To exceed a quota or goal.
Hit one's stride. To reach one's usual or expected speed, efficiency, or performance.
Hit the jackpot. To have a stroke of very good luck or make any highly successful move.
Hurdle. To overcome (an obstacle or difficulty).

Make the grade. To reach any goal, meet a required standard.
Parlay. To make strikingly successful use of (one's talents, possessions, etc.).
Ring the bell. To succeed, win a prize.
Shellac. To beat, drub, defeat completely and decisively.
Walk off with. To win; to take, get, or gain easily.

FAILURE

Flop. A failure.
Turkey. A flop, a failure.
Washout. An utter failure, a disappointment, a fiasco.

FAILURE—Verbs

Backfire. To get an unexpected and wrong result.
Conk out. To fail (said of an engine).
Flop. To fail.
Fold, fold up. To fail, collapse, go out of existence.
Wash out. To fail and be dropped from a course of studies or training.

FAILURE—Adjectives, Adverbs

In the cellar. In last place.
Washed-up. Unsuccessful, done for, finished, discarded, rejected.

sul'-fa drugs or **sul'-pha drugs.** A group of drugs derived from coal tar and used in the treatment of infections and bacterial diseases. REMEDY-BANE.

sun'-dae. An individual serving of ice cream covered with syrup, fruit, nuts, or the like. NUTRIMENT-EX-CRETION.

su"-per-e'-go. In psychoanalysis, the part of the personality formed by external authority, especially the influence of parents in the early years, and functioning as an unconscious check on the id and the ego. *MIND-IMBECILITY, SUBJECTIVENESS-OBJECTIVENESS.

su"-per-het'-er-o-dyne. Relating to a type of heterodyne radio reception in which the incoming wave is changed to a fixed frequency for ease and efficiency of amplification and detection. #RADIO-TELEVISION.

su"-per-high'-way". A high-speed highway, usually of four or more lanes, often with separations between the two directions, and constructed so as to avoid crossings at grade. WAY.

*su-pe"-ri-or'-i-ty. **Superiority feeling** or, popularly, **superiority complex,** an exaggerated feeling of self-importance, often a reaction to or defense against an inferiority complex, EQUALITY-INEQUALITY, *MIND-IM-BECILITY, SUPREMACY-SUBORDINACY.

su'-per-man". A hypothetical ideal man of the future (in Nietzsche's philosophy) with superior strength and ability to dominate; a man of superhuman powers or much greater than ordinary abilities. MIGHT-IMPO-TENCE.

su'-per-mar"-ket. A large cash-and-carry grocery store at which customers select their purchases from open shelves. MARKET.

su"-per-son'-ic. Above the limit of human audibility; greater than or faster than the speed of sound in air. SOUND-SILENCE, SWIFTNESS-SLOWNESS.

sur-re'-al-ism. A movement in art and literature, influenced by psychoanalysis, which undertakes to express the activities of the subconscious mind, including dreams: images and juxtapositions thus usually appear bizarre and irrational. *MIND-IMBECILITY, NATURE-ART, REGULARITY-IRREGULARITY.

*sweat. **Sweat out,** to wait impatiently but helplessly for the end or attainment of (something one cannot control or influence), EMOTION, PERSISTENCE-WHIM.

*swing. Jazz music, especially in a recent style with free improvisations on melody and accompaniment; to play (music) in swing style, MUSIC; **swing shift,** the working hours in a factory between the day shift and the night shift, e.g., from 4 P.M. to midnight.

syn'-chro–cy'-clo-tron. A modification of the cyclotron which will produce beams of protons or other particles at much higher energies. #NUCLEAR PHYSICS.

syn'-chro-tron. An atomic accelerator, combining features of the betatron with those of the cyclotron, which accelerates electrons to a speed almost as great as the speed of light. #NUCLEAR PHYSICS.

syn'-di-cal-ism. A theory and movement which proposed to transfer the means of production and distribution to unions of the workers, the transfer to be accomplished by general strikes and violence. LABOR-CAPITAL, TYRANNY-ANARCHY.

***syn-thet'-ic.** A material produced by chemical synthesis; artificial, not genuine, not real. CRAFT-ARTLESSNESS, MATERIALS, *TRUTHFULNESS-FRAUD.

T

tab. An account, reckoning, check, bill. ACCOUNTS; **keep tab on,** to keep account of, keep watch on, keep a check on, HEED-DISREGARD: **pick up the tab,** to pay the bill or cost, OUTLAY-INCOME, SETTLEMENT-DEFAULT.

tab'-loid. A newspaper of about half the usual page size, with many pictures and comparatively short news stories. MISSIVE-PUBLICATION.

***tag. Tag day,** a day on which contributions to a charitable or other special fund are collected, each donor getting a tag to show that he has contributed, GIVING-RECEIVING, PETITION-EXPOSTULATION.

***tail.** To follow secretly and keep watch on, to shadow, INVESTIGATION-ANSWER, LEADING-FOLLOWING, QUEST-EVASION; **tail spin,** a steep fall or descent of an airplane with the nose pointed down and the tail moving in circles, ASCENT-DESCENT, #AVIATION; **tail wind,** a wind blowing in the direction an airplane or ship is moving and giving it additional speed, RIVER-WIND.

tai'-lor. To shape or make so as to meet a particular need or requirement. FORM-FORMLESSNESS.

***take. Take off,** to go up into the air; to get started, ARRIVAL-DEPARTURE, #AVIATION.

take'–home" pay. A worker's pay after deduction of taxes and any fixed payments or contributions. RECOMPENSE-PUNITION.

talk'-ie or **talk'-ing pic'-ture.** A motion picture accompanied by sound. #MOTION PICTURES.

tan'-go. A ballroom dance adopted from South America, or the music for it. ENTERTAINMENT-WEARINESS, MUSIC.

***tank.** An armored military vehicle moving on caterpillar treads and armed with cannon or machine guns or both, WEAPON; **tank farming,** hydroponics: the growing of plants by immersing the roots in water containing nutritive materials, DOMESTICATION-AGRICULTURE.

***tape. Tape recorder,** a machine in which sound is recorded on and played back from magnetic tape, HEARING-DEAFNESS.

***task. Task force,** a temporary group of naval vessels, or a temporary group of naval, military, and aviation units formed for a particular operation, BELLIGERENT, GATHERING-SCATTERING.

taupe. The color of moleskin: a dark brownish gray. GRAY-BROWN.

tax'-i. To ride in a taxicab; (of an airplane) to move about or run on the ground or water, #AVIATION, MOVEMENT-REST, TRAVELING-NAVIGATION; **taxi** or **taxicab,** an automobile carrying passengers for hire and provided with a meter which indicates the fare due, CONVEYANCE-VESSEL: **taxi dancer,** a girl or woman who dances with men for a certain fee paid for each dance. ENTERTAINMENT-WEARINESS.

Tech'-ni-col"-or. A process of making color motion pictures (a trademark). COLOR-ACHROMATISM, #MOTION PICTURES.

tech-noc'-ra-cy. A theory and movement proposing that a country's economic resources and political system be controlled by scientists and technologists. RULE-LICENSE.

tech"-no-log'-i-cal un"-em-ploy'-ment. Unemployment resulting from the replacement of hand labor by machines.

teen'–age". Relating to persons in their teens. INFANCY-AGE.

teen'-ag"-er. A young person in his teens. INFANT-VETERAN.

tel'-e-cast". To broadcast by television; a television broadcast. #RADIO-TELEVISION.

tel"-e-gen'-ic. Suitable for telecasting, making a good appearance on television. #RADIO-TELEVISION.

tel'-e-thon. A television program lasting several hours or around the clock, soliciting contributions to a charitable or other special fund. PETITION-EXPOSTULATION, #RADIO-TELEVISION.

Tel'-e-type. A system of sending and receiving telegraphic messages by machines which resemble typewriters (a trademark); to send (a message) by Teletype. MESSENGER.

tel'-e-view". To see or watch by television. #RADIO-TELEVISION.

tel'-e-vi"-sion. A process of converting images into radio waves which are broadcast over the air and changed back into images in the receiving apparatus, usually on the surface of a large vacuum tube. #RADIO-TELEVISION.

tem-blor'. An earthquake. GEOLOGY, TURBULENCE-CALMNESS.

tem'-po. Time (in music), rate or rhythm of any activity. MELODY-DISSONANCE, MOVEMENT-REST, MUSIC, PERIODICITY-IRREGULARITY.

***the'-a-ter. Little theater,** a small theater, usually operated at low cost by a private group or institution, with amateur or student actors, presenting plays not within the scope of the commercial theater: a movement of theatrical experimentation involving the activities of such theaters, ACTING; **theater-in-the-round,** a theater in which the stage is in the center of the auditorium, ACTING.

therm'-i"-on. An ion or electron emitted by a hot body. #ELECTRONICS.

therm"-i-on'-ic. Thermionic emission, the emission of electrons from an incandescent filament or other hot body; **thermionic valve** is a British term for a vacuum tube. #ELECTRONICS.

ther"-mo-nu'-cle-ar. Relating to the extremely high temperatures generated in atomic reactions and required in order to bring about atomic fusion (e.g., *thermonuclear reaction*); relating to atomic fusion or the fusion bomb (e.g., *thermonuclear weapon, thermonuclear war*). #NUCLEAR PHYSICS.

Ther'-mos bot'-tle. An insulated jug or flask for carrying hot or cold liquids and keeping them hot or cold (a trademark). OVEN-REFRIGERATOR.

thi'-a-min or **thi'-a-mine.** A vitamin (Vitamin B_1) available in many foods or as a synthetic chemical. BIOLOGY.

***think. Think up,** to conceive, plan, invent, DESIGN, FANCY, REFLECTION-VACANCY.

***third. Third degree,** harsh treatment, brutality, or torture of a person by police (or other authorities) in order to make him give information or make a confession, CHARITABLENESS-MALEVOLENCE, INVESTIGATION-ANSWER, PLEASURE-PAIN.

***three. 3-D,** three-dimensional; stereoscopic, giving the effect or illusion of three dimensions, as in certain motion-picture processes, #MOTION PICTURES; VISIBILITY-

INVISIBILITY; **three-point landing,** a perfect landing of an airplane: the two main wheels and the tail wheel or skid touch the ground at the same time, #AVIATION, FAULTLESSNESS-FAULTINESS.

*thresh'-old. A dividing point between stimuli or differences which can be perceived and those which cannot. DIFFERENTIATION-INDISCRIMINATION, *MIND-IMBECILITY.

thru'-way. An expressway, a high-speed highway. WAY.

throw'-a-way". An advertising leaflet, circular, publication, or the like, given to persons on the streets or distributed from house to house. *PUBLICITY.

*thumb. To hitchhike, to solicit rides in automobiles by signaling with the thumb. #AUTOMOBILE, PETITION-EXPOSTULATION, TRAVELING-NAVIGATION.

thumb'-nail". Brief, concise, small-scale, very small. GREATNESS-LITTLENESS, MAGNITUDE-SMALLNESS.

tie'-in" sale. A requirement that a buyer take an unpopular item in order to buy a popular or scarce item which he wants; a combination sale at a reduced price. COERCION, COSTLINESS-CHEAPNESS, EXCHANGE.

*tight. Stingy, tight-fisted, parsimonious, EXTRAVAGANCE-AVARICE; **sit tight,** to do nothing until someone else acts or something expected happens; to remain firm, to keep the same position or the same opinion, ACTION-PASSIVENESS, DETERMINATION-VACILLATION, MUTABILITY-STABILITY.

tight'-lipped'. Not talking, uncommunicative, secretive. *ENLIGHTENMENT-SECRECY, TALKATIVENESS-TACITURNITY.

tight'-wad". A stingy person, miser, skinflint. EXTRAVAGANCE-AVARICE.

*time. **On time,** punctual, at the right time, not late; on credit, CREDIT-DEBT, EARLINESS-LATENESS.

tin'-pan" al'-ley. A section (specifically, of New York City) where writers and publishers of music, especially of theatrical music and popular songs, work; the business of producing and publishing popular music. CITY-COUNTRY, MUSICIAN.

*tip. A hint, suggestion, warning, secret information; **tip** or **tip off,** to give a hint, suggestion, warning, or secret information. *ENLIGHTENMENT-SECRECY, EXPOSURE-HIDINGPLACE, WARNING.

tip'-off". A warning, secret information. *ENLIGHTENMENT-SECRECY, EXPOSURE-HIDINGPLACE, WARNING.

tiz'-zy. A dither, a state of agitation or excitement, especially over a trifling matter. AGITATION.

TNT or T.N.T. Trinitrotoluene, a high explosive. TURBULENCE-CALMNESS.

*toe. **Toe hold,** a place to put one's toe in climbing; an opening, an initial advantage, a means of support or access; in wrestling, a hold which enables a wrestler to twist his opponent's foot, ENTRANCE-EXIT, OBSTRUCTION-HELP, SUSPENSION-SUPPORT.

*to'-ken. Partial, incomplete, nominal, slight; serving merely to indicate a right, obligation, intention, or the like. EVIDENCE-COUNTEREVIDENCE, PURPOSE-LUCK, WHOLE-PART; **token payment,** a small payment which acknowledges a debt and indicates an intention to pay it, SETTLEMENT-DEFAULT; **token resistance,** resistance for the sake of form but with no expectation of success, REPRISAL-RESISTANCE.

Tom'-my gun. A portable automatic weapon (strictly, a Thompson submachine gun; a trademark). WEAPON.

tom'-my-rot". Nonsense, bosh, rubbish, foolishness. *ADAGE-NONSENSE, MEANING-JARGON.

ton-neau'. An enclosed rear part of an automobile body containing the passenger seats; an automobile body including such a compartment. #AUTOMOBILE.

*top. **Go over the top,** to climb out of a trench for an attack; to exceed a quota or goal, as in raising funds or makin' sales, ATTACK-DEFENSE, *SUCCESS-FAILURE, TRANSCURSION-SHORTCOMING.

top'-flight'. Leading, eminent, excellent, first-rate. GOODNESS-BADNESS.

top'-lev'-el. Describing or relating to persons in highest rank or authority. SUPREMACY-SUBORDINACY.

top'-notch". First-rate, tiptop, best. GOODNESS-BADNESS.

top'-se'-cret. Highly secret or confidential. *ENLIGHTENMENT-SECRECY.

toss'-up". An even chance. PURPOSE-LUCK, RATIONALE-LUCK.

to-tal"-i-tar'-i-an. Describing or relating to a highly centralized government controlled by one party which does not permit or tolerate any other parties. RULE-LICENSE, TYRANNY-ANARCHY.

*touch. **Touch off,** to fire, detonate; to set off, start, initiate, BEGINNING-END, TURBULENCE-CALMNESS.

tour'-ing car. An open automobile with front and rear seats and often with a folding top. #AUTOMOBILE.

*tow. To pull by a chain or rope, haul. PUSH-PULL.

trac'-er. An inquiry sent out for a missing person or lost article; a radioactive isotope (e.g., radiocarbon) incorporated into a chemical compound so that the behavior of the compound can be followed in biological or chemical investigations or experiments, INVESTIGATION-ANSWER, #NUCLEAR PHYSICS; **tracer bullet** or **tracer shell,** a bullet or shell whose course is marked by a trail of smoke or fire, WEAPON.

trac'-tor. A self-propelled vehicle for pulling farm machinery or doing other pulling or pushing work; a truck unit without a body, which can be attached to a trailer or semitrailer (a trailer in which part of the weight is carried on the tractor) in which a load is carried. #AUTOMOBILE.

*trade. **Trade acceptance,** a bankable acknowledgement of indebtedness arising from a specific purchase, MONEY, SETTLEMENT-DEFAULT.

trade'-in". An article given as part payment on another. EXCHANGE.

*traf'-fic. **Traffic circle,** an intersection at which all traffic from and to any of the roads moves in one direction around a central plot; a rotary, CROSSING, WAY.

trail'-er. A vehicle for hauling loads, pulled by an automobile, truck, or tractor; a vehicle containing living quarters, pulled by an automobile; scenes from a motion picture shown in another program to arouse interest in the picture, a prevue. #AUTOMOBILE, CONVEYANCE-VESSEL, #MOTION PICTURES.

train-ee'. A person who is being trained, especially a recent recruit in the army or a new employee in a business organization. INSTRUCTOR-PUPIL.

tran-scribe'. To make a phonograph record of (music or other parts or all of a program) for reproduction by radio. #RADIO-TELEVISION.

tran-scrip'-tion. A phonograph record on which a radio program (or part of one) is recorded and from which it is reproduced in the broadcast; the use of such a record. #RADIO-TELEVISION.

tran-sis'-tor. An electronic device in which an electric current passes through a crystal (of germanium) at a rate controlled by a much smaller current: it serves much the same purposes as a vacuum tube but is smaller and lasts longer. #ELECTRONICS.

trans-son'-ic. Relating to the speed of sound in air, or traveling at approximately that speed. SOUND-SILENCE, SWIFTNESS-SLOWNESS.

trans"-u-ran'-ic el'-e-ment. Any chemical element with an atomic number higher than that of uranium (92). CHEMISTRY.

trau'-ma. An injury or wound, either physical or psychic, or the condition resulting from it. GOOD-EVIL, *MIND-IMBECILITY, PLEASURABLENESS-PAINFULNESS.

trav'-e-logue. A description of travels, especially an illustrated lecture or a motion picture describing travels. ACCOUNT, #MOTION PICTURES.

*tri'-al. **Trial balloon,** a balloon sent up to get information on air conditions and movements; a tentative project, preliminary statement, etc., announced in order to see how people react to the idea or plan. INVESTIGATION-ANSWER, TRIAL, VENTURE.

*trig'-ger. To set off, start, initiate. BEGINNING-END.

tri-phib'-i-an or tri-phib'-i-ous. Relating to military operations by land, water, and air. FIGHTING-CONCILIATION.

trit'-i-um. An isotope of hydrogen heavier even than "heavy hydrogen" (deuterium): it does not occur in nature but can be produced in a nuclear reactor. CHEMISTRY, #NUCLEAR PHYSICS.

tri'-ton. The nucleus of a tritium atom. #NUCLEAR PHYSICS.

trou'-ble-mak"-er. A person who stirs up trouble; a person who meddles maliciously in another's affairs. GOOD MAN-BAD MAN.

trou'-ble-shoot"-er. A person skilled at or charged with locating the source of and correcting trouble in any mechanism or operation. ADEPT-BUNGLER, SKILL-UNSKILFULNESS.

troup'-er. A member of a theatrical troupe; an experienced actor; an actor who can be relied upon in difficult situations. ACTING, ADEPT-BUNGLER.

trust'-bust"-er. A government official who is zealous in enforcement of the laws restraining the formation of business trusts. LABOR-CAPITAL.

*TRUTH-ERROR

TRUTH

The low-down. The whole truth, the real facts, a confidential report.

The McCoy, the real McCoy. The geniune article or person, the real thing.

On the beam. On course, on the right track, right.

ERROR

Blooper. An error made in some public utterance.

Boner. A blunder, a foolish error.

Miss the boat, miss the bus. To let an opportunity slip by, to make a wrong decision.

Off the beam. Off the course, wrong.

Spoonerism. An accidental mix-up of parts of two or more words.

*TRUTHFULNESS-FALSEHOOD; -FABRICATION; -FRAUD

TRUTHFULNESS

Come clean. To confess, tell the whole truth.

Debunk. To take the "bunk" away from.

Talk turkey. To speak frankly and plainly.

FALSEHOOD

Baloney. Nonsense. (See *ADAGE-NONSENSE.)

Bunk. Buncombe, nonsense.

Camouflage. To disguise, deceive.

Misbrand. To label or mark falsely or deceptively.

Runaround. Deliberate avoidance or evasion, evasive answers, equivocation.

FABRICATION

Camouflage. Disguise, deception.

Double talk. Deceptive or ambiguous statements.

Ersatz. Substitute, imitation, inferior.

Smoke screen. Any action, speech, etc., intended to conceal the truth.

Weasel words. Deliberately ambiguous or equivocal words which keep a statement from having any real meaning or force.

FRAUD

Bait advertising. Advertising an article at a very low price with intent to sell a more expensive article.

Booby trap. A practical joke; a trap for the unsuspecting.

Phony. A fake, a sham.

Razzle-dazzle. Fast and bewildering or spectacular action or performance.

Rubber check. A check which is not covered by money on deposit.

Spoof. A trick, hoax, deception.

FRAUD—Verbs

Crash. To get into without being invited or without paying.

Crash the gate. To get in without paying or being invited.

Finagle. To deceive, cheat, get by craft or slyness, wangle.

Short-change. To give less than the right amount of change; to cheat, defraud.

Spoof. To joke, fool, trick, deceive.

Take for a ride. To betray, victimize, hoax, swindle.

Wangle. To get or accomplish by scheming, persuading, etc.; to manipulate or juggle (records, accounts, etc.).

FRAUD—Adjectives, Adverbs

Phony. False, counterfeit, fake, fraudulent.

Razzle-dazzle. Tricky, confusing; flashy, showy.

Synthetic. Artificial, not genuine, not real.

Under the counter. Surreptitious(ly), illicit(ly).

*tube. **Vacuum tube,** a glass bulb enclosing electrodes in almost a vacuum, used to modify or control a flow of electricity in a radio, television apparatus, or other electronic device, #ELECTRONICS.

tur'-bine. An engine or motor driven by the force of water, steam, air, or other fluid against the blades of a wheel. INSTRUMENT.

tur'-bo-jet". A jet engine in which the hot gases of combustion drive a turbine providing the power to compress the air used in combustion and then are ejected to the rear. #AVIATION.

tur'-bo-prop". A jet engine in which hot gases of combustion drive a propeller and an air compressor and exhaust gases are ejected to the rear. #AVIATION.

tur'-key. A flop, a failure (a play or other theatrical production or motion picture), *SUCCESS-FAILURE; talk turkey. to speak frankly and plainly, CRAFT-ARTLESSNESS, *TRUTHFULNESS-FALSEHOOD.

*turn. **Turn down,** to refuse, deny, reject, decline. CHOICE-REJECTION, PROFFER-REFUSAL.

tux-e'do. A man's tailless evening jacket, less formal than a full-dress coat; a suit including such a jacket. DRESS-UNDRESS.

TV. Television. #RADIO-TELEVISION.

tweet'-er. A small loudspeaker which reproduces only the sound of high pitch (see also *woofer*). HEARING-DEAFNESS.

twelve'-tone". Relating to music based on the twelve-tone chromatic scale (arranged in some specific order as the basis for a particular composition) rather than the seven-tone diatonic scale. MELODY-DISSONANCE, MUSIC.

twen'-ty-twen'-ty vi'-sion. Normal human eyesight, according to a commonly used scale. SIGHT-BLINDNESS.

*twi'-light". **Twilight sleep,** a semiconscious condition produced by injection of drugs to lessen the pains of childbirth, REMEDY-BANE.

two'-time". To be unfaithful to, deceive, betray (especially, a wife, husband, or lover, by making love to another person). PURITY-IMPURITY, UPRIGHTNESS-DISHONESTY.

*ty-coon'. A businessman in a position of great financial or industrial power. CHIEF-UNDERLING.

tyke, tike. A small child. INFANT-VETERAN.

type'-cast". To cast (an actor or actress) in a part which physical, temperamental, or other characteristics he or she actually has. ACTING, LIKENESS-UNLIKENESS.

U

UHF, U. H. F., or **ul'-tra-high' fre'-quen-cy.** Any radio or television broadcasting frequency of 300 megacycles or more, that is, above the range of *VFH* (*very high frequency*). #RADIO-TELEVISION.

u"-ku-le'-le. A small four-stringed guitar introduced from Hawaii. MUSICAL INSTRUMENTS.

ul"-tra-son'-ic. Relating to sound waves above the limit of human audibility; supersonic. SOUND-SILENCE.

ul"-tra-vi'-o-let rays. Electromagnetic waves with shorter waves lengths than the violet part of visible light. LIGHT-DARKNESS.

ump-teen'. An indefinite (but ordinarily fairly large) number. MULTIPLICITY-PAUCITY.

ump-teenth'. Occurring at some indefinite but fairly high point in a series, e.g., *for the umpteenth time.* RECURRENCE.

UN or **U. N.** United Nations. ASSOCIATION.

un-clas'-si-fied. Not secret, open, publicly revealed or available for public announcement or discussion. *ENLIGHTENMENT-SECRECY.

un"-con-di'-tioned. Natural, innate, inborn, not learned or acquired, NATURE-ART, SUBJECTIVENESS; **unconditioned reflex** or **response,** a response produced by its normal or natural stimulus, *MIND-IMBECILITY.

*un-con'-scious. The unconscious, in psychoanalysis, all of a person's mental make-up which does not enter into consciousness but which influences his behavior, *MIND-IMBECILITY.

un'-der-car"-riage. The landing gear of an airplane. #AVIATION.

un'-der-pass". A passage through which a road goes under a railroad or another road. CROSSING, WAY.

un"-der-priv'-i-leged. Lacking, because of poverty or low social status, some of the rights and opportunities to which all members of a society are believed to be entitled. AFFLUENCE-PENURY, WELFARE-MISFORTUNE.

U-NES'-CO or **U-nes'-co.** The United Nations Educational, Scientific, and Cultural Organization, an organization related to the United Nations, promoting collaboration among nations through education, science, and culture. ASSOCIATION.

un-freeze'. To remove controls of prices or of trade in a commodity or product. RELEASE-RESTRAINT.

u"-ni-cam'-er-al. Having only one legislative chamber, e.g., the unicameral legislature of Nebraska. PRESIDENT-MEMBER.

U-nit'-ed Na'-tions. The nations allied against Germany, Italy, and Japan in World War II; a world organization of nations formed in 1945. ASSOCIATION.

un-quote'. To end a quotation; the punctuation indicating the end of a written quotation; the word is said aloud to indicate the end of a spoken quotation. BEGINNING-END, DISCONTINUANCE-CONTINUANCE.

un"-re-con-struct'-ed. Clinging to ideas, especially political and economic ideas, that are out of date, stubbornly refusing to recognize change (said originally of persons who were not reconciled to the consequences of the Civil War). BIGOTRY-APOSTASY, MUTABILITY-STABILITY, NOVELTY-ANTIQUITY.

un-scram'-ble. To bring order out of a confusion; to interpret a coded message. INTERPRETATION-MISINTERPRETATION, ORGANIZATION-DISORGANIZATION.

up'-grade". Uphill; an upward slope or incline; to raise in rank, salary, or importance, ASCENT-DESCENT, ELEVATION-DEPRESSION, REPUTATION-DISCREDIT; **on the upgrade,** rising, improving, progressing, BETTERMENT-DETERIORATION.

*up'-stairs'. (In aviation) in the air, especially at a high elevation. HEIGHT-LOWNESS.

up'-surge". A surging up, welling out, gush (especially of feelings or ideas). EMOTION, ENTRANCE-EXIT.

up'-to-date', up to date. Up to the present time; keeping up with the times and latest developments in style, ideas, etc.; modern. NOVELTY-ANTIQUITY.

up'-trend". A showing of improvement, an upward tendency, especially in business conditions. BETTERMENT-DETERIORATION.

u-ra'-ni-um. A radioactive metallic element, found in various ores and rocks, and important as a source of atomic energy. CHEMISTRY, #NUCLEAR PHYSICS.

ur"-ban-i-za'-tion. Conversion of an area into the status and conditions of a city or cities or a metropolitan area. CITY-COUNTRY.

*use. Use tax, a tax, supplementing a state sales tax, imposed on goods bought outside the state and brought into the state without payment of the sales tax, PRICE-DISCOUNT.

U-turn. A turn (of a vehicle) through half of a complete rotation so that the vehicle heads back in the direction from which it came. CIRCULATION.

V

V-1. A jet-propelled bomb used by the Germans against England in the spring of 1944, also called *buzz bomb, flying bomb,* or *robot bomb.* WEAPON.

V-2. A rocket-propelled bomb used by the Germans against England in the late summer of 1944, also called the *rocket bomb.* WEAPON.

*vac'-u-um. Vacuum tube, see **tube.** #ELECTRONICS.

val"-or-i-za'-tion. The fixing of a value or price, especially the maintenance of prices for a commodity by government action and assistance. RELEASE-RESTRAINT.

*vamp. To entice, captivate, or seduce (a man) by means of feminine charms and sexual attractiveness, BLANDISHMENT, LOVE-HATE, PURITY-IMPURITY; ***vamp** or ***vampire,** a woman who vamps a man or men; an actress noted for vampire roles, ACTING, MOTIVE-CAPRICE, PURITY-RAKE.

V-Day. Day of victory; specifically. December 31, 1946, proclaimed as the date of complete victory of the Allies in World War II. *SUCCESS-FAILURE.

veep. Vice-president. PRESIDENT-MEMBER.

*vel'-vet. Clear profit, gain, winnings. GAIN-LOSS, OUTLAY-INCOME.

vers libre [F.]. Free verse; verse of free rather than fixed patterns of rhythm and rhyme. POETRY-PROSE.

*ver'-ti-cal. Vertical union, a labor union made up of workers in a particular industry even though different skills or crafts are involved, LABOR-CAPITAL.

ves-tig'-i-al. Remaining or surviving as a trace of something that has disappeared; surviving in an undeveloped or imperfect or useless form. INCREMENT-REMNANT.

vest'-pock'-et. Very small, miniature. GREATNESS-LITTLENESS, MAGNITUDE-SMALLNESS.

VHF, V. H. F., or **very high fre'-quen-cy.** Any radio or television broadcasting frequency between 30 and 300 megacycles, that is, below the range of *UHF* (*ultrahigh frequency*). #RADIO-TELEVISION.

vic-tro'-la. A phonograph (a trademark: Victrola). HEARING-DEAFNESS.

vid'-e-o. Television; relating to television. #RADIO-TELEVISION.

vim. Vigor, energy, force, spirit, dash. VIGOR-INERTIA.

vin'-e-gar-ish or **vin'-e-gar-y.** Sour disposition, temper, or behavior; sharp, tart, caustic, crabbed, ill-natured.

Favorite-Quarrelsomeness, Politeness-Impoliteness.

Vip or **V. I. P.** Very important person: a visiting official to whom special attentions are paid. Gentility-Commonalty.

vis'-u-al-ize. To form a mental image or picture of. Fancy, Reflection-Vacancy.

vi'-ta-min. Any of a number of substances (present in certain foods, or available in concentrated form as commercial drug products) which the body must have in order to grow and to function properly: they are identified by letters and numbers, e.g., Vitamin A, Vitamin B_1, etc. Biology.

vol'-plane". To glide (in aviation), to come down slowly in an airplane without using the motor. Ascent-Descent, #Aviation.

W

WAC or **Wac.** A member of the Women's Army Corps (WAC) of the United States Army. Belligerent.

wack'-y, whacky. Eccentric, unconventional, erratic, irrational, crazy. *Adage-Nonsense, Conventionality-Unconventionality, *Sagacity-Incapacity.

***wag'-on.** On the wagon, abstaining from alcoholic liquor, Teetotalism-Intemperance.

***walk.** Walk away from, to surpass easily, to make better progress than, Supremacy-Subordinacy, Transcursion-Shortcoming; walk off with, to win; to take, get, or gain easily, Gain-Loss, *Success-Failure; walk out, to go on strike; to leave (a meeting) abruptly as a means of protest, Assent-Dissent, Labor-Capital, Reprisal-Resistance; walk out on, to desert, leave in the lurch, Duty-Dereliction.

walk'-a-way". An easy victory. Difficulty-Facility, *Success-Failure.

walk'-ie-talk'ie. A light, portable radio sending and receiving set. #Radio-Television.

walk'-out". A workers' strike; an abrupt departure from a meeting, in protest against the proceedings. Assent-Dissent, Labor-Capital, Reprisal-Resistance.

walk'-up". An apartment house which has no elevator. Dweller-Habitation.

wall'-board". An artificial board replacing wood or plaster as a covering for walls and ceilings. Materials.

wan'-der-lust". A strong desire or urge to travel or wander. Traveling-Navigation.

wan'-gle. To get or accomplish by scheming, contriving, or persuading, or by indirect or dishonest means; to manipulate or juggle (records, accounts, etc.) dishonestly or to personal advantage. Craft-Artlessness, *Truthfulness-Fraud.

***want.** Want ad, a small advertisement grouped with others of the same sort, offering or asking for employment or services or merchandise, *Publicity.

***war.** War of nerves, a conflict waged by the building up of tensions by intimidation, propaganda, obstructive or delaying tactics, or the like, rather than the use of arms or violence, Harmony-Discord, Strife-Peace, Variance-Accord.

***war horse.** A veteran, a person who has taken part in many battles, struggles, campaigns, etc. Adept-Bungler, Belligerent, Infant-Veteran.

war'-mon"-ger. A person (or group) who advocates war or tries to stir up a war. Attack-Defense.

***wash.** Wash out, to fail and be dropped from a course of studies or training; to dismiss (a student or trainee) for failure, Choice-Rejection, Commission-Abrogation, *Success-Failure.

washed'-up'. Tired, fatigued, exhausted; unsuccessful, done for, finished, discarded, rejected. Choice-Rejection, *Success-Failure, Weariness-Refreshment.

wash'-out". An utter failure, a disappointment, a fiasco. *Success-Failure.

WAVE or **Wave.** A member of the Women's Reserve (the WAVES) of the United States Naval Reserve. Belligerent.

weap"-on-eer'. The person who sets off the mechanism which leads to the detonation of an atomic bomb. Belligerent.

wea'-sel words. Deliberately ambiguous or equivocal words which keep a statement from having any real meaning or force. Ambiguity, Meaning-Jargon, *Truthfulness-Fabrication.

***wel'-fare.** Welfare state, a state in which the government takes direct responsibility for its citizens' welfare by providing medical care, health and unemployment insurance, old-age pensions, and the like, Humanitarianism-Misanthropy, Welfare-Misfortune.

wet'-back". A Mexican who enters the United States illegally. Constituent-Alien, Entrance-Exit.

whack'-y. Wacky. *Adage-Nonsense, Conventionality-Unconventionality, *Sagacity-Incapacity.

wheel'-base". The length between front and rear axles (centers) of an automobile. #Automobile.

whis'-per-ing cam-paign'. A systematic spreading of rumors to discredit or defame a person or group. Adulation-Disparagement, Reputation-Discredit.

***whis'-tle.** Whistle stop, a small town, especially a town on a railroad but not a regular stop, City-Country; whistle-stop campaign, a political campaign which includes brief visits to great numbers of small communities, Traveling-Navigation.

***white.** White dwarf, a star of comparatively small size but of great density and high temperature, Astronomy; white elephant, a burdensome or embarrassing possession, a possession which costs too much to take care of, Excess-Lack, Obstruction-Help; white noise, the sound heard when all audible frequencies are sounded together, as in the operation of some very fast aircraft, Sound-Silence; white slave, a woman forced into prostitution. Purity-Rake.

white'-col'-lar. Relating to office and professional workers or employment, as contrasted with manual workers or work. Labor-Capital, Occupation.

***whiz.** A person who is clever, adroit, skillful, or expert (at an art, science, craft, game, etc.); an outstanding person or thing. Adept-Bungler, Skill-Unskilfulness.

who-dun'-it. A mystery or detective story, play, or motion picture. Account.

wild'-cat" strike. A strike begun in violation of established procedure and without authorization by the responsible union officials. Labor-Capital, Reprisal-Resistance.

wil'-lies. The willies, nervousness, uneasiness, the jitters, Sanguineness-Timidity.

win'-ter-ize. To prepare (an automobile) for winter operation; to treat (cloth, equipment, etc.) so as to resist winter weather. Conservation.

***wire.** Wire recorder, a machine in which sound is recorded on and played back from magnetized wire, Hearing-Deafness.

wire'-pho"-to. A system for sending photographs (especially for newspaper reproduction) by means of electric signals transmitted by wire; a photograph transmitted by this system (a trademark: Wirephoto). *Publicity.

wise'-crack". A witticism; a smart, facetious, or flippant remark or reply; to make a wisecrack; to make wisecracks. Presumption-Obsequiousness, Wittiness-Dulness.

***wish'-ful.** Wishful thinking, belief in something not

necessarily because it is true but because it is what one wishes to believe; mental activity governed by one's wishes rather than by realistic consideration of the facts and circumstances, FANCY, *MIND-IMBECILITY, REFLECTION-VACANCY.

*witch. **Witch hunt,** a search for and publicizing of charges of disloyalty or subversive activities among one's political opponents with the main purpose of embarrassing or defaming the opposition, ADULATION, JUSTIFICATION-CHARGE, REPUTATION-DISCREDIT.

with-drawn'. Retiring, preoccupied with one's own affairs, not responsive to social contacts. SOCIABILITY-PRIVACY.

with-hold'-ing tax. An amount roughly equal to the amount of an income tax, deducted from wages or other payments and turned over directly to the government. PRICE-DISCOUNT.

*wolf. A man persistent and aggressive in his attentions to women; a libertine, Lothario, philanderer, seducer. PURITY-RAKE.

woof'-er. A loudspeaker which reproduces only the sounds of low pitch (see also *tweeter*). HEARING-DEAFNESS.

wooz'-y. Befuddled, confused; tipsy. HEED-DISREGARD, TEETOTALISM-INTEMPERANCE.

work'-out". A strenuous exertion, especially in physical activity; a trial or test; practice or exercise in athletic activities. *ACTIVITY-INDOLENCE, TOIL-RELAXATION, TRIAL.

*world. **World Court,** an international court established in 1921 to settle certain disputes between nations, ASSOCIATION, TRIBUNAL; **world island,** in geopolitics, the land mass which includes Asia, Europe, and Africa, EXTENSION-DISTRICT.

wow. An exclamation expressing astonishment, admiration, pleasure, anxiety, etc.; a hit, a sensational success; to arouse enthusiastic approval in (an audience); a distortion of sound due to variations in speed of a record, tape, or other reproducing device. EXCITATION, JUBILATION-LAMENTATION, MOTIVE-CAPRICE, SOUND-SILENCE, *SUCCESS-FAILURE.

wrick. A wrench, strain, or sprain; to wrench, sprain, twist, strain. MIGHT-IMPOTENCE, STRENGTH-WEAKNESS.

*write. **Write off,** to cancel (bad debts, etc.); to give up and forget (an unsuccessful attempt or the like); to charge the cost of (equipment, etc.) against income for tax accounting, ACCOUNTS, GAIN-LOSS, REMEMBRANCE-FORGETFULNESS; **write up,** to write an account or description of (an event, a thing, a place, a person), ACCOUNT.

write'-in". A vote for a person not named on a ballot by writing his name in a space on it; a name written in on a ballot.

write'-up". A newspaper or magazine account or description. ACCOUNT, MISSIVE-PUBLICATION.

X

xen"-o-pho'-bi-a. Hatred or fear of foreigners. AMITY-HOSTILITY.

Y

yegg or **yegg'-man.** A safebreaker, safecracker, burglar; a criminal, thug. BENEFACTOR-EVILDOER, ROBBER.

*yel'-low. Cowardly, unreliable; mean, contemptible; (of newspapers or other publications) vulgarly sensational, BRAVERY-COWARDICE, REGARD-SCORN, TASTE-VULGARITY; **yellow journalism,** vulgarly sensational methods of reporting the news and of displaying the contents of a newspaper or other periodical, MISSIVE-PUBLICATION.

*yes. **Yes man,** a person who agrees enthusiastically and uncritically with his superior's ideas and opinions; a toady, sycophant, FLATTERER-DEFAMER, PRESUMPTION-OBSEQUIOUSNESS.

yip. A yelp; a sharp, high-pitched bark; a sharp, high-pitched sound, cry, peep, or the like; to make any such sound. CRY-ULULATION.

Z

zep'-pe-lin. A large dirigible airship. #AVIATION.

*ze'-ro. Describing extremely limited conditions of visibility either vertically (the ceiling) or horizontally or both (*zero-zero*), VISIBILITY-INVISIBILITY; **zero hour,** the time set for beginning an attack; a crucial or critical moment, the beginning of any exertion, trial, or the like, BEGINNING-END.

zing. A shrill hum, especially of something moving very fast; to make such a sound. RESONANCE-SIBILATION.

zip. A high, short buzzing or hissing sound; to make such a sound (especially, of a bullet or something else moving very fast); to move very fast and energetically; energy, vigor; to fasten with a zipper. RESONANCE-SIBILATION, SWIFTNESS-SLOWNESS, UNION-DISUNION, VIGOR-INERTIA.

zip'-per. A slide fastener: a device of interlocking metal strips which takes the place of buttons, hooks, or lacings; a trademark (Zipper) for boots and overshoes fastened with zippers. CONNECTIVE.

zip'-py. Energetic, brisk, lively, vigorous. *ACTIVITY-INDOLENCE, VIGOR-INERTIA.

zom'-bi or **zom'-bie.** In the voodoo cult of the West Indies, a supernatural power supposed to be able to reanimate a corpse; a corpse brought back to physical life but having no intelligence or will, DEVOTION-MAGIC; **zombie,** a person who shows no animation, drive, intelligence, or will, a dull or stupid person; a group or institution which has no initiative or powers, *ACTIVITY-INDOLENCE, MIGHT-IMPOTENCE, *SAGE-FOOL, VOLITION-OBLIGATION.

zoom. To make a loud, low buzz or hum; (of an airplane) to climb suddenly and steeply (using the momentum gained in a level flight to rise more sharply than is possible in a steady climb); to make (an airplane) zoom; a sudden climb. ASCENT-DESCENT, #AVIATION, RESONANCE-SIBILATION.

zoot suit. A flashy style of man's suit with a knee-length coat, padded shoulders, and baggy trousers of exaggeratedly high waist and very narrow cuffs. DRESS-UNDRESS.